KU-546-581

France

Nicola Williams, Steve Fallon, Miles Roddis, Daniel Robinson,
Jonathan Knight, Oliver Berry, Andrew Stone, Annabel Hart

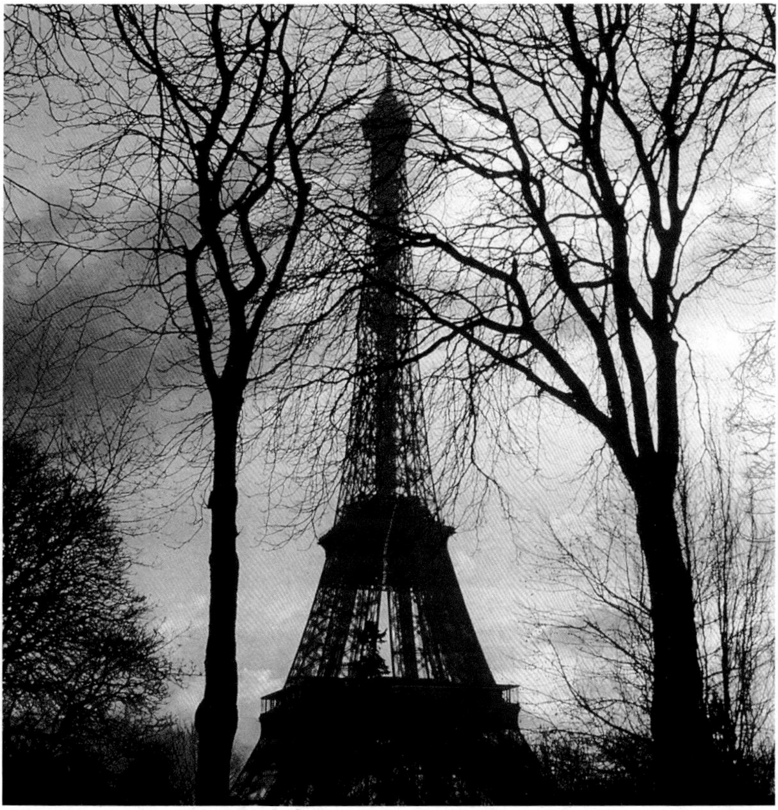

Contents

FAR NORTHERN FRANCE p200

PARIS p85

NORMANDY p235

CHAMPAGNE p323

ALSACE-LORRAINE p341

AROUND PARIS p177

BRITTANY p277

THE LOIRE p387

BURGUNDY p425

FRENCH ALPS & JURA p489

ATLANTIC COAST p609

LIMOUSIN, THE DORDOGNE & QUERCY p570

MASSIF CENTRAL p546

LYON & THE RHÔNE VALLEY p466

FRENCH BASQUE COUNTRY p646

THE PYRENEES p667

TOULOUSE AREA p693

LANGUEDOC-ROUSSILLON p717

PROVENCE p760

CÔTE D'AZUR & MONACO p815

CORSICA p860

Destination France

France is maddening and beautiful, infuriating and inspiring. It is Europe's land of good food and good wine, of royal chateaux and renovated farmhouses, of landmarks known the world over and hidden landscapes few really know. Matisse, Renoir and Picasso painted it. Hemingway wrote about it. Descartes and Sartre defined modern thought in it. And Sinatra sang about it.

People here have *joie de vivre* and savoir-faire. They know how to look good and live well. They eat like there is no tomorrow and drink red wine by the barrelful – with grace and panache. They perfect the art of living. They madden and they inspire.

Their cultural heritage is gargantuan and inexhaustible: savour the multitude of museums, striking architecture and precious works of art packed into the shining capital on the timeless River Seine. See glorious pasts blaze forth at Versailles and in the royal chateaux of the Loire Valley. Travel south for Roman civilisation and the sparkling blue sea. Sense the subtle infusion of language, music and mythology in Brittany brought by 5th-century Celtic invaders. Smell ignominy on the beaches of Normandy and battlefields of Verdun and the Somme. And know that this is but the icing on the cake. How very infuriating.

France's dizzying landscape ensnares mountain peaks and giddy glaciers, jagged ridges and rivers, lakes, white-water canyons, canals and orchards, vineyards and forests and endless coastline. Biking, boating, ballooning and boarding are four of the zillion and one ways to see it, taste it, feel it, love it, hate it. A love-hate relationship it might be, but that is all part of 'old' Europe's French charm.

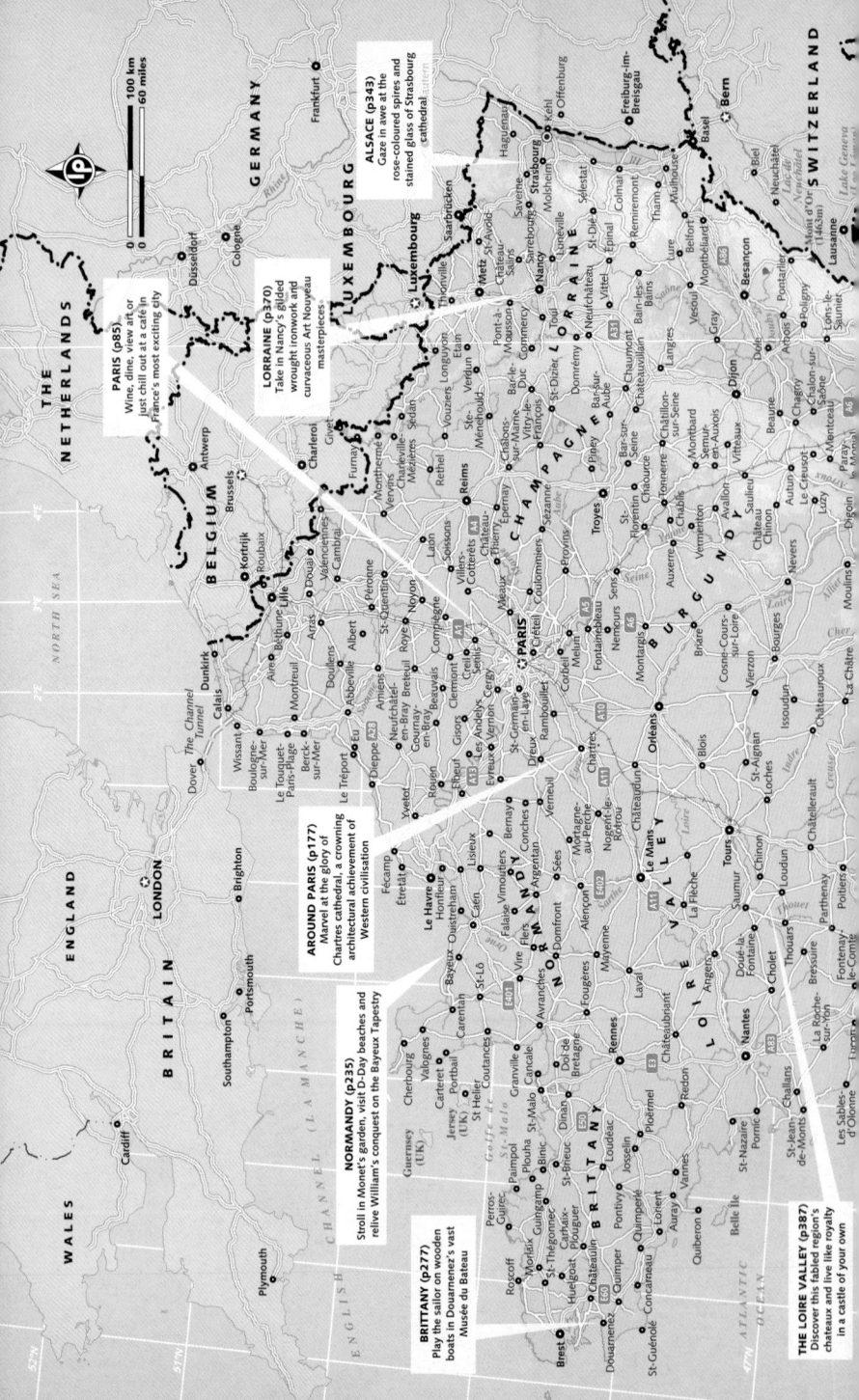

ALSACE (p343)
Gaze in awe at the rose-coloured spires and stained glass of Strasbourg cathedral

PARIS (p85)
Wine, dine, view art or just chill out at a café in France's most exciting city

LORRAINE (p370)
Take in Nancy's gilded wrought ironwork and curvaceous Art Nouveau masterpieces

AROUND PARIS (p177)
Marvel at the glory of Chartres cathedral, a crowning architectural achievement of Western civilisation

NORMANDY (p235)
Stroll in Monet's garden, visit D-Day beaches and relive William's conquest on the Bayeux Tapestry

BRITTANY (p277)
Play the sailor on wooden boats in Douarnenez's vast Musée du Bateau

THE LOIRE VALLEY (p387)
Discover this fabled region's chateaux and live like royalty in a castle of your own

100 km
60 miles

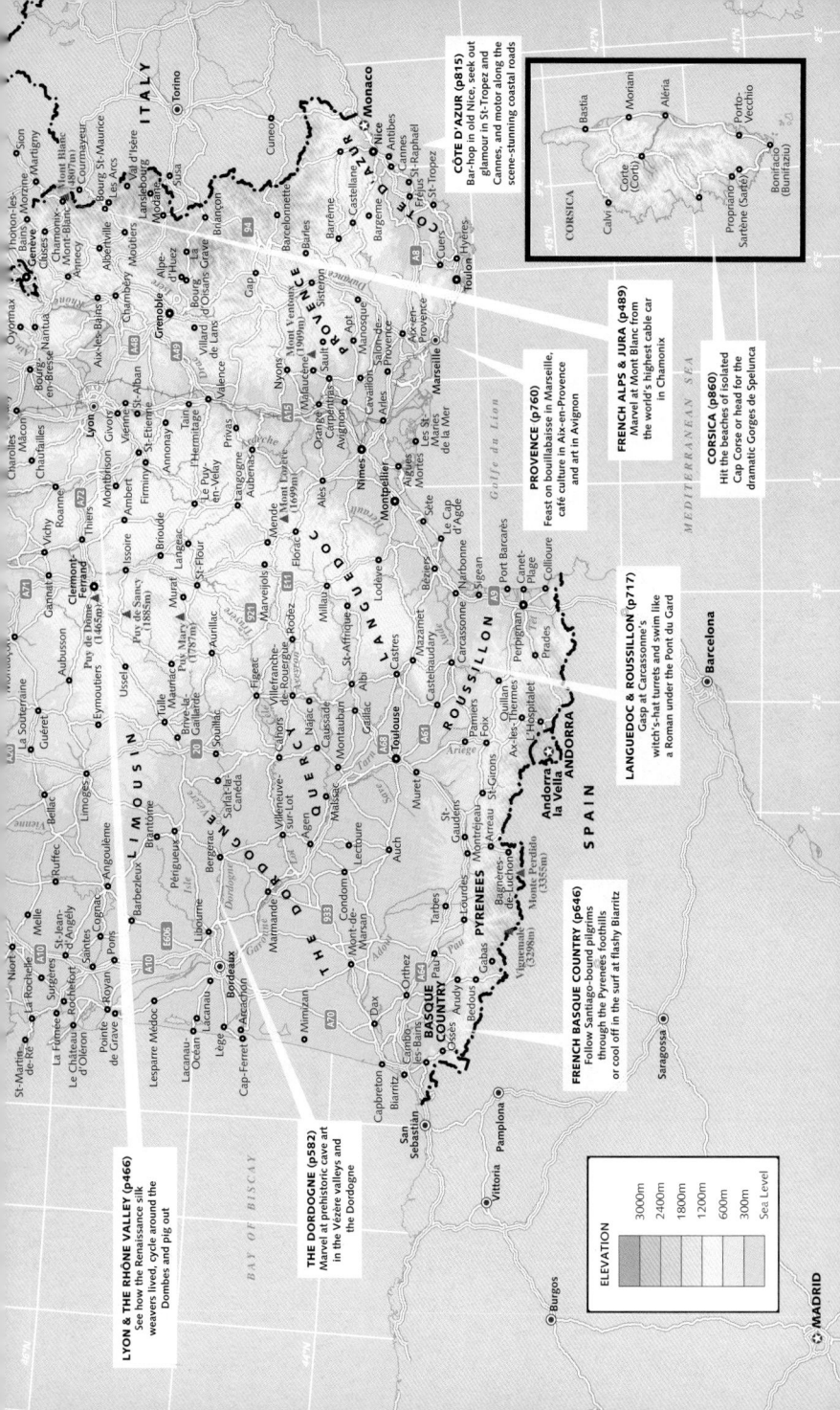

CÔTE D'AZUR (p815)
Bar-hop in old Nice, seek out glamour in St-Tropez and Cannes, and motor along the scene-stunning coastal roads

FRENCH ALPS & JURA (p489)
Marvel at Mont Blanc from the world's highest cable car in Chamonix

CORSICA (p860)
Hit the beaches of isolated Cap Corse or head for the dramatic Gorges de Spelunca

PROVENCE (p760)
Feast on bouillabaisse in Marseille, café culture in Aix-en-Provence and art in Avignon

LANGUEDOC & ROUSSILLON (p717)
Gasp at Carcassonne's witch's-hat turrets and swim like a Roman under the Pont du Gard

FRENCH BASQUE COUNTRY (p646)
Follow Santiago-bound pilgrims through the Pyrenees foothills or cool off in the surf at flashy Biarritz

THE DORDOGNE (p582)
Marvel at prehistoric cave art in the Vézère valleys and the Dordogne

LYON & THE RHÔNE VALLEY (p466)
See how the Renaissance silk weavers lived, cycle around the Dombes and pig out

ELEVATION

3000m
2400m
1800m
1200m
600m
300m
Sea Level

Whichever chunk of the country you choose, there's no escaping the France of the past. Paris is only the start of a history tour. Prehistory takes the shape of cave art in the **Dordogne** (p591); and there are no better places for Roman relics than the **Rhône Valley** (p486), **Provence** (p792) and **Languedoc** (p733). Medieval and Renaissance old towns abound, **Lyon** (p472), **Lille** (p203), **Strasbourg** (p348) and **Dijon** (p445) among them; while the **Loire Valley chateaux** (p395, p409) make a glorious blast to France's royal past. The **Bayeux Tapestry** (p262), northern France's **WWI battlefields** (p223) and **D-Day landing beaches** (p266) evoke grisly war images.

RICHARD NEBESKY

Revel in *belle époque* Montmartre (p130), the Paris of song and story

Reflect on the ravages of war at the Omaha Beach Memorial (p267)

MICHELLE LEW

Envisage royal courts of the past as you explore the glorious Chateau de Chambord (p401)

CHRIS MELLO

DIANA MAYFIELD

Take a pictorial journey through history as you view favourite masterpieces in the Louvre (p113), Paris, the world's richest art depository

JEAN-BERNARD CARILLET

Contemplate the meaning of the mysterious megaliths at Carnac (p310)

Imagine 17th-century life passing by in the narrow streets of Annecy (p508), on the River Thiou

GLENN VAN DER KNIJFF

There's no end to art and architecture must-sees, Paris alone promising something fabulous around every corner with its architecture and art from all eras. Other treasures – invariably with a generous dose of romance thrown in – include chateaux at **Versailles** (p187), **Chambord** (p401), **Chenonceau** (p410) and **Cheverny** (p402); **Strasbourg** (p348) and **Chartres** (p196) cathedrals; **Vichy's** *belle époque* spa buildings (p556); Avignon's medieval **Palais des Papes** (p786); and Matisse's minimalist chapel in **Vence** (p834). **Provence** (p803) and the **Côte d'Azur's** (p822) modern art portfolio is unsurpassable.

FRANCES LINZEE GORDON

Admire Rouen's French Gothic Cathédrale Notre Dame (p240)

Join pilgrims in Ronchamp at La Chapelle de Notre Dame du Haut (p542), by Le Corbusier

PAUL DAVID HELLANDER

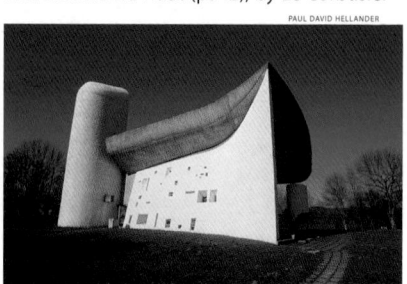

Crane your neck to take in the ultramodern skyscape of La Défense, Paris (p179)

IZZET KERIB

IZZET KERIBAR

Be drawn like the tides that surround the sea-splashed Abbaye du Mont St-Michel (p272) and explore the medley of its architectural styles

BETHUNE CARMICHAEL

Journey from impressionism to Art Nouveau at the Musée d'Orsay (p124)

Wander the witch's-capped streets of the medieval La Cité (p730) at Carcassonne

PASCALE BEROUJON

France's natural beauty – and the opportunities it presents – is a big drawcard. Skiing and snowboarding and hiking are invigorating ways to view vistas of the French Alps and the Pyrenees: the breath-taking **Chamonix Valley** (p497) and a heart-stopping **Aiguille du Midi** (p499) cable-car ride are highlights. At lower altitudes, the **Grande Corniche** (p852), with panoramas of the Côte d'Azur and Corsica's **Gorges de Spelunca** (p877) are spectacular. The cliffs and rock formations at **Étretat** (p279) in Normandy, **Brittany's sea-swept islands** (p298, p313) and the **Côte d'Opale** (p215) in far northern France are stunning chunks of coastline.

Flock to the Camargue delta (p800) to join throngs of pink flamingos

CHRISTER FREDRIKSSON

Hike close to the summer spectacle of Mont Blanc (p497) and stunning mountain tarns

GARETH McCORM.

Embrace the inspiration of Monet's garden (p243), Giverny

JOHN HAY

DAVID WALL

Enjoy a bird's-eye view of the French Riviera from the dramatic clifftop vantage point of Èze (p852)

JOHN S KING

Soar above the Pyrenees at Accous (p682)

Slow down and relish the leisurely pace of the port of Annecy (p508) on the shores of Lac d'Annecy

GLENN VAN DER KNIJFF

For many the magnet to France is its food and wine, arguably the Western world's most important and seminal cuisine. Whether it's staples – one of almost 500 types of **cheese** (p63); or the sausages, blood puddings, cured and salted meats called **charcuterie** (p65) – or regional specialities, you'll be tempted and well-fed. For dairy products, nowhere beats **Normandy** (p65). **Périgord** (p68) is famed for its duck and goose liver; produce is at its freshest in sunny **Provence** (p69). Everyone knows the wines from **Bordeaux** (p71) and **Champagne** (p72) but don't overlook those from **Alsace** (p70), the **Loire** (p71) and the **Rhône** (p72).

CHRIS MELLOR

Taste a cloudy, young wine (p71) in Burgundy

Sample oysters and other shellfish gathered in waters around Cancale (p67)

OLIVIER CIRENDINI

Salivate to the aroma of freshly baked bread (p63) and baguettes – 'the staff of life'

BETHUNE CARMICHA

Getting Started

Be it a cheap spur-of-the-moment weekend break or a carefully thought-out trip of a lifetime, travel in France requires as little – or as much – money, planning and time as you do or don't have.

WHEN TO GO

French pleasures can be savoured any time, although many Francophiles swear spring is best. Sun-worshippers bake in the hot south between June and early September and winter-sports enthusiasts soar down snow-covered mountains mid-December to late March. Festivals (p903) and gastronomic temptations (p63) around which to plan a trip abound year-round.

School holidays – Christmas and New Year, mid-February to mid-March, Easter, July and August – see millions of French families descend on the coasts, mountains and other touristy areas. Traffic-clogged roads, sky-high accommodation prices and sardine-packed beaches and ski slopes are downside factors of these high-season periods. Many shops take their *congé annuel* (annual closure) in August; Sundays and public holidays (p905) are dead everywhere.

The French climate is temperate, although it gets nippy in mountainous areas and in Alsace and Lorraine. The northwest suffers from high humidity, rain and biting westerly winds, while the Mediterranean south enjoys hot summers and mild winters.

COSTS & MONEY

Accommodation will be your biggest expense: count on a bill of at least €50 a night for a mid-range hotel double. Backpackers staying in hostels and living on bread and cheese can survive on €40 a day; those opting for mid-range hotels, restaurants and museums will spend upwards of €70. For cent savers, see p902.

TRAVEL LITERATURE

France has inspired reams of writing over the centuries. For books on French history and society see the History and Culture (p47) chapters.

An Orderly Man and **A Short Walk from Harrods** (Dirk Bogarde) British film icon renovates his farmhouse in Provence.

A Moveable Feast (Ernest Hemingway) Bohemian literary life in Paris between the wars.

Down and Out in Paris and London (George Orwell) Famous account of the time Orwell spent living with tramps in Paris and London in the late 1920s.

Tender is the Night and **Bits of Paradise** (F Scott Fitzgerald) Vivid accounts of life during the decadent 1920s Jazz Age on the Côte d'Azur.

LONELY PLANET INDEX

Litre of petrol €1.10

Litre bottle of Evian/Perrier mineral water €0.35/0.75

Cheap/expensive bottle of wine €4/as much as you want to pay

Souvenir T-shirt €15

Croissant & café au lait €2.50

HOW MUCH?

Local/foreign newspaper €1/3

Filled baguette €4

Mid-range hotel double (outside Paris) €60 to €100

Ten-minute taxi ride €15

Metro, tram or city bus ticket €1.20-1.40

DON'T LEAVE HOME WITHOUT...

- Valid travel insurance (p905)
- ID card or passport and visa if required (p911)
- Driving licence, car documents and car insurance (p923)
- Sunglasses, hat, mosquito repellent and a few clothes pegs for the hot south
- A brolly for wet 'n soggy Brittany, neighbouring northern climes and Paris
- An adventurous appetite, a pleasure-seeking palate and a thirst for good wine

TOP TENS
FESTIVALS & EVENTS

France's festival calendar dishes up something for everybody. For a comprehensive listing of events and dates, see p903.

- Carnaval de Nice (Nice) February (p825)
- Pélerinage des Gitans (Stes-Maries de la Mer) May & October (p808)
- Fête des Gardians (Arles) May (p804)
- Grand Prix Automobile de Monaco (Monaco) May (p857)
- Fête de la Musique (countrywide) 21 June (p904)
- Paris Plage (Paris) July-August (p136)
- Festival d'Avignon & Festival Off (Avignon) July (p787)
- Journées du Patrimoine (countrywide) September
- Fête des Lumières (Lyon) December (p476)
- Tour de France (countrywide) July (p45)

BUILDINGS

Ignoring the obvious (the Louvre, Eiffel Tower and so on), here are our Top 10. For a comprehensive look at famous and fascinating buildings in France, see p52.

- Vesunna Musée Gallo-Romain de Périgueux (p585)
- Le Corbusier's Chapelle de Notre-Dame du Haut, Ronchamp (p542)
- Maison Carrée & Carré d'Art, Nîmes (p733)
- Matisse's Chapelle du Rosaire, Vence (p834)
- La Piscine Musée d'Art et d'Industrie, Lille (p205)
- Chartres (p196), Reims (p327) & Strasbourg (p349) cathedrals
- Châteaux de Chambord (p401) and Chenonceau (p410) in the Loire Valley
- Château de Versailles, Versailles (p187)
- Mont St-Michel (p273)
- Fontenay (p459) and Fontevraud (p424) abbeys

OUT OF THE ORDINARY

Keen to travel France on the quirky side (see p20)? Been there, done that; we bet that you have never...

- Scaled Europe's highest sand dune (p644)
- Sailed along subterranean waters (p608)
- Scuttled like a rat through Paris' sewers (p126) and catacombs (p123)
- Celebrated Sunday mass in Breton (p302)
- Found the spring of eternal youth (p318)
- Watched 90 dogs wolf down 90kg of stinking offal in 10 seconds flat (p403)
- Been a space tourist (p700)
- Eaten silk weavers' brains or pig-intestine sausage (p478)
- Seen tender, tragic, fickle and passionate love growing in a garden (p410)
- Gone volcanic (p553)

Flaubert's Parrot (Julian Barnes) A witty homage to one of France's greatest writers.

Home and Dry in France: Or a Year in Purgatory (George East) A nightclub bouncer moves into a water mill in Normandy — and survives to tell the hilarious tale.

Tropic of Cancer and **Tropic of Capricorn** (Henry Miller) Steamy novels set in Paris, published in France in the 1930s, banned in the UK and USA until the 1960s.

A Year in Provence (Peter Mayle) Witty look at the French through English eyes.

See Climate Charts (p899) for more information

INTERNET RESOURCES

French Government Tourist Office (www.francetourism.com) Official tourist site.

Lonely Planet (www.lonelyplanet.com)

Maison de la France (www.franceguide.com) Main tourist office website.

Motorist Information (www.bison-fute.equipement.gouv.fr in French) Road conditions, closures and school holiday schedule.

Meteo France (www.meteo.fr in French) For details of nationwide weather conditions.

SNCF (www.sncf.com) France's national railways website.

Itineraries

CLASSIC ROUTES

THE TIMELESS CLASSICS
Two weeks / Paris to Nice

There's no better place to kick off a whistle-stop tour of classic French sights than Paris where the **Eiffel Tower** (p125), **Arc de Triomphe** (p127), **Notre Dame** (p119) and the **Louvre** (p113) beckon romance seekers. Stroll the banks of the Seine and gardens of **Versailles** (p185), then flee the capital for Renaissance royalty at **Châteaux de Chambord** (p401) and **Chenonceau** (p410). If castles are not your thing, skip the Loire and spend a couple of days in Normandy, not missing Rouen's **Cathédrale Notre Dame** (p240), the **Bayeux Tapestry** (p262), **Mont St-Michel** (p272) and the **D-Day landing beaches** (p266).

Then venture south, visiting the **Bordeaux wine region** (p637) en route. Surfers will find waves in **Biarritz** (p657), while the faithful or faithfully curious might enjoy world-famous **Lourdes** (p675). Otherwise, it's straight to **Carcassonne**'s (p727) turreted city walls; Roman **Nîmes** (p733) with a trip to the **Pont du Gard** (p738); and the papal city of **Avignon** (p783) with its **nursery-rhyme bridge** (p786). Finish on the Côte d'Azur, not missing Grace Kelly's **Monaco** (p854), a flutter in **Monte Carlo** (p857), a portside aperitif in **St-Tropez** (p844), a strut in **Cannes** (p834) and a stroll in **Nice** (p818).

From Paris to Nice, with a few short detours along the way, is a breathtaking 2000km that can be done in a whirlwind fortnight, but definitely merits as much time as you can give it.

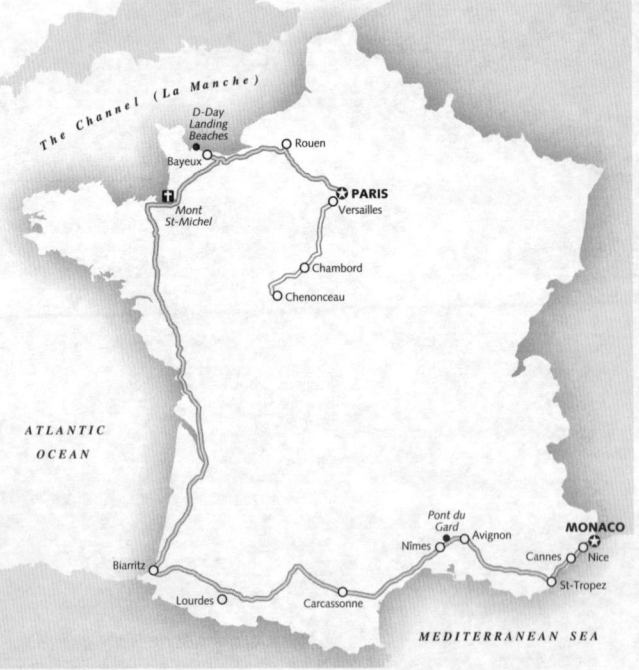

COAST TO COAST

One week / Calais to Marseille

Step off the boat in **Calais** (p209) and there's 40km of stunning cliffs, sand dunes and windy beaches – not to mention great views of those white cliffs of Dover across the Channel – on the spectacular **Côte d'Opale** (p215). Speed southwest next, taking in a fish lunch in **Dieppe** (p247), a cathedral-stop in **Rouen** (p240) or a picturesque cliff-side picnic in **Étretat** (p249) on the **Côte d'Albatre** (p248) on your way to your overnight stop: one of Normandy's prettiest seaside resorts – **Honfleur** (p251), **Deauville** (p254) or **Trouville** (p254).

Devote day two to the **D-Day landing beaches** (p266) and abbey-clad **Mont St-Michel** (p272). If island life is more your cup of tea, push on to **Brest** (p296) or **Camaret** (p300) instead, from where you can sail to Brittany's hauntingly beautiful **Île d'Ouessant** (p298). Equally tempting to Robinson Crusoes is **Belle Île** (p313), with its fantastic rock formations, caves and beaches.

A long drive south along the Atlantic Coast rewards you with chic **La Rochelle** (p620) and its lavish portside feasts of seafood and oysters. In **Royan** (p627), catch a ferry across the water to **Soulac-sur-Mer** (p637), a happening seaside resort from where it is simply a matter of wining your way through the **Médoc** (p637) to bustling **Bordeaux** (p628) – city of fine food, wine, museums and nightlife. Next morning, continue south through **Toulouse** (p695) and **Carcassonne** (p727) to the Med. The flamingo- and horse-studded **Camargue** (p806), immediately west of **Marseille** (p763), is a unique patch of coast to explore – and a far cry from the glitz and glamour of the **Riviera** (p816) further east.

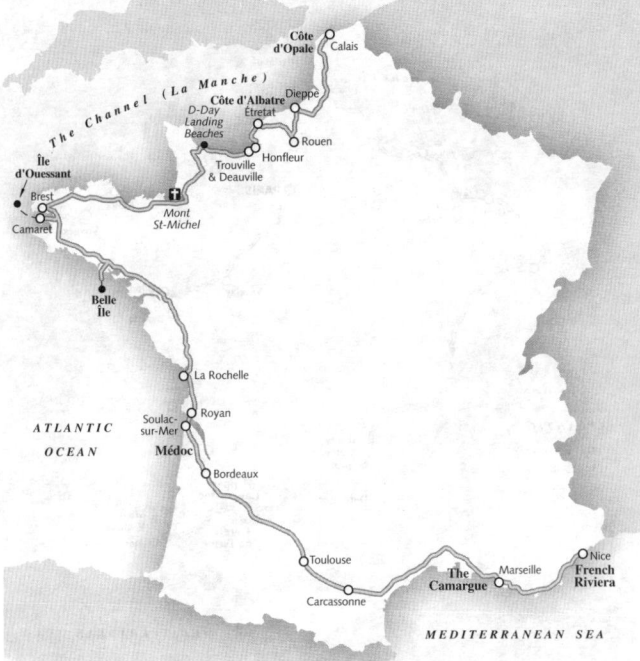

The Atlantic to the Mediterranean in a week – 2500km in all – is no mean feat, but one that rewards with stunning vistas, some superb coastal motoring and sensational seafood. For those with more time to play with, activities abound in, on and out of the sea – and there's always Corsica for the truly coast crazy.

TOUR DE FRANCE   One month / Strasbourg to Paris

Get set for your race around the country in Strasbourg: stroll canal-clad **Petite France** (p349), marvel at its **cathedral** (p349) and dine in a **winstub** (p353). Moving on to greener climes, pick up the **Route du Vin d'Alsace** (p357) and tipple your way around the **Vosges** (p367) foothills. But keep a clear head for that splendid Art Nouveau architecture in **Nancy** (p372) where you should spend at least one night to enjoy romantic **place Stanislas** (p372) illuminated. From Lorraine it is guns a-ho to champagne cellars around **Épernay** (p332), then north to the sobering **Battle of Somme memorials** (p223) in far northern France.

Devour Normandy and Brittany's best sights in week two: base yourself in **Bayeux** (p260) to see the **tapestry** (p262), **D-Day landing beaches** (p266) and **WWII memorials** (p267). **Mont St-Michel** (p272) is an astounding pit stop en route to France's Celtic **land of legends** (p279); **St-Malo** (p281) and **Dinard** (p286) are charming places to overnight. Meander around megaliths in **Carnac** (p310), then zoom south for even more prehistory in the **Vézère Valley** (p591).

The pace hots up the third week: from the **Dordogne** (p582), wiggle through the **Upper Languedoc** (p720) – through the spectacular **Gorges du Tarn** (p745) – to **Avignon** (p783). Take a break with local café culture then slog like a Tour de France cyclist up **Mont Ventoux** (p795). Explore Provence's **hilltop villages** (p798) then speed north to the majestic city of **Lyon** (p468), from where an **Alpine mountain adventure** (opposite) is doable.

The last leg takes in wine-rich Burgundy: **Beaune** (p453), **Dijon** (p444) and **Vézelay** (p440) are the obvious places to stop en route to Paris.

Tour de France cyclists take three weeks to bike 3000km around the country. This 3000km tour of France can be done in one month, but warrants much more time than that. As with the world's greatest cycling race, it labours through the Pyrenees and Alps, and finishes on Paris' Champs-Élysées.

ROADS LESS TRAVELLED

A MOUNTAIN ADVENTURE   Two weeks / Chamonix to Cauterets

Start an Alpine adventure in chic **Chamonix** (p497), at the foot of Europe's highest peak (p497): take a cable car to the **Aiguille du Midi** (p499) and **Le Brévent** (p499) or a train to the **Mer de Glace** (p500). Skiing the legendary **Vallée Blanche** (p501), **snowshoeing** (p500) and warmer-weather **paragliding** (p502) are top thrills. For the truly Alpine-dedicated there are always the **Vanoise** (p519) and **Écrins** (p529) national parks to explore.

Hopping across Lake Geneva by boat, the unexplored **Jura** (p535) looms large. Gentle land of cross-country skiing, dog-mushing and cheese dining in **Métabief Mont d'Or** (p543) – not to mention Le Corbusier's **Ronchamp** (p542) chapel – this tranquil region is perfect for peace-seekers.

Alternatively, head southwest for week two, breaking the journey in the **Parc Naturel Régional de Chartreuse** (p516) of potent pea-green liqueur fame or in the cave-riddled **Parc Naturel Régional du Vercors** (p528). Passing through the wild **Cévennes** (p741), walking a stage of Robert Louis Stevenson's **donkey trek** (p743) is a possibility before hitting the Pyrenees.

Once in the **Parc National des Pyrénées** (p680), revitalise weary bones with spa waters in **Bagnères de Luchon** (p690) before hitting the **Vallée d'Ossau** (p684) and **Vallée d'Aspe** (p681) for a heady cocktail of **mountain biking** (p691), wild **walking** (p691) and **vulture spotting** (p685). Use **Cauterets** (p686) – from where you can ski (p688) in season – as your base.

This highly energetic 1500km tour from the French Alps to the Pyrenees will leave you breathless, especially if you take a few days out to indulge in an adrenalin rush of outdoor activity up, down or on the mountain slopes.

QUIRKY FRANCE   One month / A Paris sewer to a Burgundy building site

Forget the Eiffel Tower, St-Tropez and the sweet-smelling lavender fields of Provence. This tour zooms in on France's quirky sights, sounds – and smells in the case of the **Paris sewer** (p126) where its starts. Gawp at more skulls than you can imagine in the capital's **catacombs** (p123), then venture north to the spot near **Compiègne** (p233) where WWI officially ended. Top off your day with a subterranean dose of V2 rocket technology in a **bunker** (p214) near St-Omer.

A few drops of Christ's blood in **Fécamp** (p248) on the Normandy coast inspired monks to concoct Bénédictine: visit the **Palais Bénédictine** (p248) and get a free shot – then tell yourself you're not drunk as you tour the 'laboratory of emotions' in Honfleur's wacky **Les Maisons Satie** (p252). In Brittany find the **forest** (p318) where King Arthur met Viviane.

Steering south along the Atlantic Coast, cartwheel down Europe's highest sand dune near **Arcachon** (p641). Afterwards, head east to Quercy and set sail on an underground river in **Gouffre de Padirac** (p608); then nip to Toulouse to tour **Space City** (p700) and see **Airbus planes** (p700) being built.

Seeing where silk weavers toiled in the 19th century and the tunnels they walked puts **Lyon** (p474) in a different light. Returning north, watch a son et lumière with 60 knights on horseback and 600 actors at a **Burgundy chateau** (p436) and see brickies in costume at the **Chantier Médiéval de Guédelon** (p433), near La Puisaye, build a castle using 13th-century tools.

It might well follow a predictable route – enabling it to be mixed-and-matched with other itineraries in this chapter – but that is about it. Covering 2400km in all, one month scarcely does quirky France justice. Take longer if you can.

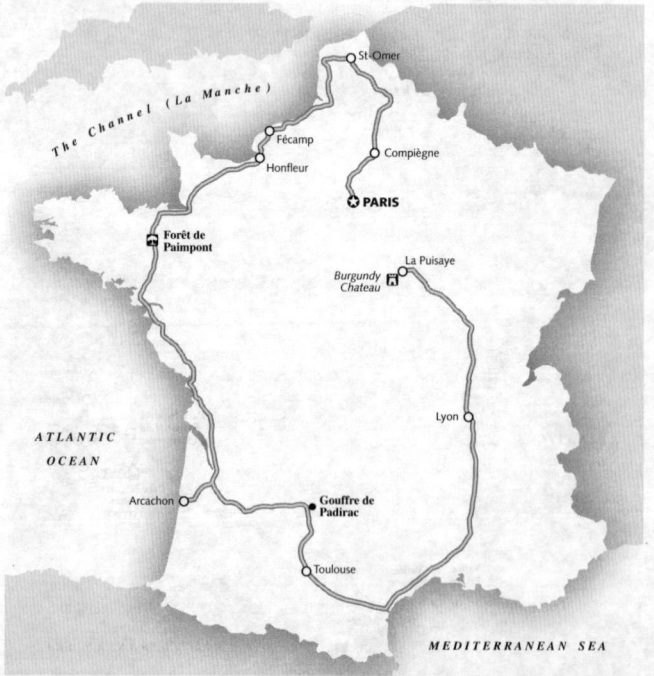

TAILORED TRIPS

TASTEBUDS ON TOUR

Eating your way around France is a fulfilling way of seeing it, although the fiercest of appetites will have trouble tasting all that's cooking. When our 'Author's Choice' tastebuds went on tour, they plumped for porky-pig *bouchon* cuisine in **Lyon** (p478), considered the gastronomic capital. Then they hit Burgundy to discover what quintessential French dishes like *escargots* (snails) and **bœuf Bourguignon** (p68) really taste like. The region's gooey, stinky, mouth-melting **époisses cheese** (p64) was a particular hit.

Next stop was Alsace with its **Strasbourg** (p351) brewery tours and wine route through the **Vosges** (p367). Lunch was a **cowherd feast** (p367), **smelly Munster** (p368) included. Then it was north to Champagne for some bubbly and *biscuits roses* in **Reims** (p328).

In Normandy authors ate *tripes à la mode de Caen* (a tripe and trotter dish) in **Caen** (p258); **St-Brieuc** (p67) in Brittany cooked sea urchins; and the Atlantic Coast proffered **oysters** (p645). Zooming south, foie gras tickled tastebuds in **Périgord** (p590); several hours was spent over *bouillabaisse* (a Provençal fish stew) in **Marseille** (p770); then it was all aboard the ferry for *charcuterie* (cold meats), *civet de sanglier* (wild boar stew) and chestnuts in **Corsica** (p69).

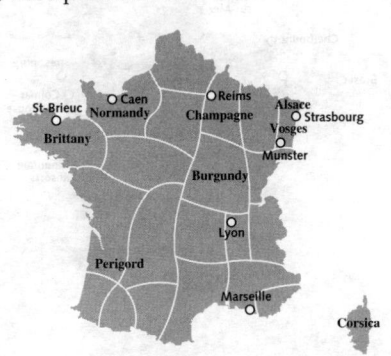

THE ARTSY WAY

Provence and the Côte d'Azur have always been an artist's paradise: Matisse lapped up the extraordinary sunlight and Mediterranean vivacity in **Nice** (p823), designing an extraordinary chapel in **Vence** (p834). Picasso set up studio in **Antibes** (p832); **Signac** and other Fauvists found inspiration in **St-Tropez** (p844); while Cézanne spent his artistic career in **Aix-en-Provence** (p779). Looking west along the coast, Dutch-born Van Gogh painted some of his most famous canvases in **Arles** (p803) and **St-Rémy de Provence** (p791).

The Fauvist-favoured port of **Collioure** (p758) on the Côte Vermeille in Roussillon is an essential stop on any art lover's itinerary; as is Henri de Toulouse-Lautrec's hometown of **Albi** (p705), near Toulouse. Moulin Rouge cancan girls and prostitutes the bohemian artist painted in Paris hang in the town's **Musée Toulouse-Lautrec** (p706).

A day trip to Monet's spectacular garden-clad home and studio (now a museum) in **Giverny** (p243) is irresistible for anyone doing France the artsy way from Paris – where, incidentally, Monet's famous painting of **Rouen cathedral** (p240) in the **Musée d'Orsay** (p124) is a must. Renoir hung out with his impressionist buddies in and around **Le Havre** (p249, p252, p244) on the serene Normandy coast, and is buried in **Essoyes** (p340) in Champagne.

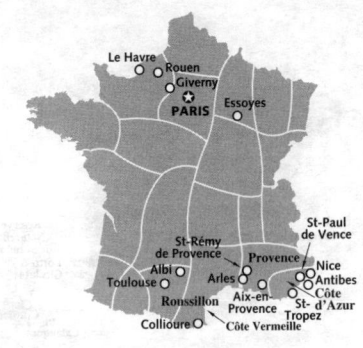

KIDDING AROUND

Kidding around France need not be an endurance test: amusements aimed at the biggest and smallest of budgets and ages abound.

Paris offers the **Jardin du Luxembourg** (p123) with play areas and the activity-driven **Cité des Sciences et de l'Industrie** (p131), not to mention **Disneyland Resort Paris** (p184). Heading north, there are fish to be felt in **Boulogne** (p217); ships models in **Dunkirk** (p220); horses in **Compiègne** (p233); and **Nigloland** theme park (p339) in Champagne. Older children might enjoy Alsace's trio of kid-orientated museums: science in **Strasbourg** (p351), cars in **Mulhouse** (p369) and toys in **Colmar** (p364).

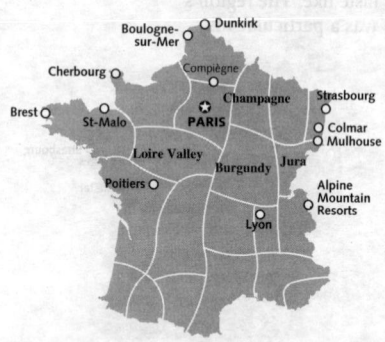

Beaches, boats and islands in Brittany and along the Atlantic Coast are the stuff that idyllic childhood holidays are made from. And for rainy days, there are aquariums in **Cherbourg** (p269), **St-Malo** (p284) and **Brest** (p297), and **Futuroscope** theme park (p619) near Poitiers.

Hot-air ballooning (p401, p428), **cycling** (p390, p428) and **canal-cruising** (p428) are big in the Loire Valley and Burgundy. **Lyon** (p473), with its green city parks and puppet theatres, suits kids of all ages; as do the **Alpine mountain resorts** (p495) where supervised *jardins de neige* (snow gardens) take kids from the age of three. At lower altitudes, children can visit farms and ride dog sledges in the **Jura** (p544), and on the island of Corsica **horse-riding** (p864), **snorkelling** (p875) and **sea cruises** (p867) entertain.

WORLD HERITAGE SITES

France is home to 28 World Heritage Sites (http://whc.unesco.org). So put on your historical hat for a tour of the country's most precious treasures.

In Paris revel in the most romantic city on earth from the banks of the **River Seine** (p113) and in royal palaces at **Versailles** (p187) and **Fontainebleau** (p189). In **Chambord** (p401), take your hat off to François I for the 440-room hunting lodge he had built. Cathedrals in **Bourges** (p396) and **Chartres** (p196) make other fine forays from the capital.

Those needing a break from Paris life could consider Burgundy with its medieval abbey in **Fontenay** (p459) and Romanesque basilica in **Vézelay** (p440). The latter – a fortified village – has been the starting point for French pilgrims heading to **Santiago de Compostela** (p440) in Spain for centuries. Their well-trodden paths in France are protected as World Heritage Sites.

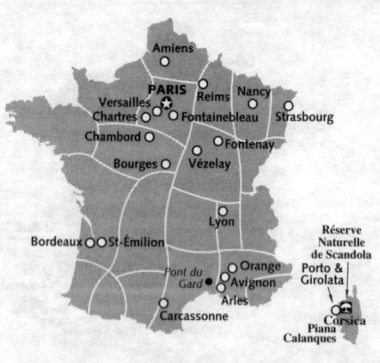

Northern gems include Strasbourg's **Grande Île** (p348); a trio of fine squares in **Nancy** (p372); the cathedral, palace-museum and basilica in **Reims** (p327); and **Amiens** (p227) cathedral. Sea-splashed **Mont St-Michel** (p272) and its bay is yet another priceless world treasure.

In the south, taste **St-Émilion** (p640), a Bordeaux red produced from listed vineyards. Other jewels include **Carcassonne** (p727); the Roman **Pont du Gard** (p738), **Arles** (p800) and **Orange** (p791); and the historical centres of **Avignon** (p783) and **Lyon** (p468). Several capes and natural beauty spots in **Corsica** (p860) are also protected.

The Authors

NICOLA WILLIAMS Coordinating Author; Lyon & Rhône Valley

Living in Lyon – crossroads to the Alps and the Mediterranean, not to mention the fabulous 19th-century silk-weaving *canut* she lives in – Nicola considers herself well and truly spoilt. A journalist by training, she worked in the Baltic region as a newspaper features editor and later city-guide series editor for several years before trading in Lithuanian *cepelinai* for Lyonnaise *andouillette* in 1997. Nicola has authored many Lonely Planet titles, including *The Loire* and *Provence & the Côte d'Azur*.

My Favourite Trip

It has to be *Le Train Bleu* (p34): Paris to Marseille at TGV-lightning speed (p918), then along the coast to Nice by snail-slow seaside train. Lingering on steps and squares – at the Sacré Cœur (p130), in front of the Pompidou (p116), beneath the Grande Arche de la Défense (p180) and so on – is the *only* way to see Paris. At Gare de Lyon (p171), lavish frescoes inside the restaurant named after the 1920s train tell a thousand tales of *belle époque* train travel. Then it's southbound for a port-side aperitif and *bouillabaisse* in Marseille (p770), and sunset over the stunning red rocks and coves of Massif de l'Estérel (p841) en route to Nice (p818).

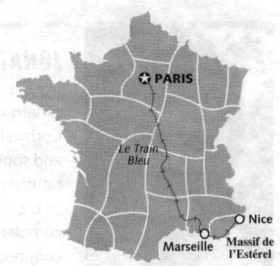

OLIVER BERRY Burgundy; French Alps & the Jura; Corsica

Oliver graduated from University College London with a degree in English and now works as a writer and journalist in Cornwall and London. His first trip to France was at the tender age of two, and subsequent travels have carried him from the streets of Paris to the Alpine mountains and from the wine regions of southern France to the chestnut forests of Corsica. He is a regular contributor to various film and travel publications and in 2001 he was named *The Guardian* Young Travel Writer of the Year.

STEVE FALLON Food & Drink; Paris; Around Paris

A native of Boston, Steve graduated from Georgetown University with a Bachelor of Science in modern languages and then taught English at the University of Silesia near Katowice in Poland. After working for several years for a daily newspaper in the USA and earning a master's degree in journalism, his fascination with the 'new' Asia led him to Hong Kong, where he lived for more than a dozen years, working for a variety of media and running a travel bookshop. Steve lived in Budapest for several years before moving in 1994 to London, from where he travels to Paris as often as he can. He has contributed to or written more than two dozen Lonely Planet titles, including *Paris* and *World Food France*.

ANNABEL HART
Normandy; Directory; Transport

Tired of university, Annabel left her home town of Melbourne and set off for a four-month trip to Paris to study French. Four years on she's still there, addicted to the ups and downs of life in Paris – where she has spent most of her time working as a freelance writer and practising her Parisian slang. Annabel has contributed to Lonely Planet's Web content and various guidebooks including *Paris Condensed* and *Bretagne*, and has now embarked on a master's degree in world politics. Her travels have taken her throughout France and Europe, Southeast Asia, New Zealand and Australia.

JONATHAN KNIGHT
The Loire; Limousin, the Dordogne & Quercy; Atlantic Coast; French Basque Country

Jonathan's interest in France began at 15 after meeting a sassy French girl in Cornwall. She smoked, swore and spoke wiz a Franch accent. Despite her glamour and sophistication, the distance and language proved problematic, and the relationship ended. But an intrigue with all things French had taken hold and holidays to the Alps, Cannes and Paris were followed by a year studying in Nice. Studies complete, he took a job at a radio station in Monte Carlo, enjoying a morning commute along the shores of the Mediterranean. Jonathan now lives in London where he works as a freelance advertising copywriter and travel writer.

DANIEL ROBINSON
Far Northern France; Champagne; Alsace & Lorraine

Over the past 15 years, Daniel's articles and books – published in six languages – have covered every French region, but he has a particular fondness for those bits of the *Hexagone* in which Romance and Germanic cultures have mingled for over a thousand years. Seeking out enchanting corners of rust belt France is a long-time hobby, and he takes particular interest in the creativity and panache of dynamic northern cities such as Lille, Nancy and Strasbourg.

Daniel grew up in the United States and Israel and holds a BA in Near Eastern Studies from Princeton University. He is based in Tel Aviv.

MILES RODDIS
Brittany; Massif Central; The Pyrenees; Langedoc-Roussillon

Miles' involvement with France began when, 15 and spotty, he noisily threw up the night's red wine in a Paris café. Undeterred by the subsequent monumental hangover, he mainlined in French at university, becoming seriously hooked and spending an idyllic sandwich year in Neuville-sur-Saône, a place quite rightly overlooked by the best guidebooks, including the one in your hand.

Living over the Pyrenees in Valencia, Spain, he and his wife, Ingrid, make a point of visiting France, for work or for sheer fun, at least once a year.

Miles has written or contributed to more than 25 Lonely Planet titles including *France*, *Brittany & Normandy* and *Walking in France*.

ANDREW STONE   Toulouse Area; Provence; Côte d'Azur & Monaco

Andrew's first experience of southern France was as a schoolboy barely out of short trousers and he has never forgotten it. Having arrived late and woken early at his aunt's house, he threw back the shutters on a dazzling Côte d'Azur dawn of cobalt sky and pungent, dark-green pine forest. A large French family (10 cousins) has given Andrew ample opportunities to come back regularly and stay all over the south since then. Trips to France today are divided evenly between recapturing the wonder of that first moment and snuffling out new regional food and wine treats.

Snapshot

Presidential elections aren't until 2007 but contenders are already jockeying for position in a political race riddled with back-stabbing drama and intrigue. Jacques Chirac (1932–) has never recovered from the fact that his old mate Nicolas Sarkozy (1955–) didn't back him in his 1995 run for the Élysée Palace (p127). Since then it has been all-out *guerre froide* (cold war) between the two politicians who – despite being on the same right-wing side of the political fence – make no bones about their dislike for each another.

FAST FACTS

Population: 60.2 million

Area: 551,000 sq km

GDP: €1557.2 billion

GDP growth: 0.5%

Inflation: 2.1%

Unemployment: 9.8%

Highest point: Mt Blanc (4807m)

Internet domain: fr

Mobile phone users: 65% of the population, the lowest percentage of the original 15 countries in the EU at the start of 2004

Annual alcohol consumption (average per person over 15 years): wine 78.9L, beer 41L, cider 6.9L and spirits 9.1L

Unfortunately for French president *Le Grand Jacques,* he is already in his 70s, has two terms under his presidential belt and is too old and too old-hat say critics. And then there is Sarko (as the French press nickname him). A man of the masses and the man of the moment, finance minister Nicolas Sarkozy is dynamic, high-profile, highly ambitious – and short. As interior minister (until April 2004), he put more police on French streets, cracked down on crime and drugs and spoke a lot (but didn't do anything) about helping the country's substantial immigrant population (p45) get on in French life (Sarkozy himself is the son of a Hungarian immigrant).

Enter Alain Juppé (1945–), a Chirac loyalist set to take over the presidential helm until February 2004 when he landed an 18-month suspended jail sentence for his role as Paris deputy mayor in a party funding scam. The scandal – all the more shady given Chirac's job as mayor of Paris (p39) at the time – saw Chirac's centre-right Union pour un Movement Populaire (UMP) party sent to the slaughterhouse by the socialists in countrywide regional elections the following month. European elections in June 2004 were equally disastrous for the UMP. Juppé is expected to be replaced by Sarko as UMP chairman in November 2004.

François Hollande (1954–) might chair France's left-wing Parti Socialiste, but it is Paris mayor Bertrand Delanoë (1948–) who is the Socialist Party's brightest political spark – and its hottest contender for the 2007 race. The dynamo politician – openly gay and survivor of an assassination attempt a couple of years back – brought to an end 130 years of right-wing rule in the capital by landing the Paris mayorship in 2001. Creating a summertime sandy beach (p136) on the banks of the Seine is but one of the fabulously innovative touches he has brought to the French capital.

France's outright opposition to the US-led war in Iraq in 2003 stirred up widespread anti-French sentiment among Americans: many restaurants in the US changed 'French fries' to 'freedom fries on their menus, to avoid having to mention the unspeakable, while US defence secretary Donald Rumsfeld publicly dismissed France (along with Germany) as 'old Europe'.

The government's greatest challenge is to put some wind back in the sails of a sluggish economy. A strong engine for EU growth, rivalled only by Germany, the French economy nonetheless only grew by 0.5% in 2003 – its lowest growth rate since 1993. Despite widespread privatisation in the 1990s, public spending and the public deficit (4.1% of GDP in 2003) are still high. More privatisation, trimming down the state sector (employer of one in four French workers) and slashing costs in France's much-revered healthcare system are among the heavyweight tasks faced by the government.

And all eyes are on it (not least the nation's smokers who watched a packet of their favourite cigarettes hiked up in price by 40% in 2003–04) for what promises to be a thrilling ride.

History

PREHISTORIC PEOPLE

Neanderthals were the first to live in France. Out and about during the Middle Palaeolithic period (about 90,000 to 40,000 BC), these early *Homo sapiens* hunted animals, made crude flake-stone tools and lived in caves. In the late 19th century Neanderthal skeletons were found in caves at Le Moustier (p591) and Le Bugue in the Vézère Valley (p591) in Dordogne.

Cro-Magnons, a taller *Homo sapien* variety who notched up 1.70m on the height chart, followed 35,000 years ago. These people had larger brains than their ancestors, long and narrow skulls, and short, wide faces. Their hands were nimble and with the aid of improved tools they hunted reindeer, bison, horses and mammoths to eat. They played music, danced, performed assorted ceremonies and had fairly complex social patterns. View archaeological finds (decorated tools, primitive musical instruments and so on) from this period in museums in Strasbourg (p350) and Dijon (p448).

Significantly, Cro-Magnons also drew, painted and sculpted, marking the birth of prehistoric. A tour of Grotte de Lascaux II (p591) – a replica of the Lascaux cave where one of the world's best examples of Cro-Magnon drawings were found in 1940 – demonstrates how initial simplistic drawings and engravings of animals gradually became more detailed and realistic. Dubbed 'Périgord's Sistine Chapel', the Lascaux cave is one of 25 known decorated caves in Dordogne's Vézère Valley, the prehistory of which is covered in Les Eyzies de Tayac's Musée National de Prehistoire (p591).

The Neolithic period (about 7500 to 4000 years ago), also called the New Stone Age, created France's incredible collection of menhirs and dolmens: the Morbihan Coast in Brittany (p310) is an ode to megalithic monuments. During this era, warmer weather caused great changes in flora and fauna, and ushered in farming and stock rearing. Cereals, peas, beans and lentils were grown; communities became more settled and villages were established. Decorated pottery, woven fabrics and polished stone tools became commonplace household items.

GAULS & ROMANS

The Celtic Gauls moved into the region between 1500 and 500 BC, establishing trading links by about 600 BC with the Greeks whose colonies included Massilia (Marseille) on the Mediterranean coast. About 300 years later the Celtic Parisii tribe built a few wattle and daub huts on what is now Paris' Île de la Cité (p119).

It was from Wissant (p215) on the Côte d'Opale in far northern France that Julius Caesar launched his invasion of Britain in 55 BC. Centuries of conflict between the Gauls and Romans ended in 52 BC when Julius Caesar's legions crushed a revolt led by Gallic chief Vercingétorix (p551) in Gergovia near present-day Clermont-Ferrand. See Vercingétorix on Clermont-Ferrand's place de la Jaude (p549) and

DID YOU KNOW?

France's oldest prehistoric cave paintings (drawn 31,000 years ago) adorn the Grotte Chauvet-Pont d'Arc (Ardèche, Rhône Valley) and the underwater Grotte Cosquer (near Marseille). Neither can be visited.

Shut to everyone bar a privileged handful of scientists, the Grotte Chauvet-Pont d'Arc makes for a fascinating electronic visit at www .culture.gouv.fr/culture /arcnat/chauvet/en.

It took several years for TV producer and historian Mario Ruspli to come up with the images and texts for *Cave of Lascaux: The Final Photographs*, a rare pictorial insight into what the real Lascaux cave looks like.

TIMELINE

c90,000–30,000 BC

Around 30,000 BC, Cro-Magnons start decorating the caves in the Vézère Valley (Dordogne) with a riot of bestial scenes

1500–500 BC

The Celtic Parisii tribe set up camp on the Île de Cité in Paris

Caesar in action on the façade of the Roman triumphal arch (p792) in Orange.

The subsequent period gave rise to magnificent public baths, temples, aqueducts like the Pont du Gard (p738), arenas and amphitheatres and other splendid public buildings: stand like a plebeian or sit like a Roman patrician in awe-inspiring theatres and amphitheatres at Autun (p461), Lyon (p473), Vienne (p486), Arles (802) and Orange (p792). Lyon also has an excellent Gallo-Roman civilisation museum (p473). In the Dordogne Périgueux's 1st-century Roman amphitheatre (p585) was dismantled in the 3rd century and its stones used to build the city walls. The town's stunningly contemporary Vesunna Musée Gallo-Romain (p586) is a feast to behold.

France remained under Roman rule until the 5th century, when the Franks (thus the name 'France') and the Alemanii overran the country from the east. These peoples adopted important elements of Gallo-Roman civilisation (including Christianity) and their eventual assimilation resulted in a fusion of Germanic culture with that of the Celts and the Romans.

DYNASTY

The Frankish Merovingian and Carolingian dynasties ruled from the 5th to the 10th centuries, the Carolingians wielding power from Laon (p233) in northern France. The Frankish tradition by which the king was succeeded by all of his sons led to power struggles and the eventual disintegration of the kingdom into a collection of small feudal states. In Poitiers (p671) in 732 Charles Martel defeated the Moors, thus preventing France from falling under Muslim rule as Spain had done.

Martel's grandson, Charlemagne (742–814), extended the power and boundaries of the kingdom and was crowned Holy Roman Emperor (Emperor of the West) in 800. But during the 9th century, Scandinavian Vikings (also called Norsemen, thus Normans) raided France's western coast, settling in the lower Seine Valley and forming the duchy of Normandy a century later.

With the crowning of Hugh Capet by the nobles as king in 987, the Capetian dynasty was born. The king's then-modest domain – a paltry parcel of land around Paris and Orléans – was hardly indicative of a dynasty that would rule one of Europe's most powerful countries for the next 800 years.

The tale of how William the Conqueror and his Norman forces occupied England in 1066 (making Normandy and, later, Plantagenet-ruled England, a formidable rival of the kingdom of France) is told on the Bayeux Tapestry, showcased inside Bayeux's Musée de la Tapisserie de Bayeux (p262). In 1152 Eleanor of Aquitaine wed Henry of Anjou (see ornate polychrome effigies of the royal couple in Abbaye de Fontevraud, p424), bringing a further third of France under the control of the English crown. The subsequent rivalry between France and England for control of Aquitaine and the vast English territories in France lasted three centuries.

In Clermont-Ferrand in 1095 Pope Urban II preached the First Crusade, prompting France to play a leading role in the Crusades and giving rise to

DID YOU KNOW?

Between 816 and 1825, 34 sovereigns – among them, 25 kings of France – were crowned in Reims Cathedral in Champagne. Most French monarchs are buried in the Basilica of St-Denis in the Parisian suburb of St-Denis.

For an in-depth study of the Crusades, including suggested further reading, log-on to *Medieval Crusades* at www.medievalcrusades.com.

'As finely woven as the Bayeux tapestry' is how critics sum up David Bates' excellent biography of *William the Conqueror.*

55–52 BC

Julius Caesar launches his invasion of Britain from the Côte d'Opale in northern France; the Gauls defeat the Romans at Gergovia

c AD 455–70

The Franks invade and kick out the Romans; Alsace is overrun by the Alemanii

some splendid cathedrals – Reims (p327), Strasbourg (p349), Metz (p377) and Chartres (p196) among them – between the 12th and 14th centuries. In 1309 French-born Pope Clement V moved the papal headquarters from Rome to Avignon, Avignon's third pope Benoît XII (1334–42) starting work on the resplendent Palais des Papes (p786). The Holy See remained in the Provençal city until 1377.

Two Lives of Charlemagne, edited by Betty Radice, is a striking Charlemagne biography, beautifully composed by a monk who spent 23 years in Charlemagne's court.

THE HUNDRED YEARS' WAR

Incessant struggles between the Capetians and England's King Edward III (a Plantagenet) over the powerful French throne degenerated into the Hundred Years' War (1337–1453). The French suffered particularly nasty defeats at Crécy and Agincourt (home to a great multimedia battle museum; p214). Abbey-studded Mont St-Michel (p272) was the only place in northern and western France not to fall into English hands.

Five years later, the dukes of Burgundy (allied with the English) occupied Paris and in 1422 John Plantagenet, duke of Bedford, was made regent of France for England's King Henry VI, then an infant. Less than a decade later he was crowned king of France at Paris' Notre Dame (p119).

Luckily for the French, a 17-year-old virginal warrior in the shape of Jeanne d'Arc (Joan of Arc) came along, the tale of whom is told at Orléans' Maison de Jeanne d'Arc (p391). At Château de Chinon (p416) in 1429, she persuaded French legitimist Charles VII that she had a divine mission from God to expel the English from France and bring about Charles' coronation in Reims. Convicted of witchcraft and heresy by a tribunal of French ecclesiastics following her capture by the Burgundians and subsequent sale to the English in 1430, Joan was burned at the stake in Rouen in 1431: one tower of the castle (p240) where the teenager was imprisoned and the square (p240) where she was burned as a witch remain.

Charles VII returned to Paris in 1437, but it wasn't until 1453 that the English were entirely driven from French territory (with the exception of Calais). At Château de Langeais (p411) in 1491, Charles VIII wed Anne de Bretagne, marking the unification of independent Brittany with France.

Jeanne d'Arc (Joan of Arc, 1999) by Paris-born film director Luc Besson is the seventh film to immortalise the 15th-century virginal warrior on the silver screen. The only scene to be shot in France (at Château de Blois in the Loire Valley) was part of Joan's trial.

RENAISSANCE TO REFORMATION

With the arrival of Italian Renaissance culture during the reign of François I (r 1515–47), the focus shifted to the Loire Valley. Italian artists were recruited in droves to decorate royal castles in Amboise (p412), Blois (p397), Chambord (p401) and Chaumont (403), Leonardo da Vinci making Le Clos Lucé (which can be visited; p413) in Amboise his home from 1516 until his death. Artist and architect disciples of Michelangelo and Raphael were influential, as were writers like Rabelais, Marot and Ronsard. Renaissance ideas of scientific and geographic scholarship and discovery assumed a new importance, as did the value of secular over religious life.

The Reformation swept through Europe in the 1530s, the ideas of Jean (John) Calvin (1509–64) – a Frenchman born in Noyon (Picardie) but exiled to Geneva – strengthening it in France. Following the Edict

Letters, testimonies and trial notes from the 15th century document the meteoric rise and fall of Joan of Arc in *Joan of Arc: By Herself and her Witnesses* by Régine Pernoud (English translation by Edward Hyams).

Five centuries of Merovingian and Carolingian rule ends with the crowning of Hugh Capet as king; the Capetian dynasty is born

Duke of Normandy William the Conqueror and his Norman forces occupy England

of Jan (1562), which afforded the Protestants certain rights, the Wars of Religion (1562–98) broke out between the Huguenots (French Protestants who received help from the English), the Catholic League (led by the House of Guise) and the Catholic monarchy. In 1588 the Catholic League forced Henri III (r 1574–89) to flee the royal court at the Louvre (p113) and the next year the monarch was assassinated.

Henri IV (r 1589–1610) kicked off the Bourbon dynasty, issuing the controversial Edict of Nantes (1598) to guarantee the Huguenots many civil and political rights, notably the freedom of conscience. Ultra-Catholic Paris refused to allow the new Protestant king entry to the city, and a siege of the capital continued for almost five years. Only when Henri IV embraced Catholicism at the cathedral in St-Denis (p182) did the capital submit to him.

Throughout most of his undistinguished reign, Fontainebleau-born Louis XIII (r 1610–43) remained firmly under the thumb of his ruthless chief minister, Cardinal Richelieu, best known for his untiring efforts to establish an all-powerful monarchy in France and French supremacy in Europe.

THE SUN KING

At the tender age of five, *le Roi Soleil* (the Sun King) ascended the throne as Louis XIV (r 1643–1715). Bolstered by claims of divine right, he involved France in a rash of wars that gained it territory but terrified its neighbours and nearly bankrupted the treasury. At home, he quashed the ambitious, feuding aristocracy and created the first centralised French state. In Versailles, 23km southwest of Paris, Louis XIV built an extravagant palace and made his courtiers compete with each other for royal favour, reducing them to ineffectual sycophants. In 1685 he revoked the Edict of Nantes.

Sun-king grandson Louis XV (r 1715–74) was an oafish buffoon whose regent, the duke of Orléans, shifted the royal court back to Paris. As the 18th century progressed, the *ancien régime* (old order) became increasingly out of step with the needs of the country. Enlightened anti-establishment and anticlerical ideas expressed by Voltaire, Rousseau and Montesquieu further threatened the royal regime.

The Seven Years' War (1756–63), fought by France and Austria against Britain and Prussia, was one of a series of ruinous wars pursued by Louis

Listen to the French national anthem (p349), what de Gaulle said when Paris was liberated in 1944 and Chirac's defence of nuclear testing in 1995 on the BBC News website (follow the Europe/Country Profile/France/Time line link) at http://news.bbc.co.uk.

For the classic work on Louis XIV and the country he ruled from Versailles, look no further than *The Sun King* by Nancy Mitford.

VAUBAN'S CITADELS

From the mid-17th century to the mid-19th century, the design of defensive fortifications around the world was dominated by the work of one man: Sébastien le Prestre de Vauban (1633–1707).

Born to a relatively poor family of the petty nobility, Vauban worked as a military engineer during almost the entire reign of Louis XIV, revolutionising both the design of fortresses and siege techniques. To defend France's frontiers, he built 33 immense citadels, many of them star-shaped and surrounded by moats, and he rebuilt or refined over 100 more. Vauban's most famous citadel is situated at Lille, but his work can also be seen at Antibes, Belfort, Belle Île, Bensançon, Concarneau, Perpignan, St-Jean Pied de Port, St-Malo and Verdun.

1309	1431
The Holy See moves from Rome to Avignon in southern France, the Popes staying in southern France until 1377	Jeanne d'Arc (Joan of Arc) is burnt at the stake for heresy in Rouen; the English are not driven out of France until 1453

OFF WITH HIS HEAD

In a bid to make public executions more humane (hanging and quartering – roping the victim's limbs to four oxen which then ran in four different directions – was the favoured method of the day for commoners), French physician Joseph Ignace Guillotin (1738–1814) came up with the guillotine.

Several tests on dead bodies down the line, highwayman Nicolas Jacques Pelletie was the first in France to have his head sliced off by the 2m-odd long falling blade on 25 April 1792 on place de Grève on Paris' Right Bank. His head rolled into a strategically placed wicker basket. During the Reign of Terror, at least 17,000 met their death by guillotine.

By the time the last person in France (murderer Hamida Djandoubi in Marseille) to be guillotined had the chop in 1977 (behind closed doors – the last public execution was in 1939), the lethal contraption had been sufficiently refined to slice off a head in 2/100 of a second. France abolished capital punishment in 1981.

XV, leading to the loss of France's flourishing colonies in Canada, the West Indies and India to the British. The war cost a fortune and, even more ruinous for the monarchy, it helped to disseminate in France the radical democratic ideas that the American Revolution thrust onto the world stage.

REVOLUTION TO REPUBLIC

Social and economic crisis marked the 18th century. With the aim of warding off popular discontent, Louis XVI called a meeting of the *États Généraux* (Estates General) in 1789 made up of representatives of the nobility (First Estate), clergy (Second Estate) and the remaining 90% of the population (Third Estate). When the Third Estate's call for a system of proportional voting failed, it proclaimed itself a National Assembly and demanded a constitution. On the streets, a Parisian mob took the matter into their own hands by raiding the Invalides (p124) for weapons and storming the prison at Bastille (now a very busy roundabout; p119).

France was declared a constitutional monarchy and various reforms enacted. But as the new government armed itself against the threat posed by Austria, Prussia and the many exiled French nobles, patriotism and nationalism mixed with revolutionary fervour. Before long, the moderate republican Girondins lost power to the radical Jacobins led by Robespierre, Danton and Marat, and in September 1792 France's First Republic was declared. Louis XVI was publicly guillotined in January 1793 on Paris' place de la Concorde (p127) and the head of his queen, the vilified Marie-Antoinette, rolled several months later.

The terrifying Reign of Terror between September 1793 and July 1794 saw religious freedoms revoked, churches closed, cathedrals turned into 'Temples of Reason' and thousands incarcerated in dungeons in Paris' Conciergerie (p120) before being beheaded (see above).

Afterwards, a five-man delegation of moderate republicans led by Paul Barras set itself up as a *Directoire* (Directory) to rule the Republic – until a dashing young Corsican general named Napoleon Bonaparte (1769–1821) came along.

DID YOU KNOW?

Portrayed as something of a clueless idiot, Louis XVI is reckoned to have written 'rien' (nothing happened) in his diary the day the Bastille was stormed.

From Joan of Arc to the Eurostar, *Cross Channel* by Julian Barnes is a witty collection of key moments in shared Anglo-French history.

With the reign of François I, the royal court moves to the Loire Valley where a rash of regal chateaux and hunting lodges are built

Henry IV gives French Protestants freedom of conscience with the Edict of Nantes

NAPOLEON BONAPARTE

Napoleon Bonaparte's skills and military tactics quickly turned him into an independent political force and in 1799 he overthrew the Directory and assumed power as consul of the First Empire. A referendum in 1802 declared him consul for life, his birthday became a national holiday and in 1804 he was crowned emperor of the French by Pope Pius VII at Paris' Notre Dame (p119). Two years on he commissioned the world's largest triumphal arch (p127) to be built.

To consolidate and legitimise his authority, Napoleon waged several wars in which France gained control of most of Europe. In 1812 his troops captured Moscow, only to be killed off by the brutal Russian winter. Two years later, Allied armies entered Paris, exiled Napoleon to Elba and restored the House of Bourbon to the French throne at the Congress of Vienna (1814–15).

But in 1815 Napoleon escaped from the Mediterranean island-kingdom, landed at Golfe Juan in southern France and proceeded north, triumphantly entering Paris on 20 May. His glorious 'Hundred Days' back in power ended with the Battle of Waterloo and his return to exile (to the South Atlantic island of St-Helena, where he died in 1821). In 1840 his remains were moved to a very grand tomb in the Église du Dôme (p125) on Paris' Esplanade des Invalides.

SECOND REPUBLIC TO SECOND EMPIRE

A struggle between extreme monarchists who sought a return to the *ancien régime*, people who saw the changes wrought by the Revolution as irreversible, and the radicals of the poor working-class neighbourhoods of Paris dominated the reign of Louis XVIII (r 1815–24). Charles X (r 1824–30) responded to the conflict with ineptitude and was overthrown in the so-called July Revolution of 1830. Those who were killed in the Paris street battles that accompanied the Revolution are buried in vaults under the Colonne de Juillet in the centre of place de la Bastille (p119).

DID YOU KNOW?

The *Code Napoléon* (or Civil Code), instituted by French hero Napoleon Bonaparte, forms the basis of the French legal system and many others in Europe.

A History of Modern France by Alfred Cobban is a very readable, three-volume history covering the period from Louis XIV to 1962.

REPUBLICAN CALENDAR

During the Revolution, the Convention adopted a calendar from which all 'superstitious' associations (such as saints' days) were removed. Year 1 began on 22 September 1792, the day the Republic was proclaimed. The 12 months – renamed Vendémiaire, Brumaire, Frimaire, Nivôse, Pluviôse, Ventôse, Germinal, Floréal, Prairial, Messidor, Thermidor and Fructidor – were divided into three 10-day weeks called *décades*.

The poetic names of the months were seasonally inspired: the autumn months, for instance, were Vendémiaire (derived from *vendange*, grape harvest or vintage), Brumaire (from *brume*, mist or fog) and Frimaire (from *frimas*, frost). The last day of each *décade* was a rest day, and the five or six remaining days of the year were used to celebrate Virtue, Genius, Labour, Opinion and Rewards. These festivals were initially called *sans-culottides* in honour of the *sans-culottes*, the extreme revolutionaries who wore pantaloons rather than the short breeches favoured by the upper classes.

While the Republican calendar worked well in theory, it caused no end of confusion and on 1 January 1806 Napoleon switched back to the Gregorian calendar.

1643–1715	1789–94
The Sun King assumes the French throne and shifts the royal court from Paris to a fabulous palace 23km west of the city in Versailles	Revolutionaries storm the Bastille, leading to the public beheading of Louis XVI and Marie Antoinette and the Reign of Terror

FRENCH INVENTIONS

- The first digital calculator (Blaise Pascal, 1642)
- The hot-air balloon (Jospeh and Étienne Montgolfier, 1783)
- A printed language that blind people could read (Louis Braille, 1829)
- Margarine (Mège Mouriés, 1869)
- Etch-a-Sketch children's toy (Arthur Granjean, 1958)
- The installation of a silicon chip computer memory on credit cards (Roland Moreno, 1974)
- Minitel, the first public interactive computer network (1980)

Louis-Philippe (r 1830–48), a constitutional monarch of bourgeois sympathies and tastes, was subsequently chosen by parliament, only to be ousted by the 1848 Revolution. The Second Republic was established and elections brought in Napoleon's almost useless nephew, Louis Napoleon Bonaparte, as president. But in 1851 Louis Napoleon led a coup d'état and proclaimed himself Emperor Napoleon III of the Second Empire (1852–70).

A *Social History of the French Revolution* by Christopher Hibbert is the book to buy for those seeking an easy-to-digest social account of the period.

France enjoyed significant economic growth at this time. Paris was transformed under urban planner Baron Haussmann (1809–91) who, among other things, created the 12 huge boulevards radiating from the Arc de Triomphe (p127). Napoleon III threw glittering parties at the royal palace (p232) in Compiègne, and breathed in the sea air at fashionable Biarritz (p654) and Deauville (p254).

As his uncle had done before him, Napoleon III embroiled France in various catastrophic conflicts, including the Crimean War (1853–56) and the humiliating Franco-Prussian War (1870–71), which ended with Prussia taking the emperor prisoner. Upon hearing the news, defiant Parisian masses took to the streets demanding a republic; the so-called Wall of the Federalists in Paris' Cimetière du Père Lachaise (p129) serves as a deathly reminder of the subsequent bloodshed.

A BEAUTIFUL AGE

There was nothing beautiful about the start of the Third Republic. Born as a provisional government of national defence in September 1870, it was quickly besieged by the Prussians who laid siege to Paris and demanded National Assembly elections be held. Unfortunately, the first move made by the resultant monarchist-controlled assembly was to ratify the Treaty of Frankfurt (1871), the harsh terms of which – a five-billion-franc war indemnity and surrender of the provinces of Alsace and Lorraine – prompted immediate revolt. During *La Semaine Sanglante* (Bloody Week), several thousand rebel Communards (supporters of the hard-core insurgent Paris Commune) were killed and a further 20,000 or so executed.

DID YOU KNOW?

Starving citizens baked bread laced with sawdust and ate most of the animals in the city zoo during Prussia's siege of Paris (1870–71).

Despite this bloody start, the Third Republic ushered in the glittering *belle époque* (beautiful age), with Art Nouveau architecture, a whole field of artistic 'isms' from impressionism onwards, and advances in science and engineering, including the construction of the first metro line in

1799–1815	1858
The rise and fall of dashing Corsican soldier Napoleon Bonaparte	A 14-year-old peasant girl in Lourdes sees the Virgin Mary in a series of 18 visions; the town becomes a world pilgrimage site

THE DREYFUS AFFAIR

The greatest moral and political crisis of the day in the Third Republic was the infamous Dreyfus Affair, sparked off in 1894 when Jewish army officer Captain Alfred Dreyfus was accused of betraying military secrets to Germany. Dreyfus was court-martialled and sentenced to life imprisonment on Devil's Island, a notoriously hideous penal colony in French Guiana, South America, where some 56,000 French prisoners were sent between 1864 and 1946.

Despite bitter opposition from the army command, right-wing politicians and many Catholic groups, the case was eventually reopened and Dreyfus vindicated. The affair greatly discredited both the army and the Catholic Church. The result was more rigorous civilian control of the military and, in 1905, the legal separation of Church and State.

Documents relating to the Dreyfus Affair are exhibited at the Musée d'Art et d'Histoire du Judaïsme (p118) in Paris.

Paris. World exhibitions were held in the capital in 1889 (showcased by the Eiffel Tower, p125) and again in 1901 in the purpose-built Petit Palais (p127). Bohemia Paris, with its nightclubs and artistic cafés, was conceived around this time.

Discover the type of life Alfred Dreyfus would have led on Devil's Island with *Dry Guillotine: 15 Years among the Living Dead*, a gripping account of the South American French penal colony by René Belbenoît, first published in 1938.

Colonial rivalry between France and Britain in Africa ended in 1904 with the *Entente Cordiale* (literally 'Cordial Understanding'), marking the start of a cooperation that has continued, more or less, to this day.

THE GREAT WAR

A trip to the Somme (p223) or Verdun (p384) battlefields – places synonymous with wartime slaughter – goes some way to revealing the unimaginable human cost of WWI. Of the eight million French men called to arms, 1.3 million were killed and almost one million crippled. Much of the war took place in northeastern France, trench warfare using thousands of soldiers as cannon fodder to gain a few metres of territory: trenches at the battle ground of Le Linge in Alsace form part of a memorial museum (p368).

Central to France's entry into war against Austria-Hungary and Germany had been its desire to regain Alsace and Lorraine, lost to Germany in 1871. The Great War officially ended in November 1918 with Germany and the Allies signing an armistice in a clearing (p233) near Compiègne. But the details were not finalised until 1919 when the so-called 'big four' – French Prime Minister Georges Clemenceau, British Prime Minister Lloyd George, Italian Premier Vittorio Orlando and US President Woodrow Wilson – gathered in the Palace of Versailles (p187) to sign the Treaty of Versailles. Its harsh terms included the return of Alsace-Lorraine to France and a reparations bill of US$33 billion for Germany.

Battles, battleground tours, a who's who, propaganda posters, diaries and war timeline are among the impressive range of features to be found on this comprehensive site examining the Great War at www.firstworldwar.com.

WWI saw industrial production drop by 40% and France thrown into financial crisis. Yet somehow Paris still sparkled as the centre of the avant-garde in the 1920s and 1930s, with artists pushing into the new fields of cubism and surrealism, Le Corbusier (p53) rewriting the architectural textbook, foreign writers like Ernest Hemingway and F Scott Fitzgerald attracted by the liberal atmosphere of Paris, and nightlife establishing a cutting-edge reputation for everything from jazz to striptease. In 1922 the luxurious *Train Bleu* (Blue Train) made its first run from Calais, via

1870	1914–18
The Third Republic ushers in the *belle époque*	Eight million French men are called to arms during WWI; of these, 1.3 million are killed and almost one million are crippled

Paris, to the Côte d'Azur. The train only had 1st-class carriages and was quickly dubbed the 'train to paradise'.

WWII

The naming of Adolf Hitler as Germany's chancellor in 1933 signalled the end of a decade of accommodation and compromise between France and Germany. Initially the French tried to appease Hitler, but two days after Germany invaded Poland in 1939, France joined Britain in declaring war on Germany.

By June 1940 France had capitulated. The British expeditionary force sent to help the French barely managed to avoid capture by retreating to Dunkirk and crossing the English Channel in small boats. The Maginot Line (p344) had proved useless, German armoured divisions outflanking it by going through Belgium.

Germany divided France into a zone under direct German occupation (in the north and along the western coast) and a puppet state led by ageing WWI hero General Pétain in the spa town of Vichy; the demarcation line between the two ran through Château de Chenonceau (p410) in the Loire Valley. Life in the Nazi-occupied north is examined at La Coupole (p214), a WWII museum inside a subterranean Nazi-built rocket launch site.

The Vichy regime was viciously anti-Semitic, local police invariably proving very helpful to the Nazis in rounding up French Jews and others for deportation to Auschwitz and other death camps. Museums in Grenoble (p524) and Lyon (p475), among others, examine these deportations. The only Nazi concentration camp on French soil was Natzweiler-Struthof (p357); it can be visited.

An 80km-long stretch of beach (p226, p264) and Bayeux's Musée Mémorial 1944 Bataille de Normandie (p262) tell the tale of the D-Day landings on 6 June 1944 when 100,000-plus Allied troops stormed the coastline to liberate most of Normandy and Brittany. Paris was liberated on 25 August by a force spearheaded by Free French units, sent in ahead of the Americans, so the French would have the honour of liberating their own capital.

The US general's war room in Reims (p327) where Nazi Germany officially capitulated in May 1945 is open to the public.

POST-WAR DEVASTATION

France was ruined by the time it was liberated. Over one-third of industrial production fed the German war machine during WWII, the

> A detailed history of WWII with Nazi leader biographies and a Holocaust timeline with over 150 images make this website stand out www .historyplace.com

> *WWI: Trenches on the Web* (www.worldwar1 .com) provides dozens of hot links to other Great War-related websites.

> 'A simple story of the nightmare of Flanders mud' is how one critic reviewed *Birdsong* by Sebastian Faulks, a gripping novel about trench warfare in northern France during WWI. The novel spans 1910 to the Armistice.

THE FRENCH RESISTANCE

Despite the myth of *'la France résistante'* (the French Resistance), the underground movement never actually included more than 5% of the population. The other 95% either collaborated or did nothing. Resistance members engaged in railway sabotage, collected intelligence for the Allies, helped Allied airmen who had been shot down and published anti-German leaflets, among other activities. The impact of their pursuits might have been modest but the Resistance served as an enormous boost to French morale – not to mention fresh fodder for numerous literary and cinematic endeavours.

1939	1944
Nazi Germany occupies France and establishes a Vichy regime	Normandy and Brittany are the first to be liberated by Allied troops following the June 1944 D-Day landings

occupiers requisitioning practically everything that wasn't (and was) nailed down: ferrous and nonferrous metals, statues, iron grills, zinc bar tops, coal, leather, textiles and chemicals. Agriculture, strangled by the lack of raw materials, fell by 25%.

In their retreat, the Germans burned bridges (2600 destroyed) and the Allied bombardments tore up railroad tracks (40,000km). The roadways hadn't been maintained since 1939, ports were damaged, and nearly half a million buildings and 60,000 factories destroyed. The French had to pay for the needs of the occupying soldiers to the tune of 400 million francs a day, prompting an inflation riptide.

France's humiliation at the hands of the Germans was not lost on its restive colonies. As the war economy tightened its grip, the native-born people, poorer to begin with, noticed that they were taking the brunt of the pain. In North Africa, the Algerians coalesced around a movement for greater autonomy that blossomed into a full-scale independence movement by the end of the war. The Japanese moved into strategically important Indochina in 1940. A Vietnamese resistance movement that developed quickly took on an anti-French, nationalistic tone setting the stage for Vietnam's eventual independence.

Wine & War by Don & Petie Kladstrup is the cliffhanger story of how France's wine-makers saved their country's greatest treasure – its vineyards – from destruction during WWII.

THE FOURTH REPUBLIC & POST-WAR PROSPERITY

After the liberation, General Charles de Gaulle (1890–1970) – France's undersecretary of war who had fled Paris for London in 1940 after France capitulated – faced the delicate task of setting up a viable government. Vichy officials were disqualified but what to do about the resistance fighters who had already installed themselves in many municipal offices? Using his personal prestige, de Gaulle kept reprisals to a minimum, convincing resistance fighters to disarm and join a temporary government of national unity.

DID YOU KNOW?
Women in France gained the right to vote in 1944.

Elections on 21 October 1945 created a national assembly composed largely of pro-resistant communists. De Gaulle was appointed head of the government, but quickly sensed that the tide was turning against his idea of a strong presidency and in January 1946 he resigned.

The magnitude of France's post-war economic devastation required a strong central government with broad powers to rebuild its industrial and commercial base. Soon after the liberation, most banks, insurance companies, car manufacturers and energy-producing companies passed into the hands of the government. Other businesses remained in private hands, the objective being to combine the efficiency of state planning with the dynamism of private initiative. But progress was slow. By 1947 rationing remained and France was forced to turn to the USA for loans as part of the Marshall Plan to rebuild Europe.

DID YOU KNOW?
Charles de Gaulle was a record breaker: he is included in the *Guinness Book of Records* as surviving more assassination attempts – 32 to be precise – than anyone else in the world.

One of the aims of the Marshall Plan was to stabilise post-war Europe financially and politically, thus thwarting the expansion of Soviet power. As the Iron Curtain dropped over Eastern Europe, the pro-Stalinist bent of the Communist Party put it in a politically untenable position. Seeking at once to exercise power within the government and at the same time oppose its measures as insufficiently Marxist, the communists found themselves on the losing end of disputes involving the colonies, workers' demands and American aid. In 1947 they were booted out of government.

1949	1954–62
France signs the Atlantic Pact uniting North America and Western Europe in a mutual defence alliance (NATO)	The Algerian War of Independence marks the end of French colonialism

While the Communist Party fulminated against the 'imperialism' of American power, de Gaulle founded a new party, the Rassemblement du Peuple Français (RPF), which argued for the containment of Soviet power. In 1949 France signed the Atlantic Pact uniting North America and Western Europe in a mutual defence alliance (NATO). The fear of both communism and a resurgent Germany also led to the first steps towards European integration with the birth of the Council of Europe in 1949, the European Coal and Steel Community in 1951 and military accords in 1954.

The economy gathered steam in the 1950s, helped in part by a worldwide economic expansion. The French government invested in hydroelectric plants, nuclear power plants, oil and gas exploration, petrochemical refineries, steel production, naval construction, auto factories, building construction to accommodate a baby boom and consumer goods.

For a vivid, in-depth and provocative portrait of de Gaulle go to www .charles-de-gaulle.org.

WAR IN THE COLONIES

The 1950s spelled the end of French colonialism. When Japan surrendered to the Allies in 1945, the nationalist Ho Chi Minh launched a drive for an autonomous Vietnam that became a drive for independence. Under the brilliant General Giap, the Vietnamese perfected a form of guerrilla warfare that proved highly effective against the French army (and later the Americans). After their defeat at Dien Bien Phu in 1954, the French threw in the towel and withdrew from Indochina.

The struggle for Algerian independence was nastier. Technically a French *département* (p906), Algeria was in effect ruled by a million or so French settlers who wished to protect their privileges at all costs. Heads stuck firmly in the Saharan sands (especially in the south where the oil was), the colonial community and their supporters in the army and the right wing refused all Algerian demands for political and economic equality.

The Algerian War (1954–62) was brutal. Nationalist rebel attacks were met with summary executions, inquisitions, torture and massacres that only made Algerians more determined to gain their independence. The government responded with half-hearted reform and reorganisation programmes that failed to address the fact that most people no longer wished to be a part of France.

International pressure on France to pull out of Algeria came from the UN, the USSR and the USA, while *pieds noirs* (literally 'black feet' –

Past Imperfect: French Intellectuals, 1944–1956 by Tony Judt studies the lively intellectual life of post-war France with flair and authority.

THE BIRTH OF THE BIKINI

Almost called *atome* (French for atom) rather than bikini after its pinprick size, the scanty little two-piece bathing suit was the 1946 creation of Cannes fashion designer Jacques Heim and automotive engineer Louis Réard.

Top-and-bottom swimsuits had existed for centuries, but it was the French duo who plumped for the name, bikini – after Bikini, an atoll in the Marshall Islands chosen by the USA in 1946 as the testing ground for atomic bombs.

Once wrapped around the curvaceous buttocks of 1950s sex-bomb Brigitte Bardot on St-Tropez' Plage de Pampelonne, there was no looking back. The bikini was born.

1968	1981
Anti-authoritarian student protests at de Gaulle's style of government by decree escalate into countrywide strike	The super-speedy TGV makes it first commercial journey (Paris to Lyon)

as Algerian-born French people are known in France), elements of the military and extreme right-wingers became increasingly enraged at what they saw as defeatism in dealing with the problem. A plot to overthrow the government and replace it with a military-style regime, raising the serious risk of a civil war in France, was narrowly avoided when de Gaulle agreed to assume the presidency in 1958.

THE FIFTH REPUBLIC & YESTERDAY'S MAN

While it could claim to have successfully reconstructed and expanded the economy and created a certain political stability, the Fourth Republic was ultimately hampered by a weak presidential branch and the debilitating situation in Algeria. De Gaulle remedied the first problem by drafting a new constitution – the Fifth Republic – which gave considerable powers to the president at the expense of the National Assembly.

Algeria was a greater problem, de Gaulle's initial attempts at reform – according the Algerians political equality and recognising their right in principle to self-determination – only serving to further infuriate right-wingers without quenching the Algerian thirst for independence. Following a failed coup attempt by a bunch of military officers in 1961, the Organisation de l'Armée Secrète (OAS; a group of French settlers and sympathisers opposed to Algerian independence) resorted to terrorism. It tried to assassinate de Gaulle several times and in 1961 violence broke out on the streets of Paris. Police violently attacked Algerian demonstrators, murdering more than 100. In 1962 de Gaulle negotiated an end to war in Algeria with the lakeside signing of the *Accord d'Évian* (Evian Accord) in Évian-les-Bains.

By the late 1960s de Gaulle was appearing more and more like yesterday's man. The loss of the colonies, the surge in immigration (p45) and rise in unemployment had weakened his government, while de Gaulle's government by decree was starting to gall the anti-authoritarian baby-boomer generation, which was now at university and gagging for social change. Students reading Herbert Marcuse and Wilhelm Reich found much to admire in Fidel Castro, Che Guevara and the black struggle for civil rights in America and vociferously denounced the American war in Vietnam.

Student protests of 1968 climaxed with a brutal overreaction by police to a protest meeting at Paris' most renowned university(p121). Overnight, public opinion turned in favour of the students, while the students themselves occupied the Sorbonne and erected barricades in the Latin Quarter. Within days, a general strike by 10 million workers countrywide paralysed France.

But such comradeship between worker and student did not last long. While the former wanted a greater share of the consumer market, the latter wanted to destroy it. After much hesitancy, de Gaulle took advantage of this division by appealing to people's fear of anarchy. Just as the country seemed on the brink of revolution and an overthrow of the Fifth Republic, stability returned. The government immediately decentralised the higher education system and followed through in the 1970s with a wave of other reforms (lowering the voting age to 18, an abortion law and so on). De Gaulle meanwhile resigned from office in 1969 after losing

DID YOU KNOW?

L'Imagination au Pouvoir (Power to the Imagination) and *Sous les Pavés, la Plage* (Under the Cobblestones, the Beach) – a reference to Parisians' favoured material for building barricades and what they could expect to find beneath – were slogans drummed up in 1968.

DID YOU KNOW?

France has had 11 constitutions since 1789. The present one, instituted by de Gaulle in 1958, is known as the Fifth Republic.

1994	1995
The 50km-long Channel Tunnel linking mainland France with Britain opens after seven years of hard graft by 10,000 workers	After twice serving as prime minister, Jacques Chirac becomes president of France

an important referendum on regionalisation and suffered a fatal heart attack the following year.

POMPIDOU TO LE PEN

Georges Pompidou (1911–74), prime minister under de Gaulle, stepped onto the podium as president. Despite embarking on an ambitious modernisation programme, investing in aerospace, telecommunications and nuclear power, he failed to stave off inflation and social unrest following the global oil crisis of 1973.

Valéry Giscard d'Estaing (1926–) inherited a deteriorating economic climate and sharp divisions between the left and right upon assuming presidential power in 1974. Hampered by a lack of media nous and an arrogant demeanour that left him ill-equipped to marshal a consensus, d'Estaing proved unpopular. His friendship with emperor and accused child-eater Jean Bédel Bokassa of the Central African Republic did little to win him friends and in 1981 he was ousted by long-time head of the Parti Socialiste (PS; Socialist Party), François Mitterrand (1916–96). As the only surviving French president to remain in politics, the French media nicknamed d'Estaing *l'Ex* (the Ex).

Despite France's first socialist president instantly alienating the business community (the Paris stock market index fell by 30% on news of his victory) by setting out to nationalise 36 privately owned banks, industrial groups and other parts of the economy, Mitterrand did give France a new sparkle. The Minitel – a potent symbol of France's advanced technological savvy – was launched in 1980 and a clutch of *grands projets* (great works; p52) were embarked upon in the French capital. The death penalty was abolished, homosexuality was legalised, a 39-hour work week was instituted, annual holiday time was upped from four to five weeks and the right to retire at 60 was guaranteed.

Yet by 1986 the economy was weakening and in parliamentary elections that year the right-wing opposition, led by Jacques Chirac (Paris mayor since 1977), won a majority in the National Assembly. For the next two years Mitterrand worked with a prime minister and cabinet from the opposition, an unprecedented arrangement known as *cohabitation*. The extreme-right Front National (FN; National Front) meanwhile quietly gained ground by loudly blaming France's economic woes on immigration.

Presidential elections in 1995 ushered Jacques Chirac (an ailing Mitterrand did not run) into the Élysée Palace, the former mayor winning immediate popular acclaim for his direct words and actions in matters relating to the EU and the war raging in Bosnia. Whizz-kid foreign minister Alain Juppé was appointed prime minister and several women were placed in top cabinet positions. Unfortunately, Chirac's attempts to reform France's colossal public sector in order to meet the criteria of European Monetary Union (EMU) were met with the largest protests since 1968, and his decision to resume nuclear testing on the Polynesian island of Mururoa and a nearby atoll was the focus of worldwide outrage.

Always the maverick, Chirac called early parliamentary elections in 1997 – only for his party, the Rassemblement pour la République (RPR;

View pics of all the French presidents, take a virtual tour of the presidential pad and see the Arman-studded room where visiting heads of state are received in the online office of the French president at www .elysee.fr.

In *The Extreme Right in France*, JG Shields digs deep into France's political past to trace the rise of the far right and find out just how Le Pen managed to make such an impact in the 2002 presidential race (p40).

Follow the moves and motions of the National Assembly at www .assemblee-nat.fr.

1999	2002
A fire in the Alpine Mont Blanc tunnel kills 41 people	The French franc, first minted in 1360, is dumped as France adopts the euro (€) as its official currency

Rally for the Republic), to lose out to a coalition of socialists, communists and greens. Another period of *cohabitation* ensued, this time with Chirac on the other side.

Presidential elections in 2002 were a shocker. Not only did the first round of voting see left-wing Socialist Party leader Lionel Jospin eliminated. It also saw racist demagogue Jean-Marie Le Pen (1928–) of the FN scoop 17% of the national vote. In the fortnight preceding the subsequent run-off ballot, demonstrators took to the streets with cries of 'Vote for the crook, not the fascist' ('crook' referring to the various party financing scandals floating around Chirac). On the big day itself, left-wing voters – without a candidate of their own – hedged their bets with the 'lesser-of-two-evils' Chirac to give him 82% of votes. Chirac's landslide victory was echoed in parliamentary elections a month later when the president-backed coalition UMP (Union pour un Mouvement Populaire) won 354 of the 577 parliamentary seats, ending years of *cohabitation* and leaving a seatless Le Pen-led FN feeling very sorry for its xenophobic self. Subsequent claims of nepotism in response to Le Pen trying to pass the party leadership automatically to his daughter weakened the party further.

France is one of the five permanent members of the UN Security Council. It withdrew from NATO's joint military command in 1966 and has maintained an independent arsenal of nuclear weapons since 1960. Despite ritual denunciations of globalisation by politicians and pundits, its economy is heavily dependent on the global marketplace – its export market is Europe's fourth largest and its agricultural sector, the largest in the EU, thanks to generous subsidies awarded to the high-voting, sympathy-inducing agricultural sector.

Keep abreast with the policies, speeches and actions of the *premier ministre* (prime minister) at www.premier-ministre .gouv.fr.

2003	2004
A heatwave across Europe brings sizzling temperatures of 40°C to Paris in August, killing an estimated 14,800 (mainly elderly) people	The National Assembly says yes to a controversial bill banning overtly religious symbols such as the Islamic headscarf in state schools

The Culture

THE NATIONAL PSYCHE

There is nothing more maddening than the shop assistant who unabashedly chats to her mate while you wait, or the post-office clerk who greets you with complete lack of recognition. Dumb insolence some say.

France is a country whose people have attracted more stubborn myths and stereotypes than any other in Europe. Arrogant, rude, bolshy, unbelievably bureaucratic (which, incidentally, is true: you try getting a *carte grise* or car-ownership papers), sexist, chauvinistic, super chic and stylish are among the dozens of tags – true or otherwise – donned on the garlic-eating, beret-wearing French over the centuries. The French, by the way, don't wear berets these days.

Most people are extremely proud to be French and staunchly nationalistic to boot, a result of the country's republican stance that places nationality – rather than religion, for example – at the top of the self-identity list. This has created an overwhelmingly self-confident nation, both culturally and intellectually – a French superiority complex that manifests itself in a pompous refusal to speak any language other than French, according to many Anglophones.

Contrary to popular belief, a surprisingly large number of French speak English or another foreign language very well, are open to travel and are perfectly happy to use their language skills should the need arise. Of course, if monolingual English-speakers don't even attempt '*bonjour*', then there is no way proud French linguists will let on they speak great English with a great sexy accent. French men, by the way, deem an English gal's heavily accented French as downright sexy as many women deem a Frenchman speaking English.

On the subject of sex, not all French men ooze romance or light Gitanes all day. Nor are they as civilised about adultery as French cinema would have you believe. Despite the insouciance with which film-makers treat infidelity, surveys reveal that only 7% of those in a couple strayed in the previous 12 months. *Adieu 'French Lover'* bemoaned *Le Monde* in reporting this unsettling news when it first came out. Adultery, illegal in France until 1975, was actually grounds for automatic divorce until as late as mid-2004.

Suckers for tradition, the French are slow to embrace new ideas and technologies: it took the country an age to embrace the Internet, clinging on to their own Minitel system for dear life. Yet the French are also incredibly innovative (p33) – a dichotomy reflected in practically every facet of French life: they drink and smoke more than anyone else, yet live longer. They eat like kings, but are not fat, and so on…

By looking at history, Jean-Benoit Nadeau and Julie Barlow find solutions to puzzling dichotomies such as how the French can be so horribly bureaucratic, archaic and inventive all at the same time in *Sixty Million Frenchmen can't be Wrong: What Makes the French so French*.

Gals seeking French chic could try donning Debra Ollivier's *Entre Nous: A Woman's Guide to Finding Her Inner French Girl*, an imaginative little number that delves into the secret of inner (and outer) French beauty.

LIFESTYLE

Peek into the 5th-floor bourgeois apartment of Monsieur et Madame Tout le Monde and you'll see them dunking croissants in bowls of *café au lait* for

---

SACRE BLEU!

'*Ooooo la la*' they do say, but '*sacre bleu*' they don't. A favourite of writers seeking to add colour to a 'French' scene, this chestnut hasn't been heard in France since the Franco-Prussian War. '*Mon Dieu!*' is one of the gentler expressions of surprise. More popular expletives can't be printed but just sit in a café some afternoon and watch Parisians slip on dog-droppings.

breakfast, buying a baguette every day from the bakery (Monsieur nibbles the top off on his way home) and not recycling bar a few glass bottles. They go to the flicks once a month, work not a second more than 35 hours a week and have a 20-year-old daughter who is 'oh so BCBG, darling'.

Madame buys a clutch of hot-gossip weekly mags, Monsieur enjoys *boules* and August is the *only* month a summer holiday is considered. Dodging dog poo on pavements is a sport practised from birth, Minitel remains the best way to find telephone numbers and in shops everything goes on the *carte bleue*: this *is* the society after all that microchipped credit cards long before anyone else even dreamt of scrapping the swipe-and-sign system.

The couple have a landlord: with a longstanding tradition of renting rather than buying (38% of households rent the property they live in), home ownership is low. Rented accommodation in cities and towns tends to be high-rise apartment blocks.

Jospin's slashing of the standard French working week from 39 to 35 hours in 2000 (applicable to employers of more than 20 from 2002) created jobs, boosted domestic tourism and redefined peak hours as pleasure-thirsty workers headed out to the country on Thursday night (instead of Friday) and returned to urban life on Monday evening. While most French workers, given the choice, would plump for less income and more leisure time, a sizeable chunk of the population still toils 39 hours or more a week. (Since 2003 employers can enforce a 39-hour work week for a negotiable extra cost.)

Rich in play time (a 35-hour work week, five weeks annual holiday and every religious holiday in the book) they might be, but one out of three French can't afford to travel on holiday. Of those that do, only 10% holiday abroad. Women overall earn 12% less than men.

The family plays a vital role, 85% of French defining themselves in terms of their family (rather than profession or friends). Nonetheless, couples are marrying later (men at the age of 30, women at 28) and waiting longer to have children. More children are born out of wedlock (44% in 2002 compared to 11% in 1980) and divorce is on the rise (37% of marriages end in divorce). The traditional sense of duty towards the elderly is also diminishing claim critics who cite the shocking number of elderly Parisians who died during the 2003 heatwave without any relative coming forward to bury them.

Abortion is legal during the first 12 weeks of pregnancy, girls under 16 not needing parental consent providing they are accompanied by an adult of their choice: 30 abortions take place in France for every 100 live births.

Civil unions between two members of the same (or different) sex have been legal since 2000, although this falls short of legal marriages say gay lobbyists who want homosexual couples to be granted the same fiscal advantages and adoptive rights in marriage as heterosexuals. A petition calling for the legal recognition of same-sex marriages in early 2004 was topped off in June that year by the civil wedding of two gay men in Bègles town hall in

DID YOU KNOW?

One out of two French practise a sport regularly, walking being the vastly preferred activity. Five million smooth-movers cruise around on in-line skates.

Find out everything you need to know about buying or selling a home in France, setting up a business, marriage, inheritance and so on, under French law with Notaires de France (French Notaries) at www.notaires.fr (click on the minuscule Union Jack for English).

In *Le Divorce*, Diane Johnson explores expatriate society and French manners through the eyes of a young American woman in 1990s Paris, embroiled in her sister's divorce.

WHAT KIDS DO

French kids start *école maternelle* (nursery) at the age of three; move to *école primaire* (primary school) when they are six; and go to *lycée* (secondary school) from 11 to 16 or 18. The grand finale for academically minded pupils is the *baccalauréat*.

Anyone who's passed the *bac* bags a free place at one of France's 77 overcrowded universities – where 30% of students flunk the compulsory end-of-first-year exams and leave. One-third of French students plump for the University of Paris (p121), of which the historic Sorbonne is part; while the country's top 5% study at one of 140 elite *grandes écoles*.

FRENCH KISSING

Kissing is an integral part of French life. (The expression 'French kissing', as in tongues, doesn't exist in French incidentally.) That said, put a Parisian in Provence and there's no saying they will know when to stop.

Countrywide, people who know each other reasonably well, really well, a tad, barely at all, greet each other with a glancing peck on each cheek. Southern France aside (where everyone kisses everyone), two men rarely kiss (unless they are related or artists) but always shake hands. Boys and girls start kissing as soon as they're out of nappies, or so it seems.

Kissing French-style is not completely straightforward, 'how many' and 'which side first' potentially being problematic. In Paris it is definitely two: unless parties are related, *very* close friends or haven't seen each other in an age, anything more is deemed affected. That said, in certain trendy 20-something circles friends swap three or four cheek-skimming kisses, as do many young teenagers at school *parce qu'ils ont que ça à faire…*

Travel south and the *bisous* (kisses) multiply, three or four being the norm in Provence. The bits of France neighbouring Switzerland around Lake Geneva tend to be three-kiss country (in keeping with Swiss habits); and in the Loire Valley it is four. Corsicans, bizarrely, stick to two but kiss left cheek first – which can lead to locked lips given everyone else in France starts with the right cheek.

Bordeaux. The ground-breaking ceremony, conducted by local mayor and former Green party presidential candidate, Noël Mamère, was the first in France. The gay scene thrives in Paris, Marseille and Lyon (see p904).

POPULATION

France is not that densely populated – 107 people inhabit every square kilometre (compared to 235 in Germany, 240 in the UK and 116 in the EU), although a fat 20% wedge of the national population is packed into the greater metropolitan area of Paris.

The last 10 years have seen rural and suburban areas steadily gaining population; and Paris and the northeast (except Alsace) losing inhabitants to southern France, an increasingly buoyant part of the country where populations are predicted to rise by 30% over the next 30 years.

In keeping with European trends, France's overall population is ageing: by 2050 one in three will be 60 or more (compared to one in five in 2000) – a demographic phenomenon that will be less marked in urban areas like Paris, Lyon and the Rhône Alpes and on the Mediterranean coast where increasing work opportunities ensures a younger, more active population.

For much of the last two centuries, France has had a considerably lower rate of population growth than its neighbours. In the last decade, that trend has changed and the birth rate now equals 2.1 children per woman. By 2050 the population of mainland France is expected to notch up 64 million – five million more than in 2000.

See p45 for a snapshot of France's foreign population.

SPORT

Most French wouldn't be seen dead walking down the street in trainers and tracksuit bottoms. Contrary to appearances though, they do love sport. Shaved-leg cyclists toil up Mont Ventoux (p795) in good weather; anyone who is anyone flits off for the weekend to ski; and football fans fill stadiums during home matches.

France has achieved a strikingly high level in international judo, four-time world champion David Douillet being the star. Les 24 Heures du

A New Yorker transplanted to Paris with a wife and small child takes a wry look at French politics, habits and society in Adam Gopnick's recommended *Paris to the Moon*.

DID YOU KNOW?

French life expectancy is among the world's highest – 82.9 for women and 75.8 for men.

Mans and the F1 Grand Prix in Monte Carlo are the world's raciest dates in motor sports.

With the exception of mogul champion, *le boss des bosses* Edgar Gospiron, skiing bizarrely hasn't produced any stars since the 1968 Alpine sweep of Jean-Claude Killy. Chamonix snowboarder Karine Ruby (1978–) won the discipline's first Olympic gold medal in 1998 and holds more World Cup titles than any other boarder. On ice, Marina Anissina and Gwendal Peizerat scooped ice-dancing gold at Salt Lake City in 2002, and Brian Joubert finished second in the 2004 world figure-skating championships.

Paris will know in 2005 if its bid to host the 2012 Summer Olympics is successful. The French capital last hosted the gargantuan event in 1924.

Football

France's greatest sporting moment came at the 1998 World Cup, which the country hosted and won.

DID YOU KNOW?

Marseille-born Zinedane Zidane transferred from Juventus to Real Madrid in 2001 for US$64.45 million, making him the most expensive player in football history.

At club level, Marseille was the first French side in 1991 to win the European Champions League. In 1994 Paris–St-Germain won the European Cup Winners' Cup. Since the 1995 Bosman decision allowing European clubs to field as many European players as they wish, French football greats (including Zidane and Petit) have been lured to richer clubs in Italy, Britain, Spain and Germany. Other hotshots out of France include Arsenal's French manager Arsène Wenger and striker Thierry Henry.

France's home matches (friendlies and qualifiers for major championships) kick off at St-Denis' magnificent 80,000-capacity Stade de France (p183), built for the World Cup. Other noteworthy stadiums (there are 250-odd in all in France) include the Stade de Gerland (p482) in Lyon, home to national champions Olympique Lyonnais.

Read all about French rugby and keep tabs with the scores on the board at www.francerugby.fr (in French)

Rugby

Rugby league has a strong following in the south and southwest of France, favourite teams being Toulouse, Montauban and St-Godens. Rugby union is more popular still, as the enduring success of the powerful Paris–St-Germain club testifies.

DOS & DON'TS

Many visitors to France conclude it would be a great place if it weren't for the French. Adopt some simple dos and don'ts of French etiquette yourself and you could well find your relations with the French so vastly improved you actually start liking them.

- Say *'Bonjour, monsieur/madame/mademoiselle'* when you walk into a shop or café, and *'Merci, monsieur…au revoir'* when leaving. Use *'Monsieur'* for any male person who isn't a child; *'Madame'* for those you'd call 'Mrs' in English; and *'mademoiselle'* for unmarried women.

- Touching, fondling or picking up fruit, vegetables, flowers or a piece of clothing in shops attracts immediate killer stares from shop assistants. Ask if you want to look at something.

- Take a gift – flowers (not chrysanthemums, which are only brought to cemeteries) or wine for more informal gatherings – when invited to someone's home.

- Going 'Dutch' (splitting the bill) in restaurants is an uncivilised custom for many French. The person who invites generally pays, although close friends often share the cost.

- Never discuss money, particularly income, over dinner.

- Knock what your French textbook at school taught you on the head. These days *'s'il vous plaît'* – never *'garçon'* (meaning 'boy') – is the *only* way to summon a waiter in restaurants.

FRENCH BALLS

France's most traditional ball games are *pétanque* and the similar, though more formal, *boules*, which has a 70-page rule book. Both are played by village men in work clothes on a rough gravel or sandy pitch known as a *boulodrome*, scratched out wherever a bit of flat and shady ground can be found. World championships are held for both sports. In the Basque Country, the racquet game of *pelote* (p653) is the thing to do.

France's home games in the Tournoi des Six Nations (Six Nations Tournament) are held in March and April. The finals of the Championnat de France de Rugby take place in late May and early June.

Cycling

In July the world's most prestigious bicycle race, the **Tour de France**, brings together 189 of the world's top male cyclists (21 teams of nine) and 15 million spectators for a spectacular 3000-plus kilometre cycle around the country. The three-week route changes each year, but always labours through the Alps and Pyrenees and finishes on the Champs-Élysées in Paris. The publicity caravan preceding the cyclists showers roadside spectators with coffee samples, logo-emblazoned balloons, pens and other free junk-advertising gifts. Annual tour dates and routes are listed at www.letour.fr.

Drug scandals reduced the 1998 Tour de France to a 'tour of shame', less than 100 riders crossing the finishing line after several teams were disqualified for doping. Since then the race has cleaned up its act, although 2004 started badly with the withdrawal of the French team and banning of the Spanish, both on doping grounds. Brittany-born biking legend Bernard Hinault (1954–), nicknamed *le blaireau* (the badger), won the Tour de France five times before retiring in 1986.

France is the world's top track cycling nation and has a formidable reputation in mountain biking: Christian Taillefer holds the world speed record on a mountain bike, 212.39km/h, which he hit by flying down a snow-covered ski slope.

Tennis

The French Open, held in Paris's Roland Garros Stadium in late May and early June, is the second of the year's four Grand Slam tennis tournaments. Marseille-born Sébastien Grosjean (1978–) has been the highest-ranking French player on the men's circuit for the last few years, and WTA No 1 (September 2004) player Amélie Mauresmo is the French star on the women's circuit.

MULTICULTURALISM

Multicultural France has always drawn immigrants: 4.3 million from other parts of Europe arrived between 1850 and WWI and another three million came between the world wars. During the post-WWII economic-boom years, several million unskilled workers followed from North Africa and French-speaking sub-Saharan Africa. Large-scale immigration peaked in the early 1960s when, as the French colonial empire collapsed, French settlers returned to metropolitan France from Algeria, other parts of Africa and Indochina.

Immigrants today form 7.4% (4.3 million) of the population – a constant since 1975 when France implemented its first immigration law. The largest communities are Algerians (13%), Portuguese (13%), Moroccans (12%) and Italians (9%). Of this ethnic community, only one-third (36%)

Belt up with Les 24 Heures du Mans at www.lemans.org and Monte Carlo's F1 Grand Prix at www.acm.mc.

DID YOU KNOW?

French journalist and cyclist, Henri Desgrange, came up with the Tour de France in 1903 as a means of promoting his sports newspaper *L'Auto* (*L'Équipe* today). With the exception of two world war–induced intervals, it has been held every year since.

Make the Fédération Française de Tennis (French Tennis Federation) your first stop in court for everything to do with tennis in France, including the French Open website www.fft.fr in French).

has French citizenship, which is not conferred at birth but subject to various administrative requirements.

Racial tensions are fuelled by the extreme-right Front National (FN; National Front), whose leader Jean-Marie Le Pen makes no bones about his party's anti-foreigner stance. The politician outraged millions with his dismissal of the Holocaust as a 'mere detail of history' in the 1980s and his 'inequality of races' jargon in the late 1990s. Yet he got through to the second round of elections in the 2002 presidential race (p40), making a right-wing takeover of France a possibility. Though Paris may at times appear to be multiracial heaven, racism does exist here, and what may appear to be exotic to the outsider (an elderly Maghreb man selling salted nuts in the metro) is simply a tough struggle for survival for those who can't find employment. Racist acts of violence have not been uncommon in recent years, particularly in Paris' crowded suburbs. In the workplace, young people of non-French origin face widespread discrimination. How many black waiters do you see in central Paris cafés and restaurants?

The French republican code, while inclusive and nondiscriminatory on the one hand, does little to accommodate a multicultural society. This dichotomy exploded in a riot of demonstrations in 2004 when the Islamic headscarf (along with Jewish skullcaps, crucifixes and other religious symbols) was banned in French schools. The law, intended to place all schoolchildren on an equal footing in the classroom, was slammed by Muslims as intolerant and yet more proof that the French state is not prepared to integrate Muslims into French society.

Some 90% of France's Muslim community are noncitizens; many are illegal immigrants; and most live in depressing poverty-stricken *bidonvilles* (tinpot towns) surrounding major metropolitan centres.

DID YOU KNOW?

Both parents of 10% of children born in France are foreign; another 10% of French children have one foreign parent.

MEDIA

Public licence fees subsidise public broadcaster France Télévisions, which controls 40% of the market with its three TV channels – France 2, 3 and 5 (Arte after 7pm), see p893. Yet in the face of increasingly stiff competition from private broadcasters such as TF1 and M6, its future looks bleak.

Until 2003 cable TV operators could not transmit to more than eight million households each. With this restriction lifted, cable and satellite TV services are expected to grow 127% by 2007 to reach 15.9 million households. TV via broadband ADSL is the other big sell: France Télécom's video-driven MaLigne tv was launched in Lyon in 2003 and Paris the year after.

As in Britain, there is a strong distinction between broadcasting and print media. The press, like TV and radio broadcasters, are independent and free of censorship.

Find out about the public broadcaster behind France 2, 3 and 5 (Arte) with www.francetelevi sions.fr (in French) and its biggest private competitor at www.tf1.fr (in French).

RELIGION

Secular France maintains a rigid distinction between the church and state – to the horror of certain religious groups for whom the state ban on the wearing of religious symbols (above) in schools in 2004 was offensive and discriminative.

Some 55% of French identify themselves as Catholic, although no more than 10% attend church regularly. Another one million people are Protestant, concentrated in Alsace, the Jura, the Massif Central and along the Atlantic Coast.

Coexisting uneasily with this nominally Christian majority is France's five million-strong Muslim community. Most Muslims adhere to a moderate Islam, although the deportation (and subsequent return) in 2004 from Lyon of an Algerian iman in favour of stoning unfaithful wives – one

Listen to the voice of French Jews online at www.col.fr (in French).

of 27 radical Muslim prayer leaders to be deported since 2001 – renewed fears that Islamic fundamentalists are gaining ground. It also prompted calls from more moderate Muslims for the state to help train imans in a French-style Islam and build more mosques. Most of the 1500 or so imans in France are self-taught or have been educated in more radical climes. Almost 90% are employees of Algeria, Saudi Arabia or another Islamic country and work in mosques funded by these countries.

Over half of France's 600,000-strong Jewish population (Europe's largest) lives in and around Paris. Marseille has the next-largest Jewish community. French Jews, the first in Europe to achieve emancipation, have been represented by the Paris-based umbrella organisation the Consistoire since 1808. The number of anti-Semitic incidents is rising.

DID YOU KNOW?

French Muslims were only given a national voice in 2003 with the election of the French Muslim Council (FCMC), an umbrella organisation of 18 representatives from Muslim associations and mosques in France.

WOMEN IN FRANCE

Women were given the right to vote in 1945 by de Gaulle's short-lived post-war government, but until 1964 a woman needed her husband's permission to open a bank account or get a passport. Younger French women especially are quite outspoken and emancipated, but self-confidence has yet to translate into equality in the workplace, where women are often kept out of senior and management positions. The problem of sexual harassment *(harcélement sexuel)* in the workplace is finally beginning to be addressed with a new law imposing financial penalties on the offender.

A great achievement in the last decade has been *Parité*, the law requiring political parties to fill 50% of their slates in all elections with female candidates.

Feminism in France from 1968 to the mid-1980s is charted by Claire Duchen in *Feminism in France*.

ARTS
Literature
COURTLY LOVE TO SYMBOLISM

Lyric poems of courtly love composed by troubadours dominated medieval French literature, while the *roman* (literally 'the romance') drew on old Celtic tales like King Arthur, the search for the Holy Grail and so on. With the *Roman de la Rose*, a 22,000-line poem by Guillaume de Lorris and Jean de Meung, the allegorical figures of Pleasure and Riches, Shame and Fear popped on the scene.

La Pléiade, Rabelais and Montaigne made French Renaissance literature great: La Pléiade was a group of lyrical poets active in the 1550s and 1560s, of whom the best known is Pierre de Ronsard. The highly exuberant narrative of Loire Valley-born François Rabelais (1494–1553) blends coarse humour with encyclopaedic erudition in a vast panorama that includes every kind of person, occupation and jargon existing in mid-16th-century France. Michel de Montaigne (1533–92) meanwhile wrote essays on everything from cannibals, war horses and drunkenness to the uncanny resemblance of children to their fathers.

'*Le grand siècle*' ushered in the great French classical writers with their lofty odes to tragedy. François de Malherbe (1555–1628) brought a new rigour to the treatment of rhythm in poetry; and Parisian Marie de La Fayette (1634–93) penned the first major French novel, *La Princesse de Clèves* (1678).

The chateau on the French–Swiss border in the Jura where Voltaire (1694–1778) lived from 1759 can be visited (p545). His philosophical work, together with that of Swiss-born philosopher Jean-Jacques Rousseau, dominated the 18th century. A century on, Besançon (p536) gave birth to Victor Hugo – the key figure of French Romanticism. The breadth of interest and technical innovations exhibited in his poems

DID YOU KNOW?

On Victor Hugo's 80th birthday, the street on which he lived in Paris was renamed avenue Victor Hugo. After he died his coffin was laid overnight beneath the Arc de Triomphe for an all-night vigil.

PRIZES FOR THE LITERARY

Slammed as conservative (greats like Flaubert, Molière and Balzac weren't allowed in) and chauvinistic (just three of its current 38 members are women) it might be, but there's no disputing one fact: the Paris-based Académie Française (French Academy), founded in 1635 by Cardinal Richelieu to discuss rhetoric and literary criticism, is one of the country's grandest and oldest institutions. Each year it awards 70 or so different literary prizes to the brightest and best writers in French.

Literary prizes awarded outside the academy include the Prix Fémina for works by women writers; the Prix Goncourt for imaginative prose; the Prix Médicis for writers 'whose fame does not match their talent'; and the Prix Interallié, won in 2003 by Frederic Beigbeder's *Windows on the World*, a September 11-inspired novel set in New York in 2002 and named after the World Trade Centre's 107th-floor restaurant.

France honours its literary talent with almost 200 different prizes and awards in all. For a complete list of prizes and authors – present and past – see www.prix-litteraires.net.

---

and novels – *Les Misérables* and *Notre Dame de Paris* (The Hunchback of Notre Dame) among them – was phenomenal.

In 1857 two literary landmarks were published: *Madame Bovary* by Gustave Flaubert (1821–80) and Charles Baudelaire's (1821–67) collection of poems, *Les Fleurs du Mal* (The Flowers of Evil). Émile Zola (1840–1902) meanwhile strove to convert novel-writing from an art to a science in his powerful series, *Les Rougon-Macquart*.

The expression of mind states rather than the detailing of day-to-day reality was the aim of the symbolists, Paul Verlaine (1844–96) and Stéphane Mallarmé (1842–98). Verlaine's poems – alongside those of Arthur Rimbaud (1854–91), with whom Verlaine shared a tempestuous homosexual relationship – are seen as French literature's first modern poems.

MODERN LITERATURE

The world's longest novel – a seven-volume 9,609,000-character giant by Marcel Proust (1871–1922) – dominated the early 20th century: *À la Recherche du Temps Perdu* (Remembrance of Things Past) explores in evocative detail the true meaning of past experience recovered from the unconscious by 'involuntary memory'.

Surrealism proved a vital force until WWII, André Breton (1896–1966) capturing its spirit – a fascination with dreams, divination and all manifestations of 'the marvellous' – in his autobiographical narratives. In Paris the bohemian Colette (1873–1954) captivated and shocked with her titillating novels detailing the amorous exploits of heroines such as schoolgirl Claudine. Of her many Parisian addresses, it is the apartment where she died in the Palais Royal (p115) that is the most illustrious. Otherwise, there's a small museum (p433) in the Burgundian village where she was born.

After WWII, existentialism developed around the lively debates of Jean-Paul Sartre (1905–80), Simone de Beauvoir (1908–86) and Albert Camus (1913–60) in Paris' Left-Bank cafés of St-Germain des Prés. View the graves of Sartre and Beauvoir in the Cimetière du Montparnasse (p123).

The 1950s' *nouveau roman* saw experimental young writers seek new ways of organising narratives, Nathalie Sarraute slashing identifiable characters and plot in *Les Fruits d'Or* (The Golden Fruits). *Histoire d'O* (Story of O), an erotic sadomasochistic novel written by Dominique Aury under a pseudonym in 1954, meanwhile sold more copies than any other contemporary French novel outside France. In the 1960s it

A Penguin Classic worth devoting several days of reading time is *Gargantua and Pantagruel* by François Rabelais (translated by JM Cohen), a farcical epic about the adventures of the giant Gargantua and his son Pantagruel.

Les Poètes du 19ème Siècle (Poets of the 19th Century) is an excellent online resource (in French) for anyone interested in reading in-depth about Verlaine, Baudelaire, Rimbaud et al. Go to www.poetes.com.

was the forbiddingly experimental novels of Philippe Sollers (1936–) that raised eyebrows.

Contemporary authors include Françoise Sagan, Pascal Quignard, Jean Auel, Emmanuel Carrère and Stéphane Bourguignon. Also popular are Frédéric Dard (alias San Antonio), Léo Malet and Daniel Pennac, widely read for his witty crime fiction such as *Au Bonheur des Ogres* (The Scapegoat) and *La Fée Carabine* (The Fairy Gunmother).

Cinema & TV
CINEMA
Watching French classics in the Lyonnaise factory (p475) where those cinematographic pioneers, the Lumière brothers, shot the world's first-ever motion picture in March 1895, is a must for cinema buffs.

French film flourished in the 1920s, Abel Gance (1889–1981) being king of the decade with his powerful antiwar blockbuster *J'Accuse* (I Accuse; 1918) – all the more impressive for its location filming on actual WWI battlefields (p223). The switch to sound ushered in René Clair (1898–1981) and his world of fantasy and satirical surrealism: his exuberant *À Nous La Liberté* (For Us, Liberty; 1931) clearly influenced Charlie Chaplin's famous assembly-line scene in *Modern Times*.

WWI was inspired the 1930s classic, *La Grande Illusion* (The Great Illusion; 1937), a devastating portrayal of the folly of WWI based on the trench warfare experience of director Jean Renoir (1894–1979). Indeed, portraits of ordinary people and their lives dominated film until the 1950s when realism was eschewed by surrealist Jean Cocteau (1889–1963) in two masterpieces of cinematic fantasy: *La Belle et la Bête* (Beauty and the Beast; 1945) and *Orphée* (Orpheus; 1950) are unravelled in Menton's Musée Jean Cocteau (p853) on the Côte d'Azur.

Sapped of talent and money after WWII, France's film industry begged new energy by the 1950s. And so the *nouvelle vague* (new wave) burst forth. With small budgets and no extravagant sets or big-name stars, film-makers produced uniquely personal films using real-life subject matter: Claude Chabrol (1930–) explored poverty and alcoholism in a French village in *Le Beau Serge* (Bitter Reunion; 1958); Alain Resnais (1922–) portrayed the problems of time and memory in his *Hiroshima, Mon Amour* (1959); and François Truffaut (1932–84) dealt with love in its many permutations.

By the 1970s the new wave had lost its experimental edge, handing over the limelight to lesser known directors like Eric Rohmer (1920–), who made beautiful but uneventful films in which the characters endlessly analyse their feelings. Two 1960s movies ensured France's invincibility as land of romance: Claude Lelouch's *Un Homme et une Femme* (A Man and a Woman; 1966), a beautifully photographed love story set in Deauville (p254) and

The vast labour-intensive series of novels, known under the general title of *La Comédie Humaine*, by Tours-born Honoré de Balzac is nothing short of a social history of France.

André Gide found his voice in the celebration of homosexual sensuality and left-wing politics, exposing the hypocrisy and self-deception with which people try to avoid sincerity in his novel *Les Faux-Monnayeurs* (The Counterfeiters).

CÉSARS
The little golden statues handed to actors at the Césars – the French Oscars – are named after the man who made them.

One of the most influential sculptors to emerge after WWII, Marseille-born César Baldaccini (1921–98) used scrap metal and iron to sculpt larger-than-life insects and animals. Proof of the pudding stands on his grave in Paris' Cimetière du Montparnasse (p123).

César was the first to use motorised vehicles as an artistic medium, crushing no less than 23 cars in the name of art between 1960 and 1989; a couple are in Nice's Musée d'Art Moderne et d'Art Contemporain (p822).

Jacques Demy's *Les Parapluies de Cherbourg* (The Umbrellas of Cherbourg; 1964), a wise and bittersweet love story likewise filmed in Normandy.

Existentialist Camus stresses the importance of the writer's political engagement in his work *L'Étranger* (The Outsider), which scooped him the Nobel Prize for Literature in 1957.

Big-name stars, slick production values and a strong sense of nostalgia were the dominant motifs in the 1980s as generous state subsidies to film-makers switched to costume dramas, comedies and 'heritage movies' in the face of growing competition from American thrillers and action flicks. Claude Berri's depiction of prewar Provence in *Jean de Florette* (1986), Jean-Paul Rappeneau's *Cyrano de Bergerac* (1990) and *Bon Voyage* (2003) set in 1940s Paris, and *Astérix et Obélix: Mission Cléopâtre* (2001) – all starring France's best known (and biggest-nosed) actor Gérard Depardieu – found huge audiences in France and abroad.

In 2001 the delightfully uncontroversial *Le Fabuleux Destin de Amélie Poulain* (Amélie; 2001), a feel-good story of a winsome Parisian do-gooder directed by Jean-Pierre Jeunet of *Delicatessen* (1991) fame, proved an instant hit – everywhere. French film has enjoyed a massive renaissance ever since, French-film cinema-goers outside of France rising from 17 million in 2000 to a current 37.5 million a year.

DID YOU KNOW?

Colette was the first woman in France to be honoured with a state funeral.

Subjects broached by box-office smash hits are wide and varied, among them Jacques Perrin's beautifully photographed animal film *Le Peuple Migrateur* (Winged Migration; 2001) about bird migration; the big-name (Omar Sharif and Isabelle Adjani) *Monsieur Ibrahim et les Fleurs du Coran* (Mr Ibrahim and the Flowers of Coran; 2003) about an Arab grocer living on rue Bleue; and the giggle-guaranteed, Marseille comedy *Taxi 3* (2003).

A HISTORY OF FRENCH CINEMA IN 10 FILMS

Grab a bottle of Burgundy, glue yourself to the screen and take a whirlwind tour through French cinematic history (all available on video or DVD) with:

- *La Règle du Jeu* (The Rules of the Game; 1939) Shunned by the public and censored, Jean Renoir's story of a 1930s bourgeoisie hunting party in the Loire Valley's soggy Sologne (p396) is a dark satirical masterpiece.

- *Les Enfants du Paradis* (Children of Paradise; 1945) Made during the Nazi occupation of France, Marcel Carné celebrates the vitality and theatricality of a Paris without Nazis.

- *Et Dieu Créa la Femme* (And God Created Woman; 1956) Roger Vadim's tale of the amorality of modern youth set in St-Tropez made a star out of Brigitte Bardot.

- *Les Quatre Cents Coups* (The 400 Blows; 1959) Partly based on the rebellious adolescence of the best loved of new-wave directors François Truffaut.

- *Les Vacances de M Hulôt* (Mr Hulôt's Holiday; 1953) and *Mon Oncle* (My Uncle; 1958) Two films starring the charming, bumbling figure of Monsieur Hulot and his struggles to adapt to the modern age by non-new-wave 1950s director Jacques Tati.

- *Diva* (1981) & *37°2 le Matin* (Betty Blue; 1986) Two visually compelling films by Jean-Jacques Beineix. *Diva* stars French icon Richard Bohringer.

- *Shoah* (1985) Claude Lanzmann's 9½-hour-long B&W documentary – interviews with Holocaust survivors worldwide – is disturbing. It took 11 years to make.

- *Indochine* (Indochina; 1993) An epic love story set in 1930s French Indochina with Catherine Deneuve – timeless beauty et al – as a French plantation owner.

- *Subway* (1985), *Le Grand Bleu* (The Big Blue; 1988), *Nikita* (1990) and *Jeanne d'Arc* (Joan of Arc; 1999) Take your pick from these box-office hits directed by Luc Besson.

- *Code Inconnu* (Code Unknown; 2001) Intellectual art-house film starring Oscar-winning French actress Juliette Binoche as an actress in Paris.

An increasing number of French film directors are turning to Hollywood to make big commercial productions and also forsaking their mother tongue to reach wider audiences. French films made in English include Louis Leterrier's *The Transporter* (2002) with a script written by Parisian film director Luc Besson; Michel Gondry's *Eternal Sunshine of the Spotless Mind* (2004) starring Kate Winslet and Jim Carrey; and Jean-Jacques Annaud's *Two Brothers* (2004), about two tiger cubs separated at birth.

The Palme d'Or, awarded each year at Cannes (p836), is the world's most coveted film prize. The French film industry honours its film-makers, actors and so on with Césars (p49).

TV

Most French know you don't phone your friends at 8pm, so sacred is *Le Journal*, the evening news slots on TF1 and France 2. Many turn on the box at 7.55pm to enjoy a five-minute satirical summary of world events with the witty Spitting Image-style *Les Guignols de l'Info*. So revered are the sharp-tongued puppets that Canal Plus repeats the entire week's episodes on Sunday around 1pm.

La télé-realité (reality TV) sees TF1 and M6 vying for prime-time viewers. Not without controversy, reality TV is barred from the public channels, while *Loft Story* – the first such show – outraged viewers when it was aired in 2001. Such was the furore that the Conseil Supérieur de l'Audiovisuel (CSA; www.csa.fr) limited the time cameras in the loft could film. Contestants needed time and a space away from the public eye, the French broadcasting authority ruled.

Jumel Debouzze (1976–; www.jamel.fr) is French TV's funniest man, a feat all the more impressive given the mischievous comic's upbringing as one of five children in an immigrant Moroccan family in a Parisian suburb.

Music

There's more to it than accordions and Edith Piaf.

French baroque music influenced European musical output enormously in the 17th and 18th centuries, while French musical luminaries – Charles Gounod (1818–93), César Franck (1822–90) and Carmen-creator Georges Bizet (1838–75), among them – were a dime a dozen in the 19th century. Modern orchestration was founded by Hector Berlioz (1803–69), the greatest figure in the French Romantic movement, born near Grenoble (p521), who demanded gargantuan forces: his ideal orchestra included 240 stringed instruments, 30 grand pianos and 30 harps.

Claude Debussy (1862–1918) revolutionised classical music with his *Prélude à l'Après-Midi d'un Faune* (Prelude to the Afternoon of a Fawn), creating a light, almost Asian musical impressionism; while impressionist comrade Maurice Ravel (1875–1937) peppered his work, including *Boléro*, with sensuousness and tonal colour. Contemporary composer Olivier Messiaen (1908–92) combined modern, almost mystical music with natural sounds such as birdsong. His student Pierre Boulez (1925–) works with computer-generated sound.

Jazz hit 1920s Paris in the banana-clad form of Josephine Baker, a cabaret dancer from the USA (the 15th-century chateau in the Dordogne where the African-American lived after the war can be visited; p597). Post-WWII ushered in a much-appreciated bunch of musicians – Sidney Bechet, Kenny Clarke, Bud Powell and Dexter Gordon, among them. In 1934 a chance meeting between Parisian jazz guitarist Stéphane Grappelli and three-fingered Roma guitarist Django Reinhardt in a Montparnasse

The unofficial André Bazin website features reams of colourful insight into the *nouvelle vague* www.unofficialbazini antrib.com.

TV news, views, the latest in reality TV, what's on and loads more about French TV is online (in French) at www .toutelatele.com.

DID YOU KNOW?

By law the lyrics of two out of five songs played on French radio must be French. One in five has to be that of a newcomer.

nightclub led to the formation of the Hot Club of France quintet. Claude Luter and his Dixieland Band was the hot sound of the 1950s.

The *chanson française,* a tradition dating from the troubadours of the Middle Ages, was eclipsed by the music halls and burlesque of the early 20th century, but revived in the 1930s by Piaf and Charles Trenet. In the 1950s the Left Bank cabarets nurtured *chansonniers* (cabaret singers) such as Léo Ferré, Georges Brassens, Claude Nougaro, Jacques Brel and Serge Gainsbourg.

French pop music has evolved massively since the 1960s *yéyé* (imitative rock) days of Johnny Halliday. Particularly strong is world music, from Algerian raï and other North African music (artists include Cheb Khaled, Natacha Atlas, Jamel, Cheb Mami, Racid Taha) to Senegalese *mbalax* (Youssou N'Dour), West Indian *zouk* (Kassav, Zouk Machine). One musician who combines many of these elements to stunning effect is Manu Chao (www.manuchao.net), the Paris-born son of Spanish parents whose albums are bestsellers worldwide.

Another hot musical export is Parisian electro-dance duo, Daft Punk, whose debut album *Homework* (1997) fused disco, house, funk and techno. *Discovery* (2001) adopts a more eclectic approach. Electronica duo, Air, around since the mid-1990s, remains sensational with its third album *Talkie Walkie* (2004). French rap was spearheaded in the 1990s by Senegal-born Paris-reared rapper MC Solaar.

Immigrant life in the French *banlieue* (suburbs) finds expression in the hip-hop lyrics of countless French artists, among them Marseille's hugely successful IAM; Brittany's Manau trio that fuses hip-hop with traditional Celtic sounds; and the Paris-based Triptik trio from Nantes who released its third album *TR-303* in 2003. Hard-core rappers include five-piece rap band KDD from Toulouse and Paris' Suprême NTM (NTM being an abbreviation for a French expression far too offensive to include here).

The worldly-wide travels of Will – misogynist American journalist, woman seducer and high-profile intellectual in Paris – form the basis of Philippe Sollers' novel *Women* (Femmes). Wrapped around the storyline are philosophical reflections on a variety of subjects, including the art of the modern novel and women.

Architecture
PREHISTORIC TO ART NOUVEAU

From the prehistoric megaliths around Carnac (p311) to Vauban's 33 star-shaped citadels (p30, p205, p382 and p537) built to defend France's 17th-century frontiers, French architecture has always been of *grand-projet* proportions.

For anyone who reads French, aVoir-aLire.com: l'œil culturel (www.avoir-alire.com) is an essential tool for keeping tabs of the latest literature, music, comic strips and films to be released.

Southern France is the place to find France's Gallo-Roman legacy: the Pont du Gard (p738), amphitheatres in Nîmes (p733) and Arles (p802), the theatre at Orange (p792) and Nîmes' Maison Carrée (p733).

Several centuries later, architects adopted architectural elements from Gallo-Roman buildings to create *roman* (Romanesque) masterpieces such as Toulouse's Basilica St-Sernin (p697), Poitier's Église Notre Dame la Grande (p618) and Caen's two famous Romanesque abbeys (p258). Eleventh- and 12th-century Romanesque buildings have round arches, heavy walls whose few windows let in very little light, and a lack of ornamentation bordering on the austere.

Northern France's extraordinary wealth in the 12th century lured the finest architects, engineers and artisans who created impressive Gothic structures with ribbed vaults carved with great precision, pointed arches, slender verticals, chapels along the nave and chancel, refined decoration and stained-glass windows. Avignon's pontifical palace (p786) is Gothic architecture on a gargantuan scale. With the discovery of flying buttresses around 1230, Gothic masterpieces such as the seminal cathedral at Chartres (p196) and its successors at Reims (p327), Amiens (p227) and Strasbourg (p349) appeared.

By the 15th century architects had shelved size for ornamentation, conceiving the beautifully lacy Flamboyant Gothic. For an example of such decorative overkill, look at the spire of Strasbourg cathedral. To trace the shift from late Gothic to Renaissance, travel along the Loire Valley: Château de Chambord (p401) illustrates the mix of classical components and decorative motifs typical to early Renaissance architecture. In the mid-16th century, François I had Italian architects design Fontainebleau (p189).

In 1635 early-baroque architect François Mansart (1598–1666) designed the classical wing of Château de Blois (p397), while his younger rival, Louis Le Vau (1612–70), started work on Louis XIV's palace at Versailles (p187).

A quest for order, reason and serenity through the adoption of the forms and conventions of Graeco-Roman antiquity defined neoclassical architecture from 1740 until well into the 19th century. Nancy's place Stanislas (p372) is France's loveliest neoclassical square.

Under Napoleon, many of Paris's best-known sights – the Arc de Triomphe (p127), La Madeleine (p128), the Arc du Carrousel at the Louvre (p113) and the Assemblée Nationale building – were designed.

Art Nouveau (1850–1910) combined iron, brick, glass and ceramics in ways never before seen. See for yourself in Paris with Hector Guimard's noodle-like metro entrances; the fine Art Nouveau interiors in the Musée d'Orsay (p124); and the glass roof over the Grand Palais (p127).

CONTEMPORARY

Chapelle de Notre-Dame du Haut in the Jura (p542) and Couvent Ste-Marie de la Tourette near Lyon (p485) are architectural icons of the 20th century. Designed in the 1950s by France's most celebrated architect, Le Corbusier (1887–1965), the structures rewrote the architectural stylebook with their sweeping lines and functionalised forms perfectly adapted to fit the human form.

French political leaders have long sought to immortalise themselves through the erection of big huge public edifices, otherwise called *grands projects*. Georges Pompidou commissioned the now much-revered Centre Beaubourg (Centre Pompidou; p116) in Paris in 1977; Giscard d'Estaing

The French Civil Service website contains thousands of invaluable hot links, covering everything from child benefit and family allowance in France to pension information, museum listings, art and architectural sites, cultural services, NGOs and so on www .service-public.fr

LOOK TO THE FUTURE

A hat trick of magnificent architectural projects are in the making in the capital – with treasures inside as fabulous as the design outside. Target date for all three is 2006.

The Musée du Quai Branly, named after the riverside quay on which it stands, will showcase 300,000 objects dedicated to arts and civilisations of Africa, Asia, Oceania and the Americas. Designed by French architect Jean Nouvel (www.jeannouvel.fr) in his Paris *atelier* (workshop), the state-of-the-art museum embraces 700,000 sq metres of exhibition space and resembles a huge wooden bridge. Glass walls and display cases place objects against a natural backdrop of foliage. Web cams (www.quaibranly.fr) are rigged up on-site.

West along the Seine in Boulogne-Billancourt, what was a Renault car factory is being transformed by Japanese architect Tadao Ando into an art gallery of proportions sufficiently gigantic to house the contemporary art collection of French multibillionaire François Pinault of Gucci, Yves Saint Laurent, Samsonite and Christie's auction-house fame (he owns the lot). The futuristic building, trapezoid in shape, will appear as a 'spaceship suspended over the Seine'. It is anticipated to be the next big thing after London's Tate Modern.

The 120m-tall metallic tower planned for Le Havre's rejuvenated 19th-century docks on the Frissard peninsula will be impossible to miss. Another Jean Nouvel creation, the striking tower – complete with sky-high exhibition and conference rooms – tops a 12,000-sq-metre aquatic centre with a design inspired by Roman baths.

was instrumental in transforming a derelict train station into the glorious Musée d'Orsay (p124); while François Mitterrand commissioned the capital's best-known contemporary architectural landmarks, including IM Pei's glass pyramid (p114) at the Louvre; the Opéra-Bastille (p119); the Grande Arche (p180) in the skyscraper district of La Défense; Jean Nouvel's Institut du Monde Arabe; and the controversial home of the Bibliothèque Nationale (p129). Paris' 80,000-capacity Stade de France (p183), built for the 1998 football World Cup, has rarely been more than half-full since.

In the provinces, notable buildings include Strasbourg's European Parliament (p350), Dutch architect Rem Koolhaas' Euralille and Jean Nouvel's glass-and-steel Vesunna Musée Gallo-Romain in Perigueux (p586). Otherwise, there's a 1920s Art Deco swimming pool-turned-art museum to see in Lille (p205); an 11th-century abbey-turned-monumental sculpture gallery in Angers (p420); and – come 2007 – a contemporary art museum in Metz (p379) that will blow your mind away.

Painting

French painting began with Nicolas Poussin (1594–1665) according to Voltaire, who clearly rated the classical mythological and biblical scenes bathed in golden light that the baroque painter created. Forward-wind a couple of centuries and modern still life pops onto the scene with the work of Jean-Baptiste Chardin (1699–1779), the first to see still life as an essay in composition rather than a show of skill in reproduction. A century later, neoclassical artist Jacques Louis David (1748–1825) wooed the public (not to mention Napoleon) with his vast portraits; several are in the Louvre.

While Romantics like Eugène Delacroix (buried in Paris' Cimetière du Père Lachaise; p129) revamped the subject picture, the Barbizon School effected a parallel transformation of landscape painting. Barbizons included landscape artist Camille Corot (1796–1875) and Jean-François Millet (1814–75). The son of a peasant farmer from Normandy, Millet took many of his subjects from peasant life and reproductions of his L'Angélus (The Angelus; 1857) – the best-known French painting after the Mona Lisa – are strung above mantelpieces all over rural France. The original hangs in Paris' Musée d'Orsay (p124).

The latter is also the place to see the Realists, among them Édouard Manet (1832–83) who zoomed in on Parisian middle-class life and Gustave Courbet (1819–77) who depicted the drudgery of manual labour and difficult lives of the working class. The artist himself came from a privileged family; see where he lived at the Musée Courbet (p540), his family home in the Jura.

It was in a flower-filled garden in a Normandy village (p243) that Claude Monet (1840–1926) expounded impressionism, a term of derision taken from the title of his experimental painting Impression: Soleil Levant (Impression: Sunrise; 1874). A trip to the Musée d'Orsay unveils a rash of other members of the school – Boudin, Sisley, Pissarro, Renoir, Degas and so on.

BMPT

The anti-Establishment BMPT took its acronymic name from its members (Daniel **B**uren, Swiss-born Olivier **M**osset, Parisian Michel **P**armentier and Italian artist Niele **T**oroni). Founded in France in the mid-1960s, the four-man band painted commune-style, rendering any work they produced the property of the group rather than the individual – a political statement on art ownership that, ironically, backfired given issues of ownership lingered long after the rebels split.

An arthritis-crippled Renoir painted out his last impressionist days in a villa (p833) on the Côte d'Azur. With a warmth and astonishing intensity of light hard to equal, the French Riviera inspired dozens of artists post-Renoir: Paul Cézanne (1839–1906) is particularly celebrated for his postimpressionist still lifes and landscapes done in Aix-en-Provence where he was born and worked (visit his studio; p779); Paul Gauguin (1848–1903) worked in Arles; while Dutch artist Vincent van Gogh (1853–90) painted Arles and St-Rémy de Provence (p803). In St-Tropez pointillism took off: Georges Seurat (1859–91) was the first to apply paint in small dots or uniform brush strokes of unmixed colour, producing fine mosaics of warm and cool tones, but it was his pupil Paul Signac (1863–1935) who is best known for his pointillist works; see them in St-Tropez's Musée de l'Annonciade (p844).

Twentieth-century French painting is characterised by a bewildering diversity of styles, including Fauvism and cubism. Henri Matisse (1869–1954) was the man behind the former (a Fauvist trail around Collioure takes you past scenes he captured on canvas in Roussillon; p758) and Spanish prodigy Pablo Picasso (1881–1973), the latter. Both chose southern France to set up studio, Matisse living in Nice (visit the Musée Matisse; p823) and Picasso opting for a 12th-century chateau (now the Musée Picasso; p832) in Antibes. Cubism, as developed by Picasso and Georges Braque (1882–1963) deconstructed the subject into a system of intersecting planes and presented various aspects of it simultaneously.

No piece of French art better captures Dada's rebellious spirit than Marcel Duchamp's *Mona Lisa* complete with moustache and goatee. In 1922 German Dadaist Max Ernst moved to Paris and worked on surrealism, a Dada offshoot that drew on the theories of Freud to reunite the conscious and unconscious realms and permeate daily life with fantasies and dreams.

With the close of WWII, Paris' role as artistic world capital ended, leaving critics wondering ever since where all the artists have gone. The focus shifted back to southern France in the 1960s with new realists like Arman (1928–) and Yves Klein (1928–62), both from Nice and well represented in contemporary art museums in Paris (p116), Lyon (p475), St-Étienne (p485), Nice (p822), Lille (p203) and Strasbourg (p350).

In 1960 Klein famously produced *Anthropométrie de l'Époque Bleue,* a series of blue imprints made by naked women (covered from head to toe in blue paint) rolling around on a white canvas – in front of an orchestra of violins and an audience in evening dress. A decade on the supports-surfaces movement deconstructed the concept of a painting, transforming one of its structural components (such as the frame or canvas) into a work of art instead.

Artists in the 1990s threw in the towel as far as the grandeur of early French art was concerned, looking to the minutiae of everyday urban life to express social and political angst and turning to mediums other than paint to let rip. Conceptual artist Daniel Buren (1938–) reduced his painting to a signature series of vertical 8.7cm-wide stripes that he applies to every surface imaginable – white marble columns in the courtyard of Paris's Palais Royal (p115) included. The painter (who in 1967, as part of the Radical *groupe BMPT,* signed a manifesto declaring he was not a painter) was the *enfant terrible* of French art in the 1980s. Partner-in-crime Michel Parmentier (1938–2000) insisted on monochrome painting for a while – blue in 1966, grey in 1967 and red in 1968.

Current trends are best expressed by the Palais de Tokyo, a contemporary art space in Paris that opens noon to midnight or thereabouts; encourages art visitors to feel, touch, talk and interact; and bends over backwards to turn every expectation of painting and art on its head.

DID YOU KNOW?

Fauvism took its name from the slur of a critic who compared the exhibitors at the 1906 autumn salon in Paris with *fauves* (wildcats) because of their radical use of intensely bright colours.

Gem-up with what's happening tomorrow in the contemporary art scene in Paris with www.paris -art.com (in French).

Environment

THE LAND

Hexagon-shaped France, the largest country in Europe after Russia and Ukraine, is hugged by water or mountains along every side except its northeastern boundary – a relatively flat frontier abutting Germany, Luxembourg and Belgium.

Its 3200km-long coastline embraces everything from white chalk cliffs (Normandy) and treacherous promontories (Brittany) to fine-sand (Atlantic Coast) and pebble (Mediterranean Coast) beaches. Five major river systems criss-cross the country: the Garonne (which includes the Tarn, Lot and Dordogne) empties into the Atlantic; the Rhône links Lake Geneva and the Alps with the Mediterranean; Paris is licked by the Seine, which snakes through the city en route from Burgundy to the English Channel; while tributaries of the North Sea-bound Rhine drain much of the area north and east of the capital. Then there's France's longest river, the chateau-studded Loire, which meanders from the Massif Central to the Atlantic.

Mountains run riot. Europe's highest peak, Mont Blanc (4807m), spectacularly tops the French Alps that stagger along France's eastern border from Lake Geneva to the Côte d'Azur. North of Lake Geneva the gentle limestone Jura Range runs along the Swiss frontier to reach heights of around 1700m, while the rugged Pyrenees lace France's entire 450km-long border with Spain and peak at 3404m.

Stunning as they are, the Alps, Jura and Pyrenees are mere babies compared to France's ancient massifs, formed 225 to 345 million years ago. The Massif Central covers one-sixth (91,000 sq km) of the country and is renowned for its chain of extinct volcanoes: Puy de Dôme (1465m) last erupted in 5760 BC, the volcanic history and geology of which is explained in the Vulcania centre near Clermont-Ferrand (p553). Other golden oldies, worn down by time, include the forested upland of the Vosges in northeast France; the Ardennes on Champagne's northern edge; and Brittany and Normandy's backbone, the Massif Armoricain.

WILDLIFE

France is blessed with a rich variety of flora and fauna, although few habitats have escaped human impact: urbanisation, pollution, intensive agriculture, wetland draining, hunting, the encroachment of industry and tourism infrastructure developments menace dozens of species.

RESPONSIBLE TOURISM

Follow the local code of ethics and common decency in nature reserves and national parks:

- Pack up your litter.
- Minimise waste by taking minimal packaging and no more food than you need.
- Don't use detergents or toothpaste, even if they are biodegradable, in or near watercourses.
- Stick to designated paths in protected areas, particularly in sensitive biospheres, Alpine areas and coastal dunes where flora and fauna may be seriously damaged if you stray.
- When camping in the wild (check first with the landowners or a park ranger to see if it's allowed), bury human waste in catholes at least 15cm deep and at least 100m from any watercourse.
- Obey the 'no dogs, tents and motorised vehicles' rule in national parks.

WHERE TO WATCH WILDLIFE

The national parks and their smaller siblings encourage green-eyed visitors to hook up with a naturalistic guide to watch wildlife; details are in the regional chapters. Otherwise, the following observation posts are worth a gander:

- Bisons in Languedoc at the Reserve de Bisons d'Europe near Mende (p745).
- Vultures in the Pyrenees at La Falaise aux Vautours in the Vallée d'Ossau (p685) and in Languedoc at the Belvédère des Vautours in the Parc Naturel Régional des Grands Causses (p747).
- Storks in Alsace at the Centre de Réintroduction des Cigognes in Hunawihr (p361) and the Enclos Cigognes in Munster (p368); on the Atlantic Coast at the Parc Ornithologique in Le Tech (p645) and at the Parc des Oiseaux outside Villars-les-Dombes near Lyon (p645).
- Wolves in Languedoc at the wolf reserve in the Parc du Gévaudan near Mende (p745) and in the Alps with a wolf-watching expedition organised by the Parc National du Mercantour (p822).

Animals

France has more mammals to see (around 110) than other country in Europe. Couple this with its 363 bird species, 30 amphibian types, 36 varieties of reptiles and 72 kinds of fish and wildlife watchers are in paradise.

High-altitude plains in the Alps and Pyrenees shelter the marmot (it hibernates October to April) with its shrill and distinctive whistle; the nimble *chamois* (mountain antelope) with its dark-striped head; and the *bouquetin* (Alpine ibex) that can be seen in large numbers in the Parc National de la Vanoise (p519). The mouflon, introduced in the 1950s, clamber over stony sun-lit scree slopes in the mountains; and the red and roe deer and wild boar are common in lower-altitude forested areas. Winter welcomes the Alpine hare with its white coat, while 19 of Europe's 29 bat species hang out in the dark in the Alpine national parks.

The wolf, which disappeared from France in the 1930s, was spotted in the Parc National du Mercantour in 1992 – much to the horror of the mouflon (on which its preys) and local sheep farmers. Dogs, corrals and sound machines to frighten the 60-odd wolves believed to freely roam in the mountains today are effective alternatives to more murderous means of getting rid of the unwanted predator.

The brown bear also disappeared from the Alps in the mid-1930s. The 300 or so that lived in the Pyrenees at that time have dwindled to no more than five today; see p683 for more details.

A rare but wonderful treat is the sighting of a golden eagle: 40 pairs nest in the Parc National du Mercantour, 20 pairs nest in the Vanoise, 37 in the Écrins and a good handful in the Pyrenees. Other birds of prey include the peregrine falcon, kestrel, buzzard and bearded vulture with its unsavoury bone-breaking habits. The latter – the largest bird of prey with an awe-inspiring wingspan of 2.8m – was extinct in the Alps from the 19th century until the 1980s when it was reintroduced. More recently, the small pale-coloured Egyptian vulture (worshipped by the Egyptians, hence its name) has been spotted; 50 pairs inhabit the Pyrenees.

Even the eagle-eyed will have difficulty spotting the ptarmigan, a chicken-like species around since the Ice Age that moults three times a year to ensure a fool-proof camouflage for every season (brown in summer, white in winter). It lives on rocky slopes and in Alpine meadows above 2000m. The nutcracker with its loud and buoyant singsong

DID YOU KNOW?

Of the 39,000 insect species identified in France, 10,000 creep and crawl around the Parc National du Mercantour in the French Alps.

The Ligue de Protection des Oiseaux (LPO; League for the Protection of Birds) advises birders on what to see where and when. Visit its website (in French) at www.lpo.fr.

Those interested in birds of prey will also enjoy http://percnoptere.lpo.fr and http://balbuzard .lpo.fr.

and larch-forest habitat, the black grouse, rock partridge, eagle owl and three-toed woodpecker are among the other 120-odd species to keep bird-watchers on their toes in mountainous realms.

Elsewhere on the French watch-the-birdie front, there are storks (p361) to see in Alsace; 10% of the world's flamingo population to see in the Camargue (p806); giant black cormorants – some with a wingspan of 170cm – on an island (p289) off the north coast of Brittany; and unique seagull and fishing eagle populations in the Réserve Naturelle de Scandola (p876) on Corsica. The osprey – a once-widespread migratory bird that winters in Africa and returns to France in February or March – only inhabits Corsica and the Loire Valley today.

Identify birds in France by their songs and calls or listen to the sounds of the Jura forests, and so on, with CDs produced by French 'voices of nature' publisher Sitelle www .sittelle.com.

Plants

About 14 million hectares of forest – beech, oak and pine in the main – cover 20% of France, while 4200 different species of plants and flowers are known to grow countrywide (2250 alone grow in the Parc National des Cévennes). In forests near Reims in the Champagne region, beech trees grow in a bizarrely stunted, malformed shape (p331).

The Alpine and Pyrenean regions nurture fir, spruce and beech forests on north-facing slopes between 800m and 1500m. Larch trees, mountain and arolla pines, rhododendrons and junipers stud shrubby subalpine zones between 1500m and 2000m; and a brilliant riot of spring- and summer-time wildflowers carpets grassy meadows above the tree line in the Alpine zone (up to 3000m).

Alpine blooms include the single golden-yellow flower of arnica, still used in herbal and homeopathic bruise-relieving remedies; the flame-coloured fire lily that flowers from December to May; and the hardy Alpine columbine with its delicate blue petals. The rare twinflower only grows in the Parc National de la Vanoise. Of France's 150 orchids, the black vanilla orchid is one to look out for – its small red-brown flowers exude a sweet vanilla fragrance. At Les Fermes de Marie in Megève (p506), dozens of Alpine plants and seeds – gentian, St John's wort, melissa, pulsatilla, pimpernel, cyclamen, hazel seeds and so on – go into beauty care products.

Trip through France's forests with the Office National des Forêts (National Forestry Commission), online (in French) at www.onf.fr.

Corsica and the Massif des Maures, west of St-Tropez on the Côte d'Azur, are closely related botanically: both have chestnut and cork oak trees (the bark of which gets stuffed in bottles) and are thickly carpeted with *maquis* – a heavily scented scrubland where dozens of orchids, herbs (the secret behind Provençal cooking) and heathers find shelter: particularly enchanting are the rock rose (a shrub with white flowers with yellow centres or pinkish-mauve flowers), the white-flowering myrtle that blossoms in June and is treasured for its blue-black berries (used to make some excellent liqueurs) and the blue-violet flowering Corsican mint with its heady summertime aroma.

DID YOU KNOW?

The protected 'queen of the Alps' (alias the Alpine eryngo) might well bear an uncanny resemblance to a purple thistle. It is in fact a member of the Parsley family (to which the carrot also belongs). Find it on grassy ledges.

NATIONAL PARKS

The proportion of land protected in France is low relative to the country's size: six small national parks *(parcs nationaux)* fully protect just 0.8% of the country. Another 7% is protected to a substantially lesser degree by 42 *parcs naturels régionaux* (regional nature parks) and a further 0.4% by 136 smaller *réserves naturelles* (nature reserves), some of which are under the eagle eye of the Conservatoire du Littoral (p60).

While the central zones of national parks are uninhabited and fully protected by legislation (dogs, vehicles and hunting are banned and camping is restricted), the ecosystems they protect spill into populated periph-

Park	Features	Activities	Best Time to Visit	Page
Parc National des Cévennes	wild peat bogs, causses, granite peaks, ravines and ridges bordering the Massif Central and Languedoc (910 sq km); red deer, beavers, vultures, wolves, bison	walking, trekking with donkeys, mountain-biking, horse-riding, cross-country skiing, caving, canoeing, botany (2250 plant species)	spring & winter	p741
Parc National des Écrins	glaciers, glacial lakes and mountain tops soaring up to 4102m in the French Alps (1770 sq km); marmots, lynx, ibex, chamois, bearded vultures	walking, climbing, hang-gliding	spring & summer	p529
Parc National du Mercantour	Provence at its most majestic with 3000m-plus peaks and dead-end valleys along the Italian border; marmots, mouflons, chamois, ibex, wolves, golden and short-toed eagles, bearded vultures	skiing (alpine), white-water sports, mountain-biking, walking, donkey trekking	spring, summer & winter	p822
Parc National de Port Cros	Island marine park off the Côte d'Azur forming France's smallest national park and Europe's first marine park (700 hectares and 1288 hectares of water); puffins, shearwaters, migratory birds	snorkelling, bird-watching, swimming, gentle strolling & sunbathing	summer (water activities) & autumn (bird-watching)	p848
Parc National des Pyrénées	100km of mountains along the Spanish border (457 sq km); marmots, izards, brown bears, golden eagles, vultures, buzzards	skiing (alpine & cross-country), walking, mountaineering, rock-climbing, white-water rafting, canoeing, kayaking mountain-biking	spring, summer & winter (skiing)	p680
Parc National de la Vanoise	post-glacial mountain landscape of Alpine peaks, 80 sq km of glaciers and beech-fir forests, forming France's first national park (530 sq km): chamois, ibex, marmots, golden eagles	skiing (alpine & cross-country), walking, mountaineering, mountain-biking	spring, summer & winter (skiing)	p519

eral zones in which tourism and other (often environmentally unfriendly) economic activities run riot.

Most regional nature parks and reserves were established, not only to improve (or at least maintain) local ecosystems, but to encourage economic development and tourism in areas (such as the Massif Central and Corsica) suffering from diminishing populations and increasing economic problems.

Select pockets of nature – the Pyrenees, Mont St-Michel and its bay, part of the Loire Valley and a clutch of capes on Corsica – are Unesco World Heritage Sites (p22).

ENVIRONMENTAL ISSUES

Summer forest fires are an annual hazard. Great tracts of land sizzle each year, often because of careless day-trippers but occasionally, as is sometimes the case in the Maures and Estérel ranges on the Côte d'Azur, because they are intentionally set alight by people wanting to get licences to build on the damaged lands. Since the mid-1970s, between 67 sq km and 883 sq km of land a year has been reduced to a burnt black stubble by

Get the green low-down (in French) on France's 42 regional nature parks with the Fédération des Parcs Naturels Régionaux de France (Federation of French Regional Natural Parks) at www.parcs-naturels-regionaux.tm.fr.

an average of 540 fires annually – although the number of fires is falling according to the Office National des Forêts (ONF), the national forestry commission responsible for public forests in France. In the Vosges forests in northern France, acid rain is the bigger menace.

Wetlands – incredibly productive ecosystems that are essential for the survival of a number of bird species, reptiles, fish and amphibians – are shrinking. More than two million hectares – 3% of French territory – are considered important wetlands, but only 4% of this land is protected. The vulnerability of these areas was highlighted in 2003 when lumps of oil landed on beaches in southwestern France following the sinking of the *Prestige* oil tanker off Spain's northwestern coast in late 2002. The slick wrecked beaches, crippled local fishing and seafood industries, and killed hundreds of birds and marine life – to the horror of French environmentalists who were still seething with anger over the 1999 *Erika* oil tanker disaster that fouled more than 400km of shoreline in Brittany and cost US$860 million to clean up.

Men with dogs and guns pose an equally big threat to French animal life. While the number of hunters in France has fallen by 20% in the last decade, there are still way more hunters in France (almost 1.5 million) than in other Western European countries (around 1 million in Spain and Italy, 625,000 in Britain). Despite the Brussels Directive being introduced in 1979 to protect wild birds, their eggs, nests and habitats in the EU, the French government didn't bother to make its provisions part of French law – meaning birds that can safely fly over other countries can still be shot as they cross France. A good handful of those not shot – at least 1000 birds of prey a year – are electrocuted to death by high-voltage power lines instead.

Many traditional animal habitats have been destroyed by huge recreational lakes, created by the state-owned electricity company, Electricité de France (EDF), which dams rivers to produce electricity. Since the 1980s however, almost 80% of the country's electricity has been produced by 19 nuclear power plants. (The French nuclear-power station programme is the most ambitious in the world.) Most are on main rivers or near the coast – the environmental cost of which is high. Radioactive emissions spewed out by the four nuclear plants on the banks of the River Loire alone represent more than 25% of rare gas emissions in France. Blistering hot temperatures in summer 2003 prompted calls for a new round of nuclear plants to be built in a bid to cope with ever-increasing energy demands.

Nuclear waste from France and elsewhere is treated at a plant on the Cotentin Peninsula in Normandy and then pumped into the Channel.

HIGH-FACTOR PROTECTION BY THE SEA

Some 10% of the coastline of mainland France and Corsica is managed by the **Conservatoire du Littoral** (Coastal Protection Agency; ☎ 05 46 84 72 50; www.conservatoire-du-littoral.fr in French; Corderie Royale, BP 13 7, F-1 7306 Rochefort Cedex), an association that acquires threatened natural areas by the sea to restore, rejuvenate and protect.

Rare orchid-studded sand dunes east of Dunkirk (p220), a Corsican desert (p875), the Baie de la Somme with its ornithological park (p217) and several wet and watery pockets of the horse-studded Camargue (p806) rank among the conservatoire's rich pageant of *espaces naturels protégés* (protected natural areas).

Books, guides and maps on the 300 sites and 70,100 hectares managed by the Conservatoire du Littoral sites are sold in its online boutique.

TOP FIVE NATURAL CURIOSITIES

Several up hill and down dales later, here's what tickled us most in France's 42 regional parks:

- Dwarf-mutant beech trees that have grown in all their stunted glory around Reims and Champagne, since the 6th century and are protected today by the Parc Naturel Régional de la Montagne de Reims (p331) in Champagne.

- Europe's highest sand dune (which also happens to move, swallow trees and so on), the Dune de Pyla near Arcachon on the Atlantic Coast (p644).

- Europe's largest extinct volcano (by area), Monts du Cantal, the balding slopes of which can be hiked up in summer and skied down in winter. It falls within the Parc Naturel Régional des Volcans d'Auvergne (p554) in the Massif Central.

- Lunar landscape of underground sink-hills, caves and streams beneath the *causses* (limestone plateaus) of the Parc Naturel Régional des Grands Causses (p746) in Languedoc.

- Prehistoric bird footprints and marine-reptile fossil skeletons in the Réserve Naturelle Géologique de Haute-Provence in the Alps (p811).

Throughout the 1980s and 1990s France's nuclear activity was a particularly hot potato: French agents blew up the Greenpeace ship *Rainbow Warrior* in New Zealand's Auckland harbour in 1985 in an attempt to derail the organisation's campaign against nuclear testing on the Polynesian island of Moruroa and a nearby atoll. France did not sign a worldwide test-ban treaty until 1998.

Cadarache in southeast France is the favoured European contender for the construction of a thermonuclear experimental reactor – a US$5 billion engineering project between the EU, the USA, China and Japan among others that will revolutionise the production of world power should it succeed. Unlike conventional nuclear power plants, fusion reactors produce energy through the fusion of light atom nuclei and produce dramatically less radioactive waste. The cleaner, new-generation reactor will only start churning out energy in 2014.

Environmentalists in Languedoc are none too happy to have one of the world's tallest bridges (p747) slicing across one of their quiet valleys. A motorway will race along it from 2005.

> Find out more about France's role in the world quest to develop fusion power at www.iter.org.

Conservation Organisation

A growing network of environmental organisations in France watchdog trouble spots:

- **Les Amis de la Nature** (☎ 01 46 27 53 56; www.amisnature-colombes.org in French; 197 rue Championnet, 75018 Paris) Cycle or walk instead of taking the car. For further tips on how to reduce your impact on the environment, contact nature's friends.

- **Association Nationale de Protection des Eaux de Rivières** (TOS; ☎ 01 43 75 84 84; www.anpertos.org in French; 67 rue de Seine, 94140 Alfortville) Help clean up French rivers with the National Association for the Protection of River Waters.

- **Espaces Naturels de France** (ENF; ☎ 02 38 24 55 00; www.enf.asso.fr in French; 6 rue Jeanne d'Arc, 45000 Orléans) Safeguards 40,000 hectares split across 1350 sites.

- **Fondation Ligue Française des Droits de l'Animal** (LFDA; www.league-animal-rights.org; 39 rue Claude Bernard, 75005 Paris) No to force feeding and foie gras is one of the animal-friendly calls made by the French League for Animal Rights.

- **France Nature Environnement** (☎ 02 38 62 44 48; www.fne.asso.fr in French; 6 rue Dupanloup, 45000 Orléans) Umbrella organisation for 3000-odd nature-protection and environmental groups countrywide.

> **DID YOU KNOW?**
>
> France's last working coal mine (near Creutzwald on the French-German border) closed in April 2004, marking the end of a traditional 300-year-old industry that employed 300,000 until the 1960s when nuclear power took over.

A DEGRADING PROCESS

Make sure that whatever you bring to the mountains leaves with you. Decomposition, always slow, is even more protracted in the high mountains. Typical times:

- paper handkerchief: three months
- apple core: up to six months
- cigarette butt: three to five years
- wad of chewing gum: five years
- lighter: 100 years

- plastic bag: 450 years
- aluminium can: up to 500 years
- plastic bottle: up to 1000 years
- glass bottle: up to 4000 years

- **Greenpeace** (☎ 01 44 64 02 17; www.greenpeace.org; 22 rue des Rasselins, 75020 Paris) For all the environmental hotspots in France.
- **Ligue pour la Préservation de la Faune Sauvage** (ROC; www.roc.asso.fr; 26 rue Pascal, 75005 Paris) The French League for the Protection of Wild Animals also fights for the rights of non-hunters in France (98% of the population).

Food & Drink

'The French think mainly about two things – their two main meals,' a well-fed *bon-vivant* French friend once told us. 'Everything else is in parentheses.' And it's true. While not every French man, woman and child is a walking *Larousse Gastronomique,* the gastronomic Bible of French cuisine, eating and drinking well is still of prime importance to most people in this country and they continue to spend an inordinate amount of time thinking about, talking about and consuming food and wine.

But don't suppose for a moment that this obsession with things culinary means dining out in France has to be a ceremonious occasion or one full of pitfalls for the uninitiated. Approach food and wine here with even half the enthusiasm the French themselves do, and you will be warmly received, encouraged and very well fed.

For a full culinary tour of France, including tips on how to prepare your own French banquet, pick up a copy of Lonely Planet's *World Food France.*

STAPLES & SPECIALITIES

Every nation or culture has its own staples, dictated by climate, geography and tradition. French cuisine has long stood apart for its great use of a variety of foods – beef, lamb, pork, poultry, fish and shellfish, cereals, vegetables and legumes – but its staple 'trinity' is bread, cheese and *charcuterie* (cured, smoked or processed meat products). And as for national and regional specialities, well, *tout est possible* (the sky's the limit).

Staples

BREAD

Nothing is more French than *pain* (bread). More than 80% of all French people eat it at every meal, and it comes in an infinite variety.

All bakeries have *baguettes* (and the similar but fatter *flûtes*), which are long and thin and weigh 250g, and wider loaves of what are simply called *pains*. A *pain,* which weighs 400g, is softer on the inside and has a less crispy crust than a baguette. Both types are at their best if eaten within four hours of baking; if you're not very hungry, ask for a half-loaf: a *demi baguette* or a *demi pain*. A *ficelle* is a thinner, crustier 200g version of a baguette – not unlike a very thick breadstick, really.

Bread has experienced a renaissance in France in recent years and most bakeries also carry heavier, more expensive breads made with all sorts of grains and cereals; you will also find loaves studded with nuts, raisins or herbs. These heavier breads keep much longer than baguettes and standard white-flour breads.

Bread is baked at various times during the day, so it's available fresh as early as 6am and also in the afternoon. Most bakeries close for one day a week, but the days are staggered so that a town or neighbourhood is never left without a place to buy a loaf (except, perhaps, on Sunday afternoon).

CHEESE

France has nearly 500 varieties of *fromage* (cheese) produced at farms, dairies, mountain huts, monasteries and factories. They're made from either cow's, goat's or ewe's milk, which can be raw, pasteurised or *petit-lait* ('little milk', the whey left over after the milk fats and solids have been curdled with rennet, an enzyme derived from the stomach of a calf or young goat).

The choice on offer at a *fromagerie* (cheese shop) can be overwhelming, but *fromagers* (cheese merchants) always allow you to sample before you buy and are usually very generous with their advice and guidance. The following list divides French cheeses into five main groups as they are usually presented in a *fromagerie* and recommends several types to try.

Fromage de chèvre

'Goat's milk cheese' is usually creamy and both sweet and a little salty when fresh, but hardens and gets much saltier as it matures. Among the best are: Ste-Maure de Touraine, a creamy, mild cheese from the Loire region; Crottin de Chavignol, a classic though saltier variety from Burgundy; Cabécou de Rocamadour from Midi-Pyrénées, often served warm with salad or marinated in oil and rosemary; and St-Marcellin, a soft white cheese from Lyon.

Fromage à pâté persillée

'Veined' or 'blue cheese' is so called because the veins often resemble *persille* (parsley). Roquefort is a ewe's-milk veined cheese that is to many the king of French cheese. Fourme d'Ambert is a very mild cow's-milk cheese from the Rhône Valley. Bleu du Haut Jura (also called Bleu de Gex) is a mild blue-veined mountain cheese.

Fromage à pâté molle

'Soft cheese' is moulded or rind-washed. Camembert de Normandie, a classic moulded cheese that for many is synonymous with French cheese, and the refined Brie de Meaux are both made from raw cow's milk; Munster from Alsace and the strong Époisses de Bourgogne are rind-washed, fine-textured cheeses.

Fromage à pâté demi-dure

'Semi-hard cheese' denotes uncooked, pressed cheese. Among the finest are Tomme de Savoie, made from either raw or pasteurised cow's milk; Cantal, a cow's-milk cheese from Auvergne that tastes something like Cheddar; St-Nectaire, a strong-smelling pressed cheese that has a strong and complex taste; and Ossau-Iraty, a ewe's milk cheese made in the Basque Country.

Fromage à pâté dure

'Hard cheese' in France is always cooked and pressed. Among the most popular are: Beaufort, a grainy cow's milk cheese with a slightly fruity taste from Rhône-Alpes; Comté, a cheese made with raw cow's milk cheese in Franche-Comté; Emmental, a cow's-milk cheese made all over

DID YOU KNOW?

President Charles de Gaulle, commenting on the near impossibility of uniting the French on a single issue after WWII, famously grumbled: 'You cannot easily bring together a country that has 265 kinds of cheese'. And did you know that the number has now almost doubled to 500?

SERVING CHEESE

When cutting cheese at the table, remember that a small circular cheese like a Camembert is cut in slices like a pie. If a larger such cheese (eg Brie) has been bought pre-sliced, cut from the tip to the rind; cutting off the top is considered rude. Slice cheeses whose middle is the best part (eg the blue or veined cheeses) in such a way as to take your fair share of the rind. A flat piece of semi-hard cheese like Emmental is usually just cut horizontally in chunks.

Wine and cheese is a match made in heaven. It's a matter of taste but in general, strong, pungent cheeses require a young, full-bodied red or a sweet wine, while soft cheeses with a refined flavour call for more quality and age in the wine. Some classic pairings include: Alsatian Gewürztraminer and Munster; Côtes du Rhône red and Roquefort; Côte d'Or (Burgundy) red with Brie or Camembert; and mature Bordeaux with Emmental or Gruyère.

France; and Mimolette, an Edam-like bright-orange cheese from Lille that can be aged for up to 36 months.

CHARCUTERIE

Traditionally *charcuterie* is made only from pork, though a number of other meats – from beef and veal to chicken and goose – are used in making sausages, blood puddings, hams and other cured and salted meats. Pâtés, terrines and *rillettes* are essentially *charcuterie* and are prepared in many different ways.

The difference between a pâté and a terrine is academic: a pâté is removed from its container and sliced before it is served or sold while a terrine is sliced from the container itself. *Rillettes*, on the other hand, is potted meat (pork, goose, duck or rabbit) or even fish that is not ground, chopped or sliced but shredded with two forks, seasoned, mixed with fat and spread cold like pâté over bread or toast.

While every region in France produces standard *charcuterie* favourites as well as its own specialities, Alsace, Lyon and the Auvergne produce the best sausages and Périgord and the north of France some of the most acclaimed pâtés and terrines. Among the basic types of *charcuterie* you'll encounter at a *charcuterie* or *charcuterie-traiteur* (see p77):

andouille – large smoked tripe (chitterling) sausage cooked and ready to eat (usually cold) when bought

andouillette – soft raw sausage made from the pig's small intestines that is grilled and sometimes eaten with onions and potatoes

boudin blanc – smooth white sausage made from poultry, veal, pork or even rabbit, which is cooked and can be served with, say, haricot beans or apples

boudin noir – blood sausage or pudding made with pig's blood, onions and spices and usually eaten hot with stewed apples and potatoes

fromage de tête – brawn or head cheese

jambon – ham; smoked or salt-cured pork made from a pig's hindquarters

saucisse – usually a small fresh sausage that is boiled or grilled before eating

saucisson – a large salami usually eaten cold

saucisson sec – air-dried salami

Regional Specialities

There are all sorts of reasons for the amazing variety of France's regional cuisine. Climatic and geographical factors have been particularly important: the hot south tends to favour olive oil, garlic and tomatoes, while the cooler, pastoral northern regions prefer cream and butter. Coastal areas specialise in mussels, oysters and saltwater fish, while those near lakes and rivers make full use of the freshwater fish available.

Diverse though it is, French cuisine is typified by certain regions, most notably Normandy, Burgundy, Périgord, Lyon and, to a lesser extent, the Loire region, Provence and Alsace. Still others such as Brittany, the Auvergne, the Basque Country, Languedoc and Corsica have made incalculable contributions to what can generically be called French food.

NORMANDY

The large fertile region that stretches along the English Channel from northeastern Brittany in the west to Picardy in the east, Normandy is famous for the incredible richness and superior quality of its local produce, but three staples are all-important in the Norman kitchen: milk and other dairy products, apples and seafood.

Each Norman cow produces an average 5000L of milk annually, supplying France with half its milk, cream, butter and cheese. Among the

The Food of France by Waverley Root is the seminal work on la cuisine française in English, with much focus on historical development, by a long-time American correspondent based in France.

REGIONAL SPECIALITIES

| 0 | 200 km |
| 0 | 120 miles |

WALES

Cardiff

LONDON

ENGLAND

NETHERLANDS

GERMANY

BELGIUM
Brussels

LUXEMBOURG

The Channel (La Manche)

Straits of Dover

Lille
13

Somme

Picardie Aisne

Oise

♥ CHAMPAGNE

LORRAINE

Meuse

♥ ALSACE

3

Strasbourg

1

2

ALSACE

Rhine

29

Trouville Honfleur

Caen **27**

28

NORMANDY

Meaux

Châlons-en-Champagne

12

CHAMPAGNE

30

PARIS **31**

Seine

♥ LOIRE

♥ BURGUNDY

9

SWITZERLAND

Golfe de St-Malo

8

7 St-Brieuc Cancale

Camaret BRITTANY

6 Concarneau

Quiberon

Morbihan Coast

Langeais

Loire Chênehutte

36

Saumur

Chinon

LOIRE VALLEY

37

Cher

BURGUNDY

Saône

Dijon

10

11

Côte d'Or
Chalonnais

Doubs

THE JURA & THE ALPS

Lake Geneva

CORSICA

♥ CORSICA

15

14

4

Vienne

Creuse

Loire

♥ CHABLIS

Vichy

FRANCHE-COMTÉ

Charolles

Mâcon **25**

Savoy

16

Mont Blanc (4807m)

Rochefort

LIMOUSIN

Cognac

AUVERGNE

MASSIF CENTRAL

Lyon **24**

RHÔNE-ALPES

Dauphiné

17

Médoc

33 32

St-Émilion

♥ BORDEAUX

Bordeaux

5

THE DORDOGNE

Dordogne

Lot

Garonne

QUERCY

Tarn

26

ARDÈCHE

Rhône

35

♥ RHÔNE

ITALY

ATLANTIC OCEAN

Bay of Biscay

♥ PÉRIGORD

23 Toulouse

Millau

LANGUEDOC

PROVENCE

CÔTE D'AZUR

MONACO

19

18 BASQUE COUNTRY

20

MIDI-PYRÉNÉES

Adour

Garonne

21 22

ROUSSILLON

34

Marseille

Golfe du Lion

LANGUEDOC-ROUSSILLON

SPAIN

ANDORRA

MEDITERRANEAN SEA

22 HIGHLIGHTS   **♥** WINE REGION

ALSACE & LORRAINE
1 Choucroute Alsacienne
2 Gewürztraminer Wine
3 Quiche Lorraine

BORDEAUX & THE ATLANTIC COAST
4 Deux-Sèvres Butter
5 Sauternes Wine

BRITTANY
6 Belon Oysters
7 Crêpes & Galettes
8 Primeurs (Spring Vegetables)

BURGUNDY
9 Chablis Wine
10 Dijon Mustard
11 Escargots de Bourgogne (Burgundy Snails)

CHAMPAGNE & FAR NORTHERN FRANCE
12 Dom Pérignon Champagne
13 Mimolette Cheese

CORSICA
14 Charcuterie
15 Chestnut Sweets

FRENCH ALPS & THE JURA
16 Fondue Savoyarde (Cheese Fondue)
17 Grenoble Walnuts

GASCONY & THE BASQUE COUNTRY
18 Bayonne Ham
19 Espelette Chillies
20 Garbure Stew

LANGUEDOC-ROUSSILLON
21 Cassoulet
22 Roquefort Cheese
23 Toulouse Sausage

LYON & THE RHÔNE
24 Crème de Cassis (Blackcurrant Liqueur)
25 Quenelles
26 Valrhona Chocolate

NORMANDY
27 Apples & Cider
28 Camembert Cheese
29 Scallops & Mussels

PARIS & ÎLE DE FRANCE
30 Argenteuil Asparagus
31 Brie de Meaux Cheese

PÉRIGORD & THE AUVERGNE
32 Duck & Goose Liver
33 Truffles

PROVENCE
34 Bouillabaisse
35 Olives & Olive Oil

THE LOIRE
36 Rillettes de Tours
37 Tarte Tatin

cheeses, Camembert (produced in Normandy since the time of William the Conqueror) reigns supreme, but there are a great many others, including the heart-shaped Neufchâtel, salty Pont l'Évêque and smelly Livarot. Cream and butter go into the creation of the many rich, thick sauces that accompany fish, meat and vegetable dishes in the region.

Trouville and Honfleur are the places to go for fish and seafood; market barrows there are laden with lobsters, crayfish, langoustines, prawns, scallops, oysters, mussels and an endless variety of fish. Specialities include *matelote,* a kind of fish stew made with white wine and cream, and *sole à la normande* served with tiny shrimps.

Apples are the third essential of Norman cuisine, and light, refreshing, slightly alcoholic *cidre* (cider) – be it *doux* (sweet) or *brut* (dry) – is popular. It is also used extensively in cooking, particularly in meat and poultry dishes, including a dish not to everyone's taste: *tripes à la mode de Caen,* tripe combined with ox or calf's trotters, cider or Calvados, carrots, leeks, onions and herbs and slow-cooked in a sealed clay pot.

Calvados is to the apple what Cognac is to the grape. The most celebrated variety of this strong apple brandy comes from the Vallée d'Auge and is widely used in the preparation of sauces and in desserts.

BRITTANY

At the westernmost tip of France and surrounded by open sea on three sides, Brittany is a paradise for lovers of seafood, especially shellfish: oysters from Cancale and the Morbihan Gulf coast; scallops and sea urchins from St-Brieuc; crabs from St-Malo; and lobsters from Camaret, Concarneau and Quiberon. The region enjoys a very mild (though wet) Atlantic climate, which helps to produce some of the finest *primeurs* (spring or early vegetables) in France.

Without a doubt the *crêpe* and the *galette* are the royalty of Breton cuisine. A crepe is made from wheat flour and almost always sweet; the *crêpe beurre-sucre,* made with butter and sugar, is the classic variety but anything ranging from fruit and jam to liqueurs can be added. The flour used in a *galette* is made from buckwheat, a traditional staple of the region, and the fillings are always savoury. A *galette complète,* for example, comes with ham, egg and cheese.

ALSACE

In a traditional Alsatian restaurant you're likely to find *baeckeoffe* (baker's oven), a stew made of several kinds of meat (often pork, mutton and beef) and vegetables that have been marinated for several days. *Choucroute alsacienne* (or *garnie*) is sauerkraut served hot with sausage, bacon, pork loin and/or ham knuckle and accompanied by cold beer or chilled Pinot Noir.

Alsatians love savoury pies and tarts. The most popular is the *flammeküche* (or *tarte flambée*), a thin layer of pastry topped with cream, onion, bacon and sometimes cheese or mushrooms and cooked in a wood-fired oven. *Zwiebelküche* (or *tarte à l'oignon*) is an onion tart, while a *tourte* is a raised pie with ham, bacon or ground pork, eggs and leeks and often flavoured with Riesling. Alsace produces some excellent *charcuterie,* prepared from what is known in these parts as *le seigneur cochon* (the noble pig).

Due to the abundance of fruits and nuts in the region, Alsace's patisseries (pastry shops) are particularly well stocked with scrumptious cakes, tarts and pies, including *kugelhopf,* a mildly sweet, domed sultana-and-almond cake. *Tarte alsacienne* is a custard tart made with local fruits, which also includes the distinctive purple plums called *quetsches.*

DID YOU KNOW?

In Normandy Calvados is sometimes drunk in the middle of a meal as a *trou norman,* a 'Norman hole', to allow room for more courses.

LOIRE REGION

The cuisine of this region should be familiar to most since it was the cooking of the Loire, refined in the kitchens of the region's chateaux from the 16th century onward, that became the cuisine of France as a whole: *rillettes, coq au vin,* basic *beurre blanc* sauce and *tarte Tatin.*

Don't miss the opportunity to try *rillons,* chunks of fatty pork or duck cooked until crisp and crunchy and sometimes mixed with *rillettes* or foie gras. Also try *jambon d'Amboise,* an especially fine ham; *boudin blanc,* a smooth white sausage stuffed with chicken; and some of the freshwater fish (pike, shad, gudgeon, perch and smelt) that abound in the Loire and its many tributaries.

The Loire region has been called the 'garden of France' and quality produce of all types is grown here. But it is especially known for its mushrooms and prunes. The misnamed *champignons de Paris* are raised in 'caves' (actually quarries from where stones for the chateaux were mined) at Langeais and Chênehutte; the *pruneaux de Tours,* prunes dried from luscious Damson plums, are often cooked in poultry, pork or veal dishes or end up stuffed.

BURGUNDY

The cuisine of Burgundy, based on beef, wine and mustard, is solid, substantial and served in generous portions. The region's signature dish, *bœuf bourguignon,* is beef marinated and cooked in red wine with mushrooms, onions, carrots and bits of bacon. Any dish described as *à la bourguignonne* will be prepared with a similar sauce. Quite a few other Burgundian dishes are prepared with cream-based sauces, although *andouillette de Mâcon* (a small pork sausage) is served with a sauce made with the region's most famous condiment, Dijon mustard. The large, black and very tasty *escargots de Bourgogne* are raised on grape leaves.

Other traditional Burgundian products include *pain d'épices,* a gingerbread that traditionally takes up to eight weeks to prepare, and blackcurrants, which are used to make both jams and *crème de cassis,* a sweet blackcurrant liqueur that is combined with white wine (traditionally Aligoté) to make the aperitif known as a *kir.*

LYON

The city of Lyon, at the crossroads of some of France's richest agricultural regions (Burgundy and its wines, Charolles and its beef cattle, Dauphiné and its dairy products), enjoys a supply of quality foodstuffs unequalled in France. Indeed, it is considered by many to be France's *temple de gastronomie;* some of France's most talented chefs work here.

Some typical Lyonnaise dishes include *saucisson de Lyon* pan-fried with apples and *quenelles,* light poached dumplings made of pike (or less frequently chicken) and often served in a *sauce Nantua,* a creamy crayfish sauce. The *marrons glacés,* candied chestnuts from nearby Ardèche, are superb and with Valrhona chocolate (p486) being made at Tain l'Hermitage just downriver, it's no surprise that Lyon's proudest boast is its chocolates, particularly those made by the firm Bernachon (p481).

PÉRIGORD

Better known to many English speakers as the Dordogne (the name of the most important of the region's rivers and of its chief *département*), Périgord is celebrated for its truffles and poultry. Most prized among the latter are the ducks and geese whose fattened livers are turned into *pâté de foie gras* (duck or goose liver pâté) or cooked and stored in their own fat as *confit de canard* and *confit d'oie*. Goose fat is very important in the region's traditional cuisine, and walnut oil is used as a seasoning and in salads.

La cuisine périgourdine is very diverse and also includes freshwater fish (which can be stuffed with foie gras or cooked with truffles, grilled, marinated or cooked in ashes), crayfish, rabbit and beef. One of the best desserts is *gâteau aux châtaignes* (chestnut cake), but also look out for flans and tarts made with plums, quinces, grapes, cherries or pears.

THE AUVERGNE
The terrain, the climate and even the people of the Auvergne (the Massif Central area) are often described in French as *rude* – 'rugged', 'harsh' or 'tough'. In a word this, too, is its cuisine, including *potée auvergnate,* a hearty soup-stew of cabbage, bacon, pork sausages and potatoes, and lots of *charcuterie,* with the celebrated *salaisons d'Auvergne* (salt-cured meats) sold and consumed throughout France.

Specialities of the Auvergne include *lentilles vertes du Puy aux saucisses fumées,* smoked pork sausages with green Puy lentils, and *truffade,* a sticky blend of potatoes, cheese (usually Cantal) and garlic not unlike the *aligot* enjoyed in Languedoc and eaten with sausages.

PROVENCE
The Roman legacy of olives, wheat and wine remain the triumvirate of *la cuisine provençale,* and many dishes are prepared with olive oil and generous amounts of garlic. Provence's most famous dish is *bouillabaisse,* a chowder made with at least three kinds of fresh fish, cooked for 10 minutes or so in broth with onions, tomatoes, saffron and various herbs, and eaten as a main course with toasted bread and *rouille,* a spicy mayonnaise of olive oil, garlic and chilli peppers. Tomatoes, aubergine and squash, stewed together with green peppers, garlic and various aromatic herbs, produce that perennial Provençal favourite, *ratatouille.*

BASQUE COUNTRY
Among the essential ingredients of Basque cooking are the deep-red chillies you'll see hanging out to dry in summer, brightening up houses and adding that extra bite to many of the region's dishes, including the area's signature *jambon de Bayonne,* the locally prepared Bayonne ham. Fish dishes abound on the coast, especially those made with hake; the 'Basque bouillabaisse' called *ttoro* may include hake, eel and monkfish as well as tomatoes, white wine and chillies. Basques love cakes and pastries but the most popular of all is *gâteau basque,* a relatively simple layer cake filled with cream or cherry jam.

Le Grand Atlas des Cuisines de Nos Terroirs from Éditions Atlas is a beautifully illustrated atlas of regional cooking in France with emphasis on *cuisine campagnarde* (country cooking).

LANGUEDOC
No dish is more evocative of Languedoc than *cassoulet,* a casserole or stew with beans and meat. There are at least three major varieties but a favourite is the cassoulet from Toulouse, which adds *saucisse de Toulouse,* a fat, mild-tasting pork sausage. *Saucisse de Toulouse* often comes *à la languedocienne,* sautéed in goose fat and served with tomato, parsley and capers. But 'in the Languedoc style' is not an immutable recipe; it can also mean a garlicky garnish of tomatoes, aubergines and *cèpes* (boletus mushrooms). France's most famous blue cheese is made at Roquefort, south of Millau.

CORSICA
The hills and mountains of the island of Corsica have always been ideal for raising goats, sheep, cows and pigs; kitchen gardens produce a bounty

of courgettes, small, purplish artichokes, asparagus and aubergines. The *maquis,* the dense Corsican underbrush made up of shrubs mixed with wild rosemary, laurel, lavender and thyme, flavours many dishes, along with olive oil, wild mint, fennel, tomatoes, honey, oranges and *cédrat,* a sweeter variety of lemon.

These raw materials have all come together to create such trademark Corsican foods as *stufatu,* a fragrant mutton stew, *premonata,* beef braised with juniper berries, and *lonzo aux haricots blancs,* a Corsican sausage cooked with white beans, white wine and herbs.

The island's most popular cheese is *brocciu,* which can be eaten fresh, when it is almost like ricotta, or as a rather mild and creamy, crumbly cheese when drained, salted and aged. Many sweets are prepared with chestnut flour (once a staple of the island), including *falculelli,* pressed and frittered Corsican *brocciu* cheese served on a chestnut leaf, and *castagnacci,* chestnut-flour pudding.

DRINKS
Alcoholic Drinks

Although alcohol consumption has dropped by a third in less than two decades, France still ranks sixth in the world in the boozing stakes behind Luxembourg, Romania, Portugal, Ireland and the Czech Republic.

WINE

Grapes and the art of wine-making were introduced to Gaul by the Romans. In the Middle Ages, important vineyards developed around monasteries as the monks needed wine to celebrate Mass. Large-scale wine production later moved closer to the ports (eg Bordeaux) from it could be exported.

In the middle of the 19th century, phylloxera aphids were accidentally brought to Europe from the USA. The pests ate through the roots of Europe's grapevines, destroying some 10,000 sq km of vineyards in France alone. European wine production appeared to be doomed until root stocks resistant to phylloxera were brought from California and original cuttings grafted onto them.

Wine-making is a complicated chemical process, but ultimately the taste and quality of the wine depend on four key factors: the type(s) or blend of grape, the climate, the soil and the art of the *vigneron* (wine-maker).

Some viticulturists have honed their skills and techniques to such a degree that their wine is known as a *grand cru* (literally, 'great growth'). If this wine has been produced in a year of optimum climatic conditions it becomes a *millésime* (vintage) wine. *Grands crus* are aged first in small oak barrels and then in bottles, sometimes for 20 years or more, before they develop their full taste and aroma. These are the memorable (and pricey) bottles that wine experts talk about with such passion.

There are dozens of wine-producing regions throughout France, but the seven principal regions are Alsace, Bordeaux, Burgundy, Champagne, Languedoc-Roussillon, the Loire region and the Rhône. Areas such as Burgundy comprise many well-known districts, including Chablis, Beaujolais and Mâcon, while Bordeaux encompasses Médoc, St-Émilion and Sauternes – to name just a few of its many subregions.

With the exception of Alsatian ones, wines in France are named after the location of the vineyard rather than the grape varietal.

Alsace

Alsace has been producing wine since about AD 300. These days, the region produces almost exclusively white wines – mostly varieties produced

DID YOU KNOW?

Each year, some 3% of the volume of the casks fermenting in Cognac – the so-called *part des anges* (angels' share) – evaporates through the pores in the wood.

nowhere else in France – that are known for their clean, fresh taste and compatibility with the often heavy local cuisine. The vineyards closest to Strasbourg produce light red wines from Pinot Noir that are similar to rosé. This wine is best served chilled.

Alsace's four most important varietal wines are Riesling, known for its subtlety; the more pungent and highly regarded Gewürztraminer; the robust, high-alcohol Pinot Gris; and Muscat d'Alsace, which is not as sweet as that made with Muscat grapes grown further south.

Bordeaux

Bordeaux has been synonymous with full-bodied red wine since the time of the Romans. Britons, who call Bordeaux reds clarets, have had a taste for the wines of this region since the mid-12th century when King Henry II, who controlled the region through marriage, tried to gain the favour of the locals by granting them tax-free trade status with England. Thus began a roaring business in wine exporting that continues to this day.

The reds of Bordeaux, which produces more fine wine than any other region in the world, are often described as well balanced, a quality achieved by blending several grape varieties. The grapes predominantly used are Merlot, Cabernet Sauvignon and Cabernet Franc. Bordeaux's foremost wine-growing areas are Médoc, Pomerol, St-Émilion and Graves; the sweet whites of the Sauternes area are the world's finest dessert wines.

Burgundy

Burgundy has produced wines since the time of the Celts but developed its reputation during the reign of Charlemagne, when monks first began to produce wine here.

Burgundy's red wines are produced with Pinot Noir grapes; the best vintages need 10 to 20 years to age. White wine is made from the Chardonnay grape. The five main wine-growing areas of Burgundy are Chablis, Côte d'Or, Côte Chalonnais, Mâcon and Beaujolais, which alone produces 13 different types of light Gamay-based red wine.

Languedoc

This region is the country's most important wine-growing area, with up to 40% of France's wine – mainly cheap red *vin de table* (table wine) produced here. About 300,000 hectares of the region is 'under vine', which represents one-third of France's total.

In addition to the well-known Fitou label, the area's other quality wines are Coteaux du Languedoc, Faugères, Corbières and Minervois. The region also produces about 70% of France's *vin de pays*, 'country wine' from a particular named village or region, most of which is labelled Vin de Pays d'Oc.

Loire Region

The vineyards of the fertile Loire Valley are small and wine-makers are used to selling directly to day-trippers who make their way here to buy their favourite wines. The Loire's 75,000 hectares of vineyards rank the region as the third-largest area in France for the production of quality wines. Although sunny, the climate is moist and not all grape varieties thrive here.

The most common grapes are the Muscadet, Cabernet Franc and Chenin Blanc varieties. Wines tend to be light and delicate. The most celebrated areas are Pouilly-Fumé, Vouvray, Sancerre, Bourgueil, Chinon and Saumur.

'Bordeaux has been synonymous with full-bodied red wine since the time of the Romans.'

Rhône Region

The Rhône region is divided into northern and southern areas. The different soil, climate, topography and grapes used means there is a dramatic difference in the wines produced by each.

On steep hills by the river, the northern vineyards make red wines from the ruby-red Syrah grape; the aromatic Viognier grape is the most popular for white wines. The south is better known for the quantity rather than quality of the wine it produces. The Grenache grape, which ages well when blended, is used in the reds, while the whites use the Ugni Blanc grape.

CHAMPAGNE

Champagne is made from the red Pinot Noir, the black Pinot Meunier or the white Chardonnay grape. Each vine is vigorously pruned and trained to produce a small quantity of high-quality grapes. Indeed, to maintain exclusivity (and price), the amount of champagne that can be produced each year is limited to between 160 and 220 million bottles, most of which is consumed in France and the UK.

The process of making champagne – carried out by innumerable *maisons* (houses) – is a long and complex one. There are two fermentation processes, the first in casks and the second after the wine has been bottled and had sugar and yeast added.

In the two months that the bottles are aged in cellars kept at 12°C, the wine turns effervescent. The sediment that forms in the bottle is removed by *remuage,* a painstakingly slow process in which each bottle – stored horizontally – is rotated slightly every day for weeks until the sludge works its way to the cork. Next comes *dégorgement:* the neck of the bottle is frozen, creating a blob of solidified Champagne and sediment, which is then removed.

At this stage, the champagne's sweetness is determined by adding varying amounts of syrup dissolved in old champagne. Then the bottles of young champagne are laid in a cellar and aged for between two and five years (sometimes longer), depending on the *cuvée* (vintage).

If the final product is labelled *brut,* it is extra dry, with only 1.5% sugar content. *Extra-sec* means it's very dry (but not as dry as brut), *sec* is dry and *demi-sec* is slightly sweet. The sweetest Champagne is labelled *doux.*

Some of the most famous champagne houses are Dom Pérignon, Möet et Chandon, Veuve Cliquot, Mercier, Mumm, Krugg, Laurent-Perrier, Piper-Heidsieck and Taittinger.

APERITIFS & DIGESTIFS

Meals in France are often preceded by an appetite-stirring *apéritif* such as *kir* (white wine sweetened with cassis or blackcurrant syrup), *kir royale* (champagne with cassis) or *pineau* (cognac and grape juice). *Pastis,* a 90-proof, anise-flavoured alcoholic drink that turns cloudy when you add water, is especially popular at cafés and with your author.

After-dinner drinks are often ordered with coffee. France's most famous brandies are Cognac and Armagnac, both of which are made from grapes in the regions of those names. *Eaux de vie,* literally 'waters of life', can be made with grape skins and the pulp left over after being pressed for wine (Marc de Champagne, Marc de Bourgogne), apples (Calvados), pears (Poire William) as well as such fruits as plums *(eau de vie de prune)* and raspberries *(eau de vie de framboise).*

BEER & CIDER

The *bière à la pression* (draft beer) served by the *demi* (about 33cL) in bars and cafés across the land is usually one of the national brands such as

DID YOU KNOW?

Part of the reason the 17th-century monk Dom Pierre Pérignon's technique for making sparkling wine was more successful than earlier efforts was because he put his product in strong, English-made bottles and capped them with corks brought from Spain.

Kronenbourg, 33 or Pelforth and totally forgettable. Alsace, with its close cultural ties to Germany, produces some excellent local beers (eg Bière de Scharrach, Schutz Jubilator and Fischer, a hoppy brew from Scilligheim). Northern France, close to Belgium and the Netherlands, has its own great beers as well, including St-Sylvestre Trois Monts, Colvert, Terken Brune and Brasserie Jeanne d'Arc's Grain d'Orge made from barley.

Cidre (apple cider) is made in many parts of France, including Savoy, Picardy and the Basque Country, but its real home is Normandy and Brittany. You'll find *poiré* (perry, or pear cider) in Picardy and Normandy.

Nonalcoholic Drinks

The most popular nonalcoholic beverages consumed in France are coffee and mineral water.

WATER & MINERAL WATER

All tap water in France is safe to drink, so there is no need to buy bottled water. People in cities don't agree, however; less than 1% of the water consumed by a typical Parisian household each day, for example, is actually drunk. Tap water that is not drinkable (eg at most public fountains and on trains) will usually have a sign reading '*eau non potable*'.

If you prefer tap water rather than pricey bottled water, make sure you ask for *de l'eau* (some water), *une carafe d'eau* (a jug of water) or *de l'eau du robinet* (tap water). Otherwise you'll most likely get bottled *eau de source* (spring water) or *eau minérale* (mineral water), which comes *plate* (flat or still) or *gazeuse* (fizzy or sparkling). Popular mineral waters in France:

Badoit – France's oldest bottled mineral water with the tiniest of bubbles and medium taste, from the Loire Valley

Évian – A light, still Alpine mineral water from the spa town Évian-les-Bains, the 'pearl of Lake Geneva' (p508)

Perrier – Well-known, very carbonated mineral water in a distinctive green bottle from Languedoc (p737)

Vittel – Popular still mineral water from Lorraine sold in vending machines everywhere

Volvic – A very neutral still water from the Auvergne (p554)

COFFEE

The most ubiquitous form of coffee here is espresso, made by forcing steam through ground coffee beans. A small espresso, served without milk, is called *un café noir, un express* or simply *un café*. You can also ask for a *grand* (large) version.

Café crème is espresso with steamed milk or cream. *Café au lait* is lots of hot milk with a little coffee served in a large cup or, sometimes, a bowl. A small *café crème* is a *petit crème*. A *noisette* (literally, 'hazelnut') is an espresso with just a dash of milk. Decaffeinated coffee is *café décaféiné*.

CELEBRATIONS

At the risk of sounding facile, food in itself makes French people celebrate, and they'll accept any excuse for a party. There are birthdays and engagements and weddings and christenings and, like everywhere, there are special holidays.

One tradition that is very much alive is called the *jour des rois,* which falls on 6 January and marks the feast of the *Épiphanie* (Epiphany), when the Three Wise Men paid homage to the Infant Jesus. A *galette des rois* (kings' cake), a puff pastry with frangipane cream, a little dried *fève* bean (or plastic or silver figurine) and topped with a gold paper crown that goes on sale in patisseries throughout France after the new year, is placed

'Food in itself makes French people celebrate, and they'll accept any excuse for a party.'

on the table. The youngest person in the room ducks under the table and calls out which member of the party should get each slice. The person who gets the bean is named king or queen, dons the crown and chooses his or her consort. This tradition is popular not just at home among families but also at offices and dinner parties.

At *Chandeleur* (Candlemas, marking the Feast of the Purification of the Virgin Mary) on 2 February, family and friends gather together in their kitchens to make *crêpes de la Chandeleur* (sweet pancakes).

Pâques (Easter) is marked here as elsewhere with *œufs au chocolat* (chocolate eggs) filled with candy fish and chickens and there is always an egg hunt for the kids. The traditional meal at Easter lunch is *agneau* (lamb) or *jambon de Pâques*, which – like hot-cross buns in Britain – seems to be available throughout the year nowadays.

After the *dinde aux marrons* (turkey stuffed with chestnuts) eaten at lunch on *Noël* (Christmas), a *bûche de Noël*, a 'log' of chocolate and cream or ice cream, is served.

WHERE TO EAT & DRINK

There's a vast number of eateries in France where you can get breakfast or brunch, a full lunch or dinner, and a snack between meals. Most have defined roles, though some definitions are becoming a bit blurred.

Auberge

An *auberge* (inn), which may also appear as an *auberge de campagne* and *auberge du terroir* (country inn), is usually attached to a rural inn or small hotel and serves traditional country fare.

Bar

'Unlike the vast majority of restaurants in France, brasseries serve full meals, drinks and coffee from morning till late at night.'

A *bar* or *bar américain* (cocktail bar) is an establishment dedicated to elbow-bending and rarely serves food beyond pre-made sandwiches or snacks. A *bar à vins* is a 'wine bar', which may or may not (usually the former) serve full meals at lunch and dinner. A *bar à huîtres* is an 'oyster bar'.

Bistro

A *bistro* (often spelled *bistrot*) is not clearly defined in France. It can be simply a pub or bar with snacks and light meals or a fully fledged restaurant.

Brasserie

Unlike the vast majority of restaurants in France, *brasseries* – which can look very much like cafés – serve full meals, drinks and coffee from morning till late at night. The dishes served almost always include *choucroute* and sausages because the brasserie, which actually means 'brewery' in French, originated in Alsace.

Buffet

A *buffet* (or *buvette*) is a kiosk usually found at train stations and airports selling drinks, filled baguettes and snacks.

Café

The main focus of a café is, of course, *café* (coffee) and only basic food is available at most. Common options include a baguette filled with Camembert or pâté and *cornichons* (gherkins), a *croque-monsieur* (grilled ham and toasted cheese sandwich) or a *croque-madame* (a toasted cheese sandwich topped with a fried egg).

Cafétéria

Many cities in France have *cafétérias* (cafeteria restaurants), including Flunch, that offer a decent selection of dishes you can see before ordering – a factor that can make life easier if you're travelling with kids.

Creperie

Creperies (sometimes seen as *galetteries*) specialise in sweet crepes and savoury *galettes* (see p67).

Ferme-Auberge

A *ferme-auberge* (literally 'farm inn') is usually a working farm that serves diners traditional regional dishes made from ingredients produced on the farm itself. The food is usually served *table d'hôte* (literally 'host's table'), meaning in set courses with little or no choice.

Relais Routier

A *relais routier* is a transport café or truck stop, usually found on the outskirts of towns and along major roads, which caters to truck drivers and can provide a quick, hearty break from cross-country driving.

Restaurant

The *restaurant* comes in many guises and price ranges in France. Generally they specialise in a particular variety of food (eg regional, traditional, North African, Vietnamese). There are lots of restaurants where you can get an excellent French meal for under €30 – Michelin's *Guide Rouge* is filled with them – and they usually offer what the French call a *bon rapport qualité-prix* (good value for money). Some of the best French restaurants in the country are attached to hotels, and are usually open to nonguests. Chain restaurants with standard *menus* are a definite step up from fast-food places and usually offer good-value (though uninspired) *menus*. Among the most common are Hippopotamus, Bistrot Romain and Léon de Bruxelles.

Almost all restaurants close for at least 1½ days (ie a full day and either one lunch or one dinner period) each week and this schedule will be posted on the front door. Chain restaurants are usually open throughout the day, seven days a week.

Restaurants almost always have a *carte* (menu) posted outside so you can decide before going in whether the selection and prices are to your liking. Most offer at least one fixed-price, multicourse meal known in French as a *menu, menu à prix fixe* or *menu du jour* (daily menu). A *menu* (not to be confused with a *carte*) almost always costs much less than ordering à la carte.

When you order a *menu*, you usually get to choose an entree, such as salad, paté or soup; a main dish (several meat, poultry or fish dishes, including the *plat du jour*, or 'the daily special', are generally on offer); and one or more final courses (usually cheese or dessert). In some places, you may also be able to order a *formule*, which usually has fewer choices but allows you to pick two of three courses – a starter and a main course, say, or a main course and a dessert.

Boissons (drinks), including wine, cost extra unless the *menu* says *boisson comprise* (drink included), in which case you may get a beer or a glass of mineral water. If the *menu* has *vin compris* (wine included), you'll probably be served a 25cL *pichet* (jug) of wine. The waiter will always ask if you would like coffee to end the meal, but this will almost always cost extra.

Restaurant meals here are almost always served with bread, which is rarely accompanied by butter. If you run out of bread in your basket, don't be afraid to ask the waiter for more (*'Pourrais-je avoir encore du pain, s'il vous plaît'*).

Restaurant Libre-Service

A *restaurant libre-service* is a 'self-service restaurant' similar to a *cafétéria* (see p75).

Restaurant Rapide

A *restaurant rapide* is a fast-food restaurant be it imported (McDonald's, Pizza Hut and KFC) or home-grown such as Quick.

Restaurant Universitaire

All French universities have several *restaurants universitaires* (refectories or canteens) subsidised by the Ministry of Education and operated by the Centre Régional des Œuvres Universitaires et Scolaires, better known as 'Crous'. They serve very cheap meals (typically under €5) and are usually open to nonstudents.

Salon de Thé

A *salon de thé* (tearoom) is a trendy and somewhat pricey establishment that usually offers quiches, salads, cakes, tarts, pies and pastries in addition to black and herbal teas.

VEGETARIANS & VEGANS

Vegetarians and vegans make up a small minority in a society where *viande* (meat) once also meant 'food', and they are not particularly well catered for; specialist vegetarian restaurants are few and far between. In fact, the vegetarian establishments that do exist in France often look more like laid-back, 'alternative lifestyle' cafés than restaurants. On the bright side, more and more restaurants are offering vegetarian choices on their set *menus*, and *produits biologiques* (organic products) are all the rage nowadays, even among carnivores. Other options include *saladeries*, casual restaurants that serve a long list of *salades composées* (mixed salads).

DINING WITH CHILDREN

It is sometimes said here that France treats its children as adults until they reach puberty – at which time they revert to being children again. You'll see a few *petits hommes* (little men) and *petites dames* (little ladies) dining decorously on the town with their parents, but most restaurants here do not have highchairs, children's menus or children's portions. In fact, children are rarely seen in most Parisian restaurants, which may explain the popularity of American-style fast-food restaurants and French chain restaurants such as Hippopotamus and Buffalo Grill (see p151), which cater to parents with kids in tow.

HABITS & CUSTOMS

French people do not eat in the clatter-clutter style of the Chinese or with the exuberance and sheer gusto of, say, the Italians. A meal is an artistic and sensual delight to most people here, something to be savoured and enjoyed with a certain amount of style and *savoir-vivre*.

When shopping for provisions, follow the example of the French and shop at speciality stores, whose managers can always offer advice.

When the French Eat

BREAKFAST

What the French call *petit déjeuner* is not every Anglo-Saxon's cup of tea. Masters of the kitchen throughout the rest of the day, French chefs don't seem up to it in the morning. Perhaps the idea is not to fill up – *petit déjeuner* means 'little lunch' and the real *déjeuner* (lunch) is just around the corner!

In the Continental style, people here traditionally start the day with a bread roll or a bit of baguette left over from the night before eaten with butter and jam and followed by a *café au lait* (coffee with lots of hot milk), a small black coffee or even a hot chocolate. Some people also eat cereal, toast, fruit and even yogurt in the morning – something they never did before.

Contrary to what many foreigners think, the French do not eat croissants every day but usually reserve these for a treat at the weekend when they may also choose *brioches, pains au chocolat* or other *viennoiserie* (baked goods).

> 'Contrary to what many foreigners think, the French do not eat croissants every day'

LUNCH & DINNER

Many French people still consider *déjeuner* (lunch) to be the main meal of the day. But as the pace of life is as hectic here as it is elsewhere in the industrialised world nowadays, the two-hour midday meal has become increasingly rare, at least on weekdays. Dinners, however, are still turned into elaborate affairs whenever time and finances permit. A fully fledged, traditional French meal at home is an awesome event, often comprising six distinct *plats* (courses). They are always served with wine – red, white or rosé (or a combination of two or all three), depending on what you're eating. A meal in a restaurant almost never consists of more than three or four courses: the *entrée* (starter or first course), the *plat principal* (main course), *dessert* and perhaps *fromage* (cheese).

Where the French Shop

Most French people buy a good part of their food from a series of small neighbourhood shops, each with its own speciality (though like everywhere more and more people are relying on supermarkets). At first, having to go to four shops and stand in four queues to fill the fridge (or assemble a picnic) may seem a waste of time, but the ritual is an important part of the way many French people live their daily lives. Note that many food shops are closed Sunday afternoon and all day Monday.

It's perfectly acceptable to purchase only meal-size amounts: a few *tranches* (slices) of meat to make a sandwich, perhaps, or a *petit bout*

FRITES

To make perfectly fried French fries or chips *(frites)* you'll need a *friteuse,* a deep-fryer (either stove-top or electric). Slice the potatoes uniformly, relatively thin (2cm) and about 8cm long. Put them in a bowl of cold salted water and let them soak for an hour, changing the water once or twice to remove some of the excess starch. Then dry them thoroughly on kitchen towels or on a tea towel/dish cloth.

Begin to heat the oil and put the potatoes in a *grille* (deep-frying basket). When the oil reaches 180°C plunge the *grille* into the *friteuse,* which will cause the temperature to drop. After about 10 minutes, when the potatoes start to take on a slightly waxy look and glisten, remove the basket from the oil and let it rest for about five minutes and allow the oil to heat back up. Put the basket back in the deep-fryer and cook till the chips are golden brown (about 10 minutes).

(small hunk) of sausage. You can also request just enough *pour une/deux personne(s)* (for one/two person/s).

BOUCHERIE

A *boucherie* is a general butcher's shop selling fresh beef, lamb, pork, chicken etc, but for specialised poultry you have to go to a *marchand de volaille* (also called a *volailler*), where *poulet fermier* (free-range chicken) and *poulet de grain* (corn-fed chicken) are also sold. A *boucherie chevaline,* easily identifiable by the gilded horse's head above the entrance, sells horsemeat, which some people prefer to beef or mutton, in part because it is less likely to have been produced using artificial hormones and has less fat. A *triperie* has tripe, either fresh or in various sauces.

BOULANGERIE

Fresh bread is baked and sold at France's 36,000 *boulangeries,* which supply three-quarters of the country's bread. Along with bread, bakeries usually sell croissants, *brioches, pains au chocolat* etc – baked goods that are lumped together under the term *viennoiserie.*

CHARCUTERIE

A *charcuterie* is a delicatessen offering sliced meats, pâtés, terrines, *rillettes* etc, though they sometimes do other things like seafood salads and even casseroles like *traiteurs* (opposite) do. Most supermarkets have a *charcuterie* counter.

CHOCOLATERIE

This is a shop selling only chocolate; most specialise in their own bonbons made on the premises.

'Most chocolateries specialise in their own bonbons on the premises'

CONFISERIE

Sweets including chocolate made with the finest ingredients can be found at *confiseries,* which are sometimes combined with *boulangeries* and patisseries.

ÉPICERIE

Literally 'spice shop', this is a small grocery store with a little bit of everything, including fruit and vegetables, and also known as an *alimentation générale.* Some *épiceries* are open on days when other food shops are closed, and many family-run operations close late at night.

FROMAGERIE

If you buy your cheese in a supermarket, you're likely to end up with unripe and relatively tasteless products unless you know how to select each variety. Here's where a *fromagerie,* also known as a *crémerie,* comes in. The owner, a true expert on matters dairy, can supply you with cheese that is *fait* (ripe) to the exact degree that you request and will almost always let you taste before you decide what to buy.

MARCHAND DE LÉGUMES ET DE FRUITS

Fruits and vegetables are sold by a *marchand de légumes et de fruits* (greengrocer) and at food markets and supermarkets. Most *épiceries* have only a limited selection. You can buy whatever quantity of produce suits you, even if it's just three carrots and a peach. *Biologique* (or *bio*) means grown organically (ie without chemicals).

MARCHAND DE VIN

Wine is sold by a *marchand de vin* (or *caviste*), such as the shops of the Nicolas chain. Wine shops in close proximity to the vineyards of Burgundy, Bordeaux, the Loire region and other wine-growing areas are often called *vinothèques* and offer tastings.

MARCHÉ

In most towns and cities, many of the aforementioned products are available one or more days a week at a *marché en plein air* (open-air market), also known as a *marché découvert*, and up to six days a week at a *marché couvert* (covered marketplace), often known as *les halles*. Markets are cheaper than food shops and supermarkets and the merchandise, especially fruit and vegetables, is much more fresh and of better quality.

PATISSERIE

Mouth-watering pastries are available at patisseries. Some of the most common pastries include *tarte aux fruits* (fruit tarts), *pain aux raisins* (a flat, spiral pastry made with custard and sultanas) and *religieuses* (eclairs that – vaguely – resemble a nun's habit).

POISSONERIE

Fresh fish and seafood are available from a *poissonnerie* (fishmonger). People have such a taste for fish in France that fish shops in big cities and towns inland often have as big a selection of fresh fish and crustaceans as the ones closer to the coast do.

SUPERMARCHÉ

Both town and city centres usually have at least one department store with a large *supermarché* (supermarket) section in the basement or on the 1st floor. Most larger supermarkets have *charcuterie* and cheese counters, and many also have in-house *boulangeries*.

TRAITEUR

A *traiteur* (caterer) sells ready-to-eat dishes to take home: casseroles, salads of all shades and hues and many more elaborate dishes. *Traiteurs* are a picnicker's delight and a godsend to people at home who want something better than takeaway but can't be bothered to cook.

COOKING COURSES

What better place to discover the secrets of *la cuisine française* than in front of a stove? Cooking courses are available at different levels and lengths of time and the cost of tuition varies widely. In Paris one of the most popular – and affordable – is **Cours de Cuisine Françoise Meunier** (Map pp96-8; ☎ 01 40 26 14 00; www.fmeunier.com; 7 rue Paul Lelong, 2e; metro Bourse), which offers three-hour courses at 2.30pm on Tuesday and at 10.30am from Wednesday to Saturday for adult/child aged 12 to 14 €90/60. 'Carnets' of five/20 courses cost €400/1500. Other major cooking schools in Paris:

École de Gastronomie Française Ritz Escoffier (Map pp93-5; ☎ 01 43 16 30 50; www .ritzparis.com; 38 rue Cambon, 1er; metro Concorde)

École Le Cordon Bleu (Map pp99-101; ☎ 01 53 68 22 50; www.cordonbleu.edu; 8 rue Léon Delhomme, 15e; metro Vaugirard or Convention)

École Lenôtre (Map pp93-5; ☎ 01 45 02 21 19; www.lenotre.fr; Pavillon Élysée, 10 av des Champs-Élysées, 8e; metro Champs-Élysées Clemenceau)

DID YOU KNOW?

French homemakers have never been averse to letting the experts take care of the more complicated dishes and have used the services of *traiteurs* and *pâtissiers* for centuries.

SOUPE À L'OIGNON GRATINÉE

Nothing is more Parisian than onion soup with a crust of oven-browned grated cheese.

225g onions, thinly sliced   salt and pepper
60g butter   thin rounds of bread
1 tablespoon flour   thin slices of Gruyère cheese
1.5L water

Cook the sliced onions in butter. When they are golden, sprinkle with flour. Mix well with a wooden spoon and gradually blend in the water. Season with salt and pepper and simmer for 15 minutes. Slice the bread thinly and brown in butter. Ladle the soup into individual earthenware bowls, top with a crouton and cheese and heat in the oven until the cheese begins to brown. Serves 6.

There are a number of regional cooking schools around France:

Domaine de la Tortinière (☎ 02 47 34 35 00; www.tortiniere.com; route de Ballan Miré, Les Gués de Veigné, 37250 Montbazon) Traditional Touraine cuisine courses in a chateau setting.

La Cuisine du Soleil (☎ 04 93 75 78 24; www.moulin-mougins.com; Notre Dame de Vie, 06250 Mougins) Mediterranean cuisine taught by a top chef.

La Manoir d L'Aufragère (☎ 02 32 56 91 92; www.laufragere.com; L'Aufragère, La Croisée, 27500 Fourmetot) Courses are held in a Norman manor house.

Mas de Cornud (☎ 04 90 92 39 32; www.mascornud.com; Petite Route de Mas Blanc, 13210 St-Rémy de Provence) Provençal home cooking.

EAT & DRINK YOUR WORDS

For pronunciation guidelines see p932.

Useful Phrases

I'm hungry/thirsty.
  J'ai faim/soif.   zhay fum/swaf

A table for two, please.
  Une table pour deux, s'il vous plaît.   ewn ta·bler poor der seel voo play

Do you have a menu in English?
  Est-ce que vous avez la carte en anglais?   es·ker voo za·vay la kart on ong·lay

What's the speciality of this region?
  Quelle est la spécialité de la région?   kel ay la spay·sya·lee·tay de la ray·zhon

What is today's special?
  Quel est le plat du jour?   kel ay ler pla doo zhoor

I'd like the set menu, please.
  Je prends le menu, s'il vous plaît.   zher pron ler mer·new seel·voo·play

I'd like some...
  Je voudrais du/de la...   zher voo·dray doo/de la...

May I have another...please?
  Puis-je avoir encore un/une...   pwee zher a·vwa ong·kor un/oon...
  s'il vous plaît?   seel voo play

I'm a vegetarian.
  Je suis végétarien/végétarienne. (m/f)   zher swee vay·zhay·ta·ryun/
        vay·zhay·ta·ryen

I don't eat (meat).
  Je ne mange pas de viande.   zher ne monzh pa de vyond

Is service included?
  Le service est compris?   ler sair·vees ay kom·pree

The bill, please.
  L'addition, s'il vous plaît.   la·dee·syon seel voo play

Menu Decoder
STARTERS (APPETISERS)

assiette anglaise	plate of cold mixed meats and sausages
assiette de crudités	plate of raw vegetables with dressings
soufflé	a light, fluffy dish of egg yolks, stiffly beaten egg whites, flour and cheese and other ingredients

SOUP

bouillabaisse	Mediterranean-style fish soup, originally from Marseille, made with several kinds of fish, including *rascasse* (spiny scorpion fish); often eaten as a main course
bouillon	broth or stock
bourride	fish stew; often eaten as a main course
potage	thick soup made with puréed vegetables
soupe au pistou	vegetable soup made with a basil and garlic paste
soupe de poisson	fish soup
soupe du jour	soup of the day

MEAT & POULTRY

aiguillette	thin slice of duck fillet
andouille or **andouillette**	sausage made from pork or veal tripe
bifteck	steak
bleu	nearly raw
saignant	very rare (literally: 'bleeding')
à point	medium rare but still pink
bien cuit	literally: 'well cooked', but usually like medium rare
blanquette de veau	veal stew with white sauce
bœuf bourguignon	beef and vegetable stew cooked in red wine
bœuf haché	minced beef
boudin noir	blood sausage (black pudding)
brochette	kebab
canard	duck
caneton	duckling
cassoulet	Languedoc stew made with goose, duck, pork or lamb fillets and haricot beans
charcuterie	cooked or prepared meats (usually pork)
chevreuil	venison
choucroute	sauerkraut with sausage and other prepared meats
civet	game stew
confit de canard (d'oie)	duck (goose) preserved and cooked in its own fat
coq au vin	chicken cooked in wine
côte	chop of pork, lamb or mutton
côtelette	cutlet
cuisses de grenouille	frogs' legs
entrecôte	rib steak
escargot	snail
faisan	pheasant
faux-filet	sirloin steak
filet	tenderloin
foie	liver
foie gras de canard	duck liver pâté
fricassée	stew with meat that has first been fried
gibier	game
gigot d'agneau	leg of lamb
grillade	grilled meats

jambon	ham
langue	tongue
lapin	rabbit
lard	bacon
lardon	pieces of chopped bacon
lièvre	hare
mouton	mutton
oie	goose
pieds de cochon/porc	pigs' trotters
pintade	guinea fowl
quenelles	dumplings made of a finely sieved mixture of cooked fish or (rarely) meat
rognons	kidneys
sanglier	wild boar
saucisson	large sausage
saucisson fumé	smoked sausage
steak	steak
steak tartare	raw ground meat mixed with onion, raw egg yolk and herbs
tournedos	thick slices of fillet
volaille	poultry

FISH & SEAFOOD

anchois	anchovy
anguille	eel
brochet	pike
cabillaud	cod
calmar	squid
chaudrée	fish stew
coquille St-Jacques	scallop
crabe	crab
crevette grise	shrimp
crevette rose	prawn
écrevisse	freshwater crayfish
fruits de mer	seafood
hareng	herring
homard	lobster
huître	oyster
langouste	crayfish
langoustine	very small saltwater 'lobster' (Dublin Bay prawn)
maquereau	mackerel
merlan	whiting
morue	cod
moules	mussels
palourde	clam
rouget	mullet
sardine	sardine
saumon	salmon
thon	tuna
truite	trout

COOKING METHODS, SAUCES & CONDIMENTS

à la vapeur	steamed
aïoli	garlic mayonnaise
au feu de bois	cooked over a wood-burning stove
au four	baked

béchamel	basic white sauce
en croûte	in pastry
farci	stuffed
fumé	smoked
gratiné	browned on top with cheese
grillé	grilled
huile d'olive	olive oil
moutarde	mustard
pané	coated in breadcrumbs
pistou	pesto (pounded mix of basil, hard cheese, olive oil and garlic
provençal(e)	tomato, garlic, herb and olive oil dressing or sauce
rôti	roasted
sauté	sautéed (shallow fried)
tartare	mayonnaise with herbs
vinaigrette	salad dressing made with oil, vinegar, mustard and garlic

DESSERTS & SWEETS

crêpes suzettes	orange-flavoured pancakes flambéed in liqueur
dragées	sugared almonds
éclair	pastry filled with cream
flan	egg-custard dessert
frangipane	pastry filled with cream and flavoured with almonds
gâteau	cake
gaufre	waffle
glace	ice cream
île flottante	literally: 'floating island'; beaten egg white lightly cooked, floating on a creamy sauce
macaron	macaroon (sweet biscuit of ground almonds, sugar and egg whites)
sablé	shortbread biscuit
tarte (aux pommes)	apple tart or pie
yaourt	yogurt

SNACKS

croque-monsieur	grilled ham and cheese sandwich
croque-madame	croque-monsieur with a fried egg
frites	chips (French fries)
quiche	quiche

Food Glossary

BASICS

breakfast	petit déjeuner	**lunch**	déjeuner
dinner	dîner	**food**	nourriture
menu	carte	**set menu**	menu/formule
starter/appetiser	entrée	**main course**	plat principal
wine list	carte des vins	**market**	marché
grocery store/		**waiter/**	
delicatessen	épicerie/traiteur	**waitress**	serveur/serveuse
knife	couteau	**fork**	fourchette
spoon	cuillère	**bottle**	bouteille
glass	verre	**plate/dish**	plat/assiette
hot/cold	chaud/froid	**with/without**	avec/sans

MEAT & FISH

beef	boeuf	**meat**	viande
chicken	poulet	**pork**	porc

fish	*poisson*	**turkey**	*dinde*
lamb	*agneau*	**veal**	*veau*

FRUIT & VEGETABLES

apple	*pomme*	**lemon**	*citron*
apricot	*abricot*	**lentils**	*lentilles*
artichoke	*artichaut*	**lettuce**	*laitue*
asparagus	*asperge*	**mushroom**	*champignon*
banana	*banane*	**onion**	*oignon*
beans	*haricots*	**peach**	*pêche*
beetroot	*betterave*	**peas**	*petit pois*
bilberry		**pepper**	
(blueberry)	*myrtille*	(red/green)	*poivron (rouge/vert)*
blackcurrant	*cassis*	**pineapple**	*ananas*
cabbage	*chou*	**plum**	*prune*
carrot	*carotte*	**potato**	*pomme de terre*
celery	*céleri*	**prune**	*pruneau*
cepe (boletus		**pumpkin**	*citrouille*
mushroom)	*cèpe*	**raspberry**	*framboise*
cherry	*ceris*	**rice**	*riz*
cucumber	*concombre*	**shallot**	*échalotte*
French (string)		**spinach**	*épinards*
beans	*haricots verts*	**strawberry**	*fraise*
gherkin (pickle)	*cornichon*	**sweet corn**	*maïs*
grape	*raisin*	**tomato**	*tomate*
grapefruit	*pamplemousse*	**turnip**	*navet*
leek	*poireau*	**vegetable**	*légume*

OTHER

bread	*pain*	**jam**	*confiture*
butter	*beurre*	**oil**	*huile*
cheese	*fromage*	**pepper**	*poivre*
cream	*crème*	**salt**	*set*
egg	*œuf*	**sugar**	*sucre*
honey	*miel*	**vinegar**	*vinaigre*

DRINKS

beer	*bière*	**milk**	*lait*
coffee	*café*	**mineral water**	*eau minérale*
with milk	*au lait*	**tea**	*thé*
with sugar	*avec sucre*	**water**	*eau*
juice (apple)	*jus (de pomme)*	**wine (red)**	*vin (rouge)*
juice (orange)	*jus (d'orange)*	**wine (white)**	*vin (blanc)*

Paris

Paris is to many people the most beautiful and romantic city in the world. The architecture, the parks and squares, the timeless Seine, the café life and the people's *joie de vivre* – and dress sense – all combine to make the 'City of Light' a monumental, handsome and fascinating place in which to live and to visit. But the uninitiated may find it all a bit daunting at first.

Paris has more landmarks familiar to people who have never visited than any other city. First-time visitors often arrive in the French capital with all sorts of expectations and trepidations: of grand vistas, of intellectuals discussing weighty matters in cafés, of romance along the Seine, of sexy cabaret revues and of rude people who don't (or won't) speak English but will happily rip you off. If you look, you'll find all those things – there's no doubt about that. But set aside your preconceptions and explore the city's avenues and backstreets as if the Eiffel Tower and Notre Dame weren't about to pop into view at any moment.

Parisians believe they have savoir-faire – the inherent knowledge of how to live well – and you'll find that Paris is a feast for the senses. It's a city to view: wide boulevards, monuments, works of art and magical lights. It's a city to taste: cheese, wine, *charcuterie*. It's a city to hear: opera, jazz or world music, or just the sound of metro cars whooshing by. It's a city to smell: perfume boutiques, cafés with fresh coffee and croissants, chestnuts roasting in winter. It's a city to feel: the wind in your face as you cycle by the Seine, the *frisson* of fear and pleasure as you peer from the top of the Eiffel Tower. Above all, it's a city to discover. This chapter is designed to whet your appetite and guide you when you arrive. But remember: it's just a guidebook Leave it behind from time to time and wander to find your very own personal Paris.

HIGHLIGHTS

- Take in the contents and rooftop view at the art and cultural complex of **Centre Pompidou** (p116)

- Play 'spot the departed' at **Cimetière du Père Lachaise** (p129), the world's most visited necropolis

- Ascend the **Eiffel Tower** (p125) the image that has become more Parisian than Paris itself

- Visit the **Louvre** (p113) to view old favourites such as the *Mona Lisa* and *Venus de Milo*

- Check out the **Marais** (p117) for stately *hôtels particuliers* (private mansions) by day and the pulsating nightlife after dark

- Say ooooh-la-la to **Montmartre** (p130), the Paris of story, song and myth

- Marvel at the incomparable collection of impressionist art and the architectural beauty of the **Musée d'Orsay** (p124)

- Come to **Notre Dame** (p119) for both the sacred (rose windows, medieval statuary) and the profane (gargoyles, tourist hordes)

- Admire the sublime stained glass of Christ's Passion on a sunny day at **Ste-Chapelle** (p120)

■ POPULATION: 2.1 MILLION	■ AREA: 105 SQ KM

HISTORY

What is now the Île de la Cité was settled in the 3rd century BC by a tribe of Celtic Gauls known as the Parisii. Centuries of conflict between the Gauls and Romans ended in 52 BC, when Julius Caesar's legions crushed a Celtic revolt led by Vercingétorix. Christianity was introduced in the 2nd century AD, and Roman rule ended in the 5th century with the arrival of the Germanic Franks. In 508 Frankish king Clovis I united Gaul as a kingdom and made Paris his seat.

The Middle Ages brought prosperity to Paris. Construction began on the cathedral of Notre Dame in the 12th century, and the marshy Marais area north of the Seine – what would become known as the Right Bank – was drained and settled. The Louvre began as a riverside fortress around 1200, the beautiful Ste-Chapelle was consecrated in 1248 and the Sorbonne opened its doors in 1253.

Scandinavian Vikings (also known as Norsemen or Normans) had begun raids on France's west coast in the 9th century; after three centuries of conflict, they started to push towards Paris. These conflicts heralded the Hundred Years' War between Norman England and Paris' Capetian dynasty, eventually bringing the French defeat at Agincourt in 1415 and English control of the capital in 1420. In 1429 the 17-year-old Jeanne d'Arc (Joan of Arc) rallied the French troops to defeat the English at Orléans. With the exception of Calais, the English were finally expelled from France in 1453.

At the end of the 15th century the Renaissance helped Paris get back on its feet, and many of the city's most famous buildings and monuments were erected at this time. But in less than a century Paris was again in turmoil, this time in the name of religion. Clashes between the Huguenot Protestants and Catholic groups became increasingly commonplace, culminating with the 1572 St Bartholomew's Day massacre of 3000 Huguenots who had gathered in Paris to celebrate the wedding of Henri of Navarre (later King Henri IV).

Louis XIV (le Roi Soleil, or the Sun King) ascended the throne in 1643 at the age of five and held the crown until 1715. During his long reign, he nearly emptied the national coffers with his ambitious building and battling. His most tangible legacy is the palace at Versailles, 21km southwest of Paris. The excesses of Louis XVI and his queen Marie-Antoinette, led to an uprising of Parisians on 14 July 1789 and the storming of the Bastille prison – kick-starting the French Revolution.

After a few short years the populist visions of the Revolution gave way to a Reign of Terror, during which even a few of the original patriots were executed. The unstable post-Revolution government was consolidated in 1799 under a young Corsican general named Napoleon Bonaparte, who declared himself First Consul. In 1804 he had the Pope crown him Emperor of the French and then swept most of Europe under his wing. Napoleon's hunger for more victories and glory led to his defeat, first in Russia in 1812 and later at Waterloo in Belgium in 1815.

After the defeated Napoleon was exiled, France struggled under a string of mostly inept rulers until a coup d'état in 1851 brought emperor Napoleon III to power. He oversaw the construction of a more modern Paris, with wide boulevards, sculptured parks and – not insignificantly – a modern sewer system. Like his uncle, however, this Napoleon and his penchant for pugnacity led to a costly and eventually unsuccessful war, this time with the Prussians in 1870. When the masses in Paris heard of their emperor's capture by the enemy, they took to the streets, demanding that the republic be restored. Despite its bloody beginnings, the Third Republic ushered in the glittering and very creative period known as the *belle époque* (beautiful era).

The *belle époque* was famed for its Art Nouveau architecture and advances in the arts and sciences. By the 1930s Paris had become a centre for the artistic avant-garde and had established its reputation among freethinking intellectuals. This was all cut short by the Nazi occupation of 1940; Paris would remain under direct German rule until 25 August 1944. After the war Paris regained its position as a creative centre and nurtured a revitalised liberalism that reached a climax in the student-led uprisings of 1968. The Sorbonne was occupied, barricades were set up in the Latin Quarter and some nine million people nationwide were inspired to join in a general strike that paralysed the country.

During the 1980s President François Mitterrand initiated several costly *grands projets,* a series of building projects that garnered widespread approval even when the results were popular failures. Responses to the flashier examples, such as the glass pyramids in the courtyard of the Louvre and the Bibliothèque Nationale, have ranged from shock horror to doting rapture; if nothing else, the *projets* provoked dialogue about the Parisian aesthetic.

In May 2001 Bertrand Delanoë, a Socialist with support from the Green Party, became Paris' – and a European capital's – first openly gay mayor. He continues to enjoy widespread popularity, particularly for his efforts to make Paris more liveable by promoting bicycles and buses and to create a more approachable and responsible city administration.

ORIENTATION

Central Paris is relatively small: approximately 9.5km (north to south) by 11km (east to west). Within the 'oval' of central Paris, which Parisians call *intra-muros* (Latin for 'within the walls'), the Rive Droite (Right Bank) is north of the Seine, while the Rive Gauche (Left Bank) is south of it since the river flows from east to west.

Paris is quite an easy city to negotiate, but this chapter offers you three ways to find the addresses listed: by district, map reference and metro station.

Arrondissements

Paris is divided into 20 arrondissements (districts), which spiral out clockwise from the centre like a conch shell. City addresses always include the number of the arrondissement, as streets with the same name exist in different districts.

In this chapter, arrondissement numbers are given after a street address using the usual French notation: 1er for *premier* (1st), 2e for *deuxième* (2nd), 3e for *troisième* (3rd) and so on. On some signs or commercial maps, you will see the variation 2ème, 3ème etc.

Maps

The most useful map of Paris is the 1:10,000-scale *Paris Plan* published by Michelin. It

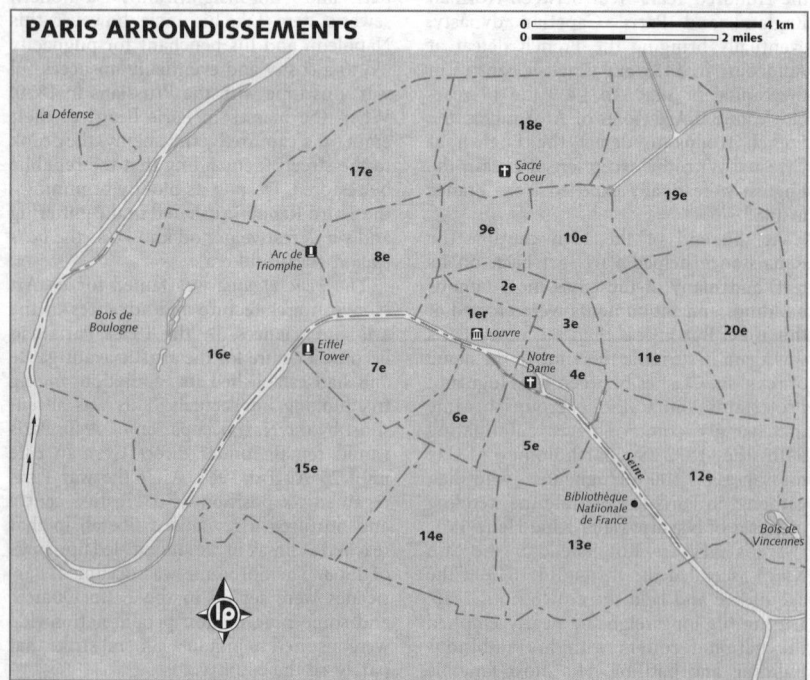

PARIS ARRONDISSEMENTS

0 — 4 km
0 — 2 miles

La Défense

18e

Sacré Coeur

17e

19e

9e   10e

Arc de Triomphe   8e

2e

1er   3e   20e

Louvre

Bois de Boulogne

16e   Eiffel Tower   Notre Dame

11e

7e   4e

6e

5e   Seine

15e   12e

Bibliothèque Nationale de France

14e

13e   Bois de Vincennes

PARIS

PARIS IN...

Two days

If you've got just a couple of days in Paris you should definitely join a morning tour and then concentrate on the most Parisian of sights and attractions: Notre Dame (p119), the Louvre (p113), the Eiffel Tower (p125) and the Arc de Triomphe (p127). In the late afternoon have a coffee or a pastis on the av des Champs-Élysées (p154) and then make your way to Montmartre (p130) for dinner. The following day take in such sights as the Musée d'Orsay (p124), Ste-Chapelle (p120), Conciergerie (p120), Musée National du Moyen Âge (p121) and/or the Musée Rodin (p125). Have brunch on the place des Vosges (p148) and enjoy a night of mirth and gaiety in the Marais (p158).

Four days

With another day to look around the city, you should consider a cruise (p134) along the Seine or the Canal St-Martin and visit some place further afield – the Cimetière du Père Lachaise (p129), say, or the Parc de la Villette (p130). Take in a concert, opera or ballet (p162) at the Palais Garnier or Opéra Bastille or a play at the Comédie Française (p166). Why not head to a destination in the Île de France on the following day such as Versailles (p185) or Chartres (p196)? Be back in time for a farewell pub and club crawl through Ménilmontant (p160), though.

A week

If you have a full week here you can see a majority of the sights listed in this chapter, visit places 'outside the walls' such as La Défense (p179) and St-Denis (p182), and leave Paris for a couple of days' excursion. Vaux-le-Vicomte (p192) can be easily combined with Fontainebleau (p189), Senlis (p195) with Chantilly (p193) and, if you travel hard and fast, Chartres (p189) with Versailles (p185).

---

comes in booklet form (No 11 or 14; €5.25) or as a fold-out sheet (No 10 or 12; €4.25 to €6) or, under the name *Atlas Paris 15*, in large format (€9). The Lonely Planet *Paris City Map* is available from bookshops in the UK and France.

For a more user-friendly street atlas than the venerable old *Paris par Arrondissement* (€13.50), choose L'Indispensable's *Paris Pratique par Arrondissement* (€5.50), which is a slim, pocket-sized atlas. The larger *Le Petit Parisien* (€7) has three maps for each arrondissement, showing streets, metro lines and bus routes.

The best place to find a full selection of maps is the Espace IGN (p906).

Metro Stations

Paris counts some 372 metro stations and there is always one station within a maximum of 500m of wherever you need to go in Paris (see the Metro map, opposite p108). Thus all the offices, museums, hotels and restaurants mentioned here have the nearest metro stop written immediately after the contact details. Metro stations usually have a useful *plan du quartier* (map of the neighbourhood) on the wall near the exits.

INFORMATION
Bookshops

Abbey Bookshop (Map pp105-7; ☎ 01 46 33 16 24; 29 rue de la Parcheminerie, 5e; metro Cluny-La Sorbonne; ☷ 10am-7pm Mon-Sat) Mellow Canadian-owned bookshop not far from place St-Michel celebrated for its free tea and coffee and good selection of new and used books.

Les Mots à la Bouche (Map pp105-7; ☎ 01 42 78 88 30; www.motsbouche.com in French; 6 rue Ste-Croix de la Bretonnerie, 4e; metro Hôtel de Ville; ☷ 11am-11pm Mon-Sat, 2-8pm Sun) 'On the Tip of the Tongue' is Paris' premier gay bookshop. If you're feeling naughty, go down – stairs, that is.

Red Wheelbarrow Bookstore (Map pp105-7; ☎ 01 48 04 75 08; 22 rue St-Paul, 4e; metro St-Paul; ☷ 10am-7pm Mon-Sat, 2-6pm Sun) This relatively new English-language bookshop has arguably the best selection of literature and 'serious reading' in Paris.

Shakespeare & Company (Map pp105-7; ☎ 01 43 26 96 50; 37 rue de la Bûcherie, 5e; metro St-Michel; ☷ noon-midnight) Paris' most famous English-language bookshop has a varied collection of new and used books in English, including paperback novels for as little as €1.

(Continued on page 109)

A B C D

1

See La Défense
Map (p181)

A14

La Défense
Grande Arche
La Défense
Esplanade de
la Défense
Blvd Circulaire
R. de la République

Stade de
Courbevoie

Cimetière de
Lavallois

Mairie
de Clichy

St Ouen

Cimetière
Parisien des
Batignolles

Île de la
Grande Jatte

Pont de
Levallois
Bécon

Cimetière
Sud

21
Porte de
Clichy

Blvd Bessières

1
3

Anatole
France

Pablo
Neruda
Louison
Bobet

Blvd Victor Hugo

2

Pont de
Neuilly

Av Charles de Gaulle

Les Sablons

Blvd Maurice Barrès

Blvd Maillot

Av du Roule

Blvd Péreire

See Central Paris - NW Map (pp94-5)

Blvd Victor Hugo
Blvd Périphérique

Av de Wagram

17e

R de Courcelles

R de Rome

Av de Clichy

Blvd Malesherbes

Gare S
Lazare
Blvd Haussman

Seine

Île de
Puteaux

Mare St
James

Arc de
Triomphe

Av de Friedland

8e

Av Foch

Av des Champs Élysées

3

Lac Pour
le Patinage

Parc de
Bagatelle

Lac Inférieur

Racing
Club de
France

Garde
Républicaine
I Cheval

Bois de
Boulogne

Lac
Supérieur

Hippodrome
de Longchamp

Étang de
Boulogne

A13

Avenue
Foch

Ave Henri
Martin
Av Henri Martin

Av Victor Hugo

Av Kléber

Av Marceau

Triangle
d'Or

Cimetière
de Passy

Q d'Orsay Q Anatole Franc

15

La
Muette

16e

Av Paul Doumer

Q Branly

Av de la Bourdonnais

Q de la Bourdonnais

Eiffel
Tower

7e

Faubourg
St Germain

4

BoulainVilliers

Ranelagh

Jasmin

Hippodrome
d'Auteuil

Michel
Ange
Auteuil

Porte
d'Auteuil

Église
d'Auteuil

Javel

Stade
Rolland
Garros

13

Michel Ange
Molitor

Stade
Jean Bouin

Chardon
Lagache

30

Blvd Suchet

Blvd Lannes

R de la Pompe

R de Passy

R Raynouard

Blvd Grenelle

Q de Grenelle

Seine

Q d'Issy

R du Théâtre

R de la Croix Nivert

16e

R de la Convention

R St-Dominique

R de l'Université

Blvd Garibaldi

Blvd des Invalides

15e

R Lecourbe

R de Sèvres

Necker

Left
Bank

Gare
Montparnasse

Av du Maine

5

Parc
des
Princes

Exelmans

Ancien
Cimetière

Porte
de St Cloud

Boulevard
Victor

Blvd Victor

Av de Versailles

R Baland

R Balard

R de Vaugirard

Cimetière
de
Vaugirard

See Central Paris - SW Map (pp100-1)

Blvd Périphérique

Porte de
Versailles

Blvd Lefebvre

R de Vaugirard

Stade de
la Porte de
la Plaine

Stade Charles
Rigoulot
(Centre Sportif)

25

Pernety

Plaisance

Porte
de Vanves

14e

Stade
Didot

Stade
Jules
Noel

Porte
d'Orleans

Cimetière de
Montrouge

17

16

Billancourt

Marcel
Sembat

N10

Pont de
Sèvres

Île
Seguin

Nouveau
Cimetière

Île St
Germain

Stade
Jean
Bouin

Stade
G Voisin

Issy-
Val de
Seine

Centre Sportif
Suzanne
Lenglen

Corentin
Celton

Mairie d'Issy

Seine

Q de Stalingrad

Île de
Billancourt

Jacques
Henri
Lartigue

Issy Ville

André
Roche

Malakoff
Plateau
de Vanves

Malakoff
Rue E Dolet

Chatillon Montrouge

Cimetière
des Longs
Réages

6

INFORMATION
American Hospital in Paris.........................**1** B1
Bureau des Objets Trouvés....................**2** C5
Hertford British Hospital..........................**3** C1
SOS Dentaire...**4** E5

SIGHTS & ACTIVITIES   (pp113-32)
Bibliothèque Nationale de France -
   François Mitterrand.............................**5** F5
Catacombes..**6** E5
Cité de la Musique....................................**7** G1
Cité des Sciences et de l'Industrie.......**8** G1
Hippodrome d'Auteuil..............................**9** B4
Manufacture des Gobelins....................**10** E5
Musée de la Musique..........................(see 7)
Parc de Bercy...**11** G5

Porte de Choisy.......................................**12** F6
Stade Roland Garros..............................**13** B4

SLEEPING   [icon]   (pp136-47)
Auberge de Jeunesse Le D'Artagnan.....**14** H3
Camping du Bois de Boulogne.............**15** A3
Hôtel de Blois...**16** D5
Petit Palace Hôtel....................................**17** D5

EATING   [icon]   (pp147-58)
L'Avant-Goût...**18** F5
La Fleuve de Chine.................................**19** F6
Sinorama..**20** F5

ENTERTAINMENT   [icon]   (pp160-7)
Ateliers Berthier......................................**21** D1

Cité de la Musique Box Office...............**22** G2
Le Batofar..**23** G5
Le Zénith...**24** G1

SHOPPING   [icon]   (pp167-70)
Marché aux Puces de la Porte de
   Vanves..**25** D5
Marché aux Puces de Montreuil...........**26** H4
Marché aux Puces de St Ouen...............**27** E1
Musée & Compagnie..............................**28** G5

TRANSPORT   (pp170-6)
Gare Routière Internationale de Paris
   Galliéni..**29** H3
Rent a Car Système.................................**30** B4

A B C D

1 2 3 4 5 6

R St Paul
R de Lesseps
Blvd Victor Hugo
R Voltaire
R Barbès
R Aristide Briand
R Louis Rouquier
R Danton
R Carnot
R Gabriel Péri
R Henri Barbusse
R Jacques Ibert
R d'Alsace
R de Reims
R Bruneteau
Boulogne

Av Bineau
R de Villiers
R Louise Michel
Louise Michel
R de la Somme
Av Paul Adam
Place Paul Leantaud
Blvd Pereire (Nord)
Blvd Pereire (Sud)

R Borghèse
R des Dames-Augustines
Porte de Villiers
Jardin de l'Amérique Latine
Place Stuart Merrill
Square J Bellat
Pereire-Levallois
Place d'Israel

R Madeleine Michelis
R Perronet
Porte de Champerret
Place du Mal Juin
Péreire
Av de Villiers
Place du Brest

Square du Cardinal Petit de Julleville
Blvd Gouvion St Cyr
Villa Aublet
Place A Maillart
R de Prony
Av de Wagram

Av du Roule
Porte des Ternes
Place Tristan Bernard
Av des Ternes
Ternes
Place des Ternes
Blvd de Courcelles

Porte Maillot
Place de la Porte Maillot
Neuilly Porte Maillot Palais des Congrès
Porte Maillot
Place St Ferdinand

Square de l'Amiral Bruix
Square Anna de Noailles
TEP Jean Pierre Wimille
Blvd de l'Amiral Bruix
Place du Gal Patton
Av de la Grande Armée
Charles de Gaulle-Étoile
Av Hoche
Av de Friedland

Porte Dauphine
Av Foch
Place Charles de Gaulle
Av des Champs Élysées
George V

R de Presbourg
Kléber
R Newton
R Euler

Victor Hugo
Place Victor Hugo
R Copernic
R La Pérouse

Av Victor Hugo
R St Didier
Place des États Unis
Place Amiral de Grasse

Boissière
Lycée Assomption

Place de Mexico
Place d'Iéna
Iéna
Square Brignole Galliera
Alma Marceau
Place de la Reine Astrid

Av Henri Martin
Rue de la Pompe
Av Georges Mandel
Trocadéro
Av du Président Wilson
Pont de l'Alma
Place de la Résistance

Cimetière de Passy
Palais de Chaillot
Jardins du Trocadéro
Av de New York
Seine
Q Branly

0   400 m
0   0.2 miles

Parc de la Villette
Grande Halle
Parc de la Villette

R de Torcy
R Buzelin
E
R Curial
R Archereau
R Mathis
R de Crimée
F
R de Joinville
R de Flandre
Crimée
G
Q de Marne
H
Porte de Pantin

R de Tanger
R Riquet
Av de Flandre
R Duvergier
R Jomard
Canal de l'Ourcq
Q de l'Oise
Q de la Marne
R des Ardennes
R Adolphe Mille
R Edgar Varèse
Allée du Zénith
Porte de Pantin
1

Riquet
•4
R de Rouen
Passage de Flandre
Q de la Seine
R Léon Giraud
R de l'Ourcq
R de Lorraine
R Delesseux
R Euryale Dehaynin
Ourcq
Allée Darius Milhaud

R du Maroc
R d'Aubervilliers
R Bellot
R Cail
Bassin de la Villette
•18
R Pierre Reverdy
R de la Loire
R Tandou
Av Jean Jaurès
R Léon Giraud
R Thionville
R André Danjon
Cimetière de la Villette
Allée Darius Milhaud
R Manin

Stalingrad
Blvd de la Villette
R Chaudron
Place de la Bataille de Stalingrad
Q de la Loire
R de la Moselle
Laumière
•2
Av de Laumière
R du Rhin
R Megnadier
Place F Poulenc
R de la Solidarité
R Gaston Pinot
R David d'Angers
2

33
Jaurès
R Bouret
R de Meaux
R Cavendish
R Armand Carrel
Place A Carrel
R de Crimée
R Compans du Général Brunet
R Miguel Hidalgo
Danu

Louis Blanc
38
R La Fayette
R Louis Blanc
Q de Valmy
Cité Lepage
Bolivar
R Édouard Pailleron
Av Secrétan
R Henri Murger
Parc des Buttes Chaumont
R de Crimée
Botzaris
3

55
81
R Eugène Varlin
Q de Jemmapes
Place du Colonel Fabien
Colonel Fabien
R des Chaufourniers
Av Mathurin Moreau
Buttes Chaumont
R Botzaris
R du Plateau
R Pradier
R de la Villette
R des Alouettes
R Carducci
R des Annelets
R Arthur Rozier
R Louise
Place des Fête

Place Raoul Follereau
Canal St-Martin
R Vicq d'Azir
R de la Grange aux Belles
R Juliette Dodu
R de Sambre et Meuse
Blvd de la Villette
R Burnouf
R de l'Atlas
R Laurin
R des Dunes
R Rébeval
R de Belleville
R Clavel
R Fessart
R Mélingue
R des Solitaires
R de l'Ermitage
Place des Fête

70
St Louis
Av Richerand
Av Claude Vellefaux
R Ste Marthe
R du Chalet
R Sté Marthe
Square de Rebeval
R Jules Romains
R Rampal
R de la Guerre
R Simon Bolivar
R Piat
Pyrénées
R de Belleville
Jourdain
R Levert
R Olivier Mét
4

67
Q de Valmy
R de Lancry
R Dieu
R Alibert
R du Buisson St Louis
R Civale
Belleville
R Déloyre
R de Tourtille
R Lesage
R Jouye Rouve
R Pali
R Piat
R des Envierges
R des Cascades
R de la Mare
R des Rigoles
R des Pyrénées
R de l'Ermitage

Place de la République
R Léon Jouhaux
R Yves Toudic
75
R Jacques Louvel Tessier
R Tesson
R Louis Bonnet
R du Faubourg du Temple
85
Marché Belleville
59
51
Ramponeau
Place A Allais
14
Square Alexandre Luquet
R Henri Chevreau
R Bisson
R Jullien Lacroix
R Boyer

Goncourt
44
Square J Ferry
72
74
22
République
Oberkampf
43
•1
R de la Fontaine au Roi
R de l'Orillon
R de Vaucouleurs
R Deguerry
R Morand
R des Trois Couronnes
66
7•
Couronnes
R du Moulin Joly
Place A Allais
R Ramponeau
Belleville
Blvd de Belleville
R Julien Lacroix
R des Maronites
R Étienne Dolet
R d'Eupatoria
R de Ménilmontant
Ménilmontant
R des Panoyaux
R Max Ernst
R Sorbier
R Soleillet
R des Partants
5

République
R Rampon
Oberkampf
88
Parmentier
R de Nemours
78
76
R Oberkampf
St Maur
Av Jean Aicard
R du Chemin Vert
R des Bluets
R des Nanettes
R de Tourtille
R de Ménilmontant
Blvd de Ménilmontant
R des Cendriers
R des Amandiers
R de Tlemcen
Av Gambetta
6

R Chaligny
R de Turenne
Blvd Voltaire
R du Temple
R Amelot
Filles du Calvaire
54
56
R Jean Pierre Timbaud
69
49
R des Trois Couronnes
R Jean Pierre Timbaud
Blvd Richard Lenoir
Av Parmentier
St Maur
Av de la République
R Servan
Square Maurice Gardette
Père Lachaise
Cimetière du Père Lachaise

R Vieille du Temple
R de Crussol
R St Sébastien
Passage St Pierre Amelot
R Commines
Blvd Voltaire
Blvd Beaumarchais
St Ambroise
R Lacharrière
Passage St Sébastien
R Pasteur
R Servan
Cour Joly

See pp102-3

A B C D

1

Rue de la Pompe
Av Georges Mandel
R Greuze
R Scheffer
Trocadéro
Av du Président Wilson
Iéna
Place de l'Alma
Pont de l'Alma

R Decamps
R Cortambert
Place du Trocadéro et du 11 Novembre
Cimetière de Passy
48
27
Jardins du Trocadéro
Av Albert de Mun
Av d'Iéna
R Fresnel
Av de New York
Pont de l'Alma

See pp94-5
Place de la Résistance
R Cognacq
25

Villa Gilbert
R Nicolo
R de la Tour
R Louis David
R Bellini
R Vineuse
Av du Président Wilson

Place de Varsovie
24
Jardins du Trocadéro
Av des Nations Unies
Pont d'Iéna
Pont de la Bourdonnais
Allée Paul Deschanel
57
Cité de l'Alma
Av Franco Russe
R de Montessuy
Av Rapp
R de l'Université

2

Place Possoz
Av Paul Doumer
R Eugène Manuel
R Benjamin Franklin
Blvd Delessert
Champ de Mars-Tour Eiffel
Branly
9
Eiffel Tower
17
19
Place Jacques Rueff
Parc du Champ de Mars

Boulain Villiers
R Bois le Vent
R de Passy
Place de Costa Rica
Square Dickens
R Raynouard
Passy
Champ de Mars-Tour Eiffel
Stade Émile Anthoine
5
R Jean Rey
3

Place des Martyrs Juifs du Vélodrome d'Hiver
Bir Hakeim

3

R du Ranelagh
Kennedy Radio-France
Maison de Radio France
Seine
Allée des Cygnes
R du Docteur Finlay
R de la Fédération
Blvd de Grenelle
Place A Sauvy
18
R Gros
R Félicien David
Voie Georges-Pompidou
Pont de Grenelle
Place de Brazzaville
Place Dupleix
Dupleix
La Motte Picquet Grenelle
Square Cambronne

4

Javel
Rond Point du Pont Mirabeau
Q André Citroën
Square Pablo Casals
Place St Charles
Place Charles Michels
Charles Michels
Av Émile Zola
Avenue Émile Zola
R Frémicourt
Cambronne
Place du Commerce
Commerce

5

Square des Cévennes
Parc André Citroën
Cimetière de Grenelle
Rond Point St Charles
R de la Convention
Jardin Duranton
Boucicaut
Square Violet
Félix Faure
Square St Lambert
Square Gerbert
Place et Square Adolphe Chérioux
Vaugirard

6

Balard
Place Balard
Blvd du Général Martial Valin
Balard
Lourmel
Cimetière de Vaugirard
R de Lourmel
R de la Croix Nivert
Convention
7

0 ——————— 400 m
0 ——————— 0.2 miles

E · Pont des Invalides · Pont Alexandre III · **F** · Seine · **G** · Jardin des Tuileries · **H**

Q d'Orsay · Place de Finlande · Assemblée Nationale (Palais Bourbon) · Q des Tuileries · Tuileries

Av Robert Schuman · Invalides · Assemblée Nationale · Q Anatole France · Musée d'Orsay · Jardin du Carrousel · Place du Carrousel

R de l'Université · Esplanade des Invalides · Place du Palais Bourbon · Place du Prés E Harriot · R de Lille · R de la Légion d'Honneur · Q du Louvre

Passage Commun · R St Dominique · R de Constantine · Square S Rousseau · R de Poitiers · Q Voltaire

Place Santiago du Chili · Place des Invalides · R de Bourgogne · R Las Cases · R de Villersexel · R de l'Université

La Tour Maubourg · Square Santiago du Chili · Square d'Ajaccio · Solférino · R du Bac

Varenne · Hôtel des Invalides · R de Grenelle · R de Bellechasse · Rue du Bac

École Militaire · Jardin de l'Intendant · Faubourg St Germain · Place St Germain des Prés · St Germain des Prés

Place Vauban · Blvd des Invalides · R de Babylone · R de Varenne · Square Chaise Récamier · R du Four

Place de Fontenoy · Square des Missions Etrangères · R du Dragon · St Sulpice · Place St Sulpice

Left Bank · Jardin Catherine Labouré · Square Boucicaut · Sèvres Babylone · R de Mézières

Unesco Building · Place du Prés Mithouard · St François Xavier · Square de l'Abbé Esquerré · Laennec · R de Sèvres · R de Rennes

Av de Saxe · Esplanade du Souvenir Français · Vaneau · St Placide · Rennes · R de Vaugirard

Ségur · Place de Breteuil · Duroc · Necker · St Placide · R de Fleurus

Blvd Garibaldi · Sèvres Lecourbe · Place Henri Queuille · Falguière · Notre Dame des Champs · Place P Lafue

Pasteur · Place J et T Trefouel · Montparnasse Bienvenüe · Place du 18 Juin 1940 · Place et Square Ozanam

Square Blomet · Volontaires · Porte Océane · Vavin · Blvd du Montparnasse

Square Necker · Pl R Dautry · Gare Montparnasse · Square Gaston Baty · Edgar Quinet · Raspail

Jardin de l'Atlantique · Gaité · Place des Cinq Martyrs du Lycée Buffon · Cimetière du Montparnasse

Place d'Alleray · Square Cardinal Wyszynski · Place de Catalogne · R Jean Zay · Square Georges Lamarque

Square de l'Abbé Lemire · Hôpital St Vincent de Paul

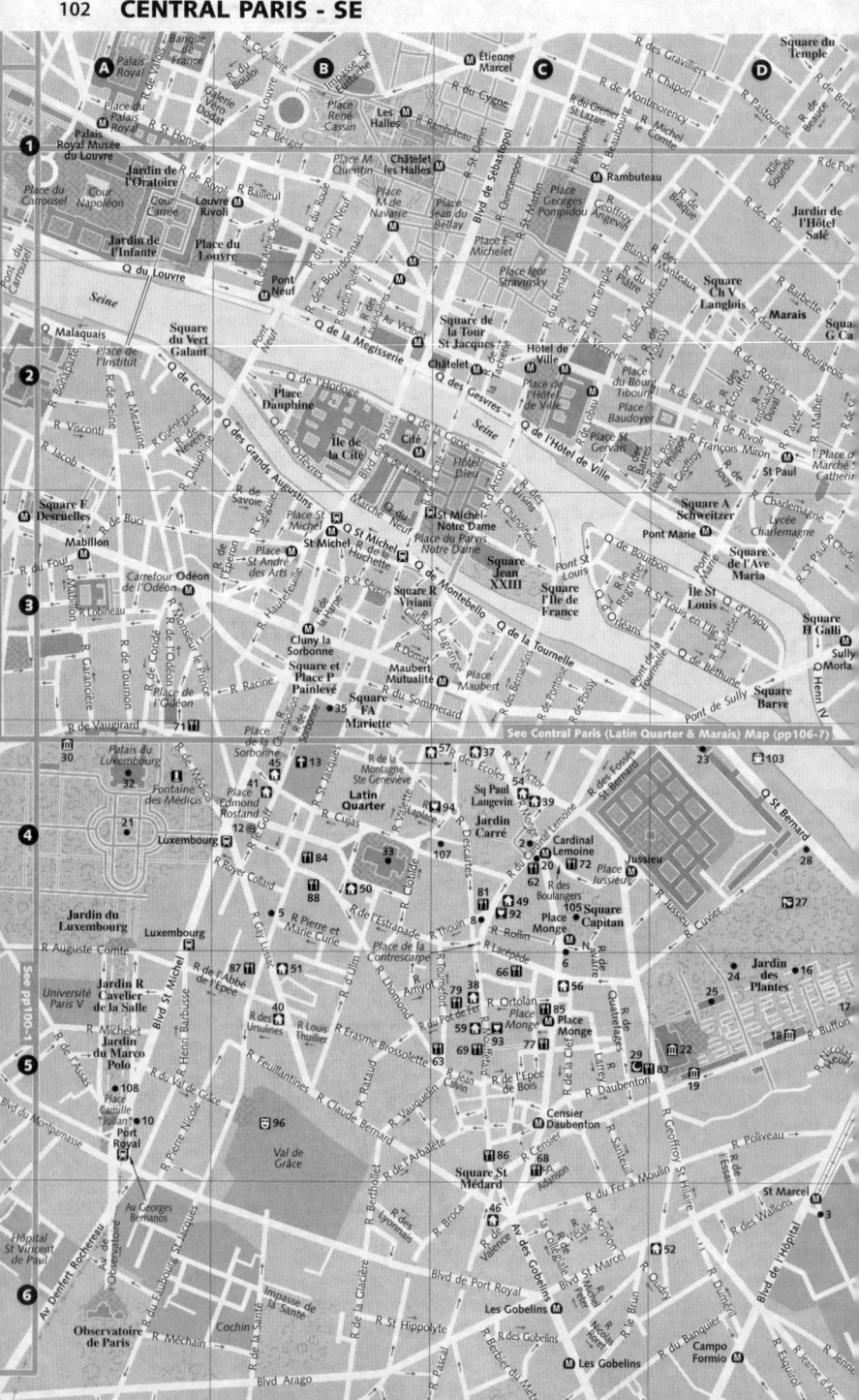

See Central Paris (Latin Quarter & Marais) Map (pp106-7)

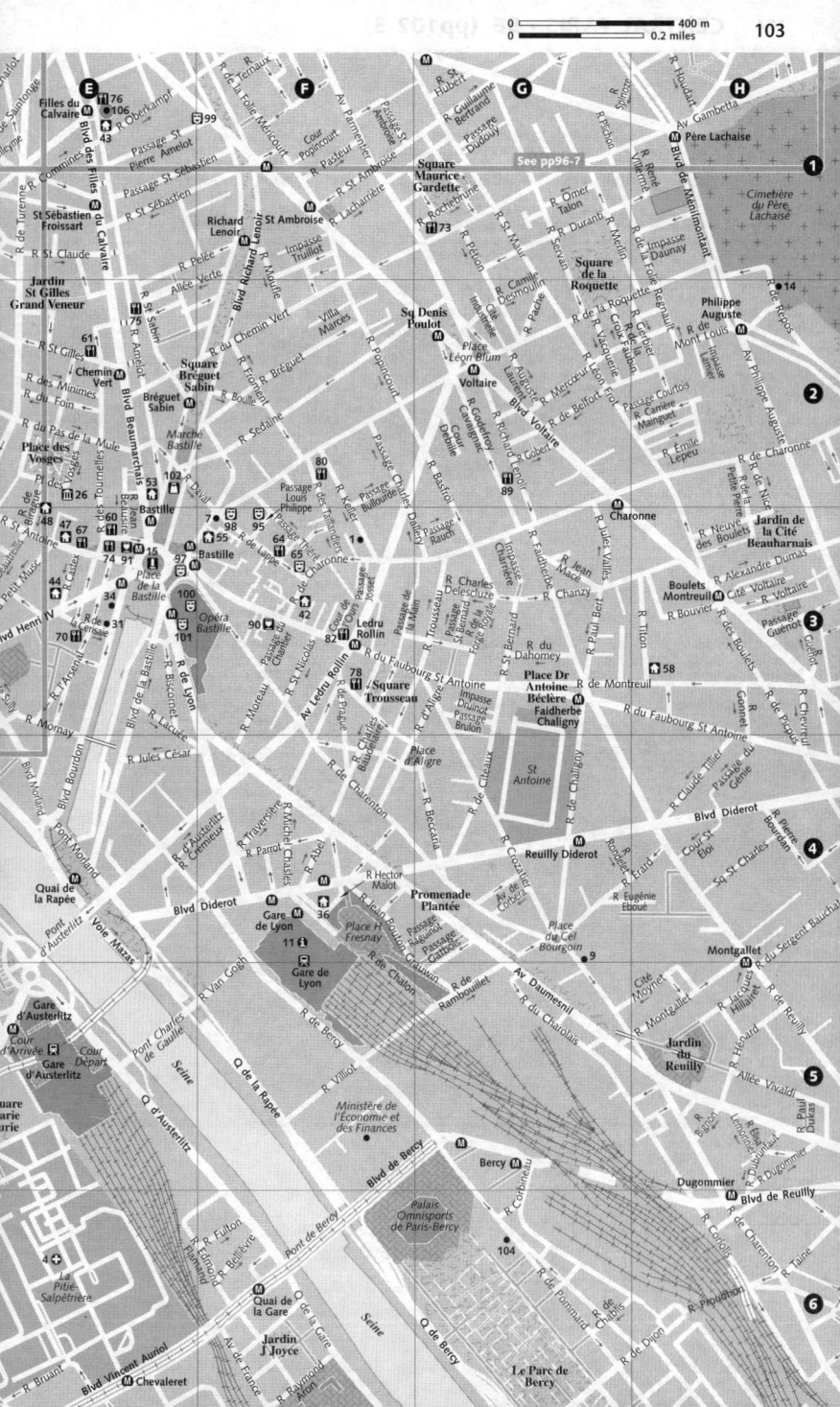

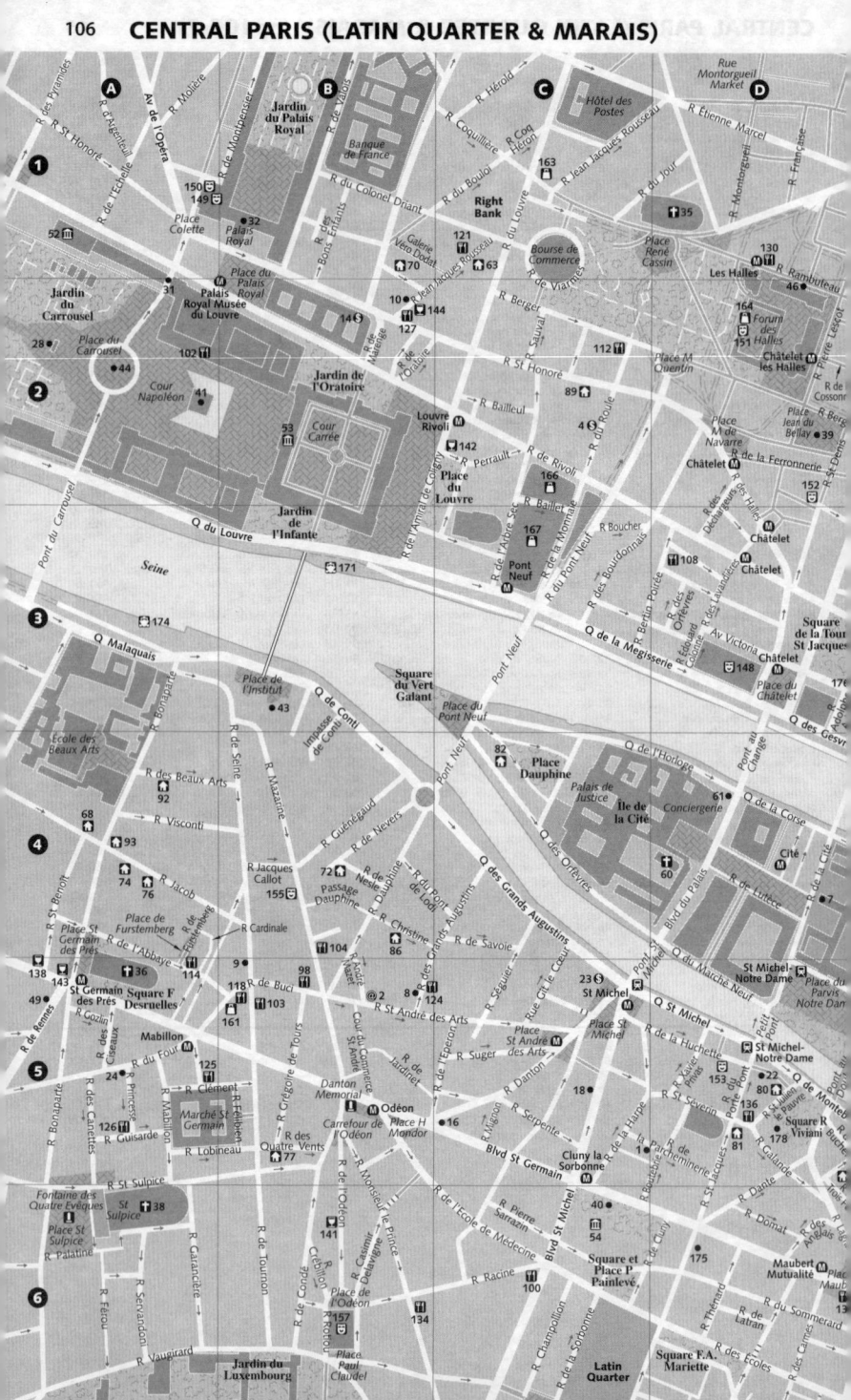

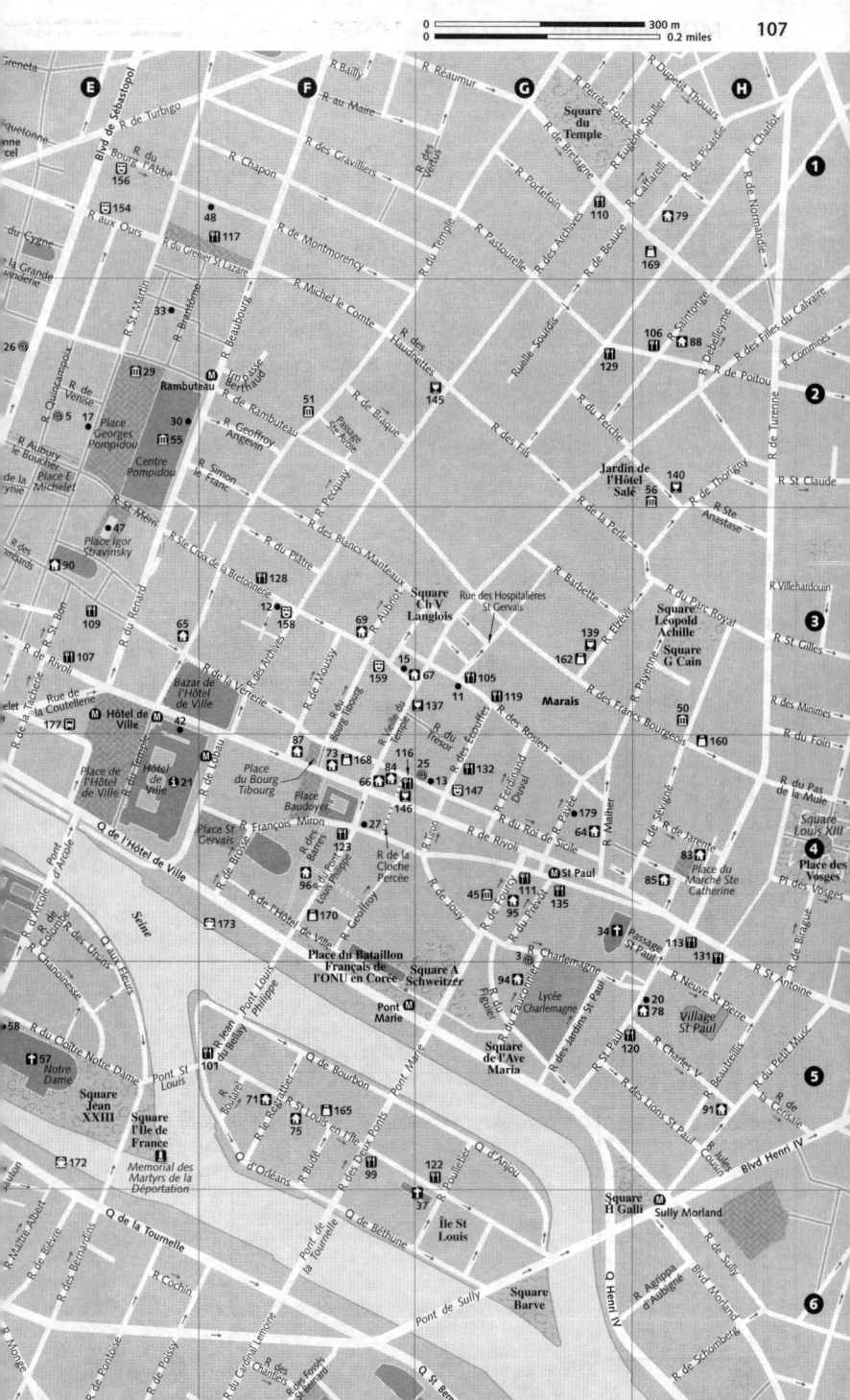

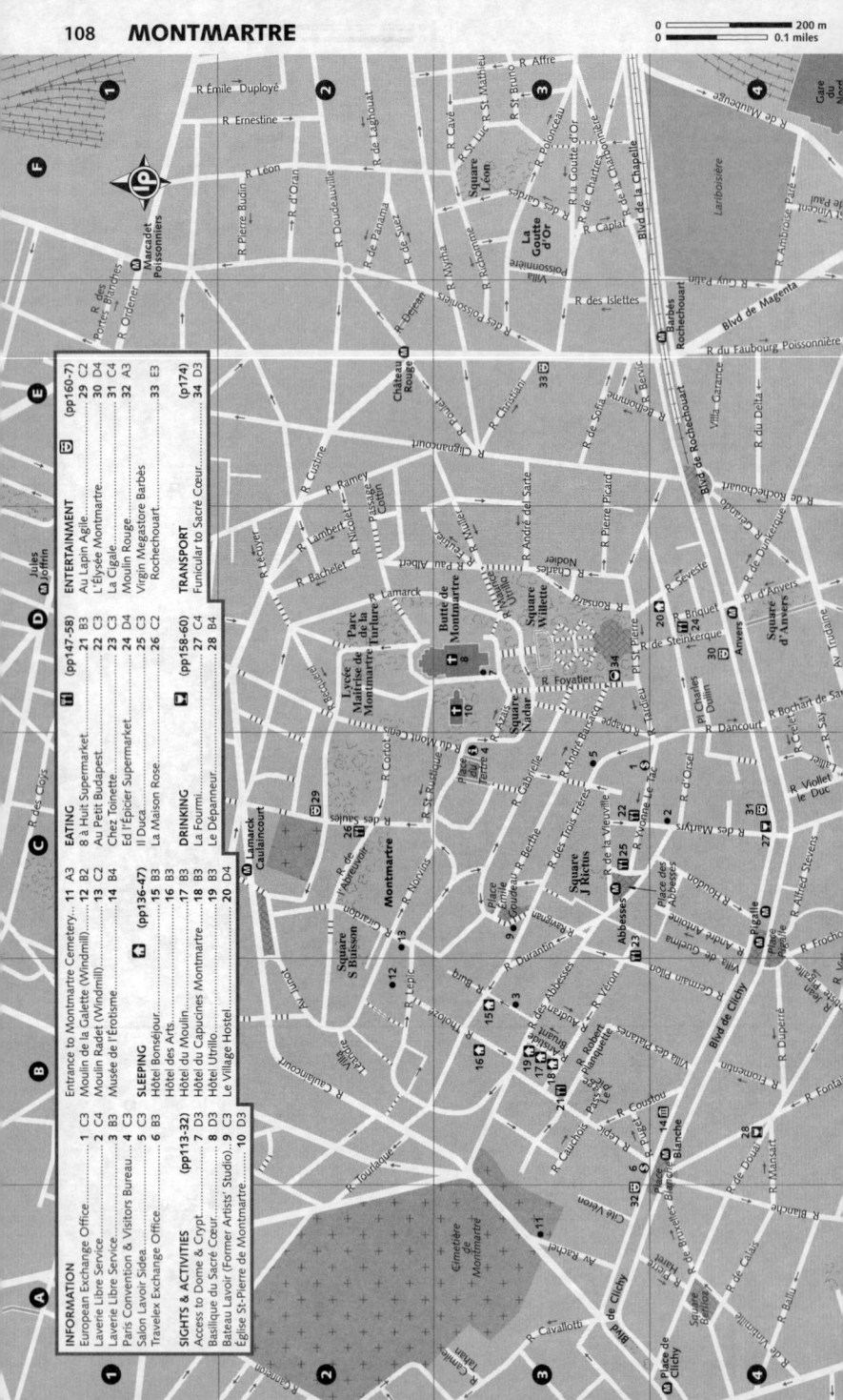

0 — 200 m
0 — 0.1 miles

INFORMATION
European Exchange Office..................1 C3
Laverie Libre Service..........................2 C4
Laverie Libre Service..........................3 B3
Paris Convention & Visitors Bureau....4 C3
Salon Lavoir Sidea...............................5 C3
Travelex Exchange Office....................6 B3

SIGHTS & ACTIVITIES (pp113-32)
Access to Dome & Crypt......................7 D3
Basilique du Sacré Cœur.....................8 D3
Bateau Lavoir (Former Artists' Studio)..9 C3
Église St-Pierre de Montmartre..........10 D3

Entrance to Montmartre Cemetery..11 A3
Moulin de la Galette (Windmill)........12 B2
Moulin Radet (Windmill)...................13 C2
Musée de l'Érotisme...........................14 B4

SLEEPING (pp136-47)
Hôtel Bonséjour.................................15 B3
Hôtel des Arts....................................16 B3
Hôtel du Moulin.................................17 B3
Hôtel du Capucines Montmartre.......18 B3
Hôtel Utrillo.......................................19 B3
Le Village Hostel................................20 D4

EATING (pp147-58)
8 à Huit Supermarket.........................21 B3
L'Élysée Montmartre..........................22 C2
La Cigale...23 C4
Ed l'Épicier Supermarket...................24 D4
Il Duca..25 C3
La Maison Rose..................................26 C2

DRINKING (pp158-60)
La Fourmi...27 C4
Le Dépanneur.....................................28 B4

ENTERTAINMENT (pp160-7)
Au Lapin Agile....................................29 C2
L'Élysée Montmartre..........................30 D4
Moulin Rouge.....................................31 C4
Virgin Megastore Barbès
Rochechouart.....................................32 A3

TRANSPORT (p174)
Funicular to Sacré Cœur....................33 E3
....34 D3

PARIS METRO MAP

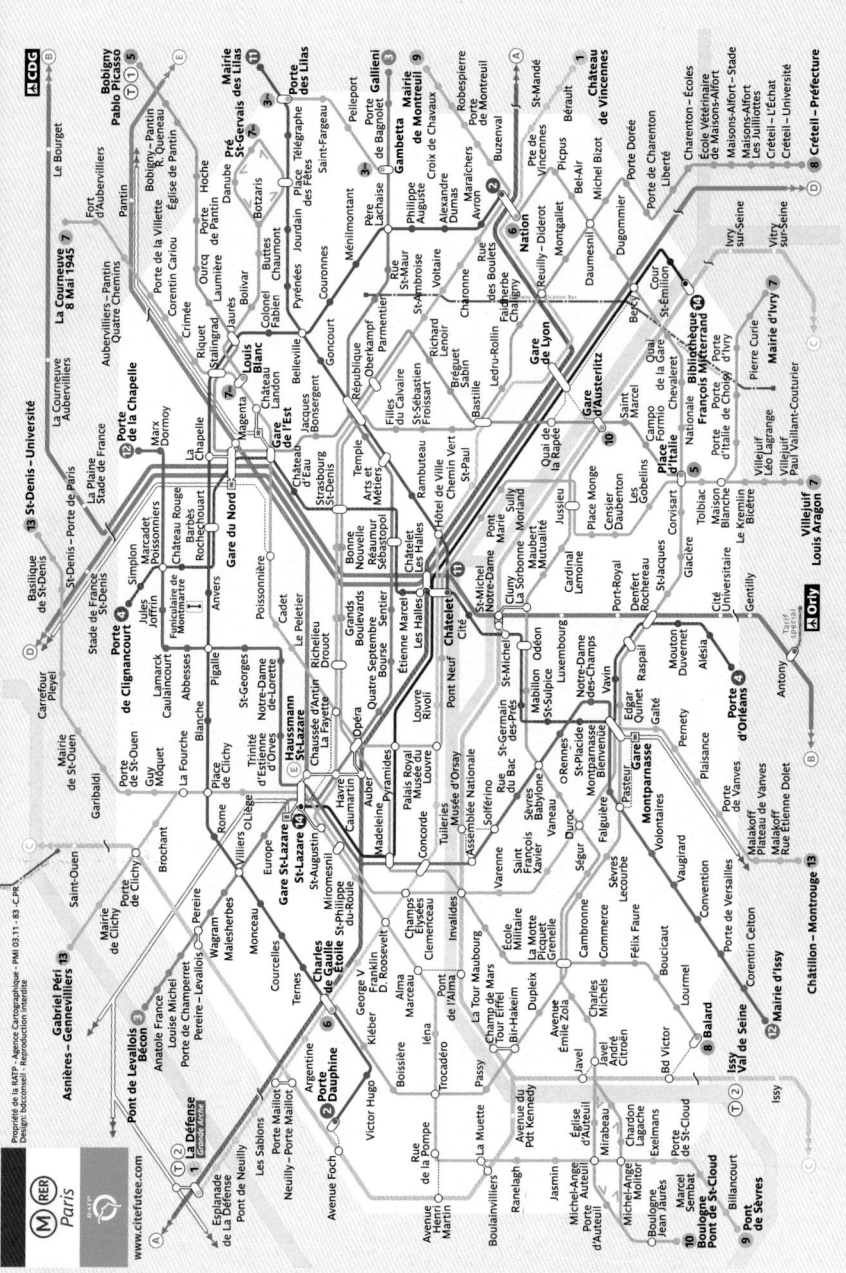

CHRISTOPHER GROEN

Aerial view of Paris (p85) and the Seine

Ste-Chapelle (p120), Paris

MARTIN MOOS

JONATHAN SMITH

Eiffel Tower (p125)

Centre Pompidou (p116), Paris

MARTIN MOOS

(Continued from page 89)

Tea & Tattered Pages (Map pp99-101; ☎ 01 40 65 94 35; 24 rue Mayet, 6e; metro Duroc; ⏰ 11am-7pm Mon-Sat, noon-6pm Sun) T&TP is by far the best and most comprehensive shop selling used English-language books in Paris, with some 15,000 volumes squeezed into two floors.

Village Voice (Map pp105-7; ☎ 01 46 33 36 47; www.villagevoicebookshop.com; 6 rue Princesse, 6e; metro Mabillon; ⏰ 2-8pm Mon, 10am-8pm Tue-Sat, 2-6pm Sun) The Voice has an excellent selection of contemporary North American fiction and European literature in translation, lots of readings and helpful knowledgeable staff.

Emergency

The numbers below are to be dialled in an emergency. See p110 for hospitals with 24-hour accident and emergency departments. For nationwide emergency numbers, see inside the front cover.

Ambulance (SAMU Paris; ☎ 01 45 67 50 50)
SOS Médecins (☎ 01 47 07 77 77) 24hr house calls.
SOS Helpline (☎ 01 47 23 80 80) In English.
Urgences Médicales de Paris (Paris Medical Emergencies; ☎ 01 53 94 94 94, 01 48 28 40 40) 24hr house calls.

Internet Access

Some metro and RER stations (eg St-Michel, Miromesnil) offer free Internet access but there's always a queue a mile long. At the same time, some 50 post offices in Paris – up to five in a few arrondissements – have Internet centres called Cyberposte (p905). The centres generally are open from 8am or 9am to 7pm weekdays and till noon Saturday.

The best and most central commercial Internet cafés in Paris:

Access Academy (Map pp105-7; ☎ 01 43 25 23 80; www.accessacademy.com in French; 60-61 rue St-André des Arts, 6e; metro Odéon; per hr approx €3.50, per day/week/month €6.80/14.90/35.70; ⏰ 8am-2am) This is France's largest Internet café, with some 400 screens in the heart of St-Germain. Hourly rates depend on what time you log on.
Akyrion Net Center (Map pp105-7; ☎ 01 40 27 92 07; www.akyrion.com in French; 19 rue Charlemagne, 4e; metro St-Paul; adult per 15/30/60min €2.50/4.10/7.30 student €2/3.30/5.90; ⏰ 11am-midnight Mon-Sat, 2pm-midnight Sun) This centre in the Marais is popular with students at the nearby university.
Cyberbe@ubourg Internet C@fé (Map pp105-7; ☎ /fax 01 42 71 49 80; 38 rue Quincampoix, 4e; metro Châtelet-Les Halles; per 15/30/45/60min €1.50/3/4.60/6, per 10/20/40hr €29/44/75; ⏰ 9am to 11pm)

Web 46 (Map pp105-7; ☎ 01 40 27 02 89; fax 01 40 27 03 89; 46 rue du Roi de Sicile, 4e; metro St-Paul; per 15/30/60min €2.50/4/7, 5hr €29; ⏰ 9.30am-midnight) This is a very pleasant, well-run café in the heart of the Marais with 15 modules.
XS Arena Luxembourg (Map pp105-7; ☎ 01 43 44 55 55; 17 rue Soufflot, 5e; metro Luxembourg; per 1/2/3/4/5hr €3/6/8/10/12; ⏰ 24hr) This minichain of Internet cafés is bright, buzzy and open round the clock. The **XS Arena Les Halles** (Map pp105-7; ☎ 01 40 13 02 60; 43 rue Sébastopol, 1er; metro Les Halles) branch is just down from the Forum des Halles.

Internet Resources

Mairie de Paris (www.paris.fr) Statistics plus city and tourist information direct from the Hôtel de Ville.
Metropole Paris (www.metropoleparis.com) Excellent online magazine in English.
Paris Pages (www.paris.org) Good links to museums and cultural events.
Paris Tourist Office (www.paris-touristoffice.com) Super site with more links than you'll ever need.

Laundry

There's a *laverie libre-service* (self-service laundrette) around just about every corner in Paris; your hotel or hostel can point you to one in the neighbourhood. Machines usually cost €2.80 to €3.70 for a small load (5kg to 7kg) and €5 to €5.50 for a larger (10kg to 13kg) one. Drying costs €1 for 10 to 12 minutes.

LOUVRE & LES HALLES

Laverie Libre Service (Map pp105-7; 7 rue Jean-Jacques Rousseau, 1er; metro Louvre-Rivoli; ⏰ 7.30am-10pm) Near the Centre International BVJ Paris-Louvre hostel.

MARAIS & BASTILLE

Laverie Libre Service (Map pp105-7; 35 rue Ste-Croix de la Bretonnerie, 4e; metro Hôtel de Ville; ⏰ 7am-10pm)
Laverie Libre Service (Map pp105-7; 25 rue des Rosiers, 4e; metro St-Paul; ⏰ 7.30am-10pm)
Laverie Libre Service Primus (Map pp105-7; 40 rue du Roi de Sicile, 4e; metro St-Paul; ⏰ 7.30am-8.30pm)
Laverie Miele Libre Service (Map pp102-4; 2 rue de Lappe, 11e; metro Bastille; ⏰ 7am-10pm)

LATIN QUARTER & JARDIN DES PLATES

Laverie Libre Service (Map pp102-4; 216 rue St-Jacques, 5e; metro Luxembourg; ⏰ 7am-10pm) Three blocks southwest of the Panthéon.
Le Bateau Lavoir (Map pp102-4; 1 rue Thouin, 5e; metro Cardinal Lemoine; ⏰ 7am-10pm) Near place de la Contrescarpe.

ST-GERMAIN, ODÉON & LUXEMBOURG
Julice Laverie (Map pp105-7; 56 rue de Seine, 6e; metro Mabillon; ⌚ 7am-11pm)
Julice Laverie (Map pp105-7; 22 rue des Grands Augustins, 6e; metro St-André des Arts; ⌚ 7am-9pm)

GARE DU NORD, GARE DE L'EST & RÉPUBLIQUE
Laverie Libre Service (Map pp96-8; 14 rue de la Corderie, 3e; metro République or Temple; ⌚ 8am-9pm)
Laverie SBS (Map pp96-8; 6 rue des Petites Écuries, 10e; metro Château d'Eau; ⌚ 7am-10pm)

MÉNILMONTANT & BELLEVILLE
C'Clean Laverie (Map pp96-8; 18 rue Jean-Pierre Timbaud,11e; metro Oberkampf; ⌚ 8am-10pm)
Laverie Libre Service Primus (Map pp96-8; 83 rue Jean-Pierre Timbaud, 11e; metro Couronnes; ⌚ 7.30am-8pm)

MONTMARTRE & PIGALLE
Laverie Libre Service (Map p108; 92 rue des Martyrs, 18e; metro Abbesses; ⌚ 7.30am-10pm)
Laverie Libre Service (Map p108; 4 rue Burq, 18e; metro Blanche; ⌚ 7.30am-10pm) West of the Butte de Montmartre.
Salon Lavoir Sidea (Map p108; 28 rue des Trois Frères, 18e; metro Abbesses; ⌚ 7am-8.50pm)

Left Luggage

All the train stations (see p171) have left-luggage offices or lockers. They charge €3.40/5/7.50 for 48 hours for a medium/large/extra-large bag. After that the fee is a flat €4.50 per day. Be warned that most of these left-luggage offices and lockers are closed to the public from about 11.15pm to between 6.15am and 6.45am.

Media

There are no local English-language newspapers in Paris although freebies such as *Paris Voice, Paris Where* and *The Irish Eyes* proliferate and are available at English-language bookshops, pubs and so on. The Paris-based *FUSAC* (short for *France USA Contacts*), a freebie issued every fortnight, consists of hundreds of ads placed by both companies and individuals. It is distributed free at the same places as well as at the **American Church in Paris** (Map pp99-101; ☎ 01 40 62 05 00; www.acparis.org; 65 quai d'Orsay, 7e; metro Pont de l'Alma or Invalides; reception ⌚ 9am-noon & 1-10.30pm Mon-Sat, 9am-noon & 1-7pm Sun), which functions as a community centre for English speakers and

is an excellent source of information on au pair work, short-term accommodation etc.

Paris Live Radio (www.parislive.net), the city's first all-English station, can be heard via the Internet, cable, satellite and DAB digital radio (1463.232MHz LG) throughout the day.

Medical Services
DENTAL SURGERIES

For emergency dental care contact either of the following:
Hôpital de la Salpêtrière (Map pp102-4; ☎ 01 42 16 00 00; rue Bruant, 13e; metro Chevaleret) This is the only dental hospital with extended hours. After hours use the **emergency entrance** (Map pp102-4; 83 blvd de l'Hôpital, 13e; metro St-Michel; ⌚ 5.30pm-8.30am).
SOS Dentaire (Map pp90-2; ☎ 01 43 36 36 00; 87 blvd de Port Royal, 14e; metro Port Royal) This is a private dental office that also offers services when most dentists are off duty – from 8.30pm to 11pm weekdays and from 9.30am to 11pm at the weekend.

HOSPITALS

There are some 50 *assistance publique* (public health service) hospitals in Paris. Major hospitals in the city:
American Hospital in Paris (Map pp90-2; ☎ 01 46 41 25 25; www.american-hospital.org; 63 blvd Victor Hugo, 92200 Neuilly-sur-Seine; metro Pont de Levallois Bécon) Offers emergency 24-hour medical and dental care.
Hertford British Hospital (Map pp90-2; ☎ 01 46 39 22 22; www.british-hospital.org; 3 rue Barbès, 92300 Levallois-Perret; metro Anatole France) This is a less expensive, English-speaking option than the American Hospital.
Hôtel Dieu (Map pp105-7; ☎ 01 42 34 81 31; place du Parvis Notre Dame, 4e; metro Cité) After 8pm use the **emergency entrance** (rue de la Cité).

PHARMACIES

Some pharmacies with extended hours:
Pharmacie Bader (Map pp105-7; ☎ 01 43 26 92 66; 12 blvd St-Michel, 5e; metro St-Michel; ⌚ 9am-9pm)
Pharmacie des Champs (Map pp93-5; ☎ 01 45 62 02 41; Galerie des Champs, 84 av des Champs-Élysées, 8e; metro George V; ⌚ 24hr)
Pharmacie des Halles (Map pp105-7; ☎ 01 42 72 03 23; 10 blvd de Sébastopol, 4e; metro Châtelet; ⌚ 9am-midnight Mon-Sat, 9am-10pm Sun)

Money

Post offices generally offer the best exchange rate and accept both cash and travellers cheques. *Bureaux de change* are faster and easier, open longer hours and give better rates than most banks. For general advice on exchanging money, see p908.

Among some of the better *bureaux de change* in Paris are the following:

LOUVRE & LES HALLES
Best Change (Map pp105-7; ☎ 01 42 21 46 05; 21 rue du Roule, 1er; metro Louvre Rivoli; ☺ 10am-1pm & 2-7pm Mon-Sat) This *bureau de change* is three blocks southwest of Forum des Halles.

Le Change du Louvre (Map pp105-7; ☎ 01 42 97 27 28; 151 rue St-Honoré, 1er; metro Palais Royal-Musée du Louvre; ☺ 10am-6pm Mon-Sat) This moneychanger is just north of the Louvre.

LATIN QUARTER & JARDIN DES PLANTES
Société Touristique de Services (STS; Map pp105-7; ☎ 01 43 54 76 55; 2 place St-Michel, 6e; metro St-Michel; ☺ 9am-8pm Mon-Sat, 10am-3pm Sun)

ÉTOILE & CHAMPS-ÉLYSÉES
Bureau de Change (Map pp93-5; ☎ 01 42 25 38 14; 25 av des Champs-Élysées, 8e; metro Franklin D Roosevelt; ☺ 9am-8pm)

Thomas Cook (Map pp93-5; ☎ 01 47 20 25 14; 125 av des Champs-Élysées, 8e; metro Charles de Gaulle-Étoile; ☺ 9.15am-8.30pm)

MONTMARTRE & PIGALLE
European Exchange Office (Map p108; ☎ 01 42 52 67 19; 6 rue Yvonne Le Tac, 18e; metro Abbesses; ☺ 10am-6.30pm Mon-Fri, 10.30am-6pm Sat)

Travelex (Map p108; ☎ 01 42 57 05 10; 82-86 blvd de Clichy, 18e; metro Blanche; ☺ 10am-8.30pm Mon-Sat, 9.45am-8.30pm Sun)

Post
The **main post office** (Map pp96-8; ☎ 01 40 28 76 00; 52 rue du Louvre, 1er; metro Sentier or Les Halles; ☺ 24hr), five blocks north of the eastern end of the Louvre, is open round the clock, but only for basic services such as sending letters and picking up poste restante mail (window Nos 5 to 7; €0.46 per letter). Other services, including currency exchange, are available only during regular opening hours. Be prepared for long queues after 7pm. Poste restante mail not specifically addressed to a particular branch post office will be delivered here. There is a one-hour closure from 6.20am to 7.20am Monday to Saturday and from 6am to 7am on Sunday.

Each arrondissement has its own five-digit postcode, formed by prefixing the arrondissement number with '750' or '7500' (eg 75001 for the 1er arrondissement, 75019

for the 19e etc). The only exception is the 16e, which has two postcodes: 75016 and 75116.

You can also buy stamps from *tabacs* (tobacconists).

Telephone
For information on how to use phones in France, see p910. All public telephones in Paris require a *télécarte* (phonecard), which can be purchased at post offices, *tabacs*, supermarket check-out counters, SNCF ticket windows, metro stations and anywhere you see a blue sticker reading '*télécarte en vente ici*'.

Toilets
The public toilets in Paris are signposted as *toilettes* or *WC*. The tan-coloured, self-cleaning cylindrical toilets you see on Paris' pavements are open 24 hours and cost €0.40.

Café owners do not appreciate use of their facilities if you are not a paying customer. If you are desperate, try ducking into a fast-food place, a major department store, Forum des Halles (Map pp105-7) or even a big hotel. There are public toilets (€0.40) underground in front of Notre Dame cathedral (Map pp105-7), near the Arc de Triomphe (Map pp93-5), east down the steps at Sacré Cœur (Map p108) and in a few metro stations. Check out the wonderful Art Nouveau public toilets below place de la Madeleine, 8e (Map pp93-5). They were built in 1905.

In older cafés and bars, the amenities may consist of a *toilette à la turque* (Turkish-style toilet), which is what the French call a squat toilet.

Tourist Information
The main branch of the **Office de Tourisme et de Congrès de Paris** (Paris Convention & Visitors Bureau; Map pp93-5; ☎ 0 892 683 000; www.paris-touristoffice .com; 25-27 rue des Pyramides, 1er; metro Pyramides; ☺ 9am-8pm Apr-Oct, 9am-8pm Mon-Sat & 11am-7pm Sun Nov-Mar) is about 500m northwest of the Louvre. It closes on 1 May only.

In addition the bureau maintains five centres (telephone numbers and website are the same as the main office) elsewhere in Paris.

Eiffel Tower (Map pp99-101; Pilier Nord, Parc du Champ de Mars, 7e; metro Champ de Mars-Tour Eiffel; ☺ 11am-6.45pm 2 May-Sep) In the base of the Eiffel Tower's North Pillar.

Gare de Lyon (Map pp102-4; Hall d'Arrivée, 20 blvd Diderot, 12; metro Gare de Lyon; ☺ 8am-6pm Mon-Sat, closed Sun & holidays) In the mainline trains arrivals hall.
Gare du Nord (Map pp96-8; 18 rue de Dunkerque, 10; metro Fare du Nord; ☺ 12.30-8pm, closed Christmas Day & 1 May) Under the glass roof of the Île de France departure and arrival area at the eastern end of the station.
Montmartre (Map p108; 21 place du Tertre, 18e; metro Abbesses; ☺ 10am-7pm, closed Christmas Day & 1 May)
Opéra/Grands Magasins (Map pp93-5; 11 rue Scribe, 9e; metro Gare de Lyon; ☺ 9am-6.30pm Mon-Sat, closed Sun, Christmas Day, 1 Jan & 1 May) In the same building as Opéra's landmark American Express office.

Espace du Tourisme d'Île de France (p179) is responsible for the areas around Paris.

Travel Agencies
You'll find travel agencies everywhere in Paris, but the following are among the largest and offer the best service and (usually) deals.
Forum Voyages (www.forum-voyages.fr in French); Latin Quarter branch (Map pp102-4; ☎ 01 53 10 50 50; 28 rue Monge, 5e; metro Cardinal Lemoine); Opéra branch (Map pp96-8; ☎ 01 42 61 20 20; 11 av de l'Opéra, 1er; metro Pyramides) Forum has nine outlets in Paris that are usually open 9.30am to 7pm Monday to Saturday.
Nouvelles Frontières (☎ 0 825 000 825; www .nouvelles-frontieres.fr in French); Odéon branch (Map pp105-7; ☎ 01 43 25 71 35; 116 blvd St-Germain, 6e; metro Odéon); Opéra branch (Map pp96-8; ☎ 01 42 61 02 62; 13 av de l'Opéra, 1er; metro Pyramides) There are 22 outlets around the city open 9am to 7pm Monday to Saturday.
OTU Voyages (☎ 0 820 817 817; www.otu.fr in French); Luxembourg branch (Map pp102-4; ☎ 0 825 004 027; 39 av Georges Bernanos, 5e; metro Port Royal; ☺ 9am-6.30pm Mon-Fri, 10am-noon & 1.15-5pm Sat) There is also a branch opposite the Centre Pompidou (p137).
Voyageurs du Monde (Map pp96-8; ☎ 01 42 86 16 00; www.vdm.com in French; 55 rue Ste-Anne, 2e; metro Pyramides or Quatre-Septembre; ☺ 9.30am-7pm Mon-Sat) 'World Travellers' is an enormous agency with more than 10 departments dealing with different destinations.

DANGERS & ANNOYANCES
Crime
In general Paris is a safe city and random street assaults are rare; in fact, criminal acts fell by 7% between 2002 and 2003, with thefts involving violence dropping by almost 10%. The so-called Ville Lumière (City of Light) is generally well lit, and there's no reason not to use the metro before it stops running at some time between 12.30am and just past 1am. As you'll notice, women *do* travel alone on the metro late at night in most areas, though not all who do so report feeling 100% comfortable.

Metro stations that are probably best avoided late at night include: Châtelet-Les Halles and its seemingly endless corridors; Château Rouge in Montmartre; Gare du Nord; Strasbourg St-Denis; Réaumur Sébastopol; and Montparnasse Bienvenüe. *Bornes d'alarme* (alarm boxes) are located in the centre of each metro/RER platform and in some station corridors.

Nonviolent crime such as pickpocketing and thefts from handbags and packs is a problem wherever there are crowds, especially tourists. Places to be particularly careful include Montmartre (especially around Sacré Cœur); Pigalle; the areas around Forum des Halles and Centre Pompidou; the Latin Quarter (especially the rectangle bounded by rue St-Jacques, blvd St-Germain, blvd St-Michel and quai St-Michel); below the Eiffel Tower; and on the metro during rush hour.

Lost Property
All objects found anywhere across Paris – except those picked up on the trains or in train stations – are eventually brought in to the city's **Bureau des Objets Trouvés** (Lost Property Office; Map pp90-2; ☎ 01 55 76 20 20; fax 01 40 02 40 45; 36 rue des Morillons, 15e; metro Convention; ☺ 8.30am-7pm Mon-Fri Jul & Aug, 8.30am-5pm Mon & Wed, 8.30am-8pm Tue & Thu, 8.30am-5.30pm Fri Sep-Jun), which is run by the Préfecture de Police. Since telephone enquiries are impossible, the only way to find out if a lost item has been located is to go there and fill in the forms.

Items lost on the **metro** (☎ 01 44 68 20 20) are held by station agents for three days before being sent to the Bureau des Objets Trouvés.

Anything found on trains or in train stations is taken to the lost-property office – usually attached to the left-luggage office – of the relevant station. Telephone enquiries (in French) are possible:
Gare d'Austerlitz (☎ 01 53 60 71 98)
Gare de l'Est (☎ 01 40 18 88 73)
Gare de Lyon (☎ 01 53 33 67 22)
Gare du Nord (☎ 01 55 31 58 40)

Gare Montparnasse (☎ 01 40 48 14 24)
Gare St-Lazare (☎ 01 53 42 05 57)

Litter & Dog Dirt

In theory Parisians can be fined over €150 for littering but we've never seen (or heard of) anyone ever having to pay up. Don't be nonplussed if you see locals drop paper wrappings or other detritus along the side of the pavement, however; the gutters in every quarter of Paris are washed and swept out daily and Parisians are encouraged to use them where litter bins are not available.

A much greater annoyance are all those dog droppings on the pavements. The Paris municipality spends €11 million each year to keep them relatively free of dog dirt, but it seems that repeated campaigns – including threats of heavy fines (up to €450) and free plastic bags distributed in parks and along the quays – to get people to clean up after their pooches, owned by 160,000 households in Paris, have been less than a howling success, with only an estimated 60% of dog owners doing so.

SIGHTS

Paris' major sights are distributed more or less equally on the Right and Left Banks of the Seine. We start in the heart of the Right Bank in the area around the Louvre and Les Halles, which largely takes in the 1er and follows, more or less, the order of the arrondissements (see p88), ending in the Parc de la Villette in the 19e.

Louvre & Les Halles

The area around the Louvre in the 1er contains some of the most important sights for visitors in Paris. To the northeast, the mostly pedestrian zone between the Centre Pompidou and the Forum des Halles, with rue Étienne Marcel to the north and rue de Rivoli to the south, is filled with people by day and by night, just as it was for the 850-odd years when part of it served as Paris' main marketplace known as *les halles*.

MUSÉE DU LOUVRE

The vast Palais du Louvre was constructed as a fortress by Philippe-Auguste in the early 13th century and rebuilt in the mid-16th century for use as a royal residence. In 1793 the Convention turned it into the **Musée du Louvre** (Louvre Museum; Map pp105–7; ☎ 01 40 20 53

> **AH, LA CARTE!**
>
> The **Carte Musées-Monuments** (Museums-Monuments Card; ☎ 01 44 61 96 60; for 1/3/5 days €18/36/54) is valid for entry to some three dozen sights in Paris – including the Louvre, the Centre Pompidou and the Musée d'Orsay – and another two dozen 22 in the Île de France, including parts of the chateaux at Versailles, Fontaine and Chantilly. The pass is available from the participating venues as well as tourist offices, Fnac outlets, RATP information desks and major metro stations.

17, 01 40 20 51 51; www.louvre.fr; metro Palais Royal-Musée du Louvre; admission to permanent collections/permanent collections & temporary exhibits €7.50/11.50, after 3pm & all day Sun €5/9.50, under 18 free, 1st Sun of month free; 9am-6pm Thu-Sun, 9am-9.45pm Mon & Wed).

The paintings, sculptures and artefacts on display in the Louvre Museum have been assembled by French governments over the past five centuries. Among them are works of art and artisanship from all over Europe and important collections of Assyrian, Etruscan, Greek, Coptic and Islamic art and antiquities. Traditionally the Louvre's *raison d'être* is to present Western art from the Middle Ages to about the year 1848 (at which point the Musée d'Orsay takes over) as well as the works of ancient civilisations that formed the starting point for Western art. However, in recent years it has acquired or begun to exhibit other important collections as well.

The Louvre may be the most actively avoided museum in the world. Daunted by the richness and sheer size of the place (the side facing the Seine is some 700m long and it is said that it would take nine months just to glance at every piece of art here), both local people and visitors often find the prospect of an afternoon at a smaller museum far more inviting. Eventually, most people do their duty and come, but many leave overwhelmed, unfulfilled, exhausted and frustrated at having got lost on their way to da Vinci's *La Joconde*, better known as *Mona Lisa* (Denon Wing, 1st floor, Rm 13). Since it takes several serious visits to get anything more than a brief glimpse of the works on offer, your best bet – after checking out a few you really want to see – is to choose a particular period or section of the Louvre and pretend that the rest is in another museum somewhere across town.

The most famous works from antiquity include the *Seated Scribe* (Sully Wing, 1st floor), the *Code of Hammurabi* (Richelieu Wing, ground floor) and that armless duo, the *Venus de Milo* (Sully Wing, ground floor) and the *Winged Victory of Samothrace* (Denon Wing, 1st floor). From the Renaissance, don't miss Michelangelo's *The Dying Slave* (Denon Wing, ground floor) and works by Raphael, Botticelli and Titian (Denon Wing, 1st floor). French masterpieces of the 19th century (Sully Wing, 2nd floor) include Ingres' *The Turkish Bath*, Géricault's *The Raft of the Medusa* and works by Corot, Delacroix and Fragonard.

When the museum opened in the late 18th century it contained 2500 paintings; today there are around 30,000 on display. The 'Grand Louvre' project, inaugurated by the late President Mitterrand in 1989, doubled the museum's exhibition space. In recent years new and renovated galleries have opened devoted to *objets d'art* such as Sèvres porcelain and the crown jewels of Louis XV (Sully Wing, 1st floor).

The main entrance and ticket windows in the Cour Napoléon are covered by a 21m-high **Grande Pyramide**, a glass pyramid designed by the Chinese-born American architect IM Pei. You can avoid the queues outside the pyramid or at the Porte des Lions entrance by entering the Louvre complex via the Carrousel du Louvre shopping area or by following the 'Louvre' exit from the Palais Royal-Musée du Louvre metro station. Those in the know buy their tickets in advance by ringing ☎ 0 892 697 073, from the *billeteries* (ticket offices) of Fnac or Virgin Megastores (p161) or from any of the major department stores (see p168), and walk straight in without queuing. Tickets are valid for the whole day, so you can come and go as you please. If planning to visit during one of the two weekly *nocturnes*, remember that on Wednesday virtually the entire museum remains open after 6pm but on Monday evening there's only a *circuit court* (short tour) of selected galleries.

The Musée du Louvre is divided into four sections: the Sully, Denon and Richelieu Wings and the Hall Napoléon. **Sully** creates the four sides of the Cour Carrée (literally 'square courtyard') at the eastern end of the complex. **Denon** stretches along the Seine to the south; **Richelieu** is the northern wing along rue de Rivoli.

The split-level public area under the glass pyramid is known as the **Hall Napoléon** (🕑 9am-10pm Thu-Mon). It has an exhibit on the history of the Louvre, a bookshop, a restaurant, a café, auditoriums for concerts, lectures and films and **CyberLouvre** (🕑 10am-6.45 Wed-Mon), an Internet salon with monitors that allow virtual-reality access to some 20,000 works of art. The centrepiece of the **Carrousel du Louvre shopping centre** (Map pp105-7; ☎ 01 40 20 67 30; 99 rue de Rivoli; 🕑 8.30am-11pm), which runs underground from the pyramid to the Arc de Triomphe du Carrousel in the Jardin du Carrousel, is an **inverted glass pyramid** *(pyramide inversée)*, also created by Pei.

Free maps in English of the complex called *Louvre Plan/Information* are available at the information desk in the centre of the Hall Napoléon. Excellent publications to guide you if you are doing the Louvre on your own are *Destination Louvre: A Guided Tour* (€7.50), *Louvre: The Visit* (€7.90) and *The Louvre: Key Art Works* (€15). All are available from the museum bookshop.

English-language guided tours (☎ 01 40 20 52 63) lasting 1½ hours depart from the area marked 'Acceuil des Groupes' (Group Welcome) under the glass pyramid at 11am, 2pm and 3pm Monday to Saturday. Tickets cost €6 (€3.50 for those aged 13 to 18, free for under 12s) in addition to the cost of admission. Groups are limited to 30 people, so it's a good idea to sign up at least 30 minutes before departure time. Audioguide tours in six languages and lasting 1½ hours can be rented for €5 under the pyramid at the entrance to each wing until 4.30pm.

OTHER PALAIS DU LOUVRE MUSEUMS
The Palais du Louvre contains three other museums run by the **Union Centrale des Arts Décoratifs** (UCAD; ☎ 01 44 55 57 50; www.ucad.fr; 107 rue de Rivoli, 1er; metro Palais Royal-Musée du Louvre; adult/18-25 yrs/under 18 €6/4.50/free; 🕑 11am-6pm Tue-Fri, 10am-6pm Sat & Sun) in the Rohan Wing of the Louvre complex. These were revamped or created under the Grand Louvre project. Admission includes entry to all three museums (Map pp105-7).

Musée des Arts Décoratifs The Applied Arts Museum on the 3rd floor displays furniture, jewellery and such *objets d'art* as ceramics and glassware from the Middle

Ages and the Renaissance through the Art Nouveau and Art Deco periods to modern and contemporary. Some departments may be closed over the next several years as the museum undergoes extensive renovations.

Musée de la Publicité The Advertising Museum, which shares the 3rd floor, contains some 100,000 posters dating as far back as the 13th century and innumerable promotional materials touting everything from 19th-century elixirs and early radio advertisements to Air France and electronic publicity. Only certain items are on exhibit at any one time.

Musée de la Mode et du Textile The Museum of Fashion and Textiles on the 1st and 2nd floors warehouses some 16,000 costumes dating from the 16th century till today, but only displays them in unusual themed exhibitions.

JARDIN DES TUILERIES

The formal, 28-hectare **Jardin des Tuileries** (Tuileries Garden; Map pp93-5; metro Tuileries or Concorde; 7am-9pm late Mar-late Sep, 7am-7.30pm late Sep-late Mar), which begins just west of the Jardin du Carrousel, was laid out in its present form – more or less – in the mid-17th century by André Le Nôtre, who also created the gardens at Vaux-le-Vicomte (p192) and Versailles (p185). The Tuileries soon became the most fashionable spot in Paris for parading about in one's finery; today it is a favourite of joggers.

The **Voie Triomphale** (Triumphal Way), also called the Axe Historique (Historic Axis), the western continuation of the Tuileries' east–west axis, follows the av des Champs-Élysées to the Arc de Triomphe and, ultimately, to the Grande Arche in the skyscraper district of **La Défense** (p179).

JEU DE PAUME & ORANGERIE

The **Galerie Nationale du Jeu de Paume** (Jeu de Paume National Gallery; Map pp93-5; ☎ 01 47 03 12 52; www.rmn.fr; 1 place de la Concorde, 1er; metro Concorde; adult/senior, student, senior & 13-18 yrs/under 13 €6/4.50/free; noon-9.30pm Tue, noon-7pm Wed-Fri, 10am-7pm Sat & Sun) is housed in an erstwhile *jeu de paume* (real, or royal, tennis) court built in 1861 during the reign of Napoleon III in the northwestern corner of the Jardin des Tuileries. Once the home of a good part of France's national collection of impressionist art, now housed across the Seine in the Musée d'Orsay (p124), the two-storey Jeu de Paume stages innovative exhibitions of contemporary art.

The **Musée de l'Orangerie** (Orangery Museum; Map pp93-5; ☎ 01 42 97 48 16; www.rmn.fr; place de la Concorde, 1er; metro Concorde) in the southwestern corner of the Jardin des Tuileries is, with the Jeu de Paume, all that remains of the once palatial Palais des Tuileries, which was razed during the Paris Commune in 1871 (see p33). It exhibits important impressionist works, including a series of Monet's exquisite *Décorations des Nymphéas* (Water Lilies) and paintings by Cézanne, Matisse, Picasso, Renoir, Sisley, Soutine and Utrillo, but was undergoing extensive renovations at the time of research is due to reopen at the beginning of 2005.

PLACE VENDÔME

The octagonal **place Vendôme** (Map pp93-5; metro Tuileries or Opéra) and the arcaded and colonnaded buildings around it were constructed between 1687 and 1721. In March 1796 Napoleon married Josephine, Viscountess Beauharnais, in the building at No 3. Today, the buildings surrounding the square house the posh Hôtel Ritz Paris (p137) and some of the city's most fashionable boutiques. The 43.5m-tall **Colonne Vendôme** (Vendôme Column), that stands in the centre of the square, consists of a stone core wrapped in a 160m-long bronze spiral made from 1250 Austrian and Russian cannons captured by Napoleon at the Battle of Austerlitz in 1805. The statue on top depicts Napoleon as a Roman emperor.

PALAIS ROYAL

The **Palais Royal** (Royal Palace; Map pp105-7; Place du Palais Royal, 1er; metro Palais Royal-Musée du Louvre), which briefly housed a young Louis XIV in the 1640s, lies to the north of place du Palais Royal and the Louvre. Construction was begun in the 17th century by Cardinal Richelieu, though most of the present neoclassical complex dates from the latter part of the 18th century. It now contains the governmental **Conseil d'État** (State Council) and is closed to the public.

The colonnaded building that is opposite place André Malraux is the **Comédie Française** (p166), which was founded in 1680 and is the world's oldest national theatre.

Just north of the palace is the **Jardin du Palais Royal** (Map pp105-7; 7.30am-11pm Jun-Aug, 7.30am-9.30pm Sep, 7.30am-8.30pm Oct-Mar, 7.30am-10.15pm Apr & May), a lovely park surrounded by 19th-century shopping arcades, including **Galerie de Valois** on the eastern side and **Galerie de**

PARIS

Montpensier to the west. Don't miss the zany Palais Royal-Musée du Louvre **metro entrance** on the place du Palais Royal.

CENTRE POMPIDOU

The **Centre National d'Art et de Culture Georges Pompidou** (Georges Pompidou National Centre of Art & Culture; Map pp105-7; ☎ 01 44 78 12 33; www .centrepompidou.fr; place Georges Pompidou, 4e; metro Rambuteau) is the most successful art and cultural centre in the world. An extensive €85-million renovation was completed at the start of the new millennium, with expanded exhibition space, a new cinema, CD and video centre, and dance and theatre venues, making it even more popular.

The Centre Pompidou, also known as the Centre Beaubourg, has amazed and delighted visitors since it was inaugurated in 1977, not just for its outstanding collection of modern art, but also for its radical architectural statement; it was among the first buildings to have its 'insides' turned outside. But it all began to look somewhat *démodé* by the late 1990s, hence the refit.

The **Forum du Centre Pompidou** (admission free; ☼ 11am-10pm Wed-Mon), the open space at ground level, has temporary exhibits and information desks.

The 4th and 5th floors of the centre exhibit about a third of the 50,000-plus works of the **Musée National d'Art Moderne** (MNAM, National Museum of Modern Art; adult/senior & 18-25 yrs/under 18 €7/5/free, 1st Sun of month free; day pass incl MNAM & temporary exhibits adult/senior & 18-25 yrs €10/8; permanent collection ☼ 11am-9pm Wed-Mon), France's national collection of art dating from 1905 onwards and including the work of the Surrealists and Cubists, as well as pop art and contemporary works. The huge (and free) **Bibliothèque Publique d'Information** (BPI; ☎ 01 44 78 12 33; www.bpi.fr in French; ☼ noon-10pm Mon & Wed-Fri, 11am-10pm Sat & Sun) takes up the 3rd, 2nd and part of the 1st floors, while the 6th floor has three galleries for **temporary exhibitions** (admission usually €7/5).

The **Atelier Brancusi** (Map pp105-7; place Georges Pompidou; ☼ 2-6pm Wed-Mon), west of the main building, contains some 140 examples of the work of Romanian-born sculptor Constantin Brancusi (1876–1957) as well as drawings, paintings and glass photographic plates. An MNAM ticket includes entry.

Place Georges Pompidou, west of the centre, and the nearby pedestrian streets attract buskers, street artists, musicians, jugglers and mime artists, and can be as much fun as the centre itself. The fanciful **mechanical fountains** (Map pp105-7; place Igor Stravinsky) of skeletons, dragons, G clefs and a big pair of ruby-red lips, just south of the centre and created by Jean Tinguely and Niki de St-Phalle, are a positive delight.

Le Défenseur du Temps (Map pp105-7; Defender of Time; 8 rue Bernard de Clairvaux; ☼ 9am-10pm), a mechanical clock (1979) whose protagonist does battle on the hour with the elements (air, water and earth in the form of a phoenix, crab and dragon), is a block north of the Centre Pompidou, just off Rue Brantôme (3e) in a development known as Quartier de l'Horloge.

FORUM DES HALLES

Les Halles, the city's main wholesale food market, occupied the area just south of the Église St-Eustache from the early 12th century until 1969, when it was moved to the southern suburb of Rungis. In its place, the unspeakable **Forum des Halles** (Map pp105-7; ☎ 01 44 76 96 56; 1 rue Pierre Lescaut, 1er; metro Les Halles or Châtelet Les Halles), a huge underground shopping centre, was constructed in the glass-and-chrome style of the early 1970s.

Atop the Forum des Halles is a popular **park**. During the warmer months, street musicians, fire-eaters and other performers display their talents throughout the area, especially at **place du Jean du Bellay**, whose centre is adorned by a multitiered Renaissance fountain, the **Fontaine des Innocents**, erected in 1549. It is named after the Cimetière des Innocents, a cemetery on this site from which two million skeletons were disinterred and transferred to the Catacombes (p123) in the 14e after the Revolution.

ÉGLISE ST-EUSTACHE

The majestic **Église St-Eustache** (Map pp105-7; ☎ 01 42 36 31 05; www.st-eustache.org in French; 2 impasse St-Eustache, 1er; metro Les Halles; ☼ 9am-7.30pm), one of the most beautiful churches in Paris and consecrated to an early Roman martyr who is the patron saint of hunters, is just north of the gardens above the Forum des Halles. Constructed between 1532 and 1640, St-Eustache is primarily Gothic, though a neoclassical façade was added on the western side in the mid-18th century. Inside, there are some exceptional

Flamboyant Gothic arches holding up the ceiling of the chancel, although most of the interior ornamentation is Renaissance and classical. The gargantuan organ above the west entrance, with 101 stops and 8000 pipes, is used for concerts (long a tradition here) and during High Mass on Sunday (11am and 6pm).

TOUR ST-JACQUES

The Flamboyant Gothic, 52m-high **Tour St-Jacques** (St James' Tower; Map pp105–7; place du Châtelet, 4e; metro Châtelet) is all that remains of the Église St-Jacques la Boucherie, built by the powerful butchers guild in 1523 and demolished by the Directory in 1797. The tower is topped by a weather station. It is closed to the public.

LA SAMARITAINE ROOFTOP TERRACE

For an amazing 360-degree, panoramic view of central Paris, head for the roof of this department store's **main building** (Map pp105–7; ☎ 01 40 41 20 20; www.lasamaritaine.com; 19 rue de la Monnaie, 1er; metro Pont Neuf; ☒ 9.30am-7pm Mon-Wed & Fri, 9.30am-10pm Thu, 9.30am-8pm Sat). A lift will take you to the 9th floor; you then walk two flights up to the 11th floor. At the time of research the terrace was closed for security reasons.

Marais & Bastille

The Marais, the area of the Right Bank north of Île St-Louis in the 3e and 4e, was exactly what its name implies – 'marsh' or 'swamp' – until the 13th century, when it was put to agricultural use. In the early 17th century, Henri IV built the place Royale (today's place des Vosges), turning the area into Paris' most fashionable residential district and attracting wealthy aristocrats who then erected their own luxurious *hôtels particuliers* (private mansions) and less expensive *pavillons* (smaller residences). Today many of them house museums and government institutions.

When the aristocracy moved out of Paris to Versailles and Faubourg St-Germain during the late 17th and the 18th centuries, the Marais and its townhouses passed into the hands of ordinary Parisians. The 110-hectare area was given a major face-lift in the late 1960s and early 1970s. The Marais has become a much desired address in recent years; it also remains home to a long-established Jewish community and is the centre of Paris' gay life.

Today, the Marais is one of the few neighbourhoods of Paris that still has most of its pre-Revolution architecture. Examples include the **oldest house in Paris** at 3 rue Volta (Map pp96–8) in the 3e, parts of which date back to 1292; the medieval one at 51 rue de Montmorency (Map pp105–7) in the 3e dating back to 1407 and the 16th-century half-timbered buildings at 11 and 13 rue François Miron (Map pp105–7) in the 4e.

After years as a run-down immigrant neighbourhood notorious for its high crime rate, the contiguous Bastille district (11e and 12e) has undergone a fair degree of gentrification, largely due to the opening of the Opéra Bastille back in 1989. Though the area is not the hip nightlife centre it was throughout most of the 1990s, it still has quite a bit to offer after dark, with numerous pubs, bars and clubs lining rue de Lappe and rue de la Roquette.

HÔTEL DE VILLE

After having been gutted during the Paris Commune of 1871, Paris' **Hôtel de Ville** (city hall; Map pp105–7; ☎ 0 820 007 575; www.paris.fr; place de l'Hôtel de Ville, 4e; metro Hôtel de Ville) was rebuilt in the neo-Renaissance style (1874–82). The ornate façade is decorated with 108 statues of noteworthy Parisians. There's a **Salon d'Accueil** (reception hall; 29 rue de Rivoli, 4e; ☒ 9.30am–6-7pm Mon-Sat), which dispenses copious amounts of information and brochures and is used for temporary exhibitions.

The Hôtel de Ville faces the majestic **place de l'Hôtel de Ville**, used from the Middle Ages to the 19th century to stage many of Paris' celebrations, rebellions, book burnings and public executions. Known as place de Grève (Strand Square) until 1830, it was in centuries past a favourite gathering place of the unemployed, which is why a strike is called *une grève* in French to this day.

PLACE DES VOSGES

Place des Vosges (Map pp102–7; metro St-Paul or Bastille), inaugurated in 1612 as place Royale, is an ensemble of 36 symmetrical houses with ground-floor arcades, steep slate roofs and large dormer windows arranged around a large square. Only the earliest houses were built of brick; to save time and money, the rest were given timber frames and faced with plaster, which was then painted to resemble brick.

The author Victor Hugo lived at the square's Hôtel de Rohan-Guéménée from 1832 to 1848, moving here a year after the publication of *Notre Dame de Paris* (The Hunchback of Notre Dame). The **Maison de Victor Hugo** (Victor Hugo House; Map pp102-4; ☎ 01 42 72 10 16; www.paris.fr/musees/maison_de _victor_hugo in French; permanent collections admission free, temporary exhibitions adult/senior & student/14-25 yrs/under 14 €5.50/4/2.50/free; ☼ 10am-6pm Tue-Sun) is now a municipal museum devoted to the life and times of the celebrated novelist and poet, with an impressive collection of his drawings and portraits.

MUSÉE CARNAVALET

This museum, also called **Musée de l'Histoire de Paris** (Paris History Museum; Map pp105-7; ☎ 01 44 59 58 58; www.paris.fr/musees/musee_carnavalet in French; 23 rue de Sévigné, 3e; metro St-Paul or Chemin Vert; permanent collections admission free, temporary exhibits adult/senior & student/14-25 yrs/under 14 €5.50/4/2.50/free; ☼ 10am-6pm Tue-Sun), is in two *hôtels particuliers*. It charts the history of Paris from the Gallo-Roman period to the 20th century. Some of the nation's most important documents, paintings and other objects from the French Revolution are here (Rooms 101 to 113), as is Fouquet's magnificent Art Nouveau jewellery shop from the rue Royale (Room 142) and Marcel Proust's cork-lined bedroom from his apartment on blvd Haussmann (Room 147), in which he wrote most of the 7350-page *À la Recherche du Temps Perdu*.

MUSÉE PICASSO

The **Picasso Museum** (Map pp105-7; ☎ 01 42 71 25 21; 5 rue de Thorigny, 3e; metro St-Paul or Chemin Vert; adult/18-25 yrs/under 18 €6.70/5.20/free, 1st Sun of month free; ☼ 9.30am-6pm Wed-Mon Apr-Sep, 9.30am-5.30pm Wed-Mon Oct-Mar), housed in the mid-17th-century Hôtel Salé, is one of Paris' best-loved art museums and includes more than 3500 of the *grand maître*'s engravings, paintings, ceramic works, drawings and sculptures. You can also see part of Picasso's personal art collection, which includes works by Braque, Cézanne, Matisse, Modigliani and Degas.

MUSÉE D'ART ET D'HISTOIRE DU JUDAÏSME

The **Musée d'Art et d'Histoire du Judaïsme** (Art & History of Judaism Museum; Map pp105-7; ☎ 01 53 01 86

<table>
<tr><td>

MUSEUM CLOSING TIMES

The vast majority of museums in Paris close on Monday though more than a dozen (including the Louvre, Centre Pompidou and Musée Picasso) are closed on Tuesday instead. It is also important to remember that *all* museums and monuments in Paris shut their doors or gates between a half-hour and an hour before their actual closing times, which are the ones listed in this chapter. Therefore if we say a museum or monument closes at 6pm, don't count on getting in much later than 5pm or 5.30pm.

</td></tr>
</table>

60; www.mahj.org; 71 rue du Temple, 3e; metro Rambuteau; adult/student & 18-25 yrs/under 18 €6.10/3.80/free; ☼ 11am-6pm Mon-Fri, 10am-6pm Sun) is housed in the sumptuous, 17th-century Hôtel de St-Aignan. It was formed by combining the crafts, paintings and ritual objects from Eastern Europe and North Africa of the Musée d'Art Juif (Jewish Art Museum) in Montmartre with medieval Jewish artefacts from the Musée National du Moyen Âge (p121). It traces the evolution of Jewish communities from the Middle Ages to the present, with particular emphasis on the history of the Jews in France. Highlights include documents relating to the Dreyfus Affair (1894–1900) and works by Paris-based Jewish artists Chagall, Modigliani and Soutine. Expect a very high level of security at the entrance.

MAISON EUROPÉENNE DE LA PHOTOGRAPHIE

The **Maison Européenne de la Photographie** (European House of Photography; Map pp105-7; ☎ 01 44 78 75 00; www.mep-fr.org in French; 5-7 rue de Fourcy, 4e; metro St-Paul or Pont Marie; adult/senior & 9-25 yrs/under 9 €5/2.50/free, plus 5-8pm Wed free; ☼ 11am-8pm Wed-Sun), housed in the rather overwrought Hôtel Hénault de Cantorbe dating from the early 18th century, has cutting-edge temporary exhibits (usually retrospectives on single photographers) and a huge permanent collection on the history of photography, with particular reference to France.

MUSÉE DES ARTS ET MÉTIERS

The **Musée des Arts et Métiers** (Arts & Crafts Museum; Map pp96-8; ☎ 01 53 01 82 00; 60 rue de Réaumur, 3e; metro

Arts et Métiers; adult/5-18 yrs/family €5.50/3.80/15.25; 🕙 10am-6pm Tue, Wed & Fri-Sun, 10am-9.30pm Thu) is a must for anyone with a scientific (or mechanical) bent. Instruments, machines and working models from the 18th to 20th centuries are displayed across three floors, with Foucault's original pendulum (1855) taking pride of place.

PLACE DE LA BASTILLE

The Bastille, built during the 14th century as a fortified royal residence, is the most famous monument in Paris that no longer exists; the notorious prison – the quintessential symbol of monarchical despotism – was demolished by a Revolutionary mob on 14 July 1789 and all seven prisoners were freed. **Place de la Bastille** (Map pp102-4; metro Bastille) in the 12e, where the prison once stood, is now a very busy traffic roundabout.

In the centre of the *place* is the 52m-high **Colonne de Juillet** (July Column), whose shaft of greenish bronze is topped by a gilded and winged figure of Liberty. It was erected in 1833 as a memorial to those killed in the street battles that accompanied the July Revolution of 1830; they are buried in vaults under the column. It was later consecrated as a memorial to the victims of the February Revolution of 1848 (see p32).

OPÉRA BASTILLE

Paris' giant 'second' **opera house** (Map pp102-4; ☎ 0 892 899 090, 01 44 61 59 65; www.opera-de-paris .fr in French; 2-6 place de la Bastille, 12e; metro Bastille), designed by the Canadian architect Carlos Ott, was inaugurated on 14 July 1989, the 200th anniversary of the storming of the Bastille. There are **guided tours** (☎ 01 40 01 19 70; adult/senior & student/under 19 €10/8/5; 1½hr), which usually depart at 1pm and 5pm Monday to Saturday. Tickets go on sale 15 minutes before departure at window No 4 of the **box office** (120 rue de Lyon, 11e; 🕙 11am-6.30pm Mon-Sat).

Île de la Cité

The site of the first settlement in Paris around the 3rd century BC and later the Roman town of Lutèce (Lutetia), the Île de la Cité remained the centre of royal and ecclesiastical power even after the city spread to both banks of the Seine during the Middle Ages. The buildings on the middle part of the island were demolished and rebuilt during Baron Haussmann's great urban renewal scheme of the late 19th century.

NOTRE DAME CATHEDRAL

The **Cathédrale de Notre Dame de Paris** (Cathedral of Our Lady of Paris; Map pp105-7; ☎ 01 42 34 56 10; place du Parvis Notre Dame, 4e; metro Cité; 🕙 8am-6.45pm Mon-Fri, 8am-7.45pm Sat & Sun) is the true heart of Paris; in fact, distances from Paris to all parts of metropolitan France are measured from **place du Parvis Notre Dame**, the square in front of Notre Dame. A bronze star, set in the pavement across from the main entrance, marks the exact location of **point zéro des routes de France** (point zero of French roads).

Notre Dame is not only a masterpiece of French Gothic architecture but has also been the focus of Catholic Paris for seven centuries. In recent years its western façade has had a thorough cleaning, which makes it even more attractive and inspiring.

Constructed on a site occupied by earlier churches – and, a millennium before that, a Gallo-Roman temple – it was begun in 1163 and largely completed by the mid-14th century. Architect Eugène Emmanuel Viollet-le-Duc carried out extensive renovations in the 19th century. The interior is 130m long, 48m wide and 35m high and can accommodate more than 6000 worshippers.

Notre Dame is known for its sublime balance, though if you look closely you'll see all sorts of minor asymmetrical elements introduced to avoid monotony, in accordance with standard Gothic practice. These include the slightly different shapes of each of the three main portals, whose statues were once brightly coloured to make them more effective as a *Biblia pauperum* – a 'Bible of the poor' to help the illiterate understand the Old Testament stories, the Passion of the Christ and the lives of the saints. One of the best views of Notre Dame is from **Square Jean XXIII**, the lovely little park behind the cathedral, where you can see the mass of ornate **flying buttresses** that encircle the chancel and support its walls and roof.

Inside, exceptional features include three spectacular **rose windows**, the most renowned of which is the 10m-wide one over the western façade above the 7800-pipe organ, and the window on the northern side of the transept, which has remained virtually unchanged since the 13th century. The central choir with its carved wooden stalls and statues representing the Passion of the Christ is also noteworthy. There are free guided tours (in English) of the cathedral at noon on Wednesday and Thursday and at 2.30pm on Saturday.

The **trésor** (treasury; adult/student/3-12 yrs €2.50/2/1; 9.30am-6pm Mon-Sat, 1.30-5.30pm Sun) in the southeastern transept contains artwork, liturgical objects, church plate and relics, some of them of questionable origin. Among these is the Ste-Couronne, the 'Holy Crown', which is purportedly the wreath of thorns placed on Jesus' head before he was crucified and was brought here in the mid-13th century. It is exhibited at 4.45pm on each Friday of Lent and on the first Friday of each month during the rest of the year.

The entrance to the **tours de Notre Dame** (Notre Dame towers; ☎ 01 53 10 07 00; www.monum.fr; rue du Cloître Notre Dame; adult/student & 18-25 yrs/under 18 €6.10/4.10/free, 1st Sun Oct-Mar free; 9.30am-7.30pm Mon-Fri, 9am-9pm Sat & Sun Jul & Aug, 10am-5.30pm Oct-Mar, 9.30am-7.30pm Apr-Jun & Sep), which can be climbed, is from the **North Tower**, to the right and around the corner as you walk out of the cathedral's main doorway. The 387 spiralling steps bring you to the top of the west façade, where you'll find yourself face-to-face with many of the cathedral's most frightening gargoyles, the 13-tonne bell Emmanuel (all the cathedral's bells are named) in the **South Tower** and a spectacular view of Paris.

STE-CHAPELLE

Ste-Chapelle (Holy Chapel; Map pp105-7; ☎ 01 53 40 60 97; www.monum.fr; 4 blvd du Palais, 1er; metro Cité; adult/18-25 yrs/under 18 €6.10/4.10/free, 1st Sun Oct-Mar free, joint ticket with Conciergerie €10.40/7.40/free; 9.30am-6pm Mar-Oct, 9am-5pm Nov-Feb), the most exquisite of Paris' Gothic monuments, is tucked away within the walls of the **Palais de Justice** (Law Courts). The 'walls' of the **upper chapel** are sheer curtains of richly coloured and finely detailed **stained glass**, which bathe the chapel in an extraordinary light.

Built in just under three years (compared with nearly 200 years for Notre Dame), Ste-Chapelle was consecrated in 1248. The chapel was conceived by Louis IX to house his personal collection of sacred relics (now kept in the treasury of Notre Dame).

CONCIERGERIE

The **Conciergerie** (Map pp105-7; ☎ 01 53 40 60 97; www.monum.fr; 2 blvd du Palais, 1er; metro Cité; adult/18-25 yrs/under 18 €7.50/5.50/free, 1st Sun Oct-Mar free, joint ticket with Conciergerie €10.40/7.40/free; 9.30am-6pm Mar-Oct, 9am-5pm Nov-Feb), built in the 14th century for the concierge of the Palais de la Cité, was the main prison during the Reign of Terror (p31) and used to incarcerate alleged enemies of the Revolution before they were brought before the Revolutionary Tribunal in the Palais de Justice next door. Among the 2700 prisoners held in the **cachots** (dungeons) here before being sent in tumbrels to the guillotine were Queen Marie-Antoinette and, as the Revolution began to turn on its own, the Revolutionary radicals Danton and Robespierre.

The Gothic **Salle des Gens d'Armes** (Cavalrymen's Hall) dates from the 14th century and is a fine example of the Rayonnant Gothic style. It is the largest surviving medieval hall in Europe. The **Tour de l'Horloge** (clock tower; cnr blvd du Palais & quai de l'Horloge), built in 1353, has held a public clock aloft since 1370.

PONT NEUF

The sparkling-white stone spans of Paris' oldest bridge, **Pont Neuf** (Map pp105-7; metro Pont Neuf) – literally 'New Bridge' – have linked the western end of the Île de la Cité with both banks of the Seine since 1607, when King Henri IV inaugurated it by crossing the bridge on a white stallion. The seven arches, best seen from the river, are decorated with humorous and grotesque figures of barbers, dentists, pickpockets, loiterers etc.

Île St-Louis

The smaller of the Seine's two islands, Île St-Louis is just downstream from the Île de la Cité. In the early 17th century, when it was actually two uninhabited islets (Île Notre Dame and Île aux Vaches), a building contractor and two financiers worked out a deal with Louis XIII to create one island out of the two and build two stone bridges to the mainland. In exchange they would receive the right to subdivide and sell the newly created real estate. This they did with great success, and by 1664 the entire island was covered with fine new houses.

Today, the island's 17th-century, greystone houses and the shops that line the streets and quays impart a village-like, provincial calm. The central thoroughfare, **rue St-Louis en l'Île**, is home to a number of upmarket art galleries, boutiques and the

French baroque **Église St-Louis en l'Île** (Map pp105-7; ☎ 01 46 34 11 60; 19bis rue St-Louis en l'Île, 4; metro Pont Marie; ☺ 9am-noon & 3-7pm Tue-Sun), built between 1656 and 1725. The area around **Pont St-Louis**, the bridge linking the island with the Île de la Cité, and **Pont Louis Philippe**, the bridge to the Marais, is one of the most romantic spots in all of Paris.

Latin Quarter & Jardin des Plantes

Known as the Quartier Latin because all communication between students and professors here took place in Latin until the Revolution, this area of the 5e has been the centre of Parisian higher education since the Middle Ages. It still has a large population of students and academics affiliated with the Sorbonne (now part of the University of Paris system), the Collège de France, the École Normale Supérieure and other institutions of higher learning. To the southeast, the Jardin des Plantes, with its tropical greenhouses and Muséum National d'Histoire Naturelle, offers a bucolic alternative to cobbles and chalkboards.

MUSÉE NATIONAL DU MOYEN ÂGE

Sometimes called the Musée de Cluny, the **Musée National du Moyen Âge** (National Museum of the Middle Ages; Map pp105-7; ☎ 01 53 73 78 16, 01 53 73 78 00; www.musee-moyenage.fr in French; Thermes de Cluny, 6 place Paul Painlevé, 5e; metro Cluny-La Sorbonne or St-Michel; adult/senior, student & 18-25 yrs/under 18 €5.50/4/free, 1st Sun of month free; ☺ 9.15am-5.45pm Wed-Mon) is housed in two structures: the **frigidarium** (cooling room) and other remains of Gallo-Roman baths dating from around AD 200, and the late-15th-century Hôtel de Cluny, considered the finest example of medieval civil architecture in Paris.

The spectacular displays at the museum include statuary, illuminated manuscripts, armaments, furnishings and objects made of gold, ivory and enamel. A sublime series of late-15th-century tapestries from the southern Netherlands known as *La Dame à la Licorne* (The Lady with the Unicorn) is hung in Room 13 on the 1st floor. The **Forêt de la Licorne**, a medieval-style garden, is north of the museum.

SORBONNE

Paris' most renowned university, the **Sorbonne** (Map pp102-4; 12 rue de la Sorbonne, 5; metro Luxembourg or Cluny-La Sorbonne) was founded in 1253 by Robert de Sorbon, confessor to Louis IX, as a college for 16 impoverished theology students. Today, the Sorbonne's main complex (bounded by rue de la Sorbonne, rue des Écoles, rue St-Jacques and rue Cujas, 5e) and other buildings in the vicinity house most of the 13 autonomous universities that were created when the University of Paris was reorganised after violent student protests in 1968.

Place de la Sorbonne links blvd St-Michel and the **Chapelle de la Sorbonne**, the university's gold-domed church constructed between 1635 and 1642. The chapel holds the remains of Cardinal Richelieu (1585–1642).

PANTHÉON

The domed landmark now known simply as the **Panthéon** (Map pp102-4; ☎ 01 44 32 18 00; www.monum.fr; place du Panthéon, 5e; metro Luxembourg; adult/18-25 yrs/under 18 €7/4.50/free, 1st Sun Oct-Mar free; ☺ 9.30am-6.30pm Apr-Sep, 10am-6.15pm Oct-Mar) was commissioned around 1750 as an abbey church dedicated to Ste Geneviève, but because of financial and structural problems it wasn't completed until 1789 – not a good year for churches to open in France. Two years later, the Constituent Assembly converted it into a secular mausoleum for the *grands hommes de l'époque de la liberté française* (great men of the era of French liberty).

The Panthéon is a superb example of 18th-century neoclassicism but its ornate marble interior is gloomy in the extreme. The 80-odd permanent residents of the crypt include Voltaire, Jean-Jacques Rousseau, Victor Hugo, Émile Zola, Jean Moulin and Nobel Prize winner Marie Curie.

JARDIN DES PLANTES

Paris' 24-hectare **Jardin des Plantes** (Botanical Gardens; Map pp102-4; ☎ 01 40 79 30 00; 57 rue Cuvier, 5e; metro Gare d'Austerlitz, Censier Daubenton or Jussieu; ☺ 7.30am-5.30 to 8pm according to the season) was founded in 1626 as a medicinal herb garden for Louis XIII. Here you'll find the Eden-like **Jardin d'Hiver** (Winter Garden; adult/senior & 16-25 yrs €2.30/1.50; ☺ 1-5pm Mon & Wed-Fri, 1-6pm Sat & Sun Apr-Sep, 1-5pm Wed-Sun Oct-Mar), which is also called the **Serres Tropicales** (Tropical Greenhouses); the **Jardin Alpin** (Alpine Garden; admission free; ☺ 8-11am & 1.30-5pm Mon-Fri Apr-Sep), with 2000 mountain plants; and the gardens of the **École de Botanique** (admission free; 8-11am & 1.30-5pm Mon-Fri), which is where students of the School of Botany 'practice'.

The **Ménagerie du Jardin des Plantes** (Botanical Garden Zoo; ☎ 01 40 79 37 94; 57 rue Cuvier & 3 quai St-Bernard, 5e; metro Jussieu or Gare d'Austerlitz; adult/senior, student & 4-15 yrs €6/3.50; 9am-6pm Mon-Sat, 9am-6.30pm Sun Apr-Sep, 9am-5pm Mon-Sat, 9am-5.30pm Sun Oct-Mar), a medium-sized (5.5-hectare) zoo in the northern section of the garden, was founded in 1794. During the Prussian siege of Paris in 1870, most of the animals were eaten by starving Parisians. The **Microzoo** (10am-noon & 2-5.15pm Apr-Sep, 10am-noon & 1.30-4.45pm Oct-Mar), entry to which is included in the admission fee, features microscopic animals and is open to those over 11.

MUSÉE NATIONAL D'HISTOIRE NATURELLE

The **Musée National d'Histoire Naturelle** (National Museum of Natural History; ☎ 01 40 79 30 00; www.mnhn .fr in French; 57 rue Cuvier, 5e; metro Censier Daubenton or Gare d'Austerlitz), created by a decree of the Revolutionary Convention in 1793, was the site of important scientific research during the 19th century. It is housed in four different buildings (all on Map pp102–4) along the southern edge of the Jardin des Plantes.

The **Grande Galerie de l'Évolution** (Great Gallery of Evolution; 36 rue Geoffroy St-Hilaire, 5e; adult/senior & 16-25 yrs €7/5; 10am-6pm Wed-Mon) has some imaginative exhibits on evolution and mankind's effect on the global ecosystem spread over four floors and 6000 sq metres of space. The **Salle des Espèces Menacées et des Espèces Disparues** on level 2 displays extremely rare specimens of endangered and extinct species while the **Salle de Découverte** (Room of Discovery) on level 1 houses interactive exhibits for kids. There's a guided tour in English (€5) at 3pm on Saturday but it depends on demand.

The **Galerie de Minéralogie, de Géologie et de Paléobotanie** (36 rue Geoffroy St-Hilaire; adult/senior & 16-25 yrs €5/3; 10am-5pm Mon-Fri, 10am-6pm Sat & Sun Apr-Oct, 10am-5pm Wed-Mon Oct-Mar), which covers mineralogy, geology and palaeobotany (fossilised plants), has an amazing exhibit of giant natural crystals and a basement display of jewellery and other objects made from minerals. The **Galerie de Botanique** (10-18 rue Buffon, 5e), the Botany Gallery to the east, is used for temporary exhibits. The **Galerie d'Anatomie Comparée et de Paléontologie** (2 rue Buffon; adult/senior & 16-25 yrs €5/3; 10am-5pm Mon-Fri, 10am-6pm Sat & Sun Apr-Sep, 10am-5pm Wed-Mon Oct-Mar) has displays on comparative anatomy and palaeontology (the study of fossils).

MOSQUÉE DE PARIS

The central **Mosquée de Paris** (Paris Mosque; Map pp102-4; ☎ 01 45 35 97 33; www.mosquee-de-paris .org; 39 rue Geoffroy St-Hilaire, 5e; metro Censier Daubenton or Place Monge; adult/senior & 7-25 yrs €2.30/1.50; 9am-noon & 2-6pm Sat-Thu), with its striking 26m-high minaret, was built in 1926 in the ornate Moorish style so popular at the time. Visitors must be modestly dressed and remove their shoes at the entrance to the prayer hall. The complex includes a North African-style **salon de thé** (tearoom) and **restaurant** (p152) and a **hammam** (☎ 01 43 31 18 14, 01 43 31 38 20; admission €15; men 2-9pm Tue & 10am-9pm Sun, women 10am-9pm Mon, Wed, Thu & Sat, 2-9pm Fri), a traditional Turkish-style bathhouse where a massage costs €10/20/30 for 10/20/30 minutes.

St-Germain, Odéon & Luxembourg

Centuries ago the Église St-Germain des Prés and its affiliated abbey owned most of today's 6e and 7e. The neighbourhood around the church began to develop in the late 17th century, and these days it is celebrated for its heterogeneity. Cafés such as Les Deux Magots and Café de Flore (p159) were favourite hangouts of postwar, Left Bank intellectuals and the places where existentialism was born.

ÉGLISE ST-GERMAIN DES PRÉS

Romanesque **Église St-Germain des Prés** (Church of St Germanus of the Fields; Map pp105-7; ☎ 01 43 25 41 71, 01 55 42 81 33; 3 place St-Germain des Prés, 6e; metro St-Germain des Prés; 8am-7pm Mon-Sat, 9am-8pm Sun), which is the oldest church in Paris, was built in the 11th century on the site of a 6th-century abbey and was the dominant church in Paris until the advent of Notre Dame. It has since been altered many times, but **Chapelle de St-Symphorien**, to the right as you enter, was part of the original abbey and is the final resting place of St Germanus (AD 496–576), the first bishop of Paris. Columns in the chancel were taken from the Merovingian abbey. The bell tower over the western entrance has changed little since 990, although the spire dates only from the 19th century.

INSTITUT DE FRANCE

Bringing together five of France's academies of arts and sciences, the august **Institut de**

France (French Institute; Map pp105-7; ☎ 01 44 41 44 41; www.institut-de-france.fr in French; 23 quai de Conti, 6e; metro Mabillon or Pont Neuf) was created in 1795. The most famous of these is the **Académie Française**, founded by Cardinal Richelieu in 1635. Its 40 members, known as the Immortels (Immortals), are charged with the Herculean (some might say impossible) task of safeguarding the purity of the French language.

The domed building housing the Institut de France, across the Seine from the eastern end of the Louvre, is a masterpiece of 17th-century French neoclassical architecture. There are usually **guided tours** (adult/under 25 €9/6) at 10.30am and 3pm on the first Saturday of the month and occasionally on Sunday. Check *Pariscope* or *L'Officiel des Spectacles* (see p160) under 'Conférences' or ring the institute for details.

JARDIN DU LUXEMBOURG
When the weather is fine Parisians of all ages flock to the formal terraces and chestnut groves of the 23-hectare **Jardin du Luxembourg** (Luxembourg Garden; Map pp102-4; metro Luxembourg; 7am-9.30pm Apr-Oct, 8am-sunset Mar-Nov) to read, relax and sunbathe. There are a number of activities for children here, and in the southern part of the garden you'll find urban **orchards** as well as the honey-producing **Rucher du Luxembourg** (Luxembourg Apiary).

Palais du Luxembourg (Luxembourg Palace; rue de Vaugirard, 6e), at the northern end of the garden, was built for Marie de Médicis, Henri IV's consort; it has been the **Sénat** (Senate), the upper house of the French parliament, since 1958. There are **guided tours** (reservations ☎ 01 44 61 20 89; adult/under 25 €9/6) of the interior at 10am on the first Sunday of each month, but you must book by the preceding Wednesday.

The **Musée du Luxembourg** (Luxembourg Museum; ☎ 01 42 34 25 95; 19 rue de Vaugirard, 6e; metro Luxembourg or St-Sulpice; adult/student & 13-26 yrs/8-12 yrs from €9/6/4; 11am-7pm Tue-Thu, 11am-10.30pm Fri-Mon), which opened at the end of the 19th century in the orangery of the Palais du Luxembourg as an exhibition space for living artists, now hosts prestigious temporary art exhibitions. Admission price depends on the exhibit.

Montparnasse
After WWI, writers, poets and artists of the avant-garde abandoned Montmartre

and crossed the Seine, shifting the centre of artistic ferment to the area around blvd du Montparnasse. Chagall, Modigliani, Léger, Soutine, Miró, Kandinsky, Picasso, Stravinsky, Hemingway, Ezra Pound and Cocteau, as well as such political exiles as Lenin and Trotsky, all used to hang out in the cafés and brasseries for which the quarter became famous. Montparnasse remained a creative centre until the mid-1930s; the boulevard's many restaurants, cafés and cinemas still attract large numbers in the evening.

TOUR MONTPARNASSE
A steel-and-smoked-glass eyesore built in 1974, the 210m-high **Tour Montparnasse** (Montparnasse Tower; Map pp99-101; ☎ 01 45 38 52 56; www.tourmontparnasse56.com; rue de l'Arrivée, 15e; metro Montparnasse Bienvenüe; to 56th fl adult/senior & student/under 14 €7/6/4.50, to 59th fl €8/6.80/5.50; 9.30am-11.30pm Apr-Sep; 9.30am-10.30pm Sun-Thu, 9.30am-11pm Fri & Sat Oct-Mar) affords spectacular views over the city – a view, we might add, that does not take in this ghastly oversized lipstick tube. A lift takes you up to the 56th-floor enclosed **observatory**, with an exhibition centre and a video about Paris. You can combine the lift trip with a hike up the stairs to the **open-air terrace** on the 59th floor.

CIMETIÈRE DU MONTPARNASSE
Cimetière du Montparnasse (Montparnasse Cemetery; Map pp99-101; blvd Edgar Quinet & rue Froidevaux, 14e; metro Edgar Quinet or Raspail; 8am-6pm Mon-Fri, 8.30am-6pm Sat, 9am-6pm Sun mid-Mar–early Nov; 8am-5.30pm Mon-Fri, 8.30am-5.30pm Sat, 9am-5.30pm Sun early Nov–mid-Mar) received its first 'resident' in 1824. It contains the tombs of such illustrious personages as Charles Baudelaire, Guy de Maupassant, Samuel Beckett, Constantin Brancusi, Chaim Soutine, Man Ray, André Citroën, Alfred Dreyfus, Jean Seberg, Simone de Beauvoir, Jean-Paul Sartre and the crooner Serge Gainsbourg. Maps showing the location of the tombs are available free from the **conservation office** (☎ 01 44 10 86 50; 3 blvd Edgar Quinet, 14e).

CATACOMBES
In 1785 it was decided to solve the hygiene and aesthetic problems posed by Paris' overflowing cemeteries by exhuming the bones and storing them in the tunnels of three disused quarries. One ossuary created

---

STRANGERS IN PARIS

Foreigners (*étrangers*, or strangers, to the French) of a literary bent have found inspiration in Paris since Charles Dickens used it with London as the setting for his novel on the French Revolution, *A Tale of Two Cities* (1859). The glory days of Paris as a magnet for writers, however, were the years between WWI and WWII.

Ernest Hemingway's *The Sun Also Rises* and *A Moveable Feast* both portray bohemian life in Paris between the wars; many of the vignettes in the latter – dishing Ford Maddox Ford in a café, 'sizing up' F Scott Fitzgerald in a toilet in the Latin Quarter, and overhearing Gertrude Stein and her lover, Alice B Toklas, bitching at one another from the sitting room of their salon near the Jardin du Luxembourg – are classics.

Language guru Stein, who could be so tiresome with her word plays and seemingly endless repetitions (eg 'A rose is a rose is a rose is a rose') in books like *The Making of Americans*, was able to let her hair down by assuming her lover's identity in *The Autobiography of Alice B Toklas*. It's a fascinating account of the author's many years in Paris, her salon on rue de Fleurus and her friendships with Hemingway, Matisse, Picasso, Braque, Juan Gris and others.

Down and Out in Paris & London is George Orwell's account of the time he spent working as a *plongeur* (dishwasher) in Paris and living with tramps in both cities in the early 1930s. *Tropic of Cancer* and *Quiet Days in Clichy* by Henry Miller are steamy novels set in the French capital; his *Max and the White Phagocytes* and *Black Spring* are among some of his less raunchy Parisian writings. Anaïs Nin's voluminous diaries, fiction and published correspondence with Miller are highly evocative of 1930s Paris. Jack Kerouac's *Satori in Paris* can be extremely irritating but it does have its moments (eg the scene in the Montparnasse gangster bar).

---

in 1810 is now known as the **Catacombes** (☎ 01 43 22 47 63; Map pp90-2; www.paris.fr/musees /musee_carnavalet in French; 1 place Denfert Rochereau, 14e; metro Denfert Rochereau; adult/senior & student/ 14-25 yrs/under 14 €5/3.30/2.60/free; ☿ 10am-5pm Tue-Sun), which can be visited. After descending 20m (130 steps) from street level, visitors follow 1.6km of underground corridors in which the bones and skulls of millions of Parisians are neatly stacked along the walls. During WWII these tunnels were used as a headquarters by the Resistance.

The route through the Catacombes begins at a small, dark-green *belle époque*-style building in the centre of place Denfert Rochereau. The exit is on rue Remy Dumoncel (metro Mouton Duvernet), 700m southwest of place Denfert Rochereau.

Faubourg St-Germain & Invalides

Faubourg St-Germain in the 7e, the area between the Musée d'Orsay and, a kilometre to the south, rue de Babylone, was Paris' most fashionable neighbourhood during the 18th century. Some of the most interesting mansions, many of which now serve as embassies, cultural centres and government ministries, are along three streets running east to west: rue de Lille, rue de Grenelle and rue de Varenne. The **Hôtel Matignon** (Map pp99-101; 57 rue de Varenne, 7e) has been the official residence of the French prime minister since the start of the Fifth Republic in 1958.

MUSÉE D'ORSAY

The **Musée d'Orsay** (Orsay Museum; Map pp99-101; ☎ 01 40 49 48 84; www.musee-orsay.fr; 1 rue de la Légion d'Honneur, 7e; metro Musée d'Orsay or Solférino; adult Mon-Sat/Sun €5/3 senior & 18-25 yrs €3, under 18 free, 1st Sun of month free; ☿ 9am-6pm Tue, Wed, Fri & Sat, 9am-9.45pm Thu, 9am-6pm Sun late Jun-Sep, 10am-6pm Tue, Wed, Fri & Sat, 10am-9.45pm Thu, 9am-6pm Sun Oct-late Jun) is housed in a former train station (1900) facing the Seine from quai Anatole France. It displays France's national collection of paintings, sculptures, *objets d'art* and other works produced between the 1840s and 1914, including the fruits of the impressionist, postimpressionist and Art Nouveau movements. The Musée National d'Art Moderne (p116) at the Centre Pompidou then picks up the torch.

Many visitors to the museum go straight to the upper level (lit by a skylight) to see the famous **impressionist paintings** by Monet, Pissarro, Renoir, Sisley, Degas and Manet and the **postimpressionist works** by Gauguin, Cézanne, Van Gogh, Seurat and Matisse, but there's also lots to see on the ground floor, including some early works by Manet,

Monet, Renoir and Pissarro. The middle level has some superb **Art Nouveau rooms**.

English-language tours (information ☎ 01 40 49 48 48; admission fee plus €6/4.50; 1½hr) include the 'Masterpieces of the Musée d'Orsay' tour, departing at 11.30am Tuesday to Saturday, with an additional one at 4pm on Thursday from February to August. There's an in-depth tour focusing on the impressionists at 2.30pm on Tuesday and 4pm on Thursday at least once a month. The 1½-hour **audioguide tour** (€5), available in six languages, points out around 80 major works. Be aware that tickets are valid all day so you can leave and re-enter the museum as you please.

MUSÉE RODIN

The **Musée Rodin** (Rodin Museum; Map pp99–101; ☎ 01 44 18 61 10; www.musee-rodin.fr; 77 rue de Varenne, 7e; metro Varenne; adult Mon-Sat/Sun €5/3 senior & 18-25 yrs €3, under 18 free, 1st Sun of month free, garden only €1; ⊙ 9.30am-5.45pm Apr-Sep, 9.30am-4.45pm Oct-Mar) is both a sublime museum and one of the most relaxing spots in the city, with a lovely **garden** full of sculptures and shade trees in which to rest and contemplate *The Thinker*. Rooms on two floors of this 18th-century residence display extraordinarily vital bronze and marble sculptures by Rodin, including casts of some of his most celebrated works: *The Hand of God*, *The Burghers of Calais*, *Cathedral*, that perennial crowd-pleaser *The Thinker* and the incomparable *The Kiss*.

HÔTEL DES INVALIDES

The **Hôtel des Invalides** (Map pp99–101; metro Varenne or La Tour Maubourg) was built in the 1670s by Louis XIV to provide housing for 4000 *invalides* (disabled war veterans). On 14 July 1789 a mob forced its way into the building and, after fierce fighting, seized 28,000 rifles before heading on to the prison at Bastille and revolution.

North of the Hôtel des Invalides' main courtyard, the so-called **Cour d'Honneur**, is the **Musée de l'Armée** (Army Museum; ☎ 01 44 42 37 72; www.invalides.org; 129 rue de Grenelle, 7e; adult/senior, student & 18-25 yrs/under 18 €7/5.50/free; ⊙ 10am-6pm Apr-Sep, 10am-5pm Oct-Mar, closed 1st Mon of month), which holds the nation's largest collection on the history of the French military. To the south are the **Église St-Louis des Invalides**, once used by soldiers, and the **Église du Dôme**, with its sparkling dome (1677–1735) visible throughout the city, which received

the remains of Napoleon in 1840. The very extravagant **Tombeau de Napoléon 1er** (Napoleon's Tomb; ⊙ 10am-6pm Apr-Sep, 10am-5pm Oct-Mar, closed 1st Mon of month), in the centre of the church, consists of six coffins that fit into one another like a Russian *matryoshka* doll. Admission to the Army Museum allows entry to all the other sights in the Hôtel des Invalides.

A 500m-long expanse of lawn called the **Esplanade des Invalides** (metro Invalides, Varenne or La Tour Maubourg) separates Faubourg St-Germain from the Eiffel Tower area.

Eiffel Tower Area & 16e Arrondissement

Paris' very symbol, the Eiffel Tower, is surrounded by open areas on both banks of the Seine, which take in both the 7e and 16e, which is perhaps the most chichi and snobby part of Paris. It's not everyone's *tasse de thé* but there are several outstanding museums and sights in this part of the Right Bank.

EIFFEL TOWER

The **Tour Eiffel** (Map pp99–101; ☎ 01 44 11 23 23; www.tour-eiffel.fr; metro Champ de Mars-Tour Eiffel or Bir Hakeim; ⊙ lifts 9am-midnight mid-Jun–Aug, 9.30am-11pm Sep–mid-Jun; stairs 9am-midnight mid-Jun–Aug, 9.30am-6.30pm Sep–mid-Jun) faced massive opposition from Paris' artistic and literary elite when it was built for the 1889 Exposition Universelle (World Fair), marking the centenary of the Revolution. The 'metal asparagus', as some Parisians snidely called it, was almost torn down in 1909 but was spared because it proved an ideal platform for the transmitting antennas needed for the new science of radiotelegraphy. It welcomed two million visitors the year it opened and three times as many climb to the top each year today.

The Eiffel Tower, named after its designer, Gustave Eiffel, is 324m high, including the TV antenna at the tip. This figure can vary by as much as 15cm, however, as the tower's 10,000 tonnes of iron, held together by 2.5 million rivets, expand in warm weather and contract when it's cold.

Three levels are open to the public. The lifts (west and north pillars), which follow a curved trajectory, cost €4 to the 1st platform (57m above the ground), €7.30 to the 2nd (115m) and €10.40 to the 3rd (276m). Children aged three to 11 pay €2.20/4/5.70, respectively; there are no youth or student discounts and children under three are free.

You can avoid the lift queues by taking the stairs (€3.50) in the south pillar to the 1st and 2nd platforms.

CHAMP DE MARS
Running southeast from the Eiffel Tower, the grassy **Champ de Mars** (Field of Mars; Map pp99–101; metro Champ de Mars-Tour Eiffel or École Militaire) is named after the Roman god of war. It was originally a parade ground for the cadets of the 18th-century **École Militaire** (Military Academy), the vast, French-classical building (1772) at the southeastern end of the park, which counted Napoleon among its graduates.

PALAIS DE CHAILLOT
The two curved, colonnaded wings of the **Palais de Chaillot** (Chaillot Palace; Map pp99–101; metro Trocadéro), built for the 1937 World Exhibition held here, and the terrace in between them afford an exceptional panorama of the Jardins du Trocadéro, the Seine and the Eiffel Tower.

At the far eastern tip of the Palais de Chaillot is the main branch of the **Cinémathèque Française** (p161). In its western wing there are two interesting museums. The **Musée de l'Homme** (Museum of Mankind; ☎ 01 44 05 72 72; www.mnhn.fr in French; 17 place du Trocadéro, 16e; adult/senior & student/4-16 yrs €7/5/3; ♥ 9.45am-5.15pm Wed-Mon) contains an excellent display on population growth linked with UN databases, as well as anthropological and ethnographical exhibits from Africa and Europe (1st floor) and the Americas, the Pacific and the Arctic (2nd floor). The **Musée de la Marine** (Maritime Museum; ☎ 01 53 65 69 53; www.musee-marine.fr; 17 place du Trocadéro; adult/senior or student/under 18 €7/5.40/free; ♥ 10am-6pm Wed-Mon) focuses on France's naval adventures from the 17th century until today and boasts one of the world finest collections of carved model ships.

JARDINS DU TROCADÉRO
The **Trocadero Gardens** (Map pp99–101; metro Trocadéro), whose fountains and statue garden are grandly illuminated at night, are across Pont d'Iéna from the Eiffel Tower. They are named after a Spanish stronghold near Cádiz that was captured by the French in 1823.

MUSÉE GUIMET DES ARTS ASIATIQUES
The **Musée Guimet des Arts Asiatiques** (Guimet Museum of Asian Art; Map pp93–5; ☎ 01 56 52 53 00; www.museeguimet.fr; 6 place d'Iéna; metro Iéna; permanent collections adult Mon-Sat/Sun €5.50/4 student, senior & 18-25 yrs €4, under 18 free, 1st Sun of month free; ♥ 10am-6pm Wed-Mon) is France's foremost repository for sculptures, paintings, *objets d'art* and religious articles from Afghanistan, India, Nepal, Pakistan, Tibet, Cambodia, China, Japan and Korea. The core of the collection – Buddhist paintings and sculptures brought to Paris in 1876 by collector Émile Guimet – is housed in the annexe called the **Galleries du Panthéon Bouddhique du Japon et de la Chine** (Buddhist Pantheon Galleries of Japan & China; ☎ 01 47 23 61 65; 19 av d'Iéna; metro Iéna), in the scrumptious Hôtel Heidelbach a short distance to the north. Don't miss the wonderful Japanese garden here.

FLAME OF LIBERTY MEMORIAL
Southeast of the Musée Guimet and over the border to the 8e is **place de l'Alma** (Map pp93–5; metro Alma-Marceau). This is where on 31 August 1997 in the underpass running parallel to the Seine Diana, Princess of Wales, was killed in an automobile accident along with her companion, Dodi Fayed, and their chauffeur, Henri Paul. The bronze **Flame of Liberty** is a replica of the one topping the torch of the Statue of Liberty and was placed here by Paris-based US firms in 1987 on the centenary of the *International Herald Tribune* newspaper as a symbol of friendship between France and the USA. It became something of a memorial to Diana and was decorated with flowers, photographs, graffiti and personal notes for almost five years. In 2002 it was renovated and cleaned and, this being an age of short memories, there are now very few reminders of the tragedy that happened so close by.

MUSÉE DES ÉGOUTS DE PARIS
The **Musée des Égouts de Paris** (Paris Sewers Museum; Map pp99–101; ☎ 01 53 68 27 81; place de la Résistance, 7e; metro Pont de l'Alma; adult/student & 5-16 yrs/under 5 €3.80/3.05/free; ♥ 11am-6pm Sat-Wed May-Sep, 11am-5pm Sat-Wed Oct-Apr) is a working museum whose entrance – a rectangular maintenance hole topped with a kiosk – is across the street from 93 quai d'Orsay, 7e. Raw sewage flows beneath your feet as you walk through 480m of odoriferous tunnels, passing artefacts illustrating the development of Paris' wastewater disposal system. It'll take your breath away, it will.

Étoile & Champs-Élysées

A dozen avenues radiate out from place de l'Étoile – officially place Charles de Gaulle – and first among them is the av des Champs-Élysées. This broad boulevard, whose name refers to the 'Elysian Fields' where happy souls dwelt after death, according to Greek mythology, links place de la Concorde with the Arc de Triomphe. Symbolising the style and *joie de vivre* of Paris since the mid-19th century, the avenue remains a popular tourist destination.

Some 400m north of av des Champs-Élysées is rue du Faubourg St-Honoré (8e), the western extension of rue St-Honoré. It is home to some of Paris' most renowned couture houses, jewellers, antique shops and the 18th-century **Palais de l'Élysée** (Map pp93–5; cnr rue du Faubourg St-Honoré & av de Marigny, 8e; metro Champs Élysées Clemenceau), the official residence of the French president.

ARC DE TRIOMPHE

The **Arc de Triomphe** (Triumphal Arch; Map pp93–5; ☎ 01 55 37 73 77, 01 44 95 02 10; www.monum.fr; metro Charles de Gaulle-Étoile; viewing platform adult/ 18-25 yrs/under18 €7/4.50/free, 1st Sun of month free; ☽ 9.30am-11pm Apr-Sep, 10am-10.30pm Oct-Mar) is 2.2km northwest of place de la Concorde in the middle of place Charles de Gaulle or place de l'Étoile), the world's largest traffic roundabout. It was commissioned in 1806 by Napoleon to commemorate his imperial victories but remained unfinished when he started losing battles and then entire wars. It was not completed until 1836. Since 1920, the body of an **Unknown Soldier** from WWI, taken from Verdun in Lorraine, has lain beneath the arch; his fate and that of countless others is commemorated by a **memorial flame** that is rekindled each evening around 6.30pm.

From the **viewing platform** on top of the arch (up 284 steps and well worth the climb) you can see the 12 avenues – many of them named after Napoleonic victories and illustrious generals (including ultra-exclusive av Foch, which is Paris' widest boulevard) – radiating towards every part of the city. Tickets are sold in the underground passageway beneath place de l'Étoile that surfaces on the even-numbered side of av des Champs-Élysées.

GRAND & PETIT PALAIS

Erected for the 1900 World Exposition, the **Grand Palais** (Great Palace; ☎ 01 44 13 17 17; Map pp93–5; www.rmn.fr; 3 av du Général Eisenhower, 8e; metro Champs-Élysées Clemenceau; without/with booking adult Thu-Mon €9/10 Sun €7/8, student & senior €7/8 Thu-Sun, under 18 free, 1st Sun of month free; ☽ without booking 1-8pm Thu-Mon, 1-10pm Wed, with booking 10am-8pm Thu-Mon, 10am-10pm Wed) was houses the **Galeries Nationales du Grand Palais** beneath its huge, Art Nouveau glass roof. Special exhibitions, among the biggest the city stages, last three or four months here.

The **Petit Palais** (Little Palace; ☽ 01 42 65 12 73, 01 44 51 19 31; www.paris.fr/musees in French; av Winston Churchill, 8e; metro Champs-Élysées Clemenceau), which was also built for the 1900 fair, is home to the **Musée des Beaux-Arts de la Ville de Paris**, the Paris municipality's Museum of Fine Arts, with medieval and Renaissance *objets d'art*, tapestries, drawings and 19th-century French painting and sculpture. It was closed at the time of research and is expected to reopen in 2005.

PALAIS DE LA DÉCOUVERTE

The **Palais de la Découverte** (Palace of Discovery; Map pp93–5; ☎ 01 56 43 20 21; www.palais-decouverte.fr in French; av Franklin D Roosevelt, 8e; metro Champs-Élysées Clemenceau; adult/senior, student & 5-18 yrs/under 5 €6/3.90/free; ☽ 9.30am-6pm Tue-Sat, 10am-7pm Sun) is a fascinating science museum with interactive exhibits on astronomy, biology, medicine, chemistry, mathematics, computer science, physics and earth sciences. The **planetarium** (admission €3.50 extra) usually has four shows a day in French; ring or consult the website for current schedules.

Concorde & Madeleine

The cobblestone expanses of 18th-century place de la Concorde are sandwiched between the Jardin des Tuileries and the parks at the eastern end of av des Champs-Élysées. Delightful place de la Madeleine is to the north. Both are in the 8e arrondissement.

PLACE DE LA CONCORDE

This square (Map pp93–5; metro Concorde) was laid out between 1755 and 1775. The 3300-year-old pink granite **obelisk** with the gilded top in the middle of the square once stood in the Temple of Ramses at Thebes (today's Luxor) and was given to France in 1831 by Muhammad Ali, viceroy and pasha of Egypt. The **female statues** adorning the four corners of the square represent France's eight largest cities.

In 1793 Louis XVI's head was lopped off by a guillotine set up in the northwest corner of the square, near the statue representing Brest. During the next two years, a guillotine built near the entrance to the Jardin des Tuileries was used to behead some 1343 more people, including Marie-Antoinette and, six months later, the Revolutionary leaders Danton and Robespierre. The square was given its present name after the Reign of Terror (p31), in the hope that it would be a place of peace and harmony.

The two imposing buildings on the north side of the square are the **Hôtel de la Marine**, headquarters of the French navy, and the **Hôtel de Crillon** (p144), one of Paris' swankiest hotels.

ÉGLISE DE LA MADELEINE

The neoclassical **Église de la Madeleine** (Church of St Mary Magdalene; Map pp93-5; ☎ 01 44 51 69 00; rue Royale, 8e; metro Madeleine; ☼ 7.30am-7pm Mon-Sat, 7.30am-1.30pm & 3.30-7pm Sun) is 350m northeast of place de la Concorde. Built in the style of a Greek temple, what is simply called La Madeleine was consecrated in the year 1845 after almost a century of design changes and construction delays. It is surrounded by 52 Corinthian columns, and the marble and gilt interior is topped by three sky-lit cupolas.

Opéra & Grands Boulevards

Place de l'Opéra (Map pp93-5) is the site of Paris' world-famous (and original) opera house. It abuts the Grands Boulevards, the eight contiguous 'Great Boulevards' – Madeleine, Capucines, Montmartre, Poissonnière, Italiens, Bonne Nouvelle, St-Denis and St-Martin – that stretch from elegant place de la Madeleine in the 8e eastwards to the less-than-desirable place de la République in the 3e, a distance of just under 3km.

The Grands Boulevards were laid out in the 17th century on the site of obsolete city walls and served as a centre of café and theatre life in the 18th and 19th centuries, reaching the height of fashion during the *belle époque*. North of the western end of the Grands Boulevards is blvd Haussmann (8e and 9e), the heart of the commercial and banking district and known for some of Paris' most famous department stores, including **Galeries Lafayette** and **Le Printemps** (p168).

PALAIS GARNIER

Palais Garnier (Garnier Palace; Map pp93-5; place de l'Opéra, 9e; metro Opéra), one of the most impressive monuments erected in Paris during the 19th century, stages operas, ballets and classical-music concerts (p162). In summer it can be visited on English-language **guided tours** (☎ 01 40 01 22 63; admission €10; ☼ 10.30am & noon late Jul-early Sep).

Palais Garnier houses the **Musée de l'Opéra** ☎ 01 47 42 07 02, 01 40 01 22 63; www.opera-de-paris .fr in French; adult/senior, student & 10-26 yrs €6/3, under 10 free; ☼ 10am-6pm Jul & Aug, 10am-5pm Sep-Jun), which contains a lot of documentation (it also functions as an important research library) and some memorabilia. More interestingly admission to the museum includes a visit to the opera house itself as long as there's not a daytime rehearsal or performance.

COVERED ARCADES

There are several **passages couverts** (covered shopping arcades; Map pp96-8) off blvd Montmartre (9e) and walking through them is like stepping back into early-19th-century Paris. The **passage des Panoramas** (11 blvd Montmartre, 2e; metro Grands Boulevards), which was opened in 1800 and received Paris' first gas lighting in 1817, was expanded in 1834 with the addition of four other interconnecting passages: Feydeau, Montmartre, St-Marc and Variétés. The arcades are open till about midnight daily.

On the northern side of blvd Montmartre, between Nos 10 and 12, is **passage Jouffroy** (metro Grands Boulevards), which leads across rue de la Grange Batelière to **passage Verdeau**. Both contain shops selling antiques, old postcards, used and antiquarian books, gifts, pet toys, imports from Asia and the like. The arcades are open until 10pm.

MUSÉE GRÉVIN

Inside passage Jouffroy, the **Musée Grévin** (Grévin Museum; Map pp96-8; ☎ 01 47 70 85 05; www .grevin.com in French; 10 blvd Montmartre, 9e; metro Grands Boulevards; adult/student/6-14 yrs €16/13.80/9; ☼ 10am-6.30pm Mon-Fri, 10am-7pm Sat & Sun) boasts some 250 wax figures that look more like caricatures than characters, but where else do you get to see Marilyn Monroe and Charles de Gaulle face to face or the real death masks of French Revolutionary leaders? The admission charge is positively outrageous and just keeps growing.

Ménilmontant & Belleville

A solidly working-class *quartier* with little to recommend it until just a few years ago, Ménilmontant in the 11e now boasts a surfeit of restaurants, bars and clubs. On the other hand, Belleville (20e), home to large numbers of immigrants, especially Muslims and Jews from North Africa and Vietnamese and ethnic Chinese from Indochina), remains for the most part unpretentious and working-class. **Parc de Belleville** (Map pp96-8; metro Couronnes), which opened in 1992 a few blocks east of blvd de Belleville, occupies a hill almost 200m above sea level amid 4.5 hectares of greenery and offers superb views of the city, especially from the **Maison de l'Air** (☎ 01 43 28 47 63; 27 rue Piat, 20e; metro Pyrénées; adult/senior & student €2/1; ⏱ 1.30-5.30pm Tue-Sat, 1.30-6.30pm Sun Apr-Sep, 1.30-5pm Tue-Sun Oct-Mar), which stages temporary exhibitions related to ecology and the environment. Paris' most famous necropolis lies just to the south of the park.

CIMETIÈRE DU PÈRE LACHAISE

The world's most visited graveyard, **Cimetière du Père Lachaise** (Père Lachaise Cemetery; Map pp102-4; ☎ 01 55 25 82 10; metro Philippe Auguste, Gambetta or Père Lachaise; ⏱ 8am-6pm Mon-Fri, 8.30am-6pm Sat, 9am-6pm Sun mid-Mar–early Nov; 8am-5.30pm Mon-Fri, 8.30am-5.30pm Sat, 9am-5.30pm Sun early Nov–mid-Mar) opened its one-way doors in 1804. Its 70,000 ornate, even ostentatious tombs form a verdant, open-air sculpture garden.

Among the mortal remains of the one million people buried in the cemetery are Chopin, Molière, Apollinaire, Oscar Wilde, Balzac, Proust, Gertrude Stein, Colette, Simone Signoret, Pissarro, Seurat, Modigliani, Sarah Bernhardt, Yves Montand, Delacroix, Edith Piaf, Isadora Duncan and even the immortal 12th-century lovers, Abélard and Héloïse. One particularly frequented grave is that of 1960s rock star **Jim Morrison** (1943–71), who is buried in division No 6.

Père Lachaise has four entrances, two of which are on blvd de Ménilmontant. Maps indicating the location of noteworthy graves are posted around the cemetery including one by the **conservation office** (Map pp102-4; 16 rue du Repos, 20e) on the western side of the cemetery. Better yet, newsstands and flower kiosks in the area, especially those by the metro stations, sell the primitive but useful *Plan Illustré du Père Lachaise* (Illustrated Map of Père Lachaise; €2).

13e Arrondissement & Chinatown

The 13e begins a few blocks south of the Jardin des Plantes in the 5e and is undergoing a true renaissance following the opening of the Bibliothèque Nationale de France François Mitterrand, the arrival of the high-speed Météor metro line (No 14) and the start of the ZAC Paris Rive Gauche project, the massive redevelopment of the old industrial quarter along the Seine. The stylishness of the neighbouring 5e extends to the av des Gobelins, while further south, between av d'Italie and av de Choisy, the succession of Asian restaurants, stalls and shops in the capital's version of Chinatown gives passers-by the illusion of having imperceptibly changed continents.

BIBLIOTHÈQUE NATIONALE DE FRANCE FRANÇOIS MITTERRAND

Rising up from the banks of the Seine are the four glass towers of the controversial, €2 billion **Bibliothèque Nationale de France** (National Library of France; Map pp90-2; ☎ 01 53 79 53 79; www .bnf.fr; 11 quai François Mauriac, 13e; metro Bibliothèque Fr Mitterrand; admission per 2 days/1 yr €4.50/46; ⏱ 10am-8pm Tue-Sat, noon-7pm Sun), which was conceived by the late President François Mitterrand as a 'wonder of the modern world' and opened in 1988.

No expense was spared to carry out a plan that many said defied logic. While many of the books and historical documents were shelved in the sun-drenched, 23-storey towers – shaped like half-open books – readers sat in artificially lit basement halls built around a 'forest courtyard' of 140 50-year-old pines, trucked in from the countryside. The towers have since been fitted with a complex (and expensive) shutter system, but the basement is prone to flooding from the Seine. The national library contains around 12 million tomes stored on some 420km of shelves and can accommodate 2000 readers and 2000 researchers.

MANUFACTURE DES GOBELINS

The **Manufacture des Gobelins** (Gobelins Factory; Map pp90-2; ☎ 01 44 08 52 00; 42 av des Gobelins, 13e; metro Les Gobelins; adult/8-25 yrs/under 7 €8/6/free; ⏱ guided tour 2pm & 2.45pm Tue-Thu) has been weaving *haute lisse* (high-relief) tapestries on specialised looms since the 18th century, along with Beauvais-style *basse lisse* (low-relief) ones and Savonnerie rugs. The factory can be visited by guided tour only three days a week.

Montmartre & Pigalle

During the late 19th and early 20th centuries the bohemian lifestyle of Montmartre in the 18e attracted a number of important writers and artists, including Picasso, who lived at the studio called **Bateau Lavoir** (Map p108; 11bis Émile Goudeau) from 1908 to 1912 during his so-called Blue Period. Although the activity shifted to Montparnasse after WWI, Montmartre retains an upbeat ambience that all the tourists in the world couldn't spoil.

Only a few blocks southwest of the tranquil, residential streets of Montmartre is lively, neon-lit Pigalle (9e and 18e), one of Paris' two main sex districts (the other, which is *much* more low-rent, is along rue St-Denis and its side streets north of Forum des Halles in the 1er). But Pigalle is more than just a sleazy red-light district; there are plenty of trendy nightspots, including clubs and cabarets, here as well.

The easiest way to reach Montmartre is via the RATP's sleek funicular (p173). Montmartrobus, a bus run by the RATP. It makes a circuitous route from place Pigalle through Montmartre to the 18e Mairie on place Jules Joffrin. Detailed maps are posted at bus stops.

BASILIQUE DU SACRÉ CŒUR

The **Basilique du Sacré Cœur** (Basilica of the Sacred Heart; Map p108; ☎ 01 53 41 89 00; www.sacre-coeur -montmartre.com; place du Parvis du Sacré Cœur, 18e; metro Anvers; ☼ 6am-11pm), perched at the very top of the Butte de Montmartre (Montmartre Hill), was built from contributions pledged by Parisian Catholics as an act of contrition after the humiliating Franco-Prussian War of 1870–71. Construction began in 1873, but the basilica was not consecrated until 1919.

Some 234 spiralling steps lead you to the basilica's **dome** (admission €5; ☼ 9am-7pm Apr-Sep, 9am-6pm Oct-Mar), which affords one of Paris' most spectacular panoramas; they say you can see for 30km on a clear day.

PLACE DU TERTRE

Half a block west of the **Église St-Pierre de Montmartre**, which once formed part of a 12th-century Benedictine abbey, is **place du Tertre**

(Map p108; metro Abbesses), once the main square of the village of Montmartre. These days it's filled with cafés, restaurants, portrait artists and tourists and is always animated. Look for the **Moulin de la Galette** and **Moulin Radet**, two old-style windmills to the west of the square on rue Lepic.

CIMETIÈRE DE MONTMARTRE

Established in 1798, **Cimetière de Montmartre** (Montmartre Cemetery; Map p108; ☎ 01 43 87 64 24; metro Place de Clichy; ☼ 8am-6pm Mon-Fri, 8.30am-6pm Sat, 9am-6pm Sun mid-Mar–early Nov, 8am-5.30pm Mon-Fri, 8.30am-5.30pm Sat, 9am-5.30pm Sun early Nov–mid-Mar) is perhaps the most famous cemetery in Paris after Père Lachaise. It contains the graves of Zola, Alexandre Dumas the younger, Stendhal, Heinrich Heine, Jacques Offenbach, Hector Berlioz, Degas, François Truffaut and Vaslav Nijinsky – among many others. The entrance closest to Butte de Montmartre is at the end of av Rachel, just off blvd de Clichy or down the stairs from 10 rue Caulaincourt.

MUSÉE DE L'ÉROTISME

The **Musée de l'Érotisme** (Museum of Erotic Art; Map p108; ☎ 01 42 58 28 73; 72 blvd de Clichy, 18e; metro Blanche; adult/student €7/5; ☼ 10am-2am) tries to put some 2000 titillating statuary and stimulating sexual aids and fetishist items from days gone by on a loftier plane, with erotic art – both antique and modern – from four continents spread over seven floors. But most of the punters know why they are here.

La Villette

The Buttes Chaumont, the Canal de l'Ourcq and especially the Parc de la Villette, with its wonderful museums and other attractions, create the winning trifecta of the 19th arrondissement.

PARC DE LA VILLETTE

The whimsical, 35-hectare **Parc de la Villette** (La Villette Park; Map pp90-2; ☎ 01 04 03 75 75, 01 40 03 75 03; www.villette.com; metro Porte de la Villette or Porte de Pantin) in the city's far northeastern corner, which opened in 1993, stretches from the Cité des Sciences et de l'Industrie (metro Porte de la Villette) south to the Cité de la Musique (metro Porte de Pantin). Split into two sections by the Canal de l'Ourcq (p135), the park is enlivened by shaded walkways, imaginative street furniture, a series of themed gardens for kids and fanciful, bright-red pavilions known as *folies*.

CITÉ DES SCIENCES ET DE L'INDUSTRIE

The huge **Cité des Sciences et de l'Industrie** (City of Science & Industry; Map pp90-2; ☎ 01 40 05 80 00, ☎ reservations 0 892 697 072; www.cite-sciences.fr; 30 av Corentin Cariou, 19e; metro Porte de la Villette; 🕑 10am-6pm Tue-Sat, 10am-7pm Sun), at the northern end of Parc de la Villette, has all sorts of high-tech exhibits. Free attractions:

Aquarium (level -2; 🕑 10am-6pm Tue-Sat, 10am-7pm Sun)

Cité des Métiers (level -1; 🕑 10am-6pm Tue-Fri, noon-6pm Sat) Information about trades, professions and employment.

Cyber-base (level 1; 🕑 noon-7.30pm Tue, noon-6.30pm Wed-Sun) Internet centre.

Médiathèque (levels 0 & -1; 🕑 noon-7.45pm Tue, noon-6.45pm Wed-Sun) With multimedia exhibits dealing with childhood, the history of science and health.

A free (and very useful) map/brochure in English called *The Keys to the Cité* is available from the information counter at the main entrance to the complex. If you really want to know what's what and what's where, buy a copy of the detailed, 80-page *Guide to the Permanent Exhibitions* (€3) at reception. An audioguide costs €4.

The huge and rather confusingly laid-out – **Explora** (adult/7-25 yrs/under 7 €7.50/5.50/free) exhibitions are on levels 1 and 2 and cover everything from train technology and space to biology and sound. Tickets are valid for a full day and allow you to enter and exit up to four times.

The **Planétarium** (level 1; admission €3, 3-7 yrs free, under 3 not admitted; 🕑 11am-5pm Tue-Sun) has six shows a day on the hour (except at 1pm) on a screen measuring 1000 sq metres.

The highlight of the Cité des Sciences et de l'Industrie is the brilliant **Cité des Enfants** (Children's Village; level 0), whose colourful and imaginative hands-on demonstrations of basic scientific principles are divided into three sections: one for three- to five-year-olds, and two for five- to 12-year-olds. In the first, kids can explore, among other things, the behaviour of water (waterproof lab ponchos provided). The second allows children to build toy houses with industrial robots and stage news broadcasts in a TV studio equipped with video cameras. The

third, **Électricité**, is a special electricity exhibition devoted to the five-to-12 age group.

Visits to Cité des Enfants lasting 1½ hours begin four times a day: at 9.45am, 11.30am, 1.30pm and 3.30pm on Tuesday, Thursday and Friday and at 10.30am, 12.30pm, 2.30pm and 4.30pm on Wednesday, Saturday and Sunday. Each child is charged €5 and must be accompanied by an adult (maximum two per family). During school holidays it's a good idea to make reservations two or three days in advance by telephone or via the Internet.

CITÉ DE LA MUSIQUE

The **Cité de la Musique** (Music Village; Map pp90-2; ☎ 01 44 84 44 84; www.cite-musique.fr; 221 av Jean Jaurès, 19e; metro Porte de Pantin), on the southern edge of Parc de la Villette, is a striking triangular-shaped concert hall whose brief is to bring non-elitist music from around the world to Paris' multiethnic masses. In the same complex, the **Musée de la Musique** (Music Museum; ☎ 01 44 84 44 84; adult/senior, student & 18-25 yrs/under 18 €6.10/4.80/free; 🕑 noon-6pm Tue-Sat, 10am-6pm Sun) displays some 900 rare musical instruments out of a collection of 4500 warehoused, and you can hear many of them being played through the earphones included in the admission cost.

ACTIVITIES

The best single source of information on sports in Paris (but in French only) is the 500-page *Parisports: Le Guide du Sport à Paris* (www.sport.paris.fr) available free from the **Mairie de Paris** information centre in the **Hôtel de Ville** (Map pp105-7; ☎ 0 820 007 575; www.paris.fr; 29 rue de Rivoli, 4e; metro Hôtel de Ville).

Cycling

Paris has some 220km of bicycle lanes running throughout the city as well as a dedicated lane paralleling some two-thirds of the blvd Périphérique. On Sundays and holidays throughout most of the year, large sections of road are reserved for pedestrians, cyclists and skaters under a scheme called 'Paris Respire' (Paris Breathes).

Maison Roue Libre (Map pp105-7; ☎ 0 810 441 534; www.rouelibre.fr; Forum des Halles, 1 passage Mondétour, 1er; metro Les Halles; 🕑 9am-7pm mid-Jan–mid-Dec), sponsored by RATP, the city's public transport system, is the best place to rent a

PARIS

bicycle in Paris. Bicycles cost €3/8/12/14/20 per hour/half-day/10-hour day/24-hour day/weekend and include insurance, helmet and baby seat.

Other outfits that rent bicycles:

Bike 'n' Roller (Map pp99-101; ☎ 01 45 50 38 27; 38 rue Fabert, 7e; metro Invalides; per 3 hr/day €9/12; ⏲ 10am-8pm Mon-Sat, 10am-6.30pm Sun)

Fat Tire Bike Tours (see p134)

Gepetto & Vélos (Map pp102-4; ☎ 01 43 54 19 95; www.gepetto-et-velos.com in French; 59 rue du Cardinal Lemoine, 5e; metro Cardinal Lemoine; per ½ day/day/weekend/week €7.50/15/23/50; ⏲ 9am-1pm & 2-7.30pm Tue-Sat, 9am-1pm & 2-7pm Sun)

Paris à Vélo, C'est Sympa! (Map pp102-4; ☎ 01 48 87 60 01; www.parisvelosympa.com in French; 37 blvd Bourdon, 4e; metro Bastille; per ½ day/day/weekend/week €9.50/12.50/24/59; ⏲ 9.30am-1pm & 2-6pm Mon-Fri, 9am-6pm Sat & Sun Nov-Mar, 9.30am-1pm & 2-6.30pm Mon-Fri, 9am-7pm Sat & Sun Apr-Oct)

Skating

Those into in-line skating might want to join in one of the two so-called Skating Rambles *(Randonnées en Roller)* organised each week throughout the year that attract up to 10,000 participants. The **Pari Roller** ramble (information ☎ 01 43 36 89 81; www.pari -roller.com in French) leaves **place Raoul Dautry** (Map pp99-101; metro Montparnasse Bienvenüe), the plaza between gare Montparnasse and Tour Montparnasse in the 14e, at 10pm Friday, returning at 1am. The **Rollers & Coquillages** ramble (☎ 01 44 54 07 44; www.rollers-coquillages.org) departs from **blvd Bourdon** (Map pp102-4; metro Bastille) in the 4e every Sunday at 2.30pm, returning at between 5.30pm and 6pm.

Nomades (Map pp102-4; ☎ 01 44 5 54 07 44; www .nomadeshop.com in French; 37 blvd Bourdon, 4e; metro Bastille; ⏲ 11am-1pm & 2-7pm Mon-Fri, 10am-7pm Sat, 10am-6pm Sun) is the Harrods of shops for roller heads and, in addition to renting out skates, it sells equipment and accessories and gives courses at five different levels. Skates rent for €5/8 per half-day/day during the week and €6/9 at the weekend. A weekend/week (Monday to Friday)/full week costs €16/23/30. Elbow and knee guards/helmets cost €1/2.

Swimming

Paris has 35 swimming pools that are open to the public; check with the **Mairie de Paris** (☎ 0 820 007 575; www.paris.fr) for the one that's nearest you. Most are short-length pools and finding a free lane for lengths can be nigh on impossible. Opening times vary widely, but avoid Wednesday afternoon and Saturday when kids off from school take the plunge. Unless noted otherwise the entry cost for municipal pools in Paris is €2.40/1.35 for adults/under 21. A carnet of 10 tickets costs €19.80/11.40.

WALKING TOUR

And you thought it was all berets, baguettes and bistros…To be sure Paris is and will always be *français* – the *couturiers* will continue to spin their glad rags, the *boulangeries* will churn out those long, crispy loaves and the terrace cafés will remain the places from which to watch the world go by. But it's a much more international world nowadays, and *Paris Mondial* (literally 'World Paris'), a diverse, dynamic, multicultural city, vibrates to its rhythms.

France ruled a considerable part of the world until as recently as the middle of the 20th century, and today its population includes a large number of immigrants and their descendants from its former colonies and protectorates in Africa, Indochina, the Middle East, India, the Caribbean and the South Pacific. At the same time, France has continued to accept significant numbers of exiles and refugees. Most of these immigrants have settled in specific areas of the capital, especially Belleville in the 19e and 20e, rue du Faubourg St-Denis in the 10e and La Goutte d'Or and Château Rouge in the 18e. A stroll through these quarters will have you touring the globe without even boarding an aeroplane.

Begin the walk at the Pyrénées metro stop in Belleville, a district where Jewish kosher and Muslim halal butchers share the same streets with cavernous Chinese eating establishments, their windows festooned with dripping *cha siu* (roast pork). Walk west on rue de Belleville past the **birthplace of Edith Piaf (1**; see p51) at No 72 and turn left (south) onto rue Piat, which you will be forgiven for thinking says 'Piaf'. Rue Piat will bring you to the **Parc de Belleville** (p129) which, at 200m above sea level, offers wonderful views of what is a very flat city. Descend the steps at the end of rue du Transvaal that lead to the **Maison de l'Air (2**; p129) nature centre exhibition space and follow the path to rue de Pali Kao and blvd de Belleville.

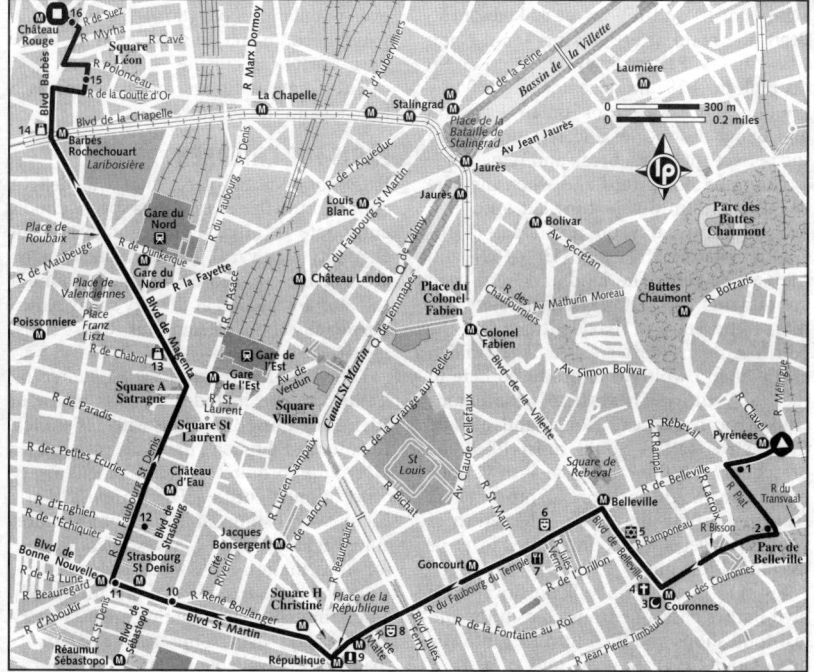

Blvd de Belleville is like a microcosm of Paris Mondial and on market mornings (p169), you might think you've been transported to the Mediterranean, Africa or even Asia. Watch the elegant, turbaned African women in Technicolor *boubous* (West African dress) brush past frenzied, young Asians with mobile phones glued to their ears, and more relaxed Orthodox Jews wearing yarmulkes alongside North Africans in *jellabas* (hooded cloak) on their way to the mosque. At No 39 is the **Mosquée Abou-Bakr (3)** just a few doors down from the modern **Église Notre Dame Réconciliatrice (4)** at the corner of rue de la Fontaine du Roi. About 100m up on the right-hand – or Tunisian – side of blvd de Belleville is the **Synagogue Michkan-Taachov (5)** at No 110. In nearby **rue Ramponeau** you'll encounter a Jewish shop called La Maison du Taleth at No 10 with religious tomes and articles and a kosher butcher Boucherie Zlassi at No 7.

The walk down rue du Faubourg du Temple (11e), left (west) at the top of blvd de Belleville, to place de la République is a long one and you can take the metro for a

couple of stops. But in doing so you'd miss the vibrancy and assorted sights: **La Java (6**; p163) at No 105, where Piaf once warbled, and the **Épicerie Asie, Antilles, Afrique (7)** at No 88 that sells edibles from three continents.

Once you've crossed the placid **Canal St-Martin** and walked past the decrepit entrance to the popular clubs **La Favela Chic** and **Gibus (8**; p164), enormous **place de la République** and its ever-present **statue of the Republic (9)**, erected in 1883, pop into view. This is where many political rallies and demonstrations in Paris start, end or are taking place. Make your way to the square's northwestern corner and follow blvd St-Martin past **Porte St-Martin (10)** and **Porte St-Denis (11)**, two triumphal arches dating from the late 17th century. Turn right (north) and follow **rue du Faubourg St-Denis**, the main artery linking Tamil Nadu with Turkey. **Passage Brady (12**; p156) at No 46, built in 1828 and once housing 100 tiny boutiques, is a warren of Indian, Pakistani and Bangladeshi cafés and restaurants and the perfect spot for a break and refuelling.

Continue northward and when the **Gare de l'Est** comes into view turn left onto blvd Magenta and carry on north past 19th-century **Marché St-Quentin (13**; p169) and the **Gare du Nord**. The landmark pink sign announcing the **Tati department store (14)** marks the start of La Goutte d'Or, the North African quarter called 'The Golden Drop' after a white wine produced here in the 19th century. The district is contiguous with African Château Rouge and outside the metro station you'll most likely be presented with the calling cards of various mediums *(médiums)* or fortune tellers *(voyants)* promising to effect the return of your estranged spouse, unrequited lover or misplaced fortune.

From the metro stop walk northwards up blvd Barbès past numerous goldsmiths and fast-food shops and then turn east into rue de la Goutte d'Or, a great *souk* of a street selling everything from gaudy tea glasses and pointy-toed leather *babouches* (slippers) to colourful belly dancers' costumes. From every direction the sounds of *rä* (a fusion of Algerian folk music and rock) fill the air.

Cut up **villa Poissonnière (15)**, a cobbled street that looks straight out of the 19th-century daguerreotype, and turn left and then right onto **rue des Poissoniers**, the 'Street of Fishermen' that is anything but: here you're more likely to find halal butchers offering special deals on sheep heads and 5kg packets of chicken.

Rue Myrha is the frontier between Central and West Africa and the Maghreb; raï music quickly gives way to Cameroonian *bikutsi* (a fusion of ancestral rhythms and speedy electric guitars) and Senegalese *mbalax*. After crossing over rue Myrha, turn left (west) into **rue Dejean (16)**, where an open-air market is held from 8am to 1pm and 3.30pm to 7.30pm Tuesday to Saturday and 8am to 1pm on Sunday. Here you *will* find fish and lots of it, especially fresh *capitaine* and *thiof* from Senegal, alongside stalls selling fiery Caribbean Scotch Bonnet chillies, plantains and the ever-popular *dasheen* (taro). It's everything you'd need, in fact, to succeed in the art of Afro-Caribbean cuisine.

The Château Rouge metro station is a few steps to the southwest.

PARIS FOR CHILDREN

Paris abounds in places that will delight children, and there is always a special child's entry rate to attractions (though ages of eligibility may vary). Family visits to many areas of the city can be designed around a rest stop (or picnic) at the city's may parks. For details about Disneyland Resort Paris, see p184.

Lonely Planet's *Travel with Children* by Cathy Lanigan includes all sorts of useful advice for those travelling with little ones. If you read French, the daily newspaper *Libération* produces a supplement every other month entitled *Paris Mômes* (Paris Kids), with listings and other information aimed at kids to age 12. An excellent website for information is www.babygoes2.com. *L'Officiel des Spectacles* (p160), the weekly entertainment magazine that appears every Wednesday, lists some *gardes d'enfants* (babysitters) available in Paris.

TOURS
Bicycle

An English-speaking company that consistently gets rave reviews from readers is **Fat Tire Bike Tours** (Map pp99-101; ☎ 01 56 58 10 54; www .fattirebiketoursparis.com; 24 rue Edgar Faure, 15e; metro La Motte-Piquet Grenelle; office ⓨ 9am-7pm), formerly Mike's Bike Tours. Fat Tire offers day tours of the city (adult/student €24/22) lasting about four hours at 11am in March and April and September to November, and at 11am and 3.30pm from May to August. Night bicycle tours (adult/student €28/26) depart at 7pm on Sunday, Tuesday and Thursday in March and November and at 7pm daily from April to October. Tours depart from av Gustave Eiffel, 7e (Map pp99–101), just opposite the Eiffel Tower's South Pillar at the start of the Champ de Mars. Costs include bicycle hire and, if necessary, raingear. Three-speeds are also available to rent for €2/15/25/50/65 per hour/day/weekend/week/month.

Boat

Based on the Right Bank just east of the Pont de l'Alma **Bateaux Mouches** (Map pp93-5;

☎ 01 42 25 96 10; www.bateauxmouches.com; Port de la Conférence, 8e; metro Alma Marceau; adult/senior & 4-12 yrs/under 4 €7/4/free), the most famous riverboat company in Paris, runs 1000-seat tour boats, the biggest on the Seine. The tours leave every half-hour from 10am to 8pm and every 20 minutes from 8pm to 11pm between mid-March and mid-November. For the rest of the year, there are five daily at 11am, 2.30pm, 4pm, 6pm and 9pm. There may be additional cruises in winter, depending on demand. The cruise lasts an hour and commentary is in several prerecorded languages.

If you prefer to see Paris from one of its reconditioned canals, **Paris Canal Croisières** (Map pp96-8; ☎ 01 42 40 96 97; www.pariscanal.com in French; Bassin de la Villette, 19-21 quai de la Loire, 19e; adult/senior & 12-25 yrs/4-11 yrs €16/12/9 Mon-Sun morning, adult, senior & 12-25 yrs/4-11 yrs €16/9 Sun afternoon) has daily three-hour cruises from quai Anatole France (7e), just northwest of the Musée d'Orsay (Map pp99–101) to Parc de la Villette, 19e (Map pp90–2) via the charming Canal St-Martin and Canal de l'Ourcq. Departures are 9.30am from quai Anatole France and at 2.30pm from Bassin de la Villette.

Bus
Balabus (in French ☎ 0 892 687 714, in English 6am-9pm ☎ 0 892 684 114; www.ratp.fr in French; €1.30 or 1 metro/bus ticket; 🕐 12.30-8pm Sun Apr-Sep) run by RATP follows a 50-minute route from Gare de Lyon to La Défense that passes by many of central Paris' most famous sights. Buses depart about every 20 minutes.

L'Open Tour (Map pp93-5; ☎ 01 42 66 56 56; www.paris-opentour.com; 13 rue Auber, 9e; metro Havre Caumartin or Opéra; 1 day adult/4-11 yrs €25/12, 2 consecutive days €28/12) operates open-deck buses along four circuits (central Paris, 2¼ hours; Montmartre-Grands Boulevards, 1¼ hours; Bastille-Bercy, one hour; and Montparnasse-St-Germain one hour) daily year-round. You can jump on and off at more than 50 stops. Schedules vary but buses depart roughly every 10 to 15 minutes from 9.30am to 6pm April to October and every 25 to 30 minutes from 9.30am to 4.30pm November to March.

Walking
Paris Walking Tours (☎ 01 48 09 21 40; www.paris-walks.com; adult/students under 25/10-18 yrs €10/7/5) has

English-language tours of several different districts and along different themes, including Montmartre at 10.30am on Sunday and Wednesday (leaving from metro Abbesses; Map p108) and the Marais at 10.30am on Tuesday and Saturday and 2.30pm on Sunday (departing from metro St-Paul, north of Île St-Louis; Map pp105–7). There are other tours focusing on Hemingway, impressionism, Thomas Jefferson, the French Revolution and so on.

FESTIVALS & EVENTS
Innumerable cultural and sporting events take place in Paris throughout the year; weekly details appear in *Pariscope* and *L'Officiel des Spectacles* (p160). You can also find them listed month by month under the heading 'Évènements' (Events) on the tourist office's website (www.paris -touristoffice.com).

The following abbreviated list gives you a taste of what to expect throughout the year.

January & February
La Grande Parade de Paris (www.parisparade.com) The city's New Year's Day parade originated in Montmartre but takes place in different venues (eg along the Grands Boulevards) depending on the year. Check the website for details.

Chinese New Year (www.paris.fr) Dragon parades and other festivities are held in late January or early February in Chinatown, the area of the 13e between av d'Ivry and av de Choisy (metro Porte de Choisy or Tolbiac), with an abridged version along rue Au Maire (metro Arts et Métiers) in the 3e.

Salon International de l'Agriculture (www.salon -agriculture.com) A 10-day international agricultural fair with lots to eat and drink, including dishes and wine from all over France. Held at the Parc des Expositions at Porte de Versailles in the 15e (metro Porte de Versailles) from late February to early March.

March & April
Jumping International de Paris (www.bercy.fr in French) Annual showjumping tournament, held in early March, featuring the world's most celebrated jumpers at the Palais Omnisports de Paris-Bercy in the 12e (metro Bercy).

Banlieues Bleues (www.banlieuesbleues.org) 'Suburban Blues' jazz and blues festival (with world, soul, funk and R&B thrown in for good measure) held in March and April in St-Denis and other Paris suburbs and attracting big-name talent.

Marathon International de Paris (www.paris marathon.com) The Paris International Marathon in early April starts on place de la Concorde, 1er, and finishes on av Foch, 16e. The **Semi-Marathon de Paris** is a half-marathon held in March (see the marathon website for details).

Foire du Trône (www.foiredutrone.com in French) Huge fun fair (350 attractions) held on the pelouse de Reuilly of the Bois de Vincennes (metro Porte Dorée) for eight weeks during April and May.

May & June
Foire de Paris (www.comexpo-paris.com) Huge modern living fair, including crafts, gadgets, food and wine, held in early May at the Parc des Expositions at Porte de Versailles in the 15e (metro Porte de Versailles).

Internationaux de France de Tennis (www.french open.org) The glitzy French Open tennis tournament takes place from late May to early June at Stade Roland Garros (metro Porte d'Auteuil) at the southern edge of the Bois de Boulogne in the 16e.

Fête de la Musique (www.fetedelamusique.culture.fr) A national music festival welcoming in summer on 21 June. Caters to a great diversity of tastes (jazz, reggae, classical etc) and features staged and impromptu live performances all over the city.

Gay Pride March (www.gaypride.fr in French) A colourful, Saturday afternoon parade held in late June through the Marais to Bastille celebrates Gay Pride Day, with various bars and clubs sponsoring floats and participants in some pretty outrageous costumes.

Paris Jazz Festival (www.parcfloraldeparis.com) Free jazz concerts every Saturday and Sunday afternoon in June and July in Parc Floral (metro Château de Vincennes).

La Goutte d'Or en Fête (www.gouttedorenfete.org in French) World-music festival (raï, reggae, rap and so on) running from late June to early July at square Léon, 18e (metro Barbès Rochechouart or Château Rouge).

July & August
Bastille Day Paris is *the* place to be on France's national day. Late on the night of the 13th, *bals des sapeurs-pompiers* (dances sponsored by Paris' fire brigades, who are considered sex symbols in France) are held at fire stations around the city. At 10am on the 14th, there's a military and fire-brigade parade along av des Champs-Élysées, accompanied by a fly-over of fighter aircraft and helicopters. In the evening a huge display of *feux d'artifice* (fireworks) is held at around 11pm on the Champ de Mars, 7e.

Tour de France (www.letour.fr) The last stage of the world's most prestigious cycling event ends with a race up av des Champs-Élysées on the 3rd or 4th Sunday of July.

Paris Plage (www.paris.fr) 'Paris Beach', one of the most unique and successful, city recreational events in the world sees 3km of embankment from the quai Henri IV (metro

Sully Morland) in the 4e to the quai des Tuileries (metro Tuileries) in the 1er transformed into three sand and pebble beaches, with sun beds, umbrellas, atomisers and plastic palm trees from mid-July to mid-August.

September & October
Jazz à La Villette (www.cite-musique.fr) Super 10-day jazz festival with sessions in Parc de la Villette, at the Cité de la Musique and in surrounding bars in early September.

Festival d'Automne (www.festival-automne.com in French) 'Autumn Festival' of arts – including painting, music, dance and theatre – held in venues throughout the city from mid-September for three months.

November & December
Christmas Eve Mass Celebrated at midnight on Christmas Eve at many Paris churches, including Notre Dame, but get there by 11pm to find a place.

New Year's Eve Blvd St-Michel (5e), place de la Bastille (11e), the Eiffel Tower (7e) and especially av des Champs-Élysées (8e) are the places to be.

SLEEPING
There is a wide choice of accommodation for all budgets throughout much of Paris. When calculating accommodation costs in Paris, assume you'll spend €15 to €25 per person per night in a hostel and at least €30 for a wash-basin-equipped double in a budget hotel (count on closer to €50 if you want your own shower). Bear in mind that you may be charged €2 to €5 to use communal showers in budget hotels. If you can't go without your daily ablutions, it is often a false economy staying at such places.

Mid-range hotels in Paris offer some of the best value for money of any European capital. Hotels at this level always have en suite facilities. All rooms have showers or baths unless noted otherwise. These hotels charge between €65 and €150 for a double and are generally excellent value, especially at the higher end.

Top-end places run the full gamut from tasteful and discreet boutique hotels that will usually cost two people up to €250 a night to deluxe-style palaces with rack rates equivalent to the GNP of a medium-sized Latin American republic.

Breakfast (usually a simple continental affair of bread, croissants, butter, jam and coffee or tea) is served at most hotels with two or more stars and costs from about €6.

Like most cities and towns elsewhere in France, Paris levies a *taxe de séjour* (tourist tax) of between €0.20 (camp site, unclassified hotels) to €1.20 (four-star hotels) per person per night on all forms of accommodation.

Accommodation Services

The Paris tourist office, notably the Gare du Nord branch (p112), can find you a place to stay for the night of the day you stop by. The price for booking a hostel is €1.20, a one-star hotel costing between €40 and €70 for a double is €3 and a two-star (€60 to €100) costs €4. For a three-star hotel costing €100 to €150, you'll pay €6 to book, it's €7.60 for a four-star (€150 to €450) and for a four-star deluxe hotel costing from €260 to €730 it's €8.

Some travel agencies (see p112) can book you reasonably priced accommodation. The student travel agency **OTU Voyages** (Map pp105-7; ☎ 01 40 29 12 22, 0 825 004 024; www.otu.fr in French; 119 rue St-Martin, 4e; metro Rambuteau; 9.30am-6.30pm Mon-Fri, 10am-5pm Sat), directly across the *parvis* (square) from Centre Pompidou, can *always* find you accommodation, even in the summer. You pay for the accommodation plus a finder's fee of €12, and the staff give you a voucher to take to the hotel. Prices for singles are around €35, doubles start at about €40. Be prepared for long queues in the high season.

An agency that can arrange bed-and-breakfast accommodation in Paris and gets good reviews from readers is **Alcôve & Agapes** (☎ 01 44 85 06 05; fax 01 44 85 06 14; info@paris-bedandbreakfast.com). Expect to pay between €45 and €100 for a double. **Frendy** (www.frendy .com) is an accommodation booking service (mostly apartments and B&Bs) for gays and lesbians.

Louvre & Les Halles

The very central area encompassing the Musée du Louvre and the Forum des Halles, effectively the 1er and a small slice of the 2e, is more disposed to welcoming top-end travellers, but there are some decent mid-range places to choose from as well. Both airports are linked to nearby metro Châtelet-Les Halles by the RER.

BUDGET

Centre International BVJ Paris-Louvre (Map pp105-7; ☎ 01 53 00 90 90; bvj@wanadoo.fr; 20 rue Jean-Jacques Rousseau, 1er; metro Louvre-Rivoli; dm €25, d per person €28;) This modern hostel run by the

Bureau des Voyages de la Jeunesse (Youth Travel Bureau), has bunks in a single-sex room for two to eight people; rates include breakfast. Guests should be aged under 35. Rooms are accessible from 2.30pm on the day you arrive and all day after that. There are no kitchen facilities and showers are in the hallway. There is usually space in the morning, even in the summer, so stop by as early as you can.

Hôtel de Lille Pélican (Map pp105-7; ☎ 01 42 33 33 42; 8 rue du Pélican, 1er; metro Palais Royal-Musée du Louvre; s/d/tr with washbasin €35/43/65, d with shower €50;) This old-fashioned but clean 13-room hotel down a quiet side street has recently been given a face-lift. Some of its rooms have just a washbasin and bidet, with communal showers in the hallway (€4.50), but most now have their own shower. The friendly and helpful manager speaks good English.

MID-RANGE

Hôtel St-Honoré (Map pp105-7; ☎ 01 42 36 20 38; paris@hotelsthonore.com; 85 rue St-Honoré, 1er; metro Châtelet; s/d/tw/q €59/74/83/92) This upgraded, 29-room hotel is between the Palais Royal and the Seine and at the eastern end of a very upmarket shopping street. It offers some fairly cramped rooms and a few more spacious ones for three and four people.

TOP END

Hôtel Ritz Paris (Map pp93-5; ☎ 01 43 16 35 29; www.ritzparis.com; 15 place Vendôme, 1er; metro Opéra; s & d Jul, Aug & Nov-Apr €580-680, May, Jun, Sep & Oct €630-730, junior ste €800-1030, 1-bedroom ste €1050-1500;) One of the world's most celebrated hotels, the Ritz Paris – is there any other? – has sparkling rooms and suites. Its **L'Espadon** restaurant has two Michelin stars and the **Hemingway Bar** is where the American author imbibed once he'd made a name for himself – and could afford it.

Marais & Bastille

There are quite a few top-end hotels in the heart of the lively Marais as well as in the vicinity of the elegant place des Vosges, and the choice of lower-priced one- and two-star hotels is excellent. Two-star comfort is less expensive closer to the Bastille in the neighbouring 11e, however. Despite massive gentrification in recent years, there are some fine hostels and some less expensive hotels in the Marais as well. East of Bastille, the relatively untouristed 11e is generally made up of unpretentious, working-class areas and is a good way to see the 'real' Paris up close.

BUDGET

Maison Internationale de la Jeunesse et des Étudiants (☎ 01 42 74 23 45; www.mije.com; ✕ 🖳) The MIJE runs three hostels in attractively renovated 17th- and 18th-century *hôtels particuliers* (private mansions) in the heart of the Marais, and it's difficult to think of a better budget deal in Paris. Costs are the same for all three. A bed in a shower-equipped, single-sex dorm sleeping four to eight people is €27 and €42/32/28 per person in a single/double/triple. Rooms are closed from noon to 3pm, and the curfew is 1am to 7am. The maximum stay is seven nights. Individuals can make reservations at any of the three MIJE hostels listed below (all Map pp105–7) by calling the central switchboard or emailing; they'll hold you a bed till noon. During the summer and other busy periods, there may not be space after about mid-morning. There's an annual membership fee of €2.50.

MIJE Le Fourcy (6 rue de Fourcy, 4e; metro St-Paul) The largest of the three branches. There's a cheap eatery here called **Le Restaurant** with a three-course *menu* including a drink for €10.50 and a two-course *formule* plus drink for €8.50.

MIJE Le Fauconnier (11 rue du Fauconnier, 4e; metro St-Paul or Pont Marie) This hostel is two blocks south of MIJE Le Fourcy.

MIJE Maubuisson (12 rue des Barres, 4e; metro Hôtel de Ville or Pont Marie) The pick of the three in our opinion is half a block south of the *mairie* (town hall) of the 4e.

Maison Internationale des Jeunes pour la Culture et la Paix (Map pp102–4; ☎ 01 43 71 99 21; mij.cp@wanadoo.fr; 4 rue Titon, 11e; metro Faidherbe Chaligny; dm €20; ✕ 🖳) About 1.3km east of place de la Bastille, this hostel offers accommodation in comfortable but rather institutional rooms for up to eight people, and there's a curfew between 2am and 6am. The upper age limit of 30 is not strictly enforced. Telephone reservations are accepted, but your chance of finding a bed is greatest if you call or stop by between 8am and 10am. The maximum stay is theoretically three days but you can usually stay for a week if there is room.

Hôtel de la Herse d'Or (Map pp102–4; ☎ 01 48 87 84 09; hotel.herse.dor@wanadoo.fr; 20 rue St-Antoine, 4e; metro Bastille; s/d with washbasin €38/45, d with shower/bath & toilet €58/60) This friendly, 35-room place on busy rue St-Antoine has unsurprising, serviceable rooms down a long stone corridor that have been partially renovated. Hall showers cost €2. And, BTW, *herse* is not 'hearse' in French but 'portcullis'. So let's just call it the 'Golden Gate Hotel'.

Hôtel Rivoli (Map pp105–7; ☎ 01 42 72 08 41; 44 rue de Rivoli or 2 rue des Mauvais Garçons, 4e; metro Hôtel de Ville; s/d with washbasin €27/35, s/d with shower €35/39, d with bath & toilet €49) Long an LP favourite, the Rivoli is forever cheery but not as dirt cheap as it once was, with 20 basic, somewhat noisy rooms. Showers are free. The front door is locked from 2am to 7am.

MID-RANGE

Hôtel du Septième Art (Map pp105–7; ☎ 01 44 54 85 00; hotel7art@wanadoo.fr; 20 rue St-Paul, 4e; metro St-Paul; s with washbasin €59, s & d with shower or bath & toilet €75-130, tw €85-130; 🖳) This heavily themed 23-room hotel on the south side of rue St-Antoine is a fun place for film buffs (*le septième art*, or 'the seventh art', is what the French call cinema), with a black-and-white-movie theme throughout, right down to the tiled floors and bathrooms. Oddly, almost all the posters and memorabilia relate to old Hollywood films, with not a reference to a *film français* in sight.

Hôtel Baudelaire Bastille (Map pp102–4; ☎ 01 47 00 40 98; www.tonichotel.com; 12 rue de Charonne, 11e; metro Bastille or Ledru Rollin; s with shower €62-65, d with shower & toilet €65-72, tr €72-82, q €90-100; Ⓟ) Formerly the Pax and now part of the small chain called Tonic Hotels, with three properties elsewhere in France, the one-star Baudelaire Bastille offers large and spotless rooms but does not have a lift.

Hôtel de la Bretonnerie (Map pp105–7; ☎ 01 48 87 77 63; www.bretonnerie.com; 22 rue St-Croix de la Bretonnerie, 4e; metro Hôtel de Ville; s & d €110-145, tr & q €170, ste €180-205) A very charming three-star in the heart of the Marais nightlife area dating from the 17th century. Decorations in each of the 22 rooms and seven suites are unique and some rooms have four-poster and canopy beds.

Hôtel Caron de Beaumarchais (Map pp105–7; ☎ 01 42 72 34 12; www.carondebeaumarchais.com; 12 rue Vieille du Temple, 4e; metro St-Paul; d €120-152; ✖) You have to see this award-winning, themed hotel to believe it. Done up like a private house in the Marais contemporary with the eponymous dramatist – who happens to have written his *chef d'œuvre Le Mariage de Figaro* (The Marriage of Figaro) at No 47 of the same street – the hotel has a prized 18th-century pianoforte, gilded mirrors and candelabras in its front room and stylish (though somewhat small) guest rooms.

Hôtel Castex (Map pp102-4; ☎ 01 42 72 31 52; www .castexhotel.com; 5 rue Castex, 4e; metro Bastille; s €95-115, d €120-140, ste €190-220; ☒) Once a budget hotel, equidistant from Bastille and the Marais, the Castex has had a major face-lift, but retained some of its 17th-century elements, including a vaulted stone cellar used as a breakfast room, terracotta floor tiles and Toile de Jouy wallpaper. Unusual for a small hotel in Paris, the Castex is fully air-conditioned.

Hôtel Central Marais (Map pp105-7; ☎ 01 48 87 56 08; www.hotelcentralmarais.com; 2 rue Ste-Croix de la Bretonnerie, 4e; metro Hôtel de Ville; r €87, ste €110) This small, seven-room hotel in the centre of gayland caters essentially for gay men, though lesbians are also welcome. Be aware that there is only one bathroom for every two rooms, and the suite for up to four people demands a minimum stay of three nights.

Hôtel Le Compostelle (Map pp105-7; ☎ 01 42 78 59 99; fax 01 40 29 05 18; 31 rue du Roi de Sicile, 4e; metro Hôtel de Ville; s/d with shower & toilet €60/89, d with bath €96) A tasteful 25-room place at the more tranquil end of the Marais not far from place des Vosges and surrounded by excellent restaurants, but the welcome could be a titch warmer.

Hôtel Jeanne d'Arc (Map pp105-7; ☎ 01 48 87 62 11; www.hoteljeannedarc.com; 3 rue de Jarente, 4e; metro St-Paul; small/large s €57/70, d €80, tw/tr/q €95/112/140) This charming hotel near lovely place du Marché Ste-Catherine is a great little *pied-à-terre* for your peregrinations among the museums, bars and restaurants of the Marais, Village St-Paul and Bastille. But everyone knows about it so book early. Do not confuse this two-star place with the two-star Grand Hôtel Jeanne d'Arc in the unlovely 13e.

Grand Hôtel Malher (Map pp105-7; ☎ 01 42 72 60 92; www.grandhotelmalher.com; 5 rue Malher, 4e; metro St-Paul; s low season €86-95, high season €103-115, d €103-112 & €118-132, ste €155-175) With a pretty courtyard in the back, this is a friendly, family-run establishment with nicely appointed rooms. Some of the public areas have been recently renovated, including the lobby.

Hôtel Lyon Mulhouse (Map pp102-4; ☎ 01 47 00 91 50; www.1-hotel-paris.com; 8 blvd Beaumarchais, 11e;

metro Bastille; s €60-85, d €68-75, tw €80-85, tr €90-95, q €100-115) As a former post house, from where carriages would set out for Lyon and Mulhouse in Alsace, this place has been a hotel since the 1920s and has quiet and comfortable rooms. Place de la Bastille and the delightful market on blvd Richard Lenoir (p169) are just around the corner.

Hôtel de Nice (Map pp105-7; ☎ 01 42 78 55 29; fax 01 42 78 36 07; 42bis rue de Rivoli, 4e; metro Hôtel de Ville; s/d/tr €65/100/120) Reception is on the first floor of this especially warm, family-run hotel with 23 comfortable rooms. Some rooms have balconies high above busy rue de Rivoli.

Hôtel de la Place des Vosges (Map pp102-4; ☎ 01 42 72 60 46; hotel.place.des.vosges@gofornet.fr; 12 rue de Birague, 4e; metro Bastille; s €101, d with shower €101-120, tw with bath €106-120, ste 140) This superbly situated two-star hotel due south of sublime place des Vosges has rather average rooms though the public areas are quite impressive. There's a tiny lift from the 1st to 4th floors. Rates include breakfast.

Hôtel Pratic (Map pp105-7; ☎ 01 48 87 80 47; www.hotelpratic.com; 9 rue d'Ormesson, 4e; metro St-Paul; s/d with washbasin & toilet €59/77, with shower €87/98, with bath & toilet €102/117, tr with bath & toilet €135) Opposite the delightful place du Marché Ste-Catherine, this hotel has been thoroughly renovated and the *vieux Marais* theme – exposed beams, gilt frames, striped wallpaper – is almost too much. Rather pricey for what you get, frankly.

Hôtel Royal Bastille (Map pp102-4; ☎ 01 48 05 62 47; hroyalbastille@hotmail.com; 14 rue de la Roquette, 11e; metro Bastille; s/d/tr/q from €78/87/104/123) More upmarket than most of the other lower-priced hotels along lively rue de la Roquette in Bastille, the Royal Bastille is a pleasant 29-room place with good-value rooms.

Hôtel St-Louis Marais (Map pp105-7; ☎ 01 48 87 87 04; www.saintlouismarais.com; 1 rue Charles V, 4e; metro Sully Morland; small/large s €59/91, d/tw/tr €107/125/140) This especially charming hotel in an 17th-century convent is more Bastille than Marais but still within easy walking distance of the latter. Wooden beams, terracotta tiles and heavy drapes tend to darken the 16 rooms but certainly add to the atmosphere.

Hôtel Saintonge (Map pp105- ; ☎ 01 42 77 91 13; www.hotelmarais.com; 16 rue Saintonge, 3e; metro Filles du Calvaire; s €90-105, d €110-115, ste €170) Exposed beams, vaulted cellar and period furniture, makes the 23-room Saintonge

Marais really more Oberkampf/République than the Marais. But with the Musée Picasso practically next door, let's not quibble. You'll get much more bang for your buck here than in the more central parts of Marais, including at the Saintonge's sister property, **Hôtel St-Merry** (below).

TOP END

Hôtel Axial Beaubourg (Map pp105-7; ☎ 01 42 72 72 22; www.axialbeaubourg.com; 11 rue du Temple, 4e; metro Hôtel de Ville; s €110-125, d €155, tw €165; ☒ ▯) With newly refurbished 'new look' rooms in the heart of the Marais, the Axial Beaubourg has a name that says it all: modern mixed with historic. It's a very upbeat place to stay and convenient to almost everything.

Hôtel St-Merry (Map pp105-7; ☎ 01 42 78 14 15; www .hotelmarais.com; 78 rue de la Verrerie, 4e; metro Châtelet; d & tw €160-230, tr €205-275, ste €335-407) The inside of this 11-room hostelry with beamed ceilings, church pews and confessionals and wrought-iron candelabra is a Gothic historian's wet dream; you have to see the architectural elements of room No 9 and the furnishings of No 20 to believe them. In reality, it's all a bit of fee-fie *faux* fun.

Île de la Cité & Île St-Louis

Believe it or not, the only hotel on the Île de la Cité is a budget one. However, Île St-Louis, the smaller of the two islands in the Seine, is by far the more romantic and has a string of excellent top-end hotels. It's an easy walk from central Paris.

BUDGET

Hôtel Henri IV (Map pp105-7; ☎ 01 43 54 44 53; 25 place Dauphine, 1er; metro Pont Neuf or Cité; s €24-31, d €31-36, tr €42 with washbasin, d with shower €44, d with shower/bath & toilet €55/68) This decrepit place, with 20 tattered and worn rooms, is popular for its location, location and location right on the tip of the Île de la Cité. It would be impossible to find something this romantic at such a price elsewhere; just don't stay in bed too long. Hall showers cost €2.50 but breakfast is included. Be sure to book well in advance.

TOP END

Hôtel des Deux Îles (Map pp105-7; ☎ 01 43 26 13 35; www.hotel-ile-saintlouis.com; 59 rue St-Louis en l'Île, 4e; metro Pont Marie; s/d & tw €140/158; ☒) While this atmospheric 17-room hotel has rustic

furnishings and an open fire in the lobby, some of the guest rooms are disappointingly small.

Hôtel de Lutèce (Map pp105-7; ☎ 01 43 26 23 52; www.hotel-ile-saintlouis.com; 65 rue St-Louis en l'Île, 4e; metro Pont Marie; s/d/tr €133/158/172; ☒) An exquisite 23-room hotel and more country than city, the Lutèce is under the same friendly and helpful management as the **Hôtel des Deux Îles** (left). The comfortable rooms are tastefully decorated and the location is among the most desirable in the city.

Latin Quarter & Jardin des Plantes

The northern section of the 5e close to the Seine has been popular with students and young people since the Middle Ages.

There are dozens of attractive two- and three-star hotels in the Latin Quarter, including a cluster near the Sorbonne and another group along the lively rue des Écoles. Mid-range hotels in the area are very popular with visiting academics so rooms are hardest to find when conferences and seminars are scheduled (usually from March to July and October). In general this part of the city offers better value among top-end hotels than the neighbouring 6e does. The Luxembourg and Port Royal RER stations are linked to both airports by RER and Orlyval.

BUDGET

Centre International de Séjour BVJ Paris-Quartier Latin (Map pp102-4; ☎ 01 43 29 34 80; bvj@wanadoo.fr; 44 rue des Bernardins, 5e; metro Maubert Mutualité; 1/2/6-bed r per person €35/28/26; ☒) This Left Bank hostel is a branch of the **Centre International BVJ Paris-Louvre** (p137) and has the same rules. All of the rooms here have en suite showers and telephones.

Grand Hôtel du Progrès (Map pp102-4; ☎ 01 43 54 53 18; fax 01 56 24 87 80; 50 rue Gay Lussac, 5e; metro Luxembourg; basic s/d/tr €35/42/55, s/d with shower & toilet €46/54) A budget, 26-room hotel that's been a favourite of students for generations. There are washbasin-equipped singles and large, old-fashioned doubles with a view and a lot of morning sun. Rates include breakfast and the hall showers are free.

Young & Happy Hostel (Map pp102-4; ☎ 01 47 07 47 07; www.youngandhappy.fr; 80 rue Mouffetard, 5e; metro Place Monge; dm €20-22, d per person €23-25; ☒ ▯) Although slightly tatty, this is a friendly spot

CHARLOTTE HINDLE

Street café scene, Lille (p202)

NEIL SETCHFIELD

Window details of the Grand' Place (p221), Arras

STEPHEN SAKS

Grandes Écuries, Chateau de Chantilly (p193)

Chateau de Versailles (p187)

BRENT WINEBRENNER

ROCCO FASANO

River Rance, Dinan (p289)

The white cliffs of Étretat
(p249)

BETHUNE CARMICHAEL

Plage de Bon Secours (p284), St-Malo

ROCCO FASANO

in the centre of the most happening area of the Latin Quarter. It's popular with a slightly older crowd nowadays. The rooms are closed from 11am to 4pm, but the reception remains open; the 2am curfew is strictly enforced. Beds are in smallish rooms for two to four people with washbasins. Rates differ according to the season. In summer the best way to get a bed is to stop by at about 9am.

MID-RANGE

Hôtel Cluny Sorbonne (Map pp102-4; ☎ 01 43 54 66 66; www.hotel-cluny.fr; 8 rue Victor Cousin, 5e; metro Luxembourg; s €69-74, d/tr/q €78/122/130) This hotel, where Rimbaud and Verlaine dallied – and how – in 1872, has 23 pleasant, well-kept rooms; room No 63 has fabulous views of the college and the Panthéon. The lift may only be the size of a telephone box but it will accommodate most travellers and their hat boxes. Service could be better, though.

Comfort Inn Mouffetard (Map pp102-4; ☎ 01 43 36 17 00; www.mouffetard.paris.comfort-inn.fr; 56 rue Mouffetard, 5e; metro Place Monge; s/d €89/119) A chain-like hotel may not be what you had in mind when you decided on Paris, but this one is not entirely without charm on a lovely pedestrians-only street – and it's a hop, skip and a jump from delightful place de la Contrescarpe and one of the best food markets in Paris.

Hôtel La Demeure (Map pp102-4; ☎ 01 43 37 81 25; www.hotel-paris-lademeure.com; 51 blvd St-Marcel, 13e; metro Gobelins; s/d €119-141, ste €198; ⓟ ⓧ ⒧) This self-proclaimed 'hotel de caractère', owned and operated by a charming father-son team, is just a bit away from the action at the bottom of the 5e. But the refined elegance of its 43 rooms, the almost 'clubby' public areas and the wraparound balconies of the corner rooms make it worth going that extra distance.

Hôtel Esmeralda (Map pp105-7; ☎ 01 43 54 19 20; fax 01 40 51 00 68; 4 rue St-Julien le Pauvre, 5e; metro St-Michel; s with washbasin/shower/bath €35/65/80, d with shower & toilet €80, with bath & toilet €85-95, tr/q from €110/180) The renovated, 19-room Esmeralda is tucked away in a quiet street with full views of Notre Dame. It has been everyone's secret 'find' for years now so book well in advance. This is about as central Latin Quarter as you're ever going to get.

Hôtel de l'Espérance (Map pp102-4; ☎ 01 47 07 10 99; hotel.esperance@wanadoo.fr; 15 rue Pascal, 5e; metro

Censier Daubenton; s with shower/bath & toilet €68/76, d with shower/bath & toilet €73/84, tw €84, tr €99) The 'Hotel of Hope', just a couple of minutes' walk south of lively rue Mouffetard, is a quiet and immaculately kept place with *faux* antique furnishings and a warm welcome. Larger rooms have two double beds.

Familia Hôtel (Map pp102-4; ☎ 01 43 54 55 27; www.hotel-paris-familia.com; 11 rue des Écoles, 5e; metro Cardinal Lemoine; s/d with shower & toilet €73.50/90, d/tw/tr/q with bath & toilet €100/102/143.50/180) This very welcoming and well-situated hotel has attractive sepia murals of Paris' landmarks in its rooms. Eight rooms have little balconies, from which you can glimpse Notre Dame. The flower-bedecked windows make the front of the hotel one of the most attractive in the quarter. Rates include breakfast.

Hôtel Gay-Lussac (Map pp102-4; ☎ 01 43 54 23 96; fax 01 40 51 79 49; 29 rue Gay Lussac, 5e; metro Luxembourg; s/d €33/49, with shower €55/64, with shower & toilet €59/68.50, tr/q with shower & toilet €90/95) The Gay-Lussac is a family-run hotel with a lot of character in the southern part of the Latin Quarter. Though the single rooms are small, the others are large and have high ceilings. Rates include breakfast.

Hôtel des Grandes Écoles (Map pp102-4; ☎ 01 43 26 79 23; www.hotel-grandes-ecoles.com; 75 rue du Cardinal Lemoine, 5e; metro Cardinal Lemoine or Place Monge; s & d €105-130, tr €125-150; ⓟ) This wonderful hotel, just north of place de la Contrescarpe, has one of the loveliest situations in the Latin Quarter, tucked away in a courtyard off a medieval street with its own garden; if the weather isn't suitable to have breakfast there, you'll enjoy the old-fashioned breakfast just as much. The Irish writer James Joyce lived in one of the courtyard flats in 1921. The owners are especially welcoming and will make you feel at home.

Hôtel Henri IV (Map pp105-7; ☎ 01 46 33 20 20; www.henri-paris-hotel.com; 9-11 rue St-Jacques, 5e; metro St-Michel Notre Dame or Cluny La Sorbonne; s/d/ tr €128/146/165) A three-star place awash in antiques, old prints and fresh flowers, the Henri IV is a Latin Quarter oasis mere steps from Notre Dame and the Seine. It's part of the same group as the **Hôtel de Lutèce** and the **Hôtel des Deux Îles** (opposite) on the Île de St-Louis but do *not* confuse this hotel with the bare-bones budget hotel of the same name on the Île de la Cité (see opposite).

Hôtel St-Christophe (Map pp102-4; ☎ 01 43 31 81 54; www.charm-hotel-paris.com; 17 rue Lacépède, 5e;

metro Place Monge; s €104-113, d €115-125) With well-equipped rooms this classy small hotel is on a quiet street between rue Monge in the Latin and the Jardin des Plantes. It's part of the Logis de France umbrella association, always a sign of quality.

Hôtel St-Jacques (Map pp102-4; ☎ 01 44 07 45 45; www.hotel-saintjacques.com in French; 35 rue des Écoles, 5e; metro Maubert Mutualité; s €50-75, d €85-112, tr €105-135; 🖳) An adorable place whose balconies overlook the Panthéon. Audrey Hepburn and Cary Grant, who filmed some scenes of *Charade* here a half-century ago, would commend the mod cons that now complement the original 19th-century details (ornamented ceilings, iron staircase and so on), but sadly the service seems to have slipped a notch or two since our last visit. The singles are relatively spacious but not all rooms have toilets.

TOP END

Grand Hôtel St-Michel (Map pp102-4; ☎ 01 46 33 33 02; www.grand-hotel-st-michel.com; 19 rue Cujas, 5e; metro Luxembourg; s/d €120/170, ste €220) Far away from the din of blvd St-Michel, the location of this hotel feels almost remote. Some of the rooms have a balcony and the attached *salon de thé* (tearoom) is quite pleasant.

Mélia Colbert Boutique Hotel (Map pp105-7; ☎ 01 56 81 19 00; melia.colbert@solmelia.com; 7 rue l'Hôtel Colbert, 5e; metro Maubert Mutualité; s & d €260-390, tr & q €442-549, ste €494-602; 🗶 🔀 🖳) Unabashedly calling itself a 'boutique hotel', the Colbert has a glorious front courtyard and a namesake address. Well-heeled friends swear by this discreet property.

Hôtel du Panthéon (Map pp102-4; ☎ 01 43 54 32 95; www.hoteldupantheon.com; 19 place du Panthéon, 5e; metro Luxembourg; s €99-213, d €99-223, tr €184-244, f €198-426; 🔀 🖳) In the shadow of the capital's largest secular mausoleum and just up the hill from the Jardin du Luxembourg, the Panthéon is a attractive property that feels almost more 'deluxe' than 'top end'. Rates vary so widely according to the season that staff are wary of giving them out. In any case, booking on the web will save you at least 15% on the cost.

Hôtel Relais Christine (Map pp105-7; ☎ 01 40 51 60 80; www.relais-christine.com; 3 rue Christine, 6e; metro Mabillon or St-Michel; s & d €325-425, ste from €475; 🗶 🖳) Part of the prestigious Chateaux et Hôtels de France chain, the Relais Christine has an unforgettable courtyard entrance

off a quiet street, a back garden and a spa and fitness centre built in and around an original 13th-century cellar.

St-Germain, Odéon & Luxembourg

The well-heeled St-Germain des Prés is a delightful area to stay but has very little in the way of budget offerings. On the other hand there are some excellent mid-range three-star hotels here.

MID-RANGE

Hôtel des Deux Continents (Map pp105-7; ☎ 01 43 26 72 46; www.2continents-hotel.com; 25 rue Jacob, 6e; metro St-Germain des Prés; s €135, d €145-155, tw €155, tr €190; 🔀) The 'Two Continents Hotel' (surely the name is to lure all the Yanks over) is a very pleasant establishment with spacious rooms in a quiet street. The mural in the breakfast room is an early morning eye-opener.

Hôtel de Danemark (Map pp99-101; ☎ 01 43 26 93 78; www.hoteldanemark.com; 21 rue Vavin, 6e; metro Vavin; s €112-145, d €125-145; 🗶) This positively scrumptious boutique hotel southwest of the Jardin du Luxembourg has 15 very tastefully furnished rooms – there's original artwork in each, some gaze onto Henri Sauvage's Carreaux Métro, an Art Nouveau tiled apartment building designed in 1912, and the higher priced rooms have Jacuzzis. Montparnasse and all its bars and brasseries are a short walk away.

Hôtel du Globe (Map pp105-7; ☎ 01 43 26 35 50; fax 01 46 33 62 69; 15 rue des Quatre Vents, 6e; metro Odéon;

r with toilet €55, with shower & toilet €70-90, with bath & toilet €105) The Globe is an eclectic, if somewhat dusty, caravansarie with 15 rooms, each with its own theme. We especially like room No 12 and its canopy bed.

Hôtel de Nesle (Map pp105-7; ☎ 01 43 54 62 41; fax 01 43 54 31 88; 7 rue de Nesle, 6e; metro Odéon or Mabillon; s with shower €50-60, d with shower €75, d with bath €100) The Nestle is a relaxed, colourfully decorated hotel with 20 rooms and different themes – from Molière and Africa to 1001 Nights theme – in a quiet street west of place St-Michel. There's also a lovely garden in the back. Reservations are only accepted by telephone and usually only up to a few days in advance.

TOP END

Hôtel d'Angleterre (Map pp105-7; ☎ 01 42 60 34 72; www.hotel-dangleterre.com; 44 rue Jacob, 6e; metro St-Germain des Prés; s €130-220, d €140-230, ste €270-300; 🖵) The 'England Hotel' is a beautiful 27-room property in a quiet street close to busy blvd St-Germain and the Musée d'Orsay. The loyal clientele breakfast or brunch in the courtyard garden patio of this former British Embassy where the Treaty of Paris that ended the American Revolution was signed on 3 September 1783 and where Hemingway spent his first night in Paris (in room No 14 on 20 December 1921, to be precise). Duplex suite No 51 (€300) at the top has beamed ceilings and is the finest in the house.

L'Hôtel (Map pp105-7; ☎ 01 44 41 99 00; www.l-hotel.com; 13 rue des Beaux Arts, 6e; metro St-Germain des Prés; s & d low season €248-529, high season €272-625, ste from €529/625; 🗙 🔀 🖵 🌊) With 20 rooms and tucked away in a quiet quay-side street, the place with the most minimal of names is the stuff of romantic Paris legends. Rock and film star patrons alike fight to sleep in room No 16 where Oscar Wilde died a century ago or in the mirrored Art Deco room (No 36) of legendary dancer Mistinguett. This was also a home away from home for the Argentine writer Jorge Luis Borges (1899–1986), who stayed here many times in the late 1970s and early '80s.

Hôtel des Marronniers (Map pp105-7; ☎ 01 43 25 30 60; fax 01 40 46 83 56; 21 rue Jacob, 6e; metro St-Germain des Prés; s €110, d €150-165, tw €155-170, tr €185-205, q €245; 🔀) At the end of a small courtyard, the 'Chestnut Trees Hotel' has less-than-huge rooms and a magical garden

around the back with a veranda. It's a real oasis in the heart of St-Germain.

La Villa St-Germain des Prés (Map pp105-7; ☎ 01 43 26 60 00; www.villa-saintgermain.com; 29 rue Jacob, 6e; metro St-Germain des Prés; s & d from €240-335, ste from €440; 🗙 🔀) This hotel helped set what has become almost a standard of the Parisian accommodation scene: small, minimalist, discreet. Fabrics, lighting, soft furnishings – all are of the utmost quality and taste.

Montparnasse

Just east of Gare Montparnasse, there are a number of two- and three-star places on rue Vandamme and rue de la Gaîté – though the latter street is rife with sex shops and peep shows. Gare Montparnasse is served by Air France buses from both airports. Place Denfert Rochereau is also linked to both airports by Orlybus, Orlyval and RER. The budget places here don't usually see many foreign tourists.

BUDGET

Hôtel de Blois (Map pp90-2; ☎ 01 45 40 99 48; fax 01 45 40 45 62; 5 rue des Plantes, 14e; metro Mouton Duvernet; s/d with washbasin €40/42, with shower €43/45, with shower & toilet €46/49, tr €61; 🅿) This very friendly, 25-room establishment just off av du Maine offers smallish singles and doubles with both washbasin and bidet and with shower. Triples are fully equipped and have bathtubs.

Celtic Hôtel (Map pp99-101; ☎ 01 43 20 93 53; hotelceltic@wanadoo.fr; 15 rue d'Odessa, 14e; metro Edgar Quinet; s with washbasin/shower €43/54, d with shower & toilet €57-63, tr with shower & toilet €72) An old-fashioned, 29-room place that has undergone only partial modernisation. The Celtic has pretty bare singles and doubles but the Gare Montparnasse is only a convenient 200m away from the hotel.

MID-RANGE

Hôtel Delambre (Map pp99-101; ☎ 01 43 20 66 31; www.hoteldelambre.com; 35 rue Delambre, 14e; metro Montparnasse; s €65-85, d €80-95, tr & q €140) This attractive 30-room hotel just east of the Gare Montparnasse takes wrought-iron as a theme and uses it both in functional pieces and decorative items throughout.

Hôtel de Paris (Map pp99-101; ☎ 01 43 22 10 13; fax 01 40 47 07 58; 51 av du Maine, 14e; metro Montparnasse Bienvenüe; s €68-80, d €75-90, tr €83-90) A simple hotel with the equally simple name; the rooms have little balconies overlooking the Gare Montparnasse.

Petit Palace Hôtel (Map pp90-2; ☎ 01 43 22 05 25; petitpalace@hotelsparisonline.com; 131 av du Maine, 14e; metro Gaîté; s €54-61, d €61-69, tr €69; (P)(X)) Run by the same family for half a century, this friendly (though rather ambitiously named) two-star hotel has 44 smallish but spotless rooms. All the rooms have showers and toilets.

Faubourg St-Denis & Invalides

The 7e is a lovely arrondissement in which to stay, but apart from the northeastern section – the area east of Invalides and opposite the Louvre – it's fairly quiet here.

MID-RANGE

Hôtel Lenox St-Germain (Map pp99-101; ☎ 01 42 96 10 95; hotel@lenoxsaintgermain.com; 9 rue de l'Université, 7e; metro Rue du Bac; s €115-120, d €140-150, tw €142-160, ste €255-270; (X)) This mid-range hotel in the posh 7e has simple, uncluttered and comfortable rooms upstairs and a late-opening 1930s-style bar downstairs, which attracts a chic clientele. The Art Deco décor is a treat and the leather armchairs more than comfortable.

Concorde & Madeleine

This area boasts two of Paris' finest hotels – one relatively new and one vintage.

TOP END

Hôtel Costes (Map pp93-5; ☎ 01 42 44 50 00; fax 01 42 44 50 01; www.hotelcostes.com; 239 rue St-Honoré, 1er; metro Concorde; s & d €350-800, ste from €1200; (X)(X)(Q)(Q)) The eponymous hotel of Jean-Louis Costes offers a 'luxurious and immoderate home away from home' to the style Mafia. Outfitted in over-the-top camp Second Empire cast-offs, it's the darling of the rich and famous and their hangers-on.

Hôtel de Crillon (Map pp93-5; ☎ 01 44 71 15 00; www.crillon.com; 10 place de la Concorde, 8e; metro Concorde; s €480-575, d €575-855, ste from €945, larger ste from €1400; (X)(X)(Q)) This colonnaded, 200-year-old palace is the epitome of French luxury. Its sparkling public areas (including **Les Ambassadeurs** restaurant, with its two Michelin stars) are sumptuously decorated with chandeliers, original sculptures, gilt mouldings, tapestries and inlaid furniture. The rooms are spacious and most of them have floor-to-ceiling marble bathrooms to luxuriate in.

Clichy & Gare St-Lazare

These areas offer some excellent mid-range hotels. The better deals are away from Gare St-Lazare but there are several places along rue d'Amsterdam beside the station worth checking out. There's also an unusual place to stay in the budget category.

BUDGET

Hôtel Eldorado (Map pp93-5; ☎ 01 45 22 35 21; eldorado hotel@wanadoo.fr; 18 rue des Dames, 17e; metro Place de Clichy; s/d/tr with shower €45/60/80) This boho place is one of Paris' grooviest finds: a welcoming, well-run place with 40 colourfully decorated rooms in a main building on a quiet street and in an annexe with a private garden at the back. Is this really Paris?

MID-RANGE

Hôtel Britannia (Map pp93-5; ☎ 01 42 85 36 36; fax 01 42 85 16 93; 24 rue d'Amsterdam, 9e; metro St-Lazare; s & d with shower/bath €78/85, tr with shower or bath €94) The Britannia has narrow hallways but pleasant, clean rooms. It's just opposite Gare St-Lazare and an easy walk to the *grands magasins* on blvd Haussmann. The triples are a bit on the small side though.

Hôtel Favart (Map pp96-8; ☎ 01 42 97 59 83; www .hotel-paris-favart.com; 5 rue Marivaux, 2e; metro Richelieu Drouot; s/d/tr €85/108/130) With rooms facing the Opéra Comique, the Favart is a stylish Art Nouveau hotel that feels like it never let go of the *belle époque*. If you're interested in shopping at the big department stores on blvd Haussmann, this is an excellent choice.

Opéra & Grands Boulevards

The avenues around blvd Montmartre are a popular nightlife area and a lively district in which to stay.

MID-RANGE

Hôtel des Arts (Map pp96-8; ☎ 01 42 46 73 30; hdag@ free.fr; 7 Cité Bergère, 9e; metro Grands Boulevards; s with shower/bath €68/74, d €74/82, tr €92/98; (P)) The new management of this hotel has transformed what was once a funky place to stay with loads of character (and resident parrot) into just any other old two-star hotel in the area. But some things never change. The 'Arts Hotel' still has 25 rooms and it remains in a quiet little alley off rue du Faubourg Montmartre. There are some seven other hotels on this street alone.

Hôtel Chopin (Map pp96-8; ☎ 01 47 70 58 10; fax 01 42 47 00 70; 46 passage Jouffroy, entrance at 10 blvd Montmartre, 9e; metro Grands Boulevards; s €57, s with shower & toilet €64-72, d with shower & toilet €73-84, tr with shower & toilet €97) The Chopin, dating back to 1846, is down one of Paris' most delightful 19th-century *passages couverts* (covered shopping arcades; see p128). It may be a little faded around the edges, but it's still enormously evocative of the *belle époque* and the welcome is always warm. After the arcade closes at 10pm, ring the *sonnette de nuit* (night doorbell).

Hôtel Langlois (Map pp93-5; ☎ 01 48 74 78 24; www.hotel-langlois.com; 63 rue St-Lazare, 9e; metro Trinité; s €79-89, d €89-99, tw €99, ste €132) Built in 1870, the hotel formerly known as the Hôtel des Croisés has retained its charming *belle époque* look and feel despite a massive makeover in 1997. The 27 rooms and suites are unusually large for a small-ish hotel in Paris and its very convenient to the department stores on blvd Haussmann.

Hôtel Peletier-Haussmann-Opéra (Map pp96-8; ☎ 01 42 46 79 53; www.peletieropera.com; 15 rue Le Peletier, 9e; metro Richelieu Drouot; s €70-75, d €78-86, tr €86-100; ✗) This is a pleasant, 26-room hotel just off blvd Haussmann and close to the big department stores. There are attractive packages available at weekends, depending on the season.

Gare du Nord, Gare de l'Est & République

The areas east and northeast of the Gare du Nord and Gare de l'Est have always had a more than ample selection of hotels and now you'll also find a hostel within striking distance. At the same time, there are quite a few two- and three-star places around the train stations in the 10e that are convenient if you're catching an early-morning train to London or want to crash immediately upon arrival. Place de la République is convenient for the nightlife areas of Ménilmontant.

Gare du Nord is linked to Charles de Gaulle airport by RER and RATP bus No 350 and to Orly airport by Orlyval. Bus No 350 to/from Charles de Gaulle airport also stops right in front of the Gare de l'Est.

BUDGET

Auberge de Jeunesse Jules Ferry (Map pp96-8; ☎ 01 43 57 55 60; www.fuaj.fr; 8 blvd Jules Ferry, 11e; metro République or Goncourt; dm €19.50, d per person €20; ✗ ▢) This official hostel, three blocks east of place de la République, is somewhat institutional and rooms could be cleaner, but the atmosphere is fairly relaxed. Beds are in two- to six-person rooms, which are locked between 10.30am and 2pm for housekeeping, and there is no curfew. You'll have pay an extra €3 per night if you don't have a Hostelling International card or equivalent. The only other official hostel in central Paris is the **Auberge de Jeunesse Le D'Artagnan** (Map pp90-2; ☎ 01 40 32 34 56; www .fuaj.fr; 80 rue Vitruve, 20e; metro Porte de Bagnolet; dm €20.60; ✗ ▢), which is far from the centre of the action but just one metro stop from the Gare Routière Internationale de Paris-Gallieni (international bus terminal). The largest hostel in France, with 439 beds on seven floors, the D'Artagnan has rooms with two to eight beds, big lockers, laundry facilities, a bar, a cinema and the same rules and regulations as the Jules Ferry hostel.

Peace & Love Hostel (Map pp96-8; ☎ 01 46 07 65 11; www.paris-hostels.com; 245 rue La Fayette, 10e; metro Jaurès or Louis Blanc; dm €17-21, d per person €21-26; ▢) This modern-day hippy hang-out (not an oxymoron, it would appear) is a groovy though chaotically run hostel with beds in smallish, shower-equipped rooms for two to four people. There's a great kitchen and eating area but most of the action seems to revolve around the ground-floor bar (open till 2am) that boasts more than 10 types of beer, including the cheapest *blonde* (that's lager) in Paris.

Sibour Hôtel (Map pp96-8; ☎ 01 46 07 20 74; sibour .hotel@wanadoo.fr; 4 rue Sibour, 10e; metro Gare de l'Est; s & d with washbasin €35, s & d with toilet €40, s/d/tr/q with shower & toilet €50/58/63/80; ℗) A homely and friendly place with well-kept rooms, including some old-fashioned ones. Hall showers cost €3.

Hôtel La Vieille France (Map pp96-8; ☎ 01 45 26 42 37; la.vieille.france@wanadoo.fr; 151 rue La Fayette, 10e; metro Gare du Nord; d with washbasin €42, d with shower/ bath & toilet €58/64, tr €78-90) 'The Old France' has relatively spacious and pleasant rooms. At least one reader has written to complain about the noise, however. Hall showers are free.

MID-RANGE

Hôtel Français (Map pp96-8; ☎ 01 40 35 94 14; www .hotelfrancais.com; 13 rue du 8 Mai 1945, 10e; metro Gare de l'Est; s €77-81, d €84-91, tr €109-116; ℗ ✗ ▢) This two-star hotel facing the Gare de l'Est has attractive, almost luxurious rooms (some with balconies). Parking – always difficult around the train stations – in the hotel garage costs a steep €8.

Grand Hôtel de Paris (Map pp96-8; ☎ 01 46 07 40 56; grand.hotel.de.paris@gofornet.com; 72 blvd de Strasbourg, 10e; metro Gare de l'Est; s/d/tr/q €74/79/96/112) A well-run establishment just south of the Gare de l'Est, the Grand has pleasant, soundproofed rooms and a tiny lift.

Nord Hôtel (Map pp96-8; ☎ 01 45 26 43 40; www.nordhotel.com; 37 rue de St-Quentin, 10e; metro Gare du Nord; s €60-79, d €89, tr €109) Just opposite the Gare du Nord, the 'North Hotel' has 46 clean and quiet rooms with shower or bath.

Nord-Est Hôtel (Map pp96-8; ☎ 01 47 70 07 18; hotel.nord.est@wanadoo.fr; 12 rue des Petits Hôtels, 10e; metro Poissonnière; s/d/tr/q €62/72/92/115) This unusual 30-room hotel, charmingly located on the 'Street of Little Hotels', is set away from the street and fronted by a small terrace. It is convenient to both the Gare du Nord and the Gare de l'Est.

Ménilmontant & Belleville

The Ménilmontant nightlife district is an excellent area in which to spend the evening, but the selection of accommodation in all price categories is surprisingly limited.

MID-RANGE

Hôtel Beaumarchais (Map pp102-4; ☎ 01 53 36 86 86; www.hotelbeaumarchais.com; 3 rue Oberkampf, 11e; metro Filles du Calvaire; s €69-85, d €99, ste 140) This brighter-than-bright boutique hotel with its emphasis on sunbursts and bold colours, particularly orange and yellows, is just this side of kitsch. But it makes for a different Paris experience and fits in with its surroundings very well indeed. Some rooms look onto a small leafy courtyard.

Hôtel du Vieux Saule (Map pp105-7; ☎ 01 42 72 01 14; www.hotelvieuxsaule.com; 6 rue Picardie, 3e; metro Filles du Calvaire; s low season €76-91, high season €91-106, d €106-136 & €121-151, VIP r €121-151 & €136-166; P X X) The flower-bedecked 'Old Willow Tree' is a hostelry in the northern Marais and something of a 'find' because of its slightly unusual location. There's a tranquil little garden and the original 16th-century vaulted cellar (now breakfast room) has antique copper utensils on display. The five rooms on the VIP (4th) floor have been renovated.

CAMPING IN PARIS

Camping du Bois de Boulogne (Map pp90-2; ☎ 01 45 24 30 81; www.abccamping.com/boulogne.htm; 2 allée du Bord de l'Eau, 16e; sites off/mid-/peak season €11/14.20/15.40, with vehicle, tent & 2 people €18.50/22.50/24.50, with electricity €22.50/26.50/31.70, first-time booking fee €12; ☽ 6am-2am) The Bois de Boulogne camping ground, the only one within the Paris city limits, measures 7 hectares and lies along the Seine at the far western edge of the Bois de Boulogne, opposite Île de Puteaux. With upwards of 500 camping places, it gets very crowded in the summer, but there's always space for a small tent. Fully equipped caravans accommodating four to five people are available for rent; rates – €49 to €85 – are dependent on the type and the season.

Porte Maillot metro station (Map pp93-5), 4.5km to the northeast through the wood, is linked to the site by RATP bus No 244, which runs from 6am to 8.30pm daily, and from April to October also by a privately operated shuttle bus that costs about €2.

Gare de Lyon, Nation & Bercy

The neighbourhood around the Gare de Lyon has a few budget hotels as well as a popular independent hostel.

BUDGET

Blue Planet Hostel (Map pp102-4; ☎ 01 43 42 06 18; www.hostelblueplanet.com; 5 rue Hector Malot, 12e; metro Gare de Lyon; dm €18.30-21; ▯) This hostel is very close to Gare de Lyon – convenient if you're heading south or west at the crack of dawn. Dorm beds are in rooms for three or four people; the place is closed between 11am and 3pm but there there's no curfew.

Montmartre & Pigalle

Montmartre, encompassing the 18e and the northern part of the 9e, is one of the most charming neighbourhoods in Paris. There is a bunch of top-end hotels in the area and the attractive two-star places on rue Aristide Bruant are generally less full in July and August than in spring and autumn.

The flat area around the base of the Butte Montmartre has some surprisingly good budget deals. The lively, ethnically mixed area east of Sacré Cœur can be a bit rough;

some say it's prudent to avoid Château Rouge metro station at night. Both the 9e and the 18e have fine and recommended hostels.

BUDGET

Hôtel Bonséjour (Map p108; ☎ 01 42 54 22 53; fax 01 42 54 25 92; 11 rue Burq, 18e; metro Abbesses; s with washbasin €22-25, d with washbasin €30-32, d with shower €38-40, tr €53) The 'Good Stay' is at the end of a quiet street in Montmartre. Some rooms (eg Nos 14, 23, 33, 43 and 53) have little balconies and at least one of the rooms (No 55) offers a fleeting glimpse of Sacré Cœur. It's a simple place to stay – no lift, linoleum floors etc – but comfortable and very friendly. Hall showers cost €2.

Le Village Hostel (Map p108; ☎ 01 42 64 22 02; www.villagehostel.fr; 20 rue d'Orsel, 18e; metro Anvers; dm mid-Mar–Oct/Nov–mid-Mar €21.50/20, d per person €25/23, tr €23/21.50; 🖳) 'The Village' is a fine 25-room hostel with beamed ceilings and views of Sacré Cœur. Dorm beds are in rooms for four to six people and all rooms have showers and toilets. Kitchen facilities are available, and there is a lovely outside terrace. Rooms are closed between 11am and 4pm and curfew is 2am.

Woodstock Hostel (Map pp96-8; ☎ 01 48 78 87 76; www.woodstock.fr; 48 rue Rodier, 9e; metro Anvers; dm Oct-Mar/Apr-Sep €15/20, d per person €17/23; 🖳) Woodstock is just down the hill from raucous Pigalle in a quiet, residential quarter. Dorm beds are in rooms for four to six people and there's a kitchen. The rooms are shut from 11am to 3pm; the curfew is 2am. It's a pleasant place with a spoiled feline in residence. The high-season rates also apply over Christmas and the New Year holidays.

MID-RANGE

Hôtel des Arts (Map p108; ☎ 01 46 06 30 52; www .arts-hotel-paris.com; 5 rue Tholozé, 18e; metro Abbesses or Blanche; s/d & tw/tr €64/78/94; 🅿) Part of the Logis de France group, the 'Arts Hotel' is a friendly and attractive place convenient for both Pigalle and Montmartre. Towering over it is the old-style Moulin de la Galette windmill.

Hôtel des Capucines Montmartre (Map p108; ☎ 01 42 52 89 80; fax 01 42 52 29 57; 5 rue Aristide Bruant, 18e; metro Abbesses or Blanche; s €45-50, d €54-60, tr €60-70) This is a decent, family-run hotel with 30 rooms on a small street awash with places to stay.

Hôtel du Moulin (Map p108; ☎ 01 42 64 33 33; www.hotelmoulin.com; 3 rue Aristide Bruant, 18e; metro Abbesses or Blanche; s €54-66, d €59-76, tw €73-79) There are 27 good-sized rooms with toilet and bath or shower at this quiet little hotel. The Korean family who owns the place is very kind. Check out the excellent (and crazy) website.

Hôtel Utrillo (Map p108; ☎ 01 42 58 13 44; adel .utrillo@wanadoo.fr; 7 rue Aristide Bruant, 18e; metro Abbesses or Blanche; s €61, d with shower/bath €73/79, tr €91; 🖳) This friendly 30-room hotel is very nicely decorated and can even boast a small sauna.

TOP END

Hôtel les Trois Poussins (Map pp96-8; ☎ 01 53 32 81 81; www.les3poussins.com; 15 rue Clauzel, 9e; metro St-Georges; s €130-175, d & tw €145-175, tr & q €210, studio for 1 €140-190, for 2 €155-190, for 3 & 4 €225; ✗ 🖳) The 'Hotel of the Three Chicks' (as in little chickens) is a lovely property due south of place Pigalle. Half of the rooms are small studios with their own cooking facilities.

EATING

When it comes to food, Paris has everything – and nothing. As the culinary centre of the most aggressively gastronomic country in the whole world, the city has more 'generic French', regional and ethnic restaurants than any other place in France. But *la cuisine parisienne* (Parisian cuisine) is a poor relation of that extended family known as *la cuisine des provinces* (provincial cuisine). That's because those greedy country cousins have consumed most of what was once on Paris' own plate, claiming it as their own. Today very few French dishes except maybe *vol-au-vent* (light pastry shell filled with chicken or fish in a creamy sauce), *potage St-Germain* (thick green pea soup), onion soup and the humble pig's trotters are associated with the capital.

That said, like the Indian curry and Turkish kebabs of London, over the years ethnic food has become as Parisian as that ubiquitous onion soup; the *nems* and *pâtés impérials* (spring or egg rolls) and *pho* (soup noodles with beef) of Vietnam, the couscous and tajines of North Africa, the *boudin antillais* (West Indian blood pudding) from the Caribbean and the *yassa* (meat or fish grilled in onion and lemon sauce) of Senegal are all eaten with relish throughout the capital. Ethnic food is what

Paris does better than any other city in the country.

Louvre & Les Halles

The area between Forum des Halles (1er) and the Centre Pompidou (4e) is filled with scores of trendy restaurants, but few of them are particularly good and mostly cater to tourists, both foreign and French. Streets lined with places to eat include rue des Lombards, the narrow streets north and east of Forum des Halles and pedestrians-only rue Montorgueil, a market street and probably your best bet for something quick.

If you're in search of Asian food, Japanese businesspeople flock to rue Ste-Anne just west of the Jardin du Palais Royal for the freshest sushi and soba (noodles). There are also some good-value restaurants serving other Asian cuisine in the area.

FRENCH

Café Marly (Map pp105-7; ☎ 01 46 26 06 60; cour Napoléon du Louvre, 93 rue de Rivoli, 1er; metro Palais Royal-Musée du Louvre; starters €8-21, pasta €13-23, sandwiches & snacks €10-14, mains €16-30; ☒ lunch & dinner to 1am) A classic venue that serves contemporary French fare under the colonnades of the Louvre and overlooks the glass pyramid.

L'Épi d'Or (Map pp105-7; ☎ 01 42 36 38 12; 25 rue Jean-Jacques Rousseau, 1er; metro Louvre-Rivoli; starters €5-15, mains €14-20, menu €18; ☒ lunch & dinner Mon-Fri, Sat evening till 10pm) This oh-so-Parisian bistro serves well-prepared, classic dishes – such as gigot d'agneau (leg of lamb) cooked for seven hours – to a surprisingly well-heeled crowd.

Le Petit Mâchon (Map pp105-7; ☎ 01 42 60 08 06; 158 rue St-Honoré, 1er; metro Palais Royal-Musée du Louvre; starters €6.50-12.50, mains €14-21, lunch menu €16.50; ☒ lunch & dinner to 11pm Tue-Sun) An upbeat bistro with Lyon-inspired specialities; it's convenient to the Louvre.

AMERICAN

Joe Allen (Map pp105-7; ☎ 01 42 36 70 13; 30 rue Pierre Lescot, 1er; metro Étienne Marcel; brunch €11.90-15, lunch menu €12.90, dinner menus €18 & €22.50; ☒ noon-midnight) An institution in Paris for some three decades, Joe Allen is little bit of New York in Paris. There's an excellent brunch from noon to 4pm on weekends.

ASIAN

Baan Boran (Map pp96-8; ☎ 01 40 15 90 45; 43 rue de Montpensier, 1er; metro Palais Royal-Musée du Louvre;

lunch menu €12.50, meals from €30; ☒ lunch Mon-Fri, dinner to 11.30pm Mon-Sat) This informal eatery just opposite the Théâtre du Palais Royal is run by two Thai women.

Kunitoraya (Map pp96-8; ☎ 01 47 03 33 65; 39 rue Ste-Anne, 1er; metro Pyramides; soups €8.50-15, noodles €9-16, lunch menu €12.50; ☒ 11.30am-10pm) With seating on two floors, this simple place has a wide and excellent range of Japanese noodle dishes and set lunches and dinners.

QUICK EATS

L'Arbre à Cannelle (Map pp96-8; ☎ 01 45 08 55 87; 57 passage des Panoramas, 2e; metro Grands Boulevards; dishes €6.50-9.50; ☒ noon-6.30pm Mon-Sat) A lovely tearoom with original 19th-century décor, tartes salées (savoury pies; €6.50 to €7) and excellent salads (€6.25 to €9.30).

SELF-CATERING

There are a number of supermarkets along av de l'Opéra and rue de Richelieu, as well as around Forum des Halles, including a large one in the basement of **Monoprix** (Map pp93-5; 21 av de l'Opéra, 2e; ☒ 9am-9.50pm Mon-Fri, 9am-8.50pm Sat). Other supermarkets include the following:

Ed l'Épicier (Map pp105-7; 80 rue de Rivoli, 4e; ☒ 9am-8pm Mon-Sat)

Franprix (Map pp105-7; 35 rue Berger, 1er; ☒ 8.30am-7.50pm Mon-Sat); Franprix Châtelet branch (Map pp105-7; 16 rue Bertin Poirée, 1er; metro Châtelet; ☒ 9am-8pm Mon-Sat)

Marais & Bastille

The Marais, filled with small restaurants of every imaginable type, is one of Paris' premier neighbourhoods for eating out. In the direction of place de la République there's a decent selection of ethnic places. If you're looking for authentic Chinese food but can't be bothered going all the way to Chinatown in the 13e or Belleville in the 20e, check out any of the small noodle shops and restaurants along rue Au Maire, 3e (Map pp96–8, metro Arts et Métiers), which is southeast of the Musée des Arts et Métiers. The kosher and kosher-style restaurants along rue des Rosiers, 4e (Map pp105–7), the so-called Pletzel, serve specialities from North Africa, Central Europe and Israel. Many are closed on Friday evening, Saturday and Jewish holidays. Takeaway falafel and shwarma (kebabs) are available at several places along the street.

Bastille is another area chock-a-block with restaurants, some of which have added a star or two to their epaulets in recent years. Narrow rue de Lappe and rue de la Roquette, 11e (Map pp102–4), just east of place de la Bastille, may not be as hip as they were a dozen years ago, but they remain popular streets for nightlife and attract a young, alternative crowd.

FRENCH

L'Alivi (Map pp105-7; ☎ 01 48 87 90 20; 27 rue du Roi de Sicile, 4e; metro St-Paul; starters €8-15, mains €14-19.50, lunch menu €15, dinner menu €20; ☺ lunch & dinner to 11.30pm) This is a rather fashionable Corsican restaurant serving such delectables as *starzapreti* (brocciu cheese and spinach quenelles) and *cabri rôti* (roast kid).

L'Ambassade d'Auvergne (Map pp105-7; ☎ 01 42 72 31 22; 22 rue du Grenier St-Lazare, 3e; metro Rambuteau; starters €9-18, mains €14-19, menu €27; ☺ lunch & dinner to 10.30pm) The 'Auvergne Embassy', is the place to go if you're really hungry; the sausages and hams of this region are among the best in France, as are the lentils from Puy and the sublime *clafoutis*, a custard and cherry tart baked upside down like a *tarte Tatin* (caramelised apple pie).

Le Bistrot du Dôme Bastille (Map pp102-4; ☎ 01 48 04 88 44; 2 rue de la Bastille, 4e; metro Bastille; starters €8.70-12, mains €18.70-23; ☺ lunch & dinner till 11pm) This lovely restaurant, little sister to the more established Dôme in Montparnasse (p154), specialises in superbly prepared fish and seafood dishes.

Bofinger (Map pp102-4; ☎ 01 42 72 87 82; 5-7 rue de la Bastille, 4e; metro Bastille; lunch menu €21.50, dinner menu €31.50; ☺ noon-1am, closed 3-6.30pm Mon-Fri) Founded in 1864, Bofinger is reputedly the oldest brasserie in Paris. Ask for a seat downstairs, under the *coupole* (stained-glass dome); it's the prettiest part of the restaurant.

Chez Nénesse (Map pp105-7; ☎ 01 42 78 46 49; 17 rue Saintonge, 3e; metro Filles du Calvaire; starters €3.50-14.50, mains €12-15, plat du jour €9.50; ☺ lunch & dinner to 10.30pm Mon-Fri) The atmosphere at Chez Nénesse, an oasis of simplicity and good taste, is 'old Parisian café' and the dishes are prepared with fresh, high-quality ingredients.

Les Galopins (Map pp102-4; ☎ 01 47 00 45 35; 24 rue des Taillandiers, 11e; metro Bastille or Voltaire; starters €6-10.50, mains €11.50-18, lunch menus €11.50 & €15; ☺ lunch Mon-Fri, dinner to 11pm Mon-Thu, to 11.30pm Fri & Sat) This cute little neighbourhood bistro serves dishes in the best tradition of French

cuisine: *poêlée de pétoncles* (pan-fried queen scallops), *magret de canard* (fillet of duck breast) and *cœur de rumsteck* (tenderloin rump steak).

Le Petit Picard (Map pp105-7; ☎ 01 42 78 54 03; 42 rue Ste-Croix de la Bretonnerie, 4e; metro Hôtel de Ville; lunch menu €12, dinner menus €14.50 & €21.50; ☺ lunch Tue-Fri, dinner till 11pm Tue-Sun) This popular little restaurant in the centre of the Marais serves traditional French cuisine. If you're very hungry, try the generous *menu traditionel* (€21.50).

Le Réconfort (Map pp105-7; ☎ 01 49 96 09 60; 37 rue de Poitou, 3e; metro St-Sébastien Froissart; starters €6-10, mains €14-20, lunch menus €13 & €17, plat du jour €10, brunch €19; ☺ lunch & dinner to 11pm Mon-Sat, brunch noon-4pm Sun) 'The Comfort' has generous space between tables, is quiet enough to chat without shouting and the kitchen turns out some very tasty and inventive dishes.

Le Square Trousseau (Map pp102-4; ☎ 01 43 43 06 00; 1 rue Antoine Vollon, 12e; metro Ledru Rollin; starters €6-10, mains €19-16, lunch menu €20, dinner menu €25; ☺ lunch & dinner to 11.30pm Tue-Sat) This vintage bistro with etched glass, zinc bar and polished wood panelling is comfortable rather than trendy, and attracts a jolly and mixed clientele. Most people come to enjoy the lovely terrace overlooking a small park.

NORTH AFRICAN & MIDDLE EASTERN

404 (Map pp96-8; ☎ 01 42 74 57 81; 69 rue des Gravilliers, 3e; metro Arts et Métiers; couscous & tajines €13-23, lunch menu €17, brunch menu €21; ☺ lunch Mon-Fri, dinner to midnight daily, brunch to 4pm Sat & Sun) As comfortable a Maghrebi (North African) caravanserai as you'll find in Paris, the 404 not only has excellent couscous and tajines but superb grills (€10 to €21). You'll just love the *One Thousand and One Nights* décor.

La Soummam (Map pp105-7; ☎ 01 43 54 12 43; 25 rue des Grands Augustins, 6e; metro Odéon or St-Michael; starters €3.70-7.30, mains €11.50-19, lunch menu €10.50, dinner menus €14.30-24.50; ☺ lunch & dinner to 11.30pm Mon-Sat) In this restaurant decorated with carpets, pottery and artworks, you can taste the unusual *tammekfoult*, a Berber-style couscous of steamed vegetables accompanied by milk curds, as well as a superb veal tajine with olives, artichokes, prunes and other vegetables.

VEGETARIAN

Grand Apétit (Map pp102-4; ☎ 01 40 27 04 95; 9 rue de la Cerisaie, 4e; metro Bastille or Sully Morland; meals from €15, menus €10-15; ☺ lunch Mon-Fri, dinner to 9pm Mon-Wed) 'The Big Appetite', a simple place near Bastille, offers light fare such as miso soup and cereals, as well as strength-building dishes for big eaters only. There's an excellent organic and macrobiotic shop attached.

Piccolo Teatro (Map pp105-7; ☎ 01 42 72 17 79; 6 rue des Écouffes, 4e; metro St-Paul; lunch menus €8.20-15.10, dinner menu €21.50; ☺ lunch & dinner till 11.30pm) This is an intimate place with exposed stone walls, a beamed ceiling and cosy little tables. Try the *assiette végétarienne* (vegetarian plate; €12.10) or the gratin, the speciality of the house, which combines vegetables, cream and cheese.

OTHER CUISINES

Caves St-Gilles (Map pp102-4; ☎ 01 48 87 22 62; 4 rue St-Gilles, 3e; metro Chemin Vert; tapas €5.50-15.70, platters €8-13; ☺ lunch & dinner till 11.30pm) This Spanish wine bar a short distance northeast of place des Vosges is the most authentic place on the Right Bank for tapas, paella (at the weekend only; €18) and sangria (€27 for 1L).

Chez Marianne (Map pp105-7; ☎ 01 42 72 18 86; 2 rue des Hospitalières St-Gervais, 4e; metro St-Paul; sandwiches €5.50-8, dishes €3.50-20; ☺ noon-midnight) Chez Marianne serves Sephardic-style kosher platters with four/five/six different meze (eg falafel, humus) and purées of eggplant, chickpeas and so on cost (€12/14/16). The window of the adjoining deli dispenses killer takeaway falafel sandwiches for €4 and there's an excellent bakery attached.

Coffee India (Map pp102-4; ☎ 01 48 06 18 57; 33-35 rue de Lappe, 11e; metro Bastille; starters €5.40-8.40, mains €12-22, lunch menu €9; ☺ lunch & dinner to 2am) Despite its confusing name, this restaurant (and cocktail bar/lounge/tearoom/café) serves surprisingly authentic southern Indian fare.

L'Enoteca (Map pp105-7; ☎ 01 42 78 91 44; 25 rue Charles V, 4e; metro Sully Morland or Pont Marie; starters €8-13, pasta €10-13, mains €17-20; ☺ lunch & dinner to 11.30pm) This trattoria in the historic Village St-Paul quarter, serves *haute cuisine à l'italienne*, and there's an excellent list of Italian wines by the glass (€3 to €9).

La Perla (Map pp105-7; ☎ 01 42 77 59 40; 26 rue François Miron, 4e; metro St-Paul or Hôtel de Ville; starters 6.30-8.50, mains €11-15, lunch platters €6-9; ☺ lunch & dinner to midnight) A favourite with younger Parisians, 'The Pearl' is a Californian-style Mexican bar-restaurant serving guacamole (€6.30), nachos (€5.50 to €8.50) and burritos

(€7.90 to €8.40). The margaritas (€8.50 to €9.30) are excellent.

Waly Fay (Map pp102-4; ☎ 01 40 24 17 79; 6 rue Godefroy Cavaignac, 11e; metro Charonne; starters €5.50-6.50, meze & platters €4.50-10, mains €11.50-15; ☺ dinner to 11pm Mon-Sat) For African food with a West Indian twist to the sounds of soul and jazz, try this easygoing 'loungin' restaurant'.

QUICK EATS

L'As de Felafel (Map pp105-7; ☎ 01 48 87 63 60; 34 rue des Rosiers, 4e; metro St-Paul; dishes €3.50-7; ☺ 11am-midnight Sun-Thu, noon-sunset Fri) This has always been our favourite place for deep-fried balls of chickpeas and herbs (€3.50 to €4).

Crêpes Show (Map pp102-4; ☎ 01 47 00 36 46; 51 rue de Lappe, 11e; metro Ledru Rollin; lunch menu €7, dinner menu €11; ☺ lunch Mon-Fri, dinner to 1am) An unpretentious little restaurant specialising in sweet crepes and savoury buckwheat *galettes* priced between €3 and €7. There are lots of vegetarian choices, including great salads from €7.

SELF-CATERING

In the Marais, there are a number of food shops and Asian delicatessens on the odd-numbered side of rue St-Antoine, 4e (Map pp105-7) as well as several supermarkets. For cheese, try the excellent **Fromagerie G Millet** (Map pp105-7; ☎ 01 42 78 48 78; 77 rue St-Antoine, 4e; ☺ 7.30am-1pm & 3.30-8pm Mon-Fri, 7.30am-1pm Sat) and there's a branch of the famous **Fauchon** (Map pp102-4; ☎ 01 53 01 91 91; 10 rue St-Antoine, 4e; metro Bastille; ☺ 8am-11pm) nearby.

Closer to Bastille, there are lots of food shops along **rue de la Roquette** (Map pp102-4; metro Voltaire or Bastille) up towards place Léon Blum.

Supermarkets include the following:

Franprix (Map pp105-7; 135 rue St-Antoine, 4e; ☺ 9am-8.30pm Mon-Sat); Franprix Marais branch (Map pp105-7; 87 rue de la Verrerie, 4e; ☺ 9am-8.15pm Mon-Fri, 9am-8.30pm Sat)

Monoprix (Map pp105-7; 71 rue St-Antoine, 4e; ☺ 9am-9pm Mon-Sat); Monoprix Bastille branch (Map pp102-4; 97 rue du Faubourg St-Antoine, 11e; metro Ledru Rollin; ☺ 9am-10pm Mon-Sat).

Supermarché G20 (Map pp105-7; 115 rue St-Antoine, 4e; ☺ 9am-8.30pm Mon-Sat)

Île St-Louis

Famed for its ice cream as much as anything else, the Île St-Louis is generally a pricey place to eat and restaurants are few and far between. It's best suited to those looking for a light snack at one of the lovely tearooms along rue St-Louis en l'Île such as **La Charlotte en Île** (Map pp105-7; ☎ 01 43 54 25 83; rue St-Louis en l'Île 24, 4e; metro Pont Marie; ☽ noon-8pm Thu-Sun) or for ingredients for a picnic along the Seine.

FRENCH
Brasserie de l'Îsle St-Louis (Map pp105-7; ☎ 01 43 54 02 59; 55 quai de Bourbon, 4e; metro Pont Marie; ☽ 5pm-1am Thu, noon-1am Fri-Tue) Established in 1870, this brasserie enjoys a spectacular location on the Seine and serves standard brasserie favourites such as *choucroute garnie*, *jarret* (veal shank) (€16.50 each) and *onglet de boeuf* (prime rib of beef).

QUICK EATS
Berthillon (Map pp105-7; ☎ 01 43 54 31 61; 31 rue St-Louis en l'Île, 4e; metro Pont Marie; 1/2/3/4 scoops €2/3.50/4.50/5.50; takeaway & shop ☽ 10am-8pm Wed-Sun, café ☽ 1-8pm Wed-Fri, 2-8pm Sat & Sun) While the fruit flavours (eg cassis) produced by this celebrated *glacier* (ice-cream maker) are justifiably renowned, the chocolate, coffee, *marrons glacés* (candied chestnuts), *Agenaise* (Armagnac and prunes), *noisette* (hazelnut) and *nougat au miel* (honey nougat) are much richer. Make your choice from among 70 flavours.

SELF-CATERING
On rue St-Louis en l'Île there are **fromageries** and **groceries** (usually closed on Sunday afternoon and all day Monday). There are more **food shops** on rue des Deux Ponts.

Latin Quarter & Jardin Des Plantes
Rue Mouffetard, 5e (Map pp102-4; metro Place Monge or Censier Daubenton), and its side streets are filled with places to eat. It's especially popular with students because of the number of stands and small shops selling baguettes, Italian *panini* and crepes.

Avoid rue de la Huchette and the labyrinth of narrow streets in the 5e across the Seine from Notre Dame (Map pp105–7). The restaurants between rue St-Jacques, blvd St-Germain and blvd St-Michel attract mainly foreign tourists, who appear to be unaware that some people refer to the area as 'Bacteria Alley' because of the meat and seafood ripening in the windows. To add insult to injury, many of the poor souls who eat here are under the impression that this little maze is the celebrated Latin Quarter.

FRENCH
Bouillon Racine (Map pp105-7; ☎ 01 44 32 15 60; 3 rue Racine, 6e; metro Cluny La Sorbonne; starters €7-11.50,

---

FAST-FOOD & CHAIN RESTAURANTS
American fast-food chains have busy branches all over Paris as does the local hamburger chain **Quick**. In addition, a number of restaurants have outlets around Paris with standard menus. They are definitely a cut above fast-food outlets and can be good value in areas such as along the av des Champs-Élysées, where restaurants tend to be over-priced or bad value (or both).

Bistro Romain (starters €4.70-9.50, pasta €9.90-13.40, mains €8.90-17.50, lunch €10.95, dinner menus €14.90 & €22.70; ☽ usually 11.30am-1am) This ever popular bistro-restaurant chain, with some 16 branches in Paris proper, is surprisingly upmarket for its price category. The **Champs-Élysées Bistro Romain** (Map pp93-5; ☎ 01 43 59 93 31; 122 av des Champs-Élysées, 8e; metro George V), one of three along the city's most famous thoroughfare, is a stone's throw from place Charles de Gaulle.

Buffalo Grill (www.buffalo-grill.fr in French; mains €8-15; menus from €8; ☽ usually 11am-11pm Sun-Thu, 11am-midnight Fri & Sat) Buffalo Grill counts some 10 branches in Paris, including the **Gare du Nord Buffalo Grill** (Map pp96-8; ☎ 01 40 16 47 81; 9 blvd de Denain, 10e; metro Gare du Nord). The emphasis here is on grills and steak – from T-bone (€16) to ostrich (€13.50).

Hippopotamus (www.hippopotamus.fr in French; starters €3.90-8.50, mains €9.80-17.50, menus €9.9-22.90; ☽ usually 11.45am-12.30am Sun-Thu, 11.45am-1am Fri & Sat) This chain, which has 10 branches in Paris proper, specialises in solid, steak-based meals. Four of the outlets stay open to 5am daily, including the **Opéra Hippopotamus** (Map pp96-8; ☎ 01 47 42 75 70; 1 blvd des Capucines, 2e; metro Opéra).

Léon de Bruxelles (www.leon-de-bruxelles.com in French; starters €3.80-6, mains €9.50-15, menus €9.90-13.60; ☽ usually 11.45am-11pm) Léon de Bruxelles focuses on one thing: *moules* (mussels). Meal-size bowls of the bivalves, served with chips and bread, start at under €10. There are a 13 Léons in Paris, including the **Les Halles Léon de Bruxelles** (Map pp105-7; ☎ 01 42 36 18 50; 120 rue Rambuteau, 1er; metro Châtelet-Les Halles).

mains €12-17, lunch menu €15, dinner menu €25; ☽ lunch & dinner to 11pm) This 'soup kitchen' built in 1906 to feed city workers is an Art Nouveau palace though the classic French dishes like *caille confite* (preserved quail) and *cochon de lait* (milk-fed pork) can't hold a candle to the surrounds.

Chez Léna et Mimille (Map pp102-4; ☎ 01 47 07 72 47; 32 rue Tournefort, 5e; metro Censier Daubenton; lunch starters/mains/desserts €7/14/7, dinner menu with wine €35; ☽ lunch Tue-Fri, dinner till 11pm Mon-Sat) Here is a cosy but elegant French restaurant with excellent food and one of the most fabulous terraces in Paris, overlooking a little park with a fountain.

Perraudin (Map pp102-4; ☎ 01 46 33 15 75; 157 rue St-Jacques, 5e; metro Luxembourg; starters €6-15, mains €14-23, lunch menu €18, dinner menu €26; ☽ lunch & dinner to 10.30pm Mon-Fri) Perraudin is a traditional French restaurant that hasn't changed much since the late 19th century. If you fancy classics such as *bœuf bourguignon* (€14), *gigot d'agneau* (€15) or *confit de canard* (€15), try this reasonably priced place.

Le Vigneron (Map pp102-4; ☎ 01 47 07 29 99; 18-20 rue du Pot de Fer, 5e; metro Place Monge; starters €6-18, mains €11-24, lunch menus €10.50 & €13.50, dinner menus €16.50 & €25; ☽ lunch & dinner till midnight) 'The Wine Grower' is one of the better French restaurants in the Mouffetard quarter, specialises in the cuisine of the southwest.

ASIAN
Tao (Map pp102-4; ☎ 01 43 26 75 92; 248 rue St-Jacques, 5e; metro Luxembourg; soups & salads €7-8, mains €8.50-13; ☽ lunch & dinner to 10.30pm Mon-Sat) A decidedly upmarket Asian restaurant with Zen-ish – Taoist? – décor, this place serves some of the best Vietnamese cuisine in the Latin Quarter.

Tashi Delek (Map pp102-4; ☎ 01 43 26 55 55; 4 rue des Fossés St-Jacques, 5e; metro Luxembourg; soups €3-4, Tibetan bowls €5.35-6.25, lunch menu €12, dinner menu €18; ☽ lunch & dinner to 11pm Mon-Sat) An intimate little place whose name approximates *tashi dele*, or 'bonjour' in Tibetan, Tashi Delek offers Himalayan dishes that may not be gourmet but are certainly tasty and inexpensive. There are also four vegetarian choices (€6.40 to €8.40).

NORTH AFRICAN & MIDDLE EASTERN
Founti Agadir (Map pp102-4; ☎ 01 43 37 85 10; 117 rue Monge, 5e; metro Censier Daubenton; lunch menus €15 & €18; ☽ lunch & dinner to 10.30pm Tue-Sun) This popular Moroccan restaurant serves some of the best couscous and tajines (€12.90 to €17) and *pastillas* (chicken pie; €7 to €8) on the Left Bank.

Mosquée de Paris (Map pp102-4; ☎ 01 43 31 38 20; 39 rue Geoffroy St-Hilaire, 5e; metro Censier Daubenton or Place Monge; starters & small dishes €4-12, mains €11-25; ☽ lunch & dinner to 10.30pm) The central Mosque of Paris (p122) has an authentic restaurant serving couscous (€11 to €25) and tajines (€12 to €16). There's also a North African-style **tearoom** (☽ 9am-midnight) where you can enjoy a cup of peppermint tea (€2.50).

VEGETARIAN
La Petit Légume (Map pp102-4; ☎ 01 40 46 06 85; 36 rue des Boulangers, 5e; metro Cardinal Lemoine; salads €10.70-12.90, dishes €6.90-9, menus €8.55-14; ☽ lunch & dinner to 10pm Mon-Sat) 'The Little Vegetable', a tiny place on a narrow road, is a great choice for house-made vegetarian fare.

Les Quatre et Une Saveurs (Map pp102-4; ☎ 01 43 26 88 80; 72 rue du Cardinal Lemoine, 5e; metro Cardinal Lemoine; lunch menu €13, dinner menus €22 & €25; ☽ lunch Sun-Fri, dinner to 10.30pm Sun-Thu & Sat) Set back from place de la Contrescarpe, this bright macrobiotic restaurant is extremely popular among health-food lovers. All ingredients are guaranteed 100% organic.

Quick Eats
Le Foyer du Vietnam (Map pp102-4; ☎ 01 45 35 32 54; 80 rue Monge, 5e; metro Place Monge; dishes €3.10-6.50, menu €8.40; ☽ lunch & dinner to 10pm Mon-Sat) This little place is a favourite meeting spot among the capital's Vietnamese community and serves simple one-dish meals in medium and large portions.

Tea Caddy (Map pp105-7; ☎ 01 43 54 15 56; 14 rue St-Julien le Pauvre, 5e; metro St-Michel; salads €9.50-11, sandwiches €7.50-9, light meals €8.50-11.80; ☽ noon-7pm Wed-Mon) The most English of 'English' tearooms in Paris, this institution founded in 1928 is a fine place to break for tea (€5.50 to €7.50) and pastries (about €7) after a tour of nearby Notre Dame, Ste-Chapelle or the Conciergerie.

SELF-CATERING
Place Maubert, 5e (Map pp105-7), becomes a lively **food market** four mornings a week. There are also some great provisions shops here, including a cheese shop called **Crémerie des Carmes** (Map pp105-7; ☎ 01 43 54 50 93; 47ter blvd

St-Germain, 5e; metro Maubert Mutualité; ⏰ 7.30am-1pm & 3.30-8pm Mon-Fri, 7.30am-1pm Sat).

There's a particularly lively **food market** along rue Mouffetard (see p169). On place Monge there's a much smaller **market** (Map pp102-4; place Monge, 5e; metro Place Monge; ⏰ 8am-2pm Wed, Fri & Sun).

Supermarkets in the area:

Champion (Map pp102-4; 34 rue Monge, 5e; metro Place Monge; ⏰ 8.30am-9pm Mon-Sat)

Ed l'Épicier (Map pp102-4; 37 rue Lacépède, 5e; ⏰ 9am-1pm & 3-7.30pm Mon-Fri, 9am-7.30pm Sat)

Franprix (Map pp102-4; 82 rue Mouffetard, 5e; metro Censier Daubenton or Place Monge; ⏰ 9am-8pm Mon-Sat)

St-Germain, Odéon & Luxembourg

Rue St-André des Arts (Map pp105-7; metro St-Michel or Odéon) is lined with restaurants, including a few down the covered passage de Rohan. There are lots of eateries between Église St-Sulpice and Église St-Germain des Prés as well, especially along rue des Canettes, rue Princesse and rue Guisarde. Carrefour de l'Odéon (metro Odéon) has a cluster of lively bars, cafés and restaurants. Place St-Germain des Prés itself is home to celebrated cafés such as **Les Deux Magots** and **Café de Flore** (p159) as well as the equally celebrated Brasserie Lip.

FRENCH

L'Arbuci (Map pp105-7; ☎ 01 44 32 16 00; 25 rue de Buci, 6e; metro Mabillon; meals from €35, lunch menus €15.50 & €20; ⏰ noon-1am) Though this retro-style brasserie recently got an all-marble, all-glass makeover (boo!), the specialities remain: seafood (especially oysters) and spit-roasted beef, chicken, pork and salmon and – for dessert – pineapple.

Brasserie Lipp (Map pp99-101; ☎ 01 45 48 53 91; 151 blvd St-Germain, 6e; metro St-Germain des Prés; starters €7.70-17.70, mains €15.50-18; ⏰ noon-1am) The Lipp is a wood-panelled café-brasserie (1880) where politicians rub shoulders with intellectuals, editors and media moguls, and waiters in black waistcoats, bowties and long white aprons serve such brasserie favourites as *choucroute garnie* (€16.60), *tête de veau* and *bœuf gros sel*.

Le Mâchon d'Henri (Map pp105-7; ☎ 01 43 29 08 70; 8 rue Guisarde, 6e; metro St-Sulpice or Mabillon; starters €6-8, mains €12-13; ⏰ lunch & dinner until 11.15pm) A very Parisian bistro in an area awash with bars, this *mâchon* (Lyon-style restaurant)

serves up Lyon-inspired dishes with – go figure – a Mediterranean twist.

Polidor (Map pp105-7; ☎ 01 43 26 95 34; 41 rue Monsieur le Prince, 6e; metro Odéon; starters €4-12, mains €7-12, lunch menu €9, dinner menus €18 & €26; ⏰ lunch & dinner till 12.30am Mon-Sat, to 11pm Sun) A meal at this quintessentially Parisian *crémerie-restaurant* is like a quick trip back to Victor Hugo's Paris – the restaurant and its décor date from 1845 – but everyone knows about it and it's pretty touristy. Specialities include *bœuf bourguignon* (€10), *blanquette de veau* (veal in white sauce; €11) and the most famous *tarte Tatin* (€5) in Paris.

OTHER CUISINES

Chez Albert (Map pp105-7; ☎ 01 46 33 22 57; 43 rue Mazarine, 6e; metro Odéon; starters €6-24, mains €17-22, lunch menu €17, dinner menu €28; ⏰ lunch & dinner to 10.30pm Tue-Sat) This place offers authentic Portuguese food. Try *porc Alentejana aux palourdes* (pork cooked with clams in a casserole), any of the numerous *bacalhau* (salt-dried cod) dishes such *brandade de morue* (creamed salt cod) or prawns sautéed in lots of garlic.

Le Golfe de Naples (Map pp105-7; ☎ 01 43 26 98 11; 5 rue de Montfaucon, 6e; metro Mabillon; starters €8-13, pizza & pasta dishes €9.50-14, mains €11-18.50; ⏰ lunch & dinner to 11pm) The 'Gulf of Naples' has some of the best pizza and fresh, shop-made pasta in Paris – though more elaborate main courses are something of a disappointment. Don't forget to try the *assiette napolitaine*, a plate of grilled fresh vegetables (€13.50).

Indonesia (Map pp102-4; ☎ 01 43 25 70 22; 12 rue de Vaugirard, 6e; metro Luxembourg; lunch menus €9-12.50, dinner menus €13-19; ⏰ lunch Sun-Fri, dinner to 10.30pm) One of only a couple of Indonesian restaurants in town, this unimaginatively named eatery has all the old favourites – from an elaborate, nine-dish *rijstafel* (€23) to *lumpia* (€4.50), *rendang* (€8.50) and *gado-gado* (€5).

QUICK EATS

Amorino (Map pp105-7; ☎ 01 43 26 57 46; 4 rue Buci, 6e; metro St-Germain des Prés; ice creams €3.40-5; ⏰ noon-midnight Sun-Thu, 1pm-midnight Fri & Sat) We're told that Berthillon (p151) has some serious competition and that Amorino's home-made ice cream (yogurt, forest fruits, caramel, kiwi, strawberry etc) is, in fact – egad! – better. Expect a long wait in the queue.

Guen Maï (Map pp105-7; ☎ 01 43 26 03 24; cnr rue Cardinale & rue de l'Abbaye, 6e; metro St-Germain des Prés or Mabillon; soups €4.50, mains €7-10.50; ☺ lunch Mon-Sat) Guen Maï is a health-food shop that also serves macrobiotic and organic *plats du jour* and soups.

SELF-CATERING

With the Jardin du Luxembourg nearby, this is the perfect area for putting together a picnic lunch. There is a large cluster of **food shops** on rue de Seine and rue de Buci, 6e (Map pp105-7; metro Mabillon). The renovated and covered **Marché St-Germain** (Map pp105-7; rue Lobineau, 6e; metro Mabillon), just north of the eastern end of Église St-Sulpice, has a huge array of produce and prepared food. Nearby supermarkets:

Champion (Map pp105-7; 79 rue de Seine, 6e; metro Mabillon; ☺ 1-9pm Mon, 8.40am-9pm Tue-Sat, 9am-1pm Sun)

Monoprix (Map pp105-7; 52 rue de Rennes, 6e; metro St-Germain des Prés; ☺ 9am-10pm Mon-Sat)

Montparnasse

Since the 1920s the area around blvd du Montparnasse has been one of the city's premier avenues for enjoying that most Parisian of pastimes: sitting in a café and checking out the scenery on two legs. Many younger Parisians, however, now consider the area somewhat *démodé* and touristy, which it is to a certain extent, and avoid it.

Montparnasse offers all types of eateries but especially traditional creperies. As Gare Montparnasse is where Bretons arriving in Paris to look for work would disembark (and apparently venture no further), there is no shortage of creperies in the area. There are three at 20 rue d'Odessa (Map pp99–101) alone and at least half a dozen more round the corner on rue du Montparnasse.

FRENCH

La Coupole (Map pp99-101; ☎ 01 43 20 14 20; 102 blvd du Montparnasse, 14e; metro Vavin; starters €7.50-12.50, mains €13.50-18.50, lunch menu €17.50, dinner menus €22.90 & €32.90; ☺ 8am-1am Sun-Thu, to 1.30am Fri & Sat) This 450-seat brasserie, which opened in 1927, has mural-covered columns painted by such artists as Brancusi and Chagall. Its dark-wood panelling and indirect lighting have hardly changed since the days of Sartre, Soutine, Man Ray and the dancer Josephine Baker.

Dix Vins (Map pp99-101; ☎ 01 43 20 91 77; 57 rue Falguière, 15e; metro Pasteur; menu €18.50; ☺ lunch Tue-Sat,

dinner to 11pm Mon-Sat) This tiny little restaurant, which offers a set menu only, is so popular you will probably have to wait at the bar even if you've booked. Be sure to sample one of the carefully chosen wines that the owner will decant into a carafe.

Le Dôme (Map pp99-101; ☎ 01 43 35 25 81; 108 blvd du Montparnasse, 14e; metro Vavin; starters €12.50-23, mains €30.50-56; ☺ lunch & dinner to 12.30am) An Art Deco extravaganza dating from the 1930s, The Dôme is a monumental place for a meal, with the emphasis on the freshest of oysters, shellfish and fish dishes such as *sole meunière*.

QUICK EATS

Mustang Café (Map pp99-101; ☎ 01 43 35 36 12; 84 blvd du Montparnasse, 14e; metro Montparnasse Bienvenüe; starters €6-13.50, salads €6.70-9, mains €7.50-13.30; ☺ 8am-5am) A café that almost never sleeps, the Mustang has passable Tex-Mex combination platters and nachos from €7.50 to €13.30, fajitas for €12.50 and burgers €8.90 to €10.60.

SELF-CATERING

Opposite the Tour Montparnasse there's an outdoor **food market** (Map pp99-101; blvd Edgar Quinet; ☺ 7am-1.30pm Wed & Sat) open two days a week. Supermarkets convenient to the area:

Franprix (Map pp99-101; 55 av du Maine, 14e; metro Gaité; ☺ 8.30am-8pm Mon-Sat); Franprix Delambre branch (Map pp99-101; 11 rue Delambre; metro Vavin; ☺ 8.30am-7.50pm Mon-Sat)

Inno (Map pp99-101; 29-31 rue du Départ, 14e; metro Montparnasse Bienvenüe; ☺ 9am-9.50pm Mon-Fri, 9am-8.50pm Sat)

Étoile & Champs-Élysées

With very few exceptions, eateries lining the touristy 'Avenue of the Elysian Fields' offer little value for money. Restaurants in the surrounding areas can be excellent, however.

FRENCH

L'Ardoise (Map pp93-5; ☎ 01 42 96 28 18; 28 rue du Mont Thabor, 1er; metro Concorde or Tuileries; menu €30; ☺ lunch & dinner to 11pm Wed-Sun) This is a little bistro with no menu as such (*ardoise* means 'blackboard', which is all there is) and the food – rabbit stuffed with plums and beef fillet with morels – is superb.

P'tit Bouchon Gourmand (Map pp93-5; ☎ 01 40 55 03 26; 5 rue Troyon, 17e; metro Charles de Gaulle-Étoile; mains €16-28, menu €25; ☺ lunch Mon-Fri, dinner to 11pm

Mon-Sat) An institution on the Breton coast for almost a quarter, 'Greedy's Little Wine Bar' has at last arrived in *la capitale*. Try the voluptuous *camembert rôti sur son lit de salade* (roasted camembert with salad) and the *millefeuille de boudin noir aux pommes* (black pudding in layered pastry with apples).

QUICK EATS

Lina's (Map pp93-5; ☎ 01 40 15 94 95; 4 rue Cambon, 1er; metro Concorde; salads €4.50-6.10, sandwiches €3.50-7; ⏰ 9.30am-4.30pm Mon-Fri, 10am-5.30pm Sat) This branch of a popular chain of sandwich and soup bars across Paris (some 19 outlets at last count) has upmarket sandwiches, salads and soups. There's also an **Opéra branch** (Map pp96-8; ☎ 01 47 03 30 29; 7 av de l'Opéra, 1er; metro Pyramides).

SELF-CATERING

The huge **Monoprix** (Map pp93-5; 62 av des Champs-Élysées, 8e; metro Franklin D Roosevelt; ⏰ 9am-midnight Mon-Sat) at the corner of rue La Boétie has a big supermarket section in the basement. Nearby **place de la Madeleine** (metro Madeleine) is the luxury food centre of one of the world's food capitals (see p168).

Opéra & Grands Boulevards

The neon-lit blvd Montmartre (metro Grands Boulevards or Richelieu Drouot) and nearby sections of rue du Faubourg Montmartre (neither of which are anywhere near the neighbourhood of Montmartre) form one of the Right Bank's most animated café and dining districts. A short distance to the north there's a large selection of kosher Jewish and North African restaurants on rue Richer, rue Cadet and rue Geoffroy Marie, 9e, south of metro Cadet.

FRENCH

Julien (Map pp96-8; ☎ 01 47 70 12 06; 16 rue du Faubourg St-Denis, 10e; metro Strasbourg St-Denis; starters €6-16, mains €13.50-28, menus with wine €22.90 & €32.90; ⏰ lunch & dinner to 1am) In the less-than-salubrious neighbourhood of St-Denis, Julien offers brasserie food that you wouldn't cross town for, but – mon Dieu! – the décor and the atmosphere: it's an Art Nouveau extravaganza perpetually in motion and a real step back in time.

Le Roi du Pot au Feu (Map pp93-5; ☎ 01 47 42 37 10; 34 rue Vignon, 9e; metro Havre Caumartin; starters €4-6,

mains €15-17, 2-/3-course menus €21 & €25; ⏰ noon-10.30pm Mon-Sat) The typical Parisian bistro atmosphere adds immensely to the charm of 'The King of Hotpots', but why you really want to come here is for a genuine *pot au feu*, a stockpot of beef, aromatic root vegetables and herbs stewed together.

JEWISH & NORTH AFRICAN

Les Ailes (Map pp96-8; ☎ 01 47 70 62 53; 34 rue Richer, 9e; metro Cadet; starters €6-17, mains €18-23; ⏰ lunch & dinner till 11.30pm) Just next door to the celebrated Folies-Bergère, 'The Wings' is a kosher North African (Sephardic) place that offers superb couscous with meat or fish (€18 to €23) and grills. Don't even consider a starter; you'll be inundated with little plates of salad, olives etc before you can say 'L'chaim'.

Wally le Saharien (Map pp96-8; ☎ 01 42 85 51 90; 36 rue Rodier, 9e; metro St-Georges or Cadet; lunch menu €23.50, dinner menu €40.40; ⏰ lunch & dinner to 10.30pm Tue-Sat) This place is several notches above most Maghrebi restaurants in Paris, offering couscous in its pure Saharan form – without any stock or vegetables, just a finely cooked grain served with a delicious sauce, as well as excellent tajines.

Gare du Nord, Gare de l'Est & République

These areas offer all types of food but most notably Indian and Pakistani, which can be elusive elsewhere in Paris. There's a cluster of traditional brasseries and bistros around the Gare du Nord.

FRENCH

Chez Papa/Espace Sud-Ouest (Map pp96-8; ☎ 01 42 09 53 87; 206 rue La Fayette, 10e; metro Charles Dupont; starters €9.15-10.20, salads €7.05-12.30, mains €13.05-16.15; ⏰ 11.30am-1am) Although this place serves southwestern specialities like *cassoulet* and *garbure* (€15.80), most people are here for the famous *salade Boyarde*, an enormous bowl filled with lettuce, tomato, sautéed potatoes, two types of cheese and ham (€7.05; €7.80 if you want two fried eggs thrown in).

Terminus Nord (Map pp96-8; ☎ 01 42 85 05 15; 23 rue de Dunkerque, 10e; metro Gare du Nord; starters €6.50-15.50, mains €13.50-28, menus with wine €22.90 & €32.90; ⏰ 8am-1am) The 'North Terminus' has a copper bar, waiters in white uniforms, brass fixtures and mirrored walls that look as they did when it opened directly opposite the

PARIS

Gare du Nord in 1925. Breakfast (from €8) is served from 8am to 11am daily, and full meals continuously from 11am to 12.30am.

QUICK EATS

Passage Brady (Map pp96-8; 46 rue du Faubourg St-Denis & 33 blvd de Strasbourg, 10e; metro Château d'Eau; ☺ usually lunch & dinner to 11pm) This derelict covered arcade, which could easily be in Calcutta, has dozens of incredibly cheap Indian, Pakistani and Bangladeshi cafés offering excellent value lunches (meat curry, rice and a tiny salad from €5, chicken or lamb biryani for €5 to €8, thalis for €12) and dinners (from €7.60). The pick of the crop: **Pooja** (☎ 01 48 24 00 83; 91 passage Brady)
Roi du Kashmir (☎ 01 48 00 08 85; 76 passage Brady)
Shalimar (☎ 01 45 23 31 61; 59 passage Brady)

SELF-CATERING

Rue du Faubourg St-Denis, 10e (metro Strasbourg St-Denis or Château d'Eau), which links blvd St-Denis and blvd de Magenta, is one of the cheapest places in Paris to buy food, especially fruit and vegetables (shop Nos 23, 27-29 and 41-43). It has a distinctively Middle Eastern air, and quite a few of the groceries offer Turkish, North African and subcontinental specialities. Many of the food shops, including the **fromagerie** at No 54, are open Tuesday to noon on Sunday. Further north, you'll find **Marché St-Quentin** (Map pp96-8; metro Gare de l'Est); for details see p169.

There are three Franprix supermarkets convenient to this area:

Franprix (Map pp96-8; 25 rue du Faubourg St-Denis, 10e; metro Strasbourg St-Denis; ☺ 9am-7.50pm Mon-Sat)
Franprix (Map pp96-8; 57 blvd de Magenta, 10e; metro Gare de l'Est; ☺ 9am-8pm Mon-Sat)
Franprix (Map pp105-7; 49 rue de Bretagne, 3e; metro Arts et Métiers; ☺ 9am-8.30pm Tue-Sat, 9am-1.20pm Sun)

Ménilmontant & Belleville

In the northern section of the 11e and into the 19e and 20e arrondissements, rue Oberkampf and its extension, rue de Ménilmontant (Map pp96-8), are popular with diners and denizens of the night though rue Jean-Pierre Timbaud, running parallel to the north, is stealing some of their glory these days. Rue de Belleville and the streets running off it are dotted with Chinese, Southeast Asian and a few Middle Eastern places; blvd de Belleville has some kosher couscous restaurants, most of which are closed on Saturday.

FRENCH

Le C'Amelot (Map pp102-4; ☎ 01 43 55 54 04; 50 rue Amelot, 11e; metro St-Sébastien Froissart; lunch menus €16 & €23, dinner menu €32; ☺ lunch Tue-Fri, dinner to midnight Mon-Sat) 'The Street Peddler' is the perfect little neighbourhood bistro but on everyone's list so book well in advance.

Le Clown Bar (Map pp102-4; ☎ 01 43 55 87 35; 114 rue Amelot, 11e; metro Filles du Calvaire; starters €10, lunch menu €13.50, dinner menu €18; ☺ lunch Mon-Sat, dinner to midnight) A wonderful wine bar-cum-bistro next to the Cirque d'Hiver, the Clown Bar is like a museum with its painted ceilings, mosaics on the wall, lovely zinc bar and circus memorabilia that touches on one of our favourite themes: the evil clown. The food is simple and unpretentious traditional French.

Juan et Juanita (Map pp96-8; ☎ 01 43 57 60 15; 82 rue Jean-Pierre Timbaud, 11e; metro Parmentier or Couronnes; starters €5.50, mains €13-15, menu €15; ☺ dinner to 2am Tue-Sat) Run by two young women, this place stands out for its over-the-top, slightly camp décor and the exceedingly high standards of its kitchen. Expect innovative dishes and unusual tastes.

Le Villaret (Map pp96-8; ☎ 01 43 57 89 76; 13 rue Ternaux, 11e; metro Parmentier; starters €7-15, mains €18-25, lunch menus €20 & €25, dinner sampling menu €46; ☺ lunch

---

AUTHOR'S CHOICE

Le Chansonnier (Map pp96-8; ☎ 01 42 09 40 58; 14 rue Eugène Varlin, 10e; metro Château Landon or Pierre Dupont; starters €6-12, mains € 13.50-15, lunch menu €10.50, dinner menu €23.50; ☺ lunch Mon-Fri, dinner to 11pm Mon-Sat) It may not be the best restaurant in Paris, but if ever there was the perfect example of a *restaurant du quartier*, 'The Singer', named after Lyonnais socialist singer/songwriter Pierre Dupont (1821-70), is it. With its curved zinc bar and Art Nouveau mouldings and windows, it could be a film set. The food is authentic, very good and very substantial; the dinner menu includes *terrine maison à valonté* – essentially all you can eat of four types of terrine. The *saucisson de Lyon* (Lyon sausage) studded with pistachios is an excellent starter while the *daube de joue de bœuf* (beef cheek stewed in a Dutch oven in a rich, wine-laden broth with herbs and vegetables) is the main course of choice. Expect a lot of repeat custom.

Mon-Fri, dinner to 11.30pm Mon & Tue, to 1am Wed-Sat)
An excellent neighbourhood bistro serving
very rich food, this place has diners coming
from across Paris till late to sample such
specialities as *velouté de cèpes à la mousse de
foie gras* (cepe mushroom soup with foie gras
mousse) and *gigot d'agneau de Lozère rôti et
son gratin de topinambours* (roast lamb with
Jerusalem artichoke gratin).

ASIAN
New Nioullaville (Map pp96-8; ☎ 01 40 21 96 18; 32
rue de l'Orillon, 11e; metro Belleville or Goncourt; starters
€5.30-6, rice & noodles €6.90-9, mains €7-14, menus
€7.30-12; ☉ lunch & dinner to 12.45am) This cavernous, 500-seat place resembles the Hong
Kong Stock Exchange on a busy day. The
food is a bit of a mishmash – *dim sum*
sits next to beef satay, as do scallops with
black bean alongside Singapore noodles.
Order carefully and you should be able to
approach authenticity.

Krung Thep (Map pp96-8; ☎ 01 43 66 83 74; 93 rue
Julien Lacroix, 20e; metro Pyrénées; starters €7-8.50, veg
dishes €5.50-7, mains €8.50-18; ☉ dinner till 11pm) The
'Bangkok' (in Thai, anyway) is a small Asio-
kitsch place with all our favourites (and
then some – there are 130 dishes on the
menu): green curries, *tom yam gung* and
fish or chicken steamed in banana leaves.

OTHER
L'Ave Maria (Map pp96-8; ☎ 01 47 00 61 73; 1 rue
Jacquard, 11e; metro Parmentier; dishes €11-14; ☉ lunch
Mon-Fri & dinner to midnight) This fusion place
is just like a Brazilian or African canteen,
a chic, imaginary and colourful greasy
spoon combining flavours of the Southern
Hemisphere and creating hearty, hybrid and
harmonious dishes. Music livens up towards
midnight and dancing carries on to 2am.

La Piragua (Map pp102-4; ☎ 01 40 21 35 98; 6 rue
Rochebrune, 11e; metro St-Ambroise; starters €4-6.50,
mains €10-13, menus €16 & €18; ☉ dinner to 11.30pm
Mon-Thu, to midnight Fri & Sat) La Piragua is a small,
brightly coloured eatery with Colombian
favourites like *ceviche* (fish marinated in
lemon juice) and *badeja paisa*, a concoction
of chopped meat, kidney beans, rice and
the kitchen sink. The list of Chilean wines
is excellent.

SELF-CATERING
Supermarkets in the area include **Franprix**
(Map pp96-8; 28 blvd Jules Ferry, 11e; metro République

or Goncourt; ☉ 8am-8pm Mon-Sat) and a **Franprix
branch** (Map pp96-8; 23 rue Jean-Pierre Timbaud, 11e;
metro Oberkampf; ☉ 8am-8pm Mon-Sat).

13e Arrondissement & Chinatown
Dozens of Asian restaurants – not just
Chinese ones – line the main streets of
Paris' Chinatown (Map pp90-2), including
av de Choisy, av d'Ivry and rue Baudricourt.
Another wonderful district for an evening
out is the Butte aux Cailles area, just southwest of place d'Italie. It's chock-a-block with
interesting addresses.

FRENCH
L'Avant-Goût (Map pp90-2; ☎ 01 53 80 24 00; 26 rue
Bobillot, 13e; metro Place d'Italie; starters €8, mains €15,
lunch menu €12, dinner menu €26; ☉ lunch & dinner to
11pm Tue-Fri) This prototype of the Parisian
'neo-bistro' (classical yet modern) in the
Butte aux Cailles serves some of the most
inventive modern cuisine around. It can
get noisy at times and there are occasional
lapses in the service, but the food is well
worth it.

ASIAN
La Fleuve de Chine (Map pp90-2; ☎ 01 45 82 06 88; 15
av de Choisy, 13e; metro Porte de Choisy; dishes €7.60-16.50;
☉ lunch & dinner to 11pm Fri-Wed) 'The River of
China', which can also be reached through
the Tour Bergame housing estate at 130 blvd
Masséna, has some of the most authentic
Cantonese and Hakka food to be found in
Paris and, as is typical, both the surroundings
and service – but definitely not the food –
are forgettable.

Sinorama (Map pp90-2; ☎ 01 53 82 09 51; 118 av de
Choisy & 23 rue du Docteur Magnan, 13e; metro Tolbiac or
Place d'Italie; starters €4-15, mains €8.50-17, rice & noodles
€4.50-8, lunch menu €9; ☉ lunch & dinner to 2am) This
airport hangar of a Chinese restaurant with
two entrances and a camp name serves good
Shanghainese dishes, with a smattering of
Cantonese choices.

Montmartre & Pigalle
The 18th arrondissement, where you will
find Montmartre and the northern half of
place Pigalle, thrives on crowds and little
else. When you've got Sacré Coeur, place
du Tertre and its portrait artists and Paris
literally at your feet, who needs decent
restaurants? But that's not to say everything
is a write-off in this well-trodden tourist

PARIS

area. You just have to pick and choose a bit more carefully.

FRENCH

Chez Toinette (Map p108; ☎ 01 42 54 44 36; 20 rue Germain Pilon, 18e; metro Abbesses; meals from €23; ☽ dinner to 11pm Tue-Sat) The atmosphere of this convivial restaurant, which has somehow managed to keep alive the tradition of old Montmartre in one of the capital's most touristy neighbourhoods, is rivalled only by its fine cuisine.

La Maison Rose (Map p108; ☎ 01 42 57 66 75; 2 rue de l'Abreuvoir, 18e; metro Lamarck Caulaincourt; starters €7.80-13, mains €14.50-16.50, menu €14.50; ☽ lunch & dinner to 10.30pm daily Mar-Oct, lunch Thu-Mon & dinner to 9pm Mon, Thu-Sat Nov-Feb) If you are looking for the quintessential intimate Montmartre bistro, head for the tiny 'Pink House' just north of place du Tertre.

OTHER CUISINES

Au Petit Budapest (Map p108; ☎ 01 46 06 10 34; 96 rue des Martyrs, 18e; metro Abbesses; starters €7.50-15, mains €10.50-16, lunch menu €13.50, dinner menu €17.50; ☽ lunch Thu-Sun, dinner to midnight Tue-Sun) The old etchings and the requisite Gypsy music here re-create something of the atmosphere of a Hungarian csárda of the late 19th century but the food – from the *paprikash au bœuf épicé* (beef paprika) to the *gâteau au fromage blanc* (cream cheese cake) – is a refined version of popular Hungarian dishes.

Il Duca (Map p108; ☎ 01 46 06 71 98; 26 rue Yvonne le Tac, 18e; metro Abbesses; starters €7-12, pasta €10-13, mains €15-17, menu €14; ☽ lunch & dinner to 11pm Mon-Fri, to midnight Sat & Sun) 'The Duke' is an intimate little Italian restaurant with good, straightforward food, including shop-made pasta. The selection of Italian wine and cheese is exceptional.

SELF-CATERING

Towards place Pigalle there are lots of grocery stores, many of them open until late at night; try the side streets leading off blvd de Clichy (eg rue Lepic). Heading south from blvd de Clichy, rue des Martyrs, 9e (Map p108), is lined with food shops almost all the way to metro Notre Dame de Lorette. Supermarkets in the area:

8 à Huit (Map p108; 24 rue Lepic, 18e; metro Abbesses; ☽ 8.30am-9pm Mon-Sat)

Ed l'Épicier (Map p108; 31 rue d'Orsel, 18e; metro Anvers; ☽ 9am-8pm Mon-Sat)

DRINKING

Traditionally drinking in Paris revolved around a café, where a *demi* looked more like an eyewash than 330mL of beer. But all that has changed and the number of drinking establishments has mushroomed in recent years, especially in the Marais and along the Grands Boulevards. Happy hour – sometimes extending to as late at 9pm – has brought the price of a pint of beer, a glass of wine or a cocktail down to pricey, rather than extortionate, levels.

Louvre & Les Halles

Le Fumoir (Map pp105-7; ☎ 01 42 92 00 24; 6 rue de l'Amiral Coligny, 1er; metro Louvre-Rivoli; ☽ 11am-2am) 'The Smoking Room' is a huge bar/café just opposite the Louvre with a gentleman's club/library theme. It's a friendly, lively place and quite good fun. Happy hour is 6pm to 8pm daily.

Papou Lounge (Map pp105-7; ☎ 01 44 76 00 03; 74 rue Jean-Jacques Rousseau, 1er; metro Louvre-Rivoli; ☽ 10am-2am Mon-Fri, 11am-2am Sat, 5pm-midnight Sun) The brothers who own this place share a fascination for les Papous (Papuans) and Papua New Guinea, and the tribal masks, carvings and photos on the wall may give you itchy feet.

Marais & Bastille

L'Apparement Café (Map pp105-7; ☎ 01 48 87 12 22; 18 rue des Coutures St-Gervais, 3e; metro St-Sébastien Froissart; ☽ noon-2am Mon-Fri, 4pm-2am Sat, 12.30pm-midnight Sun) Tucked not so 'Apparently' behind the Musée Picasso, this oasis of peace looks like a private living room.

Barrio Latino (Map pp102-4; ☎ 01 55 78 84 75; 46-48 rue du Faubourg St-Antoine, 11e; metro Bastille; ☽ 11.30am-2am) Squeezing the salsa craze for everything it's worth, the 'Latin Quarter' is an enormous bar and restaurant spread over three floors that attracts Latinos, Latino wannabes and Latino wanna-haves.

Café des Phares (Map pp102-4; ☎ 01 42 72 04 70; 7 place Bastille, 4e; metro Bastille; ☽ 7am-3am Sun-Thu, 7am-4am Fri & Sat) The 'Beacons Café' is best known as the city's original philocafé (philosophers' café), established by the late philosopher and Sorbonne professor Marc Sautet (1947–98). If you feel like debating such topics as 'What is a fact?' and 'Can people communicate?', head for the Phares at 11am on Sunday.

Jokko Bar (Map pp105-7; ☎ 01 42 74 35 96; 5 rue Elzévir, 3e; metro St-Paul or Chemin Vert; ☽ 5pm-12.30am

Wed-Sun) Part of the CSAO group (p170), the Jokko is a delightful spot with colourful African décor, great world music and rum-based cocktails from €8. There are concerts most nights at 7.30pm.

Au Petit Fer à Cheval (Map pp105-7; ☎ 01 42 72 47 47; 30 rue Vieille du Temple, 4e; metro Hôtel de Ville or St-Paul; ☺ 9am-2am) A slightly offbeat bar-restaurant named after its horseshoe-shaped zinc (counter), this tiny place is often filled to overflowing with friendly regulars and boasts one of the best people-watching vantage points in the Marais.

Quiet Man (Map pp105-7; ☎ 01 48 04 02 77; 5 rue des Haudriettes, 3e; metro Rambuteau; ☺ 5pm-2am Sun-Thu, 4pm-2am Fri & Sat) This is about the most authentic Irish pub Paris has to offer, with a real live Irish owner and musicians playing Irish music. There are trad sets every night from 8pm to 1am and happy hour is from 5pm to 8pm daily.

Stolly's Stone Bar (Map pp105-7; ☎ 01 42 76 06 76; 16 rue de la Cloche Percée, 4e; metro Hôtel de Ville; ☺ 4.30pm-2am) This Anglophone bar on a tiny street just above rue de Rivoli is always crowded, particularly during the 4.30pm to 8pm happy hour, when a 1.6L pitcher of cheap *blonde* (house lager) costs €11 and cocktails are €4.60.

Latin Quarter & Jardin des Plantes

Piano Vache (Map pp102-4; ☎ 01 46 33 75 03; 8 rue Laplace, 5e; metro Maubert Mutualité; ☺ noon-2am Mon-Fri, 9pm-2am Sat & Sun) Just down the hill from the Panthéon, 'The Mean Piano' is 'underground' as the films would have us understand the term. Great music (guest DJs) and a good crowd of very mixed ages. Happy hour is from opening to 9pm Monday to Friday.

Le Salon Égyptien (Map pp102-4; ☎ 01 43 25 58 99; 77 rue du Cardinal Lemoine, 5e; metro Cardinal Lemoine; ☺ 11.30am-2am) People come here mainly to smoke hookahs (€4.60), and you'll smell the intoxicating aromas of apricot, honey, apple or strawberry as soon as you walk through the door. Settle into a large pouf and sip tea or the unusual *karkadet* (a hibiscus-derived beverage).

Le Vieux Chêne (Map pp102-4; ☎ 01 43 37 71 51; 69 rue Mouffetard, 5e; metro Place Monge; ☺ 4pm-2am Sun-Thu, 4pm-5am Fri & Sat) 'The Old Oak', popular with students and long a Mouffetard institution (some people believe it is the oldest bar in the city) has jazz at the weekend. Happy hour is from opening until 9pm daily.

St-Germain, Odéon & Luxembourg

Le 10 (Map pp105-7; ☎ 01 43 26 66 83; 10 rue de l'Odéon, 6e; metro Odéon; ☺ 5.30pm-2am) This is a popular cellar pub with smoke-darkened posters on the walls, an eclectic jukebox with everything from jazz and the Doors to Yves Montand, and sangria, the house speciality, always at the ready. Happy hour is from 6pm to 9pm daily.

Café de Flore (Map pp105-7; ☎ 01 45 48 55 26; 172 blvd St-Germain, 6e; metro St-Germain des Prés; ☺ 7.30am-1.30am) The Flore is an Art Deco café where the red, upholstered benches, mirrors and marble walls haven't changed since the days when Sartre, de Beauvoir, Camus and Picasso bent their elbows here. The terrace is a much sought-after place to sip beer (€7.50 for 400mL), the house Pouilly Fumé (€7.50 a glass or €29 a bottle) or coffee (€4).

Les Deux Magots (Map pp105-7; ☎ 01 45 48 55 25; 170 blvd St-Germain, 6e; metro St-Germain des Prés; ☺ 7am-1am) This erstwhile literary haunt, whose name derives not from a couple of disgusting white worms but from the two *magots* (grotesque figurines) of Chinese dignitaries at the entrance, dates from 1914 although it is best known as the favoured hang-out of Sartre, Hemingway, Picasso and André Breton. Everyone has to sit on the terrace here at least once and have a coffee (€4), beer (€5.50) or the famous hot chocolate served in porcelain jugs (€6).

Montparnasse

The most popular places to while away the hours over a drink or coffee in Montparnasse are large café-restaurants like **La Coupole** and **Le Dôme** (p154) on blvd du Montparnasse.

Cubana Café (Map pp99-101; ☎ 01 40 46 80 81; 47 rue Vavin, 6e; metro Vavin; ☺ 11am-3am Sun-Wed, 11am-5am Thu-Sat) The 'Cuban Café' is the perfect bar-restaurant for a couple of 'starter' drinks before carrying on to the nearby Coupole, with Cuban cocktails (€7.30) reduced to €5.30 at happy hour (5pm to 7.30pm daily).

Opéra & Grands Boulevards

Bushwacker's (Map pp93-5; ☎ 01 44 94 95 64; 10 rue de Caumartin, 9e; metro Havre-Caumartin or Opéra; ☺ noon-2am) The name notwithstanding, this very upmarket, Australian-themed bar in the financial district is no den of thieves. Stuffed wallabies, didgeridoos and flat computer screen TVs predominate, and the circular bar encourages interaction.

Harry's New York Bar (Map pp93-5; ☎ 01 42 61 71 14; 5 rue Daunou, 2e; metro Opéra; ☒ 10.30am-4am) One of the most popular American-style bars in the prewar years, Harry's once welcomed such habitués as writers F Scott Fitzgerald and Hemingway, who no doubt sampled the bar's unique cocktail and creation: the Bloody Mary (€9.60). The Cuban mahogany interior dates from the mid-19th century and was brought over from a Manhattan bar in 1911. There's light jazz in the basement piano bar from 10pm to 2am Monday to Saturday.

Gare du Nord, Gare de l'Est & République

Chez Prune (Map pp96-8; ☎ 01 42 41 30 47; 71 quai de Valmy, 10e; metro République; ☒ 8am-2am Mon-Sat, 10am-2am Sun) This Soho-boho café is the venue that put the Canal St-Martin on the map. Most people come here for the vibe and the mojito cocktails.

Chez Wolf Motown Bar (Map pp96-8; ☎ 01 46 07 09 79; 81-83 blvd de Strasbourg, 10e; metro Gare de l'Est; ☒ 24hr except 6am-7pm Sat) This is the place to come in the lonely wee hours when you've got a thirst and a few bob but, alas, no friends; the Motown can sometimes feel like a club.

Ménilmontant & Belleville

L'Autre Café (Map pp96-8; ☎ 01 40 21 03 07; 62 rue Jean-Pierre Timbaud, 11e; metro Parmentier; ☒ 8am-1.30am Mon-Fri, 11.30am-1.30am Sat & Sun) 'The Other Café', which helped move some of the after-dark action north of rue Oberkampf to rue Jean-Pierre Timbaud, attracts a mixed young crowd of locals, artists and party-goers with its long bar, huge open space, relaxed environment and reasonable prices.

Cannibale Café (Map pp96-8; ☎ 01 49 29 95 59; 93 rue Jean-Pierre Timbaud, 11e; metro Couronnes; ☒ 8.30am-2am) The name of this place isn't suggesting that you bring condiments. In fact 'Cannibal Café' couldn't be more welcoming, with its grand rococo-style bar topped with worn zinc, decrepit mirrors, peeling mouldings, wood panelling, Formica tables and red leatherette bench seats. It is a laid-back, almost frayed alternative to the groovy pubs and bars of rue Oberkampf and the perfect place to linger over a coffee (€2) or beer at the bar (€2 a demi or €6.50 a pint).

Montmartre & Pigalle

Le Dépanneur (Map p108; ☎ 01 40 16 40 20; 27 rue Fontaine, 9e; metro Blanche; ☒ 24hr) 'The Repairman',

an American diner with postmodern frills open round the clock, has plenty of tequila and fancy cocktails (from €6) and there are DJs after 11pm from Thursday to Saturday.

La Fourmi (Map p108; ☎ 01 42 64 70 35; 74 rue des Martyrs, 18e; metro Pigalle; ☒ 8am-2am Mon-Thu, 10am-4am Fri-Sun) A trendy Pigalle hang-out, the trendy 'Ant' buzzes (marches?) all day and night and is a convenient place to meet before heading off to the clubs.

ENTERTAINMENT
Listings

It's virtually impossible to sample the richness of Paris' entertainment scene without first studying *Pariscope* (€0.40) or *Officiel des Spectacles* (€0.35), both of which come out on Wednesday and are available at newsstands everywhere in the city. *Pariscope* includes a six-page insert in English at the back, courtesy of London's *Time Out* magazine. The weekly magazine *Zurban* (www.zurban.com in French; €0.80), which also appears on Wednesday, offers a fresher look at entertainment in the capital. *Les Inrockuptibles* (www.lesinrocks. com in French; €2.90) is a national culture and entertainment weekly but, predictably, the lion's share of the information concerns Paris.

For up-to-date information on clubs and the music scene, pick up a copy of *LYLO* (an acronym for *Les Yeux, Les Oreilles*, literally 'Ears and Eyes'), a free magazine booklet with excellent listings of rock concerts and other live music. It is available at many cafés, bars and clubs across town. The monthly magazine *Nova* (www.novaplanet .com in French; €2) is an excellent source for information on clubs and the music scene; its *Hot Guide* listings insert is particularly useful. Visit any of the Fnac outlets (see opposite) for free flyers, schedules and programmes.

Other excellent sources for finding out what's on include Radio FG on 98.2MHz FM (www.radiofg.com in French) and Radio Nova on 101.5MHz FM. You can also try www.france-techno.fr (French only) or www .flyersweb.com (French only) for up-to-date information on clubbing.

Tickets & Bookings

You can buy your tickets for cultural events at numerous ticket outlets, including Fnac (rhymes with 'snack') and Virgin Megastore branches, for a small commission. Both accept reservations, ticketing by phone and the Internet and most credit cards. Tickets generally cannot be returned or exchanged unless a performance is cancelled.

Fnac (☎ 0 892 68 36 22; www.fnac.com in French) has 10 outlets in Paris with *billeteries* (ticket offices) including the following:

Fnac Musique Bastille (Map pp102-4; ☎ 01 43 42 04 04; 4 place de la Bastille, 12e; metro Bastille; ☺ 10am-8pm Mon-Sat)

Fnac Champs-Élysées (Map pp93-5; ☎ 01 53 53 64 64; 74 av des Champs-Élysées, 8e; metro Franklin D Roosevelt; ☺ 10am-midnight Mon-Sat, 11am-midnight Sun)

Fnac Forum des Halles (Map pp105-7; ☎ 01 40 41 40 00; Forum des Halles shopping centre, Level 3, 1-7 rue Pierre Lescot, 1er; metro Châtelet-Les Halles; ☺ 10am-7.30pm Mon-Sat)

Virgin (www.virginmega.fr in French) has a half-dozen 'megastores' in the capital; central locations:

Virgin Megastore Champs-Élysées (Map pp93-5; ☎ 01 49 53 50 00; 52-60 av des Champs-Élysées, 8e; metro Franklin D Roosevelt; ☺ 10am-midnight Mon-Sat, noon-midnight Sun)

Virgin Megastore Carrousel du Louvre (Map pp105-7; ☎ 01 44 50 03 10; 99 rue de Rivoli, 1er; metro Palais Royal-Musée du Louvre; ☺ 10am-8.30pm Mon & Tue, 10am-9.30pm Wed-Sun)

Virgin Megastore Barbès (Map p108; ☎ 01 56 55 53 70; 15 blvd Barbès, 18e; metro Barbès Rochechouart; ☺ 10am-10pm Mon-Sat)

DISCOUNT TICKETS

On the day of any play or musical performance, **Kiosque Théâtre** (Map pp93-5; opp 15 place de la Madeleine, 8e; metro Madeleine; ☺ 12.30-7.45pm Tue-Sat, 12.30-3.45pm Sun) sells tickets to plays and other events (concerts, operas, ballets etc) at half-price plus commission of about €2.50. Seats are almost always the most expensive ones in the stalls or 1st balcony. There's also a **Kiosque Théâtre Montparnasse branch** (Map pp99-101; parvis Montparnasse, 15e; metro Montparnasse Bienvenüe) between Gare Montparnasse and Tour Montparnasse, open the same hours. There are no telephone bookings.

Cinemas

Pariscope and *L'Officiel des Spectacles* (see opposite) list Paris' cinematic offerings alphabetically by their French title followed by the English (or other foreign) one.

Visiting to the cinema in Paris is not cheap: expect to pay between €6 and €8 for a first-run film. Students and those aged under 18 or over 60 usually get discounts of about 25% except on Friday, Saturday and Sunday nights. On Wednesday (and some Mondays) most cinemas give discounts of 20% to 30% to everyone.

Cinémathèque Française (☎ 01 56 26 01 01; www.cinemathequefrancaise.com in French; adult/student & child €4.70/3, 10-ticket carnet €44/27) This national cultural institution almost always leaves its foreign offerings – often rarely screened classics – in their original versions. There are two *salles*, the main one at the **Palais de Chaillot** (Map pp99-101; 7 av Albert de Mun, 16e; metro Trocadéro or Iéna; ☺ screenings Wed-Sun), which you enter from the Jardins du Trocadéro, and the more convenient but less dramatic **Grands Boulevards branch** (Map pp96-8; 42 blvd Bonne Nouvelle, 10e; metro Bonne Nouvelle; ☺ screenings).

Gay & Lesbian Venues

The Marais, especially those areas around the intersection of rue Ste-Croix de la Bretonnerie and rue des Archives and eastwards to rue Vieille du Temple, has been Paris' main centre of gay and lesbian nightlife for two decades. There are a few other addresses scattered elsewhere on the Right Bank.

Bliss Kfé (Map pp105-7; ☎ 01 55 34 98 81; 30 rue du Roi de Sicile, 4e; metro St-Paul; ☺ 5.30pm-2am) This dike café-cum-lounge bar is a stylish newcomer to the Marais, with a New York vibe and a somewhat mixed – guys are welcome – crowd.

La Champmeslé (Map pp96-8; ☎ 01 42 96 85 20; 4 rue Chabanais, 2e; metro Pyramides; ☺ 2pm-2am Mon-Thu, 2pm-dawn Fri & Sat) The oldest (established in 1979) lesbian bar in the city that plays mellow music and has regular theme nights, including a cabaret of French chansons commencing at 10pm on Thursday and sometimes Saturday.

Le Dépôt (Map pp105-7; ☎ 01 44 54 96 96; 10 rue aux Ours, 3e; metro Rambuteau or Étienne Marcel; admission €6-12; ☺ 2pm-8am) A huge place with both conversation bars and obscure cruising space. DJ theme nights are scheduled throughout the week.

Open Café (Map pp105-7; ☎ 01 42 72 26 18; 17 rue des Archives, 4e; metro Hôtel de Ville; ☺ 11am-2am) This is where most boyz of most ages head after work before moving on to bigger (maybe) and better (doubtful) things. It's packed but more social than cruisy. Happy hour is 6pm to 9pm daily.

Red Light (Map pp99-101; ☎ 01 42 79 94 94; 34 rue du Départ, 14e; metro Montparnasse Bienvenüe; admission €20; ☽ 11pm-6am Thu-Sun) This underground (literally) venue at the foot of the Tour Montparnasse has become the destination of choice for the young gay crowd, especially on Saturday house nights.

Le Scorp (Map pp96-8; ☎ 01 40 26 28 30; 25 blvd Poissonnière, 2e; metro Grands Boulevards; admission free-€15; ☽ 11.45pm-6.30am Wed & Thu, midnight-7.30am Fri & Sat) The Scorp – short for 'Scorpion' – is one of the more relaxed, mixed gay dance clubs in Paris. On the ground floor is **Le Pulp** (☎ 01 40 26 01 93; admission €9-10; ☽ midnight-6am Thu-Sun), the city's pre-eminent girls-only club (mixed on Thursday).

Live Music
OPERA & CLASSICAL

The **Opéra National de Paris** (ONP; ☎ 0 892 899 090; www.opera-de-paris.fr in French) splits its performance schedule between the Palais Garnier, its original home built in 1875, and the modern Opéra Bastille, which opened in 1989. Both opera houses also stage ballets and classical-music concerts performed by the ONP's affiliated orchestra and ballet companies. The season runs from September to July.

Opéra Bastille (Map pp102-4; 2-6 place de la Bastille, 12e; metro Bastille) Tickets are available from the adjacent **box office** (130 rue de Lyon, 12e; ☽ 11am-6.30pm Mon-Sat) 14 days before the date of the performance, but the only way to ensure a seat is by **post** (120 rue de Lyon, 75576 Paris CEDEX 12) some two months in advance. Operas cost €6 to €114. Ballets cost €13 to €70; seats with limited or no visibility available at the box office only are €6 to €9. Chamber-music concerts, which are also held here throughout the season, cost €6 to €16. If there are unsold tickets, people aged under 26 or over 65 and students can get excellent seats for €20 only 15 minutes before the curtain goes up.

Palais Garnier (Map pp93-5; place de l'Opéra, 9e; metro Opéra) Ticket prices and conditions (including last-minute discounts) at the **box office** (place de l'Opéra, 9e; ☽ 11am-6.30pm Mon-Sat) of the city's original opera house are almost exactly the same as those at the Opéra Bastille.

Along with opera, Paris plays host to dozens of orchestral, organ and chamber-music concerts each week. From October to June the excellent Orchestre de Paris performs at the Châtelet-Théâtre Musical

de Paris and the **Théâtre Mogador** (Map pp93-5; ☎ 01 53 32 32 00; 25 rue de Mogador, 9e; metro St-Lazare) while renovation of the Salle Pleyel is completed.

Châtelet-Théâtre Musical de Paris (Map pp105-7; ☎ 01 40 28 28 40; www.chatelet-theatre.com in French; 2 rue Édouard Colonne, 1er; metro Châtelet; concert tickets €9-60; box office ☽ 11am-7pm) This central venue hosts concerts (including ones by the Orchestre de Paris) as well as operas (€20 to €106; €11 for seats with no visibility), ballets (€21 to €62 or €9 for the cheapest seat), and theatre performances. Classical music is also performed at 11am on Sunday (€20) and at 12.45pm on Monday, Wednesday and Friday (€9). Tickets go on sale 14 days before the performance date; subject to availability, anyone aged under 26 or over 65 can get reduced-price tickets (eg €10 for the Sunday morning concert) from 15 minutes before curtain time. There are no performances in July and August.

Salle Pleyel (Map pp93-5; ☎ 01 45 61 53 00; 252 rue du Faubourg St-Honoré, 8e; metro Ternes) Dating from the 1920s, this highly regarded hall hosts many of Paris' finest classical music concerts and recitals. It was closed in July 2002 for a three-year renovation.

CHURCH CONCERT VENUES

The churches of Paris are popular venues for classical music concerts and organ recitals. The concerts held at **Notre Dame Cathedral** (Map pp105-7; ☎ 01 42 34 56 10; tickets €10-€40) don't keep to any fixed schedule but are advertised on posters around town. There's usually a free organ concert some time between 4.30pm and 5.15pm on Sunday, especially in winter. From April to October classical concerts are also held in **Ste-Chapelle** (Map pp105-7; ☎ 01 53 73 78 51; Île de la Cité, 1er); the cheapest seats cost around €17 (€12 for students aged under 26). From November to June concerts are also held at the exquisite **Église Royale du Val-de-Grâce** (Map pp102-4; ☎ 01 42 01 47 67; 277bis rue St-Jacques, 5e; metro Port Royal; adult/child €18.30/12.20).

ROCK, POP & INDIE

There's rock, pop and indie at bars, cafés and clubs around Paris, and a number of venues regularly host acts by international performers. It's often easier to see big-name Anglophone acts in Paris than in their home countries. The most popular stadiums or other big venues for international acts are the **Palais Omnisports de Paris-Bercy** (Map pp102-4; ☎ 0 825 030 031, 01 46 91 57 57; www.bercy.fr in French; 8 blvd de Bercy, 12e; metro Bercy) in Bercy; the **Stade de France** (Map p182; ☎ 0 892 700 900, 01 55 93 00 00; www.stadedefrance.fr; rue Francis de Pressensé, ZAC du Cornillon Nord, 93216 St-Denis La Plaine; metro St-Denis-Porte de Paris) in St-Denis; and **Le Zénith** (Map pp90-2; ☎ 01 42 08 60 00; www.le-zenith.com in French; 211 av Jean Jaurès, 19e; metro Porte de Pantin) at the Cité de la Musique in the Parc de la Villette, 19e.

Le Bataclan (Map pp102-4; ☎ 01 43 14 35 35; 50 blvd Voltaire, 11e; metro Oberkampf or St-Ambroise; admission €15-50; box office ☺ 11am-7pm Mon-Sat) Built in 1864 and Maurice Chevalier's debut venue in 1910, this small concert hall draws some French and international acts. It also masquerades as a theatre and dance hall. Le Bataclan usually opens from 8pm for concerts.

Café de la Danse (Map pp102-4; ☎ 01 47 00 57 59; www.cafédeladanse.com in French; 5 Passage Louis-Philippe, 11e; metro Bastille; admission €10-20; box office ☺ noon-6pm Mon-Fri) Just a few metres down a small passage from 23 rue de Lappe, 'The Dance Café' is a large auditorium with 300 to 500 seats. Almost every day from sometime between 7.30pm and 9pm, it plays host to rock and world music concerts, dance performances, musical theatre and poetry readings.

La Cigale (Map p108; ☎ 01 49 25 89 99; 120 blvd de Rochechouart, 18e; metro Anvers or Pigalle; admission €22-45; box office ☺ noon-7pm Mon-Fri) 'The Cicada' is an enormous old music hall seating up to 2000 people and hosting international rock acts, jazz and folk groups and full-on dance and variety performances. There's seating in the balcony and dancing up front.

L'Élysée Montmartre (Map p108; ☎ 01 44 92 45 36, 01 55 07 16 00; www.elyseemontmartre.com; 72 blvd de Rochechouart, 18e; metro Anvers; admission €10-34) A huge old music hall with a great sound system, this is one of the better venues in Paris for one-off rock and indie concerts. It opens at 7.30pm for concerts and becomes a popular club on Friday and Saturday from midnight to 6am.

La Java (Map pp96-8; ☎ 01 42 02 20 52; 105 rue du Faubourg du Temple, 10e; metro Goncourt; admission €8-16; ☺ 11pm-5am Thu-Sat, 2-7pm Sun) The dance hall (1922) where Édith Piaf got her first break now reverberates to the sound of live salsa and other Latino music. There's a *thé dansant* (tea dance) here on Sunday.

JAZZ & BLUES

After WWII Paris was Europe's most important jazz centre and it is again very much à la mode; the city's better clubs attract top international stars.

Le Baiser Salé (Map pp105-7; ☎ 01 42 33 37 71; 58 rue des Lombards, 1er; metro Châtelet; admission free-€22) 'The Salty Kiss' is one of several jazz clubs on the same street. The *salle de jazz* on the 1st floor has concerts of pop rock and *chansons* at 7pm and Afro-jazz and jazz fusion at 10pm. The cover charge depends on the act; it's free during the *soirée bœuf* (jam session) on Monday night. Try to catch the incomparable Pierre Chabrèle on trombone.

Le Caveau de la Huchette (Map pp105-7; ☎ 01 43 26 65 05; 5 rue de la Huchette, 5e; metro St-Michel; adult Sun-Thu €10.50, Fri & Sun €13, student €9; ☺ 9pm-2.30am Sun-Thu, 9pm-3.30am Fri, 9pm-4am Sat) Housed in a medieval *caveau* (cellar) that was used as a courtroom and torture chamber during the Revolution, this club is where virtually all the jazz greats have played since the end of WWII. It's touristy but the atmosphere can often be more electric than at the more serious jazz clubs. Sessions start at 9.30pm.

New Morning (Map pp96-8; ☎ 01 45 23 51 41; www.newmorning.com in French; 7-9 rue des Petites Écuries, 10e; metro Château d'Eau; admission €14.50-21; ☺ 8pm-2am) This informal auditorium hosts jazz concerts as well as blues, rock, funk, salsa, Afro-Cuban and Brazilian music three to seven nights a week at 9pm, with the second set ending at about 1am. Tickets (€18.30 to €22.80) are available at the box office (open 4.30pm to 7.30pm) and at the door.

Opus (Map pp96-8; ☎ 01 40 34 70 00; 167 quai de Valmy, 10e; metro Louis Blanc; admission free-€15; ☺ 8pm-2am Sun & Tue-Thu, 8pm-4am Fri & Sat) Located within a former officers' mess by the Canal St-Martin, this place has moved on from hip-hop to jazz, soul, blues, gospel and *zouk* (a blend of African and Latin American dance rhythms). It's a club-cum-concert venue and there are menus for €33 and €40 (obligatory Thursday to Saturday).

FRENCH CHANSONS

When French music comes to mind, most people hear accordions and *chansonniers* (cabaret singers) such as Edith Piaf, Jacques Brel, Georges Brassens and Léo Ferré. But although you may stumble upon buskers performing *chansons françaises* or playing *musette* (accordion music) in the market, it can sometimes be difficult to catch traditional French music in a more formal setting in Paris. We list a handful of venues where you're sure to hear it – both the traditional and the modern forms.

Au Lapin Agile (Map p108; ☎ 01 46 06 85 87; www .au-lapin-agile.com; 22 rue des Saules, 18e; metro Lamarck Caulaincourt; adult €24, students Sun & Tue-Fri only €17; ☯ 9pm-2am Tue-Sun) This rustic cabaret venue in Montmartre was favoured by artists and intellectuals in the early 20th century and *chansons* are still performed here and poetry read six nights a week starting at 9.30pm. Admission includes one drink.

Chez Adel (Map pp96-8; ☎ 01 42 08 24 61; 10 rue de la Grange aux Belles, 10e; metro Jacques Bonsergent; admission free; ☯ lunch & dinner to 2am Tue-Fri, noon-2am Sat & Sun) Chez Adel is a truly Parisian concept: Syrian hosts with guest *chansonniers* (as well as Gypsy, folk and world) performing most nights to a mixed and enthusiastic crowd.

Le Limonaire (Map pp96-8; ☎ 01 45 23 33 33; 18 cité Bergère, 9e; metro Grands Boulevards; admission free; ☯ 6pm-midnight Tue-Sun) This little wine bar is one of the best places to listen to traditional French bistro music, but come here only if you're serious about the genre; the crowd is almost reverential. Singers (who change regularly) perform at 10pm Tuesday to Saturday and at 7pm on Sunday.

Clubs

The clubs and other dancing venues that are favoured by the Parisian party people change frequently and many are officially private. Single men may not be admitted – even if their clothes are subculturally appropriate – simply because they're men on their own. Women, on the other hand, get in for free on some nights. It's always easier to get into the club of your choice during the week, when things may be hopping even more than they are at the weekend. Remember that Parisians tend to go out in groups and don't mingle as much as Anglo-Saxons do. The truly trendy crowd considers showing up before 1am a serious breach of good taste. Admission fees almost always include one alcoholic drink.

Paris is great for music (techno remains very popular) and there are some mighty fine DJs based here. Latino and Cuban salsa music is also huge. Theme nights at clubs are as common here as they are in, say, London so it's best to consult the sources mentioned earlier (see p160) before making plans

Les Bains (Map pp105-7; ☎ 01 48 87 01 80; www .lesbains-club.com in French; 7 rue du Bourg l'Abbé, 3e; metro Étienne Marcel; admission €16-20; ☯ 11pm-5am Mon-Sat) Housed in a refitted old Turkish hamman, 'The Baths' is still renowned for its surly, selective bouncers on the outside though celebrities and star-struck revellers are thinner on the ground inside. What happened to all the BMWs, Porsches and Rollers waiting at the kerb?

Le Balajo (Map pp102-4; ☎ 01 47 00 07 87; 9 rue de Lappe, 11e; metro Bastille; admission €8-17; ☯ 9-4.30pm Tue-Thu, 11pm-5.30am Fri & Sat, 3-7.30pm Sun) A mainstay of Parisian nightlife since 1936, this ancient ballroom is a bit lower shelf these days but still hosts a number of popular theme nights. Tuesday to Thursday is salsa and Latino music, on Friday and Saturday DJs play rock, disco, R 'n' B and house and from 3pm to 7.30pm on Sunday, DJs play old-fashioned musette (accordion music).

Le Batofar (Map pp90-2; ☎ 01 56 29 10 33; www .batofar.net in French; opposite 11 quai François Mauriac, 13e; metro Quai de la Gare or Bibliothèque; admission free-€12; ☯ 9pm-midnight Mon & Tue, 9 or 10pm-4, 5 or 6am Wed-Sun) What looks like an unassuming tug boat moored near the imposing Bibliothèque Nationale de France is a rollicking dancing spot that attracts some top international techno and funk DJ talent. Jazz concerts usually take place on Monday and Tuesday evening.

Le Cithéa (Map pp96-8; ☎ 01 40 21 70 95; 114 rue Oberkampf, 11e; metro Parmentier or Ménilmontant; admission free-€4; ☯ 5pm-5.30am Tue-Thu, 10pm-6.30am Fri & Sat) This popular and ever-hopping concert venue has bands playing soul, Latin and funk but especially world music and jazz, usually from 10.30pm, with DJs from 1am.

La Favela Chic (Map pp96-8; ☎ 01 40 21 38 14; www .favelachic.com in French; 18 rue du Faubourg du Temple, 10e; metro République; admission free; ☯ 7.30pm-2am Tue-Fri, 9.30pm-4am Sat) The ambience is more *favela* (shantytown) than chic in this restobar-cum-dancehall next to Gibus (following) where Brazilians and French alike get down to the frenetic mix of samba, *baile* funk and classic Brazilian pop.

Gibus (Map pp96-8; ☎ 01 47 00 78 88; www.gibus .fr in French; 18 rue du Faubourg du Temple, 11e; metro République; admission free-€18; ☯ 11pm-dawn Tue-Sat) Gibus, an enormously popular cave-like venue that is halfway between the Canal St-Martin and place de la République, has hard techno on Tuesday with Thermo Tek, acid and trance on Wednesday with Virtual Moon, and techno on Thursday with Parisjuana Night.

Le Nouveau Casino (Map pp96-8; ☎ 01 43 57 57 40; www.nouveaucasino.net in French; 109 rue Oberkampf, 11e; metro Parmentier; admission free-€18; ☺ 9pm or 11pm– btwn 2am & 6am) 'The New Casino' has made quite a splash since opening in 2000, with its electronic live music concerts and DJs. It has a huge dance floor and some pretty impressive acoustic and video systems.

Rex Club (Map pp96-8; ☎ 01 42 36 10 96; 5 blvd Poissonnière, 2e; metro Bonne Nouvelle; admission €8-13; ☺ 11.30pm-6am Wed-Sat) This huge club remains the hottest spot in town for house (Thursday and Saturday) and techno (Friday) and attracts Paris' top DJ talent.

Studio 287 (off Map pp90-2; ☎ 01 48 34 00 00; 33 av de la Porte d'Aubervilliers, 18e; metro Porte de la Chapelle; admission €10-16; ☺ 11pm-5am Tue-Thu, 11pm-noon Fri & Sat) The city's biggest dance club, with a capacity for 2000 gyrating and sweating bods, Studio 287 in the northern reaches of Paris may be a bit too commercial for some but Thursday's Studio 54 disco packs them in and Kit-Kat afters at the weekend often last till midday.

Le Wagg (Map pp105-7; ☎ 01 55 42 22 00; 62 rue Mazarine, 6e; metro Odéon; admission €10-12; ☺ 11pm-5am Wed-Sun) Clerkenwell meets St-Germain in the former Whisky a Go-go and now a UK-style Conran club. Dress light; the temperature rises considerably as the night wears on. Friday is house and electro.

Cabaret

Paris' risqué cabaret revues – those dazzling, pseudo-bohemian productions where the women all wear two beads and a feather (or was it two feathers and a bead?) – are about as representative of the Paris of the 21st century as crocodile-wrestling is of Australia or bronco-busting of the USA. But they continue to draw in the crowds as they did in the days of Toulouse-Lautrec and Aristide Bruant.

Crazy Horse (Map pp93-5; ☎ 01 47 23 32 32; www .lecrazyhorseparis.com; 12 av George V, 8e; metro Alma Marceau) This popular cabaret, whose dressing (or, rather, undressing) rooms were featured in Woody Allen's film *What's New Pussycat?* (1965), has been promoting what it calls *l'art du nu* (nudity) for over half a century. Shows (1¾ hours) are at 8.30pm and 11pm Sunday to Friday and at 7.30pm, 9.45pm and 11.50pm Saturday. Admission

(including two drinks) is €49/69/90 in the bar/mezzanine/orchestra and €110 in the orchestra with a half-bottle of champagne. Students are €29 with one drink.

Le Lido de Paris (Map pp93-5; ☎ 01 40 76 56 10; www .lido.fr; 116bis av des Champs-Élysées, 8e; metro George V) Founded at the close of WWII, the Lido gets top marks for its ambitious sets and the lavish costumes of its 70 artistes. Nightly shows cost €80 at 9.30pm and €60 (€80 on Friday and Saturday) at 11.30pm; €69 to watch from the bar (with two drinks). With dinner, entry to the 9.30pm show costs €140, €170 and €200, depending on the menu chosen, and includes a half-bottle of champagne per person.

Moulin Rouge (Map p108; ☎ 01 53 09 82 82; www .moulinrouge.fr; 82 blvd de Clichy, 18e; metro Blanche) This legendary cabaret founded in 1889, whose dancers appeared in Toulouse-Lautrec's celebrated posters, sits under its trademark red windmill (actually a 1925 copy of the 19th-century original). Champagne dinner shows (at 7pm) cost €130, €145 or €160. The show at 9pm with half a bottle of champers costs €92; at 11pm it drops to €82.

Sport

Parisians are mad about sport. For details of upcoming sporting events, consult the sports daily *L'Équipe* (€0.80; www.lequipe.fr in French) or *Figaroscope* (www.figaroscope .fr in French), an entertainment and activities supplement published with *Le Figaro* daily newspaper each Wednesday.

Most big international sporting events are held at the magnificent **Stade de France** (Map p182; ☎ 0 892 700 900; www.stadefrance .com; rue Francis de Pressensé, ZAC du Cornillon Nord, 93216 St-Denis La Plaine) at St-Denis, which was built for the 1998 World Cup.

FOOTBALL

France's home matches (friendlies and qualifiers for major championships) are held at the **Stade de France** (tickets €12 to €70).

The city's only top-division football team, **Paris-St-Germain** (☎ 01 47 43 71 71; www.psg.fr in French) plays its home games at the 45,500-seat **Parc des Princes** (Map pp90-2; ☎ 0 825 075 078; 24 rue du Commandant Guilbaud, 16e; metro Porte de St-Cloud; tickets €12-80; box office ☺ 9am-9pm Mon-Sat), near Stade Roland Garros. Tickets are also available at the more central **Boutique PSG** (Map pp93-5; ☎ 01 56 69 22 22; www.psg.fr in French; 27 av Champs Elysées, 8e; metro Franklin D Roosevelt;

PARIS

10am-7.45pm Mon-Thu, 10am-9.45pm Fri & Sat, noon-7.45pm Sun).

TENNIS

In late May/early June the tennis world focuses on the clay surface of the 16,500-seat **Stade Roland Garros** (Map pp90-2; ☎ 01 47 43 48 00, 01 47 43 52 52; www.frenchopen.org, www .rolandgarros.com; av Gordon Bennett, 16e; metro Porte d'Auteuil) in the Bois de Boulogne for Les Internationaux de France de Tennis (The French Open), the second of the four Grand Slam tournaments. Tickets are expensive and hard to come by; bookings must usually be made by the previous March at the latest.

The top indoor tournament is the Open de Tennis de la Ville de Paris (Paris Tennis Open), which usually takes place sometime in late October or early November at the **Palais Omnisports de Paris-Bercy** (Map pp102-4; ☎ 01 40 02 60 60; www.bercy.fr in French; 8 blvd de Bercy, 12e; metro Bercy). Tickets are available from the **box office** (☎ 0 892 390 490, from abroad ☎ 33-1 46 91 57 57; 11am-6pm Mon-Sat).

CYCLING

Since 1974 the final stage of the **Tour de France** (www.letour.fr), the world's most prestigious cycling event, has ended on the av des Champs-Élysées. The final day varies from year to year but is usually the 3rd or 4th Sunday in July, with the race finishing sometime in the afternoon. If you want to see this exciting event, find a spot at the barricades before noon.

Track cycling events, a sport at which France excels, are usually held in the *vélodrome* of the Palais Omnisports de Paris-Bercy.

HORSE RACING

One of the cheapest ways to spend a relaxing afternoon in the company of Parisians of all ages and backgrounds is to go to the races. The most accessible of the Paris areas' seven racecourses is **Hippodrome d'Auteuil** (Map pp90-2; ☎ 01 40 71 47 47; www.france-galop.com in French; Champ de Courses d'Auteuil, Bois de Boulogne, 16e; metro Porte d'Auteuil), in the southeastern corner of the Bois de Boulogne. It hosts steeplechases from February to late June/early July and early September to early December.

Races are held about six times a month (check the *France Galop* website for the exact days), with half a dozen or so heats

scheduled from 2pm to 5.30pm. There's no charge to stand on the *pelouse* (lawn) in the middle of the track but a seat in the *tribune* (stands) costs around €3/1.50 for adults/students and seniors on weekdays and €4/2 on Sunday; those under age 18 get in free. Race schedules are published in almost all national newspapers. If you read French, pick up a copy of *Paris Turf* (€1.15), the horse-racing daily.

Theatre

Almost all of Paris' theatre productions, including those written in other languages, are performed in French. There are a few English-speaking troupes around, though; look for ads on metro poster boards and in English-language periodicals such as *FUSAC* (p110), *Paris Voice* and *The Irish Eyes*, which are free at English-language bookshops, pubs, and so on, as well as the website www.parisfranceguide.com.

Comédie Française (Map pp105-7; ☎ 0 825 101 680; www.comedie-francaise.fr; place Colette, 1er; metro Palais Royal-Musée du Louvre; tickets €5-32; box office 11am-6pm Tue-Sat, 1-6pm Sun & Mon) Founded in 1680 during the reign of Louis XIV, the 'French Comedy' theatre bases its repertoire around works of the classic French playwrights such as Molière, Racine and Corneille, though in recent years contemporary and even non-French works have been staged. There are three venues: the main **Salle Richelieu** on place Colette just west of the Palais Royal; the **Comédie Française Studio Théâtre** (Map pp105-7; ☎ 01 44 58 98 58; Galerie du Carrousel du Louvre, 99 rue de Rivoli, 1; metro Palais Royal-Musée du Louvre; box office 1-5pm Wed-Mon); and the **Théâtre du Vieux Colombier** (Map pp99-101; ☎ 01 44 39 87 00; 21 rue du Vieux Colombier, 6e; metro St-Sulpice; box office 11am-6pm Tue-Sat, 1-6pm Sun & Mon). Discount tickets for 95 places near the ceiling (€5) go on sale one hour before curtain time (usually 8.30pm), which is when those aged under 27 years can purchase any of the better seats remaining for €7.50 to €10. The discount tickets are available from the window around the corner from the main entrance and facing place André Malraux.

Odéon-Théâtre de l'Europe (Map pp105-7; ☎ 01 44 41 36 36; www.theatre-odeon.fr; place de l'Odéon, 6e; metro Odéon) This huge, ornate theatre built in the early 1780s, often puts on foreign plays in their original languages (subtitled in French) and hosts theatre troupes from abroad. It was undergoing complete renovation until 2005 during which time plays were being staged at the **Ateliers Berthier** (Map pp90-2; ☎ 01 44 85 40 40; 8 blvd Berthier, 17e; metro Porte de Clichy; tickets €13-26; box office ✹ 11am-6.30pm Mon-Sat).

Point Virgule (Map pp105-7; ☎ 01 42 78 67 03; 7 rue Ste-Croix de la Bretonnerie, 4e; metro Hôtel de Ville; 1/2/3 shows €15/24/27, student Sun-Fri €12) The tiny 'Semicolon' is a popular comedy spot in the Marais offering café-theatre at its best – stand-up comics, performance artists and sometimes musical acts. The quality is variable but it's great fun nevertheless and the place has a reputation of discovering new talent. There are three shows daily at 8pm, 9.15pm and 10.30pm.

SHOPPING

Paris is a wonderful place to shop, whether you're someone who can afford an original Cartier diamond bracelet or you're an impoverished *lèche-vitrine* (literal meaning: 'window-licker') who just enjoys what you see from the outside looking in. From the ultrachic couture houses of av Montaigne and the cubby-hole boutiques of the Marais to the vast underground shopping centre at Les Halles and the flea-market bargains at St-Ouen, Paris is a city that knows how to make it, how to display it and how to charge for it.

Opening Hours

Opening times in Paris are notoriously anarchic, with each store setting its own hours. Most shops will be open at least from 10am to 6pm five days a week (including Saturday) but they may open earlier, close later, close for lunch (usually 1pm to 2 or 2.30pm) or for a full or half-day on Monday or Tuesday. In general, only shops in tourist areas (eg the Champs-Élysées and the Marais) open on Sunday. Many larger shops and department stores also have a *nocturne* – one late shopping night (usually to 10pm and on Thursday) a week.

Clothing & Fashion
HAUTE COUTURE & DESIGNER WEAR

Most of the major French couturiers and ready-to-wear designers have their own boutiques in the capital, but it's also possible to see labelled, ready-to-wear collections at major department stores such as Le Printemps, Galeries Lafayette and Le Bon Marché. The Right Bank, especially the so-called **Triangle d'Or** (Map pp93-5; metro Franklin D Roosevelt or Alma Marceau, 1er & 8e), **rue du Faubourg St-Honoré** (Map pp93-5; metro Madeleine or Concorde, 8e) and its eastern extension, **rue St-Honoré** (metro Tuileries), **place des Victoires** (Map pp96-8; metro Bourse or Sentier, 1er & 2e) and the Marais' **rue des Rosiers** (Map pp105-7; metro St-Paul, 4e), is traditionally the epicentre of Parisian fashion though **St-Germain** (Map pp105-7; metro St-Sulpice or S-Germain des Prés) on the Left Bank also boasts its fair share of boutiques.

FASHION EMPORIA

There are fashion shops offering creations and accessories from a variety of cutting-edge designers.

Abou Dhabi Bazar (Map pp105-7; ☎ 01 42 77 96 98; 10 rue des Francs Bourgeois, 3e; metro St-Paul; ✹ 2-7pm Sun & Mon, 10.30am-7.15pm Tue-Sat) This fashionable boutique with the odd name is a treasure-trove of smart and affordable ready-to-wear pieces from young designers including Paul & Joe, Isabel Marant and Vanessa Bruno.

Colette (Map pp93-5; ☎ 01 55 35 33 90; 213 rue St-Honoré, 1er; metro Tuileries; ✹ 10.30am-7.30pm Mon-Sat) This highly successful concept store is Japanese-inspired and has an exquisite selection of clothes, accessories and odds and ends. Featured designers include Alexander McQueen, Marko Matysik and Lulu Guinness but it doesn't stop there. Check out the limited edition Nike sneakers, Prada handbags, designer hairpins and cutting-edge clocks.

Kiliwatch (Map pp96-8; ☎ 01 42 21 17 37; 64 rue Tiquetonne, 2e; metro Étienne Marcel; ✹ 2-7pm Mon, 11am-7pm Tue-Sat) This enormous barn of a shop is filled with rack after rack of colourful, original street and club wear, plus a startling range of second-hand clothes and accessories in reasonable condition.

Réciproque (Map pp93-5; ☎ 01 47 04 30 28, 01 47 04 82 24; 88 & 95 rue de la Pompe, 16e; metro Rue de la Pompe; ✹ 11am-7pm Tue-Fri, 10.30am-7pm Sat) The biggest *dépôt-vente* (resale stores that sell used or barely used clothes and accessories from one-quarter to one-half off the original price) has rack after rack of Chanel suits as well as bits and pieces from Christian Lacroix, Hermès, Prada, Thierry Mugler, Issey Miyake, Christian Dior, John Galliano, Gucci and Dolce & Gabbana. It's an excellent place to pick up bags and shoes.

Department Stores

Paris boasts a number of *grands magasins* (department stores) including those listed here. *Soldes* (sales) are generally held in January and June/July.

Le Bon Marché (Map pp99-101; ☎ 01 44 39 80 00; www.bonmarche.fr; 24 rue de Sèvres, 7e; metro Sèvres Babylone; ☼ 9.30am-7pm Mon-Wed & Fri, 10am-9pm Thu, 9.30am-8pm Sat) Opened by Gustave Eiffel as Paris' first department store in 1852, 'The Good Market' (which also means 'bargain') is less frenetic than its rivals across the river, but no less chic. Men's as well as women's fashions are sold.

Galeries Lafayette (Map pp93-5; ☎ 01 42 82 34 56; www.galerieslafayette.com; 40 blvd Haussmann, 9e; metro Auber or Chaussée d'Antin; ☼ 9.30am-7.30pm Mon-Wed, Fri & Sat; 9.30am-9pm Thu) A vast *grand magasin* in two adjacent buildings, Galeries Lafayette features a wide selection of fashion and accessories. A fashion show (☎ 01 42 82 30 25 to book a seat) takes place at 11am every Tuesday year-round with another show at 2.30pm on Friday April to October.

Le Printemps (Map pp93-5; ☎ 01 42 82 50 00; www.printemps.com; 64 blvd Haussmann, 9e; metro Havre Caumartin; ☼ 9.35am-7pm Mon-Wed, Fri & Sat, 9.35am-10pm Thu) 'The Spring' (as in the season) is actually three separate stores – one each for women's fashion (De la Mode), one for men (De l'Homme) and one for beauty and household goods (De la Beauté et Maison) – offering a staggering display of perfume, cosmetics and accessories, as well as established and up-and-coming designer wear. There's a fashion show under the 7th-floor cupola at 10am on Tuesday.

La Samaritaine (Map pp105-7; ☎ 01 40 41 20 20; www.lasamaritaine.com; 19 rue de la Monnaie, 1er; metro Pont Neuf; ☼ 9.30am-7pm Mon-Wed & Fri, 9.30am-10pm Thu, 9.30am-8pm Sat) 'The Samaritan' is in two buildings between Pont Neuf and 142 rue de Rivoli, 1er. The main store's biggest draw is the outstanding view from the rooftop restaurant and café (p117); the building devoted to men's fashion has a large sports department in the basement.

Flea Markets

Paris' *marchés aux puces* (flea markets) can be great fun if you're in the mood to browse for unexpected diamonds in the rough through all the *brocante* (second-hand goods) and bric-a-brac on display. Some new items are also available, and a bit of bargaining is expected. Closing times depend on the season.

Marché aux Puces de Montreuil (Map pp90-2; av du Professeur André Lemière, 20e; metro Porte de Montreuil; ☼ 7.30 or 8am-6 or 7pm Sat-Mon) This flea market is renowned for its good-quality second-hand clothes and designer seconds. The 500 stalls also sell engravings, jewellery, linen, crockery, old furniture and appliances.

Marché aux Puces de la Porte de Vanves (Map pp90-2; av Georges Lafenestre & av Marc Sangnier, 14e; metro Porte de Vanves; ☼ 7am-6 or 7pm Sat & Sun) The Porte de Vanves flea market is the smallest and, some say, friendliest of the big three. Av Georges Lafenestre looks like a giant car-boot sale, with lots of 'curios' that aren't quite old (or curious) enough to qualify as antiques. Av Marc Sangnier is lined with stalls with new clothes, shoes, handbags and household items for sale.

Marché aux Puces de St-Ouen (Map pp90-2; www.les-puces.com; rue des Rosiers, av Michelet, rue Voltaire, rue Paul Bert & rue Jean-Henri Fabre, 18e; metro Porte de Clignancourt; ☼ 9am or 10am-7pm Sat-Mon) This vast flea market founded in the late 19th century and said to be Europe's largest has some 2500 stalls grouped into 10 *marchés* (market areas), each with its own speciality (eg Marché Serpette and Marché Biron for antiques, Marché Malik for second-hand clothing). Check the websites www.libertys .com and www.vernaison.net for further information.

Food & Wine

The food and wine shops of Paris are legendary and well worth seeking out. Many places will vacuum pack or shrink wrap certain food items to guard against spoilage.

Boutique Maille (Map pp93-5; ☎ 01 40 15 06 00; 6 place de la Madeleine, 8e; metro Madeleine; ☼ 10am-7pm Mon-Sat) This shop specialises in mustards, of which it stocks and/or can make up for you some two dozen different varieties.

Cacao et Chocolat (Map pp105-7; ☎ 01 46 33 77 63; 29 rue du Buci, 6e; metro Mabillon; ☼ 10.30am-7.30pm Mon-Sat, 11am-1.30pm & 2.30-7pm Sun) You have not tasted chocolate (a veritable religion in France) till you've tasted this stuff. 'Cocoa and Chocolate' is an exotic and contemporary take on chocolate, showcasing the cocoa bean in all its guises, both solid and liquid. The added citrus flavours, spices and even chilli are guaranteed to tease you back for more.

TO MARKET, TO MARKET...

Paris counts some five dozen *marchés découverts* (open-air markets) that pop up in public squares around the city two or three times a week and there are another 19 *marchés couverts* (covered markets) that keep more regular hours: 8am to 1pm and 3.30pm or 4pm to 7pm or 7.30pm from Tuesday to Saturday and till lunchtime on Sunday. Completing the picture are numerous independent *rues commerçantes*, pedestrian streets where the shops set up outdoor stalls. To find out when there's a market near your hotel or hostel, ask the staff or anyone who lives in the neighbourhood.

The following are favourite Paris markets rated according to the variety of their produce, their ethnicity and the neighbourhood. They are *la crème de la crème*.

Marché Bastille (Map pp102-4; blvd Richard Lenoir, 11e; metro Bastille; ☺ 7am or 8am-1pm Tue & Sun) Stretching as far north as Richard Lenoir metro station, this is arguably the best roving street market in Paris.

Marché Belleville (Map pp96-8; blvd de Belleville btwn rue Jean-Pierre Timbaud & rue du Faubourg du Temple, 11e & 20e; metro Belleville or Couronne; ☺ 7am or 8am-1pm Tue & Fri) This market offers a fascinating (and easy) entry into the large, vibrant ethnic communities of the *quartiers de l'est* (eastern neighbourhoods), home to African, Middle Eastern and Asian immigrants as well as artists and students.

Rue Cler (Map pp99-101; metro École Militaire; ☺ 7am or 8am-7pm or 7.30pm Tue-Sat, 8am-noon Sun) This street in the 7e is a breath of fresh air in a sometimes stuffy *quartier* and can almost feel like a party at the weekend when the whole neighbourhood turns out en masse to squeeze, pay and cart away.

Marché aux Enfants Rouges (Map pp105-7; 39 rue de Bretagne, 3e; metro Temple or Arts et Métiers; ☺ 8am-1pm & 4-7.30pm Tue-Sat, 8am-1pm Sun) This recently reopened covered market south of place de la République has both ethnic (Italian, North African etc) stalls as well as French ones.

Rue Montorgueil (Map pp96-8; rue Montorgueil btwn rue de Turbigo & rue Réaumur, 2e; metro Les Halles or Sentier; ☺ 7am or 8am-7pm or 7.30pm Tue-Sat, 8am-noon Sun) This is the closest market to Paris' 700-year-old wholesale market, Les Halles, which was moved from this area to the southern suburb of Rungis in 1969.

Rue Mouffetard (Map pp102-4; rue Mouffetard around rue de l'Arbalète; metro Censier Daubenton or Place Monge; ☺ 7am or 8am-7pm or 7.30pm Tue-Sat, 8am-noon Sun) Rue Mouffetard is the city's most photogenic market street – the place where Parisians send tourists.

Marché St-Quentin (Map pp96-8; 85 blvd de Magenta, 10e; metro Gare de l'Est; ☺ 8am-1pm & 3.30-7.30pm Tue-Sat, 8am-1pm Sun) This iron-and-glass covered market built in 1866 is a maze of corridors lined mostly with gourmet food stalls.

Les Caves Augé (Map pp93-5; ☎ 01 45 22 16 97; 116 blvd Haussmann, 8e; metro St-Augustin; ☺ 1-7.30pm Mon, 9am-7.30pm Tue-Sat) 'The Augé Cellars' should be the *marchand de vin* (wine shop) for you if you're following the advice of Marcel Proust. It's now under the stewardship of a passionate and knowledgeable *sommelier*.

Fauchon (Map pp93-5; ☎ 01 47 62 60 11; 26-30 place de la Madeleine, 8e; metro Madeleine; ☺ 8.30am-7pm Mon-Sat) Paris' most famous caterer has six departments in two buildings selling the most incredibly mouth-watering delicacies from pâté de foie gras to designer *confiture* (jam). Fruit – the most perfect you've ever seen – includes exotic items from Southeast Asia (mangosteens, rambutans etc).

Fromagerie Alléosse (Map pp93-5; ☎ 01 46 22 50 45; 13 rue Poncelet, 17e; metro Termes; ☺ 9am-1pm & 4-7pm Tue-Sat, 9am-1pm Sun) This is without a doubt the best cheese shop in Paris and well worth a trip across town.

La Petite Scierie (Map pp105-7; ☎ 01 55 42 14 88; 60 rue St-Louis en l'Île, 4e; metro Pont Marie; ☺ 11am-8pm) This little hole-in-the-wall sells every edible produced by and made from ducks, with the emphasis on foie gras (€30 for 180g).

Les Ruchers du Roy (Map pp105-7; ☎ 01 42 72 02 96; 37 rue du Roi de Sicile, 4e; metro St-Paul; ☺ 11am-1pm & 3-8pm Tue-Sun) 'The Apiaries of the King' sells dozens of types of honey and apiarian products fit for a king.

Gifts & Souvenirs

Paris has a huge number of speciality shops offering gift items.

Anna Joliet (Map pp96-8; ☎ 01 42 96 55 13; passage du Perron, 9 rue de Beaujolais, 1er; metro Pyramides; ☺ 10am-7pm Mon-Sat) This wonderful (and tiny) shop at the northern end of the Jardin du Palais Royal specialises in music boxes, both new and old. Just open the door and see if you aren't tempted in.

CSAO Boutique (Map pp105-7; ☎ 01 44 54 55 88; 1-3 rue Elzévir, 3e; metro St-Paul or Chemin Vert; ☽ 11am-7pm Tue-Fri, 11am-7.30pm Sat, 2-7pm Sun) This wonderful gallery and shop distributes the work of African artists and craftspeople. Many of the colourful fabrics and weavings are exquisite and the handmade recycled items – small watering cans from old tuna tins, handbags and caps from soft-drink cans, lamp shades from tomato paste tins – are both amusing and heartbreaking.

E Dehillerin (Map pp105-7; ☎ 01 42 36 53 13; 18-20 rue Coquillière, 1er; metro Les Halles; ☽ 8am-12.30pm & 2-6pm Mon, 8am-6pm Tue-Sat) Spread over two floors and dating back to 1820, E Dehillerin carries the most incredible selection of professional-quality *matériel de cuisine* (kitchenware) in the world. You're sure to find something even the most well-equipped kitchen is lacking.

Mélodies Graphiques (Map pp105-7; ☎ 01 42 74 57 68; 10 rue du Pont Louis-Philippe, 4e; metro Pont Marie; ☽ 2-7pm Mon, 11am-7pm Tue-Sat) 'Graphic Melodies' carries all sorts of items made from exquisite Florentine *papier à cuve* (paper hand-decorated with marbled designs). There are several other fine stationery shops along the same street.

Musée & Compagnie (Map pp90-2; ☎ 01 40 02 98 72; 40-42 Cour St-Émilion, 12e; metro Cour St-Émilion; ☽ 11am-9pm) This large shop sells top-end copies of all those knickknacks and dust-collectors you admired in the museum but couldn't have: Mona Lisa, Venus de Milo, Celtic jewellery and so on. All fakes, of course – but good ones.

GETTING THERE & AWAY

For information on the transport options between the city and Paris' airports, see opposite. For information on international air links to Paris, see p914.

Air
AÉROPORT D'ORLY

Orly (ORY; Map p179; ☎ 01 49 75 15 15, flight info ☎ 0 892 681 515; www.adp.fr), the older and smaller of Paris' two major international airports, is 18km south of the city. Air France and some other international carriers (eg Iberia and TAP Air Portugal) use Orly-Ouest (the west terminal). A driverless overhead train linking Orly-Ouest with Orly-Sud, which is part of the Orlyval system, functions as a free shuttle between the terminals.

AÉROPORT PARIS-BEAUVAIS

The international airport at **Beauvais** (BVA; off Map p179; ☎ 03 44 11 46 86; www.aeroportbeauvais .com), 80km north of Paris, is used by charter companies and discount airline Ryanair for its European flights, including those between Paris and Dublin, Shannon and Glasgow.

AÉROPORT ROISSY CHARLES DE GAULLE

Roissy Charles de Gaulle (CDG; Map p179; ☎ 01 48 62 22 80, 0 892 681 515; www.adp.fr), 30km northeast of Paris in the suburb of Roissy, consists of three terminal complexes, appropriately named Aérogare 1, 2 and 3. Aérogares 1 and 2 are used by international and domestic carriers. Aérogare 3 is used mainly by charter companies.

AIRLINE OFFICES

Contacts for airline offices in Paris can be found in the *Yellow Pages* under 'Transports aériens', among them:

Aer Lingus (☎ 01 70 20 00 72; www.aerlingus.com)
Air Canada (☎ 0 825 880 881; www.aircanada.com)
Air France (☎ arrivals 0 820 820 820, departures ☎ 0 892 681 048; www.airfrance.com)
Air New Zealand (☎ 01 40 53 82 83; www.airnz.com)
British Airways (☎ 0 825 825 400; www.british airways.com)
British Midland (☎ 01 41 91 87 04; www.flybmi.com)
Continental Airlines (☎ 01 42 99 09 09; www .continental.com)
Delta Air Lines (☎ 0 800 354 080; www.delta.com)
easyJet (☎ 0 825 082 508; www.easyjet.com)
Northwest Airlines (☎ 0 890 710 710; www.klm.com)
Qantas Airways (☎ 0 820 820 500; www.qantas.com)
Ryanair (☎ 0 892 682 073; www.ryanair.com)
United Airlines (☎ 0 810 727 272; www.ual.com)
US Airways (☎ 0 810 632 222; www.usairways.com)
Virgin Atlantic (☎ 0 800 528 528; www.virgin-atlantic .com)

Bus
DOMESTIC

Because French transport policy is biased in favour of the excellent state-owned rail system, **Société Nationale des Chemins de Fer Français** (SNCF), the country has extremely limited inter-regional bus services and there are no internal intercity bus services to or from Paris.

INTERNATIONAL

Eurolines (p917) links Paris with destinations in all parts of Western and Central Europe,

Scandinavia and Morocco. The main **Eurolines office** (Map pp105-7; ☎ 01 43 54 11 99, 0 892 899 091; www.eurolines.fr; 55 rue St-Jacques, 5e; metro Cluny-La Sorbonne; ⏰ 9.30am-6.30pm Mon-Fri, 10am-1pm & 2-6pm Sat) books seats and sells tickets. The **Gare Routière Internationale de Paris-Gallieni** (Map pp90-2; ☎ 0 892 899 091; 28 av du Général de Gaulle; metro Gallieni), the city's international bus terminal, is in the inner suburb of Bagnolet.

Train

SNCF (www.sncf.fr; ☎ 0 892 353 535) mainline train information is available round the clock.

Paris has six major train stations, each of which handles passenger traffic to different parts of France and Europe and also has a metro station bearing its name. For more information on the breakdown of regional responsibility of trains from each station, see the ferries and train map (p918).

Gare d'Austerlitz (Map pp102-4; blvd de l'Hôpital, 13e; metro Gare d'Austerlitz) Spain and Portugal; Loire Valley and non-TGV trains to southwestern France (eg Bordeaux and Basque Country).

Gare de l'Est (Map pp96-8; blvd de Strasbourg, 10e; metro Gare de l'Est) Luxembourg, parts of Switzerland (Basel, Lucerne, Zurich), southern Germany (Frankfurt, Munich) and points further east; areas of France east of Paris (Champagne, Alsace and Lorraine).

Gare de Lyon (Map pp102-4; blvd Diderot, 12e; metro Gare de Lyon) Parts of Switzerland (eg Bern, Geneva, Lausanne), Italy and points beyond; regular and TGV Sud-Est trains to areas southeast of Paris, including Dijon, Lyon, Provence, the Côte d'Azur and the Alps.

Gare Montparnasse (Map pp99-101; av du Maine & blvd de Vaugirard, 15e; metro Montparnasse Bienvenüe) Brittany and places en route from Paris (eg Chartres, Angers, Nantes), TGV Atlantique trains to Tours, Nantes, Bordeaux and other destinations in southwestern France.

Gare du Nord (Map pp96-8; rue de Dunkerque, 10e; metro Gare du Nord) UK, Belgium, northern Germany, Scandinavia, Moscow etc (terminus of the high-speed Thalys trains to/from Amsterdam, Brussels, Cologne and Geneva and Eurostar to London); trains to the northern suburbs of Paris and northern France, including TGV Nord trains to Lille and Calais.

Gare St-Lazare (Map pp93-5; rue St-Lazare & rue d'Amsterdam, 8e; metro St-Lazare) Normandy (eg Dieppe, Le Havre, Cherbourg).

GETTING AROUND
To/From the Airports
AÉROPORT D'ORLY

There a half-dozen public-transport options to get to and from Orly airport. Apart from

RATP bus No 183, all services call at both terminals. Tickets for the bus services are sold on board. With certain exceptions, children between the ages of two and 11 pay half price. You can also choose to go by shuttle van and taxi.

Air France Bus No 1 (☎ 0 892 350 820; www.cars-airfrance.com in French; one way/return €7.50/12.75; every 15min 6am-11.30pm to Paris, 5.45am-11pm to Orly; journey time 30-45min) This *navette* (shuttle bus) runs to/from the eastern side of Gare Montparnasse (Map pp99-101; rue du Commandant René Mouchotte, 15e; metro Montparnasse Bienvenüe) as well as Aérogare des Invalides (Map pp99-101; metro Invalides) in the 7e. On your way into the city, you can ask to get off at metro Porte d'Orléans or metro Duroc.

Jetbus (☎ 01 69 01 00 09; €5.15; every 15-20min 6.43am-10.49pm to Paris, 6.15am-10.15pm to Orly; journey time 55min) With the exception of RATP bus No 183, Jetbus is the cheapest way to get to/from Orly. It runs to/from metro Villejuif Louis Aragon, which is a bit south of the 13e on the city's southern fringe. From there a regular metro/bus ticket will get you into the centre of Paris.

Orlybus (☎ 0 892 687 714; €5.70; every 15-20min 6am-11.30pm to Paris, 5.35am-11pm to Orly; journey time 30min) This RATP bus runs to/from metro Denfert Rochereau (Map pp90-2) in the 14e and makes several stops in the eastern 14e in each direction.

Orlyval (☎ 0 892 687 714; €8.80 to/from Paris, €10.65 to/from La Défense; every 4-12min 6am-11pm each direction; journey time 33min to Paris, 50min to La Défense) This RATP service links Orly with the city centre via a shuttle train and the RER (p173). A driverless shuttle train runs between the airport and Antony RER station (eight minutes) on RER line B, from where it's an easy journey into the city; to get to Antony from the city (26 minutes), take line B4 towards St-Rémy-lès-Chevreuse. Orlyval tickets are valid for travel on the RER and for metro travel within the city.

RATP Bus No 183 (☎ 0 892 687 714; €1.30 or 1 metro/ bus ticket; every 35min 5.35am-8.35pm each direction; journey time 1hr) This is a is a slow public bus that links Orly-Sud (only) with metro Porte de Choisy (Map pp90-2), at the southern edge of the 13e.

RER C (☎ 0 890 361 010; €5.35; every 12-20min 5.45am-11pm each direction; journey time 50min) An Aéroports de Paris (ADP) shuttle bus links the airport with RER line C at Pont de Rungis-Aéroport d'Orly RER station. From the city, take a C2 train towards Pont de Rungis or Massy-Palaiseau. Tickets are valid for onward travel on the metro.

Along with public transport the following private options are available:
Allô Shuttle (☎ 01 34 29 00 80; www.alloshuttle.com)
Paris Airports Service (☎ 01 46 80 14 67; www.paris airportservice.com)

Shuttle Van PariShuttle (☎ 0 800 699 699; www .parishuttle.com)

World Shuttle (☎ 01 46 80 14 67; www.world -shuttles.com)

These companies all provide door-to-door service for about €25 for a single person (from about €15 to €18 per person for two or more). Book in advance and allow for numerous pick-ups and drop-offs. Some readers have written to say that some shuttle-van services are less than reliable.

A taxi between central Paris and Orly will cost about €40 and take 20 to 30 minutes

AÉROPORT ROISSY CHARLES DE GAULLE

Roissy Charles de Gaulle has two train sta-tions: Aéroport Charles de Gaulle 1 (CDG1) and the sleek Aéroport Charles de Gaulle 2 (CDG2). Both are served by commuter trains on RER line B3. A free shuttle bus links all of the terminals with the train stations.

There are various public-transport options for travel between Aéroport Roissy Charles de Gaulle and Paris. Tickets for the bus services are sold on board. With certain exceptions, children between age two and 11 pay half-price. As for Orly, shuttle vans and taxis are also available.

Air France bus No 2 (☎ 0 892 350 820; www.cars -airfrance.com in French; one way/return €10/17; every 15min 5.45am-11pm each direction; journey time 35-50min) Air France bus No 2 links the airport with two locations on the Right Bank: near the Arc de Triomphe just outside 2 av Carnot, 17e (Map pp93-5; metro Charles de Gaulle-Étoile) and the Palais des Congrès de Paris (Map pp93-5; blvd Gouvion St-Cyr, 17e; metro Porte Maillot).

Air France bus No 4 (☎ 0 892 350 820; www.cars-air france.com in French; one way/return €11.50/19.55; every 30min to Paris 7am-9pm, to Roissy Charles de Gaulle 7am-9.30pm; journey time 45-55min) Air France bus No 4 links the airport with Gare de Lyon (Map pp102-4; 20bis blvd Diderot, 12e; metro Gare de Lyon) and with the Gare Montparnasse (Map pp99-101; rue du Commandant René Mouchotte, 15e; metro Montparnasse Bienvenüe).

RATP Bus No 350 (☎ 0 892 687 714; €3.90 or 3 metro/ bus tickets; every 30min 5.45am-7pm each direction; journey time 1¼hr) This public bus links Aérogares 1 & 2 with Gare de l'Est (Map pp96-8; rue du 8 Mai 1945, 10e; metro Gare de l'Est) and with Gare du Nord (Map pp96-8; 184 rue du Faubourg St-Denis, 10e; metro Gare du Nord).

RATP Bus No 351 (☎ 0 892 687 714; €3.90 or 3 metro/bus tickets; every 30min 6am-9.30pm to Paris, 6am-8.20pm to Roissy Charles de Gaulle; journey time 55min) This public bus links the eastern side of place de la Nation

(Map pp90-2; av du Trône, 11e; metro Nation) with the Roissy Charles de Gaulle.

RER B (☎ 0 890 361 010; €7.75; every 4-15min 4.56am-11.40pm in each direction; journey time 30min) RER line B3 links CDG1 and CDG2 with the city. To get to the airport take any RER line B train whose four-letter destination code begins with E (eg EIRE) and a shuttle bus (every five to eight minutes) will ferry you to the appropriate terminal. Regular metro ticket windows can't always sell RER tickets as far as the airport so you may have to buy one at the RER station where you board.

Roissybus (☎ 0 892 687 714; €8.20; every 15-20min 5.45am-11pm in each direction; journey time 60min) This public bus links both terminals with rue Scribe (Map pp93-5; metro Opéra) behind the Palais Garnier in the 9e.

The four shuttle-van companies listed in the Orly section (p171) will take you from Roissy Charles de Gaulle to your hotel for €25 for a single person or €15 to €18 for two or more people. Book in advance.

Taxis to/from the city centre cost from €40 to €55, depending on the traffic and time of day.

BETWEEN ORLY & ROISSY

Air France bus No 3 (☎ 0 892 350 820; www.cars -airfrance.com in French; €15.50; every 30min 6am-10.30pm; journey time 50-60min) runs between Orly and Roissy Charles de Gaulle and is free for connecting Air France passengers.

The taxi fare from one airport to the other should cost around €56. Count on one hour's travel time.

AÉROPORT PARIS-BEAUVAIS

An **express bus** (☎ 0 892 682 064; ⏱ 8.40am-10.10pm to Paris, 5.45am-7.15pm to Beauvais; journey time 1-1¼hr) leaves Parking Pershing (Map pp93-5; 1 blvd Pershing, 17e; metro Porte Maillot) just west of Palais des Congrès de Paris three hours before Ryanair departures (you can board up to 15 minutes before) and leaves the airport 20 to 30 minutes after each arrival, dropping off just south of Palais des Congrès on Place de la Porte Maillot. Tickets can be bought from the **Ryanair** (☎ 03 44 11 41 41) counter at the airport or from a kiosk in the parking lot.

A taxi between central Paris and Beauvais will cost Paris €110 during the day and €150 at night and all day Sunday.

Boat

From late March to October, a river shuttle called **Batobus** (☎ 01 44 11 33 99; www.batobus.com;

1-day pass adult/2-6 yrs, €11/6, 2-day pass €13/7; every 25min 10am-7pm late Mar-May & Oct, 10am-9pm Jun-Sep) docks at the following eight locations. As you can jump on and off at will, Batobus can be used as a form of transport.

Champs-Élysées (Map pp93-5; port des Champs-Élysées, 8e; metro Champs-Élysées Clemenceau)

Eiffel Tower (Map pp99-101; port de la Bourdonnais, 7e; metro Champ de Mars-Tour Eiffel)

Hôtel de Ville (Map pp105-7; quai de l'Hôtel de Ville, 4e; metro Hôtel de Ville)

Jardin des Plantes (Map pp102-4; quai St-Bernard, 5e; metro Jussieu)

Musée d'Orsay (Map pp99-101; quai de Solférino, 7e; metro Musée d'Orsay)

Musée du Louvre (Map pp105-7; quai du Louvre, 1er; metro Palais Royal-Musée du Louvre)

Notre Dame (Map pp105-7; quai Montebello, 5e; metro St-Michel)

St-Germain des Prés (Map pp105-7; quai Malaquais, 6e; metro St-Germain des Prés)

Car & Motorcycle

While driving in Paris is nerve-racking, it is not impossible, except for the faint-hearted or indecisive. The fastest way to get across the city by car is usually via blvd Périphérique (Map pp90-2), the ring road that encircles the city.

In many parts of Paris you pay €1.50 or €2 an hour to park your car on the street. Large municipal parking garages usually charge €2.60 an hour and between €20 and €23 for 24 hours.

Parking fines are €11 to €33, depending on the offence and its gravity, and parking attendants dispense them with great abandon. You pay them by purchasing a *timbre amende* (fine stamp) for the amount written on the ticket from any *tabac* (tobacconist), affixing the stamp to the pre-addressed coupon and dropping it in a letter box.

RENTAL

You can get a small car (eg a Renault Twingo) for one day, without insurance and 250km mileage, from around €71 with Budget. Most of the larger companies listed below have offices at the airports and several are also represented at **Aérogare des Invalides** (Map pp99-101; metro Invalides) in the 7e.

Avis (☎ 0 802 050 505; www.avis.fr)

Budget (☎ 0 825 003 564; www.budget.fr in French)

Europcar (☎ 0 825 358 358; www.europcar.fr in French)

Hertz (☎ 0 825 861 861; www.hertz.fr)

Smaller agencies can offer much more attractive deals. For example, Rent A Car Système has an economical-class car for from €30 per day and €0.30 per kilometre, €45/69 a day with 100/300km, €90 for a weekend with 500km and €199 for seven days with 800km. The companies below offer reasonable rates; for a wider selection check the *Yellow Pages* under 'Location d'Automobiles: Tourisme et Utilitaires'. It's a good idea to reserve at least three days ahead, especially for holiday weekends and during the summer.

ADA (☎ 0 825 169 169; www.ada-location.com in French); 8e arrondissement branch (Map pp93-5; ☎ 01 42 93 65 13; 72 rue de Rome, 8e; metro Rome); 11e arrondissement branch (Map pp96-8; ☎ 01 48 06 58 13; 34 av de la République, 11e; metro Parmentier) ADA has a dozen bureaus in Paris.

easyCar (www.easycar.com); Montparnasse branch (Map pp99-101; Parking Gaîté, 33 rue du Commandant René Mouchotte, 15e; metro Gaîté); place Vendôme branch (Map pp93-5; ☎ /fax 01 40 15 60 17; metro Tuileries or Opéra) Britain's budget car-rental agency hires mini Mercedes from €13 a day plus extras and Smart cars (from €8). Both branches are in underground car parks and are fully automated systems; you must book in advance and fill in all the forms online on location.

Rent A Car Système (☎ 0 891 700 200; www.rentacar .fr); Gare du Nord branch (Map pp96-8; ☎ 01 42 80 31 31; 2 rue de Compiègne, 10e; metro Gare du Nord); Bercy branch (Map pp102-4; ☎ 01 43 45 98 99; 79 rue de Bercy, 12e; metro Bercy); 16e arrondissement branch (Map pp90-2; ☎ 01 42 88 40 04; 84 av de Versailles, 16e; metro Mirabeau) Rent A Car has 16 outlets in Paris.

Public Transport

Paris' public transit system, most of which is operated by the **RATP** (Régie Autonome des Transports Parisians; in French ☎ 0 892 687 714, in English ☎ 0 892 684 114; www.ratp.fr in French; ☒ 6am-9pm), is one of the cheapest and most efficient in the Western world.

Transport maps of various sizes and degrees of detail are available for free at metro ticket windows. RATP's *Paris 1* provides plans of metro, RER, bus and tram routes in central Paris; *Paris 2* superimposes the same plans over street maps; and *Île-de-France 3* covers the area surrounding Paris. For itineraries, traffic and so on, log onto www.citefutee.com (French only).

BUS

Paris' bus system, also operated by the RATP, runs between 5.45am and 12.30am Monday to Saturday. Services are drastically reduced on Sunday and public holidays (when buses run from 7am to 8.30pm) and from 8.30pm to 12.30am daily when a *service en soirée* (evening service) of 20 buses – distinct from the Noctambus overnight services described below – goes into operation.

Fares

Short bus rides (ie rides in one or two bus zones) cost one metro/bus ticket; longer rides require two tickets. Transfer to other buses or the metro is not allowed on the same ticket. Travel to the suburbs costs up to three tickets, depending on the zone. Special tickets valid only on the bus can be purchased from the driver.

Whatever kind of single-journey ticket you have, you must cancel *(oblitérer)* it in the *composteur* (cancelling machine) next to the driver. If you have a Carte Orange, Mobilis or Paris Visite pass, just flash it at the driver when you board. Do not cancel your magnetic coupon accompanying your pass.

A single ride on a Noctambus costs €2.60 and allows one immediate transfer onto another night bus. Noctambus services are free if you have a Carte Orange, Mobilis or Paris Visite pass for the zones in which you are travelling.

Night Buses

After the metro lines have finished their last runs at about 1am, the Noctambus network of night buses lines links the place du Châtelet (1er) and av Victoria just west of the Hôtel de Ville (Map pp105-7) in the 4e with most parts of the city and the suburbs. Look for the symbol of a little black owl silhouetted against a yellow quarter moon. All 18 Noctambus lines depart every hour weekdays and every half-hour at the weekend from 1am to 5.30am daily.

METRO & RER

Paris' underground network consists of two separate but interlinked systems: the **Métropolitain**, known as the *métro*, with 14 lines and 372 stations; and the **RER** (Réseau Express Régional), a network of suburban lines designated A to E and then numbered that pass through the city centre. In this book, the term 'metro' is used to cover both the Métropolitain and the RER system within Paris proper.

Fares

The same RATP tickets are valid on the metro, the RER (for travel within the city limits), buses, the Montmartre funicular and Paris' two tram lines. They cost €1.30 if bought individually and €10 (€5 for children aged four to 11) for a carnet of 10. Tickets are sold at all metro stations, though not always at every entrance. Ticket windows and vending machines accept most credit cards.

One metro/bus ticket lets you travel between any two metro stations for a period of two hours, no matter how many transfers are required. You can also use it on the RER for travel within zone 1. However, a single ticket cannot be used to transfer from the metro to a bus, from a bus to the metro or between buses.

Always keep your ticket until you exit from your station; you may be stopped by a *contrôleur* (ticket inspector) and will have to pay a fine (€20 to €40 on the spot) if you are found to be without a ticket or are holding an invalid one.

Metro Network

Each metro train is known by the name of its terminus. On maps and plans each line has a different colour and number (from 1 to 14).

Blue-on-white directional signs in metro and RER stations indicate the way to the correct platform for your line. On lines that split into several branches (eg line Nos 3, 7 and 13), the terminus served by each train is indicated on the cars with back-lit panels.

Older black-on-orange *correspondance* (transfer) signs and newer ones listing the lines in their individual colours show how to reach connecting trains. In general, the more lines that stop at a station, the longer the transfer will take – and some (eg those at Châtelet and Montparnasse Bienvenüe) are very long indeed.

White-on-blue *sortie* signs indicate the station exits from which you have to choose. You can get your bearings by checking the *plan du quartier* (neighbourhood map) posted at each exit.

The last metro train on each line begins its run sometime between 12.35am and 1.04am. The metro starts up again around 5.30am.

RER Network

The RER is faster than the metro, but the stops are much further apart. Some of Paris'

PARIS

UNDERGROUND ART

Few underground railway systems are as convenient, as reasonably priced or, at the better stations, more elegant than the Paris one. The following list is just a sample of the most interesting stations from an artistic perspective. The specific platform is mentioned for those stations served by more than one line.

Abbesses (Map p108; line No 12) The noodle-like pale-green metalwork and glass canopy of the station entrance is one of the finest examples of the work of Hector Guimard (1867–1942), the best-known French Art Nouveau architect, whose signature style once graced most metro stations.

Arts et Métiers (Map pp96-8; line No 11 platform) The copper panelling, portholes and mechanisms of this station recall Jules Verne, Captain Nemo and the nearby Musée des Arts et Métiers.

Bastille (Map pp102-4; line No 5 platform) A large ceramic fresco features scenes taken from newspaper engravings published during the Revolution.

Bibliothèque François Mitterrand (Map pp90-2; line No 14) This enormous station – all screens, steel and glass, and the terminus of the high-speed Météor line that opened in 1998 – resembles a high-tech cathedral.

Carrefour Pleyel (Map p182; line No 13) This station just south of St-Denis, and named in hour of composer and piano-maker Ignace Joseph Pleyel (1757–1831), has been reconfigured as a 'contemporary musical instrument', with the rumble of the trains the 'music' and no doubt commuters the 'picks'.

Cluny-La Sorbonne (Map pp105-7; line No 10 platform) A large ceramic mosaic replicates the signatures of intellectuals, artists and scientists from the Latin Quarter through history.

Concorde (Map pp93-5; line No 12 platform) On the walls of the station, what look like children's building blocks in white and blue ceramic are 45,000 tiles spelling out the text of the *Déclaration des Droits de l'Homme et du Citoyen* (Declaration of the Rights of Man and of the Citizen), the document setting forth the principles of the French Revolution.

Louvre-Rivoli (Map pp105-7; line No 1 platform & corridor) Statues, bas-reliefs and photographs offer a small taste of what to expect at the Musée du Louvre above ground.

Palais Royal-Musée du Louvre (Map pp105-7) The unusual modern entrance on the place du Palais Royal, a kind of back-to-the-future look at the Guimard works and designed by young artist Jean-Michel Othoniel, is made up of 800 red, blue, amber and violet glass balls and resembles a crown.

Parmentier (Map pp96-8; line No 3) The theme in this station is agricultural crops, particularly the potato since it was the station's namesake, Antoine-Auguste Parmentier (1737–1817), who brought the potato into fashion in France.

Pont Neuf (Map pp105-7; line No 7) With the old mint and the Musée de la Monnaie de Paris just above, the focus here is on coins: obsolete francs and all-too-current euros.

---

attractions, particularly those on the Left Bank (eg the Musée d'Orsay, Eiffel Tower and Panthéon), can be reached far more conveniently by the RER than by metro.

RER lines are known by an alphanumeric combination – the letter (A to E) refers to the line, the number to the spur it will follow somewhere out in the suburbs. As a rule of thumb, even-numbered RER lines head for Paris' southern or eastern suburbs while odd-numbered ones go north or west. All trains whose four-letter codes (indicated both on the train and on the light board) begin with the same letter share the same terminus. Stations served are usually indicated on electronic destination boards above the platform.

Suburban Services
The RER and **SNCF commuter lines** (☎ 0 891 362 020, 0 891 676 869; www.sncf.fr) serve suburban destinations outside the city limits (ie zones

2 to 8). Buy your ticket *before* you board the train or you won't be able to get out of the station when you arrive. You are not allowed to pay the additional fare when you get there.

If you are issued with a full-sized SNCF ticket for travel to the suburbs, validate it in one of the time-stamp pillars *before* you board the train. You may also be given a *contremarque magnétique* (magnetic ticket) to get through any metro/RER-type turnstiles on the way to/from the platform. If you are travelling on a multizone Carte Orange, Paris Visite or Mobilis pass, do *not* punch the magnetic coupon in one of SNCF's time-stamp machines. Most – but not all – RER/SNCF tickets purchased in the suburbs for travel to the city allow you to continue your journey by metro.

For some destinations, a ticket can be purchased at any metro ticket window; for others you'll have to go to an RER station on the line you need in order to buy a ticket.

TOURIST PASSES

The rather pricey Mobilis and Paris Visite passes are valid on the metro, the RER, the SNCF's suburban lines, buses, night buses, trams and the Montmartre funicular railway. They do not require a photo but you should write your card number on the ticket. They can be purchased at larger metro and RER stations, at SNCF offices in Paris and at the airports.

The Mobilis card and its coupon allows unlimited travel for one day in two to eight zones (€5.20 to €18.30). It is available at all metro and RER ticket windows as well as SNCF stations in the Paris region but you would have to make at least six metro trips in a day (based on the carnet price) in zones 1 and 2 to break even on this pass.

Paris Visite passes, which allow the holder discounted entry to certain museums and activities as well as discounts on transport fares, are valid for one, two, three or five consecutive days of travel in either three, five or eight zones. The version covering one to three zones costs €8.35/13.70/18.25/26.65 for one/two/three/five days. Children aged four to 11 pay €4.55/6.85/9.15/13.70.

TRAVEL PASSES

The cheapest and easiest way to use public transport in Paris is to get a Carte Orange, a combined metro, RER and bus pass whose accompanying magnetic coupon comes in weekly and monthly versions. You can get tickets for travel in two to eight urban and suburban zones but, unless you'll be using the suburban commuter lines extensively, the basic ticket valid for zones 1 and 2 should be sufficient.

A weekly Carte Orange *(coupon hebdomadaire)* costs €14.50 for zones 1 and 2 and is valid from Monday to Sunday and can be purchased from the previous Thursday until Wednesday; from Thursday weekly tickets are available for the following week only. Even if you'll be in Paris for only three or four days, it may work out cheaper than

buying carnets and it will certainly cost less than buying a daily Mobilis or Paris Visite pass (opposite). The Carte Orange monthly ticket *(coupon mensuel;* €48.60 for zones 1 and 2) begins on the first day of each calendar month; you can buy one from the 20th of the preceding month. Both are sold in metro and RER stations from 6.30am to 10pm and at some bus terminals. You can also buy a Carte Orange coupon from vending machines.

To buy your first Carte Orange, take a passport-size photograph (four photos are available from photo booths in train and many metro stations for €4) of yourself to any metro or RER ticket window. Request a Carte Orange (which is free) and the kind of coupon (weekly or monthly) you'd like. To prevent tickets from being used by more than one person, you must write your family name *(nom)* and first name *(prénom)* on the Carte Orange, and the number of your Carte Orange on the weekly or monthly coupon you've bought.

Taxi

The *prise en charge* (flag-fall) in a Parisian taxi is €2. Within the city limits, it costs €0.62 per kilometre for travel between 7am and 7pm Monday to Saturday (Tarif A; white light on meter), and €1.06 per kilometre from 7pm to 7am at night, all day Sunday and on public holidays (Tarif B; orange light on meter). Travel in the suburbs (Tariff C) costs €1.24 per kilometre.

There's an extra €2.60 charge for taking a fourth passenger, but most drivers refuse to accept more than three people anyway for insurance reasons. Each piece of baggage over 5kg costs €0.90 extra, an animal costs €0.60 and for pick-ups from SNCF mainline stations there's supplement of €0.70.

Radio-dispatched taxi companies, on call 24 hours:

Alpha Taxis (☎ 01 45 85 85 85)
Artaxi (☎ 01 42 41 50 50)
Taxis Bleus (☎ 01 49 36 10 10)
Taxis G7 (☎ 01 47 39 47 39)
Taxis Radio 7000 (☎ 01 42 70 00 42)
Taxis-Radio Étoile (☎ 01 42 70 41 41)

Around Paris

AROUND PARIS

Paris is encircled by the Île de France (Island of France), the seed from which France the kingdom grew, beginning about AD 1100. Today, the excellent rail and road links between the French capital and the exceptional sights of this region and neighbouring *départements* make it especially popular with day-trippers from Paris.

The Île de France can boast some of the nation's most beautiful and ambitious cathedrals. Closest to Paris, a mere 4km from Porte de la Chapelle, is St-Denis, the last resting place for France's kings until the Revolution. Senlis, just east of Chantilly, has a magnificent Gothic cathedral said to have inspired elements of the (holy) mother of all basilicas: the cathedral at Chartres. The latter, with its breathtaking stained glass and intricately carved stone portals, is arguably the most beautiful in all of Christendom.

While not exactly the Loire Valley, the Île de France counts some of the nation's most extravagant chateaux. Foremost is the palace at Versailles, whose opulence and extravagances were partly what spurred the revolutionary mob to storm the Bastille in July 1789. The chateau at Fontainebleau is one of the most important Renaissance palaces in France while the one at Chantilly is celebrated for its gardens and the artwork it contains. The woodlands and forests surrounding Fontainebleau and Chantilly offer unlimited outdoor activities.

But the Île de France is not stuck in the past. The modern cityscape of La Défense, just over the border from the 17th arrondissement, stands in stark contrast to the Paris of the imagination and reminds visitors that the capital has at least one of its feet firmly in the 21st century. And then there's every kid's favourite, Disneyland Resort Paris, which has added more attractions to its stable and is even easier to reach from central Paris by train.

Other destinations within easy striking distance of Paris include Beauvais (p230) and Compiègne (p231) in Far Northern France and Giverny (p243) in Normandy.

HIGHLIGHTS

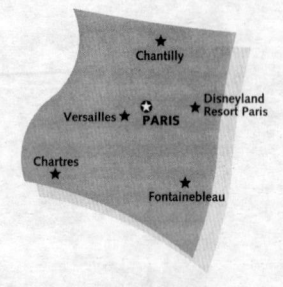

- Relive the glory, the over-the-top excess exemplified in the 18th-century **Château de Versailles** (p187)

- Contemplate the awesome stained glass and inspirational west portal of **Cathédrale Notre Dame de Chartres** (p196)

- Get behind the scenes at a new film being shot at Walt Disney Studios, **Disneyland Resort Paris** (p184)

- Wonder at the richness of the 15th-century *Très Riches Heures du Duc de Berry* illuminated manuscript at **Château de Chantilly** (p193)

- Get physical in the **Forêt de Fontainebleau** (p191), the Île de France region's most beautiful and diverse forest

---

POPULATION: 10.9 MILLION (ÎLE DE FRANCE)	AREA: 12,000 SQ KM

Orientation & Information

The Île de France is shaped by five rivers: the Epte in the northwest, the Aisne in the northeast, the Eure in the southwest, the Yonne in the southeast and the Marne in the east.

Espace du Tourisme d'Île de France (Map pp105-7; ☎ 0 826 166 666 or from abroad ☎ 33-1 44 50 19 98; www.pidf.com; Galerie du Carrousel du Louvre; 99 rue de Rivoli, 1er; metro Palais Royal-Musée du Louvre; ☒ 10am-7pm) is the central tourist office for the Île de France. It is located in the lower level of the Carrousel du Louvre shopping centre next to IM Pei's famous inverted glass pyramid. This tourist office provides a wealth of information about Île de France and its attractions.

MAPS

If you're visiting the area under your own steam, pick up a copy of IGN's 1:250,000 scale map *Île de France* (€4.90) or the more compact 1:100,000-scale *Paris et Ses Environs* (€3.70), both available from the Espace IGN outlet (see p906) just off the av des Champs-Élysées.

LA DÉFENSE

pop 40,800 (including Park District)

The ultramodern architecture of La Défense, Paris' skyscraper district on the Seine and 3km west of the 17th arrondissement, is so strikingly different from the rest of centuries-old Paris that it's worth a brief visit to put it all in perspective. When

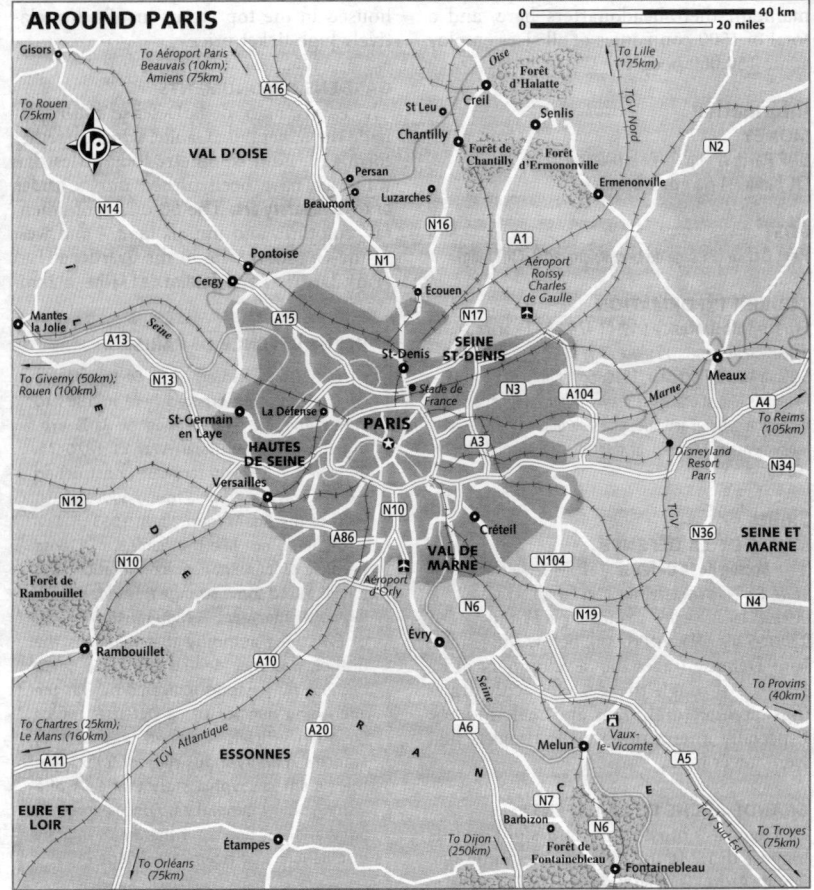

AROUND PARIS

development of the 750-hectare site began in the late 1950s, it was one of the world's most ambitious civil-engineering projects. Its first major structure was the vaulted, largely triangular-shaped **Centre des Nouvelles Industries et Technologies** (CNIT; Centre for New Industries and Technologies), a giant 'pregnant oyster' inaugurated in 1958 and extensively rebuilt 30 years later. But after the economic crisis of the mid-1970s office space in La Défense became hard to sell or lease. Buildings stood empty and further development of the area all but ceased.

Things picked up in the following decades, and today La Défense counts more than 100 buildings, the tallest of which is the 187m **Total Fina Elf Coupole** (1985). Fourteen of France's 20 largest corporations maintain their headquarters here, and a total of 1500 companies of all sizes employ some 150,000 people.

Information
MONEY
BNP Paribas (4 place de la Défense)
CIC bank (11 place de la Défense)

POST
Post Office (Passage du Levant; ground fl, CNIT Bldg)

TOURIST INFORMATION
Espace Info-Défense (☎ 01 47 74 84 24; www.la defense.fr in French; 15 place de la Défense; ☼ 9.30am-5.30pm Mon-Fri Oct-Mar, 10am-6pm Apr-Sep) La Défense's tourist office has reams of free information, details on cultural activities and sells guides to the area's monumental art (€2.30), architecture (€5.40) and history (€6.10).

Sights
MUSÉE DE LA DÉFENSE
The **Musée de la Défense** (La Défense Museum; ☎ 01 47 74 84 24; www.ladefense.fr in French; 15 place de la Défense; admission free; ☼ 10am-6pm Mon-Fri Apr-Sep, 9.30am-5.30pm Mon-Fri Oct-Mar), below the Espace Info-Défense traces the development of La Défense through the decades with drawings, architectural plans and scale models. Especially interesting are the projects that were never built.

GRANDE ARCHE DE LA DÉFENSE
La Défense's most important sight and its biggest draw is the remarkable, cube-like **Grande Arche** (Great Arch; ☎ 01 49 07 27 27; 1 parvis

de le Défense; adult/child & student/family €7.50/6/€16-22; ☼ 10am-6.30pm). Designed by Danish architect Johan-Otto von Spreckelsen and housing government and business offices, it is made of white Carrara marble, grey granite and glass, and measures 110m exactly along each side. Inaugurated on 14 July 1989, the arch marks the western end of the 8km-long **Axe Historique** (Historic Axis), begun in 1640 by André Le Nôtre of Versailles fame and stretching from the Louvre's glass pyramid. The structure, which symbolises a window open to the world, is slightly out of alignment with the Axe Historique – on purpose. Lifts will whisk you up to the 35th floor of the arch, but (frankly) neither the views from the rooftop nor the temporary exhibitions housed in the top storey justify the relatively high ticket price.

GARDENS & MONUMENTS
The Parvis, place de la Défense and Esplanade du Général de Gaulle, which together form a pleasant, kilometre-long pedestrian walkway, have been turned into a **garden of contemporary art**. The 60-odd monumental sculptures and murals here – and west of the Grande Arche in the **Quartier du Parc** (Park District) and **Jardins de l'Arche**, a 2km-

---

IN THE DEFENCE OF PARIS

La Défense is named after *La Défense de Paris,* a sculpture erected here in 1883 to commemorate the defence of Paris during the Franco-Prussian War of 1870–71. Removed in 1971 to facilitate construction work, it was placed on a round pedestal just west of the Agam fountain in 1983.

Many do not like the name La Défense because of its militaristic connotation, and it has caused some strange misunderstandings over the years. A high-ranking official of EPAD, the authority that manages the district, was once denied entry into Egypt because his passport indicated he was the 'managing director of La Défense', which Egyptian officials assumed was part of France's military-industrial complex. And there's an apocryphal story that tells of a visiting Soviet general who once expressed admiration at how well the area's military installations had been camouflaged.

long westward extension of the Axe Historique – include colourful and imaginative works by Calder, Miró, Agam, Torricini and others.

In the southeastern corner of place de la Défense and opposite the Info-Défense office is a much older **La Défense de Paris monument** honouring the defence of Paris during the Franco-Prussian War of 1870–71 (see opposite). Behind is the **Bassin Agam**, a pool with colourful mosaics and computer-controlled fountains; *ballets muets* take place between noon and 2pm and 5pm and 6pm weekdays, and from 3pm to 6pm at the weekend. Water displays accompanied by music are at 1pm on Wednesday and 4pm at the weekend.

Eating

For the most part La Défense is fast-food territory, including the ever-popular **Bistro Romain** (☎ 01 40 81 08 08; 37 Le Parvis; lunch menu €10.95, dinner menus €15.90 & €22.70; ☻ 11.30am-10pm) overlooking the Parvis, but there are a number of independent outlets from which to choose.

Brasserie du Toit de la Grande Arche (☎ 01 49 07 27 27; lunch menu €15; ☻ lunch noon-3.30pm, bar with snacks 10am-7pm) Sitting at the top the Grande Arche, this brasserie offers acceptable French standards at lunch and some of the best views in Paris from 110m up.

Le Petit Bofinger (☎ 01 46 92 46 46; 1 place du Dôme; menus €19.50 & €24; ☻ lunch & dinner until 11pm) Formerly Le Petit Dôme (as it sits

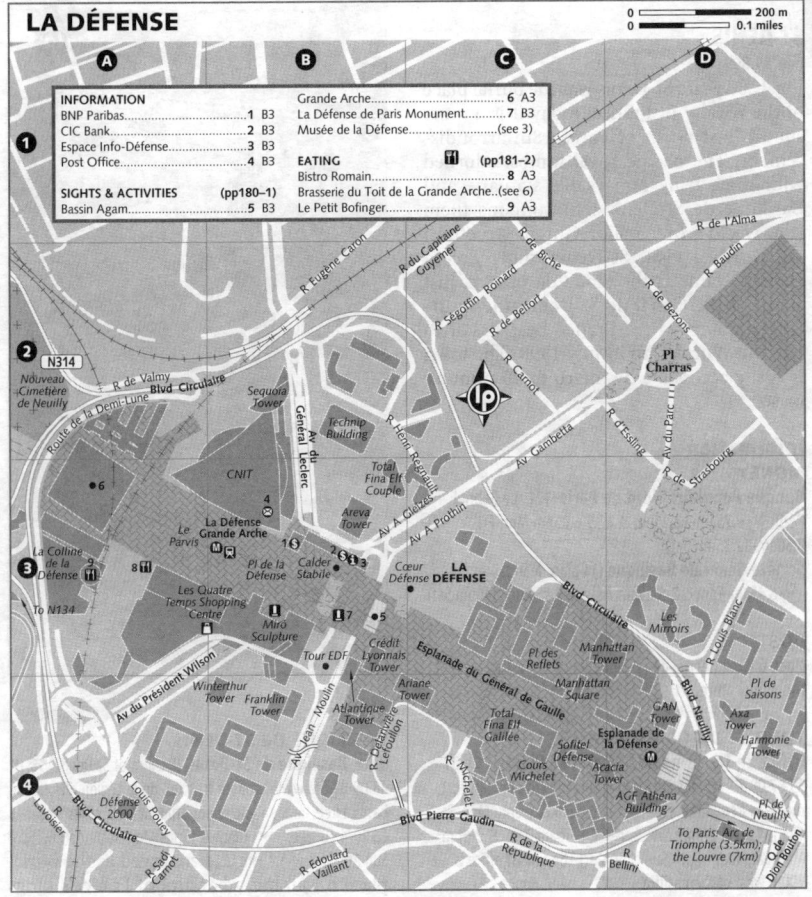

LA DÉFENSE

INFORMATION		Grande Arche	6 A3
BNP Paribas	1 B3	La Défense de Paris Monument	7 B3
CIC Bank	2 B3	Musée de la Défense	(see 3)
Espace Info-Défense	3 B3		
Post Office	4 B3	EATING	(pp181–2)
		Bistro Romain	8 A3
SIGHTS & ACTIVITIES	(pp180–1)	Brasserie du Toit de la Grande Arche	(see 6)
Bassin Agam	5 B3	Le Petit Bofinger	9 A3

AROUND PARIS

under what was once the IMAX Dôme), this glassed-in dining room with its out-of-the-way feel is a perennial favourite of La Défense *gens d'affaires* (businesspeople).

Getting There & Away

La Défense Grande Arche metro station is the western terminus of metro line No 1; the ride from the Louvre takes about 15 minutes. If you take the faster RER line A, remember that La Défense is in zone 3 and you must pay a supplement (€1.95) if you are carrying a travel pass for zones 1 and 2 only.

Bus 73 from Musée d'Orsay, place de la Concorde and place Charles de Gaulle links central Paris with La Défense Grande Arche (terminus).

ST-DENIS

pop 85,800

For 1200 years St-Denis was the burial place of the royalty of France; today it is a quiet suburb just north of Paris' 18th arrondissement. The ornate royal tombs, adorned with some truly remarkable statuary, and Basilique de St-Denis that contains them (the world's first major Gothic structure) are worth a visit. St-Denis' more recent claim to fame is the Stade de France, just south of the Canal de St-Denis, the futuristic stadium where France beat Brazil to win the World Cup in July 1998. The town is easily accessible by metro in 20 minutes or so.

Information

MONEY

Banque Populaire Nord de Paris (121 rue Gabriel Péri; ⏲ 9.25am-12.25pm & 1.35-6.05pm Mon-Fri, 8.50am-12.35pm Sat)

Société Générale Basilique (11 place Jean Jaurès; ⏲ 8.45am-1pm & 2-5.15pm Tue-Fri, 8.45am-12.40pm Sat)

POST

Post Office (59 rue de la République) Just 200m west of the tourist office.

TOURIST INFORMATION

Office de Tourisme de St-Denis La Plaine (☎ 01 55 87 08 70; www.saint-denis-tourisme.com in French; 1 rue de la République; ⏲ 9.30am-1pm & 2-6pm Mon-Sat, 10am-1pm & 2-4pm Sun Apr-Oct, 9.30am-1pm & 2-6pm Mon-Sat, 10am-2pm Sun Nov-Mar) The tourist office is 100m west of the basilica.

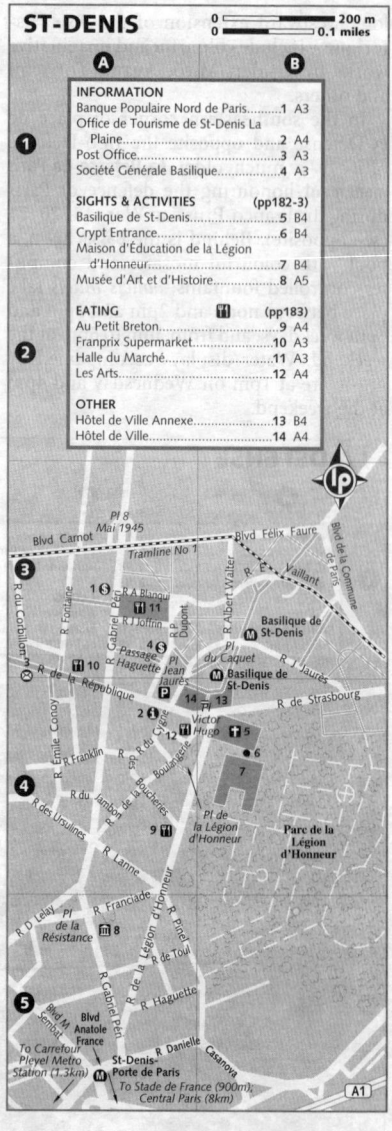

ST-DENIS

INFORMATION	
Banque Populaire Nord de Paris..........1	A3
Office de Tourisme de St-Denis La	
Plaine...2	A4
Post Office...3	A3
Société Générale Basilique.................4	A3

SIGHTS & ACTIVITIES	(pp182-3)
Basilique de St-Denis...........................5	B4
Crypt Entrance......................................6	B4
Maison d'Éducation de la Légion	
d'Honneur...7	B4
Musée d'Art et d'Histoire....................8	A5

EATING	(pp183)
Au Petit Breton.....................................9	A4
Franprix Supermarket.........................10	A3
Halle du Marché..................................11	A3
Les Arts..12	A4

OTHER	
Hôtel de Ville Annexe.........................13	B4
Hôtel de Ville......................................14	A4

Sights

BASILIQUE DE ST-DENIS

The **Basilique de St-Denis** (Basilica of St Denis; ☎ 01 48 09 83 54; www.monum.fr; 1 rue de la Légion d'Honneur; basilica free, tombs adult/senior, student & 18-25 yrs/under 18 €6.10/4.10/free; ⏲ 10am-6.15pm Mon-Sat, noon-6.15pm Sun Apr-Sep, to 5.15pm Oct-Mar) served as the burial place for all but a handful of France's kings and queens from Dagobert I (r 629–39) to Louis XVIII (r 1814–24). Their tombs and mausoleums constitute one of Europe's most important collections of funerary sculpture.

The single-towered basilica, begun around 1135, changed the face of Western architecture. It was the first major structure to be built in the Gothic style and served as a model for many other 12th-century French cathedrals, including the one at Chartres (p196). Features illustrating the transition from Romanesque to Gothic can be seen in the **choir** and **ambulatory**, which are adorned with a number of 12th-century **stained-glass windows**.

During the Revolution and the Reign of Terror, the basilica was devastated; human remains were removed from the royal tombs and dumped into two pits outside the church. The mausoleums were put into storage in Paris, however, and survived. They were brought back in 1816, and the royal bones were reburied in the crypt a year later. Restoration of the structure was begun under Napoleon, but most of the work was carried out by the Gothic Revivalist architect Eugène Viollet-le-Duc from 1858 until his death in 1879.

The **tombs** are decorated with life-size figures of the deceased. Those built before the Renaissance are adorned with *gisants* (recumbent figures). Those made after 1285 were carved from death masks and are thus fairly, well, lifelike; the 14 figures commissioned under Louis IX (St Louis; r 1214–70) are depictions of how earlier rulers might have looked. The oldest tombs (dating from around 1230) are those of **Clovis I** (d 511) and his son **Childebert I** (d 558). Self-paced 1¼-hour tours using CD-ROM headsets (€4; €5.50 for two people sharing) are available at the crypt ticket kiosk.

Just south of the basilica is the former royal abbey and now the **Maison d'Éducation de la Légion d'Honneur**, a school for 500 pupils.

MUSÉE D'ART ET D'HISTOIRE

The excellent **Musée d'Art et d'Histoire** (Museum of Art & History; ☎ 01 42 43 05 10; 22bis rue Gabriel Péri; adult/student & senior/under 16 €4/2/free; ☿ 10am-5.30pm Mon, Wed & Fri, 10am-8pm Thu, 2-6.30pm Sat & Sun) occupies a restored Carmelite convent southwest of the basilica that was founded in 1625 and later presided over by Louise de France, the young-

est daughter of Louis XV. Displays include reconstructions of the Carmelites' cells, an 18th-century apothecary and fascinating items found during excavations around St-Denis. There's a section on modern art and politically charged posters, cartoons, lithographs and paintings from the 1871 Paris Commune.

STADE DE FRANCE

The 80,000-seat, cunningly named **Stadium of France** (☎ 0 892 700 900; www.stadefrance.com; rue Francis de Pressensé, ZAC du Cornillon Nord, 93216 St-Denis La Plaine; adult/student/6-11 yrs €10/8.50/7; ☿ tours on the hour in French 10am-5pm year-round, in English 10.20am & 2.30pm Jun-Aug), just south of central St-Denis and in full view from rue Gabriel Péri, was built for the 1998 World Cup, which the French football team won by miraculously defeating Brazil 3-0. The futuristic and quite beautiful structure, with a roof the size of place de la Concorde, is now used for football and rugby matches, major gymnastic events and big-ticket music concerts. It can be visited on a guided tour from Porte H (Gate H), but they are conducted in English only in summer.

Eating

Les Arts (☎ 01 43 43 22 40; 6 rue de la Boulangerie; starters €4.90-9.50, couscous €7.90-19.20, tajines €9.50-12.50; ☿ lunch Tue-Sun, dinner to 10.30pm Mon-Sat) This is a central restaurant with French and Maghrebi cuisine that comes recommended locally.

Au Petit Breton (☎ 01 48 20 11 58; 18 rue de la Légion d'Honneur; plat du jour €8, menus €10 & €12; ☿ 8.30am-3.30pm Mon-Sat) 'At the Little Breton' is a decent choice for a light lunch of *galettes* (a savoury version of crepes) and dry cider or a snack of sweet crepes.

The large, multiethnic **food market** (place Jean Jaurès; ☿ 8am-2pm Tue, Fri & Sun) across the street from the tourist office and in the **Halle du Marché**, the large covered market a short stroll away to the northwest, is known in particular for its selection of spices.

There's a **Franprix supermarket** (34 rue de la République; ☿ 9am-1pm & 3-7.15pm Tue-Sat, 8.30am-1pm Sun) in the centre of town near the post office.

Getting There & Away

Take metro line No 13 to the penultimate station, Basilique de St-Denis, for the basilica and tourist office, or to St-Denis-Porte de Paris for the Musée d'Art et d'Histoire and the Stade de France; the latter can also be reached via RER line B (station: La Plaine-Stade de France). When taking metro line No 13, make sure you board a train heading for St-Denis Université and *not* for Gabriel Péri/Asnières-Gennevilliers, as the line splits at La Fourche station.

DISNEYLAND RESORT PARIS

It took almost €4.6 billion and five years of work to turn the beet fields east of the capital into Europe's first Disney theme park, which opened in 1992 amid much fanfare and controversy. Although Disney stockholders were less than thrilled with the park's performance for the first few years, what was originally known as Euro-Disney is now very much in the black, and the many visitors – mostly families with young children – can't seem to get enough.

Orientation

Disneyland Resort Paris consists of three main areas: commercial Disney Village, with its five hotels, shops, restaurants and clubs; Disneyland Park, with its five theme parks; and Walt Disney Studios Park, which brings film, animation and TV production to life. The first two are separated by the RER and TGV train stations; Walt Disney Studios Park is next to Disneyland Park.

Information
MONEY

Bureaux de change are everywhere, including a **branch** (10am-7pm) at the main entrance to Disneyland Park.

TOURIST INFORMATION

Espace du Tourisme d'Île de France et de Seine et Marne (☎ 01 60 43 33 33; www.pidf.com; place des Passagers du Vent, Disneyland Resort Paris, 77705 Marne-la-Vallée; 10am-7pm) The Île de France tourist office branch in the heart of the resort shares space with an office dispensing information on the *département* of Seine et Marne.

Sights

One-day admission fees at **Disneyland Resort Paris** (☎ 01 60 30 60 30, UK ☎ 0 870 503 0305, USA ☎ 407-WDISNEY, 407-934 7639; www.disneylandparis .com, www.needmagic.com) include unlimited access to all rides and activities in either Dis-

neyland Park or Walt Disney Studios Park. Those who opt for the latter, however, can enter Disneyland Park three hours before it closes. Multiple-day passes are also available: a **Passe-Partout** (adult/child €49/39) allows entry to both parks for one day while a **Hopper Ticket** (adult/child high season €109/84, low season €105/78) allows you to enter and leave both parks as you like over three days, which need not be consecutive but must be used within three years.

Disneyland Park (adult/3-11 yrs €40/30 Apr-Oct, €39/29 Nov-Mar; 9am-11pm daily early Jul-Aug, 10am-8pm Mon-Fri, 9am-8pm Sat & Sun Sep-Mar, 9am-8pm daily Apr-early May, 10am-8pm Mon-Fri, 9am-8pm Sat & Sun early May–mid-Jun, 9am-8pm daily mid-Jun–early Jul) is divided into five *pays* (lands). **Main Street, USA**, just inside the main entrance and behind Disneyland Hotel, is a spotless avenue reminiscent of Norman Rockwell's idealised small-town America c1900, complete with Disney characters let loose among the crowds. Adjoining **Frontierland** is a re-creation of the 'rugged, untamed American West'. **Adventureland**, meant to evoke the Arabian Nights and the wilds of Africa (among other exotic lands portrayed in Disney films), is home to that old favourite, Pirates of the Caribbean, as well as Indiana Jones and the Temple of Peril: a roller coaster that spirals through 360° – in reverse! **Fantasyland** brings fairy-tale characters such as Sleeping Beauty, Pinocchio, Peter Pan and Snow White to life; you will also find 'It's a Small World' here. **Discoveryland** features a dozen high-tech attractions and rides (including Space Mountain and Orbitron) and futuristic films at Videopolis that pay homage to Leonardo da Vinci, George Lucas and – for a bit of local colour – Jules Verne.

Walt Disney Studios Park (adult/3-11 yrs €40/30 Apr-Oct, €39/29 Nov-Mar; 9am-6pm daily late Jun-early Sep, 10am-6pm Mon-Fri, 9am-6pm Sat & Sun early Sep-late Jun), which opened in March 2002, has a sound stage, a production backlot and animation studios that help illustrate up close how films, TV programmes and cartoons are produced.

Sleeping & Eating

There are 50 restaurants at Disneyland Resort Paris, including such memorable venues as the **Silver Spur Steakhouse** in Frontierland, the **Blue Lagoon Restaurant** in Fantasyland and **Annette's Diner** in Disney Village. Most have adult menus for between €20 and €28 and a children's one for €10. Restaurants in Disneyland Park open for lunch and dinner according to the season; those in Disney Village open from 11am or 11.30am to about midnight daily. You are not allowed to picnic on resort grounds.

Each of the resort's half-dozen **hotels** (☎ 01 60 30 60 30; www.disneylandparis.com; P ⊠ ☒ ▣ ☎) has its own all-American theme, reflected in the architecture, landscaping, décor, restaurants and entertainment. All of the rooms have two double beds (or, in the case of the Hôtel Cheyenne, one double bed and two bunk beds) and can sleep up to four people. Free shuttle buses link the hotels with the parks.

Rates vary. The vast majority of guests stay on some sort of package. Prices are highest during July and August and around Christmas; on Friday and Saturday nights and during holiday periods from April to October; and on Saturday nights from mid-February to March. The least expensive rates are available on most weeknights (ie Sunday to Thursday or, sometimes, Friday) from January to mid-February, from mid-May to June, for most of September, and from November to mid-December.

THE TENNIS COURT OATH

At Versailles in May 1789, in an effort to deal with the huge national debt and to moderate dissent by reforming the tax system, Louis XVI convened the États-Généraux (States General), a body made up of over 1000 deputies representing the three 'estates': the nobility, the clergy and the so-called Third Estate, representing the middle classes.

When the Third Estate's representatives, who formed the majority of the delegates, were denied entry to the usual meeting place of the États-Généraux, they met in the Salle de Jeu de Paume (Royal Tennis Court), where they constituted themselves as the National Assembly on 17 June. Three days later they took the famous *Serment du Jeu de Paume* (Tennis Court Oath), swearing not to dissolve the assembly until Louis XVI had accepted a new constitution. This act of defiance sparked demonstrations of support and, less than a month later, a mob in Paris stormed the prison at Bastille.

Disneyland Hôtel (d per person €258-599) This property at the entrances to the two parks bills itself as a 'lavish Victorian fantasy' and is the pinnacle of Disney Resort Paris accommodation.

Hôtel Cheyenne (d per person €105-184) The 14 timber-framed buildings of this hotel – each with its own hokey name – are arranged to resemble a Wild West frontier town.

Hôtel Santa Fe (d per person €69-139) Offering the most affordable accommodation in the resort itself, the Santa Fe has an American Southwest style.

Getting There & Away

Marne-la-Vallée/Chessy (Disneyland's RER station) is served by RER line A4; trains run every 15 minutes or so from central Paris (€6, 35 to 40 minutes). The last train back to Paris leaves at about 12.20am.

VERSAILLES
pop 85,300

The prosperous, leafy and very bourgeois suburb of Versailles, 21km southwest of Paris, is the site of the grandest and most famous chateau in France. It served as the kingdom's political capital and the seat of the royal court for more than a century, from 1682 to 1789 – the year Revolutionary mobs massacred the palace guard and dragged Louis XVI and Marie-Antoinette back to Paris where they eventually had their heads lopped off.

Because so many people consider Versailles a must-see destination, the chateau attracts upwards of three million visitors a year. The best way to avoid the queues is to arrive first thing in the morning; if you're interested in just the Grands Appartements, another good time to get here is about 3.30pm or 4pm. The queues are longest on Tuesday, when many of Paris' museums are closed, and on Sunday.

Information

CCF bank (17-19 rue du Maréchal Foch)

Office de Tourisme de Versailles (☎ 01 39 24 88 88; www.versailles-tourisme.com; 2bis av de Paris; ☼ 9am-7pm daily Apr-Oct, 9am-6pm Tue-Sat, 9am-5pm Sun & Mon Nov-Mar) The tourist office has themed guided tours (adult/child €8/4) of the city and chateau throughout the week year-round.

Post Office (av de Paris) On the opposite side of av de Paris from the tourist office.

AROUND PARIS

VERSAILLES

0			600 m
0			0.4 miles

INFORMATION
CCF Bank.....................................1 D5
Office de Tourisme de Versailles......2 C5
Post Office..................................3 C5

SIGHTS & ACTIVITIES (pp187-8)
Bassin d'Appollon.........................4 A4
Bassin de Neptune........................5 C4
Entrée A (Ticket Office)..................6 C5
Entrée C......................................7 C5
Entrée D......................................8 C5
Entrée F.......................................9 C5
Grand Trianon.............................10 A3
Hameau de la Reine......................11 A2
Orangerie...............................(see 12)
Parterre du Midi..........................12 B5

Petit Trianon...............................13 A3
Salle de Jeu de Paume..................14 C5

SLEEPING (p188)
Hôtel d'Angleterre........................15 C5
Hôtel du Palais............................16 C5
Royal Hôtel.................................17 C6

EATING (p188)
À la Ferme..................................18 C6
Crêperie St-Louis.........................19 C5
Le Falher....................................20 C5
Marché Notre Dame &
  Food Halls................................21 D4
Monoprix Supermarket..................22 D5
Pizzeria Via Veneto......................23 C5

TRANSPORT (pp188-9)
Bicycle Hire.................................24 A4
Bicycle Hire............................(see 32)
Bus No 171 To/From Paris..............25 C5
Local Bus Station.........................26 C5
Phébus Bicycle Rental...................27 D6

OTHER
Cathédrale St-Louis......................28 C6
Cour des Ministres.......................29 C5
Cour Royale................................30 C5
Église Notre Dame........................31 C4
Grille de la Reine.........................32 B4
Grille de Neptune.........................33 C4
Grille du Dragon..........................34 C4
Hôtel de Ville..............................35 D5
Les Manèges Versailles Shopping
  Centre.....................................36 C5
Préfecture...................................37 D5

LE CHESNAY

PARC DE VERSAILLES

Château de
Versailles

Grand Canal

Bassin
du Miroir

Pièce
d'Eau des
Suisses

Parc
Balby

Sights
CHÂTEAU DE VERSAILLES

The splendid and enormous **Château de Versailles** (Palace of Versailles; ☎ 01 30 83 78 00, 01 30 83 77 77; www.chateauversailles.fr; Passport adult/10-17 yrs €20/6 Apr-Oct, €14.50/4 Nov-Mar; ☽ 9am-6.30pm Tue-Sun Apr-Oct, 9am-5.30pm Tue-Sun Nov-Mar) was built in the mid-17th century during the reign of Louis XIV – the Roi Soleil (Sun King) – to project the absolute power of the French monarchy, which was then at the height of its glory. Its scale and décor also reflect Louis XIV's taste for profligate luxury and his boundless appetite for self-glorification. Some 30,000 workers and soldiers toiled on the structure, the bills for which all but emptied the kingdom's coffers. The chateau has undergone relatively few alterations since its construction, though almost all the interior furnishings disappeared during the Revolution and many of the rooms were rebuilt by Louis-Philippe (r 1830–48).

About two decades into his long reign (1643–1715), Louis XIV decided to enlarge the hunting lodge his father had built at Versailles and turn it into a palace big enough for the entire court, which numbered about 6000 people at the time. To accomplish this he hired three supremely talented men: the architect Louis Le Vau (Jules Hardouin-Mansart took over from Le Vau in the mid-1670s); the painter and interior designer Charles Le Brun; and the landscape artist André Le Nôtre, whose workers flattened hills, drained marshes and relocated forests as they laid out the seemingly endless gardens, ponds and fountains.

Le Brun and his hundreds of artisans decorated every moulding, cornice, ceiling and door of the interior with the most luxurious and ostentatious of appointments: frescoes, marble, gilt and woodcarvings, many with themes and symbols drawn from Greek and Roman mythology. The **Grand Appartement du Roi** (King's Suite), for example, includes rooms dedicated to Hercules, Venus, Diana, Mars and Mercury. The opulence reaches its peak in the **Galerie des Glaces** (Hall of Mirrors), a 75m-long ballroom with 17 huge mirrors on one side and, on the other, an equal number of windows looking out on the gardens and the setting sun.

The chateau complex comprises four main sections: the palace building, a 580m-long structure with multiple wings, grand halls and sumptuous bedchambers (only parts of which are open to the public); the vast gardens, canals and pools to the west of the palace; and two outbuildings, the **Grand Trianon** and, a few hundred metres to the east, the **Petit Trianon**.

The so-called 'Passport' allows entry (via Entrée B2) to the State Apartments, King's Chamber, the Trianons, the gardens, Coach Museum and fountain displays or you can visit sections and sights on a guided tour or individually. The **Grands Appartements** (State Apartments; admission before/after 3.30pm €7.50/5.30, under 18 free; ☽ 9am-6.30pm Tue-Sun Apr-Oct, 9am-5.30pm Tue-Sun Nov-Mar), the main section of the palace that can be visited without a guided tour, include the Galerie des Glaces, the Appartement de la Reine (Queen's Suite) and several other sights. Tickets are on sale at Entrée A (Entrance A), which is off to the right from the equestrian statue of Louis XIV as you approach the palace. If you have a Carte Musées-Monuments (see p113) you don't have to wait in the queue – go straight to Entrée B2.

The section of the vast **chateau gardens** (adult/under 18 €3/free, after 6pm free Apr-Oct, free Nov-Mar; ☽ 9am-sunset Apr-Oct, 8am-5.30pm or 6.30pm Nov-Mar) nearest the palace, laid out between 1661 and 1700 in the formal French style, is famed for its geometrically aligned terraces, flowerbeds, tree-lined paths, ponds and fountains. The many statues of marble, bronze and lead were made by the most talented sculptors of the era. The English-style **Jardins du Petit Trianon** are more pastoral and have meandering, sheltered paths.

The **Grand Canal**, 1.6km long and 62m wide, is oriented to reflect the setting sun. It is traversed by the 1km-long **Petit Canal**, creating a cross-shaped body of water with a perimeter of more than 5.5km. Louis XIV used to hold boating parties here. In season, you too can paddle around the Grand Canal in four-person **rowing boats** (☎ 01 39 66 97 66; per ½hr/hr €8/11; ☽ Mar-Nov); board them at the canal's eastern end. The **Orangerie**, built under the Parterre du Midi (flowerbed) on the southwestern side of the palace, is used to store tropical plants in winter.

The gardens' largest fountains are the 17th-century **Bassin de Neptune** (Neptune's Fountain), 300m north of the palace, whose straight side abuts a small pond graced by a winged dragon, and the **Bassin d'Apollon**, at the eastern end of the Grand Canal, in the centre of which Apollo's chariot, pulled by rearing horses, emerges from the water.

Try to time your visit for the **Grande Perspective** and **Grandes Eaux Musicales** (adult/student & over 11 €6/4.50, after 4.50pm free; ⊗ 11am-noon & 3.30-5pm Sat early May-late Sep, Sun early Apr-early Oct) fountain displays.

In the middle of the park, approximately 1.5km northwest of the main building, are Versailles' two smaller palaces, each of which is surrounded by neatly tended flowerbeds. The pink-colonnaded **Grand Trianon** (adult/concession/under 18 €5/3/free; ⊗ noon-6.30pm Apr-Oct, noon-5.30pm Nov-Mar) was built in 1687 for Louis XIV and his family as a place of escape from the rigid etiquette of the court. Napoleon I had it redone in the Empire style. The much smaller, ochre-coloured **Petit Trianon** (entry incl with Grand Trianon; ⊗ noon-6.30pm Mar-Oct, noon-5.30pm Nov-Feb), built in the 1760s, was redecorated in 1867 by Empress Eugénie, the consort of Napoleon III, who added Louis XVI-style furnishings similar to the uninspiring pieces that now fill its 1st-floor rooms.

Further north is the **Hameau de la Reine** (Queen's Hamlet), a mock village of thatched cottages constructed from 1775 to 1784 for the amusement of Marie-Antoinette, who liked to play milkmaid here.

The **Appartement de Louis XIV** and **Appartements du Dauphin et de la Dauphine** – also called the King's Chamber – can be toured with a one-hour **audioguide** (adult/under 10 €4/free) available at Entrée C. You can begin your visit between 9am and 5pm (4pm from November to March). This is also a good way to avoid the queues at Entrée A.

Several different **guided tours** (☎ 01 30 83 77 88; 1/1½/2hr adult €4/6/8, 10-17 yrs €2.70/4.20/5.50; ⊗ 9am-4pm Tue-Sun Apr-Oct, 9am-3.45pm Tue-Sun Nov-Mar) are available in English. Tickets are sold at Entrée D; tours begin across the courtyard at Entrée F and must be booked ahead. All tours require you to purchase a ticket to the Grands Appartements. If you buy a tour ticket at Entrée C or Entrée D you can later avoid the Grands Appartements queue at Entrée A by going straight to Entrée B.

Sleeping

Hôtel d'Angleterre (☎ 01 39 51 43 50; hotel-angleterre@voila.fr; 2bis rue de Fontenay; s & d with washbasin & toilet €35, with shower & toilet €65-71, tr & q €86; Ⓟ)

Less than 300m from the chateau entrance, the 'England' has 18 charming and up-to-date rooms.

Royal Hôtel (☎ 01 39 50 67 31; www.royalhotelversailles.com; 23 rue Royale; s/d with shower & toilet €49-58, d/tr with bath & toilet €61/70) With basic but adequate rooms, the Royal is a central choice, with friendly staff.

Hôtel du Palais (☎ 01 39 50 39 29; hotelpalais@ifrance.com; 6 place Lyautay; d with washbasin €38, with shower €50-55) This well-kept 24-room hotel is an inexpensive option opposite Versailles-Rive Gauche train station.

Eating

Le Falher (☎ 01 39 50 57 43; 22 rue Satory; starters €14-20, mains €23-25, lunch menu €22, dinner menus €29 & €46; ⊗ lunch Mon-Fri & dinner to 10.30pm Tue-Sat) This quiet and elegant place not far from the palace has French gastronomic menus.

À la Ferme (☎ 01 39 53 10 81; 3 rue du Maréchal Joffre; starters €6-10, mains €10.50-15, 2-/3-course menus €15.50/19; ⊗ lunch & dinner to 11pm Wed-Sun) 'At the Farm' specialises in grilled meats and the cuisine of southwestern France.

Crêperie St-Louis (☎ 01 39 53 40 12; 33 rue du Vieux Versailles; menus €9-14; ⊗ lunch & dinner to 11pm) This is a cosy place with Breton specialities including sweet and savoury crêpes and galettes (€3 to €7.50).

Pizzeria Via Veneto (☎ 01 39 51 03 89; 20 rue Satory; pizzas & pasta dishes €7-11; ⊗ lunch & dinner to 11pm) A good choice for the specialities.

Marché Notre Dame (place du Marché Notre Dame; ⊗ 7.30am-1.30pm Tue, Fri & Sun) This outdoor market north of the tourist office is worth a visit. There are also **food halls** (⊗ 7am-1pm & 3.30-7.30pm Tue-Sat, 7am-2pm Sun) surrounding the market place.

Monoprix (9 rue Georges Clemenceau; ⊗ 8.30am-8.55pm Mon-Sat) This department store north of av de Paris has a large supermarket section.

Getting There & Away

RATP Bus No 171 (€1.30 or one metro/bus ticket, 35 minutes) links Pont de Sèvres (15e) in Paris with the place d'Armes every eight to 15 minutes daily, with the last bus leaving Versailles just before 1am. Be aware that it's faster to go by RER and you'll have to get to/from Pont de Sèvres metro station on line No 9 if you take the bus.

RER line C5 (€2.35) takes you from Paris' Left Bank RER stations to Versailles-Rive Gauche station, which is only 700m southeast of the chateau and close to the tourist office. The last train to Paris leaves shortly before midnight. RER line C8 links Paris' Left Bank with Versailles-Chantiers station, a 1.3km walk from the chateau.

SNCF operates 70 trains a day from Paris' Gare St-Lazare (€3.20) to Versailles-Rive Droite, which is 1.2km from the chateau. The last train to Paris leaves just after midnight. Versailles-Chantiers station is also served by some 30 SNCF trains a day (20 on Sunday) from Gare Montparnasse; all trains on this line continue to Chartres (€9.90; 45 to 60 minutes).

Getting Around

From February to November, bicycles can be hired from **kiosks** (☎ 01 39 66 97 66; per ½hr/ hr/½ day/day €2.50/5/10.50/12; ⏰ 10am-close Mon-Fri, 1pm-close Sat & Sun Jun-mid–Sep, 10am-close Sat & Sun Feb-May & mid-Sep–Nov) at Petite Venise at the eastern end of the Grand Canal and next to Grille de la Reine. You can also rent bikes from **Phébus** (☎ 01 39 20 16 60; www.phebus.tm.fr in French; place Raymond Poincaré; per 1hr/2hr/day/week/ month €5/10/12/16/25; ⏰ 7.15am-7.45pm Mon-Fri, 11am-5pm Sat & Sun) in front of the Versailles-Chantiers metro station.

FONTAINEBLEAU

pop 15,800

The town of Fontainebleau, 67km southeast of Paris, is renowned for its elegant Renaissance chateau – one of France's largest royal residences – whose splendid furnishings make it particularly worth visiting. It's much less crowded and pressured than Versailles. The town itself has a number of fine restaurants and nightspots and is surrounded by the beautiful Forêt de Fontainebleau, a favourite hunting ground of many French kings and today an important recreational centre in the Île de France.

Information

Office de Tourisme de Pays de Fontainebleau (☎ 01 60 74 99 99; www.fontainebleau-tourisme.com; 4 rue Royale; ⏰ 10am-6pm Mon-Sat, 10am-12.30pm & 3-5pm Sun Apr-Oct, 10am-1pm Sun Nov-Mar) The tourist office, in a converted petrol station a couple of hundred metres west of the chateau, hires out **bicycles** (per ½ day/day €15/19), as well as self-paced English-language **audioguide tours** (€4.60; 1½hr) of both the palace and the Forêt de Fontainebleau.

Post Office (2 rue de la Chancellerie)

Société Générale (102 rue Grande; ⏰ 8.35am-12.30pm & 1.30-5.25pm Mon-Fri, 8.35am-12.30pm & 1.30-4.25pm Sat)

Sights

CHÂTEAU DE FONTAINEBLEAU

The enormous, 1900-room **Château de Fontainebleau** (Palace of Fontainebleau; ☎ 01 60 71 50 70; www.chateaudefontainebleau.net; adult/18-25 yrs/under 18 €5.50/4/free, 1st Sun of month free; ⏰ 9.30am-6pm Wed-Mon Jun-Sep, 9.30am-5pm Wed-Mon Oct-May), whose list of former tenants or visitors reads like a who's who of French royalty, is one of the most beautifully decorated and furnished chateaux in France. Every centimetre of wall and ceiling space is richly adorned with wood panelling, gilded carvings, frescoes, tapestries and paintings. The parquet floors are of the finest woods, the fireplaces ornamented with exceptional carvings, and many of the pieces of furniture are originals dating back to the Renaissance era.

The first chateau on this site was built sometime in the early 12th century and enlarged by Louis IX a century later. Only a single medieval tower survived the energetic Renaissance-style reconstruction undertaken by François I (r 1515–47), whose superb artisans, many of them brought from Italy, blended Italian and French styles to create what is known as the First School of Fontainebleau. The *Mona Lisa* once hung here amid other fine works of art of the royal collection.

During the latter half of the 16th century, the chateau was further expanded by Henri II (r 1547–59), Catherine de Médicis and Henri IV (r 1589–1610), whose Flemish and French artists created the Second School of Fontainebleau. Even Louis XIV got in on the act: it was he who hired Le Nôtre to redesign the gardens.

Fontainebleau, which was not damaged during the Revolution (though its furniture was stolen or destroyed), was beloved by Napoleon, who had a fair bit of restoration work carried out. Napoleon III was another frequent visitor.

During WWII the chateau was turned into a German headquarters. After it was liberated by Allied forces under US General George Patton in 1944, part of the complex served as the Allied and then NATO's headquarters from 1945 to 1965.

AROUND PARIS

The **Grands Appartements** (State Apartments) include a number of outstanding rooms. The spectacular **Chapelle de la Trinité** (Trinity Chapel), whose ornamentation dates from the first half of the 17th century, is where Louis XV married Marie Leczinska in 1725 and where the future Napoleon III was christened in 1810. **Galerie François 1er**, a jewellery box of Renaissance architecture, was decorated from 1533 to 1540 by Il Rosso, a Florentine follower of Michelangelo. In the wood panelling, François I's monogram appears repeatedly along with his emblem, a dragon-like salamander.

The **Salle de Bal**, a 30m-long ballroom dating from the mid-16th century that was also used for receptions and banquets, is renowned for its mythological frescoes, marquetry floor and Italian-inspired coffered ceiling. Large windows afford views of the Cour Ovale and the gardens. The gilded bed found in the 17th- and 18th-century **Chambre de l'Impératrice** (Empress' Bedroom) was never actually used by Marie-Antoinette, for whom it was built. The gilding in the **Salle du Trône** (Throne Room), the royal bedroom before the Napoleonic period, is in three shades: gold, green and yellow. Conducted tours of the Grands Appartements in English usually depart at 2.30pm from July to September from the staircase near the ticket windows, but check with staff.

The **Petits Appartements** (Small Apartments) were the private rooms of the emperor and

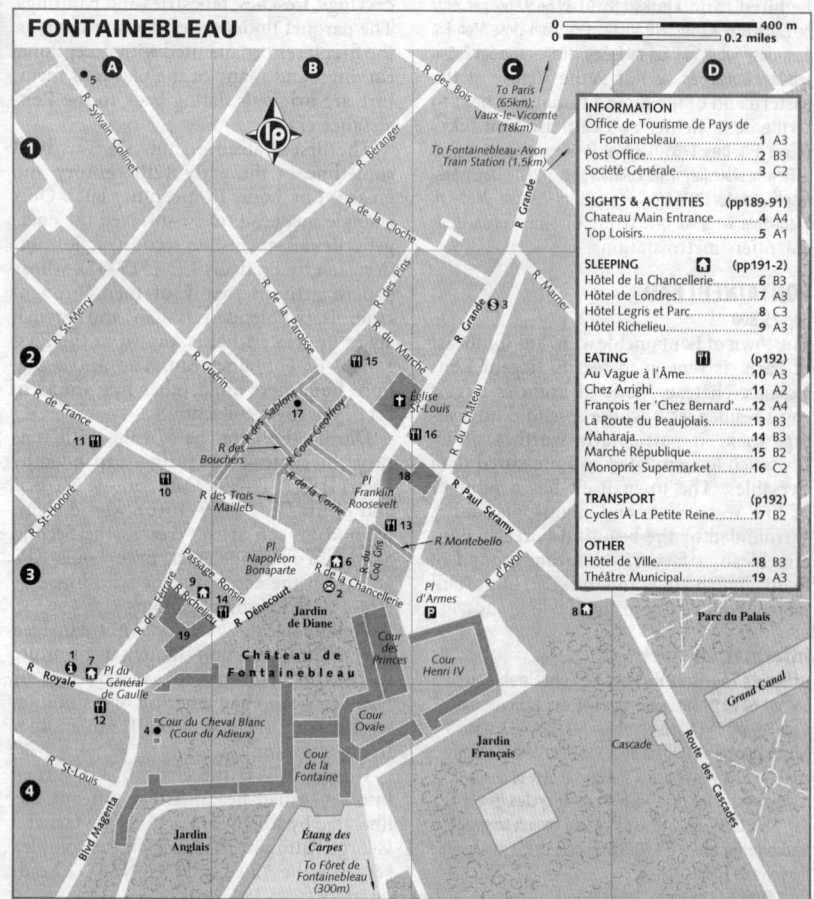

FONTAINEBLEAU

0 — 400 m
0 — 0.2 miles

empress, and the **Musée Napoléon 1er** (Napoleon I Museum) contains personal effects – such as uniforms, hats, coats, ornamental swords – and knick-knacks that belonged to Napoleon and his relatives. Neither has fixed opening hours and entry is an additional €3/2.30 for adults/ 18 to 25 years (free for those under 18).

As successive monarchs added their own wings to the chateau, five irregularly shaped courtyards were created. The oldest and most interesting is the **Cour Ovale** (Oval Courtyard), no longer oval but U-shaped due to Henri IV's construction work. It incorporates the keep, the sole remnant of the medieval chateau. The largest courtyard is the **Cour du Cheval Blanc** (Courtyard of the White Horse), from where you enter the chateau. Napoleon, about to be exiled to Elba in 1814, bade farewell to his guards from the magnificent 17th-century **double-horseshoe staircase** here. For that reason the courtyard is also called the Cour des Adieux (Farewell Courtyard).

The **chateau gardens** (admission free; ☼ 9am-7pm May-Sep, 9am-6pm Mar, Apr & Oct, 9am-5pm Nov-Feb) are quite extraordinary. On the northern side of the chateau is the **Jardin de Diane**, a formal garden created by Catherine de Médicis. Le Nôtre's formal, 17th-century **Jardin Français** (French Garden), or Grand Parterre, is east of the **Cour de la Fontaine** (Fountain Courtyard) and the **Étang des Carpes** (Carp Pond). The **Grand Canal** was excavated in 1609 and predates the canals at Versailles by more than half a century. The informal **Jardin Anglais** (English Garden), laid out in 1812, is west of the pond.

FORÊT DE FONTAINEBLEAU
This 20,000-hectare **Forêt de Fontainebleau** (Fontainebleau Forest) forest, which begins 500m south of the chateau and surrounds the town, is one of the prettiest woods in the region. The many trails – including parts of the **GR1** and **GR11** (see p897 for general information about walking trails) – are excellent for jogging, walking, cycling, horse riding and climbing. The area is covered by IGN's 1:25,000-scale *Forêt de Fontainebleau* map (No 2417OT; €9). The tourist office sells the *Guide des Sentiers de Promenades dans le Massif Forestier de Fontainebleau* (€7.60), whose maps and text (in French) cover almost 20 walks in the forest, as well as the

comprehensive *La Forêt de Fontainebleau* (€12.50), published by the Office National des Forêts, with almost three dozen walks.

Rock-climbing enthusiasts have long come to the forest's sandstone ridges, rich in cliffs and overhangs, to hone their skills before setting off for the Alps. If you want to give it a go, contact **Top Loisirs** (☎ 01 60 74 08 50; www.toploisirs.fr; 16 rue Sylvain Collinet) about equipment hire and instruction. The tourist office sells the comprehensive *Fontainebleau Climbs* (€25) in English.

Sleeping
Hôtel de Londres (☎ 01 64 22 20 21; www.hotel delondres.com; 1 place du Général de Gaulle; s & d €90-105, ste €125-150; ℗) This fine 12-room hotel opposite the chateau's main entrance dates back to at least the Second Empire and is a very comfortable place to stay. Some rooms (including Nos 2 and 10) have balconies with stunning views of the chateau.

Hôtel Richelieu (☎ 01 64 22 26 46; fax 01 64 23 40 17; 4 rue Richelieu; s €41-57, d €46-62; ℗) The 18-room Richelieu, just north of the chateau, is part of the Logis de France group – always a sign of quality – and has an excellent wine bar and bistro attached.

Hôtel de la Chancellerie (☎ 01 64 22 21 70; hotel .chancellerie@gofornet.com; 1 rue de la Chancellerie; s/d/tr €35/40/58) This hotel opposite the post office

---

AUTHOR'S CHOICE

Hôtel Legris et Parc (☎ 01 64 22 24 24; legris.et.parc@wanadoo.fr; 36 rue Paul Séramy & 6 rue d'Avon; s €46-50, d €61-95, tr €102-145; ℗ ▯ ☒) This lovely 32-room hotel, situated in a 17th-century residence where Racine apparently once laid his head, abuts the palace park and boasts its own verdant garden. The hotel has a lovely open-air swimming pool and an excellent restaurant called **L'Éden** (starters €9.50-19, mains €14-35, menu €29). History is all around you at Legris et Parc. Just next door is a synagogue built in 1861 and razed by the Nazis in 1941 and, on the hotel grounds, is a Pavillon de Chasse, a 'Hunting Pavilion' done up in what the French call *style gentleman farmer* where Field Marshal Bernard Montgomery, Commander-in-Chief of all Allied Forces in Europe, held Scottish reels while based here after the war.

has 25 old-fashioned but comfortable and spotless rooms. Rates are about €10 more from April to October.

Eating

Chez Arrighi (☎ 01 64 22 29 43; 53 rue de France; starters €9-20, mains €13.50-23.50, menus €18.80, €23.50 & €31.80; ⊗ lunch & dinner to 11pm Tue-Sun) An elegant place – arguably the best restaurant in Fontainebleau – with traditional gastronomic cuisine.

François 1er 'Chez Bernard' (⊗ 01 64 22 24 68; 3 rue Royale; starters €6.90-18.90, mains €14.50-18.60, lunch menu €15, dinner menu €28; ⊗ lunch & dinner to 11pm) This double-barrelled eatery has excellent specialities from Normandy, with an emphasis on seafood.

Maharaja (☎ 01 64 22 14 64; 15 rue Dénecourt; starters €3.50-7.50, mains €5.50-17.50, lunch menus €9 & €14, dinner menu €15; ⊗ lunch & dinner to midnight Mon-Sat) The Maharajah has curries (€7.50 to €9) and tandoori dishes (€5.50 to €17.50) as well as standard starters such as pakoras and samosas.

La Route du Beaujolais (☎ 01 64 22 27 98; 3 rue Montebello; starters €7-14, mains €12-20, lunch menu €12, dinner menus €17 & €24; ⊗ lunch & dinner to 11pm) 'The Beaujolais Way' is no great shakes, but it's central and serves reliable Lyonnaise-style dishes.

Au Vague à l'Âme (☎ 01 60 72 10 32; 39 rue de France; galettes & crêpes €2.50-7.50, menus €25 & €35; ⊗ lunch Tue-Sun, dinner to 1am Tue-Sat) This café-restaurant is the place to come for Breton specialities including fresh oysters and an oyster terrine to die for.

Marché République (rue des Pins; ⊗ 8am-1pm Tue, Fri & Sun) Fontainebleau's covered food market is just north of the central pedestrian area.

Monoprix (58 rue Grande; ⊗ 8.45am-7.45pm Mon-Sat, 9am-1pm Sun) This department store has a supermarket section on the 1st floor.

Getting There & Around

Up to 30 daily commuter trains link Paris' Gare de Lyon every hour with Fontainebleau-Avon station (€7.30, 40 to 60 minutes); the last train returning to Paris leaves Fontainebleau a bit after 9.45pm weekdays, just after 10pm on Saturday and sometime after 10.30pm on Sunday. SNCF has a package €20/16/8 for adults/ 10 to 17 years/four to nine years that includes return transport from Paris, bus transfers and admission to the chateau.

Local buses (€1.30) link the train station with central Fontainebleau, 2km to the southwest, every 10 minutes from about 6am until about 9.30pm (11.30pm on Sunday). The tourist office hires out normal bicycles (see p189). For mountain bike hire try **Cycles À La Petite Reine** (☎ 01 60 74 57 57; 32 rue des Sablons; per hr/½ day/day/week €5/10/13/54 Mon-Fri, €13/16 Sat & Sun; ⊗ 9am-7.30pm Mon-Sat, 9am-6pm Sun).

VAUX-LE-VICOMTE

Privately owned **Château de Vaux-le-Vicomte** (☎ 01 64 14 41 90; www.vaux-le-vicomte.com; adult/senior, student & 6-16 yrs €12/9.50, candlelight visit €15/13, exhibit, garden & museum only €7; ⊗ 10am-1pm & 2-6pm Mon-Fri, 10am-6pm Sat & Sun late Mar–mid-Nov, candlelight visit 8pm-midnight Fri Jul & Aug, Sat May–mid-Oct) and its magnificent **formal gardens** (⊗ 10am-6pm late Mar–mid-Nov), 20km north of Fontainebleau and 61km southeast of Paris, were designed and built by Le Brun, Le Vau and Le Nôtre between 1656 and 1661 as a precursor to their more ambitious work at Versailles.

Unfortunately the beauty of Vaux-le-Vicomte's turned out to be the undoing of its owner, Nicolas Fouquet, Louis XIV's minister of finance. It seems that Louis, seething with jealousy that he had been upstaged at the chateau's official opening, had Fouquet thrown into prison, where the unfortunate *ministre* died in 1680. Today visitors can view the interior of the chateau, and wander through the gardens and the **Musée des Équipages** (Carriage Museum; ⊗ 10am-1pm & 2-6pm Mon-Fri, 10am-6pm Sat & Sun late Mar–mid-Nov).

On the second and the last Saturday of every month from late March to October, there are elaborate *jeux d'eau* (fountain displays) in the gardens from 3pm to 6pm.

Getting There & Away

Unfortunately, Vaux-le-Vicomte is not an easy place to get to by public transport. The chateau is 6km northeast of Melun, which is served by RER line D2 from Paris (€7, 45 minutes). You will have to take a taxi to the chateau from Melun, which will cost between €15 and €20. If you are travelling by car, take the N6 from Paris and the A5a (in the direction of Melun) and exit at Voisenon. From Fontainebleau, follow the N6 and the N36.

CHANTILLY

pop 10,900

The elegant town of Chantilly, 48km north of Paris, has a heavily restored but imposing chateau, surrounded by parkland, gardens, lakes and a vast forest. There's more than ample opportunity here for walking, cycling and horse riding.

Information

Office de Tourisme de Chantilly (☎ 03 44 67 37 37; www.chantilly-tourisme.com; 60 av du Maréchal Joffre; ⏰ 9.30am-12.30pm & 1.30-5.30pm Mon-Sat, 10.30am-1.30pm Sun May-Sep, 9.30am-12.30pm & 1.30-5.30pm Mon-Sat Oct-Apr) Ask the staff for a copy of *Circuit Touristique en Ville*, a pamphlet with a 23-stop walk around town starting at the tourist office.

Post Office (26 av du Maréchal Joffre)

Société Générale (1 av du Maréchal Joffre; ⏰ 8.30am-12.15pm & 1.45-5.30pm Mon-Thu, 8.30am-12.15pm & 1.45-6.30pm Fri, 9.30am-3.25pm Sat)

Sights

CHÂTEAU DE CHANTILLY

The **Château de Chantilly** (☎ 03 44 62 62 62; www.chateaudechantilly.com; adult/12-17yrs/4-11 yrs €7/6/2.80; ⏰ 10am-6pm daily Jul-Aug, 10am-6pm Wed-Mon Mar-Jun, Sep & Oct, 10.30am-12.45pm & 2-5pm Wed-Mon Nov-Feb), left in a shambles after the Revolution, is of interest mainly because of its gardens and a number of superb paintings. It consists of two attached buildings, which are entered through the same vestibule. The **Petit Château** was built around 1560 for Anne de Montmorency (1492–1567), who served six French kings as *connétable* (high constable), diplomat and warrior and died fighting Protestants in the Counter-Reformation. The attached Renaissance-style **Grand Château** was rebuilt 100 years after the Revolution by the Duke of Aumale, son of King Louis-Philippe. It served as a French military headquarters during WWI.

The Grand Château, to the right as you enter the vestibule, contains the **Musée Condé**. Its unremarkable 19th-century rooms are adorned with furnishings, paintings and sculptures haphazardly arranged according to the whims of the duke, who donated the chateau to the Institut de France at the end of the 19th century on the condition that the exhibits not be reorganised and

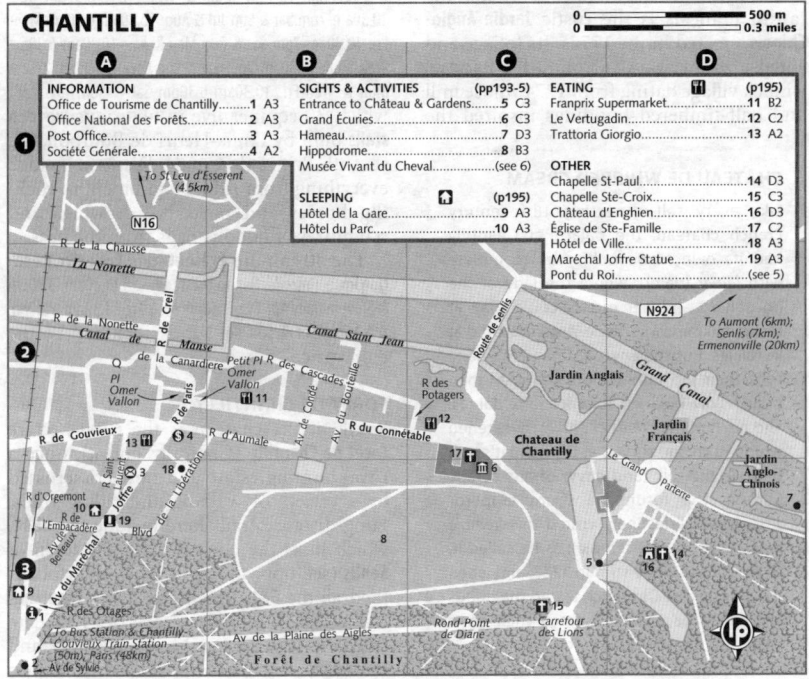

CHANTILLY

0 _____ 500 m
0 _____ 0.3 miles

INFORMATION	
Office de Tourisme de Chantilly	1 A3
Office National des Forêts	2 A3
Post Office	3 A3
Société Générale	4 A2

SIGHTS & ACTIVITIES	(pp193-5)
Entrance to Château & Gardens	5 C3
Grand Écuries	6 C3
Hameau	7 D3
Hippodrome	8 B3
Musée Vivant du Cheval	(see 6)

SLEEPING	(p195)
Hôtel de la Gare	9 A3
Hôtel du Parc	10 A3

EATING	(p195)
Franprix Supermarket	11 B2
Le Vertugadin	12 C2
Trattoria Giorgio	13 A2

OTHER	
Chapelle St-Paul	14 D3
Chapelle Ste-Croix	15 C3
Château d'Enghien	16 D3
Église de Ste-Famille	17 C2
Hôtel de Ville	18 A3
Maréchal Joffre Statue	19 A3
Pont du Roi	(see 5)

that they remain open to the public. The most remarkable works are hidden away in a small room called the **Sanctuaire**, including paintings by Raphael, Filippino Lippi and Jean Fouquet.

The Petit Château contains the **Appartements des Princes** (Princes' Suites), which are straight ahead from the entrance. The highlight here is the **Cabinet des Livres**, a repository of 700 manuscripts and more than 30,000 volumes, including a Gutenberg Bible and a facsimile of the *Très Riches Heures du Duc de Berry*, an illuminated manuscript dating from the 15th century that illustrates the calendar year for both the peasantry and the nobility. The **chapel**, to the left as you walk into the vestibule, has woodwork and stained-glass windows dating from the mid-16th century and was assembled by the duke in 1882.

The chateau's excellent gardens were once among the most spectacular in France. The formal **Jardin Français**, with flowerbeds, lakes and **Grand Canal** laid out by Le Nôtre in the mid-17th century, is northeast of the main building. To the west, the 'wilder' **Jardin Anglais** was begun in 1817. East of the Jardin Français is the rustic **Jardin Anglo-Chinois**, created in the 1770s. Its foliage and silted-up waterways surround the **Hameau**, a mock village dating from 1774 whose mill and half-timbered buildings inspired the

Hameau de la Reine at Versailles. Crème Chantilly – cream beaten with icing and vanilla sugar and dolloped on everything sweet that doesn't move in France – was born here (see left).

A normal ticket allows entry to the chateau, Musée Condé and park, though you can visit just the **park** and **gardens** (adult/4-11 yrs €3/2; ☼ 10am-6pm Mar-Oct, 10am-12.45pm & 2-6pm Nov-Feb) separately. Combination tickets include the park and canal boat ride (adult/four to 11 years €8/5); the chateau, museum, park and boat adult/12 to 17 years/four to 11 years €13/11/7); and the chateau, museum, park, boat and minitrain ride through the park (adult/12 to 17 years/four to 11 years €15/13/9).

The **Grandes Écuries** (Grand Stables) of the chateau, built between 1719 and 1740 to house 240 horses and more than 400 hunting hounds, stand apart from the chateau to the west and close to Chantilly's famous **Hippodrome** (racecourse), inaugurated in 1834. They house the **Musée Vivant du Cheval** (Living Horse Museum; ☎ 03 44 57 13 13; www.musee-vivant-du-cheval.fr; adult/12-17 yrs/4-11 yrs €8/6.50/5.50; ☼ 10.30am-6.30pm Mon & Wed-Fri, 2-6.30pm Tue, 10.30am-7pm Sat & Sun Jul & Aug; 10.30am-6.30pm Mon-Fri, 10.30am-7pm Sat & Sun May & Jun; 10.30am-6.30pm Wed-Mon, 10.30am-7pm Sat & Sun Apr, Sep & Oct; 2-6pm Mon & Wed-Fri, 10.30am-6.30pm Sat & Sun Nov-Mar), whose 30 equines live in luxurious **wooden stalls** built by Louis-Henri de Bourbon, the seventh Prince de Condé. Displays include everything from riding equipment to rocking horses and portraits, drawings and sculptures of famous nags from the past.

The 30-minute **Présentation Équestre Pédagogique** (Introduction to Dressage; ☼ 11.30am, 3.30pm & 5.30pm daily Apr-Oct, 3.30pm Mon-Fri, 11.30am, 3.30pm & 5.15pm Sat & Sun Nov-Mar) is included in the entry price.

FORÊT DE CHANTILLY
South of the chateau is the 6300-hectare **Forêt de Chantilly** (Chantilly Forest), once a royal hunting estate and now crisscrossed by a variety of walking and riding trails. Long-distance trails here include the **GR11**, which links the chateau with the town of **Senlis** (see opposite) and its wonderful cathedral; the **GR1**, which goes from **Luzarches** (famed for its cathedral, parts of which date from the 12th century) to **Ermenonville**; and the **GR12**, which goes northeast from four

---

CHÂTEAU DE WHIPPED CREAM

Like every self-respecting 18th-century French chateau, the palace at Chantilly had its own *hameau* (hamlet) complete with *laitier* (dairy), where the lady of the household and her guests could play at being milkmaids, as Marie-Antoinette did at Versailles. But the cows at Chantilly's dairy took their job rather more seriously than their fellow bovines at other faux dairies, and news of the *crème chantilly* (sweetened whipped cream) served at the hamlet's teas became the talk (and envy) of aristocratic Europe. The future Habsburg emperor Joseph II clandestinely visited this *'temple de marbre'* (marble temple), as he called it, to try out the white stuff in 1777, and when the Baroness of Oberkirch tasted the goods she cried, 'Never have I eaten such good cream, so appetising, so well prepared'.

lakes known as the **Étangs de Commelles** to the **Forêt d'Halatte**.

The area is covered by IGN's 1:25,000-scale *Forêts de Chantilly, d'Halatte and d'Ermenonville* map (No 2412OT; €9). The 1:100,000-scale *Carte de Découverte des Milieux Naturels et du Patrimoine Bâti* (€6.50), available at the tourist office, indicates sites of interest (eg churches, chateaux, museums and ruins). The **Office National des Forêts** (☎ 03 44 57 03 88; www.onf.fr in French; 1 av de Sylvie; ⏰ 8.30am-noon & 2-5pm Mon-Fri), just southeast of the tourist office, publishes a good walking guide for families called *Promenons-Nous dans les Forêts de Picardie: Chantilly, Halatte & Ermenonville* (€7.50). Mountain bikers might want to pick up a copy of the detailed *Les Cahiers de la Randonnée VTT: Forêts de Chantilly et d'Ermenonville* (€13) at the tourist office.

Sleeping & Eating

Hôtel du Parc (☎ 03 44 58 20 00; www.bestwestern.fr; 36 av du Maréchal Joffre; s €78-88, d €86-96, tr €98-108, ste €112; **P**) This architecturally bankrupt place is no great shakes, but it's part of the Best Western chain so you can expect a reasonable standard of service. Cheaper rooms face the street.

Hôtel de la Gare (☎ 03 44 62 56 90; fax 03 44 62 56 99; place de la Gare; s & d €49) Opposite the train station, this rambling hotel with a dozen rooms is a surprisingly pleasant place with renovated shower-equipped doubles.

Le Vertugadin (☎ 03 44 57 03 19; 44 rue du Connétable; starters €8-15, mains €15-25, lunch menu €15, dinner menu €23; ⏰ lunch daily, dinner to 11pm Mon-Sat) This very friendly and highly recommended restaurant has excellent menus and a walled-in garden that is a delight in summer.

Trattoria Giorgio (☎ 03 44 57 00 48; av du Maréchal Joffre; starters €6.90-11.50, pasta €7.90-11, mains €11.50-1810, lunch menu €9.90; ⏰ lunch & dinner to 11.30pm) Giorgio's is a very central Italian bistro – just the ticket for a pizza or more ambitious meal en route to/from the train station.

Franprix (132 rue du Connétable; ⏰ 8.30am-12.30pm & 2.30-7.30pm Tue-Thu, 8.30am-7.30pm Fri & Sat, 8.30am-1pm Sun) The supermarket is midway between the train station and the chateau.

Getting There & Away

Château de Chantilly is just over 2km east of the train station (next to the bus station); the most direct route from there is to walk along av de la Plaine des Aigles through a section of the Forêt de Chantilly. You'll get a better sense of the town, however, by taking av du Maréchal Joffre and rue de Paris to connect with rue du Connétable, Chantilly's principal thoroughfare.

Paris' Gare du Nord links with Chantilly-Gouvieux train station (€7.45, 30 to 45 minutes) by a mixture of RER and SNCF commuter trains (almost 40 a day; 20 on Sunday). The last train back to Paris departs daily just before midnight.

SENLIS
pop 16,250

Senlis, just 10km northeast of Chantilly, is an attractive medieval town of winding cobblestone streets, Gallo-Roman ramparts and towers. It was a royal seat from the time of Clovis to Henri IV and contains four small but fine **museums**, devoted to such diverse subjects as art, archaeology, hunting and the French cavalry in North Africa, and an important 12th-century cathedral.

The Gothic **Cathédrale de Notre Dame** (place Notre Dame; ⏰ 8am-6pm), which is entered through the south portal, was built between 1150 and 1191. The cathedral is unusually bright, but the stained glass, though original, is generally unexceptional. The magnificent carved stone **Grand Portal** (1170), on the western side facing place du Parvis Notre Dame, has statues and a central relief relating to the life of the Virgin Mary. It is believed to have been the inspiration for the portal at the cathedral in Chartres.

The **Office de Tourisme de Senlis** (☎ 03 44 53 06 40; off.tourisme-senlis@wanadoo.fr; place du Parvis Notre Dame; ⏰ 10am-12.30pm & 2-5pm Mon-Sat, 11.15am-1pm & 2.30-5pm Sun Nov-Feb, 10am-12.30pm & 2-6.15pm Mon-Sat, 10.30am-1pm & 2.30-6.15pm Sun Mar-Oct) is just opposite (and west of) the cathedral.

Sleeping & Eating

Hostellerie de la Porte Bellon (☎ 03 44 53 03 05; www.portebellon.com; 51 rue Bellon; s with shower €52-65, with bath €65-70, d with shower €55-68, with bath €68-73; **P**) This wonderful 18-room hotel is housed in an 18th-century manor a couple of hundred metres east of the cathedral.

Le Scaramouche (☎ 03 44 53 01 26; 4 place Notre Dame; starters €10-22, mains €14-35, menus €24, €35 & €58; ⏰ lunch & dinner to 10.30pm Thu-Mon) The up-market Scaramouche is the best and most central place for a meal while visiting the cathedral or museums.

Surrounding the open-air **market** (rue St-Hilaire; 8am-1pm Tue & Fri) southwest of the cathedral are a number of relatively cheap places to eat including pizzerias, creperies and cafés.

Getting There & Away

Buses (€3.10, 25 minutes) link Senlis with Chantilly's bus station just next to its train station about every half-hour on weekdays and hourly on Saturday with about a half-dozen departures on Sunday. The last bus returns to Chantilly at 8pm on weekdays (just after 7pm at the weekend).

CHARTRES

pop 40,250

The magnificent 13th-century cathedral of Chartres, crowned by two very different spires – one Gothic, the other Romanesque – rises from rich farmland 88km southwest of Paris and dominates the medieval town around its base. The cathedral's varied collection of relics, particularly the Ste-Voile (the 'Holy Veil' said to have been worn by the Virgin Mary when she gave birth to Jesus), attracted many pilgrims during the Middle Ages, who contributed to the building and extensions of the cathedral. With its astonishing blue stained glass and other treasures, the cathedral at Chartres is a must-see for any visitor to Paris.

Information

MONEY

Crédit Agricole (1 Cloître Notre Dame; 8.45am-12.30pm & 1.50-5.30pm Tue-Fri, 8.45am-12.30pm & 1.50-4pm Sat)
BNP Paribas (7-9 place des Épars; 8.30am-noon & 1.30-5.35pm Tue, 8.50am-noon & 1.45-5.35pm Wed-Fri, 8.30am-noon & 1.30-4.45pm Sat)

POST

Post Office (place des Épars) Housed in an impressive neogothic building with *fin-de-siècle* mosaics adorning the front.

TOURIST INFORMATION

Office de Tourisme de Chartres (02 37 18 26 26; info@otchartres.fr; place de la Cathédrale; 9am-7pm Mon-Sat, 9.30am-5.30pm Sun Apr-Sep; 10am-6pm Mon-Sat, 10am-1pm & 2.30-4.30pm Sun Oct-Mar) The tourist office, across the square from the cathedral's main

entrance, rents self-paced English-language **audioguide tours** (for 1/2 people €5.50/8.50; 1½hr) of the medieval city.

Sights

CATHÉDRALE NOTRE DAME DE CHARTRES

The 130m-long cathedral **Cathédrale Notre Dame de Chartres** (Cathedral of Our Lady of Chartres; 02 37 21 22 07; www.cathedrale-chartres.com in French; place de la Cathédrale; 8.30am-7.30pm), one of the crowning architectural achievements of Western civilisation, was built in the Gothic style during the first quarter of the 13th century to replace a Romanesque cathedral that had been devastated – along with much of the town – by fire on the night of 10 June 1194. Because of effective fundraising among the aristocracy and donated labour from the common folk, construction took only 30 years, resulting in a high degree of architectural unity.

Excellent English-language **guided tours** (adult/senior/student €6/4/3; noon & 2.45pm Mon-Sat Apr-early Nov; 1½hr) are conducted by Chartres expert Malcolm Miller (02 37 28 15 58; fax 02 37 28 33 03). English-language **audioguide tours** (25/45/70min €2.90/3.80/5.65) with three different themes can be hired from the cathedral bookshop. French-language **guided tours** (adult/senior/student & over 10 €6/4/3; 10.30am Tue-Sat, 3pm daily Apr-Oct, 2.30pm daily Nov-Mar) also depart from here.

The cathedral's west, north and south entrances have superbly ornamented triple **portals**, but the west entrance, known as the **Portail Royal**, is the only one that predates the 1194 fire. Carved from 1145 to 1155, its superb statues, whose features are elongated in the Romanesque style, represent the glory of Christ in the centre, and the Nativity and Ascension to the right and left, respectively. The structure's other main Romanesque feature is the 103m-high **Clocher Vieux** (Old Bell Tower; also called the Tour Sud, or 'South Tower'), which was begun in the 1140s. It is the tallest Romanesque steeple still standing anywhere.

A visit to the 112m-high **Clocher Neuf** (New Bell Tower; adult/18-25 yrs/under 18 €4.60/3.10/free, 1st Sun of certain months free; 9.30am-noon & 2-5.30pm Mon-Sat, 2pm-5.30pm Sun May-Aug, to 4.30pm Sep-Apr), which is also known as the Tour Nord (North Tower), is well worth the ticket price and the climb up the long spiral stairway. Access is just behind the cathedral

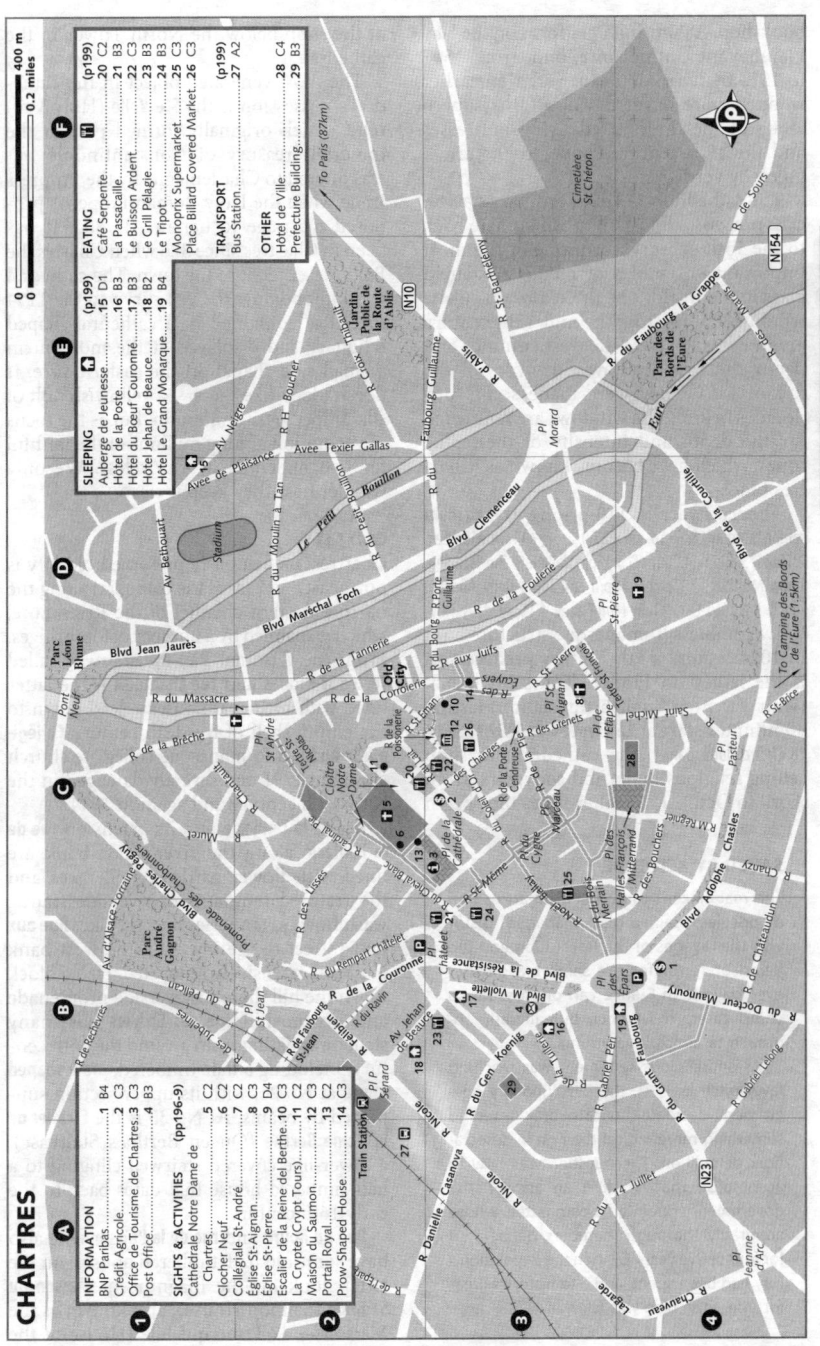

CHARTRES

AROUND PARIS

bookshop. A 70m-high platform on the lacy Flamboyant Gothic spire, built from 1507 to 1513 by Jehan de Beauce after an earlier wooden spire burnt down, affords superb views of the three-tiered flying buttresses and the 19th-century copper roof, turned green by verdigris.

The cathedral's 172 extraordinary **stained-glass windows**, almost all of which date back to the 13th century, form one of the most important ensembles of medieval stained glass in the world. The three most exquisite windows dating from the mid-12th century are in the wall above the west entrance and below the rose window. Survivors of the fire of 1194 (they were made some four decades before), the windows are renowned for the depth and intensity of their blue tones, which have become known as 'Chartres blue'.

The cathedral's 110m-long **crypt** (adult/senior, student & 7-18 yrs €2.60/2; ☾ 11am Mon-Sat, 2.15pm, 3.30pm, 4.30pm & 5.15pm daily late Jun-late Sep, 11am Mon-Sat, 2.15pm, 3.30pm & 4.30pm daily Apr-late Jun & late Sep-Oct, 11am Mon-Sat & 4.15pm daily Nov-Mar), a tombless Romanesque structure built in 1024 around a 9th-century predecessor, is the largest in France. Tours in French (with a written English translation) lasting 30 minutes start at **La Crypte** (☎ 02 37 21 56 33; 18 Cloître Notre Dame), the cathedral-run shop selling religious items and souvenirs, from April to October. At other times they begin

SAVED BY RED TAPE

The magnificent cathedral at Chartres and its priceless stained glass managed to survive the ravages of the Revolution and the Reign of Terror for the same reason that everyday life in France can often seem so complicated: the French bureaucratic approach to almost everything.

As antireligious sentiment was reaching fever pitch in 1791, the Revolutionary government decided the cathedral deserved something more radical than mere desecration: demolition. The question was how to accomplish that. To find an answer, the government appointed a committee, whose admirably thorough members deliberated for four or five years. By then the Revolution's fury had been spent, and – to history's great fortune – the plan was shelved.

at the shop below the North Tower in the cathedral.

The most venerated object in the cathedral's possession is the **Ste-Voile** (Holy Veil) relic, which originally formed part of the imperial treasury of Constantinople but was offered to Charlemagne by the Empress Irene when the Holy Roman Emperor proposed marriage to her in AD 802. It has been in Chartres since 876 when Charles the Bald presented it to the town. The cathedral was built because the veil survived the 1194 fire. It is contained in a cathedral-shaped reliquary and displayed at the moment in a small side chapel off the eastern aisle. It doesn't look like much – a yellowish bolt of silk draped over a support – but as the focus of veneration among millions of the faithful for two millennia it is priceless. We only wonder how they keep it clean.

OLD CITY

Chartres' meticulously preserved old city is northeast and east of the cathedral along the narrow western channel of the River Eure, which is spanned by a number of footbridges. From rue Cardinal Pie, the stairway called **Tertre St-Nicolas** and **rue Chantault** – the latter lined with medieval houses – lead down to the empty shell of the 12th-century **Collégiale St-André**, a Romanesque collegiate church closed in 1791 and severely damaged in the early 19th century and again in 1944.

Rue de la Tannerie and its extension **rue de la Foulerie** along the river's east bank are lined with flower gardens, mill races and the restored remnants of riverside trades: wash houses, tanneries and the like. **Rue aux Juifs** (Street of the Jews) on the west bank has been extensively renovated. Half a block down the hill there's a riverside promenade and up the hill **rue des Écuyers** has many structures dating from around the 16th century, including a half-timbered, **prow-shaped house** at No 26, with its upper section supported by beams. At No 35 is the **Escalier de la Reine Berthe** (Queen Bertha's Staircase), a tower-like covered stairwell clinging to a half-timbered house that dates back to the early 16th century.

Rue du Bourg and **rue de la Poissonnerie** also have some old half-timbered houses; on the latter, look for the magnificent **Maison du Saumon** (Salmon House), also known as the Maison de la Truie qui File (House of the

Spinning Sow), at No 10-12 with its carved consoles of the Angel Gabriel and Mary, Michael the Archangel slaying the dragon and, of course, the eponymous salmon. It is now a restaurant.

From **place St-Pierre**, you get a good view of the flying buttresses holding up the 12th- and 13th-century **Église St-Pierre** (place St-Pierre; 9am-noon & 2-6pm). Once part of a Benedictine monastery founded in the 7th century, it was outside the city walls and thus vulnerable to attack; the fortress-like, pre-Romanesque **bell tower** attached to it was used as a refuge by monks and dates from around 1000. The fine, brightly coloured **clerestory windows** in the nave, choir and apse date from the early 14th century.

Église St-Aignan (place St-Aignan; 9am-noon & 2-6pm), first built in the early 16th century, is interesting for its wooden barrel-vault roof (1625), arcaded nave and painted interior of faded blue and gold floral motifs (c 1870). The stained glass and the Renaissance **Chapelle de St-Michel** date from the 16th century.

Sleeping

Hôtel Le Grand Monarque (02 37 18 15 15; www .bw-grand-monarque.com; 22 place des Épars; s €85-107, d €105-120, tr €145-155; P X □) This three-star hotel is supposedly Chartres' finest but some of the public areas and the guest rooms have a frayed feel and look to them.

Hôtel de la Poste (02 37 21 04 27; fax 02 37 36 42 17; 3 rue du Général Koenig; s with shower/bath €57/62, d €71.50/77.50, tr €94/117; P □) A two-star property just off the place des Épars, this place offers superb service and a central location.

Hôtel du Bœuf Couronné (02 37 18 06 06; fax 02 37 21 72 13; 15 place Châtelet; s/d with washbasin & toilet €27/30, with shower €40/50, with bath €43/57) This cosy, Logis de France–affiliated guesthouse in the centre of everything offers excellent value and has a memorable **restaurant** (menus €22 & €26; lunch & dinner to 11pm) with generous menus.

Hôtel Jehan de Beauce (02 37 21 01 41; www .contact-hotel-chartres.com; 19 av Jehan de Beauce; s/d with washbasin & toilet €29/36, s with shower €43-48, d with shower €50-55, s with bath €48-52, d with bath €55-59, tr €55-61; □) If you're looking for budget accommodation, this hotel has relatively clean, but very spartan singles, doubles and triples.

Auberge de Jeunesse (02 37 34 27 64; fax 02 37 35 78 85; 23 av Neigre; dm €11; X □) Reception at the hostel, which is about 1.5km east of

the train station via blvd Charles Péguy and blvd Jean Jaurès, opens from 2pm to 10pm daily and curfew is 10.30pm in winter and 11.30pm in summer. To get there from the train station, take bus No 5 (direction: Mare aux Moines) to the Rouliers stop.

Eating

Le Tripot (02 37 36 60 11; 11 place Jean Moulin; starters €11-19, mains €13.50-24, lunch menu €15, dinner menus €22.50, €28.50 & €37.50; lunch Tue-Sun, dinner till 9.30pm Tue-Sat) This wonderful little place just down from the cathedral is one of the best bistros in Chartres.

Le Buisson Ardent (02 37 34 04 66; 10 rue au Lait; starters €9.50-16, mains €13-22, lunch menu €18, dinner menu €22; lunch Thu-Tue, dinner to 10.30pm Mon, Tue, Thu-Sat) 'The Burning Bush' is a charming, old-style place with good-value menus.

La Passacaille (02 37 21 52 10; 30 rue Ste-Même; starters €3.70-8.10, mains €9.90-12.40; lunch & dinner until 10.30pm) This welcoming Italian place has particularly good pizzas (€7.10 to €10.10) and fresh pasta (€8.10 to €9.50).

Le Grill Pélagie (02 37 36 07 49; 1 av Jehan de Beauce; starters €3.70-7.90, mains €9.90-14.80, menus €11.50-18.50; lunch & dinner till 11pm Mon-Sat) This is a popular place specialising in grills and Tex-Mex dishes such as guacamole and quesadillas (€6.50) and fajitas (€13.80 to €15.60).

Café Serpente (02 37 21 68 81; 2 Cloître Notre Dame; salads & omelettes €5.20-1150, dishes €13.50-15; 10am-1pm) The atmospheric Serpente brasserie and *salon de thé* (tearoom) is conveniently located opposite the cathedral.

There are a lot of food shops surrounding the **covered market** (place Billard; 7am-1pm Sat), just off rue des Changes south of the cathedral. The market itself dates from the early 20th century.

The **Monoprix** (21 rue Noël Ballay & 10 rue du Bois Merrain; 9am-7.30pm Mon-Sat) department store with two entrances has a supermarket on the ground floor.

Getting There & Away

Some 30 SNCF trains a day (20 on Sunday) link Paris' Gare Montparnasse (€11.80, 55 to 70 minutes) with Chartres, all of which pass through Versailles-Chantiers (€9.90, 45 to 60 minutes). The last train back to Paris leaves Chartres a bit after 9pm weekdays, just before 9pm on Saturday and sometime after 10pm on Sunday.

200

Far Northern France

The first bit of France seen by visitors coming from the UK is often Le Nord de France, densely populated and laden with declining rust-belt industries. One of the country's more fabled corners it isn't, but the area – made up of three historical regions, Flanders (Flandre or Flandres), Artois and Picardy (Picardie) – has lots to offer those willing to do a bit of exploring.

In the Middle Ages, France's far northern tip, together with much of Belgium and part of the Netherlands, made up a feudal principality known as Flanders. Many people in the area still speak Flemish – essentially Dutch with some variances in pronunciation and vocabulary – and, unlike anywhere else in France, the locals drink more beer than wine. This is especially true during the region's many annual festivals and *braderies* (carnivals; see p29 and p32).

It takes only two hours on the Eurostar to get from London to Lille, the region's surprisingly friendly commercial, cultural and culinary capital. Some 50km to the south, the 17th- and 18th-century Flemish-style buildings in picturesque Arras have no equal anywhere in France. Amiens, not far from a number of moving WWI memorials, is graced by one of France's most magnificent Gothic cathedrals.

Calais' prosperity as the premier trans-Channel port has come partly at the expense of Boulogne-sur-Mer, endowed with a picturesque old city, and Dunkirk (Dunkerque). The spectacular Côte d'Opale stretches from Calais to Boulogne along the Strait of Dover (Pas de Calais), the narrowest bit of the English Channel (La Manche). Inland, you'll find WWII sites, St-Omer, known for its basilica, and hilltop Cassel.

Just outside Greater Paris, Napoleon III's Compiègne is a popular destination for day trippers from Paris, Beauvais is known for its huge, unfinished cathedral, and Laon offers panoramic views from the walls of its hilltop old town.

FAR NORTHERN FRANCE

HIGHLIGHTS

- Visit Lille's superb **museums** (p203), explore the city's **old town** (p203) and partake of its **restaurants** and **nightlife** (p206, p207)

- Ramble along the spectacular windswept **Côte d'Opale coastline** (p215) and gaze across the Channel to the white cliffs of Dover

- Explore Arras' Flemish-style **Grand' Place** and **place des Héros** (p221)

- Admire Amiens' breathtaking **Gothic cathedral** (p227) both inside and out

- Ponder the horrors and sacrifices of WWI at the evocative **Battle of the Somme memorials** (p223)

- Amble around Laon's hilltop fortifications and picturesque **old city** (p234)

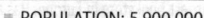

Côte d'Opale
Lille
Arras
Battle of the Somme Memorials
Amiens
Laon

| POPULATION: 5,900,000 | AREA: 31,969 SQ KM |

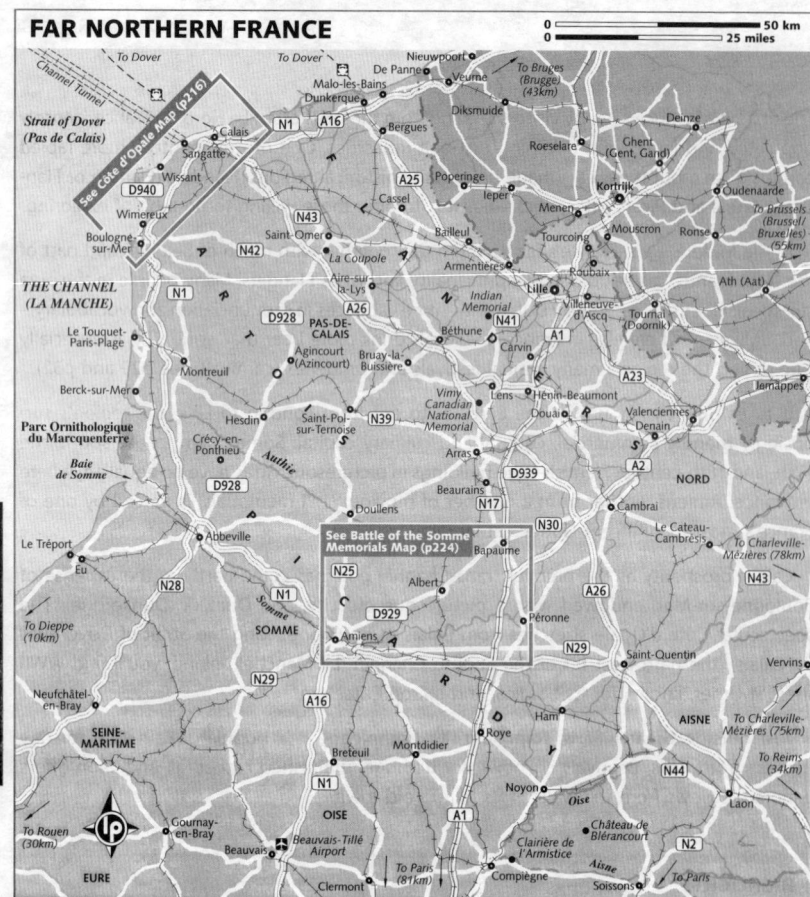

FAR NORTHERN FRANCE

LILLE

pop 1 million

Lively, forward-looking Lille (Rijsel in Flemish) may be France's most underrated major city. Long an industrial centre, Lille's recent history shows how a grimy metropolis, its economy based on declining technologies, can transform itself – with the help of generous government investment – into a glittering and self-confident cultural hub. Highlights for the visitor include an attractive old town with a strong Flemish flavour, two renowned art museums, stylish shopping, some fine dining options and a happening, student-driven nightlife scene. In 2004 Lille (along with Genoa) was the EU's Cultural Capital of Europe.

Orientation

At the heart of Lille are three public squares: place du Général de Gaulle (also called the Grand' Place), place du Théâtre and place Rihour. The area of narrow streets north of place du Général de Gaulle is known as Vieux Lille (Old Lille).

Gare Lille-Flandres is about 400m southeast of place du Général de Gaulle; ultramodern Gare Lille-Europe is 500m east of the square.

Information

BOOKSHOPS

Le Furet du Nord (☎ 03 20 78 43 43; 15 place du Général de Gaulle) The largest bookstore in Europe. Has a wide selection of English-language works.

INTERNET ACCESS

Cybercafé Le Smiley (☎ 03 20 21 12 19; 2 rue Royale; per hr €6.10; 🕑 noon-3am Mon-Sat, 4pm-midnight Sun) A lively, gay-friendly and very popular bar with a DJ on Friday nights. Lots of fun, though probably a bit too noisy for writing your thesis.

LAUNDRY

Zombified by too much art and culture? You can stare at the machines going round and round… There are laundrettes at 57 rue du Molinel, 4 rue Ovigneur and 13 rue de la Collégiale. They are open 7am to 7pm or 8pm.

MEDICAL SERVICES

Hôpital Roger Salengro (☎ 03 20 44 61 40/41; rue du Professeur Émile Laine; metro CHR B Calmette; 🕑 24hr) The *accueil urgences* (emergency room/casualty ward) of Lille's vast, 15-hospital Cité Hospitalière is 4km southwest of the city centre.

SOS Médecins (☎ 03 20 29 91 91; day/weekend/night/ late-night €30/42.56/58.50/63.50) Doctors make house calls 24 hours a day.

MONEY

There are lots of commercial banks along rue Nationale. The tourist office changes money but the exchange rate is poor.

Exchange bureaus at the train stations: **Lille-Europe** (ICE Bureau de Change; 🕑 7.30am-8pm Mon-Sat, 10am-8pm Sun) Near Accès (track access) C. **Lille-Flandres** (Travelex bureau; 🕑 8am-8pm Mon-Fri, 10am-6pm Sat & Sun) Next to counter No 14.

POST

Branch Post Office (1 blvd Carnot) In the Chambre de Commerce building; changes money and has a Cyberposte. **Main Post Office** (8 place de la République) Changes money and has a Cyberposte.

TOURIST INFORMATION

Tourist Office (☎ 03 59 57 94 00; www.lilletourism .com; place Rihour; 🕑 9.30am-6.30pm Mon-Sat, 10am-noon & 2-5pm Sun & holidays) Occupies a remnant of the 15th-century Palais Rihour, a former residence of the dukes of Burgundy; a war memorial forms the structure's eastern side. A brochure (€1) outlines four walking tours.

Sights

CITY CENTRE

North of place du Général de Gaulle, **Vieux Lille** gleams with restored 17th- and 18th-century houses. The old, brick residences along **rue de la Monnaie** now house chic shops (see also Musée de l'Hospice Comtesse, p205). Other equally atmospheric streets include **rue de la Grande Chaussée** and **rue Esquermoise**.

The ornate, Flemish-Renaissance **Vieille Bourse** (Old Stock Exchange; place du Général de Gaulle), built in 1652, actually consists of 24 separate buildings. The courtyard in the middle hosts a **book market** (🕑 2-7pm Tue-Sun).

On the southern side of place du Général de Gaulle, the Art Deco home of **La Voix du Nord** (1932), the leading regional daily, has a gilded sculpture of the Three Graces on top. The goddess-topped **column** (1845) in the square's fountain commemorates the Austrian siege of Lille in 1792.

Nearby, place du Théâtre is dominated by the neoclassical **Opéra** and the tower-topped, neo-Flemish **Chambre de Commerce**, both of which date from the early 20th century.

PALAIS DES BEAUX-ARTS

The world-renowned **Fine Arts Museum** (☎ 03 20 06 78 00; place de la République; metro République Beaux Arts; adult/12-25 yrs/under 12 €4.60/3/free; 🕑 2-6pm Mon, 10am-6pm Wed, Thu, Sat & Sun, 10am-7pm Fri) possesses a superb collection of 15th- to 20th-century paintings, including works by Rubens and Van Dyck and a recently acquired Manet. On the ground floor, there's exquisite porcelain and faïence, much of it of local provenance; the basement houses classical archaeological finds, medieval statuary and intricate 18th-century models of the fortified cities of northern France and Belgium. Tickets are valid for the whole day. An audioguide costs €4.60; information sheets are available in each hall.

MUSÉE D'ART MODERNE

The highly regarded **Museum of Modern Art** (☎ 03 20 19 68 68; www.nordnet.fr/mam in French; 1 allée du Musée, Villeneuve-d'Ascq; adult/12-25 yrs €6.50/1.50,

---

LILLE MÉTROPOLE ALL INCLUSIVE

This pass, which comes in one-/two-/three-day versions (€20/30/45), gets you access to most of the museums in greater Lille, discounts on tickets to cultural events and unlimited use of public transport. The three-day version includes various sites in the Nord-Pas-de-Calais region and the use of regional TER trains. It is on sale at the Lille, Roubaix, Tourcoing and Watrelos tourist offices.

LILLE

0 ▬▬▬▬▬ 400 m
0 ▬▬▬▬▬ 0.2 miles

10am-2pm 1st Sun of the month admission free; ☼ 10am-6pm Wed-Mon), situated in a sculpture park 8km east of central Lille, displays colourful, playful and just plain weird works by artists including Braque, Calder, Léger, Miró, Modigliani and Picasso. To get there, take metro line No 1 to Pont de Bois and then bus No 41 to Parc Urbain-Musée.

LA PISCINE MUSÉE D'ART ET D'INDUSTRIE
If Paris can turn a disused train station into a world-class museum, why not take an Art Deco municipal swimming pool (built 1927–32) – an architectural masterpiece inspired by civic pride and hygienic high-mindedness – and transform it into a temple of the arts? This innovative **museum** (☎ 03 20 69 23 60; http://museeroubaix.free.fr in French; 23 rue de l'Espérance, Roubaix; metro Gare Jean Lebas; adult €3, incl temporary exhibit €5; ☼ 11am-6pm Tue-Thu, 11am-8pm Fri, 1-6pm Sat & Sun), 11km northeast of central Lille, showcases fine arts, applied arts and sculpture in a delightful watery environment. The amusing website is worth a surf, even if you don't understand French.

MUSÉE DE L'HOSPICE COMTESSE
Housed in an attractive 17th-century poorhouse, the **Hospice Comtesse Museum** (☎ 03 28 36 84 00; 32 rue de la Monnaie; adult/12-25 yrs €2.30/1.50; ☼ 2-6pm Mon, 10am-12.30pm & 2-6pm Wed-Sun) features ceramics, faïence wall tiles and 17th- and 18th-century paintings, furniture and religious art. The **Salle des Malades** (Hospital Hall) is decorated with Lille tapestries.

CHARLES DE GAULLE'S BIRTHPLACE
The upper-middle-class house in which Charles André Marie Joseph de Gaulle (WWII Resistance leader, architect of the Fifth Republic and ferocious defender of French interests) was born in 1890 is being made into an interactive **museum** (☎ 03 28 38 12 05; www.maison-natale-degaulle.org in French; 9 rue Princesse; adult/child/under 9 €9/5/3) intended to present the French leader in the context of his times. Displays (supposed to be open from June 2005) include a dainty baptismal robe and the Citroën in which de Gaulle narrowly escaped an assassination attempt in 1961.

CITADELLE
The world's greatest 17th-century military architect, Sébastien le Prestre de Vauban (see p30), constructed this massive five-pointed, star-shaped **fortress** after the capture of Lille by French forces in 1667. It still functions as a military base but the outer ramparts (2.2km) are open to the public. On the southeastern side, the tree-shaded park has a **children's amusement park**.

Tours
The tourist office (p203) runs English-language **tours of Vieux Lille** (adult/under 16 €7/6; ☼ 2.30pm Sat). There are also **French-language tours** (☼ 3pm Sun May-Aug) of the Citadelle; the meeting point is Porte Royale, the citadel's main gate.

Bike tours (adult/under 16 €7/6) get rolling at 3pm on two Wednesdays a month from May to August.

Festivals & Events
The giants (p208) come out to cavort at the **Fêtes de Lille** street festival, which takes place on the third weekend of June. A flea market extraordinaire, the **Braderie** (below), is held on the first weekend of September. Christmas decorations and other goodies are sold at the **Marché de Noël** (Christmas market; place Rihour; ☼ late Nov-late Dec).

Sleeping
Thanks to the business market, many of the hotels are at their fullest from Monday

---

BRADERIE DE LILLE

During the first weekend in September, Lille's entire city centre is transformed into an enormous flea market – with stands selling antiques, local delicacies, handicrafts and more – called the Braderie de Lille. The extravaganza is believed to date from the Middle Ages, when the Lillois were permitted to hawk old garments from sundown to sunup for some extra cash.

Lille's biggest event of the year, the Braderie runs from 3pm on Saturday to midnight on Sunday, when street sweepers emerge to tackle the mounds of mussel shells and old *frites* (French fries) left behind by the merrymakers. Before the festivities, you can make room for all those extra calories by joining in the half-marathon held at 9am on Saturday. A free map of the market, *Braderie de Lille – Le Plan*, is available from the tourist office (p203).

to Thursday. There are lots of hotels facing Gare Lille-Flandres.

BUDGET

Auberge de Jeunesse (☎ 03 20 57 08 94; lille@fuaj.org; 12 rue Malpart; metro Mairie de Lille; dm with breakfast 1st night/subsequent nights €16.25/13.45; ☽ reception closed 11am-3pm, hostel closed late Dec–late Jan) The spartan rooms of a former maternity hospital, which are locked from 10am to 4.30pm, now house 165 beds (up to six beds per room). Toilets and showers are down the hall.

Hôtel de France (☎ 03 20 57 14 78; fax 03 20 57 06 01; 10 rue de Béthune; s/d from €30/35, with shower & toilet €39/46) You can't get more central than this two-star place; its 32 airy, functional rooms are one of the best deals in town. To get there by car, drive via place Rihour.

Central Hôtel (☎ 03 20 54 64 63; centralhotel@club -internet.fr; 91 rue Boucher de Perthes; s/d €32/40; ☽ reception closed noon-7pm Sun) With one star and 12 spacious rooms, this place – a short walk from the city centre – is a great option if you're looking for peace, quiet and the ambience of days gone by.

Hôtel Faidherbe (☎ 03 20 06 27 93; fax 03 20 55 95 38; 42 place de la Gare; d from €30, with shower & toilet €45) The one-star rooms are cheerful, compact and well-designed – but very simply furnished.

AUTHOR'S CHOICE

À l'Huîtrière (☎ 03 20 55 43 41; www.huitriere .fr; 3 rue des Chats Bossus; lunch menus €43, mains €30-48; ☽ noon-2pm & 7-9.30pm, closed Sun evening & 21 Jul-22 Aug) In 1928, the grandfather of the present owners turned to the nascent Art Deco movement – first exhibited (and named) in Paris just three years earlier – to find suitably elegant decoration for his fish shop, situated in the heart of Vieux Lille on the 'Street of the Hunchback Cats'. The sea-themed mosaics, stained glass and ceramics haven't changed since then, nor has the family's commitment to culinary excellence: the oak-panelled restaurant has held one or two Michelin stars continuously since 1930. Worth a look-in, even if you're not in the mood to dine on super-fresh seafood, accompanied by a wine or two from the 40,000-bottle cellar. Booking ahead is recommended on Friday night, Saturday and holidays.

Hôtel Le Globe (☎ 03 20 57 29 58; 1 blvd Vauban; d/q €35/50.50) The large rooms have French windows that look out on the Citadelle and (in most cases) chimneys that add a dollop of old-fashioned charm.

MID-RANGE

Hôtel Brueghel (☎ 03 20 06 06 69; www.hotel-brueghel .com in French; 5 parvis St-Maurice; d with shower from €44, s/d with shower & toilet €65/71) The two-star rooms are a mix of modern and antique, though they don't have as much Flemish charm as the lobby. The tiny wood-and-wrought-iron lift dates from the 1920s.

Hôtel Flandre-Angleterre (☎ 03 20 06 04 12; www .hotel-flandre-angleterre.fr in French; 13 place de la Gare; s/d €53/63) England certainly isn't bland and neither is Flanders, but the two-star rooms at this place, though comfortable, clean and pastel-hued, are rather lacking in character. Convenient for rail travellers.

Small two-star options near Gare Lille-Flandres include:

Hôtel Le Floréal (☎ 03 20 06 36 21; hotel-le-floreal@ wanadoo.fr; 21 rue Ste-Anne; s/d €50/65; ☒) A friendly nine-room place with linoleum floors.

Hôtel Moulin d'Or (☎ 03 20 06 12 67; francine.boidin@ wanadoo.fr; 15 rue du Molinel; s/d/tr €48/60/68) The 13 rooms are space efficient and unsurprising.

TOP END

Grand Hôtel Bellevue (☎ 03 20 57 45 64; grand.hotel .bellevue@wanadoo.fr; 5 rue Jean Roisin; d from €110) This three-star Best Western–affiliated establishment was grandly built in the early 20th century. A charmingly creaky *belle époque* lift trundles guests to the spacious rooms, which have high ceilings and antique-style French furnishings.

Eating

Lille – and especially Vieux Lille – has an excellent and varied selection of restaurants, many serving Flemish specialities such as *carbonnade* (braised beef stewed with beer and brown sugar); note that not many are open on Sunday.

VIEUX LILLE

Amid this brick-built area's cornucopia of eateries, rue Royale is *the* place for ethnic cuisine.

La Voûte (☎ 03 20 42 12 16; 4 rue des Débris St-Étienne; weekday lunch menus €9, other menus €12-16; ☽ closed Sun & Mon evening) The specialities of

Flanders, including *carbonnade* (€11), are served in a classic bistro ambience.

Le Hochepot (☎ 03 20 54 17 59; 6 rue du Nouveau Siècle; menus €18-25; ❤ closed Sun & lunch Sat) This rustic but elegant restaurant specialises in Flemish dishes such as *coq à la bière* (chicken cooked in beer) and *carbonnade*.

La Pâte Brisée (☎ 03 20 74 29 00; 63-65 rue de la Monnaie) This relaxed and ever-popular eatery serves savoury and sweet tarts, salads, meat dishes and gratin in one-/two-/three-course *menus* (€7.90/11.30/14.70), including a glass of wine, *cidre* or beer.

El-Koutoubia (☎ 03 20 55 58 97; 16 rue Royale; mains €9-15; ❤ closed lunch Sun) Moroccan treats such as couscous and tajines are brought steaming to your table amid rich decoration.

SOUTH OF PLACE DE GAULLE

South of place du Général de Gaulle, the rue d'Amiens area is full of restaurants and pizzerias. West of the main post office, there are lots of cheap eats on lively, studenty rue d'Inkermann, rue Solférino and rue Masséna.

Brasserie La Chicorée (☎ 03 20 54 81 52; 15 place Rihour; menus €9.50-25.50; ❤ meals served 10-4.30am Sun-Thu, 10-6.30am Fri & Sat) Dine on regional treats such as *carbonnade* and *waterzoë* (three kinds of fish prepared with beer) at practically any time of the day or night.

Aux Moules (☎ 03 20 57 12 46; 34 rue de Béthune; ❤ meals served noon-midnight) An informal, brasserie-style place specialising in Flemish dishes such as rabbit in Kriek beer sauce with *frites* (€9), and, of course, mussels (€10 to €11.50). Kriek beer, a Flanders speciality, is made with sour cherries.

La Source (☎ 03 20 57 53 07; 13 rue du Plat; 2-course menus €7.50-11; ❤ meals served 11.30am-2pm Mon-Sat, 7-9pm Fri) This organic food shop serves vegetarian and fish *plats du jour* (daily specials).

SELF-CATERING

The old-time *flûtes* (thin baguette) and *pain à l'ancienne* (traditionally baked bread) at **Boulangerie Notre Dame de la Treille** (26 rue Basse; ❤ 7.30am-7.30pm, closed Sun & holidays) are especially scrumptious.

Wazemmes food market (place Nouvelle Aventure; metro Gambetta; ❤ 7am-6pm Tue-Thu, to 8pm Fri & Sat, to 2pm Sun) is a lively covered market 1.2km southwest of the centre. The city's largest **outdoor market** (❤ until 1.30pm or 2pm Tue, Thu & Sun) is outside, and there's another **outdoor market**

(place Sébastopol; ❤ Wed & Sat mornings) a bit nearer the centre than Wazemmes. Other shopping options:

Carrefour hypermarket (upper level, Euralille shopping centre; ❤ 9am-10pm Mon-Sat)

Fromagerie Philippe Olivier (3 rue du Curé St-Étienne; ❤ Tue-Sat)

Match supermarket (97 rue Solférino; ❤ 9am-9pm Mon-Sat)

Monoprix supermarket (31 rue du Molinel; ❤ 8.30am-8.30pm Mon-Sat)

Drinking

Lille has two main nightlife zones: Vieux Lille, where bars – including a number of gay places – tend to be small and oriented towards a fairly chic clientele; and, 750m southwest of the tourist office, rue Masséna and rue Solférino, where inexpensive high-decibel bars draw mainly students.

Café Oz (☎ 03 20 55 15 15; 33 place Louise de Bettignies; ❤ 2pm-3am Apr-Oct, 5pm-3am Nov-Mar, happy hour 6-9pm Mon-Sat) A branch of Paris' famous Australian bar, the Oz attracts lots of international students. Footy on the wide screen, Australiana on the walls, Fosters on tap (€2.60) – what more could you ask for?

L'Illustration Café (☎ 03 20 12 00 90; 18 rue Royale; ❤ 12.30pm-3am) This mellow but smoky bar, decorated with Art Nouveau woodwork and paintings by local artists, attracts *artistes* and *intellectuels* in the mood to exchange weighty ideas – or just shoot the breeze.

Le Balatum (☎ 03 20 57 41 81; 13 rue de la Barre; ❤ 4pm-2am, to 3am Fri & Sat) This laid-back, funky, dimly lit place is ideal for a tête-à-tête. The paintings and lamps were made by the very creative owner; theme nights occur frequently. Gay friendly.

La Clave (☎ 03 20 30 09 61; 31 rue Masséna; ❤ 6pm-3am Mon-Sat) The tone at this unpretentious bar is set by Caribbean-style murals, salsa, rumba and rum (€4). Draws a mixed-age crowd. Occasionally hosts live concerts.

Entertainment

Lille's free French-language entertainment guide, *Sortir*, is issued each Wednesday and available at the tourist office, cinemas and event venues.

Tickets for Lille's rich cultural offerings can be purchased at the **Fnac billetterie** (ticket agency; ☎ 03 20 15 58 59; www.fnac.com in French; ❤ 10am-7.30pm Mon-Sat), opposite 15 rue du Sec-Arembault.

CINEMAS

For nondubbed films:

Cinéma Majestic (☎ 08 92 08 00 73; 54 rue de Béthune) Has six projection spaces.

Cinéma Metropole (☎ 03 20 15 92 20, 08 36 68 00 73; 26 rue des Ponts des Comines) An art cinema.

GAY & LESBIAN

Lille has an open and active gay scene.

Vice Versa (☎ 03 20 54 93 46; 3 rue de la Barre; 11am-3am Mon-Fri, 2pm-3am Sat, 4pm-midnight Sun) This mellow and very popular place is a mainly gay *café alternatif* that takes eclectic décor – created by the staff and changed regularly – in bold new directions.

LIVE MUSIC

The **Orchestre National de Lille** (☎ 03 20 12 82 40; www.onlille.com in French) plays in the **Nouveau Siècle concert hall** (place Pierre Mendès-France; concert tickets adult €10-34, over 60 €16-29, under 26 from €8).

Le 30 (☎ 03 20 30 15 54; www.le30club-concert.fr.st in French; 30 rue de Paris; admission free; 9.30pm-4am Mon-Sat) With its soft modular couches, this bar looks like a 1960s airport VIP lounge. There's live jazz, blues and Latin American music nightly from 10.30pm to 1.30am (to 2.30am on Friday and Saturday).

NIGHTCLUBS

Thanks to a change in local bylaws, you no longer have to cross the Belgian frontier (eg to Gand) to dance past 4am, though some locals still do because, they say, the techno is edgier, the prices lower, substances more available and the closing time even later (1pm!).

La Scala (☎ 03 20 42 10 60; 32 place Louise de Bettignies; admission free; 11pm-8am Mon-Sat) Pulsating music and gyrating bodies under the arches of a brick cellar. Music and ages are varied.

Shopping

Lille's snazziest clothing and house-wares shops are in the old city and are especially thick along rue de la Monnaie and rue de la Grande Chausée.

The cavernous Euralille shopping centre, a project of the 90s designed by Dutch architect Rem Koolhaas, lies between the two train stations.

Getting There & Away

BUS

Eurolines (☎ 03 20 78 18 88; 23 parvis St-Maurice; 9.30am-12.30pm & 1.30-6pm, in summer to 7pm Mon-Fri, 1-6pm Sat) destinations include Brussels (€10, 1½ to two hours), Amsterdam (€34, six hours) and London (€39, six hours). Buses depart from the unsignposted bus parking lane on rue de Turin, on the northeast side of Gare Lille-Europe.

CAR

Driving into and out of Greater Lille is incredibly confusing, even with a good map.

THE GIANTS

In far northern France, *géants* (giants) – wickerwork body masks up to 8.5m tall animated by someone (or several someones) inside – emerge for local carnivals and on feast days to dance and add to the general merriment. Each has a name and a personality, usually based on the Bible, legends or local history. Giants are born, grow up, marry and have children (though never really die), creating, over the years, complicated family relationships. They serve as important symbols of town, neighbourhood and village identity.

Medieval in origin and also found in places as far afield as the Iberian Peninsula (eg in Catalonia, www.gegants.org), the Austrian Tyrol, Mexico, Brazil and India, giants have been a tradition in this region since the 16th century. Over 300 of the creatures, also known as *reuze* (in Flemish) and *gayants* (in Picard), now 'live' in French towns, including Arras, Boulogne, Calais, Cassel, Douai, Dunkirk and Lille; local associations look after their every need. Giants make appearances year-round, but your best chance to see them is at pre-Lenten carnivals, during Easter and at summer festivals: dates and places – as well as the latest marriages and births – appear in the annual French-language brochure *Le Calendrier des Géants* (www.geants-carnaval.org), available at tourist offices.

At the **Maison des Géants** (☎ 32-68 26 51 70; www.ath.be/maisondesgeants in French; 18 rue de Pintamont, Ath, Belgium; adult/student €4/3; 10am-noon & 1-5pm or 6pm Tue-Fri, 2-6pm Sat, Sun & holidays), 60km due west of Lille, you can see how the popular creatures are brought to life.

Parking at the Champ de Mars (the huge car park just east of the Citadelle) costs €2, including travel to the city centre on the Citadine bus line. Parking is free along the streets southwest of rue Solférino and up around the house where Charles de Gaulle was born (p205).

Car hire for less than the biggies charge is available at:

ADA (☎ 03 20 57 03 25; 2 rue Gustave Delory)

DLM (☎ 03 20 06 18 80; 32 place de la Gare)

France Cars (☎ 03 20 57 58 99; 114 rue du Molinel)

Rent-A-Car Système (☎ 03 20 40 20 20; 113 rue du Molinel)

TRAIN

Lille's two train stations are one stop apart on metro line No 2.

Gare Lille-Flandres is used by almost all regional services and most TGVs to Paris' Gare du Nord (€33.70 or €45.80 depending on service, 62 minutes, one to two hourly).

Gare Lille-Europe – topped by what looks like a 20-storey ski boot – handles pretty much everything else, including Eurostar trains to London, TGVs/Eurostars to Brussels (weekday/weekend €22.40/14.40, 38 minutes, 12 to 14 daily) and TGVs to Nice (€104.90 or €123.70, 7¼ hours, two direct daily). Fares are higher in peak periods.

For details on getting to/from Amiens, Arras, Boulogne, Calais, Dunkirk and St-Omer, see those sections.

Getting Around

There are plans to pedestrianise virtually the whole city centre by 2006 or 2007.

BICYCLE

Not-for-profit **Ch'ti Vélo** (☎ 03 28 53 07 49; 10 av Willy Brandt; ⏰ 7.30am-7.30pm Mon-Fri, 9am-7.30pm Sat, Sun & holidays), on the northern side of Gare Lille-Flandres, rents city bikes for €5 per day.

BUS, TRAM & METRO

Lille's two speedy metro lines, two tramways and bus lines – several of which cross into Belgium – are run by **Transpole** (☎ 08 20 42 40 40), which has an **information window** (⏰ closed Sun) in the Gare Lille-Flandres metro station.

Tickets (single/10 €1.15/10) are sold on buses but must be purchased (and validated in the orange posts) *before* boarding

a metro or tram. A Pass' Journée day pass costs €3.35. To buy a weekly pass (€11), valid from Monday to Sunday, you'll need a Carte Blanche photo ID (€1.50), available at the Transpole office.

CALAIS

pop 75,000

Never in the history of tourism have so many travellers passed through a place, and so few stopped to visit. Except for some better-than-expected restaurants, two small museums and Rodin's *The Burghers of Calais* (below), there's not very much to encourage the 22 million people who travel by way of Calais each year to stop and explore. However, the town – a mere 34km from the English town of Dover (Douvres in French) – does make a convenient base for visiting French Flanders and the Channel coast.

In the 14th century the English were so covetous of Calais – in part to control its audacious pirates – that King Edward III took over the town in 1347, thus beginning over two centuries of English rule.

THE BURGHERS OF CALAIS

Rodin sculpted *Les Bourgeois de Calais* in 1895 to honour six local citizens who, in 1347, after eight months of holding off the besieging English forces, surrendered themselves and the keys to the starving city to Edward III of England. Their hope: that by sacrificing themselves they might save the town and its people. Moved by the entreaties of his consort, Philippa, Edward eventually spared both the Calaisiens and their six brave leaders.

Actually, you don't have to visit Calais' Flemish Renaissance-style town hall (1911–25) to see Rodin's masterpiece. Other casts of the six emaciated but proud figures, with varying degrees of copper-green patina (many were made posthumously), can be seen in London (next to the Houses of Parliament), the USA (New York, Washington, Philadelphia, Omaha, Pasadena, Stanford University) and even Japan (Shizuoka Prefecture). So moved by the work that you want one at home? You can buy a 66cm-high copy from www.bronzedirect.com – a bargain at US$2500!

CALAIS

The Channel (La Manche)

0 ———— 400 m
0 ———— 0.2 miles

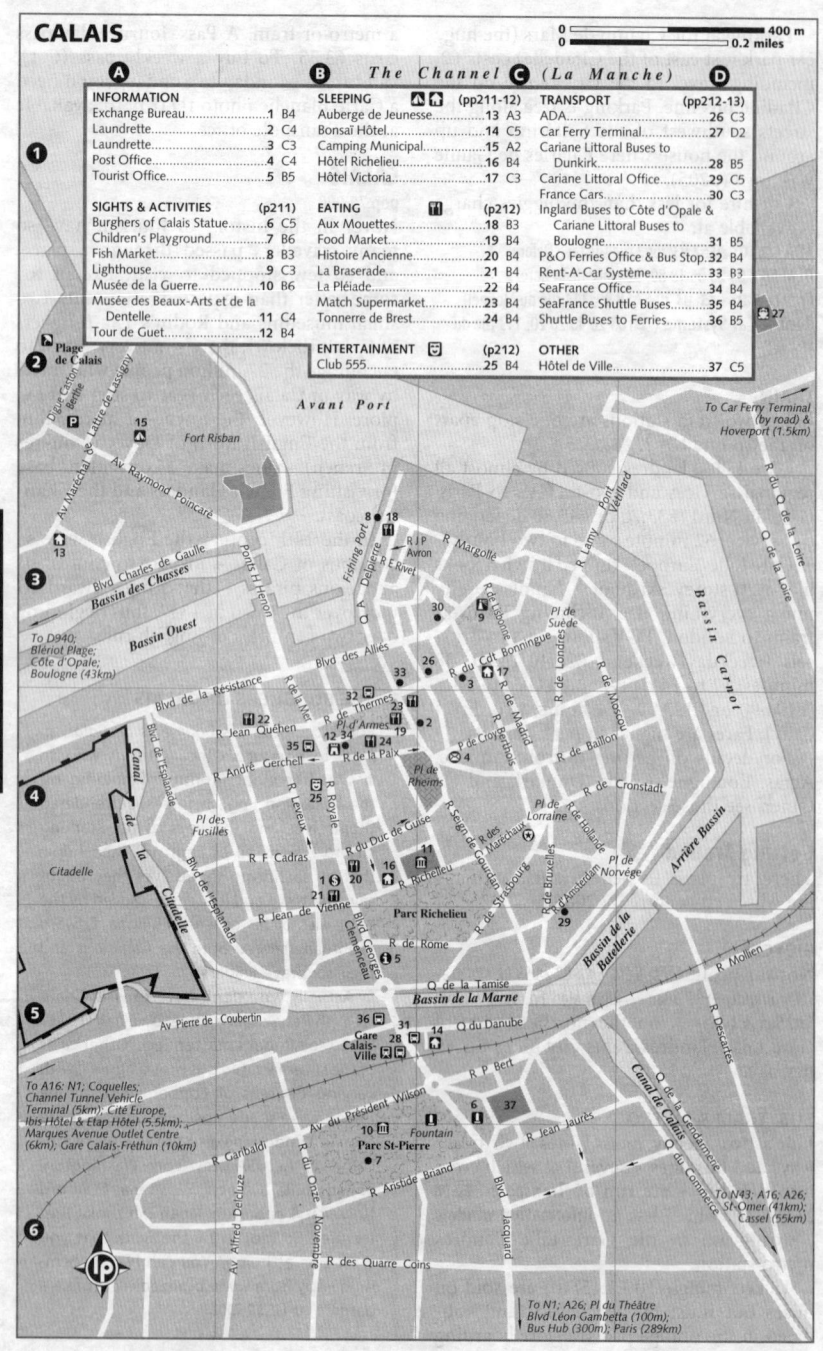

INFORMATION
Exchange Bureau..........................1 B4
Laundrette...................................2 C4
Laundrette...................................3 C3
Post Office...................................4 C4
Tourist Office...............................5 B5

SIGHTS & ACTIVITIES (p211)
Burghers of Calais Statue..............6 C5
Children's Playground....................7 B6
Fish Market..................................8 B3
Lighthouse...................................9 C3
Musée de la Guerre.....................10 B6
Musée des Beaux-Arts et de la
   Dentelle..................................11 C4
Tour de Guet..............................12 B4

SLEEPING (pp211-12)
Auberge de Jeunesse...................13 A3
Bonsaï Hôtel...............................14 C5
Camping Municipal.......................15 A2
Hôtel Richelieu............................16 B4
Hôtel Victoria..............................17 C3

EATING (p212)
Aux Mouettes.............................18 B3
Food Market................................19 B4
Histoire Ancienne.........................20 B4
La Braserade...............................21 B4
La Pléiade...................................22 B4
Match Supermarket......................23 B4
Tonnerre de Brest........................24 B4

ENTERTAINMENT (p212)
Club 555.....................................25 B4

TRANSPORT (pp212-13)
ADA..26 C3
Car Ferry Terminal.......................27 D2
Cariane Littoral Buses to
   Dunkirk..................................28 B5
Cariane Littoral Office..................29 C5
France Cars.................................30 C3
Ingland Buses to Côte d'Opale &
   Cariane Littoral Buses to
   Boulogne................................31 B5
P&O Ferries Office & Bus Stop....32 B4
Rent-A-Car Système....................33 B3
SeaFrance Office..........................34 B4
SeaFrance Shuttle Buses...............35 B4
Shuttle Buses to Ferries................36 B5

OTHER
Hôtel de Ville..............................37 C5

Orientation

Gare Calais-Ville (the train station) is 650m south of the main square, place d'Armes, and 700m north of Calais' relatively untouristed commercial district (around blvd Léon Gambetta and the place du Théâtre bus hub).

The car ferry terminal is 1.5km northeast of place d'Armes; the Hoverport (for SeaCats) is another 1.5km further out. The Channel Tunnel's vehicle loading area is about 6km southwest of the town centre.

Information

LAUNDRY

Be fully prepared for British border formalities – cross the Channel with clean undies. There are laundrettes on the eastern side of place d'Armes (open 7am to 9pm) and at 36 rue de Thermes (open 7am to 7pm and longer in summer).

MONEY

Currency exchange is possible aboard car ferries and SeaCats. In town, banks (open Tuesday to Friday and Saturday morning) are clustered along rue Royale.

Exchange Bureau (5 rue Royale; ☉ 9.30am-6pm Mon-Sat)

POST

Post Office (place de Rheims) Has a Cyberposte terminal.

TOURIST INFORMATION

Tourist Office (☎ 03 21 96 62 40; www.calais-cotedo pale.com; 12 blvd Georges Clemenceau; ☉ 9am-7pm Mon-Sat, 10am-1pm Sun & holidays Easter-Aug, 10am-1pm & 2-6.30pm Mon-Sat Sep- Easter)

Sights & Activities

You can watch huge car ferries sailing majestically towards Dover from Calais' sandy cabin-lined **beach**, which begins 1km northwest of place d'Armes and is linked to town by a **bike path**. The sand continues westward along 8km-long, dune-lined **Blériot Plage**, named after pioneer aviator Louis Blériot, who began the first ever trans-Channel flight from here in 1909. Both beaches are served by bus No 3.

If you're willing to burn calories for a superb panorama, you can climb the 271 stairs to the top of the **lighthouse** (☎ 03 21 34 33 34; blvd des Alliés; adult/5-15 yrs €2.50/1.50; ☉ 10am-noon & 2-5.30pm or 6.30pm Sat, Sun & holidays year-round,

2-5.30pm or 6.30pm Mon-Fri Jun-Sep, Wed Oct-May & during school holidays), built in 1848.

You won't be exhausted by a visit to the **Musée des Beaux-Arts et de la Dentelle** (Museum of Fine Arts & Lace; ☎ 03 21 46 48 40; 25 rue Richelieu; adult/student €3/1.50, admission free Wed; ☉ 10am-noon & 2-5.30pm Mon & Wed-Fri, 10am-noon & 2-6.30pm Sat, 2-6.30pm Sun), with exhibits that focus on mechanised lace-making (the first machines were smuggled to Calais from England in 1816), 15th- to 20th-century painting and modern sculptures, including pieces by Rodin.

World War II artefacts (uniforms, weapons, proclamations) fill the display cases of the **Musée de la Guerre** (☎ 03 21 34 21 57; adult/ student/family of 4 incl audioguide €6/5/14; ☉ 10am-6pm May-Aug, 11am-5.30pm Apr & Sep, 11am-5pm Wed-Mon mid-Feb–Mar, noon-5pm Wed-Mon Oct–mid-Nov), housed in a concrete bunker that used to be German naval headquarters. It sits incongruously in **Parc St-Pierre**, next to a *boules* ground and a **children's playground**.

The 13th-century **Tour de Guet** (watchtower; place d'Armes) is a rare remnant of pre–20th-century Calais – the rest of the town was virtually demolished during WWII.

Sleeping

A number of two-star hotels can be found along rue Royale.

Auberge de Jeunesse (☎ 03 21 34 70 20; www .auberge-jeunesse-calais.com in French; av Maréchal de Lattre de Tassigny; dm with breakfast €15.20; ☉ 24hr; **P**) Modern and well equipped, and just 200m from the beach, its a good source of information on local events. Bikes can be rented in the warm season. It is served by bus No 3.

Hôtel Richelieu (☎ 03 21 34 61 60; www.hotel richelieu-calais.com; 17 rue Richelieu; d/2-room q from €46/92) At this quiet two-star place, the 15 cheery rooms, each one unique, are outfitted with antique furniture redeemed by the owner from local markets.

Bonsaï Hôtel (☎ 03 21 96 10 10; www.bonsai -hotel.tm.fr; 2 quai du Danube; d/tr €27/31) This prefab place is the ultimate in charmless tickytacky cheapness. Sneezing within 20cm of the pressboard walls could possibly result in structural damage to the building. In triple rooms, the third bed is a bunk above the double bed.

In Coquelles next to the Cité Europe shopping mall (and near the Channel Tunnel vehicle loading area) are **Ibis Hôtel** (☎ 03 21 46 37

AUTHOR'S CHOICE

Hôtel Victoria (☎ 03 21 34 38 32; hotelvictoria@wanadoo.fr; 8 rue du Commandant Bonningue; d from €26, with shower & toilet €37) The 14 well-lit and comfortable two-star rooms have walls thin enough to let you get a good sense of how your fellow guests are getting on with each other. One theory has it that the mere act of crossing the Channel does wonders for the ardour of many Brits, though it's not clear whether the hotel's namesake would approve of this, or even understand what you were talking about if you tried to explain it to her. The joyous sounds of schoolchildren carousing in the school playground across the street greet you bright and early, a reminder of the many happy children on both sides of the Channel who owe their very existence to the seductive romance of this seemingly average hotel.

FAR NORTHERN FRANCE

00; place de Cantorbéry; d €49) and **Etap Hôtel** (☎ 08 92 68 30 59; place de Cantorbéry; s/d €29/35).

CAMPING

Camping Municipal (☎ 03 21 97 89 79; av Raymond Poincaré; per adult/site €3.24/2.27; ☿ year-round) Occupies a grassy but souless site inside Fort Risban. Served by bus No 3.

Eating

Calais is a good place for a first or last meal on the Continent. Rue Royal and place d'Armes are lined with eateries.

La Pléiade (☎ 03 21 34 03 70; 32 rue Jean Quéhen; 3-/4-/6-course menus €22/35/50; ☿ closed Sun & Mon) Some loyal customers come over from England just to dine here on *filet de bar rôti* (sea bass with almond sauce and a dollop of *pistou*) and other fish dishes.

Aux Mouettes (☎ 03 21 34 67 59; 10 rue Jean Pierre Avron; menus €15-32; ☿ closed Mon & dinner Sun) Fisherfolk sell their daily catch across the street at the quay – easy to see why this unassuming place is known for serving only the very freshest fish.

Histoire Ancienne (☎ 03 21 34 11 20; 20 rue Royale; 2-/3-/5-course menus €11/17.50/30; ☿ closed Sun & dinner Mon) Specialising in meat and fish dishes grilled over a wood fire, this Paris-style bistro also has *pieds de cochon* (pigs' trotters) and *escargots à l'ail* (snails with garlic).

La Braserade (☎ 03 21 97 02 59; 8 rue Jean de Vienne; menus from €14.94; ☿ closed lunch Mon & Sat) Gussied up like an Alpine chalet, this restaurant serves reasonably priced Savoyarde dishes such as *raclette* (melted cheese with cold cuts and pickles) and *braserade* (meat dishes you barbecue yourself at the table). The pricier *menus* (€17.53 to €29.73) include access to an all-you-can-eat seafood buffet and a bottomless glass of red wine, beer or soft drink.

Tonnerre de Brest (☎ 03 21 96 95 35; 16 place d'Armes; crepes €2.50-6.80; ☿ closed Mon except Jul & Aug) At this rustic informal eatery, run by two sisters, you can wash down with *cidre* 19 kinds of savoury *galettes* and 27 sorts of sweet crepes.

SELF-CATERING

Feed yourself by shopping at the **food market** (place d'Armes; ☿ Wed & Sat morning) or **Match supermarket** (place d'Armes; ☿ 9am-7.30pm Mon-Sat year-round, 9am-noon Sun Jul & Aug)

Entertainment

Club 555 (☎ 03 21 34 74 60; www.le555.com in French; 63 rue Royale; admission incl one drink €10; ☿ 11pm-5am Tue-Sun) This spot, one of the nightspots and bars along rue Royale, is a '70s-style discotheque with flashing lights, space for 700 revellers and plenty of banquettes for hanging out. The music is mixed; there's a theme party every Friday.

Getting There & Around

For details on getting across the Channel, see p917 and p920.

BOAT

Every day, 45 to 54 car ferries from Dover dock at the busy car ferry terminal, about 1.5km northeast of place d'Armes. Company bureaus:

P&O Ferries car ferry terminal (☎ 03 21 46 10 10; ☿ 24hr); place d'Armes (☎ 01 55 69 82 28; 41 place d'Armes)

SeaFrance car ferry terminal (☎ 03 21 46 80 05; ☿ 6am-10.45pm); place d'Armes (☎ 03 21 19 42 42; 2 place d'Armes)

Shuttle buses (€1.50 for P&O) coordinated with departure times link Gare Calais-Ville and each company's office at place d'Armes with the car ferry terminal.

Hoverspeed's car-carrying SeaCats to Dover (operational from mid-March to 22

December) use the **Hoverport** (high-speed ferry terminal; ☎ 03 21 46 14 00, 008 00 12 11 12 11), which is 3km northeast of the town centre. Alas, hovercraft – the pride of British maritime engineering in the 1960s – no longer lumber up the beach here. *Some* SeaCat arrivals and departures are met by shuttle buses to/from Gare Calais-Ville (€1.50).

BUS
Inglard (☎ 03 21 96 49 54; car ferry terminal) links Calais' train station with the beautiful Côte d'Opale (p215) and Boulogne (€4.70, 1¼ hours; three daily except Sunday and holidays), stopping at 75 blvd Daunou in Boulogne.

Cariane Littoral (☎ 03 21 34 74 40; office 10 rue d'Amsterdam) operates express services from Calais' train station to Boulogne (€6.40, 40 minutes, five daily Monday to Friday, two on Saturday), where bus stops are at the train station and place Dalton, and Dunkirk (€7, 40 minutes, 12 daily Monday to Friday, three on Saturday).

CAR & MOTORCYCLE
To reach the Channel Tunnel's vehicle loading area at Coquelles, follow the road signs on the A16 to the Tunnel Sous La Manche (Tunnel under the Channel) at exit No 13.

The following companies generally have cheaper walk-in rates than the car ferry terminal offices of Avis, Budget, Europcar, Hertz and National-Citer, which – like their Hoverport outlets – are not always staffed.

ADA (☎ 03 21 36 50 12; 15 rue de Thermes)
France Cars (☎ 03 21 96 08 00; 47 blvd des Alliés)

Rent-A-Car Système (☎ 03 21 34 41 99; 1 rue de Thermes)

TAXI
To order a cab, call **Taxis Radio Calais** (TRC; ☎ 03 21 97 13 14).

TRAIN
Calais has two train stations: Gare Calais-Ville in the city centre; and Gare Calais-Fréthun, a TGV station 10km southwest of town near the Channel Tunnel entrance. They are linked by the free Navette TER, which is a bus service operated by Cariane Littoral.

From Gare Calais-Ville you can travel to Amiens (€19.70, two to 2½ hours, two or three direct Monday to Saturday), Arras (€16.90, two hours, 10 daily Monday to Friday, six or seven daily Saturday and Sunday), Boulogne (€6.60, 27 to 48 minutes, 15 to 19 daily Monday to Saturday, nine daily Sunday), Dunkirk (€7, 50 minutes, four daily Monday to Friday, two on Saturday) and Lille-Flandres (€14, 1¼ hours, 18 daily Monday to Friday, 11 on Saturday, seven on Sunday).

Calais-Fréthun is served by TGVs to Paris' Gare du Nord (€35.50 or €47.90, 1½ hours, five daily Monday to Saturday, two on Sunday) as well as the Eurostar to London.

INLAND ATTRACTIONS
You don't have to stray far from the Channel to find beautiful countryside, typical French towns and WWII relics.

SHOP TILL YOU DROP IN CALAIS

Calais' shops and hypermarkets supply day-tripping *rosbifs* (Britons) with everything except, perhaps, roast beef. Items eagerly sought 'on the Continent' include delicious edibles (terrines, cheeses, gourmet-prepared dishes) and drinks (wine, champagne, beer and spirits) that are hard to find – or much more expensive – in the land of the pound sterling.

The enormous steel-and-glass shopping centre **Cité Europe** (☎ 03 21 46 47 48; www.cite-europe .com; boulevard du Kent; ⏲ 10am-8pm Mon-Thu, 10am-9pm Fri, 9am-8pm Sat) is in Coquelles, next to the vehicle-loading area for the Channel Tunnel. Its 130 shops include a vast **Carrefour hypermarket** (⏲ 9am-10pm Mon-Sat) and wine shops where buying alcohol in bulk to carry home in the boot is made easy.

Right nearby is the new **Marques Avenue** (☎ 03 21 17 07 70; www.marquesavenue.com; ⏲ 10am-8pm Mon-Thu, 10am-9pm Fri, 9am-8pm Sat) outlet centre, which boasts discount clothing and accessories by 80 designer brands.

To get to Cité Europe by car, take the A16 to exit Nos 12 or 14; for Marques Avenue, use exit No 12.

FAR NORTHERN FRANCE

St-Omer

pop 14,400

St-Omer, said to be the first truly French town you come to after landing at Calais – its river, the Aa, is the certainly first one you'll come across in any alphabetised list of the world's waterways – is justly renowned for its richly furnished 13th- to 15th-century **basilica** (⊙ until at least 5pm), formerly a cathedral. The only major Gothic church in the region, it's a real gem: much of the woodwork, including the main altar and breathtaking baroque organ, dates from the 1700s. The mechanism of the mechanical clock, in the north transept, was put together back in 1558.

The **tourist office** (☎ 03 21 98 08 51; www.tour isme.fr/saint-omer; 4 rue du Lion d'Or; ⊙ 9am-6pm Mon-Sat, 10am-1pm Sun & holidays Easter-Sep, 9am-12.30pm & 2-6pm Mon-Sat except holidays Oct-Easter) is one block north of place Foch, the vast square in front of the **town hall** (1830).

The **Musée Sandelin** (☎ 03 21 38 00 94; http://m3.dnsalias.com/sandelin in French; 14 rue Carnot; adult/15-25 yrs €4.50/3; ⊙ 10am-noon & 2-6pm Wed-Sun, to 8pm Thu), with its recently renovated displays that include ceramics, *objets d'art* and paintings, is housed in a harmonious townhouse built in 1776; a number of rooms are furnished in the style that suited the refined lifestyle of the Enlightenment elite. To get there from place Foch, walk a block south and then a long block east.

The **Musée Henri Dupuis** (☎ 03 21 38 24 13; 9 rue Henri Dupuis; adult/15-25 yrs €2.50/1.50; ⊙ 10am-noon & 2-6pm Wed-Sun), midway between place Foch and the basilica, displays bric-a-brac (ceramics, minerals) assembled during the late 19th century by a wealthy local.

A bit northeast of town, the market gardens of the swampy **Marais Audemarois**, rich in wildlife (including 250 kinds of bird, 19 species of dragonfly and 11 types of bat), can be visited on foot or by rowboat.

There are many good-value restaurants (lunch *menus* €10 to €13), frequented by repeat visitors from the UK, around the perimeter of place Foch and adjacent place P Bonhomme, and along rue Louis Martel.

Le Vivier (☎ 03 21 95 76 00; levivier@wanadoo.fr; 22 rue Louis Martel; d €52), a block south of the town hall, has seven comfortable but standard two-star rooms and a fine fish and seafood **restaurant** (menus €16-35; ⊙ closed Sun evening). A lively **food market** (place Foch) is held every Saturday morning.

St-Omer's train station, 1.5km northeast of the town hall, is on the rail line (15 daily Monday to Friday, seven daily Saturday and Sunday) linking Calais (€6.40, 30 minutes) with Lille-Flandres (€9.50, 50 minutes).

La Coupole

A subterranean V2 launch site just five minutes' flying time from London – almost (but not quite) put into operation in 1944 – now houses **La Coupole** (☎ 03 21 12 27 27; www.lacoupole .com; adult/5-16 yrs €9/6; ⊙ 9am-6pm, to 7pm Jul & Aug, closed 25 Dec-2 Jan), an exhibition centre that uses the latest museological techniques and lots of moving images to present:

- Life in northern France during the Nazi occupation
- The German's secret programmes to build V1 and V2 rockets (which could fly at 650km/h and an astounding 5780km/h respectively).
- The post-war conquest of space with the help of V2 rocket technology – and V2 engineers.

Built by POWs (mainly Soviets), the complex is buried deep in a hillside and is topped by a 72m-wide concrete dome (thus the name). English commentary is provided by a headset; a full tour of the site takes about 2½ hours.

La Coupole is 5km south of St-Omer (the circuitous route is signposted but confusing) just outside the town of Wizernes, near the intersection of the D928 and the D210. From the A26, take exit No 3 or 4.

Cassel

pop 2200

The compact and very Flemish village of Cassel, on a hilltop 57km east of Calais, affords panoramic views of the verdant Flanders plain. It served as Maréchal Ferdinand Foch's headquarters at the beginning of WWI and, in 1940, was the site of intensive rearguard resistance by British troops defending Dunkirk during the evacuation.

The **tourist office** (☎ 03 28 40 52 55; www.ot-cas sel.fr in French; 23 Grand' Place; ⊙ 8.30am-noon & 1.30-5.30pm Mon-Fri year round, plus 9am-noon & 2-5.30pm Sat May-Sep & 2.30pm-5.30pm Sun Jun-Sep) is on the main square.

Eight or 10 generations ago, wheat flour was milled and linseed oil pressed just as it is today at the wooden **moulin** (windmill; adult/

child €2.80/2.40; 10am-noon & 2-5.30pm Apr-Sep & during school holidays, open Sat noon & Sun Oct–mid-Dec & mid-Jan–Mar), perched on the highest point in town to catch the wind. The 30-minute, hands-on tour is noisy but interesting.

Le Foch (☎ 03 28 42 47 73; www.hotel-foch.net; 41 Grand' Place; d €72, if you also take dinner €62) has six charming rooms with an antique feel. The elegant **restaurant** (menus €16-32; closed dinner Sun & perhaps Tue) specialises in traditional French cuisine.

Taverne Flamande (☎ 03 28 42 42 59; 34 Grand' Place; menus €14-22; closed Wed & dinner Tue) serves tasty Flemish dishes in a dining room that dates from 1933.

CÔTE D'OPALE

The 40km of cliffs, sand dunes and beaches between Calais and Boulogne, known as the Opal Coast because of the ever-changing interplay of greys and blues in the sea and sky, are a dramatic and beautiful introduction to France. The coastal peaks (frequently buffeted by gale-force winds), wide beaches

---

THE BATTLE OF AGINCOURT

Agincourt (Azincourt) entered the history books on 25 October 1415 when English archers and men-at-arms – led by King Henry V – inflicted an overwhelming defeat on superior French forces in one of the bloodiest engagements of the Hundred Years' War. Against minimal losses of their own, the axe- and sword-wielding English killed 6000 of their opponents, whose cavalry and foot soldiers were weighed down by heavy armour made all the more cumbersome by the soggy terrain.

The **Centre Historique Médiéval Azincourt** (☎ 03 21 04 41 12; www.azincourt-medieval .com; adult/under 16 €6.50/5; 9am-7pm Jul & Aug, 10am-5pm or 6pm Sep-Jun) uses the latest audiovisual technology (English available) and copies of 15th-century armaments to bring alive both the battle and its context. Is the steep admission fee belated (if partial) revenge for France's battlefield debacle?

The **Champ de Bataille** (battlefield), 2.5km southeast of the museum, along the D71 (at the intersection of the D107-E2 and the D104), is marked by a granite column and a viewpoint indicator showing the battle's progression.

---

and rolling farmland are dotted with the remains of Nazi Germany's Atlantic Wall, a chain of fortifications and gun emplacements built to prevent the Allied invasion that in the end took place in Normandy. The seashore has been attracting British beach lovers for over a century.

Part of the **Parc Naturel Régional Nord-Pas-de-Calais**, the Côte d'Opale area is criss-crossed by hiking paths, including the GR Littoral trail that hugs the coast. Some routes are also suitable for mountain biking and horse riding. Each village along the Côte d'Opale has at least one camping ground.

By car, the D940 offers some spectacular vistas. Inglard buses link all the sights and villages mentioned below with Calais and Boulogne (see p213).

Sights

The Channel Tunnel slips under the Strait of Dover 8km west of Calais at the village of **Sangatte**, known for its wide beach. Southwest of there, the coastal dunes give way to cliffs that culminate in windswept, 134m-high **Cap Blanc-Nez**, which affords spectacular views of the Bay of Wissant, the port of Calais, the Flemish countryside (pockmarked by Allied bomb craters) and the cliffs of Kent. The grey **obelisk** honours the WWI Dover Patrol.

The well-off and very French seaside resort of **Wissant** (☎ tourist office 03 21 82 48 00), a good base for walks in the rolling countryside, boasts a vast fine-sand beach – in 55 BC Julius Caesar launched his invasion of Britain from here. **Hôtel Le Vivier** (☎ 03 21 35 93 61; www.levivier.com; place de l'Église; d with breakfast from €54), across the street from the church, has mid-sized pastel rooms and a nautically themed **restaurant** (menus €25-35; closed Tue & Wed) specialising in fish and seafood.

Topped by a lighthouse and a radar station serving the 600 ships that pass by each day, the 45m-high cliffs of **Cap Gris-Nez** are only 28km from the English coast. The name 'Grey Nose' is a corruption of the archaic English 'craig ness', meaning 'rocky promontory'. The area is a stopping-off point for millions of migrating birds.

The village of **Ambleteuse**, on the northern side of the mouth of Slack River, is blessed by a lovely beach once defended from attack by 17th-century **Fort Mahon**. Just south of town is a protected area of grass-covered dunes known as **Dunes de la Slack**.

CÔTE D'OPALE

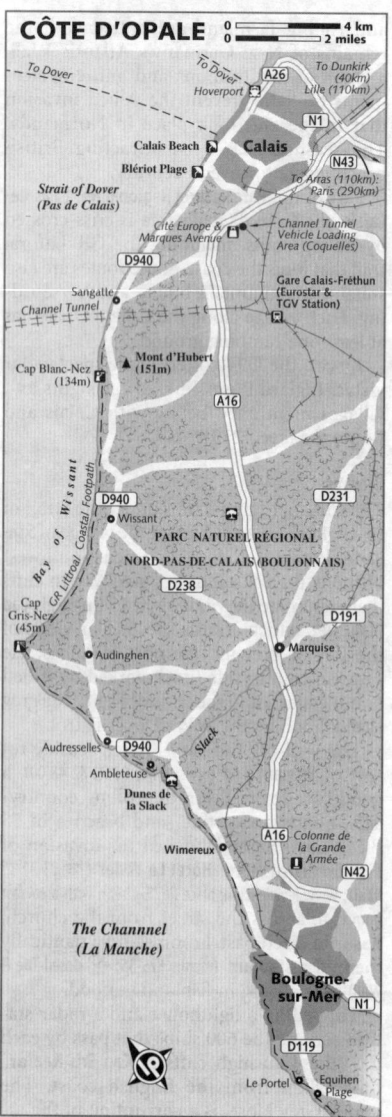

The well-organised **Musée 39-45** (☎ 03 21 87 33 01; http://musee3945.com; adult/7-14 yrs €6/4.30; ⏱ 9.30am or 10am-6pm Apr–mid-Oct, Sat & Sun only Mar & mid-Oct–Nov), devoted to the wartime period, has a 30-minute English-language film and oodles of authentic paraphernalia. Make sure you see the displays of field rations – yum!

BOULOGNE-SUR-MER

pop 44,000

Boulogne, by far the most interesting of France's Channel ports, makes a decent first stop in France, especially if combined with a swing through the Côte d'Opale. Most of the city is an uninspiring mass of postwar reconstruction, but the attractive Ville Haute (Upper City), perched high above the rest of town, is girded by a 13th-century wall. The city is also home to one of France's premier aquariums.

Orientation

Central Boulogne consists of the hilltop Ville Haute and, on the flats below, the Basse Ville (Lower City). The main train station, Gare Boulogne-Ville, is 1.2km southeast of the centre.

Information

There are laundrettes at 235 rue Nationale and 62 rue de Lille. Both are open 7am to 8pm. Several commercial banks can be found on or near rue Victor Hugo.

Main Post Office (place Frédéric Sauvage) Changes money and has a Cyberposte.

Tourist Office (☎ 03 21 10 88 10; www.tourisme -boulognesurmer.com in French; 24 quai Gambetta; ⏱ 9am-7pm Mon-Sat, 10am-1pm & 3-6pm Sun Jul & Aug, 9.15am-12.30pm & 1.45-6pm Mon-Sat Sep-Jun, 10.15am-1pm Sun Apr, May & Jun, 3-5.30pm Sun Sep-Nov)

Sights

VILLE HAUTE

You can walk all the way round the Upper City – an island of centuries-old buildings and cobblestone streets – on top of the rectangular, tree-shaded **ramparts**, a distance of just under 1.5km. Among the impressive buildings around place Godefroy de Bouillon are the neoclassical **Hôtel Desandrouin**, built in the 1780s and later used by Napoleon, and the **town hall** (1735), with its square medieval belfry.

Basilique Notre Dame (⏱ 9am-noon & 2-6pm Apr-Aug, to 5pm Sep-Mar), with a towering, Italianate dome visible from all over town, was built from 1827 to 1866 with little input from trained architects. The partly Romanesque **crypt** and **treasury** (⏱ 2-5pm Tue-Sun; admission €2) are eminently skippable.

Everything from Egyptian mummies to 19th-century Inuit masks to Oceanic art, with an *in situ*, 4th-century Roman wall thrown in for good measure, is on view at **Château-Musée** (☎ 03 21 10 02 20; adult €3.50, student & senior €2.50; ☼ 10am-5pm Mon & Wed-Sat, 10am-5.30pm Sun), which is being renovated but should reopen in early 2005. The whole eclectic collection is housed in a 13th-century fortified castle built by the counts of Boulogne.

And now for something completely unexpected: the house where José de San Martín, the exiled hero of Argentine, Chilean and Peruvian independence, died in 1850 has been turned into the **Musée Libertador San Martín** (☎ 03 21 31 54 65; 113 Grande Rue; admission free; ☼ 10am-noon & 2-6pm Fri-Tue), owned by the Argentine government. Ring the bell for a free English tour of this piece of South America, complete with memorabilia related to San Martín's life and lots of fancy military uniforms.

VILLE BASSE

The most interesting thing to do in the Lower City is to stroll along the **fishing port** (Quai Gambetta), where you'll find fish vendors – and hungry seagulls diving and squawking overhead. The **shopping precinct** is centred around rue Victor Hugo and rue Adolphe Thiers.

NAUSICAÄ

This first-class **marine aquarium** (☎ 03 21 30 99 99; www.nausicaa.fr; blvd Ste-Beuve; adult/3-12 yrs Apr-Sep €12.50/9, Oct-Mar €11/8, audioguide €3; ☼ 9.30am-8pm Jul & Aug, 9.30am-6.30pm Sep-Jun, closed 3 weeks in mid-Jan) focuses on the sustainable use of marine resources, comes with lots of kid-friendly activities (fish petting, a sea-lion tank, feeding sessions) and has signs in English. Educational in the best sense of the word, you

---

BIRD-WATCHERS' PARADISE

South of Boulogne on the Baie de la Somme, **Parc Ornithologique du Marquenterre** (☎ 03 22 25 68 99; www.baiedesomme.org/mar quenterre; St-Quentin-en-Tourmont; adult/6-16 yrs €9.60/7.10; ☼ 10am-7.30pm Apr-Sep, to 5.30pm Oct-Mar) is a stopover for hundreds of spe cies of migrating birds on their way from northern and central Europe to warmer climes around the Mediterranean and Africa. The Somme estuary, which is 5km wide, is the largest in northern France. Several walk ing routes are available for bird-watchers and guided visits are also available.

---

can see everything from sharks to speckled caimans (in a tropical forest) to see-through jellyfish up close; the new **Maison Planetaire** focuses on energy efficiency in the home. From April 2005 through the end of 2006, a special exhibit will cover South Africa and its two oceans, the Pacific and the Atlantic.

At the cafés you can buy tuna sandwiches – kind of like a zoo that sells lionburgers, some might say, but don't forget that Boulogne is Europe's most important fish-processing centre. If the prices look like they'll do to your pocket what drag nets do to the oceans, remember that you'd pay about the same to see two Hollywood movies.

BEACHES

Boulogne's beach begins just north of Nausicaä, across the mouth of the Liane from the vaguely menacing steelworks, now closed and set for demolition and decontamination. There are other fine beaches 4km north of town at **Wimereux** (bus 1 and 2, two to four times per hour), a partly *belle époque*–style resort founded by Napoleon in 1806; 2.5km southwest at **Le Portel** (bus 23); and 5km south at **Equihen Plage** (bus 11).

A bit further afield, the beach resort of **Le Touquet** (Paris Plage; ☎ tourist office 03 21 06 72 00; www.letouquet.com), 30km south of Boulogne, was hugely fashionable in the interwar period, when the English upper crust found it positively smashing (in 1940 a politically oblivious PG Wodehouse was arrested here by the Germans). These days it offers a wide selection of year-round outdoor activities for the whole family.

Sleeping

Auberge de Jeunesse (☎ 03 21 99 15 30; boulogne -sur-mer@fuaj.org; place Rouget de Lisle; dm with breakfast & sheets €15.50; ☼ closed Jan; 🖳) This modern outfit has spacious rooms with shower, toilet and three or four beds – fairly luxurious as far as hostels go. Kitchen facilities are available; there's a billiard table near the bar.

Hôtel Faidherbe (☎ 03 21 31 60 93; fax 03 21 87 01 14; 12 rue Faidherbe; d €45-60, Oct-Mar €5 less) The doors of the 34 modern, smallish rooms are upholstered so, at least upstairs, you won't hear Victor, the talking (or squawking) mynah bird who greets guests in the lobby. The new owners of this two-star place are wine connoisseurs and invite their guests to sample selected vintages at reasonable prices.

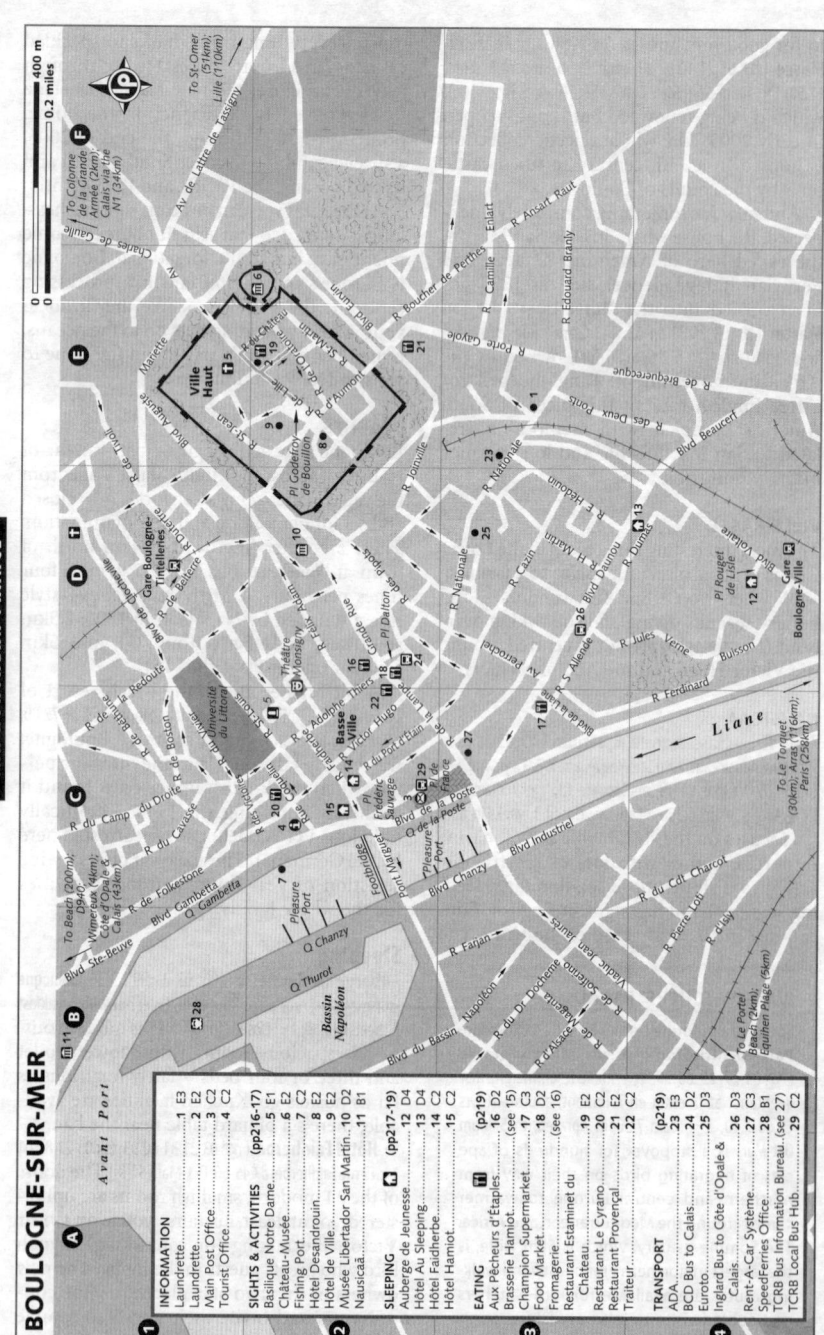

BOULOGNE-SUR-MER

INFORMATION	
Laundrette.................................1	E3
Laundrette.................................2	E2
Main Post Office........................3	C2
Tourist Office.............................4	C2

SIGHTS & ACTIVITIES	(pp216-17)
Basilique Notre Dame................5	E1
Château-Musée..........................6	F1
Fishing Port...............................7	C2
Hôtel Desandrouin....................8	E2
Hôtel de Ville............................9	E2
Musée Libertador San Martin...10	D2
Nausicaä...................................11	B1

SLEEPING	(pp217-19)
Auberge de Jeunesse...............12	D4
Hôtel Au Sleeping....................13	D4
Hôtel Faidherbe.......................14	C2
Hôtel Hamiot...........................15	C2

EATING	(p219)
Aux Pêcheurs d'Étaples............16	D2
Brasserie Hamiot...............(see 15)	
Champion Supermarket............17	C3
Food Market.............................18	D2
Fromagerie........................(see 16)	
Restaurant Estaminet du	
Château.................................19	E2
Restaurant Le Cyrano...............20	C2
Restaurant Provençal...............21	E2
Traiteur...................................22	C2

TRANSPORT	(p219)
ADA...23	E3
BCD Bus to Calais.....................24	D2
Euroto.....................................25	D3
Ingland Bus to Côte d'Opale &	
Calais.....................................26	D3
Rent-A-Car Système.................27	C3
SpeedFerries Office..................28	B1
TCRB Bus Information Bureau..(see 27)	
TCRB Local Bus Hub.................29	C2

Hôtel Hamiot (☎ 03 21 31 44 20; hotelrestaurant hamiot@wanadoo.fr; 1 rue Faidherbe; d from €55) This three-star place has 12 very comfortable wood-panelled rooms with gleaming tile bathrooms.

Hôtel Au Sleeping (☎ 03 21 80 62 79; fax 03 21 10 63 97; 18 blvd Daunou; s/d €30/34; ☽ reception closed after 1pm Sun except Jul & Aug) It may have only one star and the furnishings may be simple, but the welcome is warm and the 12 rooms are well lit and clean.

Eating
VILLE HAUTE
There are quite a few intimate restaurants – most of them moderately priced – along rue de Lille.

Restaurant Estaminet du Château (☎ 03 21 91 49 66; 2 rue du Château; menus €10-30; ☽ closed Thu & Wed evening; ☒) Meat dishes are an option but this place – a veteran French-style restaurant with an informal rustic feel – is especially strong on fish and seafood.

Restaurant Provençal (☎ 03 21 80 49 03; 107 rue Porte Gayole; ☽ Wed-Mon) Serves tasty Moroccan couscous with raisins (vegetarian €7.60, meat €11 to €19.80) and tajines (€15) amid over-the-top Oriental décor.

VILLE BASSE
Thanks to its ready supply, Boulogne is an excellent place for fresh fish. The area between rue Coquelin and place Dalton has a good choice of eateries.

Aux Pêcheurs d'Étaples (☎ 03 21 30 29 29; 31 Grande Rue; menus €13-24; ☽ closed Sun evening) Walk in past the fresh fish on ice and you arrive at a fine seafood restaurant with a modern nautical ambience. Cabillaud (cod), caught nearby, is a speciality.

Brasserie Hamiot (☎ 03 21 31 44 20; plat du jour €7.50, 3-course menus €16-28, kids' menus €6.50; ☽ noon-midnight) This bustling and hugely popular wood-panelled brasserie has a terrace in summer. See also Hôtel Hamiot (above).

Restaurant Le Cyrano (☎ 03 21 31 66 57; 9 rue Coquelin; 3-course menus from €8.25; ☽ 11.30am-10pm Mon-Sat) At this unpretentious but welcoming place, a full meal – for example, mussels, steak and dessert – comes at a good price.

SELF-CATERING
Food shops are sprinkled around rue de la Lampe and rue Adolphe Thiers and, in the Ville Haute, along rue de Lille.

Food market (place Dalton; ☽ Wed & Sat mornings) Held the day before if Wednesday or Saturday is a holiday.

Fromagerie (23 Grande Rue; ☽ closed Sun & Mon morning) This place is next door to Aux Pêcheurs d'Étaples.

Traiteur (1 Grande Rue; ☽ closed Mon & Sun afternoon) Ready-to-eat delicacies.

There's also a **Champion supermarket** (53 blvd Daunou).

Getting There & Around
BOAT
SpeedFerries (UK ☎ 01304-20 3000, France ☎ 03 21 10 50 00; www.speedferries.com) offers an ultramodern, ultrafast catamaran service between Boulogne and Dover (50 minutes, five daily). Foot passengers without cars cannot be accommodated.

BUS
For details on bus service to the beautiful Côte d'Opale and Calais, see p212.

Most local bus lines, run by **TCRB** (☎ 03 21 83 51 51), stop at place de France.

CAR
Discount rental agencies include:
ADA (☎ 03 21 80 80 82; 211 rue Nationale)
Euroto (☎ 03 21 30 32 23; 96 rue Nationale)
Rent-A-Car Système (☎ 03 21 80 97 34; 26 rue de la Lampe)

TAXI
To order a cab, ring ☎ 03 21 91 25 00.

TRAIN
Gare Boulogne-Ville has services to Amiens (€15.70, 1½ hours, five to eight daily), Calais-Ville (€6.60, 27 to 48 minutes, 15 to 19 daily Monday to Saturday, nine daily Sunday), Étaples-Le Touquet (€4.70, 20 minutes, 10 to 21 daily), Lille-Flandres or Lille-Europe (€17.80, one to two hours, 10 to 13 daily) and Paris' Gare du Nord (€27.50, 2¾ hours, six to nine daily).

DUNKIRK
pop 209,000
Dunkirk (Dunkerque), flattened during WWII, was rebuilt during one of the most uninspired periods in Western architecture, so unless you're the world's only fan of 1950s brick low-rise, want to hang out on

FAR NORTHERN FRANCE

the Malo-les-Bains beach or plan to join in a colourful pre-Lent carnival, there's little reason to spend much time here.

Under Louis XIV, Dunkirk – whose name means 'church of the dunes' in Flemish – served as a base for French privateers, including the infamous Jean Bart (1650–1702), whose daring attacks on English and Dutch ships have ensured his status as a local hero: the city centre's main square, suitably adorned with a dashing statue, bears his name.

Orientation & Information

The train station is 600m southwest of Dunkirk's main square, place Jean Bart. The beach and its waterfront esplanade, Digue de Mer, are 2km northeast of the centre – via av des Bains – in the faded, turn-of-the-20th-century seaside resort of Malo-les-Bains.

The **tourist office** (☎ 03 28 66 79 21; www.ot -dunkerque.fr; rue de l'Amiral Ronarc'h; 🕙 9am-12.30pm & 1.30-6.30pm Mon-Fri, 9am-6.30pm Sat, 10am-noon & 2-4pm Sun & holidays, no midday closure Jul & Aug) is in the base of a medieval belfry.

THE EVACUATION OF DUNKIRK

In May and June 1940, Dunkirk earned a place in the history books when the British Expeditionary Force and French and Belgian units found themselves almost completely surrounded by Hitler's armies, which had advanced into far northern France.

In an effort to salvage what it could, Churchill's government ordered British units to make their way to Dunkirk, where naval vessels and hundreds of fishing boats and pleasure craft – many manned by civilian volunteers – braved intense German artillery and air attacks to ferry 340,000 men to the safety of England. Conducted in the difficult first year of WWII, this unplanned and chaotic evacuation – dubbed Operation Dynamo – failed to save any of the units' heavy equipment but was, nevertheless, seen as a key demonstration of Britain's resourcefulness and determination.

Dunkirk's wide, promenade-lined beach, Plage des Alliés, named in honour of the Allied troops evacuated to England from here in 1940, is in the seaside Dunkirk suburb of Malo-les-Bains.

Sights & Activities

The **Musée Portuaire** (Harbour Museum; ☎ 03 28 63 33 39; 9 quai de la Citadelle; adult/under 18 €4/3; 🕙 10am-12.45pm & 1.30-6pm, probably closed Tue, no midday closure Jul & Aug), housed in a one-time tobacco warehouse, will delight ship-model lovers of all ages. Forty-five minute guided **tours** (adult/under 18 €4/3.50) take visitors aboard a barge, a lighthouse ship (to open 2005) and the *Duchesse Anne*, a three-masted merchant marine training ship built in Germany in 1901 and acquired by France as WWII reparations.

Stretching east of Dunkirk to the Belgian border, *les dunes flamandes* (Flemish dunes) represent a unique ecosystem harbouring hundreds of plant species, including rare orchids. The area – including the **Dewulf and Marchand dunes** – is served by bus No 2B (3B on Sunday and holidays), which continues on to Adinkerke in Belgium (€1.30, an extra €0.80 to cross the border).

Tours

The tourist office has details on **boat tours** (adult €7.50; 🕙 Tue-Sun Jul & Aug) of Dunkirk's huge port (France's third largest) and some of the country's most important (and odoriferous) steel and petroleum works; departures are from place du Minck.

Festivals & Events

Dunkirk's **carnival**, held at the beginning of Lent, originated as a final fling for the town's cod fishermen before they set out for months on the waters off Iceland. The biggest celebration is on the Sunday right before Mardi Gras, when costumed citizens march around town behind fife-and-drum bands, and general merriment reigns. At the climax of the festivities, the mayor and other dignitaries stand on the town hall balcony and pelt the assembled locals with dried salted herrings.

Getting There & Away

For details on links to Calais, see p212. Almost all trains to Lille stop at Lille-Flandres (€11.60, 1¼ hours, nine to 21 daily).

Ferries run by **Norfolk Line** (☎ 03 28 59 01 01; www.norfolkline.com) link Loon Plage, about 25km west of the town centre, with Dover (from €155 one way for car and five passengers, two hours, 10 daily).

ARRAS

pop 40,000

Arras (the final 's' is pronounced), former capital of Artois, is worth seeing mainly for its harmonious ensemble of Flemish-style arcaded buildings; the rest of the city, seriously damaged during both world wars, is a mixture of 19th-century and postwar architecture. The city is a good base for visits to the Battle of the Somme memorials, especially if you have a car.

Orientation

The centre of Arras is the historic Grand' Place and the almost-adjoining place des Héros (the Petite Place), where you'll find the town hall. The train station is 600m to the southeast. The pedestrianised area southeast of place des Héros, including rue Ronville, is the commercial centre.

Information

Banks can be found along rue Gambetta and its continuation, rue Ernestale.

Laundrette (17 place d'Ipswich; ☻ 7am-8pm)

Post Office (rue Gambetta) Has a Cyberposte and changes money.

Tourist Office (☎ 03 21 51 26 95; www.ot-arras .fr; place des Héros; ☻ 9am or 10am-noon & 2-6pm or 6.30pm Mon-Sat, no midday closure May-Sep, 10am-12.30pm or 1pm & 2.30pm or 3-6pm or 6.30pm Sun & holidays) Inside the town hall.

Sights & Activities

Arras' two market squares, **place des Héros** and the **Grand' Place**, with a history stretching back to the 11th century, are surrounded by Flemish-Baroque houses build in the 1600s and 1700s. These vary in all sorts of decorative details but their 345 sandstone columns form a common arcade unique in France. The tourist office offers a **self-guided tour** (adult/student €5.35/3.05) of the city centre.

The Flemish-Gothic **Hotel de Ville** (town hall, place des Héros) dates from the 16th century but was completely rebuilt after WWI. Three giants (see p208) – Colas, Jacqueline and their son Dédé – make their home in the lobby.

The basement of the town hall is a veritable hub of activity. If you're in the mood for a panoramic view, this is the place to hop on the lift to the top of the 75m **belfry** (adult/student €2.30/1.60; ☻ 9am or 10am-noon & 2-6pm or 6.30pm Mon-Sat, no midday closure May-Sep, 10am-12.30pm or 1pm & 2.30pm or 3-6pm or 6.30pm Sun & holidays). The **Histo-**rama (adult €2.30, student & child €1.55) presents the city's history in a 20-minute slide show (in English). But for a truly unique perspective on Arras, head into the slimy **souterrains** (tunnels; adult €4.40, student & child €2.40). Also known as *boves* (cellars), they run under place des Héros and were turned into British command posts, hospitals and barracks during WWI. Each spring, in a brilliant juxtaposition of underground gloom and horticultural exuberance, plants and flowers turn the tunnels into the life-affirming **Jardin des Boves** (☻ 20 Mar-20 Jun). Tours of the *souterrains* (40 to 50 minutes, English translation available) *generally* begin at 10am, 11am, 2.30pm, 3.30pm and 4.30pm from Monday to Friday, and every 30 minutes or so on Saturday and Sunday. All three attractions can be visited with the **combined ticket** (forfait; adult €6.80, student & child €4).

Highlights at the **Musée des Beaux-Arts** (Fine Arts Museum; ☎ 03 21 71 26 43; 22 rue Paul Doumer; adult €4, student, over 65 & teacher €2; ☻ 9.30am-noon & 2-5.30pm Wed-Mon, no midday closure Thu), housed in a neoclassical former Benedictine abbey, include the original copper lion from the town hall belfry, medieval sculpture (including a 15th-century skeletal figure whose stomach is being devoured by worms) and 17th-century religious paintings. **Le City Pass** (adult €9.80, student & child €6) gets you into the museum, belfry, Historama and *souterrains*.

The 18th-century house where Arras-born lawyer and Jacobin radical Maximilien Robespierre lived just before the Revolution, the **Maison Robespierre** (9 rue Maximilien Robespierre; admission free; ☻ 2-5.30pm Tue & Thu, 3.30-6.30pm Sat & Sun), houses a small exhibit on traditional construction crafts prepared by an association of master craftsmen.

Sleeping

BUDGET

Auberge de Jeunesse (☎ 03 21 22 70 02; arras@fuaj.org; 59 Grand' Place; bed 1st night/subsequent nights €11.70/8.90; ☻ reception open 7.30am-noon & 5-11pm, hostel closed Jan & perhaps Dec) Modern and superbly situated in the town centre, this has cheerful rooms for two to 10; almost all beds are bunks. Full kitchen facilities are available.

Hôtel du Beffroi (☎ 03 21 23 13 78; fax 03 21 23 03 08; 28 place de la Vacquerie; s/d from €30/34, with shower & toilet €40/45; ☻ reception closed after noon Sun) Only one star hangs by the door but the 15 rooms are tasteful and squeaky clean. Room No 16, a veritable suite, comes with a romantic view.

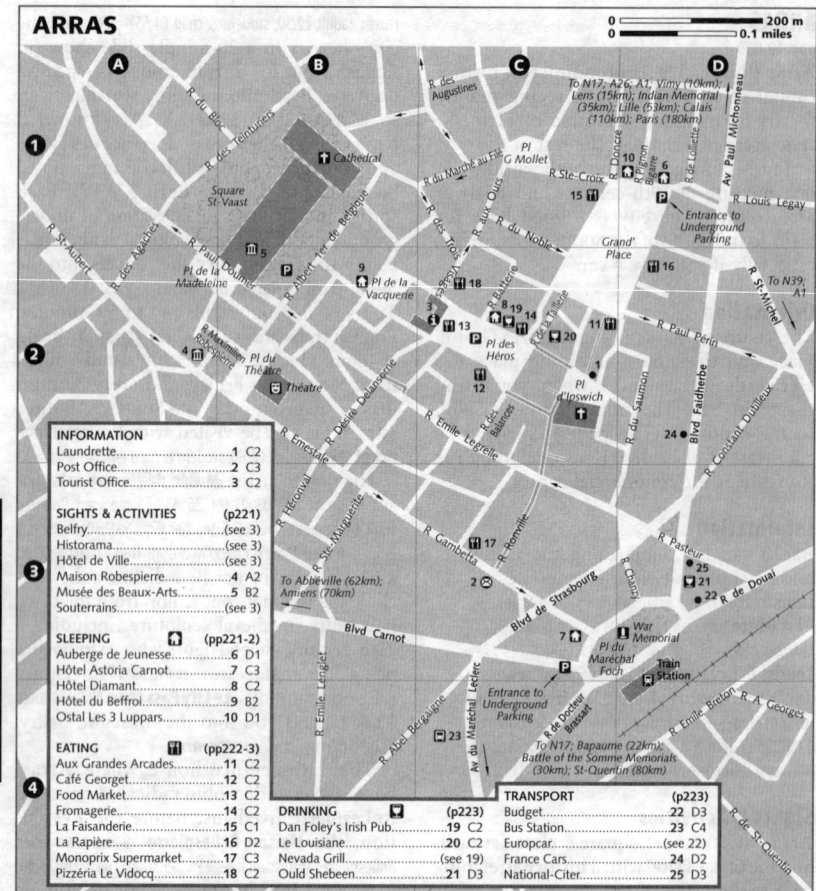

ARRAS

0 ——— 200 m
0 ——— 0.1 miles

To N17; A26; A1; Vimy (10km);
Lens (15km); Indian Memorial
(35km); Lille (53km); Calais
(110km); Paris (180km)

To N39;
A1

To N1;
A1

To Abbeville (62km);
Amiens (70km)

To N17; Bapaume (22km);
Battle of the Somme Memorials
(30km); St-Quentin (80km)

INFORMATION	
Laundrette	1 C2
Post Office	2 C3
Tourist Office	3 C2

SIGHTS & ACTIVITIES	(p221)
Belfry	(see 3)
Historama	(see 3)
Hôtel de Ville	(see 3)
Maison Robespierre	4 A2
Musée des Beaux-Arts	5 B2
Souterrains	(see 3)

SLEEPING	(pp221-2)
Auberge de Jeunesse	6 D1
Hôtel Astoria Carnot	7 C3
Hôtel Diamant	8 C2
Hôtel du Beffroi	9 B2
Ostal Les 3 Luppars	10 D1

EATING	(pp222-3)
Aux Grandes Arcades	11 C2
Café Georget	12 C2
Food Market	13 C2
Fromagerie	14 C2
La Faisanderie	15 C1
La Rapière	16 D2
Monoprix Supermarket	17 C3
Pizzéria Le Vidocq	18 C2

DRINKING	(p223)
Dan Foley's Irish Pub	19 C2
Le Louisiane	20 C2
Nevada Grill	(see 19)
Ould Shebeen	21 D3

TRANSPORT	(p223)
Budget	22 D3
Bus Station	23 C4
Europcar	(see 22)
France Cars	24 D2
National-Citer	25 D3

MID-RANGE

A number of city-centre hostelries offer good value for money.

Ostel Les 3 Luppars (☎ 03 21 60 02 03; www .ostel-les-3luppars.com in French; 47 Grand' Place; s/d/q from €44/60/75) Homy and centred on a courtyard, this 'ho(s)tel' occupies the Grand' Place's only non-Flemish-style building (it is Gothic and dates from 1370). The rooms are comfortable, if a tad too standard. Ostel Les 3 Luppars has a sauna, which costs €5 per person.

Hôtel Astoria Carnot (☎ 03 21 71 08 14; www.ho telcarnot.com; 10 place du Maréchal Foch; s/d/q €47/51/66) The well-lit, two-star rooms are spiffy and quite modern and come with spacious tile bathrooms.

Hôtel Diamant (☎ 03 21 71 23 23; www.arras-hotel -diamant.com; 5 place des Héros; s/d from €50/56 🖵) The 12 two-star rooms are compact but pleasant; the buffet breakfast costs €7.50.

Eating

Lots of eateries are hidden away under the arches of the Grand' Place.

La Faisanderie (☎ 03 21 48 20 76; 45 Grand' Place; menus €25-65; 🕑 12.15-2pm & 7.30-9.15pm, closed Mon, lunch Tue & Sun evening) An exceptionally elegant French restaurant under vaulted brick ceilings. The menu changes with the seasons so the ingredients are always fresh.

La Rapière (☎ 03 21 55 09 92; 44 Grand' Place; menus €17-27; 🕑 closed Sun evening) Regional cuisine, including *flan de maroilles* (flan made with a local cows' milk cheese), is elegantly served in a contemporary ambience.

Aux Grandes Arcades (☎ 03 21 23 30 89; 10 Grand' Place; menus €15-35, plat du jour €11; ☽ daily) This brasserie-style place focuses on regional dishes such as *potje vleesch* (Flemish terrine made with veal, rabbit and fowl, €15).

Café Georget (☎ 03 21 71 13 07; 42 place des Héros; plat du jour €7.50; ☽ noon-2pm Mon-Sat) An unpretentious eatery serving hearty, homemade French dishes.

Pizzéria Le Vidocq (☎ 03 21 23 79 50; 24 rue des Trois Visages; pizzas €6.35-9.90; ☽ closed Sun, dinner Wed & lunch Sat) The pizzas arrive steaming from a wood-fired oven. Also on offer are pasta, 12 kinds of veal and 12 varieties of salad (about €8).

SELF-CATERING

There's a **food market** (☽ Wed & Sat mornings) in the square around the Hôtel de Ville, and a **Monoprix supermarket** (30 rue Gambetta).

Fromagerie (37 place des Héros; ☽ 9.30am-12.30pm & 2.30-7.15pm Tue-Thu, 8.30am-7.15pm Fri & Sat) Several other food shops are right nearby.

Drinking

Cafés and pubs line the northern side of place des Héros and adjacent rue de la Taillerie. **Dan Foley's Irish Pub** (7 place des Héros) doesn't have much that's authentically Irish except Guinness; a quintessentially French eatery, the Nevada Grill, is next door.

Ould Shebeen (☎ 03 21 71 87 97; 6 blvd Faidherbe; ☽ 11am-1am Mon-Thu, until 2am Fri & Sat) This down-to-earth Irish pub, with its rough-hewn décor, attracts native English speakers as well as Francophone locals. Thursday is trivia night (at about 10.30pm); questions are in English and French.

Le Louisiane (☎ 03 21 23 18 00; 12 rue de la Taillerie; ☽ noon-1am or 2am, from 3pm on Sun) This yuppyish café-bar comes with mellow background music and two billiard tables.

Getting There & Away

BUS

For details on buses from Arras' **bus station** (☎ 03 21 51 34 64; rue Abel Bergaigne; ☽ office 7am-6.30pm Mon-Fri, to 12.30pm Sat) to the Vimy Canadian National Memorial and Albert, see p225 and p227.

TRAIN

Arras is on the main line linking Lille-Flandres (€8.60, 40 minutes to one hour,

11 to 17 daily) with Paris' Gare du Nord (€27.20 or €36.90 by TGV, 52 minutes, 12 to 15 daily). Other destinations include Amiens (€9.60, 50 minutes, seven to 11 daily) and Calais-Ville (€16.90, two hours, 10 daily Monday to Friday, six or seven daily Saturday and Sunday).

CAR

Budget (☎ 03 21 60 76 76; 5 rue de Douai)
Europcar (☎ 03 21 07 29 54; 5 rue de Douai)
France Cars (☎ 03 21 50 22 22; 31 blvd Faidherbe) Less expensive than the majors.
National-Citer (☎ 03 21 71 49 14; 14 blvd Faidherbe)

TAXI

Companies available pretty much 24 hours include **Taxis GT** (☎ 03 21 71 64 32) and **Alliance Taxi** (☎ 03 21 23 69 69). Both can take you to Somme battlefield sites.

BATTLE OF THE SOMME MEMORIALS

The First Battle of the Somme, a WWI Allied offensive waged in the villages and woodlands northeast of Amiens, was designed to relieve pressure on the beleaguered French troops at Verdun (see p382). On 1 July 1916, British, Commonwealth and French troops 'went over the top' in a massive assault along a 34km front. But German positions proved virtually unbreachable, and on the first day of the battle an astounding 21,392 British troops were killed and another 35,492 were wounded. Most casualties were infantrymen mown down by German machine guns.

By the time the offensive was called off in mid-November, 1.2 million lives had been lost on both sides. The British had advanced 12km, the French 8km. The Battle of the Somme has become a metaphor for the meaningless slaughter of war and its killing fields have since become a site of pilgrimage.

INFORMATION

A variety of brochures, including *A Guide to Australian Memorials on the Western Front*, can be picked up at area tourist offices. For information on the Commonwealth War Grave Commission see p225.

TOURS

Touring the area is easiest by car, but quite a few sites can be visited by train or bus from

FAR NORTHERN FRANCE

BATTLE OF THE SOMME MEMORIALS

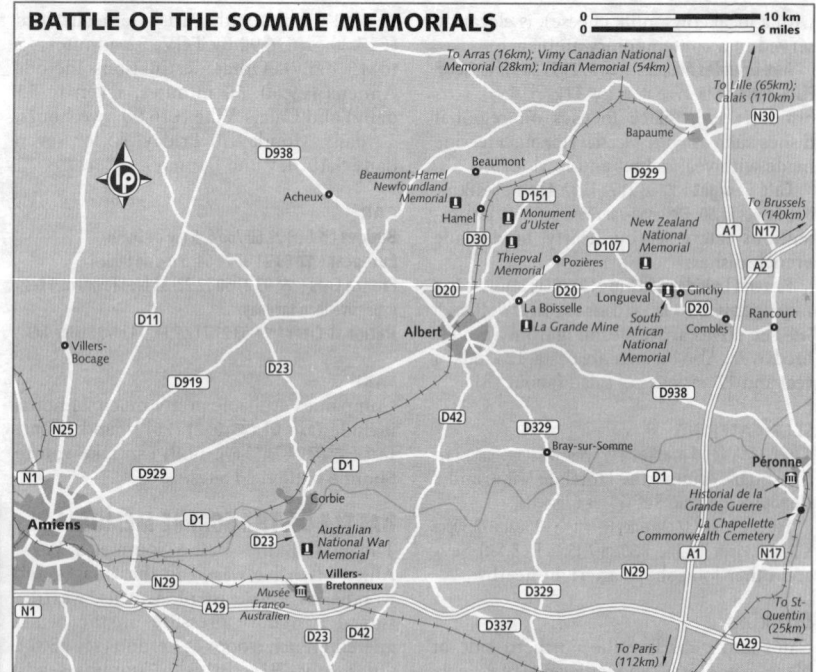

Amiens and/or Arras – details on public transport options appear after each listing. Cycling is also an option.

Experienced companies offering minibus tours from Albert include:

Battlefield Tours (☎ /fax 03 21 50 18 87, 06 87 43 10 49; www.somme-normandy-tours.com; half-/full day per person from €22/52; ☼ tours begin 10am & 3pm year-round) Pick-up in Arras or Amiens is an option.

Salient Tours (☎ France 06 86 05 61 30, ☎ UK 01225-812299; www.salienttours.com; half-day per person from €22; ☼ tours begin 10am & 3pm Tue-Sun Easter-late Oct)

North of Arras

The area north of Arras has a couple of noteworthy memorials and numerous military cemeteries.

VIMY CANADIAN NATIONAL MEMORIAL & PARK

Whereas the French, right after the war, attempted to erase all signs of battle and return the Somme region to agriculture and normalcy, the Canadians decided that the most evocative way to remember their fallen

was to preserve pieces of the crater-pocked battlefields. As a result, the best place to get some sense of the unimaginable hell known as the Western Front is at the chilling, eerie moonscape of **Vimy Ridge**. Visitors can also see **tunnels** (☼ May-Nov) and reconstructed **trenches**.

Of the 66,655 Canadians who died in WWI, 3589 lost their lives in April 1917 taking this ridge, a German defensive line, the highest point of which was later chosen as the site of Canada's **WWI memorial** (inaccessible due to repairs until mid-2006). The allegorical figures, carved from huge blocks of limestone, include a cloaked, downcast female figure representing a young Canada mourning her fallen. The base is inscribed with the names of 11,285 Canadians who went missing in action. The 1-sq-km park also includes two **Canadian cemeteries** and, at the vehicle entrance to the main memorial, a **monument to the Moroccan Division** (in French and Arabic).

The **Historical Interpretive Centre** (☎ 03 21 58 19 34; www.vac-acc.gc.ca; ☼ 10am-6pm May-Dec, 9am-5pm Jan-Apr), staffed by Canadian students, will at some point be replaced by a new museum near the trenches. The **Canadian Virtual War Memorial** (www.virtualmemorial.gc.ca) has details on over 116,000 Canadian war dead.

Getting There & Away

From Arras, you can take bus No 91 (about €2, 20 minutes, six or seven daily Monday to Saturday) towards Lens; ask the bus driver to stop at Vimy Ridge, 3.2km from the memorial.

Trains link Arras with the town of Vimy (€2.50, 12 minutes, six daily Monday to Friday, two on Saturday), 6km east of the memorial.

A taxi from Arras costs about €20 return, plus €19 for each hour the driver spends waiting.

INDIAN MEMORIAL

The fascinating and seldom-visited **Mémorial Indien**, vaguely Moghul in architecture, records the names of Commonwealth soldiers from the Indian subcontinent who 'have no known grave'. The units (31st Punjabis, 11th Rajputs, 2nd King Edward's Own Gurkha Rifles) and the ranks of the fallen (sepoy, havildar, *naik, sowar*, labourer, follower) engraved on the walls evoke the pride, pomp and exploitation on which the British Empire was built.

To get there from La Bassée, take the northbound D947 to its intersection with the D171.

South of Arras

Some of the bloodiest fighting of WWI took place around the town of Albert (p227). The farmland north and east of the town is dotted with dozens of Commonwealth cemeteries.

PÉRONNE

The best place to start a visit to the Somme battlefields is in the river port of Péronne, at the well-designed and informative **Historial de la Grande Guerre** (☎ 03 22 83 14 18; www .historial.org; Château de Péronne; adult/senior €7/6, student, teacher & ex-serviceman €3.50; ☑ 10am-6pm Apr-Sep, 10am-6pm Tue-Sun Oct–mid-Dec & mid-Jan–Mar). This innovative museum tells the story of the war chronologically, with equal space given to the German, French and British perspectives on what happened, how and why. A great deal of visually engaging material, including period films and the bone-chilling engravings of Otto Dix, capture the aesthetic sensibilities, enthusiasm, naive patriotism and unimaginable violence of the time. The proud uniforms of various units and armies are shown laid out on the ground, as if on freshly – though bloodless – dead soldiers. Not much glory here.

On the N17 at the southern edge of town, **La Chapellette Commonwealth Cemetery** has separate British and Indian sections.

One bus line links Péronne with Albert (€3.50, 50 minutes, three or four a day Monday to Saturday); another goes to both Villers-Bretonneux (€4.50, 50 minutes, one

COMMONWEALTH CEMETERIES & MEMORIALS

Over 750,000 soldiers from Australia, Canada, the Indian subcontinent, New Zealand, South Africa, the UK, the West Indies and other parts of the British Empire died on the Western Front, two-thirds of them in France. By Commonwealth tradition, they were buried where they fell, in over 1000 military cemeteries and 2000 civilian cemeteries. Today, hundreds of neatly tended Commonwealth plots – marked by white-on-dark-green signs – dot the landscape along a wide swathe of territory running roughly from Albert and Cambrai north via Arras and Béthune to Armentières and Ypres (Ieper) in Belgium. Many of the headstones bear inscriptions composed by family members. Twenty six memorials (20 of them in France) bear the names of over 300,000 Commonwealth soldiers whose bodies were never recovered or identified. French, American and German war dead were reburied in large cemeteries after the war.

Except where noted, all the monuments listed in this section are always open. Many Commonwealth cemeteries have a plaque with historical information. The bronze Cemetery Register boxes contain a booklet with details of the site; you can record your impressions in the visitors' book.

The website of the **Commonwealth War Graves Commission** (www.cwgc.org) has a search function that can find details on individual war dead.

or two daily Monday to Saturday) and Amiens' bus station (€4.50, 1¼ hours).

THIEPVAL MEMORIAL

Dedicated to 'the Missing of the Somme', this **memorial** – the region's most visited place of pilgrimage – was built in the early 1930s on the site of a German stronghold that was stormed on 1 July 1916 with unimaginable casualties. The columns of the arches are inscribed with the names of 73,367 British and South African soldiers whose remains were never found. The modern but discreet **Thiepval Visitors Centre** (www.thiepval.org.uk), built almost entirely below ground level, opened its doors in mid-2004, on the 90th anniversary of the start of WWI.

AUSTRALIAN NATIONAL WAR MEMORIAL

During WWI, 313,000 Australians (out of a total population of 4.5 million) volunteered for military service; 46,000 met their deaths on the Western Front (14,000 others perished elsewhere). The **Australian National War Memorial**, a 32m tower engraved with the names of 10,982 soldiers who went missing in action, stands on a hill where Australian and British troops repulsed a German assault on 24 April 1918. It was dedicated in 1938; two years later its stone walls were scarred by the guns of Hitler's invading armies.

The nearest town is **Villers-Bretonneux**, an ugly bourg that still hasn't completely recovered from the war. For Aussies, though, it's a heart-warming place that bills itself as *l'Australie en Picardie*, and Anzac Day is religiously commemorated. In 1993, the unidentified remains of an Australian soldier were transferred from Adelaide Cemetery, on the N29 at the western edge of town, to the Tomb of the Unknown Soldier in Canberra.

The **Musée Franco-Australien** (☎ 03 22 96 80 79; www.villers-bretonneux.com/Australian.htm; École Victoria, 9 rue Victoria, Villers-Bretonneux; adult/student €3.05/1.55; ☒ 10am-12.30pm & 2-6pm Wed-Sun & Tue afternoon, plus 2-6pm on 1st & 3rd Sun of month) has intimate, evocative displays of WWI Australiana, including letters, photographs of life on the Western Front, and a small Anzac library. The front steps are a favoured trysting spot for local teens.

The Villers-Bretonneux train station, linked to Amiens (€3, 12 minutes, five to eight daily), is 700m south of the museum (along rue de Melbourne) and an easily walkable 3km south of the Australian National War Memorial. Bus No 13 links Villers-Bretonneux with Amiens (€3.40, 25 minutes, three daily Monday to Saturday) and Péronne (€4.50, 50 minutes, one or two daily Monday to Saturday).

A **taxi** (☎ 03 22 48 49 49) to the memorial from Villers-Bretonneux costs €12 return, plus €3 for every 10 minutes spent waiting at the site.

BEAUMONT-HAMEL NEWFOUNDLAND MEMORIAL

Like Vimy (p224), the evocative **Mémorial Terre-Neuvien** preserves part of the Western Front in the state it was in at fighting's end. The zigzag trench system, which still fills with mud in winter, is clearly visible, as are countless shell craters and the remains of barbed-wire barriers.

On 1 July 1916, the volunteer Royal Newfoundland Regiment stormed entrenched German positions and was nearly wiped out; a sign explains blandly that 'strategic and tactical miscalculations led to a great slaughter'. You can survey the whole battlefield from the **caribou statue**, surrounded by plants native to Newfoundland. Canadian students based at the **visitors centre** (☎ 03 22 76 70 87; ☒ 10am-6pm May–mid-Nov, to 5pm mid-Nov–Apr, closed late Dec-early Jan), designed to look like a typical Newfoundland fisher's house, give free guided tours from May to mid-November (and on some days the rest of the year).

MONUMENT DE L'ULSTER

Built on a German frontline position assaulted by the overwhelmingly Protestant 36th (Ulster) Division on 1 July 1916, the **Tour d'Ulster** (Ulster Tower) is a replica of Helen's Tower near Bangor, County Down, where the unit did its training. Dedicated in 1921, it has long been a Unionist pilgrimage site. An obelisk known as the **Orange Memorial to Fallen Brethren** stands near the entrance.

SOUTH AFRICAN & NEW ZEALAND NATIONAL MEMORIALS

The **South African National Memorial** (Mémorial Sud-Africain) stands in the middle of shell-pocked **Delville Wood**, which was almost captured by a South African brigade in the third week of July in 1916. The avenues through the trees are named after streets in London and Edinburgh. The star-shaped **museum** (☎ 03 22 85 02 17; 10am-5.45pm Apr–mid-Oct, to 3.45pm in winter, closed Mon, holidays & 11 Nov-early Feb) was dedicated amid much apartheid-related controversy in 1986.

The **New Zealand National Memorial** is 1.5km due north of Longueval.

LA GRANDE MINE

This enormous **crater** – one of many made by tunnelling under enemy (in this case German) trenches and planting vast quantities of explosives – looks like the site of a meteor impact. Some 100m across and 30m deep and officially known as the Lochnagar Crater Memorial, it was created at 7.30am on 1 July 1916, and is a testament to the boundless ingenuity human beings show when determined to kill their fellow creatures.

ALBERT

The most noteworthy landmark in this rather unfetching town (population 10,000), virtually flattened during WWI, is neo-Byzantine-style **Basilique Notre-Dame de Brebières**, topped by a gilded statue of the Virgin Mary, famously left dangling by a German shell. For great views, you can climb the 70m-high belfry from April to September.

Right next to the basilica, the **Musée des Abris Somme 1916** (☎ 03 22 75 16 17; www.somme-1916.org; rue Anicet Godin; adult/under 18 €4/2.50; 9am-noon & 2-6pm Feb–mid-Dec, no midday closure Jun-Sep), housed in dank underground galleries, does a good job of evoking the grim lives of soldiers and local civilians at the front line.

The **tourist office** (☎ 03 22 75 16 42; www.tourisme-albert.net in French; 9 rue Gambetta; 9am-noon or 12.30pm & 1.30pm or 2pm-6.30pm Mon-Sat, 10am-12.30pm Sun & holidays Apr-Sep, to 5pm Mon-Sat Oct-Mar) is 50m towards the train station from the basilica. Year-round, it arranges tours of the WWI memorials (phone ahead for reservations) and rents out bicycles (per day €12).

Trains (six to 12 daily) link Albert's train station – the monoplane hanging in the waiting hall is a Potez 36 from 1933 – with Amiens (€5.40, 25 minutes) and Arras (€6.30, 25 minutes).

AMIENS
pop 132,000

Amiens, the comfy if reserved former capital of Picardy, boasts one of France's most magnificent Gothic cathedrals. Local people out for a quick bit of shopping, a bite or just a stroll animate the post-war city centre, a mostly pedestrianised precinct with clean-lined, modernist buildings that have aged remarkably well. The city is a good base for visits to the Battle of the Somme memorials – and its 26,000 students give the place a young, lively feel.

Orientation

Commercial life is based around place Gambetta, two blocks west of the cathedral. The train station is about 1km southeast of place Gambetta; you can find it from most anywhere in town by looking for the 26-storey Tour Perret.

Information

Banks can be found around place René Goblet and along pedestrianised rue des Trois Cailloux.

Laundrette (10 rue André; 8am-7pm)

Main Post Office (7 rue des Vergeaux) Has currency exchange and a Cyberposte.

Neurogame Cybercafé (☎ 03 22 72 68 79; 16 rue des Chaudronniers; per hr €3.50; 10am-midnight Mon-Sat, 2-8pm Sun) Internet access.

Tourist Office (☎ 03 22 71 60 50; www.amiens.com /tourisme; 6bis rue Dusevel; 9.30am-6pm or 7pm Mon-Sat, 10am-noon & 2-5pm Sun) Can supply details on visiting the Somme war monuments, including minibus tours, and on summer boat tours of St-Leu.

Sights & Activities
CATHÉDRALE NOTRE DAME

This spectacular **Gothic cathedral** (place Notre Dame; 8.30am-6.15pm Apr-Sep, 8.30am-noon & 2pm-5.15pm Oct-Mar), the largest in France and a Unesco World Heritage site, was begun in 1220 to house the (purported) head of St John the Baptist, now enclosed in gold in the northern outer wall of the ambulatory. Connoisseurs rave about the soaring Gothic arches, unity of style and immense interior but for locals, the 17th-century statue known as the **Ange Pleureur** (Crying Angel), in the ambulatory opposite the axial chapel, remains a favourite.

The nave is lined with beautifully decorated chapels and graced by 13th-century **bronze figures** of the bishops who built the

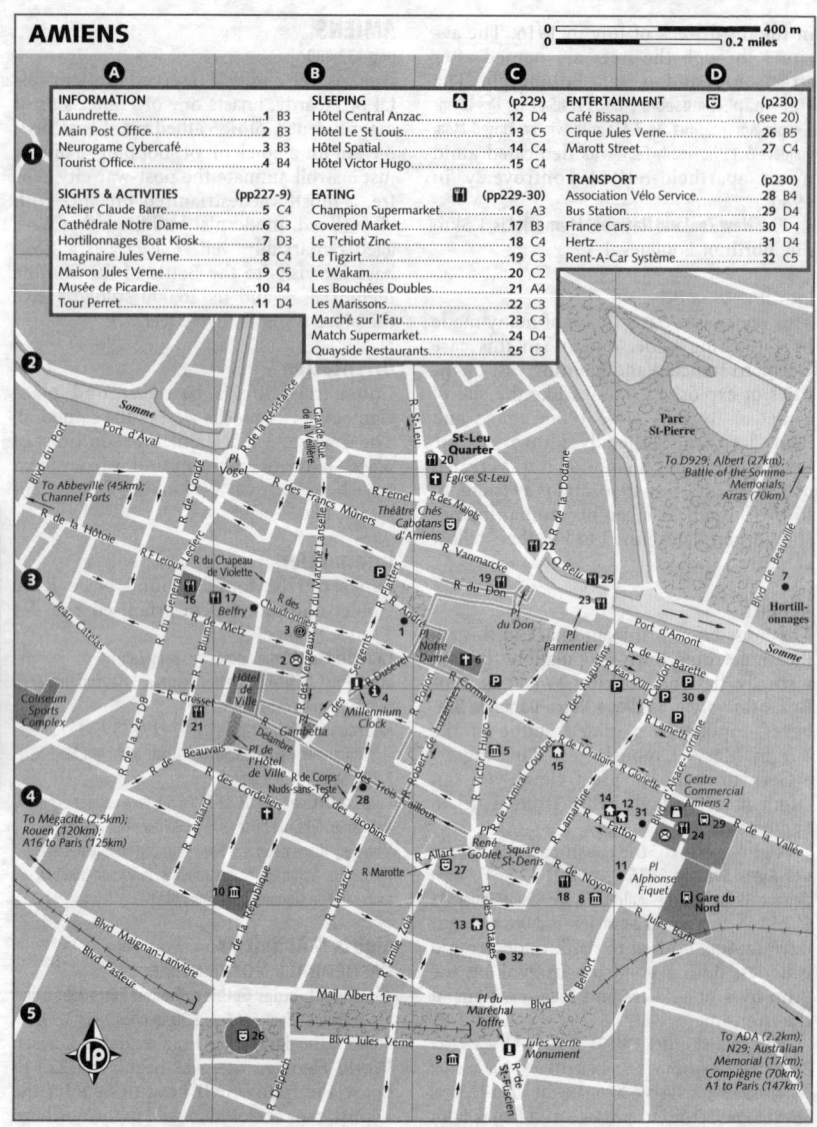

AMIENS

0 ————— 400 m
0 ————— 0.2 miles

cathedral. The choir, with its 110 sumptuously carved oak **choir stalls** (1508–22), is separated from the ambulatory by gilded wrought-iron grates and choir screens with painted, haut-relief stone figures that illustrate the lives of St John the Baptist (1531) and the first bishop of Amiens and patron saint of Picardy, St Firmin (1495). The black-

and-white 234m-long **maze** embedded in the floor of the nave is easy to miss as the soaring vaults draw the eye ever upward. Plaques in the south transept arm commemorate Australian, British, Canadian, New Zealand and US troops who died in WWI.

A free 45-minute light show bathes the cathedral façade in vivid medieval colours nightly from 15 June to 30 September and 15 December to 6 January; the photons start flying at 8pm in winter and sometime between 9.45pm (September) and 10.45pm (June) in summer.

OTHER SIGHTS & ACTIVITIES
The medieval **St-Leu Quarter**, north of the cathedral along the Somme, is the best place in town for a riverside stroll. Postwar renovations have left parts of the area too cute by half, but the many neon-lit quayside restaurants and pubs make it especially lively at night. Another product of postwar exuberance, the concrete **Tour Perret** (built 1948–54), at one time the tallest building in Europe, faces the train station.

The lawns, lakes, waterways and bridges of **Parc St-Pierre** stretch eastwards from St-Leu all the way to the **Hortillonnages** – also known as the Jardins Flottants (Floating Gardens) – a 330-hectare area of market gardens that have supplied the city with vegetables and flowers since the Middle Ages. From April to October, one-hour **cruises** (adult/11-16 yrs/4-10 yrs €5/4.20/2.50) of the peaceful canals – in 12-person gondola-like boats – depart from a riverside **kiosk** (☎ 03 22 92 12 18; 54 blvd de Beauvillé) daily from 2pm until between 5pm and nightfall; get there before 4pm to buy tickets.

The **Musée de Picardie** (☎ 03 22 97 14 00; 48 rue de la République; adult/6-18 yrs €4/2.50; ☻ 10am-12.30pm & 2-6pm Tue-Sun), housed in a dashing Second Empire structure (1855–67), is surprisingly well-endowed with archaeological exhibits, medieval art, 18th-century French paintings (including royal commissions) and Revolution-era ceramics. Some 80 works from here spent part of 2004 hanging out in California – at the Santa Barbara Museum of Art.

Ever wonder how stained glass is actually designed and put together? You can see firsthand at **Atelier Claude Barre** (☎ 03 22 91 81 18; 40 rue Victor Hugo; adult €4, child & student €2; ☻ 3pm Mon-Sat). Visitors get to see the workshop – the eight artisans fill commissions from both churches and private collectors – and a collection of 11th- to 20th-century stained glass.

Jules Verne (1828–1905) wrote many of his best-known works of brain-tingling – and eerily prescient – science fiction during the two decades he lived in Amiens. His grand turreted house is now the **Maison Jules Verne** (☎ 03 22 45 37 84; www.jules-verne.net in French; 2 rue Charles Dubois; adult/student €3/1.50; ☻ 10am-noon & 2-6pm Tue-Fri, 2-6pm Sat, Sun & holidays), the furnished rooms of which have been left just as they were back when going round the world in 80 days sounded utterly fantastic. Verne fans may also want to check out the changing exhibitions at the new **Imaginaire Jules Verne** (☎ 03 22 45 37 84; 36 rue de Noyon; adult/student €2/1; ☻ 11am-7pm mid-Jun–Sep, 3-7pm Tue-Sun Oct–mid-Jun), the bookshop of which carries Verne classics in English. The centenary of his death will be celebrated across France in 2005.

Sleeping
Amiens' hotels often fill up with business-people from Monday through Thursday.

Hôtel Victor Hugo (☎ 03 22 91 57 91; fax 03 22 92 74 02; 2 rue de l'Oratoire; d/tw €38/44) Just a block from the cathedral, this charming family-run hostelry has two stars and 10 modern stylish rooms that retain touches of days gone by.

Hôtel Le St Louis (☎ 03 22 91 76 03; www.le-saint louis.com in French; 24 rue des Otages; d/q from €47/76) All the mod cons with more than a dash of 19th-century French class. The 16 two-star rooms are spacious and tasteful.

Hôtel Spatial (☎ 03 22 91 53 23; www.hotelspatial .com; 15 rue Alexandre Fatton; s/d from €28/33, with shower & toilet €38/43; P) Staying here is hardly a scintillating aesthetic experience, but this two-star place is practical, welcoming and spotless.

Hôtel Central Anzac (☎ 03 22 91 34 08; hotel-central2@wanadoo.fr; 17 rue Alexandre Fatton; s/d from €26/30, with shower & toilet €36/40; P) Founded decades ago by an Australian ex-serviceman, this bland two-star place is now run by a friendly French family. The rooms are clean and comfortable, although small. Hall showers cost €2.50.

Eating
The area right around place du Don and the quays across the river in St-Leu (quai Bélu) are bursting with dozens of restaurants and cafés.

Les Marissons (☎ 03 22 92 96 66; pont de la Dodane; menus €18.50-49; ☻ closed Sun & lunch Sat) Occupying a 14th-century boatwright's workshop, this may well be the finest eatery in town; it's certainly the most elegant. Traditional French dishes and *cuisine du marché*, tailor-made to take advantage of fresh seasonal ingredients available in the market, are the specialities; the chef's personal favourite – it's his own invention – is *lotte rotie aux abricots* (monkfish roasted with apricots, €25).

Le T'chiot Zinc (☎ 03 22 91 43 79; 18 rue de Noyon; menus €11.40-27.70; ☾ closed Sun & lunch Mon) Inviting, bistro-style décor – banquettes, light fixtures and mirrored walls reminiscent of the *belle époque* – provides a perfect backdrop for the tasty French and Picard cuisine, including lots of fish and seafood.

Les Bouchées Doubles (☎ 03 22 91 00 85; 11bis rue Gresset; dishes €9.20-18.20; ☾ noon-2.30pm & 7.30-11.30pm) A contemporary brasserie that specialises in succulent beef dishes.

Le Wakam (☎ 03 22 72 51 50; 48 rue St-Leu; lunch menus €10-16; ☾ 12.30-2pm Mon-Fri, 7.30pm-midnight) At this chic and very mellow place, mouthwatering 'Afrotropical' (mainly West African) dishes can be washed down with fine South African wines and rums shipped in from Guyana and Jamaica.

Le Tigzirt (☎ 03 22 91 42 55; courtyard, 7 place du Don; dishes €9.50-20; ☾ closed Mon, dinner Sun & lunch Sat) The Algerian Berber-style couscous and tajines are steamed, boiled, grilled and baked to perfection. Often crowded. To get in, press intercom button No 6.

SELF-CATERING

Fruit and vegetables grown in the Hortillonnages are sold at the **marché sur l'eau** (floating market; place Parmentier; ☾ until 12.30pm Sat, to 1pm in summer), now held on dry land.

Other places to stock up for a picnic include **Champion supermarket** (22bis rue du Général Leclerc; ☾ 9am-7.30pm Mon-Sat), the **covered market** (Halles du Beffroi; rue de Metz; ☾ 9am-1pm & 3-7pm Tue-Thu, 9am-7pm Fri & Sat, 8.30am-12.30pm Sun) and **Match supermarket** (Centre Commercial Amiens 2; ☾ 9am-8pm Mon-Sat).

Entertainment

Café Bissap (☎ 03 22 92 36 41; 50 rue St-Leu; ☾ noon-3am Tue-Sat, to 1am Sun & Mon) A mixed and very laid-back crowd, including lots of students, sips West African beers amid décor from the Senegalese proprietor's native land. There's live jazz every Sunday from 9pm to midnight; the rest of the time, the beat is Afrosalsa.

Marott Street (☎ 03 22 91 14 93; 1 rue Marotte; ☾ 11am-1am) This building started out as an insurance office, designed by Gustave Eiffel's architectural firm in 1892. It has since has been turned into a chic bar where the trendy sip champagne, suspended – on clear glass tiles – over the wine cellar.

Concerts are often held at **Cirque Jules Verne** (place Longueville), a 16-sided circus venue built in 1889 for the centennial of the French Revolution, and **Mégacité** (www.megacite.com; av Hippodrome), about 2km west of the centre.

Getting There & Away

For details on visiting the Battle of the Somme memorials by public transport, see p225.

BUS

The **bus station** (☎ 03 22 92 27 03; ☾ office 6am-7pm Mon-Fri, 7am-6.45pm Sat), in the basement of the Centre Commercial Amiens 2, is accessible only from rue de la Vallée.

TRAIN

From the train station in the town centre, Amiens is linked to Arras (€9.60, 50 minutes, seven to 11 daily), Boulogne (€15.70, 1½ hours, five to eight daily), Calais-Ville (€19.70, two to 2½ hours, two or three direct Monday to Saturday), Lille-Flandres (€16.20, 1½ hours, six to nine daily) and Paris' Gare du Nord (€16.50, 1¼ to two hours, 25 daily Monday to Friday, 15 daily Saturday and Sunday). SNCF buses (45 minutes) go to the Haute Picardie TGV station, 42km east of the city.

CAR

ADA (☎ 03 22 46 49 49; 387 chaussée Jules Ferry) Situated 2.4km southeast of the train station and served by bus No 1.
France Cars (☎ 03 22 72 52 52; 75 blvd d'Alsace-Lorraine)
Hertz (☎ 03 22 91 26 24; 3 blvd d'Alsace-Lorraine)
Rent-A-Car Système (☎ 03 22 82 44 55; 19 rue des Otages)

Getting Around

There's free parking one or two blocks northeast of the Victor Hugo, Spatial and Central Anzac Hotels, on rue Lameth, rue Cardon, rue Jean XXIII and rue de la Barette.

Association Vélo Service (☎ 03 22 72 55 13; 3 rue des Corps Nuds-sans-Teste; per hr/day €1/5, tandems €2/8; ☾ 9am-12.30pm & 1.30-7pm) is a nonprofit group that rents bikes. A €100 deposit is required; helmets are free.

BEAUVAIS
pop 547,000

For the French, the name 'Beauvais' conjures up images of medieval Picardy at its most extravagant. Famed for the titanic hubris of its cathedral, doomed to remain forever unfinished, it has been a tapestry-making centre since the time of Louis XIV and is often mentioned in the same breath as Gobelins (p129) and Aubusson (p578). Alas, the modern-day town, rebuilt after being bombed in 1940, is far from enchanting.

Information
The **tourist office** (☎ 03 44 15 30 30; ot.beauvaisis@wanadoo.fr; 1 rue Beauregard; ☻ 9.30am or 10am-6pm or 6.30pm Mon-Sat, 10am-5pm Sun & holidays May-Sep, to 1.30pm Sun & holidays Oct-Apr) is about 200m southeast of the cathedral.

Sights
The history of the unfinished (but nevertheless stunning) **Cathédrale St-Pierre** (☻ 9am-12.15pm & 2-6.15pm Apr-Sep, 9am-12.15pm & 2-5.30pm Oct-Mar, no midday closure Jul & Aug) has been one of insatiable ambition and colossal failure. When Beauvais' Carolingian cathedral (parts of which can still be seen) was partly destroyed by fire in 1225, the bishop and local nobles decided that its replacement should surpass anything ever built. Unfortunately, their richly adorned creation also surpassed the limits of technology, and in 1284 the 48m-high vaults – the highest ever built – collapsed. There was further damage in 1573 when the 153m spire, the tallest of its era, came a-tumblin' down. Today, the flamboyant Gothic choir and transept stand nave-less, seemingly held up by huge wood beams (in fact, these have helped stabilise the building – so did pouring tonnes of concrete under the floor – and are to be removed as soon as funding comes through). One of the **astronomical clocks** (adult/17-25 yrs/6-16 yrs €4/2.50/1) dates from the 14th century; the other, finished in 1868, does its thing at 10.40am, 11.40am, 2.40pm, 3.40pm and 4.40pm, with additional demonstrations at 12.40pm and 5.40pm in July and August.

Just west of the cathedral, head through the two round bastions – a relic of the early 1300s – to the excellent **Musée Départemental de l'Oise** (☎ 03 44 11 11 30; 1 rue du Musée; adult €2, 18-25 yrs & senior €1, under 18 free; ☻ 10am-noon & 2-6pm Wed-Mon, no midday closure in summer). Highlights in this former bishops' palace include the *Dieu Guerrier Gaulois*, a slender and aristocratic Celtic warrior made of hammered sheet brass in the 1st century AD; a sinuous Art Nouveau dining room; a rich selection

of 19th-century French painting; and medieval wood carvings (in the reception area).

Tapestries made in the workshops of Beauvais and Gobelins are presented in themed temporary exhibitions at France's national tapestry museum, **Galerie Nationale de la Tapisserie** (☎ 03 44 15 39 10; rue St-Pierre; adult €4.60, 18-25 yrs & senior €3.10, under 18 free; ☻ 9.30am or 10am-12.30pm & 2-6pm Tue-Sun Apr-Sep, to 5pm Oct-Mar, closed btwn exhibitions), just east of the cathedral.

You can see strikingly modern tapestries actually being made, using techniques perfected over centuries, at the state-owned **Manufacture Nationale de la Tapisserie** (☎ 03 44 14 41 90; 24 rue Henri Brispot; tours adult/7-17 yrs €3.20/1; ☻ tours approximately 2pm & 3pm Tue-Thu), 1km south of the cathedral. All the projects underway have been commissioned by the French government to add panache to embassies and other official buildings.

Sleeping & Eating
JP Pub Hôtel (☎ 03 44 45 07 51; fax 03 44 45 71 25; 15 place Jeanne Hachette; d €38) Burned out in a fire started by someone's mobile-phone charger, this place, 250m south of the tourist office, should be back in action (and fireproofed) by the time you read this. Reception (at the bar) is closed until 2pm on Sunday.

Nouvelles Galeries supermarket (2 rue Carnot) Two short blocks east of the tourist office; the food section is in the basement.

Getting There & Away
Beauvais-Tillé Airport (☎ 08 92 68 20 66; www.aeroportbeauvais.com), a few kilometres northeast of the centre, is thriving thanks to cheap Ryanair flights; destinations include Dublin, Glasgow and Shannon.

Rail destinations include Paris' Gare du Nord (€10.70, 1¼ hours, 11 to 16 daily).

COMPIÈGNE
pop 45,000
Favoured by French rulers as a country retreat since Merovingian times, Compiègne reached its glittering zenith under Napoleon III (ruled 1852–70). These days the city, 80km northeast of Paris, is a favourite day trip for Parisians, particularly on Sunday.

On 23 May 1430, Joan of Arc (Jeanne d'Arc) – honoured by two statues in the city centre – was captured at Compiègne by the Burgundians, who later sold her to their allies, the English.

FAR NORTHERN FRANCE

During WWII, 49,860 people – *résist-ants*, political prisoners and Jews – were held in a transit camp in the Compiègne suburb of Royallieu before being shipped by train to Buchenwald, Mauthausen, Dachau and other Nazi concentration camps. A memorial-museum is planned to open in late 2006.

Information

The **tourist office** (☎ 03 44 40 01 00; compiegne .tourisme.infos@wanadoo.fr; place de l'Hôtel de Ville; 🕐 9.15am-12.15pm & 1.45-6.15pm Mon-Sat, 10am-1pm & 2.30-5pm Sun Apr-Sep, to 5.15pm & closed Mon morning Oct-Mar) is next to the ornate, 15th-century Gothic town hall, and opposite a statue of Jeanne d'Arc.

Sights

CHÂTEAU DE COMPIÈGNE

Napoleon III's glittering hunting parties drew well-connected participants from all around the continent to the vast **royal palace** (☎ 03 44 38 47 00; www.musee-chateau-comp iegne.fr in French; place du Général de Gaulle; adult/18-25 yrs/under 18 €4.50/3/free, adult Sun €3; 🕐 tours 10am-5.15pm Wed-Mon, to 3.45pm Nov-Feb). The chateau's sumptuously decorated **Grands Appartements** (Imperial Apartments), including the empress' bedroom and a ballroom lit by 15 chandeliers, can be seen on a one-hour tour (in French, English brochure are available; departures every 15 or 20 minutes). The **Musée du Second Empire** (open by request only – ask if a staff member is available to accompany you) illustrates the life of Napoleon III and that of his family (mid-1800s) amid a lot of gaudy gilding.

Vehicles that predate the internal combustion engine and early motorcars are the main attraction at the **Musée de la Voiture** (Vehicle Museum; adult/under 18 €2.60/free, incl the Grands Appartements adult/18-25 yrs/under 18 €5.50/4/free). Tours are in French only and last one hour.

To the east of the chateau, the English-style **Petit Parc** gardens link up with the **Grand Parc** and the **Forêt de Compiègne**, which surrounds Compiègne from the east and southeast, and is a favourite venue for hiking, cycling and horse riding.

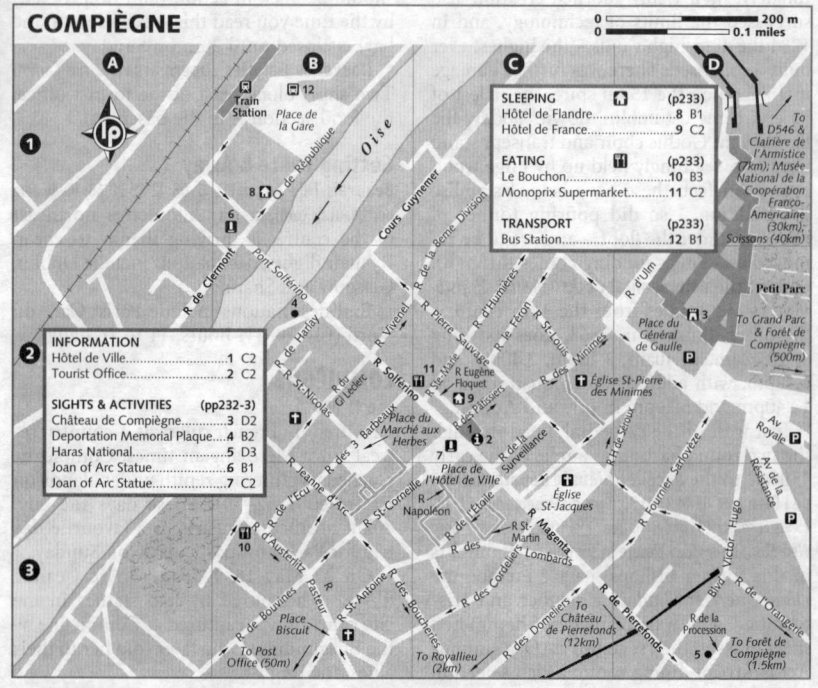

COMPIÈGNE

0   200 m
0   0.1 miles

SLEEPING	🛏	(p233)
Hôtel de Flandre	...8 B1
Hôtel de France	...9 C2

EATING	🍴	(p233)
Le Bouchon	...10 B3
Monoprix Supermarket	...11 C2

| TRANSPORT | | (p233) |
| Bus Station | ...12 B1 |

INFORMATION	
Hôtel de Ville	...1 C2
Tourist Office	...2 C2

SIGHTS & ACTIVITIES	(pp232-3)
Château de Compiègne	...3 D2
Deportation Memorial Plaque	...4 B2
Haras National	...5 D3
Joan of Arc Statue	...6 B1
Joan of Arc Statue	...7 C2

HARAS NATIONAL

You can wander among stalls housing magnificent thoroughbreds, trotters, saddle horses, ponies and draught horses at the **National Stud Farm** (☎ 03 44 38 54 50; 6 rue de la Procession; admission free; ⏰ 2–4.30pm Mon–Fri except holidays, closed Mar–mid-Jul). It was established in 1876 in the chateau's former stables, built for Louis XV in 1738, and is now run by the Ministry of Agriculture.

CLAIRIÈRE DE L'ARMISTICE

The armistice that came into force on 'the 11th hour of the 11th day of the 11th month' – the year was 1918 – and finally put an end to WWI was signed 7km northeast of Compiègne (towards Soissons) in the railway carriage of the Allied supreme commander, Maréchal Ferdinand Foch.

On 22 June 1940, in the same railway car, the French – with Hitler looking on smugly – were forced to sign the armistice that recognised the German conquest of France. Taken for exhibition to Berlin, the carriage was destroyed in April 1945 on the Führer's personal orders lest it be used for a third surrender – his own.

In the middle of a thick forest, the **Armistice Clearing** (☎ 03 44 85 14 18; adult/7–13 yrs €3/1.50; ⏰ 9am–12.15pm & 2–6pm Wed–Mon Apr–Sep, 10am–noon & 2–5pm Wed–Mon Oct–Mar), staffed by volunteers (mainly French army veterans), commemorates these events with monuments and a museum with 700 stereoscopic (3D) photos that give you an eerie feeling of being right there in the mud, muck and misery of WWI. The wooden rail wagon now on display is of the same type as the original; the furnishings, hidden away during WWII, were the ones actually used in 1918. Since 1927, only visiting heads of state and government, along with a few very lucky ministers or ambassadors, have been allowed to go inside the wagon. By tradition, the president of France pays an official visit to the site every year ending in eight (1998, 2008 etc).

Festivals & Events

One of the world's most gruelling one-day cycling races, **Paris-Roubaix** (www.letour .com/indexus.html), starts at place du Général de Gaulle on the first Sunday after Easter. The 261km competition is famous for its 50km of bone-jarring sections over *pavé*

(cobblestone) roads, including an especially tough 2.4km bit through the Forêt d'Arenberg.

Sleeping

Most of the hotels are situated between the train station and the chateau.

Hôtel de France (☎ 03 44 40 02 74; contact@restaur anthoteldefrance.fr; 17 rue Eugène Floquet; s/d from €50/60) A lovingly looked-after two-star place with chintz and antiques everywhere.

Hôtel de Flandre (☎ 03 44 83 24 40; fax 03 44 90 02 75; 16 quai de la République; s/d from €27/30, with shower & toilet €42/52) This straightforward two-star hotel offers more convenience than charm. Some of the rooms have river views.

Eating

The streets southwest of Église St-Jacques, including rue Magenta and rue des Lombards, are home to lots of restaurants.

Le Bouchon (☎ 03 44 20 02 03; 4 rue d'Austerlitz; menus €10.50-25) An old-style bistro and wine bar, this place has a sunny terrace and stick-to-the-ribs main courses such as duck *cassoulet* (casserole, €12).

Picnic supplies are sold at the **Monoprix supermarket** (37 rue Solférino).

Getting There & Around

Trains link Compiègne to Amiens (€10.50, 1½ hours, five to eight daily) and Paris' Gare du Nord (€11.40, 40 minutes to one hour 20 minutes, 15 to 26 daily).

Local buses are free except on Sunday, when service is limited. Lines No 1 and 2 link the train station with the chateau.

There's nonmetered parking in front of the chateau (place du Général de Gaulle) and along av Royale and av de la Résistance southeast of there.

LAON

pop 26,300

Laon (the name has one syllable and rhymes with *enfant*) served as the capital of the Carolingian Empire until it was brought to an end in 987 by Hugh Capet, who was rather partial to Paris. The walled, hilltop Ville Haute (Upper Town) commands fantastic views of the surrounding plains and has a fine Gothic cathedral. About 100m below sits the Ville Basse (Lower Town), completely rebuilt after being flattened in WWII.

WHEN BENNY MET LOUIE

In these days of 'freedom fries' and diplomatic hauteur, it's something of a relief to glance back at times gone by when relations between France and the USA were warmer, if not always free of rivalry. From the American Revolution (when French generals led American patriots, and Benjamin Franklin lobbied Louis XVI) through WWI (when American volunteers carried out humanitarian work long before the Doughboys arrived) and WWII (when the Parisians didn't exactly liberate themselves, whatever de Gaulle might have proclaimed), the USA and France have had a prickly but ardent love affair. All this and more is presented through art and artefacts at the **Musée National de la Coopération Franco-Américaine** (☎ 03 23 39 60 16; adult/18-25 yrs/under 18 €3/2.30/free; ☼ 10am-12.30pm & 2-5.30pm Wed-Mon), 30km northeast of Compiègne in the 17th-century Château de Blérancourt. The **Jardins du Nouveau Monde** (☼ 8am-7pm) showcase 'exotic' flowers, shrubs and trees (eg the sequoia) that are native to the Americas.

Information

In the Ville Haute, the **tourist office** (☎ 03 23 20 28 62; tourisme.info.laon@wanadoo.fr; place de la Cathédrale; ☼ 9.30 or 10am-12.30pm & 2-6pm Mon-Sat, 1-5pm or 6pm Sun & holidays, no midday closure & open Sun morning Jul & Aug) is next to the cathedral in a 12th-century hospital. It holds a 1/600-scale model of Laon as it looked in 1854 and has excellent English brochures.

Sights & Activities

A model for a number of its more famous Gothic sisters – Chartres, Reims and Dijon among them – **Cathédrale Notre Dame** (☼ 9am-6pm or 6.30pm) was built (1150–1230) in the transitional Gothic style on Romanesque foundations. The 110m-long interior has a gilded wrought-iron choir screen and is remarkably well lit; some of the stained glass dates from the 12th century. A memorial plaque for Commonwealth WWI dead hangs inside the west façade. Underneath the cathedral (and much of the town) there are three levels of **caves and quarries** (☼ tours daily Jul & Aug, Sat & Sun Jun, Sep & Oct).

The Ville Haute's narrow streets are rich in historic buildings, making Laon a particularly rewarding place for keen-eyed wandering. The octagonal 12th-century **Chapelle des Templiers** is in the garden of the archaeologically orientated **Musée de Laon** (☎ 03 23 20 19 87; 32 rue Georges Ermant; admission €3.20; ☼ 11am-6pm Tue-Sun Jun-Sep, 2-6pm Tue-Sun Oct-May).

The 7km-long **ramparts**, with their three fortified gates, are lovely for a stroll; paths known as *grimpettes* take you along the steep forested slopes. For panoramic views, head to the 13th-century **Porte d'Ardon**, circular **Batterie Morlot** and **rue du Rempart St-Rémi**. Local Jesuit missionary Jacques Marquette (1637–75), a pioneer explorer of the Mississippi River and the first European to live in what later became Chicago, is commemorated by a **statue** on rue de la Libération.

Sleeping & Eating

Rue Chatelaine, which links the cathedral with place du Général Leclerc, is home to several food shops.

Hôtel Les Chevaliers (☎ 03 23 27 17 50; hotel chevaliers@aol.com; 3-5 rue Sérurier; s from €28, d with shower & toilet €58; ☼ mid-Jan–mid-Nov) Parts of this two-star 14-room hostelry, around the corner from the Haute Ville's town hall, date from the Middle Ages. Rooms are simple, with a touch of rusticity and rates include breakfast.

Hôtel du Commerce (☎ 03 23 79 57 16; hotel.com merce.laon@wanadoo.fr; 11 place de la Gare; d from €26, with shower & toilet €37) Facing the train station, this welcoming two-star hotel has rooms that are modestly furnished but offer good value.

Getting There & Around

There are direct rail services to Amiens (€14, 1½ hours, four or five daily), Paris' Gare du Nord (€17.40, 1¾ hours, 13 daily Monday to Friday, seven on Saturday, four on Sunday) and Reims (€7.70, 40 minutes, eight daily Monday to Friday, three or four daily Saturday and Sunday).

The Ville Haute is a steep 20-minute walk from the train station – the stairs begin at the upper end of av Carnot. More fun is the overhead **Poma funicular railway** (return €1; ☼ every 3min 7am-8pm Mon-Sat except holidays year-round, 2.30-7pm Sun Jul & Aug), which links the train station with the Ville Haute.

Normandy

CONTENTS

NORMANDY

236

Normandy is a land of tradition, of quintessential grey farmhouses rising out of rolling green pastures, of blackberried hedgerows lining patchwork fields of artichokes, cauliflower and corn. It's a land of apples and crustaceans, of generous meals, half-timbered houses and honest fishing villages where deep rural countryside meets the bracing sea.

Normandy is a land steeped in history, the subject of successive invasions and decisive battles. A place where monasteries rise up from the sea and where tapestries recount historical watersheds, home to the thighbone of William the Conqueror, the garden of Claude Monet and over six million cows.

And while you can feel the proximity to English history and geography, the region retains its own distinctive culture and identity. With its swish seaside resorts, postwar reconstructions and busy universities, it is not at odds with modernity but is a place that has had to re-create itself constantly, all the while maintaining its strong link with the past.

For the visitor the charm is twofold: the peaceful country and coastal landscape, and the fascinating cities and towns. The city of Rouen is well endowed with medieval architecture, including a spectacular cathedral; Caen boasts some fine Norman Romanesque abbeys; Bayeux, home to the 11th-century Bayeux Tapestry, is only a dozen kilometres from the D-Day landing beaches. The Battle of Normandy (1944) left its mark on the region, reducing many towns to rubble. In cities such as Le Havre and Caen, postwar architecture predominates.

The coastline stretches 600km from the dramatic chalk cliffs of the Côte d'Albâtre to the celebrated island abbey of Mont St-Michel. Impressionist artists were drawn to Normandy's shores, lined with picturesque seaside resorts such as Fécamp, Honfleur and the fashionable twin towns of Deauville-Trouville. Inland lie fertile farmland and wooded valleys.

HIGHLIGHTS

- Soak everything, from your coffee to your Camembert, in local **Norman Calvados** (p251), an apple liqueur

- Fresh, fine seafood at the picturesque port of **Honfleur** (p251), where explorers set sail for the New World

- Stroll around **Giverny** (p243), the luxuriant garden planted and painted by Monet

- **D-Day landing beaches** (p266) – pay homage to those who fell during Operation Overlord in WWII

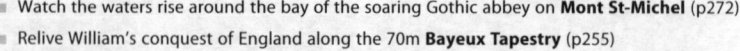

- Watch the waters rise around the bay of the soaring Gothic abbey on **Mont St-Michel** (p272)

- Relive William's conquest of England along the 70m **Bayeux Tapestry** (p255)

- Swing with the movers and shakers when Hollywood descends on seaside **Deauville** (p249)

- View the stunning Manneporte rock arch from the top of the white cliffs at Étretat (p249)

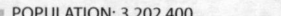

| POPULATION: 3,202,400 | AREA: 29,900 SQ KM |

NORMANDY

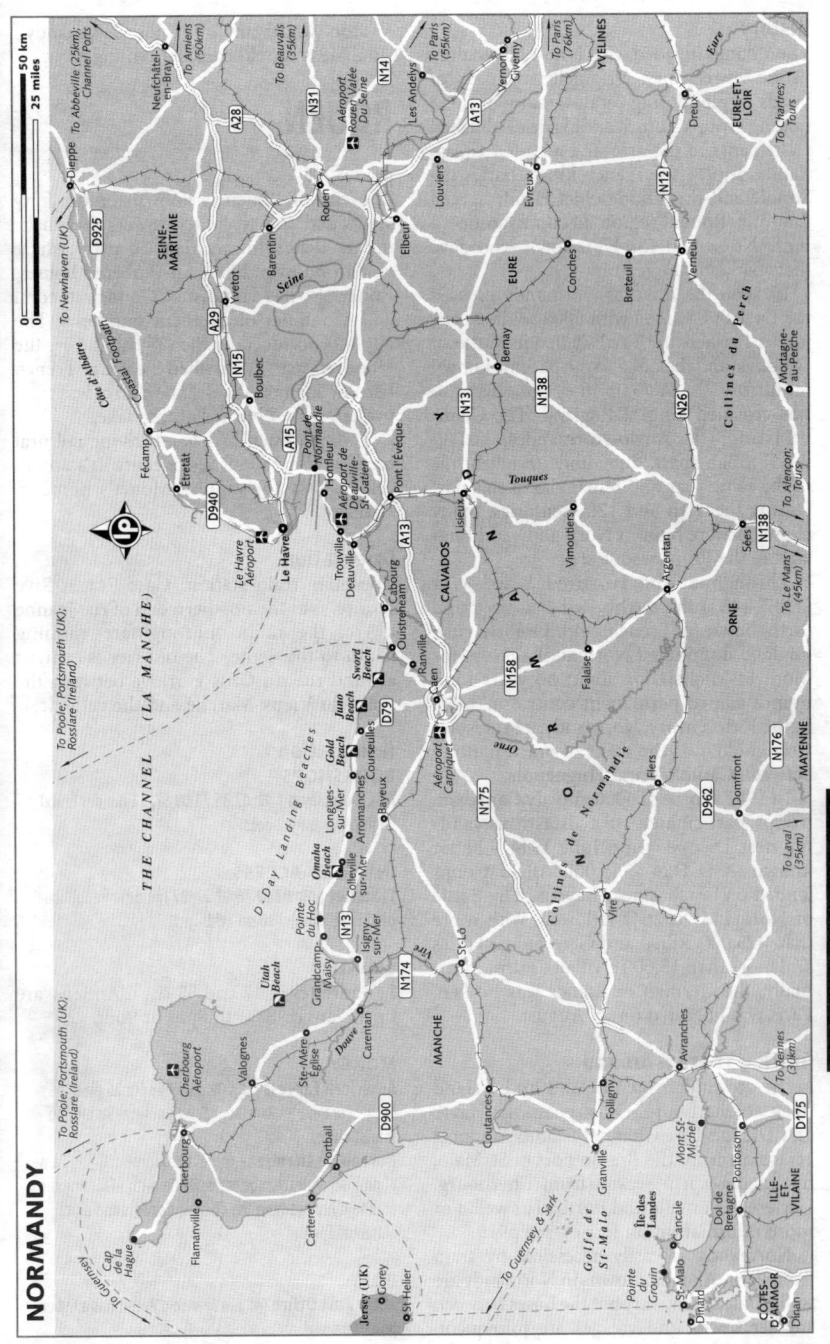

History

The Vikings invaded what is now Normandy in the 9th century. Originally made up of bands of plundering pirates, many of these raiding groups from Scandinavia established settlements in the area and adopted Christianity. In 911 the French king Charles the Simple and the Viking chief Hrölfr agreed that the Rouen region become home to these Norsemen (or Normans), who gave their name to the region.

In 1066 the duke of Normandy crossed the English Channel with 6000 soldiers. His forces crushed the English in the Battle of Hastings, and the duke – who became known in history as William the Conqueror – was crowned king of England. The Channel Islands (Îles Anglo-Normandes), just off the Norman coast, came under English rule in the same year and remain so to this day. During the 11th and 12th centuries, many churches were built in Normandy and England in the Romanesque style.

Throughout the Hundred Years' War (1337–1453) the duchy switched back and forth between French and English rule. England dominated Normandy (except for Mont St-Michel) for about 30 years until France gained permanent control in 1450. In the 16th century, Normandy, a Protestant stronghold, was the scene of much fighting between Catholics and Huguenots.

In 1942 a force of 6000, mostly Canadian, troops participated in a disastrous landing near Dieppe. On 6 June 1944 – better known as D-Day – 45,000 Allied troops landed on beaches near Bayeux. The Battle of Normandy (p264) followed, with more than 425,000 Allied and German casualties and more than 15,000 civilian deaths. Eventually, the German resistance was broken. Paris was liberated on 25 August.

Getting There & Around

Ferries to and from England and Ireland dock at Cherbourg, Ouistreham, Le Havre and Dieppe. The Channel Islands are most accessible from the Breton port of St-Malo, but in the warm season from Cherbourg, Carteret, Granville and Portbail as well. For more information on ferries, see p919.

Normandy is easily accessible by train from Paris. All major towns in Normandy are well connected by rail, but the buses between smaller towns and villages are infrequent.

Visitors who want to explore Normandy's rural areas should consider renting a car.

ROUEN

pop 108,750

The city of Rouen is known for the lofty spires and craggy church towers that make up its delightful medieval centre, where you'll find over 2000 half-timbered houses. Rouen also has a renowned Gothic cathedral and a number of excellent museums. The city was occupied by the English during the Hundred Years' War when the young French heroine Joan of Arc (Jeanne d'Arc) was tried for heresy and burned at the stake.

Today, Rouen boasts a thriving cultural scene and excellent restaurants. It's an excellent base for visiting Monet's home in Giverny.

Orientation

The main train station (Gare Rouen-Rive Droite) is at the northern end of rue Jeanne d'Arc, the main thoroughfare running south to the Seine. The old city is centred around rue du Gros Horloge between the place du Vieux Marché and the cathedral.

Information

BOOKSHOPS
ABC Bookshop (☎ 02 35 71 08 67; 11 rue des Faulx) English-language books.

INTERNET ACCESS
PlaceNet (☎ 02 32 76 02 22; 37 rue de la République; per 15min €1; ☻ 10am-midnight)

LAUNDRY
Laundrettes at 47 and 55 rue d'Amiens, are open 7am or 8am to 8pm or 9pm.

MONEY
American Express (☎ 02 35 89 48 60; 25 place de la Cathédrale; ☻ 9am-1pm & 2-6pm Mon-Sat) In the tourist office.
Bureau de Change (7-9 rue des Bonnetiers; ☻ 7am-10pm) Decent exchange rates. Banks with ATMs line rue Jeanne d'Arc between the Théâtre des Arts and place Maréchal Foch.

POST
Main Post Office (45 rue Jeanne d'Arc) It has a Cyber-poste terminal.

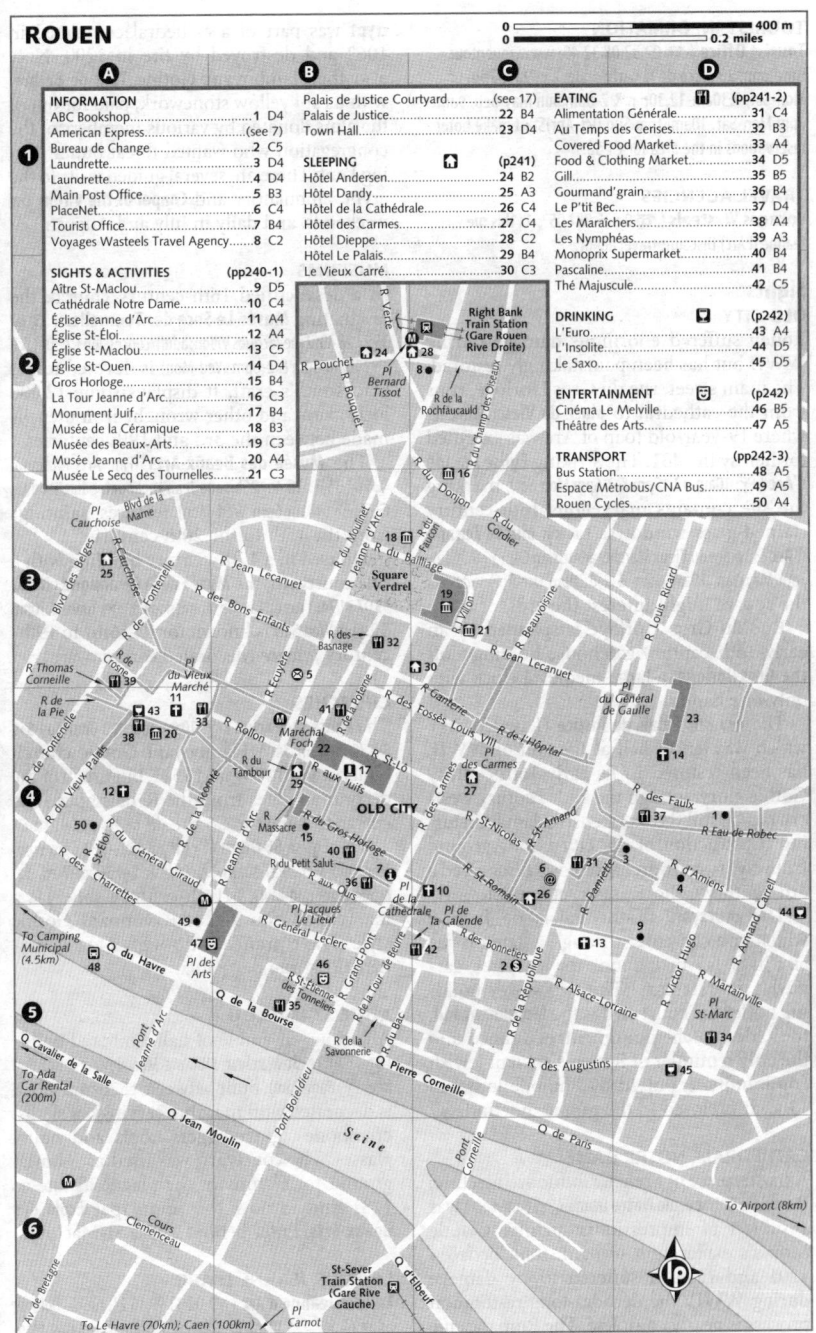

TOURIST INFORMATION

Tourist Office (☎ 02 32 08 32 40; www.rouentour isme.com; 25 place de la Cathédrale; ☉ 9am-7pm Mon-Sat, 9.30am-12.30pm & 2-6pm Sun May-Sep, 9am-6pm Mon-Sat, 10am-1pm Sun Oct-Apr)Staff make hotel reservations in the area for €1.50.

TRAVEL AGENCIES

Voyages Wasteels (☎ 0 825 887 057; 111bis rue Jeanne d'Arc) Discount travel agent.

Sights

OLD CITY

Rouen suffered enormous damage during WWII but has been painstakingly restored. The main street, rue du Gros Horloge, runs from the cathedral to **place du Vieux Marché**, where 19-year-old Joan of Arc was executed for heresy in 1431. The striking **Église Jeanne d'Arc** (☉ 10am-12.15pm & 2-6pm Mon-Sat), marking the site contains marvellous 16th-century stained-glass windows. Tacky **Musée Jeanne d'Arc** (33 place du Vieux Marché; admission €4; ☉ 9.30am-7pm May-Sep, 10am-noon & 2-6.30pm Oct-Apr) across the square might interest the kids.

Rue du Gros Horloge is spanned by an early-16th-century gatehouse holding aloft the **Gros Horloge**, a large medieval clock with only one hand.

The ornate **Palais de Justice** (Law Courts), which was left a shell at the end of WWII, has been restored to its early-16th-century Gothic glory, though the 19th-century western façade still shows extensive damage. During construction of the city's underground (subway) system, archaeologists discovered a 3rd-century Gallo-Roman settlement.

The **courtyard** of the Palais de Justice, which you can enter through a gate on rue aux Juifs, is worth a look for its spires, gargoyles and statuary. The two-storey building under the courtyard is the **Monument Juif**, the oldest such monument in France and the only reminder of Rouen's ancient Jewish community, expelled by Philippe le Bel in 1306. It is closed to the public indefinitely.

CATHÉDRALE NOTRE DAME

A masterpiece of French Gothic architecture, Rouen's **Cathédrale Notre Dame** (☉ 8am-6pm) was a subject of impressionist painter Claude Monet's exploration of light. Built between 1201 and 1514, it suffered severe damage during WWII; the decades-long restoration process is nearly complete. The Romanesque

crypt was part of a cathedral completed in 1062 and destroyed by fire in 1200. Note also the Flamboyant Gothic **Tour de Beurre**, with its apt yellow stonework, paid for out of the alms donated by various members of the congregation who wanted to eat butter during Lent. There are several guided visits to the crypt, ambulatory and **Chapel of the Virgin** on weekends, and daily in July and August.

MUSEUMS

In a desanctified 16th-century church, the fascinating **Musée Le Secq des Tournelles** (☎ 02 35 71 28 40; 2 rue Jacques Villon; adult/concession €2.30/1.55; ☉ 10am-1pm & 2-6pm Wed-Mon) is devoted to the blacksmith's craft. It displays some 12,000 locks, keys and other wrought-iron utensils made between the 3rd and 19th centuries.

The **Musée des Beaux-Arts** (Fine Arts Museum; ☎ 02 35 71 28 40; 26bis rue Jean Lecanuet; adult/student €3/2; ☉ 10am-6pm Wed-Mon) features paintings from the 15th to the 20th centuries.

Housed in a 17th-century building with a fine courtyard, the **Musée de la Céramique** (☎ 02 35 07 31 74; 1 rue du Faucon; admission €3; ☉ 10am-1.30pm & 2-6pm Wed-Sat) is known for its 16th- to 19th-century *faïence* (decorated earthenware).

CHURCHES

The **Église St-Maclou** (☉ 10am-noon & 2-6pm Mon-Sat, 3-5.30pm Sun) is a Flamboyant Gothic church built between 1437 and 1521, but much of the decoration dates from the Renaissance. The entrance is next to 56 rue de la République.

The **Église St-Ouen** (☉ 10am-noon & 2-6pm Wed-Mon mid-Mar-Oct, 10am-12.30pm & 2-4.30pm Wed, Sat & Sun Nov-mid-Mar), a 14th-century abbey, is a marvellous example of Rayonnant Gothic style. The entrance is through a lovely garden along rue des Faulx.

AÎTRE ST-MACLOU

A curious ensemble of half-timbered buildings, **Aître St-Maclou** (186 rue Martainville; admission free; ☉ 8am-8pm), built between 1526 and 1533, is decorated with macabre carvings of skulls, crossbones, gravediggers' tools and hourglasses. The courtyard was used as a burial ground for victims of the plague as late as 1781 and is now the municipal **École des Beaux-Arts**. Enter behind Église St-Maclou.

LA TOUR JEANNE D'ARC

La Tour Jeanne d'Arc (☎ 02 35 98 16 21; rue du Donjon; adult €1.50; ☉ 10am-12.30pm & 2-6pm Wed-Sat & Mon,

2-6.30pm Sun Apr-Sep; 10am-12.30pm & 2-5pm Wed-Sat & Mon, 2-5.30pm Sun Oct-Mar) is the sole survivor of eight towers that once ringed a huge 13th century chateau built by Philippe Auge. Joan of Arc was imprisoned here before her execution. The tower has two exhibition rooms.

Tours

The tourist office runs **guided tours** (French only; adult/student €6/4; 2hr) of the city at 2.30pm at least twice a week from March to November, and daily in July and August.

Festivals & Events

The next **Rouen Armada** (www.armada.org), a big week-long festival with concerts, fireworks and a parade of sailing boats and warships, will be in 2007. Accommodation is booked up about a year in advance.

Sleeping

If you're staying over a weekend, ask the tourist office about its 'Bon Week-end' offer of two nights for the price of one in some hotels.

BUDGET

Hôtel Le Palais (☎ 02 35 71 41 40; 12 rue du Tambour; r €28-40) This hotel is in a highly advantageous location right near the Palais de Justice and the Gros Horloge. The rooms, all of which have showers, are good value. For an extra €2 you can have an en suite toilet.

Camping Municipal (☎ 02 35 74 07 59; rue Jules Ferry, Déville-lès-Rouen; camping €9.70) Modern facilities just 5km northwest of the city. From the Théâtre des Arts or the bus station, take bus No 2 and get off at the *mairie* (town hall) of Déville-lès-Rouen.

MID-RANGE

Hôtel de la Cathédrale (☎ 02 35 71 57 95; www.hotel-de-la-cathedrale.fr; 12 rue St-Romain; s/d from €49/59) Behind the beautiful 17th-century timber-panelled façade and the plant-filled inner courtyard you'll find small but comfortable, prettily decorated rooms. All in all a wonderful and atmospheric hotel.

Hôtel des Carmes (☎ 02 35 71 92 31; www.hotel descarmes.fr.st in French; 33 place des Carmes; r €42-58; P) In a 19th-century building, this romantic place is the sweetest little hotel in town. The rooms of varying sizes are decorated with colour and flair. Some are equipped with a huge and gleaming bath.

Hôtel Andersen (☎ 02 35 71 88 51; www.hoteland ersen.com; 4 rue Pouchet; d from €40) A welcoming, family-run establishment housed in an elegant 19th-century mansion. The bright, airy rooms are surprisingly large and comfortable, decorated in the Directory style of post-Revolutionary France.

Le Vieux Carré (☎ 02 35 71 67 70; www.vieux-carre .fr; 34 rue Ganterie; d €58) This gorgeous, half-timbered hotel is a true gem. The elegant rooms manage to simultaneously embrace tradition and avoid tackiness, and many give onto the tranquil inner courtyard.

TOP END

Hôtel Dieppe (☎ 02 35 71 96 00; place Bernard Tissot; d €77-90; P ✗ ▯) This attractive hotel has been lovingly restored and is well worth its three stars. The rooms are smallish but plush and very well equipped, and the service is top notch. Special weekend rates are available.

Hôtel Dandy (☎ 02 35 07 32 00; www.hotels-rouen .net; 93 rue Cauchoise; r €72-95; P) A delightful option in a quiet location, decorated in Old Normandy style with much polished wood, gleaming mirrors and plush furnishings. The rooms are exceedingly comfortable and have their own coffee maker.

Eating

BUDGET

Gourmand'grain (☎ 02 35 98 15 74; 3 rue du Petit Salut; menus from €8.10; ☽ lunch only, closed Mon) This lunch-time vegetarian café with good salads and health-food *menus* is about the only place in town with vegan options.

Le P'tit Bec (☎ 02 35 07 63 33; 182 rue Eau de Robec; lunch menus €11-13.50, mains €7-9; ☽ lunch Mon-Sat, dinner Fri & Sat) Good news for the weight-conscious traveller: here you can fill up on things fresh and light, such as tarts, poached fish and steamed vegetables.

MID-RANGE

Les Maraîchers (☎ 02 35 71 57 73; 37 place du Vieux Marché; menu €18) While the food here is great, it is clearly outdone by the magnificent décor. Gleaming with mirrors, polished wood, pewter and tiles, the restaurant has been classified a *café historique d'Europe*.

Pascaline (☎ 02 35 89 67 44; 5 rue de la Poterne; menus €12.95-21.90) This atmospheric bistro has a Pianola. It has wonderful duck dishes – the chef is a master *canardier* who prepares the famous *caneton à la Rouennaise*.

Au Temps des Cerises (☎ 02 35 89 98 00; 4-6 rue des Basnage; lunch menu €10.50, dinner menus from €15; ☿ closed Sun, Mon & lunch Sat) Cheese, cheese and more cheese: turkey breast with Camembert, *oeufs cocotte* (eggs cooked in ramekins and topped with a cheese sauce) and, of course, fondue. There's a vegetarian menu.

Thé Majuscule (☎ 02 35 71 15 66; 8 place de la Calende; tartes €6.95; ☿ noon-6.30pm Mon-Sat) A tearoom and second-hand bookshop that serves up home-made tarts, desserts and exotic teas in a smoke-free environment.

TOP END

Gill (☎ 02 35 71 16 14; 8 quai de la Bourse; weekday menu €38, weekend menus €54-74; ☿ Tue-Sat) This is the finest restaurant in these parts. The food is of exceptional quality, as witnessed by the scallops served with finely sliced truffles or ravioli with fennel and crayfish in a sauce of divine inspiration.

Les Nymphéas (☎ 02 35 89 26 69; 7 rue de la Pie; weekday menu €27, weekend menus €34-44; ☿ Tue-Sat) Patrice Kukrudz, the chef of this superb establishment, is one of the stars of Norman cuisine. He succeeds in using cider and Calvados to amplify the refined flavours of foie gras and soufflés.

SELF-CATERING

Rue Rollon has several good fruit stalls, cake shops and bakeries. The **covered food market** (place du Vieux Marché; ☿ 6am-1.30pm Tue-Sun) offers dairy products, fish and fresh produce. But there's a more lively daily **food and clothing market** (place St-Marc).

There's an **Alimentation Générale** (78 rue de la République) and a **Monoprix supermarket** (65 rue du Gros Horloge).

Drinking

L'Euro (☎ 02 35 07 55 66; 41 place du Vieux Marché; ☿ around 4pm-2am) You can nibble and sip the evening away on the terrace sampling tapas and tropical cocktails. When the sun goes down a DJ spins house for the upstairs lounge and dance floor.

Le Saxo (☎ 02 35 98 24 92; 11 place St-Marc; ☿ 9am-2am) This place moves to the tune of jazz and blues – it's a must on the nightcrawler's itinerary, especially on weekends when there are sometimes live concerts.

L'Insolite (☎ 02 35 88 62 53; 58 rue d'Amiens) This is the newest bar on the gay and lesbian scene in Rouen but heteros are also welcome.

Check out the 'vivarium' that includes reptiles and a parrot.

Entertainment

Cinéma Le Melville (☎ 02 32 76 73 21; 12 rue St-Étienne des Tonneliers) occasionally runs non-dubbed English-language films.

Théâtre des Arts (☎ 02 35 71 41 36; place des Arts; tickets from €20) Rouen's premier music venue and home to the Opéra de Normandie, the theatre also runs concerts and ballets.

Getting There & Away

The **Aéroport Rouen Vallée du Seine** (☎ 02 35 79 41 00) is 8km southeast of town at Boos. There are weekday direct flights to Lyon that connect with other cities in France as well as to international destinations.

CNA (☎ 0 825 076 027; 9 rue Jeanne d'Arc) runs services throughout Seine-Maritime, including Dieppe (€10.65, two hours, three daily), and towns along the coast west of Dieppe, including Fécamp (€14.45, 3¼ hours, one daily) and Le Havre (€12.65, three hours, five daily). Buses to Dieppe and Le Havre are slower and pricier than the train. Buses leave from quai du Havre and quai de la Bourse.

From Gare Rouen-Rive Droite, an Art-Nouveau edifice built in 1912–28, there's a frequent express train to/from Paris' Gare St-Lazare (€17.40, 70 minutes). Other services include Amiens (€15.50, 1¼ hours), Caen (€19.40, two hours), Dieppe (€9, 45 minutes) and Le Havre (€11.80, one hour). Gare Rouen-Rive Gauche has regional services.

Getting Around

There is no public transport into town from the airport; a taxi costs about €20.

Both Rouen's extensive local bus network and its metro line are operated by **TCAR** (Espace Métrobus). The metro runs from 5am (6am Sunday) to 11.30pm and is most useful for getting from the train station to the centre of town. A ticket valid for an hour of unlimited travel costs €1.30, a 10-ticket magnetic card costs €10. A Carte Découverte (one/two/three days €3.50/5/6.50) public transport pass is available at the tourist office.

For taxis, **Radio Taxi** (☎ 02 35 88 50 50) operates 24 hours.

Rouen Cycles (☎ 02 35 71 34 30; 45 rue St-Éloi) rents mountain bikes for €12 per day.

For car rental, try **ADA** (☎ 02 35 72 25 88; 34 av Jean Rondeaux). **Avis** (☎ 02 35 88 60 94) and **Hertz**

(☎ 02 35 70 70 71) are both in the Gare Rouen-Rive Droite train station.

AROUND ROUEN

Lovely day trips can be made from Rouen, particularly in the landlocked Eure *département*. The beautiful gardens of Claude Monet are at Giverny. From the 12th-century Château Gaillard in Les Andelys, a breathtaking panorama takes in the bend of river banks that rise to forested hills and white bluffs.

Les Andelys
pop 8500

Some 39km to the southeast of Rouen lies Les Andelys, a small, elongated town at the confluence of the mighty Seine and the tiny Gambon. The main reason for coming to the town is to visit the ruins of Château Gaillard, a 12th-century stronghold of English king Richard the Lion-Heart.

ORIENTATION & INFORMATION

The town is split into two parts: Grand Andely, whose main square is place Poussin, and to the west the older Petit Andely, which lies on the banks of the mighty Seine.

The tiny **tourist office** (☎ 02 32 54 41 93; 24 rue Philippe-Auge; ☼ 9.30am-noon & 2-6pm Mon-Sat, to 5.30pm Sun Jun-Sep; 2-5.30pm Mon-Fri Oct-May) is in Petit Andely at the foot of the cliffs, which form the base of the chateau.

CHÂTEAU GAILLARD

Built in 1196-97, **Château Gaillard** (☎ 02 32 54 04 16; admission €3; ☼ 10am-1pm & 2-6pm Wed-Mon) secured the western border of English territory along the Seine until Henry IV ordered its destruction in 1603. More impressive than the ruins is the fantastic view over the Seine, whose white cliffs are best seen from the platform north of the castle. The chateau is a 20-minute climb via a path that begins about 100m north of the tourist office. By car, take the turn-off opposite Église Notre Dame in Grand Andely and follow the signs.

SLEEPING & EATING

The tourist office has a list of *chambres d'hôtes* (B&Bs).

Hôtel Normandie (☎ 02 32 54 10 52; 1 rue Grande; d €54) Watch the boats and ducks go by along the Seine from the flowery terrace of this pleasant establishment. The hotel offers comfortable, nicely fitted rooms.

Hôtel and Restaurant de la Chaine d'Or (☎ 02 32 54 00 31; www.lachainedor.com; 27 rue Grande; r €72-122; P ⌨) This romantic hideaway in Petit Andely has peaceful, comfortable rooms, many of which look out on the Seine. The hotel has a **restaurant** (menus €27-55.50; ☼ closed Mon & dinner Sun) that offers fine regional specialties. A buffet breakfast on the terrace is an extra €12 but is well worth it.

Camping Château Gaillard (☎ 02 32 54 18 20; route de la Mare; adult/tent €5/4.20; ☼ Feb-Dec) A good choice for camping, 800m southeast of the chateau and 200m from the Seine.

Villa du Vieux Château (☎ 02 32 54 30 10; 78 rue G Nicolle; menus €25 & €31; ☼ closed Sun dinner, Mon & Tue) In Petit Andely, this restaurant does excellent fish *menus*. There are restaurants around place Poussin in Grand Andely.

GETTING THERE & AWAY

There's no train station in Les Andelys. **CNA buses** (☎ 0 825 076 027) link Grand Andely (place Poussin) and Rouen at least twice daily (€7.49, 1¼ hours).

Giverny
pop 550

Between Paris and Rouen and an ideal day trip from either, this small village contains the Musée Claude Monet. First opened to the public in 1980, the garden museum is immensely popular with visitors, many of whom also come to view the fine impressionist collection of the Musée d'Art Américain.

MUSÉE CLAUDE MONET

Musée Claude Monet (☎ 02 32 51 28 21; adult/student/child €5.50/4/3; ☼ 9.30am-6pm Tue-Sun Apr-Oct, Mon if public holiday) was Monet's home and studio. The hectare of land that Monet owned has become two distinct areas cut by the Chemin du Roy, a train line that was unfortunately changed into what is now the D5 road.

The northern part is the **Clos Normand** where Monet's famous pastel pink and green house and Water Lily studio stand. His studio is now the entrance hall, adorned with reproductions of his works and ringing with cash register bells from busy souvenir stands. Outside are the symmetrically laid-out gardens.

From the Clos Normand's far corner, a tunnel leads under the D5 to the **Jardin d'Eau** (Water Garden). Having bought this piece of land in 1895 after his reputation had been established, Monet dug a pool (fed by the Epte, a tributary of the nearby Seine), planted water lilies and constructed the Japanese bridge, which has since been rebuilt. Draped with purple wisteria, the bridge blends into the asymmetrical foreground and background, creating the intimate atmosphere for which the 'Painter of Light' was famous.

Seasons have an enormous effect on the gardens at Giverny. From early to late spring, daffodils, tulips, rhododendrons, wisteria and irises appear, followed by poppies and lilies. By June, nasturtiums, roses and sweet peas are in flower. Around September, there are dahlias, sunflowers and hollyhocks.

MUSÉE D'ART AMÉRICAIN
The **Musée d'Art Américain** (American Impressionist Museum; ☎ 02 32 51 94 65; www.maag.org; 99 rue Claude Monet; adult/student/child €5.50/4/3; ☺ 10am-6pm Tue-Sun Apr-Oct) contains works of American impressionist painters who flocked to France in the late 19th and early 20th centuries. It's housed in a garish building 100m down the road from Musée Claude Monet.

GETTING THERE & AWAY
Giverny is 76km northwest of Paris and 66km southeast of Rouen. The nearest town is Vernon, nearly 7km to the west on the Paris–Rouen train line.

From Paris' Gare St-Lazare (€10.80, 50 minutes) there are two early trains to Vernon. For the return trip there's about one direct train an hour between 5pm and 9pm. From Rouen (€8.60, 40 minutes), four trains leave before noon; to get back, there's about one train every hour between 5pm and 10pm.

Once in Vernon it's still a hike to Giverny. **Shuttle buses** (☎ 02 35 71 32 99) meet most trains and cost €2 each way. You can rent a bike from the **Café de Chemin de Fer** (☎ 02 32 21 16 01) for €12 a day.

CLAUDE MONET

Everyone discusses my art and pretends to understand, as if it were necessary to understand, when it is simply necessary to love.

Claude Monet

The undisputed leader of the impressionists, Claude Monet was born in Paris in 1840 and grew up in Le Havre, where he found an early affinity with the outdoors. Monet disliked school and would spend his time drawing and caricaturing his professors in the margins of his exercise books. By 15 his skills as a caricaturist were known throughout Le Havre, where he sold his portraits. Eugène Boudin, his first mentor, convinced him to turn his attention to the landscapes, light, shadows and nature that later defined Monet's work.

In 1860 military service interrupted Monet's studies at the Académie Suisse in Paris and took him to Algiers, where the intense light and colours further fuelled his imagination. The young painter became fascinated with capturing a specific moment in time, the immediate impression of the scene before him, rather than the precise detail.

From 1867 Monet's distinctive style began to emerge, focusing on the effects of light and colour and using the quick, undisguised broken brushstrokes that would characterise the impressionist period. His contemporaries were Pissarro, Renoir, Sisley, Cézanne and Dégas. The young painters left the studio to work outdoors, experimenting with the shades and hues of nature, arguing and sharing ideas. Their work was far from welcomed by critics; one of whom condemned it as 'impressionism', in reference to Monet's *Impression: Sunrise* (1874), which became the name of their movement.

From the late 1870s Monet concentrated on painting in series, seeking to re-create a landscape by showing its transformation under different conditions of light and atmosphere. *Haystacks* (1890–91) and *Rouen Cathedral* (1891–95) are some of the best-known works of this time. In 1883 he moved to Giverny, planting his property with a variety of flowers around an artificial pond, in order to paint the subtle effects that varying tones of sunlight had on nature. Here he painted the *Nymphéas* (Water Lilies) series. The huge dimensions of some of these works, together with the fact that the pond's surface takes up the entire canvas, meant the abandonment of composition in the traditional sense and the virtual disintegration of form. Despite his failing eyesight, Monet completed the series just before his death in 1926.

DIEPPE

pop 35,700

Dieppe is an ancient seaside town and a favourite among British weekenders. It's not the prettiest place in Normandy, but its location – set between two limestone cliffs – and its medieval castle are dramatic. Dieppe also has the attractive, gritty appeal of an old-fashioned port.

Privateers based in Dieppe pillaged Southampton in 1338 and blockaded Lisbon two centuries later. The first European settlers in Canada included many Dieppois. The town was one of France's most important ports during the 16th century, when ships regularly sailed from Dieppe to West Africa and Brazil.

Orientation

The town centre is largely surrounded by water. Boulevard de Verdun runs along the lawns – a favourite spot for kite flyers – that border the beach. Most of the Grande Rue and rue de la Barre has been turned into a pedestrianised area. Quai Duquesne and its continuation quai Henri IV follow the western and northern sides of the port area. Ferries dock at the terminal on the northeastern side of the port, just under 2km on foot from the tourist office.

Information

INTERNET ACCESS

La Au Bar (☎ 02 35 40 48 35; 19 rue de Sygogne; ◷ 10am-2am Mon-Sat, 2-7pm Sun; per 15min/hr €1/4)

LAUNDRY

Laundrette (44 rue de l'Épée; ◷ 7am-9pm)

MONEY

Banque Populaire (15 place Nationale) One of several on place Nationale.
Crédit Maritime Mutuel (3 rue Guillaume Terrien) One of the few banks open Monday.

POST

Main Post Office (2 blvd Maréchal Joffre) It has Cyberposte.

TOURIST INFORMATION

Tourist Office (☎ 02 32 14 40 60; www.dieppetour isme.com; Pont Jehan Ango; ◷ 9am-1pm & 2-8pm Mon-Sat, 10am-1pm & 3-6pm Sun Jul & Aug, 9am-1pm & 2-7pm Mon-Sat, 10am-1pm & 3-6pm Sun May-Jun & Sep, 9am-noon & 2-6pm Mon-Sat Oct-Apr) On the western side of the port area. Hotel reservations in the area cost €3.50.

Château Musée

High over the city to the west, **Château Musée** (☎ 02 35 84 19 76; adult/student €3/1.50; ◷ 10am-noon 2-6pm Jun-Sep, 10am-noon & 2-5pm Wed-Mon Oct-May) is Dieppe's most impressive landmark. Dating from the 15th century it offers sweeping views over the sea. The museum is devoted to Dieppe's maritime and artistic history, a large portion of which involved the dubious practice of separating African elephants from their tusks and shipping the ivory back to Dieppe. The craft of ivory-carving reached extraordinary heights in Dieppe during the 17th century and the results are on display.

Cité de la Mer

Exhibits at the **Cité de la Mer** (☎ 02 35 06 93 20; 37 rue de l'Asile Thomas; adult/under-16s €5/3; ◷ 10am-12.30pm & 2-6.30pm Jun-Aug, 10am-noon & 2-6pm Sep-May) are devoted to fishing techniques, shipbuilding, cliffs and even pebbles. The visit ends with five large aquariums filled with happy living examples of sea creatures that are usually found on French plates: octopus, lobsters, turbot and cod.

Other Sights

Although the white cliffs on either side of Dieppe have been compared to those at Dover, the **beach** is gravelly and at times very windy.

The vast **lawns** between blvd de Verdun and the beach were laid out in the 1860s by that seashore-loving imperial duo, Napoleon III and his wife, Eugénie. **Église St-Jacques**, a Norman Gothic church at place St-Jacques, has been reconstructed several times since the early 13th century.

The **Canadian Military Cemetery** is 4km towards Rouen. Take av des Canadiens (the continuation of av Gambetta) south and follow the signs.

The **GR21 hiking trail** follows the Côte d'Albâtre southwest from Dieppe all the way to Le Havre. Maps and topoguides for hikes and easy walks in the surrounding area are available from the tourist office.

Water in the Olympic-sized **swimming pool** (☎ 02 35 06 05 66; promenade Plage; ◷ 10am-7.30pm) is heated to 25°C and there are diving boards.

Sleeping

BUDGET

Auberge de Jeunesse (☎ 02 35 84 85 73; 48 rue Louis Fromager; dm €8.90; ◷ mid-May–mid-Sep; **P**)

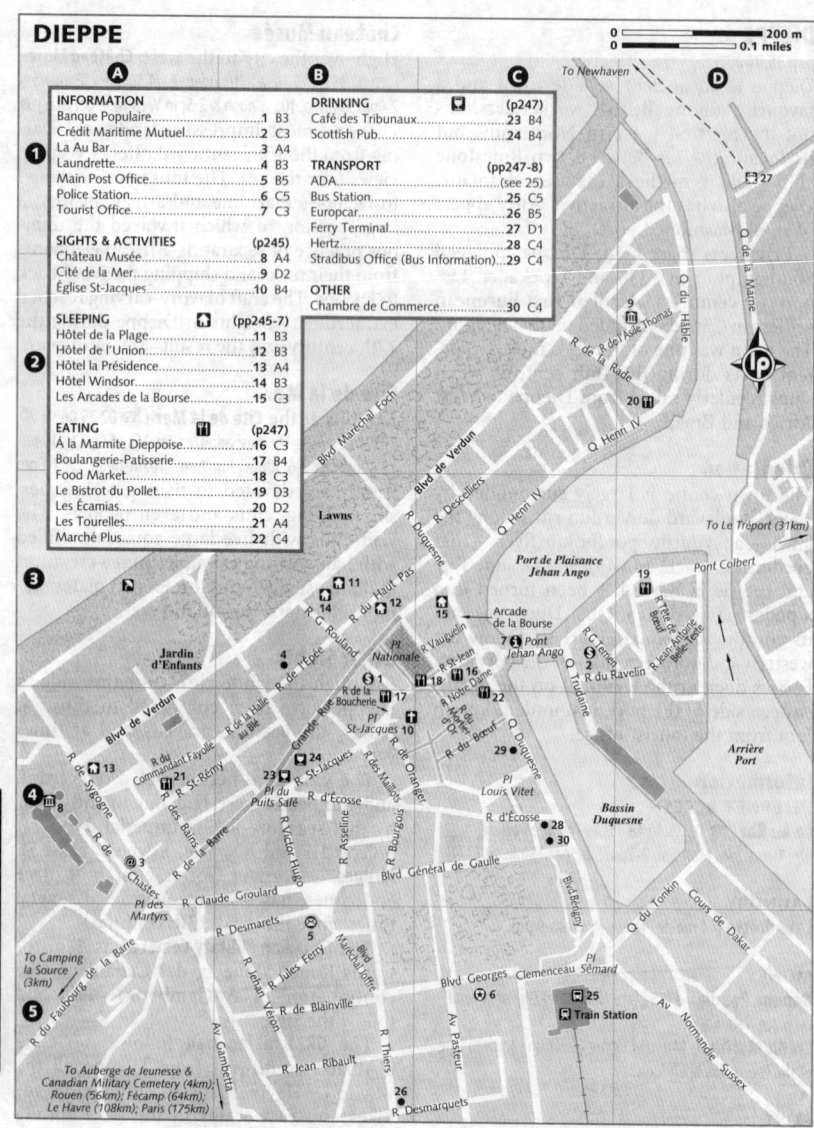

DIEPPE

INFORMATION		
Banque Populaire	1	B3
Crédit Maritime Mutuel	2	C3
La Au Bar	3	A4
Laundrette	4	B3
Main Post Office	5	B5
Police Station	6	C5
Tourist Office	7	C3

SIGHTS & ACTIVITIES		(p245)
Château Musée	8	A4
Cité de la Mer	9	D2
Église St-Jacques	10	B4

SLEEPING		(pp245-7)
Hôtel de la Plage	11	B3
Hôtel de l'Union	12	B3
Hôtel la Présidence	13	A4
Hôtel Windsor	14	B3
Les Arcades de la Bourse	15	C3

EATING		(p247)
Á la Marmite Dieppoise	16	C3
Boulangerie-Patisserie	17	B4
Food Market	18	C3
Le Bistrot du Pollet	19	D3
Les Écamias	20	D2
Les Tourelles	21	A4
Marché Plus	22	C4

DRINKING		(p247)
Café des Tribunaux	23	B4
Scottish Pub	24	B4

TRANSPORT		(pp247-8)
ADA	(see 25)	
Bus Station	25	C5
Europcar	26	B5
Ferry Terminal	27	D1
Hertz	28	C4
Stradibus Office (Bus Information)	29	C4

OTHER		
Chambre de Commerce	30	C4

About 4km southwest of the train station, this hostel provides a kitchen and laundry. From the train station, walk straight up blvd Bérigny to the Chambre de Commerce from where you take bus No 2 Val Druel to the Château Michel stop.

Hôtel de l'Union (☎ 02 35 84 35 52; 47-49 rue du Haut Pas; s/d from €22.90/24.50) This family-run

establishment has somewhat faded rooms of varying sizes. It also hosts a good little restaurant.

Camping

Camping La Source (☎ 02 35 84 27 04; adult/site €4/6; ☼ mid-Mar–mid-Oct) This camping ground is 3km southwest of Dieppe in a lovely creekside location, just off the D925 (well signposted). Take bus No 4 to the Petit-Appeville train station (10 minutes), walk beneath the railway bridge and up the marked gravel drive.

MID-RANGE & TOP END

Les Arcades de la Bourse (☎ 02 35 84 14 12; fax 02 35 40 22 29; 1-3 Arcade de la Bourse; r from €49; **P**) This is an elegant, old-style hotel in the centre of town, by the port. All rooms have a private bathroom, TV and telephone, and the more expensive ones have views over the port.

Hôtel Windsor (☎ 02 35 84 15 23; 18 blvd de Verdun; r from €58; **P**) This hotel *is* on the seafront, though you'll have to walk across all those lawns to get to the water. The décor is a little garish but the rooms are comfortable and many offer sea views and balconies.

Hôtel de la Plage (☎ 02 35 84 18 28; 20 blvd de Verdun; r €48-73; **P** **▣**) These well-equipped rooms either give onto the seafront, or onto the interior garden and courtyard. Some are more attractively decorated than others; those with sea views are larger (and more expensive).

Hôtel La Présidence (☎ 02 35 84 31 31; www .hotel-la-presidence.com in French; blvd de Verdun; r €78-93; **P** **✗** **▣**) This large, sleek, modern hotel has all the comforts you would expect. The huge restaurant has sea views, as do many of the rooms. Some apartments with kitchenettes are available.

Eating

Les Tourelles (☎ 02 35 84 15 88; 43 rue du Commandant Fayolle; menus €9.50-19; ☉ closed Mon & dinner Sun) This is an old-fashioned restaurant with an ever-changing array of simple, generous dishes and a decent selection of wines. Its fresh seafood and convivial atmosphere attract tourists, families and local office workers alike.

Le Bistrot du Pollet (☎ 02 35 84 68 57; 23 rue Tête de Boeuf; weekday lunch menu €11.50; ☉ closed Sun & Mon) A gem for fish lovers, hidden away from the tourist crowds in the old fishermen's quarter. The à la carte offerings might include *lotte* (monkfish) marinated in wine and *daurade* (sea bream) with herbs. The restaurant is small so it's best to reserve.

Les Écamias (☎ 02 35 84 67 67; 129 quai Henri IV; menus €13.50-20; ☉ closed Mon, dinner Sun & Tue) This is a simple, family-style place serving fresh, tasty seafood at reasonable prices. You can't go wrong with a delicious pile of mussels or the *raie* (ray) with butter sauce.

À la Marmite Dieppoise (☎ 02 35 84 24 26; 8 rue St-Jean; menus €26-39; ☉ closed Mon & dinner Sun) If you really want to taste Dieppe's *fruits de la mer* at their best, head for this intimate establishment in the old city. Their speciality is *marmite Dieppoise*, a delicious fish stew.

SELF-CATERING

There's a **food market** (☉ 6am-1pm Tue & Thu, 7am-5pm Sat) between place St-Jacques and place Nationale and two wonderful **boulangeries** (15 quai Henri IV; ☉ Tue-Sun; 14 rue de la Boucherie; ☉ Thu-Tue). The **Marché Plus supermarket** (22 quai Duquesne) is open long hours.

Drinking

Dieppe has loads of pubs and bars full of interesting characters, but don't be surprised if you have to buzz to be let in.

Scottish Pub (☎ 02 35 84 13 16; 12 rue St-Jacques) This is a good place to kick off a pub crawl, and the friendly bar staff will point you in the right direction.

Café des Tribunaux (☎ 02 32 14 44 65; place du Puits Salé) This sprawling 18th-century building was a preferred hang-out for impressionist painters in the late 19th century. It remains an impressive venue to this day.

Getting There & Away

The bus station is in the same cavernous building as the train station. CNA runs services to Fécamp (€11.40, 2¼ hours, at least two daily) and Rouen (€10.65, two hours, three daily). No buses run on Saturday or Sunday afternoons.

The first ferry service from Dieppe to the UK began in 1790. These days **Hoverspeed** (☎ 08 20 00 35 55) runs car and pedestrian ferries between Dieppe and Newhaven. Boats depart from the ferry terminal on the northeastern side of the port area at the end of quai de la Marne. For further ferry information, see p919.

From Dieppe's **train station** (☉ 02 35 06 69 33), the paucity of direct trains to Paris' Gare St-Lazare (€22.80, 2¼ hours, four daily) is offset by frequent services to Rouen (€9, 50 minutes, 10 daily), where there is a connecting service to Le Havre (€16, two hours from Dieppe).

Getting Around

Stradibus (☎ 02 32 14 03 03) operates 13 local lines that run until 6pm or 8pm. All buses

NORMANDY

stop at either the train station or the nearby Chambre de Commerce, on quai Duquesne. It has an information office on this road. A single ticket costs €1.05, a 10-ticket carnet €7. Buses shuttle foot passengers between the ferry terminal and the tourist office (€2).

ADA (☎ 02 35 84 32 28; train station)

Europcar (☎ 02 35 04 97 10; 33 rue Thiers)

Hertz (☎ 02 32 14 01 70; 5 rue d'Écosse)

Taxis (☎ 02 35 84 20 05) Fare from the ferry pier to the city centre is about €7.50.

CÔTE D'ALBÂTRE

Stretching 100km southwest from Dieppe to Étretat are the tall white cliffs and pebbled beaches of the Côte d'Albâtre (Alabaster Coast). Small villages and resorts nestle in the dry valleys leading down from the Pays de Caux, a chalky inland plateau. Towards the southwest are the Côte d'Albâtre's two main centres: Fécamp and Étretat.

Without a car, the Côte d'Albâtre is rather inaccessible. However, walkers can follow the coastal GR21 footpath from Dieppe to Le Havre. If you are driving, take the coastal road, which starts at the D75 west of Dieppe, and not the inland D925.

Fécamp
pop 21,500

Fécamp was a fishing village until the 6th century, when a few drops of Christ's blood miraculously found their way here and attracted hordes of pilgrims. Benedictine monks soon established a monastery and the 'medicinal elixir' they concocted in the early 16th century helped keep Fécamp on the map. The recipe, lost during the Revolution, was rediscovered in the 19th century and the after-dinner liqueur was produced commercially. Today, Bénédictine is one of the most widely marketed *digestifs* in the world.

INFORMATION

Tourist Office (☎ 02 35 28 51 01; www.fecamp.com in French; 113 rue Alexandre Le Grand; ⏰ 9am-12.30pm & 2.30-6pm Apr-Sep, 9am-noon & 2.30-6pm Oct-Mar) In the town centre, this is the main source of information.

Tourist Office (☎ 02 35 29 16 94; quai de la Vicomté; ⏰ 11am-2pm & 3-7.30pm Jul & Aug) Another, smaller office at the port that opens over the summer months.

PALAIS BÉNÉDICTINE

In an ornate 1900 building, mixing Flamboyant Gothic and other eclectic styles, is the **Palais Bénédictine** (☎ 02 35 10 26 10; 110 rue Alexandre Le Grand; adult/student €5/3.70; ⏰ 10am-6pm Jul & Aug, 10am-noon & 2-5pm Apr-Jun & Sep, 10.30-11.45am & 2-5pm Feb, Mar & Oct-Dec, closed Jan). It was inspired by the 15th-century Hôtel de Cluny in Paris. It's geared up to tell you everything about the history and making of its aromatic liqueur – except the exact recipe.

Tours start in the art museum, which houses the private collection of founder Alexandre Le Grand, and continues through a hall where hundreds of bottles of bootlegged Bénédictine are proudly displayed. In the fragrant Plant & Spice Room, you can smell a handful of some of the ingredients used to make the potent drink. The tour ends in the attractive modern art gallery, which has changing exhibits.

The admission price includes a free shot of Bénédictine.

ABBATIALE DE LA STE-TRINITÉ

Built from 1175 to 1220 under the instigation of Richard the Lion-Heart, the **Abbatiale de la Ste-Trinité** (☎ 02 35 28 84 39; place des Ducs Richard; ⏰ 9am-6pm) was the most important pilgrimage site in Normandy until the construction of Mont St-Michel, thanks to the drop of holy blood that miraculously floated to Fécamp in the trunk of a fig tree. Among the many treasures inside is the late-15th-century *Dormition de la Vierge*.

Across from the abbey are the remains of the **fortified chateau** built by the earliest dukes of Normandy in the 10th and 11th centuries.

SLEEPING & EATING

Hôtel de la Mer (☎ 02 35 28 24 64; 89 blvd Albert 1er; r €35-53) A cool, modern establishment, this place is the pick of the bunch of the various beachfront hotels. The rooms are very comfortably outfitted, and many have balconies with sea views.

Camping Renéville (☎ 02 35 28 20 97; Côte de Renéville; site €9.50) Dramatically situated on the western cliffs overlooking the beach, this is a prime position for camping.

Marée (☎ 02 35 29 39 15; 75 quai Bérigny; menus €17.60-34; ⏰ closed Sun, Mon & dinner Thu) An extension of a fish shop, this place offers the freshest, tastiest fish in town. The *choucroute de la mer* (seafood with sauerkraut) has just the right touch of tang but all the fish and seafood is prepared with a minimum of fuss. Finish off with *crème brûlée à la Bénédictine*.

GETTING THERE & AWAY

Fécamp is accessible by bus from Dieppe, Le Havre and Rouen, and by train from Le Havre. The **train station** (☎ 02 35 28 24 82) is conveniently located. **Autocars Gris** (☎ 02 35 22 34 00) has 10 buses daily to Le Havre (€7.30, 1½ hours) via Étretat and five on Sunday.

Étretat

pop 1650

The small village of Étretat, which is 20km southwest of Fécamp, is renowned for its two cliffs: the Falaise d'Amont and the Falaise d'Aval. Featuring the most unusual rock formations in the area, you'll see them long before you arrive. They appear somewhat deceivingly to be one rock.

Beyond the Falaise d'Aval, southwest of the village, is the stunning Manneporte rock arch and the 70m-high Aiguille (Needle), which pierces the surface of the water behind the arch. From the western end of Étretat's stony beach, a steep path leads to the top of the cliff, which affords fine views. On the Falaise d'Amont opposite, a memorial marks the spot where two aviators were last seen before their attempt to cross the Atlantic in 1927. Do *not* explore the base of the cliffs outside low tide.

The **tourist office** (☎ 02 35 27 05 21; www.etretat .net; place Maurice Guillard; ☺ 10am-7pm mid-Jun–mid-Sep, 10am-noon & 2-6pm mid-Mar–mid-Jun & mid-Sep–mid-Nov, 10am-noon & 2-6pm Fri & Sat mid-Nov–mid-Mar) posts accommodation lists for the area on the door outside opening hours. It also has a map of the cliff trails and rents bicycles.

The only way to reach Étretat is on the bus line that runs from Fécamp to Le Havre, stopping at Yport. See p250.

LE HAVRE

pop 193,250

Le Havre is France's second-most important port and a bustling gateway for ferries to Britain, but it wouldn't win any prizes in a beauty contest.

All but obliterated by WWII bombing raids, Le Havre was rebuilt by Auguste Perret, who also designed the city's 100m-high 'Stalinist Baroque' church. While the regimented boulevards and concrete buildings make this urban landscape uninviting, the very newness of the city can be intriguing. The sophisticated André Malraux fine-arts museum is one of the best in Normandy. You can also enjoy the wide, rocky beach, good seafood restaurants, lots of parking and a number of good-value hotels.

Orientation

The main square is the enormous place de l'Hôtel de Ville. Avenue Foch runs westwards to the sea and the Port de Plaisance recreational area. Boulevard de Strasbourg goes eastwards to the train and bus stations. Rue de Paris cuts south past Espace Oscar Niemeyer, a square named after the Brazilian who designed two cultural centre buildings (which have been compared to a truncated cooling tower and a toilet bowl).

Rue de Paris ends at the quai de Southampton and the Bassin de la Manche, from where ferries to Britain set sail out of the Terminal de la Citadelle, southeast of the central square. Within easy walking distance of the terminal is the Quartier St-François, Le Havre's 'old city'.

Information

INTERNET ACCESS

Microminute (☎ 02 35 22 10 15; 7 rue Casimir Periér; per hr €3.60; ☺ 2-7pm Mon, 10am-7pm Tue-Sat)

LAUNDRY

Laundrette (5 rue Georges Braque)

MONEY

Exchange Bureau (41 Chaussée Kennedy) Opposite the old Irish Ferries terminal.

Société Générale (2 place Léon Meyer) Plus other banks along blvd de Strasbourg.

POST

Main Post Office (62 rue Jules Siegfried) It has Cyber poste.

TOURIST INFORMATION

Tourist Office (☎ 02 32 74 04 04; www.lehavretour isme.com in French; 186 blvd Clemenceau; ☺ 9am-7pm Mon-Sat, 10am-12.30pm & 2.30-6pm Sun Jun-Sep, 9am-6.30pm Mon-Fri, 9am-12.30pm & 2-6.30pm Sat, 10am-1pm Sun Oct-May) On the waterfront about 650m southwest of city hall. Staff reserve local accommodation for free.

Sights

The main highlight of Le Havre is the hypermodern **Musée des Beaux-Arts André-Malraux**

NORMANDY

(☎ 02 35 19 62 62; 2 blvd Clemenceau; adult/student €3.80/2.20; ⌚ 11am-6pm Mon-Wed, 11am-7pm Sat & Sun), about 800m south of the tourist office. There is an excellent collection of impressionist art, including paintings from Monet, Sisley, Renoir and Le Havre native Eugène Boudin. Another large section is devoted to Fauvist Raoul Dufy who was also born in Le Havre.

Sleeping

Hôtel Celtic (☎ 02 35 42 39 77; www.hotel-celtic.com in French; 106 rue Voltaire; r €31-48) Rooms in varying in size are brightly painted and furnished in a traditional style. The more expensive have views over the Bassin du Commerce but all are equipped with private facilities and satellite TV.

Le Petit Vatel (☎ 02 35 41 72 07; www.multimania.com/lepetitvatel; 86 rue Louis Brindeau; s/d €35/43) A modern, efficient and comfortable choice, this hotel lacks character but offers small, bright rooms that are good value for money. All rooms have satellite TV and windows are double glazed to assure a sound night's sleep. More expensive rooms are available with bathtubs and views.

Hôtel Vent d'Ouest (☎ 02 35 42 50 69; www.ventdouest.fr; 4 rue de Caligny; r €75-105; Ⓟ) This carpeted and comfortable three-star hotel is very big on décor. Each of the rooms has its own personalised style based upon the themes of mountain, countryside or sea.

CAMPING

Camping de la Forêt de Montgeon (☎ 02 35 46 52 39; chlorophile1@wanadoo.fr; camping €12.20; ⌚ year-round) Nearly 3km north of town in a 250-hectare forest, this is a lovely shaded site. From the station, take bus No 11 and alight after the 700m-long Jenner Tunnel. Then walk north 1.5km through the park.

Eating

La Marine Marchande (☎ 02 35 25 11 77; 27 blvd Amiral Mouchez; lunch menu €10; ⌚ lunch only Mon-Sat) Here you can chow down with hungry sailors at a full buffet table of hors d'oeuvres, plus a main course, cheese, dessert and wine. They might open for dinner if you call ahead. To get there take rue Charles Laffitte from the train station, follow it to the right as it becomes rue Marceau, and onto blvd Amiral Mouchez.

L'Odyssée (☎ 02 35 21 32 42; 41 rue du Général Faidherbe; menus €21-34; ⌚ closed Mon, lunch Sat & dinner Sun) This refined dining room is one of the best spots in Le Havre for superb fish dishes. The cheaper *menus* are only available during the week.

Les Trois Pics (☎ 02 35 48 20 60; Promenade des Régates, Sente Alphonse Karr, Ste-Adresse; weekday lunch menus €13-17, dinner menus €23 & €35; ⌚ closed Mon & dinner Sun) When the locals of Le Havre are looking for the very best in seafood, they head out to Ste-Adresse for a whiff of salt air, excellent service and piles of shells.

La Villa (☎ 02 35 54 70 80; 66 blvd Albert 1er; weekday lunch menu €29.50, dinner menus €46-125; ⌚ closed Mon & dinner Sun & Wed) People come from miles around for the astonishing cuisine of master chef Jean-Luc Tartarin. The marvellous *menus* changes according to the market and the chef's inspiration.

For self-caterers, there's a **Champion** supermarket (cnr rue de la République & rue Turenne).

Drinking & Entertainment

Le Camp Gourou (☎ 02 35 22 00 92; 163 rue Victor Hugo) As its play-on-words name suggests, this raucous and highly popular student bar attracts lots of Australians.

Le Havana Café (☎ 02 35 42 35 77; 173 rue Victor Hugo) The Havana will brighten your day with its tropical ambience and reasonably priced drinks. The musical programme is varied, although there is a Latin night once a month.

L'Agora (☎ 02 32 74 09 70; Espace Oscar Niemeyer) Not only do you get to see the inside of Le Havre's most striking building but there's a bar and concert hall that hosts an eclectic selection of musical acts from hip-hop to something called celtic-rock-latino.

Getting There & Away

AIR

The **airport** (☎ 02 35 54 65 00), 6km north of town in Octeville-sur-Mer, mainly serves Lyon.

BOAT

P&O European Ferries (☎ 0 803 013 013; ⌚ information desk 9am-7pm), which links Le Havre with Portsmouth, uses the new Terminal de la Citadelle on av Lucien Corbeaux, just over 1km southwest of the train station.

BUS

Caen-based **Bus Verts du Calvados** (☎ 08 10 21 42 14) and Rouen's **CNA** (☎ 0825 07 60 27) run frequent services from the bus station (be-

NORMANDY

hind the train station) to Honfleur (€6.80, 30 minutes), Rouen (€12.65, 2½ hours), Deauville-Trouville (€9.35, 1¾ hours) and Caen (€20, two to three hours). **Autocars Gris** (☎ 02 35 22 34 00) has 10 buses daily to Le Havre (€7.30, 1½ hours) via Étretat (one hour) and five on Sunday.

TRAIN
Le Havre's **train station** (cours de la République) is east of the city centre. Chief destinations are Rouen (€11.80, one hour, 15 daily) and Paris' Gare St-Lazare (€25.20, 2¼ hours, 10 daily). A secondary line goes north to Fécamp (€6.70, 1¼ hours, five daily) with a change at Bréauté-Beuzeville.

Getting Around
There's no public transport to town from the airport. A taxi will cost about €12.

Bus Océane (☎ 02 35 22 35 00; place de l'Hôtel de Ville) runs 14 lines in Le Havre. Single tickets cost €1.40 and a carnet of 10 is €9.20; a day ticket costs €3.20 and gives unlimited bus travel for that day.

To order a **taxi**, call (☎ 02 35 25 81 81) or (☎ 02 35 25 81 00).

CALVADOS

The *département* of Calvados stretches from Honfleur in the east to Isigny-sur-Mer in the west. It's famed for its rich pastures and farm products: butter, cheese, cider and an apple-flavoured brandy called Calvados. The D-Day beaches extend along almost the entire coast of Calvados.

HONFLEUR
pop 8350

The gateway to the sea, the picturesque harbour town of Honfleur recalls a time when fishermen, pirates and explorers set sail to seek their fortunes over the seas. It has long been popular with Parisian weekenders, who flock to the pretty town and its sandy beaches.

The stone dwellings constructed at the height of Honfleur's glory in the 17th and 18th centuries survive largely intact in a warren of streets around its old harbour. Because of extensive siltation, centuries-old wooden houses that once lined the seafront quay now lie several hundred metres inland.

In the 19th century Honfleur attracted a steady stream of artists, among them many impressionists.

The graceful 2km-long Pont de Normandie over the Seine, linking Honfleur with Le Havre for the first time, opened in 1995. Just 15km southwest are the coastal resorts of Deauville and Trouville.

History
Honfleur's seafaring tradition dates back over a millennium. After the Norman invasion of England in 1066, goods bound for the conquered territory were shipped across the Channel from Honfleur.

In 1608 Samuel de Champlain left from here on his way to found Quebec City. In 1681 Cavelier de la Salle started out from Honfleur to explore what is now the USA. He reached the mouth of the Mississippi and named the area Louisiana in honour of King Louis XIV, ruler of France at the time. During the 17th and 18th centuries, Honfleur achieved a degree of prosperity through trade with the West Indies, the Azores and the colonies on the western coast of Africa.

Orientation
Honfleur is centred around the Vieux Bassin (old harbour). To the east is the heart of the old city, known as the Enclos because it was once enclosed by fortifications. To the north is the Avant Port (outer harbour) where the fishing fleet is based. Quai Ste-Catherine fronts the Vieux Bassin on the west, and rue de la République runs southwards from it. The Plateau de Grâce, with Chapelle Notre Dame de Grâce on top, is west of town.

Information
Lavomatic (4 rue Notre Dame; ⏰ 8am-9pm) Laundry.
Léviathan (☎ 02 31 87 92 95; 11 blvd Charles V; per 30min €1.50; ⏰ 2.30pm-1am Mon-Sat) Internet access.
Main Post Office (rue de la République) Southwest of the centre, just past place Albert Sorel. It has a Cyberposte terminal.

PASSE MUSÉE

The **Passe Musée** (adult/student €9/6) is on sale in museums and allows one visit to each of the town's four museums, except the Clocher. Bought at any museum, you can use it over a one-year period.

NORMANDY

Tourist Office (☎ 02 31 89 23 30; www.ot-honfleur.fr; quai Lepaulmier; ☿ 10am-7pm Mon-Sat, 10am-5pm Sun Jul & Aug, 10am-12.30pm & 2-6.30pm Mon-Sat 10am-5pm Sun Apr-Jul & Sep, 10am-12.30pm & 2-6pm Mon-Sat 10am-5pm Sun Oct-Mar) Helps visitors find accommodation.

Sights

ÉGLISE STE-CATHERINE

Wooden **Église Ste-Catherine** (place Ste-Catherine; ☿ 10am-noon & 2-6pm, except during services), whose stone predecessor was destroyed during the Hundred Years' War, was built by the people of Honfleur during the late 15th and the early 16th centuries. It is thought that they chose wood, which could be worked by local shipwrights, in an effort to save stone for strengthening the fortifications of the Enclos. The structure that the town's carpenters created, which was intended to be temporary, has a vaulted roof that looks like an overturned ship's hull. The church is also remarkable for its twin naves, each topped by vaulted arches supported by oak pillars.

CLOCHER STE-CATHERINE

The church's free-standing wooden bell tower, **Clocher Ste-Catherine** (☎ 02 31 89 54 00; adult/student incl admission to Musée Eugène Boudin €4.40/2.70; ☿ 10am-noon & 2-6pm Wed-Mon mid-Mar–Sep, 2.30-5pm Mon-Fri, 10am-noon & 2.30-5pm Sat & Sun Oct–mid-Mar), dates from the second half of the 15th century. It was built apart from the church for both structural reasons (so the church roof would not be subject to the bells' weight and vibrations) and for safety (a high tower was more likely to be hit by lightning). The former bell-ringer's residence at the base of the tower houses a small museum of liturgical objects, but the huge, rough-hewn beams are of more interest.

MUSÉE EUGÈNE BOUDIN

Named in honour of the early impressionist painter born here in 1824, **Musée Eugène Boudin** (☎ 02 31 89 54 00; rue de l'Homme de Bois; adult/student incl admission to Clocher Ste-Catherine €4.40/2.70, Jun-Nov €5.10/3.60; ☿ 10am-noon & 2-6pm Wed-Mon mid-Mar–Sep, 2.30-5pm Mon-Fri, 10am-noon & 2.30-5pm Sat & Sun Oct–mid-Mar) has a good collection of impressionist paintings from Normandy, including works by Dubourg, Dufy and Monet. An entire room is devoted to the works of Eugène Boudin, whom Baudelaire called the 'king of skies' for his luscious skyscapes.

LES MAISONS SATIE

The delightful **Les Maisons Satie** (☎ 02 31 89 11 11; 67 blvd Charles V; adult/student €5.10/3.60; ☿ 10am-7pm Wed-Mon Jun-Sep, 11am-6pm Wed-Mon Oct-May) imaginatively captures the spirit of composer Erik Satie (1866–1925) who lived and worked in Honfleur. 'Esoteric' Satie was known for his surrealistic wit as much as for his starkly beautiful piano compositions. Located in Satie's birthplace, visitors wander through the museum with a headset playing Satie's music and excerpts from his writings (in French or English). Each room is a surprise. One features a winged pear. Another, the Laboratory of Emotions, has a whimsical contraption that is pedalled.

HARBOURS

The **Vieux Bassin**, from where ships bound for the New World once sailed, now shelters mainly pleasure boats. The nearby quays and streets, especially **quai Ste-Catherine**, are lined with tall, narrow houses dating from the 16th to 18th centuries. The **Lieutenance**, once the residence of the town's royal governor, is at the mouth of the old harbour.

The **Avant Port**, on the other side of the Lieutenance, is home to Honfleur's 50 or so fishing vessels. Further north, dikes line both sides of the entrance to the port.

Either harbour makes a pleasant route for a walk to the seashore. Honfleur is a good launching pad for boat tours of the region.

MUSÉE DE LA MARINE

Honfleur's small **Musée de la Marine** (☎ 02 31 89 14 12; adult/student €3/1.80, incl admission to Musée d'Ethnographie et d'Art Populaire Normand €4.20/2.60; ☿ 10am-noon & 2-6pm Tue-Sun Apr-Sep, 2-6pm Mon-Fri, 10am-noon & 2-6pm Sat & Sun Oct–mid-Nov & mid-Feb–Mar, closed mid-Nov–mid-Feb) is on the eastern side of the Vieux Bassin in the deconsecrated Église St-Étienne, which was begun in 1369 and enlarged during the English occupation of Honfleur (1415–50). Displays include assorted model ships, ships' carpenters' tools and engravings.

MUSÉE D'ETHNOGRAPHIE ET D'ART POPULAIRE NORMAND

Next to the Musée de la Marine on rue de la Prison (an alley off quai St-Étienne), the **Musée d'Ethnographie et d'Art Populaire Normand** (☎ 02 31 89 14 12; adult/student €3/1.80, incl admission to Musée de la Marine €4.20/2.60; ☿ 10am-noon & 2-6pm

Tue-Sun Apr-Sep, 2-6pm Mon-Fri, 10am-noon & 2-6pm Sat & Sun Oct–mid-Nov & mid-Feb–Mar, closed mid-Nov–mid-Feb) occupies a couple of houses and a former prison dating from the 16th and 17th centuries. Its rooms re-create the homes and furnishings of Honfleur in the 16th to 19th centuries.

GRENIERS À SEL

The two huge **Greniers à Sel** (salt stores; ☎ 02 31 89 02 30; rue de la Ville), along from the tourist office, were built in the late 17th century to store the salt needed by the fishing fleet to cure its catch of herring and cod. During July and August the stores host art exhibitions and concerts.

CHAPELLE NOTRE DAME DE GRÂCE

Built between 1600 and 1613, the **Chapelle Notre Dame de Grâce** is at the top of the Plateau de Grâce, a wooded, 100m-high hill about 2km west of the Vieux Bassin. There's a great view of the town and port.

Tours

Within Honfleur, the tourist office runs two-hour **guided tours** (adult/student €6/4; ☼ 3pm Mon) of the town in English and a variety of themed tours in French.

Fifty-minute **boat tours** of the Vieux Bassin and the port area with Vedettes Stéphanie, Alphée and Evasion cost €6.50. Vedette la Jolie France goes to the Pont de Normandie (€8). Tours run from March to mid-October. Boarding is from the quai des Passagers or the quai de la Quarantaine. The schedule depends upon the tides.

Sleeping

BUDGET & MID-RANGE

Auberge de la Claire (☎ 02 31 89 05 95; 77 cours Albert Manuel; apt from €70) Those keen to do their own cooking – with fresh local produce – will be pleased to find these tidy apartments with kitchenettes about 900m southwest of the Vieux Bassin.

Hôtel Belvédère (☎ 02 31 89 08 13; 36 rue Emile Renouf; s/d €51/62; P) Less than 1km east of the town centre, this tranquil retreat has a relaxing garden and terrace. Ask for room 11 to secure a view of the Pont de Normandie.

Hôtel des Loges (☎ 02 31 89 38 26; www.hoteldesloges.com; 18 rue Brûlée; r from €90; P) A romantic choice with soft lighting and elegant design. Rooms are minimalist but comfortable and

the ambience is friendly and fuss-free. Families will like the baby-sitting service (per hour €8).

Camping

Camping du Phare (☎ 02 31 89 10 26; blvd Charles V; site €10.65; ☼ Apr-Sep) This camping ground is the closest to town. From the town centre, follow rue Haute about 500m northwest of the Vieux Bassin.

TOP END

Hôtel du Dauphin (☎ 02 31 89 15 53; www.hotel-du-dauphin.com; 10 place Pierre-Berthelot; r €66-151; P ☒ ▢) Behind a 17th-century, half-timbered façade lies this modern and charming hotel. The colourful rooms are bound to cheer you up on a grey Norman day, and the more expensive rooms even have spa baths.

Hôtel Le Cheval Blanc (☎ 02 31 81 65 00; www.hotel-honfleur.com; 2 quai des Passagers; r €70-230; P ☒) This luxurious establishment is in a 15th-century mansion overlooking the port. The rooms, which have views over the Vieux Bassin, are modern with plush furniture and exposed beams.

Eating

Places to dine in Honfleur are abundant, especially along quai Ste-Catherine.

La Cidrerie (☎ 02 31 89 59 85; 26 place Hamelin; menu €9; ☼ closed Tue-Wed Oct-Jun) The crepes and *galettes* are sure to please, but the main attraction is the wide selection of beverages that are based almost exclusively on apples and pears. *Cidre* (cider), *pommeau*, *poiré* (perry or pear cider) and Calvados are served in surprising ways.

La Tortue (☎ 02 31 89 04 93; 36 rue de l'Homme de Bois; menus €16-30; ☼ closed Tue & dinner Mon) Mmmm… fried fois gras in truffle juice! Here you can enjoy fine cuisine in a refreshingly relaxed and informal setting. Vegetarians will be relieved to discover a decent meat-free *menu*.

L'Absinthe (☎ 02 31 89 39 00; 10 quai de la Quarantaine; menus €29/€48/€63) Located in a ravishing 18th-century mansion, this is one of the finest restaurants in Normandy. The cuisine is sumptuous and sophisticated, even on its cheapest *menu*. Do reserve in advance.

SELF-CATERING

The **market** (place Ste-Catherine; ☼ 9am-1pm Sat) has an excellent selection of local products and an organic food market. There's a Champion supermarket just west of rue de la République, near place Albert Sorel.

Drinking

Café L'Albatros (☎ 02 31 89 25 30; 32 quai Ste-Catherine) Sailors, students, philosophers and layabouts are all at home at this café-bar, from breakfast through beer and sandwiches and on to nightcaps.

Le Perroquet Vert (☎ 02 31 89 14 19; 52 quai Ste-Catherine) The 'green parrot' has an excellent selection of beer and a good terrace for people-watching.

Getting There & Around

The **bus station** (☎ 02 31 89 28 41) is southeast of the Vieux Bassin on rue des Vases. **Bus Verts** (☎ 0 810 214 214 Caen) No 20 runs via Deauville-Trouville (€3.40, 30 minutes, five per day) to Caen (€11.05, €13.70 by express bus, one hour). The same line goes northwards to Le Havre (€6.80, 30 minutes, five per day) via the Pont de Normandie.

Honfleur is very small and can be visited on foot. A small tourist train does take people up the hill as part of a guided tour.

TROUVILLE & DEAUVILLE

pop 5600 (Trouville) / pop 4300 (Deauville)
Roughly 15km southwest of Honfleur lie Trouville and Deauville, two seemingly similar seaside resorts that maintain distinctly different personalities. Chic Deauville has been a playground of the wealthy ever since it was founded by Napoleon III's cousin, the duke of Morny, in 1861. Often called the '21st *arrondissement*' for its masses of Parisian weekenders, Deauville cultivates this 'lifestyles of' reputation with its designer boutiques, casino, racetrack and annual Festival of American Film.

Trouville is more down to earth, offers better-value accommodation and some decent restaurants. The town attracted a series of painters and writers during the 19th-century, such as Mozin and Flaubert. One thing both towns have in common are wide, sandy beaches lined with bathhouses.

Orientation

The towns are separated only by the River Touques, with Trouville on the eastern bank and Deauville on the western bank, respectively, and linked by the Pont des

Belges. The combined train and bus station is situated just west of the bridge. Beaches line the coast to the north of both towns on either side of the port.

Information

INTERNET ACCESS

Gestimedia (☎ 02 31 14 04 61; 6 rue Thiers, Deauville; per hr €6; ⊙ 9am-1pm & 2-6pm Mon-Fri)

MONEY

Crédit du Nord (84 rue Eugène Colas, Deauville) Has an ATM.
Société Générale (9 place Morny, Trouville) Has an ATM.

POST

Deauville Post Office (rue Robert Fossorier) Has Cyberposte and exchanges currency.
Trouville Post Office (16 rue Amiral de Maigret)

TOURIST INFORMATION

Deauville Tourist Office (☎ 02 31 14 40 00; www .deauville.org; place de la Mairie; ⊙ 9am-7pm Jul-Sep, 9am-6.30pm May & Jun, 9am-12.30pm & 2-6.30pm Mon-Sat, 10am-1pm & 2-5pm Sun mid-Sep–Apr) Pick up a copy of the free, outlandishly glossy magazine *Deauville Passions* for an overview of annual events.
Trouville Tourist Office (☎ 02 31 14 60 70; www .trouvillesurmer.org; 32 blvd Fernand Moureaux; ⊙ 9.30am-7pm Mon-Sat, 10am-4pm Sun Jul & Aug, 9.30am-noon & 2-6.30pm Mon-Sat Apr-Jun & Sep-Oct, 9.30am-noon & 1.30-6pm Mon-Sat Nov-Mar)

Sights & Activities

In Deauville, the rich, famous and assorted wannabes strut along the beachside **Promenade des Planches**, a 500m-long boardwalk lined with private swimming huts, before losing a wad at the **Casino de Deauville** 200m to the south.

About 1km to the northeast of the Trouville tourist office is the **Musée de Trouville** (☎ 02 31 88 16 26; 64 rue du Général Leclerc; adult/student €2/1.50; ⊙ 2-6.30pm Wed-Mon Apr-Sep), in the magnificent Villa Montebello. The villa has a panoramic view over the beaches, and the museum recounts the history of Trouville and features work from Charles Mozin and Eugène Boudin. There are temporary exhibitions by local artists.

On Trouville's beachside promenade, you'll see several illustrious **19th-century villas**. The beach is also home to the remarkably varied **Aquarium Vivarium de Trouville** (☎ 02 31 88 46 04; adult/student €6.50/4.50; ⊙ 10am-noon &

2-6.30pm Easter-Jun & Sep-Oct, 10am-7pm Jul & Aug, 2-6pm Nov-Easter), which aside from wild and wonderfully colourful fish also houses some fearsome reptiles (snakes, crocodiles and iguanas among them) and weird insects.

Festivals & Events

Deauville's answer to Cannes is the **American Film Festival** (www.festival-deauville.com), which is open to all and attracts a procession of Hollywood stars in the first week of September.

Trouville's **Festival Folklorique** fills the streets with colourfully clad musicians and dancers in the third week of June.

Deauville is renowned for its equestrian tradition. The **horse-racing season**, which runs from early July to mid-October, is held at two local racetracks: Hippodrome La Touques for gallop races and jumping events and Hippodrome Clairfontaine with galloping, trotting and steeplechase.

Sleeping

The best-value hotels are all in Trouville, and the town participates in the 'Bon Week-end' two-nights-for-the-price-of-one programme from November to March.

Hôtel de la Paix (☎ 02 31 88 35 15; hoteldela paix@hotmail.com; 4 place Fernand Moureaux, Trouville; d €50-61) Quite recently – and tastefully – renovated, this hotel has retained its traditional features while brushing up its amenities. The more expensive rooms overlook the port.

La Maison Normande (☎ 02 31 88 12 25; www .maisonnormande.com in French; 4 place de Lattre de Tassigny, Trouville; r with shower €44, with bathroom €52-64) A real Norman house in quintessential Norman style, with crisscrossing beams, flowery furnishings and traditional touches. You'll feel like you're visiting your new Norman grandma.

The most luxurious establishments in Deauville are the **Hôtel Normandy** (☎ 02 31 98 66 22; www.lucienbarriere.com; 38 rue Jean Mermoz; r from €238; P ☒) and the **Hôtel Royal Barrière** (☎ 02 31 98 66 33; www.lucienbarriere.com; 14 blvd Cornuché; r €229-1165; P ☒ ▢ ☒), which are as much tourist attractions as hotels.

CAMPING

Le Chant des Oiseaux (☎ 02 31 88 06 42; fax 02 31 98 16 09; 11 route d'Honfleur; adult/site €2.50/5; ☽ Apr-Oct) About 1km east of Trouville, this camping ground has a sweeping view of the coast.

Eating

Deauville has a somewhat overpriced dining scene. For better value, head to Trouville.

Bistrot Sur Le Quai (☎ 02 31 81 28 85; 68 blvd Fernand Moureaux, Trouville; lunch menu €12, dinner menus €15-25; ☽ closed Wed) One of the better choices of the waterfront eateries in Trouville, Bistro Sur Le Quai serves great seafood and has a very agreeable terrace.

Brasserie Le Central (☎ 02 31 88 13 68; 158 blvd Fernand Moureaux, Trouville; menus from €16.20) Parisians will feel right at home in this large dining room reminiscent of some of the capital's most celebrated brasseries. Portions are quite copious; one main course is usually sufficient.

La Petite Auberge (☎ 02 31 88 11 07; 7 rue Carnot, Trouville; menus €25-42; ☽ closed Tue & Wed) It doesn't get much more Norman than this, from the traditional décor to the well-chosen *menu*. Prices are reasonable considering the quality of the cuisine.

SELF-CATERING

Mamy Crêpe (☎ 02 31 14 96 44; 16 rue Désiré-le-Hoc, Deauville) sells excellent crepes and sandwiches. There is also a **Monoprix** (blvd Fernand Moureaux; ☽ closed Sun) and a **food market** (place du Maréchal Foch; ☽ Wed & Sat mornings).

Drinking & Entertainment

Zoo Bar (☎ 02 31 81 02 61; 53 rue Désiré-le-Hoc, Deauville) Dim lighting, deep house and designer-clad clients make this postmodern-style bar popular with the fashionable fauna of Deauville.

La Maison (☎ 02 31 81 43 10; 66 rue des Bains, Trouville) A welcome exception to the snooty seaside vibe is this casual, atmospheric wine bar where you can drink vintage wine by the glass and enjoy cheese and *charcuterie* platters. Concerts and art exhibitions are held regularly.

Casino de Deauville (☎ 02 31 14 31 14; av Lucien Barrière, Deauville; ☽ 11am-2am Mon-Fri, 10am-4am Sat, 10am-3am Sun) Dress is formal, but men can borrow a jacket and tie from reception.

Louisiane Follies (☎ 02 31 87 75 00; place du Maréchal Foch, Trouville; ☽ 10am-2am) This beachfront casino is a more relaxed affair with an adjoining cinema and nightclub.

Getting There & Around

Aéroport de Deauville-St-Gatien (☎ 02 31 65 65 65) is 10km northeast of Deauville-Trouville. There is no public transport into town.

Bus Verts (☎ 0 810 214 214) has very frequent services to Caen (€8.50, 1¼ hours), Honfleur (€3.40, 30 minutes) and Le Havre (via Honfleur; €9.35, one hour).

Train services from Deauville-Trouville require changes at Lisieux (€5.10, 20 minutes, 10 daily). Trains go to Caen (€12.40, one to 1½ hours, 13 daily), Rouen (€19.90, 3¼ hours, four daily) and Dieppe (via Rouen; €28.90, 3½ hours, four daily).

CAEN

pop 117,000

Today, Caen is a bustling university city with some fine museums and historical sites and a massive 11th-century chateau. Unfortunately, it has little else of great interest to visitors, having been decimated during WWII and rebuilt in a utilitarian, though not entirely unpleasing, style.

The capital of Basse Normandie, Caen was bombed on D-Day and burned for over a week before being liberated by the Canadians – only to be then shelled by the Germans. The only vestiges of the past to have survived are the ramparts around the chateau and the two abbeys, all built by William the Conqueror when he founded the city in the 11th century. Much of the medieval city was built from 'Caen stone', a creamy local limestone exported for centuries to England.

Caen makes a good base for exploring the D-Day beaches. Linked to the sea by a canal running parallel to the River Orne, Caen is gateway for Ouistreham, a minor passenger port for ferries to England.

Orientation

Caen's modern heart is made up of a few pedestrianised shopping streets and some busy boulevards. The largest, av du 6 Juin, links the centre, which is based around the southern end of the chateau, with the canal and train station to the southeast. What's left of the old city is centred around rue du Vaugueux, a short distance east of the chateau.

Information

BOOKSHOPS

Hemisphères (☎ 02 31 86 67 26; 15 rue des Croisières) Guidebooks in English, including Lonely Planet titles.

INTERNET ACCESS

M.I.G. (☎ 02 31 93 09 09; 74-76 av de la Libération; per hr €3; ⏱ 2.30-7pm Mon, 10am-noon & 2.30-7pm Tue-Sat)

LAUNDRY

Laundrette (127 rue St-Jean)

MONEY

Crédit Agricole (1 blvd Maréchal Leclerc) There's an exchange bureau here.

POST

Main Post Office (place Gambetta) It has Cyberposte.

TOURIST INFORMATION

SNCF Boutique (8 rue St-Pierre) For train information and reservations.

Tourist Office (☎ 02 31 27 14 14; www.caen.fr/tourisme; place St-Pierre; ⏱ 9am-7pm Mon-Sat, 10am-1pm & 2-5pm Sun Jul & Aug, 9.30am-6.30pm Mon-Sat & 10am-1pm Sun Jun & Sep) Information on sites and entertainment.

Mémorial – Un Musée pour la Paix

Caen's best-known museum, **Mémorial – Un Musée pour la Paix** (Memorial – A Museum for Peace; ☎ 02 31 06 06 44; www.memorial-caen.fr in French; adult /student €18/16, WWII veterans free; ⏱ 9am-8pm Jun-Sep, 9am-7pm Oct-May, closed 1st 2-3 weeks of Jan), provides an outstanding and vivid account of the Battle of Normandy and the challenges to world peace from WWII to today.

The visit begins with a history of Europe's descent into total war, tracing events from the end of WWI through the rise of Fascism to the Battle of Normandy in 1944. Telling the story through artefacts, sound, lighting, film footage, documents and animation, the exhibits graphically evoke the horrors of war, the occupation and the battle for liberation. A recently installed section of the museum focuses on the Cold War, decolonisation and the emergence of the European Union. The exhibition is poignant and stirring; the hordes of noisy school children certainly aren't. All signs are in French, English and German.

The memorial is about 3km northwest of the tourist office on Esplanade Dwight Eisenhower. To reach it, take bus No 17 from opposite the tourist office at place St-Pierre; the last bus back departs at 8.45pm (earlier on Sunday). By car, follow the multitude of signs with the word 'Mémorial'.

Château de Caen

An enormous fortress surrounded by a dry moat, **Château de Caen** (www.chateau.caen.fr; ⏱ 6am-10pm May-Sep, 6am-7.30pm Oct-Apr) was begun by

CAEN

0   400 m
0   0.2 miles

NORMANDY

William the Conqueror in 1060 and extended by his son Henry I. It has been used over the centuries by royals, revolutionaries, townsfolk and the military.

Take a walk around the **ramparts** and visit the 12th-century **Chapelle de St-Georges** and the **Échiquier** (Exchequer), which dates from about AD 1100 and is one of the oldest civic buildings in Normandy. Of special interest is the **Jardin des Simples**, a garden of medicinal and aromatic herbs cultivated during the Middle Ages – some of which are poisonous. A book (written in French) on the garden is on sale inside the **Musée de Normandie** (☎ 02 31 30 47 50; adult/student €1.50/0.80; ☒ 9.30am-6pm Wed-Mon), which contains historical artefacts illustrating life in Normandy. There are explanatory signs in English.

The **Musée des Beaux-Arts** (☎ 02 31 30 47 70; admission €3.80, Wed free; ☒ 9.30am-6pm Wed-Mon) is based in a modern building nearby. It houses an extensive collection of paintings dating from the 15th to 20th centuries (including the wonderful *Marriage of the Virgin* painted by Pietro Vannucci in 1504), ceramics and a noteworthy collection of engravings.

Abbeys

Caen's two Romanesque abbeys were built by William the Conqueror and his wife, Matilda of Flanders, after the distant cousins had been absolved by the Roman Catholic church for marrying. The **Abbaye aux Hommes** (☎ 02 31 30 42 81; adult/student €2/1, free Sun, guided visit €4; ☒ 8.50am-noon & 2-7.30pm, guided visits 9.30am, 11am, 2.30pm & 4pm), with its multiturreted Église St-Étienne, is at the end of rue Écuyère and was William's resting place. The tomb was destroyed in turn by a 16th-century Calvinist mob and by 18th-century revolutionaries – a solitary thighbone is all that's left of Will's mortal remains. The convent buildings are today home to the town hall.

The starker **Abbaye aux Dames** (☎ 02 31 06 98 98; admission free; guided tours 2.30pm & 4pm), at the eastern end of rue des Chanoines, incorporates the Église de la Trinité. Access to the abbey, which houses regional government offices, is by guided tour only. Look for Matilda's tomb behind the main altar.

Sleeping

BUDGET

Cité de Lébisey (☎ 02 31 46 74 74; fax 02 31 46 74 76; Cité de Lébisey, 114-116 rue de Lébisey, BP 5153, 14070 Caen Cedex 5; student/nonstudent per day €7.50/11, per 2 weeks €60.25/78.85, per month €120.45/153; ☐) These university dormitories offer a good deal for clean doubles with showers in the hall. Reservations must be made by mail or fax. The dormitories are just north of the chateau.

Hôtel Bernières (☎ 02 31 86 01 26; www.hotelberni eres.com; 50 rue de Bernières; s/d €35/45) This friendly place is a particularly good find for the price with cosy, comfortable rooms. Bear in mind that in some rooms there's only a curtain separating the shower from the sleeping area.

MID-RANGE & TOP END

Hôtel des Cordeliers (☎ 02 31 86 37 15; fax 02 31 39 56 51; 4 rue des Cordeliers; d from €45) One of the rare Caen hotels in an 18th-century building, this hotel has more character than most. The rooms are attractive with white walls and plain pine furniture, and open directly onto a relaxing interior garden.

Hôtel du Château (☎ 02 31 86 15 37; www.hotel -chateau-caen.com; 5 av du 6 Juin; s/d €45/55; ☒) This is an excellent location just a stone's throw from the chateau. The rooms are simple but quite generous in size, each painted a different colour of the rainbow. Front windows are double glazed and there's an elevator.

Hôtel des Quatrans (☎ 02 31 86 25 57; www .hotel-des-quatrans.com; 17 rue Gémare; s/d €48/58; ☒) Taking care not to break that unspoken agreement among hotel owners to match the bedspreads with the curtains, this hotel offers calm, fairly plush rooms and modern comforts such as satellite TV.

Hôtel Le Dauphin (☎ 02 31 86 22 26; www.le-dau phin-normandie.com; 29 rue Gémare; r €70-150; ☒ ☒) With warm, calming colours and discerning details such as antiques, polished wood doors and exposed beams, this former priory offers a touch of class (Rm 310 is particularly romantic). There's also a fancy restaurant.

Eating

In one of Caen's few remaining old quarters, the area around rue du Vaugueux is a popular dining spot offering a wide range of prices and cuisines.

La Petite Auberge (☎ 02 31 86 43 30; 17 rue des Équipes d'Urgence; menus €12 & €19; ☒ closed Sun & Mon) This is a cosy little place for a home-style meal. The dishes are simple and delicious, including, of course, the ubiquitous tripe, a local Caen speciality. The €11 *menu* is available on weekdays only.

L'Alcide (☎ 02 31 44 18 06; 1 place Courtonne; menus €14.50-22.50; ☒ closed Sat) This is an excellent address for sampling Caen cuisine, especially the infamous *tripes à la mode de Caen*. Connoisseurs say that the tripe here are served in a sauce so flavoursome you can almost forget you're eating intestines.

Le Météor (☎ 02 31 82 31 35; 55 rue d'Auge; menu €10; ☒ lunch only Mon-Sat) A good three-course *menu* for €10 is already a great find. At this little restaurant by the train station, they'll also throw in a glass of wine. We're not complaining.

Dolly's Café & Tea Rooms (☎ 02 31 94 03 29; 16-18 av de la Libération; breakfast €6-12, dishes around €8.50; ☒ 10am-7.30pm Tue-Sat, 9.30am-6pm Sun) Just what you've been craving after all those croissants: a full, hearty, savoury English breakfast that is served all day. Daily specials can include fish and chips. Cross-Channel products such as tea, jam and newspapers are available next door at The English Shop.

Le Costa (☎ 02 31 86 28 28; 13 rue Guilbert; menus from €21; ☒ closed Sun) Slide through the revolving door into the sleek, Art-Deco interior of this chic restaurant, where you will dine on modern French classics. The *saumon sauvage* (wild salmon) is a particularly fine choice.

WILLIAM CONQUERS ENGLAND

The son of Robert I of Normandy and his concubine Arlette, William 'the Conqueror' (commonly referred to as 'William the Bastard') ascended the throne of Normandy at the tender age of five. Thwarting several attempts by rivals – including members of his own family – to kill him and his advisers, William took over the reign of Normandy aged 15. He soon set about regaining his lost territory and feudal rights, quashing several rebellions along the way.

William had twice been promised the throne of England: once from the king himself, Edward the Confessor (William's relative), and once from the most powerful Saxon lord in England, Harold Godwinson of Wessex, who had the misfortune of being shipwrecked on the Norman coast.

In January 1066 Edward died without an heir. Harold was immediately crowned king, with the support of the great nobles of England (and very likely the majority of the Saxon people).

One of several pretenders to the throne, William was preparing to send an invasion fleet across the Channel, when a rival army (consisting of an alliance between Harold's estranged brother Tostig and Harold Hardrada of Norway) landed in the north of England. In a September battle at Stamford Bridge, near York, Harold defeated and killed both Hardrada and Tostig.

Meanwhile, William had crossed the Channel unopposed with an army of about 6000 men, including a large cavalry force. They landed at Pevensey before marching to Hastings on 13 October, where Harold faced William with about 7000 men from a strong defensive position. The battle began the next day.

Although William's archers scored many hits among the densely packed and ill-trained Saxon peasants, the latter's ferocious defence ended a charge by the Norman cavalry and drove them back in disarray. William faced the real possibility of losing the battle. Summoning the knowledge and tactical ability he had gained in numerous campaigns against rivals in Normandy, he used the cavalry's rout to draw the Saxon infantry out from their defensive positions, whereupon the Norman infantry turned and caused heavy casualties on the undisciplined Saxon troops. The battle started to turn against Harold, who was slain (by an arrow through the eye, according to the Bayeux Tapestry) late in the afternoon. The embattled Saxons fought on until sunset and then fled. William immediately marched to London, ruthlessly quelled the opposition, and was crowned king of England on Christmas Day.

William thus became the ruler of two kingdoms, bringing England's feudal system of government under the control of Norman nobles. Ongoing unrest among the Saxon peasantry soured William's opinion of the country and he spent the rest of his life after 1072 in Normandy, only going to England when compelled to do so. William left most of the governance of the country to the bishops.

In Normandy William continued to expand his influence through military campaigns, strategic marriages and the ruthless elimination of all opposition. In 1087 he was injured during an attack on Mantes. He died at Rouen a few weeks later and was buried at Caen.

SELF-CATERING

There's a downstairs supermarket at **Mono-prix** (45 blvd Maréchal Leclerc; 🕙 8.30am-8.30pm Mon-Sat). Late-night purchases can be made at **Épicerie de Nuit** (23 rue Porte au Berger; 🕙 8pm-2am Tue-Sun).

For food markets check out place St-Sauveur on Friday, blvd Leroy (behind the train station) on Saturday and place Courtonne on Sunday.

Drinking & Entertainment

We're not sure where this Caen–Havana connection originated, but Cuban-style bars are all the rage here. The general idea is cool, rum-laced cocktails, hot Latin music and the odd cigar. Some of the better places include **El Che Guevara** (☎ 02 31 85 10 75; 53 rue de Geôle), popular with young beer drinkers early in the evening and smart 30-somethings later on, and **Le Farniente** (☎ 02 31 86 30 00; 13 rue Paul Doumer) where a cool crowd dances it up.

Students always know where to find good vibes and cheap drinks: in Caen they flock to **6X** (☎ 02 31 86 36 98; 7 rue St-Sauveur; 🕙 noon-1am Mon-Sat, 4pm-1am Sun) and **Le Vertigo** (☎ 02 31 85 43 12; 14 rue Écuyère).

Le Carré (☎ 02 31 38 90 90; 32 quai Vendeuvre) This is one of the region's the slickest discos, with theme nights and a strict, selective door policy. The décor is kind of disco-baroque and the music mainly '70s and '80s. You must be over 27 and dressed smartly.

Le Zinc (☎ 02 31 93 20 30; 12 rue du Vaugueux) This is one of the better gay bars in town. It can get quite packed with a young, sometimes mixed, crowd. The DJ spins house and techno and there's a terrace in summer.

Théâtre de Caen (☎ 02 31 30 48 00; 135 blvd Maréchal Leclerc) In the centre of town, this hall offers a season of opera, dance, jazz and classical concerts that runs from October to May.

Getting There & Away

AIR

Caen's **airport** (☎ 02 31 71 20 10) is 5km west of town in Carpiquet.

BOAT

Brittany Ferries (☎ 02 31 36 36 36) sail from Ouistreham, 14km northeast of Caen, to Portsmouth in England. For more information see p919.

BUS

Bus Verts (☎ 0 810 214 214; information kiosk place Courtonne) serves the entire Calvados *département*, including Bayeux (€5.80, 50 minutes), Courseulles-sur-Mer (€4.80, 30 minutes) as well as Deauville-Trouville (€8.50, 1¼ hours), Honfleur (€10.20 via Cabourg and Deauville, or €13.70 by express bus) and the ferry port at Ouistreham (€3.40, 25 minutes). It also runs two buses a day to Le Havre (€20, 1½ hours).

See p268 for details on getting to the D-Day beaches.

Most buses stop at the bus station and in the centre of town at place Courtonne. When leaving or arriving at Caen by bus, your ticket will be valid for public transport to/from the bus station.

CAR

Rental places include **Hertz** (☎ 02 31 84 64 50; 34 place de la Gare), **Europcar** (☎ 02 31 84 61 61; 36 place de la Gare), **Avis** (☎ 02 31 84 73 80; 44 place de la Gare) and **ADA** (☎ 02 31 34 88 89; 26 rue d'Auge).

TRAIN

Caen is on the Paris–Cherbourg line. There are regular connections to Paris' Gare St-Lazare (€26.20, 2½ hours, 13 daily), as well as Bayeux (€5.10, 20 minutes, 15 per day), Cherbourg (€16.60, 3¼ hours, four daily), Pontorson (€20.40, 2½ hours, daily), Rennes (€27.30, three hours, two daily), Rouen (€19.40, two hours, 10 daily) and Tours (via Le Mans; €28.40, 3¾ hours, five daily).

Getting Around

A bus links the airport with Caen's train station. A taxi costs about €15.

CTAC (☎ 02 31 15 55 55) runs city bus No 7 and the more direct No 15 between the train station and the tourist office (stop: St-Pierre). There's also a tram line connecting the train station with the university, stopping at quai de Juillet, rue de Bernières, place St-Pierre and the chateau. A single ride on either costs €1.05 and a carnet of 10 tickets costs €9. Services end between 6pm and 8pm.

There are a couple of options for **taxis** (☎ 02 31 26 62 00, 02 31 52 17 89).

BAYEUX

pop 15,400

Stately Bayeux proudly possesses the only pictorial record of William the Conqueror's trans-Channel invasion in 1066 – the Bayeux Tapestry. This invaluable stretch of embroidered cloth is the magnet for several million tourists each year and, with a majestic cathedral, the British War Cemetery and some excellent museums, a visitor can easily pass an absorbing few days here. Bayeux was the first town liberated after the D-Day landings and is one of the few in Calvados to have survived WWII unscathed.

Orientation

The Cathédrale Notre Dame, the major landmark in the centre of Bayeux and visible throughout the town, is 1km northwest of the train station. The River Aure, with

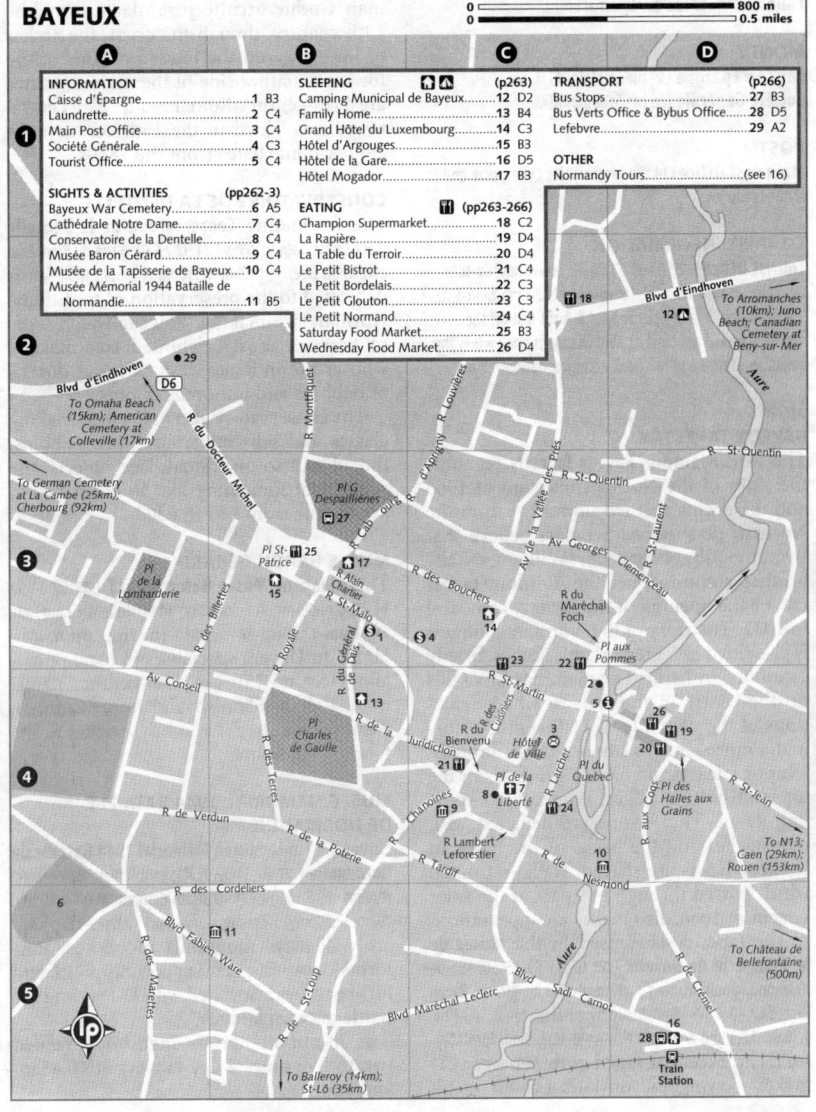

BAYEUX

0 — 800 m
0 — 0.5 miles

To Arromanches
(10km); Juno
Beach; Canadian
Cemetery at
Beny-sur-Mer

Blvd d'Eindhoven

Aure

R St-Quentin

Av Georges Clemenceau

To Omaha Beach
(15km); American
Cemetery at
Colleville (17km)

Blvd d'Eindhoven

To German Cemetery
at La Cambe (25km);
Cherbourg (92km)

Pl G
Despaillières

Pl St-
Patrice

Pl
de la
Lombarderie

R des Bouchers

R du
Maréchal
Foch

Pl aux
Pommes

Av Conseil

Pl
Charles
de Gaulle

R du
Bienvenu

Hôtel
de Ville

Pl du
Québec

Pl des
Halles aux
Grains

R St-Jean

To N13;
Caen (29km);
Rouen (153km)

R de Verdun

Pl de la
Juridiction

Pl de la
Liberté

R Lambert
Leforestier

R Tardif

R de
Nesmond

Aure

R des Cordeliers

Blvd Fabien Ware

Blvd Maréchal Leclerc

Blvd
Sadi Carnot

To Château de
Bellefontaine
(500m)

To Balleroy (14km);
St-Lô (35km)

Train
Station

several attractive little mills along its banks, flows northwards on the eastern side of the centre.

Information

INTERNET ACCESS

You can log on at the tourist office for €10 per 1½ hours.

LAUNDRY

Laundrette (13 rue du Maréchal Foch)

MONEY

Caisse d'Épargne (59 rue St-Malo) ATM.
Société Générale (26 rue St-Malo) ATM.

POST

Main Post Office (14 rue Larcher) Has Cyberposte and changes money.

TOURIST INFORMATION

Tourist Office (☎ 02 31 51 28 28; www.bayeux-tour ism.com; pont St-Jean; ☒ 9am-noon & 2-6pm Mon-Sat, 9.30am-noon & 2.30-6pm Sun Jul & Aug) Just off the northern end of rue Larcher. Will change money when the banks are closed and can book accommodation (€2 fee).

Sights

BAYEUX TAPESTRY

The world-famous **Bayeux Tapestry** recounts the story of the Norman invasion of 1066 and the events that led up to it – from the Norman perspective. Scholars believe that Bishop Odo of Bayeux, William's half-brother, commissioned the 70m-long tapestry for the opening of the Bayeux cathedral in 1077. The story of the Norman conquest is presented in 58 remarkable scenes, briefly captioned in Latin. The main narrative fills up the centre of the canvas, while depictions of the daily life of 11th-century Norman France – men's labours, dress, animals, weapons, feasts and battles – unfolds in the top and bottom edges, rendered in startling detail. The Saxons are depicted with moustaches and the backs of the Norman soldiers' heads are shaved. Halley's Comet, which passed through our part of the solar system in 1066, also makes an appearance.

The tapestry is housed in the **Musée de la Tapisserie de Bayeux** (☎ 02 31 51 25 50; rue de Nesmond; adult/student incl admission to Musée Baron Gérard €7.40/3; ☒ 9am-6.30pm mid-Mar–Apr & Sep-Nov, 9.30am-12.30pm & 2-6pm Nov–mid-Mar, 9am-7pm May-Aug). The excellent taped commentary (€1) makes viewing the upstairs exhibits a bit unnecessary. A 14-minute film on the 2nd floor is screened eight to 13 times a day in English (last showing 5.15pm, or 5.45pm May to August).

CATHÉDRALE NOTRE DAME

Most of Bayeux's spectacular **Cathédrale Notre Dame** (place de la Liberté; ☒ 8.30am-6pm Oct-Jun, 8.30am-7pm Jul-Sep), a fine example of Norman Gothic architecture, dates from the 13th century, though the crypt, the arches of the nave and the lower portions of the towers on either side of the main entrance are 11th-century Romanesque. The central tower was added in the 15th century; the copper dome dates from the 1860s.

CONSERVATOIRE DE LA DENTELLE

The fascinating **Conservatoire de la Dentelle** (Lace Conservatory; ☎ 02 31 92 73 80; 6 rue du Bienvenu; admission free; ☒ 10am-12.30pm & 2-6pm Mon-Sat) is dedicated to the preservation of traditional Norman lace-making. You can watch some of France's most celebrated lace-makers, who create intricate designs using dozens of bobbins and hundreds of pins.

The conservatory also offers lace-making classes and sells materials (pins, bobbins, thread and so on). Small lace objects, the product of something like 50 hours' work, are on sale from €30 to €300.

MUSÉE BARON GÉRARD

The pleasant **Musée Baron Gérard** (☎ 02 31 92 14 21; 6 rue Lambert Leforestier; adult/student €2.60/1.60; ☒ 10am-12.30pm & 2-6pm), in the mansion, Hôtel du Doyen, specialises in local porcelain, lace and 15th- to 19th-century paintings (Italian, Flemish and impressionist). Admission is free if you buy a ticket to the tapestry museum.

MUSÉE MÉMORIAL 1944 BATAILLE DE NORMANDIE

Bayeux's huge **Musée Mémorial 1944 Bataille de Normandie** (☎ 02 31 92 93 41; blvd Fabien Ware; adult/student €5.50/2.60; ☒ 9.30am-6.30pm May–mid-Sep, 10am-12.30pm & 2-6pm mid-Sep–Apr) rather haphazardly displays thousands of photos, uniforms, weapons, newspaper clippings and lifelike scenes associated with D-Day and the Battle of Normandy.

A 30-minute film in English is screened two to five times a day (always at 10.45am and 5pm).

BAYEUX WAR CEMETERY

This peaceful cemetery, on blvd Fabien Ware a few hundred metres west of the war museum, is the largest of the 18 Commonwealth military cemeteries in Normandy. It contains 4868 graves of soldiers from the UK and 10 other countries. Many of the 466 Germans buried here were never identified, and the headstones are simply marked 'Ein Deutscher Soldat' (A German Soldier). There is an explanatory plaque in the small chapel to the right as you enter the grounds. The large structure across blvd Fabien Ware commemorates the 1807 Commonwealth soldiers missing in action.

Festivals & Events

The first weekend in July, **Fêtes Médiévales de Bayeux** holds parades and medieval song and dance for the anniversary of the Battle of Formigny, which put an end to the Hundred Years' War.

Sleeping

BUDGET

Family Home (☎ 02 31 92 15 22; fax 02 31 92 55 72; 39 rue du Général de Dais; dm incl breakfast €18-20) This is an excellent, friendly old hostel and a great place to meet other travellers. Multicourse French dinners with wine (€11) are often served. Vegetarian dishes are available on request or you can cook for yourself.

Hôtel de la Gare (☎ 02 31 92 10 70; fax 02 31 51 95 99; 26 place de la Gare; r €24.50-48; P) This is a fair compromise: it's old but well maintained; the rooms are slightly cramped but well-equipped; and it's by the station but still quiet at night (as there are few late trains). Normandy Tours (see p268) operates from the hotel.

Camping

Camping Municipal de Bayeux (☎ 02 31 92 08 43; blvd d'Eindhoven; adult/site €2.90/3.60; ☾ mid-Mar–mid-Nov) This camping ground is about 2km north of the town centre. Bus No 3 stops three times daily at nearby Les Cerisiers.

MID-RANGE

The tourist office has a list of *chambres d'hôtes* in the Bayeux area. The cheapest cost is about €34 for two people, with breakfast.

Hôtel Mogador (☎ 02 31 92 24 58; hotel.mogador@wanadoo.fr; 20 rue Alain Chartier; d €45-50; P) Exposed ceiling beams and old-fashioned décor add a touch of warmth and character to this two-star establishment. The rooms are restful and comfortable and many face a pleasant interior courtyard.

Hôtel d'Argouges (☎ 02 31 92 88 86; dargouges@aol.com; 21 rue St-Patrice; r €80-100; P) The former 18th-century mansion of the d'Argouges family, this stately residence is now a graceful hotel. The rooms are elegant, while the inner garden allows for some peaceful time out.

Grand Hôtel du Luxembourg (☎ 02 31 92 00 04; hotel.luxembourg@wanadoo.fr; 25 rue des Bouchers; r €99-115; P ✗) This hotel combines businesslike comfort with a warm and friendly welcome. It manages to connect with tradition without appearing old-fashioned, and contains an excellent restaurant.

Château de Bellefontaine (☎ 02 31 22 00 10; hotel.bellefontaine@wanadoo.fr; 49 rue de Bellefontaine; s/d €108/120; P ✗) Surrounded by five acres of groomed parkland, this majestic 18th-century castle makes for some very luxurious accommodation. Rooms Nos 4, 5 and 6 have their own chimney and boast a fine view over the park.

Eating

Le Petit Normand (☎ 02 31 22 88 66; 35 rue Larcher; menus €9.50-23; ☾ closed Thu Oct-Apr) That ever-present regional staple, apple cider, makes it into most of the traditional Norman recipes at this popular little restaurant, which has a view over the cathedral.

La Table du Terroir (☎ 02 31 92 05 53; 42 rue St-Jean; menus lunch €11, dinner €14-26; ☾ closed Sun & Mon) The extension of a butcher shop, this is a no-go for vegetarians but the cuts are of high quality. The big wooden tables fill up with a carnivorous crowd who come for the excellent *menus*.

La Rapière (☎ 02 31 21 05 45; 53 rue St-Jean; lunch menu €15, dinner menus €24 & €30; ☾ closed Wed & Thu) A real highlight here is the quite extraordinary salad Rapière, with foie gras, *gesiers* (gizzards – sounds better in French!) and langoustines. And why not conclude with a Camembert in Calvados?

Le Petit Bistrot (☎ 02 31 51 85 40; 2 rue du Bienvenu; menus €16 & €28; ☾ closed Sun & Mon Sep-Jun) This is a charming little eatery whose strong suit is the intelligent use of fresh local ingredients. The fish and duck *menus* are an excellent choice.

Le Petit Bordelais (☎ 02 31 92 06 44; 15 rue du Maréchal Foch; dishes €7.20-16; ☾ lunch to 2.30pm, drinks

THE BATTLE OF NORMANDY

In early 1944 an Allied invasion of Continental Europe seemed inevitable. Hitler's folly on the Russian front and the Luftwaffe's inability to control the skies had left Germany vulnerable.

Normandy was to be the spearhead into Europe. Codenamed 'Operation Overlord', the invasion entailed an assault by three paratroop divisions and five seaborne divisions, along with 13,000 aeroplanes and 6000 vessels. The total initial invasion force was 45,000, and 15 divisions were to follow once successful beachheads had been established.

The Straits of Dover seemed the most likely invasion spot to the Germans who set about heavily reinforcing the area around Calais and the large Channel ports. Allied intelligence went to extraordinary lengths to encourage the German belief that the invasion would be north of Normandy, even creating phoney airfields and military bases across from the Pas de Calais.

Because of the tides and unpredictable weather patterns, Allied planners had only a few days available each month in which to launch the invasion. On 5 June, the date chosen, very bad weather set in, delaying the operation. The weather had only improved slightly the next day, but General Dwight D Eisenhower, Allied commander-in-chief, gave the go-ahead: 6 June would be D-Day.

In the very early hours of 6 June the first troops were on the ground. British commandos captured key bridges and destroyed German communications, while the paratroops weren't far behind them. Although the paratroops' tactical victories were few, they caused enormous confusion in German ranks. More importantly, because of their relatively small numbers, at first, the German high command didn't believe that the real invasion had begun.

Sword, Juno & Gold Beaches

These beaches, stretching for about 35km from Ouistreham to Arromanches, were attacked by the British 2nd Army, which included sizable detachments of Canadians and smaller groups of Commonwealth, Free French and Polish forces.

At Sword Beach, initial German resistance was quickly overcome by the Allies and the beach was secured after approximately two hours. Infantry pushed inland from Ouistreham to link up with paratroops around Ranville, but it wasn't long before they suffered heavy casualties as their supporting armour fell behind, trapped in a massive traffic jam on the narrow coastal roads. Nevertheless, they were within 5km of Caen by 4pm, but a heavy German armoured counterattack forced them to dig in. Thus, in spite of the Allies' successes, Caen was not taken on the first day as planned.

At Juno Beach, Canadian battalions landed quickly but had to clear the Germans trench by trench before moving inland. Mines took a heavy toll on the infantry, but by noon they were south and east of Creuilly. Late in the afternoon the German armoured divisions that had halted the British coming from Sword Beach were deflected towards the coast and held Douvres, thus threatening to drive a wedge between the Sword and Juno forces. But the threat of encirclement made them withdraw by the next day.

At Gold Beach, the attack by the British forces was at first chaotic as unexpectedly high waters obscured German underwater obstacles. By 9am, though, Allied armoured divisions were on the beach and several brigades pushed inland. By afternoon they'd joined up with the Juno forces and were only 3km from Bayeux. On all three of these beaches, odd-looking 'Funnies' – specially designed armoured amphibious vehicles made to clear minefields, breach walls and wire entanglements, and provide support and protection for the infantry – proved their worth. Their construction and successful deployment was due to the ingenuity and foresight of British Major-General Hobart.

Omaha & Utah Beaches

The struggle on Omaha Beach (Vierville, St-Laurent and Colleville beaches) was by far the bloodiest of the day. Omaha Beach stretched 10km from Port-en-Bessin to the mouth of the River Vire and was backed by 30m-high cliffs. The beach was heavily defended by three battalions of heavily armed, highly trained Germans supported by an extensive trench system, mines and underwater obstacles. Men disembarked their landing craft in choppy seas and under heavy German fire; the naval bombardment had done little damage to German positions at the top of the cliffs and only two of the 29 Sherman tanks expected to support the troops made it to shore. Man by man, metre by metre, the GIs gained a precarious toehold on the beach and scaled the cliffs. A naval destroyer finally opened fire and the Germans, lacking reserves, had to fall back a short distance. Nevertheless, 1000 soldiers were killed at Omaha on D-Day, out of a total of 2500American casualties.

At Utah, US forces faced little resistance, and got off the beach after two hours. By noon, the beach had been cleared with the loss of only 12 men. Pockets of troops held large tracts of territory to the west of the landing site, and the town of Ste-Mère-Église was captured.

The Beginning of the End
Four days later, the Allies held a coastal strip about 100km long and 10km deep. British Field Marshal Montgomery's plan successfully drew the weight of German armour towards Caen, where fierce fighting continued for more than a month and reduced the city to rubble. This enabled the US army who were stationed further west to consolidate and push northwards up the Cotentin Peninsula.

The prized port of Cherbourg fell to the Allies on 27 June, after a series of fierce battles. However, its valuable facilities were blown up by the Germans so it remained out of service until autumn. To overcome such logistical problems, the Allies had devised the remarkable 'Mulberry Harbours'. These were enormous floating harbours that were towed from England, and set up off the Norman coast. They were indispensable in allowing large amounts of supplies to be quickly taken off ships and onto the roads leading to the front. A big storm from 19 to 22 June, however, destroyed the harbour stationed at Omaha Beach and damaged the Gold Beach installation.

The fierce Battle of the Hedgerows was fought mainly by the Americans up and down the Cotentin Peninsula. The *bocage* (farmland crisscrossed by walled roads and hedgerows) made ideal territory for defending and the Germans made good use of it. Nevertheless, once the Allies finally broke out from the beachheads, their superior numbers prevailed.

By the end of July, US army units had smashed through to the border of Brittany. By mid-August, two German armies had been surrounded and destroyed near Falaise and Argentan, and on 20 August, US forces crossed the Seine at several points about 40km north and south of Paris.

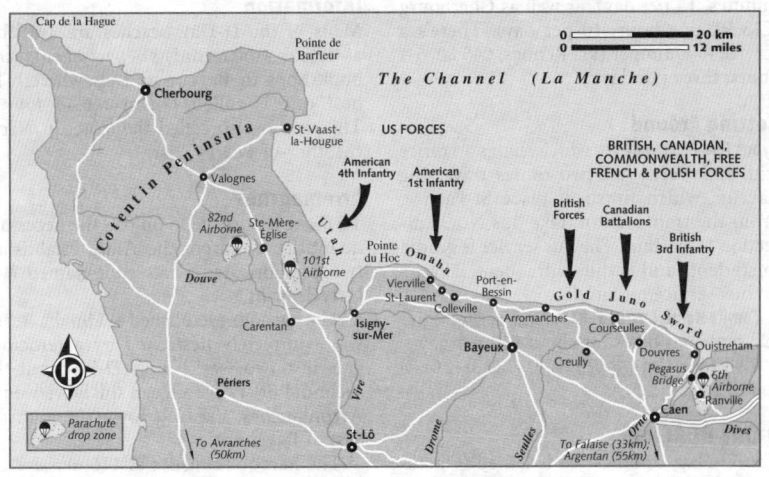

NORMANDY

to 7pm Tue-Sat) This little wine cellar makes a brilliant lunch destination. You can enjoy the plat du jour or sample an assortment of cheeses, all complemented with excellent – and inexpensive – vintages.

SELF-CATERING

Takeaway shops are near rue St-Martin and rue St-Jean, including **Le Petit Glouton** (☎ 02 31 92 86 43; 42 rue St-Martin). There's also a **Champion supermarket** (blvd d'Eindhoven).

Rue St-Jean has an open-air food market on Wednesday morning, as does place St-Patrice on Saturday morning. Don't miss *tergoule*, a sweet, cinnamon-flavoured rice pudding typical of the Bayeux region.

Entertainment

Bayeux is not known for its hot nightlife, but there are frequent concerts and theatrical events staged in venues around town. Check the free booklet *Sorties Plurielles* for listings.

Getting There & Away

Bus Verts (☎ 0 810 214 214; opposite the train station in Bayeux) offers rather infrequent services from the train station and place St-Patrice to Caen, the D-Day beaches (see p268), Vire and elsewhere in the Calvados *département*. The schedules are arranged for school children coming into Bayeux in the morning and going home in the afternoon.

Train services from Bayeux include Paris' Gare St-Lazare (€28.80) via Caen (€5.10, 20 minutes, 15 per day), as well as Cherbourg (€13.30, one hour, 10 per day). There's a service to Quimper (via Rennes; €45.80, 5¾ hours, three per day).

Getting Around

Bybus (☎ 02 31 92 02 92), which shares an office with Bus Verts, has two routes traversing Bayeux, which finish at place St-Patrice. From the train station, take bus No 3 (direction J Cocteau). The bus service is geared to students and is thus infrequent. There's no bus service on Sunday.

Family Home (☎ 02 31 92 15 22; 39 rue du Général de Dais) rents out bikes for about €12 per day.

Call for a **taxi** (☎ 02 31 92 92 40, 02 31 92 04 10) round the clock.

D-DAY BEACHES

The D-Day landings, codenamed 'Operation Overlord', were the largest military operation in history. Early on the morning of 6 June 1944, swarms of landing craft – part of a flotilla of over 6000 boats – hit the beaches, and tens of thousands of soldiers from the USA, UK, Canada and elsewhere began pouring onto French soil.

The majority of the 135,000 Allied troops stormed ashore along 80km of beaches north of Bayeux codenamed (from west to east) Utah, Omaha (in the US sector), Gold, Juno and Sword (in the British and Canadian sectors). The landings on D-Day – called Jour J in French – were followed by the Battle of Normandy, which would lead to the liberation of Europe from Nazi occupation. In the 76 days of fighting, the Allies suffered 210,000 casualties, including 37,000 troops killed. German casualties are believed to be around 200,000; and another 200,000 German soldiers were taken prisoner. Caen's memorial museum provides the best introduction to the history of what took place here and also attempts to explain the rationale behind each event. Once on the coast, travellers can take a well-marked circuit that links the battle sites, close to where holiday-makers sunbathe.

Fat Norman cows use the bombed-out bunkers to shield themselves from the wind. Many of the villages near the D-Day beaches have small museums with war memorabilia on display collected by local people after the fighting.

Information

Maps of the D-Day beaches are available at *tabacs* (tobacconists), newsagents and bookshops in Bayeux and elsewhere. The best one is called *D-Day 6.6.44 Jour J*. The area is also called the Côte du Nacre (Mother-of-Pearl Coast).

Arromanches

To make it possible to unload the necessary quantities of cargo, the Allies established two prefabricated ports code-named **Mulberry Harbours**.

The harbour established at Omaha Beach was completely destroyed by a ferocious gale just two weeks after D-Day, but the second, Port Winston, can still be viewed at Arromanches, a seaside town 10km northeast of Bayeux.

The harbour consists of 146 massive cement caissons towed from England and sunk to form a semicircular breakwater in which floating bridge spans were moored. In the three months after D-Day, 2.5 million men, four million tonnes of equipment and 500,000 vehicles were unloaded there. At low tide you can walk out to many of the caissons. The best view of Port Winston is from the hill, east of town, topped with a statue of the Virgin Mary.

The well-regarded **Musée du Débarquement** (Invasion Museum; ☎ 02 31 22 34 31; place de 6 Juin; adult /child €6/4; 🕙 9am-7pm Jul & Aug, 9.30am-12.30pm & 1.30-5.30pm Sep-Jun), right in the centre of Arromanches, explains the logistics and importance of Port Winston and makes a good first stop before visiting the beaches. The last guided tour (in French, with text in English) leaves 45 minutes before closing time.

Longues-sur-Mer

The massive casemates and 152mm German guns on the coast near Longues-sur-Mer, 6km west of Arromanches, were designed to hit targets some 20km away, which in June 1944 included both Gold Beach (to the east) and Omaha Beach (to the west). Half a century later, the mammoth artillery pieces are still sitting there in their colossal concrete emplacements. (In wartime they were covered with camouflage nets and tufts of grass.)

Parts of an American film about D-Day, *The Longest Day* (1962), were filmed both here and at Pointe du Hoc. On clear days, Bayeux's cathedral, 8km away, is visible to the south.

Omaha & Juno Beaches

The most brutal fighting on D-Day took place 15km northwest of Bayeux along 7km of coastline known as Omaha Beach.

A memorial marks the site of the first US military cemetery on French soil, which contained the bodies of soldiers killed on the beach as they ran inland towards German positions on the nearby ridge. Their remains were later reinterred at the American Military Cemetery at Colleville-sur-Mer or in the USA.

These days, Omaha Beach is lined with holiday cottages and is popular with swimmers and sunbathers. Little evidence of the war remains apart from a single concrete boat used to carry tanks ashore and, 1km further west, the bunkers and munitions

sites of a German fortified point (look for the tall obelisk on the hill).

Dune-lined Juno Beach, 12km east of Arromanches, was stormed by Canadian troops on D-Day. A Cross of Lorraine marks the spot where General Charles de Gaulle came ashore shortly after the landings.

Military Cemeteries

The bodies of the American soldiers who lost their lives during the pivotal Battle of Normandy were either sent back to the USA (if their families so requested) or buried in the **American Military Cemetery** (☎ 02 31 51 62 00; 🕙 9am-6pm mid-Apr–Sep, 9am-5pm Oct–mid-Apr) at Colleville-sur-Mer, 17km northwest of Bayeux. The cemetery contains the graves of 9386American soldiers and a memorial to 1557 others whose remains were never found.

The huge, immaculately tended expanse of lawn, with white crosses and Stars of David set on a hill overlooking Omaha Beach, testifies to the extent of the killings that took place around here in 1944. There's a large colonnaded memorial, a reflecting pond and a chapel for silent meditation. The staff at the welcome centre are highly efficient at finding specific graves.

By tradition, soldiers from the Commonwealth killed in the war were buried near where they fell. As a result, the 18 **Commonwealth Military Cemeteries** in Normandy follow the line of advance of British and Canadian troops.

Many of the gravestones bear epitaphs written by the families of the dead. The Commonwealth cemeteries are always open. There is a **Canadian Military Cemetery** at Bény-sur-Mer, a few kilometres south of Juno Beach and 18km east of Bayeux. See p263 for information on the mostly British Bayeux War Cemetery.

Some 21,000 German soldiers are buried in the **German Military Cemetery** near the village of La Cambe, 25km west of Bayeux. Hundreds of other German dead were buried in the Commonwealth cemeteries, including the one in Bayeux.

Pointe du Hoc Ranger Memorial

At 7.10am on 6 June 1944, 225 US Army Rangers scaled the 30m cliffs at Pointe du Hoc, where the Germans had a battery of huge artillery guns. However, the guns had been transferred elsewhere, but the Americans captured the gun emplacements (two huge circular cement structures) and the German command post (next to the two flag poles), and then fought off German counterattacks for two days. By the time they were relieved on 8 June, 81 of the rangers had been killed and 58 more had been wounded.

Today the site, which France turned over to the US government in 1979, looks much as it did half a century ago. The ground is still pockmarked with 3m bomb craters. Visitors can walk among and inside the German fortifications, but they are warned not to dig: mines and explosive materials may remain below the surface. In the German command post, you can see where the wooden ceilings were charred by American flame-throwers. As you face the sea, Utah Beach, which runs roughly perpendicular to the cliffs, is 14km to the left. Pointe du Hoc, which is 12km west of the American Military Cemetery, is always open. The command post is open the same hours as the cemetery.

Tours

A bus tour is an excellent way to see the D-Day beaches. **Normandy Tours** (☎ 02 31 92 10 70; Hôtel de la Gare, Bayeux; per person €35 incl museum admission) has four-hour tours stopping at Longues-sur-Mer, Arromanches, Omaha Beach, the American Military Cemetery and Pointe du Hoc for €35.

D-Day Tours (☎ 02 31 22 00 08; fax 02 31 51 74 74; www.d-daybeaches.com; BP 48525, 14400 Bayeux; per adult/student €45/40 incl museum admission) are best booked through the Family Home hostel (see p266). They'll collect you from place du Quebec in Bayeux.

The Mémorial museum tours include a combined ticket that includes a visit to the Mémorial – Un Musée pour la Paix (p256) and a half-day tour of the landing beaches for €67.50 (€55.50 for veterans, those under 18 and morning departures). The visit and tour can be done separately or on the same day but must be booked in advance. Tours leave at 1pm daily from mid-January to March and October to December; and at 9am and 2pm daily from April to September.

Getting There & Away
BUS
From Bayeux, bus No 70, run by **Bus Verts** (☎ 0 810 214 214), goes west to the American Military Cemetery at Colleville-sur-Mer and Omaha Beach, and on to Pointe du Hoc and the town of Grandcamp-Maisy. Bus No 74 (No 75 during summer) serves Arromanches, Gold and Juno Beaches, and Courseulles. Bus No 30 will get you from Caen to Bayeux.

During July and August, the Côte de Nacre line goes to Caen via Arromanches, Gold, Juno and Sword Beaches, and Ouistreham; Circuit 44 links Bayeux and Caen via Pointe du Hoc, the American Military Cemetery, Arromanches and Mémorial – Un Musée pour la Paix. You can start the journey in Caen (€17 return), Courseulles (€15 return), Arromanches (€12 return) or Bayeux (€13 return). Prices are for all bus lines.

D-Day Lines (☎ 0 810 214 214; www.busverts14.fr /dday60) runs summer services along the coast from Bayeux, past all the major the beaches to Grand Caen.

Local transport company Bus Verts runs a summer service from Caen, Bayeux and Deauville. The day circuits visit one of the major landing beaches, stopping at points of interest, major cemeteries and museums along the way (discounts are offered for museum entry). Cost is €14 for all of them.

Caen – to Arromanches and Omaha Beach. Leaves from place Courtonne at 9.35am.

Bayeux – two circuits leave from place St-Patrice at 9.42am: one to Arromanches and Omaha Beach, and the other to Utah Beach via St-Mère-Église.

Deauville – to Sword Beach and Ouistreham. Leaves from the station at 9.20am.

CAR
For three or more people, renting a car can be cheaper than a tour. **Lefebvre Car Rental** (☎ 02 31 92 05 96; blvd d'Eindhoven), at the Esso petrol station in Bayeux, charges €78 per day with 200km free (more than enough for a circuit to the beaches along coastal route D514), or €135 for two days with 400km free.

MANCHE

The Manche *département* includes the entire Cotentin Peninsula from Utah Beach to the magnificent Mont St-Michel. The peninsula's northwest corner is especially captivating, with unspoiled stretches of rocky coastline sheltering tranquil bays and villages. Due west lie the Channel Islands of Jersey and Guernsey. The fertile inland areas, crisscrossed with hedgerows, produce an abundance of cattle, dairy products and apples.

Sadly, over the past two decades, the Manche region has become known as Europe's nuclear dump due to its uranium waste treatment plant (Cap de la Hague), its sprawling power plant (Flamanville) and its nuclear submarines construction (at the Cherbourg shipyards).

CHERBOURG

pop 26,750

At the very tip of the Cotentin Peninsula sits Cherbourg, the largest but hardly the most appealing town in this part of Normandy. Transatlantic cargo ships, passenger ferries from Britain, yachts and warships pass in and out of Cherbourg's monumental port. The port took on an enormous strategic importance during the D-Day landings, as it was indispensable in resupplying the invasion forces.

Don't expect to find any of the romance portrayed in Jacques Demy's 1964 classic film *Les Parapluies de Cherbourg* (The Umbrellas of Cherbourg) here.

Orientation

The Bassin du Commerce, a wide central waterway, separates the 'living' half of Cherbourg to the west from the deserted streets to the east. The attractive Avant Port (Outer Harbour) lies to the north.

Information

INTERNET

Forum Espace Culture (☎ 02 33 78 19 30; place Centrale; per 10/30min €1.50/2.35; ☷ 2-7pm Mon, 10am-7pm Tue-Sat) The Internet café is on the upper floor of this cultural centre.

LAUNDRY

Laundrette (62 rue au Blé)

MONEY

Crédit Lyonnais (16 rue Maréchal Foch) ATM.

POST

Main Post Office (1 rue de l'Ancien Quai) It has a Cyberposte and exchanges currency.

TOURIST INFORMATION

Tourist Office (☎ 02 33 93 52 02; www.ot-cherbourg -cotentin.fr in French; 2 quai Alexandre III; ☷ 9am-

6.30pm Mon-Sat, 10am-12.30pm Sun Jul & Aug, 9am-12.30pm & 2-6.30pm Mon-Sat Sep-Jun)
Tourist Office Annexe (☎ 02 33 44 39 92; ferry terminal) Open for ferry arrivals.

Sights & Activities

Upstairs in a cultural centre, **Musée Thomas Henry** (☎ 02 33 23 02 23; 4 rue Vastel; adult/child €2.3/1.10; ☷ 10am-noon & 2-6pm Tue-Sat, 2-6pm Sun & Mon May-Sep, 2-6pm Wed-Sun Oct-Apr) has 200 works by French, Flemish, Italian and other artists. Highlights include *Atalante et Maleagre* by Van Dyck, *Conversion de St-Augustin* by Fra Angelico and 30 paintings by Jean-François Millet.

The new **Cité de la Mer** (☎ 02 33 20 26 26; www .citedelamer.com; Gare Maritime Transatlantique adult/child €13/9.50; ☷ 9.30am-7pm Jun–mid-Sep, 10am-6pm mid-Sep–May), north of the city centre, contains half a million litres of water and is the largest aquarium in Europe. There is also a former nuclear submarine – children under six cannot visit it.

Cherbourg is a big sailing centre. At the entrance to the Port de Plaisance Chantereyne, **Station-Voile Cherbourg-Hague** (☎ 02 33 78 19 29; www.cherbourg-hague-nautisme.com in French) runs half-day beginners sailing courses (€92) and a range of other activities such as kayaking, rowing and paragliding.

Sleeping

Auberge de Jeunesse (☎ 02 33 78 15 15; cherbourg@ fuaj.org; 55 rue de l'Abbaye; dm €16.05) This comfortable, ultramodern hostel opened in 1998 and is still going strong. Take bus No 3 or 5 to the Hôtel de Ville stop.

Quai de Caligny has plenty of mid-range options. There are cheaper places in the backstreets north of the tourist office.

Hôtel Moderna (☎ 02 33 43 05 30; www.moderna -hotel.com; 28 rue de la Marine; r €39-48; P ☒) The comfortable, well-equipped rooms (ask for a port view) are decorated in soft pastels and come with satellite TVs and telephones. A good spot for a stopover before catching the ferry.

Hôtel Renaissance (☎ 02 33 43 23 90; fax 02 33 43 96 10; 4 rue de l'Église; r €49-58) This large hotel has modern facilities and a prime location: smack in the centre of town and right near the ferry terminals. Recently renovated, the rooms have views of the port.

Hôtel La Croix de Malte (☎ 02 33 43 19 16; hotel .croix.malte@wanadoo.fr; 5 rue des Halles; r €35-48) Near

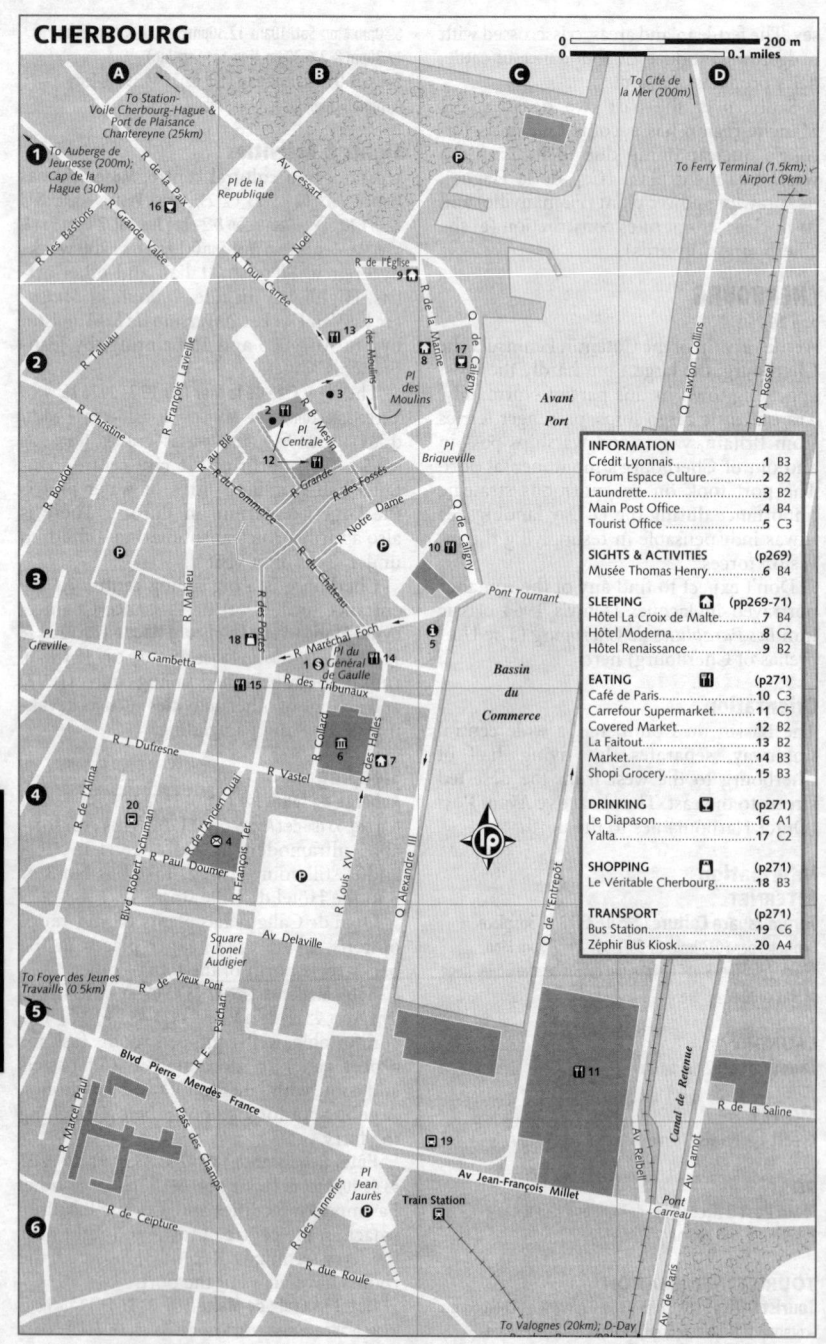

CHERBOURG

0	200 m
0	0.1 miles

To Station-
Voile Cherbourg-Hague &
Port de Plaisance
Chantereyne (25km)

To Cité de
la Mer (200m)

To Auberge de
Jeunesse (200m);
Cap de la
Hague (30km)

To Ferry Terminal (1.5km);
Airport (9km)

Avant
Port

Pl
des
Moulins

Pl
Briqueville

Pont Tournant

Pl
Greville

Bassin
du
Commerce

Pl du
Général
de Gaulle

Square
Lionel
Audigier

To Foyer des Jeunes
Travaille (0.5km)

Blvd Pierre Mendes France

Pl
Jean
Jaurès

Train Station

To Valognes (20km); D-Day

INFORMATION
Crédit Lyonnais........................1 B3
Forum Espace Culture..............2 B2
Laundrette................................3 B2
Main Post Office......................4 B4
Tourist Office...........................5 C3

SIGHTS & ACTIVITIES   (p269)
Musée Thomas Henry..............6 B4

SLEEPING   (pp269-71)
Hôtel La Croix de Malte............7 B4
Hôtel Moderna.........................8 C2
Hôtel Renaissance...................9 B2

EATING   (p271)
Café de Paris..........................10 C3
Carrefour Supermarket............11 C5
Covered Market.......................12 B2
La Faitout...............................13 B2
Market....................................14 B3
Shopi Grocery.........................15 B3

DRINKING   (p271)
Le Diapason............................16 A1
Yalta.......................................17 C2

SHOPPING   (p271)
Le Véritable Cherbourg............18 B3

TRANSPORT   (p271)
Bus Station.............................19 C6
Zéphir Bus Kiosk.....................20 A4

NORMANDY

the Théâtre de Cherbourg (built in 1882), this hotel has well-equipped doubles.

Eating

Rue Tour Carrée, rue de la Paix and around place Centrale offer a wide choice in both cuisine and price.

Café de Paris (☎ 02 33 43 12 36; 40 quai de Caligny; menus €17-21; ☒ closed Mon & dinner Sun Oct-May) It's not the place for a romantic tête-à-tête with the constant crowds and bustle, but the seafood is the freshest in town.

La Faitout (☎ 02 33 04 25 04; 25 rue Tour Carrée; menu €19; ☒ closed Sun & Mon) Of course the other dishes are great, but at this popular and atmospheric restaurant it's all about the show-stopping crusty duck. On weekends it's best to reserve a table.

SELF-CATERING

Cherbourg's market days are Tuesday and Thursday until 5pm at place de Gaulle and the covered place Centrale. The latter operates on Saturday morning. There's **Carrefour supermarket** (Centre Continent quai de l'Entrepôt) and the **Shopi grocery store** (57 rue Gambetta).

Entertainment

Yalta (☎ 02 33 43 02 81; 46 quai de Caligny) This is the sizzling centre of Cherbourg nightlife, attracting sailors, students and sophisticates alike. There are usually two or three jazz, rock or blues concerts a month and occasionally French singers.

Le Diapson (☎ 02 33 01 21 43; 21 rue de la Paix) This place has a little bit of everything – a philosophy night, art exhibits and the occasional concert. There's a good selection of beer and a varied musical programme.

Shopping

The umbrellas of Cherbourg are beautifully made and the best place to buy them is at **Le Véritable Cherbourg** (☎ 02 33 93 66 60; 30 rue des Portes), which has a stunning selection starting at €85.

Getting There & Away

AIR

Cherbourg's airport is 9km east of town at Maupertus-sur-Mer.

BOAT

The three companies with services to either England or Ireland have bureaus in the ferry terminal *(gare maritime)*. Their desks are open two hours before departure and for 30 minutes after the arrival of each ferry.

Brittany Ferries (☎ 02 33 88 44 44) covers the route to Poole in England; **Irish Ferries** (☎ 02 33 23 44 44) sails to Rosslare, Ireland; and **P&O** (☎ 02 33 88 65 70) handles the link to Portsmouth. For further details and schedules see p919.

BUS

The main regional bus line (which stops at the station on av Jean-François Millet) is **STN** (☎ 02 33 44 32 22). It has services to Valognes (€3.90, 30 minutes, six daily) and Barfleur (€4.30, 40 minutes, two daily).

TRAIN

Services from the **train station** (☎ 02 33 57 50 50; ☒ 6am-10pm) include one direct to Paris' Gare St-Lazare (€36.60, 3½ hours, seven daily) and another via Caen (€60, 1½ hours, eight daily). There are also trains to Rennes and Pontorson. Most destinations require a change at either Caen or Lisons.

Getting Around

There's no public transport from the airport into town. A taxi will cost about €20.

City buses are run by **Zéphir** (☎ 08 10 81 00 50; 40 blvd Robert Schuman). Buses leave from either outside the kiosk or at various points around place Jean Jaurès, in front of the train station. Single tickets cost €1 and a carnet of 10 is €8. There's a shuttle-bus service linking the ferry terminal, the town centre and the train station.

Taxis can be called on ☎ 02 33 53 36 38. The trip between the train station and ferry terminal costs about €8. **Station-Voile** (see p269) rents mountain bikes.

COUTANCES

pop 9700

The medieval hilltop town of Coutances, 77km south of Cherbourg, has two major sights: a remarkable cathedral and a stunning landscape garden. Together they justify a day trip from Bayeux, or a pleasant stopover on the road to Mont St-Michel further south.

Orientation & Information

The town centre is compact and confined by blvd Alsace-Lorraine in the northwest and blvd Jeanne Paynel to the east. At the centre of town is the cathedral and town hall. The train and bus stations are about 1km southeast of the town centre.

Post Office (10 rue St-Dominique) Exchanges money and has a Cyberposte terminal.

Société Générale (8 rue Daniel) Bank opposite the tourist office.

Tourist Office (☎ 02 33 19 08 10; tourisme-coutan ces@wanadoo.fr; place Georges Leclerc; ☽ 10am-12.30pm & 2-5.30pm Mon, 10am-12.30pm & 2-6pm Tue, Wed & Fri, 10am-6pm Thu, 10am-12.30pm & 2-5pm Sat)

Sights & Activities

The lofty 13th-century Gothic **Cathédrale de Coutances** (admission free; ☽ 9am-7pm) is one of France's finest, prompting Victor Hugo to call it the prettiest he'd seen after the one at Chartres. Its airy Norman-Romanesque design is enhanced by the use of light-hued limestone. There are several frescoes worth a look, including a 13th-century St George slaying the beast. There are **tours** (adult/student €5/3; ☽ 3.30pm Mon-Fri summer) in English available, which also afford sweeping views from the galleries in the lantern tower.

Opposite place Leclerc lies the splendid **Jardin des Plantes** (☽ 9am-8pm mid-Sep–Oct & Apr-Jun, 9am-11.30pm Jul–mid-Sep, 9am-5pm Oct-Mar), a grand 19th-century landscape garden that blends symmetrical French lines with Italianate terraces, English-style copses, a maze and fountains. Its varied stock of ornamental trees includes giant redwood, cedar of Lebanon, New Zealand beech and Canadian nut. Like the cathedral, the grounds are illuminated on summer nights. During the day it's ideal for picnics.

Sleeping & Eating

Hôtel des Trois Piliers (☎ 02 33 45 01 31; 11 rue des Halles; r €25) Rooms are small but well equipped. The bar downstairs draws a young, noisy crowd and the hotel is often booked out by students during holiday periods.

Hôtel le Parvis (☎ 02 33 45 13 55; fax 02 33 45 68 00; place de la Cathédrale; r €42-67) This is an unremarkable but resolutely comfortable hotel, where all the rooms have en suites and English TV. If you're a die-hard fan of *choucroute*, you might like to try their restaurant, which specialises in the Alsacian dish commonly known as sauerkraut.

Restaurant le Vieux Coutances (☎ 02 33 47 94 78; 55 rue Geoffroy de Montbray; menus €10.70-32;

☽ closed Mon) This former post office is a small, intimate Norman eatery with excellent fish or meat *menus*. We think this is the best address in town.

The market is held on Thursday morning. Look for the delicious local Coutances cheese with its creamy centre.

Getting There & Away

The SNCF runs buses to Granville (€7.40, 30 minutes, up to five daily). In July and August there are buses to the beaches (20 minutes, three daily). Regular train services include Cherbourg (€15.30, two hours, six daily), Caen (€13.50, 1½ hours, six daily) and Paris' Gare du Nord (€34.70, four hours, twice daily).

MONT ST-MICHEL
pop 42

It's difficult not to be impressed with your first sighting of Mont St-Michel. Covering the summit is the massive abbey, a soaring ensemble of buildings in a hotchpotch of architectural styles. The abbey (80m above the sea) is topped by a slender spire with a gilded copper statue of Michael the Archangel slaying a dragon. Around the base are the ancient ramparts and a jumble of buildings that house the handful of true residents. At night the whole structure is brilliantly illuminated.

Mont St-Michel's fame derives equally from the bay's extraordinary tides. Depending on the gravitational pull of the moon and, to a lesser extent, the sun, the difference between low and high tides can reach 15m. The Mont either looks out onto bare sand stretching many kilometres into the distance or, at high tide (only about six hours later), the same expanse under water. However, the Mont and its causeway are completely surrounded by the sea only at the highest of tides, which occur at seasonal equinoxes.

Most people will stay at Pontorson, the town opposite.

History

According to Celtic mythology, Mont St-Michel was one of the sea tombs to which the souls of the dead were sent. In 708 the saint appeared to Bishop Aubert of Avranches and told him to build a devotional chapel at the summit. In 966, Richard I, duke of Normandy, gave Mont St-Michel to the Benedictines, who turned it into an important centre of learning and, in the 11th century, into something of an ecclesiastical fortress, with a military garrison at the disposal of the abbot and the king.

In the 15th century, during the Hundred Years' War, the English blockaded and besieged Mont St-Michel three times. The fortified abbey withstood these assaults; it was the only place in western and northern France not to fall into English hands. After the Revolution, Mont St-Michel was turned into a prison. In 1966 the abbey was symbolically returned to the Benedictines as part of the celebrations marking its millennium. Mont St-Michel and the surrounding bay became a Unesco World Heritage Site in 1979.

Orientation

There is only one opening in the ramparts, Porte de l'Avancée, immediately to the left as you walk down the causeway. The Mont's single street – Grande Rue – is lined with restaurants, a few hotels, souvenir shops and entrances to some rather tacky exhibits in the crypts below. There are several large car parks (€4 per day) close to the Mont.

Pontorson (population 4200), the nearest town to Mont St-Michel, is 9km south and the base for most travellers. Route D976 from Mont St-Michel runs right into Pontorson's main thoroughfare, rue du Couësnon.

Information

MONEY

There is an ATM next to the tourist office in Mont St-Michel.

CIN bank (98 rue du Couësnon, Pontorson; ⊙ Tue-Sat) Better exchange rates than the Mont.

Société Générale ATM just inside the Porte de l'Avancée.

POST

Pontorson Post Office (place de l'Hôtel de Ville)
Mont St-Michel Post Office (Grande Rue)

TOURIST INFORMATION

Mont St-Michel Tourist Office (☎ 02 33 60 14 30; www.ot-montsaintmichel.com; ⊙ 9am-7pm Jul & Aug, 9am-noon & 2-5.30pm Sep-Jun) Up the stairs to the left as you enter Porte de l'Avancée. If you're interested in what the tides will be doing, look for the table of tides *(horaire des marées)* posted outside. A detailed map of the Mont is available at the tourist office for €3.50.

Pontorson Tourist Office (☎ 02 33 60 20 65; fax 02 33 60 85 67; mont.st.michel.pontorson@wanadoo.fr; place

de l'Église; ⊙ 9am-noon & 2-7pm Mon-Fri, 10am-noon & 3-6pm Sat, 10am-noon Sun Apr-Sep, 9am-noon & 2-6pm Mon-Fri, 10am-noon & 3-6pm Sat Oct-Mar) Friendly staff and heaps of information about local walks, tours and events.

Walking Tour

When the tide is out, you can walk all the way around Mont St-Michel, a distance of about 1km. Straying too far from the Mont could be risky: you might get stuck in wet sand – from which Norman soldiers are depicted being rescued in one scene of the Bayeux Tapestry.

Abbaye du Mont St-Michel

The Mont's major attraction is the renowned **abbey** (☎ 02 33 89 80 00; adult/18-25/under 18 incl 1hr guided tour €7/4.50/free; ⊙ 9am-7pm May-Sep, 9.30am-6pm Oct-Apr). To reach it, walk to the top of the Grande Rue and then climb the stairway. From Monday to Saturday between mid-May and September, there are self-paced illuminated night-time visits of Mont St-Michel complete with music from 9pm to midnight.

Most rooms can be visited without a guide, but it's worthwhile taking the tour included in the ticket price. One-hour tours in English depart three to eight times daily (the last leaves about 1½ hours before closing). It is also possible to rent an audioguide with recorded commentary (€4) if you miss the tour.

The **Église Abbatiale** (Abbey Church) was built at the rocky tip of the mountain cone. The transept rests on solid rock while the nave, choir and transept arms are supported by the massive rooms below. The church is famous for its mixture of architectural styles: the nave and south transept (11th and 12th centuries) are Norman Romanesque, while the choir (late 15th century) is Flamboyant Gothic. Mass is at 12.15pm from Tuesday to Sunday.

The buildings on the northern side of the Mont are known as **La Merveille** (literally 'the marvel'). The famous **cloître** (cloister) is surrounded by a double row of delicately carved arches resting on granite pillars. The early-13th-century **réfectoire** (dining hall) is illuminated by a wall of recessed windows – remarkable, given that the sheer drop precluded the use of flying buttresses – which diffuses the light beautifully. The Gothic

NORMANDY

Salle des Hôtes (Guest Hall), dating from 1213, has two giant fireplaces. Watch out for the **promenoire** (ambulatory), with one of the oldest ribbed vaulted ceilings in Europe, and **La Chapelle de Notre Dame sous Terre** (Underground Chapel of Our Lady), one of the earliest rooms built in the abbey and rediscovered in 1903.

The masonry used to build the abbey was brought to the Mont by boat and pulled up the hillside using ropes. What looks like a treadmill for gargantuan gerbils was in fact powered in the 19th century by half a dozen prisoners who, by turning the wheel, hoisted the supply sledge up the side of the abbey.

Église Notre Dame de Pontorson

Though no match for its dramatic sister to the north, the 12th-century Church of Our Lady in Pontorson is a good example of the Norman Romanesque style of architecture. To the left of the altar is a 15th-century relief of Christ's Passion, which was mutilated during the Religious Wars and again during the Revolution.

Grande Rue

Of the several so-called **museums** (adult/child per museum €4/2) along the street, two might merit a visit. Children may find the **Archéoscope**, a smart 20-minute multimedia history of the Mont with lights, video and even smoke, as exciting as the actual bricks and mortar. The **Musée de la Mer et de l'Écologie** is informative about Mont St-Michel's complex tidal patterns and merits a visit if model ships excite you.

Sleeping

There are eight hotels within the walls of Mont St-Michel and several more at the end of the causeway. All tend to be fully booked in summer, often by large coach parties. We recommend that you beat a retreat further afield. The following hotels are in Pontorson:

Centre Duguesclin (☎ /fax 02 33 60 18 65; aj@ville-pontorson.fr; blvd du Général Patton; r per person €7.30; ☙ year-round) About 1km west of the train station, this modern, newly renovated hostel offers four- to six-bed rooms and kitchen facilities. The hostel closes from 10am to 6pm, but there's no curfew. It is in an old three-storey stone building opposite No 26.

Hôtel de Bretagne (☎ 02 33 60 10 55; www.le bretagnepontorson.com; 59 rue du Couësnon; s €35-48, d €39-64) Rooms in this attractive mid-range option are brighter than its rather dreary reception area. Its quite formal **restaurant** offers excellent service and food, from the two-course *formule* (€11) to a gourmet *menu* (€38).

Hôtel Montgomery (☎ 02 33 60 00 09; www.hotel-montgomery.com; 13 rue du Couësnon; r €77-225; (P)) A lovely 16th-century mansion with a vine-covered Renaissance façade. Each room is different and has been decorated with period furnishings and equipped with modern amenities. The restaurant is excellent.

CAMPING

Camping Haliotis (☎ 02 33 68 11 59; www.camping-haliotis-mont-saint-michel.com in French; adult/site €4.20/3.50; ☙ Apr-Oct; 🏊) Just off blvd Général Patton, this complex has a heated pool.

Eating
MONT ST-MICHEL

Tourist restaurants around the base of the Mont have lovely views, but although *menus* start at about €12 the quality can be mediocre. Cosy **Crêperie La Sirène** (☎ 02 33 60 08 60; galettes €6.40-8.20) offers reasonable value.

La Mère Poulard (☎ 02 33 89 68 68; Grande Rue; lunch menus €29-39, dinner menus €45-55; ☙ 11am-10pm) Established in 1888, this tourist institution turns out its famous *omelettes à la Mère Poulard* (soufflé omelettes cooked in a wood-fired oven) at astronomical prices. Autographed photos of visiting film stars and politicians adorn the walls. The choices also include seafood, free-range chicken and *agneau pré-salé* (lamb from animals that have grazed the salt meadows in the surrounding area).

PONTORSON

You'll find a few cheap, unexceptional eateries along main rue du Couësnon but if you're looking for anything special, choose a hotel restaurant.

In addition to the eateries listed above, the **Hôtel La Tour Brette** (☎ 02 33 60 10 69; latourbrette@wanadoo.fr; 8 rue du Couësnon) and **Hôtel La Cave** (☎ 02 33 60 11 35; www.hotel-la-cave.com; 37 rue Libération) both have lovely restaurants with traditional French *menus* for €12 to €20.

SELF-CATERING
The nearest supermarket is across from the Hôtel Mercure on the causeway, 2km from the Mont. In Pontorson, there's the **8 à Huit** (5 rue du Couësnon).

Getting There & Away
BUS
Courriers Bretons (☎ 02 33 60 11 43) runs between Pontorson and Mont St-Michel (€1.70, 15 minutes, seven to 10 daily) and also to/from St-Malo (€7.80, one hour).

TRAIN
Services from Pontorson include Caen (via Folligny; €19.20, 2¼ hours, two daily), Rennes (via Dol; €10.50, 50 minutes, two daily) and Cherbourg (€20.70, 2½ hours, two daily). To get to Pontorson, from Paris, take the train to Caen (from Gare St-Lazare), to Rennes (from Gare Montparnasse), or travel directly to Pontorson via Folligny (from Gare Montparnasse; €35.60).

Getting Around
You can rent bicycles from **Camping Haliotis** (☎ 02 33 68 11 59; off blvd Général Patton) and **VMPS** (☎ 02 33 60 28 76, 06 86 90 95 01). VMPS delivers to your hotel or camp site. For a taxi, call ☎ 02 33 60 33 23.

ALENÇON
pop 30,400

In the far south of Normandy, on the edge of the Normandie-Maine nature reserve, lies the former lace-making hub of Alençon. The town exudes an aura of genteel wealth – harking back to its days as a Norman tax-collecting centre in the 17th century – and makes a nice breather en route to/from Paris, 193km to the south.

Orientation
The old town and its sights are about 1.5km southwest of the train station, via av du Président Wilson and rue St-Blaise. The River Sarthe snakes past the old quarter to the south.

Information
Crédit Mutuel (89bis rue aux Sieurs) ATM.
Espace Internet (☎ 02 33 32 40 33; 6-8 rue des Filles Notre Dame; ✆ 8.30am-7pm Mon-Sat) Internet access.
Laundrette (5 rue du Collège)

Post Office (16 rue du Jeudi) It has Cyberposte and exchanges currency.
Tourist Office (☎ 02 33 80 66 33; alencon.tourisme@ wanadoo.fr; place La Magdelaine; ✆ 9.30am-6pm Mon-Sat, 10am-12.30pm & 3-5.30pm Sun Jul & Aug, 9.30am-noon & 2-6.30pm Mon-Sat Sep-Jun) In the turreted Maison d'Ozé, this tourist office will book accommodation for free. Ask for the walking tour brochure *Alençon Foot*.

Sights
The old town, especially along the **Grande Rue**, is full of atmospheric Second Empire houses and wrought-iron balconies dating from the 18th century. To the southeast looms the crowned turret of the **Château des Ducs**, which was used by the Nazis as a prison during WWII (closed to the public).

Occupying an old Jesuit schoolhouse, the **Musée des Beaux-Arts et de la Dentelle** (☎ 02 33 32 40 07; 12 rue Charles Aveline; adult/child €2.90/2.40; ✆ 10am-noon & 2-6pm Jul & Aug, Tue-Sun Sep-Jun) has a so-so collection of Flemish, Dutch and French artworks from the 17th to 19th centuries and an exhaustive (some might say exhausting) exhibit on the history of lace-making. There's also an unexpected section of Cambodian artefacts – including buddhas, spears and tiger skulls – donated by a former (French) governor of Cambodia.

The **Église Notre Dame** (Grande Rue; ✆ 8.30am-noon & 2-5.30pm) has a stunning Flamboyant Gothic portal from the 16th century and some superb stained glass in the chapel where St Theresa was baptised. The house in which St Theresa was born is next door.

The **Musée Leclerc** (☎ 02 33 26 27 26; 33 rue du Pont Neuf; adult/child €2.25/1.20; ✆ 10am-noon & 2-6pm Apr-Sep, 10.30am-noon & 2-5.30pm Oct-Mar) details the history of Alençon during WWII, including some fascinating wartime photos. The town was liberated in August 1944 by General Leclerc, whose statue stands guard out front.

Sleeping & Eating
Hôtel Le Grand St-Michel (☎ 02 33 26 04 77; fax 02 33 26 71 82; 7 rue du Temple; r with washbasin/bathroom €32/43; Ⓟ) In the centre of old Alençon and on a quiet street, this place has the air of a traditional country house. The rooms are comfortable in a casual, thrown-together way.

Hôtel-Restaurant Le Grand Cerf (☎ 02 33 26 00 51; 21 rue St-Blaise; s/d €51/59; Ⓟ ✗ ▢) This stately old building on the edge of the old

NORMANDY

town offers more luxury, with plush rooms and a delightfully traditional décor. It has a garden patio and a good **restaurant** (menus from €13.50; ⊗ closed Sat & Sun).

Camping Municipal (☎ 02 33 26 34 95; 69 rue de Guéramé; adult/site €2.10/2.45) Southwest of town on the Sarthe, this well-outfitted location has only 87 sites.

Restaurant Au Petit Vatel (☎ 02 33 26 23 78; 72 place du Commandant-Desmeulles; menus €18.50-69; ⊗ closed Wed & dinner Sun) Recently taken over by new owners, this well-known restaurant serves refined cuisine in an equally refined dining room. Go on, try the *beignet de Camembert* (Camembert fritters).

Getting There & Around

STAO (☎ 02 33 26 06 35) buses connects Alençon with Sées (€4.60, 20 minutes, once daily) and Mortagne-au-Perche (€6.10, one hour, four daily).

From Alençon there are frequent train services to Gare Montparnasse in Paris (€47.20, 1¾ hours), Caen (€14.50, 1¾ hours), Pontorson (€30.40, four hours) and Le Mans (€8.10, 45 minutes), among other destinations.

Altobus (☎ 08 00 50 02 29) has three routes that serve the city including one, Line A, which runs from the train station to the town centre.

Brittany

CONTENTS

Brittany stands slightly aloof from the rest of France, set apart by its Celtic roots and a stubborn independent streak. Even on the map it seems to want to break away – a granite prow yearning westwards into the Atlantic, reaching towards Canada, the Caribbean and Cape Horn.

Much of the region's charm lies in its Celtic culture and intimate relationship with the sea. Brittany's intricately fretted shoreline – mirrored in the Gothic tracery of its cathedrals and the patterns of its traditional lace headdresses – has some of France's finest coastal scenery, while its music and cultural festivals are among the liveliest and most colourful in Europe.

Although for centuries the ocean has been a hard taskmaster for Breton sailors, for today's visitor it is both playground and larder. Brittany boasts dozens of classic seaside resorts, such as Dinard, Perros-Guirec and Bénodet, and offers some of the best yachting, windsurfing, sea-kayaking and coastal hiking in France. When it's time to eat, the harvest of the sea – from mussels and oysters to lobster and sea bass – is on the menu. Washed down, of course, with a glass of Breton cider or a crisp Muscadet wine from the vineyards of Nantes, to the south.

The Celtic culture planted in Brittany 1500 years ago put down strong roots, which neither union with France nor Revolution was able to rip out. Bretons care for and cherish their past. You'll sense it in the serried megaliths of Carnac, the stone calvaries of Finistère and the upholding of the ancient traditions of *pardons* (religious pilgrimages). You see it in the old wooden sailing boats, redolent of tar and turpentine, straining at their moorings in Breton harbours, and hear it in the strident wail of traditional musical instruments, the *biniou* and *bombarde*.

It's a past leavened with the spice of myth and legend. The region abounds with tales of lost, sunken cities; and of Ankou (Death) prowling darkened villages in his creaking, wooden cart.

Brittany may show a French face to the world but it possesses a Celtic soul all its own.

HIGHLIGHTS

- Walk the rugged coastline of the **Île d'Ouessant** (p298) or another of Brittany's seaswept islands
- Ponder the meaning of Carnac's **megaliths** (p311)
- Cycle forest trails in the **Forêt de Paimpont** (p318)
- Wander the streets of St-Malo's old **walled city** (p281)
- Cruise up the River Rance to the medieval city of **Dinan** (p289)
- Play the sailor on the traditional wooden boats in Douarnenez's vast **Musée du Bateau** (p302)
- Sprawl on Dinard's swanky **beach** (p286)
- Dance till you drop at Lorient's **Festival Interceltique** (p309)

★ Île d'Ouessant   Dinard ★★ St-Malo
                           ★ Dinan
★ Douarnenez
                           ★ Forêt de Paimpont
Lorient ★
      Carnac ★

POPULATION: 2,905,000	AREA: 27,210 SQ KM

BRITTANY

History

Brittany's earliest known inhabitants were Neolithic tribes whose menhirs and dolmens still poke skywards (see p311). In the 6th century BC, the first wave of Celts swept in and named their new homeland 'Armor', the land beside the sea. In 56 BC Julius Caesar conquered the region, which remained in Roman hands until the 5th century AD.

After the Romans withdrew, a second wave of Celts – driven from what is now Britain and Ireland by the Anglo-Saxon invasions – crossed the Channel and settled in Brittany. They brought with them Christianity, spread by Celtic missionaries, after whom many Breton towns, such as St-Malo and St-Brieuc, were named.

In the 9th century, Brittany's national hero, Nominoë, revolted against French rule. But, sandwiched geographically between two more powerful kingdoms, the duchy of Brittany was contested by both France and England throughout the Middle Ages until, after a series of strategic royal weddings, the region became part of France in 1532.

Over the centuries, Brittany has retained a separate regional identity. To this day, some Bretons retain the hope that their region might one day regain its independence.

KING ARTHUR

Breton culture abounds in mysterious legends and the most famous of all is that of King Arthur, which spread to England in the Middle Ages via Celtic Cornwall. In Brittany many sites still recall Arthur, Lancelot his favourite knight, Merlin the magician and the fairies Vivian and Morgan le Fay.

Île Grande and Île d'Aval, close to Perros-Guirec, both lay claim to be the island of Avalon where, legend says, Arthur is buried. Deep in the Forêt d'Huelgoat, one of the last vestiges of the old, vast inland forest, is where Arthur searched in vain for the Holy Grail. Merlin's mistress, Vivian (the mysterious Lady of the Lake), prowled the Forêt de Paimpont (or Brocéliande), southwest of Rennes; deep within it, the wizard's spring of eternal youth still trickles. Vannes, for its part, was the capital of the kingdom ruled by Ban, Lancelot's father, while Nantes, in many versions of the myth, is where King Arthur held court.

The latest violent manifestation of Breton nationalism was in April 2000, when a bomb attack on a McDonald's fast-food restaurant in Quévert, near Dinan, left one person dead. Despite this isolated, tragic event, the overwhelming body of nationalist sentiment in Brittany is entirely peaceful.

Most Bretons retain a strong bond with their native culture without feeling the need to belong to any separatist movement. Nowadays, there's a drive for cultural and linguistic renewal – and a consciousness of Brittany's place within a wider Celtic culture that embraces Ireland, Wales, Scotland, Cornwall and Galicia in Spain, with all of whom stronger ties have been established.

Climate

Brittany's coast is washed by the Gulf Stream, a warm ocean current flowing from the Gulf of Mexico towards northwest Europe. As a result, the region enjoys a gentle climate with warm, but never too warm, summers and mild winters. Even though Brittany records France's highest annual rainfall, it rarely pours for many consecutive days, even during the wettest months (January to May).

The Culture

Breton customs and language are more evident in Basse Bretagne (lower Brittany), the western half of the peninsula, and particularly in Cornouaille, its southwestern tip. Haute Bretagne (upper Brittany), the eastern half (which includes St-Malo), has retained little of its traditional way of life.

You might be lucky enough to see traditional costumes, including the tall lace headdresses of the women, at a *fest-noz* (night-time dance and music fiesta) or *pardon*. Brittany's two major cultural festivals are Quimper's Festival de Cornouaille in late July and Lorient's Festival Interceltique in early August.

Language

Breton (Breiz) is a Celtic language related to Cornish and Welsh and, more distantly, to Irish and Scottish Gaelic. You might well hear Breton in western Brittany (especially in Cornouaille), where as many as 600,000 people have some degree of fluency. However, as with so many minority languages, the number of Breton-speaking households is diminishing.

BRITTANY

50 km
25 miles

CALVADOS
ORNE
MANCHE
MAYENNE
MAINE-ET-LOIRE
ILLE-ET-VILAINE
LOIRE-ATLANTIQUE
CÔTES D'ARMOR
FINISTÈRE
MORBIHAN
BRITTANY
CORNOUAILLE

To Caen (32km)
To Domfront (32km)
To Le Mans (100km)

Vire
Avranches
Mont St-Michel
Fougères
Vitré
Laval
Château-Gontier
Ancenis
Granville
Pontorson
Rennes
Châteaubriant
Nantes
Îles Chausey
Île des Landes
Cancale
Pointe du Grouin
St-Malo
Dinard
St-Briac
St-Cast
Dinan
Redon
St-Nazaire
Côte d'Émeraude
Cap Fréhel
St-Lunaire
Dol-de-Bretagne
Forêt de Paimpont
La Baule
Golfe de Saint Malo
Le Val-André
Lamballe
Ploërmel
Josselin
Vilaine
Le Croisic
Île de Bréhat
Binic
St-Brieuc
Loudéac
Etang au Duc
Vannes
Le Palais
Côte de Granite Rose
Paimpol
Guingamp
Pontivy
Lac de Guerlédan
Auray
Carnac
Locmariaquer
Port Navalo
Île d'Houat
Ploumanac'h
Perros-Guirec
Trégastel-Plage
Trébeurden
Lannion
Plouha
Carhaix-Plouguer
Plouharnel
Quiberon
Gulf of Morbihan
Île de Hoëdic
Belle Île
Bird Sanctuary
Roscoff
Île de Batz
Morlaix
St-Thégonnec
Guimiliau
Huelgoat
Montagnes Noires
Lorient
Île de Groix
St-Pol-de-Léon
Lesneven
Landivisiau
Lampaul-Guimiliau
Landerneau
Sizun
Menez Hom
Parc d'Armorique
Monts d'Arrée
Quimperlé
Pont-Aven
Port-Manec'h
Île de Glénan
Île d'Ouessant
Île Molène
Le Conquet
Brest
Plougastel
Crozon
Châteaulin
Concarneau
Bénodet
Lampaul
Presqu'île de Crozon
Camaret-sur-Mer
Lochrist
Douarnenez
Quimper
Pont-l'Abbé
Pointe du Raz
Audierne
St-Guénolé
Île de Sein
ATLANTIC OCEAN
Presqu'île de Crozon

To Plymouth, Rosslare (UK); Cork (Ireland)
To The Channel Islands; Plymouth; Poole (UK)

N12
N24
N137
N157
N164
N165

Loire
Oust
Nantes-Brest

THE GWENN HA DU: BRITTANY'S FLAG

Wherever you go in Brittany, you'll see the distinctive monochrome Breton flag, the *Gwenn ha Du* (White and Black). Invented in 1923, it took its inspiration from the USA's stars and stripes. The nine horizontal stripes – five black and four white – represent the five ancient bishoprics of Haute Bretagne (Upper Brittany) and the four of Basse Bretagne (Lower Brittany). In the upper left corner is a field of stylised ermines, the device on the coat of arms of the former duchy of Brittany.

Legend has it that Anne de Bretagne adopted the ermine as a symbol of Brittany. The duchess was watching an ermine (a stoat in its white winter coat) being chased by hunters, when the tiny animal stopped and accepted death rather than cross a patch of muddy ground and stain its pure white fur. The motto of the duchy of Brittany was *'Plutôt la mort que la souillure'* – 'Rather death than the stain (of dishonour)'.

After the Revolution, the new government made a concerted effort to suppress the Breton language and replace it with French. Indeed, no more than 25 years ago, if school children spoke Breton in class they might have been punished. Things have changed, however, and nowadays some 20 privately subsidised schools – including several at the secondary level – teach in Breton.

Activities

On the coast, even quite small resorts offer the opportunity for sailing, windsurfing, canoeing and kayaking – and scuba diving around the rocky archipelagos is among the best in France.

A leisurely way to tour the region is by canal boat along the waterways from Brest or Dinan to Nantes. For information on boats, moorings and locks contact the **Service de la Navigation** (in Rennes ☎ 02 99 59 20 60, in Lorient ☎ 02 97 64 85 20).

Getting There & Around

Ferries link St-Malo with the Channel Islands and the English ports of Portsmouth, Poole and Weymouth. From Roscoff, there are ferries to Plymouth (UK) and Cork (Ireland).

Brittany's major towns and cities are linked by rail but routes leave the interior poorly served. The bus network is extensive, but services are often infrequent.

It's well worth renting a car or motorbike or bringing your own, especially if you're keen on exploring out-of-the-way destinations. Brittany – especially Cornouaille and the interior – is an excellent area for cycling, and bike-rental places are never hard to find.

NORTH COAST

The central swathe of Brittany's north coast is shared between the *départements* of Ille-et-Vilaine and Côtes d'Armor. It's as wild or tame, as family-friendly or look-at-me cool as you care to make it.

All along the Côte d'Émeraude (Emerald Coast), which transcends both *départements,* are promontories with spectacular sea views, emerald-green shallows and aquamarine deeps. The long, broad, safe strands of golden sand are backed by small, well-resourced resorts, each ideal for a family holiday. Smarter and more substantial are exclusive Perros-Guirec and its rival, Dinard, chic as they come with its casino and distinctive striped bathing tents.

Eastwards, across the Rance Estuary (do take the scenic passenger ferry across its mouth if you're travelling light) is St-Malo, with the ramparts and narrow streets of Intra-Muros, its old quarter, faithfully reconstructed after the devastation of WWII. Nearby, Cancale, famous for its oyster beds, is a must for all serious seafood scoffers.

Allow a full day too to venture inland and visit the charming walled medieval city of Dinan, left behind a bit by the tide of coastal development but still hugely – excessively in high summer – popular with day visitors.

ST-MALO

pop 52,700

The port of St-Malo is one of Brittany's most popular tourist destinations. Squatting at the mouth of the River Rance, it's famed for its walled city, nearby beaches – and one of the world's highest tidal ranges.

BRITTANY

BRITTANY

ST-MALO & ST-SERVAN

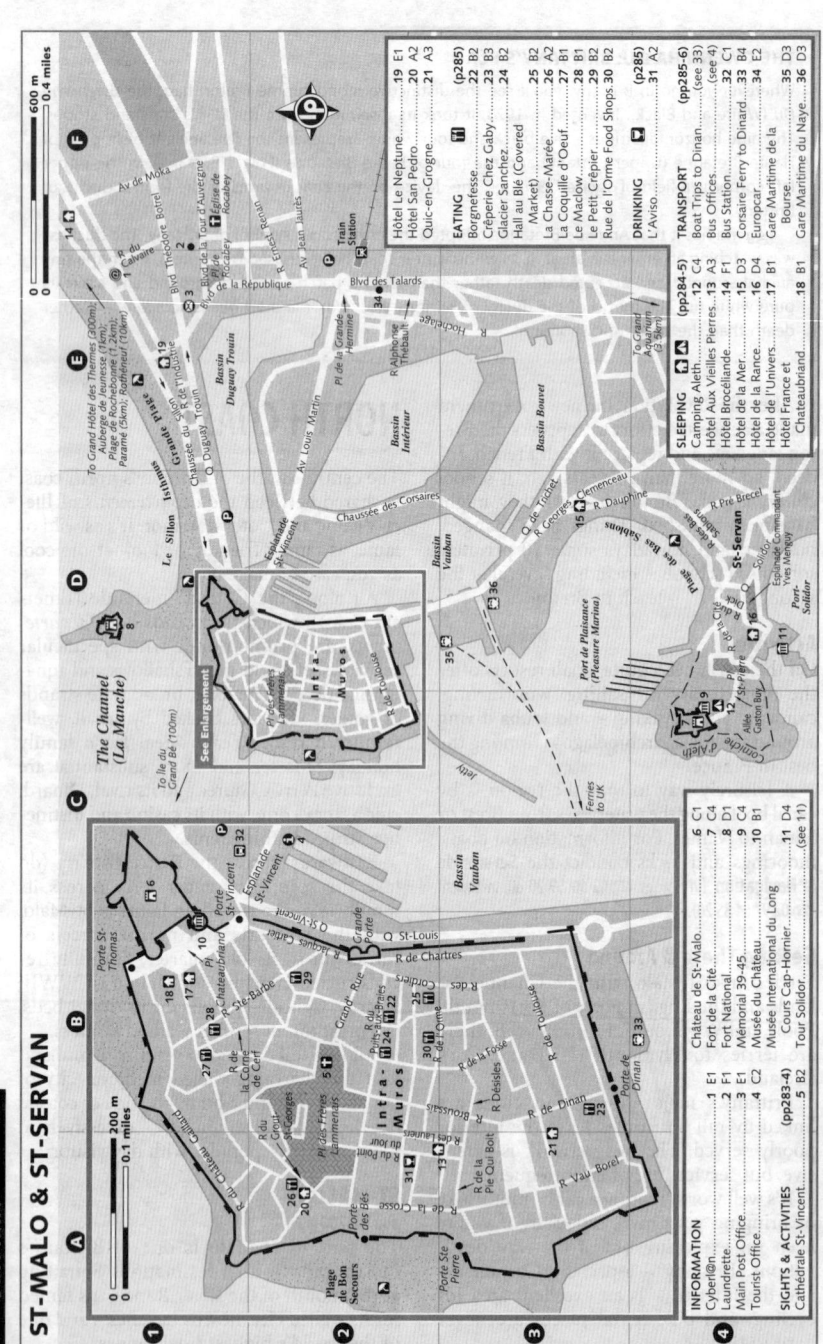

INFORMATION	**(pp283-4)**	
Cyber@n........................1	E1	
Laundrette........................2	F1	
Main Post Office........................3	E1	
Tourist Office........................4	C2	
SIGHTS & ACTIVITIES		
Cathédrale St-Vincent........................5	B2	
Château de St-Malo........................6	C1	
Fort de la Cité........................7	C4	
Fort National........................8	D1	
Mémorial 39-45........................9	C4	
Musée du Château........................10	B1	
Musée International du Long		
Cours Cap-Hornier........................11	D4	
Tour Solidor........................(see 11)		

SLEEPING	**(pp284-5)**	
Camping Aleth........................12	C4	
Hôtel Aux Vieilles Pierres........................13	A3	
Hôtel Brocéliande........................14	F1	
Hôtel de la Mer........................15	D3	
Hôtel de la Rance........................16	D4	
Hôtel de l'Univers........................17	B1	
Hôtel France et		
Chateaubriand........................18	B1	

Hôtel Le Neptune........................19	E1	
Hôtel San Pedro........................20	A2	
Quic-en-Grogne........................21	A3	
EATING	**(p285)**	
Borgnefesse........................22	B2	
Crêperie Chez Gaby........................23	B3	
Glacier Sanchez........................24	B2	
Hall au Blé (Covered		
Market)........................25	B2	
La Chasse-Marée........................26	A2	
La Coquille d'Oeuf........................27	B1	
Le Maclow........................28	B1	
Le Petit Crêpier........................29	B2	
Rue de l'Orme Food Shops........................30	B2	
DRINKING	**(p285)**	
L'Aviso........................31	A2	

TRANSPORT	**(pp285-6)**	
Boat Trips to Dinan........................(see 33)		
Bus Offices........................(see 4)		
Bus Station........................32	C1	
Corsaire Ferry to Dinard........................33	B4	
Europcar........................34	E2	
Gare Maritime de la		
Bourse........................35	D3	
Gare Maritime du Naye........................36	D3	

St-Malo was a key port during the 17th and 18th centuries, serving as a base for both merchant ships and government-sanctioned pirates, known euphemistically as privateers. Although fortification began in the 12th century, the most imposing military architecture dates from the 17th and 18th centuries, when the English, the favourite targets of Malouin privateers, posed a constant threat.

Orientation

The St-Malo conurbation consists of the harbour towns of St-Malo and St-Servan plus the modern suburbs of Paramé and Rothéneuf to the east. The old walled city of St-Malo is known as Intra-Muros ('within the walls') or Ville Close. From the train station, it's a 15-minute walk westwards along av Louis Martin.

Information

Cyberl@n (☎ 02 99 56 07 78; 68 chaussée de Sillon; per hr €4; 🕑 noon-1am Mon-Sat, 3pm-1am Sun) Internet access.

Laundrette (25 blvd de la Tour d'Auvergne; 🕑 7.30am-9pm)

Main Post Office (1 blvd de la Tour d'Auvergne)

Tourist Office (☎ 02 99 56 64 48; www.saint-malo -tourisme.com; esplanade St-Vincent; 🕑 9am-7.30pm Mon-Sat, 10am-6pm Sun Jul & Aug, 9am-12.30pm & 1.30-6pm or 6.30pm Mon-Sat Sep-Jun, 10am-12.30pm & 2.30-6pm Sun Easter-Jun & Sep)

Sights & Activities

OLD CITY

The old walled city was originally an island, which became linked to the mainland by the sandy isthmus of Le Sillon in the 13th century.

During August 1944, the battle to drive German forces out of St-Malo destroyed around 80% of it. The main historical monuments were faithfully reconstructed, while the rest of the area was rebuilt in the style of the 17th and 18th centuries.

Constructed between the 12th and 18th centuries, the town's centrepiece, **Cathédrale St-Vincent** (place Jean de Châtillon; 🕑 9.30am-6pm), was severely damaged by the 1944 bombing. Highlights are the striking modern bronze altar and the glowing, harlequin colours of the modern stained glass in the traceried windows of the east wall.

If the narrow streets become claustrophobic, escape to the **ramparts**, constructed

at the end of the 17th century under the great military architect Vauban. You can make a complete circuit (around 2km); there's free access at several places, including all the main city gates.

From their northern stretch, you can look across to the remains of **Fort National** (admission free; 🕑 Jun-Sep). Accessible only at low tide, this fort, also Vauban-designed, was long used as a prison. Within **Château de St-Malo**, built by the dukes of Brittany in the 15th and 16th centuries, is the **Musée du Château** (☎ 02 99 40 71 57; adult/child €4.80/2.40; 🕑 10am-noon & 2-6pm Apr-Sep, Tue-Sun Oct-Mar). Covering the history of the city and the St-Malo region, the museum's most interesting exhibits are in the Tour Générale – the history of cod fishing on the Grand Banks on the ground floor and the photos of St-Malo after WWII.

> ### COMBINED TICKET
>
> A combined ticket (adult/child €11.75/5.90) gives access to St-Malo's three major monuments: the Musée du Château de St-Malo, Musée International du Long Cours Cap-Hornier and Mémorial 39-45. It can be purchased at any of the three participating museums and is valid for the duration of your stay in St-Malo.

ÎLE DU GRAND BÉ

You can walk to the rocky islet of Île du Grand Bé, where the great 18th-century writer Chateaubriand is buried, via the Porte des Bés. Once the tide rushes in, the causeway remains impassable for about six hours so check tide times with the tourist office.

ST-SERVAN

Fort de la Cité was constructed in the mid-18th century and used as a German base during WWII. One of the bunkers now houses **Mémorial 39-45** (☎ 02 99 82 41 74; adult/child €4.8/ 2.40; guided visits 2pm, 3.15pm & 4.30pm Tue-Sun Apr-Jun & Sep-Mar, 6 times daily Jul & Aug), which depicts St-Malo's violent WWII history and liberation and includes a 45-minute film in French.

Musée International du Long Cours Cap-Hornier (Museum of the Cape Horn Route; ☎ 02 99 40 71 58; adult/ child €4.8/2.40; 🕑 10am-noon & 2-6pm Apr-Sep, Tue-Sun Oct-Mar) is in the 14th-century Tour Solidor. Presenting the life of the hardy sailors who

BRITTANY

followed the Cape Horn route, it offers superb views from the top of the tower.

AQUARIUM

The **Grand Aquarium** (☎ 02 99 21 19 00; av Général Patton; adult/child €13/9.50; ☎ at least 10am-6pm Feb-Dec), about 4km south of the city centre, is an excellent wet-weather alternative for kids with its mini-submarine descent and *bassin tactile* (touch pool), where you can fondle rays, turbot – even a baby shark (don't fear for their fingers; it's small and not noticeably carnivorous!). Bus No 5, direction Grassinais, passes by every half-hour.

BEACHES

West of the city walls is **Plage de Bon Secours** with a protected tidal pool for bathing. St-Servan's **Plage des Bas Sablons** has a cement wall to keep the sea from receding completely at low tide. The **Grande Plage**, much larger, stretches northeast along the isthmus of Le Sillon. **Plage de Rochebonne** is another 1km to the northeast. The stretch from Grande Plage to Plage des Bas Sablons via the ramparts of the old city makes a wonderful sunset stroll.

BOAT TRIPS

Corsaire (☎ 02 23 18 15 15) runs ferries from just outside the Porte de Dinan to Îles Chausey (adult/child €26/15.60 return, 1½ hours, July to August), the Île Cézembre (€12/7 return, 20 minutes, April to September) and Dinan (adult/child one way €18/11, return €24/14.50, 2½ hours, May to September). For ferries to Dinard see p288.

Sleeping

Auberge de Jeunesse (☎ 02 99 40 29 80; info@centre varangot.com; 37 av du Père Umbricht; dm €13.20, s €20.70-22, d €29.40-32, all with breakfast) Choose the more expensive option for a considerably more luxurious stay than the usual hostel fare. Take bus No 5 from the train station or No 1 (July and August only) from the bus station and tourist office.

BEYOND THE WALLS

There are plenty of hotels for all budgets near the train station and around the beaches of Sillon and Grande Plage.

Hôtel Le Neptune (☎ 02 99 56 82 15; 21 rue de l'Industrie; d €20-27.50, with bathroom €27-42) Close to the Grande Plage, this comfortable, family-run place is above a small, cheerful bar.

Hôtel Brocéliande (☎ 02 99 20 62 62; 43 chaussée du Sillon; d €84-125) The Brocéliande is a delightful, cosy place. Most rooms – including the breakfast room with its picture window – directly overlook the Grande Plage and bedrooms are individually and tastefully decorated.

HOTELS – INTRA-MUROS

Hôtel Aux Vieilles Pierres (☎ 02 99 56 46 80; 4 rue des Lauriers; d €29, with bathroom €45) This friendly, intimate, family-run hotel, the cheapest in the old city, has only six rooms so it's wise to reserve in advance. For dinner, step no further than its equally cosy downstairs restaurant.

Hôtel San Pedro (☎ 02 99 40 88 57; www.san pedro-hotel.com; 1 rue Ste-Anne; s/d €50/55; ☒ Feb-Nov) Tucked at the back of the old city, the San Pedro, extensively renovated in 2003, offers impeccable rooms, the warmest of welcomes and sea views.

Hôtel France et Chateaubriand (☎ 02 99 56 66 52; www.hotel-fr-chateaubriand.com; place Chateaubriand; s €64-73, d €74.50-95.50) This smart, two-star establishment faces the entrance to the chateau. Its 80 rooms – the more expensive ones overlook the sea – are plush, speaking of the baroque, and several have wheelchair access.

Hôtel de l'Univers (☎ 02 99 40 89 52; www.hotel -univers-saintmalo.com in French; place Chateaubriand; s €44-71.50, d €58-81) Also attractive, in the same square and more modestly priced, it may lack the France et Chateaubriand's sea views but oh, what a bar (see opposite)!

Quic-en-Groigne (☎ 02 99 20 22 20; www.quic-en -groigne.com; 8 rue d'Estrées; s €48, d €53-62; ℗) This tranquil, mid-range choice occupies two floors (there's no lift so be prepared to flex your muscles and drag your bags) in a quiet street off main rue de Dinan.

HOTELS – ST-SERVAN

Hôtel de la Rance (☎ 02 99 81 78 63; www.larance hotel.com; 15 quai Sébastopol; d €55-81) This small, welcoming 11-room hotel overlooking Port Solidor has spacious and stylish rooms – try to get one at the front with a balcony and sea view.

Hôtel de la Mer (☎ 02 99 81 61 05; 3 rue Dauphine; d €31) This hotel, with a couple of public car parks nearby, is an excellent deal and particularly convenient if you've been decanted from an evening ferry from the UK. It's small – so best to book ahead.

CAMPING

Camping Aleth (☎ 02 99 81 60 91; camping@ville -saint-malo.fr; allée Gaston Buy, St-Servan; camping €11.10; Apr-Sep) Camping Aleth (also spelt Alet), next to Fort de la Cité, enjoys an exceptional view in all directions. Take bus No 1 in July and August or No 6 year-round.

Eating

The old city has lots of tourist restaurants, creperies and pizzerias in the area bounded by Porte St-Vincent, the cathedral and the Grande Porte.

Le Maclow (☎ 02 99 56 50 41; 22 rue Ste-Barbe; sandwiches €2.50-4) Although it looks like a burger chain clone, this little sandwich bar is fine for cheap, no-nonsense takeaway grub.

Le Petit Crêpier (☎ 02 99 40 93 19; 6 rue Ste-Barbe; dishes €5.50-8; closed Tue-Wed except Jul & Aug) This famous creperie is known for its gourmet specialities such as a *galette* with plaice in a seaweed and Muscadet sauce or a crepe with a mousse of dates and spices.

Other worthwhile places for a snack include the tiny, hole-in-the-wall **Crêperie Chez Gaby** (2 rue de Dinan), which has excellent *galettes* and crepes costing from €1.75 to €5.50, and **Glacier Sanchez** (☎ 02 99 56 67 17; 9 rue de la Vieille Boucherie), serving up great ice cream (€4 for three scoops).

La Chasse-Marée (☎ 02 99 40 85 10; 4 rue du Grout-St-Georges; mains €12-23, menus €14-23) Here you can enjoy excellent seafood, beef and lamb in a dining room with exposed timber beams. The dinner *menu* includes half a dozen oysters, a main course and cheese.

La Coquille d'Oeuf (☎ 02 99 40 92 62; 20 rue de la Corne de Cerf; menus €12-23.50) Neat, trim and with a nautical theme, this small restaurant with its tables for two makes for intimate, good value dining.

Borgnefesse (☎ 02 99 40 05 05; 10 rue du Puits-aux-Braies; mains €11.50, full meal €21; closed lunch Sat-Mon) Fish and seafood are the main elements on the short but impressive menu. Ask the owner, an exuberant Captain Haddock figure, to explain just why his restaurant is called Borgnefesse (But One Buttock)...

SELF-CATERING

Among the food shops along rue de l'Orme is a truly excellent **cheese shop** (Tue-Sat) at No 9. Just down the street is **Hall au Blé**, once the town's grain store and now its **covered market**.

Drinking

Hôtel de l'Univers (see opposite) has a magnificent, snug bar, all in wood and clad with maritime photos and prints.

L'Aviso (☎ 02 99 40 99 08; 12 rue Point du Jour; 5pm-2am) With 300 beers on offer, over 10 of them on draught, this cheerful place is for serious hopheads. It sometimes has live music.

Entertainment

In summer, classical music concerts are held in Cathédrale St-Vincent and elsewhere in the city.

Getting There & Away

AIR

See Dinard Getting There & Away (p288) for flight details.

BOAT

Brittany Ferries (☎ reservations France 08 25 82 88 28, ☎ UK 0870 556 1600; www.brittany-ferries.com) sail between St-Malo and Portsmouth and **Condor Ferries** (☎ France 08 25 16 03 00, ☎ UK 0845 345 2000; www.condorferries.co.uk) run to/from both Poole and Weymouth via Jersey or Guernsey.

Hydrofoils and catamarans depart from the Gare Maritime de la Bourse; car ferries leave from the Gare Maritime du Naye.

From April to September, **Corsaire** (☎ 02 23 18 15 15) runs the Bus de Mer (Sea Bus; adult/child €5.90/3.60 return, 10 minutes, hourly) shuttle service between St-Malo and Dinard.

BUS

All intercity buses stop by both train and bus stations.

Courriers Bretons (☎ 02 99 19 70 80) has services to Cancale (€3.80, 30 minutes), Fougères (€13.90, 1¾ hours, one to three daily), Pontorson (€8.30, one hour) and Mont St-Michel (€9.20, 1½ hours, three to four daily). It also offers all-day tours to Mont St-Michel (return €25, Tuesday and Saturday June to September).

TIV (☎ 02 99 82 26 26) has buses to Dinard (€3.40, 30 minutes, hourly) and Rennes (€9.90, one to 1½ hours, three to six daily).

BRITTANY

CAT (☎ 02 99 82 26 26) bus No 10 goes to Dinan (€5.70, 50 minutes, three to eight daily) via the Barrage de la Rance.

CAR & MOTORCYCLE

Avis (☎ 02 99 40 18 54) has a desk at both the main train station and Gare Maritime du Naye. **ADA** (☎ 02 99 56 06 15) has a booth in the train station, while **Europcar** (☎ 02 99 56 75 17; 16 blvd des Talards) is across the street.

TRAIN

Trains or SNCF buses run between St-Malo and Rennes (€11.40, one hour, frequent), Dinan (€7.60, one hour, five daily) and Lannion (€21.60, four hours, seven daily). Change at Rennes for Paris' Gare Montparnasse (€53, 4¼ hours, eight to 10 daily).

Getting Around

St-Malo city buses (single journey €1.10, 10-trip carnet €7.80, 24hr pass €3.20) operate until about 8pm with some lines extending until around midnight in summer. Between esplanade St-Vincent and the train station, take bus Nos 1 (July to August only), 2, 3 or 4.

Call ☎ 02 99 81 30 30 for a taxi.

DINARD

pop 10,100

Dinard has attracted a well-heeled clientele, especially from the UK, since the mid-19th century. Indeed, it retains something of the feel of a late-19th-century beach resort with its striped bathing tents, beachside carnival and pinnacled *belle époque* mansions perched above the water. And there's an annual festival of British cinema, held in early October.

Orientation

Dinard's focal point is Plage de l'Écluse (also called Grande Plage), flanked by Pointe du Moulinet and Pointe de la Malouine. To get to this beach from the Embarcadère (where boats from St-Malo dock), climb the stairs and walk 200m northwest along rue Georges Clemenceau.

Information

Cyberk@w@ (☎ 02 99 46 79 01; 32 rue de la Gare; per hr €4; 11am-1am Tue-Sat, 2-11pm Sun-Mon)
Lavomatic de la Poste (10 rue des Saules; 8am-7pm Jun-Sep, Mon-Sat Oct-May)
Main Post Office (place Rochaid)

Tourist Office (☎ 02 99 46 94 12; www.ville-dinard .fr; 2 blvd Féart; 9.30am-7.30pm Jul & Aug, core hours 9am-12.15pm & 2-6pm Mon-Sat Sep-Jun) Staff will book accommodation for free.

Sights

As befits a classic seaside resort, Dinard's main attractions are its beaches, cafés and waterfront walks. Take a stroll along **promenade du Clair de Lune** (Moonlight promenade). With a free sound-and-light spectacle in summer, it runs from just north of place Général de Gaulle to the Embarcadère, offering views of St-Malo's old city across the River Rance estuary.

Guided walks (2.30pm & 4.30pm, Mon & Wed-Sat) covering the town's history, art and architecture, depart from the tourist office.

BARRAGE DE LA RANCE

This 750m bridge over the Rance estuary carries the D168 between St-Malo and Dinard, lopping a good 30km of the journey. The **Usine Marémotrice de la Rance**, jutting below it, generates over 3% of Brittany's electricity. Its 24 turbines churn out over 600 million kWh annually by exploiting the lower estuary's extraordinary high tidal range – a difference of 13.5m between high and low tide.

If you're even slightly mechanically minded, visit **Espace Découverte** (admission free; 1-7pm Tue-Sun) on the Dinard bank. Illustrating the power station's construction and environmental impact, it runs an interesting film in English.

Activities

SWIMMING

Wide, sandy **Plage de l'Écluse** is fringed with Dinard's trademark blue-and-white striped bathing tents and overlooked by fashionable hotels, a casino and some attractive neo-Gothic villas. Picasso used the beach as the setting for several canvases in the 1920s and you may see reproductions of them planted in the sand. A **statue** of film director Alfred Hitchcock, with a seagull perched on each shoulder, stands near the beach's entrance in honour of the annual festival of British film.

The **Piscine Olympique** (☎ 02 99 46 22 77; promenade des Alliés; adult/student €4/2.55), an indoor Olympic-sized swimming pool right beside the beach, is filled with heated sea water.

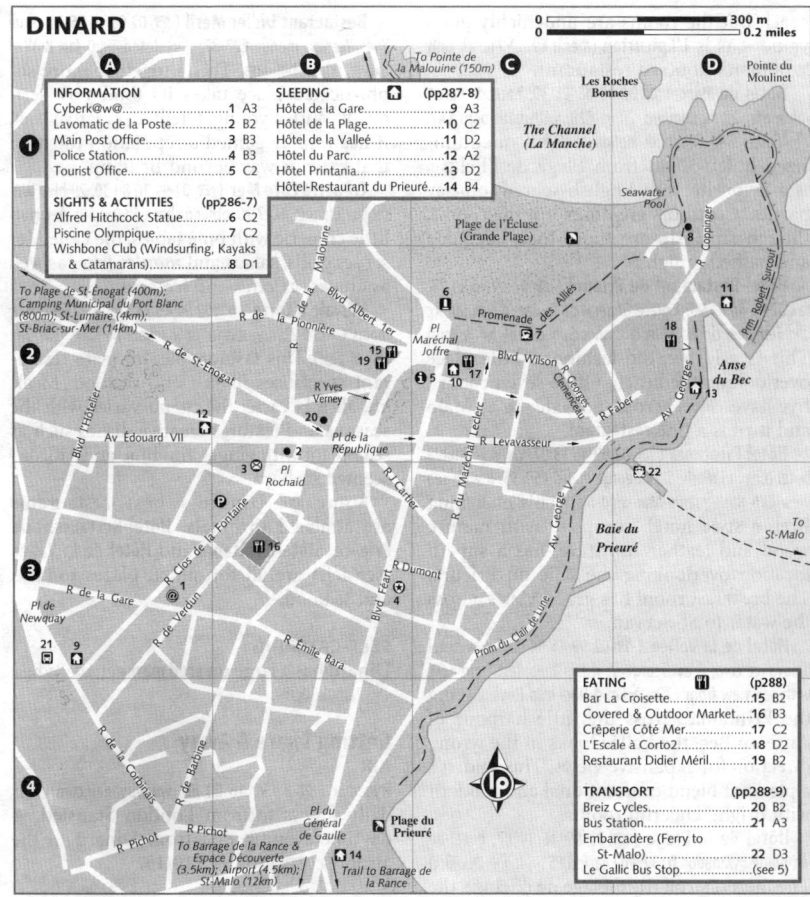

DINARD

0 — 300 m
0 — 0.2 miles

To Pointe de
la Malouine (150m)

Pointe du
Moulinet

Les Roches
Bonnes

INFORMATION	
Cyberk@w@	1 A3
Lavomatic de la Poste	2 B2
Main Post Office	3 B3
Police Station	4 B3
Tourist Office	5 C2

SIGHTS & ACTIVITIES	(pp286-7)
Alfred Hitchcock Statue	6 C2
Piscine Olympique	7 C2
Wishbone Club (Windsurfing, Kayaks	
& Catamarans)	8 D1

SLEEPING	(pp287-8)
Hôtel de la Gare	9 A3
Hôtel de la Plage	10 C2
Hôtel de la Valleé	11 D2
Hôtel du Parc	12 A2
Hôtel Printania	13 D2
Hôtel-Restaurant du Prieuré	14 B4

The Channel
(La Manche)

Seawater
Pool

Plage de l'Écluse
(Grande Plage)

Anse
du Bec

Baie du
Prieuré

To
St-Malo

To Plage de St-Énogat (400m);
Camping Municipal du Port Blanc
(800m); St-Lunaire (4km);
St-Briac-sur-Mer (14km)

To Barrage de la Rance &
Espace Découverte
(3.5km); Airport (4.5km);
St-Malo (12km)

Trail to Barrage de
la Rance

EATING	(p288)
Bar La Croisette	15 B2
Covered & Outdoor Market	16 B3
Crêperie Côté Mer	17 C2
L'Escale à Corto2	18 D2
Restaurant Didier Méril	19 B2

TRANSPORT	(pp288-9)
Breiz Cycles	20 B2
Bus Station	21 A3
Embarcadère (Ferry to	
St-Malo)	22 D3
Le Gallic Bus Stop	(see 5)

Plage du Prieuré, 1km to the south, may not be as chic as Plage de l'Écluse but you'll find it less crowded. **Plage de St-Énogat** is 1km west of Plage de l'Écluse, on the far side of Pointe de la Malouine.

WALKING & CYCLING
Beautiful seaside trails extend along the coast in both directions. Particularly spectacular is a traverse of the splendid shoreline from Plage du Prieuré to Plage de St-Énogat via Pointe du Moulinet. For other hiking opportunities throughout the *département*, pack the Institut National Géographique (IGN) 1:50,000 map *Ille-et-Vilaine: Randonnées en Haute Bretagne,* which highlights walking trails.

WINDSURFING & KAYAKING
At Plage de l'Écluse, **Wishbone Club** (☎ 02 99 88 15 20; ☽ 9am-9pm Jun-Sep, 10am-noon & 2-6pm Oct-May), next to the open-air swimming pool, offers windsurfing lessons (€30 per hour) and also hires out boards (€14 to €19 per hour, €30 to €40 per half-day) and catamarans/kayaks (€30/10 per hour).

Sleeping
Dinard can be an expensive place to stay; you might want to base yourself in St-Malo and hop over on the ferry.

Hôtel de la Gare (☎ 02 99 46 10 84; 28 rue de la Corbinais; d €20-26) Station Hotel, still so called even though trains no longer pass and the station is long demolished, is a fair hike from the beach but the rooms are undeniably good value – as is **L'Épicurien** (menu €9, ☺ lunch only Mon-Fri), its Routard restaurant.

Hôtel du Parc (☎ 02 99 46 11 39; hotel.du.parc@ infonie.fr; 20 av Édouard VII; d €28, with bathroom €47; ☺ Easter-Sep & school holidays) This medium-sized hotel, 500m from Plage de l'Écluse, is a favourite with English school journey parties. Corridors are dingy but the rooms, though smallish, are more than adequate and bathed in light.

Hôtel-Restaurant du Prieuré (☎ 02 99 46 13 74; fax 02 99 46 81 90; 1 place Général de Gaulle; d €38.50-46; ☺ Feb-Dec, closed Mon & dinner Sun except Jul & Aug) This is a lovely, old-fashioned little place overlooking the beach. Of its seven rooms, five have views across the water to St-Malo and it runs a fine **restaurant**.

Hôtel Printania (☎ 02 99 46 13 07; www.printania hotel.com in French; 5 av George V; s/d €50/55, d with sea view €75-85; ☺ mid-Mar–mid-Nov) This charming Breton-style hotel, complete with mature wood and leather furniture, has a superb location overlooking the Baie du Prieuré. The breakfast room has grand views across the water to St-Servan.

Hôtel de la Vallée (☎ 02 99 46 94 00; www.hotel delavallee.com; 6 av George V; d incl breakfast from €60, with sea view from €70; ☺ mid-Dec–mid-Nov) Facing the Printania across the little harbour of Anse du Bec, the Vallée looks in the wrong direction for expansive views. This said, it's a pleasant blend of traditional and modern with bright, cheerful rooms.

Hôtel de la Plage (☎ 02 99 46 14 87; hotel-de -la-plage@wanadoo.fr; 3 blvd Féart; d €51-84; ☺ Dec-Oct) The merest stroll from Plage de l'Écluse, the 'Beach Hotel' is a fine, stone-built structure with 18 well-appointed rooms. The dearer ones have a balcony with sea views.

CAMPING

Camping Municipal du Port Blanc (☎ 02 99 46 10 74; camping.dinard@free.fr; rue Sergeant Boulanger; camping €18.70; ☺ Apr-Sep) It's close to the beach, about 2km west of Plage de l'Écluse.

Eating

Bar La Croisette (☎ 02 99 46 43 32; 4 rue Yves Verney; menus €11 & 17; ☺ mid-Dec–mid-Nov, closed Tue Oct-Mar) La Croisette, easily recognised by the blonde, bikini-clad mannequin on the roof, is a cheerful eatery and bar where portions are ample. It carries a wide selection of wines by the glass.

Restaurant Didier Méril (☎ 02 99 46 95 74; 6 rue Yves Verney; menus €27-37; ☺ closed 5-20 Jan & Wed except school holidays) This altogether more so-phisticated place takes its food *very* seriously. With a young, talented, creative chef, it has rapidly gained a reputation for itself that extends way beyond Brittany.

Crêperie Côte Mer (☎ 02 99 16 80 30; 29 blvd Wilson; galettes €2.60-7.20, other dishes €4.60-7.80) A crisp little creperie with pine tables, the Côte Mer serves grills, salads and *moules-frites* as well as crepes, galettes and ice cream.

L'Escale à Corto (☎ 02 99 46 78 57; 12 av George V; mains €10.20-22; ☺ dinner only school holidays, Tue-Sun rest of year) This fashionable, intimate restaurant specialises in fish and seafood. Meals are all à la carte; the menu varies with the seasons and features creative dishes such as sea bream with ginger and lime and saffron-scented scallops.

Some of Dinard's best restaurants are attached to hotels. **Hôtel-Restaurant du Prieuré**, **Hôtel Printania** and **Hôtel de la Vallée** (see left) are all top-notch places for fish and seafood.

SELF-CATERING

Dinard has a large **covered market** (place Rochaid; ☺ 7am-1.30pm).

Getting There & Away

AIR

Ryanair (☎ 02 99 16 00 66; www.ryanair.com) has daily flights to/from London Stansted. A daytime/evening taxi from Dinard to the airport costs around €10/15.

BOAT

From April to September, **Corsaire** (☎ 02 23 18 15 15) runs the Bus de Mer (Sea Bus; adult/child €5.90/3.60 return, 10 minutes, hourly) shuttle service between Dinard and St-Malo.

BUS

TIV (☎ 02 99 82 26 26) buses (€3.40, 30 minutes, hourly) connect Dinard and the train station in St-Malo via the Barrage de la Rance. Dinard's bus station is southwest of the town centre at place de Newquay; Le Gallic bus stop, outside the tourist office, is more convenient.

TAE (☎ 02 99 26 16 00) runs five buses daily between Dinard and Rennes (€11.80, two hours) via Dinan (€3.80, 25 minutes).

Getting Around

You can hire bicycles (€5.50/8 per half-/full day) and motor scooters (€11/38 per hour/ day) to get around at **Breiz Cycles** (☎ 02 99 46 27 25; 8 Rue St-Énogat).

For a taxi, telephone ☎ 02 99 46 88 80 or ☎ 02 99 88 15 15.

CANCALE
pop 5200

Cancale, a relaxed fishing port 14km east of St-Malo, is famed for its offshore *parcs à huîtres* (oyster beds), which each year yield around 4000 tonnes of prize mollusc. The town even has a small museum dedicated to oyster farming and shellfish, the **Ferme Marine** (Marine Farm; ☎ 02 99 89 69 99; Corniche de l'Aurore; adult/child €6.10/3.10; ❧ mid-Feb–Oct, tours in English 2pm mid-Jun–mid-Sep), southwest of the port, where you can take a guided tour.

The *marché aux huîtres* (oyster market) is just a cluster of little stalls in the shadow of the Pointe des Crolles lighthouse. Numbered according to size and quality, oysters cost from €2.50 per dozen for the smallest *huîtres creuses* (No 5) to as much as €20 for saucer-sized *plates de Cancale*.

The **tourist office** (☎ 02 99 89 63 72; www.ville -cancale.fr; ❧ 9.30am-12.30pm & 2-6pm or 7pm Mon-Sat, 9.30am-12.30pm Sun) is at the top of rue du Port. Startlingly uninformed – even about its own opening hours – it does, however, rent bicycles (per half-day/day from €8/11).

There's a seasonal tourist office **annexe** on quai Gambetta in the wooden house where the fish auction takes place.

Sleeping

Auberge de Jeunesse (☎ 02 99 89 62 62; cancale@fuaj .org; Port Pican; dm €9.30; ❧ Feb–mid-Dec). Cancale's HI-affiliated youth hostel overlooks the beach at Port Pican, 3km north of the town, to where the St-Malo–Cancale bus continues.

Hôtel La Mère Champlain (☎ 02 99 89 60 04; 1 quai Thomas; interior d €30-45, with sea view €50-65) Rooms at this recently renovated hotel have great sea views. There's a nice **restaurant** deck, complete with crisp linen, heavy cutlery and smart waiters with black bow ties.

CAMPING
Camping Municipal Le Grouin (☎ 02 99 89 63 79; fax 02 99 89 96 31; Pointe du Grouin; camping €12.70; ❧ Mar-Oct) This area, 6km north of Cancale

near Pointe du Grouin, overlooks a fine beach and is one of several in the area.

Eating

Cancale boasts over 50 restaurants, most of which specialise in – you've guessed it – oysters, starting at around €6.50 per dozen.

Le Surcouf (☎ 02 99 89 61 75; 7 quai Gambetta; menus €18-50, mains €19-24; ❧ closed Wed-Thu except Jul & Aug) Le Surcouf is among the best of the many quality seafood restaurants that line the waterfront.

Au Pied d'Cheval (☎ 02 99 89 76 95; 10 quai Gambetta; ❧ 9am-9pm) At this rustic little place, the *assiette du capitaine* (captain's plate; €5.60) gives you half a dozen oysters, direct from their farm, washed down with a glass of Muscadet while their *super plateau* (a mixed seafood platter) for two costs a bargain €30.50.

Getting There & Away

Buses stop behind the church on place Lucidas and at Port de la Houle, next to the pungent fish market. **Courriers Bretons** (☎ 02 99 19 70 70) and **TIV** (☎ 02 99 82 26 26) have year-round services to/from St-Malo (€3.80, 30 minutes). At least three Courriers Bretons buses daily continue to Port Pican and Port Mer, near Pointe du Grouin.

POINTE DU GROUIN

This nature reserve lies on a headland at the tip of the wild, beautiful coast between Cancale and St-Malo. Cancale tourist office's free map covers the coastline well. **Île des Landes**, just offshore, is home to a colony of giant black cormorants, whose wingspan can reach 170cm.

Via the GR34 coastal hiking trail, Pointe du Grouin is a stunning 7km hike from Cancale and 18km from St-Malo. By the D201 road, it's 4km from Cancale.

DINAN
pop 11,000

Perched above the River Rance 22km south of Dinard, this walled, medieval city has some beautiful 15th-century half-timbered houses. During Fête des Remparts, held every second year in late July, Dinannais decked out in medieval garb are joined by some 40,000 visitors for a rollicking two-day festival in the tiny old city.

Orientation

Nearly everything of interest – except the picturesque port area on the River Rance – is within the tight confines of the old city, at its heart place des Cordeliers and adjacent place des Merciers.

Information

@rospace (☎ 02 96 87 04 87; 9 rue de la Chaux; per 15 min €1.50; ⓨ 10am-12.30pm & 1.30-7pm Tue-Sat) Internet access.

Main Post Office (7 place Duclos)

Tourist Office (☎ 02 96 87 69 76; www.dinan-tour isme.com; 9 rue du Château; ⓨ 9am-7pm Mon-Sat, 10am-12.30pm & 2.30-6pm Sun mid-Jun–mid-Sep, 9am-12.30pm & 2-6pm Mon-Sat mid-Sep–mid-Jun)

Sights

OLD TOWN

Within the cobbled streets of the old town, attractive half-timbered houses overhang place des Cordeliers and place des Merciers. A few paces south, the **Tour de l'Horloge** (adult/ under 18 €2.60/1.65; ⓨ 10am-6.30pm Jun-Sep, 2-6.30pm Apr-May), a 15th-century clock tower whose tinny chimes ping every quarter-hour, rises from rue de l'Horloge. It's well worth the climb up to its tiny balcony.

In the north transept of **Basilique St-Sauveur** (place St-Sauveur; ⓨ 9am-6pm), with soaring Gothic chancel, is a 14th-century grave slab, reputed to contain the heart of Bertrand du Guesclin, a 14th-century knight noted for his hatred of the English and his fierce battles to expel them from France.

Just east of the church, beyond the tiny **Jardin Anglais** (English Garden), a former cemetery and nowadays a pleasant little park, is the 13th-century **Tour Ste-Cathérine**, with great views down over the viaduct and port.

Rue du Jerzual and its continuation, steep **rue du Petit Fort**, both lined with art galleries, antiques shops and restaurants, lead down to the **Vieux Pont** (Old Bridge), from where the little **port** extends northwards while the 19th-century **Viaduc de Dinan** soars high above to the south.

CHÂTEAU & MUSÉE DE DINAN

Dinan's **museum** (☎ 02 96 39 45 20; rue du Château; adult/child €4/1.55; ⓨ 9am-noon & 2-7pm mid-Jun–Aug, 1.30-5.30pm Sep-Dec & Feb–mid-Jun) is in the keep of the ruined 14th-century castle. It presents the town's history, especially its textile industry, together with a collec-

tion of 16th-century polychrome wooden statues and a fine collection of *coiffes* (traditional lace headdresses).

Activities

BOAT TRIPS

Between May and September, **Corsaire** (☎ 02 96 39 18 04) runs boats along the River Rance to Dinard and St-Malo (one way/return €17.30/23, 2½ hours). There's usually one sailing a day, the morning departure time linked to the tide and the return trip (by boat) occurring the following day. From Dinard or St-Malo, you can easily return to Dinan by bus (and, from St-Malo, by train too).

WALKING

Ask at the tourist office for its leaflet *Discovery Tours*, in English, which plots three walking itineraries around town.

Sleeping

Auberge de Jeunesse Moulin de Méen (☎ 02 96 39 10 83; dinan@fuaj.org; Vallée de la Fontaine des Eaux; dm €9.30) Dinan's HI-affiliated youth hostel is in a lovely old water mill about 750m north of the port. It has limited camping space and five much-coveted double rooms.

Hôtel Duchesse Anne (☎ 02 96 39 09 43; fax 02 96 87 57 26; 10 place Duguesclin; d €28, with bathroom €36-40) This inexpensive, central place has cramped yet acceptable accommodation. It runs a reasonable restaurant and there's public parking right opposite.

Hôtel Les Grandes Tours (☎ 02 96 85 16 20; carregi@wanadoo.fr; 6 rue du Château; d €35, with bathroom €45-50; ⓨ Feb–mid-Dec; Ⓟ) Venerable, altogether larger and once upon a time called Hôtel des Messageries; it was here that Victor Hugo slept with his very good friend Juliette Drouet in 1836. It has smallish but attractively renovated rooms.

Hôtel Tour de l'Horloge (☎ 02 96 39 96 92; hil iohotel@wanadoo.fr; 5 rue de la Chaux; d €48-54) The 12-room Horloge occupies a charming 18th-century house on a cobbled, car-free lane. Top-floor rooms have exposed wooden beams and a splendid view of the clock tower.

Hôtel Le d'Avaugour (☎ 02 96 39 07 49; www .avaugourhotel.com; 1 place du Champ; d with breakfast €119-176; ⓨ mid-Feb–mid-Nov) In an elegant 18th-century town house just inside the city walls, the Avaugour is a peaceful luxury hotel with tastefully decorated rooms and

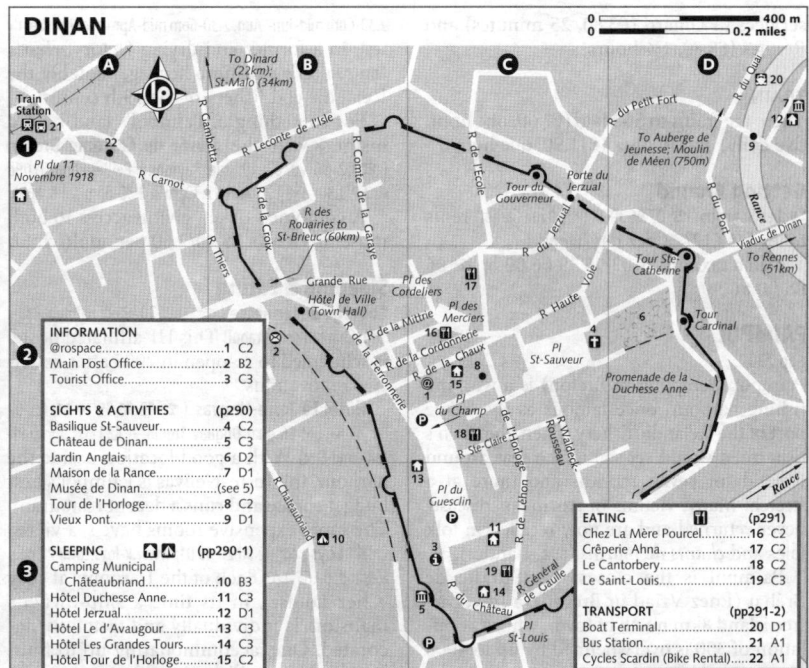

DINAN

0 _____ 400 m
0 _____ 0.2 miles

To Dinard (22km); St-Malo (34km)

Train Station

Pl du 11 Novembre 1918

To Dinard (22km); St-Malo (34km)

R du Petit Fort

To Auberge de Jeunesse; Moulin de Méen (750m)

R du Quai

Porte du Jerzual

Tour du Gouverneur

R des Rouairies to St-Brieuc (60km)

Grande Rue

Hôtel de Ville (Town Hall)

Pl des Cordeliers

Pl des Merciers

Tour Ste-Catherine

To Rennes (51km)

Tour Cardinal

Pl St-Sauveur

Promenade de la Duchesse Anne

Pl du Champ

Pl du Guesclin

Pl St-Louis

Rance

Viaduc de Dinan

INFORMATION

@rospace	1 C2
Main Post Office	2 B2
Tourist Office	3 C3

SIGHTS & ACTIVITIES (p290)

Basilique St-Sauveur	4 C2
Château de Dinan	5 C3
Jardin Anglais	6 D2
Maison de la Rance	7 D1
Musée de Dinan	(see 5)
Tour de l'Horloge	8 C2
Vieux Pont	9 D1

SLEEPING (pp290-1)

Camping Municipal Châteaubriand	10 B3
Hôtel Duchesse Anne	11 C3
Hôtel Jerzual	12 D1
Hôtel Le d'Avaugour	13 C3
Hôtel Les Grandes Tours	14 C3
Hôtel Tour de l'Horloge	15 C2

EATING (p291)

Chez La Mère Pourcel	16 C2
Crêperie Ahna	17 C2
Le Cantorbery	18 C2
Le Saint-Louis	19 C3

TRANSPORT (pp291-2)

Boat Terminal	20 D1
Bus Station	21 A1
Cycles Scardin (Bike Rental)	22 A1

a pretty rear garden. There's ample public parking right opposite.

Hôtel Jerzual (☎ 02 96 87 02 02; www.bestwestern .com/fr/jerzual; 26 quai des Talards; s €75-108, d €80-148; P ⊗) Outside the city walls, the Jerzual overlooks the port. Modern and sensitively constructed in stone and slate, its 52 rooms have every last comfort while the restaurant merits a visit for its own sake. They rent bikes – ideal for a towpath spin – to guests.

CAMPING

Camping Municipal Châteaubriand (☎ 02 96 39 11 96; fax 02 96 85 06 97; 103 rue Chateaubriand; camping €7; ⊗ Easter-Sep) The nearest camping ground is this small, unexceptional two-star place, at the foot of the ramparts.

Eating

Le Cantorbery (☎ 02 96 39 02 52; 6 rue Ste-Claire; menus €22-32; ⊗ closed Wed & dinner Sun Oct-Apr) Occupying a magnificent 17th-century house, this elegant, intimate restaurant changes its menu regularly, according to the rhythm of the seasons, and does an excellent-value lunch *formule* (€15).

Chez La Mère Pourcel (☎ 02 96 39 03 80; 3 place des Merciers; menus €28-62.50, mains €18-33; ⊗ Tue-Sat & lunch Sun) La Mère Pourcel is a Dinan institution: a wonderful beamed dining room, mostly 15th-century, that serves specialities of the region such as salt-marsh lamb.

Le Saint-Louis (☎ 02 96 39 89 50; 9-11 rue de Léhon; lunch menus Mon-Fri €11.50, dinner menus €16.50 & €20; ⊗ closed Wed & lunch Mon) This popular place is famous for its good-value, all-you-can-eat buffets. In season, walk through to the charming floral patio at the rear.

Crêperie Ahna (☎ 02 96 39 09 13; 7 rue de la Poisonnerie; galettes €6-7.85; ⊗ Mon-Sat) This excellent place, in the family for three generations, tosses up gourmet, inventive crepes and galettes; the speciality of the house is a galette filled with duck breast and cooked with garlic-and-herb butter.

Getting There & Away
BUS

Buses leave from place Duclos and the bus station. **CAT** (☎ 02 96 39 21 05) bus No 10 goes to St-Malo (€5.70, 50 minutes, three to eight daily). **TAE** (☎ 02 99 26 16 00) runs five daily services to Dinard (€3.80, 25 minutes) and Rennes (€8.80, 1½ hours).

TRAIN
There are trains to St-Malo (€7.60, one hour, five daily) and Rennes (€11.90, one hour).

Getting Around
Cycles Scardin (☎ 02 96 39 21 94; 30 rue Carnot) rents bikes for €12/72 per day/week.

Call a taxi on ☎ 02 96 39 06 00 or ☎ 06 08 00 80 90.

PAIMPOL
pop 7900
Paimpol (Pempoull in Breton) is a working fishing harbour, once famous as the home port of the Icelandic fishery. Then, the town's fishermen would set sail to the seas around Iceland for seven months and more at a stretch. Many, victims of storms or disease, never returned and are now recalled in folk tales and *chants de marins* (sea shanties).

Paimpol is the closest port to Île de Bréhat (Enez Vriad in Breton), a tiny, car-free island 8km north of town, whose population of 350 is overwhelmed by up to 4000 tourists daily in summer.

The centre of Paimpol, to the south of the two harbours, is around the market square of place du Martray. Bus and train stations are both 100m south of this square.

The **tourist office** (☎ 02 96 20 83 16; www.paimpol-goelo.com; 9.30am-7.30pm Mon-Sat & 10am-6pm Sun Jun-Sep, 9.30am-12.30pm & 1.30-6.30pm Mon-Sat Oct-May) is on place de la République.

Sights
The splendid **Musée de la Mer** (☎ 02 96 22 02 19; rue Labenne; adult/child €4.25/2.10; 10.30am-noon &

2.30-6pm mid-Jun–Aug, 2.30-6pm mid-Apr–mid-Jun & early Sep), in a former cod-drying factory, charts the region's maritime heritage, notably the Icelandic cod fishery of the 19th century.

For something of Paimpol's land-bound history, visit the **Musée du Costume Breton** (☎ 02 96 22 02 19; rue Raymond Pellier; adult/child €2.50/1.30; 10.30am-12.30pm & 2.30-6pm Jul & Aug).

A combined ticket, giving access to both museums, costs €5.40/2.60 per adult/child.

Sleeping & Eating
Auberge de Jeunesse (☎ 02 96 20 83 60; paimpol@fuaj .org; Château de Kerraoul) This HI-affiliated hostel is scheduled to re-open in 2005 after extensive renovations.

Hôtel Le Terre-Neuvas (☎ 02 96 55 14 14; fax 02 96 20 47 66; 16 quai Duguay Trouin; d €31-37; mid-Jan–mid-Dec) With a good location beside the harbour, the Terre-Neuvas is Paimpol's best budget choice and runs a decent restaurant. The more expensive rooms have sea views.

K″ Loys (☎ 02 96 20 40 01; www.k-loys.com; 21 quai Morand; d €65-120) Each of the 15 rooms at cosy 'Chez Louise', in its time a ship-owner's mansion, is individually and tastefully decorated. One, accommodating up to four, has disabled facilities.

Crêperie-Restaurant Morel (☎ 02 96 20 86 34; 11 place du Martray; galettes €4.20-6.90) On Paimpol's main square, the Morel is much favoured by locals during the low season. Help your galette down with a glass of their refreshing draught cider.

L'Islandais (☎ 02 96 20 93 80; 19 quai Morand; menus €16.50 & €24.50) This attractive, bustling harbourside restaurant serves, predominantly and appropriately, fish and seafood. For something lighter, try their salads (€7.70) or a galette (€3.40 to €6.10).

LA GRANDE PÊCHE

It was the fishermen of Brittany who, way back in the 16th century, pioneered *La Grande Pêche à la Morue* (The Great Cod Fishery), long-lining for cod on the Grand Banks of Newfoundland. Braving the stormy waters of the north Atlantic, the *morutiers* (cod-fishing boats) would be away from their home ports for up to six months at a time, their crews suffering lives of unimaginable hardship – a tradition that continued until the 1930s.

During the peak of *La Grande Pêche* in the late 19th and early 20th centuries, boats from St-Malo favoured the Newfoundland (Terre-Neuve) fishing grounds, while the fishermen of Paimpol and nearby Binic frequented the Icelandic fishery. Their *goélettes* (schooners), with a crew of only a dozen or so men, were small and fast but often exposed to dangerous conditions. In the 19th and early 20th centuries, the Paimpol region lost a total of 100 ships and more than 2000 men to the sea in only 80 years.

Paimpol's Tuesday **market** spreads over place Gambetta and place du Martray. At the weekend, vendors sell freshly-shucked oysters at quai Duguay Trouin.

CAMPING
Camping Municipal de Cruckin (☎ 02 96 20 78 47; rue de Cruckin; camping €12.40; ⚑ Easter-Sep) This quiet, two-star camping ground is on the beautiful Baie de Kérity, 2km southeast of town off the road to Plouha.

Getting There & Around
BICYCLE
Cycles du Vieux Clocher (☎ 02 96 20 83 58; place Verdun) rents bikes (per day €11). It's south of the tourist office near the Vieux Clocher (Old Bell Tower).

BOAT
Vedettes de Bréhat (☎ 02 96 55 79 50; www.vedettesdebrehat.com) operates ferries (adult/child €7.50/6.50 return, 15 minutes, hourly sailings 8.30am to 7pm April to September, at least eight daily October to March) goes to Île de Bréhat from Pointe L'Arcouest, 6km north of Paimpol.

BUS & TRAIN
CAT (☎ 02 96 68 31 20) runs buses to/from St-Brieuc (€7.60, 1½ hours). In summer most continue to Pointe L'Arcouest.

There are several trains or SNCF buses daily between Paimpol and Guingamp (€5.80, 45 minutes), where you can pick up connections to Brest, St-Brieuc and Rennes.

PERROS-GUIREC
pop 7900
The chic resort of Perros-Guirec sits on a rocky peninsula at the eastern end of the Côte de Granit Rose (Pink Granite Coast). It's an exclusive town, flanked by a new marina to the southeast and the old fishing port of Ploumanac'h, about 3km to the northwest; in between lie granite cliffs and coves where sea otters still feel at home.

Orientation
Perros has two distinct parts: the upper town on the hill and the marina area at its base, to the south. They're about 1km apart if you make your way up through the back streets, or double that distance if you follow the main coastal road (blvd de la Mer and

blvd Clemenceau) around Pointe du Château, at the eastern end of town.

Information
Laverie du Port (7 rue Anatole le Braz; ⚑ 9.15am-7.15pm) For your laundry needs.
Main Post Office (rue de la Poste)
Tourist Office (☎ 02 96 23 21 15; www.perros-guirec.com; 21 place de l'Hôtel de Ville; ⚑ 9am-7.30pm Mon-Sat, 10am-12.30pm & 4-7pm Sun Jul & Aug, 9am-12.30pm & 2-6.30pm Mon-Sat Jun-Sep)

Activities
SWIMMING & WALKING
Of several beaches close to Perros, the main one is **Plage de Trestraou**, to the north about 1km from the tourist office. The others, attractive **Plage de Trestrignel** and **Plage du Château**, on either side of Pointe du Château, are smaller, prettier but often more crowded.

The **sentier des douaniers** (custom officer's trail) follows the spectacular 5km coastline from Plage de Trestraou to Ploumanac'h through a wilderness of massive, pink granite boulders and outcrops.

Sleeping
Hôtel du Port (☎ 02 96 23 21 79; www.caféduport.fr; 85 rue Ernest Renan; d €38-47) This hotel has a dozen modern, double-glazed rooms, with bathroom, TV and telephone. The pricier ones have balconies overlooking the marina.

Hôtel Le Gulf Stream (☎ 02 96 23 21 86; www.gulf-stream-hotel-bretagne.com; 26 rue des Sept-Îles; d €40-48, with bathroom €55-68) The Gulf Stream is a lovely villa perched above the eastern end of Plage de Trestraou. Its 12 modest – and very pleasant – rooms (eight with sea views) contrast with its grand and decidedly up-market **restaurant**.

Hostellerie les Feux des Îles (☎ 02 96 23 22 94; www.feux-des-iles.com; 53 blvd Clemenceau; s €61-90, d €92-112; ⚑ closed 1-15 Oct) Surrounded by a large, flower-filled, clifftop garden looking out towards the Sept-Îles, 'Island Lights' is a magnificent stone villa with a modern wing attached. Its **restaurant** specialises in gourmet seafood.

CAMPING
Camping de Trestraou (☎ 02 96 23 08 11; fax 02 96 23 26 06; 89 av du Casino; camping €20; ⚑ May–mid-Sep) Ideally positioned, this camping area is close to the centre of Perros-Guirec and only a few minutes' walk from Plage de Trestraou.

Eating

Crêperie du Trestraou (☎ 02 96 23 04 34; blvd Thalassa; galettes €3-9.40; ☽ closed Mon & Thu except Jul & Aug) Although this creperie looks more like a standard pizza joint from the outside, it has an excellent selection of crepes and galettes, as well as salads, seafood and grills.

Crêperie Les Vieux Gréements (☎ 02 96 91 14 99; 19 rue Anatole Le Braz; galettes €5.50-9; ☽ Tue-Sun, closed 2 weeks in Oct, 1-15 Dec) In an old shipowner's house overlooking the marina, this creperie has a pleasant outdoor terrace. On the 1st floor is a *moulerie*, serving mussels, mussels and more mussels.

Digor Kalon (☎ 02 96 49 03 63; 89 rue du Maréchal Joffre; menus €12-17.50; ☽ dinner only, closed Mon & Tue except Jul & Aug) This Celtic-themed pub-cum-restaurant is an Aladdin's cave of bric-a-brac. The food – snacky stuff such as mixed tapas (€6.50), mussels (€8.50 to €9.50) and Breton cakes – is good and they do a great line in local beers.

SELF-CATERING

At the **Marché des Pêcheurs** (Marina; ☽ 8.30am-12.30pm Jul & Aug, 2-3 times weekly Sep-Jun), the fisherfolk sell their catch directly. Nearby, **Biocoop** (67 rue Anatole le Braz) is a neat little co-operative that sells only organic produce.

Getting There & Around

CAT (☎ 02 96 68 31 20) bus No 15 (€3, 30 minutes, five to eight daily) links Perros-Guirec with Lannion's train station, calling at Ploumanac'h, Trégastel and Trébeurden. From Lannion, there are rail links via Plouaret Trégor eastwards to Guingamp (€7, 40 minutes) and on to St-Brieuc (€10.30, one hour); and westwards via Morlaix (€7, one hour) to Roscoff (€22.10, three hours) and Brest (€13.90, 1¾ hours).

Perros-Cycles (☎ 02 96 23 13 08; 129 rue Maréchal Joffre) rents out city/mountain bikes for €12/23 per day.

FINISTÈRE

To really delve into Breton culture and tradition, push west to Finistère (Land's End), its heartland. On the northern knuckle of this fist thrust into the Atlantic, you stand the greatest chance of hearing native Breton spoken. Here is the greatest concentration of *enclos paroissiaux* (parish closes), intricately sculpted groups decorating village churchyards and peculiar to Brittany.

The islands off the coast are buffeted by wild seas and strong tidal currents while some 350 lighthouses, beacons, buoys and radar installations stand watch over the busy, treacherous sea lanes leading into the Channel.

Cornouaille (meaning Cornwall) differs in mood from the wilder, more sparsely populated north of Finistère. Holiday resorts are livelier, fishing ports bigger and more bustling and the coastline is more dramatic.

Build in time to visit Quimper, capital of the *département*, with its cobbled streets, half-timbered houses and waterways, and Brest, host to the world's largest boat festival. You'll find the tang of salt strong too in the still active fishing ports and seaside resorts of Concarneau and Douarnenez (give yourself a good half-day to explore its huge maritime museum).

ROSCOFF

pop 3600

Protected from the furious seas by the little island of Batz, Roscoff (Rosko in Breton), whose 16th-century granite houses cluster around a bay, is the southernmost – and arguably the most attractive – French channel ferry port.

Beneath the waters around Roscoff grow a wide variety of algae, some of which are used in *thalassothérapie*, a health and beauty treatment based on sea water.

Roscoff's fertile hinterland is known for its *primeurs* (early fruits and vegetables), such as cauliflower, onions, tomatoes, new potatoes and artichokes. Before the advent of large roll-on ferries, Roscoff farmers, known as 'Johnnies', would load up boats with the small pink onions grown locally, cross the Channel, then peddle – and pedal; they strung their onions from the handlebars of their bikes – them around the towns of the UK.

Orientation

Roscoff ranges around a north-facing bay, with its fishing port and pleasure harbour on the western side. Quai d'Auxerre leads northwest – becoming quai Charles de Gaulle, then rue Amiral Réveillère – to the main place Lacaze-Duthiers.

THE SEAWEED HARVESTERS

All along much of the north coast of Brittany, the receding tide exposes vast areas of sea bed covered in a thick growth of seaweed (goémon). For centuries, a small band of seaweed harvesters (goémoniers) have collected the weed washed up along the shore or set out in boats to dredge it fresh from its rocky bed. Long used as an agricultural fertiliser, the seaweed is today dried and used for various purposes in the food and cosmetics industries.

Roscoff's **Centre de Découverte des Algues** (☎ 02 98 69 77 05; 5 rue Victor Hugo; admission free; 🕑 9am-noon & 2-7pm Mon-Sat) has a small permanent display (in French) about the history, harvesting and multiple uses of seaweed and also organises guided walks.

The car ferry terminal is at Port de Bloscon, 2km east of the town centre.

Information

LAUNDRY
Ferry Laverie (23 rue Jules Ferry; 🕑 9am-8pm)

MONEY
The **ferry terminal** has a 24hr banknote exchange and ATM.

POST
Post Office (19 rue Gambetta)

TOURIST INFORMATION
Tourist Office (☎ 02 98 61 12 13; www.roscoff-tourisme.com; 46 rue Gambetta; 🕑 9am-12.30pm & 1.30-7pm Mon-Sat, 10am-12.30pm Sun Jul & Aug, 9am-noon & 2-6pm Mon-Sat Sep-Jun) Occupies a fine old stone building just north of place de la République.

Sights & Activities
The 16th-century flamboyant Gothic **Église Notre Dame de Kroaz-Batz** (place Lacaze-Duthiers) with its Renaissance belfry is one of Brittany's most spectacular churches.

Aquarium de Roscoff (☎ 02 98 29 23 25; place Georges Teissier), just northwest of the church, was closed for extensive renovations at the time of writing.

Maison des Johnnies (☎ 02 98 61 25 48; 48 rue Brizeux; admission €4; 🕑 afternoons Jun–mid-Sep, Sat & Sun mid-Feb–May & late Sep) is a museum devoted

to the itinerant onion vendors of times past who enjoy near-hero status hereabouts.

Thalasso Roscoff (☎ 08 25 00 20 99; www.thalasso.com in French; rue Victor Hugo) offers a huge range of health-inducing activities including a heated seawater pool, hammam and Jacuzzi (each €9 or all three for €16).

Sleeping
Hôtel Les Arcades (☎ 02 98 69 70 45; lesarcadesroscoff@wanadoo.fr; 15 rue Amiral Réveillère; d with toilet €32-36, with bathroom €48-60; 🕑 Mar–mid-Nov) This two-star hotel, run by the same family for nearly a century, overlooks the bay. It has simple but modern rooms and – who knows – you may find yourself in the same bed that Jane Fonda and Roger Vadim once shared.

Hôtel Les Chardons Bleus (☎ 02 98 69 72 03; www.chardonsbleus.fr.st in French; 4 rue Amiral Réveillère; d 48-55; 🕑 Mar-Jan, closed Sat & Sun except Jul & Aug) The 'Thistles', a Logis de France, is also good value, with quiet rooms and a pleasant restaurant.

Hôtel Talabardon (☎ 02 98 61 24 95; www.talabardon.fr in French; place de l'Église; s €84-127, d €112-174; 🕑 Mar-Oct) Roscoff's oldest hotel, established in 1890, offers spacious, comfy rooms, many with balconies looking over the sea. You may find the welcome rather frostier than the weather.

CAMPING
Camping de Perharidy (☎ 02 98 69 70 86; www.aquacamp.fr in French; Le Ruguel; per person/tent/car €2.70/2.45/1.15; 🕑 Easter-Sep) This spot is close to a sandy beach in the grounds of a lovely 19th-century mansion. It's approximately 3km southwest of Roscoff.

Eating
In Roscoff, France's premier crabbing port, seafood reigns supreme.

La Moule au Pot (☎ 02 98 19 33 60; 13 rue Édouard Corbière; 🕑 May-Oct, closed Wed except Jul & Aug) With fresh flowers, wooden beams, a huge fireplace and a leafy rear terrace, the 'Mussel in the Pot' is a wonderful place for a substantial snack, such as a platter of mussels or one of their giant salads (€8).

L'Écume des Jours (☎ 02 98 61 22 83; quai d'Auxerre; menus €18-43; 🕑 closed Wed Jul & Aug, Tue-Wed Sep-Jun) In a beautiful 16th-century house overlooking the harbour, this is one of Roscoff's top seafood restaurants with a warm, friendly atmosphere. Highly recommended.

Le Surcouf (☎ 02 98 69 71 89; 14 rue Amiral Réveillère; ☉ Feb-Dec, closed Wed Jul & Aug, Tue-Wed Sep-Dec & Feb-Jun) This pleasant, brasserie-style restaurant specialises in seafood, drawing strongly upon local produce and culinary tradition.

Hôtel Les Arcades (see p295) has a quality restaurant, strong on seafood, does a particularly good value lunch *menu* and has superb views of the harbour. The gourmet restaurant (*menus* €19 to €44) of **Hôtel Talabardon** (see p295) also has stunning views over the bay.

Getting There & Away

BOAT
Brittany Ferries (☎ reservations 08 25 82 88 28; www .brittany-ferries.com) links Roscoff to Plymouth in England (five to nine hours, one to three daily, year-round) and Cork in Ireland (14 hours, once weekly, June to September). Boats leave from Port de Bloscon, about 2km east of the town centre.

BUS & TRAIN
The combined bus and train station is on rue Ropartz Morvan.

Cars Bihan (☎ 02 98 83 45 80) operates buses from Roscoff to Brest (€9.70, 1½ to two hours; up to four daily) departing from the ferry terminal (Port de Bloscon) and passing by the town centre.

There are regular trains and SNCF buses to Morlaix (€8.60, 45 minutes), where you can make connections to Brest, Quimper and St-Brieuc.

AROUND ROSCOFF
Île de Batz
pop 600

A 20-minute ferry trip north of Roscoff, Île de Batz (pronounced ba; Enez Vaz in Breton) is a charming little island with some good beaches. Just 4 sq km, it's one big, fertile vegetable garden with soil fertilised by seaweed.

Jardins Georges Delaselle (☎ 02 98 61 75 65; adult/child €4/2; ☉ 1-6pm Jul & Aug, 2-6pm Wed-Mon Apr-Jun & Sep-Oct), founded in the 19th century, has a luxuriant display of over 1500 plants from all five continents.

GETTING THERE & AROUND
The ferry (adult/child €6.50/3.50 return, bike €6 return) between Roscoff and Île de Batz runs every 30 minutes between 8am and 8pm from late-June to mid-September;

there are about eight sailings daily during the rest of the year.

On the island, **Vélos et Nature** (☎ 02 98 61 75 75), **Le Saout** (☎ 02 98 61 77 65) and **Prigent** (☎ 02 98 61 77 65) all rent bicycles.

BREST
pop 149,600

Rainy Brest, sheltered by its magnificent natural harbour, is one of France's most important naval and commercial ports. Flattened by air attacks during WWII, it was rebuilt as a modern – and not particularly attractive – city. Even though the medieval port area and its narrow streets are long gone, you'll still see the crisp, white uniforms of French sailors everywhere.

History
Brest grew up around its castle, built to defend the harbour on the River Penfeld. Following the 1532 union of Brittany and France, both the castle and its harbour became a royal fortress.

During the reign of Louis XIV, Brest and its naval dockyards became one of France's four main military ports. In WWII, this strategically important city, occupied by German forces, was bombarded intensively and virtually razed by allied aircraft. These days, Brest is still a major port and naval base. And, although its shipbuilding and heavy industries have waned, it is re-inventing itself as a centre for high-tech, tourism and service industries.

Orientation
Brest sprawls along the northern shore of the deep natural harbour known as the Rade de Brest. Its castle, the naval base (Arsenal Maritime) and Port de Commerce are on the waterfront. From the castle, rue de Siam runs northeast to place de la Liberté, the city's main square, then it intersects with av Georges Clemenceau, the main northwest to southeast traffic artery.

Information
Laverie du Père Denis (8 place de la Liberté; ☉ 7am-8.30pm) Laundry.
Main Post Office (place Général Leclerc)
Net@rena (☎ 02 98 33 61 11; 30 rue Yves Collet; per hr €3.50; ☉ 11am-1am Mon-Thu, 11-4am Fri & Sat, 1-11pm Sun) Internet access.

Tourist Office (☎ 02 98 44 24 96; office.de.tourisme
.brest@wanadoo.fr; place de la Liberté; ⏰ 9.30am-7pm
Mon-Sat & 10am-noon Sun mid-Jun–mid-Sep, 9.30am-
12.30pm & 2-6pm Mon-Sat mid-Sep–mid-Jun)

Sights & Activities
OCÉANOPOLIS
Within the huge aquariums of Brest's ultramodern **Océanopolis** (☎ 02 98 34 40 40; www
.oceanopolis.com in French; port de Plaisance; adult/child
€14.50/10; ⏰ 9am-6pm Apr-Aug, 10am-5pm Tue-Sun
Sep-Mar), about 3km east of the city centre,
are kelp forests, seals, crabs, anemones,
penguins, sharks and so much more that
swims or crawls. Take bus No 7 from place
de la Liberté.

MUSÉE DE LA MARINE
The **Naval Museum** (☎ 02 98 22 12 39; adult/child
€4.60/free; ⏰ 10am-6.30pm Apr–mid-Sep, 10am-noon & 2-
6pm Wed-Mon mid-Sep–Mar) is within the fortified,
13th-century **Château de Brest** (one of the few
buildings to survive WWII bombing), from
whose ramparts there are striking views of
the harbour and naval base.

TOUR TANGUY
The paintings, photographs and dioramas
in this 14th-century **tower** (☎ 02 98 00 88 60;
place Pierre Péron; admission free; ⏰ 10am-noon & 2-
7pm Jun-Sep, 2-5pm Wed-Thu & 2-6pm Sat & Sun Oct-
May) trace the history of Brest – in particular
how it was on the eve of WWII. Don't miss
the documented visit of three Siamese ambassadors in 1686 who presented gifts to
the court of Louis XIV; rue de Siam was
renamed to commemorate the occasion.

Tours
Between April and September, **La Société
Maritime Azenor** (☎ 02 98 41 46 23) offers cruises
(adult/child €14/10, 1½ hours, two or three
times daily) around the harbour and naval
base, departing from both the Port de Commerce (near the castle) and the Port de
Plaisance (opposite Océanopolis). **Vedettes
Armoricaines** (☎ 02 98 44 44 04) operates similar
cruises, sailing from the Port de Commerce.
The tourist office sells tickets for both.

Festivals & Events
The big summer attraction is **Les Jeudis du
Port** (Harbour Thursdays; admission free; 7.30pm-midnight
Thu mid-Jul–late Aug) with live bands, concerts,
street theatre and children's events.

Brest 2008 is the title of the next mega-
moot of around 2000 traditional sailing craft
from around the world that the city hosts in
an intensive week of July every four years.

Sleeping
Auberge de Jeunesse (☎ 02 98 41 90 41; brest.aj.cis@
wanadoo.fr; rue de Kerbriant; dm B&B €12.10) Brest's
modern youth hostel is near Océanopolis
and a stone's throw from the artificial beach
at Moulin Blanc. Take bus 7 from the train
station to the terminus (Port de Plaisance).

Hôtel Le Régent (☎ 02 98 44 29 77; www.brestle
-regent.fr.st in French; 22 rue d'Algésiras; s/d from €30/33)
With its lovely Art-Nouveau café-bar, this
place speaks attitude and offers excellent
value. All 18 rooms have private bathrooms
and at weekends rates fall as low as €24.

Hôtel Continental (☎ 02 98 80 50 40; continental
-brest@hotel-sofibra.com; rue Émile Zola; s €101-133, d 109-
141) The Continental is the smartest spot in
Brest city centre. The exterior is just plain
dull but the Art-Deco interior will suck
your breath away.

CAMPING
Camping du Goulet (☎ 02 98 45 86 84; camping
dugoulet@wanadoo.fr; Ste-Anne du Portzic; per person/
tent/car €3.50/4/1.30) This huge, hilly camping
ground is in Ste-Anne du Portzic, 6km
southwest of Brest and 400m from the sea.
Take bus No 14 from the train station to Le
Cosquer stop.

Eating
Amour de Pomme de Terre (☎ 02 98 43 48 51; 23 rue
Halles St-Louis; menus €9-26) 'Potato Love' serves
up all manner of dishes – just as long as
they have potatoes. You also get a delightful
mini-salad of the freshest fruit and veg from
the covered market opposite – and a dip
into a basket of rich dried sausages, from
which you hack off a hunk.

Fleur de Sel (☎ 02 98 44 38 65; 15bis rue de Lyon;
mains €16-23.50; ⏰ closed Sun & lunch Sat) This
stylish Art-Deco restaurant, its minimalist décor contrasting with the warm atmosphere, serves creative French cuisine,
with dishes such as veal kidneys sizzled in
truffle vinegar.

Ma Petite Folie (☎ 02 98 42 44 42; Port de Plaisance;
menus €18-25; ⏰ Mon-Sat) This superb seafood
restaurant is in an old lobster-fishing boat,
forever beached at Moulin Blanc, near the
auberge de jeunesse.

Le Ruffé (☎ 02 98 46 07 70; 1bis rue Yves Collet; menus €25-30, mains €13.50-18; ☺ closed dinner Sun) With its unostentatious maritime décor, Le Ruffé, airy, friendly and highly regarded, is among the best places in town for seafood and quality, creative fish dishes.

Les Halles Ste-Marie, Brest's covered market, is a rich resource for self-caterers.

Getting There & Away

AIR
Ryanair has a daily flight to/from London (Stansted).

BOAT
Ferries to Île d'Ouessant (see p300) leave from the Port de Commerce.

BUS
Brest's bus station (☎ 02 98 44 46 73) is beside the train station. Routes include Le Conquet (€4.45, 45 minutes, six daily) and Roscoff (€9.70, 1½ to two hours, four daily).

CAR & MOTORCYCLE
Hire companies include **ADA** (☎ 02 98 44 44 88; 9 av Georges Clemenceau) and **Europcar** (☎ 02 98 44 66 88; rue Voltaire).

TRAIN
There are frequent trains or SNCF buses to Quimper (€13.80, 1¼ hours) and Morlaix (€8.80, 45 minutes), which has connections to Roscoff (€12, 1½ hours). There are also around 15 TGV trains daily to Rennes (€29.40, two hours) and Paris (Gare Montparnasse; €66.30, 4½ hours).

Getting Around
The local bus network **Bibus** (☎ 02 98 80 30 30) sells tickets for €1, carnets of 10 for €8.30 and day passes for €3. It also has an information kiosk on place de la Liberté.

Torch'VTT (☎ 02 98 46 06 07; 93 blvd Montaigne) rents bicycles.

To order a taxi call ☎ 02 98 80 43 43 or ☎ 02 98 42 11 11.

LE CONQUET
pop 2150

Perched on the westernmost tip of Brittany, the pretty fishing village of Le Conquet (called, engagingly, Konk Leon in Breton) lies close to some pristine beaches and lovely coastal paths. It's largely ignored by tourists, who generally leave their cars here, then pile onto the Île d'Ouessant ferry.

Information
The **tourist office** (☎ 02 98 89 11 31; www.leconquet .fr in French; ☺ 9am-1pm & 3-7pm Mon-Sat, 9am-1pm Sun Jul & Aug, 9am-noon Tue-Sat Sep-Jun) is in the town hall in the Parc de Beauséjour.

Activities
The tourist office's free town plan details a couple of good **walks** in and around Le Conquet. A clifftop stride leads to **Phare de Kermorvan**, a 37m-high lighthouse perched on the Kermorvan Peninsula, which guards the harbour entrance. To its north lies **Plage des Blancs Sablons**, a lovely, wide beach.

A 5km hike along the coastal path south of Le Conquet leads to **Pointe St-Mathieu**. At the foot of its conspicuous lighthouse are the spectacular ruins of the 16th-century Benedictine **Abbaye St-Mathieu**.

Sleeping & Eating
Le Relais du Vieux Port (☎ 02 98 89 15 91; 1 quai du Drellac'h; d €37-55) Le Relais, with seven comfortable rooms (three with four-poster beds), enjoys an appealing setting beside the waterfront at the old (inner) harbour and represents excellent value. Staff are friendly and there's a cosy creperie and restaurant on the ground floor.

Hostellerie de la Pointe St-Mathieu (☎ 02 98 89 00 19; www.pointe-saint-mathieu.com; Pointe St-Mathieu; s €58-66, d €63-80; dinner menus €25-64) Five kilometres south of Le Conquet, this lovely hotel has a swimming pool, stylish bar and gourmet restaurant with a Gothic fireplace and stone vaulting.

Getting There & Away
Buses operated by **Les Cars St-Mathieu** (☎ 02 98 89 12 02) link Brest with Le Conquet (€4.65, 45 minutes, six daily).

Ferries to Île d'Ouessant depart from the *embarcadère* (ferry terminal) in the outer harbour.

ÎLE D'OUESSANT
pop 950

Île d'Ouessant (Enez Eusa in Breton, meaning 'Island of Terror'; Ushant in English) is rugged and hauntingly beautiful. About 20km from the mainland and some 7km by 4km, it serves as a beacon for over 50,000 ships entering the English Channel each year.

Traditionally, the sea provided the islanders with both a livelihood and resources. The menfolk, mostly sailors, would be away for as much as two years at a time and it was the women who tilled the fields and pulled in the seaweed. The interior of the houses, partitioned by little more than wooden panels, could almost be the inside of a boat, the furniture often fashioned from driftwood. To mask its imperfections, it was usually painted in bright colours – green for hope or blue and white symbolising the Virgin Mary.

Although the island is no longer isolated (day visitors by the thousand pour from the ferries in high summer), a few local traditions persist. Old women still make delicate lace crosses in memory of husbands who never returned from the sea, little black sheep are free to roam as they please and the delicious local dish, *ragoût de mouton* (lamb roasted in an extempore peat oven), is prepared on special days.

The entire island is ideal for windy walks. A 45km path follows the craggy, rocky coastline amid some very grand scenery.

Orientation & Information

The ferry landing is at Port du Stiff on the east coast. The island's only village is Lampaul, 4km away. On the west coast, there's a handful of hotels, restaurants and shops.

The tiny **tourist office** (☎ 02 98 48 85 83; www .ot-ouessant.fr in French; ☻ 10am-noon & 1.30-6pm Mon-Sat, 10am-noon Sun) is on place de l'Église in Lampaul. It sells an English-language version of its brochure *Circuits de Randonnée Pédestre* (€2.30) with stylised maps and descriptions of four coastal walks varying between 10km and 16km.

Sights & Activities

MUSEUMS

Black-and-white striped Phare de Créac'h is the world's most powerful lighthouse, its beam (two white flashes every 10 seconds) visible for over 50km. Beneath is the island's main museum, the **Musée des Phares et des Balises** (Lighthouse & Beacon Museum; ☎ 02 98 48 80 70; adult/child €4/2.50; ☻ 10.30am-6.30pm Apr-Sep, 1.30-5pm or 5.30pm Oct-Mar). In the old lighthouse generator rooms, it tells the story of these vital navigation aids. Unless you're of a technical bent, you'll probably find the section on shipwrecks and underwater archaeology more interesting.

The small **Écomusée d'Ouessant** (☎ 02 98 48 86 37; Maison du Niou; adult/child €3.20/2; ☻ as Musée des Phares et des Balises) occupies two typical local houses, one recreating a traditional homestead, the other exploring the island's history and customs.

A combined ticket giving entry to both museums costs €6.30/2.

CYCLING

The most practical and enjoyable way to get around the island is by bike (for details of bicycle hire, see p300).

BEACHES

Plage de Corz, 600m south of Lampaul, is the island's best beach. Other good spots to stretch out are **Plage du Prat**, **Plage de Yuzin** and **Plage Ar Lan**. All are easily accessible by bike from Lampaul or Port du Stiff.

Sleeping & Eating

Auberge de Jeunesse (☎ 02 98 48 84 53; fax 02 98 48 87 42; La Croix-Rouge, Lampaul; dm B&B €13.70; ☻ closed last 3 weeks Jan) This friendly hostel, on the hill above Lampaul, has two- to six-person bedrooms. Reservations are essential since it's very popular with school and walking groups.

Hôtel Roc'h Ar Mor (☎ 02 98 48 80 19; www .rocharmor.com in French; d €59-82.50; ☻ mid-Feb–Dec) This modern 15-room hotel has bright, cheerful rooms, enjoys a superb location next to the Baie de Lampaul and runs a good **restaurant** with a terrace overlooking the sea.

Camping Municipal (☎ 02 98 48 84 65; fax 02 98 48 83 99; Stang Ar Glan, Lampaul; per person/site €2.65/2.70; ☻ Apr-Sep) About 500m east of Lampaul, it looks more like a football field than a camping ground.

Crêperie Ti A Dreuz (☎ 02 98 48 83 01; Lampaul; galettes €3-9; ☻ Easter–mid-Sep) This pretty little blue-and-white creperie (named 'the slanting house' because of its somewhat wonky walls) serves delicious galettes. Try the *ouessantine*, with its creamy potato, cheese and sausage topping.

Ty Karn (☎ 02 98 48 87 33; Lampaul; lunch menu €12-15, dinner €20-28) The ground floor of this hyperfriendly place is a bar, offering tasty midday snacks in summer, while upstairs there's an agreeable restaurant.

If you forgot the sandwich filling, you'll find three minimarkets in Lampaul.

Getting There & Away

AIR

Finist'air (☎ 02 98 84 64 87; www.finistair.fr) flies from Brest's small airport to Ouessant in a mere 15 minutes. There are two flights daily (adult/child €61/35).

BOAT

Two companies operate ferries to Ouessant year-round. Fares quoted are all return.

Penn Ar Bed (☎ 02 98 80 80 80; www.pennarbed.fr) sails from the Port de Commerce in Brest (adult/child €30/18, 2½ hours) and from Le Conquet (€25.90/15.50, 1½ hours). Boats run between each port and the island two to five times daily from May to September and once daily between October and April.

In season, Penn Ar Bed also operates from Camaret (€26.80/16.10, two hours, once daily mid-April to mid-September).

Finist'mer (☎ 02 98 89 16 61; www.finist-mer.fr in French) runs faster boats to the island up to six times daily from Le Conquet (€25.50/14, 40 minutes, mid-April to September) and from Camaret (adult/child €26.50/15, one hour, daily mid-July to mid-August, Wednesday only Easter to mid-July).

Buy ferry tickets at the ports or at the Brest or Le Conquet tourist offices. In high summer, it's prudent to reserve at least one day in advance and check in 30 minutes before departure.

Getting Around

BICYCLE

Several bike hire operators have kiosks at the Port du Stiff ferry terminal and compounds just up the hill. They also have outlets in Lampaul. The going rate for town/mountain bikes is €10/14.

Cycling on the coastal footpath is forbidden – the fragile turf is strictly for walkers.

MINIBUS

Several islanders – including **Lucien Malgorn** (☎ 06 84 42 12 70) and **Dominique Etienne** (☎ 06 07 90 07 43) – run minibus services. They meet the ferry at Port du Stiff and will shuttle you to Lampaul or your accommodation for a flat fare of €1.50 (in July and August, book ahead to guarantee a seat). For the return journey, the pick-up point is the car park beside Lampaul's church.

Minibus owners also offer two-hour guided tours (€12 per person) of the island.

PRESQU'ÎLE DE CROZON

The tempting Crozon Peninsula, part of the Parc Naturel Régional d'Armorique, offers wild and spectacular sea cliffs at Pointe de Dinan and Pointe de Pen-Hir and, in Morgat and Camaret, a pair of sheltered resort towns with beaches.

Ménez-Hom

The rounded, 330m-high, heather- and grass-clad hump of Ménez-Hom guards the eastern end of the peninsula. The summit – a surfaced road leads right to the top – offers a superb panorama over the Baie de Douarnenez and is also a popular hang-gliding and paragliding site. The **Club Celtic de Vol Libre** (☎ 02 98 81 50 27; www.vol-libre-menez-hom.com in French) offers half-day hang-gliding and *parapente* sessions for €70.

Landévennec

To the north of Ménez-Hom, the River Aulne flows into the Rade de Brest beside the pretty little village of Landévennec, famous for its ruined Benedictine **Abbaye St-Guenolé**. The abbey **museum** (☎ 02 98 27 35 90; admission €4; ☼ 10am-7pm Jul–mid-Sep, 2-6pm Sun-Fri May-Jun & late Sep) records the history of the settlement, founded by St Guenolé in AD 485 and the oldest Christian site in Brittany. Nearby, a new abbey is home to a contemporary community of monks, who run a little shop selling, among the usual tourist paraphernalia, delicious, home-made fruit jellies.

Camaret-sur-Mer

Until early last century, Camaret was France's biggest crayfish port, its boats roaming as far as the Indian Ocean in search of this expensive crustacean. Today, the carcasses of abandoned fishing boats line the harbour, sad testimony to this once-thriving local industry. But it's a lively place in summer and a popular yachting harbour that depends on the annual flood of summer visitors for a living.

The **Chapelle Notre-Dame-de-Rocamadour**, its timber roof like an inverted ship's hull, is dedicated to the sailors of Camaret, who have adorned it with votive offerings of oars, lifebuoys and model ships.

The **tourist office** (☎ 02 98 27 93 60; www.camaret-sur-mer.com in French; 15 quai Kléber; ☼ 9am-7pm Mon-Sat & 10am-1pm Sun Jul & Aug, 10am-noon & 2-5pm Mon-Sat Sep-Jun) is on the waterfront.

Pointe de Pen-Hir

Pointe de Pen-Hir, 3km south of Camaret, is a spectacular headland bounded by steep sea cliffs. It bears two WWII memorials; one commemorates the Bretons who died, the other, a bunker, is to soldiers and sailors who perished during the Battle of the Atlantic. The line of sea stacks off the point is known as the Tas de Pois – rather more euphonic in French than its translation, 'Pile of Peas'.

Crozon & Morgat

pop 7800

Crozon, the largest town on the peninsula, provides shops and services for the more alluring resort of Morgat, 2km south, which makes a good base for exploring this outstandingly beautiful peninsula.

INFORMATION

The **Crozon tourist office** (☎ 02 98 27 07 92; croz on.maison.du.tourisme@wanadoo.fr; blvd Pralognan; ⏰ 9.15am-12.30pm & 2-7pm Mon-Sat, 10am-noon Sun Jul & Aug, 9.15am-noon & 2-5.30pm or 6pm Mon-Sat Sep-Jun) is on the main road to Camaret 500m west of the church.

The seasonal **Morgat tourist office** (☎ 02 98 27 29 49; ⏰ Jul & Aug) overlooks the promenade at the corner of blvd de la Plage.

ACTIVITIES

Beyond the marina at the southern end of Morgat's fine sandy **beach**, the coastal path offers an excellent 8km hike along the sea cliffs to **Cap de la Chèvre**.

A couple of Morgat-based companies, **Vedettes Rosmeur** (☎ 02 98 27 10 71) and **Vedettes Sirènes** (☎ 02 98 26 20 10) operate 45-minute boat trips to the colourful **sea caves** along the coast. Tours (adult/child €9/6) depart from Morgat harbour several times daily from April to September.

SLEEPING & EATING

Hôtel de la Baie (☎ 02 98 27 07 51; hotel.delabaie@ presquile-crozon.com; 46 blvd de la Plage, Morgat; d with shower €33, with bathroom €37-45.50; P) This jolly, family-run place on Morgat's promenade is one of the best deals in town; parking's free and it's also one of the very few hotels to remain open year-round.

Camping Les Pieds Dans l'Eau (☎ 02 98 27 62 43; St-Fiacre; per person/tent/car €3.75/3.75/2; ⏰ mid-Jun–mid-Sep) 'Camping feet in the water' (almost literally so at high tide since the beach is only a well-cast pebble away) is one of nine camping grounds along the peninsula.

La Grange de Toul-Boss (☎ 02 98 27 17 95; 1 place d'Ys; galettes €3-7.50, menus €13, mains €10-18.50) Near the Morgat tourist office, this restaurant, creperie and tearoom occupies an old traditional Breton barn. The *menu* is exceptionally good value; starters include half a crab or six oysters and the mains are principally large portions of fish.

Les Échoppes (☎ 02 98 26 12 63; 24 quai du Kador, Morgat; menus €15-30; ⏰ lunch & dinner Jul & Aug, dinner only May, Jun & Sep) This unassuming stone cottage at the southern end of the waterfront specialises in seafood – the catch of the day is advertised on a sign outside. It's so small that we advise reserving, whatever the day.

GETTING THERE & AROUND

There are five buses daily from Quimper to Crozon (€9.30, 1¼ hours), continuing to Camaret (€9.50) and up to four from Camaret and Crozon to Brest (€9, 1¼ hours, daily). Buses also run between Morgat, Crozon and Camaret several times daily (€1.70, 10 minutes).

To rent a bike, contact **Presqu'îles Loisirs** (☎ 02 98 27 00 09; 13 rue de la Gare, Crozon), opposite Crozon's tourist office, **Point Bleu** (☎ 02 98 27 09 04; Quai Kador, Morgat) or, in summer, the open-air stall in front of Morgat's tourist office. The going rate is about €10 per day.

HUELGOAT

pop 1750

Huelgoat (An Uhelgoat in Breton), 30km south of Morlaix, makes an excellent base for exploring what's left of the forested Argoat. The village borders the unspoiled Forêt d'Huelgoat – where King Arthur's treasure is said to be buried – with its unusual rock formations, caves, menhirs and abandoned silver and lead mines. To the east and northeast are the Forêt de St-Ambroise and the Forêt de Fréau. All have a good network of walking trails.

Orientation & Information

Huelgoat sits beside a small Y-shaped lake that empties into the Argent, a mere trickle of a river. Between June and September, the **tourist office** (☎ 02 98 99 72 32; fax 02 98 99 75 72; ⏰ 10am-12.30pm & 2-5.30pm Mon-Sat Jul & Aug, 10am-noon & 2-4.30pm Mon-Fri Sep-Jun) is in the Moulin du Chaos, an old mill beside the bridge at the eastern end of the lake. During the rest of the year it operates within the town hall (place Alphonse Penven).

Activities
WALKING
Huelgoat gets busy in summer and the network of forest tracks is best appreciated in the relative calm of spring and autumn. An undemanding walking trail (45 minutes round trip) heads downstream from the bridge, initially on the opposite bank to the tourist office. Here, the river disappears into a picturesque, wooded valley where giant granite boulders lie pell mell, each upholstered with shaggy green moss.

Longer hikes (1½ to two hours) lead along the Promenade du Canal to some old silver mines and to the unremarkable Grotte d'Artus (Arthur's Cave).

Sleeping & Eating
Hôtel-Restaurant du Lac (☎ 02 98 99 71 14; fax 02 98 99 70 91; 9 rue Général de Gaulle; d €45-58; ☼ mid-Feb–mid-Dec) Huelgoat's only hotel, a Logis de France that's a mere 200m from the tourist office, is fine, if not as charming as its name and lakeside location might suggest. Its popular **restaurant** serves steaks, pizzas and salads.

Camping Municipal du Lac (☎ 02 98 99 78 80; rue Général de Gaulle; per person/site €2.90/3.40; ☼ mid-Jun–mid-Sep) This camping ground is on the lakeside around 500m west of the town centre.

Crêperie des Myrtilles (☎ 02 98 99 72 66; 26 place Aristide-Briand; crepes €2-6, menus from €8; ☼ Jan-Oct, closed Mon except Jul & Aug) This pretty little creperie on the town's main square has a pleasant summer terrace. Try their juicy, signature *crêpe aux myrtilles* (crepes with bilberry, picked locally).

Getting There & Away
EFFIA (☎ 02 98 93 06 98) runs at least two services daily to Morlaix (€8.70, one hour) to the north and Carhaix to the southeast. Buses stop in front of the Chapelle de Notre-Dame in place Aristide-Briand.

DOUARNENEZ & LOCRONAN
In Breton, the good folk of Douarnenez are called *penn sardin* (sardine head), a nickname derived from former days when it was home port to more than 1000 sardine boats, whose catch was processed by over 30 canneries. Today it's still an important fishing

port, but it has also re-invented itself as a guardian of Brittany's – and France's – maritime traditions.

The action part of Douarnenez sits on a stubby peninsula. From it, streets fall steeply west to the narrow, river-mouth harbour of Port Rhu. Eastwards, the narrow alleys of the old town lead more gently down to the old port of Rosmeur.

The **tourist office** (☎ 02 98 92 13 35; www.douarnenez-tourisme.com in French; 2 rue Docteur Mével; ☼ 10am-noon & 2-7pm Mon-Sat, 10am-1pm Sun Jul & Aug, 10am-noon & 2-5pm or 6pm Mon-Sat Sep-Jun) is beside place Édouard Vaillant.

On Port Rhu's lively waterfront are **Port-Musée** and the **Musée du Bateau** (☎ 02 98 92 65 20; quai du Port Rhu; combined ticket adult/child €6.20/3.85; ☼ 10am-7pm mid-Jun–mid-Sep, 10am-12.30pm & 2-6pm Tue-Sun Apr–mid-Jun & mid-Sep–Oct). Moored at open-air Port-Musée are around 20 traditional vessels, ranging from a Breton *langoustier* (cray-fishing boat) to a Norwegian masted sailing ship. Within the vast Musée du Bateau, occupying a former sardine cannery, are around 40 smaller traditional boats such as an Inuit kayak and a Welsh coracle as well as local craft.

On the other side of town is the old port area of **Rosmeur**, an attractive waterfront lined with fishermen's bars and touristy restaurants.

CAT (☎ 02 98 90 68 40) runs buses to/from Quimper (€6, 35 minutes, six to 10 daily).

To the east of Douarnenez, Locronan has changed little outwardly since the 18th century – and so has been much in demand as a film location, most famously in 1979 for Roman Polanski's *Tess*.

It may have evaded the passage of time, but Locronan certainly doesn't escape the passage of thousands of tourists every year. To savour the atmosphere of *les temps perdus*, it's best to visit very early in the morning or outside the summer season.

Locronan's **tourist office** (☎ 02 98 91 70 14; www.locronan.org in French; place de la Mairie; ☼ Apr-Sep) is on the main square.

Between two and seven buses daily run to Locronan from both Quimper and Camaret.

QUIMPER
pop 59,400
Quimper (kam-pair), lying where the small Rivers Odet and Steïr meet, takes its name

from the Breton word *kemper,* meaning 'confluence'. Strongly Breton in character and administrative capital of the *département* of Finistère, it's very much the cultural and artistic capital too, with its cobbled streets, half-timbered houses, waterways and magnolias, imparting a pleasing village feel.

Orientation
The old city, much of it pedestrianised, clusters around the cathedral on the north bank of the Odet, overlooked by Mont Frugy on the south bank.

Information
Eixxos (☎ 02 98 64 40 56; 12 blvd Dupleix; per hr €3.50; ☉ 11am-10pm Mon-Thu, 11am-1am Fri & Sat, 2-10pm Sun) Internet access.
Laverie de la Gare (4 av de la Gare; ☉ 8am-8pm) Laundry.
Main Post Office (blvd Amiral de Kerguélen)
Tourist Office (☎ 02 98 53 04 05; www.quimper-tour isme.com in French; place de la Résistance; ☉ 9am-7pm Mon-Sat, 10am-1pm & 3-5.45pm Sun Jul & Aug, 9.30am-12.30pm & 1.30-6pm or 6.30pm Mon-Sat Sep-Jun, 10am-12.45pm Sun Jun & 1-15 Sep) Can reserve accommodation. Arranges weekly guided city tours in English, July-August.

Sights & Activities
CATHÉDRALE ST-CORENTIN
The twin spires and soaring vertical lines of Quimper's **cathedral** dominate the city centre. Begun in 1239, it wasn't fully completed until the 1850s, when those spires that meld so harmoniously into the original structure were added. The inside, recently scrubbed, renovated and repainted, gives an extraordinary feeling of light and space. High up on the west façade, between the spires, is an equestrian statue of King Gradlon, the city's mythical 5th-century founder.

MUSEUMS
Musée Départemental Breton (☎ 02 98 95 21 60; 1 rue du Roi Gradlon; adult/child €3.80/2.50; ☉ 9am-6pm Jun-Sep, 9am-noon & 2-5pm Tue-Sat & 2-5pm Sun Oct-May) is in what used to be the bishop's palace, beside the cathedral. It has superb exhibits on the history, furniture, costumes, crafts and archaeology of the area. Adjoining the museum is the **Jardin de l'Évêché** (Bishop's Palace Garden; admission free; ☉ 9am-5pm/6pm).
Musée de la Faïence (☎ 02 98 90 12 72; 14 rue Jean-Baptiste Bousquet; adult/child €4/2.30; ☉ 10am-6pm Mon-Sat mid-Apr–mid-Oct) occupies a one-

time ceramics factory and displays over 2000 pieces of choice china.
Musée des Beaux-Arts (☎ 02 98 95 45 20; 40 place St-Corentin; adult/child €4/2.50; ☉ 10am-7pm Jul & Aug, 10am-noon & 2-6pm Wed-Mon Apr-Jun & Sep-Oct, 10am-noon & 2-6pm Wed-Sat & Mon, 2-6pm Sun Nov-Mar) in the town hall displays European paintings from the 16th to early 20th centuries.

WALKING
A nice way to get the feel of Quimper is to simply stroll along the banks of River Odet, where flowers cascade from its numerous foot bridges, or around place Médard, rue Kéréon, rue des Gentilhommes and its continuation, rue du Sallé, to place au Beurre. Most of old Quimper's **half-timbered houses** are concentrated in this tight triangle.

If you're feeling a little more energetic, climb 72m-high **Mont Frugy**, which offers great views of the city. Follow the switchback path that starts just east of the tourist office.

Tours
From May to September **Vedettes de l'Odet** (☎ 02 98 57 00 58) runs boat trips (adult/child €21.50/13, 1¼ hours) from Quimper along the wonderfully scenic Odet estuary to Bénodet, departing from quai Neuf.

Festivals & Events
The **Festival de Cornouaille** (www.festival-cornouaille .com in French), a showcase for traditional Celtic music, costumes and culture, takes place between the third and fourth Sundays of July. After the traditional festival, classical music concerts are held at different venues around town. Ask the tourist office for times and venues of a local *fest-noz* (night festival).

Sleeping
Auberge de Jeunesse (☎ 02 98 64 97 97; quimper@fuaj .org; 6 av des Oiseaux; dm €8.90) Quimper's youth hostel, with self-catering facilities, is beside Camping Municipal (see below), on the edge of a wooded park.
Hôtel TGV (☎ 02 98 90 54 00; www.hoteltgv.com in French; 4 rue de Concarneau; d €36-42) One among several hotels around the train station, the TGV, recently under new ownership, has small but well-appointed rooms. A reader reports that noise from the bar beneath can be intrusive so aim high, for one of the top-floor rooms.
Hôtel Gradlon (☎ 02 98 95 04 39; www.hotel-gra dlon.com in French; 30 rue de Brest; d €82-99; ☉ closed

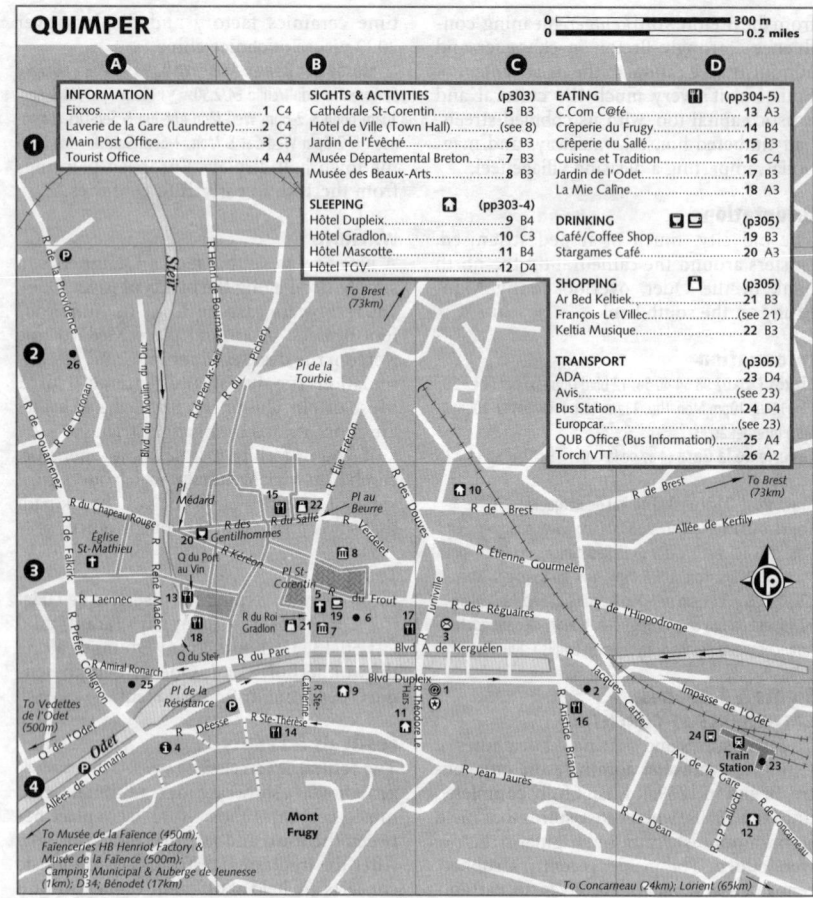

QUIMPER

INFORMATION	
Eixxos	1 C4
Laverie de la Gare (Laundrette)	2 C4
Main Post Office	3 C3
Tourist Office	4 A4

SIGHTS & ACTIVITIES	(p303)
Cathédrale St-Corentin	5 B3
Hôtel de Ville (Town Hall)	(see 8)
Jardin de l'Évêché	6 B3
Musée Départemental Breton	7 B3
Musée des Beaux-Arts	8 B3

SLEEPING	(pp303-4)
Hôtel Dupleix	9 B4
Hôtel Gradlon	10 C3
Hôtel Mascotte	11 B4
Hôtel TGV	12 D4

EATING	(pp304-5)
C.Com C@fé	13 A3
Crêperie du Frugy	14 B4
Crêperie du Sallé	15 B3
Cuisine et Tradition	16 C4
Jardin de l'Odet	17 B3
La Mie Câline	18 A3

DRINKING	(p305)
Café/Coffee Shop	19 B3
Stargames Café	20 A3

SHOPPING	(p305)
Ar Bed Keltiek	21 B3
François Le Villec	(see 21)
Keltia Musique	22 B3

TRANSPORT	(p305)
ADA	23 D4
Avis	(see 23)
Bus Station	24 D4
Europcar	(see 23)
QUB Office (Bus Information)	25 A4
Torch VTT	26 A2

20 Dec-20 Jan) This comfortable place, full of character, is almost a home from home. Rooms are set around a pretty courtyard with a rose garden at its heart and there's a convivial bar with an open fire for winter evenings.

Hôtel Dupleix (☎ 02 98 90 53 35; www.hotel-dup leix .com in French; 34 blvd Dupleix; d €82-105; P) The Dupleix, reliable if bland, is part of a business complex overlooking the River Odet opposite the town hall. All rooms are modern and well equipped and some have a balcony and view of the cathedral.

Hôtel Mascotte (☎ 02 98 53 37 37; www.hotel-sofi bra.com; 6 rue Théodore Le Hars; s €55-77, d €64-77) The Mascotte is spruce and reliable, if short on character. Rooms are double glazed and size-

able and there's adjacent public parking. Just don't expect anything out of the ordinary.

CAMPING

Camping Municipal (☎ /fax 02 98 55 61 09; av des Oiseaux; per person/tent/car €3.26/0.75/1.55) This park is 1km west of the old city. From quai de l'Odet follow rue Pont l'Abbé northwestwards and continue straight ahead where it veers left. Alternatively, take bus No 1 from the train station to the Chaptal stop.

Eating

Crêperie du Frugy (☎ 02 98 90 32 49; 9 rue Ste-Thérèse; galettes €3.70-6.55; closed Sun & lunch Mon) This tiny place, in the shadow of Mont Frugy, dishes up excellent inexpensive crepes and galettes.

Crêperie du Sallé (☎ 02 98 95 95 80; 6 rue du Sallé; galettes €3-9; ⏱ Tue-Sat) Locals crowd into this bright and breezy creperie at lunchtime so arrive early to guarantee a table. Sample some real Breton specialities, tucked away inside your galette, such as *saucisse fumée* (smoked sausage; €6.60) and coquilles St-Jacques (scallops; €8.60).

Jardin de l'Odet (☎ 02 98 95 76 76; 39 blvd Amiral de Kerguélen; menus €19-35; ⏱ Mon-Sat) This stylish Art-Deco restaurant overlooks part of the Jardin de l'Évêché. Specialising in Breton and French cuisine, it takes familiar dishes, then twists and modifies them creatively.

SELF-CATERING
La Mie Câline (14 quai du Steir) is a hugely popular bakery where you can get a whopping filled baguette, pastry and soft drink for only €5.20. If the midday line is too long – or if you want something a bit more subtle – just cross the stream to **C.Com C@fé** (9 quai du Port au Vin). Here, they do great sandwiches and garnished salads – so the midday queues are likely to be just as long.

Cuisine et Tradition (45 av de la Gare) is a delicatessen with a huge choice of cured meats, tarts, pies and ready-prepared dishes.

Drinking
Rue du Frout near the cathedral has a couple of small pubs that attract a Breton-speaking clientele.

Stoke up a hookah at **Stargames Café**. Primarily an Internet café, Stargames has a lovely little oriental café, all cushions and low seating, on the ground floor.

Café/Coffee Shop (20 Rue du Frout; ⏱ 6pm-1am) is a popular gay venue.

Entertainment
From late June to the first week in September, there's traditional Breton music and dance (admission €4) every Thursday evening at 9pm in the Jardin de l'Évêché.

Shopping
Ar Bed Keltiek (Celtic World; ☎ 02 98 95 42 82; 2 rue du Roi Gradlon) has a wide selection of Celtic books, music, pottery and jewellery.

Keltia Musique (☎ 02 98 95 45 82; 1 place au Beurre) carries an excellent range of CDs and books on Breton and Celtic music and art.

François Le Villec (☎ 02 98 95 31 54, 4 rue du Roi Gradlon) is an excellent place to shop for

faïence and creative textiles based upon traditional Breton designs.

Getting There & Away
BUS
CAT (☎ 02 98 90 68 40) bus destinations include Brest (€13.30, 1¼ hours) and Douarnenez (€6, 35 minutes, six to 10 daily).

Caoudal (☎ 02 98 56 96 72) runs buses to Concarneau (€4.60, 45 minutes, seven to 10 daily); three daily continue to Quimperlé (€8.90, 1½ hours).

CAR
ADA (☎ 02 98 52 25 25), **Europcar** (☎ 02 98 65 10 05) and **Avis** (☎ 02 98 90 31 34) all have offices right outside the train station.

TRAIN
There are frequent trains to Brest (€13.80, 1¼ hours, up to 10 daily), Lorient (€9.70, 40 minutes, six to eight daily), Vannes (€15.90, 1½ hours, seven daily), Rennes (€27.60, 2½ hours, five daily) and Paris (Gare Montparnasse; €63.30, 4¾ hours, eight daily).

Getting Around
BICYCLE
Torch VTT (☎ 02 98 53 84 41; 58 rue de la Providence; ⏱ Tue-Sat) rents mountain bikes for €15 per day. The friendly owner is a fount of information about local cycle routes.

CAR & MOTORCYCLE
Leave your car in the vast Parking de la Providence, which can accommodate over 1000 vehicles.

PUBLIC TRANSPORT
The information office of **QUB** (☎ 02 98 95 26 27; 2 quai de l'Odet), the local bus company, is opposite the tourist office.

TAXI
For a taxi, call ☎ 02 98 90 21 21.

CONCARNEAU
pop 18,600

Concarneau (Konk-Kerne in Breton), 24km southeast of Quimper, is France's third-most important trawler port after Boulogne and Lorient. Much of the tuna brought in here is caught in the Indian Ocean or off the coast of Africa; look out for handbills announcing the size of the incoming fleet's catch.

BRITTANY

The city has the refreshingly unpretentious air of a working fishing port, its charms supplemented by Ville Close, the walled old town perched on a rocky islet, and several good nearby beaches.

Orientation

Concarneau hugs the western side of the harbour at the mouth of the River Moros. Ville Close and its ramparts separate the Port de Plaisance, to the south, from the busy fisheries area of the Port de Pêche. Quai d'Aiguillon, becoming quai Peneroff, runs from north to south beside the harbour.

Information

Laundrette (21 av Alain Le Lay; ⏱ 7am-8pm)
Post Office (14 quai Carnot)
Tourist Office (☎ 02 98 97 01 44; www.ville-concarneau .fr in French; quai d'Aiguillon; ⏱ 9am-7pm Jul & Aug, 9am-12.30pm & 1.45-6.30pm Mon-Sat, 9.30am-12.30pm Sun April-Jun & 1-15 Sep, 9am-noon & 2-6pm Mon-Sat mid-Sep–March) Our sole candidate for the least friendly tourist office in Brittany award.

Sights

VILLE CLOSE

The **walled town**, fortified between the 14th and 17th centuries, is on a small island linked to place Jean Jaurès by a footbridge. Heed that timely warning on a sundial by the entrance: 'Time passes like a shadow'.

Savour rue Vauban and place St-Guénolé, their old stone houses converted into shops, restaurants and galleries, then return via the **ramparts** on the southern side of the island for views over the town, port and bay.

MUSEUMS & VISITS

The excellent **Musée de la Pêche** (Fisheries Museum; ☎ 02 98 97 10 20; 3 rue Vauban; adult/child €6/4; ⏱ 9.30am-8pm Jul & Aug, 10am-noon & 2-6pm Sep-Jun, closed 3 weeks in Jan) has offshore fishing boats, a retired trawler, model ships and exhibits on everything you might want to know about the fishing industry.

The **Marinarium** (☎ 02 98 50 81 64; place de la Croix; adult/child €5/3; ⏱ 10am-7pm Jul & Aug, 10am-noon & 2-6pm Apr-Jun & Sep, 2-6pm Oct-Dec & Feb), founded in 1859, is the world's oldest institute of marine biology. It has 10 aquariums and exhibits on oceanography and marine flora and fauna.

Maison Courtin (☎ 02 98 97 01 80; 3 quai du Moros; adult/child €2/free; ⏱ tours 9.30am, 10.30am, 11.30am & 2.30pm Tue-Sun Jun-Sep, 10.30am & 11.30am Tue-Fri Sep-

Jun), one of Concarneau's last functioning canning factories, does cannery tours that include a film of the cannery in peak production and free sampling.

BEACHES

Plage des Sables Blancs is on Baie de la Forêt, 1.5km northwest of the town centre; take bus No 2, northbound, from the tourist office. For Plage du Cabellou, 5km south of town, take bus No 2, southbound.

Activities

WALKING

The tourist office sells a walking guide, *Balades au Pays des Portes de Cornouaille* (€4; in French), that describes half-a-dozen walks around Concarneau. One good walk, the *Boucle de Moros* (5km), is a loop trail following the banks of the River Moros upstream.

SEA ANGLING

If you fancy catching your own fish, the **Santa Maria** (☎ 02 98 50 69 01; adult/child €31/16 incl equipment hire; sailing 8am Mon, 8am & 1.30pm or 2pm Tue-Fri) does four-hour sea-angling trips daily in July and August. It's moored alongside quai d'Aiguillon near the tourist office.

Tours

In July and August, **Vedettes Glenn** (☎ 02 98 97 10 31) does four-hour river trips (adult/child €24/12, sailing 2.15pm Tuesday to Friday and Sunday) from Concarneau along the gorgeously scenic estuary of the River Odet.

Sleeping

Auberge de Jeunesse (☎ 02 98 97 03 47; concar neau.aj.cis@wanadoo.fr; quai de la Croix; dm €10) This friendly hostel is right on the waterfront, next to the Marinarium.

Hôtel des Halles (☎ 02 98 97 11 41; www.hotel deshalles.com; place de l'Hôtel de Ville; s €42, d €47-56) A quiet, older-style hotel with comfortable, renovated rooms, the Halles is only a few minutes' stroll from Ville Close.

Hôtel de France et d'Europe (☎ 02 98 97 00 64; hotel.france-europe@wanadoo.fr; 9 av de la Gare; d €48-59; Ⓟ) The 26 rooms at this conveniently central place, a member of the Citôtel group, are all bright and modern.

Hôtel Modern (☎ 02 98 97 03 36; fax 02 98 97 89 06; 5 rue du Lin; d €40, with bathroom €55-60; Ⓟ) With its friendly landlady, this is a cosy, 1950s, put-your-feet-up kind of place.

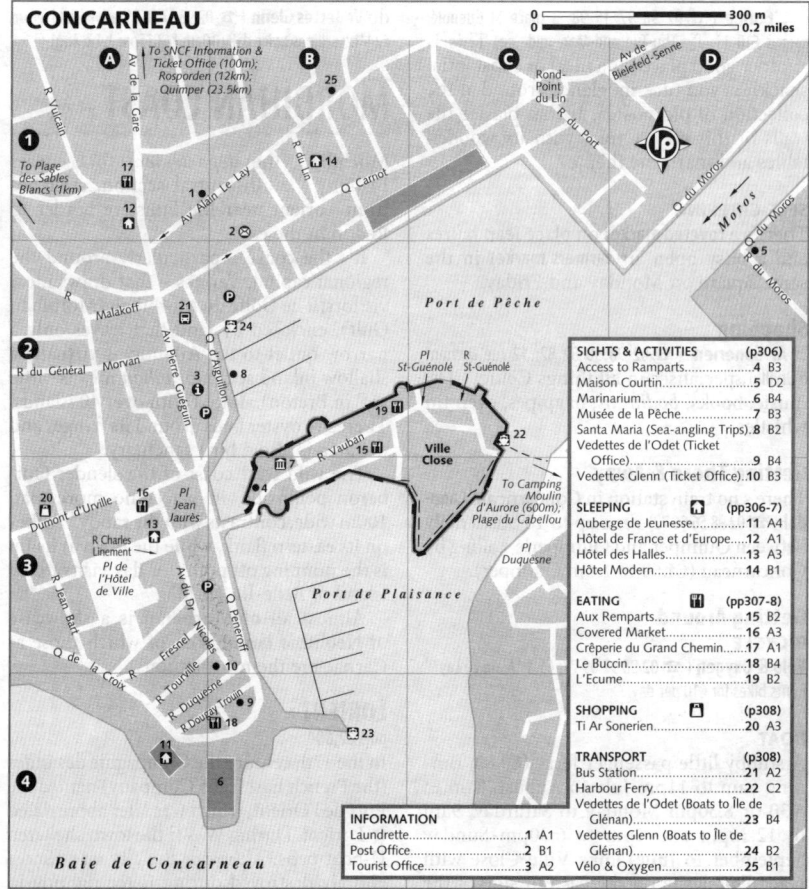

CONCARNEAU

SIGHTS & ACTIVITIES (p306)
Access to Ramparts.................**4** B3
Maison Courtin....................**5** D2
Marinarium........................**6** B4
Musée de la Pêche.................**7** B3
Santa Maria (Sea-angling Trips)..**8** B2
Vedettes de l'Odet (Ticket
Office)...........................**9** B4
Vedettes Glenn (Ticket Office)..**10** B3

SLEEPING (pp306-7)
Auberge de Jeunesse..............**11** A4
Hôtel de France et d'Europe......**12** A1
Hôtel des Halles.................**13** A3
Hôtel Modern.....................**14** B1

EATING (pp307-8)
Aux Remparts.....................**15** B2
Covered Market...................**16** A3
Crêperie du Grand Chemin.........**17** A1
Le Buccin........................**18** B4
L'Ecume..........................**19** B2

SHOPPING (p308)
Ti Ar Sonerien...................**20** A3

TRANSPORT (p308)
Bus Station......................**21** A2
Harbour Ferry....................**22** C2
Vedettes de l'Odet (Boats to Île de
Glénan)..........................**23** B4
Vedettes Glenn (Boats to Île de
Glénan)..........................**24** B2
Vélo & Oxygen....................**25** B1

INFORMATION
Laundrette.......................**1** A1
Post Office......................**2** B1
Tourist Office...................**3** A2

CAMPING

Camping Moulin d'Aurore (☎ 02 98 50 53 08; www
.moulinaurore.com in French; 49 rue de Trégunc; per person/site €4/4; ⊗ Apr-Sep) This area is only 600m
southeast of the harbour and a mere 50m
from the sea. Take bus No 1 or 2 to Le
Rouz stop from the tourist office or the
ferry from Ville Close, then walk southeast
along rue Mauduit Duplessis.

Eating

Crêperie du Grand Chemin (☎ 02 98 97 36 57; 17 av
de la Gare; crepes €1.30-3.80; ⊗ closed Mon except Jul
& Aug) For excellent Breton crepes, try this
unpretentious little place. Your basic *crêpe
au beurre* (buttered crepe) costs only €1.30
or you can make a meal of it with crepes

from starter to finish (three-course *menus*
€8 to €12.30).

Le Buccin (☎ 02 98 50 54 22; 1 rue Dougay Trouin;
menus €16-34; ⊗ closed Thu, lunch Sat & dinner Sun except Jul & Aug) Elegant Le Buccin (The Whelk)
is the place where Concarneau's gourmets
gather to enjoy whatever harvest of the
sea has been landed at the Port de Pêche
that morning.

You can eat well in La Ville Close – and
prices aren't necessarily top-tourist.

Aux Remparts (☎ 02 98 50 65 66; 31 rue Théophile
Louarn; ⊗ Easter-Oct) Enjoy their very Breton
lunchtime *menu* (€11) of fish soup, *moules
frites* and *far breton*. Or, for something
lighter, choose from their inventive range
of galettes (€6 to €8.45).

BRITTANY

L'Écume (☎ 02 98 97 15 98; 3 place St-Guénolé; menus €10-13; ✎ Thu-Tue mid-Mar–mid-Sep) This is another good place for a meal or substantial snack. As you tuck in, glance around at the collection of old postcards that plaster the walls of this cosy retreat with its wooden tables and maritime theme.

SELF-CATERING
There's a **covered market** on place Jean Jaurès and a busy open-air **farmers market** in the same square on Monday and Friday.

Shopping
Ti Ar Sonerien (☎ 02 98 50 82 82; 12 rue Dumont d'Urville) specialises in all things Celtic: CDs, music, books, *bodhrans*, bagpipes, even tin whistles.

Getting There & Away
There's no train station in Concarneau. **Caoudal** (☎ 02 98 56 96 72) runs up to 10 buses daily between Quimper and Quimperlé, calling by Concarneau (€4.60 to/from Quimper).

Getting Around
BICYCLE
Vélo & Oxygen (☎ 02 98 97 09 77; 65 av Alain Le Lay) Rents bikes for €10 per day.

BOAT
A stubby little passenger ferry (€0.80; running 8am to 11pm July to August, 8am to 6.30 or 8.30pm Monday to Saturday, 9am to 12.30pm and 2pm to 6.30pm Sunday September to June) links Ville Close with place Duquesne on the eastern side of the harbour.

TAXI
Call ☎ 02 98 97 10 93 or ☎ 02 98 50 70 50.

AROUND CONCARNEAU
The **Îles de Glénan** are a cluster of nine little islands about 20km south of Concarneau. Several are nature reserves; **Île de St-Nicolas**, a mere 900m by 300m, is the only one accessible to visitors.

Vedettes de l'Odet (☎ 02 98 57 00 58; adult/child return €25/13; sailings 1-4 daily May-Sep, Wed-Thu Apr & Oct) sails from Bénodet. It also does a guided cruise (adult/child €38.50/20) around the islands with English commentary.

Vedettes de l'Odet (sailings twice daily mid-Jul–Aug, Thu Jun–mid-Jul) also sails from Concarneau, as

do **Vedettes Glenn** (☎ 02 98 97 10 31; adult/child return €24/12; sailings twice daily 10am & 2.15pm Jul & Aug).

MORBIHAN COAST

Morbihan, the *département* that covers Brittany's south-central section, stretches from Lorient near the Finistère border to Redon in the east.

It's the coast – particularly around the regional capital, Vannes – that draws most visitors. The Golfe du Morbihan (Morbihan Gulf), enclosed by land that leaves only a narrow outlet to the Atlantic, is virtually a shallow inland sea (*mor bihan* means 'little sea' in Breton), dotted with over 40 islands. There are oyster beds around its fringes and the area is also a bird sanctuary.

The wild west coast of the slender Quiberon peninsula, in places no more than 100m wide, contrasts with the sandy beaches on its eastern flank, while the town at its tip is the jumping off point for day visits to the island of Belle-Île-en-Mer.

Almost all of Morbihan is a showcase of Neolithic landmarks, of which those at Carnac are the most famous.

LORIENT
pop 62,000
In the 17th century the Compagnie des Indes (the French East India Company) named the Port de l'Orient, which was later abbreviated to Lorient. During WWII the town sheltered U-boat pens. Although the city was almost entirely destroyed during fierce fighting in 1945, it remains an important port.

Lorient (An Oriant in Breton) is not a particularly pretty city – like Brest, it was almost completely rebuilt after its hammering in WWII – and it has few specific attractions. All the same, its tidy streets, upbeat atmosphere and large student community make it worth a visit. Fans of Celtic music and culture will enjoy the Festival Interceltique, which takes place every summer.

Orientation
Lorient creeps along the western side of a large natural harbour, the Rade de Lorient, at the mouth of the River Scorff. The centre of town is near the canal-like Port de Plaisance, about 1km south of the train and bus stations. From these terminals, you can

reach it by walking down cours de Chazelles and its continuation, rue Maréchal Foch, or by taking bus No D, direction Carnel.

Information

INTERNET ACCESS
No Work Tech (☎ 02 97 84 72 09; 5 place de la Libération; per hr €4; ◷ 2pm-1am Mon, 10am-1am Tue-Sat, 3-11pm Sun)

LAUNDRY
There are two laundrettes on blvd Cosmao Dumanoir beside the bus station.

POST
Main Post Office (9 quai des Indes)

TOURIST INFORMATION
Tourist Office (☎ 02 97 21 07 84; www.lorient-tour isme.com; quai de Rohan; ◷ 9am-7pm Mon-Sat, 10am-1pm Sun Jul & Aug, 9am or 10am-12.30pm & 1.30-5pm or 6pm Mon-Fri Sep-Jun, 9am-noon & 2-6pm Sat Apr-Jun & Sep, 10am-12.30pm Sat Oct-Mar)

Sights
The oceanographic research vessel **Thalassa** (☎ 02 97 35 13 00; quai de Rohan; adult/child €6.30/4.90; ◷ 9am-7pm Jul & Aug, 9am-12.30pm & 2-6pm Tue-Fri, 2-6pm Sat-Mon Sep-Jun), permanently moored at the Port de Plaisance, enjoys life as an oceanography museum and hands-on exhibition.

In Port Louis, 5km south of Lorient, the magnificent 16th-century **citadel** (adult/student/child €4.60/3/free; ◷ 10am-6.30pm Wed-Mon Apr–mid-Sep, 2-6pm Wed-Mon mid-Sep–mid-Dec & Feb-Mar) has two worthwhile museums. **Musée de la Compagnie des Indes** (☎ 02 97 82 19 13) traces the history of the French East India Company and its lucrative trade with India, China, Africa and the New World from 1660 to the end of the 18th century through its fascinating display of documents, maps and artefacts.

Musée National de la Marine (☎ 02 97 82 56 72) illustrates the themes of safety at sea and underwater archaeology, with a rich treasure trove from the world's oceans.

To reach Port Louis and the museum, take the **Batobus** (☎ 02 97 21 28 29; one way €1.15) ferry, which runs between Lorient and Port Louis, leaving every half-hour between 6.45am and 8pm. It departs from Lorient's Port de Pêche from Monday to Saturday and from the Embarcadère de la Rade on Sunday.

Île de Groix, 8km long by 3km wide and about 14km offshore, was once a major tuna fishing port. With its excellent beaches and a 25km coastal footpath, it makes a great day trip (for ferries, see p310).

Festivals & Events
For 10 days in early August, Lorient throbs to the **Festival Interceltique** (☎ 02 97 21 24 29; www.festival-interceltique.com). At this celebration of Celtic music, literature and dance, which attracts around 500,000 visitors, folk from the Celtic countries and regions – Ireland, Scotland, Wales, Cornwall, Isle of Man and Galicia (in northwest Spain) – join the Bretons in celebrating their common heritage.

Sleeping
Auberge de Jeunesse (☎ 02 97 37 11 65; lorient@fuaj .org; 41 rue Victor Schoelcher; dm €9.30) Lorient's HI-affiliated hostel is 4km from town in a beautiful waterside setting on the banks of the River Ter. From the bus stop on cours de Chazelles, outside the bus station, take bus No B2.

Bar-Hôtel Les Pêcheurs (☎ 02 97 21 19 24; fax 02 97 21 13 19; 7 rue Jean Lagarde; d €18-21, with shower or toilet €23-29, with bathroom €34; ◷ Mon-Sat; **P**) The cheery 'Fishermen', with rooms above a cosy neighbourhood bar, is excellent value. Ask for a room at the bar, which usually closes well before bedtime.

Hôtel Victor Hugo (☎ 02 97 21 16 24; hotelvic torhugo.lorient@wanadoo.fr; 36 rue Lazare Carnot; d €27, with bathroom €42-48; **P**) The 30-room Victor Hugo is warm and welcoming. Rooms overlooking the street are soundproofed, public areas are bright and rooms are tasteful and spotless.

Rex Hôtel (☎ 02 97 64 25 60; www.rex-hotel-lorient .com; 28 cours de Chazelles; s €43, d €46-54; **P**) Rooms positively gleam at this tautly run ship – almost literally so; the reception desk has the shape of a boat's prow, there's woodwork everywhere and a tape of waves breaking and seagulls mewing plays in the small lounge.

Eating
Bistro Le Clos des Vignes (☎ 02 97 64 15 72; 7 cours de la Bôve; menus €11, weekdays €15.75) All polished wood, brass rails and crisp white tablecloths, this lively bistro dishes up seafood and Lyonnais specialities. Finish off with a selection from their splendid cheeseboard.

Restaurant Les Papilles (☎ 02 97 21 08 44; 63 rue Maréchal Foch; mains €9.50-11, menus €20-25; ◷ closed Mon, Sat & dinner Sun) Les Papilles serves classic French cuisine at reasonable prices; the lunch *menu* at €11.50 is particularly good value.

Le Jardin Gourmand (☎ 02 97 64 17 24; 46 rue Jules-Simon; meals €18-48; ☻ Tue-Sat) The minimalist décor at this highly regarded restaurant, a couple of blocks north of the train station, contrasts with the rich, subtle cuisine. The menu, based upon what's best in the market that morning, changes regularly.

SELF-CATERING
Stock up at the **Halles de Merville**, one of Lorient's two covered markets.

Getting There & Away
BOAT
The **Société Morbihannaise de Navigation** (SMN; ☎ 08 20 05 60 00; www.smn-navigation.fr in French) operates car ferries between the Gare Maritime and Île de Groix (adult/child €24.15/15.30 return, 45 minutes, seven to eight daily). From mid-July to the end of August, SMN runs a passenger-only ferry to Sauzon on Belle Île (adult/child €29.25/15.55 return, one hour, once daily).

BUS
The **bus station** (☎ 02 97 21 28 29) is linked to the train station by a footbridge. Destinations include Josselin (€11) and Pontivy (€9.20).

TRAIN
There are several trains a day from Lorient to Quimper (€9.70, 40 minutes), Vannes (€8.10, 40 minutes) and Rennes (€22.70), plus TGVs to Paris (Gare Montparnasse; €59.10 to €69.70, four hours).

Getting Around
City **buses** (☎ 02 97 21 28 29; ticket €1.15, 10-trip carnet €10, 24hr pass €3.50) run until around 8pm.
For a taxi, call ☎ 02 97 21 29 29.

CARNAC
pop 4600
Carnac (Garnag in Breton) has the world's greatest concentration of megalithic sites, erected between 5000 BC and 3500 BC. About 32km west of Vannes, it consists of an attractive old village, Carnac-Ville, and a modern seaside resort, Carnac-Plage, with its 2km-long sandy beach.

Orientation
Carnac-Ville is 1.5km north of Carnac-Plage. The megalithic sites of Le Ménec and Kermario are 1km north of Carnac-Ville.

Information
INTERNET ACCESS
Le Bao-Bab (3 allée du Parc, Carnac-Plage; per hr €4) A friendly bar with four terminals.

POST
Main Post Office (av de la Poste, Carnac-Ville)

TOURIST INFORMATION
Main Tourist Office (☎ 02 97 52 13 52; www.carnac.fr; 74 av des Druides, Carnac-Plage; ☻ 9am-7pm Mon-Sat & 3-7pm Sun Jul & Aug, 9am-noon or 12.30pm & 2-6pm Mon-Sat Sep-Jun)
Tourist Office Annexe (☎ 02 97 52 13 52; place de l'Église, Carnac-Ville; ☻ Apr-Sep & school holidays)

Sights
MUSÉE DE PRÉHISTOIRE
To set the scene, pass by the **Museum of Prehistory** (☎ 02 97 52 22 04; 10 place de la Chapelle, Carnac-Ville; adult/child €5/2.50; ☻ 10am-12.30pm & 1.30-6pm or 7pm Thu-Tue & Wed morning Oct-May) A block northeast of place de l'Église, it chronicles life in and around Carnac from the Palaeolithic and Neolithic eras to the Middle Ages. There's a free English-language booklet to guide you through the exhibits.

MAISON DES MÉGALITHES
Opposite the Alignements du Ménec is the **Maison des Mégalithes** (☎ 02 97 52 89 99; route des Alignements; admission free; ☻ 9am-8pm Jul & Aug, to 5.15pm Sep-Apr, to 7pm May-Jun), where you sign on for guided visits to the alignments. This recently opened information centre has rolling video, topographic models and a good selection of books about the sites (including the official *The Carnac Alignments* in English; €6). Its rooftop terrace gives a good view of the menhirs.

THE MEGALITHS
The best way to get a feel for the alignments is to walk or bike between the Le Ménec and Kerlescan groups, with menhirs almost constantly in view. Between June and September, seven buses a day run between the two sites and both Carnac-Ville and Carnac-Plage.

Because of severe erosion, the sites are fenced off to allow the vegetation to regenerate. However, between 10am and 5pm from October to May, you can wander freely through parts (exactly where changes so check the frequent site billboards or ask at the Maison des Mégalithes). For the rest of the year, there are **guided visits** (€4; regularly in French, at least once daily in English, Jul & Aug, Sat & Sun Apr-Jun).

Tumulus St-Michel, at the end of rue du Tumulus and 400m northeast of the Carnac-Ville tourist office, dates back to at least 5000 BC. From the top, capped by a much weathered 16th-century cross, there's a fine view of the estuary and inland plain.

The largest menhir field – with no less than 1099 stones – is the **Alignements du Ménec**, 1km north of Carnac-Ville, its rows of stones easily seen from the road. From here, the D196 heads northeast for about 1.5km to the equally impressive **Alignements de Kermario**. Climb the stone observation tower midway along the site to see the alignment from above, threading like rows of pulled teeth. Another 500m further on are the **Alignements de Kerlescan**, a smaller grouping.

Between Kermario and Kerlescan and 500m to the south of the D196 is the small, well-preserved **Tumulus de Kercado** (admission €1), dating from 3800 BC and the burial site of a Neolithic chieftain. During the French Revolution it was used as a hiding place for Breton royalists.

From the parking area 300m further along the D196, a 15-minute walk brings you to the **Géant du Manio**, highest menhir in the whole complex, and the **Quadrilatère**, a group of mini-menhirs, close-set in a rectangle.

Near Locmariaquer, 13km southeast of Carnac-Ville, the major monuments are the **Table des Marchands**, a 30m-long dolmen,

and the **Grand Menhir Brisé** (adult/student/child €4.70/3/free; 9am-8pm Jul & Aug, 9am-7pm May-Jun, 9.30am-12.30pm & 2-5.15pm Sep-Apr), the region's largest menhir, which once stood 20m high but now lies broken on its side. Both are off the D781, just before the village.

Just south of Locmariaquer and by the sea is the **Dolmen des Pierres Plates**, a 24m-long chamber whose rocky walls are decorated with still visible engravings.

Sleeping
Auberge Le Ratelier (02 97 52 05 04; www.le-ratelier.com; 4 Chemin du Douet, Carnac-Ville; d with shower €38-46, with bathroom €43-55; Feb-Dec) This delightfully rustic eight-room hotel – a former farmhouse that's all low ceilings with traditional timber furnishings – is in a quiet street one block southwest of place de l'Église.

Hôtel Ho-Ty (02 97 52 11 12; fax 02 97 52 89 52; 15 av de Kermario, Carnac-Plage d €37-59; Easter–mid-Nov) A mere minute's walk from the beach, the Ho-Ty is a traditional family seaside hotel in a lovely blue and white 1930s building. Given its location, its eight rooms, recently renovated, represent great value.

Hôtel Le Bateau Ivre (02 97 52 19 55; fax 02 97 52 84 94; 71 blvd de la Plage, Carnac-Plage; d with breakfast €83-113.50;) Set in landscaped gardens with a small heated swimming pool, the Bateau Ivre is one of Carnac's more luxurious hotels. All rooms have a balcony and overlook the beach. Avoid August, when it's significantly overpriced at €160.

CAMPING

There are over 15 camping grounds around Carnac.

Camping des Menhirs (☎ 02 97 52 94 67; www .lesmenhirs.com; 7 allée St-Michel, Carnac-Plage; per peson/ site €7.20/27; ☼ May–late-Sep; ☒) This luxury complex – complete with pool, sauna, massage and cocktail bar – is just 300m north of the beach.

Eating

Le Jardin de Valentin (☎ 02 97 52 19 12; 2 rue St-Cornély, Carnac-Ville; menus €8.50-12, salads €9; ☼ Jan–mid-Nov) You can eat in the stylishly decorated restaurant or in the courtyard of this delightful little place, tucked away down a short alley. Save room for one of their desserts.

Auberge Le Ratelier (see Sleeping; menus €17-40; ☼ May-Sep, Thu-Mon Oct-Apr) This hotel restaurant serves gourmet *menus* in a pleasant low-beamed dining room with whitewashed walls. The English version of the menu, with its 'banana greediness to rhum' and other verbal tidbits, is also to be savoured.

Crêperie St-George (☎ 02 97 52 18 34; 8 allée du Parc, Carnac-Plage; galettes, buckwheat pancakes €3.20-6.70, menu €9; ☼ Apr-Sep & school holidays) Set in the Galeries St-George shopping centre, this chic, modern creperie is one of the best-value eating places in town.

Getting There & Away
BUS

The main bus stops are in Carnac-Ville outside the police station on rue St-Cornély and in Carnac-Plage beside the tourist office. Buses go to Auray (€4), Vannes (€6.90) and Quiberon (€3.80).

TRAIN

The nearest year-round train station is in Auray, 12km to the northeast. SNCF has an office above the Carnac-Plage tourist office.

Getting Around

You can hire bikes from **Lorcy** (☎ 02 97 52 09 73; 6 rue de Courdiec, Carnac-Ville) and **Le Randonneur** (☎ 02 97 52 02 55; 20 av des Druides, Carnac-Plage).

For a taxi, call ☎ 02 97 52 75 75.

QUIBERON
pop 4600

At the tip of a slim, 14km-long peninsula, Quiberon (Kiberen in Breton) is a popular seaside town fringed by sandy beaches and a wild sea-swept coastline. It's the major port for ferries to Belle Île.

Orientation & Information

The D768, leads along the peninsula and into Quiberon, ending at the train station. From here rue de Verdun winds down to the sheltered bay of Port-Maria, pincered by the town's main beach, La Grande Plage, to its east and the ferry harbour to the west.

The **tourist office** (☎ 02 97 50 07 84; www .quiberon.com; 14 rue de Verdun; ☼ 9am-1.30pm & 2-7pm Mon-Fri, to 5pm Sat, 10am-1pm & 2-5pm Sun Jul & Aug, 9am-12.30pm & 2-6pm Mon-Sat Sep-Jun) is between the train station and Grande Plage.

Sights & Activities

Conserverie La Belle-Iloise (☎ 02 97 50 08 77; rue de Kerné; ☼ 9-11.30am & 2-6pm Jul & Aug, 10-11am & 3-4pm Mon-Fri Sep-Jun), north of the train station and one of only two remaining sardine canning factories, offers guided visits around its former cannery.

Grande Plage attracts families; bathing spots towards the peninsula's tip are larger and less crowded. The peninsula's rocky western flank is known as the **Côte Sauvage** (Wild Coast). It's great for a windy walk though usually too rough for swimming.

Sleeping

Many hotels close between November and March or April.

Auberge de Jeunesse – Les Filets Bleus (☎ 02 97 50 15 54; 45 rue du Roch Priol; dm €7.70; ☼ Apr-Sep) Quiberon's HI-affiliated hostel is in a quiet part of town 800m east of the train station. There's limited camping in the grounds.

Hôtel Le Roc'h Priol (☎ 02 97 50 04 86; www .hotelrochpriol.fr; 1-5 rue des Sirènes; d €54-89; ☼ mid-Feb–mid-Nov; ℗) The bright, modern Roc'h Priol is in a quiet corner of town, 800m east of the centre.

Hôtel L'Océan (☎ 02 97 50 07 58; hotel-de-locean .com in French; 7 quai de l'Océan; d €34-60; ☼ Easter-Sep) You can't miss this pleasant family hotel, overlooking the harbour. Look for the big white house with multicoloured shutters. The top rate gets you a harbour view.

Hôtel Albatros (☎ 02 97 50 15 05; fax 02 97 50 27 61; 24 quai de Belle-Île; d €54-82) The modern, 35-room Albatros looks over the waterfront between the harbour and Grande Plage. Paying top whack will secure a comfy room with a big balcony and a view of Belle-Île.

CAMPING

Camping du Conguel (☎ 02 97 50 19 11; www
.campingduconguel.com; blvd de la Teignouse; camping
€15-33; ☼ Apr-Oct; ☒) This luxury four-star
option, with aquapark, is one of the peninsula's 15 camping grounds. Just 2km
east of the town centre, it's beside Plage du
Conguel. Rates rocket in July and August.

Eating

Creperies, pizzerias and snack bars line
quai de Belle-Île, promenade de la Plage
and rue de Port Maria.

La Closerie de St-Clément (☎ 02 97 50 40 00; 36
rue de St-Clément; galettes €4-8.20; ☼ closed Wed & dinner Sun except Jul & Aug) This rustic creperie, with
gnarled timber beams and chunky wooden
furniture, has a garden terrace for summer
and a cosy fireplace for winter.

Restaurant-Créperie du Vieux Port (☎ 02 97
50 01 56; 42-44 rue Surcouf; menu €11, mains around €12,
galettes €4-7; ☼ mid-Feb–Oct) Overlooking Port-
Haliguen, 1km northeast of Grande Plage,
this eatery occupies an old stone house
with a beautiful, flower-filled garden.

La Criée (☎ 02 97 30 53 09; 11 quai de l'Océan; mains
€15-18; ☼ Tue-Sun Feb-Dec) On the seafront and an
easy walk from the ferry terminal, this splendid restaurant offers quite the finest seafood
(laid out enticingly on a table for you to take
your pick) and freshest fish in town.

Getting There & Away

BOAT

For ferries between Quiberon and Belle-Île,
see p314.

BUS

Quiberon is connected by **Cariane Atlantique**
(☎ 02 97 47 29 64) buses with Carnac (€3.80),
Auray (€6.30) and Vannes (€9.10, 1¾ hours).
Buses stop at the train station and place
Hoche near the tourist office and beach.

CAR & MOTORCYCLE

Drive your car into Quiberon town centre
during July and August and you'll spend
the day stuck in a traffic jam. During high
summer, we strongly recommend leaving
your vehicle at the 1200-place Sémaphore
car park (up to four hours €3.40, 24 hours
€9), 1.5km north of the beach, then walking or taking the free shuttle bus into town.
Even better: leave the car at Auray station
and hop on the Tire-Bouchon train.

TRAIN

A shuttle train called the 'Tire-Bouchon'
(corkscrew) runs several times a day between Auray and Quiberon in July and
August only (€2.60, 40 minutes). From September to June a SNCF bus service links
Quiberon and Auray train stations (€6.20,
50 minutes) four times a day.

Getting Around

Cycles Loisirs (☎ 02 97 50 31 73; 3 rue Victor Golvan),
200m north of the tourist office, charges
€8/13 a day to rent a touring/mountain bike.
Cyclomar (☎ 02 97 50 26 00; 47 place Hoche) rents
both bikes and scooters. The shop, which
is around 200m south of the tourist office,
also runs an operation from the train station
during July and August.

To order a taxi ring ☎ 02 97 50 11 11.

BELLE ÎLE

pop 5200

Belle-Île-en-Mer, about 15km south of Quiberon, is just what its name suggests: a beautiful island. About 20km by 9km and the
biggest of Brittany's islands, it's exposed to
the full force of Atlantic storms to the west.
Its eastern waters are relatively sheltered.

Although the summer daytime population can swell to over 35,000, the island
rarely feels crowded.

Information

Turn left as you leave the ferry in Le Palais
for the main **tourist office** (☎ 02 97 31 81 93;
www.belle-ile.com; quai Bonnelle; ☼ 8.45am-7.30pm
Mon-Sat & 8.45am-1pm Sun Jul & Aug, 9am-12.30pm &
2-6pm Mon-Sat, 10-12.30pm Sun Sep-Jun).

There's a summer-only **information kiosk**
(☎ 02 97 31 69 49; ☼ Easter-Sep) on the quay in
Sauzon.

Sights & Activities

Le Palais is a cosy port dominated by the
citadel, which Vauban strengthened in 1682
after centuries of Anglo-French dispute over
control of the area. The citadel now houses
the **Musée Historique** (☎ 02 97 31 84 17; adult/child
€6.10/3.05; ☼ 9.30am-6pm May-Oct, 9.30am-noon & 2-
5pm Nov-Apr), which examines Belle Île's past.

Belle-Île's wild, deeply eroded southwestern coast, known with reason as the **Côte Sauvage**, has spectacular rock formations and a
number of caves. The most famous, **Grotte
de l'Apothicairerie** (Cave of the Apothecary's

Shop), is an awesome cavern where the waves roll in from two sides.

Port de Donnant has a beautiful beach, popular with surfers, though swimming here is dangerous. **Port Kérel** is the best one for children is **Plage des Grands Sables**, 2km long, is the island's biggest and busiest strand.

The large-scale maps in *Guide des Randonnées Pédestres et Cyclistes* (Walking and Cycling Trail Guide; €8), on sale at the tourist office, are excellent for navigation. The ultimate hike is a circuit of the 95km **coastal footpath** that follows the island's coastline.

Sleeping

Auberge de Jeunesse Haute Boulogne (☎ 02 97 31 81 33; belle-ile@fuaj.org; Le Palais; dm €9.30; ❧ closed Oct) This modern HI-affiliated hostel is to the north of the citadel.

Hôtel La Frégate (☎ 02 97 31 54 16; fax 02 97 31 33 13; quai de l'Acadie, Le Palais; d €29, with bathroom €39; ❧ Apr–mid-Nov) Facing the ferry dock, the Frégate is a good economical choice though the interior décor doesn't live up to the appeal of the colourful exterior. There's a lively bar beneath and a spacious guest living room overlooking the harbour.

Hôtel Vauban (☎ 02 97 31 45 42; www.hotelvauban .com in French; 1 rue des Ramparts, Le Palais; s €39, d €1-70; ❧ mid-Feb–Oct) The Vauban has 16 comfortable, spacious rooms and a grand location, perched beside the coastal path high above the ferry landing. By car, it's signed from place de la République. On foot, turn second left up a steep, narrow alley that becomes rue des Remparts.

CAMPING

There are 10 camping areas around Belle-Île; most open from April or May to September or October.

Camping Municipal Les Glacis (☎ 02 97 31 41 76; Le Palais; per person/tent/car €4/4.50/2, site €2; ❧ Apr-Sep) This camping area is at the base of the citadel in Le Palais.

Eating

Le Goéland (☎ 02 97 31 81 26; 3 quai Vauban, Le Palais; mains €10-16; ❧ Thu-Mon Mar–mid-Nov) The Goéland (seagull) in Le Palais is an excellent restaurant, whether you choose the lively bar-brasserie on the ground floor or the more formal restaurant upstairs. The menu concentrates on seafood, augmented by local lamb, fattened on the island, and salads.

Getting There & Away

FROM QUIBERON

The shortest crossing to Belle-Île is from Quiberon. **SMN** (☎ 08 20 05 60 00; www.smn-navigation.fr in French) operates car ferries (45 minutes, year-round) and fast passenger ferries (20 minutes, July to August) to Le Palais, and fast passenger ferries to Sauzon (April to mid-September). An adult/child return fare is €25.50/16.10 for boats and €28/17.65 for the fast ferry. There are five crossings a day – more than double that in July and August.

FROM VANNES

Navix operates a ferry at least daily between May and mid-September from Vannes.

FROM LORIENT

From mid-July to the end of August, **SMN** runs a fast passenger-only ferry (adult/child €29.25/15.55 return, one hour, once daily) from Lorient to Sauzon.

Getting Around

There are lots of places in Le Palais where you can hire bicycles/motor scooters for around €12/35 a day.

VANNES

pop 55,000

Gateway to the islands of the Golfe du Morbihan, Vannes (Gwened in Breton) is a lovely town – small enough to feel intimate, close enough to the sea to taste the salt air and old enough to have an interesting history. Its medieval heart, lively with students from the Vannes branch of the Université de Rennes, must be as vital as it was centuries ago.

History

In pre-Roman times Vannes was the capital of the Veneti, a Gaulish tribe of sailors who fortified their town with a sturdy wall (some of which remains) and built a formidable fleet of sailing ships. The Veneti were conquered by Julius Caesar in the 1st century BC. Under the 9th-century Breton hero Nominoë, the town became the centre of Breton unity, while in 1532 the union of the duchy of Brittany with France was proclaimed here in Vannes.

Orientation

Vannes' small marina sits at the end of a canal-like waterway about 1.5km from the gulf's entrance. Roughly 3.5km south of town, the Île de Conleau, also known as the Presqu'île de Conleau (Conleau Peninsula) is linked to the mainland by a causeway.

Information

Futur i Média (☎ 02 97 01 84 09; 14 rue de la Boucherie; €4 per hr; ☾ noon-1am Mon-Fri, 2pm-1am Sat & Sun) Internet access.

Laverie Automatique (5 av Victor Hugo; ☾ 7am-9pm) For washing those clothes.

Main Post Office (2 place de la République)

Tourist Office (☎ 02 97 47 24 34; www.tourisme-vannes .com in French; 1 rue Thiers; ☾ 9am-7pm Jul & Aug, 9.30am-12.30pm & 2-6pm Mon-Sat Sep-Jun) Occupies a lovely 17th-century half-timbered house.

Sights

Vannes' **old town** is a maze of narrow alleys ranged around the Gothic splendour of **Cathédrale St-Pierre**, built in the 13th century and remodelled several times since.

Part of the **ramparts**, which afford views over the manicured gardens, is accessible for wandering (the stairs are tucked away behind rue des Vierges). You can see the black-roofed **Vieux Lavoirs** (Old Laundry Houses), though you'll get a better view from the **Tour du Connétable** or **Porte Poterne** to the south.

Musée de la Cohue (☎ 02 97 47 35 86; 9-15 place St-Pierre; adult/child €4/2.50; ☾ 10am-6pm Jul-Sep, 1.30-6pm Oct-Jun), named after the venerable 14th-century building that houses it, has been, over the centuries, a produce market, a law

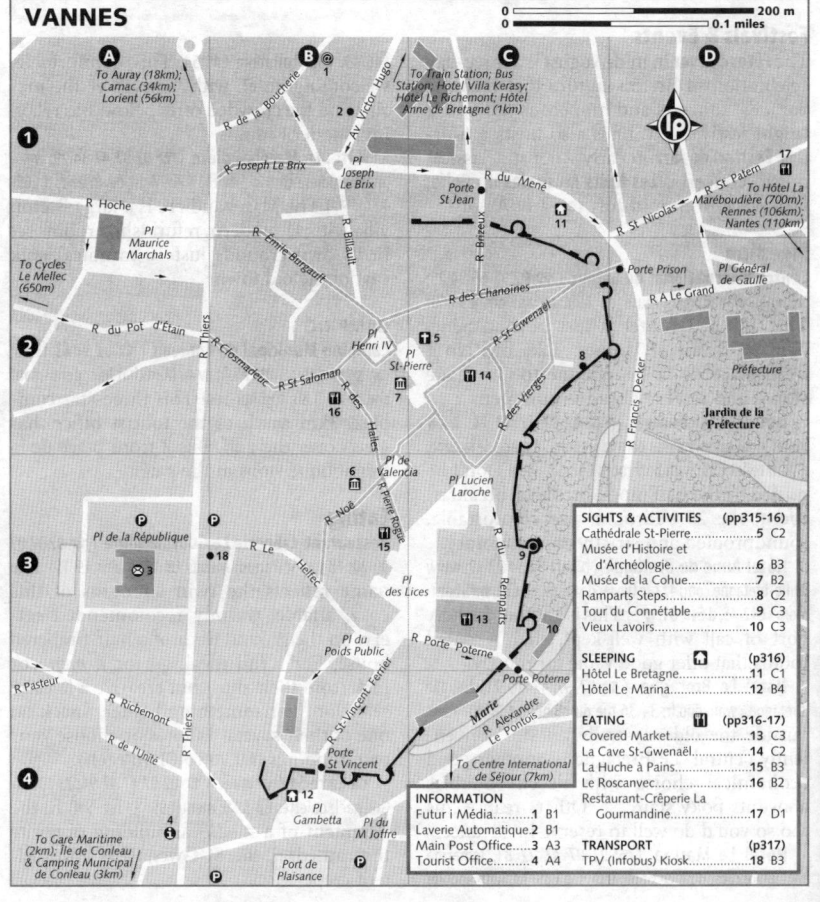

VANNES

0	200 m
0	0.1 miles

INFORMATION
Futur i Média..........1 B1
Laverie Automatique..2 B1
Main Post Office........3 A3
Tourist Office..........4 A4

SIGHTS & ACTIVITIES (pp315-16)
Cathédrale St-Pierre..............5 C2
Musée d'Histoire et
  d'Archéologie....................6 B3
Musée de la Cohue................7 B2
Ramparts Steps....................8 C2
Tour du Connétable................9 C3
Vieux Lavoirs....................10 C3

SLEEPING (p316)
Hôtel Le Bretagne................11 C1
Hôtel Le Marina..................12 B4

EATING (pp316-17)
Covered Market..................13 C3
La Cave St-Gwenaël..............14 C2
La Huche à Pains................15 B3
Le Roscanvec....................16 B2
Restaurant-Crêperie La
  Gourmandine..................17 D1

TRANSPORT (p317)
TPV (Infobus) Kiosk..............18 B3

BRITTANY

court and the seat of the Breton parliament. Today it's a museum of fine arts, displaying mostly 19th-century paintings, sculptures, engravings and temporary exhibits.

Musée d'Histoire et d'Archéologie (☎ 02 97 47 35 86; 2 rue Noë; adult/child €3/1.50; ☿ 10am-6pm mid-Jun–mid-Sep), in the 15th-century Château Gaillard, exhibits primarily artefacts from the megalithic sites at Carnac and Locmariaquer plus Roman and Greek finds. Outside the summer season, it's closed for extensive renovation works.

Tours
From April to September **Navix** (☎ 02 97 46 60 00) offers a range of cruises on the Golfe du Morbihan, departing from the Gare Maritime, 2km south of the tourist office.

Festivals & Events
The **Fêtes d'Arvor** in mid-August is a three-day celebration of Breton culture that includes parades, concerts and numerous *festoú noz* (night festivals). Vannes also hosts a four-day **Festival de Jazz** in early August. Classical music concerts, **Les Nuits Musicales du Golfe**, take place from mid-July to early August.

Sleeping
Centre International de Séjour (☎ 02 97 66 94 25; cis.sene@wanadoo.fr; route de Moustérian; dm €10.60) This 100-bed hostel is just beyond Séné, 7km southeast of Vannes. Take bus No 4 from place de la République to Le Stade stop – and reserve ahead in summer.

Hôtel Le Richemont (☎ 02 97 47 17 24; www .hotel-richemont-vannes.com in French; 26 place de la Gare; d with toilet €33, with bathroom €47-52; P) Don't be misled by the naff mock-medieval breakfast room; the 28 bedrooms are comfortable, soundproofed and strictly contemporary.

Hôtel Anne de Bretagne (☎ 02 97 54 22 19; www .anne-bretagne.com; 42 rue Olivier de Clisson; d €32, with bathroom s €42-45, d €48-61; P) This is another friendly port of call with well-kept, slightly dated rooms that offer good value for money.

Hôtel Le Bretagne (☎ 02 97 47 20 21; hotel.le .bretagne@wanadoo.fr; 34-36 rue du Mené; d €35-40) Just outside the old city walls yet still conveniently central, Le Bretagne is another good economical choice with decent doubles above its poky staircase. Others realise this too so you'd do well to reserve in advance.

Hôtel Le Marina (☎ 02 97 47 22 81; lemarina hotel@aol.com; 4 place Gambetta; s/d €35/38, with shower

€46/49, with bathroom €49/54) This comfortable, welcoming hotel, with views over the marina and the crowded cafés below, has relaxing, modern rooms.

Hôtel La Marébaudière (☎ 02 97 47 34 29; www .marebaudiere.com in French; 4 rue Aristide-Briand; d €62-107; P) The Marébaudière is a large Breton villa with 41 modern, refurbished rooms set in its own grounds just 10 minutes' walk east of the old town.

CAMPING
Camping Municipal de Conleau (☎ 02 97 63 13 88; camping.conleau@tiscali.fr; av du Maréchal Juin; per person/ site €4.10/8.80; ☿ Apr-Sep) This three-star complex, 3km south of the tourist office, has views over the gulf. Bus 2 from place de la République stops at the gate.

Eating
Restaurant-Crêperie La Gourmandine (☎ 02 97 01 00 20; 18 rue St-Patern; menus €8-15, mains €9-15) The name reflects the twin strengths of this cosy, affable, warmly recommended eatery, on the ground floor of a half-timbered house. For a full meal, go for a *menu* or pick from their short but creative à la carte selection. For something lighter, snack on one of their special galettes or choose your own toppings (€0.90 to €1.90 each).

La Cave St-Gwenaël (☎ 02 97 47 47 94; 23 rue St-Gwenaël; galettes €3-6.50; menu €9; ☿ Tue-Sat) In the basement of a medieval building opposite the cathedral, the St-Gwenaël is an excellent creperie.

Le Roscanvec (☎ 02 97 47 15 96; 17 rue des Halles; menus €17-74; ☒ Mon-Sat Jul & Aug, Tue-Sat Sep-Jun) The Roscanvec is the best of several tempting eateries along rue des Halles. Set in a lovely 16th-century timbered house, it has a superb menu of seafood and game. The cheapest menu is available for weekday lunches only while the most expensive offers lobster in just about every way it can be prepared.

SELF-CATERING

On Wednesday and Saturday mornings, a **produce market** takes over place du Poids Public and the surrounding area. Vannes' **covered market** is just around the corner.

La Huche à Pains (23 place des Lices) is a popular patisserie that sells *kouign amann* (butter cake) and other enticing Breton pastries.

Getting There & Away
BUS

TIM (☎ 02 97 01 22 10) buses serve Pontivy (€8.50, 50 minutes, three daily) while **Cariane Atlantique** (☎ 02 97 47 29 64) runs via Auray to Carnac (€6.90 1¼ hours) and on to Quiberon (€9.10, 1¾ hours). A SNCF express bus goes to/from St-Brieuc (€15.30, two hours, four daily) via Pontivy (€8.85, 55 minutes).

The small bus station is opposite the train station.

CAR & MOTORCYCLE

Europcar (☎ 02 97 42 43 43) and **ADA** (☎ 02 97 42 59 10) are in the train station. **Budget** (☎ 02 97 54 25 22) is opposite, in the bus station.

TRAIN

There are frequent trains westwards to Auray (€3.40, 12 minutes), Lorient (€8.10, 40 minutes) and Quimper (€15.90, 1½ hours). Eastbound trains serve Rennes (€16.50, 1½ hours) and Nantes (€17.40, 1½ hours). For Quiberon (€9.50 to €11), take the train to Auray and continue by SNCF bus or, in July and August, train.

Getting Around

TPV (☎ 02 97 01 22 23; ticket €1.10, 10-trip carnet €8.50) runs eight city bus lines till 8.15pm. Its Infobus kiosk is on place de la République. Bus Nos 3 and 4 link the train station with place de la République.

You can hire bikes from **Cycles Le Mellec** (☎ 02 97 63 00 24; 51ter rue Jean Gougaud) for €12 a day.

To order a taxi, ring ☎ 02 97 54 34 34.

AROUND VANNES
Golfe du Morbihan Islands

Of the 40 inhabited islands in the Golfe du Morbihan, **Île d'Arz** and **Île aux Moines**, the two largest, are popular day-trip destinations from Vannes.

From the Vannes' Gare Maritime, **Navix** (☎ 02 97 46 60 00; www.navix.fr in French) offers a range of cruises on the Golfe du Morbihan between April and September. Its 'Grand Tour du Golfe' (adult/child €21.50/14, 3¼ hours) includes optional visits to Île aux Moines and Île d'Arz (supplementary €5/4).

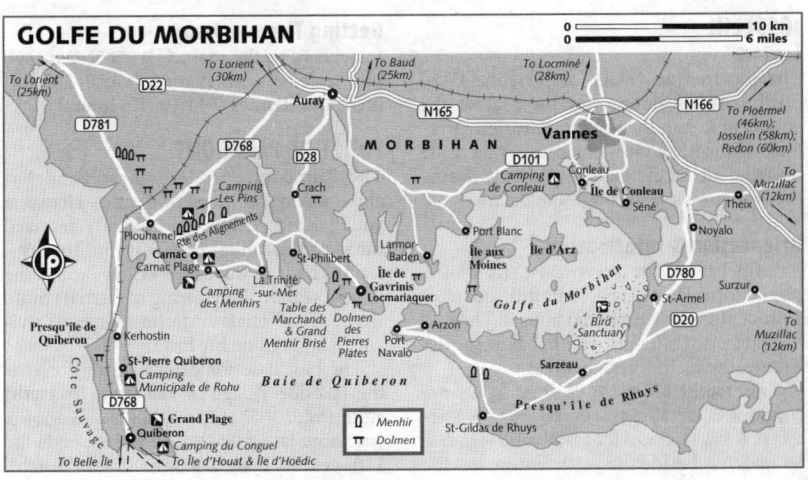

GOLFE DU MORBIHAN

Le Passeur de l'Île d'Arz (☎ 02 97 50 83 83) runs ferries from Île de Conleau, 3.5km south of Vannes, to Île d'Arz (adult/child return €6/3.50, 15 minutes, hourly year-round).

Izenah (☎ 02 97 26 31 45) boats make the short crossing from Port Blanc, 13km southwest of Vannes, to Île aux Moines (adult/child return €3.5/2, five minutes, half-hourly year-round).

EASTERN & CENTRAL BRITTANY

Eastern Brittany encompasses the inland portion of the *département* of Ille-et-Vilaine. A region of fertile farmland and gently rolling countryside, it marks the one-time frontier between Brittany and France. Rennes, capital of Ille-et-Vilaine and of Brittany as a whole, may not feel all that Breton but it's a bustling university city in its own right and has an attractive old quarter.

Central Brittany is split between the *départements* of Côtes d'Armor and Morbihan. The Forêt de Paimpont (or Brocéliande), where King Arthur and his court once held sway and Merlin wove his magic, is wonderful for cycling and walking. Throughout, small villages with character are tucked away, far from any tourist track – though today charming Josselin with its stunning 14th-century chateau has been very much 'discovered'.

JOSSELIN
pop 2400
The picturesque village of Josselin, 43km northeast of Vannes, was the seat of the counts of Rohan for several centuries. Overlooking the River Oust, their imposing castle hosted many of the dukes of Brittany during their progressions through the duchy.

Orientation & Information
Josselin lies on the River Oust. Its centre, place Notre Dame, is a beautiful square of 16th-century half-timbered houses. The castle and tourist office are south, below rue des Trente, the main through street.

The **tourist office** (☎ 02 97 22 36 43; www .paysdejosselin.com; place de la Congrégation; 🕙 10am-6pm Jul & Aug, 10am-noon & 2-6pm Mon-Fri, 10am-noon Sat Sep-Jun) is beside the castle entrance.

Sights & Activities
The three huge round towers of the 14th-century **Château de Josselin** (☎ 02 97 22 36 45; adult/child €6.60/4.50; 🕙 10am-6pm mid-Jul–Aug, 2-6pm Jun–mid-Jul & Sep, Sat & Sun Apr-May & Oct) dominate the riverbanks. Behind them, the elegant Gothic-Renaissance building dates from the late 15th and early 16th centuries.

The **Basilique Notre Dame du Roncier** (place Notre Dame), parts of which date from the 12th century, has some superb 15th- and 16th-century stained glass in the south aisle. In the chapel northeast of the choir is the finely carved marble tomb of Olivier de Clisson, who fortified the chateau during the Hundred Years' War, together with his wife.

Sleeping & Eating
Hôtel-Restaurant du Château (☎ 02 97 22 20 11; www.hotel-chateau.com in French; 1 rue Général de Gaulle; d €31, with shower €43, with bathroom €55.50-60; 🕙 closed Sun-Mon Nov-Mar; **P**) Pay top whack to enjoy a room with the most magnificent view of the chateau, looming above this delightfully cosy hotel. Its **restaurant** (menus €14-40) also has a gorgeous picture window.

Camping du Bas de la Lande (☎ 02 97 22 22 20; campingbasdelalande@wanadoo.fr; Guégon; per person/tent/car €3/3/2; 🕙 Apr-Oct) This spot is about 2km west of Josselin, on the south bank of the Oust.

There are several popular creperies on and around place Notre-Dame. Down the hill, **Crêperie-Grill Sarrazine** (☎ 02 97 22 37 80; 51 rue Glatinier; menus from €9, galettes & salads from €6) packs in the locals.

Getting There & Away
Josselin is on the main **CTM** (☎ 02 97 01 22 01) bus route between Pontivy (€6.20, 30 minutes) and Rennes (€11.10, 1½ hours).

FORÊT DE PAIMPONT
The Paimpont Forest (or Brocéliande) is about 40km southwest of Rennes. Here, the young King Arthur traditionally received the sword Excalibur from Viviane, the mysterious Lady of the Lake. Visitors still come here in search of the spring of eternal youth, where the magician Merlin first met Viviane, who became his lover.

The best base for exploring the forest is the lakeside village of **Paimpont**. Its **tourist office** (☎ 02 99 07 84 23; 🕙 10am-noon & 2-5pm or 6pm Jun-Sep, Tue-Sun Oct-Dec & Feb-May) is beside the 12th-century **Église Abbatiale** (Abbey Church).

It has a free walking/cycling map detailing over 50km of trails, or you can buy the more complete *Brocéliande à Pied* walking guide, which describes over 30 forest paths. In July and August the tourist office leads guided tours (half/full day €8/10) of the forest.

Sleeping & Eating

Auberge de Jeunesse (☎ 02 97 22 76 75; dm €7.70; ☺ Jun–mid-Sep) This hostel occupies a lovely stone farmhouse at Choucan-en-Brocéliande, 5km north of Paimpont.

Hôtel Le Relais de Brocéliande (☎ 02 99 07 84 94; www.le-relais-de-broceliande.fr; 7 rue du Forges, Paimpont; d €34, with shower €42, with bathroom €48, menus €16-68.60) This 24-room hotel has pleasantly rustic rooms with all mod cons, as well as an excellent restaurant.

Camping Municipal de Paimpont (☎ 02 99 07 89 16; rue du Chevalier Lancelot du Lac; per person/tent/car €2.50/2.20/1; ☺ May-Sep) This small camping ground is near the lake.

For a cheaper bite, try the **Crêperie au Temps des Moines** (☎ 02 99 07 89 63; 16 av Chevalier Ponthus) in a pleasing granite house overlooking the lake.

Getting There & Around

TIV (☎ 02 99 30 87 80) runs buses to/from Rennes (€2.85, one hour).

You can rent mountain bikes (per half/full day €9/14) from **Bar Le Brécilien** (☎ 02 99 07 81 13; rue Général de Gaulle), beside Paimpont's tourist office.

RENNES

pop 203,500

The attractive university town of Rennes has been an important crossroads from Roman times onwards. Capital of Brittany since its incorporation into France in the 16th century, it developed at the junction of the highways linking the northern and western ports of St-Malo and Brest with the former capital, Nantes (see p612), and the inland city of Le Mans.

Orientation

The city centre is divided by La Vilaine, a river channelled into a cement-lined canal that disappears underground just before the central square, place de la République. The northern area includes the pretty, pedestrianised old city, while the south is garishly modern.

Information

France Telecom (place de la République, beside the post office; per 20 min €1; ☺ noon-7pm Mon-Sat) Internet access.

Laundrette (23 rue de Penhoët; ☺ 7am- 8pm)

Main Post Office (place de la République)

Tourist Office (☎ 02 99 67 11 11; www.ville-rennes.fr; 11 rue St-Yves; ☺ 9am-6pm/7pm Mon-Sat, 11am-6pm Sun) Staff will book local accommodation for a fee of €1.

Sights & Activities

OLD CITY

Much of medieval Rennes was gutted by the great fire of 1720, started by a drunken carpenter who accidentally set alight a pile of shavings. The half-timbered houses that survived now make up the old city, Rennes' most picturesque quarter.

Among the prettiest streets are **rue St-Michel** and **rue St-Georges**. The latter bisects the enormous place de la Mairie and place du Palais, site of the 17th-century **Palais du Parlement de Bretagne**, the former seat of the rebellious Breton parliament and more recently, the Palais de Justice. In 1994 this building too was destroyed by fire, started by demonstrating fishermen. Now restored, it houses the Court of Appeal.

One of the most stylish half-timbered houses is **Maison du Guesclin** (3 rue St-Guillaume), named after the 14th-century Breton warrior. Nearby is 17th-century **Cathédrale St-Pierre** (☺ 9.30am-noon & 3-6pm) with its pure neoclassical interior.

MUSEUMS

The city's former university building now houses the **Musée des Beaux-Arts** (☎ 02 99 28 55 85; 20 quai Émile Zola; adult/child €4/2; ☺ 10am-noon & 2-6pm Wed-Mon), unexceptional except for rooms devoted to the Pont-Aven school.

Temporarily sharing premises are the most important elements of the **Musée de Bretagne** (☎ 02 99 28 55 84), with displays on Breton history and culture. It's scheduled to move to a new cultural complex – the futuristic **Champs Libres** (cours des Alliés), due to open in 2005, which will also house **Espace des Sciences**, an interactive science museum.

ACTIVITIES

To see Rennes from a special perspective, hire an electric boat from **urbaVag** (☎ 02 99 33 16 88; rue Canal St Martin; per hr €15-25) and cruise its waterways. Boats take up to seven

RENNES

| 0 | 300 m |
| 0 | 0.2 miles |

INFORMATION
France Telecom..............................1 B4
Laundrette.....................................2 B2
Main Post Office............................3 B4
Tourist Office................................4 A3

SIGHTS & ACTIVITIES (pp319-21)
Cathédrale St-Pierre......................5 A3
Champs Libres (Opens 2005)........6 C5
Maison du Guesclin.......................7 A3
Musée de Bretagne...................(see 8)
Musée des Beaux Arts...................8 C4
Palais du Parlement de Bretagne.9 C2

SLEEPING (p321)
Hôtel d'Angleterre.......................10 C4
Hôtel de la Tour d'Auvergne........11 A5
Hôtel des Lices.............................12 A2
Hôtel-Restaurant Au Rocher de
    Cancale...................................13 B2

EATING (p321)
Bistrot des Alibantes...................14 C2
Hôtel-Restaurant Au Rocher de
    Cancale e............................(see 13)
L'Ouvrée.....................................15 A2
Léon le Cochon...........................16 C4
Les Halles Centrales (Covered
    Market).................................17 B4
St-Germain-des-Champs.............18 C3

ENTERTAINMENT (p322)
Ciné TNB....................................19 D4
Cinéma Arvor..............................20 C1
Théâtre National de Bretagne..(see 19)

TRANSPORT (p322)
Allo Stop Bretagne......................21 B5
Bus Station.................................22 D6
Car Hire.....................................23 D6
City Bus Station..........................24 C3
STAR Office................................25 C3
STAR Office................................26 B4

To Auberge de
Jeunesse (600m);
urbaVag boat
hire (1.5km);
Hédé (25km);
Bécherel (33km);
St-Malo (60km)

To Camping des
Gayeulles (3km);
Mont St-Michel
(50km)

R St-Malo
R d'Échange
Pl Ste-Anne
Ste-Anne
R d'Antrain
R St-Louis
R St-Michel
Pl R de St-Michel
Penboët
R de la Visitation
R le Bastard
R St-Guillaume
Monnaie
R St-
Guillaume
Pl des Lices
Pl du
Champ-
Jacquet
R de la
R Victor Hugo
Pl du
Parlement
de Bretagne
R St-Georges
R du Chapitre
Pl de
la Mairie
R de Rohan R de l'Horloge
Pont de
Nemours
R F Buisson
Pl St-
Germain
Pl du
Maréchal Foch
R St-Yves
Q Duguay Trouin
Pl de la
République
République
La Vilaine
Q Chateaubriand
Q Lamennais
R Chalotais
Q Émile Zola
Pl de
Bretagne
R Poullain Duparc
R du Pré Botté
R Toullier
R Dupont des Loges
R de Léon
La Vilaine
Blvd de la Tour d'Auvergne
R Chicogné
Blvd de la Liberté
Pl Honoré
Commeurec
R de Nemours
R Jules Simon
R Maréchal Joffre
R Vasselot
Blvd de la Liberté
Av Jean Janvier
Blvd Magenta
R M Duhamel
R St-Hélier
R Thiers
R de Plélo
Charles de Gaulle
R du Puits Mauger
R d'Isly
Pl Charles
de Gaulle
Shopping
Centre
Cours des Alliés
Pl du
Colombier
To Airport (6km);
Forêt de Paimpont
(40km); Vannes
(111km)
R de l'Alma
R Gurvand
Blvd de Beaumont
Blvd Solférino
Pl
de la
Gare
Gares
Train
Station
Blvd du Colombier
To Nantes (107km)
To Nantes (107km)

BRITTANY

passengers and the price drops significantly by each extra hour of rental.

Festivals & Events

Rennes is at its most lively during the **Tombées de la Nuit** festival in the first week of July when the old city is lively with music, theatre and locals togged out in medieval costume.

Yaouank (☎ 02 99 30 06 87) is a huge *fest-noz* (night festival), held on the third Saturday in November.

Sleeping

Auberge de Jeunesse (☎ 02 99 33 22 33; rennes@fuaj .org; 10-12 Canal St-Martin; dm with breakfast €13.25) Rennes' youth hostel has a canal-side setting. Take bus No 18 from place de la Mairie.

Hôtel de la Tour d'Auvergne (☎ 02 99 30 84 16; fax 02 23 42 10 01; 20 blvd de la Tour d'Auvergne; d €25, with bathroom €38) The spick-and-span rooms at this warm, inviting place, only a 10-minute walk from the old town, are a real bargain.

Hôtel d'Angleterre (☎ 02 99 79 38 61; fax 02 99 79 43 85; 19 rue Maréchal Joffre; s €23, d with shower €32, with bathroom €38-47) The Angleterre occupies a grand old town house with monumental staircases, echoing corridors and spacious, if somewhat tired, rooms.

Hôtel-Restaurant Au Rocher de Cancale (☎ 02 99 79 20 83; 10 rue St-Michel; d €37-46) Set in a half-timbered house and one of the few options in the old town, this fine restaurant (see right) has four pretty, renovated rooms upstairs.

Hôtel des Lices (☎ 02 99 79 14 81; www.hotel-des -lices.com in French; 7 place des Lices; s/d €54/57) Bright and breezy Hôtel des Lices offers comfortable, attractive, soundproofed rooms in a superb location; the ones on the upper floors have good views over the old town.

CAMPING

Camping des Gayeulles (☎ 02 99 36 91 22; fax 02 23 20 06 34; rue Professeur Audin; per person/tent/car €3.35/5/40/1.50) Rennes' only camping ground is in Parc des Bois, about 4.5km northeast of the train station. Take bus No 3 from place de la République to the Gayeulles stop.

Eating

Rue St-Georges and rue St-Malo are lined with creperies and ethnic eateries – from Indian to Brazilian.

L'Ouvrée (☎ 02 99 30 16 38; 18 place des Lices; menus €15-32; ☯ Tue-Fri, lunch Sun & dinner Sat) You'll relish highly-reputed L'Ouvrée for the subtle blends of its main dishes, so attractively presented that it's almost a shame to tuck into them.

St-Germain-des-Champs (☎ 02 99 79 25 52; 12 rue Vau St-Germain; mains €9, menu €15; ☯ lunch Tue-Fri, dinner Fri & Sat) Even ardent carnivores will enjoy this organic-food-only vegetarian restaurant with its tranquil rear terrace. It also does sandwiches and dishes to take away (€4.50 to €6).

Bistrot des Alibantes (☎ 02 99 84 02 02; 36 rue de la Visitation; lunch menu €10, dinner menu €17; ☯ closed Sun, dinner Mon & Tue) This attractive bistro, all antique furniture and wooden floors, serves great classic French and Breton dishes. The lunch *menu* is particularly good value.

Hôtel-Restaurant Au Rocher de Cancale (see Sleeping; mains €9-13, menus €14-25; ☯ Mon-Fri) This delightful restaurant serves mainly fish. Settle into their *plateau du rocher* (€20), a seafood platter that includes oysters, winkles, whelks and *amandes de mer*, a kind of giant clam.

SELF-CATERING

Les Halles Centrales (place Honoré Commeurec) is the larger of Rennes' two covered markets. On Saturday morning there's a huge fresh produce market on place des Lices.

Drinking

Students usually head to Rue St-Michel – renamed 'Rue de la Soif' (Street of Thirst) – for bars, pubs and cafés. Rue St-Malo also has lots of music bars and cafés, of a slightly scruffier, more eclectic nature.

BRITTANY

Entertainment

Nondubbed films are screened at both **Cinéma Arvor** (☎ 02 99 38 72 40; 29 rue d'Antrain) and **Ciné TNB** (☎ 02 99 30 88 88; 1 rue St-Hélier) at the Théâtre National de Bretagne. *Ciné Spectacles* is the free weekly guide.

Getting There & Away

Cariane Atlantique (☎ 02 40 18 42 00) offers services to Nantes (€14.50, two hours). **CTM** (☎ 02 97 01 22 01) runs an express bus service to/from Pontivy (€15, two hours, eight daily). **TAE** (☎ 02 99 26 16 00) runs five times daily to Dinard (€11.80, two hours) via Dinan (€8.80, 1½ hours); **TIV** (☎ 02 99 26 11 26) serves St-Malo (€9.90, one to 1½ hours, three to six daily), Fougères (€8.50, one hour) and Paimpont (€2.85, one hour).

CAR & MOTORCYCLE

ADA (☎ 02 99 67 43 79), **Europcar** (☎ 02 23 44 02 72), **National Citer** (☎ 02 23 44 02 78) and **Hertz** (☎ 02 23 42 17 01) all have offices at the train station.

TRAIN

Destinations with frequent services include St-Malo (€11.40, one hour), Dinan (€11.90, one hour), Vannes (€16.50, 1½ hours), Nantes (€18.90, 1¼ hours), Brest (€29.40, two hours), Quimper (€27.60, 2½ hours) and Paris' Gare Montparnasse by TGV (€59.80, 2¼ hours).

HITCHING

Allo Stop Bretagne (☎ 02 99 67 34 67; www.allosto prennes.com in French; 20 rue d'Isly; ☉ 9.30am-12.30pm & 2-6pm Mon-Sat), in the Trois Soleils shopping centre, matches up hitchers with drivers for a fee of €6.10.

Getting Around

Rennes has an efficient local bus network and a very smart, 22nd-century single-line metro, both run by **STAR** (☎ 08 20 03 20 02; www.star.fr in French). Bus and metro tickets (single journey €1, 10-trip carnet €9.20, 24hr pass €3) are interchangeable.

To get to the town centre from the train or bus station, take bus No 17 to place de la République.

The metro line runs northwest to southeast. Main stations of interest to visitors are Gares (train stations), République (place de la République) and Ste-Anne (old town).

Ring ☎ 02 99 30 79 79 for a taxi.

Champagne

The name Champagne comes to us from the Latin *campania*, literally 'Land of Plains'. It is fitting, then, that a region famed around the world for the sparkling wines that have been made here since the days of Dom Pérignon. A comfortable train trip east from Paris, this largely rural and undramatic area, impregnated and imbued with tradition, is where the world-renowned *vin de Champagne* – nothing will convince the locals that their own homegrown brew is anything less than liquid gold – is produced.

Champagne, known in Roman times as Campania (literally 'Land of Plains'), is a largely agricultural region famed around the world for the sparkling wines that have been made here since the days of Dom Pérignon. According to French law, only bubbly from the region – grown in designated areas, then aged and bottled according to the strictest standards – can be labelled as champagne. Nothing will drive the locals into fits of righteous indignation faster – or will elicit more searing expressions of contempt mixed with pity – than a mention of that absurd liquid marketed as 'California champagne'!

The production of the celebrated wine takes place mainly in two *départements:* Marne, whose metropolis is the 'Coronation City' of Reims, famed for its medieval churches; and the less prestigious Aube, whose *préfecture* is the ancient and picturesque city of Troyes, one of the best places in France to stroll among half-timbered houses.

The town of Épernay, a bit south of Reims, is the de facto capital of champagne (the drink) and is the best place to head for *dégustation* (tasting). The Route Touristique du Champagne (Champagne Tourist Route) wends its way through the region's diverse vineyards, taking visitors from one picturesque – and prosperous – village to the next. A number of big *maisons* (champagne houses) have achieved international renown, but much of the region's liquid gold is made by 5000 small-scale *vignerons* (wine producers), many of whose family-run facilities welcome visitors. The regional tourism committee's website is www.tourisme-champagne-ardenne.com.

HIGHLIGHTS

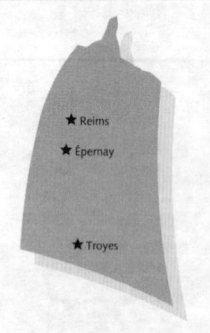

- Inhale the heady odours of maturing champagne on a cellar tour in **Épernay** (p332) or **Reims** (p328)
- Explore the rolling vineyards along Champagne's scenic **wine route** (p331, p340)
- Stroll among half-timbered houses and duck into Gothic churches in Troyes' medieval **old city** (p336)
- Admire modern and medieval paintings and ancient hand tools in Troyes' fine **museums** (p337)

★ Reims

★ Épernay

★ Troyes

■ POPULATION: 1.3 MILLION　　　　■ AREA: 25,720 SQ KM

REIMS
pop 206,000

Meticulously reconstructed after WWI and WWII, Reims (pronounced something like 'rance') is a neat and orderly city with wide avenues and well-tended parks. Together with Épernay, it's the most important centre of champagne production.

After Clovis I, founder of the Frankish kingdom, was baptised here in AD 496, Reims (often anglicised as Rheims) became the traditional site of French coronations. From 816 to 1825, 34 sovereigns – among them 25 kings – began their reigns as Christian rulers in the city's famed cathedral.

Orientation

In the commercial centre (northwest of the cathedral), the main streets are rue Carnot, rue de Vesle, rue Condorcet and, for shopping, rue de Talleyrand. The train station is about 1km northwest of the cathedral, across square Colbert from place Drouet d'Erlon, the city's major nightlife centre. Virtually every street in the city centre is one way.

Information

INTERNET ACCESS

Clique et Croque Cybercafé (☎ 03 26 86 93 92; 27 rue de Vesle; per hr €4.20; ⏰ 10am-12.30am Mon-Sat, 2-9pm Sun) In the courtyard of the shopping arcade.

LAUNDRY

Laundrette (59 rue Chanzy; ⏰ 7am-9.30pm)

MONEY

There's a cluster of commercial banks on rue Carnot; several more can be found at the southern end of place Drouet d'Erlon. The tourist office changes money on Sunday and holidays.

POST

Branch Post Office (2 rue Cérès) Through the arches on the eastern side of place Royale. Has currency exchange and a Cyberposte.
Main Post Office (2 rue Olivier Métra; ⏰ 8am-7pm Mon-Fri, 8am-noon Sat) Has a Cyberposte.

TOURIST INFORMATION

Tourist Office (☎ 03 26 77 45 00; www.reims-tourisme .com; 2 rue Guillaume de Machault; ⏰ 9am-7pm Mon-Sat, 10am-6pm Sun & holidays early Apr–mid-Oct, 10am-5pm

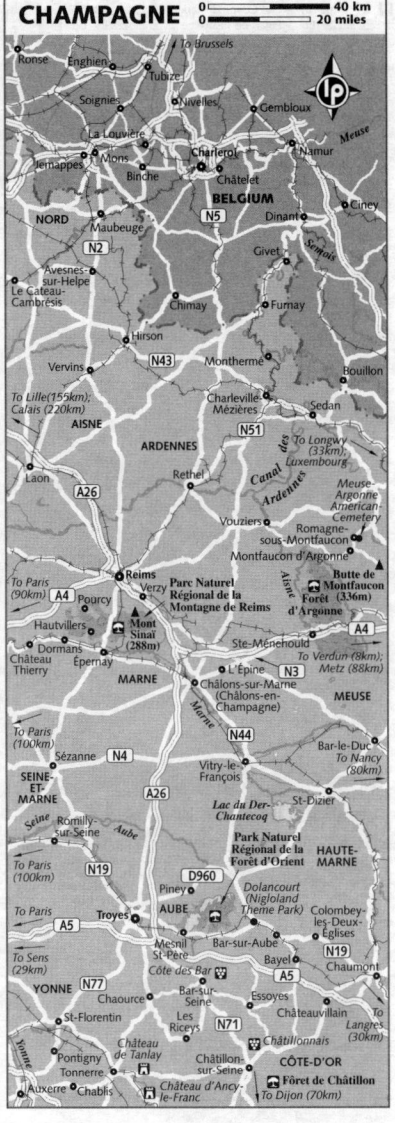

CHAMPAGNE

MUSEUM PASS

All four museums run by the municipality – St-Rémi, Reddition, Beaux-Arts and the Ancienne Collège des Jésuites – as well as the Chapelle Foujita are covered by a single entry fee of €3 (free for students; valid one month).

REIMS

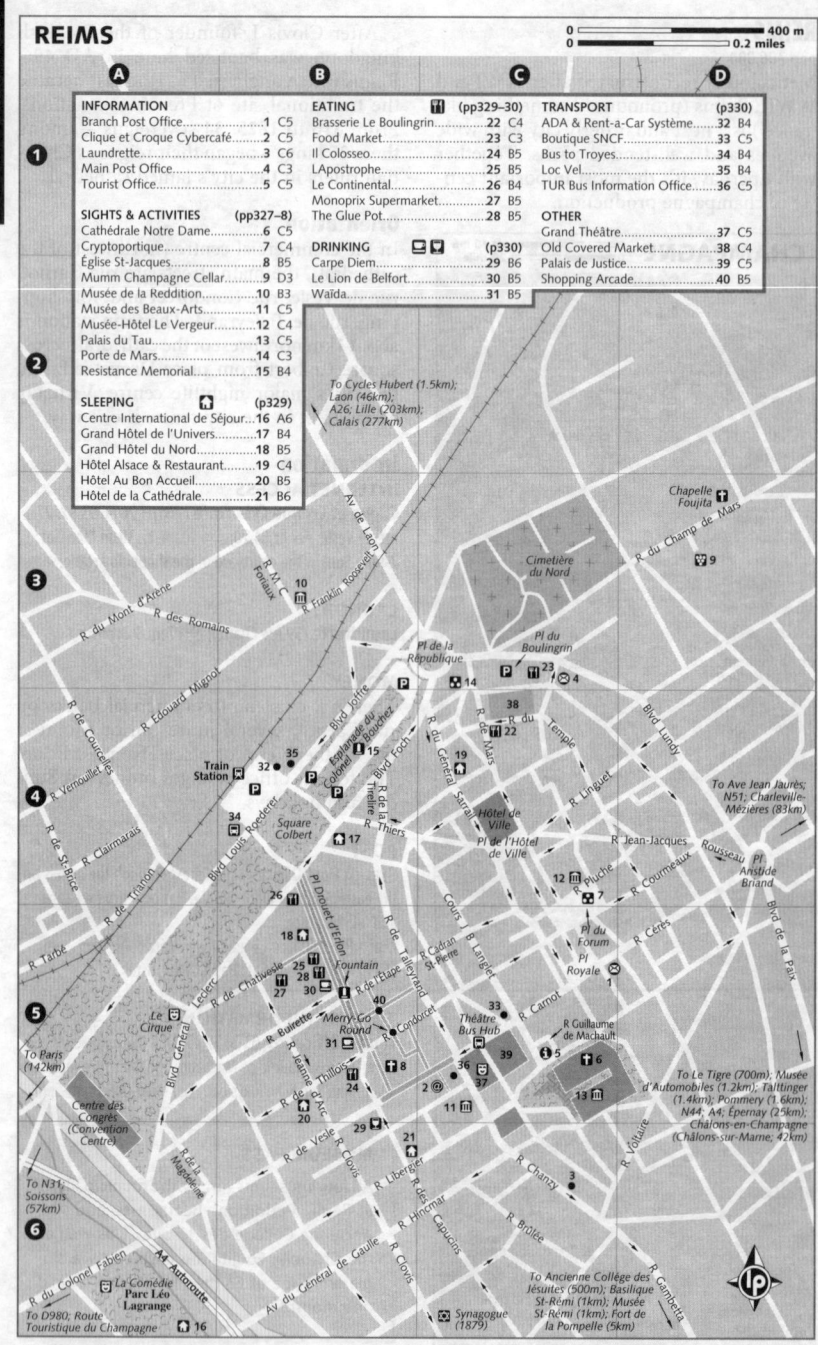

0 — 400 m
0 — 0.2 miles

INFORMATION
Branch Post Office.....................1 C5
Clique et Croque Cybercafé........2 C5
Laundrette................................3 C6
Main Post Office........................4 C3
Tourist Office............................5 C5

SIGHTS & ACTIVITIES (pp327-8)
Cathédrale Notre Dame..............6 C5
Cryptoportique..........................7 C4
Église St-Jacques......................8 B5
Mumm Champagne Cellar...........9 D3
Musée de la Reddition...............10 B3
Musée des Beaux-Arts................11 C5
Musée-Hôtel Le Vergeur.............12 C4
Palais du Tau...........................13 C5
Porte de Mars..........................14 C3
Resistance Memorial..................15 B4

SLEEPING (p329)
Centre International de Séjour.....16 A6
Grand Hôtel de l'Univers............17 B4
Grand Hôtel du Nord..................18 B5
Hôtel Alsace & Restaurant..........19 C4
Hôtel Au Bon Accueil.................20 B5
Hôtel de la Cathédrale...............21 B6

EATING (pp329-30)
Brasserie Le Boulingrin..............22 C4
Food Market............................23 C3
Il Colosseo..............................24 B5
L'Apostrophe...........................25 B5
Le Continental.........................26 B4
Monoprix Supermarket..............27 B5
The Glue Pot...........................28 B5

DRINKING (p330)
Carpe Diem.............................29 B6
Le Lion de Belfort.....................30 B5
Waïda....................................31 B5

TRANSPORT (p330)
ADA & Rent-a-Car Système.........32 B4
Boutique SNCF..........................33 B4
Bus to Troyes...........................34 B4
Loc Vel...................................35 B4
TUR Bus Information Office.........36 C5

OTHER
Grand Théâtre..........................37 C5
Old Covered Market...................38 C4
Palais de Justice.......................39 C5
Shopping Arcade.......................40 B5

To Cycles Hubert (1.5km);
Laon (46km);
A26; Lille (203km);
Calais (277km)

Chapelle
Foujita

Cimetière
du Nord

R. du Champ de Mars

Pl de la
République

Pl du
Boulingrin

Train
Station

Square
Colbert

Hôtel de
Ville

Pl de l'Hôtel
de Ville

To Ave Jean Jaurès;
N51; Charleville-
Mézières (83km)

Rousseau Pl
Aristide
Briand

Pl du
Forum

Pl
Royale

Le
Cirque

Merry-Go
Round

Fountain

Théâtre
Bus Hub

R Guillaume
de Machault

To Le Tigre (700m); Basilique
d'Automobiles (1.2km); Taittinger
(500m); Pommery (1km);
N44; A4; Épernay (25km);
Châlons-en-Champagne
(Châlons-sur-Marne, 42km)

To Paris
(142km)

Centre des
Congrès
(Convention
Centre)

To N31;
Soissons
(57km)

La Comédie
Parc Léo
Lagrange

To D980; Route
Touristique du Champagne

Synagogue
(1879)

To Ancienne Collège des
Jésuites (1km); Basilique
St-Rémi (1km); Musée
St-Rémi (1km); Fort de
la Pompelle (5km)

Mon-Sat, 11am-4pm Sun & holidays mid-Oct–early Apr) Has an Internet post that runs on a France Télécom *télécarte*.

Churches & Museums

Imagine the pomp, the extravagance, the over-the-top costumes and the egos writ large of a French royal coronation. For centuries, the focal point of such affairs was Reims' **Cathédrale Notre Dame** (🕑 approx 7.30am-7.30pm, closed during Sun morning Mass), a Gothic edifice begun in 1211 – on a site occupied by churches since the 5th century – and mostly completed a century later.

The most famous event in the cathedral's history was the coronation of Charles VII – with Joan of Arc at his side – on 17 July 1429. Very badly damaged (like the whole city) by artillery and fire during WWI, it was restored with funds donated largely by John D Rockefeller; reconsecration took place in 1938, just in time for the next world war.

The 138m-long cathedral is more interesting for its dramatic history than for its heavily restored architectural features. The finest stained-glass windows are the western façade's 12-petalled **great rose window**, its smaller downstairs neighbour, and the rose window in the north transept arm, above the Flamboyant Gothic organ case (15th and 18th centuries). Nearby is a 15th-century **astronomical clock**. There's a window by Chagall in the axial chapel (behind the high altar) and, two chapels to the left, a statue of Joan of Arc.

The hearty might want to climb to the **cathedral roof** (adult €4.60, incl Musée du Tau €7.50; 🕑 Tue-Sat & Sun afternoon early May-early Sep, Sat & Sun afternoon mid-Mar–early May & early Sep-Oct) on a one-hour tour – the Palais du Tau has details.

Palais du Tau (☎ 03 26 47 81 79; adult/18-25 yrs/under 18 €6.10/4.10/free; 🕑 9.30am-6.30pm Tue-Sun early May-early Sep, 9.30am-12.30pm & 2-5.30pm Tue-Sun early Sep-early May), a former archbishop's residence constructed in 1690, was where French princes stayed right before their coronations – and where they played host to a sumptuous banquet right afterwards. Now a museum, it displays truly exceptional statues, ritual objects and tapestries from the cathedral, some in the impressive Salle du Tau.

Way back in the AD 400s, Bishop Remigius baptised Clovis and 3000 Frank-

ish warriors; 121m-long **Basilique St-Rémi** (place St-Rémi) is named in his honour. Once a Benedictine abbey church and now a Unesco World Heritage Site (along with the cathedral and the Palais du Tau), its Romanesque nave and transept – worn but stunning – date mainly from the mid-11th century. The choir (constructed between 1162 and 1190) is in the early Gothic style, with a large triforium gallery and, way up top, tiny clerestory windows. The 12th-century-style chandelier has 96 candles, one for each year of the life of St-Rémi, whose tomb (in the choir) is marked by a mausoleum from the mid-1600s.

An **evocation lumière** (a sort of sound & light show; admission free) takes place inside at 9.30pm on Saturday from July to September. The basilica is about 1.5km southeast of the tourist office; to get there by bus take the Citadine 1 or 2 lines to St-Rémi.

Just 100m from the western façade of Basilique St-Rémi, **Musée St-Rémi** (☎ 03 26 85 23 36; 53 rue Simon; 🕑 2-6.30pm Mon-Fri, 2-7pm Sat & Sun) displays archaeological items, tapestries and 16th- to 19th-century weapons.

Musée-Hôtel Le Vergeur (☎ 03 26 47 20 75; 36 place du Forum; adult/student/10-18 yrs €3.90/2.80/1; 🕑 tours begin 2-5pm or 5.30pm Tue-Sun, also at 10am Tue-Fri Jun-Aug), in a 13th- to 16th-century town house, displays some lovely furniture and art objects.

About 1.5km southeast of the cathedral, the **Musée d'Automobiles** (☎ 03 26 82 83 84; 84 av Georges Clemenceau; adult/student/6-10 yrs/family of 4 €5/4/2.50/15; 🕑 10am-noon & 2-6pm Wed-Mon) displays 140 motor vehicles from the 1920s to the 1970s. To get there by public transport, take bus D to the Boussinesq stop.

WWII IN EUROPE ENDED IN REIMS

Nazi Germany capitulated on 7 May 1945 in US General Dwight D Eisenhower's war room (another surrender document was signed two days later near Berlin), now a museum known as the **Musée de la Reddition** (Surrender Museum; ☎ 03 26 47 84 19; 12 rue Franklin Roosevelt; 🕑 10am-noon & 2-6pm Wed-Mon).

The original Allied battle maps are still affixed to the walls of the one-time technical college, now known as Lycée Franklin Roosevelt. Signs are in French.

CHAMPAGNE & MORE

Le Pass Citadine (€12), sold at the tourist office, gets you a champagne house tour, an all-day local bus ticket, entry to all four municipal museums and a box of *biscuits roses* (pink biscuits), traditionally eaten with champagne.

Other Sights

Reims' main nightlife can be found at **place Drouet d'Erlon**, a huge pedestrianised square with runway lights, almost as much neon as Times Square and dozens of places to eat and drink. Southeast of the **fountain** – crowned by a gilded statue of Winged Victory – is a covered **shopping arcade**. At rue Condorcet, the 12th- to 14th-century **Église St-Jacques** has some pretty awful post-war stained glass.

The handsome **place Royale**, surrounded by neoclassical arcades, reflects the magnificence of Louis XV's France (that's him on the pedestal).

Relics of the Roman period include **Porte de Mars** (place de la République), a Roman triumphal arch from the 3rd century AD and the **Cryptoportique** (place du Forum; admission free; ⏲ 2-5pm Tue-Sun mid-Jun–mid-Sep), a 3rd-century Roman gallery that was apparently used for grain storage.

Champagne Cellars

The musty *caves* (cellars) and dusty bottles of about a dozen Reims-area champagne houses can be visited on guided tours. The following places all have fancy websites, cellar temperatures of 8°C to 10°C and offer frequent English-language tours that end with a tasting session. For details of the champagne production process see p72.

The headquarters of the **Taittinger** (☎ 03 26 85 84 33; www.taittinger.com; 9 place St-Niçaise; tours adult/under 12 €7/free) empire is 1.5km southeast of the cathedral. It is an excellent place to come for a clear, straightforward presentation on how champagne is actually made – no clap-trap about 'the champagne mystique' here! On the one-hour tours visitors are shown everything from *remuage* (bottle turning) to *dégorgement* (sediment removal at -25°C) to the corking machines. Parts of the cellars occupy 4th-century Roman stone quarries; other bits were made by 13th-century Benedic-

tine monks. For €270 you can purchase a 6L Mathusalem, though for a really big bash you'll surely want a Nabuchodonosor (15L) – and a Bible to figure out why oversized champagne bottles have such bizarre names! Tours begin from 9.30am to 11.45am and 2pm to 4.20pm (closed on weekends from December to mid-March).

Mumm (pronounced moom; ☎ 03 26 49 59 70; www.mumm.com; 34 rue du Champ de Mars; tours adult/under 16 €7/free) was founded in 1827 and is now the world's third-largest producer (eight million bottles a year). Mumm offers edifying, one-hour cellar tours – completely revamped in 2004 – that end with a *flûte* of Cordon Rouge. They run from 9am to 11am and 2pm to 5pm from March to October, and also take place on weekend and holiday afternoons – and (if you reserve in advance) from Monday to Friday – from November to February. A tasting session with oenological commentary is available for €13/18 for two/three champagnes.

Pommery (☎ 03 26 61 62 55; www.pommery.com; 5 place du Général Gouraud; tours adult/student/under 12 €7.50/6/free) is located in an Elizabethan-style hilltop campus (built 1868–78) 1.8km southeast of the cathedral, Pommery has cellar tours that take you 30m underground to Gallo-Roman quarries and 25 million bottles of bubbly; they operate from 10am to 5pm (to 4pm or 4.30pm from mid-November to March). Weekends can get crowded so phoning ahead is a good idea. The complex often hosts contemporary art exhibitions.

Tours

Mumm (see above) arranges **vineyard visits** (per person €25; ⏲ Mar-Oct) by six-person minibus; reserve in advance.

The tourist office offers a self-guided tour of the cathedral and the city centre (about €8 for one or two people) and English-language guided tours of the cathedral (in summer, around 2.30pm).

THE EXPLOSIVE SIDE OF FIZZY WINE

The pressure in a champagne bottle can reach six atmospheres at the end of the second fermentation. As a result, about one in 10,000 bottles explodes. Ask to see an unlucky one on a cellar tour!

Festivals & Events

In June, the six-day **Les Sacres du Folklore**, one of northern France's most colourful folk festivals, takes place concurrently with **Les Fêtes Johanniques**, an over-the-weekend medieval celebration that re-enacts Joan of Arc's arrival in Reims.

From July to early August, **Les Flâneries Musicales d'Été** brings over 100 concerts (most of them free) to historic venues all over town.

Sleeping

The city centre offers a wide range of good-value accommodation options.

BUDGET

Centre International de Séjour (CIS; ☎ 03 26 40 52 60; www.cis-reims.com; chaussée Bocquaine; dm in a 2- or 3–5-bed room €12/11, with shower & toilet €16/13, s €28; 🕑 24hr; 🖳) The 189 rooms are institutional, brightly painted and have not a drop of charm – but the friendly atmosphere more than makes up for it. A great place to meet people! To get there take bus B, K, M or N to the Comédie stop or bus H to the Pont de Gaulle stop.

Hôtel Alsace (☎ 03 26 47 44 08; fax 03 26 47 44 52; 6 rue du Général Sarrail; s/d/tr with shower from €26/29/34, with shower & toilet €29/32/37) Run by the friendly son of a Yorkshireman who married a Frenchwoman during the war, this 24-room place has large rooms that are being redecorated as we go to press. In winter reception is closed on Sunday afternoon – call ahead if you'll be arriving then.

Hôtel Au Bon Accueil (☎ 03 26 88 55 74; fax 03 26 05 12 38; 31 rue de Thillois; s from €22, d with shower & toilet €35) This place almost (but not quite) lives up to its name, but it does offer clean, eminently serviceable rooms. Hall showers cost €1.50.

MID-RANGE

There are a number of two- and three-star hotels at place Drouet d'Erlon and along adjacent rue Buirette.

Hôtel de la Cathédrale (☎ 03 26 47 28 46; fax 03 26 88 65 81; 20 rue Libergier; d/q from €56/77) Charm, graciousness – and some very shiny brass, lovingly polished – greet guests at this family-run two-star place, whose tasteful rooms have high ceilings.

Grand Hôtel du Nord (☎ 03 26 47 39 03; www.hotel reims.com; 75 place Drouet d'Erlon; d from €55) Has a sunny breakfast room and cheerful, upbeat rooms, some with views of the square.

Grand Hôtel de l'Univers (☎ 03 26 88 68 08; hotel-univers@ebc.net; 41 blvd Foch; d from €68, Nov–mid-Mar from €62.50) This venerable three-star place has large rooms, tastefully appointed, with high ceilings, bathrooms with space to move around and odd plastic keys.

Eating

Place Drouet d'Erlon is lined with pizzerias, brasseries, cafés, pubs and sandwich places.

FRENCH

The restaurant attached to the **Hôtel Alsace** (see left; 3-course menu €9.90; 🕑 lunch Mon-Sat) has one of the best midday deals in town.

Le Continental (☎ 03 26 47 01 47; 95 place Drouet d'Erlon; menus, some with wine €18.50-36; 🕑 noon-2.30pm & 7-11pm or later) Built in the early 20th century, this marble-floored place serves up panoramic views and classic French dishes such as *magret de canard* (fillet of duck breast); seafood is the speciality from September to May. The tablecloths are very pink.

Brasserie Le Boulingrin (☎ 03 26 40 96 22; 48 rue de Mars; menus €16-23; 🕑 Mon-Sat) Offers a mini-trip back in time with original 1920s décor, including an old-time zinc bar. The culinary focus is on meat and fish.

OTHER

Il Colosseo (☎ 03 26 47 68 50; 9 rue de Thillois; 🕑 11.30am-2.30pm & 6.30-11.30pm Tue-Sat) Reached through a dilapidated – one could even say decadent – Art Nouveau theatre façade, this place serves pizzas and pastas (€7.70 to €11.50) as well as salads (€8 to €10.50).

The Glue Pot (☎ 03 26 47 36 46; 49 place Drouet d'Erlon; 🕑 10am-3am, meals served noon-2.30pm & 7-11pm, until 1.30am Fri & Sat nights) An eatery that

---

AUTHOR'S CHOICE

L'Apostrophe (☎ 03 26 79 19 89; 59 place Drouet d'Erlon; 2-course weekday menu €13, salads €11-14, mains €12.50-23) This bustling café-brasserie serves generous portions of very French intellectual pretension (the walls are lined with books!) – and some mean cocktails – along with its very international cuisine. Don't feel you have to discuss metaphysics, though: the arty types and local literary figures who flock here are more interested in the chic atmosphere, summertime terrace and good value.

CHAMPAGNE

only the French genius for eclecticism could have created: this Irish pub doubles as a Tex-Mex restaurant (*fajitas* are €13.60, *quesadillas au chèvre* €13.15) that serves burgers (the Big Boy has an egg on top) and pizzas (€6.60 to €9.90) to patrons seated on bright red banquettes. Believe it or not, the food is pretty good!

SELF-CATERING
Facing the cathedral's western front, a bunch of **shops** sell champagne. Fresh food choices include the **food market** (place du Boulingrin; ⟳ until 1.30pm Wed) and **Monoprix Supermarket** (21 rue de Chativesle; ⟳ 9am-8pm Mon-Sat).

Drinking
Terraced brasseries and cafés line brightly lit place Drouet d'Erlon, the focal point of Reims' nightlife; some places stay open till 3am. *Les Rendez-Vous*, a free guide published each Wednesday, lists concerts and other cultural events.

Waïda (☎ 03 26 47 44 49; 5 place Drouet d'Erlon; ⟳ 7.30am-7.30pm Tue-Sat, 7.30am-1pm & 3.30-7pm Sun) An old-fashioned patisserie with mirrors, mosaics and marble from 1960.

Le Lion de Belfort (☎ 03 26 47 48 17; 37 place Drouet d'Erlon; ⟳ 7am-3am) This quintessentially French café-bar is, oddly, outfitted with tea-related British colonial memorabilia.

Carpe Diem (☎ 03 26 02 00 41; http://lecarpediem .free.fr in French; 6 rue des Capucins; ⟳ from 9pm) This gay, bi and transsexual bar, situated above a kebab place, flies its rainbow flags proudly and has frequent theme nights.

Le Tigre (☎ 03 26 82 64 00; 2bis av Georges Clemenceau; ⟳ 5pm-4am Mon-Thu, 5pm-5am Fri & Sat, weekends only Aug) Funky, sprawling and student-oriented, this bar-disco is about 1km east of the cathedral, has live rock and reggae bands (€5) on Friday and Saturday starting at 9pm (but not in July and August). At 11pm from Thursday to Saturday, Le Tigre becomes a disco (Thursday free, Friday and Saturday €6).

Getting There & Away
BUS
The best way to get to Troyes (€19.70, 1¾ to 2¼ hours, three or four daily weekdays, two on Saturday, one on Sunday except during university breaks, none on holidays) is to take a bus operated by **TransChampagne** (STDM; ☎ 03 26 65 17 07). The stop is next to the train station; hours are posted.

CAR
Rental companies with offices facing the train station car park:
ADA (☎ 03 26 50 08 40)
Loc Vel (☎ 03 26 40 43 38)
Rent-a-Car Système (☎ 03 26 77 87 77)

TRAIN
Reims' train station is on the secondary Paris–Longwy line. Destinations with direct services include Épernay (€5.20, 21 to 45 minutes, 23 daily weekdays, 14 daily weekends), Laon (€7.70, 40 minutes, eight daily Monday to Friday, three or four daily Saturday and Sunday) and Paris' Gare de l'Est (€20.30, 1¾ hours, 12 to 16 daily).

In the city centre, information and tickets are available at the **Boutique SNCF** (1 cours JB Langlet; ⟳ 10am-7pm Mon-Sat).

Getting Around
BICYCLE
The **Centre International de Séjour** (see p329) rents city bikes to the public for €10/15 for a half/whole day.

BUS
The local bus company is **TUR** (☎ 03 26 88 25 38; office at 6 rue Chanzy; ⟳ closed Sun & holidays). Two circular lines, Citadine 1 and Citadine 2 (single ticket €0.80), serve most of the sights mentioned in this section. Most lines begin their last runs at about 8.50pm.

PARKING
Just east of the train station, the car park at esplanade du Colonel Bouchez is unmetered (at least it was at the time of writing). There's plenty of free parking north and northwest of the train tracks.

TAXI
For a taxi, call ☎ 03 26 47 05 05.

FLIGHT OF THE HUMBLED KING

Louis XVI's attempt to escape from Paris in 1791 ended at **Ste-Ménehould** (pronounced Saint Menoo), 79km east of Reims, when the soon-to-be-beheaded monarch and Marie-Antoinette were recognised by the postmaster thanks to the king's portrait printed on a banknote.

AROUND REIMS

The **Route Touristique du Champagne** (Champagne Route) weaves its way among neatly tended vines covering the slopes between small villages, some with notable churches or speciality museums, some quite ordinary. All along the route, beautiful panoramas abound and small-scale *producteurs* (champagne producers) welcome travellers in search of bubbly; many are closed during the *vendange* (grape harvest), ie September and into October. Tourist offices can supply you with an excellent colour-coded booklet, *The Sparkling Vinyards*, which lists up-to-date addresses, emails and websites. In this region you must phone before stopping by.

The signposted tertiary roads that make up the Champagne Route – 600km in all, divided into six circuits – meander through the Marne's three most important wine-growing areas:

- **Montagne de Reims** – between Reims and Épernay
- **Côte des Blancs** – south of Épernay towards Sézanne
- **Vallée de la Marne** – west of Épernay towards Dormans and Château Thierry

For details on the Côte des Bar region, see p340.

Hautvillers

Three centuries ago it was in this tidy and conspicuously prosperous village (population 860), 7km north of Épernay, that Dom Pérignon created champagne as we know it. His tomb is next the altar of the **Église Abbatiale** (abbey church), which has lots of 17th-century woodwork; the abbey itself was burnt down by the English during the Hundred Years' War. Great vineyard views await a few hundred metres north of the centre along route de Fismes (D386); and south along route de Cumières (a road leading to the D1). Hautvillers is twinned with Eguisheim in Alsace, which may help explain why two **storks** live in a cage 800m towards Épernay along the D386.

Details on the village and region are available at the **tourist office** (☎ 03 26 57 06 35; www.ccgvm.com in French; place de la République; ☷ 9.30am-1pm & 1.30-6pm Mon-Sat, 10am-5pm Sun mid-Apr–Oct, 10am-noon & 2-5pm Mon-Sat Nov–mid-Apr, 11am-4pm Sun Nov & mid-Mar–mid-Apr).

DWARF-MUTANT BEECH TREES

No one knows why the forests on a plateau above the village of Verzy (see below) are home to some 700 *hêtres tortillards* (twisted beech trees), also known as **faux de Verzy** (see http://k.collinet.free.fr or http://verzy .verzenay.free.fr for photos), but their presence has been documented since at least the 1600s. Scientists have determined that the phenomenon is genetic and apparently natural, but that hardly explains why so many of these trees are to be found in this small area (similar mutants grow in Sweden and Germany and elsewhere in France in ones and twos) – or why the vertically challenged beeches has as neighbours 13 dwarf-mutant oaks and three chestnuts. Is it a virus? Some property of the soil? One thing is certain though: the faux, whose gnarled and contorted branches droop towards the ground to form an umbrella-shaped dome, suffer in the competition for light with their non-mutant companions and need to be protected.

Parc Naturel Régional de la Montagne de Reims

The section of the Route Touristique nearest Reims skirts the Montagne de Reims Regional Park, endowed with lush forests and a botanical curiosity, the mutant beech trees known as **faux de Verzy** (see above). To get to the faux from the village of Verzy, follow the signs up the D34; the first trees can be seen about 1km from 'Les Faux' car park.

Across the D34, a short trail leads through the forest to the *point de vue* (panoramic viewpoint) atop 288m-high **Mont Sinaï**. Visitors are asked to refrain from worshipping golden calves, roasting marshmallows over the burning bush and doing impious impressions of Charlton Heston.

ÉPERNAY

pop 26,000

Épernay, a well-to-do provincial town 25km south of Reims, is home to some of the world's most famous champagne houses. Beneath the streets in some 100km of subterranean cellars, 200 million of bottles of champagne, just waiting to be popped open for some sparkling celebration, are being aged. In 1950, one such cellar – owned by

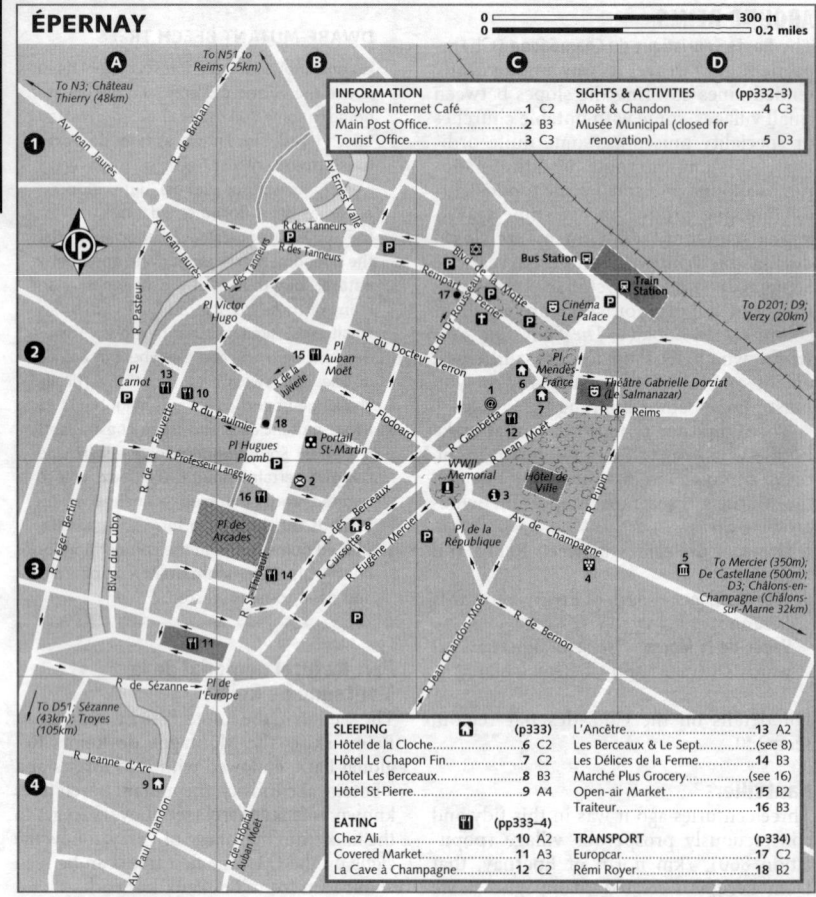

ÉPERNAY

INFORMATION	
Babylone Internet Café	1 C2
Main Post Office	2 B3
Tourist Office	3 C3

SIGHTS & ACTIVITIES	(pp332–3)
Moët & Chandon	4 C3
Musée Municipal (closed for renovation)	5 D3

SLEEPING	(p333)
Hôtel de la Cloche	6 C2
Hôtel Le Chapon Fin	7 C2
Hôtel Les Berceaux	8 B3
Hôtel St-Pierre	9 A4

EATING	(pp333–4)
Chez Ali	10 A2
Covered Market	11 A3
La Cave à Champagne	12 C2

L'Ancêtre	13 A2
Les Berceaux & Le Sept	(see 8)
Les Délices de la Ferme	14 B3
Marché Plus Grocery	(see 16)
Open-air Market	15 B3
Traiteur	16 B3

TRANSPORT	(p334)
Europcar	17 C2
Rémi Royer	18 B2

the irrepressible Mercier – hosted a car rally without the loss of a single bottle!

The town, set amid the gentle, vineyard-covered slopes of the Marne Valley, is the best place in Champagne to tour cellars and sample fizzy wine. It can easily be visited as a day trip from Reims – or even Paris.

Orientation

Mansion-lined av de Champagne, where many of Épernay's champagne houses are based, stretches east from the town's commercial heart (around place des Arcades), whose liveliest streets are rue Général Leclerc and rue St-Thibault. The area south of place de la République is given over to car parks.

Information

Babylone Internet Café (☎ 03 26 55 96 44; 25 rue Gambetta; per hr €4; ☼ noon-10pm Tue-Thu, noon-1am Fri & Sat, 3-10pm Sun)

Main Post Office (place Hugues Plomb; ☼ 8am-7pm Mon-Fri, 8am-noon Sat) Has currency exchange and a Cyberposte.

Tourist Office (☎ 03 26 53 33 00; www.ot-epernay.fr; 7 av de Champagne; ☼ 9.30am-12.30pm & 1.30-7pm Mon-Sat, 11am-4pm Sun & holidays mid-Apr–mid-Oct, 9.30am-12.30pm & 1.30-5.30pm Mon-Sat mid-Oct–mid-Apr) Has details on activities in the region, including cellar visits and options for walking and cycling.

Champagne Houses

Épernay's champagne houses cannot be accused of cowering behind excessive modesty or aristocratic understatement. When it comes to PR for brand-name bubbly, dignified razzle-dazzle is the name of the game. Many of the well-touristed *maisons* on or near av de Champagne offer interesting, informative tours, followed by tasting and a visit to the factory-outlet bubbly shop. For details on the champagne production process, see p72).

The prestigious **Moët & Chandon** (☎ 03 26 51 20 20; www.moet.com; adult/12-16 yrs €7.50/4.50; 18 av de Champagne) produces more champagne (25 to 30 million bottles a year) than anyone else and offers one-hour tours that are among the region's most impressive. They depart every 10 or 20 minutes from 9.30am to 11.30am and 2pm to 4.30pm (closed weekends from mid-November to mid-March). Super-premium Dom Perignon will set you back at least €94 a bottle; a 1962 vintage is a bargain at €650.

The 45-minute tours at **De Castellane** (☎ 03 26 51 19 19; www.castellane.com in French; 64 av de Champagne; adult/10-18 yrs €6/4.50) take in the *maison's* informative bubbly **museum**, dedicated to elucidating the *méthode champenoise* and its diverse technologies. The reward for climbing the 237 steps up the 60m tower: a panoramic view. Tours run from 10.30am to 11.15am and 2.30pm to 5.15pm, April to November.

Mercier (☎ 03 26 51 22 22; www.champagnemercier.com; 68-70 av de Champagne; adult/12-15 yrs €6.50/3; ☣ mid-Jan–about 20 Dec, closed Tue & Wed except mid-Mar–mid-Nov), the most popular brand in France (and No 2 in overall production), has thrived on unabashed self-promotion since it was founded in 1847 by Eugène Mercier, a trailblazer in the field of eye-catching publicity stunts and the virtual creator of the cellar tour. Everything here is flashy, including the 160,000L barrel that took two decades to build (for the Universal Exposition of 1889) and the lift that transports you 30m underground to a laser-guided train that gets confused by forward-facing camera flashes and has been known to veer into the bottles that line its route. There are entertaining 45-minute tours from 9.30am to 11.30am and 2pm to 4.30pm.

Vineyard Tour

Champagne Domi Moreau (☎ 06 30 35 51 07 or after 6.30pm 03 26 59 45 85; www.champagne-domimoreau .com; adult €20; departures 9.30am &/or 2.30pm except

---

THE JOYS OF NOT SHARING

Unlike cognac, 95% of which is consumed outside France, two-thirds of the 270 million bottles of champagne produced each year are popped open, sipped and savoured in France itself. That doesn't leave much for the rest of us!

Large *maisons*, which have global brand recognition, export a high percentage of their production (Moët & Chandon exports 80% of its bubbly), whereas the many of small *producteurs* generally serve an almost exclusively domestic clientele.

Wed & during the 2nd half of Aug, the Christmas period & Feb school holidays) runs three-hour minibus tours to nearby vineyards. Pick-up is across the street from the tourist office. Call ahead for reservations.

Sleeping

Épernay's hotels are especially full on weekends from Easter to September and on weekdays in May, June and September.

Hôtel St-Pierre (☎ 03 26 54 40 80; fax 03 26 57 88 68; 1 rue Jeanne d'Arc; s/d from €21/24, d with shower & toilet from €34; ☐) Occupying an early-20th-century mansion that has hardly changed in half a century, this place has simple rooms that retain the charm and atmosphere of yesteryear. Reception *may* be closed on Sunday from 2pm to 6pm.

Hôtel Les Berceaux (☎ 03 26 55 28 84; les.berceaux@wanadoo.fr; 13 rue des Berceaux; d €66-75) The rooms of this three-star institution, founded in 1889, are endowed with a certain Champenoise ambience.

Hôtel de la Cloche (☎ 03 26 55 15 15; hotel-de-la -cloche.c.prin@wanadoo.fr; 5 place Mendès-France; d from €39) Has two stars and 19 cheerful, pastel rooms.

Hôtel Le Chapon Fin (☎ 03 26 55 40 03; fax 03 26 54 94 17; 2 place Mendès-France; d €34) The rooms are plain but perfectly serviceable; the floors are not linoleum, we're told, but imitation wood.

Eating

Rue Gambetta is home to four pizzerias.

L'Ancêtre (☎ 03 26 55 57 56; 20 rue de la Fauvette; menus €15.50-29; ☣ closed Tue, Wed lunch & in Jul) An intimate, country-style eatery with traditional French cuisine and just six tables.

La Cave à Champagne (☎ 03 26 55 50 70; 16 rue Gambetta; menus €14.50-28; ⏰ Thu-Tue) Designed to look like a wine cellar, this place specialises in Champenoise cuisine.

Chez Ali (☎ 03 26 51 80 82; 27 rue de la Fauvette; menus €12-18.50; ⏰ closed Mon & dinner Sun) Serves up steaming Algerian couscous.

The venerable **Hôtel Les Berceaux** (see p333) has two in-house eateries. **Les Berceaux** (weekday menu with/without wine €38/28, other menus €46 & €61; ⏰ Wed-Sun) is a sparklingly elegant *gastronomique* restaurant. As we went to press the staff was in mourning over having lost their Michelin star (one of the authors made the unpardonable faux pas of asking about it) but we're betting that the shock and humiliation will inspire them to try even harder. **Le Sept** (menus €16-22) is a more popularly priced place with traditional French cuisine.

SELF-CATERING
Fresh food is abundant at the **covered market** (Halle St-Thibault; rue Gallice; ⏰ 8am-noon Wed & Sat) and the modest **open-air Market** (place Auban Moët; ⏰ Sun morning).

Traiteur (9 place Hugues Plomb; ⏰ 8am-12.45pm & 3-7.30pm except Sun & Wed) sells scrumptious prepared dishes and **Les Délices de la Ferme** (19 rue St-Thibault; ⏰ approximately 9am-noon & 3-7pm Tue-Sat) has wonderful cheeses.

Another option is **Marché Plus Grocery** (13 place Hugues Plomb; ⏰ 7am-9pm Mon-Sat, 9am-1pm Sun).

Getting There & Around
The **train station** (place Mendès-France) has direct services to Nancy (€23.80, two hours, four or five daily), Reims (€5.20, 21 to 45 minutes, 23 daily weekdays, 14 daily weekends) and Paris' Gare de l'Est (€17.50, 1¼ hours, 10 to 16 daily).

Cars can be hired from **Europcar** (☎ 03 26 54 90 61; 20 rempart Perrier).

Parking in the lots south of place de la République is free for the first hour and costs about €1.50 per hour after that.

Mountain bikes can be rented from **Rémi Royer** (☎ 03 26 55 29 61; 10 place Hugues Plomb; half-/whole day €10/17; ⏰ 9am-noon & 2-7pm Tue-Sat). The tourist office sells cycling maps.

TROYES
pop 123,000
Troyes – like Reims, one of the historic capitals of Champagne – has a lively old city that is graced with one of France's finest ensembles of medieval and Renaissance half-timbered houses. It is thus one of the best places in France to get a sense of what Europe looked like back when William Shakespeare was alive. Several unique and very worthwhile museums and a number of ancient churches provide further reasons to spend some time here.

Troyes does not have any champagne cellars. However, you can shop till you drop in its scores of outlet stores specialising in brand-name clothing and accessories.

Orientation
Although Troyes hardly benefits from the champagne trade, the medieval city centre– bounded by blvd Gambetta, blvd Victor Hugo, blvd du 14 Juillet and the Seine – is, ironically, shaped like a champagne cork *(bouchon)*. The main commercial street is rue Émile Zola. Most of the city's sights and activities are in the old city, centred on the 17th-century town hall and Église St-Jean.

Information
INTERNET ACCESS
Open Games Cybercafé (☎ 03 25 41 58 71; 24 rue Claude Huez; per hr €2.80; ⏰ 2-10pm Mon, 11am-10pm Tue-Thu, 11am-midnight Fri & Sat, 2-8pm Sun) You can order a *really* tacky tombstone down the block at No 14.

LAUNDRY
Laundrette (9 rue Georges Clemenceau; ⏰ 7am-8pm) Duds meet suds in a gripping contest of wills.

MONEY
The tourist office annexe changes money when the banks are closed but the rate is poor.

BNP Bank (53 rue Général de Gaulle, ⏰ 8.30am-12.15pm & 1.30-6pm)

PASS' TROYES

This new discount pass (€12), on sale at the tourist office and (oddly) packaged differently for men and women, is a great deal. Among its benefits: free entry to all five of the old city's museums; a champagne tasting session; a guided or audioguided tour of the old city; a horse-drawn carriage ride (in summer); and discounts at various factory outlet shops.

TROYES

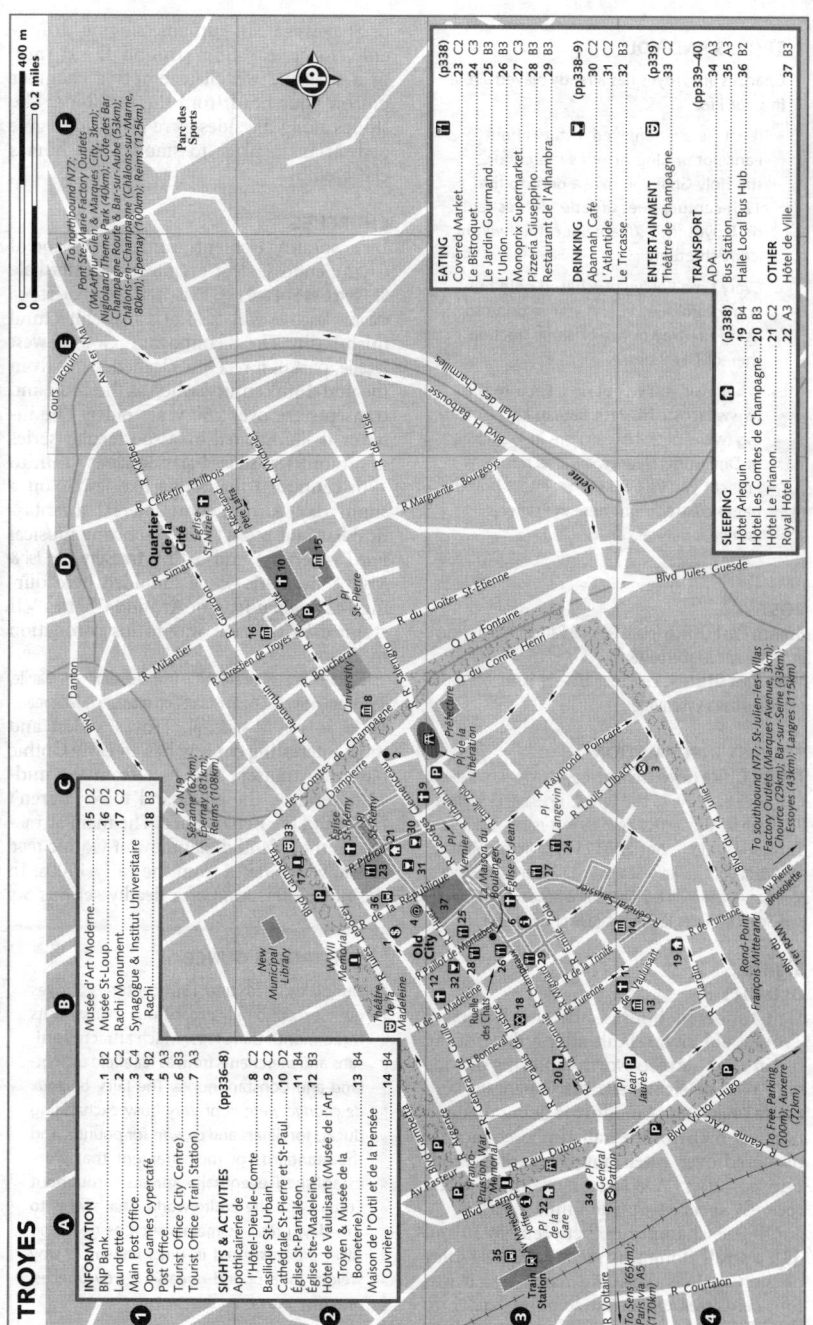

To north-bound N77;
Pont Ste-Marie Factory Outlets
(McArthur Glen & Marques City, 3km);
Nigloland Theme Park (40km); Côte des Bar
Champagne Route & Bar-sur-Aube (53km);
Châlons-en-Champagne (Châlons-sur-Marne,
80km); Épernay (110km); Reims (125km)

INFORMATION

BNP Bank	1 B2
Laundrette	2 C2
Main Post Office	3 C4
Open Games Cypercafé	4 B2
Post Office	5 A3
Tourist Office (City Centre)	6 B3
Tourist Office (Train Station)	7 A3

SIGHTS & ACTIVITIES (pp336–8)

Apothicairerie de l'Hôtel-Dieu-le-Comte	8 C2
Basilique St-Urbain	9 C2
Cathédrale St-Pierre et St-Paul	10 D2
Église St-Pantaleon	11 B4
Église Ste-Madeleine	12 B3
Hôtel de Vauluisant (Musée de l'Art Troyen & Musée de la Bonneterie)	13 B4
Maison de l'Outil et de la Pensée Ouvrière	14 B4
Musée d'Art Moderne	15 D2
Musée St-Loup	16 D2
Rachi Monument	17 C2
Synagogue & Institut Universitaire Rachi	18 B3

EATING (p338)

Covered Market	23 C2
Le Bistroquet	24 C3
Le Jardin Gourmand	25 B3
L'Union	26 B3
Monoprix Supermarket	27 C3
Pizzeria Giuseppino	28 B3
Restaurant de l'Alhambra	29 B3

DRINKING (pp338–9)

Abannah Café	30 C2
L'Atlantide	31 C2
Le Tricasse	32 B3

ENTERTAINMENT (p339)

Théâtre de Champagne	33 C2

TRANSPORT (pp339–40)

ADA	34 A3
Bus Station	35 A3
Halle Local Bus Hub	36 B2

OTHER

Hôtel de Ville	37 B3

SLEEPING (p338)

Hôtel Arlequin	19 B4
Hôtel Les Comtes de Champagne	20 B3
Hôtel Le Trianon	21 C2
Royal Hôtel	22 A3

To Sens (65km);
Paris via A5
(170km)

To N19
Sézanne (62km);
Épernay (81km);
Reims (108km)

To Free Parking
(200m); Auxerre
(72km)

To southbound N77; St-Julien-les-Villas
Factory Outlets (Marques Avenue, 3km);
Chource (29km); Bar-sur-Seine (33km);
Essoyes (43km); Langres (115km)

Parc des
Sports

0   400 m
0   0.2 miles

TROYES AND YOU

Chances are Troyes has already played a role in your life:

■ If you've ever enjoyed a story about Lancelot or King Arthur's search for the Holy Grail you owe a debt to the 12th-century poet Chrétien (Chrestien) de Troyes (http://camelot.celtic-twilight .com/chretien).

■ Every time you've purchased gold bullion (or gold jewellery) you've done so using the troy ounce or some fraction thereof (see right).

■ Whenever you've put on a Lacoste shirt (www.lacoste.fr), Petit Bateau kids clothing (www.petit-bateau.com in French) or Dim underwear (www.dim.fr in French) you've paid homage to a brand name created right here in France's knitwear capital.

POST

Branch Post Office (place Général Patton) Has currency exchange and a Cyberposte.

Main Post Office (38 rue Louis Ulbach) Exchanges currency and has a Cyberposte.

TOURIST INFORMATION

Tourist Office (www.tourisme-troyes.com) Train Station (☎ 03 25 82 62 70; 16 blvd Carnot; ⏱ 9am-12.30pm & 2-6.30pm Mon-Sat except holidays year-round, 10am-1pm Sun Nov-Mar) City Centre (☎ 03 25 73 36 88; rue Mignard; ⏱ 10am-7pm Jul–mid-Sep, 9am-12.30pm & 2-6.30pm Mon-Sat, 10am-noon & 2-5pm Sun & holidays May, Jun & mid-Sep–Oct) Faces the west façade of Église St-Jean.

Sights

OLD CITY

Half-timbered houses line the streets of Troyes' old city, rebuilt after a devastating fire in 1524 – streets worth exploring include **rue Paillot de Montabert**, **rue Champeaux** and **rue de Vauluisant**. An effort is being made to uncover many of the half-timbered façades plastered over when buildings were 'modernised' after WWII (for example, along recently spruced-up rue Émile Zola).

Off rue Champeaux (between No 30 and 32), a stroll along tiny **ruelle des Chats** (Alley of the Cats), as dark and narrow as it was four centuries ago, is like stepping back into the Middle Ages. You half expect a group

of Shakespearean ruffians, singing drunkenly, to appear from around the corner, or a sneering wench to empty a chamber pot on your head from the top floor. The stones along the sides were installed to give pedestrians a place to stand when horses clattered by.

CHURCHES

Incorporating elements from every period of Champenois Gothic architecture, **Cathédrale St-Pierre et St-Paul** (⏱ 10am-1pm & 2-6pm except Mon morning, longer hours Jul–mid-Sep) is an architectural mishmash. The Flamboyant Gothic **west façade**, part of it recently cleaned, dates from the mid-16th century, whereas the choir and transepts are over 250 years older. The interior is illuminated by a spectacular series of around 180 **stained-glass windows** (13th to 17th centuries) that shine like jewels on a sunny day. Also of some interest: a fantastical baroque **organ** (1730s) sporting musical *putti* (cherubs) and a tiny **treasury** (⏱ Jul & Aug). A dramatic scene unfolded here during 1429, when Joan of Arc and Charles VII stopped by on their way to his coronation in Reims.

Église Ste-Madeleine (rue Général de Gaulle; ⏱ 10am-noon & 2-5pm except Sun morning & Mon morning, longer hours Jul–mid-Sep), Troyes' oldest and most interesting church, has an early Gothic nave and transept that date from the mid-12th century; the choir and tower weren't built until the Renaissance. The main attraction is the splendid Flamboyant Gothic **rood screen**, which dates from the early 1500s. In the nave, the statue of a deadly serious **Ste**

THE TROYES OUNCE

During the 12th and 13th centuries, Troyes grew exceptionally prosperous thanks to its three-month trade fairs, which attracted artisans and merchants from as far afield as Scotland and Constantinople. The fairs' *bureaux de change* were kept very busy exchanging ducats for dinars and crowns for pounds, and the standards of measurement that were established eventually spread throughout Europe and the entire world. That's why, to this day, precious metals such as gold and silver are measured in units known as troy weight (one pound equals 12 troy ounces, one troy ounce equals 31.1g).

Marthe (St Martha), around the pillar from the wooden pulpit, is considered a masterpiece of the 15th-century Troyes School.

Other churches worth a visit include **Église St-Pantaléon** (rue de Turenne; ☺ same as Église Ste-Madeleine). Built from 1508 to 1672 in the Renaissance-style on the former site of a synagogue. The interior is decorated with dozens of 16th-century statues, most of them carved locally.

Basilique St-Urbain (place Vernier; ☺ same as Église Ste-Madeleine) is a Gothic structure begun in 1262 by Pope Urban IV, who was born in Troyes and whose father's shoemaker shop once stood on this spot. It has some fine 13th-century stained-glass windows. In the choir is *La Vierge au Raisin*, a graceful early-15th-century stone statue of the Virgin.

MUSEUMS

Centuries-old hand tools, worn to a sensuous lustre by generations of skilled hands, bring to life a world of manual skills largely destroyed by the Industrial Revolution at the **Maison de l'Outil et de la Pensée Ouvrière** (Museum of Tools & Crafts; ☎ 03 25 73 28 26; www.maison-de-l-outil.com; 7 rue de la Trinité; adult/student €6.50/5; ☺ 10am-6pm). A new exhibit features locksmithing. Videos show artisans at work. Run by a national crafts guild, this unique and – if you'll excuse the expression – riveting museum is housed in the magnificent Renaissance-style Hôtel de Mauroy (mid-1500s).

Musée d'Art Moderne (☎ 03 25 76 26 80; place St-Pierre; adult/student under 25 €5/free; ☺ 11am-6pm except Mon & holidays) owes its existence to all those alligator shirts, whose global success allowed the museum's benefactors, Lacoste entrepreneurs Pierre and Denise Lévy, to amass this outstanding collection. Housed in a one-time bishop's palace (16th to 18th centuries), the museum focuses on glass, ceramics and French painting (including lots of Fauvist works) created between 1850 and 1950. Featured artists include Derain, Dufy, Matisse, Modigliani, Picasso, Soutine and local favourite Maurice Marinot.

Musée St-Loup (☎ 03 25 76 21 68; 1 rue Chrestien de Troyes; adult/student under 25 €4/free; ☺ 10am-noon & 2-6pm except Tue & holidays), across the street from the cathedral, has a varied and sometimes surprising collection of medieval sculpture, enamel, archaeology and natural history. The stuffed mammals and birds at the entrance give the completely wrong impression!

If you come down with an old-fashioned malady – scurvy, perhaps, or unbalanced humours – the place to go is the **Apothicairerie de l'Hôtel-Dieu-le-Comte** (☎ 03 25 80 98 97; quai des Comtes de Champagne; ☺ irregular hours), a fully outfitted, wood-panelled pharmacy from the early 1700s.

Hôtel de Vauluisant (☎ 03 25 73 05 85; 4 rue de Vauluisant; adult/student under 25 €3/free; ☺ 10am-noon or 1pm & 2-6pm except Tue & holidays, also closed Mon Oct-May), a haunted-looking Renaissance-style mansion-turned-museum, has two sections:

■ **Musée de l'Art Troyen** (Museum of Troyes Art) Features the evocative paintings, stained glass and statuary (stone and wood) of the Troyes School, which flourished here during the economic prosperity and artistic ferment of the 1500s.

RASHI

During the 11th and 12th centuries, a small Jewish community was established in Troyes under the protection of the counts of Champagne. Its most illustrious member was Rabbi Shlomo Yitzhaki (Solomon son of Isaac; 1040–1105), better known as Rashi (Rachi in French).

Rashi's commentaries on the Bible and the Talmud, which combine literal and non-literal methods of interpretation and make extensive use of allegories and parables as well as symbolic meanings, are still vastly important to Jews; they have also had an impact on Christian Bible interpretation. Rashi's habit of explaining difficult words and passages in the local French vernacular – transliterated into Hebrew characters – has made his writings an important resource for scholars of Old French. In 1475 (a mere 30 years after Gutenberg) Rashi's Bible commentary became the first book to be printed in Hebrew.

In Troyes (pronounced 'Troysh' in Rashi's transliteration), the striking **Rachi monument** (next to the Théâtre de Champagne) stands on the site of a medieval Jewish cemetery. A local institute of Jewish studies, the **Institut Universitaire Rachi** (www.institut-rachi-troyes.com), is named in his honour. The 900th anniversary of his death will be marked with a big bash in June 2005.

■ **Musée de la Bonneterie** (Hosiery & Knitwear Museum) Showcases the sock-strewn story of Troyes' 19th-century knitting industry. Some of the machines on display look like enormous Swiss watches.

Festivals & Events

A celebrity musical performer helps select the theme and artists featured at the week-long **Nuits de Champagne** (www.nuitsdecham pagne.com in French), held in late October or early November.

La Ville en Musique brings music of all sorts (classical, jazz, rock, organ etc) to Troyes from late June to late August.

Sleeping

Hôtel Les Comtes de Champagne (☎ 03 25 73 11 70; www.comtesdechampagne.com; 56 rue de la Monnaie; d from €28, with shower & toilet €37; P) This super-welcoming place has been held up for centuries by the same massive wooden ceiling beams. A huge and very romantic double with balcony costs €60 – an excellent deal!

Royal Hôtel (☎ 03 25 73 19 99; www.royal-hotel -troyes.fr; 22 blvd Carnot; d from €70; ☷ closed for 3 weeks around New Year) This family-run hostelry has restrained rooms with bright, shiny bathrooms and the usual three-star comforts.

Hôtel Le Trianon (☎ 03 25 73 18 52; 2 rue Pithou; d from €25, with shower €34; ☷ reception 11am-8pm Mon, 6.30am-8pm Tue-Sat, 9am-1pm Sun) At this gay-friendly place the French tricolour flies proudly from the balcony, a rainbow flag next to it. The eight rooms, above a jaunty yellow bar, are spacious but ordinary.

Eating

Rue Champeaux is lined with eateries. Ethnic restaurants, cafés and student-oriented takeaways can be found just west of the cathedral along rue de la Cité.

FRENCH

Le Bistroquet (☎ 03 25 73 65 65; place Langevin; menus €16.90-26.90; ☷ closed dinner Sun, also lunch Sun mid-Jun–mid-Sep) This Parisian-style brasserie, hugely popular with locals, offers excellent French dining value. Among the specialities: *andouillette de Troyes* (chitterling sausages), not for the fainthearted but nevertheless the city's culinary pride and joy.

Le Jardin Gourmand (☎ 03 25 73 36 13; 31 rue Paillot de Montabert; menu €16.50; ☷ closed Sun & lunch Mon) Elegant without being overly formal,

this intimate eatery uses only the freshest ingredients for its French and Champenoise dishes (meat and fish). The estimable wine list includes 25 vintages available by the glass. There's a terrace in summer.

L'Union (☎ 03 25 40 35 76; 34 rue Champeaux; 2-/3-course menus €12.50/18.50; ☷ Mon-Sat) Suffused with the atmosphere of 1950s Paris – with just a touch of the classic American diner – this place serves solid brasserie-style food.

OTHER

Pizzeria Giuseppino (☎ 03 25 73 92 44; 26 rue Paillot de Montabert; pasta & pizzas €6.50-9; ☷ Tue-Sat) Troyes' best pizza – ultrathin and crispy – is on offer at this chummy student hang-out.

Restaurant de l'Alhambra (☎ 03 25 73 18 41; 31 rue Champeaux) Amid Moorish-style décor (brought over from Morocco), you can sip Algerian wines and dine on couscous (€12 to €16) and tajines.

SELF-CATERING

There is a **covered market** (☷ 8am-12.45pm & 3.30-7pm Mon-Thu, 7am-7pm Fri & Sat, 9am-12.30pm Sun) for self-caters.

The **Monoprix Supermarket** (71 rue Émile Zola; ☷ 8.30am-8pm Mon-Sat) may be the most beautiful supermarket in France – the upper floors recently got their half-timbers buffed and shined.

Drinking

Abannah Café (☎ 03 25 73 99 02; 12 rue Pithou; ☷ 2pm-3am Mon-Sat) When live bands drop by to play jazz, rock and Cuban music (two Fridays a month from about 9.30pm), patrons – a mix of students and factory workers – dance on the chairs of this vaguely Cuban-style bar, which also doubles as a Tex-Mex restaurant.

It is shirts-optional for the bar guys. There's a theme night each Thursday at 8pm. The people caricatured in the murals – drawn by one of the *serveurs* – are Abannah *habitués*. This place regularly produces champion darts teams.

Le Tricasse (☎ 03 25 73 14 80; 16 rue Paillot de Montabert; ☯ 3pm-3am Mon-Sat) For decades, revellers with bourgeois tendencies – including students, both foreign and domestic – have headed to this bar, named after a local Gallic tribe. DJs spin CDs on Friday and Saturday from 10pm (and often on Thursday, too). You can try your skill in a genteel game of pool.

L'Atlantide (☎ 03 25 73 85 83; 2 place Claude Huez; admission free Thu, €5-10 Fri-Sun; ☯ 11pm-4am or 5am Thu-Sun) Enter the rounded plate-metal entrance, walk down the stairs to the cellar and you could almost be in Berlin or Zurich. The 18-to-25 crowd – their white T-shirts fluorescing in the black light – boogie to house, techno and R&B in one vast space, while the over-25s congregate in the quieter **Privilege** enjoying the sweet sounds of the '80s and '90s. The stats: three bars, two DJs and lots of locals out to party.

Shopping

Troyes is famous across France for its **magasins d'usine** (factory outlets; ☯ generally 10am-7pm, closed most Sun, some also closed Mon until 2pm), a legacy of the local knitwear industry. Brand-name sportswear, underwear, baby clothes, shoes and so on – discontinued styles, unsold stock, returns, prototypes – attract bargainhunters by the coachload.

Most stores are situated in two main zones:
- **St-Julien-les-Villas** – About 3km south of the city centre on blvd de Dijon (the N71

to Dijon). **Marques Avenue** (☎ 08 25 85 86 87; www.marquesavenue.com; av de la Maille) boasts 240 name brands.
- **Pont Ste Marie** – About 3km northeast of Troyes' city centre along rue Marc Verdier, which links av Jean Jaurès (the N77 to Châlons-en-Champagne) with av Jules Guesde (the D960 to Nancy). **McArthur Glen** (☎ 03 25 70 47 10; www.mcarthurglen.fr in French) is a huge strip mall with some 84 shops. Close to McArthur Glen **Marques City** (☎ 03 25 46 37 48; 35 rue Danton; www.marquescity.com in French) houses 30 more stores.

Getting There & Away

BUS

Coach services fill some of the gaping holes left by Troyes' rather pathetic rail services. The **bus station office** (☎ 03 25 71 28 42; ☯ 8.30am-12.30pm & 2-6.30pm Mon-Fri), run by Courriers de l'Aube, is in a corner of the train station building. Schedules are posted on the uprights next to each bus berth. For details on getting to Reims, see p330.

CAR

Vehicles can be rented from **ADA** (☎ 03 25 73 41 68; 2 rue Voltaire).

TRAIN

Troyes is on the rather isolated line linking Basel (Bâle) with Paris' Gare de l'Est (€19.90, 1½ hours, 13 to 15 daily). A change of trains gets you to Dijon (€24.40, 2½ to four hours, three to five daily).

Getting Around

Old-city street improvements will continue through to 2006 so there may be changes to the one-way street grid.

NIGLOLAND THEME PARK

The third most popular amusement park in France (Disneyland Resort Paris, p184, is No 1), **Nigloland** (☎ 03 25 27 94 52; www.nigloland.fr; adult/under 12 & over 60 €15.50/14; ☯ 10am-6pm or 7pm mid-Jun–Aug & during Apr school holidays, to 5.30pm or 6pm on most weekends & some weekdays May, Jun, Sep & Oct) may be even cheesier than its competitors, but the place is still a huge hit with kids, especially those aged three to 12. Homesick Americans can drop by 1950s-style **Hollywood Boulevard** and take a road trip (without autoroute tolls!) along **Route Nationale 66**, both in the **Village Rock'n'Roll**. It's not clear why there's a Caribbean pirate galleon (a giant swing), a California gold rush-style roller coaster and a paddlewheel river steamer named the *King of Mississippi* in the **Village Canadien** (Canadian Village), but you might want to mention this arrangement the next time you hear a snooty European making condescending noises about North Americans' ignorance of world geography. The park is on the N19 40km east of Troyes in Dolancourt. If you're on the A5 take exit No 22 or 23.

All city-centre parking is metered except for one free segment at the western end of blvd Gambetta. There's a large free car park a block south of blvd du 1er RAM.

TCAT (☎ 03 25 70 49 00; www.tcat.fr in French) has its main bus hub, known as Halle, next to the covered market.

To order a taxi, call ☎ 03 25 78 30 30 or ☎ 03 25 76 06 60.

CÔTE DES BAR

Although the Aube *département,* of which Troyes is the capital, is a major producer of champagne (it has 65 sq km of vineyards), it gets little of the recognition accorded the Marne *département* and the big *maisons* around Reims and Épernay. Much of the acrimony dates from 1909, when the Aube growers were excluded from the growing area for Champagne's Appellation d'Origine Contrôlée (AOC). Two years later, they were also forbidden to sell their grapes to producers up north, resulting in months of strikes and chaos; eventually the army was called in. It was another 16 years before the Aube wine growers could again display the prestigious (and lucrative) AOC tag on their labels, but by then the producers in the region's north had come to dominate the champagne market.

Today, champagne production in the southeastern corner of the Aube – about 35km southeast of Troyes and just north of Burgundy's Châtillonnais vineyards (see p459) – is relatively modest in scale, though the reputation of the area's wines has been on an upward trajectory in recent years.

The Côte des Bar section of the **Route Touristique du Champagne** (see p331) passes through **Bar-sur-Aube** (☎ tourist office 03 25 27 24 25), graced by a medieval quarter and two churches, and **Colombey-les-Deux-Églises**, Charles de Gaulle's burial place. **La Boisserie** (☎ 03 25 01 52 52; adult/under 12 €4/free, incl memorial adult/student €7/6; ☯ 10am-12.30pm & 2-6.15pm mid-Apr–mid-Oct, 10am-12.30pm & 2-4.45pm mid-Oct–Nov, 20 Dec-4 Jan & Feb–mid-Apr), the general's family home from 1934 to 1970, is now a museum and place of Gaullist pilgrimage. The 43.5m-high Lorraine cross (1972), symbol of the Resistance, was paid for by public subscription.

Also along the route is **Essoyes**, Renoir's burial place. **Maison de la Vigne** (☎ 03 25 29 64 64; ☯ 2.30-6.30pm Easter-1 Nov) has exhibits on wine-growing in Champagne. **Bayel** (☎ tourist office 03 25 92 42 68; www.bayel-cristal.com) is a village known for its long tradition of crystal-making. Tours of the **Cristalleries Royales de Champagne** (Champagne Royal Glassworks) generally begin at 9.30am and 11am Monday to Friday.

Les Riceys (☎ tourist office 03 25 29 15 38; www .les-riceys-champagne.com) is a *commune* noted for its three churches, three different AOCs and exceptional rosé wines.

Langres
pop 10,000 / elevation 466m

Langres, 75km southeast of Bar-sur-Aube and about the same distance north of Dijon, is both an elongated hilltop bastion, with six towers and seven fortified gates, and a cheese with an orangey-yellow crust. The town's most famous son is Denis Diderot (1713–84), the great encyclopaedist; his statue graces place Diderot, the main square in the centuries-old, stone town centre.

Two blocks north of place Diderot is **Cathédrale St-Mammès**, whose classical façade (1758), with its mammoth columns, hides a late-Romanesque and early-Gothic interior. The modern **Musée d'Art et d'Histoire** (☎ 03 25 87 08 05; place du Centenaire; admission free; ☯ 10am-noon & 2-5pm or 6pm Wed-Mon), two short blocks west of the cathedral, has a collection that ranges from archaeology to the local faïence, cutlery and tinware industries. Circumambulating the **ramparts** – on the inside or the outside – is a 3.5km affair.

The **tourist office** (☎ 03 25 87 67 67; office .tourisme.pays.de.langres@wanadoo.fr; square Olivier Lahalle; ☯ Mon-Sat year-round, Sun & holidays May-Sep) is next to one of the town gates, **Porte des Moulins** (1647).

The two-star, Logis de France-affiliated **Grand Hôtel de l'Europe** (☎ 03 25 87 10 88; hotel -europe.langres@wanadoo.fr; 23 rue Diderot; s/d from €45/55), in a one-time post house two blocks north of place Diderot, has rooms that boast 'bourgeois comfort'. The rustic **restaurant** (menus €14.50-46) specialises in game (in season) and dishes made with local cheese.

Langres' train station, on the flats about 3km west of the old town centre, has services to Dijon (€12.10, one hour, two to four daily), Reims (€25.70, 2½ hours, two to four daily) and Troyes (€16.90, 1¼ hours, five to seven daily). It's linked to the city centre by bus (every 60 to 90 minutes from 6.22am to 6.44pm Monday to Saturday).

Alsace & Lorraine

ALSACE & LORRAINE

Though often spoken of as if they were one, Alsace and Lorraine, neighbouring regions in France's northeastern corner, are linked by little more than a common border through the Vosges Mountains and the imperial ambitions of late-19th-century Germany. In 1871, after the Franco-Prussian War, the newly created German Reich annexed Alsace and part of Lorraine, making the regions' return to rule from Paris a rallying cry of French nationalism.

The charming and beautiful region of Alsace, long a meeting place of Europe's Latin and Germanic cultures, is nestled between the Vosges Mountains and the River Rhine – along which the long-disputed Franco-German border has found a final resting place. Popularly known as a land of storks' nests and colourful half-timbered houses sprouting geraniums, Alsace also offers a wide variety of outdoor activities – including hiking, mountain biking and skiing – in and around its gentle, forested mountains. Throughout France, the people of Alsace have a reputation for being hard-working, well organised and tax-paying.

Lorraine, a region of prairies and forests popularly associated with quiche and de Gaulle's double-barred cross *(croix de Lorraine)*, has little of the picturesque quaintness of Alsace. However, it is home to two particularly handsome cities, both former capitals. Nancy, one of France's most refined and attractive cities, is famed for its Art Nouveau architecture, while Metz, 54km to the north, is a dynamic place known for its Germanic architecture and the stunning stained glass in its marvellous cathedral. The town of Verdun bears silent testimony to the destruction and insanity of WWI.

HIGHLIGHTS

- Crane your neck to see the rose-coloured spires and stained glass of Strasbourg's splendiferous **cathedral** (p349)
- Take in Nancy's supremely refined **wrought iron grillwork** (p372) and **Art-Nouveau masterpieces** (p372)
- Watch storks glide majestically above their rooftop nests in **Hunawihr** (p361), **Munster** (p368) and along the **Route du Vin d'Alsace** (p357)
- Marvel at Colmar's medieval **Issenheim Altarpiece** (p364)
- Be dazzled by the curtains of stained glass in the **Gothic cathedral** (p377) at Metz
- Gaze out on the Vosges, the Rhine, the Black Forest and the Alps from the **Grand Ballon** or the **Ballon d'Alsace** (p368)

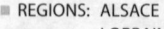

■ REGIONS: ALSACE LORRAINE	■ POPULATION: 1.7 MILLION ■ POPULATION: 2.3 MILLION	■ AREA: 8332 SQ KM ■ AREA: 23,669 SQ KM

ALSACE

Alsace occupies an area 190km long and no more than 50km wide and is made up of two rival *départements*: Bas-Rhin (Lower Rhine; www.tourisme67.com in French), the area around the dynamic regional (and European) capital, Strasbourg; and Haut-Rhin (Upper Rhine; www.tourisme68.com), which covers the region's more southerly reaches, including the picturesque *département* capital, Colmar, and the industrial city of Mulhouse. Germany is just across the busy, barge-laden Rhine, whose left bank is Alsatian as far south as the Swiss city of Basel.

History

French influence in Alsace began in the 1500s during the Wars of Religion (1562–98) and increased during the Thirty Years' War (1618–48) when Alsatian cities, caught between opposing Catholic and Protestant factions, turned to France for assistance. Most of the region was attached to France in 1648 under the Treaty of Westphalia. Today one-fifth of Alsatians are Protestants.

By the time of the French Revolution, the Alsatians felt far more connected to France than to Germany, but the passage of time did little to dampen Germany's appetite for the region known in German as Elsass (Elsaß). The Franco-Prussian War of 1870–71, a supremely humiliating episode

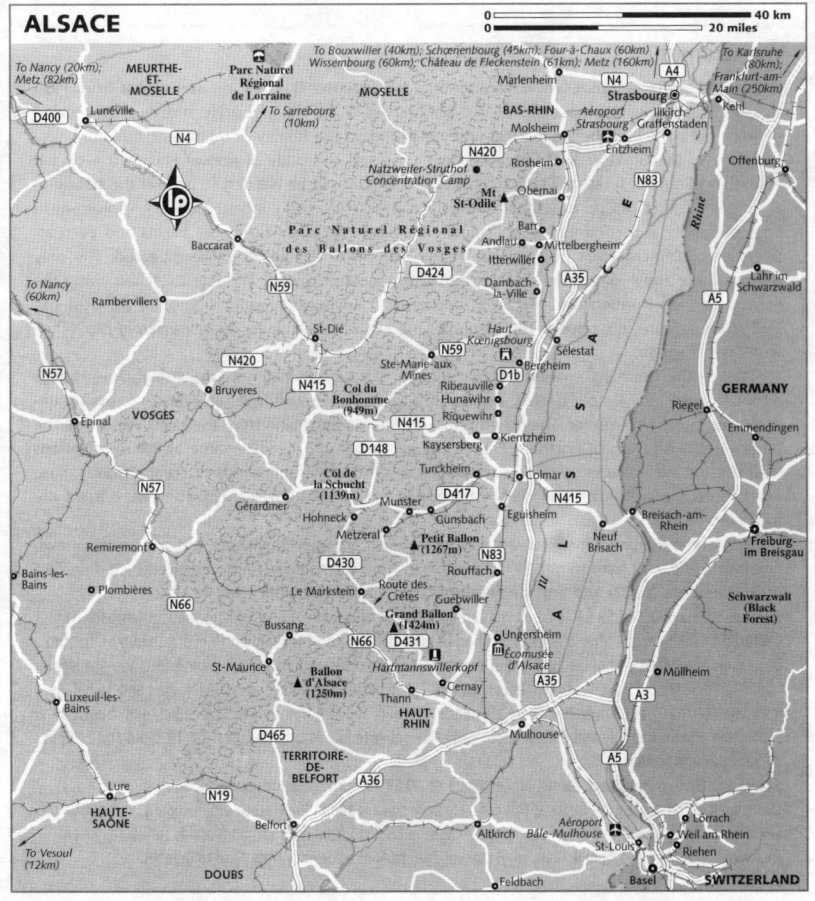

in French history, ended with the Treaty of Frankfurt (1871), by which an embittered France was forced to cede Alsace and the northern part of Lorraine (Lothringen) to the Second Reich.

Following Germany's defeat in WWI, Alsace and Lorraine were returned to France, but the French government's programme to reassimilate the area (eg by banning German-language newspapers) gave rise to a strong home-rule movement. These days, similar sentiments fuel support for the far-right Front National party, at 22% (in the first round of the 2004 regional elections) the highest in the country.

Germany's second annexation of Alsace and Lorraine in 1940 (and indeed the occupation of all of France) was supposed to have been made impossible by the state-of-the-art Maginot Line (see below). Immediately after Nazi Germany took over the area, about half a million Alsatians fled to occupied France. This time, the Germanisation campaign was particularly harsh: anyone caught speaking French was imprisoned, and even the Alsatian language was banned.

After the war, Alsace was once again returned to France. Intra-Alsatian tensions ran high, however, as those who had left came back and confronted neighbours whom they suspected of having collaborated with the Germans: 140,000 Alsatians, as annexed citizens of the Third Reich, had been conscripted into Hitler's armies. Known as the 'Malgré-Nous' because the vast majority

THE MAGINOT LINE

The famed **Ligne Maginot** (www.maginot.org), named after France's minister of war from 1929 to 1932, was one of the most spectacular blunders of WWII. This elaborate, mostly subterranean defence network, built between 1930 and 1940 (and, in the history of military architecture, second only to the Great Wall of China in sheer size), was the pride of prewar France. It included everything France's finest military architects thought would be needed to defend the nation in a 'modern war' of poison gas, tanks and aeroplanes: reinforced concrete bunkers, subterranean lines of supply and communication, minefields, antitank canals, floodable basins and even artillery emplacements that popped out of the ground to fire and then disappeared. The only things visible above ground were firing posts and lookout towers. The line stretched along the Franco–German frontier from the Swiss border all the way to Belgium where, for political and budgetary reasons, it stopped. The Maginot Line even had a slogan: *'Ils ne passeront pas'* (They won't get through).

'They' – the Germans – never did. Rather than attack the Maginot Line straight on, Hitler's armoured divisions simply circled around through Belgium and invaded France across its unprotected northern frontier. They then attacked the Maginot Line from the rear. Against all the odds – and with most of northern France already in German hands – some of the fortifications held out for a few weeks. When resistance became hopeless, thousands of French troops managed to escape to Switzerland, where the Swiss promptly interned them (they were freed the following year).

Parts of the Maginot Line – remarkably preserved – are open to visitors, but without your own wheels they're a bit hard to get to. In Lorraine, visitors can tour over a dozen sites, including Fort du Hackenberg (p382) and Fort de Fermont (p386). Major Maginot sites in Alsace:

Four-à-Chaux (☎ 03 88 94 48 62, at the Lembach tourist office ☎ 03 88 94 43 16; www.ot-lembach.com) Captured by the Germans after a week of fighting in June 1940, this fort is 60km north of Strasbourg on the tiny D65 (a few kilometres east of Lembach). **Guided tours** (in French and German with English text; adult/student/under 12 €4.50/3.50/2) last 1½ to two hours, involve 1.7km of walking and begin at 10am, 2pm and 3pm daily from late March to early November. There are additional tours at 11am from July to September, 4pm from May to September and 5pm in July and August. From early November to late March, tours start at 10.30am and 2.30pm on Saturday and Sunday.

Schœnenbourg (Hunspach tourist office ☎ 03 88 80 59 39; www.lignemaginot.com; adult/6-18 yrs €5/3) The largest visitable Maginot fortress, this concrete behemoth is about 45km north of Strasbourg. You can begin a self-guided tour of the two-hour, 2.5km route (signs in English) from 2pm to 4pm Monday to Saturday from Easter to September and from 9.30am to 11am and 2pm to 4pm on Sunday from April to October.

had gone off to war against their will, over half never returned from the Russian front and post-war Soviet prison camps. To make Alsace a symbol of hope for future Franco-German (and pan-European) cooperation, Strasbourg was chosen as the seat of the Council of Europe (in 1949) and, later, of the European Parliament.

Language

Alsatian (Elsässisch; www.heimetsproch.org), the language of Alsace, is an Alemannic dialect of German not unlike the dialects spoken in nearby parts of Germany and Switzerland. It has no official written form (spelling – including on menus – is something of a free-for-all), and pronunciation varies considerably from one area to another (especially between the north and south). Despite a series of heavy-handed attempts by both the French and the Germans to impose their languages on the region, in part by restricting (or even banning) the use of Alsatian, it is – miraculously – still used in everyday life by people of all ages, in the villages as well as the cities. You're likely to hear its sing-songy cadences whenever you happen upon locals who are just being themselves – for instance, in a *boulangerie*.

STRASBOURG

pop 427,000

Prosperous, cosmopolitan Strasbourg (City of the Roads) is France's great northeastern metropolis and the intellectual and cultural capital of Alsace. Situated only a few kilometres west of the Rhine, the city is aptly named, for it is on the vital transport arteries that have linked northern Europe with the Mediterranean since Celtic times. Strasbourg continues to serve as an important European crossroads thanks to the presence of the European Parliament, the Council of Europe, the European Court of Human Rights, the Eurocorps (www.eurocorps.org), the Franco-German TV network Arte (www.arte-tv.com in French) and a student population of some 48,000, 20% from outside France.

Towering above the restaurants, *winstubs* (traditional Alsatian eateries) and pubs of the lively old city – a wonderful area to explore on foot – is the cathedral, a medieval marvel in pink sandstone. Nearby you'll find one of the finest ensembles of museums anywhere in France.

Accommodation is extremely difficult to find during European Parliament sessions (p352).

History

Before it was attached to France in 1681, Strasbourg was effectively ruled for several centuries by a guild of citizens whose tenure accorded the city a certain democratic character. A university was founded in 1566 and several leaders of the Reformation took up residence here. Johannes Gutenberg worked in Strasbourg from about 1434 to 1444, perfecting his printing press and the moveable metal type that made it so revolutionary. Three centuries later, the German poet, playwright, novelist and philosopher Johann Wolfgang von Goethe (1749–1832) studied law here.

Orientation

Strasbourg's train station is 400m west of the Grande Île (Big Island), the core of ancient and modern Strasbourg, whose main squares are place Kléber, place Broglie (pronounced **broag**-lee), place Gutenberg and place du Château. The quaint Petite France area in the Grande Île's southwestern corner is subdivided by canals. Much of the city centre is for pedestrians only.

The European Parliament building and Palais de l'Europe are about 2km northeast of the cathedral.

The city centre is about 3.5km west of Pont de l'Europe, the bridge that links the French bank of the Rhine with the German city of Kehl.

Information
BOOKSHOPS

Géorama (☎ 03 88 75 01 95; 20-22 rue du Fossé des Tanneurs; ❤ closed Sun & Mon morning) Has a huge selection of hiking maps and topoguides.

The Bookworm (☎ 03 88 32 26 99; 3 rue de Pâques; tram stop Ancienne Synagogue) Carries new and used English-language books, including Lonely Planet guides.

INTERNET ACCESS

L'Utopie (☎ 03 88 23 89 21; 21-23 rue du Fossé des Tanneurs; per hr €3; ❤ 7am-11.30pm Mon-Sat, 8am-10pm Sun) The computers are in the basement. A Wireless Internet connection for your laptop costs €3 per hour.

NeT SuR CouR (☎ 03 88 35 66 76; 18 quai des Pêcheurs; tram stop Gallia; per hr €2; ❤ 9.30am-9.30pm Mon-Fri, 2-8pm Sat & Sun) At the end of a narrow courtyard.

STRASBOURG

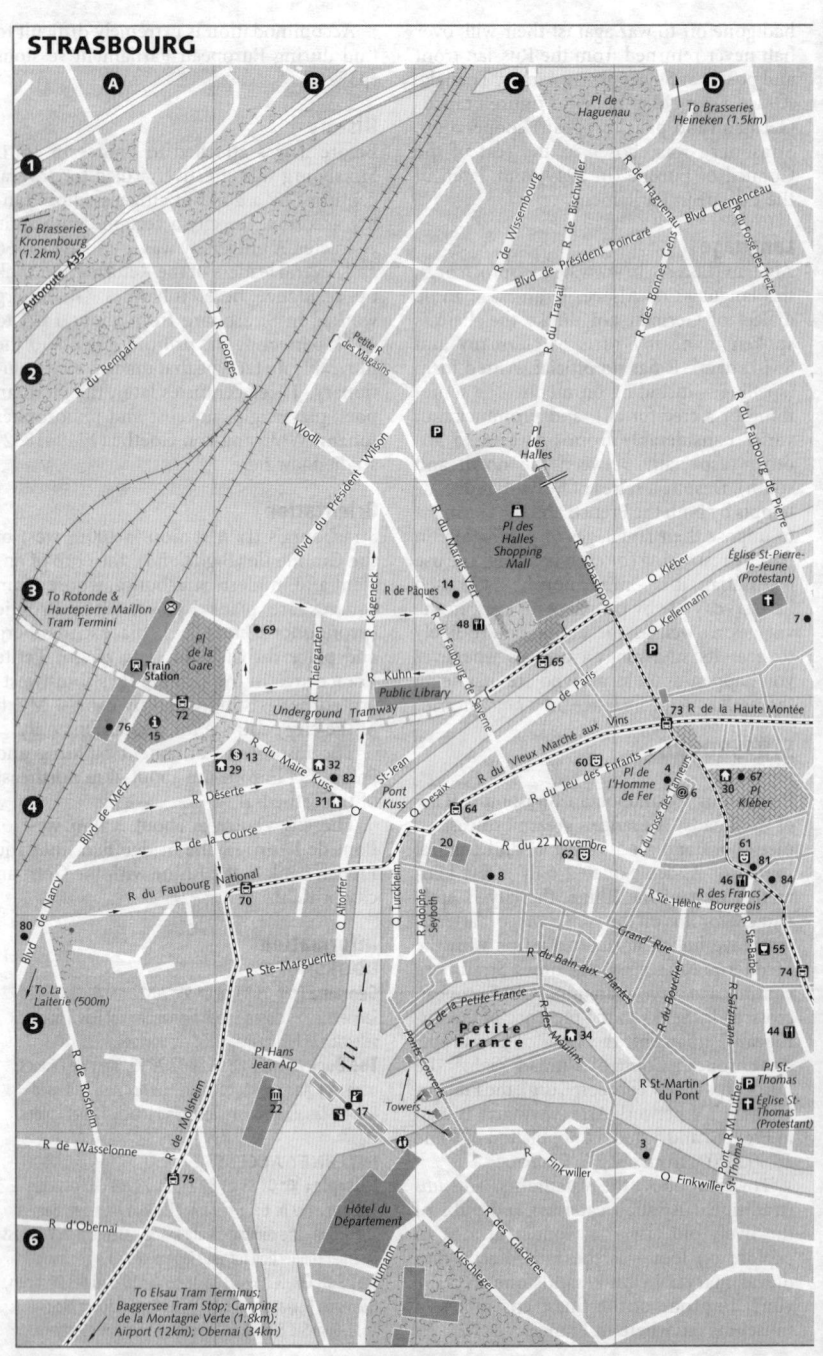

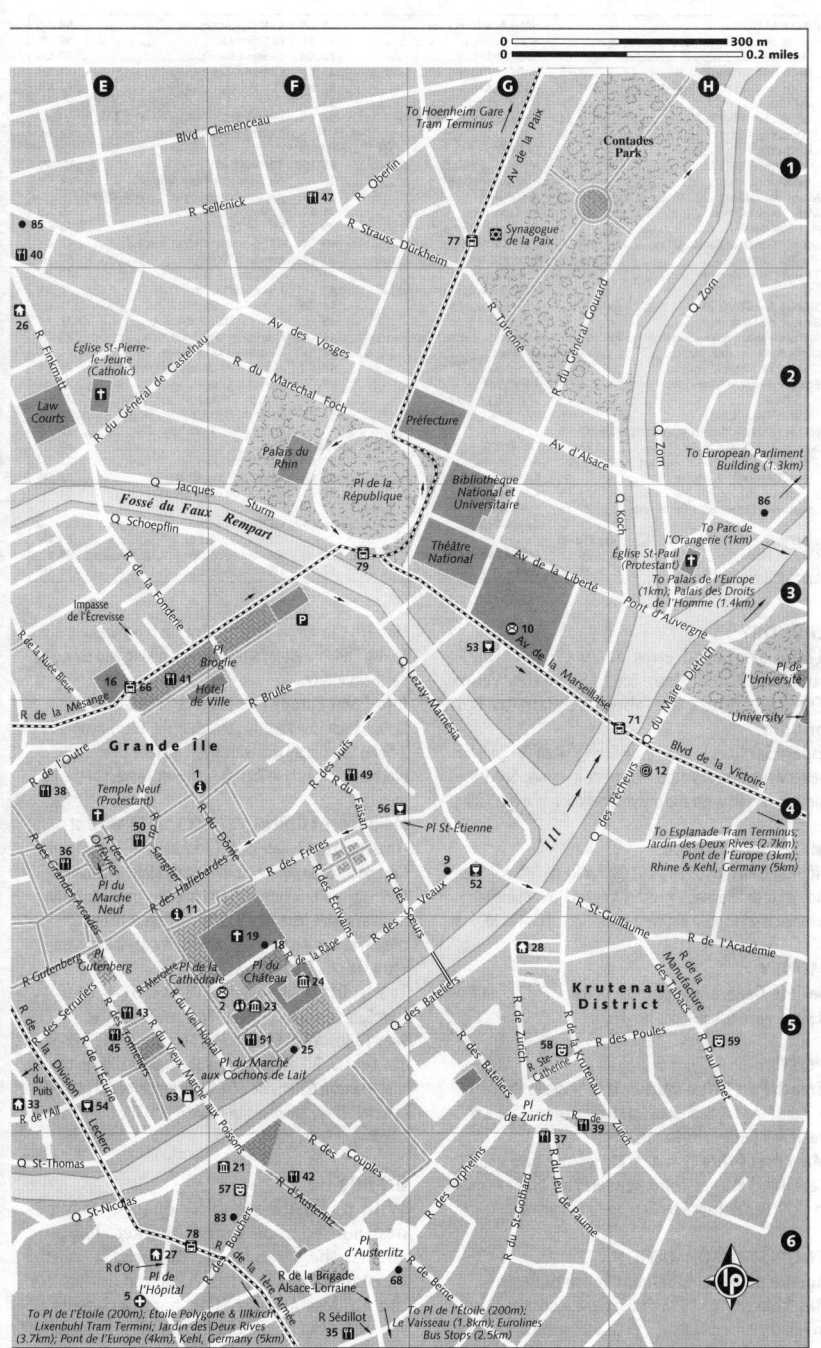

ALSACE & LORRAINE

ALSACE & LORRAINE

INFORMATION	
Agence de Développement Touristique en	
Bas-Rhin...1	E4
Branch Post Office...2	F5
Espace Services (Laundrette)............................3	D6
Géorama..4	D4
Hôpital Civil (Hospital)....................................5	E6
L'Utopie..6	D4
Laundrette...7	D3
Laundrette...8	C4
Laundrette...9	G4
Main Post Office..10	G3
Main Tourist Office..11	E4
NeT SuR CouR...12	H4
Société Générale Bank.....................................13	B4
The Bookworm..14	C3
Tourist Office Annexe......................................15	A4

SIGHTS & ACTIVITIES	(pp348–52)
Banque de France..16	E3
Barrage Vauban & Terrasse Panoramique...17	B5
Cathedral's South Entrance............................18	F5
Cathédrale Notre Dame...................................19	F5
Église St-Pierre-le-Vieux (Protestant &	
Catholic)...20	C4
Musée Alsacien...21	F6
Musée d'Art Moderne et Contemporain..22	B5
Musée de l'Œuvre Notre Dame..............23	F5
Palais Rohan (Musée Archéologique, Musée des	
Arts Décoratifs & Musée des	
Beaux-Arts)..24	F5
Strasbourg Fluvial Boat Excursions........25	F5

SLEEPING	(pp352–3)
CIARUS Hostel...26	E2
Hôtel Au Cerf d'Or...27	E6

Hôtel Aux Trois Roses....................................28	G5
Hôtel du Rhin..29	B4
Hôtel Kléber..30	D4
Hôtel Le Colmar..31	B4
Hôtel Le Grillon..32	B4
Hôtel Patricia..33	E5
Hôtel Régent Petite France...........................34	C5

EATING	(pp353–4)
Adan..35	F6
Atac Supermarket..36	E4
Au Cèdre...37	G6
Au Crocodile...38	D4
Au Renard Prêchant...39	G5
Cash' Center Supermarket..............................40	E1
Food Market..41	E3
Food Shops..42	F6
Fromagerie des Tonneliers.............................43	E5
L'Assiette du Vin..44	D5
La Cloche à Fromage..45	F6
Lafayette Gourmet Supermarket...............46	D4
Le King..47	F1
Le Sahara...48	C3
Tiger Wok...49	F4
Winstub Le Clou...50	E4
Winstubs s'Muenstertstuewel.................51	F5

DRINKING	(pp354–5)
Au Brasseur...52	D5
La Taverne Française.......................................53	D3
Route 66..54	E5
The Irish Times...55	D5
Zanzibar...56	F4

ENTERTAINMENT	(pp355–6)
Bar Le Zoo...57	F6

Café des Anges...58	G5
La Salamandre..59	H5
Le Star Cinema...60	C4
Odyssée Cinema...61	D4
Star St Exupéry Cinema..................................62	C4

SHOPPING	(p356)
Marché de Brocante...63	D5

TRANSPORT	(pp356–7)
Alt Winmärik Tram Stop..................................64	C4
Ancienne Synagogue-Les Halles Tram	
Stop...65	C3
Broglie Tram Stop..66	D3
CTS Bus Information Bureau...........................67	D4
Eurolines Office..68	F6
Europcar..69	B3
Faubourg National Tram Stop.......................70	B4
Gallia Tram Stop..71	H4
Gare Centrale Tram Stop................................72	A4
Homme de Fer Tram Hub................................73	D4
Langstross Grand' Rue....................................74	D5
Musée d'Art Moderne Tram Stop..............75	A4
National-Citer & Avis......................................76	A4
Parc du Contades Tram Stop..........................77	G1
Porte de l'Hôpital Tram Stop.........................78	E6
République Tram Stop.....................................79	F3
Sixt..80	A5
SNCF Boutique...81	A5
Vélocation Bicycle Rental...............................82	B4
Vélocation Bicycle Rental...............................83	F6

OTHER	
German Consulate..84	D4
Strasbourg Section of Club Vosgien............85	E1
US Consulate...86	H3

LAUNDRY

There are laundrettes at 29 Grand' Rue, 8 rue de la Nuée Bleue and 15 rue des Veaux. Opening hours are about 7.30am to 8pm or 9pm.

Espace Services (2 quai Finkwiller; 8am-7.45pm) Has better views than any other laundrette in France. Special facilities let you wash and dry your *petit* or *grand chien* (dog).

MEDICAL SERVICES

Hôpital Civil (03 88 11 67 68; 1 place de l'Hôpital; tram stop Porte de l'Hôpital; 24hr) A new 15-block hospital complex is set to open just west of the Hôpital Civil in 2006.

MONEY

Société Générale (8 place de la Gare; 2-6pm Mon, 8.30am-noon & 1.30-6pm Tue-Fri)

POST

Branch Post Office (place de la Cathédrale; 8am-6.30pm Mon-Fri, 8am-5pm Sat) Has extended Saturday hours and currency exchange.

Main Post Office (5 av de la Marseillaise; tram stop République) In a neo-Gothic structure built by the Germans in 1899. Has exchange services and a Cyberposte.

TOURIST INFORMATION

Agence de Développement Touristique en Bas-Rhin (03 88 15 45 80; www.tourisme67.com in French; 9 rue du Dôme; 9.30am-noon & 1.30-6pm Mon-Fri) Can supply excellent English brochures on Jewish and Protestant sites, cycling, hiking and skiing in northern Alsace.

Info-Point Europe (03 88 15 70 80; 26a av de la Paix; tram stop Parc du Contades; 10am-noon & 2-5pm) Can supply you with a vast number of official brochures – mostly in French – on every aspect of the EU project.

Main Tourist Office (03 88 52 28 28; www.ot -strasbourg.fr; 17 place de la Cathédrale; 9am-7pm) Next door to the ornate, 16th-century Maison Kammerzell. Walking-tour brochure (€1) and free bus/tram and cycling maps available here. The Strasbourg Pass (€10.60), a coupon book valid for three consecutive days, may save you a fair bit of cash.

Tourist Office Annexe (03 88 32 51 49; tram stop Gare Centrale; 9am-7pm Jun-Sep & Dec, 9am-12.30pm & 1.45-6pm Apr, May, Oct & Nov, closed Sun Jan-Mar & Nov) In front of the train station in the subterranean Galerie de l'En-Verre (underneath place de la Gare). There are plans to move it into the train station building at some point.

Grande Île

With its bustling public squares, busy pedestrianised areas and upmarket shopping streets, the Grande Île, declared a World Heritage Site by Unesco, is a paradise for the aimless ambler. The narrow streets of the **old city**, particularly right around the cathedral, are especially enchanting at night. There are watery views from the paths along the **River Ill** and its canalised branch, the **Fossé du Faux Rempart**; the grassy quays, frequented by swans, are a great venue for a picnic or a romantic stroll.

Crisscrossed by narrow lanes, canals and locks, **Petite France** is the stuff of fairy tales. The half-timbered houses, meticulously maintained and sprouting veritable thickets of geraniums, and the riverside parks attract multitudes of tourists. However, the area still manages to retain its Alsatian atmosphere and charm, especially in the early morning and late evening.

The romantic Terrasse Panoramique on top of **Barrage Vauban** (admission free; 9am-7.30pm), a dam built to prevent river-borne attacks on the city, affords panoramas of the River Ill.

Cathédrale Notre Dame

Strasbourg's lacy, almost fragile-looking Gothic **Cathédrale Notre Dame** (7am-7pm) is one of the marvels of European architecture. The west façade, most impressive if approached from rue Mercière, was com-

pleted in 1284, but the 142m spire – the tallest of its time – was not in place until 1439; its southern companion was never built. The cathedral served as a Protestant church from 1521 to 1681.

On a sunny day, the 12th- to 14th-century **stained-glass windows** – especially the rose window over the western portal – shine like jewels. The colourful **organ case** on the northern side dates from the 14th century, while the 30m-high Gothic and Renaissance contraption just inside the southern entrance is the **horloge astronomique** (astronomical clock), a late-16th-century clock (the mechanism dates from 1842) that strikes solar noon every day at 12.30pm. There's a €1 charge to see the carved wooden figures whirl through their paces, which is why only the cathedral's **south entrance** is open from a bit after 11.40am until the end of the show.

The 66m-high **platform** (03 88 43 60 40; adult/student & under 18 €3/1.50; 9am-5pm Mon-Fri, 10am-5pm Sat & Sun Apr-Oct, 9am-4.30pm Mon-Fri, 10am-4.30pm Sat & Sun Nov-Mar) above the façade – from which the **tower** and its Gothic openwork **spire** soar another 76m – affords a spectacular stork's-eye view of Strasbourg. The entrance to the 330 spiral steps is at the base of the bell tower that was never built.

Musée de l'Œuvre Notre-Dame

Occupying a group of magnificent 14th- and 16th-century buildings, the renowned **Musée de l'Œuvre Notre-Dame** (03 88 32 88 17; 3 place du Château; adult/student under 26 & senior/under 18 & disabled incl audioguide €4/2/free; 10am-6pm Tue-Sun) houses one of Europe's premier collections of Romanesque, Gothic and Renaissance sculptures (including many originals from the cathedral), 15th-century paintings and stained glass. *Christ de Wissembourg* (c1060; Room 2) is the oldest work of stained glass in France. The celebrated figures of a downcast and blindfolded *Synagogue* (representing Judaism) and a serenely victorious *Église* (the Church), which date from approximately 1230 and once flanked the southern entrance to the cathedral (the statues that stand there now are copies), are on the right and left walls, respectively, of Room 7.

Hollywood gore seems pretty milquetoasty compared to what they came up with back when Hell really was hell. *Les Amants Trépassés* (the Deceased Lovers; Room 23),

LA MARSEILLAISE

Though you'd never know it from the name, France's stirring national anthem, 'La Marseillaise', was written in Strasbourg. In April 1792, at the beginning of the war with Austria, the mayor of Strasbourg – in whose city a garrison was preparing for battle – suggested that the revolutionary army could use a catchy and patriotic tune to sing while marching off to spread the blessings of liberty throughout Europe. He approached Claude Rouget de Lisle, a young army engineer with a minor reputation as a composer, who after a furious all-night effort came up with a marching song entitled 'Chant de Guerre de l'Armée du Rhin' (War Song of the Rhine Army). The mayor himself first performed it in his home, which stood at the western end of place Broglie (on the site of the present Banque de France building). The soul-stirring tune and its bloody lyrics became popular immediately, and by August were on the lips of volunteer troops from Marseille as they marched northwards to defend the Revolution.

painted in 1470, shows a remarkably ugly couple being punished for their illicit lust: both of their entrails are being devoured by dragon-headed snakes while a toad feasts on her pudenda. If this work isn't enough to scare you into a life of chastity nothing will!

Musée d'Art Moderne et Contemporain

The outstanding **Musée d'Art Moderne et Contemporain** (Museum of Modern & Contemporary Art; ☎ 03 88 23 31 31; place Hans Jean Arp; tram stop Musée d'Art Moderne; adult/student/over 60 & under 18 €5/2.50/free; ☷ 11am-7pm Tue, Wed, Fri & Sat, noon-10pm Thu, 10am-6pm Sun) has an exceptionally diverse collection of works representing every major art movement of the past century or so, including impressionism, symbolism, Fauvism, cubism, Dadaism and surrealism. Laminated cards provide background in English (except for temporary exhibits).

Palais Rohan

Palais Rohan (☎ 03 88 52 50 00; 2 place du Château; for the whole complex adult/student under 26 & senior/under 18 & disabled €6/3/free, for each museum €4/2/free; ☷ 10am-6pm Wed-Mon) was built between 1732 and 1742 as a residence for the city's princely bishops. In the basement the **Musée Archéologique** (audioguide included in ticket price) takes you from the Palaeolithic period to AD 800. On the ground floor is the **Musée des Arts Décoratifs**, which has a series of lavish rooms featuring the lifestyle of the rich and powerful during the 18th century. Louis XV and Marie-Antoinette once slept here – in 1744 and 1770, respectively. On the 1st floor the **Musée des Beaux-Arts** has a rather staid collection of French, Spanish, Italian, Dutch and Flemish masters from the 14th to the 19th centuries.

MUSEUMS

The **Pass Musées** (one-day/three-day/annual €6/8/20, one-day version for students under 26 & seniors €3) gets you into all of Strasbourg's museums, including temporary exhibitions.

All of Strasbourg's **museums** (www.musees -strasbourg.org) are free on the first Sunday of the month. On other days tickets are valid all day long so you can enter and re-enter as you please.

Musée Alsacien

Housed in three typical houses from the 1500s and 1600s, the **Musée Alsacien** (☎ 03 88 52 50 01; 23 quai St-Nicolas; tram stop Porte de l'Hôpital; adult/student under 26 & senior/under 18 & disabled €4/2/free; ☷ 10am-6pm Mon & Wed-Sun Jan-Mar, Jul & Aug, noon-6pm Mon & Wed-Sat, 10-6pm Sun rest of year), affords a fascinating glimpse of Alsatian life over the centuries. Displays in the museum's two dozen rooms include kitchen equipment (stoves, ceramics, biscuit cutters), children's toys, colourful furniture and even a tiny 18th-century synagogue.

European Institutions

The home of the relatively toothless 785-member **European Parliament** (Parlement Européen; ☎ 03 88 17 20 07; www.europarl.eu.int; rue Lucien Febvre; tram stop Wacken), used just 12 times a year for four-day 'part-sessions' (plenary sessions), is 2km northeast of the cathedral. When it's in session (dates are available from the tourist office or on the EU website under 'Plenary Sessions' in the Activities section), you can sit in on debates for up to one hour; it's first-come first-served and no reservations are possible. The best times to come (with ID) are from 5pm to 6pm on Monday (the session often continues until late at night) and from 9am (10am on Thursday) to noon and 3pm to 6pm Tuesday to Thursday. The rest of the time the building is inaccessible because of strict post-9/11 security measures.

Across the Ill, the Council of Europe's **Palais de l'Europe** (☎ 03 88 41 20 29; www.coe.int), once used by the European Parliament, can be visited on free one-hour weekday tours; ring a day ahead for reservations. During the four annual sessions of the council's 45-country *assemblée parlementaire* you can sit in on debates (no reservations required). To get there by bus, take No 6, 30 or 72.

Just across the Canal de la Marne, the striking **Palais des Droits de l'Homme** (☎ 03 88 41 34 95; www.echr.coe.int), home of the European Court of Human Rights since 1995, completes the city's ensemble of major European institutions. Sitting in on one of the two to five monthly court sessions, which begin at 9am or 9.30am Tuesday to Thursday and last about 90 minutes, is possible if there's space – check the website under 'pending cases' for dates and get there with ID a half-hour ahead. The *palais* is served by bus Nos 6, 30 and 72.

JEWISH ALSACE

Interest in Alsace's rich Jewish heritage (www.sdv.fr/judaisme in French), spanning a thousand years, has grown tremendously in recent times. Indeed, the European Day of Jewish Culture (www .jewisheritage.org), marked in early September in 23 countries, grew out of a local initiative in northern Alsace. Famous people of Alsatian-Jewish origin include the Marx Brothers and the actress Julia Louis-Dreyfus, who played Elaine Benes on *Seinfeld*.

Towns all over the region, including many along the Route du Vin d'Alsace (p357), have historic **synagogues**. Museums with exhibits related to Alsatian Judaism include Strasbourg's Musée de l'Œuvre Notre Dame (p349) and Musée Alsacien (p350); Colmar's Musée Bartholdi (p364); and the **Musée Judéo-Alsacien** (☎ 03 88 70 97 17; 62 Grand' Rue; ☷ 9am-noon & 2-5pm Tue-Fri mid-Mar–mid-Sep) in Bouxwiller, 40km northeast of Strasbourg. Several tourist offices (eg Strasbourg and Colmar) offer walking tours of Jewish sites, though these are usually in French.

The Agence de Développement Touristique en Bas-Rhin (p348) has published an excellent brochure *Discovering Alsatian Judaism*.

East & South of the Grande Île

Many of Strasbourg's most impressive (and German-built) public buildings are just northeast of the Grande Île around **place de la République** (tram stop République). The neighbourhood that stretches from there eastwards to Parc de l'Orangerie is dominated by solid, stone buildings inspired by late-19th-century Prussian tastes. Most are some sort of 'neo' – Romantic, Gothic or Renaissance – and you can see that some had the initials RF (République Française) hastily added after 1918 to replace the original German insignia.

Across av de l'Europe from Palais de l'Europe, the flowerbeds, playgrounds, shaded paths and swan-dotted lake of **Parc de l'Orangerie** are hugely popular with local families, especially on sunny Sunday afternoons. In the warm months you can rent **rowing boats** on Lac de l'Orangerie. To get there by bus, take No 6, 30 or 72.

Le Vaisseau (the Vessel; pont d'Ankara; http://levais seau.cg67.fr), an interactive, hands-on science and technology museum inspired by Paris' La Villette, is due to open in late 2004/early 2005. Situated 2.5km southeast of the cathedral, its exhibits – all of them trilingual (English, French and German) – are aimed at kids aged three to 15.

As a concrete (but very green) expression of Franco-German friendship, Strasbourg and its German neighbour Kehl have turned areas once used by customs posts and military installations into the 60-hectare **Jardin des Deux Rives** (Two-Shores Garden; opened April 2004), whose play areas, promenades and gardens stretch along both banks of

the Rhine just south of Pont de l'Europe. The centrepiece is a sleek (and hugely expensive) **suspension bridge** for pedestrians and cyclists, designed by the French architect Marc Mimram (www.mimram.com in French); one of the walkways is 275m long, the other 387m long.

Tours
CITY TOURS

Boat excursions (70 minutes in length) that take in Petite France and the European institutions are run by **Strasbourg Fluvial** (☎ 03 88 84 13 13, 03 88 32 75 25; behind the Palais Rohan; adult/student €6.80/3.40, at night €7.20/3.60; at least 4 times daily).

The tourist office offers 1½-hour Walkman tours of the cathedral and the old city (adult/student €6/3).

BREWERIES

Brasseries Kronenbourg (☎ 03 88 27 41 59; siege .visites@kronenbourg-fr.com; 68 route d'Oberhausbergen; tram stop Ducs d'Alsace), which sells one billion litres of beer in France every year (that is enough beer to fill over 300 Olympic swimming pools!), has a brewery 2.5km northwest of the Grande Île in the suburb of Cronenbourg. Interesting and thirst-quenching tours (adult/12 to 18 years €3/2) take place on weekdays and, from May to September and in December, on Saturday; call ahead for times and reservations.

Brasseries Heineken (☎ 03 88 19 57 55; 4 rue St-Charles) is 2.5km north of the Grande Île in Schiltigheim, near the intersection of rue St-Charles and route de Bischwiller. Free, two-hour tours in French, German or English (depending on group bookings) are held on weekdays; phone ahead for times and reservations. Take the No 4 bus (northbound) to the Schiltigheim Mairie stop.

HIKING, CYCLING & SNOW-SHOEING

The Strasbourg section of the **Club Vosgien** (☎ 03 88 35 30 76; www.club-vosgien-strasbourg.net in French; 71 av des Vosges; ☺ staffed 4-6.30pm Mon-Fri, 10am-noon Sat), a regional walking organisation founded in 1872, runs walks, cycling excursions and snow-shoe trips for its members (guests welcome) in the Vosges and other parts of Alsace; there are departures at around 8am each Sunday and sometimes on other days too. No reservations are needed for trips by private car (passengers pay €0.06 per kilometre) or train; reserve a few days ahead for bus trips (€12). Insurance costs €4.

Festivals & Events

The **Festival International de Musique** (International Music Festival; ☎ 03 88 15 44 66) is held in mid-June and **Musica** (☎ 03 88 23 46 46), a feast of contemporary music runs from mid-September to early October.

Marché de Noël (Christkindelsmärik in Alsatian, ie Christmas Market; place Kléber, place de la Cathédrale, place Broglie & place de la Gare) is a huge and justifiably renowned outdoor market selling Christmas decorations and seasonal treats such as mulled wine. It's held from the last weekend in November until 31 December (until 24 December at place Broglie).

Sleeping

It is *extremely* difficult to find last-minute accommodation from Monday to Thursday when the European Parliament is in plenary session (generally for one week each month; see p350). Because of the Christmas Market, weekends in December are also a problem. If you're stuck, the tourist office can provide details of same-night room availability and may be able to reserve a room. Hotel reservations can also be made via www.strasbourg.com/hotels.

BUDGET

Centre International d'Accueil et de Rencontre Unioniste de Strasbourg (CIARUS; ☎ 03 88 15 27 88; www.ciarus.com; 7 rue Finkmatt; dm in 8-/4-/2-bed rooms incl breakfast €16.50/20/22.50; P ☐) This welcoming Protestant-run hostel, outfitted

with 295 beds, is so stylish it even counts a few European Parliament members among its regular clients. The 700 groups it puts up (with) every year are equally international. There are frequent social events in the evening. No HI card is necessary. Dorm rooms have industrial-strength furniture, toilets and showers; facilities for the disabled are available. By bus, take No 2, 4 or 10 to the Place de Pierre stop

Hôtel Patricia (☎ 03 88 32 14 60; www.hotelpatricia.fr.st; 1a rue du Puits; d from €30, with shower & toilet €40; ☺ reception 8am-8pm Mon-Sat, 8am-2pm Sun) The dark, rustic interior and Vosges sandstone floors – the 16th-century structure was once a convent – fit in well with the local ambience. Rooms are simply furnished but spacious and soundproofed; some also have great views. Hall showers cost €2. The best budget bet on the island.

Hôtel Le Colmar (☎ 03 88 32 16 89; hotel.le.colmar@wanadoo.fr; 1 rue du Maire Kuss; tram stop Alt Winmärik; s/d from €24.50/27.50, with shower & toilet €37/40; ☺ reception closed 1.30-5.30pm Sun) This cheapie offers a unique combination of light, linoleum and loquaciousness – it ain't stylish but it's convenient and good value. Showers are €2.50.

Camping

Camping de la Montagne Verte (☎ 03 88 30 25 46; 2 rue Robert Forrer; per adult/site €3.35/4.50; ☺ mid-Mar–Oct & late Nov-early Jan) A grassy municipal camping ground a short walk from the Nid de Cigognes stop on bus line No 2.

MID-RANGE

Two- and three-star hotels line place de la Gare.

Hôtel du Rhin (☎ 03 88 32 35 00; www.hotel-du-rhin.com; 7-8 place de la Gare; tram stop Gare Centrale; d from €34, with shower & toilet €60) This two-star establishment, run by the same family since 1941, makes at least token efforts at being stylish (tatami mats line the hallways). The rooms are comfortable and soundproofed; thanks to the timeless décor, some of them would make a good set for a French film about a tawdry love affair, c 1972.

Hôtel Le Grillon (☎ 03 88 32 71 88; www.grillon.com; 2 rue Thiergarten; tram stop Gare Centrale; s/d from €30/37, old room with shower & toilet €40/47, new room €55/62; ☐) This informal two-star place has old-style rooms that are bland and have prefab bathroom modules, and new-style rooms that come with wooden floors, proper tiled bathrooms and sleeker furnishings. Internet access is free for the first 15 minutes.

Hôtel Au Cerf d'Or (☎ 03 88 36 20 05; fax 03 88 36 68 67; 6 place de l'Hôpital; tram stop Porte de l'Hôpital; s/d from €50.30/61; 🏊) A Jacuzzi, small swimming pool and sauna (half-hour €8) are the cherry on the icing of this Logis de France-affiliated hotel, a golden *cerf* (stag) hanging proudly out front. On the ground floor there's a traditional French restaurant and a homey sitting area with two pianos; upstairs, the spacious and very comfortable rooms have solid all-tile bathrooms.

Hôtel Aux Trois Roses (☎ 03 88 36 56 95; www .hotel3roses-strasbourg.com; 7 rue de Zurich; s/d from €47/63; P) Housed in a handsome building classified as a historic monument, this two-star hotel has cheery rooms with lots of pine; the cheaper ones are on the small side. A sauna costs €5. Two rooms are outfitted for disabled guests.

Hôtel Kléber (☎ 03 88 32 09 53; hotel.kleber@gofornet .com; 29 place Kléber; s/d with shower €32/37, with shower & toilet €40.50/47.50) You're likely to be disappointed by this superbly situated two-star unless you've got a thing for loveably bad taste. The public areas retain echoes of the 1970s, while the rooms – cramped unless you pay €69 – have laughably cheap wood-panel ceilings and plastic faux-plaster walls.

TOP END

Hôtel Régent Petite France (☎ 03 88 76 43 43; 5 rue des Moulins; www.regent-hotels.com; s/d from €223/243, ste for 2 €366-455; P 🛈) Guests of this luxurious four-star hotel enjoy romantic watery views, a sauna and marble bathrooms worthy of a Roman emperor. If you're in one of the rooms over the lock your stay will be accompanied by the rush of water, which can be either calming (no need to bring along a relaxation CD) or nerve-wracking (New Yorkers might try pre-recording the sound of honking cars and ambulance sirens). The breakfast room is decorated with giant paintings inspired by angry underclass graffiti, so paying €18.50 is both an act of self-indulgence and a safe and sophisticated way of slumming it. Bringing along Fido or Mitzi will set you back €18.50. Facilities for the disabled are available.

Eating

Strasbourg is a gastronomer's dream. Just south of place Gutenberg, pedestrianised rue des Tonneliers is lined with mid-range restaurants of all sorts, both ethnic and French. Inexpensive student eateries can be found northeast of the cathedral along rue des Frères, especially towards place St-Étienne.

WINSTUBS & FRENCH

Winstub Le Clou (☎ 03 88 32 11 67; 3 rue du Chaudron; 🕑 meals served 11.45am-2pm & 5.30pm-midnight except Sun, holidays & lunch Wed) Diners sit together at long tables with paisley tablecloths, so come here for an evening in the company of fellow diners, not an intimate tête-à-tête. Specialities include *baeckeoffe* (€16.50) and *wädele braisé au pinot noir* (€14.50). The selection of Alsatian and French wines is quite good.

L'Assiette du Vin (☎ 03 88 32 00 92; 5 rue de la Chaîne; lunch menu €19.90, 2-/3-course menus €21/26, 4-course menu with 4 wines €45; 🕑 closed Sun, lunch Mon & Sat) At this mellow and elegant French restaurant, the décor changes with the seasons (the summer flowers come from the chef's mother's garden) as does the cuisine, inspired by what's available fresh in the marketplace. The wine list is extensive, with over 180 options; 12 to 15 vintages can be sampled by the glass (€3 to €7).

La Cloche à Fromage (☎ 03 88 23 13 19; 27 rue des Tonneliers; 🕑 closed lunch Tue) The world's largest cheese platter – with some 90 different cheeses – greets you at the door of this haven for the lactose addicted, a perennial favourite of local *fromage* connoisseurs. A plate of 15 cheeses matured and selected by a master *fromager* costs €21.50; *fondue Savoyarde* (cheese fondue) will warm your insides for €20.50.

WINSTUBS

A *winstub* (literally 'wine room') is a traditional Alsatian restaurant renowned for its warm, homey atmosphere. Most dishes are based on pork and veal; specialities include *baeckeoffe* (meat stew), *jambonneau* (knuckle of ham), *wädele braisé au pinot noir* (ham knuckles in wine) and *jambon en croûte* (ham wrapped in a crust). Vegetarians can usually order *Bibeleskas* (*fromage blanc;* soft white cheese mixed with fresh cream) and *pommes sautées* (sautéed potatoes). Few *winstubs* offer fixed-price *menus;* many have nonstandard opening hours.

ALSACE & LORRAINE

Au Renard Prêchant (☎ 03 88 35 62 87; 33 place de Zurich; mains €9-16; ⊙ closed lunch both Sat & Sun) Occupying a 16th-century chapel, this convivial and often crowded restaurant offers excellent, reasonably priced French and regional cuisine. The atmosphere is warm, woody and very Alsatian; décor includes stained glass, a stuffed *renard* (fox) and a mural of historic Strasbourg. *Gibier* (game) is a seasonal speciality.

Winstub s'Muensterstuewel (☎ 03 88 32 17 63; 8 place du Marché aux Cochons de Lait; lunch menu €23; ⊙ Tue-Sat) Though in the middle of a touristy area, this *winstub* has an excellent reputation – for mains and desserts – thanks to its English-speaking, Paul Bocuse-trained owner, who's happy to whip up vegetarian options on demand.

ASIAN & NORTH AFRICAN

Tiger Wok (☎ 03 88 36 44 87; 8 rue du Faisan; lunch incl a drink €13, dinner €14, all-you-can-eat €22; ⊙ noon-2.15pm & 7-10.30pm, to 11.30pm Fri & Sat) Locals chic-sters tired of pigs' knuckles and fois gras flock to this wokkery, where you choose your ingredients (vegies, fish, meat) and then tell your personal *wokeur* (wok guy) – muscular and short-sleeved – how to prepare them and with which sauces. The result: a quick crunchy meal eaten with giant wooden tweezers (is someone afraid of chop sticks?) Chic and modern in a Zen sort of way.

Au Cèdre (☎ 03 88 25 14 69; 1 rue St-Gothard; meat mains €12.20-16; ⊙ closed lunch both Sat & Sun) Au-

thentic Lebanese cuisine and a good selection of vegetarian dishes have made this somewhat formal restaurant hugely popular. The multidish *mezza menu* costs €19 (minimum two people).

Le Sahara (☎ 03 88 22 64 50; 3 rue du Marais Vert; tram stop Ancienne Synagogue; lunch menu €9; ⊙ closed Sun) A favourite of people who work in the neighbourhood, this unpretentious Berber restaurant serves copious portions of steaming couscous (€6.20 to €14.50).

VEGETARIAN & KOSHER

Adan (☎ 03 88 35 70 84; 6 rue Sédillot; menu €11; ⊙ 11.30am-2pm Mon-Sat) Adan is an informal vegetarian-organic restaurant serves tasty soups, salads and four kinds of quiches, including two without milk products.

Le King (☎ 03 88 52 17 71; 28 rue Sellénick; tram stop Parc du Contades; 2-course menu €10; ⊙ closed Sat & dinner Fri) In the heart of Strasbourg's Jewish neighbourhood, this kosher place specialises in Moroccan-style grilled meats and fish.

SELF-CATERING

A few blocks south of the cathedral, pedestrianised rue d'Austerlitz is home to quite a few **food shops**.

The **food market** (place Broglie; ⊙ until at least 4pm, often until 6pm Wed & Fri) moves to place Kléber during the Christmas market.

Stock up on cheese at **Fromagerie des Tonneliers** (32 rue des Tonneliers; ⊙ 9.15am-12.15pm & 2.30-7pm Mon-Fri, 8.15am-6.30pm Sat).

Supermarkets in Strasbourg:

Atac supermarket (47 rue des Grandes Arcades; ⊙ 8.30am-8pm Mon-Sat)

Cash' Center (22 rue Finkmatt; ⊙ 9am-7.30pm Mon-Thu, 8.30am-3pm or 4pm Fri, 9am-1pm & 3-7pm Sun) An all-*cacher* (kosher) supermarket that serves Strasbourg's large Jewish community.

Lafayette Gourmet supermarket (34 rue du 22 Novembre; ⊙ 9am-8pm Mon-Sat) On the ground floor of the Galeries Lafayette department store.

Drinking

La Taverne Française (☎ 03 88 24 57 89; 12 av de la Marseillaise; tram stop République or Gallia; ⊙ 8.30am-2am Mon-Thu, 8.30am-3am Fri, 2pm-3am Sat) At this mellow café – favoured by actors from the nearby theatre, musicians and students – a mixture of the old-fashioned and the endearingly tacky creates the ideal atmosphere for stimulating conversation. Bring along some

---

AUTHOR'S CHOICE

Au Crocodile (☎ 03 88 32 13 02; 10 rue de l'Outre; 3-/4-course weekday lunch menus €53/74, with wine €77/104, dinner menus €80 & €122; ⊙ Tue-Sat) This restaurant, holder of two Michelin stars (the third was lost a few years back, creating a national scandal), has the hushed solemnity of a true temple of French gastronomy. Elegant down to the tiniest detail (the table settings, for example, are exquisite), it offers all-out *gastronomique* indulgence and sophisticated elegance at a surprisingly reasonable price. Specialities include *foie de canard cuit en croûte de sel* (duck liver cooked in a crust of salt crystals; €49). Reservations are a good idea in the evening, especially on Friday and Saturday.

fresh salmon and by the end of the evening you'll have lox.

Zanzibar (☎ 03 88 36 66 18; 1 place St-Étienne; ☺ 5pm-4am) A friendly laid-back bar in the heart of the Grande Île's student quarter. Local groups (plus a few from abroad) play rock, reggae, pop, jazz etc in the funky cellar starting at 10pm on Thursday, Friday and Saturday (except from mid-July to August). Admission is usually free.

The Irish Times (☎ 03 88 32 04 02; 19 rue St-Barbe; ☺ 4pm-1.30am Mon-Fri, 2pm-1.30am Sat & Sun) A congenial and genuinely Irish pub with a very international clientele. There's live music (mainly Irish) from about 9.30pm to 12.30am on Friday and Saturday; Thursday is open-mike night (9pm), Wednesday features a trivia quiz with prizes (9.30pm). Major sports events – shown on the two wide screens – often push back Sunday opening to kick-off time.

Au Brasseur (☎ 03 88 36 12 13; 22 rue des Veaux; ☺ 11am-1am) Four beers – *brune, ambrée, blonde* and *blanche* – are brewed on the premises of this warm, dimly lit microbrewery, which also has some of the best deals in town on Alsatian treats: *baeckhoffe* is €13.50, while all-you-can-eat *Flammekueche* (served at all hours) with 0.9L of beer will set you back just €12.50. Local groups play rock and blues from 9.30pm to 1am on Friday and Saturday.

Route 66 (☎ 03 88 32 89 79; 15 rue de la Division Leclerc; ☺ 3pm-4am Tue-Sun) Mercifully short on ersatz Americana (despite the name), the student crowd at this friendly down-to-earth bar is sprinkled with American year-abroaders and players from Étoile Noire (the local 1st-division ice-hockey team). As for the background music, almost anything that sounds good loud – except techno and rap – goes, especially if it is rock.

Entertainment

The Strasbourgeois may head to bed earlier than their counterparts in other major French cities but the city's entertainment options are legion – despite a new ordinance that killed the late-late scene by forcing nightspots to close between 4am and 6am. Details on cultural events appear in the free monthly *Spectacles* (www.spectacles-publications.com in French), available at the tourist office.

CINEMAS
Nondubbed film venues:

Le Star (☎ 03 88 32 44 97; www.cinema-star.com in French; 27 rue du Jeu des Enfants)

Odyssée (☎ 03 88 75 10 47; www.cinemaodyssee .com in French; 3 rue des Francs Bourgeois) An art-house cinema.

Star St-Exupéry (☎ 03 88 22 28 79; www.cinema-star .com in French; 18 rue du 22 Novembre)

GAY & LESBIAN VENUES
Bar Le Zoo (☎ 03 88 24 55 33; www.lezoobar.com in French; 6 rue des Bouchers; tram stop Porte de l'Hôpital; ☺ 6pm-2am) This friendly mostly gay bar has a mellow cellar lounge with sofas and frequent theme nights. On Wednesday from 9pm there's a *soirée poste*, during which patrons post letters to each other. *Kfé Kuchen*, a coffee and cake combo, is served up on Sunday (6pm to 9pm). In summer you can sit out on the terrace.

LIVE MUSIC
A number of the places listed under Drinking (above) host live concerts.

Strasbourg's most vibrant venue for live music of every sort is **La Laiterie** (☎ 03 88 23 72 37; www.artefact.org in French; 11-13 rue du Hohwald; tram stop Laiterie; ☺ closed Jul, Aug & around Christmas), about 1km southwest of the train station. It puts on about 20 concerts a month. Tickets (€5 to €25) are available either at the door (telephone bookings aren't accepted) or for a slight surcharge at an Fnac or Virgin ticket outlet in the city. On Friday nights from midnight to 6am, La Laiterie turns into a techno disco (€5).

NIGHTCLUBS
La Salamandre (☎ 03 88 25 79 42; www.lasalamandre -strasbourg.fr in French; 3 rue Paul Janet; adult/student incl a drink €10/6; ☺ 10pm-4am Wed-Sun) Billed as a *bar-club-spectacles*, this discotheque – warmly lit, friendly and with a marble fountain in the middle – has theme nights each Friday (salsa, disco, 1980s etc). Wednesday and Thursday are student nights (open to all). From October and April there's a *bal musette* (dancing to live French accordion music, salsa, tango and 1950s rock and roll; adult/student €12/8) on Sunday from 5pm to 10pm.

Café des Anges (☎ 03 88 37 12 67; 5 rue Ste Catherine; admission generally free; ☺ 9pm-4am Mon-Sat, 7pm-4am Sun) On the ground floor – that is, *au paradis* (in paradise) – the DJ spins disks (everything from gypsy to *bal musette*) from inside a psychodelic Austin Mini amid décor inspired by Austin Powers: welcome (back) to the early 1970s. In the cellar – *en enfer* (in hell) – the darker world of *A Clockwork Orange* sets the tone: stage lights sweep the dance floor and drinks can be ordered at the bright red bar. Things don't start until midnight or 1am. There salsa every Sunday starting at 7pm.

Shopping

The city's fanciest shopping can be found on and around **rue des Hallebards**; the super-elegant window displays are real eye candy.

Second-hand goods and antiques are on sale at the small **Marché de Brocante** (southern end of rue du Vieux Marché aux Poissons; ☒ 9am-6pm Wed & Sat).

Getting There & Away

AIR

Strasbourg's **airport** (☎ 03 88 64 67 67; www.strasbourg.aeroport.fr) is 12km southwest of the city centre (towards Molsheim) near the village of Entzheim.

Ryanair (www.ryanair.com) no longer has cheap flights to Strasbourg (they were deemed a violation EU rules against state subsidies) but the company does link London Stansted with Karlsruhe–Baden Baden airport (www.badenairpark.de), about 50km to the northeast; both cities are linked to Strasbourg by train (about €15; 35 minutes).

BUS

As part of the French government's relentless campaign to restrict private-sector competition with the state-owned SNCF and 44.7% state-owned Air France, Eurolines buses must now stop 2.5km south of the **Eurolines office** (☎ 03 90 22 14 60; 6D place d'Austerlitz; ☒ 10am-6.30pm Mon-Fri, 10am-noon & 2-5pm Sat) near Stade de la Meinau (the city's main football stadium), on rue du Maréchal Lefèbvre about 200m west of av de Colmar and the Lycée Couffignal tram stop.

Strasbourg city bus No 21 (€1.20) links place Gutenberg with the Stadthalle in Kehl, the German town just across the Rhine.

CAR

Rental options:

Avis (☎ 03 88 32 30 44) In the train station's arrival hall.

Europcar (☎ 03 88 15 55 66; 16 place de la Gare)

National-Citer (☎ 03 88 23 60 76) In the train station's arrival hall.

Sixt (☎ 03 88 23 72 72; 31 blvd de Nancy)

TRAIN

Train information and tickets are available on the Grande Île at the **SNCF Boutique** (5 rue des France-Bourgeois; ☒ 10am-7pm Mon-Fri, to 5pm Sat).

The train station, built in 1883 and now being given a pre-TGV upgrade, is linked to Metz (€19.10, 1¼ to 1¾ hours, five to nine daily), Nancy (€18.40, 1¼ hours, nine to 12 daily), Lyon (€42.30, five hours, four or five direct daily) and Paris' Gare de l'Est (€40.90, four to 4½ hours, eight to 12 daily); and, internationally, to Basel (Bâle; €17.40, 1¼ hours, 15 direct each weekday, 11 daily on weekends), Frankfurt (€35.60, 2½ hours, six to eight nondirect daily) and Budapest (€147.80, 14 hours, nightly).

Route du Vin destinations include Colmar (€9.30, 31 to 60 minutes, 36 each weekday, 20 daily weekends), Dambach-la-Ville (€6.80, 45 to 70 minutes, 16 daily on weekdays, nine on Saturday, three on Sunday), Obernai (€4.70, 27 to 50 minutes, 20 daily weekdays, 10 on Saturday, three on Sunday) and Sélestat (€6.70, 20 to 40 minutes, 43 each weekday, 21 daily weekends).

In 2007, when the long-planned TGV-Est line (at 320km/h the fastest TGV yet) is supposed to go into operation, the trip from Strasbourg to Paris will take a mere two hours 20 minutes.

Getting Around

TO/FROM THE AIRPORT

CTS's **Navette Aéroport** (☎ 03 88 77 70 70) links the Baggersee tram stop with the airport (€4.80, 12 minutes). It runs every 20 minutes (every 20 or 30 minutes on weekends) until at least 9.50pm.

BICYCLE

Strasbourg, a European leader in bicycle-friendly planning, has an extensive and ever-expanding *réseau cyclable* (network of cycling paths and lanes; www.strasbourg.fr/Strasbourgfr/GB/SeDeplacer/Avelo). Free maps are available at the tourist office.

The city government's **Vélocation system** can supply you with a well-maintained one-speed bike for €4/7 per half-/whole day (plus a €100 deposit) – and just €18 a month for students! Outlets:

City Centre (☎ 03 88 24 05 61; 10 rue des Bouchers; tram stop Porte de l'Hôpital; 🕑 9.30am-noon & 2-6.30pm Mon-Fri, to 7pm Sat, Sun & holidays Apr-late Oct, 10am-5pm Mon-Fri late Oct-Mar)

Train Station (☎ 03 88 23 56 75; 4 rue du Maire Kuss; tram stop Alt Winmärik; 🕑 6am-7.30pm Mon-Fri, 9.30am-noon & 2-7pm Sat year-round, 9.30am-noon & 2-7pm Sun & holidays Apr-late Oct)

BUS & TRAM

Four highly civilised tram lines – to which a fifth line, 13.5km of track and 22 stations are to be added by 2007 – form the centrepiece of Strasbourg's excellent public transport network, run by **CTS** (☎ 03 88 77 70 70; information bureau 31 place Kléber). The main hub is at place de l'Homme de Fer. Buses – few of which pass through the Grande Île – run until about 11.30pm; trams generally operate until about 12.30am. This being earnest, hard-working Strasbourg there are no night buses.

Single bus/tram tickets, sold by bus drivers and the ticket machines at tram stops, cost €1.20. The Tourpass (€3), valid for 24 hours from the moment you time-stamp it, is sold at tourist offices and ticket machines. The weekly Hebdopass (€11, free

CTS photo ID required) is good from Monday to Sunday.

In this chapter, tram stops are mentioned for places outside of the Grande Île, where relevant.

PARKING

Virtually the whole city centre is either pedestrianised or a hopeless maze of one-ways, so don't even think of getting around the Grande Île by car – or parking there for more than a couple of hours. For details on parking options check out www.parcus.com.

At Strasbourg's eight Park-and-Ride (Parking-Relais) lots, all on tram lines, the €2.40 all-day fee gets the driver and each passenger a free round-trip tram ride into the city centre. If you'd like to visit the city without car hassles this is the way to do it. To get to a Park-and-Ride lot from the autoroute, follow the signs marked 'P+R Tram'.

TAXI

Round-the-clock companies:
Alsace France Taxi (☎ 03 88 22 19 19)
Taxi Treize (☎ 03 88 36 13 13)

ROUTE DU VIN D'ALSACE

Meandering for some 120km along the eastern foothills of the Vosges, the Alsace Wine

---

NATZWEILER-STRUTHOF CONCENTRATION CAMP

A mere 50km southwest of Strasbourg stands the only Nazi concentration camp on French soil, Natzweiler-Struthof. The site was chosen by Hitler's personal architect, Albert Speer, because of the nearby deposits of valuable pink granite, in whose extraction – in the **Grande Carrière** (Large Quarry) – many inmates were worked to death as slave labourers. In all, some 10,000 to 12,000 of the camp's prisoners died; many were shot or hung and some were gassed. In early September 1944, as the Allies were approaching, the 5517 surviving inmates were sent to Dachau.

The camp provided the Reichsuniversität (Reich University) in Strasbourg with inmates for use in often lethal pseudo-medical experiments involving chemical warfare agents (mustard gas, phosgene) and infectious diseases such as hepatitis and typhus. In April 1943 86 Jews (including 30 women) specially brought from Auschwitz were gassed here to supply the university's anatomical institute with skulls and full skeletons for its anthropological and racial skeleton collection. After liberation, their bodies, preserved in alcohol, were found by Allied troops in Strasbourg.

Today, visitors can see the remains of the **camp** (☎ 03 88 97 04 49; adult/under 16 €1.52/free; 🕑 10am-6pm Jul & Aug, 10am-noon & 2-5.30pm Mar-Jun, 10am-noon & 2-5pm Sep-24 Dec), whose barracks – one housing a **museum** – are still surrounded by guard towers and two rows of barbed wire. The **chambre à gaz** (gas chamber), an ordinary-looking building 1.7km down the D130 from the camp gate, the **four crématoire** (crematorium oven) and the **salle d'autopsie** (autopsy room) bear grim witness to the unspeakable atrocities committed here.

To get to Natzweiler-Struthof from Obernai, take the D426, D214 and D130; follow the signs to 'Le Struthof' or 'Camp du Struthof'.

Route passes through villages guarded by ruined hilltop castles, surrounded by vine-clad slopes and coloured by half-timbered houses. Combine such charms with numerous roadside *caves* (wine cellars), where you can sample Alsace's crisp white varietal wines (in particular Riesling and Gewürtztraminer – the accent is on the 'tra'), and you have one of France's busiest tourist tracks. Local tourist offices can supply you with an English-language map-brochure, *The Alsace Wine Route*.

The Route du Vin, at places twee and commercial, stretches from Marlenheim, about 20km west of Strasbourg, southwards to Thann, about 35km southwest of Colmar. En route are some of Alsace's most picturesque villages (and some very ordinary ones, too), many extensively rebuilt after being flattened in WWII. Ramblers can take advantage of the area's *sentiers viticoles* (signposted vineyard trails) and the paths leading up the eastern slopes of the Vosges to the remains of medieval bastions.

The villages mentioned below – listed from north to south – all have plenty of hotels, camping areas and restaurants. *Chambres d'hôtes* (B&Bs) can cost as little as €25 (plus breakfast) for a double – tourist offices can provide details on local options.

Tours
For minibus tours of the Route du Vin:
LCA Top Tour (☎ 03 89 41 90 88, after hours ☎ 06 88 40 21 02; www.alsace-travel.com; 6 place de la Gare, Colmar; half-day €47.50) Reservations can be made via the Colmar tourist office.

Regioscope (☎ 06 88 21 27 15; www.regioscope.com; morning/afternoon tour €39/48) Based in Mulhouse. Also offers visits to the Vosges.

Getting There & Around
The Route du Vin, which is not just one road but also a composite of several (the D422, D35, D1bis and so on), can be followed by car or bicycle. It is well signposted but you might want to pick up a copy of Blay's colour-coded map, *Alsace Touristique* (€5.65). Cyclists will find IGN maps such as *Le Haut-Rhin à Vélo* (€5.40) invaluable.

Parking can be a nightmare in the high season, especially in Ribeauvillé and Riquewihr. Your best bet is to park outside town centres and walk.

It's possible to get around the Route du Vin by public transport since most of the towns and villages mentioned below are served by train and/or bus from Strasbourg (see p356) and Colmar (see p367). On many trains you can take along a bicycle.

Obernai
pop 9600
This walled town, 35km south of Strasbourg, is centred on the picturesque place du Marché, an ancient market square that's still put to use each Thursday morning. Around the square you'll find the mainly 16th-century **hôtel de ville** (town hall), decorated with baroque trompe l'œil; the Renaissance **Puits aux Six Seaux** (Well of the Six Buckets), across rue du Général Gouraud (the main street); and the partly stone **Halle aux Blés** (Corn Exchange; 1554), from whose flanks pedestrianised rue du Marché and tiny parallel ruelle du Canal de l'Ehn – just a hand's breadth wide – lead to the Vosges-sandstone **synagogue** (1876). The cool and flower-bedecked courtyards and alleyways (such as little ruelle des Juifs, next to the tourist office) are fun to explore, as are the 1.75km-long, 13th-century **ramparts**.

A number of wine cellars are just a short walk from town. From the hilltop cross north of town, the 1.5km **Sentier Viticole du Schenkenberg** takes you through vineyards.

The **tourist office** (☎ 03 88 95 64 13; www.obernai.fr; place du Beffroi; ⏲ 9.30am-12.30pm & 2-7pm daily Jul & Aug, 9am-noon & 2-6pm daily Apr-Jun, Sep & Oct, 9am-noon & 2-5pm Mon-Sat Nov-Mar) is behind the *hôtel de ville*, opposite the 59m **Kapellturm** (Belfry), completed in 1280.

La Cloche (☎ 03 88 95 52 89; 90 rue du Général Goraud; s/d from €30/37.50, with shower & toilet €39/47), a two-star Logis de France-affiliated hotel facing the *hôtel de ville*, has 20 spacious, wood-furnished rooms, some with classic views of the ancient town centre. Charming and atmospheric, its rustic **restaurant** (menus €13-26; ⏲ closed dinner Sun Dec-Feb) serves delicious bourgeois Alsatian cuisine.

The train station is about 300m east of the old town.

Mont Ste-Odile
Occupied by a convent originally founded in the 8th century (it's been destroyed and rebuilt several times since), the 763m-high summit of Mont Ste-Odile is a place of great

spiritual meaning for many Alsatians, in part because it affords spectacular views of the wine country and, nearer the Rhine, the fields of white cabbage (for sauerkraut) around Krautergersheim. Vestiges of the 10km **Mur Païen** (Pagan Wall), built by the Celts around 1000 BC and fixed up by the Romans, are nearby. The summit, surrounded by conifer forests, can be reached on foot via a network of trails that come from every direction, including Obernai, 12km to the northeast.

Mittelbergheim
pop 620

A solid hillside village with no real centre, Mittelbergheim is awash with Sylvaner grape vines, its tiny streets lined with ancient houses in subdued tones of tan, mauve and terra cotta. From **Parking de Zotzenberg** (northern edge of the village on the D362), named after the local *grand cru* (a wine grown in a vineyard bearing the region's most prestigious AOC classification), a paved *sentier viticole* heads across the slopes toward the two towers of the Château du Haut Andlau and the Vosges. A stroll along rue Principale (the main street) will take you past the red sandstone **Catholic Église St-Martin** (next to No 17) built in 1893 and, a block down, the Protestant **Église St-Étienne** (next to No 30) dating from the 12th to the 17th centuries.

The two-star **Hôtel Gilg** (☎ 03 88 08 91 37; www.reperes.com/gilg; 1 route du Vin - the D362; d €47-68; ☺ reception closed Tue & Wed), built in 1614 (the trompe l'oeil dates from 2001), has wood-panelled rooms – reached via a spiral stone staircase – that are as almost as romantic as the village. Reserve well in advance for May, September and October. The rustically elegant **restaurant** (menus €18-66; ☺ closed Tue & Wed) serves classic French and Alsatian cuisine.

Private accommodation is easy to come by – you'll see '*chambres/zimmer*' signs in windows all over town; a list of about two dozen options is posted outside the Renaissance **hôtel de ville** (☎ tourist office 03 88 08 01 66; 2 rue Principale).

Dambach-la-Ville
pop 2000

Surrounded by vines, this village has plenty of wine cellars but manages to avoid touristic overload. The best-preserved sections of the 14th-century, pink-granite **ramparts** are along the southwestern side of the old

town; three of the four original watchtowers still stand. Some of the superb half-timbered houses date from before 1500.

The neo-Romanesque **Église St-Étienne** (place de l'Église) and the **synagogue** (rue de la Paix), unused since WWII, both date from the 1860s.

The **tourist office** (☎ 03 88 92 61 00; www.pays-de-barr.com; place du Marché; ☺ 9am-noon & 2-6pm Mon-Sat, 10am-12.30pm Sun Jul & Aug, 10am-noon & 2-6pm Mon-Fri, 2-6pm Sat rest of year), in the mid-16th-century Renaissance-style **hôtel de ville**, can supply you with a walking-tour brochure.

The renowned Frankstein *grand cru* vineyards cover the southern and southeastern slopes of four granitic hills west and southwest of Dambach. The two-hour **Sentier Viticole du Frankstein** meanders among the hallowed vines, passing by the hillside **Chapelle St-Sebastien** (☺ 9am-7pm May-Oct, 9am-4pm or 5pm Sat, Sun & holidays Nov-Apr), known for its Romanesque tower, Gothic choir, Renaissance windows and baroque high altar. The granite 12th-century **Château du Bernstein**, with its pentagonal tower, is about an hour's walk westwards up the hill.

The train station is about 1km east of the old town.

Sélestat
pop 17,500

Sélestat is the largest town between Strasbourg, 50km to the north, and Colmar, 23km to the south. Its claim to cultural fame is the 15th- and 16th-century **Bibliothèque Humaniste** (Humanist Library; ☎ 03 88 58 07 20; 1 rue de la Bibliothèque; adult/student €3.60/2; ☺ 9am-noon & 2-6pm Mon & Wed-Fri, Sat morning year-round, also open 2-5pm Sat & Sun Jul & Aug), whose displays include a 7th-century book of Merovingian liturgy, a 10th-century treatise on Roman architecture and a copy of *Cosmographiae Introductio*, printed in 1507 in the Vosges town of St-Dié, in which the New World was referred to as 'America' for the very first time. An audioguide costs €1.55; explanatory sheets are available in six languages.

Maison du Pain (☎ 03 88 58 45 90; rue du Sel; admission €4.60; ☺ 10am-noon & 2-6pm Tue-Fri, 2-6pm Sat, 10am-1pm & 2-5pm Sun year-round, also 10am-1pm Sat Jul & Aug), 50m from the Bibliothèque Humaniste, showcases not S&M but rather the art of bread-making. It is run by local *boulangers*.

The 13th- to 15th-century **Église St-Georges**, one of Alsace's loveliest Gothic churches, has curtains of stained glass – some from the 1300s and 1400s – in the choir. Nearby, the 12th-century Romanesque **Église St-Foy** was heavily restored in the 19th century.

Vieux Sélestat, the old town area south and southwest of the churches, is a mainly post-war commercial precinct dotted with half-timbered and *trompe-l'œil* shop buildings. An **outdoor market**, held since 1435, takes over the streets around Église St-Foy from 8am to noon every Tuesday.

The turn-off to the **cimetière israélite** (Jewish cemetery; ☺ 8am-6pm Apr-Sep except Sat & Jewish holidays, to 4pm Oct-Mar) is 1.8km north of Sélestat's water tower along the N83. The key is kept by the people in the house facing the entrance.

The usual information is available at the **tourist office** (☎ 03 88 58 87 20; www.selestat-tourisme.com in French; blvd du Général Leclerc; ☺ 9am-noon & 2-5.45pm, to 5pm Sat, closed Sun & holidays year-round, longer hours & open 11am-3pm Sun & holidays Jul & Aug).

The train station is 1km west of the Bibliothèque Humaniste.

Bergheim
pop 1830

The delightful walled town of Bergheim – overflowing with geraniums, dotted with flowerbeds and enlivened by half-timbered houses in shocking pastels – is more spacious than its neighbours. But things have not always been so cheerful: over the centuries, the town has passed from one overlord to another – having been sold, ceded or captured – some 20 times; and between 1582 and 1630, 35 women and one man were burnt at the stake here for witchcraft. **Maison des Sorcières** (House of the Witches; ☎ 03 89 73 85 20; rue de l'Église; adult €3; ☺ 2-6pm Wed-Sun Jul & Aug, 2.30-6.30pm Sun & holidays May, Jun, Sep & Oct) takes a hard look at the local witch hunts.

The centre, spared the ravages of WWII, is dominated by the 14th-century, early-Gothic **church**, significantly modified in the early 1700s. The wall-mounted **sundial** at 44 Grand' Rue has its origins in 1711. The tile-roofed, 14th-century, Gothic **Porte Haute** is the only one of the village's original three main gates still extant; across the car park, the **Herrengarten lime tree**, planted around 1300, is hanging in there but looks like it could use a hug. Bergheim's *grands crus* are Kanzlerberg and Altenberg de Bergheim.

The tiny **tourist office** (☎ 03 89 73 31 98; ☺ most days Jun-Sep), staffed by volunteers, is between the well-proportioned **hôtel de ville**, constructed of red sandstone in 1767, and the **synagogue**, built in 1863 on the site of an early-14th-century synagogue.

Just inside the Porte Haute, **La Cour du Bailli** (☎ 03 89 73 73 46; www.cour-bailli.com; 57 Grand' Rue; 2–8-person studio mid-Jun–early Oct & Dec €65-110, rest of year €56-99; ☺ reception 10am-6pm) is a three-star apartment hotel built around a flowery, 16th-century courtyard. Its 24 spacious and very comfortable studios come with kitchenettes. There are several reasonable **restaurants** between here and the *hôtel de ville*.

Haut Kœnigsbourg

Perched on a lushly forested promontory and offering superb vistas, the imposing red-sandstone **Château du Haut Kœnigsbourg** (☎ 03 88 82 50 60; adult/student under 26/under 18 €7/4.50/free, adult €5.50 if you buy your ticket at the Riquewihr or Ribeauvillé tourist offices; ☺ 9.30am-6.30pm Jun-Aug, 9.30am-5.30pm Apr, May & Sep, 9.45am-5pm Mar & Oct, 9.45am-noon & 1-5pm Nov-Feb) makes a very medieval impression despite having been reconstructed in the early 1900s – with German imperial pomposity – by Kaiser Wilhelm II (r 1888–1918).

Ribeauvillé
pop 4750

Ribeauvillé, some 19km northwest of Colmar, is arguably the most heavily touristed of all the villages on the Route du Vin. It's easy to see why: this little village, nestled in a valley and brimming with 18th-century overhanging houses and narrow alleys, is picture-perfect.

Don't miss the 17th-century **Pfifferhüs** (Fifers' House; 14 Grand' Rue), which once housed the town's fife-playing minstrels and is now home to a friendly *winstub*; the **hôtel de ville** (town hall; across from 64 Grand' Rue) and its Renaissance fountain; or the nearby clock-equipped **Tour des Bouchers** (Butchers' Bell-tower; 13th and 16th centuries).

Just across the traffic roundabout from the tourist office, the **Cave Vinicole** (☎ 03 89 73 61 80; www.cave-ribeauville.com; 2 route de Colmar; admission & tasting free; ☺ 9am-noon & 2-6pm), a winegrowers' cooperative founded way back in 1895, has a small museum and very informative brochures in English.

West and northwest of Ribeauvillé, the remains of three 12th- and 13th-century hilltop castles – **St-Ulrich** (530m), **Giersberg** (530m) and **Haut Ribeaupierre** (642m) – can be reached on a three-hour hike. The local *grands crus* are Kirchberg de Ribeauvillé, Osterberg and Geisberg.

The **tourist office** (☎ 0 820 360 922, from abroad ☎ 03 89 49 08 40; www.ribeauville-riquewihr.com; 1 Grand' Rue; ☉ 9.30am-noon & 2-6pm Mon-Sat Apr-Oct & Dec, 10am-1pm Sun May-Oct & Dec, 10am-noon & 2-5pm Mon-Fri & alternate Sat rest of year), the area's best equipped, is at the southern end of the main street, the one-way (south-to-north) Grand' Rue.

Hunawihr
pop 515

About 1km on foot south of Ribeauvillé, this quiet hamlet, surrounded by a 14th-century wall and vineyards, feels more solid and se-rious than its neighbours do. On a hillside just outside the centre, the 16th-century fortified **church**, surrounded by a hexagonal wall, has been a *simultaneum* – that is, it has served both the Catholic and Protestant communities – since 1687.

About 500m east of Hunawihr, the **Centre de Réintroduction des Cigognes** (Stork Reintroduction Centre; ☎ 03 89 73 28 48; adult/5-14 yrs €7.50/5; ☉ 10am-noon & 2pm-btwn 5pm & 7pm, no midday clo-sure weekends & Jun-Aug, closed mid-Nov–late Mar) is *the* place in Alsace to see storks up close (see below). Home base for about 150 free-flying storks (who gobble up 45 tonnes of chopped meat each year), the centre is also working to reintroduce otters to the area. Cormorants, penguins, otters and a sea lion show off their fishing prowess several times each afternoon.

At the nearby **Jardins des Papillons** (Butterfly Gardens; ☎ 03 89 73 33 33; ☉ Apr-1 Nov) you can stroll among exotic free-flying butterflies.

Riquewihr
pop 1080

This largely pedestrianised village is every bit as popular with visitors as Ribeauvillé, 5km to the north, but feels much more medieval. The 16th-century **ramparts** are great for ex-ploring, as are the alleys and courtyards. The *grands crus* here are Schoenenbourg (north of town) and Sporen (southeast of town).

The late-13th-century **Dolder** (admission €2; ☉ daily Jul & Aug, Sat, Sun & holidays Easter-Jun & Sep-2 Nov) is a stone and half-timbered gate – topped by a bell tower – with a small local-history mu-seum inside. From there, rue des Juifs leads to the **Tour des Voleurs** (Thieves' Tower; admission incl

---

STORKS

White storks *(cigognes)*, long a feature of Alsatian folklore, are one of the region's most beloved symbols. Believed to bring luck (as well as babies), they winter in Africa and then spend the warmer months in Europe, feeding in the marshes (their favourite delicacies include worms, insects, small rodents and even frogs) and building their nests of twigs and sticks on church steeples, rooftops and tall trees.

When mid-August arrives, instinct tells young storks – at the age of just a few months – to fly south for a two- or three-year, 12,000km trek to sub-Saharan Africa (Alsatian storks are par-ticularly fond of Mali and Mauritania), from where they return to Alsace ready to breed – if they return at all. Research has shown that over 90% die en route because of electrocution, hunting, exhaustion and dehydration. In subsequent years, the adult storks – 1m long, with a 2m wingspan and weighing 3.5kg – make only a short trek south for the winter, returning to Alsace to breed after a few months in Africa.

Since about 1960, however, the draining of the marshes along the Rhine, hunting and droughts in Africa, chemical poisons and – most lethal of all – high-tension lines have reduced stork numbers catastrophically. By the early 1980s there were only two pairs left in the wild in all of Alsace.

In the 1970s and 1980s, research and breeding centres were set up with the goal of establishing a permanent, year-round Alsatian stork population. The young birds spend the first three years of their lives in captivity, which causes them to lose their migratory instinct and thus avoid the rigours and dangers of migration. The programme has been a huge success, and today Alsace – the western extremity of the storks' range – is home to 250 pairs.

See above and p368 for details of stork-breeding centres.

the Dolder €3; (Easter-2 Nov), a former dungeon containing some extremely efficient-looking implements of torture. The **Château des Princes de Wurtemberg-Montbéliard**, (1540), now houses the **Musée de la Communication** (☎ 03 89 47 93 80; (Wed-Mon early Apr-1 Nov), which traces the development of written and voice communications, especially in Alsace, from the Roman period to the present. A must for fans of mail coaches!

The **tourist office** (2 rue de la Première Armée) has the same contact details and opening hours as its Ribeauvillé colleague.

Le Sarment d'Or (☎ 03 89 86 02 86; www.riquewihr -sarment-dor.com; 4 rue du Cerf; d €57-77), a two-star hotel with 10 rooms, has a very local atmosphere and charming touches in every corner. The attached **restaurant** (menus €18-52; (closed Mon, lunch Tue & dinner Sun) is resolutely French. To get there walk down the narrow medieval street across from 60 rue du Général de Gaulle.

Kaysersberg
pop 3000

In the middle of the picture-perfect centre of Kaysersberg, 10km northwest of Colmar, stands the red-sandstone Catholic **church** (12th to 15th centuries), which has the ornate Renaissance **hôtel de ville** (1605) on one side and a Renaissance **fountain** on the other. Up the main street, av du Général de Gaulle (one way going west to east, ie downhill), there are lots of colourful old houses, many half-timbered, others showing baroque influences; further along is the squat, **fortified bridge** (next to No 84), built to span the River Weiss in 1514.

You can see master glass-blowers practising their magic at **Verrerie d'Art** (☎ 03 89 47 14 97; 30 rue du Général de Gaulle; (10am-12.15pm & 2-5.45pm Tue-Sat year-round, 2-5.45pm Sun mid-Apr–late Dec).

The house where the musicologist, medical doctor and 1952 Nobel Peace Prize winner **Albert Schweitzer** (1875–1965) was born is now a **museum** (☎ 03 89 47 36 55; 126 rue du Général de Gaulle; adult/child €2/1; (9am-noon & 2-6pm Apr-11 Nov & weekends late Nov-late Dec) with exhibits on the good doctor's life in Alsace and Gabon.

On the hill above town, the remains of a massive, crenellated **chateau** stand surrounded by vines. Footpaths lead in all directions from Kaysersberg through glen and vineyard; possible destinations include

Riquewihr (1½ hours), Labaroche (2½ hours) and Ribeauvillé (three hours).

The **tourist office** (☎ 03 89 78 22 78; www.kayser sberg.com; 37 rue du Général de Gaulle; (9am-12.30pm & 1.30-6.30pm Mon-Sat, 10am-2pm Sun Jul & Aug, 8.30am-noon & 1-5.30pm Mon-Sat Sep-Jun) is inside the *hôtel de ville*.

Painted yellow-orange and very Alsatian in ambience, the **Hôtel Arbre Vert** (☎ 03 89 47 11 51; http://perso.wanadoo.fr/arbrevertbellepromenade; 1 rue Haute du Rempart; d from €61; (reception closed 11am-2pm or 3pm Mon, Tue & Thu-Sat, closed after 7pm Mon, hotel closed Jan), with two stars and 22 rooms, is at the western edge of the town centre next to 135 rue du Général de Gaulle.

COLMAR
pop 67,000

The centre of the harmonious town of Colmar, capital of the Haut-Rhin *département*, is a maze of cobbled pedestrian malls and Alsatian-style buildings from the late Middle Ages or the Renaissance. Many of the half-timbered houses are painted in tones of blue, orange, red or green. The Musée d'Unterlinden is renowned worldwide for the profoundly moving *Issenheim Altarpiece*.

The Route du Vin (p357) can be explored by bike, car and even bus using Colmar as a base. And for something a bit different, it's easy to take day trips to the German university city of Freiburg and the Swiss city of Basel, each about an hour away.

Orientation

Avenue de la République links the train station and the intercity bus terminal with the Musée d'Unterlinden and the nearby tourist office, a distance of about 1km. The old city, much of it pedestrianised, is southeast of the Musée d'Unterlinden. The Petite Venise quarter runs along the River Lauch, at the southern edge of the old city.

Information

Cyber Didim (☎ 03 89 23 20 44; 9 rue du Rempart; per hr €2.70; (theoretically 10am-midnight Mon-Sat, 2-11pm Sun) Upstairs at the döner kebab place.

Hôpital Pasteur; ☎ 03 89 12 40 94; 39 av de la Liberté; (24hr) Situated 700m west of the train station and served by bus lines 1, 3, 10, A, C and S.

Laundrette (1b rue Ruest; (7am-9pm)

Le Poussin Vert cybercafé (☎ 03 89 41 18 58; 37 route de Neuf-Brisach; per hr €2; (1pm-1.30am Mon-Sat, 3pm-1.30am Sun)

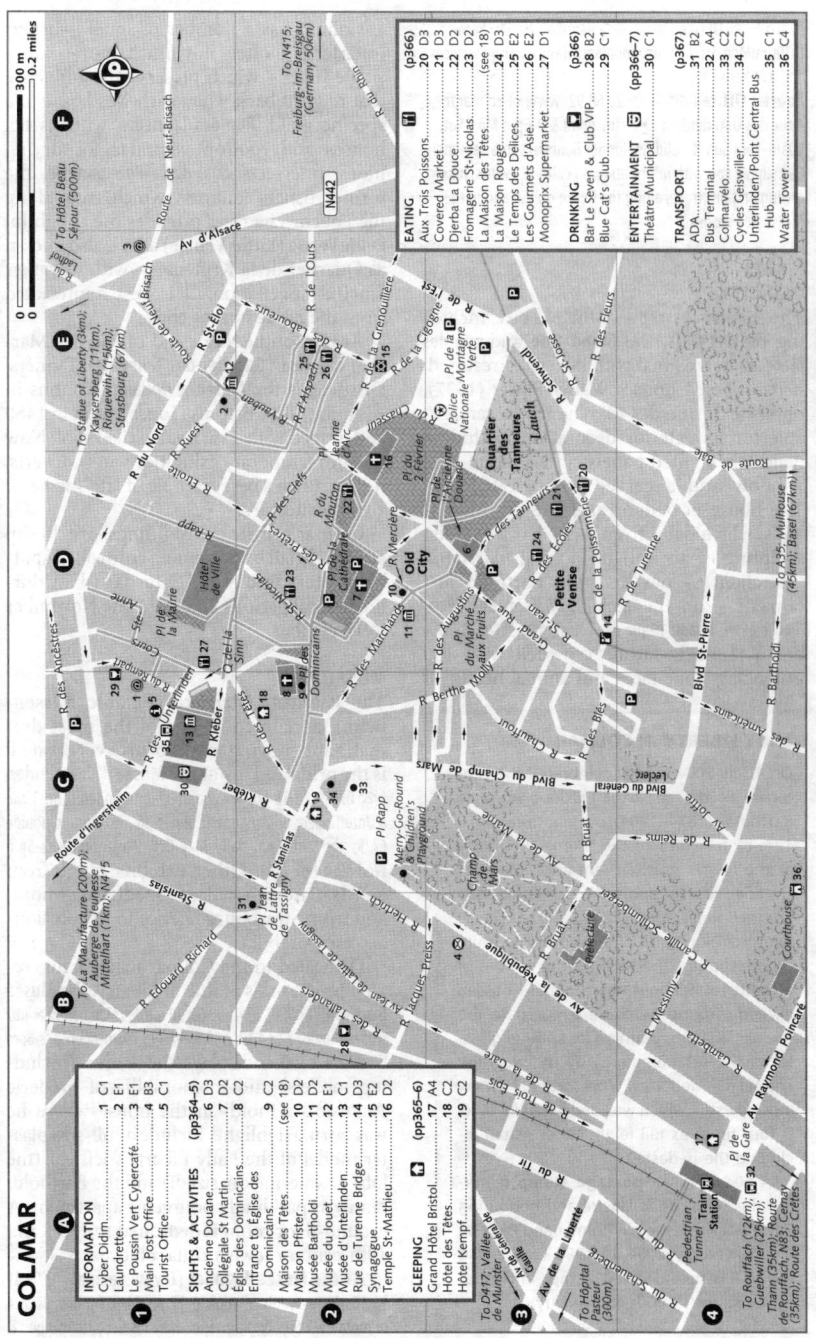

COLMAR

Main Post Office (36 av de la République; 8am-6.30pm Mon-Fri, 8.30am-noon Sat) Has exchange services and a Cyberposte.

Tourist Office (03 89 20 68 92; www.ot-colmar.fr; 4 rue des Unterlinden; 9am-noon & 2-6pm Mon-Sat, 10am-1pm Sun & holidays, longer hours in some seasons) Can supply you with information on cultural events, hiking, cycling and bus travel along the Route du Vin and in the Massif des Vosges.

Sights

OLD CITY

The medieval streets of the old city, including **rue des Clefs**, the **Grand' Rue** and **rue des Marchands**, are lined with dozens of restored, half-timbered houses. **Maison Pfister** (1537), opposite 36 rue des Marchands, is remarkable for its exterior decoration, including delicately painted panels, an elaborate oriel window and a carved wooden balcony. The house next door at 9 rue des Marchands, which dates from 1419, has a wooden sculpture of an uptight-looking *marchand* (merchant) – has his tulip portfolio just tanked? – on the corner. **Maison des Têtes** (House of the Heads; 19 rue des Têtes), built in 1609, has a fantastic façade crowded with 106 grimacing stone faces and animal heads.

LADY LIBERTY IN COLMAR

On 4 July 2004 Colmar celebrated the centenary of the death of Frédéric Auguste Bartholdi (1834–1904) by inaugurating a 12m-high replica of the Statue of Liberty at the town's northern entrance. Made of stratified resin supported by an Eiffelesque internal metal frame, Lady Liberty II bears her torch 3km north of the old city on route de Strasbourg (the N83), in the middle of a traffic roundabout near Colmar-Houssen airfield. Around her base congregate the huddled masses, yearning for another glassful of Gewürztraminer... By the way, the copper-skinned New York original (www.nps.gov/stli), which was dedicated in 1886, is four times as tall (eight times as tall including the pedestal).

A €0.90 French **postage stamp** featuring the *Statue de la Liberté* and honouring Bartholdi was issued in Colmar and Paris on 21-22 February 2004. In 1986 France and the USA issued identical stamps in honour of the statue's 100th anniversary.

Colmar has a number of small *quartiers* (quarters) – often not much more than a single street – which preserve the ambience that reigned back when each was home to a specific guild. **Rue des Tanneurs**, with its tall houses and rooftop verandas for drying hides, intersects **quai de la Poissonnerie**, the former fishers' quarter, which runs along the Lauch. The river provides the delightful **Petite Venise** (Little Venice) area – also known as Quartier de la Krutenau – with its rather fanciful appellation. It is best appreciated from the **rue de Turenne bridge**.

At the southeastern end of rue des Marchands, near **Quartier des Tanneurs** ('Tanners' District), is the **Ancienne Douane** (Koïfhus in Alsatian; Old Customs House), built in 1480 and topped with a variegated tiled roof. Now used for temporary exhibitions and concerts, it is the town's best example of late-medieval civil architecture.

Colmar's historic buildings are lit up after nightfall by computer-controlled spotlights every Friday and Saturday (daily during festival periods and from late November to December).

MUSEUMS

The **Issenheim Altarpiece** (Rétable d'Issenheim), acclaimed as one of the most dramatic and moving works of art ever created, is the pride and joy of the **Musée d'Unterlinden** (03 89 20 15 50; www.musee-unterlinden.com; 1 rue d'Unterlinden; adult/student under 26 incl an audioguide €7/5; 9am-6pm daily May-Oct, 9am-noon & 2-5pm Wed-Mon Nov-Apr). Other exhibits range from an Alsatian wine cellar to medieval armour, and from Strasbourg faïence to Revolutionary memorabilia.

Dedicated to the Colmar native who created New York's Statue of Liberty, the **Musée Bartholdi** (03 89 41 90 60; 30 rue des Marchands; adult/student/under 12 €4.10/2.50/free; 10am-noon & 2-6pm Wed-Mon Mar-Dec) displays the works (including models) and memorabilia of Frédéric Auguste Bartholdi in the house where he was born. Highlights include a full-size plaster model of the Lady Liberty's left ear (the lobe is watermelon-sized!) and the Bartholdi family's sparklingly bourgeois apartment. A ground-floor room is dedicated to 18th- and 19th-century Jewish ritual objects.

At the **Musée du Jouet** (Toy Museum; 03 89 41 93 10; 40 rue Vauban; adult/6-17 yrs €4/3, for groups of 4 or more €3/1.50; 9am-6pm daily Jul-Sep, 10am-noon &

2-6pm Wed-Mon Oct-Jun), kids of every age will be delighted to see toys, dolls and trains from generations past.

HOUSES OF WORSHIP
The 13th- and 14th-century Gothic **Collégiale St-Martin** (place de la Cathédrale; ⏰ 8am-6.30pm except during services) has a sombre ambulatory and a peculiar, Mongol-style copper spire (1572).

The celebrated triptych *La Vierge au Buisson de Roses* (The Virgin in the Rose Bush), painted by Martin Schongauer in 1473, can be seen inside the desanctified Gothic **Église des Dominicains** (adult/student €1.30/1; ⏰ 10am-1pm & 3-6pm Apr-Dec). In 1972 the work made world headlines when it was stolen, not to be recovered until 18 months later. The stained glass is from the 14th and 15th centuries.

Temple St-Mathieu (Grande' Rue; ⏰ 10am-noon & 3-5pm around Easter, 20 May-about 7 Jun & end Jul-about 17 Oct), typically Protestant in its austerity, has something of a split personality. From 1715 to 1987, a wall cut off the soaring 14th-century Gothic choir – a Catholic hospital chapel until 1937 – from the nave, long a Protestant church. Thanks to this odd architectural arrangement, the 14th-century *jubé* (rood screen) – such structures were removed from most Catholic churches during the counter-Reformation – survived. The elaborate Silbermann organ is used for concerts.

God only knows why Colmar's classical-style 1843 **synagogue** (3 rue de la Cigogne) has its very own belfry (Jews have no tradition of ringing bells), but if 19th-century neo-Moorish synagogues (eg the Great Synagogue of Budapest) can have minarets, why not?

Festivals & Events
From mid-May to mid-September, **Soirées Folkloriques** (free performances of Alsatian music and dancing) are held at 8.30pm on Tuesday at place de l'Ancienne Douane.

Vintners display their creations at the **Foire Régionale des Vins d'Alsace** (Regional Wine Fair of Alsace), which attracts large numbers of visitors from the weekend before 15 August until the following weekend. Local food specialities are also on offer. During the summer, villages all over Alsace hold **Fêtes du Vin** (Wine Festivals) featuring wine and song; the tourist office supplies details.

During the first two weeks of July, Colmar plays host to a number of music festivals, including the Western-classical **Festival International de Colmar** (www.festival-colmar .com). The **Festival de Jazz** takes place in early or mid-September.

Colmar's magical **Marché de Noël** (Christmas Market; www.noel-colmar.com) runs from the last Saturday in November to 31 December.

Sleeping
In December (during the Christmas market), around Easter and from mid-July to mid-August (especially during the wine fairs) most hotels are booked up well in advance.

BUDGET
Auberge de Jeunesse Mittelhart (☎ 03 89 80 57 39; fax 03 89 80 76 16; 2 rue Pasteur; dm/d with 2 bunks incl breakfast €11.65/28.30; ⏰ reception 8-10am & 5-11pm, to midnight during daylight savings time, closed mid-Dec–mid-Jan) This one-time orphanage isn't cheery (it's not hard to imagine lonely children crying themselves to sleep) but the management does its best. An old-style place with 110 beds, hall showers and kitchen facilities, it's situated 1.2km northwest of the tourist office, just around the corner from 76 route d'Ingersheim. Curfew is 11pm (midnight during daylight savings time). By bus take No 4, 5, 6, 12 or 15 to the Pont Rouge stop.

Hôtel Kempf (☎ 03 89 41 21 72; www.chez.com /mawo/kempf.html; 1 av de la République; d from €28, with shower & toilet €40) The phone system may date from before Sputnik and the rooms may be plain Jane, but the mattresses at this family-run two-star place are especially comfortable and the showers squirt torrents of hot water. To get there by car, follow the signs to the Rapp car park.

MID-RANGE & TOP END
Hôtel Beau Séjour (☎ 03 89 20 66 66; www.beausejour .fr; 25 rue du Ladhof; d depending on size & season €49-85, apt-style d per week €180-330; ℗ ✗) This venerable and very classy three-star hostelry, built in 1913, has been run by the Keller family for five generations. Everything about it oozes charm, from the rooms, some with Provençal or Louis XV décor, to the elegant restaurant. Situated about 1km northeast of the centre.

ALSACE & LORRAINE

Grand Hôtel Bristol (☎ 03 89 23 59 59; www
.grand-hotel-bristol.com; 7 place de la Gare; d from €75;
P) A marble stairway leads from the plush
lobby of this Best Western-affiliated three-
star place (built in 1925) to grand hallways and rooms in which you're unlikely
to bump your head: not only are the ceilings sky-high and the floor padded with
leafy carpeting, but hanging pillows protect
guests who collapse onto the bed after one
too many varietals. Handicapped facilities
available.

Hôtel des Têtes (☎ 03 89 24 43 43; www.la-maison
-des-tetes.com; 19 rue des Têtes; d €131-269, low season
€91-209; P ⊠ ⊠) This impeccable four-star
hostelry, luxurious but never flashy, is definitely honeymoon material. Situated in and
around the magnificent Maison des Têtes
(p364), each of its 21 rooms offers rich wood
panelling, an elegant sitting area, a mostly
marble bathroom and romantic views.

Eating
Restaurants are sprinkled all over Colmar's old city, especially around place de
l'Ancienne Douane.

ALSATIAN & FRENCH
La Maison des Têtes (☎ 03 89 24 43 43; 19 rue des
Têtes; menus €28-60; closed Mon, lunch Tue & dinner Sun) Behind the leaded windows of the
spectacular Maison des Têtes (p364) awaits
a truly grand dining room, built in 1898
and decorated with grape bunches in wood,
wrought iron and stained glass. The chef's
cuisine française actuelle includes *foie gras
au Riesling* and, in season, fish and game.
Known for its superb wine list.

La Maison Rouge (☎ 03 89 23 53 22; 9 rue des Écoles;
menus €16.90-34.30; Mon-Sat; ⊠) A good variety of hearty Alsatian specialities, including
mouthwatering *jambon braisé* (spit-roasted
ham; €10.90), are on offer at this rustic city
restaurant.

Aux Trois Poissons (☎ 03 89 41 25 21; 15 quai de la
Poissonnerie; menus €21-45; closed Wed, dinner both
Sun & Tue) Oil paintings on the walls and Persian carpets on the floor give this mainly
fish restaurant an atmosphere of hushed and
very civilised elegance. The chef's speciality
is *sandre à la choucroute* (pike-perch with
sauerkraut; €20). Provençal frogs' legs will
hop onto your plate for €15.

Le Temps des Délices (☎ 03 89 23 45 57; 23
rue d'Alspach; lunch menu €18, other menus €23-50;
noon-1.30pm & 7-9pm, closed Mon, dinner both Sun
& Thu; ⊠) A classy Franco-Italian restaurant with space for just 15 to 20 diners. All
ingredients are fresh, and there's a terrace
in summer.

OTHER
Les Gourmets d'Asie (☎ 03 89 41 75 10; 20b rue
d'Alspach; menus €11.75-21.20; closed Mon & lunch
Tue) Authentic Vietnamese cuisine is served
with exceptional elegance.

Djerba La Douce (☎ 03 89 24 17 12; 10 rue du
Mouton; Mon-Sat) You'll be given a welcome
as warm and gentle as the beaches of Jerba.
Steaming Tunisian couscous costs €9.50
to €17.50.

SELF-CATERING
Buy fresh ingredients at **food markets** (place
de l'Ancienne Douane & in the covered market on rue des
Écoles; 8am-noon or to 12.30pm Thu). Market
gardeners once unloaded their produce
directly from boats at the handsome sandstone *marché couvert* (1865).

Prepare yourself to be overcome by the
heady odours of unpasteurised cheese at
Fromagerie St-Nicolas (18 rue St-Nicolas; 9am-
12.30pm & 2-7pm Mon afternoon & Tue-Fri, 9am-7pm Sat)
and there is a **Monoprix supermarket** (8am-
8pm Mon-Sat) across the square from Musée
d'Unterlinden.

Drinking
Blue Cat's Club (☎ 03 89 23 31 57; 17 rue du Rempart;
5pm-1.30am) Colmar may be pretty con-
servative but this relaxed bar, where Cuban
and American themes mix promiscuously,
is pretty hip. The mint juleps are highly
recommended.

Bar Le Seven (☎ 03 89 23 32 72; www.seven-vip
.com in French; 6 rue des Trois Épis; admission free;
6pm-2.30am) Rock concerts play on huge
TVs while under-30s play darts or down
pints at high, round tables. Wednesday
is karaoke night (from 8.30pm). *Soirées à
thème* (theme nights) often begin at 10pm
on Friday or Saturday; there are live concerts about once a month. The adjacent **Club
VIP** is a cosy, dimly lit lounge that attracts a
mainly over-30 crowd.

Entertainment
Colmar's main concert and theatre venues
are **La Manufacture** (☎ 03 89 24 31 78; www.atelier
durhin.com in French; 6 route d'Ingersheim), housed in a

former factory 400m northwest of the tourist office, and the **Théâtre Municipal** (☎ 03 89 20 29 02), next to the Musée d'Unterlinden.

Getting There & Away
BUS
Public bus may not be the quickest way to explore Alsace's Route du Vin but it *is* a viable option; destinations served include Riquewihr, Hunawihr, Ribeauvillé, Kaysersberg and Eguisheim. In the Vosges you can bus it to Munster, Col de la Schlucht and Col du Bonhomme.

Buses and bus-train combos (via Breisach) also serve the German city of Freiburg (€6.15, 1¼ hours, seven daily weekdays, four daily weekends and holidays). From Monday to Friday the last bus back leaves Freiburg at 10.10pm.

The bus terminal – little more than a car park – is to the right as you exit the train station. Timetables are posted and available at the tourist office or online (www.l-k.fr in French). Services are severely reduced on Sunday and holidays.

CAR
Cars can be hired from **ADA** (☎ 03 89 23 90 30; 22bis rue Stanislas).

TRAIN
Colmar has train connections to Basel (Bâle; €10.20, 50 minutes, 11 to 17 daily), Mulhouse (€6.60, 20 to 40 minutes, 32 each weekday, 20 daily weekends), Paris' Gare de l'Est (€46.20, five to six hours via Strasbourg) and Strasbourg (€9.30, 31 to 60 minutes, 36 each weekday, 20 daily weekends).

Route du Vin destinations accessible by train include Dambach-la-Ville (€4.90) and Obernai (€6.70), both of which require a change of trains at Sélestat (€3.80, 11 to 20 minutes, 33 daily weekdays, 21 daily weekends). About 16 daily autorails or buses (10 daily on weekends) link Colmar with the Vallée de Munster towns of Munster (€3.10, 35 minutes) and Metzeral (€3.90, 45 minutes); the last run back begins at 7.24pm.

Getting Around
BICYCLE
Colmarvélo (☎ 03 89 41 37 90; place Rapp; per half-/whole day €3/4.50; ☼ 8.30am-noon & 2-8pm Jun-Sep, 9am-noon & 2-7pm Apr, May & Oct), run by the municipality, rents city bikes (deposit €50).

Hybrid bikes for Route du Vin touring can be rented from **Cycles Geiswiller** (☎ 03 89 41 30 59; 4-6 blvd du Champ de Mars; per half-/whole day €5/9.50; ☼ Tue-Sat).

BUS
Colmar's 16 local bus lines, which run until sometime between 6pm and 8.30pm Monday to Saturday, are operated by **TRACE** (☎ 03 89 20 80 80). The main hub is Unterlinden-Point Central.

PARKING
Unmetered parking can be found a few blocks east of the train station (around the water tower) and in *part* of the lot at place de la Montagne Verte.

TAXI
For a cab call **Taxi Gare** (☎ 03 89 41 40 19) or **Radios Taxis** (☎ 03 89 80 71 71).

MASSIF DES VOSGES
The delightful and sublime **Parc Naturel Régional des Ballons des Vosges** covers about 3000 sq km in the southern part of the Vosges range. In the warm months, the gentle, rounded mountains, deep forests, glacial lakes and rolling pastureland are a walker's paradise, with an astounding 10,000km of marked trails, including GRs (GR5, GR7, GR53 etc) and their variants. Cyclists also have hundreds of kilometres of idyllic trails. In winter 36 inexpensive skiing areas offer modest downhill pistes and cross-country options.

For details of outings sponsored by the Strasbourg section of the Club Vosgien, see p352.

For information on bus and train connections to access towns in the Vosges region, see left.

MOUNTAIN DINING

On weekends, many Alsatians head to a *ferme-auberge* (farm restaurant) in the Vosges for a *repas marcaire* (cowherd's meal), which usually includes *tourte* (pork pie), *Roïgabrageldi* (potatoes with bacon and onion), *Schiffala* (smoked pork), *Siesskass* (soft white cheese with cream and Kirsch brandy) and, of course, a cheese such as Munster – made right on the farm!

Vallée de Munster

This lush, verdant river valley – its pastureland dotted with tiny villages, its upper slopes thickly forested – is one of the loveliest in the Vosges range. Walking and cycling trails abound.

MUNSTER

The quiet streamside town of Munster (population 5000; the name means 'monastery'), famed for its eponymous cheese, is a good base for exploring the valley. It grew up around Abbaye St-Grégoire, a Benedictine abbey founded by monks from Ireland in AD 660.

At **place du Marché** (food market on Tuesday and Saturday mornings), the roof and chimneys of the **Maison du Prélat** (former prelate's quarters) are the year-round home of about a dozen pairs of storks. About 250m behind the Renaissance **hôtel de ville** (across the square from the Maison du Prélat) is the **Enclos Cigognes** (Stork Enclosure; see p361), where a half-a-dozen frisky young birds dine on chopped meat, fish and day-old male chicks (sorry cuddly chick lovers, but storks are avid carnivores).

Information

Maison du Parc (☎ 03 89 77 90 34; www.parc-ballons -vosges.fr in French; 1 rue du Couvent; ☉ 10am-noon & 2-6pm Tue-Sun May–mid-Sep, 2-6pm Mon-Fri mid-Sep–Apr, also open 10am-noon Mon-Fri during school holidays) The regional park's visitor centre has ample

---

THE CONTINENTAL DIVIDE

The Massif des Vosges serves as a *ligne de partage des eaux* (continental divide): a raindrop that falls on the range's eastern slopes will flow to the Rhine and eventually make its way to the icy waters of the North Sea, but a drop of rain that lands on the southern slopes of the Ballon d'Alsace – perhaps only a few metres from its Rhine-bound counterpart – will eventually end up in the Rhône before merging with the warm waters of the Mediterranean. The Vosges' western slopes feed the Moselle, which joins the Rhine at Koblenz.

The Danube (Donau), which meanders through Vienna and Budapest on its way to the Black Sea, rises 100km east of the Vosges in the mountains of the Black Forest.

---

information in English. To get there walk through the arch of the Maison du Prélat.

Tourist Office (☎ 03 89 77 31 80; www.la-vallee-de -munster.com; 1 rue du Couvent; ☉ 9.30am-12.30pm & 1.30-6pm or 6.30pm Mon-Sat, 10am-12.30pm Sun Jul & Aug, 9.30am-12.30pm & 2-6pm Mon-Fri, 10am-noon & 2-4pm Sat Sep-Jun) Has information – some in English – on the whole Munster Valley, including visits to cheese-makers. In the same building as the Maison du Parc but around the other side.

Sleeping & Eating

Hôtel des Vosges (☎ 03 89 77 31 41; hotelbardesvosges@ wanadoo.fr; 58 Grand' Rue; d with toilet & with/without shower €47/34; ☉ reception closes at 1pm Sun except Jul & Aug) This family-run two-star place, on the main commercial street, has rather bland soundproofed rooms with huge bathrooms. There are several **restaurants** in the immediate vicinity.

Super U supermarket (☉ 8am-7pm Mon-Sat, to 8pm Fri, to 6.30pm Sat) Situated on the southern outskirts of Munster (towards Colmar) on the D417.

LE LINGE

Carved into the sandstone hilltop, the German fortifications at Le Linge (986m) were the object of a French offensive launched in July 1915. Some 10,000 French troops and 7000 Germans died in the assaults and subsequent hand-to-hand warfare between trenches only metres apart. The battle site, which has one of the best-preserved WWI trench networks in France, is still surrounded by rusted tangles of the original barbed wire. Some areas have yet to be cleared of live munitions and still contain human remains.

The forested memorial site, on the D11-VI, affords gorgeous views of tree-covered hills and pastoral hamlets – making for a jarring contrast with the trenches and rifle slits. WWI relics are displayed in the small **memorial museum** (adult/under 16 €2/free; ☉ 9am-12.30pm & 2-6pm 15 Apr-1 Nov).

Route des Crêtes

The Route of the Crests, part of it built during WWI to supply French frontline troops, takes you to (or near) the Vosges' highest *ballons* (bald, rounded mountain peaks) as well as to several WWI sites. Mountaintop lookouts afford spectacular views of the Alsace plain, the Schwartzwald (Black Forest) across the Rhine in Germany, the Jura and, on clear days, the Alps.

Starting in Cernay, the Route des Crêtes continues northeast and then north along the D431, D430, D61 and D148 to the **Col du Bonhomme** (949m), often impassable due to snow in the winter months and early spring.

The site of the bloodiest WWI fighting in Alsace, **Hartmannswillerkopf** – known as **Vieil Armand** to the French troops – saw the deaths of some 30,000 French and German soldiers as the strategic hilltop fortress changed hands several times. The remains of trenches and fortifications, most of them German, can be seen near the hilltop fortress (956m), marked by a 22m-high white cross.

At the dramatic, windblown summit of the **Grand Ballon** (1424m), the highest point in the Vosges, a trail takes you to a radar ball and a weather station. If the unsurpassed panorama doesn't blow you away, the howling wind just might.

From **Col de la Schlucht** (1139m), home to a small ski station, trails lead in various directions; walking north along the GR5 will take you to three lakes, **Lac Vert**, **Lac Noir** and **Lac Blanc** (Green, Black and White Lakes).

The **Ballon d'Alsace** (1250m), 20km southwest of the Grand Ballon as the crow flies (by road, take the D465 from St-Maurice), is the meeting point of four *départements* (Haut-Rhin, Territoire de Belfort, Haute-Saône and Vosges) and of three regions (Alsace, Franche-Comté and Lorraine). Between 1871 and WWI, the border between France and Germany passed by here, attracting French tourists eager to catch a glimpse of France's 'lost province' of Alsace from the heroic equestrian **statue of Joan of Arc** (1909) and the cast-iron **orientation table** (1888). During WWI the mountaintop was heavily fortified, but the trenches, whose shallow remains can still be seen, were never used in battle.

The Ballon d'Alsace is a good base for day walks. The GR5 passes by here, as do other trails; possible destinations include **Lac des Perches** (four hours).

MULHOUSE

pop 234,000

The industrial city of Mulhouse (pronounced 'moo-**looze**'), 43km south of Colmar, was al-

lied with the cantons of nearby Switzerland before voting to join revolutionary France in 1798. Largely rebuilt after the ravages of WWII, it has none of the quaint Alsatian charm that you find further north – but the city's world-class industrial museums are well worth a stop.

Information

The **tourist office** (☎ 03 89 35 48 48; www.tourism-mulhouse.com; 9 av du Maréchal Foch; ☾ 9am-noon & 2-6pm Mon-Fri) is 250m due north of the train station. In the heart of the old city, the **tourist office annexe** (place de la Réunion; ☾ 10am-6pm Mon-Sat, 10am-noon & 2-6pm Sun & holidays year-round, to 7pm Jul, Aug & Dec) is in the 16th-century former **hôtel de ville** (town hall). English-language brochures detail walking tours of medieval **Vieux Mulhouse** and the 19th-century **Nouveau Quartier**.

Museums

The wonderful **Musée National de l'Automobile** (☎ 03 89 33 23 23; www.collection-schlumpf.com; 192 av de Colmar; tram stop Musée de l'Auto; adult/7-17 yrs/student/family incl an English audioguide €10/5/7.50/27.50; ☾ 10am-6pm Apr-Oct, to 5pm Nov-May, from 1pm Mon-Fri early Jan-early Feb) displays 400 rare and beautiful European motorcars produced since 1878 by over 100 different companies, including Bugatti, whose factory was in nearby Molsheim. The collection was secretly assembled by Fritz Schlumpf, a self-made textile magnate whose passion – indeed, obsession – for fast cars only grew as his worsted-wool empire nosedived. In 1977, after he had gone bust and fled to Switzerland, outraged former workers occupied the one-time factory that housed the glittering collection, which they saw as a symbol of capitalist greed. By car, exit the A36 at the Mulhouse Centre exit.

A gricer's dream, the **Musée Français du Chemin de Fer** (☎ 03 89 42 83 33; 2 rue Alfred de Glehn) displays the SNCF's superb collection of locomotives and carriages, perhaps the finest in Europe. It should have reopened by the time you read this.

One long block northeast of the station, **Musée de l'Impression sur Étoffes** (Museum of Textile Printing; ☎ 03 89 46 83 00; www.musee-impression.com; 14 rue Jean-Jacques Henner; adult/student €6/3; 🕑 10am-noon & 2-6pm Tue-Sun) covers the history of the industry that made Mulhouse – the 'French Manchester' – incredibly wealthy. Its unique collection of over six million printed fabric samples, assembled since 1833 and now the most extensive in the world, is a mecca for fabric designers. There are printing demonstrations at 3pm on Wednesday, Friday and Sunday.

Has wallpaper always been something of a wallflower in your life? The delightful **Musée du Papier Peint** (Wallpaper Museum; ☎ 03 89 64 24 56; www.museepapierpeint.org; 28 rue Zuber, Rixheim; adult/student over 12 €6/4.50; 🕑 9am or 10am-noon & 2-6pm daily Jun-Sep, closed Tue Oct-May), home to an unparalleled collection of wallpaper and the machines used to make it since the 18th century, will change all that. Situated a couple of kilometres southeast of central Mulhouse on the D66, it's easy to get to: by car take the A36 and get off at Rixheim; by bus take line No 10 from place de l'Europe to the Commanderie stop.

Getting There & Around

France's second train line, linking Mulhouse with Thann, opened in 1839. Today, the **train station** (10 av du Général Leclerc), just south of the city centre, has direct services to Colmar (€6.60, 20 to 40 minutes, 32 each weekday, 20 daily weekends) and Strasbourg (€14.10, one hour, 19 to 25 daily).

Mulhouse is getting a two-line, 20km tram system; until construction of the first phase is finished sometime in 2005, the city centre will remain in a state of traffic chaos.

ÉCOMUSÉE D'ALSACE

In Ungersheim about 17km northwest of Mulhouse (off the A35 to Colmar), **Écomusée d'Alsace** (☎ 03 89 74 44 74; www.ecomusee-alsace.com

in French; adult/4-14 yrs/student €14.50/9.50/13, slightly less in winter; 🕑 tickets sold & artisans at work 9.30am-7pm Jul & Aug, 10am-6pm late Feb-Jun, Sep & Oct, to 5pm Nov-early Jan, closed early Jan-late Feb, restaurant & park open until 11pm) is a 'living museum' in which some 20 smiths, cartwrights, coopers and other craftspeople do their thing in and among 70 centuries-old Alsatian buildings – a veritable village – brought here for preservation (and so storks can build nests on them) from seven different Alsatian subregions. The whole thing is much less hokey than it sounds and in fact inspires real enthusiasm from Alsatians proud of their heritage. Traditional agriculture and its implements are showcased on Sundays. By the time you read this there should be signs in English.

That industrial relic next door is the **Rodolphe Potassium Mine**, shut down in 1976. Now affiliated with the Écomusée, parts can be visited with a retired miner (additional fee).

LORRAINE

Lorraine is fed by the Rivers Meurthe, Moselle and Meuse – hence the names of three of its four *départements* (the fourth is Vosges).

NANCY
pop 331,000

Delightful Nancy has an air of refinement found nowhere else in Lorraine. With a magnificent central square, several fine museums and sparkling shop windows, the former capital of the dukes of Lorraine seems as opulent today as it did in the 16th to 18th centuries, when much of the city centre was built.

Nancy has long thrived on a combination of innovation and sophistication. The Musée de l'École de Nancy features the dream-like sinuous works of the Art Nouveau movement, which flourished here (as the Nancy School) thanks to the rebellious spirit of local artists – including Émile Gallé (1846–1904) – who set out to prove that everyday objects could be drop-dead gorgeous. Further examples of their work can be found at the Musée des Beaux-Arts and throughout the city: keep an eye out for the stained-glass windows and elaborate

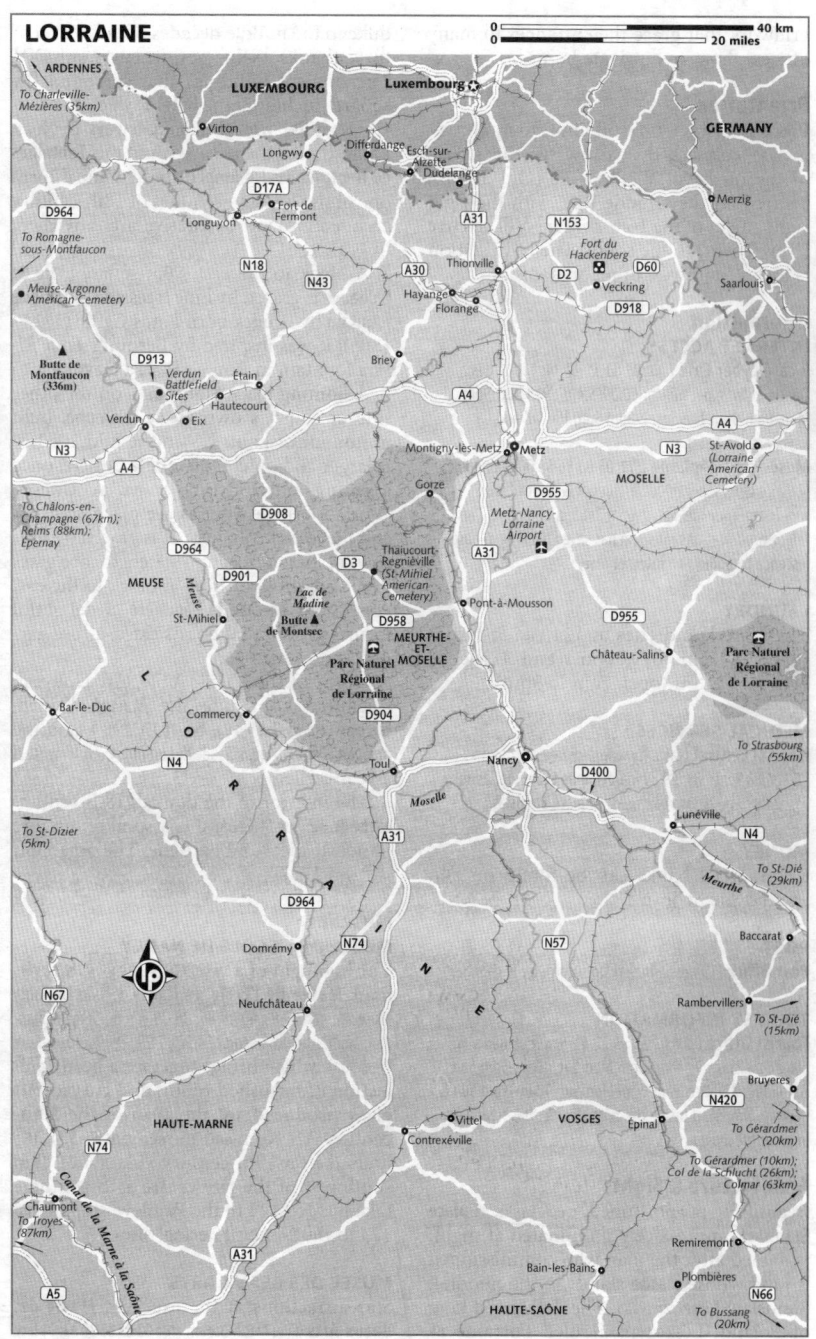

LORRAINE

0   40 km
0   20 miles

ARDENNES

To Charleville-Méziéres (35km)

LUXEMBOURG

Luxembourg

GERMANY

Virton

Longwy

Differdange
Esch-sur-Alzette
Dudelange

Merzig

D964

D17A

Fort de Fermont

A31

N153

Fort du Hackenberg

D2

D60

Saarlouis

To Romagne-sous-Montfaucon

Longuyon

N18

N43

A30

Thionville

Veckring

D918

Meuse-Argonne American Cemetery

A4

Hayange
Florange

Butte de Montfaucon (336m)

D913

Verdun Battlefield Sites

Étain

Briey

A4

A4

Verdun

Hautecourt

Eix

N3

Montigny-lès-Metz

Metz

N3

St-Avold
(Lorraine American Cemetery)

A4

Gorze

D955

MOSELLE

To Châlons-en-Champagne (67km); Reims (88km); Épernay

D908

Metz-Nancy-Lorraine Airport

D964

D901

MEUSE

D3

Thiaucourt-Regniéville *(St-Mihiel American Cemetery)*

A31

Lac de Madine

Butte de Montsec

D958

Pont-à-Mousson

D955

St-Mihiel

MEURTHE-ET-MOSELLE

Château-Salins

Parc Naturel Régional de Lorraine

Bar-le-Duc

Commercy

Parc Naturel Régional de Lorraine

D904

N4

Toul

Nancy

D400

To Strasbourg (55km)

Moselle

Lunéville

N4

To St-Dizier (5km)

A31

To St-Dié (29km)

Meurthe

D964

Baccarat

Domrémy

N74

N57

Rambervillers

To St-Dié (15km)

N67

Neufchâteau

Bruyères

HAUTE-MARNE

Vittel

VOSGES

Épinal

N420

To Gérardmer (20km)

N74

Contrexéville

To Gérardmer (10km); Col de la Schlucht (26km); Colmar (63km)

Canal de la Marne à la Saône

Chaumont
To Troyes (87km)

Remiremont

A5

A31

Bain-les-Bains

Plombières

N66

HAUTE-SAÔNE

To Bussang (20km)

grillwork that grace the entrances to many offices, shops and private homes.

Orientation

Place Stanislas – now off limits to motor vehicles – connects the narrow, twisting streets of the medieval Vieille Ville (Old Town), centred on the Grande Rue, with the rigid right angles of the 16th-century Ville Neuve (New Town) to the south. The train station is 800m southwest of place Stanislas.

Information

INTERNET ACCESS

E-café Cyber Café (☎ 03 83 35 47 34; 11 rue des Quatre Églises; per min/hr €0.09/5.40; ☺ 11am-9pm Mon, 9am-9pm Tue-Sat, 2-8pm Sun) Has UK and US keyboards on hand.

Musée du Téléphone (☎ 03 83 86 50 00; 11 rue Maurice Barrès; per hr adult/student & senior €4/3; ☺ 10am-7pm Tue-Sat, 2-6pm 1st Sun of month) This telecommunications museum has saved itself from obsolescence by adding an Internet café.

LAUNDRY

There are laundrettes at 124 rue St-Dizier (open 7.45am to 9.30pm) and 1 rue de l'Armée Patton (open 7am to 9pm).

MEDICAL SERVICES

Hôpital Central (casualty ward/emergency room ☎ 03 83 85 14 61; 29 av Maréchal de Lattre de Tassigny; ☺ 24hr) About 1km southeast of place Stanislas.

MONEY

Commercial banks can be found on and around rue St-Jean.

POST

Post Office (10 rue St-Dizier) Does currency exchange.

TOURIST INFORMATION

Tourist Office (☎ 03 83 35 22 41; www.ot-nancy.fr; place Stanislas; ☺ 9am-7pm Mon-Sat, 10am-5pm Sun & holidays Apr-Oct, 9am-6pm Mon-Sat, 10am-1pm Sun & holidays Nov-Mar) Inside the *hôtel de ville*. Has free walking tour brochures.

Architecture & Sights

Beautifully proportioned, neoclassical **place Stanislas**, impressively illuminated at night, is named after the man who commissioned it (and whose **statue** stands in the middle), Stanislaw Leszczynski. The dethroned king of Poland, Leszczynski ruled Lorraine as duke in the middle decades of the 17th century, thanks to his son-in-law Louis XV. The opulent buildings that surround the square (including the **hôtel de ville**), the dazzling gilded **wrought-iron gateways** by Jean Lamour, and the rococo fountains **Fontaines de Neptune** and **d'Amphitrite** by Guibal form one of the finest ensembles of 18th-century architecture and decorative arts anywhere in France.

A block to the east, 90m-square **place de l'Alliance** is graced by lime trees and a **baroque fountain** by Bruges-born Louis Cyfflé (1724–1806); it was inspired by Bernini's *Four Rivers* fountain in Rome's Piazza Navona.

Adjoining place Stanislas – on the other side of Nancy's own **Arc de Triomphe**, built in honour of Louis XV in the mid-1750s – is larger and quieter **place de la Carrière**, once a riding and jousting arena. A Unesco World Heritage Site (as are place Stanislas and place de l'Alliance), it is graced by four rows of linden trees and stately rococo gates in gilded wrought iron. A block to the east you'll find **Parc de la Pépinière**, a delightful formal garden that boasts cafés, a rose garden and a small zoo.

North of the Vieille Ville, Art Nouveau townhouses include the **Maison Weissenburger** (1 blvd Charles V), built in 1904, and the **Maison Huot** (92 quai Claude de Lorrain), constructed a year earlier.

The interior of the domed, 18th-century **cathédrale** (rue St-Georges) is a sombre mixture of neoclassical and baroque. The organ loft is from 1757.

Museums

MUSÉE DE L'ÉCOLE DE NANCY

The highlight of a visit to Nancy is the brilliant **Musée de l'École de Nancy** (School of Nancy Museum; ☎ 03 83 40 14 86; 36-38 rue du Sergent Blandan; adult/student & senior €4.575/2.29; ☺ 10.30am-6pm Wed-Sun), which brings together a heady collection of furnished rooms and curvaceous glass produced by the turn-of-the-20th-century Art Nouveau movement (p53). It's housed in a 19th-century villa about 2km southwest of the city centre – to get there take bus No 122 to the Painlevé stop or No 123 to the Nancy Thermal stop.

MUSÉE DES BEAUX-ARTS

Star attractions at the excellent **Musée des Beaux-Arts** (Fine Arts Museum; ☎ 03 83 85 30 72; 3 place

Suite-hotel.com
(Tel.0870 240 4825)

Stanislas; adult/student & senior €5.34/3.05; 10am-6pm Wed-Mon) include a superb collection of Daum-made Art Nouveau glass and a rich and varied selection of paintings from the 14th to 18th centuries. Laminated information sheets in English are available.

MUSÉE HISTORIQUE LORRAIN
The mostly 16th-century Palais Ducal, splendid former residence of the dukes of Lorraine, now houses the **Musée Historique Lorrain** (Lorraine Historical Museum; ☎ 03 83 32 18 74; 64 & 66 Grande Rue; adult/student for both sections €4.60/3.10, for 1 section €3.10/2.30; 10am-12.30pm & 2-6pm Wed-Mon). The part dedicated to **fine arts and history** (at No 64) has rich collections of medieval statuary, engravings and faïence, as well as Judaica from before and after the Revolution; the section dedicated to **regional art and folklore** (at No 66) is housed in the 15th-century **Couvent des Cordeliers**, a former Franciscan monastery. Inside, the late-15th-century Gothic **Église des Cordeliers** and the adjacent **Chapelle Ducale** (Ducal Chapel; 1607) modelled on the Medici Chapel in Florence, served as the burial place of the dukes of Lorraine.

Tours
The tourist office offers MP3 tours (€5) of the historic centre (two hours) and the Art-Nouveau quarters (three hours).

Sleeping
SUITE HOTEL (ACCOR)
MODERN - ROOM ONLY
BUDGET
Auberge de Jeunesse Château de Remicourt (☎ 03 83 27 73 67; aubergeremicourt@mairie-nancy.fr; 149 rue de Vandœuvre in Villers-lès-Nancy; dm in 3-10-bunk room €13.50, in double with shower €15.50, rates incl sheets & breakfast) Surrounded by a peaceful park, this fantastic old chateau, with 60 beds, is 4km south of the centre. Check-in is between 2pm (5.30pm on Sunday) and 9pm. By bus, take No 126 to the St-Fiacre stop or Nos 134 and 135 to Villers Lycée Stanislas.

Hôtel de l'Académie (☎ 03 83 35 52 31; fax 03 83 32 55 78; 7bis rue des Michottes; s/d with shower from €23.50/26.50, r with shower & toilet from €29.50) This offbeat place has a tacky fountain that sounds like a broken urinal and cheaply furnished rooms with acoustic tile ceilings. Gallé would have been appalled but you can't beat the price.

MID-RANGE
Hôtel de Guise (☎ 03 83 32 24 68; www.hoteldeguise .com; 18 rue de Guise; s/d/q €46/56/73; **P**) A grand

MUSEUM PASSES
The discount **Pass Nancy 3 Musées** (€8) gives you entry to the Musée de l'École de Nancy, Musée Historique Lorrain and the Musée des Beaux-Arts; it is sold at the tourist office and each museum.

Le **Pass Nancy** (€13), available only at the tourist office, affords holders a variety of museum options, a guided tour of the city and a half-day bike rental.

stone staircase leads to extra-wide hallways and bright, spacious rooms. The bathrooms are as modern as the 18th-century hardwood floors are charmingly creaky. The building, in the heart of the old city, dates from 1680.

Hôtel des Portes d'Or (☎ 03 83 35 42 34; www .hotel-lesportesdor.com; 21 rue Stanislas; d from €51) This welcoming and very cosy two-star hostelry, superbly situated just metres from place Stanislas, has charming rooms of almost three-star quality. Often full so call ahead.

Hôtel des Prélats (☎ 03 83 32 11 52; fax 03 83 37 58 74; 56 place Monseigneur Ruch; tram stop Cathédrale; r €51-88) In a grand historic building that has served as a hotel since 1906, this place is being completely restored and renovated.

Eating
No less than 20 reasonably priced eateries of all sorts line rue des Maréchaux, just west of the Arc de Triomphe; lunch *menus* start at just €9. North of there, intimate eateries can be found all along the Grande Rue. There are lots of cheapies in the vicinity of the covered market.

Brasserie Excelsior (☎ 03 83 35 24 57; 50 rue Henri Poincaré; tram stop Nancy Gare; lunch & after-10pm menu €20.50, other menu €29.90; 8am-12.30am Mon-Sat, 8am-11pm Sun; meals served noon-3pm & 7pm-closing time) Built in 1910, this sparkling brasserie's sumptuous Art Nouveau décor makes every meal memorable. Six kinds of pork are on offer; the sauerkraut options include one *choucroute à trois poissons* with salmon, haddock and scallops.

Restaurant Le Gastrolâtre (☎ 03 83 35 51 94; 1 place Vaudémont; lunch menu €18, other menus €30-40; closed Sun, lunch Mon & dinner Thu) Warm and lived-in, this restaurant has been serving Lorraine cuisine – with some Provençal touches – since 1970. Specialities with deep regional roots include *boekoffe à foie gras*

food average Good to sit

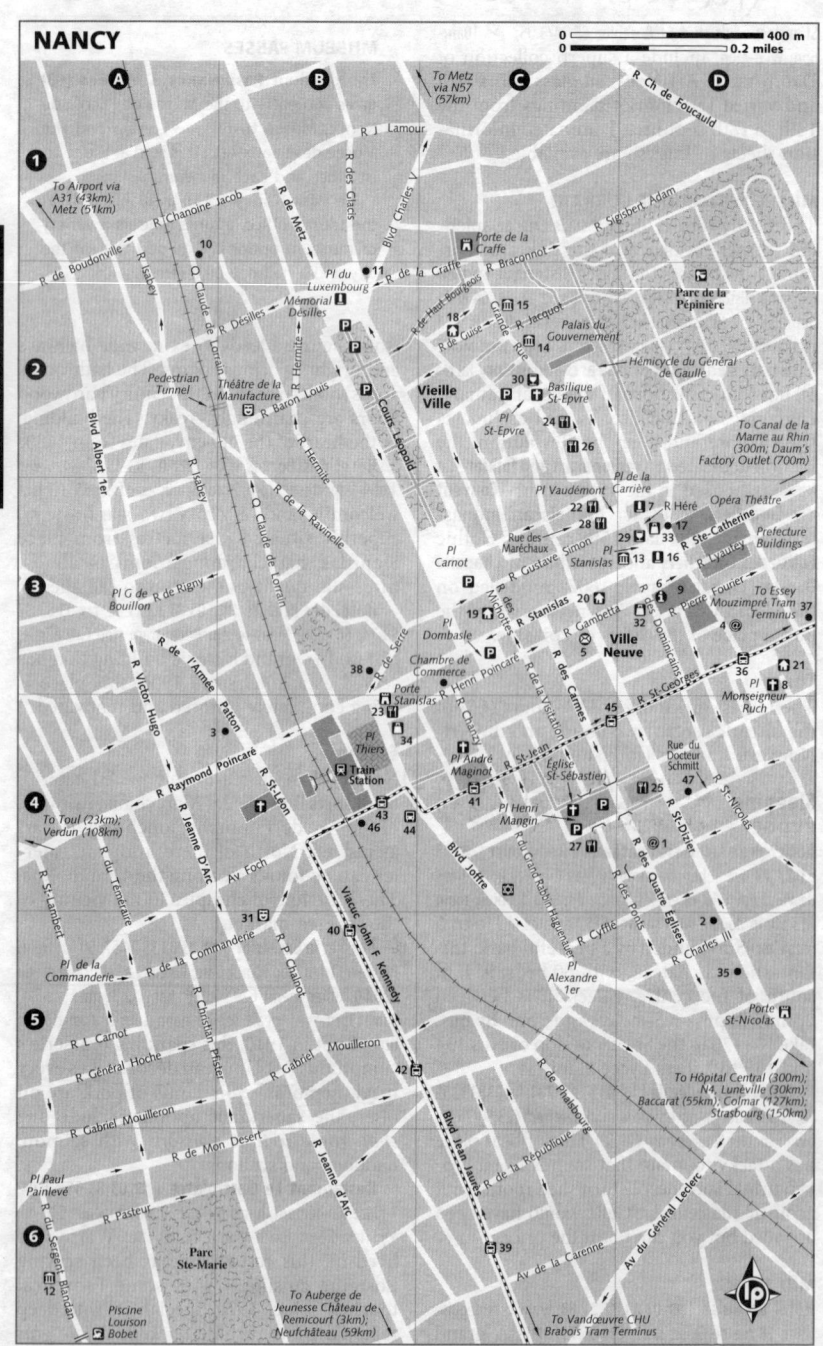

NANCY

0 _____ 400 m
0 _____ 0.2 miles

To Metz
via N57
(57km)

R Ch de Foucauld

To Airport via
A31 (43km);
Metz (51km)

R J Lamour

R des Clercs

R Chanoine Jacob

R de Metz

R de Boudonville

R Isabey

O Claude de Lorraine

10

Pedestrian
Tunnel

Théâtre de la
Manufacture

Mémorial
Désilles

Pl du
Luxembourg

11

R de la Craffe

Porte de la
Craffe

R Bracannot

R Sigisbert Adam

Parc de la
Pépinière

18
R du Haut Bourgeois

R du Guise

R Jacquot

15

Palais du
Gouvernement

14

Blvd Albert 1er

R Désilles

R Hermite

R Baron Louis

Cours Léopold

Vieille
Ville

30

Basilique
St-Epvre

Hémicycle du Général
de Gaulle

Pl
St-Epvre

24

26

To Canal de la
Marne au Rhin
(300m); Daum's
Factory Outlet (700m)

Pl G de
Bouillon

R Victor Hugo

R de Rigny

R de la Ravinelle

O Claude de Lorrain

R Isabey

Pl
Carnot

Rue des
Maréchaux

R Gustave Simon

Pl Vaudémont

Pl de la
Carrière

22

28

R Héré

7

17

29

33

13

16

Opéra Théâtre

Rue Ste-Catherine

Préfecture
Buildings

R Lyautey

To Essey
Mouzimpré Tram
Terminus

R de l'Armée Patton

R de Serre

R des Dominicains

R des Carmes

R Stanislas

R Gambetta

R de la Visitation

Pl
Stanislas

Ville
Neuve

20

6

9

32

5

R Fourier

R Pierre

4

37

38

R Jeanne D'Arc

R Raymond Poincaré

R St-Léon

Chambre de
Commerce

Porte
Stanislas

23

34

Pl
Dombasle

19

R Henri Poincaré

Pl
Thiers

3

Train
Station

43

46

44

R Charles III

Pl André
Maginot

41

Eglise
St-Sébastien

Pl Henri
Mangin

27

25

R St-Georges

45

Rue du
Docteur Schmitt

47

Pl
Monseigneur
Ruch

36

21

8

To Toul (23km);
Verdun (108km)

Av Foch

R St-Lambert

R du Téméraire

31

Viaduc John F Kennedy

40

R St-Jean

Blvd Joffre

R du Grand Rabbin Haguenauer

R des Ponts

R des Quatre Eglises

R St-Dizier

R St-Nicolas

R Cyffle

1

2

35

Porte
St-Nicolas

Pl de la
Commanderie

R L Carnot

R Général Hoche

R de la Commanderie

R P Chalnot

R Christian Pfister

R Gabriel
Mouilleron

Mouilleron

42

Pl
Alexandre
1er

To Hôpital Central (300m);
N4, Lunéville (30km);
Baccarat (55km); Colmar (127km);
Strasbourg (150km)

Pl Paul
Painlevé

R du Sergent Blandan

R Pasteur

R de Mon Desert

R Jeanne d'Arc

Blvd Jean Jaurès

Parc
Ste-Marie

12

Piscine
Louison
Bobet

To Auberge de
Jeunesse Château de
Remicourt (3km);
Neufchâteau (59km)

39

Av de la Garenne

Av du Général Leclerc

R de la République

To Vandœuvre CHU
Brabois Tram Terminus

ALSACE & LORRAINE

de canard (meat stew with duck foie gras). Black truffles take centre stage from December to March.

La Basse Cour (☎ 03 83 36 67 29; 23 Grande Rue; menu €16; ⏲ 6.30-11pm or later Mon-Sat) A bourgeois apartment in a 16th- and 17th-century townhouse has been transformed into a homey, intimate eatery specialising in mouth-watering Lorraine-style cuisine de campagne (farm-fresh country cuisine). One of the chef's favourites is vol-au-vent filled with lamb sweetbread, ham and morilles mushrooms, but it's poultry that rules the roost, on the menu as well the walls.

Chez Bagot-Le Chardon Bleu (☎ 03 83 37 42 43; 45 Grande Rue; lunch menu €14.50, other menus €21.50-31; ⏲ 12.15-1.45pm & 7.15-10pm, closed Mon, lunch Tue & dinner Sun) This very popular restaurant, elegant yet convivial, is known for its creative French cuisine. Specialities include fish.

SELF-CATERING
Aux Croustillants (10 rue des Maréchaux; ⏲ 24hr except from 9pm Sun to 5.30am Tue) is an almost-24/7 boulangerie. Other options are the **covered market** (place Henri Mangin; tram stop Point Central; ⏲ 7am-6pm Tue-Thu, 7am-6.30pm Fri & Sat) and the **Monoprix supermarket** (⏲ 8.30am-8.30pm Mon-Sat), inside the St-Sébastien shopping mall.

Drinking
Le Ch'timi (☎ 03 83 32 82 76; 17 place St-Epvre; ⏲ 9am-2am Mon-Sat, 9am-8pm Sun) At this unpretentious mellow bar, spread out over three brick-and-stone storeys, you can choose from 200 different beers, 16 of them on tap.

L'Arquebuse (☎ 03 83 32 11 99; 13 rue Héré; ⏲ 6.30pm-4am Tue-Sat) This very stylish candle-lit bar has superb views of place Stanislas and, from about 11pm, dancing to salsa, zouk etc; the clientele comes mainly from the over-35 demographic. Sushi (about €1 per piece) is served until 10pm.

Entertainment
Details on cultural events appear in the free monthly Spectacles (www.spectacles-publications.com in French).

CINEMA
There's a good selection of nondubbed films at the **Caméo** (☎ 03 83 28 41 00; www.cine-cameo.com in French; 16 rue de la Commanderie; tram stop Kennedy), a four-screen art cinema.

LIVE MUSIC
Blue Note III Club (☎ 03 83 30 31 18; 3 rue des Michottes; ⏲ 10pm-4am Wed, Thu & Sun, 11pm-5am Fri & Sat) This vaulted subterranean discotheque, at the far end of the courtyard, has concerts (€3 to €5) and student nights (€2) – and after 2am a disco – on Wednesday and Thursday; live jazz and blues (until 1am) and two dance floors (one Latino, the other disco; €10) on Friday and Saturday; and karaoke (and after 2am a disco) on Sunday. Twenty-somethings predominate.

Le Varadero (☎ 03 83 36 61 98; 27 Grande Rue; admission free; ⏲ 6pm-2am Mon-Sat Apr-Sep, 8pm-2am Tue-Sat Oct-Mar) Named after a beach in Cuba, this laid-back radical-chic student hangout has live Joan Baez-style folk music from 8.30pm to 10pm every Friday and Saturday; after that a Latino-oriented DJ takes over. There are often student nights on Wednesdays.

Shopping

The main commercial thoroughfares in the city are rue St-Dizier, rue St-Jean and rue St-Georges.

Exquisite crystal and jewellery is on display at the **Baccarat shops** (☎ 03 83 30 55 11; 2 rue des Dominicains & next door at 3 rue Gambetta; ☽ closed Mon morning & Sun), where the cheapest wine glass – impossibly delicate – costs €54. At **Daum** (☎ 03 83 22 21 65; 14 place Stanislas; ☽ closed Mon morning & Sun), you can watch a video showing crystal artisans at work and visit a small **museum** of early-20th-century pieces.

Daum's factory outlet (☎ 03 83 32 14 55; 17 rue des Cristalleries; tram stop Cristalleries; ☽ 9.30am-12.30pm & 2.30-6.30pm Mon-Sat), about 1km northeast of place Stanislas, sells discontinued designs and unsigned seconds.

Bergamotes de Nancy, the local confectionery speciality, are hard candies made with bergamot, a citrus fruit – also used to flavour Earl Grey tea – that grows on the slopes of Mt Etna. The only confectioner allowed to sell *bergamottes* (with two Ts) is **Lefèvre-Lemoine** (Au Duché de Lorraine; ☎ 03 83 30 13 83; 47 rue Henri Poincaré; tram stop Nancy Gare; ☽ 8.30am-7pm Mon-Sat, 9.30am-12.30pm Sun), founded in 1840 and last redecorated – with Gilded Age panache – way back in 1928. One of its old-fashioned sweets tins made a cameo appearance in the film *Amélie*.

Getting There & Away

CAR

Rental options:

ADA (☎ 03 83 36 53 09; 138 rue St-Dizier)

Europcar (☎ 03 83 37 57 24; 18 rue de Serre)

National-Citer (☎ 03 83 37 38 59; in the train station departure hall; tram stop Nancy Gare)

TRAIN

The **train station** (place Thiers; tram stop Nancy Gare) is on the line linking Paris' Gare de l'Est (€35.30, three hours, 12 to 14 daily) with Strasbourg (€18.40, 1¼ hours, nine to 12 daily). Other destinations include Baccarat (€8.50, 40 to 70 minutes, six to nine daily) and Metz (€8.30, 40 to 70 minutes, 34 daily Monday to Friday, 22 on Saturday, 14 on Sunday).

Getting Around

BICYCLE

Cyclotop (☎ 03 83 40 31 31; 89 rue St-Georges; tram stop Cathédrale; per half-/full day €5/7; ☽ 9am-noon & 2-6pm except Sat afternoon, Mon morning & Sun), run by the municipality, rents distinctive yellow-and-red city bikes.

BUS & TRAM

The local public transport company, **STAN** (☎ 03 83 30 08 08; www.reseau-stan.com in French; offices at 3 rue du Docteur Schmitt & place de la République; ☽ 7am-7.25pm Mon-Sat), has its main hubs at Nancy République and Point Central. The tram line – the first of three planned – uses innovative new technology that's based on rubber-tyred street cars guided by a single rail. One/10 tickets cost €1.15/8.20.

PARKING

There's free parking 600m northeast of place Stanislas on the other side of Canal de la Marne au Rhin, and in the working-class neighbourhoods west of the train tracks.

TAXI

A **taxi** (☎ 03 83 37 65 37) is just a telephone call away.

BACCARAT

pop 5000

For centuries Nancy and southern Lorraine have produced some of the world's finest crystal and glassware. The most famous *cristallerie* (crystal glassworks) of all, founded in 1764, is at Baccarat, 55km southeast of Nancy. At the **Musée du Cristal** (☎ 03 83 76 61 37; www.baccarat.fr; adult/under 10 €2.50/free; ☽ 9.30am-12.30pm & 2-6.30pm Apr-Oct, 10am-noon & 2-6pm Nov-Mar), on the grounds of the Baccarat glassworks, you can admire 1100 exquisite pieces.

Across the River Meurthe, the concrete **Église St-Rémy**, built in the mid-1950s to replace an earlier church destroyed by Allied bombing in 1944, is decorated with over 4000 panels of coloured Baccarat crystal.

The **tourist office** (☎ 03 83 75 13 37; www.ville-baccarat.fr/accotgb.htm; ☽ 9am-noon & 2-5.30pm Mon-Sat year-round, 10am-noon Sun & holidays Jul & Aug) is in the car park behind the church.

Hôtel La Renaissance (☎ 03 83 75 11 31; www.hotel-la-renaissance.com; 31 rue des Cristalleries; s/d €43/47), just down the block from the museum, is a two-star Logis de France-affiliated hotel with attractive rooms and an excellent French restaurant.

Baccarat's train station is a few hundred metres north of the Musée du Cristal, with trains to Nancy (€8.50, 40 to 70 minutes, six to nine daily).

METZ

pop 322,000

Present-day capital of the Lorraine region and an important high-tech centre, Metz is a dignified city with stately public squares, shaded riverside parks, a large university and a historic commercial centre. The Gothic cathedral, with its stunning stained glass, is the most outstanding attraction.

Metz became part of France in 1648. When Germany annexed the city in 1871, a quarter of the population fled to French territory; many went to nearby Nancy, which remained French. Quite a few of the most impressive buildings date from the 48-year period when Metz was part of the German empire.

Orientation

The cathedral, on a hill above the River Moselle, is a bit over 1km north of the train station. The city centre's main public squares are place d'Armes, next to the cathedral; place St-Jacques, in the heart of the pedestrianised commercial precinct; place St-Louis; and, 400m to the west, place de la République.

Information

EMERGENCY

Police (Hôtel de Police; ☎ 03 87 16 17 17; 6 rue Belle Isle; ⚕ 24hr)

INTERNET ACCESS

Diacom Internet Café (☎ 03 87 63 08 85; 20 rue Gambetta; per hr €3; ⚕ 10am-9pm Mon-Sat, 11am-9pm Sun)

LAUNDRY

There are laundrettes at 11 rue de la Fontaine, 4 rue des Allemands, 22 rue du Pont des Morts and 23 rue Taison. All are open 7am to 8pm.

MEDICAL SERVICES

Notre Dame de Bonsecours CHR (Bldg F emergency room/casualty ward ☎ 03 87 55 34 91/2; 1 place Philippe de Vigneulles; ⚕ 24hr)

MONEY

There are commercial banks at place St-Louis and on the southeastern side of place de la République. The tourist office charges a 5.5% commission to change money.

POST

Main Post Office (9 rue Gambetta) Has currency exchange and a Cyberposte.

TOURIST INFORMATION

Tourist Office (☎ 03 87 55 53 76; http://tourisme.mairie-metz.fr; place d'Armes; ⚕ 9am-8.30pm Mon-Sat Jul & Aug, to 7pm Mar-Jun & Sep-Nov, to 6.30pm Dec-Feb, plus 10am-3pm Sun & holidays year-round) In a one-time guardroom built in the mid-1700s. The free monthly *Ce Mois-Ci à Metz* lists cultural events. Has a free walking and cycling map and an Internet terminal that works with a *télécarte*.

Cathédrale St-Étienne

Metz' spectacular Gothic **Cathédrale St-Étienne** (⚕ 8am-7pm May-Sep, to 6pm Oct-Apr), built between 1220 and 1522, is famed for its veritable curtains of 13th- to 20th-century stained glass, among the finest in France. The superb **Flamboyant Gothic windows** (1504), on the main wall of the north transept arm, provide a remarkable stylistic contrast with the glorious **Renaissance windows** on the main wall of the south transept arm, created a mere two decades later. There are distinctive windows by **Chagall** on the western wall of the north transept arm and in the nearby section of the ambulatory (over the entrance to the Grande Sacristie), where you'll also find the **treasury** (adult/student €1.50/1). In the 15th-century **crypt** (below the altar; adult/student €1.50/1) you can see a 15th-century sculpture of the Graoully ('**grau**-lee' or '**grau**-yee'), a dragon that is said to have terrified pre-Christian Metz. Try to visit on a bright day. Like the city centre's other major monuments, the cathedral is beautifully illuminated at night (until 1am).

Musée La Cour d'Or

The truly excellent **Musée La Cour d'Or** (☎ 03 87 68 25 00; 2 rue du Haut Poirier; adult/senior & student under 26/under 12 €4.60/2.30/free, 1st Sun of month free; ⚕ 9am-5pm Mon & Wed-Fri, 10am-5pm Sat & Sun) has an outstanding collection of Gallo-Roman antiquities, paintings, and early-medieval religious art and stonework. It is housed in a maze of 60 rooms that were originally part of a 15th-century granary and a 17th-century convent.

City Centre

On the eastern edge of the city centre, triangular **place St-Louis** is surrounded by medieval arcades and merchants' houses dating from the 14th to 16th centuries.

Neoclassical **place de la Comédie**, bounded by one of the channels of the Moselle, is home to the city's **théâtre** (1738–53), the oldest theatre building in France that's still in

METZ

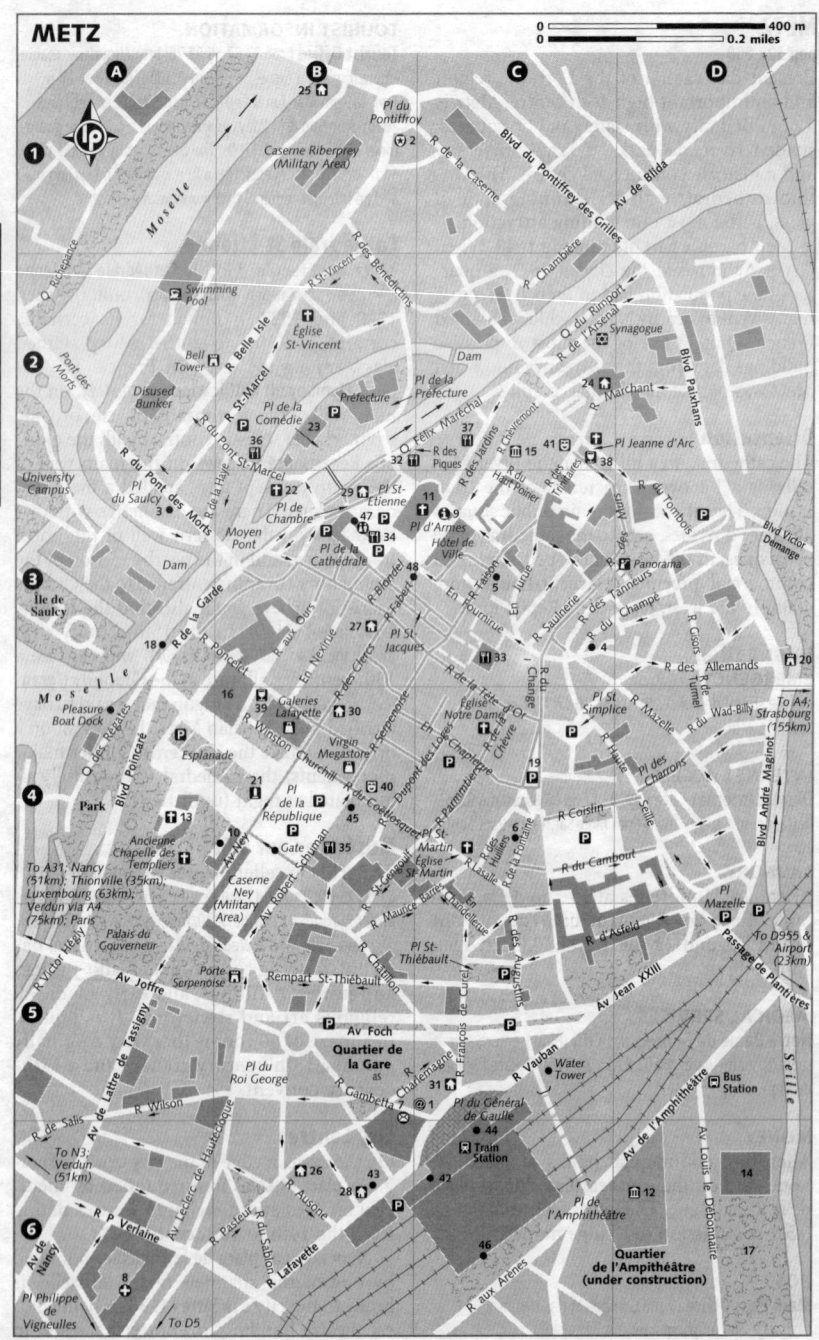

use. During the Revolution, place de l'Égalité (as it was then known) was the site of a guillotine that lopped the heads off 63 'enemies of the people'. The neo-Romanesque **Temple Neuf** (Protestant Church), sombre and looming, was constructed under the Germans in 1903.

The formal flowerbeds of the **Esplanade** – and its **statue** of a gallant-looking Marshall Ney, sword dangling at his side (1859) – are flanked by imposing public buildings, including the **Arsenal Cultural Centre** (1863) and the sober, neoclassical **Palais de Justice** (late 18th century). **Église St-Pierre-aux-Nonains** (admission free; ☾ 1-6pm Tue-Sat & 2-6pm Sun mid-Jun–21 Sep, 1-6pm Sat & 2-6pm Sun late Sep-early May) was originally built around AD 400 as part of a Gallo-Roman spa complex (the wall sections that have horizontal red-brick stripes are Roman originals). For a thousand centuries – from the 6th to the 16th centuries – the structure served as the abbey church of a women's monastery.

West and northwest of the Esplanade, on both sides of blvd Poincaré, is a lovely **riverside park** graced with statues, ponds, swans and a fountain. **Pedal boats** can be rented on quai des Régates in the warm months.

The crenellated **Porte des Allemands** (Gate of the Germans; interior closed) was first erected around 1230 when a wall to surround this part of the city was constructed. It owes its name, not (heaven forbid!) because of a fondness for the Germans, but to the friars of Notre-Dame-des-Allemands, who ran a hospital near here in the Middle Ages. The gate, overlooking the River Seille, was severely damaged during the liberation of the city by Allied forces in November 1944.

Quartier de la Gare

The solid and bourgeois buildings and broad avenues of Quartier de la Gare, including rue Gambetta and av Foch, were constructed in the decades leading up to WWI. Built with the intention of Germanising the city by emphasising Metz' post-1871 status as an integral part of the Second Reich, its neo-Romanesque and neo-Renaissance buildings are made of dark-hued sandstone, granite and basalt, rather than the yellow-tan Jaumont limestone characteristic of French-built neoclassical structures.

The massive, grey-sandstone **train station**, completed in 1908 and decorated with Teutonic sculptures whose common theme is German imperial might, was designed with military needs clearly in mind. With a length of 300m, it could handle the loading or unloading of 20,000 troops and their equipment in just 24 hours. The massive **main post office**, built in 1911 of red Vosges sandstone, is as solid and heavy as the cathedral is light and lacy.

Quartier de l'Amphithéâtre

'The wrong side of the tracks', until recently a wasteland of abandoned hangars and depots, is undergoing a complete transformation thanks to Metz' seemingly boundless cultural ambitions (and development budget). The Amphitheatre Quarter already boasts **Les Arènes** (Palais Omnisports), a vast steel-and-glass venue for sports events and concerts, and the green riverside lawns of **Parc de la Seille**. But you ain't seen nothin' yet: come 2007, the **Centre Pompidou-Metz** – a branch of the inside-out original in Paris –

is supposed to open its doors. The winning design, by Shigeru Ban (Tokyo), Jean de Gastines (Paris) and Philip Gumuchdjian (London), is like nothing else ever conceived by the human mind. Suffice it to say that the whole thing will be covered by an undulating, translucent 'membrane' of Teflon-coated fibreglass. The project may just do for Metz what the Guggenheim did for Bilbao.

Tours

The tourist office's 1½-hour *visites audioguidées* (Walkman tours; €7) of the city centre are available in six languages.

Sleeping

In general, Metz' hotels offer excellent value. Except in summer, they are at their fullest from Monday to Thursday.

BUDGET

Auberge de Jeunesse Carrefour (☎ 03 87 75 07 26; ascarrefour@wanadoo.fr; 6 rue Marchant; dm in 3–4-bedroom €12.35, s/d €14.10/28.20, rates incl breakfast) This hostel for young working people has plain rooms, accessible all day long, in which showers and toilets are being installed. There's no curfew. From the train station, take bus Nos 3 or 11 to the St-Georges stop.

Auberge de Jeunesse Metz-Plage (☎ 03 87 30 44 02; aubjeumetz@aol.com; dm €12.30, s €15.30, rates incl breakfast ; ⊗ check-in 8am-10am & 5-10pm) This old-time hostel, with 62 beds, has decades-old facilities but offers room access (with a code) all day long; there's no curfew. Kitchen facilities are available. By bus, take the No 3 or 11 to the Pontiffroy stop.

Hôtel Lafayette (☎ 03 87 75 21 09; fax 03 87 75 66 87; 24 rue des Clercs; d with toilet or shower €28, d/tr with shower & toilet €33/41) The spotless rooms, many with old-fashioned touches (eg chimneys), are a bit ragged around the edges but the staff is welcoming and you can't beat the location.

MID-RANGE

Hôtel Métropole (☎ 03 87 66 26 22; www.hotel metropole-metz.com; 5 place du Général de Gaulle; s/d/q from €38/45/57; ✗) Built as a hotel at the tail end of the German period (1912), this two-star place has rooms that are so bright and cheery they're almost spiritually uplifting. Excellent value for money.

Cécil Hôtel (☎ 03 87 66 66 13; www.cecilhotel-metz .com; 14 rue Pasteur; d €54) Built in 1920, right after Metz was returned to France, this charming two-star hotel has modern, pastel rooms with spacious tile bathrooms. From Thursday to Sunday nights, the buffet breakfast (€6) is free if you stay at least two days.

Hôtel Bristol (☎ 03 87 66 74 22; www.hotel-bristol -57.com; 7 rue Lafayette; s/d from €28/32, larger d €45) Bring your bell-bottoms and nose plug – at the Bristol it's still the 1970s, the period authenticity certified by the fusty odour of furnishings undisturbed since Elvis didn't die. The two-star rooms can charitably be termed compact (in the cheaper ones the word 'cramped' also comes to mind).

Grand Hôtel de Metz (☎ 03 87 36 16 33; www .grandhotelmetz.com in French; 3 rue des Clercs; d from €59) At this two-star place, you can luxuriate in a two-person bathtub in one of the romantic minisuites (€90), big enough for ballroom dancing (our advice to management: lose the plastic plants), and make your own eggs at the buffet breakfast (€6.50). By car, take rue Fabert from the cathedral, push the button on the 'appel' upright and explain you're going to the hotel.

Eating

Place St-Jacques is taken over by cafés in the warmer months. Cheap student eats are available near the university on grungy rue du Pont des Morts.

À la Ville de Lyon (☎ 03 87 36 07 01; next to 13 rue des Piques; menus €19-45.80, children's menu €6.90; ⊗ closed Mon & dinner Sun) This elegant and very formal restaurant features traditional French dishes as well as the cuisine of Lorraine. Specialities include quiche Lorraine and *soufflé glacé à la mirabelle* (chilled soufflé with mirabelle plums).

Restaurant du Pont St-Marcel (☎ 03 87 30 12 29; 1 rue du Pont St-Marcel; menus €18-29) Everything

---

AUTHOR'S CHOICE

Hôtel de la Cathédrale (☎ 03 87 75 00 02; www.hotelcathedrale-metz.fr in French; 25 place de Chambre; d €55-80, ste €90). Ensconced in a gorgeous 17th-century townhouse, this three-star place positively oozes romance! The 20 large rooms are tastefully furnished with antiques and silks that perfectly complement the ancient wooden beams overhead. The wrought ironwork is by Jean Lamour (1698–1771), creator of the gilded masterpieces that adorn Nancy's place Stanislas.

AUTHOR'S CHOICE

L'Étude (☎ 03 87 36 35 32; www.l-etude.com in French; 11 av Robert Schuman; 2-/3-course menus €19.80/23.80, when there's live music €22.60/26.30; 🕑 Mon-Sat) Hugely popular with local cognoscenti, this eatery is a real quintessential French mixture of the intellectual (with book-lined walls) and the gastronomic (French, of course). There's live music (jazz, blues, Roma, Cuban – the website has the schedule) commencing at 8.30pm on Friday and Saturday (reservations recommended).

here is typical of Lorraine, from the succulent dishes to the white cotton hats, billowy shirts, black vests and long skirts worn by the waitresses.

Taj Mahal (☎ 03 87 74 33 23; 16 rue des Jardins) This place has a weekday, all-you-can-eat Indian lunch buffet for just €8.50 and vegetarian mains for €7.

SELF-CATERING

For food supplies there is the **covered market** (place de la Cathédrale; 🕑 approx 7am-6pm Tue-Sat) or the **Atac supermarket** (place St-Jacques; 🕑 8.30am-7.30pm Mon-Sat), on the lower level of the Centre St-Jacques shopping mall.

Drinking

Café Jehanne d'Arc (☎ 03 87 37 39 94; place Jeanne d'Arc; 🕑 noon-2.30am Mon-Fri, 3pm-3.30am Sat) This establishment bears its long history – the roof beams are from the 1500s, the frescoes two or three centuries older – with good humour and mellowness. The sound track is pure jazz. There's a refreshing terrace in the warm months.

L'Appart (☎ 03 87 18 59 26; 2 rue Haute Pierre; 🕑 5pm-3am Sun-Thu, 7pm-7am or 8am Fri & Sat) The house in which the poet Paul Verlaine – Arthur Rimbaud's lover and almost his assassin – was born in 1844 is now a laid-back mainly gay bar with campy chandeliers, a retro 1950s ceiling, a bright orange floor and centuries-old carved wood panelling (protected by law). It is a disco on Sunday.

Entertainment

The city's main concert venues are the **Arsenal cultural centre** (☎ 03 87 39 92 00; av Ney), **Les Arènes** (☎ 03 87 62 82 93 60; www.arenes-de-metz.com in French), and the smaller **Salle des Trinitaires**

(place Jeanne d'Arc). Details on cultural events appear in the free monthly *Spectacles* (www .spectacles-publications.com in French).

The gyrating bodies and ultramodern décor of **Le Tiffany** (☎ 03 87 75 23 32; 24 rue du Coët-losquet; admission free except Fri/Sat €10/12; 🕑 11pm-5am Wed-Sat) would have knocked the socks off the medieval people who built the vaulted cellar it has occupied since 1972. Each of the three dance halls features a different type of music (soul, R&B, house, retro etc).

Getting There & Away
CAR
Rental options:

Budget (☎ 03 87 66 36 31; 5 rue Lafayette)
Europcar (☎ 03 87 62 26 11; in the train station's arrival hall)
National-Citer (☎ 03 87 38 09 99; in the train station's arrival hall)

TRAIN

Metz' train station is on the line linking Paris' Gare de l'Est (€35.30, three hours, seven to nine daily) with Luxembourg (€11.20, 50 minutes, 11 to 19 daily). Direct trains also go to Nancy (€8.30, 40 to 70 minutes, 27 to 37 daily Monday to Saturday, 15 on Sunday), Strasbourg (€19.10, 1¼ to 1¾ hours, five to nine daily) and Verdun (€11.40, 1¼ hours, three each weekday, one daily weekends).

Getting Around
BICYCLE

Three-speed city bikes can be rented from non-profit **Vélocation** (per half-/whole day €3/5) outlets:

Train station (☎ 03 87 62 61 79; in the arrival hall; 🕑 9am-8pm, to 6pm Sat & Sun, closed Sat & Sun Christmas-Feb)
Under the covered market (☎ 03 87 74 50 43; rue d'Estrées 🕑 8am-7pm, to 6pm Sat & Sun)

BUS

The local bus system, run by **TCRM** (☎ 03 87 76 31 11; office at 1 av Robert Schuman; 🕑 Mon-Sat) operates from 6am to about 8pm daily (bus No 11 also has runs at about 10pm, 11pm and midnight). One/six rides cost €0.90/4.10 and the all-day Visipass is €3.

PARKING

Near the train station, there's free parking under the trees on av Foch and, to the northeast, at place Mazelle.

TAXI

You can order a **taxi** (☎ 03 87 56 91 92) day or night.

FORT DU HACKENBERG

The largest single Maginot Line bastion (p344) in the Metz area was the 1000-man **Fort du Hackenberg** (☎ 03 82 82 30 08), which is 30km northeast of Metz near the village of Veckring, whose 10km of galleries were designed to be self-sufficient for three months and, in battle, to fire four tonnes of shells a minute. Two-hour tours (adult/child under 16 €5/2.50) begin every 15 minutes between 2pm and 3.30pm on Saturday and Sunday from April to October. An electric trolley takes visitors along 4km of the fortress' underground tunnels – always at 12°C – past a variety of subterranean installations (kitchen, hospital, electric plant etc).

VERDUN

pop 21,000

The horrific events that took place in and around Verdun between February 1916 and August 1917 – *l'enfer de Verdun* (the hell of Verdun) – have turned the town's name into a byword for wartime slaughter. During the last two years of WWI, over 800,000 soldiers – some 400,000 French and almost as many Germans, along with thousands of the Americans who arrived in 1918 – lost their lives here.

After the annexation of Alsace and part of Lorraine by Germany in 1871, Verdun became a frontline outpost. Over the next four decades, it was turned into the most important – and most heavily fortified – element in France's eastern defensive line. During WWI Verdun itself was never taken by the Germans, but the evacuated town was almost totally destroyed by artillery bombardments. In the hills to the north and east of Verdun, where most of the fighting took place, the brutal combat (carried out with artillery, flame-throwers and poison gas) completely wiped out nine villages.

These days, Verdun is an economically depressed and profoundly provincial backwater, though the dispatch of French troops based near Verdun to peacekeeping missions abroad has made world politics a very local – and for some, personal – affair.

Orientation

Central Verdun straddles the River Meuse and its two canals, but the livelier Ville Haute (Upper Town) is on the river's western bank, which rises to the cathedral. The train station is 700m northwest of the cathedral. The main drag is known as rue St-Paul and rue Mazel.

Information

Commercial banks can be found around the intersection of rue Mazel and rue Beaurepaire. The tourist office exchanges US dollars and pounds sterling on weekends and holidays.

Laundrette (2 place Chevert; ⏲ 6.30am-8pm, to 9pm Jun-Sep)

Main Post Office (av de la Victoire) Has currency exchange and a Cyberposte.

Tourist Office (☎ 03 29 86 14 18; www.verdun-tourisme.com; place de la Nation; ⏲ 8.30am-6.30pm Mon-Sat May-Sep, 9am-noon & 2-5pm or 6pm Mon-Sat Oct-Apr, 9.30am-5pm Sun & holidays Apr-Sep, 10am-1pm Sun & holidays Oct-Mar)

Citadelle Souterrraine

In 1916 Verdun's huge **Citadelle Souterrraine** (Underground Citadel; ☎ 03 29 86 62 02; tourist entrance on av du 5e RAP; adult/5-15 yrs €5.40/2.30), with its 7km of underground galleries, was turned into an impregnable command centre in which 10,000 *poilus* (French WWI soldiers) lived, many while waiting to be dispatched to the front. About 10% of the galleries have been converted into an imaginative audiovisual re-enactment of the war, making this an excellent introduction to the WWI history of Verdun. The citadel was designed by Vauban (p30) in the 17th century and completed in 1838.

Half-hour tours, in battery-powered cars and available in six languages, depart every five minutes from 9am (10am from December to March) to 11.30am or noon and 2pm to 4.30pm (5pm in October and November, 6pm or 6.30pm from April to September, when there's no midday closure). The citadel is closed during the second and third weeks of January.

Centre Mondial de la Paix

The **Centre Mondial de la Paix** (World Centre for Peace; ☎ 03 29 86 55 00; place Monseigneur Ginisty; adult/student €5.50/3; ⏲ 9.30am-7pm Jun–mid-Sep, 9.30am-noon & 2-6pm mid-Sep–May, closed Jan) has imaginative and moving exhibits – accompanied by English commentary (via headsets) and video images – on the themes of peace and human rights in light of the horrific carnage of WWI. The exhibits are different from what many people expect as the focus here is on human beings rather than political or military developments – or army hardware. The centre is housed in Verdun's handsomely classical (and classically handsome) former bishop's palace built in 1724.

Other Sights

Inside **Cathédrale Notre Dame** (place Monseigneur Ginisty; 8am-6pm or 7pm), a gilded baroque **baldachin** and 18th-century furnishings add

some character to the heavily restored Romanesque and Gothic structure. Much of the most-colourful stained glass is from the interwar period.

The colossal **Monument à la Victoire** (Victory Monument), built from 1920 to 1929 and overlooking rue Mazel, portrays a warrior and is flanked by two cannons. Its almost Fascist-looking countenance is softened somewhat by the new cascading fountain.

Two one-time city gates are the **Porte Chaussée** (rue Chaussée), built in the 14th century and later used as a prison, and **Porte St-Paul** (rue St-Paul), built in 1877 and rebuilt between 1919 and 1929. The Rodin bronze was given to the city by the Netherlands.

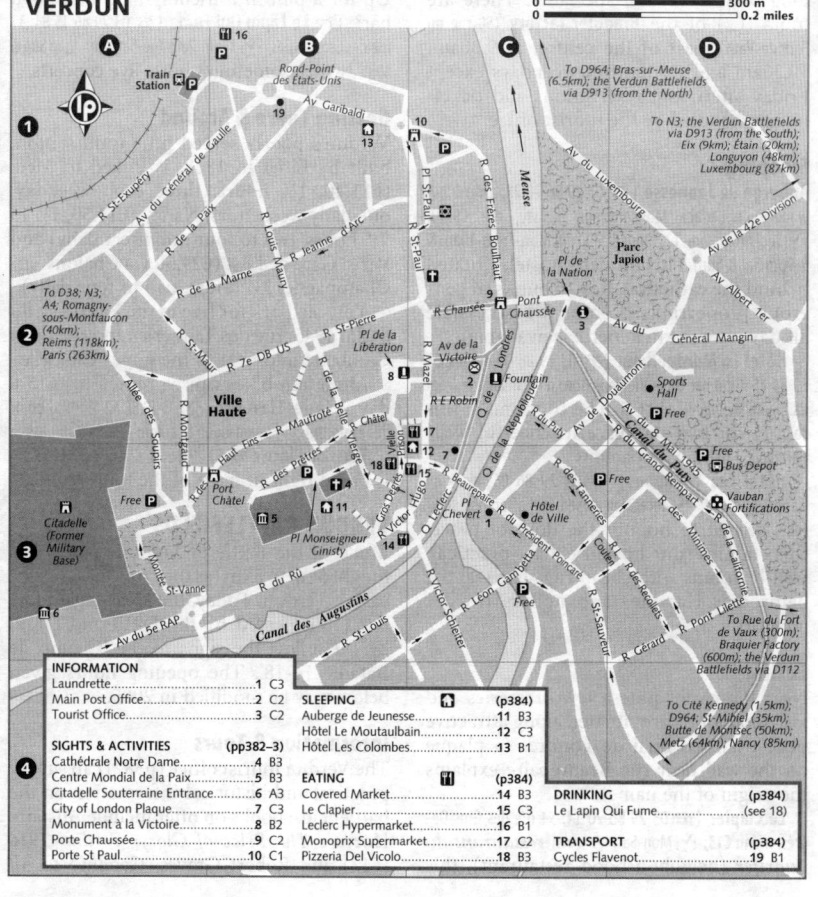

VERDUN

0 — 300 m
0 — 0.2 miles

INFORMATION
Laundrette	1 C3
Main Post Office	2 C2
Tourist Office	3 C2

SIGHTS & ACTIVITIES (pp382–3)
Cathédrale Notre Dame	4 B3
Centre Mondial de la Paix	5 B3
Citadelle Souterraine Entrance	6 A3
City of London Plaque	7 C3
Monument à la Victoire	8 B2
Porte Chaussée	9 C2
Porte St Paul	10 C1

SLEEPING (p384)
Auberge de Jeunesse	11 B3
Hôtel Le Moutaulbain	12 C3
Hôtel Les Colombes	13 B1

EATING (p384)
Covered Market	14 B3
Le Clapier	15 C3
Leclerc Hypermarket	16 B1
Monoprix Supermarket	17 C2
Pizzeria Del Vicolo	18 B3

DRINKING (p384)
Le Lapin Qui Fume	(see 18)

TRANSPORT (p384)
Cycles Flavenot	19 B1

LA PETITE AMERIQUE

Verdun had a significant American military presence until Charles de Gaulle pulled France out of NATO's integrated military command in 1966. In **Cité Kennedy**, a neighbourhood that once housed American military families, the streets still bear names such as av d'Atlanta, av de Floride, av de Géorgie and impasse de Louisiane.

Tours

For details on tours of the Verdun Battlefields, see p384.

Dragées (pronounced 'dra-**zhay**'; sugared almonds) – not to be confused with *draguer* (dra-**gay**), which means to chat up – have long been a Verdun speciality. There are tours (€2) of the **Braquier factory** (50 rue du Fort de Vaux), east of the centre, at 9.30am, 10.30am and 2.30pm on weekdays except Friday afternoon; reservations and ticketing are handled by the tourist office.

Sleeping

Auberge de Jeunesse (☎ 03 29 86 28 28; ajverdun@ wanadoo.fr; place Monseigneur Ginisty; dm €9.30; 🕒 reception 8am-12.30pm & 5-11pm Mon-Fri, 8-10am & 5-9pm Sat & Sun) This modern hostel, situated behind the cathedral, has 70 bunks of generous proportions. Rooms are accessible all day long; a kitchenette is available.

Hôtel Le Montaulbain (☎ 03 29 86 00 47; fax 03 29 84 75 70; 4 rue de la Vieille Prison; d with shower from €32, with shower & toilet €38) The 10 rooms at this family-run two-star place are cheerful, well-tended and fairly spacious.

Hôtel Les Colombes (☎ 03 29 86 05 46; 9 av Garibaldi; d €34; 🕒 reception closed Sun afternoon Nov-Feb) Named to honour the dove of peace, this family-run hostelry has practical, well-lit rooms with cheap rugs but real tile bathrooms. Has one star but offers two-star comfort.

Eating

Near the river, quite a few brasseries and fast-food joints are situated along attractive pedestrianised quai de Londres (a plaque on the wall near rue Beaurepaire explains the origin of the name).

Le Clapier (☎ 03 29 86 20 14; 34 rue des Gros Degrés; menu €13; 🕒 Mon-Sat) A real *restaurant du quartier* (neighbourhood restaurant), this

intimate place serves up traditional home cooking in a homey atmosphere.

Pizzeria Del Vicolo (☎ 03 29 83 93 93; 33 rue des Gros Degrés; 🕒 closed Sun & lunch Mon) Tasty pizzas from the wood-fired oven (€6.30 to €9.70), pasta dishes (€6.50 to €7.90) and meat mains (€8.20 to €11.90) are the specialities.

SELF-CATERING

The **food market** (rue Victor Hugo; 🕒 7am-12.30pm Fri & perhaps other days), renovated in 2004, is under the arches of the old covered market. The **Leclerc hypermarket** (🕒 9am-8pm Mon-Sat) is across the car park from the train station and there is a **Monoprix supermarket** (rue Mazel; 🕒 9am-noon & 2-7pm Mon-Sat, to 8.30pm Fri).

Drinking

Up for a pint in a friendly neighbourhood bar? Try **Le Lapin Qui Fume** (☎ 03 29 86 15 84; 31 rue des Gros Degrés; 🕒 11am-2am Tue-Sat, 6pm-2am Sun & Mon), which sometimes hosts live concerts.

Getting There & Around

Verdun's poorly served little train station, built by Eiffel in 1868, is linked to Metz (€11.40, 1¼ hours, three each weekday, one daily weekends), Nancy (€14.50, 1½ hours, two to four nondirect daily) and Paris' Gare de l'Est (€29.50 via Châlons-en-Champagne, 3½ hours, two to four daily).

You can park for free in the lots on av du 8 Mai 1945, rue des Tanneries and rue Léon Gambetta and next to the upper Citadelle.

Mountain bikes can be rented for €15 a day at **Cycles Flavenot** (☎ 03 29 86 12 43; rond-point des États-Unis; 🕒 9am-noon & 2-7pm Tue-Sat).

Taxis de Place (☎ 03 29 86 05 22 or 03 29 84 53 59) is based right in front of the tourist office.

VERDUN BATTLEFIELDS

Much of the Battle of Verdun (p385) was fought 5km to 8km (as the crow flies) northeast of Verdun. Today, the area – again forested – is served by the D913 and D112; by car follow the signs to the 'Champ de Bataille 14-18'. The opening hours given below may be modified in 2005.

Information & Tours

The Verdun tourist office (p382) can supply practical and historical information on the battlefields; books on offer include Alistaire Horne's *The Price of Glory: Verdun 1916* (€13) and Robert Graves' *Goodbye to All*

That (€9). The tourist office's four-hour minibus tours (€25.50 including entrance fees; English text available) of the five main battle sites begin at 2pm from May to mid-September.

Mémorial de Verdun

The village of Fleury, wiped off the face of the earth in the course of being captured and recaptured 16 times, is now the site of the **Mémorial de Verdun** (Musée Mémorial de Fleury; ☎ 03 29 84 35 34; adult/11-16 yrs €7/3.50; 🕑 9am-6pm Apr-early Sep, 9am-noon & 2-6pm early Sep-late Dec, Feb & Mar). The story of the battle is told using evocative (and in some cases gruesome) photos, documents, weapons and other objects; downstairs is a re-creation of the battlefield as it looked on the day the guns finally fell silent. Admission includes a film, available in English.

In the grassy crater-pocked centre of **Fleury**, a few hundred metres down the road from the memorial, signs among the low ruins indicate the village's former layout.

Ossuaire de Douaumont

The sombre, 137m-long **Douaumont Ossuary** (☎ 03 29 84 54 81), inaugurated in 1932, is one of France's most important WWI memorials. It contains the remains of about 130,000 unidentified French and German soldiers collected from the battlefields after the war. An excellent, 20-minute **audiovisual presentation** (adult/8-12 yrs €4/3; 🕑 no screenings in Jan or mornings in Dec & Feb) on the battle and its participants begins every 30 minutes from 9am to 11.30am and 2pm to sometime between 4.30pm (in November) and 6pm (May to August); there's no midday break from April to September. With the same ticket you can climb the 46m-high **bell tower**, which houses a small museum.

Fort de Douaumont

About 2km northeast of the Douaumont Ossuary on the highest of the area's hills stands **Fort de Douaumont** (☎ 03 29 84 41 91; adult/8-15 yrs €3/1.50; 🕑 9am-6.30pm Apr-Aug, 10am-noon & 2-6pm Sep-Mar, to 5pm Dec, closed Jan), the strongest of the 39 fortresses and bastions built along a 45km front to protect Verdun. Because the French high command disregarded warnings of an impending German offensive, Douaumont – whose 3km network of cold, dripping galleries was built between 1885 and 1912 – had only a skeleton crew when the Battle of Verdun began. By the fourth day it had been captured easily; four months later it was retaken by colonial troops from Morocco.

Tranchée des Baïonnettes

On 12 June 1916 two companies of the 137th Infantry Regiment of the French army were

---

THE BATTLE OF VERDUN

The outbreak of WWI in August 1914 was followed on the Western Front by a long period of trench warfare in which neither side made any significant gains. To break the stalemate, the Germans decided to change tactics, attacking a target so vital for both military and symbolic reasons that the French would throw every man they had into its defence. These troops would then be slaughtered, 'bleeding France white' and causing the French people to lose their will to resist. The target selected for this bloody plan by the German general staff was the heavily fortified city of Verdun.

The Battle of Verdun began on the morning of 21 February 1916. After the heaviest shelling of the war to that date (something like two million shells were fired in 10 hours), German forces went on the attack and advanced with little opposition for four days, capturing, among other unprepared French positions, Fort de Douaumont. Thus began a 300-day battle fought by hundreds of thousands of cold, wet, miserable and ill-fed men, sheltering in their muddy trenches and foxholes amid a moonscape of craters.

French forces were regrouped and rallied by General Philippe Pétain (later the leader of the collaborationist Vichy government during WWII), who slowed the German advance by launching several French counterattacks. He also oversaw the resupply of Verdun via the **Voie Sacrée** (Sacred Way), the 75km road from Bar-le-Duc, maintained by territorial troops from Senegal. The Germans weren't pushed back beyond their positions of February 1916 until American troops and French forces launched a coordinated offensive in September 1918.

sheltering in their *tranchées* (trenches), *baïonnettes* (bayonets) fixed, waiting for a ferocious artillery bombardment to end. It never did – the incoming shells covered their positions with mud and debris, burying them alive. They weren't found until three years later, when someone spotted several hundred bayonet tips sticking out of the ground. The victims were left where they died, their bayonets still poking through the soil. The site is always open. The tree-filled valley across the D913 is known as the **Ravin de la Mort** (Ravine of Death).

Fort de Vaux

On 1 June 1916 German troops managed to enter the tunnel system of the **Fort de Vaux** (☎ 03 29 88 32 88; adult/8-15 yrs €3/1.50; ⏰ 9am-6.30pm Apr-Sep, 10am-5pm Oct-Mar, closed Jan), attacking the French defenders from inside their own ramparts. After six days and seven nights of brutal, metre-by-metre combat along the narrow passageways (the most effective weapons were grenades, flame throwers and poison gas) the steadfast French defenders, dying of thirst (drops of moisture off the walls had become their only water source), were forced to surrender. The fort was re-captured by the French five months later.

The interior of Vaux, built between 1881 and 1912 and encased in 2.5m of concrete, is smaller, more reconstructed and less dreary – and thus less interesting – than Douaumont.

Fort de Souville

This unrestored fort (built 1875–77), some of whose underground galleries have collapsed, sits in the **Forêt Domaniale de Verdun** (Verdun Forest) on a gravel track linked to the D112 and D913. All around, post-war trees and undergrowth sprout from shell craters and traces of the trench lines. Nature heals all – but very, slowly.

AMERICAN MEMORIALS

The largest US military cemetery in Europe, the WWI **Meuse-Argonne American Cemetery**, is at Romagne-sous-Montfaucon, 41km north-west of Verdun along the D38 and D123. Just east of Montfaucon d'Argonne (about 10km southeast of the cemetery), a 58m-high column atop the 336m-high **Butte de Montfaucon** commemorates the US 1st Army's Meuse-Argonne offensive of 1918.

About 40km southeast of Verdun, the WWI **St-Mihiel American Cemetery** is on the outskirts of Thiaucourt-Regniéville. From there, a 15km drive to the southwest takes you to the 375m-high **Butte de Montsec**, site of a US monument with a bronze relief map surrounded by a round, neoclassical colonnade.

The WWII **Lorraine American Cemetery** is about 45km east of Metz just outside of St-Avold.

These sites are managed by the **American Battle Monuments Commission** (www.abmc.gov).

FORT DE FERMONT

One of the larger underground fortresses on the Maginot Line (p344), **Fermont** (☎ 03 82 39 35 34; www.ligne-maginot-fort-de-fermont.asso.fr) is approximately 56km north of Verdun. Around 30m deep, it withstood three days of heavy bombardment when the Germans attacked on 21 June 1940 but surrendered a few days later. During the 2½-hour tour (adult/seven to 12 years €5/3), in English for Anglophone groups (the rest of the time a written translation is available), a small electric trolley transports you from one subterranean army block to another. Tours begin between 2pm and 4.30pm daily from July to 19 September, at 3pm Monday to Friday in May and June and at 2pm and 3.30pm on Saturday, Sunday and holidays from April to June and 20 September to October.

The Loire

THE LOIRE

Some French words are understood the world over. 'Chateau' is one of them. Its very mention inspires images of grand towers rising to the heavens, of extravagant dining rooms for hundreds of guests, of exquisite gardens and shimmering moats. It says banquets, balls and decadence; crystal chandeliers and candelabras. It encapsulates both the intrigue of French history and our vision of romantic France. It's a word that belongs to the Loire Valley.

From the 15th to the 18th centuries, this area served as the playground of kings, princes, dukes and nobles, who expended family fortunes and the wealth of the nation to turn it into a vast neighbourhood of lavish (and not-so-lavish) chateaux. The result is a rich and concentrated collection of architectural treasures – indeed, its historical importance was recognised in 2000 when Unesco named the entire region a World Heritage Site. The Renaissance architecture to be found at Chambord, Chaumont, Chenonceau and Azay-le-Rideau is truly stunning; earlier defensive fortresses, simpler in design but no less significant, can be glimpsed at Angers, Chinon and Loches. Numerous other chateaux, big and small, dot the landscape.

The Loire is France's longest, most regal river. From its source in the Massif Central, it follows a 1020km course through Bourgogne, Orléanais, Blésois, Touraine and Anjou, into the Atlantic. It cuts a wide, flat valley through stunning countryside, making cycling a popular way to get around, although amateur cyclists should be aware that up to 50km can be clocked up for a return trip to just one chateau.

There are other attractions here too – religious architecture, curious caves and regional gastronomy in particular – but make no mistake, the real stars of the Loire are, in a word, the chateaux.

HIGHLIGHTS

- Explore the lifestyle of early royalty at the huge, gracious **Château de Chambord** (p401)
- Enjoy the quiet grandeur of **Chenonceau** (p410), a beautiful château built on the River Cher
- Splash out on a luxurious stay at **Château de Brissac** (p395)
- Take in the views of the Loire Valley from on high with a **hot-air balloon ride** (p401)
- Sniff out the vineyards and of **Sancerre** (p395) & **Vouvray** (p409)
- Try out the numerous restaurants in **Tours** (p407) and drinking at bustling **place Plumereau** (p408)
- Experience history through the sound-and-light show at eclectic **Château de Blois** (p397)
- Marvel at the control of the dog trainers at La Soupe des Chiens at **Château de Cheverny** (p402)

- POPULATION: 2,220,039
- AREA: 26,411 SQ KM

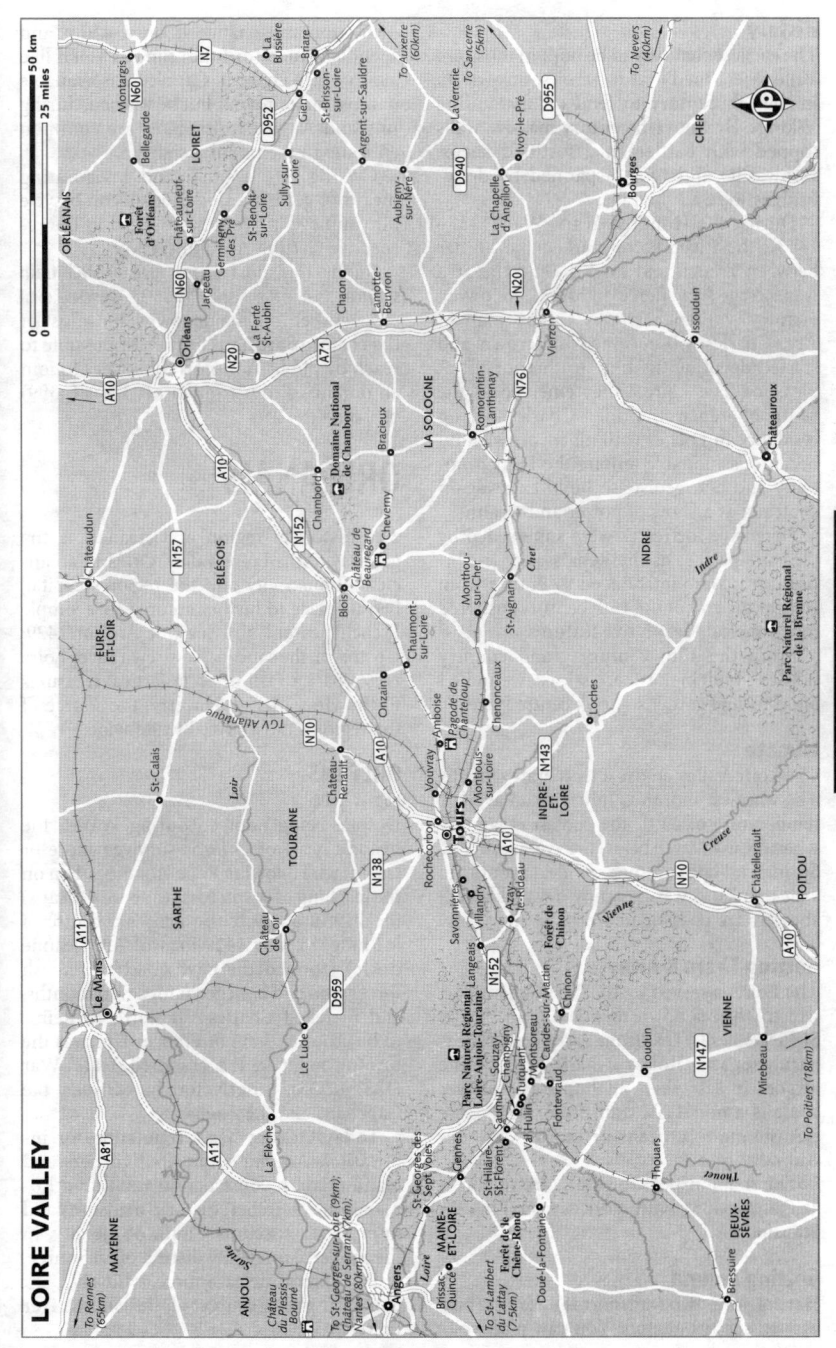

LOIRE VALLEY

THE LOIRE

History

The earliest chateaux to be built in the Loire Valley were medieval fortresses, thrown up in the 9th century to fend off marauding Vikings. By the 11th century massive walls topped with battlements, fortified keeps, arrow slits and moats spanned by drawbridges were all the rage.

During the Hundred Years' War (1337–1453), the River Loire marked the border between French and English, and the area was ravaged by fierce fighting. Following victory by French troops led by Joan of Arc, Charles VII regained his crown and started devoting his time to the pursuit of pleasure. The Loire Valley emerged as the centre of French court life – Charles took up residence in Loches with his mistress and it became fashionable among the French nobility and bourgeoisie to build extravagant chateaux as a show of power and wealth.

Defensive fortresses were superseded by pleasure palaces as the Renaissance (its innovations were introduced to France from Italy at the end of the 15th century) ushered in whimsical, decorative features.

From the 17th century grand country houses – built in the neoclassical style and set amid formal gardens – took centre stage.

Climate

The Loire Valley enjoys a temperate climate. The warmest month is July with an average temperature of 25°C, the coolest is January when it can fall well below the average of 5°C. Spring and late summer are ideal months to visit thanks to warm, sunny days, although showers are possible in any season.

Getting There & Away

The Loire is served by the TGV Atlantique, which whizzes down to Tours (and nearby St-Pierre des Corps) from Paris' Gare Montparnasse and Roissy Charles de Gaulle airport in less than an hour. The slower route is a non-TGV train from Paris' Gare d'Austerlitz to Orléans or nearby Gare des Aubrais-Orléans.

The main airport for the Loire region is at Tours (p408), with services from London Stansted.

Getting Around

Having your own transport is by far the best way to see the region. You can plan your own itinerary, change it on a whim and spend as much (or little) time as you'd like at any given chateau. Car rental is available in most major towns, but be warned, during July and August traffic jams are common en route to the popular sights.

Cycling is a popular and invigorating means of getting around; details on bicycle hire and cycling routes are listed in the respective Getting Around sections.

Public transport is not great. **SNCF train services** (national enquiries ☎ 36 35; www.sncf.com) run between the major towns, but most of the chateaux are hard or even impossible to reach by public transport. It's easier to join an organised tour from either Blois (p399) or Tours (p410).

ORLÉANAIS

The historical region of Orléanais is the gateway to the Loire Valley. Orléans, an ancient Roman city and the region's capital, had its place in history secured by a simple French peasant girl, Joan of Arc, in 1429. Upstream, the sand-bank-strewn River Loire twists past a rash of ecclesiastical treasures to the vineyards of Sancerre, the source of the region's most prized white wine.

ORLÉANS

pop 112,600

Despite being bombed during WWII, the historic heart of Orléans survived more or less intact. Following Pope Honorius' ban on the teaching of law in Paris (but not Orléans) in 1219, the city blossomed as a centre of learning. In May 1429 Joan of Arc (Jeanne d'Arc) stormed the city, smashed English forces who had besieged it for seven months, and marched Charles VII north to Reims to be crowned king of France. This was the turning point in the Hundred Years' War (1337–1453), bitterly fought between the Capetians and the English.

Today Orléans has a reputation for innovation. Among some tired corners and bland modern construction you'll find Romanesque churches, historic mansions and impressive museums. South of the city, in the modern university district of La Source, is Parc Floral de la Source, a lovely park containing the source of the short river Loiret.

Orientation

The River Loire snakes along the southern fringe of the city centre. Rue de la République links place du Martroi, the main square, with the central train station (Gare d'Orléans) and the adjoining Centre Commercial place d'Arc, a shopping complex that lies 400m to the north. The station for trains to and from Paris (Gare des Aubrais-Orléans) is 2km further north from Gare d'Orléans. The historic quarter of the city is east of place du Martroi, along rue Jeanne d'Arc.

Information

INTERNET ACCESS

BSP Info (☎ 02 38 77 02 82; 125 rue Bannier; per hr €4; ☽ 10am-8pm Tue-Sat, 2-8pm Sun & Mon)

Médiatheque (☎ 02 38 65 45 37; per hr €3.60; 1 place Gambetta; ☽ 10am-6pm Tue, Wed, Fri & Sat, 1-8pm Thu)

Odysseus Cyber Café (☎ 02 38 77 98 48; 32 rue du Colombier; per hr €4.50; ☽ 9am-9pm Mon-Wed, 9am-1am Thu & Fri, 11am-1am Sat)

MONEY

There are several commercial banks on place du Martroi. The post office at place du Général de Gaulle deals with currency exchange.

POST

Post Office (place du Général de Gaulle)

TOURIST INFORMATION

Espace d'Accueil Touristique (☎ 02 38 53 33 44; 6 rue Jeanne d'Arc; ☽ 2-5pm Tue-Sat, 10am-noon Sun)

Tourist Office (☎ 02 38 24 05 05; www.ville-orleans.fr; 6 rue Albert 1er; ☽ 10am-1pm & 2-6.30pm Mon, 9am-1pm & 2-6.30pm Tue-Sat)

Sights

HÔTEL GROSLOT

A flamboyant, Renaissance-style *hôtel particulier* (private mansion), **Hôtel Groslot** (☎ 02 38 79 22 30; place de l'Étape; admission free; ☽ 10am-noon & 2-6pm Sun-Fri, 4.30-6pm Sat Oct-Jun, 5-8pm Sat Jul-Aug) was built between 1550 and 1552 for Jacques Groslot, a city bailiff whose family lived here until 1790 when the French Revolution turned it into the town hall. Its lavish interior dates from 1850–54. The bedroom in which the 17-year-old king of France François II died in 1560 is today used as a marriage hall. Guided tours are possible on request.

MUSÉE DES BEAUX ARTS

The **Musée des Beaux Arts** (Museum of Fine Arts; ☎ 02 38 79 21 55; 1 rue Fernand Rabier; adult/student €3/1.60; ☽ 9.30am-12.15pm & 1.30-5.45pm Tue-Sat, 2-6pm Sun) houses an impressive collection of European art from the 15th to 20th centuries. Numerous religious works of art and treasures from surrounding chateaux that were seized during the French Revolution are among the displays.

CATHÉDRALE STE-CROIX

Orléans' Flamboyant Gothic **Cathédrale Ste-Croix** (☎ 02 38 77 87 50; place Ste-Croix; admission free; ☽ 9.15am-noon & 2.15-6pm), was built under Henri IV from 1601. Louis XIII (1610–43) had the choir and nave restored, Louis XIV (1638–1715) built the transept, and the next two Louis (1715–74) rebuilt the western façade and its towers. The spire (1858) completed the project. **Stained-glass windows** (1895) in the lower nave depict the life of Joan of Arc, France's patron saint who was canonised in 1920.

MAISON DE JEANNE D'ARC

The timber-framed **Maison de Jeanne d'Arc** (☎ 02 38 52 99 89; 3 place du Général de Gaulle; adult/student €2/1; ☽ 10am-12.15pm & 1.30-6pm Tue-Sun May-Oct, 1.30-6pm Tue-Sun Nov-Apr) is a reconstruction of the 15th-century house where Joan of Arc stayed for 11 days in April and May 1429. The original building was destroyed during WWII. Timber beams from a house dating from the same era were used to build the current edifice in 1965. The building houses an exhibition dedicated to the 17-year-old virgin warrior.

Festivals & Events

Since 1430 the Orléanais have celebrated the annual **Fête Johanniques**, which falls around 8 May and commemorates Joan of Arc's liberation of the city. A week of street parties, medieval costume parades and concerts climaxes with a solemn Mass at the cathedral.

Sleeping

Decent budget accommodation is scarce in Orléans, although a few cheaper hotels can be found on rue du Faubourg Bannier just north of place Gambetta. Better to spend a bit more on the good-value mid-range options. Most hotel reception desks close on Sunday afternoons.

THE LOIRE

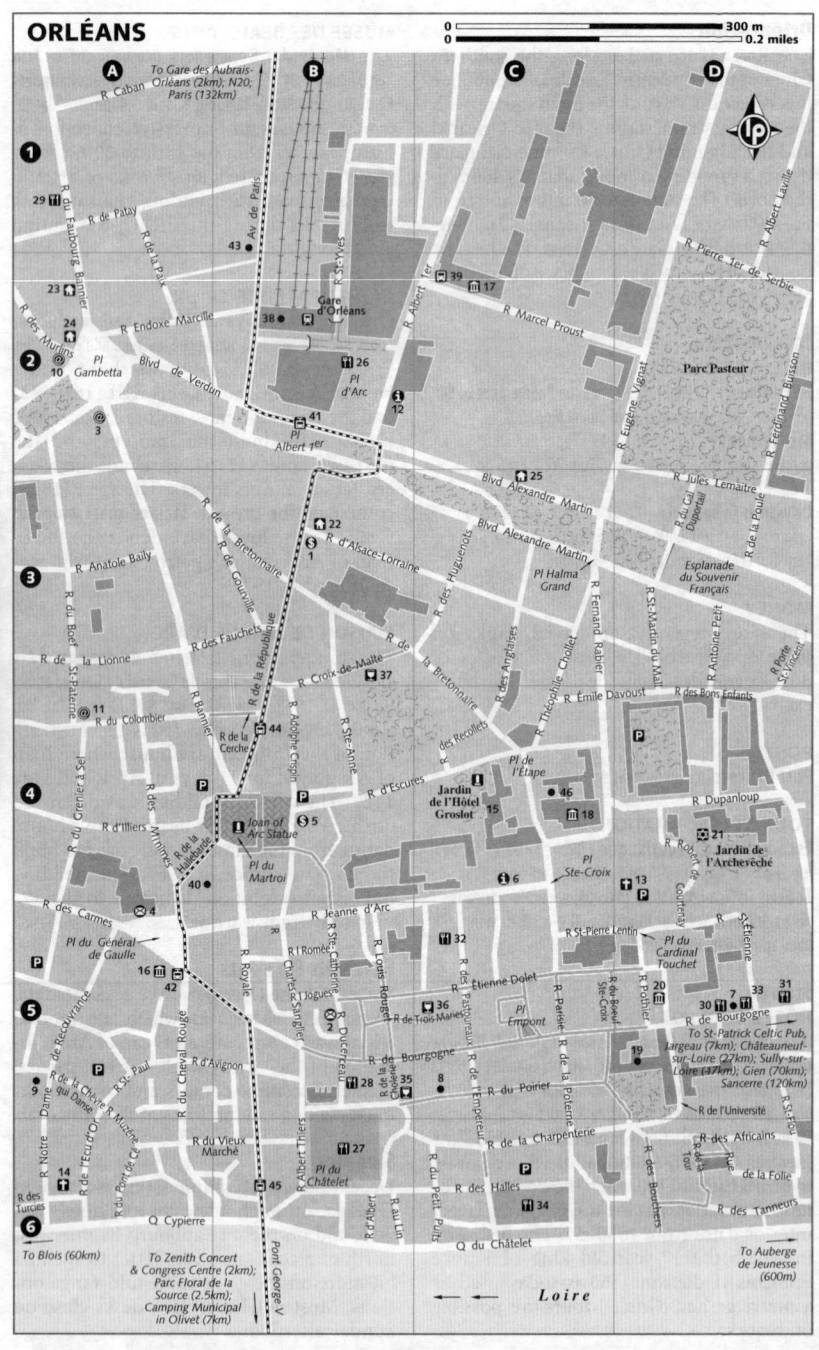

ORLÉANS

To Gare des Aubrais-Orléans (2km); N20; Paris (132km)

INFORMATION		Musée des Beaux Arts	18 C4	L'Estaminet	33 D5
Banque de France	1 B3	Prefecture	19 D5	Marché de la Charpenterie	34 C6
Branch Post Office	2 B5	Salle des Thèses	20 D5		
BSP Info	3 A2	Synagogue	21 D4	DRINKING	(p394)
Central Post Office	4 A5			Bel Air	35 B5
Crédit Lyonnais	5 B4	SLEEPING	(pp391–3)	Cats des Trois Maries	36 C5
Espace d'Acceuil Touristique	6 C4	Hôtel de l'Abeille	22 B3	Le Saint-Andrews	37 B3
Laundrette	7 D5	Hôtel Le Bannier	23 A2		
Laundrette	8 C5	Hôtel St Aignan	24 A2	TRANSPORT	(p394)
Laundrette	9 A5	Hôtel St-Martin	25 C3	Avis	38 B2
Médiatheque	10 A2			Bus Station	39 C2
Odysseus Cyber Café	11 A4	EATING	(pp393–4)	Espace Transport	40 A4
Tourist Office	12 B2	Carrefour Supermarket	(see 26)	Gare d'Orléans Tram Stop	41 B2
		Centre Commercial Place d'Arc	26 B2	Général de Gaulle Tram Stop	42 A5
SIGHTS & ACTIVITIES	(p391)	Covered Market	27 B6	Rent-Van & Car Ecoto	43 B1
Cathédrale Ste-Croix	13 D4	Espace Canal	28 B5	République Tram Stop	44 B4
Église Notre Dame de Recouvrance	14 A6	Intermarché Supermarket	29 A1	Royale Châtelet Tram Stop	45 B6
Hôtel Groslot	15 C4	La Petite Marmite	30 D5		
Maison de Jeanne d'Arc	16 A5	Le Gargantua	31 D5	OTHER	
Musée d'Orléans	17 C2	Le KT	32 C5	Hôtel de Ville	46 C4

BUDGET

Auberge de Jeunesse (☎ 02 38 53 60 06; asse.crjs@
libertysurf.fr; 1 blvd de la Motte-Sanguin; dm €7, sheets €2.50;
reception ⏰ 8am-9.30pm) Occupying an impos-
ing neoclassical building in a park east of
the town centre, this hostel has mainly small
dorms with two beds and a shower. Take bus
SY to the 'Pont Bourgogne' stop.

Hôtel Le Bannier (☎ 02 38 53 25 86; 13 rue du
Faubourg Bannier; r with shower €25, with bath & toilet €28)
This zero-star hotel above a bar is a cheer-
ful place for budget travellers, once you get
past the moody cigar-smoking patron. The
simple rooms hold the record for world's
thinnest walls.

Camping

Camping Municipal (☎ 02 38 63 53 94; fax 02 38 63
58 96; rue du Pont Bouchet; camping €14.20; ⏰ Apr–mid-
Oct) This camping ground is 7km south of
Orléans in Olivet.

MID-RANGE

Hôtel St Aignan (☎ 02 38 53 15 35; www.contact
-hotel.com; 3 place Gambetta; s/d from €45/51; ℗) This
high-rise two-star hotel is modern, comfortable and spacious – the bathrooms are
as big as some bedrooms in town. Popular
with business travellers.

Hôtel de l'Abeille (☎ 02 38 53 54 87; www.ho
teldelabeille.com in French; 64 rue Alsace-Lorraine; r with
toilet/shower from €37/42) On the edge of the
pedestrian zone, this lovingly restored,
century-old hotel is furnished with beautiful antiques and Jeanne d'Arc memorabilia. The creaky floorboards can definitely
be excused; this is good value for such a
charming place.

Hôtel St-Martin (☎ 02 38 62 47 47; www.hotel
-orleans-st-martin.com; 52 blvd Alexandre Martin; d with/

without shower & toilet €43/35) This friendly, tidy
hotel near the station has well-furnished
rooms and showers of the small, plastic capsule variety. It's on a main road; rooms at
the back are quieter.

Eating

The stretch of rue du Bourgogne between
the *préfecture* and rue St-Etienne is loaded
with places to eat. Take your pick from
Moroccan, Indian, Chinese and plenty of
French eateries.

Le Gargantua (☎ 02 38 54 30 80; 136 rue Bourgogne; menus €13-25) Among an appropriate
setting of wooden beams and red-checked
tablecloths you can sample the cuisine of
times gone by such as veal's head, tongue
and *andouille* (tripe sausage). Not for the
faint-hearted – or vegetarian.

L'Estaminet (☎ 02 38 54 27 57; 148 rue Bourgogne;
mains €8-14) A small, atmospheric place serving French fare with an international twist.
The delicious foie gras tagliatelle is a popular
speciality. With only seven tables, it's wise to
book ahead in busy periods.

La Petite Marmite (☎ 02 38 54 23 83; 178 rue de
Bourgogne; mains €14-22, menus €20 & €32; ✗) Warm,
cosy and always busy, this nonsmoking restaurant in a beautiful old timber-framed
house serves up tasty regional fare.

Espace Canal (☎ 02 38 62 04 30; 6 rue Ducerceau;
dishes €11-13; ⏰ lunch Mon-Fri, dinner Thu-Sat) A unique cellar restaurant where you can swirl,
sip and swallow or spit local wines while
feasting on fine French food. A prestigious
place, let down only by the uncomfortable
chrome chairs.

Le KT (☎ 02 38 52 90 69; 13 rue des Pastoureaux;
menu €5.30, plat du jour €5; ⏰ 11.30am-2pm Mon-Fri) A
canteen run by catering students.

THE LOIRE

SELF-CATERING
Snack food and cafés abound along Rue de Bourgogne. **Marché de la Charpenterie** (rue des Halles; 4-10.30am Tue, Thu & Sat) is an outdoor market. The **covered market** (place du Châtelet; 7.30am-7pm Tue-Sun) also has a good selection of fresh produce.

There is an **Intermarché supermarket** (49 rue du Faubourg Bannier), as well as a massive **Carrefour supermarket** inside the Centre Commercial place d'Arc.

Drinking
Bel Air (02 38 77 08 06; 44 rue du Poirier; 6pm-1am Tue-Sat) The bar of the moment is the sophisticated Bel Air. All atmospheric red lights, soft furnishings, mellow house tunes and €10 cocktails.

Cats des Trois Maries (02 38 54 68 68; 2 rue des Trois Maries; 6pm-3am Wed-Sat) The spot for jazz, blues and funk, with live bands from 9.30pm Friday and Saturday.

Other busy drinking holes include the Irish **St-Patrick Celtic Pub** (02 38 54 53 50; 1 rue de Bourgogne; noon-1am) and **Le St-Andrews** (02 38 54 44 00; 15 rue Croix-de-Malte; 1pm-1am Tue-Sat), a very British pub.

Entertainment
What's-on listings fill **Orléans Poche** (www.orleanspoche.com in French), a free monthly events magazine available at the tourist office.

The tourist office **billetterie** (02 38 24 05 05) sells tickets for choral concerts at Cathédrale Ste-Croix and classical (and occasionally rock) concerts at **Zénith** (02 38 25 05 05; 1 rue President Schuman), the city's concert and congress centre.

Getting There & Away
BUS
From the **bus station** (02 38 53 94 75; 1 rue Marcel Proust), **Les Rapides du Val de Loire** (02 38 61 90 00; www.rvl-info.com in French) operates buses to/from Châteauneuf-sur-Loire (€5.40, 35 minutes, four to six daily), Gien (€11.40, 1¾ hours, one daily) and Jargeau (€4.30, 45 minutes, three daily).

CAR
There is an office of **Avis** (02 38 62 27 04; 8am-noon) inside the central train station. **Rent-Van & Car Ecoto** (02 38 77 92 92; 19 av de Paris), which is behind the Ibis hotel, offers competitive rates.

TRAIN
Shuttle trains (every eight minutes) link the **central train station** (Gare d'Orléans; 02 38 79 91 00; 1 rue St-Yves) with Gare des Aubrais-Orléans, 2km north.

From Orléans, most westbound trains along the Loire Valley stop at both train stations, including trains to/from Blois (€8.60, 30 minutes, about 20 trains daily), St-Pierre des Corps (€14.70, one to two hours, six daily), Nantes (€32.10, 2½ hours, three daily) and Tours (€14.80, 1¼ to 1¾ hours, four daily).

Most trains to/from Paris' Gare d'Austerlitz use Gare des Aubrais-Orléans (€15.50, one hour, 10 to 15 daily) but some continue on to central Gare d'Orléans.

Getting Around
Tickets and timetables for Semtao city buses and trams are available at **Espace Transport** (02 38 71 98 38; rue de la Hallebarde; 9am-6.30pm Mon-Sat). It sells Liberté tickets (€3) allowing unlimited travel on buses and trams. Otherwise one-way tram/bus tickets purchased from the driver cost €1.20.

Orléans' 18km north–south tramline links Gare des Aubrais-Orléans with the central train station, rue de la République and place du Général de Gaulle in the centre of town, and the Parc Floral de la Source on the Loire's southern banks.

ORLÉANS TO SULLY-SUR-LOIRE
Medieval chateaux are overshadowed by ecclesiastical treasures along the eastern stretch of the River Loire between Orléans and Sully-sur-Loire. Its northern bank is flanked by the elk-rich **Forêt d'Orléans**, 38,234 hectares and the only place in France to shelter nesting osprey.

The riverside town of **Jargeau** (population 3561), which is 20km east of Orléans, is home to the Confrèrie des Chevaliers du Goûte Andouille (Tripe Sausage Brotherhood), dedicated to *andouille* – a fat tripe sausage, typical to the region, and sold at Monsieur Guibet's *charcuterie* at 14 place du Matroi.

The history of trade along the mighty River Loire comes alive in the **Musée de la Marine** (02 38 46 84 46; 1 place Aristide Briand; adult/child €5/2.50; 10am-6pm Wed-Mon Apr-Oct, 2-6pm Wed-Mon Nov-Mar), a marine museum that is housed in an 11th- to 17th-century chateau in **Châteauneuf-sur-Loire**, 7km further east. The **tourist office** (☎ 02 38 58 44 79; 3 place Aristide Briand; 9.30am-12.30am & 2-7pm Mon-Sat Jun-Sep, to 6pm Oct-Mar) has information on cycling routes in the area.

In **Germigny des Prés**, 6km further east, the historically significant **Église de Germigny des Prés** is a rare example of Carolingian architecture. Dating to AD 806, this is one of France's oldest churches. The Greek-cross-shaped floor plan and 9th-century mosaic in its eastern apse are unique.

The 11th-century Romanesque **Basilique de St-Benoît** in **St-Benoît-sur-Loire**, 12km further east, shelters the relics of St Benedict (480–547). The heavily ornamented capitals supporting the monumental porch tower illustrate scenes from the Bible's Book of Revelations.

Château de Sully-sur-Loire (☎ 02 38 36 36 86; adult/child €5/3.50; 10am-6pm Apr-Sep, 10am-noon & 2-5pm Feb-Mar & Oct-Dec), with its fairy-tale moats and its thick-set towers, is a quintessential medieval fortress. It was built at the end of the 14th century to defend one of the River Loire's few crossings.

Sleeping & Eating

The **tourist office** (☎ 02 38 36 23 70; ot.sully.sur .loire@wanadoo.fr; place du Général de Gaulle; 9.30am-12.30pm & 2-7pm Mon-Sat May-Sep, 9.30am-noon & 2.30-6.30pm Tue-Sat Oct-Apr) in Sully-sur-Loire has accommodation details.

Hôtel de la Poste (☎ 02 38 36 26 22; fax 02 38 36 39 35; 11 rue Faubourg St-Germain; d from €46; P) in the village has comfortable rooms. The lovely courtyard **restaurant** (menu €15) dishes up memorable cuisine.

La Ferme des Châtaigniers (☎ 02 38 36 51 98; chemin des Châtaigniers; lunch menu €18, dinner menus €19-34) restaurant is run by a young couple who enthusiastically welcome guests to their rustic old chestnut farm, 2.5km west of Sully-sur-Loire off the D951.

LIVE LIKE A KING

Living in a château may be beyond the reach of most of us, but it is possible to experience the romantic magic of château life by staying in one of these *châteaux chambres d'hôtes*. You can't send the staff to the gallows on a whim but in most cases you'll get a queen-size bed, and breakfast fit for a king. These are our top five choices; a useful website for others is www .chateaux-france.com.

Château de Brissac (☎ 02 41 91 22 21; www.chateau-brissac.fr; r incl breakfast €390, dinner €77; P) The huge, extravagantly furnished rooms have to be seen to be believed: antique four-poster beds, wood panelling, hidden doors and historically significant tapestries are unique extras you won't get anywhere else. The chateau itself is grand, tall and set in well-tended gardens. All round, an exceptional experience and worth the royal price tag for the finest rooms, and setting, in the Loire.

Château de Verrieres (☎ 02 41 38 05 15; http://chateau-verrieres.com; 53 rue d'Alsace, Saumur; r €120-240, dinner €38; P   ) An elegant town chateau in the southwest of Saumur (p423) set in four acres of a tree-filled English park. It was built in 1890 and inside, the furnishings and décor remain pretty much as they were then – graceful, refined and ornate.

Château des Réaux (☎ 02 47 95 14 40; www.allchateaux.com/chateau-reaux.html; d incl breakfast €120-250; P) With its moat, brick and stone cheeseboard-effect towers and flower-filled garden this little chateau is undeniably beautiful. The rooms are not as grand as at some of the other chateau on offer, but it is a family home rather than a royal residence. Also open to day visitors between March and November. It's 12km north of Chinon (p416); take the D749 towards Bourgueil, and turn off onto the D238.

Château de la Verrerie (☎ 02 48 81 51 60; www.chateaux-france.com/verrerie; d €140-395; P) This 16th-century chateau was built as a summer house for the Scottish Stuart clan. It's in an idyllic spot, edging a tranquil lake and surrounded by forest. There are 12 luxury rooms, a 1.6km lake-side walking trail and a handy heliport on site. It's 8km north of Château d'Ivoy in Aubigny-sur-Nère.

Château d'Ivoy (☎ 02 48 58 85 01; chateau.divoy@wanadoo.fr; d incl breakfast €170; P   ) A modestly sized 16th to 17th-century chateau set in 10 hectares of prime hunting land. The six spacious rooms are exquisitely decorated with period furnishings. Dogs can be accommodated in the kennels. It's 30km west of Sancerre (p396) on the D12 in Ivoy-le-Pré.

GIEN TO SANCERRE

Corn and asparagus fields line the southern banks of the Loire from Sully-sur-Loire to picture-postcard **Gien** (population 16,477), 23km east. The town is known for its distinctive *bleu de Gien* earthenware, and bridle paths, ideal for cycling, skirt the river.

From Gien, the GR3 shadows the river on its course to Briare. Privately owned 17th-century **Château de la Bussière** (☎ 02 38 35 93 35; adult/child €7/4; ⏱ Apr-Sep), which showcases fishing memorabilia and a 13th-century vegetable garden, and **Château de St-Brisson** (☎ 02 38 36 71 29; €7/4; ⏱ Apr-Sep), known for its display of medieval stone-fed war machines, can be visited en route.

The industrial town of **Briare**, 15km east of Gien, is of little interest beyond its magnificent Art Nouveau canal bridge that spans the Loire. Built from iron between 1604 and 1642, the 662m canal bridge is Europe's longest. **Cruises** (adult/child €6/1; ⏱ Apr-Nov) depart from **Port de Commerce** (☎ 02 38 37 12 75), in Briare and take 1½ hours.

The vineyards around **Sancerre** produce the region's best-known white wine. The **tourist office** (☎ 02 48 54 08 21; www.sancerre.net; Nouvelle Place; ⏱ 10am-12.30pm & 2.30-5.30pm daily Apr–mid-Nov, closed Sun rest of year), in the village, has a list of places where you can taste and buy the local vintage.

Château d'Ivoy (p395) and Château de la Verrerie (p395), both west of Sancerre, are two remarkable places to stay and eat.

BOURGES

pop 76,000

The bustling city of Bourges is in the Berry region, southwest of Sancerre on the D955. Not part of the Loire Valley castle circuit, Bourges is known for its maze of cobbled streets, its culinary specialities and – above all – its magnificent cathedral. First settled by the Gauls, Bourges was the home of the future king Charles VII and later the centre of arms production under Napoleon III. Evening illuminations between May and August show the town in its best light.

The **tourist office** (☎ 02 48 23 02 60; www.ville-bourges.fr; 21 rue Victor Hugo; ⏱ 9am-7pm Apr-Sep, 9am-6pm Mon-Fri & 2-5pm Sun Oct-Mar) is opposite the cathedral. Bourges is south of Gien along the D940, and on direct train lines from Orléans, Nantes and Tours; from Paris, change at Vierzon.

Cathédrale St-Étienne (☎ 02 48 65 49 44; place Étienne Dolet), a gothic masterpiece begun by Henri de Sully in 1195, has impressive medieval stained-glass windows and an incredible astronomical clock, designed in 1424 as a wedding present to Charles VII and Marie d'Anjou.

Hotel Le Berry (☎ 02 48 65 99 30; www.le-berry.com in French; 3 place Général Leclerc; r €55-62; P 🐾), opposite the station, is a large hotel with modern rooms.

There are a few lively places to eat on rue Porte Jaune, just north of the cathedral, including **Le Latino** (☎ 02 48 65 26 37; 17 rue Porte Jaune; menus €10-15) with Latin American specialities and English *menus*.

LA SOLOGNE

The French associate the soggy wetland of La Sologne with one thing: hunting. A vast 490,000 hectares of ponds and woodland between the Rivers Loire and Cher, it has forests rich in deer, while eels, carp and pike fill its lakes and rivers.

La Sologne's 'capital' is Romorantin-Lanthenay, 41km southeast of Blois on the D765, a pretty little town straddling the River Sauldre. The **tourist office** (☎ 02 54 76 43 89; www.tourisme-romorantin.com in French; ⏱ 10am-12.15pm & 2-6.30pm Mon, 8.45am-12.15pm & 1.30-6.30pm Tue-Fri, 8.45am-12.15pm & 2-6pm Sat year-round, plus 1am-noon Sun & holidays) has free brochures on driving and walking tours in the area.

La Sologne became a royal hunting playground under François I (r 1515–47). Years of war, disease and floods turned the area into waterlogged, malaria-infested swamp until the mid-19th century, when the plateau was drained by Napoleon III and regained its hunting prestige. Today the private hunting lifestyles of the rich and famous are unapologetically revealed in the **Maison du Braconnage** (House of Poaching; ☎ 02 54 88 68 68; adult/7-18 yrs €3/2.30; ⏱ 2-6pm Wed-Mon Jul-Sep, 2-6pm Wed, Sat, Sun & holidays Apr-Jun & Oct–mid-Nov), which is in Chaon (about 11km east of Lamotte-Beuvron).

Aside from hunting, La Sologne is known for *tarte Tatin*, the famous and delicious upside-down apple tart accidentally created in 1888 by the Tatin sisters from Lamotte-Beuvron a small town south of Orléans on the N20.

There's an unexpectedly stylish hotel in town, the four-star **Grand Hotel du Lion d'Or**

MICHAEL GEBICKI

Vineyards along the scenic Route Touristique du Champagne (p331) near Reims

Cathédrale Notre Dame (p348), Strasbourg

CHRIS MELLOR

ELLIOT GERARD DANIEL

Half-timbered houses in the old city of Troyes (p336)

CHRIS MELLOR

Street cafés and wrought ironworks, place Stanislas, (p372) Nancy

SALLY D

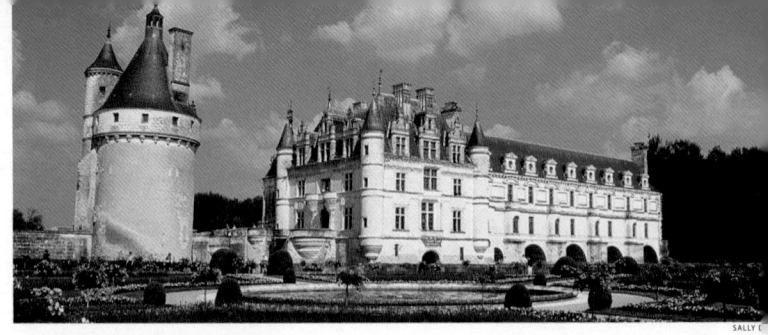

Château de Chenonceau (p410), Loire Valley

RUSSELL MOUNTFORD

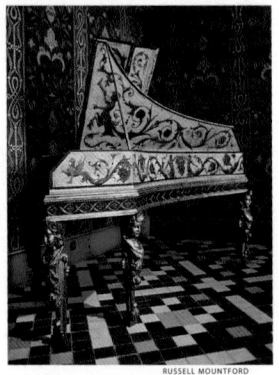

Ornate keyboard, Château de Blois (p397), Loire Valley

BETHUNE CARMICHAEL

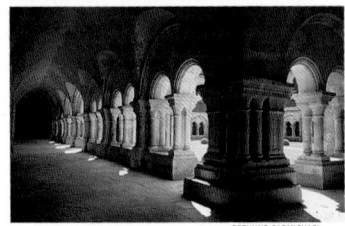

Cloisters of Abbaye de Fontenay (p459), near Dijon

Hôtel-Dieu des Hospices de Beaune (p454) on the Côte d'Or

CHRISTOPHER

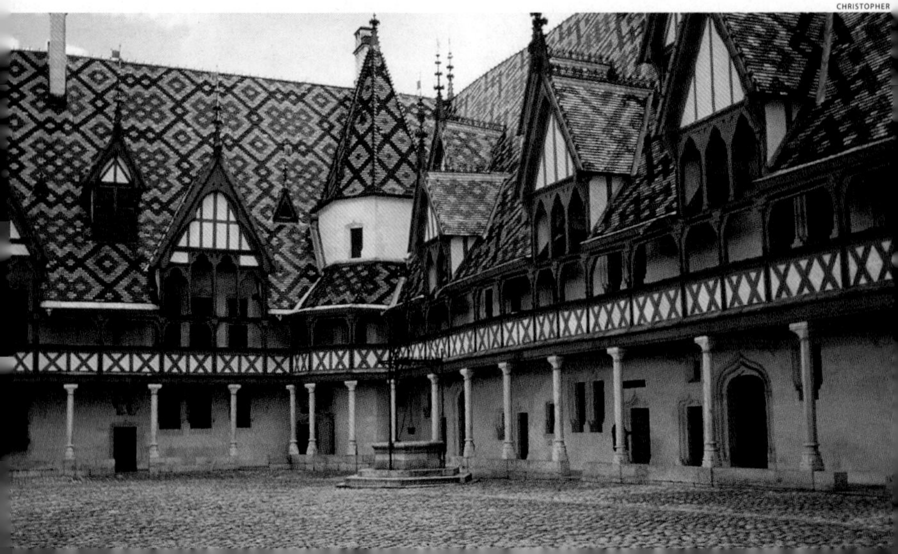

(☎ 02 54 94 15 15; www.hotel-liondor.fr; 69 rue Georges Clemenceau; r from €122; ⓨ closed mid-Feb–mid-Mar; ℗ ⊠ ⬚), which occupies a 16th-century *hôtel particulier*. Rooms have been individually refurbished to an exceptionally high standard in keeping with the buildings origins. The hotel's acclaimed **restaurant** (menus €79-115; ⓨ lunch closed Tue) has two Michelin stars.

There are daily trains to Romorantin-Lanthenay from Tours (€12.40, 1¼ to 1½ hours, three daily) and Orléans (€12, 1½ to 1¾ hours, three daily).

BLÉSOIS

Blésois is graced with some of the Loire's finest chateaux, including stunning Chambord, magnificently furnished Cheverny, romantic Chaumont and modest Beauregard. Blois' tourist office has information on son et lumières (sound-and-light shows) hosted by these and other chateaux.

BLOIS
pop 49,300
Medieval Blois (pronounced blwah) was once the seat of the powerful counts of Blois, from whom France's Capetian kings were descended. From the 15th to the 17th century, Blois was a hub of court intrigue, and in the 16th century it served as a second capital of France. Several dramatic events – involving some of the most important personages in French history such as kings Louis XII, François I and Henri III – took place inside the city's outstanding attraction, Château de Blois.

The old city, seriously damaged by German attacks in 1940, retains its steep, twisting medieval streets.

Orientation
Blois, on the northern bank of the Loire, is a compact town – almost everything is within 10 minutes' walk of the train station. The old city is the area south and east of Château de Blois, which towers over place Victor Hugo. Blois' modern commercial centre is focused around pedestrianised rue du Commerce, rue Porte Chartraine and rue Denis Papin, which is connected to rue du Palais by a monumental staircase built in the 19th century.

Information
Several commercial banks face the river along quai de la Saussaye near place de la Résistance.

3'me Monde (☎ 02 54 74 38 22; 39 av Jean Laigret; per hr €4; ⓨ 11am-9pm) Internet access.

Centre Hospitalier de Blois (☎ 02 54 55 66 33; mail Pierre Charlot) Two kilometres northeast of the town centre.

Post Office (rue Gallois) Has a Cyberposte.

Tourist Office (☎ 02 54 90 41 41; www.ville-blois .fr in French & www.loiredeschateaux.com; 23 place du Château; ⓨ 9am-7pm Mon-Sat, 10am-7pm Sun Apr-Sep, 9am-12.30pm & 2-6pm Mon-Sat, 9.30am-12.30pm Sun Oct-Mar) Charges €2.30 to make hotel or B&B reservations.

Sights
CHÂTEAU DE BLOIS
The ornate and serendipitous **Château de Blois** (☎ 02 54 90 33 32; adult/student/child €6.50/4.50/2; ⓨ 9am-7pm Jul & Aug; 9am-6pm Apr-Jun, Sep & Oct; 9am-12.30pm & 2-5.30pm Nov-Mar) is a useful crash course in château architecture of the Loire. It's formed of four distinct wings constructed around a central courtyard, each reflecting the favoured style of the period in which it was built: medieval (13th century); Flamboyant Gothic (1498–1503), from the reign of Louis XII; early Renaissance (1515–24), from the reign of François I; and classical (17th century).

During the Middle Ages, the counts of Blois meted out justice in the huge **Salle des États Généraux** (Estates General Hall), a part of the feudal castle that survived wars, rebuilding and, most dangerous of all, changes in style and taste. It was used as a film set by the French film director Luc Besson for the trial scene in his box-office hit *Jeanne d'Arc* (1999).

A few steps away, but worlds apart in terms of design, the distinctive brick-and-stone **Louis XII section**, which includes the hall where entrance tickets are sold, is ornamented with porcupines – Louis XII's heraldic symbol. The king himself is also featured among the intricate decoration on the façade, cutting a dashing figure on horseback. The royal apartments on the first floor house the **Musée des Beaux-Arts**.

Started just 15 years later, the **François I wing** illustrates the speed at which Italian-influenced Renaissance design gained popularity in France. The famous projecting **spiral staircase**, a magnificent structure decorated

THE LOIRE

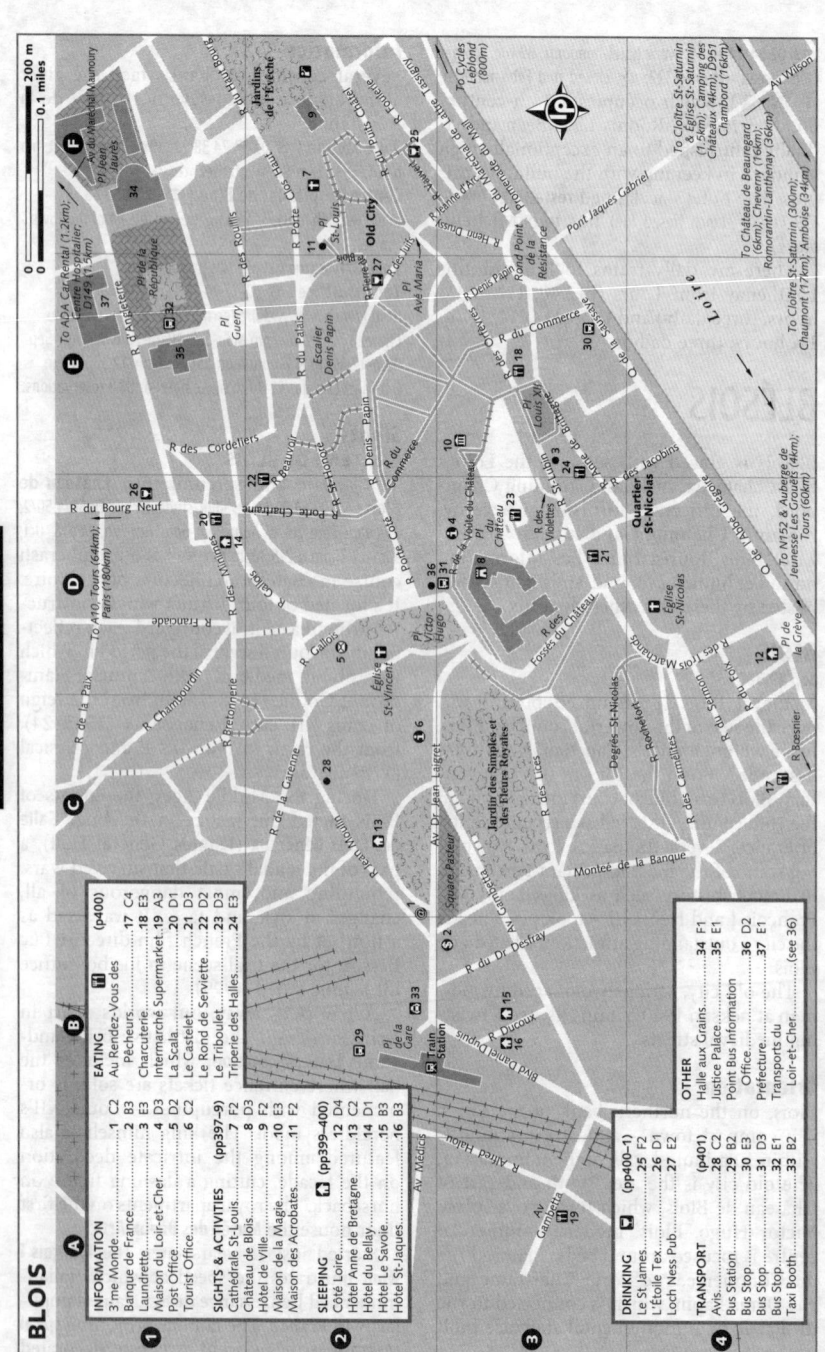

BLOIS

with François I's insignia, a capital 'F' and a salamander, dominates the exterior.

The fourth wing to be built, the **Gaston d'Orléans wing**, is an impressive example of French classical architecture. Again, the monumental staircase is the most notable aspect of the construction, a double-vaulted design adorned with allegorical sculpture.

The most infamous episode in the history of the chateau occurred during the chaotic 16th century. King Henri III summoned his great rival, the ultra-powerful duke of Guise – a leader of the Catholic League (which threatened the authority of the king, himself a Catholic) – to his Counsel Chamber. There, he was set upon by 20 royal bodyguards armed with daggers and swords. When the violence was over, the joyous king, who had been hiding behind a tapestry, stepped into the room to inspect the duke's perforated body. Henri III was himself assassinated eight months later.

There's a **son et lumière** (☎ 02 54 78 72 76; adult/student/child €9.50/6/4.50; ☼ 9.30pm, 10pm, 10.15pm & 10.30pm early May–mid-Sep) and a show in English on Wednesday in May, June, August and September. Tickets are sold 30 minutes before the show starts. Combined same-day tickets (€12/8.50/5.50) are available for the show and chateau.

MAISON DE LA MAGIE
The **Maison de la Magie** (House of Magic; ☎ 02 54 55 26 26; 1 place du Château; adult/12-17 yrs/6-11 yrs €7.50/6.50/5; ☼ 10am-12.30pm & 2-6.30pm Jul & Aug, 10am-12.30pm & 2-6pm Tue-Sun Apr-Jun, 10am-noon & 2-6pm Wed, Thu, Sat & Sun Sep-Mar) faces Château de Blois and has magic shows, interactive exhibits and displays of clocks invented by the Blois-born magician Jean-Eugène Robert-Houdin (1805–71), after whom the great Houdini named himself. Tickets combining magic and *son et lumière* shows are available.

OLD CITY
Around the old city, large brown explanatory signs indicate tourist sights. **Cathédrale St-Louis** (☼ 7.30am-6pm) was rebuilt in a late Gothic style following the devastating hurricane of 1678.

Immediately behind is the **Hôtel de Ville**. Note the unusual double-aspect **sundial**, across the courtyard in a corner of the

Ecclesiastical Tribunal building. There's a great view of Blois and the Loire from the lovely **Jardins de l'Évêché** (Gardens of the Bishop's Palace), behind the cathedral.

Across the square from the cathedral, 15th-century **Maison des Acrobates** (House of the Acrobats; 3bis rue Pierre de Blois), is so-named because its timbers are decorated with characters taken from medieval farces. It was one of the few medieval houses to survive the bombings of WWII.

Tours
Transports du Loir-et-Cher (TLC; ☎ 02 54 58 55 55; adults/student & child €10/8; ☼ mid-May–early-Sep) operates chateau excursions from Blois to Chambord and Cheverny. Tours depart twice daily from Blois train station at 9.10am and 1.20pm, arriving back in Blois at 1.10pm and 6pm respectively. Admission fees to the two chateaux are not included but tour participants are eligible for reduced tariffs. Tickets are sold on the bus, or in advance from the tourist office and the TLC's **Point Bus information office** (☎ 02 54 78 15 66; 2 place Victor Hugo) in Blois.

Sleeping
Reservations for Gîtes de France *chambres d'hôtes* (B&Bs) can be made at the **Maison du Loir-et-Cher** (☎ 02 54 58 81 64; www.gites-de-france-blois.com in French; 5 rue de la Voûte du Château; ☼ 9am-5pm Mon-Fri).

BUDGET
The **Auberge de Jeunesse Les Grouëts** (☎ 02 54 78 27 21; blois@fuaj.org; 18 rue de l'Hôtel Pasquier; dm €7, sheets €2.70, breakfast €3.20; ☼ Mar–mid-Nov) is in Les Grouëts, 4.5km southwest of Blois train station. Be sure to call before arriving as it's often full. Beds are in two 24-bed, single-sex dorms and kitchen facilities are available. To get there, take local TUB bus No 4 (runs until 7pm) from place de la République (linked to the train station by TUB bus No 1).

Hôtel du Bellay (☎ 02 54 78 23 62; http://hotel dubellay.free.fr; 12 rue des Minimes; d with washbasin €23-25, d/tr/q with shower & toilet €35/45/55) It's easy to miss the tiny entrance to this ancient stone house, the original doorway obviously having been built in times when people were much smaller. Some of the rooms are tiny too, but all have charm, lovingly adorned with older-style, mumsy wallpaper.

Hôtel St-Jacques (☎ 02 54 78 04 15; www.hotel saintjacquesblois.com; 7 rue Ducoux; s/d with washbasin €25/27, with shower & toilet €35/37) A functional one-star hotel next to the station where friendly, helpful staff will show you to amply sized but uninspiring rooms. There are bicycles to rent for €12.50 per day.

Camping

Camping des Châteaux (☎ 02 54 78 82 05; camping with/without electricity €10/8; ☙ Jul-Sep) This two-star camping ground is in Vineuil, about 4km south of Blois. There is no bus service from town except in July and August (phone the camping ground or the tourist office for details).

MID-RANGE

Côté Loire (☎ 02 54 78 07 86; www.coteloire.com; 2 place de la Grève; r from €39, Apr-Oct €46) Full of wooden-beamed character, this small, higgledy-piggledy hotel has had a recent spruce-up with new beds, carpets and a colour scheme. A good choice, if you can get one of the seven rooms.

Hôtel Anne de Bretagne (☎ 02 54 78 05 38; fax 02 54 74 37 79; 31 av Jean Laigret; s/d with shower or bath & toilet from €33/48) A pretty, two-star hotel with bright, comfortable rooms overlooking a leafy crescent. The location is handy for the chateau and there's a small terrace for breakfast.

Hôtel Le Savoie (☎ 02 54 74 32 21; hotel.le.sa voie@wanadoo.fr; 6 rue Ducoux; s/d with shower & toilet from €37/41) A quiet, family-run hotel, conveniently located for the station. The two-star rooms are well equipped with extras like English TV channels.

Eating

In addition to those mentioned below, popular restaurants line rue Foulerie and several café-brasseries dot place de la Résistance.

Au Rendez-Vous des Pêcheurs (☎ 02 54 74 67 48; 27 rue du Foix; mains €21-28; ☙ Tue-Sat) Perhaps the finest seafood restaurant in town, this pretty cottage-style place specialises in fish from the River Loire and the Atlantic Ocean. The setting may be relaxed, but the food is of the highest quality.

La Scala (☎ 02 54 74 88 19; 8 rue des Minimes; pizza & pasta €6-10; ☙ noon-11pm) Prompt service and decent, good value Italian food are what makes this pizzeria popular and lively. If the *quatrro fromaggio* pizza isn't cheesy

enough for you, the huge Venice mural and life-size gondola will be!

Le Triboulet (☎ 02 54 74 11 23; Place du Château; menus €16.50-23.50; ☙ closed Sun & Mon) A busy restaurant right by the château offering traditional French dining. The tasty *menu du terroir* (€23.50) showcases seasonal Loire area specialities. After the architectural delights of its neighbour, the simple interior is nothing to get excited about but there's a pleasant garden and terrace nice on hotter days.

Le Castelet (☎ 02 54 74 66 09; 40 rue de Saint Lubin; menus €15.40-24.80; ☙ closed Wed & Sun) A convivial restaurant with the motto '*classic cooking in tune with the seasons*'. This translates to traditional French cuisine with a regional market-fresh twist. It has a vegetarian *menu* (€15.40) on offer. One of the two dining rooms is nonsmoking.

Le Rond de Serviette (☎ 02 54 74 48 04; 18 rue Beauvoir; menus €5.50 & €7.80, mains €5-7; ☙ closed Sun lunch) This cosy little pizzeria markets itself as Blois' cheapest and most humorous restaurant. The €5.50 *menu* is certainly unbeatable, but the Lonely Planet sign out the front has nothing to do with us.

SELF-CATERING

There is an **Intermarché supermarket** (av Gambetta; ☙ 9am-12.30pm & 3-7.15pm Mon-Sat). In the old city, a food market fills rue Anne de Bretagne on Tuesday, Thursday and Saturday until 1pm. There are a number of **charcuteries** in the area around Place Louis XII offering cold meats and prepared dishes. For tasty tripe, try the **Triperie des Halles** (☎ 02 54 78 14 63; 5 rue Anne de Bretagne).

Drinking

The best of the bars can be found in the old town, particularly in the small alleys and squares off rue Foulerie. Several pubs overlook place Av Maria.

Le St James (☎ 02 54 74 44 99; 50 rue Foulerie; ☙ 10pm-5am Thu-Sun) A lively bar with a choice of 162 cocktails and an atmospheric courtyard in which to install yourself while you try them all.

Loch Ness Pub (☎ 02 54 56 08 67; cnr rue des Juifs & rue Pierre de Bois) Another popular watering hole with a younger crowd and Guinness on tap. The two floors get busier and noisier as the night gets longer, especially on karaoke Thursdays.

THE LOIRE

L'Étoile Tex (☎ 02 54 78 46 93; 9 rue du Bourg Neuf)
For a student vibe, head to this busy bar/
Tex-Mex place at the top of the hill hosting rock concerts every Saturday night at
9.30pm (free entry). Modern, trendy and
sophisticated it's not, but the unpretentious
vibe is refreshing. Good fun.

Getting There & Away

For information on transport to/from Blésois
chateaux, see p399. Further details appear
under each chateau listing.

BUS

The **TLC bus network** (☎ 02 54 58 55 44) has a
very limited service, reduced further during the holidays and on Sunday. TLC buses
to destinations around Blois leave from in
front of the **Point Bus information office** (☎ 02
54 78 15 66; 2 place Victor Hugo; ✆ 1.30-6pm Mon, 8am-
noon & 1.30-6pm Tue-Fri, 1.30-4.30pm Sat) and the bus
station – a patch of car park with schedules
posted – in front of the train station. Verify
departure times before travelling.

Bus No 2 travels between Chambord and
Blois (€3.25, 45 minutes), from Monday to
Saturday. It departs from Blois station at
12.15pm, and leaves Chambord at 6.45pm
for the return trip. On Sunday buses leave
Blois at 1.45pm.

Your other option is the TLC's tourist bus
(p399), or hiring a minibus (see right).

CAR

On the D149, **ADA** (☎ 02 54 74 02 47; 108 av du
Maréchal Maunoury) is 3km northeast of the train
station. Take bus No 1 from the train station
or bus No 4 from place de la République to
the Cornillettes stop. **Avis** (☎ 02 54 74 48 15; 6 rue
Jean Moulin) also has an office in Blois.

TRAIN

The **train station** (av Dr Jean Laigret) is at the western end of the street.

There are frequent trains to/from Amboise (€5.50, 20 minutes, hourly), Tours
(€8.30, 40 minutes, 11 to 17 daily) and the
nearest TGV station, St-Pierre des Corps
(€8, 25 to 35 minutes, half-hourly).

There are four direct non-TGV trains
daily from Blois to Paris' Gare d'Austerlitz
(€20.80, 1½ to two hours), plus several
more if you change trains in Orléans. There
are also direct trains to Nantes (€27.10, two
hours, three daily).

HOT-AIR BALLOONING

Hop aboard a hot-air balloon to view the
Loire Valley from an aerial perspective.

France Montgolfière (☎ 02 54 32 20 48;
www.franceballoons.com) is based at La Ribou-
lière in Monthou-sur-Cher (30km south of
Blois). Weather permitting, hot-air balloon
flights are arranged year-round from almost
anywhere in the Loire Valley.

A one- to 1½-hour flight, including champagne at the end, costs €230 per person
(children six to 12 years, €145) for a fully
flexible ticket, which can be reimbursed
should your flight be cancelled due to ad-
verse weather conditions. A variety of other
deals is also on offer. Make reservations several days ahead for weekday flights, four
weeks ahead for weekend flights, especially
Saturday night.

Getting Around

BICYCLE

Hire two wheels from **Cycles Leblond** (☎ 02
54 74 30 13; 44 levée des Tuileries; bike hire per day/week
€12.50/80; ✆ 9am-9pm). Levée des Tuileries is
the continuation of promenade du Mail.

BUS

TUB (☎ 02 54 78 15 66) operates buses around
Blois. Buses run until about 8pm and a one-
way ticket costs €1; bus No 5 links the train
station with the chateau. Point Bus information office (see left) has information and
timetables.

TAXI

The **taxi booth** (Taxi Radio; ☎ 02 54 78 07 65; place
de la Gare) is in front of the train station. For
chateau trips, air-conditioned eight-person
minibuses can be hired. A return trip to
Chambord and Cheverny with an hour
at each costs €74; to Chaumont, Amboise
and Chenonceau €115. Prices go up 50%
on Sundays and holidays. You can choose
which chateau to visit; it's best to book well
in advance.

AROUND BLOIS
Château de Chambord

The pinprick village of Chambord is dominated by the spectacular **Château de Chambord**
(☎ 02 54 50 50 02; www.chambord.org; adult/18-25 yrs/
child €7/4.50/free; ✆ 9am-6.15pm Apr-Sep, 9am-5.15pm

Oct-Mar), which François I had built from 1519 as a base for hunting game in the Sologne forests. Ironically, the king chose the site for its easy two-day ride by horse and carriage from Paris, but he stayed here a total of only 42 days during his reign (1515–47).

The Renaissance chateau has a feudal ground plan. You'll see the king's emblems – the royal monogram (a letter 'F') and salamanders of a particularly fierce disposition – adorning many parts of the building. Though forced by liquidity problems to leave his two sons unransomed in Spain and to help himself to both the wealth of his churches and his subjects' silver, François I kept 1800 workers and artisans busy for 15 years.

The chateau's famed **double-helix staircase**, attributed by some to Leonardo da Vinci who lived in Amboise (34km southwest) at the invitation of François I from 1516 until his death three years later, consists of two spiral staircases that wind around a central axis but never meet. The ornamentation is early French Renaissance.

The double-helix staircase leads up to the Italianate **rooftop terrace**. Standing here, surrounded by towers, cupolas, domes, chimneys, mosaic slate roofs and lightning rods, is rather like standing on an overcrowded chessboard. It was on the terrace that the royal court assembled to watch military exercises, tournaments and the hounds and hunters returning from a day of stalking deer.

Ticket sales end 30 minutes before the chateau closes. As well as free mini-guides in English distributed on arrival, you can rent an audioguide (€4). Free, one-hour guided tours are available daily in French (and often in English) from around 10am.

DOMAINE NATIONAL DE CHAMBORD

The chateau is in the middle of the **Domaine National de Chambord**, a 54-sq-km hunting preserve reserved solely for the use of the president of France (a right that Jacques Chirac has chosen not to exercise). A 32km stone wall built between 1542 and 1645 surrounds the estate. **Walking and mountain bike trails** crisscross 12 sq km on the western side and there's **aires de vision** (observation towers) where you can spot animals.

The **estate** (☎ 02 54 50 50 00) runs fun and informative **4WD forest tours** (up to 8 people €125; ☽ Apr-Sep) and bike tours (see right).

ENTERTAINMENT

Night promenades (adult/child €12/7, combination show & chateau ticket €14/9; ☽ nightfall Mon-Sat Jun-Aug, Fri & Sat Sep) Chambord runs 'metamorphose' night promenades, where the chateau is lit up with a variety of images and scenes, with music playing in the background. Visitors are then free to wander around at their own leisure; the grounds stay open until 10pm or midnight.

GETTING THERE & AWAY

Chambord is 16km east of Blois and 20km northeast of Cheverny. To/from Blois there are TLC buses during the school year (p401) and coach tours to Chambord and Cheverny between mid-May and 31 August (p399).

In Chambord TLC public buses use the stop on the westbound D33.

GETTING AROUND

Bicycles, perfect for exploring Forêt de Chambord and around, can be rented in Chambord from the **Echapée Belle kiosk** (☎ 02 54 33 37 54; bike hire per hr/day/weekend €5.50/13/24) next to Pont St-Michel in the castle grounds. From July to September the estate authorities (p402) organise two-hour **cycling tours** (adult €10), not including bike hire.

Château de Cheverny

The elegant, perfectly symmetrical **Château de Cheverny** (☎ 02 54 79 96 29; www.chateau-cheverny .fr; adult/student/child €6.10/4.10/3; ☽ 9.15am-6.45pm Jul & Aug, 9.15am-6.15pm Apr-Jun & Sep, 9.30am-noon & 2.15-5.30pm Oct & Mar, 9.30am-noon & 2.15-5pm Nov-Feb), built between 1625 and 1634, is the region's most magnificently furnished chateau. Sitting like a sparkling white ship amid a sea of beautifully manicured gardens, the chateau is graced with a finely proportioned neoclassical façade. Inside visitors are treated to room after sumptuous room fitted out with the finest of period appointments. The most richly furnished rooms are the **Chambre du Roi** (in which no king ever slept because no king ever stayed at Cheverny) and the **Grand Salon**. In the 1st-floor dining room, 36 panels illustrate the story of *Don Quixote*.

The grounds shelter the 18th-century **Orangerie**, where Leonardo da Vinci's *Mona Lisa* was hidden during WWII.

The château was also the inspiration for the mythical Marlinspike Hall, home of French fictional favourite *Tintin*. It features in many of Tintin's adventures and in honour of this, a permanent Tintin exhibition, **Les Secrets de Moulinsart** (The Secrets of Marlinspike Hall; adult/student/child combined chateau & exhibition ticket €10.50/8.40/6.20), has been created in the grounds; opening hours are the same as Château de Cheverney. The colourful, interactive display, aimed squarely at kids and Tintin fans, re-creates scenes from some of the character's best-known adventures.

GETTING THERE & AWAY
Cheverny is 16km southeast of Blois and 20km southwest of Chambord. The TLC bus No 4 from Blois to Villefranche-sur-Cher stops at Cheverny (€2.40, 25 to 35 minutes). Buses leave Blois at 12.25pm Monday to Friday. Returning to Blois, the last bus leaves Cheverny at 6.52pm. Departure times can vary and are different on Sundays and holidays; check with TLC or the Blois tourist office (p397). Between mid-May and 31 August, TLC operates coach tours (p399) from Blois.

Château de Chaumont
It's a short, healthy climb up to **Château de Chaumont** (☎ 02 54 51 26 26; adult/18-25 yrs/child €5.50/3.50/free; ⏰ 9.30am-6pm mid-Mar–mid-Oct, 10am-4.30pm mid-Oct–mid-Mar), which is set on a bluff overlooking the Loire. The entrance, across a wooden drawbridge between two wide towers, opens onto an inner courtyard from where there are stunning views. The building itself, resembling a feudal castle, is modestly sized for a chateau. It's easy to imagine enjoying a family meal in the homely dining room, or popping into the tiny chapel for prayer and solitude. Opposite the main entrance are the luxurious **stables**, built in 1877.

In 1560 Catherine de Médicis (France's powerful queen mother) took revenge on Diane de Poitiers, the mistress of her late husband, Henry II, by forcing her to accept Chaumont in exchange for her much more favoured residence, Château de Chenonceau (p410).

GETTING THERE & AWAY
Chaumont-sur-Loire is 17km southwest of Blois and 20km northeast of Amboise, on the Loire's southern bank. The path leading to the park and chateau starts at the intersection of rue du Village Neuf and rue Maréchal Leclerc (D751).

By public transport, the only way to get to Chaumont-sur-Loire is via local train on the Orléans–Tours line. Get off the train at Onzain (10 minutes), from where it is about a 20-minute, 2km walk across the river to the chateau. Single rail fares to Onzain from Blois/Tours/Orléans cost €2.80/6.60/10.30.

THE LOIRE

LA SOUPE DES CHIENS

As was the custom among the nobility of centuries past, the Viscount de Sigalas – whose family has owned Cheverny since it was built – hunts with hounds. His 100 dogs – most a cross between English fox terriers and French *poitevins* – are quite beautiful, no matter what you think of the practice of using them to kill stags.

Each dog has a name, posing a fantastic memory feat for the two dog trainers who do, indeed, know every dog and its name. The *soupe des chiens* (feeding of the dogs) is an awe-inspiring demonstration of the exact control they exercise over the pack. A massive 90kg of animal parts is brought by wheelbarrow into the cement enclosure each day and methodically arranged in a 2m-wide mountain while the hounds whimper and sniff from inside the kennel. The tiny kennel door is then opened and 100 dogs bundle and squeeze out as fast as they can – but not until the dog master cracks the whip does the pack dare so much as sniff at their daily 1kg ration. The stinking offal is then ripped to shreds and gobbled up in minutes. Double portions are doled out after the twice-weekly winter hunt.

The *soupe des chiens* takes place in the *chenils* (kennels) at 5pm daily in summer. In January, February and between mid-September and December, the dogs are fed at 3pm on Monday, Wednesday, Thursday and Friday only. The pack hunts every Tuesday and Saturday between September and March, departing from the majestic front entrance of the chateau if hunting in the Forêt de Cheverny.

By bicycle, the sleepy back roads on the southern bank of the river are a tranquil option. The Chaumont-sur-Loire **tourist office** (☎ 02 54 20 91 73; 24 rue du Maréchal Leclerc; ⏰ 9.30am-7.30pm mid-Jun–Sep, 9.30am-12.30pm & 1.30-6pm Apr–mid-Jun, Sep & Oct, 9.30am-12.30pm & 1.30-5.30pm Nov-Mar) rents bicycles for €10 per day.

Château de Beauregard

Built in the early 16th century to serve as a hunting lodge for François I, the most famous feature of **Château de Beauregard** (☎ 02 54 70 36 74; adult/student & child €6.50/4.50; ⏰ 9.30am-7.30pm Jul & Aug, 9.30am-12.30pm & 2-6.30pm Apr-Jun & Sep, 9.30am-12.30pm & 2-5pm Thu-Tue Oct-Dec & mid-Feb–Mar) is its **Galerie des Portraits**, the walls of which are plastered with 327 portraits of notable faces dating from the 14th to 17th century.

GETTING THERE & AWAY

Beauregard is 6km south of Blois. It can also be reached via a pleasant 15km cycle ride through the forest from Chambord. There is road access to the chateau from the Blois–Cheverny D765 and the D956 (turn left at the village of Cellettes).

The **TLC** (☎ 02 54 58 55 44) bus from Blois to St-Aignan stops at Cellettes (€1.50), 1km southwest of the chateau, Monday to Friday at 7.50am and on Wednesday, Friday and Saturday; the first bus from Blois to Cellettes leaves at 12.25pm.

Unfortunately, there's no afternoon bus back except for the Châteauroux–Blois line operated by **Transports Boutet** (☎ 02 54 34 43 95), which passes through Cellettes around 6.15pm on Monday to Saturday, and – except during August – at roughly 6pm on a Sunday.

TOURAINE

With the exception of the medieval fortresses at Chinon and Loches, the castles of Touraine – Azay-le-Rideau, Chenonceau, Langeais and Villandry – date to the Renaissance. They were designed purely to pamper the soul and pander to the physical pleasures of the queen, king and his multitude of royal mistresses.

Tours is the historical capital of Touraine and an inexpensive base from which to explore the region.

TOURS

pop 270,000

Lively Tours has the cosmopolitan, bourgeois air of a miniature Paris, with wide 18th-century avenues, formal public gardens, café-lined boulevards and a thriving university – home to 30,000 students. The French spoken in Tours is said to be the purest in France. Twice in its history Tours briefly hosted the French government: in 1870 during the Franco-Prussian War and again in 1940, with the onset of WWII. Since then, it has become better known for its crisp white Vouvray and Montlouis wines.

Orientation

Thanks to the spirit of the 18th century, Tours is efficiently laid out. Its focal point is place Jean Jaurès, where the city's major thoroughfares – rue Nationale, blvd Heurteloup, av de Grammont and blvd Béranger – meet. The train station is 300m east of place Jean Jaurès. The old city is centred on place Plumereau, which is about 400m west of rue Nationale. The northern boundary of the city is demarcated by the River Loire, which flows roughly parallel to the River Cher, 3km south.

Information

BOOKSHOPS

Géothèque (☎ 02 47 05 23 56; 6 rue Michelet) Travel bookshop selling maps and guides.
La Boîte à Livres de l'Étranger (☎ 02 47 05 67 29; 2 rue du Commerce) English-language fiction and nonfiction.

EMERGENCY

Police Station (☎ 02 47 33 80 69; 70-72 rue Marceau; ⏰ 24hr)

INTERNET ACCESS

Alli@nce Micro (☎ 02 47 05 49 50; calliance-micro@wanadoo.fr; 7ter rue de la Monnaie; per hr €3; ⏰ 9.30am-7pm Mon-Sat)
CyberGate (☎ 02 47 05 95 94; 11 rue du Président Merville; per hr €3; ⏰ 11am-midnight Tue-Sat, 2-10pm Sun & Mon)

LAUNDRY

Laundrette (22 rue Bernard Palissy; ⏰ 7am-8.30pm)

MONEY

The post office has an exchange service. There are commercial banks around place Jean Jaurès.

Credit Agricole (av de Grammont)
Exchange Kiosk (☎ 8.45am-6pm Mon-Sat; closed Jan)
In the train station. Offers good rates.

POST
Post Office (1 blvd Béranger) Has a Cyberposte.

TOURIST INFORMATION
Tourist Office (☎ 02 47 70 37 37; www.ligeris.com;
78-82 rue Bernard Palissy; ☺ 8.30am-7pm Mon-Sat,
10am-12.30pm & 2.30-5pm Sun mid-Apr–mid-Oct;
9am-12.30pm & 1.30-6pm Mon-Sat, 10am-1pm Sun
mid-Oct–mid-Apr)

Sights
MUSÉE DES BEAUX-ARTS
Occupying three floors of an impressive
17th- to 18th-century archbishop's palace,
the **Musée des Beaux-Arts** (☎ 02 47 05 68 73;
18 place François Sicard; adult/student/child €4/2/free;
☺ 9am-12.45pm & 2-6pm Wed-Mon) has an excellent collection of paintings, furniture and
objets d'art from the 14th to the 20th century. Contemporary works include *le Jardin
de la France* by local artist Max Ernst, an
abstract marriage of a Loire Valley landscape and the female form.

CATHÉDRALE ST-GATIEN
Various parts of Tours' Gothic-style **Cathédrale St-Gatien** (☺ 9am-7pm, closed during services)
represent the 13th century (the choir), 14th
century (the transept), 14th and 15th centuries (the nave) and 15th and 16th centuries
(the west façade). The domed tops of the
two 70m-high **towers** (closed to the public)
date from the Renaissance. There's a fine
view of the **flying buttresses** from behind the
cathedral. Spectacular exterior aside, the interior is renowned for its marvellous 13th-
to 15th-century **stained-glass windows**.
    You can also visit the Renaissance **Cloître
de la Psallette** (☎ 02 47 47 05 19; adult/child €2.50/
free; ☺ 9.30am-12.30pm & 2-6pm Mon-Sat, 2-6pm Sun
Apr-Sep, 2-5pm daily Oct-Mar).

MUSÉUM D'HISTOIRE NATURELLE
Housed in an 18th-century bailiff's tribunal,
the modern **Muséum d'Histoire Naturelle** (☎ 02
47 64 13 31; 3 rue du Président Merville; adult/student & child
€4/2; ☺ 10am-noon & 2-6pm Tue-Fri, 2-7pm Sat & Sun)
has a colourful collection of permanent and
temporary exhibits. Kids can get up close to
all kinds of (stuffed) creatures; hedgehogs,
badgers, otters and plenty of birds and fish.

There are also life-size lions, crocodiles and
bears to scare any pint-size visitors. Long-
term temporary exhibits include dinosaur-
and volcano- themed displays. There are no
explanations in English, but that doesn't detract from this largely visual experience.

JARDIN BOTANIQUE
About 1km west of the city centre, the **Jardin
Botanique** (blvd Tonnelle; admission free; ☺ 7.45am-
sunset) is a great place for a stroll or a picnic.
Created between 1831 and 1843 on reclaimed
land on the banks of St Anne stream, the
five-hectare landscaped park has a tropical
greenhouse, medicinal herb garden and petting zoo. There are also emus and kangaroos
bouncing around. To get there, it's a short
walk or take Bus No 4 (€1.05, every 10 minutes) along blvd Béranger.

MUSÉE DE L'HÔTEL GOÜIN
This archaeological museum, **Musée de l'Hôtel
Goüin** (☎ 02 47 66 22 32; 25 rue du Commerce; adult/
child €3.50/2.60; ☺ 9.30am-12.30pm & 1.15-6.30pm Apr-
Sep, 9.30am-12.30pm & 2-5.30pm Oct-Mar) is housed in
Hôtel Goüin, a Renaissance residence built
around 1510 for a wealthy merchant. Its
Italian-style façade is worth seeing, even if
the eclectic assemblage of prehistoric, Gallo-
Roman, medieval, Renaissance and 18th-
century artefacts doesn't interest you.

Tours
For details on chateau tours, see p400.

Sleeping
There are lots of good value hotels and
other accommodation options to be found
in Tours.

BUDGET
Auberge de Jeunesse du Vieux Tours (☎ 02 47 37
81 58; tours@fuaj.org; 5 rue Bretonneau; dm HI members/
nonmembers €12.70/15.60; reception ☺ 8am-12.30pm,
6-10pm; 🖳) A new and well-equipped hostel
near the old town. It's a large place with a
friendly feel, and has a decent-size kitchen
for cooking and a lounge for hanging out
and playing foosball.
    Hôtel Val de Loire (☎ 02 47 05 37 86; hotel.val
.de.loire@club-Internet.fr; 33 blvd Heurteloup; r €29-40) A
delightful two-star hotel in a century-old
bourgeois home near the station. The cheaper
rooms are quite simple, but the larger rooms
are individually furnished with the occasional

TOURS

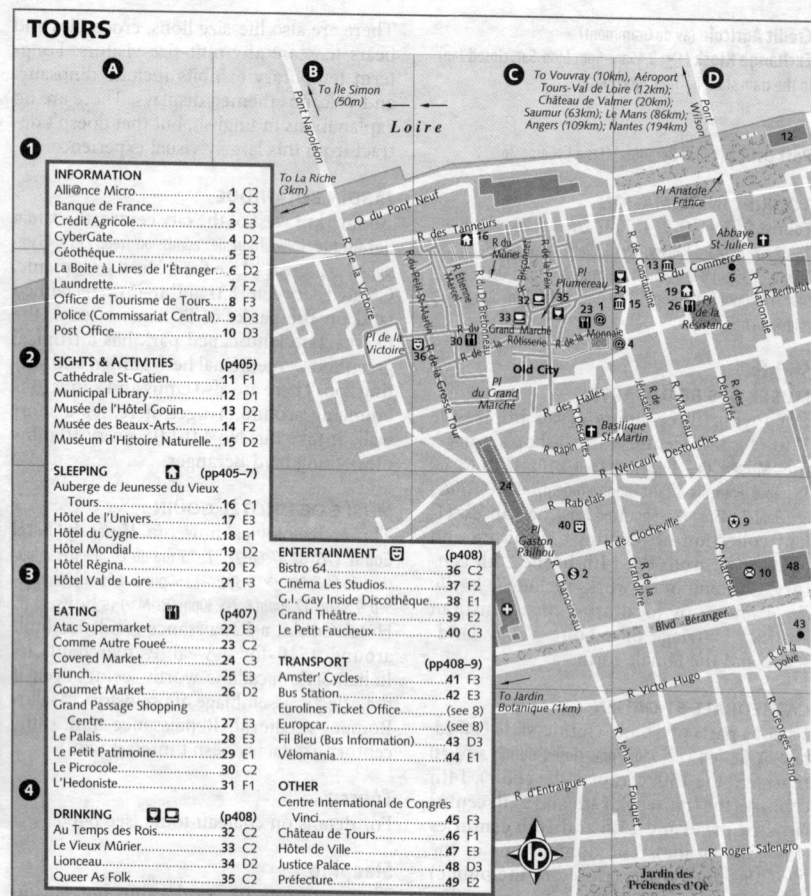

To Île Simon (50m)

To Vouvray (10km), Aéroport Tours-Val de Loire (12km); Château de Valmer (20km); Saumur (63km); Le Mans (86km); Angers (109km); Nantes (194km)

Loire

Pont Napoléon

To La Riche (3km)

Pl Anatole France

Abbaye St-Julien

Old City

To Jardin Botanique (1km)

Jardin des Prébendes d'Oé

INFORMATION

Alli@nce Micro	1 C2
Banque de France	2 C3
Crédit Agricole	3 E3
CyberGate	4 D2
Géothèque	5 E3
La Boîte à Livres de l'Étranger	6 D2
Laundrette	7 F2
Office de Tourisme de Tours	8 E3
Police (Commissariat Central)	9 D3
Post Office	10 D3

SIGHTS & ACTIVITIES (p405)

Cathédrale St-Gatien	11 F1
Municipal Library	12 D1
Musée de l'Hôtel Goüin	13 D2
Musée des Beaux-Arts	14 F2
Muséum d'Histoire Naturelle	15 D2

SLEEPING (pp405–7)

Auberge de Jeunesse du Vieux Tours	16 C1
Hôtel de l'Univers	17 E3
Hôtel du Cygne	18 E1
Hôtel Mondial	19 D2
Hôtel Régina	20 E2
Hôtel Val de Loire	21 F3

EATING (p407)

Atac Supermarket	22 E3
Comme Autre Foueé	23 C2
Covered Market	24 E3
Flunch	25 E3
Gourmet Market	26 D2
Grand Passage Shopping Centre	27 E3
Le Palais	28 E3
Le Petit Patrimoine	29 E1
Le Picrocole	30 C2
L'Hedoniste	31 F1

DRINKING (p408)

Au Temps des Rois	32 C2
Le Vieux Mûrier	33 C2
Lionceau	34 D2
Queer As Folk	35 C2

ENTERTAINMENT (p408)

Bistro 64	36 C2
Cinéma Les Studios	37 F2
G.I. Gay Inside Discothèque	38 E1
Grand Théâtre	39 E2
Le Petit Faucheux	40 C3

TRANSPORT (pp408–9)

Amster' Cycles	41 F3
Bus Station	42 E3
Eurolines Ticket Office	(see 8)
Europcar	(see 8)
Fil Bleu (Bus Information)	43 D3
Vélomania	44 E1

OTHER

Centre International de Congrès Vinci	45 F3
Château de Tours	46 F1
Hôtel de Ville	47 E3
Justice Palace	48 D3
Préfecture	49 E2

ornate fireplace, antique wardrobe or writing desk. The 1st-floor rooms have high ceilings and full-length windows.

Hôtel Régina (☎ 02 47 05 25 36; fax 02 47 66 08 72; 2 rue Pimbert; s/d with washbasin €21/24, s/d/q with shower from €25/29/38) The best of the lower-priced options, this popular and good value hotel has a range of rooms depending on your budget. It's clean, if a little smoky-smelling and the matronly manageress doesn't stand for any mischief.

Camping

Camping Municipal des Rives du Cher (☎ 02 47 27 27 60; fax 02 47 25 82 89; 61 rue de Rochpinard, St-Avertin; camping €11; ☼ Apr–mid-Oct) This three-star camping ground is 5km south of Tours.

To get there, take bus No 5 from place Jean Jaurès to the St-Avertin bus terminal, then follow the signs.

MID-RANGE

Hôtel du Cygne (☎ 02 47 66 66 41; hotelcygne .tours@wanadoo.fr; 6 rue du Cygne; r €40-60; P) A pretty hotel on a quiet side street in the old town; wooden-shuttered windows, high ceilings, blooming flowerboxes, chandeliers and period detail. The spacious 1st-floor rooms tick all the boxes, but it loses a couple of marks for the dreary reception/breakfast room and its smaller upper-floor rooms.

Hôtel Mondial (☎ 02 47 05 62 68; www.hotel mondialtours.com; 3 place de la Résistance; s/d from €34/40, breakfast €6) A modern two-star option with

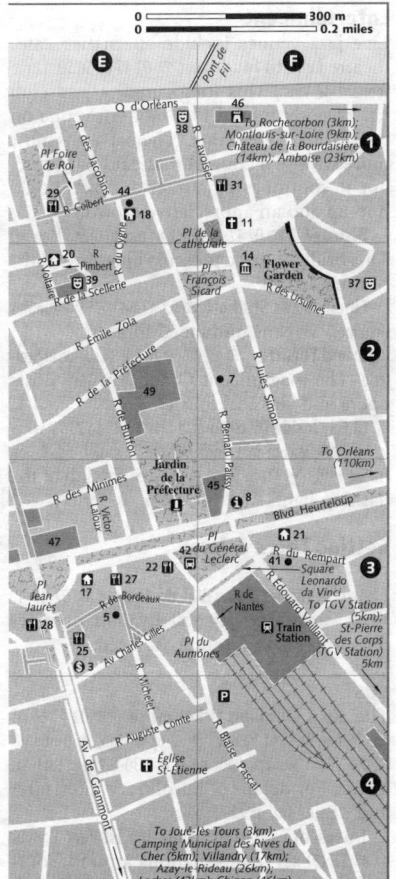

immaculate, carpeted rooms overlooking place de la Résistance. There's a sunny room on the second floor to enjoy the buffet breakfast, which could take all morning with the spread they provide here.

TOP END

Hôtel de l'Univers (☎ 02 47 05 37 12; www.hotel-univers-loirevalley.com; 5 blvd Heurteloup; standard €185, superior €255; ☒ ☒ ☐) Tours' swishest town-centre hotel is unapologetically old-fashioned, from the wood-panelled whisky-and-cigar bar to the Chesterfield-scattered reception. The grand old building dates from 1846; upstairs the refined rooms offer spaciousness and a good level of four-star comfort.

Eating

In the old city, place Plumereau and nearby rue du Grand Marché and rue de la Rôtisserie are loaded with restaurants, cafés, creperies and *boulangeries* – many have lovely street terraces. Another cluster of places serving tasty food grace rue Colbert.

L'Hedoniste (☎ 02 47 05 20 40; 16 rue Lavoisier; lunch/dinner menus from €11/16) In this convivial, cave-like place, a regional French menu is enhanced by an exhaustive range of wines and the viticultural knowledge of the proprietor. He can advise on the perfect glass of wine to have with every dish, selecting from row upon row of bottles decorating the stone walls.

Le Picrocole (☎ 02 47 20 68 13; 28-30 rue du Grand Marché; menus €11 & €17) Occupying a series of cosy rooms in an old house, this popular place serves regional and French specialities. It's a good place to try *rillons*; another popular choice is their renowned chocolate *fondant* cake.

Le Palais (☎ 02 47 61 48 54; 15 place Jean Jaurès; lunch/dinner menus €9.90/15.90) Trendy pizzeria/brasserie serving the usual pizzas and salads plus more unusual mains (€8 to €9) including rabbit, and marinated salmon. Cool music, relaxed surroundings and attentive service all add to the vibe and there's a terrace outside for people-watching.

Le Petit Patrimoine (☎ 02 47 66 05 81; 58 rue Colbert; lunch menu €9, dinner menus €12-26) This relaxed eatery is always busy and is excellent value for such tasty, well-presented French food. The restaurant, simple but atmospheric with stone walls and a wood-beamed ceiling, may be small, but the portions are not.

Flunch (☎ 02 47 64 56 70; 14 place Jean Jaurès; menu €6, mains €4-10; ☺ 11am-10pm) A canteen chain with cheap prices and décor.

SELF-CATERING

Sandwich stalls sell filled baguettes and pastries in the **Grand Passage shopping centre** (18 rue de Bordeaux).

Tours has some 30 markets around town on various days of the week; your best bet is the large, permanent **covered market** (place Gaston Pailhou), or the open-air **gourmet market** (place de la Résistance; ☺ 4-10pm 1st & 3rd Fri of month).

There is also an **Atac supermarket** (5 place du Général Leclerc; ☺ 8.30am-8pm Mon-Sat & 9.30am-12.30pm Sun).

AUTHOR'S CHOICE

Comme Autre Fouée (☎ 02 47 05 94 78; 11 rue de la Monnaie; lunch/dinner menus from €10/19.50) *Fouée* (or *fouaces*), is an age-old regional speciality, a small disc of dough thrown into a woodfired oven for 45 seconds and served immediately, piping hot. The pitta-like bread is used to scoop up *fouéefuls* of *rillettes*, *haricots blanc* or farmhouse goat's cheese for a hearty, filling, country-style meal. At Comme Autre Fouée, a pun on Comme Autre Fois (just like the old days), you can install yourself in this old stone building for a good few hours while they constantly replenish your basket with oven-fresh *fouée*.

Drinking

You don't need to look very hard for bars and cafés in Tours – the old town is full of them. A good starting point is place Plumereau, which fills to bursting in the summer with tourists and locals sipping wine or espresso.

There are also a few lively student bars situated along rue de la Longue Echelle and the southern strip of adjoining rue du Dr Bretonneau.

Le Vieux Mûrier (☎ 02 47 61 04 71; 11 place Plumereau; ☽ 11am-midnight) This stylish place is favourite for people-watching in the bustling heart of the old town, with tables spilling out into place Plumereau.

Au Temps des Rois (☎ 02 47 05 04 51; 3 place Plumereau; ☽ 11am-2am) Also with a great location in place Plumereau, this café attracts a younger, livelier student-type crowd. It is quite a popular place to hang out and look cool.

Le Palais (☽ 11am-2am) The ground floor bar at Le Palais is a trendy place for a drink and there are tables outside so patrons can enjoy a beer in the sunshine. Things liven up after about 11pm with regular DJs and karaoke evenings.

Queer As Folk (☎ 02 47 75 04 27; 108 rue de Commerce; ☽ 6pm-2am) Unashamedly camp bar, with blue neon lights, zebra-print soft furnishings and plenty of trash techno, euro-pop and '80s disco.

Lionceau (55 rue de Commerce; ☽ 7pm-2am) Ole-in-the-wall gay bar favoured by a slightly older crowd than Queer As Folk.

Entertainment

Live jazz venues include alternative café-theatre **Le Petit Faucheux** (☎ 02 47 64 50 50; 12 rue Leonard de Vinci) This long-running jazz club has recently moved to a modern venue on rue Leonard de Vinci. The set-up is now more sit-down concert than laid-back café, but it continues to attract an exceptional line-up and an appreciative crowd.

Bistro 64 (☎ 02 47 38 47 40; 64 rue du Grand Marché) This brilliant place presents blues in a 16th-century setting.

Cinémas Les Studio (☎ 02 47 64 42 61; 2 rue des Ursulines) Screens undubbed films.

Grand Théâtre (☎ 02 47 60 20 20; 34 rue de la Scellerie) The magnificent Grand Théâtre hosts opera and classical music.

GI Gay Inside Discothêque (☎ 02 47 66 29 96; www .gidiscotheque.com in French; 13 rue Lavoisier; admission Fri/Sat €5/8; ☽ 11pm-5am) A gay nightclub of the flashing-lights-and-nude-torsos variety.

Getting There & Away

AIR

From **Aéroport Tours-Val de Loire** (☎ 02 47 49 37 00; www.tours-aeroport.com) Ryanair operates direct flights to London Stansted.

BUS

There's a **Eurolines ticket office** (☎ 02 47 66 45 56; 76 rue Bernard Palissy; ☽ 2-6pm Mon, 9am-noon & 1.30-6.30pm Tue-Fri, 9am-noon & 1.30-5.30pm Sat) in Tours. For details of Eurolines routes, fares and deals, see p917.

Buses operated by **Touraine Fil Vert** (☎ 02 47 47 17 18) serve destinations around Tours and the Indre-et-Loire department, including Amboise (€2.10). They leave from the **bus station** (☎ 02 47 05 30 49; place du Général Leclerc), which has an **information desk** (☎ 02 47 05 30 49; ☽ 7am-7pm Mon-Sat), only drivers sell tickets.

In July and August you can make an all-day circuit by public bus from Tours to Chenonceaux and Amboise by taking the 10am bus to Chenonceaux (€2.10, 1¼ hours), then the 12.40pm bus from Chenonceaux to Amboise (€1.05, 25 minutes). Return buses from Amboise to Tours (€2.10) leave at 4.25pm, 5.25pm and 6.20pm. Double-check times and schedules before departing.

CAR

Car-rental offices:

Avis (☎ 02 47 20 53 27) At the train station.

Europcar (☎ 02 47 64 47 76; 76 blvd Bernard Palissy)

TRAIN

The **train station** (place du Général Leclerc) has an **information office** (⊙ 8.30am-6.30pm Mon-Sat, closed public holidays). Tours is linked to St-Pierre des Corps (Tours' TGV train station) by shuttle train.

Local trains run between Tours and Orléans at least hourly (€15, 1¼ hours). Stops on this route include St-Pierre des Corps (€1.20, five minutes), Montlouis-sur-Loire (€2.20, 12 minutes), Amboise (€4.40, 20 minutes) and Blois (€8.30, 35 minutes). There are trains southbound to Loches (€7.20, one hour, two daily) and westbound to Saumur (€9.20, 40 minutes, 13 daily).

To get from Paris to Tours by rail take a TGV from Gare Montparnasse (€35 to €45, 1¼ hours, 10 to 15 daily). This trip often requires a change of trains at St-Pierre des Corps; or a direct non-TGV from Gare d'Austerlitz (€25.80, two to three hours, five to eight daily). There are TGV and non-TGV services to Bordeaux (€37, 2½ hours by TGV), Poitiers (€16, one hour) and Nantes (€22.50, two hours). Change trains in Poitiers to get to/from La Rochelle (€29.80, two to three hours).

Getting Around
TO/FROM THE AIRPORT

A **shuttle bus** (one way €5) leaves Tours bus station at 3.45pm daily, stopping at the train station (3.55pm) before continuing to the airport in time for the daily Ryanair departure at 5.20pm. Arriving passengers can catch it back into town at 5.30pm.

BICYCLE

From May to September friendly **Amster' Cycles** (☎ 02 47 61 22 23; 5 rue du Rempart; 1-/2-/7-day bike hire €14/21/55), rents out road and mountain bikes. Staff provide cyclists with a puncture-repair kit and map.

Vélomania (☎ 02 47 05 10 11; 109 rue Colbert) is another bike-rental outlet charging the same.

BUS

The network serving Tours and its suburbs is run by **Fil Bleu** (☎ 02 47 66 70 70), which has an **information office** (5bis rue de la Dolve). Most lines stop around the periphery of place Jean Jaurès. Tickets, which are valid for one hour after being stamped, cost €1.05.

AROUND TOURS

Vineyards carpet **Vouvray** (population 2900) and **Montlouis-sur-Loire** (population 8000), 10km east of Tours on the northern and southern bank respectively of the Loire. For centuries wine growers have stored their wines in *caves* (wine cellars), hewn out of the white tufaceous cliffs that line this stretch. Neither village is overly attractive, but each offers ample opportunity to taste and buy Appellation d'Origine Contrôlée (AOC) Vouvray and Montlouis wines.

The **Vouvray tourist office** (☎ 02 47 52 68 73; cnr route du Vignoble on the N152 & av Brulé, the D46; ⊙ 9am-6pm Mon-Sat, 9am-1pm Sun Apr-Sep, 9am-1pm Tue-Sat rest of year), has information on wine-tasting options and rents bicycles. Opposite, the **Maison du Vouvray** (☎ 02 47 52 72 51; 24 av Brulé; ⊙ 9am-12.30pm & 1.45-7pm) is a good place to kick off a *dégustation* (tasting) spree.

In Montlouis-sur-Loire the **tourist office** (☎ 02 47 45 00 16; www.ville-montlouis-loire.fr in French; place de la Mairie; ⊙ 9am-12.30pm & 2-6.30pm Mon-Sat May-Sep, plus 10am-1pm Sun Jul & Aug, 10am-noon & 2-5pm Mon-Sat Oct-Apr) and the **Maison de la Loire** (☎ 02 47 50 97 52; 60 quai Albert Baillet; ⊙ 2-6pm) can provide information.

A unique spot to stay and eat in the surrounds is **Les Hautes Roches** (☎ 02 47 52 88 88; www.leshautesroches.com; 86 quai de la Loire; d €125-255; menus €45-61) in the northern suburb of Rochecorbon. Dug by monks as a haven during the Wars of Religion, the caves now form part of a four-star hotel/restaurant. (For more troglomania see p423.)

GETTING THERE & AWAY

Fil Bleu's bus No 61 links Tours' place Jean Jaurès with Vouvray (€1.05, 20 minutes). Montlouis-sur-Loire is served by bus line C2 (€2.20, 45 minutes) operated by Fil Vert.

TOURS AREA CHATEAUX

A number of the most interesting Loire chateaux make an easy day trip from Tours. Those accessible by train or SNCF bus from Tours include Chenonceau, Villandry, Azay-le-Rideau, Langeais, Amboise (p412), Chaumont (p403), Chinon (p416) and Saumur (p423). Transport details are listed at the end of each chateau listing.

The tourist office in Tours has details of *son et lumières*, medieval re-enactments, and other spectacles performed at the chateaux during summer.

Tours

Touring chateaux by public transport can be horribly slow and expensive, so even veteran backpackers should consider taking an organised bus tour. The interesting English-language tours are surprisingly relaxed and informal. Most allow you between 45 minutes and one hour at each chateau. Tour prices do not include entrance fees, but if you're part of a group you may be entitled to discounts. If you can get five to seven people together, you can design your own minibus itinerary.

There are three companies offering minibus tours from Tours: **Acco-Dispo** (☎ 06 82 00 64 51; www.accodispo-tours.com), **Quart de Tours** (☎ 06 85 72 16 22; www.quartdetours.com) and **St-Eloi Excursions** (☎ 02 47 37 08 04; www.saint-eloi.com). Typical prices are from €18 to €31 for a half-day trip to various chateaux sharing a minibus for up to eight people. Reservations can be made at the Tours tourist office or via its website.

Services Touristiques de Touraine (STT; ☎ 02 47 05 46 09; www.stt-millet.fr) runs full-sized coaches for individuals rather than groups from April to mid-October. Many tours include wine tasting in Vouvray or Montlouis-sur-Loire. Afternoon/day tours taking in three chateaux cost €34, which includes admission fees.

For something a bit different and to get away from peak-season crowds, it's possible to take to the air for a birds-eye view of the chateaux. The Tours tourist office has details of **aerial excursions** by helicopter, plane, microlight and hot-air balloon (p401).

See p399 for information about tours departing from Blois.

Château de Chenonceau

With its stylised moat, turrets, drawbridge and towers from the 16th-century, **Château de Chenonceau** (☎ 08 20 20 90 90; www.chenonceau .com; adult/student & child €8/6.50; ⏰ 9am-7pm mid-Mar–mid-Sep, 9am-4.30pm to 6.30pm rest of year) is everything a fairy-tale castle should be, although its interior – crammed with period furniture, tourists, paintings, tourists, tapestries and tourists – is only of moderate interest. If you are visiting during the low season, check on opening hours because they vary.

Chenonceau's vast park, with landscaped gardens and forests, covering 70 hectares either side of the River Cher, affords some stunning vistas of the chateau exterior. Diane de Poitiers, mistress of King Henri II, one of the series of remarkable women who created Chenonceau, planted the garden to the left (east) as you approach the chateau. After Henri's death in 1559 she was forced to give up Chenonceau by Henri II's widow, the vengeful Catherine de Médicis, who applied her own energies to the chateau and laid out the garden to the right (west) as you approach the castle.

In the 18th century, Madame Dupin, the chateau's owner at the time, brought Jean-Jacques Rousseau to Chenonceau as a tutor for her son. During the French Revolution, the affection with which the peasantry regarded Madame Dupin saved the chateau from the violent fate of its neighbours.

GETTING THERE & AWAY

Château de Chenonceau, in the town of Chenonceaux (the village has an 'x' at the end), is 34km east of Tours, 10km southeast of Amboise and 40km southwest of Blois.

Chenonceaux SNCF train station is in front of the chateau. Between Tours and Chenonceaux there are four to six trains daily (€5.20, 30 minutes).

Château de Villandry

Château de Villandry (☎ 02 47 50 02 09; www.cha teauvillandry.com; admission chateau & gardens adult/child €7.50/5, gardens only €5/3.50; ⏰ chateau 9.30am-5pm or 6.30pm mid-Feb–mid-Nov, gardens 9am-dusk year-round) has some of the most spectacular formal gardens in France. **Jardin d'Ornement** (Ornamental Garden) comprises intricate, geometrically pruned hedges and flowerbeds loaded with romantic symbolism so abstract that you can tour the entire garden without comprehending its true meaning (even with the aid of the free English-language brochure available at the entrance). Between the chateau and the village church, the **potager** (kitchen garden) is a cross between the vegetable plots in which medieval monks grew their food and the formal gardens so beloved of 16th-century France.

All told, Villandry's gardens occupy five hectares and include in excess of 1150 lime trees, hundreds of grape trellises and 52km of landscaped plant rows. Villandry is at its most colourful from May to mid-June and August to October, but is worth a visit year-round.

The chateau itself was completed in 1536, making it the last of the major Renaissance chateaux to be built in this area. The interior has undergone extensive refurbishment and although not yet finished, it's worth exploring. Furnished in comfortable 18th-century style, the rooms and hallways are adorned with dark and moody Spanish paintings and large, faded tapestries. An unusual 13th-century **Moorish ceiling** is thought to have been bought here from Toledo, Spain.

The corner **tower** is all that remains of the original medieval structure on which the current chateau was built. From the tower, the intricate gardens can be seen in their entirety, as can the parallel Rivers Loire and Cher.

GETTING THERE & AWAY
Villandry is 17km southwest of Tours, 31km northeast of Chinon and 11km northeast of Azay-le-Rideau. By road the shortest route from Tours is the D7, but cyclists will find less traffic on the D88 (which runs along the southern bank of the Loire) and the D288 (which links the D88 with Savonnières). If heading southwest from Villandry towards Langeais, the best bike route is the D16; it has no verges and only light traffic. Villandry is included on most organised tour circuits (p405).

By public transport the only way of travelling between Tours and Villandry is the largely inconvenient train to Savonnières (€2.60, 13 minutes), about 4km east of Villandry. During the week the first train from Tours is at 12.28pm; heading back, there is a direct train to Tours at 1.42pm (13 minutes) and another at 5.40pm via Langeais (1¼ hours). On Saturday there is an additional direct train from Savonnières to Tours at 5.37pm. On Sunday the only train to Tours is at 1.42pm.

Château d'Azay-le-Rideau
Château d'Azay-le-Rideau (☎ 02 47 45 42 04; adult/18-25 yrs/child €6.10/4.10/free; ☯ 9.30am-6pm Apr-Jun & Sep-Oct, 9.30am-7pm Jul & Aug, 9.30am-12.30pm & 2-5.30pm Nov-Mar), built on an island in the River Indre and surrounded by a quiet pool and park, is harmonious and elegant. It is adorned with stylised fortifications and turrets intended both as decoration and to indicate the rank of the owners. Inside, seven rooms are open to the public, but, beyond a few 16th-century Flemish tapestries, they

are disappointing. Forty-five minute **tours** (adult €4) in several languages take place at regular intervals.

The bloodiest incident in the chateau's history occurred in 1418. During a visit to Azay, then a fortified castle, the crown prince (later King Charles VII) was insulted by the Burgundian guard. Enraged, he had the town burned and executed some 350 soldiers and officers. The present chateau was begun exactly a century later by Giles Berthelot, one of François I's less-than-selfless financiers. When the prospect of being audited and hanged drew near, Berthelot fled abroad. The finishing touches were added in the 19th century.

GETTING THERE & AWAY
Château d'Azay-le-Rideau, 26km southwest of Tours, features on most tour itineraries from Tours (p405). The D84 and D17, either side of the Indre, are a delight to cycle along.

Azay-le-Rideau is on the SNCF Tours-Chinon line (four or five daily Monday to Saturday and one on Sunday). From Tours the 30-minute trip (50 minutes by SNCF bus) costs €4.40; the station is 2.5km from the chateau. The last train/bus to Tours leaves Azay at about 6.35pm (8pm on Sunday).

Château de Langeais
Built in the late 1460s to cut off the most likely invasion route from Brittany, **Château de Langeais** (☎ 02 47 96 72 60; adult/senior/student & child €6.50/5.50/4; ☯ 9.30am-8pm mid-July-mid-Aug, 9.30am-6.30pm Apr-mid-Jul & mid-Aug-mid-Oct, 10am-5.30pm mid-Oct-Mar), in flowery Langeais presents two faces to the world. From the town it appears a 15th-century fortified castle – nearly windowless with machicolated ramparts (ie walls from which missiles and boiling liquids could be dropped on attackers) rising forbiddingly from the drawbridge. The sections facing the courtyard, however, are outfitted with the large windows, dormers and decorative stonework characteristic of later chateaux designed for more refined living. The **ruined dungeon** in its grounds dates from around 944 and is the oldest such structure in France.

Langeais has a truly interesting interior. The unmodernised configuration of the rooms and the **period furnishings** give you a pretty good idea of what the place looked like during the 15th and 16th centuries. The walls are decorated with fine but somewhat faded Flemish and Aubusson **tapestries**, representing the most extensive and significant tapestry collection in France other than at the Louvre.

In one room, wax figures re-enact the marriage of King Charles VIII and Duchess Anne of Brittany, held here on 6 December 1491. The event brought about the final union of France and Brittany.

GETTING THERE & AWAY

Langeais is 14km west of Villandry and about 24km southwest of Tours. Its **train station** (☎ 02 47 96 82 19), 400m from Château de Langeais, is on the Tours–Savonnières–Saumur line. The last train to Tours (€4.30, 15 to 25 minutes, three to six daily) is at 6.37pm (5.30pm on Saturday, 7.15pm or 8.20pm on Sunday and holidays). Tickets from Langeais cost €2.20 to Savonnières (4km from Villandry) and €6.20 to Saumur (25 minutes).

AMBOISE

pop 11,000

The picturesque town of Amboise, nestling under its fortified chateau on the southern bank of the Loire, reached its peak during the decades around 1500, when the luxury-loving King Charles VIII enlarged it and King François I held raucous parties here. These days the town makes the most of its association with Leonardo da Vinci, who lived his last years here under the patronage of François I.

Amboise is protected from the river by a dyke, and its flower-covered heights are a great place for a riverside promenade. Tours, 23km downstream, and Blois, 34km upstream, are easy day trips from here. Amboise makes a good base for visiting the chateaux east of Tours (p410).

Orientation

Amboise train station, across the river from the town centre, is about 800m north of Château d'Amboise. Le Clos Lucé, Leonardo da Vinci's former home, is 500m southeast of the chateau along rue Victor Hugo. The island in the middle of the Loire is called Île d'Or.

Place Michel Debré – effectively an extension of rue Victor Hugo and sometimes called place du Château – stretches westwards from the northern end of rue de la Tour to pedestrian rue Nationale, Amboise's main commercial and touristy street.

Information

Several banks dot rue Nationale.

Playconnect (119 rue Nationale; ☎ 02 47 57 18 04; ⏰ 1-10pm Mon, 10am-10pm Tue-Thu, 10am-midnight Fri & Sat) In addition to Internet and games, Playconnect will transfer your digital photos onto CD.

Post Office (20 Quai du Général de Gaulle)

Tourist Office (☎ 02 47 57 09 28; www.amboise-valdeloire.com; ⏰ 10am-1pm & 2-6pm Mon-Sat, 10am-1pm & 3-6pm Sun Apr-Jun & Sep, 9am-8pm Mon-Sat & 10am-6pm Sun Jul & Aug, 10am-1pm & 2-6pm Mon-Sat & 10am-1pm Sun Oct-Mar) In a pavilion opposite 7 quai du Général de Gaulle, stocks walking and cycling maps, and supplies a free English-language brochure for walking around Amboise.

Sights & Activities

CHÂTEAU D'AMBOISE

The fortified rocky outcrop topped by **Château d'Amboise** (☎ 02 47 57 00 98; place Michel Debré; adult/student/7-14 yrs €7.50/6.50/4.20; ⏰ 9am-7.30pm Jul & Aug, 9am-6.30pm Apr-Jun, Sep & Oct, 9am-noon & 2-5pm Nov-May). Charles VIII (r 1483–98), who was born and brought up here, enlarged the chateau in 1492 after a visit to Italy, where he was impressed by that country's artistic creativity and luxurious lifestyle. He died six years later after hitting his head on a low lintel while on his way to a *jeu de paume* (the precursor to tennis) game. His widow, the 22-year-old Anne de Bretagne, was obliged by contract to marry the new king of France, Louis XII.

King François I (r 1515–47) also grew up here as did his sister, the reform-minded French Renaissance author Margaret of Angoulême (also known as Margaret of Navarre). François I lived in the chateau during the first few years of his reign, a lively period marked by balls, masquerade parties, tournaments and festivities of all sorts.

Today just a few of the 15th- and 16th-century structures survive. These include the Flamboyant Gothic **Chapelle St-Hubert** and the **Salle des États** (Estates Hall), where a group of Protestant conspirators were tried before being hanged from the balcony in 1560. From 1848 to 1852, Abdelkader, the military and political leader of the

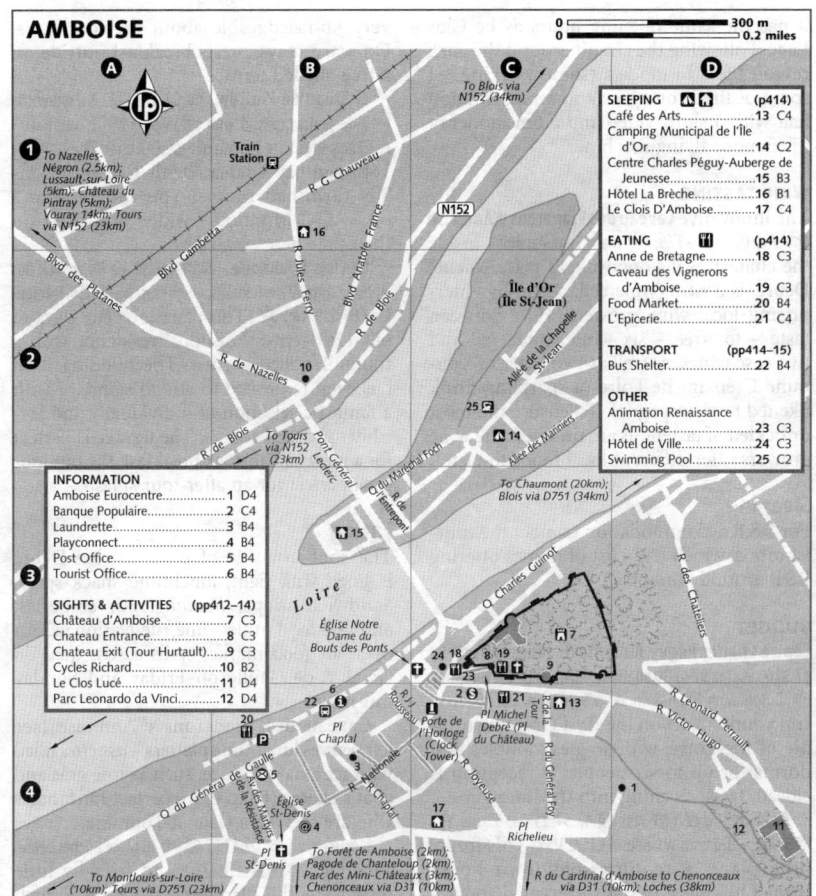

AMBOISE

0 — 300 m
0 — 0.2 miles

Algerian resistance to French colonialism, was imprisoned here. The chapel is said to be the final resting place of Leonardo da Vinci, a modest monument to such a great man.

The **ramparts** afford a panoramic view of the town and the Loire Valley.

The entrance to the chateau is located at the end of rampe du Château. On Wednesday and Saturday evenings between mid-June and the end of August, the chateau stages an evening show – a re-enactment of the life and times of François I – in its courtyard. Tickets can be bought in advance from **Animation Renaissance Amboise** (☎ 02 47 57 14 47; www.renaissance-amboise.com; adult grandstand/stalls €16/13, child €16/7).

LE CLOS LUCÉ

Leonardo da Vinci came to Amboise in 1516 at the invitation of François I. Until his death three years later at the age of 67, Leonardo lived and worked in **Le Clos Lucé** (☎ 02 47 57 62 88; 2 rue du Clos Lucé; adult/student/6-15 yrs €9.50/7.50/5; 🕑 9am-8pm Jul & Aug, 9am-7pm Apr, Jun, Sep & Oct, 9am-6pm Nov, Dec, Feb & Mar, 9am-5pm Jan), a brick manor house, which contains restored rooms and scale models of Leonardo's inventions, including a proto-automobile, armoured tank, parachute and hydraulic turbine. It's a fascinating place offering a unique insight into the mind of the genius.

The house is set in the lovely **Parc Leonardo da Vinci** (🕑 Apr-Nov; adult/student/6-15 yrs combined ticket for Le Clos Lucé & Parc Leonardo da Vinci €11/9/6.50);

it has the same opening hours as Le Clos Lucé. Following the circuit around the park reveals life-size models (some working) of some of the prototypes and a presentation hall with a short video and a 6m model of his famous flying machine.

WINE TASTING

The innovative **Caveau des Vignerons d'Amboise** (☎ /fax 02 47 57 23 69; 10am-7pm Mar-Nov), inside the chateau walls opposite 42 place Michel Debré, is a *cave* (wine cellar) run by enterprising local wine growers. Here you can taste – for free – six white, three red and two rosé wines, as well as two types of Touraine Crémant de Loire (a sparkling drink likened to champagne). To ensure the most untickled of tastebuds are titillated, the wine growers offer different local foods to taste.

Sleeping

For B&B accommodation contact the tourist office, which has a list of homes offering B&B around Amboise.

BUDGET

Centre Charles Péguy-Auberge de Jeunesse (☎ 02 47 30 60 90; fax 02 47 30 60 91; Île d'Or; dm €8.60; reception 2-8pm Mon-Fri, 6-8pm Sat & Sun) An efficiently run youth hostel on the Île d'Or in the middle of the Loire, with singles, doubles and dorms for up to six people. If reception is closed, try screeching into the intercom.

Café des Arts (☎ /fax 02 47 57 25 04; 32 rue Victor Hugo; s/d/q with washbasin €15/29/52; This funky little place, a centuries-old town house turned hip place to stay, is situated above a happening café. It's the best budget deal in town by a margin.

Camping

Camping Municipal de l'Île d'Or (☎ 02 47 57 23 37; Île d'Or; camping €9.25; Apr-Sep) There is minigolf, a mountain bike circuit and on-site tennis courts at this camping ground. Admission to the neighbouring swimming pool costs €2/1.20 for adults/children.

MID-RANGE

Hôtel La Brèche (☎ 02 47 57 00 79; www.labreche -amboise.com; 26 rue Jules Ferry; d with shower & toilet €50-64; Feb-Nov) Across the river from the town centre this hotel, with red sun-shades and colourful flower boxes, is comfortable and full of charm. The friendly owner is

very knowledgeable about the local area. On warm days guests breakfast outside on a tree-shaded terrace.

Château de Pintray (☎ 02 47 23 22 84; www.chateau-de-pintray.com; d with breakfast €95) Five kilometres west in Lussault-sur-Loire, is a small 16th-century chateau with five traditionally furnished rooms. You can taste and buy AOC Montlouis wines produced on the estate here.

Le Clois D'Amboise (☎ 02 47 30 10 20; www.leclos amboise.com; 27 rue Rabelais; r high season €75-150, low season €65-129; P) This place is a gem; a grand old 17th-century bishops' residence with a tranquil walled garden. The building itself has been renovated to a high standard with a fantastic selection of individually and lavishly furnished rooms. The terrace is perfect for a pre-chateau-tour breakfast, the outdoor pool perfect for an after-tour splash.

Eating

The southern side of place Michel Debré is lined with light, lunchtime snack spots. Sandwich shops, *boulangeries*, creperies, and fast-food outlets line rue Nationale. An open-air food market spills across quai du Général de Gaulle on Friday and Sunday morning.

Caveau des Vignerons d'Amboise (see left) serves lunchtime platters – *assiettes* filled with regional produce, such as foie gras and goat's cheese (€6 to €7) – perfect for foodies who are seeking a taste of Touraine.

L'epicerie (☎ 02 47 57 08 94; 46 place Michel Debré; menus €10.50-35) A quaint and friendly little restaurant, this place serves regional French cuisine. Fish is a speciality; you'll often find *sandre* from the River Loire on the *menu*.

Anne de Bretagne (☎ 02 47 57 05 46; 1 rampe du Château; mains €7-10) Big salads, pasta and *galettes*, as well as a vegetarian *menu* and a host of tempting, alcohol-soaked crepes. It's also a good spot to grab coffee and an outside table, and watch the world go by.

Getting There & Around

BICYCLE

Hire mountain bikes at **Cycles Richard** (☎ 02 47 57 01 79; 2 rue de Nazelles; bike hire per day €11; 9am-noon & 2.30-7pm Mon-Sat).

BUS

Buses to/from Amboise stop at the bus shelter across the car park from the tourist office.

CAT's line No 10 links the town with Tours' bus terminal (one way €2.10, 30 to 50 minutes, eight daily Monday to Saturday, six daily during summer holidays). There are likewise round trips, from Monday to Saturday, between Amboise and Château de Chenonceau). Buses depart from outside the central post office at 10.52am (one way €1.05, 25 minutes) and return from Chenonceaux at 5pm.

TRAIN
The **train station** (☎ 02 47 23 18 23; blvd Gambetta), across the river from the centre of town, is served by trains from Paris' Gare d'Austerlitz (€24.20, 2¼ to three hours, 11 daily).

About three-quarters of the trains on the Blois–Tours line (11 to 17 daily) stop at Amboise. Fares are €5.50 to Blois (20 minutes) and €4.40 to Tours (20 minutes).

PAGODE DE CHANTELOUP
The 44m-high, Chinese-style **Pagode de Chanteloup** (☎ 02 47 57 20 97; adult/student/7-15 yrs €6/5/4; ☽ 10am-6.30pm May, Jun & Sep, 9.30am-7.30pm Jul & Aug, 10am-noon & 2-5.30pm Mar, Apr & Oct, 2-5pm Mon-Fri, 10am-noon & 2-5pm Sat & Sun Feb & Nov) is one of the 18th century's more pleasing follies. Built between 1775 and 1778, it combines contemporary French architectural fashions with elements from China, a subject of great fascination at the time. From the top of the pagoda, visitors are rewarded with an impressive view of the Loire Valley.

This eccentric pagoda is a delightful picnic venue. **Hampers** (€10) bursting with regional treats are sold at the May-to-October entrance. You can hire a **boat** (per hour €6) to row your sweetheart around the lake and there is a fun collection of old-fashioned games to play for free.

The pagoda is about 2km south of Amboise. Take rue Bretonneau and follow the plentiful signs to 'La Pagode'. Public buses between Amboise (see p414) and Tours (see p408) stop at the 'Pagode' stop.

LOCHES
pop 6550
Medieval Loches, with its cobbled streets and imposing keep perched on a rocky spur, could be a film set. The 11th-century keep was built by Foulques Nerra (Falcon the Black; r 987–1040), while its feudal chateau witnessed Joan of Arc persuade Charles VII

to march north in June 1429 to be crowned. The royal court he consequently established here was notorious for its wild banquets, thrown primarily to woo the scandalously wicked yet stunningly beautiful Agnès Sorel, a royal mistress who died aged 28. Her tomb lies in Loches. The town's golden age ended in 1461 with the ascension of Louis XI to the throne. The new king turned the keep into a state prison.

Orientation & Information
Loches is about 40km southeast of Tours. The citadel sits south of the old town, on the western bank of the Indre. The train and bus stations are across Pont Pierre Senard on the eastern bank of the river.

Post Office (rue Descartes) Has a Cyberposte.
Tourist Office (☎ 02 47 91 82 82; www.lochesentou raine.com; place de la Marne; ☽ 9.30am-7pm Mon-Sat mid-Jun–mid-Sep, 9.30am-12.30pm & 2-6.30pm Mon-Sat mid-Sep–mid-Jun) The tourist office is wedged between Pont Pierre Senard and rue de la République, the main commercial street.

Sights
CITADEL
The 11th-century **Porte Royale** (Royal Gate), up the hill on rue de la Porte, is flanked by two 13th-century towers and remains the only opening in the sturdy 2km wall that encircles the citadel.

Inside, the **Donjon** (Castle Keep; adult/7-18 yrs €5/3.50; ☽ 9am-7pm Apr-Sep, 9am-12.30pm & 2-5pm Oct-Mar) at the southernmost point of the rocky promontory is the oldest structure within the citadel (built 1010–35). The notorious **Round Tower** and **Martelet** were built under Louis XI as prisons. Inmates were tortured in a cage weighing 2.5 tons, a replica of which is on display.

The northern end of the citadel contains the **Logis Royal** (Royal Residence; adult/7-18 yrs €3.80/2; ☽ 9am-7pm Apr-Sep, 9am-12.30pm & 2-5pm Oct-Mar). The 15th-century funerary urn of Agnès Sorel is in the northern wing of the residence, built for Charles VIII and Anne de Bretagne in the 16th century. A **combined ticket** (adult/7-14 yrs €7/4.50) to Donjon and Royal Lodge is available.

In summer **son et lumières** (☎ 02 47 59 01 76) are held in the citadel at 10pm Friday and Saturday. The terrace offers a fine panorama of Loches village tumbling down the hillside towards the Indre Valley.

THE LOIRE

Sleeping & Eating

The tourist office has plenty of information on camping grounds and *chambre d'hôtes* in the area.

Hôtel de France (☎ 02 47 59 00 32; hoteldefrance@aol.com; 6 rue Piçois; r €42-64; **P**) In the centre of the medieval district, this imposing two-star hotel has an impressive entranceway and a pleasant courtyard **restaurant** (menus €15-43). The rooms, by comparison, are cheaply decked-out, although perfectly comfortable.

La Crêpicoise (☎ 02 47 59 25 59; 3 rue Picois; mains €8-15; ☺ lunch Fri-Wed, dinner Fri-Tue) Decent, simple food such as crepes, salads and grills in unfussy surroundings.

CAK'T (☎ 02 47 59 39 35; 6 Grande Rue; set lunch €8, cakes from €1.50; ☺ lunch noon-7pm daily, dinner Jul & Aug) Quirky little tearoom with art hanging on the walls and tempting cakes displayed on the trolley. The lunch *menus* are good value.

A **food market** fills place du Marché and rue St-Antoine on Wednesday morning.

Getting There & Around

Loches is on the Tours–Châteauroux train line. The train and bus stations are across Pont Pierre Senard on place des Cordeliers. There are trains to and from Tours (€7.20, 45 minutes, two daily) and SNCF buses (€10.70, 50 minutes, three or four daily).

Peugeot Cycles-JM Jourdain (☎ 02 47 59 02 15; 7 rue des Moulins; road/mountain bike hire per day €8/12, per week €40/65) rents out road and mountain bikes.

CHINON

pop 8627

Chinon's massive fortress – 400m long – looms above the town's medieval quarter. The uneven, cobblestone streets are lined with ancient houses, some built of decaying tufa stone, others half-timbered and brick. The contrast between the triangular, black slate roofs and the whitish-tan tufa gives the town its distinctive appearance.

Villandry, Azay-le-Rideau and Langeais all can easily be visited from Chinon if you are using your own transport. The Forêt de Chinon (Chinon Forest), which is a wooded area ideal for walking and cycling, begins a couple of kilometres northeast of town and stretches along the D751 all the way to Azay-le-Rideau.

Chinon's vineyards stretch north, south and east of the town, on both banks of the Vienne.

Orientation & Information

Rue Haute St-Maurice, the main street in the medieval quarter, becomes rue Voltaire as you move east. The train station is 1km east of the town's commercial hub, place du Général de Gaulle (also called place de l'Hôtel de Ville).

Internet access is available at Hôtel le Menestrel (see p417) for €0.40 per minute and there are several banks near the post office.

Post Office (quai Jeanne d'Arc)

Tourist Office (☎ 02 47 93 17 85; www.chinon.com; place Hofheïm; ☺ 10am-7pm May-Sep, 10am-noon & 2-6pm Mon-Sat Oct-Apr)

Sights

CHÂTEAU DE CHINON

Perched atop a rocky spur high above the River Vienne, this huge, mostly ruined medieval fortress, **Château de Chinon** (☎ 02 47 93 13 45; adult/student or child €6/4.50; ☺ 9am-7pm Apr-Sep, 9.30am-5pm Oct-Mar), consists of three parts separated by waterless moats: the 12th-century **Fort St-Georges** (of which little remains), which protected the chateau's vulnerable eastern flank; the **Château du Milieu** (the Middle Castle); and, at the western tip, the **Château du Coudray**. From the ramparts there are great views in all directions.

After crossing the moat (once spanned by a drawbridge) and entering Château du Milieu, you pass under the **Tour de l'Horloge** (Clock Tower). The four rooms inside are dedicated to the career of Joan of Arc, who picked out Charles VII from among a crowd of courtiers in 1429 in the castle's **Salle du Trône** (Throne Room). Other parts of the almost undecorated **Grand Logis Royal** (Royal Apartments), built during the 12th, 14th and 15th centuries, are in slightly better condition.

To get to the chateau, walk up the hill to rue du Puits des Bancs and turn left. By car, route de Tours (the continuation of the D751 from Tours) will take you to the rear of the chateau.

MUSÉE ANIMÉ DU VIN

The kitsch **Musée Animé du Vin** (Animated Wine Museum; ☎ 02 47 93 25 63; 12 rue Voltaire; adult/child €3.80/3.20; ☺ 10.30am-12.30pm & 2-7pm Apr-Sep) has

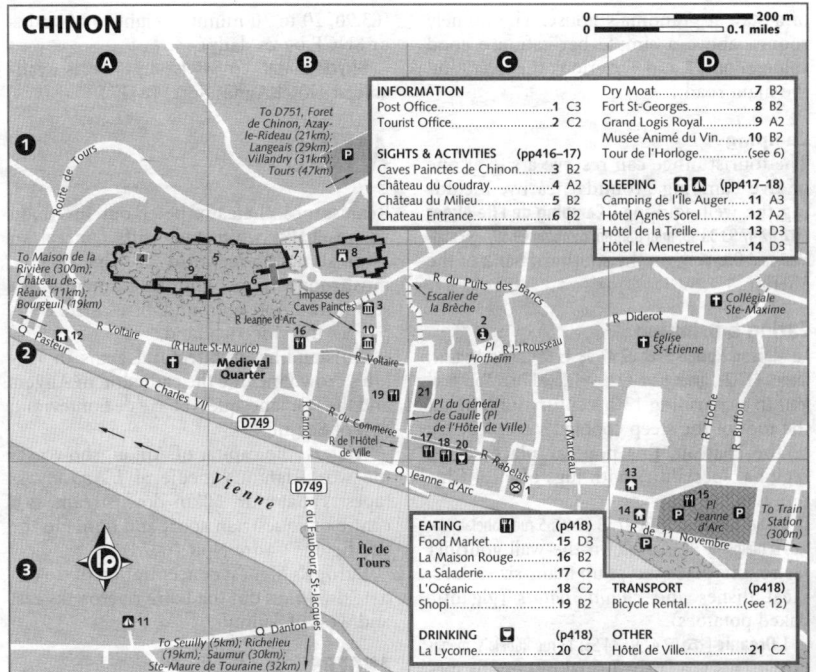

CHINON

0	200 m
0	0.1 miles

INFORMATION
Post Office.........................**1** C3
Tourist Office.....................**2** C2

SIGHTS & ACTIVITIES (pp416–17)
Caves Painctes de Chinon....**3** B2
Château du Coudray............**4** A2
Château du Milieu...............**5** B2
Chateau Entrance................**6** B2

Dry Moat...........................**7** B2
Fort St-Georges..................**8** B2
Grand Logis Royal..............**9** A2
Musée Animé du Vin.........**10** B2
Tour de l'Horloge...........(see 6)

SLEEPING (pp417–18)
Camping de l'Ile Auger......**11** A3
Hôtel Agnès Sorel.............**12** D3
Hôtel de la Treille.............**13** D3
Hôtel le Menestrel............**14** D3

EATING (p418)
Food Market....................**15** D3
La Maison Rouge..............**16** B2
La Saladerie....................**17** C2
L'Océanic.......................**18** B2
Shopi.............................**19** B2

TRANSPORT (p418)
Bicycle Rental.............(see 12)

DRINKING (p418)
La Lycorne......................**20** C2

OTHER
Hôtel de Ville..................**21** C2

THE LOIRE

life-size mechanical figures that demonstrate how wine and wine barrels are made, accompanied by a piped commentary in English. The admission price includes a sample of local wine and *confiture de vin* (sweet wine jam or jelly).

CAVES PAINCTES DE CHINON
Underneath the ruins of the chateau are the **Caves Painctes de Chinon** (☎ 02 47 93 30 44; impasse des Caves Painctes; admission €3; ☷ guided tours 11am, 3pm, 4.30pm & 6pm, Tue-Sun Jul–mid-Sep), former quarries converted into wine cellars during the 15th century and hardly touched since. The extensive network of caves is filled with row upon row of bottles; guided tours conclude with a free glass of the local produce. This is also a good source of information on regional wines, local growers and possible *dégustations*.

Festivals & Events
On the third weekend in August, musicians, dancers and locals dress up in period costume for the **Marché à l'Ancienne**, a recreation of a 19th-century farmers' market,

where wines and traditional food products from the Loire region are sold.

Sleeping
The tourist office has a list of *chambres d'hôtes* in the area including Château des Réaux (p395) 11km north of town.

Hôtel Agnès Sorel (☎ 02 47 93 04 37; www.agnes-sorel.com; 4 quai Pasteur; d €46-56, with private terrace €72) A lovely riverside spot run by a friendly family; choose from older-style rooms, immaculately furnished with sturdy wooden beds in the original building, or comfortable, modern rooms with terrace in the annexe. Access for disabled guests.

Hôtel de la Treille (☎ 02 47 93 07 71; fax 02 47 93 94 10; 4 place Jeanne d'Arc; d with washbasin €28, with shower & toilet €36-40; ℗) Simple, but rustic with a 14th-century stone staircase leading to five cosy rooms. The bustling downstairs **restaurant** (menus €11-18) is a great value place to eat.

Hôtel le Menestrel (☎ 02 47 93 07 20; fax 02 47 93 48 75; place Jeanne d'Arc; d with shower from €28; ▯) Wooden beams, fussy bedspreads and flowery wallpaper all contribute to the feel of a stay at grandma's house. The homely rooms, above a simple bar-café are good value; rooms 2 and 3 overlook the river (and the main road).

Camping
The tourist office can reserve a site at one of five camping grounds nearby, including the well-equipped **Camping de l'Île Auger** (☎ 02 47 93 08 35; quai Danton; camping €9.50; ☼ mid-Mar–mid-Oct; ☒), on the southern bank of the Vienne.

Eating & Drinking
La Maison Rouge (☎ 02 47 98 43 65; 38 rue Voltaire; menus €17-23, lunch from €12; ☼ closed Fri & Nov–mid-Mar) In a charming 13th-century building at the foot of the steep cobbled street leading to the chateau, this popular place serves regional specialities with jugs of local Chinon wine.

La Saladerie (☎ 02 47 93 99 93; 5 rue Rabelais; salads & mains €8-10) A hole-in-the-wall gourmet bistro, this place serves up main-size salads, meat dishes and *chaud' patats* (gigantic baked potatoes).

L'Océanic (☎ 02 47 93 44 55; 13 rue Rabelais; menus €21-50) This is a fairly formal restaurant specialising in fresh and tasty seafood. There's a small terrace outside; reserve a table if you're planning to visit for a summertime lunch.

Rue Rabelais is the most likely spot for an evening tipple or two.

La Lycorne (☎ 02 47 93 94 94; 15 rue Rabelais; ☼ noon-midnight, closed Mon) A large, lively pub-brasserie with occasional live music.

SELF-CATERING
A handy supermarket is **Shopi** (22 place du Général de Gaulle). At the northern end of place du Général de Gaulle, there's an **outdoor market** (☼ 8am-6pm Thu, to 1pm Sat & Sun). Place Jeanne d'Arc plays host to a **food market** on Thursday morning.

Getting There & Around
Chinon is 47km southwest of Tours, 21km southwest of Azay-le-Rideau and 80km north of Poitiers.

The **train station** (☎ 02 47 93 11 04), 300m east of place Jeanne d'Arc, is linked with Tours (€7.40, 50 minutes, 11 trains or SNCF buses on weekdays, five on Saturday and two on Sunday and holidays) and Azay-le-Rideau

(€3.90, 20 to 30 minutes, eight to 12 trains or SNCF buses daily).

Bicycle rental (per half-/full-day €8/14) is available at Hôtel Agnès Sorel (p417).

ANJOU

Renaissance chateaux peter out in Anjou where chalky-white tufa cliffs conceal an astonishing underworld of wine cellars, mushroom farms and monumental art sculptures. Above ground, black slate roofs pepper the vine-rich land.

Outstanding architectural gems in Anjou's crown include the cathedral in Angers and the Romanesque Abbaye de Fontevraud east of Saumur.

Angers, the capital of Anjou, showcases the world-famous medieval *L'Apocalypse* tapestry. Saumur, 50km downstream, is a centre of equestrian sport and home to the prestigious Cadre Noir (p424).

Europe's highest concentration of troglodyte dwellings dot the Loire riverbanks east and west of Saumur.

ANGERS
pop 141,500
Angers, 70km west of Chinon, straddles the River Maine. The city was settled by the Andes Celtic tribe and became an administrative capital under the Romans. In the 9th century it served as the seat of the powerful counts of Anjou who controlled a vast territory embracing most of southwestern France by the 12th century.

Much of the city was bombed during WWII; the city housed an exiled Polish government in 1940 and the regional headquarters of the Gestapo in 1942.

Angers is pleasantly walkable. Its richest treasure, displayed inside its mighty chateau, is a medieval tapestry depicting scenes from the Apocalypse.

The city hosted the royal court until the 12th century when Henri II shifted it east to Chinon.

Orientation
Angers' historic quarter lies on the eastern bank of the Maine, bordered by blvd Ayrault and its continuation, blvd Carnot, to the north; blvd du Maréchal Foch to the east; and blvd du Roi René to the south.

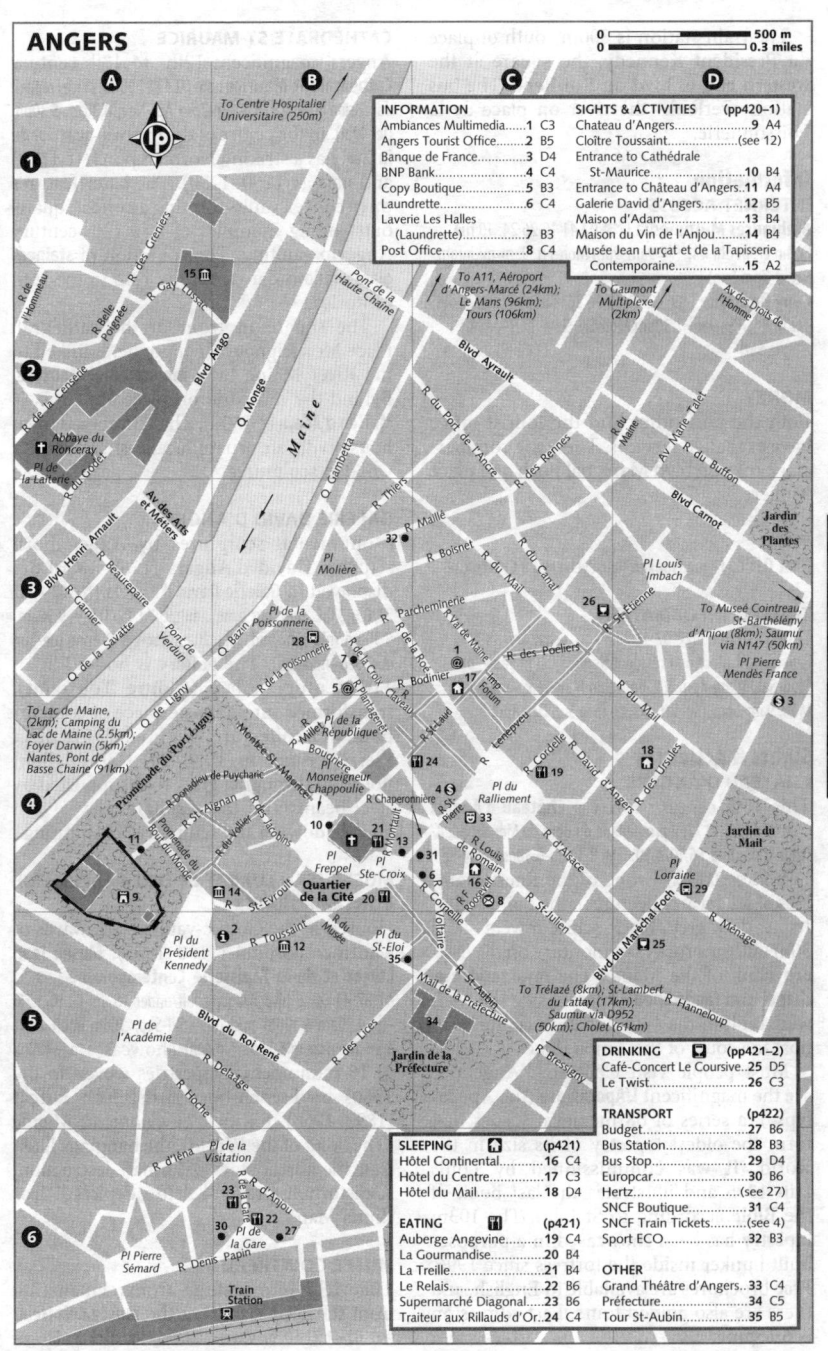

ANGERS

| 0 | 500 m |
| 0 | 0.3 miles |

INFORMATION
Ambiances Multimedia......**1** C3
Angers Tourist Office.......**2** B5
Banque de France............**3** D4
BNP Bank......................**4** C4
Copy Boutique................**5** B3
Laundrette.....................**6** C4
Laverie Les Halles
  (Laundrette).................**7** B3
Post Office.....................**8** C4

SIGHTS & ACTIVITIES (pp420–1)
Chateau d'Angers.............**9** A4
Cloître Toussaint...............(see 12)
Entrance to Cathédrale
  St-Maurice...................**10** B4
Entrance to Château d'Angers..**11** A4
Galerie David d'Angers.......**12** B5
Maison d'Adam................**13** B4
Maison du Vin de l'Anjou....**14** B4
Musée Jean Lurçat et de la Tapisserie
  Contemporaine..............**15** A2

THE LOIRE

DRINKING (pp421–2)
Café-Concert Le Coursive..**25** D5
Le Twist.......................**26** C3

TRANSPORT (p422)
Budget...........................**27** B6
Bus Station.....................**28** B3
Bus Stop........................**29** D4
Europcar........................**30** B6
Hertz.............................(see 27)
SNCF Boutique................**31** C4
SNCF Train Tickets...........(see 4)
Sport ECO......................**32** B3

OTHER
Grand Théâtre d'Angers.....**33** C4
Préfecture......................**34** C5
Tour St-Aubin.................**35** B5

SLEEPING (p421)
Hôtel Continental.............**16** C4
Hôtel du Centre...............**17** C3
Hôtel du Mail.................**18** D4

EATING (p421)
Auberge Angevine............**19** C4
La Gourmandise...............**20** B4
La Treille.......................**21** B4
Le Relais.......................**22** B6
Supermarché Diagonal.......**23** B6
Traiteur aux Rillauds d'Or...**24** C4

The train station is 800m south of place du Président Kennedy, the square at the western end of blvd du Roi René. The bus station overlooks the river on place de la Poissonnerie.

Information

INTERNET ACCESS

Ambiances Multimedia (☎ 02 41 18 26 24; 10 rue Bodinier; per hr €3; ☻ 9am-9pm Mon-Fri, 9am-midnight Sat, 3-7pm Sun)

Copy Boutique (☎ 02 41 88 96 26; 48 rue Plantagenêt; per hr €4; ☻ 9am-7.30pm Mon-Fri, 9am-12.30pm & 2-7pm Sat)

MONEY

Both the post office and the tourist office have exchange services. There are commercial banks on blvd Maréchal Foch and place Molière.

POST

Post Office (1 rue Franklin Roosevelt) Has a Cyberposte.

TOURIST INFORMATION

Tourist Office (☎ 02 41 23 50 00; www.angers-tourisme.com; 7 place du Président Kennedy; ☻ 9am-7pm Mon-Sat, 10am-1pm & 2-6pm Sun May-Sep; 9am-1pm Mon, 9am-6pm Tue-Sat, 10am-1pm Sun Oct-Apr)

Sights & Activities

CHÂTEAU D'ANGERS

This 13th-century fortress **Château d'Angers** (☎ 02 41 86 48 77; 2 promenade du Bout du Monde; adult/student & child €6.10/4.10; ☻ 9.30am-6.30pm May-Sep, 10am-5.30pm Oct-Apr) is one of the finest examples of feudal architecture in the Loire Valley. Its 17 dark-grey, black schist towers stand 30m tall, on a rocky promontory on the eastern bank of the Maine. The **royal residence**, **chapel** and **landscaped gardens** inside the walls were built in the 14th and 15th centuries to host the court of the Anjou dukes.

Most people visit Château d'Angers to see the magnificent **L'Apocalypse** (the Apocalypse), a series of 68 medieval scenes that form the oldest tapestry of its size in the world. It was commissioned by Louis I in 1375 and illustrates the last book of the Bible according to St John. The 103m tapestry has been showcased in a purpose-built bunker inside the fortress since 1996. Free brochures are available in English, and there are also guided tours. Last admission is 6.15pm.

CATHÉDRALE ST-MAURICE

Angers' magnificent 12th- to 13th-century **Cathédrale St-Maurice** (☎ 02 41 87 58 45; place Freppel; admission free; ☻ 8.30am-7pm Apr-Nov, 8.30am-5.30pm Dec-Mar), in the centre of the historic **quartier de la Cité**, has a striking Norman porch (c 1170) and nave (c 1150–1250). The latter features three convex vaults forming a perfect square, outstanding examples of mid-12th-century Angevin vaulting. The collection of **stained-glass windows** date from the 12th to the 16th centuries.

The square in front of the cathedral, Place Monseigneur Chappoulie, is linked to the River Maine by a **monumental staircase**. Behind the cathedral on place Ste-Croix is **Maison d'Adam** (c 1500), a half-timbered town house with an ornate façade studded with wooden sculptures.

GALERIE DAVID D'ANGERS

Monumental sculptures by Angers-born sculptor David d'Angers (1788–1856) are displayed in **Galerie David d'Angers** (☎ 02 41 87 21 03; 33bis rue Toussaint; adult/child €2/1; ☻ 9.30am-6.30pm mid-Jun–mid-Sep, 10am-noon & 2-6pm Tue-Sun mid-Sep–mid-Jun). The gallery is housed in an 11th-century abbey (Cloître Toussaint), transformed into a masterpiece of contemporary architecture by French architect Pierre Prunet in 1980–94. Natural light floods in through a glass roof supported by steel beams and the resultant play of sun and shadow on the sculptures is stunning.

MUSÉE JEAN LURÇAT ET DE LA TAPISSERIE CONTEMPORAINE

Housed in the Gothic-vaulted sick wards of a former hospital (1180–1865), **Musée Jean Lurçat et de la Tapisserie Contemporaine** (☎ 02 41 87 41 06; 6 blvd Arago; adult/under 18 yrs €3.50/1.75; ☻ 9.30am-6.30pm mid-Jun–mid-Sep, 10am-noon & 2-6pm Tue-Sun mid-Sep–mid-Jun) showcases a series of 10 monumental tapestries woven in the 1960s by French-born artist Jean Lurçat (1892–1966). Entitled *Le Chant du Monde* (The Song of the World), the hangings illustrate the horror story of human destruction. A disturbing green skeleton depicts 'Hiroshima Man'.

MUSÉE COINTREAU

The rich, intoxicating aroma emanating from the copper stills at the **Musée Cointreau** (☎ 02 41 31 50 50; www.cointreau.com; blvd des Bretonnières; adult/12-18 yrs €5.50/2.60; tours ⊙ 10.30am, 2.30pm, 3.30pm & 4.30pm Jul & Aug, 10.30am & 3pm Mon-Sat plus additional tour 4.30pm Sun May, Jun, Sep & Oct, 3pm Mon-Sat plus additional tour 4.30pm Sun Nov-Apr) is enough to send anyone running for the gift shop to stock up. The exact ingredients required for the famous orange liquor are top secret, known to just a select few. As such, every bottle of Cointreau sold anywhere in the world is produced right here; 30 million bottles a year. The displays and thorough guided tour are interesting and professional, but it's that sublime aroma – of orange peel and summertime – that lingers.

The museum is off the ring road to the east of Angers. Take bus No 7 from Angers bus station to the 'Cointreau' stop.

WINE TASTING

The **Maison du Vin de l'Anjou** (☎ 02 41 88 81 13; www.vins-valdeloire.com in French; 5bis place du Président Kennedy; admission free; ⊙ 9.30am-1pm & 3-6.30pm Tue-Sun Apr-Sep, 9am-1pm & 3-6.30pm Tue-Sat Oct-Mar), across from the chateau, is the perfect spot to sample Anjou and Saumur wines.

Sleeping
BUDGET

Foyer Darwin (☎ 02 41 22 61 20; contact@foyerdarwin .com; 3 rue Darwin; dm €10.50) Five kilometres west of Angers and not far from the lake, Foyer Darwin is a large, 300-bed hostel on the Bellebeille Cité Université campus. Facilities here are good; there's a decent lounge with billiards and foosball, plus a self-service canteen and mountain bikes for hire. To get there, take bus No 6 or No 8 from Angers train station.

Hôtel du Centre (☎ 02 41 87 45 07; 12 rue St-Laud; d with shower & toilet €28) In a pretty pedestrian street, it has ordinary rooms above a popular, comfy-leather-sofa-filled bar of the same name.

Camping

Camping du Lac de Maine (☎ 02 41 73 05 03; fax 02 41 73 02 20; av du Lac de Maine; camping €9.70-13; ⊙ mid-Mar–mid-Oct) overlooking a lake, is approximately 2.5km southwest of Angers. To get to this 162-site area from town, take bus No 6 from the stop at the train station.

MID-RANGE

Hôtel du Mail (☎ 02 41 25 05 25; hoteldumailangers@ yahoo.fr; 8-10 rue des Ursules; s/d from €37/49; Ⓟ) This

fantastic not-quite-boutique hotel fills a lovely townhouse set around a quiet courtyard. The beautiful, well-furnished interior is immaculate and the overall experience is better than its two-star rating would imply.

Hôtel Continental (☎ 02 41 86 94 94; www .hotellecontinental.com; 12-14 rue Louis de Romain; s/d €42/56) Right in the centre of town, this reliable two-star has a stylised 1920s logo, but modern, if unspectacular rooms. The buffet breakfast (€6) is good value. It is accessible to disabled travellers.

Eating

Auberge Angevine (9 rue Cordelle; ⊙ noon-2pm, 6-11pm Tue-Sat) Wenches in medieval costume serve up platters of wild boar and goblets of red wine in this themed restaurant that doesn't take itself too seriously. The venue is a cavernous old chapel, with wooden benches and candelabras. Good fun and great value; Tuesday evening sees kids entertainment.

La Treille (☎ 02 41 88 45 51; 12 rue Montault; lunch menu €10, dinner menus €14-19; ⊙ Tue-Sat) A traditional, homely little restaurant at the back of the cathedral, boasting a terrace opposite Maison d'Adam and a good value lunch *menu*. Known locally for top-notch food and service.

Le Relais (☎ 02 41 88 42 51; 9 rue de la Gare; lunch menu €14.50, dinner menus €18.80-30; ⊙ Tue-Sat) A refined, turn-of-the-century ambience is to be found at this classy restaurant, but it's in an odd choice of area, down by the station. Traditional gourmet *plats* (specials), excellent fresh market cuisine and an extensive wine list.

SELF-CATERING

For top-rate sandwiches, filled baguettes and other satisfying lunchtime bites, head to **La Gourmandise** (cnr place Ste-Croix & rue St-Aubin; ⊙ 7am-7.30pm Mon-Sat). Count on a long queue at peak meal times.

Near the train station, **Supermarché Diagonal** (4 rue de la Gare; ⊙ 8am-8pm Mon-Sat) is a small grocery store.

Traiteur aux Rillauds d'Or (☎ 02 41 88 03 13; 59 rue St-Laud) sells prize-winning *rillons* (fat-fried pork cubes) and other meaty treats.

Drinking

Pubs and bars bespeckle the southern end of rue St-Laud. Irish bars dot the pedestrian section of nearby rue des Poeliers.

THE LOIRE

Le Twist (☎ 02 41 88 72 00; 8 rue St-Étienne; ⏰ 11.30am-2am Tue-Sat) Slick back your hair and head down to this fun – if a little kitsch – 50's style American bar. Traditional cocktails and tequila shots get this place buzzing until the early hours.

Café-Concert Le Coursive (☎ 02 41 25 13 87; 7bis blvd du Maréchal Foch; ⏰ 5pm-2am Mon-Sat) Live concerts are held regularly at this laid-back venue. The music is predominately on a jazz tip, but it's worth checking the listings for other genres.

Entertainment

For the latest information on cinema, music, and theatre, pick up a copy of *Angers Poche*, a free weekly gig guide available at the tourist office.

Getting There & Away

AIR

Aéroport d'Angers-Marcé (☎ 02 41 33 50 00) is 24km northeast of the centre in Marcé, off the A11.

BUS

Eurolines buses depart from quai H at Angers **bus station** (place de la Poissonnerie).

Regional services from the bus station are operated by **Anjou Bus** (☎ 02 41 88 59 25). Destinations include Brissac-Quincé (€1.40, 25 minutes, six daily); St-Georges-sur-Loire (€1.40, 40 minutes, about five daily), take bus No 7; and Saumur (€6.50, 1½ hours, about 10 daily), take bus No 11.

TRAIN

Angers' sparkling new glass and steel **SNCF train station** (Angers St-Laud; place de la Gare) is well served, and there is an **SNCF Boutique** (5 rue Chaperonnière). There is at least one train hourly to/from Tours (€14/16.90 for a non-TGV/TGV, 50 minutes to 1½ hours), Saumur (€6.80, 20 minutes) and St-Pierre des Corps (€16.90, one hour). Change trains in Tours or St-Pierre des Corps to get to/from Blois (€19.40, 1½ hours), Orléans (€24.60, two hours), and various other eastern Loire destinations. Trains run daily to/from Nantes (€13.50, 30 minutes, at least half-hourly), from where there are connecting southbound rail services to La Rochelle, Bordeaux and Toulouse.

There are TGV services between Angers and Paris' Gare Montparnasse (€41.40 to €52.50, 1½ hours, 10 to 15 daily).

Getting Around

BICYCLE

Sport ECO (☎ 02 41 87 07 77; 45 rue Maillé; per day/weekend/week €11/20/45; ⏰ 10am-noon & 2-7pm Tue-Sat) rents bicycles or rollerblades.

CAR

Car-rental companies:

Budget (☎ 02 41 88 23 16; 16 rue Denis Papin) Opposite the station.

Europcar (☎ 02 41 87 87 10; place de la Gare)

Hertz (☎ 02 41 88 15 16; rue Denis Papin) Also opposite the station.

AROUND ANGERS

South of Angers, the River Maine joins the Loire for the final leg of its journey to the Atlantic. The river banks immediately west of this confluence remain the source of some of the valley's most noble wines – Savennières, Coteaux du Layon and so on.

The **Musée de la Vigne et du Vin d'Anjou** (Museum of Anjou Wine and Vines) 17km south of Angers in St-Lambert du Lattay, is the best place to learn more about these wines.

The 13th-century **Prieuré de l'Epinay** (☎ 02 41 39 14 44; bernard.gaultier3@wanadoo.fr; d with breakfast €70; ⏰ Easter-Sep; 🚲) in St-Georges-sur-Loire, 1km southwest of Serrant, is a delightful place to stay (and eat) for wine lovers. The *chambre d'hôte* is run by a wine connoisseur who takes guests on tours of surrounding wine cellars. The priory rents bicycles.

Château de Serrant

Château de Serrant (☎ 02 41 39 13 01; adult/child €8.40/4.60; ⏰ Apr–mid-Nov), 15km west of Angers, is a perfect example of Renaissance architecture, with an unusually well-furnished interior. Its library has over 12,000 books. The 17th-century ebony cabinet in the drawing room conceals 33 secret drawers and is one of four known to exist in the world (the others are in Windsor Castle, Château de Fontainebleau and Amsterdam's Rijksmuseum). Guided tours depart at 20 minutes past the hour from 10.20am to 5.20pm, with extra tours at 10 minutes to the hour in July and August (no tours 11.20am to 2.20pm).

GETTING THERE & AWAY

Château de Serrant is 15km west of Angers on the N23. It's an easy cycle from Angers. Bus Nos 18 and 18B to St-Georges-sur-Loire (40 minutes, five daily) stop nearby.

Château de Brissac

This highly ornate chocolate-box folly **Château de Brissac** (☎ 02 41 91 22 21; adult/student & child €7/5.50; 🕙 10am-6pm Jul–mid-Sep, 10am-noon & 2.15-5.15pm Apr-Jun & Sep-Oct) is 15km south of Angers in Brissac-Quincé. Home to the dukes of Brissac since 1502, it is the tallest castle in the Loire at seven storeys and sits regally amid grounds studded with cedar trees and stretching across 800 hectares.

Inside, flamboyant furnishings and ornamentation coat its 203 rooms. The theatre, lit with chandeliers, was the whimsical creation of the Vicomtesse de Trèdene, a soprano with a passion for the arts. Château de Brissac can be visited with an hourly guided tour.

You can stay at the château (p395).

GETTING THERE & AWAY

Travelling from Angers, Brissac-Quincé can be reached via the D748 and its continuation, the D761. Bus Nos 9 and 9B link Angers bus station with Brissac-Quincé (€3, 25 minutes, six daily); the village bus stop is on place de la République, in front of the chateau.

SAUMUR & TROGLODYTE VALLEY

pop (Saumur) 30,100

The notability of small-town Saumur, 70km southeast of Angers, rides on the renowned National Equestrian School, stabled in St-Hilaire-St-Florent on its western outskirts. In the town centre, military personnel from the calvary school – stationed here since 1599 – buzz around town on bicycles, creating a pleasant old-fashioned atmosphere.

In the Revolution, *troglodytes* – Swisscheese-like caves hollowed in the chalky buffs that dominate the river banks around Saumur – provided a refuge for 75% of the populations of Angers and Saumur. Today the caves are used to store wine, grow mushrooms and bake *fouaces*, a kind of pitta bread that is typical of this valley.

Information

Doué-la-Fontane Tourist Office (☎ 02 41 59 20 49; tourisme@ville-douelafontaine.fr; 30 place des Fontaines) On the central square.

Saumur Tourist Office (☎ 02 41 40 20 60; www.saumur-tourisme.com; place de la Bilange; 🕙 9.15am-7pm Mon-Sat, 10.30am-12.30pm & 2.30-5.30pm Sun mid-May–mid-Oct; 9.15am-12.30pm & 2-6pm Mon-Sat mid-Oct-Apr) Near the bridge (Pont Cessart), inside the old theatre.

Saumur

The historic heart of Saumur, on the south bank of the Loire, is dominated by **Château de Saumur** (☎ 02 41 40 24 40; adult/child €6/4; 🕙 9.30am-6pm Jul & Aug, 10am-1pm & 2-5.30pm Sep-Jun, closed Tue Nov-Mar & Mon Jan), a stunning, fairy-tale castle cornered by pointed towers. It was built under Louis XI from 1246 and has been used as a dungeon, a fortress and a country residence. Today it houses two museums, one dedicated to horses and the other to decorative arts.

The **École Nationale d'Équitation** (National Equestrian School; ☎ 02 41 53 50 60; www.cadrenoir.fr), 3km west of the town centre in St-Hilaire–St-Florent, trains instructors and riders at competition level, prepares teams for the Olympic Games and is home to the elite Cadre Noir (p424). The school sports Europe's largest indoor riding arena. Guided **tours** (morning/afternoon €7/5; 🕙 9.30am Tue-Sat, btwn 2-4pm Sat & Sun Apr-Sep) include watching a Cadre Noir training session. Advance reservations are essential; tours are held in English when there are enough Anglophones.

Surrounding **mushroom farms** recycle the 10 tonnes of droppings dumped daily by the school's 400 horses. The **Musée du Champignon** (☎ 02 41 50 31 55; adult/student/children €6.50/5/4; 🕙 10am-7pm), tucked in a cave in St-Hilaire-St-Florent, is a living example of the area's thriving button-mushroom industry that occupies 800km of Saumurois caves and accounts for 65% of national production.

West of Saumur

Caves riddle this stretch, dubbed 'Troglodyte Valley'. **St-George des Sept Voies**, 23km west of Saumur, is home to the **Hélice Terrestre de l'Orbière** (☎ 02 41 57 95 92; Espace d'Art Plastique Contemporain; admission €4; 🕙 11am-8pm May-Sep, 2-6pm Oct-Apr), a startling piece of monumental art, sculpted underground by local artist Jacques Warminski (1946–96). The screw-shaped subterranean gallery, duplicated in reverse above ground, can be explored on foot.

In **Gennes**, 8km southeast, there's a **Gallo-Roman amphitheatre** (☎ 02 41 51 55 04), built around AD 150, which in summer hosts lively (bloodless) re-enactments of the bloody spectacles once staged by the Romans. From here, the scenic D69 cuts south through the green **Forêt de le Chêne-Rond** to **Doué-la-Fontaine** (population 7200), an ideal base for exploring Troglodyte Valley. In the town **zoo** (☎ 02 41 59

THE LOIRE

CADRE NOIR

Three moves set the Cadre Noir apart from its equestrian counterparts in Vienna: the *croupade*, which requires the horse to stretch its hind legs 45° into the air while its front legs stay on the ground; the *courbette*, which sees its front legs raised and tucked firmly into its body; and the demanding *cabriole*, which elevates the horse into the air in a powerful four-legged leap. These acrobatic feats, far from being crude or cruel, are considered the height of grace, elegance and Classicism. They are achieved after 5½ years of training, which starts when a horse is three years old. Daily training sessions last 1½ hours, following which the horse is untacked, washed down, dried and boxed for the remaining 22hrs of the day.

A black cap and jacket, gold spurs and three golden wings on the rider's whip are the distinctive trademarks of the elite Cadre Noir rider.

18 58; adult/child €12/6; ☻ 9am-7pm Apr-Sep, 10am-6pm Oct-Mar), off route de Cholet (D960), giraffes hang out in former falun pits and crocodiles bathe in pools inside clammy caves. Other troglodyte sites here include **Les Perrières** (☎ 02 41 59 71 29; 545 rue des Perrières), where falun rock was quarried in the 18th century; and the **Cave aux Sarcophages** (☎ 02 41 59 24 95; 1 rue Croix Mordret), an ancient Merovingian mine where 35,000-odd Monolithic sarcophagi were manufactured from the 6th to the 9th centuries.

The abandoned troglodytic village of **Rochemenier**, about 6km north of Doué via the D761, is also open to visitors from April to October.

East of Saumur

Saumur's eastern Troglodyte Valley is dominated by underground wine cellars. Fruity Saumur-Champigny red wine, the most respected Saumurois appellation, can be sampled at various cave cellars in **Souzay-Champigny**, 6km east of Saumur.

Subterranean **Musée de la Pomme Tapée** (Museum of Tapped Apples; ☎ 02 41 51 48 30; adult/child €4.80/2.80; ☻ 2.30-6pm Tue-Fri, 10am-noon & 2.30-6pm Sat & Sun Jul & Aug, Sat & Sun only Apr-Jun & Sep-Nov) in Val Hulin, 3km further east along the riverside D947, demonstrates how apples

were dried, squashed and rehydrated into spiced mulled wine in the 19th century.

Button mushrooms are the gastronomic speciality of the **Cave à Champignons** in Le Saut aux Loups, a few kilometres east of Musée de la Pomme Tapée.

The neighbouring medieval villages of **Montsoreau** (population 560) and **Candes-sur-Martin** (240) are a blend of mellow-hued rooftops, snug on the confluence of the Loire and the Vienne.

The breathtaking, 12th-century Romanesque **Abbaye de Fontevraud** (☎ 02 41 51 71 41), 4km south of Montsoreau, forms the largest monastic ensemble in France. Until it closed in 1793, it was unique in that its nuns and monks were governed by a woman: the abbess. It was also one of France's harshest prisons between 1804 and 1963 – now people pay to stay in luxury at this Unesco World Heritage Site.

Sleeping & Eating

See p395 for information on staying at the grand Château de Verrieres in Saumur.

Prieuré St-Lazare (☎ 02 41 51 73 16; www.hotelfp-fontevraud.com; d €60-85), a converted priory in the grounds of Abbaye de Fontevraud, is a prestigious choice. Despite its 12th-century origins, the rooms are modern and comfortable. The cloister restaurant is renowned for its gastronomic menu and wine list.

Auberge de la Route d'Or (☎ 02 41 95 81 10; 2 place de l'Église, Candes-sur-Martin; lunch menu €12.90, dinner menus €19.90-31; ☻ daily Jul & Aug, Thu-Mon Sep-May), just under the church in Candes-sur-Martin, is well worth a gastronomical detour: it has a roaring fire in winter, a terrace in summer and delicious *menus*.

Other options in town include **Camping Caravaning l'Île d'Offard** (☎ 02 41 40 30 00; fax 02 41 67 37 81; rue de Verden, Saumer; camping €13.50-18.50; ☻ Mar-Nov) on the island at Saumur and **Centre International de Séjour l'Île d'Offard** (dm incl breakfast €10.50, d with shower €31) next door.

Getting There & Away

From Angers, **Anjou Bus** (☎ 02 41 88 59 25) operates regular daily buses to/from Saumur (1½ hours) and Doué-la-Fontaine (€5, 55 minutes, about six daily).

Saumur is on the train line between Tours (€9.20, 30 to 50 minutes) and Angers (€6.80, 30 minutes) with regular trains – at least hourly – in both directions.

Burgundy

CONTENTS

Bordered to the south and east by the snow-crowned Alps, and to the north and west by the hills and flat plains of Champagne and the Massif Central, Burgundy is in many ways the real heartland of France. It's also at the epicentre of two of the country's greatest passions: food and wine. Some of the most prestigious vintages are produced in northern Burgundy around Chablis, and along the sun-baked Côte d'Or south of Beaune. It's certainly a place where you can eat and drink to your heart's content, but there's more to Burgundy than gastronomic greatness.

Until the 15th century Burgundy was an independent kingdom from the rest of France, with a vast territory that extended far beyond its own borders. The remnants of its rich heritage are scattered across the region, from the glorious medieval and Renaissance architecture of Dijon and Beaune to the grand chateaux of Tanlay, St-Fargeau and Ancy-le-Franc. In the Middle Ages Burgundy was also one of the most important religious centres in France. Nearly every town boasts an impressive church, and the magnificent abbeys of Auxerre, Vézelay, Pontigny and Fontenay are some of the best preserved in the country.

Burgundy is also a great place to experience the French countryside. Whether exploring the wild reaches of the Parc Naturel Régional du Morvan, floating down the waterways of the Yonne or sailing across the Côte d'Or vineyards in a hot-air balloon, you'll find Burgundy is one of France's most varied *départements* – an enticing blend of hilltop villages and bustling market towns, grand chateaux and tiny churches, patchwork fields and abandoned abbeys.

Burgundy is divided into four *départements:* Yonne (capital: Auxerre) in the northwest, Côte d'Or (capital: Dijon) in the northeast, Saône-et-Loire (capital: Mâcon) in the south, and the southwestern Nièvre *département*, which is mostly taken up by the Parc Naturel Régional du Morvan.

BURGUNDY

HIGHLIGHTS

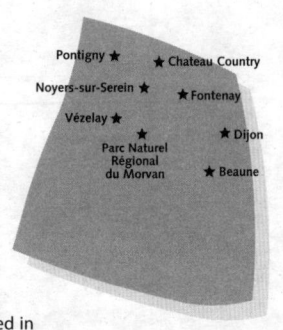

- Wander through the lavish mansions of **Ancy-le-Franc** (p436), **Tanlay** (p436) and **St-Fargeau** (p436)

- Sample the local wines in the cellars of **Beaune** (p454) and the **Côte d'Or** (p453)

- Explore the walled village of **Noyers-sur-Serein** (p435)

- The hilltop town of **Vézelay** (p440)

- Imagine the life of Cistercian monks at the abbeys of **Fontenay** (p459) and **Pontigny** (p434)

- Hike and bike in the **Parc Naturel Régional du Morvan** (p442)

- Delve into Dijon's medieval and Renaissance past captured in the city's **museums** and **architecture** (p445)

| POPULATION: 1.6 million | AREA: 31,582 SQ KM |

History

At its height in the 14th and 15th centuries, the dukedom of Burgundy (Bourgogne in French) was one of the richest and most powerful states in Europe, second only to Venice in terms of wealth. The Valois Dukes commanded a vast swathe of territory encompassing Holland, Flanders, Luxembourg, Belgium, Picardy, Alsace and Lorraine, and their rivalry with their French neighbours was bitter (during the Hundred Years War, it was the Burgundians who sold Joan of Arc to the English). At the time, it seemed more likely that the kingdom of France would become part of Burgundy, rather than the other way around. But in the

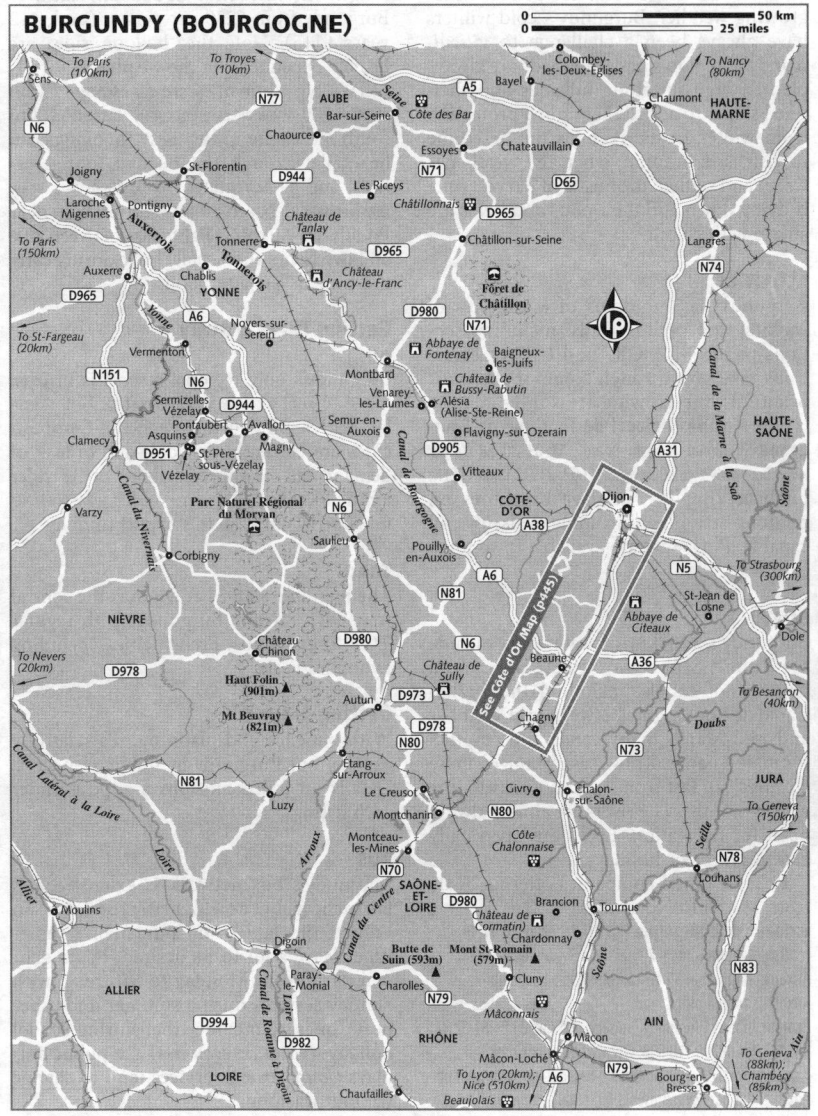

BURGUNDY (BOURGOGNE)

end, when Duke Charles the Bold was killed during the siege of Nancy, it was Burgundy that became part of France, in 1477.

Climate

Burgundy shares a similar climate to much of the rest of the country. The mixture of sunshine and showers in spring and the long, hot summers make for perfect wine-growing weather. Burgundy's cold winters have always been a challenge to *viticulteurs;* the region's best vineyards are always planted high up along hillsides and sheltered slopes to afford them some protection from winter frosts. Perhaps the best time to visit is in autumn, when the weather is warm and settled, the bustle of harvest time is dying down and the woods and fields are ablaze with colour.

Activities

Burgundy has hundreds of kilometres of walking and cycling trails, including sections of the GR2, GR7 and GR76. Several trails take you through some of the most beautiful wine-growing areas in France.

The **Comité Régional de Tourisme de Bourgogne** (Regional Tourism Board; ☎ 03 80 28 02 80; www.burgundy-tourism.com; BP 1602, 21035 Dijon CEDEX) publishes English-language brochures on outdoor activities (including walking and canal boating) that are available from tourist offices.

BOATING

Burgundy's 1200km of waterways include the Yonne, Saône and Seille Rivers and a network of canals, including the 242km Canal de Bourgogne. Between mid-October and mid-March many canals are emptied for maintenance. Known as *chômages,* these closures can last from several weeks to one or two months. The rivers are almost always open for navigation. Locks are open daily except on major holidays.

Reliable rental companies offering boats from March to November:

Bateaux de Bourgogne (☎ 03 86 72 92 10; sla@tourisme-yonne.com; 1-2 quai de la République, 89000 Auxerre) A group of 15 rental companies based above Auxerre's tourist office.

France Afloat (Burgundy Cruisers; ☎ /fax 03 86 81 67 87, UK ☎ /fax 08700 110 538; www.franceafloat.com; 1 quai du Port, 89270 Vermenton) Based 23km southeast of Auxerre, this agency represents 10 rental companies.

Locaboat Plaisance (☎ 03 86 91 72 72; www.locaboat.com; Port au Bois, BP 150, 89303 Joigny CEDEX) Offers boats from many locations in France, including Joigny (27km northwest of Auxerre) and Venarey-les-Laumes (67km northwest of Dijon).

HOT-AIR BALLOONING

From April to October you can take a stunning *montgolfière* (hot-air balloon) ride over Burgundy from €230 per person (under 12 years €115). Note that balloon rides are heavily dependent on the weather.

Two big companies are **Air Escargot** (☎ 03 85 87 12 30; www.air-escargot.com), based 16km south of Beaune in Remigny (bookings can be made through the Beaune tourist office); and **Air Adventures** (☎ 03 80 90 74 2; www.airadventures.fr), based 50km west of Dijon near Pouilly-en-Auxois. Flights last between one and two hours and usually leave during early morning or late afternoon.

Getting There & Away

AIR

Burgundy's only regional airport is in **Dijon** (☎ 03 80 67 67 67; www.dijon.aeroport.fr), but regular chartered flights to French and European cities are currently on hold, due to lack of demand and the unpredictability of the wider airline industry. Plans are under way to find new carriers to keep the airport running.

TRAIN

The mainline station at Dijon is the central transport hub for Burgundy, with regular TGV links to most French cities, including Lyon and Paris.

Getting Around

With patience and planning, it's relatively easy to tour Burgundy by public transport. Details on trains and buses appear under each listing.

BUS

Burgundy's bus network is extensive and fairly cheap, but as with many rural areas in France, timetables and punctuality sometimes leave a lot to be desired. Buses generally run from Monday to Saturday, with Sunday services during summer and other peak times. Remember that during school holidays *(vacances scolaires)* and public holidays *(jours feriés),* services tend to change without warning.

GARETH McCORMACK

Parc National de la Vanoise (p519),
Rhône-Alpes

GLENN VAN DER KNIJFF

Cathédrale St-Jean (p472), Vieux Lyon

NICOLA WILLIAMS

Pont d'Arc p488),
Rhône Valley

Vineyards of the Beaujolais region (p484)

PASCALE BEROUJON

Musée d'Histoire Naturelle
(p612), Nantes

Le Thot – Espace Cro-Magnon
(p594), Vézère Valley

The *bastide* village of Najac (p606), Quercy

Seafood harvest at La Rochelle (p620) on the Atlantic Coast

CAR

As always, the most convenient way to get around is by car, which will allow you to get off the beaten track and explore some of the lesser known areas of Burgundy. Major car-hire firms are found in most large towns.

CYCLING

Since most of Burgundy is (fairly) flat, cycling is also a great way of getting around. Tourist offices stock a selection of guidebooks and leaflets detailing possible routes – the most popular criss-cross through the Morvan National Park and the wine territory of the Côte d'Or. Bikes are widely available for hire.

TRAIN

The train is probably the best way of getting around if you're planning on taking public transport. Services connect Auxerre, Avallon, Beaune and Montbard, from where you can catch regional trains to most areas around Burgundy.

YONNE

The Yonne *département,* roughly midway between Dijon and Paris, has long been the gateway to Burgundy. The region is home to the riverside city Auxerre; the white-wine centre, Chablis; medieval towns Pontigny, Noyers-sur-Serein and Tonnerre; the chateaux of Tanlay and Ancy-le-Franc; Avallon's hilltop city; and the medieval village of Vézelay.

AUXERRE

pop 37,800

Auxerre (pronounced oh-*sair*) is one of the oldest and most alluring towns in the Yonne. The city's varied architecture reflects its age; wandering through the maze of cobbled streets in the old city, you'll pass Roman remains, Gothic churches, and timber-framed medieval houses, and gaze across a jumble of belfries, spires and steep tiled rooftops all the way to the wide River Yonne.

Auxerre makes a good base for visiting northern Burgundy, and the city's pleasure-boat port makes it an excellent place to rent a canal boat (p428).

History

The area around Auxerre has been inhabited since long before the birth of Christ, but the first significant settlement grew up under the auspices of the Romans, and the city still retains some of its Gallo-Roman architecture. Auxerre became an important religious centre from the 4th century, especially following the construction of the town's impressive abbey, built to house the tomb of St-Germain. The town found much of its wealth in the Middle Ages as a river-port and centre for the wine-growing industry, but after the coming of the railways, most of the heavy industry moved elsewhere and the town slipped into economic decline.

These days Auxerre has reinvented itself as a pleasure port and a bustling provincial town, and also boasts one of the country's top football teams.

Orientation

The old city climbs from the left bank of the River Yonne, while the train station is 700m east of the river in the industrial zone. The commercial centre stretches uphill from Cathédrale St-Étienne to the post office, with shops lining rue de Paris and rue du Temple. The liveliest areas are around pedestrianised rue de l'Horloge and place Charles Surugue.

Information

INTERNET ACCESS

Maison de la Jeunesse (pl de l'Arquebuse; Internet access free; ⏰ Mon-Fri 10am-12pm & 2-6pm) Youth centre (inside the France Telecom building) offering free Internet access.

LAUNDRY

Laundrette (138 rue de Paris; ⏰ 8am-9pm)

MONEY

Banks can be found between place Charles Surugue and place Charles Lepère. The tourist office changes small amounts of money on Sunday and holidays.

POST

Post Office (pl Charles Surugue)

TOURIST INFORMATION

Tourist Office (☎ 03 86 52 06 19; www.ot-auxerre.fr; 1-2 quai de la République; ⏰ 9am-1pm & 2-7pm Mon-Sat,

AUXERRE

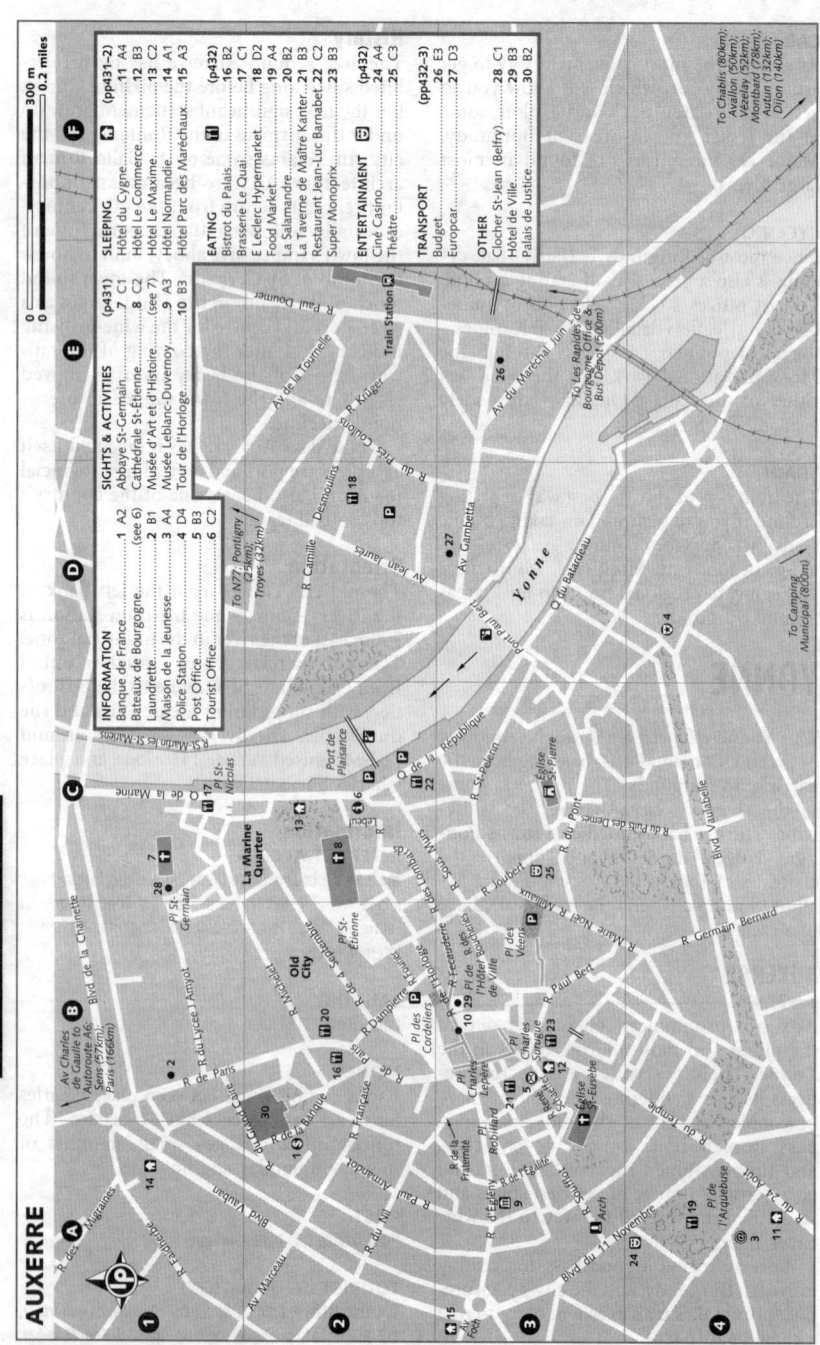

INFORMATION
Banque de France........................	**1** A2
Bateaux de Bourgogne.................	(see 6)
Laundrette....................................	**2** B1
Maison de la Jeunesse..................	**3** A4
Police Station...............................	**4** D4
Post Office...................................	**5** B3
Tourist Office..............................	**6** C2

SIGHTS & ACTIVITIES (p431)
Abbaye St-Germain......................	**7** C1
Cathédrale St-Étienne..................	**8** C2
Musée d'Art et d'Histoire............	(see 7)
Musée Leblanc-Duvernoy............	**9** A3
Tour de l'Horloge........................	**10** B3

SLEEPING (pp431-2)
Hôtel du Cygne............................	**11** A4
Hôtel Le Commerce......................	**12** B3
Hôtel Le Maxime..........................	**13** C2
Hôtel Normandie.........................	**14** A1
Hôtel Parc des Maréchaux............	**15** A3

EATING (p432)
Bistrot du Palais..........................	**16** B2
Brasserie Le Quai.........................	**17** C1
E Leclerc Hypermarket.................	**18** D2
Food Market................................	**19** A4
La Salamandre..............................	**20** B2
La Taverne de Maître Kanter........	**21** B3
Restaurant Jean-Luc Barnabet......	**22** C2
Super Monoprix...........................	**23** B3

ENTERTAINMENT (p432)
Ciné Casino.................................	**24** A4
Théâtre.......................................	**25** C3

TRANSPORT (pp432-3)
Budget..	**26** E3
Europcar......................................	**27** D3

OTHER
Clocher St-Jean (Belfry)...............	**28** C1
Hôtel de Ville..............................	**29** B3
Palais de Justice..........................	**30** B2

9.30am-1pm & 3-6.30pm Sun mid-Jun–mid-Sep; 9.30am-12.30pm & 2-6pm Mon-Fri, 9.30-12.30pm & 2-6.30pm Sat, 10am-1pm Sun mid-Sep–mid-Jun)

Sights & Activities

Wonderful views of the city are available from **Pont Paul Bert** (1857) and the arched footbridge opposite the tourist office. Both bridges are ideal places for starting a walk around the city. Auxerre's oldest architecture is found along the streets leading from the river towards the abbey and the cathedral.

ABBAYE ST-GERMAIN

The ancient **Abbaye St-Germain** (☎ 03 86 18 05 50; pl St-Germain; adult €4.20; ⏰ 10am-6.30pm Wed-Mon Jun-Sep, 10am-noon & 2-6pm Wed-Mon Oct-May) began as a basilica above the tomb of St Germain, founder of the first monastery in Auxerre. Over the centuries, as the site's importance grew, so did the abbey. During the Middle Ages, it attracted pilgrims from all over Europe.

The atmospheric **crypts** (last tour at 5pm or 5.30pm) contain some of the only surviving examples of Carolingian architecture in France. Supported by 1000-year-old oak beams, the walls and vaulted ceiling are decorated with 9th-century frescoes, and the far end of the crypt houses the tomb of St Germain himself. Guided tours (in French) are provided several times daily. Excavation has uncovered sarcophagi from as early as the 6th century, as well as the foundations of previous buildings. Left in situ, they now form a fascinating exhibit.

MUSÉE D'ART ET D'HISTOIRE

Housed in the eastern section of Abbaye St-Germain, and included in the abbey's admission price, this intriguing museum displays prehistoric artefacts, Gallo-Roman remains and sculpture and pottery discovered in and around Auxerre.

The same ticket includes entry to **Musée Leblanc-Duvernoy** (☎ 03 86 52 44 63; 9bis rue d'Églény; separate admission €2.10; ⏰ 2-6pm Wed-Mon), which has a fine collection of china and *faïence* (decorated pottery).

CATHÉDRALE ST-ÉTIENNE

The vast Gothic **Cathédrale St-Étienne** (place St-Germain; ⏰ 7.30am-7pm summer, 7.30am-5.30pm winter) and its stately 68m-high bell tower dominate Auxerre's skyline (and most of

the postcards, too). The building was mainly constructed between the 13th and 16th centuries, though the choir, ambulatory and vivid **stained-glass windows** date from the 1200s. The Gothic western front was badly damaged by the hammer-happy Huguenots, who decapitated most of the statues during the Wars of Religion.

The **crypt** (admission €2.30; ⏰ 9am-noon & 2-6pm, closed Sun morning in summer) contains frescoes dating from the 11th to 13th centuries, including a scene of Christ on horseback unknown anywhere else in Christendom. Sitting in the underground chapel, with light filtering through the little windows and faint echoes of voices in the cathedral above, it's easy to imagine the power such places held for medieval pilgrims.

Upstairs, the modest **treasury** (admission €1.50) displays what was left of the cathedral's riches after the revolutionary mobs came calling.

From June to September a 75-minute sound-and-light show is held nightly in the cathedral, and from June to August hour-long organ concerts are held every Sunday.

TOUR DE L'HORLOGE

The spire-topped **Tour de l'Horloge** (clock tower; rue de l'Horloge) was built in 1483 as part of the city's fortifications. On the 17th-century clock faces (there's one on each side), the sun-hand indicates the time of day; the moon-hand shows what day of the lunar month it is, making a complete rotation every 29½ days. Look out for the fibre-glass statue of Marie Noël, Auxerre's best known poet, near the clock tower.

Sleeping

BUDGET

Hôtel Le Commerce (☎ 03 86 52 03 16; hotel_du _commerce@ipoint.fr; 5 rue René Schaeffer; s/d/f €41/45/55) A cheap, welcoming place in the centre of town. The rooms are hardly luxurious, but the old building is full of character with original beams and a timber-framed frontage. The **restaurant** (mains €8-12) serves up Italian and French cuisines.

Camping Municipal (☎ 03 86 52 11 15; 8 route de Vaux; camping from €2.30; ⏰ Apr-Sep) A shaded, grassy place 1.5km south of the train station (and across the street from the football stadium). From place de l'Arquebuse, take bus A (two to three per hour until 7pm) to the Stades Arbre Sec stop.

MID-RANGE

Hôtel Parc des Maréchaux (☎ 03 86 51 43 77; www
.hotel-parcmarechaux.com; 6 av Foch; s €70, d €75-90;
ⓟ) One of Auxerre's best hotels, housed
in a former private mansion near the old
city. The 25 rooms are all named after
French marshals, and the best have balconies overlooking the peaceful garden,
where you can enjoy a luxurious summertime breakfast.

Hôtel Le Maxime (☎ 03 86 52 14 19; www.lemax
ime.net; 2 quai de la Marine; s/d €65/75, ste €100-120;
ⓟ 🐾) In a wonderful spot with views over
the River Yonne, this upmarket place offers
impeccable rooms and first-class service.
The attached restaurant is also very good,
if a little pricey.

Hôtel Normandie (☎ 03 86 52 57 80; normandie@
acom.fr; 41 blvd Vauban; s €49-55, d €55-75; 🕙 closed early
Feb; ⓟ) On the tree-lined square of blvd
Vauban, this is a great value hotel just outside the old city. The ivy-covered frontage,
friendly staff and understated rooms make
it feel like a much more expensive country
hotel.

Hotel du Cygne (☎ 03 86 52 26 51; fax 03 86 51
68 33; 14 rue du 24 Août; s/d €47/52; ⓟ) A cheaper
place outside the city centre, in a modern
building near place Arquebuse. The 30
plain rooms have all the mod-cons including satellite TV and minibars.

Eating

Bistrot du Palais (☎ 03 86 51 47 02; 69 rue de Paris;
mains €10; 🕙 lunch & dinner Tue-Sat) A classic
French bistro with tiny tables, checked
tablecloths and the essential sound of clat-
tering saucepans. It offer homely country
cooking, Lyonnaise sausages and Burgundian stews are specialities.

La Salamandre (☎ 03 86 52 87 87; 84 rue de Paris;
lunch menu €22, dinner menus €30-51; 🕙 closed Sun, dinner Wed, lunch Sat) A refined seafood restaurant,
with dishes ranging from pan-fried scallops
and *fruits de mer* (seafood) to wild turbot
and skate wing.

La Taverne de Maître Kanter (☎ 03 86 52 16 21;
11 pl Charles Lepère; mains €12-16; 🕙 lunch & dinner)
A reliable restaurant that serves enormous
plates of *sauerkraut* and more kinds of sausages than you knew existed.

Brasserie Le Quai (☎ 03 86 51 66 67; 4 pl St-Nicolas;
pizzas €8-10.50, menus €16-23; 🕙 lunch & dinner) Situated in a gorgeous fountainside setting
within a stone's throw of the river, this chic,

contemporary brasserie serves a good selection of salads, pizzas and pasta classics.

Restaurant Jean-Luc Barnabet (☎ 03 86 51 68
88; 14 quai de la République; menus €34-66, children's menu
€16; 🕙 lunch Wed-Sun, dinner Wed-Sat) Auxerre's
finest food is along the quay at Restaurant
Jean-Luc Barnabet. The owner's innovative versions of traditional French dishes
have earned many accolades, including a
Michelin star.

SELF-CATERING

A large **food market** (pl de l'Arquebuse) springs to
life on Tuesday and Friday mornings. There
are plenty of food shops along rue de Paris.

Supermarkets include a **Super Monoprix** (pl
Charles Surugue; 🕙 8.30am-8pm Mon-Sat) and a vast
E Leclerc hypermarket (14 av Jean Jaurès; 🕙 9am-8pm
Mon-Fri).

Entertainment

CINEMAS

Ciné Casino (☎ 03 86 52 36 80; 1 blvd du 11 Novembre)
This cinema has eight screens and shows
mainstream releases and art-house films
(often nondubbed).

THEATRE & MUSIC

Théâtre (☎ 03 86 72 24 24; 54 rue Joubert) The city's
Art Deco style theatre produces dance,
drama and theatre, and hosts Le Studio, a
regular event that brings top jazz talent to
the town from mid-October to early June.

Getting There & Away

BUS

Buses run by **Les Rapides de Bourgogne** (☎ 03
86 94 95 00; 3 rue des Fontenottes; 🕙 9am-noon Mon-Fri,
9am-noon Sat afternoon) link the train station and
place de l'Arquebuse with Chablis (€4.20,
35 minutes, two daily Monday to Friday
and usually one on Saturday) and Pontigny
(€3, 35 minutes, one or two daily except
Sunday). The tourist office has timetables.

CAR

Car-rental companies:
Budget (☎ 03 80 18 00 88; 32 av Gambetta)
Europcar (☎ 03 86 46 99 08; 9 av Gambetta)

TRAIN

Trains run from the Auxerre–St-Gervais **station** (rue Paul Doumer) to the mainline Laroche-
Migennes station (€3.30, 20 minutes, 12 to 15
daily), where you can change for Paris' Gare

de Lyon (€20.60, two to three hours, eight to 10 daily); Dijon (€20.80, two hours, three direct and 10 nondirect daily); and Montbard (€13.70 from Auxerre, 1½ hours, six to 10 daily), which is near Abbaye de Fontenay. Trains also go to Sermizelles-Vézelay (€6.40, 45 minutes, three to five daily) and Avallon (€8.10, one hour, three to five daily).

Getting Around

Free parking is available on quai de la Marine and quai de la République, and on the *boulevards périphériques* around the old city: de la Chainettes, Vauban, du 11 Novembre and Vaulabelle. The city's one-way system can be very confusing – bring a good map if you're driving.

For a taxi call ☎ 03 86 94 02 02 or ☎ 03 86 46 95 67.

AROUND AUXERRE

Between the River Yonne and the Canal de Bourgogne lie the Auxerrois and the Tonnerrois, rural areas covered with forests, fields, pastures and vineyards. The quiet back roads, such as the D124, and many of the walking trails make for excellent cycling.

La Puisaye

The countryside west of Auxerre is known as **La Puisaye**, a sparsely-populated landscape of woods, winding creeks and dark hills. The area is best-known as the birthplace of Colette (1873–1954), author of *La Maison de Claudine* and *Gigi*, and still one of France's most popular women writers. Colette was born in the tiny town of St-Sauveur-en-Puisaye, southwest of Auxerre, and much of her work explores her rural childhood in Burgundy. The **Musée Colette** (Colette Museum; ☎ 03 86 45 61 95; admission €4.30; ☯ 10am-6pm Wed-Mon Apr-Oct, weekends & public holidays only Nov-Mar), on the outskirts of St-Sauveur-en-Puisaye, houses a collection of her manuscripts, letters and belongings.

Other sights include the chateaux of **St-Fargeau** and **Ratilly** (see p436), and the **Chantier Médiéval de Guédelon** (☎ 03 86 45 66 66; www .guedelon.org; adult/child €8/6; ☯ 10am-6pm Thu-Tue & 10am-7pm Sun Mar-Jun, 10am-7pm Jul & Aug, 10am-5.30pm Thu-Tue Sep-Nov), near St-Fargeau, where for the last six years, a huge team of builders, stonemasons and carpenters (in period costume) have been constructing a medieval

castle with only 13th-century tools and materials. No-one seems to have any idea when the project is likely to be finished.

The **Musée de la Reproduction du Son** (☎ 03 86 74 13 06; musee.son@wanadoo.fr; St-Fargeau; admission €5.50; ☯ 10am-noon & 2-6pm Apr-Nov, to 7pm Jul & Aug, also open 2-6pm school holidays year-round), in St-Fargeau itself, is also well worth investigating. This extraordinary little museum houses one of the country's finest collections of early sound-recording equipment, from pump-operated barrel organs to self-playing pianos – the noise when they're all going at once is unforgettable (and quite deafening).

Chablis

pop 2600

The well-to-do but sleepy town of Chablis, 19km east of Auxerre, has made its fortune growing, ageing and marketing the white wines that bear its name. True Chablis derives its character from the area's unique clay and limestone soil, which contains millions of fossilised oyster shells.

Most of Chablis' shops are closed on Monday and from noon to 3pm on other days. In winter many cellars and *domaines* close down, but in summer, especially around harvest-time, it's a great place to come to watch the wine industry in full swing.

HISTORY

The village of Chablis originally grew up around a small monastery in the 9th century. The original building was replaced by the present-day Église St-Martin, (modelled on the Gothic cathedral in Sens) during the 12th century. Monks from Chablis and the nearby Abbatiale at Pontigny were among the first to perfect the process of making white wine, and the town's vintages were highly prized as far back as the Middle Ages. The town grew rich on the proceeds of the wine industry, and its reputation for making some of France's best white wines continues to this day.

ORIENTATION & INFORMATION

Chablis' main street is known as rue Auxerroise (west of the main square, place Charles de Gaulle) and rue du Maréchal de Lattre de Tassigny (east of place Charles de Gaulle).

BURGUNDY

CHABLIS CLASS

Chablis is one of the largest wine-producing areas in Burgundy. The dry, light white wine is made exclusively from Chardonnay grapes, and is divided into four Appellations d'Origine Contrôlées (AOC): Petit Chablis, Chablis, Chablis Premier Cru and, most prestigious of all, Chablis Grand Cru. The seven *grands crus*, lovingly grown on just 1 sq km of land on the hillsides north of town, are Blanchot, Bougros, Les Clos, Grenouilles, Preuses, Valmur and Vaudésir.

Wine can be sampled and bought at dozens of places – the tourist office has a comprehensive list. One of the largest is **La Chablisienne** (☎ 03 86 42 89 89; blvd Pasteur; ☿ 9am-12.30pm & 2-7pm), a cooperative cellar 1km south of town on the D91 towards Noyers-sur-Serein. Free *dégustation* is possible year-round. Another good house is the family-run **Cave du Connaisseur** (☎ 03 86 42 87 15; www.chablis.net/caveduconnaisseur in French; rue des Moulins; ☿ 9am-noon & 2-6pm).

The **tourist office** (☎ 03 86 42 80 80; www.chablis .net; 1 quai du Biez; ☿ 10am-12.30pm & 1.30-6pm Mon-Sat, 10am-12.30pm Sun Dec-Mar) is just east of place Charles de Gaulle.

SIGHTS & ACTIVITIES

The 12th- and 13th-century early Gothic **Église St Martin** (☿ Jul & Aug), founded in the 9th century by monks fleeing the Norman attacks on Tours, is north of place Charles de Gaulle. South along rue Porte Noël are the twin bastions of **Porte Noël** (1778), which hosts art exhibitions from mid-June to mid-September. Nearby is the shell of a 16th-century building known (inaccurately) as the **synagogue** (12 rue des Juifs). **Petit Pontigny** (rue de Chichée) was once used by the Cistercian monks of Pontigny as a fermentation cellar.

Vineyard walks from Chablis include the **Sentier des Grands Crus** (8km) and the **Sentier des Clos** (13km to 24km, depending on your route). The tourist office sells a French-language topoguide (€5.50).

Cycling is a popular way to tour the surrounding countryside, and the tourist office helpfully hires **bikes** (2hr/full-day €3.80/12) from Easter to early October.

Nearby villages worth exploring include **Courgis**, which offers great views; **Chichée** and **Chemilly**, both on the River Serein; and **Chitry-le-Fort**, famous for its fortified church.

SLEEPING & EATING

Hôtel Bergerand's (☎ 03 86 18 96 08; www.bergerand -chablis-france.com; 4 rue des Moulins; d €55-75) A pleasant, rustic hotel within stumbling distance of the centre of Chablis – a bonus if you've gone a little wild on the wine-tasting.

Hostellerie des Clos (☎ 03 86 42 10 63; www.hos tellerie-des-clos.fr; rue Jules-Rathier; s €50-71, d €58-84; ☿ mid-Jan–mid-Dec; P ☒) A luxurious, three-

star hotel housed in the town's former hospices, with lavish rooms and enclosed gardens. A separate building offers suites and apartments (€100 to €183). The **restaurant** (menus €33-70) bears one Michelin star, and as you'd expect, the wine-list is rather impressive.

Many restaurants around place Charles de Gaulle have outside terraces. **Le Syracuse** (☎ 03 86 42 19 45; 19 rue du Maréchal de Tassigny; menus €12-23.50; ☿ closed Sun night & Mon) This place serves regional specialities and pizzas (from €7.50) in a vaulted, 13th-century dining room.

Except for the **Petit Casino grocery** (rue du Maréchal Leclerc; ☿ Mon-Sat), all the food shops along rue Auxerroise are closed on Sunday afternoon and Monday.

Chablis has an **outdoor food market** (place Charles de Gaulle; ☿ until 1pm Sun).

GETTING THERE & AWAY

Place Charles de Gaulle is linked to Auxerre by **Les Rapides de Bourgogne** (☎ 03 86 94 95 00) bus (€4.20, 35 minutes, two daily on weekdays, usually one on Saturday).

Pontigny

pop 825

Rising from flat fields 25km north of Auxerre, Pontigny's **Abbatiale** (abbey church; ☎ 03 86 47 54 99; ☿ 9am-6pm), is one of the last surviving examples of Cistercian architecture in Burgundy. The simplicity and purity of its construction reflects the austerity of the Cistercian order. On summer days sunshine filtering through the high windows bathes the abbey in light, creating an amazing sense of peace and tranquillity.

The Gothic sanctuary, 108m long and lined with 23 chapels, was built in the mid-

12th century, but the wooden choir screen, stalls and organ loft were added in the 17th and 18th centuries. Monks from the abbey were the first to perfect the production of Chablis wine.

The **tourist office** (☎ 03 86 47 47 03; pontigny@ wanadoo.fr; 22 rue Paul Desjardins; ⏰ 10am-12.30pm & 2-6pm Mon-Fri Apr-Oct, to 4.30pm Tue-Fri Nov-Mar), across the road from the Abbatiale, has information on accommodation and walking trips.

The only hotel in Pontigny is **Le Relais de Pontigny** (☎ 03 86 47 96 74; d from €30), a roadside bar 400m along the N77 from the tourist office. The 10 upstairs rooms are bland but cheap, and you can find food at the attached truckers' **restaurant** (menus €13-16). Or try the nearby **Moulin de Pontigny** (☎ 03 86 47 44 98; menus €20, €27 & €33; ⏰ lunch Mon-Sat, dinner Fri & Sat) offers fine rural cooking in the town's old mill – frog's legs, braised ham and *andouillette* (tripe sausage) are on the menu.

Supplies are available at the **Proximarché grocery** (43 rue Paul Desjardins; ⏰ 8.30am-1pm & 3-7.30pm, closed Sun afternoon).

Les Rapides de Bourgogne (☎ 03 86 94 95 00) runs daily buses to Pontigny from Auxerre (€3, 35 minutes).

Noyers-sur-Serein
pop 810

Surrounded by rolling pastureland and wooded hills, the tiny medieval village of Noyers (pronounced nwa-*yer*) is 30km southeast of Auxerre. Stone ramparts and fortified battlements hem the village in on every side, and from the imposing stone gateway, cobbled streets lead past 15th- and 16th-century gabled houses and half-timbered buildings. Many of the streets still bear their medieval names – look out for rue du Grenier-à-Sel (Salt Store) and place du Marché-au-Blé (Flour Market).

THE ENGLISH CONNECTION

Three archbishops of Canterbury played a role in the history of Pontigny Abbey: Thomas à Becket spent the first three years of his exile here (1164–66); Stephen Langton, a refugee from political turmoil in England, lived here for six years (from 1207 to 1213); and Edmund Rich, who fell ill and died at Soissy in 1240 while on his way to the Vatican, was brought here for burial.

A KNIGHT IN SHINING PETTICOATS

Speculation about the cross-dressing habits of the French secret agent Charles Chevalier d'Éon de Beaumont (1728–1810), born in Tonnerre, has been rife for centuries, especially in sex-obsessed England, where he spent much of his life wearing the latest women's fashion and spying for Louis XV. The locals, at least, have no doubt about the brave chevalier's suitability as a role model for today's youth: they've named the local secondary school after him.

Lines carved into the façade of the 18th-century **village hall**, next to the library, mark the level of historic floods. Across the street you'll find the **tourist office** (☎ 03 86 82 66 06; 22 pl de l'Hôtel de Ville; ⏰ 9am-noon & 2.30-6.30pm, closed Sat & Sun Oct-Easter).

Musée de Noyers (☎ 03 86 82 89 09; rue de l'Église; admission €3.05; ⏰ 11am-6.30pm Wed-Mon Jun-Sep, 2.30-6.30pm Sat & Sun Oct-May), along a back-street near the 15th-century church, displays a collection of **naive art** assembled by a local art historian.

Just outside the clock-topped southern gate, Chemin des Fossés leads eastwards towards the River Serein and a **riverside walk** around Noyers' 13th-century **fortifications.**

The only place to stay in the village is **Hôtel de la Vieille Tour** (☎ 03 86 82 87 69; fax 03 86 82 66 04; 59 place du Grenier-à-Sel; d €40-55; ⏰ Apr-Sep), a charming, ivy-covered hotel along one of the cobbled streets. The nicest rooms look onto the river behind the village, and there's a sweet garden where you can relax in summer.

There's a **camping ground** outside the city walls, on the left as you approach the southern gates, near the post office. The two grocery stores inside the gates are closed on Sunday afternoon.

Les Rapides de Bourgogne (☎ 03 86 94 95 00) runs buses from Avallon (€6, one or two daily and none on Sunday or during school holidays).

Tonnerre
pop 6000

The town of Tonnerre is best known for **Hôtel-Dieu** (rue de l'Hôpital; adult/concession €3.50/2.50; ⏰ 9am-11.30 & 2-5.30pm Mon-Sat), a charity hospital founded in 1293 by Marguerite de

BURGUNDY

Bourgogne, sister-in-law of St Louis. At the eastern end of the barrel-vaulted patients' hall, near the chapel and Marguerite's tomb, is an extraordinary 15th-century Entombment of Christ, carved from a single stone. The **tourist office** (☎ 03 86 55 14 48; ⏰ 9am-12.30pm & 2-6.30pm Mon-Sat, 10am-noon & 2-5pm Sun) is housed inside.

About 400m west, some 100L of water per second gush from **Fosse Dionne**, a natural spring – its weird blue-green tint hints at its great depth. The pool is surrounded by an 18th-century washing house and a semicircle of ancient houses. Legend has it that a serpent lurks at the bottom of the spring.

The nicest place to stay in town overlooks the Fosse Dionne. **La Ferme de Fosse Dionne** (☎ 03 86 54 82 62; www.fermefossedionne.com; 11 rue de la Fosse Dionne; d from €48) has six tasteful rooms of varying sizes. Downstairs, the owner runs a café and antique shop; ask nicely and he might play one of his old gramophones.

Budget accommodation can be found at the dingy **Hotel du Centre** (☎ 03 86 55 10 56; 65 rue de l'Hôpital; s €21.50-32, d €22-40, tr €35.10) on the main road through town.

Tonnerre, 19km to the northeast of Chablis, is on the train line linking Dijon (€30.60, one hour, eight to 10 daily) with Laroche–Migennes.

Les Rapides de Bourgogne (☎ 03 86 94 95 00) has buses (one or two daily except Sunday and Saturday during school holidays) to Auxerre (€6, 80 minutes) and to Chablis (€2.40, 35 minutes).

Château de Tanlay

The French Renaissance–style **Château de Tanlay** (☎ 03 86 75 70 61; adult/child €7/3; ⏰ Wed-Mon Apr–mid-Nov), an elegant product of the 17th century, is surrounded by a wide moat and elaborately carved outbuildings. Interior highlights include the Grande Galerie, whose walls and ceiling are completely covered with trompe l'œil. One-hour tours are offered from 9.30am to 11.30am and 2.15pm to 5.15pm. The chateau is 10km east of Tonnerre in the village of Tanlay.

Château d'Ancy-le-Franc

The Italian Renaissance makes an appearance at the square **Château d'Ancy-le-Franc**

MOATS & MANSIONS

The following are five chateaux off Burgundy's beaten track.

St-Fargeau (☎ 03 86 74 05 67; www.chateau-de-st-fargeau.com in French; 40km southwest of Auxerre on the D965; admission €7; ⏰ 10-noon & 2-6pm Apr-Sep) This fabulous pentagonal red-brick chateau, set around a vast central courtyard, dates mainly from the 15th century. From mid-July to mid-August a huge outdoor spectacle involving 60 mounted knights and 600 actors takes place every Friday and Saturday at 10pm in the chateau's grounds.

Ratilly (☎ 03 86 74 79 54; 12km southeast of St Fargeau; admission €3.50; ⏰ 10am-noon & 2-5pm Mon-Fri Sep-Jun, 10am-6pm Jun-Sep) A 13th-century stone castle surrounded by dense forests and a dry moat. The chateau is privately owned and displays sculptures, stonework and pottery exhibitions in its grounds.

Bussy-Rabutin (☎ 03 80 96 00 03; 15km northeast of Semur-en-Auxois, just off D954; admission €6.10; ⏰ 9am-noon & 2-6pm Tue-Sun mid-May–mid-Sep, 9am-noon & 2-5pm Tue-Sat mid-Sep–mid-May) A 16th- to 17th-century chateau with twin turrets bordered by formal gardens. Inside you'll find over 200 17th-century paintings collected by Roger Bussy-Rabutin, a scurrilous member of Louis XIV's court. Entry includes a guided tour.

La Rochepot (☎ 03 80 21 71 37; www.larochepot.com; 22km southeast of Beaune, off the N6; admission €5.50; ⏰ 10am-6pm Wed-Mon Jul-Aug, 10-11.30am & 2-5.30pm Wed-Mon Sep-Apr) The conical towers of this 15th-century chateau rise from thick woods above the ancient village of Rocheport. Inside you can view the chateau's beautifully-preserved architecture, including the dining room, former guard's room and chapel.

Sully (☎ 03 85 82 10 27; www.chateaudesully.com; 15km northeast of Autun along the D973; admission €6, gardens €2.50; ⏰ 10am-6pm Apr-Nov) On the outskirts of the village of Sully, this chateau was the birthplace of Marshall Mac-Mahon, duke of Magenta and president of France from 1873 to 1879; today it is still occupied by his descendants. The four wings are decorated with elaborate towers and spiky turrets. Hourly guided tours are available.

(☎ 03 86 75 00 25; www.chateau-ancy.com; adult/ student/under 15 €6/5/3; ☑ Apr-early Nov), built in the 1540s by the celebrated Italian architect Serlio. The richly painted interior was mostly completed by Italian artists brought to Fontainebleau by François I. One-hour tours begin at 10.30am, 11.30am, 2pm, 3pm and 4pm (and at 5pm from June to August). Overlooking huge stables, a large park and the Canal de Bourgogne, the chateau is 19km southeast of Tonnerre. In summer there are outdoor classical concerts followed by tours of the chateau.

AVALLON
pop 9500
The walled town of Avallon, set on a picturesque hilltop overlooking the River Cousin and the far reaches of the Parc Naturel Régional du Morvan, has been an important strategic site since Roman times. Over the centuries the town has witnessed many bloody conflicts but the majority of its 15th- and 16th-century fortifications are still standing, and are best appreciated from the lush river valley below the city. Avallon is at its most animated during the Saturday morning market. The city makes a good base for exploring Parc Naturel Régional du Morvan and Vézelay.

Orientation
The old city is built on a triangular granite hilltop, with steep ravines to the east and west. The train station is 900m northeast of place Vauban. The main commercial thoroughfare is Grande Rue Aristide Briand, which runs through town to the old city gates, passing the tourist office en route.

Information
INTERNET ACCESS
Tourist Office (per 15min €3) See Tourist Information.

MONEY
Banks are dotted along Grande Rue Aristide Briand.

POST
Post Office (9 place des Odebert)

TOURIST INFORMATION
Tourist Office (☎ 03 86 34 14 19; www.avallonnais -tourisme.com in French; 6 rue Bocquillot; ☑ 10am-7.30pm Jul & Aug, 10am-noon & 2-6pm Mon afternoon-Sat morning Sep-Jun) In a 15th-century house near the old city gates.

Sights
WALLED CITY
Construction of Avallon's fortifications, which tower over the green terraced slopes of the Cousin Valley, was begun in the 9th century. The city was contested by the first French kings, the dukes of Burgundy and English armies during the Hundred Years' War, and was pillaged during the Wars of Religion for good measure. A stroll around the walls, past the 15th- to 18th-century towers, ramparts and bastions, is an excellent way to appreciate the town's battle-scarred past.

Église St-Lazare (rue Bocquillot; ☑ Easter-Sep) was built in the 12th century. Soon after the huge numbers of pilgrims drawn here by a piece of the skull of St Lazarus (believed to provide protection from leprosy) rendered the structure inadequate. As a result, the façade was moved 20m west. The church once had three **portals**, but one was crushed when the northern belfry collapsed in 1633. The two remaining portals are grandly decorated in the Burgundian Romanesque style, though much of the exterior carving has been damaged. Nearby, the 15th-century **Tour de l'Horloge** (clock tower) spans the southern end of Grande Rue Aristide Briand.

South of the church is the city's ancient gateway, the **Bastion de la Petite Porte**. A pathway meanders from the gateway and gives fine views over the Cousin Valley. On clear days you can see all the way to the hilltops of the Parc Naturel Régional du Morvan.

OTHER SIGHTS
Regular art exhibitions are held in the **Église St-Pierre**, next door to Église St-Lazare, and across the street in the 18th-century **Grenier à Sel** (Salt Store).

Musée de l'Avallonnais (☎ 03 86 34 03 19; pl de la Collégiale; adult/student/under 18 €3/1.50/free; ☑ 2-6pm Wed-Mon May-Oct), founded in 1862, displays religious art, fossils and expressionist sketches by Georges Rouault (1871–1958).

About 100 costumes from the 18th to 20th centuries are displayed at the **Musée du Costume** (☎ 03 86 34 19 95; 6 rue Belgrand; adult/ student €4/2.50; ☑ 10.30am-12.30pm & 1.30-5.30pm Easter-Oct).

AVALLON

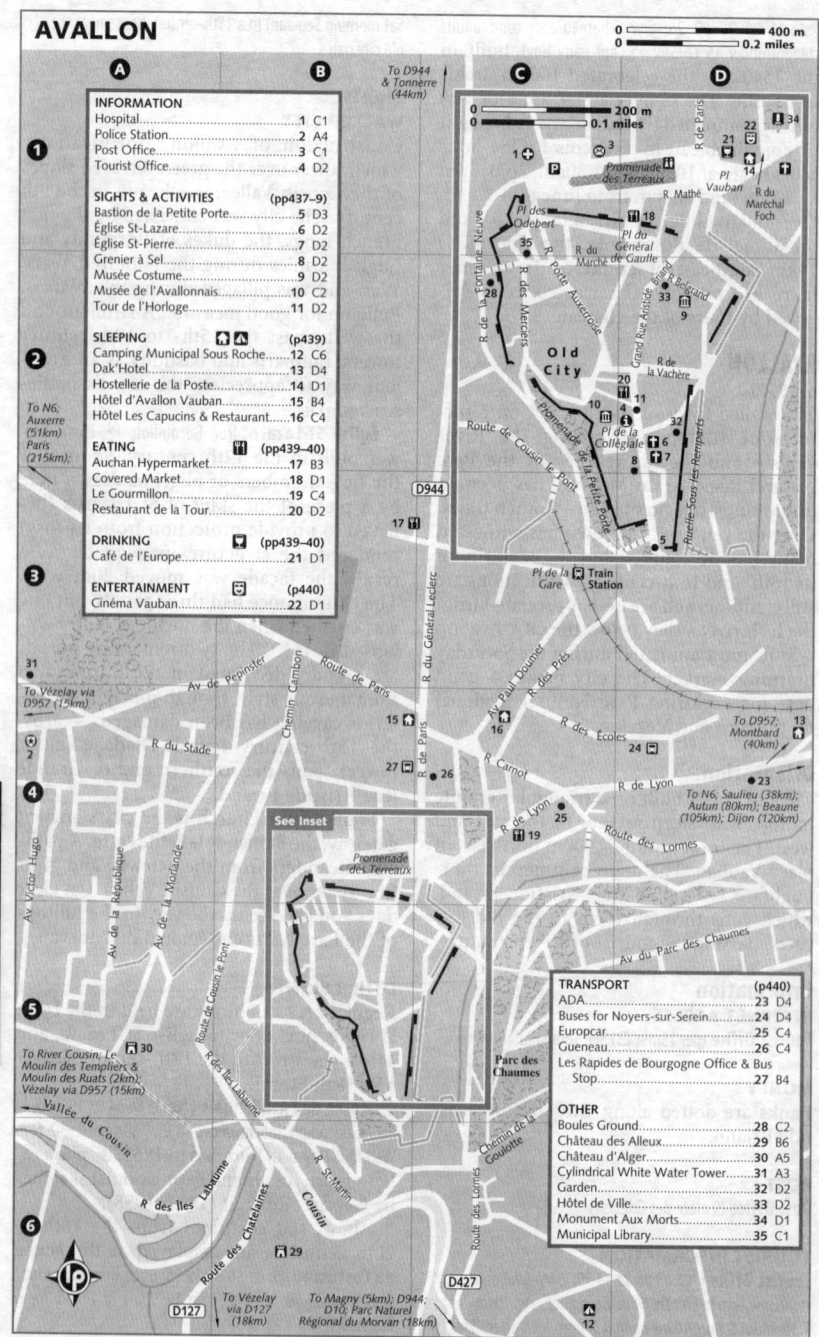

0 ————— 400 m
0 ————— 0.2 miles

INFORMATION
Hospital...**1** C1
Police Station...**2** A4
Post Office...**3** C1
Tourist Office...**4** D2

SIGHTS & ACTIVITIES (pp437–9)
Bastion de la Petite Porte.....................**5** D3
Église St-Lazare...................................**6** D2
Église St-Pierre....................................**7** D2
Grenier à Sel..**8** D2
Musée Costume....................................**9** D2
Musée de l'Avallonnais........................**10** C2
Tour de l'Horloge................................**11** D2

SLEEPING (p439)
Camping Municipal Sous Roche..........**12** C6
Dak'Hotel..**13** D4
Hostellerie de la Poste.........................**14** D1
Hôtel d'Avallon Vauban.......................**15** B4
Hôtel Les Capucins & Restaurant........**16** C4

EATING (pp439–40)
Auchan Hypermarket...........................**17** B3
Covered Market...................................**18** D1
Le Gourmillon......................................**19** C4
Restaurant de la Tour..........................**20** D2

DRINKING (pp439–40)
Café de l'Europe..................................**21** D1

ENTERTAINMENT (p440)
Cinéma Vauban....................................**22** D1

TRANSPORT (p440)
ADA..**23** D4
Buses for Noyers-sur-Serein................**24** D4
Europcar..**25** C4
Gueneau..**26** C4
Les Rapides de Bourgogne Office & Bus
  Stop..**27** B4

OTHER
Boules Ground.....................................**28** C2
Château des Alleux..............................**29** B6
Château d'Alger...................................**30** A5
Cylindrical White Water Tower............**31** A3
Garden...**32** D2
Hôtel de Ville......................................**33** D2
Monument Aux Morts...........................**34** C1
Municipal Library.................................**35** C1

To D944
& Tonnerre
(44km)

Promenade
des Terreaux

R. de Paris

Pl
Vauban

R du
Maréchal
Foch

Pl des
Odebert

R. Mathé

Pl du
Général
de Gaulle

R. du
Marché au

Grand Rue Aristide Briand

R de
la Vachère

Old
City

Route de Cousin le Pont

Promenade de la Petite Porte

Ruelle Sous les Remparts

Pl de la
Collégiale

D944

Pl de la
Gare

Train
Station

To N6;
Auxerre
(51km)
Paris
(215km);

To Vézelay via
D957 (15km)

Av de Pepinder

Chemin Cambon

Route de Paris

R. du Général Leclerc

R des Prés

Av de Paul Douener

R. des Écoles

To D957; 13
Montbard
(40km)

R. du Stade

R. de Paris

R. Carnot

R de Lyon

To N6; Saulieu (38km);
Autun (80km); Beaune
(105km); Dijon (120km)

Av de Victor Hugo

Av de la République

Av de la Morlande

R de Lyon

Route des Lormes

See Inset

Promenade
des Terreaux

Av. du Parc des Chaumes

Parc des
Chaumes

To River Cousin; Le
Moulin des Templiers &
Moulin des Ruats (2km);
Vézelay via D957 (15km)

Vallée du Cousin

R. des Îles Labaume

R. des Îles

R. St-Martin

Cousin

Route des Chatelaines

R des Lormes

Chemin de la
Goulotte

To Vézelay
via D127
(18km)

D127

To Magny (5km); D944;
D10; Parc Naturel
Régional du Morvan (18km)

D427

Activities

An excellent route for a walk or bike ride in the Vallée du Cousin is the shaded, one-lane D427, which follows the River Cousin through dense forests and open meadows. You can head west towards Pontaubert and Vézelay, or east towards Magny.

The tourist office provides maps for walking tours, as well as information on Parc Naturel Régional du Morvan. You can also pick up the *Passeport Cœur en Bourgogne* (€5) booklet, which offers discounts on sights and activities, including museums and chateaux.

Sleeping

BUDGET

Dak'Hotel (☎ 03 86 31 63 20; www.dak-hotel.com in French; route de Saulieu; s/d €46/51; **P** **⚍**) This functional chain hotel is a little way out of town towards Saulieu. The concrete exterior is far from beautiful, and the modern bedrooms might be a little boxy and bland, but there's an onsite swimming pool and it's a handy option for those with their own car.

Hôtel Le St Vincent (☎ 03 86 34 04 53; 3 rue de Paris; d €28-60; reception 🕐 usually closed Sun) Above a busy restaurant on a main roundabout, this is an acceptable alternative if everywhere else is full.

Camping

Camping Municipal sous Roche (☎ /fax 03 86 34 10 39; per adult/tent/car €2/2/2; 🕐 mid-Mar–mid-Oct) Two kilometres southeast of the old city on the banks of the Cousin.

MID-RANGE

Hotel d'Avallon Vauban (☎ 03 86 34 36 99; www .avallonvaubanhotel.com; 53 rue de Paris; s/d €45/51, tr €61-88; **P**) The best deal near the city centre, housed inside an old coaching inn on the road towards Tonnerre. The 26 rooms all have private phones and satellite TV, and there are four self-contained apartments in the attached garden.

Hôtel les Capucins (☎ 03 86 34 06 52; hotelles capucins@aol.com; 6 av Paul Doumer; d/tr €50/60; **P**) Eight simple rooms are offered above its stylish restaurant (see right), which is quite handy if you've sipped a little too much *vin rouge* over supper.

Le Moulin des Templiers (☎ 03 86 34 10 80; www .hotel-moulin-des-templiers.com; 10 route de Cousin; s €42-52, d €52-60; **P**) This beautifully converted mill is tucked away in a shady location in the Cousin Valley, about 5km south of town. The cosy bedrooms, rustic dining room and country furnishings are brimming with charm, and there's a delightful outside terrace next to the rushing river, which makes an ideal place for sipping an early evening aperitif.

TOP-END

Hostellerie de la Poste (☎ 03 86 34 14 19; www.hos telleriedelaposte.com; 13 pl Vauban; s/d €98/114, ste €167; **P**) Set around a quaint cobbled courtyard where horse-drawn carriages once clattered, this has been Avallon's top hotel for 200 years. The rooms are lavishly furnished, and the only downside is its position on busy place Vauban.

Le Moulin des Ruats (☎ 03 86 34 97 00; www .moulin-des-ruats.com; Vallée du Cousin; d €70-140) This former flour mill is a little closer to town than Moulin des Templiers, and a lot more expensive, but the fantastic wooded location, luxurious rooms and riverside terraces justify the price.

Eating & Drinking

Hôtel des Capucins restaurant (☎ 03 86 34 06 52; 6 av Paul Doumer; menus €23-52; 🕐 closed Wed year-round & Tue Sep-Jun) This elegant hotel serves French cuisine with a modern twist – roast rabbit and rump steak in red butter are some of the items you might find on its *carte*.

Restaurant de la Tour (☎ 03 86 34 24 84; 84 Grande Rue Aristide Briand; pizza & pasta €5.50-8, plats du jour €7-8; 🕐 lunch & dinner Mon-Sat) A lively bistro that serves good antipasti, pizza and pasta, and has a tempting selection of *plats du jour*.

Le Gourmillon (☎ 03 86 31 62 01; 8 rue de Lyon; menus €13-27; 🕐 closed dinner Sun) French and Burgundian dishes are served in the bright dining room of this down-to-earth restaurant: try the country paté and delicious *crème brûlée*.

Café de l'Europe (☎ 03 86 34 04 45; 7 place Vauban; 🕐 8am-2am) The often-crowded Café de l'Europe is a lively café-bar-brasserie with billiards, lottery tickets and meals available at all hours.

SELF-CATERING

The **covered market** (marché couvert; 🕐 until 1pm Sat) and place du Général de Gaulle fill with food stalls on Saturday morning. There are several food shops nearby.

BURGUNDY

The vast **Auchan hypermarket** (rue du Général Leclerc; ◷ 8.30am-9pm Mon-Sat) is north of the town centre.

Entertainment

Cinéma Le Vauban (☎/fax 03 86 34 22 87; 1 rue du Maréchal Foch) Shows new release films (usually in French) in an endearingly run-down old building near the town centre.

Getting There & Away

BUS

Service No 49 run by **Transco** (☎ 03 80 42 11 00) goes to Dijon (€15.77, two hours, two or three daily). **Les Rapides de Bourgogne** (☎ 03 86 34 00 00; 39 rue de Paris; ◷ 8am-noon & 3-5pm Mon-Fri, 9.30am-11.30am Sat) buses travel to Noyers (€6, one hour, one or two daily except Sunday and school holidays). Timetables are available from the tourist office.

CAR

Car-rental companies include **ADA** (☎ 03 86 34 20 38; 64 rue de Lyon) and **Europcar** (☎ 03 86 34 39 36; 28 rue de Lyon).

TRAIN

Trains link Avallon with Auxerre (€8.10, one hour, three to five daily) and the mainline Laroche–Migennes station (€10.10, two hours, three to five daily). Change at Laroche–Migennes for Paris' Gare de Lyon (€25.40, three to four hours, three or four daily) and Dijon (€14.90, two hours, two or more daily).

SNCF buses go to Montbard (€7.30, 50 minutes, two or three daily), also on the Paris–Dijon line (near the Abbaye de Fontenay). Trains/buses serve Saulieu (€6.60, one hour, two or three daily) and Autun (€11.70, 1¾ hours, one daily).

Getting Around

Parking marked by blue lines require a timer *disque* (disk) available at tobacconists; spaces with white lines are unrestricted.

VÉZELAY

pop 570

Despite the hordes of tourists who descend on Vézelay in summer, this tiny, hilltop village is one of France's architectural gems. Perched on a rocky spur crowned by slender buildings and the ancient abbey church of Basilique Ste-Madeleine, surrounded by a patchwork of vineyards, sunflower fields, and grazing sheep, Vézelay seems to have been lifted from another age.

History

Thanks to the relics of St Mary Magdalene, Vézelay's Benedictine monastery became an important pilgrimage site in the 11th and 12th centuries, and served as the starting point for one of the four pilgrimage routes to Santiago de Compostela in Spain. The town reached the height of its renown in the 12th century, when St Bernard, leader of the Cistercian order, preached the Second Crusade in Vézelay, and King Philip Augustus of France and King Richard the Lion-Heart of England met up here before setting out on the Third Crusade.

Information

MONEY

There are no banks in Vézelay, but there is an ATM by the post office.

POST

Post Office (pl Charles Surugue)

TOURIST INFORMATION

Tourist Office (☎ 03 86 33 23 69; www.vezelaytour isme.com in French; rue St-Pierre; ◷ 10am-1pm & 2-6pm Jun-Oct, closed Thu Nov-Apr) A new location on place du Champ-de-Foire is under construction.

Sights & Activities

BASILIQUE STE-MADELEINE

Originally established in the 880s, Vézelay's abbey, **Basilique Ste-Madeleine**, has had a very turbulent history. The original basilica was rebuilt between the 11th and 13th centuries, trashed by the Huguenots in 1569, desecrated during the Revolution and, to top off the human ravages, repeatedly struck by lightning.

By the mid-1800s it was on the point of collapse. In 1840 the architect Viollet-le-Duc undertook the daunting task of rescuing the structure. His work, which included reconstructing the western façade and its doorways, helped Vézelay – previously a ghost town – spring back to life.

On the 12th-century **tympanum** inside the church, Romanesque carvings show Jesus radiating his holy spirit to the Apostles. The **nave**, rebuilt following the great fire of 1120, has round arches and tiny windows, typical

VÉZELAY

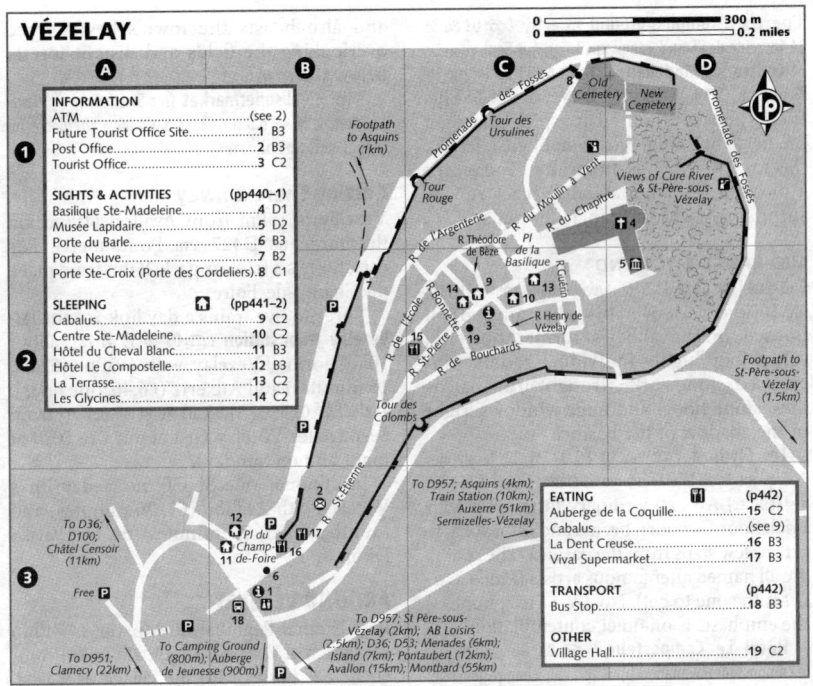

INFORMATION
ATM...(see 2)
Future Tourist Office Site.......................**1** B3
Post Office...**2** B3
Tourist Office..**3** C2

SIGHTS & ACTIVITIES   **(pp440–1)**
Basilique Ste-Madeleine........................**4** D1
Musée Lapidaire....................................**5** D2
Porte du Barle.......................................**6** B3
Porte Neuve..**7** B2
Porte Ste-Croix (Porte des Cordeliers).**8** C1

SLEEPING   **(pp441–2)**
Cabalus...**9** C2
Centre Ste-Madeleine..........................**10** C2
Hôtel du Cheval Blanc.........................**11** B3
Hôtel Le Compostelle..........................**12** B3
La Terrasse...**13** B3
Les Glycines...**14** C2

EATING   **(p442)**
Auberge de la Coquille.........................**15** C2
Cabalus...(see 9)
La Dent Creuse....................................**16** B3
Vival Supermarket................................**17** B3

TRANSPORT   **(p442)**
Bus Stop..**18** B3

OTHER
Village Hall...**19** C2

---

features of the Romanesque style; the transept and choir (1185) have ogival arches and larger windows, hallmarks of Gothic architecture. Under the transept there is a mid-12th-century **crypt** with a reliquary dedicated to Mary Magdalene.

The abbey can be visited all day except during prayers (sometimes held in the cloister chapel), which visitors are welcome to attend. Services are sung in haunting four-voice harmonies by the monks and nuns of the Fraternité Monastique de Jérusalem several times daily. Prayers last 30 to 40 minutes (1¼ hours for the 6pm Mass and, on Sunday and holidays, the 11am Mass). From April to September concerts are held in the main nave.

The **park** behind Ste-Madeleine affords wonderful views of the Cure Valley and nearby villages, including St-Père-sous-Vézelay. From the northern side, a dirt road leads down to the **old cemetery**. The **Promenade des Fossés** circumnavigates Vézelay's medieval ramparts.

While you're wandering around Vézelay, look out for the brass shells on the cobbled street – they mark the original pilgrims' trail to the abbey.

CANOEING & CYCLING
Bicycles can be rented and kayak trips can be arranged at **AB Loisirs** (☎ 03 86 33 38 38; www .abloisirs.com in French; route du Camping, St-Père-sous-Vézelay; ⏰ 9.30am-6.30pm), 400m southeast of the D957 along the D36.

Sleeping
BUDGET
Hôtel du Cheval Blanc (☎ 03 86 33 22 12; fax 03 86 33 34 29; pl du Champ-de-Foire; d €32-38; ⏰ Feb-Nov, reception closed Mon & after 5.30pm Sun) Good basic hotel at the bottom of the hill from town, with eight rooms and a homely restaurant.

La Terrasse (☎ 03 86 33 25 50; pl de la Basilique; d €25-35; ⏰ Easter–mid-Nov) This handy option for those on a tight budget has seven rooms, some with toilets across the garden.

Auberge de Jeunesse (☎ /fax 03 86 33 24 18; route de l'Étang; dm €8-10; ⏰ Apr-Oct) Nine hundred metres southwest of place du Champ-de-Foire towards Étang-sur-Arroux. Kitchen facilities are available, but sheets aren't.

There's a **camping ground** nearby (☎ 03 86 33 24 18; route de l'Étang; camping €7; ☺ Apr-Sep).

Centre Ste Madeleine (☎ 03 86 33 22 14; rue St-Pierre; dm €8.50, s/d €13.50/19; ☺ year-round) This friendly hostel is housed in a spick-and-span medieval building, once inhabited solely by the town's religious fraternity. Today, it's a pleasant (if rather starchy) place run by surprisingly with-it Franciscan nuns.

MID-RANGE & TOP-END
Cabalus (☎ 03 86 33 20 66; www.cabalus.com in French; rue St-Pierre; d €38-54) This charming B&B, housed in the abbey's former hostelry, offers four highly individual rooms with exposed stonework, wrought-iron balconies, stone floors and huge windows, right in the shadow of the basilica.

Les Glycines (☎ /fax 03 86 32 35 30; lesglycines .bourgogne@club-Internet.fr; rue St-Pierre; s €35, d €50-80; ☺ Feb-Dec) An extraordinary little hotel with brick floors, wooden beams and offbeat character a few steps from the basilica. The rooms are all named after famous artists (*Paul Claudet* is the one to get). No TV or telephones – the emphasis is on quiet contemplation.

Hôtel Le Compostelle (☎ 03 86 33 28 63; le.compostelle@wanadoo.fr; 1 pl du Champ-de-Foire; d €46-56, f €66-78; ☺ mid-Feb–Dec) The 18 spotless rooms overlook the valley or the garden, but the ones facing uphill towards the basilica are the ones to choose.

Eating
There are lots of lively restaurants, cafés and delicatessens along rue St-Pierre. **Cabalus** runs an excellent tearoom with an open fire in the hostelry's old kitchens. Delicious *croques-monsieurs*, crepes, bruschetta and cakes are all under €8, and the coffee, tea and hot chocolate come in little earthenware cups. It's highly recommended.

Auberge de la Coquille (☎ 03 86 33 35 57; 81 rue St-Pierre; crepes €3-8, menus €13-23; ☺ lunch & dinner Feb-Nov, Sat & Sun & some lunch Nov-Jan) A traditional country creperie that also serves hearty French cuisine in its small low-ceilinged dining room. Budget diners can go for the standard selection of sweet and savoury crepes; those with deeper pockets could try *coq au vin* and *jambon persillé*.

La Dent Creuse (☎ 03 86 33 36 33; pl du Champ-de-Foire; menus €13-30; ☺ lunch & dinner) A large and rather formal restaurant that specialises in Burgundian roasts, fish and chicken dishes,

and also boasts the town's best terrace overlooking the fields and distant forests below the town.

The **Vival supermarket** (rue St-Étienne; ☺ 9am-12.30pm daily, 4-7pm Tue, Thu & Sat & most afternoons Jul & Aug) sells groceries.

Getting There & Away
Vézelay is 15km from Avallon (19km via the gorgeous D427 via Pontaubert). For cars, there's a free car park 250m from place du Champ-de-Foire.

Three to five trains a day link **Sermizelles-Vézelay train station** (☎ 03 86 33 41 78), about 10km north of Vézelay, with Avallon (€2.60, 15 minutes) and Auxerre (€6.40, one hour). **Taxis** (☎ 03 86 32 31 88, 03 86 88 19 06) to/from Sermizelles-Vézelay cost about €16 (€20 at night and on Sunday).

In summer one SNCF bus a day links Vézelay with Avallon (€3, 20 minutes) and Montbard (€3, 70 minutes) on the Paris–Dijon line.

AROUND VÉZELAY
Parc Naturel Régional du Morvan is within easy reach of Vézelay. A footpath links Promenade des Fossés with the village of **Asquins**, from where trails lead to the River Cure.

Southeast of Vézelay at the base of the hill, **St Père-sous-Vézelay** contains a Flamboyant Gothic church and several upmarket restaurants. Three kilometres south along the D958 are the **Fontaines Salées** (☺ Thu-Tue Easter-Oct), saltwater hot springs where excavations have uncovered a Celtic sanctuary (2nd century BC) and Roman baths (1st century). A few kilometres south is **Pierre-Perthuis**, named after a natural stone arch; nearby, a graceful stone bridge (1770) spans the forested River Cure Gorge.

PARC NATUREL RÉGIONAL DU MORVAN (NIÈVRE)

In the Nièvre *département*, the 2304-sq-km **Parc Naturel Régional du Morvan** is a granite plateau bounded by Vézelay, Avallon, Saulieu, Autun and Chateau Chinon. It includes 700 sq km of dense woodland, 13 sq km of lakes, and rolling farmland broken by hedgerows, stone walls and stands of beech, hornbeam and oak. The majority of the area's 34,000 residents earn their living from farming, ranching, logging and even growing Christmas trees. The time when the impoverished Morvan (a Celtic name meaning 'Black Mountain') supplied wet nurses to rich Parisians has passed long ago.

Visitors to the park can now enjoy walking, mountain biking, horse riding, rock climbing, fishing and water sports. Rafting, canoeing and kayaking are possible on the Rivers Chalaux, Cousin, Cure and Yonne.

St-Brisson Visitors Centre

Surrounded by hills, forests and lakes, the **Maison du Parc** (☎ 03 86 78 79 00; http://parcdumorvan.org in French) is 14km west of Saulieu in St-Brisson. General information, including hiking and cycling guides, is available either in the **Accueil building** (⏰ 9.30am-5pm Mon-Sat & 10am-1pm & 2.30-6pm Sun Easter-Oct, longer hours Jul & Aug) or in the **Administration building** (⏰ 8.30am-noon & 1.30-5pm Mon-Fri Nov-Easter), both in the Maison du Parc complex. Guided walks of the park are arranged in July and August.

The **Écomusée du Morvan** (☎ 03 86 78 79 06; admission free; ⏰ 10.15am-6pm Easter-Nov), which explores traditional Morvan life and customs, has five sites around the park with two more planned.

Morvan was a major stronghold for the Resistance in WWII; the **Musée de la Résistance en Morvan** (☎ 03 86 78 72 99; adult/student €4/2.50; ⏰ 10.15am-6pm Easter–mid-Nov) chronicles key events and characters.

The **Verger Conservatoire**, established in 1995, is an orchard that cultivates 200 varieties of rare fruit trees. Half a dozen **trails** pass by St-Brisson.

SAULIEU
pop 2900

Once an overnight stop on the Paris–Lyon coach road, the village of Saulieu – approximately 40km from Avallon and Autun – has been renowned for its cooking for a long time, and today remains a gastronomic centre.

The **tourist office** (☎ 03 80 64 00 21; saulieu .tourisme@wanadoo.fr; 24 rue d'Argentine; ⏰ 9am-12.30pm & 2-7pm daily mid-Jun–mid-Sep, 9am-noon &

> **EDIBLE ESCARGOT**
>
> In France *helix pomatia* (otherwise known as the edible snail) is known as *escargot de Bourgogne* – the Burgundy snail. The humble crawler was once a regular – and unwelcome – visitor to the vineyards of Burgundy (hence the name) and was all but killed off after the introduction of industrial-strength pesticides in the 19th and 20th centuries. Ironically, the vast majority of the snails eaten in France are now imported from Eastern Europe.

2-5pm Tue-Sat mid-Sep–Feb, 9am-noon & 2-6pm Tue-Sat Mar–mid-Jun), on the N6, covers the Parc Naturel Régional du Morvan including cycling and hiking.

Musée François Pompon (☎ 03 80 64 19 51; 3 rue du Docteur Roclore; adult/student €4/2.50; ⏰ 10am-noon & 2-6pm Mon & Wed-Sat, 10.30am-noon & 2-5.30pm Sun & holidays, closed Jan & Feb) displays medieval statuary and work by the local animal sculptor François Pompon (1855–1933). Next to the museum, the **Basilique St Andoche** is known for its carved capitals depicting flora, fauna and Biblical stories.

Sleeping & Eating

La Vieille Auberge (☎ 03 80 64 13 74; 15 rue Grillot; menus €12-29; ⏰ closed Jan & Feb) This is a traditional inn serving Burgundy cooking at a fair price. Rustic rooms are available upstairs.

La Côte d'Or (☎ 03 80 90 53 53; www.bernard-loiseau.com; 2 rue d'Argentine; menus €122-185) The main restaurant of one of France's renowned chefs, Bernard Loiseau. The sophisticated country cuisine has earned three Michelin stars: despite the price, you won't get a table without a reservation.

Atac supermarket (rue Jean Bertin; ⏰ 8.45am-12.15pm & 2.45-7pm Mon-Sat) is 300m downhill from the Restaurant Bernard Loiseau, on the D26.

Getting There & Away

SNCF trains and/or buses go to Autun (€6.90, 50 minutes, four or five daily and two on Sunday and holidays) and Avallon (€11.70, 50 to 60 minutes, three daily). **Transco** (☎ 03 80 42 11 00) runs bus No 48 to Dijon (€12, 1½ hours, once daily except on Sunday and holidays).

BURGUNDY

CHATEAU CHINON

pop 2720

Château Chinon is best known for having had François Mitterrand as its mayor from 1959 to 1981, and it was once a key strategic point for defending upper Burgundy. It now makes a convenient base for exploring the Morvan, but the modern town hasn't got much to offer.

The **tourist office** (☎ 03 86 85 06 58; otsi.chateau -chinon@wanadoo.fr; pl Notre Dame; 🕑 9am-12.30pm & 2-6pm Mon-Thu, 9am-12.30pm & 2-5pm Fri year-round) supplies brochures, maps and topoguides.

Jean Tinguely and Niki de St-Phalle's **fountain** in front of the town hall resembles the one at the Centre Pompidou in Paris.

The **Musée du Septennat** (☎ 03 86 85 19 23; 6 rue du Château; adult/concession €4/2; 🕑 10am-noon & 2-6pm Wed-Mon mid-Feb–Jun & Sep-Dec, 10am-1pm & 2-7pm Jul & Aug) displays official trinkets presented to Mitterrand during his two *septennats* (seven-year presidential terms, now reduced to five). Next door the **Musée du Costume** (☎ 03 86 85 18 55; 4 rue du Château; adult/student €4/2; 🕑 10am-noon & 2-6pm Wed-Mon Apr-Jun & Sep, 10am-1pm & 2-7pm Jul & Aug) explores French fashion since the 18th century.

Hôtel Le Vieux Morvan (☎ 03 86 85 05 01; fax 03 86 85 02 78; 8 place Gudin; d from €45; 🕑 closed mid-Dec–mid-Jan, reception closed Sun night & Mon approx Nov-Apr) long served as Mitterrand's official local residence. The attached **restaurant** (menus €15-39) serves French and regional cuisine.

Hôtel Lion d'Or (☎ 03 86 85 13 56; fax 03 86 79 42 22; 10 rue des Fossés; d from €25-40; reception 🕑 closed Fri evening & often Sun evening approx Nov-Mar), through the arch from place Notre Dame, is an older place with seven plain, one-star rooms.

For buses see Autun (p462).

MAQUIS BERNARD RÉSISTANCE CEMETERY

Seven RAF airmen – the crew of a bomber shot down near here in 1944 – and 21 *résitants* are buried in the neatly tended **Maquis Bernard Résistance Cemetery**, surrounded by the dense forests in which British paratroops operated with Free French forces. The nearby **drop zone** is marked with signs.

The cemetery is about 8km southwest of Montsauche-les-Settons (along the D977) and 5.6km east of Oroux-en-Morvan (along the D12), near the tiny hamlet of Savelot. From the D977, go 2.8km along the narrow dirt road to Savelot.

CÔTE D'OR

The Côte d'Or *département* is named after one of the world's foremost wine-growing regions, which stretches from Dijon south to the wine town of Beaune and beyond. In the far northwest, Châtillon-sur-Seine displays spectacular Celtic treasures, while in the west you can visit Abbaye de Fontenay and the walled town of Semur-en-Auxois. South of Dijon is Abbaye de Cîteaux, once hugely influential.

DIJON

pop 230,000

Dijon, mustard capital of the universe, is one of France's most appealing provincial cities, with an inviting centre graced by elegant medieval and Renaissance buildings. Despite its long history, modern Dijon is a lively, dynamic city with 24,000 university students and a thriving cultural scene.

History

Dijon served as the capital of the dukes of Burgundy from the 11th to 15th centuries, reaching its golden age during the 14th and 15th centuries under Philippe-le-Hardi (Philip the Bold), Jean-sans-Peur (John the Fearless) and Philippe-le-Bon (Philip the Good). During their reigns Dijon was turned into one of the great centres of European art, but the chasm between rich and poor was always vast, and the city endured a turbulent time during the Revolution.

Orientation

Dijon's commercial centre stretches from the tourist office eastwards to Église St Michel; the main shopping streets are rue de la Liberté and rue du Bourg. Place Grangier, with its many bus stops, is north of rue de la Liberté, while the train station is at the western end of av Maréchal Foch. The old city is around place François Rude and the surrounding streets.

Information

EMERGENCY

Police Station (☎ 03 80 44 55 00; 2 place Suquet; 🕑 24hr) Access between 6pm and 7.30am is on rue du Petit Cîteaux.

INTERNET ACCESS

Multi-Rezo (☎ 03 80 66 33 21; 74 rue Vannerie; per 12min/hr €1/5; 🕑 9am-midnight Mon-Sat, 2-10pm Sun)
Netwave (☎ 03 80 30 55 16; 10 rue de la Liberté; per hour €4; h10am-10pm Mon-Sat, 4-8pm Sun)

LAUNDRY

There are laundrettes at 41 rue Auguste Comte, 28 and 55 rue Berbisey and 8 place de la Banque They are generally open 7.30am to 9pm.

MEDICAL SERVICES

The duty pharmacy and doctors are listed outside the tourist office.
Hôpital Général (☎ 03 80 29 30 31; 3 rue du Faubourg Raines; 🕑 24hr)

MONEY

Banque de France (2 place de la Banque) Usually changes money on weekday mornings.

POST

Main Post Office (pl Grangier)

TOURIST INFORMATION

Tourist Office (☎ 03 80 44 11 44; www.dijon-tourism .com; place Darcy; 🕑 9am-7pm May–mid-Oct, 10am-6pm mid-Oct–Apr) There's a branch at the airport open for incoming flights.
Tourist Office Annexe (☎ 03 80 44 11 44; 34 rue des Forges; 🕑 9am-noon & 2-6pm Mon-Sat)

UNIVERSITIES

The main **Dijon University** campus is 2km east of the centre.

Sights

MEDIEVAL & RENAISSANCE ARCHITECTURE

Once home to the region's rulers, the **Palais des Ducs et des États de Bourgogne** (Palace of the Dukes & States of Burgundy) is an elaborate complex in the heart of old Dijon. The building received its neoclassical façade in the 17th and 18th centuries when it was the seat of Burgundy's parliament. The palace overlooks **place de la Libération**, a public arcade designed by Jules Hardouin-Mansart (an architect of Versailles) in 1686.

The west wing is occupied by Dijon's **city hall**. The eastern wing houses the Musée des Beaux-Arts (see later); its entrance is next to the **Tour de Bar**, a squat 14th-century tower that once served as a prison.

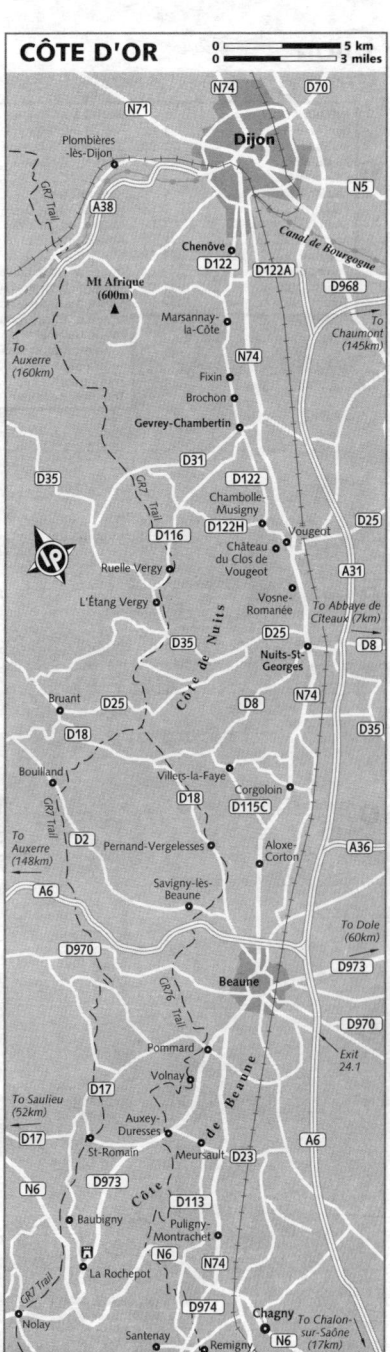

BURGUNDY

DIJON

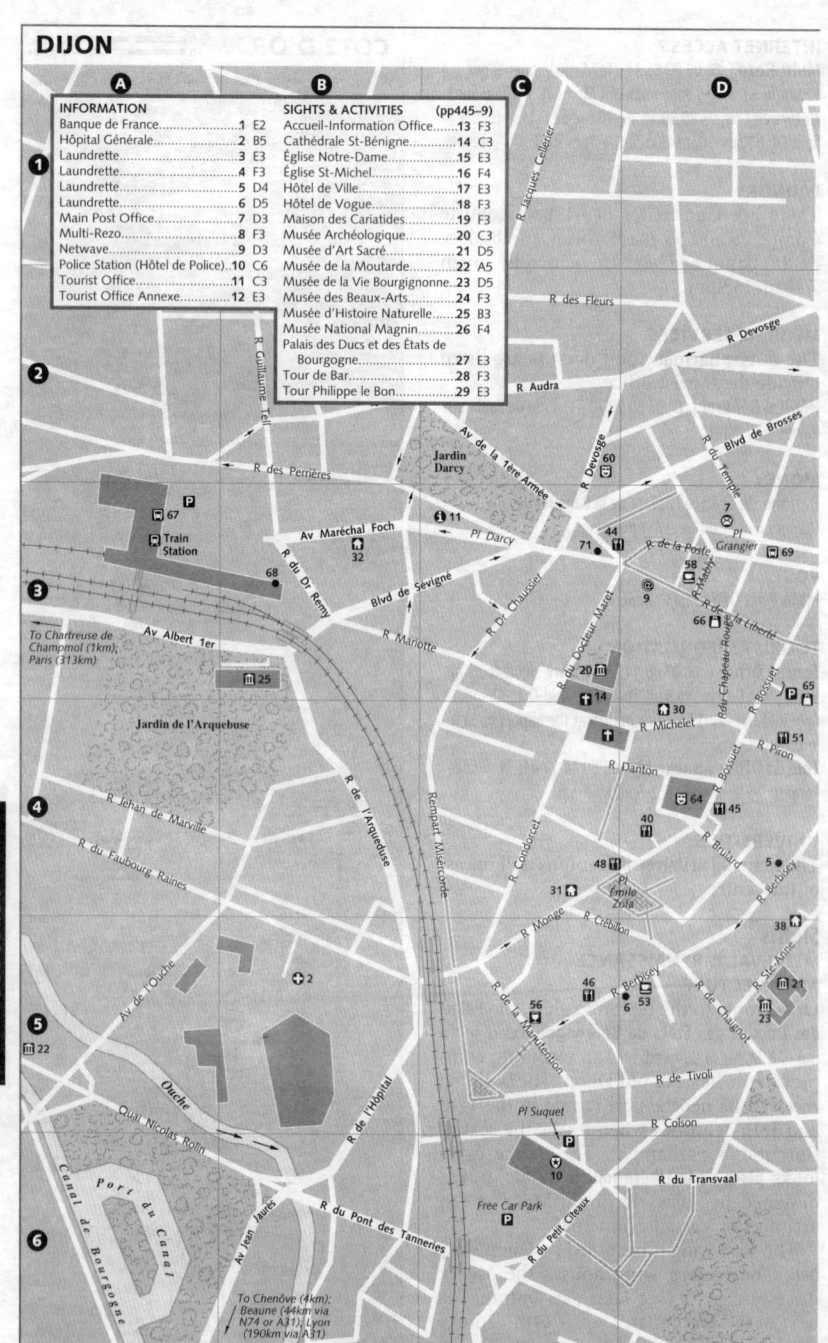

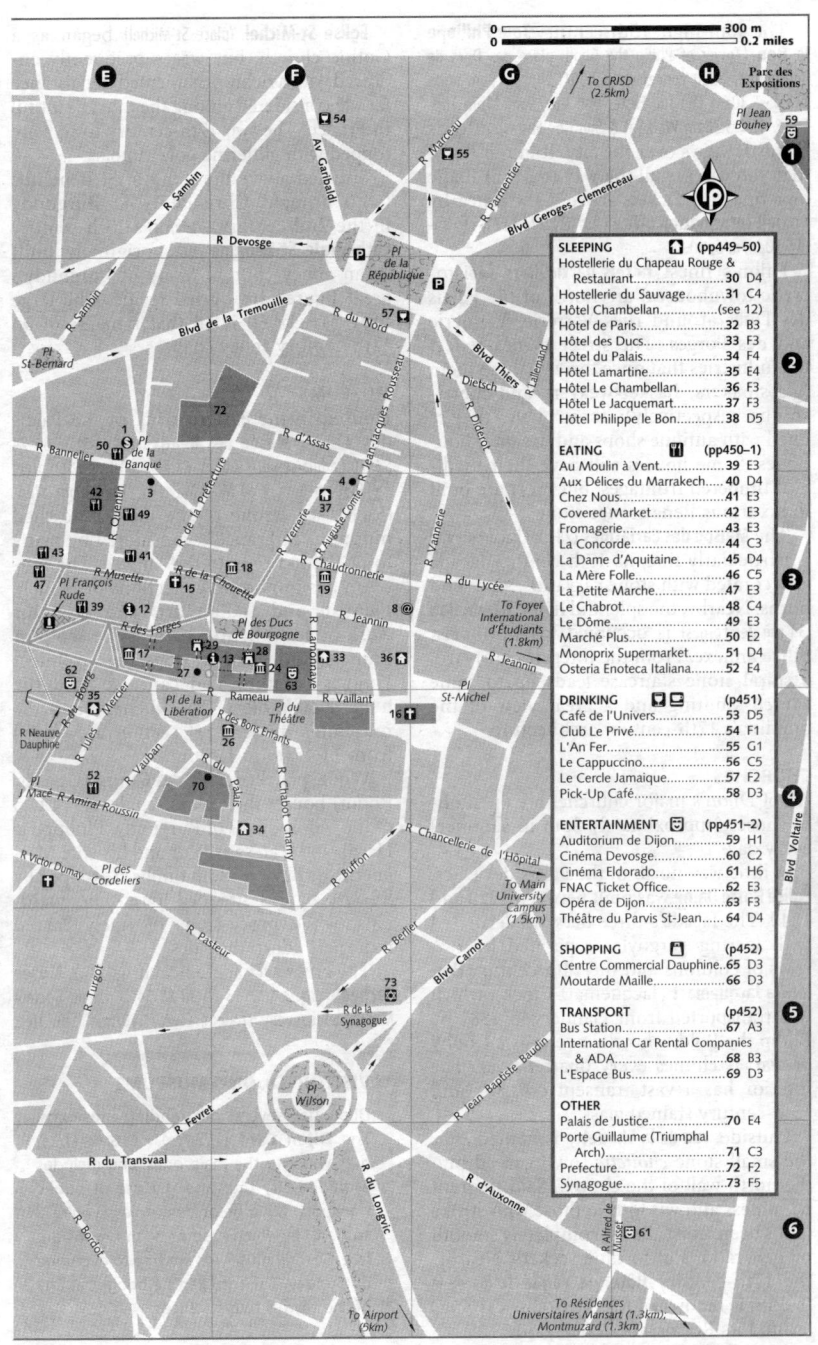

To CRISD
(2.5km)

Parc des
Expositions

Pl Jean
Bouhey

SLEEPING (pp449–50)
Hostellerie du Chapeau Rouge &
Restaurant..................30 D4
Hostellerie du Sauvage..........31 C4
Hôtel Chambellan.............(see 12)
Hôtel de Paris..................32 B3
Hôtel des Ducs................33 F3
Hôtel du Palais................34 F3
Hôtel Lamartine...............35 E4
Hôtel Le Chambellan...........36 F3
Hôtel Le Jacquemart...........37 F3
Hôtel Philippe le Bon..........38 D5

EATING (pp450–1)
Au Moulin à Vent..............39 E3
Aux Délices du Marrakech......40 D4
Chez Nous...................41 E3
Covered Market...............42 E3
Fromagerie...................43 E3
La Concorde.................44 C3
La Dame d'Aquitaine...........45 D4
La Mère Folle................46 C5
La Petite Marche.............47 E3
Le Chabrot..................48 C4
Le Dôme...................49 E3
Marché Plus.................50 E2
Monoprix Supermarket.........51 D4
Osteria Enoteca Italiana.......52 E4

DRINKING (p451)
Café de l'Univers.............53 D5
Club Le Privé................54 F1
L'An Fer...................55 G1
Le Cappuccino...............56 C5
Le Cercle Jamaique...........57 F2
Pick-Up Café................58 D3

ENTERTAINMENT (pp451–2)
Auditorium de Dijon...........59 H1
Cinéma Devosge..............60 C2
Cinéma Eldorado.............61 H6
FNAC Ticket Office...........62 E3
Opéra de Dijon..............63 F3
Théâtre du Parvis St-Jean......64 D4

SHOPPING (p452)
Centre Commercial Dauphine...65 D3
Moutarde Maille.............66 D3

TRANSPORT (p452)
Bus Station.................67 A3
International Car Rental Companies
& ADA..................68 B3
L'Espace Bus................69 D3

OTHER
Palais de Justice.............70 E4
Porte Guillaume (Triumphal
Arch)...................71 C3
Prefecture.................72 E2
Synagogue.................73 F5

BURGUNDY

The 46m-high, 15th-century **Tour Philippe le Bon** (Tower of Philip the Good; place des Ducs de Bourgogne; adult/concession €2.30/1.20; ☺ 9am-noon & 1.45-5.30pm Thu-Tue Easter-end Nov, 9am-11pm Thu-Tue & 1.30-3.30pm Wed Sat & Sun Nov-Easter) affords fantastic views over the city. Rumour has it that you can see all the way to Mont Blanc on a fine day. Tickets are sold at the nearby **Accueil-Information office** (☎ 03 80 74 52 71; ☺ until 5.30pm or 6pm).

Dijon's finest **hôtels particuliers** (aristocratic townhouses) are north of the Palais des Ducs around rues Verrerie, Vannerie and des Forges. The street names reflect the industries that once thrived along them (glassmakers, basket-weavers and metalsmiths respectively); these days, they're lined with antique shops and designer boutiques. Some houses still have their medieval timbered frontages, but most are built in luxurious Renaissance stone.

The **Maison des Cariatides** (28 rue Chaudronnerie) is particularly fine; its 17th-century façade is decorated with stone caryatids, vines and horns. Nearby, the splendid **Hôtel Chambellan** (34 rue des Forges) is occupied by the tourist office annexe. From the interior courtyard, a spiral stone staircase leads up to some carved vaulting and a great view of the building's 17th-century architecture.

CHURCHES

All of Dijon's major churches are open until sunset (approximately 8pm in summer) every day.

A little way north of the Palais des Ducs, **Église Notre Dame** was built between 1220 and 1240. The façade's three tiers are decorated with leering gargoyles separated by two rows of columns and the 14th-century **Horloge à Jacquemart** (Jacquemart Clock), which was transported from Flanders in 1382 by Philip the Bold, who claimed it as a trophy of war. It chimes every quarter-hour. The interior has a vast transept crossing and 13th-century stained glass.

Outside, **rue de la Chouette** is named after the small stone *chouette* (owl) carved into the north wall of the church. Said to grant happiness and wisdom to those who stroke it, it's been worn almost completely smooth by generations of fortune-seekers. Nearby, the 17th-century **Hôtel de Vogüé** (8 rue de la Chouette) is renowned for the ornate carvings around its Renaissance courtyard.

Église St-Michel (place St-Michel) began as a Gothic church, but was subsequently endowed with a richly ornamented Renaissance façade considered among the most beautiful in France. The two 17th-century towers are topped with glittering gold cupolas.

Situated above the tomb of St Benignus (who brought Christianity to Burgundy in the 2nd century), Dijon's 13th-century **Cathédrale St-Bénigne** was originally built as an abbey church. Many of Burgundy's great figures are buried inside. The large **crypt** (admission €1) is all that remains of an 11th-century abbey chapel.

MUSEUMS

Housed in the eastern wing of the Palais des Ducs, **Musée des Beaux-Arts** (☎ 03 80 74 52 70; adult/senior/student €3.40/1.60/free, Sun free; ☺ 9.30am-6pm Wed-Mon May-Oct, 10am-5pm Wed-Mon Nov-Apr) is one of the most renowned museums in France – considered by many to be second only to the Louvre. The museum has important collections of French, Flemish and Italian art, and contains work by local figures such as the sculptor Francis Rude and the designer/architect Hugues Sambin. You can also visit the huge **ducal kitchens**. The kitchens and the museum's modern art section are closed from 11.45am to 1.45pm.

Wood-panelled **Salle des Gardes** (Guards' Room) houses the carved sepulchres of two of the Valois dukes of Burgundy, Philippe le Hardi, and Jean sans Peur and his wife Marguerite de Bavière. Both tombs are topped by life-size figures attended by angelic guardians, while processions of finely carved mourners adorn the sides.

The city's archaeological museum, **Musée Archéologique** (☎ 03 80 30 88 54; 5 rue du Docteur Maret; adult/senior/student €2.20/1.10/free, Sun free;

VISITING DIJON'S MUSEUMS

Dijon has several outstanding museums. The **Dijon Card** (1-/2-/3-day pass €8/11/14) gets you into the main ones, and includes a guided city tour and the use of public transport. It's a great deal unless you're a student, in which case most museums are free. Several museums are free to everyone on Sunday. The card can be bought at any of the town's tourist offices.

9.30am-12.30pm & 1.30-6pm Wed-Sun Oct-May, 9.30am-6pm Jun-Sep), displays Celtic artefacts and a particularly fine 1st-century bronze of the goddess Sequana standing on a boat. The 11th-century chamber on the lowest level was once part of a Benedictine abbey.

Housed in a 17th-century *hôtel particulier*, **Musée National Magnin** (☎ 03 80 67 11 10; 4 rue des Bons Enfants; adult/student €3/2.30, Sun €2.30, first Sun of month free; 10am-noon & 2-6pm Tue-Sun) displays works of art donated to the city in 1938 by the brother and sister team of Jeanne and Maurice Magnin.

In the copper-domed chapels of a neoclassical church (1709), the ecclesiastical **Musée d'Art Sacré** (☎ 03 80 44 12 69; 15 rue Ste Anne; adult/senior/student €2.80/1.60/free, Sun free; 9am-noon & 2-6pm Wed-Mon) displays objects from the 12th to 19th centuries. Almost next door and included in the ticket price, **Musée de la Vie Bourguignonne** (☎ 03 80 44 12 69; 17 rue Ste Anne; 9am-noon & 2-6pm Wed-Mon) occupies a 17th-century Cistercian convent and explores rural life in Burgundy in past centuries.

Finally, you can't leave Dijon without paying homage to the city's most famous export, **Musée de la Moutarde** (Musée Amora; 48 quai Nicolas Rolin; adult/under 12 incl tour €3/free; tours 3pm Mon-Sat Jun-Sep, Wed & Sat Oct). Visits to the mustard museum at the factory of Amora, Dijon's main mustard company, must be arranged at the tourist office on place Darcy.

In Dijon's botanical park, **Jardin de l'Arquebuse**, you'll find a stream, pond and formal gardens. The city's **Musée d'Histoire Naturelle** (Natural History Museum; ☎ 03 80 76 82 76; adult/student €2/free, Sun free; 9am-noon & 2-6pm except Tue, Sat & Sun morning) is near the entrance.

OTHER SIGHTS

Dijon has plenty of green spaces. Try **Jardin Darcy** (next to the tourist office), **Jardin de l'Arquebuse**, **place des Ducs de Bourgogne** (just north of the Palais des Ducs) and **place St-Michel** (next to Église St Michel).

Founded in 1383 **Chartreuse de Champmol** (Carthusian monastery; 1 blvd Chanione Kir; 8am-6pm) was almost completely destroyed during the Revolution. The famous **Puits de Moïse** (Well of Moses), a grouping of six Old Testament figures by Claus Sluter between 1395 and 1405, is undergoing restoration. Another Sluter work, the **Portail de la Chapelle** (Chapel

Doorway) is nearby. The site, 1.2km west of the train station, is now occupied (bizarrely) by a psychiatric hospital.

Tours

The tourist office (p445) publishes the *Owl's Trail* (€2), a brochure detailing a self-guided walking tour of the city centre; the route is marked on the pavement by red arrows. The tourist office also runs English-language walking tours of the city, including *nocturnes* at 10pm in July and August. They cost €6/9/3 for adults/ couples/concessions. The two-hour Visite Audioguidée (Walkman tour) costs €6.

Circuits des Châteaux bus tours to the region's chateaux, churches and abbeys run most Sundays from late June to September. They cost €40/50 per half-/full day. Commentary is in French. Tickets are arranged through the tourist office. You can also reserve places for Couleurs Bourgogne, two- or three-day trips around Burgundy with a gastronomic theme.

Wine & Voyages (☎ 03 80 61 15 15; www.winean dvoyages.com; 2/3hr tours €45/50, full day €95; early Mar–mid-Dec) runs minibus tours in French and English, including circuits of the Côte de Nuits vineyards. It's essential to reserve ahead.

Festivals & Events

The **Folkloriades Internationales et Fêtes de la Vigne** is week-long dance festival held in August or September. **Foire Internationale et Gastronomique**, in late-October to November and held at the Parc des Expositions, gives visitors the chance to sample cuisines from Burgundy and around the world. **L'Estivade** brings theatre, ballet and concerts to town in late June to July.

Sleeping

The best hotels in Dijon are around the old city or near the restaurants and bars southwest of the centre. Considering the city's size and prosperity, hotels in Dijon are surprisingly affordable.

BUDGET

Centre de Rencontres Internationales et de Séjour de Dijon (CRISD; ☎ 03 80 72 95 20; reservation@ auberge -cri-dijon.com; 1 blvd Champollion; s/d/q per person €26/16/14) An institutional, 260-bed place 2.5km northeast of the centre. By bus, take

BURGUNDY

No 5 (towards Épirey) from place Grangier; at night take line A to Épirey.

Hôtel le Chambellan (☎ 03 80 67 12 67; hotel chambellan@aol.com; 92 rue Vannerie; s €34-48, d €42-52) A great deal on one of the city's oldest streets. The pretty building is typical of the area, with flower boxes and shuttered windows, and there is a small 17th-century courtyard where breakfast is served in summer.

Hôtel Lamartine (☎ 03 80 30 37 47; www.ot-dijon.fr; 12 rue Jules Mercier; s/d €31/47; reception ☻ closed noon-3pm) On a shabby backstreet just off rue du Bourg. The 14 rooms are plain and the street views are uninspiring, but the location is unbeatable – the Palais des Ducs is a few steps from the front door.

Hôtel de Paris (☎ 03 80 43 41 88; hoteldeparis dijon@minitel.net; 9-11 av du Maréchal Foch) This hotel is on the traffic-thronged road to the train station, so it can get noisy, but it's a useful option if you're got an early connection. Pastel shades and boxy rooms make for a cosy night's sleep.

MID-RANGE

Hôtel du Palais (☎ 03 80 67 16 26; fax 03 80 65 12 16; 23 rue du Palais; s with shower €30-37, d with shower €34-43, s with bath €40-45, d with bath €48-65, tr with bath €52-70) One of Dijon's best-kept secrets, a smart hotel housed in a former *hôtel particulier* near the Quartier d'Antiquaires. The rooms are spacious and welcoming (the best are on the first floor), and the place oozes old-fashioned charm from every corner.

Hostellerie du Sauvage (☎ 03 80 41 31 21; hotel dusauvage@free.fr; 64 rue Monge; d from €41) On a charming cobbled courtyard in a 15th-century *relais de poste* (relay posthouse), this great value hotel is off buzzy rue Monge. Parking is available in the old carriage-houses for €4 per day.

Hôtel Le Jacquemart (☎ 03 80 60 09 60; www.hotel-lejacquemart.fr; 32 rue Verrerie; d €28-54, ste €60) Right in the heart of old Dijon in a 17th-century building, this hotel offers 31 quaint and comfortable rooms. The window boxes make it a pretty place to arrive in summer.

Hôtel des Ducs (☎ 03 80 67 31 31; fax 03 80 67 19 51; 5 rue Lamonnaye; d €54-74, tw €79-87, ste €106; P ✖) A modern hotel, opposite the Opéra de Dijon and around the corner from Église St-Michel. Most rooms have small balconies onto the street. If you're looking for a city-style hotel, this is a good choice.

TOP END

Hôtel Philippe le Bon (☎ 03 80 30 73 52; www.hotel philippelebon.com in French; 18 rue Ste-Anne; d €79-103; P ✖) Thirty-six stylish, contemporary rooms in a buzzy setting near the cafés and restaurants of rue Berbisey. There is a small garden, a decent restaurant and parking is included.

Hostellerie du Chapeau Rouge (☎ 03 80 50 88 88; www.chapeau-rouge.fr; 5 rue Michelet; d €130-197; ✖) A Dijon institution since 1847, and one of the city's most luxurious places to stay, with four stars, 30 Jacuzzi-equipped rooms and an inevitably stuffy atmosphere. The attached restaurant is one of the city's best.

Eating

As Burgundy's foremost city, Dijon has no shortage of excellent places to eat, ranging from cheap creperies to the highest *haute cuisine*. The best restaurants are around rue Berbisey and place Émile Zola, and along rue Bannelier and rue Quentin, next to the covered market.

RESTAURANTS

Hostellerie du Chapeau Rouge (see above; menus with/without wine €42/35) Features bold, creative French cuisine based on traditional ingredients and top-quality local produce. For gastrophiles, the restaurant offers two gourmet menus; €75 buys seven sumptuous courses, while €100 gets a belt-busting 11.

La Dame d'Aquitaine (☎ 03 80 30 45 65; 23 pl Bossuet; menus €18-36; ☻ closed Sun & lunch Mon) Excellent Burgundian and southwestern French cuisine and the atmospheric location in a vaulted 13th-century cellar make this one of Dijon's most renowned restaurants.

Le Chabrot (☎ 03 80 30 69 01; 36 rue Monge; menus €11-27; ☻ lunch & dinner Mon-Sat) An attractive wine bar serving traditional French cooking. The relaxed atmosphere, candle-lit tables and rustic décor make it popular with gourmets and wine-lovers alike.

Aux Délices du Marrakech (☎ 03 80 30 82 69; 20 rue Monge; dishes €10-25; ☻ closed lunch Mon), On the same street as Le Chabrot, this excellent Moroccan restaurant boasts an ornately decorated dining room with an unmistakably North-African ambiance, and the huge portions of tajine and couscous are just as authentic.

La Mère Folle (☎ 03 80 50 19 76; 102 rue Berbisey; menus €12-22; ☻ closed lunch Sat) A relaxed and rather camp French restaurant serving unusual variations on traditional dishes, such as *bœuf bourguignon* with tagliatelle. The restaurant itself is crammed with character, from the baroque mirrors on the walls to the pineapple-shaped lights on the tables – even the drinking water is different (appropriately enough, it's served in watering cans).

La Petite Marche (☎ 03 80 30 15 10; 27-29 rue Musette; menus €10-15; 🕐 lunch Mon-Sat) Vegetarians tired of Burgundy's meat-heavy menus should head for this popular organic restaurant, renowned as one of the best in France.

Osteria Enoteca Italiana (☎ 03 80 50 07 36; 32 rue Amiral Roussin; lunch menu €14; 🕐 Tue-Sun) A small Italian diner with delicious pasta and fish dishes.

CAFÉS & QUICK EATS
Au Moulin à Vent (☎ 03 80 30 81 43; 8 pl François Rude; 🕐 closed Mon & dinner Sun) A quintessentially French street-side café opposite the fountain on place François Rude. There's a large terrace outside and a snug restaurant upstairs serving local specialities.

La Concorde (☎ 03 80 30 69 43; 2 pl Darcy) This classic Art Deco styled café and brasserie occupies a great position overlooking busy Darcy. The pavement conservatory is the place for morning coffee and late-night drinking, and inside there's a fine restaurant serving excellent bistro food.

Le Dôme (☎ 03 80 30 58 92; 16bis, rue Quentin; menus from €12, formule midi €12; 🕐 closed dinner Sun) In the dynamic area around the covered market, this smart café has lots of outside tables where you can sit and watch the city go by. The *formule midi* includes entrée, plat du jour and coffee.

SELF-CATERING
For picnic treats head for the 19th-century **covered market** (Halles du Marché; rue Quentin; 🕐 until 1pm Tue & Thu-Sat) and the nearby **fromagerie** (28 rue Musette; 🕐 closed Sun & Mon morning). Supermarkets include **Monoprix supermarket** (11-13 rue Piron; 🕐 9am-9pm Mon-Sat) and **Marché Plus** (rue Bannelier; 🕐 7am-9pm Mon-Sat, 9am-noon Sun).

Drinking
Pick-Up Café (☎ 03 80 30 61 44; 9 rue Mably; 🕐 8am-2am) A typically French idea of an American bar-diner, complete with jukeboxes and pinball machines.

Le Cercle Jamaïque (Rhumerie; ☎ 03 80 73 52 19; 14 place de la République; 🕐 2pm-4am Tue-Sat) A large bar that specialises in rum cocktails and is decked out with tacky Chinese-baroque décor. There's often live music (ranging from Cuban to jazz) from about 11pm to 3.30am. Downstairs, there's a **club** (🕐 11pm-4am Thu-Sat) that plays everything but techno (cover charge from €6).

Café de l'Univers (☎ 03 80 30 98 29; 47 rue Berbisey; 🕐 9am-2am) One of many convivial café-bars along rue Berbisey. Downstairs there's a cellar with a small **dance floor** (🕐 10pm-2am Thu-Sun, to noon weekends).

Le Cappuccino (☎ 03 80 41 06 35; 132 rue Berbisey; 🕐 3pm-2am) Despite the name, this is one of Dijon's most popular beer bars, with a varied selection of bottled and draught beers from all over Europe. The dimly lit interior regularly hosts bands and live music events, and it's always jammed with a lively crowd on weekends.

Entertainment
For the latest on Dijon's cultural scene, pick up *Spectacles*, available free from the tourist office. Events tickets are sold at the **Fnac ticket office** (☎ 08 92 68 36 22; www.fnac.com in French; 24 rue du Bourg; 🕐 10am-7pm Tue-Fri, 9.30-7pm Sat, 1-7pm Mon).

NIGHTCLUBS
Dijon's club scene is centred around place de la République.

L'An-Fer (☎ 03 80 70 03 69; 8 rue Marceau; admission with/without drink Wed & Thu €7/5, Fri €9.50, Sat & Sun €8; 🕐 11pm-5am Wed-Sun, closed Wed mid-Jul-mid-Sep) L'An-Fer achieved fame for pioneering techno music (Laurent Garnier worked here for four years); house takes centre stage on Saturday.

Club Le Privé (☎ 03 80 73 39 57; 20 av Garibaldi; admission Sun-Thu €5, Fri & Sat €8; 🕐 10pm-5am) The bright lights and leopard-skin banquettes say it all – this is a cheesy club popular with Dijon's students and bright young things.

CINEMAS
Cinéma Eldorado (☎ 03 80 66 51 89; 21 rue Alfred de Musset; 🕐 closed mid-Jul–mid-Aug) A three-screen arts cinema where nondubbed films flicker nightly.

Cinéma Devosge (☎ 03 80 30 74 79; 6 rue Devosge) Usually has a nondubbed film playing next to the new releases.

BURGUNDY

THEATRE

Théâtre du Parvis St-Jean (☎ 03 80 30 12 12; www
.tdb-cdn.com in French; rue Monge) In the converted
Église St-Jean on rue Monge, presents
dance, music and theatre, including classics and new work.

CLASSICAL MUSIC & DANCE

Auditorium de Dijon (☎ 03 80 60 44 44; www.leduo
dijon.com in French; 11 blvd de Verdun) Presents concerts, opera and dance from September
through to June.

Shopping

Moutarde Maille (☎ 03 80 30 41 02; 32 rue de la Liberté; ☺ 9am-7pm Mon-Sat) Buy gourmet mus-
tard at this factory shop of the company
that makes Grey-Poupon. You can even
have it dispensed from the pump.

Mulot & Petitjean (☎ 03 80 30 07 10; mulot
.petitjean@wanadoo.fr; 13 place Bossuet; ☺ 9am-noon
& 2-7pm, closed Sun morning) Dijon has lots of
sumptuous patisseries; one of the best-
known is Mulot & Petitjean, which sells the
finest *pains d'épices* in town.

Getting There & Away

AIR

Aéroport Dijon-Bourgogne airport (☎ 03 80 67
67 67; www.dijon.aeroport.fr) is 5km southeast of
the city centre, but lack of demand has
meant regular scheduled flights are currently suspended.

BUS

The bus station is in the train station complex. Details on services are available at the
Transco information counter (☎ 03 80 42 11 00;
☺ 5.30am-8.30pm Mon-Fri, 6.45am-12.30pm & 4-8.30pm
Sat, 10am-1pm & 4pm-8.30pm Sun). Timetables are
posted on the platforms; tickets are sold
on board.

Lines to the Côte d'Or include No 44 to
Beaune and No 60, which serves Gevrey-
Chambertin (€1.70, 30 minutes, 15 to 18
Monday to Saturday, fewer on Sundays) via
Fixin and Marsannay-la-Côte. See the following sections for details about Transco
transport to/from Autun (p462), Avallon
(p440), Châtillon-sur-Seine (p459), Saulieu
(p443) and Semur-en-Auxois (p458).

CAR

Major rental companies and **ADA** (☎ 03 80 53
15 56) have *bureaux* in the train station.

TRAIN

The **train station** (rue du Docteur Remy) is in the
western part of Dijon. Paris' Gare de Lyon
is just 1¾ hours away by TGV (€46.20, nine
to 16). Most trains to Lyon (€22.50, two
hours, at least 12 daily) go to Gare de la
Part-Dieu. Other long-haul destinations
include Nice (€76.20, six hours, two daily)
and Strasbourg (€34.60, four hours, three or
four non-direct daily).

Getting Around

BUS

Details on Dijon's bus network, operated by
STRD, are available from **L'Espace Bus** (☎ 03
80 30 60 90; pl Grangier; ☺ 7.15am-7.15pm Mon-Fri,
7.15am-12.15pm & 2.15-7.15pm Sat). Single tickets,
sold by drivers, cost €0.80 and last for an
hour; a Forfait Journée ticket is valid all day
and costs €2.70 (available from the tourist
office or L'Espace Bus).

Bus lines are known by their number and
destination. In the city centre, seven lines
stop along rue de la Liberté, and five more
have stops around place Grangier. Most lines
operate until 8.30pm; after that, the six lines
of the Réseau du Soir (A, B, C, D, E and F)
run every 30 minutes or so until 12.15am.
The train station is linked with the city centre
(rue de la Liberté) by bus Nos 1, 9 and 12.

CAR & MOTORCYCLE

All city centre parking is metered. Free spots
are available (clockwise from the train station): northwest of rue Devosge, northeast
of blvd Thiers, southeast of blvd Carnot
and south of rue du Transvaal. There's a
big free car park at place Suquet, just south
of the police station. As in many French
cities, the one-way system is hellish –
a detailed city map (such as Michelin) is a
very good idea.

TAXI

A taxi is just a phone call away on ☎ 03 80
41 41 12, available 24 hours a day.

CÔTE D'OR VINEYARDS

Burgundy's finest vintages come from the
vine-covered Côte d'Or (Golden Hillside;
p445), the narrow, eastern slopes of a limestone, flint and clay ridge that run south
from Dijon for about 60km. The north-
ern section, the **Côte de Nuits**, stretches from
the village of Fixin south to Corgoloin and

produces reds known for their full-bodied, robust character. The southern section, the **Côte de Beaune**, lies between Aloxe-Corton and Santenay and produces great reds and great whites.

The wonderful wine-making villages of the Côted'Or include (from north to south): Marsannay-la-Côte, Fixin, Brochon, Gevrey-Chambertin, Vougeot, Vosne-Romanée, Nuits-St-Georges, Pernand-Vergelesses, Aloxe-Corton and Savigny-lès-Beaune, all north of Beaune; and Pommard, Volnay, St-Romain, Auxey-Duresses, Meursault, Puligny-Montrachet, Rochepot and Santenay, all south of Beaune. Just hearing these names makes wine-buffs go weak at the knees.

Wine Tasting

Look for signs reading *dégustation* (tasting), *domaine* (wine-making estate), *chateau,* or *cave* (wine cellar) around the villages of Côte d'Or. Another key term is *gratuit* (free); visitors are still expected to be serious about making a purchase. Places offering more than a few wines to try usually charge a fee.

Walking & Cycling

The GR7 and GR76 run along sections of the Côte d'Or. Much of the route follows tertiary roads west of the N74. The Beaune tourist office sells cycling guides covering Côte d'Or villages.

To get from Dijon to Beaune by bike, follow the quiet D122 through the vineyards until Nuits-St-Georges, and then take the D8 and the D115C. The ride takes three or four hours and covers about 40km. To avoid cycling both ways, you can take your bike on the train for the return trip, but this is possible only on certain runs – contact the SNCF for details.

Getting Around

Apart from hiring a hot-air balloon or cycling, the best way to see the Côte d'Or is by car. Getting around by bus and train is possible but can be taxing.

The best trail for wine-lovers to follow is the 'Route des Grands Crus', a signposted route that winds through the region's most famous villages – though if you're tasting wine at every stop, you might not get very far in a day.

BURGUNDY WINE: TOP FIVE FACTS

- Red wines in Burgundy are made only with the Pinot Noir grape; whites are made with the Chardonnay grape.
- Burgundy has 37,500 hectares of vineyards, which produce around 40m gallons of wine every year.
- Cistercian monks were the first to plant vines on the Côte d'Or in the 12th century.
- The outbreak of the phylloxera bug in 1878 decimated the majority of Burgundy's vineyards.
- The best wines come from the higher slopes of the Côte d'Or.

BEAUNE

pop 22,000

Beaune (pronounced similarly to bone) is the unofficial capital of the Côte d'Or. The thriving town's *raison d'être* is wine – making it, tasting it, selling it, but most of all, drinking it. Consequently Beaune is one of the best places in France for wine-tasting. The old city also contains the magnificent Hôtel-Dieu, France's most beautiful medieval charity hospital.

History

Like many other towns in Burgundy, Beaune was founded on the site of a Roman fort (named Belen after a Gaulish sun god). For a short time during the reign of the dukes of Burgundy, Beaune became the region's capital, but declined in political importance following the death of the last Valois dukes. Beaune later became a centre for the cloth and wine industries, and remains a hugely prosperous commercial centre, but the town's fortified walls and martial architecture (as well as its vast medieval hospices) are reminders of more unsettled times.

Orientation

The old city is partly enclosed by ramparts and encircled by a one-way boulevard. The train station is 1km east of the tourist office, and most of the town's sights. The main commercial area centres on place Carnot. Rue Monge and rue Carnot are pedestrianised.

Information

BOOKSHOPS
Athenaeum de la Vigne et du Vin (☎ 03 80 25 08 30; 7 rue de l'Hôtel-Dieu; ☺ 10am-7pm) Specialist bookseller with thousands of oenological titles (the art and science of wine-making).

LAUNDRY
Laundrette (19 rue du Faubourg St-Jean; ☺ 7.00am-9pm)

MONEY
The tourist office changes money on Saturday, Sunday and holidays in summer.
Banque de France (26 pl Monge) May change money from 8.45am to noon Monday to Friday.

POST
Post Office (7 blvd St Jacques)

TOURIST INFORMATION
Tourist Office (☎ 03 80 26 21 30; www.beaune -burgundy.com; 1 rue de l'Hôtel-Dieu; ☺ 9.30am-8pm Mon-Sat 21 Jun-21 Sep, 9.30am-7pm Mon-Sat Apr-20 Jun & 22 Sep–mid-Nov, 10am-6pm Mon-Sat mid-Nov–Mar, 10am-12.30pm & 2-5pm or 6pm Sun year-round)

Sights
Hôtel-Dieu des Hospices de Beaune (☎ 03 80 24 45 00; rue de l'Hôtel-Dieu; adult/student/under 18 €5.40/ 4.50/2.60; ☺ 9am-6.30pm Easter–mid-Nov, 9am-11.30am & 2pm-5.30pm mid-Nov–Easter), Beaune's celebrated charity hospital, was founded in 1443 by Nicolas Rolin (chancellor to Philip the Good). Behind the Gothic frontage, the hospice opens into a stone courtyard, surrounded by ornate turrets and pitched rooftops covered in multicoloured tiles.

PASS BEAUNE

This pick-and-mix pass, offered by the Beaune tourist office, offers discounts on local attractions. Sample itineraries include **Pass Beaune Maxi** (€21.20), which gives admission to Hôtel-Dieu, Beaune's museums, a wine cellar visit and a tourist train-ride; and **Pass Chateau Trio** (€14.85), which gives admission to the chateaux of Sully, Rochepot and Demigny. Alternatively, you can devise your own itinerary (possible items include hot-air balloon flights, abbey visits and cellar tours). In general the passes offer 5%, 10% or 15% off for two, three or four attractions.

You can also visit the Grande Salle, the hospice's main sick room (look out for dragon-motifs on the roof-beams) and the 18th-century pharmacy, lined with pottery flasks once filled with newt's eyes and vomit-nut powder. Another highlight is the graphic **Polyptych of the Last Judgement** (1443), an ornate altar-piece by the Flemish painter Roger van der Weyden.

Basilique Collégiale Notre Dame (admission tapestries €2.30; ☺ 9am-7pm, tapestries 9.30am-12.30pm & 2-5pm Mon-Sat mid-Apr–mid-Nov), a 11th- to 15th-century church affiliated with the Cluny Monastery, it displays medieval tapestries commissioned by the Rolin clan.

Musée du Vin de Bourgogne (Museum of Burgundy Wines; ☎ 03 80 22 08 19; rue d'Enfer; admission €5.40; ☺ 9.30am-5pm Wed-Mon Jan-Mar, 9.30am-6pm Wed-Mon Apr-Dec) has exhibits on wine production.

Musée des Beaux-Arts (☎ 03 80 24 98 70; 6 blvd Perpreuil; admission €5.40; ☺ 2-6pm Apr-Sep) features Gallo-Roman carvings and assorted paintings, including works by Beaune-born Félix Ziem (1821–1911).

Musée Marey (☎ 03 80 24 56 92; rue de l'Hôtel de Ville; admission €5.40; ☺ 2-6pm Apr-Oct), in the southern wing of the Hôtel de Ville (town hall), is dedicated to early cinematography.

Beaune's stone **ramparts**, which shelter private wine cellars and wild, overgrown gardens, are ringed by a pathway that makes a lovely afternoon stroll.

Activities
WINE TASTING
Underneath Beaune, millions of dusty bottles of wine are being aged to perfection in cool, dark, cobweb-lined cellars. Everyone in town seems to be cultivating their own personal *cave* – to get you started, there are many places in town where you can sample fine wines.

Marché aux Vins (☎ 03 80 25 08 20; www .marcheauxvins.com in French; 2 rue Nicolas Rolin; tastings ☺ 10-11am & 2-5pm mid-Sep–mid-Jun, 9.30am-5.45pm mid-Jun–mid-Sep) During this tour, using a *tastevin* (a flat metal cup with shiny surfaces, which help you admire the wine's colour) you'll sample 18 wines in the candle-lit former Église des Cordeliers and its cellars. Tastings last an hour.

Reine Pédauque (☎ 03 80 22 23 11; www.reine -pedauque.com in French; rue de Lorraine; tastings ☺ 10-11.30am & 2-4pm mid-Nov-Mar, 9.30-11.30am & 2-5.30pm Apr–mid-Nov) During a 45-minute

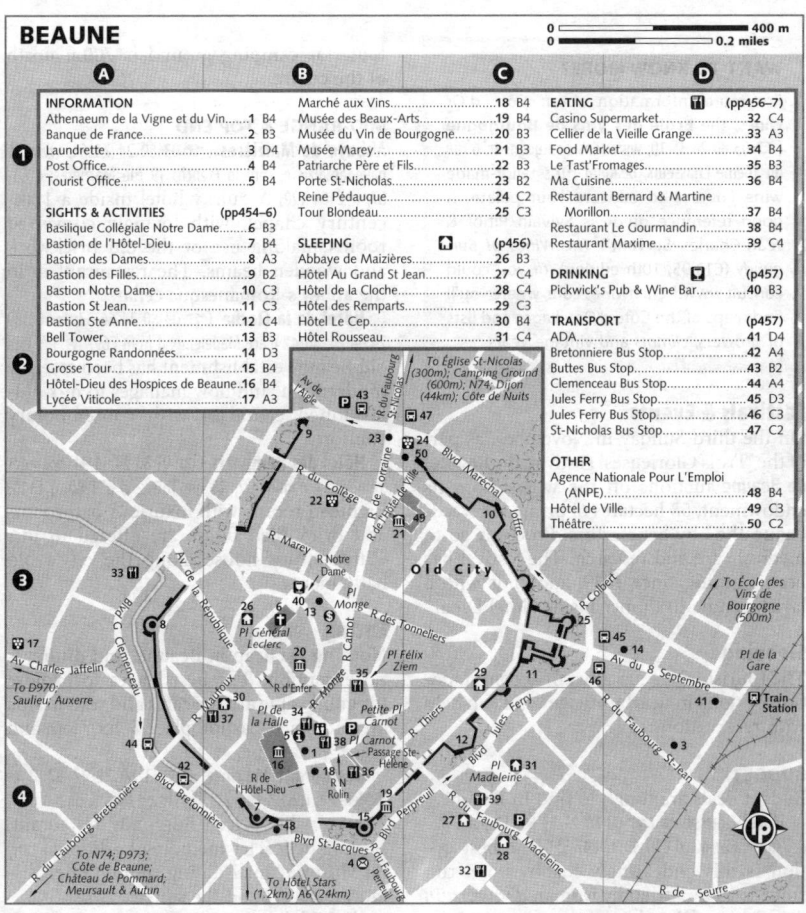

BEAUNE

INFORMATION
Atheneaum de la Vigne et du Vin......1 B4
Banque de France.............................2 B3
Laundrette......................................3 D4
Post Office.....................................4 B3
Tourist Office.................................5 B4

SIGHTS & ACTIVITIES (pp454–6)
Basilique Collégiale Notre Dame........6 B3
Bastion de l'Hôtel-Dieu....................7 B4
Bastion des Dames..........................8 A3
Bastion des Filles............................9 B2
Bastion Notre Dame.......................10 C3
Bastion St Jean.............................11 C3
Bastion Ste Anne..........................12 C4
Bell Tower....................................13 B4
Bourgogne Randonnées..................14 D3
Grosse Tour..................................15 B4
Hôtel-Dieu des Hospices de Beaune.16 B4
Lycée Viticole...............................17 A3

Marché aux Vins............................18 B4
Musée des Beaux-Arts....................19 B4
Musée du Vin de Bourgogne............20 B3
Musée Marey................................21 B3
Patriarche Père et Fils....................22 B3
Porte St-Nicholas..........................23 B2
Reine Pédauque............................24 C2
Tour Blondeau..............................25 C3

SLEEPING (p456)
Abbaye de Maizières.....................26 B3
Hôtel Au Grand St Jean..................27 C4
Hôtel de la Cloche........................28 C4
Hôtel des Remparts......................29 C3
Hôtel Le Cep...............................30 B4
Hôtel Rousseau............................31 C4

EATING (pp456–7)
Casino Supermarket.......................32 C4
Cellier de la Vieille Grange.............33 A3
Food Market.................................34 B4
Le Tast'Fromages..........................35 B3
Ma Cuisine...................................36 B4
Restaurant Bernard & Martine
   Morillon...................................37 B4
Restaurant Le Gourmandin.............38 B4
Restaurant Maxime.......................39 C4

DRINKING (p457)
Pickwick's Pub & Wine Bar.............40 B3

TRANSPORT (p457)
ADA..41 D4
Bretoniere Bus Stop......................42 A4
Buttes Bus Stop............................43 B2
Clemencaus Bus Stop....................44 A4
Jules Ferry Bus Stop......................45 D3
Jules Ferry Bus Stop......................46 C3
St-Nicholas Bus Stop.....................47 C2

OTHER
Agence Nationale Pour L'Emploi
   (ANPE)....................................48 B4
Hôtel de Ville..............................49 C3
Théâtre......................................50 C2

guided tour (in English upon request) of the 18th-century cellar you'll be able to sample one white, three reds and Belen, an aperitif. Given the thick cobwebs on the ceiling, you wouldn't want to be in here if gravity reversed itself.

Patriarche Père et Fils (☎ 03 80 24 53 78; www .patriarche.com; 5 rue du Collège; guided audio tour & tastings €9; tastings ⏲ 9.30-11.30am & 2-5.30pm) The largest cellars in Beaune are rather like Paris' Catacombs except that the corridors are lined with dusty wine bottles instead of human bones. You have the opportunity to compare 13 wines during the audio tour; circuits take 40 minutes.

Lycée Viticole (☎ 03 80 26 35 81; 16 av Charles Jaffelin; ⏲ 8am-noon & 2-5.30pm Mon-Fri, 8am-noon Sat) One of 14 French secondary schools that

train young people to grow vines and ferment, age and bottle wine. You can visit the cellars and taste the excellent wines made by the students as part of their studies.

Tours

The tourist office (p454) hosts English-language **walking tours** (per person/couple €6.50/11) from July to mid-September. It also arranges **minibus tours** (tours €40-66) of the vineyards and hot-air balloon rides (p428).

CYCLING

Bourgogne Randonnées (☎ 03 80 22 06 03; 7 av du 8 Septembre; ⏲ 9am-noon & 1.30-7pm Mon-Sat, 10am-noon & 2-7pm Sun Apr-Oct) arranges tailor-made bike tours around the Côte d'Or. Bikes cost €15/69/170 per day/week/month.

BURGUNDY

WANT TO KNOW MORE?

For more information about Côte d'Or wines, the **École des Vins de Bourgogne** (☎ 03 80 26 35 10; www.vins-bourgogne.fr; 6 rue du 16eme Chasseurs, Beaune) runs tailor-made wine courses to educate your palate. A good reference guide is Sylvain Pitiot & Jean-Charles Servant's The Wines of Burgundy (€13.95, 10th edition), or you could consult www.frenchwines.com, where you'll find maps of the Côte d'Or villages and lists of growers, climats and vintage years.

Festivals & Events

On the third Sunday in November, as part of the 'Trois Glorieuses' Festival, the **Hospices de Beaune** auctions off the wines from its endowment, 58 hectares of prime vineyards bequeathed by benefactors. Proceeds go to medical care and research. The festival has been running since 1859, and ends with a lavish candle-lit dinner inside Hôtel Dieu.

Sleeping

The tourist office has a list of accommodation options in nearby villages and can help with reservations.

BUDGET

Budget deals are tough to find in Beaune.

Hôtel Rousseau (☎ 03 80 22 13 59; 11 place Madeleine; s €24-40, d €30-50, tr €47-55) The best option is this endearingly shabby hotel run since 1959 by a friendly woman d'un certain âge. Some of the old-fashioned rooms have showers or toilets. Reception occasionally shuts for a while without warning.

Hôtel Au Grand St Jean (☎ 03 80 24 12 22; hotel-au-grand-st-jean@wanadoo.fr; 18 rue du Faubourg Madeleine; d/q from €41/51; ⏰ Jan–mid-Nov) This big, institutional hotel has lots of plain rooms and it's cheap – at least for Beaune.

Hôtel de France (☎ 03 80 24 10 34; fax 03 80 24 96 78; 35 av du 8 Septembre; s €38-65, d €51-75, tr €61-75; P) Perhaps not the period hotel you were dreaming of in Beaune, but it's comfortable enough and affordable. The sparse modern rooms are clean and it's near the train station.

Camping

Camping ground (☎ 03 80 22 03 91; 10 rue Auguste Dubois; per adult/tent €3/4; ⏰ mid-Mar–Oct) This four-star camping ground is 700m north of the centre.

MID-RANGE & TOP END

Abbaye de Maizières (☎ 03 80 24 74 64; www.abbayedemaizieres.com in French; 19 rue Maizières; d 65-87, tr €104-120) A quirky hotel inside a 12th-century chapel, with lovingly converted rooms making use of the old brickwork and wooden beams. The restaurant is in the abbey's Romanesque cellar.

Hôtel de la Cloche (☎ 03 80 24 66 33; fax 03 80 24 04 24; 40/42 place Madeleine; d from €69; P) This old Beaune establishment has been recently modernised, and now manages to mix old-fashioned character with contemporary comfort.

Hôtel des Remparts (☎ 03 80 24 94 94; hotel.des.remparts@wanadoo.fr; 48 rue Thiers; d €51-80, q €110) Eighteen rooms with luxurious bathrooms and brick-tiled floors are offered in this 17th-century house along the city's old battlements.

Eating

Nothing is cheap in Beaune, and dining is no exception. The best places to explore for good value are the cafés and restaurants around place Carnot, place Félix Ziem and place Madeleine.

Restaurant Maxime (☎ 03 80 22 17 82; 3 pl Madeleine; menus €16-28; ⏰ closed Mon & dinner Sun) A reasonably priced Burgundy restaurant, serving delicacies including traditional coq au vin in a small dining room. Other restaurants surround the square.

Ma Cuisine (☎ 03 80 22 30 22; passage Ste Hélène; menu €16; ⏰ lunch & dinner Mon-Fri, closed lunch Wed, Sat & Sun) Excellent French and Burgundian dishes offer good value at this busy bistro, and there's a nice outdoor terrace.

Restaurant Bernard & Martine Morillon (☎ 03 80 24 12 06; 31 rue Maufoux; menus €35-77; ⏰ closed lunch Mon, Tue & Fri & Jan) This restaurant provides sophisticated French dining with a substantial price-tag. Gastrophiles might try the lobster, oysters, or pigeon with fresh figs, and in season, could even order truffles (€84).

Restaurant Le Gourmandin (☎ 03 80 24 07 88; 8 pl Carnot; lunch menu €14, other menus €20-54) An intimate place that offers regional specialities, including bœuf bourguignon and jambon persillé, cooked with loving care and attention.

SELF-CATERING

The covered market in place de la Halle hosts a **food market** (until 1pm Sat) and a much smaller **marché gourmand** (gourmet market; Wed morning). The nearest *fromagerie* is **Le Tast' Fromages** (23 rue Carnot; closed Sun & Mon mid-Nov–mid-Apr).

Casino supermarket (28 rue du Faubourg Madeleine; 8.30am-7.30pm Mon-Sat) is through an archway on rue Faubourg Madeleine.

Wine can be purchased *en vrac* (in bulk) for as little as €1.10 per litre (from €3.40 per litre for AOC vintages), not including the container, at **Cellier de la Vieille Grange** (27 blvd Georges Clemenceau; closed Sun afternoon).

Drinking

Pickwick's Pub & Wine Bar (03 80 24 72 59; 2 rue Notre Dame; 11am-3pm & 5pm-2am Mon-Sat, 12.30-2.30pm & 5-9pm Sun) A convincingly English-style pub, with leather armchairs, an open fireplace and lots of beers and whiskies behind the counter. There's live music most Saturdays.

Getting There & Away

BUS

Service No 44 run by **Transco** (03 80 42 11 00) links Beaune with Dijon (€5.80, one hour, six to nine daily, two on Sunday and holidays), stopping at wine-growing villages such as Vougeot, Aloxe-Corton and Nuits-St-Georges. Buses serve villages south of Beaune (eg Pommard, Volnay, Meursault and Rochepot). In Beaune, buses stop along the boulevards around the old city. The tourist office has timetables.

CAR

You can rent cars from **ADA** (03 80 22 72 90; 26 av du 8 Septembre).

TRAIN

Beaune's **train station** (pl de la Gare) is outside the city walls, about 500m east of the town centre.

There are frequent trains to Dijon (€6, 20 minutes, 15 to 20 daily) and the Côte d'Or village of Nuits-St-Georges (€3, 10 minutes, 15 to 20 daily). The last train from Beaune to Dijon leaves at about 11.20pm.

Other destinations include Paris' Gare de Lyon (from €35.30, two direct TGVs daily), Autun (€11.90 via Étang, 1¾ hours, two daily), Mâcon (€11.60, one hour, 11 to 15 daily) and one or both of Lyon's train stations (€19.20, 1½ to 2¼ hours, seven to nine daily).

AUTHOR'S CHOICE

Hôtel le Cep (03 80 22 35 48; www.hotel-cepbeaune.com; 27 rue Maufoux; s €125, d €160-190, ste €240-320) Quite simply, this is one of France's very finest hotels. Housed in an absolutely stunning 16th-century mansion in the old quarter of Beaune, Le Cep offers the kind of old-fashioned luxury and effortless grandeur you don't find very often these days. The hotel is furnished in lavish Renaissance style, with grand salons, four-poster beds, marble statues, enormous open fireplaces, original wooden beams and a colonnaded courtyard, and the bedrooms are all named after famous wines of the Côte d'Or. If all that is not enough to convince you, rumour has it that Louis XIV preferred staying here, rather than at the Hôtel-Dieu. Now that is some recommendation!

Getting Around

Parking is free outside the town walls. When your legs get tired you can take a **taxi** (06 09 42 36 80, 06 09 43 12 08).

From April to October, Bourgogne Randonnées (p455) hires bikes.

NORTHWEST OF DIJON

The area northwest of Dijon is a mainly rural landscape of broad fields, sharp hills and wooded escarpments dotted with fortified towns perched on the hilltops, notably at Flavigny and Semur-en-Auxois. This region was once one of the main Celtic strongholds in Burgundy, and one of the country's most important pre-Roman treasure troves (the Trésor de Vix) was discovered near Chatillon-sur-Seine. Its strategic position also made it an important military site – Gaulish resistance against Roman rule was crushed once and for all on the plains below the village of Alice-Ste-Reine.

Semur-en-Auxois

pop 4500

Surrounded by a hairpin curve in the River Armançon, this beautiful fortified town is criss-crossed by cobbled lanes and arched

ABBAYE DE CÎTEAUX

It was largely due to St Bernard (1090–1153) that the **Abbey of Cîteaux** (☎ 03 80 61 32 58; www
.citeaux-abbaye.com in French), south of Dijon, became the headquarters of a vast monastic order, the
Cistercians, which once had 600 abbeys stretching from Sweden to the Near East.

In contrast with the showy Benedictines of Cluny, the Cistercian order was known for its discipline and humility. Monks were required to engage in manual labour, and as a result became
expert wine-growers, farmers, builders and metal-workers. Founded in 1098 Cîteaux was mostly
destroyed during the Revolution, so there are few historic buildings left. Monks didn't return to
the abbey until 1898.

From early May to mid-October, you can visit the monastery on a 1¾-hour guided **tour** (adult/
student €7/3.50; tours ⏱ 10.30am, 11.30am, 2.30pm, 3.15pm, 4pm & 4.45pm Tue-Sat, except Fri from mid-Jun–mid-
Sep; 12.15pm, 1pm, 2pm, 3pm, 4pm & 5pm Sun). It's in French (English text supplied) and is described as
'more spiritual than architectural'; a 30-minute audiovisual presentation offers wordless insights
into the life of the abbey's 30 modern-day monks. Phone ahead for reservations.

arcades, guarded by four massive, 13th- and
14th-century pink-granite bastions. Dotted
with artists' galleries, timber-framed houses
and antique shops, it is a lovely place to
while away a summer afternoon.

The **tourist office** (☎ 03 80 97 05 96; www.ville
-semur-en-auxois.fr; 2 pl Gaveau; ⏱ 9am-7pm Mon-Sat
mid-Jun–Sep, 2-6pm Mon, 9am-noon & 2-6pm Tue-Sat
Oct–mid-Jun, 10am-noon & 3-6pm Sun Apr-Sep) has a
free brochuredetailing walking tours.

The handsome buildings in the **old city** were
built when Semur was an important religious
centre, boasting no less than six monasteries. The **Promenade du Rempart** affords panoramic views from the medieval battlements.

Inside the twin-towered **Église Notre-
Dame** (⏱ 9am-noon & 2-6.30pm, until 5.45pm in winter), restored in the mid-19th century, are a
stained-glass window (1927) and a plaque
commemorating American soldiers who
fell in WWI.

The exhibits of the **Musée Municipal** (☎ 03
80 97 24 25; rue Jean-Jacques Collenot; adult/concession
€3.15/1.35; ⏱ 2-6pm Wed-Mon May–mid-Jun, 10am-noon
& 2-6pm Wed-Mon mid-Jun–mid-Sep, 2-5pm except Tue &
Sat & Sun mid-Sep–Apr), which range from fossils
and stuffed fauna to archaeology, sculpture
and oil paintings, are still arranged much as
they were in the 19th century.

SLEEPING & EATING

Hôtel Cymaises (☎ 03 80 97 21 44; www.proveis
.com/lescymaises in French; rue du Renandot; d from
€35) A good, uncomplicated hotel housed
in an 18th-century *maison bourgeoise*, set
around a quiet courtyard. The rooms are
simple and there's a bright conservatory for
breakfast.

Hôtel de la Côte d'Or (☎ 03 80 97 28 28; 3 pl Gaveau;
low/high season €45/58; **P**) This attractive hotel,
housed in a pretty white building with blue
shuttered windows opposite the tourist office, offers carefully-kept rooms with a hint
of bygone days.

Le Calibressan (☎ 03 80 97 32 40; 16 rue Févret;
menus €13-28; ⏱ closed Mon, lunch Sat & dinner Sun)
A rustic eatery that mixes old Burgundian
favourites with modern Californian cuisine, run by a Franco-American husband
and wife team.

Hôtel Les Gourmets (☎ 03 80 97 09 41; 4 rue Varenne; ⏱ closed Tue & dinner Mon) In a 16th-century
house in the old city, this family-run restaurant serves home-style cooking made to traditional Burgundy recipes. Plain bedrooms
are available upstairs.

Pub Le Lion (☎ 03 80 97 26 68; 4 rue de l'Ancienne
Comédie; ⏱ 9am-2am Mon-Sat) The centre of local
nightlife, with five billiard tables and a good
wine and beer selection.

GETTING THERE & AWAY

Two or three SNCF buses a day go to Saulieu (€4.80, 34 minutes) and Montbard (on
the Paris–Dijon line; €3.10, 21 minutes).
Transco (☎ 03 80 42 11 00) runs bus No 49 to/
from Dijon (€9.60, one hour 20 minutes,
two or three daily).

Flavigny-sur-Ozerain & Alésia

Flavigny, 16km east of Semur, is a delightful
hilltop village surrounded by ramparts and
rolling pastureland. Neither over-restored
nor touristy, it's straight out of the Middle
Ages, which is why movies such as *Chocolat* have been filmed here. The local sweet,

anis de Flavigny, consists of an anise seed wrapped in rock-hard candy.

Flavigny's only hotel, the seven-room **Le Relais de Flavigny** (☎ 03 80 96 27 77; www.le-relais .fr; rue des Anciennes Halles; d from €31; ☺ closed Jan), is above a local bar and restaurant in the middle of the old city. Rooms are very simple, but have a certain rustic charm.

Local farmers cook up their produce at **La Grange** (☎ 03 80 96 20 62; mains €8-10; ☺ Sun & holidays Mar-Nov, 12.30-5pm Tue-Fri, 12.30-6pm Sat, 12.30-8pm Sun Jul-Sep), next to the church. In recent years this place has started drawing diners from far and wide, and it's a fantastic way to try traditional Burgundy cooking.

Diehard fans of Roman military history should drop by **Alésia** (Alice-Ste-Reine), a few kilometres northwest of Flavigny, where the Celtic chief Vercingétorix was defeated by Julius Caesar in 52 BC. In addition to the **archaeological excavations** (☺ closed winter) a few hundred metres from the village, there's a small **museum** and a hilltop **statue of Vercingétorix** erected on the orders of Napoleon III. The nearby viewpoint indicator shows the presumed battle lines.

Abbaye de Fontenay

Fontenay Abbey (☎ 03 80 92 15 00; adult/concession €7.50/3.75), founded in 1118 and restored to its medieval glory over the past century, offers a fascinating glimpse of how the Cistercian monks once lived. Set in a wooded riverside valley, the abbey grounds include a beautifully simple chapel, the barrel-vaulted monks' dormitory, landscaped gardens, and even the old forge, bakery and trout farm. Guided **tours** (☺ hourly 10am-noon & 2-5pm Mar-Nov) are in French (printed information in English is available); unguided visits are possible year-round.

A **taxi** (☎ 06 08 82 20 61) from Montbard's train station – served from Dijon (€9.90, 40 minutes) and Paris' Gare de Lyon (non-TGV/TGV train €25.70/30.60, two to 2½ hours) – costs €8 to €10.

Châtillon-sur-Seine
pop 6800

Châtillon's main claim to fame is the **Trésor de Vix**, a treasure trove of Celtic, Etruscan and Greek objects found in the tomb of a Celtic princess believed to have controlled the trade in British tin and Baltic amber. The collection is displayed at the **Musée du Châtil-**

lonnais (☎ 03 80 91 24 67; rue du Bourg; adult/under 15 €4.30/2.30; ☺ 9.30am-noon & 2-5pm Wed-Mon Sep-Jun, 10am-6pm Jul & Aug) and includes the princess' gold tiara and a 1.64m-high, bronze Greek vase (krater) that held a bladder-bursting 1100L of wine.

Châtillon's **tourist office** (☎ 03 80 91 13 19; tourism-chatillon-sur-seine@wanadoo.fr; pl Marmont; ☺ 2-5pm Mon, 9am-noon & 2-5pm Tue-Sat) is at the fountain roundabout. The town was heavily bombed during WWII; the postwar commercial centre is bordered by two branches of the Seine, here hardly more than a stream.

Near the **Source de la Douix**, you can climb up to the 16th-century **Tour de Gissey**, where there's a fine view of the whole town; access is via the cemetery. Overlooking the village is the 10th-century **Église St-Vorles**. The **Châtillonnais vineyards**, northwest of town, produce wines including Burgundy's own bubbly, *crémant de Bourgogne.*

Accommodation is limited: there's **Hotel de la Côte d'Or** (☎ 03 80 97 28 28; 2 rue Charles-Ronot; s/d €45/58; **P**), a pleasant hotel with shuttered windows off the main street, and the ultra-budget rooms above the run-down bar-restaurant of **Hotel Le Cheval Rouge** (☎ 03 80 81 53 70; pl du 8 Mai; d from €28).

Transco (☎ 03 80 42 11 00) has buses to Dijon (line No 50; €13.28, 1½ hours, two or three daily).

SAÔNE-ET-LOIRE

The Saône-et-Loire *département,* in Burgundy's south, has important Gallo-Roman ruins in Autun, glorious Romanesque churches (or what's left of them) in Cluny and Paray-le-Monial, a fascinating industrial heritage in Le Creusot, and vineyards around Mâcon and between Tournus and Cluny. Several rivers and the Canal du Centre meander among its green hills.

AUTUN
pop 18,000

Eighty-five kilometres southwest of Dijon, Autun is a quiet provincial town but two millennia ago – under the name Augustodunum – it was one of the most important cities in Roman Gaul, boasting 6km of ramparts, two theatres, an amphitheatre and a system of aqueducts. From AD 269

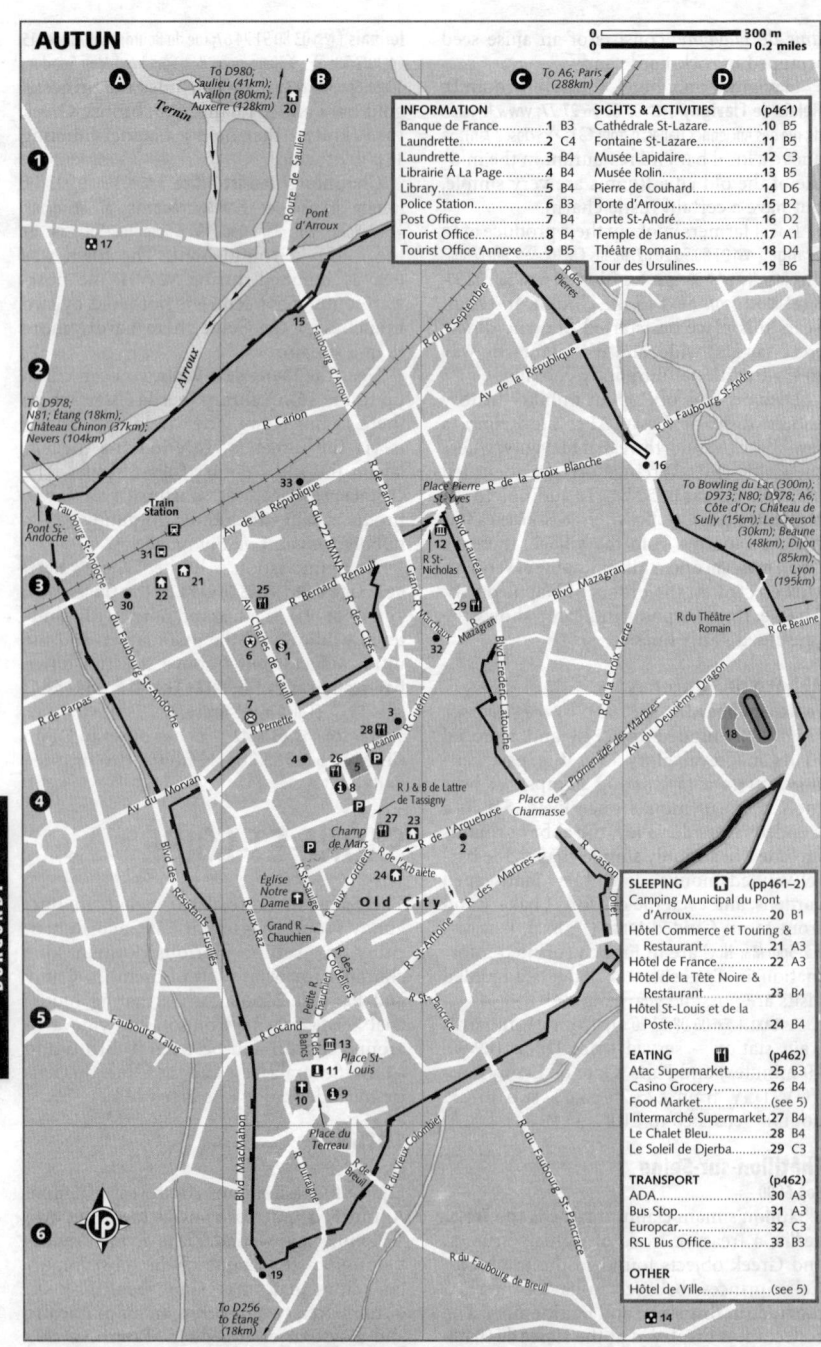

AUTUN

0 — 300 m
0 — 0.2 miles

INFORMATION	
Banque de France	**1** B3
Laundrette	**2** C4
Laundrette	**3** B4
Librairie Á La Page	**4** B4
Library	**5** B4
Police Station	**6** B3
Post Office	**7** B4
Tourist Office	**8** B4
Tourist Office Annexe	**9** B5

SIGHTS & ACTIVITIES	(p461)
Cathédrale St-Lazare	**10** B5
Fontaine St-Lazare	**11** B5
Musée Lapidaire	**12** C3
Musée Rolin	**13** B5
Pierre de Couhard	**14** D6
Porte d'Arroux	**15** B2
Porte St-André	**16** D2
Temple de Janus	**17** A1
Théâtre Romain	**18** D4
Tour des Ursulines	**19** B6

SLEEPING	(pp461–2)
Camping Municipal du Pont d'Arroux	**20** B1
Hôtel Commerce et Touring & Restaurant	**21** A3
Hôtel de France	**22** A3
Hôtel de la Tête Noire & Restaurant	**23** B4
Hôtel St-Louis et de la Poste	**24** B4

EATING	(p462)
Atac Supermarket	**25** B3
Casino Grocery	**26** B4
Food Market	(see 5)
Intermarché Supermarket	**27** B4
Le Chalet Bleu	**28** B4
Le Soleil de Djerba	**29** C3

TRANSPORT	(p462)
ADA	**30** A3
Bus Stop	**31** A3
Europcar	**32** C3
RSL Bus Office	**33** B3

OTHER	
Hôtel de Ville	(see 5)

onwards the city was repeatedly sacked by Barbarian tribes, but its fortunes turned in the Middle Ages, when an impressive cathedral was built. Many of the town's buildings date from the 17th and 18th centuries.

Autun is an excellent base for exploring the southern Parc Naturel Régional du Morvan.

Orientation
The train station is linked to Autun's common-turned-car park, the Champ de Mars, by the town's main thoroughfare, av Charles de Gaulle. The hilly area around Cathédrale St-Lazare, reached via narrow cobblestone streets, is known as the old city. The main shopping area is around rue St-Saulge.

Information
BOOKSHOPS
Librairie À La Page (☎ 03 85 52 24 72; 17bis av Charles de Gaulle; ⊗ closed Mon morning & Sun)

EMERGENCY
Police Station (☎ 03 85 86 01 80; 29ter av Charles de Gaulle; ⊗ 24hr)

LAUNDRY
There are laundrettes at 18 rue de l'Arquebuse (open 7am to 9pm) and 1 rue Guérin (7am to 8pm).

POST & MONEY
The Post Office is opposite 8 rue Pernette.

TOURIST INFORMATION
Tourist Office (☎ 03 85 86 80 38; www.autun.com; 2 av Charles de Gaulle; ⊗ 9am-7pm Jun-Sep, 9am-noon & 2-6pm Mon-Fri, 9am-12.30pm & 2.30-6pm Sat Oct-May) Offers a self-guided walking-tour brochure and pamphlets on Parc Naturel Régional du Morvan.
Tourist Office Annexe (☎ 03 85 52 56 03; 5 pl du Terreau; ⊗ 10am-noon & 2-6pm Jun–mid-Oct)

Sights
Built during the reign of Constantine, **Porte d'Arroux** was one of Augustodunum's four gates. Constructed entirely without mortar, it has four arches: two for vehicles and two for pedestrians. **Porte St-André** is similar in design.

The **Théâtre Romain** (Roman Theatre), designed to hold 16,000 people, was damaged in the Middle Ages (much of its stone was plundered for new buildings). Thanks to

19th-century restorations it's now possible to imagine the place filled with cheering (or jeering) spectators. From the top of the theatre, you can see southwest to **Pierre de Couhard** (Rock of Couhard), the 27m-high remains of a Gallo-Roman pyramid that was probably a tomb.

Long associated (wrongly) with the Roman god Janus, the 24m-high **Temple de Janus** – in the middle of farmland 800m north of the train station – is thought to have been a site for Celtic worship. Only two of its massive walls are still standing.

Cathédrale St-Lazare (place du Terreau; ⊗ 8am-8pm) was built in the 12th century to house the sacred relics of St Lazarus. Later additions include the 15th to 16th bell tower, upper choir and chapels, and the 19th-century square towers over the entrance. The Romanesque **tympanum** – inhabited by tiny chirping bats – over the main doorway shows the Last Judgement, and was carved in the 1130s by Gislebertus, whose name is written below Jesus' right foot. Across the bottom, the saved are on the left while the damned – including a woman whose breasts are being bitten by snakes (symbolising lust) – are on the right. The Renaissance-style fountain next to the cathedral, **Fontaine St-Lazare**, dates from the 16th century.

Musée Rolin (☎ 03 85 52 09 76; 5 rue des Bancs; adult/student €3.05/1.50; ⊗ 9.30am-noon & 1.30-6pm Wed-Mon Apr-Sep, 10am-noon & 2-5pm Wed-Mon Oct-Mar) displays Gallo-Roman artefacts, Romanesque sculptures and 15th- and 16th-century French and Flemish paintings.

For a **stroll** along the city walls (part-Roman but mostly medieval), walk from av du Morvan south to the 12th-century **Tour des Ursulines** and follow the walls to the northeast. You can also walk to the Pierre de Couhard, where you can pick up the Circuit des Gorges, three marked forest trails ranging from 4.7km to 11.5km – ask for a brochure at the tourist office.

Tours
From July to mid-September, there are daily **walking tours** (€5.50), sometimes in English, of the old city and the cathedral. They are run by the tourist office.

Sleeping
Hôtel Commerce et Touring (☎ 03 85 52 17 90; fax 03 85 52 37 63; 20 av de la République; d €32-42) A

BURGUNDY

tidy, simple 21-room hotel at the bottom of town, near the train station, with neat and unremarkable rooms.

Hôtel de France (☎ 03 85 52 14 00; fax 03 85 86 14 52; 18 av de la République; d €22-39) Near the Hotel Commerce, this 26-room, family-run hostelry is another basic option for tight purse strings.

Hôtel de la Tête Noire (☎ 03 85 86 59 99; www .hoteltetenoire.fr; 3 rue de l'Arquebuse; d €44-65) This great value hotel is in an excellent position between old and new cities. The newly renovated rooms are spacious and comfortable, and the buffet breakfast is huge. There's a lift to the upper floors.

Hôtel St-Louis et de la Poste (☎ 03 85 52 01 01; louisposte@aol.com; 6 rue de l'Arbalète; d €70-100, deluxe ste from €200) A luxurious four-star establishment, justly proud of its lavish lobby – and the fact that Napoleon once slept here. The Suite Napoléon costs a mere €230.

Camping

Camping Municipal du Pont d'Arroux (☎ 03 85 52 10 82; route de Saulieu; per adult/tent/car €2.50/2.15/1.30; 🕙 1 week before Easter-Oct) In a beautiful (if cramped) spot on the River Ternin.

Eating

Le Chalet Bleu (☎ 03 85 86 27 30; 3 rue Jeannin; menus €14-43; 🕙 closed Tue, dinner Mon) Creative French cuisine served in a light, modern dining room decorated with potted plants. Regional produce forms the heart of the varied menu.

Le Soleil de Djerba (☎ 03 85 86 17 77; 17 rue Mazagran; menus €10-19; 🕙 Mon-Sat) Very popular with the Autunois, this small Tunisian restaurant serves generous portions of excellent couscous as well as good French menus.

SELF-CATERING

The square outside the town hall hosts a **food market** (🕙 until noon or 12.30pm Wed & Fri).

Other grocery options include an **Atac supermarket** (av Charles de Gaulle; 🕙 8.30am-7pm Mon-Sat); a **Casino grocery** (6 av Charles de Gaulle; 🕙 7.30am-12.30pm & 3-7.30pm Tue-Sat, 8.30am-noon & 4-6pm Sun); and an **Intermarché supermarket** (21 rue J&B de Lattre de Tassigny; 🕙 8am-7.30pm Mon-Sat).

Getting There & Away

BUS

From the bus stop next to the train station, RSL buses travel to Château Chinon

(€5.35, one hour, one daily Monday to Friday, Saturday during school terms) and other towns in the Parc Naturel Régional du Morvan. There's an **RSL Bus Office** (☎ 03 85 86 92 55; 13 av de la République; 🕙 8.15am-noon & 2-6pm Mon-Thu, to 5pm Fri). Timetables are available at the tourist office or the bus station.

Transco (☎ 03 80 42 11 00) has daily buses to Dijon (€12.84, 2¼ hours) via Beaune and the Côte d'Or wine-making villages.

CAR

You can rent cars from **ADA** (☎ 03 85 52 64 03; 8 av de la République) and **Europcar** (☎ 03 85 52 13 31; 3 Grande rue Marchaux).

TRAIN

Autun's **train station** (av de la République; 🕙 until 6.30pm most days) is on a very slow line that requires a change of train (or bus) to get anywhere except Saulieu (€6.90, 50 minutes, four or five daily, two on Sunday) and Avallon (€11.70, 1¾ hours, two or three daily, one on Sunday).

Except on Sunday and holidays, one or two trains a day go to Auxerre (€17.60, 2¾ hours).

LE CREUSOT
pop 28,900

Le Creusot is, frankly, an ugly industrial town, but the story of how it got that way is fascinating (at least if you like industrial history). After all, this is where the power hammer was invented in 1841 – the towering gadget at the southern entrance to town was the mightiest power hammer in the world when it was built in 1876.

Thanks to abundant coal deposits and cheap transport via the Canal de Charolais (1793), Le Creusot became a major steelmaking centre during the 19th century. The story of the smoke-belching Schneider steelworks is told at **Château de la Verrerie** (☎ 03 85 73 92 00; adult/student/f €5.95/3.80/15.25; 🕙 10am-7pm Mon-Fri, 2-7pm Sat & Sun Jun-Sep, 10am-noon & 2-6pm Mon-Fri, 2-6pm Sat & Sun Sep-May), an 18th-century glassworks turned into a private mansion by the Schneiders, undisputed masters of the town.

The chateau's **Musée de l'Homme et de l'Industrie** (🕙 10am-noon & 2-6pm Mon-Fri, 2-6pm Sat & Sun) tells the story of the Schneider dynasty and exhibits some marvellous 1:14-scale steam locomotives. Across the courtyard, the **Académie François Bourdon** (⏲ 11am-12.30pm & 3-6pm Mon-Fri, 3-6pm Sat & Sun, longer hours in summer) has models of various flagship Schneider products (including railway locomotives, bridges, naval vessels and nuclear power plants).

The **tourist office** (☎ 03 85 55 02 46; lecreusot.net; ⏲ 9am-noon & 2-6pm Mon-Fri, 2-5pm Sat & Sun) can be found in the chateau's gatehouse.

The town is linked to the Le Creusot TGV station by **TGV Bus** (☎ 03 85 73 01 10) (€1, 20 minutes, two to four daily) and to Autun by the **SNCF** (€6, 45 minutes, six to eight daily, two on Sunday).

CLUNY

pop 4400

The remains of Cluny's great abbey – which was Christendom's largest church until the construction of St Peter's Basilica in the Vatican – are fragmentary and scattered, barely discernible among the houses and green spaces of the modern-day town. But with some imagination, it's possible to picture how things looked in the 12th century, when Cluny's Benedictine abbey, answerable only to the Pope, held sway over 1100 priories and monasteries stretching from Poland to Portugal. A smaller version of Cluny's lost abbey can be seen 30km west in the little town of **Paray-le-Monial**.

Orientation & Information

Cluny's main street is known (from southeast to northwest) as place du Commerce, rue Filaterie, rue Lamartine and rue Mercière.

Post Office (rue de la Levée)

Tourist Office (☎ 03 85 59 05 34; cluny@wanadoo.fr; 6 rue Mercière; ⏲ 10am-12.30pm & 2.30-7pm Apr-Sep, 10am-7pm Jul & Aug, 10am-12.30pm & 2.30-5pm Mon-Sat Nov-Mar) Has good English-language brochures.

Sights

The vast **Église Abbatiale** (☎ 03 85 59 89 99; adult/18-25 yrs/under 18 €6.10/4.10/free; ⏲ 9.30am-6.30pm May-Aug, 9.30am-noon & 1.30-5pm Sep-Apr, closed major holidays), built between 1088 and 1130, once stretched from the **map table** in front of Musée Ochier to the trees near the **Clocher de l'Eau Bénite** (Tower of the Holy Water) and its neighbour, **Tour de l'Horloge** – a distance of 187m. The original building boasted two towers, several belfries and some 300 windows, but as the influence of the Cluny order waned, so did the abbey's importance, and

the building fell into disrepair and was finally closed in 1790. During the Revolution, angry mobs set out to sack the building but lost interest (it took them a week just to burn the archives), and the abbey was instead sold to a local property developer, who carved it up piece by piece and auctioned off the stone for building material.

Cluny has two other churches: the **Église St Marcel** (rue Prud'hon; ⏲ closed to public), topped by an octagonal, three-storey belfry; and the 13th-century **Église Notre Dame**, across the street from the tourist office.

Tickets and guide leaflets are purchased at **Musée Ochier** near the abbey ruins, and open at the same times. Much of the remaining site (including the southern transept and 18th-century chapel) is occupied by the **École Nationale Supérieure d'Arts et Métiers** (ENSAM; place du 11 Août), an institute for training engineers. You can wander around the grounds at noon and for around an hour after closing time. Free guided tours in English take place in July and August.

The best place to appreciate the abbey's scale is from the top of the **Tour des Fromages** (Tower of Cheeses; adult/student €1.25/0.80), once used to ripen cheeses. Access to the tower's 120 steps is through the tourist office.

The **Haras National** (National Stud Farm; 2 rue Porte des Prés; ⏲ 9am-7pm), founded by Napoleon in 1806, houses some of France's finest thoroughbreds, ponies and draught horses. Visitors are welcome to wander the grounds.

Sleeping

Hôtel Bourgogne (☎ 03 85 59 00 58; www.hotel-cluny .com; pl de l'Abbaye; d €78-150; **P**) Tucked away beside the remains of the abbey, this smart brick-fronted hotel is the most comfortable place to stay in Cluny, with modern rooms and a flowery outside terrace.

Hôtel de l'Abbaye (☎ 03 85 59 11 14; hotel@abbaye -cluny.fr; av Charles de Gaulle; s €38-48, d €48-52; **P**) Hard to miss thanks to its vicious peach exterior, this is a more affordable option on the outskirts of town. The rural atmosphere and cosy rooms are pleasant, and the regional restaurant is good too.

Hôtel du Commerce (☎ 03 85 59 03 09; fax 03 85 59 00 87; 8 pl du Commerce; s/d €24-39) A very central, one-star, 17-room hotel that has little to recommend it apart from the price. Reception closes from noon to 4.30pm.

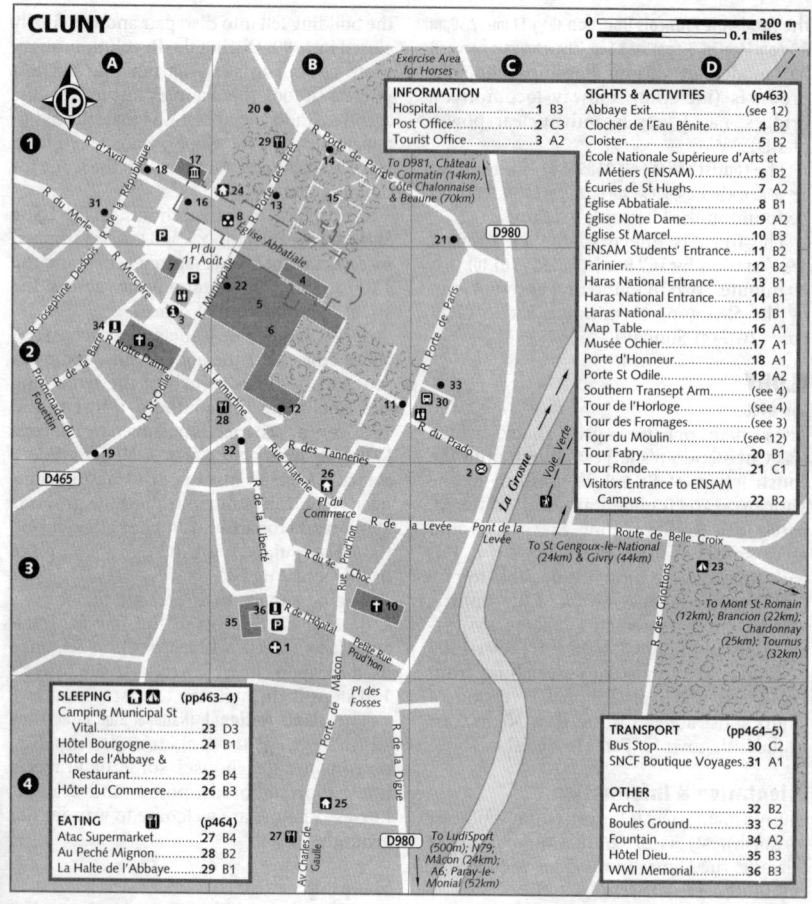

CLUNY

0 ————————— 200 m
0 ————————— 0.1 miles

Exercise Area
for Horses

INFORMATION
Hospital.............................1 B3
Post Office........................2 C3
Tourist Office...................3 A2

SIGHTS & ACTIVITIES (p463)
Abbaye Exit.......................(see 12)
Clocher de l'Eau Bénite.....4 B2
Cloister.............................5 B2
École Nationale Supérieure d'Arts et
Métiers (ENSAM)..............6 B2
Écuries de St Hughs............7 A2
Église Abbatiale.................8 B1
Église Notre Dame.............9 A2
Église St Marcel...............10 B3
ENSAM Students' Entrance..11 B2
Farinier...........................12 B2
Haras National Entrance....13 B1
Haras National Entrance....14 B1
Haras National.................15 B1
Map Table........................16 A1
Musée Ochier....................17 A1
Porte d'Honneur...............18 A1
Porte St Odile..................19 A2
Southern Transept Arm......(see 4)
Tour de l'Horloge..............(see 4)
Tour des Fromages............(see 3)
Tour du Moulin.................(see 12)
Tour Fabry.......................20 B1
Tour Ronde......................21 C1
Visitors Entrance to ENSAM
Campus...........................22 B2

To D981, Château
de Cormatin (14km);
Côte Chalonnaise
& Beaune (70km)

D980

To D981, Château

D980

D465

La Grosne

Voie Verte

Route de Belle Croix

To St Gengoux-le-National
(24km) & Givry (44km)

To Mont St-Romain
(12km); Brancion (22km);
Chardonnay
(25km); Tournus
(32km)

SLEEPING (pp463–4)
Camping Municipal St
Vital................................23 D3
Hôtel Bourgogne...............24 B1
Hôtel de l'Abbaye &
Restaurant.......................25 B4
Hôtel du Commerce...........26 B3

EATING (p464)
Atac Supermarket.............27 B4
Au Peché Mignon..............28 B2
La Halte de l'Abbaye..........29 B1

TRANSPORT (pp464–5)
Bus Stop..........................30 C2
SNCF Boutique Voyages....31 A1

OTHER
Arch................................32 B2
Boules Ground..................33 C2
Fountain...........................34 A2
Hôtel Dieu.......................35 B3
WWI Memorial..................36 B3

To LudiSport
(500m); N79;
Mâcon (24km);
A6, Paray-le-
Monial (52km)

D980

CAMPING
Camping Municipal St Vital (☎ 03 85 59 08 34; rue des Griottons; camping €10.20; ☼ May-Sep) A grassy camping area slightly east of town.

Eating
La Halte de l'Abbaye (☎ 03 85 59 28 49; 3 rue Porte des Prés; 4-course lunch menu €10; ☼ 9am-6pm Thu-Tue, lunch 11.30am-2.30pm) A classic little French bistro that specialises in Charolais beef dishes. The dining room is packed with wooden tables and overhead beams, and there are regional beers on tap.

Au Péché Mignon (☎ 03 85 59 11 21; 25 rue Lamartine; ☼ 7.30am-8pm) Cluny's gourmet patisserie offers all kinds of sweet and sticky delights – home-made nougat, jams, choc-

olate, sumptuous cakes and a house speciality – 'monk's truffles'. There's also an attached teashop.

There are several other cafés and restaurants around place de l'Abbaye and rue Lamartine. Cluny's food shops – virtually all closed on Monday – are along place du Commerce, rue Lamartine and rue Mercière. There's also an **Atac supermarket** (av Charles de Gaulle; ☼ 8.45am-7.15pm Tue-Sat, 9am-noon Sun).

Getting There & Away
The bus stop on rue Porte de Paris is served by the SNCF coach line between Chalon-sur-Saône's train station (€7.50, 1-1½ hours, four daily), Mâcon's train station (€3.90, 45 minutes, six daily) and the Mâcon-Loché

BURGUNDY

TGV station. Tickets are available at the **SNCF's Boutique Voyages** (☎ 03 85 59 07 72; 9 rue de la République; ☺ 9am-noon & 1.30-5.30pm Tue-Fri & Sat morning).

NORTH OF CLUNY

An old railway line stretching 44km from Cluny to Givry and a former canal towpath form the flat **Voie Verte** (Green Road), which is perfect for walking, cycling and in-line skating.

Tournus, known for its 9th- to 12th-century church, is 33km northeast of Cluny. The medieval village of **Brancion** sits at the base of its chateau, while **Chardonnay** is surrounded by vineyards. There's a panoramic view from 579m **Mont St-Romain**.

The **Côte Chalonnaise** wine-growing area runs from St-Gengoux-le-National northwards to **Chagny** (south of the vineyards of the Côte de Beaune); tourist offices have wine route maps.

Fourteen kilometres north of Cluny, the Renaissance-style **Château de Cormatin** (☎ 03 85 50 16 55; adult/student/under 17 €6.50/5/4; ☺ 10am-noon & 2-5.30pm Apr-May & Oct–mid-Nov, 10am-noon & 2-6.30pm Jun-Sep; 10am-6.30pm mid-Jul–mid-Aug) is renowned for its opulent 17th-century, Louis XIII-style interiors. Cormatin is linked to Cluny by seven SNCF buses daily (€2.80, 25 minutes).

MÂCON

pop 37,200

The town of Mâcon, on the right bank of the Saône, is a good base for exploring the **Mâconnais**, Burgundy's southernmost wine-growing area. The area's best vintage is Pouilly Fuissé, a renowned white produced southwest of Mâcon.

The **tourist office** (☎ 03 85 21 07 07; www.macon -tourism.com; 1 place St-Pierre; ☺ 10am-7pm Mon-Sat, 3-7pm Sun & holidays Jun-Sep, 10am-12.30pm & 2-6pm Mon-Sat Oct-May) has information on the Mâconnais and Beaujolais vineyards. It's across

the street from the **town hall**, part of which was built around 1750 as the most splendid mansion in town. You can visit some of the interior.

The shops in Mâcon's pedestrianised centre reflect the town's prosperity. The 16th-century **Maison de Bois** (☎ 03 85 38 37 70; rue Dombey) is decorated with carved wooden figures, some of them on the cheeky side – these days it's an upmarket pub. The early-19th-century **Cathédrale St Vincent** (pl Lamartine) was briefly known as Église St-Napoléon.

Musée Lamartine (☎ 03 85 38 96 19; 41 rue Sig-orgne; adult/student €2.30/free; ☺ 10am-noon & 2-6pm Mon-Sat, 2-6pm Sun & holidays) explores the life and times of the Mâcon-born Romantic poet and left-wing politician Alphonse de Lamartine (1790–1869). **Musée des Ursulines** (☎ 03 85 39 90 38; adult/student €2.30/free; ☺ 10am-noon & 2-6pm, closed Sun morning & Mon), housed in a 17th-century Ursuline convent, features Gallo-Roman archaeology and 16th- to 20th-century paintings.

You'll find restaurants and bars near the tourist office on rue Joseph Dufour, and along the river south of Pont St Laurent.

Mâcon's elegant riverfront and proximity to the Alps made it a popular destination with 19th-century tourists – when Queen Victoria visited, she took up an entire floor of the **Hôtel d'Europe et d'Angleterre** (☎ 03 85 38 27 94; fax 03 85 39 22 54; 92-109 quai Jean Jaurès; d €50-70). The hotel's old-world grandeur may have faded a little since then, but it's still an atmospheric place to stay, with a lovely 19th-century lobby, extravagant spiral staircase and quaint rooms.

The Mâcon-Ville train station is linked to Dijon (€15.90, 1½ hours, 15 to 20 daily) and Lyon's two stations (€11.70, 30 to 45 minutes, 14 to 23 daily). SNCF buses travel daily to Cluny from the train station (€3.90, 45 minutes).

The Mâcon-Loché TGV station is 5km southwest of town.

BURGUNDY

Lyon & the Rhône Valley

CONTENTS

Plumb at the crossroads to central Europe and the Atlantic, the Rhineland and the Mediterranean, the Rhône Valley has been the envy of many a soul for centuries. Roman Lyon – the region's cultural highlight – is majestic and elegant with artistic and culinary riches exceeded only by those of Paris; gastronomy-wise, it is on a par – if not better. The city is, after all, France's gastronomic capital, say gourmets. Nearby, you can visit the Gallo-Roman ruins at Vienne (of jazz festival fame), the industrial museums of St-Étienne, and medieval Pérouges.

The Rhône wiggles through Lyon on its 813km-long journey from Lake Geneva to the Mediterranean. Around 2000 BC during the Bronze Age, its waters were a prime trade route for amber and tin. Under the Romans, wine-making flourished in the region, and it continues to do so – highly regarded Côtes du Rhône appellations grow between Vienne and the unassuming town of Valence, as well as in vineyards south of sweet Montélimar.

The Gorges de l'Ardèche (Ardèche Gorges) bring the River Ardèche tumbling to the gates of Provence and Languedoc. For Rhône Valley sights further south (eg, Orange, Avignon), see the Provence chapter.

HIGHLIGHTS

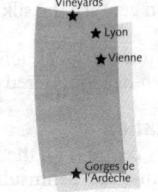

Beaujolais Vineyards
★ Lyon
★ Vienne
★ Gorges de l'Ardèche

- Explore the diverse neighbourhoods of **Vieux Lyon** (p472) or the **Croix Rousse** *canuts* (p474)
- Ride the funicular railway up **Fourvière hill** (p473)
- Step back in time with a visit to the Roman archaeological museums in **Lyon** (p473) and **Vienne** (p486)
- Salivate over some mouth-watering **Valrhona chocolate** (p486) and **Montélimar nougat** (p487)
- Enjoy some porky piggy-part cuisine in Lyon's traditional **bouchons** (p478)
- Exercise legs and wine palates visiting **Beaujolais vineyards** (p484) by pedal-power
- Rush headlong into white-water sports in **Gorges de l'Ardèche** (p488)

■ POPULATION: 5,645,407   ■ AREA: 43,698 SQ KM

LYON & THE RHÔNE VALLEY

LYON

pop 415,000

Grand old Lyon (Lyons in English) – the focal point of a prosperous urban area of almost two million people, France's second-largest conurbation – has spent the last 500 years as a commercial, industrial and banking powerhouse. At the forefront of scientific research, it produced physicist André-Marie Ampère (1775–1836), after whom the basic unit of electrical current was named, and the Lumière brothers, creators of the world's first motion picture in 1895.

Outstanding museums, a dynamic cultural life, a hotter-than-hot clubbing and bar scene, a thriving university and fantastic shopping endow this thriving metropolis – making it no mean surprise for anyone who ventures its way. Green parks, riverside paths and a historical centre sufficiently precious to be protected as a Unesco World Heritage Site is there to be explored on foot or by bicycle, while gourmets can indulge their wildest gastronomic fantasies with a dining scene that is both sharp and savvy.

History

Founded in 43 BC as a Roman military colony called Lugdunum, Lyon served as the capital of the Roman territories known as the Three Gauls under Augustus. The city's extraordinary prosperity took root in the 15th century when, with the arrival of moveable type in 1473, Lyon became one of Europe's foremost publishing centres, with several hundred resident printers. By the mid-18th century, the city's silk weavers emerged as a force to be reckoned with, making what had been a textiles centre since the 15th century the silk-weaving capital of Europe.

The international police agency Interpol has been headquartered here since 1989.

Orientation

The city centre is on the Presqu'île, a 500m- to 800m-wide peninsula bounded by the Rhône and the Saône. Public squares running down the peninsula from north to south include place de la Croix Rousse, in the hilltop neighbourhood of Croix Rousse; place Louis Pradel, just north of the opera house; place des Terreaux; place de la République, attached to pedestrianised rue de la République; vast place Bellecour; and place

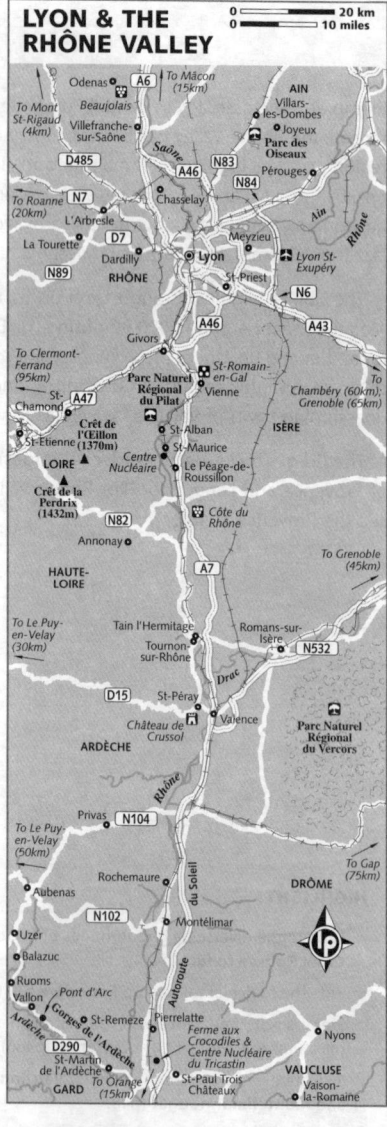

Carnot, just north of Gare de Perrache, one of Lyon's two mainline train stations.

On the western bank of the Saône, Vieux Lyon (Old Lyon) is sandwiched between the river and the hilltop area of Fourvière.

The districts east of the Rhône are known as Lyon-Rive Gauche (Lyon-Left Bank). Gare de la Part-Dieu, the city's other mainline

THE BUTCHER OF LYON

Klaus Barbie (1913–91) – 'the butcher of Lyon' – was Lyon's Gestapo commander from 1942 to 1944. Under him, some 4000 people (including Resistance leader Jean Moulin) were killed and 7500 others – including many *résistants* and Jews – were deported to Nazi death camps. The bloody years of Nazi rule ended in September 1944, when the retreating Germans blew up all but two of Lyon's 28 bridges.

After the war, Barbie worked for US counter-intelligence (1947–51) then settled in Bolivia with his family under the name Klaus Altmann. In 1952 and again in 1954, he was sentenced to death in absentia by a Lyonnais court but it was not until 1987, following his extradition from Bolivia, that he was tried in person for crimes against humanity. Barbie was sentenced to life imprisonment and died of leukaemia in prison three years later.

The life and times of Klaus Barbie are the subject of the epic 4½-hour film *Hôtel Terminus*.

train station, is 1.5km east of the Rhône in La Part-Dieu, a modern commercial centre dominated by *le crayon* – the pencil-shaped Crédit Lyonnais tower.

Lyon is divided up into nine arrondissements (districts); the arrondissement number appears after each street address in this chapter.

Information

BOOKSHOPS

Decitre (Map pp470-2; ☎ 04 26 68 00 30; 6 place Bellecour, 2e; metro Bellecour; ☯ 9.30am-7pm Mon-Sat) English-language fiction, travel guides and maps.

Raconte-Moi La Terre (Map pp470-2; ☎ 04 78 92 60 20; www.raconte-moi.com; 38 rue Thomassin, 2e; metro Cordeliers; ☯ 10am-7.30pm Mon-Sat) Travel bookshop, predominantly French titles.

EMERGENCY

Police Station (Map pp470-2; Commissariat de Police; ☎ 04 78 42 26 56; 47 rue de la Charité, 2e; metro Perrache or Ampère)

INTERNET ACCESS

The Albion (Map pp470-2; ☎ 04 78 28 33 00; 12 rue Ste-Catherine, 1er; metro Hôtel de Ville; ☯ 7pm-2am Sun-Thu, 7pm-3am Fri & Sat) English pub with free WiFi zone and free Internet access on two terminals.

Connectik Café (Map pp470-2; ☎ 04 72 77 98 85; 19 quai St-Antoine, 2e; metro Cordeliers; per 15min/hr/10hr €3/6/45; ☯ 10am-7pm Mon-Sat)

Raconte-Moi La Terre (Map pp470-2; see Bookshops above; per hr/3hr €4/10) First-floor Internet café.

INTERNET RESOURCES

www.lyon.fr Official city of Lyon website.

www.lyonclubbing.com The very latest (in French) on Lyon's nightlife scene; bars, clubs, live music, celebrities, hot gossip and so on.

www.lyonresto.com Restaurant listings with reviews, menu prices and ratings for food, atmosphere, service, quality and quantity (in French).

www.petitpaume.com Search electronically through the best city guide (in French) on Lyon, compiled by university students and distributed for free just one day a year in October.

www.rhonealpes-tourisme.com Regional tourist information site.

LAUNDRY

Laundrette (Map pp470-2; 10 rue Ste-Catherine, 1er; metro Hôtel de Ville; ☯ 6.30am-8.30pm)

Lav' + (Map pp470-2; rue Terme, 1er; metro Hôtel de Ville; ☯ 6am-9pm)

MEDICAL SERVICES

Duquesne Pharmacy (off Map pp470-2; ☎ 04 78 93 70 96; 30 rue Duquesne, 6e; metro Foch; ☯ 24hr)

CENT SAVER

The **Lyon City Card** (€15/25/30 for 1/2/3 days) gains you admission into every museum in Lyon, onto the roof of Basilique Notre Dame de Fourvière, and up Fourvière's Tour de l'Observatoire. It also includes the cost of one of the tourist office's guided or audioguided city tours, and – between April and October – you can also set sail on a river excursion. Last but not least, the Lyon City Card – sold by the tourist office and also available at certain hotels – gets you unlimited travel on buses, trams, the funicular and the metro.

Cent savers note that the Musée de la Civilisation Gallo-Romaine in Fourvière and the Musée de la Poupée are free on Thursday.

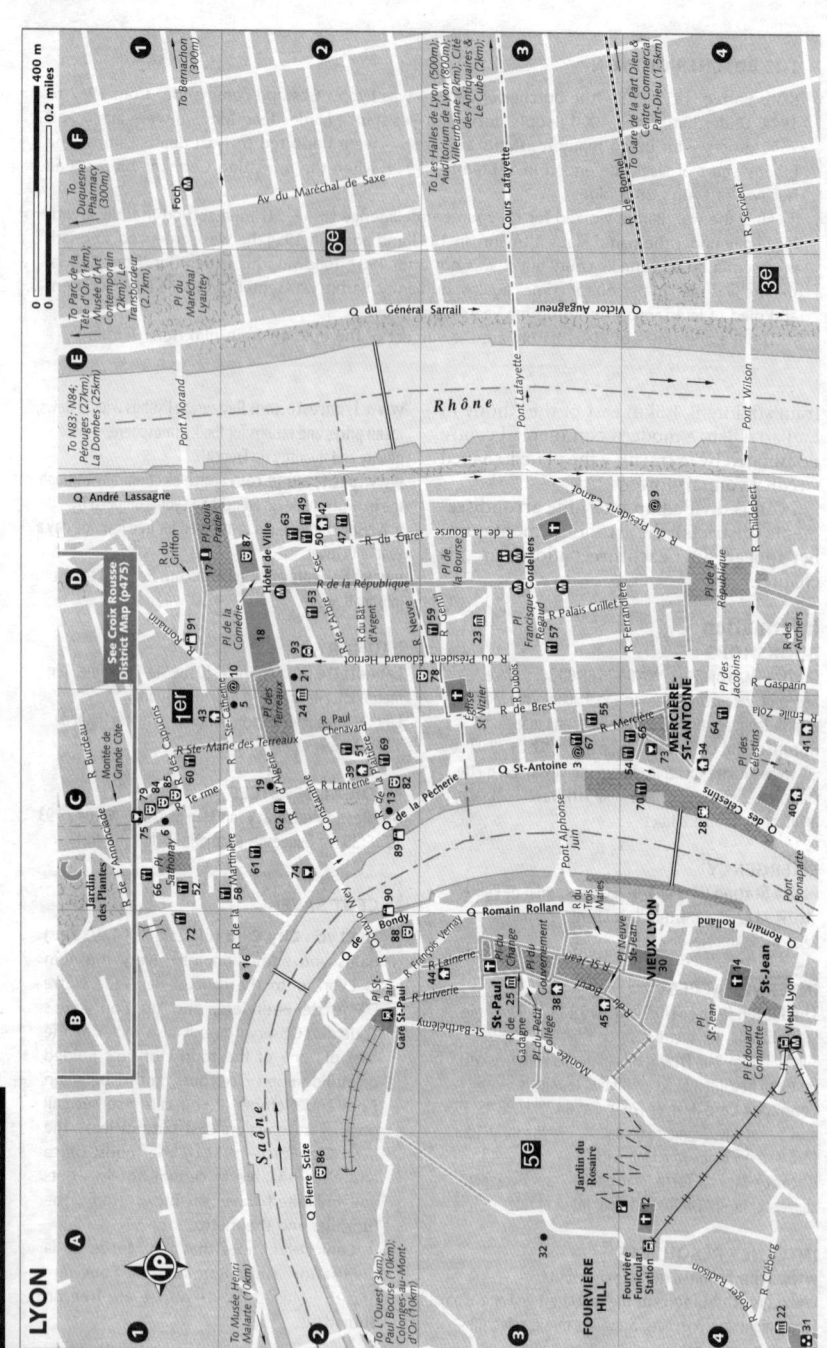

LYON

5
6
7
8

To Hôtel de Noailles
(150m); Le Fridge;
Musée Lumière;
Hangar du Premier Film &
Mur du Cinema Mural (3km);
Hôpital Edouard Herriot (4km);
Grande Mosquée de Lyon (4km)

Guillotière

Cours de la Liberté

Cours Gambetta

LYON-
RIVE
GAUCHE

7e

Victor Augagneur

R de Marseille

R Pasteur

83
80

Q Claude Bernard

R de l'Université

R Pasteur

R Chevreul

Rhône

University

To Musée Urbain (2.5km);
Tony Garnier (2.5km);
Maison de la
Danse (3km); A43
to Lyon St-Exupéry
Aérodont (25km);
Grenoble (110km)

R de la Barre
68

Pont de l'Université

R des Marronniers

Pl Antonin
Poncet

Q du Docteur Gailleton

To Au Bureau (500m);
Ninkasi (3km);
Fresque de Gerland
Mural (3km); Parc &
Stade de Gerland;
Skate Park (3km)

27

115

Q Claude Bernard

26
81

PRESQU'ÎLE

20   Bellecour
1

Bellecour

11
36

R de la Charité

Pl Bellecour

71
56
76

R Sala

R Auguste Comte

R des Remparts d'Ainay

2e

7

R de Condé

46
8

R Duhamel

Pont Galliéni

To Vienne
(32km); Valence
(106km); Montélimar
(152km); Marseille
(315km via the A7)

Quartier
Auguste Comte

R Ste-Hélène

R Jarente

Pl
Ampère   Ampère

R Henri IV

37

R Franklin

Av Berthelot

R Victor Hugo

Av Berthelot

Q de Tilsitt

Q du Plat

Saône

77

Pl
Carnot

R de Condé

ramp

Cours de Verdun

R du Bélier

48

Perrache

92

R St-Georges

St-Georges

Q Fulchiron

Q du Doyenné

Église
St-Georges

33

R Vauban

R Général Plessier

35

Gare de
Perrache

Minimes
Funicular
Stop

Monte du Chemin Neuf

To St-Just
Funicular Station

29
5

To Musée de la Poupée
(5km); Camping Municipal
International (10km);
Beaujolais (40km);
A6 to Paris (460km)

A6

A7

To Aquarium du
Grand Lyon (3km)

Q Rambaud

To Musée des
Confluences (200m)

6
7
8

Hôpital Édouard Herriot (off Map pp470-2; ☎ 08 20 08 20 69; 5 place d'Arsonval, 3e; metro Grange Blanche) 24hr emergency room; 4km southeast of place Bellecour.

Maisons Médicales de Garde (☎ 04 72 33 00 33; ⏱ 7pm-midnight Mon-Fri, noon-midnight Sat, Sun & holidays) After-hours medical care.

MONEY

Commercial banks abound on rue Victor Hugo, 2e; rue du Bât d'Argent, 1er; and rue de la République, 1er.

AOC Exchange (Map pp470-2; 20 rue Gasparin, 2e; metro Bellecour; ⏱ 9.30am-6.30pm Mon-Sat)

POST

Central Post Office (Map pp470-2; 10 place Antonin Poncet, 2e; metro Bellecour)

TOURIST INFORMATION

Tourist Office (Map pp470-2; ☎ 04 72 77 69 69; www .lyon-france.com; place Bellecour, 2e; metro Bellecour; ⏱ 9am-7pm Mon-Sat, 10am-6pm Sun mid-Apr–mid-Oct, 10am-6pm Mon-Sat, 10am-5.30pm Sun mid-Oct–mid-Apr)

Sights

VIEUX LYON

Old Lyon (Map pp470-2), with its cobblestone streets and **medieval and Renaissance houses** below Fourvière hill, is divided into three quarters: St-Paul at the northern end, St-Jean in the middle and St-Georges in the south. Facing the river is the **Palais de Justice** (Law Courts; quai Romain Rolland).

Lovely old buildings languish on **rue du Bœuf**, **rue St-Jean** and **rue des Trois Maries**. Look up to see the gargoyles and other cheeky stone characters that sit on the window ledges along **rue Juiverie**, home to Lyon's Jewish community in the Middle Ages.

The partly Romanesque **Cathédrale St-Jean** (place St-Jean, 5e; metro Vieux Lyon; ⏱ 8am-noon & 2-7.30pm Mon-Fri, 8am-noon & 2-5pm Sat & Sun), seat of Lyon's 133rd bishop, was built from the late 11th to the early 16th centuries. The portals of its Flamboyant Gothic façade (completed in 1480) are decorated with 280 square stone medallions (early 14th century). The **astronomical clock** in the north transept arm chimes at noon, 2pm, 3pm and 4pm. Organ concerts (free) are held at 6pm on the third Sunday of each month.

The **Musée Gadagne** (☎ 04 78 42 03 61; www .museegadagne.com in French; place du Petit Collège, 5e; metro Vieux Lyon; adult/under-18 €3.80/free; ⏱ 10.45am-6pm Wed-Mon), housed in the 16th-century mansion once owned by two rich Florentine bankers, houses a local history museum and a puppet museum.

FOURVIÈRE

Over two millennia ago, the Romans built the city of Lugdunum on the slopes of Fourvière (Map pp470–2). Today, Lyon's 'hill of prayer' – topped by a basilica and the **Tour Métallique**, a grey, Eiffel Tower-like structure built in 1893 and used as a TV transmitter – affords spectacular views of Lyon and its two rivers. Several footpaths wind uphill but the funicular departing from place Édouard Commette in Vieux Lyon is the easiest way up; use a metro ticket or buy a funicular return ticket (€2.20).

Crowning the hill is the ornate **Basilique Notre Dame de Fourvière** (www.lyon-fourviere.com in French; 8am-7pm), a superb example of the exaggerated enthusiasm for embellishment that dominated French ecclesiastical architecture during the late 19th century. **Guided tours** (04 78 25 86 19; adult/child €4/2.50; 2.30pm & 4pm Mon-Sun Jun-Sep, 2.30pm Oct & Nov, 2.30pm & 4pm Apr & May) last 1¼ hours and take in the roof and various bits inside, and end up at the top of the **Tour de l'Observatoire** (Observatory Tower). There's an equally stunning city view from the less-giddying terrace below.

Extraordinary artefacts found in the Rhône Valley, including the remains of a four-wheeled vehicle from around 700 BC, several sumptuous mosaics and lots of Latin inscriptions are displayed in the **Musée de la Civilisation Gallo-Romaine** (Museum of Gallo-Roman Civilisation; 04 72 38 81 90; 17 rue Cléberg, 5e; Fourvière funicular station; adult/under 18 €3.80/free, free for everyone Thu; 10am-6pm Tue-Sun Mar-Oct, 10am-5pm Tue-Sun Nov-Feb). Next door is the **Théâtre Romain**, built around 15 BC and enlarged in AD 120 to seat an audience of 10,000, and the smaller **odéon** where Romans held poetry readings and musical recitals.

PRESQU'ÎLE

The centrepiece of Presqu'île's (Map pp470–2) beautiful **place des Terreaux** (metro Hôtel de Ville), 1er, is a 19th-century fountain made of 21 tonnes of lead and sculpted by Frédéric-Auguste Bartholdi, creator of New York's Statue of Liberty. The four horses pulling the chariot symbolise rivers galloping seawards. The contemporary fountains dotting the square were designed by Burden. The **Hôtel de Ville** (City Hall) fronting the square was built in 1655 but given its present ornate façade in 1702.

Next door, the **Musée des Beaux-Arts** (Museum of Fine Arts; 04 72 10 17 40; 20 place des Terreaux, 1er; metro Hôtel de Ville; adult/under 18 €6/free; 10am-6pm Wed-Mon, from 10.30pm Fri) showcases France's finest collection of sculptures and paintings from every period of European art outside Paris. The free **cloister garden** is a great picnic venue.

Lyon's neoclassical, glass-topped **opera house** (place de la Comédie, 1er; metro Hôtel de Ville) was

---

TOP FIVE: LYON FOR KIDS

There's no end to kidding around Lyon, proof of the pudding being in the city's quarterly what's-on-for-kids listings magazine *Bulles de Gones* (www.bullesdegones.com in French). Parks, biking and boats aside, how about …

Aquarium du Grand Lyon (off Map pp470-2; 04 72 66 65 66; www.aquariumlyon.fr in French; 6 place du Général Leclerc, La Mulatière; adult/child €11/7; 10am-5pm Mon-Fri, 10am-6pm Sat & Sun school holidays, 10am-6pm Sat & Sun rest of year) Watch sharks and feel fish at this well thought-out aquarium, 4km south of the city centre in La Mulatière. Bus No 15 from place Bellecour.

A Puppet Show in Parc de la Tête d'Or (off Map pp470-2; 04 78 71 75) at Vieux Lyon's Théâtre Le Guignol (Map pp470-2; 04 78 28 92 57; 2 rue Louis Carrand, 5e; metro Vieux Lyon; adult/child €8/6); or at the Théâtre de la Croix Rousse (off Map p475; 04 72 32 11 55; 65 blvd des Canuts, 4e; metro Hénon).

A Nature Workshop Making a barometer, mini-vegetable garden, star spotting and the like – organised by Nature & Découvertes (Map pp470-2; 04 78 38 38 74; 58 rue de la République, 2e; metro Bellecour).

Musée de l'Automobile Henri Malartre (Car Museum; off Map pp470-2; 04 78 22 18 80; Château de Rochetaillée; adult/under 18 €5.30/free; 9am-6pm Tue-Sun) Ogle at 120 vintage cars and 50-odd motorbikes at this 15th-century chateau-museum, 10km north in Rochetaillée-sur-Saône. Bus No 40 or 70.

Musée de la Poupée (Doll Museum; off Map pp470-2; 04 78 87 87 00; www.lacroix-laval.com in French; Parc de Lacroix-Laval, route de St-Bel, Marcy l'Étoile; adult/under 18 €3.80/free, everyone free on Thu; 10am-5pm Tue-Sun) Little girls will love with this fairy-tale castle, surrounded by a dreamy 115-hectare park, where dolls from all eras and countries live.

erected in 1832. Skateboarders and roller-bladers buzz around the fountains of riverside **place Louis Pradel**, surveyed by the figure of **Homme de la Liberté** (Man of Freedom) on roller-skates, sculpted from scrap metal by Marseille-born César (1921–98).

The **Musée de l'Imprimerie** (Printing Museum; ☎ 04 78 37 65 98; 37 rue de la Poulaillerie, 2e; metro Cordeliers; adult/under 18 €3.80/free; ⌚ 9.30am-noon & 2-6pm Wed-Sun) focuses on a technology established in Lyon by the 1480s.

Extraordinary Lyonnais silks, French and Asian textiles, and carpets are included in the collection of the **Musée des Tissus** (Textile Museum; ☎ 04 78 38 42 00; www.musee-des-tissus.com; 34 rue de la Charité, 2e; metro Ampère; adult/under 18 €4.60/free; ⌚ 10am-5.30pm Tue-Sun). Next door, the **Musée des Arts Décoratifs** (Decorative Arts Museum; free with Textile Museum ticket; ⌚ 10am-noon & 2-5.30pm Tue-Sun) showcases 18th-century furniture, tapestries, wallpaper, ceramics and silver.

Laid out in the 17th century, **place Belle-cour** (metro Bellecour) – one of Europe's largest public squares – is pierced by an equestrian **statue of Louis XIV**. From here, pedestrianised **rue Victor Hugo** runs southwards to place Carnot and Gare de Perrache.

South of the train station lies the **Confluent de Lyon** (off Map pp470-2; www.lyon-confluence.fr), one of the city's most exciting urban areas where the Rhône and the Saône meet.

Watch this space for the spacey science-orientated **Musée des Confluences** to open in 2007. As much a stunning piece of contemporary architecture as museum, it will be housed in a gigantic glass riverside crystal. The exhibition space inside will be shaped like a cloud.

CROIX ROUSSE

The hilltop neighbourhood of Croix Rousse (Map opposite), to the north up the steep *pentes* (slopes) from central Lyon, is known for its village air, bohemian inhabitants and outdoor market. Following the introduction of the mechanical Jacquard loom in 1805, Lyonnais *canuts* (silk weavers) built workshops here with beamed ceilings high enough to accommodate the new machines. During the bitter 1830–31 *canut* uprisings, triggered by low pay and dire working conditions, hundreds of weavers were killed.

The labour-intensive life of 19th-century silk weavers comes to life at the riveting **Atelier de Passementerie** (off Map pp475; ☎ 04 78 27 17 13; www.soierie-vivante.asso.fr; 21 rue Richan, 4e; metro Croix Rousse; adult/child €1.90/1.40; ⌚ 2-6.30pm Tue, 9am-noon & 2-6.30pm Wed-Sat), an authentic workshop where *canuts* (weavers) weaved until as late as 1979. The Passementerie workshop is one of three that can be visited by guided tour only. In the **Atelier de Tissage**

TROMPE-L'ŒIL MURALS

Famous Lyonnais, past and present, beckon from a series of huge wall murals painted by Cité de la Création (www.cite-creation.fr), a local artists' group set up in the early 1980s.

Some 25 local personalities stare out from the seven-storey **Fresque des Lyonnais** (Map pp470-2; cnr rue de la Martinière & quai de la Pêcherie, 1er; metro Hôtel de Ville). More-familiar faces include loom inventor Joseph-Marie Jacquard (1752–1834), Renaissance poet Maurice Scève (c 1499–c 1560), superstar chef Paul Bocuse (see p479) and explorer Giovanni da Verrazzano, a Florentine shipmaster and navigator who discovered what is now New York in 1524 (he left it untouched, enabling the Dutch to settle it a century later, though he did earn a narrows and a bridge for his efforts). The yellow-haired Little Prince is a tribute to his creator, author Antoine de St-Exupéry, born in Lyon in 1900. Up the hill in Croix Rousse, the **Mur des Canuts** (Map opposite; cnr blvd des Canuts & rue Denfert-Rochereau, 4e; metro Hénon) celebrates the quarter's silk-weaving tradition.

At the **Musée Urbain Tony Garnier** (off Map pp470-2; ☎ 04 78 75 16 75; www.museeurbaintonygarnier .com; 4 rue des Serpollières, 8e; admission free; ⌚ 2-6pm Tue-Fri & Sun, 10am-noon & 2-7pm Sat), 25 murals painted on apartment blocks illustrate different aspects of 'the ideal city' as perceived by Tony Garnier (1869–1948), the Lyonnais architect who designed the 1930s housing estate in which the urban museum is housed. Bus No 53 from Gare de Perrache stops outside the museum.

Other monumental murals include **Bibliothèque de la Cité** (Map pp470-2; cnr quai de la Pêcherie & rue de la Platière, 1er; metro Hôtel de Ville) featuring five storeys of shelved books; and **Mur du Cinéma** (off Map pp470-2; cnr cours Gambetta & Grand Rue de la Guillotière, 7e; metro Guillotière), which illustrates the city's marvellous cinematic history.

Mécanique (Mechanical Weaving Workshop) an entire family of weavers lived and worked in just 65 sq metres for decades.

RIVE GAUCHE

Lyon's 117-hectare **Parc de la Tête d'Or** (off Map right; ☎ 04 72 69 47 60; blvd des Belges, 6e; metro Masséna; ☾ 6am-11pm mid-Apr–mid-Oct, to 9pm mid-Oct–mid-Apr), landscaped in the 1860s, is graced by a lake, a botanical garden with greenhouses, an Alpine garden, rose garden and zoo. When it's warm you can rent boats, ride ponies and play miniature golf. The park is served by bus No 41 or 47 from metro Part-Dieu.

The park's northern realms snug up to the brick-and-glass **Cité Internationale**, designed by Italian architect Renzo Piano to host the G7 summit in 1996. Inside, the **Musée d'Art Contemporain** (off Map right; Museum of Contemporary Art; ☎ 04 72 69 17 17; www.moca-lyon.org; 81 quai Charles de Gaulle, 6e; adult/under 18 €3.80/free; ☾ noon-7pm Wed-Sun) displays works created after 1960.

The WWII headquarters of Gestapo chief Klaus Barbie (see p469) houses the evocative **Centre d'Histoire de la Résistance et de la Déportation** (Map pp470-2; ☎ 04 78 72 23 11; 14 av Berthelot, 7e; metro Perrache or Jean Macé; adult/under 18 €3.80/free; ☾ 9am-5.30pm Wed-Sun). Multimedia exhibits present the history of Nazi atrocities and the heroism of French Resistance fighters.

Cinema's glorious beginnings are featured at the **Musée Lumière** (off Map pp470-2; ☎ 04 78 78 18 95; www.institut-lumiere.org; 25 rue du Premier Film, 8e; metro Monplaisir-Lumière; adult/student €6/5; ☾ 11am-6.30pm Tue-Sun), 3km southeast of place Bellecour on cours Gambetta. It's in the home of Antoine Lumière who, with his sons Auguste and Louis, shot the first reels of the world's first motion picture, *La Sortie des Usines Lumières* (Exit of the Lumières Factories) on 19 March 1895. Classic films are screened at the **Hangar du Premier Film** (p482).

The **Grande Mosquée de Lyon** (off Map pp470-2; ☎ 04 78 76 00 23; 146 blvd Pinel, 8e; metro Laënnec; ☾ 9am-noon Sat-Thu), 5km east of Presqu'île, fuses traditional North African architecture and calligraphy with contemporary Western styles.

Activities

BLADING

Rollerbladers (www.generationsroller.asso.fr) meet on Fridays at 9pm on place Bellecour for a mass swirl around the city. Otherwise, they

CROIX ROUSSE DISTRICT

SIGHTS & ACTIVITIES	(pp472–6)
Mur des Canuts	1 A2

SLEEPING	🏠 (pp476–8)
Hôtel de la Croix Rousse	2 A3
Hôtel de la Poste	3 A3

EATING	🍴 (pp478–81)
Aux 7 Péchés du Plateau	4 A3
Outdoor Food Market	5 B3
Plato	6 A3

DRINKING	🍷 (pp481–2)
Bistro Fait Sa Broc'	7 B3

blade by the rivers; in Parc de la Tête d'Or (off Map pp475); and in the **skate park** (off Map pp470-2; ☎ 04 78 69 17 86; 24 rue Pierre de Coubertin, 7e; metro Gerland) in Parc de Gerland, south of the city at the confluence of the Rhône and the Saône.

Le Cri du Kangourou (Map pp470-2; ☎ 04 78 39 59 26; 21 rue d'Algérie, 1er; metro Hôtel de Ville) rents blades.

CYCLING

Cycle paths run beside both rivers; the tourist office has details. Bicycles can be rented from **Lyon Parc Auto** (Map pp470-2; ☎ 04 78 30 11 10; 23 place des Terreaux, 1er; metro Hôtel de Ville; €7/12 per half/full day; ☾ 9am-7pm), the subterranean car park underneath place des Terreaux.

LYON & THE RHÔNE VALLEY

Motorists who park in the **car park** (☎ 04 78 42 50 09; www.vincipark.com; parking per hr/24hr €1.50/20.50; ☒ 24hr) beneath place Bellecour can borrow a bike for free.

Tours

The tourist office runs thematic English-language **walking tours** (adult €9 or €12) of Vieux Lyon and Croix Rousse. Alternatively, DIY with a set of headphones (€8/12 per half-/full day) or a copy (€1.50) of *Lyon Balades: Decouvrez Lyon à pied* (Lyon Walks: Discover Lyon on foot) or *à vélo* (by bike) in hand. The tourist office stocks both.

Navig-Inter (☎ 04 78 42 96 81; www.naviginter.fr in French) runs 1¼-hour afternoon **river excursions** (Map pp470–2; from the dock at 3 quai des Célestins, 2e; metro Bellecour or Vieux Lyon; adult/child €7/5) from April to October. Advance bookings are vital for its **lunch** and **dinner cruises** (adult/child from €24/37), departing from 23 quai Claude Bernard, 7e (Map pp470–2).

Festivals & Events

In June and July, **Les Nuits de Fourvière** (☎ 04 72 32 00 00; www.nuitsdefourviere.fr in French) brings a multitude of open-air concerts to Fourvière's Théâtre Romain (Map pp470–2).

For several days around 8 December, Lyon is lit up by the **Fête des Lumières** (Festival of Lights), marking the Feast of the Immaculate Conception. Sound-and-light shows are projected onto the city's most important buildings (place des Terreaux is always a key festival venue; Map p475) and

everyone puts candles in the windows of their homes.

Even-numbered years host the month-long **Biennale de la Danse** (Dance Biennial) in September and odd-numbered years hail the **Biennale d'Art Contemporain** (Contemporary Art Biennial) between July and September.

Sleeping

BUDGET

Auberge de Jeunesse du Vieux Lyon (Map pp470–2; ☎ 04 78 15 05 50; lyon@fuaj.org; 41-45 montée du Chemin Neuf; metro Vieux Lyon, 5e; dm €12.70; reception ☒ 7am-1pm & 9m or 10pm-1am) Rates include breakfast at this superbly located hostel above Vieux Lyon. Its 180 beds are split between rooms for two to seven people.

Hôtel Iris (Map pp470–2; ☎ 04 78 39 93 80; hoteliris@freesurf.fr; 36 rue de l'Arbre Sec, 1er; metro Hôtel de Ville; s/d with hand basin €29/32, with shower & toilet from €36/39). The location of this two-star hotel inside a wonderful, four-centuries-old convent could not be better – so get in quick to snag one of its 11 simple rooms overlooking a quiet courtyard.

Hôtel de la Poste (Map p475; ☎ /fax 04 78 28 62 67; 1 rue Victor Fort, 4e; metro Croix Rousse; s/d/q with shared shower from €17/17/33, d/tr with shower €33/46; reception ☒ 6.30am-8.30pm) Rooms share toilets on the corridor (some showers too) at this back-to-basics hotel where price – not prettiness – pulls in the punters. Fourth-floor rooms command a bird's-eye view of Croix Rousse's central square.

TRABOULES

There's more to Lyon than meets the eye. Beneath and between the city's chic shops and cafés, dark and dingy (and invariably smelly) *traboules* (secret passages) wind their way through apartment blocks, under streets and into courtyards. In all, 315 passages link 230 streets and have a combined length of 50km.

Although a couple of Vieux Lyon's *traboules* date from Roman times, most were constructed by *canuts* (silk weavers) in the 19th century to facilitate the transport of silk in inclement weather. Resistance fighters found them equally handy during WWII.

Genuine *traboules* (derived from the Latin *trans ambulare* meaning 'to pass through') cut from one street to another, often wending their way up fabulous spiral staircases en route. Passages that fan out into a courtyard or lead into a cul de sac are not *traboules*, but rather *miraboules*.

Vieux Lyon's most celebrated *traboules* include those linking 54 rue St-Jean with 27 rue du Bœuf (push the intercom button to buzz open the door), 24 rue St-Jean with 1 rue du Bœuf and 10 quai Romain Rolland with 2 place du Gouvernement. In Croix Rousse, step into the city's underworld at 9 place Colbert, crossing cours des Voraces – renowned for its monumental staircase that zigzags up seven floors – and emerging at 29 rue Imbert Colomès.

The tourist office runs *traboules* guided tours (above).

Camping

Wanting to pitch up on a farm around Lyon? Contact Gîtes de France (see below).

Camping Municipal International (off Map pp470-2; ☎ 04 78 35 64 55; camping-lyon@marie-lyon.fr; allée du Camping, Portes de Lyon; camping €13.70; reception 🕑 8am-8pm Mon-Fri, 12.30-8pm Sat & Sun 🔌) About 10km northwest of central Lyon in Dardilly, this 215-site area can be reached by bus No 3 from metro Hôtel de Ville or bus No 89 from metro Gare de Vaise.

MID-RANGE

From a room above a village *épicerie* to a suite in a Second Empire mansion in Beaujolais, **Gîtes de France** (Map pp470-2; ☎ 04 72 77 17 50; www.gites-de-france-rhone.com; 1 rue Général Plessier, 2e; metro Perrache; B&B for 2 people €40-100; 🕑 9am-noon & 1-6pm Mon-Fri, 10am-1pm Sat) organises B&B around Lyon to suit all budgets and tastes. Many places cook dinner (€10 to €25 per person).

Hôtel St-Paul (Map pp470-2; ☎ 04 78 28 13 29; www.hotelstpaul.fr; 6 rue Lainerie, 5e; metro Vieux Lyon; d with shower €38, d/q with shower & toilet €45/68) Two stars stud this 20-room inn in Vieux Lyon where medieval stonework mixes with modern blandness. Rooms facing the shabby but interior courtyard promise a quieter night's sleep than those facing the street.

Hôtel Alexandra (Map pp470-2; ☎ 04 78 37 75 79; 49 rue Victor Hugo, 2e; metro Ampère; d with shower/shower & toilet €43.50/49.50) Another one-star establishment with a smidgen of old-fashioned charm thrown.

Hotel des Artistes (Map pp470-2; ☎ 04 78 42 04 88; www.hoteldesartistes.fr; 8 rue Gaspard André, 2e; metro Bellecour or Hôtel de Ville; s €70-102, d €79-108) Theatrically furnished rooms are the trademark of this very red, very charming, three-star pad in the heart of Presqu'île shopping land. Rates reflect what's in the bathroom (shower or bath) and the view.

Hôtel de Paris (Map pp470-2; ☎ 04 78 28 00 95; www.hoteldeparis-lyon.com; 16 rue de la Platière, 1er; metro Hôtel de Ville; small s/d €42/49, lux d €53-68). Middle-of-the-road sums up this mid-range hotel bang slap in central Lyon's commercial heart. The priciest doubles have a minibar and a big bath to wallow in as well as a shower.

Hôtel de la Croix Rousse (Map p475; ☎ 04 78 28 29 85; 157 blvd de la Croix Rousse, 4e; metro Croix Rousse; d €46; 🅿) Croix Rousse's simple, village-style hotel touts 18 rooms – furnished several decades ago but spick, span and spotlessly

HAVE A GOOD WEEKEND

City-breakers arriving in Lyon on Friday or Saturday can take advantage of the city's 'Bon Week-end à Lyon' deal, whereby selected hotels offer the second night free to guests staying in a single or double room for two consecutive nights. *Bon* weekenders also get a free Lyon City Card (see p469). Book at least 24 hours in advance directly through the hotel, mentioning 'Bon Week-end à Lyon'.

clean. Reception shuts for the night around midnight; ask for the code to get back in if you intend staying out late.

Hôtel de Noailles (off Map pp470-2; ☎ 04 78 72 40 72; hotel-de-noailles-lyon@wanadoo.fr; 30 cours Gambetta, 7e; metro Saxe-Gambetta; s/d from €54/62; 🔌 🅿) This charming 24-room place is a comfortable choice for those seeking a bed on the *rive gauche* (left bank). Part of the Logis de France association (always a safe bet), everything about this place is reassuringly unsurprising.

Hôtel des Celestins (Map pp470-2; ☎ 04 72 56 08 98; www.hotelcelestins.com; 4 rue des Archers, 2e; metro Bellecour; courtyard s/d €56/60, theatre d €63) Families with kids – cot or camp-bed size (both provided for free) – are welcome at this friendly, theatre-side hotel; it goes out of its way to ensure guests get the most out of their stay in Lyon.

Comfort Hôtel St-Antoine (Map pp470-2; ☎ 04 78 92 91 91; www.hotel-saintantoine.com; 1 rue du Port du Temple, 2e; metro Cordeliers; s/d from €63/66; 🔌 🅿 💻) A stylish mix of old and new – a WiFi Internet zone and period furnishings – greet guests at this thoroughly modern hotel that occupies an 18th-century townhouse.

Hôtel Ste-Cathérine (Map pp470-2; ☎ 04 78 37 44 91; fax 04 78 42 90 17; 28 rue Ste-Cathérine, 1er; metro Hôtel de Ville; street-facing s/d €50/55, garden-facing €58/63) This charming old 29-room pile in the heart of kebab land is slowly getting a contemporary face-lift, meaning things get shabbier the higher you ascend. Pricier but quieter 'garden'-facing rooms peep out onto a pocket-sized interior courtyard with a couple of flowerbeds.

TOP END

Hôtel Cour des Loges (Map pp470-2; ☎ 04 72 77 44 44; www.courdesloges.com; 2-8 rue du Bœuf, 5e; metro Vieux

BOUCHONS

A *bouchon* might be a 'bottle stopper' or 'traffic jam' elsewhere in France, but in Lyon it's a small, friendly, more local-than-local bistro that cooks up the city's traditional cuisine.

Kick-start what will definitely be a memorable gastronomic experience with a *communard*, an aperitif of red Beaujolais wine and *crème de cassis* (blackcurrant liqueur), named after the supporters of the Paris Commune killed in 1871. Blood-red in colour, the mix would be considered criminal elsewhere in France. When ordering wine, don't bother asking for a wine list. Simply order a *pot* – a thick glass bottle adorned with an elastic band to prevent wine drips – of red Côtes du Rhône or Beaujolais.

Next comes the entrée of *tablier de sapeur* (literally 'fireman's apron', but actually meaning breaded, fried stomach) or *salade de cervelas* (salad of boiled pork sausage, sometimes studded with pistachio nuts or specks of black truffle perhaps). Hearty main dishes to sink meat-frantic gnashers into include *boudin blanc* (veal sausage), *boudin noir aux pommes* (blood sausage with apples), *quenelle* (a lighter-than-light flour, egg and cream dumpling), *quenelle de brochet* (pike quenelle, usually served in a creamy crayfish sauce) and *andouillette* (sausages made from pigs' intestines). If none of those appeal, try wrapping your lips around some *pieds de mouton/veau/couchon* (sheep/calf/piggie trotters).

The cheese course usually comprises a choice of three things: a bowl of *fromage blanc* (a cross between cream cheese and natural yogurt) with or without cream; *cervelle de canut* (literally 'brains of the silk weaver'), *fromage blanc* mixed with chives and garlic that originated in Croix Rousse and accompanied every meal for 19th-century weavers; or a round of local St-Marcellin ripened to perfection by the legendary Mère Richard for three generations. Desserts are unadventurous and rarely that inspiring. Think *tarte aux pommes* (apple tart) or *fromage blanc* (again) with a fruit coulis dribbled on top.

Little etiquette is required to eat in *bouchons*. Seldom do you get clean cutlery for each course, mopping your plate with a chunk of bread is fine; and, if the tablecloth is of the paper variety, that's probably where your bill will be added up.

In keeping with tradition, many *bouchons* are closed weekends and in August.

Lyon; ste from €230/440; (P ✕ ✕ 💻) This haven of peace and tranquillity languishes in four beautiful Renaissance mansions wrapped around a *traboule*. Some suites have a fireplace and *plafond à la française* (a hefty wooden-beamed ceiling typical to Lyon), and there's a sauna to sweat it out. Kenzo, Kissinger and Phil Collins star in the *livre d'or* (guest book).

La Tour Rose (Map pp470-2; ☎ 04 78 92 69 10; 22 rue du Bœuf, 5e; metro Vieux Lyon; d €230-540; P ✕ ✕ 💻) The 12 lavishly appointed suites in this four-star beauty built from three 13th- to 18th-century buildings honour Lyon's silky traditions. Prices reflect room size. One restaurant spectacularly reclines in an old chapel with cobbled floor and glass roof.

Sofitel Royal Lyon (Map pp470-2; ☎ 04 78 37 57 31; H2952@accor-hotels.com; 20 place Bellecour, 2e; metro Bellecour; s/d from €136/150, lux from €215/241, ste €492; P ✕ ✕ 💻) The most prestigious address on place Bellecour has lavished tender loving luxurious care upon its guests ever since

1895 when it first opened (at that time under the name Hôtel Royal). Service is four star and royal here, and 24-hour hotel parking costs €16.

Hilton Lyon (Map pp470-2; ☎ 04 78 17 50 50; www .hilton-lyon.com; 70 quai Charles de Gaulle, 6e; s/d from €136/150, lux s/d from €215/241, ste €492; P ✕ ✕ 💻) The city's other big-name hotel is a shimmering, state-of-the-art, sun-lit glass palace with 201 rooms wedged between the River Rhône and Parc de la Tête d'Or. Suites on the top floor command a stunning city panorama.

Eating
BOUCHONS
Reservations are recommended at these quintessentially Lyonnais establishments (see above).

Café des Fédérations (Map pp470-2; ☎ 04 78 28 26 00; www.lesfedeslyon.com in French; 8 rue Major Martin, 1er; metro Hôtel de Ville; dinner menu €23; ☾ Mon-Fri) For proof of the pudding that some things never change, plop yourself down at this splendid *bouchon* and feast on *caviar de la Croix Rousse* (lentils dressed in a creamy sauce) and other age-old dishes.

Chez Hugon (Map pp470-2; ☎ 04 78 28 10 94; 12 rue Pizay, 1er; metro Hôtel de Ville; menu €22; ☼ Mon-Fri) Madame Hugon serves typical meaty treats on red-and-white checked tablecloths in an interior that can only be described as a blast from the past – 1937 to be precise.

Café-Restaurant des Deux Places (Map pp470-2; ☎ 04 78 28 95 10; 5 place Fernand Rey, 1er; metro Hôtel de Ville; menu €22; ☼ Mon-Fri) Checked curtains and an interior crammed with antiques and old photographs contribute to the overwhelmingly traditional feel of this well-placed *bouchon*. Its pavement-terrace beneath trees on a quiet village-like square is a major drawcard.

Le Garet (Map pp470-2; ☎ 04 78 28 16 94; 7 rue du Garet, 1er; metro Hôtel de Ville; lunch menu €17, dinner menu €21; ☼ Mon-Fri) Yet another in the great cluster of typical *bouchons*, Le Garet – named after the small street on which it stands no less – is within spitting distance of the opera house, making it a particularly tasty choice for the city's cultural set.

La Meunière (Map pp470-2; ☎ 04 78 28 62 91; 11 rue Neuve, 1er; metro Hôtel de Ville; lunch menu €17, dinner menus €22 & €27; ☼ Tue-Sat) Excellent trotter selection, snails and ox muzzle.

FRENCH

Plato (Map p475; ☎ 04 72 00 01 30; 1 rue Villeneuve, 4e; metro Croix Rousse; lunch menus €15 & €19.50; ☼ Mon-Sat) Sweep through thick pink curtains into this stylish plateau restaurant, decked out in with contemporary flair and oozing theatre. Creative dishes – think mussel carpaccio, a whole roasted Bourg en Bresse chicken and the like – are just divine, darling.

Aux 7 Péchés du Plateau (Map p475; ☎ 04 78 28 48 82; place Tapis 3, 4e; metro Croix Rousse; menus €18 & €30; ☼ Mon-Sat) Make no bones about it – diners come here for the meat, not the décor which is strictly bare-bones. This butcher's restaurant serves *salade de rognons blancs et ris d'agneau* (white kidney salad with sweet breads), *tête de veau* (calf's head) and several beef cuts.

Commanderie des Antonins (Map pp470-2; ☎ 04 78 37 19 21; www.commanderie-antonons.fr in French; 30 quai St-Antoine, 2e; metro Bellecour; lunch menu €15, dinner menu €19.90) Another meaty choice, albeit it a highly refined one, this ode to the carnivorous cooks meat the old-fashioned way – slowly over a low heat in a wood-burning oven – and serves it with a flourish in a medieval banquet hall. Once a month it hosts thematic meal-accompanied, gastronomy lectures.

La Soup'ente (Map pp470-2; ☎ 04 78 39 32 64; 6 place des Capucins, 1er; metro Hôtel de Ville; plat du jour €8; ☼ Tue-Sun) A charming traffic-free courtyard terrace is the main draw of this unpretentious art, sound and food concept restaurant where a cultured crowd munches simple food platters (€9).

La Table d'Hippolyte (Map pp470-2; ☎ 04 78 27 75 59; 22 rue Hippolyte Flandrin, 1er; lunch menu €17, full dinner around €45; ☼ closed Sun, Mon & lunch Sat) Traditional French cuisine is concocted with the freshest seasonal ingredients at this pocket-sized place with a pocket-sized pavement terrace in summer. What's at the market dictates what is chalked up on the board.

Restaurant Albert (Map pp470-2; ☎ 04 78 27 95 56; 10 place Fernand Rey, 1er; metro Hôtel de Ville; menu €27; ☼ Tue-Sat) Albert fuses the eclectic with the traditional to create an intimate,

---

AUTHOR'S CHOICE

L'Ouest (off Map pp470-2; ☎ 04 37 64 64 64; www.bocuse.com; 1 quai du Commerce, 9e; metro Gare de Vaise; starters/mains around €14/20; ☼ lunch & dinner) No other chef has done more to secure Lyon's reputation as French gastronomic capital than Paul Bocuse, one of the oldest and most respected names in the business who has revolutionised fine dining in the city with his four-card pack of contemporary dining spaces. (He still runs his self-named, 'old-school' haute cuisine restaurant in Collonges-au-Mont d'Or, 10km north, too.) With the focus at Ouest (meaning 'west') being on island cuisine – any island that is – Bocuse-trained chefs cook up everything from crab 'n' saffron soup to Indonesian-inspired cod and straight-forward lamb chops – all in front of diners' eyes in a state-of-the-art stainless-steel open kitchen. Décor is minimalist and avant garde (think glass and wood), fashion TV flashes (rather annoyingly so) across flat wall TV screens, and a vast decking space outside overlooks the murky grey waters of the Saône.

bistro where delicious fare rules. Service veers on the bohemian and Albert's *raviolis d'escargots maison* (snail-stuffed pasta cushions) followed by *rognons de veau au vinaigre de zérès* (veal kidneys in sherry vinegar) are memorable musts.

Cobbled rue Mercière (2e) is crammed with eating options, terraces overflowing in summer.

Gaston Restaurant Agricole (Map pp470–2; ☎ 04 72 41 87 86; 41 rue Mercière, 2e; metro Cordeliers; lunch buffet €12; ✆ Mon-Sat) Pack a hearty thirst and giant-sized appetite before venturing into this feisty agricultural restaurant complete with rusty old tractor parked up front and a liberal scattering of vegie-filled wheelbarrows. Dining is around shared wooden tables and the feast-until-you're-full lunchtime buffet of cold meat and vegies is a steal.

Lolo Quoi (Map pp470–2; ☎ 04 72 77 60 90; 40-42 rue Mercière, 2e; metro Cordeliers; pasta €12, starters €5, mains €15; ✆ noon-2pm & 7pm-midnight) Sleekly kitted

out in wood and slate, Italianate Lolo Quoi is hugely trendy and very chic. Pastas with innovative sauces are the speciality.

Brasserie Georges (Map pp470–2; ☎ 04 72 56 54 54; 30 cours de Verdun, 2e; metro Perrache; menus €19 & €21.50; ✆ 11.30am-11.15pm Sun-Thu, 11.30am-12.15am Fri & Sat) Going strong since 1836, this brasserie seats over 500 people amid ornate 1920s Art Deco ceiling murals, floor tiles and upholstered red banquettes. Food is of the onion soup, mussels and sauerkraut variety.

ETHNIC & VEGETARIAN

Alyssaar (Map pp470–2; ☎ 04 78 29 57 66; 29 rue du Bât d'Argent, 1er; metro Hôtel de Ville; menus €12, €15 & €19; ✆ dinner Tue-Sat) Aleppo is undoubtedly 'the gastronomic capital of the Middle East' as far as the Syrian-born owner of this cheap, cheerful and tasty joint is concerned.

Le Pâtisson (Map pp470–2; ☎ 04 72 41 81 71; www .lepatisson.com in French; 17 rue du Port du Temple, 2e; metro Bellecour; menus €15.50 & €18.50; ✆ closed Sun, lunch Sat & dinner Fri) A *médaillon de tofu* and *escalope d'aubergine* are among the refreshingly imaginative dishes cooked up with flair at this well established vegetarian restaurant.

Rue Ste-Marie-des-Terreaux and rue Ste-Catherine, 1er (metro Hôtel de Ville), are lined with Chinese, Turkish and Indian places offering cheap eats.

CAFÉS

Outdoor cafés spill across place des Terreaux (metro Hôtel de Ville) and seemingly every square and street in Vieux Lyon (metro Vieux Lyon) in summer. Our perennial favourites follow.

Maison Perroudon (Map pp470–2; ☎ 04 78 37 37 56; 6 rue de la Barre, 2e; metro Bellecour; ✆ 7am-7.30pm Tue-Sun; ✘) Smoking is no go in this cake shop's contemporary-styled café where a predominantly female crowd lunches on light salads. Its cakes are to die for.

Giraudet (Map pp470–2; ☎ 04 72 77 98 58; www .giraudet.fr; 2 rue Colonel Chambonnet, 2e; metro Bellecour; ✆ lunch 11.30am-2.30pm Mon-Sat) Essentially a small sleek boutique selling *quenelles* (flour, egg and cream dumplings), Giraudet also has tables and a bar where you can taste the Lyonnais speciality and unusual soups (watercress, curry, broad bean and cumin etc).

Café 203 (Map pp470–2; ☎ 04 78 28 66 65; 9 rue du Garet, 1er; metro Hôtel de Ville; 1-/2-/3-course menu €7/9.50/12; ✆ 7am-2am) One of the most popular addresses in city-slick circles, 203 oozes

---

BREAKFAST & BRUNCH

A clutch of inspired breakfast and brunch joints guarantees to drag the laziest of bones out of bed. **Café 203** (see right) cooks up a simple croissant or waffle, juice and coffee breakfast (€5); and the **Modern Art Café** (see opposite) does weekend brunch. Otherwise try:

■ **Les Enfants Gâtés** (Map pp470–2; ☎ 04 78 30 91 14; 3 place Sathonay, 1er; metro Hôtel de Ville; breakfast from €6, lunch menu €8.50; ✆ Tue-Sun) The Spoilt Children leaves breakfast and brunch lovers feeling thoroughly spoilt. Pick from a French breakfast, English breakfast or giant-sized mix of both at this unpretentious café with a pavement terrace on one of the city's prettiest squares.

■ **L'Épicérie** (Map pp470–2; ☎ 04 78 37 70 85; 2 rue de la Monnaie, 2e; metro Cordeliers; breakfasts €4.90 & €6.90; ✆ 8am-1am) Enjoy breakfast *comme à la maison* (like at home) – bread with jam, honey and nutella, plus coffee, tea or chicory – or indulge in *brioche* (sweet bread) too *comme chez mémé* (like at grandma's) at this family-run bistro, decked out like a 1950s grocery store.

TASTEBUD TICKLERS

Titillate your tastebuds or those of Granny's back home with...

- *Boudins, andouillettes* and other porky piggy Lyonnais sausages from **Moinon** (Map pp470-2; 18 rue de la Plaitière, 1er; metro Hôtel de Ville; ☻ Tue-Sat & Sun morning), the best sausage maker in town.

- The best Côte du Rhône money can buy from **La Vieille Réserve** (Map pp470-2; 1 place Tobbie Robatel, 1er; metro Hôtel de Ville; ☻ Tue-Sat), an exclusive wine shop.

- Hand-painted spice chocolates from **Richart** (Map pp470-2; 1 rue du Plat, 2e; metro Bellecour; ☻ Mon-Sat).

- A strawberry, peach, blueberry or other fruity liqueur from **Pagès Védrenne** (Map pp470-2; 5 place Bellecour, 2e; metro Bellecour; ☻ Tue-Sat).

- Lyon's finest cakes and pastries from **Bernachon** (off Map pp470-2; www.bernachon.com in French; 42 cours Franklin Roosevelt, 6e; metro Foch; ☻ Tue-Sun).

---

atmosphere and is simply a great place to breakfast (see opposite), lunch, dine in the evening or just drink. It also runs **Café 100 Tabac** (Map pp470-2; 23 rue de l'Arbre Sec; ☒) around the corner – same hours, prices, genre but no smoking.

Grand Café des Négociants (Map pp470-2; ☎ 04 78 42 50 05; 2 place Francisque Regaud, 2e; metro Cordeliers; ☻ 7am-1am) Mirror-lined walls and impeccable service characterise this refined café-cum-brasserie where Lyonnais have met for coffee or to lunch since 1864. Its buzzing pavement terrace makes it a popular choice.

SELF-CATERING

Central Lyon has two fantastic **outdoor food markets** (Riverfront Map pp470-2; quai St-Antoine, 2e; metro Bellecour or Cordeliers; ☻ Tue-Sun morning; Croix Rousse Map p475; blvd de la Croix Rousse, 4e; metro Croix Rousse; ☻ Tue-Sun morning), stuffed with fruits, vegetables, meats, cheese, bread and so on.

Les Halles de Lyon (off Map pp470-2; 102 cours Lafayette, 3e; metro Part-Dieu; ☻ 7am-noon & 3-7pm Tue-Thu, 7am-7pm Fri & Sat, 7am-noon Sun) and **La Halle de la Martinière** (Map pp470-2; 24 rue de la Martinière, 1er; metro Hôtel de Ville; ☻ 8am-12.30pm & 4-7.30pm Tue-Sun) are the main indoor food markets. Mère Richard (see Bouchons, p478) has a stall at Les Halles.

Drinking

The bounty of café-terraces on place des Terreaux, 1er, buzz with drinkers day and night. English-style pubs are clustered on rue Ste-Cathérine, 1er (metro Hôtel de Ville) and in Vieux Lyon.

Modern Art Café (off Map p475; ☎ 04 72 87 06 82; www.modernartcafé.net; 65 blvd de la Croix Rousse, 4e; metro Croix Rousse; ☻ 5am-1am Mon-Fri, 11am-1am Sat & Sun) Retro furnishings, changing art on the walls, a *plage* (beach) with deckchairs, weekend brunch and a clutch of music- and video-driven happenings make this art bar one cool place to lounge.

Bistro Fait Sa Broc' (Map p475; ☎ 04 72 07 93 97; 1-3 rue Dumenge, 4e; metro Croix Rousse; ☻ 5.30pm-1am Mon-Sat) A rainbow greets punters at this colourful wine bar, known for its retro furnishings (you try spotting two chairs that match), changing wall art and occasional live bands. Regional cheeses, cold meats and light snacks are served all hours.

Elle (Map pp470-2; ☎ 04 78 42 92 83; 2 rue de la Monnaie, 2e; metro Cordeliers; ☻ 10.30am-12.30am Tue-Sat) A Moroccan-inspired interior means floor poufs, comfy sofas with an abundance of cushions, and low tables bedecked with pots of complimentary almonds and raisins for this oh-so-chic bar.

Le Voxx (Map pp470-2; ☎ 04 78 28 33 87; 1 rue d'Algérie, 1er; metro Hôtel de Ville; ☻ 8am-2am Mon-Sat, 10am-2am Sun) What adds up to one of the Presqu'île's most hip and trendy bars boasts a minimalist interior – only really visible by day when there's less of a crowd – and a Saône-side pavement terrace where you can watch impatient motorists wait for the lights to turn green.

Palais de la Bière (Map pp470-2; ☎ 04 78 27 94 00; 1 rue Terme, 1er; metro Hôtel de Ville; ☻ 6pm-2am Tue-Thu, 6pm-3am Fri & Sat) With 15 beers on tap (€3.40/4.20 for a 25cL glass before/after 9pm) and 300 different types of bottled beers, pint lovers won't go thirsty. An Ardèche-brewed *bière aux marrons* (chestnut beer) is about the only beer produced in the wine-loving

LYON & THE RHÔNE VALLEY

Rhône Valley. The truly thirsty can embark on a 15-beer *tour du monde* (world tour).

Thé Cha Yuan (Map pp470–2; ☎ 04 72 41 04 60; 7-9 rue des Remparts d'Ainay, 2e; metro Ampère; ☺ 9am-7pm Tue-Sat) Some 300 kinds of tea are brewed at this tea room that also serves dim sum – a sublime combination of French elegance and traditional Chinese serenity.

Entertainment

The tourist office has loads of information on Lyon's rich and varied entertainment scene. Locally published listings guides include the weekly *Lyon Poche* (www.lyonpoche.com in French; €1 at newsagents); the quarterly *Progrescope* (www.progrescope.com) distributed every three months with the local daily newspaper *Le Progrès* (www.leprogres. fr; €0.80 at newsagents); and the free weekly *Le Petit Bulletin* (www.petit-bulletin.fr) available at the tourist office. See p469 for online entertainment information.

Tickets for most events are sold at the **Fnac Billetterie** (ticket office; Map pp470–2; ☎ 04 72 40 49 49; 85 rue de la République, 2e; metro Bellecour; ☺ 10am-7.30pm Mon-Sat).

CINEMAS

Nondubbed films are the staple diet at **CNP-Terreaux** (Map pp470–2; ☎ 08 92 68 69 33; 40 rue du Président Édouard Herriot, 1er; metro Hôtel de Ville).

Hangar du Premier Film (off Map pp470–2; ☎ 04 78 78 18 95; www.institut-lumiere.org; 25 rue du Premier Film, 8e; metro Monplaisir Lumière) screens films of every sort and from every era, moving onto the square outside the theatre on Tuesday evenings from June to September.

In summer films (usually with a musical or pop slant) are shown on a big screen outside at Ninkasi (see below).

LIVE MUSIC

Hot Club de Lyon (Map pp470–2; ☎ 04 78 39 54 74; www .hotclubjazz.com in French; 26 rue Lanterne, 1er; metro Hôtel de Ville; adult €9-12, student €7-9; ☺ 9pm-1am Tue-Thu, 9.30pm-1am Fri, 4-7pm & 9.30pm-1am Sat) This nonprofit musical landmark since 1948 stages five weekly concerts of live jazz (big band, swing, bebop, contemporary etc), plus a free Saturday afternoon jamming session.

Ninkasi (off Map pp470–2; ☎ 04 72 76 89 00; www .ninkasi.fr in French; 267 rue Marcel Mérieux, 7e; tram stop Stade de Gerland; ☺ 10am-1am Mon-Wed, 10am-3am Thu-Sat & 4-11pm Sun) This micro-brewery near the stadium lures a frenetic crowd who steam

in to drink beer, listen to DJ beats and jive to bands. In summer everything (including films on Tuesday and Wednesday) spills onto the vast bamboo terrace outside. Ninkasi runs three other joints in town

Le Transbordeur (off Map pp470–2; ☎ 04 72 43 09 99; www.transbordeur.fr; 3 blvd de Stalingrad, Villeurbanne) Lyon's prime concert venue in an old industrial building is on the big-time European concert-tour circuit and draws international stars. Take bus No 59 or 70 from metro Part-Dieu or No 4 from metro Foch.

NIGHTCLUBS

Fish (Map pp470–2; ☎ 04 72 84 98 98; 21 quai Victor Augagneur, 3e; metro Guillotière; admission €10; ☺ 8pm-5am Wed & Thu, 8pm-6am Fri & Sat). Hugely popular with the trendy set, this huge *discothèque* (capacity over 1000) occupies a boat moored on the Rhône's left bank. DJs spin varied sounds.

Le Fridge (off Map pp470–2; ☎ 04 72 61 13 61; 67 rue des Rancy, 3e; metro Guillotière; admission €10, free for women Wed & Fri; ☺ 10.30pm-5am Wed-Sat) Hip hop, house, groove and techno are the order of the day at this DJ-driven club.

La Marquise (Map pp470–2; ☎ 04 37 40 13 93; www .marquise.net; 20 quai Victor Augagneur, 3e; metro Guillotière; admission free; ☺ 10pm-5am Wed-Sat) A 'good vibes generator' is how this moored barge sells itself. Come here for electronic music of all sorts – drum and bass, soul, rap etc.

Le Cube (off Map pp470–2; ☎ 04 78 17 29 84; 115 blvd Stalingrad, Villeurbanne; admission free; ☺ 8pm-5.30am Wed-Sat) The Cube is just that – a glass box where the Lyonnais jet set flock to jive the night away. House reigns at this trend temple.

Edy'ns Club (☎ 04 78 30 02 01; 3 rue Terme, 1er; free; ☺ 10pm-12.30am Thu-Sat), **Le Madras** (☎ 04 78 30 62 30; 3 rue Terme, 1er; ☺ 10pm-late Fri & Sat) and karaoke club **L'Opéra Rock** (☎ 04 78 39 99 88; 7 rue Terme, 1er; admission €11; ☺ 10.30pm-late Tue-Sat) are a trio of dancing venues near the opera (Map pp470–2). Otherwise, nightclubs dot the length of quai Pierre Scize, 5e, along the Saône north of Vieux Lyon.

SPORT

When at home, the national football champions **Olympique Lyonnais** (http://olweb.fr) kick off at the **Stade de Gerland** (off Map pp470–2; ☎ 04 72 76 01 70; 353 av Jean Jaurès, 7e), the city stadium built in 1926 and overhauled for the 1998 World Cup. Match tickets (☎ 08 92 46 12 30) are sold online.

THEATRE, DANCE & CLASSICAL MUSIC

Opera House (Map pp470–2; ☎ 0472004545; www.opera
-lyon.com in French; place de la Comédie, 1er; metro Hôtel de
Ville; box office ☯ 11am-7pm Mon-Sat) Opera, ballet
and classical concerts are presented mid-
September to early July.

Maison de la Danse (off Map pp470–2; ☎ 04 72
78 18 00; www.maisondeladanse.com in French; 8 av Jean
Mermoz, 8e; tram stop Bachut-Mairie du 8e; box office
☯ 11.45am-6.45pm Mon-Fri, 2-6.45pm Sat) Stunning performances of contemporary dance,
tango, flamenco etc.

Auditorium de Lyon (off Map pp470–2; ☎ 04 78 95
95 95; www.auditoriumlyon.com in French; 82 rue de Bonnel,
3e; metro Part-Dieu; box office ☯ 11am-6pm Mon-Fri, 2pm
Sat) Home to the Orchestre National de Lyon;
also hosts workshops and jazz and world
music concerts September to late June.

Shopping

The **Presqu'île** (Map pp470–2) is the place
to shop: Mainstream shops line rue de la
République and rue Victor Hugo, its continuation south of place Bellecour. Upmarket
boutiques and big-name design houses stud
parallel rue du Président Édouard Herriot,
rue de Brest and the trio of streets fanning
from place des Jacobins to place Bellecour.
Lyon-créateur.com (33 rue Romarin, 1er; metro Hôtel de
Ville) sells clothes by Lyon designers.

More big-name fashion designers are
clustered alongside art galleries and antique
shops in **Quartier Auguste Comte** (Map pp470–
2), an exclusive quarter around rue Auguste
Comte, 2e, south of place Bellecour. At least a
hundred antique dealers operate from **La Cité
des Antiquaires** (off Map pp470–2; www.cite-antiquaires
.fr; 117 blvd Stalingrad, Villeurbanne; metro Charpennes;
☯ 9.30am-12.30pm & 2.30-7pm Thu, Sat & Sun).

Centre Commercial La Part-Dieu (off Map pp470–2;
metro Part-Dieu; ☯ 9.30am-7.30pm Mon-Sat) is Lyon's
vast indoor shopping centre, with a large
supermarket, cafés and dozens of shops.

Markets for browsing away sunny days:
Book Market (Map pp470–2; quai de la Pêcherie, 1er;
metro Hôtel de Ville; ☯ 7am-6pm Sat & Sun)

Crafts Market (Map pp470–2; quai de Bondy, 5e; metro
Vieux Lyon; ☯ 9am-noon Sun)

Getting There & Away
AIR

Flights from cities around Europe land at
Aéroport Lyon–St-Exupéry (formerly Lyon-Satolas; off
Map pp470–2; ☎ 0 800 826 826; www.lyon.aeroport.fr),
25km east of the city.

BUS

In the Perrache complex (Map pp470–2),
Eurolines (☎ 04 72 56 95 30), **Intercars** (☎ 04 78
37 20 80) and Spain-oriented **Linebús** (☎ 04 72
41 72 27) have offices on the bus-station level
of the Centre d'Échange (follow the 'Lignes
Internationales' signs).

CAR & MOTORCYCLE

Major car-rental companies have offices at
Gare de la Part-Dieu, east of the centre, and
Gare de Perrache.

TRAIN

Lyon has two mainline train stations: **Gare
de la Part-Dieu** (off Map pp470–2; metro Part-Dieu),
1.5km east of the Rhône, which handles all
long-haul trains; and **Gare de Perrache** (Map
pp470–2; metro Perrache), on the Presqu'île, which
is becoming just a regional station. Many
long-distance trains stop at both. Just a few
local trains stop at **Gare St-Paul** (Map pp470–2;
metro Vieux Lyon) in Vieux Lyon. Tickets are sold
at all three stations and in town at the **SNCF
Boutique** (Map pp470–2; 2 place Bellecour, 2e; metro Bellecour; ☯ 9am-6.45pm Mon-Fri, 10am-6.30pm Sat).

Destinations by direct TGV include Paris'
Gare de Lyon (€55.60, two hours, every 30
to 60 minutes), Lille-Europe (€85.80, three
hours, nine daily), Nantes (€102.20, 4¾
hours, six daily), Beaune (€19.20, 1½ hours
to 2¼ hours, seven to nine daily), Dijon
(€24.20, 1¾ hours to two hours, at least 12
daily) and Strasbourg (€42.30, five hours,
four or five direct daily).

Getting Around
TO/FROM THE AIRPORT

Lyon–St-Exupéry airport is linked to the city
by **Satobus** (☎ 04 72 68 72 17; www.satobus.com; adult
one way/return €8.40/14.90; every 20min 5am-9pm from the
centre, 6am-11.20pm from the airport). The trip takes
45 minutes from Gare de Perrache (from
the international bus station in the Centre
d'Échange) and 35 minutes from Gare de
la Part-Dieu. A one-way/return Rhône Pass
(€9.30/18.60) covers a one-hour ride on the
metro as well as the trip to/from the airport.

By taxi, the 30-minute trip from the airport to the city centre costs upwards of €45
depending on the time of day.

PUBLIC TRANSPORT

Public transport – buses, trams, a four-line
metro and two funiculars linking Vieux

Lyon to Fourvière and St-Just – is run by **TCL** (☎ 08 20 42 70 00, www.tcl.fr in French; office at 17bis blvd Vivier Merle, 3e; metro Part-Dieu; 🕙 8.30am-5pm Mon-Fri). It operates from around 5am to midnight.

Tickets cost €1.40/11.50 for one/10 and are available from bus and tram drivers and from machines at metro entrances. Tickets allowing unlimited travel for two hours/one day €2/4.20 are also available, as are a couple of *tickets jumelés* which combine a return public-transport ticket with admission to the Musée Lumière (adult/child €7/6) or aquarium (€11/7). On all forms of public transport tickets must be time-stamped; a regular single ticket is valid for one hour after being stamped and allows up to three transfers (but no return journey).

TAXI

Taxis hover at stands in front of both train stations; on the place Bellecour end of rue de la Barre, 2e; and at the northern end of rue Chenavard, 1er. Otherwise call:

Allo Taxi (☎ 04 78 28 23 23; www.allotaxi.fr in French)
Taxis Lyonnais (☎ 04 78 26 81 81)
Taxi-Radio (☎ 04 78 28 13 14)

NORTH & WEST OF LYON

Hills, lakes and vineyards are but a short ride away from cosmopolitan Lyon.

Beaujolais

Hilly Beaujolais is a land of streams (all tributaries of the Saône), granite peaks (the highest is 1012m Mont St-Rigaud), pastures

---

> **AUTHOR'S CHOICE**
>
> There's no better spot to lunch à la Dombes than at **La Bicyclette Bleue** (☎ 04 74 98 21 48; www.labicyclettebleue.fr in French; lunch menu from €10, dinner menu €18; 🕙 closed Wed & dinner Tue), an intimate family-run place 7.5km southeast of Villars-les-Dombes in Joyeux. As well as serving delicious local fare – including must-try *grenouilles fraîches en persillade* (frogs legs cooked up in butter and parsley) – it rents kids, adults and tandem bicycles (bikes/tandems per hr €4.50/8, per half-day €12.50/20) to explore the many surrounding *étangs*. Cyclists can pick from 11 different mapped circuits, 12km (one hour) to 59km (four hours) long.

---

and forests northwest of Lyon. The region is famed for its fruity red wines, especially its 10 premium *crus*, and the Beaujolais *nouveau*, drunk at the tender age of just six weeks. Vineyards stretch south from Mâcon (see p465) along the right bank of the Saône for some 50km.

At the stroke of midnight on the third Thursday in November (late Wednesday night) – as soon as French law permits – the *libération* or *mise en perce* (tapping; the opening) of the first bottles of cherry-bright Beaujolais *nouveau* is celebrated with much hype and circumstance around France and the world. In the town of **Beaujeu**, 64km northwest of Lyon, there's free Beaujolais *nouveau* for all at a grand street party known as the Sarmentelles de Beaujeu.

For details on B&Bs and chateaux where you can taste and buy wine, contact Beaujeu's **tourist office** (☎ 04 74 69 22 88; www.beaujeu .com in French; place de l'Église; 🕙 10am-noon & 2-6pm) next to the church. Down the block, the giant statue – with arms outstretched – honours **Gnafron**, a puppet character known for his exceptional fondness for Beaujolais wine.

The region's other gastronomic highlights include fine oils – such as pecan, almond and pine kernel – available at the **Huilerie Beaujolaise** (☎ 04 74 69 28 06; 29 rue des Echarmeaux), on Beaujeu's northern edge; and the prize-winning honey sold at the **Miellerie du Fût** (☎ 04 74 69 92 03) in **Avenas**, a village surrounded by pastures and forests and endowed with a 12th-century Romanesque church.

Exploring Beaujolais by **mountain bike** is uplifting, its gentle hills suitable for the least experienced of cyclists. Fifteen routes (230km) for two-wheelers are detailed in the topoguide *Le Beaujolais à VTT*. **Évasion Beaujolaise** (☎ 04 74 02 06 84) in Marchampt, 10km south of Beaujeu, rents bicycles and maps showing thematic circuits for cyclists. **Walking** the area's many footpaths is another delightful option.

Rewarding spots to sleep, wine and dine include the two-star, seven-room **Anne de Beaujeu** (☎ 04 74 04 87 58; 28 rue de la République; d from €57; 🕙 closed Mon, lunch Tue & dinner Sun), a charming hotel-restaurant in Beaujeu; and **Restaurant Christian Mabeau** (☎ 04 74 03 41 79; menus €34-54.50; 🕙 closed Mon, dinner Sun & most of Jan & Sep) in Odenas, 10km south of Beaujeu via the D37. Its French *gastronomique* cuisine, including lots of fish dishes, can be enjoyed on the extraordinary rear terrace overlooking a vineyard.

Your own wheels or a sturdy set of walking boots is really the only way to explore Beaujolais.

Pérouges & La Dombes

The medieval village of **Pérouges** (population 850), a bit too perfectly restored, has starred in a number of films. In the warm months, day-trippers flock here to stroll its cobbled alleys, admire its half-timbered and stone houses, and devour *galettes de Pérouges* (sweet tarts, served warm and crusted with sugar) with cider. The old **liberty tree** at place de la Halle, planted in 1792, has seen better days but is still hanging in there. Bus Nos 126 and 130 link the village, perched on a hill 27km northeast of Lyon, with Gare de Perrache.

Northwest is **La Dombes**, a marshy area whose hundreds of *étangs* (shallow lakes), created from malarial swamps over the past six centuries by local farmers, are used as fish ponds and then drained so crops can be grown on the fertile lake bed. The area, famed for its production of frogs' legs, attracts lots of wildlife, particularly waterfowl. Local and exotic birds, including dozens of pairs of storks, can be observed at the more kid-friendly **Parc des Oiseaux** (☎ 04 74 98 05 54; www.parc-des-oiseaux.com in French; admission depending on season €7.50-11; ☼ 10am-nightfall), an extremely well-run and beautifully landscaped bird park and ornithological research centre just outside Villars-les-Dombes on the N83.

Couvent Ste-Marie de la Tourette

This modernistic **convent** (☎ 04 74 26 79 70; www.couventlatourette.com; guided tour adult/child €5/free), 30km west of Lyon in La Tourette, is a mecca for dedicated fans of the architect Le Corbusier (p53), renowned for his stark, concrete buildings and innovative furniture design. The convent is currently under renovation – meaning no overnight accommodation or guided tours by the white-robed Dominican monks living here. Until work is complete only parts of the building will be open to visitors; check its website for the latest update.

From Lyon's Gare de Perrache (10 daily) and Gare St-Paul (20 daily), trains go to L'Arbresle (€3.90, 40 minutes), 2km north of La Tourette; call ☎ 04 74 26 90 19 for a taxi or walk (around 25 minutes). By car

---

NUCLEAR TOURISM

Nuclear tourism enjoys a twist at the **Ferme aux Crocodiles** (☎ 04 75 04 33 73; www.lafermeauxcrocodiles.com; adult/child €8.30/6; ☼ 9.30am-7pm Mar-Sep, 9.30am-5pm Oct-Feb), a crocodile farm, which is 20km south of Montélimar in Pierrelatte, where 350-odd grouchy Nile crocodiles slumber in tropical pools heated by a neighbouring nuclear power plant.

The **Centre Nucléaire du Tricastin** plant has four 915-megawatt reactors, sufficiently productive to heat 42 hectares of greenhouses and 2400 local homes. Nearby, the **Centre Nucléaire de St-Alban–St-Maurice**, 20km south of Vienne on the Rhône's left bank, has two pressurised water reactors rated at a mighty 1300 megawatts, enough to supply the needs of Lyon 10 times over.

---

follow the westbound N7 out of Lyon or the more scenic D7.

ST-ÉTIENNE
pop 200,000

The best bits of St-Étienne – an unpretentious, down-to-business industrial city 62km southwest of Lyon – look like the dullest bits of Paris, but don't let the greyness scare you off: the city has three excellent museums that merit a visit.

The city's industrial heritage, including the local bicycle industry founded in 1886, feature at the **Musée d'Art et d'Industrie** (☎ 04 77 33 04 85; 2 place Louis Comte; adult/child €4.40/free; ☼ 10am-6pm Wed-Mon) and the **Musée de la Mine** (☎ 04 77 43 83 26; 3 blvd Franchet d'Espérey; adult/child €5.60/free; ☼ Wed-Mon), a mine active from 1910 to 1973 where you can see coal-extraction technology in situ and get a sense of what it was like to work as a collier. Underground tours departing several times daily are by train.

On a considerably brighter note, the internationally renowned **Musée d'Art Moderne** (☎ 04 77 79 52 52; adult/child €4.40/free; ☼ 10am-6pm Wed-Mon) has a flamboyant collection of paintings, sculptures and photographs including classics from the early 20th century as well as contemporary works. It is in La Terrasse, a neighbourhood on the northern edge of the city. To get there, take tram No 4.

Should you need to spend the night in St-Étienne, the **tourist office** (☎ 08 92 70 05 42;

www.tourisme-st-etienne.com; 16 av de la Libération; 9am-7pm Mon-Sat, 9am-noon Sun Apr-Sep, 9am-6pm Mon-Sat, 9am-noon Sun Oct-Mar), 1km southwest of the main train station, St-Étienne Châteaucreux, has accommodation lists.

Getting There & Around

Ryanair flies from London Stansted to/from tiny **Aéroport de St-Étienne-Bouthéon** (☎ 04 77 55 7171; www.saint-etienne.aeroport.fr), 15km northwest of the city. Local bus No 100 (€2.80, 14 to 17 daily Monday to Saturday, five on Sunday) links the roundabout outside the airport with place Chavanelle, near the St-Étienne tourist office. Ryanair buses to Lyon are coordinated with the flight times (adult one way/return €20/30).

France's very first train line, which was built between 1824 and 1833, connected St-Étienne with Lyon. Today, trains linking St-Étienne Châteaucreux with Lyon (€8.60, 50 minutes) go to either Gare de la Part-Dieu or Gare de Perrache (both at least hourly).

DOWNSTREAM ALONG THE RHÔNE

South of Lyon, vineyards meet nuclear power plants – not the most auspicious juxtaposition perhaps, but worth a stop for Lyon-based day-trippers or those bound south.

TAIN'S CHOCOLATE FACTORY

There's more to Tain l'Hermitage than just revered red wine. Its other *grand cru* is **Valrhona chocolate**, produced in the village in all its guises – be it bitter dark, milky caramel, with orange slices or hazelnut slivers – since 1924. Indulge your wildest chocolate fantasy at its **shop** (14 av du Président Roosevelt; 9am-7pm Mon-Fri, 9am-6pm Sat) in Tain.

As well as running workshops for professional pastry chefs and chocolate-makers, the prestigious chocolate-maker of world renown runs sweet courses for individuals in its **École du Grand Chocolate** (☎ 04 75 07 90 90; www.valrhona.com; quai du Général de Gaulle). A sweet tooth for chocolate is about the only qualification you need to sign up for Valrhona's four-day 'Chocolate Experience' course (€822) devoted to the use of chocolate in pastries, or its three-day 'Basic Chocolate Candies' course (€632).

Vienne

pop 29,900

This one-time Gallo-Roman city, now a disappointingly average town 30km south of Lyon, is only worth a stop if you're an aficionado of the Romans, or you're around during its famous two-week **jazz festival** (☎ 08 92 70 20 07; www.jazzavienne.com) at the end of June.

The Corinthian columns of the superb **Temple d'Auguste et de Livie** (place Charles de Gaulle), built about 10 BC to honour the Emperor Augustus and the lovely Livia (his wife), in the small old town are a fine sight. Across the river in St-Romain-en-Gal, the excavated remains of the Gallo-Roman city form the archaeological **Musée Gall-Romain** (☎ 04 74 53 74 01; 2 chemin de la Plaine Gal; adult/under 18 €3.80/free, free 1st Sun of month; 10am-6pm Tue-Sun Mar-Oct, 10am-5pm Tue-Sun Nov-Feb). There are great town views from the **Belvédère de Pipet**, a viewing balcony with a 6m-tall statue of the Virgin Mary, immediately above Vienne's fabulous **Théâtre Romain** (☎ 04 74 85 39 23; rue du Cirque; admission €2, free 1st Sun of month; 9.30am-1pm & 2-6pm Apr-Aug, 9.30am-1pm & 2-6pm Tue-Sun Sep & Oct, 9.30am-12.30pm & 2-5pm Tue-Sat, 1.30-5.30pm Sun Jan-Mar, Nov & Dec). The vast Roman amphitheatre, built around AD 40–50, tumbles majestically down the hillside and is a key jazz-festival venue.

The **tourist office** (☎ 04 74 53 80 30; www.vienne-tourisme.fr; 3 cours Brillier; 9am-noon & 1.30-6pm Mon-Sat, 10am-noon & 2-5pm Sun) has information on guided walking tours of the city, festivals, markets and other sights and activities in and around town.

SLEEPING & EATING

Auberge de Jeunesse (☎ 04 74 53 21 97; 11 quai Riondet; dm €10; reception 5-8pm Mon-Thu, 2-5pm Fri) Vienne's 54-room riverside hostel is a two-minute strut south of the tourist office. At weekends and in winter, call ahead to make sure someone is in when you arrive.

Grand Hôtel de la Poste (☎ 04 74 85 02 04; 47 cours Romestang; d/tr/q €45/55/65; P) This old-time, two-star hotel with 36 spacious rooms sits plumb on the main, tree-lined avenue. Night owls beware; the front door closes at midnight (11pm weekends).

Hôtel de la Pyramide (☎ 04 74 53 01 96; www.lapyramide.com in French; 14 blvd Fernand-Point; s/d/ste from €160/175/240; menus €49, €85 & €130; restaurant Thu-Mon; P ⊠ ❄ 🖳) So called because of its location overlooking La Pyramide de la Cirque (a 15.5m-tall obelisk that in Roman

AS NUTTY AS NOUGAT

There is just one sweet reason to stop in Montélimar – to eat its nutty chewy nougat.

Produced in the otherwise ordinary town, 46km south of Valence, since the 17th century, *nougat de Montélimar* took off after WWII when holidaying motorists on their way to Provence and the Côte d'Azur stopped off in the Rhône-side town to buy the sweeter-than-sweet treat.

Traditional Montélimar nougat consists of at least 28% almonds, 25% lavender honey, 2% pistachio nuts, sugar, egg white and vanilla. Nougat varies in texture (more or less tender), honey taste (more or less strong) and crispness of the nuts. Some nougats are coated in chocolate and others have fruit (try the one with figs), but traditional Montélimar nougat is quite simply off-white.

A dozen nougat producers in Montélimar offer free tours of their sweet factories; pick a small (rather than an industrial) confectioner and arrange your visit to coincide with the morning cooking session. Most producers spend the afternoon cutting and packing their morning's production.

- **Le Gavial** (☎ 04 75 01 67 19; 6 chemin de Géry; ◷ 8-11.30am & 2-5pm) Four-person workshop producing the best nougat according to a taste test by the French *Gault & Millau* food guide.

- **Le Chaudron d'Or** (☎ 04 75 01 03 95; www.chaudron-dor.com; 7 av du 52e Regiment d'Infanterie; ◷ 8am-7pm) The Golden Cauldron warrants a peek for the 'show' by the loveable confectioner.

- **Diane de Poytiers** (☎ 04 75 01 67 02; www.diane-de-poytiers.fr; 99 av Jean Jaurès; ◷ 8.30-11.45am & 2-5.15pm) Slightly south of town but the trip through this refurbished factory is worth it.

- **Musée du Nougat Arnaud Soubeyran** (☎ 04 75 51 01 35; www.nougatsoubeyran.com; Quartier des Blaches, RN7; shop ◷ 9am-7pm Mon-Sat, 10am-noon & 2.30-6.30pm Sun, guided tours 9.30am, 10.30am & 11.30am, 2pm, 3pm, 4pm & 5pm) Large factory-cum-museum and shop with a café where you can sample fruit-flavoured nougats.

The **tourist office** (☎ 04 75 01 00 20; www.montelimar-tourisme.com; allées Provençales; ◷ 9am-12.15pm & 2-6.30pm Mon-Sat), across the park from the train station, has more detailed information on visiting nougat producers. In town, souvenir and nougat shops on allées Provençales sell 200g bags of *papillotes* (bite-sized nougat chunks wrapped in shiny paper) for €4 to €5.50.

Montélimar is on the train line linking Valence-Ville (€6.90, 23 minutes, five daily) with Avignon-Centre (€10.90, 45 minutes, hourly).

---

times pierced the centre of a hippodrome), this apricot villa with powder-blue shutters is a four-star haven of peace and tranquillity. French chef Patrick Henriroux works wonders in the kitchen with lobsters, foie gras, fresh black truffles (in season), *coquilles St-Jacques* (mussels) and other gourmet treats.

Less-grand eating options abound along cours Romestang and cours Brillier near the tourist office.

GETTING THERE & AWAY

Trains and buses link Vienne with Lyon's Gare de Perrache (€5.40, 20 to 32 minutes, at least hourly) and Valence (€10.20, 45 minutes, at least hourly).

Towards Valence

The **Parc Naturel Régional du Pilat** spills across 650 sq km southwest of Vienne and offers some breathtaking panoramas of the Rhône Valley from its highest peaks, Crêt de l'Œillon (1370m) and Crêt de la Perdrix (1432m). The Montgolfier brothers, inventors of the hot-air balloon in 1783, were born – and held their first public *montgolfière* demonstration – in **Annonay**, 50km northwest of Valence on the park's southeastern boundary.

The north section of the Côtes du Rhône wine-growing area, known for vintages offering particularly good value, stretches from Vienne south to Valence. Two of the area's most respected *appellations*, St-Joseph and Hermitage, grow around **Tain l'Hermitage**, an ordinary bourg on the Rhône's left bank. Its **tourist office** (☎ 04 75 08 06 81; place de l'Église; ◷ 9am-noon & 2-6pm Mon-Sat) has a list of cellars where you can taste and buy wine.

One or two trains every hour link Tain l'Hermitage with Valence (€3.10, 12 minutes) and Lyon (most trains use Gare de Perrache; €11.70, one hour).

Valence

pop 63,400

Several Rhône Valley towns claim to be the gateway to Provence, but Valence has a better claim than most. Alas, the threshold is rather less interesting than what slumbers inside…

In Vieux Valence, the city's old town, the main landmark is **Cathédrale St-Apollinaire**, a late-11th-century pilgrimage church (thus the ambulatory), largely destroyed in the Wars of Religion and rebuilt in the 17th century. Nearby, allegorical sculpted heads adorn **Maison des Têtes** (57 Grande Rue), a blend of Flamboyant Gothic and Renaissance built in 1530. The main commercial streets are rue Émile Augier and Grande Rue.

Grand panoramas of the Rhône Valley can be enjoyed from the clifftop ruins of 12th-century **Château de Crussol** (admission free; ⏲ 24hr), accessible from **St-Péray**, a village 5km northwest along the N532.

The local shortbread speciality, le Suisse, is a crunchy, orange-rind-flavoured biscuit shaped like one of the Vatican's Swiss guards. Said to commemorate Pope Pius VI's imprisonment and death in Valence in 1799, it's available at patisseries.

The Valence **tourist office** (☎ 04 75 44 90 40; www.tourisme-valence.com; ⏲ 9am-6.30pm Mon-Fri, 9am-5pm Sat, also 9am-noon Sun Jul & Aug) is in the train-station building. There is a complete list of accommodation options available online at www.hotels-valence.com.

SLEEPING & EATING

Hôtel des Senteurs (☎ 04 75 44 15 32; www.pic-valence.com; 285 av Victor Hugo; d low/high season from €145/165; P ⊠ ⊠ ⊠ ⊠) Run with loving tender care by the Pic family since the late 19th century, this Provençal-style Relais & Châteaux hotel stuns. Relax in the reading room or billiard room, or over a gastronomic feast in the gourmet **Restaurant Pic** (☎ 04 75 44 15 32; 285 av Victor Hugo; lunch menu €50, dinner menus €75-135; ⏲ closed Mon, dinner Sun year-round plus Tue Nov-Mar) or on the terrace of the less-formal **Auberge du Pin** (☎ 04 75 44 53 86; 285bis av Victor Hugo; menus €26 & €30; lunch & dinner year-round). Anne-Sophie Pic, the gourmet force behind Pic, is the only female chef in France with two Michelin stars.

GETTING THERE & AWAY

Train destinations include Montélimar (€6.90, 23 minutes, five daily), Lyon (€13.70,

1¼ hours, 12 daily), Avignon-Centre (€15.90, 1¼ hours, four to six direct daily) and Grenoble (€12.80, 1¼ hours, nine daily).

Frequent trains and buses (€2) link the city centre train station (Valence-Ville) with the Valence TGV Rhône-Alpes Sud station, 10km east.

Gorges de l'Ardèche

The serpentine River Ardèche slithers and churns past towering cliffs of mauve, yellow and grey limestone – dotted with vegetation typical of the Midi – as it makes its way from near **Vallon Pont d'Arc** to **St-Martin de l'Ardèche**, a few kilometres west of the Rhône. Eagles nest in the cliffs and there are numerous grottes (caves) – some inhabited as far back as 40,000 years ago – to explore. One of the area's most famous features is the **Pont d'Arc**, a natural stone bridge created by the river's torrents.

About 300m above the canoeable waters of the gorge (half- and full-day river expeditions can be arranged in Vallon Pont d'Arc and St-Martin de l'Ardèche) is the **Haute Corniche** (D290), which affords a magnificent series of belvédères (panoramic views). It turns into a huge and chaotic traffic jam in summer. On the plateaus above the gorges, typically Midi villages (eg St-Remèze) are surrounded by garrigue, lavender fields and vineyards.

From Vallon Pont d'Arc, the scenic D579 takes cyclists and motorists northwest to **Ruoms**; across the river, the D4 (signposted 'Largentière') snakes wildly along the **Défilé de Ruoms** (a narrow tunnel of rock) and the **Gorges de la Ligne** for 8km. From Bellevue, bear north on the D104 for 2km to Uzer, then east on the D294 to **Balazuc**, one of France's prettiest villages.

From Balazuc the D579 leads northwards to **Aubenas**, from which point a multitude of scenic roads fans out into the surrounding Cévenol countryside. This is a land of chestnuts where the dark brown fruit is turned into everything from crème de châtaigne (a sweet purée served with ice cream, crepes or cake) to bière aux marrons (chestnut beer). Unique to the region is liqueur de châtaigne, a 21% alcohol-by-volume liqueur which makes a sweet aperitif when mixed with white wine. Buy a bottle at the **Palais du Marron** (☎ 04 75 64 35 16; 10 cours de l'Esplanade) in **Privas**.

French Alps & the Jura

CONTENTS

'Lances des glaciers fiers, rois blancs' (Lances of proud glaciers, white kings)
from Voyelles, Arthur Rimbaud (1854–91)

The French Alps, where green valleys meet soaring peaks topped with craggy, snowbound summits, form one of the most awesome mountain ranges in the world. Created by the impact of two huge continental plates over 200 million years ago, the icy spikes, needles and snowy peaks of the Alpine mountains have inspired Roman generals, Romantic poets and madcap mountaineers alike. These days, the region may no longer be an isolated wilderness, but the Alps continue to excite and inspire their visitors all the same.

Blanketed by snow and ice in winter, and bathed with warm sunshine and blue skies in summer, the mountains and valleys of the French Alps contain some of the country's top tourist destinations. The Alps are the spiritual home of winter sports, and skiing and snowboarding are the region's main attractions, especially around the high-octane resorts of Chamonix, Megève and Val d'Isère. But the mountains are also a hugely popular destination in summer, when the snow melts away to reveal lush valleys, green meadows and fields of wildflowers, as well as hundreds of kilometres of walking trails.

While thrill-seekers indulge in warm-weather sports ranging from paragliding to white-water rafting, hikers can head out into one of the region's many national parks in search of golden eagles, mountain goats and the elusive ibex. History buffs should head for the medieval towns of Annecy and Chambéry, and big city thrills can be found in the dynamic capital of the Alps, Grenoble. North of Lake Geneva (Lac Léman), in the Jura region, the old city of Besançon and the villages of Arbois and Baume-les-Messieurs make ideal bases for exploring the little-visited Franche-Comté region and the wild reaches of Parc Naturel Régional du Haut-Jura.

HIGHLIGHTS

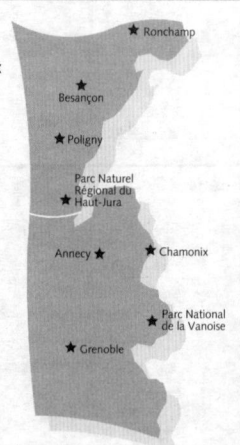

- Riding the world's highest, scariest **cable car** (p500) in Chamonix
- Stroll the lantern-lit lanes of **Annecy** (p508)
- Absorb the big-city ambience of **Grenoble** (p521), capital of the Alps
- Explore the high mountain trails of the **Parc National de la Vanoise** (p519)
- Pass some time exploring the clocks and citadel of **Besançon** (p536)
- Get back to nature in the mountains, forests and waterfalls of the **Jura** (p544)
- Sample freshly made cheese in **Poligny** (p541)
- Join the architects' pilgrimage to Le Corbusier's futuristic chapel at **Ronchamp** (p542)

■ POPULATION: 5,600,000	■ AREA: 210,000 SQ KM

History

For much of their history, the French Alps have been a place of transition, a bridge between the warmer climes of the Mediterranean and the cooler regions of northern Europe. Little is known of the earliest settlers of the Alps (mainly thought to be Neolithic tribes, who arrived around 3000 BC, and later Bronze Age settlers). Migrant tribes of Celtic, Gaulish and Teutonic origin also made their home in various places around the Alps, and by the time of Christ permanent communities were well established, especially around the lakes of Geneva, Bourget and Annecy, and the Tarentaise and Maurienne valleys.

The Alps became an important strategic stronghold during the years of Roman conquest and, after years of struggle, were finally placed under Roman control during the reign of Augustus. Over the following centuries, the Frankish kings of the Merovingian and Carolingian empires laid the foundations for the modern Alps and its distinctive dialects, traditions and cultures.

During the 13th and 14th centuries, the Alps were fiercely contested by the feudal houses of Savoy, the Dauphiné and Provence, but by the end of the 14th century only the house of Savoy remained as serious opposition to the kingdom of France and its Italian rivals. The ensuing centuries were marked by successive wars and occupations, with each side swapping and reoccupying towns and territories – a cycle which was only finally ended with the union of Savoy with France in 1860. Savoy was divided into two *départements* (Savoie and Haute-Savoie), and the Alps were finally integrated into the wider French Republic.

During the Industrial Revolution, the abundant natural resources of the Alps led to the growth of heavy industry, especially hydroelectric power, mining, metalworking and agriculture. Tourism had also been a growing industry since the first holiday-makers made their way to the area around Chamonix and Mont Blanc in the late 19th century, a trend which continued in the early 20th century with the foundation of the first spa towns and holiday resorts.

During WWII, the Alps were occupied by German and Italian forces, but much of the population despised the Vichy French regime and the mountains became one of the main strongholds for the French resistance. Liberation finally came in 1944, but the region had been badly scarred by the years of occupation, and it took many years for the region to recover its economic strength. Modern industry, huge urban development and large-scale tourism all contributed to the regeneration of the Alps in the post-war years. Though its rural traditions and heritage may have largely disappeared today, the Alps remain one of the most popular and economically successful areas in France.

Geography

The Alps have served as a barrier between Europe's peoples since ancient times. Formed some 44 million years ago, the peaks and valleys of the Alpine ranges have been sculpted by erosion and massive glaciers. Both have endowed the river valleys with mild climates and rich soils, making them very suitable for human settlement. The Alps stretch for 370km from Lake Geneva (Lac Léman) in the north, almost to Provence in the south. France's border with Italy follows the Alps' highest ridges and peaks.

The two major historic regions are Savoy and Dauphiné. Savoy covers the northern area and culminates in Europe's highest mountain, Mont Blanc (4807m), with the town of Chamonix at its base. To the west, Annecy is the gateway to Savoy, while further south sits the region's historic capital, Chambéry. Dauphiné, which is south of Savoy and stretches eastwards all the way to Briançon and the Italian border, is home to Grenoble, the main city of the Alps.

North of Lake Geneva, the Jura Mountains form an arc that extends northwards along the River Doubs towards Alsace.

The Alps are characterised by extreme climatic diversity. There's enough snow most years from December to April for skiing even at lower-altitude stations. In spring (and late spring and summer at higher elevations), carpets of flowers bloom beside the magnificent forests. Throughout the year, weather conditions can change rapidly.

For weather information, call the **météo** (weather bureau; regional report ☎ 08 36 68 00 00, snow & mountain report ☎ 08 36 68 04 04; www.meteo.fr in French). For the departmental report, dial ☎ 08 36 68 02 followed by the two-digit

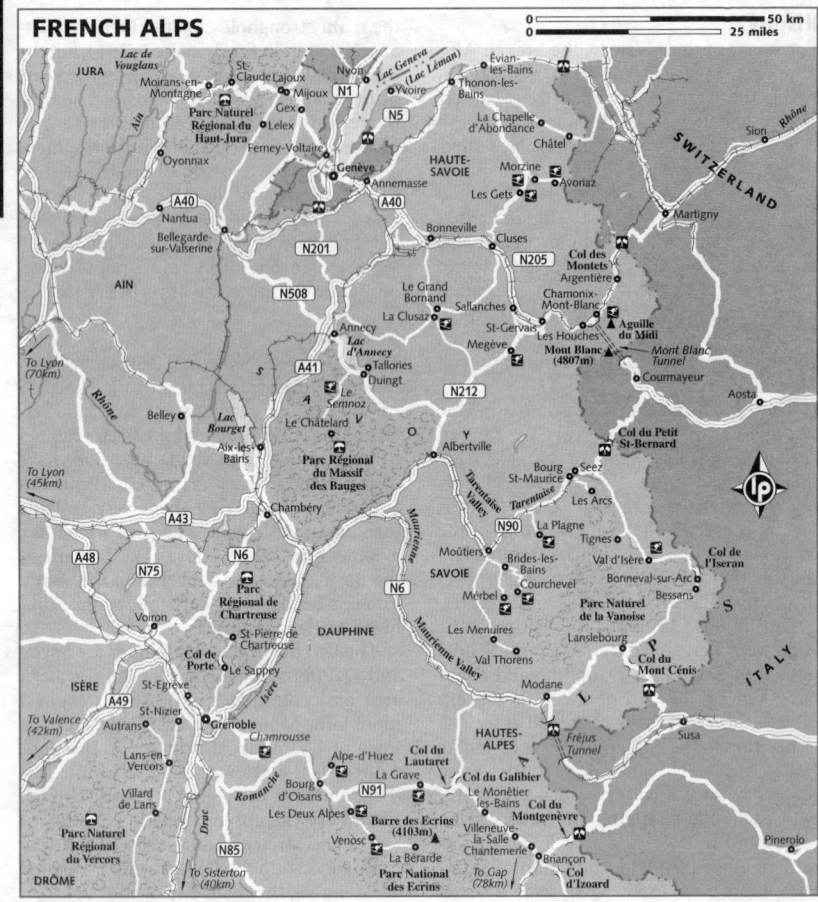

departmental number (p907). Year-round, daily weather bulletins are pinned outside the tourist office in ski resorts.

National & Regional Parks

Unlike other similar-size mountain ranges around the world, the Alps are not a pristine wilderness. In fact, the habitable parts of the French Alps support a dense population, and the region's villages, towns and ski resorts are linked by an extensive network of roads (and motorways). Fortunately, parts of the Alps are within the boundaries of three national and four regional parks, in which wildlife is carefully protected (p58).

The national parks – Vanoise (in Savoy), Écrins (in Dauphiné) and Mercantour (in Provence, along the Italian border) – are surrounded by larger zones where industry and human habitation are permitted. Including the regional parks of Queyras (on the Italian border south of Briançon), the Vercors (southwest of Grenoble), Chartreuse (north of the Vercors) and Massif des Bauges (north of Chartreuse), the Alps are endowed with the greatest concentration of parks in France.

The Jura region is home to the Parc Naturel Régional du Haut-Jura.

Dangers & Annoyances

Despite precautions such as anti-avalanche fences and tunnels, avalanches pose a very real danger in snowbound areas. Every year people are killed as a result of these disasters, and whole valleys can be cut off for days.

The daily avalanche risk is announced through signs and coloured flags outside all ticket kiosks, at the base of most ski lifts and dotted around resorts and slopes:

- yellow=low risk,
- black/yellow=heightened risk
- black=severe risk.

All avalanche warning signs should be heeded, whether they are along roads or on ski slopes. They are there for a reason.

On glaciers, be careful of crevasses. An accident in an isolated area can be fatal, so never ski, hike or climb alone. At high altitudes, where the sun's ultraviolet radiation is much stronger than at sea level (and is intensified by reflection off the snow), wear sunglasses and put sunscreen on exposed skin.

The air is often dry in the Alps – carry water when hiking, and drink more than you would at lower altitudes. Also, be aware of the possibility of hypothermia after a long climb or a sudden storm, as you'll cool off quickly while enjoying the cold, windy panorama.

Skiing & Snowboarding

Snow sports, once reserved for the truly wealthy, are now accessible to most people. Each winter millions of holiday-makers head to the 200-plus resorts in the French Alps for Alpine (downhill) skiing, cross-country treks, ski touring, and snowboarding – not to mention the après-ski.

The ski season starts just before Christmas and finishes at the end of April. In years of heavy snowfall, it's possible to ski from November until mid-May in higher-altitude resorts. At the beginning and end of the season, and in January, accommodation and lift tickets are discounted, and many resorts offer deals. Give the slopes a wide berth over Christmas and New Year, and during school holidays in late February and early March, when prices are sky-high and accommodation is scarce.

Summer skiing on high-altitude glaciers is usually possible in July and August in some areas. Most resorts have a combination of cross-country areas, Alpine runs and snowboard parks.

Off-piste skiing, known in French as *hors piste* (skiing outside groomed trails on fresh or powder snow), is popular, but off-piste skiers should exercise extreme caution as these areas usually do not have any warning signs. Take a guide with you.

Experienced off-piste skiers can ski tour – skiing and climbing the less accessible peaks, ridges and glaciers outside resort areas. Most tours last from three to seven days with accommodation in mountain *refuges*. Depending on the exact itinerary, three-day tours start at around €400. Experienced guides can be contacted in most resorts at the Bureau des Guides (p494) and ESF (p495).

Known in French as *ski de fond,* cross-country skiing is most popular in the Jura. Cross-country stations are more relaxed and casual than the higher ski resorts, with prices reflecting the lower altitudes, smaller snowfalls and shorter ski season.

Snowboarding is a fast-growing Alpine sport. Chamonix, Chamrousse, Les Arcs, Espace Killy, Les Deux Alpes, La Plagne and Méribel all have large snowparks equipped with half-pipes, quarter-pipes, gaps, rails and ramps.

INFORMATION

Every ski station has a tourist office that provides information on skiing, indoor

WEB WORLD

- **www.natives.co.uk** Excellent website aimed at seasonal ski workers.
- **www.planetmountain.com** Comprehensive website with advice on classic Alpine ski routes.
- **www.planetsubzero.com** Book seasonal and long-term ski accommodation online.
- **www.skifrance.fr** Official website for the main Alpine ski resorts.
- **www.thealps.com** Useful resort guide with some great photo galleries.

SKIING & SNOWBOARDING IN THE ALPS

Resort	Trademarks	Alpine runs	Cross-country trails	Difficulty level	Ski lifts	Ski pass (6 days)
Chamonix-Mont Blanc	High in altitude & attitude; young, trendy & full of fun	155km	45km	Intermediate, advanced, off-piste	47	€176
Portes du Soleil	Exclusive resort attracting a more sedate crowd	650km	130km	All abilities, off-piste	209	€176
St-Gervais & Megève	Pricey, chic & full of Alpine charm	300km	76km	Beginners, intermediate	79	€154
La Clusaz	A cheaper spot, popular locally	132km	70km	Beginners, intermediate	55	€137.50
Trois Vallées	Méribel: heavy traffic & bars packed with Brits	600km	130km	All abilities	200	€198
La Plagne	The family choice; Olympic bobsleigh run	225km	85km	Beginners, intermediate	111	€176
Les Arcs	Top skiing & snow-boarding; car-free but little charm	200km	30km	All abilities, off-piste	54	€181
Val d'Isère	Unrivalled Alpine skiing; buzzy nightlife	300km	44km	Intermediate, advanced, off-piste	97	€181
Les Deux Alpes	Snowboarders' delight; summer skiing; lively bar scene	220km	20km	Intermediate, advanced	54	€158
Alpe d'Huez	Snowboarding park; longest black run; summer skiing	236km	50km	All abilities	87	€178.50
Le Grand Serre Chevalier	Door-to-door skiing from several resorts	250km	35km	All abilities, off-piste	74	€160
Métabief Mont d'Or	Low altitude; snow not guaranteed	40km	250km	Predominantly cross-country	23	€97.20
Les Rousses	Popular with French & Swiss day-trippers	42km	260km	Predominantly cross-country	38	€94

and outdoor activities, and public transport. The local accommodation service, ski school and **Bureau des Guides**, an association of professional, independent guides, are often conveniently located in the same building (usually known as the Maison de la Montagne). Nearly all resorts have post offices, banks, bakeries and supermarkets.

SkiFrance (☎ 01 47 42 23 32; skifrance.fr; 61 blvd Haussmann, F-75008 Paris) and the **Fédération Française de Ski** (☎ 04 50 51 40 34; www.ffs.fr; 50 rue des Marquisats, BP 2451, F-74011 Annecy) provide information on all French ski resorts.

Downhill runs range in length from a few hundred metres to 20km and are colour-coded to indicate the level of difficulty of the runs: green (beginners), blue (intermediate), red (advanced) and black (very advanced). Summer skiing on glaciers tends to be on short green or blue runs.

Cross-country ski trails are designated as easy or difficult. The resorts charge fees for the upkeep of the trails. Single resort ski passes for cross-country skiing only are usually around €6/27 per day/week (Métabief Mont D'Or; website: www.montdor-2lacs .com/actihiver.htm).

EQUIPMENT

Skis, snowboards, boots and poles can be hired in every resort. Alpine equipment starts at €18/50 per day/week. Cross-country equipment ranges per day from €6.50 to €33 and per week from €14 to €65, and snowboards and boots per day from around €17 to €25 and per week from €140 to €190. You can hire monoskis and telemark skis in most resorts, too.

Take a note of the serial number marked on your skis. If you lose them, you have to pay for a replacement pair (take out insurance to cover this cost). Most ski shops have a locker room where you can leave your skis free of charge overnight. Always equip yourself with UV-protective sunglasses, gloves, a piste map (free from tourist offices), warm and water-resistant clothing, and sunscreen.

If you're looking to purchase your gear, one of the best ideas is to head for the resorts towards the end of the winter season, when many shops clear out last year's stock at rock-bottom prices. Look out for shop windows announcing *liquidation* or *fin de serie*.

LIFT PASSES

A daunting range of contraptions *(remontées mécaniques)* cover the slopes to whisk skiers uphill. Lifts include *téléskis* (drag lifts), *télésièges* (chair lifts), *télécabines* (gondolas), *téléphériques* (cable cars) and *funiculaires* (funicular railways).

Daily, weekly, monthly or seasonal ski passes – *forfaits* – offer the best value. Passes give access to one or more ski sectors and sometimes include neighbouring resorts. Passes are cheaper for children and seniors, and many resorts offer package deals covering a six-day ski pass and six half-day group lessons. Others offer packages incorporating a six-day ski pass with accommodation or ski school.

For prices see opposite.

SCHOOLS

France's leading ski school, the **École de Ski Français** (ESF; www.esf.net) has branches in most stations and generally offers tuition at better rates than the smaller, independent ski schools. ESF also offers group or private snowboarding lessons.

Prices vary greatly between resorts: in general, the more expensive the resort, the pricier the lessons are likely to be. If you're looking to learn from scratch, the smaller ski resorts will offer much better value. A six-day course (three hours of group tuition daily) costs between €80 and €300; private one- or two-hour lessons cost between €30 and €80. All resorts offer lessons for children; some have snow gardens for toddlers aged from three to five to play in.

PACKAGE DEALS

Package deals are by far the cheapest way to ski. Most resorts offer excellent-value discount packages that usually include a week's accommodation, ski pass, and sometimes equipment hire and ski lessons.

The FUAJ (p894) has 17 hostels in the French Alps and offers some good-value package deals in winter, starting from about €300/420 in the low/high season for six days' hostel accommodation, meals, ski pass and equipment hire.

INSURANCE

Insurance is a necessity if you're planning a trip to the snow. If you're hurt on the slopes, all the services that come to your aid – from the ambulance that ferries you down the mountainside to the doctor who treats you – will charge. If you require evacuation by helicopter, the bill you receive on your hospital bed might do you more lasting damage than your injuries.

Most package deals include insurance, but *Carte Neige* is a flexible policy (available for a few days to a full season) offered by nearly all resorts. It often entitles the holder to extra deals, such as discounted ski lessons and lift passes. Full cover includes mountain rescue costs and medical treatment. It costs between €40 and €60 per year (€20 to €30 for cross-country skiers), depending on the level of cover you choose and where you buy the insurance.

All resorts also offer *Carré Neige,* a daily insurance scheme that offers similar cover to the *Carte Neige.* It can be purchased from ticket kiosks at the same time as your lift pass, and costs €2.50 to €3 per day. Insurance is also available from most equipment hire shops to cover the cost of any damage to your equipment – it's usually a wise purchase.

Warm-Weather Activities

The Alps come alive in spring and summer, when the snow cover melts and carpets of wildflowers reclaim the mountainsides. Fantastic hiking trails criss-cross national parks; the GR5 traverses the entire Alps. Rafting, canoeing and mountain biking are also popular, as are the more sedate pastimes of horse riding and ice-skating. Warm-weather activities can be enjoyed at most larger ski resorts.

A popular Alpine activity is *parapente* (paragliding), the sport of floating down from somewhere high suspended from a wing-shaped, steerable parachute. The ESF in most resorts offers courses: an initiation flight costs from €60 to €90. A five-day beginner course costs from €360 to €550. A second five-day course, which prepares you to pursue the sport on your own, costs the same.

Skydiving costs a lot more: €200 to €220 for a day of instruction and a first jump from 1200m.

Sleeping & Eating

Most resorts have a central reservation service that books accommodation in hotels, studios, apartments and chalets. Prices vary drastically between the low and high seasons, and hotels generally offer full or half-board. Most apartments and studios have kitchenettes – the cheapest option for budget travellers. Gîtes de France publishes the annual *Gîtes de Neige* guide (p894).

The **Club Alpin Français** (Map p333-33; ☎ 01 53 72 87 00; www.clubalpin.com; 24 av de Laumière, 19e, Paris; metro Laumière) has numerous mountain *refuges* in the Alps, for which advance reservations are usually required. Contact the relevant office in the place you are visiting.

Restaurants in ski resorts tend to offer poor-quality cuisine at heightened prices. On the slopes, you'll ski past plenty of restaurants with prices that reflect the high altitude.

Getting There & Around

The Alps' closest international airport is Aéroport International de Genève (Geneva international airport), near Geneva, and Lyon St-Exupéry, just outside Lyon. Allow ample time to check in as the airport can become almost impassable with the hordes of skiers, snowboarders and their oversized luggage.

Geneva airport is split into Swiss and French sectors and you may have to travel between both sides (to pick up or drop a hire car, for example), which means negotiating customs, police and baggage reclaim – often with lengthy queues – all over again.

On a clear day and with the right flight path, the view through the plane window is the best introduction to the Alps you can possibly have. In winter there are direct bus connections from both airports to numerous ski resorts with **Geneva's Aeroski bus** (☎ 022-798 20 00; www.gva.ch/en/inst/aeroskibus.htm) and **Lyon's Satobus-Alpes** (☎ 04 37 25 52 55; www .satobus-alps .com).

The Eurostar speeds its way through the Channel Tunnel from London (Waterloo station) to Moûtiers (8¾ hours) and Bourg St-Maurice (9½ hours) on Saturday during the ski season. Train services within France to many parts of the Alps are excellent. Full details are published in the SNCF's *La Neige en Direct* brochure, which you can pick up at most stations.

To reach some ski resorts by car you may need snow chains after heavy snowfalls, and in the high season, traffic on the high mountain passes leading to the resorts can be hellish. The Fréjus road tunnel connects the French Alps with Italy, as do a number of major passes: Col du Petit St-Bernard (2188m) near Bourg St-Maurice, Col du Mont Cénis (2083m) in the Haute Maurienne Valley, and Col du Montgenèvre (1850m) near Briançon. Certain high-altitude passes, such as the Col du Galibier

(2558m) and the Col de l'Iseran (2770m), are usually closed between November and June, although this depends on snowfall. Road signs indicate well in advance if passes are blocked.

SAVOY

Bordered by Switzerland and Italy, Savoy (Savoie; pronounced sav-*wa*) rises from the southern shores of Lake Geneva (Lac Léman) and keeps rising until it reaches the massive Mont Blanc, which dominates the town of Chamonix. To the southwest, long U-shaped valleys are obvious relics of ancient glaciers that created lakes such as Lac d'Annecy, as well as France's largest natural lake, Lac Bourget, near Aix-les-Bains.

Savoy is divided into two *départements,* Haute-Savoie and Savoie, and the people of the region are known as Savoyards. Despite centuries of French cultural influence, they have managed to keep their identity and often speak their own dialect, which reveals Provençal influences. In the remote valleys, such as in the Haute Maurienne, rural life goes on as it has for centuries, and the people continue to struggle with the harsh climate and the ever-present threat of avalanches.

History
Savoy was long ruled by the House of Savoy, founded by Humbert I (the Whitehanded) in the mid-11th century. During the Middle Ages, the dukes of Savoy extended their territory eastwards to other areas of the western Alps, including the Piedmont region of what is now Italy.

In the 16th century the dukes of Savoy turned towards their Italian territories; in 1563 they moved their capital from Chambéry to Turin. However, they continued to rule Savoy and resisted repeated French attempts to take over the region. Savoy was annexed by France in 1792 but was returned 23 years later.

In 1720 Victor Amadeus II, duke of Savoy, became king of Sardinia and over the next century important territories in northern Italy, including Genoa, came under Savoyard control. In the mid-19th century the House of Savoy worked to unify Italy under Piedmontese leadership, a goal they achieved in 1861 with the formation of the Kingdom

of Italy under King Victor Emmanuel II of the House of Savoy. However, in exchange for Napoleon III's acceptance of this new arrangement and the international agreements that led up to it, Savoy – along with the area around Nice – was ceded to France.

CHAMONIX
pop 10,000 / elevation 1037m

The town of Chamonix is surrounded by the most spectacular scenery in the French Alps. The area, a leading mountaineering centre, is almost Himalayan: deeply crevassed glaciers point towards the valley from the icy crown of Mont Blanc, which soars 4.8km above sea level. Chamonix has been a summer resort since the 18th century and a winter one from 1903. It's also gained a reputation as one of the top spots in the Alps for heli-skiing (p501). Since 1965, when the 11.6km Mont Blanc tunnel – the world's highest rock-covered tunnel (2480m) – was opened, Chamonix has been linked by road to Courmayeur in Italy.

The tunnel was closed in March 1999 following a devastating fire, which started when a goods lorry carrying flour and margarine burst into flames and quickly spread to nearby vehicles. The blaze burned for over two days and killed 39 people. A massive investigation was launched after the fire had been extinguished. The tunnel's safety systems and emergency procedures were completely overhauled, and after three years of exhaustive repairs, it finally reopened to cars and other vehicles in 2002.

Orientation
Chamonix runs along the banks of the River Arve for about 2km. The Mont Blanc massif looms over the east side of the valley, while the Aiguilles Rouges range lines the western edge. The two main streets, rue du Docteur Paccard and rue Joseph Vallot, contain most of the town's shops and restaurants. The bus and train stations are across the river, 500m east of the town centre at the end of av Michel Croz.

Information
BOOKSHOPS
Librairie VO (☎ 04 50 53 24 41; 20 av Ravanel -le-Rouge; ☺ 9am-noon & 2-7.30pm Mon-Sat) Sells English books, including many (as you might expect) with a mountaineering theme.

Photo Alpine Tairraz (☎ 04 50 53 14 23; 162 av Michel Croz) A photographic shop that also sells mountaineering books and prints.

EMERGENCY

PGHM (Peloton Gendarmerie Haute Montagne; ☎ 04 50 53 16 19; 69 rue de la Mollard) The main mountain rescue service for the Mont Blanc area.

Police Station (☎ 04 50 53 00 55; 111 rue de la Mollard)

INTERNET ACCESS

As well as the following internet cafés, there are a number of bars and restaurants in Chamonix that offer Internet access at around 15 to 20 cents a minute.

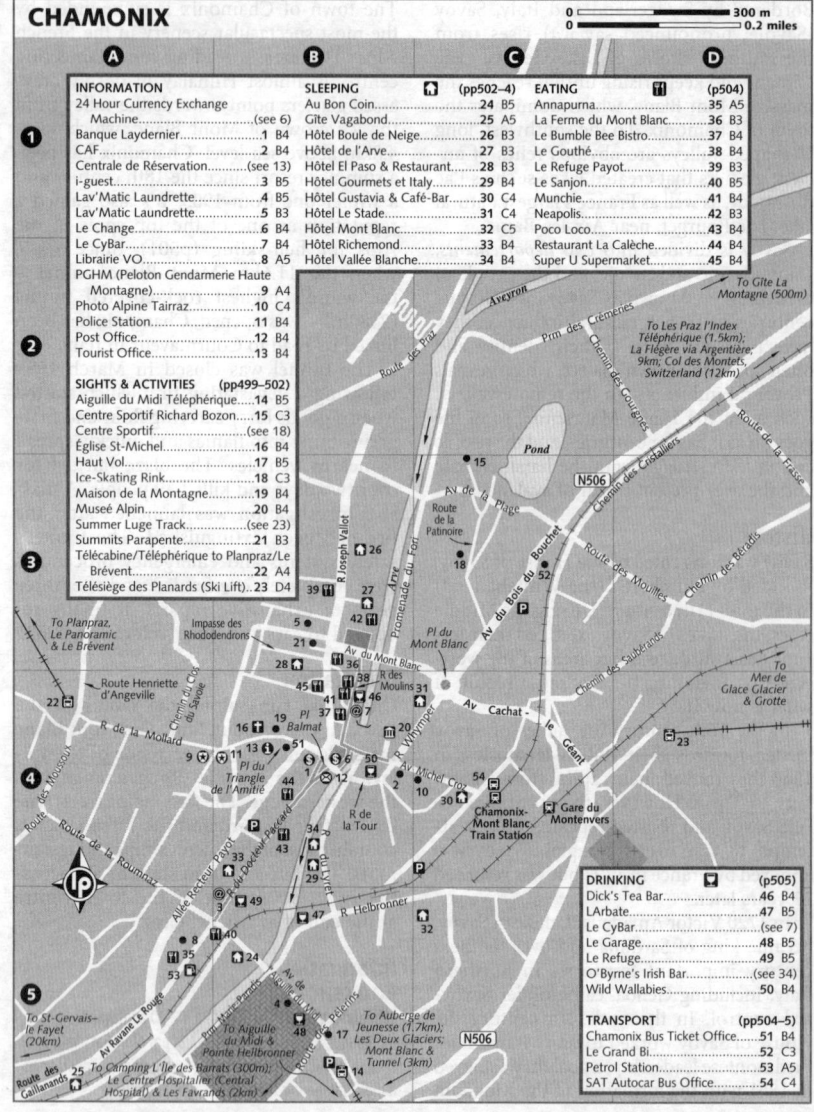

CHAMONIX

0 ——— 300 m
0 ——— 0.2 miles

INFORMATION	
24 Hour Currency Exchange Machine	(see 6)
Banque Laydernier	1 B4
CAF	2 B4
Centrale de Réservation	(see 13)
i-guest	3 B5
Lav'Matic Laundrette	4 B5
Lav'Matic Laundrette	5 B3
Le Change	6 B4
Le CyBar	7 B4
Librairie VO	8 A5
PGHM (Peloton Gendarmerie Haute Montagne)	9 A4
Photo Alpine Tairraz	10 C4
Police Station	11 B4
Post Office	12 B4
Tourist Office	13 B4

SIGHTS & ACTIVITIES	(pp499–502)
Aiguille du Midi Téléphérique	14 B5
Centre Sportif Richard Bozon	15 C3
Centre Sportif	(see 18)
Église St-Michel	16 B4
Haut Vol	17 B5
Ice-Skating Rink	18 C3
Maison de la Montagne	19 B4
Museé Alpin	20 B4
Summer Luge Track	(see 23)
Summits Parapente	21 B3
Télécabine/Téléphérique to Planpraz/Le Brévent	22 A4
Télésiège des Planards (Ski Lift)	23 D4

SLEEPING	(pp502–4)
Au Bon Coin	24 B5
Gîte Vagabond	25 A5
Hôtel Boule de Neige	26 B3
Hôtel de l'Arve	27 B3
Hôtel El Paso & Restaurant	28 B3
Hôtel Gourmets et Italy	29 B4
Hôtel Gustavia & Café-Bar	30 C4
Hôtel Le Stade	31 C4
Hôtel Mont Blanc	32 C5
Hôtel Richemond	33 B4
Hôtel Vallée Blanche	34 B4

EATING	(p504)
Annapurna	35 A5
La Ferme du Mont Blanc	36 B3
Le Bumble Bee Bistro	37 B4
Le Gouthé	38 B4
Le Refuge Payot	39 B3
Le Sanjon	40 B5
Munchie	41 B4
Neapolis	42 B3
Poco Loco	43 B4
Restaurant La Calèche	44 B4
Super U Supermarket	45 B4

DRINKING	(p505)
Dick's Tea Bar	46 B4
L'Arbate	47 B5
Le CyBar	(see 7)
Le Garage	48 B5
Le Refuge	49 B5
O'Byrne's Irish Bar	(see 34)
Wild Wallabies	50 B4

TRANSPORT	(pp504–5)
Chamonix Bus Ticket Office	51 B4
Le Grand Bi	52 C3
Petrol Station	53 A5
SAT Autocar Bus Office	54 C4

i-guest (☎ 04 50 55 98 58; iguestchx@yahoo.fr;
22 Galerie Blanc Neige; per min around €0.10-0.15, per hr
around €7.50; ⏰ 2-8pm) In a small shopping arcade just
off rue Docteur Paccard.

Le CyBar (☎ 04 50 53 69 70; www.cybarchamonix
.com; 80 rue des Moulins; per min from €0.10; ⏰ 10am-
1.30am) Has computers spread over two floors. You can
also bring your own laptop to connect.

INTERNET RESOURCES
www.chamonix.com Official website for the Chamonix
valley, with comprehensive information on staying and
playing in the Mont Blanc massif.
www.chamonix.net Companion site, which offers more
advice on accommodation, entertainment and nightlife in
Chamonix.
www.compagniedumontblanc.com The company
that handles most tourist activities in Chamonix.

LAUNDRY
Lav'Matic Laundrette (40 impasse des Primevères;
⏰ 9am-8pm)
Lav'Matic Laundrette (174 av de l'Aiguille du Midi;
⏰ 9am-8pm)

MEDICAL SERVICES
Duty Chemist (☎ 04 50 53 36 79)
Duty Dentist (☎ 04 50 66 17 19)
Duty Doctor (☎ 04 50 53 48 48)
Le Centre Hospitalier (Central Hospital; ☎ 04 50 53
84 00; 509 route des Pélerins) In Les Favrands about 2km
south of Chamonix centre. A list of medical practitioners
can be obtained from the tourist office.

MONEY
There are several seasonal exchange places
between the tourist and post offices. Most
banks in town have an ATM.
Le Change (21 place Balmat; ⏰ 9am-1pm & 3-7pm
May, Jun & early Sep–Nov, 8am-8pm Jul–early Sep &
Dec-Apr) Generally offers the best rate in town. Outside, a
24-hour ATM accepts banknotes in 15 currencies.

POST
Post Office (place Balmat; ⏰ 8am-noon & 2-6pm Mon-
Fri, 8am-noon Sat Sep-Jun, 8am-7pm Mon-Fri, until noon
Sat Jul & Aug) Right in the centre of town.

TOURIST INFORMATION
Centrale de Réservation (☎ 04 50 53 23 33;
reservation@chamonix.com; Tourist Office; ⏰ 24hr)
Usually takes accommodation bookings for stays of three
nights minimum.
Club Alpin Français (CAF; ☎ 04 50 53 16 03; fax 04 50
53 27 52; 136 av Michel Croz; ⏰ 3.30-7.30pm Mon, Tue &

Fri, 3-6.15pm Thu, 9am-noon Sat) Looks after most Mont
Blanc *refuges*, and runs climbing excursions and tours.
Seasonal hours vary.
Tourist Office (☎ 04 50 53 00 24; www.chamonix.com;
85 place du Triangle de l'Amitié; ⏰ 8.30am-12.30pm &
2-7pm Jun-Sep & Dec-Apr, 9am-12.30pm & 2-6.30pm Oct,
Nov & May) Offers hundreds of brochures on accommoda-
tion and activities, and also sells ski passes.

Sights
AIGUILLE DU MIDI
A jagged pinnacle of rock rising above
glaciers, snowfields and rocky crags, 8km
from the domed summit of Mont Blanc, the
Aiguille du Midi is one of Chamonix's most
famous landmarks. If you can handle the
height, the panoramic views from the summit are absolutely breathtaking and should
not be missed.

Cable-car tickets (advance reservations 24hr ☎ 08 92
68 00 67; adult/child return €34/24, one way/return to Plan
de l'Aiguille €12.30/14.40; ⏰ 7am-5.30pm summer, 8am-
3.30pm winter) from Chamonix to Aiguille du
Midi are available; a ride to the *téléphérique's*
halfway point, Plan de l'Aiguille (2317m) is
an excellent place to start hikes in summer.

The *téléphérique* leaves from the end of av
de l'Aiguille du Midi and runs year-round.
Be prepared for long queues. Note that making advance reservations on the 24-hour
number incurs a booking fee of €2.

From the Aiguille du Midi, between May
and September, you can make the 5km ride
in the panoramic Mont Blanc cable car to
Pointe Helbronner (3466m) on the Italian
border, crossing a vista of glaciers, snow
plains and shimmering ice-fields en route.
Another *téléphérique* from Pointe Helbronner descends to the Italian ski resort
of Courmayeur, but the views alone are
worth the trip.

LE BRÉVENT
The highest peak on the western side of the
valley, **Le Brévent** (2525m) has fabulous views
of the Mont-Blanc massif. It can be reached
by **télécabine** (larger than a *téléphérique*) and
téléphérique (☎ 04 50 53 13 18; adult/child return
€15.50/11; ⏰ 8am-5.45pm summer, 9am-5pm winter),
from the end of rue de la Mollard.

Several hiking trails can be picked up at
Le Brévent or at the *télécabine*'s midway
station, **Planpraz** (one way/return €8.50/10.50), at
2000m. There is a great restaurant at the
summit of Le Brévent (p504).

MER DE GLACE

The **Mer de Glace** (Sea of Ice), the second-largest glacier in the Alps, is 14km long, 1800m wide and up to 400m deep. During a visit to Chamonix in 1741, Englishman William Windham was the first foreigner to set eyes on the glacier, which he described as 'a sort of agitated sea that seemed suddenly to have become frozen' (hence the name). The glacier moves 45m a year at the edges, and up to 90m a year in the centre, and has become a popular tourist attraction thanks to the rack-and-pinion railway line built between 1897 and 1908.

Since 1946, the **Grotte de la Mer de Glace** (ice cave; ◷ late May-late Sep) has been carved every spring – work begins in February and takes three months. The interior temperature is between -2°C and -5°C. Look down the slope for last year's cave to see how far the glacier has moved.

With avalanche proofing over parts of the tracks, the train – which leaves from **Gare du Montenvers** (☎ 04 50 53 12 54; 35 place de la Mer de Glace; adult return €14; ◷ 10am-4pm winter, 8.30am-5.30pm May-Jun & Sep, 6.30am-6pm Jun & Jul, 6am-7.30pm Aug) in Chamonix and creeps up to Montenvers (1913m) – runs year-round and takes 20 minutes. From Montenvers, a *téléphérique* takes tourists to the cave. A **combined ticket** (adult/child €21/15) is valid for the train, *téléphérique* and admission to the cave.

The Mer de Glace can be reached on foot via the Grand Balcon Nord trail from Plan de l'Aiguille. The uphill trail from Chamonix (two hours) begins near the summer luge track. Traversing the glacier and its crevasses requires proper equipment and an experienced guide.

MUSÉE ALPIN

The **Musée Alpin** (☎ 04 50 53 25 93; 89 av Michel Croz; adult/child €4/1.50; ◷ 2-7pm summer, 10am-noon school holidays, closed rest of year), just off av Michel Croz, occupies a grand building that once housed one of Chamonix's most luxurious hotels. Exhibits include artefacts, lithographs and photos illustrating the history of mountain climbing and other Alpine sports.

Activities
WINTER ACTIVITIES
Maison de la Montagne

The **Maison de la Montagne** (190 place de l'Église) is across the square from the tourist office, and should be your first port of call for finding out about the Mont Blanc area.

On the ground floor, the **Compagnie des Guides** (☎ 04 50 53 00 88; www.chamonix-guides.com; ◷ 8am-noon & 3.30-7.30pm Jul & Aug, closed Sun Sep-Jun) is the central base for Chamonix' professional mountain guides. Guides for skiing, mountaineering, hiking, mountain-biking and just about every other alpine pastime can be hired year-round (starting from €250 per day for four people).

École Ski Français (ESF; ☎ 04 50 53 22 57; www .esf-chamonix.com; per hr from €20; ◷ 8.15am-7pm Mon-Sat in winter) is on the 1st floor and offers tailor-made programmes for all levels, from complete novices to seasoned skiers looking to improve their technique. Discounts are available for longer courses.

On the 2nd floor, the **Office de Haute Montagne** (☎ 04 50 53 22 08; www.ohm-chamonix.com

---

CHAMONIX'S CABLE-CAR

The **téléphérique** (☎ 04 50 53 30 80) from Chamonix to the Aiguille du Midi (3842m) has deservedly earned its reputation as the highest (and scariest) cable car in Europe. The idea of a floor-to-peak cable-car was first conceived in 1909, but the technical challenges proved enormous, and engineers initially had to settle for a lower-altitude version, completed in 1924. After WWII, the original dream was revived and the spectacular full-altitude cable car finally swung into action in 1955.

It's an amazing feat of engineering, climbing from the valley floor to a terrace beneath the Aiguille at 3777m in just 20 minutes. From far below, the Aiguille looks like a single peak; in fact, it has twin spires connected by a gravity-defying footbridge. There is even a restaurant where you can savour the afternoon tea of a lifetime: the **3842** (☎ 04 50 55 82 23; mains from €6; ◷ late morning-téléphérique closing).

The last few metres to the summit itself are by elevator. From the viewing platform at the top, there are stunning 360° views of the surrounding mountains. Often you can watch mountain climbers on nearby ridges or brave skiers setting out for the daunting Vallée Blanche descent.

COMPAGNIE DES GUIDES

Founded between 1821 and 1823, the Compagnie des Guides is the oldest organisation of its kind in the world. Its members are all highly skilled mountain experts with unparalleled experience in the Alpine ranges. The selection process is famously gruelling – until recently, only young men born in the Chamonix valley were even considered for selection. The present membership is more diverse, and includes a number of female guides – a major shift pioneered by women mountaineers like climber and guide Sylviane Tavernier.

The guides take their work (and reputation) very seriously – the annual **Fête des Guides,** when new members are welcomed and lost colleagues remembered, is one of the highlights of the Chamonix year. The son-et-lumière show usually takes place in mid-August, with fireworks, concerts and mountaineering displays, and culminates in a solemn ceremony at the Église St-Michel in Chamonix.

in French; 🕑 9am-12.30pm & 2.30-6.30pm Mon-Sat), which serves walkers, hikers and mountain climbers, provides information on trails, hiking conditions and *refuges* (staff can help make reservations).

Skiing & snowboarding

Chamonix is most famous for its world-class skiing and snowboarding. Of the nine main areas, the best for beginners are Le Tour, Les Planards, Le Brévent and La Flégère (the latter two are connected by *téléphérique*). Les Chosalets and Les Grands Montets, accessible from Argentière 9km north of Chamonix, offer accomplished skiers the most challenging skiing. There are also more advanced runs in most areas.

Les Grands Montets has a snowpark equipped with a half-pipe, kicker ramps and other obstacles for snowboarders, and most of Chamonix's runs are open to boarders and skiers. The valley has produced several champion snowboarders in recent years.

The region also has a large number of marked but ungroomed trails suitable for skiers looking for off-piste thrills. The famous 20km **Vallée Blanche descent** is one of the world's most celebrated runs, and remains a life-long dream for most serious skiers. The route leads from the Aiguille du Midi over the Mer de Glace and through the forests back to Chamonix, covering a drop in altitude of just under 2760m (9200ft). It should *only* be tackled with a guide – the route crosses the crevasse-riddled glacier and passes through avalanche-prone areas. It takes four to five hours and a guide costs €235 for up to four people, but this is one skiing experience you will never forget. Contact the ESF or Compagnie des Guides for details.

Lift Passes

The tourist office and the kiosks next to ski-lifts sell several ski-passes for the Chamonix area. The most popular is the **Cham' Ski pass** (per day/week/season €40/176/650), valid for all the valley lifts and free bus transport. Family, seniors' and beginners' passes are available too. You can also buy passes for a single ski area. The more expensive Ski-Pass Mont Blanc covers Megève–St-Gervais as well as the Chamonix Valley.

Ski Touring & Heli-skiing

One of Chamonix's great attractions is the possibility for *ski de randonnée* (ski touring). The range of tours is almost endless. It's possible to travel for a week or longer, skiing all the way to Switzerland or Italy, staying in mountain *refuges* (or if you're really unhinged, tents) along the way. A three-day *stage* package starts at around €400 per person. During winter, it's illegal to make overnight trips in the Chamonix–Mont Blanc area without the permission of the Compagnie des Guides, due to the danger of avalanches.

The king of ski tours is the classic six-day **Haute Route** (per person incl guide 730; 🕑 Mar & Apr) between Chamonix and Zermatt in Switzerland, opened by guides in 1927. Skiers should be experienced in off-piste skiing and will need to be very fit.

Other classic routes include the **Oberland** to Switzerland (six days, from €830), which traverses steep mountain descents and glacial areas including the famous Konkordiaplatz, and the **Tour des Jorasses** from Argentière to the Géant glacier through the rocky spires of the Grandes Jorasses range (five days, starting from €640).

Heli-skiing is also possible: contact **Chamonix Mont-Blanc Helicopters** (☎ 04 50 54 13 82; info@helico.fr), **SAF Chamonix Helicopters** (☎ 04 50 54 07 86; www.saf-helico.com) or the Compagnie des Guides for details. Prices range from €230 to €370. A 10-minute panoramic **helicopter flight** (per person from €65) is available with a minimum of four people.

SUMMER ACTIVITIES
Walking
In late spring and summer (about mid-June to October), 310km of spectacular walking trails open up around Chamonix. The most rewarding are the high-altitude trails reached by cable car. The *téléphériques* shut down in the late afternoon, but in June and July there is enough light to walk until 9pm or later.

Combined map and guide *Carte des Sentiers du Mont Blanc* (Mountain Trail Map; €4) is ideal for straightforward day walks. The most useful map is the 1:25,000 IGN map entitled *Chamonix-Massif du Mont Blanc* (No 3630OT; €9). Both are sold at Photo Alpine Tairraz (p498).

The **Grand Balcon Sud** trail along the western side of the valley stays at around 2000m and affords great views of Mont Blanc. On foot, it can be reached from behind Le Brévent's *télécabine* station. For less uphill walking, take either the Planpraz or La Flégère lifts.

A number of routes start from Plan de l'Aiguille, including the **Grand Balcon Nord**, which takes you to the Mer de Glace, from where you can walk or take the train down to Chamonix.

There are also trails to **Lac Blanc** (White Lake) at 2350m, a turquoise lake (despite its name) surrounded by mountains, from either the top of Les Praz-l'Index cable car (€12) or La Flégère (€1), the line's midway point.

Canyoning
Chamonix Guide (☎ 04 50 53 05 16; www.chamonix guide.com; 44 chemin de l'Ordon) offers summer canyoning expeditions in the mountains around Mont Blanc and other destinations in the Alps.

Summer Luge
The **summer luge track** (☎ 04 50 53 08 97; per ride €5.50; 🕑 1.30-6.30pm Sat & Sun Jun, 10am-7.30pm Jul & Aug) is near the *télésiège des Planards*. If there is no snow the luge also opens in May.

Cycling
Many lower-altitude trails (like the Petit Balcon Sud) are perfect for mountain biking. See p505 for information on bike rental. The Compagnie des Guides can organise one-day mountain-bike tours for €50 per person per day, and also offers three-, four- or five-day tours of Mont Blanc.

Paragliding
The sky above Chamonix is often dotted with colourful paragliders wheeling down from the snowy heights. Starter flights from Planpraz (2000m) cost €90 (€220 from the Aiguille du Midi). A five-day course starts at €420. Contact **Haut Vol** (☎ 04 50 53 98 01; haut.vol@tiscali.fr; 14 place de Chamonix Sud) or **Summits Parapente** (☎ 04 50 53 50 14; www.summits.fr; 28 impasse des Primevères).

Ice-Skating & Other Sports
An indoor **ice-skating rink** (patinoire; adult/child €4.10/3.30, skate rental €3; 🕑 10am-noon & 3-6pm Mon-Tue & Thu-Sun, 2-6pm & 9-11pm Wed) is located near the **Centre Sportif Richard Bozon** (☎ 04 50 53 09 07; 214 av de la Plage), where you'll also find a huge outdoor swimming pool and squash and tennis courts. *Location patins* is French for skate rental.

Sleeping
The cheapest way to visit Chamonix is through a package deal. If you decide to go it alone, Chamonix has no shortage of hotels – though finding one with an available bed might be the greatest challenge of your season.

During July, August and the ski season, hotels are heavily booked, so reserve ahead. Many prefer guests who take full or half-board. Accommodation can be booked in advance through Centrale de Réservation (p499).

Les Carnets de l'Hébergement, available free from the tourist office, lists most of the region's camping grounds, *refuges, gîtes d'étape, chambres d'hôtes*, apartments and hotels. In the low/high season expect to pay from €160/245 per week for a two-person studio.

Most mountain *refuges* (€14 to €20 a night) are accessible to hikers, though some can be reached only by mountain climbers. Breakfast and dinner, prepared by the warden, are often available for an extra fee.

It's essential to reserve a place – you don't want to hike halfway across Mont Blanc to find the refuge full. For information, contact the CAF (p499). When the office is closed, pick up a list detailing CAF *refuges* from outside the office. Many are minor architectural miracles, built at crazy angles or teetering precariously over stomach-churning drops.

BUDGET

Budget accommodation is always scarce in Chamonix, and in high season you'll have to book several months in advance. Gîte accommodation can be a good way to cut costs, though space to dry your gear after a day's skiing can be hard to find.

There are some 14 camping grounds in the Chamonix region, but you'd be a brave soul (or have an industrial-strength sleeping bag) to make use of them in winter. Because of the altitude, it's nearly always chilly at night.

Auberge de Jeunesse (☎ 04 50 53 14 52; chamonix@fuaj.org; 127 montée Jacques Balmat; dm incl breakfast summer €13.25-17; check-in ☒ 8am-noon & 5-10pm, closed early May & Oct–mid-Dec) About 2km southwest of Chamonix in Les Pélerins, this hostel can be reached by bus. Take the Chamonix–Les Houches line and get off at the Pélerins École stop. In winter, only weekly packages are available, including bed, food, ski pass and ski hire for six days. There's no kitchen.

Gîte La Montagne (☎ 04 50 53 11 60; 789 promenade des Crémeries; dm €12; ☒ closed 11 Nov–20 Dec) An attractive *gîte* in a traditional alpine-style building on a forested site, about 1.5km north of the train station (near La Frasse bus-stop).

Gîte Vagabond (☎ 04 50 53 15 43; www.levagabond.co.uk; 365 av Ravanel-le-Rouge; dm €12.50, half-board €28; ☒) A neat hostelry with a kitchen, bar-restaurant with Internet access, BBQ area, climbing wall and parking. Beds are in four- or six-person dorms.

Au Bon Coin (☎ 04 50 53 15 67; hotelauboncoin@wanadoo.fr; 80 av de l'Aiguille du Midi; d with bath & view €55-62; ℗) One of the best year-round deals in Chamonix. Perched above busy shops, it looks drab from the front, but the rear rooms are south-facing, and most have small balconies offering views of Mont Blanc. There are no TVs – but with views like this, who needs light entertainment?

Hôtel Le Stade (☎ 04 50 53 05 44; 79 rue Whymper; s/d from €34/46) Dull but pleasant rooms, though its position above shops on a busy roundabout can be a headache in high season. The entrance is around the back, up steps to the 1st floor.

Hôtel Boule de Neige (☎ 04 50 53 04 48; 362 rue Joseph Vallot; s/d from €36/56) A chalet-style hotel halfway up the lively rue Joseph Vallot. The rooms are as basic as they come, but there's an attractive mountain-town feel helped by the little local bar downstairs.

Hôtel El Paso (☎ 04 50 53 64 20; fax 04 50 53 64 22; 37 impasse des Rhododendrons; d with shared bath low/high season €42/50) Looks like a cheap hotel in a Mexican border-town, but the rowdy atmosphere and Tex-Mex *menu* in the downstairs bar are just the trick for young boarders abroad – and it comes at a price that's hard to beat.

Camping

L'Île des Barrats (☎ 04 50 53 51 44; 185 chemin d'Île des Barrats; ☒ May-Oct) A three-star camping ground in a quiet clearing, near the base of the Aiguille du Midi *téléphérique*.

Les Deux Glaciers (☎ 04 50 53 15 84; glaciers@clubInternet.fr; 80 route des Tissières; ☒ closed mid-Nov–mid-Dec) Another three-star camping ground in Les Bossons, 3km south of Chamonix. To get there, take the train to Les Bossons or the Chamonix bus to the Tremplin-le-Mont stop.

MID-RANGE

Most of Chamonix's hotels fall into this bracket, and what you get for your money can vary wildly.

Hôtel de l'Arve (☎ 04 50 53 02 31; www.hotelarve-chamonix.com; 60 impasse des Anémones; d high season €78-104; ℗) Built to resemble a traditional mountain chalet, this hotel is tucked away in a quiet courtyard off rue Joseph Vallot. All the rooms have lots of Alpine atmosphere and the best have a stunning view down the valley to Mont Blanc.

Hôtel Vallée Blanche (☎ 04 50 53 04 50; www .vallee-blanche.com; 36 rue du Lyret; d low/high season €67/130; ℗) This place is hard to miss, thanks to its shocking pink exterior and the bright-red telephone box outside, but inside, the hotel has a sophisticated feel that wouldn't be out of place in the smarter ski resorts. The nicest rooms look onto the river or the Mont Blanc range.

Hôtel Gourmets et Italy (☎ 04 50 53 01 38; www .hotelgourmets-chamonix.com; 96 rue du Lyret; d low/high season €75/157) Just along the street from Hôtel Vallée Blanche, this smart hotel sometimes offers good deals in the shoulder months. The rooms are decorated in plain, warm tones and all have minibars, bathrobes and satellite TV, and there's a lovely flower-filled garden to enjoy in summer.

Hôtel Gustavia (☎ 04 50 53 00 31; fax 04 50 55 86 39; www.hotel-gustavia.com; 272 av Michel Croz; d low/high season from €71/144) A large, three-star hotel with attractive double rooms, the best of which have mountain views. It's popular with young skiers and snowboarders, with a busy après ski bar, and is near the train station.

Hôtel Richemond (☎ 04 50 53 08 85; www.riche mond.fr; 228 rue du Docteur Paccard; s low season €53-60, high season €83-96; **P**) A vast, austere hotel where the prices stay low even in high season, which means it's nearly always full. The best rooms have mountain views; the worst have views of the car park.

TOP END

Hôtel Mont Blanc (☎ 04 50 53 05 64; www.bestmont blanc.com; 62 allée du Majestic; d with half-board per person low/high season €103/183; **P** ⊠ 🎿 🖳) South of the tourist office, this is one of Chamonix's top hotels, boasting four stars and all the luxury you could possibly wish for.

Eating
RESTAURANTS

In season, most of Chamonix's restaurants are open daily for lunch and dinner.

Neapolis (☎ 04 50 53 98 41; 79 Gallerie Alpina; pizza & pasta €6.40-9.90; ⊙ Mon-Sat) This simple Italian restaurant overlooks the river and has cheap, wholesome cooking – which makes it very popular.

Restaurant La Calèche (☎ 04 50 55 94 68; 18 rue du Docteur Paccard; evening menus from €17) One of many restaurants around place Balmat aimed squarely at undiscriminating holiday makers. Still, the fondue is very good, which is more than can be said for the décor.

Annapurna (☎ 04 50 55 81 39; 62 av Ravanel-Le Rouge; mains €6-15) If you're feeling chilly after the snow, how about a volcanic curry? This snazzy Indian place has a good vegetarian selection – try the chickpea curry or the vegetarian platter.

Le Sanjon (☎ 04 50 53 56 44; 5 av Ravanel Le Rouge; menus €15-25, fondue €11-21) A picturesque

wooden chalet restaurant serving *raclette* – a block of melted cheese, usually eaten with potatoes and cold meats and fondue.

Munchie (☎ 04 50 53 45 41; 87 rue des Moulins; mains €10-25; ⊙ closed lunch) A trendy hang-out with great pan-Asian food. Mains include blackened salmon *sashimi,* authentic sushi and Thai Chicken with pimento and ginger.

Le Panoramic (☎ /fax 04 50 53 44 11; Le Brévent; menus from €15) At Le Brévent cable station, this is the place to choose for a lofty lunch with an incredible view of Mont Blanc. The selection of *menus* include local cheese, cured meat, potatoes and salad, and a warming glass of *vin chaud* will perk you up on a snowy winter's day.

CAFÉS & QUICK EATS

Le Gouthé (☎ 04 50 53 58 95; 95 rue des Moulins; cakes & pastries €1-4; hot drinks €1.50-3) Head here for the best cakes, pastries and hot chocolate in town.

Le Bumble Bee Bistro (☎ 04 50 53 50 03; 65 rue des Moulins; mains €5-10) A tiny, welcoming café that serves hot, hearty meals throughout the day. Cod fritters, chargrilled chicken, steak and ale pie, and potato wedges are ideal after a hard day on the slopes, but vegetarians should try the Red Dragon Pie, stuffed full of vegetables, lentils and spicy beans.

Poco Loco (☎ 04 50 53 43 03; 47 rue du Docteur Paccard; crepes from €1.50, pizza €5-7, menus from €7) One of several sandwich shops near place Balmat, with hot paninis, sweet crepes and huge burgers.

SELF-CATERING

There's a **Super U Supermarket** (117 rue Joseph Vallot; ⊙ 8.15am-7.30pm Mon-Sat, 8.15am-12.45pm Sun winter). **Le Refuge Payot** (☎ 04 50 53 18 71; 166 rue Joseph Vallot) and **La Ferme du Mont Blanc** (☎ 04 50 53 37 13; 202 rue Joseph Vallot) stock an excellent range of cheeses, meats and other local products.

Getting There & Away
BUS

The bus station is in the train station building. The office of **SAT Autocar** (☎ 04 50 53 01 15; www.satobus-alps.com in French; ⊙ 6.45am-10.30am & 1.25-4.45pm Mon-Fri, 6.45am-11.00am & 1.25-4.45pm Sat & Sun winter) is near the train station entrance; seasonal hours vary. Buses operate to Geneva bus station (€33, 1½ to two hours), Annecy (€15.30, three hours) and Geneva airport (€33, 2¼ hours). Services to Italy, through

APRÈS-SKI IN CHAMONIX

Chamonix's humming nightlife is one of its main attractions, and there are enough bars and clubs to keep you going for a whole season.

Popular places include the café-bar of **Hôtel Gustavia** (see p504), which has a happy hour most evenings, and a lively terrace outside, and **O'Byrne's Irish Bar** at Hôtel Vallée Blanche (see p503), which does a decent Murphy's and attracts an older crowd.

Le Cybar (p499) regularly hosts après-ski bands and comedy nights and usually has a happy hour from 6pm to 7pm. You can grab a warming snack (tortillas, jacket potatoes, burgers and paninis for €4 to €8) or watch a DVD in the upstairs lounge.

Dick's Tea Bar (☎ 04 50 53 19 10; www.dicksteabar.com; rue des Moulins), is Chamonix's outpost of the Alpine nightclub chain. Club classics and weird cocktails are the order of the day.

Wild Wallabies (☎ 04 50 53 01 31; 1 rue de la Tour) is a grungy Australian-themed joint that offers pool, table football and bar snacks. As you might imagine it's a popular place with the snow-crowd from Down Under.

Le Refuge (☎ 04 50 53 00 94; 275 rue du Docteur Paccard) and **L'Arbate** (☎ 04 50 53 80 23; www.arbate .com; 80 chemin du Sapi) are buzzy late-night destinations. Chamonix's biggest, cheesiest disco is **Le Garage** (☎ 04 50 53 64 49; 200 av de l'Aiguille du Midi), down an alleyway off av Michael Croz.

the Mont Blanc tunnel, include Courmayeur (€18 return) and Aoste (€22 return).

CAR

If you're coming to Chamonix from Italy, you'll arrive via the **Mont Blanc Tunnel** (cars single/return €29/36), which enters town in the southern suburb of Les Pélerins. From France, the N205 travels to Les Houches and Les Bossons before arriving in Chamonix.

Parking in town can be tricky. Car parks (some free) are scattered along Route du Bouchet, around Rue des Allobroges and in Chamonix Sud, but in season they're likely to be full. Another option is to park outside town and connect by bus or train: contact **Chamonix Parc-Auto** (☎ 04 50 53 65 71; weekly rates from €31).

TRAIN

Chamonix–Mont Blanc **train station** (☎ 04 50 53 12 98; ticket counter ✆ 6am-8pm) is at the end of av Michel Croz. It has a **left-luggage counter** (1st/additonal piece luggage €3/1.50; ✆ 6am-8pm).

Major destinations include Paris' Gare de Lyon (€87, six to seven hours, five daily), Lyon (€32, 4½ hours via Annecy), Annecy (€18, 2½ hours), Geneva (€17, four hours via Annecy or Chambéry), and Grenoble (€28, five hours via Annecy). There's an overnight train to Paris (€99, 10 hours) year-round.

The narrow-gauge train line from St-Gervais–le Fayet (23km west of Chamonix) to Martigny, Switzerland (42km north of Chamonix), stops at 11 towns in the valley including Argentière. There are nine to 12 return trips a day. From St-Gervais–le Fayet, there are trains to all parts of France.

Getting Around

BICYCLE

Between June and September, **Le Grand Bi** (☎ 04 50 53 14 16; 240 av du Bois du Bouchet; 3-/10-speed mountain bike hire per day €15/22; ✆ 9am-12.30pm & 2.30-7pm Tue-Sat) rents bikes.

BUS

Bus transport is handled by **Chamonix Bus** (☎ 04 50 53 05 55; place du Triangle de l'Amitié; ✆ 7am-7pm winter, 8am-noon & 2-7pm Jun-Aug).

Bus stops are marked by black-on-yellow roadside signs. From mid-December to mid-May, there are numerous lines to the ski lifts. During the rest of the year there are only two lines, both leaving from place de l'Église and passing by the Chamonix Sud stop. One line goes south to Les Houches; the other goes north via Argentière to Col des Montets. Buses stop running between 6pm and 7pm, depending on the season. In winter, buses are free for holders of ski passes; others pay €1.50 for one sector during the day, €2 at night.

TAXI

There's a **taxi stand** (☎ 04 50 53 13 94) outside the train station. Tariffs are posted inside the station. Minibuses for two to eight people are available from **Chamonix Transfer** (☎ 06 07 67 88 85; www.chamonix-transfer.com in French).

MEGÈVE & ST-GERVAIS

Megève (population 4700, elevation 1113m), 36km southwest of Chamonix, and neighbouring St-Gervais (population 5400, elevation 810m) sit below Mont Blanc and are connected by a common network of ski lifts. These tiny ski villages are among the oldest in the Alps.

Megève was developed as a resort in the 1920s for a French baroness following her disillusionment with Switzerland's crowded St-Moritz. Today it remains an expensive, trendy resort with an old square accessed by old narrow medieval-style streets and lanes. On the eastern outskirts of the village are some chapels and oratories that trace the Stations of the Cross in baroque, rococo, and Tuscan-style woodcarvings.

Summer hiking trails in the Bettex, Mont d'Arbois and Mont Joly areas are accessible from both villages. Mountain biking is equally popular; some of the best terrain is found along marked trails between Val d'Arly, Mont Blanc and Beaufortain.

Information

Megève has a **tourist office** (☎ 04 50 21 27 28; www.megeve.com; rue de Monseigneur Conseil; � 9am-12.30pm & 2-7pm Mon-Sat, 9am-12.30pm & 4-7pm Sun winter). The **accommodation service** (☎ 04 50 21 29 52; reservation@megeve.com) is based here too.

Megève's **ESF** (☎ 04 50 21 00 97; www.megeve-ski.com; 76 rue Ambroise Martin) and the **Bureau des Guides** (☎ 04 50 21 55 11; www.bureaudesguides.com; 76 rue Ambroise Martin) are inside Maison de la Montagne. Megève's **International Ski School** (ESI; ☎ 04 50 58 78 88; www.esimegeve.com) is at the bottom of the Mont d'Arbois cable car.

In St-Gervais the **tourist office** (☎ 04 50 47 76 08; fax 04 50 47 75 69; 115 av Mont Paccard; � 9am-noon & 2.30-7.30pm high season, 9am-noon & 2-6pm low season) also has an **accommodation service** (☎ 04 50 93 53 63). There are also **ESF** (☎ 04 50 47 7621; promenade du Mont Blanc) and **Bureau des Guides** (☎ 04 50 47 76 55; place du Mont Blanc) offices here.

Sleeping

Both tourist offices stock lists of accommodation, but Megève isn't cheap. Studios for two people per week in the low/high season start at €230/310.

Bookings for CAF *refuges* in St-Gervais and Megève can be made through the CAF office in Chamonix (p499) or through the

Refuge du Val-Monjoie (☎ 04 50 47 76 70; 73 av de Miage, St-Gervais).

Alp Hôtel (☎ 04 50 21 07 58; www.alp-hotel.fr; 434 route de Rochebrune; half-board d €53-62) A friendly chalet-style place in Megève with comfortable, rustic two-star rooms.

Hôtel Au Coeur de Megève (☎ 04 50 21 25 30; www.hotel-megeve.com; rue Charles Feige; r €104-163) Near the centre of Megève, this three-star hotel has pleasant rooms and balconies looking onto the street.

Au Vieux Moulin (☎ 04 50 21 22 29; www.vieux moulin.com; 188 rue Ambroise-Martin; d €146-250; P ⊠) One of Megève's oldest hotels, housed in a beautiful refurbished alpine chalet with lots of luxurious touches.

Eating

Les Fermes de Marie (☎ 04 50 93 03 10; www.fermes demarie.com; chemin de Riante Colline; mains €12-20, menus from €35; ☺ lunch & dinner) A renowned Alpine spa-resort boasting not one but three of the top restaurants in Megève – a formal dining room, a traditional Alpine rotisserie, and a cheese restaurant serving fondue and *raclette*.

La Ferme de mon Père (☎ 04 50 21 01 01; www.marc-veyrat.com; 367 route du Crêt; mains €75-105, menus €270/360; ☺ lunch & dinner Dec-Apr) This celebrated gastronomic restaurant is owned by one of France's top chefs, Marc Veyrat. In keeping with the rest of Megève, the prices are sky-high, but with dishes such as *sirène de macaron meringuée* (mermaid macarooned meringue) and *coquillages en folie* (joyous shellfish) on the menu, you're guaranteed a truly unique dining experience

Getting There & Away

There's a **SAT bus** and **SNCF office** (☎ 04 50 47 73 88) opposite the tourist office in St-Gervais. In Megève, contact the **bus station** (☎ 04 50 21 25 18) and **train station** (☎ 08 92 35 35 39) for further information on transfers to and from Megève.

Many trains to/from Paris via Annecy stop at Sallanches (13km from Megève) and St-Gervais–le Fayet (16km from Megève and 2km from St-Gervais). All trains terminate in St-Gervais–le Fayet.

There are four buses daily between St-Gervais, Megève and Chamonix (€8.50, 55 minutes). Seven buses daily link Megève and St-Gervais with St-Gervais–le Fayet and Sallanches train stations. There are also five buses daily in winter to/from Geneva airport (€33, 1½ hours).

From St-Gervais–le Fayet and St-Gervais, the **Mont Blanc tramway** (☎ 04 50 47 51 83) rattles its way up to Bellevue (1800m), offering staggering mountain views en route. A return ticket costs €15.

LES PORTES DU SOLEIL

The dozen villages linked by lifts along the French–Swiss border in the northern Chablais – dubbed the Portes du Soleil (Gates of the Sun) – comprise the largest ski area in France. Some 650km of slopes and trails criss-cross the region. You can buy a ski pass covering some or all of them.

The largest village is **Morzine** (population 3000, elevation 1000m) in Haute Savoie, retaining some (but not much) of its traditional Alpine village atmosphere. Accommodation can be booked through the **accommodation service** (☎ 04 50 79 11 57; reservation@morzine-avoriaz .com) inside the **tourist office** (☎ 04 50 74 72 72; www.morzine-avoriaz.com in French; place de la Crusaz; ☼ 8.30am-7.30pm Sun-Fri, plus 8am-8pm Sat during winter & summer seasons). There's also an **Auberge de Jeunesse** (☎ 04 50 79 14 86; morzine@fuaj.org; dm €12; ☼ Christmas-Apr & Jun-Sep).

Avoriaz (1800m), a few kilometres up the valley from Morzine, is among the most expensive of the French ski resorts. Built in the 1960s, Morzine's high-rise apartment blocks manage to blend into their surroundings because each one is covered with wooden shingles. Apart from two four-star hotels and a **Club Méditerranée** (☎ 04 50 74 28 70; fax 04 50 74 03 61; all-inclusive package per week from €805), all accommodation is in studios or apartments, which can be booked through the **tourist office** (☎ 04 50 74 02 11; www.avoriaz .com; ☼ 8.30am-7pm). Avoriaz is a car-free resort but there are outdoor and covered car parks. Transport is by horse-and-sleigh in winter. There's a special course for mountain bikes with jumps and other obstacles. It's free, but only open in summer.

If you're arriving by road via Cluses, **Les Gets** (population 1300, elevation 1172m) is the first village of the Portes du Soleil. Quieter than Morzine and cheaper than Avoriaz, it has plenty of accommodation; contact the **tourist office** (☎ 04 50 75 80 80; www .lesgets.com; place de la Mairie; ☼ 8.30am-7pm in winter, 8.30am-12.30pm & 2-7pm Mon-Fri, 8.30am-7pm Sat & Sun in summer) or the **accommodation booking office**

(☎ 04 50 75 80 51; reservations@lesgets.com) housed in the same building.

Getting There & Away

Free shuttle buses serve the lifts of Télécabine Super Morzine, Télécabine du Pléney and Téléphérique Avoriaz.

During the ski season, Morzine is linked by bus to Geneva airport (€29), 50km north. From Morzine there are regular **SAT buses** (☎ 04 50 79 15 69) to Les Gets and Avoriaz. There are also buses from Morzine to its closest train stations: Thonon-les-Bains (34km to the north) and Cluses (31km to the south).

THONON-LES-BAINS

pop 30,000 / elevation 430m

Thonon-les-Bains is the largest town on the French side of Lake Geneva (Lac Léman), and the capital of the Chablais area. Just across the water from the Swiss city of Lausanne, the modern town sits on a bluff above the lake and is linked to the marina (port des Rives) by a 230m-long **funiculaire** (☎ 04 50 71 21 54; one way/return €1/1.80; ☼ 8am-12.30pm & 1.30-6.30pm, 8am-11pm summer). Thonon makes for a peaceful overnight stop in summer, with serene lake cruises and pleasant lakefront walks – but the town itself hasn't got much to offer. From the port, quai de Ripaille follows the lake 1km east to **Château de Ripaille** (☎ 04 50 26 64 44; admission incl tour €6; tours 3pm).

The **tourist office** (☎ 04 50 71 55 55; www.thonon lesbains.com; place du Marché; ☼ 9am-noon & 2-6pm Mon-Sat Sep-Jun, 8.30am-12.30pm & 1.30-7pm Mon-Sat, 10am-noon Sun Jul & Aug) operates a lakeside **annexe** (☎ 04 50 26 19 94; port des Rives; ☼ 10.30am-12.30pm & 2-7pm Jul & Aug) during summer. The annexe sells tickets for Lake Geneva cruises, run mainly by the Swiss **CGN company** (☎ 04 50 71 14 71) and **Navirives** (☎ /fax 04 50 71 52 42).

Accommodation can be found at the old **Hôtel à l'Ombre des Marronniers** (☎ 04 50 71 26 18; fax 04 50 26 27 47; 17 place de Crète; d €44-46), beside the train station, or the modern **Hôtel Ibis** (☎ 04 50 71 24 24; fax 04 50 71 87 76; 2ter av d'Évian; d €55-75) near the town centre.

SAT (☎ 04 50 71 00 88; 11 av Jules Ferry) has regular buses to/from Thonon to Évian (€1.50, 15 minutes) and into the Chablais Mountains, including to Morzine. The **train station** (☎ 08 36 35 35 35; place de la Gare) is southwest of place des Arts, the main square. Trains go to Geneva (€6.30, 40 minutes) and Bellegarde (€9.60, 1¼ hours) via Thonon-les-Bains.

HEALTH FARMS & HOT WATER

Nine kilometres east of Thonon is **Évian-les-Bains**, famous for its mineral water. Known as the 'Pearl of Lake Geneva', Évian was a favourite country retreat of the dukes of Savoy, but was razed during the Wars of Religion. It reinvented itself as a luxury tourist resort in the 18th century when the fashion for spa baths reached its height. Though the health benefits of sitting in tubs of mineral water were never quite established, drinking the stuff caught on in a big way: bottled mineral water now accounts for most of Évian's economy. The water takes 15 years to trickle down through the Chablais mountains, gathering minerals en route, before emerging at a constant temperature of 11.4°C (52.8°F).

If you're interested, it's possible to visit the Évian factory; ask at the **tourist office** (☎ 04 50 75 04 26; www.eviantourism.com; place d'Allinges; ☜ 8.30am-12.30pm & 2-7pm Mon-Fri, 9am-noon & 3-7pm Sat, 10am-noon & 3-6pm Sun Jul & Aug, to 6pm mid-May–mid-Sep, 8.30am-noon & 2-6pm Mon-Fri Oct-Apr) for details or head straight for the factory's **Public Relations Office** (☎ 04 50 26 80 80; 22 av des Sources). Tours are free but must be booked in advance. You might even get a free sample.

ANNECY

pop 50,000 / elevation 448m

Annecy, the chic capital of Haute-Savoie, is a pretty lakeside town, criss-crossed with ancient canals and lined with medieval houses and arched alleyways. Visitors can stroll along the lakefront or mosey around the old city, admiring the Alpine peaks and the geranium-covered bridges or take to the waters of Lac d'Annecy in *pedalos*, canoes and cruise-boats. Annecy makes the perfect place to kick back and relax after the adrenaline-fuelled Alpine resorts – except in summer, when the bumper-to-bumper traffic can be a little taxing.

Orientation

The train and bus stations are 500m northwest of the Vieille Ville (old town), which is huddled around the River Thiou (split into Canal du Thiou to the south and Canal du Vassé to the north). The town centre is between the post office and the purpose-built Centre Bonlieu, which houses the city's theatre and the tourist office, near the shores of Lac d'Annecy.

Information

INTERNET ACCESS

Syndrome Cybercafé (☎ 04 50 45 39 75; infos@syndrome.com; per 15min/hr €2/6; 3bis av de Chevène; ☜ noon-midnight)

LAUNDRY

Lav' Confort Express (4 rue de la Gare; ☜ 7am-9pm)

MONEY

Convenient branches include Crédit Lyonnais in the Bonlieu Centre and Banque Populaire (Faubourg Ste-Claire), with an ATM and currency-exchange machine.

Banque de France (9bis av de Chambéry; ☜ 8.45am-noon & 1.45-3.45pm Mon-Fri)

POST

Post Office (4bis rue des Glières)

TOURIST INFORMATION

Annecy Sport Information (☎ 04 50 33 88 31; ☜ 3-7pm Mon, 2.30-7pm Tue-Fri, 10am-noon Sat) Also in Centre Bonlieu.

Tourist Office (☎ 04 50 45 00 33; www.lac-annecy .com; 1 rue Jean Jaurès; ☜ 9am-12.30pm & 1.45-6pm Mon-Sat mid-Sep–mid-May, 9am-6.30pm Mon-Sat mid-May–mid-Sep, Sun summer) In Centre Bonlieu.

Sights & Activities

Wandering around the old town and the lakefront are the essence of a visit to Annecy. Just east of the Vieille Ville, behind the town hall, are the flowery **Jardins de l'Europe**, shaded by Californian giant redwoods. **Champ de Mars** is a popular park across the Canal du Vassé from the redwoods. Both are linked by the elegant arch of the Pont des Amours.

VIEILLE VILLE

The Vieille Ville, a warren of narrow streets and colonnaded passageways, retains much of its 17th-century appearance. On the central island, the imposing **Palais de l'Isle** (☎ 04 50 33 87 31; adult/student €3.05/0.75; ☜ 10am-6pm Jun-Sep, 10am-noon & 2-6pm Wed-Mon Oct-May) was once a prison, but is now home to local-history displays. Between mid-June and September there are guided tours in English around Vieille Ville – contact the tourist office for details.

CHÂTEAU D'ANNECY

In the 13th- to 16th-century castle above town, the **Musée Château** (☎ 04 50 33 87 30; adult/student €4.70/1.60; ☒ 10am-noon & 2-6pm Wed-Mon Oct-May, 10.30am-6pm Jun-Sep) is a fine museum that explores traditional Savoyard art and crafts, and has a display on Alpine natural history. It also holds frequent special exhibitions. The climb to the chateau is worth it just for the view over the old town's crowded rooftops.

SUNBATHING & SWIMMING

The lakefront is lined with parks and grassy areas where you can picnic, sunbathe and swim in the warm months. **Plage d'Annecy-le-Vieux** (admission free) is 1km east of the

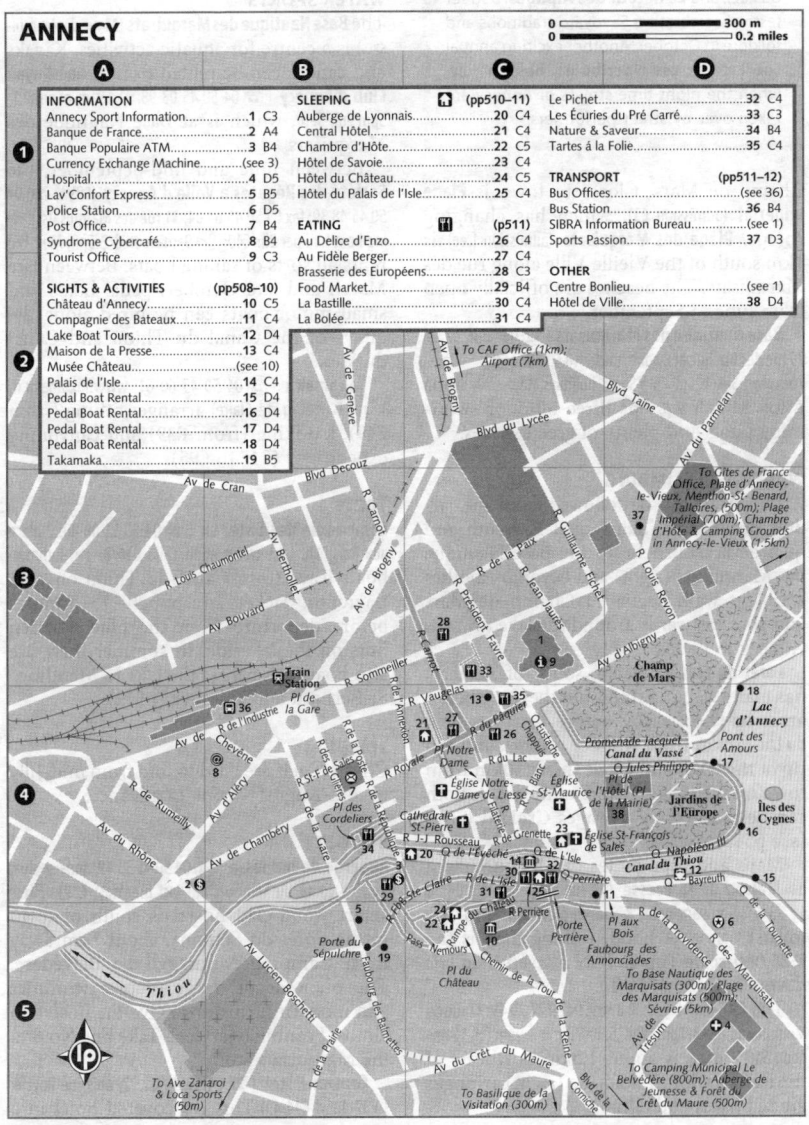

ANNECY

| | | 0 | 300 m |
| | | 0 | 0.2 miles |

INFORMATION
Annecy Sport Information	1 C3
Banque de France	2 A4
Banque Populaire ATM	3 B4
Currency Exchange Machine	(see 3)
Hospital	4 D5
Lav'Confort Express	5 B5
Police Station	6 D5
Post Office	7 B4
Syndrome Cybercafé	8 B4
Tourist Office	9 C3

SIGHTS & ACTIVITIES (pp508-10)
Château d'Annecy	10 C5
Compagnie des Bateaux	11 C4
Lake Boat Tours	12 D4
Maison de la Presse	13 C4
Musée Château	(see 10)
Palais de l'Isle	14 C4
Pedal Boat Rental	15 D4
Pedal Boat Rental	16 D4
Pedal Boat Rental	17 D4
Pedal Boat Rental	18 D4
Takamaka	19 B5

SLEEPING ☐ (pp510-11)
Auberge de Lyonnais	20 C4
Central Hôtel	21 C4
Chambre d'Hôte	22 C5
Hôtel de Savoie	23 B5
Hôtel du Château	24 C5
Hôtel du Palais de l'Isle	25 C4

EATING ☐ (p511)
Au Delice d'Enzo	26 C4
Au Fidèle Berger	27 C4
Brasserie des Européens	28 C3
Food Market	29 B4
La Bastille	30 C4
La Bolée	31 C4

Le Pichet	32 C4
Les Écuries du Pré Carré	33 C3
Nature & Saveur	34 C4
Tartes à la Folie	35 C4

TRANSPORT (pp511-12)
Bus Offices	(see 36)
Bus Station	36 B4
SIBRA Information Bureau	(see 1)
Sports Passion	37 D3

OTHER
Centre Bonlieu	(see 1)
Hôtel de Ville	38 D4

OUT & ABOUT IN ANNECY

Annecy hosts many events and exhibitions throughout the year. Highlights include a **Venetian carnival** in March, Spanish and Italian **film festivals** in March and October, a major **animation festival** in June, a **fireworks display** over the lake in August (Fête du Lac), and **Le Retour des Alpages**, a street festival celebrating Savoyard traditions and folklore in October. Another exciting annual spectacle is **Les Noctibules,** held in July, when the night-time streets of Annecy are taken over by street performers.

Champ de Mars. Closer to town is **Plage Impérial** (admission €3), which has changing rooms. **Plage des Marquisats** (admission free) is 1km south of the Vieille Ville along rue des Marquisats. The beaches are officially open from June to September.

Base Nautique des Marquisats (☎ 04 50 45 39 18; 29 rue des Marquisats; adult/under 18 €3.50/2.50; ☽ 9am-7pm Mon-Sat, 10am-7pm Sun & holidays May–early Sep, to 7.30pm Jul–early Sep) has three outdoor swimming pools and plenty of green spaces.

WALKING & CLIMBING
A fine stroll can be followed from the Jardins de l'Europe along quai Bayreuth and quai de la Tournette to the Base Nautique des Marquisats (right) and beyond. Another excellent walk begins at Champ de Mars and goes eastwards around the lake towards Annecy-le-Vieux.

Forêt du Crêt du Maure, south of Annecy, has many walking trails, but there are better areas in two nearby nature reserves: **Bout du Lac** (20km from Annecy on the southern tip of the lake) and **Roc de Chère** (10km from town on the eastern shore of the lake). Both can be reached by Voyages Crolard buses (see p512).

Maps and topoguides can be purchased at **Maison de la Presse** (13 rue Vaugelas; ☎ 04 50 51 73 51; ☽ 9am-noon & 2-6pm Mon-Sat) and the tourist office. A good walking map is the 1:25,000-scale Top 25 IGN map entitled *Lac d'Annecy* (No 3431OT).

The **CAF** (☎ 04 50 09 82 09, 04 50 27 29 45; 77 rue du Mont Blanc; ☽ 3-7pm Wed, 5.30-7pm & 8-9pm Fri, 10am-noon Sat) office is about 1.5km northeast of the train station. Takamaka (right) arranges guided hikes and climbs.

CYCLING & IN-LINE SKATING
There's a cycling path (also popular with in-line skaters) along the western shore of the lake. It starts 1.5km south of Annecy (on rue des Marquisats) and travels to Duingt, 12km further south. See p512 for information on bicycle and in-line skate rental.

WATER SPORTS
The **Base Nautique des Marquisats** (31 rue des Marquisats) is a centre for aquatic activities. Kayaks and canoes can be rented from **Canoë-Kayak Club d'Annecy** (☎ 04 50 45 03 98; ☽ 9am-noon & 1-5pm Jun-Sep), which is at Base Nautique des Marquisats.

Between June and mid-September, the **Société des Régates à Voile d'Annecy** (SRVA; ☎ 04 50 45 48 39; fax 04 50 45 64 64; 31 rue des Marquisats; sailing boat hire per 2hr €40; ☽ 9am-noon & 2-5pm Mon-Fri) rents all sorts of sailing boats. Between late March and late October, pedal boats and small motor-boats can be hired along the quays of the Canal du Thiou and Canal du Vassé.

Takamaka (☎ 04 50 45 60 61; www.takamaka.fr; 17 rue Faubourg Ste-Claire) arranges rafting (from €49), kayaking (from €39) and canyoning expeditions (€47 to €95).

Tours
Compagnie des Bateaux (☎ 04 50 51 08 40; 2 place aux Bois; 1hr lake cruise adult/child €10/8; ☽ summer) boats leave from Canal du Thiou on quai Bayreuth. Tickets are bought 15 minutes before departure from the blue wooden huts on the lakeside. In summer there are also boat trips across the lake to Menthon-St-Bernard and Talloires (p512).

Sleeping
Cheap hotels are hard to find from mid-July to mid-August – book in advance.

BUDGET
Auberge de Jeunesse (☎ 04 50 45 33 19; annecy@fuaj .com; 4 route du Semnoz; dm incl breakfast €12) This smart wood-clad hostel is south of town in the Forêt du Semnoz, about 1km away from Camping Municipal Le Belvédère. The plain décor, large picture windows and modern furnishings give the hostel an almost Scandinavian feel. Take bus No 6 to the Marquisats stop.

Central Hôtel (☎ 04 50 45 05 37; 6bis rue Royale; s €37-42, d €44-49) This ivy-covered hotel in a quiet, shabby courtyard is one of the cheapest places close to the Vieille Ville – but the rooms are a little basic.

Auberge du Lyonnais (☎ 04 50 51 26 10; fax 04 50 51 05 04; 14 quai de l'Évêché; r €29-45) In the heart of the old city, this hotel-restaurant occupies an idyllic setting next to the canal – but there are only nine rooms, so be quick.

Camping
There are several camping grounds near the lake in Annecy-le-Vieux.

Camping Municipal Le Belvédère (☎ 04 50 45 48 30; fax 04 50 45 55 56; camping €13) In the Forêt du Crêt du Maure, is 2.5km south of the train station.

MID-RANGE & TOP END
One **chambre d'hôte** (☎ 04 50 23 34 43; 2 av de la Mavéria; d €35-50) overlooks the lake next to the Impérial Palace. Alternatively, there's a **chambre d'hôte** (☎ 04 50 45 72 28; rampe du Château; d €60-80) in a big period house next to Hôtel du Château.

Hôtel du Château (☎ 04 50 45 27 66; fax 04 50 52 75 26; 16 rampe du Château; r €45-60; P) Just below one of the towers of the chateau, this small, hilltop hotel is hard to beat for a serene view over Annecy's lantern-lit lanes. The rooms are cosy and there's a great terrace overlooking the city's rooftops.

Hôtel du Palais de L'Isle (☎ 04 50 45 86 87; fax 04 50 51 87 15; 13 rue Perrière; d €69-88) Next to Le Pichet restaurant, this is an upmarket hotel with 26 well-kept modern rooms, many of which look over the canal.

Hôtel de Savoie (☎ 04 50 45 15 45; fax 04 50 45 11 99; 1 place de St-François; s/d €45/70) Once a convent, this charterful little hotel has its entrance on the left side of Église St-François de Sales. It's a small, friendly place with simple rooms and in a great location.

Eating
RESTAURANTS
In the Vieille Ville, the quays along both sides of Canal du Thiou are lined with cafés and restaurants. There are lots of cheap places along rue du Pâquier.

Au Delice d'Enzo (☎ 04 50 45 35 36; 17 rue du Pâquier; pizza or pasta €6.50-10; ☺ lunch & dinner) One of several restaurants under the arched colonnades of rue du Pâquier, this tiny little Italian joint has a streetside terrace and serves good, simple pizza and pasta.

Brasserie des Européens (☎ 04 50 51 30 70; 23 rue Sommeiller; mains €8-20; ☺ lunch & dinner) A popular brasserie with a 1920s ambience, specialising in mussels; try the *Moules Spéciales Brasserie* cooked in beer. It also has a fresh seafood takeaway counter.

Les Écuries du Pré Carré (☎ 04 50 45 59 14; 10 rue Vaugelas; menus €15-25; ☺ Mon-Sat) South of Brasserie des Européens in a small courtyard off rue Vaugelas, this is a pricey, classy place which usually has lake fish on its varied menu.

La Bolée (☎ 04 50 45 26 62; 14 rue de l'Isle; crepes €7-9.15; ☺ Thu-Tue May-Sep) A simple Breton creperie with regional variations on the theme. Try the *Savoyard*, with bacon and local *reblochon* cheese.

Le Pichet (☎ 04 50 45 32 41; 13 rue Perrière; menus €18-29; ☺ Thu-Mon) Next door to the Hôtel du Palais de L'Isle, this restaurant has a big terrace and a range of Savoyard dishes, including delicious, diet-busting *tartiflette* (sliced potatoes and *reblochon* cheese baked in the oven).

La Bastille (☎ 04 50 45 09 37; 3 quai des Vieilles Prisons; menus €11-20; ☺ lunch & dinner) A great little canalside restaurant with a sheltered terrace, opposite the old city prison. *Tartiflette*, steaks and Savoyard fondues are all delicious.

CAFÉS
Rue Perrière and rue de l'Isle have several cheap sandwich shops.

Tartes à la Folie (7-9 rue Vaugelas) Sweet and savoury tarts are on offer at this little café – don't miss out on the scrumptious rhubarb and nut tarts.

Au Fidèle Berger (cnr rue Royale & rue Carnot; ☺ 9.15am-7pm Tue-Fri, 9am-7.30pm Sat) A traditional tearoom and patisserie with a fantastic old-world feel.

Nature & Saveur (place des Cordeliers; ☺ 8.30am-7pm Tue-Sat) A cosy organic café with a terrace on the quayside, offering smoothies, fresh juices and organic salads and snacks.

SELF-CATERING
In the Vieille Ville, there is a popular **food market** (rue Faubourg Ste-Claire; ☺ 8am-noon Sun, Tue & Fri).

Getting There & Away
AIR
Annecy's small **airport** (☎ 04 50 27 30 06; www .annecy.aeroport.fr; 8 route Côte Merle) is north of the

city in Meythet, just west of the autoroute to Geneva. The airport has daily flights to Paris' Orly Sud (from €250, one hour 20 minutes).

BUS

The bus station, **Gare Routière Sud** (rue de l'Industrie), is next to the train station. Exits from the train station platforms lead directly to the bus station. Tickets can be purchased from the bus offices at the bus station.

Voyages Crolard (☎ 04 50 45 08 12; ⏰ 7.15am-12.30pm & 1.45-7.30pm Mon-Sat, also Sun in peak seasons), based at the bus station, serves various points around Lac d'Annecy, including Menthon, Talloires and Roc de Chère on the eastern shore; Sévrier on the western shore; and Bout du Lac on the southern tip. Other destinations include La Clusaz (€9.20, 50 minutes), Albertville (€7.70, 1¼ hours) and Chamonix (€16, two hours).

Autocars Frossard (☎ 04 50 45 73 90; ⏰ 7.45-11am & 2-7.15pm Mon-Fri, 7.45am-1pm Sat), at the bus station, sells tickets to Annemasse, Chambéry, Évian, Geneva, Grenoble, Nice and Thonon.

TRAIN

There are information counters at the **train station** (☎ 08 36 35 35 35; place de la Gare; information counters ⏰ 9am-noon & 2-7pm, ticket windows ⏰ 5am-10.30pm Mon-Fri, 9am-7.30pm Sat & Sun).

There are frequent trains to Paris' Gare de Lyon (€77 by TGV, 3¾ hours), Nice (€66, 7½ hours), Lyon (€19, three hours), Chamonix (€18, 2½ to three hours), Aix-les-Bains (€6.20, 30 minutes) and Chambéry (€9.60, one hour).

The night train to Paris (€70, eight hours), often full on weekends, leaves between 9pm and 10pm. Couchettes cost extra.

Getting Around
BICYCLE & IN-LINE SKATING

Bikes can be hired from **Loca Sports** (☎ 04 50 45 44 33; 2 av de Zanaroli), southwest of the Vieille Ville. **Sports Passion** (☎ 04 50 51 46 28; 3 av du Parmelan) rents out tandems, mountain bikes and in-line skates.

BUS

The municipal bus company is **SIBRA** (☎ 04 50 51 72 72). The **SIBRA information bureau** (☎ 04 50 10 04 04; Centre Bonlieu; ⏰ 8.30am-7pm Mon-Sat) is at Centre Bonlieu.

Buses run from 6am to 8pm Monday to Saturday. On Sunday, 20-seat minibuses (identified by letters rather than numbers) provide a limited service. Tickets cost €1, an eight-ride carnet costs €6.50 and weekly coupons cost €10.

TAXI

Taxis (☎ 04 50 45 05 67) are based at the bus station; otherwise call **Taxi Plus** (☎ 04 50 68 93 33).

AROUND ANNECY

When the sun shines, the villages of **Sévrier**, 5km south on Lake Annecy's western shore, and **Menthon-St-Bernard**, 7km south on the lake's eastern shore, make good day trips. **Talloires**, just south of Menthon, is Annecy's most exclusive lakeside spot.

Skiing is the Annéciens' main weekend activity in winter. Eighteen km south is the cross-country resort of **Le Semnoz** (1700m). Further afield are **La Clusaz** (1100m), 32km east of Annecy, and **Le Grand Bornand** (1000m), 34km northeast. Accommodation in La Clusaz is handled by the **tourist office** (☎ 04 50 32 65 00; www.laclusaz.com).

CHAMBÉRY
pop 58,000

Chambéry, which lies in a wide valley between Annecy and Grenoble, has long served as one of the principal gateways between France and Italy. Occupying the entrance to the valleys that lead to the main Alpine passes, the town was the capital of Savoy from the 13th century until 1563. Its charming old quarter, crammed with courtyards and cobbled streets, grew up around the castle, which once served as the seat of power for the dukes of Savoy.

Orientation

Busy dual carriageways along a narrow canal separate the town's compact old section from the northern sprawl, which starts near the train station at the northern end of rue Sommeiller. Place des Éléphants – the old city's focal point – is at the northeastern end of rue de Boigne.

Information
LAUNDRY

Laverie Automatique (1 rue Doppet; ⏰ 7.30am-8pm).
Lavomatique (37 place Monge; ⏰ 7am-10pm)

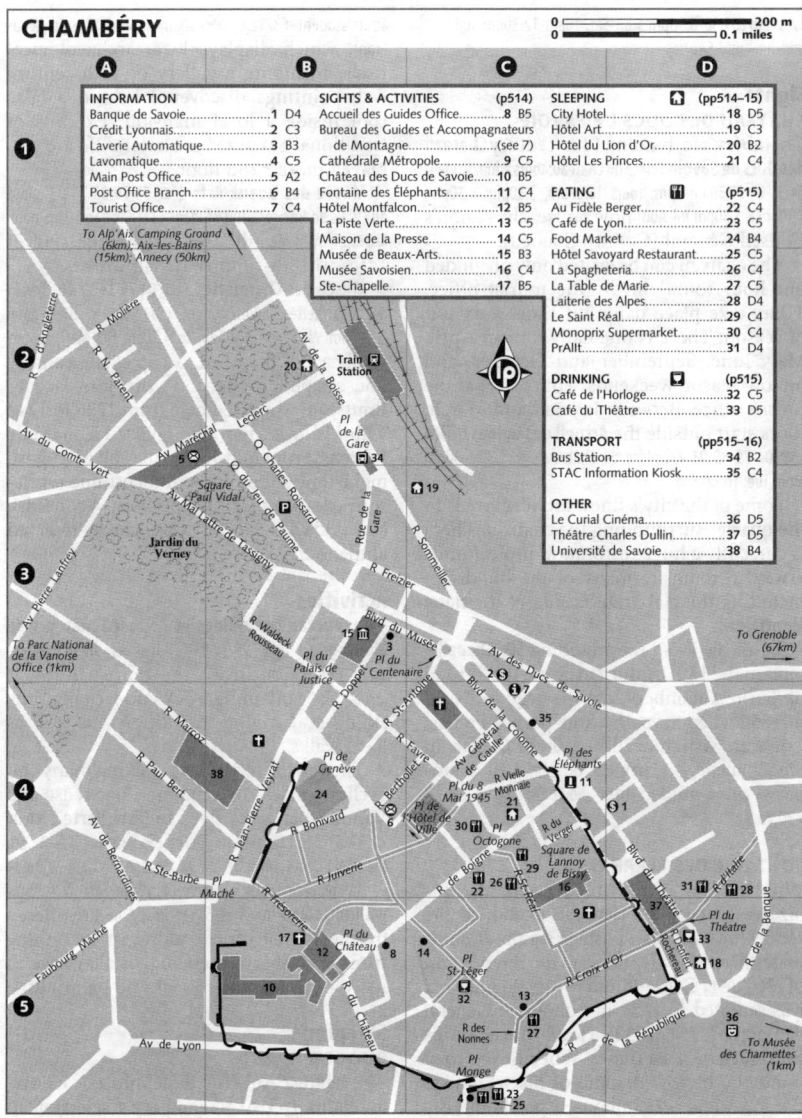

CHAMBÉRY

INFORMATION	
Banque de Savoie	1 D4
Crédit Lyonnais	2 C3
Laverie Automatique	3 B3
Lavomatique	4 C5
Main Post Office	5 A2
Post Office Branch	6 B4
Tourist Office	7 C4

SIGHTS & ACTIVITIES	(p514)
Accueil des Guides Office	8 B5
Bureau des Guides et Accompagnateurs de Montagne	(see 7)
Cathédrale Métropole	9 C5
Château des Ducs de Savoie	10 B5
Fontaine des Éléphants	11 C4
Hôtel Montfalcon	12 B5
La Piste Verte	13 C5
Maison de la Presse	14 C5
Musée de Beaux-Arts	15 B3
Musée Savoisien	16 C4
Ste-Chapelle	17 B5

SLEEPING	(pp514–15)
City Hotel	18 D5
Hôtel Art	19 C3
Hôtel du Lion d'Or	20 B2
Hôtel Les Princes	21 C4

EATING	(p515)
Au Fidèle Berger	22 C4
Café de Lyon	23 C5
Food Market	24 B4
Hôtel Savoyard Restaurant	25 C5
La Spaghetteria	26 C5
La Table de Marie	27 C5
Laiterie des Alpes	28 C4
Le Saint Réal	29 C4
Monoprix Supermarket	30 C4
PrAllt	31 D4

DRINKING	(p515)
Café de l'Horloge	32 C5
Café du Théâtre	33 D5

TRANSPORT	(pp515–16)
Bus Station	34 B2
STAC Information Kiosk	35 C4

OTHER	
Le Curial Cinéma	36 D5
Théâtre Charles Dullin	37 D5
Université de Savoie	38 B4

MONEY

Most branches in the city have ATMs.

Banque de Savoie (6 blvd du Théâtre)

Crédit Lyonnais (26 blvd de la Colonne)

POST

Post Office (sq Paul Vidal)

Post Office Branch (place de l'Hôtel de Ville)

TOURIST INFORMATION

Parc National de la Vanoise Office (☎ 04 79 62 30 54; fax 04 79 96 37 18; 135 rue du Docteur Julliand; ☑ 8am-noon & 2-6pm Mon-Fri) Parc National de la Vanoise's main headquarters.

Tourist Office (☎ 04 79 33 42 47; www.chambery -tourisme.com in French; 24 blvd de la Colonne; ☑ 9am- noon & 1.30-6pm Mon-Sat mid-Sep–mid-Jun, 9am-

12.30pm & 1.30-6.30pm Mon-Sat, 10am-12.30pm Sun mid-Jun–mid-Sep)

Sights

CHÂTEAU DES DUCS DE SAVOIE

Chambéry's forbidding 14th-century **Château des Ducs de Savoie** (place du Château; tours adult/student €4/3; ☎ 7.30am-7pm, tours 10.30am, 2.30pm, 3.30pm, 4.30pm & 5.30pm Jul-Aug) now houses the region's Conseil Général (County Council).

The château can be visited only on guided one-hour tours run by the tourist office. Tours take place daily but times vary out of season. There is one daily tour in April, May, June, September and October, and on low-season weekends. Tours start at the tourist office. Between January and March, tours start outside the **Accueil des Guides office** (☎ 04 79 85 93 73; place du Château; ☎ 1.30-5.30pm Mon, Tue, Thu & Fri).

Some of the city's finest architecture is in the quarter surrounding the chateau. There is currently a huge restoration project underway to renovate many of the buildings, including the elaborate façade of the **Hôtel Montfalcon**.

Tours also visit the adjoining **Ste-Chapelle**, built in the 15th century to house the Shroud of Turin. Chambéry lost the relic to Turin in 1860 when Savoy became part of France. You can visit the 70-bell **Grand Carillon** in Ste-Chapelle – Europe's largest bell chamber – on a guided **tour** (adult €4; ☎ 10.30am & 5.30pm Sat).

FONTAINE DES ÉLÉPHANTS

With its four huge carved elephants, this bizarre **Fontaine des Éléphants** could be the model for an Indian postage stamp. It dominates place des Éléphants at the intersection of blvd de la Colonne and rue de Boigne, and was sculpted in 1838 in honour of Général de Boigne (1751–1830), a local who made his fortune in the East Indies. When he returned home, he bestowed some of his wealth on the town and was honoured posthumously with this monument. The arcaded street that leads from the fountain to Château des Ducs and bears his name was one of his most important local projects.

MUSEUMS

South of the fountain, near the 15th- and 16th-century **Cathédrale Métropole**, is **Musée Savoisien** (☎ 04 79 33 44 48; sq de Lannoy de Bissy; adult/student €3/1.50; ☎ 10am-noon & 2-6pm Wed-Mon), which displays local archaeological finds, including a gallery of 13th-century wall paintings discovered behind a false roof inside a local mansion. Exhibits of traditional Savoyard mountain life are displayed on the 2nd floor.

Musée des Beaux-Arts (☎ 04 79 33 75 03; place du Palais de Justice; adult/student €3/1.50; ☎ 10am-noon & 2-6pm Wed-Mon) houses a rich collection of 14th- to 18th-century Italian works.

Musée des Charmettes (☎ 04 79 33 39 44; chemin des Charmettes; adult/student €3/1.50; ☎ 10am-noon & 2-6pm Wed-Mon Apr-Sep, to 4.30pm Oct-Mar), 1km southeast of the town, occupies the country house of philosopher and writer Jean-Jacques Rousseau, who lived here from 1736 to 1742 with his lover, Baronne Louise Éléonore de Warens. From mid-July to the end of August, night-time shows in period costume (visite-spectacle costumée) take place on Wednesday and Friday evenings. Tickets can be reserved at the tourist office.

Activities

The **Bureau des Guides et Accompagnateurs de Montagne** (☎ 04 79 33 81 62) has an **information desk** (☎ 2-6pm) inside the tourist office. It arranges canyoning, rock and ice climbing, skiing and caving expeditions, as well as local walks.

The tourist office sells walking maps and cycling guides covering the Chartreuse and Vanoise parks, as does **La Piste Verte** (☎ 04 79 33 57 31; 172 rue Croix d'Or; ☎ 9am-noon & 2-6pm Mon-Sat) and **Maison de la Presse** (☎ 04 79 33 41 62; 139 place St-Léger; ☎ 9am-6pm Mon-Sat). Various **walking tours** (tours €4-5; ☎ Jul & Aug) are offered by the tourist office, taking in everything from Chambéry's network of alleyways to its colourful trompe-l'oeil wall paintings.

Sleeping

BUDGET

The nearest Auberge de Jeunesse is in Aix-les-Bains (p516). Chambéry's selection of hotels leaves a lot to be desired. The best places are nearer the town centre.

City Hotel (☎ 04 79 85 76 79; fax 04 79 85 86 11; 9 rue Denfert Rochereau; d €35-50) Southeast of the centre, this is a functional, modern place near the theatre. The best rooms overlook place du Théâtre.

Hôtel du Lion d'Or (☎ 04 79 69 04 96; fax 04 79 96 93 20; 13 av de la Boisse; s €22-32, d €33-42) One of several hotels opposite the train station, with large, drab rooms and a busy brasserie adjoining the hotel.

Camping

There are several camping grounds outside Chambéry.

Alp'Aix (☎ 04 79 88 97 65; 20 blvd du Port-aux-Filles, Le Bourget du Lac; camping €11-15; ☯ Apr-Sep) A good choice just north of Chambéry. Take bus H from the place des Éléphants stop or the train station to the terminus, from where it's a 400m walk.

MID-RANGE

Hôtel Art (☎ 04 79 62 37 26; fax 04 79 62 49 98; 154 rue Sommeiller; d €44-51; [P]) Though the concrete façade looks uninspiring, this modern hotel has nicely furnished rooms with bath and TV, and is one of the city's better options.

Hôtel Les Princes (☎ 04 79 33 45 36; fax 04 79 70 31 47; 4 rue de Boigne; s/d €60/70; [P] [⚅]) Housed in one of the arcaded buildings close to the centre, this is by far the nicest hotel in Chambéry. Rooms are tastefully furnished and very comfortable.

Eating
RESTAURANTS

La Spagheteria (☎ 04 79 33 27 62; 43 rue St-Réal; pizza & pasta €5.95-10.35, menus €12 & €16; ☯ lunch & dinner Mon-Sat) Lively little Italian restaurant tucked away down a narrow alleyway, with flowers on the tables, plenty of Mediterranean atmosphere and a great range of pizzas and pastas.

Hôtel Savoyard (☎ 04 79 33 36 55; 35 place Monge; menus €12-21; ☯ lunch & dinner) The place to come in Chambéry for Savoyard specialities: its *tartiflette* (oven-cooked potatoes and *reblochon* cheese) and *gratin de crozets* (Savoyard pasta with cheese) are out of this world. It also has a children's *menu*. Try Mondeuse, Savoy's almost berry-like red wine.

La Table de Marie (☎ 04 79 85 99 76; 193 rue Croix d'Or; menus €13-18; ☯ dinner) An excellent little home-style restaurant at the end of busy place St-Léger, with Savoyard mains and an intimate, candle-lit atmosphere.

Le St-Réal (☎ 04 79 70 09 33; 10 rue St-Réal; mains €25-90; ☯ Mon-Sat) The best restaurant in Chambéry, with several menus exploring a varied range of Alpine and French cuisine. It's a little starchy, and expensive too, but the food is wonderful. The €90 *menu* includes seven courses.

CAFÉS

Au Fidèle Berger (☎ 04 79 33 06 37; rue de Boigne; ☯ Mon-Sat) This traditional *salon de thé* has exquisite chocolates and cakes.

Café de Lyon (place Monge; lunch menu €8.50-11; ☯ 7am-midnight Mon-Sat) This is a busy brasserie that overlooks a main thoroughfare of Chambéry.

SELF-CATERING

On Saturday morning a **food market** (place de Genève) is held. There's a **Monoprix supermarket** (place du 8 Mai 1945; ☯ 8.15am-7.30pm Mon-Sat). **Laiterie des Alpes** (88 rue d'Italie) stocks a wide variety of local cheeses and dairy products. Italian products are sold at **Pr.Al.It** (67 rue d'Italie).

Drinking

The huge open square of place St-Leger is the heart of Chambéry's night-time scene.

Café de l'Horloge (☎ 04 79 33 39 26; 107 place St-Léger) This great old-world café offers 200 brands of bottled beer, 30 brands of whisky and nine draught beers, as well as a fine selection of ice-cream sundaes.

Café du Théâtre (☎ 04 79 33 16 53; place du Théâtre) A lively café-bar with a large outside terrace in front of the Théâtre Charles Dullin, great for people-spotting and soaking up the Alpine sunshine.

Entertainment

Le Curial Cinéma (☎ 04 79 85 55 43; commalraux@wanadoo.fr; place François Mitterrand; tickets adult/concession €7/5) Part of the Éspace Malraux arts and exhibition complex located just south of rue de la République.

Getting There & Away
BUS

There's a **ticket office** (☯ 6.15am to 7pm) at **Chambéry bus station** (☎ 04 79 69 11 88; place de la Gare), south of the train station. From the station, there are buses to Aix-les-Bains (€2.80, 35 minutes, five daily), Annecy (€8.20, 50 minutes, seven daily) and Grenoble (€8.90, 1½ hours, 10 daily). There's one bus to Geneva and Nice every day, and five buses to Lyon St-Exupéry airport (€20, one hour).

TRAIN

The Chambéry **train station** (☎ 08 36 35 35 35; place de la Gare; ticket office ☯ 5.45am-8.30pm Mon-Sat, 6.45am-9.30pm Sun) is located at the end of rue Sommeiller.

There are major rail connections to Paris' Gare de Lyon (€76 by TGV via Lyon or Aix-les-Bains, 3¾ hours, 11 daily), Lyon (€14, 1¼ hours, 12 daily), Annecy (€7.90, one hour, 25 daily) and Grenoble (€9, one hour, 10 to 13 daily).

There are also trains up the Maurienne Valley to Modane (€13, one hour, nine daily), which continue to Turin, Rome and Naples in Italy.

Getting Around
BUS
The main hub for local buses is run by **STAC** (☎ 04 79 68 67 00; blvd de la Colonne), near Fontaine des Éléphants; there's also a **STAC information kiosk** (☎ 04 79 70 26 27; blvd de la Colonne; ⏰ 7.15am-7.15pm Mon-Fri, 8.30am-12.15pm & 2.30-6.30pm Sat). Many buses also stop at the train station. In general, they run Monday to Saturday until about 8pm. Single tickets cost €1 and a carnet of 10 costs €6.20.

AROUND CHAMBÉRY
Chambéry town is wedged in between two regional nature parks – **Parc Naturel Régional de Chartreuse** in the southwest and **Parc Naturel Régional du Massif des Bauges** to the northeast. Covering an area of 800 sq km, the Massif des Bauges offers some excellent hiking opportunities. The nature reserve in the north of the park is home to more than 600 chamois and mouflon.

The **main tourist office** (☎ 04 79 54 84 28; www.lesbauges.com; ⏰ 9am-noon & 2-6pm Mon-Sat) for the Massif des Bauges is in Le Châtelard. The **Chartreuse national park headquarters** (☎ 04 76 88 75 20; www.parc-chartreuse.net) is located in St-Pierre-de-Chartreuse.

From the thermal spa of **Aix-les-Bains**, 11km northwest of Chambéry, you can tour **Lac Bourget** – France's largest natural lake – by boat. Contact **Bateaux d'Aix-les-Bains** (☎ 04 79 88 92 09) at the Grand Port or **Aix-les-Bains tourist office** (☎ 04 79 88 68 00; www.aixlesbains.com; place Maurice Mollard; ⏰ 9am-6pm or 6.30pm daily Apr-Sep, Mon-Sat Oct, Nov & Mar, to 5.30pm Mon-Sat Dec-Feb), next to the port.

Albertville, 39km from Chambéry on the eastern park boundary, played host to the 1992 Winter Olympics. The Olympic highs and lows are colourfully told at the **Maison des Jeux Olympiques** (☎ 04 79 37 75 71; 11 rue Pargoud; ⏰ 9am-7pm Mon-Sat, 2-7pm Sun Jul & Aug, 9am-noon & 2-6pm Mon-Sat Sep-May).

MÉRIBEL
elevation 1450m
Méribel lies at the heart of one of the largest skiable areas in the world – the Trois Vallées (Three Valleys), which also includes the resorts of Courchevel and Belleville. The wealthy, purpose-built ski station, 42km southeast of Albertville and 88km from Annecy and Chambéry, was established in 1938 by Scotsman Colonel Peter Lindsay, and today remains one of the most 'British' resorts in France.

Despite the circus of pubs and shops that have cropped up to appease its predominantly British clientele, Méribel has just about managed to retain an Alpine village atmosphere, thanks to a decision made in the mid-1940s to use only traditional Savoyard building styles.

Information
Méribel's central **Maison du Tourisme** (www.meribel.net; ⏰ 9am-7pm winter, closed noon-3pm summer) houses the **tourist office** (☎ 04 79 08 60 01; info@meribel.net), the **accommodation service** (☎ 04 79 00 50 00; reservation@meribel.net) and the **ESF** (☎ 04 79 08 60 31; www.esf-meribel.com; ⏰ 9am-noon Mon-Fri), as well as a transport information counter.

The glossy French-English booklet *Méribel – Very Belle!* is available free from the tourist office and has a full listing of all the resort's facilities. Alternatively, consult www.meribel.net for the latest prices.

Activities
SKIING & SNOWBOARDING
One of the best skiing resorts in France, the vast area around Méribel can satisfy skiers of all levels. Above Val Thorens, there is summer skiing on the Glacier de Péclet.

Méribel Valley alone has 73 Alpine ski runs (150km), 47 ski lifts, two snowboarding parks, a slalom stadium, and two Olympic downhill runs built for the 1992 Winter Olympics. Many of these runs pass through Mottaret, a transit point 300m above the town, from where the valley's highest lift (2910m) climbs Mont Vallon.

The Trois Vallées pass (one/six days €41/198) allows use of all the area's lifts. Passes valid for more than six days also allow one day of skiing at Espace Killy, La Plagne, Les Arcs, Peisey Vallandry, Pralognan la

Vanoise or Les Saisies. Cheaper ski passes that only cover Méribel Valley are available (€34/161).

SUMMER ACTIVITIES

The *Guide des Sentiers* (available at the tourist office) details 20 marked walking trails in Méribel Valley. Particularly enticing is the botanical trail around Lake Tueda in the Réserve Naturelle de Tueda (Tueda Nature Reserve).

The **Bureau des Guides** (☎ 04 79 00 30 38; guides .meribel@laposte.net; ⊙ 9.30am-noon & 4-7pm Sun-Fri) inside the tourist office organises rock climbing, walking and mountain-biking expeditions. Contact **AN Rafting** (☎ 04 79 09 72 79; www.an-rafting.com in French; per day €95) about courses on white-water rafting.

Sleeping

Of the seven hotels built for the 1992 Olympics, all but two have three or four stars – one-star hotels became almost extinct in Méribel long ago. Accommodation prices are high, but studio and apartment prices are around €330 to €450 per week for two people. Contact the reservation service for more details.

The cheapest options are **Hôtel du Moulin** (☎ 04 79 00 52 23; fax 04 79 00 58 84; d €73) and **Hôtel Le Doron** (☎ 04 79 08 60 02; hotel-doron@wanadoo.fr; d from €92), both no-star hotels within reach of the town centre. At the other end of the scale is **Hôtel Mont Vallon** (☎ 04 79 00 44 00; montvallon -meribel@laposte.fr; r with half-board €150-700), one of Méribel's oldest and best hotels.

Getting There & Away

The four-lane A43, built for the 1992 Olympics, links Chambéry (88km northwest) with the nearest town, Moûtiers, 18km north of Méribel.

There are shuttle buses from Méribel to Geneva airport (€64, four hours) and Lyon St-Exupéry airport (€57, three to four hours). There's a **SNCF information bureau** (☎ 04 79 00 53 28) at the tourist office. The closest **train station** (☎ 08 36 35 35 35) is in Moûtiers from where there are connections to Paris (€59.30, 4½ hours) and Chambéry (€10.40, 1¼ hours).

Regional buses are operated by **Transavoie** (☎ 04 79 24 21 58) and run between Méribel and Moûtiers (€10.30, four to six Monday to Friday, 10 to 12 Saturday and Sunday).

VAL D'ISÈRE

pop 1738 / elevation 1850m

It's hip to be seen in Val d'Isère, a trendy resort in the upper Tarentaise Valley, 31km southeast of Bourg St-Maurice. Until the 1930s, Val d'Isère – a former hunting ground for the dukes of Savoy – was a remote village in the upper reaches of the eastern Alps. Today, Val d'Isère offers everything the discerning snow-junky could wish for – vast areas of groomed snow, plenty of off-piste thrills, modern lift systems allowing easy access to the slopes, a thriving commercial centre, and an animated après-ski scene.

On the other hand, if you're looking for a traditional Alpine atmosphere, then Val d'Isère is hardly ideal – the town's oldest building is the 11th-century church, with the rest of the village made up of Savoyard stone houses, chalet-style hotels and apartment blocks. But serious snow-goers rate Val d'Isère as one of the Alps' best all-round resorts, which accounts for the thousands of British, German and Scandinavian tourists who flock here every year, while French skiers head for quieter slopes.

Along with the high-altitude, purpose-built resort of **Tignes** (2100m), Val d'Isère and four other villages combine to form **Espace Killy** – named after local skiing legend Jean-Claude Killy, a triple gold medallist at the 1968 Winter Olympics.

The resort's most famous run is **La Face de Bellevarde**, a 63% black ski slope peaking at 2809m, used for the men's downhill skiing events in the 1992 Winter Olympics. Anyone daring or reckless enough to do it can. The Olympic gold medallist, Austrian Patrick Ortlieb, completed the enormous run in one minute 50.37 seconds.

Orientation

The majority of Val d'Isère is concentrated along the main central street, which runs directly on from the D902 into town. The bus station is at the bottom of the village, while most of the bars, restaurants and hotels are in the centre. The nearby resorts of Tignes and Val Claret are reached by the twisting D87, which branches off the main road just before the Lac du Chevril.

Information

The **tourist office** (☎ 04 79 06 06 60; www.valdisere .com; place Jacques Mouflier; ⊙ 8.30am-7.30pm Sun-Fri,

8.30am-8pm Sat) is in the village centre and the Bureau des Guides has a desk inside during summer. The **Val Hôtel Accommodation Service** (☎ 04 79 06 18 90; valhotel@valdisere.com) makes bookings for four days and over.

There are ATMs in the village and a couple of seasonal exchange offices.

Activities
WINTER ACTIVITIES
Espace Killy offers some of the best skiing in the country between 1550m and 3450m. Ski touring is also excellent, especially in the Parc National de la Vanoise. The snowboarders' Snowspace Park in La Deille has a half-pipe, tables, gaps, quarter-pipes, and kicker ramps, while the runs around Tignes are popular with both snowboarders and skiers. In July and August you can ski on the glacier.

Val d'Isère has no less than 11 ski schools and many more independent instructors. The **ESF** (☎ 04 79 06 02 34; esf.valdisere@wanadoo .fr; ☼ 8.30am-7pm) is housed in a large building off place Jacques Mouflier. Nearby **Misty Fly Snowboard School** (☎ 04 79 40 08 74; lionel .surf@infonie.fr; place Jacques Mouflier) specialises in snowboarding while **Alpine Experience** (☎ 04 79 06 28 81; www.alpineexperience.com) runs courses in off-piste skiing.

During special periods, Espace Killy ski passes (one/six days €39/187) include one day's skiing in La Plagne, Les Arcs, Les Trois Vallées or Valmorel.

Heli-skiing, ice diving, ice climbing, snow-shoeing, snowmobiling and husky-drawn sledge rides are some of the more unusual activities on offer in Val d'Isère. The tourist office has full details.

SUMMER ACTIVITIES
One of the best walks from Val d'Isère is to the village of Tignes along the Gorges de la Daille or the high road along Vallon de la Tovière. Other walks include the classic route across the high mountain pass of Col de l'Iseran, or the trek to the Glacier des Sources d'Isère, but there are many more trails in the nearby Parc National de la Vanoise.

The valleys and trails from Val d'Isère into the Vanoise National Park offer many possibilities for mountain biking and fishing. The Bureau des Guides organises, among other things, visits to a local cheese farm and Alpine bird-watching treks. **Safaris Vanoise** (☎ 04 79 06 00 03; www.valgliss.com in French)

organises animal photography and filming expeditions. The ESF runs *parapente* (paragliding) lessons in summer.

Sleeping
Accommodation in Val d'Isère is geared towards package skiers, which makes independent travelling expensive. Advance bookings are essential and can be made through Val Hôtel Accommodation Service (left).

Apartments, ranging from private short-term lets to purpose-built apartment blocks, are more accommodating to a range of budgets. Val Hôtel Accommodation Service is the best place to find out what's available. Two-person apartments in the low/high season start at €190/330 per week, but prices vary widely so shop around.

There are really no budget hotels in Val d'Isère, so unless you plan well ahead, accommodation is likely to take a major bite out of your budget.

MID-RANGE
Hôtel l'Avancher (☎ 04 79 06 02 00; route Fornet; d with half-board €77-100; ☼ usually closed summer; P) One of several hotels on the more affordable east side of town. The alpine chalet-style building looks just the ticket, especially when it's covered in snow and icicles are hanging from the eaves.

Hôtel Les Chardons (☎ 04 79 06 00 15; www .hotel-les-chardons.com; d €91-124, with half-board €98-142; P) Twenty-seven unfussy rooms in an attractive timber-clad building a short walk from the town centre.

Relais du Ski (☎ 04 79 06 02 06; fax 04 79 41 10 64; d winter €57-65, summer €50-58) An affordable hotel with nine basic double rooms. The in-house restaurant is also good, with an *Assiette Montagnarde* for €13, which includes local cheeses and cold meats.

TOP END
If you feel like doing Val d'Isère in style, there are plenty of top-end hotels to choose from. Try the refurbished **Hôtel Christiania** (☎ 04 79 06 08 25; www.hotel-christiania.com; d €169-277; P ✸ ♨) with its roaring fireplace, or the lavish **Hôtel Tsanteleina** (☎ 04 79 06 12 13; www.hoteltsanteleina.com; d €103-243; P ✸).

Eating
Eating in Val d'Isère is a hit-and-miss affair. With 70 restaurants in the village catering

---

THE DISAPPEARING LAKE

Look out for Lac du Chevril on your right as you approach Val d'Isère. The lake and dam were created amid much controversy between 1947 and 1955 by the French Electricity company EDF to generate hydroelectric power. The village of Tignes-le-Lac, once home to 500 people, was abandoned as a result of the project and now lies at the bottom of the lake. You can hardly miss Lac du Chevril – that is, if it's there…

Every 10 years the EDF drain the lake to carry out dam maintenance, leaving a huge hole where the lake used to be. In the mud you can still spot the remains of the doomed Tignes-le-Lac – houses, tree trunks and even an old car, and on the southern side the remains of a couple of bridges. Sightseers flock to the muddy floor of Lac du Chevril to wander among the debris of this bizarre spectacle and a solemn commemorative Mass is held on the lake bed before it is refilled, a process that takes two months. The lake was last emptied in March 2000 and won't be emptied again until 2010.

---

to a largely English clientele, the quality of cuisine is varied and unpredictable. Better deals are to be had opting for half- or full-board in your hotel.

Nonetheless, try the central **Samovar** (☎ 04 79 06 13 51; mains €12-20) for French and Savoyard cuisine, or **Bananas** (☎ 04 79 06 04 23; mains €8-15), near the bottom of the Olympic run, for a selection of Tex-Mex food.

SELF-CATERING
At the eastern end of the village is a **Spar supermarket** (☒ 8am-noon & 2-7pm) with a well-stocked wine cellar, cheese and meat counter and plenty of DIY meal items.

Drinking
Val d'Isère has gained a reputation as one of the biggest party towns in the Alps, and there are loads of bars in the village.

Dick's Tea Bar (☎ 04 79 06 14 87; www.dicksteabar.com; admission €12, free before 11.30pm; ☒ 3pm-4am) The Val d'Isère outpost of the Alpine nightclub chain. If you've been to any of the others – or to a student night in a British nightclub – you'll know what to expect.

Café Face (☎ 04 79 06 29 80) Opposite Dick's, this chic après-ski bar is something of an institution in Val d'Isère, boasting moody lighting, stylish retro furniture and enough cocktails to keep you going all season.

Warm'Up Cafés (☎ 04 79 06 27 00; ☒ from 10am) A big, pub-style drinking hole on the main street, with live music, lots of tables and a large central bar.

Getting There & Away
Autocars Martin (☎ 04 79 06 00 42; ☒ 9.15am-12.30pm & 1.15-7pm) runs four buses daily to Val

d'Isère and Tignes (€10.50, 20 to 30 minutes) from Bourg St-Maurice, the nearest train station. There is a **SNCF counter** (☒ 9am-noon & 3-7pm) here too.

Satobus-Alpes (☎ 04 37 25 52 55) operates four buses every day (three on Sunday) from Val d'Isère to Lyon St-Exupéry airport via Bourg St-Maurice (€50, three to four hours). The service runs only from mid-December to April and on Saturday in July and August.

Getting Around
Val d'Isère is served by free buses operating around the resort. The *train rouge* (red train), a network of 23 shuttle buses, connects Val d'Isère with Tignes and other villages, including Les Boisses and the Grand Motte funicular. Timetables are posted at bus stops.

PARC NATIONAL DE LA VANOISE
A wild mix of high mountains, steep valleys and vast glaciers, the Parc National de la Vanoise was declared the country's first national park in 1963. It covers 530 sq km between the Tarentaise Valley to the north and the Maurienne Valley to the south. The park is a hiker's heaven, with 500km of waymarked trails (including the GR5 and GR55) and 42 remote *refuges* for overnight shelter. The scenery is spectacular – snowcapped peaks mirrored in icy lakes are only just the start of what you can expect to see here. Marmots and chamois, as well as France's largest colony of Alpine ibex, graze free and undisturbed among the larch trees, and above them all reigns the mighty eagle.

A SHAGGY GOAT STORY

The animal most synonymous with the French Alps is without a doubt the Alpine ibex, a hardy mountain goat identifiable by its huge, curly horns and fondness for sickeningly high mountain ledges. In the 16th century, the Alps were full of ibex (*bouquetin* in French), but unfortunately their extravagant horns – which can measure one metre in length and weigh over five kilograms – became the must-have item for every self-respecting gentleman's trophy cabinet in the 19th century, and within a few years the animals had been hunted to the brink of extinction. Following lengthy conservation campaigns and the foundation of national reserves such as the Parc National de la Vanoise, populations have steadily recovered. But don't be surprised if you don't see one – thankfully, the ibex seems to have learned that humans can be bad for its health.

Orientation

The park is divided into two main areas: the *zone central* (central zone), which is highly protected and is bordered by five designated nature reserves, and the *zone périphérique* (peripheral zone), where the nearest villages and tourist centres to the park are located. The most convenient bases are along the southern edge of the park in Bonneval-sur-Arc and Lanslebourg, and to the southwest around Modane and Saint-André.

Information

The Parc National de la Vanoise Office (p513) in Chambéry has information on the park and a list of *refuges*. To book *refuges* in June, July or August call ☎ 04 79 08 71 49. The park newspaper, *Estive*, contains a full listing of all *refuges* complete with direct contact numbers, and is available free from tourist offices.

Park information is available at the **Tourist Office** (☎ 04 79 05 95 95; www.bonneval-sur-arc .com; ☼ 9am-noon & 2-6.30pm Mon-Sat in season, to 6pm rest of year) in Bonneval-sur-Arc and **Maison du Val Cénis** (☎ 04 79 05 23 66; www.valcenis.com; ☼ 9am-noon & 3-7pm) in Lanslebourg. A good regional map is the 1:50,000-scale IGN map *Parc de la Vanoise* (No 11).

Activities

SKIING

Lanslebourg and Bonneval-sur-Arc are popular cross-country skiing resorts. Both offer limited Alpine skiing as well. The **ESF** (☎ 04 79 05 95 70) is inside the Bonneval-sur-Arc tourist office.

In summer it's possible to ski on the Grand Pissaillas glacier at Col de l'Iseran, 23km northeast of Lanslebourg. The best skiing is between March and early May.

WALKING

Walkers have a network of small trails to choose from – the Maison du Val Cénis (see Information) has a trails booklet. The **Bureau des Guides** (☎ 04 79 05 95 70) inside Bonneval-sur-Arc tourist office and **Guide de Haute-Montagne** (☎ 04 79 05 94 74) run guided walks and climbs.

The trail from Lanslebourg up to the Turra Fort (2500m), from where there are great views over the Lac du Mont Cénis, generally takes about three hours. To really take in the region, you can follow all or part of Le Grand Tour de Haute Maurienne – a hike of five days or more around the upper reaches of the valley. There are 15 *refuges* or *gîtes d'étape* en route.

The GR5 and GR55 pass through the park and there are also trails linked to the Écrins National Park to the south and Grand Paradiso National Park in Italy. Tracks are usually passable from June to October.

Sleeping

Auberge de Jeunesse Hameau des Champs (☎ 04 79 05 90 96; fax 04 79 05 82 52; dm €7.30, breakfast €2.90; ☼ mid-Dec–mid-Sep), which is located in the hamlet of Les Champs, is on the eastern side of Lanslevillard.

There are five hotels in Lanslebourg, including **Hôtel La Vieille Poste** (☎ 04 79 05 93 47; fax 04 79 05 86 85; d €40-44; ☼ closed mid-Apr–Jun & Nov-Jan). This warm and welcoming two-star place is on the main road through town.

Hôtel La Bergerie (☎ 04 79 05 94 97; fax 04 79 05 93 24; d €48; ☼ closed May–mid-Jun & Oct–mid-Dec) is in pretty Bonneval-sur-Arc.

Camping Les Balmasses (☎ 04 79 05 82 83; ☼ Jun-Sep) is in Lanslebourg.

Getting There & Away

The trains serving the valley leave from Chambéry and run as far as the **Modane train**

station (☎ 08 36 35 35 35), 23km southwest of Lanslebourg.

From Modane, **Transavoie buses** (☎ 04 79 05 01 32) go to Lanslebourg (€9.30, one hour). Once daily (in the evening) they continue to Bessans and Bonneval-sur-Arc. In winter a shuttle bus runs several times daily between Lanslebourg and Bonneval-sur-Arc.

DAUPHINÉ

Dauphiné, which encompasses the territories south and southwest of Savoy, stretches from the River Rhône in the west to the Italian border in the east. It includes the city of Grenoble and, a little further east, the mountainous Parc National des Écrins. The gentler terrain of the western part of Dauphiné is typified by the Parc Naturel Régional du Vercors, much loved by cross-country skiers. In the east, the town of Briançon stands guard on the Italian frontier.

History

The area now known as Dauphiné was first inhabited by the Celts and the Romans. By the 11th century it was under the rule of Guigues I, the count of Albon, whose great-grandson Guigues IV (ruled 1133–42) was the first count to bear the name of 'dauphin'. By the end of the 13th century, the name 'dauphin' had become a title and the fiefs held by the region's ruling house, La Tour du Pin, were known collectively as Dauphiné. The rulers of Dauphiné continued to expand their territories, which gave them control of all the passes through the southern Alps.

In 1339 Humbert II established a university at Grenoble. A decade later, lacking money and a successor, he sold Dauphiné to the French king, Charles V, who started the tradition whereby the eldest son of the king of France (the crown prince) ruled Dauphiné and bore the title 'dauphin'. The region was annexed to France by Charles VII in 1457.

GRENOBLE
pop 156,000

The elegant, modern city of Grenoble is the intellectual and economic capital of the Alps. Spectacularly sited in a broad valley surrounded by snow-capped mountains – the Chartreuse to the north, the Vercors to the southwest and the Italian Alps to the east – the city is also the centre of the Dauphiné region. The modern shops, broad boulevards and varied architecture make it a great place to spend a few days soaking up the big-city atmosphere.

Grenoble gained a reputation for progress in the 1960s, when the Socialist Hubert Dubedout served as mayor. People from all over France were attracted by the city's social, artistic and technological innovations. The large university serves a student body of 50,000 and has a thriving foreign student exchange programme. Grenoble also has important facilities for nuclear and microelectronic research.

The city hosts a jazz festival in March, a rock festival in April, and a theatre festival in June and July. Given Grenoble is the capital of Dauphiné, this is *the* place to sample the popular French dish *gratin dauphinois* (finely-sliced potatoes cooked with milk and Gruyère cheese). *Noix de Grenoble* (a sweet walnut candy) and *gâteau aux noix* (walnut cake) are the local specialities for those with a sweet tooth.

Orientation

Grenoble can be a difficult city to negotiate, especially from behind the wheel, thanks to the bewildering one-way system. The old city is centred around place Grenette and place Notre Dame, both about 1km east of the train and bus stations. The main university campus is a couple of kilometres east of the old centre on the southern side of the River Isère.

Information
BOOKSHOPS
Arthaud (☎ 04 76 42 49 81; 23 Grande Rue; ◷ 10.30am-7pm Mon, 9.30am-7pm Tue-Sat) The best bookshop in Grenoble for new titles, although mostly French.

Librairie le Sphinx (☎ 04 76 44 55 08; genevieve .journault@wanadoo.fr; 6 place Notre Dame; ◷ noon-8.30pm Mon-Fri, Sat noon-7pm) A wonderful, chaotic place above the Tonneau de Diogène café that specialises in French philosophy books.

EMERGENCY
Duty Pharmacy (☎ 04 76 63 42 55)
Grenoble University Hospital (☎ 04 76 76 75 75; www.chu-grenoble.fr in French) There are two main sites: Hôpital Nord La Tronche and Hôpital Sud.
Police Station (☎ 04 76 69 48 00; 21 av Leon Blum)

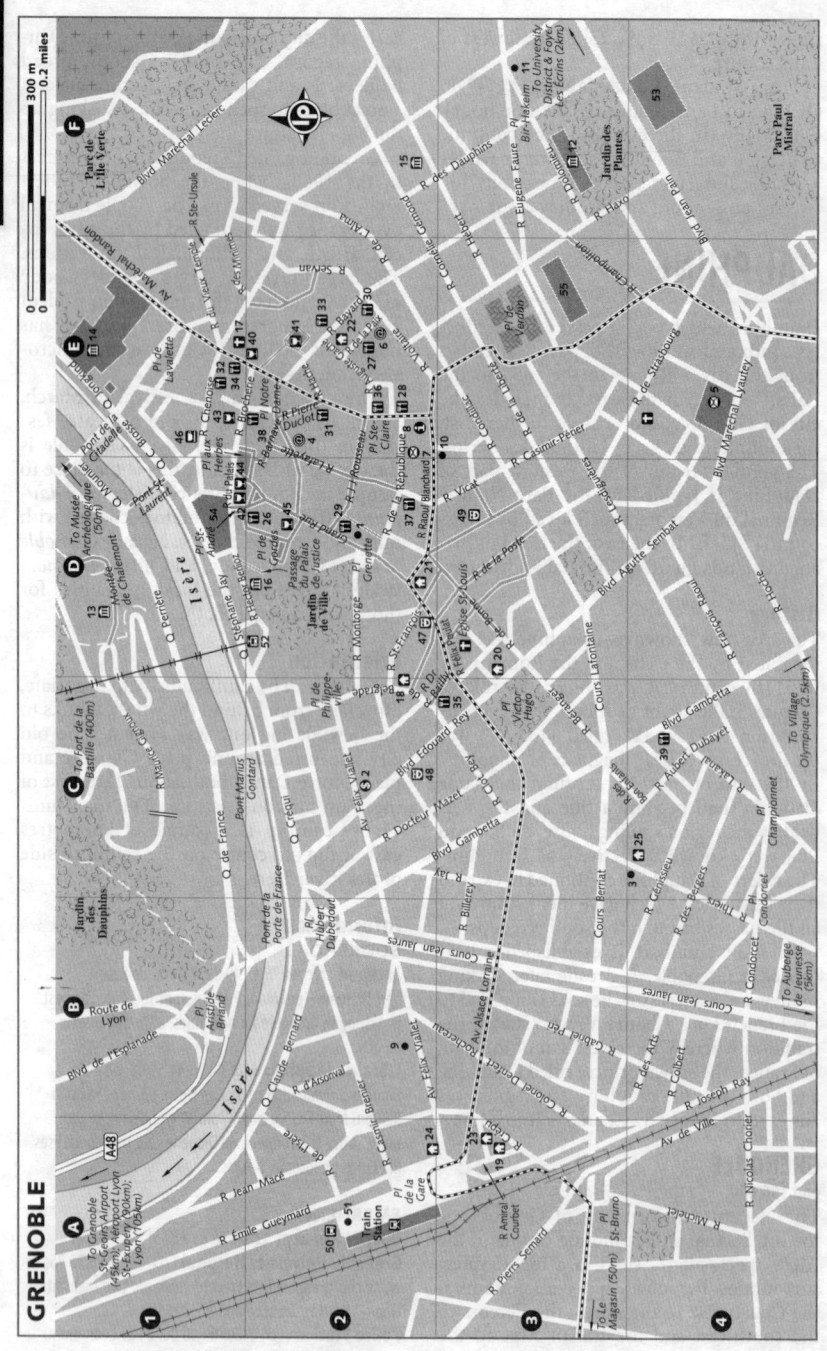

GRENOBLE

INTERNET ACCESS

Le New Age Cyber Café (☎ 04 76 51 94 43; 1 rue Bernave; per 15min/hr €2/3.50; ⊗ 8am-10pm Mon-Sat, 10am-9pm Sun) Cheap access noon-2pm.

Neptune Internet Services (☎ 04 76 63 94 18; salle -Internet@neptune.fr; 2 rue de la Paix; per 15min/hr €2/3.50, discounts noon-2pm & 7-9pm; ⊗ 9am-9pm Mon-Fri, 9am-8pm Sat, 1-8pm Sun) WiFi and laptop connection points.

INTERNET RESOURCES

www.grenoble-isere.info Official site for the Grenoble tourist office.

LAUNDRY

Lavomatique (14 rue Thiers; ⊗ 7am-10pm) Opposite Hôtel Victoria.

MEDIA

Le Petit Bulletin Published every Wednesday. Free listings guide to the week's events.

MONEY

ATMs are found at most main banks.

Banque de France (cnr blvd Édouard Rey & av Félix Viallet; ⊗ 8.45am-12.15pm & 1.30-3.30pm Mon-Fri) Usually changes money at a good rate.

POST

Post Office (7 blvd Maréchal Lyautey; ⊗ 8am-6.45pm Mon-Fri, until noon Sat).

Post Office Branch (rue de la République; ⊗ 8am-6.30pm Tue-Sat) Next to the tourist office.

TOURIST INFORMATION

Cargo Kiosk (⊗ 1-6.30pm Tue-Sat) For events tickets.

SNCF Counter (⊗ 8.30am-6.30pm Mon-Fri, 9am-6pm Sat) For train information.

TAG Office (⊗ 8.30am-6.30pm Mon-Fri, 9am-6pm Sat) For local bus information.

Tourist Office (☎ 04 76 42 41 41; www.grenoble-isere .info; 14 rue de la République; ⊗ 9am-6.30pm Mon-Sat, 10am-1pm Sun, longer hours in summer) Inside the large purpose-built Maison du Tourisme on rue de la République.

Sights
FORT DE LA BASTILLE

Looming above the old city on the northern side of the River Isère, the **Fort de la Bastille** is Grenoble's best known landmark. Constructed during the 16th century (and expanded in the 19th) to control the approaches to the city, the stronghold has long been a focus of military and political action.

These days, its strategic importance may have waned, but the views are as spectacular as ever, with vast mountains on every side, the bridges and grey waters of the Isère river below, and the wide streets of modern Grenoble stretching out into the south. On clear days, you can even catch a glimpse of Mont Blanc, northeast along the jagged Grésivaudan valley. Three viewpoint indicators – one west of the *téléphérique* station, the other two on the roof of the building just to the east – explain the surrounding vistas, and a sign near the disused Mont Jalla chairlift indicates nearby hiking trails.

To get to the fort, a **téléphérique** (☎ 04 76 44 33 65; adult/student one way €3.80/3, return €5.50/4.40; ⊗ 10.45am-6.30pm Nov-Feb, 9.30am-11.45pm Mar-May, 9.15-12.15am Jun-Aug) leaves from quai Stéphane Jay between the Marius Gontard and St-Laurent bridges. The rapid ascent in egg-shaped pods, which climb 264m from the quay over the swift waters of the river, is almost more fun than the fort itself. Unsurprisingly, it gets crowded in summer – leave early to avoid the worst queues.

The *téléphérique* hours vary on Sundays and in high season – check the time for the last return car before you leave, as it's a long walk back to town if you miss it. A number of trails and a road lead up the hillside to the fort.

MUSEUMS

Dauphiné's foremost city has no shortage of excellent museums, ranging from world-renowned arts collections to exhibits on local culture and history.

Several of Grenoble's museums offer free entry. The **MultiPass Grenoble** (per day €10) is also a good deal. It's available from the tourist office and includes admission to one of the city's (paying) museums or Le Magasin arts centre (below), a return ticket on the Grenoble–Bastille *téléphérique*, guided city tour, day pass for Grenoble's public transport, and a parking ticket worth €2 for the Museum or Verdun car parks.

Musée de Grenoble

The sleek glass and steel exterior of Grenoble's boldest museum stands at the southern end of place Notre Dame. Also known as the Musée des Beaux-Arts, **Musée de Grenoble** (☎ 04 76 63 44 44; 5 place de Lavalette; www.museede grenoble.fr; adult/student €5/2; ☉ 10am-6.30pm, closed Tue) is renowned for its distinguished modern collection, including various works by famous artists Chagall, Matisse, Modigliani, Monet, Picasso, Pissaro, Gauguin among others. There are 1½-hour guided **tours** (adult €3; ☉ Sat & Sun 3pm) available.

Musée d'Histoire Naturelle

Alpine flora and fauna, a 'carnival of insects' and an aquarium are housed in the **Musée d'Histoire Naturelle** (Museum of Natural History; ☎ 04 76 44 05 35; 1 rue Dolomieu; adult/student €2.20/1.50; ☉ 9.30am-noon & 1.30-5.30pm Mon-Fri, 2-6pm Sat & Sun), overlooking the Jardin des Plantes. The grounds also include a botanical garden.

Musée Dauphinois

The **Musée Dauphinois** (☎ 04 76 85 19 01; www .musee-dauphinois.fr in French; 30 rue Maurice Gignoux; ☉ 10am-7pm Wed-Mon May-Oct, until 6pm Nov-Apr) documents the cultures, crafts and traditions of Alpine life. The museum occupies a beautiful 17th-century convent, nestled at the foot of the hill below Fort de la Bastille. From the city centre, it is most easily reached by the Pont St-Laurent footbridge.

East of the museum, also in the historic St-Laurent quarter, is **Musée Archéologique** (☎ 04 76 44 78 68; www.musee-archeologique-grenoble .com in French; ☉ 9am-6pm Wed-Mon), housed in a 12th-century church.

Musée de l'Ancien Évêché

The **Notre Dame and St-Hugues Cathedral** (place Notre Dame) and the adjoining 14th-century **Bishop's Palace** (☎ 04 76 03 15 25; www.ancien -eveche-isere.com in French; 2 rue Très Cloîtres; admission free; ☉ 9am-6pm Mon-Sat except Tue, 10am-7pm Sun) have had complete facelifts and now contain three museums: the **crypte archéologique**, with Roman walls and a baptistery dating from the 4th to 10th centuries; the **Musée d'Art Sacré**, which contains liturgical and religious objects; and the **Centre Jean Achard**, with exhibits of art from the Dauphiné region.

Musée de la Résistance et de la Déportation de l'Isère

This moving **Musée de la Résistance et de la Déportation de l'Isère** (☎ 04 76 42 38 53; 14 rue Hébert; admission free; ☉ 9am-7pm Wed-Mon Jun-Aug, 9am-noon & 2-6pm Wed-Mon, from 10am Sun Sep-May) examines the deportation of Jews and other 'undesirables' from Grenoble to Nazi camps during WWII, and explores the role of the Vercors region in the French Resistance. Captions are in French, English and German.

LE MAGASIN

Grenoble has lots of art galleries and exhibition places, but the most impressive (and not just in terms of size) is **Le Magasin** (the Shop; ☎ 04 76 21 95 84; www.magasin-cnac .org in French; 155 cours Berriat; adult/concession €3.50/2), one of Europe's leading centres of contemporary art, created in 1986 in a vast warehouse built by employees of Gustave Eiffel. There are two exhibition areas – 'The Rue', a permanent 1000 sq m space with a huge glass roof, and 'The Galleries', a flexible space of about 900 sq m. Exhibitions change almost daily – call to find out the latest news and opening hours. Charles Saatchi would be green with envy.

Musée Stendhal

Stendhal, author of *Le Rouge et le Noir* (The Red and the Black), was born in Grenoble in 1783. The tourist office distributes a free brochure called *Route Historique – Stendhal*, which traces the life and works of the author from his birthplace to the outlying villages where he found inspiration. **Musée Stendhal** (☎ 04 76 54 44 14; 1 rue Hector Berlioz; ☺ 9am-noon & 2-6pm Tue-Sat), overlooks the formal Jardin de Ville, only opens in the afternoon in winter.

Activities

SKIING

The tourist office has comprehensive information, including accommodation lists, for Grenoble and all of its surrounding ski resorts.

WALKING

For information on outdoor activities, head for the **Maison de la Montagne** (☎ 08 25 82 55 88; www.grenoble-montagne.com in French; 3 rue Raoul Blanchard). All the main organisations are housed under one roof. The **Bureau Info-Montagne** (☎ 04 76 42 45 90; fax 04 76 42 87 08; ☺ 9am-noon & 2-6pm Mon-Fri, 10am-1pm & 2-6pm Sat) can give advice on just about every imaginable mountain activity except skiing. It sells hiking maps and has information on *gîtes d'étape* and *refuges*. The **Bureau des Guides de Grenoble** (☎ 04 38 37 01 71; www .guide-grenoble.com in French; ☺ 9am-noon & 1-6pm; Mon afternoon-Sat) and the **Accompagnateurs en Montagne Alpes-Dauphiné** both provide guiding services in the Dauphiné region and further afield.

The **Club Alpin Français** (CAF; ☎ 04 76 87 03 73; 32 av Félix Viallet; www.clubalpin-grenoble.com in French; ☺ 2-6pm Tue-Wed, 2-8pm Thu-Fri) manages *refuges* and organises walking, mountain-biking and skiing trips. Other walking clubs include **Mountain Wilderness** (☎ 04 76 84 54 42; fax 04 76 84 54 44; 5 place Bir-Hakeim) in the Maison de la Nature et de l'Environnement.

Festivals & Events

Grenoble Jazz Festival (☎ 04 76 51 65 32; www .jazzgrenoble.com in French; 3-/5-night pass €42/75) has been bringing a wide selection of jazz greats and outdoor concerts to Grenoble for the last 30 years. The festival is held annually in March; full details are available from the tourist office or the festival website.

Sleeping

Grenoble's hotels are expensive, but compared to the sky-high prices of nearby ski resorts, many offer good value. Special deals are available at certain hotels through the '**Bon Weekend en Ville' scheme** (www.bon-week-end -en-villes.com). In general, if you reserve your room at a participating hotel in advance, and stay for two nights, arriving on a Friday or Saturday, the second night is free. Make sure you receive confirmation before arrival.

Parking in Grenoble can often be a problem. Few hotels have private garages, which means you'll have to factor in the cost of a city car park (usually between €6 to €10 for 24 hours). Some hotels have special arrangements with local car parks – ask when you book your room.

BUDGET

Auberge de Jeunesse (☎ 04 76 09 33 52; grenoble@fuaj .org; 10 av du Grésivaudan; B&B €12; reception ☺ 7.30am-11pm) Five kilometres south of the train station in the Echirolles district. From Cours Jean Jaurès, take bus No 1 to the Quinzaine stop (look for the Casino supermarket).

Hôtel de l'Europe (☎ 04 76 46 16 94; www.hotel europe.fr; 22 place Grenette; s €26-53, d €28-59) One of the city's oldest establishments, housed in a classic Grenoblois building above place Grenette. It's a great value hotel, with big rooms and a fabulous spiral staircase to the top floor. The front rooms have balconies offering views of Fort Bastille and the mountains beyond.

Hôtel du Moucherotte (☎ 04 76 54 61 40; fax 04 76 44 62 52; 1 rue Auguste Gaché; s/d from €28/30) The murky Moucherotte is one of the cheapest options near the city centre. Despite its dingy exterior, the rooms are clean but basic in the extreme.

Hôtel Alizé (☎ 04 76 43 12 91; fax 04 76 47 62 79; 1 rue Amiral Courbet; s/d €31/36, tr €44-48) In the area near the train station, this hotel is small, simple and very cheap, which makes it popular – book in advance if you can.

Hôtel Victoria (☎ 04 76 46 06 36; 17 rue Thiers; r with shower from €32-36; ☺ Sep-Jul; P) Located in the place Condorcet area, this is the best of the bunch – tucked away in a quiet courtyard, with old-fashioned floral décor and friendly owners. The lively place Condorcet area has lots of low-rent restaurants and scruffy bars.

MID-RANGE

The following hotels are in the city centre.

Hôtel Angleterre (☎ 04 76 87 37 21; www.hotel -angleterre.fr; 5 place Victor Hugo; d €91-155) The pick of several three-star hotels in the area, thanks to its luxurious rooms and a great location opposite the fountain-adorned place Victor Hugo. It accepts reservations for 'Bon-Weekend' packages.

Hôtel Acacia (☎ 04 76 87 00 71; fax 04 76 47 21 25; 13 rue de Belgrade; s/d/tw €36/49/56) As boxy and boring as they come, but the city-centre position is ideal. If you've ever stayed in a city motel you'll know what to expect. Accepts 'Bon-Weekend' reservations.

The following hotels are in the area around the train station.

Hôtel Lux (☎ 04 76 46 41 89; www.hotel-lux.com in French; 6 rue Crépu; s/d/tw €41/44/47) A tidy, friendly two-star place on a quiet back street near the station. It looks utilitarian from the outside, but the rooms are pleasant and there's a car park close by.

Hôtel Suisse et Bordeaux (☎ 04 76 47 55 87; www .hotel-sb-grenoble.com; 6 place de la Gare; s/d/tr €41/48/58) One of three huge hotels facing the station. In its heyday it must have been a fine establishment, with big balconies and lavish décor; these days it's a little run-down, but still nicer than some hotels nearby.

Eating

Eating out in style is easy in Grenoble. The main food thoroughfares are around place Grenette, place Notre Dame, place St-André and rue Brocherie, but there are interesting places scattered all over the city.

RESTAURANTS

Le Mal Assis (☎ 04 76 54 75 93; 9 rue Bayard; evening menu €21; ☽ lunch & dinner Tue-Sat) A cosy, upmarket restaurant serving delicious *cuisine bourgeoise*. The surrounding streets are packed with antique shops and art galleries, so expect a smart, cultured crowd. Reservations are recommended.

La Panse (☎ 04 76 54 09 54; 7 rue de la Paix; lunch menu €11, all-day menu €13; ☽ lunch & dinner Mon-Sat) A relaxed option, popular with the architects and media types who have offices in this quarter of the city. The lunchtime and all-day menus offer traditional dishes with a contemporary twist.

La Voile Blanche (☎ 04 76 44 22 62; 4 rue Pierre Duclot; menus €15-35; ☽ closed Mon & dinner Sun) Recommended by readers and locals alike. The restaurant has been refurbished (and has changed its name) but still offers the same seasonal cuisine, with seafood and local dishes a speciality. The €15 menu includes two courses, wine and coffee.

La Mère Ticket (☎ 04 76 44 45 40; 13 rue Jean-Jacques Rousseau; lunch menu €11; ☽ lunch & 8-11pm Mon-Sat) A tiny, traditional French restaurant tucked away on a busy shopping street. The homely country cooking is fantastic value, especially at lunchtime. The delicious *poulet aux écrevisses* (chicken with crayfish) and *gratin dauphinois* come highly recommended.

Restaurant des Montagnes (☎ 04 76 15 20 72; 5 rue Brocherie; salads from €5.90, fondue per person €12.50-21; ☽ 7pm-midnight Sep-Jun) Grenoble's premier place for fondue and *tartiflette*. This is a restaurant where waistline worries should be left at the door. Loosen your belt and order one of the 13 kinds of sumptuous fondue instead. You need a minimum of two people for the fondue.

Les Archers (☎ 04 76 46 27 76; 2 rue Docteur Bailly; mains €8-15; ☽ 11am-1am) A brasserie with great outside seating in summer. Fish and seafood are especially good, with delicacies including pan-fried trout and grilled sea bass.

Ciao a Te (☎ 04 76 42 54 41; 2 rue de la Paix; salads from €10; ☽ Tue-Sat) A vibrant Italian restaurant that serves great pasta. If you're feeling hungry, try the filling, delicious cannelloni.

L'Amphitryon (☎ 04 76 51 38 07; 9 rue Chenoise; couscous €9-13; ☽ Mon-Sat) With its stark, minimalist décor, this is one of Grenoble's funkiest restaurants, serving great, generous couscous and North African cuisine.

CAFÉS

Le Tonneau de Diogène (☎ 04 76 42 38 40; 6 place Notre Dame; menu from €6, plat du jour €10; ☽ 8.30am-1am) Grenoble's best known philo-café, a cramped, wonderfully atmospheric place, decked out with polished wood, leather booths, and lots of tightly packed tables. If you feel like strutting your philosophical stuff, discussions are usually held on Thursday evenings.

Café de la Table Ronde (☎ 04 76 44 51 41; 7 place St-André; lunch menu €10, dinner €10-28; ☽ 7am-midnight Mon-Sat) Another of Grenoble's most famous cafés. The establishment, which dates from 1739, was a favoured haunt of Stendhal and Rousseau, and the old-world atmosphere and period furnishings don't seem to have changed much since they were around. In summer, place St-André is one of the city's liveliest squares, especially after dark.

Subway (☎ 04 76 87 31 67; cnr rue Lakanal & blvd Gambetta; salads €3.50-7.60; ☾ 10am-1am Mon-Sat, from 5pm Sat & Sun) The best breakfast option in town for late risers. The sandwiches are cheap and generous, the beer is cold, and there's usually reggae, dub or rock on the stereo – which makes this a popular student hangout by night.

La Forêt Noire (☎ 04 76 44 54 98; 5 rue Alphand; cakes €2-6, mains €6-12) A Grenoble institution for afternoon tea. The café serves a lavish range of cakes, tarts and *viennoiseries*, as well as light meals. Look no further for something sweet and sticky.

SELF-CATERING

Les Halles Ste-Claire (place Ste-Claire; ☾ 6am-1pm Tue-Sun) is Grenoble's lovely old covered market. Even if you're not going there to shop, the market atmosphere is worth investigating. There's also a busy **food market** (place Ste-Claire; ☾ Wed-Mon).

The **Monoprix supermarket** (cnr rue de la République & rue Lafayette; ☾ 8.30am-7.30pm Mon-Sat) has a basement grocery section and a *boulangerie*. For cake fiends, patisseries can be found around place Notre Dame.

Drinking

Barberousse (☎ 04 76 57 14 53; 8 rue Hache; ☾ 5pm-1am) There are 33 sorts of aromatic rum fermenting in giant glass flasks behind the counter at Barberousse. Try downing a shot of cherry, apple, papaya or other fruit-flavoured liqueurs.

Bar 1900 (place Notre Dame; ☾ 5pm-1am) Right next door to the chiming clock-tower of the Notre Dame cathedral, this is an atmospheric little bar with a great outdoor terrace onto the square.

Le Twenty (☎ 04 76 51 13 74; 20 rue Chenoise; ☾ 11am-1am Mon-Sat) A funky bar in the heart of the old city with kitsch, colourful décor and an equally colourful management. The huge lunchtime platters have a national theme (Italian, Savoyard, Chinese etc) and are great value. By night, you can sample house-special Chartreuse cocktails in the company of a relaxed, friendly crowd.

Le Couche Tard (☎ 04 76 44 18 79; 1 rue du Palais; ☾ 4pm-1am) and **Le Saxo Pub** (☎ 04 76 51 06 01;

5 rue d'Agier; ☾ 6pm-2am) are two of Grenoble's popular late-night drinking spots, but there are loads more to discover – Rue Brocherie, place St-André, and the streets around rue Thiers are all good places for night-owls to explore.

Also worth a look are **Café Tamara** (☎ 04 76 63 85 88; 3 rue du Palais; ☾ 1pm-2am Mon-Sat, 2pm-1am Sun), a chic piano-bar with great coffee and cocktails, and **Chorus Café** (☎ 04 76 15 22 89; 8 rue Brocherie; ☾ 6pm-1am Tue-Sun), a fun place where the walls are covered with graffiti.

Entertainment

Grenoble's best art cinema is the seven-screen **La Nef** (☎ 04 76 46 53 25; 18 blvd Edouard Rey; ☾ from 7pm), which shows a great selection of art-house and independent films. For new releases, **Les 6 Rex** (☎ 08 92 68 00 31; 13 rue St-Jacques; ☾ from 7pm) is the most central.

As a thriving student city, Grenoble has lots of music venues. The best place to find out what's on is the huge **Fnac** (☎ 04 76 85 85 85; www.fnac.com in French; 4 rue Félix Poulet), just off place Grenette, which has an in-store ticket booking agency.

Getting There & Away

AIR

Domestic flights are handled by **Grenoble -St-Geoirs airport** (☎ 04 76 65 48 48), 45km north-west of Grenoble. International flights operate to/from **Lyon St-Exupéry airport** (☎ 08 26 80 08 26), 90km from the city off the A43 to Lyon.

BUS

The **bus station** (☎ 04 76 87 90 31; rue Émile Gueymard; ☾ 6.30am-7pm Mon-Sat, 7.15am-7pm Sun) is next to the train station, and is the main terminus for several bus companies. **VFD** (☎ 08 20 83 38 33; www.vfd.fr in French; ☾ 8am-6pm Tue-Fri, 8am-noon & 1.30-4.30pm Sat & Mon) serves most Alpine destinations; tariffs are worked out on a zone system according to how far you travel. Destinations include Chambéry (€4.90, 1¾ hours), Chamrousse (€6, 1¼ hours), Bourg d'Oisans (€4.90, 50 minutes), Les Deux Alpes (€4.90, 1¾ hours) and the Vercors ski stations.

Intercars (☎ 04 76 46 19 77; www.intercars.fr in French; station office ☾ 9am-noon & 2-6pm Mon-Fri, 9am-noon & 2-5pm Sat) handles long-haul destinations including Berlin (€87, 21 hours), Munich (€72, 10 hours), Rome (€48, 10 hours), Milan

(€23, 5½ hours), Zurich (€31, eight hours) and Geneva (€12, four hours). It operates buses departing from Annecy, Chambéry, Chamonix and Lyon too.

TRAIN
The huge, modern **train station** (☎ 08 36 35 35 35; rue Émile Gueymard; ☻ 4.30am-2am) is next to the Gare Europole tram stop, which is served by both tramlines (see Getting Around).

Destinations served include Paris' Gare de Lyon (from €64, 3½ hours by TGV), Chambéry (€9, one hour, 14 daily) and Lyon (€16, 1½ hours, five daily), from where you can catch trains to Nice and Monaco. There are also daily trains to Turin (€44, 3½hours), Milan (€54, five hours, change at Chambéry), and Geneva (€20, two hours).

Getting Around
TO/FROM THE AIRPORT
The bus to **Lyon St-Exupéry airport** (☎ 04 76 87 90 31) stops at the bus station (one way/return €20/30, 65 minutes). Buses to the Grenoble-St-Geoirs domestic airport depart from the bus station (one way/return €13/20, 45 minutes).

BICYCLE
If you can't face another tram-ride into town, **Métro-Vélo** (☎ 08 20 22 38 38; bike hire per day €5; ☻ 7am-8pm Mon-Fri, 9am-noon & 2-7pm Sat & Sun), opposite the car-hire offices underneath the station, rent out bikes.

BUS & TRAM
The pride of Grenoble's public transport system are its two pollution-free tram lines – sensibly called A and B (plans are underway for a third). Both stop at the tourist office and the train station, and run through the heart of town. They're fast, reliable and almost silent, which makes you wonder why all big cities don't have them – until you've almost been run over for the nineteenth time.

Bus and tram tickets cost €1.20 and are available from ticket machines at tram stops or from drivers. They must be time-stamped in the blue machines located at each stop before boarding. Tickets are valid for transfers – but not return trips – within one hour.

A carnet of 10 tickets costs €9.50. Daily/five-day passes (Visitag) are available for

€3.20/11 from the **TAG information desk** (☎ 04 76 20 66 66) at the tourist office, or from the TAG office outside the train station. Family passes are also available.

The majority of the buses on the 20 different lines stop running quite early, usually between 6pm and 9pm. Trams run daily from 5am (6.15am on Sunday) until just after midnight.

CAR
Having a car in the city is of little benefit, since the roads are confusing and parking is expensive. If you're looking for four wheels to explore the surrounding countryside, all the main agencies are underneath the station, including **ADA** (☎ 04 67 43 00 36; ☻ 8am-noon &1-6.30pm Mon-Fri, 8am-noon & 2-5pm Sat).

TAXI
Taxis can be ordered by calling the central reservation line on ☎ 04 76 54 42 54.

AROUND GRENOBLE
The low-altitude regions surrounding Grenoble attract a relaxed crowd in search of cheap winter skiing or summer walking. Stations known for their cross-country skiing include Lans-en-Vercors and Villard de Lans, southwest of Grenoble in the Vercors range; and Col de Porte and Le Sappey, north of Grenoble in the Chartreuse. Summer skiing can be found further east in **Les Deux Alpes** and **Alpe d'Huez**.

Chamrousse, the nearest ski resort to Grenoble, was built for the 1968 Winter Olympics. The family resort, popular for its wide and gentle slopes, hosts the snowboarding World Cup and the French freestyle ski championships every March. Chamrousse's **tourist office** (☎ 04 76 89 92 65; www.chamrousse .com; 42 place de Belledonne; ☻ 9am-6pm ski season, 9am-noon & 1.30-5pm rest of year) can help with accommodation. There are several VFD buses daily from Grenoble to Chamrousse (€6, 1¼ hours).

Parc Naturel Régional du Vercors
Immediately southwest of Grenoble the Parc Naturel Régional du Vercors (1750 sq km) is a large cross-country skiing, caving and hiking area. During WWII it became a stronghold of the Resistance movement and was given the name the 'Fortresse de la Résistance'.

Lans-en-Vercors (population 1450, elevation 1020m), 25km southwest of Grenoble, is the leading ski village on the Vercors plateau. There's none of the adrenaline of the high-Alpine descents here, nor is there a bustling nightlife. From Lans-en-Vercors, hourly shuttle buses travel to the Stade de Neige (Snow Stadium), an area of wooded slopes crowned by Le Grand Cheval (1807m), about 4km east.

The equally sedate village of **Villard de Lans** (population 3350, elevation 1050m), 9km up the valley from Lans-en-Vercors, is linked by ski lifts and roads to neighbouring resort **Corrençon-en-Vercors** (1111m).

INFORMATION

The **park headquarters** (☎ 04 76 94 38 26; www.pnr-vercors.fr; 255 chemin des Fusillés; ⊗ 8.30am-12.30pm & 2-5pm Mon-Fri) is inside the Maison du Parc in Lans-en-Vercors. The **tourist office** (☎ 04 76 95 42 62; www.ot-lans-en-vercors.fr; place de la Mairie; ⊗ 9am-12.30pm & 1.30-6pm daily high seasons, 9am-noon & 2-6pm Mon-Fri, 10am-noon & 2-5pm Sat & Sun rest of year) in Lans-en-Vercors and the **tourist office** (☎ 04 76 95 10 38; www.villarddelans.com; place Mure Ravaud; ⊗ 9am-12.30pm & 2-7pm summer, 9am-7pm winter; 9am-noon & 2-6pm Mon-Sat rest of year) in Villard de Lans provide extensive information on activities in the park.

The free brochure *Welcome to Vercors* lists walks as well as driving and caving tours; *Site National Historique de la Résistance en Vercors* traces the footsteps of the Resistance movement.

GETTING THERE & AWAY

From Lans-en-Vercors, **VFD** (☎ 04 76 95 11 24) runs six buses daily (five at the weekend) to and from Grenoble (€6, 50 minutes), Villard de Lans (€1.80, 10 minutes) and Corrençon (€1.40, 15 minutes).

Parc National des Écrins

The spectacular Parc National des Écrins (930 sq km) was created in 1973. Stretching between the towns of Bourg d'Oisans, Briançon and Gap, it is France's second-largest national park, The area is enclosed by steep, narrow valleys, sculpted by the Romanche, Durance and Drac rivers and their erstwhile glaciers.

The **main park headquarters** (☎ 04 92 40 20 10; ecrins-parcnational@espaces-naturels.fr; ⊗ 8am-noon & 1-5pm Mon-Fri) is at the Domaine de la Cha-

rance, F-05000 Gap. There's a large **park office** (☎ 04 92 21 08 49; ecrins.briançonnais@espaces-naturels.fr; place Médecin Général Blanchard; ⊗ 9.30am-7pm Jul & Aug; 9.30am-noon & 2-7pm Sep-Jun) in Briançon.

Bourg d'Oisans (population 3000, elevation 720m), 50km southeast of Grenoble, and Briançon, another 67km in the same direction, make good bases for exploring the park. The **Maison du Parc** (☎ 04 76 80 00 51; ecrins.oisans@espaces-naturels.fr; rue Gambetta; ⊗ 8am-noon & 1.30-7pm summer, 8am-noon & 1.30-5.30pm Mon-Fri rest of year) sells maps and guides including the invaluable IGN 1:25,000 *Les Deux Alpes–Le Parc National des Écrins* (No 3336ET) and *Bourg d'Oisans-Alpe d'Huez* (No 3335ET). The town's **tourist office** (☎ 04 76 80 03 25; www.bourgdoisans.com; ⊗ 8.30am-noon & 2-5.30pm Mon-Sat, 8.30am-noon Sun winter; 9am-7pm Mon-Sat, 10am-noon & 3-6pm Sun summer) is well stocked too. You'll find it on the main road just before the River Romanche at quai Girard.

ACTIVITIES
Walking

There are plenty of zigzagging paths used for centuries by shepherds and smugglers from points all along the Romanche Valley.

From Bourg d'Oisans there is a path up to Villard Notre Dame (1525m, two hours). From Vénosc, a tiny mountain village in the Vénéon Valley, about 12km southeast of Bourg d'Oisans, there is a trail to the popular skiing resort of Les Deux Alpes (1660m, 1½ hours).

Dix Itinéraires (a publication in French) is a good companion for 10 different treks and climbs of up to seven hours. *Venosc/Vallée de Vénéon* is another good publication.

The Bourg d'Oisans tourist office sells six different walking maps (in English and French) entitled *Oisans au Bout des Pieds* (Oisans Under Your Feet).

Other Activities

Air Écrins Club de Parapente de l'Oisans (☎ /fax 04 76 11 00 35; 23 rue Général de Gaulle, Bourg d'Oisans) runs canoeing, kayaking and *parapente* schools.

At St-Christophe, near Venosc, **Vénéon Eaux Vives** (☎ 04 76 80 23 99) organises similar activities and hires out mountain bikes.

SLEEPING & EATING

Most of the park's 32 **refuges** (dm €10-12) are run by the CAF. Several **gîtes d'étape** (dm €12-15) on the outskirts of the park are open year-round. For a full listing, ask at the Bourg d'Oisans tourist office for the free *Guide des Hébergements*.

Maison des Jeunes Le Paradis (☎ 04 76 80 01 76; 50 rue Thiers; dm €10; ☷ closed May & Oct), in Bourg d'Oisans, has dorm beds in rooms for 12 people and can also arrange mountain biking, kayaking, canoeing etc.

Bourg d'Oisans also has about 10 hotels, the cheaper ones being around the bus station on rue de la Gare. You can find simple doubles at **Le Moulin des Fruites Bleues** (☎ 04 76 80 00 26; d €30-50), **Hôtel Le Rocher** (☎ 04 76 80 01 53; fax 04 76 79 11 94; d from €35) and **Hôtel de l'Oberland Français** (☎ 04 76 80 24 24; d from €35).

Hôtel Le Florentin (☎ 04 76 80 01 61; fax 04 76 80 05 49; rue Thiers; s €43-52, d €55-59; ☷ closed mid-Dec–Sep) is a family-run hotel with a friendly welcome.

There are plenty of camping grounds in Bourg d'Oisans – the best is **La Cascade** (☎ 04 76 80 02 42; fax 04 76 80 22 63; camping €18; ☷ mid-Dec–Sep), near the tourist office. Most of the cheaper camping grounds are only open from June to September.

There are plenty of small supermarkets and grocery stores in Bourg d'Oisans to stock up on supplies.

GETTING THERE & AWAY

VFD buses (☎ 04 76 80 00 90; Bourg d'Oisans) serve the Romanche Valley and Briançon. They operate from the **bus station** (av de la Gare), on the main road into Bourg d'Oisans. From Grenoble, VFD bus No 3000 goes to Bourg d'Oisans (€2.70, 80 minutes) up to eight times a day, while the No 3030 and the No 3020 from Grenoble stop in Bourg d'Oisans on their way to Les Deux Alpes and Alpe d'Huez.

LES DEUX ALPES
elevation 1600m

Les Deux Alpes, 28km southeast of Bourg d'Oisans, has the largest summer skiing area in Europe. From mid-June to early September, you can ski on the Glacier du Mont de Lans (3200m to 3425m), which offers panoramic views of Mont Blanc, Massif Central and Mont Ventoux.

Les Deux Alpes is a popular winter skiing resort too, as well as one of France's top snowboarding spots. The never-ending stream of traffic clogging up the main street belies its lowly beginnings as a mountain pasture for local sheep flocks.

Orientation
Les Deux Alpes is mostly centred around the long main street (av de la Muzelle), which cuts north-south through town from the road from Grenoble. The central square of place des Deux Alpes is about 700m into the resort. The Maison de la Montagne is a short way north, while the main car parks and bus stops are further south towards the end of the street.

Information
Everything in town revolves around the **Maison des Deux Alpes** (place des Deux Alpes). It houses the **tourist office** (☎ 04 76 79 22 00; www.les2alpes .com; ☷ 8am-7pm high season, 9am-noon & 2-6pm Mon-Fri rest of year) and **accommodation service** (☎ 04 76 79 24 38; res2alp@les2alpes.com), as well as the **ESF** (see opposite).

The main **Bureau des Guides** (☎ 06 11 32 71 88) inside the **Maison de la Montagne** (av de la Muzelle), north of the main tourist office, arranges ice climbing, rock climbing, walking, rafting and mountain-bike expeditions with experienced guides.

The *les2alpes Magazine* and the annual *Winter Guide*, both available free from the tourist office, have stacks of useful information in English about the resort.

Sights
A 6m-tall dinosaur, Alpine flowers and shepherds are just some of the ice-sculptures you'll find in the **grotte de glace** (ice cave; cable-car & cave entry adult/child €20/15; ☷ 9.30am-4.30pm) carved into the Glacier du Mont de Lans at Dôme de Puy Salié (3425m). Take the Jandri Express *télécabine* to 3200m (change of *télécabine* at 2600m), from where you can take the underground Dôme Express funicular to 3400m.

For a glimpse of traditional Alpine life as it once was, visit the **Maison de la Montagne** (☎ 04 76 79 53 15; av de la Muzelle; admission €2; ☷ 10am-noon & 3-7pm summer, 2-6pm winter).

Activities
SKIING & SNOWBOARDING
The main skiing domain lies below La Meije (3983m), one of the highest peaks in the Parc National des Écrins. There are 200km of marked pistes, 20km of cross-country trails, and in the snowpark (2600m), a 600m-long axe pipe, 110m-long half-pipe and numerous jumps.

ESF (☎ 04 76 79 21 21; esf.les2alpes@wanadoo.fr) and the **École de Ski International St-Christophe** (☎ 04 76 79 04 21; ecole.ski.internationale@wanadoo.fr; av de la Muzelle), close to place des Deux Alpes, run skiing and snowboarding schools for all levels.

WARM-WEATHER ACTIVITIES
Numerous walks are listed in the free brochure *Le Guide des Randonnées Pédestres au Départ des Deux Alpes* available at the tourist office.

Parapente ESF (☎ 06 07 72 26 60; ☼ 6-7.30pm; parapente@2alpes.com; 1-day course €60), inside the Maison des Deux Alpes, offers paragliding courses.

Sleeping
The accommodation service (see Information opposite) inside the Maison des Deux Alpes arranges accommodation within the resort. Two-person apartments cost around €190/250 a week in the low/high season – bookings, as usual, should be made well in advance.

Off-piste skiers wishing to tackle the challenge of the fearsome La Grave descent should consider basing themselves in the village of La Grave, 21km to the east of Les Deux Alpes.

The **Auberge de Jeunesse** (☎ 04 76 79 22 80; les-deux-alpes@fuaj.org; Les Brûleurs de Loups; dm €11) is in the heart of town. It only offers weekly packages in winter, including seven days' accommodation, food and a ski-lift pass. Prices start at €290/400 in the low/high season.

Auberge Edelweiss (☎ 04 76 79 90 93; edelweiss@waw.com; s/d high season €40/52) is a homely little hotel that caters to individual and small groups. Rooms here are cosy. There is also a restaurant and a Jacuzzi to thaw out tired skiers.

Getting There & Away
VFD operates buses running to Les Deux Alpes from Grenoble (€2.70, 1¾ hours, eight daily), 77km northwest.

In Les Deux Alpes, reserve tickets in advance from the **VFD office** (☎ 04 76 80 51 22; 112 av de la Muzelle) or from the tourist office. Buses stop at Bourg d'Oisans (40 minutes) en route to Grenoble. There are also services to Lyon St-Exupéry, Alpe d'Huez, Briançon and Geneva airports.

ALPE D'HUEZ
elevation 1860m
The ski resort of Alpe d'Huez sits 13km above Bourg d'Oisans, and is reached by a steep road (La Montée de l'Alpe d'Huez) which is best known as one of the 'classic' ascents often included in the Tour de France cycle race.

Alpe d'Huez has winter runs for skiers and snowboarders of all abilities. At 16km, La Sarenne is the longest black run in the French Alps. Experienced skiers can also ski in July and August on glaciers (ranging from 2530m to 3330m). The panoramic view from Pic du Lac Blanc (3330m), the highest point accessible year-round from the village by the Tronçon *télécabines*, is particularly impressive.

Information
The **tourist office** (☎ 04 76 11 44 44; info@alpedhuez .com; ☼ 9am-12.30pm & 2.30-6pm), **accommodation centre** (☎ 04 76 11 44 44; resa@alpedhuez.com; ☼ 9am-12.30pm & 2.30-6pm) and **ESF** (☎ 04 76 80 31 69; ☼ 9am-12.30pm & 2.30-6pm) are inside the **Maison de l'Alpe** (place Joseph Paganon).

The **Bureau des Guides** (☎ 04 76 80 42 55) and the **Taburle École du Snowboard Français** (☎ 04 76 80 95 82) are both off place du Cognet at the Rond Point des Pistes, the northernmost point of the village. The annual *Le Guide de l'Alpe* booklet, free from the tourist office, has a full listing of all facilities in the resort.

Sleeping
The accommodation centre (see Information above) takes accommodation bookings. Expect to pay €215/350 in the low/high season for a small, two-person studio. With some 28 hotels and another 27 rental places, accommodation is plentiful but demand is high in season.

One of the least expensive hotels in Alpe d'Huez, **Gai Vallon** (☎ 04 76 80 98 37; rue de l'Église; r from €37, half-board from €41) is one-star and offers simple, neat rooms.

Hôtel Alp'Azur (☎ 04 76 80 34 02; place Jean Molin; d €67-82; ☼ closed Apr-Jun) is a friendly, helpful, two-star place. Its rates include breakfast.

Getting There & Away
VFD buses (☎ 04 76 80 31 61) run from Grenoble to Alpe d'Huez (€15.50, 1¾ hours, eight daily) via Bourg d'Oisans.

BRIANÇON

pop 11,300 / elevation 1026m

Jutting out from a rocky outcrop at the meeting of five valleys, the hilltop city of Briançon stands like a sentinel between the French Alps and Italy, which is 20km to the northeast.

Long a frontier post, the fortified old city of Briançon overlooks the road to the Col de Montgenèvre (1850m), an ancient Roman mountain pass that was made into a reliable road by Napoleon. Briançon's lofty ramparts and sheer walls are more reminiscent of the towns of northern Burgundy than its Alpine neighbours, but the town's main claim to fame is its altitude – at 1320m, it is the highest town in Europe and boasts approximately 300 days of sunshine a year.

During the late 17th century, the military architect Vauban was called in to make the town impregnable to attack after it had been razed during a regional war. Since then, the town has crept down the slopes to encompass the Durance Valley. The lower town has a lift station to the ski resort of Le Grand Serre Chevalier. Sadly, it's inherited none of the charm of the old town, and generally looks its best covered with a blanket of snow.

Briançon is sandwiched between Parc National des Écrins to the west and Parc Naturel Régional du Queyras to the south, making it an excellent base for outdoor pursuits.

Orientation

The town is divided into two sections: the Vieille Ville (old city), with its pedestrianised streets and battlements, and the modern Ville Basse (lower town), which sprawls out beneath the old city at the junction of two rivers. The upper and lower towns are connected by the steep hill of av de la République.

Entry to the Vieille Ville is from place du Champ de Mars (on the old city's northern side) or, if you're walking up the hill from the lower town, through the Porte d'Embrun. The train station is in the suburb of Ste-Catherine.

Information

LAUNDRY

LavPlus (Central Parc; 7am-7pm)

MONEY

Banque Populaire (20 av Maurice Petsche) Exchanges currency.

Crédit Agricole (10 Grande Rue; 8am-noon & 1.55-5pm Mon-Fri, until 4.30pm Sat) The branch in the old city.

Crédit Agricole (Le Moulin shopping mall)

POST

Post Office (place du Champ de Mars) Opposite the entrance to the old town.

Post Office Branch (Parc Chancel) In the lower town just off av du 159 RIA.

TOURIST INFORMATION

Maison du Parc (04 92 21 42 15; ecrins.briançonnais@espaces-naturels.fr; Place Médecin Général Blanchard; 9.30am-7pm Jul & Aug, 9.30am-noon & 2-7pm Sep-Jun) At the southern end of Grande Rue in the Vieille Ville, provides information on the Parc National des Écrins.

Tourist Office (04 92 21 08 50; office-tourisme-briancon@wanadoo.fr; 1 place du Temple; 9am-noon & 2-6pm Mon-Sat, 10am-12.30pm & 3-5pm Sun Sep-Jun, 9am-7pm Jul & Aug) In Vieille Ville.

Sights

VIEILLE VILLE

The old city is a fine place to spend an afternoon drinking in the mountain air and admiring the views from the city's battlements. In high summer the throngs of tourists can be troublesome, but off-season the town is quiet and the atmosphere is tranquil. If you've spent a week in the sardine-can ski resorts of the central Alps, it makes an ideal place to rest those weary bones before the journey home.

At the top of the old city is the **Porte de Pignerol**, a daunting gateway hewn from dark stone. The steep main street, Grande Rue, is known as the Grande Gargouille (Great Gargoyle) because of the drain that gushes down its middle, and there are several fountains in the old part of town, spouting water from underground springs. The brightly coloured buildings, all earthy reds, rich pinks and ochre yellows, lend the town an almost Tuscan air – a reminder that the Italian border lies just a few miles east. There are also a couple of tiny, tumbledown chapels along Briançon's back streets.

The coral-pink **Collégiale** (Church of Our Lady & St Nicholas) is a more permanent relic. Built by Vauban in the early 18th century, the twin-towered church is characteristically heavy and fortified. The baroque

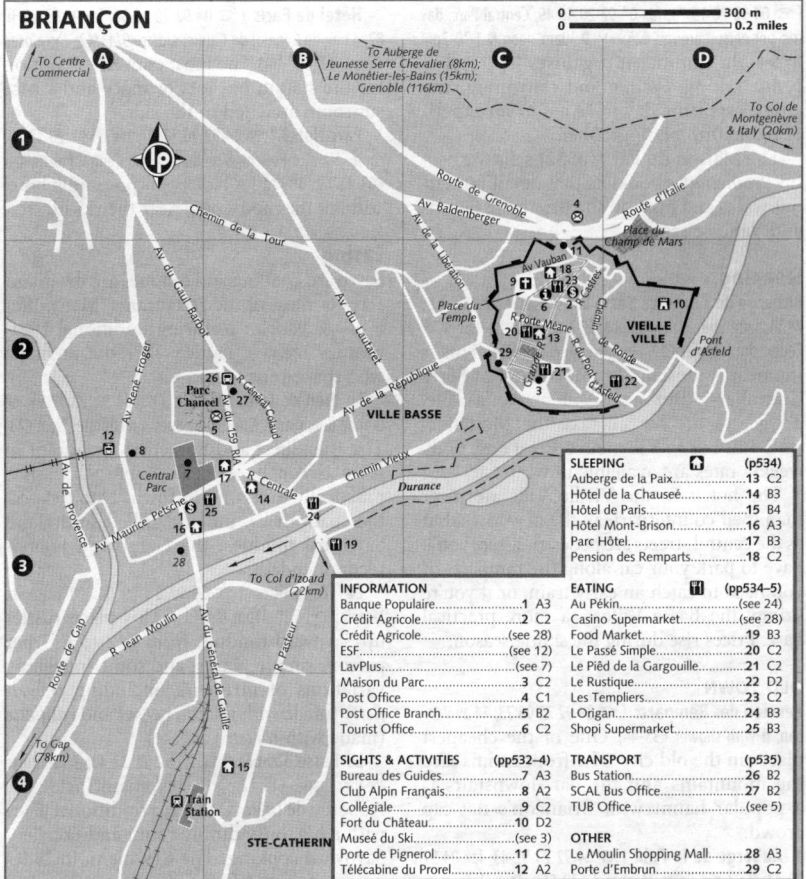

BRIANÇON

paintings and gilt chapels inside are worth a closer look.

The 18th-century **Fort du Château** sits above the old city and offers magnificent views of the surrounding mountains. Guided **tours** (adult/concessions €4.50/3; ☺ Jul-Aug) are organised by the tourist office, but if you don't think you're up to the uphill climb, av Vauban, which runs along the town's ramparts, affords fine views of the snowy peaks of the Écrins national park.

TÉLÉCABINE DU PROREL

The **télécabine du Prorel** (av René Froger; return ticket/day pass €5.30/9; ☺ 8.45am-4.15pm Mon-Fri, 7am-5.15pm Sat & Sun ski season & summer mid-Jun–mid-Sep), which leaves from the Briançon-Serre-

Chevalier 1200 station in the lower town, climbs to Le Prorel (2566m), one of the highest points of Le Grand Serre Chevalier mountain range.

Activities

In winter there is skiing at Le Grand Serre Chevalier (p535), the range that stretches from Briançon to Le Monêtier-les-Bains, 15km northwest. The **ESF** (☎ 04 92 20 30 57; www.esf-serrechevalier.com; 7 av René Froger) and various ski-hire shops are inside the *télécabine* du Prorel station. **CAF** (☎ 04 92 20 16 52; 6 av René Froger; ☺ 5-7pm Tue-Sat) is near the ski-lift station.

During winter, ice climbing and ski tours can be organised by the **Bureau des Guides**

(☎ 04 92 20 15 73; fax 04 92 20 46 49; Central Parc; day trip per person around €25; ☽ 9.30am-noon & 1.30-7pm Jul-Sep). In summer it organises treks, *parapente*, rafting, cycling and canyoning, and animal-spotting day treks led by an experienced nature photographer.

The Maison du Parc (p532) sells the useful *Promenades* booklets that detail numerous walks and hikes in the Briançon, Oisans and Vanoise region.

Sleeping

Auberge de Jeunesse Serre Chevalier (☎ 04 92 24 74 54; serre-chevalier@fuaj.org; BP 2, 05240 Serre-Chevalier Cedex; dm summer €12; ☽ Dec-Apr & Jun-Nov) This is the nearest hostel, 8km northwest at Serre Chevalier-le-Bez near Villeneuve-la-Salle. To get to the hostel, take the Monêtier-les-Bains bus to Villeneuve-Pre-Long. Only weekly rates are available in winter.

The hotels in the Vieille Ville are nicer than their counterparts in the new town, but as the central streets are pedestrianised, you'll have to park your car along the ramparts. If you need to catch an early train, or if you're skiing, the Basse Ville is a more practical base. Prices rise during the skiing season.

OLD TOWN

Pension des Remparts (☎ 04 92 21 08 73; 14 av Vauban; d with shower €35-44) One of the cheapest places in the old city. The front rooms face the mountains and the bar downstairs is a popular haunt with Briançon's flat-cap crowd.

Auberge de la Paix (☎ 04 92 21 37 43; fax 04 92 20 44 45; 3 rue Porte Méane; d €39-55; P) Twenty comfortable rooms in an old inn near the Grande Rue, though some of the rooms are quite dark because of the minuscule windows. The attached restaurant is one of the best in town.

NEW TOWN

Hôtel de la Chaussée (☎ 04 92 21 10 37; fax 04 92 20 03 94; 4 rue Centrale; d €37-42, tw/tr €51/58; P) An alpine-style hotel in the lower town that has better than two-star rooms and is usually very quiet.

Hôtel Mont-Brison (☎ 04 92 21 14 55; 3 av du Général de Gaulle; d €30-49; ☽ Jan-Oct) Another two-star place at the bottom of the hill from the old city. The rooms are showing their age and it's on a busy roundabout, but it's clean and central.

Hôtel de Paris (☎ 04 92 20 15 30; fax 04 92 20 30 82; 41 av du Général de Gaulle; s/d/tr 39/43/42; ☽ closed early Oct & end Apr) The most convenient option for the station has lots of space and a nice sunroom attached to the side.

Parc Hôtel (☎ 04 92 20 37 47; fax 04 92 20 53 74; cnr av Maurice Petsche & av du 159 RIA, Central Parc; s/d/tr €63/71/79; P ☒) A blocky purpose-built hotel with all the mod-cons, near the ski-lift.

Eating

Savoyard cooking and fondues are the mainstays of most of the restaurants. Many offer a *menu Vauban* featuring traditional 18th-century recipes, named after the architect who shaped the town.

Le Pied de la Gargouille (☎ 04 92 20 12 95; 64 Grande Rue; menus €16-18, fondues & tartiflettes from €13) The friendliest and homeliest restaurant in town is run by a local couple who know practically everyone in town. Don't expect too many frills, but for grilled meats and Savoyard fondues, the Gargoyle's Foot is recommended.

Les Templiers (☎ 04 92 20 29 04; 20 place du Temple; ☽ 6.30-11pm Dec-Oct) This place rustles up Savoyard fondues from €12 to €15 per person, simple pizzas, and some intriguing variations of *tartiflette*, including *chèvriflette* (made with goats' cheese) and *ratiflette* (made with *raclette* cheese).

Le Passé Simple (☎ 04 92 21 37 43; 3 rue Porte Méane; menus €15-22; ☽ lunch & dinner) Inside the Auberge de la Paix, this is a traditional place with a big, busy dining room and excellent Savoyard cooking. The €19 menu includes onion soup and *filet de boeuf*.

Le Rustique (☎ 04 92 21 00 10; 36 rue du Pont d'Asfeld; ☽ until 11pm) For local dishes and traditional fondue, try this cavernous place. It has a non-smoking room, and house specialities include locally caught trout. Gourmands should try its apple tart with *foie gras* or quail roasted in honey.

L'Origan (☎ 04 92 20 10 09; 25 rue Centrale; pizza from €5.80) is a pizzeria with lots of varieties. **Au Pékin** (☎ 04 92 21 24 22; menus from €10; ☽ 11am-2pm & 6-11pm) is in the same building as L'Origan, and offers the usual Chinese favourites.

SELF-CATERING

There's a **food market** (☽ Wed) in the car park next to the fire station, just off rue Centrale. Numerous food shops line Grande Rue in the Vieille Ville.

Briançon has a **Shopi supermarket** (av Maurice Petsche; ☎ 8.30am-12.30pm & 2.30-7.30pm Mon-Sat, 8.45am-noon Sun) and a huge **Casino supermarket** (Le Moulin shopping mall).

Getting There & Away
BUS
The **bus station** (cnr av du 159 RIA & rue Général Colaud) is simply a bus stop marked Autocar Arrêt. **SCAL** (☎ 04 92 21 12 00; 14 av du 159 RIA; ☎ 8am-noon & 2-6pm Mon-Fri) has an office next door. It runs a daily bus to Gap (€9.25, two hours), Digne (€17, 3¼ hours, no bus on Sunday), Marseille (€26, 5¾ hours), and Aix-en-Provence (€23, five hours).

VFD buses (p527) in Grenoble travel from Briançon via Bourg d'Oisans (€12, 1¾ hours) to Grenoble (€25, 2¼ hours) twice daily.

TRAIN
Briançon's **train station** (☎ 04 92 51 50 50; av du Général de Gaulle) is at the southern end of the street, about 1.5km from the Vieille Ville. There are **ticket windows** (⏰ 5.30am-12.20am Mon-Fri, until 10pm Sat & Sun). Left luggage costs €2 per piece.

To Paris' Gare d'Austerlitz, a direct overnight train leaves at 8.30pm (€90, 10 hours). Faster daytime services go via Grenoble or Valence (€69.50, 6½-seven hours). Other destinations include Gap (€11, 1¼ hours), Grenoble (€25, 4½ hours) and Marseille (€33, four hours).

Getting Around
BUS
Local buses run by TUB – Nos 1, 2 and 3 – connect the train station to place du Champ de Mars, from about 7am to 6pm Monday to Saturday. Line 1 runs slightly later. On Sunday, Line D runs from around 9am to 5pm. A single ticket costs €1 and a carnet of 10, €7 (available from the TUB office, *tabacs* and the tourist office). The **TUB office** (☎ 04 92 20 47 10; tub@wanadoo.fr; place de Suse; ☎ 9am-noon & 1.30-5.30pm Tue-Fri) is in Parc Chancel.

TAXI
You can also call a **taxi** (☎ 04 92 21 14 42).

AROUND BRIANÇON
Le Grand Serre Chevalier
Le Grand Serre Chevalier is a ski area above the Serre Chevalier Valley in the Hautes-Alpes. There are 13 villages along the valley

floor, but the lift system only reaches Briançon and the villages of Chantemerle, Villeneuve-la-Salle and Le Monêtier-les-Bains. Chantemerle (Serre Chevalier 1350) and Villeneuve-la-Salle (Serre Chevalier 1400) are the central resorts. Le Monêtier-les-Bains (Serre Chevalier 1500) is quieter, while Briançon has the cheapest accommodation.

The main tourist office is in Briançon, but there is a small **tourist office** (☎ 04 92 24 98 97) in Chantemerle, a **tourist office** (☎ 04 92 24 98 98) in Villeneuve-la-Salle and a **tourist office** (☎ 04 92 24 98 99) in Le Monêtier-les-Bains. All are open 9am to noon and 2pm to 7pm daily in high season, but close an hour earlier and on Sunday the rest of the year. Accommodation can be booked through the **central reservation office** (☎ 04 92 24 98 90; resa@ot-serrechevalier .fr) at Briançon tourist office.

There are lots of passes available covering the different ski areas – ask at any of the ski-lift stations or pick up the free guidebook *(Guide d'Accueil)*, which lists tariffs. A pass for Serre Chevalier costs €32/160 per day/six days.

The Bureau des Guides in Briançon (p535) and the **Maison de la Montagne** (☎ 04 92 24 75 90) in Villeneuve-la-Salle offer winter ski tours and summer mountaineering trips.

GETTING AROUND
There are buses from Briançon (€4.15, 20 minutes, 10 daily) to Villeneuve-la-Salle. In winter, lifts operate and free shuttle buses ply the route between Le Monêtier-les-Bains and Briançon.

THE JURA

The dark wooded hills and granite plateaus of the Jura Mountains stretch for 360km along the Franco-Swiss border from the Rhine to the Rhône. Part of the historic Franche-Comté region, the Jura is one of the least explored regions in France, which makes it a fine place to escape the Alpine crowds. If you're looking for a taste of traditional mountain life, the Jura makes a far better destination than the ruthlessly modernised and tourist-orientated resorts elsewhere in the Alps.

The Jura – from a Gaulish word meaning 'forest' – is an important agricultural area, best known for its unique wines and cheeses. It is

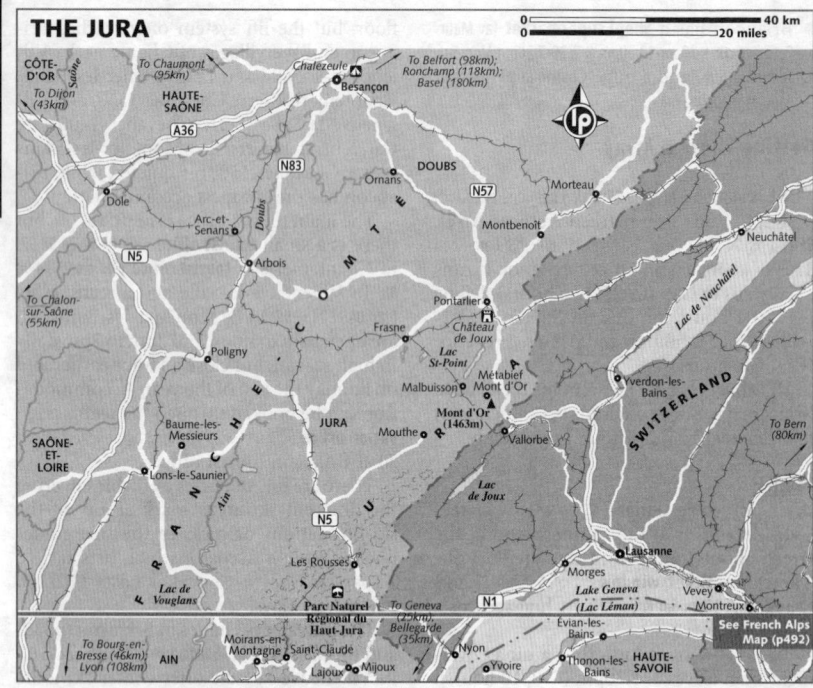

THE JURA

also France's premier cross-country skiing area. The range is dotted with ski stations from Pontarlier south to Bellegarde; Métabief Mont d'Or, north of the Parc Naturel Régional du Haut-Jura, is the main station, as popular for its superb hiking and nature trails as for its gentle slopes. Every year the region hosts the Transjurassienne, one of the world's toughest cross-country skiing events.

BESANÇON
pop 125,000

Besançon, capital of the Franche-Comté region, is surrounded by hills on the northern reaches of the Jura range. First settled in Gallo-Roman times, it became an important stop on the early trade routes between Italy, the Alps and the Rhine.

Since the 18th century, it has been a noted clock-making centre. Victor Hugo, author of *Les Misérables*, and the film-pioneering Lumière brothers, were all born on the square now known as place Victor Hugo in Besançon's old town.

Noted for its vast parks, clean streets and few tourists, Besançon is considered one of the most liveable cities in France. It has one of the country's largest foreign student populations and the old town's cobbled streets hum with bars and bistros. The Battant quarter, originally settled by wine-makers, is the most historic area of town.

Orientation
Besançon's old city is neatly encased by the curve of the River Doubs called the Boucle du Doubs. The tourist office and train station are both just outside this loop to the north and northwest. The Battant quarter straddles the northwest bank of the river around rue Battant. Grande Rue, the pedestrianised main street, slices through the old city from the river to the gates of the citadel.

Information
INTERNET ACCESS
Optimum (☎ 03 81 82 13 07; www.optimum.fr; 31 rue d'Arènes; per 10min/1hr €1/3.50; ⌚ 10am-10.30pm Mon-Sat, 2-10pm Sun)

LAUNDRY
Blanc-Matic (14 rue de la Madeleine; ⌚ 7am-8pm)

MONEY

Foreign currency can be changed at the tourist office, post office and the train-station information office. Most banks have ATMs.
Banque de France (19 rue de la Préfecture) Usually changes money.

POST

Post Office (23 rue Proudhon; ⏱ 9am-noon & 2-6pm) In the old city.
Post Office Branch (rue Battant)

TOURIST INFORMATION

Tourist Office (☎ 03 81 80 92 55; www.besancon -tourisme.com; 2 place de la 1ère Armée Française; ⏱ 10am-7pm Mon, 9am-7pm Tue-Sat, 10am-noon & 3-5pm Sun Apr-Sep, 10am-6pm Mon, 9am-6pm Tue-Sat Oct-Mar, 10am-noon Sun mid-Sep–mid-Jun)

Sights & Activities
MUSÉE DES BEAUX-ARTS ET D'ARCHÉOLOGIE

Thought to be France's oldest museum, the **Musée des Beaux-Arts** (☎ 03 81 87 80 49; 1 place de la Révolution; adult/student €3/free; ⏱ 9.30am-noon & 2-6pm Wed-Mon) houses an impressive collection of paintings, including primitive and Renaissance works. Franche-Comté's long history of clock-making is also displayed here.

CITADEL

Built by Vauban for Louis XIV between 1688 and 1711, Besançon's **citadel** (☎ 03 81 87 83 33; rue des Fusillés de la Résistance; adult/concession/ child €7/6/4; ⏱ 9am-7pm Jul & Aug, 9am-6pm Apr-Jun, Sep & Oct, 10am-5pm Nov-Mar) sits at the top of rue des Fusillés de la Résistance. It's a steep 15-minute walk from the **Porte Noire** (Black Gate; rue de la Convention), a triumphal arch left over from Besançon's Roman days, dating from the 2nd century AD.

Inside the walls of the citadel, and open at the same times, are three museums focusing on local culture: the **Musée Comtois**, the **Musée d'Histoire Naturelle** (Natural History Museum) and the **Musée de la Résistance et de la Déportation**, which examines the rise of Nazism and fascism and the French Resistance movement.

Less sobering are the colourful collections of insects, fish and nocturnal rodents exhibited in the **insectarium**, **aquarium** and **noctarium**. Siberian tigers prowl the **parc zoologique**. Admission to the citadel includes entry to all the museums.

HORLOGE ASTRONOMIQUE

Housed in the 18th-century **Cathédrale St-Jean** (rue de la Convention; admission €2.50; ⏱ closed Tue Apr-Sep, Tue & Wed Oct-Mar, closed Jan), this incredible astronomical clock has 30,000 moving parts, 62 dials and, among other things, tells the time in 16 places, the tides in eight different ports, and the time of sunrise and sunset. It really has to be seen to be believed. There are guided **tours** (⏱ 9.50-11.50am & 2.50-5.50pm).

Activities

Club Alpin Français (CAF; ☎ 03 81 81 02 77; 14 rue Luc Breton; ⏱ 5-7pm Tue-Fri) provides information on walking, skiing and mountain biking, and sells useful topoguides and maps.

Tours

Two boat companies based in Villers-le-Lac with vessels docked beneath the Pont de la République in Besançon – **CNFS** (☎ 03 81 68 05 34; fax 03 81 68 01 00; adult/child €8/7; ⏱ Jul & Aug) and **Les Vedettes Bisontines** (☎ 03 81 68 13 25; fax 03 81 68 09 85; adult/child €8/7; ⏱ Apr-Oct depending on weather conditions) – offer 1¼-hour river trips along the Boucle du Doubs. In summer there are usually three trips a day.

Sleeping

Auberge de Jeunesse Les Oiseaux (☎ 03 81 40 32 00; 48 rue des Cras; dm incl breakfast €20) Two kilometres east of the train station is this hostel. Rates include breakfast and bedding; subsequent nights cost €2 less. Take bus No 7 from the tourist office in the direction of Orchamps and get off at Les Oiseaux.

Hôtel du Nord (☎ 03 81 81 34 56; 8 rue Moncey; d €30-52; **P**) Excellent city hotel along a smart street in the old quarter. The more expensive rooms are huge and have great, spacious bathrooms. Parking is off-site in an underground garage.

Hôtel de Paris (☎ 03 81 81 36 56; hoteldeparis@ hotmail.com; 33 rue des Granges; d €45-60; **P**) One of the best deals in Besançon, this efficient and comfortable hotel has 60 rooms that vary in quality – ask to see a couple before you choose. The ample car park is a real bonus – entry to the car park is from rue de la République

Hôtel Regina (☎ 03 81 81 18 30; 91 Grande Rue; d €35-50; **P**) Down a quiet alley in the heart of the old city, this two-star hotel offers cosy, floral rooms with shower, toilet and TV. There's

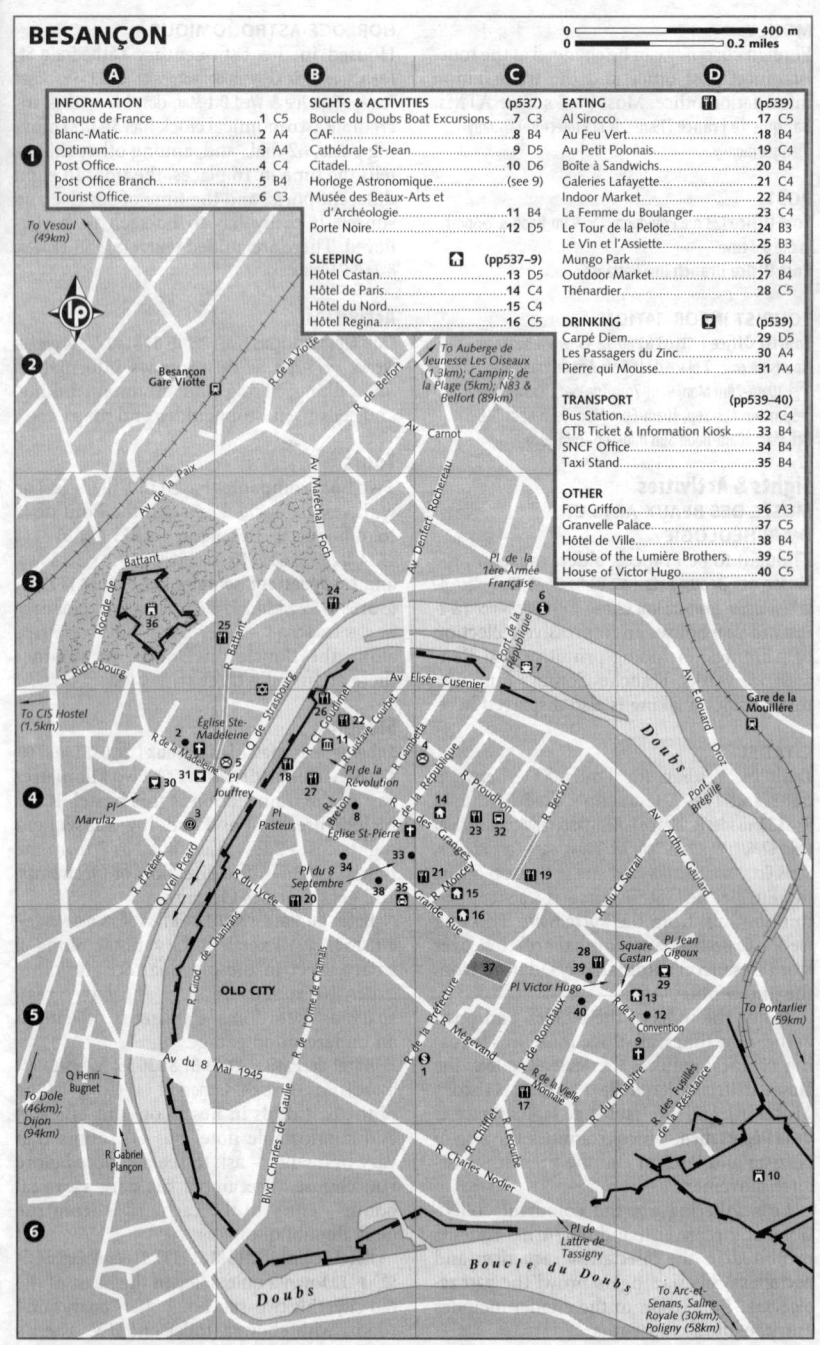

BESANÇON

0   400 m
0   0.2 miles

INFORMATION
Banque de France...............................1 C5
Blanc-Matic...2 A4
Optimum...3 A4
Post Office...4 C4
Post Office Branch..............................5 B4
Tourist Office......................................6 C3

SIGHTS & ACTIVITIES (p537)
Boucle du Doubs Boat Excursions....7 C3
CAF...8 B4
Cathédrale St-Jean.............................9 D5
Citadel..10 D6
Horloge Astronomique..............(see 9)
Musée des Beaux-Arts et
   d'Archéologie................................11 B4
Porte Noire.......................................12 D5

SLEEPING (pp537–9)
Hôtel Castan.....................................13 D5
Hôtel de Paris...................................14 C4
Hôtel du Nord...................................15 C4
Hôtel Regina.....................................16 C5

EATING (p539)
Al Sirocco...17 C5
Au Feu Vert......................................18 B4
Au Petit Polonais..............................19 C4
Boîte à Sandwichs............................20 B4
Galeries Lafayette.............................21 C4
Indoor Market..................................22 B4
La Femme du Boulanger..................23 C4
Le Tour de la Pelote.........................24 B3
Le Vin et l'Assiette...........................25 B3
Mungo Park......................................26 B4
Outdoor Market...............................27 B4
Thénardier.......................................28 C5

DRINKING (p539)
Carpé Diem......................................29 D5
Les Passagers du Zinc......................30 A4
Pierre qui Mousse............................31 A4

TRANSPORT (pp539–40)
Bus Station.......................................32 C4
CTB Ticket & Information Kiosk.......33 B4
SNCF Office......................................34 B4
Taxi Stand..35 B4

OTHER
Fort Griffon......................................36 A3
Granvelle Palace...............................37 C5
Hôtel de Ville...................................38 B4
House of the Lumière Brothers.......39 C5
House of Victor Hugo......................40 C5

To Vesoul
(49km)

Besançon
Gare Viotte

To Auberge de
Jeunesse Les Oiseaux
(1.3km); Camping; de
la Plage (5km); N83 &
Belfort (89km)

R de la Viotte

R de Belfort

Av Carnot

Av de la Paix

Av Maréchal Foch

Av Denfert Rochereau

Rocade de Battant

Battant

R Richebourg

Pl de la
1ère Armée
Française

To CIS Hostel
(1.5km)

Église Ste-
Madeleine

R de la Madeleine

Q de Strasbourg

R Battant

R de la République

Av Elisée Cusenier

Pont de la
République

R de la Préfecture

Pl
Jouffrey

Pl
Marulaz

R d'Arènes

R Gambetta

R Proudhon

Pl de la
Révolution

R Charles Nodier

Q Vel Picard

R du Lycée

Église St-Pierre

R des Granges

Grande Rue

R Mégevand

R Moncey

Pl du 8
Septembre

Doubs

Gare de la
Mouillère

Av Edouard Droz

Pont
Bregille

Av Arthur Gaulard

R du Chateau

OLD CITY

Square
Castan

Pl Jean
Gigoux

Pl Victor Hugo

R de la
Convention

To Pontarlier
(59km)

Av du 8 Mai 1945

R Griod de Chamars

R Tome de Chamars

Blvd Charles de Gaulle

Q Henri
Bugnet

R Gabriel
Plançon

To Dole
(46km);
Dijon
(94km)

R Chifflet

R Ronchaux

R de la Vieille
Monnaie

R du Chapitre

R des Fusillés
de la Résistance

Pl de
Lattre de
Tassigny

Boucle du Doubs

Doubs

To Arc-et-
Senans, Saline
Royale (30km);
Poligny (58km)

enough parking space for just three cars in the lane.

Hôtel Castan (☎ 03 81 65 02 00; fax 03 81 83 01 02; 6 square Castan; d €65-95) Housed in an ivy-covered 18th-century townhouse on a little shaded square in the old city, this is one of the nicest places to stay in town. Book well ahead for one of the 10 tastefully furnished rooms.

CAMPING

Camping de la Plage (☎ 03 81 88 04 26; route de Belfort; camping €11; ☺ May-Sep) The closest camping ground is at Chalezeule, 5km northeast of Besançon on the N83.

Eating
RESTAURANTS

Au Petit Polonais (☎ 03 81 81 23 67; 81 rue Granges; mains €8-15; ☺ closed Sun & dinner Sat) One of Besançon's oldest restaurants, founded in 1870 by Polish émigrés and still pulling in the punters with delicious offerings of cooked meats, fondues and sausages.

Au Feu Vert (☎ 03 81 82 17 20; 11 place de la Révolution; menus from €9; ☺ noon-10.30pm) A simple restaurant with a colourful dining room and a cheap and generous *menu,* offering regional specialities such as *gratin de saucisse de Morteau* (a cheesy potato and sausage bake).

Thénardier (☎ 03 81 82 06 18; 11 place Victor Hugo; menus from €8) A good option for lunch, with cheap, filling salads, light meals, good coffee and speedy service.

Al Sirocco (☎ 03 81 82 24 05; 1 rue Chifflet; ☺ closed Sun & lunch Mon) Great, traditional Italian diner with little tables and fishing nets hanging from the ceiling. Locals come here for the best pizza and pasta in Besançon.

La Tour de la Pelote (☎ 03 81 82 14 58; 41 quai de Strasbourg; menus from €22; ☺ Tue-Sun) Popular with tourists and housed in a 16th-century stone tower. Offers the usual selection of French cuisine mixed with local specialities.

Le Vin et l'Assiette (☎ 03 81 81 48 18; 97 rue Battant; menu €18; ☺ Tue-Sat) An intimate bistro and wine bar, above the Caves Marcellin (Marcellin wine cellars). Sample local Jura wine accompanied by meats and cheeses.

Mungo Park (☎ 03 81 81 28 01; 11 rue Jean Petit; menus from €39-89; ☺ noon-3.30pm & 5.30-9.30pm Tue-Sat) Named after a Scottish explorer, this is one of the town's most renowned restaurants. Braised fish in peppered artichokes and Charollais beef fillet are just some of the items you might try.

QUICK EATS

La Femme du Boulanger (☎ 03 81 82 86 93; 6 rue Morand; cakes €2-5, breakfast €4-8) Scrumptious bakery and coffee bar, offering home-made breads, sweet and savoury tarts, healthy breakfasts and not-so-healthy cakes. There is no obvious sign outside, so look for the blackboard and the bread displays.

Boîte à Sandwichs (☎ 03 81 81 63 23; 21 rue du Lycée; sandwiches €2.80-4.50) Offers cheap, filling sandwiches.

SELF-CATERING

Fresh fish, meat, vegetables and cheeses are sold at the large **indoor market** (cnr rue Paris & rue Claude Goudimel). The nearby **outdoor market** (place de la Révolution) sells mainly fresh fruit and vegetables.

Galeries Lafayette (☺ 9am-7pm Mon-Sat) Enter from 69 Grande Rue or opposite the Hôtel de Paris on rue des Granges. There's a grocery section in the basement.

Drinking

Besançon is an old town with a young heart. The nightlife is mostly concentrated around the river and in the old Battant quarter.

Carpé Diem (☎ 03 81 83 11 18; 2 place Jean Gigoux; salads from €2.60 & plats du jour €8) A small, rough-and-ready café-bar. The wooden bar, smoky atmosphere and tattered posters covering the wall make it an ideal hangout for lost bohemians.

Pierre qui Mousse (☎ 03 81 81 15 25; 1 place Jouffrey; ☺ 9am-1am) A popular bar-brasserie right on the riverfront, where you can sup Belgian beer (€3.50) under low wooden beams. Happy hour is usually from 6pm to 7pm.

Les Passagers du Zinc (☎ 03 81 81 54 70; 5 rue de Vignier; ☺ 5pm-1am Tue-Fri, 5pm-2am Sat & Sun) A grungy bar and club that hosts tapas nights, live bands and music nights; it's where Besançon's hip brigade can be found by night. Step through the bonnet of an old Citröen DS to reach the cellar.

Getting There & Away
BUS

Buses operated by **Monts Jura** (☎ 08 25 00 22 44) depart from the **bus station** (9 rue Proudhon; ☺ 8-10am & 4-6.30pm Mon-Fri, 8am-1pm & 2.30-5.30pm Sat). There are daily services to Ornans and Pontarlier.

TRAIN

Around 800m uphill from the city centre is **Besançon Gare Viotte** (☎ 08 36 35 35 35; ticket office ☽ 5am-10.30pm). Train tickets can be bought in advance at the **SNCF office** (44 Grande Rue).

Major connections include Paris' Gare de Lyon (from €45 non-TGV, three hours, three daily), Dijon (€14, 50 minutes, 20 daily), Lyon (€32, three hours, eight daily), Belfort (€13, 1¼ hours, six daily), Arbois (€7.40, six to eight daily) and Arc-et-Senans (€5.60, 35 minutes, four daily). To get to Frasne (near Métabief), change trains in Mouchard (€12.90, 2½ hours).

Getting Around

BUS

Local buses are run by **CTB** (☎ 03 81 48 12 12), which has a **ticket & information kiosk** (place du 8 Septembre; ☽ 9am-12.30pm & 1-7pm Mon-Sat). A single ticket/day ticket/carnet of 10 costs €1/3.20/8.50. Bus Nos 8 and 24 link the train station with the centre.

TAXI

You can phone for a **taxi** (☎ 03 81 88 80 80) or pick one up next to the town hall.

AROUND BESANÇON

Saline Royal

Envisaged by its designer, Claude-Nicolas Ledoux, as the 'ideal city', the 18th-century **Saline Royale** (Royal Salt Works; ☎ 03 81 54 45 45; fax 03 81 54 45 46; adult/student/child €7/4.50/2.80; ☽ 9am-7pm Jul-Aug, 9am-6pm Jun & Sep, 9am-noon & 2-6pm Apr, May & Oct, 10am-noon & 2-5pm Nov-Dec, Jan-Mar) at **Arc-et-Senans**, 30km southwest of Besançon, is a showpiece of early Industrial Age town planning. Although his urban dream was never realised, Ledoux's semicircular salt-works is now listed as a Unesco World Heritage site.

The **tourist office** (☎ 03 81 57 43 21; www.ot -arcetsenans.fr; Saline Royale; ☽ 2-5pm Mon-Wed, 10am-noon & 2-5pm Fri & Sat, closed Thus & Sun) is housed inside the gateway of the Salt Works, and can help with finding local homestays and B&Bs. One option nearby is **Hotel Relais** (☎ 03 81 57 40 60; fax 03 81 57 46 17; d €32-35), a family-run place in the centre of the village, with 10 cosy double rooms in a traditional red-roofed house.

Camping des Bords de Loue (☎ 03 81 57 42 20, 03 81 57 43 21; camping €12-18; ☽ May-Oct) is a 1.5km-hike signposted off the main road.

There are regular trains running from Besançon (€5.60, 35 minutes, eight to 10 daily) to Arc-et-Senans.

Ornans

pop 4015

Ornans, 25km southeast of Besançon, is known as Franche-Comté's 'Little Venice'. The River Loue cuts through the heart of the pretty old town, above which towers the **Château d'Ornans**.

Realist painter Gustave Courbet (1819–77) was born in Ornans, and his house is now occupied by the **Musée Courbet** (☎ 03 81 62 23 30; summer/winter €6.70/3.40; ☽ 10am-noon & 2-6pm, closed Tue Nov-Mar), which displays some of the famous works of Courbet, including a self-portrait painted while he was in prison.

Chocoholics should aim to hit Ornans in March for the annual **Chocolate Festival** (☎ 03 81 40 21 01; www.rec-production.com).

The best hotel in Ornans is the smart **Hôtel de France** (☎ 03 81 62 24 44; hoteldefrance@euro post.org; 51-53 rue Pierre-Vernier; **P**), opposite the bridge across the river Loue.

Close to Ornans, the **Vallée de la Loue** (Loue Valley) is a popular destination for mountain biking, canoeing and kayaking enthusiasts. Contact the **Syratu sports club** (☎ 03 81 57 10 82; fax 03 81 57 18 49; 2 route de Montgesoye) for information. Ornans' **tourist office** (☎ 03 81 61 21 50; 7 rue Pierre Vernier; ☽ 9.30am-noon & 3-5.30pm Mon-Fri, 9.30am-noon & 2-6pm Sat) has plenty of walking and cycling information.

There are nine buses daily (€3.30, 45 minutes) from Besançon to Ornans.

Route Pasteur & Route du Vin

Nearly every town in the Jura seems to have a street, square or garden (sometimes all three) named after Louis Pasteur, the great 19th-century chemist who invented pasteurisation and developed the first rabies vaccine (he also made great leaps in the treatment of ailing silkworms). And rightly so – though much of his working life was spent in Paris, Pasteur was born and raised in the Jura, and he returned for holidays until his death in 1895.

Pasteur was born in **Dole**, 20km west of Arc-et-Senans along the D472. His childhood home, **La Maison Natale de Pasteur** (☎ 03 84 72 20 61; www.musee-pasteur.com; 43 rue Pasteur; adult/child €4.50/2; ☽ 10am-6pm Mon-Sat, 2-6pm Sun Jul & Aug, 10am-noon & 2-6pm Mon-Sat, 2-6pm Sun Apr-Jun, Sep & Oct,

10am-noon & 2-6pm Sat & Sun Nov-Mar), overlooking the Canal des Tanneurs in the old town, is now an atmospheric museum housing letters, artefacts and exhibits including his university cap and gown.

In 1827, the Pasteur family settled in the rural community of **Arbois**, about 35km east of Dole. His laboratory and workshops in Arbois are on display at **La Maison de Louis Pasteur** (☎ 03 84 66 11 72; 83 rue de Courcelles; adult/child €5.50/2.80). Visits are only by **tour** (☙ hourly 9.45-11.45am & half-hourly 2.15-6.15pm Jun-Sep, hourly 2.15-5.15pm Apr, May & 1-15 Oct). The house is still decorated with its original 19th-century fixtures and fittings.

Despite his international reputation, Pasteur was an active member of village life, and often found himself called upon to dispense neighbourly advice on subjects ranging from sickly vines to sickly children (despite the fact that he was a chemist by profession). He also regularly took part in the **Fête de Bou**, a traditional harvest festival that still takes place every year in Arbois.

No visit to Arbois, the wine capital of the Jura, would be complete without sampling a glass of *vin jaune*. The history of this nutty 'yellow wine', which is matured for six years in oak casks, is recounted in the **Musée de la Vigne et du Vin** (☎ 03 84 66 26 14; percee@jura.vins .com; ☙ 10am-noon & 2-6pm Wed-Mon Feb-Jun & Sep, 10am-6pm Wed-Mon Jul & Aug) inside the restored

Château Pécaud, a turreted mansion that once formed part of the city's fortifications.

High above Arbois, along the twisting Route du Vin, is **Pupillin**, a quaint, yellow-brick village (population 220) famous for its wine production. Some 10 different *caves* are open to visitors, but there is no public transport to Pupillin and it's a long 2.5km walk uphill from Arbois.

The **tourist office** (☎ 03 84 37 47 37; www.arbois .com; rue de l'Hôtel de Ville; ☙ 9.30am-noon & 2-6pm Sep-Easter, 9am-12.30pm & 2-6.30pm Easter-Sep) offers advice on cycling routes in the Arbois area. The SNCF office is housed in the same building. There are regular trains to Arbois from Besançon via Mouchard (€14.80, 40 minutes, eight to 10 daily).

Poligny & Baume-les-Messieurs

Whereas much of nearby Burgundy relies on the fruits of the vine for its livelihood, the Jura is best known for its cheese. Poligny is the capital of the Comté cheese-making industry, and you can find out all about this venerable cheese at the **Maison du Comté** (☎ 03 84 37 23 51; av de la Résistance; admission free; ☙ 9.30am-noon & 2.30-5pm Tue-Sun summer).

Some 40 million tonnes of Comté are produced each year, mostly by *fruitières* (cheese dairies) located in the Franche-Comté area. The **tourist office** (☎ 03 84 37 24 21; tourisme.poligny@ wanadoo.fr; rue Victor Hugo; ☙ 9am-noon & 2-6pm Mon-Fri,

---

THE CHEESE ROUTE

One of the best ways to taste the Jura's cheeses is to head to a traditional *fruitière* (cheese dairy). Not only will you be able to see cheeses being made in the traditional way, you'll also get to sample regional varieties including Comté, Morbier, Bleu de Gex and Mont d'Or.

Le Hameau du Fromage (☎ 03 81 62 41 51; Cleron, 7km west of Ornans; www.hameaudufromage.com; ☙ 9am-7pm year-round) This is a good place to start your tour, with two films on cheese-making (in English on request), a cheese museum, cheese restaurant and huge cheese shop.

Fructeries Vagne de Château-Chalon (☎ 03 84 44 92 25; vagne-fromageries@wanadoo.fr; Château-Chalon, 10km southwest of Poligny; ☙ 11am-12.30pm & 2-7pm mid-Jun–mid-Sep, 11am-12.30pm & 2-6pm Fri-Sun rest of year) Traditional village *fruitière* offering guided tours and tastings of most of the region's main cheeses.

Musées des Maisons Comtoises (☎ 03 81 55 29 77; maisons-comtoises.org; Nancray, 10km east of Besançon; ☙ 10am-7pm Apr-Oct, 2-5pm mid-Mar–Apr & Oct–mid-Nov) Reconstructed cheese farm dating from the 19th century, now turned into an intriguing museum.

La Fruitière du Massif Jurassien (☎ 03 84 51 24 00; juraterroir.com; Pont-du-Navoy, 10km southeast of Poligny; ☙ 8am-noon & 2-6pm) One of the largest Comté producers in the Jura. Tasting and tours available.

Fruitière bio de la Chaux de Gilley (☎ 03 81 43 30 35; La Chaux, 20km northeast of Pontarlier; ☙ 9am-noon & 6-7pm) One of the only entirely organic cheese farms in the region. English, German and Spanish tours available.

For further info, check out **www.lesroutesducomte.com**, where you'll find other theme tours around the Jura, including suggested routes through the region's lakes, forests, and clock-making centres.

9am-noon & 2-5.30pm Sat) in Poligny has a list of local cheese shops that visitors can tour.

Baume-les-Messieurs (population 200) is an extraordinarily pretty village of cob houses and red-tiled rooftops, nestled between three glacial valleys, 20km south of Poligny. The town is best known for its abandoned **Benedictine abbey** (☎ 03 84 44 99 28; admission €3; ☉ 10am-6pm mid-Jun–mid-Sep). Nearby, the **Grottes de Baume** (Baume Caves; ☎ 03 84 44 61 58), are accessible by road from the foot of the 10m-tall **Cascade de Baume** (Baume Waterfall). Guided **tours** (☉ 10am-5.30pm Apr-Sep) of the 30 million-year-old caves are available.

Immediately to the east of Baume-les-Messieurs is the Jura's **Région des Lacs** (Lakes District).

SLEEPING & EATING
Opposite Baume-les-Messieurs' abbey is **Le Grand Jardin** (☎ 03 84 44 68 37; d €45-60), a traditional village house offering quaint double rooms. Book well ahead in summer.

Café de l'Abbaye (☎ 03 84 44 63 44; ☉ lunch & dinner Mon-Sat summer) is a lovely little café in one of the abbey's old buildings which offers salads, cheese tarts, *tartiflette* and a delicious *cassolette franc-comtoise* (a casserole of potatoes, onions, cheese and local sausage).

Le Comptois (☎ /fax 03 84 25 71 21; d €35-55) is some 5km east in Doucier. Don't miss out on its Jurassien fondue. Le Comptois also organises gastronomic tours of the region.

BELFORT & AROUND
Belfort (population 50,125), just across the border from Germany and Switzerland, is as Alsatian as it is Jurassien. Historically part of Alsace, it became part of the Franche-Comté region in 1921. Today the city is best known as the manufacturer of the TGV train.

Belfort's **tourist office** (☎ 03 84 55 90 90; www.ot-belfort.fr; 2 rue Clemenceau; ☉ 9am-noon & 2-6pm Mon-Fri) can provide city maps and accommodation lists.

The **Musée d'Art et d'Histoire** (☎ 03 84 54 25 51; ☉ 10am-6pm, Wed-Mon Apr-Sep, 10am-noon & 2-6pm Wed-Mon Oct-Apr) is inside the **Vauban citadel**. Open-air concerts are held on Wednesday in summer. At the foot of the citadel stands **Le Lion de Belfort**, created by Frédéric-Auguste Bartholdi, who also designed the Statue of Liberty in New York. The 11m-tall lion commemorates Belfort's resistance to the Prussians in 1870–71 – while the rest of Alsace was annexed as part of the greater German Empire, Belfort stubbornly remained a part of France.

In July, Belfort hosts **Les Eurockéennes** (☎ 03 84 57 01 92; fax 03 84 28 15 12), a three-day open-air rock festival. In **Sochaux**, 12km south of Belfort near Montbéliard , car enthusiasts can visit the **Musée Peugeot** (☎ 03 81 99 42 03; adult/child €7/3.50; ☎ 10am-6pm). The modernist **Sacré-Coeur church** at Audincourt, 4km southeast, is a must for architecture buffs.

The **Massif du Ballon d'Alsace** (1247m), 20km north of Belfort in the southern Vosges Mountains, offers winter skiing, summer walking, mountain biking, kayaking and hot-air ballooning.

Ronchamp
Ronchamp has a **tourist office** (☎ 03 84 63 50 82; 14 place du 14 Juillet; ☎ 9am-noon & 2-6pm Mon & Fri, 9am-noon & 2-5pm Sat Jun-Oct).

La Chapelle de Notre Dame du Haut (Chapel of our Lady of the Height; ☎ 03 84 20 65 13; admission €2; ☎ 9.30am-6.30pm Apr-Sep, to 4pm Oct-Mar), Ronchamp's striking modernist chapel, sits on a hill overlooking the old mining town, 20km west of Belfort. Designed by the Swiss architect Le Corbusier between 1950 and 1955 to replace a church destroyed in WWII, the chapel is considered one of the 20th century's architectural masterpieces – making it a pilgrimage site for thousands of architects every year. The chapel's surreal design and sweeping concrete roof are said to have been inspired by a hermit crab shell.

In summer, Sunday service is at 11am. Over 3000 pilgrims gather here each year on 8 September. A 15-minute walking trail leads uphill from the centre of Ronchamp to the chapel.

Sleeping & Eating
In Ronchamp, **Hôtel à la Pomme d'Or** (☎ 03 84 20 62 12; fax 03 84 63 59 45; d €38-45) is at the foot of the hill leading up to the chapel, while the rustic **Hôtel Carrer** (☎ 03 84 20 62 32; fax 03 84 63 57 08; d €35-40) is 2km north of Ronchamp in Le Rhien.

Don't leave Belfort without biting into a Belfore, a scrumptious almond-flavoured pastry filled with raspberries and topped with hazelnuts.

HOT BOX, CHRISTMAS ICE & JESUS

It's hot, it's soft and it's packed in a box. *Vacherin Mont d'Or* is the only French cheese to be eaten with a spoon – hot (or cold for that matter). Made between 15 August and 15 March with *lait cru* (unpasteurised milk), it derives its unique nutty taste from the spruce bark in which it's wrapped.

Louis XV adored it. In the 18th century it was called fat cheese, wood cheese or box cheese. Today, *vacherin Mont d'Or* is named after the mountain village from which it originates. Connoisseurs top the soft-crusted cheese with chopped onions, garlic and white wine, wrap it in aluminium foil and bake it for 45 minutes to create a *boîte chaude* (hot box).

Only 11 factories in the Jura are licensed to produce *vacherin Mont d'Or* which, ironically, has sold like hot cakes since 1987, when 10 people in Switzerland died from listeriosis after consuming the Swiss version of Mont d'Or. Old-fashioned cheese buffs in Mont d'Or believe the bacterial tragedy, which claimed 34 lives between 1983 and 1987, only happened because the Swiss copycats pasteurised their milk.

Mouthe, 15km south of Métabief Mont d'Or, is the mother of *liqueur de sapin* (fir-tree liqueur). *Glace de sapin* (fir-tree ice cream) also comes from Mont d'Or, known as the North Pole of France due to its seasonal sub-zero temperatures (record low –38°C). Sampling either is rather like ingesting a Christmas tree. Then there's Jesus. *Jésus* – a small, fat version of *saucisse de Morteau* (Morteau sausage) – is the gastronomic delight of the village of Morteau. *Jésus* is easily identified by the wooden peg on its end, attached after the sausage is smoked with pine-wood sawdust in a traditional *tuyé* (mountain hut). Morteau residents claim their sausage is bigger and better than any other French sausage. They host a **sausage festival** (☎ 03 81 50 69 43) every August.

Getting There & Away

Major connections from Belfort's train station include Paris' Gare de Lyon via Besançon (from €53, 4½ hours, three daily), Montbéliard (€3.10, 15 minutes, 20 daily) and Besançon (€13, 1¼ hours, six daily).

From Belfort there are one or two trains a day to/from Ronchamp (€3.80, 20 minutes). On weekdays there are also two buses a day to/from Ronchamp (€3.60, 35 minutes).

MÉTABIEF MONT D'OR

pop 700 / elevation 1000m

Métabief Mont d'Or, 18km south of Pontarlier on the main road to Lausanne, is the region's leading cross-country ski resort. All year, lifts take you almost to the top of Mont d'Or (1463m), the area's highest peak, from where a fantastic 180° panorama stretches over the foggy Swiss plain to Lake Geneva (Lac Léman) and from the Matterhorn all the way to Mont Blanc. Métabief is famed for its unique *vacherin Mont d'Or* cheese.

Orientation & Information

The main lift station for downhill skiers is in Métabief. There are smaller lifts in Les Hôpitaux Neufs, 2km northeast.

In Métabief, the local **tourist office** (☎ 03 81 49 16 79; ot@metabief-montdor.com; 9am-noon

& 2-5pm, closed Sun Sep–mid-Dec) and **École du Ski Français** (ESF; ☎ 03 81 49 04 21; 9am-noon & 2-5pm) are housed in the **Centre d'Accueil** (6 place Xavier Authier).

There is another **tourist office** (☎ 03 81 49 13 81; fax 03 81 49 09 27; 1 place de la Mairie) in Les Hôpitaux Neufs, open until 6pm daily in season.

Fromagerie du Mont d'Or

Comté, *morbier* and *vacherin Mont d'Or* cheese have been produced by the Sancey-Richard family in Métabief since 1953. The **Fromagerie du Mont d'Or** (☎ 03 81 49 02 36; www .fromageriedumontdor.fr; rue Moulin; admission free; cheese shop 9am-12.15pm & 3-7pm Mon-Sat, 9am-noon Sun), which produces over 200 tonnes of cheese a year, is open to visitors. Guided **tours** (9.30am) include a visit to the dairy's salting rooms, where the *vacherin Mont d'Or* cheeses are washed with salt water, and the maturing cellars where the 45kg rounds of Comté cheese are turned by hand twice weekly for up to 12 months. If you want to see cheese being made, arrive with the milk lorry before 10.30am.

Sleeping & Eating

Both tourist offices have comprehensive lists of hotels and apartments to rent in Métabief.

GRANDE TRAVERSÉE DU JURA

The Grande Traversée du Jura (GTJ) – the Grand Jura Crossing – is a 210km cross-country skiing track from Villers-le-Lac (north of Pontarlier) to Hauteville-Lompnes (southwest of Bellegarde). The path peaks at 1500m near the town of Mouthe (south of Métabief) and follows one of the coldest valleys in France. After the first 20km the route briefly crosses into Switzerland, but mostly runs along the border on the French side. Well maintained and very popular, the track takes 10 full days of skiing to cover – a feat even for the ultrafit.

Part of the GTJ – the 76km from Lamoura to Mouthe – is traversed each year during the world's second-largest cross-country skiing competition, the Transjurassienne. Held in late February, the challenge is taken up by more than 4000 skiers, who charge off in a blaze of colour.

For information on the GTJ and accommodation along the route, contact **Relais de Randonnée Étapes Jura** (☎ 03 84 41 20 34; F-39310 Lajoux); or **GTJ-Espace Nordique Jurassien** (☎ 03 84 52 58 10; rue Baronne-Delort, F-39300 Champagnole). The best map of the area is the IGN 1:50,000-scale map entitled *Ski de Fond – Massif du Jura*.

Hôtel Étoile des Neiges (☎ 03 81 49 11 21; fax 03 81 49 26 91; rue du Village; s/d/tr low season €49/59/72; menus €10-28), in Métabief, is a family-run chalet with good, cosy rooms. Local dishes such as *raclette*, fondue Comtoise, *Mont d'Or chaud* and *la saucisse Jésus de Morteau* are served in its excellent restaurant, which is also open to nonguests. Tickle your taste-buds first with a hearty shot of *anis de Pontarlier* (a liquorice-flavoured aperitif), the Jura's answer to Provençal pastis.

Getting There & Away
The closest **train station** (☎ 08 36 35 35 35) is at Frasne, 25km northwest on the rail line between Dijon, Arc-et-Senans and Vallorbe (9km east in Switzerland). From Frasne, there are daily buses that pass through Métabief and Les Hôpitaux Neufs.

AROUND MÉTABIEF MONT D'OR
Winter skiers keen for a break from the slopes should head a few kilometres south to **L'Odyssée Blanche – Parc du Chien Polaire** (White Odyssey Polar Dog Park; ☎ 03 81 69 20 20; fax 03 81 69 13 02; adult/child €6.50/4.90; ☺ 10am-noon & 2-6pm Tue-Sun) in Chaux Neuve. Try your hand at 'mushing' on a dog-drawn sledge, or simply tour the kennels and coo over the huskies and malamutes instead. A 90-minute dog sleigh expedition costs €45 to €50.

The **Château de Joux** (☎ 03 81 69 47 95; adult/student/child €5/4.25/2.55; ☺ 9am-6pm Jul-Aug, 10-11.30am & 2-4.30pm Apr-Jun, tours 10am, 11.30am, 2pm, 3.15pm & 4.15pm Oct-May), 10km north of Métabief, guards the entrance from Switzerland into northern and central France. It sits atop Mont Larmont (922m), overlooking a dramatic **cluse**

(transverse valley). Part of *Les Misérables* (1995) was filmed here, and during the First Empire, the castle was a state prison. Today it houses France's most impressive arms museum. The music and theatre festival, **Festival des Nuits de Joux**, takes place here in mid-July.

Montbenoît (population 230), 20km further north, is the capital of the tiny **Saugeais Republic**. The folkloric republic, declared in 1947, has its own flag, national anthem, postage stamp and a 94-year-old president, Gabrielle Pourchet, who is featured on the Saugeais banknote. During summer a customs officer greets tourists as they enter the town.

PARC NATUREL RÉGIONAL DU HAUT-JURA
The Haut-Jura Regional Park covers an area of 757 sq km, stretching from Chapelle-des-Bois in the north almost to the western tip of Lake Geneva. Each year in February its abundant lakes, mountains and low-lying valleys play host to the Transjurassienne, the world's second longest cross-country skiing race (above). Exploring this region is difficult without private transport.

The largest town in the park, **Ste-Claude** (population 12,704), is best known for its illustrious wooden pipe-making and diamond-cutting traditions, the history of which unfolds in the local pipe and diamond museum. The **CAF** (☎ 03 84 45 58 62; fax 03 84 60 36 88; 8 blvd de la République) provides information on its *refuges* in the Jura. Dubbed the French capital of wooden toys, **Moirans-en-Montagne**, 14km west, is an apt home for the playful **Musée du Jouet** (Toy Museum).

Les Rousses (population 2850, elevation 1100m) on the northeastern edge of the park, is the main centre for winter sports, walking and mountain biking. Three of its four small, gently sloped downhill ski areas – Les Jouvencelles, Le Noirmont and La Serra – are in France; the fourth – La Dole – is in Switzerland. Extensive cross-country trails take skiers as far north as Métabief Mont d'Or as well as eastwards across the Swiss border.

The **tourist office** (☎ 03 84 60 02 55; www.les rousses.com; rue Pasteur), **SNCF bureau** (☎ 03 84 60 01 90) and the **Club des Sports** (☎ 03 84 60 35 14) are inside the **Maison du Tourisme** (route Blanche), next to the bus station.

The Jura's most staggering view can be savoured from the **Col de la Faucille**, 20km south of Les Rousses. As the N5 twists and turns its way down the Jura Mountains past the small ski resort of **Mijoux**, the panoramic view of Lake Geneva embraced by the French Alps and Mont Blanc beyond is startling. For the best vantage point, take a *télécabine* from Mijoux or head for the terrace restaurant of La Mainaz (right).

Continuing a further 25km southeast you arrive at the French–Swiss border, passing through **Ferney-Voltaire**, 5km north of Geneva

en route. Following his banishment from Switzerland in 1759, Voltaire lived in Ferney until his return to Paris and death in 1778. There are guided **tours** (admission €4; ⊙ 10am-6pm Oct-Apr, closed Mon May-Sep) of his estate, which includes a chateau, chapel and seven-hectare park. Past visitors include Auden, Blake and Flaubert, all of whom wrote about the philosopher's home in exile.

AUTHOR'S CHOICE

La Mainaz (☎ 04 50 41 31 10; mainaz@club -Internet.fr; 5 route du Col de la Faucille; d €57-89) What better way to round off your journey in the Jura than at this beautiful, classy hotel, at the edge of the Haut-Jura National Park? There are lots of luxury hotels in the Alps, but you'll need a second mortgage to pay for most of them – the Mainaz manages to combine old-fashioned Alpine charm, modern-day comfort and fantastic value. The rooms are spacious and beautifully presented, but the real draw is the absolutely unbelievable view of the Alps, which you can savour either from your room or the panoramic restaurant terrace. By sunset it's a sight never forgotten.

Massif Central

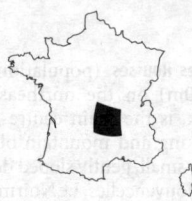

CONTENTS

The Massif Central is France's spine, its vertebrae the spiky plugs and rounded grassy cones of extinct volcanoes called *puys*, (pronounced 'pwee'). Down in the relatively rich volcanic soil of its plains and valleys, maize, tobacco and vines all thrive. Its rumpled slopes are clad in either dense forest or pasture, offering sweet grazing for the cattle and sheep that are the source of Auvergnat cheeses, some of France's finest.

At valley level too you'll find spa towns that these days pull in both the hale and those seeking health. Vichy is for those who treasure a touch of faded elegance while St-Nectaire, home to the smooth, eponymous cheese, and Le Mont-Dore, ski resort in winter and summertime trekking base, both still speak of *la belle époque*.

Clermont-Ferrand is the only city of consequence. It's home to the Michelin tyre giant – though you'd never guess it as you roam the narrow streets of the old quarter. It's a great base for exploring the northern *puys* – and for visiting Vulcania, a breathtaking multimedia exhibition about all things volcanic.

But the Massif Central, with its superb walking and mountain biking, is above all for those who love the great outdoors. Two large regional parks, the dramatic Parc Naturel Régional des Volcans d'Auvergne and its tamer eastern neighbour, the Parc Naturel Régional du Livradois-Forez, together make up France's largest environmentally protected area. And from the Massif Central, which is roughly coextensive with the Auvergne, trickle the myriad streams that band together to form some of France's mightiest rivers such as the Dordogne, Allier and Loire.

HIGHLIGHTS

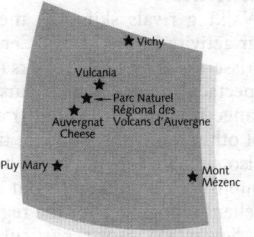

- Drink in views of all southeastern France from **Mont Mézenc's summit** (p569)
- Live a little of the *belle époque* life in the spa town of **Vichy** (p554)
- Puff your way to the tiptop of spectacular **Puy Mary** (p562)
- Survive a virtual volcanic eruption at state-of-the-art **Vulcania** (p553)
- Crunch across **volcanic cinders** (p554), tiny and light as Rice Krispies
- Tuck into windy picnics up high, sampling each day a different **Auvergnat cheese** (p562)

- POPULATION: 1,310,000
- AREA: 26,015 SQ KM

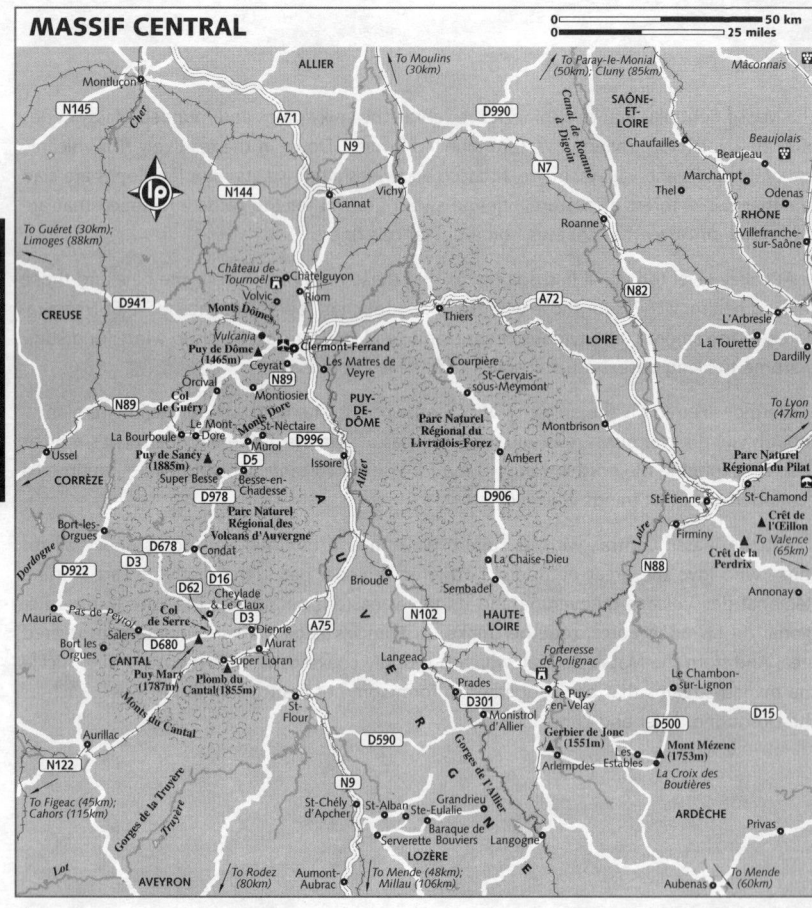

MASSIF CENTRAL

Activities

Walking rivals skiing as the most popular activity in the Massif Central, which is crisscrossed by 13 GR tracks (including the spectacular GR4, which cuts through the range from north to south) and hundreds of other footpaths. Some of these trails are also suitable for mountain biking and the publisher Chamina puts out a series of excellent topoguides for the region.

Several ski resorts, particularly Le Mont-Dore, Super Besse and Super Lioran (near Murat), provide full Alpine skiing facilities and the Massif Central's undulating terrain is great for cross-country skiing.

The region's topography and thermal currents also mean it's ideal for hang-gliding and *parapente* (paragliding), for which the *puys* are used as take-off platforms (p553).

CLERMONT-FERRAND
pop 137,000 / elevation 400m

The lively city of Clermont-Ferrand, the Massif Central's principal urban centre, makes a good base for exploring the north of the region. A student population of some 30,000 gives vitality to the town centre, built on top of a long-extinct volcano.

Clermont-Ferrand is the centre of France's rubber industry, better known to the world as the Michelin tyre empire. The company got into the sideline of guidebook publishing in 1898 to promote motor-car tourism – and thus the use of its pneumatic tyres.

Orientation

The old city is bounded by av des États-Unis, rue André Moinier and blvd Trudaine. The partly pedestrianised commercial centre stretches westwards from the cathedral to av des États-Unis and place de Jaude, then along rue Blatin.

Information

BOOKSHOP

Book'in (☎ 04 73 36 40 06; 38 av des États-Unis) Has a small selection of used English-language books.

INTERNET ACCESS

Lepton (16 av des Paulines; per hr €2.50; ☉ 11am-midnight Mon-Sat, 2pm-midnight Sun; from 2pm school holidays)

Visio2 Paulines (14 av des Paulines; per hr €2.50; ☉ 10am-midnight Mon-Sat, 1-8pm Sun) Carnot (11 av Carnot; per hr €2.50; ☉ 10am-midnight Mon-Sat)

LAUNDRY

Laundrette (6 place Hippolyte Renoux; ☉ 7am-8.30pm)

POST

Main Post Office (rue Maurice Busset)

TOURIST INFORMATION

Espace Massif Central (☎ 04 73 42 60 00; ☉ Mon-Sat) In the same building as the tourist office and observing similar hours. Provides information on the region's outdoor activities. Partly run by Chamina, the excellent Massif Central topoguide publisher, it carries a full range of walking guides.

Tourist Office (☎ 04 73 98 65 00; www.clermont-fd .com; place de la Victoire; ☉ 9am-7pm Mon-Fri, 10am-6pm Sat & Sun May-Sep; 9am-6pm Mon-Fri, 10am-1pm & 2-7pm Sat, 9.30am-12.30pm & 2-6pm Sun Oct-Apr) Espace Art Roman downstairs is an excellent free exhibition highlighting the region's outstanding Romanesque churches. There's a 30-minute film with optional English audio.

Sights

The soaring, Gothic **Cathédrale Notre Dame** (☉ 8am-6pm Jun–mid-Sep, 8am-noon & 2-6pm mid-Sep–May) looks smog-blackened and grim. But the structure's volcanic stones, dug from the quarries of nearby Volvic, were the same blackish-grey hue the day the finishing touches were put to the choir seven centuries ago.

The twin towers are from the 19th century, when the west façade too was restored by the Gothic revivalist Viollet-le-Duc. The ar-

chitects took full advantage of the strength yet lightness of Volvic stone to create a vast, double-aisled nave, held aloft by particularly slender pillars and vaults. Stand before the altar steps and marvel at the glowing 14th-century rose windows at each end of the transept. Several stained glass windows in the choir and side-chapels are also from the 13th and 14th centuries.

From place de la Poterne and its early-16th-century **Fontaine d'Amboise**, two blocks north of the cathedral, there's a fine view of the Puy de Dôme and nearby peaks.

Flanking the narrow streets east of the cathedral are some of Clermont-Ferrand's finest 17th- and 18th-century townhouses, including **Hôtel Reboul-Sadourny** (9 rue Savaron), fronting a small courtyard, and **Hôtel de Chazerat** (4 rue Blaise Pascal).

Rue Blaise Pascal, with several antique shops that merit a browse, leads, via rue du Port, to the 12th-century **Basilique Notre Dame du Port** (☉ 8am-8pm May-Sep, 8am-6pm Oct-Apr), a Unesco World Heritage Site. The highlight of this truly magnificent example of Auvergnat-Romanesque is its choir, into which the light streams on a summer's day. Notice too the delightfully naive carving on the capitals of the four easternmost pillars.

The **Musée Bargoin** (☎ 04 73 91 37 31; 45 rue Ballainvilliers; adult/student/child €4/2.50/free; ☉ 10am-noon & 1-6pm Tue-Sat, 2-5pm Sun) has excellent prehistory and Gallo-Roman sections on the ground floor. Between November and March it mounts temporary exhibitions upstairs.

Just down the street, **Musée Lecoq** (☎ 04 73 91 93 78; 15 rue Bardoux; adult/student/under 18 €4/2/free; ☉ 10am-noon & 2-6pm Mon-Sat May-Sep, to 5pm Oct-Apr; 2-6pm Sun year-round) is a natural history museum with an impressive collection of rocks, fossils, stuffed fauna and pickled things that creep.

The most striking feature of **Place de Jaude**, the city's main square, is the equestrian statue of Vercingétorix, the Celtic chief who almost foiled Julius Caesar's conquest of Gaul (p551).

The quiet, none-too-prosperous suburb of **Montferrand**, 2.5km northeast of the cathedral, beyond the vast Michelin works, is worth a visit for its many **Gothic and Renaissance houses**, especially around where rue de la Rodade meets rue des Cordeliers. Many have stone-built ground floors and overhanging, half-timbered upper floors.

CLERMONT-FERRAND

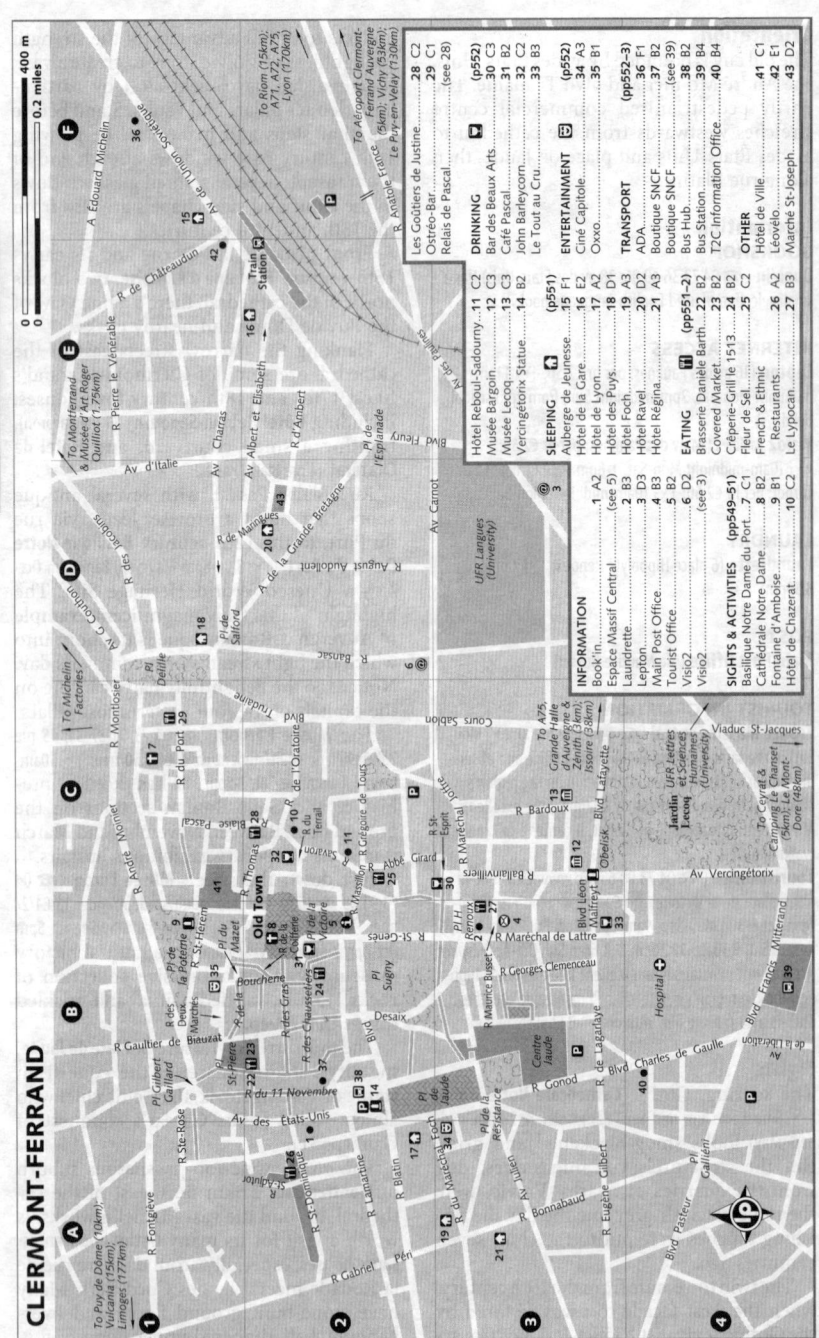

INFORMATION		
Book'in......................................	1	A2
Espace Massif Central.................	(see 5)	
Laundrette.................................	2	B3
Lepton......................................	3	D3
Main Post Office.........................	4	B3
Tourist Office.............................	5	B2
Visio2..	6	D2
Visio2..	(see 3)	

SIGHTS & ACTIVITIES (pp549–51)		
Basilique Notre Dame du Port......	7	C1
Cathédrale Notre Dame................	8	B2
Fontaine d'Amboise....................	9	B1
Hôtel de Chazerat.......................	10	C2

SLEEPING		(p551)
Auberge de Jeunesse...................	15	F1
Hôtel de la Gare.........................	16	E2
Hôtel de Lyon............................	17	A2
Hôtel des Puys...........................	18	D1
Hôtel Foch................................	19	A3
Hôtel Ravel...............................	20	D2
Hôtel Régina..............................	21	A3

EATING		(pp551–2)
Brasserie Danièle Barth................	22	B2
Covered Market..........................	23	B2
Crêperie-Grill Le 1513..................	24	B2
Fleur de Sel...............................	25	C2
French & Ethnic..........................	26	A2
Le Lypocan...............................	27	B3

Hôtel Reboul-Sadourny...............	11	C2
Musée Bargoin...........................	12	C3
Musée Lecoq..............................	13	C3
Vercingétorix Statue....................	14	B2

| Les Goûters de Justine................ | 28 | C2 |
| Ostréo-Bar................................ | 29 | C1 |

DRINKING		(p552)
Bar des Beaux Arts......................	30	C3
Café Pascal...............................	31	B2
John Barleycorn..........................	32	B2
Le Tout au Cru...........................	33	B3

ENTERTAINMENT		(p552)
Ciné Capitole.............................	34	A3
Oxoo..	35	B1

TRANSPORT		(pp552–3)
ADA..	36	F1
Boutique SNCF...........................	37	B2
Boutique SNCF...........................	(see 39)	
Bus Hub....................................	38	B4
Bus Station...............................	39	B4
T2C Information Office.................	40	B4

OTHER		
Hôtel de Ville.............................	41	C1
Léovélo.....................................	42	E1
Marché St-Joseph........................	43	D2

CELTIC HERO

Vercingétorix, chief of the Celtic Arverni tribe, almost foiled Julius Caesar's conquest of Gaul. With most of Gaul overrun and Caesar slyly playing one tribe off against the other, Vercingétorix pulled together the tribes between the Loire and Garonne rivers and forged a force that could match the Roman legions in discipline.

In the summer of 52 BC, it thrashed Caesar's troops at Gergovia near Clermont-Ferrand, in the tribe's heartland. Glimpsing hope, all but five of the Gallic tribes rose against Rome and joined forces, led by Vercingétorix.

For a couple of years, the Gauls hounded the Romans with guerrilla warfare and stood up to them in several match-drawn pitched battles. But gradually Gallic resistance collapsed and Roman rule in Gaul reigned supreme.

Vercingétorix was captured and taken to Rome, where he was paraded in chains in Caesar's triumphal procession. As a final insult, he was left languishing in prison for six years before being put to death by strangulation.

The **Musée d'Art Roger Quilliot** (☎ 04 73 16 11 30; place Louis Deteix; adult/child €4/free; 10am-6pm Tue-Sun) is an excellent fine arts museum in an architecturally superb complex in Montferrand. It has a fascinating, chronologically arranged collection of sculpture, painting and art objects from the late Middle Ages to the 20th century. To get to Montferrand, take the bus No 16 from place de Jaude or Nos 1 and 9 from the bus station.

Sleeping

Auberge de Jeunesse (☎ 04 73 92 26 39; fax 04 73 92 99 96; 55 av de l'Union Soviétique; dm €8.90; May-Oct) The Auberge du Cheval Blanc (White Horse Inn), Clermont's HI-affiliated hostel, is only 100m from the bus and train stations.

Hôtel Ravel (☎ 04 73 91 51 33; hotelravel63@ wanadoo.fr; 8 rue de Maringues; s/d €35/42) With its eccentric mosaic façade and pleasant old-fashioned rooms, the Ravel is a good bet if you like your accommodation with character – something the landlady too has, in spades! It's in a quiet part of town, where the only bustle comes from the St-Joseph morning market, around which there's free parking, once evening falls.

Hôtel de la Gare (☎ 04 73 92 07 82; garehotel63@aol .com; 76 av Charras; s/d €35/40) One of several hotels in a quiet street near the train station, the 19-room Hôtel de la Gare, fully renovated in 2003, is a good two-star choice.

Hôtel Régina (☎ 04 73 93 44 76; regina.foch@ wanadoo.fr; 14 rue Bonnabaud; d €36, s/d with bathroom €46/52;) On a quiet street, just off place de Jaude in the heart of town, Hôtel Régina has trim, comfortable rooms and private parking (€6) right opposite.

Hôtel Foch (☎ 04 73 93 48 40; regina.foch@wanadoo .fr; 22 rue Maréchal Foch; d €32, s with bathroom €37-46, d €42-50;   ) Owned by the same family as the Régina, Hôtel Foch is an equally central, marginally more economical choice with smaller rooms, some of which have air-con.

Hôtel de Lyon (☎ 04 73 17 60 80; hotelde.lyon@ wanadoo.fr; 16 place de Jaude; s €53.50-60.50, d €67-75;   ) This 33-room hotel on place de Jaude couldn't possibly be more central – and it has private parking so your car needn't be an encumbrance. Most rooms overlook the square and are double glazed throughout so you needn't be apprehensive about noise from the square-side pub.

Hôtel des Puys (☎ 04 73 91 92 06; www.hoteldespuys .fr; 16 place Delille; s €67-75, d €83-90;   ) In most rooms, toilet and bathroom are separate and the majority share a balcony overlooking busy place Delille. All have been recently and comprehensively renovated and – rare for France – one floor is reserved for non-smokers. Equally recently renamed, this three-star hotel still features in many information sources as Hôtel des Puys d'Arverne.

CAMPING

Camping Le Chanset (☎ 04 73 61 30 73; camping .lechanset@wanadoo.fr; av Jean Baptiste, Ceyrat; per person/tent/car €2.60/4/1.50; year-round) The nearest camping ground is in Ceyrat, virtually a suburb of Clermont-Ferrand. Bus No 4 stops right outside.

Eating

RESTAURANTS

Two blocks north of place de Jaude, rue St-Dominique and nearby rue St-Adjutor sprawl with reasonably priced **French and ethnic restaurants**, including Tunisian, Indian, Vietnamese, Italian, Tex-Mex, Portuguese and Cuban.

Brasserie Danièle Bath (☎ 04 73 31 23 22; place St-Pierre; menu €21, mains €15-25; ☷ Tue-Sat, closed mid-end Feb & 18-31 Aug) This classy little place serves top-quality dishes based on fresh local ingredients from the central market opposite. Dining is a delight on its summer terrace.

Fleur de Sel (☎ 04 73 90 30 59; 8 rue Abbé Girard; menus €25 & €40, mains €25-30; ☷ Tue-Sat Sep-Jul) Fleur de Sel specialises in fine fish and seafood, which feature in every dish except the desserts. It's small, stylishly furnished and popular so you'll need to reserve.

Relais de Pascal (☎ 04 73 92 21 04; 15 rue Blaise Pascal; weekday lunch menus €8-10.50, dinner €19.50; ☷ Tue-Sat) This seething *bar-restaurant du quartier* serves pork-based Auvergnat dishes on marble tables. Ample platters of pig-based *charcuterie* (€5.60 to €9.20) are dished up any old time.

Crêperie-Grill le 1513 (☎ 04 73 92 37 46; 3 rue des Chaussetiers; menus €13.50-23, crepes €2.50-5.50) This cavernous restaurant occupies the ground floor of a sumptuous mansion built in 1513 – hence the name. For a hefty snack, go for a *galette* (savoury buckwheat pancake). For the ravenous, the French fries that accompany the mains must have depleted half a potato field. Go downstairs to the lovely internal terrace for summer dining.

Ostréo Bar (☎ 04 73 91 58 28; 63bis rue du Port; ☷ 7.30am-8pm Mon-Sat) This tiny hole in the wall offers oysters (€13 per dozen, €8.50 to take away) whenever there's an 'r' in the month.

Le Lypocan (☎ 04 73 92 67 24; 16 place Hippolyte Renoux; ☷ lunch & dinner Sat, dinner Tue-Fri, lunch Mon) This is an informal, immensely popular pizza and pasta joint that also does meaty mains with an Italian touch.

CAFÉS

Les Goûters de Justine (☎ 04 73 92 26 53; 11bis rue Blaise Pascal; ☷ noon-7pm Tue-Sat) This charming tearoom – it's rather like stepping into your great aunt's parlour – is a haven of calm and mellowness in the heart of the city that also does a range of snacks.

SELF-CATERING

The city's **covered market** (☷ 6am-7pm Mon-Sat) is a jumble of blue, yellow and grey cubes splaying over place St-Pierre.

Drinking

Café Pascal (4 place de la Victoire) This favourite exchange-student hang-out is most times packed to the gunnels inside and you'll be lucky to find a chair on its popular summertime terrace.

Bar des Beaux Arts (4 rue Ballainvilliers) This bar too pulls in the student crowd, here to enjoy its recently renovated interior or to sit and sip at the tables that take over most of the adjacent square.

Le Tout au Cru (9 blvd Léon Malfreyt; dishes €8) This pleasant, intimate wine bar with its wooden counter and tables serves a variety of wines by the glass and snacks. You'll enjoy its plate of cold cuts and salad.

John Barleycorn (9 rue du Terrail; ☷ 2pm-2am Mon-Sat May-Aug, 5pm-2am Mon-Sat Sep-Apr) This long-established Celtic pub serves liquids brewed from both barley and corn.

Entertainment

Oxxo (☎ 04 73 14 11 11; 14-16 rue des Deux Marchés; admission €5; ☷ 10pm-4am Wed-Sat) The downstairs dance floor at this rough-hewn discotheque-bar, popular with students, only begins to fill up after 11pm.

There are nondubbed films at the five-screen **Ciné Capitole** (☎ 08 92 68 73 33; 32 place de Jaude).

The city's main venue for concerts and spectacles is the striking, ultramodern **Zénith** (☎ 04 73 77 24 24), which can accommodate up to 8500 spectators. Inaugurated in late 2003 and part of the Grande Halle d'Auvergne complex, it's southeast of the city centre.

Getting There & Away

AIR

The **Clermont-Ferrand Auvergne airport** (☎ 04 73 62 71 00), a major Air France hub for domestic and European flights, is 7km east of the city centre.

BUS

The **bus station** (69 blvd François Mitterrand) has an efficient **information office** (☎ 04 73 93 13 61).

Bus No 73 runs to Riom (€3.60, 15-30 minutes, nine daily) and No 1 serves Thiers (€7.90, 1¼ hours, up to 10 daily). For Vichy, you're better off by train.

Intercars (☎ 04 73 29 70 05) handles Eurolines ticketing. **Linebus** (☎ 04 73 34 81 16; ☷ 10am-7pm Mon-Sat) has buses to a wide number of destinations in Spain.

CAR & MOTORCYCLE

Try **ADA car rental** (☎ 04 73 91 66 07; 79 av de l'Union Soviétique).

TRAIN

Clermont-Ferrand is the Massif Central's most important rail junction. It has two **boutiques SNCF** (ticketing offices; ☎ 08 92 35 35 35; 43 rue du 11 Novembre & bus station).

Destinations include Paris' Gare de Lyon (€39, 3½ hours, six to nine daily) and Lyon (€23.20 via St-Étienne, three hours, up to 12 daily). The route through the Gorges de l'Allier to Nîmes (€31.80, five hours, two or three daily) via Langeac (€13.40) and Monistrol d'Allier (€16.10), known as Le Cévenol, is one of the most scenic in France.

Short-haul trains run to/from Le Mont-Dore (€10.70, 1¼ hours, four or five daily), Le Puy-en-Velay (€18.10, 2¼ hours, four daily), Murat (€14.50, 1½ hours, six to 10 daily), Riom (€2.60, 10 minutes, frequent), Vichy (€8.10, 40 minutes, frequent) and Thiers (€7.30, 40 to 55 minutes, eight to 10 daily).

Getting Around

Léovélo (☎ 04 73 14 12 36; av de l'Union Soviétique; ☷ 7am-7pm Mon-Sat), a splendid public sector initiative, rents bikes for a bargain €3/5 per half-/full-day. You need to drop a refundable deposit of €150.

The local bus company, **T2C** (☎ 04 73 28 56 56), has an information office on place de Jaude.

Call **Allo Taxi** (☎ 04 73 19 53 53).

AROUND CLERMONT-FERRAND
Puy de Dôme

Covered in outdoor adventurers in summer and snow in winter, the balding Puy de Dôme (1465m) gives a panoramic view of Clermont-Ferrand and scores of volcanoes. The Celts, then Romans, worshipped their gods from the summit. Nowadays, dominated by a TV transmission tower resembling a giant rectal thermometer, it's a popular launching platform for *parapente* and hang-gliding enthusiasts.

You can reach the summit either by the 'mule track' – a steepish hour's climb starting at the Col de Ceyssat, 4km off the D941A – or by the 4km **toll road** (per vehicle €4.50; ☷ 8am-dusk Mar-Nov, weekends only Dec). This road is closed to private cars from 10am to 6pm daily in July and August and between 12.30pm and 6pm on weekends in May, June and September – then, you take a shuttle bus (per adult/child €3.50/1.40 return).

Vulcania

Vulcania (☎ 08 20 82 78 28; www.vulcania.com; adult/child €19/12; ☷ 9am-6pm or 7pm Apr-Aug, Wed-Sun mid-Feb–Mar & Sep–mid-Nov) is 15km to the west of Clermont-Ferrand on the D941B. A hugely spectacular multimedia visitors centre in an architecturally innovative site, it illustrates the workings of volcanoes and their role in the development of our planet.

Riom
pop 18,800

Riom, 15km north of Clermont-Ferrand on the train line to Vichy, makes a convenient day or half-day trip from Clermont-Ferrand. The streets of the austere old city, in the Middle Ages the capital of the Auvergne region, are lined with magistrates' mansions built of dark Volvic stone.

ORIENTATION & INFORMATION

The main arteries of the old city are the north–south rue du Commerce, plus its northern extension, rue de l'Horloge, and the east–west rue de l'Hôtel de Ville. The train station is 400m southeast of the old city at the end of av Virlogeux.

The **tourist office** (☎ 04 73 38 59 45; www.riom -auvergne.com in French; 16 rue du Commerce; ☷ 9.30am-noon & 2-5.30pm Tue, Wed, Fri & Sat, 2-5.30pm Mon & Thu Sep-Jun, 9.30am-12.30pm & 2-6.30pm Mon-Sat, 10am-1pm Sun Jul & Aug), 100m south of rue de l'Hôtel de Ville, supplies an English-language walking-tour brochure.

SIGHTS

The 15th-century **Église Notre Dame du Marthuret** (rue du Commerce), about 200m from the tourist office, has a fine pair of 14th-century statues of the Virgin: the *Vierge à l'Oiseau* (Virgin with Bird; the figure over the entrance is a copy – the original is inside, in the first chapel to the right) – and the squat *Vierge Noire* (Black Virgin), in the next chapel eastwards.

Transitional **Église St-Amable** (rue St-Amable) has a Gothic choir and a Romanesque nave, its pillars topped by wonderful painted capitals.

Riom has two **museums** (combined ticket adult/child €5.60/2.60; ☺ 10am-noon & 2.30-6pm Tue-Sun Jun-Sep, 10am-noon & 2-5.30pm Tue-Sun Oct-May), both of which merit a visit. The **Musée Francisque Mandet** (☎ 04 73 38 18 53; 14 rue de l'Hôtel de Ville) has a collection of classical antiquities, medieval sculptures and 17th- to 19th-century paintings while the excellent **Musée d'Auvergne** (☎ 04 73 38 17 31; 10bis rue Delille) has displays documenting rural life in Auvergne.

Volvic

About 7km southwest of Riom is the town of **Volvic**, famous for its spring water and quarries which provided the lightweight but strong volcanic stone used in so many local buildings, including Clermont-Ferrand's cathedral.

Even if you don't go inside, it is well worth the walk up to the ruins of the nearby **Château de Tournoël** (adult/child €5/3; ☺ Apr-Sep) to enjoy the splendid panoramic view from its base.

PARC NATUREL RÉGIONAL DES VOLCANS D'AUVERGNE

An ideal area for great walking is the 3950-sq-km, 120km- long **Parc Naturel Régional des Volcans d'Auvergne** (information office ☎ 04 73 65 64 00). Volcanic activity started about 20 million years ago, with the last eruptions petering out about 5000 years ago.

The northernmost range, the **Monts Dômes**, are a chain of some 80 'recent' cinder cones, the best known being the Puy de Dôme (see p553). Three million years older, the **Monts Dore** culminate in the Puy de Sancy (1885m), the Massif Central's highest point and a popular downhill ski station in winter. At its foot lies the spa town of Le Mont-Dore, an ideal base from which to explore the area.

The wilder, rugged **Monts du Cantal**, all that remains of a super-volcano worn down over the millennia, dominate the south of the park. The highest point is the Plomb du Cantal (1855m), a desolate peak often shrouded in heavy, swirling clouds, even in summer.

VICHY
pop 27,000

The spa resort of Vichy exudes faded *belle époque* charm. The town became enormously fashionable after visits by Napoleon III in the 1860s. These days, however, the average age of *curistes* (patients taking the waters) must equal that of any old folk's home. Most come seeking relief from rheumatism, arthritis and digestive ailments under France's generous social security system.

Since July 1940, Vichy has enjoyed dubious fame as the wartime capital of Marshal Philippe Pétain's collaborationist 'Vichy French' government, attracted to the town by the availability of hotel rooms and phone lines.

Orientation

Vichy is centred around triangular Parc des Sources, 800m west of the train station along rue de Paris. Rue Georges Clemenceau, the main shopping thoroughfare, crosses the partly pedestrianised city centre.

Information

Échap (☎ 04 70 32 28 57; 12 rue Source de l'Hôpital; per hr €4; ☺ noon-midnight Tue-Sat, 2pm-midnight Sun) Internet access.
Main Post Office (place Charles de Gaulle)
Multi-Nett (12 rue Source de l'Hôpital; ☺ 7am-9pm) Laundrette.
Tourist Office (☎ 04 70 98 71 94; www.vichytourisme .com; 19 rue du Parc; ☺ 9am-7.30pm Mon-Sat, 9.30am-12.30pm & 3-7pm Sun Jul & Aug, 9am-12.30pm & 1.30-7pm Mon-Sat, 9.30am-12.30pm & 3-7pm Sun Apr-Jun & Sep, 9am-noon & 1.30-6pm Mon-Fri, 9am-noon & 2-6pm Sat, 2.30- 5.30pm Sun Oct-Mar)

Sights & Activities

To savour the full richness of Vichy's Second Empire and *belle époque* heritage, pick up a couple of flimsy pamphlets (in French but very visual) from the tourist office. *Vichy Pas à Pas* describes a couple of walking routes while *Quartier Thermal Vichy: Exercices de Styles* explores the spa area in more depth.

The bench-lined walkways of **Parc des Sources**, created in 1812, are enclosed by a covered promenade. At the park's northern end is the glass-enclosed **Hall des Sources** (☺ 6.15am-6/7/8.30pm), whose taps deliver six types of mineral water, three of them warm (up to 43.3°C). There's no charge to sit in

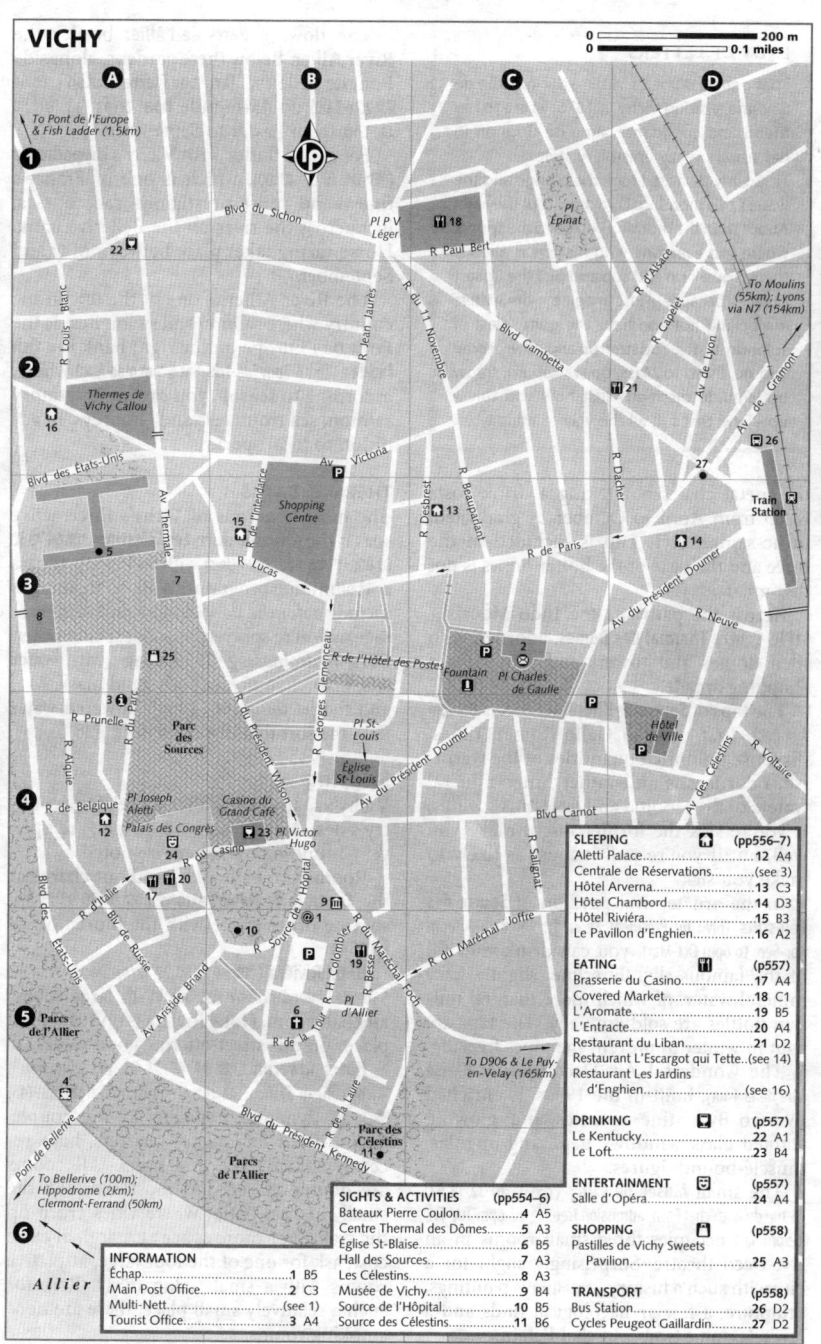

VICHY

| 0 | 200 m |
| 0 | 0.1 miles |

MASSIF CENTRAL

SLEEPING 🛏 (pp556–7)
Aletti Palace.....................................**12** A4
Centrale de Réservations.............(see 3)
Hôtel Arverna...................................**13** C3
Hôtel Chambord...............................**14** D3
Hôtel Riviéra....................................**15** B3
Le Pavillon d'Enghien......................**16** A2

EATING 🍴 (p557)
Brasserie du Casino..........................**17** A4
Covered Market................................**18** C1
L'Aromate..**19** B5
L'Entracte..**20** A4
Restaurant du Liban.........................**21** D2
Restaurant L'Escargot qui Tette....(see 14)
Restaurant Les Jardins
    d'Enghien....................................(see 16)

DRINKING 🍷 (p557)
Le Kentucky.....................................**22** A1
Le Loft...**23** B4

ENTERTAINMENT 🎭 (p557)
Salle d'Opéra...................................**24** A4

SHOPPING 🛍 (p558)
Pastilles de Vichy Sweets
    Pavilion......................................**25** A3

TRANSPORT (p558)
Bus Station......................................**26** D2
Cycles Peugeot Gaillardin................**27** D2

SIGHTS & ACTIVITIES (pp554–6)
Bateaux Pierre Coulon.......................**4** A5
Centre Thermal des Dômes.................**5** A3
Église St-Blaise.................................**6** B5
Hall des Sources................................**7** A3
Les Célestins.....................................**8** A3
Musée de Vichy.................................**9** B4
Source de l'Hôpital...........................**10** B5
Source des Célestins.........................**11** B6

INFORMATION
Échap..**1** B5
Main Post Office................................**2** C3
Multi-Nett.....................................(see 1)
Tourist Office....................................**3** A4

Allier

LADY OF LETTERS

That *grande dame* of letter writing, Mme de Sévigné, visiting Vichy in 1676, wrote to her friend and confidante Mme de Grignon in her usual breezy epistolary style:

'So, my dearest, I took the plunge and the waters this morning. Lord, how foul they are! About six in the morning you go to the spring, where just everyone who matters is already there. You all sip and sup and pull the ugliest of faces because – just imagine – the waters are boiling hot and have the quite vilest of sulphury tastes. You stroll up and down, come and go, listen to Mass, go walkabout, throw up, confide discreetly just how you threw up – and that's it, all the way to midday...'

the metal chairs but taking a drink costs €1.65 from April to October. A graduated, urine-sample-style cup is included in the price and the taste of the hotter brews is not dissimilar.

Across the path sits the Indo-Moorish-style **Centre Thermal des Dômes**, adorned with tiled domes and towers and nowadays a shopping arcade.

The taps of **Source de l'Hôpital** (8am-8.30pm Apr-Dec), first used in Gallo-Roman times, dispense unlimited quantities of the warmish, odoriferous and rather bitter mineral waters of the Hôpital and Célestins springs. If you're sick the former might make you well, but if you're well it's just as likely to make you sick.

In the ornate, oval pavilion of **Source des Célestins** (blvd du Président Kennedy; 8am-8.30pm Apr-Sep, to 6pm Oct-Mar), you can drink your fill of the famous slightly saline, slightly fizzy mineral water, of which more than 60 million bottles are sold annually. The taps are shut in winter to prevent the pipes freezing.

The wonderful Art-Deco **Église St-Blaise** (rue de la Tour), built in the 1930s, is enriched by neo-Byzantine mosaics and glowing stained-glass windows depicting angular, muscle-bound figures.

The small **Musée de Vichy** (04 70 32 12 97; 15 rue du Maréchal Foch; admission free; 2-6pm Tue-Fri, 2-5pm Sat) occupies three small rooms in an Art-Deco theatre. Surprisingly slight for a city with such a history, it displays paintings, sculpture, a few archaeological finds and a few telegrams from Marshal Pétain.

The flowery **Parcs de l'Allier** border the River Allier. Below these gardens, alongside Pont de Bellerive, **Bateaux Pierre Coulon** (04 73 26 62 00) do 45-minute **boat trips** (adult/child €6/4.50) from Easter to September.

For a little flutter, visit Vichy's **Hippodrome** (04 70 32 47 00), which is one of France's finest and most prestigious racecourses, just across the river on the Bellerive bank. Horse racing takes place between May and September.

The River Allier is one of the few in the country where salmon still swim. Beside the Pont de l'Europe on the right bank is a **fish ladder** (3-7pm Tue-Thu, Sat & Sun Mar-Aug) where, according to season, you can see migratory salmon, sea trout, eels and lampreys, in addition to local species.

THERMAL BATHS

The most luxurious of Vichy's three active spas is the ultramodern **Les Célestins** (04 70 30 82 00; 111 blvd des États-Unis) with its beauty, fitness and slimming programs. Walk-in treatments include a *douche de Vichy* (a four-hand massage as you're sprayed with hot spring water; €41), *hydromassage* (a massage with water jets; €28), *illutation* (a body mud mask; €41) and the *jet tonifiant* (a high-powered water jet – the sort that disperses riots; €28).

Sleeping

Vichy's many hotels offer some of the country's best deals. Those we include are open year-round unless otherwise noted.

Rooms can be booked without charge at the **Centrale de Réservations** (04 70 98 23 83), sharing office space with the tourist office (p554).

Hôtel Riviéra (04 70 98 22 32; fax 04 70 96 14 09; 5 rue de l'Intendance; s/d €30/33) With large rooms and bathroom, Hôtel Riviéra is one of several places on this street offering good value.

Hôtel Arverna (04 70 31 31 19; www.hotels -vichy.com in French; 12 rue Desbrest; s/d from €39/45;) A dynamic, engaging young couple, fleeing Paris for quieter quarters, have recently taken over this hotel. All rooms are double glazed and most overlook the small internal patio, where vines creep up the walls. For more space at marginal extra cost, ask for one of the four large, attractive rooms with a small salon (€51). Rare for such a relatively small place, there are non-smoking rooms.

Pavillon d'Enghien (☎ 04 70 98 33 30; www.pavil londenghien.com; 32 rue Callou; s €45-70, d €57-76; closed 20 Dec–1 Feb; P ⓔ) Rooms in this converted mansion are trim and attractive. Each is individually furnished without one square centimetre of plastic in sight, except for the minibar. Nearly all rooms have a bathtub and most overlook the internal garden and small pool. Next door is its fantastic restaurant, **Les Jardins d'Enghien**, whose *menu terroir et découverte* (€18), an ample selection of local specialities, is quite outstanding value.

Hôtel Chambord (☎ 04 70 30 16 30; le.chambord@ wannadoo.fr; 82-84 rue de Paris; s €35-42, d €38-51) This hotel, handy for the station, has been run by the same family for three generations. Welcoming and relaxed, it runs a decent restaurant, **L'Escargot qui Tette** (The Suckling Snail; menus €26 & 33).

Aletti Palace (☎ 04 70 30 20 20; www.aletti.fr; 3 place Joseph Aletti; s €92-138, d €107-153; ☒ ☒ ▢ ⓔ) This is *the* place to stay to get a sense of what a visit during the *belle époque* must have been like for the affluent. Nothing could be more of the era and more French – except that, as a sign of more modern times, it has now become part of a multinational chain. But no chain-smoking here – an impressive 40% of the rooms are tobacco-free.

Eating

For two excellent hotel restaurants, see Les Jardins d'Enghien, at Le Pavillon d'Enghien, and L'Escargot qui Tette, at Hôtel Chambord (above).

Brasserie du Casino (☎ 04 70 98 23 06; 4 rue du Casino; lunch menu €14, fish menu €24; ☾ Thu-Mon, closed mid-Oct–mid-Nov & mid-end-Feb) This is a wonderful pre-WWII brasserie, its walls plastered with signed photos of the once-famous artistes who dropped in from the Opéra, just across the road. Count on around €35 for an à la carte meal with wine.

Restaurant du Liban (☎ 04 70 31 14 79; 51 blvd Gambetta; mezze €3-4.30; closed lunch Mon) This unpretentious place serves tasty Lebanese food, offering more than 50 different kinds of mezze. For a variety of taste sensations, go for the *mini mezze* (€22 for two people), a selection of 10 of the best.

L'Entracte (☎ 04 70 59 85 68; 10 rue du Casino; ☾ Tue-Sat) Essentially a wine bar clad in attractive antique wood panelling, this is a great place for an open toasted sandwich (€7.50) or a platter of Auvergnat cheese (€6), sluiced down with fine wine from the select wine list, available by the glass.

SELF-CATERING

The cavernous **covered market**, built in the mid-1930s in a heavy, unadorned Stalinist style, is on place PV Léger.

Drinking

There's little after dark in Vichy to make young blood tingle.

Le Kentucky (14 blvd du Sichon; ☾ 5pm-2am Mon-Sat) pulls in a young crowd and has a decent range of draught beers. Thursday night is student night.

Le Loft (☎ 04 70 97 16 46; 7 rue du Casino; admission €8; ☾ from 11pm Thu-Sun), below the Casino du Grand Café, is a popular discotheque.

Entertainment

Grab *Vichy Mensuel*, a free monthly what's-on guide, at the tourist office or around town.

Vichy was once known as the 'French Bayreuth', and even today operas, operettas, dance performances and concerts are regularly staged in the ornate 1902 **Salle d'Opéra** (☎ 04 70 30 50 50; rue du Casino) in the Palais des Congrès (formerly Vichy's Grand Casino).

AUTHOR'S CHOICE

L'Aromate (☎ 04 70 32 13 22; 9 rue Besse; menus €13.50-31, mains €16-18; ☾ mid-Aug–mid-Jul, closed Wed, dinner Tue & Sun) With its pillars topped by ornate capitals holding up the high ceiling – which, it must be said, bears a crack or two – its softly piped classical music and tall, gilded mirrors, L'Aromate speaks of a lost elegance. But the food is imaginative, stylishly presented and strictly contemporary. It's a fairly formal place; reservations are all but essential and even if you strike lucky with a lunchtime walk-in, you won't be all that well regarded. And don't expect lightning service; good food, as the menu points out, takes time. So set aside a good two hours of your life. By the end, you won't regret it and, as a souvenir of a special meal, you can take away a pot of one of their exotic home-made jams.

Shopping

You can sample and purchase the octagonal mint, aniseed and lemon lozenges known as *pastilles de Vichy*, pride of the city since 1825, at the **sweets pavilion** of the **Parc des Sources** (Apr-Oct).

Getting There & Around

Major train destinations include Paris' Gare de Lyon (€36.20, three hours, six to eight daily), Clermont-Ferrand (€8.10, 40 minutes, frequent), Riom (€6.20, 25 minutes, frequent) and Lyon (€20.50, 2½ hours, six to eight daily).

Cycles Peugeot Gaillardin (☎ 04 70 31 52 86; 48 blvd Gambetta) hires both town and mountain bikes year-round (half-/full-day €5/8) and requires a refundable deposit of €80.

ORCIVAL
pop 290 / elevation 860m

The delightful, slate-roofed village of Orcival lies midway between the Puy de Dôme and Le Mont-Dore. Beside the gurgling River Sioulet, it's a perfect base for day hikes and, despite the coachloads of quick-fix tourists, a lovely spot to spend a few soothing days.

Hanging over the entrance of the superb 12th-century Auvergnat-Romanesque **basilica** are balls and chains left in gratitude by released prisoners. Perched on a pillar behind the altar is a squat 12th-century statue of the Virgin, fashioned from gilded silver over wood.

Turreted 15th-century **Château de Cordès** (☎ 04 73 65 81 34; adult/student/child €4/3/2.30; 10am-noon & 2-6pm Easter-Oct) is about 2.5km to the north. It's well worth the short detour to enjoy the rich 18th-century furnishings and the formal gardens, laid out by Le Nôtre, designer of the gardens of Versailles and of London's Greenwich and St James's parks.

The **tourist office** (☎ 04 73 65 89 77; terresdomes .sancy@wanadoo.fr; 10am-noon & 2-7pm Mon-Sat, 10am-noon Sun Jul & Aug, 10am-noon & 2-6pm Tue-Sat Jun & Aug, 2-6pm Tue-Sat other school holidays) is opposite the church.

Sleeping & Eating

Les Bourelles (☎ 04 73 65 82 28; d €25; Easter-Sep) Set back from the road, Les Bourelles has a lovely, flowery terrace and seven simple rooms giving beautiful views.

Hôtel Notre Dame (☎ /fax 04 73 65 82 02; d €32-36; Feb-Dec) This hotel belongs to the same friendly couple who run Les Bourelles and is excellent value. All seven rooms have views of the basilica and have been recently renovated. Ask for No 26, which has its own large terrace. The **restaurant** has filling *menus* (€10.50 to €19.50).

COL DE GUÉRY

The D27 from Orcival to the Col de Guéry (1268m), 8.5km to its south, passes through spectacular scenery.

In summer, the **Maison des Fleurs d'Auvergne** (☎ 04 73 65 20 09; 10am-7pm mid-Jun–mid-Sep, Sat & Sun only May–mid-Jun) presents the area's flora. Although in French, the display is highly visual and in the *jardin écologique* grow many of the plants and trees you'll encounter on walks in the area. From the first snowfall, the centre becomes the **Foyer Ski de Fond Orcival Guéry** (9am-7pm), a cross-country skiing centre from which radiate nearly 30km of groomed pistes. Hire of cross-country equipment costs €9.20 per day and snowshoes are €5.50.

Auberge du Lac de Guéry (☎ 04 73 65 02 76; www .auberge-lac-guery.fr in French; d €50; mid-Jan–mid-Oct) Rooms are relatively plain but the site, on the southern shore of **Lac de Guéry**, is unbeatable. You'll eat well in its **restaurant** (menus from €10.50), where the fish, selected from the nearby fish farm, couldn't come fresher.

LE MONT-DORE
pop 1800 / elevation 1050m

This lovely little spa town, 44km southwest of Clermont-Ferrand, is ideal for exploring the Puy de Sancy area on foot, by bicycle or by car. It stretches along a narrow, wooded valley beside the Dordogne, not far from the river's source. Built from locally quarried dark stone, the town bustles with skiers in winter, then hikers and *curistes*, attracted by the hot springs and spa, in summer.

Information

Laundrette (place de la République; 9am-7pm)
Post Office (place Charles de Gaulle)
Tourist Office (☎ 04 73 65 20 21; www.mont-dore .com; av de la Libération; 9am-12.30pm & 2-6.30pm Mon-Sat, 9am-noon Sun, also 2-5pm Sun school holidays) Has a France Telecom Internet post.

Sights & Activities

The waters (37°C to 40°C) of the huge **Établissement Thermal** (hot springs complex; ☎ 04 73 65 05 10; place du Panthéon; ☉ May–mid-Oct) soothe respiratory ailments and rheumatism. The spa also offers fitness programmes for the hale and hearty (from €91, minimum three days), or you can test the waters with its one-day introductory programme (€43). There are 45-minute **guided tours** (adult/child €3/2; hourly 2-5pm Mon-Sat May–mid-Oct; 3pm Mon-Fri mid-Oct–Apr), of the sumptuous 19th-century neo-Byzantine interior, which retains vestiges from Gallo-Roman times.

The **Funiculaire du Capucin** (☎ 04 73 65 01 25; av René Cassin; single/return €3.30/4.20; ☉ May–mid-Oct) runs to Les Capucins, a 1270m-high wooded plateau above town. France's oldest funicular railway, built in 1898, it creeps up at precisely one metre per second. From the upper station, multiple signed walking possibilities open up such as linking with the GR30, which wends its way southwards towards the Puy de Sancy, continuing to the Pic du Capucin (1450m; about 45 minutes one way) or dropping steeply back to town.

A cable-car lift, the **Téléphérique du Sancy** (☎ 04 73 65 02 73; single/return €5.20/6.50; ☉ 9am-6pm Jul & Aug, 9.30am-12.30pm & 1.30-5pm May, Jun & Sep, ski-season hours vary with daylight & operation of other lifts), about 3.5km south of town, swings to the summit of the Puy de Sancy (also known as the Pic de Sancy). Here, you can take in the stunning panorama of the northern puys and the southern Monts du Cantal before starting a hike or, in winter, slip-sliding down the slopes.

A session at the town's **ice-skating rink** (☎ 04 73 65 06 55; allée Georges Lagaye; ☉ Dec-Aug) costs €6.15, including skate hire.

Mont-Dore Aventures (☎ 04 73 65 00 00; www .montdoreaventures.com in French; le Salon du Capucin; adult/under 14/under 10 €19/14/10; ☉ 9am or 10am-7pm Jun-Aug; 1-7pm Sat & Sun Apr-May & Sep-Nov) is great for playing Tarzan for an hour or two, as you clamber and swing your way around the circuits up in the trees. It's 150m from the Funiculaire du Capucin's upper station. Alternatively, take the winding 4km road via the D465.

SKIING

The northern side of the spectacular Puy de Sancy has 42km of runs. Another 45km splay over the hill down to **Super Besse**, on the

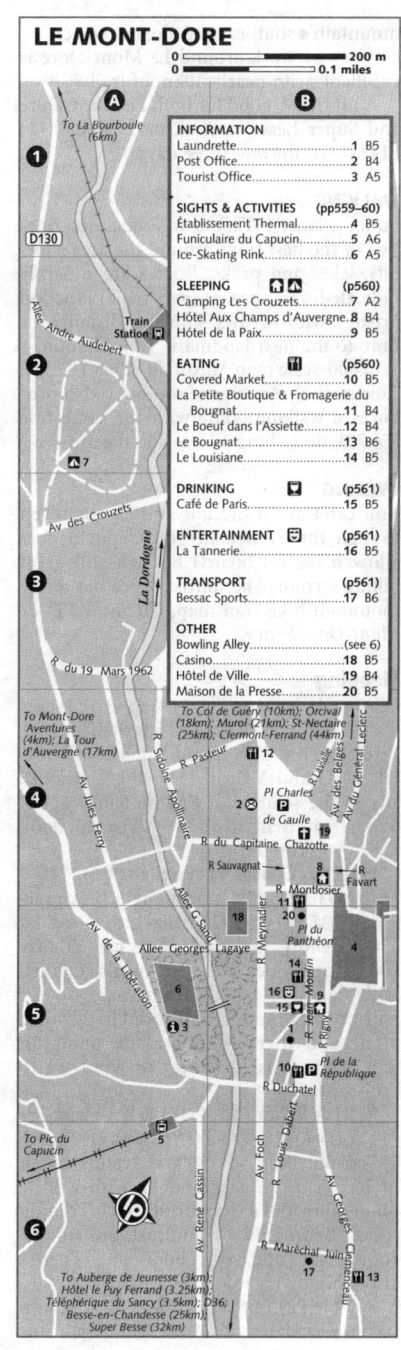

LE MONT-DORE

INFORMATION	
Laundrette...............................1	B5
Post Office..............................2	B4
Tourist Office..........................3	A5

SIGHTS & ACTIVITIES	(pp559–60)
Établissement Thermal.............4	B5
Funiculaire du Capucin.............5	A6
Ice-Skating Rink.......................6	A5

SLEEPING	
Camping Les Crouzets...............7	A2
Hôtel Aux Champs d'Auvergne.8	B4
Hôtel de la Paix.......................9	B5

EATING	(p560)
Covered Market......................10	B5
La Petite Boutique & Fromagerie du	
Bougnat..............................11	B4
Le Boeuf dans l'Assiette..........12	B4
Le Bougnat............................13	B6
Le Louisiane...........................14	B5

DRINKING	(p561)
Café de Paris...........................15	B5

ENTERTAINMENT	(p561)
La Tannerie.............................16	B5

TRANSPORT	(p561)
Bessac Sports.........................17	B6

OTHER	
Bowling Alley.......................(see 6)	
Casino....................................18	B5
Hôtel de Ville.........................19	B4
Maison de la Presse................20	B5

MASSIF CENTRAL

mountain's southeastern slopes. The cross-country network around Le Mont-Dore is excellent, with nearly 40km of trails.

A lift ticket, good for both Le Mont-Dore and Super Besse, costs €20/52 (under 12s €14/37.50) for one/three days.

WALKING

Lonely Planet's *Walking in France* describes two of the best trails around the area's forests, lakes and peaks. Routes are superbly indicated; a signpost at every major junction bristles with arrows showing distance or time to the next landmark. Buy Chamina's 1:30,000-scale map *Massif du Sancy* (€5.35). This sterling Auvergnat company also produces a walking guide with the same title (€6.70), describing 30 hikes in the area.

CYCLING

You can't avoid the ups and downs (even though the Funiculaire du Capucin *does* allow bikes on board) but it's still great biking terrain. The tourist office has a free mountain bike trail map, *Circuit VTT: Le Mont-Dore Sancy*.

Sleeping

Auberge de Jeunesse (☎ 04 73 65 03 53; le-mont-dore@fuaj.org; route du Sancy; dm with breakfast €11.70; ☾ Dec–mid-Nov) This HI-affiliated youth hostel, Le Grand Volcan (The Big Volcano), sits in the shadow of Puy de Sancy about 3.5km south of town. It's wise to book ahead in summer.

Hôtel Aux Champs d'Auvergne (☎ 04 73 65 00 37; fax 04 73 65 00 30; 18 rue Favart; s/d €18/25, with bathroom €29/36, half-board €30/39; ☾ late Dec–mid-Oct) This friendly, laid-back place has 23 cosy rooms and does plentiful meals, cooked with flair and strictly for guests. Go for half-board; dinner is a splendid five-course affair and there's home-made pumpkin jam at breakfast to smear on your warm croissant.

Hôtel de la Paix (☎ 04 73 65 00 17; www.hotel-de-la-paix.info; 8 rue Rigny; s/d €37/47; menu €19; ☾ mid-Dec–mid-Oct) Built in 1880, it retains much of its *fin de siècle* grandeur with a little bijou salon and a wonderfully lavish dining room. Bedrooms, by contrast, are simple, comfortable and very good value. There's also a highly regarded restaurant.

Hôtel le Puy Ferrand (☎ 04 73 65 18 99; www.hotel-puy-ferrand.com; d €45-78; ☾ Dec-Sep) This

cosy mid-range hotel, 150m below the Puy de Sancy cable car, has an excellent restaurant, sauna and year-round covered pool.

CAMPING

Camping Les Crouzets (☎ & fax 04 73 65 21 60; per person/site €2.60/2.35; ☾ mid-Dec–mid-Oct) It's municipal and conveniently opposite the train station.

Camping L'Esquiladou (☎ 04 73 65 23 74; camping.esquiladou@wanadoo.fr; per person/site €3/2.45; ☾ May–mid-Oct) About 1.5km north of town and signposted from the train station, L'Esquiladou, also municipal, is altogether more tranquil and roomy.

Eating

Several hotels (including the three we recommend) offer good *menus*.

Le Bougnat (☎ 04 73 65 28 19; 23 rue Georges Clemenceau; menus €15-23; closed Nov–early Dec) With its low-beamed wooden interior hung with appealing farmhouse clutter and an attractive, flowery terrace, this splendid place offers rich Auvergnat dishes confected from local produce. A recent change of ownership does not seem to have affected quality.

Le Louisiane (☎ 04 73 65 03 14; 2 rue Jean Moulin; menus €12-25; closed Wed mid-Oct–Apr) Spacious and airy, Le Louisiane is an odd yet pleasing marriage with its décor, which owes much to the deep south of the US, grafted onto the vast dining room of what was once the largest luxury hotel in the region. Go for a *brochette* (skewer) of succulent meat (€16) or fish (€17). Also surprising for a restaurant that couldn't possibly be farther from the sea, the quality of its fish dishes is superb.

Le Bœuf dans l'Assiette (Beef on the Plate; ☎ 04 73 65 01 23; 9 av Michel Bertrand; mains €7-11.50, menus €10.40-14.50; ☾ Tue-Sun) As its name suggests, this place is for serious carnivores as photographs of cows gaze down on you from the walls like film stars' portraits.

SELF-CATERING

There's a small **covered market** (place de la République, ☾ 8am-1pm Tue-Sun).

La Petite Boutique du Bougnat (1 rue Montlosier), sister to the restaurant of the same name, positively bursts with the best local cured and canned meats, hams, sausages and over 30 varieties of Auvergnat wine. Right opposite, its *fromagerie* is just as enticing.

Drinking

Café de Paris (8 rue Jean Moulin) is a convivial, crowded old-time café where clients, mainly from the town, play cards, flirt and chat until the cows come home.

Entertainment

La Tannerie (☎ 04 73 65 02 67; rue du Docteur Perpère) is the town's sole discotheque.

Getting There & Around

From the sleepy Le Mont-Dore **train station** to Paris' Gare de Lyon (€42.80, 5½ hours), change at Clermont-Ferrand (€10.70, 1¼ hours, up to four or five daily).

In winter, a free skiers **shuttle bus** *(navette)* regularly plies between Le Mont-Dore and the cable car. From mid-May to September, the service operates four or five times daily (single/return €2/3), continuing to La Bourboule (single/return €3/5.50).

Bessac Sports (☎ 04 73 65 02 25; 3 rue Maréchal Juin) hires out mountain bikes from €10/15 per half-/full-day and can also put you wise about the most attractive routes.

The Téléphérique du Sancy and Funiculaire du Capucin are other means of transport (p559).

AROUND LE MONT-DORE

Only 7km downriver westwards, **La Bourboule**, Le Mont-Dore's slightly larger sister spa, has some lovely *belle époque* buildings. The **tourist office** (☎ 04 73 65 57 71; www.bourboule.com in French; place de la République) is in the town hall. The train trip to/from Le Mont-Dore (€1.30, seven daily) takes eight minutes.

About 10km east of Le Mont-Dore, the 12th-century **Château de Murol** (☎ 04 73 88 67 11; www.chateaudemurol.com in French; adult/child €4/3; ☻ daily Apr–mid-Nov & school holidays, Sat & Sun mid-Nov–Mar) sits squat atop a knoll overlooking the village of the same name. In July and August, actors in period costume recreate medieval castle life.

Lac Chambon

This pleasant little beach resort, beside the natural lake of the same name, is 1.5km west of Murol. Among its string of hotels, a couple at the northern end that are just that little bit higher offer the best views of the lake.

Try **Hôtel La Mouteroun** (☎ 04 73 88 63 18; fax 04 73 88 61 07; d with shower €35, with bathroom €45; ☻ year-round) and its equally impressive

neighbour, **Hôtel Restaurant Beau Site** (☎ 04 73 88 61 29; fax 04 73 88 66 73; d €40-48; menus €16-24; ☻ Feb-Oct), which also runs a fine, highly recommended restaurant.

Also at the northern end are **Sancy Loisirs** (☎ 04 73 88 67 07), which rents canoes, dinghies and windsurfs.

Besse-en-Chandesse

Picturesque Besse-en-Chandesse is 25km southeast of Le Mont-Dore. There's a small **tourist office** (☎ 04 73 79 52 84; place du Docteur Pipet; ☻ 9am-noon & 2-6pm Dec-Sep, Mon-Sat Oct-Nov).

With cobbled streets and houses of solid rectangular basalt block, it's known for its cheese production (in fact processing much more St-Nectaire cheese than the town of St-Nectaire itself). Several of the 15th- to 18th-century houses along rue de la Boucherie were built of basalt quarried right beside each home – and the quarry became the cheese cellar.

The 15th-century **Maison de la Reine Margot** is home to a small **ski museum** (☎ 04 73 79 57 30; admission €2.50; ☻ 9am-noon & 2-7pm school holidays). Pierre-André, who's collected more than 300 pairs of vintage skis and other mountain gear, will himself guide you around with his charmingly eccentric English.

The mostly Romanesque **Église St-André** has a 12th-century nave with finely carved capitals.

The ski station of **Super Besse** (p559), established in the 1960s as a purpose-built resort, is 7km west. On the way, pause after 4km at **Lac Pavin**, an attractive near-circular lake, Auvergne's deepest, in the hollow of an extinct volcano. A gentle walk around its perimeter takes about 45 minutes.

St-Nectaire

Famed for its 50 natural springs and eponymous soft and flavoursome cheese, St-Nectaire merits a visit. Straggling for more than 2km from St-Nectaire-le-Haut (the upper) to St-Nectaire-le-Bas (the lower), it's a lively place with still a whiff of faded charm from its days as a spa town.

The efficient **tourist office** (☎ 04 73 88 50 86; ☻ 9-11.45am & 2-4.45pm Jul & Aug, Mon-Sat Sep-Jun) is in St-Nectaire-le-Bas.

The Romans were the first to steep themselves in the waters, both hot and cold, of the **Grottes du Cornadore** (☎ 04 73 88 57 97; adult/child

AUVERGNAT CHEESES

From as early as the 1st century AD, the lush grasses of Auvergne's volcanic soils have fed the cows that gave the milk that farmers ferment into its range of excellent cheeses. The region has no less than five classified as Appellation d'Origine Contrôlée (AOC; the highest category of French cheese, with an officially controlled declaration of origin): Cantal, white and full flavoured; Salers, similar, from the same area but made only from the milk of cows that graze on high summer pastures; St-Nectaire, rich-scented, flat and round like a discus; Fourme d'Ambert, a mild, smooth blue cheese; and Bleu d'Auvergne, also blue and stronger, with a creamier texture than its much-touted cousin, Rocquefort.

Take your pick; each in its distinct way makes a delightful sandwich filling.

€5.80/4.30; ☽ mid-Feb–Oct). Perfect natural baths, these caves today make an impressive underground spectacle.

At the **Grottes de Jonas** (☎ 04 73 88 57 98; adult/child €5.80/4.30; ☽ mid-Feb–Oct), 6km south of town, are more than 60 interconnecting troglodyte caves hewn into the cliff, several retaining traces of medieval frescoes.

Maison du St-Nectaire (☎ 04 73 88 57 96; adult/child €4.40/3.40; ☽ mid-Dec–mid-Nov) is a small exhibition that takes you through the cheese-making process and includes a guided tasting and introductory film.

At the top of the town, highlights of the delightful Romanesque **church** (☽ 9am-7pm Apr-Oct, 10am-12.30pm & 2-6pm Nov-Mar) are its 103 carved polychrome capitals and a fine 12th-century statue of the virgin.

PUY MARY

Majestic Puy Mary (1787m) is an easy, 30-minute ascent from **Pas de Peyrol**, a 1582m pass on the D680 that's blocked by snowdrifts between late October and May.

North of Puy Mary is **Col de Serre** (1364m), a notch 3km northeast of the Pas de Peyrol. From here the D62 drops tortuously to the green River Cheylade valley, passing through rich pasture and deciduous forests.

Alternatively, take the D680 from Col de Serre to follow the gentle Santoire Valley eastwards to the tidy little village of **Dienne**, and continue to the town of Murat.

MURAT

pop 2400 / elevation 930m

Murat sits at the foot of a basaltic crag topped by a giant white statue of the Virgin Mary. It makes a good base for exploring the Monts du Cantal, including **Puy Mary** and the 1855m **Plomb du Cantal**. Walks bagging each peak, starting from the ski station of **Super Lioran**, are described in Lonely Planet's *Walking in France*.

The friendly **tourist office** (☎ 04 71 20 09 47; www.ville-de-murat.com in French; 2 rue du Faubourg Notre-Dame; ☽ 9am-12.30pm & 1.30-7pm Mon-Sat, 9.30am-1pm & 2.30-6.30pm Sun Jul & Aug, 9am-noon & 2-6pm Mon-Sat Sep-Jun) is beside the town hall.

Armed with its free pamphlet, *The Picturesque Visit in the Old Murat* (sic; the text flows better than the title), you can happily spend a pleasant hour or so browsing Murat's steep, narrow streets.

Maison de la Faune (☎ 04 71 20 00 52; just off place de l'Hôtel de Ville; adult/child €4/2.40; ☽ 10am-12.30pm & 2-7pm Mon-Sat, 10am-noon & 3-7pm Sun Jul & Aug, 10am-noon & 2-6pm Mon-Sat, 2-6pm Sun other school holidays) occupies an elegant 16th-century house. On the ground floor are more than 10,000 mounted insects, starring some truly dazzling tropical butterflies. Upper levels display local stuffed and mounted wildlife in a natural, well documented – in French – setting. This said, there's a chilling irony – the frequent green spots on individual labels denote endangered species; lift your eyes and there's the hapless creature, staring back at you in death.

AUTHOR'S CHOICE

Auberge du Maître Paul (☎ 04 71 20 14 66; fax 04 71 20 22 20; 14 place du Planol; s/d €30/36) Upstairs, this jolly, family-friendly *gîte* with attitude has winding corridors and spruce, charmingly decorated rooms that put many a pension to shame. Popular with walkers in summer and skiing families when the snow's on the heights, its restaurant is worth dropping into even if you're lodged elsewhere. Pick up a pizza (€6.90; to eat in or take away) the size of a flying saucer or indulge in the excellent *menu* (€17) that's rich in local specialities. If you're overnighting, find space in the small, free public parking lot just behind the *auberge*. If you're just visiting, leave your car in the square beside the town hall.

A steepish ascent (45 minutes round trip from the tourist office) takes you up to Rocher de Bonne Vie with its statue of the Virgin. Follow the red-and-white GR flashes northwestwards out of town, then signs for the Rocher, to enjoy a magnificent view of the town and the higher peaks to the west.

Sleeping & Eating

Hostellerie Les Breuils (☎ 04 71 20 01 25; fax 04 71 20 33 20; 34 av du Docteur Mallet; d €62-76; Ⓨ mid-May–mid-Oct; Ⓟ Ⓡ) Converted from a private 19th-century mansion and still in the hands of the original family, Les Breuils' more modern features include a heated pool. Ivy-clad and welcoming with a lovely garden, it makes a excellent mid-range choice. The pricier rooms are very large and those on the 1st floor still have the original furniture.

Hôtel Les Messageries (☎ 04 71 20 04 04; www .hotel-les-messageries.com in French; 18 av Docteur Mallet; s/d €35/41; menus €12-25; closed Nov-Christmas; Ⓡ) Overlooking the train station, this Logis de France is more characterful than its bland exterior suggests. Its restaurant is strong on Auvergnat dishes and there's a sauna (€3.80), pool and mini-gym, should you still have energy to expend after a day's hiking.

CAMPING

Camping Municipal Stalapos (☎ 04 71 20 01 83; rue du Stade; person/pitch €2/1.60; Ⓨ May-Sep) Beside the River Alagnon, this attractive camping area is 750m south of the train station.

Getting There & Away

Trains running between Clermont-Ferrand (€14.50, 1½ hours) and Aurillac (€7.50, 45 minutes) call by Murat six to 10 times daily. One or two continue beyond Aurillac to Toulouse (€28.50, 4½ hours).

PARC NATUREL RÉGIONAL LIVRADOIS-FOREZ

One of France's largest protected areas, this nature park slopes away gently to the west to the plains of Limagne while the Monts du Forez, dropping abruptly to the upper Loire valley, form a natural eastern limit.

The **park information office** (☎ 04 73 95 57 57; www.parc-livradois-forez.org in French; Ⓨ 9am-12.30pm & 1.30-4.40pm or 5.30pm Mon-Fri year-round, 3-7pm Sat & Sun May–mid-Sep) is just off the D906 in St-Gervais-sous-Meymont. It produces an excellent brochure, *La Route des Métiers* (The Cottage Industry Trail). This describes and pinpoints on the map 40 small museums and cottage industries, all open to the public, which produce items as diverse as lace, honey, medicinal plants and perfumes. Its *Guide de la Randonnée et des Loisirs de Plein Air* gives a host of suggestions for treks and mountain bike routes, cross-referring to the relevant topoguides. Both are in French and free.

Getting Around

The observation car of the **Discovery Train** (Train de la Découverte; ☎ 04 73 82 43 88) is a superb way to see the heart of the park. In July and August, it runs for 85km between Courpière (15km south of Thiers) via Ambert (adult/child €11/7) to Sembadel (6km south of La Chaise-Dieu; adult/child €18/13). From Ambert to Sembadel is €12/9. Check the variable timetable with the park office, or Ambert and La Chaise Dieu tourist offices.

THIERS

pop 14,800 / elevation 420m
Down below, beside the Gorges de la Durolle, you could convince yourself that Thiers is a town seriously on the skids. The thundering river that once drove the mills that ground the knives roars on but the abandoned factories along its banks are a sad testament to an outmoded way of production.

Nevertheless, Thiers remains Steel City with more than 60 workshops and factories producing some 70% of knives sold in France. To understand its unique industrial history, you need to visit the Musée de la Coutellerie and the Vallée des Rouets.

The **Musée de la Coutellerie** (Cutlery Museum; ☎ 04 73 80 58 86; 23 & 58 rue de la Coutellerie; adult/child €4.75/2.30; Ⓨ year-round, tours & demonstrations 10am-6.30pm Jul & Aug, 10am-noon & 2-6pm Tue-Sun Sep-Oct & Mar-Jun, Wed-Sun Nov-Dec & Feb) presents cottage-industry cutlery manufacturing with demonstrations by skilled craftspeople.

The **Vallée des Rouets** (Valley of the Waterwheels; Ⓨ noon-6.30pm Jul & Aug, noon-6pm Tue-Sun Jun & Sep), about 10km upstream from Thiers, is an open-air museum to the self-employed knife grinders who spent their working

MASSIF CENTRAL

days stretched along a wooden plank above their grindstone. You can follow either an easy 1km signed walking trail or another, scarcely more arduous, of 2.5km. In July and August a shuttle bus runs hourly from opposite the town hall. Otherwise, take the N89 towards Lyon.

A combined ticket (adult/child €5.80/2.50) covers the shuttle bus and admission to both the museum and Vallée des Rouets.

The friendly **tourist office** (☎ 04 73 80 65 65; www.ville-thiers.fr in French; 1 place du Pirou; ☿ 9am-1pm & 1.30-7pm Mon-Sat, 10am-noon & 2-6pm Sun mid-Jun–mid-Sep, 9.30am-noon & 2-6pm Mon-Sat mid-Sep–mid-Jun) is in the Château du Pirou. Nearby is the **Maison de l'Homme de Bois** (21 rue de la Coutellerie), named after the bizarre figure in skins carved in wood on the left of the façade. It's one of several fine wood and half-timbered 15th-century mansions in the old quarter.

AMBERT

Back in the 16th century, Ambert, 30km north of La Chaise-Dieu, had more than 300 small water-powered mills. The little town fed the printing presses of Lyon and was France's most important paper producer until the Industrial Revolution. Today it's renowned for the fine Fourme d'Ambert cheese and is a centre for the surrounding agricultural area.

The **tourist office** (☎ 04 73 82 61 90; 4 place de l'Hôtel de Ville; ☿ 9am-6pm Mon-Sat, 10am-noon Sun Jul & Aug, 9am-noon & 2-6pm Mon-Fri, 10am-noon Sat Sep-Jun) is opposite the town hall. At 3pm on Thursdays during July and August, it organises **guided walks** (adult/child €4/2) in English around old Ambert.

Maison de la Fourme d'Ambert (☎ 04 73 82 49 23; rue des Chazeaux; adult/child €4.20/3.40; ☿ 9am-7pm Jul & Aug, 9am-noon & 2-7pm Tue & Thu-Sat Oct-Jun) explains via a short video in French the production process of rich, mellow blue Fourme d'Ambert cheese. It has a display of traditional cheese-making implements – and also graciously displays Auvergne's other fine cheeses.

Musée Agrivap (☎ 04 73 82 60 42; rue de l'Industrie; adult/child €4.80/3; ☿ 10am-1pm & 2-7pm Jul & Aug; 2-6pm Easter-Jun & Sep–mid-Oct) is a collection of vintage agricultural machinery and traction engines.

Moulin Richard de Bas (☎ 04 73 82 03 11; adult/child €5.50/3.60; ☿ 9am-8pm Jul & Aug, 9am-noon & 2-6pm Sep-Jun) occupies a 14th-century mill and produces handmade paper using traditional

techniques. It's 4km out of town on the D57 towards Valeyre.

Ambert's round **town hall** was originally the town's grain store. Notice the grotesque gargoyles sprouting like warts all along the exterior southern wall of Gothic **Église St-Jean**. There are some lovely half-timbered, mainly 15th-century houses along rue du Château, rue de la République and place Minimes.

LA CHAISE DIEU

Early in the 14th century, an 11-year-old novice monk, Pierre Roger de Beaufort, joined the **Église Abbatiale de St-Robert** (adult/student/child €3/2/1; ☿ 9am-noon & 2-7pm Jun-Sep, 10am-noon & 2-5pm Mon-Sat, 10am-noon Sun Oct-May). Later, as Pope Clement VI, he bequeathed funds for a fundamental reconstruction of this abbey church, originally built in 1044 – and for the placing of his tomb at its heart.

Although sacked by Huguenots in 1562, ravaged by fire in 1695 and despoiled by revolutionary mobs in the late 18th century, it's still deeply impressive.

At the west end is an elaborately carved 18th-century wooden organ gallery. Plumb in the centre of the choir sits the black-and-white marble tomb of the good pope, surrounded by 144 14th-century choir stalls in pale oak. Lift your eyes to take in the magnificent 17th-century Flemish tapestries above them.

By the northern aisle is an unfinished 15th-century fresco of the **Dance of Death** where sinuous skeletons mock human figures representing the various classes of society.

Outside, the **Salle de l'Écho** has led to all sorts of speculation. Whisper, facing the wall, in one corner and someone listening in the opposite corner will hear you perfectly. Was it, as some maintain, for hearing the confession of lepers? Or of indiscreet fellow monks? Or is it no more than an unanticipated architectural and acoustic fluke?

The abbey and village of La Chaise Dieu are internationally renowned for their annual festival of sacred music, held during the last 10 days of August.

LE PUY-EN-VELAY
pop 20,500 / elevation 630m

From Le Puy-en-Velay protrude a trio of striking volcanic plugs. Surrounded by a fertile valley, the city, capital of the Haute- Loire *département*, is proud of its lace-making tradition – and its pedigree green lentils, which have earned Appellation d'Origine Contrôlée status, just like a fine wine, thanks to the area's uniquely rich volcanic soil.

In medieval times, the cathedral of Le Puy was one of four French departure points for pilgrim routes to Santiago de Compostella in Spain. Known as the Via Podiensis, it's today called, more prosaically, the GR65, a 1600km long-distance walking trail.

From nearby Le Monastier-sur-Gazeille begins an equally famous and much less arduous trail, the GR70, following in the donkey tracks of Robert Louis Stevenson (p743).

Orientation

North of the main square, place du Breuil, lies the pedestrianised old city, its narrow streets leading uphill to the cathedral. Le Puy-en-Velay's commercial centre is around the town hall and between blvd Maréchal Fayolle and rue Chaussade.

Information

INTERNET ACCESS
Cyb'Aire (17 rue Général Lafayette; per hr €3.50; 10am-midnight Mon-Sat, 2pm-midnight Sun)

LAUNDRY
There are laundrettes at 24 rue Portail d'Avignon (open daily) and 12 rue Chèvrerie (open Monday to Saturday).

POST
Main Post Office (8 av de la Dentelle)

TOURIST INFORMATION
Main Tourist Office (☎ 04 71 09 38 41; www.ot-lep uyenvelay.fr; place du Breuil; 8.30am-7.30pm Jul & Aug, 8.30am-noon & 1.30-6.15pm Sep-Jun, closed Sun pm Oct-Easter) Has good walking tour leaflet in English, *Historical Visits*, describing three walks around town.
Tourist Office Annexe (23 rue des Tables; late Jun–early-Sep)

Sights & Activities

Medieval, Gothic and Renaissance houses of dark volcanic stone border rue Chaussade, rue du Collège, rue Porte Aiguière and rue Pannessac.

God beams down from each of Le Puy's three lava pinnacles: the largest, around whose skirts the old city fans, has the cathedral; the highest bears a giant statue of the Virgin; and on the steepest, a few hundred metres further north, perches a 10th-century gravity-defying chapel.

Cathédrale Notre Dame is a heavily restored Romanesque cathedral. The most impressive way to enter it is through the massive arches at the top of cobbled rue des Tables. Byzantine and Moorish elements include the six domes over the nave and the ornately patterned stonework. A 17th-century **Black Virgin** takes pride of place on the high altar.

The beautiful 12th-century **cloister** (adult/18-25 yrs/under 18 €4.60/3.10/free; 9am-6.30pm Jul & Aug, 9am-noon & 2-6.30pm mid-May–Jun & Sep, to 5pm Oct–mid-May) with its multicoloured building blocks would look perfectly at home in Moorish Spain.

The massive **Rocher Corneille** (adult/child €3/1.50; 9am-6/7/7.30pm mid-Mar–Sep; 10am-5pm Oct–mid-Nov & Feb–mid-Mar) is just north of the cathedral and accessible via rue du Cloître. It was crowned in 1860 by a jarringly red, 16m-high statue of Notre Dame de France made from melted-down cannons captured in the Crimean War. She looks for all the world like something in raspberry from the top of a wedding cake but the view from her feet is superb.

Chapelle St-Michel d'Aiguilhe (adult/child €2.50/1; 9.30am-6.30pm May-Sep, 9.30am-noon & 2-5.30pm mid-Mar–Apr & Oct–mid-Nov, 2-5pm Feb–mid-Mar) perches at the summit of an 85m-high volcanic plug. The 10th-century choir is pre-Romanesque and you can still see traces of the 12th-century murals. It's an easy walk – as far as the base, that is! Or take bus No 6 to the base.

You can admire antique and modern lace and take lace-making classes (€8 per hour) at the **Centre d'Enseignement de la Dentelle au Fuseau** (☎ 04 71 02 01 68; 38-42 rue Raphaël; admission €2; 9am-noon & 1.30-5.30pm Mon-Fri, 9.30am-4.30pm Sat mid-Jun–mid-Sep, 10am-noon & 2-5pm Mon-Fri mid-Sep–mid-Jun), a nonprofit museum and educational centre that seeks to preserve what

---

DISCOUNT ADMISSION

Between February and October you can visit Le Puy's four major sights – the cathedral cloister, Rocher Corneille, Chapelle St-Michel d'Aiguilhe and the Musée Crozatier – with an open-dated discount combination ticket (€7.50), available at the tourist office and each location.

MASSIF CENTRAL

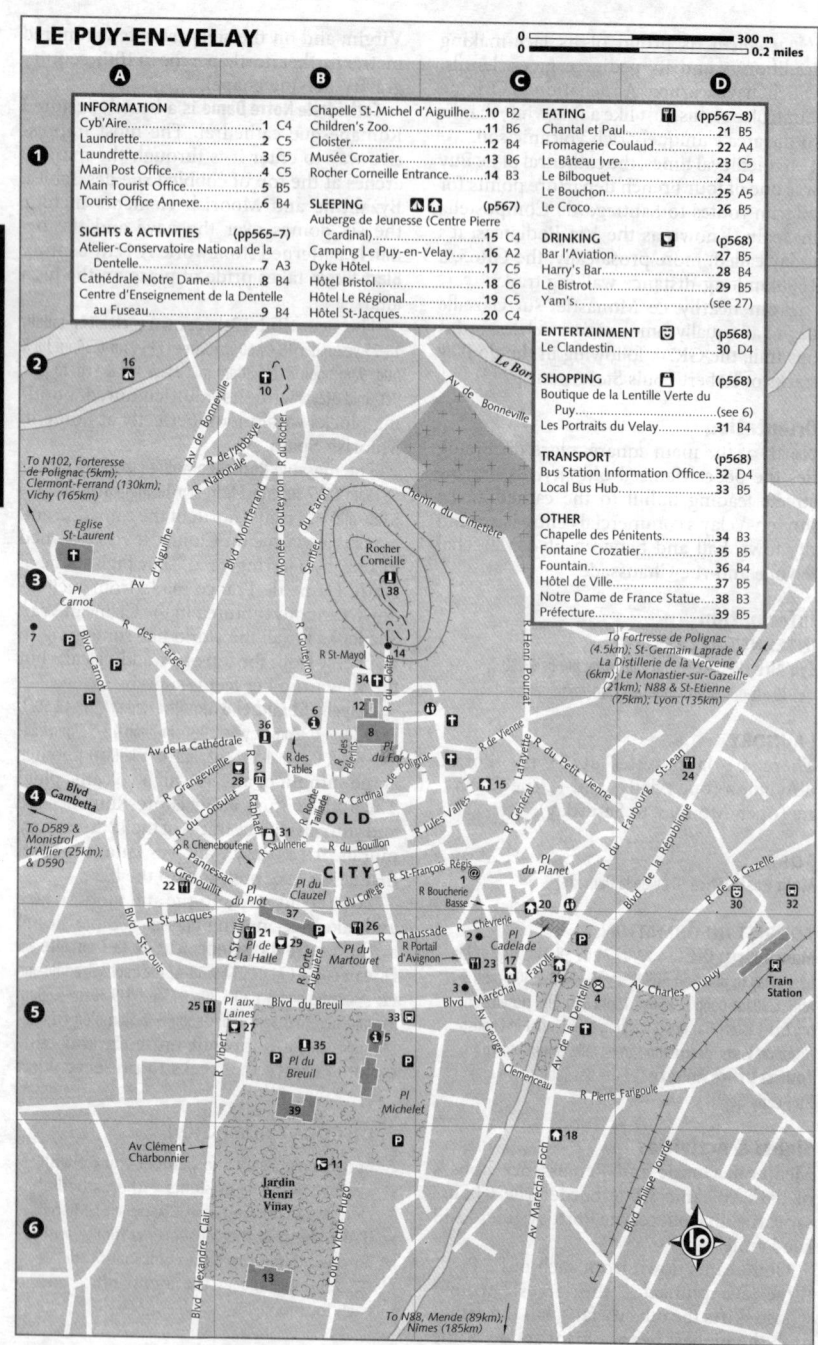

LE PUY-EN-VELAY

0 — 300 m
0 — 0.2 miles

INFORMATION
Cyb'Aire..1 C4
Laundrette...2 C5
Laundrette...3 C5
Main Post Office................................4 C5
Main Tourist Office............................5 B5
Tourist Office Annexe........................6 B4

SIGHTS & ACTIVITIES (pp565–7)
Atelier-Conservatoire National de la
Dentelle..7 A3
Cathédrale Notre Dame.....................8 B4
Centre d'Enseignement de la Dentelle
au Fuseau......................................9 B4

Chapelle St-Michel d'Aiguilhe....10 B2
Children's Zoo..................................11 B6
Cloister...12 B4
Musée Crozatier..............................13 B6
Rocher Corneille Entrance..........14 B3

SLEEPING (p567)
Auberge de Jeunesse (Centre Pierre
Cardinal)..15 C4
Camping Le Puy-en-Velay............16 A2
Dyke Hôtel.......................................17 C5
Hôtel Bristol....................................18 C6
Hôtel Le Régional.............................19 C5
Hôtel St-Jacques.............................20 C4

EATING (pp567–8)
Chantal et Paul................................21 B5
Fromagerie Coulaud.......................22 A4
Le Bâteau Ivre.................................23 C5
Le Bilboquet....................................24 D4
Le Bouchon......................................25 A5
Le Croco...26 B5

DRINKING (p568)
Bar l'Aviation...................................27 B5
Harry's Bar.......................................28 B4
Le Bistrot..29 B5
Yam's...(see 27)

ENTERTAINMENT (p568)
Le Clandestin...................................30 D4

SHOPPING (p568)
Boutique de la Lentille Verte du
Puy...(see 6)
Les Portraits du Velay.....................31 B4

TRANSPORT (p568)
Bus Station Information Office....32 D4
Local Bus Hub.................................33 B5

OTHER
Chapelle des Pénitents....................34 B3
Fontaine Crozatier...........................35 B5
Fountain...36 B4
Hôtel de Ville...................................37 B5
Notre Dame de France Statue....38 B3
Préfecture...39 B5

Le Bor

Av de Bonneville

To N102, Forteresse
de Polignac (5km);
Clermont-Ferrand (130km);
Vichy (165km)

Eglise
St-Laurent

Pl
Carnot

Rocher
Corneille

R St-Mayol

To Fortresse de Polignac
(4.5km); St-Germain Laprade &
La Distillerie de la Verveine
(6km); Le Monastier-sur-Gazeille
(21km); N88 & St-Etienne
(75km); Lyon (135km)

Blvd
Gambetta

To D589 &
Monistrol
d'Allier (25km);
& D590

Av de la Cathédrale

R des
Tables

Pl
du Fort

R de Vienne

OLD

CITY

Pl
du Planet

Pl
du Plot

Pl du
Clauzel

Chaussade
R Portail
d'Avignon

R Chèvrerie

Pl
Cadelade

Fayolle

Av Charles Dupuy

Train
Station

Pl aux
Laines

Pl du
Breuil

Pl
Michelet

R Pierre Farigoule

Av Clément
Charbonnier

Jardin
Henri
Vinay

To N88, Mende (89km);
Nîmes (185km)

was once an important local industry (in 1900 the Haute-Loire *département* had 5000 lace workshops).

You might also want to take a look at the state-owned **Atelier-Conservatoire National de la Dentelle** (☎ 04 71 09 74 41; 2 rue Duguesclin), just west of place Carnot. Here, the French government orders some of the prestigious gifts it gives to visiting heads of state. Free hour-long visits start at 10am and 2pm on Monday, Tuesday, Thursday and Friday.

Jardin Henri Vinay, in the heart of town, is a pleasant park with a swan lake and small children's zoo. At its southern end is **Musée Crozatier** (☎ 04 71 09 38 90; adult/18-25 yrs/under 18 €3/1.20/free; ☽ 10am-noon & 2-6pm mid-Jun–mid-Sep, Wed-Mon mid-Sep–mid-Jun, to 4pm Oct-Apr). Exhibits include some impressive Romanesque capitals, local folk costumes and lace, a sad collection of stuffed birds and animals and some ingenious late-19th-century mechanical devices, among them the first patented sewing machine.

La Distillerie de la Verveine du Velay (☎ 04 71 03 04 11; 45min tour adult/student/child €5.30/4/2; ☽ 10am-noon & 1.30-6.30pm Jul & Aug, Tue-Sat Mar-Jun & Sep-Dec) is famous for its bright green firewater, first brewed in 1859. It's 6km east of town in St-Germain Laprade; take the N88 then the C150.

Festivals & Events

The **Fêtes Renaissance du Roi de l'Oiseau** are four days of street fun in mid-September. The tradition dates to 1524 when the title of King (*Roi*) was first accorded to the archer who brought down a straw bird, the *oiseau*. Among other concessions, the winner was exempt from all local taxes for the following year. Today's prize, alas, is markedly less generous but there's still heaps of fun for all.

Interfolk, Le Puy's annual week-long folk festival, in the second half of July, is nearly 40 years old but remains as fresh as ever.

Sleeping

Auberge de Jeunesse (☎ 04 71 05 52 40; auberge@ maire-le-puy-en-velay.fr; 9 rue Jules Vallès; dm €7.70; ☽ Apr-Sep, Mon-Fri Oct-Mar) The youth hostel, which occupies part of Centre Pierre Cardinal, has a members kitchen.

Hôtel Le Régional (☎ 04 71 09 37 74; 36 blvd Maréchal Fayolle; d €21.50, with bathroom €26-34) This is a good budget option whose 12 rooms are altogether cosier than the hotel's stark exterior might suggest.

Hôtel St-Jacques (☎ 04 71 07 20 40; www.hotel -saint-jacques.com; 7 place Cadelade; s €43, d €43-50; **P**) Hôtel St-Jacques, intimate, friendly and well maintained, has 12 tidy rooms, one with disabled access, on four floors overlooking a pedestrian square.

Hôtel Bristol (☎ 04 71 09 13 38; www.hotelbris tol-lepuy.com; 7-9 av Maréchal Foch; s €38, d €42-49; ☽ closed 1-15 Jan & 2 weeks in Mar; **P**) This Logis de France, its 40 rooms recently and comprehensively refurbished, is a good two-star option with a garden, attractively retro restaurant and small, cosy bar.

Dyke Hôtel (☎ 04 71 09 05 30; fax 04 71 02 58 66; 37 blvd Maréchal Fayolle; d €40-48; **P**) This warm, welcoming place has 15 attractive, modern rooms, some with balconies. That name may be something of a *faux ami* – or *fausse amie*; *dyke* (pronounced 'deek') here means a volcanic spire.

CAMPING

Camping Le Puy-en-Velay (☎ 04 71 09 55 09; chemin de Bouthezard; camping €9.10; ☽ Easter-Sep) Le Puy's camping ground is attractively situated beside the River Borne. Bus No 6 delivers you outside.

Eating

Chantal et Paul (☎ 04 71 09 09 16; 8 place de la Halle; menus €9 & €12.20; ☽ closed Sun, dinner Sat) Popular with downtown workers, this unpretentious husband-and-wife restaurant offers unbeatable value for the few euros you drop.

Le Bateau Ivre (☎ 04 71 09 67 20; 5 rue Portail d'Avignon; menus €18-29; ☽ Tue-Sat) This long, thin place exudes elegance with polished wooden tables and stylish cutlery – each fork a miniature Neptune's trident. Portions are generous and the cuisine is imaginative; the *fricassée de cailles*, sautéed quail nestling in a green salad sprinkled with a variety of nuts, makes a superb starter. For dessert indulge yourself with the *assiette gourmande*, a selection of exotic fruits, mousses and other soft, calorie-rich temptations.

Le Croco (☎ 04 71 02 40 13; 5 rue Chaussade; lunch menus €11-13; ☽ Tue-Sat) While not eschewing red meat, Le Croco (The Crocodile; tuck into your cheek the pair of croc jelly babies/ jellybeans that come with your bill) is particularly strong on bushy salads and equally

MASSIF CENTRAL

enormous, mainly vegetarian *plats compo-sés* (mixed platters).

Le Bouchon (☎ 04 71 05 41 42; 3 blvd St-Louis; menus €13-22; closed dinner Tue & Wed) Le Bouchon is another highly popular venue, rich in local fare. The *menu du terroir* (€16) is a stimulating four-course exploration of local specialities.

Le Bilboquet (☎ 04 71 09 74 24; 52 rue du Faubourg St-Jean; menus €15-45; closed Sun dinner Sep-Apr) It pulls in the diners by the sheer quality of its regional cuisine and the friendliness of the family owners. Australian readers are assured of a special welcome; just ask the *patronne* about her brother in Brisbane.

SELF-CATERING
Just west of the town hall, there's a good Saturday morning **food market** sprawling over place du Plot, place de la Halle and rue St-Jacques. **Fromagerie Coulaud** (24 rue Grenouillit; ☼ Tue-Sat) is one of France's disastrously declining number of specialist cheese shops and merits your patronage.

Drinking
Harry's Bar (37 rue Raphaël), a congenial place for a drink, these days pounds to a Latin beat. **Bar l'Aviation** (place aux Laines) and its neighbour **Yam's** pack in a youthful crowd. **Le Bistrot** (7 place de la Halle) is a great watering hole if you've a taste and thirst for good beer.

Entertainment
Le Clandestin (☎ 04 71 05 77 53; 20 rue de la Gazelle; ☼ Fri & Sat plus Wed & Thu school holidays) is Le Puy-en-Velay's only discotheque.

Shopping
Several shops sell handmade lace. Pieces marked *dentelle du Puy* were made in Le Puy-en-Velay many years ago (there's no longer any commercial lace production here); lace marked *fait main* (handmade) has probably been imported from China.

Les Portraits du Velay (☎ 04 71 06 00 94; www .dentelledupuy.com in French; 10 rue Raphaël; ☼ Easter-Sep, afternoons only Mon-Sat Oct-Easter), a lace shop, has lace-making demonstrations between Easter and August.

Le Puy's other Big L is the humble lentil. But not just any old pulse. To be sure of the real AOC thing – and to learn more than you ever thought you wanted to know about lentils – visit **Boutique de la Lentille**

Verte du Puy (☎ 04 71 02 60 44; 23 rue des Tables; ☼ Jun-Sep), sharing an address with the tourist office's summer annexe (p565).

Getting There & Away
The bus station and its **information office** (☎ 04 71 09 25 60) is just north of the train station. Three buses run to/from Mende on weekdays, and two travel to/from St-Étienne, which has good onwards bus and rail connections.

Le Puy-en-Velay's sleepy **train station** (av Charles Dupuy) has limited rail services. Destinations include Lyon (€18.10, 2½ hours, three daily), Clermont-Ferrand (€18.10, 2¼ hours, four daily) and St-Étienne (€11.10, 1½ hours, five to seven daily), which connects with the TGV network.

Getting Around
All six lines of the local **TUDIP** bus network (single ticket/10-trip carnet €1/7) pass by place Michelet.

For a taxi call ☎ 04 71 05 42 43.

AROUND LE PUY-EN-VELAY
Forteresse de Polignac
Perched atop yet another volcanic plug, about 5km northwest of Le Puy centre, are the crumbling remains of this 11th-century fortress whose 32m-high **Donjon** remains nearly intact, if much restored over the years. Once home to the powerful Polignac family, who virtually ruled Velay from the 11th to the 14th centuries, it's scheduled to re-open to the public in 2005.

Gorges de l'Allier
About 30km west of Le Puy-en-Velay, the salmon-filled River Allier – paralleled by the scenic Langeac-Langogne stretch of the Clermont-Ferrand–Nîmes rail line (two to three trains daily) – weaves between rocky, scrub-covered hills and steep cliffs. Above the river's right (eastern) bank, the narrow D301 gives fine views as it passes through wild countryside and a number of remote, mud-puddle hamlets. Several villages in the area have Romanesque churches. The one in **Prades** – where you can laze on the village's small sand beach – has an expressive 15th-century polychrome wood entombment of Christ, and a rich baroque altarpiece.

AN Rafting (☎ 04 71 57 23 90; www.an-rafting.com in French), in scenic **Monistrol d'Allier**, does river

---

QUIET HEROISM IN LE CHAMBON-SUR-LIGNON

The village of Le Chambon-sur-Lignon is in the Montagne Protestante, a remote highland area with a long-standing Protestant majority. Its tradition of sheltering the persecuted began in the 17th century, when Huguenots fled here. Throughout WWII, Chambon and nearby hamlets 'hid, protected and saved' around 3000 refugees, including hundreds of Jewish children, being hunted by French police and the Gestapo. A crucial role in this resistance to the Nazis was played by the local religious leadership, led by Pastor André Trocmé.

Today Chambon continues its venerable tradition of welcoming the disadvantaged by taking in orphans and children from troubled families, both in institutions (such as the Collège-Lycée International Cévenol) and in local homes.

---

descents to Prades by raft and inflatable canoe (€40) between April and September and also organises canyon descents and rock climbing.

Hôtel des Gorges (☎ 04 71 57 24 50; fax 04 71 57 25 36; d with shower/bathroom €35/38; ☺ Apr-Sep) does a special deal for pilgrims and hikers: €20 for dinner and a bunk bed in a double room – it'll want to see your backpack to confirm that you're more than a motorist on the scrounge, though. The hotel does a plentiful *menu* for all comers at €12.

In tidy **Langeac** (population 4500), at the northern extremity of the Allier's most interesting stretch, drop into the **Collégiale St-Gal**, a 15th-century Gothic church, and, beside it, **Le Jaquemard**, a small museum of local traditions.

Langeac has a well-equipped **tourist office** (☎ 04 71 77 05 41; place Aristide Briand; ☺ 9am-noon & 2-7pm Mon-Fri, 5pm Sat, 10am-noon Sun May-Sep, 9am-noon & 2-5.30pm Tue-Sat Oct-Apr).

Le Chambon-sur-Lignon
'L'espace ouvert, l'esprit aussi' (open space, open mind) is the motto of this quiet, neat village, 45km east of Le Puy-en-Velay, which played a courageous role in WWII.

Across the street from the Protestant **temple** is a bronze **plaque** erected in Chambon's honour by Jews sheltered here as children. Every July and August there's an exhibition on the town's WWII history. Ask at the **tourist office** (☎ 04 71 59 71 56; www.ot-lechambonsurlignon .fr; rue des Quatre Saisons; ☺ 9am-noon & 2-6.30pm Mon-Sat, 10am-noon Sun Jun-Sep, 9am-noon & 3-6pm Mon-Sat Oct-May) for details.

Mont Mézenc
South of Le Chambon-sur-Lignon, the D500 and D262 take you to the scenic D410, from which the D400 winds its way up to the col of La Croix des Boutières (1508m). Here you can link up with the GR7 and GR73 trails for the half-hour hike to the summit of Mont Mézenc (1753m; pronounced meh-*zang*).

On a clear day, you can see the entire southeastern quarter of France, from Mont Blanc, 200km to the northeast, right around to Mont Ventoux, 140km in the southeast of the region.

Limousin, the Dordogne & Quercy

The adjacent regions of Limousin, the Dordogne and Quercy are tucked away in southwestern France between the Massif Central and the vineyard-covered lowlands around Bordeaux. Although they share similar histories and are firmly steeped in rural life, each has its own distinctive landscape, ambience and cuisine.

Limousin is the least densely populated region in France. Its main city, Limoges, known for fine china and enamelware, is a good staging post. But the real draw is the countryside; a verdant landscape of hills, rivers and woodland dotted with tiny hamlets. The beautiful village of Gimel-les-Cascades, surrounded by brooks and pine-clad hills, is idyllic enough to inspire visitors to move here. Indeed, plenty of Britons now have homes or second homes in this region.

The Brits, however, were not the first to discover these parts. Around the Dordogne River (known as Périgord), prehistoric paintings in limestone caves point to the existence of civilisations some 14,000 years ago. Paintings, such as those at Lascaux, are among the most significant examples of prehistoric art in the world. More recent attractions include hilltop chateaux and fortified *bastide* villages, so there's plenty above ground to explore too.

Quercy, the southernmost area, is warmer and drier, being not far from Toulouse and the Pyrenees. It's not as well-known as its neighbours to the north, but this area also harbours magnificent prehistoric art, majestic castles and pretty villages alongside the steep, dramatic limestone canyons cut by the River Lot.

The best way to experience the beauty of this river-rich region is by boat. Whether it's a white-knuckle canoe ride down the Dordogne or a few days relaxing on a houseboat on the River Lot, the glistening waters offer a raft of opportunities for fun and adventure.

LIMOUSIN, THE DORDOGNE & QUERCY

HIGHLIGHTS

- Marvel at incredible prehistoric cave paintings in the **Vézère Valley** (p591)
- Taste the local foie gras and truffles at the medieval town of **Sarlat-la-Canéda** (p587)
- Shop at the open-air market in **Villefranche de Rouergue** (p605)
- Stroll through the pretty villages of **Gimel-les-Cascades** (p580) and **Collongnes-la-Rouge** (p581)
- Explore the *bastides* of **Domme** (p595), **Monpazier** (p597) and **Najac** (p606)
- Relax on a houseboat on the River Lot near **Cahors** (p599)
- Take a cruise on the underground river at **Gouffre de Padirac** (p608)

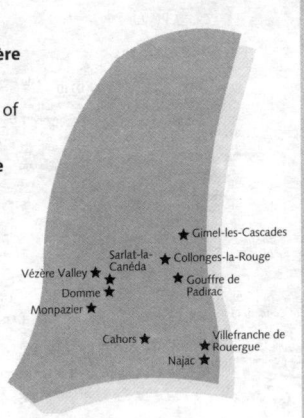

★ Gimel-les-Cascades
Sarlat-la-Canéda ★ ★ Collonges-la-Rouge
Vézère Valley ★ ★ ★ Gouffre de
Domme ★ Padirac
Monpazier ★
Cahors ★ Villefranche de
★ Rouergue
Najac ★

- POPULATION: 1,134,959
- AREA: 25,654 SQ KM

LIMOUSIN, THE DORDOGNE & QUERCY

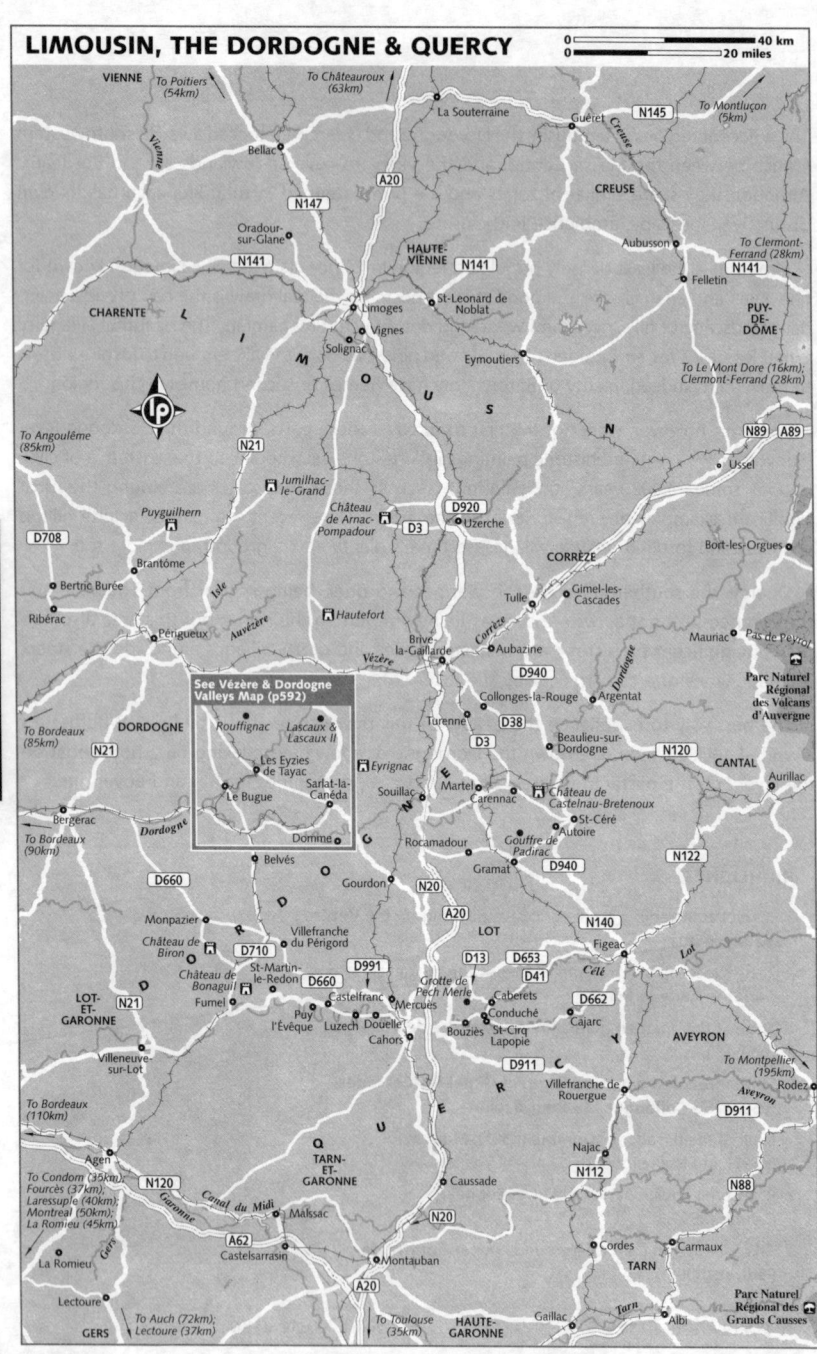

Getting There & Around

The major transportation hub for the region is Limoges (p577): the A20 motorway heads northwards from here to Paris and continues south through the region to Toulouse, trains serve Paris and neighbouring regions, and planes arrive from around France and across the channel in the UK. Bergerac airport (p598) also has services to and from the UK.

The best way to see the region is by car, although there is a useful rail link that wiggles down to Toulouse from Limoges via Brive, Souillac and Cahors. Train services are supplemented by SNCF buses.

LIMOUSIN

The tranquil, green hills of Limousin, dotted with old churches and castles, present the quintessential image of rural France. Long overlooked by tourists, the region's many rivers, springs and lakes now attract visitors interested in such outdoor pursuits as sailing, canoeing, kayaking and fishing. The local economy is based on agriculture, in particular cattle and sheep farming.

Limousin is made up of three *départements*: Haute-Vienne, in the west, whose *préfecture* is the city of Limoges; the rural Creuse, in the northeast; and, in the southeast, the Corrèze, blessed with many of the region's most beautiful sights.

LIMOGES
pop 200,000

The pleasant, although hardly compelling, city of Limoges has long been acclaimed for its production of enamelware and fine porcelain. Museums and galleries dedicated to these arts are among the city's main attractions. Known around Europe for its top-flight basketball team, Limoges also has a small but animated nightlife scene, thanks largely to the presence of some 17,000 university students.

Orientation

The train station is located 500m northeast of place Jourdan. The Cité Quarter and its cathedral are southeast of place Jourdan and east of the partly pedestrianised commercial centre, the chateau-less Château Quarter.

Information
INTERNET ACCESS
Le Cybar (☎ 05 55 32 31 71; 33 rue Delescluze; per hr €4; 🕑 10am-1am Mon-Wed, 10am-2am Thu-Sat)

LAUNDRY
There are laundrettes at 28 rue Delescluze and 9 rue Monte a Regret; both are open until 9pm.

MONEY
There are several banks on place Jourdan and place Wilson and the post office also changes money.
Banque de France (8 blvd Carnot; money exchange 🕑 8.45am-noon Mon-Fri)

POST
Main Post Office (29 av de la Libération) Offers currency exchange services, a Cyberposte and an ATM.
Post Office (6 blvd de Fleurus) Has Cyberposte and ATM.

TOURIST INFORMATION
Maison du Tourisme (☎ 05 55 79 04 04; 4 place Denis Dussoubs; 🕑 8.30am-noon & 1.30-6.30pm Mon-Sat) Provides information on the Haute-Vienne, including B&B reservations and organised cycling and hiking trips.
Tourist Office (☎ 05 55 34 46 87; otlimoges.haute -vienne@en-france.com; 12 blvd de Fleurus; 🕑 9am-7pm Mon-Sat, 10am-6pm Sun mid-Jun–mid-Sep, 9am-noon & 2-7pm Mon-Sat mid-Sep–mid-Jun) The office also organises guided walks of the town from February to June.

Sights
PORCELAIN & ENAMEL
The **Musée National Adrien Dubouché** (☎ 05 55 33 08 50; 8bis place Winston Churchill; adult/18-25 yrs/under 18 €4/2.60/free; 🕑 10am-12.30pm & 2-5.45pm Wed-Mon, no lunch break Jul & Aug) has one of France's two most outstanding ceramics collections (the other is in Sèvres, southwest of Paris). An English-language brochure is available at the entrance.

The **Bernardaud porcelain factory** (☎ 05 55 10 55 91; 27 av Albert Thomas), 1km northwest of the Musée National Adrien Dubouché, can be visited daily June to September; **tours** (adult/under 12 €4/free) are from 9.15am to 11am and 1pm to 4.30pm and include a demonstration. The rest of the year tours take place Monday to Friday (and sometimes on Saturday), but you have to phone ahead.

In Limoges *émail* (eh-*my*) has nothing to do with the Internet, it means 'enamel', which has been produced here since the 12th

LIMOGES

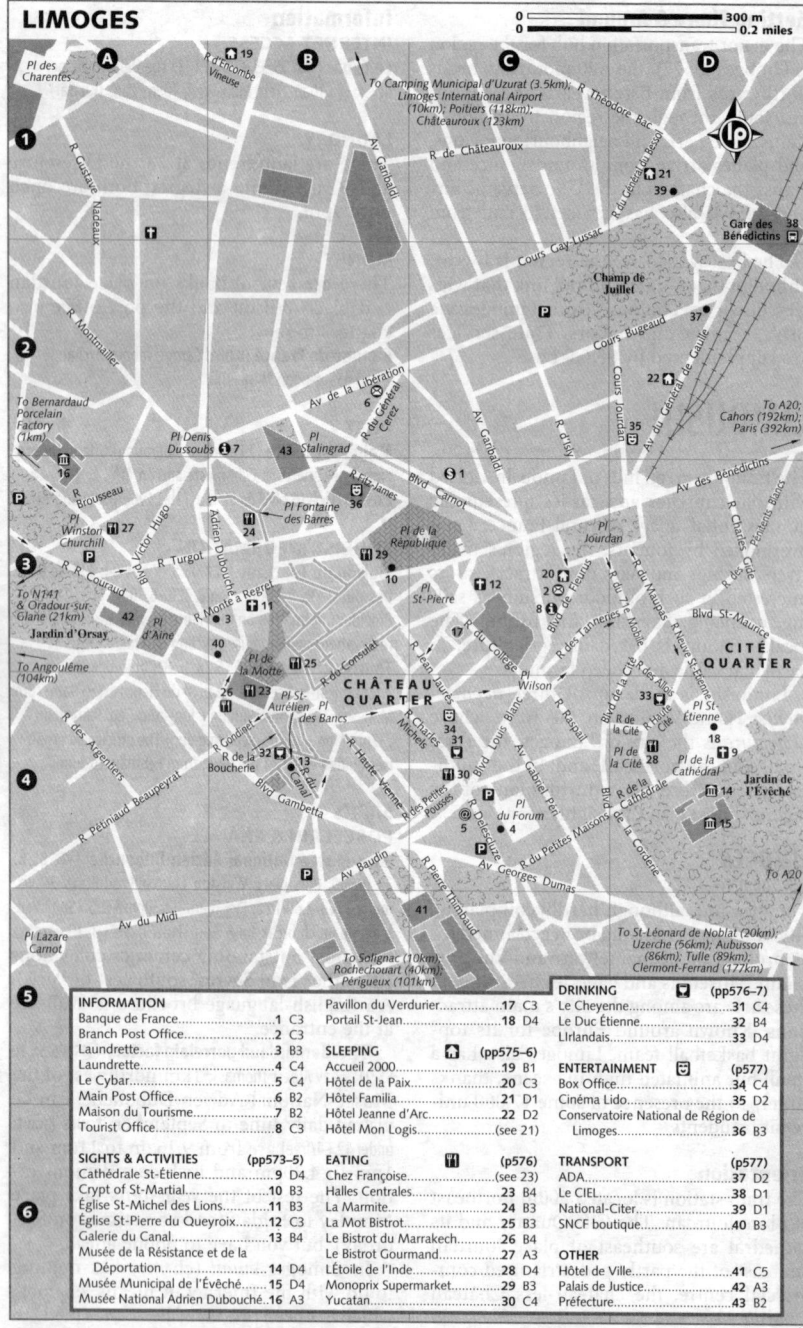

century. The Musée Municipal (below) has a fine collection of *émaux* (plural). Stunning (but pricey) contemporary works can be admired at **Galerie du Canal** (☎ 05 55 33 14 11; 15 rue du Canal; 10am-noon & 2-7pm Tue-Sat; also Mon in Jul, Aug & Dec), a cooperative gallery run by six master enamellists.

Traditional porcelain and enamel galleries can be found south of the tourist office along blvd Louis Blanc.

CHÂTEAU QUARTER

All that remains of the great pilgrimage abbey of St-Martial, founded in AD 848, is an outline on place de la République. The **Crypt of St-Martial** (mid-Jun–mid-Sep), from the 9th-century, contains the tomb of Limoges' first bishop, who converted the population to Christianity. It can be visited.

Église St-Pierre du Queyroix (place St-Pierre) half a block southeast of place de la République, has an impressive 13th-century tower. Across place St-Pierre is the **Pavillon du Verdurier**, an octagonal, porcelain-faced structure that dates from 1900.

Église St-Michel des Lions (rue Adrien Dubouché), named for the two granite lions standing on either side of the tower door, has a huge copper ball perched atop its 65m-high spire. Built between the 14th and 16th centuries, it contains St-Martial's relics (including his head) and a number of beautiful 15th-century stained-glass windows.

Just off place St-Aurélien, the pedestrianised **rue de la Boucherie** – so named because of the butcher's shops that lined the street in the Middle Ages – and nearby streets are graced with half-timbered houses.

CITÉ QUARTER

The crumbly granite **Cathédrale St-Étienne** – one of the few Gothic churches built south of the Loire – was begun in 1273 and completed in 1888. Facing place St-Étienne, the Flamboyant Gothic **Portail St-Jean** (the carved portal of the northern transept arm) dates from the early 1500s. Inside, the richly decorated Renaissance rood screen, once situated at the entrance to the choir (c 1300), is now in a less conspicuous location at the far end of the nave. Note the cathedral's remarkably slender pillars.

The **Musée Municipal de l'Évêché** (☎ 05 55 45 98 10; place de la Cathédrale; admission free; 10-11.45am & 2-6pm Wed-Mon, to 5pm Oct-May, also Tue Jul-Sep) spe-

cialises in 12th- to 20th-century enamel but also has a handful of lesser-known works by Pierre-Auguste Renoir, born in Limoges in 1841. Across the courtyard, the **Musée de la Résistance et de la Déportation** (☎ 05 55 45 98 10; admission free; 10-11.45am & 2-6pm Wed-Mon Jun–mid-Sep, 2-5pm mid-Sep–May, also Tue Jul-Sep) illustrates the exploits of the Resistance and the suffering of the deportees with the help of photos, handbills, maps and military equipment. Both 18th-century buildings are in a peaceful, terraced garden.

The cathedral is surrounded by the **Jardin de l'Évêché**, Limoges' botanical garden, whose formal beds include both medicinal and toxic herbs and lots of flowers. Nearby **rue Haute Cité** is lined with 16th- and 17th-century houses that have granite lower floors and half-timbered upper storeys.

Sleeping
BUDGET
Hôtel Mon Logis (☎ 05 55 77 41 43; www.hotel-limoges-monlogis.com in French; 16 rue du Général du Bessol; s from €24, s/d with shower from €26/29.50;) Don't be put off by the fierce-looking Alsatian guard dog – this one-star hotel, close to the station, is about the best budget option. The simple, brown-carpeted rooms have toilet cubicles and hairdryers; some have TVs.

Accueil 2000 (☎ 05 55 77 63 97; fjt.accueil-2000@wanadoo.fr; 20 rue d'Encombe Vineuse; s incl breakfast €14; reception 24hr) A charmless 93-room co-ed

---

hostel for young working people. It accepts travellers year-round, though rooms are most likely to be available in summer.

Camping

Camping Municipal d'Uzurat (☎ 05 55 38 49 43; av d'Uzurat; sites 2 people & tent €9; ⊗ Jul-Aug) This is a three-star camping ground on the edge of the Bastide forest about 3.5km north of the train station. By bus, take No 20 to av Louis Armand stop and then walk along the lake for about 400m.

MID-RANGE

Hôtel de la Paix (☎ 05 55 34 36 00; fax 05 55 32 37 06; 25 place Jourdan; d with shower/& toilet from €36/47; **P**) This is the place where time has stood still. Antique gramophones and related memorabilia clutter the corridors, floral print runs wild and the impeccable, courteous service can only be from times gone by. A delightful old hotel with modern, comfortable rooms; the spacious ones on the 2nd floor have balconies. Free parking out the front.

Hôtel Jeanne d'Arc (☎ 05 55 77 67 77; www.hotel jeannedarc-limoges.fr; 17 av du Général de Gaulle; s/d with shower €53/62.50, s/d with bath €68/78; **P**) This old blue-shuttered coaching inn has been transformed into a charming three-star hotel. The elegant, traditionally furnished rooms come with big beds, armchairs and desks.

Hôtel Familia (☎ 05 55 77 51 40; 18 rue du Général du Bessol; d with shower & toilet €40) A very well-maintained, two-star hotel in a quiet spot close to the station. The rooms are spotless and fully equipped although the building itself is nothing special.

Eating

Two areas in particular have a good concentration of restaurants; around Halles Centrales in the Château Quarter, and around rue Haute Cité in the Cité Quarter.

Chez Françoise (☎ 05 55 32 32 79; Halles Centrales; menus €8.50/15; ⊗ lunch only, closed Sun & holidays) Fast food, local style. Find a space between the friendly market workers on these long benches and tuck in to a hearty, three-course feed for €8.50. There's a limited choice – usually a couple of meat options plus a fish choice for the main – but it's great value.

Le Bistrot du Marrakech (☎ 05 55 34 49 68; 11 place de la Motte; mains €12-16) Despite tacky Moroccan décor and sloppy presentation, this intimate restaurant serves delicious sizzling tagines.

The melt-in-the-mouth lamb and prune tagine (€12) is an absolute winner.

La Mot Bistrot (☎ 05 55 34 47 19; 22 place de la Motte; mains €7.50-12) In a sunny corner overlooking bustling place de la Motte, this is a good place to people-watch and work on the facial tan while tucking into traditional French café-bistro fare or sipping an espresso.

Yucatan (☎ 05 55 33 67 77; 3 rue Charles Michels; mains €6-9.80; ⊗ Tue-Sun) Sombrero lamp shades, fake cacti and colourful ponchos fill this lively Tex-Mex place; fajitas, tacos, burgers and cocktails fill the menu. This is one of a handful of busy eateries at the bottom of rue Charles Michels.

La Marmite (☎ 05 55 33 38 34; 1 place Fontaine des Barres; menus €16.50-37; ⊗ Tue-Sat) In a pretty square of lop-sided medieval houses, this intimate place occupying a rustic, 17th-century building, offers traditional Périgord specialities.

Le Bistrot Gourmand (☎ 05 55 10 29 29; 5-7 place Winston Churchill; ⊗ noon-3pm & 7-11.30pm Mon-Sat; mains €7.90-16.50) This large and popular bistro-style restaurant serves tasty fish and meat mains. Choose from the cosy inside room or the sunny conservatory.

L'Étoile de l'Inde (☎ 05 55 32 46 95; 7 rue Haute Cité) French waitresses finely dressed in full Indian regalia serve up tasty tandoori and curry dishes (some vegetarian) from €5, though the screeching Goa techno is a bit unnecessary.

SELF-CATERING

Stock up at the **Halles Centrales** (covered market; place de la Motte; ⊗ to 1pm), or the **Monoprix supermarket** (42 rue Jean Jaurès; ⊗ 8.30am-8pm Mon-Sat).

Drinking

Rue Charles Michels, with its many watering holes, has been nicknamed 'rue de la Soif' (Thirst St) by local students.

Le Cheyenne (☎ 05 55 32 32 62; 4 rue Charles Michels; ⊗ 7pm-1am Mon-Sat) A small, lively spot for cowboys and cowgirls.

Le Duc Étienne (place St-Aurélien; ⊗ 2pm-2am Mon-Sat, 6pm-2am Sun) Also in the Cité Quarter area is this small, mellow bar popular with students.

Le Trompe L'Oeil (☎ 05 55 32 51 03; 26 place de la Motte; ⊗ 11am-midnight Tue-Sat) A trendy new café-bar in a charming medieval building, with tables that spill out onto the square.

L'Irlandais (☎ 05 55 32 46 47; 2 rue Haute Cité; ☻ 5pm-1am Tue-Fri, 3pm-2am Sat & Sun) In the hip Quartier de la Cathédrale, L'Irlandais is run by a Breton and is a friendly little place. In an atmospheric old building with a wooden interior, it has live music on Friday and Saturday and seats outside in summer.

Entertainment

Tickets for cultural events all over south-western France are available from **box office** (☎ 05 55 33 28 16; 15 rue Jean Jaurès; ☻ Tue-Sat).

Conservatoire National de Région de Limoges (☎ 05 55 45 95 50; 9 rue Fitz-James) holds regular concerts and lessons in traditional musical instruments.

Cinéma Lido (☎ 05 36 68 20 15; 3 av du Général de Gaulle) screens nondubbed films.

Getting There & Away
AIR

Just off the A20, **Limoges International Airport** (☎ 05 55 43 30 30; www.aeroportlimoges.com in French) is 10km west of Limoges. It is served by domestic flights and Ryanair flights from the UK.

BUS

Buses to destinations such as Oradour-sur-Glane (€3), St-Léonard de Noblat (€3 by SNCF bus), Tulle (€16.30 by SNCF bus), Solignac (€2) and Rochechouart (€5) depart from **Le CIEL** (Centre Intermodal d'Échanges de Limoges;

☎ 05 55 45 10 10), the bus terminal that is situated right across the tracks from the train station.

CAR

Hire cars from **ADA** (☎ 05 55 79 61 12; 27 av du Général de Gaulle) or **National-Citer** (☎ 05 55 77 10 10; 8 cours Gay-Lussac).

TRAIN

The green-domed, Art Deco-style **Gare des Bénédictins** (☎ 0 836 353 535), completed in 1929, is one of the most striking train stations in France.

Train destinations include Paris' Gare d'Austerlitz (€39.50, three hours, 12 daily), Aubusson (€12.30, 1¾ hours, three daily, one on Sunday), Cahors (€23.30, 2¼ hours, five daily), Périgueux (€13.30, one hour, 13 daily) and Uzerche (€9, 40 minutes, 11 daily).

Tickets are also available from the **SNCF boutique** (4 rue Othon Péconnet).

AROUND LIMOGES
Oradour-sur-Glane

This village, site of a horrific SS massacre in 1944 (below), has been turned into a moving and evocative memorial.

Seven buses daily link Le CIEL in Limoges with Oradour-sur-Glane (€3, 30 minutes). By car, take the D9 and follow the road signs to the *village martyr* (martyred village).

LIMOUSIN, THE DORDOGNE & QUERCY

SILENCE BEARS WITNESS

Oradour-sur-Glane, 21km northwest of Limoges, was an unexceptional Limousin town until the afternoon of 10 June 1944, when German lorries bearing an SS detachment rumbled into town.

The town's entire population was ordered to assemble at the market square. The men were divided into groups and forced into *granges* (barns), where they were gunned down before the structures were set alight. Several hundred women and children were herded into the church, inside which a bomb was detonated; those who tried to escape through the windows were shot before the building was set on fire. The Nazi troops then burned down the entire town; inside the 328 buildings left smouldering that evening were the corpses of dozens of civilians who had hidden to avoid capture. Of the people rounded up that day – among them refugees from Paris and a couple of Jewish families living under assumed names – only one woman and five men survived; 642 people, including 205 children, were killed.

Since these events, the entire **village** (admission free; ☻ 9am-5pm, to 7pm mid-May–mid-Sep) has been left untouched to serve as a memorial. The tram tracks and overhead wires, the prewar-style electricity lines and the rusting hulks of 1930s automobiles give a pretty good idea of what the town must have looked like on the morning of the massacre.

Entry to the village is via the **Centre de la Mémoire** (adult/child, student & war veteran €6/4; ☻ same as the village) which describes the village before the massacre and shows survivors' testimonies and executioners' confessions.

After the war, a larger Oradour was built a few hundred metres west of the ruins.

Solignac

pop 1350

The pretty medieval village of Solignac, 10km south of Limoges on the River Briance, owes its outsized, 75m-long granite **church** to its popularity as a stopover on the pilgrimage route to Santiago de Compostela (Spain; p604). Built during the second quarter of the 1100s in the Limousin-Romanesque style, the sober, one-time abbey church is – thanks to the domed roof – remarkably wide (14m) and (considering that it's pre-Gothic) pretty well lit. The **stalls** in the nave, made for the Benedictines in the late 1400s, are decorated with carved human heads, bizarre animals and a monk mooning the world. Above the stalls, the **capitals** of the columns – intended to further the moral education of the faithful – are decorated with human figures being devoured by dragons and serpents. There's a 15th-century **fresco** of St-Christophe on the southern (right-hand) wall of the choir. One of the transept arms is crowned with a dome, the other by a barrel arch.

The 12km-long **Sentier de la Briance**, with yellow trail markings, leads you through the surrounding countryside, much of it forested. Shorter trails are also marked; maps are available at the tourist office. The **Parc du Reynou** (☎ 05 55 00 40 00; www.parczooreynou.com in French; exit 37 off the A20; adult/child €9/6.50; ⏰ 10am-8pm Apr-Sep; 1-5pm Wed, Sat & Sun Oct-Mar) is a free-range exotic animal park a few kilometres away in Le Vigen, popular with children.

Solignac's **tourist office** (☎ 05 55 00 42 31; tourisme-solignac@wanadoo.fr; ⏰ 10am-1pm & 2.30-6.30pm Tue-Sat, 10am-1pm & 3-6pm Sun May-Sep; 9am-noon & 2-6pm Tue-Fri & 9am-noon Sat Oct-Apr) is in the car park across the street from the church. When it's closed, brochures are available from the Secretariat on the 1st floor of the *mairie* (village hall) at 57 av St-Eloi, 150m west of the church.

Hôtel Le St-Eloi (☎ 05 55 00 44 52; fax 05 55 00 55 56; 66 av St-Eloi; r from €43), 150m from the church's western front, has 15 Provençal-style rooms. It has an attached **restaurant** (menus from €14; ⏰ closed Sun evening, Mon lunch & Jan).

When school is in session, three buses daily (except Sunday) link Le CIEL in Limoges with Solignac (€3, 25 minutes, two the rest of the year); and the neighbouring hamlet of Le Vigen (€3, 35 minutes, two or three daily year-round). The Solignac–Le Vigen train station is linked to Limoges (€2.50, 10 minutes) and Uzerche (€9, 40 minutes) by one or two trains daily.

AUBUSSON

pop 5000

Aubusson, about 90km from both Limoges and Clermont-Ferrand, has been acclaimed for its exquisite tapestries and carpets for over 500 years.

Sights

These days the town, in something of an economic slump, and nearby Felletin (10km to the south) are home to about 30 tapestry workshops. Their products, both traditional and contemporary, are on display in season at the **L'Exposition Tapisseries d'Aubusson-Felletin** (admission €3; ⏰ 9am-12.30pm & 2-6pm Jun-Sep, no lunch break Jul & Aug), held inside the town hall on the Grande Rue (the main drag).

Across the curvaceous River Creuse, on the other side of the hill (on top of which sit the ruins of a chateau), is the modest **Musée Départemental de la Tapisserie** (☎ 05 55 83 08 30; adult/child €4/2.50; ⏰ 9.30am-noon & 2-6pm Wed-Mon, no lunch break Jul & Aug). The museum houses changing exhibits of antique and modern tapestries. The town's tapestry workshops include the large **Manufacture St-Jean** (☎ 05 55 66 10 08; av des Lissiers; ⏰ 9am-noon & 2-5.30pm Mon-Fri), 200m from the Musée Départemental, which can be toured for €6.50. Call in advance to book a tour.

Aubisson's **tourist office** (☎ 05 55 66 32 12; ⏰ 10am-7pm Mon-Sat, 10am-noon & 2.30-5.30pm Sun & holidays mid-Jun–mid-Sep; 9.30am-12.30pm & 2-6pm Mon-Sat mid-Sep–Easter; to 6.30pm Mon-Sat & to 5.30pm Sun Easter–mid-Jun), down the alley from 65 Grande Rue, has details about visiting many of the area's other tapestry *ateliers*, most of which have no admission fee. Next door, the 16th-century **Maison du Tapissier** (admission €3) houses a museum of the history of tapestry-making. Opening hours are the same as those of the tourist office, which handles ticket sales.

Sleeping & Eating

Hôtel du Lissier (☎ 05 55 66 14 18; fax 05 55 66 33 87; 84 Grande Rue; s/d with shower & toilet €34/39; reception ⏰ closed Sun, & Mon night in winter) The Hôtel du Lissier has brand-new colour-coordinated rooms that are bright and spacious. The attached restaurant downstairs has a small selection of standard, good-value dishes (€7.50 to 11.50).

Hôtel Le France (☎ 05 55 66 10 22, 05 55 66 88 64; 6 rue des Déportés; r from €46) This is a charming hotel occupying an 18th-century *hôtel particulier* with an imposing white-shuttered façade. The spotlessly clean rooms are comfortable and well-equipped.

Getting There & Away

Aubusson is linked to Limoges by four SNCF buses each day (€12.10, 1¾ hours), except on Sunday.

UZERCHE

pop 3500

Set on a promontory high above the River Vézère, the picturesque town of Uzerche – much quieter now the A20 diverts most traffic around the town – is known for its 15th- and 16th-century **Maisons à Tourelles**, which look like small castles thanks to their turrets. Some fine examples can be seen around **Porte Bécharie**, a 14th-century town gate near place Marie Colein.

At the top of the hill, high above the steep, dark-grey slate rooftops, is **Église St-Pierre**. A barrel-vaulted, Romanesque abbey church, it has a typically Limousin-style belfry and an 11th-century crypt, reached through a squat door in the outside wall of the choir.

Take the D3 under the railway viaduct to get a panoramic view of the town.

Orientation & Information

The old city is perched on a hill almost entirely surrounded by a hairpin curve in the Vézère. The only street into the old city is at shop-lined place Marie Colein, which is about 500m up the D920 (av de Paris) from the D3.

Tourist Office (☎ 05 55 73 15 71; ot.uzerche@wanadoo.fr; place de la Libération; ☀ 10am-12.30pm & 2.30-6.30pm Mon-Sat, 10am-12.30pm & 2.30-6pm Sun Jun-Sep, 10am-noon & 2-5.30pm Mon-Fri Apr, May & Oct, 10am-noon Mon-Fri Nov-Mar) Behind the church.

Sleeping & Eating

Hôtel Jean Teyssier (☎ 05 55 73 10 05; http://hotel teyssier.free.fr in French; rue du Pont-Turgot; d from €47; ☀ reception closed Tue & Wed, except from 5pm mid-Jul–mid-Sep) At an attractive, two-star place with 14 rooms, at the intersection of the N20 and D3; it has a **restaurant** (menus €18-33; ☀ closed Wed).

Hôtel Ambroise (☎ 05 55 73 28 60; fax 05 55 98 45 73; 34 av de Paris; r with shower €38) A rustic family

hotel with a pretty garden right on the river. The two-star rooms have older-style furnishings and lovely river views.

Getting There & Away

Uzerche is linked to Limoges, 56km to the north, by train (€9, 40 minutes, 11 daily). The train station is 2km north of the old city along the N20.

BRIVE-LA-GAILLARDE

pop 51,590

Brive-La-Gaillarde (Brive), known for its champion rugby team, is sprawling, ugly and of little interest to most travellers. However, nearby areas of the Corrèze *département* include some of Limousin's most attractive towns and villages. A major rail junction, Brive can be used as a transport, provisioning and accommodation base.

The **tourist office** (☎ 05 55 24 08 80; www.brive -tourisme.com in French; place du 14 Juillet; ☀ 9am-7pm Mon-Sat, 10am-1pm Sun Jul & Aug, 9am-noon & 2-6pm Mon-Sat except holidays Sep-Jun) is housed in a 19th-century water tower.

A cluster of cheap hotels near the train station includes the **Hôtel Le France**(☎ 05 55 74 08 13; 60 av de la Gare; r from €32) with tiny rooms into which a shower and toilet have been squeezed. For more comfort, the three-star **Hôtel Le Quercy** (☎ 05 55 74 09 26; fax 05 55 74 06 24; r €49; P ✿) offers spacious rooms with carpeted walls, cable TV and large baths. It's opposite the tourist office.

Brive is the region's major rail and bus hub – see the relevant town and city listings for details. The **bus station** (☎ 05 55 17 91 19; place du 14 Juillet; ☀ 8.15am-noon & 2-6.15pm Mon-Sat) is next to the tourist office. Local and intercity buses do not run on Sunday or holidays.

The train station is linked to the tourist office and bus station, 1.3km to the southwest, by the hourly bus No 5, which runs until a little before 7pm.

NORTHEAST OF BRIVE
Aubazine

The restful, idyllic village of Aubazine sits on a hilltop surrounded by forests, sloping pastures and verdant valleys. The small **tourist office** (☎ 05 55 25 79 93; place de l'Église) is in the village hall on the main square. Opening hours vary.

The 12th-century Romanesque **church** contains an extremely rare oak **armoire liturgique** (liturgical chest) from the late 1100s, as well as the elaborately carved, 13th-century limestone **tomb** of Étienne d'Obazine, founder of the Cistercian abbey to which the church once belonged. About 300m north, along route de Tulle, the small, Greek Melchite (Catholic) monastery has a modern, Byzantine-style **Chapelle Grecque** (Greek Chapel).

One of the area's footpaths heads up the hill to the **Puy de Pauliac** (or Pauliat; 520m), which has a *cromlech* (dolmen) at the top and affords fine views. For part of the way it follows the abbey's one-time aqueduct, the **Canal des Moines**.

Hôtel Le Saint Étienne (☎ 05 55 25 71 01; hotel .saint-etienne@netcourrier.com; place du Bourg; r from €43; Mar-Nov), a two-star inn, is housed in a 14th-century chateau in the centre of the village. Its 41 rooms are simply designed but comfortable. The adjoining **restaurant** (menus €15-19.50; closed Mon & dinner Sun) serves traditional French cuisine in a sunny courtyard.

Tulle
pop 15,500

The town of Tulle (pronounced with a long 'Toole'), prefecture of the Corrèze *département* and home of France's last accordion factory, stretches along both banks of the River Corrèze for some 3km. The river itself is hard to spot, as it's choked with lines of traffic along both banks. The train station is 2km southwest of the cathedral.

Opposite the cathedral (and next to the ornate **Maison de Loyac**) is Tulle's **tourist office** (☎ 05 55 26 59 61; office-de-tourisme-de-tulle@wanadoo .fr; 2-6pm Mon, 9am-noon & 2-6pm Tue-Sat & 10am-noon Sun Jul & Aug).

There's a busy market selling local produce, lace and clothes in front of the cathedral on Wednesday mornings.

Next door to the Romanesque and Gothic **cathedral**, which consists of just a nave (the transept collapsed in 1796), a 13th-century cloister leads to the **Musée du Cloître** (☎ 05 55 26 91 05; adult/student/under 7 yrs €2.35/1.10/free; closed Wed morning & Sat), which displays an eclectic collection that includes lace, ceramics and religious sculpture. Walking around the tranquil cloistered courtyard is free.

At the other end of town and across the river from the train station, the **Musée des Armes Anciennes** (Armaments Museum; ☎ 05 55 20 28 28; 1 rue du 9 Juin 1944; 9am-noon & 2-6pm Mon-Fri Jul & Aug, 2-6pm Wed & 9am-noon & 2-6pm Thu & Fri Sep-Jun)

displays firearms collected over the last two centuries by the city's national armaments manufactory.

Hôtel Le Bon Accueil (☎ /fax 05 55 26 70 57; 8-10 rue du Canton; d €30; reception usually closed Sat night & Sun), right across the river from the cathedral, is a one-star place whose average rooms are brightened up with cheesy photos of cats and fast cars. The attached rustic **restaurant** (menus from €12) has hearty, family-style French meals.

Despite its position overlooking the station, the brightly painted **Hôtel de la Gare** (☎ 05 55 20 04 04; 25 av Winston Churchill; d from €39) is a good mid-range option worth its two stars.

Le Richlieu (☎ 05 55 26 42 18; 8 av Charles de Gaulle) is a friendly, traditional bar where locals hang out. You can buy a sandwich at the adjacent patisserie and eat it at the bar's outdoor tables.

Tulle is linked by train and SNCF bus to Brive (€4.40, 25 minutes, nine to 15 daily) and Clermont-Ferrand (€19.60, three hours, three to seven daily).

Gimel-les-Cascades
pop 650

This tiny, flower-filled village, lying 37km northeast of Brive-la-Gaillarde, is set amid some of the most spectacular scenery in Limousin. It's an ideal spot to come for a picturesque stroll and a picnic.

A few hundred metres down the hill from the late-15th-century **Église St-Pardoux**, known for its late-12th-century enamel reliquary, are the **Cascades**, three waterfalls that drop 143m into a gorge aptly named the Inferno. They're within a privately owned **park** (☎ 05 55 21 26 49; adult/6-14 yrs €4/3; 10am-6pm Mar-Oct).

Other sights in and around Gimel-les-Cascades include the **Pont de Péage**, a medieval toll bridge rebuilt in the 1700s; the ruins of the **Château de Roche Haute**; the remains of the Romanesque **Église St-Étienne de Braguse**; and the Big Dipper–shaped, 20-hectare **Étang de Ruffaud**, a lake that offers a refreshing dip and a shady retreat for a picnic. Walking options include the trails along the **Gorges de la Vallée de la Montane**. Details are available at the **tourist office** (☎ 05 55 21 44 32; 10am-6pm Jul & Aug), 50m up the hill from the church.

Hostellerie de la Vallée (☎ 05 55 21 40 60; fax 55 21 38 74; d with shower/bath €41/43; Mar-Dec) is a two-star place between the church and the tourist office. Its nine simple, newly renovated rooms are small but the view and sound of the nearby cascades from the bedroom windows more than make up for the lack of space. The attached **restaurant** (menus €19.50-30; ☺ Thu-Tue), overlooking the gorge, offers delicious home-cooked food using local produce.

SOUTHEAST OF BRIVE
This part of Limousin is very near Carennac (p608), Rocamadour (p607), Château de Castelnau-Bretenoux (p608) and the Gouffre de Padirac (p608).

Turenne
pop 755
The pretty hilltop village of Turenne, 11km west of Collonges-la-Rouge on the D8 road, and 28km south of Brive, enjoyed considerable independence – under a viscount – from about 1000 until 1738. However, it was sold to Louis XV, whose taxation sent the town into precipitous decline as the artisan class fled. Dominating the village is the **chateau** (☎ 05 55 85 90 66; adult/under 18 €3/2; ☺ 10am-7pm Jul & Aug, 10am-noon & 2-6pm Apr-Jun, Sep & Oct, 2-5pm Sun Nov-Mar), on a sheer limestone outcrop that affords superb panoramas of the surrounding countryside. The massive 17th-century **Collégiale** (Collegiate Church) is in the style of the Counter-Reformation. Turenne is on the GR46 footpath.

The **tourist office** (☎ 05 55 85 94 38; ☺ 9am-12.30pm & 3-6.30pm Jul & Aug, 10am-12.30pm & 3-6pm Apr-Jun & Sep) is a few metres from place du Foirail (on the D8). The rest of the time, brochures can be picked up at the village hall, 200m to the west, on weekday and Saturday mornings and in the afternoon on Tuesday, Thursday and Friday.

La Maison des Chanoines (☎ 05 55 85 93 43; d €60-85; ☺ Apr-Oct), surrounded by 15th- to 18th-century slate-roofed houses, is a charming, six-room hotel in the centre of the village. It has stylish accommodation and there is an attached **restaurant** (menus €30-36) with a tree-shaded terrace, serving creative French food.

Turenne Gare, 3km southeast of the village, is served by a daily train from Brive (€2.80, 14 minutes). From Monday to Saturday there are buses from Brive (€2.80, 25 minutes, one or two daily).

Collonges-la-Rouge
pop 50
On a gently angled slope above a tributary of the Dordogne, the narrow alleyways of 'Collonges-the-Red', built entirely of bright red sandstone, squeeze between wisteria-covered houses topped with round turrets. Surrounded by lush greenery, and in the spring flowers of every colour, this tiny hamlet is a delightful place for a stroll.

The part Romanesque **church**, constructed from the 11th to the 15th centuries on the foundations of an 8th-century Benedictine priory, was an important resting place on the pilgrimage to Santiago de Compostela (p604). In the late 16th century local Protestants held prayers in the southern nave and their Catholic neighbours prayed in the northern nave, where there is still a gilded-wood retable erected in the 17th century. Nearby, the ancient wood and slate roof of the **old covered market**, held up by stone columns, shelters an ancient baker's oven.

The **tourist office** (☎ 05 55 25 47 57; ☺ 10am-7pm Jul & Aug, 10am-12.30pm & 2.30-7pm Jun & Sep, 11am-noon & 2-5pm Mon-Fri Oct-Mar) is next to the town hall on the village's 'main' road, a turning from the D38.

Relais de St-Jacques de Compostelle (☎ 05 55 25 41 02; fax 05 55 84 08 51; d with shower & toilet €50-65; ☺ mid-Mar–mid-Nov), the only place to stay, has 11 rooms. It's in a partly medieval building in the centre of the village. The attached **restaurant** (menus from €18-45) has traditional regional fare.

Collonges is linked by bus with Brive, 18km to the northwest along the D38 (€3, 30 minutes, six on weekdays and one only on Saturday).

Beaulieu-sur-Dordogne
pop 1300
The verdant, aptly named town of Beaulieu (literally 'beautiful place'), one of the most attractive medieval villages along the upper Dordogne, is well worth at least an overnight visit.

INFORMATION
Tourist Office (☎ 05 55 91 09 94; www.beaulieu -sur-dordogne.fr in French; place Marbot; ☺ 9am-7pm Jul & Aug, 10am-12.30pm & 2.30-5pm Mon-Sat Sep-Jun, 10am-12.30pm & 2.30-5pm Apr-Sep) On the D940, it has an English-language walking guide (€2) and Internet access (€6 per hour).

LIMOUSIN, THE DORDOGNE & QUERCY

SIGHTS

Beaulieu is famed for the majestic **Abbatiale St-Pierre**, a 12th-century Romanesque abbey church that was a stop on the Santiago de Compostela pilgrimage (p604). The southern portal's brilliant **tympanum** (c 1130), based upon prophecies from the books of Daniel and the Apocalypse, illustrates the Last Judgement with vivid scenes including monsters devouring the condemned. The **treasury**, with its 12th-century gilded Virgin and 13th-century enamel reliquary, is on view inside. The nearby streets have picturesque houses that date from the 14th and 15th centuries.

Lovely areas for a stroll include **Faubourg de la Chapelle**, a neighbourhood of 17th- and 18th-century houses on the banks of the Dordogne, especially up towards **Chapelle des Pénitents**, a Romanesque chapel. The river can be crossed on foot at the dam. The GR480, a spur of the GR46, passes by here.

SLEEPING

Auberge de Jeunesse de la Riviera Limousine (☎ 05 55 91 13 82; www.fuaj.org/aj/beaulieu; place du Monturu; dm €9.20; ⊗ Apr-Nov, reception 6-9pm) This is a homey, 28-bed place idyllically situated along the river, occupying a partly 14th-century building. Kitchen facilities are available. Bags can be left during the day.

Auberge Les Charmilles (☎ 05 55 91 29 29; charme@club-Internet.fr; 20 blvd Rodolphe de Turenne; d with large bathroom €52) Housed in a lovely old building overlooking the river, Auberge Les Charmilles has eight delightful rooms and a garden.

Hôtel L'Étape Fleurie (☎ 05 55 91 11 04; 17 place du Champ de Mars; s from €28, d with shower/bath €38/42). A welcoming 18-room, one-star place with bright, modern rooms.

Camping

Camping des Îles (☎ 05 55 91 02 65; per person €5-7, per car €2.50; ⊗ Apr-Oct) On the other side of the old city from the tourist office, this lovely, shaded camping ground is on an island sandwiched between two branches of the Dordogne. Its three-star facilities include tennis, children's play area and fishing.

EATING

Hôtel L'Étape Fleurie (☎ 05 55 91 11 04; 17 place du Champ de Mars; lunch/dinner menus from €10/16.50) This rustic restaurant in the hotel serves family-style regional specialities in a central spot overlooking the main square.

Auberge Les Charmilles (☎ 05 55 91 29 29; charme@club-Internet.fr; 20 blvd Rodolphe de Turenne; ⊗ closed Tue & Wed Oct-Apr) This place offers delicious, classic French cuisine. Try a dozen oysters or pork in balsamic vinegar.

Au Beau Lieu Breton (☎ 05 55 91 20 46; rue du Presbytère; crepes €4-7; ⊗ closed Mon Sep-Mar) On an alley behind (west of) the church, Au Beau Lieu Breton serves sweet and savoury crepes as well as omelettes and salads.

On Wednesday and Saturday mornings, an open-air market is held next to the village church. At least one of the two grocery stores on place Marbot – the Suprette and the Casino – are open daily (closed Sunday afternoon except in July and August); midday closure for both lasts from 12.30pm to 2.30pm or 3pm.

GETTING THERE & AWAY

Beaulieu is situated 70km east of Sarlat-la-Canéda and 47km northeast of the Gouffre de Padirac (p608).

From Monday to Saturday, there are buses linking Beaulieu with Brive (€5.90, one hour, one to three daily, none to two daily during school holidays). Schedules are posted at the bus shelter on place du Champ de Mars (opposite Hôtel L'Étape Fleurie) and outside the tourist office.

THE DORDOGNE

Known to the French as Périgord, the Dordogne *département*, named after the most important of the region's seven rivers, was one of the prehistoric cradles of human civilisation. The remains of Neanderthal and Cro-Magnon people have been discovered throughout the region, and quite a number of local caves, including the world-famous Lascaux, are decorated with extraordinary works of prehistoric art. Périgord's numerous hilltop chateaux (p585) and *bastides* (opposite) bear witness to the bloody battles waged here during the Middle Ages and the Hundred Years' War.

To make the region's attractions more accessible to visitors, Périgord has been divided into four areas, each assigned a colour according to its most prominent feature. The fields and forests to the north and northwest are known as Périgord Vert (green). In the centre, the area of limestone surrounding the capital, Périgueux, and along the River Isle is known as Périgord Blanc (white). The wine-growing area of Périgord Pourpre (purple) lies to the southwest, around Bergerac. Périgord Noir (black), known for its dark forests and many chateaux, encompasses the Vézère Valley and, to the south, part of the Dordogne valley; between the two valleys lies the attractive medieval town of Sarlat-la-Canéda.

Warm-weather sports that are popular within the region include canoeing, kayaking, fishing, rock climbing, horse riding and cycling. Tourist offices have details and can supply you with informative, English-language brochures.

During the warmer months, the Dordogne, famed for its rich cuisine, attracts vast numbers of tourists, including many from the UK. In winter the region goes into deep hibernation, and many hotels, restaurants and tourist sites close.

PÉRIGUEUX
pop 33,294

Périgueux, prefecture of the Dordogne *département,* has a restored medieval and Renaissance quarter, much of it built of dazzling white limestone, and one of France's best museums of prehistory. Founded over 2000 years ago on a hill bounded by a curve in the gentle River Isle, the city is at its liveliest during the Wednesday and Saturday truffle and foie gras markets (p586).

Périgueux is located 45km northwest of the Vézère Valley.

Orientation

The medieval and Renaissance old city, known as Puy St-Front, is on the hillside between the Isle (to the east), blvd Michel Montaigne and place Bugeaud (to the west). On the other side of place Bugeaud is the old city's historic rival, the largely residential Cité, centred around the ruins of a Roman amphitheatre. The train station is about 1km northwest of the old city.

Information
EMERGENCY
Hôtel de Police (police station; ☎ 05 53 06 44 44; place du Président Roosevelt; ☼ 24hr) Across from 20 rue du 4 Septembre.

BASTIDES

In the early 1200s the population of southwestern France was growing, as was a certain discontent with feudalism. Local suzerains and bishops, seeing in the new demographics an opportunity to enhance their authority and increase their income from rents, tolls and tariffs, turned to ancient Roman models of urban planning. Over the next 150 years they established more than 300 towns and villages known as *bastides*.

Generally surrounded by defensive walls, these 'new towns' had a regular street grid (terrain permitting), numbered building lots of uniform shape and size (to facilitate tax collection) and a charter granting various privileges to the inhabitants; the arcaded market square – which was the centre of the town's commercial life – often had a church in one corner. *Bastides* that are covered in this chapter include Villefranche de Rouergue (p605), Najac (p606), Monpazier (p597) and Domme (p595).

INTERNET ACCESS
Cybertek (☎ 05 53 06 89 65; 14 cours Fénelon; ☼ Tue-Sat)

LAUNDRY
There are laundrettes at place Hoche (open 8am to 8pm), 18 rue des Mobiles de Coulmiers (open to 9pm) and 61 rue Gambetta (open to 9pm, except Saturday to 8pm).

MONEY
There are several banks on place Bugeaud.
Banque de France (1 place du Président Roosevelt; money exchange ☼ 8.45am-12.15pm Mon-Fri)

POST
Main Post Office (1 rue du 4 Septembre) Offers money exchange and a Cyberposte.

TOURIST INFORMATION
Espace Tourisme Périgord (☎ 05 53 35 50 24; 25 rue du Président Wilson; ☼ 9am-noon & 2-5pm Mon-Fri) Provides information on the Dordogne département.
Tourist Information Kiosk (place André Maurios; ☼ 9am-8pm Jun-Sep)
Tourist Office (☎ 05 53 53 10 63; tourisme .perigueux@perigord.tm.fr; 26 place Francheville; ☼ 9am-1pm & 2-6pm Mon-Sat year-round & 10am-1pm & 2-6pm Sun mid-Jun–mid-Sep) The main tourist office.

PÉRIGUEUX

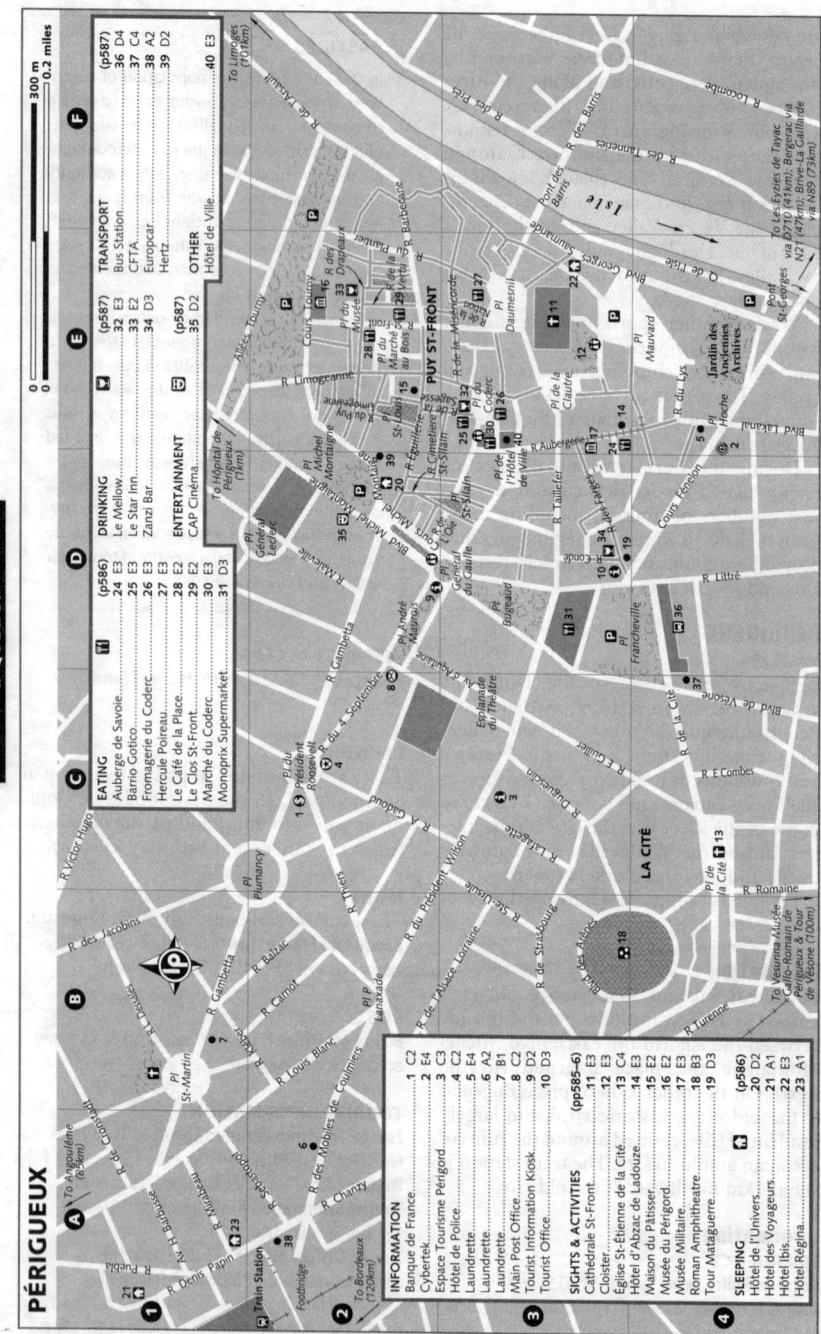

INFORMATION
Banque de France..................1	C2
Cybertek...............................2	E4
Espace Tourisme Périgord......3	C3
Hôtel de Police....................4	C2
Laundrette............................5	E4
Laundrette............................6	A2
Laundrette............................7	B1
Main Post Office..................8	C2
Tourist Information Kiosk......9	D2
Tourist Office......................10	D3

SIGHTS & ACTIVITIES (pp585-6)
Cathédrale St-Front.............11	E3
Cloister..............................12	E3
Église St-Étienne de la Cité..13	C4
Hôtel d'Abzac de Ladouze....14	E3
Maison du Pâtissier.............15	E2
Musée du Périgord...............16	E2
Musée Militaire....................17	E3
Roman Amphitheatre............18	B3
Tour Mataguerre..................19	D3

SLEEPING (p586)
Hôtel de l'Univers................20	D2
Hôtel des Voyageurs.............21	A1
Hôtel Ibis............................22	E3
Hôtel Régina.......................23	A1

EATING (p586)
Auberge de Savoie................24	C2
Barrio Gotico.......................25	E3
Fromagerie du Codec............26	E3
Hercule Poireau....................27	E3
Le Café de la Place..............28	E2
Le Clos St-Front..................29	E2
Marché du Codec.................30	E3
Monoprix Supermarket..........31	D3

DRINKING (p587)
Le Mellow...........................32	E3
Le Star Inn.........................33	E2
Zanzi Bar............................34	D3

ENTERTAINMENT (p587)
CAP Cinéma........................35	D2

TRANSPORT
Bus Station.........................36	D4
CFTA..................................37	C4
Europcar.............................38	A2
Hertz..................................39	D2

OTHER
Hôtel de Ville......................40	E3

Sights

PUY ST-FRONT

The **Musée du Périgord** (☎ 05 53 06 40 70; 22 cours Tourny; adult/student/under 18 €4/2/free; 🕑 11am-6pm Mon, Wed-Fri, 1-6pm Sat & Sun Apr-Sep, 10am-5pm Mon, Wed-Fri, 1-6pm Sat & Sun Oct-Mar, closed holidays) is well known for its rich collection of prehistoric tools and implements; Gallo-Roman and medieval artefacts are also on display. There's free admission from midday to 2pm Monday to Saturday between mid-September and mid-June.

When seen against the evening sky, the **Cathédrale St-Front** (place de la Clautre; admission free; 🕑 8am-12.30pm & 2.30-7.30pm), topped with five bump-studded domes and many more equally bumpy domelets, looks like something you might come across in Istanbul. However, by day, the sprawling structure, 'restored' by Abadie (the creator of Paris' Sacré Cœur) in the late 19th century, looks contrived and overwrought in the finest pseudo-Byzantine tradition. The carillon sounds the same hour chime as Big Ben. The best views of the cathedral (and the town) are from **Pont des Barris**.

The ancient cobblestone streets north of the cathedral are lined with centuries-old limestone houses, such as along **rue du Plantier**. A few short blocks to the west, the area's main thoroughfare, **rue Limogeanne**, has graceful Renaissance buildings at Nos 3 and 12. There are more such structures on nearby streets, including **rue Éguillerie** (such as the Renaissance-style **Maison du Pâtisser** at place St-Louis) and **rue de la Miséricorde**. The 15th- and 16th-century houses along **rue Aubergerie** include the **Hôtel d'Abzac de Ladouze** (across from No 19) with its two octagonal towers.

The **Musée Militaire** (☎ 05 53 53 47 36; 32 rue des Farges; admission €3.50; 🕑 1-6pm Mon-Sat Apr-Sep, 2-6pm Mon-Sat Oct-Dec, Wed & Sat Jan-Mar, closed holidays), founded right after WWI, has a varied collection of swords, firearms, uniforms and insignia from the Napoleonic wars and the two world wars.

Of the 28 towers that once formed Puy St-Front's medieval fortifications, only **Tour Mataguerre**, a stout, round bastion next to the main tourist office, remains. It was given its present form in the late 15th century.

LA CITÉ

Only a few arches of Périgueux's 1st-century **Roman amphitheatre** are still standing – the rest of the massive structure, designed to hold 30,000 spectators, was disassembled and carried off to construct the city walls in the 3rd century.

The **Église St-Étienne de la Cité** (place de la Cité), constructed in the 11th and 12th centuries, served as Périgueux's cathedral until 1669. Only two cupolas and two bays survived the

---

CHATEAUX

The Dordogne and Quercy aren't in the same league as the Loire Valley, but they do have quite a few impressive chateaux, many of them massive fortresses built in the Middle Ages. This chapter provides details on visiting the chateaux of Beynac (p596), Biron (p597), Bonaguil (p607), Carennac (p608), Castelnau-Bretenoux (p608), Castelnaud (p596), Milandes (p597) and Najac (p606), as well as Turenne (p581) in southern Limousin.

There are a number of other chateaux in the region:

Jumilhac-le-Grand (☎ 05 53 52 42 97; adult/child €6/4; 🕑 Jun-Sep, weekends & holidays May, Oct–mid-Nov) A turreted 15th- to 17th-century chateau about 50km northeast of Périgueux along the N21 and D78.

Puyguilhem (☎ 05 53 54 82 18; adult/child €5.20/3.20) A Renaissance-influenced chateau 30km north of Périgueux near Villars.

Hautefort (☎ 05 53 50 51 23; adult/child €8/4; 🕑 late Mar–Oct, Sun afternoons Nov–mid-Mar, closed mid-Dec–mid-Jan) An imposing neoclassical chateau 40km east of Périgueux. It has an English-style garden and French flower terraces.

Eyrignac (☎ 05 53 28 99 71; adult/child €8/4) Around 13km northeast of Sarlat, this chateau is famed for its exquisite 18th-century French-style gardens.

Puymartin (☎ 05 53 59 29 97; adult/child €6/3; 🕑 Apr-Nov) A castle-like and partly furnished chateau 8km northwest of Sarlat.

Losse (☎ 05 53 50 80 08; adult/student/child €6/5/3; 🕑 Easter-Oct) In the Vézère Valley 5km southwest of Montignac, Losse is decorated with 16th- and 17th-century tapestries and furniture.

devastation wrought by the Huguenots during the Wars of Religion (1562–98). Two blocks to the south, the **Vesunna Musée Gallo-Romain de Périgueux** (☎ 05 53 53 00 92; rue Claude Bernard; adult/child €5.50/3.50; 🕙 10am-7pm Jul & Aug, 10am-12.30pm & 2-5.30pm Sep-Jun) is a new museum built to showcase the ruins of a 1st-century Roman villa uncovered in pretty good nick in 1959. The excavations have revealed a treasure-trove of Roman artefacts, jewellery, cooking utensils and some incredible murals. In the grounds stands the **Tour de Vésone**, shaped like a gargantuan anklet, the only remaining section of a Gallo-Roman temple thought to have been dedicated to the goddess Vessuna, protector of the town (and the Roman name for Périgueux).

Tours

There are French-language **guided tours** of the city with guides who speak English two to four times a week (daily in summer). Tickets cost €5 (12 to 18 years and students €3.80); the details are available at the tourist office. Ask also about the less regular **bicycle tours**.

Sleeping

There's a lack of decent accommodation in town in every price range; options are functional rather than memorable. The tourist office can provide details of camping grounds, *chambres d'hôtes* (B&Bs) and youth hostels.

Hôtel de l'Univers (☎ 05 53 53 34 79; fax 05 53 06 70 76; 18 cours Michel Montaigne; s €42.70, d €45-53.35; 🕙 Feb-Dec) This welcoming, two-star hotel has a varied selection of generously sized rooms. Most have high ceilings and bathrooms; the two attic rooms are a touch cheaper. There's a decent restaurant (right) downstairs.

Hôtel des Voyageurs (☎ 05 53 53 17 44; 26 rue Denis Papin; s/d from €14/16) This is one of half a dozen inexpensive hotels near the train station, along rue Denis Papin and rue des Mobiles de Coulmiers. The rock-bottom prices here mean tiny rooms and flimsy furniture, but the rooms are perfectly clean, and the creaky staircase helps to drown out the noise from the rowdy bar next door.

Hôtel Régina (☎ 05 53 08 40 44; comfort.perigueux@ wanadoo.fr; 14 rue Denis Papin; d from €42/46; P) This place is one of the better two-star options

in the hotel ghetto around the station, but it may not be to everyone's taste, with pastel walls and brightly coloured soft furnishings. Comfortable, modern and good value. Suitable for disabled guests.

Hôtel Ibis (☎ 05 53 53 64 58; H0636@accor.hotels .com; 8 blvd Georges Saumande; s/d from €41/50; P) The Ibis is a comfortable chain hotel.

Eating

Hercule Poireau (☎ 05 53 08 90 76; 2 rue de la Nation; mains €15-25; 🕙 Mon-Fri) An exceptionally stylish eatery in an old stone-arched building opposite the cathedral, serving delicious Périgord specialities. The restaurant has a trendy anteroom for drinks next door.

Le Clos St-Front (☎ 05 53 46 78 58; 12 rue St-Front; menus €16-20; 🕙 Tue-Sat) Tucked away in a quiet corner of town, this upmarket place has French *menus* that vary depending on the fresh produce available in the marketplace. The pretty garden is perfect for a long summer lunch.

Auberge de Savoie (☎ 05 53 09 58 32; 19 rue Aubergerie; menus €10-24) Reliable, good-value regional specialities are offered by this mini-chain that prides itself on friendly service as well as tasty food. The sunny terrace, surrounded by medieval buildings, is a winner in season.

Le Café de la Place (☎ 05 53 08 21 11; 7 place du Marché au Bois; mains €11-15) A bohemian, old-style bar where artists and students hang out on the terrace. It serves a large selection of tasty regional dishes, (including the house speciality foie gras) plus salads and local wines by the glass.

Hôtel de l'Univers (☎ 05 53 53 34 79; fax 05 53 06 70 76; 18 cours Michel Montaigne; menus €15-35; 🕙 closed Mon & lunch Tue) A refined restaurant popular for its tasty Périgord and Breton specialities (including fish and lobster). Inside, the restaurant lacks atmosphere, but there's a delightful vine-covered terrace.

Barrio Gotico (☎ 05 53 05 07 33; 12 rue de la Sagesse; tapas €1.50-4; 🕙 6.30pm-1am Tue-Sat) A funky little tapas bar, off place St-Louis, serving cheap hot and cold tapas to the strain of Latin beats. There's a lively vibe, with DJs playing later in the evening.

SELF-CATERING

On Wednesday and Saturday mornings from mid-November to mid-March, black truffles, wild mushrooms, foie gras, *confits* (duck or goose conserve), cheeses and other local delicacies are sold at the Marché de Gras (on place St-Louis) in Puy St-Front.

On Wednesday and Saturday mornings year-round, there's a food market on place de la Clautre, near the cathedral. Not far from the southern end of rue Limogeanne is the **Marché du Coderc** (covered market; 🕑 to about 1.30pm). Across the square is **Fromagerie du Coderc** (🕑 Tue-Sat & Sun morning).

There's an upstairs **Monoprix supermarket** (🕑 8.30am-8pm Mon-Sat) between place Bugeaud and place Francheville.

Drinking

Le Mellow (☎ 05 53 08 53 97; 4-6 rue de la Sagesse; 🕑 5pm-2am Tue-Sat) One of a handful of bars along this stretch in Puy St-Front, this is by far the trendiest, with a good-looking crowd enjoying cool music and cocktails.

Zanzi Bar (☎ 05 53 53 28 99; 2 rue Condé; 🕑 6.30pm-2am Tue-Sat) A lively place with a tropical ambiance and exotic cocktails. The salsa lessons on Wednesday evenings at 8pm and 9.30pm get easier in direct proportion to the number of cocktails drunk!

Le Star Inn (☎ 05 53 08 56 83; place du Musée; 🕑 8pm-2am Mon-Sat May-Sep, 8pm-1am Mon-Sat Oct-Apr) A welcoming pub across from 23 rue St-Front, run by a British couple and something of a hang-out for English speakers. English books are available to borrow.

Entertainment

The seven-screen **CAP Cinéma** (☎ 05 53 09 40 99; 19 blvd Michel Montaigne) screens nondubbed films.

Getting There & Away
BUS

The Périgueux **bus station** (place Francheville) is on the southern side of the square; hours are posted at the bus stops. One of the carriers, **CFTA** (☎ 05 53 08 43 13; 🕑 Mon-Fri), has an office on the storey overlooking the waiting room. The tourist office and the train station information office can supply you with schedules.

Except on Sunday and holidays, destinations include Bergerac (€6.80, 70 minutes, three daily), Ribérac (€5.15, one hour, four daily, one on Saturday) and Sarlat-la-Canéda (€8.35, 1½ hours, two daily, fewer in July and August) via the Vézère Valley town of Montignac (€5.85, 55 minutes).

CAR
Hire cars from **Europcar** (☎ 05 53 08 15 72; 7 rue Denis Papin) or **Hertz** (☎ 05 53 53 88 88; 20 cours Michel Montaigne).

TRAIN
The **train station** (rue Denis Papin) is served by local bus Nos 1, 4 and 5. Destinations with direct services include Bordeaux (€16.30, 1¼ hours, nine to 13 daily), Brive-La-Gaillarde (€10.30, one hour, three to five daily), Les Eyzies de Tayac (€6.30, 30 minutes, two to four daily) and Limoges (€10, one hour, seven to 11 daily, three on Saturday).

Train services to Paris' Gare d'Austerlitz (€45.90, three to five hours, 12 to 16 daily) are via Limoges. To get to Sarlat-la-Canéda (€12) you have to change at Brive.

Getting Around
Allo Taxi (☎ 05 53 09 09 09) is available 24 hours a day.

BERTRIC BURÉE
This tiny village (population 399), 35km northwest of Périgueux between Ribérac and Verteillac on the D708, draws thousands of gourmands and onlookers for the annual **snail festival** (☎ 05 53 91 94 96), held on the first Monday in May.

SARLAT-LA-CANÉDA
pop 10,000
The beautiful, well-restored town of Sarlat, administratively twinned with nearby La Canéda, is the capital of Périgord Noir. Its medieval and Renaissance townscape, much of it built of tan sandstone in the 16th and 17th centuries, attracts large numbers of tourists, especially for the year-round Saturday market.

Sarlat is an excellent base for car trips to the prehistoric sites of the Vézère Valley and to the Dordogne Périgourdine.

Orientation
The heart-shaped Cité Médiévale (Medieval Town) is bisected by the ruler-straight rue de la République (La Traverse), which (along with its continuations) stretches 2km north from the viaduct and nearby train station to the Auberge de Jeunesse. The Cité Médiévale is centred on place de la Liberté, rue de la Liberté and place du Peyrou.

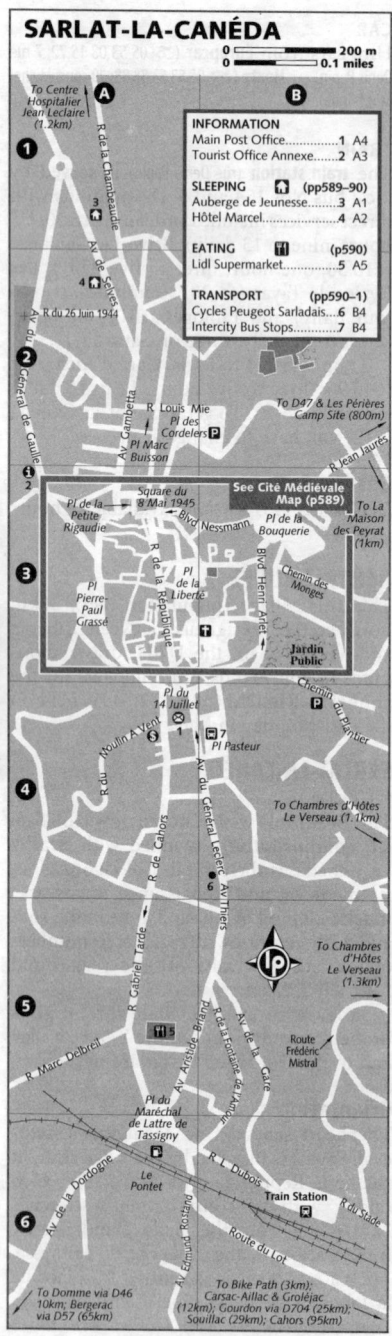

SARLAT-LA-CANÉDA

INFORMATION		
Main Post Office	1	A4
Tourist Office Annexe	2	A3

SLEEPING	(pp589–90)	
Auberge de Jeunesse	3	A1
Hôtel Marcel	4	A2

EATING	(p590)	
Lidl Supermarket	5	A5

TRANSPORT	(pp590–1)	
Cycles Peugeot Sarladais	6	B4
Intercity Bus Stops	7	B4

Information

MONEY

There are several banks along rue de la République.

POST

Main Post Office (Map left; place du 14 Juillet) Currency exchange and a Cyberposte.

TOURIST INFORMATION

Main Tourist Office (Map left; ☎ 05 53 31 45 45; www.ot-sarlat-perigord.fr in French; rue Tourny; 9am-7pm Mon-Sat, 10am-noon Sun Apr-Oct, 9am-noon & 2-7pm Mon-Sat Nov-Mar) In a building attached to the cathedral. Staff can supply the *Visitors' Map of the Medieval Town*, which takes you on a walking tour of the historic centre, and brochures on hikes and car tours in the area. In summer there is a €2 charge for making hotel and B&B bookings.
Tourist Office Annexe (Map p588; ☎ 05 53 59 18 87; av du Général de Gaulle; 9am-noon & 2-6pm Mon-Sat Jul & Aug).

Sights & Activities

Once part of Sarlat's Cluniac abbey, **Cathédrale St-Sacerdos** (Map opposite) is a real hotchpotch of styles. The wide, airy nave and its chapels date from the 17th century; the cruciform chevet (at the far end from the entrance) is from the 14th century; and the western entrance and much of the belfry above it are 12th-century Romanesque. The organ dates from 1752.

Behind the town's cathedral is **Jardin des Enfeus** (Map opposite), Sarlat's first cemetery, and the 12th-century **Lanterne des Morts** (Lantern of the Dead; Map opposite), a short tower that looks like the top of a missile. It may have been built to commemorate St-Bernard, who visited Sarlat in 1147 and whose relics were given to the abbey.

Across the square from the front of the cathedral is the ornate façade of the Renaissance **Maison de la Boétie** (Map opposite), the birthplace of the writer Étienne de la Boétie (1530–63).

The alleyways of the quiet, largely residential area west of rue de la République, many of them lined with centuries-old stone houses, are also worth exploring. **Rue Jean-Jacques Rousseau** makes a good starting point.

A **bicycle path** *(piste cyclable)* begins 3km southeast of Sarlat (near the intersection of the D704 and the D704A), and takes you along an old railway grade to Carsac-Aillac (12km from Sarlat) and across the river to

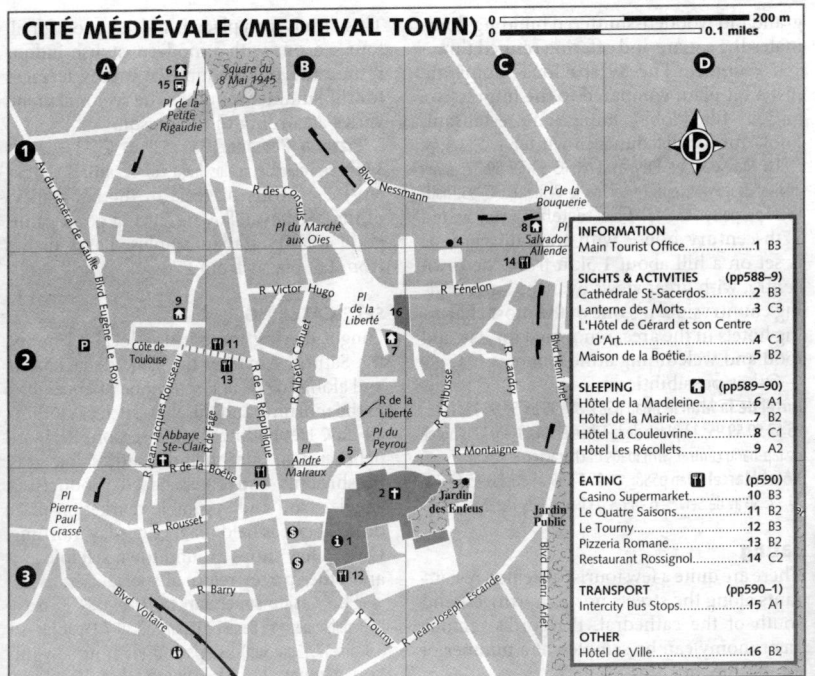

CITÉ MÉDIÉVALE (MEDIEVAL TOWN)

INFORMATION	
Main Tourist Office...................**1** B3	

SIGHTS & ACTIVITIES	(pp588–9)
Cathédrale St-Sacerdos............**2** B3	
Lanterne des Morts...................**3** C3	
L'Hôtel de Gérard et son Centre	
d'Art.................................**4** C1	
Maison de la Boétie..................**5** B2	

SLEEPING	(pp589–90)
Hôtel de la Madeleine..............**6** A1	
Hôtel de la Mairie.....................**7** B2	
Hôtel La Couleuvrine................**8** C1	
Hôtel Les Récollets...................**9** A2	

EATING	(p590)
Casino Supermarket..................**10** B3	
Le Quatre Saisons.....................**11** B2	
Le Tourny................................**12** B3	
Pizzeria Romane.......................**13** B2	
Restaurant Rossignol................**14** C2	

TRANSPORT	(pp590–1)
Intercity Bus Stops....................**15** A1	

OTHER	
Hôtel de Ville...........................**16** B2	

Groléjac. It will eventually reach Souillac (about 30km from Sarlat).

L'Hôtel de Gérard et son Centre d'Art (Map above; ☎ 05 53 59 57 97; 1 passage de Gérard du Barry) is an arts centre housed in a beautiful medieval building off rue Fénelon, which offers week-long painting courses in the first week of July and September.

Sleeping

Sarlat has no really cheap hotels. On holiday weekends during spring and in July and August, virtually everything is booked up way in advance. The tourist office has a full list of the area's many *chambres d'hôtes*.

BUDGET

Auberge de Jeunesse (Map opposite; ☎ 05 53 59 47 59, 05 53 30 21 27; 77 av de Selves; dm €10) is a modest but friendly 15-bed hostel with cooking facilities; call ahead for a reservation.

Chambres d'Hôtes Le Verseau (☎ 05 53 31 02 63; 49 route des Pechs; d incl breakfast €24-44) Just four rooms are available in this friendly place, with a leafy garden ideal for breakfast, picnics and barbecues. It's 2.2km north of the train station

along route Frédéric Mistral – if you call from the station the owner will pick you up.

Hôtel Les Récollets (Map above; ☎ 05 53 31 36 00; www.hotel-recollets-sarlat.com; 4 rue Jean-Jacques Rousseau; d from €39) Lost in narrow alleys of the Medieval Town, this delightful old building has been renovated inside with 18 fully equipped two-star rooms. While some of the charm of the building has been lost, the larger rooms (and breakfast room) retain some stone-walled character. The nearest parking is a block up the hill on blvd Eugène Le Roy.

MID-RANGE

Hôtel La Couleuvrine (Map above; ☎ 05 53 59 27 80; www.la-couleuvrine.com; 1 place de la Bouquerie; d from €55; P) A beautiful, chateau-like, three-star place, parts of which date from the 13th to 15th centuries. The accommodation, beautifully furnished with old, dark wood furniture, combines rustic comfort and medieval minimalism. Try room No 19, an atmospheric family room in the turret.

Hôtel de la Madeleine (Map above; ☎ 05 53 59 10 41; www.hoteldelamadeleine-sarlat.com; 1 place de la Petite Rigaudie; s/d from €62/71; Feb-Dec; P) This grand old wooden-shuttered building dominates the square and offering refined three-star comfort. The 39 spacious rooms are just a bit plain compared to the impressive, antique-filled lobby, lounge and restaurant. Look out for discounts in winter.

La Maison des Peyrat (☎ 05 53 59 00 32; www .maisondespeyrat.com; Le Lac de la Plane; r €47-95, half-board per person €51-75) This tastefully renovated 17th-century house with tranquil gardens is set on a hill about 1.5km from the town centre, with great views over the surrounding countryside. It's one of the most charming hotels in the area, renowned for its good food and welcoming atmosphere.

Other possibilities:

Hôtel de la Mairie (Map p589; ☎ 05 53 59 05 71; fax 05 53 59 59 95; 13 place de la Liberté; d €43-45) This hotel is slap-bang central with loads of character.

Hôtel Marcel (Map p588; ☎ 05 53 59 21 98; fax 05 53 30 27 77; 50 av de Selves; d €45-55) Cheerful two-star rooms.

Eating

There are quite a few tourist-oriented restaurants along the streets north, northwest and south of the cathedral. Périgord's famous gastronomy can be sampled at a number of establishments.

Hôtel La Couleuvrine (Map p589; see Sleeping; menus €18-32; ☒ mid-Feb–mid-Jan) The popular restaurant here is a bit special. A huge medieval fireplace, glowing chandeliers and a scattering of French antiques help to create a traditional country atmosphere. The gastronomic and regional *menus* are superb, and there's a great value lunch *menu* on Tuesday, Wednesday and Friday with two courses and a glass of wine for €14.

Restaurant Rossignol (Map p589; ☎ 05 53 31 02 30; 15 rue Fénelon; menus €19-60; ☒ Fri-Wed) A spacious, refined restaurant with starched white tablecloths and sparkling wine glasses. The service is exemplary, but the real attraction is the delicious €60 menu, full of Périgord specialities including foie gras and truffles.

Le Tourny (Map p589; ☎ 05 53 29 17 80; 1 rue Tourny; menus €16-22.50; ☒ Tue-Sun) A few doors down from the tourist office, this friendly little restaurant, popular with the locals, is renowned for Basque specialities as well as traditional Périgord cuisine. The dish to try is the succulent duck-based *confit de canard en croûte* (€13.50).

Le Quatre Saisons (Map p589; ☎ 05 53 29 48 59; 2 Côte de Toulouse; menus €18-29; ☒ closed Wed Sep-Jun)

This family-run place is indeed good for all four seasons with a modern, stylish indoor restaurant and a couple of breezy terraces for the summer months. The regional menu varies according to the season.

Pizzeria Romane (Map p589; ☎ 05 53 59 23 88; 3 Côte de Toulouse; mains from €6) A small, pack-em-in, no-frills pizzeria in the back alleys of the Medieval Town, serving good value, good quality Italian staples. Pasta dishes from €6, pizzas from €7.

SELF-CATERING

Long a driving force in the local economy, the Saturday market on place de la Liberté and along rue de la République offers edibles in the morning and durables such as clothing all day. Depending on the season, Périgord delicacies on offer include truffles, foie gras, mushrooms and goose-based products. A smaller fruit and vegetable market on place de la Liberté is held on Wednesday morning. Quite a few shops around town sell foie gras and other pricey regional specialities.

The **Casino supermarket** (Map p589; 32 rue de la République; ☒ 8am-12.15pm & 2.30-7.15pm Tue-Sat, 8.30am-12.15pm Sun) keeps longer hours in July and August. The **Lidl supermarket** (Map p588; av Aristide Briand; ☒ 9am-12.30pm & 2.30-7.30pm Mon-Fri, 9am-7pm Sat) is at the southern end of the avenue.

Getting There & Away

BUS

Services are very limited; schedules are available at the tourist office. There's no bus station – departures are from the train station, place Pasteur or place de la Petite Rigaudie, depending on where you're going. There are one or two buses daily (fewer in July and August) to Périgueux (€6.80, 1½ hours) via the Vézère Valley town of Montignac.

TRAIN

The **train station** (☎ 05 53 59 00 21), 1.3km south of the old city at the southern end of av de la Gare, is poorly linked with the rest of the region. The ticket windows are staffed until 7pm.

Destinations include Bordeaux (€19.90, 2½ hours, two to four direct daily) which is on the same line as Bergerac, Périgueux (change at Le Buisson; €12.00, 1½ hours, two daily), and Les Eyzies de Tayac (trains at Le Buisson; €7.10, 50 minutes to 2¼ hours depending on connections, two daily). The SNCF bus to Souillac (€4.90, 40 minutes, two to four daily) passes through Carsac-Aillac (on the scenic D703) and links up with trains on the Paris (Gare d'Austerlitz)–Limoges–Toulouse line.

Getting Around
BICYCLE
The Sarlat area has nine bike-rental outlets including **Cycles Peugeot Sarladais** (Map p588; ☎ 05 53 28 51 87; 36 av Thiers).

CAR & MOTORCYCLE
Free parking is available around the perimeter of the Medieval Town along blvd Nessmann, blvd Voltaire and blvd Henri Arlet. Cars are banned from the Medieval Town from June to September, and rue de la République is pedestrianised in July and August.

PREHISTORIC SITES & THE VÉZÈRE VALLEY
Of the Vézère Valley's 175 known prehistoric sites, the most famous ones, including the world-renowned cave paintings in Lascaux, are situated between **Le Bugue** (near the confluence of the Vézère and Dordogne) and Montignac, 25km to the northeast. The sites mentioned here are just the highlights and are listed roughly from southwest to northeast.

Many of the villages that are situated in the area, including Les Eyzies de Tayac and Montignac, have one or more hotels. You can also use Périgueux (p583) and Sarlat-la-Canéda (p587) as bases to explore the area. Most of the valley's sites are closed in winter; the best time to visit is in spring or autumn, when the sites are open but the crowds are not overwhelming.

Getting Around
The Vézère Valley is well signed; arrows at every crossroads direct you to both major and minor sights. Public transport in the area is limited, see p587, opposite and p592.

Les Eyzies de Tayac
pop 850
The two museums in the one-street touristy village of Les Eyzies de Tayac provide an excellent introduction to the valley's prehistoric legacy.

INFORMATION
Tourist Office (☎ 05 53 06 97 05; www.leseyzies.com; ☒ 9am-7pm Mon-Sat, 10am-noon & 2-6pm Sun Jul & Aug, 9am-noon & 2-6pm Mon-Sat, 10am-noon & 2-5pm Sun Sep-Jun, closed Sun Oct-Apr) On Les Eyzies' main street, the D47, right below the most prominent part of the cliff.
Librairie de la Préhistoire (☒ 8.30am-12.30pm & 3-7pm Mar-Nov, no lunch break Jun-Aug, 8.30am-noon Dec-Feb) Sells IGN maps and topoguides; across from the tourist office.

SIGHTS
The very interesting **Musée National de Préhistoire** (National Museum of Prehistory; ☎ 05 53 06 45 45; adult/18-25 yrs/under 18 yrs €4.50/3/free, on Sun adults €3; ☒ 9.30am-6.30pm Jul & Aug, 9.30am-noon & 2-5.30pm Wed-Mon Sep-Jun) is built into the cliff above the tourist office (with an expanded exhibition space that opened in mid-2004). Its well-presented collection of artefacts provides a great introduction to the area's prehistoric human habitation.

About 250m north of Musée National de Préhistoire along the cliff face is the **Abri Pataud** (☎ 05 53 06 92 46; adult/6-12 yrs €5.20/3.20; ☒ 10am-7pm Jul & Aug, 10am-7pm Tue-Thu & Sun Sep-Jun), a Cro-Magnon shelter *(abri)* inhabited over a period of 15,000 years starting some 37,000 years ago; bones and other artefacts discovered during the excavations are on display. The ibex carved into the ceiling dates from about 19,000 BC. The admission price includes a one-hour guided tour (the guides generally know some English).

SLEEPING & EATING
Hostellerie du Passeur (☎ 05 53 06 97 13; www.hostellerie-du-passeur.com; place de la Mairie; d €62-85; ☒ Feb-Oct; **P**) In a great spot overlooking the Vézère, this superb two-star hotel, in an old bourgeois mansion house, has pretty country-style rooms. The **restaurant** (menus from €22; ☒ closed Mon & Tue lunch), with a shady terrace, serves traditional Périgord and French fare. It's next door to the tourist office.

Hôtel des Roches (☎ 05 53 06 96 59; hotel@roches-les-eyzies.com; 15 av de la Forge; d €75-85; ☒ Apr-Nov; **P** **⊠**) On the edge of town, this comfortable 41-room, three-star place is set in pretty gardens. It also has a swimming pool.

Camping & Caravanning Le Vézère Périgord (☎ 05 53 06 96 31; fax & off season 05 53 06 79 66; route de Montignac, Tursac; camping for 2 people €16, extra person €5; ☒ Apr-Oct; **P** **⊠**) This excellent three-star place is in the middle of a forest 6km

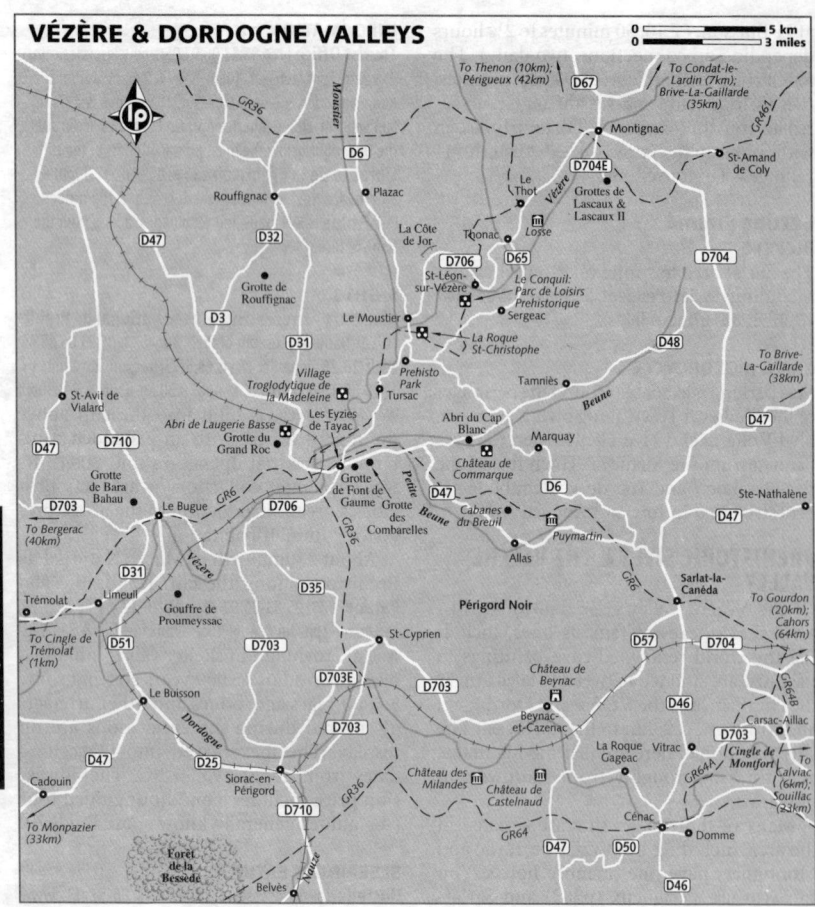

north of Les Eyzies (on the D706). It's quiet, well maintained and in a beautiful setting with swimming pool, tennis courts and children's playground.

GETTING THERE & AWAY

The **train station** (☎ 05 53 06 97 22) is 700m north of the tourist office (and 200m off the D47). The ticket windows are staffed until at least 6pm (but closed until noon at the weekend).

Destinations include Bordeaux (change trains at Le Buisson; €28.40, two to three hours, eight or nine daily), Sarlat-la-Canéda (change at Le Buisson; €7.50, 50 minutes to two hours depending on connections, three daily), Périgueux (€6.30, 30 minutes, four

or five daily) and Paris' Gare d'Austerlitz (€48.70, five hours, three daily).

GETTING AROUND

Bicycles can be rented at the tourist office for €8 per half-day or €12 per day.

Limeuil

This charming walled village, perched high above the confluence of the Rivers Vézère and Dordogne, is known for its municipal gardens. **Hôtel Au Bon Accueil** (☎ 05 53 63 30 97; d with/without shower €35/27; ⊗ Easter-Oct), with 10 rooms, is just down the one-way street from place des Fosses. The attached **restaurant** (menus €15-23; ⊗ closed Mon Sep & Oct) serves traditional Périgord-style *menus*.

AUTHOR'S CHOICE

Domaine de la Vitrolle (☎ 05 53 61 58 58; beaugier@perigord.com; r €60-100, apt per night/ week from €40/255) A short distance outside Limeuil on the D31 towards Le Bugue is this Périgord manor house, an imposing building surrounded by 110 hectares of apple orchards and vines. The estate has been transformed into a residential leisure complex and is an ideal base for an extended stay in the region, especially for families. Bedrooms and suites within the main building are beautifully furnished with antiques; the neighbouring apartments and *gîtes* (cottages) are of a more functional, country-style design with small kitchens. Facilities include tennis, badminton, volleyball, foosball and a swimming pool.

Grotte de Font de Gaume

Just over 1km northeast of Les Eyzies on the D47, this **cave** (☎ 05 53 06 86 00; www.leseyzies .com/grottes-ornees; adult/18-25 yrs/under 18 €6.10/4.10/ free; ☷ 9am-12.30pm & 2-5.30pm Sun-Fri, no lunch break Jun-Sep) has one of the most astounding collections of prehistoric paintings still open to the public. About two dozen of its 230 remarkably sophisticated polychrome figures of mammoths, bison, horses, reindeer, bears and other creatures, created by Cro-Magnon people 14,000 years ago, can be visited. A number of the animals, engraved and/or painted in red and black, are depicted in movement or in three dimensions.

To protect the cave, discovered in 1901, the number of visitors is limited to 200 per day, and the 45-minute group tours (explanatory sheets in English available) are limited to 20 participants and must be reserved a few days ahead (a week or two ahead from July to September) by phone or via the website.

Grotte des Combarelles

The long and very narrow Combarelles Cave, 3km northeast of Les Eyzies and 1.6km east of Grotte de Font de Gaume, averages only 80cm in width. Discovered in 1894 it is renowned for its 600 often-superimposed engravings of animals, especially reindeer, bison and horses; there are also some human or half-human figures. The works date from 12,000 to 14,000 years

ago. To reserve a place in a six-person group (tours last 45 to 60 minutes), call the Grotte de Font de Gaume – opening hours, admission costs and reservation guidelines are the same for both sites.

Abri du Cap Blanc

High-relief and low-relief figures of horses, reindeer and bison, created 14,000 years ago, decorate this natural shelter, formed by an overhanging rocky outcrop. Situated on a pristine, forested hillside, the privately owned **shelter** (☎ 05 53 59 21 74; adult/7-15 yrs €5.90/3.50; ☷ Apr-Nov) can be visited on guided tours lasting an hour (English explanatory sheets available), between 10am and noon and between 2pm and 6pm (7pm in July and August, when there's no midday closure).

The Abri, 8km east of Les Eyzies along the beautiful D48, is a fine place to begin a day hike.

Grotte du Grand Roc

The **Grand Roc Cave** (☎ 05 53 06 92 70; www.grand roc.com; adult/child €7/3.50; ☷ 10am-6pm Jul & Aug, 10am-5pm Sep-Jun), known for its masses of delicate, translucent stalactites and stalagmites, is a few kilometres northwest of Les Eyzies along the D47. Nearby is the prehistoric site of **Abris de Laugerie Basse** (adult/child €6/3; ☷ same as Grand Roc) and a still-inhabited troglodytic hamlet.

Grotte de Rouffignac

About 15km north of Les Eyzies, the cave at **Rouffignac** (☎ 05 53 05 41 71; adult/child €6/3.50; ☷ tours in French 9am-11.30am & 2-6pm Jul & Aug, from 10am Sep-Nov & Apr-Jun), the largest in the area (it has some 10km of galleries), is known for its 250 engravings and paintings of mammoths and other animals.

Village Troglodytique de la Madeleine

This cave-dwelling **village** (☎ 05 53 06 92 49; adult/family/5-12 yrs €5/16/3; ☷ 9.30am-7pm Jul & Aug, 10am-6pm Sep-Jun, to 5pm Dec & Jan), 8km north of Les Eyzies along the D706, is in the middle of a delightfully lush forest overlooking a hairpin curve in the River Vézère. The site has two levels: 10,000 to 14,000 years ago, prehistoric people lived on the bank of the river in an area now closed to the public; and 500 to 700 years ago, medieval French people built a fortified village – which is now lies in ruins – halfway up the cliff face. Their chapel, dedicated to Ste-Madeleine, gave its name to the site, and to the entire Magdelenian era. On the plateau above the cliff are the ruins of a 14th-century castle (closed to the public). Many of the artefacts discovered here are at the prehistory museum in Les Eyzies. Several walking trails pass by the site.

Guided tours (in French; 50 minutes) begin every half-hour or so; a free English-language brochure is available.

La Roque St-Christophe

This 900m-long series of terraces and **caves** (☎ 05 53 50 70 45; www.roque-st-christophe.com; adult/student/5-11 yrs €6/5/3; ☿ 10am-6pm Apr-Oct, to 7pm Jul & Aug, 11am-5pm Nov-Mar) sits on a sheer cliff face 30m above the Vézère. It has had an extraordinary history as a natural bastion, serving Mousterian (Neanderthal) people some 50,000 years ago, enemies of the Normans in the 10th century, the English from 1401 to 1416, as well as Protestants in the late 16th century.

La Roque St-Christophe is on the D706, 9km northeast of Les Eyzies. At the ticket kiosk, you can borrow an informative brochure that makes a valiant effort to make the now-empty caverns come alive.

Le Moustier

Across the River Vézère from La Roque St-Christophe is Le Moustier – the findings here gave the Mousterian era its name.

Dhagpo Kagyu-Ling (☎ 05 53 50 70 75; www .dhagpo-kagyu.org; s/d from €10.70/12.20; meals from €2.30), a centre for Tibetan Buddhist studies and meditation that was founded in 1975, is 1km up the hill from the church – you will know you have found it when you see the gold-topped stupa, the small, Tibetan-style temple, a row of prayer wheels and lots of fluttering prayer flags. The centre offers day, weekend and longer courses (from €9 per day) on Buddhist philosophy and meditation, many in English, and also hosts inter-religious dialogue. Accommodation is available for varying prices; advance reservations are essential.

St-Léon-sur-Vézère
pop 427

This quiet, one-time river port, on a picturesque loop of the River Vézère 10km southwest of Montignac, is a good base for day hikes. It has two small castles (both closed to the public): the 14th-century **Manoir de la Salle**, with its squat, square donjon; and the more refined, 16th-century **Château de Clérens**, adorned with Renaissance turrets. The interior of the 11th- and 12th-century Romanesque **church** has a wooden ceiling; the half-dome above the choir shows remnants of medieval frescoes.

The **Auberge du Pont Restaurant** (☎ 05 53 50 73 07; menu €21-35; ☿ closed Wed) serves Périgord and Provençal specialities.

Le Thot

The museum and animal park known as **Le Thot – Espace Cro-Magnon** (☎ 05 53 50 70 44; adult/6-12 yrs €5/3; ☿ 9am-7pm Jul & Aug, 10am-noon & 2-5.30pm Tue-Sun Sep-Jun, closed Jan), intended as an introduction to the world of prehistoric people, has models of animals that appear in prehistoric art, live specimens of similar animals, and exhibits on the creation of Lascaux II. See Lascaux II (opposite) for details of combined tickets.

Montignac
pop 3101

The relaxing and picturesque town of Montignac, on the Vézère 25km northeast of Les Eyzies, achieved sudden fame after the discovery of the nearby Grotte de Lascaux. The attractive old city and commercial centre is on the river's right bank, but of more use for touristic logistics is the left-bank area around place Tourny. Rue du 4 Septembre links the D65 with the D704 and the D704E to Lascaux.

ORIENTATION & INFORMATION

There are three banks right around the tourist office.

Maison de la Presse (☿ closed Sun afternoon except Jul & Aug) Across the street from the tourist office, it sells IGN maps and topoguides.

Post Office (place Tourny) Offers currency exchange.

Tourist Office (☎ 05 53 51 82 60; www.bienvenue -montignac.com in French; place Bertrand de Born; ☿ 9am-7pm Jul-Sep, 9am-noon & 2-6pm Mon-Sat Oct-Jun) Around 200m west of place Tourny and next to the 14th-century Église St-Georges le Prieuré.

SLEEPING & EATING

Hôtel de la Grotte (☎ 05 53 51 80 48; fax 05 53 51 05 96; place Tourny; d with shower/bath €42/47) With a very pleasant garden on the banks of the river, this charming place, 200m east of the tourist office, offers 10 very comfortable rooms. Its restaurant has traditional and creative Périgord-style *menus* from €18 (€11.50 at lunch) to €38.

Le Relais du Soleil d'Or (☎ 05 53 51 80 22; www.le-soleil-dor.com in French; 16 rue du 4 Septembre; d €81-110; ⓨ closed mid-Jan–mid-Feb; P ⓡ) An old post house that is now home to a swish three-star hotel and restaurant. There's a large shaded garden with a swimming pool, and a charming, antique-filled lounge for relaxing. The rooms are not quite as exciting, but are well-equipped with minibars and satellite TVs. Its fine dining restaurant has regional *menus* from €19.

Bar des Arcades (☎ 05 53 51 95 73; 37 rue du 4 Septembre; ⓨ 8am-8pm in winter, to 2am in summer) A cosy, traditional café, popular with locals, serving good snacks and regional specialities such as *cassoulet de canard* (duck casserole; €8.50).

Le Tourny (☎ 05 53 51 59 95; place Tourny) This is both a brasserie and a bar with DJs, sports on the TV and regular concerts. It usually opens 7.30am to 1am in winter (2.30am in summer), but stays open to 4am or 5am when there's a live concert, which is generally on Saturday night and, from April to September, on Friday night from 10pm to 2am.

Casino supermarket (place Tourny; ⓨ Tue-Sat & Sun morning, closed 12.30-3pm) Next to the post office.

ENTERTAINMENT
Nondubbed films are screened at **Cinéma Vox** (☎ 05 53 51 87 24), across the car park from the tourist office.

GETTING THERE & AWAY
For information on buses to/from Montignac, see p587 and p590. There's a bus stop (hours posted) at place Tourny.

Grottes de Lascaux & Lascaux II
Lascaux Cave, 2km southeast of Montignac at the end of the D704E, is adorned with some of the most extraordinary prehistoric paintings ever found. Discovered in 1940 by four teenage boys who, it is said, were out searching for their dog, the cave's main room and a number of steep galleries are decorated with figures of wild oxen, deer, horses, reindeer and other creatures depicted in vivid reds, blacks, yellows and browns. The drawings and paintings, shown

by carbon dating to be between 15,000 and 17,000 years old, are thought to have been done by members of a hunting cult.

The cave, in pristine condition when found, was opened to the public in 1948 but was closed 15 years later when it became clear that human breath and the resulting carbon dioxide and condensation were causing the colours to fade and a green fungus – and even tiny stalactites – to grow over the paintings.

In response to massive public curiosity about prehistoric art, a precise replica of the most famous section of the original cave was meticulously re-created a few hundred metres away. **Lascaux II** (☎ 05 53 51 95 03; adult/6-12 yrs €8/4.50; ⓨ 9am-7pm Jul & Aug, 10am-noon & 2-5.30pm Tue-Sun Sep-Jun, closed Jan) opened in 1983, and although the idea sounds kitschy, the reproductions are surprisingly evocative and well worth a look.

The 40m-long Lascaux II can handle 2000 visitors daily (in guided groups of 40). The last tours (40 minutes) begin about an hour before the morning and afternoon closing times. From April to October, tickets are sold *only* in Montignac (next to the tourist office). Reservations are not necessary except for groups. Combined tickets (€9/5) are available for Lascaux II and Le Thot (opposite).

DORDOGNE PÉRIGOURDINE
The term Dordogne Périgourdine is used to describe the part of Périgord that stretches along the River Dordogne.

Domme
pop 1030
Set on a steep promontory high above the Dordogne, the trapezoid-shaped walled village of Domme is one of the few *bastides* to have retained most of its 13th-century ramparts, including three fortified gates. A bit too perfectly restored, it attracts more than its share of coach tours, but they in no way spoil the stunning panorama from the cliff-side **Esplanade du Belvédère** and the adjacent **Promenade de la Barre**, which stretches west along the forested slope to the Jardin Public (a public park).

Across from the **tourist office** (☎ 05 53 31 71 00; place de la Halle; ⓨ 10am-7pm Jul & Aug, 10am-noon & 2-6pm Feb-Jun & Sep–mid-Nov, 2-5pm Mon-Fri mid-Nov–Dec, closed Jan) is the 19th-century reconstruction of a 16th-century *halle* (covered market).

This houses the entrance to the **grottes** (adult/student/child €6/5/3.50; ☼ guided tours every 20-30min 10.30am-6.40pm), 450m of stalactite-filled galleries below the village; a lift whisks you back up at the end of the 30-minute tour. Except in January, tours take place whenever the tourist office, which sells tickets, is open; the last tour leaves 30 minutes before closing time in the morning and the afternoon.

On the far side of the square from the tourist office, the **Musée d'Arts et Traditions Populaires** (adult/student/child €3/2.50/2; ☼ Apr-Sep) has nine rooms of artefacts (clothing, toys and tools), mainly from the 19th century.

ACTIVITIES

From March to September or mid-October (unless the river is too high), **canoe and kayak trips** can be arranged through **Randonnée Dordogne** (☎ 05 53 28 22 01; randodordogne@wanadoo.fr), a highly professional, English-speaking outfit whose base is in Cénac, 300m to the right as you approach the D46 bridge over the River Dordogne from the south (ie from Domme). Day trips cost €22 per person or €38 for a double kayak, including transport. Half-day trips are available from €14 per person.

SLEEPING

Hôtel Les Quatre Vents (☎ 05 53 31 57 57; fax 05 53 31 57 59; d with shower & toilet €40-48; ☎) A two-star place with 26 comfortable rooms, two swimming pools and gardens.

Château de Castelnaud

The 12th- to 16th-century **Château de Castelnaud** (☎ 05 53 31 30 00; adult/10-17 yrs €6.60/3.30; ☼ 9am-8pm Jul & Aug, 10am-7pm May, Jun & Sep, 10am-6pm Mar, Apr & Oct–mid-Nov, 2-5pm Sun-Fri mid-Nov–Feb), 11km west of Domme along the D50 and D57, has everything you'd expect from a cliff-top castle: walls up to 2m thick (as you can see from the loopholes, some designed for crossbows, others for small cannons); a superb panorama of the meandering Dordogne; and fine views of the fortified chateaux (including arch rival Château de Beynac) that dot the nearby hilltops. The interior rooms are occupied by a **museum of medieval warfare**, whose displays range from daggers and spiked halberds to huge catapults. The houses of the medieval village of Castelnaud cling to the steep slopes below the fortress. An English-language guidebook can be borrowed at the ticket counter.

La Roque Gageac

This hamlet of tan stone houses is built halfway up the cliff face on the right bank of one of the *cingles* (hairpin curves) in the River Dordogne. When the tiny **tourist office** (☎ 05 53 29 17 01; ☼ 9am-12.30pm & 2-6pm Easter-Oct) shed in the car park is closed, brochures can be picked up at the post office.

The **Fort Troglodyte** (☎ 05 53 31 61 94; adult/child €4/2; ☼ 10am-7pm Mon-Fri, Apr–mid-Nov & usually in off season, also Sat Jul & Aug) consists of a number of medieval military positions built into the cliff. There's some tropical foliage in the small, free **Jardin Exotique** (Exotic Garden), next to the tiny **church**. Down below, the quay serves as a launch point for short **river cruises** – contact **Gabares Norbert** (☎ 05 53 29 40 44).

Canoes can be rented from **Canoë Dordogne** (☎ 05 53 29 58 50; 1-person canoe travelling 7/14/21km €12/18/24, 2-person canoe €20/25/32), next to the car park, which also offers rock climbing and spelunking daily from April to October (often booked out in July and August).

East of La Roque Gageac, the beautiful D703 follows the northern bank of the serpentine Dordogne, passing by the **Cingle de Montfort** (a particularly sharp hairpin curve). Unfortunately, it's too narrow and busy for cycling – bikers are much better off taking the old railroad tracks, sections of which have been turned into a bike path (look for signs to the *piste cyclable*).

The place with the sign that reads **Bar-Hôtel** (☎ 05 53 29 51 63; d with shower €29; ☼ Easter-Oct) offers basic accommodation.

Hôtel La Belle Étoile (☎ 05 53 29 51 44; fax 05 53 29 45 63; d €46-70; ☼ Apr-Oct) has 16 two-star rooms.

Château de Beynac

This dramatic **fortress** (☎ 05 53 29 50 40; adult/5-11 yrs €7/3; ☼ 10am-6pm) is perched on a sheer cliff, dominating a strategic bend in the Dordogne. A steep trail links it to the centre of the village of **Beynac-et-Cazenac**, 150m below on the river bank (and the D703). Opening times may vary slightly according to the owners' discretion.

Loyal to the king of France, the fort, built from the 12th to 14th centuries (and later modified), was long a rival of Castelnaud, just across the river, which owed its allegiance to the king of England. The interior is architecturally interesting – you get a good idea of the layout of a medieval fortress – but is only partly furnished. From mid-March to mid-November, one-hour guided tours (in French) take place every half-hour.

In a stunning spot, with the château high above and the river just below, is the stylish **Hôtel-Restaurant du Château** (☎ 05 53 29 19 20; www.hotelduchateau-dordogne.com; d from €50; ☯ Feb-Dec), with spacious rooms. The rooms at the front have been redecorated with minimalist chic; four rooms have castle views. The **restaurant** (menus €17.50-22) specialises in traditional Périgord cuisine. It's on the main road through Beynac.

Château des Milandes

The claim to fame of the smallish, late-15th-century **Château des Milandes** (☎ 05 53 59 31 21; adult/4-15 yrs €7.50/5.50; ☯ 9am-7pm Jul & Aug, 10am-6pm Apr-Jun, Sep & Oct) is its post-war role as the home of the African-American dancer and music-hall star Josephine Baker (1906–75), who helped bring black American culture to Paris in the 1920s with her *Revue Nègre* and created a sensation by appearing on stage wearing nothing but a skirt of bananas.

Baker was awarded the Croix de Guerre and the Legion of Honour for her work with the French Resistance during WWII and was later active in the US civil rights movement. She established her Rainbow Tribe here in 1949, adopting 12 children from around the world as 'an experiment in brotherhood'.

The last obligatory, bilingual guided tour (lasting about 60 minutes) begins about an hour before closing time. The fierce-looking birds of prey in the courtyard are the stars of falconry displays several times a day (only in the afternoon in April, September and October).

MONPAZIER
pop 560

Of all the *bastides* in southwestern France, Monpazier (about 45km from both Sarlat-la-Canéda and Bergerac), founded by a representative of the king of England in 1284, is one of the most attractive, and popular with warm-season tourists.

The arcaded market square, **place des Cornières** (place Centrale) is surrounded by a motley assemblage of well-preserved stone houses that reflect centuries of building and rebuilding. The rectangular street grid is no longer enclosed by ramparts, but

three of the town **gates** still stand. Thursday is market day, as it has been since the Middle Ages.

The **tourist office** (☎ 05 53 22 68 59; www.pays-des-bastides.com in French; place des Cornières; ☯ 10am-7pm Jul & Aug, 10am-12.30pm & 2-6.30pm Apr-Jun & Sep, to 6pm Mon-Sat, 2.30-6pm Sun Oct-Mar), in the southeastern corner of the square, has an informative historical brochure in English.

Two-star **Hôtel de Londres** (☎ 05 53 22 60 64; fax 05 53 22 61 98; Foirail Nord; d with shower & toilet €35-45), on the way into Monpazier (on the D53), has 10 spacious rooms that are in need of a lick of paint. Even a good clean would help. The attached **restaurant** (menus from €17), with shaded terrace, serves traditional French and Périgord dishes and also has a vegetarian *menu* (€14.50).

The **Casino grocery** (place des Cornières; ☯ 8am-12.30pm & 2.30-7pm Tue-Sat & Sun morning, also Mon in Jul & Aug) is on the northern side of the square.

CHÂTEAU DE BIRON

Over the course of eight centuries, the Gontaud (or Gontaut) Biron family built, expanded and rebuilt this **castle** (☎ 05 53 63 13 39; adult/student & child €4.60/2.60; ☯ 10am-12.30pm & 2-6pm end Apr–mid-Oct, closed Mon, Fri & Sat end Oct–mid-Apr & Jan). In the early 1900s the castle was sold off, along with its contents, to pay for the extravagant lifestyle of a particularly irresponsible heir.

The castle's gloriously eclectic mixture of architectural styles, the oldest from the 12th century, is a bit hard to fathom if you don't take one of the free, French-language tours (a sheet in English is available). The realistic re-creations of medieval life that fill some of the rooms were once movie sets (the chateau itself is frequently used as a backdrop for films).

The GR36 links Biron with Monpazier, 8km to the north.

BERGERAC
pop 27,000

The less-than-thrilling town of Bergerac, the capital of the Périgord Pourpre wine-growing area, is surrounded by 125 sq km of vineyards. A Protestant stronghold in the 16th century, it sustained heavy damage during the Wars of Religion, but the old city and the old harbour quarter have retained some of their old-time ambience and are worth a stroll. Bergerac makes a convenient stopover on the way from Périgueux (47km to the northeast) to Bordeaux (93km to the west).

The dramatist and satirist Savinien Cyrano de Bergerac (1619–55) may have put the town on the map, but his connection with his namesake is extremely tenuous: it is believed that during his entire life he stayed here a few nights at most.

Information

The **tourist office** (☎ 05 53 57 03 11; www.bergerac -tourisme.com; 97 rue Neuve d'Argenson; ⏰ 9.30am-7.30pm Mon-Sat, 10.30am-1pm & 2-7pm Sun Jul & Aug, 9.30am-1pm & 2-7pm Mon-Sat Sep-Jun) supplies useful brochures in English, including information on cycling and wine-tasting in the region.

Sights

Bergerac has long been an important centre for tobacco-growing, which is why it has the **Musée du Tabac** (Tobacco Museum; ☎ 05 53 63 04 13; 10 rue de l'Ancien Port; adult/child €3/1.50; ⏰ 10am-noon & 2-6pm Tue-Fri Jan-Dec, 2-6pm Sat & Sun Mar-Nov & Mon Jul & Aug), housed in the early-17th-century, elegant Maison Peyrarède.

The **Musée du Vin et de la Batellerie** (☎ 05 53 57 80 92; place de la Mirpe; adult/child €1/0.60; ⏰ 10am-noon & 2-5.30pm Tue-Fri, 10am-noon Sat) showcases local wine-making and the historic role of the river as a vital transport artery.

Cloître des Récollets (☎ 05 53 63 57 55; admission free; ⏰ 10am-12.30pm & 2-6pm Mon-Sat May-Sep, Tue-Sat Oct-Apr), a 16th-century cloister along the river, is occupied by the local Maison des Vins, which offers free wine-tasting.

Sleeping & Eating

The tourist office can provide a full list of *chambres d'hôtes* in the area.

Le Colombier de Cyrano & Roxane (☎ 05 53 57 96 70; bluemoon2@club-Internet.fr; 17 place de la Mirpe; d incl breakfast from €45) About the only *chambre d'hôte* in town, and the most attractive place to stay, this quirky 16th-century building with sloping floors and rickety stairs is the oldest house still standing in Bergerac. The rooms are true to the period theme, though the bathrooms are modern.

Le Moderne (☎ 05 53 57 19 62; 19 av du 108e RI; d from €26, with shower & toilet €36) One of a few small hotels near the station offering good value, this two-star option has 11 rooms above a fairly quiet bar.

Restaurant La Treille (☎ 05 53 57 60 11; 12 quai Salvette; mains €12-18) This restaurant occupies

a scenic spot near the riverbank at the edge of the old town. It serves tasty traditional French food on an outside terrace.

Getting There & Away

Bergerac is on the tertiary train line that links Bordeaux and St-Émilion with Sarlat. The airport, 4km southeast of town, is served by flights from Paris (Air France) and the UK (Ryanair).

QUERCY

Southeast of the Dordogne *département* lies the warm, unmistakably southern region of Quercy, many of whose residents still speak Occitan (Provençal). The dry limestone plateau that is found in the northeast is covered with oak trees and cut by dramatic canyons created by the serpentine River Lot and its tributaries. The main city of Cahors is not far away from some of the region's finest vineyards.

Boating

One of the most relaxing ways to see the cliffs and villages along the 64km, navigable stretch of the Lot between St-Cirq Lapopie and Luzech – Cahors is about midway between the two – is to rent a houseboat. Over the next few years, there are plans to open up more of the River Lot to navigation, making it possible to travel downstream to Fumel and upstream to Cajarc.

For detailed information, contact the Centrale de Réservation Loisirs Accueil (p601); or **Les Bateaux Safaraid** (☎ 05 65 30 22 84; fax 05 65 35 98 89) in Bouziès; **Baboumarine** (☎ 05 65 30 08 99; fax 05 65 23 92 59) in Cahors; **Crown Blue Line** (☎ 05 65 20 08 79; fax 05 65 30 97 96) in Douelle; or **Locaboat Plaisance** (head office ☎ 03 86 91 72 72; fax 03 86 62 42 41) in Luzech.

For general information on boating in France, see p922.

Walking & Cycling

In addition to the GR36 and the GR65, both of which pass through Cahors, Quercy has numerous marked trails for day walks. Other Grande Randonnée trails that cross the Lot *département* include the GR6, GR46 and GR652. A variety of topoguides for walkers and cyclists are available from tourist offices.

CAHORS

pop 21,432

Cahors, former capital of the Quercy region, is a quiet town with a relaxed Midi atmosphere. Surrounded on three sides by a bend in the River Lot and ringed by hills, it is endowed with a famous medieval bridge, a large (if unspectacular) medieval quarter and a couple of minor Roman sites. The weather is mild in winter, hot and dry in summer and generally delightful in the spring and autumn. Cahors makes an excellent base for exploring Quercy.

Orientation

The town's main commercial thoroughfare, the north–south oriented blvd Léon Gambetta, is named in honour of Cahors-born Léon Gambetta (1838–82), one of the founders of the Third Republic and briefly premier of France (1881–82). It divides Vieux Cahors (Old Cahors) to the east from the new quarters to the west. At its northern end is place Général de Gaulle, essentially a giant car park; about 500m to the south is place François Mitterrand, home of the tourist office. An even-numbered street address is often blocks away from a similar odd-numbered one.

Information

INTERNET ACCESS

INIT (☎ 05 65 22 00 81; 100 rue Jean Vidal; per hr €2; ۞ 8.30am-noon & 1.30-5pm Mon-Fri)
Les Docks (see Entertainment; per hr €3; ۞ 2-8pm Mon & Tue, 2-10pm Wed-Fri, 2-6pm Sat & Sun)

LAUNDRY

There are laundrettes at place de la Libération and 208 rue Georges Clemenceau; both are open 7am to 9pm.

MEDICAL SERVICES

Centre Hospitalier Jean Rougier (☎ 05 65 20 50 50) The ramp to the 24-hour Urgences (casualty ward) is just across from 428 rue Président Wilson.

MONEY

There are banks offering money exchange along blvd Léon Gambetta, open either Tuesday to Saturday or Monday to Friday.

POST

Main Post Office (257 rue Président Wilson) Has a Cyberposte.

TOURIST INFORMATION

Tourist Office (☎ 05 65 53 20 65; cahors@wanadoo.fr; place François Mitterrand; ۞ 9am-12.30pm & 1.30-6pm Mon-Sat, 10am-noon Sun & holidays Jul & Aug) Efficient, with several excellent brochures in English on offer.
Comité Départemental du Tourisme (☎ 05 65 35 07 09; www.tourisme-lot.com; 1st fl, 107 quai Eugène Cavaignac; ۞ 8am-12.30pm & 1.30-6pm Mon-Thu, to 5.30pm Fri) Provides information on the Lot *département*.

Sights & Activities

It is possible to walk around three sides of Cahors by following the **quays** along the town's riverside perimeter. Sights below are listed more or less anticlockwise from the bridge. **Pont Valentré**, one of France's finest fortified medieval bridges, consists of six arches and three tall towers, two of them outfitted with machicolations (projecting parapets equipped with openings that allow defenders to drop missiles on attackers below). Built in the 14th century (the towers were added later), it was designed as part of the town's defences, not as a traffic bridge.

Two millennia ago, the **Fontaine des Chartreux** was used in the worship of Divona, the namesake of Gallo-Roman Cahors. A large number of coins, minted between 27 BC and AD 54 and apparently thrown into the water as offerings, were discovered by archaeologists a few years back. The flooded cavern under the pool has been explored by divers to a depth of 137m.

In the Middle Ages Cahors was a prosperous commercial and financial centre. To this day **Vieux Cahors**, the medieval quarter east of blvd Léon Gambetta, is densely packed with old (though not necessarily picturesque) four-storey houses linked by streets and alleyways that are so narrow you can almost touch both walls. At place St-Urcisse, there's a fascinating **mechanical clock** (1997) that drops metal balls through a series of improbable contraptions.

The cavernous nave of the Romanesque-style **Cathédrale St-Étienne** (admission free), which was consecrated in 1119, is crowned with two 18m-wide cupolas (the largest in France) that were inspired by the architecture of the Near East. The chapels along the nave (repainted in the 19th century) are Gothic, as are the choir and the massive western façade. The wall paintings between the organ and the interior of the western façade are early 14th-century originals.

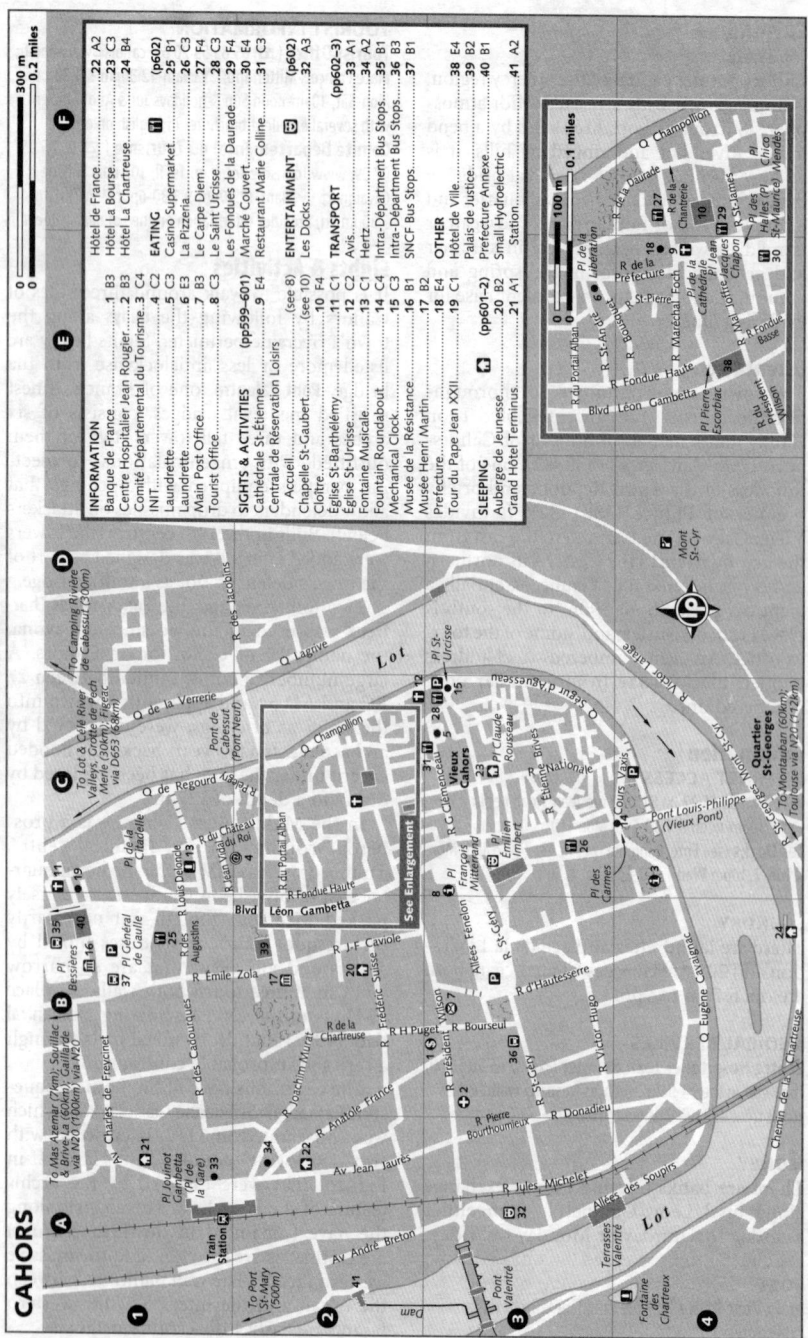

CAHORS

See Enlargement

INFORMATION
Banque de France..........................1	B3
Centre Hospitalier Jean Rougier........2	B3
Comité Départemental du Tourisme..3	C4
INIT..4	C2
Laundrette....................................5	C3
Laundrette....................................6	E3
Main Post Office............................7	B3
Tourist Office................................8	C3

SIGHTS & ACTIVITIES (pp599–601)
Cathédrale St-Étienne..............(see 8)	
Centrale de Réservation Loisirs	
Accueil......................................9	E4
Chapelle St-Gaubert....................10	F4
Cloître..11	C1
Église St-Barthélémy...................12	C1
Église St-Urcisse.........................13	C2
Fontaine Musicale.......................14	C4
Fountain Roundabout..................15	C1
Mechanical Clock........................16	B1
Musée de la Résistance................17	B2
Musée Henri Martin.....................18	E4
Préfecture..................................19	C1
Tour du Pape Jean XXII................20	B2

SLEEPING (pp601–2)
Auberge de Jeunesse..................21	A1
Grand Hôtel Terminus.................22	A2
Hôtel de France..........................22	A2
Hôtel La Bourse..........................23	C3
Hôtel La Chartreuse....................24	B4

EATING (p602)
Casino Supermarket.....................25	B1
La Pizzeria..................................26	C3
Le Carpe Diem............................27	F4
Le Saint Urcisse..........................28	C3
Les Fondues de la Daurade...........29	F4
Marché Couvert..........................30	E4
Restaurant Marie Colline..............31	C3

ENTERTAINMENT (p602)
Les Docks...................................32	A3

TRANSPORT (pp602–3)
Avis..33	A1
Hertz..34	A2
Intra-Department Bus Stops..........35	B1
Intra-Department Bus Stops..........36	B3
SNCF Bus Stops...........................37	B1

OTHER
Hôtel de Ville.............................38	E4
Palais de Justice..........................39	B2
Prefecture Annexe.......................40	B1
Small Hydroelectric	
Station....................................41	A2

Accessible from the cathedral's choir or through the arched entrance opposite 59 rue de la Daurade de la Chantrerie, the heavily mutilated **cloître** (cloister; Jun-Sep), is in the Flamboyant Gothic style of the early 16th century. Off the cloister, **Chapelle St-Gausbert** (admission €3), named after a late-9th-century bishop of Cahors, houses a small collection of liturgical objects. The frescoes of the Final Judgement date from around 1500.

The **Musée Henri Martin** (Musée Municipal; ☎ 05 65 30 15 13; 792 rue Émile Zola; Wed-Mon) has some archaeological artefacts and a collection of works by the Cahors-born pointillist painter Henri Martin (1893–1972). It opens only when there are temporary exhibitions, usually from June to September.

To get to the 1989 **Fontaine Musicale** (Musical Fountain), go down the alley next to 70 rue Louis Deloncle.

The **Tour du Pape Jean XXII** (1-3 blvd Léon Gambetta), a square, crenellated tower – at 34m the tallest structure in town – was built in the 14th century as part of the home of Jacques Duèse, later Pope John XXII from 1316 to 1334. The second of the Avignon popes, he established a university in Cahors in 1331. The interior is closed to the public. Across the street is the 14th-century **Église St-Barthélémy**, with its massive brick and stone belfry.

The small **Musée de la Résistance** (☎ 05 65 22 14 25; place Général de Gaulle; admission free; 2-6pm), on the northern side of the square, presents illustrated exhibits on the Resistance, the concentration camps and the liberation of France.

WALKING

The 264m-high antenna-topped hill of **Mont St-Cyr**, across the river from Vieux Cahors, affords excellent views of the town and the surrounding countryside. It can easily be climbed on foot with some sturdy shoes, the trail begins near the southern end of Pont Louis-Philippe (1838).

Tours

The **Centrale de Réservation Loisirs Accueil** (☎ 05 65 53 20 90; loisirs.accueil.lot@wanadoo.fr; place François Mitterrand; 8am-noon & 1.30-6.30pm Mon-Fri, also Sat Jun-Sep), in the tourist office building, arranges canoe, bicycle and horse-riding excursions, cookery courses and houseboat rental. If you want a hassle-free walk, it can provide an itinerary and arrange for accommodation, meals and even the transport of your bags. Activities can often be booked at short notice.

Festivals & Events

Around Bastille Day (14 July), the week-long **Festival de Blues** brings big-name jazz stars to town.

Sleeping

Rooms are hardest to come by in July and August. Many cheapies do not register new guests on Sunday unless you make advance arrangements by phone.

The staff at Centrale de Réservation Loisirs Accueil (left) can organise accommodation in the area's many *chambres d'hôtes* and *gîtes*.

BUDGET

Auberge de Jeunesse (☎ 05 65 35 64 71; fax 05 65 35 95 92; 20 rue Frédéric Suisse; dm €9.30; check-in 24hr;) The 40-bed youth hostel is located in the same building as the Foyer des Jeunes Travailleurs. The hostel's staff are helpful and efficient and there's a cheap canteen. Smaller rooms for one or two people are often full, so accommodation is usually in dorms of four to 10 beds; telephone reservations advisable.

Hôtel La Bourse (☎ /fax 05 65 35 17 78; 7 place Claude Rousseau; d from €28) Despite the entrance being down a dark, dingy alleyway around the corner from the bar/reception, the 10 rooms here are all spacious and clean. It's also the only decent budget option in the medieval quarter.

Camping

Camping Rivière de Cassebut (☎ 05 65 30 06 30; www.cabessut.com; sites €8 & per person €3; Apr-Oct;) This three-star camping ground is situated on the left bank of the River Lot about 1km north of Pont de Cabessut (the bridge just east of Vieux Cahors).

MID-RANGE

Grand Hôtel Terminus (☎ 05 65 53 32 00; terminus .balandre@wanadoo.fr; 5 av Charles de Freycinet; d €60-160;) Not your run-of-the-mill station hotel, this exceptional place is both luxurious and full of character. Built around 1920, the hotel has recently been refurbished to a high standard with period detail including ornamental radiators, stained-glass windows and roll-top baths. The rooms are beautifully furnished and the huge beds are perfect for holiday lie-ins.

Hôtel La Chartreuse (☎ 05 65 35 17 37; www.hotel-la-chartreuse.com; chemin de la Chartreuse; d with shower/bath from €49/62; P X N R) This comfortable three-star hotel, although in an ugly, modern building, occupies a great spot on the southern bank of the River Lot. The rooms (some with balconies) have the usual three-star comforts and views across the river and to the town on the far side.

Hôtel de France (☎ 05 65 35 16 76; www.hotel defrance-cahors.fr in French; 252 av Jean Jaurès; d from €42; P X N) Near the train station and the Pont Valentré is this modern, reliable three-star hotel with good-sized rooms. Facilities include minibars and international TV channels. Good value.

Eating

Les Fondues de la Daurade (☎ 05 65 35 27 27; place Jean Jacques Chapon; lunch menus from €8.60, dinner menus from 14.50) For something quick and hearty, this snackery gets the thumbs up. Fondues (€14) are its speciality, but it's also good for *tartines*, crepes, omelettes and other snacks and there's a sunny terrace overlooking the square.

Le Carpe Diem (☎ 05 65 35 68 28; 219 rue Maréchal Foch; mains €10-15; ☼ Wed-Sat) A quirky little place whose speciality is cooking with tea. Tea is used as a spice to liven up mainly traditional French dishes and to create unusual combinations such as river perch infused with Egyptian tea (€13.80) – it's tastier than it sounds!

Le Saint Urcisse (☎ 05 65 35 06 06; place St-Urcisse; mains €15-22; ☼ Tue-Sat) With a delightful walled

---

AUTHOR'S CHOICE

Restaurant Marie Colline (☎ 05 65 35 59 96; 173 rue Clemenceau; ☼ noon-2pm Tue-Fri) This is a rarity in France – a fantastic vegetarian restaurant! Choose from a changing menu of just two or three delicious dishes such as *Aubergine Lasagne* or *Dauphinois of Pumpkin*. Mains are €7; entrées and desserts are €3.50 each. The white wooden floors and garden chairs create a rustic ambiance, and there are three tables outside in the sunshine. Advance bookings essential.

---

garden and birds chattering away, this place is hard to beat for summer lunch, especially with the weekday lunch time *menu du jour* at just €11.80. There's a good choice of traditional French cuisine, including some very moorish desserts! Just don't plan too much for the afternoon…

La Pizzeria (☎ 05 65 35 12 18; 58 blvd Léon Gambetta; pizza from €7; ☼ Mon-Sat, also Sun lunch May-Oct) An extremely popular and good value pizzeria where the pizzas are created and fired in full view – always a good sign. Pastas and large salads also on offer.

SELF-CATERING

Marché Couvert (place des Halles; ☼ 7.30am-12.30pm & 3-7pm Tue-Sat, 9am-noon Sun & most holidays) A covered market also known as Les Halles. There's an open-air market on Wednesday and Saturday mornings around the covered market and on place Jean-Jacques Chapou. Nearby, food shops can be found around place des Halles and along rue de la Préfecture.

There's a **Casino supermarket** (☼ closed Wed) on place Général de Gaulle.

Entertainment

Les Docks (☎ 05 65 22 36 38; 430 allées des Soupirs) This one-time warehouse is now a municipal cultural centre, with a concert hall, a venue for small-scale theatre productions, music lessons (€2 per hour) and practice rooms for young musicians (€1 per hour per musician), a free skate park (for fans of in-line skates and skateboards) and an Internet café (p599).

Getting There & Away

BUS

The bus services linking Cahors with destinations around Lot *département*, designed primarily to transport school children, are a mess. To check your limited options, ask at the tourist office.

There are daily SNCF bus services from Cahors' train station and place Charles de Gaulle to Bouziès (see opposite), Tour de Faure (St-Cirq Lapopie, see opposite), Figeac (see p604) and Mercuès, Castelfranc, Luzech and Puy l'Évêque (see p607).

CAR

Choose from **Avis** (☎ 05 65 30 13 10; place de la Gare) or **Hertz** (☎ 05 65 35 34 69; 385 rue Anatole France) opposite the train station.

Free parking is available all along the river and in the westernmost sections of the car parks along allées Fénelon (behind the tourist office) and also at place Charles de Gaulle.

TRAIN
Cahors' **train station** (place Jouinot Gambetta, aka place de la Gare) is on the main SNCF line (four to nine daily) linking Paris' Gare d'Austerlitz (€59.60, five hours). Trains stop at Limoges (€23.30, two hours), Souillac (€9.20, 45 minutes), Brive-La-Gaillarde (€13.20, one hour) and Toulouse (€14.70, 1½ hours). To get to Sarlat-la-Canéda, take a train to Souillac and an SNCF bus from there (€13.80, three hours, three daily).

EAST OF CAHORS
The limestone hills between Cahors and Figeac are cut by the dramatic, cliff-flanked Rivers Lot and Célé. The narrow, winding and supremely scenic D662 (signposted 'Vallée du Lot') follows the River Lot, while the even narrower and more spectacular D41 (signposted 'Vallée du Célé') follows the tortuous route of the River Célé.

Bouziès
pop 70
The quiet hamlet of Bouziès, on the left bank of the Lot between the cliffs and the river bank, is home to the welcoming, two-star **Hôtel Les Falaises** (☎ 05 65 31 26 83; www.mona lisahotels.com; r €42-58; Apr-Oct; P   ). Prices depend on the season Mountain bikes, canoes and kayaks are rented out to guests and visitors alike. The attached **restaurant** (menus from €13) serves regional meals.

Les Bateaux Safaraid (p598) rents *gabarres* (flat-bottomed river boats) and six-person houseboats.

The SNCF bus (four to six daily) that links Cahors (€4.40, 25 minutes) with Figeac (€7.50, 70 minutes) stops on the D662 just across the narrow suspension bridge from Bouziès. If you make advance reservations, the hotel will send its minivan to pick you up at Cahors' train station or drop you off at the starting point of a hike.

Grotte de Pech Merle
The spectacular, 1200m-long **Pech Merle Cave** (☎ 05 65 31 27 05; www.pechmerle.com; adult/5-18 yrs mid-Jun–mid-Sep €7/4.50, mid-Sep–mid-Jun €6/3.80),

30km northeast of Cahors, is first and foremost a natural wonder, with thousands of stalactites and stalagmites of all varieties and shapes. It also has dozens of paintings of mammoths, horses and 'negative' human handprints, drawn by Cro-Magnon people 16,000 to 20,000 years ago in red, black, blue and dark grey. Prehistoric artefacts that have been found in the area are on display in the museum.

From April to October one-hour guided tours (English text available) take place every 45 minutes (every 15 minutes in summer) from 9.30am to noon and 1.30pm to 5pm daily. It's well worth the admission price. During the months when there are lots of tourists around (especially July and August), get there early as only 700 people daily are allowed to visit. Telephone reservations are accepted.

The cave is 8km from the Bouziès bridge and 3km from Cabrerets along the D41, D13 and D198. On foot the cave is about 3km from Bouziès via the GR651.

Conduché
Le Bureau des Sports Nature (☎ 05 65 24 21 01; perso.wanadoo.fr/bureau-sports-nature; Mon-Fri year round, Sat & Sun in Jul & Aug), based in the village of Conduché (near the confluence of the Rivers Lot and Célé), offers guided **rock climbing** and **spelunking**, guided **walks**, **canoe trips** and off-road **mountain biking**, weather permitting. Prices vary depending on numbers and activities; guided canoe trips start at €19 for a half day.

St-Cirq Lapopie
pop 50
St-Cirq Lapopie, 25km east of Cahors and 44km southwest of Figeac, is perched on a cliff top 100m above the River Lot. The spectacular views and the area's natural beauty more than make up for the village's self-conscious charm.

The fortified, early-16th-century **Gothic church** is of no special interest except for its stunning location. The ruins of the 13th-century **chateau**, at the top of the hill, also afford a fine panorama. Below, along the narrow alleyways, the restored stone and half-timbered houses, topped with steep, red-tiled roofs, shelter **artisans' studios** offering leather goods, pottery, jewellery and various wooden items. The **Musée Rignault**

SANTIAGO DE COMPOSTELA

The prospect of a few less years in purgatory through the granting of a soul-cleansing plenary indulgence may have motivated the early pilgrims to Santiago de Compostela in northwest Spain. However, for the thousands of contemporary spiritualists and atheists who undertake the long and rocky road to this important medieval site each summer, the incentive may be a little more palpable.

In the early 9th century a hermit, Pelayo, led by a vision, stumbled across the 800-year-old tomb of the apostle James, brother of John the Evangelist. Soon after his remains were authenticated, a shrine was established and by the 12th century Santiago de Compostela had become as significant a site of pilgrimage as Jerusalem and Rome. Four traditional routes through France now exist, the most popular of which passes through Figeac (below) and Cahors (p599). Though you can pick up the trail from any number of points, it's possible to follow a road from Paris for an arduous 2000km hike. Numerous points of worship and *refuges* were established en route, encouraging the welcome patronage of passing pilgrims. Walkers or those on horseback who complete the final 100km to Santiago (cyclists the final 200km) qualify for a Compostela Certificate issued on arrival at the cathedral.

(admission €2; 10am-12.30pm & 2.30-6pm Apr-Oct, to 7pm Jul & Aug) has a delightful garden and an eclectic collection of French furniture and art from Africa and China.

The **tourist office** (☎ 05 65 31 29 06; saint-cirq .lapopie@wanadoo.fr; 10am-1pm & 2-7.30pm Jun-Sep, to 6pm Apr, May & Oct, to 5pm Sun & closed Mon Nov-Mar) in the village hall can supply you with an English-language brochure.

The riverside **Camping de la Plage** (☎ 05 65 30 29 51; site for 2 people with/without electricity €17.80/14.80; Apr-Nov) is on the left bank of the Lot at the bridge linking the D662 (Tour de Faure) with the road up to St-Cirq Lapopie.

The **Hôtel de La Pelissaria** (☎ 05 65 31 25 14; http://perso.wanadoo.fr/hoteldelapelissaria; r €71-130; Apr-Oct;), a short way down the hill from the tourist office, has rooms in a lovely 16th-century house, perched dramatically on the edge of the cliff. There are panoramic views of the town and the river from the terrace.

St-Cirq Lapopie is 2km across the river and up the hill from Tour de Faure (on the D662), from where SNCF buses go to Cahors (€4.80, 35 minutes, four to six daily) and Figeac (€7.90, one hour, five daily).

Figeac
pop 9500
The harmonious riverside town of Figeac, on the River Célé 70km northeast of Cahors, has a picturesque **old city**, with many houses dating from the 12th to 18th centuries. Founded in the 9th century by Benedictine monks, it became a prosperous medieval market town, an important stopping place for

pilgrims travelling to Santiago de Compostela (above) and, later, a Protestant stronghold (1576–1623).

ORIENTATION & INFORMATION
The main commercial thoroughfare is the north–south blvd Docteur G Juskiewenski, which runs perpendicular to the Célé and its right-bank quays. Pedestrianised rue Gambetta, four short blocks east, is also perpendicular to the river. The train station, about 600m to the southeast, is across the river from the centre of town, at the end of av Georges Clemenceau.

The **tourist office** (☎ 05 65 34 06 25; http://figeac .quercy-tourisme.com; place Vival; 10am-7.30pm Jul & Aug, 10am-12.30pm & 2.30-6pm Mon-Sat & 10am-12.30pm Sun May, Jun & Sep, 10am-noon & 2.30-6pm Mon-Sat Oct-Apr) is one block north of the river and two blocks east of blvd Docteur G Juskiewenski.

The **post office** (8 av Fernand Pezet), a block west of blvd Docteur G Juskiewenski, offers currency exchange. There are a couple of banks along the same street.

The **Allo Laverie laundrette** (6am-10pm) is next to the tourist office.

SIGHTS
The tourist office is housed in a handsome, 13th-century building. Upstairs is the **Musée du Vieux Figeac** (adult/child €2/1; same as tourist office), with a varied collection of antique clocks, coins, minerals and a propeller blade made by a local aerospace firm.

Figeac's most illustrious son is the brilliant linguist and founder of the science of Egyptology, Jean-François Champollion

(1790–1832), who managed to decipher the written language of the pharaohs by studying the Rosetta Stone, an edict issued in 196 BC in Greek and two Egyptian scripts, demotic and hieroglyphic. Discovered by Napoleon's forces in 1799 during their abortive invasion of Egypt, the stone was captured by the English in 1801 and taken to the British Museum, where it remains; an enlarged copy fills the ancient courtyard next to Champollion's childhood home, now the **Musée Champollion** (☎ 05 65 50 31 08; rue des Frères Champollion; adult/student & child €3.10/1.85; ☾ 10am-noon & 2.30-6.30pm Tue-Sun Mar-Oct, also Mon in Jul & Aug, 2.30-6.30pm Tue-Sun Nov-Feb) on a tiny street four blocks north of the tourist office (along pedestrianised rue de la République). There is a small collection of Egyptian antiquities. Some of the explanatory signs are in English.

North of the Musée Champollion and place Champollion, **rue de Colomb**, favoured by the local aristocracy in the 18th century, is lined with centuries-old mansions in sandstone, half-timbers and brick. Near the river on rue du Chapitre, the musty **Église St-Sauveur**, a Benedictine abbey church built from the 12th to 14th centuries, features stained glass installed during the last half of the 19th century.

SLEEPING

Hôtel-Café Champollion (☎ 05 65 34 04 37; fax 05 65 34 61 69; 3 place Champollion; d with bath €47) This is a funky, modern hotel with 10 nicely designed rooms, right in the heart of the old city. Good breakfasts with real coffee and fresh juice are available at its adjoining café.

Hôtel Le Terminus (☎ 05 65 34 00 43; www.hotel-terminus.fr; 27 av Georges Clemenceau; d with shower & toilet €46; ℗) This reasonable two-star hotel opposite the train station has 12 bright, cheery rooms and a decent **restaurant** (menus €23-50) with tender Quercy lamb a particular speciality.

Grand Hôtel Le Pont D'Or (☎ 05 65 50 95 00; hotel.pont.or@free.fr; 2 av Jean Jaurès; d €60-76; ℗ ✗ ❊ ▫ ▣) Overlooking the river Célé, this 13th-century building has been completely renovated inside to create a characterless but comfortable three-star hotel. Top-notch facilities include pool, sauna and fitness room. Riverside rooms are larger (and more expensive).

EATING

Cuisine du Marché (☎ 05 65 50 18 55; 15 rue Clermont; menus €18-35; ☾ Mon-Sat) Regional gastronomy can be sampled in the old city at this airy and refined establishment. *Menus* feature contemporary variations on Quercy cuisine and there's an extensive wine list.

Le Crepuscule (☎ 05 65 34 28 53; rue de la République) A plain but friendly diner-style place, popular with locals, serving tasty pizzas, savoury crepes and grills.

Le Marrakech (☎ 05 65 34 69 25; 7 rue des Maquisards; mains €10-15) A harem-like, dark and cosy place beside the steps of the old city, offering authentic Moroccan tagines (stews) and couscous.

There is a **Centre L Gambetta (Leclerc) supermarket** (32 rue Gambetta; ☾ 8.30am-12.30pm & 2pm-7.30pm Mon-Sat), and place Carnot hosts a food market on Saturday morning.

GETTING THERE & AWAY

Four SNCF buses daily travel to Cahors (€10.20, 1¾ hours) via Bouziès and Tour de Faure (St-Cirq Lapopie). Stops are at Figeac's train station and on av Maréchal Joffre (which runs along the river) behind Lycée Champollion.

The **train station** (☎ 05 65 04 94 79) is on two major lines: the one that links Clermont-Ferrand (€25.70, four hours) with Villefranche de Rouergue (€5.70, 40 minutes), Najac (€7.70, 50 minutes) and Toulouse (€18.60, 2½ hours); and the route from Paris' Gare d'Austerlitz (€50.10, about 4½ hours) to Limoges (€22.10, 2¼ hours), Brive (€11.80, 1¼ hours), Rocamadour-Padirac (€6.70, 35 minutes) and Rodez (€10.20, 2¼ hours). There are four or five trains daily to each destination.

Villefranche de Rouergue
pop 12,300

Villefranche, 61km east of Cahors, is – like most *bastides* – centred around an arcaded central square, **place Notre Dame**. In one corner is the Languedoc Gothic **Collégiale Notre Dame**, a flying buttress-less structure built in the 14th and 15th centuries, whose never-completed belfry is held aloft by massive supports. The 15th-century **choir stalls** are ornamented with humorous figures.

A few blocks to the southwest along streets lined with stone and half-timbered houses, the **Musée Urbain Cabrol** (☎ 05 65 45 44 37;

rue de la Fontaine; 🕙 Mon–Sat Jun–mid-Sep, Mon–Fri mid-Sep–May) has an eclectic but fascinating collection of prehistory, religious art, local folk art and 19th-century medical equipment. The **fountain** at the front, decorated with stone carvings from 1336, gushes naturally.

Approximately 500m towards Najac from the train station, the **Chartreuse St-Sauveur**, a 15th-century monastery once affiliated with the austere Carthusian order, now houses a hospital. Of interest are the vaulted Gothic **cloister** (🕙 24hr) and the **chapel** (🕙 2-5pm Mon–Fri, 9-11am Sun), topped by a square belfry.

The large Thursday morning market on place Notre Dame is a real draw for tourists and locals alike, where everything from Chinese herbal medicine to organic produce and handmade kites is sold.

Next to the town hall, the **tourist office** (☎ 05 65 45 13 18; www.villefranche.com in French; promenade du Guiraudet; 🕙 9am–noon & 2-6pm Mon–Sat May–Oct, also 10am–noon Sun Jul & Aug, 9am–noon & 2-6pm Mon–Fri Nov–Apr) has a walking tour brochure in English.

Hôtel Bellevue (☎ 05 65 45 23 17; 3 av de Segala; d from €30), at the intersection of the D922 and the D911, across the tracks and half a block up the hill from the train station, is a small, family-run place with simple rooms.

Le Relais de Farrou (☎ 05 65 45 18 11; fax 05 65 45 32 59; route de Figeac; s/d from €43/48.50; P 🐾), 4km from town, offers three-star comfort in an old *relais de poste* (postal station) at very reasonable rates.

L'Assiette Gourmande (☎ 05 65 45 25 95; place Andrée Lescur; menus €12.50-28; 🕙 closed Sun, Tue & Wed evening), just off place Notre Dame, is a snazzy restaurant with an outside terrace, offering fine regional and French cuisine. The tasty four-course *menu de saison* is good value at €17.50.

La Mestiça (☎ 05 65 45 68 20; 12 rue Prestat; mains from €4.50) is a cosy little creperie selling good value snacks and salads as well as crepes. The lunch-time menu is a bargain €4 including wine. It's half a block west of place Notre Dame.

Villefranche's train station (across the river from the tourist office) is linked with regular trains to Figeac (€5.70, 40 minutes) and Capdenac (€4.90, 30 minutes) from where there are SNCF buses to Cahors (€13.90) and Brive (€15.30).

Najac
pop 250

The beautifully preserved, fairytale-like *bastide* village of Najac grew in the 13th century around the **Fortresse Royal** (☎ 05 65 29 71 65; 🕙 Apr-Sep), also known as the Château Fort, built on a rocky, easily defensible hill high above a hairpin curve in the River Aveyron. A bit to the west is the massive, Midi-Gothic **Église St-Jean l'Évangéliste**, which the locals were forced to construct by the Inquisition in 1258 as punishment for their Catharist tendencies.

The medieval parts are spread out along one, east–west-oriented street that runs 1.2km along the crest of the hill; it links the church with the sloping **place du Faubourg**, a charming, *bastide*-style central square surrounded by houses – each unique – from as early as the 13th century.

The **tourist office** (☎ 05 65 29 72 05; otsi .najac@wanadoo.fr; place du Faubourg; 🕙 9am–noon & 2-5.45pm Mon–Sat Apr–Sep, also 10am–noon Sun Jul & Aug, 9am–noon & 2-5.45pm Mon–Fri & Sat morning Oct-Mar) is on the southern side of the square.

Najac makes a good base for kayaking, rafting, cycling and hiking (a topoguide is available at the tourist office). **Najac de la Vallée**, along the river, is 3km (by road) down the hill near the train station (see p605 for train information).

Oustal del Barry (☎ 05 65 29 74 32; www.oustaldel barry.com; place du Faubourg; d €66.50-89, 🕙 late Mar–mid-Nov), just up the hill from the tourist office, is a two-star place in an old wooden-beamed building with stunning views of the valley and the fortress. The attached **restaurant** (menus from €22.30; 🕙 closed Tue lunch & Mon Oct-Jun) has *menus* made with fresh local products.

Le Belle Rive (☎ 05 65 29 73 90; fax 05 65 29 76 88; Le Roc du Pont; d with shower or bath €50-53; P 🐾) is a two-star, family-run hotel 1.5km from the village, past the train station. It has 30 comfortable rooms, a swimming pool, tennis court and billiard room.

La Salamandre (☎ 05 65 29 74 09; rue du Barriou; menus €16-20; 🕙 closed Wed dinner Dec & Jan), just downhill from the tourist office, is a stylish, contemporary restaurant serving inventive variations on traditional cuisine. The wonderful panoramic terrace has giddying views of the roller-coaster valley below.

Il Capello (☎ 05 65 29 70 26; route de la Gare; menu €10, pizza €5.80-7.30; 🕙 closed Wed dinner) is a busy, rustic restaurant packed with locals, serving pizzas, grills and hearty homemade local dishes.

The most scenic way to get to Villefranche de Rouergue, 23km to the north, is via the twisting, one-lane D638, which intersects the D339 about 5km northeast of Najac.

WEST OF CAHORS

Downstream from Cahors, the lower River Lot follows an impossibly serpentine route through the rich vineyards of the Cahors Appellation d'Origine Contrôlée (AOC) region, passing the dams at **Luzech**, whose medieval section sits at the base of a donjon, and **Castelfranc**, with a suspension bridge.

Along (and above) the river's right bank, the D9 – too narrow and heavily trafficked for cycling – affords superb views of the vines and the river's many hairpin curves. Château de Biron and Monpazier (p597) are nearby.

Four to seven SNCF buses each day link Cahors with Luzech (€3, 20 minutes) and Puy l'Évêque (€5.50, 45 minutes).

Puy l'Évêque
pop 2200

The once-important riverside port of Puy l'Évêque, on a rocky hillside above the right bank of the Lot, has an intimate, stone centre with numerous, centuries-old stone houses. It is a good base for exploring the lower Lot area, including the Cahors AOC wineries. The town is 31km from Cahors.

The Puy l'Évêque **tourist office** (☎/fax 05 65 21 37 63; ⏰ 8.30am-12.30pm & 2-6.30pm Mon-Fri, to 6pm Sat, Sep-Jun, 9.30am-12.30pm & 2.30-6.30pm Mon-Sat, 10am-12.30pm Sun Jul & Aug), in the golden-hued village hall building – at the base of a square, 13th-century donjon – can supply you with an English-language brochure on day hikes.

About 4km north up the hill and through the forest, the austere **Église de Martignac** (⏰ 10am-7pm), topped by a peculiar half-timbered belfry, is decorated with 15th-century frescoes, protected for centuries by layers of whitewash. The surrounding area is perfect for quiet walks.

Hôtel Henry (☎ 05 65 21 32 24; www.hotel-henry .com; 23 rue du Docteur Roumat; d €32-38, with garden view €43-47; ☒) is a very well appointed two-star hotel near the old town with a leafy terrace and small garden. The attached **restaurant** (menus €15-28; ⏰ closed Sun night & some Sat in winter) has French and Quercy-style *menus*.

Château de Bonaguil

This imposing feudal **fortress** (☎ 05 53 71 90 33; adult/7-16 yrs €4.50/3; ⏰ 10am-6pm Jun-Aug, 10.30am-1pm & 2.30-5pm Sep, 11am-1pm & 2.30-5pm Oct, 11am-1pm & 2.30-5.30pm Feb & Mar, 11am-1pm & 2.30-5.30pm Apr & May; 2.30-4.30pm Sun & holidays Nov-Jan) is a fine example of late-15th-century military architecture, featuring the artful integration of cliffs, outcrops, towers, bastions, loopholes, machicolations and crenellations. It's situated about 15km west of Puy l'Évêque (and on the GR36 footpath). Optional guided tours (1½ hours), in English three times daily in July and August, generally take place on the hour, with the last one about an hour before closing time.

About 5km to the southeast is the attractive village of **St-Martin-le-Redon**, in a quiet little valley along the River Thèze (and just off the D673).

NORTHERN QUERCY

The northern edge of Quercy is not far from Collonges-la-Rouge, Beaulieu-sur-Dordogne and Turenne (p581).

Rocamadour
pop 630

Except in winter, when it's nearly dead, the spectacularly situated pilgrimage centre of Rocamadour, 59km north of Cahors and 51km east of Sarlat, is a touristic nightmare, overrun with coaches and crammed with tacky souvenir shops.

Perched on a 150m-high cliff face above the River Alzou, the old city – known as the **Cité** – was, from the 12th to 14th centuries, an important stop on one of the pilgrimage routes to Santiago de Compostela (p604). These days, coach tourists with glazed eyes obediently plod through a number of over-restored Gothic chapels, including **Chapelle Notre Dame**, home to a 12th-century Black Madonna said to have miraculous powers.

The Cité's only street is connected to the chapels and the plateau above, known as **L'Hospitalet**, by the **Grand Escalier** (Great Staircase). The pious once climbed this on their knees, and there's a path whose switchbacks are marked with graphic Stations of the Cross. At the top of the stairs is the 14th-century **chateau** (charging €2.50 for a view from the ramparts).

Sights in L'Hospitalet include the **Grotte des Merveilles** (☎ 05 65 33 67 92; ⏰ Apr–mid-Nov), a one-room cave with some mediocre stalactites and prehistoric cave paintings.

The Cité **tourist offices** (☎ 05 65 33 62 59) is on the main street, and there's another **branch** (☎ 05 65 33 22 00) at L'Hospitalet, next to the Grotte des Merveilles.

Gouffre de Padirac

The truly spectacular **Padirac Cave** (☎ 05 65 33 64 56; adult/6-9 yrs €8/5.20; ☺ 9am-6pm Jul, 8.30am-6.30pm Aug 9am-noon & 2-6pm Apr-Jun & Sep–early Oct), 15km northeast of Rocamadour and 10km southeast of Carennac, offers the closest thing – at least in *this* world – to a cruise to Hades across the River Styx. Discovered in 1889, the cave's navigable river, 103m below ground level, is reached through a 75m-deep, 33m-wide chasm.

Boat pilots, who speak only Occitan and Midi-accented French, ferry visitors along a 500m stretch of the subterranean waterway, guiding them up and down a series of stairways to otherworldly pools and vast, floodlit caverns.

The whole cave operation is unashamedly mass-market, but it retains an innocence and style reminiscent of the 1930s, when the first lifts were installed. The temperature inside the cave is a constant 13°C. The 1¼-hour visits take place from April to early October.

Château de Castelnau-Bretenoux

A stunning hilltop silhouette greets you as you approach this feudal **fortress** (☎ 05 65 10 98 00; adult/18-25 yrs/under 18 €6.10/4.10/free; ☺ 9.30am-7pm Jul & Aug, 9.30am-12.30pm & 2-6.30pm May & Jun, 10am-12.30pm & 2-5.30pm Wed-Mon Sep-Apr). One of France's most impressive, it is 9km east of Carennac. It dominates the valleys of the Rivers Dordogne, Cère and Bave, with its sandy limestone hues ranging from golden yellow to deep red. Most of the complex – which, mercifully, has not been overrestored – dates from the 12th to the 15th centuries. The site has signs in English.

Ticket sales stop 45 minutes before the morning and afternoon closing times. The seven eclectically furnished rooms must be visited with a guide (English information sheet available).

Carennac

pop 370

The narrow alleyways of this delightful medieval village, on the left bank of the Dordogne, meander among tile-roofed houses made of golden-hued stone, some built as early as the 10th century (and most occupied only in the summer).

An arched stone gate leads to the 16th-century **Château du Doyen**, which houses a heritage centre, **L'Espace Patrimoine** (☎ 05 65 33 81 36; patrimoine-vallee-dordogne@wanadoo.fr; admission free; ☺ 10am-noon & 2-6pm Tue-Fri Apr-Jun, Tue-Sun Jul-Sep), showcasing the art and history of the region. Above is the square **Tour de Télémaque**, named after the hero of Fénelon's *Les Aventures de Télémaque*, written here in 1699.

Next to the chateau is the **priory**, reached via the same stone gate. Over the entrance to the Romanesque **Église St-Pierre** is an exceptional **tympanum** depicting Jesus in majesty, carved in the Languedoc Romanesque style in the mid-12th century. Just off the **cloître** (cloister; adult/child €2.50/0.80), heavily damaged in the Revolution, is a remarkable, late-15th-century **Mise au Tombeau** (Statue of the Entombment), once brightly painted. Its opening hours are the same as the **tourist office** (☎ 05 65 10 97 01; ot.intercom.carennac@wanadoo .fr; ☺ 10am-7pm mid-Jun–Sep, 10am-noon & 2-6pm Mon-Sat, 2-6pm Sun Oct–mid-Jun) next door.

Walking options include the GR652, which links the village of Mézels (on the river to the northwest) with the Gouffre de Padirac (to the southeast). For a lovely drive, follow the D30 southeast along the Dordogne.

Hôtel des Touristes (☎ 05 65 10 94 31; www .hotel-touristes.com; d from €40; ☺ closed Christmas) is a cosy, renovated nine-room place run by the same family for four generations and open pretty much year-round. The lovely double rooms have wooden floorboards, cool blue tones and river views. Half-board (from €47 per person, including the room) may be required in July and August. The **restaurant** (menus €14.50-24; ☺ closed dinner Fri & Sat Oct–mid-Apr) features traditional regional cuisine.

The only place to buy food is the small **grocery** (☺ closed 12.30-3pm, also Sun & Mon afternoons) next to the post office.

Atlantic Coast

It may not have the glitz and glamour associated with its counterpart on the Mediterranean, but France's Atlantic coast is just as appealing. Of course, there's the scorching sunshine and miles of sandy beaches, but there's so much more to this region than bucket-and-spade summer days.

Lively Bordeaux is emerging from an ambitious makeover to become one of France's hot destinations. Rich in museums, restaurants and nightlife, the city centre has been scrubbed, polished and pedestrianised to great effect, showcasing its grand neoclassical architecture. Then there's the wine. The city is surrounded by one of the most renowned wine-growing regions, from the pompous chateaux of the Médoc to the distinguished wineries of St-Émilion.

On the coast itself, the relaxed seaside resorts of Soulac-sur-Mer and Arcachon sit at either end of the Côte d'Argent, a long stretch of virtually deserted sand beaches and dunes best explored on bicycle. If you prefer riding the waves rather than two-wheelers, you're also in luck. The surf here is about the best in Europe.

The charming, picturesque ports of La Rochelle and on nearby Île de Ré are the nearest you'll find to the yacht-glamour of the Med, but these unpretentious places are known more for *poisson* than posing, with succulent, fresh seafood on the menu. Inland diversions include the famed brandy town of Cognac, the historic and commodious city of Nantes and the superb Romanesque churches at Poitiers.

The area in this chapter straddles three regions; Pays de la Loire in the north around Nantes; Poitou-Charentes from Poitiers to the coast; and Aquitaine, south of the Gironde Estuary. That may help to explain the sheer diversity of attractions on offer here.

HIGHLIGHTS

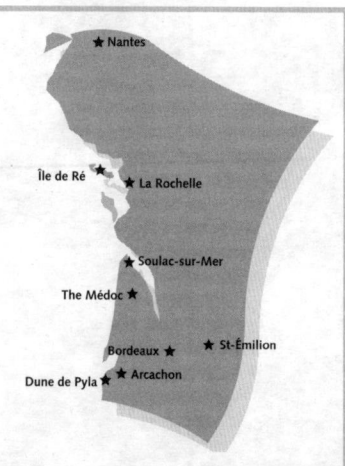

- Surf's up! Catching the waves (or a lesson) at **Arcachon** (p641) or **Soulac-sur-Mer** (p638)

- Wine tasting, chateaux visits and long lunches at **St-Émilion** (p639) and the **Médoc** (p637)

- Gorging on magnificent seafood in **La Rochelle** (p623)

- Run, jump or cartwheel down **Dune de Pyla** (p644)

- Laugh, cry and applaud at the Opera House, **Nantes** (p616)

- Explore the restaurants, bars and clubs of **Bordeaux** (p634)

- Laze around on the beaches at **Île de Ré** (p626)

■ POPULATION: 4,529,642	■ AREA: 51,597 SQ KM

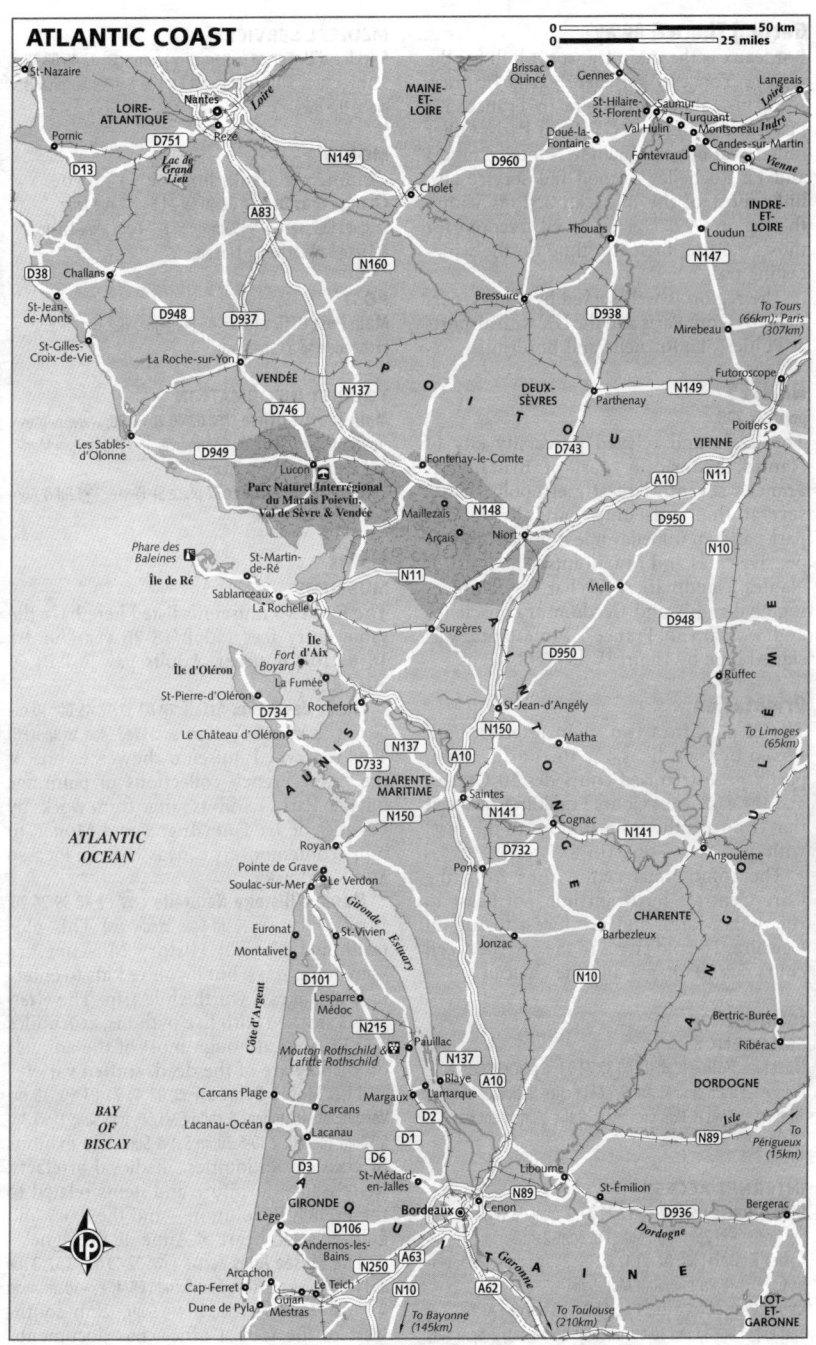

ATLANTIC COAST

0   50 km
0   25 miles

St-Nazaire

LOIRE-
ATLANTIQUE

Nantes

Rezé

Loire

MAINE-
ET-
LOIRE

Brissac
Quincé

Gennes

Langeais

Loire

Pornic

D751

D13

Lac de
Grand
Lieu

N149

Cholet

D960

Doué-la-
Fontaine

St-Hilaire-
St-Florent

Val Hulin

Saumur

Turquant
Montsoreau

Candes-sur-Martin

Fontevraud

Chinon

Indre

Vienne

INDRE-
ET-
LOIRE

D38

Challans

Thouars

Loudun

N147

St-Jean-
de-Monts

N160

Bressuire

D938

Mirebeau

To Tours
(66km); Paris
(307km)

St-Gilles-
Croix-de-Vie

D948

D937

La Roche-sur-Yon

VENDÉE

D746

N137

DEUX-
SÈVRES

Parthenay

N149

Futuroscope

VIENNE

Poitiers

Les Sables-
d'Olonne

D949

Luçon

Parc Naturel Interrégional
du Marais Poitevin,
Val de Sèvre & Vendée

Fontenay-le-Comte

Maillezais

N148

Arçais

Niort

D743

A10

N11

D950

N10

Phare des
Baleines

St-Martin-
de-Ré

Île de Ré

Sablanceaux

La Rochelle

N11

Surgères

Melle

D948

Île
Fort d'Aix
Boyard

Île d'Oléron

La Fumée

St-Pierre-d'Oléron

Rochefort

D734

Le Château d'Oléron

D733

N137

A10

CHARENTE-
MARITIME

N150

St-Jean-d'Angély

N150

Matha

Saintes

N141

Cognac

Ruffec

To Limoges
(65km)

N141

Angoulême

ATLANTIC
OCEAN

Royan

Pointe de Grave

Soulac-sur-Mer

Le Verdon

D732

Pons

Jonzac

CHARENTE

Barbezieux

N10

Bettric-Burée

Euronat

Montalivet

St-Vivien

Gironde Estuary

Côte d'Argent

D101

Lesparre-
Médoc

N215

Pauillac

N137

Ribérac

BAY
OF
BISCAY

Mouton Rothschild &
Lafitte Rothschild

Carcans Plage

Margaux

Lamarque

Blaye

A10

DORDOGNE

Lacanau-Océan

Carcans

Lacanau

D1

D2

Isle

N89

To
Périgueux
(15km)

D3

D6

St-Médard-
en-Jalles

Libourne

N89

St-Émilion

Bergerac

GIRONDE

D106

Lège

Bordeaux

Cenon

D936

Dordogne

Arcachon

Andernos-les-
Bains

N250

A63

Garonne

Cap-Ferret

Gujan
Mestras

Le Teich

N10

A62

Dune de Pyla

To Bayonne
(145km)

To Toulouse
(210km)

LOT-
ET-
GARONNE

Getting There & Away

Bordeaux is the main transport hub for the region. You can get there easily by train from just about anywhere in France; it's just three hours by TGV from Paris. Other rail arrival options include Nantes, Poitiers and La Rochelle. A good rail service also links most of the main attractions within the region. A car gives added freedom for those wanting to spend time on the wine-tasting trail.

The region is well-served by flights, particularly from Paris and the UK with airports at Poitiers, La Rochelle and Bordeaux.

NANTES

pop 277,728

The lively and relaxed university city of Nantes, historically part of Brittany, is France's seventh-largest metropolis. It has several fine museums, carefully tended parks and an unbelievable number of inexpensive cafés and restaurants. The Edict of Nantes, a landmark royal charter guaranteeing civil rights and freedom of conscience and worship to France's Protestants, was signed here by Henri IV in 1598.

Orientation

The city centre's two main arteries, both served by tram lines, are the north–south, partly pedestrianised cours des 50 Otages, and the east–west Cours Franklin Roosevelt that connects the train station (to the east) with quai de la Fosse (to the west).

The commercial centre runs from the Gare Centrale bus/tram hub northeast to rue de la Marne and northwest to rue du Calvaire. The old city is to the east, between cours des 50 Otages and the chateau.

Information

EMERGENCY

Hôtel de Police (☎ 02 40 37 21 21; 6 place Waldeck Rousseau; tram stop Motte Rouge) Police Nationale's 24-hour station is 1km northeast of the Monument des 50 Otages.

INTERNET ACCESS

Cyber House (☎ 02 40 12 11 84; 8 quai de Versailles; per hr €3; ❂ 2pm-2am Mon-Fri, 3pm-2am Sat)

Cyber Kebab (☎ 02 40 47 09 21; 30 rue de Verdun; per hr €3; ❂ 10am-midnight Mon-Sun)

Cyber Planet (☎ 02 51 82 47 97; 18 rue de l'Arche Sèche; per hr €3; ❂ 10am-midnight Mon-Sat, 2-8pm Sat)

MEDICAL SERVICES

Service d'Urgence (emergency room; ☎ 02 40 08 38 95; quai Moncousu) Of the vast CHR de Nantes hospital is along the river.

MONEY

Commercial banks line rue La Fayette.

Change Graslin (☎ 02 40 69 24 64; 17 rue Jean-Jacques Rousseau; ❂ 9am-noon & 2-6pm Mon-Fri, to 4.45pm Sat) Exchange bureau.

POST

Main Post Office (place de Bretagne) Has currency exchange and a Cyberposte.

TOURIST INFORMATION

Main Tourist Office (☎ 02 40 20 60 00; www.nantes-tourisme.com; place du Commerce; ❂ 10am-7pm Mon-Sat) In the Palais de la Bourse.

Tourist Office Annexe (2 place St-Pierre; ❂ Jul & Aug) Next to the cathedral.

Sights

MUSEUMS

The first two museums listed here have the same entry fees (adult/18-26 years/under 18 €3.10/1.60/free). Adults pay just €1.60 after 4.30pm.

Musée des Beaux-Arts (☎ 02 51 17 45 00; 10 rue Georges Clemenceau; ❂ 10am-6pm Wed-Mon, to 8pm Fri) This renowned museum showcases one of the finest French collections of paintings outside Paris. Exhibits range from works by Georges de La Tour, Ingres and Monet, to more contemporary canvasses from Picasso and Kandinsky.

Musée d'Histoire Naturelle (☎ 02 40 99 26 20; 12 rue Voltaire; ❂ 10am-6pm Wed-Mon) This old-fashioned Natural History Museum has seen better days, but if you've kids to entertain it makes a worthwhile trip. The **vivarium** is stocked with live pythons, crocodiles and iguanas although most of the animals on display are of the dead, stuffed variety.

The **Musée Dobrée** (☎ 02 40 71 03 50; 18 rue Voltaire; adult/student & child €3/1.50, free Sun; ❂ 1.30-5.30pm Tue-Fri, 2.30-5.30pm Sat & Sun) has exhibits of classical antiquities, medieval artefacts, Renaissance furniture and items related to the French Revolution – and the ivory and gold-encased heart of Anne de Bretagne!

The **Musée Jules Verne** (☎ 02 40 69 72 52; 3 rue de l'Hermitage; adult/student & child €8/4; ❂ 10am-noon & 2-6pm Mon & Wed-Sat, 2-6pm Sun), 2km southwest of the tourist office, has documents, posters, first-editions and other items connected with Jules Verne, the visionary sci-fi writer, who was born in Nantes in 1828.

OTHER ATTRACTIONS
From the outside, the **Château des Ducs de Bretagne** (Chateau of the Dukes of Brittany; ☎ 02 40 41 56 56; admission to grounds free; ☼ 10am-6pm) looks like your standard medieval castle. Inside, the parts facing the courtyard are in the style of a Renaissance pleasure palace. Walking along part of the ramparts is free.

Inside the Flamboyant Gothic **Cathédrale St-Pierre et St-Paul** (place St-Pierre), the **tomb of François II** (r 1458–88), duke of Brittany, and his second wife, Marguerite de Foix, is considered a masterpiece of Renaissance art. The statue facing the nave represents **Prudence**.

The **Jardin des Plantes**, across blvd de Stalingrad from the train station, is one of the most exquisite botanical gardens in France. Founded in the early 19th century, it has beautiful flowerbeds, duck ponds, fountains and even a few California redwoods (sequoias). There are **hothouses** and a **children's playground** at the northern end.

The channels of the Loire that once surrounded **Île Feydeau** (the neighbourhood south of the Gare Centrale) were filled in after WWII, but you can still see the area's 18th-century mansions, built by rich merchants. Some are adorned with stone carvings of the heads of African slaves.

Two blocks northwest of Île Feydeau is **Passage Pommeray**, a delightful shopping arcade that opened in 1843. Nearby are **place Royale**, laid out in 1790, and **place Graslin**, on the northern side of which stands the imposing, neoclassical **Théâtre Graslin**, built in 1788 and beautifully renovated in 2003 (see p616).

Sleeping
In addition, to the hotels reviewed, the tourist office has a list of camping grounds and hostels in town. Most places close reception on Sunday afternoons.

BUDGET
Hôtel St-Daniel (☎ 02 40 47 41 25; hotel.st.daniel@ wanadoo.fr; 4 rue du Bouffay; d from €29) In the heart of the old town, this great value budget place offers rooms with un-budget extras

like spaciousness, TV, hairdryer and double-glazing. Some rooms have been renovated and boast flashy wooden floors. There are a few family rooms for €39.

Hôtel de la Bourse (☎ 02 40 69 51 55; fax 02 40 71 73 89; 19 quai de la Fosse; d from €19, with shower & toilet €24) The emphasis here is on low prices rather than style and location, unless you like cheap pine furniture, feline art and car park views. As a place to sleep though, the clean, tidy rooms here are a steal. Hall showers cost €2.20.

Hôtel Fourcroy (☎ 02 40 44 68 00; 11 rue Fourcroy; s/d with shower & toilet €30/32; **P**) In a nondescript building tucked away down a side-street, this great value hotel has 19 exceptionally well-kept rooms, with modern bathrooms and upholstered doors.

MID-RANGE & TOP END
Hôtel de France (☎ 02 40 73 57 91; www.hotels-exclusive .com/hotels/france; 24 rue Crébillon; s €60-99, d €63-102; **P**) A three-star place in an 18th-century mansion, with Louis XVI-style furnishings. It's showing its age a bit now; some of the high-ceilinged rooms don't quite match up to the grandeur of the opulent entrance hall. Rooms with disabled access available.

Hôtel Graslin (☎ 02 40 69 72 91; fax 02 40 69 04 44; 1 rue Piron; d €57-70; ▯) Modern three-star hotel with all the in-room facilities you could wish for including bathrobes, minibar and matching yellow curtains, bedspreads and chairs. Good location off Place Graslin.

Grand Hôtel Nantes Central (☎ 02 51 82 10 00; H1985@accor-hotels.com; 4 rue du Couedic; s/d €130/140, ste €160; **P** ✕ ▮ ▯) Part of the Mercure chain, this well-appointed hotel offers very

---

AUTHOR'S CHOICE

Hôtel Pommeraye (☎ 02 40 48 78 79; www .hotel-pommeraye.com; 2 rue Boileau; s/d from €35/43 weekends, €49/59 weekdays; **P** ▯) A new, stylish boutique hotel within an older building, mixing the classic and the contemporary with great success. Relax to the gentle sounds of the water feature while using the free lobby Internet, or walk straight out into the heart of Nantes' shopping district. Comfortable, well-equipped rooms are presented in warm, modern colours. Cheaper rooms are a bit small, but you can pay extra to 'Go Large'.

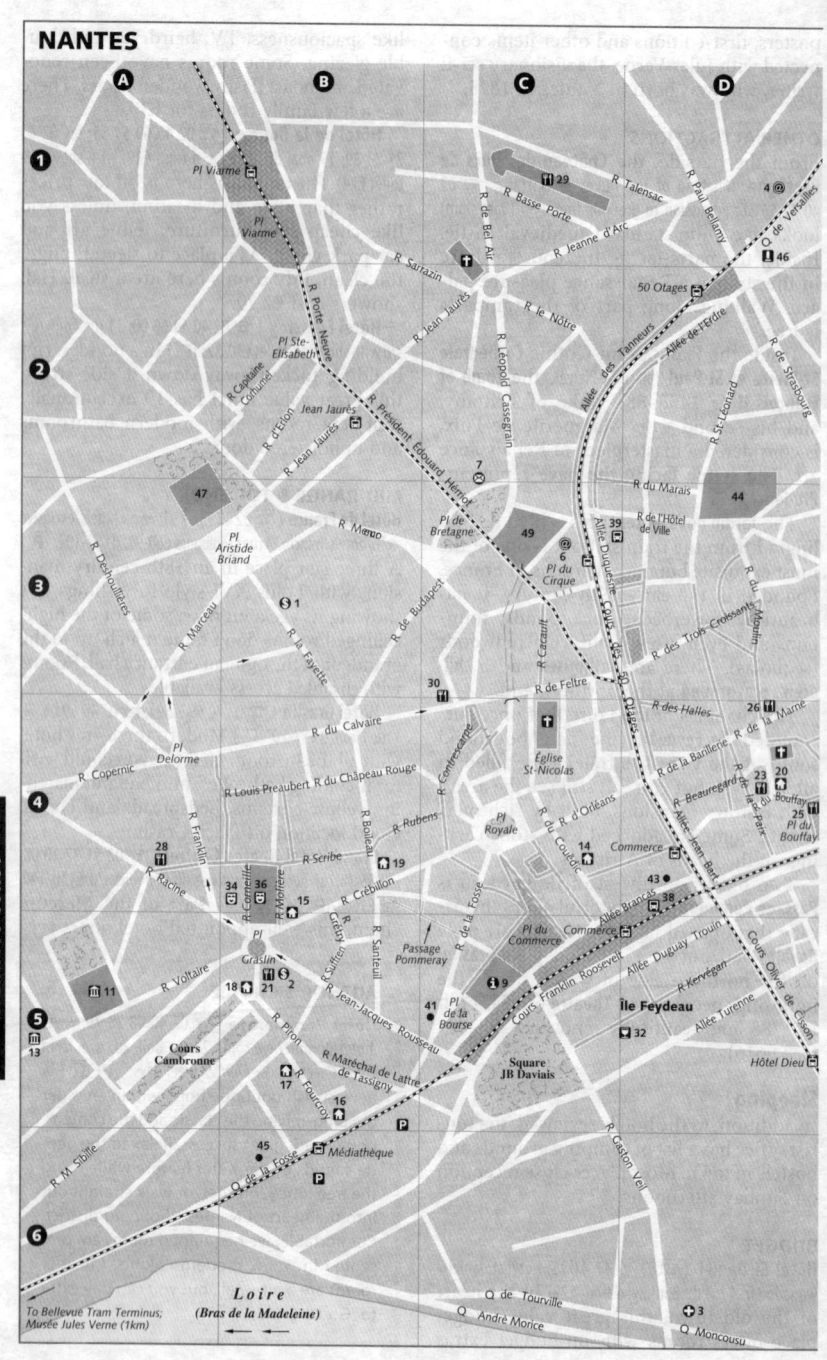

NANTES

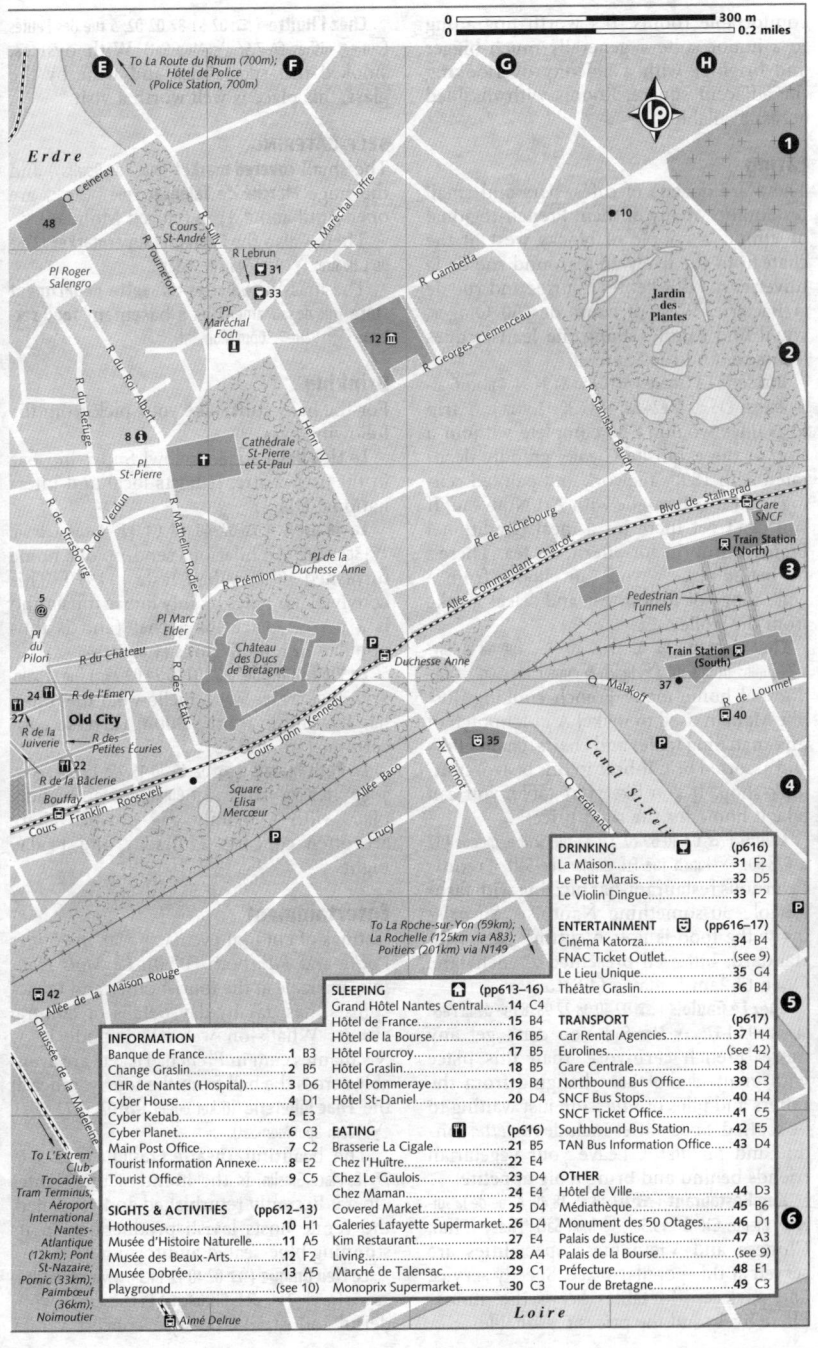

DRINKING 🍷 (p616)
La Maison.............................**31** F2
Le Petit Marais....................**32** D5
Le Violin Dingue.................**33** F2

ENTERTAINMENT 🎭 (pp616–17)
Cinéma Katorza...................**34** B4
FNAC Ticket Outlet............(see 9)
Le Lieu Unique....................**35** G4
Théâtre Graslin....................**36** B4

TRANSPORT (p617)
Car Rental Agencies...........**37** H4
Eurolines.............................(see 42)
Gare Centrale.....................**38** D4
Northbound Bus Office.......**39** C3
SNCF Bus Stops..................**40** H4
SNCF Ticket Office.............**41** C5
Southbound Bus Station......**42** E5
TAN Bus Information Office...**43** D4

OTHER
Hôtel de Ville.....................**44** D3
Médiathèque.......................**45** B6
Monument des 50 Otages....**46** D1
Palais de Justice.................**47** A3
Palais de la Bourse.............(see 9)
Préfecture...........................**48** E1
Tour de Bretagne...............**49** C3

INFORMATION
Banque de France.................**1** B3
Change Graslin.....................**2** B5
CHR de Nantes (Hospital)......**3** D6
Cyber House..........................**4** D1
Cyber Kebab.........................**5** E3
Cyber Planet..........................**6** C3
Main Post Office....................**7** C2
Tourist Information Annexe.....**8** E2
Tourist Office.........................**9** C5

SIGHTS & ACTIVITIES (pp612–13)
Hothouses...........................**10** H1
Musée d'Histoire Naturelle.....**11** A5
Musée des Beaux-Arts..........**12** F2
Musée Dobrée......................**13** A5
Playground...........................(see 10)

SLEEPING 🛏 (pp613–16)
Grand Hôtel Nantes Central...**14** C4
Hôtel de France....................**15** B4
Hôtel de la Bourse................**16** B5
Hôtel Fourcroy.....................**17** B5
Hôtel Graslin........................**18** B5
Hôtel Pommeraye.................**19** B4
Hôtel St-Daniel.....................**20** D4

EATING 🍴 (p616)
Brasserie La Cigale...............**21** B5
Chez l'Huître........................**22** E4
Chez Le Gaulois....................**23** D4
Chez Maman.........................**24** E4
Covered Market.....................**25** D4
Galeries Lafayette Supermarket..**26** D4
Kim Restaurant.....................**27** E4
Living...................................**28** A4
Marché de Talensac..............**29** C1
Monoprix Supermarket..........**30** C3

comfortable rooms. It's worth upgrading to a junior suite – generally much bigger and brighter with a balcony overlooking the adjacent square. Rooms with disabled access available.

Eating

There are dozens of cafés, bars and small restaurants, many of them French-regional or ethnic, a couple of blocks west of the chateau in the lively area around rue de la Juiverie, rue des Petites Écuries and rue de la Bâclerie. West of cours des 50 Otages, you'll find eateries along rue Jean-Jacques Rousseau and rue Santeuil.

Brasserie La Cigale (☎ 02 51 84 94 94; 4 place Graslin; menus €15.20 & €24.80; ☺ 7.30-12.30am) A trip to Nantes wouldn't be complete without a stop at the exquisite Cigale, grandly decorated with 1890s tilework and painted ceilings that mix baroque with Art Nouveau. If you can't get there for a meal (traditional French) drop in for afternoon tea. There's no better place – you can choose from a wide range of fusion teas and select a cake from the trolley.

Chez Maman (☎ 02 51 72 20 63; 2 rue de la Juiverie; mains from €10; ☺ lunch & dinner Tue-Sun) Traditional home-made French cooking, just like Maman used to make! A hotchpotch of mis-matching tables and chairs, chandeliers and assorted bric-a-brac in this bistro-cum-junk-shop. If you like your table, you can take it home for the right price!

Living (☎ 02 40 69 67 22; 32 rue Scribe; menus €17 & €28.50; ☺ lunch Tue-Fri, dinner Tue-Sat) Trendy, cavernous restaurant-bar buzzing with fashionable 30-something Nantoise. Surprisingly, the food is not so cutting-edge with standard, but well-presented French fare. Open til 2am Friday and Saturday.

Chez Le Gaulois (☎ 02 40 08 22 98; 8 rue de la Paix; mains €9.50-17; ☺ Mon-Sat) You can't get any more 'French carnivore' than this place with giant legs of ham hanging from the rafters and piles of *saucisson* just waiting to be scoffed. Specialities include *raclette*, fondue and *tartiflette*. Leave your vegetarian friends behind and bring a big appetite!

Kim Restaurant (☎ 02 40 35 18 40; 4 rue de la Juiverie; menus €10 & €15.50; ☺ Mon-Sat) Tasty Thai, Chinese and Vietnamese specialities are served at this popular place. Speedy service and pack-'em-in tables keeps the atmosphere lively and the prices reasonable.

Chez l'Huître (☎ 02 51 82 02 02; 5 rue des Petites Écuries; dishes €6-7.5; ☺ Mon-Sat) With oysters, smoked fish specialities and wine by the glass, this place is well worth a visit.

SELF-CATERING

The small **covered market** (place du Bouffay) and the huge **Marché de Talensac** (rue Talensac) are open until about 1pm (closed Monday).

There's also the **Monoprix supermarket** (2 rue du Calvaire; ☺ 9am-9pm Mon-Sat).

The massive **Galeries Lafayette department store** (rue de la Marne) has a basement **food section** (☺ 9am-7.30pm Mon-Sat).

Drinking

For the hard stuff, take your pick from the following bars.

Le Lieu Unique (see below) Super-hip bar in the arts centre. It hosts local and international DJs.

La Maison (☎ 02 40 37 04 12; 4 rue Lebrun; ☺ 3pm-2am) An hilarious send-up of a home furnished in very bad taste c 1970. This convivial bar plays mainly house music and is a perfect place for a chat (and is thus popular with loquacious students).

Le Violin Dingue (☎ 02 40 74 09 29; 1 rue Lebrun; ☺ 7.30pm-2am Tue-Sun) A mellow bar that often has live music from 8.30pm (diverse concerts cost around €5).

Le Petit Marais (☎ 02 40 20 15 25; 15 rue Kervégan; ☺ 6.30pm-4am Mon-Sat, 6pm-2am Sun) Friendly place with a mainly gay crowd. There are often concerts Thursday and Friday nights.

Entertainment

Listings of cultural events appear in *Nantes Poche* and *Pil'* (both €0.50). *Le Mois Nantais*, available at the tourist office and tobacconists, has day-by-day details of cultural events. What's-on websites include www.vivanantes.com in French. Tickets are available across the hall from the tourist office at the **Fnac billeterie** (ticket outlet; ☎ 02 51 72 47 23; ☺ 10am-8pm Mon-Sat).

The beautiful **Théâtre Graslin** (☎ 02 40 69 77 18; Place Graslin) is the home of the Nantes Opera. Recently refurbished and reopened, the venue hosts lavish productions in its stunning blue-seated auditorium.

Le Lieu Unique (☎ 02 40 12 14 34; www.lelieuunique.com in French; 2 rue de la Biscuiterie) is the city's wonderful industrial-chic-style concert venue, occupying the one-time Lu biscuit factory. This former artists squat offers dance and theatre performances, eclectic and electronic music, philosophical sessions and contemporary art. It also has a bar and restaurant.

NIGHTCLUBS

La Route du Rhum (☎ 02 40 74 48 57; quai Henri Barbusse; tram stop Motte Rouge; ☯ 8pm-4am Tue-Sun) This two-storey houseboat sitting around 1km northeast of the Monument des 50 Otages has jam sessions and concerts of blues, rock and reggae music.

L'Extrem' Club (☎ 02 28 00 11 46; 44 Bouaye, Les Landes Bigots; ☯ midnight-5am Fri-Sun) South of the Loire in Les Landes Bigots (about 10 minutes south by car from the chateau, in the direction of Pornic-Noirmoutier), is currently the area's hottest gay disco.

CINEMAS

The six-screen **Cinéma Katorza** (☎ 02 51 84 90 60; 3 rue Corneille) offers nondubbed films.

Getting There & Away

AIR

Aéroport Nantes-Atlantique International (☎ 02 40 84 80 00; www.nantes.aeroport.fr) is 12km southeast of town.

BUS

The southbound **bus station** (☎ 0 825 087 156), across from 13 allée de la Maison Rouge, is used by CTA buses serving areas of the Loire-Atlantique *département* south of the Loire River.

The northbound **bus office** (☎ 0 825 087 156; 1 allée Duquesne, on cours des 50 Otages), run by Cariane Atlantique, handles buses to destinations north of the Loire.

There's also a **Eurolines office** (☎ 02 51 72 02 03; allée de la Maison Rouge; ☯ 8am-6pm Mon-Fri, 8am-12.30pm Sat).

CAR

Budget, Europcar and Hertz have offices right outside the train station's southern entrance.

TRAIN

The **train station** (☎ 36 35; 27 blvd de Stalingrad) is well connected to most of France. Destinations include Paris' Gare Montparnasse (€49.10 to €61.40, 2¼ hours by TGV, 15 to 20 daily), Bordeaux (€37, four hours, three

or four daily) and La Rochelle (€21, 1¾ hours, three or four daily).

Tickets and information are also available at the **SNCF ticket office** (La Bourse, 12 place de la Bourse; ☯ 10am-7pm Mon, 9am-7pm Tue-Sat) in the city centre.

Getting Around

TO/FROM THE AIRPORT

A public bus known as TAN-Air links the airport with the Gare Centrale bus/tram hub and the train station's southern entrance (€6, 20 minutes) from about 5.30am (2pm Sunday) until 9pm. For information call **Allotan** (☎ 0 810 444 444).

BUS & TRAM

The **TAN network** (☎ 0 801 444 444; www.tan.fr in French), which has an **information office** (2 allée Brancas, place du Commerce; ☯ Mon-Sat), includes three modern tram lines that intersect at the Gare Centrale (Commerce), the main bus/tram transfer point. Buses run from 7.15am to 9pm. Night services continue until 12.30am.

Bus/tram tickets can be purchased individually (€1.20) from bus (but not tram) drivers and at tram stop ticket machines, and are valid for one hour after being time-stamped. A *ticket journalier*, good for 24 hours, costs €3.30; time-stamp it only the first time you use it.

CAR & MOTORCYCLE

There's free parking in the car park 200m east of the southbound bus station; in the car park across the street from the Médiathèque tram stop (except for the first few rows, marked *payant*); and south of the train station along the southern section of quai Malakoff.

TAXI

To order a taxi, call ☎ 02 40 69 22 22.

POITIERS

pop 120,000

Poitiers, the former capital of Poitou, is home to some of France's most remarkable Romanesque churches. It is not a particularly fetching city – it fits very tightly into its hilltop site – but the pedestrian-only shopping precinct has its charms.

In the year AD 732 somewhere near Poitiers (the exact site is not known), the cavalry of Charles Martel defeated the Muslim forces of Abd ar-Rahman, governor of Córdoba, thereby ending Muslim attempts to conquer France.

Orientation

The train station is about 600m west and down the slope from the old city and commercial centre, which begins just north of Poitiers' main square, place du Maréchal Leclerc, and stretches northeast to Église Notre Dame la Grande. Rue Carnot heads south from place du Maréchal Leclerc.

Information

Commercial **banks** can be found around place du Maréchal Leclerc.

Cybercafé Poitiers (☎ 05 49 39 51 87; www.cyber café-poitiers.fr in French; 171 Grand'Rue; per hr €5.50; ⏰ 10am-8pm Mon-Sat, 4-8pm Sun, to 10pm Jul & Aug) East of Église Notre Dame.

Post Office (21 rue des Écossais) Has a Cyberposte and changes money.

Tourist Office (☎ 05 49 41 21 24; accueil@ot-poitiers .fr; 45 place Charles de Gaulle; ⏰ 9.30am-7pm Mon-Sat, 10am-6pm Sun Jun-Sep; 10am-6pm Mon-Sat Oct-May) Near Église Notre Dame.

Sights

The Romanesque **Église Notre Dame la Grande** (place Charles de Gaulle; ⏰ 8.30am-7pm Mon-Sat, 2-5pm Sun) is in the pedestrianised old city. It dates from the 11th and 12th centuries, except for three of the five choir chapels (added in the 15th century) and all six chapels along the northern wall of the nave (added in the 16th century). The atrociously painted decoration in the nave is from the mid-19th century; the only original **frescoes** are the faint 12th- or 13th-century works that adorn the U-shaped dome above the choir. The celebrated **west façade** is beautifully decorated with three layers of stone carvings based on the Old and New Testaments. On summer evenings between late June and late September, the characters adorning the façade are colourfully illuminated.

At the northeastern end of rue Gambetta, the Palais de Justice (law courts) occupies a one-time palace of the counts of Poitou and the dukes of Aquitaine. Inside, you can visit the **Salle des Pas-Perdus** (⏰ 9am-6pm Jul & Aug, 8.45am-5.30pm Mon-Fri Sep-Jun), a vast, partly 14th-century hall with three huge fireplaces.

At the bottom of the street (500m east of Église Notre Dame la Grande), the vast, Angevin (or Plantagenet) Gothic-style **Cathédrale St-Pierre** (rue de la Cathédrale; ⏰ 8am-6pm) – so unlike its Gothic cousins to the north – was built from 1162 to 1271; the west façade and the towers date from the 14th and 15th centuries. At the far end of the choir, the stained-glass window of the Crucifixion and the Ascension is among the oldest in France.

Constructed in the 4th and 6th centuries on Roman foundations, **Baptistère St-Jean** (rue Jean Jaurès; admission €0.60; ⏰ 10.30am-12.30pm & 3-6pm Wed-Mon Apr-Oct, 2.30-4.30pm Wed-Mon Nov-Mar), a block south of the cathedral, was rebuilt in the 10th century and used as a parish church. The octagonal hole under the frescoes was used for total-immersion baptisms, practised until the 7th century. It now houses a museum of Merovingian sarcophagi (from the 5th to 7th centuries).

The worthwhile **Musée Ste-Croix** (☎ 05 49 41 07 53; www.musees-poitiers.org in French; 3 rue Jean Jaurès; adult/child €3.50/free; ⏰ 1.15-6pm Mon, 10am-noon & 1.15-6pm Tue-Fri, 10am-noon & 2-6pm Sat & Sun Jun-Sep; only to 5pm Mon-Fri & afternoons Sat & Sun Oct-May) is across the lawn from Baptistère St-Jean, and was built atop Gallo-Roman walls that were excavated and left *in situ*. It has exhibits on the history of Poitou from prehistoric times to the 19th century. Admission here also affords access to the **Musée Rupert de Chièvre** (☎ 05 49 41 07 53; 9 rue Victor Hugo; ⏰ same hours as Musée Ste-Croix), which displays furniture, paintings and art from the 19th century.

Sleeping

Other than a couple of unappealing places opposite the station, Poitiers is short on budget accommodation. A better option is to spend a bit extra on one of the decent mid-range options.

MID-RANGE

Hôtel de l'Europe (☎ 05 49 88 12 00; www.hotelde leuropepoitiers.com; 39 rue Carnot; s/d from €47.50/53; **P**) This charming hotel is worth more than its official two stars. The main building, dating from 1710, has a sweeping staircase, oversized rooms and pleasing older-style décor. The annex has modern rooms for the same price. Breakfast is served in the lovely garden room.

Hôtel du Plat d'Étain (☎ 05 49 41 04 80; hotelduplat detain@wanadoo.fr; 7-9 rue du Plat d'Étain; d with shower or bath & toilet €45-50; P) In a pedestrian street half a block north of place du Maréchal Leclerc (through the arch next to the theatre), is this cosy two-star hotel, next to a late-opening bar. Up three flights of narrow stairs, the tranquil third floor attic rooms look on to the adjacent church and across the town.

Le Grand Hôtel (☎ 05 49 60 90 60; www.grand hotelpoitiers.fr; 28 rue Carnot; s/d €65.50/80.50; P) Faux Art Deco furnishings and fittings give this three-star hotel character. The rooms, popular with business travellers, are spacious and well-equipped.

Eating & Drinking

The most promising area for dining is south of place du Maréchal Leclerc, especially rue Carnot. The Grand'Rue also has some good eateries.

La Serrurerie (☎ 05 49 41 05 14; 28 rue des Grandes Écoles; mains €10-14) This atmospheric, lively and hugely popular café *bistrot* does great meals and huge weekend brunches (€14). Temporary exhibitions showcase local art and sculpture.

La Joyeuse Marmite (☎ 05 49 88 14 59; 66 Grand' Rue; menu €10; ☺ lunch only Mon-Fri) A merry local bistro serving hearty lunch meals including wine. Just north of Place de la Cathédrale.

The **Marché Notre Dame** (☺ 7am-1pm Tue-Sat) is right next to Église Notre Dame la Grande. About 200m to the south, the **Monoprix supermarket** (☺ 9am-7.30pm Mon-Sat) is across from 29 rue du Marché Notre Dame (behind the Palais de Justice).

Bars and pubs can be found along rue Carnot and one block north of place du Maréchal Leclerc along rue du Chaudron d'Or.

Getting There & Away

The modern **train station** (☎ 0 836 353 535; blvd du Grand Cerf) has direct links to Bordeaux (€28.70, 1¾ hours), La Rochelle (€19.80, one hour 20 minutes), Tours (€16, one hour) and many other cities. TGV tickets from Paris' Gare Montparnasse (1½ hours, 12 daily) cost from €43. SNCF buses go to Nantes (€23, 3¼ hours).

AROUND POITIERS
Futuroscope

With striking domes, pods and towers rising from the French countryside like a James Bond movie set, **Futuroscope** (☎ 05 49 49 30 80;

www.futuroscope.com; Jaunay-Clan; adult/5-12 yrs Apr-Sep & weekends €30/22, Mon-Fri Oct-Mar €21/16; ☺ 10am-at least 10.15pm Apr-Sep, to 6pm Sun-Fri & to 10pm Sat Feb, Mar, Oct & Nov, closed mid-Nov–mid-Feb) is a unique cinema theme park whose 22 attractions make for a hugely entertaining day. There are evening lakeside **laser and firework shows** (Apr-Aug, Sat & Sun Mar-Nov) – as a result, closing times range from 6pm to 11pm. On show days, a ticket costs €15/9 if you arrive after 6pm. Allow a minimum of five hours to see all the major attractions or two days to see everything.

Attractions include **Cyberworld**, an action-packed 3D trip inside a computer with a Lara Croft-style cyber-guide. The journey features a dizzying array of spectacular 3D effects, plus a cameo appearance by the Pet Shop Boys. At **Cosmos**, board a spaceship for a journey through the solar system and beyond; back on planet earth, take a trip to the Rio Carnivale at **Couleurs Bresil**, where a 360° screen puts you in the heart of the action.

The films, which last four to 40 minutes, showcase the park's cinematic technological wizardry, so don't come expecting convincing acting or intelligent plots. A free infra-red headset lets you pick up soundtracks in English, German and Spanish.

Futuroscope is 10km north of Poitiers in Jaunay-Clan (take exit No 28 off the A10). TGV trains link the park's TGV station with Paris (€43.20, 1½ hours, three daily), Tours (€14.90, 30 minutes, three daily) and Bordeaux (€29.60, 1¾ hours, two to three daily).

Local **STP buses** (☎ 05 49 44 66 88) Nos 9, 16 and 17 (€1.30, 30 minutes) link Futuroscope (Parc de Loisirs stop) with Poitiers' train station (the stop in front of Avis car rental); there are one to two buses an hour from 6.15am until 7.30pm or 9pm.

Marais Poitevin

Known as Venise Verte (Green Venice) for its green waterways, the Marais Poitevin (*marais* means marsh) is a marvellous wetland, with a rich and varied birdlife. Part of the protected Parc Naturel Interrégional du Marais Poitevin, it covers a sprawling 80,000 hectares of wet marsh and drained marsh, interspersed with villages and woods.

The main modes of transport around the area are **canoeing** and **boating**. To rent a boat or bicycle, or to organise gîtes and *chambres* *d'hôtes* accommodation, contact **Venise Verte Loisirs** (☎ 05 49 35 43 34; www.veni severteloisirs.fr in French; 10 chemin du Charret, Arçais).

The main stepping stone to the Marais is Niort, 76km southwest of Poitiers, where there's a **tourist office** (☎ 05 49 24 18 79; 16 rue du Petit St-Jean). Niort station connects with Poitiers (€12.60, 50 minutes), and there are some bus services to villages – after that you need to explore by foot, boat or bike.

LA ROCHELLE
pop 120,000
The lively and increasingly chic port city of La Rochelle, midway down France's Atlantic coast, gets lots of tourists, especially in July and August, but most of them are of the domestic, middle-class variety: unpretentious families or young people out to have fun.

La Rochelle's focal point is the picturesque café- and restaurant-lined old port, which basks in the bright Atlantic sunlight by day and is grandly illuminated by night.

Despite a progressively more sophisticated feel, La Rochelle remains a great destination for families, with decent kid-friendly attractions and kilometres of fine-sand beaches on nearby Île de Ré.

History
La Rochelle was one of France's foremost seaports from the 14th to 17th centuries, and local shipowners were among the first to establish trade links with the New World. Many of the early French settlers in Canada, including the founders of Montreal, set sail from here in the 17th century.

During the 16th century, La Rochelle, whose spirit of mercantile independence made it fertile ground for Protestant ideas, incurred the wrath of Catholic loyalists, especially during the Wars of Religion. After the notorious St Bartholomew's Day Massacre of 1572, many of the Huguenots who survived took refuge here.

In 1627 La Rochelle – by that time an established Huguenot stronghold – was besieged by Louis XIII's forces under the personal command of his principal minister, Cardinal Richelieu. By the time they surrendered after 15 months of resistance, all but 1500 of the city's 20,000 residents had died of starvation. The city recovered slowly, but was dealt further blows by the revocation of the Edict of Nantes in 1685

and the loss of French Canada – and the right to trade with North America – to the English in 1763.

Orientation
La Rochelle is centred around the Vieux Port (Old Port), to the north of which lies the old city. The tourist office is on the southern side of the Vieux Port in an area of brightly-painted wooden buildings known as Le Gabut. The train station is linked to the Vieux Port by the 500m-long av du Général de Gaulle. Place du Marché and place de Verdun are at the northern edge of the old city.

The university campus is midway between the Vieux Port and the seaside neighbourhood of Les Minimes, 3km southwest of the city centre.

Information
BOOKSHOPS
Planète Bleue (☎ 05 46 34 23 23; 41 rue des Merciers)

EMERGENCY
Hôtel de Police (police station; ☎ 05 46 51 36 36; 2 place de Verdun; ⊗ 24hr)
Médecins d'Urgence (emergency doctors; ☎ 05 46 67 33 33)

INTERNET ACCESS
Cyber Club (☎ 05 49 76 76 76; 20 rue Cordouan; per hr €6; ⊗ noon-8pm Mon-Tue, noon-2am Wed-Sat, 2-8pm Sun)

MONEY
In the old city, there are a number of banks on rue du Palais. The post office also has exchange services.

POST
Post Office (6 rue de l'Hôtel de Ville) Has exchange services and a Cyberposte.

TOURIST INFORMATION
Tourist Office (☎ 05 46 41 14 68; http://larochelle -tourisme.com or www.ville-larochelle.fr; Le Gabut; ⊗ 9am-8pm Mon-Sat, 11am-5.30pm Sun Jul & Aug; 9am-7pm Mon-Sat, 11am-5pm Sun Jun & Sep; 9am-6pm Mon-Sat, 10am-1pm Sun Oct-May)

Sights & Activities
To protect the harbour at night and defend the city in times of war, an enormous chain used to be stretched between the two

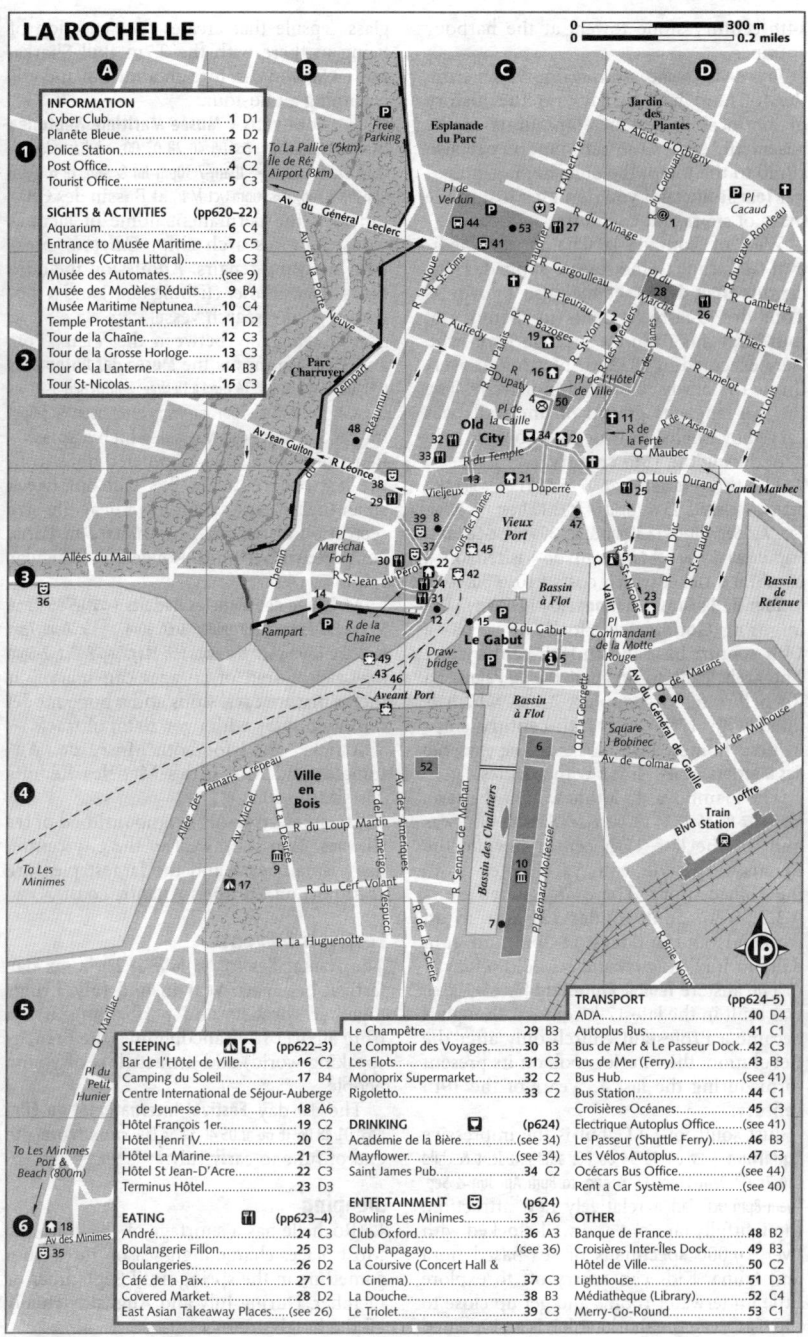

LA ROCHELLE

0 _____ 300 m
0 _____ 0.2 miles

INFORMATION
Cyber Club.............................1 D1
Planète Bleue.........................2 D2
Police Station.........................3 C1
Post Office.............................4 C2
Tourist Office.........................5 C3

SIGHTS & ACTIVITIES (pp620–22)
Aquarium...............................6 C4
Entrance to Musée Maritime.......7 C5
Eurolines (Citram Littoral).........8 C3
Musée des Automates..............(see 9)
Musée des Modèles Réduits.......9 B4
Musée Maritime Neptunea........10 C4
Temple Protestant...................11 D2
Tour de la Chaîne....................12 C3
Tour de la Grosse Horloge........13 C3
Tour de la Lanterne.................14 B3
Tour St-Nicolas......................15 C3

Jardin
des
Plantes

Free
Parking

Esplanade
du Parc

To La Pallice (5km);
Île de Ré;
Airport (8km)

Pl de
Verdun

Pl
Cacaud

Old
City

Pl de
la Caille

Vieux
Port

Bassin
à Flot

Le Gabut

Bassin
de
Retenue

Canal Maubec

Bassin
de
Retenue

Aveant Port

Bassin
à Flot

Ville
en
Bois

Train
Station

To Les
Minimes

To Les
Minimes
Port &
Beach (800m)

ATLANTIC COAST

TRANSPORT (pp624–5)
ADA.......................................40 D4
Autoplus Bus..........................41 C1
Bus de Mer & Le Passeur Dock...42 C3
Bus de Mer (Ferry)..................43 B3
Bus Hub...............................(see 41)
Bus Station............................44 C1
Croisières Océanes...................45 C3
Electrique Autoplus Office.......(see 41)
Le Passeur (Shuttle Ferry)........46 C3
Les Vélos Autoplus..................47 C3
Océcars Bus Office.................(see 44)
Rent a Car Système.................(see 40)

SLEEPING (pp622–3)
Bar de l'Hôtel de Ville.............16 C2
Camping du Soleil...................17 B4
Centre International de Séjour-Auberge
de Jeunesse...........................18 A6
Hôtel François 1er...................19 C2
Hôtel Henri IV.........................20 C2
Hôtel La Marine.......................21 C3
Hôtel St Jean-D'Acre...............22 C3
Terminus Hôtel.......................23 D3

EATING (pp623–4)
André....................................24 C3
Boulangerie Fillon...................25 D3
Boulangeries...........................26 D2
Café de la Paix.......................27 C1
Covered Market......................28 D2
East Asian Takeaway Places.....(see 26)

Le Champêtre.........................29 B3
Le Comptoir des Voyages.........30 B3
Les Flots...............................31 C3
Monoprix Supermarket.............32 B3
Rigoletto................................33 C2

DRINKING (p624)
Académie de la Bière............(see 34)
Mayflower............................(see 34)
Saint James Pub......................34 C3

ENTERTAINMENT (p624)
Bowling Les Minimes................35 A6
Club Oxford...........................36 A3
Club Papagayo.....................(see 36)
La Coursive (Concert Hall &
Cinema)................................37 C3
La Douche.............................38 B3
Le Triolet..............................39 C3

OTHER
Banque de France....................48 B2
Croisières Inter-Îles Dock.........49 C3
Hôtel de Ville........................50 C2
Lighthouse............................51 C3
Médiathèque (Library).............52 C4
Merry-Go-Round......................53 C1

14th-century stone towers at the harbour entrance.

Tour de la Chaîne affords fine views from the top and has displays on the history of the local Protestant community in the basement. Across the harbour you can also climb to the top of the 36m-high, pentagonal **Tour St-Nicolas** if you don't get lost in the maze of stairs and corridors.

West of Tour de la Chaîne, the medieval wall leads to the steeple-topped, 15th-century **Tour de la Lanterne**, also known as Tour des Quatre Sergents in memory of four sergeants from the local garrison who were executed in 1822 for plotting to overthrow the newly reinstated monarchy. The English-language graffiti on the walls was carved by English privateers who were held here during the 18th century.

The three **towers** (☎ 05 46 34 11 81; admission per tower adult/18-25 yrs/child €4.60/3.10/free; ☾ 10am-7pm Apr-Sep, 10am-12.30pm & 2-5.30pm Tue-Sun Oct-May, closed during holidays) can be visited on a combined ticket costs €10/6.50.

Tour de la Grosse Horloge (Quai Duperré), the imposing Gothic-style clock tower, has a 14th-century base and an 18th-century top. The arch leads to arcaded **rue du Palais**, La Rochelle's main shopping street, which is lined with 17th- and 18th-century shipowners' homes. Two blocks to the east, **rue des Merciers** is also lined with arcades.

The Flamboyant Gothic wall of the **town hall** (☎ 05 46 41 14 68; place de l'Hôtel de Ville) was built in the late 15th century, while the Renaissance-style courtyard dates from the 16th century. There are guided tours (€3/1.50 for adults/under 12) at 3pm on weekends and holidays; at 3pm and 4pm daily in July, August and school holidays.

The austere **Temple Protestant** (2 rue St-Michel) was built in the late 17th century, though it became a Protestant church only after the Revolution; the interior took on its present form during the last 75 years of the 19th century.

Just south of Le Gabut is the impressive **Aquarium** (☎ 05 46 34 00 00; adult/student & child €10/7; ☾ 9am-11pm Jul & Aug, to 8pm Apr-Jun & Sep, 10am-8pm Oct-Mar) a relatively new attraction, thoughtfully laid-out and well-stocked with over 10,000 specimens of sea-based flora and fauna. Kids can scurry off to explore little underwater rooms and get up close to the fish; even the shark tank has an indented

glass capsule that creates the sensation of being in there with the 2.7m Bull Sharks. For €3.50 you can hire an amusing and entertaining audio-tour.

The innovative **Musée Maritime Neptunea** (Maritime Museum; ☎ 05 46 28 03 00; adult/student & child €7.60/5.30; ☾ 10am-7.30pm Jul & Aug, til 6.30pm Apr-Jun & Sep, 2-6.30pm Oct-Mar) at Bassin des Chalutiers is the permanent home of Jacques Cousteau's research ship, *Calypso*, presently awaiting repairs. Admission includes tours of a *chalutier* (fishing boat) and a meteorological research vessel.

About midway between the Vieux Port and Les Minimes is the **Musée des Automates** (☎ 05 46 41 68 08; 14 rue La Désirée; adult/child 3-10 yrs €6.50/4; ☾ 9.30am-7pm Jun-Aug; 10am-noon & 2-6pm Feb-May, Sep & Oct; 2-6pm Nov-Jan), which displays – in action – some 300 automated dolls from the last two centuries. It's laid out like a small theme park, including a near-life-size recreation of bygone Montmartre in Paris, complete with Moulin Rouge and funicular railway.

At **Musée des Modèles Réduits** (☎ 05 46 41 64 51; rue La Désirée; adult/under 10 €6.50/4; ☾ 9.30am-7pm Jun-Aug; 10am-noon & 2-6pm Feb-May, Sep & Oct; 2-6pm Nov-Jan), children of all ages can marvel at the miniature cars, ships and a huge model railway display with over 200m of track.

A ticket good for both Musée des Automates and Musée des Modèles Réduits costs €10/5.50.

The modern resort neighbourhood of **Les Minimes**, 3km southwest of the city centre, has a small **beach** and the largest pleasure craft port on Europe's Atlantic coast.

Festivals & Events

The **Francofolies** (☎ 05 46 28 28 28), a six-day festival held each year in mid-July, brings together vocalists and performing artists from all over La Francophonie (the French-speaking world) and attracts lots of young people.

The 10-day **Festival International du Film** (☎ 01 48 06 16 66 or 05 46 51 54 00) runs from the end of June to early July.

Sleeping

La Rochelle has a shortage of cheap hotels. Most places charge high-season rates from sometime in the spring until September or October. During July and August, virtually all the hotels are full.

BUDGET

Centre International de Séjour-Auberge de Jeunesse (☎ 05 46 44 43 11; fax 05 46 45 41 48; av des Minimes; bus No 10; dm/d with breakfast €13/32) This place is 2km southwest of the train station in Les Minimes. Check-in is possible from 8am to midnight.

Bar de l'Hôtel de Ville (☎ 05 46 41 30 25; 5 rue St-Yon; d from €32, with shower & toilet €39; 1-3-person studio per night/week €54/305) This busy nine-room hotel attached to the Bar de l'Hôtel de Ville represents the only budget accommodation in town. The simple rooms are popular with students on long-stays, so it's often difficult to bag a bed. The studio apartments are available only in July and August.

Camping

During the warmer months, dozens of camping areas open up around La Rochelle and on the Île de Ré, but most are full during July and August. The tourist office has a list of those outside the town.

Camping du Soleil (☎ 05 46 44 42 53; av Marillac; bus No 10; camping €16.65; ⊙ mid-May–mid-Sep) Nearest camping area to the city centre but it is often completely full.

MID-RANGE

Hôtel La Marine (☎ 05 46 50 51 63; www.hotel-marine .com in French; 30 quai Duperré; r May-Sep €70-95, Oct-May €59-75) This two-star hotel is in a fantastic location overlooking the port. Most rooms have recently been refurbished with neutral tones and designer furniture – rooms 1, 6, 9 and 13 stand out, with first class views.

Hôtel François 1er (☎ 05 46 41 28 46; www .hotelfrancois1er.fr; 15 rue Bazoges; d €50-85; P) Charming, quiet hotel with a cobbled courtyard entrance and traditionally furnished rooms. In the 15th and 16th centuries a number of French kings stayed in this building. It certainly has some king-size rooms, but you pay more for the extra space.

Terminus Hôtel (☎ 05 46 50 69 69; hotel.termi nus@tourisme-francais.com; 7 rue de la Fabrique; s/d from low season €39/47, high season €53/53) Near to the tourist office, this welcoming hotel has 32 comfortable rooms that vary in price depending on the season. Each room is named after one of the offshore islands; the bright, sunny ones at the front are the best. Access for disabled guests.

Hôtel St Jean-D'Acre (☎ 05 46 41 73 33; www .hotel-la-rochelle.com; 4 place de la Chaîne; r high/low

season from €65/60; 🖳) Situated near a cluster of good seafood restaurants, this modern three-star hotel has views of the port and the Tour de la Chaîne. Part of the Inter Hotel chain.

Hôtel Henri IV (☎ 05 46 41 25 79; henriIV@wanadoo .fr; 31 rue des Gentilshommes; d low/high season from €40/54, with shower & toilet €50/77) In a late-16th-century building in the middle of the pedestrianised old city.

Eating

According to locals, La Rochelle has so many restaurants, you could dine out every day of the year and never eat at the same place twice. Dozens of eateries can be found along the northern side of the Vieux Port, especially on quai Duperré, cours des Dames, rue de la Chaîne and rue St-Jean du Pérot. The place du Marché area has several inexpensive restaurants and pizzerias.

Café de la Paix (☎ 05 46 41 39 79; 54 rue Chaudrier; menus €14 & €19, children €8, mains €15-20; ⊙ 7am-9.30pm) This century-old place is a grand, atmospheric brasserie-bar with high, painted ceilings, gold-edged mirrors and all the traditional choices: beef, duck, foie gras and salads. Also a good spot for breakfast (€6.50) or afternoon tea.

Le Comptoir des Voyages (☎ 05 46 50 62 60; 22 rue St-Jean du Perot; menu €22, mains €11) A chic and ambient new place. The emphasis is on 'world food', meaning international flavours

---

AUTHOR'S CHOICE

André (☎ 05 46 41 28 24; 5 rue St-Jean du Perot; mains €12-22) Something of an institution, this restaurant has been serving up fresh seafood for more than 50 years. It started life as a small bar serving seafood; as its popularity grew, André began buying adjacent shops. There are now eight interconnecting rooms, each with its own individual ambience from traditional bistro to contemporary café to port-holed cabin. Each one is packed with fish-hungry punters, and in each the menu is the same – not just traditional dishes, but innovative creations like monkfish infused with mango and Indian spices (delicious) or the knock-out *cassate Charentaise* (regional fruit flan) both on the €35 menu. An exceptional dining experience.

(Madrid, Madras, Madagascar) but regional produce. The colourful food contrasts fittingly with the cool, understated design.

Le Champêtre (☎ 05 46 41 12 17; 22 rue Verdière; menu €22, mains around €12; ☺ dinner only from 7.30pm Tue-Sat) An unfussy and intimate little place away from the main restaurant strips, but worth seeking out. You'll find classic (mainly meat-based) French dishes and an enthusiastic patron.

Les Flots (☎ 05 46 41 32 51; 1 rue de la Chaîne; mains €12-22; ☺ closed dinner Sun) Serves up stylish seafood. Overlooks the port.

Rigoletto (☎ 05 46 41 05 00; 12-14 rue Chef de Ville; pizzas & pasta €6-9; ☺ closed dinner Sun) What more can we say – it's a busy pizzeria.

SELF-CATERING
The best place to pick up your own edibles is the lively, 19th-century **covered market** (place du Marché; ☺ 7am-1pm).

Food shops in the vicinity include two cheap East Asian **takeaway places** (4 & 10 rue Gambetta) and **boulangeries** (8 & 29 rue Gambetta).

In the old city, there's **Monoprix supermarket** (30-36 rue du Palais; ☺ 8.30am-8pm Mon-Sat) and **Boulangerie Fillon** (18 quai Louis Durand; ☺ 6am-10.30pm Mon & Thu, to 8pm Tue, to 1pm Sun, 6am-2am Fri & Sat).

Drinking
For *salon de thé* ambience, make for the beautifully traditional **Café de la Paix** (p623) where smart waiters will bring you any number of speciality teas.

During the day, the best place for a drink is around the port. For an evening tipple, there are three trusty drinking holes side by side in tiny cour Temple: the **Saint James Pub** (☎ 05 46 41 72 11), the **Mayflower** (☎ 05 46 50 51 39) and the cosy **Académie de la Bière** (☎ 05 46 41 03 44).

Entertainment
The discos **Club Oxford** and **Club Papagayo** (☎ 05 46 41 51 81 for both; admission with one drink €10; ☺ 11pm-5am Tue-Sun, plus Mon in Jul & Aug) are on the waterfront about 500m west of Tour de la Lanterne, dishing out a standard, eclectic French soundtrack. A newer, more trendy option in the area is **La Douche** (☎ 05 46 41 24 79; 14 rue Léonce; admission €10, free on Thu & Sun; ☺ 11pm-5am Thu-Sun) spinning house tunes to a mixed gay and straight crowd.

In the port area, **Le Triolet** (☎ 05 46 41 03 58; 8 rue des Carmes; ☺ 7pm-3am) is known as *le*

cool club for over 25s. There's a laid-back jazzy vibe earlier in the evening but the music gets livelier after 11pm when the disco kicks off.

In Les Minimes, **Bowling Les Minimes** (☎ 05 46 45 40 40; rue Trinquette; ☺ 10am-2am daily) is situated in an alley next to the youth hostel.

The two auditoriums of **La Coursive** (☎ 05 46 51 54 00; 4 rue St-Jean du Pérot; ☺ early Sep-late Jul) host concerts and nondubbed art films.

Getting There & Away
AIR
From **La Rochelle Airport** (☎ 05 46 42 30 26; www .larochelle.aeroport.fr in French; north of city centre off the N237) there are flights throughout France and to London Stansted (with Ryanair) and Southampton (with Flybe) in the UK.

BUS
The **bus station** and bus information offices are at place de Verdun. **Océcars** (☎ 05 46 00 95 15) runs services to regional destinations like Royan. See p626 for details on bus services to the island.

Eurolines ticketing is handled by **Citram Littoral** (☎ 05 46 50 53 57; 30 cours des Dames; ☺ closed Sat afternoon, Mon morning & Sun).

CAR
For rental, there's **ADA** (☎ 05 46 41 02 17; 19 av du Général de Gaulle) and **Rent A Car Système** (☎ 05 46 27 27 27; 27 av du Général de Gaulle).

TRAIN
The **train station** (☎ 0 836 353 535) is linked by TGV to Paris' Gare Montparnasse (€53.60, three hours, five or six direct daily). Other destinations served by direct trains include Nantes (€22, two hours, five or six daily), Poitiers (€19.80, 1½ hours, nine to 10 daily), Rochefort (€6.20, 20 minutes, five to seven daily) and Bordeaux (€22.60, two hours, five to seven daily).

Getting Around
BICYCLE
At **Les Vélos Autoplus** (☎ 05 46 34 02 22) you can hire a bike for free for the first two hours; after that the charge is €1 per hour. Child seats, but not bike helmets, are available for no extra charge. Bikes are available at the **Electrique Autoplus office** (☎ 05 46 34 84 58; place de Verdun; ☺ 7.30am-7pm Mon-Sat, 1-7pm Sun). From May to September, they can also be picked

up at the **Vieux Port** (across the street from 11 quai Valin).

BOAT
Autoplus' **Le Passeur** (€0.60; 7.45am-8pm, to 10pm Apr & May, to midnight Jul & Aug) is a ferry service that links Tour de la Chaîne with the Avant Port. It runs when there are passengers – just press the red button on the board at the top of the gangplank.

The ferry **Bus de Mer** (€1.50; €1.70 Jul & Aug), also run by Autoplus, links Tour de la Chaîne with Les Minimes (20 minutes). It runs daily April to September; at weekends and holidays only from October to March. Boats from the Vieux Port depart every hour on the hour (except at 1pm) from 10am to 7pm (every half-hour and until 11.30pm in July and August).

BUS
The innovative local transport system, **Autoplus** (☎ 05 46 34 02 22), has a main bus hub and **information office** (place de Verdun; 7am-7.30pm Mon-Sat). Most lines run until sometime between 7.15pm and 8pm. Tickets cost €1.20.

Bus No 21 runs from place Verdun to the train station, returning via the Vieux Port. No 10 links place de Verdun with the youth hostel and Les Minimes.

CAR & MOTORCYCLE
The **Electrique Autoplus office** (place de Verdun; see opposite) rents electric-powered motorcars €10/16 with a range of 50km for €10/16 per half-day/day. The deposit is €500.

There is free parking on the side streets north of place de Verdun; at esplanade des Parcs, which is a few hundred metres northwest of place de Verdun; and around Neptunea. There's an underground garage at place de Verdun.

Avoid the city centre, especially on market mornings (Wednesday and Saturday).

TAXI
Taxis can be ordered 24 hours a day on ☎ 05 46 41 55 55 or ☎ 05 46 34 02 22.

ÎLE DE RÉ
pop 16,000
This flat island, whose eastern tip is 9km west of the centre of La Rochelle, gets more hours of sunshine than any part of France away from the Mediterranean coast. In summer its many beaches and seasonal camping grounds are a favourite destination for families with young children; the water is shallow and safe and the sun is bright and warming, but less harsh than along the Mediterranean. Île de Ré can easily be visited as a day trip from La Rochelle.

Île de Ré's main town is the fishing port of St-Martin de Ré, on the northern coast about 12km from the toll bridge. In most of the island's villages, the houses are traditional in design: one- or two-storey whitewashed buildings with green shutters and red Spanish-tile roofs.

The Île de Ré boasts 70km of coastline, including 20km to 30km of fine-sand beaches. Most of the northern coast is taken up by mudflats and oyster farms. The island's western half curves around a bay known as the Fier d'Ars, which is lined with *marais salants* (salt evaporation pools), saltwater marshes and a nature reserve for birds, **Lilleau des Niges**.

There are virtually no budget hotels on the island. Every hotel and camping ground on the island is *totally* full from 14 July to 25 August.

ST-MARTIN DE RÉ
pop 2500
This picturesque little fishing village, which is entirely surrounded by 17th-century fortifications, is especially attractive when the white houses and sailboats are bathed in the bright coastal sun. You can stroll along most of the ramparts but the **citadel** (1681), which has been a prison for over two centuries is closed to the law-abiding public.

Information
In St-Martin, the **tourist office** (☎ 05 46 09 20 06; www.iledere.com; av Victor Bouthillier; 10am-1pm & 2-7pm, closes noon Sun Sep-Jun) is a block east of the port (across the street from the Rébus bus stop).

Sleeping
Hôtel de Sully (☎ 05 46 09 26 94; rue Jean Jaurès; r €32-45, Jul-Sep €39-48) Located 150m south of the port in a pretty pedestrian street, this reasonable one-star place is a cheap option with wood panelling and trippy '60s bathroom tiles. It's in an old, converted house so some of the rooms are very small.

ATLANTIC COAST

Hôtel du Port (☎ 05 46 09 21 21; iledere-hot
.port@wanadoo.fr; quai de la Poithevinière; d/q from €50/65,
Jul-Sep €60/90) A modern two-star hotel right
on the port with bright, spacious rooms.
The wonderful views from the north-facing
rooms are worth the extra outlay.

Hôtel la Jetée (☎ 05 46 09 36 36; info@hotel-lajetee
.com; 23 quai Georges Clemenceau; r €49-76, Jul-Sep €78-
99; **P**) A contemporary villa-style building
designed around a quiet courtyard. The
three-star hotel, at the eastern edge of the
port, has decent-sized doubles as well as
family rooms with a mezzanine level.

CAMPING

Camping Municipal (☎ 05 46 09 21 96; camping €14;
☼ Mar-mid-Oct) A grassy and shaded site situated a few hundred metres to the south of
the church. Pitching your tent anywhere
but in an official camping area is strictly
forbidden.

Eating

You can find touristy restaurants in the port
area. The friendly **Bistrot du Marin** (☎ 05 46 68
74 66; 10 quai Nicolas Baudin; mains €10-15) is a quaint,
bustling bar-*bistrot*.

In St-Martin, the **covered market** (rue Jean
Jaurès; ☼ 8.30am-1pm) is on the southern side
of the port with a cluster of **food shops** nearby, although it's much cheaper to buy food
in La Rochelle.

Beaches

The best beaches on the Île de Ré are
along the southern edge of the island (east
and west of La Couarde) and around the
western tip of the island (northeast and
southeast of Phare des Baleines). Near
Sablanceaux, there are sandy beaches along
the south coast towards Ste-Marie. Many
of the beaches are bordered by dunes that
have been fenced off to protect the vegetation. There's an unofficial **naturist beach** near
the outskirts of Les Portes; access is via the
Forêt du Lizay.

Getting There & Away

For automobiles, the bridge toll (paid on
your way *to* the island; nothing to leave) is
€9 (a whopping €16.50 from mid-June to
mid-September).

Year-round, excruciatingly slow buses
run by **Rébus** (☎ 05 46 09 20 15) link La Rochelle (the train station car park, Tour de

la Grosse Horloge and place de Verdun)
with all the major towns on the island. The
company also covers intra-island routes.

Getting Around

Cycling is an extremely popular way to get
around the island, which is flat and has an
extensive network of paved bicycle paths. A
biking map is available at tourist offices. In
summer practically every hamlet has somewhere to hire bikes.

At Sablanceaux, from mid-June to mid-
September, bikes can be hired at Cycland,
in a **kiosk** (☎ 05 46 09 97 54) in one of the little
buildings to the left as you come off the
bridge. It's best to call one to two days in
advance. The rest of the year, call **Cycland's
office** (☎ 05 46 09 65 27; www.cycland.fr in French) in
La Flotte and it'll deliver a bike to the bridge
in about 15 minutes. Bicycles/mountain
bikes/tandems cost €7/11.50/18 per day.

SOUTH OF LA ROCHELLE

The crescent-shaped **Île d'Aix** (pronounced
'eel day') is a 1.33-sq-km, car-free island
16km due south of La Rochelle, was fortified by Vauban and later used as a prison. It
has some very nice beaches and is served by
regular ferries from La Fumée (see opposite
for information on getting to La Fumée by
bus). **Fort Boyard**, built during the first half of
the 19th century, is an oval-shaped island/
fortress between the Île d'Aix and the **Île
d'Oléron** – the latter is a larger and less picturesque version of the Île de Ré. You can
travel to the Île d'Oléron from Rochefort
by bus.

Companies offering cruises include **Croisières Océanes** (☎ 05 46 50 68 44; cours des Dames, La
Rochelle), which has daily sailings from Easter
to early November.

About 30km southeast of La Rochelle,
Rochefort (population 25,500), founded as a
fortified town in the late 1600s has several
interesting museums and a good market
every Wednesday and Saturday. A guided
tour of the town leaves from the **tourist office** (☎ 05 46 99 08 60; av Sadi Carnot; ☼ 9am-8pm Jul
& Aug, 9am-12.30pm & 2-6pm Mon-Sat Oct-Mar) every
Thursday morning at 10am between May
and September.

In a central location, opposite the tourist
office, **Hôtel de France** (☎ 05 46 99 34 00; 55 rue du
Dr Peltier; s/d from €36/38) has standard chain-
hotel rooms at a good price.

Keolis Littoral buses (☎ 05 46 82 31 31) operates services to the Île d'Oléron and to La Fumée, from where there are ferries to the Île d'Aix. Rochefort is on the La Rochelle/Bordeaux train line.

About 40km south of Rochefort is **Royan** (population 16,800), flattened by Allied bombing in early 1945 and rebuilt after the war in the modernist style of the early 1950s. It's a good place to start a visit to the Médoc thanks to the ferry to Pointe de Grave (p638). Trains go to Cognac and, via Saintes, to Nantes and Bordeaux.

COGNAC

pop 19,500

Cognac, surrounded by rolling vineyards and quiet villages, is famed around the world for the double-distilled spirit that bears the town's name, and on which the local economy is based.

Orientation

The train station is on the southern edge of the town centre, while the four cognac distilleries mentioned below are on the other side of town, about 1.5km to the north, near the River Charente. Place François 1er, 200m northeast of the tourist office (follow rue du 14 Juillet), is linked to the river by blvd Denfert Rochereau.

Information

Cyber Espace (☎ 05 45 36 85 60; 68 blvd Denfert Rochereau; per hr €0.75; ☽ 2-6pm Mon-Fri) Internet access.
Post Office (2 place Bayard) ATM and currency exchange facilities.
Société Générale (33 rue Angoulême) With exchange facilities.
Tourist Office (☎ 05 45 82 10 71; www.tourism-cognac.com; 16 rue du 14 Juillet; ☽ 9am-7pm Mon-Sat, 10am-4pm Sun Jul & Aug; 9.30am-5.30pm Mon-Sat May, Jun & Sep; 10am-5pm Mon-Sat Oct-Apr) Can supply a town map.

Sights & Activities

The narrow streets of the **Vieille Ville** (Old City), between the partly Romanesque **Église St-Léger** (rue Aristide Briand) and the river, are lined with half-timbered 15th- to 17th-century buildings.

The **Musée de Cognac** (☎ 05 45 32 07 25; 48 blvd Denfert Rochereau; adult/student €2.20/1.20; ☽ 10am-6pm Jun-Sep, 2.30-5.30pm Wed-Mon Oct-May) has a varied collection that covers fine arts, local

---

THE PRODUCTION OF COGNAC

Cognac is made of grape *eaux de vie* (brandies) of various vintages, aged in oak barrels and blended by an experienced *maître de chai* (cellar master). Each year some 3% of the volume of the casks – *la part des anges* (the angels' share) – evaporates through the pores in the wood, nourishing the tiny black mushrooms that thrive on the walls of cognac warehouses.

---

folk traditions and, in the basement, Cognac production.

The Musée de Cognac is in the southern corner of the **Jardin Public** (Public Park). The small zoo is home to a few deer.

COGNAC HOUSES

The most famous cognac distilleries offer tours of their *chais* (cellars; pronounced 'shay') and production facilities, that end with a tasting session. Reservations are only necessary for groups.

Camus (☎ 05 45 32 28 28; www.camus.fr; 29 rue Marguerite de Navarre) is 250m northeast of the Jardin Public. From June to September, 1¾-hour tours (adult/child €5/free) begin at 9.45am, 10.45am, 1.45pm, 2.30pm, 3.15pm and 4pm daily. In May and October, tours begin at 10.45am, 2.30pm and 4pm on weekdays.

The informative tours (adult/student/child €4/2/free) of the sprawling **Martell complex** (☎ 05 45 36 33 33; place Édouard Martell), 250m northwest of the tourist office, last one hour and are sometimes in English. June to September, tours run from 9.30am to 6pm daily, last tour at 5pm; October to May, tours run on weekdays (except Friday afternoon) at 9.30am, 11am, 2.30pm, 3.45pm and 5pm. Call to check times for foreign-language tours.

The **Château de Cognac** (127 blvd Denfert Rochereau), 650m north of place François 1er, was the birthplace in 1494 of King François I and has been home to **Otard** (☎ 05 45 36 88 86; www.otard.com) since 1795. From April to October, the well-conducted, one-hour tours (adult/12 to 18 years, €5/2.50) with commentary available in seven languages begin at 10am, 11am, 2pm, 3pm, 4pm and 5pm daily. Phone in advance to find out when English tours are scheduled, and for all tours between December and March.

ATLANTIC COAST

The 1¼-hour tours (adult/student and child €6/free) of the **Hennessey facility** (☎ 05 45 35 72 68; 8 rue Richonne), 100m up the hill from quai des Flamands, which runs along the river, include a film (in English) and a boat trip across the Charente to visit the cellars. June to September they run every half-hour daily from 10am to 6pm; March to December, they begin every 45 minutes from 10am to 5pm. Private tours with fancier tastings cost €17 to €30.

The tourist office can supply you with a list of smaller cognac houses near town; most are closed from October to mid-March. **Rémy Martin** (☎ 05 45 35 76 66; www.remy.com) is a few kilometres southwest of town towards Pons. One-hour mini-train tours (adult/12 to 18 years €6/3) run from April to October (except Sunday in April and October). English tours usually leave at 3.30pm, but it is strongly advised to ring in advance to reserve tours.

Sleeping

Hôtel d'Orléans (☎ 05 45 82 01 26; fax 05 45 82 20 33; 25 rue d'Angoulême; d €42; **P**) A wonderful, rambling 17-century house in the heart of the pedestrianised district which, despite a splash of paint and a few recent improvements, hasn't lost any of its charm. Even the staircase is listed as a historic monument.

Hôtel Le Cheval Blanc (☎ 05 45 82 09 55; www.hotel-chevalblanc.fr; 6 place Bayard; s/d/tr €41/46/53; **P**) You'll get a friendly welcome at this efficiently-run two-star place, 100m west of the tourist office. Although the rooms here aren't huge, they are spotlessly clean and well-equipped. There's also a vending machine stocked with miniature bottles of cognac, for those midnight cravings! Access for disabled guests.

Hôtel François 1er (☎ 05 45 32 07 18; www.hotel-francois1er.com; 3 place François 1er; d/twn with shower €44/51; **P**) Occupying a lovely mid-19th century building in central Cognac, this three-star hotel has spacious, renovated rooms with high ceilings and wooden floors.

Eating

There are a number of restaurants and bars to be found in the immediate vicinity of place François 1er and the tourist office.

La Belle Époque (see Hôtel d'Orléans, p628; mains €12-15; ☪ lunch Mon-Sat, dinner Tue-Sat) Like Hôtel d'Orléans to which this restaurant belongs,

there's a fading, atmospheric grandeur here, enhanced by the slow ceiling fans, sweeping wooden bar and background jazz. The traditional French food on the menu is also served in the shady courtyard.

La Boune Goule (☎ 05 45 82 06 37; 42 allée de la Corderie; mains €5-11; ☪ May-Sep, Mon-Sat Oct-Apr), across the square from the Martell complex, offers local Charentaise dishes at reasonable prices.

SELF-CATERING

There is an **Ecofrais supermarket** (32 place Bayard; ☪ 9am-12.30pm & 3-7.30pm Mon-Fri, 8am-noon Sun) opposite the post office. About 300m to the north of place François 1er, the **covered market** (57 blvd Denfert Rochereau; open until 1pm) is just across from the Musée de Cognac.

The friendly and informative **Cognathèque** (☎ 05 45 82 43 31; 10 place Jean Monnet; ☪ 9am-7pm) sits 100m from the tourist office. Over 250 different cognacs costing up to €1500 a bottle are available.

Getting There & Away

Cognac's **train station**, at the southern end of av du Maréchal Leclerc, is on the line that links Angoulême with Royan (40 minutes). There are daily trains to/from La Rochelle (€13.80, 1¼ hours).

BORDEAUX

pop 735,000

Bordeaux is buzzing. Long known as *La Belle Au Bois Dormant* (Sleeping Beauty), the city developed a reputation as a dull place with neglected buildings and a chronic lack of urban planning or infrastructure. The then controversial ex-Prime Minister Alain Juppé became mayor. With his blunt, no-nonsense approach he pushed through massive investment in the city; buildings were cleaned, traffic-choked roads pedestrianised, squares re-paved and trees planted. A state-of-the-art tram system was built and plans were drawn up for the redevelopment of the run-down riverside areas. Such sweeping changes have been causing major disruption for several years but at last, the work is nearly finished, and a new, reinvigorated Bordeaux is emerging as one of the country's finest cities. Against a backdrop of neoclassical architecture, wide avenues and pretty parks, the city boasts excellent museums, a vibrant nightlife, an ethnically diverse population and a lively university community.

History
About 100km from the Atlantic at the lowest bridging point on the Garonne River, Bordeaux was founded by the Romans in the 3rd century BC. From 1154 to 1453, the city prospered under the rule of the English, whose fondness for the Bordeaux region's red wine – known across the Channel as claret – provided the impetus for the eventual creation of Bordeaux's international reputation for quality wines.

Orientation
The city centre lies between place Gambetta and the 350m- to 500m-wide Garonne, which is usually a muddy brown as it flows either towards the sea or inland, depending on the tides. From place Gambetta, place de Tourny is 500m northeast, and the tourist office is 400m to the east.

The train station, Gare St-Jean, is in a seedy area about 3km southeast of the city centre. Cours de la Marne stretches from the train station to place de la Victoire, which is linked to place de la Comédie by the long and straight pedestrianised shopping street, rue Ste-Catherine.

Information
BOOKSHOPS
Bradley's Bookshop (☎ 05 56 52 10 57; 8 cours d'Albret; 🕑 9.30am-12.30pm & 2-7pm Tue-Sat, 2-7pm Mon)
Librairie Mollat (☎ 05 56 56 40 40; 15 rue Vital Carles; 🕑 9.15am-7pm Mon-Sat)

INTERNET ACCESS
Cyberstation (☎ 05 56 01 15 15; 23 cours Pasteur; 🕑 9.30am-2am Mon-Sat, 2pm-2am Sun; per hr €3)
NetZone (☎ 05 57 59 01 25; 209 rue Ste-Catherine; 🕑 9.30am-midnight; per hr €3)
Tribal (☎ 05 56 92 99 22; 71 cours Pasteur; 🕑 8.30am-7.30pm Mon-Thu, 8.30am-7pm Fri, 9.30am-6pm Sat; per hr €4.60)

LAUNDRY
There is a full-service laundrette at 31 rue du Palais Gallien, which is open 8am to 9pm, while self-service options are at 32 rue des Augustins, 5 rue de Fondaudège and 8 rue Lafaurie de Monbadon. These are open 7am to 9pm.

MEDICAL SERVICES & EMERGENCY
Hôpital St-André (☎ 05 56 79 56 79; 1 rue Jean Burguet) 24-hour casualty ward.
Police Station (☎ 05 56 99 77 77; 29 rue Castéja; 🕑 24hr)

MONEY
Banks offering currency exchange can be found near the tourist office on cours de l'Intendance, rue de l'Esprit des Lois and cours du Chapeau Rouge.
American Express (☎ 05 56 00 63 36; 11 cours de l'Intendance; 🕑 9am-noon & 1.30-5.30pm Mon-Fri Apr-Sep, to 5pm Mon-Fri Oct-Mar, plus 9.30am-12.30pm Sat Jun-Sep)

POST
Main Post Office (37 rue du Château d'Eau) Currency exchange and Cyberposte.
Post Office (43 place Gambetta; 🕑 10am-7pm Mon & Thu, 9am-7pm Tue, Wed, Fri, 9am-5pm Sat) Extended hours here.
Post Office (place St-Projet)

TOURIST INFORMATION
Maison du Tourisme de la Gironde (☎ 05 56 52 61 40; www.tourisme-gironde.cg33.fr in French; 21 cours de l'Intendance; 🕑 9am-6pm Mon-Fri, to 7pm Apr-Oct, 10am-1pm & 2-6.30pm Sat) For brochures on Gironde *département*.

MUSEUM PRICES & PASSES
The municipal museums in Bordeaux, which include Musée d'Art Contemporain (CAPC), Musée d'Histoire Naturelle, Musée des Arts Décoratifs, Musée des Beaux-Arts and Musée d'Aquitaine, are free to those under 18 and students holding a valid student card. They're also free for everyone on the first Sunday of each month.

The admission for adult/concession is €4/2.50 for each museum's permanent collections and €5.50/3 for temporary exhibits. Concession prices refer to people over the age of 60 or under 25 (though sometimes under 25s can enter free, even without a student card).

The municipal **Carte Pass** is €15.25 and is valid for 10 admissions into the eight municipal museums – those mentioned above, plus the Centre Jean Moulin, the Musée Goupil and the Jardin Botanique – great value for museum buffs.

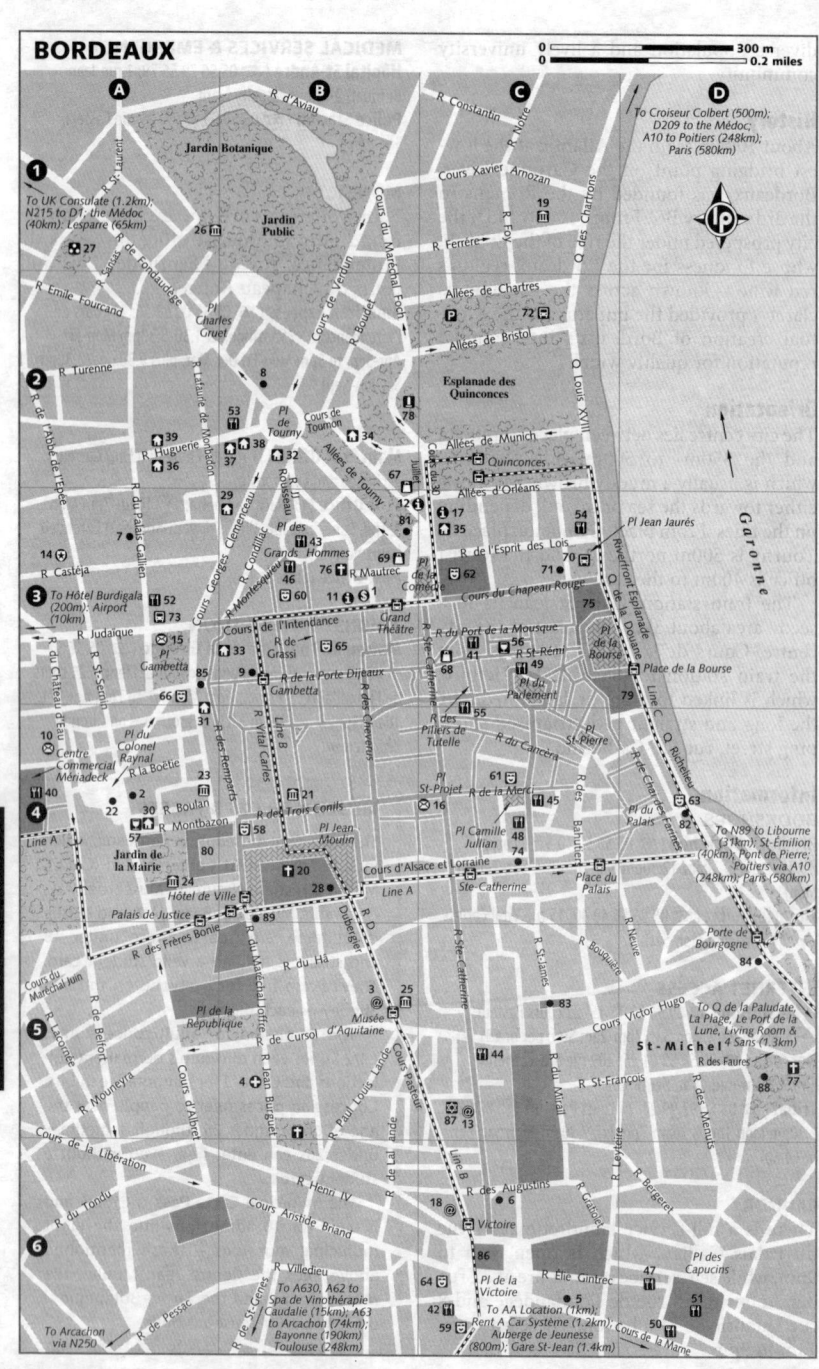

BORDEAUX

INFORMATION
American Express..............................1 B3
Bradley's Bookshop...........................2 A4
Cyberstation....................................3 B5
Hôpital St-André................................4 B5
Laundrette...................................(see 29)
Laundrette..5 C6
Laundrette..6 C6
Laundrette..7 A3
Laundrette..8 B2
Librairie Mollat..................................9 B3
Main Post Office..............................10 A4
Maison du Tourisme de la Gironde....11 B3
Maison du Vin de Bordeaux...............12 B3
Net Zone...13 C5
Police Station...................................14 A3
Post Office (extended hours)............15 A3
Post Office......................................16 C4
Tourist Office..................................17 C3
Tribal...18 C6

SIGHTS & ACTIVITIES   (pp631-2)
CAPC Musée d'Art Contemporain......19 C1
Cathédrale St-André..........................20 B4
Centre National Jean Moulin..............21 B4
École du Vin................................(see 12)
Galerie des Beaux-Arts......................22 A4
Musée des Arts Décoratifs..................23 A4
Musée des Beaux-Arts........................24 A4
Musée d'Aquitaine............................25 B5
Musée d'Histoire Naturelle.................26 A1
Palais Gallien...................................27 A1
Tour Pey-Berland..............................28 B4

SLEEPING   (pp632-4)
Hôtel Balzac.....................................29 B3
Hôtel Boulan....................................30 A4

Hôtel Bristol.....................................31 A4
Hôtel de Famille................................32 B2
Hôtel de la Tour Intendance................33 B3
Hôtel de Sèze....................................34 B2
Hôtel des 4 Soeurs.............................35 C3
Hôtel Excelsior.................................36 A2
Hôtel Studio.....................................37 B2
Hôtel Touring...................................38 B2
La Maison du Lierre...........................39 A2

EATING   (p634)
Auchan Supermarket..........................40 A4
Bodega Bodega.................................41 C3
Cassolette Café.................................42 C6
Champion Supermarket......................43 B3
Champion Supermarket......................44 C5
Claret's..45 C4
Fromagerie......................................46 B3
Fruit & Vegie Stalls...........................47 D6
La Petite Brasserie............................48 C4
Le Bistrot d'Édouard.........................49 C3
Le Fournil des Capucins.....................50 D6
Marché des Capucins.........................51 D6
Restaurant Agadir.............................52 A3
Restaurant Baud et Millet...................53 B2
Restaurant Jean Ramet......................54 C3
Taj Mahal..55 C4

DRINKING   (pp634-5)
Bodega Bodega...........................(see 41)
Café Brun...56 C3
Connemara......................................57 A4

ENTERTAINMENT   (p635)
Bar de l'Hôtel de Ville.......................58 B4
Box Office...................................(see 68)
Café des Sports................................59 C6

Centre Jean Vigo...............................60 B3
Cinéma Utopia..................................61 C4
Grand Théâtre..................................62 C3
La Reine Carotte...............................63 D4
Le Plana..64 C6
Théâtre Femina.................................65 B3
Virgin Megastore Billeterie................66 A3

SHOPPING   (p636)
Bordeaux Magnum.............................67 B2
Galerie Bordelaise.............................68 C3
L'Intendant.....................................69 B3

TRANSPORT   (pp636-7)
Bus Hub...70 B3
CGFTE Bus Information Office............71 C3
Halte Routière (Bus Station)...............72 C3
Jet'Bus (Airport Bus)........................73 A3
Le 63...74 C4

OTHER
Bourse du Commerce..........................75 C3
Église Notre Dame.............................76 B3
Église St-Michel................................77 D5
Girondins Fountain-
 Monument.....................................78 B2
Hôtel de la Douane............................79 D3
Hôtel de Ville...................................80 A4
Merry-Go-Round................................81 B3
Porte Cailhau...................................82 D4
Porte de la Grosse Cloche...................83 C5
Porte des Salinières..........................84 D5
Porte Dijeaux....................................85 A3
Porte d'Aquitaine..............................86 C6
Synagogue.......................................87 C5
Tour St-Michel..................................88 D5
Tribunal de Grande Instance...............89 B4

Tourist Office (☎ 05 56 00 66 00; www.bordeaux
-tourisme.com; 12 cours du 30 Juillet; ⊙ 9am-7.30pm
Mon-Sat Jul & Aug, to 7pm May & Jun, to 7pm Sep & Oct,
9.30am-6.30pm Sun May-Oct; 9am-6.30pm Mon-Sat,
9.45am-4.30pm Sun Nov-Apr) Right next to the tram stop
Comédie. Ask here about the *Passport Gourmand* (€50),
which offers reductions on restaurants, activities and
some museums and is worth considering if you're staying
a while in Bordeaux. The *Plan Guide du Patrimoine* (€1),
has information on the city's architectural heritage and
suggests two walking itineraries.
Tourist Office Annexe (⊙ 9am-noon & 1-6pm Mon-
Sat, 10am-noon & 1-3pm Sun May-Oct; 9.30am-12.30pm
& 2-7pm Mon-Fri Nov-Apr) At the train station.

Sights

The sights mentioned appear pretty much
from north to south.

The **Croiseur Colbert** (☎ 05 56 44 96 11; adult/
student & child €7.30/5.80; ⊙ 10am-7pm Jun-Aug;
10am-6pm Mon-Fri, 10am-6pm Sat & Sun Apr, May & Sep;
10am-6pm Wed, Sat, Sun & school holidays Oct-Mar), a
180m-long French navy missile cruiser,
was in service from 1957 to 1991. It is now
docked at quai des Chartrons, (500m north
of the Musée d'Art Contemporain) and offers a glimpse of life aboard a battleship.

Entrepôts Lainé was built in 1824 as a
warehouse for the rare and exotic products
of France's colonies (such as coffee, cocoa,

peanuts and vanilla). Its capacious spaces
now house the **CAPC Musée d'Art Contemporain**
(Museum of Contemporary Art; ☎ 05 56 00 81 50; Entrepôt
7, rue Ferrére; ⊙ 11am-6pm Tue, Thu-Sun, to 8pm Wed,
closed Mon). Most of the exhibits and installations that the museum hosts are temporary,
presenting major artistic movements over
the last 30 years.

The beautifully landscaped **Jardin Public**
(cours de Verdun), established in 1755 and laid
out in the English style a century later,
includes the meticulously catalogued **Jardin Botanique** (☎ 05 56 52 18 77; admission free;
⊙ 8.30am-6pm), founded in 1629 and at this
site since 1855; and the **Musée d'Histoire
Naturelle** (Natural History Museum; ☎ 05 56 48 29
86; ⊙ 11am-6pm Mon & Wed-Fri, 2-6pm Sat & Sun).
There's a **children's playground** on the island.

Nearby, off rue de Fondaudège, is the
city's most impressive Roman site, **Palais Gallien** (rue du Dr Albert Barraud; adult/under 12 €1.50/free;
⊙ 3-7pm Jun-Sep), the ruins of a 3rd-century
amphitheatre.

The most prominent feature of **esplanade
des Quinconces**, a vast square laid out in 1820,
is the fountain monument to the Girondins,
a group of moderate, bourgeois National Assembly deputies during the French Revolution, 22 of whom were executed in 1793 after
being convicted of Counter-Revolutionary

ATLANTIC COAST

activities. The entire 50m-high ensemble, completed in 1902, was dismantled in 1943 by the Germans so the statues could be melted down for their 52 tonnes of bronze. Restoration took years and was not completed until 1983.

The 4km-long **riverfront esplanade** is gradually being redeveloped as part of the town's facelift. The section just north of esplanade des Quinconces is the first to benefit, featuring a park with trees, playgrounds and bicycle paths. However, the six lanes of traffic that clog up adjacent Quai Louis XVIII mean that this spot isn't as peaceful as it might be.

Nowadays, **place Gambetta** is an island of greenery in the midst of the city centre's hustle and bustle, but during the Reign of Terror that followed the Revolution, a guillotine placed here severed the heads of 300 alleged counter-revolutionaries.

A few blocks south of place Gambetta, the **Musée des Arts Décoratifs** (Museum of Decorative Arts; ☎ 05 56 00 72 50; 39 rue Bouffard; museum ♥ 2-6pm Wed-Mon, temporary exhibits from 11am Mon-Fri) specialises in faïence, porcelain, silverwork, glasswork, furniture and the like.

The **Musée des Beaux-Arts** (☎ 05 56 10 20 56; 20 cours d'Albret; ♥ Wed-Mon 11am-6pm) occupies two wings of the Hôtel de Ville (city hall) complex (built in the 1770s); between them is a verdant public park, the **Jardin de la Mairie**. Founded in 1801 the museum has a large collection of paintings, including Flemish, Dutch and Italian works from the 17th century and a particularly important work by Delacroix. At nearby place du Colonel Raynal, the museum's annexe, the **Galerie des Beaux-Arts**, hosts short-term exhibitions.

In 1137 the future King Louis VII married Eleanor of Aquitaine in **Cathédrale St-André** (☎ 05 56 81 26 25; admission free; ♥ 10-11.30am & 2-6.30pm Mon, 7.30-11.30am & 2-6pm Tue-Fri, 9-11.30am & 2-7pm Sat, 8am-12.30pm Sun, but 2.30-5.30pm 1st Sun of month), now a Unesco World Heritage Site. The exterior wall of the cathedral's nave dates from 1096; most of the rest of the structure was built in the 13th and 14th centuries. Renovation of the north portal has uncovered fantastic carvings under centuries of grime. Behind the choir, the 50m-high belfry, 15th-century **Tour Pey-Berland** (adult/student/child €4.60/3.10/free; ♥ 10am-midday & 2-6pm) has a panoramic view at the top of 232 narrow steps.

The outstanding **Musée d'Aquitaine** (Museum of Aquitaine; ☎ 05 56 01 51 00; 20 cours Pasteur; ♥ 11am-6pm Tue-Sun) presents 25,000 years of Bordeaux's history and ethnography. Exceptional artefacts include several stone carvings of women and a collection of Gallo-Roman steles, statues and ceramics. The English-language catalogue is worth borrowing at the ticket counter (€1.50 deposit).

Activities
WINE-TASTING & -BATHING
For many visitors, Bordeaux is all about wine; tasting it, drinking it, and of course buying it. To get the most out of your visit, consider enrolling at the **Ecole du Vin** (☎ 05 56 00 22 88; http://ecole.vins-bordeaux.fr; 3 cours du 30 Juillet) at the Maison du Vin de Bordeaux. Introductory two-hour courses are available in English between June and September (€20), but to really develop your nose and impress dinner-party guests with your knowledge of vinification, sign up for a more extensive three- to four-day course (from €375). The courses offer an entertaining introduction to the techniques and vocabulary of tasting and wine-making. Chateaux visits are included to test your new skills.

If you've over-indulged in the local produce, try bathing in it! At the **Spa de Vinothérapie Caudalie** (☎ 05 57 83 83 83; www.sources -caudalie.com; Chemin de Smith Haut Lafitte, Martillac) you can benefit from the blood-strengthening, anti-ageing effects of vine and grape extracts. Take a red-wine bath, enjoy a Merlot wrap or order a Cabernet body scrub. It's 20 minutes south of Bordeaux next to Chateau Smith Haut Lafitte. Leave the A62 at junction 1.

Tours
The tourist office runs a range of guided tours, including a two-hour bilingual **walking tour** of the city (adult/senior or student €6.50/6) at 10am daily. From mid-April to mid-November the tours on Wednesday and Saturday are only by bus.

The tourist office also offers two-hour, bilingual 'Introduction to Wine Tasting' courses (adult/senior or student €20/17) every Thursday at 4.30pm (and on Saturday from mid-July to mid-August).

Sleeping
Budget and mid-range options are plentiful and competitive, but there's a dearth of

good top-end accommodation in town. The quality of rooms (particularly in the budget category) can vary enormously, sometimes even within the same hotel, so have a look before you sign up.

BUDGET

Most of the decent budget accommodation is in the area just west of place de Tournay. If possible, don't stay in the seedy area around the train station.

Auberge de Jeunesse (☎ 05 56 33 00 70; fax 05 56 33 00 71; 22 cours Barbey, annexe at 208 cours de l'Argonne; dm €16/17.50 HI member/nonmember incl breakfast; 🖳) Unexpectedly flash for a youth hostel, this place is ultra-modern, well-equipped and open 24 hours. There's a café-bar, kitchen, laundry and facilities for the disabled. All the rooms are dorms, but most are for just four people or less, so you won't have to share your digs with hundreds of smelly-footed students. Take bus No 7/8 to the Meunier stop.

Hôtel Boulan (☎ 05 56 52 23 62; fax 05 56 44 91 65; 28 rue Boulan; s/d €20.25/23.50, with shower €28.25/28.50) Tucked away in a quiet side-street, but still handy for many of the sights (and the Connemara bar!) this friendly place has rooms of a good standard for this price.

Hôtel Excelsior (reception at Hôtel Studio; see below) A better option than its sister hotel up the road. The simple, functional rooms here have all had a lick of paint and are larger and brighter than those at Hôtel Studio, although facilities and prices are identical.

Hôtel de Famille (☎ 05 56 52 11 28; fax 05 56 51 94 43; 76 cours Georges Clemenceau; s & d €18-22, with shower, toilet & TV €29-36) A variety of ordinary but homey rooms. There's no lift, so the higher your room, the cheaper (and smaller) it is. Light sleepers beware – there's no double-glazing.

Hôtel Studio (☎ 05 56 48 00 14; www.hotel-bordeaux.com; 26 rue Huguerie; d/tw/tr €22.80/24.40/27.50; P 🖳) This is the headquarters of Bordeaux's cheap hotel empire – the same family owns at least seven other hotels in town. This particular establishment is a bit dark and stuffy with decrepit rooms. On the upside, a shower, telephone and TV (with a couple of English channels) are all included in the cheap price. A better option from the same owners is the Excelsior, a few doors up the road. The hotel's Internet café charges guests €1.50 per hour.

Hôtel Balzac (☎ 05 56 81 85 12; 14 rue Lafaurie de Monbadon; s/d with shower & toilet €28/31) This is another budget priced option worth trying.

Hôtel Touring (☎ 05 56 81 56 73; le-touring@wanadoo.fr; 16 rue Huguerie; s/d with shower & toilet €36.90/40.30) Don't be put off by the dodgy '70s wallpaper – this place is an excellent deal. The 12 older-style rooms have comfortable beds and sturdy dark-wood furniture; those on the first floor are especially spacious.

MID-RANGE

La Maison du Lierre (☎ 05 56 51 92 71; www.maisondulierre.com; 57 rue Huguerie; s/d €63/73; P) Occupying a sympathetically restored townhouse with a beautiful Bordeaux stone staircase and a pretty courtyard for breakfast in summer, this delightful hotel has a relaxed and friendly *chambre d'hôte* feel. The 12 mid-sized rooms are nicely decorated with warm colours and parquet floors; four rooms have balconies.

Hôtel des 4 Soeurs (☎ 05 57 81 19 20; http://4soeurs.free.fr; 6 cours du 30 Juillet; s/d from €60/70; ✕ ✕ 🖳) An appealing three-star hotel in a great location with the tourist office, Maison du Vin and Grand Theatre all right on the doorstep. The very comfortable rooms boast extras such as hairdryers and English-language TV channels and some overlook place de la Comédie.

Hôtel Bristol (☎ 05 56 81 85 01; www.hotel-bordeaux.com; 14ter place Gambetta; r €32-46) An attractive two-star option from the Hôtel Studio group in a central location overlooking place Gambetta. The 27 cheerful and well-equipped rooms are priced according to size. All have showers, toilets, TVs, mini-bars and all-important double-glazing.

Hôtel de Sèze (☎ 05 56 52 65 54; hotelsezmedoc@aol.com; 7 rue de Sèze; s/d from €46/53; P) A charming three-star hotel occupying an elegant 18th-century building with 69 individually styled rooms. Some rooms are worn, but it serves to enhance the character of this place.

Hôtel de la Tour Intendance (☎ 05 56 44 56 56; fax 05 56 44 54 54; 14-16 rue de la Vieille Tour; s/d with shower & toilet €68/78; P). This place is usually a very good two-star option.\

TOP END

Hôtel Burdigala (☎ 05 56 90 16 16; www.burdigala.com; 6 cours du 30 Juillet; traditional/superior/ste from €170/200/370; P ✕ ✕ 🖳) A modern, four-star hotel, this is Bordeaux's best bet for top-end comfort, although there's nothing particularly special about it. The standard rooms, although comfortable, are a bit pokey. The larger suites are of questionable design, with red leather sofas a big feature. Wheelchair friendly.

Eating

Bordeaux has some excellent restaurants, many of which offer reasonably priced lunch *menus*. There's a good choice of places along rue St-Remi and in the streets to the south including place du Parlement and rue du Pas St Georges. There are also many inexpensive cafés and restaurants around place de la Victoire, an area that's hugely popular with students.

There's a cluster of sandwich joints around the top end of rue Ste-Catherine and along rue du Palais Gallien.

Claret's (☎ 05 56 01 21 21; 46 rue du Pas St Georges; lunch menu €10, dinner menus €16-20; 🕓 closed Sat lunch & Sun) A chic little venue on place Camille-Jullian offering an interesting selection of southwestern French and Japanese specialities. Despite the sleek wood-toned décor and smooth service, the prices here are very reasonable. In the immediate vicinity there are a number of other intimate restaurants and trendy terrace cafés.

Cassolette Café (☎ 05 56 92 94 96; www.cassolette café.com in French; 20 place de la Victoire; cassolette - 5 choices - €10.50, lunch menu €8.50, dinner menu €10.50; 🕓 noon-midnight) Extremely popular and great value, this is the place to come for hearty French family-style cooking. You order your menu or the ingredients of your *cassolette* (casserole cooked on a terracotta plate) using a check-off form and your choices appear promptly. Weekend nights have been known to get a bit rowdy with song-singing students, but it's all good fun.

Le Bistrot d'Édouard (☎ 05 56 81 48 87; 16 place du Parlement; menus €11-20; 🕓 lunch & dinner) The great-value three-course menu at €11 keeps this *bistrot* packed. Outside tables are in a calming spot by the fountain in place du Parlement. If you can't get a table here, try next door at L'Ombrière. It's run by the same owners and has an identical menu.

La Petite Brasserie (☎ 05 56 52 19 79; 43 rue du Pas St Georges; menus €25/35; 🕓 Wed-Sun) An unpretentious place offering fine brasserie-style dining in a relaxed and cosy atmosphere. The traditional bordelaise cuisine, extensive wine list and attentive service all get top marks.

Taj Mahal (☎ 05 56 51 92 05; 24 rue du Parlement Ste Catherine; lunch menu from €9.50, dinner menu from €16) Sitting on exquisite carved teak chairs, being served by waiters wearing traditional *shalwar kameez*, feasting on authentic dishes from India and Pakistan; you'll think you've been transported to the subcontinent.

Restaurant Baud et Millet (☎ 05 56 79 05 77; 19 rue Huguerie; menus €22.10-26.70; 🕓 11am-midnight Mon-Sat) For something a bit different, try this unusual, well-respected eatery with over 250 different cheeses on offer and almost as many international wines lining the walls. The mostly vegetarian cuisine includes an all-you-can-eat cheese buffet *(raclette)* for €18.50. The same street is home to a number of other reasonably priced eateries.

Restaurant Jean Ramet (☎ 05 56 44 12 51; jean. ramet@free.fr; 7 place Jean Jaurès; lunch menu €28, dinner menus €45 & €56; 🕓 Tue-Sat) This very formal establishment is a classy choice serving traditional *gastronomique* French and Bordelais cuisine amid mirrors, white tablecloths and sparkling tableware.

Other places you might like to try:

Restaurant Agadir (☎ 05 56 52 28 04; 14 rue du Palais Gallien; couscous €12-17)

Bodega Bodega (☎ 05 56 01 24 24; 4 rue des Piliers de Tutelle; 🕓 noon-3.15pm & 7pm-2am Mon-Sat, 7pm-2am Sun). Tapas bar, see opposite.

SELF-CATERING

A few blocks east of place de la Victoire is **Marché des Capucins** (🕓 6am-1pm Tue-Sun), a one-time wholesale market. Nearby rue Élie Gintrec has super-cheap **fruit and vegie stalls** on weekdays and Saturday until 1pm or 1.30pm.

Champion supermarket (place des Grands Hommes; 🕓 8.30am-7.30pm Mon-Sat) is in the basement of the Marché des Grands Hommes. Nearby, you'll find a fine **fromagerie** (2 rue Montesquieu; 🕓 closed Mon morning & Sun), while there's another **Champion supermarket** (190 rue Ste-Catherine; 🕓 8.30am-8pm Mon-Sat).

Auchan supermarket (opposite 58 rue du Château d'Eau; 🕓 8.30am-10pm Mon-Sat) is a vast, cheap place in the Centre Commercial Mériadeck.

Le Fournil des Capucins (62-64 cours de la Marne), near place de la Victoire, is a bakery that never closes.

Drinking

Connemara (☎ 05 56 52 82 57; 18 cours d'Albret; 🕓 noon-2am) Popular with both locals and expats, this lively Irish bar gets absolutely packed on major sporting occasions. Get there early to bag a seat in front of the big screen. There's also darts, pool and regular live music as well as pub food.

Bodega Bodega (☎ 05 56 01 24 24; 4 rue des Piliers de Tutelle; noon-3.15pm & 7pm-2am Mon-Sat, 7pm-2am Sun) Two floors of tapas, tunes and trendy types; this is the biggest and best Spanish bar in town. Mind your head on the giant hams hanging up above the bar when you order a drink.

Café Brun (☎ 05 56 52 20 49; 45 rue St-Rémi; 10am-2am) This bar-bistro with a warm atmosphere and cool jazz is great for an evening aperitif.

Entertainment

Bordeaux has a really vibrant nightlife scene; details of events appear in *Bordeaux Plus* and *Clubs & Concerts* (www.clubsetconcerts.com in French), both free and available at the tourist office. The fortnightly *Spectaculaire*, €0.50 at newsstands, lists music, cinema, theatre and dance events.

Student nightlife is centred around place de la Victoire, which can be somewhat seedy at night.

Tickets for events such as concerts and bullfights can be purchased from the **Virgin Megastore billeterie** (☎ 05 56 56 05 55; 17place Gambetta; 10am-7.30pm Mon-Thu, 10am-9.30pm Fri & Sat, 3-6.30pm Sun) or the **Box Office** (☎ 05 56 48 26 26; Galerie Bordelaise).

NIGHTCLUBS & LIVE MUSIC

For zoning reasons, many of the city's late-late dance venues are a few blocks northeast of Gare St-Jean along the river, on quai de la Paludate (just south of the railway bridge) and perpendicular rue du Commerce. Most places are not huge clubs but bars with DJs and dancing. Bouncers can be selective but there's normally no cover charge.

Le Port de la Lune (☎ 05 56 49 15 55; portdelalune@wanadoo.fr; 58 quai de la Paludate; 7pm-2am) Jazz club and bistrot. A dark, smoky and atmospheric place in the best jazz tradition. The large venue hosts live jazz virtually every night while the restaurant with tables either in the main room or in the quieter room next door offers seasonal menus (€18 to €20).

La Plage (☎ 05 56 49 02 46; 40 quai de la Paludate; 11pm-5am Wed-Sat) Popular local DJs serve up a mix of banging house and techno tunes to a happy crowd of 20- to 30-somethings. The tropical beach theme adds to the fun. Don't forget your sun-tan lotion.

Café des Sports (5 cours de l'Argonne) If you've had a big feed at the Cassolette Café next door, it's just a short stagger to get the drinks in at this lively student hang-out. Beer on tap, football on the telly.

4 Sans (☎ 05 56 49 40 05; 40 rue Armagnac; international/local acts €5-10/free; from midnight Thu-Sat) Trendy night club featuring top-notch local and international house, techno and drum 'n' bass DJs.

Living Room (☎ 05 56 85 71 85; 14 rue du Commerce; midnight-5am) If staying in is the new going out, this is a comfortable home from home. The cosy oriental-lounge décor (lots of rugs and couches) and techno/house sound attracts a slightly older crowd.

Le Plana (☎ 05 56 91 73 23; 22 place de la Victoire; 7am-2am Mon-Sat, 2pm-2am Sun) A lively, animated student hang-out. Except in July and August, it has live jazz every Sunday at about 10.30pm, and concerts (ranging from rock to funk and soul, some of them jam sessions) at 10.30pm Monday to Wednesday.

GAY & LESBIAN VENUES

Bar de l'Hôtel de Ville (☎ 05 56 44 05 08; 4 rue de l'Hôtel de Ville; 6pm-2am) It's often very busy and there's a spirited 95% gay crowd at this bar. Shows are held on some Sundays.

La Reine Carotte (☎ 05 56 01 26 68; 32 rue du Chai des Farines; 7pm-2am Tue & Sat) This is a mellow place attracting a clientele that's about 50% lesbian.

CLASSICAL MUSIC

Except in August and September, the 18th-century **Grand Théâtre** (☎ 05 56 00 85 95; place de la Comédie) stages operas, ballets and concerts of orchestral and chamber music; there's a **ticket office** (11am-6pm Tue-Sat). For the operettas, plays, dance performances and variety shows held at **Théâtre Femina** (10 rue de Grassi), there is a ticket office in the nearby **Galerie Bordelaise** (☎ 05 56 48 26 26; 10am-7pm Tue-Sat, 2-7pm Mon).

CINEMAS

Nondubbed films are screened at two art-house cinemas, **Centre Jean Vigo** (☎ 05 56 44 35 17; 6 rue Franklin), and the popular, five-screen **Cinéma Utopia** (☎ 05 56 52 00 03; 3 place Camille Jullian).

Shopping

The main shopping artery is the 1.2km **rue Ste-Catherine**, reputed to be the longest pedestrianised shopping street in Europe.

Galerie Bordelaise, a 19th-century shopping arcade, is at the intersection of rue de la Porte Dijeaux and rue Ste-Catherine.

The city's luxury shopping district, formed by the Allée de Tourny, Cours Georges Clemenceau and Cours de l'Intendance, is called **le triangle d'or** (the golden triangle).

Bordeaux wine in all price ranges is on sale at several speciality shops near the tourist office, including **Bordeaux Magnum** (☎ 05 56 48 00 06; 3 rue Gobineau; ☉ 10am-7.30pm Mon-Sat) and **L'Intendant** (☎ 05 56 48 01 29; 2 Allée de Tourny; ☉ 10am-7.30pm).

There are antique shops along rue Bouffard, near the Musée des Arts Décoratifs.

Getting There & Away

AIR

Bordeaux airport (☎ 05 56 34 50 50; www.bordeaux.aeroport.fr) is in Mérignac, 10km west of the city centre. In addition to domestic services operated by Air France, Ryanair (www.ryanair.com) has regular flights from the UK and low-cost Dutch airline Basiq Air (www.basiqair.com) fly from Amsterdam. A taxi from the airport into town costs €15 to €20.

BUS

Buses to places all over the Gironde (and parts of nearby *départements*) leave from the **Halte Routière** (bus terminal; allées de Chartres), in the northeast corner of esplanade des Quinconces; schedules are posted. For details on buses to the Médoc see p638 and St-Émilion see p641. **Citram Aquitaine** runs most buses to destinations in the Gironde and has an **information kiosk** (☎ 05 56 43 68 43; ☉ 1-8pm Mon-Fri, 9am-1.30pm & 5-8pm Sat) at the Halte Routière.

Eurolines (☎ 05 56 92 50 42; 32 rue Charles Domercq; ☉ Mon-Sat) faces the train station.

CAR

The big boys have offices in the train station building, all the way to the left as you exit. Inexpensive rental companies close to the train station:

AA Location (☎ 05 56 92 84 78; 185 cours de la Marne; ☉ Mon-Sat) About 400m from the station.

Rent A Car Système (☎ 05 56 33 60 75; 204 cours de la Marne; ☉ Mon-Sat)

TRAIN

Bordeaux is one of France's most important rail transit points. The station, **Gare St-Jean**, is about 3km from the city centre at the southern terminus of cours de la Marne. Be extra-careful with your bags here.

Destinations from Bordeaux include Paris' Gare Montparnasse (€58.90, three hours, at least 16 daily), Bayonne (€24.40, 1¾ hours, eight daily), Nantes (€37, four hours, five or six daily), Poitiers (€28.70, 1¾ hours, nine daily), La Rochelle (€22.50, two hours, five to seven daily) and Toulouse (€27.70, two to three hours, nine to 14 daily).

Getting Around

TO/FROM THE AIRPORT

The train station and place Gambetta are connected to the airport (single/return €6.50/11, 35 minutes, every 45 minutes at the weekend) by **Jet'Bus** (☎ 05 56 34 50 50) from 5.30am until 9.30pm (last departure from the airport 10.45pm). The trip takes approximately 45 minutes; much more if there are traffic jams.

BICYCLE

Le 63 (☎ 05 56 51 39 41, 06 74 82 27 62; 63 cours d'Alsace et Lorraine; ☉ 24hr) rents out bicycles (€3/14/18 for one/eight/24 hours) and *go-ped* motorised scooters (€15/45 per hour/day).

BUS

Bordeaux's urban buses are run by **CGFTE** (Allo Bus; ☎ 05 57 57 88 88). The company has Espace Bus information/ticket offices at the train station, place Gambetta (4 rue Georges Bonnac).

The train station is linked with the city centre by bus Nos 7 and 8; line No 1 runs along the waterfront from the train station north to Le Croiseur Colbert and beyond. Single tickets (€1.15), sold on board, are *not* valid for transfers. The Bordeaux Découverte card, available at the tourist office, allows unlimited travel for one/three/six days (€3.60/8.30/11.80). Time-stamp it only the first time you use it.

There are night bus services on nights when big shows and sporting events take place at the Grand Théâtre, Palais des Sports and Théâtre Femina. On weekends, night buses run on line S11, between place de la Victoire and the night-club zone on quai de la Paludate.

CAR
Parking in the city centre is hard to find and pricey. Places to look for free spaces include the side streets north of the Musée d'Art Contemporain and west of the Jardin Public. Many hotels provide parking for around €6 to per night. There are large parking lots to the north of esplanade des Quinconces and opposite place de la Bourse.

TAXI
To order a taxi call ☎ 05 56 99 28 41.

TRAM
The first section of the new tramway system, Line A, opened in December 2003. It starts at the Mériadeck shopping centre to the west of the city centre, and continues east along cours d'Alsace et Lorraine before crossing the river and continuing 10km eastwards to the suburb of Cenon. Another two lines were due to open as this book went to press. Line B will start at esplanade des Quinconces, heading south to place de la Victoire and on to the university. Line C will link esplanade des Quinconces with the train station via the riverside.

When the service is fully operational, trams will run every 10 minutes between 5am and 1am. Purchase a ticket (€1.15) from the machine at your tram stop and stamp it on board. Découverte cards are also valid on the trams.

BORDEAUX WINE-GROWING REGION
The 1000-sq-km wine-growing area around the city of Bordeaux is, along with Burgundy, France's most important producer of top-quality wines. The region is divided into 57 appellations (production areas whose soil and microclimate impart distinctive characteristics on the wine produced there) that are grouped into seven *familles* and subdivided into a hierarchy of designations (eg *premier grand cru classé,* the most prestigious) that often vary from appellation to appellation.

The majority of the region's many wines – reds, rosés, sweet and dry whites and sparkling wines – have all earned the right to include the abbreviation AOC (Appellation d'Origine Contrôlée) on their labels, indicating that the contents have been grown, fermented and aged according to strict regulations governing such matters as the number of vines permitted per hectare and acceptable pruning methods.

Bordeaux has over 5000 chateaux (also known as *domaines, crus* or *clos*), a term that in this context refers not to palatial residences but rather to the properties where grapes are raised, picked, fermented and then matured as wine. The smaller chateaux sometimes accept walk-in visitors, but at many places, especially the better-known ones, you have to make advance reservations by phone. Many chateaux are closed during the *vendange* (grape harvest) in October.

Information
In Bordeaux, the **Maison du Vin de Bordeaux** (☎ 05 56 00 22 88; 3 cours du 30 Juillet; ⏰ 8.30am-4.30pm Mon-Fri), across the street from the tourist office, can supply you with a free, colour-coded map of production areas, details on chateau visits, and the addresses of local *maisons du vin* (tourist offices that deal mainly with winery visits).

Tours
On Wednesday and Saturday (daily from May to October) at about 1.30pm, the Bordeaux tourist office runs five-hour bus tours in French and English to wine chateaux in the area (adult/student/child under 12 €26/23/11.50). From May to October all-day trips (adult/student/child €47/40/23.50) to wine chateaux, starting with a tour and lunch in Bordeaux, begin at 9.15am on Wednesday and Saturday.

More information on winery tours appears on p640.

THE MÉDOC
Northwest of Bordeaux, along the western shore of the Gironde Estuary – formed by the confluence of the Garonne and Dordogne Rivers – lie some of Bordeaux's most celebrated vineyards. To the west, fine-sand beaches, bordered by dunes and *étangs* (lagoons), stretch for some 200km from Pointe de Grave south along the **Côte d'Argent** (Silver Coast) to the Bassin d'Arcachon and beyond; seaside resorts include **Soulac-sur-Mer** (see later), **Carcans Plage, Lacanau-Océan** and **Cap Ferret**. The coastal dunes abut a vast pine forest planted in the 19th century to stabilise the drifting sands and prevent them from encroaching on areas further inland.

Getting There & Away

The northern tip of the Médoc, Pointe de Grave, is linked to Royan by **car ferries** (☎ 05 46 38 35 15; one-way person/bicycle/motorcycle/car €3/1.50/9.40/20; 25min) that run six times daily in winter and every 45 minutes in summer. The service runs until sometime between 6.30pm and 8.30pm (7.15pm and 9.30pm from Royan), depending on the season.

There is another **car ferry** (☎ 05 57 42 04 49; one-way person/bicycle/car/motorcycle €3/1.50/12/7) linking Lamarque (between Pauillac and Margaux on the D2) with Blaye, running five to 10 times daily (every 1½ hours June to September). This service starts around 7.30am and ends between 6.30pm and 8pm (until 9pm Saturday and Sunday June to September).

Citram Aquitaine buses (☎ 05 56 43 68 43) link Bordeaux with Margaux (€5.70, 50 minutes), Pauillac (€8.60, 1½ hours), Lesparre Médoc (€11.40, 1½ hours), Soulac-sur-Mer (€13.30, two hours) and Point de Grave (€13.30, 2¼ hours).

Soulac is also linked to Bordeaux by train (€13.60, two hours, change at Lesparre, four daily) and SNCF buses (€13.80, two hours, two to five daily).

To reach the Médoc by car from Bordeaux, take exit (sortie) 7 to get off the Bordeaux Rocade (ring road).

Pauillac & Médoc Wine Information Centre

While Pauillac is a fairly unremarkable port town by the banks of the muddy Gironde, it is at the heart of the wine country, surrounded by the distinguished Haut-Médoc, Margaux and St-Julien appellations. The Pauillac wine appellation encompasses 18 crus classés including the world-renowned Mouton Rothschild, Latour and Lafite Rothschild.

The Pauillac tourist office houses the **Maison du Tourisme et du Vin** (☎ 05 56 59 03 08; www .pauillac-medoc.com; ◷ 9am–7pm Jul–mid-Sep; 9.30am-12.30pm & 2-6.30pm Jun & mid-Sep–Nov; 9.30am-12.30pm & 2-6pm Mon-Sat, 10.30am-12.30pm & 3-6pm Sun Dec-May), an excellent centre for information about the Médoc region. They can also make appointments (for €3.90) to visit specific wine cellars, and have information on the many chambres d'hôtes (B&Bs) in the area. A good resource available here is the Médoc Guide Découverte brochure, which lists chateaux and how to visit them.

Vineyards & Chateaux

The gravelly soil of the Médoc's gently rolling hills supports orderly rows of meticulously tended grape vines (mainly Cabernet Sauvignon) that produce some of the world's most sought-after red wines. The most beautiful part of this renowned wine-growing area is north of Pauillac, along the D2 and the D204 (towards Lesparre). To the north, the vines give way to evergreen forests.

Chateaux in the Pauillac appellation that welcome visitors by appointment include the beautifully landscaped **Château Lafite Rothschild** (☎ 05 56 73 18 18; www.lafite.com; admission free; ◷ Mon-Fri Nov-Jul), famed for its premier grand cru classé, and whose free, bilingual, one-hour tours (including a tasting session) take place on weekdays; and the equally illustrious **Château Mouton Rothschild** (☎ 05 56 73 21 29; fax 05 56 73 21 28; ◷ daily Apr-Nov, Mon-Fri Jan-Dec), whose tours, frequently in English, cost €5 (more including a tasting session). Both places require you to make advance reservations.

About 20km to the south in Margaux, you can visit the celebrated **Château Margaux** (☎ 05 57 88 83 83; www.chateau-margaux.com; ◷ 10am-noon & 2-4pm Mon-Fri Sep-Jul). It is closed during the grape harvest.

Château Palmer (☎ 05 57 88 72 72; www.chateau -palmer.com), on the D2, 3km south of Margaux in Issan, has one-hour tours (€5) including tastings on weekdays (daily from April to September). Again, both chateaux require advance reservations.

Soulac-sur-Mer
pop 2800

Soulac, which is 9km south of Pointe de Grave and 90km north of Bordeaux, is a lively seaside resort in summer and an almost dead seaside town the rest of the year. The beach, fronted by a promenade, is wide and safe. The mellow waves here are ideal for learning to surf; a variety of courses are offered by **Soulac Surf School** (reservations through the tourist office) between April and October.

ORIENTATION & INFORMATION

The commercial centre is along pedestrianised rue de la Plage, which runs perpendicular to the beach. The train station is 700m south of the town's Romanesque church, buried by drifting dunes in 1757 and dug out a century later.

The **tourist office** (☎ 05 56 09 86 61; www.sou
lac.com; 68 rue de la Plage; 🕑 9am-7pm Jul & Aug; 9am-
12.30pm & 2-5.30pm Mon-Fri, 10am-12.30pm & 3-5.30pm
Sat Sep-Jun; plus 10am-12.30pm & 3-5.30pm Sun during Apr-Jun & school holidays), is across from the
marché municipal (a covered food market that
opens every morning).

The **post office** (rue du Maréchal d'Ornano), which
does currency exchange, is one block northeast of the tourist office.

SLEEPING & EATING

Ask at the tourist office about furnished
villa rental. Rooms and camping grounds
are always full in July and August.

Hôtel L'Hacienda (☎ 05 56 09 81 34; www.logis
-gironde.com in French; rue des Lacs; r in winter/summer
€42/58) The amiable, multilingual couple
that run this two-star hotel have individually decorated the rooms to a high standard. It's in a quiet spot, 150m south of the
church, with a shady garden. The **restaurant**
(closed Sunday night in winter) serves good
seafood and generous **menus** (€10/18/25).
The interior is a bit dull, but meals are also
served in the garden in season.

Hôtel La Dame de Cœur (☎ 05 56 09 80 80;
www.hotel-damedecoeur.com; 103 rue de la Plage; s/d/tr
€31/40/46, Jul & Aug €36.50/52/62.50) A two-star
hotel notable more for its giant Queen of
Hearts playing card sign than for its ordinary rooms. Reception opens at 6pm in the
low season. During July and August, the
price includes compulsory breakfast.

There are **pizzerias**, **Tex-Mex** and **seafood**
eateries along rue de la Plage.

ST-ÉMILION

pop 2500

The medieval village of St-Émilion, 39km
east of Bordeaux, is surrounded by vineyards
renowned for their full-bodied, deeply coloured red wines. It is named after Émilion,
a miracle-working Benedictine monk who
came here from Brittany and lived in a
cave between 750 and 767. The monastery
founded on this site later became a stop on
medieval pilgrimage routes.

Today, St-Émilion and seven surrounding districts have been recognised as a
Unesco World Heritage Site. Situated on
two limestone hills that look out over the
Dordogne River valley, its ramparts (dating
to the 13th century) and the rest of the town
take on a luscious golden hue as the sun

sets. Not even the vast numbers of tourists
who flock here can spoil the charm.

Information

The **tourist office** (☎ 05 57 55 28 28; www.saint
-emilion-tourisme.com; place des Créneaux; 🕑 9.30am-7pm
mid-Jun–mid-Sep, 9.30am-12.30pm & 1.45-6pm mid-Sep–
mid-Jun) has brochures in English and details
on visiting almost 100 nearby chateaux. During the summer the tourist office opens an
information kiosk (place de l'Église Monolithe), selling
tickets to places of interest. Opening times
vary (usually 10am to noon and 2pm to 6pm
Monday to Friday and some weekends).

The post office, which can exchange currency, the pharmacy, and banks are along
rue Guadet.

Sights

The town's most interesting historical sites
can only be visited with one of the tourist
office's 45-minute guided tours. The worthwhile tours (adult/student/child €5.50/3.60/
2.90, plus entry to the sites) depart regularly
throughout the day. Most are in French, although an English translation is available –
call ahead to check English tour times
(usually at 1pm).

The tour is the only way to see the astounding **Église Monolithe**, carved out of
limestone from the 9th to the 12th centuries;
and the **Grotte de l'Ermitage**, the hermit saint's
famous cave where his uncomfortable-
looking stone bed can be seen.

You can climb the **clocher** (bell tower; ☎ 05
57 55 28 28; entrance on place des Créneaux; admission €1;
🕑 9.30am-7pm mid-Jun–mid-Sep, 9.30am-12.30pm &
1.45-6pm mid-Sep–mid-Jun) above the church for
a splendid view of the village. If it's closed,
they'll give you a key at the tourist office.

The impressive former **Collégiale** (Collegiate Church) has a narrow, domed, Romanesque nave that dates from the 12th
century, and a spacious vaulted choir (14th
to 16th century) that's almost square. Free
concerts are held here during summer
(every Thursday, 6pm). **Cloître de l'Église Collégiale**, the church's tranquil 14th-century
cloister, is accessible through the tourist office building.

Several of the city's medieval gates survive, including **Porte de la Cadène** (Gate of the
Chain), off rue Guadet. Next door is **Maison
de la Cadène**, a half-timbered house from the
early 16th century.

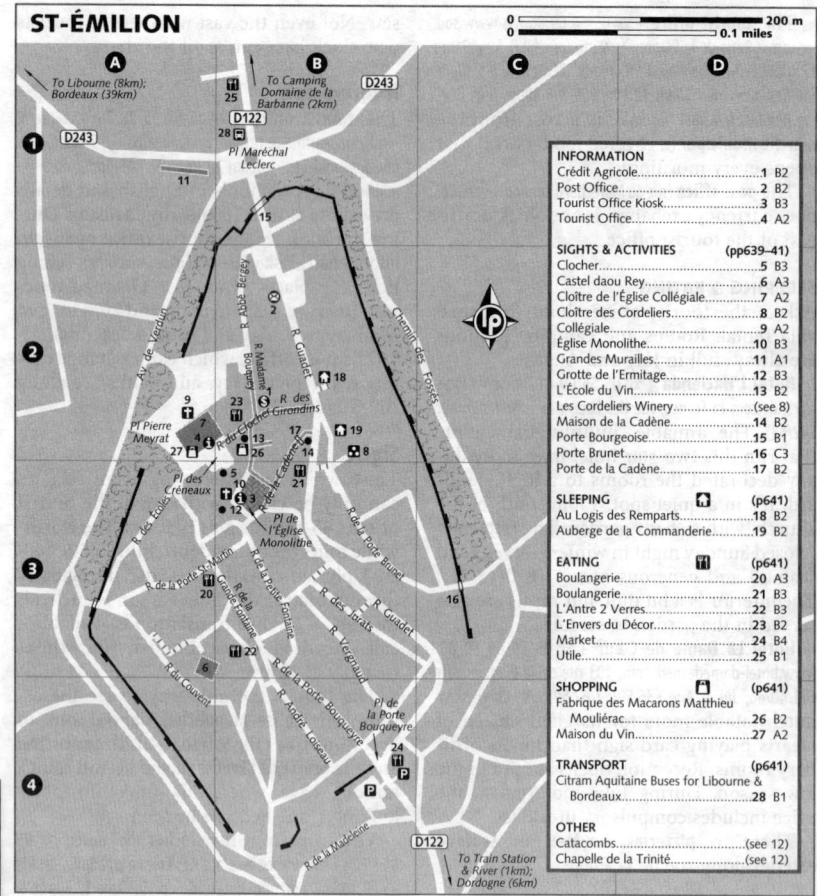

ST-ÉMILION

INFORMATION	
Crédit Agricole	1 B2
Post Office	2 B2
Tourist Office Kiosk	3 B3
Tourist Office	4 A2

SIGHTS & ACTIVITIES	(pp639–41)
Clocher	5 B3
Castel daou Rey	6 A3
Cloître de l'Église Collégiale	7 A2
Cloître des Cordeliers	8 B2
Collégiale	9 A2
Église Monolithe	10 B3
Grandes Murailles	11 A1
Grotte de l'Ermitage	12 B3
L'École du Vin	13 B2
Les Cordeliers Winery	(see 8)
Maison de la Cadène	14 B2
Porte Bourgeoise	15 B1
Porte Brunet	16 C3
Porte de la Cadène	17 B2

SLEEPING	(p641)
Au Logis des Remparts	18 B2
Auberge de la Commanderie	19 B2

EATING	(p641)
Boulangerie	20 A3
Boulangerie	21 B3
L'Antre 2 Verres	22 B3
L'Envers du Décor	23 B2
Market	24 B4
Utile	25 B1

SHOPPING	(p641)
Fabrique des Macarons Matthieu Mouliérac	26 B2
Maison du Vin	27 A2

TRANSPORT	(p641)
Citram Aquitaine Buses for Libourne & Bordeaux	28 B1

OTHER	
Catacombs	(see 12)
Chapelle de la Trinité	(see 12)

Cloître des Cordeliers (rue des Cordeliers; admission free; ☻ year-round) is a ruined monastery. **Les Cordeliers** (☎ 05 57 24 72 07), the winery that has occupied part of the site for over a century, makes sparkling wine. It runs interesting **guided cellar tours** (admission €3.80; ☻ 11am, 3pm, 5pm & 6.30pm Jun–mid-Jul, Sep & Oct; 11am, 3pm, 4.30pm, 5.30pm, 6.30pm & 7.30pm mid-Jul–Aug; 3pm & 5.15pm Apr, Nov & Dec, 4.30pm Jan-Mar) that include a wine and macaroon tasting.

The 13th-century donjon known as the **Castel daou Rey** (Tour du Roi, King's Tower; admission €1; ☻ 9.30am-8.30pm Jun-Sep; variable opening hours out of season), the only remains of what is believed to have been a royal fortress, affords exceptional views of the town and the Dordogne Valley.

Activities

Introductory wine-tasting classes are available in English every day at **L'École du Vin** (☎ 05 57 74 44 29; www.vignobleschateaux.fr; Vignobles & Châteaux, 4 rue du Clocher). The courses (3pm; 1½ hours; €20) are great fun, with games to identify aromas and tastes plus a blind tasting session. Between November and March they're by appointment only. From mid-July to mid-September, the **Maison du Vin** (opposite) also offers bilingual, 1½-hour classes daily (€17).

Tours

The tourist office organises two-hour afternoon **chateau visits** (adult/12-17 yrs €9/6; ☻ Mon-Sat May-Sep) in French and English. It also has details of concerts and wine-tasting events taking place in local chateaux.

Sleeping

Accommodation in St-Émilion can get very pricey in summer. The tourist office has a list of nearby **chambres d'hôtes**, which generally charge €40 to €70 for a double.

Auberge de la Commanderie (☎ 05 57 24 70 19; www.aubergedelacommanderie.com; rue des Cordeliers; d €60-100, q duplex apartments €120; ☯ mid-Feb–mid-Jan) Despite the building being of medieval origin, the rooms are modern and very comfortable. The relative appeal of the giant, gaudy in-room murals is a matter of personal taste. A few of the rooms have vineyard-views.

Au Logis des Remparts (☎ 05 57 24 70 43; logis-des-remparts@saint-emilion.org; 18 rue Guadet; d €68-130; ☯ mid-Jan–mid-Dec; P ⓢ) This appealing Gothic house has been completely renovated for three-star comfort, although occasional stained-glass windows and exposed stone keep it true to its origins. Facilities include 17 pleasant rooms, an air-conditioned bar and a large sunny terrace.

CAMPING

Camping Domaine de la Barbanne (☎ 05 57 24 75 80; www.camping-saint-emilion.com; route de Montagne; camping €12.50-18; ☯ Apr-Sep; ⓢ) With three stars and two swimming pools, this place is about 2km north of St-Émilion on the D122.

Eating

L'Envers du Décor (☎ 05 57 74 48 31; rue du Clocher; menus €15 & €25, mains €9-14; ☯ closed dinner Sun) Inside an attractive, ambient restaurant/wine bar; outside is a tranquil terrace backing on the Collégiale. Take a seat in either for tasty bistro-style cuisine and fine wine by the glass or the bottle.

L'Antre 2 Verres (☎ 05 57 24 09 73; escalette de la Tour du Roi; menus €14.50-25; ☯ lunch daily, dinner Sat & Sun) An atmospheric, cave-like eatery occupying limestone hollows at the foot of the *Castel daou Rey*. Traditional and creative French dishes with, unsurprisingly, a big choice of local wines.

SELF-CATERING

The grocery **Utile** (☯ 8am-7pm Mon-Sat, 8am-1pm Sun Jun–mid-Sep; 8am-12.30pm & 2-7pm Mon-Fri, 8am-1pm Sun mid-Sep–May) is on the D122, 150m north of town.

There are two **boulangeries** at rue Guadet and rue de la Grande Fontaine; both open to 6pm or 7pm.

There is a **market** every Sunday on place de la Porte Bouqueyre.

Shopping

St-Émilion's quaint streets and squares are lined with wine shops – about 50 of them, one for every eight of the old city's residents!

Maison du Vin (☎ 05 57 55 50 55; place Pierre Meyrat; ☯ 9.30am-12.30pm & 2-6pm Sep-Jul, 9.30am-7pm Aug), owned by the 250 chateaux whose wines it sells, has exhibitions and publications on local wines.

The recipe for *macarons* (macaroons) was brought to St-Émilion in the 17th century by Ursuline nuns. To this day, the local biscuits are renowned for their soft, fluffy texture and subtle almond flavour. **Fabrique des Macarons Matthieu Mouliérac** (Tertre de la Tente; ☯ closed mornings Jan-Mar) charges €5 per two dozen. There's another macaroon bakery next to the post office.

Getting There & Away

St-Émilion can be visited as a day trip from Bordeaux by bus and/or train. **Citram Aquitaine** (☎ 05 56 43 68 43) buses to/from Bordeaux's Halte Routière run at least once daily (except on Sunday and holidays from October to April) to Libourne (€5.70, 45 minutes); from there you take a **Marchesseau** (☎ 05 57 40 60 79) bus to St-Émilion (€2, 10 minutes). There's talk of operating a direct service during July and August; contact Citram Aquitaine for the latest.

The SNCF has three autorails daily (two on Sunday and holidays) from Bordeaux (€6.80, 40 minutes); the last train back usually departs at 6.26pm.

By car from Bordeaux, follow the signs for Libourne and take the D243.

Year-round, the tourist office rents out bicycles for €9.15/13.75 per half-day/day.

ARCACHON

pop 11,800

The coastal resort of Arcachon became popular with bourgeois residents of Bordeaux at the end of the 19th century. It's not hard to see why – beach lovers can frolic away sunny days on the long, sandy seashore and nearby Dune de Pyla (p644),

ARCACHON

Europe's highest sand dune. The town itself is not overly attractive but it does have a certain laid-back charm and a pretty inner-suburb of heyday villas harks back to its golden era.

Arcachon makes an easy day trip from Bordeaux, meaning it's often crowded in summer. To escape the hordes, grab a bike and explore the practically deserted out-of-town beaches.

Orientation

Arcachon is on the southern side of the triangular Bassin d'Arcachon (Arcachon Bay), which is linked to the Atlantic by a 3km-wide channel just west of town. The narrow peninsula of Cap Ferret is on the other side of the outlet. The Dune de Pyla begins 8km to the south of Arcachon along the D218.

Arcachon's main commercial streets run parallel to the beach: blvd de la Plage, cours Lamarque de Plaisance and cours Héricart de Thury. Perpendicular to the beach, busy streets include av Gambetta and rue du Maréchal de Lattre de Tassigny.

Information

Credit Agricole (252 Blvd de la Plage) Only bank that will change money.

Le Bistrot du Boulevard (☎ 05 56 83 45 67; 230 blvd de la Plage; per hr €7.50; ☿ 11am-11pm)

Post Office (place Président Roosevelt) Offers currency exchange services, has Cyberposte.

Tourist Office (☎ 05 57 52 97 97; www.arcachon.com; place Président Roosevelt; ☿ 9am-7pm Jul & Aug; 9am-6.30pm Mon-Fri, 9am-5pm Sat, 10am-noon & 1-5pm Sun Apr-Jun & Sep; 9am-6pm Mon-Fri, 9am-5pm Sat Oct-Mar)

Sights

The flat area that abuts the **Plage d'Arcachon** (the town's beach) is known as the **Ville d'Été** (Summer Quarter). The liveliest section is around **Jetée Thiers**, one of the two piers.

In front of the eastern pier, **Jetée D'Eyrac**, stands the town's appealing **casino** building, resembling a Renaissance château trans-planted from the Loire. The intricate lines of the façade are juxtaposed against brash neon signs after dark.

The **Aquarium et Musée** (☎ 05 56 83 33 32; 2 rue du Professeur Jolyet; adult/student/under 10 €4.40/3/2.80; ☿ 9.45am-12.15pm & 1.45-7pm Jun-Aug, to 6.30pm Mar-

May & Sep-Nov; closed Dec-Feb) in a wooden shack opposite the casino, is uninspiring with a collection of fish in small tanks and other basic displays.

The elegant **Ville d'Hiver** (Winter Quarter), on the tree-covered hillside south of the Ville d'Été, dates back 100 years. Over 300 villas, many decorated with delicate wood tracery, range in style from neo-Gothic through to colonial. The easy stroll up to the higher ground is aided by the unusual deco-style **public lift** (€0.15; ☯ 9am-12.45pm, 2.30-7pm). The lift is in Parc Mauresque at the southern end of rue du Maréchal de Lattre de Tassigny.

A lovely **pedestrian promenade** lined with trees and playgrounds runs west and then south from the Plage d'Arcachon to **Plage Péreire**, **Plage des Abatilles** and **Pyla-sur-Mer**.

Activities

High-quality **cycle paths** link Arcachon with the Dune de Pyla and Biscarosse (30km to the south), and go all the way around the Bassin d'Arcachon to Cap Ferret. From here, a cyclable path parallels the near-deserted beaches all the way to Pointe de Grave. You can take cycles aboard the boat to Cap Ferret.

The exposed ocean beaches to the south of town generally offer good conditions for surfing. Lessons and equipment hire are offered by **Ocean Roots** (☎ 06 62 26 04 11; 27 av Saint Francois Xavier; oceanrclub@hotmail.com).

Centre Nautique d'Arcachon (☎ 05 56 22 36 83; quai Goslar; ☯ Apr-Sep), 1.5km east of the Jetée d'Eyrac at the Port de Plaisance (Pleasure Boat Port), rents sea kayaks, windsurfing and diving equipment, and offers courses.

Tours

Les Bateliers Arcachonnais (UBA; ☎ 05 57 72 28 28; www.bateliers-arcachon.asso.fr in French) runs ferries from Jetée Thiers to the pine-shaded town of **Cap Ferret** (return ticket adult/child €10/6), across the mouth of the Bassin d'Arcachon. From April to October, boats run four to 20 times daily, depending on the season; the rest of the year there are two sailings on Monday, Wednesday and Friday and four sailings on Saturday and Sunday.

The company also runs daily, year-round cruises around the **Île aux Oiseaux** (adult/child €13/9), the uninhabited island in the middle of the bay. It's a haven for tern,

curlew and redshank, so take your binoculars. There's also an informative running commentary. In July and August there are all-day excursions to the **Banc d'Arguin**, the sand bank off the Dune de Pyla (€15/10, leaving Arcachon 11am).

Sleeping

During July and August, prices go up dramatically and it is extremely difficult to find accommodation. Some hotels require that you take half-board. The tourist office can provide information on furnished rental houses and apartments.

Hôtel La Paix (☎ 05 56 83 05 65; fax 05 56 83 05 65; 8 av de Lamartine; s/d from €25.80/28.90, with shower & toilet €33.30/36.10, half-board d €54-62, studio apartments for 2 per week from €152.40-290, in summer from €320-487; ☯ late Apr-Nov) A charming, friendly and down-to-earth place in a quaint old house, 200m from the beach. Prices vary greatly according to season; from June to September, half-board is obligatory.

Hôtel St-Christaud (☎ /fax 05 56 83 38 53; 8 allée de la Chapelle; d with washbasin €21-35, with shower & toilet €31-47; ☯ year-round) A rambling old house with a maze of simple rooms in varying states of renovation. Facilities are basic, but prices are reasonable.

Hôtel le Dauphin (☎ 05 56 83 02 89; www.dauphin-arcachon.com; 7 av Gounod; d €55-84, q €60-105; P ✕ ⌘) This attractive patterned-brick mansion house dates from 1818, although the décor, all tiling and cork panelling, is unmistakably 1970s. Back-lit mirrors and brown-toned bathrooms continue the theme. As well as spotless doubles, there are some family rooms available, all of which have satellite TV.

Grand Hôtel Richelieu (☎ 05 56 83 16 50; www.grand-hotel-richelieu.com; 185 blvd de la Plage; standard d €60-98, deluxe d €120-160; P ⌘) With a hint of the grand bourgeois Arcachon of 100 years ago, this refined hotel, just a few steps from the beach, is the best located in town. The only drawback is the smallish size of some of the rooms. Deluxe rooms are larger, with bath and fantastic bay views.

Camping

The steep, inland side of the Dune de Pyla, 10km south of town, is gradually burying five large and rather pricey camping grounds, most of them half-hidden in a forest of pine trees.

La Forêt (☎ 05 56 22 73 28; www.campinglaforet.fr; route de Biscarosse; camping €12.25-26.50; ☺ Apr–mid-Oct; 🚉) A well-run, three-star place with plenty of shade and good amenities. Prices vary depending on the season.

Eating

The beachfront promenade between Jetée Thiers and Jetée d'Eyrac is lined with **tourist restaurants** and places offering pizza and crepes. Locals tend to avoid this slightly tacky strip, but it has a lively atmosphere and competition keeps prices reasonable.

For a quick lunch-time bite or something to take to the beach, head for **Bonheur Gourmand** (☺ 10.30am-6pm), a tiny kiosk near Jetée Thiers making delicious sandwiches to order.

Chez Pierre (☎ 05 56 22 52 94; 1 blvd Veyrier Montagnères; menus from €19) One of the better (and more upmarket) restaurants on the seaside strip. As you enjoy the seafood specialities on offer, you can gaze out from the terrace to the rippling waters.

La Paix (see Sleeping; menus from €10; ☺ Jun–mid-Sep) One of the more unusual and appealing places to eat in town, this conservatory-like wood and glass enclosure is dripping with assorted greenery. Traditional French food is on the menu.

Captain Aldo (☎ 05 56 83 78 81; 22 blvd Veyrier Montagnères; menus from €19) Another popular eatery on the beach, with a relaxed and family-friendly terrace. Choose from the lobsters in the tank or from the large selection of fresh fish on display. If you're over-fished, there are Italian options too.

Aux Mille Saveurs (☎ 05 56 83 40 28; 25 blvd du Général Leclerc; menus €13.50-39; ☺ closed Sun dinner, Mon) Fine, traditional dining in genteel surroundings.

SELF-CATERING

The lively **food market** (rue Roger Expert; ☺ 8am-1pm) is just north of the Mairie on the ground floor of a parking garage.

There's a **Casino supermarket** (57 blvd du Général Leclerc; ☺ 9am-12.30pm & 3-7pm Mon-Sat, 9am-noon Sun). Other supermarkets include **E Leclerc** (224 blvd de la Plage; ☺ 9am-7.30pm Mon-Sat & 9.30am-12.30pm Sun) and **Monoprix** (46 cours Lamarque de Plaisance; ☺ 8.30am-12.30pm & 2-7.30pm Mon-Sat).

Getting There & Away

Some of the trains from Bordeaux to Arcachon (€8.60, 50 minutes, 11 to 18 daily) are coordinated with TGVs from Paris' Gare Montparnasse. The last train back to Bordeaux usually leaves Arcachon at 8.15pm (9.51pm on Sundays and holidays).

Getting Around

There is unmetered parking south of the casino along av de Général de Gaulle.

Locabeach (☎ 05 56 83 39 64; www.locabeach .com; 326 blvd de la Plage; ☺ 9am-12.30pm & 2.30-7pm) rents out scooters and motorcycles starting at €39/215 per day/week.

To order a cab, call ☎ 05 56 83 88 88.

BICYCLE

At **Dingo Vélos** (☎ 05 56 83 44 09; www.dingove los.com; rue Grenier; ☺ 9.30am-6.30pm daily Apr-Sep, until midnight July & Aug) you can rent tandems, *triplos*, *quatros* and *quintuplos* (bikes with places for two to five riders, half/full day €16/23) and pushme-pullyous (tandems whose riders face in opposite directions; 30 minutes for €4). Five-speeds/mountain bikes start at €10/13 per day.

AROUND ARCACHON
Dune de Pyla

This remarkable sand dune, also known as the Dune du Pilat, stretches from the mouth of the Bassin d'Arcachon southwards for almost 3km. Studies have shown it to be creeping eastwards at about 4.5m a year – it has already swallowed trees, a road junction and even an entire hotel, and at this rate the camping area at the base of the dune's steep eastern side appears to have a limited lifespan.

The view from the top – approximately 114m above sea level – is magnificent. To the west you can see the sandy shoals at the mouth of the Bassin d'Arcachon, including the **Banc d'Arguin bird reserve** and **Cap Ferret**. In the other direction, dense pine forests stretch from the base of the dune eastwards almost as far as the eye can see.

Caution is advised while swimming in this area: powerful currents swirl out to sea from the deceptively tranquil *baïnes* (baylets) that jut into the beach.

GETTING THERE & AWAY

There's a car park at the northern end of the dune.

The local bus company, **Autobus d'Arcachon** (☎ 05 57 72 45 00; 47 blvd du Général Leclerc), has daily buses from the SNCF station in Arcachon to the Pyla Plage (Haïtza), 1km north of the dune (€2.70).

From mid-June to mid-September, buses continue south to the dune's car park, the camping grounds and Biscarosse.

Gujan Mestras

A bit east of Arcachon, the town of Gujan Mestras sprawls along 9km of coastline. This stretch of the bay is home to seven picturesque and lively oyster ports.

The **tourist office** (☎ 05 56 66 12 65; www.ville-gujanmestras.fr; 16 av De Lattre de Tassigny) is at the western edge of town in La Hume.

About 4km to the east, **Port de Larros**, the largest of the town's seven oyster ports, is lined with weathered wood shacks, with flat-bottom oystering boats moored out the front. The small **Maison de l'Huître** (☎ 05 56 66 23 71; adult/child €2.80/2; ☽ 10am-12.30pm & 2.30-6pm Mon-Sat) has a display on oyster farming including a short film in English.

Just 100m away you'll find the little shop **Cap Noroit** (☎ /fax 05 56 66 04 15; 112 allée du Haurat), where you can buy super-fresh Banc d'Arguin oysters (the area's finest) direct from the growers. A dozen medium oysters costs just €3. Seafood restaurants nearby include **Les Viviers** (☎ 05 56 66 01 04), at the port, and **Les Pavois** (☎ 05 56 66 38 71; ☽ closed Mon), next to the Maison de l'Huitre. Both charge from around €12 for a dozen oys-

ters which they serve on their waterside terraces.

The Gujan Mestras **train station**, not far from Port de Larros, is on the train line linking Bordeaux with Arcachon. The tiny train station in La Hume is 50 metres west of the tourist office.

Le Teich Parc Ornithologique

Only 29% of the shallow Bassin d'Arcachon, a 155-sq-km tidal bay, is underwater at low tide, making it an ideal habitat for birds. Indeed, some 260 species, both migratory and nonmigratory, visit each year.

The idyllic **Parc Ornithologique** (Bird Reserve; ☎ 05 56 22 80 93; www.parc-ornithologique-du-teich .com; adult/child 5-14 yrs €6.40/4.60; ☽ 10am-8pm Jul & Aug, to 7pm mid-Apr–Jun & early Sep–mid-Sep, to 6pm mid-Sep–mid-Apr) at Le Teich, in the southeastern corner of the bay at the mouth of the multi-channelled River Leyre (l'Eyre), is an important centre for the preservation of endangered species. It's an outstanding place to see some of Europe's rarest and most beautiful birds.

It's easiest to observe the birds at high tide. Tidal schedules, available at local tourist offices, appear on the back page of the regional daily *Sud Ouest*.

The Parc Ornithologique is in Le Teich, 15km east of Arcachon on the D650. Le Teich's train station, 1.2km south of the park, is linked with Bordeaux and Arcachon.

ATLANTIC COAST

French Basque Country

The Basque Country ('Euskal Herria' in the Basque language) – the area around the western foothills of the Pyrenees (Pyrénées in French) as it slopes down to the Bay of Biscay – has been home to the Basque people for many centuries. The area straddles modern-day France and Spain (with roughly 20% on the French side) but it's still a land apart, stubbornly independent and profoundly different from either of the nation-states that have adopted it.

The French side (called 'Iparralde' in Basque or 'Le Pays Basque' in French), less populous and industrialised than the Spanish Basque region, is perhaps best known for its glitzy beach resort, Biarritz. But the medium-rise town, with bronzed surfers hooning around on mopeds and swarms of peak-season sun-seekers, is the least Basque of the area's towns.

More authentic is the cultural and administrative capital, Bayonne, where French and Basque influences successfully combine to create a unique atmosphere. Traditional Basque music, sports and festivals are a big part of the summer's entertainment and it's not just for the benefit of tourists. Bayonne is also an excellent base from which to explore the region as it has good transport links, restaurants and sleeping options.

To the southwest is St-Jean de Luz, a relaxed family beach resort. There's also a bustling fishing port there, so bring along an appetite and tuck into some tasty Basque seafood specialities.

You'll find the 'Iparralde' of old away from the coast and into the hills, with little one-street villages to discover and green valleys to explore. St-Jean Pied de Port offers a likely base for such excursions, as an age-old pit stop for pilgrims heading over the border to Santiago de Compostela.

HIGHLIGHTS

- Taste the delicious chocolates in **Bayonne** (p653)
- Surf the world-class waves at **Anglet Beach** (p654) near Biarritz
- Catch a frantic game of high-speed *pelote basque* (p653)
- Creep up the mountainside railway on **Le Petit Train de la Rhune** (p662)
- Follow the centuries-old footsteps of pilgrims near **St-Jean Pied de Port** (p665)

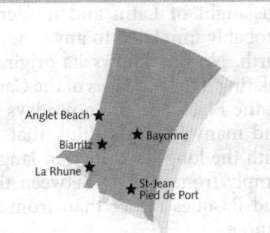

Anglet Beach ★

Biarritz ★   ★ Bayonne

La Rhune ★

★ St-Jean
Pied de Port

■ POPULATION: 574,000   ■ AREA: 13,383 SQ KM

FRENCH BASQUE COUNTRY

History

The origins and early history of the Basque people are a mystery. Roman sources mention a tribe called the Vascones living in the area and it's attested that the Basques took over what is now southwestern France in the 6th century. Converting to Christianity in the 10th century, they are still known for their strong devotion to Catholicism.

After resisting invasions by Visigoths, Franks, Normans and Moors, the Basques on both sides of the Pyrenees emerged from the turbulent Middle Ages with a fair degree of local autonomy, which they retained in France until the Revolution. The French Basque Country, then part of the duchy of Aquitaine, was under Anglo-Norman rule from the mid-12th century until the mid-15th century.

Basque nationalism flourished before and during the Spanish Civil War (1936–39). Until the death of Franco, the Spanish dictator, in 1975, many Basque nationalists and anti-Franco guerrillas from the other side of the Pyrenees sheltered in France.

Some Basques still dream of carving an Euskadi state out of the Basque areas of Spain and France, and a few support the terrorist organisation Euskadi ta Azkatasuna (ETA), whose name means 'Basque Nation and Liberty'. While France remains peaceful, bombings and other barbarities are not uncommon in the Spanish Basque Country, and Spanish ETA terrorists often seek sanctuary in France.

Language

Basque (Euskara), the only language in southwestern Europe to have withstood the onslaught of Latin and its derivatives, is probably unrelated to any other tongue on earth. No one knows its origins. Theories relating it to languages of the Caucasus, east of the Black Sea, are nowadays discredited and many linguists think that similarities with the long-dead Iberian language come simply from contact between the Iberians and Basques rather than from a common source.

The first book in Basque, marking the beginning of Basque literature, was printed in 1545. Basque is now spoken by approximately a million people throughout Spain and France, nearly all of whom are bilingual. In the French Basque Country, the

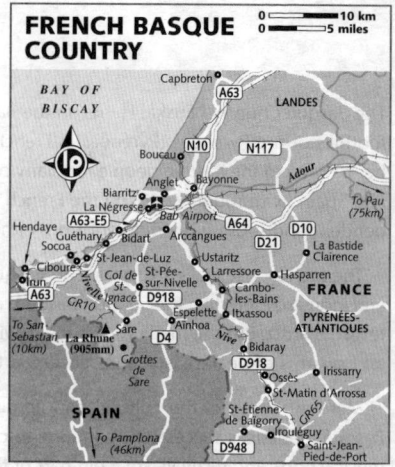

FRENCH BASQUE COUNTRY

language, widely spoken in Bayonne, is even more common in the hilly hinterland. Two TV stations in Spain and one in France broadcast in Basque, and you'll occasionally see on shop doors *'Hemen Euskara emaiten dugu'* (Basque spoken here).

Basque Symbols

The Basque flag resembles the UK's but with a red field, a white vertical cross and a green diagonal one. Another common Basque symbol – the *lauburu* – resembles a curly swastika and is a sign of good luck or protection.

Sleeping

In coastal resorts, many holiday-makers return to the same hotel year after year. It can be extremely difficult to find a room in July and August, when room prices rise substantially and some hotels will insist on half board.

Sport

For a canter through the various kinds of *pelote basque,* see p653. To find out where to see them played, turn to the Sport sections in most towns.

Corrida, Spanish-style bullfighting in which the bull is killed, has devotees all over the Basque Country. Corridas take place intermittently during summer and advance reservations are usually necessary; enquire at either the Bayonne or Biarritz tourist offices.

Getting There & Away

All roads and train lines lead to Bayonne, which is easily accessible from the rest of France.

For rail travel to Spain, switch trains at the frontier since the Spanish track gauge is narrower. Take an SNCF train to Hendaye, where you can pick up the EuskoTren, familiarly known as 'El Topo' (The Mole), a shuttle train that runs via Irún to San Sebastián every half-hour until 9pm.

Year-round, the Spanish company Sema runs twice-daily buses between Bayonne and San Sebastián via St-Jean de Luz, while ATCRB operates a summer-only service.

The airport (p653) serving Bayonne and Biarritz has domestic flights as well as services to Switzerland and the UK.

Getting Around

A good rail service links the major towns and plentiful buses connect Bayonne, Biarritz and the surrounding beaches.

BAYONNE

pop 42,000

Founded as Lapurdum by the Romans, Bayonne ('Baiona' in Basque, meaning 'the good river') is the cultural and economic capital of the French Basque Country. Together with sprawling Anglet (the final 't' is pronounced) and Biarritz, 8km to the west, Bayonne forms an urban area (population around 100,000) sometimes known as BAB.

In contrast to the more upmarket seaside resort of Biarritz, Bayonne retains much of its Basqueness: the riverside buildings with their red and green shutters are typical of the region and you'll hear almost as much Euskara as French in certain quarters. Most of the graffiti around town are the work of nationalist groups seeking an independent Basque state.

The town is known for its smoked ham, chocolate and marzipan. According to tradition, the *baïonnette* (bayonet) was developed here in the early 17th century.

Orientation

The Rivers Adour and Nive split Bayonne into three: St-Esprit, the area north of the Adour; Grand Bayonne, the oldest part of the city, on the western bank of the Nive; and the very Basque Petit Bayonne quarter to its east.

MAPS

Local bus company STAB's free local bus map gives a stylised overview of the BAB conurbation. For something more detailed, buy Blay Foldex's *Bayonne Biarritz Anglet* or the Michelin equivalent.

Information

BOOKSHOPS

Mattin Megadenda (☎ 05 59 59 35 14; place de l'Arsenal) Texts on Basque history and culture, walking in the Basque Country, maps and CDs of Basque music.

INTERNET ACCESS

Cyber Net Café (☎ 05 59 50 85 10; place de la République; per hr €4.50; ☽ 7am-11pm Mon-Sat, noon-11pm Sun)

LAUNDRY

Laverie St-Esprit (16 blvd Alsace-Lorraine; ☽ 8am-8pm)
Hallwash (6 rue d'Espagne; ☽ 8am-8pm)

POST

Main Post Office (rue de la Nouvelle Poste) About 1km northwest of the city centre.
Post Office (11 rue Jules Labat)
Post Office (21 blvd Alsace-Lorraine)

TOURIST INFORMATION

Tourist Office (☎ 05 59 46 01 46; www.bayonne-tourisme.com; place des Basques; ☽ 9am-7pm Mon-Sat, 10am-1pm Sun Jul & Aug, 9am-6.30pm Mon-Fri, 10am-6pm Sat Sep-Jun) Has useful free brochures including *Fêtes*, listing French Basque Country cultural and sporting events, and *Tout à Loisir*, for hiking, biking and other activities. From July to mid-September, the office organises guided tours of the city (€5) at 10am from Monday to Saturday (in French except for Thursday's English-language tour).

Sights & Activities

RAMPARTS

Thanks to Vauban's 17th-century fortifications (see 'Vauban's Citadels', p30), now grass-covered and dotted with trees, a slim, green belt surrounds the city centre. You can walk the stretches of the old ramparts that rise above blvd Rempart Lachepaillet and rue Tour de Sault.

CATHÉDRALE STE-MARIE

Construction of Bayonne's Gothic **cathedral** (☽ 7.30-11.45am & 3-5.45pm Mon-Sat, 3.30-5.45pm Sun) began in the 13th century, when Bayonne was ruled by the Anglo-Normans, and was completed well after France assumed control

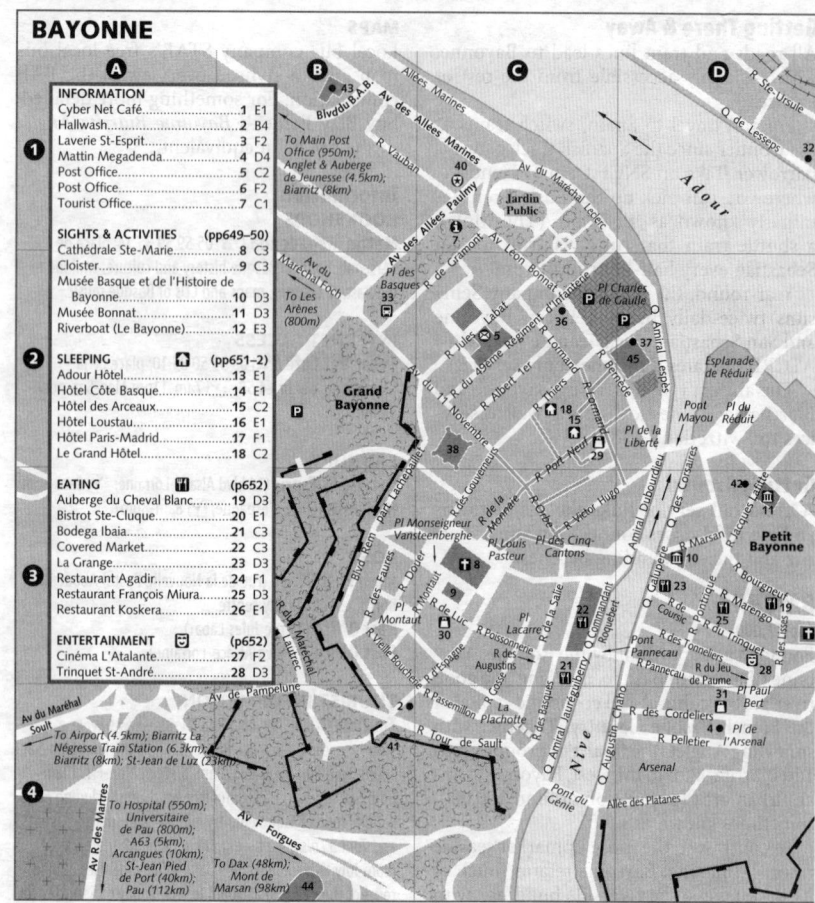

BAYONNE

INFORMATION	
Cyber Net Café	1 E1
Hallwash	2 B4
Laverie St-Esprit	3 F2
Mattin Megadenda	4 D4
Post Office	5 C2
Post Office	6 F2
Tourist Office	7 C1

SIGHTS & ACTIVITIES	(pp649–50)
Cathédrale Ste-Marie	8 C3
Cloister	9 C3
Musée Basque et de l'Histoire de Bayonne	10 D3
Musée Bonnat	11 D3
Riverboat (Le Bayonne)	12 E3

SLEEPING	(pp651–2)
Adour Hôtel	13 E1
Hôtel Côte Basque	14 E1
Hôtel des Arceaux	15 C2
Hôtel Loustau	16 E1
Hôtel Paris-Madrid	17 F1
Le Grand Hôtel	18 C2

EATING	(p652)
Auberge du Cheval Blanc	19 D3
Bistrot Ste-Cluque	20 E1
Bodega Ibaia	21 C3
Covered Market	22 C3
La Grange	23 D3
Restaurant Agadir	24 F1
Restaurant François Miura	25 D3
Restaurant Koskera	26 E1

ENTERTAINMENT	(p652)
Cinéma L'Atalante	27 F2
Trinquet St-André	28 D3

in 1451. These political changes are reflected in the ornamentation on the nave's vaulted ceiling, which includes both the English coat of arms (three lions) and that most French of emblems, the fleur-de-lys. The entrance to the stately 13th-century **cloister** (🕙 9am-12.30pm & 2-6pm Tue-Sun mid-May–mid-Sep, 9am-12.30pm & 2-5pm Tue-Sun mid-Sep–mid-May) is on place Louis Pasteur.

MUSÉE BASQUE ET DE L'HISTOIRE DE BAYONNE

This **museum** (☎ 05 59 46 61 90; 37 quai des Corsaires; adult/student/under 18 €5.50/3/free; 🕙 10am-6.30pm Tue-Sun May-Oct, 10am-12.30pm & 2-6pm Tue-Sun Nov-Apr) presents the history and culture of this unique people and also of Bayonne, their prime fishing port and maritime window on the wider world.

There is a **combined ticket** (adult/student €9/4.50) to both the Musée Basque and **Musée Bonnat** (☎ 05 59 59 08 52; 5 rue Jacques Lafitte; adult/student/child €5.50/3/free; 🕙 10am-6.30pm Wed-Mon May-Oct, 10am-12.30pm & 2-6pm Wed-Mon Nov-Apr), which is an art gallery featuring canvases by El Greco, Goya and Degas, and a roomful of works by Rubens.

RIVER TRIPS

From mid-June to mid-September, the riverboat **Le Bayonne** (☎ 06 80 74 21 51) runs two-hour cruises on the River Adour from 10am until noon and 2.45pm until 7pm, if enough passengers turn up.

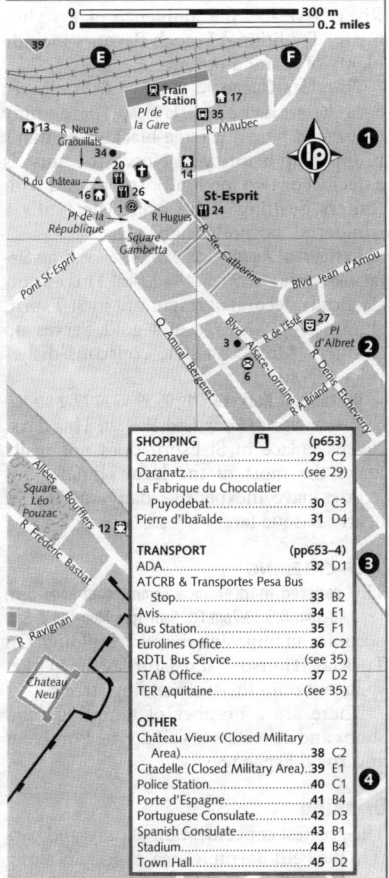

SHOPPING (p653)

Cazenave	29	C2
Daranatz	(see 29)	
La Fabrique du Chocolatier		
Puyodebat	30	C3
Pierre d'Ibaïalde	31	D4

TRANSPORT (pp653–4)

ADA	32	D1
ATCRB & Transportes Pesa Bus		
Stop	33	B2
Avis	34	E1
Bus Station	35	F1
Eurolines Office	36	C2
RDTL Bus Service	(see 35)	
STAB Office	37	D2
TER Aquitaine	(see 35)	

OTHER

Château Vieux (Closed Military		
Area)	38	C2
Citadelle (Closed Military Area)	39	E1
Police Station	40	C1
Porte d'Espagne	41	B4
Portuguese Consulate	42	D3
Spanish Consulate	43	B1
Stadium	44	B4
Town Hall	45	D2

Festivals & Events

The town's premier fiesta is the five-day **Fêtes de Bayonne**, beginning on the first Wednesday in August. It includes a 'running of the bulls', like in Pamplona, Spain, only more benign. Here, they use cows not bulls – and most of the time, participants chase the frisky beasts rather than vice versa. The festival also includes Basque music, bullfights, fireworks, a float parade and rugby.

During Easter week, the town hosts a **Ham Fair**, honouring the *jambon de bayonne*, the acclaimed local ham. The **Journées du Chocolat**, on a variable weekend in May, are a celebration of chocolate, Bayonne's other claim to gastronomic fame.

Sleeping

Accommodation is extremely difficult to find from mid-July to mid-August – and it's near impossible to find during the Fêtes de Bayonne.

BUDGET

Hôtel Paris-Madrid (☎ 05 59 55 13 98; sorbois@wanadoo.fr; place de la Gare; s/d from €16/22, r with shower from €25; **P**) This friendly place is highly recommended, especially for those arriving at the station just across the road. The owners speak English and the rooms are good value – murals and large papier-mâché animals add some colour and artistic flair.

Hôtel des Arceaux (☎ 05 59 59 15 53; hotel.arceaux@wanadoo.fr; 26 rue Port Neuf; r with washbasin/shower €28/38) The rooms are well priced, if not particularly welcoming, but the new owners are embarking on a complete overhaul so by the time you read this, they should be offering sparkling new rooms for the same price. Rooms at the front have large windows overlooking the bustling pedestrian street below.

The **Auberge de Jeunesse** (☎ 05 59 58 70 00; anglet@fuaj.org; 19 route des Vignes, Anglet; B&B €17 first night, €14.20 subsequent nights; ❍ mid-Feb–mid-Nov) in Anglet, complete with a Scottish pub, is lively and popular. Reservations are essential in summer. See p655 for details of the outdoor sports courses Anglet offers. The hostel also has some **camping** sites (per adult incl breakfast €10).

From Bayonne station, take STAB bus No 2 (direction Anglet). At the Cinq Cantons stop, change to No 72 (direction Les Plages), which stops at the hostel. Alternatively – and in high season when bus No 72 doesn't operate – take No 2 to the Moulin Barbot stop, from where the hostel is a 10-minute signed walk. On Sunday take line C from the town hall. From Biarritz station or place Clemenceau, take bus No 9 to the Moulin Barbot stop.

See p656 for details of BAB's camping grounds.

MID-RANGE

Hôtel Loustau (☎ 05 59 55 08 08; hotel.loustau@wanadoo.fr; 1 place de la République; s/d/tr/q from €72/76/82/88; ❄ ✉) A tall and attractive 18th-century building on the St-Esprit side of the town, with comfortable three-star rooms. On the southern side of the building, the full-length windows open out onto views of the River Adour.

Adour Hôtel (☎ 05 59 55 11 31; www.adourhotel .net; 13 place Ste-Ursule; d/tr/q from €47/50/64) Just north of the River Adour and conveniently near the station, this friendly and helpful establishment has bright, airy rooms decorated along regional themes including bullfighting, rugby and gastronomy.

Hôtel Côte Basque (☎ 05 59 55 10 21; fax 05 59 55 39 85; 2 rue Maubec; d €40-46, tr €46-55) This place, also near the station, has taken a leap forward under its new owners. The rooms are pleasant and, for the most part, freshly decorated.

TOP END

Le Grand Hôtel (☎ 05 59 59 62 00, www.bw-legrand hotel.com; 21 rue Thiers; s €59-112, d €65-122; 🟦 🗶) This tastefully refurbished hotel, part of the Best Western chain, offers spacious cream-toned rooms with three-star facilities, including cable TV and room service. The old building was once a convent; you'd never guess from the slick, modern interior, but the grand façade has a certain amount of character.

Eating

You'll find a good selection of medium-priced restaurants around the covered market and all along quai Amiral Jauréguiberry.

Restaurant François Miura (☎ 05 59 59 49 89; 24 rue Marengo; menus €18.30 & €29; 🟦 closed Sun dinner & Wed) This ultrastylish place contrasts original postmodern décor with the raw timelessness of a 19th-century cloister. It's the place to be seen in Petit Bayonne, where the food, such as tender pigeon stuffed with foie gras, is just as fashionable as the clientele.

Bodega Ibaia (☎ 05 59 59 86 66; 45 quai Amiral Jauréguiberry; mains €8-12; 🟦 closed Sun & Mon lunch) This atmospheric Basque restaurant/tapas bar with wooden benches, sawdust on the floor and traditional Spanish tiling is less formal than most of the terrace restaurants on this popular stretch.

Auberge du Cheval Blanc (☎ 05 59 59 01 33; 68 rue Bourgneuf; menus €22, €32 & €68; closed Sun dinner & Mon Sep-Jun) Renowned as one of the town's most exclusive restaurants, this refined eatery fully deserves its Michelin star for its mouth-watering creative French cuisine. A must with the business set at lunch times.

La Grange (☎ 05 59 46 17 84; 26 quai Galuperie; mains €12-38; 🟦 closed Sun) With a shady outside terrace, this popular place overlooking the River Nive has the ambience of a stylish bistro. Traditional French flavours include plenty of seafood options.

Bistrot Ste-Cluque (☎ 05 59 55 82 43; 9 rue Hugues; menu €16; open lunch & dinner to 10pm) There's only one *menu* here – a large blackboard that's propped up before you. Noisy (the music's a decibel or two too loud), smoky and with waiters bustling about everywhere, it's a wonderful, no-pretensions place.

Restaurant Agadir (☎ 05 59 55 66 56; 3 rue Ste-Catherine; menu €15.50; closed lunch Mon) This enthusiastically decorated restaurant in St-Esprit, shimmering with red and gold, serves up southern Moroccan-style couscous dishes priced €9 to €13.

Restaurant Koskera (☎ 05 59 55 20 79; 2 rue Hugues; menus around €10; 🟦 lunch Mon-Sat) This dark, cavelike place in St-Esprit does not really make the most of the local climate, but it does have inexpensive daily specials of hearty Basque fare.

SELF-CATERING

The **covered market** (quai Commandant Roquebert; 🟦 7am-1pm & 3.30-7pm Fri, 8am-1pm Mon-Thu & Sat) occupies an imposing riverside building. On Tuesday, Thursday and Saturday the market spills out onto the surrounding streets.

There are a number of tempting food shops and delicatessens along rue Port Neuf and rue d'Espagne.

Drinking

The greatest concentration of pubs and bars is in the Petit Bayonne area, especially along rue Pannecau, rue des Cordeliers and quai Galuperie.

Entertainment

Every Thursday in July and August, there's traditional **Basque music** (admission free) at 9.30pm in place Charles de Gaulle.

Between October and June **Trinquet St-André** (☎ 05 59 59 18 69; rue du Jeu de Paume; tickets around €9) stages *main nue* matches (see Pelota, p653) every Thursday at 4.30pm.

In summer, corridas are held from time to time at **Les Arènes** (av du Maréchal Foch), 1km west of the city centre. The tourist office has details of upcoming corridas and also sells tickets.

A filmgoers' cooperative, **Cinéma L'Atalante** (☎ 05 59 55 76 63; 7 rue Denis Etcheverry; adult/student €5.65/3.80) screens nondubbed films.

GREG JOHNSTON

Cirque de Gavarnie (p690), Pyrenees

MARTIN MOOS

Sanctuaires Notre Dame
de Lourdes (p677)

Traditional houses along the River Nive in the Basque resort of St-Jean Pied de Port (p663)

GREG JOHNSTON

CHRISTOPHER WOOD

Cathédrale St-Étienne (p688),
Toulouse

Quai de la Daurade, River Garonne,
Toulouse (p695)

CHRISTOPHER WOOD

Unesco World Heritage–protected Pont du Gard (p738), north of Nîmes

STEVE

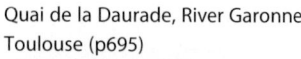

PELOTA

Pelota (*pelote basque* in French) is the generic name for a group of games native to the Basque Country, all played using a hard ball with a rubber core (the *pelote*) which is struck with bare hands (*mains nues*), a wooden paddle (*pala or paleta*), or a scoop-like racquet made of wicker, leather or wood and strapped to the wrist (*chistera*).

Cesta punta, also known as jai alai, the world's fastest ball game and the most popular variety of pelota, became faster and faster after the introduction of rubber made it possible to produce balls with more bounce. The game is played with a *chistera*, with which players catch and hurl the ball with great force. Matches take place in a jai alai, or *cancha*, a three-walled court, usually a precise 53m long.

The walls and floor are made of materials that can withstand the repeated impact of the ball, which can reach speeds of up to 300km/h. A cancha and its tiers of balconies for spectators constitute a fronton. Other types of pelota (such as *joko-garbi, main nue, pala, paleta, pasaka, rebot* and *xare*) are played in outdoor, one-wall courts, also known as frontons, and in enclosed structures called *trinquets*.

Shopping

Bayonne is famous throughout France for its ham. For the lowest prices, visit the covered market (p652). For the best quality, visit a specialist shop such as **Pierre d'Ibaïlde** (☎ 05 59 25 65 30; 42 rue des Cordeliers) where you can taste before you buy.

The town's other claim to gastronomic fame is its chocolate. Two traditional *chocolateries* are **Daranatz** (☎ 05 59 59 03 05; 15 rue Port Neuf) and **Cazenave** (☎ 05 59 59 03 16; 19 rue Port Neuf) where you'll find chocolate pralines the size of apples to challenge even the most devout chocoholics. You can also see chocolate-making in progress at **La Fabrique du Chocolatier Puyodebat** (☎ 05 59 59 20 86; 5/7 rue de Luc; ⏲ 10.30am-noon & 4.30-6pm Tue-Sat).

Getting There & Away

AIR

Biarritz-Anglet-Bayonne airport (☎ 05 59 43 83 83; www.biarritz.aeroport.fr in French) is 5km southwest of central Bayonne and 3km southeast of the centre of Biarritz. Air France flies to/from Paris Orly about eight times daily and less frequently to Lyon and Geneva. Ryanair has a daily flight to/from London Stansted.

Bus No 6 links both Bayonne and Biarritz with the airport (buses depart roughly hourly). A taxi from the town centre costs around €14.

BUS

From place des Basques, **ATCRB buses** (☎ 05 59 26 06 99) follow the coast to the Spanish border. There are 10 services daily to St-Jean de Luz (€3.60, 40 minutes) with connections for Hendaye (€5.60, one hour). Summer beach traffic can double journey times. Transportes Pesa buses leave twice a day for Irún and San Sebastián in Spain (€6.20, 1¾ hours).

From the car park at the train station, **RDTL** (☎ 05 59 55 17 59) runs services northwards into Landes. For beaches north of Bayonne, such as Mimizan Plage and Moliets Plage, get off at Vieux Boucau (1¼ hours, six or seven daily). **TER Aquitaine** (☎ 05 59 27 45 98) has two buses daily to Pau (€14.50, 2¼ hours).

Bayonne is one of three centres in southwest France for **Eurolines** (☎ 05 59 59 19 33; 3 place Charles de Gaulle). Its buses stop in the square, opposite the company office.

CAR & MOTORCYCLE

Among several rental agencies near the train station are **ADA** (☎ 05 59 50 37 10; 11 quai de Lesseps) and **Avis** (☎ 05 59 55 06 56; 1 rue Ste-Ursule). Both open Monday to Saturday.

TRAIN

TGVs run between Bayonne and Paris' Gare Montparnasse (€71.60, five hours, five daily). Within the Basque Country, there are fairly frequent trains to Biarritz (€2.10, 10 minutes), St-Jean de Luz (€3.90, 25 minutes) and St-Jean Pied de Port (€7.50, one hour), plus the Franco-Spanish border towns of Hendaye (€5.80, 40 minutes) and Irún (€6.10, 45 minutes).

There are also train sevices to Dax (€7.60, 40 minutes, up to 10 daily), Lourdes (€17.80, 1¾ hours, six daily), Bordeaux (€24.40, 2¼ hours, at least 10 daily), Pau (€13.70, 1¼ hours, eight daily) and Toulouse (€33.10, 3¾ hours, at least four daily).

Getting Around

BICYCLE

Near the train station, Adour Hôtel (p652) rents bikes, for €9/12.50/30 per half-day/ full day/three days.

BUS

STAB buses link Bayonne, Biarritz and Anglet. A single ticket costs €1.15 while carnets of five/10 are €4.75/9.50. STAB has an **information office** (☎ 05 59 52 59 52) in the northeastern corner of the town hall. Bus Nos 1, 2 and 6 run between Bayonne and Biarritz and stop at the town halls of both towns.

CAR & MOTORCYCLE

There's free parking along av des Allées Paulmy, which is within easy walking distance of the tourist office. From here there's a bright-orange shuttle bus that travels the short distance to the town centre.

TAXI

Call **Taxi Bayonne** (☎ 05 59 59 48 48) or **Taxi Gare** (☎ 05 59 55 13 15).

BIARRITZ

pop 30,000

The stylish coastal town of Biarritz, 8km west of Bayonne, took off as a resort in the mid-19th century when Napoleon III and his Spanish-born wife, Eugénie, visited regularly. These days, Biarritz is known for its beaches and some of Europe's best surfing.

The town can be expensive. If you're travelling on a budget, consider staying in Bayonne and visiting Biarritz from there, as many French holiday-makers do. Many surfers camp or stay at one of the two excellent youth hostels in Biarritz and in Anglet.

Orientation

Place Clemenceau, the heart of town, is south of the main beach (Grande Plage). Pointe St-Martin, topped with a lighthouse, rounds off Plage Miramar, the northern continuation of the Grande Plage, which is bounded on its southern side by Pointe Atalaye.

Both train station and airport are about 3km southeast of the centre.

Information

BOOKSHOPS

The Bookstore (☎ 05 59 24 48 00; place Clemenceau) Has a small selection of English books.

INTERNET ACCESS

Génius Informatique (☎ 05 59 24 39 07; 60 av Édouard VII; per hr €5; ⏱ 10am-12.30pm & 2-7.30pm Tue-Sat)
Plat-Net (☎ 05 59 24 54 48; 6 rue Guy Petit; per hr €4.50; ⏱ 10am-8pm Mon-Sat)

LAUNDRY

Laundrette (11 av de la Marne; ⏱ 7am-9pm)

POST

Main Post Office (rue de la Poste)

TOURIST INFORMATION

Tourist Office (☎ 05 59 22 37 10; www.biarritz.fr; 1 square d'Ixelles; ⏱ 8am-8pm Jul & Aug; 9am-6pm Mon-Sat, 10am-5pm Sun Sep-Jun) Publishes *Biarritzcope*, a free monthly what's-on guide.
Tourist Office Annexe At the train station in July and August.

Sights & Activities

BEACHES

Biarritz' fashionable beaches are wall-to-wall on hot summer days. In the high season, the **Grande Plage** and also **Plage Miramar** to its north are lined with striped bathing tents. Beyond Pointe St-Martin, the superb surfing beaches of **Anglet** stretch northwards for more than 4km. To get there, take the eastbound bus No 9 from place Clemenceau.

Beyond long, exposed **Plage de la Côte des Basques**, some 500m south of Port Vieux, are **Plage de Marbella** and **Plage de la Milady**. Both can be reached by westbound bus No 9.

MUSÉE DE LA MER

Biarritz' **Musée de la Mer** (Sea Museum; ☎ 05 59 22 75 40; www.museedelamer.com; Esplanade de la Vierge; adult/child €7.20/4.60; ⏱ minimum 9.30am-12.30pm, 2-6pm, closed Mon Nov-Mar) overlooks Rocher de la Vierge. The ground-floor aquarium has 24 tanks seething with underwater life from the Bay of Biscay (Golfe de Gascogne). On the 1st floor are exhibits on commercial fishing and whaling, telling stories of Biarritz' whaling past. On the 3rd floor, it's feeding time for a pair of seals at 10.30am and 5pm. A nearby pool holds a couple of sleek sharks, while the top floor has a rather mournful display of stuffed birds.

Tickets are €0.80 cheaper at the tourist office.

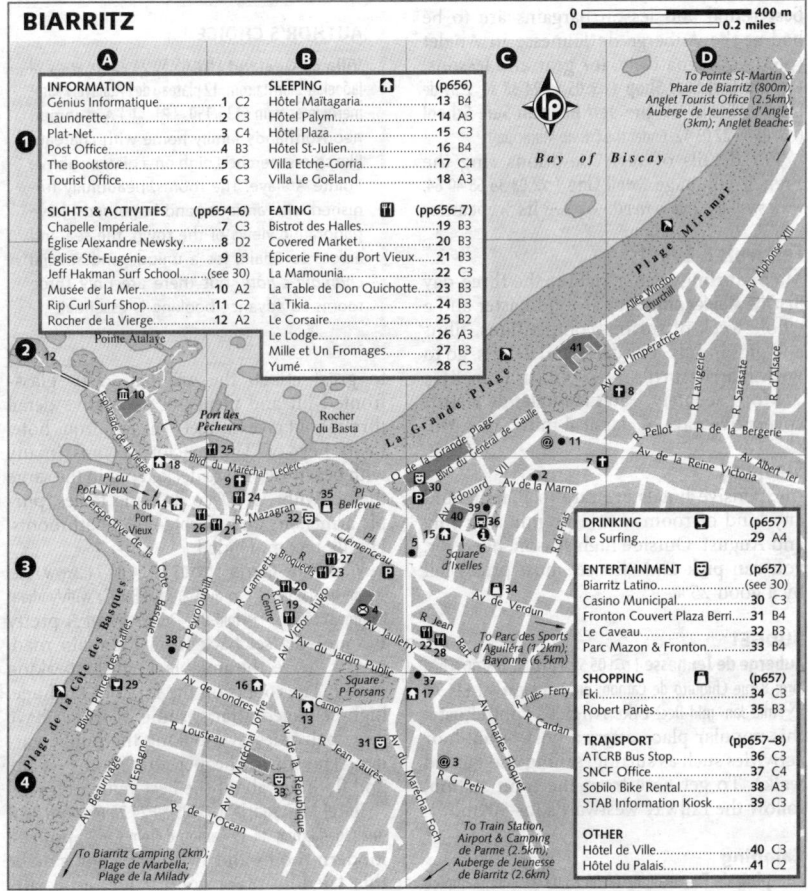

BIARRITZ

0 — 400 m
0 — 0.2 miles

INFORMATION	
Génius Informatique	1 C2
Laundrette	2 C3
Plat-Net	3 C4
Post Office	4 B3
The Bookstore	5 C3
Tourist Office	6 C3

SIGHTS & ACTIVITIES	(pp654–6)
Chapelle Impériale	7 C3
Église Alexandre Newsky	8 D2
Église Ste-Eugénie	9 B3
Jeff Hakman Surf School	(see 30)
Musée de la Mer	10 A2
Rip Curl Surf Shop	11 C2
Rocher de la Vierge	12 A2

SLEEPING	(p656)
Hôtel Maïtagaria	13 B4
Hôtel Palym	14 A3
Hôtel Plaza	15 C3
Hôtel St-Julien	16 B4
Villa Etche-Gorria	17 C4
Villa Le Goëland	18 A3

EATING	(pp656–7)
Bistrot des Halles	19 B3
Covered Market	20 B3
Épicerie Fine du Port Vieux	21 B3
La Mamounia	22 C3
La Table de Don Quichotte	23 B3
La Tikia	24 B3
Le Corsaire	25 B2
Le Lodge	26 A3
Mille et Un Fromages	27 B3
Yumé	28 C3

DRINKING	(p657)
Le Surfing	29 A4

ENTERTAINMENT	(p657)
Biarritz Latino	(see 30)
Casino Municipal	30 C3
Fronton Couvert Plaza Berri	31 B4
Le Caveau	32 B3
Parc Mazon & Fronton	33 B4

SHOPPING	(p657)
Eki	34 C3
Robert Pariès	35 B3

TRANSPORT	(pp657–8)
ATCRB Bus Stop	36 B4
SNCF Office	37 C4
Sobilo Bike Rental	38 A3
STAB Information Kiosk	39 C3

OTHER	
Hôtel de Ville	40 C3
Hôtel du Palais	41 C2

OTHER ATTRACTIONS

Stroll over the footbridge at the end of Pointe Atalaye to **Rocher de la Vierge** (Rock of the Virgin), named after the white statue of the Virgin and child. From this impressive outcrop, there are views northwards of the Landes coastline and, far to the south, the mountains of the Spanish Basque Country.

Once a lively fishing port, **Port des Pêcheurs** is nowadays a haven only to pleasure craft. Above it, the Byzantine and Moorish-style **Église Ste-Eugénie** was built in 1864 for – who else? – Empress Eugénie.

Dominating the northern end of the Grande Plage is the stately **Hôtel du Palais**, also built for Empress Eugénie in 1854 and now a luxury hotel. Opposite is **Église Alexandre Newsky** (8 av de l'Impératrice), a Russian Orthodox church built by and for the Russian aristocrats who frequented Biarritz until the Soviet Revolution. Eugénie was also the inspiration for the nearby doll's-house **Chapelle Impériale** (2-7pm Mon-Sat Jul-Sep, 3-7pm Tue, Thu & Sat Apr-Jun, 3-5pm Thu Oct-Mar), constructed in 1864.

To the north on Pointe St-Martin is the **Phare de Biarritz** (admission €1.50; 10am-noon & 3-7pm Tue-Sun Jul & Aug, 3-7pm Sat & Sun mid-Apr–Jun), the town's lighthouse, which is 73m tall and was erected in 1834.

SURFING

The 4km-long stretch of Anglet beach ranks among Europe's finest surfing venues. The best rental and lesson bargains are to be had at the Auberge de Jeunesse in Anglet (p651). Alternatively, for gear and lessons, try **Rip Curl Surf Shop** (☎ 05 59 24 38 40; 2 av de la Reine Victoria) or the **Jeff Hakman Surf School** (☎ 05 59 22 03 12; under the Casino Municipal).

For details of surf conditions ring the French-language **Swell Line** (☎ 08 36 68 40 64; www.swell-line.com in French) or see its webcam.

Festivals & Events

Major surfing events include the three-day **Biarritz Maïder Arosteguy** around Easter and a whole week of surfing competitions, films and gigs in July. For dates and details, go to www.biarritzsurffestival.com (in French).

More sedately, **Fêtes Musicales de Biarritz** covers five days of classical music in April.

Sleeping

Inexpensive hotels are rare in Biarritz and any kind of room is at a premium in July and August. Outside high season, however, you can pick and choose; most prices fall by a good 25%.

BUDGET

Auberge de Jeunesse (☎ 05 59 41 76 00; biarritz@fuaj .org; 8 rue Chiquito de Cambo; dm incl breakfast €14.90; ☒ mid-Jan–mid-Dec) Like Anglet's youth hostel this popular place offers a host of outdoor activities such as surfing, sailing and guided walks. To get here from the train station, follow the railway westwards for 800m.

Camping

Camping de Parme (☎ 05 59 23 03 00; www.camping deparme.com; route de l'Aviation; camping €15.50-23) BAB's only year-round camping ground is in a leafy spot 800m northeast of the train station. It's usually fully booked months in advance for July and August.

Biarritz Camping (☎ 05 59 23 00 12; www.biarritz -camping.fr; 28 rue d'Harcet; camping €13.50-19.50; ☒ mid-May–mid-Sep; ☒) Spacious and shady sites can be found at this summer camping ground, 3km southwest of the centre. Take westbound bus No 9 to the Biarritz Camping stop.

MID-RANGE

Hôtel Plaza (☎ 05 59 24 74 00; hotel.plaza.biarritz@ wanadoo.fr; 20 av Édouard VII; s/d from €81/103; ☒) The Plaza is a three-star Art Deco delight overlooking Grande Plage. Recently refurbished

to great effect, the original 1930s glass-fronted lift and plenty of decorative detail throughout give the feel of a glamorous hotel in its heyday. The spacious rooms (many with beach views) are decked out in the same theme, with Art Deco dressing tables, pur-ple armchairs and marble-effect bathrooms. Highly recommended.

Villa Etche-Gorria (☎ 05 59 24 00 74; www.hotel -etche-gorria.com; 21 av du Maréchal Foch; r with/without bathroom €60/35; ☒ mid-Dec–3rd week Nov) A pretty Basque villa set back from the main road, run by Pierre, the amiable, English-speaking owner. The rooms on the 1st floor are huge, high-ceilinged affairs, some of which have large balconies overlooking the public gar-den. The small, cheaper attic rooms on the 2nd floor are about the best value in town.

Hôtel Maïtagaria (☎ 05 59 24 26 65; www.hotel -maitagaria.com; 34 av Carnot; d from €56) Spotless, modern rooms and swish bathrooms make this friendly place good value, especially the large, two-roomed family suite (€99). There's an intimate garden at the rear for summer breakfasts (€6).

Hôtel St-Julien (☎ 05 59 24 20 39; www.hotel-saint -julien.com; 20 av Carnot; s/d €59/75; ☒ mid-Jan–mid-Dec) A stylish two-star option in a quiet but cen-tral location. Some rooms on the 3rd floor have mountain views.

Hôtel Palym (☎ 05 59 24 16 56; fax 05 59 24 96 12; 7 rue du Port Vieux; r with basin/bathroom from €37/49) A cosy little hotel occupying a brightly painted town house on a busy tourist street. The bedrooms are colourful but the bath-rooms are very small.

Eating

Le Corsaire (☎ 05 59 24 63 72; Port des Pêcheurs; mains €9-22; ☒ lunch & dinner Tue-Sat) The service may be excruciatingly slow at peak times, but at least you get an opportunity to enjoy the delightful harbourside setting from the terrace. It's all about seafood down here by the water's edge, with dishes including *dorade à l'espagnole* (€14.50) and *grilled cod with chorizo* (€12.20). This is one of three incredibly popular seafood restaurants here, with neighbouring **Casa Juan Pedro** (☎ 05 59 24 00 86) offering a similar *menu*, and **Chez Albert** (☎ 05 59 24 43 84; mains €17-25) offering a slightly more refined, gastronomic approach.

La Tikia (☎ 05 59 24 46 09; 1 place Ste Eugénie; menus €12.50; ☺ lunch & dinner) 'Tikia' is the Basque word for small, but although the restaurant is modestly sized, the same can't be said of the *brochettes*, giant skewers of duck (€12.50), steak (€14.50) or seafood (€13.50). For lighter appetites, there's a good selection of big and small salads. There's also a good choice of local wines, all topped off with friendly service.

Le Lodge (☎ 05 59 24 73 78; 1 rue du Port Vieux; mains €13-17; ☺ closed Sun & Mon) A buzzing new restaurant and gallery featuring traditional cuisine and contemporary art. This place dispenses with the minimalist look in favour of a clutter of zebra- and leopard-skin tablecloths and African wall art, but the overall effect works well.

Bistrot des Halles (☎ 05 59 24 21 22; 1 rue du Centre; mains €13-17; ☺ lunch & dinner until 10pm) One of a cluster of decent restaurants along rue du Centre that take their produce fresh from the nearby covered market. This bustling place serves three-course meals from the blackboard menu for about €25, including wine.

Yumé (☎ 05 59 22 01 02; 6 rue Jean Bart; menus €28-48; ☺ closed Sun) A stylish, gastronomic Japanese restaurant offering authentic, well-presented sushi, sashimi and tempura dishes.

La Mamounia (☎ 05 59 24 76 08; 4 rue Jean Bart) The extravagant North African décor, the centrepiece of which is a ridiculously huge Moroccan teapot, makes this a suitable place to tuck into delicious tagine (€15 to €16) and couscous (€13 to €19.50) dishes.

SELF-CATERING
Biarritz has a **covered market** (☺ 7am-1.30pm). Just downhill, **La Table de Don Quichotte** (12 av Victor Hugo) sells all sorts of Spanish hams, sausages and wines, while you'll find a tempting array of cheeses, wines and pâtés at nearby **Mille et Un Fromages** (8 av Victor Hugo). Down at

sea level, **Épicerie Fine du Port Vieux** (41bis rue Mazagran) is another excellent delicatessen.

Drinking
There are good bars along rue du Port Vieux and the streets radiating from it. It's also well worth snooping around place Clemenceau and the central food market area.

Le Surfing (☎ 05 59 24 78 72; 9 blvd Prince des Galles) After a hard day's surfing, this is the place to come and discuss waves and wipe-outs. The bar is full of surfing memorabilia and there's an outside terrace with decent views.

Entertainment
In high summer there are free Friday evening **classical music concerts** in front of Église Ste-Eugénie and at other venues.

If you fancy frittering away your travel money, step into the white slab of Biarritz' **Casino Municipal** (1 av Édouard VII; 10am-3am Mon-Fri, 10am-4am Sat & Sun). Constructed in 1928, gambling (slot) machines whir and chink until the wee hours.

Two discos near the town centre are **Le Caveau** (☎ 05 59 24 16 17; 4 rue Gambetta; ☺ 11pm-5am) and **Biarritz Latino** (☎ 05 59 22 77 59; ☺ 11pm-5am Tue-Sat). Both venues are within the Casino Municipal.

At the **Fronton Couvert Plaza Berri** (☎ 05 59 22 15 72; 42 av du Maréchal Foch) there's pelota (p653) at 9pm every Tuesday and Friday from June to early September. Other tournaments are held here year-round, often on Sunday afternoons. From July to mid-September, the open-air fronton at **Parc Mazon** has regular *chistera* matches at 9pm on Monday. Admission to each is around €8.

Between mid-June and mid-September, **Euskal-Jaï** (☎ 05 59 23 91 09; av Henri Haget) in the Parc des Sports d'Aguiléra complex, 2km east of central Biarritz, has regular professional *cesta punta* matches at 9pm. Tickets cost between €10 and €20, Bus No 1 stops nearby.

Shopping
For Basque music, crafts and guidebooks, visit **Eki** (☎ 05 59 24 79 64; 21 av de Verdun). For scrumptious chocolates and Basque sweets, drop in on **Robert Pariès** (1 place Bellevue).

Getting There & Away
AIR
Biarritz-Anglet-Bayonne is the nearest airport (p653). Take STAB bus No 6 or, on

Sunday, line C to/from Biarritz' town hall. Each runs once or twice hourly, from 6am until about 7pm.

BUS

Stopping outside the tourist office, there are nine daily **ATCRB buses** (☎ 05 59 26 06 99) that follow the coast southwestwards to St-Jean de Luz (€2.80, 30 to 40 minutes) and Hendaye (€4.90, one hour five minutes). For other destinations, it's better to go from Bayonne – not least in order to ensure a seat in high season.

TRAIN

Biarritz–La Négresse train station is about 3km from the town centre. Bus Nos 2 and 9 connect the two. **SNCF** (13 av du Maréchal Foch; ☒ Mon-Fri) has a town-centre office. Times, fares and destinations are much the same as those detailed on p653.

Getting Around

BUS

Most services stop beside the town hall, from where route Nos 1 and 2 go to Bayonne's town hall and station. **STAB** (☎ 05 59 24 26 53) has an information kiosk just outside the tourist office.

MOTORCYCLE & BICYCLE

You can rent several varieties of wheeled transport from **Sobilo** (☎ 05 59 24 94 47; 24 rue Peyroloubilh): mountain bikes (€12 per day), scooters (from €31) and even in-line skates (€12).

TAXI

Call **Taxis Biarritz** (☎ 05 59 23 05 50).

ST-JEAN DE LUZ & CIBOURE

pop 19,450

St-Jean de Luz ('Donibane Lohizune' in Basque), 24km southwest of Bayonne at the mouth of the River Nivelle, is the most Basque of the region's beach resorts. Hugging one side of a sheltered bay, it has a colourful history of whaling and piracy. Together with its twin town of Ciboure, it makes a pleasant day trip from either Bayonne or Biarritz.

St-Jean de Luz is still an active fishing port, renowned for large catches of sardines (from the waters off Portugal and Morocco), tuna (from the Bay of Biscay and West Africa) and anchovies (from the Bay of Biscay).

Ciboure is St-Jean de Luz' quiet alter ego. Many whitewashed Basque houses, timber-framed and shuttered in green or oxblood-red, survive just south of rue Agorette.

Places mentioned in this section are in St-Jean de Luz unless stated otherwise.

Orientation

St-Jean de Luz and its long beach is on the eastern side of Baie de St-Jean de Luz, with smaller Ciboure on the western curve of the bay. A tiny but active fishing harbour nestles at the mouth of the River Nivelle, dividing the two towns. The axis of St-Jean de Luz is pedestrianised rue Gambetta with bustling place Louis XIV at its southwestern end.

Information

Cyber-Café Azerty (☎ 05 59 51 22 50; 8 blvd Thiers; per hr €5; ☒ 9am-12.30pm & 2-7pm Mon-Fri) Has six terminals for Internet access.

Laverie du Port (place Maréchal Foch; ☒ 7am-9pm) For washing those travelling clothes.

Post Office St-Jean de Luz (cnr blvd Victor Hugo & rue Salagoity) Ciboure (quai Maurice Ravel)

Tourist Office (☎ 05 59 26 03 16; www.saint-jean-de-luz.com; place Maréchal Foch; ☒ 9am-7.30pm Mon-Sat, 10am-1pm & 3-7pm Sun Jul & Aug, 9am-12.30pm & 2.30-6.30pm Mon-Sat, 10am-1pm Sun Sep-Jun)

Sights & Activities

The promontory of **Pointe Ste-Barbe,** at the northern end of the Baie de St-Jean de Luz, is great for panoramas of the town and the wind-tossed sea. It's 1km northeast of the St-Jean de Luz beach, via blvd Thiers and the seaside promenade des Rochers.

The heart of **Socoa** is about 2.5km west of Ciboure along the continuation of quai Maurice Ravel. Its prominent **fort** was built in 1627 and later improved by Vauban. You can walk out to the **Digue de Socoa** breakwater or climb to the **lighthouse** via rue du Phare, then out along rue du Sémaphore for fabulous coastal views.

BEACHES

St-Jean de Luz' family-friendly sandy beach sprouts bathing tents (€6.25 per day) from June to September. Ciboure has its own modest beach.

Plage de Socoa, 2km west of Socoa on the corniche (the D912), is served by ATCRB buses (p662) en route to Hendaye and in high season by boats (p662).

ST-JEAN DE LUZ

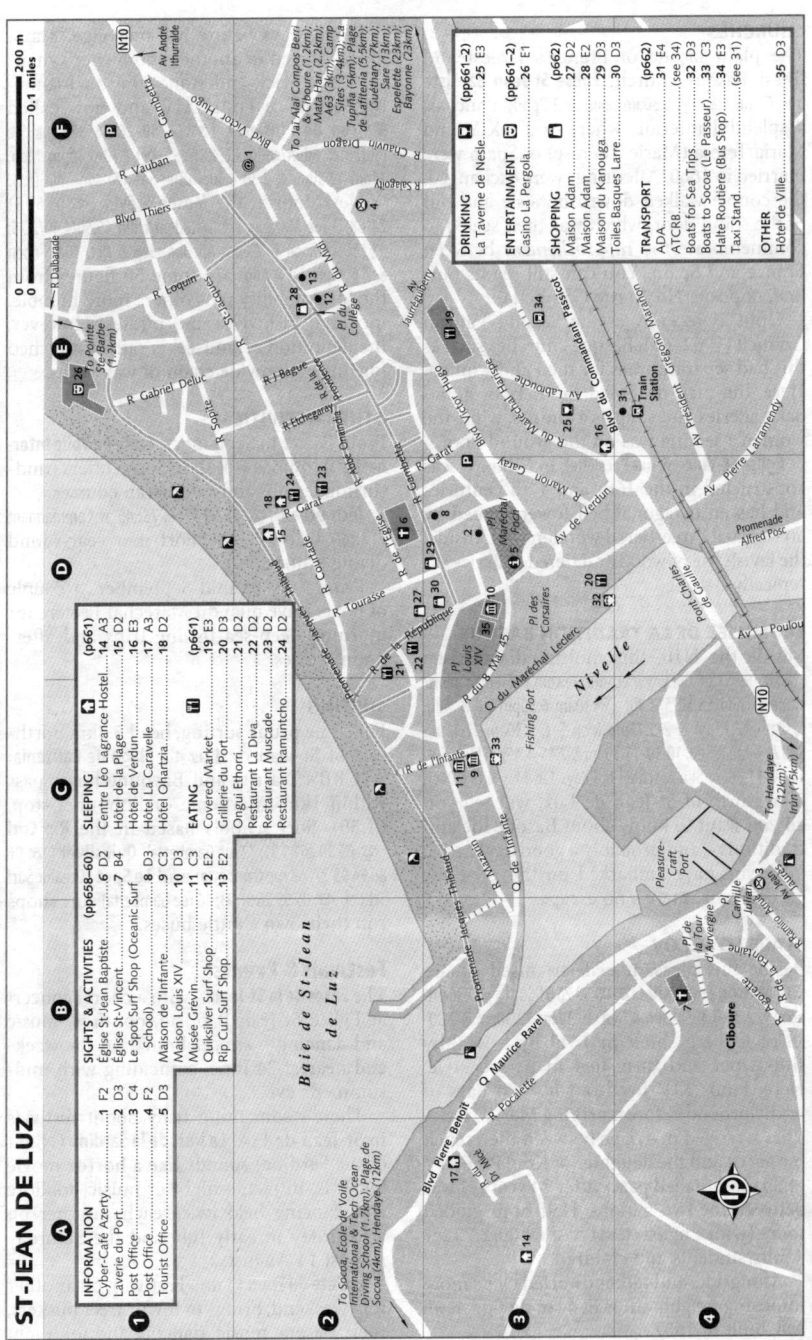

CHURCHES

The plain façade of France's largest and finest Basque church, **Église St-Jean Baptiste** (rue Gambetta; ⏰ 8.30am-noon & 2-7pm), conceals a splendid interior, where Louis XIV and Maria Teresa (Marie Thérèse) of Spain were married in 1660. After rings were exchanged, the couple walked down the aisle and out of the south door, which was then sealed to commemorate the *rapprochement* between France and Spain. You can still see its outline, opposite No 20 rue Gambetta.

Until as recently as the Second Vatican Council (1962–65), Basque churches such as this had separate areas for men and women. Here, the men occupied the tiers of grand oak galleries and sang as a chorus, while the women's seating was on the ground floor.

Église St-Vincent (rue Pocalette), in Ciboure, was constructed in the 16th and 17th centuries and has an octagonal bell tower topped by an unusual three-tiered wooden roof. Inside, the lavish use of wood and tiered galleries are typically Basque.

ÉCOMUSÉE DE LA TRADITION BASQUE

Beside the N10, this multimedia **museum** (⏰ 05 59 51 06 06; www.ecomusee.com in French; adult/student/child €5.50/5/2.30; ⏰ 10am-6.30pm Jul & Aug, 9.30am-12.15pm & 2-5.15pm Mon-Sat, 9.30am-12.15pm Sun Apr-Jun & Sep, 10.30-11.30am & 2.45-4.45pm Mon-Sat, 10.30-11.30am Sun & school holidays Jan-Mar & Oct-Dec), 2km north of St-Jean de Luz, will tell you all you want to know about Basque life and traditions – and probably a good deal more; once you have embarked on the 1½-hour guided tour, there's no escape.

PLACE LOUIS XIV

Beside this pleasant pedestrianised square sits **Maison Louis XIV** (⏰ 05 59 26 01 56; ⏰ 10.30am-noon & 2.30-5.30pm Jun & Sep, 10.30am-12.30pm & 2.30-6.30pm Jul & Aug), built in 1643 by a wealthy shipowner and furnished in period style. Here, Louis XIV lived out his last days of bachelorhood before marrying Maria Teresa. This arranged marriage between the French monarch and the daughter of King Philip IV of Spain signalled peace after 24 years of war between the two nations. Half-hour guided tours (with English text) cost €4.60/2.75 for adults/students and children.

Alongside, and rather dwarfed by its more imposing neighbour, is St-Jean de Luz' **town hall**, built in 1657.

In the days before her marriage, Maria Teresa stayed in another shipowner's mansion, the brick-and-stone Maison Joanoenia, off place Louis XIV and now called **Maison de l'Infante** (⏰ 05 59 26 36 82; quai de l'Infante; adult/child €2.30/free; ⏰ 2.30-6.30pm Mon, 11am-12.30pm & 2.30-6.30pm Tue-Sat mid-Jun–mid-Oct).

Next door at the **Musée Grévin** (⏰ 05 59 51 24 88; 3 rue Mazarin; adult/student/child €5.50/4.40/2.75; ⏰ 10am-noon & 2-6pm Apr-Jun, Sep & Oct, 10am-noon & 2-6.30pm Jul & Aug) are some 50 figures from the local nobility plus others more humble, including fishwives and pirates. However, the definition of 'musée' is rather stretched for this nationwide chain of waxworks.

OTHER ACTIVITIES

From Easter to September, **École de Voile International** (⏰ 05 59 47 06 32) in Socoa offers windsurfing lessons and catamaran courses.

Tech Ocean (⏰ 05 59 47 96 75; 45 av Commandant Passicot) below Socoa Fort is a year-round diving school.

From May to mid-September, a couple of boats leave quai du Maréchal Leclerc for morning deep-sea fishing trips and afternoon cruises.

SURFING

For some prime surfing, head 5.5km northeast of St-Jean de Luz to **Plage de Lafitenia**; ATCRB's Biarritz and Bayonne buses pass within 1km (Martienia or Bubonnet stop, €1.50). Surf schools based in the **Rip Curl** (⏰ 05 59 26 81 95; 72 rue Gambetta), **Quiksilver** (⏰ 06 86 94 95 27; 68 rue Gambetta) and **Le Spot** (Oceanic Surf School; ⏰ 05 59 26 07 93; 16 rue Gambetta) surf shops run their own shuttle buses.

Festivals & Events

The **Fêtes de la St-Jean** – with a choral concert at Église St-Jean Baptiste, bonfires, music and dancing – are celebrated on the weekend nearest 24 June, coinciding with midsummer's eve.

There's something fishy about festivals in St-Jean de Luz. **La Nuit de la Sardine** (Night of the Sardine) sounds like a horror movie but it is, in fact, a night of music, folklore and dancing held twice each summer on a Saturday in early July and the Saturday nearest 14 August.

La Fête du Thon (Tuna Festival), on another July weekend, brings to town street buskers, rock, Basque music, dancing and midnight fireworks, while numerous stands sell all sorts of tuna dishes.

Folk dancers from all across the Spanish and French Basque Country congregate for **Danses des 7 Provinces Basques** in late May or early June, while **Régates de Traînières** is a weekend of whaleboat races on the first weekend in July.

Sleeping

You will need to reserve your accommodation well in advance for visits between July and mid-September. There are very few budget hotels, although off-season prices for mid-range hotels can fall relatively low.

Centre Léo Lagrange (☎ 05 59 47 04 79; 8 rue Simone Menez; dm with breakfast €10) This cheap hostel in Ciboure offers the bare essentials. It's best to phone before arriving in high summer, when it's often full.

Hôtel Ohartzia (☎ 05 59 26 00 06; www.hotel-ohartzia.com in French; 28 rue Garat; r €75-84 high season, €59-65 low-season) This beautifully tranquil Basque house, just a few steps from the beach in St-Jean de Luz, is a world away from the bustle. The immaculate rooms are well furnished and equipped, but the highlight is the rear garden courtyard, an oasis of calm with a gentle twittering of birds: perfect background noise for a siesta.

Hôtel La Caravelle (☎ 05 59 47 18 05; www.hotel lacaravelle.com; blvd Pierre Benoît; r €50-80; P) This nautical themed place in Ciboure comprising two former fishermen's cottages has recently been updated to provide 20 modern rooms, seven of which have fantastic views over the bay.

Hôtel de la Plage (☎ 05 59 51 03 44; www.hotelde laplage.com; 33 rue Garat; r €59-118; ☼ mid-Feb–mid-Dec; P) Located right on the main stretch of beach in St-Jean de Luz, this white-painted red-shuttered building is in a fantastic spot. Most rooms have tiny balconies, enough to fit a table and two chairs. The drawback is that it can get noisy in peak season, especially when the bar downstairs is full.

Hôtel de Verdun (☎ 05 59 26 02 55; 13 av de Verdun; r €26-63) Opposite the train station in St-Jean de Luz, this simple place has a complicated pricing structure, which involves taking half board in high season, which is probably not the best option if you want to explore the town's better restaurants. At other times it's good value for relatively spacious, if plain, rooms.

CAMPING

Between St-Jean de Luz and Guéthary, 7km northeast up the coast, are no fewer than 16 camping areas. ATCRB's Biarritz and Bayonne buses stop within 1km of them all. The selection includes the four-star **Camping International Erromardie** (☎ 05 59 26 07 74; www .erromardie.com; camping €15-26; ☼ mid-Apr–Sep) in Erromardie.

Eating

There are a number of fancy restaurants along rue de la République and more, interspersed with cafés, around place Louis XIV.

Grillerie du Port (☎ 05 59 51 18 29; quai du Maréchal Leclerc; ☼ mid-Jun–mid-Sep) For the freshest seafood in town – guaranteed – join the crowds in this old shack by the port gorging themselves on fresh sardines, salads and slabs of tuna steak fresh off the boat. Informal, economical and enormously popular.

Restaurant La Diva (☎ 05 59 51 14 01; 7 rue de la République; menus €15, €18 & €25; ☼ Mar-Oct) Less hearty and more relaxed than Grillerie du Port, this restaurant's cuisine is still firmly fishy, with an emphasis on Basque and Spanish flavours. It's one of many decent options on this restaurant-packed street.

Ongui Ethorri (☎ 05 59 26 85 07; 15 rue de la République; menus €17 & €26; lunch & dinner Mar-Nov) Another popular Basque seafood place on this stretch. If you're feeling a bit peckish, try the house speciality, *parrillada de poissons* (€46 to €54), a huge seafood platter with langoustines, mussels, prawns and five types of fish!

Restaurant Ramuntcho (☎ 05 59 26 03 89; 24 rue Garat; menus €18 & €23; ☼ closed Mon low season) This lively place, whose owner hails from Normandy, successfully blends the cuisine of northern and southwestern France. Duck and fish dishes feature prominently, as do tasty jugs of sangria.

Restaurant Muscade (☎ 05 59 26 96 73; 20 rue Garat; ☼ Feb-Dec) Mixed salads (€8 to €11) and tasty pies and tarts (€5 to €€8) feature here.

SELF-CATERING

There is a food market that operates every Tuesday and Friday mornings (plus Saturdays in July and August) at the covered market, which spills into blvd Victor Hugo.

Drinking & Entertainment

La Taverne de Nesle (☎ 05 59 26 60 93; www.lataverne .best.cd in French; 5 av Labrouche; ☼ 1pm-3am Mon-Sat,

5pm-3am Sun) This cheery neighbourhood pub has a DJ every Friday year-round, and more frequently in summer.

Although swarming with people in high season, St-Jean de Luz has only two discos: **Mata Hari** (☎ 05 59 26 04 28; 48 av André Ithurralde), 2km east of the train station, and **La Tupiña** (☎ 05 59 54 73 23), 5km east on the N10.

Casino La Pergola (☎ 05 59 51 58 58; rue Dalbarade) – with slot machines operating from 11am to 3am daily, and gaming from 9pm to 3am from Tuesday to Sunday – is bang on the beach.

SPORT

In July and August, there's *cesta punta* at the **Jaï Alaï Compos Berri** (☎ 05 59 51 65 30) on route de Bayonne (the N10), 1km northeast of the train station. Matches start at 9pm every Tuesday and Friday, and half-time is spiced up with music or dancing. Tickets are available at the tourist office and are priced between €9 and €20, depending on the crowd-pulling capacity of the players.

Shopping

Agonise over the rich choice of high-calorie Basque pastries and sweets at **La Maison du Kanouga** (9 rue Gambetta). Equally tempting are the two branches of **Maison Adam** (49 rue Gambetta & 6 rue de la République), which has been making sweets since the 17th century.

St-Jean de Luz is also a good place to purchase Basque linen – for example, at **Toiles Basques Larre** (4 rue de la République). In summer, linen woven by the local manufacturer Créations Jean-Vier is on sale at **Maison de l'Infante** (see p660).

Getting There & Away

BUS

Buses run by **ATCRB** (☎ 05 59 26 06 99) pass the Halte Routière bus stop near the train station on their way northeast to Biarritz (€2.80, 30 minutes, over 10 daily Monday to Saturday, six on Sunday) and Bayonne (€3.60, 40 minutes, same frequency as to Biarritz). Southwestwards, there are around 15 services daily to Hendaye (€2.80, 25 minutes), of which four follow the coast and a couple continue to Irún (€3.10) in Spain.

Also passing Halte Routière, Spanish company Transportes Pesa has twice-daily buses to San Sebastián (€3.60, one hour), to which ATCRB runs a summer-only service.

From April to October **Le Basque Bondissant** (The Leaping Basque; ☎ 05 59 26 30 74) runs buses to La Rhune and the Grottes de Sare (p663).

TRAIN

There are frequent trains to Bayonne (€3.90, 25 minutes) via Biarritz (€2.50, 15 minutes) and to Hendaye (€2.50, 15 minutes), with connections to San Sebastián.

Getting Around

BOAT

Between June and September, the good ship **Le Passeur** (☎ 06 81 20 84 98) plies between quai de l'Infante and Socoa (€2 one way) every half-hour.

BUS

Between June and September, the Navette Intercommunale, run by ATCRB, provides a local daily bus service and a skeleton service during the rest of the year. Take Line A for Erromardie and the camping grounds north of town, and Line D for Socoa via Ciboure.

CAR

Car-rental company **ADA** (☎ 05 59 26 26 22) has an office at the train station.

MOTORCYCLE & BICYCLE

Based at the train station, **Fun Bikes** (☎ 05 59 26 75 76) rents cycles (€12 per day) and scooters (€31 per day).

TAXI

The train station has a taxi rank, or call ☎ 05 59 26 10 11 to book a car.

AROUND ST-JEAN DE LUZ
La Rhune

La Rhune ('Larrun' in Basque), a 905m-high, antenna-topped mountain, lies 10km south of St-Jean de Luz. Half in France and half in Spain, it's something of a Basque symbol. Views are spectacular from its peak, which is best approached from **Col de St-Ignace**, which is 3km northwest of Sare on the D4 (the St-Jean de Luz road). From here, you can take a pleasant if fairly strenuous walk or hop onto **Le Petit Train de la Rhune** (☎ 05 59 54 20 26; www.rhune.com; single/return adult €9/11, children €5.50/6.50). This charming little train takes 30 minutes to haul itself up the 4km from col to summit. It runs from Easter to mid-November with departures roughly every half-hour from 9am (8.30am in July and August), depending on the crowds. Be prepared for a wait of up to an hour in high summer.

Sare

Sare sits in the skirts of La Rhune. At its heart is place du Fronton, where you'll find the **tourist office** (☎ 05 59 54 20 14) sharing premises with the town hall and another sturdy Basque parish church.

Along the D306, 6km south of the village, is the **Grottes de Sare** (☎ 05 59 54 21 88; adult/child €6/3; ☽ 10am-7pm Jul & Aug, 10am-6pm Easter-Jun & Sep, 10am-5pm Oct–mid-Nov, 2-5pm mid-Nov–Dec & Mar-Easter, 2-4pm Feb), whose gaping entrance leads via narrow passages to a huge central cavern, first inhabited at least 20,000 years ago. To reach it, you need to join one of the obligatory multilingual tours.

Espelette

Whether you like your food sweet or spicy, Espelette should appeal. Above all, the village is famous for its dark red peppers, an essential ingredient of so much Basque cuisine. So prized is *le piment d'Espelette* that it's been accorded *Appellation d'Origine Contrôlée* (AOC) status, much like a fine wine. Arrive in the autumn and you can scarcely see the walls of the houses, which are masked by rows of peppers, threaded with string and hung up to dry. The last weekend in October marks Espelette's **Fête du Piment**, with processions, a formal blessing of the peppers and the ennoblement of a *chevalier du piment* (a knight of the pimento).

Although some like it hot, others may prefer sweeter pleasures. **Chocolats Anton** (☎ 05 59 93 80 58; place du Marché) is a specialist chocolate-maker that offers free tastings of its delightful wares.

The **tourist office** (☎ 05 59 93 95 02) is within a small stone chateau and shares its premises with the town hall. On the 2nd floor of the chateau is a photographic exhibition about – what else? – peppers around the world.

ST-JEAN PIED DE PORT

pop 1400

The walled Pyrenean town of St-Jean Pied de Port (Donibane Garazi in Basque), 53km southeast of Bayonne, was once the last stop in France for pilgrims who converged here from all over the country. Refreshed, they headed south over the Spanish border, a mere 8km away, and on to Santiago de Compostela in western Spain.

Nowadays the town is a popular departure point for hikers and bikers attempting the pilgrim trail.

A pretty little town, St-Jean Pied de Port desperately needs a traffic bypass but it does make for a pleasant day trip from Bayonne. Half the reason for coming here is the scenic journey south of Cambo-les-Bains, as both railway and road (the D918) pass through rocky hills, forests and lush meadows dotted with white farmhouses whose signs announce *ardi* ('cheese' in Basque) for sale.

The town can be hideously crowded in summer. Consider staying the night and exploring before breakfast or visit in low season. Even better, to leave it all behind, rent a bike or pull on your boots and head for the surrounding hills.

Information

Bar Paris (☎ 05 59 37 01 47; 33 av Renaud; per hr €4) For Internet access; a few steps from the station.

Tourist office (☎ 05 59 37 03 57; www.pyrenees -basques.com; place Charles de Gaulle; ☽ 9am-7pm Mon-Sat, 10am-4pm Sun Jul & Aug; 9am-noon & 2-6pm Mon-Sat Sep-Jun plus 10am-4pm Sun Apr-Jun)

Sights & Activities

OLD TOWN

The church of **Notre Dame du Bout du Pont**, with foundations as old as the town itself, was thoroughly rebuilt in the 17th century. Beyond **Porte de Notre Dame**, which abuts the church, is the photogenic **Vieux Pont** (Old Bridge) from where there's a fine view of whitewashed houses with balconies leaning out above the water. Fishing is forbidden where the River Nive passes through town, and the fat, gulping trout seem to know it. Over the bridge is the commercial artery of rue d'Espagne. A pleasant 500m riverbank stroll upstream brings you to the steeply arched so-called **Pont Romain** (meaning Roman Bridge, but in fact dating from the 17th century).

Rue de la Citadelle is bordered by substantial, pink-granite 16th- to 18th-century residences. Look for the construction date on door lintels (the oldest we found was 1510). A common motif is the scallop shell, symbol

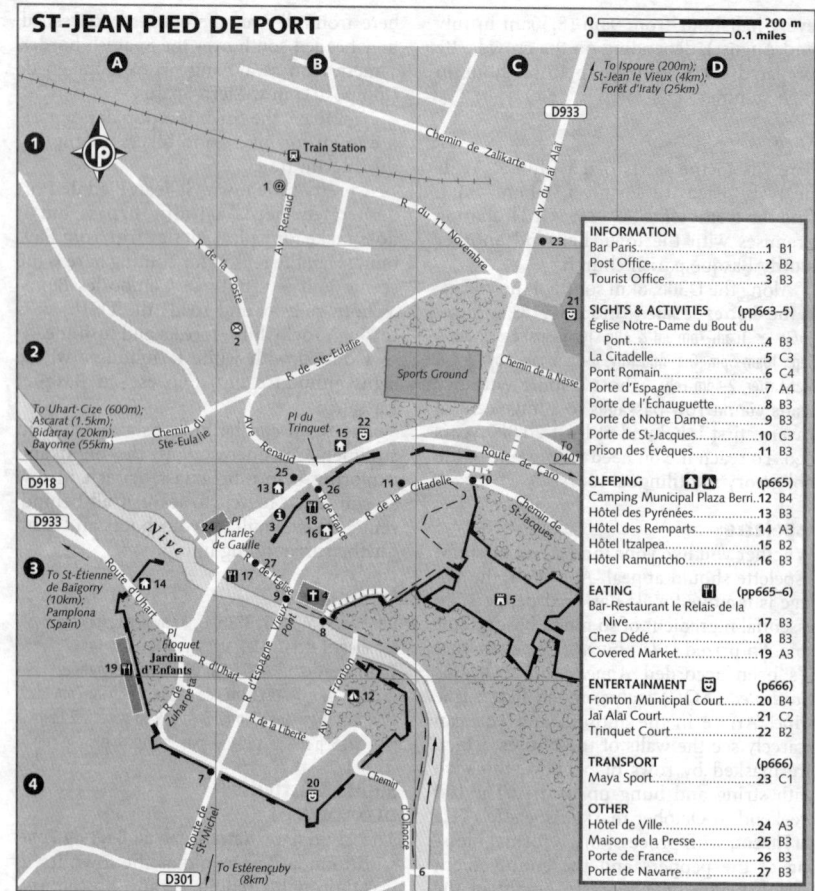

ST-JEAN PIED DE PORT

of St-Jacques (St James or Santiago) and of the Santiago de Compostela pilgrims, and perhaps an early example of come-hither advertising by the boarding housekeepers of the time. Pilgrims would enter the town through the **Porte de St-Jacques** on the northern side of town, then, refreshed and probably a little poorer, head for Spain through the **Porte d'Espagne**, south of the river.

LA CITADELLE

From the top of rue de la Citadelle, a rough cobblestone path ascends to the massive citadel itself, from where there are splendid views of the town, the River Nive and the surrounding hills. Constructed in 1628, the fort was rebuilt around 1680 by military

engineers of the Vauban school. Nowadays it serves as a secondary school and is closed to the public.

If you've a head for heights, descend by the steps signed *escalier poterne* (rear stairway). Steep and slippery after rain, they plunge beside the moss-covered ramparts to **Porte de l'Échauguette** (Watchtower Gate).

PRISON DES ÉVÊQUES

The so-called **Prison des Évêques** (Bishops' Prison; 41 rue de la Citadelle; €3; ☒ 11am-12.30pm & 2.30-6pm Easter–mid-Oct), a claustrophobic vaulted cellar, gets its history muddled. It indeed served as the town jail from 1795, as a military lock-up in the 19th century, then as a place of internment during WWII for those caught trying to flee to nominally neutral Spain. The lower section dates from the 13th century when St-Jean Pied de Port was a bishopric of the Avignon papacy, but the building above it dates from the 16th century, by which time the bishops were long gone.

WALKING & CYCLING

St-Jean Pied de Port is a fine place from which to walk or cycle into the Pyrenean foothills, where the loudest sounds you'll hear are cowbells and the wind. Both the GR10 (the trans-Pyrenean long-distance trail running from the Atlantic to the Mediterranean) and the GR65 (the Chemin de St-Jacques pilgrim route) pass through town. **Maison de la Presse** (place Charles de Gaulle) carries a good selection of walking maps.

Pick up a copy of *25 Randonnées en Pays Basque* (€6.10) from the tourist office. Written in French but with explicit maps, it gives enough ideas for walking or mountain-bike routes to keep you active and happy for a good two weeks or more.

To cycle the easy way while enjoying the best of the views of the Nive Valley, load your bicycle onto the train in Bayonne – they're carried free on most services – and roll back down the valley from St-Jean Pied de Port. If you find the ride all the way back to the coast daunting, rejoin the train at Pont-Noblia, for example, or Cambo-les-Bains. For local bike hire, see p666.

Tours

In July and August, the tourist office organises tours of the old town (in French) and Friday morning visits to the citadel.

Festivals & Events

In high summer there is a weekly handicraft and food fair, held most Thursdays, in the covered market.

Sleeping

The tourist office has details of *gîtes* and *chambres d'hôtes* in the area, primarily but not exclusively, for walkers and pilgrims.

Hôtel Itzalpea (☎ 05 59 37 03 66; itzalpea@wanadoo .fr; 5 place du Trinquet; d/tr/q with bathroom €35/46/54) This family-run budget option is sure to please.

Hôtel des Remparts (☎ 05 59 37 13 79; remparts .hotel@wanadoo.fr; 16 place Floquet; d with bathroom €40-50; Feb-Sep) A red-shuttered, chalet-style building with functional, good-sized rooms and

sturdy wooden furniture. It's the best of the cheaper options and is popular with walkers swapping tips and comparing blisters.

Hôtel Ramuntcho (☎ 05 59 37 03 91; fax 05 59 37 35 17; 1 rue de France; d with bathroom €45-59; closed Wed off-season) A pleasant Logis de France (see p895) within the old walls, this rustic place offers smallish but well-maintained rooms. Some rooms (3, 4, 10 and 11) have balconies that directly overlook the red-brown ramparts and beyond to the mountains. There's also a good restaurant (p665).

Hôtel des Pyrénées (☎ 05 59 37 01 01; hotel .pyrenees@wanadoo.fr; 19 place Charles de Gaulle; r €92-155; mid-Jan–mid-Nov; P X X) The town's classiest hotel offers large, luxurious rooms of contemporary design inside a traditional Basque building. Balconies reveal stunning views of the surrounding mountains, and there's a much-acclaimed restaurant (p665).

CAMPING

Riverside **Camping Municipal Plaza Berri** (☎ 05 59 37 11 19; av du Fronton; per adult/tent/car €2/1.50/1.50; Apr-Oct) has ample shade.

Eating

Chez Dédé (☎ 05 59 37 16 40; 3 rue de France; menu €10, full meals €14-15; closed Thu & dinner Wed) Nestled in the ramparts of the old town, this busy place, pulling in pilgrims and walkers, is hot on Basque peppers. The flexible, pick-and-mix menu includes entrees (€4), mains (€8 to €9) and desserts (€2). Try the *piquillos farcis à la morue* (sweet peppers stuffed with cod in a rich tomato sauce).

Bar-Restaurant le Relais de la Nive (☎ 05 59 37 04 22; place du Marché; menus €18.50 & €25; closed Thu & Dec-Feb) This eatery occupies a wonderful spot beside the river and has views of the Vieux Pont, which is perfectly reflected by day and floodlit at night.

Most of the hotels recommended in the Sleeping section also have worthwhile restaurants. Both **Hôtel Itzalpea** (menus €10.70-14.50) and **Hôtel Ramuntcho** (menus €11.20-17.50) offer family-style, regional cuisine at a budget price. In its own league, **Hôtel des Pyrénées** (menus €40-85) is a highly respected gastronomic establishment, with a quiet, refined ambience. The Michelin-starred French and Basque cuisine is reason enough to come to St-Jean; creations such as *raviolis de langoustines au caviar d'aquitaine* (€45) justify all the hype.

FRENCH BASQUE COUNTRY

SELF-CATERING

Farmers bring in their fresh produce for the town's **Monday market** (place Charles de Gaulle).

Entertainment

In high summer, there are performances of Basque music and dancing in the jai alai court at 9.30pm on Thursdays.

At 5pm every Monday, coinciding with market day, there's a bare-handed pelota tournament at the **trinquet court** (place du Trinquet).

In summer, variants of pelota are played according to the day of the week at the *trinquet, fronton municipal* and jai alai courts. Check schedules at the tourist office. Admission to each costs about €10.

Getting There & Away

Train is the best option; the irregular bus service to/from Bayonne is a huge detour. The train journey to/from Bayonne up the Nive Valley to the end of the line (€7.50, one hour, four daily) is just beautiful.

For a day trip, take the 8.55am from Bayonne. The last train back leaves St-Jean Pied de Port at 4.53pm (check these times, which may vary according to season).

Getting Around

BICYCLE

Maya Sport (☎ 05 59 37 15 98; 18 av du Jaï Alaï) has mountain bikes for hire.

CAR

Parking can be a real pain in summer. The car parks beside the covered market and by the jai alai pelota court, both free, are the largest.

TAXI

To order a taxi, call ☎ 05 59 37 05 00 or ☎ 05 59 37 13 37.

AROUND ST-JEAN PIED DE PORT

The village of **St-Étienne de Baïgorry** along with its outlying hamlets straggle across the Vallée de Baïgorry. Tranquillity itself, after busy St-Jean Pied de Port, and stretched thinly along a branch of the Nive, the village has, like so many Basque settlements, two focal points: the church and the fronton court.

Irouléguy is the French Basque Country's only AOC wine – and most of it comes from the Vallée de Baïgorry. Just north of town, the **wine-growers' cooperative** (☎ 05 59 37 41 33) organises vineyard visits (€3) in July and August. It's open year-round for sales and tasting.

Both St-Étienne de Baïgorry and its near-neighbour **Bidarray**, further down the valley, make excellent bases for walking. The tourist office in St-Jean Pied de Port has a booklet on walks in the area (€6.10) and accommodation details.

The Pyrenees

As the crow flies, the Pyrenees (Pyrénées) stretch for 430km, sea to sea, forming a natural boundary between France and Spain. Had you sufficient time and energy, you could follow the GR10 walking trail that bucks and twists from Hendaye beside the Bay of Biscay on France's Atlantic coast all the way to Banyuls beside the Mediterranean. But few travellers have such luxuries in abundance so you'll probably have to select from its three distinct zones.

The Pyrénées-Atlantiques rise steadily from the Atlantic, their lush green heads poking through mist and cloud, their skirts of rustling beech forest.

The Hautes Pyrénées, focus of this chapter, are wilder and higher. Their rugged peaks and ridges, deep valleys and high cols are protected territory, falling within the narrow strip of the Parc National des Pyrénées that shadows the frontier for about 100km. Here, you can disappear into the mountains for days and spot only other walkers, marmots, izards (cousin to the chamois) – and, if you're *very* lucky, one of the Pyrenees' last surviving brown bears.

Stunning valleys, such as the Vallée d'Aspe and the Vallée d'Ossau, cut laterally into the central Pyrenees, their lower reaches rich pasture, their narrow, southern necks steeper and more enclosed. Here up high, shimmering lakes and tarns are fed by swift mountain streams punctuated by gushing cascades. Towns, such as the winter ski resorts and summer walking bases of Cauterets and Bagnères de Luchon, are appropriately small, deferring to the sheer grandeur of the mountains.

To the north of their foothills sit the sedate yet dynamic cities of Pau and Lourdes, one of Christianity's most important pilgrim towns.

Eastwards, in the Pyrénées Orientales, the climate becomes warmer and drier, the vegetation pricklier, squatter and more abundant as the mountains taper down into Roussillon, then finally dip into the Mediterranean.

HIGHLIGHTS

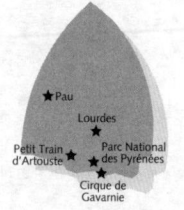

- Catch a first glimpse of **snow-capped mountains** (p669) from Pau's stylish blvd des Pyrénées
- Mingle with the faithful at **Lourdes** (p677), one of the world's most important pilgrimage sites
- Trek in the **Parc National des Pyrénées** (p680), one of western Europe's wildest areas
- Trundle along in the open-topped **Petit Train d'Artouste** (p686) at a constant 2000m
- Gasp at the magnificent wrap-around sweep of the **Cirque de Gavarnie** (p690)

★ Pau
Lourdes ★
Petit Train ★ ★ Parc National des Pyrénées
d'Artouste
Cirque de Gavarnie

- POPULATION: 3,017,200
- AREA: 8400 SQ KM

Information

Information on the Pyrenees is available in Paris, from the **Maison des Pyrénées** (☎ 01 42 86 51 86; pyrenees.paris@cg65.fr; 15 rue St-Augustin, 2e; metro Quatre Septembre).

PAU

pop 81,000

Pau (rhymes with 'so') is famed for its mild climate, flower-filled public parks and magnificent views of the Pyrenees. In the 19th century it was a favourite wintering spot for wealthy English and Americans. In recent years, the city has owed its prosperity to a high-tech industrial base and the huge natural gas field, plus spin-off chemical plants, at nearby Lacq. Nowadays, it's also at the cutting edge of communications technology and has attracted such giants of the trade as Microsoft, Intel, IBM and Toshiba.

Elegant, stylish (the shopping's great, especially if you're of a gourmet bent), it also has a fun-loving undertow, as befits a long-standing university city, and makes a good base for forays into the Pyrenees.

Orientation

The town centre sits on a small hill with the River Pau (Gave de Pau) at its base. Along its crest stretches blvd des Pyrénées, a wide promenade offering Cinemascope views of the mountains. The town's east–west axis is the thoroughfare of cours Bosquet, rue Maréchal Foch and rue Maréchal Joffre, with place Clemenceau at its heart. Small Vieille Ville (old town) surrounds the chateau.

Information

BOOKSHOP

Librairie des Pyrénées (☎ 05 59 27 78 75; 14 rue St-Louis) Carries an excellent selection of walking maps and guidebooks in French.

INTERNET ACCESS

C Cyber Café (☎ 05 59 82 89 40; 20 rue Lamothe; per hr €4.50; ☽ 10am-2am Mon-Fri, 2pm-2am Sat & Sun)
Cyber Coyote (☎ 05 59 27 04 03; 11 rue Duboué; per hr €4.80; ☽ 11.30am-11pm Mon-Thu, 11am-2am Fri & Sat, 2-8pm Sun)

LAUNDRY

Laundrette (66 rue Émile Garet; ☽ 7am-8pm)

POST

Main Post Office (21 cours Bosquet)

TOURIST INFORMATION

Tourist Office (☎ 05 59 27 27 08; www.pau.fr; place Royale; ☽ 9am-6pm Jul & Aug, closed Sun afternoon Sep-Jun) Offers the free booklet *Béarn: Leisure Activities*, a detailed summary of almost everything to do and see in the region.

Sights

CHÂTEAU

Pau's **château** (☎ 05 59 82 38 19; adult/18-25 yrs/under 18 €4.50/3/free; ☽ 9.30am-12.15pm & 1.30-5.45pm mid-Jun–mid-Sep, 9.30-11.45am & 2-4.15pm or 5pm mid-Sep–mid-Jun) was originally the residence of the monarchs of Navarre. It was transformed into a Renaissance chateau, bedecked with gardens, by Marguerite d'Angoulême in the 16th century. Marguerite's grandson, the future Henri IV, was born here – cradled, so the story goes, in an upturned tortoise shell.

Neglected in the 18th century and used as barracks after the Revolution, the chateau was in a sorry state by 1838, when King Louis-Philippe ordered a complete interior renovation, completed by Napoleon III. The whole, especially the façade, has recently been painstakingly re-restored.

The chateau holds one of Europe's richest collections of 16th- to 18th-century Gobelins tapestries and some fine Sèvres porcelain. These items apart, most of the ornamentation and furniture, including an oak dining table that can seat 100, dates from Louis-Philippe's intervention. In the room where Henry IV was born is what's claimed to be that tortoise-shell cradle.

Within the brick-and-stone **Tour de la Monnaie** below the main chateau, a free, modern lift hauls you from place de la Monnaie up to the ramparts.

Admission includes an obligatory and less than arresting guided tour in rapid-fire French or Spanish (though a printed version in English is available).

PYRENEES PANORAMA

From majestic blvd des Pyrénées, there's a breathtaking panorama of the Pyrenean summits on clear days, prevalent in autumn and winter. The **orientation table** opposite No 20 details the names of the peaks.

VIEILLE VILLE

Little is left of Pau's labyrinthine old centre. An area of around 300m in diameter is all that remains, yet it's rich in restored medieval and Renaissance buildings.

PYRENEES (PYRÉNÉES)

MUSÉE BERNADOTTE

The **Musée Bernadotte** (☎ 05 59 27 48 42; 8 rue Tran; adult/child €2/1; ☼ 10am-noon & 2-6pm Tue-Sun) has exhibits illustrating the improbable yet true story of how a French general, Jean-Baptiste Bernadotte, born in this very building, became king of Sweden and Norway (see the boxed text, p672). You'll spot the building from a distance by the blue and yellow Swedish flag fluttering outside.

MUSÉE DES BEAUX-ARTS

Pau's **Musée des Beaux-Arts** (Fine Arts Museum; ☎ 05 59 27 33 02; entrance rue Mathieu Lalanne; adult/child €2/1; ☼ 10am-noon & 2-6pm Wed-Mon) features 15th- to 20th-century European paintings, including works by Rubens, El Greco and Degas.

Activities

Romano Sport (see p675) rents equipment for a whole range of outdoor activities, including walking (you can hire a pair of mountain boots, even just for the weekend), climbing, skiing, canyon clambering – and also hires bikes.

Festivals & Events

The **Festival de Pau** is an extravaganza of dance, music and theatre, held mid-June to mid-July, with events at the Théâtre St-Louis, Palais Beaumont and several outdoor venues.

L'Été à Pau (Summer in Pau) is a time for free music concerts, often of high quality, at venues throughout the town – notably the amphitheatre in parc Beaumont.

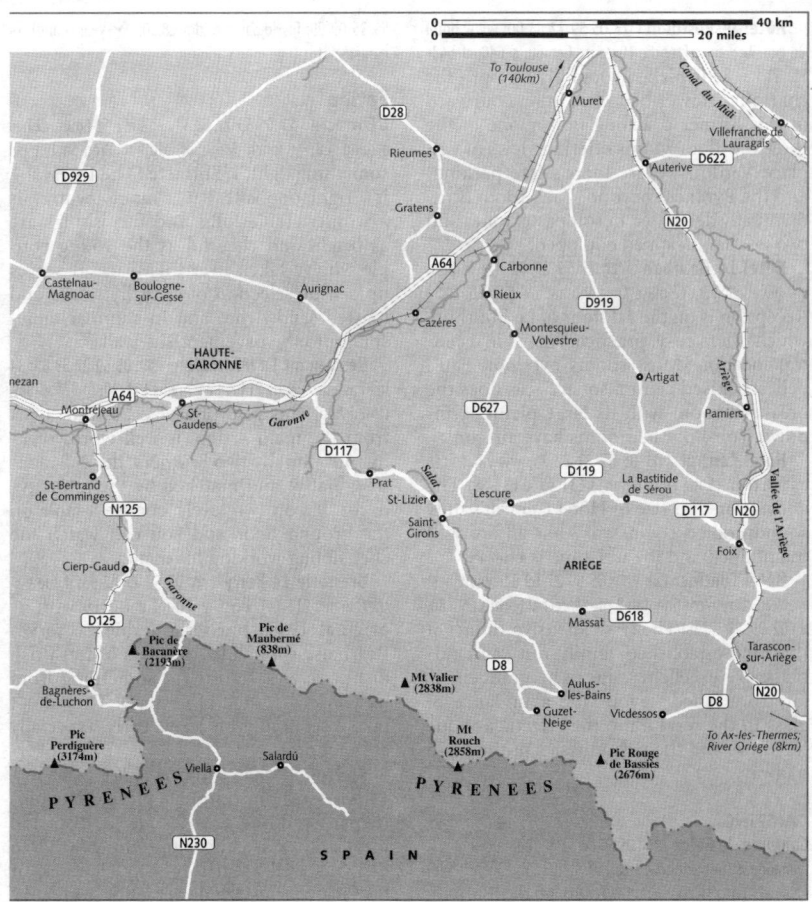

March sees both Carnival week and the month-long **Festival de Dance**, a celebration of contemporary dance.

If cars, whether they are venerable and distinguished or mean and growling, captivate you, plan to spend the week before Whitsuntide in Pau. On the first weekend, there's a parade of vintage vehicles, followed by the **Grand Prix Historique.** On the second weekend, a Formula 3 Grand Prix motor race howls and whines through the city's streets.

Every October, the **Concours Complet International** brings together some of the world's best horse riders in a gruelling competition embracing dressage, cross-country and jumping.

Sleeping

Hôtel de la Pomme d'Or (☎ 05 59 11 23 23; fax 05 59 11 23 24; 11 rue Maréchal Foch; s/d €20/23, with shower €24-28, with bathroom from €25/29) On the 1st floor of a former coaching inn, this is a decent economical choice. Ask for a room facing away from the busy street. Go into the recessed courtyard and you'll find the entrance on the left.

Hôtel Adour (☎ 05 59 27 47 41; www.hotel-adour-pau .com in French; 10 rue Valérie Meunier; s/d with shower €30/32, with bathroom from €40/42; **P** **X**) Even though the street isn't particularly noisy, rooms overlooking this central hotel are *triple* glazed. The other client-sensitive touch is its nonsmoking rooms – a welcome feature absent from many hotels with greater pretensions.

Hôtel le Postillon (☎ 05 59 72 83 00; www.hotel-le-postillon.fr in French; 10 cours Camou; s €40, d €43-52) Take your pick; a room giving onto the charming, flower-bedecked inner courtyard of this former coaching inn or one of the three top-floor rooms offering views of vast place Verdun (where there's free parking) and the Pyrenees beyond. Each room is individually decorated in soft pastel tones and two are handicapped equipped.

Hôtel Le Bourbon (☎ 05 59 27 53 12; le-bourbon@wanadoo.fr; 12 place Clemenceau; s/d €47/56; 🔀) Reception is on the 1st floor of Le Bourbon, which offers cosy, practical rooms in a central location. Most rooms overlook Pau's pedestrianised central square – as does the breakfast room with its large picture windows. Top-floor bedrooms have air-con.

Hôtel Central (☎ 05 59 27 72 75; www.hotelcentralpau.com; 15 rue Léon Daran; s €31-45, d €31-58) The decoration and size of Hôtel Central's fully soundproofed rooms vary but all are well maintained and the welcome is cheery.

Hôtel Continental (☎ 05 59 27 69 31; www.bestwestern.com/fr/continental; 2 rue Maréchal Foch; s €55-80, d €62-95; 🅿 🖳) The less expensive rooms at this long-established, family-run Pau landmark are excellent value. The grandeur is far from faded; savour the abundance of glass in the restaurant, the eclectic antique furniture and the rich mosaics in the main hallway.

CAMPING

Camping de Gelos (☎ 05 59 06 57 37; bearn.camping@wanadoo.fr; per adult/tent/car €3/4.20/1.20; 🕙 Jun-Sep) It's about 3km out of town at the Base de Plein Air recreational area. Take bus No 1 from place Clemenceau to the Mairie de Gelos stop. Pau's **Auberge de Jeunesse** (☎ 05 59 35 09 99; fjt@ldjpau.org; dm €8.50; 🕙 year-round) is beside it.

Eating

L'Entracte (☎ 05 59 27 68 31; 2bis rue St-Louis; dishes around €8; 🕙 lunch Mon-Sat, dinner Wed-Sat) For something light, L'Entracte (The Interval – it's right opposite Pau's main theatre) is a winner. Tablecloths and furnishings are as bright and cheerful as the young couple who've taken over this place. It serves up a wide selection of crunchy salads and toasted sandwiches and in summer tables spill onto the pavement/sidewalk.

Restaurant La Michodière (☎ 05 59 27 53 85; 34 rue Pasteur; menus €14 & €24; mains €11-20; 🕙 Mon-Sat, closed Aug) This gem of a place, a little apart from the main action, is well worth seeking out. Run by two brothers, the cuisine is imaginative and matched by the attractive décor. It's on two levels; choose a table on the ground floor and you can watch the chef sibling working his magic.

Brasserie Le Berry (☎ 05 59 27 42 95; 4 rue Gachet; mains €11-14) Top-value Le Berry with its original 1950s brasserie ambience serves Béarnaise specialities and lots of fresh fish dishes. Save a cranny for something from its tempting range of desserts. They don't take reservations so arrive early, especially at lunchtime.

Au Fruit Défondu (☎ 05 59 27 26 05; 3 rue Sully; 🕙 dinner only) This intimate place offers participatory dinners, with cheese, fish and meat and even chocolate fondues (€11 to €15), as well as grill-it-yourself duck or beef *pierrades*, sizzled over a hot stone (€12 to €15).

Chez Pierre (☎ 05 59 27 76 86; 16 rue Louis Barthou; menu €34; 🕙 closed Sun, lunch Sat & Mon) Chez Pierre

---

FRANCE'S SWEDISH KING

Jean-Baptiste Bernadotte, an enthusiastic supporter of the French Revolution, was a distinguished general and diplomat serving both the Revolutionary government and Napoleon and acquiring a reputation as a talented and humane administrator.

Meanwhile, in Stockholm, the Swedish Riksdag (parliament) reckoned that the only way out of the country's dynastic and political crisis was to stick a foreigner on the throne. Admiring French military prowess, they turned to Bernadotte, electing him crown prince in 1810.

Contrary to Napoleon's expectations, Bernadotte didn't follow a pro-French foreign policy. Indeed, in the Battle of Leipzig (1813), Swedish troops under his command helped the allied army give Napoleon his first serious whipping. In 1818, Bernadotte became King Charles XIV. He died in office in 1844 but his line lives on: the present king of Sweden is the seventh ruler in the Bernadotte dynasty.

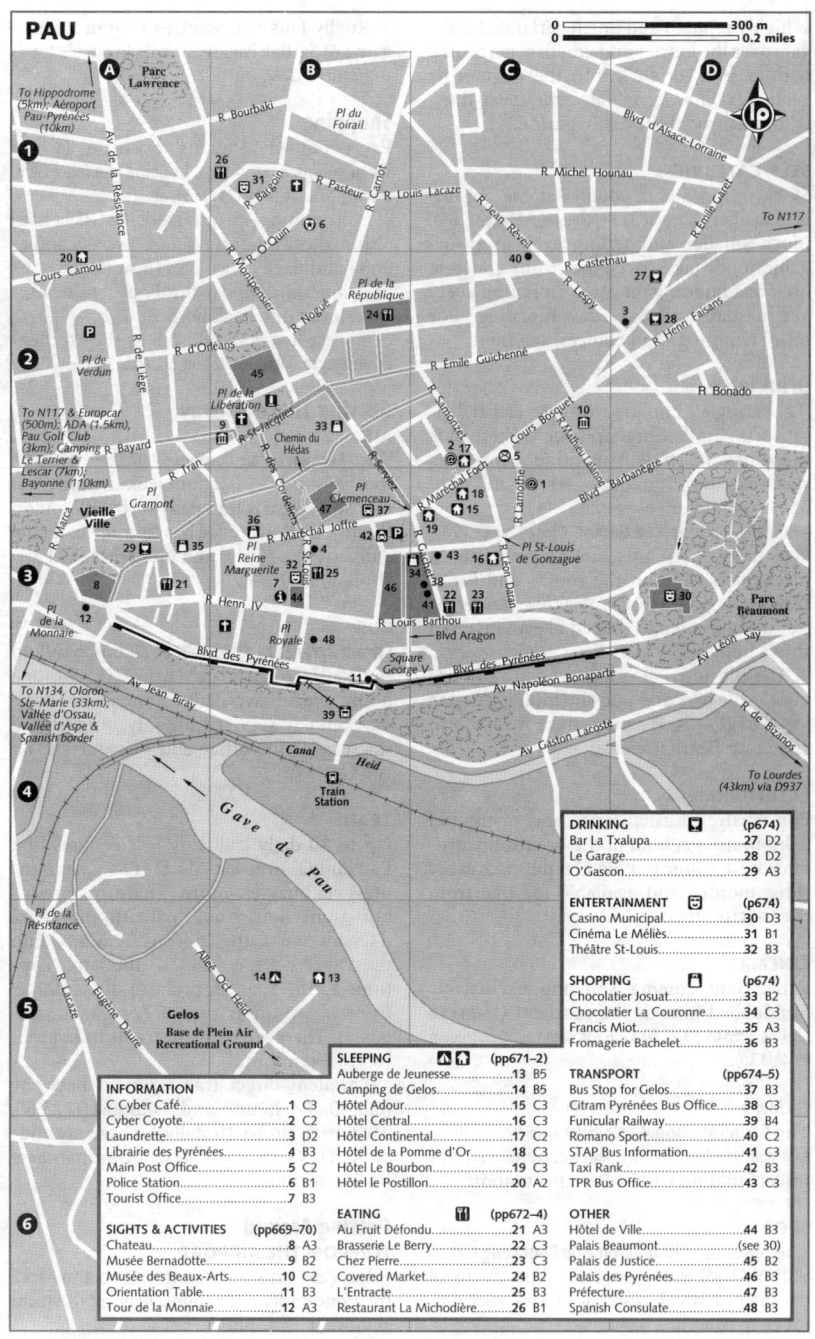

PAU

| 0 | 300 m |
| 0 | 0.2 miles |

DRINKING (p674)
Bar La Txalupa........................27 D2
Le Garage...............................28 D2
O'Gascon...............................29 A3

ENTERTAINMENT (p674)
Casino Municipal.....................30 D3
Cinéma Le Méliès.....................31 B1
Théâtre St-Louis......................32 B3

SHOPPING (p674)
Chocolatier Josuat....................33 B2
Chocolatier La Couronne............34 C3
Francis Miot............................35 A3
Fromagerie Bachelet.................36 B3

TRANSPORT (pp674–5)
Bus Stop for Gelos...................37 B3
Citram Pyrénées Bus Office........38 C3
Funicular Railway.....................39 B4
Romano Sport..........................40 C2
STAP Bus Information................41 C3
Taxi Rank...............................42 B3
TPR Bus Office.........................43 C3

OTHER
Hôtel de Ville..........................44 B3
Palais Beaumont...................(see 30)
Palais de Justice.......................45 B2
Palais des Pyrénées..................46 B3
Préfecture..............................47 B3
Spanish Consulate...................48 B3

SLEEPING (pp671–2)
Auberge de Jeunesse................13 B5
Camping de Gelos....................14 B5
Hôtel Adour............................15 C3
Hôtel Central..........................16 C3
Hôtel Continental.....................17 C2
Hôtel de la Pomme d'Or............18 C3
Hôtel Le Bourbon.....................19 C3
Hôtel le Postillon.....................20 A2

EATING (pp672–4)
Au Fruit Défondu.....................21 A3
Brasserie Le Berry....................22 C3
Chez Pierre............................23 C3
Covered Market.......................24 B2
L'Entracte..............................25 B3
Restaurant La Michodière..........26 B1

INFORMATION
C Cyber Café............................1 C3
Cyber Coyote...........................2 C2
Laundrette................................3 D2
Librairie des Pyrénées.................4 B3
Main Post Office.........................5 C3
Police Station............................6 B1
Tourist Office............................7 B3

SIGHTS & ACTIVITIES (pp669–70)
Chateau..................................8 A3
Musée Bernadotte......................9 B2
Musée des Beaux-Arts...............10 C2
Orientation Table.....................11 B3
Tour de la Monnaie...................12 A3

is highly reputed and much garlanded. Salivate over the lobster and crayfish, garnished with saffron, or tuck into the *mignon de veau aux morilles et foie gras* (veal fillet, wild mushrooms and foie gras; €24).

SELF-CATERING

Stock up on picnic goodies at the big **covered market** (place de la République). **Marché Bio**, much smaller and selling exclusively organic food, takes over the gaunt concrete hulk of a building on place du Foirail every Wednesday and Saturday morning. For other tempting food choices, see right.

Drinking

'Le Triangle', bounded by rue Henri Faisans, rue Émile Garet and rue Castetnau is the centre of student nightlife. Most bars stay open until 2am out of season and until 3am in summer.

Good bets are **Le Garage** (☎ 05 59 83 75 17; 49 rue Émile Garet) – look for the giant stucco mechanic sitting on the roof – and **Bar La Txalupa** (34 rue Émile Garet; ◷ Oct-Jun, Tue-Sat Jul-Sep), all in wood and shaped like an inverted ship's hull.

The old town also has its share of convivial little bars and pubs including **O'Gascon** (☎ 05 59 27 64 74; 13 rue du Château), which also serves up Béarnaise cuisine.

Entertainment

For theatre, music, dance and upcoming exhibitions, get hold of the beautifully produced *La Culture à Pau*, published every three months and available for free from the tourist office.

CINEMAS

Pau's only cinema showing exclusively nondubbed films is the excellent **Cinéma Le Méliès** (☎ 05 59 27 60 52; 6 rue Bargoin; adult/student €5.40/4.30).

CASINO

The **Casino Municipal** (☎ 05 59 27 06 92; ◷ 10am-3am Mon-Fri, 10am-4am Sat & Sun) occupies a sumptuous building within Parc Beaumont.

SPORT

The renowned **Hippodrome du Pont Long** (☎ 05 59 13 07 07; 462 blvd du Cami-Salié), 5km north of the town centre, has steeplechases from October to March.

Rugby fans will want to take in a home game of **Section Paloise**, one of France's leading club sides.

Shopping

Pau is renowned for its chocolate. Two of its best *chocolatiers* are **La Couronne** (place Clemenceau) and **Josuat** (23 rue Serviez).

Still on things sweet, **Francis Miot** (48 rue Joffre) also makes wonderful jams, sweets/candies and handmade chocolates (how about a box of *couilles du Pape* – the Pope's testicles – for a loved one back home?).

Cheese lovers should call by the excellent **Fromagerie Bachelet** (24 rue Maréchal Joffre).

Getting There & Away

AIR

The **Aéroport Pau-Pyrénées** (☎ 05 59 33 33 00; www.pau.aeroport.fr) is about 10km northwest of town. Ryanair flies daily to/from London (Stansted). Air France has four to six flights daily to Paris (Orly) and up to three to Paris (Roissy).

BUS

Citram Pyrénées (☎ 05 59 27 22 22) buses roll up the Vallée d'Ossau to Laruns (€7.30, one hour, two to five daily Monday to Saturday; Sunday service only July, August and ski season). Its office and bus stand is on rue Gachet.

TRAIN

Up to 10 daily trains or SNCF buses link Pau and Oloron-Ste-Marie (€5.70, 40 minutes) via Buzy-en-Béarn. There are onward bus connections from Buzy into the Vallée d'Ossau and from Oloron-Ste-Marie into the Vallée d'Aspe. Most of the latter continue to the Spanish railhead of Canfranc, from where trains run to Zaragoza (Saragossa). There are frequent trains to Lourdes (€6.10, 30 minutes).

Frequent direct trains run to Bayonne (€13.40, 1¼ hours) and Toulouse (€23.60, 2¾ hours, up to 10 daily). There are four daily TGVs to Paris' Gare Montparnasse (€74, five hours).

Getting Around

TO/FROM THE AIRPORT

A bus (€5) runs to/from the airport to serve the London Ryanair flight, leaving the train station at 12.15pm.

BICYCLE
At **Romano Sport** (☎ /fax 05 59 98 48 56; 1 rue Jean Réveil; ☺ 9am-noon & 3-7pm Mon-Sat) you can rent town bikes (€10/27/55 per day/three days/week) and mountain bikes (€15/40/85), along with other sporting equipment.

CAR & MOTORCYCLE
There's extensive free parking on place de Verdun. Rental agencies in town include **ADA** (☎ 05 59 72 94 40; 3bis route de Bayonne) and **Europcar** (☎ 05 59 92 09 09; 115 av Jean Mermoz), both in the suburb of Billère.

FUNICULAR RAILWAY
The train station is linked to blvd des Pyrénées by a free funicular railway, a wonderful creaky little contraption. But unless you're heavily laden or a railway nut, it's scarcely worth the wait; the walk itself, even uphill, takes much the same time.

PUBLIC TRANSPORT
The local bus company, **STAP** (☎ 05 59 14 15 16), has a sales and information office on rue Gachet. Single tickets/daily passes/eight-ride *carnets* cost €1/2.50/5.50.

TAXI
For a taxi call ☎ 05 59 02 22 22.

LOURDES
pop 15,000 / elevation 400m
Lourdes, 43km southeast of Pau, was just a sleepy market town until 1858, when Bernadette Soubirous (1844–79), a near-illiterate, 14-year-old peasant girl, saw the Virgin Mary in a series of 18 visions that came to her in a grotto. The Vatican eventually confirmed them as bona fide apparitions and, having lived out her short life as a nun, she was declared Ste Bernadette in 1933.

Nowadays Lourdes is one of the world's most important pilgrimage sites, descended upon annually by some five million visitors from all over the world. Well over half are pilgrims, including many invalids seeking cures. Nowadays, 45% of pilgrims come from beyond France's frontiers – and two-thirds are over 45 years old.

But accompanying the fervent piety of the pilgrims is an astounding display of tacky commercial exuberance – shake-up snow domes, baseball caps, and plastic bottles in the shape of the Virgin (just add holy water

at the shrine) are but a sample. It's easy to mock but remember that some people spend their life savings to come here.

Orientation
Lourdes' two main east–west streets are rue de la Grotte and blvd de la Grotte, both leading to the Sanctuaires Notre Dame de Lourdes. The principal north–south thoroughfare, called av Général Baron Maransin where it passes above blvd de la Grotte, connects the train station with place Peyramale, where you'll find the tourist office.

The huge religious complex that has grown up around the original cave where Bernadette's visions took place is across the River Pau, west of the town centre.

Information
BOOKSHOPS
The Book Shop (☎ 05 62 42 27 94; www.lourdes -bookshop.com; 13 rue du Bourg) Mainly stocks titles relating to the shrine of Lourdes plus a few novels, travel titles and a good range of walking maps.

INTERNET ACCESS
Difintel (5 rue de la Grotte; per hr €3; ☺ 9am-noon & 2-7pm Mon-Sat)
B&W (46 place du Champ Commun; per hr €4; ☺ 2pm-midnight)

LAUNDRY
Laundrette (10 av du Général Baron Maransin; ☎ 8am-7pm)

POST
Main Post Office (1 rue de Langelle)

PASSPORTS & PASSES
If you're intent upon doing Lourdes thoroughly, you save by picking up a *visa passeport touristique* (adults/children €34/17), giving free access to five museums, the little train that circumnavigates the town and a trip on the spectacular Pic du Jer funicular railway, plus an audio-guide to the Grotte de Massabielle.

Alternatively, pick up the free *Lourdes Pass,* pay the normal tariff for five of the seven attractions (Musée de Lourdes, Château Fort/Musée Pyrénéen, Musée de la Nativité, Musée Grévin, Funiculaire du Pic du Jer, Musée du Petit Lourdes, Le Petit Train) and get the last two free.

LOURDES

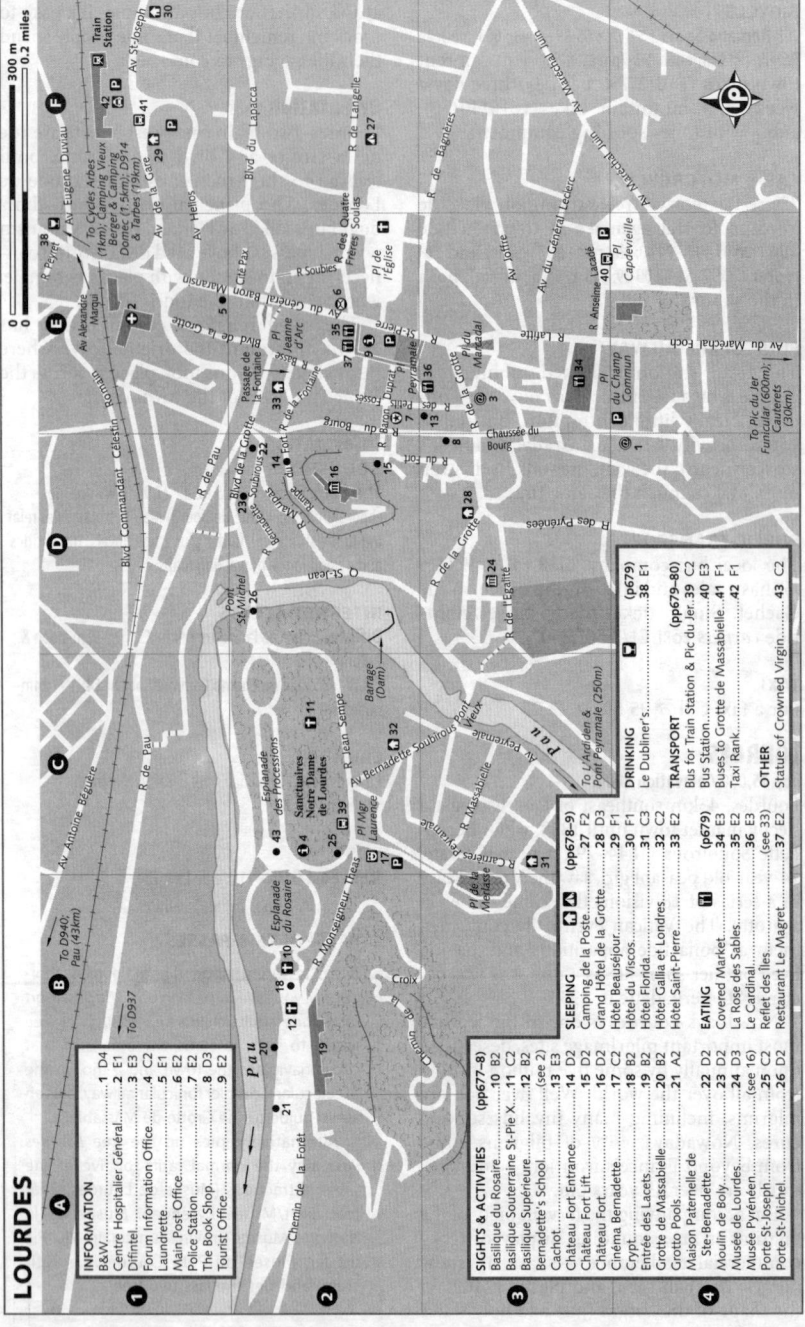

0 — 300 m
0 — 0.2 miles

TOURIST INFORMATION

Tourist Office (☎ 05 62 42 77 40; www.lourdes-info tourisme.com; place Peyramale; ⏰ 9am-7pm Mon-Sat, 10am-6pm Sun Jul & Aug, 9am-6.30pm Mon-Sat, 10am-12.30pm Sun Apr-Jun & Sep–mid-Oct, 9am-noon & 2-6pm Mon-Sat Jan-Mar & mid-Oct–Dec)

Forum Information office (☎ 05 62 42 78 78; www .lourdes-france.com; Esplanade des Processions; ⏰ 8.30am-12.15pm & 1.45-6.30pm Apr-Oct, 9am-noon & 1.30-5.30pm or 6pm Nov-Mar) For information on the Sanctuaires Notre Dame de Lourdes.

Sights

SANCTUAIRES NOTRE DAME DE LOURDES

The development of the Sanctuaries of Our Lady of Lourdes began within a decade of the miraculous events of 1858. The most revered site is known variously as the **Grotte de Massabielle** (Massabielle Cave or Grotto), the Grotte Miraculeuse (Miraculous Cave) and the Grotte des Apparitions (Cave of the Apparitions). Open 24 hours, its walls are worn smooth by the touch of millions of hands over the years. Nearby are 19 **pools** in which 400,000 pilgrims seeking cures immerse themselves each year. Miraculous cures are becoming rarer and rarer; the last medically certifiable case took place in 1987 and, after an exhaustive 12-year investigation, was recognised by the church as a miracle.

The main 19th-century section of the sanctuaries has three parts. On the western side of Esplanade du Rosaire, between the two ramps, is the neo-Byzantine **Basilique du Rosaire** (Basilica of the Rosary). One level up is the **crypt**, reserved for silent worship. Above is the spire-topped, neo-Gothic **Basilique Supérieure** (Upper Basilica).

From Palm Sunday (the Sunday before Easter) to at least mid-October, there are solemn **torchlight processions** nightly at 9pm from the Massabielle Grotto, while at 5pm there's the **Procession Eucharistique** (Blessed Sacrament Procession), where pilgrims bearing banners process along the Esplanade des Processions.

When it's wet, the latter ceremony is held inside the vast, bunker-like **Basilique Souterraine St-Pie X** (Underground Basilica of St Pius X) with a capacity for 20,000 worshippers. Built in 1959 in the fallout-shelter style then all the rage, it's redeemed to some extent by vibrantly warm back-lit works of *gemmail*, superimposed pieces of coloured glass embedded in enamel.

Visitors to the sanctuaries should dress modestly. Smoking is forbidden throughout the complex.

All four places of worship open 6am to 10pm in summer and 7am to 7pm in winter. You can enter the grounds around the clock via the Entrée des Lacets on rue Monseigneur Theas. The **Porte St-Michel** and **Porte St-Joseph** entrances are open 5am to midnight year-round.

CHEMIN DE LA CROIX

Also known by the name Chemin du Calvaire (Way of Calvary), the 1.5km **Chemin de la Croix** (Way of the Cross; ⏰ 6am-7pm Easter-Oct, 8am-6pm Oct-Easter), leading up the forested hillside from near the Basilique Supérieure, is punctuated by the 14 Stations of the Cross. Especially devout pilgrims mount to the first station on their knees.

OTHER BERNADETTE SITES

In addition, vistors can see four other places that figured prominently in the life of Ste Bernadette.

On rue Bernadette Soubirous are the **Moulin de Boly** (Boly Mill; No 12; admission free), Bernadette's birthplace, and the **Maison Paternelle de Ste-Bernadette** (No 2; admission €1), the house that the town of Lourdes bought for the Soubirous family after Bernadette saw the apparitions.

The **Cachot** (15 rue des Petits Fossés; admission free), a former prison, is where Bernadette lived during the apparitions.

Bernadette's school (av du Général Baron Maransin; admission free), where she studied and lived from 1860 to 1866 with the Sœurs de Notre Dame de Nevers (Sisters of Our Lady of Nevers), contains some of her personal effects and is now part of the town's Centre Hospitalier Général.

MUSÉE DE LOURDES

The **Musée de Lourdes** (☎ 05 62 94 28 00; adult/child €5.50/2.50; ⏰ 9-11.45am & 1.30-6.45pm Apr-Oct), west of the Cinéma Pax in the Parking de l'Égalité, portrays the life of Ste Bernadette as well as the general history of Lourdes.

CINÉMA BERNADETTE

If you've a yen to learn yet more about Ste Bernadette or simply want to rest your feet, the **Cinéma Bernadette** (☎ 05 62 42 79 19; 6 av Monseigneur Schoepfer; adult/under 18 €6/4.50) shows the same two-hour feature film entitled (you've guessed it) *Bernadette* with optional English dialogue at 2pm, 4.30pm and 8.30pm daily from Easter to October.

CHÂTEAU FORT

There are great bird's eye views of town from the **Château Fort** (Fortified Castle; adult/child €5/2.50; h 9am-noon & 1.30-6.30pm Easter-Oct, 9am-noon & 2-6pm Nov-Easter), up on its rocky pinnacle. Within is the **Musée Pyrénéen**, with displays on folk art and tradition.

Take the free lift (elevator) from rue Baron Duprat or walk up the ramp at the northern end of rue du Bourg.

PIC DU JER

There's a splendid panoramic view of Lourdes and the central Pyrenees from the summit of Pic du Jer (948m). It's but a six-minute ride from valley level by the **funicular railway** (☎ 05 62 94 00 41; blvd d'Espagne; adult/child one way €6/4.50, return €8/6; ☼ 10am-6pm Easter-Oct).

More strenuously and satisfyingly, follow the signed trail to the summit from the lower station (allow 2½ to three hours for the return journey). The ticket booth has a free stylised map.

Take bus No 2 from place Monseigneur Laurence.

Activities

To get away from Bernadette Soubirous, put on your walking shoes or hire a cycle (see p679) and do some or all of the 17km **Voie Verte des Gaves** (Mountain Streams Green route). It follows the old Lourdes–Cauterets train line (parallel to the Cauterets road) up the attractive Vallée des Gaves as far as Soulom, from where walkers can catch a bus back to town.

Festivals & Events

Lourdes' renowned **Festival International de Musique Sacrée** is two weeks of sacred music held around Easter.

Sleeping

Since Lourdes has over 350 hotels – in France, only Paris has more – you shouldn't need our help to find one of the 32,000 available beds. Even so, you may have to scout around during Easter, Whitsuntide, Ascension Day, May and from August to the first week of October. By contrast, the town is so quiet in winter, when most hotels shut down, that it would need a miracle to bring it to life. Given the nature of their clientele, a high proportion have facilities for the handicapped.

BUDGET

Hôtel du Viscos (☎ 05 62 94 08 06; fax 05 62 94 26 74; 6bis av St-Joseph; d €29, with bathroom €34; ☼ Feb–mid-Dec) This friendly, family-run place has a bustling bar for guests, offers great value and couldn't be handier for the station.

Hôtel Saint-Pierre (☎ 05 62 42 30 31; fax 05 62 94 80 32; 4-6 passage de la Fontaine; s/d €25/30; ☼ Apr-Oct) Rooms at this recently renovated hotel are smallish but quite satisfactory. There's a bar for guests, a pleasant street-side patio and a restaurant, Reflet des Îles, serving exotic fare (see p679).

Camping

Camping de la Poste (☎ 05 62 94 40 35; 26 rue de Langelle; 2 people & car €9; ☼ Easter–mid-Oct) Right in the heart of town, it's tiny, friendly – and consequently often full. It also rents eight excellent-value rooms with bathroom (d/tr/q €25/32/40).

Among the nearest of the dozen or so camping grounds ringing town are **Camping Vieux Berger** (☎ 05 62 94 60 57; ☼ mid-Jun–mid-Oct) and **Camping Domec** (☎ /fax 05 62 94 08 79; ☼ Easter-Oct). Both are on route de Julos, just off blvd de Centenaire, the eastern ring road.

MID-RANGE

Hôtel Beauséjour (☎ 05 62 94 38 18; www.hotel-beausejour.com; 16 av de la Gare; s/d €60/70; P ✕ 🖳) At the three-star Beauséjour, with its scrubbed white and ox-blood façade, parking is free and a full third of its 45 rooms are non-smoking. Recently affiliated to the Best Western group, it runs a good **restaurant** (menu €14). Rooms at the rear, though a little smaller, have an incomparable view of town and the Pyrenees beyond.

Grand Hôtel de la Grotte (☎ 05 62 94 58 87; www.hotel-grotte.com; 66 rue de la Grotte; s €66-113, d €74-140; ☼ Apr-Oct; P 🈺) Established in 1872, this charming *fin de siècle* place has belonged to the same family for four generations. With a gorgeous garden, bar and a couple of prestige restaurants, it's an excellent choice for those who like comfort, maturity and old world courtesy.

Hôtel Gallia et Londres (☎ 05 62 94 35 44; www
.hotelgallialondres.com; 26 av Bernadette Soubirous; s
€78-83, d €100-110; ☻ Apr-Oct; P ☒ ▣) Much
in the same mould, the spacious bedrooms
at this hotel too are each individually and
attractively decorated à la Louis XVI. You'll
gasp at the chandeliers and wooden panelling of the dining room with its side alcoves
for more intimate eating. Equally seductive
is the lovely little garden, a rarity in this
town of stone and concrete.

Hôtel Florida (☎ 05 62 94 51 15; flo_aca_mira
_hotels@hotmail.com; 3 rue Carrières Peyramale; s €46.50,
d €60; ☻ Apr-Oct; P ☒) All 117 rooms at this
large mid-range, renovated, family-owned
hotel have air-con and double glazing, while
as many as 20 are equipped for the disabled.
There are fine views of the sanctuaries from
its open air terrace.

Eating

Most hotels offer half- or full-board; some
even require guests to stay on those terms,
especially in high season. Restaurants close
early in this pious town; even the local Mc-
Donald's slams shut at 10.30pm.

Le Cardinal (☎ 05 62 42 05 87; 11 place Peyramale;
salads €5.50-6, menu du jour €8.50; ☻ Mon-Sat) This
unpretentious bar/brasserie is where the
staff of the tourist office lunch – and they
should know what's best. Tuck into steak,
chips and salad for only €6.50.

La Rose des Sables (☎ 05 62 42 06 82; 8 rue des
Quatre Frères Soulas; ☻ Tue-Sun) This North African restaurant – a bold Muslim presence in
such a fervently Catholic town – specialises
in couscous (€12 to €14).

Reflet des Îles (☻ Apr-Oct) This, the restaurant of Hôtel Saint-Pierre (see 678) serves

---

AUTHOR'S CHOICE

Restaurant le Magret (☎ 05 62 94 20 55;
10 rue des Quatre Frères Soulas; menus €24 & 33;
☻ Tue-Sun Feb-Dec) This pleasant restaurant,
its agreeably rustic décor embellished with
early photos of Lourdes, offers an innovative menu with a pronounced regional
flavour. The friendly, courteous _maître_ – a
dead ringer for a portly Lenin – talks you
through the dishes you've ordered and
offers informed rugby chat too, if you've
the inclination. It's prudent to reserve in
advance.

---

spicy dishes from the Indian Ocean island
of La Réunion as well as less exotic French
cuisine. Count on about €15 for a three-
course meal.

L'Ardiden (☎ 05 62 94 30 55; 48 av Peyramale; lunch
menu €10, dinner menus €12 & €16, mains €8-13; ☻ Wed-
Sun) It's well worth the short walk upstream
to L'Ardiden, pleasantly situated beside Pont
Peyramale and the river and strong on pizza
and pasta.

SELF-CATERING

Lourdes' **covered market** occupies most of
place du Champ Commun.

Drinking

There's not much to rave about after dark;
Lourdes has only one Madonna and she's
far from being a Material Girl.

However, poke your nose into **Le Dublin-
er's** (☎ 05 62 42 16 38; 7 av Alexandre Marqui) and – a
rarity for France – you stand a chance of
actually meeting an Irish drinker in an Irish
pub; every year over 250,000 Hibernians
make the pilgrimage to Lourdes.

Getting There & Away

BUS

The **bus station** (place Capdevieille) has services
northwards to Pau (€7.20, 1¼ hours, four to
six daily) and is a stop for buses running between Tarbes and Argelès-Gazost (at least
eight daily) to the south and gateway to the
Pyrenean communities of Cauterets, Luz-
St-Sauveur and Gavarnie. SNCF buses to
Cauterets (€6.10, one hour, six daily) leave
from the train station.

TRAIN

Many pilgrims arrive by rail and Lourdes
is well connected by train to cities all over
France, including Bayonne (€17.80, 1¾
hours, three to four daily), Pau (€6.20, 30
minutes, over 10 daily) and Toulouse (€20.90,
1¾ hours, seven daily). There are four daily
TGVs to Paris' Gare Montparnasse (€72.40
to €81.40, six hours).

Getting Around

BICYCLE

Opposite Leclerc supermarket, **Cycles Arbes**
(☎ 05 62 94 05 51; 51bis av Alexandre Marqui) hires
out both mountain and town bikes. **Roue
Libre** (☎ 06 87 14 93 48), at the base of the Pic du
Jer cable railway, rents mountain bikes.

CAR & MOTORCYCLE

Lourdes is one big, fuming traffic jam in summer. If you have a vehicle, your best bet is to leave it near the train or bus station, where there's free parking, and walk.

PUBLIC TRANSPORT

The local bus No 1 links the train station with place Monseigneur Laurence and the Sanctuaries.

TAXI

Call ☎ 05 62 94 31 30.

AROUND LOURDES

The **Grottes de Bétharram** (☎ 05 62 41 80 04; adult/child €9/4.50; ⏰ 9am-noon & 1.30-5.30pm Apr-Oct, 2.30-4pm Mon-Fri Jan-Mar), 14km west of town along the D937, are among France's most spectacular limestone caves. Guided visits, by mini-train and barge, last 1½ hours. In summer, it's best to arrive early in the morning to avoid long queues.

To see fauna that you'd be extremely lucky to stumble across higher up the valley in the Parc National des Pyrénées, you might want to visit **Parc Animalier des Pyrénées** (☎ 05 62 97 91 07; www.parc-animalier-pyrenees.com in French; adult/child €9/6; ⏰ 9am-7pm Jun-Aug, 9am-noon & 2-6pm Apr-May & Sep, 1-6pm Oct) at the northern entrance to the village of **Argelès-Gazost**. Residents of this small animal park include marmots, mouflons, otters and a couple of brown bears.

PARC NATIONAL DES PYRÉNÉES

The Parc National des Pyrénées (Pyrenees National Park) extends for about 100km along the Franco-Spanish border, from the Vallée d'Aspe in the west to the Vallée d'Aure in the east. Never broad, its width varies from 1.5km to 15km. Created in 1967, it covers an area of 457 sq km, within which are 230 lakes and Vignemale (3298m), whose summit is the highest in the French Pyrenees. To the south is Spain's 156-sq-km Parque Nacional de Ordesa y Monte Perdido, with which the French park collaborates closely.

Its many streams are fed by both springs and some 2000mm of annual precipitation, much of which falls as snow. The French slopes, especially in the west, are much wetter and greener than the dun-coloured Spanish side.

The vast and varied park is exceptionally rich in both fauna and plant life (over 150 species of flora are endemic). Keep glancing up: its wilder reaches rank among the best places in Europe to see large birds of prey such as golden eagles, griffon and bearded vultures, booted eagles, buzzards and falcons.

The animal population includes 42 of France's 110 species of mammal. Look out for marmots – or rather, listen out for their distinctive whistle. Having become extinct in the Pyrenees, they were successfully reintroduced from the Alps, where they thrive. Another success story is that of the izard, a close relative of the chamois, which was all but blasted out of existence half a century ago, mainly by firearms left over from WWII. Nowadays, thanks to careful control and monitoring, the park is home to about 5000 izards while numbers on both sides of the Pyrenees exceed 20,000. By contrast, brown bears, once numerous, are now extremely scarce; indeed, it's possible that the last survivors may have disappeared by the time you read this.

Each year, the park receives over two million visitors, 80% of whom increase the pressure upon three beleaguered sites: Cirque de Gavarnie, Pont d'Espagne above Cauterets and the Réserve Naturelle de Néouvielle in the eastern sector.

Park boundaries are marked by a red izard head on a rectangular white background, painted on rocks and trees.

MAPS & BOOKS

Each of the six park valleys (Vallée d'Aure, Vallée de Luz, Vallée de Cauterets, Val d'Azun, Vallée d'Ossau and Vallée d'Aspe) is covered by a national park folder or booklet in French, *Randonnées dans le Parc National des Pyrénées*, describing 10 to 15 walking itineraries. Worthwhile for the route maps alone, they're on sale at local park and tourist offices.

The park is covered by IGN's 1:25,000 Top 25 maps 1547OT *Ossau*, 1647OT *Vignemale*, 1748OT *Gavarnie* and 1748ET *Néouvielle*.

The Pyrenees chapter in Lonely Planet's *Walking in France* centres on the Vallée d'Aspe and Vallée de Cauterets. It describes in detail a variety of day walks plus a three-day tour in and around the valleys and suggests extended treks within the park.

Fleurs des Pyrénées Faciles à Reconnaître by Philippe Mayoux, published by Rando Éditions, is a handy, well-illustrated pocket guide in French.

Information

There are **national park offices** with visitors centres at (from west to east) Etsaut, Laruns, Arrens-Marsous, Cauterets, Luz-St-Sauveur, Gavarnie and St-Lary-Soulon. Most – although not the Cauterets or Gavarnie ones – close during the cold half of the year.

For information about the park, its flora and fauna and activities, go to www.parc-pyrenees.com.

Activities
WALKING

The Parc National des Pyrénées is criss-crossed by 350km of waymarked trails (including the Mediterranean to Atlantic GR10), some of which link up with trails in Spain.

The park has about 20 *refuges* (mountain huts or lodges), the majority run by the Club Alpin Français (CAF). Most are staffed only from July to September but retain a small wing year-round.

SKIING

The Pyrenees receive less snow than the much higher Alps and what snow falls is generally wetter and heavier. Despite this, there's reasonable downhill skiing and snowboarding for beginners and intermediates. The potential for cross-country skiing, ski touring and, increasingly, snowshoeing, is also good. The ski season normally lasts from December to early April, depending upon snow conditions.

Ski resorts dot both sides of the Pyrenees. The French side alone has over 20 downhill ski stations, most of them quite modest, and more than 10 cross-country areas.

One of the oldest resorts is **Cauterets**, which usually has the longest season and most reliable snow conditions. The largest is the combined resort of **Barèges-La Mongie** (tourist office ☎ 05 62 92 16 00), 39km southeast of Lourdes, with 64 runs and over 50 lifts.

For some of the best cross-country skiing, head for **Val d'Azun** (tourist office in Arrens-Marsous; ☎ 05 62 97 49 49), about 30km southwest of Lourdes. It has 110km of trails between 1350m and 1600m.

WHITE-WATER SPORTS

Rivers racing from the Pyrenean heights offer some of France's finest white water, which, as spring snowmelt is supplemented by modest year-round rain, have a fairly steady annual flow. Organisations offering rafting and canoeing within, or downstream from, the Parc National include **A Boste Sport Loisir** (☎ 05 59 38 57 58; www.aboste.com in French; rue Léon Bérard, 64390 Sauveterre de Béarn) and **Centre Nautique de Soeix** (☎ 05 59 39 61 00; fax 05 59 39 65 16; quartier Soeix, 64400 Oloron-Ste-Marie).

VALLÉE D'ASPE

The River Aspe (Gave d'Aspe) flows for some 50km from the Col du Somport, which marks the frontier with Spain, down to Oloron-Ste-Marie. Fewer than 3000 people live in the 13 villages of the valley, whose upper reaches have always been among the remotest corners of the French Pyrenees and one of the final refuges of their more timid wildlife.

But such seclusion may soon be lost as juggernauts plough through the Pyrenees' newest road tunnel, 8km long and completed in 2003. Despite concessions such as ring roads around the luckier villages of the lower valley, its impact upon the fragile higher reaches of the valley in particular can only be negative.

The Vallée d'Aspe has been a trans-frontier passage ever since Julius Caesar's Roman legionaries marched through. A railway line, completed in 1928 and a minor masterpiece of engineering, forged its way up the valley before tunnelling through to meet the Spanish railhead at Canfranc. Services stopped when a bridge collapsed in 1970 and the railway, still visible for most of its length, has been allowed to rust away.

MAPS

The 1:50,000-scale *Béarn: Pyrénées Carte No 3*, published by Rando Éditions, is a practical general trekking map of the area. A more detailed option is IGN's 1:25,000-scale Top 25 map No 1547OT, *Ossau*.

The National Park's *Randonnées dans le Parc National des Pyrénées: Aspe* is a pack of information sheets on 11 walks, varying from 1½ hours to eight hours, in and around the valley.

Information

The valley's friendly **tourist office** (☎ 05 59 34 57 57; www.aspecanfranc.com in French & Spanish; place

Sarraillé; 9am-12.30pm & 2-5.30pm or 6.30pm Mon-Sat) is in the main square of **Bedous.** It and **Librairie d'Aspe** (rue de la Caserne) both carry a reasonable selection of walking maps.

The **Maison du Parc National des Pyrénées** (park information centre; ☎ 05 59 34 88 30; 10.30am-12.30pm & 2-6.30pm May-Oct) occupies the old train station in **Etsaut** and houses a good display (in French) about the fauna of the Pyrenees.

Getting There & Away

SNCF (☎ 08 92 35 35 35) buses and trains connect Pau and Oloron-Ste-Marie up to 10 times daily (see 674). From Oloron, there are four onward bus connections into the valley via Bedous to Etsaut, the majority continuing to Somport and the Spanish railhead of Canfranc.

Two short cuts over the tops link the Aspe and Ossau valleys. Take the narrow, steeply winding D294 between Escot and Bielle for a spectacular 21km drive over the Col de Marie-Blanque (1035m). The D918, linking Asasp-Arros and Arudy is a more gentle, still attractive yet less spectacular alternative.

Bedous

Bedous, the valley's biggest village – with, despite this superlative, under 600 inhabitants – is 25km south of Oloron-Ste-Marie, where the valley's still wide.

Moulin d'Orcun (☎ 05 59 34 74 91; adult/child €4/3; visits 11am & hourly 3-6pm Jul & Aug, by appointment Sep-Jun), 0.5km out of Bedous on the Aydius road, is a working 18th-century watermill.

OUTDOOR ACTIVITIES

The tourist office in Bedous and other outlets in the valley sell the excellent locally produced guide *45 Randonnées dans la Vallée d'Aspe.*

Montagne Nature (☎ 05 59 34 75 77; montagne .nature@wanadoo.fr; 10am-12.30pm & 3-7.30pm Jul & Aug, 4-7pm Fri-Sun Sep-Jun), a cooperative of specialists in outdoor-activity, offers just about everything energetic you might want to do in the valley. It rents mountain bikes (€9/15 per half/full day), runs guided cycling outings and does canyon clambering, climbing, skiing, snowshoeing and winter mountaineering trips.

SLEEPING & EATING

Le Mandragot (☎ 05 59 34 59 33; place Sarraillé; beds €10) Accommodation in this welcoming *gîte*

d'étape with its cosy common room is in rooms for two to eight. It has self-catering facilities.

Camping Municipal de Carole (☎ 05 59 34 59 19; per person/tent/car €2.50/2/2; Mar-Oct) Around 300m west of the N134, it's well signposted from the main highway.

Chez Michel (☎ 05 59 34 52 47; abr.michel@free.fr; rue Gambetta; d €42 with breakfast; menus €10 & €16.50) On the main street, Chez Michel has a sauna, free for overnighters, and also runs a neat little **restaurant**. Go for the *menu saveur du pays* ('flavours of the region'; €13) of *garbure* (a scrumptious local pork-based gruel, thick with vegetables and pulses), trout with *cèpe* mushrooms and bilberry pie.

Restaurant des Cols (☎ 05 59 34 70 25; closed 1-15 Oct) This little place merits a 50km detour for its sumptuous *menus* (€10 to 21.50) Happily it's a mere 6.5km east of Bedous in the hamlet of Aydius. It also has three delightful doubles (€29) with self-catering facilities. The only downsides: the stuffed wildlife in the restaurant and those rabbit skin (or could it be cat?) barstool cushions…

Accous

This little village, 2.5km south of Bedous and 800m east of the highway, sits at the yawning mouth of the Vallée Berthe with a splendid backdrop of 2000m-plus peaks. North of here, the Vallée d'Aspe is broad and fertile. To the south, it closes in dramatically.

The **Fermiers Basco-Béarnais cheese centre** (☎ 05 59 34 76 06; 9am-noon & 2-6pm Mon-Fri, 10am-noon & 3-6pm Sat, plus Sun during school holidays), a farmers' cooperative and thriving *fromagerie*, is beside the N134. It has free sampling and offers a 20-minute audiovisual presentation in French, plus the opportunity to buy the best of local ewe, goat and cow's-milk cheeses.

ACTIVITIES

Tiny Accous boasts two *parapente* (paragliding) schools. **Ascendance** (☎ 05 59 34 52 07, www.ascendance.fr in French) offers accompanied 15-minute introductory flights for €65 and five-day induction courses for €366. It also advertises the valley's only Internet point although you'll be turned away if they're busy parapenting. **Air Attitude** (☎ 05 59 34 50 06; www.air-attitude.com in French), newer and offering a wider range of courses and flights, has similar prices.

Starting at Easter through to November, hiring a horse at Auberge Cavalière (see below) will cost you €43/65 per half/full day. Alternatively for an investment of €580 you can enjoy half-board and half a day's riding for the entire week. The hotel also arranges pony treks of four to seven days and walking holidays, supplying detailed maps for circular day walks based from the hotel.

SLEEPING & EATING

Auberge Cavalière (☎ 05 59 34 72 30; www.auberge -cavaliere.com; d €38.50; menus €17 & €20; ☘ year-round) About 3km south of Accous and just off the main road, this well-established place has a strong equine flavour. Dining – and you dine well – in the cosy low-beamed restaurant with sheep and goat pelts around the walls is rather like eating in a particularly cosy barn.

Camping Despourrins (☎ 05 59 34 71 16; per person/site €2.50/2.65; ☘ Mar-Oct) This tiny camping ground is just off the N134, tucked behind the Fermiers Basco-Béarnais cheese centre.

Lescun

The bridge at L'Estanguet that collapsed in 1970 and finished off the valley's train traffic is about 4km south of Bedous. Nearby, a steeply hairpinned, 5.5km detour climbs southwest to the mountain village of Lescun (900m), whose slate roofs once sheltered a leper colony.

It's worth a touch of vertigo on the ascent for the breathtaking, photogenic view westwards of the Cirque de Lescun, an amphitheatre of jagged limestone mountains, backed by the 2504m Pic d'Anie.

WALKING

A number of splendid walks can be started from Lescun. For a day walk with spectacular views back over the Vallée de Lescun and the distinctive Pic du Midi d'Ossau, follow the GR10 northwest via the Refuge de Labérouat and along the base of Les Orgues de Camplong (Camplong Organ Pipes) up to the Cabane du Cap de la Baigt, a *fromagerie* (open only in the summertime), where you can buy fresh cheese directly from the shepherd.

THE BROWN BEAR'S LAST STAND?

The brown bear *(ursos arctos)*, widespread throughout Europe 3000 years ago, was mercilessly hunted and captured for public display. Although rigorously protected for nearly half a century, its very existence is threatened by loss of habitat, tourism and road building – and not helped by its long, precarious two-year breeding cycle. Brown bears disappeared from the French Alps in 1937 while the Pyrenees sustain only a minute population, boosted by a trio from Slovenia, who have successfully bred. However, it's quite possible that, as you read this, the last brown bear will have disappeared from the Hautes-Pyrénées.

As we went to print, there were probably five at the very most roaming the Aspe and Ossau valleys. No one really knows for sure since the evidence comes primarily from footprints, often indistinct and ambiguous and nowadays on occasion supplemented by DNA traces. Best estimates are that there are a couple of youngsters out there, plus the venerable old male Papillon who, experts fear, can't manage it any more, Canelle, the only female, and Néré, imported from Slovenia and released amid great controversy.

In Pyrenean valleys, you'll see slogans daubed on rocks: 'Non aux ours' (No to the bears), 'Pas d'ours' (No bears) and, our favourite, 'Bonne année et longue vie aux ours!' (Happy New Year and long life to the bears!).

Little Borce used to have a couple of Pyrenean bears, Ségoulène and her cub, Myrtille, on display. Criticised by many yet well presented, this brought pleasure to thousands and helped to sensitise visitors to the probable extinction of their cousins in the wild.

Then, in the summer of 2004, Borce established **Espace Animalier** (☎ 05 59 34 89 33; adult/child €7/4.50; ☘ 9.30am-7pm Jul-Sep, 2-6pm Oct-Jun), a large open area above the village where the animals live in semi-captivity.

Here, Ségoulène, her cub, Myrtille, and a young male, a recent arrival (could there be romance in the air?) roam freer, together with izards, roe deer, marmots and mouflons –though higher authority, under pressure from local herders, did veto plans to introduce a small pack of wolves.

Lonely Planet's *Walking in France* describes other tempting walks from Lescun and also from Etsaut, higher up the Vallée d'Aspe.

SLEEPING

Gîte & Camping du Lauzart (☎ & fax 05 59 34 51 77; campinglauzart@wanadoo.fr; per person/tent/car €2.20/ 3.80/1; ⏰ 20 Apr-20 Sep) Spacious, friendly and beautifully situated, this pleasant camping area is 1.5km southwest of the village. A dorm bed in the *gîte* costs €9.35.

Hôtel du Pic d'Anie (☎ 05 59 34 71 54; hotel .picdanie@club-Internet; s/d €32/40; ⏰ May–mid-Sep) In the village itself, the hotel does particularly hearty meals (*menus* €15 – including a vegetarian option – and €23). A couple of doors away is its year-round *gîte* (dorm bed €11) with self-catering facilities.

Maison de la Montagne (☎ 05 59 34 79 14; les cun.dom@clubInternet.fr; dm €11, half-board €26) This cosy, rustic *gîte* has been adapted from an old barn. The owner, a qualified guide, leads mountain walks.

Etsaut & Borce

The twin villages of Etsaut and Borce are set back on either side of the N134, 11km south of Bedous. Both are popular bases for higher-elevation walks. For details of its National Park office, see p681.

Up the hill, Borce is one of the trimmest little hamlets in all the Pyrenees, restored and documented with care – just see how the telephone booth and public toilets blend harmoniously with the village's mellow stone domestic architecture! – yet still a living community, just on the right side of twee.

AUTHOR'S CHOICE

Au Château d'Arance (☎ 05 59 34 75 50; www.auchateaudarance.com in French; d €54-60) From the hamlet of Cette-Eygun, climb eastwards up a narrow, winding lane for 2.25km to reach this delightfully renovated 13th-century castle. For a castle, it's decidedly intimate with only eight rooms, one of which has facilities for the handicapped. Its **restaurant** (menus €15 & €25) is equally stylish and the sweeping view of the valley below from the terrace makes a sundowner taste all the sweeter.

One route for medieval pilgrims heading for Santiago de Compostela (nowadays the GR653 long-distance trail) was via the Vallée d'Aspe, through Borce and over the Col du Somport. **Hospitalet de St-Jacques de Compostelle** (☎ 05 59 34 88 99; admission free; ⏰ 10am-6.30pm) in Borce is a tiny museum, housed in a former pilgrims' lodging and 15th-century chapel. Pop two euros in the slot for 20 minutes of haunting plainsong.

WALKING

For a challenging half-day walk, pick up the GR10 in Borce or Etsaut and follow it south to Fort du Portalet, a 19th-century fortress used as a prison in WWII by the Germans and Vichy government. Here, head east to negotiate the Chemin de la Mâture, a vertiginous path, originally hacked into the vertical cliff face to allow bullock trains to transport timber for ships' masts from the upper slopes.

Prefer hands-in-pockets walking? **Rand'en Âne**, run by the friendly folk at La Garbure (see below) can line you up with a donkey (per hour/half-/full day €11/22/33) to take the strain.

SLEEPING & EATING

La Garbure (☎ 05 59 34 88 98; www.garbure.net; dm €11, half-board €23.50) This popular *gîte d'étape*, down the alleyway beside Etsaut's parish church, has donkeys to rent. The owners have a mountain of information about local walks and there's a kitchen for self-caterers. The same family also runs **La Maison de l'Ours** (☎ 05 59 34 86 38; prices as La Garbure) in the village square. In July and August, you can sit on its terrace and savour their lipsmacking home-made ice cream.

Hôtel des Voyageurs (☎ 05 59 34 88 05; d €31; menus €16.50 & €26; ⏰ mid-Dec–Oct, closed Sun-Mon except school holidays) This unpretentious hotel with its cosy rooms offers just about the best value cuisine in the whole valley. It's in Urdos, 5km south of Etsaut and the last village before the Spanish frontier.

VALLÉE D'OSSAU

The River Ossau makes a 60km journey from the watershed at Col du Pourtalet (1794m) to its confluence with the Aspe at Oloron-Ste-Marie. The Vallée d'Ossau, through which the river cuts a swathe, is one of contrasts. The lower, northern

JEAN-BERNARD CARILLET

Harbour at Cassis (p771), Provence

JEAN-BERNARD CARILLET

Traditional Provençal costume,
Digne-les-Bains (p810)

INGRID RODDIS

Intriguing rock formations of the Lubéron hills (p799)
of Provence

Palais des Papes (p786), Avignon

MANFRED GOTTSCHALK

EMILY RIDDELL

Limestone outcrops off the Corsican coast near Bonifacio (p886)

DAVID TOMLINSON

Casino de Monte Carlo (p859), Monaco

FRANCES LINZEE GORDON

Citadel (p872) in Calvi, Corsica

Rue Grande, St-Paul de Vence (p833), Côte d'Azur

DAN HERRICK

reaches as far as Laruns are broad, green and pastoral. Then, as it cuts more deeply and more steeply into the Pyrenees, it becomes narrow, confined, wooded and looming before broadening out again near the hamlet of Gabas.

MAPS & BOOKS

The most practical general walking map of the area is the 1:50,000-scale *Béarn: Pyrénées Carte No 3*, published by Rando Éditions. For more detail, consult three IGN 1:25,000-scale Top 25 maps – Nos 1547OT *Ossau*, 1647OT *Vignemale* and 1546ET *Laruns*.

The tourist office produces *Randonnées en Vallée d'Ossau* (€7), describing 30 signed walks between 5km and 16km, plus five mountain-bike routes. The quality of the mapping, reproduced from IGN originals, is excellent. The National Park visitor centre stocks *Randonnées dans le Parc National des Pyrénées: Vallée d'Ossau* (€6.40), describing 14 more challenging walks in the area, supported by 1:50,000-scale maps.

Information

INTERNET ACCESS

Refuge-Auberge L'Embaradère (under Laurens, right) Has an Internet point that functions with a France Telecom phonecard.

TOURIST INFORMATION

La Maison de la Vallée d'Ossau (☎ 05 59 05 31 41; ossau.tourisme@wanadoo.fr; place de La Mairie, Laruns; ☷ 9.30am-noon & 2-6pm Mon-Sat plus 9am-noon Sun school holidays only) The valley's tourist office, on Laruns' main square.

National Park Visitor Centre (☎ 05 59 05 41 59; pnpossau@espaces-naturels.fr; ☷ 9am-12.30pm & 1.30-6pm Jun-Sep, Mon-Fri Oct-May) Beside the Laruns tourist office.

Getting There & Around

Citram Pyrénées (☎ 05 59 27 22 22) runs buses from Pau to Laruns (€7.30, one hour, two to five daily Monday to Saturday – Sunday service only July, August and ski season).

SNCF trains from Pau stop at Buzy-en-Béarn from where there are at least three onward bus connections daily as far as Laruns (40 minutes).

During school holidays, **SARL Canonge** (☎ 05 59 05 30 31) runs a morning and an evening bus between Laruns and Artouste-

Fabrèges (€6.10 return, 35 minutes, daily). The summer service continues as far as Col du Pourtalet (€6 one way).

For scenic routes between the Ossau and Aspe valleys, see p682.

Falaise aux Vautours

The gliding flight of the griffon vulture *(Gyps folvus)* is once more a familiar sight over the Pyrenees. It feeds exclusively on carrion, thus acting as a kind of alpine dustman.

This 82-hectare reserve originally protected around 10 griffon vulture pairs nesting in the limestone cliffs above the villages. Now, there are more than 100 nesting pairs, plus various other raptors – notably a couple of migratory Egyptian vultures.

La Falaise aux Vautours (Cliff of the Vultures; ☎ 05 59 82 65 49; www.falaise-aux-vautours.com in French; adult/child €6/4; ☷ 10.30am-12.30pm & 2-6.30pm Jun-Aug, 2.30-5.30pm or 6.30pm May-Jun, Sep & other school holidays) in Aste-Béon shows round-the-clock live, big-screen images from nests up on the cliffs. Time it right and you can peek in on nesting, hatching and feeding in real time. There's also an interactive display about vultures with captions in English.

Laruns

pop 1500 / elevation 536m

Laruns, 6km south of Aste-Béon and 37km from Pau, is the valley's principal village.

Refuge-Auberge L'Embaradère (☎ 05 59 05 41 88; www.gite-embaradere.com in French; 13 av de la Gare; dm €10, half-board €25; menus €11 & €16; ☷ mid-Jun–mid-Sep, Tue-Sun mid-Sep–mid-Jun) This welcoming walkers' favourite has self-catering facilities – and the valley's only Internet access, open to anyone with a France Telecom phone card. Try its *assiette béarnaise* (€8.50), a rich selection of regional cold cuts.

Hôtel de France (☎ 05 59 05 33 71; fax 05 59 05 43 83; av de la Gare; r €29, with bathroom €39-44) Although no longer young (and all the more characterful for that), this place is spotless and spruce. It serves real jam in real jam pots for breakfast, unlike the usual sealed-plastic goo. The friendly family owners readily dispense information about hiking opportunities.

Camping areas sprawl nearby. At most, however, you're hemmed in by caravans and mobile homes.

Camping du Valentin (☎ 05 59 05 39 33; pelphi@infonie.fr; per person/site €3.15/4.75; ☷ May-Oct) By contrast, this highly recommended camping ground, 2.4km south of the village beside the D918, has separate zones for mobile homes, caravans and family tents. Overlooking all, and enjoying the best of the impressive views northwards, is an area for lightweight campers.

Gabas

Tiny Gabas, with less than 50 souls, is now mainly a trekking base, 13km south of Laruns. Its equally small-scale 12th-century **chapel** is the only vestige of what was once a monastery and the last Santiago de Compostela pilgrim hostel before the Spanish frontier at Col du Pourtalet. Pick up a hunk of tangy *fromage d'Ossau*, made in the high mountains from ewe's milk and matured in the hamlet.

The Club Alpin Français **refuge** (CAF; ☎ 05 59 05 33 14; dm €7.60, half-board €23; ☺ Jun–Sep & school holidays, Sat & Sun only other times, closed Nov–mid-Dec), 500m south of Gabas, offers cheery accommodation in rooms for four to 12 and a culinary reputation that extends way beyond the valley; Madame's home-made desserts are to die for.

Hôtel-Restaurant le Biscaü (☎ 05 59 05 31 37; fax 05 59 05 43 23; s/d with shower €17/32.50, with bathroom €27.50/40; menus €9.50-15; ☺ mid-Dec–Oct) Le Biscaü is Gabas' most comfortable option and offers hearty cuisine (save room for the cheese course; the owner himself matures cheeses brought in by the local shepherds).

From the CAF *refuge*, a 3.5km forest track brings you to Lac de Bious-Artigues (1420m) and a superb view southeast to Pic du Midi d'Ossau and southwest to Pic d'Ayous.

Le Petit Train d'Artouste

Winter skiers and summer holiday-makers converge upon charmless, lakeside Artouste-Fabrèges (1250m), 6km by road east of Gabas, to squeeze into the cable car which soars up the flanks of the 2032m Pic de la Sagette. Between June and September, an open-topped **train** (☎ reservations 05 59 05 49 61; adult/child €17/13), built for dam workers in the 1920s, runs for 10km at a constant 2000m from the upper cable car station to Lac d'Artouste (1991m). Views are constantly heart stopping and the 'little train' tucks away over 100,000 passengers annually in its four months of operation. Allow a good

four hours. For walkers, the one-way/return cable-car fare is €3.70/5.70.

There's a seasonal **tourist office** (☎ 05 59 05 34 00; ☺ Jun-Sep & other school holidays) beside the cable car.

CAUTERETS

pop 1300 / elevation 930m

The thermal spa and ski resort of Cauterets, less than 30km south of Lourdes, nestles in a tight valley, crowded in by steep slopes rising to 2800m. In summer, it's a superb base for exploring the forests, meadows, lakes and streams of the Parc National des Pyrénées. In winter, Cauterets is blessed with an abundance of snow; it's usually the first of France's Pyrenean ski stations to open and the last to close.

Information

INTERNET ACCESS

Pizzeria Giovanni (see p689; per hr €4 for nondiners)

LAUNDRY

Laverie Ydéaly (19 rue Richelieu; ☺ 8am-8pm)

TOURIST INFORMATION

Maison de la Presse (8 place Maréchal Foch) For walking maps and international newspapers.

Maison du Parc National des Pyrénées (☎ 05 62 92 52 56; place de la Gare; ☺ 9.30am-noon & 3-7pm Jun–mid-Sep, 9.30am- noon & 3-6pm Mon-Tue & Thu-Sat mid-Sep–Apr) Sells walking maps, has an impressive free exhibition on Pyrenean flora and fauna and shows park-related films. Organises guided walks (per half/full day €9.15/15.25; Jul & Aug).

Pont d'Espagne Information Office (☎ 05 62 92 52 19; ☺ Jun–mid-Oct & mid-Dec–Mar)

Tourist Office (☎ 05 62 92 50 50; www.cauterets.com in French; place Maréchal Foch; ☺ 9am-noon & 2-6pm Mon-Sat, 9am-noon & 2-6pm Sun)

Sights & Activities

WALKING

Cauterets makes a particularly good base for day walks since so many start right from town or from Pont d'Espagne at the end of the spectacular D920 road, 8km south, 600m higher and accessible in season by shuttle bus (see p689). For a week or more's stimulating walking in the area, consult Lonely Planet's *Walking in France*.

The area west of Cauterets is covered by IGN's 1:25,000-scale Top 25 map No 1647OT *Vignemale;* land east of town fea-

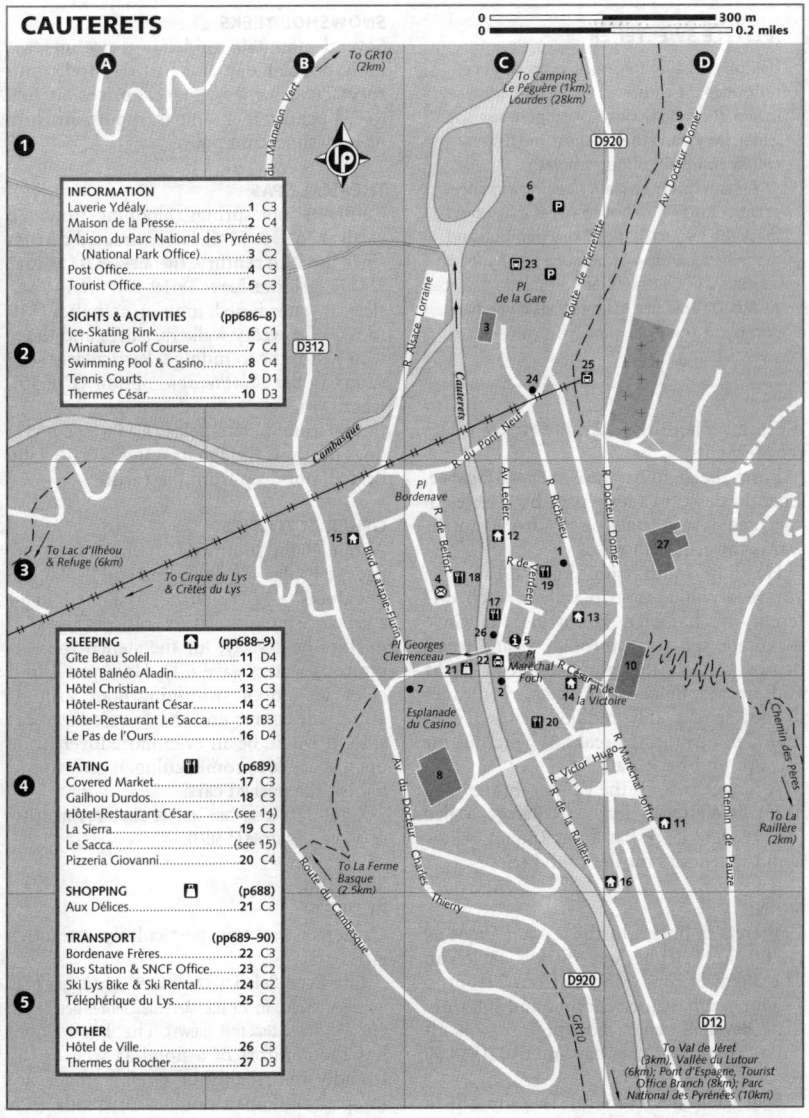

CAUTERETS

0   300 m
0   0.2 miles

To GR10
(2km)

To Camping
Le Péguère (1km);
Lourdes (28km)

D920

INFORMATION
Laverie Ydéaly...................1 C3
Maison de la Presse.............2 C4
Maison du Parc National des Pyrénées
  (National Park Office)........3 C2
Post Office.......................4 C3
Tourist Office...................5 C3

SIGHTS & ACTIVITIES   (pp686–8)
Ice-Skating Rink.................6 C1
Miniature Golf Course..........7 C4
Swimming Pool & Casino.......8 C4
Tennis Courts...................9 D1
Thermes César..................10 D3

D312

To Lac d'Ilhéou
& Refuge (6km)

To Cirque du Lys
& Crêtes du Lys

SLEEPING   (pp688–9)
Gîte Beau Soleil................11 D4
Hôtel Balnéo Aladin............12 C3
Hôtel Christian.................13 C3
Hôtel-Restaurant César........14 C4
Hôtel-Restaurant Le Sacca....15 B3
Le Pas de l'Ours...............16 D4

EATING   (p689)
Covered Market.................17 C3
Gailhou Durdos.................18 C3
Hôtel-Restaurant César.......(see 14)
La Sierra........................19 C3
Le Sacca.......................(see 15)
Pizzeria Giovanni...............20 C4

SHOPPING   (p688)
Aux Délices....................21 C3

TRANSPORT   (pp689–90)
Bordenave Frères...............22 C3
Bus Station & SNCF Office....23 C2
Ski Lys Bike & Ski Rental.....24 C2
Téléphérique du Lys...........25 C2

OTHER
Hôtel de Ville.................26 C3
Thermes du Rocher.............27 D3

To La Ferme
Basque
(2.5km)

To La
Raillère
(2km)

D920

GR10

D12

To Val de Jéret
(3km), Vallée du Lutour
(6km); Pont d'Espagne, Tourist
Office Branch (8km); Parc
National des Pyrénées (10km)

tures on No 1748OT *Gavarnie*. Rando Éditions' *Bigorre Carte No 4* covers the region
at 1:50,000.

The Parc National produces *Randonnées
dans le Parc National des Pyrénées: Vallée de
Cauterets* (€6.40), a loose-leaf pack describing, in French and with a detailed map, 15
walks. The tourist office carries *Sentiers du*

Lavaudon (€5), describing seven easy walks
in the area.

A painless way to gain height from Cauterets is to take the Téléphérique du Lys
cable car (see 689).

For a pleasant day walk from Cauterets
(allow around six hours), follow the Vallée de Lutour southwards as far as Lac

---

A LITTLE SWEETENER

Halitosis is never fun. Back in the 19th century, once the *curistes* of Cauterets had swallowed their daily dose of sulphurous spa water, they – and their nearest and dearest – would complain of dog's breath.

An enterprising villager, seeing a chance, set about making a boiled sweet that would mask the odour. Shaped like a humbug and made in a rainbow of colours, *berlingots*, a speciality of Cauterets, are on sale in town. At **Aux Délices** (place Clemenceau), if you happen by at the right time, you can see the sweets being made.

---

d'Estom, where the lakeside *refuge* offers refreshments.

From the giant car park at **Pont d'Espagne**, Chemin des Cascades passes by a series of spectacular waterfalls as it drops northwards towards Cauterets.

Heading south from Pont d'Espagne, you've a choice of two valleys, each different in character. Following the Gave de Gaube upstream through a pine wood brings you to the popular **Lac de Gaube** and, nearby, **Hôtellerie de Gaube** which does drinks, snacks and midday *menus*. Three hours, not counting breaks, is generous for this out-and-back walk.

A longer trek up the gentler, more open **Vallée de Marcadau** leads to **Refuge Wallon** (☎ 05 62 92 64 28; ☽ Mar-Oct) at 1866m. Allow about five hours for the round trip.

SKIING

Cauterets is linked to the 23-run **Cirque du Lys** by the Téléphérique du Lys cable car. The 35km of runs, ranging from 2450m to 1850m, are best for beginner and intermediate **downhill** skiers. Low/high-season lift passes cost €20/23 per day and €102/148.50 per week.

Pont d'Espagne (1450m) is primarily a **cross-country** skiing area. From it, 37km of maintained trails, paralleled in their lower reaches by a piste for walkers and snowshoers, lead up the Vallée du Marcadau. A one-day/week trail pass costs €8/39.

Several shops in Cauterets hire ski equipment. Typical prices per day are downhill €12 to €20, snowboards €19 to €25 and cross-country gear €8 to €12.

SNOWSHOE TREKS

Several mountain guides organise increasingly popular day and half-day treks into spectacular scenery. Typical prices are €20 to €31 per day including transport, and hire of snowshoes and poles.

THERMAL SPAS

Cauterets' hot springs, blooping from the earth at 36°C to 53°C, have attracted *curistes* since the 19th century. **Thermes César** (☎ 05 62 92 14 20; rue Docteur Domer; ☽ Feb-Nov) offers a variety of water-based, tone-up activities (€10 to €33) for weary walkers, skiers and those who just want to indulge. Particularly sensuous is the *pelothérapie* option (€18.50), where you get plastered in mud.

Year-round, **Hôtel Balnéo Aladin** (see p689) does the same though its water is artificially heated, not deep from the earth.

OTHER ACTIVITIES

About 200m southwest of the tourist office are Esplanade du Casino and Esplanade des Oeufs (Egg Esplanade, so named, in an age before public-relations officers and spin doctors held sway, for the stench the sulphurous waters gave off). Here you'll find cafés, an indoor swimming pool, a miniature golf course and the town's large casino. It would be an even more lovely little open space for promenading, if only they'd banish the parked cars.

Cauterets also has an **ice-skating rink** (place de la Gare; adult/child €5.50/3).

Sleeping
BUDGET

Cauterets has two particularly attractive *gîtes*:

Gîte Beau Soleil (☎ 05 62 92 53 52; gite.beau .soleil@wanadoo.fr; 25 rue Maréchal Joffre; per person €16; ☽ closed Nov-first snows) The Beau Soleil has the comfort of a hotel as well as the friendly informality of a *refuge*. Beds are in spick and span doubles or quads with bathrooms and there's also a kitchen for self-caterers.

Le Pas de l'Ours (☎ 05 62 92 58 07; www.lepas delours.com in French; 21 rue de la Raillère; dm €15, with half-board €32, d with bathroom €57-61.50, with half-board per person €42.50; ☽ mid-May–Sep & Dec–mid-Apr) 'The Bear's Footstep' is both hotel and *gîte*. Dorm prices include use of the kitchen and all guests can use the sauna (€8).

Camping

Camping Le Péguère (☎ 05 62 92 52 91; camping peguere@wanadoo.fr; 2 people & car €10.50; ☺ Apr–Sep) This grassy, shady camping ground, 1.5km north of town on the D920, has some choice sites right beside the Gave de Cauterets.

MID-RANGE

Hôtel Christian (☎ 05 62 92 50 04; www.hotel-chris tian.fr in French; 10 rue Richelieu; s/d €44/56 with breakfast; ☺ Dec–Sep) Rooms are large and comfortable at this friendly hotel, in the hands of the same Cauterets family for three generations.

Hôtel-Restaurant César (☎ 05 62 92 52 57; www .cesarhotel.com; 3 rue César; d €46–50; ☺ closed May & Oct) This cosy option, run by an engaging husband and wife team, has attractively furnished rooms and represents excellent value. They also run an impressive restaurant.

Hôtel-Restaurant Le Sacca (☎ 05 62 92 50 02; hotel.le.sacca@wanadoo.fr; 11 blvd Latapie-Flurin; d €40–46; ☺ closed 10 Oct-20 Dec) Le Sacca is another excellent mid-range choice, run by the same husband and wife team for three decades. It too has a great restaurant and most of the 48 rooms have separate bathroom and toilet.

Hôtel Balnéo Aladin (☎ 05 62 92 60 60; www .hotel-balneo-aladin.com in French; 11 av Général Leclerc; d €110-130 incl breakfast; ☺ Christmas-Apr & Jun-Sep) Cauterets' only three-star hotel, the Aladin also doubles as a private spa (see p688). Strikingly modern – brash even – in a resort where venerable hotels are closing or converting into apartments, it offers every luxury. A stay of four nights is normally expected, although this is negotiable outside peak periods.

Eating

Le Sacca (see Hôtel-Restaurant Le Sacca, above; menus €12-27) Here is by common consent the finest place to eat in Cauterets with a range of *menus* to suit most pockets. Whether you're down from the mountains or fresh from Lourdes and the plains, make a pilgrimage to savour its subtle cuisine.

Hôtel-Restaurant César (see Sleeping; menus €20-40; ☺ closed lunch in winter) With its crisp white tablecloths and napkins, the César offers elegant dining. The food is excellent and there's a good range of regional wines at reasonable prices.

La Sierra (☎ 06 61 35 57 15; 8 rue Verdun; lunch menu €10.50, dinner menu €13.50-19) This intimate little place, tucked away down a side street, of-

fers excellent value. Service is cheerful and friendly and the menu is varied.

Pizzeria Giovanni (☎ 05 62 92 57 80; 5 rue de la Raillère; menu €14; ☺ dinner only except school holidays, closed mid-May–mid-Jun & Nov–mid-Dec) Pizzas (around €9, to eat in or take away) are superior, a generous steak costs €13 and the home-cooked desserts (€4 to €5.50) are a dream. A nice touch: diners can check out their emails for free.

La Ferme Basque (☎ 05 62 92 54 32; route de Cambasque) Around 4km by road west of town, it has a superb plunging view of Cauterets from its terrace and makes a great spot for a daylight drink. But don't bother dining here: the food is indifferent and the service excruciatingly slow.

SELF-CATERING

Stalls are few but Cauterets' **Covered market** (av Leclerc) is a gastronome's delight. Inside, a stall does tasty takeaway regional dishes such as *garbure* while its neighbours sell wonderful mountain cheeses. Just follow your nose…

Gailhou Durdos (rue de Belfort), opposite the post office, has a rich selection of local wines and specialities.

Getting There & Away

The last train steamed out of Cauterets' magnificent, all-wood station in 1947. Like something left over from a cowboy film set, it now serves as the **bus station** (☎ 05 62 92 53 70).

SNCF buses run between Cauterets and Lourdes train station (€6.10, 50 minutes, five to seven daily).

Getting Around

BICYCLE

Rent mountain bikes from **Ski Lys** (☎ 05 62 92 58 30; route de Pierrefitte; per half/full day from €16/25).

CABLE CAR

The two-stage Téléphérique du Lys operates mid-June to mid-September and from December to the end of the ski season. It rises over 900m to the Cirque du Lys, where you can catch the Grand Barbat chair-lift up to Crêtes du Lys (2400m). A return trip costs €4.50/6.50 to Cirque du Lys or €5/9 to Crêtes du Lys.

TAXI

Bordenave Frères (☎ 05 62 92 53 68, 06 71 01 46 86; place Clemenceau), who also call itself Allo Taxis, operates a shuttle service between the bus station and Pont d'Espagne (single/return €3.50/5) during the ski season (twice daily) and in summer (six times daily).

Year-round, a taxi between Cauterets and Pont d'Espagne costs €13.

VALLÉE DES GAVES & AROUND

Vallée des Gaves (Valley of the Mountain Streams), gentle and pastoral, extends south from Lourdes to Pierrefitte-Nestalas. Here, the valley forks, narrows, twists and becomes more rugged. The eastern tine pokes into the Pyrenees via Gavarnie while the western prong leads up to Cauterets.

Pic du Midi de Bigorre

Lament the fact or love it, the Pic du Midi (2877m), until recently almost exclusively the preserve of astronomers and scientists, is now accessible to all by **cable car** (☎ 08 25 00 28 77; adult/student/child €23/18/12; ⊙ daily Jun-Sep, Thu-Mon Oct & Dec-May). Leaving from the ski resort of La Mongie (1800m), it gives access to one of the Pyrenees' most soul-stirring panoramas, albeit at heart-stopping prices.

Gavarnie

pop 175 / elevation 1360m

In winter, Gavarnie, 52km south of Lourdes at the end of the D921, offers limited downhill and decent cross-country skiing plus snowshoe treks. In summer, it's a popular take-off point for walkers. And take off they do, as quickly as their feet will carry them: by 10am the village and its tawdry souvenir stalls are overrun by trippers.

Consult the IGN Top 25 map No 1748OT *Gavarnie* (€9) or the National Park pack *Randonnées dans le Parc National des Pyrénées: Vallée de Luz* (€6.40) for the rich menu of routes.

The most frequented trail, accessible to all, leads to the **Cirque de Gavarnie**, a breathtaking rock amphitheatre, 1500m high, dominated by ice-capped peaks. The round-trip walk to its foot takes around two hours. Between June and September, you can sit astride a horse or donkey (about €20 round trip). In mid-July, Gavarnie hosts an arts festival in the dramatic setting of the Cirque.

The **tourist office** (☎ 05 62 92 49 10; www.gavarnie.com; ⊙ 8.30am-7pm Jul & Aug, 9am-noon & 2-6pm Sep-Jun) occupies new premises at the northern entrance to the village.

The **National Park office** (☎ 05 62 92 42 48; ⊙ 9.30am-noon & 1.30-6pm Tue-Sat school holidays, Mon-Fri rest of year) is 200m beyond.

Camping Le Pain de Sucre (☎ 05 62 92 47 55; www.camping-gavarnie.com; per person/site €3.25/3.40; ⊙ mid-Dec–mid-Apr & Jun-Sep) enjoys a lovely riverside spot a little north of town.

In summer only, two buses operate daily between Gavarnie and Luz-St-Sauveur, from where there are connections to Lourdes.

Cirque de Troumouse

From Gèdre, 6.5km north of Gavarnie, a toll road (€4 per vehicle) winds southeast up a desolate valley into the Pyrenees to the base of the Cirque de Troumouse, wilder, infinitely less trodden and almost as stunning as the Cirque de Gavarnie. Snows permitting, the road is open between May and October.

UPPER GARONNE VALLEY
St-Bertrand de Comminges

On an isolated hillock, St-Bertrand and its **Cathédrale Ste-Marie** (adult/child €4/1.50; ⊙ 9am-7pm Mon-Sat, 2-7pm Sun May-Sep, 10am-noon & 2-5pm or 6pm Mon-Sat, 2-5pm or 6pm Sun Oct-Apr) loom protectively over the Vallée de Garonne and the much-pillaged remains of the Gallo-Roman town of Lugdunum Convenarum, where you can wander at will for free.

The splendid Renaissance oak choir stalls sit below the soaring Gothic east end of the cathedral. Carved in 1535 by local artisans, they blend the serene and spiritual with an earthy realism. The adjacent **tourist office** (☎ 05 61 95 44 44; ⊙ 10am-6pm or 7pm Apr-Oct, 10am-5pm Tue-Sun Nov-Dec & Feb-Mar) has a detailed pamphlet in English.

Bagnères de Luchon

pop 3100 / elevation 630m

Bagnères de Luchon (or simply Luchon) is a trim little town of gracious 19th-century buildings, expanded to accommodate the *curistes* who came to take the waters at its splendid spa.

The **tourist office** (☎ 05 61 79 21 21; www.luchon.com; ⊙ 9am-7pm Jul & Aug & Dec-Mar, 9am-12.30pm & 1.30-7pm Sep-Nov & Apr-Jun) is at 18 allées d'Étigny.

SIGHTS & ACTIVITIES

Once only for the ailing, the **Thermes** (Health Spa; ☎ 05 61 79 22 97; ⊙ Apr-Oct), at the southern end of allées d'Étigny, now also offers relaxation and fitness sessions for weary skiers and walkers, mainstay of the town's tourism-based economy. It's €13 to loll in the scented steam of the 160m-long underground *vaporarium*, then dunk yourself in the caressing 32°C waters of its pool. Follow this with a flutter in the elegant surroundings of the casino and you'll have had a good night out.

The stylish allées d'Étigny, flanked by cafés and restaurants, links place Joffre with the Thermes. Just to the west of this boulevard is the base of the **cabin lift** (single/return €4.90/7.50), which hauls you up to **Superbagnères**, at 1860m the starting point for winter skiing and summer walking. It operates daily in the ski season and during July and August (weekends only during most other months).

Cycling

Although you'll huff and puff, the area is rich in opportunities for mountain biking. Pick up a free copy of *Guide des Circuits VTT*, prepared by the local mountain-bike club, from the tourist office. To rent a bike, see right.

Walking

An amazing 250km of marked trails, ranging from gentle valley-bottom strolls to more demanding high-mountain treks, thread their way from Luchon and Superbagnères. Lonely Planet's *Walking in France* describes five days of walks in the area and the tourist office carries a useful pamphlet, *Sentiers Balisés du Pays de Luchon*. Pick up IGN 1:25,000 map No 1848OT *Bagnères de Luchon*, pull on your boots and you're away.

Other Activities

The skies above Superbagnères are magnificent for **parapenting**. Contact **École Soaring** (☎ /fax 05 61 79 29 23; 14 rue Sylvie). More down-to-earth, **Pyrénées Aventure** (☎ 05 61 79 20 59; 9 rue Docteur Germès) arranges **canyon clambering**, plus **rafting** and **canoeing** on the River Garonne.

SLEEPING

Hôtel des Sports (☎ 05 61 79 97 80; www.hotel-des-sports.net; 12 av Maréchal Foch; s/d €30/38) This hotel is that rare institution in France – an entirely non-smoking hotel, where the friendly owner, himself a hiker, happily dispenses local walking information and advice.

Camping Beauregard (☎ 05 61 79 30 74; fax 05 61 79 04 35; 37; av de Vénasque; per person/site €4/5; Apr–mid-Oct) It's the larger and more welcoming of Luchon's two camping grounds.

EATING

Allées d'Étigny is packed with bars and restaurants, some fine delicatessens and the usual pizza-'n'-pasta joints. Two restaurants offer excellent value:

L'Arbesquens (☎ 05 61 79 33 69; 47 allées d'Étigny; menus from €13) Its speciality is *fondue* (€14, minimum two people) in 14 different varieties. Help it down with a jug of their fine Jurançon white wine.

Caprices d' Étigny (☎ 05 61 94 31 05; 30bis allées d'Étigny; menus €14 & €20; Fri-Wed) Just across the road and staffed by a young, friendly crew, it does great grilled meats (three-course *menu* €17) on its open fire.

Le Jardin des Cascades (☎ 05 61 79 83 09; menu €24.50, mains €13-20; Apr-Sep) In the hamlet of Montauban de Luchon, 1.5km east of Luchon, this restaurant more than merits the steep walk up from its parking lot. Cascading with fresh flowers and tastefully furnished in blue, it's justifiably renowned for its fine cuisine.

Self-caterers should pass by Luchon's daily **market**, established in 1897 and offering fine fresh fare ever since.

GETTING THERE & AROUND

There are SNCF trains and buses between Luchon and Montréjeau (€5.75, 50 minutes, five to seven daily), which have frequent connections to Toulouse (€16.80) and Pau (€17.70).

There's free parking around the Casino and cabin lift station.

For bicycle hire, contact **Liberty Cycles Demiguel** (☎ 05 61 79 12 87; 82 av Foch) – look for the Statue of Liberty sign. Mountain bikes cost €18/51/75 per day/three days/week.

VALLÉE DE L'ARIÈGE

The Vallée de l'Ariège offers some great pre-Pyrenean walking. Tourist offices carry *Guide Randonnée*, a useful free booklet in French that recommends hikes for all levels, including family outings.

Foix

pop 9950

Foix, county seat of the Ariège *département*, merits a small detour from the N20 to visit its castle, 11th-century church and streets lined with medieval, half-timbered houses.

The town sits in the crook of the confluence of the Rivers Ariège and Arget. Its oldest, most attractive quarter is on the west bank of the Ariège.

INFORMATION

The **tourist office** (☎ 05 61 65 12 12; www.ot-foix.fr; 9am-7pm Mon-Sat, 9.30am-12.30pm & 2-6pm Sun Jul & Aug, 9am-noon & 2-6pm Mon-Sat Sep-Jun) is beside the covered market on cours Gabriel Fauré, the wide main thoroughfare.

SIGHTS

Imposing **Château des Comtes de Foix** (☎ 05 34 09 83 83; adult/child €4/2; 9.45am-6.30pm Jul & Aug, 9.45am-noon & 2-6pm May-Jun & Sep, 10.30am-noon & 2-5.30pm Wed-Sun & daily in school holidays Oct-Dec & Feb-Apr), with its three crenellated, gravity-defying towers, stands guard over the town. Constructed in the 10th century as a stronghold for the counts of Foix, the castle served as a prison from the 16th century onwards; look for the graffiti scratched into the stones by some hapless prisoner. Today it houses a small **archaeological museum**. In July and August, there are several daily guided visits in French and one in English at 1pm.

ACTIVITIES

Go canyon clambering, mountain biking or hiking with **Pyrénévasion** (☎ 05 61 65 01 10; www.pyrenevasion.com in French) or **Maison de la Montagne** (☎ 05 61 02 68 19; e.mayodon@free.fr).

SLEEPING & EATING

Hôtel Lons (☎ 05 61 65 52 44; www.hotel-lons-foix.com; 6 place Dutilh; d €48-70) Once a coaching inn, it's now a three-star Logis de France with attractive, good-value rooms, nine of which overlook the river. The hotel's **restaurant** (closed Fri dinner & Sat lunch Sep-mid-Jul) offers similar river views through its picture windows.

Camping du Lac (☎ 05 61 65 11 58; www.camp ingdulac.com in French; 2 people & car €11-17; year-round; 🐕) Situated on the RN20 2.5km north of Foix, this attractive camp site has a pool and restaurant.

Le Sainte Marthe (☎ 05 61 02 87 87; place Lazéma; menus €24-51; Jul & Aug, Thu-Mon Sep-Jun) This gourmet restaurant specialises in Ariègeois cuisine, especially *cassoulet* (€16). It can rustle up a vegetarian menu on request and has a non-smoking room.

GETTING THERE & AWAY

Trains and buses (€12, 50 minutes, seven to 15 daily) connect Toulouse and Foix.

Around Foix

Beneath **Labouiche**, 6km northwest of Foix on the D1, flows Europe's longest navigable underground river, along which you can take a spectacular 1500m, 75-minute **boat trip** (☎ 05 61 02 90 77; adult/child €7.50/5.50; 9.30am-5.15pm Jul & Aug, 10-11.15am & 2-5.15pm Apr-Jun & Sep, 10-11.15am & 2-4.30pm Sat & Sun Oct-mid-Nov).

Ax-les-Thermes

pop 1500 / elevation 720m

Ax-les-Thermes flourishes as a small base for skiing in winter and, with over 60 hot-water springs, as a spa town. Like Foix, it lies at the confluence of two rivers: the Ariège and its near namesake the Oriège. The **tourist office** (☎ 05 61 64 60 60; www.vallees-ax.com; 9am-noon & 2-7pm Jul & Aug, to 6pm Sep-Jun) is on av Delcassé.

The heart of town is place du Breilh. On one side of the square is the faded elegance of the casino. On the other side is the **Bassin de Ladres**, a pool originally built to soothe the wounds of Knights Templar injured in the Crusades and the ulcers of the town's leper colony. Pull off your socks, follow the example of the knights and steep in its waters.

There are a couple of interesting narrow streets with overhanging buildings between place du Breilh and place Roussel. The **Thermes du Teich** (☎ 05 61 65 86 60; Apr-mid-Nov), beside the River Oriège, has a pool, sauna, hammam and aquagym (€12 per session), open to all comers.

If you are heading up to or down from Andorra and the Pyrenees, Ax makes a good meal or snack stop.

Le Grand Café (☎ 05 61 64 67 16; 1 av Delcassé) is strong on atmosphere and dishes up good salads and snacks. Its high walls, stucco ceilings and tall etched-glass windows speak of the classic French town café, while the funky music and impressive collection of beer mats and drip towels are decidedly more contemporary.

La Petite Fringale (☎ 06 87 74 03 21; 6 rue Rigal; mains €13-14.50) This popular, friendly place has a small summertime terrace. It does *fondues* (€14 to €17), lots of tempting cheese-based dishes and meaty mains.

La Pizzatière (☎ 05 61 64 33 95; 2 rue Rigal), a couple of doors away, does a huge range of takeaway pizzas, from single slice to giant (55cm across).

Most buses and trains serving Foix (see left) continue as far as Ax.

Toulouse Area

Not quite the Pyrenees (Pyrénées) and no longer part of Languedoc-Roussillon (after regional boundaries were redrawn in the 1960s), Languedoc's traditional centre, Toulouse, may be in geographical limbo but it's a fascinating region full of historical sights and activities.

Central to the area is Toulouse itself, one of France's fastest-growing cities. Bolstered by its booming hi-tech industries (most notably aerospace – this is the epicentre of the huge Europe-wide EADS aircraft manufacturing consortium) the city is an increasingly self-confident one. It has a vibrant centre with a subtle Spanish flavour and a large student population. To the south of Toulouse lie the Pyrenees, while within easy reach are four towns with strong historical connections: Albi, 75km to the northeast, birthplace of Toulouse-Lautrec; Montauban, 53km north, a Huguenot stronghold in the 16th century; Condom, 110km to the northwest, with a host of 18th-century *hôtels particuliers;* and Auch, 77km west, a key Roman trading route.

West of Toulouse city, the region of Gascony (Gascogne) rolls all the way to the Atlantic. Famous for its lush countryside, sleepy *bastides* (medieval villages), fine wines, foie gras and Armagnac liqueur, slow-paced Gascony is ideal for experiencing some of France's finest examples of medieval and Renaissance architecture.

HIGHLIGHTS

- Sample the delights of **Gascon cuisine** (p702) in Toulouse
- Trace the development of an artistic master at the **Musée Toulouse-Lautrec** (p706), in Albi
- Absorb the ambience of the **bastide villages** (p715) around Condom
- Mix with the revellers enjoying **Toulouse's busy bar scene** (p703)
- Expand your mind and universe at **Cité de l'Espace** (p700)

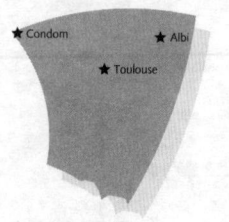

- POPULATION: 2,551,687
- AREA: 45,349 SQ KM

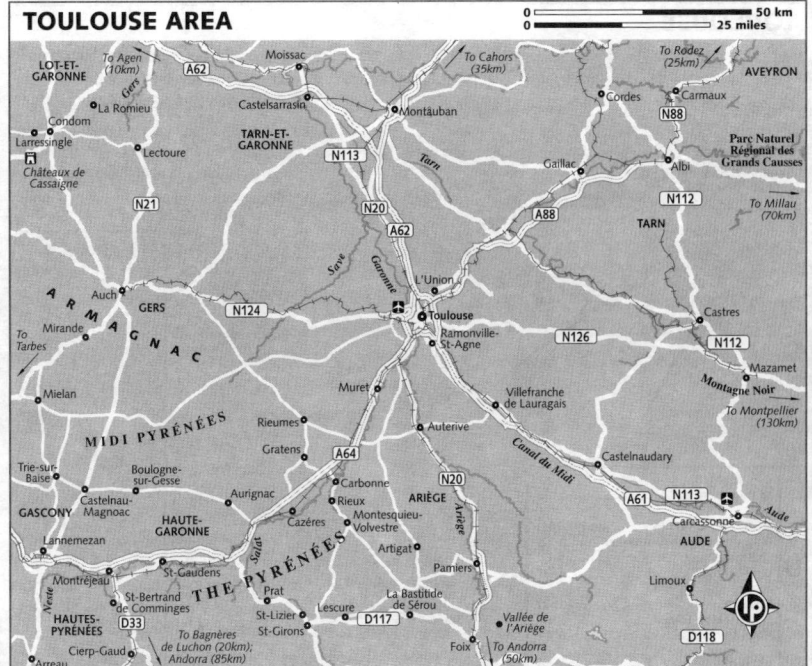

TOULOUSE AREA

TOULOUSE
pop 398,423

Be warned, even the grannies will want to fight you in Toulouse according to the lyrics of *Oh! Toulouse,* a bittersweet tribute to the city by the late crooner Claude Nougaro, a kind of Sinatra figure in France, who was born and bred here.

Nougaro may have had a hard time growing up on the streets of *la ville rose* (the pink city – so named because of the profusion of rose-red brick buildings), but these days you're more likely to find a good time in Toulouse than you are to bump into any pugilistic pensioners.

Toulouse is a lively, friendly city, with an economy bolstered by its booming aerospace industries and with plenty to offer the visitor.

Anywhere that's home to 100,000 students can't really fail to be a buzzing, busy place with a terrific café and bar scene, a decent club scene and dozens of good affordable places to eat.

Signs of a rich (and tumultuous) history crowd around you in the narrow medieval streets and inside the many churches and cathedrals of the city, which is the capital of the Midi-Pyrénées region and France's fourth-largest city.

History

Toulouse, known to the Romans as Tolosa, was the Visigoth capital from AD 419–507. In the 12th and 13th centuries the counts of Toulouse supported the Cathars (see p756). Three centuries later, during the Wars of Religion, the city sided with the Catholic League. Toulouse merchants grew rich in the 16th and 17th centuries from the woad (blue dye) trade, which collapsed when the Portuguese began importing indigo from India. The Toulouse Parliament ruled Languedoc from 1420 until the 1789 Revolution.

During WWI, Toulouse became a centre for the manufacture of arms and aircraft. In the 1920s, Antoine de St-Exupéry, author of *Le Petit Prince* (The Little Prince), and other daring pilots pioneered mail flights to northwestern Africa and South America, often staying in the city between sorties. After WWII, Toulouse became the nucleus of

TOULOUSE

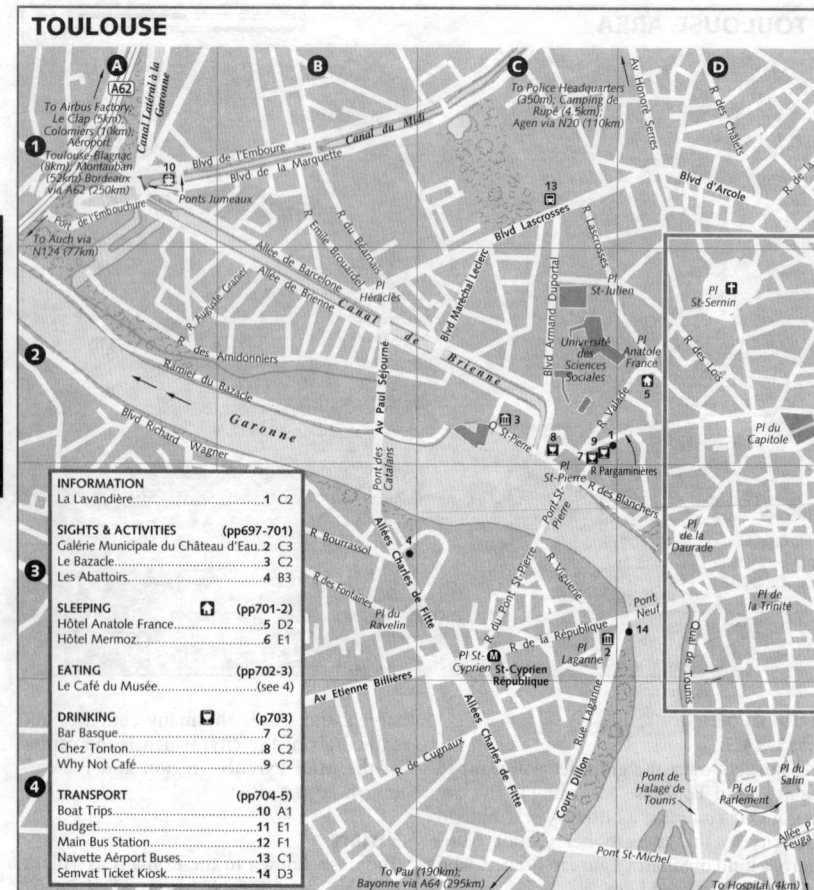

INFORMATION	
La Lavandière..............................1 C2	

SIGHTS & ACTIVITIES	(pp697-701)
Galérie Municipale du Château d'Eau.2 C3	
Le Bazacle.................................3 C2	
Les Abattoirs..............................4 B3	

SLEEPING	(pp701-2)
Hôtel Anatole France....................5 D2	
Hôtel Mermoz.............................6 E1	

EATING	(pp702-3)
Le Café du Musée.......................(see 4)	

DRINKING	(p703)
Bar Basque................................7 C2	
Chez Tonton...............................8 C2	
Why Not Café.............................9 C2	

TRANSPORT	(pp704-5)
Boat Trips................................10 A1	
Budget...................................11 E1	
Main Bus Station........................12 F1	
Navette Aérport Buses..................13 C1	
Semvat Ticket Kiosk.....................14 D3	

the country's aerospace industry. Passenger planes built here have included the Caravelle and the Concorde as well as the latest 555-seat Airbus A380, and local factories also produce the Ariane rocket. These are boom times for Airbus, and especially good ones for Toulouse, as the HQ of the consortium overtook its great US rival Boeing in 2004 in terms of sales of new aircraft. It's a rare success story of Europe outdoing the USA.

Orientation

The heart of Toulouse is bounded to the east by blvd de Strasbourg and its continuation, blvd Lazare Carnot, and, to the west, by the River Garonne. Its two principal squares are place du Capitole and, 200m east, place

Wilson. From the latter, the wide allées Jean Jaurès leads northeast to the main bus station and Gare Matabiau, the train station, both just across the Canal du Midi.

From place du Capitole, rue du Taur runs north to the Basilique St-Sernin, while pedestrianised rue St-Rome and rue des Changes lead south from the square to the transport hub of place Esquirol.

Information
BOOKSHOPS

Bookshop (Map p699; ☎ 05 61 22 99 92; 17 rue Lakanal) Has an excellent range of English-language books and operates an information board.

Ombres Blanches (Map p699; ☎ 05 34 45 53 33; 48-50 rue Gambetta) A friendly and accessible place specialising

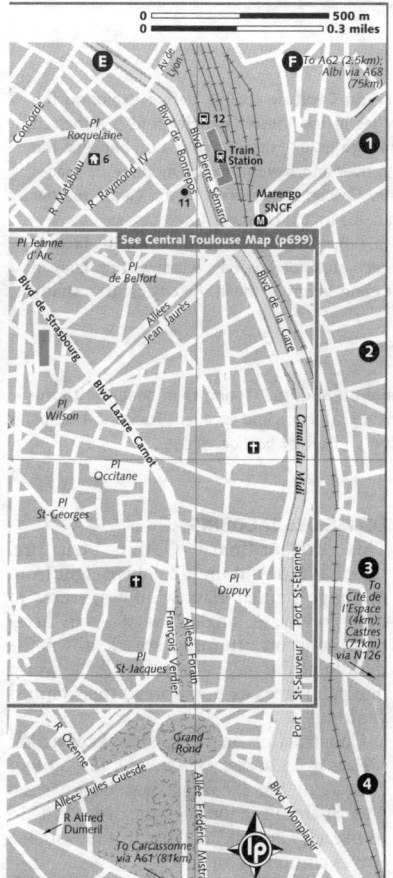

in travel guides, including a good range of Lonely Planet titles and maps.

INTERNET ACCESS
Cyber King (Map p699; 31 rue Gambetta; per hr €4.55; 11am-midnight Mon-Fri, 11.30am-2am Sat, 2-10pm Sun) Centrally located.

Résomania (Map p699; 85 rue Pargaminières; per hr €3-4; 9.30am-midnight Mon-Fri, noon-midnight Sat & Sun)

LAUNDRY
Befitting a city with so many students in digs, Toulouse is well endowed with laundrettes. Two located centrally are:

Hallwash (Map p699; 7 rue Mirepoix)
La Lavandière (Map pp696-7; 29 rue Pargaminières)

POST
Main Post Office (Map p699; 9 rue la Fayette)

TOURIST INFORMATION
Tourist Office (Map p699; ☎ 05 61 11 02 22; www.ot -toulouse.fr; square Charles de Gaulle; 9am-7pm Mon-Sat, 10am-1pm & 2-6.15pm Sun Jun-Sep, 9am-6pm Mon-Fri, 9am-12.30pm & 2-6pm Sat, 10am-12.30pm & 2-5pm Sun Oct-May) In the base of the Donjon du Capitole, a 16th-century tower. Wine lovers planning to visit *caves* and vineyards in the Toulouse region should pick up the excellent and free *Guide des Vins du Sud-Ouest* plus a free wine map here.

Sights
PLACE DU CAPITOLE
Bustling and pedestrianised **place du Capitole** (Map p699) is the city's main square. On the ceiling of the arcades on its western side are 29 vivid illustrations of the city's history, from the *Venus of Lespugue* (a prehistoric representation of woman) through to the city's role during the crusades and its modern-day status as a hub for the aeronautics industry, by contemporary artist Raymond Moretti.

On the eastern side of the square is the 128m-long façade of Toulouse's city hall, the **Capitole** (9am-5pm Mon-Fri, 9am-1pm Sat mid-Jun–mid-Sep, Mon-Fri mid-Sep–mid-Jun). Built in the early 1750s, it is a focus of civic pride. Within the Capitole is the **Théâtre du Capitole** (☎ 05 61 63 13 13), one of France's most prestigious opera and operetta venues. The interior of the Capitole also includes the over-the-top, late 19th-century **Salle des Illustres** (Hall of the Illustrious).

On the Capitole's eastern side is the green square Charles de Gaulle, or Jardin du Capitole.

VIEUX QUARTIER
The small, 18th-century **Vieux Quartier** (Old Quarter; Map p699) is a web of narrow lanes and plazas south of place du Capitole and place Wilson. Place de la Daurade is the city's 'beach' beside the River Garonne, peaceful by day and romantic by night, overlooking the floodlit Pont Neuf. Well worth the walk.

BASILIQUE ST-SERNIN
Once a Benedictine abbey church, **Basilique St-Sernin** (Map p699; ☎ 05 61 21 80 45; place St-Sernin; 8.30am-5.45pm Mon-Sat, 8.30am-7.30pm Sun Jul-Sep,

TOULOUSE IN...

Two days

Breakfast at one of the cafés on handsome **place du Capitole** (p697), before exploring the **Capitole** building (city hall), and the many churches in the **Vieux Quartier** (p697). Lunch at the cheap tasty canteens above **Les Halles Victor Hugo** (p703), then it's a toss-up between the **Musée des Augustins** (see below) or a walk to the river and beyond to the modern art spaces and café at **Les Abattoirs** (p700). Browse on hearty Gascon fodder back in the Vieux Quartier before hitting the many excellent bars (p703) and clubs (p703) in town.

Next day head out of town to **Cité de l'Espace** (p700) in the morning and the **Airbus factory** (p700) in the afternoon or, if this is too much hi-tech stuff for one day, window-shop back in the Vieux Quartier or relax back in the various cafés and *salons de thé* in the city centre's **shady squares** (p703).

Four days or more

Take a boat or a bike for a lazy day along the **Canal du Midi** (p701) and then head out to the villages in the region such as **Albi** (p705) for the striking cathedral and excellent Toulouse-Lautrec museum or the **Condom area** (p713) for fine dining and pretty *bastide* villages.

8.30-11.45am & 2-5.45pm Mon-Sat Oct-Jun) was once an important stop on the Santiago de Compostela pilgrimage route. The chancel of this vast, 115m-long brick basilica, France's largest and most complete Romanesque structure, was built between 1080 and 1096, and the nave was added in the 12th century. The basilica is topped by a magnificent eight-sided 13th-century **tower** and spire, added in the 15th century.

Directly above the double-level crypt is the 18th-century **tomb of St-Sernin** beneath a sumptuous canopy. In the north transept is a well-preserved **12th-century fresco** of Christ's Resurrection.

Visiting hours for the **ambulatory chapels** and **crypt** (admission €2; 🕑 10am-6pm Mon-Sat, 12.30-6pm Sun Jul-Sep, 10-11.30am & 2.30-5pm Mon-Sat, 2.30-5pm Sun Oct-Jun) are shorter than those for the basilica. There are also guided tours of the crypt (10am and 2.30pm Monday to Saturday).

MUSÉE DES AUGUSTINS

The **Musée des Augustins** (Augustins Museum; Map p699; ☎ 05 61 22 21 82; www.augustins.org; 21 rue de Metz; adult/child €2.20/1.10; 🕑 10am-6pm Thu-Mon, 10am-9pm Wed) houses a superb collection ranging from Roman stone artefacts to paintings by Rubens, Delacroix and Toulouse-Lautrec. The museum occupies a former Augustinian monastery, and the gardens of its two 14th-century **cloisters** are among the prettiest in southern France. A rather striking row of gargoyles lines one side of the cloister.

ÉGLISE DES JACOBINS

This extraordinary Gothic structure, flooded by day in multicoloured light from the huge stained-glass windows, seems to defy gravity. A single row of seven 22m-high columns, running smack down the middle of the nave, looks for all the world like palm trees as they spread their fanned vaulting.

Construction on the **Église des Jacobins** (Map p699; parvis des Jacobins; 🕑 9am-7pm), the mother church of the Jacobins, was begun soon after St Dominic founded the order in 1215 to preach Church doctrine to the Cathars. It was completed in 1385.

Interred below the modern, grey-marble altar on the northern side are the remains of St Thomas Aquinas (1225–74), an early head of the Dominican order. From outside, admire the 45m-high, octagonal, 13th-century **belfry**. Admission to the tranquil **cloister** costs €1.50.

The 14th-century refectory, entered via the Église des Jacobins, nowadays hosts temporary art exhibitions.

CATHÉDRALE ST-ÉTIENNE

The **Cathédrale St-Étienne** (Cathedral of St Stephen; Map p699; place St-Étienne; 🕑 7.30am-7pm) has a bizarre layout. The vast, 12th-century nave is out of kilter with the huge choir, built in northern French Gothic style as part of an ambitious and unfinished late-13th-century plan to realign the cathedral along a different

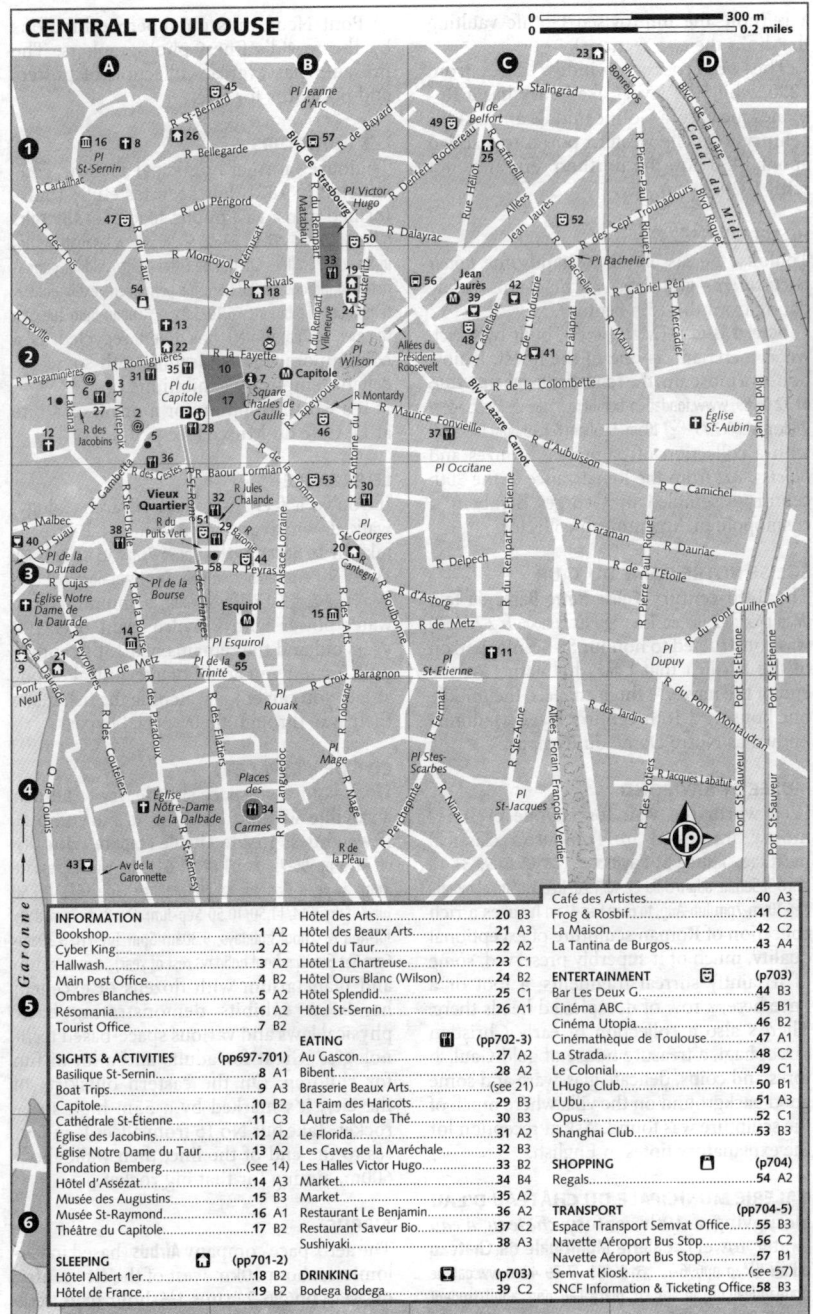

CENTRAL TOULOUSE

0		300 m
0		0.2 miles

INFORMATION	
Bookshop	1 A2
Cyber King	2 A2
Hallwalk	3 A2
Main Post Office	4 B2
Ombres Blanches	5 A2
Résomania	6 A2
Tourist Office	7 B2

SIGHTS & ACTIVITIES	(pp697-701)
Basilique St-Sernin	8 A1
Boat Trips	9 A3
Capitole	10 B2
Cathédrale St-Étienne	11 C3
Église des Jacobins	12 A2
Église Notre Dame du Taur	13 B2
Fondation Bemberg	(see 14)
Hôtel d'Assézat	14 A3
Musée des Augustins	15 B3
Musée St-Raymond	16 A1
Théâtre du Capitole	17 B2

SLEEPING	(pp701-2)
Hôtel Albert 1er	18 B2
Hôtel de France	19 B2
Hôtel des Arts	20 B3
Hôtel des Beaux Arts	21 A3
Hôtel du Taur	22 A2
Hôtel La Chartreuse	23 C1
Hôtel Ours Blanc (Wilson)	24 B2
Hôtel Splendid	25 C1
Hôtel St-Sernin	26 A1

EATING	(pp702-3)
Au Gascon	27 A2
Bibent	28 A2
Brasserie Beaux Arts	(see 21)
La Faim des Haricots	29 B3
Le Florida	31 A2
LAutre Salon de Thé	30 B3
Les Caves de la Maréchale	32 B3
Les Halles Victor Hugo	33 B2
Market	34 B4
Market	35 A2
Restaurant Le Benjamin	36 A2
Restaurant Saveur Bio	37 C2
Sushiyaki	38 A3

DRINKING	(p703)
Bodega Bodega	39 C2

Café des Artistes	40 A3
Frog & Rosbif	41 C2
La Maison	42 C2
La Tantina de Burgos	43 A4

ENTERTAINMENT	(p703)
Bar Les Deux G	44 B3
Cinéma ABC	45 B1
Cinéma Utopia	46 B2
Cinémathèque de Toulouse	47 A1
La Strada	48 C2
Le Colonial	49 C1
LHugo Club	50 B1
LUbu	51 A3
Opus	52 C1
Shanghai Club	53 B3

SHOPPING	(p704)
Regals	54 A2

TRANSPORT	(pp704-5)
Espace Transport Semvat Office	55 B3
Navette Aéroport Bus Stop	56 C2
Navette Aéroport Bus Stop	57 B1
Semvat Kiosk	(see 57)
SNCF Information & Ticketing Office	58 B3

axis (note the improvised Gothic vaulting that links the two sections).

The western rose window dates from 1230, while the layer-cake belfry has a Romanesque base, a Gothic middle and a 16th-century top. The western portal was added about 1450 and the northern entrance not until 1929.

HÔTEL D'ASSÉZAT

Toulouse boasts about 50 handsome *hôtels particuliers* – grand, private mansions mostly dating from the 16th century.

Hôtel d'Assézat (Map p699), built by a rich woad merchant, is one of the finest. It now houses a museum, the **Fondation Bemberg** (☎ 05 61 12 06 89; www.fondation-bemberg.fr; rue de Metz; adult/student €4.60/2.75; ✆ 10am-12.30pm & 1.30-6pm Tue-Sun), with a collection of paintings, bronzes and *objets d'art* from the Renaissance to the 20th century assembled by Georges Bemberg, a cosmopolitan Argentinean collector.

ÉGLISE NOTRE DAME DU TAUR

The 14th-century **Église Notre Dame du Taur** (Map p699; 12 rue du Taur; ✆ 10am-noon & 2-7.15pm) was constructed to honour St-Sernin, patron of the basilica that bears his name. At the end of the nave are three chapels, the middle one housing a 16th-century Black Madonna known as Notre Dame du Rempart.

MUSÉE ST-RAYMOND

Well worth the visit for anyone even remotely interested in Toulouse's classical heritage, **Musée St-Raymond** (☎ 05 61 22 31 44; place St Sernin; adult/child €2.40/1.20, free 1st Sun of month; ✆ 10am-7pm Jun-Aug, to 6pm Sep-May) houses a rich collection of Roman sculpture of exceptional quality, much of it superbly preserved, some of it faintly surreal fragments: a foot or a knee here, a row of decapitated heads there. There's also a collection of early Christian sarcophagi, a treasure house of gold Gaulish torcs and coins, delicate glassware and some good background on the villa where much of the sculpture was found. Ask at reception for the explanatory notes in English.

GALERIE MUNICIPALE DU CHÂTEAU D'EAU

Occupying a 19th-century *château d'eau* (water tower), **Galerie Municipale du Château d'Eau** (Map pp696-7; ☎ 05 61 77 09 40; www.galerie chateaudeau.org in French; place Laganne; adult/student €2.50/1.50; ✆ 1-7pm Tue-Sun), at the western end

of Pont Neuf, puts on superb exhibitions by the world's finest photographers. The museum has a great collection of posters and postcards for sale.

LES ABATTOIRS

Toulouse's former municipal abattoir, constructed in 1831, has been tastefully transformed into a vast public space. **Les Abattoirs** (Map pp696-7; ☎ 05 62 48 58 00; www.lesabattoirs.org in French; 76 allées Charles de Fitte; adult/child for permanent exhibitions €3.05/1.55, for permanent exhibitions & temporary exhibitions €6.10/3.05; ✆ noon-8pm Tue-Sun summer, to 7pm winter) has been recycled as a contemporary art museum, with some excellent temporary exhibitions.

It's worth stopping for a drink or a bite at Le Café du Musée (see p702).

LE BAZACLE

If you've a feel for industrial archaeology, walk downstream from Pont St-Pierre to take in **Le Bazacle** (Map pp696-7; ☎ 05 62 30 16 00; 11 quai St-Pierre; admission free; ✆ 10am-noon & 2-6pm Mon-Fri, 2-7pm Sat & Sun Sep-Jul), a monument to water power with a hydro plant over 100 years old and the remains of a 13th-century mill. Even if you aren't of a technical disposition, you can enjoy watching the fish make their way through their special bypass.

CITÉ DE L'ESPACE

Dock your own space shuttle, try to launch a satellite without crashing it and jump as if weightless inside **Cité de l'Espace** (Space City; off Map pp696-7; ☎ 05 62 71 64 80; www.cite-espace .com; av Jean Gonord; adult/student/child €16/13/11.50 Jul & Aug, €14/11.50/10.50 Sep-Jun; ✆ 9am-7pm daily Jul-Aug & school holidays, 9.30am-5pm Tue-Fri, 9.30am-6pm Sat-Sun & school holidays rest of year), a museum and planetarium with dozens of excellent hands-on exhibits demonstrating basic physical laws and various space-based technologies. Great for adults and a lot of fun for children. On the eastern outskirts of the city, it's marked by a 55m-high space rocket. Take bus No 15 from allées Jean Jaurès to the end of the line, then walk about 600m, aiming for that big rocket.

AIRBUS

The aerospace company **Airbus** (based in Colomiers, about 10km west of the city centre; off Map pp696-7) runs 1½-hour **tours** (adult/child €9/7.50, incl visit to Concorde €13.50/10.50) of its huge Clément Ader aircraft factory, where you can visit the Airbus assembly line and see large chunks of massive airliners being ferried about or unloaded from the huge, bulbous-bodied 'Beluga' transport aircraft that line the runway.

In May 2004, Airbus' A380 factory was opened. This aircraft is the world's largest airliner, with a capacity of 555 passengers. The assembly facility is one of the largest buildings in the world, measuring 490m by 250m, with a height of 46m.

To book a tour, contact **Taxiway** (☎ 05 61 18 06 01; www.taxiway.fr), ideally at least a week in advance for tours in English. Be sure to take a passport or other ID.

Activities
The city's many canalside paths are peaceful places to walk, run or cycle. Port de l'Embouchure (Map pp696-7) is the meeting point of the Canal du Midi (1681; linking Toulouse with the Mediterranean), the Canal Latéral à la Garonne (1856; flowing to the Atlantic) and the Canal de Brienne (1776).

Tours
A number of Toulouse operators run short trips on the canals, including Canal du Midi, or the River Garonne, leaving from Quai de la Daurade or Ponts Jumeaux. Most of the boats operate between 11am and 7pm daily in July and August and at weekends from April to June, September and October. Prices vary with the duration and inclusions for each tour. Try **Toulouse Croisières** (☎ 05 61 25 72 57; www.toulouse-croisieres .com in French) or **Baladines** (☎ 06 07 43 48 28; www .bateaux-toulaisans.com).

Festivals & Events
Major annual events in Toulouse include **Festival Garonne**, a riverside celebration of music, dance and theatre in July; **Piano Jacobins** featuring classical piano recitals in the Église des Jacobins during September; and **Jazz sur Son 31**, an international jazz festival held in October.

Sleeping
Many Toulouse hotels cater for business people so rooms are easiest to find at weekends, when there are great discounts in all price ranges and, surprisingly, during most of the July and August holiday period. Many mid-range places offer much better value for money than budget alternatives. Strangely for such a major city, Toulouse has no hostel.

BUDGET
Hôtel Splendid (Map p699; ☎ /fax 05 61 62 43 02; 13 rue Caffarelli; r from €17, s/d with shower €23/26, s/d/tr with bathroom €25/29/37) This is a good downtown budget choice though the price of the hall showers (€3.05) may induce temporary hydrophobia.

Hôtel des Arts (Map p699; ☎ 05 61 23 36 21; fax 05 61 12 22 37; 1bis rue Cantegril; s/d with washbasin €24/28, with shower €28/32) Just off place St-Georges and well situated for the evening action. Toilets are in the hall.

Hôtel La Chartreuse (Map p699; ☎ 05 61 62 93 39; la.chartreuse@wanadoo.fr; 4bis blvd Bonrepos; r with bathroom €29) Family-run with an intimate feel, this is a decent budget bet among some fairly scruffy offerings near the station.

Hôtel Anatole France (Map pp696-7; ☎ 05 61 23 19 96; fax 05 61 62 58 17; 46 place Anatole France; d with washbasin €19-22, with shower €22-25, with bathroom €29; **P**) Handy for place du Capitole, it has double glazing and parking spaces.

Camping
Camping de Rupé (off Map pp696-7; ☎ 05 61 70 07 35; 21 chemin du Pont de Rupé; camping €12.50; ☺ for caravans year-round, tents mid-Jun–mid-Sep) This place is often packed. It's 6km northwest of the train station. From place Jeanne d'Arc take bus No 59.

MID-RANGE
The area around place Victor Hugo has plenty of two-star hotels.

Hôtel du Taur (Map p699; ☎ 05 61 21 17 54; www .hotel-du-taur.com; 2 rue du Taur; s €38-52, d €48-56, tw/tr €56/63) Sports the naff-paintings-and-textured-wallpaper look but it's comfortable, friendly enough and rooms overlook a quiet interior courtyard. Its killer attraction is location: roll out of bed and you'll find yourself on place du Capitole.

Hôtel St-Sernin (Map p699; ☎ 05 61 21 73 08; fax 05 61 22 49 61; 2 rue St-Bernard; s/d/tr from €44/48/68; **P**) A peaceful, well-located place with private parking (€8). Ask for a room overlooking the Basilique. The fun-size baths are only for munchkins or very supple contortionists though.

Hôtel Ours Blanc (Wilson) (Map p699; ☎ 05 61 21 62 40; www.hotel-oursblanc.com; 2 rue Victor Hugo; s €43-59, d €53-65; ❸) The best and most central of the trio of Ours Blanc places in the centre. It has smart, modern rooms and satellite TV.

Hôtel de France (Map p699; ☎ 05 61 21 88 24; www .hotel-france-toulouse.com; 5 rue d'Austerlitz; s €38, d €42-50, q €64-74; ❸) It has spotless rooms, all with bathroom, some with views of the small, pretty garden. Rooms with air-con cost €4 extra.

Hôtel Albert 1er (Map p699; ☎ 05 61 21 17 91; www .hotel-albert1.com; 8 rue Rivals; r with bathroom & air-con €45-67; ❸) A pleasant, well-maintained and fairly central family hotel with satellite TV.

TOP END

Hôtel des Beaux Arts (Map p699; ☎ 05 34 45 42 42; www.hoteldesbeauxarts.com; 1 place Pont du Neuf; r with shower €88, river view with bath €110-168, suite €188; ❸) Surely the most romantic spot in town, with great views over river and bridge by day or night. The rooms are soothingly decorated and there's a smart, modern **brasserie** downstairs (see right).

Hôtel Mermoz (Map pp696-7; ☎ 05 61 63 04 04; www.hotel-mermoz.com; 50 rue Matabiau; d/tr €97/103; 🅿 ❸) Off an ugly street but in a very pretty little nook with a peaceful terrace/garden and bright, welcoming rooms.

Eating

You'll find plenty of places around town offering excellent-value lunch *menus* for under €16 including the great-value places above Les Halles Victor Hugo (see below).

Both blvd de Strasbourg and the permeter of place du Capitole are lined with restaurants and cafés. The terrace cafés of place St-Georges are lively.

Les Caves de la Maréchale (Map p699; ☎ 05 61 23 89 88; 3 rue Jules Chalande; menus €14-23, mains €18-21; 🕒 Tue-Sat & dinner Mon) Dine under the eyeless gaze of classical statues in the magnificently vaulted brick cellar of a pre-Revolution convent. The excellent lunchtime *menu* (€14) of hors d'oeuvre buffet, a *pichet* of wine and main course is an absolute steal. The *menu* at €23 has a wide choice of inventive dishes.

Au Gascon (Map p699; ☎ 05 61 21 67 16; 9 rue des Jacobins; menus €9-20; 🕒 lunch & dinner Mon-Sat) Terrific value for hearty, filling and artery-thickening Gascon comfort food comprised almost entirely of duck, foie gras and dauntingly large, oily and utterly delicious servings of *cassoulet au confit* (a haricot bean stew with confit of duck).

Restaurant Saveur Bio (Map p699; ☎ 05 61 12 15 15; 22 rue Maurice Fonvieille; menus €15 & €19.50; 🕒 lunch & dinner Mon-Sat) A mainly vegie place given to proselytising about all things organic, it serves tasty, imaginative vegetarian food, including a lunchtime mixed plate (€8) and a great-value evening buffet (€8). It also serves fresh takeaway salads and dishes (€4 to €8).

La Faim des Haricots (Map p699; ☎ 05 61 22 49 25; 3 rue du Puits Vert; menus €8 & €11; 🕒 lunch Mon-Sat, dinner Thu-Sat) Offers friendly service and a pick-'n'-mix all-vegetarian menu. There are salad and dessert bars, home-made soups (winter) and a *plat du jour*.

Restaurant Le Benjamin (Map p699; ☎ 05 61 22 92 66; 7 rue des Gestes; lunch menu €14, dinner menu €28) Serves excellent *nouvelle cuisine* rich in duck dishes with a goose variant here and there.

Sushiyaki (☎ 05 61 12 00 60; 9 rue Ste-Ursule; menus €10-20; 🕒 lunch & dinner Mon-Sat) Head for this small, intimate, reasonably priced sushi and *teppanyaki* place when you can't face any more duck or *cassoulet*.

Brasserie Beaux Arts (Map p699; ☎ 05 61 21 12 12; 1 quai Daurade; menus €20 & 32; 🕒 lunch & dinner) A smart, modern brasserie with a retro '30s feel serving fresh seafood and classic French dishes with style and bustling efficiency.

Le Café du Musée (Map pp696-7; ☎ 05 61 59 33 56; 76 allées Charles de Fitte; plat du jour €7.50, formule du jour €12; 🕒 11am-8pm Tue-Sun) A bright and light space in one of the outbuildings of Les Abattoirs museum (see p700). The *formule du jour* – the daily special, entrée or dessert, drink and coffee – is very good value. This café is also a great spot for an afternoon coffee, some home-made cake, dessert or ice cream.

CAFÉS & TEAHOUSES

L'Autre Salon de Thé (Map p699; ☎ 05 61 23 46 67; 16 place St Georges) Very civilised teahouse serving a good range of darjeelings and green teas along with rich, filling desserts inside and (if you're lucky enough to find a free seat) out in the pleasant square.

Two of the best places to linger by day or night over a coffee or something stronger in place du Capitole (Map p699) include **Le Florida** (12 place du Capitole) and **Bibent** (5 place du Capitole), with an ornate plastered, chandeliered and mirrored interior and lots of style.

SELF-CATERING

For fresh produce, visit **Les Halles Victor Hugo** (Map p699; place Victor Hugo), the large covered food market, or the **market** (Map p699; place des Carmes) to the south. Both open until 1pm, Tuesday to Sunday. Another small **market** (Map p699; place du Capitole) spreads across the square selling organically grown food on Tuesday and Saturday mornings.

Drinking
PUBS & BARS

Almost every square in the Vieux Quartier has at least one café, busy day and night. Most cafés are open from early morning until at least midnight, while the bars generally open late morning until the small hours.

Bodega Bodega (Map p699; 1 rue Gabriel Péri) A popular *bodega* (wine bar) with live music and lively crowds at weekends in this small but bustling nightlife enclave close to Jean Jaurès metro stop.

La Tantina de Burgos (Map p699; 27 av de la Garonnette) Another popular *bodega* that is an especially good bet for the strongly Spanish flavour lent by the bullfighting posters, the tapas and the buzzing atmosphere most nights. There is live music here as well at weekends. **Frog & Rosbif** (Map p699; 14 rue de l'Industrie) Very British. A lively expat pub, east of blvd de Strasbourg, with a dartboard and its own microbrewery churning out ales and stouts.

La Maison (Map p699; 9 rue Gabriel Péri) Very French. a cosy place with a log fire in winter where you can smoke while arguing animatedly, or at least watch the youngish local crowd doing so over a glass of excellent red, white or dessert wine.

Rue des Blanchers has several 'alternative' joints. Those clustered around place St-Pierre beside the Garonne pull in a predominantly young crowd. **Chez Tonton** (Map pp696-7; place St-Pierre) and Spanish-flavoured **Bar Basque** (Map pp696-7; place St-Pierre) are sports bars. Nearby are the **Why Not Café** (Map pp696-7; 5 rue Pargaminières), with its beautiful rear terrace (summer only), and **Café des Artistes** (Map p699; 13 place de la Daurade), an art-student hang-out.

Entertainment

For what's on where, grab yourself a copy of *Toulouse Hebdo, Le Flash,* both weekly, or *Intramuros* (which is free from major hotels and cinemas).

NIGHTCLUBS

Toulouse has dance venues aplenty. There are a fair few fully fledged nightclubs, but many bars in town also double up as clubs on certain nights.

Opus (Map p699; 24 rue Bachelier) Offers food until 1.30am, a huge blackboard on which to pen your thoughts and dancing all night (rock upstairs, funk and disco down below).

L'Hugo Club (Map p699; 18 place Victor Hugo) This place is a slightly smarter dance bar attracting an older crowd.

Two hot spots near the centre are **La Strada** (Map p699; 4 rue Gabriel Péri; ☼ midnight-dawn Tue-Sat) and **L'Ubu** (Map p699; ☎ 05 61 23 26 75; 16 rue St-Rome; ☼ Mon-Sat), which has a choosy door policy, so dress smartly.

Out of town, the intrepid may like to risk **Le Clap** (off Map pp696-7; 146 chemin des Étroits); take exit 24 off the A64.

GAY VENUES

Toulouse is a very gay city – it ain't called *la ville rose* just for those pink bricks. Popular **Bar Les Deux G** (Map p699; 5 rue Baronie) attracts a mixed gay and lesbian crowd. **Shanghai Club** (Map p699; 12 rue de la Pomme; ☼ midnight-dawn) is a long-established gay club, also with a mixed clientele. The sauna-like **Le Colonial** (Map p699; 8 place de Belfort; ☼ noon-1am) is much more a male haunt.

CINEMAS

The three-screen **Cinéma Utopia** (Map p699; ☎ 05 61 23 66 20; 24 rue Montardy) and **Cinéma ABC** (Map p699; ☎ 05 61 29 81 00; 13 rue St-Bernard) both show nondubbed foreign films. **Cinémathèque de Toulouse** (Map p699; ☎ 05 62 30 30 10; 69 rue du Taur) also frequently has nondubbed screenings.

THEATRE

Toulouse also has a vibrant theatre scene. The tourist office offers comprehensive information on venues and up-to-the-minute listings.

Shopping

Toulouse's main shopping district, rich in department stores and expensive boutiques, embraces rue du Taur, rue d'Alsace-Lorraine, rue de la Pomme, rue des Arts and nearby streets. Place St-Georges is also surrounded by fashionable shops.

Regals (Map p699; ☎ 05 61 21 64 86; 25 rue du Taur) sells edible specialities such as chocolates, cakes, liqueurs and sweets containing or made of violets or violet flavourings. Place du Capitole (Map p699) hosts a huge **flea market** (including books) each Wednesday and there's another on Saturday and Sunday on place St-Sernin (Map p699). You'll find an antiquarian **book market** (Map p699; place St-Étienne) on Saturday.

Getting There & Away

AIR

Aéroport Toulouse-Blagnac (☎ 05 61 42 44 00; www .toulouse.aeroport.fr) is 8km northwest of the city centre. Air France and easyJet between them have over 30 flights daily to/from Paris (mainly Orly). There are also daily or almost-daily flights to/from many other cities in France and Europe. EasyJet and BA each fly from Gatwick at least twice daily.

Flybe and BMIBaby operate services from various UK regional airports.

BUS

Toulouse's modern **bus station** (Map pp696-7; ☎ 05 61 61 67 67; blvd Pierre Sémard; information office ☘ 8am-7pm) is just north of the train station. Services are listed below.

destination	one-way fare (€)	duration (hr)	frequency
Agen	12.00	3	1 daily
Albi	12.20	1½	1 daily
Andorra	21.00	3½	1–2 Wed, Fri & Sun
Auch	12.10	1¼	2 daily
Castres	9.80	1½	5–7 daily
Foix	9.20	1½	2 daily
Millau	23.80	4	3 daily
Montauban	6.70	1¼	5–7 daily

Semvat's (☎ 05 61 61 67 67) Arc-en-Ciel buses, serving local destinations in Haute-Garonne and nearby *départements*, also use the station, as do **Intercars** (☎ 05 61 58 14 53) and **Eurolines** (☎ 05 61 26 40 04) buses.

CAR

Most car-rental agencies have desks at the train station and airport.

ADA Train Station (☎ 05 61 63 68 63) Airport (☎ 05 61 30 00 33)

Europcar Train Station (☎ 05 62 73 41 64) Airport (☎ 0825 825 514)

Budget (☎ 05 61 63 18 18; 49 rue Bayard)

TRAIN

The **train station** (Gare Matabiau; ☎ 36 35; blvd Pierre Sémard), is about 1km northeast of the city centre. Local destinations served by frequent direct trains are listed below.

destination	one-way fare (€)	duration (hr)	frequency
Albi	11.80	1¼	at least 10 daily
Bayonne	44.80	3¾	at least 5 daily
Bordeaux	27.70	2–3	9–14 daily
Carcassonne	12.10	1hr	10–15 daily
Castres	11.60	1¼	5–9 daily
Foix	11.30	1¼	3–11 daily
Lourdes	20.90	2¼	7 daily
Montauban	7.60	½	at least hourly

The fare from Toulouse to Paris is €80 by Corail (6½ hours, to Gare d'Austerlitz) and €77.10 by TGV (5½ hours, to Gare Montparnasse via Bordeaux).

There is an information and ticketing office for **SNCF** (☎ 08 92 35 35 35; 5 rue Peyras; ☘ 9.30am-6.30pm Mon-Sat) in the town centre.

Getting Around

TO/FROM THE AIRPORT

The **Navette Aéroport bus** (☎ 05 34 60 64 00) links town and airport every 20 minutes and costs €3.90/5.90 single/return. The last run to the airport is at 8.20pm, Sunday to Friday (7.40pm on Saturday). Pick it up at the bus or train station, outside Jean Jaurès metro station or place Jeanne d'Arc. From the airport, the last bus leaves at 11.30pm daily.

An airport taxi costs about €20.

BICYCLE

Semvat (see below) hires bikes for almost nothing. Call by its **Espace Transport base** (Map p699; 05 34 30 03 00; 7 place Esquirol; ☺ 6.45am-6.30pm Mon-Fri, 9am-noon Sat & Sun). Rates are €2.30/2.70 per day/24 hours, although a €260 deposit is required.

BUS & METRO

The local bus network and 15-station metro line are run by **Semvat** (☎ 05 61 41 70 70; www.sem vat.com in French). A ticket for either service costs €1.30 and a 10-ticket carnet costs €10.30.

Most of the bus lines run daily until at least 8pm. The seven 'night' bus lines all start at the train station and run from 10pm to just after midnight.

The metro runs northeast to southwest from Jolimont to Basso-Cambo. Major city stops are Jean Jaurès, Capitole, Esquirol and Marengo SNCF (the train station). These last two are also important metro/bus interchanges. It's fully automated – no driver, no conductor, just lots of short, swift trains speeding under the city. A second line is under construction.

Semvat has ticket and information kiosks across town, including at Marengo and Basso-Cambo metro stations and at 9 place du Capitole. There's also an **Espace Transport Semvat office** (Map p699; 7 place Esquirol; ☺ 8.30am-6.30pm Mon-Fri, 9am-7pm Sat & Sun). All supply route maps, as does the tourist office.

CAR

Parking is tight in the city centre. There are huge car parks under place du Capitole, beneath allées Jean Jaurès, just off place Wilson and above the covered market on place Victor Hugo. At place St-Sernin you can park for free (except Sunday) – if you can find a spot. Parking in the municipal multistoreys costs around € 1.80/11.80 per hour/day.

TAXI

There are 24-hour taxi stands at the **train station** (☎ 05 61 21 00 72), **place Wilson** (☎ 05 61 21 55 46) and **place Esquirol** (☎ 05 61 80 36 36).

ALBI

pop 49,106

The massive, fortress-like Gothic cathedral dwarfing the rest of town is an unmissable reminder of Albi's violent religious past.

Albi was the location of the so-called Albigensian heresy of the 12th and 13th centuries and the bloody crusade that crushed it (see The Cathars, p756). Almost all of central Albi, including the cathedral, is built from bricks of reddish clay, dug from the nearby Tarn River.

Two things make a trip here more than worthwhile: that extraordinary cathedral and the excellent museum dedicated to artist Henri de Toulouse-Lautrec, who hailed from Albi. It has the most extensive collection of his work anywhere.

Orientation

Cathédrale Ste-Cécile dominates the heart of the old quarter. From it, a web of narrow, semi-pedestrianised streets stretches southeast to place du Vigan, Albi's commercial hub. The train station is about 1km southwest of the city centre.

Information

INTERNET ACCESS

Ludi.com (64 rue Séré de Rivières; per hr €4.60; ☺ 11am-midnight Mon-Sat, 2pm-midnight Sun)
Mediathèque (av Général de Gaulle; per hr €3.80; ☺ 1-6pm Mon & Tue, 10am-noon & 1-6pm Wed & Sat, 10am-6pm Fri) Albi's splendid, 21st-century public-sector Internet café.

LAUNDRY

Lavomatique (10 rue Émile Grand; ☺ daily)
Lavotop (96 av Général de Gaulle; ☺ daily)

POST

Main Post Office (place du Vigan) With Cyberposte.
Post Office (place de Verdun)

TOURIST INFORMATION

Tourist Office (☎ 05 63 49 48 80; www.tourisme.fr /albi; place Ste-Cécile; ☺ 9am-7pm Mon-Sat, 10am-12.30pm & 2.30-6.30pm Sun Jul-Sep, 9am-12.30pm & 2-6pm Mon-Sat, 10am-12.30pm & 2.30-5pm Sun Oct-Jun) Has a free pamphlet in English, *Three Cultural Heritage Routes*, which describes a trio of signposted walks in the semipedestrianised old quarter.

Cathédrale Ste-Cécile

As much a fortress as a church, the mighty **Cathédrale Ste-Cécile** (place Ste-Cécile; admission free; ☺ 8.30am-6.45pm Jun-Sep, 9am-noon & 2-6.30pm Oct-May) was begun in 1282, not long after the Cathar movement was crushed. Built, to impress and subdue, of red brick in the southern (or

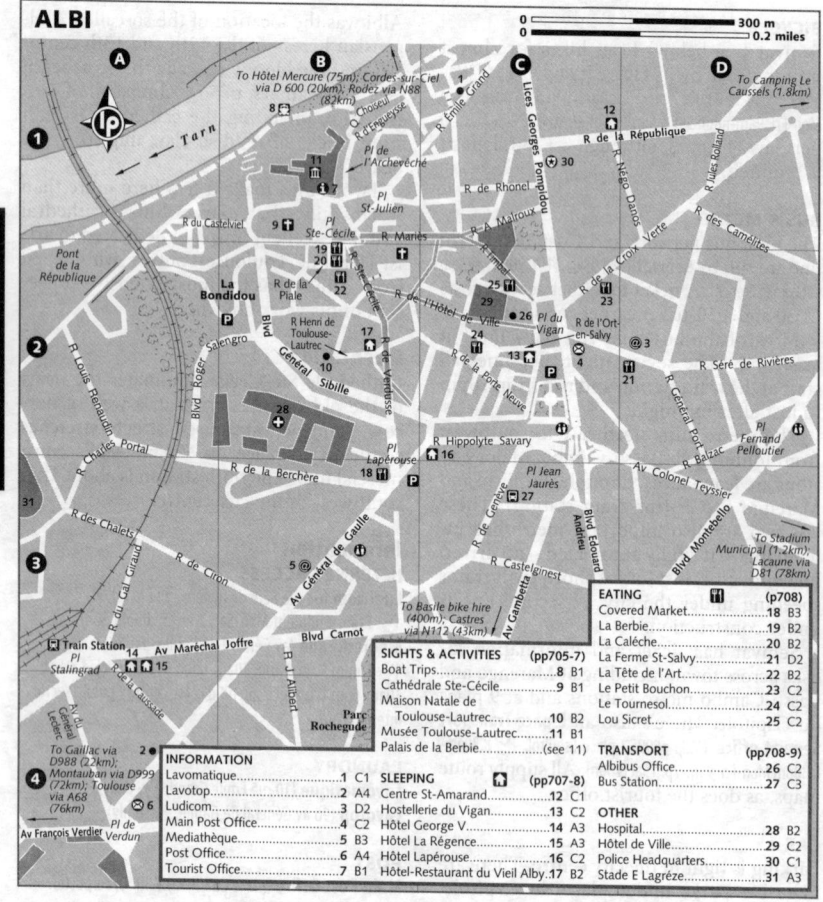

ALBI

SIGHTS & ACTIVITIES (pp705-7)
Boat Trips	8 B1
Cathédrale Ste-Cécile	9 B1
Maison Natale de Toulouse-Lautrec	10 B2
Musée Toulouse-Lautrec	11 B1
Palais de la Berbie	(see 11)

INFORMATION
Lavomatique	1 C1
Lavotop	2 A4
Ludicom	3 D2
Main Post Office	4 C2
Médiathèque	5 B3
Post Office	6 A4
Tourist Office	7 B1

SLEEPING (pp707-8)
Centre St-Amarand	12 C1
Hostellerie du Vigan	13 C2
Hôtel George V	14 A3
Hôtel La Régence	15 A3
Hôtel Lapérouse	16 C2
Hôtel-Restaurant du Vieil Alby	17 B2

EATING (p708)
Covered Market	18 B3
La Berbie	19 B2
La Caléche	20 B2
La Ferme St-Salvy	21 D2
La Tête de l'Art	22 B2
Le Petit Bouchon	23 C2
Le Tournesol	24 C2
Lou Sicret	25 C2

TRANSPORT (pp708-9)
Albibus Office	26 C2
Bus Station	27 C3

OTHER
Hospital	28 B2
Hôtel de Ville	29 C2
Police Headquarters	30 C1
Stade E Lagrèze	31 A3

Meridional) Gothic style, it was finished approximately a century later. Attractive isn't the word – indeed, the cathedral's dominant feature is its sheer mass rising over town like some Tolkeinesque dark lord's tower rather than a place of Christian worship. It's a haunting sight when illuminated at night.

When you step inside, however, the contrast with that brutal exterior is total. No surface was left untouched by the Italian artists who, in the early 16th-century, painted their way along its vast nave.

An intricately carved, lacy **rood screen**, many of its statues smashed in the Revolution, spans the sanctuary. The **stained-glass windows** in the apse and choir date from the 14th to 16th centuries.

On no account miss the **grand chœur** (great choir; admission €1) with its frescoes, chapels and 30 fine biblical polychrome figures carved in stone.

At the western end, behind today's main altar, is *Le Jugement Dernier* (The Last Judgement; 1490), a particularly vivid Doomsday horror-show of the damned being boiled in oil, beheaded or imaginatively but casually tortured by demons and monsters.

Musée Toulouse-Lautrec

Beside the tourist office, the **Musée Toulouse-Lautrec** (☎ 05 63 49 48 70; www.musee-toulouse-lautrec .com; place Ste-Cécile; adult/student/child €4.50/2.50/free; 9am-6pm Jul & Aug, 9am-noon & 2-6pm Sep, 10am-noon & 2-5pm or 5.30pm Oct-Jun, closed Tue Oct-Mar) occupies the **Palais de la Berbie**, the vast, fortress-like 13th- to 15th-century archbishop's palace.

The museum boasts over 500 examples of the artist's work, giving both an excellent idea of his development as an artist and the way individual works evolved – everything from simple pencil sketches and rough pastel drafts to the final works such as his celebrated Parisian brothel scenes, including the *Salon de la rue des Moulins* taking pride of place. On the top floor are works by artists such as Degas, Matisse and Rodin. Audioguides in English cost €3. The attractive ornamental palace gardens and courtyard outside are well worth a wander.

The tourist office runs 45-minute guided **tours** (adult/student/child €7.10/6.50/free) of the museum in French twice daily at Easter and from July to early September.

A short walk away, a plaque on the wall of the privately owned **Maison Natale de Toulouse-Lautrec** (14 rue Henri de Toulouse-Lautrec) marks the house where the artist was born.

Tours
From mid-June to mid-September you can take 35-minute **boat trips** (adult/student or child €5/3) – departures every half-hour daily – from just below the Palais de la Berbie on a *gabarre*, a flat-bottomed sailing barge of the kind that used to haul goods down the Garonne to Bordeaux.

Festivals & Events
There's music for all tastes in Albi's cultural calendar. The **Festival Albi-Jazz** is in late June, while **Musiques en Albigeois**, in the last two weeks of July, offers classical-music concerts in a variety of venues around town. Albi celebrates **Carnaval** at the beginning of Lent with particular gusto.

Sleeping
BUDGET
Centre St-Amarand (☎ 05 63 48 18 29; 16 rue de la République; s/d €16/23; ☿ year-round) A religious centre, about 300m northeast of place du Vigan, offering spotless if spartan budget accommodation to young travellers. Take bus No 1 from the train station to the République stop and look for the courtyard entrance under the 'Tarn Libre' sign.

Hôtel George V (☎ 05 63 54 24 16; www.hotel georgev.com; 29 av Maréchal Joffre; d with shower €33, with bathroom from €41) A recommended family-run place, this hotel has spacious rooms, is handy for the bus and train stations and has a small breakfast terrace.

Camping
Camping Le Caussels (☎ /fax 05 63 60 37 06; camping €12; ☿ Apr–mid-Oct) It's just off route de Millau 2km northeast of place du Vigan. Take bus No 5 from place du Vigan to the terminus. There's running water but few other facilities.

PAINTER, LITHOGRAPHER, POSTER DESIGNER &....COOK?

Henri de Toulouse-Lautrec (1864-1901), Albi's most famous son, was famously short. As a teenager he broke both legs in separate accidents, stunting his growth and leaving him unable to walk without his trademark cane.

He spent his early twenties studying painting in Paris where he mixed with other artists including Van Gogh. In 1890, at the height of the *belle époque,* he abandoned impressionism and took to observing and sketching Paris's colourful nightlife. His favourite subjects included the cabaret singer Aristide Bruant, cancan dancers from the Moulin Rouge and prostitutes from the rue des Moulins, sketched to capture movement and expression in a few simple lines.

With sure, fast strokes he would sketch on whatever was to hand – a scrap of paper or a tablecloth, tracing paper or buff-coloured cardboard. He also became a skilled and sought-after lithographer and poster designer until drinking and general overindulgence in the heady nightlife scene led to his premature death in 1901.

If you want to taste, rather than see, a Toulouse-Lautrec creation, you may find some of Albi's restaurants offering versions of the recipes devised by the keen amateur chef Lautrec (for more information, ask at the tourist office). Alternatively, try to track down the out-of-print *The Art of Cooking* (in French or English), a collection of his amusing, whimsical recipes which include advice on how to cook a squirrel or stew a 'marmot you caught that very same morning sunning himself on a rock'.

MID-RANGE

Hôtel-Restaurant du Vieil Alby (☎ 05 63 54 14 69; fax 05 63 54 96 75; 25 rue Henri de Toulouse-Lautrec; r with bathroom €45-65; closed 2nd half Jan & late Jun/early Jul; P ✕) Above an excellent restaurant (see below), this is a family-run, good-value place. Parking, difficult hereabouts, costs €7.

Hotel Mercure (☎ 05 63 46 66 66; fax 05 63 46 18 40; 41 rue Porta; s/d €72/80, with river views €80/90; P ✕ ✕) Occupying a handsome old brick building hogging a prime riverside spot, the rooms are recently and handsomely refurbished and there's a great terrace from which to gaze back across to town. There's also WiFi access.

Hostellerie du Vigan (☎ 05 63 43 31 31; fax 05 63 47 05 42; 16 place du Vigan; d/tr from €50/65; P ✕) At the heart of town this place has spacious, modern rooms and a popular brasserie below.

Hôtel La Régence (☎ 05 63 54 01 42; www.hotel laregence.com in French; 27 av Maréchal Joffre; r with shower/ bathroom from €30/42; P) Next door to Hôtel George V, this hotel is warm in its welcome and there's a small garden out the back.

Hôtel Lapérouse (☎ 05 63 54 69 22; fax 05 63 38 03 69; 21 place Lapérouse; r €35-59; P ✕) This place has cosy rooms with bathrooms and there's a small pool.

Eating & Drinking

Le Petit Bouchon (☎ 05 63 54 11 75; 77 rue de la Croix Verte; menus €8-25; ✕ lunch Mon-Sat, closed early Aug) A small, bustling joint serving simple fare at reasonable prices.

La Tête de l'Art (☎ 05 63 38 44 75; 7 rue de la Piale; menus €14-28; ✕ lunch & dinner daily May-Jul & Sep, Thu-Mon rest of year) Dishes for the adventurous such as jugged hare, tripe and pork foot mix with more traditional local stuff. It also does excellent desserts (pistachio and chocolate tart) and gourmet takeaways.

La Calèche (☎ 05 63 54 15 52; 6 rue de la Piale; menus €14-25; ✕ lunch & dinner) Opposite La Tête de l'Art, you'll also find the classics with the odd quirk among them including frogs' legs, marinated herring and a vegetarian platter (€13).

Lou Sicret (☎ 05 63 38 26 40; 1 rue Timbal; mains €12-17; ✕ lunch & dinner Tue-Sat, dinner only Sun & Mon) Tucked away down an alley at the northwestern corner of place du Vigan, this is friendly and bustling and serves delightful regional cuisine in a secluded courtyard.

Hôtel-Restaurant du Vieil Alby (see above; ☎ 05 63 38 28 23; menus €16-45, lunch €12; ✕ lunch Tue-Sun, closed late Jul) The very best in local fare is served with the local Gaillac wine. Foie gras with caramelised apples, cassoulet, filet mignon with a cep sauce and mandarin and champagne sorbet are some menu examples. There are also vegetarian options.

Le Tournesol (☎ 05 63 38 38 14; 11 rue de l'Ort-en-Salvy; plat du jour €7.50; ✕ lunch Tue-Sat) A highly popular vegetarian restaurant, airy and full of light. Mixed salad platters start at €8.

Le Grand Pontié (☎ 05 63 54 16 34; place du Vigan; pizzas from €7, menus €10-25; ✕ brasserie lunch, pizzeria lunch & dinner) A large, grand place with a pizzeria on the mezzanine floor, a brasserie below and a pleasant pavement café spilling onto the square, great for nursing a coffee and watching the action on the square.

Hostellerie du Vigan (see left; menus €16-23, salads €6-8; ✕ lunch & dinner Mon-Sat) A popular bar/brasserie.

La Berbie (☎ 05 63 54 13 86; 17 place St-Cécile; ✕ 9am-6pm Sun-Thu, 8am-3pm Fri & Sat) A cosy *salon de thé* with great cakes and a fine *tarte tatinand*. There's a great choice of teas served in heavy cast-iron pots (the Darjeeling is especially good).

SELF-CATERING

Fresh fare can be picked up from the temporary (until 2006) **covered market** (place Lapérouse; ✕ morning-early afternoon Tue-Sun) while a car park is built beneath the old and stylish market on place St-Julien. An animated Saturday morning **farmers' market** overflows from place Ste-Cécile into the surrounding streets.

Pick up the very best in cheese from **La Ferme St-Salvy** (53 rue Séré de Rivières), one of France's dwindling number of *fromageries* (specialist cheese shops).

Getting There & Away
BUS

The **bus station** (☎ 05 63 54 58 61), little more than a parking area, is on the southwestern corner of place Jean Jaurès. Ask at the tourist office for a timetable. Services include Cordes (€4.70, 50 minutes, two daily weekdays), Castres (€5.25, 50 minutes, up to 10 daily), Montauban (€11.50, 1¼ hours, two daily) and Toulouse (€11.20, 1½ hours, three daily).

TRAIN

The **train station** (place Stalingrad) is linked by Bus No 1 with the bus station and place du

Vigan. There are multiple trains to/from Rodez (€11.30, 1¼ hours), Millau (€19, 2¾ hours), Toulouse (€10.80, 1¼ hours) and Cordes (€6.50, one hour). For Montauban (€16), change in Toulouse.

Getting Around

You can rent mountain bikes from **Basile** (☎ 05 63 38 43 09; 18 av Maréchale Foch; per day/week €15/73).

Leave your vehicle in the large car park at Le Bondidou, near the cathedral.

Local bus services are run by **Albibus** (☎ 05 63 38 43 43), Monday to Saturday. It has an information office beside the Hôtel de Ville.

Phone for a **taxi** (☎ 05 63 47 99 99, 05 63 54 85 03).

CASTRES

Castres is a worthwhile detour if you are travelling between Albi and Toulouse, Carcassonne or the Mediterranean coast. It was founded by the Romans as a settlement, or *castrum*. At its heart is place Jean Jaurès, which is named in honour of Castres' most famous son and founding father of French socialism.

Castres' **tourist office** (☎ 05 63 62 63 62; 3 rue Milhau Ducommun; ⏰ 9.30am-6.30pm Mon-Sat, 3-5pm Sun, closed 12.30-2pm Sep-Jun) is on the eastern bank of the River Agoût, near Pont Vieux.

The **Musée Goya** (☎ 05 63 71 59 30; Hôtel de Ville, rue de l'Hôtel de Ville; admission Apr-mid-Sep €3, mid-Sep–Mar €2.30, under 18 free; ⏰ 9am-noon & 2-6pm daily Jul & Aug; 9am-noon & 2-5pm or 6pm Tue-Sun Sep-Jun), well worth a visit, contains France's most important collection of Spanish art, including many paintings and engravings by Goya himself.

Parc de Gourjade (av de Roquecourbe, the D89) is a vast municipal park north of the town centre with camp sites, golf course, about 15km of jogging trails, riding centre, **L'Archipel** (☎ 05 63 62 54 00) water park and an ice-skating rink. You can take bus No 6 or 7 from the Arcades stop on place Jean Jaurès but it's more fun to hop aboard **Le Miredames** (☎ 05 63 62 41 71; adult/child €4/1.60 return), a replica river barge that runs to/from the park from the quay in front of the tourist office three to five times daily from June to September.

MONTAUBAN

pop 54,421

On the right bank of the River Tarn, Montauban was founded in 1144 by Count Al-

phonse Jourdain of Toulouse who, legend has it, was so charmed by its trailing willow trees (*alba* in Occitan) that he named the place Mont Alba.

Montauban, southern France's second-oldest *bastide*, sustained significant damage during the Albigensian crusade. It became a Huguenot stronghold in 1570. The Edict of Nantes (1598) brought royal concessions to the Huguenots but, after its repeal by Louis XIV in 1685, the town's Protestants again suffered persecution.

Montauban's many classical townhouses date from the prosperous decades following the Catholic reconquest.

Orientation

Place Nationale, surrounded by attractive arcaded 17th-century brick buildings and a grid of semipedestrianised streets, sits at the heart of the old city. Place Franklin Roosevelt, overlooked by the cathedral, lies to its south.

The train station is about 1km from place Nationale, across the River Tarn at the western end of av Mayenne.

Information

3D Gamma (103 Faubourg Lacapelle; per hr €4.80; ⏰ 11am-midnight Mon-Fri, 2pm-midnight Sat) Internet access.

Laundrette (26 rue de l'Hôtel de Ville; ⏰ 7am-7.30pm)

Tourist Office (☎ 05 63 63 60 60; www.montauban -tourisme.com; place Prax-Paris; ⏰ 9.30am-6.30pm Mon-Sat Jul & Aug, 9.30am-12.30pm & 2-6.30pm rest of year) Has a free pamphlet in English, *On the Paths to Heritage*, describing an exhaustive walking tour around the old town. It also sells tickets for the town's festivals.

Sights

MUSÉE INGRES

Jean Auguste Dominique Ingres, the sensual neoclassical painter and accomplished violinist, was a native of Montauban. Many of his works, plus canvases by Tintoretto, Van Dyck, Courbet and others, are exhibited in the **Musée Ingres** (☎ 05 63 22 12 91; 19 rue de l'Hôtel de Ville; adult/student & under 18 €4/free; ⏰ 10am-6pm daily July & Aug, 10am-noon & 2-6pm Tue-Sat Sep-Jun & Sun Easter–mid-Oct), a former bishop's palace. Reception can provide explanatory notes in English.

For €4.50 you can buy a combined pass that also admits you to the nearby museums of Histoire Naturelle (natural history),

Terroir (local costumes and traditions) and Résistance et Déportation (with mementos of WWII).

CHURCHES

The 18th-century **Cathédrale Notre Dame de l'Assomption** (place Franklin Roosevelt), with its clean, classical lines, contains one of Ingres' masterpieces, *Le Vœu de Louis XIII*, depicting the king pledging France to the Virgin. The fine 13th-century **Église St-Jacques**, also in mellow pink brick, still bears cannonball marks from Louis XIII's 1621 siege of the town.

Festivals & Events

Montauban has summer music fun and historical celebrations.

Alors Chante in May is a festival of traditional French song. **Jazz à Montauban** is a giant jam in the second week of July. The **Fête des Quatre-Cent Coups** (400 Blows) is a weekend street festival in the first half of September. It commemorates the moment when, says local lore, a fortune-teller told Louis XIII, besieging Montauban in 1621, to blast off 400 cannons simultaneously against the town, which still failed to fall.

Sleeping

Hôtel du Commerce (☎ 05 63 66 31 32; 9 place Franklin Roosevelt; r with bathroom €44-70) Central and recently renovated. It does a very generous buffet breakfast (€6).

Hôtel Le Lion d'Or (☎ 05 63 20 04 04; fax 05 63 66 77 39; 22 av Mayenne; s/d from €24/48) A trim two-star option near the train station.

Hôtel d'Orsay (☎ 05 63 66 06 66; www.hotel-restaurant-orsay-com; av Roger Salengro; r with bathroom €47-54; P ⚡) Next door to Hôtel Le Lion d'Or and a notch up, this hotel offers comfortable enough, if rather dated, rooms and an upmarket restaurant (see right).

Etap Hôtel (☎ 08 92 68 00 79; www.etaphotel.com; rue Léon Cladel; s/d/tr €32/38/44; P ⚡) Just out of the town centre but reasonable value. Inside the ugly concrete bunker exterior are modern, smart (if uniform) rooms. Parking is free, breakfast is €4.

Eating

Bistrot du Faubourg (☎ 05 63 63 49 89; 111 Faubourg Lacapelle; menus €11, €17 & €23; ☾ lunch & dinner Mon-Fri, lunch Sat 15 Aug-Jul) Montauban's best value for money is perhaps found here, as its 'house full' notice regularly attests.

Brasserie des Arts (☎ 05 63 20 20 90; 4 place Nationale; menus €15-19.25, daily special €7.30; ☾ lunch only). One of several brasseries on place Nationale, this popular choice offers a good range of fish dishes.

Agora Café (☎ 05 63 63 05 74; 9 place Nationale; mains €7; ☾ lunch) Local specialities of *piperade* (sweet pepper dish), cassoulet or lentils are served alongside salads (€5.50 to €7) here.

Restaurant Au Fil de l'Eau (☎ 05 63 66 11 85; 14 quai du Dr Lafforgue; menus €24, €38 & €53; ☾ lunch Tue-Sun) Beside the River Tarn, tempting *menus* and a window full of merited recommendations from Gallic gastronomic guides beckon you in. Typical *menu* examples include: frog soufflé, foie gras terrine, pork with confit onions and mustard, *crème brûlée* with star anise.

La Cuisine d'Alain (☎ 05 63 66 06 66; Hôtel d'Orsay, av Roger Salengro; menus €22, €32 & €52; ☾ lunch & dinner Wed-Sun, lunch Mon) Trying to match Restaurant Au Fil de l'Eau in quality, it's especially strong on seafood including oysters, scallops and fish such as *rouget* and offers free wine and coffee with lunch.

Morning **farmers' markets** are on Saturday (place Prax-Paris) and Wednesday (place Lalaque), as well as a smaller, daily one (place Nationale).

Getting There & Away

BUS

Several daily buses for Toulouse (€7) are run by **Autocar Jardel** (☎ 05 63 22 55 00) and to Moissac and Agen by **Autocar Barrière** (☎ 05 63 93 34 34). Since Montauban has no bus station, intercity buses stop at a bewildering – and changing – number of points. Ask at the tourist office for the stop of the week.

From the train station, two SNCF buses run to Albi (€10.20, 1¼ hours, daily except Saturday).

TRAIN

There are Corail trains to Paris' Gare d'Austerlitz (€71, four to six hours) and TGVs to Gare Montparnasse (€71 to €81, five hours, four daily). Regional services include Toulouse (€7.60, 30 minutes, frequent), Bordeaux (€23.30, two hours, frequent) via Agen (€11.50, 45 minutes) and Moissac (€4.80, 20 minutes, up to six daily).

Getting Around

BUS

The train and bus stations are connected with the town centre by bus Nos 3 and 5.

CAR

There may be free parking under Pont Vieux when you read this (although the mayor wants to install meters). Alternatively **Parking Occitan** (place Prax-Paris), where the above-ground section – markedly cheaper than the adjacent underground park – charges €2 for a full day.

TAXI

If you need a taxi, the company to call is **Radio Taxis** (☎ 05 63 66 99 99).

MOISSAC
pop 12,744

Moissac, a day trip from Montauban or Toulouse, was once a stop for Santiago de Compostela pilgrims. **Abbaye St-Pierre** (€5; 9am-noon & 2-7pm Jul & Aug, to 6pm mid-Mar–Jun & Sep–mid-Oct, to 5pm mid-Oct–mid-Mar, but subject to change), resplendent with France's finest Romanesque sculpture, became a model for ecclesiastical buildings in southern France.

Above the **south portal**, completed around 1130, is a superb tympanum depicting St John's Vision of the Apocalypse, with Christ in majesty flanked by the apostles, angels and 24 awestruck elders.

In the **cloister** 116 delicate marble columns support wedge-shaped, deeply carved capitals, each a little masterpiece of foliage, earthy figures or biblical scenes. The Revolution's toll is everywhere – nearly every face is smashed.

You enter the cloister through the **tourist office** (☎ 05 63 04 01 85; www.moissac.fr; place Durand de Bredon; 9am-noon & 2-7pm Jul & Aug, to 6pm mid-Mar–Jun & Sep–mid-Oct, to 5pm mid-Oct–mid-Mar). It shows a free 10-minute video (English version available) and sells a detailed guidebook, also in English. Admission to the cloister also includes a museum of folk art and furnishings, and a library containing replicas of the monastery's beautiful illuminated manuscripts.

There are up to six trains daily to/from Montauban (€4.80, 20 minutes), the majority also serving Toulouse (€7.60). You can park for free in place des Récollets (the market square) and just above (north of) the tourist office.

AUCH
pop 23,501

Auch (pronounced similarly to poche or cloche) has been an important trade cross-roads since the Romans conquered a Celtic tribe called the Auscii and established Augusta Auscorum on the flats east of the River Gers. The town's heyday was in the Middle Ages when the counts of Armagnac (and their archbishops) built the city's cathedral. Its second flowering was in the late 18th century, following the building of new roads to Toulouse and into the Pyrenees. A slide into rural obscurity followed the Revolution in 1789.

Auch is the place to enjoy genuine Gascon cuisine and makes a convenient base for exploring the Gers region's underrated gentle countryside.

Orientation

Hilltop Auch, with place de la Libération, place de la République and the cathedral at its heart, has most of the sights, restaurants, shops and hotels. Pedestrianised rue Dessoles is the principal shopping street. The old town, tumbling away to the south, is a web of lanes, steps and little courtyards. Across the Gers River is the 'new' Auch and the train station.

Information

Bureau Information Jeunesse (16bis rue Rouget de Lisle; per hr €3; 11am-6.30pm Mon-Sat) Cheap Internet access.

Main Post Office (rue Gambetta) With Cyberposte.

Tourist Office (☎ 05 62 05 22 89; www.mairie-auch .fr in French; 1 rue Dessoles; 9.15am-7pm daily Jul & Aug; 9am-noon & 2-6pm Mon-Sat, 9am-noon Sun Easter–mid-Sep) In Maison Fedel, a handsomely restored 15th-century building. Its town map shows a couple of signposted walking tours. Ask for the English version of the exhaustively detailed accompanying leaflet. The office can provide some good recommendations, itineraries and leaflets for exploring the surrounding countryside, villages and public gardens.

Sights
CATHÉDRALE STE-MARIE

This magnificent building, now a Unesco World Heritage Site, moved Napoleon II to exclaim 'A cathedral like this should be put in a museum!'. Constructed over two centuries, from 1489 to 1680, **Cathédrale Ste-Marie** (☎ 05 62 05 72 71; 9.30am-noon & 2-5pm) ranges in style from pure Gothic to Italian Renaissance. To appreciate the contrast, take a look at the doorway in the external north wall; the lower part is lacy Gothic

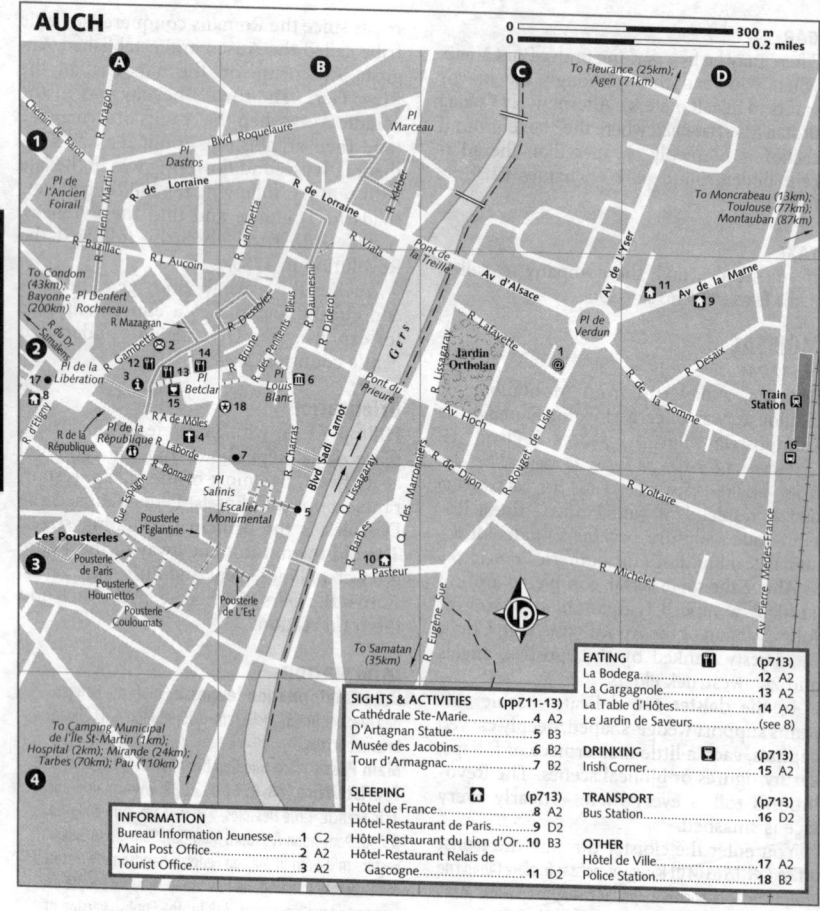

AUCH

0 - 300 m
0 - 0.2 miles

while the upper, unadorned arch is purest Florentine.

Though the heavy western façade impresses by its sheer bulk – and looks imposingly grand illuminated at night – the real splendour is within: 18 vivid 16th-century Renaissance **stained-glass windows** and the astonishing **choir** (admission €1.50 incl guide sheet in English), featuring over 1500 individual carvings of biblical scenes and mythological creatures in the 113 oak choir stalls.

Behind the cathedral, the 14th-century, 40m-high **Tour d'Armagnac** served Auch's medieval archbishops (and later Revolutionaries) as a prison. It's closed to the public.

MUSÉE DES JACOBINS

The eclectic **Musée des Jacobins** (☎ 05 62 05 74 79; 4 place Louis Blanc; adult/child €3/1.50; ☼ 10am-noon & 2-6pm daily May-Sep, to 5pm Tue-Sun Oct-Apr), sometimes referred to as the Musée d'Auch, was established in 1793, its original collection selected from property seized during the Revolution. Occupying a 15th-century Dominican monastery, it is one of France's oldest and best provincial museums. If you show your entry ticket to the cathedral's choir, you will receive a 50% reduction on the museum admission.

Highlights of this eclectic collection include frescoes and other artefacts from an early Gallo-Roman villa, landscapes by locally born painter Jean-Louis Rouméguère

(1863–1925) and a collection of the ethnography of the Americas, from pre-Colombian pottery to 18th-century religious art.

ESCALIER MONUMENTAL

Auch's 370-step, 19th-century Monumental Stairway drops to the river from place Salinis. Near the bottom swaggers a statue of d'Artagnan, the fictional swashbuckling Gascon hero immortalised by Alexandre Dumas in *Les Trois Mousquetaires* (The Three Musketeers). Nearby, a series of narrow, stepped alleyways, collectively called Les Pousterles, also plunge to the plain.

Sleeping

There's no hostel in town and budget accommodation is scarce.

Hôtel-Restaurant de Paris (☎ 05 62 63 26 22; fax 05 62 60 04 27; 38 av de la Marne; s/d from €24/27, with bathroom from €39/45; ☺ Dec-Oct; **P**)) Pleasantly old-fashioned with cosily furnished rooms and a good restaurant that serves copious quantities. Private parking costs €4.

Hôtel-Restaurant du Lion d'Or (☎ 05 62 63 66 00; fax 05 62 63 00 38; 7 rue Pasteur; r with bathroom €30-60) A rambling old place near the river whose cheaper rooms are reasonable value.

Hôtel-Restaurant Relais de Gascogne (☎ 05 62 05 26 81; fax 05 62 63 30 22; 5 av de la Marne; s/d/tr/q with bathroom €45/49/60/72; ☺ mid-Jan–mid-Dec; **P**) A member of the Logis de France chain with comfortable, well-tended rooms.

Hôtel de France (☎ 05 62 61 71 71; auchgarreau@ intercom.fr; 2 place de la Libération; s/d from €62/78, with half-board from €88/131; **P** ✄) A very comfortable three-star establishment up in the old town with a grand, old-fashioned fine dining restaurant attached (see below).

CAMPING

Camping Municipal de l'Île St-Martin (☎ 05 62 05 00 22; ☺ mid-Apr–mid-Nov) A spartan place 1.5km south of town. Take bus No 5 from place de la Libération to the Mouzon stop.

Eating & Drinking

La Table d'Hôtes (☎ 05 62 05 55 62; 7 rue Lamartine; menus €15-30; ☺ lunch & dinner, closed Wed & Sun) Usually full of locals enjoying the great food, much of it local Gascon fare with interesting twists, for example a heavenly pasta with foie gras and morels.

Le Jardin des Saveurs (☎ 05 62 61 71 71; Hôtel de France, 2 place de la Libération; menus from €25; ☺ lunch & dinner Mon-Sat, lunch Sun) Chef Roland Garreau is an acknowledged specialist in Gascon food but it needn't bust your budget: enticing *menus* begin at only €25, rising to the gastronomic revelations of his *menu gourmand du chef* at €48.

La Bodega (☎ 05 62 05 69 17; 7 rue Dessoles; lunch menu €11, mains €13 & €15; ☺ lunch & dinner Mon-Sat, dinner Sun) Serves full meals of Spanish and Basque origin by day and tapas by night and attracts a youngish crowd.

La Gargagnole (☎ 05 62 05 09 64; 10 rue Dessoles; plat du jour €7, salads €6-7, mains €9-11; ☺ lunch & dinner Mon-Sat) Bang opposite La Bodega, this is a bustling, popular place.

Irish Corner (1 place Betclar) French-run, and not an Irish accent in ear shot but convivial and lively all the same, this is a good central spot for a Guinness.

Getting There & Around

Useful bus connections include Condom (€5.80, 50 minutes, three or four daily), Montauban (€11.90, 1¾ hours, up to three daily) and Tarbes (€10.80, 1¾ hours, three daily). These services stop at both the **bus station** (☎ 05 62 05 76 37) and **train station** (☎ 05 62 60 62 12).

SNCF buses operate between Auch and Agen (€9.80, 1½ hours, six to eight services daily), while five to seven trains and two SNCF buses link Auch and Toulouse (€12.10, 1¾ hours).

There's extensive free parking along the length of allées d'Étigny.

CONDOM

pop 7555

Poor Condom, whose name has made it the butt of so many nudge-snigger, English-language jokes (the French don't even use the word, preferring *préservatif* or, more familiarly, *capote anglaise*, meaning 'English hood' – touché!).

Condom is actually a self-confident town beside the River Baïse, and is well worth a visit for its decorative cathedral, some fine restaurants and a clutch of sober neoclassical mansions.

Information

La Lavandière (5 rue Jules Ferry; ☺ 7am-10pm) Open daily to keep your clothes clean.

Tourist Office (☎ 05 62 28 00 80; place Bossuet; ☺ 9am-7pm Mon-Sat, 10am-noon Sun Jul & Aug,

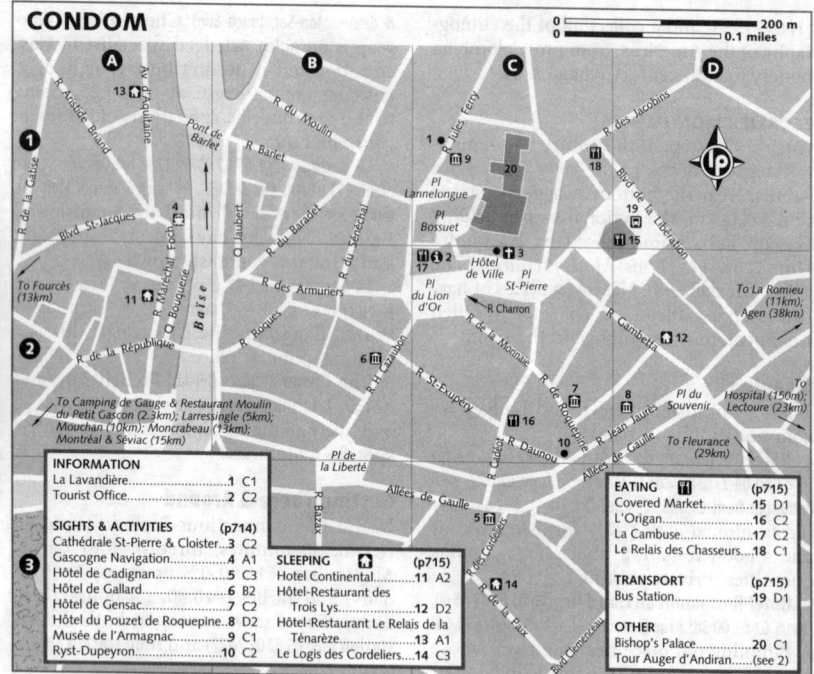

CONDOM

9am-noon & 2-6pm Mon-Sat Sep-Jun) Located in the 13th-century Tour Auger d'Andiran, just west of the cathedral. Its *Condom: Porte du Bonheur* (Condom: Gateway to Happiness) describes a walking tour of the town.

Sights

Condom's 16th-century **Cathédrale St-Pierre** (place St-Pierre), with its lofty nave and elaborately carved chancel, is a rich example of southern Flamboyant Gothic architecture. Its most richly sculpted entrance – much defaced during the Revolution – gives onto the square. Abutting the cathedral on its northern side is the delicately arched cloister, now occupied in part by the Hôtel de Ville.

Around the corner from the cathedral, **Musée de l'Armagnac** (☎ 05 62 28 47 17; 2 rue Jules Ferry; adult/child €2.20/1.10; 10am-noon & 3-6pm Wed-Mon Apr-Oct, 2-5pm Wed-Sun Nov, Dec, Feb & Mar, closed Jan) portrays the traditional production of Armagnac, Gascony's fiery rival to Cognac that's distilled to the north in the Bordeaux vineyards.

For a taste of the real stuff, head to **Ryst-Dupeyron** (☎ 05 62 28 08 08; 36 rue Jean Jaurès; 10am-noon & 2-6.30pm Mon-Fri year-round, 3.30-6.30pm Sat-Sun

Jul & Aug), one of several Armagnac producers offering free tastings. It occupies the 18th-century Hôtel de Cugnac.

Among the town's most elegant 18th-century *hôtels particuliers* mansions are **Hôtel de Gallard** (rue H Cazaubon), **Hôtel de Gensac** (rue de Roquepine), **Hôtel du Pouzet de Roquepine** (rue Jean Jaurès) and **Hôtel de Cadignan** (allées de Gaulle). None is open to the public.

Tours

During July and August, **Gascogne Navigation** (☎ 05 62 28 46 46; quai Bouquerie; adult/child €7/5.50) runs 1½-hour cruises at 3pm and 4.30pm Monday to Saturday from its quayside base, La Capitainerie. It also hires small motor boats by the hour or day (€23/92) and bigger ones by the week.

Festivals & Events

Held on the second weekend in May, **Bandas à Condom** (www.festival-de-bandas.com) brings marching and brass bands from all over Europe for 48 hours of nonstop oompah. In July and August you can listen to operetta in the cloister during **Les Nuits Musicales**.

Sleeping

Hôtel-Restaurant Le Relais de la Ténarèze (☎ 05 62 28 02 54; fax 05 62 28 46 96; 22 av d'Aquitaine; d/tr/q with bathroom €40/49/60) A family-run place with plain but comfortable rooms and an good-value restaurant (see right).

Hôtel Continental (☎ 05 62 68 37 00; www.le continen tal.net; 20 av Maréchal Foch; r with bath/shower €39/47; 😵) Modern, welcoming and fairly central with a reasonable restaurant attached. Guests benefit from discounted entry to Aquablue, the local pool and sauna. Avoid the road-facing rooms.

Le Logis des Cordeliers (☎ 05 62 28 03 68; www .logisdescordeliers.com; rue de la Paix; r €46-68; 😵 Feb-Dec; 🅿 🗶 🐾) Family-run and tranquil, with an attractive small garden, pool and bar.

Hôtel-Restaurant des Trois Lys (☎ 05 62 28 33 33; www.lestroislys.com; 38 rue Gambetta; r €80-150) Occupying an 18th-century mansion complete with pool and superb restaurant (see right), this is a good place to indulge yourself.

CAMPING

Camping de Gauge (☎ 05 62 28 17 32; fax 05 62 28 48 32; route d'Eauze; 😵 Apr–mid-Sep) Well equipped and beside the River Baïse, 2.3km south-west of town along the D931. There's a sports centre with pool nearby.

Eating

For a small town, Condom is disproportionately rich in good-value restaurants.

L'Origan (☎ 05 62 68 24 84; 4 rue Cadéot; pizzas €7-8.80, mains €7-10; 😵 lunch & dinner Tue-Sat year-round, plus dinner Mon Jul & Aug) Takes over the street in summer and does takeaways. It's good-value, offering a choice of robust Italian dishes.

Le Relais des Chasseurs (☎ 05 62 28 20 14; 3 blvd de la Libération; menus €10-28; 😵 lunch & dinner Tue-Sat, lunch Mon) An unpretentious place, popular with workers. Its midday *menu* at €10 including wine is particularly good value.

Hotel-Restaurant Le Relais de la Ténarèze (see left; 3-course dinner menus €10.50 & €22; 😵 daily Jun-Sep, lunch only Mon-Sat Oct-May) Dishes up hearty meals. Often as not, there's no menu and you take what Madame has simmering in the pot.

Hôtel-Restaurant des Trois Lys (see left; menus €20 & €30, à la carte dishes €21-35) The finest Gascon cuisine is found here, with such delights as cod terrine with ceps, crab raviolis in bisque and a *menu terroir* (regional *menu*) at €27.

Restaurant Moulin du Petit Gascon (☎ 05 62 28 28 42; menus €16-32; 😵 lunch & dinner daily Jul–mid-Sep, closed dinner Sun rest of year) Occupies an unparalleled site on the river close to Camping de Gauge and serves fine food.

La Cambuse (☎ 05 62 68 48 95; place Bossuet; salads €6-9, sandwiches €2.50-3.50, plat du jour €7.90; 😵 lunch Mon-Sat, dinner Tue, Thu & Fri) A quick-fix place beside the tourist office. Good for eating in or takeaway, the restaurant spills onto place Bossuet in summertime.

SELF-CATERING

The **farmers market**, rich in local produce, is held on Wednesday and Saturday mornings in the covered market. There's a small, Sunday morning market on blvd St-Jacques.

Getting There & Around

Condom, with the nearest train station in Auch, is ill served by public transport. There are three or four daily buses to Auch (€5.80, 50 minutes), including one that continues to Toulouse (€13.90, 2½ hours) and one early-bird run to Bordeaux (€17.70, 2¾ hours Monday to Saturday). There is also one bus a day to Pau (€19.60, 2½ hours) and also to Agen (€7.70, 45 minutes).

Camping de Gauge (see left) rents bikes for €7 per day.

AROUND CONDOM

Condom makes an excellent base for exploring the gentle Armagnac countryside and its attractive villages. Bus services, except to/from Lectoure, are nonexistent but the mild undulation makes it ideal cycling country.

VULGAR VILLAGES

The more puerile English-speaking visitors to France have long been amused by place names such as Condom (not to mention the likes of Pissy or Stains), but the French are in on the act now too. In an attempt to really put themselves on the map, in 2003 a group of French villages with names that mean silly or rude things in French staged their first summit meeting of 'Villages of lyric or burlesque names' in a tiny village outside Toulouse called Mingocebos (or 'eat onions' in the old Occitan tongue). Members include Saligos ('filthy pig'), Beaufou ('beautiful mad'), and Cocumont ('cuckold hill'), although Trecon ('very stupid') and Montcuq ('my arse') have yet to join.

Château de Cassaigne

At the 13th-century **Château de Cassaigne** (☎ 05 62 28 04 02; www.chateaudecassaigne.com; ⏰ 9am-noon & 2-7pm), the old country house of the bishops of Condom, you can enjoy a free visit, then sample Armagnac from its 18th-century distillery. It's 6.5km southwest of Condom, just off the D931 to Eauze.

Fourcès

Fourcès (pronounce that 's'), 13km northwest of Condom via the D114, is a picturesque *bastide* on the River Auzoue. Uniquely circular, its shady expanse is ringed by well-restored medieval houses. You can sip a drink or have a pleasant but none too copious lunch on the terrace of **L'Auberge** (☎ 05 62 29 40 10; menus €15, €20.50 & €30). Opposite is the tiny, dusty **Musée des Vieux Métiers** (Museum of Ancient Crafts).

The village bursts into colour during the last weekend of April as thousands pour in for its **Marché aux Fleurs**, more a flower festival than market.

The tiny seasonal **tourist office** (☎ 05 62 29 50 96; ⏰ Jun-Sep) is in the square (or, more accurately, circle).

Larressingle

Larressingle, 5km west of Condom on the D15, is probably France's cutest fortified village. It is certainly the most besieged, bravely withstanding armies of tourists and Compostela pilgrims.

This textbook bastion bears witness to the troubled times of medieval Gascony. Within the largely intact original walls are the remains of a **castle-keep**, once the principal residence of the bishops of Condom, and the very sturdy Romanesque **Église St-Sigismond**.

Montréal & Séviac

Montréal, established in 1255, was one of Gascony's first *bastides*. Its chunky Gothic church squats beside place Hôtel de Ville, the arcaded main square.

At Séviac, 1.5km southwest of Montréal, are the excavated remains of a 4th-century **Gallo-Roman villa** (admission €3.50; ⏰ 10am-7pm Jul & Aug, 10am-noon & 2-6pm Mar-Jun & Sep-Nov). Discovered by the local parish priest in 1868, the site is still being excavated. What archaeologists have revealed are the remains of a luxurious villa, including baths and outbuildings, on the agricultural estate of a 4th-century

Roman aristocrat. Large areas of the villa's spectacular mosaic floors (over 450 mosaics have been uncovered) have survived.

The admission price includes entry to the **museum**, located with Montréal's **tourist office** (☎ 05 62 29 42 85; place Hôtel de Ville; both ⏰ 10am-12.30pm & 2.30-6pm Mon-Sat, 11am-5pm Sun Feb-Dec), where artefacts from Séviac are displayed. Ask for its explanatory sheet in English.

La Romieu

La Romieu, 11km northeast of Condom and once an important stopover on the Santiago de Compostela route, takes its name from the Occitan *roumieu*, meaning pilgrim. It's dominated by the magnificent 14th-century collegiate **Église St-Pierre** (admission €3.05). Just opposite the entrance is the **tourist office** (☎ 05 62 28 86 33; ⏰ 10am-12.30pm & 2-7.30pm Jul & Aug, to 6pm Feb-May & Oct-Dec, closed Sun morning year-round), whose staff will let you into the fine Gothic cloister that gives onto the church. Left of the altar is the **sacristy** where original medieval frescoes include arcane biblical characters, black angels and esoteric symbols. Climb the 136 steps of the double-helix stairway to the top of the octagonal tower for a good view over the countryside.

About 500m west of the village is the **Arboretum Coursiana** (☎ 05 62 68 22 80; with/without guided tour €5/4; ⏰ 9am-8pm mid-Mar–Nov), an initiative of a local agricultural engineer, where over 650 trees and rare plants flourish.

Lectoure

Lectoure's main claim to fame is its superb **Musée Lapidaire** (☎ 05 62 68 70 22; place Général de Gaulle; adult/child €2.30/1.50; ⏰ 10am-noon & 2-6pm daily Mar-Sep, 10am-noon & 2-6pm Wed-Mon Oct-Feb) in the the former Episcopal palace, today the Hôtel de Ville. The museum displays finds from local Gallo-Roman sites, and includes some Roman jewellery and mosaics, as well as an early Christian marble sarcophagus.

Rearing over the museum is the bulk of the 15th-century **Cathédrale St-Gervais et St-Protais** with its curious, ornate tower.

The **tourist office** (☎ 05 62 68 76 98; www.lectoure.fr; ⏰ 9am-12.30pm & 2.30-7pm Jul & Aug, 9am-noon & 2-6pm Mon-Sat, 2-5pm Sun Sep-Jun) is next door.

Lectoure is 23km east of Condom and 36km north of Auch. SNCF's Auch–Agen buses stop here eight times daily Monday to Friday, less often at weekends (Auch €5.65, 40 minutes; Agen €5.80, 50 minutes).

Languedoc-Roussillon

Languedoc-Roussillon is something of a three-eyed hybrid, cobbled together in the 1980s by the merging, for administrative purposes, of two historic regions. Bas Languedoc (Lower Languedoc), land of bullfighting, rugby and robust red wines, looks towards the more-sedate Provence. On the plain are all the major towns, such as Montpellier, the vibrant capital, sun-baked Nîmes with its fine Roman amphitheatre – and fairy-tale Carcassonne, with its witches'-hat turrets. On the coast, good beaches abound, old Agde lies somnolent beside the River Hérault and Sète, a thriving port, adds a touch of commercial vigour.

Deeper inland, Haut Languedoc (Upper Languedoc) is quite distinct from the sun-soaked lowlands. A continuation of the Massif Central, this rugged, sparsely populated mountainous terrain shares great trekking, mountain pasture, forests and hearty cuisine with Auvergne. It's a more isolated land for lovers of solitude and the outdoors, where the small towns of Mende, Florac, Alès and Millau are like oases within the greater wilderness. The Parc National des Cévennes is a wild, mountainous area, long the refuge of hermits and exiles and criss-crossed by marked trails. Trekking country too are the bare limestone plateaus of the Grands Causses, sliced through by deep canyons such as the Gorges du Tarn, perfect for a day's canoeing.

Roussillon, abutting the Pyrenees, constantly glances over the frontier to Catalonia, in Spain, with which it shares a common language and culture. Nestling alongside the rocky coastline are attractive little resorts such as Collioure, which drew the likes of Matisse and Picasso, attracted by its special light, while the gentle Têt and Tech Valleys stretch away inland. To their south, the Pic de Canigou, highest summit in the eastern Pyrenees and symbol of Catalan identity, pokes its nose, white in winter, to the clouds while, further east, the foothills are capped by stark, lonely Cathar fortresses.

HIGHLIGHTS

■ Gasp at your first glimpse of **La Cité's witches'-hat turrets** (p727) above Carcassonne

■ Spot vultures looping and swooping high above **Gorges de la Jonte** (p747)

■ Swim under the bridge for an original perspective of the **Pont du Gard** (p738)

■ Drift lazily down the **Gorges du Tarn** (p745) in a canoe

■ Walk a stage or two of Robert Louis Stevenson's **Cévennes donkey trek** (p743)

■ Enjoy spectacular Pyrenean scenery from the trundling **Train Jaune** (Yellow Train; p757)

■ Take a slow boat along the **Canal du Midi** (p726)

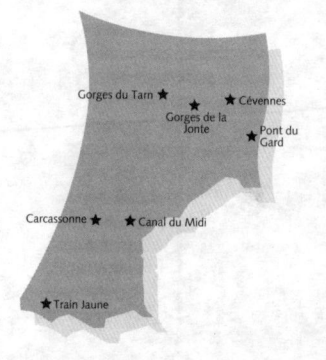

■ POPULATION: 2,295,000   ■ AREA: 27,375 SQ KM

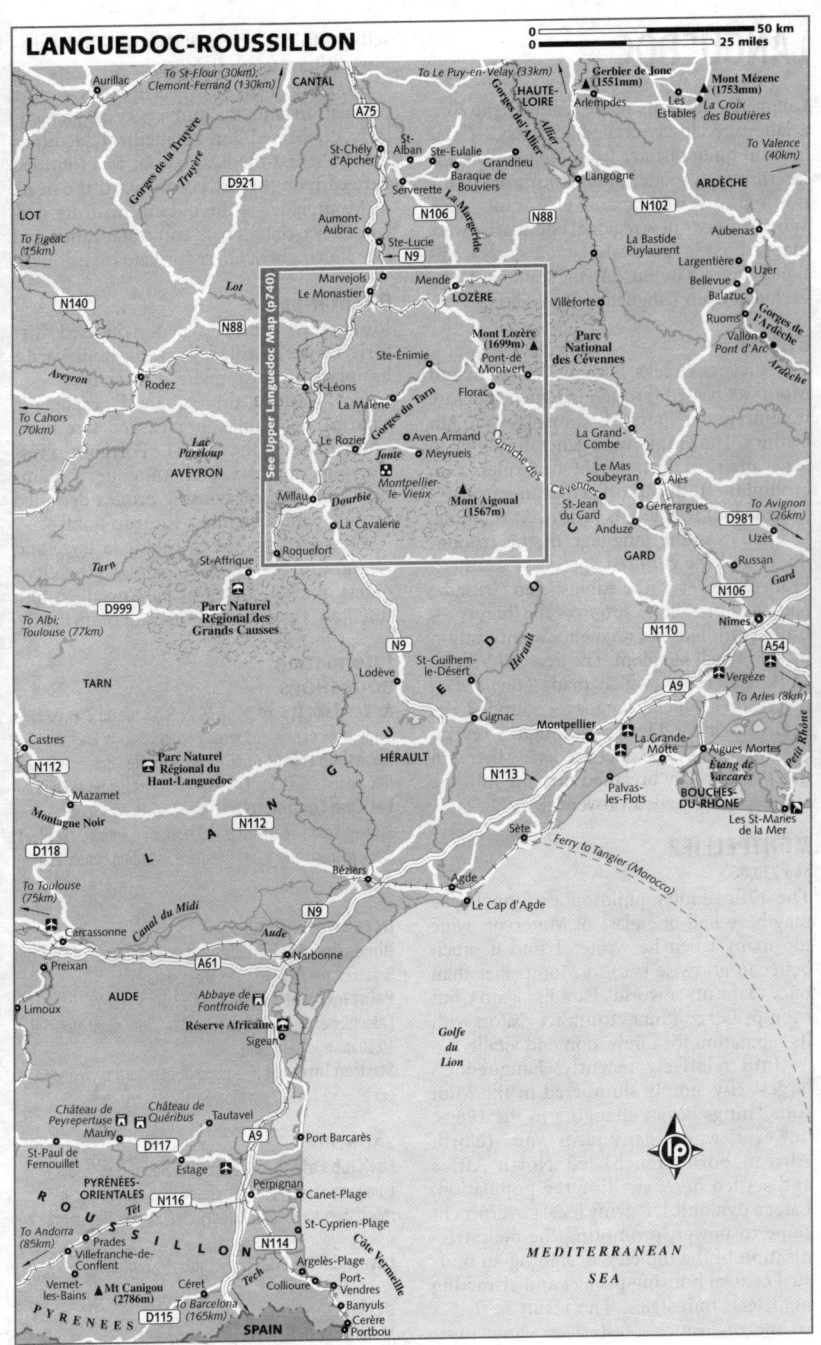

LANGUEDOC-ROUSSILLON

LANGUEDOC-ROUSSILLON

0 _____ 50 km
0 _____ 25 miles

Aurillac

To St-Flour (30km);
Clermont-Ferrand (130km)

CANTAL

To Le Puy-en-Velay (33km)

Gerbier de Jonc
(1551mm) ▲

Mont Mézenc
(1753mm) ▲

Les
Estables

La Croix
des Boutières

A75

St-Chély
d'Apcher

St-
Alban

Ste-Eulalie

Grandrieu
Baraque de
Bouviers

HAUTE-
LOIRE

Gorges de l'Allier

Allier

Arlempdes

To Valence
(40km)

LOT

To Figéac
(15km)

D921

Serverette

Aumont-
Aubrac

N106

Ste-Lucie

N9

Langogne

La Bastide
Puylaurent

ARDÈCHE

N88

N102

Aubenas

Largentière

Uzer

N140

Lot

Marvejols

Le Monastier

Mende

LOZÈRE

Villefort

Bellevue

Balazuc

Ruoms

Gorges de
l'Ardèche

Vallon
Pont d'Arc

Ardèche

N88

Rodez

Ste-Énimie

Mont Lozère
(1699m) ▲

Pont-de-
Montvert

Parc
National
des Cévennes

Aveyron

To Cahors
(70km)

St-Léons

La Malène

Florac

Gorges du Tarn

Lac
Pareloup

AVEYRON

Le Rozier

Aven Armand

Jonte

Meyrueis

Corniche des

La Grand-
Combe

Le Mas
Soubeyran

Alès

To Avignon
(26km)

Millau

Dourbie

Montpellier-
le-Vieux

Mont Aigoual
(1567m) ▲

Cévennes

St-Jean
du Gard

Générargues

D981

Uzès

La Cavalerie

Anduze

GARD

Russan

Tarn

St-Affrique

Roquefort

N106

Gard

To Albi;
Toulouse (77km)

D999

Parc Naturel
Régional des
Grands Causses

N9

St-Guilhem-
le-Désert

N110

Nîmes

A54

TARN

Lodève

Hérault

A9

Vergèze

To Arles (8km)

Castres

N112

Parc Naturel
Régional du
Haut-Languedoc

Gignac

Montpellier

La Grande-
Motte

Aigues Mortes

Étang de
Vaccarès

BOUCHES-
DU-RHÔNE

Mazamet

HÉRAULT

N113

Palvas-
les-Flots

Montagne Noire

N112

Petit Rhône

D118

Sète

Les St-Maries
de la Mer

To Toulouse
(75km)

Béziers

Agde

Ferry to Tangier (Morocco)

Canal du Midi

N9

Le Cap d'Agde

Carcassonne

Aude

A61

Narbonne

Golfe
du
Lion

Preixan

AUDE

Abbaye de
Fontfroide

Limoux

Réserve Africaine

Sigean

MEDITERRANEAN
SEA

Château de
Peyrepertuse

Château de
Quéribus

Maury

Tautavel

A9

Port Barcarès

St-Paul de
Fernouillet

D117

Estage

PYRÉNÉES-
ORIENTALES

Perpignan

Canet-Plage

R

O

U

S

N116

Têt

St-Cyprien-Plage

Côte Vermeille

To Andorra
(85km)

Prades

Villefranche-de-
Conflent

N114

Argelès-Plage

Vernet-
les-Bains

Mt Canigou
(2786m) ▲

Céret

Collioure

Port-
Vendres

Banyuls

P Y R E N E E S

D115

To Barcelona
(165km)

Tech

SPAIN

Cerère

Portbou

LANGUEDOC

Languedoc takes its name from *langue d'oc,* a language closely related to today's Catalan and quite distinct from *langue d'oïl,* the forerunner of modern French, spoken to the north (the words *oc* and *oïl* meant 'yes'). When France's new regional boundaries were mapped out in the 1980s, Languedoc's traditional centre, Toulouse, to the southwest, was excluded from Languedoc-Roussillon.

History

Phoenicians, Greeks, Romans, Visigoths and Moors all passed through Languedoc before it came under Frankish control in the 8th century. The Franks were generally happy to leave affairs in the hands of local rulers and, around the 12th century, Occitania (today's Languedoc) reached its zenith. At the time, Occitan was the language of the troubadours and the cultured speech of southern France. However, the Albigensian Crusade, launched in 1208 to suppress the 'heresy' of Catharism, led to Languedoc's annexation by the French kingdom. The treaty of Villers-Cotterêts (1539), which made *langue d'oïl* the realm's official language, sounded the death knell for Occitan, though a revival spearheaded by the poet Frédéric Mistral in the 19th century breathed new life into the language now called Provençal.

MONTPELLIER

pop 230,000

The 17th-century philosopher John Locke may have had one glass of Minervois wine too many when he wrote: 'I find it much better to go twise (sic) to Montpellier than once to the other world'. Paradise it ain't, but Montpellier continues to attract visitors with its reputation for innovation and vitality.

Until relatively recently, Languedoc's largest city simply slumbered in the Midi sun. Things began changing in the 1960s, however, when many *pieds noirs* (North African–born French) left North Africa and settled here, swelling the population. Later a dynamic left-wing local government came to power, promoting the pedestrianisation of the old city, designing an unusual central housing project and attracting high tech industries. The result is that it is one of France's fastest-growing, most

self-confident cities with a public transport system second to none.

Students form nearly a quarter of the population and the university is particularly celebrated for its medical faculties; Europe's first medical school was founded here early in the 12th century. At the heart of Montpellier is the old city with its narrow alleys, rich in bars and restaurants, and fine *hôtels particuliers* (private mansions).

Orientation

Montpellier's mostly pedestrianised historic centre, girdled by wide boulevards, has place de la Comédie at its heart.

Northeast of this square is esplanade Charles de Gaulle, a pleasant tree-lined promenade. To the east is Le Polygone, a vast shopping complex, and Antigone, a mammoth neoclassical housing project designed by the Spanish architect Ricardo Bofill.

Westwards, between rue de la Loge and Grand Rue Jean Moulin, sprawls the city's oldest quarter, a web of narrow alleys and fine *hôtels particuliers* (private mansions).

Information
BOOKSHOPS

As You Like It (☎ 04 67 66 22 90; 8 rue du Bras de Fer) Large stock of new and second-hand books in English.

Bookshop (☎ 04 67 66 09 08; 4 rue de l'Université) Carries a good selection of novels and travel guides in English.

Les Cinq Continents (☎ 04 67 66 46 70; 20 rue Jacques Cœur) Specialist travel bookshop with an excellent stock of maps and travel literature including Lonely Planet guides.

INTERNET ACCESS

Dimension 4 Cybercafé (☎ 04 67 60 57 57; 11 rue des Balances; per hr €3.85; 🕑 10am-midnight)

Point Internet (☎ 04 67 54 57 60; 54 rue de l'Aiguillerie; per hr €1.60; 🕑 9.30am-midnight Mon-Sat, 10.30am-midnight Sun)

St@tion Internet (6-8 place du Marché aux Fleurs; €4 per hr; 🕑 10am-7pm Mon-Sat)

LAUNDRY

Lav'Club Café (6 rue des Écoles Laïques; 🕑 9.30am-8pm Mon-Sat, 2-7pm Sun; closed Wed morning year-round, Sun Jun-Sep) A laundry-café; sip a coffee or grab a snack as your smalls spin.

Lavasud (19 rue de l'Université; 🕑 7am-9pm)

POST

Main Post Office (13 place Rondelet)

TOURIST INFORMATION
Main Tourist Office (☎ 04 67 60 60 60; www.ot-mont pellier.fr; ☼ 9am-6.30pm or 7.30pm Mon-Fri, 10am-6pm Sat, 10am-1pm & 2-5pm Sun) At southern end of esplanade Charles de Gaulle.
Tourist Office Annexe (train station; ☼ Jul-Aug)

Sights
HÔTELS PARTICULIERS
During the 17th and 18th centuries, Montpellier's wealthier merchants built grand private mansions with large inner courtyards. Fine examples are **Hôtel de Varennes** (2 place Pétrarque), a harmonious blend of Romanesque and Gothic, and **Hôtel St-Côme** (Grand Rue Jean Moulin), the city's first anatomy theatre for medical students and nowadays its Chambre de Commerce. The 17th-century **Hôtel des Trésoriers de France** (7 rue Jacques Cœur) today houses the Musée Languedocien. Within the old quarter are several other mansions, each marked by a descriptive plaque in French.

MUSEUMS
Musée Fabre (☎ 04 67 14 83 00; 39 blvd Bonne Nouvelle), the city's cultural showpiece, is undergoing fundamental renovation and will remain closed until at least mid-2006. In the interim the **Pavillon du Musée Fabre**, across the esplanade, continues to host temporary displays.

Musée Languedocien (☎ 04 67 52 93 03; 7 rue Jacques Cœur; adult/student €5/3; ☼ 3-6pm Mon-Sat Jul-Aug, 2-5pm Mon-Sat Sep-Jun) displays the area's rich archaeological finds as well as *objets d'art* from the 16th to 19th centuries.

Musée du Vieux Montpellier (☎ 04 67 66 02 94; 2 place Pétrarque; admission free; ☼ 9.30am-noon & 1.30-5pm Tue-Sat), a storehouse of the city's memorabilia from the Middle Ages to the Revolution, is upstairs in the Hôtel de Varennes.

Musée Atger (☎ 04 67 66 27 77; 2 rue de l'École de Médecine; admission free; ☼ 1.30-5.45pm Mon, Wed & Fri) displays a striking collection of French, Italian and Flemish drawings. Housed within the medical faculty, it's closed during university holidays.

AROUND PLACE ROYALE DU PEYROU
This wide, tree-lined esplanade is dominated by the **Arc de Triomphe** (1692) at its eastern end, and the **Château d'Eau** (Water Tower) at the other. Leading from this hexagonal water tower is the 18th-century **Aqueduc de St-Clément**, under which there's an organic food and second-hand books market on

Saturday and *pétanque* (a variant on bowls) most afternoons. To the north, off blvd Henri IV, is the **Jardin des Plantes**, France's oldest botanic garden (1593). Opposite the garden is **Cathédrale St-Pierre**, with its disproportionately large 15th-century porch.

Tours
The main tourist office offers two-hour **walking tours** (€6.50; in English 10.30am Tue & Sat Jul-Aug, 10.30am Sat Sep, 3.30pm Sat Oct-Jun; in French 10am & 5pm daily Jul-Aug, 5pm daily Sep, 3pm Wed, Sat & Sun Oct-Jun) of the old town. Ring at least 48 hours in advance to reserve.

Festivals & Events
Montpellier hosts **Le Printemps des Comédiens**, a popular theatre festival, in June and a two-week international dance festival in June/July. The **Festival de Radio France et Montpellier** in the second half of July brings in top notch classical music and jazz and the majority of events are free.

Sleeping
Auberge de Jeunesse (☎ 04 67 60 32 22; montpellier@fuaj.org; 2 impasse de la Petite Corraterie; dm €8.90; ☼ mid-Jan–mid-Dec) Montpellier's HI-affiliated youth hostel is just off rue des Écoles Laïques. The grandiose mosaic entrance contrasts with its basic dorms but who can complain when there's a friendly bar and a cheap bed? Take the tram to the Louis Blanc stop.

Hôtel des Étuves (☎ 04 67 60 78 19; www.hoteldes etuves.fr; 24 rue des Étuves; s €20.50-31, d €32-38) This welcoming, 13-room family hotel creeps around a spiral staircase like a vine. Room

---

AUTHOR'S CHOICE
Hôtel Le Guilhem (☎ 04 67 52 90 90; www .hotel-le-guilhem.com; 18 rue Jean-Jacques Rousseau; s €71-78, d €71-135; ⊠) Occupying a couple of interconnecting 16th-century buildings, the Hôtel Le Guilhem's guest rooms are exquisitely and individually furnished. Nearly all have views of the cathedral and overlook the tranquil garden of nearby Restaurant Le Petit Jardin. Room No 100 (€135) has its own little terrace and garden. All rooms have bathtubs and some have separate toilets. It's wise to reserve at any time of year since Le Guilhem has its faithful clientele who return again and again.

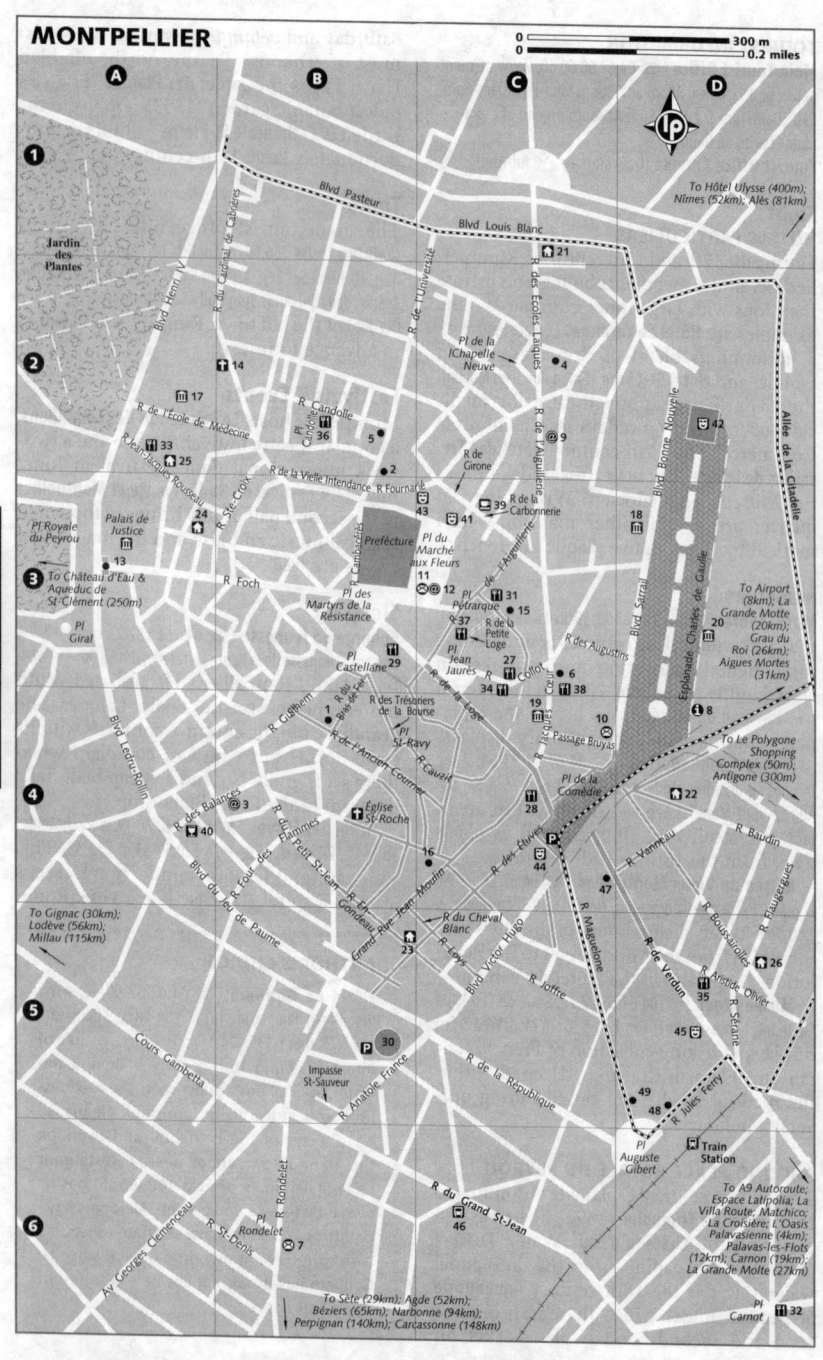

MONTPELLIER

0   300 m
0   0.2 miles

LANGUEDOC-ROUSSILLON

No 2, one of six overlooking the quiet pedestrian street, has a bath while the rest are equipped with showers.

Hôtel le Mistral (☎ 04 67 58 45 25; www.hotel-le -mistral.com in French; 25 rue Boussairolles; basic s €26, with bathroom s €37-39.50, d €38.50-46; P) This spruce, cosy, friendly 20-room place offers great value and is handy for both the station and heart of town.

Hôtel du Palais (☎ 04 67 60 47 38; fax 04 67 60 40 23; 3 rue du Palais; s €54, d €59-71; P ✕) All 26 rooms of this delightful hotel overlooking a quiet square are decorated by a local artist and tastefully and individually furnished.

Hôtel de la Comédie (☎ 04 67 58 43 64; hotel delacomedie@wanadoo.fr; 1bis rue Baudin; s €44, d €52-69; ✕) This cosy family-run place, just off place de la Comédie, is a favourite with visiting musicians and theatre troupes. All 20 rooms have air-con and heating and are double glazed.

Hôtel Ulysse (☎ 04 67 02 02 30; www.hotel-ulysse .com; 338 av St-Maur; s €49.50-54.50, d €59-66; P) The Ulysse is in a quiet neighbourhood no more than a 10 minute walk from place de la Comédie. It has a small garden and attractive breakfast salon. Each of its 23 rooms, all with bathtubs, is decorated individually and pleasingly furnished in wood and wrought iron.

CAMPING

The closest camping grounds are around the suburb of Lattes, some 4km south of the city centre.

L'Oasis Palavasienne (☎ 04 67 15 11 61; www .oasis-palavasienne.com; route de Palavas; camping according to season €16.70-24.50; ✕ mid-May–Aug) This shady camping ground has a large pool. Take bus No 17 from Montpellier bus station.

Eating

You'll find plenty of cheap and cheerful eateries on rue de l'Université, rue des Écoles Laïques and the streets interlinking them.

Roule Ma Poule (☎ 04 67 60 36 15; 20 place Candolle; plat du jour €7.50) Like most places in the area, it pulls in a mainly student crowd with its decent, uncomplicated fare. Happy-go-lucky and with rapid service, it's a little shrine to the motorbike with posters, pictures, a platoon of crash helmets and models all along the lintel above the bar.

Chez Fels (3 Grand Rue Jean Moulin; ✕ 8am-7.30pm Mon-Sat) Just off place de la Comédie, this hole-in-the-wall sandwich shop does the crunchiest of baby baguettes, stuffed with salad and Alsatian goodies.

Le Ban des Gourmands (☎ 04 67 65 00 85; 5 place Carnot; menu €25, mains €16-18; ✕ Tue-Fri & dinner Sat Sep-Jul) South of the train station and a favourite of locals in the know, this appealing restaurant, run by a young family team, serves delicious local cuisine.

Caves Jean Jaurès (☎ 04 67 60 27 33; 3 rue Collot; menu €17, mains €12-15; ✕ closed Sun, lunch Mon & Wed) Scan this attractive restaurant's range of tasty dishes on the chalkboard that the waiter props against a nearby table. A glass of wine? Select from the bottles of the day on the bar counter. Rather more? Pick from the shelves; every bottle has its price marked and the range is superlative.

Restaurant Verdi (☎ 04 67 58 68 55; 10 rue Aristide Olivier; menus €22-26; ✕ Mon-Sat) This restaurant does delicious Italian fare, especially fish dishes, in an Italian ambience – walls are plastered with posters relating to the eponymous Verdi – and has an outstanding wine list. Two doors away, **Pizzeria Aïda**

serves pasta, pizzas and salads from the same kitchen and in a more informal setting.

Tripti Kulai (☎ 04 67 66 30 51; 20 rue Jacques Cœur; salads €8.50, menus €11 & €15; ⊙ noon-9.30pm Mon-Sat) Barrel-vaulted and cosy, this popular vegetarian place stands out for the inventiveness of many of its dishes. To finish, you could drink an infusion of tea a day for more than a month and still not exhaust their selection.

Le Petit Jardin (☎ 04 67 60 78 78; 20 rue Jean-Jacques Rousseau; lunch menu €14, dinner menus €20-28; ⊙ Tue-Sun Feb-Dec) 'The Little Garden' is just that: a restaurant offering imaginative cuisine, its big bay windows overlooking a shady, fairytale greenness at the rear, where you could be 100km from Montpellier's bustle.

Restaurant Cerdan (☎ 04 67 60 86 96; 8 rue Collot; menus €12.60-32.50; ⊙ closed all Sun, lunch Sat & Mon) This much garlanded family restaurant carries a good list of local wines and offers five different *menus*, each rich in local fare with a leavening of dishes from Normandy, Mme Cerdan's home region.

La Diligence (☎ 04 67 66 12 21; 2 place Pétrarque; lunch menu €17, dinner menus €33-59; ⊙ closed all Sun, lunch Sat & Mon) Dine beneath attractive vaults and arches and savour the elegant rear patio beneath a gallery of the Hôtel de Varennes. The lunch *menu* I excellent value.

Salmon Shop (04 67 66 40 70; 5 rue de la Petite Loge; mains €12; ⊙ Mon-Sat, closed Sun & lunch Mon) For something fishy, head for the Salmon Shop with its mock log-cabin décor. Most dishes, including the plat du jour, feature salmon, prepared 11 different ways.

SELF-CATERING

The city's **food markets** include **Halles Castellane** (rue de la Loge), the biggest and **Halles Laissac** (rue Anatole France). There's a farmers market every Sunday morning on av Samuel de Champlain in the Antigone complex.

Drinking

All summer long, place de la Comédie is alive with café's where you can drink, grab a quick bite and watch street entertainers strut their stuff. Smaller, more intimate squares include place Jean Jaurès and place St-Ravy.

L'Heure Bleue (1 rue de la Carbonnerie; ⊙ Tue-Sun) At this tea salon, you can sip Earl Grey to a background of classical music. It also does light lunches with plenty of choice for vegetarians.

With more than 60,000 students, Montpellier has a profusion of places to drink and dance. You'll find dense concentrations around rue En-Gondeau, off Grand Rue Jean Moulin, around place Jean Jaurès and around the intersection of rue de l'Université and rue Candolle.

If beer is your favourite tipple, call by **Mannekin-Pis** (110 rue des Balances), a neighbourhood bar whose *patron* runs a temple to the amber nectar with eight brands on draught, approximately 100 in bottle and drip mats – a mere sample from his vast collection, built up over 25 years – plastered all over.

Entertainment

Montpellier has a busy cultural calendar. To find out what's on where, pick up the free weekly *Sortir*, available around town and at the tourist office.

Tickets for Montpellier's numerous theatres are sold at the **Opéra-Comédie box office** (☎ 04 67 60 05 45; place de la Comédie). **Le Corum** (☎ 04 67 61 67 61), at the northern end of esplanade Charles de Gaulle, is the city's prime concert venue.

In central Montpellier you'll recognise longstanding discothèque **Rockstore** (☎ 04 67 06 80 00; 20 rue de Verdun) by the rear of a classic American '70s car protruding above the entrance.

There's a critical mass of discos outside town in Espace Latipolia, about 10km out of town on route de Palavas heading towards the coast. These include **La Villa Rouge** (☎ 04 67 06 52 15), **Matchico** (☎ 04 67 64 19 20) and **La Croisière** (☎ 04 67 64 19 52).

L'Amigo, a night bus, does a circuit of these and other dance venues on the periphery of town, leaving Le Corum at midnight, 12.45am and 1.30am, returning at 2.30am, 3.30am and (yawn!) 5am.

GAY VENUES

To tune into the active men-on-men scene (many reckon Montpellier is France's most gay-friendly city), call by **Le Village** (☎ 04 67 60 29 05; 3 rue Fournarié), a shop specialising in queer gear and gay literature, or **Café de la Mer** (☎ 04 67 60 79 65; 5 place du Marché aux Fleurs), just around the corner, where the friendly staff will arm you with a map of gay venues. Right next door, **Le Heaven** (1 rue Delpech) is an exclusively men's bar, which gets busy from 8pm.

Getting There & Away

AIR

Montpellier's **airport** (☎ 04 67 20 85 00; www .montpellier.aeroport.fr) is 8km southeast of town. British Airways flies three times per week (daily in summer) to/from London (Gatwick) and Ryanair operates daily to/from London (Stansted). Air France has up to 10 daily flights to Paris.

BUS

The **bus station** (☎ 04 67 92 01 43; rue du Grand St-Jean) is an easy walk from the train station. **Hérault Transport** (☎ 08 25 34 01 34) runs hourly buses to La Grande Motte (No 106; €1.25, 35 minutes) via Carnon from Odysseum at the end of the tram line. Some continue to Aigues Mortes (€6, 1½ hours, six daily) and, in July and August, Stes-Maries de la Mer in the Camargue (€9.30, two hours).

Eurolines (☎ 04 67 58 57 59; ticketing & information office 8 rue de Verdun) has buses to most European destinations including Barcelona (€27, five hours), London (€93, 17 hours) and Amsterdam (€87, 21 hours). **Linebus** (☎ 04 67 58 95 00) mainly operates services to destinations in Spain.

TRAIN

Major destinations from Montpellier's two-storey train station include Paris' Gare de Lyon by TGV (€70 to €83, 3½ hours, 12 daily), Carcassonne (€19.50, 1½ hours, six to eight daily), Millau (€21.80, 1½ hours, two daily) and Perpignan (€19.20, two hours, frequent).

More than 20 trains daily go northwards to Nîmes (€7.50, 30 minutes) and southwards to Narbonne (€12.80, one hour) via Sète (€4.60), Agde (€7.50) and Béziers (€9.90).

Getting Around

TO/FROM THE AIRPORT

A shuttle bus (€4.80, 15 minutes, 12 daily) runs between the airport and bus station.

BICYCLE

Montpellier encourages cycling with more than 100km of bicycle track. **TaM Vélo** (☎ 04 67 92 92 67; 27 rue Maguelone; ☽ 9am-7pm Mon-Sat, 9am-1pm & 4-7pm Sun), an admirable urban initiative, rents town bikes and electric bikes per hour/half-day/full-day for €1.50/3/6 and tandems per half-day/full-day for €12/15. You'll need to leave a deposit (cheque, credit card or cash) of €150/300 per bike/ electric bike.

PUBLIC TRANSPORT

Take a ride, even just for fun, on Montpellier's high tech, high-speed leave-your-car-at-home tram. Like city buses, it's run by **TaM** (☎ 04 67 22 87 87; 6 rue Jules Ferry) and runs until midnight. Regular buses run until about 8.30pm daily.

Single-journey tickets, valid for bus or tram, cost €1.20. A one-day pass/10-ticket *carnet* costs €3/10. Pick them up from newsagents or any tram station.

TAXI

To call a cab, ring **Taxi Bleu** (☎ 04 67 03 20 00) or **Taxi 2000** (☎ 04 67 04 00 60).

AROUND MONTPELLIER

The closest beaches are at **Palavas-les-Flots**, 12km south of the city and very much Montpellier-on-Sea in summer. Take TaM bus No 17 or 28 (€2.10, 35 minutes, frequent) from the Port Marianne tram stop. Heading north on the coastal road towards Carnon, you stand a good chance of seeing flamingos snuffling the shallows of the lagoons on either side of the coastal D21.

Carnon itself comes out fairly low in the charm stakes despite its huge marina. Continue hugging the coast along the D59 (Le Petit Travers), bordered by several kilometres of white sand beach, uncrowded and without a kiosk or café in sight.

Further northwards and about 20km southeast of Montpellier is **La Grande Motte**, sitting on what was once mosquito ridden salt marsh. Purpose-built on the grand scale back in the 1960s to plug the tourist drain southwards into Spain, its architecture, considered revolutionary at the time, now comes over as fairly heavy and leaden, contrasting with the more organic growth of adjacent **Grau du Roi**, deeper rooted and a still-active fishing port.

Aigues Mortes, situated on the western edge of the Camargue (p806), is another 11km to the east.

SÈTE

pop 40,300

Twenty-six kilometres southwest of Montpellier, Sète is France's largest Mediterranean fishing port and its biggest commercial port after Marseille. Established by Louis XIV in the 17th century, it prospered as the harbours of Aigues Mortes and Narbonne, to north and south, were cut off from the sea by silt deposits.

Huddled east of Mont St-Clair, from where there are great views of town and port, Sète has lots in its favour: waterways and canals, beaches, outdoor cafés and shoals of fish and seafood restaurants.

For the **tourist office** (☎ 04 67 74 71 71; www .ot-sete.fr; 60 Grand'Rue Mario Roustan; ☼ 9.30am-7.30pm Jul-Aug; 9.30am-12.30pm & 2-6pm Mon-Sat, 10am-noon & 2-5pm Sun May-Jun & Sep; 9.30am-12.30pm & 2-5.30pm Mon-Fri, 10am-noon & 2-5pm Sat Oct-Apr), take bus No 2 from the train station.

Sète was the birthplace of the symbolist poet Paul Valéry (1871–1945), whose remains lie in the **Cimetière Marin**, inspiration for and title of his most famous poem. Overlooking this cemetery is the **Musée Paul Valéry** (☎ 04 67 46 20 98; rue François Desnoyer; adult/child €3/1.50; ☼ 10am-noon & 2-6pm daily Jul-Aug, Wed-Mon Sep-Jun), which hosts temporary exhibitions and has one room devoted to the poet.

The town was also the childhood home of singer and infinitely more accessible poet Georges Brassens (1921–81), whose mellow voice still speaks and sings over the headphones at **Espace Georges Brassens** (☎ 04 67 53 32 77; 67 blvd Camille Blanc; adult/child €5/2; ☼ 10am-noon & 2-6pm Tue-Sun), a multimedia centre set up in his memory. Ask for the English synopsis.

Sète Croisières (☎ 04 67 46 00 46; quai Général Durand) does a variety of boat trips, including a one-hour **harbour tour** (adult/child €10/5).

On the first weekend in July, Sète celebrates **La Fête de la St-Pierre**, or Fête des Pêcheurs (Fisherfolks Festival). The **Fête de la St-Louis** fills six frantic days around 25 August with *joutes nautiques*, where participants in competing boats try to knock each other into the water.

Sleeping & Eating

Auberge de Jeunesse (☎ 04 67 53 46 68; fax 04 67 51 34 01; rue Général Revest; dm €9.30; ☼ Jan–mid-Dec) It's 1km northwest of the tourist office in rather glum former administrative buildings, but enjoys a lovely wooded site with great views over the town and harbour.

Hôtel la Conga (☎ 04 67 53 02 57; plage de la Corniche; d €25-40 Sep-Jun, €38-52 Jul-Aug) This pleasant hotel overlooks the beach, 2.25km west of the port area. You'll need to reserve at its

popular restaurant **La Table de Jean** (menus €12-25), justifiably famous for its fish dishes.

Le Chalut (☎ 04 67 74 81 52; 38 quai Maximin Licciardi; menus €14-30, mains €14-20; ☼ closed Wed Oct-Jun) Right on the quayside, this is a local favourite for Sètois delicacies. You can dine in the sober, wood-panelled interior or on the colourful terrace, which teeters just the right side of kitsch.

Les Demoiselles Dupuy (☎ 04 67 74 03 46; 4 quai Maximin Licciardi) This tiny, vital place is only four doors but half a world away from Le Chalut. Crowded, rough and ready, it serves up deliciously fresh seafood at economical prices in unpretentious surroundings.

Getting There & Away

Should you want to head across the Med, both Comanav and Comarit, a pair of Moroccan companies, run ferries to the port of Tangier (Tanger) from quai d'Alger about every four days. For tickets, schedules and information, consult agents **SNCM** (☎ 04 67 46 68 00; fax 04 67 74 93 05; 4 quai d'Alger).

AGDE
pop 22,300

Originally a Phoenician, then a Greek settlement at the mouth of the River Hérault, Agde (from *agathos*, Greek for 'good') is a picturesque fishing port with a small attractive inland old quarter. Make time for a short boat trip along the Canal du Midi, which joins the River Hérault just upstream from the old quarter. The tourist office sells tickets for both **Bateaux du Soleil** (☎ 04 67 94 08 79) and **Bateau Roussillon Languedoc** (☎ 04 67 01 71 93).

The **tourist office** (☎ 04 67 94 29 68; ☼ 9am-7pm Mon-Sat, 10am-1pm Sun Jul-Aug, 9am-noon & 2-6pm Mon-Sat Sep-Jun) is at 1 place Molière.

The dark grey basalt of older buildings, such as the fortress-like, mainly 12th-century **Cathédrale St-Étienne**, motivated Marco Polo to describe the town as the 'black pearl of the Mediterranean'.

Hôtel des Arcades (☎ 04 67 94 21 64; 16 rue Louis Bages; basic rooms €30, with shower €40, with bathroom €45) is an exceptionally friendly place occupying a former convent.

There are some attractive restaurants terraces stretch along the quayside. The fish couldn't be fresher at **Restaurant du Port** (☎ 04 67 94 97 58; 24 rue Chassefière; menu €12; ☼ lunch & dinner May-Sep, lunch only Oct-Apr), which has its own boat. It also does a vegetarian *menu* (€10).

Buses ply the 6km route at least hourly to the modern tourist resort of **Le Cap d'Agde**, famed for its long beaches and large nudist colony – a little township in itself with more than 20,000 bare bodies in high season.

BÉZIERS
pop 70,000

Béziers, first settled by the Phoenicians, became an important military post in Roman times. It was almost completely destroyed in 1209 during the Albigensian Crusade, when some 20,000 'heretics', many seeking refuge in the cathedral, were slaughtered. In happier times, the local tax collector Paul Riquet (1604–80) moved heaven and earth to build the Canal du Midi, a 240km-long marvel of engineering with its aqueducts and more than 100 locks, enabling cargo vessels to sail from the Atlantic to the Mediterranean without having to circumnavigate Spain. There's a fine statue to Béziers' most famous son on allées Jean-Jaurès, a wide, leafy esplanade at the heart of the town.

The **tourist office** (☎ 04 67 76 84 00; 29 av St-Saens; ☑ 9am-7pm Jul-Aug, 9am-noon & 2-6pm Mon-Sat Sep-Jun) is in the Palais des Congrès.

Fortified **Cathédrale St-Nazaire** (☑ 9am-noon & 2.30-5.30pm), surrounded by narrow alleys, is typical of the area, with massive towers, an imposing façade and a huge 14th-century rose window.

Musée du Biterrois (☎ 04 67 36 71 01; place St Jacques; adult/child €2.35/1.60; ☑ 10am-6pm Tue-Sun Jul-Aug, 9am-noon & 2-5pm or 6pm Tue-Sun Sep-Jun) is a well displayed and illuminated museum of the town's history, its largest sections devoted to Roman artefacts and wine-making.

As the wine capital of Languedoc, Béziers holds its grape harvest festival in October. Year-round, visit **Terroirs et Cépage** (av Président Wilson) for a little *dégustation* (tasting).

Popular annual events include the week-long **Festa d'Oc**, a celebration of Mediterranean music and dance, in late July, and the **féria** (bullfighting festival) in early August.

NARBONNE
pop 48,000

Once a coastal port but now a whole 13km inland because of silting-up, Narbonne in its time was capital of Gallia Narbonensis and one of the principal Roman cities in Gaul.

The **tourist office** (☎ 04 68 65 15 60; place Roger Salengro; ☑ 8.30am-7pm Mon-Sat, 9.30am-12.30pm Sun

Jun–mid-Sep; 8.30am-noon & 2-6pm Mon-Sat mid-Sep–May) is just northwest of the massive cathedral.

The splendid **Cathédrale St-Just** (entry on rue Armand Gauthier; ☑ 10am-7pm Jul-Sep, 9am-noon & 2-6pm Oct-Jun) is, in fact, no more than its towers and a soaring choir – at 41m, one of France's highest – construction having stopped in the early 14th century. The Notre Dame de Bethlehem ambulatory chapel has a haunting alabaster Virgin and Child and fine polychrome stone carving, although it is much knocked about. The **treasury** (admission €2.20) has a beautiful Flemish tapestry of the Creation while grotesque gargoyles peer down upon the 16th-century **cloister**.

Adjoining the cathedral to the south and facing place de l'Hôtel de Ville, the fortified **Palais des Archevêques** (Archbishops' Palace) includes the **Donjon Gilles Aycelin** (admission €2.20; ☑ 11am-6pm Jul-Sep, 9am-noon & 2-6pm Oct-Jun), a large, square 13th-century keep.

The **town hall**, with its mock-Renaissance 19th-century façade by Viollet-le-Duc, is home to Narbonne's **Musée d'Art** and **Musée Archéologique**, the latter with its impressive collection of Roman mosaics and paintings on stucco. Nearby is the **Horreum**, an underground gallery of Gallo-Roman shops. A combined ticket (adult/child €5.20/3.20) gives access to all three.

Take in too Narbonne's imposing Art Nouveau **covered market**, a colourful place to stock up on food and an architectural jewel in it own right.

Just off the A9, 15km south of Narbonne, is the **Réserve Africaine de Sigean** (☎ 04 68 48 20 20; adult/child €20/16; ☑ 9am-4.30pm up to 8pm according to season), where lions, tigers and other 'safari' specimens live in semi-liberty. If you arrive by bike or on foot, there's free – in a manner of speaking – transport around the reserve. From the A9, take exit 39.

CARCASSONNE
pop 46,250

From afar, Carcassonne looks like some fairy-tale medieval city. Bathed in late-afternoon sunshine and highlighted by dark clouds, La Cité, as the old walled city is known, is truly breathtaking.

Once you're inside the fortified walls, La Cité is far less magical. Luring more than two million visitors each year, it can be a tourist hell in high summer.

LANGUEDOC-ROUSSILLON

CARCASSONNE

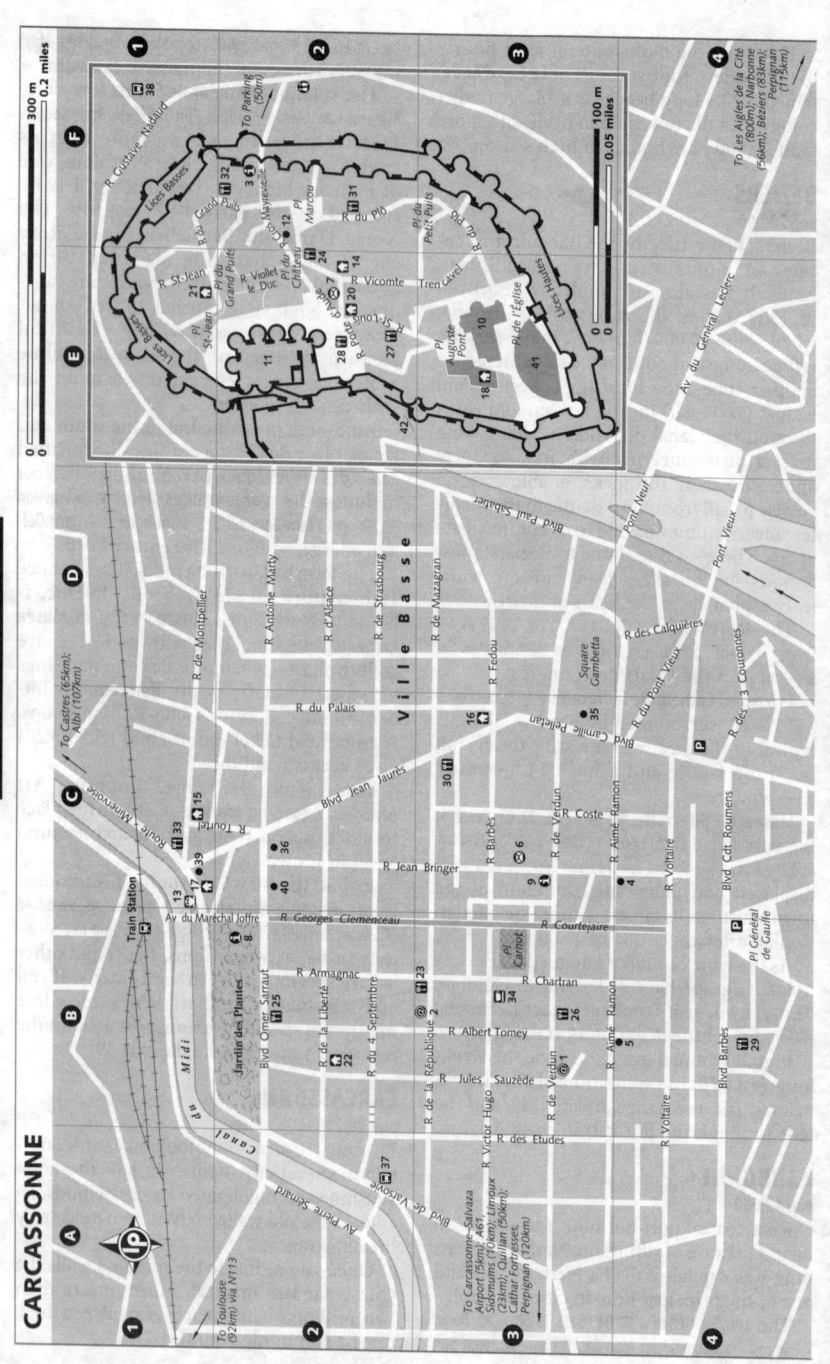

To Toulouse
(92km) via N113

To Castres (65km);
Albi (107km)

To Carcassonne-Salvaza
Airport (5km); Aragon (12km);
Sidobrun (30km); Limoux
(23km); Quillan (50km);
Cathar Fortresses;
Perpignan (120km)

To les Aigles de la Cité
(800m); Narbonne
(56km); Béziers (83km);
Perpignan
(115km)

Canal du Midi

Train Station

Jardin des Plantes

Ville Basse

Pl Carnot

Pl Gambetta

Square
Gambetta

Pont Neuf

Pont Vieux

R de Montpellier
R Antoine Marty
R d'Alsace
R de Strasbourg
R de Mazagran
R Fedou
R des Calquières
R du Pont Vieux
R des 3 Couronnés
Av du Général Leclerc
Blvd Paul Sabatier

R du Palais
Blvd Camille Pelletan
Bvd Jean Jaurès
R du Tourel
R de Verdun
R Coste
R Barbès
R Aimé Ramon
R Voltaire
Blvd Cdt Roumens
Pl Général
de Gaulle

R Jean Bringer
R Georges Clemenceau
R Courtejaire
R Chartran
R Armagnac
Av du Maréchal Joffre
Blvd Omer Sarraut
R de la Liberté
R du 4 Septembre
R de la République
R Albert Tomey
R Jules Sauzède
R Victor Hugo
R de Verdun
R des Études
R Voltaire
R Aimé Ramon
Blvd Barbès
Pl Carnot

Av Pierre Semard
Blvd de Varsovie

Route de Minervoire

Lices Basses
R Gustave Nadaud
R de la Grand Puits
R du Grand Puits
R St-Jean
Pl St-Jean
R Viollet le Duc
Dos Maisonnette
Porte
Narbonnaise
R Vicomte
R St-Louis
Pl Marcou
R du Plô
Pl du
Petit Puits
R du Petit Puits
Lices Hautes
Tren Cavel
Pl
Auguste Pont
R de l'Église

To Parking
(50m)

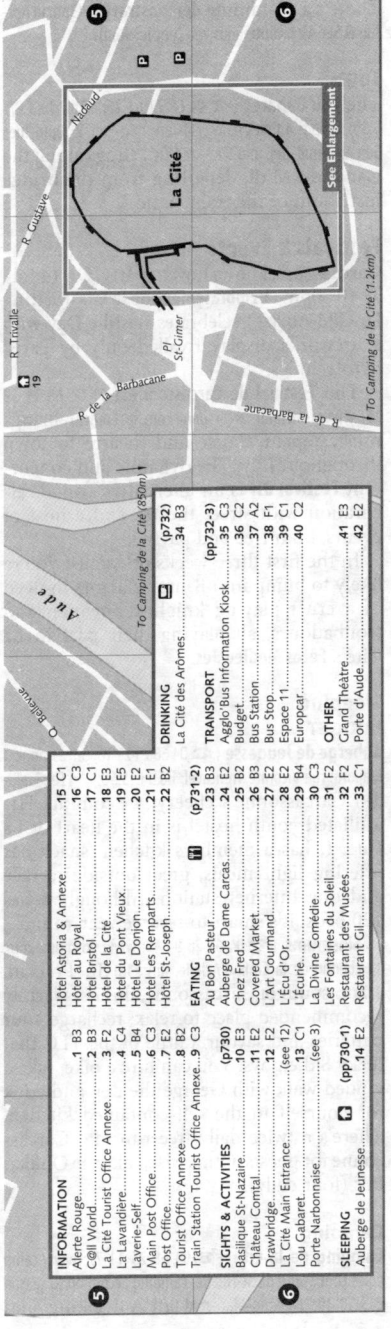

Today's city walls are but the last in a line of fortifications built by Gauls, Romans, Visigoths, Moors and Franks. In the 13th century, they protected one of the major Cathar strongholds (see p756). After 1659, when Roussillon was annexed to France, Carcassonne, no longer a frontier town, began its slow decline. By the 19th century La Cité was 'little more than a slum' and only the elaborate intervention of Viollet-le-Duc, the influential but controversial to this day 19th-century restorer, who, in addition to reworking Carcassonne, also profoundly changed, for example, the cathedrals of Notre Dame in Paris and Vézelay in the Massif Central – prevented the remaining fortifications from just tumbling away.

Carcassonne is not just La Cité, however. The Ville Basse (Lower Town), established in the 13th century and a more modest stepsister to camp Cinderella up the hill, also merits a browse.

Orientation

The River Aude separates the Ville Basse from the Cité, up on a hill 500m southeast. Pedestrianised rue Georges Clemenceau leads from the train station and Canal du Midi southwards through the heart of the lower town.

Information

INTERNET ACCESS

Alerte Rouge (73 rue de Verdun; per hr €4; ☘ 10am-11pm Mon-Sat, 1-8pm Sun)
C@ll World (32 rue de la République; per hr €3.50; ☘ 10am-11pm Mon-Sat, 2-11pm Sun)

LAUNDRY

La Lavandière (31 rue Aimé Ramon; ☘ 8am-7pm Mon-Sat)
Laverie-Self (63 rue Aimé Ramon; ☘ 7am-9pm)

POST

Main Post Office (40 rue Jean Bringer, Ville Basse)
Post Office (rue Porte d'Aude, La Cité)

TOURIST INFORMATION

La Cité Tourist Office Annexe (Porte Narbonnaise; ☘ 9am-5pm or 7pm according to season)
Main Tourist Office (☎ 04 68 10 24 30; www.carcassonne-tourisme.com; 28 rue de Verdun; ☘ 9am-7pm Jul-Aug, 9am-6pm Sep-Jun)
Train Station Tourist Office Annexe (av du Maréchal Joffre; ☘ Apr-Oct) Kiosk just south of the train station.

LANGUEDOC-ROUSSILLON

INFORMATION
Alerte Rouge.....................................1	B3
C@ll World..2	B3
La Cité Tourist Office Annexe..........3	F2
La Lavandière...................................4	C4
Laverie-Self......................................5	B4
Main Post Office...............................6	C3
Post Office.......................................7	E2
Tourist Office Annexe.......................8	B2
Train Station Tourist Office Annexe...9	C3

SIGHTS & ACTIVITIES (p730)
Basilique St-Nazaire.......................10	E2
Château Comtal.............................11	E2
Drawbridge...........................(see 12)	
La Cité Main Entrance....................12	F2
Lou Gabaret...................................13	C1
Porte Narbonnaise................(see 3)	

SLEEPING (pp730-1)
Auberge de Jeunesse......................14	E2
Hôtel Astoria & Annexe..................15	C1
Hôtel au Royal...............................16	C3
Hôtel Bristol..................................17	C1
Hôtel de la Cité..............................18	E3
Hôtel du Pont Vieux.......................19	E5
Hôtel Le Donjon.............................20	E2
Hôtel Les Remparts........................21	E1
Hôtel St-Joseph..............................22	B2

EATING (p731-2)
Au Bon Pasteur..............................23	B3
Auberge de Dame Carcas...............24	E2
Chez Fred......................................25	B2
Covered Market.............................26	B3
L'Art Gourmand.............................27	E2
L'Écu d'Or.....................................28	E2
L'Écurie..29	B4
La Divine Comédie.........................30	C3
Les Fontaines du Soleil...................31	F2
Restaurant des Musées...................32	F2
Restaurant Gil................................33	C1

DRINKING
La Cité des Arômes.........................34	B3

TRANSPORT (pp732-3)
Agglo'Bus Information Kiosk...........35	C3
Budget..36	C3
Bus Station....................................37	A2
Bus Stop.......................................38	F1
Espace 11.......................................39	C1
Europcar.......................................40	C2

OTHER
Grand Théâtre................................41	E3
Porte d'Aude..................................42	E2

Sights
LA CITÉ
Just beside the main entrance to La Cité, a magnificent reconditioned 19th-century merry-go-round (carousel) gyrates to old Julie Andrews numbers. It's emblematic of the blend of tack and charm within.

La Cité, dramatically illuminated at night and enclosed by two rampart walls punctuated by 52 stone towers, is one of Europe's largest city fortifications. But only the lower sections of the walls are original; the rest, including the anachronistic witches'-hat roofs (the originals were altogether flatter and weren't covered with slate), were stuck on by Viollet-le-Duc in the 19th century.

From square Gambetta, it's an attractive walk to La Cité across Pont Vieux, along rue de la Barbacane, then up and in through Porte d'Aude. Catching a bus is also an option (p732).

If you pass over the drawbridge and through the main entrance, you're faced with a massive bastion, the **Porte Narbonnaise** and, just inside, the tourist office annexe. Rue Cros Mayrevieille, suffocating in kitschy souvenir shops, leads up to place du Château, heart of La Cité.

Through another archway and across a second dry moat is the 12th-century **Château Comtal** (adult/student/under 18 €6.10/4.10/free; ⏱ 9.30am-6.30pm Apr-Sep, 9.30am-5pm Oct-Mar). The entrance fee lets you visit the castle itself and also join a 30 to 40-minute guided tour of both castle and ramparts. You may have to wait some time until a critical mass of visitors assembles and the quality of the guiding is variable.

South of place du Château is **Basilique St-Nazaire**. Highlights are the graceful Gothic transept arms with a pair of superb 13th- and 14th-century rose windows at each end.

There's numerous hole-in-the-wall private museums and initiatives, each eager to separate you from your money and including Memories of the Middle Ages, a Schooldays Museum, the Haunted House – and a particularly repellent exhibition of replica medieval torture instruments. All are very resistible.

FALCONRY
Birds of prey dive and swoop at **Les Aigles de la Cité** (☎ 04 68 47 88 99; adult/child €8/5; ⏱ from 2.30pm Apr-Oct), 800m south of the Cité walls.

There's a 45-minute **demonstration** (3pm in Apr-Jun & Sep-Oct, continuously 3-7pm Jul-Aug).

Tours
The **Lou Gabaret** (☎ 04 68 71 61 26; adult/child €7/5.50; sailings 4 times daily mid-Jun–mid-Sep, 2.30pm Tue-Sun Apr–mid-Jun, mid-Sep–mid-Oct) chugs along the Canal du Midi, departing from the bridge just south of the train station.

Festivals & Events
Carcassonne knows how to party. On 14 July at 10.30pm, **L'Embrasement de la Cité** (Setting La Cité Ablaze) celebrates Bastille Day with a fireworks display rivalled only by Paris' pyrotechnics.

The **Festival de Carcassonne** (☎ 04 68 11 59 15; www.festivaldecarcassonne.com in French) brings music, opera, dance and theatre to town throughout July. The dynamic and concurrent **Festival Off** is an alternative fringe celebration with street theatre and a host of events, both free and paying.

In the first three weeks of August you're likely to bump into B-movie actors in need of a crust playing knights, bowmen and troubadours, all playing their part in La Cité's **Fêtes Médiévales**.

Sleeping
BUDGET
Auberge de Jeunesse (☎ 04 68 25 23 16; carcassonne@fuaj.org; rue Vicomte Trencavel; B&B €15.50; ⏱ Feb–mid-Dec) Carcassonne's cheery, welcoming, HI-affiliated youth hostel is in the heart of La Cité. It has a members kitchen, snack bar offering light meals, great outside terrace and one Internet station. Although it has 120 beds, it's smart to reserve year-round.

Sidsmums (☎ 04 68 26 94 49; www.sidsmums.com; 11 chemin de la Croix d'Achille; dm €18) In Preixan, 10km south of Carcassonne, this is a warmly recommended place to relax, recharge your batteries and savour a little of the TLC that lucky Sid enjoys. You can hire a bike, take a guided walk with George the dog and cook for yourself in the self-contained kitchen. There's a twice daily free run into Carcassonne for guests. Otherwise, take the Quillan bus (four daily).

Camping
Camping de la Cité (☎ 04 68 25 11 77; www.campeoles.com; route de St-Hilaire; camping according to season €13.50-19; ⏱ mid-Mar–mid-Oct) A walking and

cycling trail leads from the site to both La Cité and the Ville Basse. From mid-June to mid-September, bus No 8 connects the camping ground with La Cité and the train station.

MID-RANGE – VILLE BASSE

Hôtel Astoria (☎ 04 68 25 31 38; hotel-astoria@wanadoo .fr; 18 rue Tourtel; d €20, with shower €29, with bathroom €32-36; **P**) New owners have repainted all rooms and laid fresh tiles or parquet at this hotel and its equally agreeable annexe. Bathrooms are a bit pokey but all in all it's a welcoming place that offers good value. Parking is free.

Hôtel St-Joseph (☎ 04 68 71 96 89; hotel.saint joseph@wanadoo.fr; 81 rue de la Liberté; d €35-42; **P**) A statue of the eponymous saint guards the entrance to this trim hotel, popular with cyclists riding the Canal du Midi towpath and with itinerant railway staff. The most pleasant rooms have been recently renovated in attractive blue and ochre.

Hôtel Bristol (☎ 04 68 25 07 24; hotel.bristol11@ wanadoo.fr; 7 av du Maréchal Foch; s €54-65, d €65-80; 🅨 Mar-Nov) A plaster horse's head peers down, indicating that this 19th-century inn was in its time a staging post. Choose between a room overlooking the Canal du Midi or one giving onto the quiet inner courtyard.

Hôtel du Pont Vieux (☎ 04 68 25 24 99; www .hoteldupontvieux.com; 32 rue Trivalle; d mid-Aug–mid-Jul €45-77, mid-Jul–mid-Aug €89-119; **P** 🔀) Most bedrooms, with attractively rough-hewn walls, have a bathtub. Those overlooking the large, peaceful garden have air-con while ones overlooking the street are double glazed. On the third floor are rooms 18 and 19, each with unsurpassed views of the Cité, and a small terrace, accessible to all guests. A truly gargantuan buffet breakfast (€7) is laid on.

Hôtel au Royal (☎ 04 68 25 19 12; godartcl@wanadoo .fr; 22 blvd Jean Jaurès; d €36-65; 🅨 Jan-Nov; **P**) At this attractive mid-range option too, you're guaranteed a copious, varied breakfast. Rooms are comfortable, well appointed and equipped with ceiling fans and those facing the busy street all have double glazing.

MID-RANGE – LA CITÉ

Hôtel Le Donjon et Les Remparts (☎ 04 68 11 23 00; www.hotel-donjon.fr; 2 rue du Comte Roger; d €74-145; **P** 🔀 🔀 🖵) Low-beamed, thick-walled and cosy, Le Donjon makes a most attractive top-end option with rooms overlooking

either the ramparts or its shady garden. Les Remparts, effectively its annexe (you check in at Le Donjon), is equally comfortable but shorter on charm – as, it must be said, is the madame at reception.

Hôtel de la Cité (☎ 04 68 71 98 71; www.hotelde lacite.orient-express.com; place Auguste Pont; d €250-550; 🅨 mid-Jan–Nov; **P** 🔀 🛋) Hôtel de la Cité has rooms fit for royalty (literally so: 'A favourite hideaway for Europe's crowned heads, film stars, writers and intellectuals,' proclaims its glossy brochure), should you fancy a retreat in such august company.

Eating

Even if it's a boiling summer's day, don't leave town without trying cassoulet, a piping hot dish blending white beans, juicy pork cubes, even bigger cylinders of meaty sausage and, in the most popular local variant, a hunk of duck.

VILLE BASSE

Au Bon Pasteur (☎ 04 68 25 49 63; 29 rue Armagnac; menus €13-22; 🅨 closed Sun & Mon Jul-Aug, Sun & Wed Sep-Jun) At this welcoming, intimate family restaurant, where the simple wooden tables and chairs belie the sophistication of the cooking, you can warm yourself in winter with the yummy cassoulet or *choucroute* (sauerkraut), 100% authentic since the chef hails from Alsace. Year-round, their *menu classique* (€13) and *formules de midi* (lunch specials; €9.50 to €11) both represent excellent value.

Chez Fred (☎ 04 68 72 02 23; 31 blvd Omer Sarraut; menus €18-27; 🅨 closed lunch Wed & Sat year-round, dinner Tue Sep-Jun) With its all-orange interior and pleated drapes, Chez Fred recalls a bordello while its large protected outdoor terrace makes for pleasant summer dining. The cooking has a marked Andalucian touch and its weekday lunchtime *menu bistro* (€12) is especially worthwhile.

La Divine Comédie (☎ 04 68 72 30 36; 29 blvd Jean Jaurès; pizzas €8-9.50, mains €12.50-14.50; 🅨 Mon-Sat) Beside Hôtel Central, this restaurant serves both pizzas and regional dishes on its pleasant outside terrace.

Restaurant Gil (☎ 04 68 47 85 23; 32 route Minervoise; menus €15-33, mains €9-19) Here, you'll enjoy quality, Catalan-influenced cuisine. Its particular strength is the sheer quality of its fresh sea food and fish dishes (€10 to €15), mostly served grilled and unsmothered by superfluous sauces or adornment.

L'Écurie (☎ 04 68 72 04 04; 43 blvd Barbès; menus €22-28; ☺ closed Wed & dinner Sun) Enjoy fine fare either within this attractively renovated 18th-century stable, all polished woodwork, brass and leather, or in the large, shaded garden. Pick from its long, carefully selected list of local wines.

LA CITÉ
Place Marcou is hemmed in on three sides by eateries and every second building in La Cité seems to be a café or restaurant. For those we recommend, it's wise to reserve, particularly for lunch.

Restaurant des Musées (☎ 06 17 05 24 90; 17 rue du Grand Puits) This simple unpretentious place has three rear terraces with views of the ramparts, bakes its own organic bread and offers excellent value meals, including a couple of vegetarian *menus* (€8.50). Although they don't serve alcohol, you can bring in a bottle from the excellent wine shop next door and there's no corkage charge.

Auberge de Dame Carcas (☎ 04 68 71 23 23; 3 place du Château; menus €14 & €24; ☺ Thu-Tue Feb-Dec) This casual place specialises in pork products (model piggies, large and small, displayed all around the restaurant give you a clue) and carries a fine selection of well-priced local wines. Downstairs is cosy and agreeably rustic and you can see the chefs at work while the larger upstairs room offers more light.

Les Fontaines du Soleil (☎ 04 68 47 87 06; 32 rue du Plô; menus €17-45) Seek out this restaurant, just off crowded place Marcou. With its shady terrace, attractive interior and great cooking, it has tempting *menus* to suit every pocket.

L'Écu d'Or (☎ 04 68 25 49 03; 7-9 rue Porte d'Aude; menus €20-32) This stylish place serves, among many other delightful dishes, six varieties of cassoulet and a delicious range of creative desserts.

SELF-CATERING
There's a **covered market** (rue du Verdun; ☺ Mon-Sat) and an **open-air market** (place Carnot; ☺ Tue, Thu & Sat). Chocolate fiends should head straight for the irresistible **L'Art Gourmand** (13 rue St-Louis), which sells a creative range of calorie-laced goodies. The ice cream is pretty great too – all 33 varieties of it.

Drinking
Cafés overlooking place Carnot in the Ville Basse spill onto the square in summer. In the northwestern corner, **La Cité des Arômes** indeed wafts out scents of rich *arabica* and carries a huge selection of coffees.

In La Cité, place Marcou is one big outside café.

Getting There & Away
AIR
Carcassonne-Salvaza airport (☎ 04 68 71 96 46), 5km from town, has precisely two flights daily – **Ryanair** (☎ 04 68 71 96 65) services to/from London (Stansted) and to/from Brussels (Charleroi).

BUS
We can only reiterate the advice of the tourist office: take the train. Eurolines and such intercity buses as there are stop on blvd de Varsovie, 500m southwest of the train station.

TRAIN
Carcassonne is on the main line linking Toulouse (€12.10, 50 minutes, frequent) with Narbonne (€8.60, 30 to 45 minutes), Béziers (€11.50, 50 minutes) and Montpellier (€18.90, 1½ hours). For Perpignan (€15.60), change in Narbonne.

Getting Around
TO THE AIRPORT
Agglo'Bus No 7 runs to/from the airport (€5, 20 minutes), leaving square Gambetta 90 minutes before each Ryanair departure. By car, take the Carcassonne Ouest A61 motorway exit.

BICYCLE
You can rent mountain bikes at **Espace 11** (☎ 04 68 25 28 18; 3 route Minervoise; 1 day/3 days/week €13/35/61; ☺ Tue-Sat).

CAR & MOTORCYCLE
Europcar (☎ 04 68 25 05 09; 7 blvd Omer Sarraut) and **Budget** (☎ 04 68 72 31 31; 5 blvd Omer Sarraut) are both a two-minute walk from the train station.

Cars are forbidden in La Cité during the day. Leave your vehicle in the huge car park (€3.50/5 cars/camper vans) just east of the main entrance.

PUBLIC TRANSPORT
Agglo'Bus, the city bus company, has an **information kiosk** (☎ 04 68 47 82 22; square Gambetta). Buses run until about 7pm from Monday

to Saturday. A single ticket/10-ticket *carnet* costs €0.90/6.90.

Bus No 2 runs about every 40 minutes from the Ville Basse to La Cité's main entrance. From mid-July to mid-August, a free **navette** (shuttle service; every 15 min, 9.30am-7.30pm Mon-Sat) plies between La Cité, square Gambetta and place Carnot.

TAXI
Ring ☎ 04 68 71 50 50.

NÎMES
pop 134,000
Nîmes, encircled by vineyards, *garrigue* (scrub), headily scented rosemary, lavender and thyme, is a little bit Provençal but with a soul as Languedocien as *cassoulet*. It's graced by some of France's best-preserved Roman buildings. Founded by Emperor Augustus, the Roman Colonia Nemausensis reached its zenith in the 2nd century AD, receiving its water from a Roman aqueduct system that included the Pont du Gard, a magnificent arched bridge 23km northeast of town (p738). The sacking of the city by Vandals in the early 5th century began a downwards spiral from which it never quite recovered. Mind you, lazy, laid-back Nîmes does get more than 300 days of sunshine every year.

DENIM DE NÎMES

During the 18th century, Nîmes' sizable Protestant middle class – banned from government posts and various other ways of earning a living – turned its energies to trade and manufacturing. Among the products of Protestant-owned factories was a twilled fabric known as *serge*. Soft yet durable, it became very popular among workers and, stained blue, was the uniform of the fishermen of Genoa.

When a Bavarian-Jewish immigrant to the USA, Levi Strauss (1829–1902), began to make trousers in California during the 1849 gold rush, he soon realised that the miners needed garments that would last. After trying tent canvas, he began importing *serge de Nîmes*, now better known as denim.

Orientation
Almost everything, including traffic, revolves around Les Arènes, the roman am-

phitheatre. North of here, the fan-shaped, largely pedestrianised old city is bounded by blvd Victor Hugo, blvd Amiral Courbet and blvd Gambetta. The main squares are place de la Maison Carrée, place du Marché and place aux Herbes.

Information
INTERNET ACCESS
@dd-on System (11 rue Nationale; per hr €3; ☒ 11am-midnight Mon-Fri, 11am-2am Sat)
PC Gamer (2 rue Nationale; per hr €2.50; ☒ 9.30am-1am)

LAUNDRY
There are laundrettes at 14 rue Nationale (open 7am to 9pm) and 24 rue Porte de France (8am to 8pm).

POST
Post Office (blvd de Bruxelles)

TOURIST INFORMATION
Tourist Office (☎ 04 66 58 38 00; www.ot-nimes.fr; 6 rue Auguste; ☒ 8am-8pm Mon-Fri Jul & Aug, 8.30am-7pm Mon-Fri Sep-Jun, plus 9am-7pm Sat & 10am-5pm Sun year-round)
Maison du Tourisme (☎ 04 66 36 96 30; www.cdt-gard.fr; 3 place des Arènes; ☒ 8am-7pm Jul & Aug Mon-Fri, 8.45am-6pm Mon-Fri Sep-Jun, plus 9.30am-noon Sat year-round). For information about the Gard *département*.

Sights
LES ARÈNES
The superb Roman amphitheatre **Les Arènes** (adult/child €4.65/3.40; ☒ 9am-7pm mid-Mar–mid-Oct, 10am-5pm mid-Oct–mid-Mar), built around AD 100 to seat 24,000 spectators, is wonderfully preserved, even retaining its upper storey, unlike its counterpart in Arles. The interior has a system of exits and passages (called, engagingly, *vomitories*), designed so that patricians attending animal and gladiator combats never had to rub shoulders with the plebs up top.

Covered by a removable roof in winter, Les Arènes lives on as a frequent sporting and cultural venue – an excellent thing in itself though the scaffolding and temporary barriers do detract from its appeal as a historical site. Buy your ticket at the reception point, tucked into its northern walls.

MAISON CARRÉE
The **Maison Carrée** (Square House; admission free; ☒ as Les Arènes) is a remarkably preserved

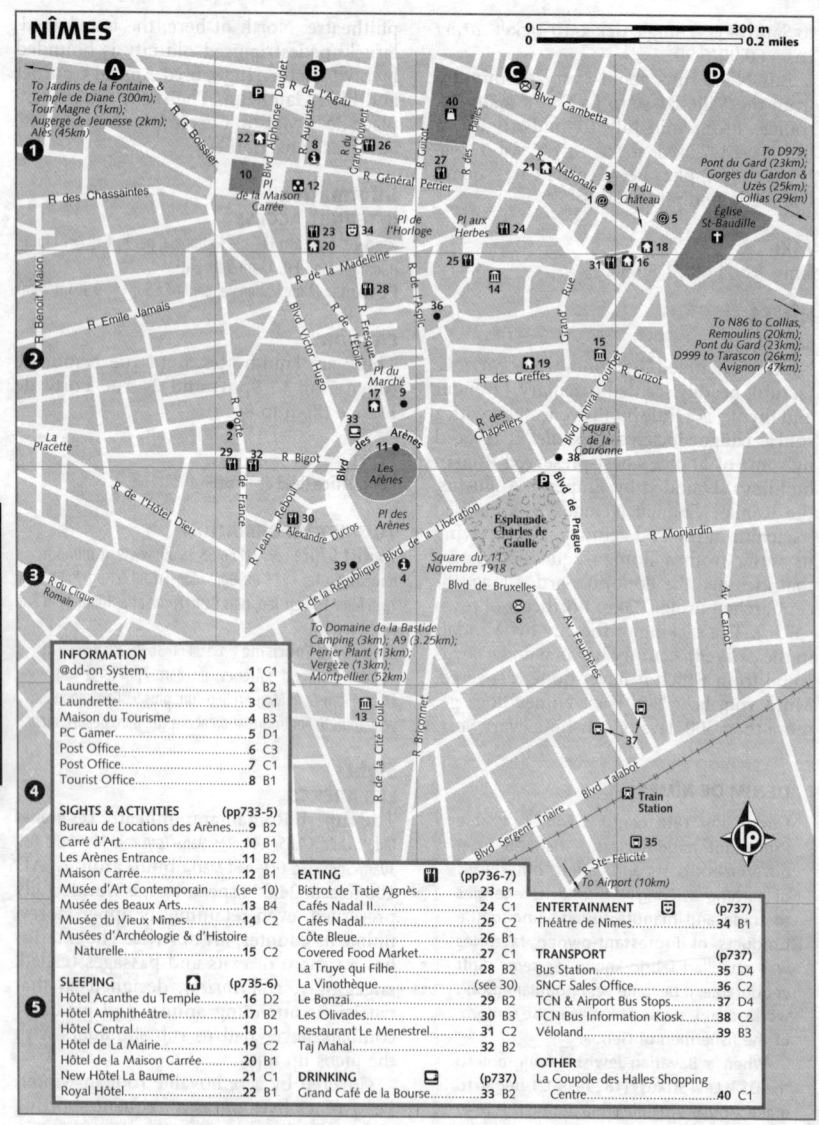

NÎMES

To Jardins de la Fontaine &
Temple de Diane (300m);
Tour Magne (1km);
Auberge de Jeunesse (2km);
Alès (45km)

To D979;
Pont du Gard (23km);
Gorges du Gardon &
Uzès (25km);
Collias (29km)

To N86 to Collias,
Remoulins (20km);
Pont du Gard (23km);
D999 to Tarascon (26km);
Avignon (47km)

To Domaine de la Bastide
Camping (3km); A9 (3.25km);
Perrier Plant (13km);
Vergèze (13km);
Montpellier (52km)

Les Arènes

Esplanade
Charles de
Gaulle

To Airport (10km)

Train
Station

INFORMATION

@dd-on System	1 C1
Laundrette	2 B2
Laundrette	3 C1
Maison du Tourisme	4 B3
PC Gamer	5 D1
Post Office	6 C3
Post Office	7 C1
Tourist Office	8 B1

SIGHTS & ACTIVITIES (pp733-5)

Bureau de Locations des Arènes	9 B2
Carré d'Art	10 B1
Les Arènes Entrance	11 B2
Maison Carrée	12 B1
Musée d'Art Contemporain	(see 10)
Musée des Beaux Arts	13 B4
Musée du Vieux Nîmes	14 C2
Musées d'Archéologie & d'Histoire Naturelle	15 C2

SLEEPING (p735-6)

Hôtel Acanthe du Temple	16 D2
Hôtel Amphithéâtre	17 B2
Hôtel Central	18 D1
Hôtel de La Mairie	19 C2
Hôtel de la Maison Carrée	20 B1
New Hôtel La Baume	21 C1
Royal Hôtel	22 B1

EATING (pp736-7)

Bistrot de Tatie Agnès	23 B1
Cafés Nadal II	24 C1
Cafés Nadal	25 C2
Côte Bleue	26 B1
Covered Food Market	27 C1
La Truye qui Filhe	28 B2
La Vinothèque	(see 30)
Le Bonzai	29 B2
Les Olivades	30 B3
Restaurant Le Menestrel	31 C2
Taj Mahal	32 B2

DRINKING (p737)

Grand Café de la Bourse	33 B2

ENTERTAINMENT (p737)

Théâtre de Nîmes	34 B1

TRANSPORT (p737)

Bus Station	35 D4
SNCF Sales Office	36 C2
TCN & Airport Bus Stops	37 D4
TCN Bus Information Kiosk	38 C2
Véloland	39 B3

OTHER

La Coupole des Halles Shopping Centre	40 C1

---

rectangular Roman temple that was constructed around AD 5 to honour Emperor Augustus' two adopted sons. It has survived the centuries as a medieval meeting hall, private residence, stable, church and, after the Revolution, archive.

The striking glass and steel building across the square, completed in 1993, is the **Carré d'Art** (Square of Art), which houses the municipal library and Musée d'Art Contemporain (opposite). The work of British architect Sir Norman Foster, it harmonises well with the Maison Carrée and is everything modern architecture should be: innovative, complementary and beautiful – a wonderful, airy building just to float around.

NÎMES DISCOUNT PASSES

A **combination ticket** (adult/child €5.70/4.65) admits you to both Les Arènes and Tour Magne. Alternatively, pick up a **three-day pass** (adult/child €10/5), giving access to all of Nîmes' museums and sites, from the tourist office or the first place you visit.

JARDINS DE LA FONTAINE

The elegant Fountain Gardens are enriched by Nîmes' other major Roman monuments. Statue-adorned paths run around inky waterways. The **Source de la Fontaine** was the site of a spring, temple and baths in Roman times. The **Temple de Diane** – 'it is strictly forbidden to escalade this monument,' says the sign in quaint near-English – is left (west) through the main entrance.

A 10- to 15-minute uphill walk brings you to the crumbling shell of the 30m high **Tour Magne** (adult/child €2.50/2; ☻ as for Les Arènes), raised around 15 BC and the largest of a chain of towers that once ran along the city's 7km-long Roman ramparts. From here, there's a magnificent view of Nîmes and the surrounding countryside.

MUSEUMS

Each of Nîmes' **museums** (☻ 10am-6pm Tue-Sun) follows a common timetable. Most are in sore need of a new broom.

Musée du Vieux Nîmes (place aux Herbes; admission free), in the 17th-century episcopal palace, is a small, eccentric museum; one room showcases denim, with smiling pin-ups of Elvis, James Dean and Marilyn Monroe, while two others are devoted entirely to what must be the world's largest – perhaps only? – collection of domestic graters and mincers.

Musée d'Archéologie (13 blvd Amiral Courbet; admission free) brings together some interesting Roman and pre-Roman artefacts unearthed around Nîmes. However, too many exhibits bear nothing more than a peeling paper label with an enigmatic number. The museum also houses a hotchpotch of artefacts from Africa, piled high and tagged with yellowing captions such as 'Abyssinia' and 'Dahomey'. In the same building, **Musée d'Histoire Naturelle** has a musty collection of stuffed animals gazing bleakly out. Only the custodians, protected from importunate visitors inside their own glass case, have life.

Musée des Beaux-Arts (rue de la Cité Foulc; adult/child €4.65/3.40) has a wonderfully preserved Roman mosaic (look down upon it from the first floor). This apart, it houses a fairly pedestrian collection of Flemish, Italian and French works.

The refreshing **Musée d'Art Contemporain** (adult/child €4.65/3.40) in the Carré d'Art makes a welcome contrast. Housing both permanent and rotating exhibitions of modern art, it merits a visit, even if only to prowl the innards of this striking building.

Tours

The tourist office runs two-hour French-language city tours (€5.50) at 10am on Tuesday, Thursday and Saturday in summer, and 2.30pm on Saturday the rest of the year.

Taxi TRAN (☎ 04 66 29 40 11) offers a one-hour tour of the city (€25 to €30 for up to six people) with a cassette commentary in English. Enquire at the tourist office.

Festivals & Events

July and August bring forth an abundance of dance, theatre, rock, pop and jazz events. The tourist office produces *Festivités à Nîmes*, a free annual calendar of events.

FÉRIAS & BULLFIGHTS

Nîmes becomes more Spanish than French during its *férias*. Each – the three-day **Féria Primavera** (Spring Festival) in February, the five-day **Féria de Pentecôte** (Whitsuntide Festival) in June, and the three-day **Féria des Vendanges** coinciding with the grape harvest on the third weekend in September – is marked by daily *corridas* (bullfights). The **Bureau de Locations des Arènes** (☎ 04 66 02 80 90; 2 rue de la Violette) sells tickets.

JEUDIS DE NÎMES

Every Thursday between 6pm and 10.30pm in July and August, artists, artisans and vendors of local food specialities take over the main squares of central Nîmes.

Sleeping

During Nîmes' *férias*, many hotels raise their prices and accommodation can be hard to find.

BUDGET

Auberge de Jeunesse (☎ 04 66 68 03 20; nimes@fuaj .org; 257 chemin de l'Auberge de Jeunesse, la Cigale; dm incl breakfast €13.25) Freshly and comprehensively renovated, it's in a lovely park 3.5km north-west of the train station. Take bus No 2, direction Alès or Villeverte, and get off at the Stade stop.

Hôtel de La Mairie (☎ 04 66 67 65 91; fax 04 66 76 07 92; 11 rue des Greffes; s with washbasin €23, with shower €30, d with bathroom €39-42; ☿ closed 15-31 Oct) Several rooms in this hyperfriendly two-star, 13-room hotel have separate toilets. Ceilings are high and rooms cool, even in high summer. To watch the world go by in the quiet street below, ask for room 3 with its tiny balcony.

Hôtel de la Maison Carrée (☎ 04 66 67 32 89; fax 04 66 76 22 57; 14 rue de la Maison Carrée; s €35, d €45) This hotel has recently changed hands. Long popular as a budget venue, its new owner is slowly pulling it more into the medium-range bracket and upgrading its facilities.

Hôtel Central (☎ 04 66 67 27 75; www.hotel-central.org; 2 place du Château; basic s €30, d with bathroom €45; P) With its creaky floorboards and bunches of wild flowers painted on each bedroom door, this hotel is full of character. Garage parking costs €6.50.

Hôtel Acanthe du Temple (☎ 04 66 67 54 61; www.hotel-du-temple.com in French; 1 rue Charles Babut; P ☒) Just opposite the Central, it has spick-and-span rooms, even if some of the wallpaper (different in every room) might induce biliousness. Room and garage prices are – more than coincidentally – within a couple of euros of its neighbours. All rooms have fans, some have separate toilets and a few are non-smoking.

Camping
Camping Domaine de la Bastide (☎ /fax 04 66 38 09 21; camping €11.85; ☿ year-round) is 4km south of town on the D13. Take bus D and get off at La Bastide, the terminus.

MID-RANGE & TOP END
Hôtel Amphithéâtre (☎ 04 66 67 28 51; hotel-amphitheatre@wanadoo.fr; 4 rue des Arènes; s €37-40, d €47-59; ☿ Feb-Dec; ☒ ☒) The welcoming Amphithéâtre, once a pair of 18th-century mansions, has recently been taken over by a young family. Rooms are decorated in warm, woody colours and named after writers or painters; we suggest dipping into Montesquieu or Arrabal (€59), both large and with a balcony overlooking pedestrian place du Marché. Some are non-smoking, most have a bathtub and those on the third floor have air-con.

Royal Hôtel (☎ 04 66 58 28 27; fax 04 66 58 28 28; 3 blvd Alphonse Daudet; s/d with shower €46/62, s with bathroom €51-66, d €67-87) With canvases just about everywhere, the huge dove cage beside reception and the local intelligentsia discoursing over coffee in **La Bodeguita** (☿ 6pm-late Mon-Sat), its very Spanish café, it's evident that *la patronne* is herself an artist. Rooms, all with ceiling fan and most with bathtubs are comfortable and furnished with flair. Some overlook pedestrian place d'Assas; fine for the view though the noise might be intrusive on summer nights.

New Hôtel La Baume (☎ 04 66 76 28 42; www.new-hotel.com; 21 rue Nationale; s/d €95/120; ☒ ☒ ▣) In fact far from new, this 34-room hotel occupies an attractive 17th-century town mansion with a glorious interior courtyard and has every comfort, though you may find it a little short on human warmth.

Eating
Nîmes' gastronomy owes as much to Provence as it does to Languedoc. Spicy southern delights, such as aïoli, rouille, are as abundant in this city as cassoulet. Sample the Costières de Nîmes wines from the pebbly vineyards to the south. If you're teetotal, your water couldn't come fresher: Perrier, the famous fizzy French mineral water, comes from nearby Vergèze (opposite).

La Truye qui Filhe (☎ 04 66 21 76 33; 9 rue Fresque; menu €8.70; ☿ noon-2pm Mon-Sat, closed Aug) Within the vaults of a restored 14th-century inn, this, the bargain of Nîmes, blends a self-service format with a homely atmosphere and does a superb-value *menu* that changes daily.

Bistrot de Tatie Agnès (☎ 04 66 21 00 81; 16 rue de la Maison Carrée; ☿ lunch only, Mon-Sat, closed 1-21 Aug) The toasted sandwiches (€7.50) at this recommended lunch spot are as original as its name and you can make a meal out of the giant salads (€7.50 to €8.50).

Côte Bleue (☎ 04 66 67 36 12; rue du Grand Couvent; menus €7.50 & 13, mains €9-11.50; ☿ Mon-Sat Jun-Sep, lunch only Oct-May) Decked in attractive Provençal blues and deep yellows, tiny and bustling, this intimate place is as attractive inside as on its summer terrace. Save a cranny for the *gâteau de marrons et noix*, a dessert that looks like sludge, tastes like ambrosia and comes with a generous squirt of Chantilly cream.

Les Olivades (☎ 04 66 21 71 78; 18 rue Jean Reboul; lunch/dinner menu €11/18.50; ☿ Tue-Sun) There's an intimate dining area to the rear of this excellent wine shop. Just one negative: the uncomfortable chairs will have you sitting ramrod straight to enjoy its excellent fare.

Restaurant Le Menestrel (☎ 04 66 67 54 45; 6 rue École Vieille; menus €15-22; ☺ closed Mon & lunch Tue) This is *the* place for quality local cuisine. Observe yourself in the giant overhead mirror as you tuck away one of its imaginative *menus*.

Rue Porte de France has a scattering of ethnic places: **Taj Mahal** (☎ 04 66 67 37 53; 15 rue Porte de France; mains €8.50-10) is an Indian place; **Le Bonzai** (☎ 04 66 21 84 76; 32 rue Porte de France; ☺ Tue-lunch Sun), opposite, is a touch of Japan.

SELF-CATERING

There are colourful Thursday **markets** in the old city in July and August. The large **covered food market** is in rue Général Perrier.

Quaint **Cafés Nadal**, overlooking place aux Herbes, specialises in local herbs, oils and spices, while its branch on rue St-Castor sells the finest coffees and chocolate. Knowledgeable staff at **La Vinothèque**, which shares premises with Les Olivades, can guide you through their unbeatable choice of local wines.

Drinking

Place aux Herbes is one communal outside café in summer. Equally bustling, beneath the huge palm tree that sprawls in its centre, is place du Marché. On the terrace or inside, **Grand Café de la Bourse**, vast, flamboyant and bang opposite Les Arènes, is great for breakfast or a quick coffee.

Entertainment

Pick up *Nîmescope*, a free fortnightly entertainment listing, available at the tourist office and major hotels. Les Arènes is a major venue for theatre performances and concerts.

Théâtre de Nîmes (☎ 04 66 36 02 04; place de la Calade) has drama, music and opera performances throughout the year.

Getting There & Away

AIR

Nîmes' **airport** (☎ 04 66 70 49 49), 10km southeast of the city on the A54, handles precisely one plane daily – the Ryanair flight to/from London Stansted.

BUS

The **bus station** (☎ 04 66 29 52 00; rue Ste-Félicité) is immediately south of the train station.

Regional destinations include Pont du Gard (€5.40, 45 minutes, up to seven daily), Uzès (€5.70, 45 minutes, eight daily) and Alès (€6.80, 1¼ hours, five daily). There are also buses to/from Avignon (€7.30, 1½ hours, seven daily).

Long-haul operator **Eurolines** (☎ 04 66 29 49 02) covers most European destinations including London (€95) and Amsterdam (€87) and, together with **Line Bus** (☎ 04 66 29 50 62), services to/from Spain.

CAR & MOTORCYCLE

Europcar (☎ 04 66 70 49 22) and **Avis** (☎ 04 66 70 49 26) have kiosks at both the airport and train station.

TRAIN

There's an **SNCF sales office** (11 rue de l'Aspic).

Ten TGVs daily run to/from Paris' Gare de Lyon (€68.90 to €82.80, three hours). There are frequent services to/from Alès (€7.60, 40 minutes), Arles (€6.60, 30 minutes), Avignon (€7.40, 30 minutes), Marseille (€16.20, 1¼ hours), Sète (€10.60, one hour) and Montpellier (€7.50, 30 minutes). Five SNCF buses or trains go to Aigues Mortes in the Camargue (€6.20, 1¼ hours).

Getting Around

TO THE AIRPORT

An airport **bus** (☎ 04 66 29 27 29; €4.50, 30min) meets and greets the daily Ryanair flight, leaving from the train station at 9.15am. To confirm times, ring.

BICYCLE

Véloland (☎ 04 66 36 01 80; 4 rue de la République; ☺ Mon afternoon & Tue-Sat) rents mountain bikes (per half-/full-day €9/15).

PUBLIC TRANSPORT

Local buses are run by **TCN**, which has an information kiosk (☎ 04 66 38 15 40) in the northeast corner of esplanade Charles de Gaulle, the main centre for buses. The cost of a single ticket/five-ticket *carnet* is €1/4.

TAXI

Ring ☎ 04 66 29 40 11.

AROUND NÎMES
Perrier Plant

Ever wondered how they get the bubbles into a bottle of Perrier water? Or why it's

LANGUEDOC-ROUSSILLON

that stubby shape? Take the one-hour tour of **Perrier's spring and bottling plant** (☎ 04 66 87 61 01; admission €5; tours at least every ½hr 9.30-10.30am & 1-3pm Mon-Thu, 2-5pm Sat & Sun Feb-Dec). It's in Vergèze, on the RN113, 13km southwest of Nîmes. We trust their tongue is firmly in their cheek when they advertise '*dégustation gratuité*' (free tasting)!

Pont du Gard

The Pont du Gard, a Unesco World Heritage Site, is an exceptionally well-preserved, three-tiered Roman aqueduct that was once part of a 50km-long system of canals built about 19 BC by the Romans to bring water from near Uzès to Nîmes. The scale is huge: the 35 arches of the 275m-long upper tier, running 50m above the River Gard, contain a watercourse designed to carry 20,000 cubic metres of water per day and the largest construction blocks weigh more than five tonnes.

From car parks either side of the River Gard, you can walk along the road bridge, built in 1743 and running parallel with the lower tier of the aqueduct. The best view of the Pont du Gard is from upstream, beside the river, where you can swim on hot days.

The complex receives many more than a million visitors each year, averaging an horrendous 15,000 or so daily in high summer. There's an **information centre** (☎ 08 20 90 33 30) on each bank.

There's a **museum** (admission €6; captions in English) featuring the bridge, aqueduct and the role of water in Roman society and a 25-minute large-screen **film** (€3; with English version). To retreat from the ever-increasing commercialism, take **Mémoires de Garrigue**, a 1.4km walking trail with interpretive signs that winds through this typical Mediterranean bush and scrubland – though you'll need the explanatory booklet in English (€4) to get the most out of it.

A combined ticket (adult/child €10/8) gives access to all three activities, plus **Ludo**, a children's activity play area.

A spectacular free **light show** (nightly Jul-Aug, Fri & Sat Jun & Sep) should again be beaming out (the installations – and much else on the right bank – were badly damaged by floods in 2002).

If you simply want to enjoy the bridge, head on down. You can ramble round for free around the clock, though the car parks close between 1am and 7am.

GETTING THERE & AWAY

The Pont du Gard is 21km northeast of Nîmes, 26km west of Avignon and 12km southeast of Uzès. Buses to/from each town stop 1km north of the bridge beside the Auberge Blanche. There are five buses daily from Nîmes, two of which continue to Collias, and three from Avignon that continue to Uzès and Alès.

The extensive car parks on each bank of the river cost a whopping €5 (reimbursed if you sign on for the combined ticket).

River Gard

The wild, unpredictable River Gard descends from the Cévennes mountains. Torrential rains can raise the water level by as much as 5m in a flash. During long dry spells, by contrast, it sometimes almost disappears.

The river has sliced itself a meandering 20km gorge (Les Gorges du Gardon) through the hills from **Russan** to the village of **Collias**, about 6km upstream from the Pont du Gard. The GR6 runs beside it most of the way.

In Collias, 4km west of the D981, **Kayak Vert** (☎ 04 66 22 80 76; www.canoefrance.com) and **Canoë Le Tourbillon** (☎ 04 66 22 85 54), both based near the village bridge, rent out kayaks and canoes.

You can paddle 7km down to the Pont du Gard (€17 per person, two hours), or arrange to be dropped 22km upstream at Russan, from where there's a great descent back through Gorges du Gardon (€26, full day), usually possible only between March and mid-June, when the river is high enough.

Uzès

pop 7650

Uzès is a laid-back little hill town 25km northeast of Nîmes. With its faithfully restored Renaissance façades, impressive Duché (Ducal Palace), narrow, semi-pedestrianised streets and ancient towers, it's a charming place for a brief wander.

The **tourist office** (☎ 04 66 22 68 88; www.ville-uzes.fr in French; ☺ 9am-6pm Mon-Fri, 10am-1pm & 2-5pm Sat & Sun Jun-Sep; 9am-noon & 1.30-6pm Mon-Fri, 10am-1pm Sat Oct-May) is on place Albert I, beside the ring road and just outside the old quarter.

SIGHTS & ACTIVITIES

The tourist office carries a useful free pamphlet in English, *Tour of the Historic Town*.

Whether you follow this guided walk or not, let your steps take you through **Place aux Herbes**, Uzès' shady, arcaded central square, its odd angles defying geometrical classification.

The **Duché** (Château Ducal; ☎ 04 66 22 18 96; 10am-1pm & 2-6.30pm Jul–mid-Sep, 10am-noon & 2-6pm mid-Sep–Jun) is a fortified chateau that has belonged to the Dukes of Uzès for more than 1000 years. Altered and expanded almost continuously from the 11th to 18th century, it has some fine period furniture, tapestries and paintings. You can take the **guided tour** (one hour, in French; adult/child €11/8) or wander at will around the **keep** (€6).

Close by, just off rue Port Royal, is the beautifully landscaped **Jardin Médiéval** (Medieval Garden; admission €2; 10.30am-12.30pm & 2-6pm daily Jul-Aug; 2-5pm or 6pm Mon-Fri, 10.30am-12.30pm & 2-5pm or 6pm Sat & Sun Apr-Jun & Sep-Oct).

Musée du Bonbon (☎ 04 66 22 74 39; Pont des Charrettes; adult/child €4.50/2.50; 10am-7pm daily Jul-Sep, 10am-1pm & 2-6pm Tue-Sun Oct-Dec & Feb-Jun) is the place for a little indulgence. As a plaque at the entrance declares, 'This museum is dedicated to all who have devoted their lives to a slightly guilty passion – greed'. Signs at this shrine to sticky sweets are multilingual and you come away with a copious goody bag.

FESTIVALS & EVENTS

Uzès is big on festivals and fairs. The town positively reeks on 24 June, the date of the **Foire à l'Ail** (Garlic Fair). On Saturday mornings between November and March, there's a **truffle market** (place aux Herbes), while the third Sunday in January sees a full-blown **Truffle Fair**. The town is also renowned for its **Nuits Musicales d'Uzès**, an international festival of baroque music held in the second half of July.

GETTING THERE & AWAY

The *gare routière* – grandly named and in fact a bus stop – is on av de la Libération. Between Avignon (€8.10) and Alès (€6.70) buses run two to four times daily. There are also six to 10 daily to/from Nîmes (€5.70).

ALÈS & AROUND
pop 41,000

Alès, 45km from Nîmes, 70km from Montpellier and snuggled against the River Gard, is the Gard *département's* second-largest town. Coal was mined here from the 13th century, when monks first dug into the surrounding hills, until the last pit closed in 1986.

The pedestrianised heart of town, having long ago shed its sooty past, is pleasant, if unexciting, to stroll through. Gateway to the Cévennes mountains and bright with flowers in summer, Alès is also a convenient base for visiting a trio of unique exhibitions close by.

The **tourist office** (☎ 04 66 52 32 15; tourisme@ville-ales.net; place Hôtel de Ville; 9am-7pm Mon-Sat, 9am-noon Sun Jul-Aug; 9am-noon & 1.30-5.30pm Mon-Sat Sep-Jun) occupies a modern building set into the shell of a baroque chapel.

Sights

Mine Témoin (☎ 04 66 30 45 15; chemin de la Cité Ste-Marie; adult/child €6.70/3.50; 10am-6pm Jul-Aug, 9am-5pm Jun, 9am-11am & 2-4pm Apr-May & Sep–mid-Nov) in Alès is no museum. Don a safety helmet and

---

THE CAMISARD REVOLT

Early in the 18th century, a guerrilla war raged through the Cévennes as Protestants took on Louis XIV's army. The revocation of the Edict of Nantes in 1685 removed rights that the Protestant Huguenots had enjoyed since 1598. Many emigrated, while others fled deep into the wild Cévennes, from where a local leader named Roland, only 22 at the time, led the resistance against the French army sent to crush them.

Poorly equipped but knowing the countryside intimately, the outlaws resisted for two years. They fought in their shirts – *camiso* in *langue d'oc;* thus their popular name, Camisards. Once the royal army gained the upper hand, the local population was either massacred or forced to flee. Roland was killed and most villages were methodically destroyed.

Each year, on the first Sunday of September, thousands of French Protestants meet at Roland's birthplace in Le Mas Soubeyran, a sleepy hamlet near the village of Mialet, just off the Corniche des Cévennes. It's now the Musée du Désert, which details the persecution of Protestants in the Cévennes between 1685 and the 1787 Edict of Tolerance, marking the reintroduction of religious freedom.

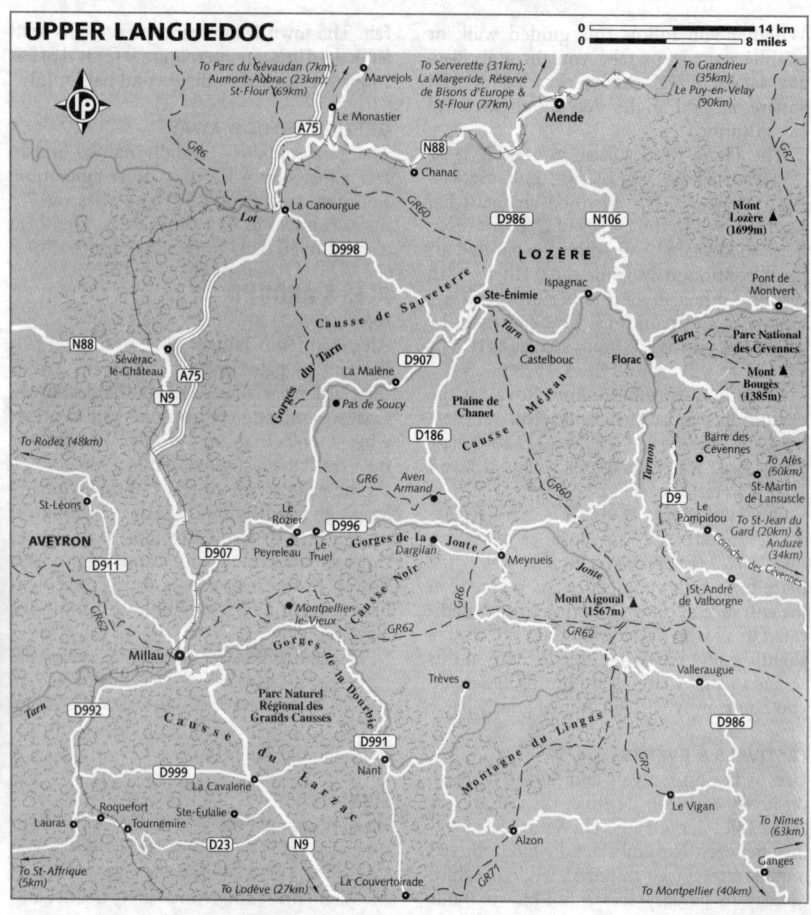

UPPER LANGUEDOC

take the cage down an actual mine. Preceded by a 20-minute video (in French), the one-hour **guided tour** (option in English, July to mid-August, if you ring to reserve; at other times, ask for the free pamphlet in English) leads you along 650m of underground galleries.

The huge **Bambouseraie de Prafrance** (Bamboo Grove; ☎ 04 66 61 70 47; adult/child €6.50/4; ☼ 9.30am-dusk Mar–mid-Nov) was founded in 1855 by a spice merchant. Here in Générargues, 12km southwest of Alès, 150 bamboo species sprout amid aquatic gardens and an Asian village. A fun way to get there is on the Cévennes steam train (opposite).

Musée du Désert (☎ 04 66 85 02 72; adult/child €4/3; ☼ 9.30am-7pm Jul-Aug, 9.30am-noon & 2-6pm

Mar-Jun & Sep–mid-Nov) portrays the clandestine way of life of the Camisards. It's in the charming hamlet of Le Mas Soubeyran, 5km north of the Bambouseraie.

Sleeping & Eating
Hôtel Le Riche (☎ 04 66 86 00 33; www.leriche.fr in French; 42 place Pierre Sémard; s €34-40 d €48; ☼ Sep-Jul; P ⊠) Opposite the train station, this hotel is highly recommended, as much for its fine restaurant (*menus* €16.50 to €47) as for its pleasant, modern rooms.

Hôtel Durand (☎ 04 66 86 28 94; fax 04 66 30 52 68; 3 blvd Anatole France; s/d €27.50/30.50; P) More modest and about 100m east of Hôtel Le Riche down a side street, it has trim rooms and also represents excellent value.

Camping

Camping la Croix Clémentine (☎ 04 66 86 52 69; www.clementine.fr in French; camping according to season €10.60-19.60; ☙ Apr–mid-Sep) This place is in Cendras, 4km northwest of Alès.

Getting There & Away

BUS

From the **bus station** (place Pierre Sémard), south of the train station, one bus daily heads into the Cévennes to Florac (€12, 1½ hours), and two to four to Uzès (€6.70, 50 minutes), continuing to Avignon (€13.80, 1¾ hours).

TRAIN

There are 10 trains daily to/from Montpellier (€13.30, 1½ hours), some requiring a change in Nîmes (€7.60, 45 minutes). Three trains daily link Alès and Mende (€15, 2¼ hours).

From April to October the little **Train à Vapeur des Cévennes** (Cévennes steam train; ☎ 04 66 60 59 00; adult/child one-way €8/6, return €10.50/7; daily Apr–mid-Sep, Tue-Sun mid-Sep–Oct) takes 40 minutes to chug the 13km between St-Jean du Gard and Anduze via the Bambouseraie, making four return trips each day.

PARC NATIONAL DES CÉVENNES

The heart of the Cévennes was designated a national park in 1970 and is also recognised as a Unesco World Biosphere Reserve. In general drier and hotter than the Auvergne to its north, it has more in common with Mediterranean lands. Sprinkled with isolated hamlets, it harbours a huge diversity of fauna and flora (an astounding 2250 plant species have been recorded). Several of its animals,

including red deer, beavers and vultures, have been successfully reintroduced over the last 25 years. The park covers four main areas: Mont Lozère, much of the Causse Méjean, the Vallées Cévenoles (Cévennes Valleys) and Mont Aigoual. Florac makes a good base for exploration.

The park has three **ecomuseums**: the Écomusées du Mont Lozère, de la Cévenne and du Causse, each of which has several different sites. For more details, ask at the excellent Maison du Parc National des Cévennes (p742).

History

The 910-sq-km park was created to bring ecological stability to an area that, because of religious and later economic upheavals, has long had a destabilising human presence. Population influxes, which saw the destruction of forests for logging and pasture, were followed by mass desertions as people gave up the fight against the inhospitable climate and terrain. Emigration led to the abandonment of hamlets and farms, many of which were snapped up in the 1960s by wealthy Parisians and foreigners.

Maps

The best overall map of the park is the IGN's *Parc National des Cévennes* (€7) at 1:100,000.

Mont Lozère

This 1699m-high lump of granite in the north of the park is shrouded in cloud and ice in winter and covered with heather and blueberries, peat bogs and flowing streams

---

CHESTNUT: THE ALL-PURPOSE TREE

In the Cévennes, the chestnut tree (known as *l'arbre à pain*, or the bread tree) was the staple food of many Auvergnat families. The nuts were eaten raw, roasted and dried, or ground into flour. Blended with milk or wine, chestnuts were the essence of *bajanat*, a nourishing soup. Part of the harvest would feed the pigs while the leaves of pruned twigs and branches provided fodder for sheep and goats.

Harvested at ground level with small forks – of chestnut wood, of course – the prickly husks (called *hèrissons*, or hedgehogs) were removed by being trampled upon in spiky boots. Nowadays, they're the favourite food of the Cévennes' wild boars and still feature in a number of local sauces and desserts.

Nothing was wasted. Sections of hollowed-out trunk would serve as beehives, smaller branches would be woven into baskets while larger ones were whittled into stakes for fencing or used to build trellises. The wood, hard and resistant to parasites was used for rafters, rakes and household furniture – everything from, quite literally, the cradle to the coffin.

in summer. **Écomusée du Mont Lozère** (☎ 04 66 45 80 73; adult/child €3.50/2.50; ☼ 10.30am-12.30pm & 2.30-6.30pm Easter-Sep) has a permanent exhibition at Pont de Montvert, 20km northeast of Florac.

Vallées Cévenoles

First planted back in the Middle Ages, *châtaigniers* (sweet-chestnut trees), carpet the Vallées Cévenoles (Cévennes Valleys), the park's central region of plunging ravines and jagged ridges, along one of which runs the breathtaking Corniche des Cévennes.

Mont Aigoual

Mont Aigoual (1567m) and the neighbouring Montagne du Lingas region are renowned for their searing winds and heavy snowfall. The area is dense with beech trees, thanks to a successful reforestation programme that has counteracted years of uncontrolled logging. The observatory atop the breezy summit has an **exhibition** (admission free; ☼ May-Sep), portraying the mountain through the seasons and the play of wind and water upon it.

Activities

In winter there's **cross-country skiing** (more than 100km of marked trails) on Mont Aigoual and Mont Lozère, and **donkey treks** are popular in the park in warmer months. There are 600km of donkey- and horse-riding trails and 200km marked out for mountain-bike enthusiasts.

An equally well-developed network of trails makes the park a **walking** paradise year-round. The free French pamphlet *Itinéraires et Sentiers Pédestres* summarises the dozen GR trails that crisscross the park. In addition, there are 22 shorter signposted walks of between two and seven hours' duration and 20 easy, educational trails.

Florac's Maison du Parc has 11 excellent wallets (€5 each) describing circular walks from various starting points within the park. Ask about the Festival Nature, a summertime mix of outdoor activities, lectures and field trips.

Getting There & Away

By car, the most spectacular route is the Corniche des Cévennes, a ridge road that winds along the mountain crests of the Cévennes for 56km from St-Jean du Gard to Florac.

FLORAC

pop 2100

Florac, 79km northwest of Alès and 38km southeast of Mende makes a great base for exploring the Parc National des Cévennes and the upper reaches of the Gorges du Tarn. Lively in summer, it's draped along the west bank of River Tarnon, one of the tributaries of the Tarn, with the fortress-like cliffs of the Causse Méjean looming 1000m overhead.

Information

Florac On-Line (1 rue du Pêcher; per hr €6) Internet access.

Laundrette (11 rue du Pêcher; ☼ 8.30am-7.30pm)

Tourist Office (☎ 04 66 45 01 14; www.mescevennes .com; av Jean Monestier; ☼ 8.30am-1.30pm & 2.30-7pm daily Jul-Aug, 9am-noon & 2-6pm Mon-Sat Sep-Jun)

Activities

The tourist office has details on a whole summer's worth of outdoor activities. For information on the park's rich walking potential, contact **Maison du Parc National des Cévennes** (☎ 04 66 49 53 01; www.cevennes-parcnational .fr; ☼ 9.30am-6pm Jul-Aug; 9.30am-12.30pm & 1.30-6.30pm Easter-Jun, Mon-Fri Sep-Easter) It occupies the handsome restored 17th-century Château de Florac, stocks an English version of the guidebook *Parc National des Cévennes* (€15) and has a splendidly informative **interactive exhibition** (admission €3.50), *Passagers du Parc*, with captions and a recorded commentary in English (delivered, alas, by a couple of glum, monotone native speakers) and a 15-minute slide show.

Activities in the Parc National des Cévennes section (left) has more information. Lonely Planet's *Walking in France* describes three varied day walks, each accessible from Florac.

DONKEY TREKS

Why not follow the lead of Robert Louis Stevenson and hire a pack animal? Several companies are in the donkey business. They include **Genti-Âne** (☎ 04 66 41 04 16; anegenti@free .fr) in Castagnols and **Tramontane** (☎ 04 66 45 92 44) in St-Martin de Lansuscle. Typical prices are €35 to €45 per day and €190 to €220 per week and both outfits can reserve accommodation along the route. Though each is outside Florac, they'll transport the dumb creatures to town or a place of your choosing for a fee (around €0.75/km).

TRAVELS WITH A DONKEY

The Cévennes were even wilder and more untamed back in October 1878, when Scottish writer Robert Louis Stevenson crossed them with only a donkey, Modestine, for company.

'I was looked upon with contempt, like a man who should project a journey to the moon, but yet with a respectful interest, like one setting forth for the inclement Pole,' Stevenson wrote in *Travels with a Donkey in the Cévennes,* published in 1879.

Accompanied by the wayward, mouse-coloured Modestine, bought for 65 francs and a glass of brandy, Stevenson took a respectable 12 days to travel the 232km on foot (Modestine carried his gear) from Le Monastier-sur-Gazelle, southeast of Le Puy-en-Velay, to St-Jean du Gard, west of Alès. Afterwards, he sold his ass – and wept.

The Stevenson trail, first retraced and marked with the cross of St Andrew by a Scottish woman in 1978, is nowadays designated the GR70.

Whether you're swaying on a donkey or simply walking, you'll find *The Robert Louis Stevenson Trail* by Alan Castle an excellent, practical, well-informed companion. Consult too www.chemin -stevenson.org and pick up the free pamphlet *Sur Le Chemin de Robert Louis Stevenson* (On The RLS Trail), stocked by tourist offices, which has a comprehensive list of accommodation en route.

OTHER ACTIVITIES

Cévennes Évasion (☎ 04 66 45 18 31; www.cevennes -evasion.com; 5 place Boyer) rents mountain bikes for €12/18 per half-/full-day and furnishes riders with handy colour route maps. In summer it'll take you for free up to the Causse Méjean, from where you can whiz effortlessly back down (minimum five persons). It also arranges caving, rock-climbing and canyon-clambering expeditions (each €42 to €50).

Sleeping

Gîte d'Étape (☎ 04 66 45 24 54; lagrave.alain@wanadoo .fr; 18 rue du Pêcher; dm €11; ☾ Feb–mid-Nov) This welcoming trekkers' favourite with doubles and quads occupies an 18th-century house and has self-catering facilities.

Hôtel Central de La Poste (☎ 04 66 45 00 01; www .archibald-hotel.com in French; 4 av Maurice Tour; d €37-42) A husband-and-wife team has taken over this ex-coaching inn (which needed a feminine touch after some years in the hands of three young men). Lower floors are renovated and they're working their way up. It runs a decent restaurant, the **Archibald**, with a summertime rear terrace overlooking the river.

Hôtel Les Gorges du Tarn (☎ 04 66 45 00 63; gorges-du-tarn.adonis@wanadoo.fr; 48 rue du Pêcher; d €30, with shower €36, with bathroom €42; ☾ Easter-Oct; 𝐏) Down a quiet side street, rooms in the main building are freshly renovated while those in the annexe are more spacious, if less sparkling. It's restaurant, **L'Adonis** (menus €17-35), merits a visit in its own right.

Grand Hôtel du Parc (☎ 04 66 45 03 05; www .grandhotelduparc.fr; 47 av Jean Monestier; d €41.50-53; ☾ mid-Mar–Nov) This venerable building with its spacious rooms enjoys its own grounds with a pool and delightful gardens. It's a great spot to recharge the batteries and also has a creditable **restaurant** (menus €15-29.50).

Camping

Florac has a pair of municipal riverside camping grounds, each 1.5km from town. **Camping Le Pont du Tarn** (☎ 04 66 45 18 26; pont dutarne@aol.com; camping €8-14; ☾ Apr–mid-Oct; 𝐞) is to the north, off the N106, while **Camping La Tière** (☎ 04 66 45 00 53; per person/tent/car €2.50/2.40/1.60; ☾ Jul-Aug) is smaller and to the south. La Tière is right beside the river and may well be less crowded.

Eating

L'Esplanade, a shady, pedestrianised allée, becomes one long dining area in summer. Here, you can eat well and economically at one of the restaurant terraces. The three hotels we recommend on this page all have impressive restaurants.

Le Chapeau Rouge (☎ 04 66 45 23 40; 3bis rue Roussel; menus €15-29) A dynamic young crew have recently taken over The Red Hat, beside the tourist office. It's excellent value and the service is friendly, though they do have trouble coping if the place is full. In summer, the shady terrace, its canopy a thick foliage of vines, is a delight.

La Source du Pêcher (☎ 04 66 45 03 01; 1 rue de Remuret; menus €25-40; ☾ Apr-Oct) With a wonderful open-air terrace, perched above the little River Pêcher, it's very good and oh, they know and show it (a Dutch family walked out the night we dined there) and they still observe the outmoded practice of handing Madame a menu with nothing so vulgar as prices indicated. This said, you'll eat very well indeed, if you can stomach a little ritual humiliation. They don't take reservations, so arrive early.

Maison du Pays Cévenol (3 rue du Pêcher) This gastronomic treasure trove sells local specialities – liqueurs, jams, Pélardon cheese and chestnuts in all their guises.

Getting There & Away

It's a pain without your own transport. One **Autocars Reilhes** (☎ 04 66 45 00 18) minibus runs to/from Alès (€12, 1½ hours), Monday to Saturday, leaving from the old railway station. And that's it for public transport, so keep your hitching thumb supple.

MENDE
pop 13,300

Mende, a quiet little place straddling the River Lot, is the capital of Lozère, France's least populous *département*. Its oval-shaped centre is ringed by a one-way road. This acts as something of a *cordon sanitaire*, leaving the old quarter relatively traffic-free.

Information

Salle Multimédia, (2nd fl, new town hall above the tourist office; place Charles de Gaulle; per hr €1.50; ☯ 2-8pm Tue-Fri, 9am-noon Sat) Internet access.

Tourist Office (☎ 04 66 94 00 23; www.ot-mende.fr; place Charles de Gaulle; ☯ 9am-12.30pm & 2-7pm Mon-Sat, 9am-noon & 2-5pm Sun Jul-Aug; 9am-12.30pm & 2-6pm Mon-Fri, 9am-noon Sat Sep-Jun)

Sights

The English tourist office brochure, *Mende: Heritage Visit of the City,* describes every nook and cranny of historical interest. The dark interior of the 14th-century, twin-towered **Cathédrale Notre Dame** (place Urbain V) makes the magnificent stained-glass windows glow but you'll have to peer hard to make out detail on the eight 17th-century Aubusson tapestries, which are hung high above the nave.

Sleeping & Eating

Hôtel le Commerce (☎ 04 66 65 13 73; www.le commerce-mende.com in French; 2 blvd Henri Bourrillon; s €31, d €37-40; ☯ closed 2 weeks in Apr) Opposite place du

Foirail on the busy ring road, this pleasantly labyrinthine hotel, run by the same family for three generations, has impeccable, tastefully furnished rooms. The owner – away on a beer tour of Germany when we last called by – is an ale fanatic and its popular **bar** carries an impressive range.

Hôtel de France (☎ 04 66 65 00 04; www.hotelde france-mende.com; 9 blvd Lucien Arnault; d €42-45; menus €21-24; ☯ mid-Jan–Dec; P ⌨) Most rooms at this Logis de France and one-time coaching inn have sweeping views over the small valley and gardens below. For the smallest of supplements, enjoy the extra space and bright, coordinated colours in room 20 or 21 (€50). The owner speaks excellent English. On the ring road, it's also a first class place to eat.

Restaurant Les Voûtes (☎ 04 66 49 00 05; 13 rue d'Aigues-Passes; menus €17-24; ☯ daily Jun-Aug, Tue-Sun Sep-May, closed 1-15 Oct) This restaurant enjoys a splendid setting, deep in the vaults of an ex-convent. Run by a cheerful young team (average age 22), it offers something for everyone: salads big enough to fill a fruit bowl (€7 to €7.50), pizzas (€6.50 to €8.40) – to eat in or takeaway – grills (€10 to €12.50) and a great, recommended lunchtime *menu express* (€12.50).

Le Mazel (☎ 04 66 65 05 33; 25 rue du Collège; menus €13-25; ☯ Wed-Mon lunch mid-Mar–mid-Nov) This stylishly decorated restaurant – do not be deterred by the bleakly modern surroundings – offers mainly local cuisine, imaginatively prepared. A recognised gourmet venue, it's true value.

Getting There & Away

Buses leave from the train station and most pass by place du Foirail. On weekdays, there's one daily to Rodez (three hours) and Le Puy-en-Velay (SNCF; two hours). Northbound, two SNCF buses run daily to/from Clermont-Ferrand in the Massif Central (€25.40, three hours).

The train station is 1km north of town across the River Lot. There are three trains daily to Montpellier (€23.80, 3½ hours) via Alès (€14.60, 2¼ hours) and Nîmes (€19.40, three hours).

Getting Around

Rent a mountain bike at **Espace Bike** (☎ 04 66 65 01 81; 1 blvd du Soubeyran; ☯ Tue-Sat) for €8/12 per half-/full-day.

AROUND MENDE
Wolf Reserve
Wolves once roamed freely through the Lozère forests but today you'll see them only in the **Parc du Gévaudan** (☎ 04 66 32 09 22; www .loupsdugevaudan.com; adult/child €6/3; ☺ 10am-7pm Jun-Aug; 10am-5pm or 6pm Apr-May & Sep-Dec) in Ste-Lucie, 7km north of Marvejols. The park sustains more than 100 Mongolian, Canadian, Siberian and Polish wolves living in semi-freedom.

Réserve de Bisons d'Europe
Above the village of Ste-Eulalie en Margeride, the **Réserve de Bisons d'Europe** (☎ 04 66 31 40 40; www.bisoneurope.com in French; ☺ 10am-5pm or 6pm or 7pm depending on season), above the village of Ste-Eulalie en Margeride, was established with 25 European bison transferred from the Bialowieza forest in Poland.

Within their 200-hectare reserve, the bison roam freely. Visitors, by contrast, must follow a 50-minute **guided tour**, either by horse-drawn carriage (adult/child €10/5.50) or by sledge (€14/8), or take a defined walking path (€5.50/4; from May to August).

GORGES DU TARN
From the village of Ispagnac, 9km northwest of Florac, the spectacular Gorges du Tarn wind southwestwards for about 50km, ending just north of Millau. En route are two villages: medieval Ste-Énimie (a good base for canoeing and walking along the gorges) and, 13km downstream, La Malène, smaller but equally attractive.

The gorge, 400m to 600m deep, marks the boundary between the Causse Méjean to the south and the Causse de Sauveterre to the north. From these plateaus, it looks like a white, limestone abyss, its green waters dotted here and there with bright canoes and kayaks. In summer the riverside road (the D907bis) is often jammed with cars, buses and caravans: every summer's day, more than 3000 cars grind through Ste-Énimie.

Activities
BOATING & CANOEING
Riding the River Tarn is at its best in high summer when the river is usually low and the descent a lazy trip over mostly calm water. You can get as far as the impassable Pas de Soucy, a barrier of boulders about 9km downriver from La Malène.

Various companies organises canoe and kayak descents. Among the longest established are **Canoë Paradan** (☎ 04 66 48 56 90) and **ADN La Cazelle** (☎ 04 66 48 46 05), both in Ste-Énimie, **Locanoë** (☎ 04 66 48 55 57) in Castelbouc and **Au Moulin de la Malène** (☎ 04 66 48 51 14) in La Malène. Prices per person vary little. Typical trips are: Ste-Énimie to La Malène (€17, 13km, 3½ hours) and Ste-Énimie to the Pas de Soucy (€23, 23km, 6½ hours).

The Ste-Énimie tourist office carries information on all companies offering rafting and canoe descents of the River Tarn.

If you'd rather someone else did the hard work, spend a lazy, effortless hour with **Les Bateliers de la Malène** (☎ 04 66 48 51 10; ☺ Apr-Oct), who, for €18 per person will punt you down an 8km stretch of the gorge, leaving from La Malène, and drive you back.

WALKING & CYCLING
The Sentier de la Vallée du Tarn trail, blazed in yellow and green, runs for around 250km, from Pont de Montvert on Mont Lozère, down the Gorges and all the way to Albi. The GR60 follows an old drovers' route, winding down from the Causse de Sauveterre to Ste-Énimie, crossing the bridge and continuing southwards up to the Causse Méjean in the direction of Mont Aigoual.

Less strenuously, there are 23 circular, signposted walks, each between four and seven hours' duration, in the stretch between Ispagnac and La Malène.

La Cazelle in Ste-Énimie (see the previous Boating & Canoeing section), rents out mountain bikes (per half/full-day €20/30).

The Ste-Énimie tourist office sells the useful *Vallée et Gorges du Tarn – Balades à Pied et à VTT* (€15), published by Chamina, which details various walking and cycling routes in the area.

HORSE RIDING
Centre Équestre La Périgouse (☎ 04 66 48 53 7; www.perigouse.com in French) in Ste-Énimie hires out horses for €13/32/48 per hour/half-/full-day.

Sleeping & Eating
Château de la Caze (☎ 04 66 48 51 01; www.cha teaudelacaze.com; d €108-162; ☺ Easter–mid-Nov) This fairy-tale 15th-century castle, next to the Tarn 2km north of La Malène, is a fabulous top-end option. Rooms are the last word

in luxury and it boasts a renowned gourmet restaurant. Accommodation in the annexe is less romantic but much easier on the pocket and guests have access to all the hotel's facilities.

Camping Les Gorges du Tarn (☎ 04 66 48 50 51, fax 04 66 48 59 37; per person/tent/car €2/1/40/1/10; ☺ Easter–mid-Sep) This park is approximately 800m upstream from Ste-Énimie and is the cheapest of the riverside camping sites. It also hires out canoes and kayaks.

Ste-Énimie
pop 200

Ste-Énimie, 27km from Florac and 56km from Millau, tumbles like an avalanche of grey-brown stone, blending into the steep, once-terraced slope behind it. Long isolated, it's now a popular destination for day-visitors from Millau, Mende and Florac and one of the starting points for descending the Tarn by canoe or kayak.

Ste-Énimie's **tourist office** (☎ 04 66 48 53 44; www.gorgesdutarn.net in French; ☺ 9am-7pm daily Jul-Aug, 9am-12.30pm & 1.30-5.30pm Mon-Fri Sep-Jun) is 100m north of the bridge. It stocks maps and walking guides, including IGN Top 25 map No 2640OT *Gorges du Tarn*. There's also a small **annexe** (☺ Jul-Aug) in La Malène.

Highlights are the Romanesque **Église de Ste-Énimie** and, just behind it, the tiny **Écomusée Le Vieux Logis** (combined ticket adult/child €2/1; ☺ visits at least 10am & 4pm Mon-Fri Jul-Aug, Wed-Sun Jun & Sep), its one vaulted room crammed with antique local furniture, lamps, tableware and costumes.

PARC NATUREL RÉGIONAL DES GRANDS CAUSSES

This nature park is mainly harsh limestone plateau. Scorched in summer and windswept in winter, the stony surface holds little moisture as water filters through the limestone to form an underground world ideal for cavers.

The Rivers Tarn, Jonte and Dourbie have sliced deep gorges through the 5000-sq-km plateau, creating four *causses* ('plateaus' in the local patois): Sauveterre, Méjean, Noir and Larzac, each different in its delicate geological forms. One may look like a dark lunar surface, another like a Scottish moor covered with the thinnest layer of grass, while the next is gentler and more fertile. But all are eerie and empty except for the occasional

shepherd and his flock – and all offer magnificent walking and mountain biking.

Millau, at the heart of the park, is a good base for venturing into this wild area. The southern part of the park, home to France's 'king of cheeses' (p750), is known as Le Pays du Roquefort (Land of Roquefort). The Gorges de la Jonte, where birds of prey wheel and swoop, skim the park's eastern boundary and rival the neighbouring, more famous Gorges du Tarn in beauty.

Information

Parc Naturel Régional des Grands Causses office (☎ 05 65 61 35 50; parc.grands.causes@wanadoo.fr; 71 blvd de l'Ayrolle, Millau; ☺ 9am-noon or 12.30pm & 2-5pm or 6pm Mon-Fri)

Causse de Sauveterre

The northernmost of the causses is a gentle, hilly plateau dotted with a few compact and isolated farms resembling fortified villages. Every possible patch of fertile earth is cultivated, creating irregular, intricately patterned wheat fields.

Causse Méjean

Causse Méjean, the highest, is also the most barren and isolated. It's a land of poor pasture enriched by occasional fertile depressions, where streams gurgle down into the limestone through sinkholes, funnels and fissures.

Underground, this combination of water and limestone has created some spectacular scenery. The cavern of **Aven Armand** (☎ 04 66 45 61 31; adult/child €8/5; ☺ 9.30am-7pm Jun-Aug; 9.30am or 10am-noon & 1.30-5pm or 6pm Apr-May & Sep-Oct) on the plateau's southwestern side lies about 75m below the surface. Stretching some 200m, it bristles with a subterranean forest of stalagmites and stalactites. A **combination ticket** (adult/child €10/6) also includes admission to the Chaos de Montpellier-le-Vieux (opposite).

Nearby is the equally spectacular, even larger cavern of **Dargilan** (☎ 04 66 45 60 20; adult/ child €8/4; ☺ Jul-Aug 10am-6.30pm, Easter-Jun & Sep-Oct 10am-noon & 2-4.30pm or 5.30pm). A one-hour tour culminates in a sudden exit to a ledge with a dizzying view of the Gorges de la Jonte (opposite) way below.

Causse Noir

Rising immediately east of Millau, the 'Black Causse' is bounded by gorges. It is known best for the **Chaos de Montpellier-le-Vieux** (☎ 05 65 60 66 30; adult/child €5/3; ☼ 9.30am-6pm or 7pm Apr-Oct), an area of jagged rocks 18km northeast of Millau overlooking the Gorges de la Dourbie. Water erosion has created more than 120 hectares of weird limestone formations with fanciful names such as the Sphinx and the Elephant. Three trails, lasting one to three hours, cover the site, as does a tourist train (adult/child €3/2).

If you're here outside official opening times, there's nothing to stop you wandering around freely.

Causse du Larzac

The Causse du Larzac (800m to 1000m) is the largest of the four causses. An endless sweep of distant horizons and rocky steppes broken by medieval villages, it's known as the 'French Desert'.

It's known in particular for old, fortified villages such as **Ste-Eulalie**, long the capital of the Larzac *région*, and **La Couvertoirade**, which were both built by the Knights Templar, a religious military order that distinguished itself during the Crusades.

Gorges de la Jonte

The dramatic Gorges de la Jonte cut east–west from Meyrueis to Le Rozier, below the western slopes of the Aigoual massif. West of Le Truel on the D996 is **Belvédère des Vautours** (Vulture Viewing Point; ☎ 05 65 62 69 69; www.vautours-lozere.com; adult/child €6/3; ☼ 10am-5pm or 6pm mid-Mar–mid-Nov), above which the birds nest high in the cliffs. Reintroduced after having all but disappeared locally, they now freely wheel and plane in the Causses skies.

The viewing point has an impressive multimedia exhibition, including live video transmission from the nesting sites of what must be the world's most heavily researched vultures. It also organises half-day **birding walks** (adult/child €6.50/3; reservation essential) to the surrounding gorges.

MILLAU

pop 22,500

Millau (pronounced mee-yo) sits between the Causse Noir and Causse du Larzac at the confluence of the Rivers Tarn and Dourbie. Falling just over the border into the Midi-Pyrénées *département* of Aveyron, it's tied to Languedoc historically and culturally. Once prosperous and still famous for glove-making, it's fairly run down these days. But as the main centre for the Parc Naturel Régional des Grands Causses, it comes to life at holiday time as a centre for hiking and other outdoor activities – particularly hang-gliding and parapente, exploiting the uplifting thermals.

Information

Laundrette (14 av Gambetta; ☼ 7am-9pm)
Main Post Office (12 av Alfred Merle)
Posanis (5 rue droite; ☼ 10am-10pm Mon-Sat) Internet access.
Tourist Office (☎ 05 65 60 02 42; www.ot-millau.fr; 1 place du Beffroi; ☼ 9am-7pm Mon-Sat Jul-Aug, 9am-12.30pm & 2-6.30pm Mon-Sat Sep-Jun, 10am-12.30pm & 3-6.30pm Sun Easter-Sep)

Sights

The 42m-tall **beffroi** (belfry; rue Droite; adult/under 19 €2.50/free; ☼ 10am-11am & 2.30-6pm Jul-Aug, 3-5pm 15-30 Jun & Sep) has a square base which dates from the 12th century and tapers into a 17th-century octagonal tower, from where there's a great view.

VIADUC DE MILLAU

This brand-new toll bridge, slung across the wide Tarn Valley to link the Causse du Larzac and Causse Rouge, takes the breath away. Designed by the British architect Sir Norman Foster and due for inauguration in January 2005, it's a true work of industrial art and an amazing feat of engineering. Only seven pylons, hollow and seemingly slim as needles, support 2.5km of four-lane motorway. Rising to 340m above the valley bottom, it ranks among the tallest road bridges in the world.

More than three years in construction, it gobbled up 127,000 cu metres of concrete, 19,000 tonnes of reinforcing steel and 5000 tonnes of cables and stays. Yet despite these heavyweight superlatives, it still looks like a gossamer thread. Far from detracting from the charms of the hitherto unspoilt countryside around the town of Millau, this vital link in the A75 motorway is a true icon for the 21st century.

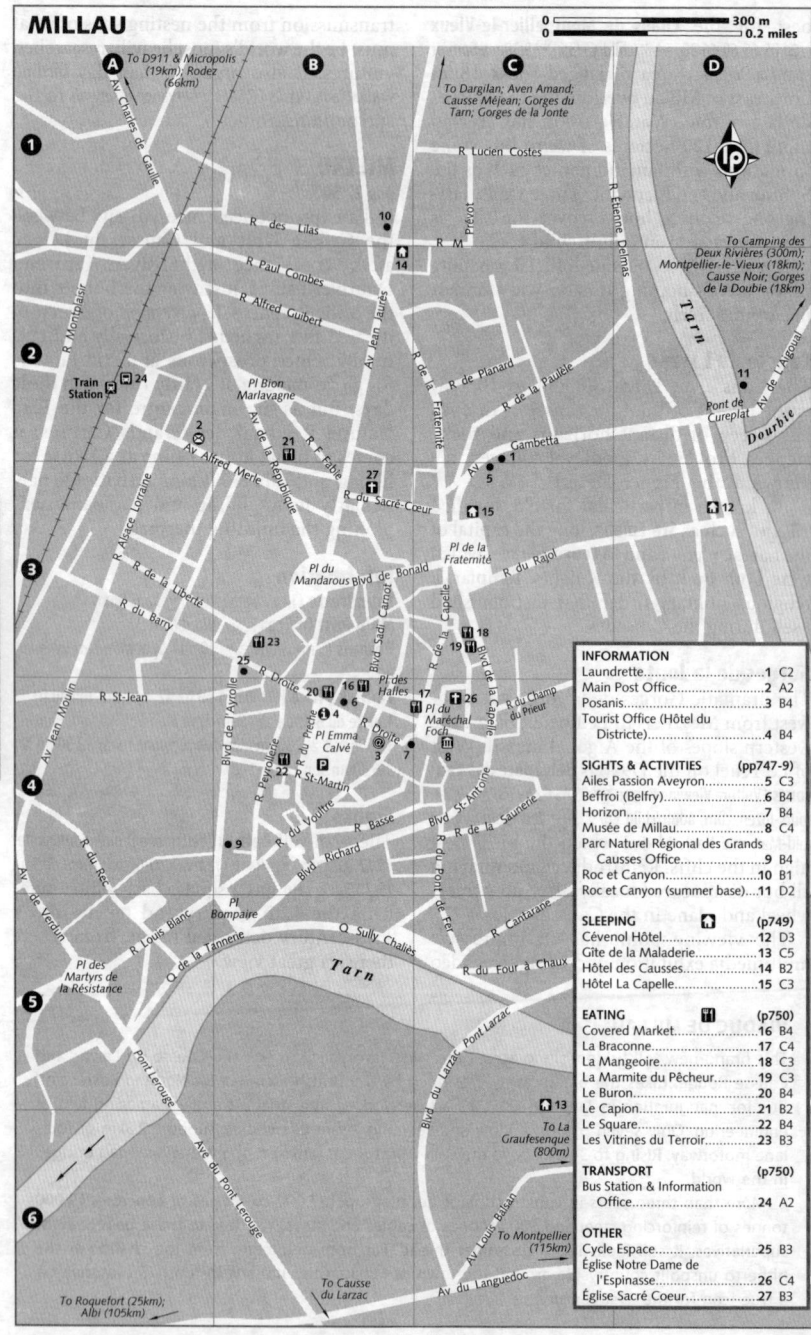

MILLAU

Musée de Millau (☎ 05 65 59 01 08; place du Maréchal Foch; adult/student/under 18 €5/3.50/free; ⏰ 10am-6pm daily Jul-Aug, 10am-noon & 2-6pm Apr-Jun & Sep, Mon-Sat Oct-Mar) has a rich collection of fossils, including mammoth molars and a dinosaur skeleton from the Causse du Larzac. In the cellar is a huge array of plates and vases from **La Graufesenque**, in its time the largest pottery workshop in the western Roman Empire. The 1st-floor leather and glove section illustrates Millau's tanneries and their products through the ages.

You can buy a **combined ticket** (€6), which also includes admission to La Graufesenque archaeological site, at the confluence of the Rivers Tarn and Dourbie.

Activities

HANG-GLIDING & PARAPENTE
Companies running introductory courses (average cost €325 to €350 for five or six days) as well as tandem flights (around €65) include:

Ailes Passion Aveyron (☎ 05 65 61 20 96; www.ailes-passion.com in French; 12 av Gambetta)

Horizon (☎ 05 65 59 78 60; www.millau-vol-libre.com; 6 place Lucien Grégoire) Just off place Maréchal Foch. Also offers caving, canyon descents and rock climbing.

Roc et Canyon (☎ 05 65 61 17 77; www.roc-et-canyon .com in French; 55 av Jean Jaurès) In summer you'll find it beside Pont Cureplat. Also on offer is caving, rock climbing, canyon descents, rafting, canoeing – and bungee jumping.

ROCK CLIMBING
The 50m- to 200m-high cliffs of the Gorges de la Jonte are an internationally renowned venue for climbers of all levels – in 2000 Millau hosted the world climbing championships. Both Horizon and Roc et Canyon offer monitored climbs and can put you in touch with local climbers.

WALKING & CYCLING
Pick up a copy of *Les Belles Balades de l'Aveyron* (€8), which is on sale at the tourist office. You can navigate by the explicit maps even if you don't read French. It describes 22 walks around Millau, the Gorges du Tarn and the Grands Causses, all waymarked and varying from 1½ to six hours, and also details 10 mountain-bike and 10 tourer routes.

If you're after more demanding trekking, the GR62 goes over the Causse Noir, passing Montpellier-le-Vieux before winding down to Millau, while the GR71 and its spurs thread across the Causse du Larzac and through its Templar villages.

Festivals & Events
During mid-August, the four-day *pétanque* world series is held in Millau. Its 16 competitions (including just one for women in this male-dominated sport) attract some 6000 players and even more spectators. Millau hosts a seven-day jazz festival in the third week of July.

Sleeping
Gîte de la Maladerie (☎ 05 65 60 41 84; chemin de la Graufesenque; dm €10) In grounds on the south bank of the Tarn, this friendly gîte is open year-round. On foot, follow the river upstream. If you're driving, turn left (east) after Pont du Larzac.

Hôtel La Capelle (☎ 05 65 60 14 72; fax 05 65 60 22 69; 7 place de la Fraternité; d €26, with bathroom €39-42; ⏰ year-round) In the converted wing of a one-time leather factory, La Capelle has new owners, long in the hotel trade and keen to make their mark. The hotel's large terrace with views towards the Causse Noir makes for a perfect breakfast spot.

Hôtel des Causses (☎ 05 65 60 03 19; fax 05 65 60 86 90; 56 av Jean Jaurès; d €40-45; menus €14.50-29) This hotel too has new owners, who have already comprehensively renovated and repainted all 19 rooms. A Logis de France with double glazing throughout, it has a good restaurant with an enticing regional *menu* and several hearty dishes from the Lyon area, the chef/owner's home town.

Cévenol Hôtel (☎ 05 65 60 74 44; www.cevenol -hotel.fr; 115 rue Rajol; d €56-59; ⏰ mid-Mar–mid-Nov; P 🏊) On the fringe of town, this modern concrete block with its uninspiring exterior is considerably more cosy within. Its 42 rooms – two with disabled access – are spacious (ask for one facing south room, with views over the Causses) and there's a pleasant open-air terrace.

Camping
For visitors in person, the tourist office will make a hotel reservation (€1.50 fee).

Camping des Deux Rivières (☎ 05 65 60 00 27; camping.deux-rivieres@wanadoo.fr; 61 av de l'Aigoual; camping €12; ⏰ Apr-Oct) Just east of Pont de Cureplat, this is the closest of several huge riverside camping sites east of town.

Eating

La Braconne (☎ 05 65 60 30 93; 7 place du Maréchal Foch; menus from €15; ⚅ closed dinner Sun) This cosy restaurant with an outside terrace overlooking Millau's main square has excellent regional *menus* and is famed for its roast lamb. It has a good selection of Faugères wines.

La Mangeoire (☎ 05 65 60 13 16; 8 blvd de la Capelle; lunch/dinner menu €16/43) This long-established place in the vaults beneath the former city walls serves delightful mainly regional dishes. The lunch *menu* is a midday special but dinner is a mouth-watering gourmet blow-out.

La Marmite du Pêcheur (☎ 05 65 61 20 44; 14-16 blvd de la Capelle; mains €11; ⚅ Thu-lunch Tue, closed 22 Jun-1 Jul) A few doors away from la Mangeoire and run by an engaging young couple, it's also attractively vaulted and has hearty regional *menus* within much the same price range. Try the innovative *salade au Roquefort et chataîgnes* (Roquefort and chestnut salad).

Le Square (☎ 05 65 61 26 00; 10 rue St-Martin; menus €16 & €24; ⚅ Thu-lunch Tue, closed Wed, dinner Tue & all Mar) It's essential to book at this intimate, highly regarded restaurant with its tempting *menus* and pleasant contemporary décor.

Le Capion (☎ 05 65 60 00 91; 3 rue J-F Alméras; mains 11.50-17, menus €16-35; ⚅ closed Wed, dinner Tue & 1-21 Jul) Peer into the kitchen to see the young team at work as you walk past on the way to the main dining room with its warm ochre and salmon colours. Portions are tasty and plentiful – none more so than the rich cheese platter (where, of course, Roquefort stars) and trolley of tempting homemade desserts.

SELF-CATERING

There are **markets** on Wednesday and Friday morning in place du Maréchal Foch, place Emma Calvé and the covered market at place des Halles.

Les Vitrines du Terroir (17 blvd de l'Ayrolle) and **Le Buron** (18 rue Droite) are *fromageries* selling local specialities including Roquefort and Perail du Larzac cheeses.

Getting There & Away

The **bus station and information office** (☎ 05 65 59 89 33) are beside the train station. Buses travel to Toulouse (€24, four hours, one daily), Montpellier (€15.90, 2¼ hours, seven daily), and Rodez (€11, 1½ hours, eight to 10 daily) via Albi (€15.30, 2½ hours).

THE KING OF CHEESES

The mouldy blue-green veins that run through Roquefort are, in fact, the spores of microscopic mushrooms, cultivated on leavened bread.

During the cheese's ripening process – which takes place in natural caves cut in the mountainside – draughts of air called *fleurines* sweep through the cave, encouraging the blue *penicillium roqueforti* to eat its way through the white cheese curds.

Roquefort is one of France's priciest and most noble cheeses. In 1407 Charles VI granted exclusive Roquefort cheese-making rights to the villagers of Roquefort and in the 17th century, the Sovereign Court of the Parliament of Toulouse imposed severe penalties against fraudulent cheese makers trading under the Roquefort name.

Connections from Millau include Béziers (€15.20, 1¾ hours, two to three daily) and Rodez (€10.30, 1½ hours, five to eight daily).

Getting Around

Millau is a compact, walkable town.

'Le Vélo est Mon Métier' ('Bikes are my Business') is the cheery slogan of the young owner of **Cycle Espace** (☎ 05 65 61 14 29; 21 blvd de l'Ayrolle), who supplies chat in plenty for free and cycles at €11/60 per day/week. Roc et Canyon (p749) also rents bikes.

AROUND MILLAU
Roquefort

In the heart of Parc Naturel Régional des Grands Causses and 25km southwest of Millau, the small village of Roquefort-sur-Soulzon turns ewe's milk into France's most famous blue cheese. Its steep, narrow streets, permeated with a cheesy smell, seethe with tourists heading for the cool natural caves, where seven different producers ripen some 22,000 tonnes of Roquefort cheese every year.

La Société (☎ 05 65 59 93 30; www.roquefort-soci ete.com) has 45-minute **guided tours** (adult/under 16 €3/free; ⚅ 9.30am-6.30pm Jul-Aug, 9.30am-noon & 1.30-5pm Sep-Jun) that include a rather feeble sound-and-light show and a sample of the three varieties the company makes. Established in 1842, it is the largest Roquefort producer, churning out 70% of the world's supply, 30% of which is exported.

Tours of the equally pungent caves of **Le Papillon** (☎ 05 65 58 50 08; www.roquefort-papillon .com in French; rue de la Fontaine; ◷ 9.30am-6.30pm Jul-Aug, 9.30am-12.30pm & 1.30-4.30pm or 5.30pm Sep-Jun) are free and include a 15-minute film.

Between mid-June and mid-September, you can also visit farms in the area, from which some 130 million litres of ewe's milk are collected annually. For details of tours, contact the **tourist office** (☎ 05 65 58 56 00; www .roquefort.com; ◷ 9am-7pm daily July & Aug; 9am-6pm Mon-Sat Apr-Jun & Sep-Oct; 10am-5pm Mon-Fri Nov-Mar) at the western entry to the village.

Micropolis

'La Cité des Insectes' (Insect City), **Micropolis** (☎ 05 65 58 50 50; www.micropolis.biz; adult/child €9.60/7.10; ◷ 10am-6pm daily Jul-Aug; 10am-5pm Tue-Sun Jun & Sep; 11am-4pm Tue-Fri, 10am-5pm Sat & Sun Mar, May & Oct) is just outside the village of St-Léons, off the D911 19km northwest of Millau.

Ever felt small? This mind-boggling high tech experience happens in a building where grass grows 6m high. The swarms of facts and statistics about insect life, all compellingly presented, seem equally tall but are all true. Admission includes an optional English audiowand and all captions are bilingual. Allow a good 1½ hours, perhaps rounding off with a meal at its pleasant, reasonably priced restaurant.

ROUSSILLON

Roussillon, sometimes known as French Catalonia, sits on Spain's doorstep at the eastern end of the Pyrenees. It's the land of the Tramontane, a violent wind which howls down from the mountains, chilling to the bone in winter and in summer strong enough to overturn a caravan. The main city is Perpignan, capital of the Pyrénées-Orientales *département*.

Long part of Catalonia (which nowadays officially designates only the autonomous region over the border in northeast Spain), Roussillon retains many symbols of Catalan identity. The *sardane* folk dance is still performed and the Catalan language (closely related to Occitan – which is also known as Provençal) is widely spoken.

History

People have lived here since prehistoric times, and one of Europe's oldest skulls was found in a cave near Tautavel (p756).

Roussillon's relatively modern history was for a long time closely bound with events over the Pyrenees in present-day Spain. In 1172 it came under the control of the realm of Catalonia-Aragon. Then, flourishing in its own right as the capital of the kingdom of Mallorca for most of the next two centuries, it again came under alien Aragonese rule for much of the late Middle Ages.

In 1640 the Catalans on both sides of the Pyrenees revolted against the Castilian kings in distant Madrid, who had engulfed Aragon. Perpignan endured a two-year siege, which was only relieved with the help of the French to the north. The subsequent 1659 Treaty of the Pyrenees defined the border between Spain and France once and for all, ceding the northern section of Catalonia, Roussillon, to the French, much to the indignation of the locals.

Geography

Roussillon occupies the southern end of the Lower Languedoc plain. Its highest point is Mont Canigou (2786m), a peak revered by the Catalan people. The flat coastline ends abruptly at the rocky foothills of the Pyrenees, backdrop to the Côte Vermeille (Vermilion Coast), a coastal area of deep-red rocks and soil that inspired Fauvist artists such as Matisse and Derain.

PERPIGNAN
pop 108,000

As much Catalan as French, Perpignan (Perpinyà in Catalan) was, from 1278 to 1344, capital of the kingdom of Mallorca, which stretched northwards as far as Montpellier and included the Balearic Islands. The town later became an important commercial centre and remains the third-largest Catalan city after Barcelona and Lleida in Spain.

It isn't southern France's most attractive city though it's far from a 'villainous ugly town' – the verdict of traveller Henry Swinburne in 1775. At the foothills of the Pyrenees and with the Côte Vermeille to the southeast, it makes a great base for day trips along the coast or to the mountains and Cathar castles of the interior.

PERPIGNAN

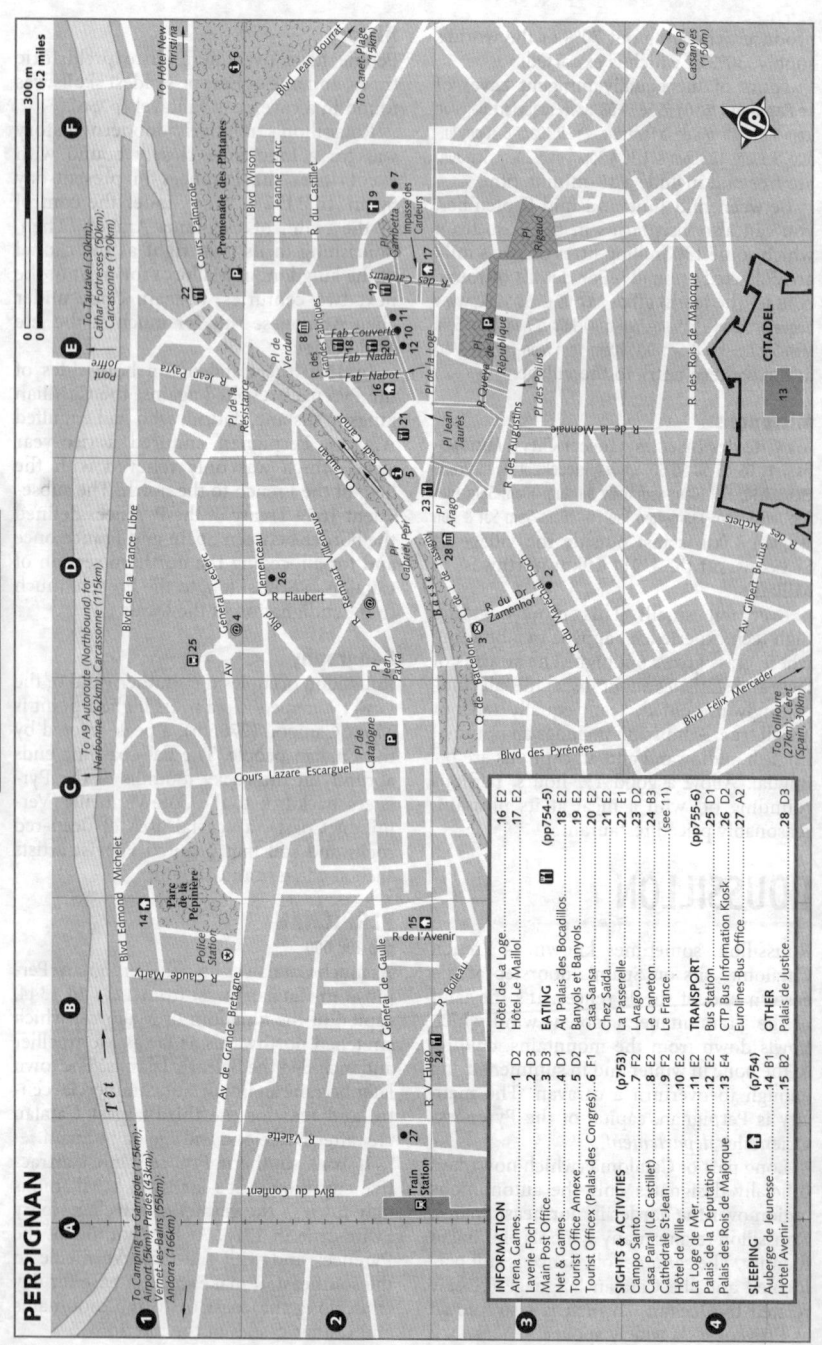

LANGUEDOC-ROUSSILLON

It's also commendably well documented – outside every major historical building is a freestanding sign with information in French, Catalan and English.

Orientation

Two rivers flow through the city: the Têt and its tributary, the narrow, crystal-clear Basse, banked with trim gardens. The heart of the partly pedestrianised old town lies around place de la Loge and place de Verdun.

Information

INTERNET ACCESS

Arena Games (9bis rue Docteur Pous; per hr €3; ⏰ 11am-2am Tue-Sat, 3pm-1am Sun & Mon)

Net & Games (45bis av Général Leclerc; per hr €3; ⏰ noon-1am Mon-Sat, 1-8pm Sun)

LAUNDRY

Laverie Foch (23 rue du Maréchal Foch; ⏰ 7am-8.30pm)

POST

Main Post Office (quai de Barcelone)

TOURIST INFORMATION

Tourist Office (☎ 04 68 66 30 30; www.perpignan tourisme.com; ⏰ 9am-7pm Mon-Sat, 10am-4pm Sun mid-Jun–mid-Sep; 9am-6pm Mon-Sat, 9am-noon Sun mid-Sep–mid-Jun) In the Palais des Congrès, off promenade des Platanes.

Tourist Office Annexe (⏰ Oct-May; Espace Palmarium, place Arago)

Sights

PLACE DE LA LOGE

Place de la Loge has three fine stone structures. **La Loge de Mer** was constructed in the 14th century and rebuilt during the Renaissance. At various times Perpignan's stock exchange and maritime tribunal, its ground floor is now occupied by the splendid café-restaurant le France (p754). Sandwiched between it and the **Palais de la Députation**, once seat of the local parliament, is the **Hôtel de Ville** with its typically Roussillon pebbled façade of river stones. Pass by on Sunday morning and you can watch locals of all ages dancing the graceful *sardane*, folk dance of the Catalans.

LE CASTILLET & CASA PAÏRAL

The museum of Roussillon and Catalan folklore, **Casa Païral** (☎ 04 68 35 42 05; place de Verdun; adult/student €4/2; ⏰ 10am-6.30pm Wed-Mon May-Sep, 11am-5.30pm Wed-Mon Oct-Apr), occupies Le Castillet, a 14th-century red-brick town gate. Once a prison, it's the only vestige of Vauban's fortified town walls, which surrounded the city until the early 1900s. The museum houses bits and pieces of everything Catalan – from traditional bonnets and lace mantillas to a 17th-century kitchen. From the rooftop terrace there are great views of the old city and citadel.

PALAIS DES ROIS DE MAJORQUE

The **Palais des Rois de Majorque** (Palace of the Kings of Mallorca; ☎ 04 68 34 48 29; entrance on rue des Archers; adult/child €4/2; ⏰ 10am-5pm or 6pm) sits on a small hill. Built in 1276 for the ruler of the newly founded kingdom, it was at one time surrounded by extensive fig and olive groves and a hunting reserve, which were lost once Vauban's formidable citadel walls enclosed the palace.

Bizarre but true: the princes of Aragon used to keep lions in the dried-up moat of the castle and the goats that constituted the lions' diet grazed the surrounding meadows, from which commoners' flocks were banned.

CATHÉDRALE ST-JEAN

Topped by a typically Provençal wrought-iron bell cage, **Cathédrale St-Jean** (place Gambetta; ⏰ 9am-noon & 3-6.30pm), begun in 1324 and not completed until 1509, has a flat façade of red brick and smooth river stones in a zigzag pattern. Inside the cavernous single nave, notice particularly the fine carving and relative sobriety of the Catalan altarpiece.

Immediately south of the cathedral (leave by a small door in the south aisle) is the early-14th-century **Campo Santo** (⏰ noon-7pm Tue-Sat Apr-Jun & Sep, 11am-5pm Oct-Mar, closed Jul & Aug), France's only cloister-cemetery, lined with white-marble Gothic niches.

Festivals & Events

As befits a town so close to the Spanish border, Perpignan is strong on fiestas.

For the Good Friday **Procession de la Sanch**, penitents wearing the *caperutxa* (traditional hooded red or black robes) parade silently through the old city. A 'sacred' flame is brought down from Mont Canigou during the week-long **Fête de la St-Jean**, marking midsummer, while in September half the town dons tights and wimples for the **Marché Médiéval** (Medieval Market).

Shutterbugs will be in their element in the first half of September, when, for a full two weeks, the town hosts **Visa Pour l'Image**, the world's major festival of photojournalism, open to the general public.

Perpignan holds a **jazz festival** throughout October and, on the third weekend in October, a **wine festival**, when a barrel of the year's new wine is ceremonially borne to Cathédrale St-Jean to be blessed.

Sleeping

Auberge de Jeunesse (☎ 04 68 34 63 32; fax 04 68 51 16 02; allée Marc Pierre; dm €8.90; ☷ late-Jan–mid-Dec) Perpignan's HI-affiliated youth hostel is just north of Parc de la Pépinière.

Hôtel Avenir (☎ 04 68 34 20 30; www.avenirhotel .com; 11 rue de l'Avenir; s/d €16/21, d with bathroom from €33.60; **P**) Among the string of budget hotels along and around av Général de Gaulle the Avenir is a particularly friendly, highly recommended place. Several rooms have a small terrace and each is uniquely and charmingly decorated by the proprietor. Savour too the delightful first-floor terrace.

Hôtel New Christina (☎ 04 68 35 12 21; www .hotel-newchristina.com; 51 cours Lassus; s/d €62/67; **P** ☷ ☷) At the excellent, family-run New Christina, rooms are attractively decorated in blue and beige and bathrooms, all with bathtubs, are separate from toilets. Those at the front overlook a public park. The open-air pool, up on the roof, has an even better view. There's also a decent restaurant (*menu* €20).

Hôtel Le Maillol (☎ 04 68 51 10 20; hotel.lemai llol@worldonline.fr; 14 impasse des Cardeurs; d €36-41) Occupying a 17th-century building, Le Maillol, at the end of a cul-de-sac off a pedestrian street, couldn't be more tranquil. Of its smallish but quite adequate rooms on three floors, those overlooking the interior patio have more light.

Hôtel de La Loge (☎ 04 68 34 41 02; www.hotel delaloge.fr; 1 rue des Fabriques Nabot; s €37 d €42-64) Disregard the threadbare stair carpet; the bedrooms themselves are a good deal more pleasant though their furniture varies from attractive and antique to flea market. Of the more expensive rooms, which have air-con and separate toilets, Nos 106 and 206 (each €57) overlook place de la Loge.

Camping

Camping La Garrigole (☎ 04 68 54 66 10; 2 rue Maurice Lévy; camping €13; ☷ year-round) This small camping ground is 1.5km west of the train station. Take bus No 2 and get off at the Garrigole stop.

Eating

Au Palais des Bocadillos (☎ 04 68 35 36 08; place de Verdun; ☷ 7.30am-9.30pm) Planted in one of the old quarter's main squares, the Sandwich Palace serves up a variety of superior sandwiches and baguettes plus a plat du jour, all of which you can eat in or take away.

Chez Saïda (☎ 06 71 82 74 82; 5 rue Lazare Escarguel; mains €10-16) Recently opened, this tiny place specialises in reasonably priced seafood plus, in summer, crunchy salads. You can slurp down a plate of oysters or indulge in a variety of seafood platters, such as their plentiful Étoile.

Le France (☎ 04 68 51 61 71; place de la Loge; mains €13-32; ☷ lunch Mon-Sun) Popular and stylish, Le France manages to blend harmoniously the modern – right down to the all-glass hand basins in the toilets – within a historical setting. Portions are smallish but attractively presented and the wine list is almost as vast as the palatial setting of what was once Perpignan's stock exchange. The lunchtime *formule rapide* (quick *menu*) at €12.50 is great value.

L'Arago (☎ 04 68 51 81 96; 1 place Arago; mains €12.50-18) Here's another restaurant that's much in demand so you may have to hang around a while for a free table. It does pizzas (€7.70 to €9.40) and has a strong and

---

AUTHOR'S CHOICE

Banyols et Banyols (☎ 04 68 34 48 40; 7 rue des Cardeurs; mains €13-18; ☷ Tue-Sat) This recently opened restaurant, stripped back to its brick and girders may be small but it's delightfully light and airy. The chef/owner moves among diners speaking with passion about his cooking before darting back to the kitchen area to stir a sauce, shake a pan and advise his minions, all in full view of the diners. The creative menu changes regularly; do start with the risotto with chestnuts and prawns if it still features. Banyols et Banyols? It's the family name of this talented father and daughter team.

LANGUEDOC-ROUSSILLON

varied à la carte selection. Sample its fine local wines, sold by the glass or bottle.

Casa Sansa (☎ 04 68 34 21 84; entrances 2 rue des Fabriques Nadal & rue des Fabriques Couvertes; mains €12.50-16) This is another highly popular place – or rather two adjacent places. Choose the older, more southerly one, its walls scarcely visible for posters and the photos of the famous and less than famous who have enjoyed its fine Catalan cuisine. It too has a great selection of wines, also available by the glass.

La Passerelle (☎ 04 68 51 30 65; 1 cours Palmarole; mains €16-22; ✆ dinner Mon-Sat) Its attractive marine décor hints at the riches within the kitchen. La Passerelle is *the* restaurant in Perpignan for Mediterranean fish, guaranteed fresh and without a whiff of freezer or fish farm.

Near the train station are plenty of cheap-and-cheerful options, including Arab, Turkish and Alsacien joints. **Le Caneton** (☎ 04 68 34 20 60; 12 rue Victor Hugo; menu €5; ✆ lunch Mon-Fri) must rank as one of France's best-value and tiniest restaurants. It's little more than a room in a private house run by a doughty old couple who do a daily three-course *menu*.

Entertainment

The tourist office publishes *L'Agenda*, a comprehensive free monthly guide to exhibitions and cultural events. *Aware, Le Mag* is one of several competing free, what's-on breakdowns of the club scene and nightlife.

Getting There & Away

AIR

Perpignan's **airport** (☎ 04 68 52 60 70) is 5km northwest of the town centre. Air France flies three to four times daily to/from Paris (Orly) while Ryanair runs a daily flight to/from London Stansted.

BUS

From the **bus station** (☎ 04 68 35 29 02; av Général Leclerc), **Courriers Catalans** services coastal resorts, running two to seven buses daily (€6.60) to/from Collioure and Port-Vendres, most continuing to Banyuls (1¼ hours).

Seven buses daily travel along the Têt Valley to Vernet-les-Bains (€9.60, 1½ hours) via Prades (€8.15) and Villefranche (€9.60) and three of these continue as far as La Tour de Carol (€12.60). Up the Tech Valley, there are up to nine buses daily to Céret (€5.80, 50 minutes).

For long-distance buses, the **Eurolines office** (☎ 04 68 34 11 46; 10 av Général de Gaulle) is just east of the train station.

CAR

Rental companies include **ADA** (airport ☎ 04 68 61 50 95) and **Budget** (airport ☎ 04 68 61 38 85).

TRAIN

Perpignan's small train station – centre of the universe according to Salvador Dalí (below) – is served by bus Nos 2 and 19.

Major destinations include Barcelona (€30 direct, €15 change at Cerbère/Portbou, up to three hours, three daily). There are frequent trains to Montpellier (€19.20, two hours) via Narbonne (€9, 45 minutes) and Béziers (€11.90). For Paris (€68 to €91), change in Montpellier; for Carcassonne (€15.60), in Narbonne.

Closer to home is Cerbère/Portbou on the Spanish border (€6.60, 40 minutes, approximately 15 daily) via Banyuls, Collioure and Port-Vendres.

The nearest you can get to Andorra by train is La Tour de Carol (€20.30, four hours, two to four daily, some changing in Villefranche) via Prades (€6.30, 40 minutes) and Villefranche (€7, at least six daily). From La Tour de Carol, a connecting bus takes you on to Andorra.

Getting Around

The local bus company, CTP, has an **information kiosk** (☎ 04 68 61 01 13; 27 blvd Clemenceau).

DALÍ'S TRAIN OF THOUGHT

You may choose to dissent from Salvador Dalí's no doubt chemically induced claim that Perpignan's train station is the centre of the universe. According to local lore (reinforced by a plaque in front of the building), the Catalan surrealist painter (1904–89) was visiting the capital of French Catalonia in 1965 when he experienced an epiphany. 'Suddenly before me, everything appeared with the clarity of lightning,' he wrote. 'I found myself in the centre of the universe.' Dalí went on to describe this nondescript place as *'la source d'illuminations'* and *'la cathédrale d'intuitions'* – no doubt putting a smile on the faces of local tourism authorities and most Perpignanais.

One ticket costs €1.10, a one-day pass *(ticket visite)* is €4.10 and a 10-ticket *carnet*, €7.80.

Bright yellow and red, *Le P'tit Bus* is a free minibus that plies a circular route around the old town. It runs about every five minutes from 8am to 7pm, Monday to Saturday, except – come on now, we're in France! – between 12.30pm and 1.30pm.

For a taxi, call **Accueil Perpignan Taxis** (☎ 04 68 35 15 15).

AROUND PERPIGNAN
Coastal Beaches
The nearest beach – all 5km of it – is at **Canet-Plage**, backed by a sprawl of hotels and apartment blocks. There's a small **tourist office** (☎ 04 68 86 72 00; 9am-7pm daily Jul-Aug; 9am-noon & 2-6pm Mon-Sat, 10am-noon & 3-5pm Sun Sep-Jun). Rent a bicycle (€12.50 per day) from **Sun Bike 66** (☎ 04 68 73 88 65) and cruise the promenade or ride around the Étang de Canet, a small inland lake and nature reserve.

From Argelès-Plage south, wide sandy beaches give way to rocky coastline as the Pyrenees tumble to the sea, their steep flanks terraced with vineyards.

Céret
It's mainly the **Musée d'Art Moderne** (☎ 04 68 87 27 76; 8 blvd Maréchal Joffre; adult/student/child €8/6/free; 10am-6pm or 7pm Wed-Mon) that draws visitors to this town of 8000 souls, settled snugly in the Pyrenean foothills just off the Tech Valley. Superbly endowed for such a small community, its collection owes much to an earlier generation of visitors and residents, including Picasso, Braque, Chagall, Matisse, Miró, Dalí, Juan Gris and Manolo, all of whom donated works (53 from Picasso alone).

Firmly Catalan, Céret is also splendidly disproportionate in the number and vigour of its festivals. Famous for its juicy cherries (the first pickings of the season are packed off to the French president), it kicks off with the **Fête de la Cerise** (Cherry Festival) in late May. Summer sees the **féria** with bullfights and roistering and **La Fête de la Sardane**, celebrating the *sardane*, folk dance par excellence of the Catalans – and, of course, yet more bullfights. More sedately, **Les Méennes** is a festival of primarily classical music. Contact the **tourist office** (☎ 04 68 87 00 53; www .ot-ceret.fr; 1 av Clemenceau) for details.

Tautavel
The Arago Cave, on the slopes above the village of Tautavel, 30km northwest of Perpignan along the D117, has yielded a human skull, estimated to be 450,000 years old, along with many other prehistoric items.

THE CATHARS

The term *le Pays Cathar* (Cathar Land) recalls the cruel Albigensian Crusade – the hounding and extermination of a religious sect called the Cathars.

Cathars (from the Greek word *katharos* meaning 'pure') believed that God's kingdom was locked in battle with Satan's evil world and that humans were evil at heart. But, they reckoned, a pure life followed by several reincarnations would free the spirit from its satanical body. The ascetic *parfaits* ('perfects') followed strict vegetarian diets and abstained from sex.

Catharism spread from the Balkans to Languedoc between the 11th and 13th centuries. Reacting against worldly Rome and preaching in *langue d'oc*, the local tongue, the sect gained many followers.

In 1208 Pope Innocent III preached a crusade against the Cathars, who were closely associated with the Albigenses, a sect based in the city of Albi. The Albigensian Crusade was a chance for northern rulers to expand their territory into Languedoc, supported spiritually by St-Dominic of Toulouse, founder of the Dominican order of monks, and in the field by the cruel Simon de Montfort.

After long sieges, the major Cathar centres at Béziers, Carcassonne, the village of Minerve and the dramatically sited fortresses of Montségur, Quéribus and Peyrepertuse were taken and hundreds of 'perfects' were burned as heretics. In Béziers as many as 20,000 of the faithful were slaughtered. Another cruel massacre took place at Montségur in 1244, when 200 Cathars, refusing to renounce their faith when the castle was captured after a 10-month siege, were burned alive in a mass funerary pyre. In 1321 the burning of the last 'perfect', Guillaume Bélibaste, marked the end of Catharism in Languedoc.

Musée de la Préhistoire (Prehistory Museum; ☎ 04 68 29 07 76; av Jean Jaurès; admission €7; ☺ 10am-8pm Jul-Aug; 10.30am-12.30pm & 1.30-5pm Apr-Jun & Sep; 1.30-5.30pm Feb-Mar, Oct-Nov; Mon only Dec-Jan) has a full-size reproduction of the cave, complete with holograms, dioramas, TVs dispensing knowledge from every corner and lots of fossilised bones and stone tools. The audio-wand (included in the admission fee) has an English channel. There's also a second-ary exhibition (ask for the English-language sheet 'The First Inhabitants of Europe'), 300m away on rue Anatole France. Allow a good 1½ hours to take in both elements.

Cathar Fortresses

When the Albigensian Crusade forced the Cathars into the arid mountains that once marked the frontier between France and Aragon, they sought refuge in these inac-cessible fortresses. The most famous are **Peyrepertuse** (adult/child €4/2; ☺ 8.30am-8.30pm Jun-Sep, 10am-5pm Feb-Mar & Nov-Dec, 9am-7pm Apr-May & Oct) and **Quéribus** (adult/child €5/2; ☺ 9am-8pm Jul-Aug, 9.30am-6.30pm or 7.30pm Apr-Jun & Sep-Oct, 10am-5pm Jan-Feb & Nov-Dec). Off the D117 about 50km northwest of Perpignan, they can be combined in a day trip that takes in the Musée de la Préhistoire in Tautavel (above) as well. Both, alas, are all but inaccessible without your own wheels.

The larger, Peyrepertuse, approached along the twisting, narrow Gorges de Gala-mus and occupying one of the most dram-atic sites of any castle anywhere, squats high on a ridge with a drop of several hundred metres on all sides. Quéribus, perched pre-cariously at 728m on a rocky spur, marked the Cathars' last stand in 1255.

It's wild country and views from both make the pulse race. They can be hot as hell in summer so be sure to pack extra water.

TÊT VALLEY

Fruit orchards carpet the lower reaches of the Têt Valley. Beyond the strategic fort-ress town of Villefranche-le-Confluent, the scenery becomes wilder, more open and undulating as the valley climbs towards Spanish Catalonia and Andorra.

Le Train Jaune

Carrying nearly half a million passengers during the three peak months of high sum-mer, **Le Train Jaune** (Yellow Train) runs from Villefranche to La Tour de Carol (return €32) through spectacular Pyrenean scen-ery. There are five trains daily in July and August, four in June and September and two between October and May. You can't reserve and it's wise to arrive an hour before departure time in high summer.

Prades

pop 6000

Prades, at the heart of the Têt Valley, is internationally famed for its annual music festival. It's an attractive town with houses of river stone and brick, liberally adorned with pink marble from nearby quarries.

The exceptionally friendly **tourist office** (☎ 04 68 05 41 02; www.prades-tourisme.com; ☺ 9am-noon & 2-6pm Mon-Sat, 10am-noon Sun Jul-Aug; 9am-noon & 2-5pm Mon-Fri Sep-Jun, 9am-noon Sat Jun & Sep) is at 4 rue des Marchands.

The belltower of **Église St-Pierre** is all that remains of the original 12th-century Ro-manesque church. The wonderfully expres-sive 17th-century *Entombment of Christ* at the western end (the light switch is just to the right) is by the Catalan sculptor Josep Sunyer, who also carved the exuberant main altarpiece, a *chef d'oeuvre* of Catalan Ba-roque and reputedly the largest in France.

The small **Musée de la Soie** (Silk Museum; ☎ 04 68 96 33 75; av Général Roques; adult/child €6/4; ☺ 10am-7pm daily Jul-Aug; 10am-noon & 2-6pm Tue-Sun Apr-Jun & Sep-Oct) evokes Prades' past as a producer of cocoons for Perpignan's silk industry.

ACTIVITIES

Hiking & Walking Around Prades details in English 20 easy-to-moderate walks lasting from 2½ to four hours. *Six Grandes Randon-nées en Conflent* in French describes six more challenging day walks, including the classic ascent of Mont Canigou (2786m). The tour-ist office sells both guides at €3 each.

VTT en Conflent details nine mountain-bike routes varying from easy to seriously tough. **Cycles Flament** (☎ 04 68 96 07 62; 8 rue Arago) rents out mountain bikes.

The **Festival Pablo Casals** (☎ 04 68 96 33 07; festival.casals@wanadoo.fr), held over two weeks in late July/early August, brings top-flight classical musicians to this small town.

Villefranche-de-Conflent

Villefranche, sitting at the strategic conflu-ence of the valley of the Rivers Têt and Cady (hence the 'de Conflent' of its name), is encircled by thick fortifications, built by Vauban in the 17th century to strengthen and augment the original 11th-century defences, which have survived intact.

The small **tourist office** (☎ 04 68 96 22 96; www.villefranche-de-conflent.com in French; 32bis rue St-Jacques; ☯ 10am-1pm & 2-6pm May-Oct; 10.30am-12.30pm & 2-5.30pm Feb-Mar & Nov-Dec, closed Jan) arranges admission to the **ramparts** (adult/student/child €4/3/free; audioguide €3).

The stronghold high above the town, built originally by Vauban (p30) and strengthened under Napoleon III, is the heavily promoted **Château-Fort Liberia** (☎ 04 68 96 34 01; admission €5.50; ☯ 10am-8pm Apr-Oct, 10am-6pm Nov-Mar), from where there are spectacular views.

Vernet-les-Bains
pop 1500

Busy in summer and almost a ghost town for the rest of the year, this small spa was much frequented by the British aristocracy in the late 19th century (there's still a small Anglican church). Nowadays, it's an alternative to Prades for hiking and, particularly, for attacking **Mont Canigou**, the Pyrenees' easternmost major peak. Three tracks wind up from Vernet. To bag the summit the easy way, bounce up in a 4x4 (about €25 per person return) with **Sport Garage Villaceque** (☎ 04 68 05 51 14; rue du Conflent) or **Jean-Paul Bouzon** (☎ 04 68 05 62 68; 17 blvd des Pyrénées) as far as Les Cortalets (2175m), from where the summit is a three-hour round trip.

Vernet's **tourist office** (☎ 04 68 05 55 35; www .ot-vernet-les-bains.fr) is on place de l'Ancienne Mairie.

CÔTE VERMEILLE

The Côte Vermeille (Vermilion Coast) runs south from Collioure to Cerbère on the Spanish border, where the Pyrenees foothills reach the sea. Against a backdrop of vineyards and pinched between Mediterranean and mountains, it's riddled with small, rocky bays and little ports. These once engaged in sardine and anchovy fishing but now have economies based primarily on tourism.

Resorts are served by regular train and less frequent bus services (p755).

Collioure
pop 2930

In picturesque Collioure, boats bob against a backdrop of houses washed in soft pastel colours. Once Perpignan's port, it found fame early this century when it inspired the Fauvist art of Henri Matisse and André Derain. Later both Picasso and Braque came here to paint (below).

The **tourist office** (☎ 04 68 82 15 47; www.col lioure.com; ☯ 9am-8pm Mon-Sat, 10am-noon & 3-6pm Sun Jul-Aug; 9am-noon & 2-7pm Mon-Sat May-Jun & Sep; 2-6pm Mon, 9am-noon & 2-6pm Tue-Fri, 9am-noon Sat Oct-Apr) is on place 18 Juin.

Across the creek is the **Château Royal de Collioure** (☎ 04 68 82 06 43; adult/child €4/2; ☯ 10am-6pm Jun-Sep, 9am-5pm Oct-May). Originally a Templar settlement built upon Roman foundations, the castle enjoyed its greatest splendour as the summer residence of the kings of Mallorca. Vauban added its towering defensive walls in the 17th century.

The medieval church tower of **Notre Dame des Anges** at the northern end of the harbour once doubled up as a lighthouse (the pink dome that gives it the air of a giant penis was

---

THE FAUVISTES & COLLIOURE

'No sky in all France is more blue than that of Collioure. I only have to close the shutters of my room and there before me are all the colours of the Mediterranean.' So effused Henri Matisse (1869–1954), instigator and chief exponent of Fauvism.

The movement briefly embraced many of the principal artists of the day such as Georges Rouault, Raoul Dufy and Georges Braque. Reacting against impressionism, *Les Fauves* (The Wild Ones) worked with pure colour. Stripping a scene to its most basic elements, they abandoned perspective, filling their canvases with firm lines and stripes, rectangles and splashes of bright colour.

The **Chemin du Fauvisme** (Fauvism Trail) is a walking route around Collioure that passes 20 reproductions of works by Matisse and his younger colleague André Derain. You can pick up a French-language guide booklet (€5.50) from the tourist office or from **Espace Fauve** (quai de l'Amirauté), which does guided tours (€6) of Collioure during school holidays.

added in 1810). Inside is a superb altarpiece, crafted by the Catalan master Josep Sunyer.

The **Musée d'Art Moderne** (☎ 04 68 82 10 19; Villa Pams, route de Port-Vendres; adult/child €2/1.50; 🕙 10am-noon & 2-6pm or 7pm; closed Tue Oct-May) is another stimulating stop for contemporary art lovers.

To sample and pick up some of the best local Collioure wine, visit **La Maison de la Vigne et du Vin** (☎ 04 68 82 49 00; 🕙 daily Jul-Sep; weekends May-Jun) in the place de la Mairie.

Collioure's Good Friday procession of hooded penitents is about the richest this side of the Pyrenees. Altogether more joyous are **Fêtes de la St-Vincent** (14-18 August), celebrations in honour of the town's patron saint, their highlight a spectacular firework display on the 16th.

From May to September, leave your car in Parking Relais and take the shuttle bus that runs to the village every 10 minutes. For the rest of the year, there's a large car park behind the castle.

Port-Vendres

Three kilometres south of Collioure, Port-Vendres, Roussillon's only natural harbour and deep-water port, has been exploited ever since Greek mariners roamed the rocky coastline. A significant entrepôt until the independence of France's North African territories in the 1960s, it remains an important coastal fishing and leisure port, though it is the least interesting of the Côte Vermeille resorts. The small **tourist office** (☎ 04 68 82 07 54; 1 quai François Joly; www.port-vendres.com) is in the port's northwestern corner.

Banyuls

pop 5000

Banyuls, 7km south of Port-Vendres, has a small pebble beach, overlooked by the **tourist office** (☎ 04 68 88 31 58; www.banyuls-sur-mer.com; av de la République; 🕙 9am-8pm daily Jul-Aug, 9am-noon & 2.30-6pm Mon-Sat Sep-Jun). The town is the starting point for the GR10, the long distance trail that snakes along the Pyrenees all the way to Hendaye, beside the Atlantic.

At the promenade's southern limit is the **Aquarium du Laboratoire Arago** (☎ 04 68 88 73 39; adult/child €4.20/2.10; 🕙 9am-1pm & 2-9pm Jul-Aug, 9am-noon & 2-6.30pm Sep-Jun). Much more than yet another commercial enterprise with smiling dolphins, it also functions as the oceanographic research station of Paris' Université Pierre et Marie Curie.

More strenuously aquatic but well worth the effort, staff of the **Réserve Naturelle Marine** (Marine Nature Reserve; ☎ 04 68 88 56 87) have mounted a splendid initiative – a 250m **underwater 'trail'** (admission free; 🕙 noon-6pm Jul-Aug) that you snorkel around. Just off Plage de Peyrefite, midway between Banyuls and Cerbère, it's punctuated by information points and you can hire fins and masks (€5) up to 5pm (if you have your own gear, you can swim the trail at any time).

Provence

CONTENTS

PROVENCE

First-time visitors may be as captivated by the beauty of this ruggedly lovely chunk of France as the painter Van Gogh was when he arrived from a gloomy Paris in 1888. 'What intensity of colours, what pure air, what vibrant serenity,' he wrote. He wasn't wrong. That colourful intensity in land, sea and sky is brought out by the glorious sun. Along the coast, its rays lend the sea gem-like blues and greens. Inland, the hues are more subtle: roofs in improbably pretty ochres and terracottas and serried rows of lavender.

It's a culturally and historically rich region, too. Van Gogh wasn't the first, or last, painter, writer or thinker to fall for Provence. Its towns and cities are dotted with galleries containing the works of Europe's most celebrated artists.

The Romans were among the first to spot its charms, invading it then sending their favourite legions to retire here. They left many unmissable monuments behind, including theatres and thermal baths (some still in use) in places such as Arles (p802), Aix (p779), Orange (p792) and Vaison-la-Romaine (p794).

Towns boast generous public spaces – just as they did under Augustus. It's an outdoor life, perhaps spent sipping *pastis* (a liquorice-flavoured aperitif) in cafés or playing *pétanque*, a type of bowls using heavy metal balls, under the shade of the region's plane trees.

The area has its own distinct smells and flavours, best experienced in the sensory trance that a visit to a Provençal market induces. The region's abundant fresh produce and seafood are best accompanied with a fresh rosé wine, a delightful and inexpensive local speciality.

HIGHLIGHTS

- Savour **bouillabaisse** (p770), Marseille's fishy speciality
- Smell, taste and buy the best local produce at one of the region's many **superb markets** (p776)
- Walking or cycling in the lovely **Parc Naturel Régional du Lubéron** (p800)
- Get down and boogy in **Aix's lively nightlife** (p782)
- Discover the many gems of Renaissance art at Avignon's **Musée du Petit Palais** (p786)
- Submerge yourself in the thermal baths and spas in **Aix-en-Provence** (p779) or **Digne-les-Bains** (p811)
- Tackle rock climbing, canyoning, canoeing and hiking in the **Gorges du Verdon** (p813)
- Peeking at the **Camargue's abundant bird life** (p806)

POPULATION: 4,632,600	AREA: 25,851 SQ KM

PROVENCE

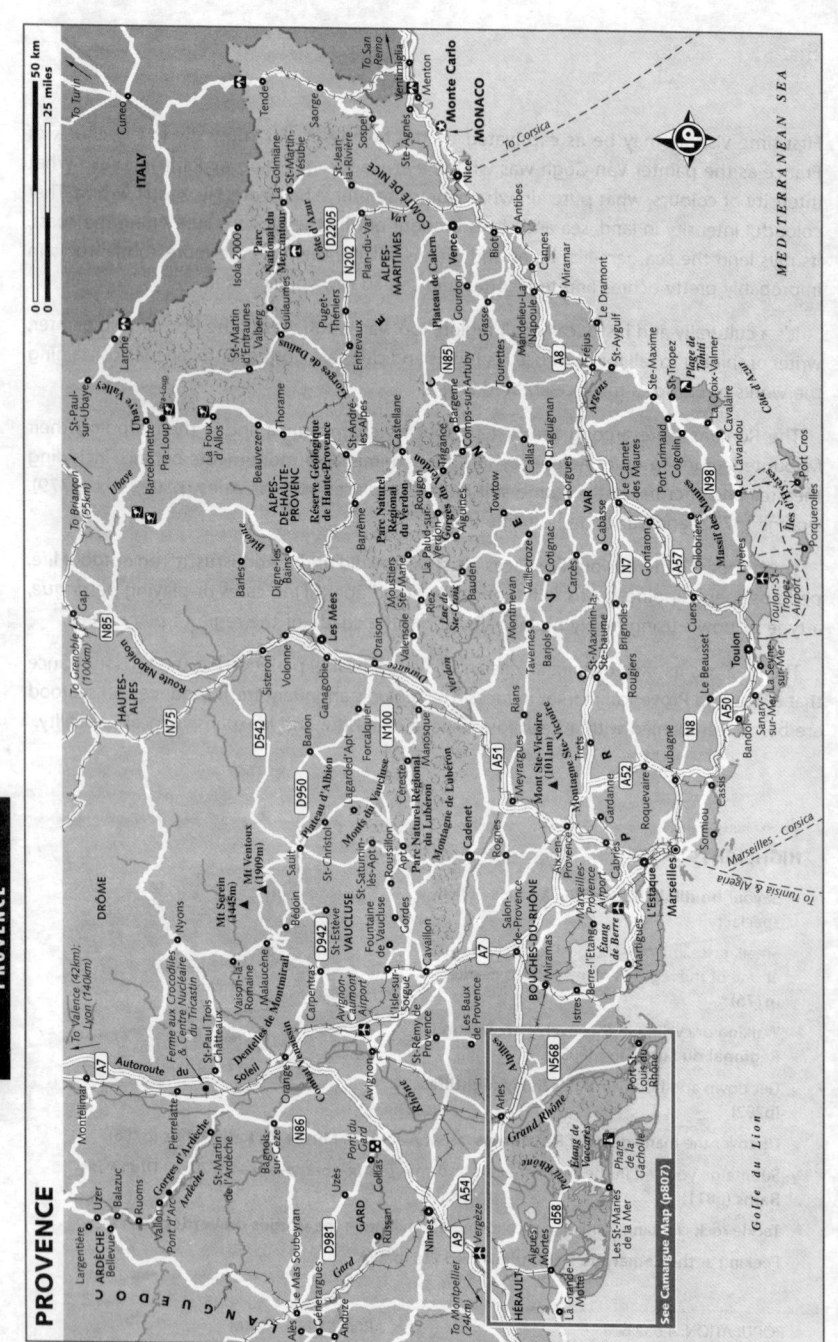

PROVENCE

See Camargue Map (p807)

History

Provence was settled over the centuries by the Ligurians, the Celts and the Greeks, but really began to flourish under the Romans after its conquest by Julius Caesar in the mid-1st century BC. The Romans called the area between the Alps, the sea and the River Rhône Provincia Romana, from which the name Provence is derived.

After the collapse of the Roman Empire in the late 5th century, Provence suffered invasions by the Visigoths, Burgundians and the Ostrogoths. The Arabs – who for some time held the Iberian Peninsula and parts of France – were defeated in the 8th century.

During the 14th century, the Catholic Church – under a series of French-born popes – moved its headquarters from feud-riven Rome to Avignon, thus beginning the most resplendent period in that city's history. Provence became part of France in 1481, but Avignon and Comtat Venaissin, with its seat at Carpentras, remained under papal control until the Revolution.

Geography

Provence stretches along both sides of the River Rhône from just north of Orange down to the Mediterranean, and along France's southern coast from the Camargue salt marshes in the west to Marseille in the east. Beyond Marseille is the Côte d'Azur, which, though historically part of Provence, appears in a separate chapter in this book along with Monaco.

South of Arles, the Camargue marsh-lands – actually the delta of the Rhône – are within a triangle formed by the Grand Rhône to the east and the Petit Rhône to the west.

Most of the region's mountains and hills lie east of the Rhône: the Baronnies; 1909m Mont Ventoux; the Vaucluse plateau; the rugged Lubéron Range and the little Alpilles. Further east is Europe's most spectacular canyon, the Gorges du Verdon.

Climate

Provence's weather is bright, sunny and dry for much of the year, although when the cold, dry winds of the mistral strike southwards down the Rhône Valley – often with surprising fury and little warning – they can turn a fine spring day into a bone-chilling wintry one.

The mistral – formed by the coincidence of high-pressure air over central France and low-pressure air over the Mediterranean – tends to blow continuously for several days. It can reach speeds of more than 100km/h, damaging crops, whipping up forest fires and generally driving everybody around the bend. It is most common in winter and spring.

Language

The various dialects of Provençal – more closely related grammatically to Catalan and Spanish than French – are still spoken every day by thousands of people across southern France, especially by older residents of rural areas.

From around the- 12th to the 14th centuries, Provençal was the literary language of France and northern Spain, and was used as far afield as Italy. During that period, it was the principal language of the medieval troubadours – poets, often courtiers and nobles – whose melodies and elegant poems were motivated by the ideal of courtly love.

A movement for the revival of Provençal literature, culture and identity began in the mid-19th century. The movement's most prominent member was the poet Frédéric Mistral (1830–1914), recipient of the Nobel Prize for literature in 1904. In recent years the language has again enjoyed something of a revival, and in many areas signs are written in Provençal and French.

Getting There & Away

For information on ferry services from Marseille to Sardinia and Tunisia see p920. For details on ferries from Marseille to Corsica see p865.

MARSEILLE REGION

MARSEILLE

pop 807,071

In parts very African, in others distinctly Middle Eastern but in its entirety unmistakeably French, the cosmopolitan port of Marseille (spelt Marseilles in English but pronounced the same) is a brusque, bustling place with bags of character. There's the pretty old port, the gritty (and often stinking) backstreets, lively markets with the atmosphere of a Moroccan souk, heavenly

MARSEILLE

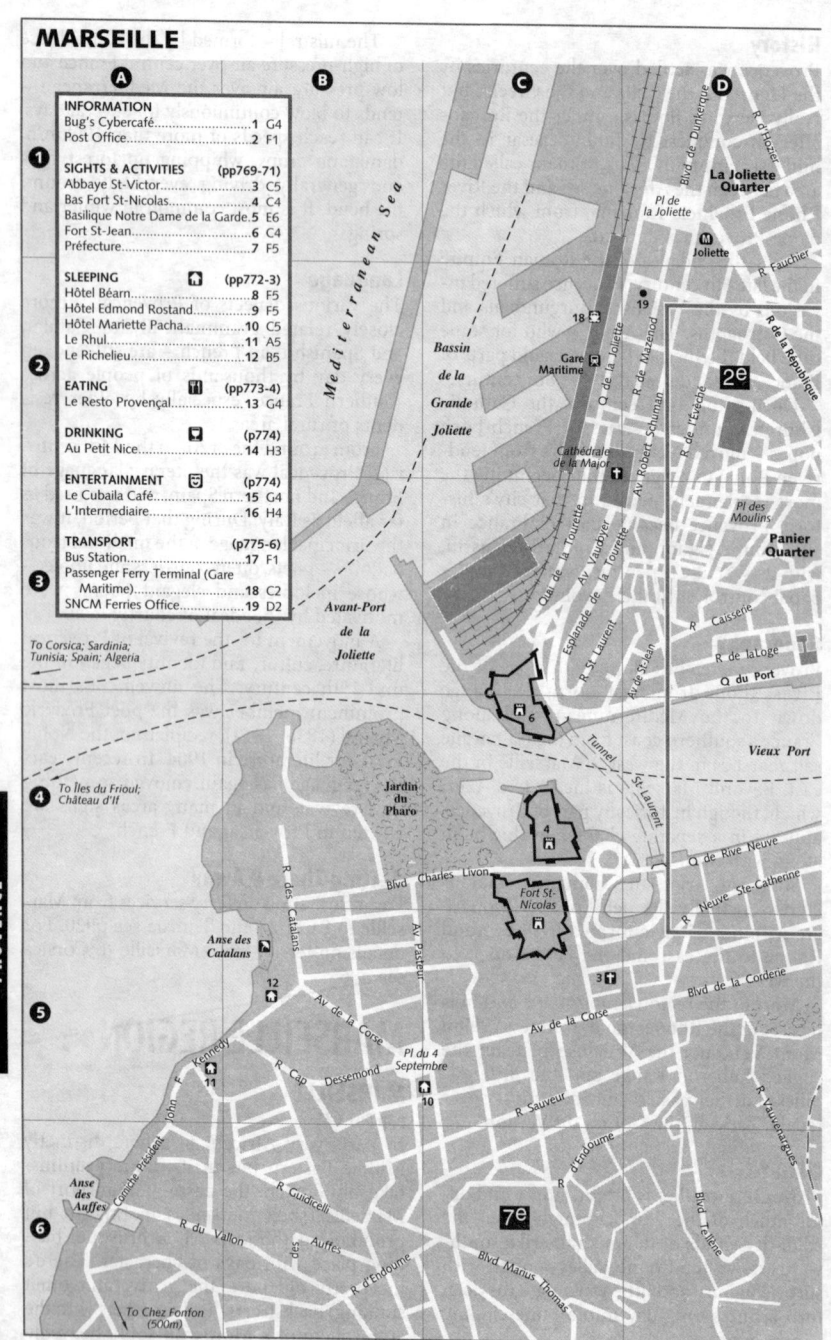

INFORMATION
Bug's Cybercafé...............................1 G4
Post Office.......................................2 F1

SIGHTS & ACTIVITIES (pp769-71)
Abbaye St-Victor.............................3 C5
Bas Fort St-Nicolas.........................4 C4
Basilique Notre Dame de la Garde.5 E6
Fort St-Jean.....................................6 C4
Préfecture..7 F5

SLEEPING (pp772-3)
Hôtel Béarn.....................................8 F5
Hôtel Edmond Rostand...................9 F5
Hôtel Mariette Pacha....................10 C5
Le Rhul..11 A5
Le Richelieu...................................12 B5

EATING (pp773-4)
Le Resto Provençal........................13 G4

DRINKING (p774)
Au Petit Nice.................................14 H3

ENTERTAINMENT (p774)
Le Cubaila Café.............................15 G4
L'Intermediaire.............................16 H4

TRANSPORT (p775-6)
Bus Station....................................17 F1
Passenger Ferry Terminal (Gare Maritime)........................18 C2
SNCM Ferries Office......................19 D2

Mediterranean Sea

To Corsica; Sardinia; Tunisia; Spain; Algeria

Bassin de la Grande Joliette

Avant-Port de la Joliette

To Îles du Frioul; Château d'If

La Joliette Quarter

Pl de la Joliette

Joliette

Gare Maritime

Cathédrale de la Major

Panier Quarter

Pl des Moulins

Vieux Port

Tunnel

2e

R de la République

R de l'Evêché

R Caisserie

R de la Loge

Q du Port

Q de Rive Neuve

R Neuve Ste-Catherine

Jardin du Pharo

Blvd Charles Livon

Fort St-Nicolas

Anse des Catalans

Av de la Corse

R Cap Dessemond

R Sauveur

Pl du 4 Septembre

Av de la Corse

Blvd de la Corderie

R Vaudragues

Anse des Auffes

Corniche Président John F Kennedy

R Guidicelli

R du Vallon

des Auffes

R d'Endoume

Blvd Marius Thomas

Blvd Tellène

7e

To Chez Fonfon (500m)

PROVENCE

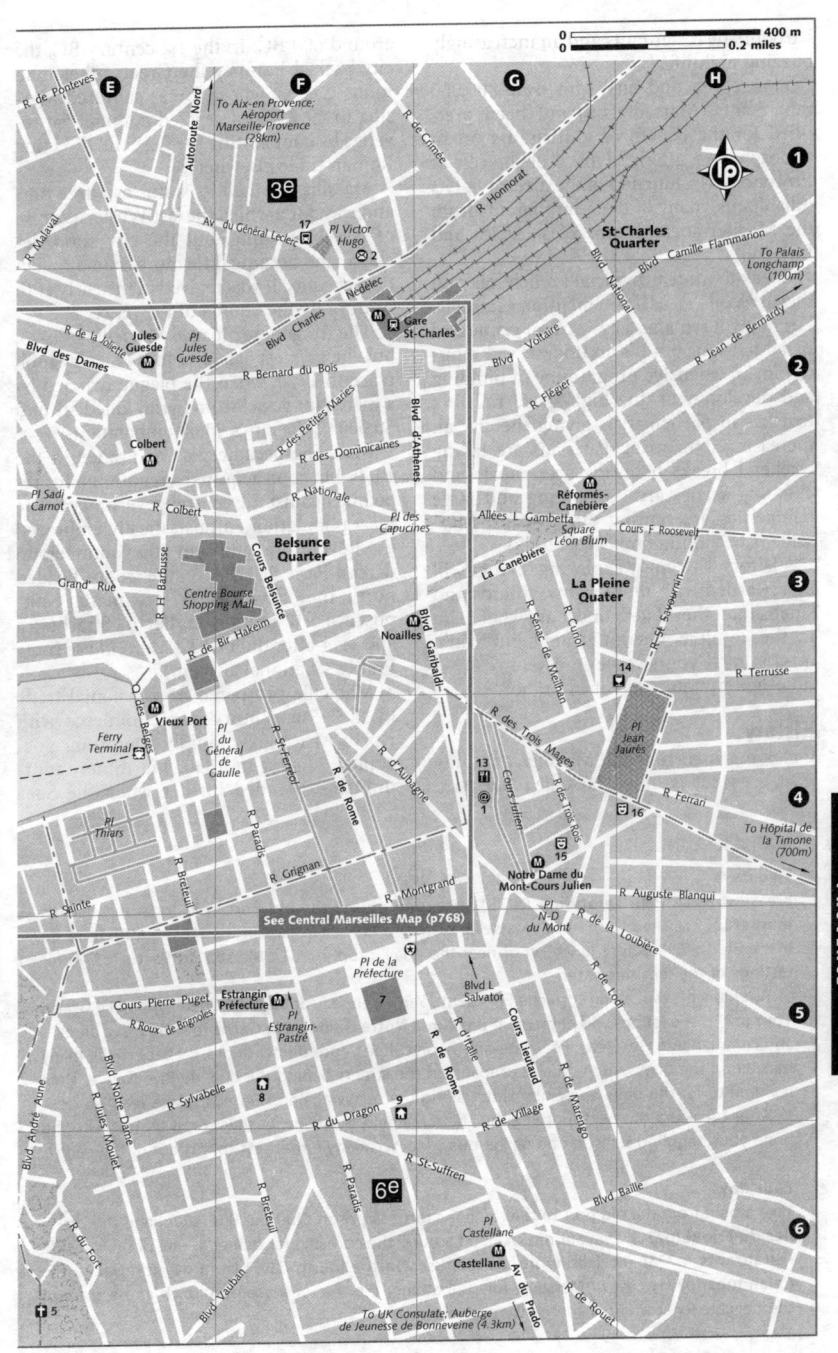

harbourside restaurants and an increasingly buzzing nightlife.

France's second city with over 800,000 inhabitants, Marseille has not been prettified for the benefit of tourists. Its urban atmosphere – utterly atypical of the rest of Provence – is a function of the diversity of its inhabitants, many of them immigrants from the Mediterranean basin, West Africa and Indochina.

Speak to more provincial French folk and they'll recoil in fear if you mention Marseille. For many it remains a byword for crime and racial tensions but it's an undeserved reputation: an extensive programme of building and development, the high-speed rail link to Paris in particular, is giving the city an increasing dynamism. Parisians are taking weekend breaks here, the arts, music and clubbing scenes are burgeoning and large companies are renting office space; Marseille is becoming *branché* (trendy).

Visitors who enjoy exploring on foot will be rewarded with more sights, sounds and smells than they'll get almost anywhere else in the country. Quaint it ain't but you'll miss a lot if you swerve it. There really is no other city quite like it in France.

History

Greek mariners founded Massilia, a trading post on what is now Marseille's old port, around 600 BC. In the 1st century BC, the city backed Pompey the Great rather than Julius Caesar, whose forces captured Massilia in 49 BC and exacted commercial revenge by confiscating the fleet and directing Roman trade elsewhere.

Massilia retained its status as a free port and was, for a while, the last Western centre of Greek learning, but the city soon declined and became little more than a collection of ruins. It was revived in the early 10th century by the counts of Provence.

The Aragonese pillaged Marseille in 1423, but the greatest calamity in its history took place in 1720, when the plague (carried by a merchant vessel from Syria) killed around 50,000 of the city's 90,000 inhabitants.

Marseille became part of France in the 1480s but soon acquired a reputation for rebelling against the central government. The local population enthusiastically embraced the Revolution, and sent 500 volunteers to defend Paris in 1792. As the troops headed north, they sang a catchy new march composed a few months earlier in Strasbourg and ever after dubbed *La Marseillaise* (now France's national anthem).

Marseille prospered from colonial trade in the 19th century and commerce with North Africa grew rapidly after France occupied Algeria in 1830. Maritime opportunities expanded further when the Suez

---

MARSEILLE IN...

Two days

Breakfast at **Le Pain Quotidien** (p773), meander around the old port's old forts and its **fish market** (p771), then learn about Marseille's Greek and Roman past in the **Musée d'Histoire de Marseille** (p769). Before lunch on or near the quay, drop in at **La Maison du Pastis** (p774) for tastings of the local firewater.

After lunch, swan along corniche Président John F Kennedy aboard the open-topped **Le Grand Tour** (p771) tourist bus and jump off at **Basilique Notre Dame de la Garde** (p770) for sea breezes and commanding city views. For a late-afternoon coffee or pre-dinner drinks, it's back to the many bars along the quays, then dinner, probably in the streets behind the quai de Rive Neuve. Then it's time to hit the pubs and clubs either along the quays again or up near place Jean Jaurès.

After breakfast the next morning, hit the remaining museums in town or, if the day is right, hone your haggling skills at one of the busy, Moroccan-style **markets** (p771) out of the centre.

Four days

Take a boat from the old port to the romantic fortress/prison **Château d'If** (p770) and the pretty **Îles du Frioul** (p770). On your return, head around the corniche for dinner at one of the **seaside restaurants** (p773) specialising in *bouillabaisse*. On the fourth day, plan a day trip out to the **Calanques** (p771) east of Marseille for sunbathing, a picnic or a seafood lunch and a glass of the delicate local white at the pretty port of Cassis.

Canal opened in 1869. During WWII, Marseille was bombed by the Germans and Italians in 1940, and by the Allies in 1943–44.

Today, Marseille is renowned as Europe's second-largest port and France's most important seaport.

Orientation

The city's main thoroughfare, the wide boulevard called La Canebière, stretches eastwards from the Vieux Port (Old Port). The train station is north of La Canebière at the northern end of blvd d'Athènes. Just a few blocks south of La Canebière is the bohemian cours Julien, a large pedestrianised square dominated by a water garden, fountains and palm trees, and lined with some of Marseille's hippest cafés, restaurants and theatres. The city's commercial heart is around rue Paradis, which gets more fashionable as you move south. The new ferry terminal is west of place de la Joliette, a few minutes walk north of the Cathédrale de la Major.

Marseille is divided into 15 arrondissements; however, most travellers will only be concerned with the central three or four. Places mentioned in the text have the arrondissement (1er, 2e, etc) listed after the street address.

Information

BOOKSHOPS

The northern end of rue Paradis (1er) is lined with bookshops.

Fnac (Map p768; ☎ 04 91 39 94 00; Centre Bourse shopping centre) On the top floor of the centre off cours Belsunce (1er).

Librairie de la Bourse (Map p768; ☎ 04 91 33 63 06; 8 rue Paradis, 1er) Best range of maps, travel books and Lonely Planet guides in Provence.

Librairie Lamy (Map p768; ☎ 04 91 33 57 91; 21 rue Paradis, 1er) A very good selection of English-language novels.

EMERGENCY

Préfecture de Police (Map p768; ☎ 04 91 39 80 00; place de la Préfecture, 1er; ☉ 24hr)

INTERNET ACCESS

Bug's Cybercafé (Map pp764-5; ☎ 04 96 12 53 43; 68 cours Julien, 6e; per hr €3.60; ☉ 9.30am-8pm Mon-Wed, 9.30am-10pm Thu-Sat)

Info Cafe (Map p768; ☎ 04 91 33 74 98; 1 quai du Rive Neuve, 1e; per 30 min/hr €2/3.60; ☉ 9am-10pm Mon-Sat, 2.30-7.30pm Sun)

LAUNDRY

Laverie des Allées (Map p768; 15 allées Léon Gambetta; ☉ 8am-8pm) Near place des Capucins.

Laverie Self-Service (Map p768; 5 rue Justice Breteuil, 1er)

MEDICAL SERVICES

Hôpital de la Timone (☎ 04 91 38 60 00; 264 rue St-Pierre, 5e) East of the city centre.

MONEY

There are a number of banks and exchange bureaus on La Canebière near the old port.

Canebière Change (Map p768; 39 La Canebière, 1er).

POST

Branch Post Office (Map p764-5; 11 rue Honnorat, 3e) Close to the train station but doesn't change money.

Main Post Office (Map p768; 1 place de l'Hôtel des Postes, 1er) Offers currency exchange.

TOURIST INFORMATION

Tourist Office (Map p768; ☎ 04 91 13 89 00; www .marseille-tourisme.com; 4 La Canebière, 1er; ☉ 9am-7pm Mon-Sat, 10am-5pm Sun, to 7.30pm mid-Jun–mid-Sep) Make hotel reservations at this often overwhelmed and understaffed place.

Tourist Office Annexe (Map p768; ☎ 04 91 50 59 18; main train station; ☉ 10am-1pm & 2-6pm Mon-Sat) Go to the central office for hotel reservations.

MARSEILLE CITY PASS

It's worth considering buying a **Marseille City Pass** (1-/2-day pass €16/23), which gives access to the city's museums, guided tours of the town, free access to all metro and bus services, and other discounts, including a reduction for Le Grand Tour tourist bus.

Dangers & Annoyances

Despite its fearsome reputation for crime, Marseille is not significantly more dangerous than other French cities. Avoid street crime by keeping your wits about you and your valuables hidden from view. *Never* leave anything you value in a parked car. Even better, leave it in a garage. It's seldom cheap, though – €14 for anything longer than nine hours and up to 24 hours in one of the central covered car parks is standard, although many hotels have cheaper parking arrangements.

PROVENCE

CENTRAL MARSEILLE

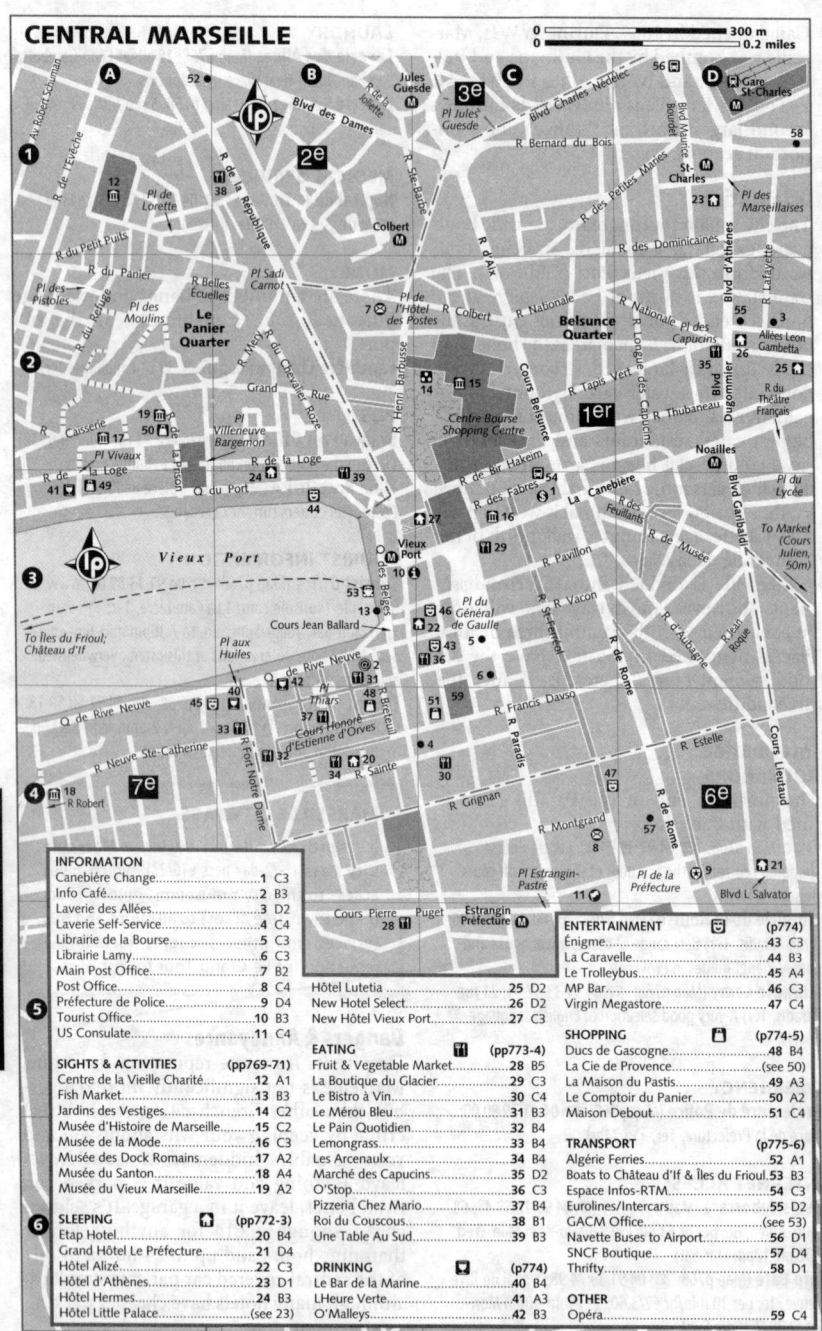

0 _____ 300 m
0 _____ 0.2 miles

At night, avoid walking alone in the Belsunce area, a poor neighbourhood southwest of the train station bounded by La Canebière, cours Belsunce and rue d'Aix, rue Bernard du Bois and blvd d'Athènes.

Sights

Marseille grew up around the old port, where ships have docked for at least 26 centuries. The majority of Marseille's sights cluster close to the port. Head along corniche Président John F Kennedy, though, for some great sea views or up to the commanding heights occupied by the striking Basilique Notre Dame de la Garde, from where you can really get a handle on Marseille's layout. The ever-circling hop-on-hop-off tourist bus service (see p771) is another good way to acquaint yourself with the city and its sights.

MUSEUMS

Unless noted otherwise, the museums listed here are open 10am to 5pm Tuesday to Sunday October to May and 11am to 6pm June to September. Admission to permanent exhibitions costs €2/1 for adults/children and temporary exhibitions usually cost €3/1.50.

Centre de la Vieille Charité

The **Centre de la Vieille Charité** (Old Charity Cultural Centre; Map opposite; ☎ 04 91 14 58 80; 2 rue de la Charité, 2e) is in the mostly North African Panier Quarter. The superb permanent exhibits and imaginative temporary exhibitions are housed in this handsome workhouse and hospice built around a monastery-like cloister between 1671 and 1745, and restored after serving as a barracks (1905), rest-home for soldiers (WWI) and low-cost housing for people who lost their homes in WWII. It is also home to **Musée d'Archéologie** (☎ 04 91 14 58 80) and **Musée des Arts Africains, Océaniens & Amérindiens** (Museum of African, Oceanic & American Indian Art; ☎ 04 91 14 58 38), which has a diverse and often striking collection, including masks from the Americas, Africa and the Pacific plus some lovingly decorated human skulls.

A combined ticket covering all of the above costs €4; individual tickets are available too at €3 for the Centre de la Vieille Charité and €2 for the others.

Musée d'Histoire de Marseille

The small **Musée d'Histoire de Marseille** (Map opposite; ☎ 04 91 90 42 22; ground fl, Centre Bourse shopping centre, 1er; ☉ noon-7pm Mon-Sat) is just north of La Canebière. It's packed with artefacts and displays that give a wonderful overview of the cultures that have made their home in Marseille and the crafts they practised over the centuries. Exhibits include the remains of a merchant vessel – discovered by chance in the old port in 1974 – that plied the waters of the Mediterranean in the early 3rd century AD. The 19m-long timbers, which include five different kinds of wood, show evidence of having been repaired repeatedly. To preserve the soaked and decaying wood, the whole thing was freeze-dried right where it now sits – hidden behind glass in a dimly lit room.

Fragments of Roman buildings, uncovered during the construction of the Centre Bourse shopping centre, can be seen outside the museum in the **Jardin des Vestiges** (Garden of Ruins), which fronts rue Henri Barbusse (1er).

Musée de la Mode

Glitz and glamour is the name of the game at the **Musée de la Mode** (Fashion Museum; Map opposite; ☎ 04 91 56 59 57; 11 La Canebière, 1er; adult/child €3/1). Housed in Marseille's superb Espace Mode Méditerranée (Mediterranean Fashion Space), the museum looks at French fashion trends over the past 30 years and displays over 2000 different items of clothing and accessories.

Musée du Santon

The private collection of 18th- and 19th-century *santon* (fingernail-sized nativity figures that are typical of Provence) gathered by *santon*-maker Marcel Carbonnel is displayed at the **Musée du Santon** (Map opposite; ☎ 04 91 54 26 58; 47 rue Neuve Ste-Catherine, 7e; admission free; ☉ 10am-noon & 2-6.30pm Tue-Sun). Entrance to the adjoining **ateliers** (workshops; ☉ 8am-1pm & 2-5.40pm Mon-Thu), where you can watch the minuscule 2.5cm- to 15cm-tall figures being crafted, is also free. Guided tours (in French only) are usually conducted on Tuesday and Thursday at 2.30pm.

Continuing 100m up the hill from the museum, you come to the imposing Romanesque **Abbaye St-Victor** (Map pp764-5; ☎ 04 91 05 84 48; ☉ 8am-7pm), built in the 12th century on the site of a 4th-century martyr's tomb. Marseille's annual sacred-music festival is held here.

PROVENCE

Palais de Longchamp

The grand, colonnaded **Palais de Longchamp** (Longchamp Palace; off Map pp764-5; blvd Philippon, 4e), constructed in the 1860s, is at the eastern end of blvd Longchamp. The palace was designed in part to disguise a *château d'eau* (water tower) built at the terminus of an aqueduct from the River Durance. The two wings house Marseille's oldest museum, the **Musée des Beaux-Arts** (☎ 04 91 14 59 30), which specialises in 15th- to 19th-century paintings, including a few by Rubens, Courbet, David and Ingres. There are also sculptures by Marseille-born Pierre Puget. The rather more missable **Musée d'Histoire Naturelle** (☎ 04 91 62 30 78) is also housed here.

BASILIQUE NOTRE DAME DE LA GARDE

Not to be missed for great panoramas and some handsome, if rather overwrought, 19th-century architecture, is a trip up to the **Basilique Notre Dame de la Garde** (Map pp764-5; ☎ 04 91 13 40 80; admission free; ⏰ basilica & crypt 7am-8pm summer, 7am-10pm mid-Jun–mid-Aug, 7am-7pm winter), an enormous Romano-Byzantine basilica 1km south of the old port. It stands on a hilltop (162m) – the highest point in the city – and provides staggering views of sprawling Marseille.

The domed basilica, ornamented with coloured marble, intricate mosaics, murals and gilded objects, was built between 1853 and 1864. The bell tower is topped by a 9.7m-tall gilded statue of the Virgin Mary on a 12m-high pedestal. The great bell inside is 2.5m tall and weighs a hefty 8324kg (the clapper alone is 387kg). Bullet marks and vivid shrapnel scars on the cathedral's northern façade mark the fierce fighting that took place here during Marseille's Battle of Liberation (15–25 August 1944).

Dress conservatively when you visit. Bus No 60 links the old port (from cours Jean Ballard) with the basilica. Count on 30 minutes each way by foot.

CHÂTEAU D'IF

Château d'If (off Map pp764-5; ☎ 04 91 59 02 30; adult/student €4.60/3.10; ⏰ 9.30am-6pm Sep-Mar, 9.30am-6.30pm Jun-Aug), the 16th-century fortress-turned-prison made infamous by Alexandre Dumas' classic work of fiction *Le Comte de Monte Cristo* (The Count of Monte Cristo) is on a 30-sq-km island 3.5km west of the entrance to the old port. Among the people incarcerated here were all sorts of political prisoners, hundreds of Protestants (many of whom perished in the dungeons), the Revolutionary hero Mirabeau, the rebels of 1848 and the Communards of 1871.

Boats run by **GACM** (Map p768; ☎ 04 91 55 50 09; www.answeb.net/gacm in French; 1 quai des Belges, 1er) to the Château d'If leave from outside the GACM office in the old port. There are boats at 9am, 10.30am, noon, 2pm and 3.30pm (€9 return, 20 minutes).

ÎLES DU FRIOUL

The islands of **Ratonneau** and **Pomègues**, each of which is about 2.5km long, are a few hundred metres west of the Château d'If. They were linked by a dyke in the 1820s. From the 17th to 19th century, the islands were used as a place of quarantine for the

---

A SIMMERING ARGUMENT

The French enjoy quarrelling about what makes a good *bouillabaisse* – Provence's seafood stew made with onions, white wine and tomatoes, flavoured with fennel and saffron and served with *rouille* (a delightful, garlicky mayonnaise) and croutons – almost as much as they do actually cooking and eating it.

Everyone agrees the soup must be boiled (*bouillir*) briefly but furiously and the heat lowered (*baisser*) thereafter. At least five or six types of Mediterranean fish plus crab or shrimp are generally held to be essential.

While some add lobster, langoustines or mussels, others regard this as unforgivable sacrilege. Many of Toulon's restaurants add potatoes too; another sinister act according to purists. Then ⸱ere's the violent schism over how it should be served: in two courses with the broth first, or ⸱en together with the broth ladled periodically over the fish to keep it warm.

⸱/hat is indisputable is that however you eat this great local dish (and be warned, some of ⸱⸱r places require you order 24 hours ahead), it's sensational accompanied by a bottle ⸱htful local Cassis white wine.

unfortunate people suspected of carrying plague or cholera.

Today, the rather barren islands (total area about 200 hectares) shelter sea birds, rare plants and bathers, and are dotted with fortifications (which were used by German troops during WWII), the ruins of the old quarantine hospital, Hôpital Caroline, and Fort Ratonneau.

Boats to the Château d'If also serve the Îles du Frioul (€14 return; €19 if you want to stop at Château d'If too). In addition to these boats, there are departures at 6.45am, 5pm and 6.30pm for the Îles du Frioul alone.

OLD PORT AREA

Although the main commercial docks were transferred to the Joliette area on the coast north of here in the 1840s, the old port remains an active and charming harbour for fishing craft, pleasure yachts and ferries to the Château d'If. Several stalls sell fresh fish, squid, octopus and spiny *oursins* (sea urchins) during the day here.

The harbour entrance is guarded by **Bas Fort St-Nicolas** (on the southern side) and, across the water, **Fort St-Jean**, founded in the 13th century by the Knights Hospitaller of St John of Jerusalem. In 1943 the neighbourhood on the northern side of the quai du Port – at the time a seedy area with a strong Resistance presence – was systematically dynamited by the Germans. This neighbourhood was rebuilt after the war.

The 17th-century **town hall** has two museums nearby: the **Musée des Docks Romains** and the **Musée du Vieux Marseille**. The **Panier Quarter**, many of whose residents are North African immigrants, is a bit further north. The **Centre de la Vieille Charité** and its museums, well worth a visit, sit at the top of the hill.

On the southern side of the old port, the large and lively **place Thiars** and **cours Honoré d'Estienne d'Orves** pedestrian zone, with its late-night restaurants and cafés, stretches south from quai de Rive Neuve.

The liveliest part of Marseille – always crowded with people of all ages and ethnic groups – is situated around the intersection of La Canebière and cours Belsunce. The area just north of La Canebière and east of cours Belsunce, which is known as **Belsunce**, is a poor immigrant neighbourhood undergoing a slow rehabilitation.

The fashionable **6th arrondissement** is well worth a stroll, especially the area between La Canebière and the **Prefecture building**. **Rue St-Ferréol** is a bustling pedestrian shopping street.

MARKETS

Marseille is home to a colourful array of markets, including the small but absorbing daily fresh **fish market** (Map p768; quai des Belges; 8am-1pm), where you can buy the makings of a *bouillabaisse*.

Cours Julien hosts a Wednesday morning fruit-and-vegetable market. Stalls laden with everything from second-hand clothing to pots and pans fill nearby **place Jean Jaurès** (8am-1pm Sat).

Tours

Le Grand Tour (☎ 04 91 91 05 82; adult/student/child €16/12/8; 10am-at least 4pm), This hop-on-hop-off, open-topped, double-decker tourist bus service, is an excellent way to get acquainted with the city or to travel between the main sights and museums in Marseille. Tours navigate the old port, head around the corniche and up to Notre Dame de la Garde. Headphones provide commentary in five languages.

The tourist office offers various guided tours, including a **walking tour** of the city (€6.50) departing from outside the tourist office at 2pm from Monday to Saturday (2.30pm Sunday).

In summer **GACM** (Map p768; ☎ 04 91 55 50 09) runs boat trips (with French commentary only) from the old port to Cassis and back (€20), which pass by the stunning

---

THE CALANQUES

If you've got wheels, get away from it all just a few miles east of busy, built-up Marseille along the Calanques: small inlets along the rocky, indented coast, sometimes with a small patch of beach on which to soak up the sun. A trip to the pretty nearby fishing village of **Cassis** makes an ideal day out and is a good place to grab lunch and sample the subtle local white wine. The **tourist office** (☎ 04 42 01 71 17; quai des Moulins; 9am-12.30pm & 2-6pm Tue-Sat) supplies a free list and map of the all the *caves* (cellars) you can visit for tastings.

PROVENCE

Calanques, dramatic formations of coastal rock that attract unusual wildlife.

Sleeping

Generally speaking, the better hotels cluster around the old port (where budget options are pretty much nonexistent) and as you head east out of the centre along the corniche. The city also has some of France's cheapest hotels, a good percentage of them dodgy dives. Establishments mentioned here are clean and reputable. Prices in Marseille hotels vary little throughout the year.

BUDGET

Auberge de Jeunesse de Bonneveine (☎ 04 91 17 63 30; fax 04 91 73 97 23; impasse du Docteur Bonfils, 8e; dm incl breakfast €14.55; ⏰ Feb-Dec) A good bet for its proximity to the sea and the Calanques, this hostel is about 4.5km south of the centre. Take bus No 44 from the Rond Point du Prado metro stop and get off at the Place Bonnefons stop.

Hôtel Béarn (Map pp764-5; ☎ 04 91 37 75 83; www .hotel-bearn.com; 63 rue Sylvabelle, 6e; s/d with shower €25/35, with shower & toilet €29/40) Although it's a bit shabby, Hôtel Béarn is clean and quiet with colourfully decorated rooms. Reception closes at 11pm or midnight and access after 11pm is via security code.

Grand Hôtel Le Préfecture (Map p768; ☎ 04 91 54 31 60; fax 04 91 54 24 95; 9 blvd Louis Salvator, 6e; r with shower €29, with shower, toilet & TV €32, with bath €37) Far from grand, this place is perfectly acceptable for the price (avoid the run-down 1st-floor rooms).

Le Richelieu (Map pp764-5; ☎ 04 91 31 01 92; hotelmer@club-Internet.fr; 52 corniche Président John F Kennedy, 7e; road-facing r €34-41, sea-facing r €41-53) An idyllic, two-star place with ace views, Le Richelieu is built onto the rocks right next to plage des Catalans. Road-facing rooms can be noisy. Some sea-facing rooms have balconies. Make sure you book ahead.

MID-RANGE

Hôtel Hermes (Map p768; ☎ 04 96 11 63 63; hotel .hermes@wanadoo.fr; 2 rue de la Bonneterie, 1er; s/d from ⁓45/67; P ✗ ✗) Right on the quayside, Hôtel ⁓rmes is bright, cheerful and good value ⁓ the location. The roof terrace and ⁓eymoon-room balcony have terrific ⁓ the harbour and out to Basilique ⁓ Nearby secure parking for

Hôtel Alizé (Map p768; ☎ 04 91 33 66 97; alize -hotel@wanadoo.fr; 35 quai des Belges, 1er; rear-facing s/d €58/63, harbour-facing s/d €75/80; ✗) An elegant, central old pile, Alizé's big draw is its location, right on the old port with great views across it up to the Basilique. The rooms are decent enough (if in need of less-dated decoration). All come with satellite TV and soundproofing.

Etap Hotel (Map p768; ☎ 0 892 680 582; fax 04 91 54 95 67; 46 rue Sainte; s €46, d & tr €50; P ✗ ✗) Set just back from the port (so no maritime views) but it's good value and close to the restaurants and cafés of place Thiers. Try to get one of the large, wood-beamed rooms in the old building (an old sea galley captain's house). Covered parking is €6.

New Hôtel Vieux Port (Map p768; ☎ 04 91 99 23 23; www.new-hotel.com; 3bis rue Reine Elisabeth, 1er; s/d from €86/92, junior ste €145; ✗ ✗) This hotel has been recently and stylishly redesigned throughout, from the lobby's impressive glass lift shaft to the large, plush rooms decked out with classy understatement in several different ethnic styles. It's very central and the pricier rooms have harbour views. Weekend deals may be available.

Hôtel Edmond Rostand (Map pp764-5; ☎ 04 91 37 74 95; www.hoteledmondrostand.com in French; 31 rue du Dragon, 6e; r with 1 or 2 beds €54; ✗) This place may be a little way out of the centre but it's small, efficient and quiet with sleek, modern rooms that come with telephone, TV and minibar.

Hôtel d'Athènes (Map p768; ☎ 04 91 90 12 93; fax 04 91 90 72 03; 37-39 blvd d'Athènes, 1er; s/d with shower €24/34, s/d/tw with shower & toilet €39/46/56) You'll find this place at the foot of the grand staircase leading from the train station into town. It has average but well-kept rooms and an elevator. It also runs the adjoining one-star **Hôtel Little Palace** (r with shower €25-34).

Hôtel Lutetia (Map p768; ☎ 04 91 50 81 78; www .hotellutetia13.com in French; 38 allées Léon Gambetta; s/d/tr from €46/51/70) Close to the New Hotel Select, the Lutetia is homely and spotless. The smallish rooms are equipped with TVs and phones.

New Hotel Select (Map p768; ☎ 04 91 95 09 09; www.new-hotel.com; 4 allées Léon Gambetta, 1er; s/d €65/72; ✗ ✗) This hotel is pleasant, modern and efficiently run. Rooms have TVs, phones and minibars. Rates are about 20% cheaper at the weekend.

Hôtel Mariette Pacha (Map pp764-5; ☎ 04 91 52 30 77; mpacha@hotelselection.com; 5 place du 4 Septembre;

r with shower & TV €56, with shower, toilet & TV €60, with bath, toilet & TV €66) Quiet and tucked away, this hotel is elegant and homely. There are some triples and adjoining rooms for families.

Le Rhul (Map pp764-5; ☎ 04 91 52 01 77, 04 91 52 49 82; 269 corniche Président John F Kennedy; s/d €75/80, bouillabaisse dinner & r for 2 €175) Enchanting sea views from all bedrooms, which are attractive, large and airy (some have balconies). The restaurant (also overlooking the sea) turns out a decent *bouillabaisse*. It's a great option if you want to escape the centre's hustle and bustle.

Eating

Marseille's restaurants offer an incredible variety of cuisines, but no trip here is complete without sampling *bouillabaisse* (see p770). For Vietnamese and Chinese fare, the many restaurants on, or just off, rue de la République are worth a visit.

RESTAURANTS

Fish is predominant and plentiful in Marseille, be it soup, *huîtres* (oysters), *moules* (mussels) or other shellfish. The quai de Rive Neuve (1er) is plastered with outdoor cafés and touristy restaurants touting *bouillabaisse*; those along quai du Port are better but pricier. Expect to pay about €50 for two people. The pedestrian streets around place Thiars are packed with terrace cafés and restaurants in the warmer months.

Chez Fonfon (off Map pp764-5; ☎ 04 91 52 14 38; 140 rue du Vallon des Auffes, 7e; bouillabaisse €40;

AUTHOR'S CHOICE

Une Table au Sud (Map p768; ☎ 04 91 90 63 53; unetableausud@wanadoo.fr; 2 quai du Port; menus €39/49/69; closed Sun & Mon) This understatedly elegant restaurant overlooking the old port, turns out inventive, delicately delicious cuisine. There's often a nod to Far Eastern flavours: light foie gras raviolis in a clear chicken broth (basically fancy French won tons) or a very faintly sweetand-sour tang to vegetables slow roasted with a red wine reduction and served with tender *rouget* fillets. The trademark sweet fennel *tatin* sounds so wrong but tastes so right. Pricey but definitely worth splashing out on.

---

closed Mon lunch & Sun) Overlooking a pretty and authentic little harbour, this restaurant has long been, and remains, legendary for serving a very fine *bouillabaisse* indeed. There's a good range of local rosés or the delicious local white Cassis to accompany it. Book ahead.

Lemongrass (Map p768; ☎ 04 91 33 97 65; 8 rue Fort-Notre-Dame, 1e; menus €20; closed Sun) A refreshingly different place among the many pizza and *bouillabaisse* places close to the old port, Lemongrass serves inexpensive and interesting menus of fusion Asian/French food using Eastern herbs and spices with restraint.

Le Mérou Bleu (Map p768; ☎ 04 91 54 23 25; 32-36 rue St-Saëns, 1er; dishes €8-19) This is a popular restaurant with a lovely terrace. It has *bouillabaisse* (€30), excellent seafood, meat and pasta.

Les Arcenaulx (Map p768; ☎ 04 91 54 85 38; 27 cours Honoré d'Estienne d'Orves, 1er; mains from €10; Mon-Sat) An unusual, beautifully restored complex wrapped around cours des Arcenaulx. It contains a delightful restaurant and *salon de thé*. Book ahead.

Le Bistro à Vin (Map p768; ☎ 04 91 54 02 20; 17 rue Sainte, 6e; dishes €12; closed Sun & Sat lunch) This rustic bistro has beamed ceilings and wooden tables. The wine selection is excellent and the accompaniments – *tapenade*, artisanal cheeses and unusual meat parts – are equally enticing.

It may also be worth following your nose to cours Julien, near the Notre Dame du Mont-Cours Julien metro station (Marseille Map) and lined with of French, Indian, Antillean, Pakistani, Thai, Armenian, Lebanese, Tunisian and Italian restaurants.

Le Resto Provençal (Map pp764-5; ☎ 04 91 48 85 12; 64 cours Julien, 1er; regional menu €21, plat du jour €9, lunch menu €12; closed Sat lunch & Sun) A winning combination of agreeable outside dining terrace and consistently good Provençal dishes.

At the snackier end of the dining spectrum are **Le Pain Quotidien** (Map p768; ☎ 04 91 33 55 00; 18 place Aux Huiles; breakfast €5-8) for a decent breakfast, **Pizzeria Chez Mario** (Map p768; ☎ 04 91 54 48 54; 8 rue Euthymènes, 1er; mains €8.50-15) for good fish, grilled meats, pizza and pasta, **Roi du Couscous** (Map p768; ☎ 04 91 91 45 46; 63 rue de la République, 2e; couscous €8-12; Tue-Sun), serving large and delicious portions of steamed semolina with meats and vegetables, and **O'Stop**

(Map p768; ☎ 04 91 33 85 34; 15 rue St-Saëns, 1er; menu €9; ✆ 24hr) for nonstop sandwiches, pasta and simple, authentic regional specialities.

CAFÉS
Quai de Rive Neuve and cours Honoré d'Estienne d'Orves (1er), a large, long, open square two blocks south of the quay, are crowded with cafés. There is another cluster overlooking place de la Préfecture, at the southern end of rue St-Ferréol (1er). There's also plenty of choice along the quaysides.

La Boutique du Glacier (Map p768; ☎ 04 91 33 76 93; 1 place du Général de Gaulle) Not a good place for people-watching but good for light and lovely daytime pastries and coffee.

SELF-CATERING
Fruit and vegetables are sold at **Marché des Capucins** (Map p768; place des Capucins, 1er; ✆ Mon-Sat), one block north of La Canebière, and at the **fruit-and-vegetable market** (Map p768; cours Pierre Puget, 6e; ✆ Mon-Sat). There are also a couple of supermarkets in the monstrously ugly concrete bunker that is the Centre Bourse shopping centre (Map p768).

Drinking
The Vieux Port is a great place to gravitate towards for a relaxed, scenic coffee by day or night. If you're after clusters of livelier, mainly night-time venues, two especially good areas are the bars and clubs around quai de Rive Neuve and, a fair hike away, the bars and cafés around place Jean Jaurès.

Le Bar de la Marine (Map p768; ☎ 04 91 54 95 42; 15 quai de Rive Neuve, 1er; ✆ 7am-2am) Chic metropolitan espresso sippers mix it with grizzled *pastis*-gulping sailor types at this gregarious bar right on the water.

O'Malleys (Map p768; ☎ 04 91 33 65 50; 9 quai de Rive Neuve, 1er) Overlooking the old port, on the corner of rue de la Paix, this is a friendly place and there are concerts on Wednesday night of Celtic and Irish music.

L'Heure Verte (Map p768; ☎ 04 91 90 12 73; 106 quai du Port; ✆ 11am-11pm high season) This is the place to go to sample many different types of *pastis*, including the house-made ones, steeped for weeks in different herbs and some fierce absinthe. The shop next door (see right) will also sell you bottles of all this stuff to take with you.

Au Petit Nice (Map pp764-5; ☎ 04 91 48 43 04; 28 place Jean Jaurès; ✆ 6am-2am) A favourite with locals for its cosy café feeling. It's more like a local British boozer than anything else.

Entertainment
Cultural event listings can be found in the monthly *Vox Mag* and weekly *Taktik* and *Sortir*, all distributed free of charge at the tourist office, cinemas and the ticket offices mentioned here. Comprehensive listings also appear in the weekly *L'Officiel des Loisirs*. It's worth consulting the website www.marseillebynight.com in French.

Tickets for most cultural events are sold at *billetteries* (ticket counters) in **Fnac** (☎ 04 91 39 94 00) on the top floor of the Centre Bourse shopping centre (Map p768), **Virgin Megastore** (Map p768; ☎ 04 91 55 55 00; 75 rue St-Ferréol, 1er) and **Arcenaulx** (Map p768; ☎ 04 91 59 80 37; 25 cours Honoré d'Estienne d'Orves, 1er).

NIGHTCLUBS
Le Trolleybus (Map p768; ☎ 04 91 54 30 45; 24 quai Rive Neuve; ✆ 11pm-dawn Wed-Sat) Inside the various sections of this tunnel-like club by the harbour there could be techno, funk and indie all playing at the same time. The sound system is great.

La Caravelle (Map p768; ☎ 04 91 90 36 64; 34 quai du Port, 2e; ✆ 7am-2am) This is a trendy place in the Hôtel Bellevue hosting jazz sessions on weekends (November to March). It's in a marvellous location overlooking the port with a small balcony. Great for predinner sundowners served with tasty (and free) bar nibbles.

Le Cubaila Café (Map pp764-5; ☎ 04 91 48 97 48; 40 rue des Trois Rois, 6e; ✆ 10.30pm-2am) This is a great place, even if all you do about Latin dancing is watch it. The food is good, too.

L'Intermediaire (Map pp764-5; ☎ 04 91 47 01 25; 39 cours Julien; ✆ 7pm-2am Mon-Sat) Intimate, vibrant, friendly and often packed, this is one of the happening bars and live-music venues in town, showcasing everything from cover bands to blues and up-and-coming local acts.

Two popular gay bars close to the centre (and attracting a youngish, male gay crowd) are **Énigme** (Map p768; ☎ 04 91 33 79 20; 22 rue Beauvau, 1er) and **MP Bar** (Map p768; ☎ 04 91 33 64 79; 10 rue Beauvau, 1e).

Shopping
La Maison du Pastis (Map p768; ☎ 04 91 90 86 77; 108 quai du Port) Run by the same proprietor as

L'Heure Verte (see opposite), La Maison du Pastis offers informative tastings in English of the southern aperitif of choice, *pastis*, and sells a wide variety of the aniseedy tipple along with it's bad big brother absinthe.

Ducs de Gascogne (Map p768; ☎ 04 91 33 87 28; 20 cours Honoré d'Estienne d'Orves) A truly mouthwatering selection of foie gras (goose liver pâté), Provençal wines and other culinary delights awaits at Ducs de Gascogne.

Maison Debout (Map p768; 46 rue Francis Davso, 1er) This traditional and very quaint shop offers a rich array of coffee, tea and chocolate.

La Cie de Provence (Map p768; ☎ 04 91 56 20 94; 1 rue Caisserie) and **La Comptoir du Panier** (Map p768; ☎ 04 91 56 20 94; 1 rue Caisserie) are both good bets for present buying or for simply treating yourself to Provençal clothes, decorations and household goodies.

Getting There & Away

AIR
Aéroport Marseille-Provence (☎ 04 42 14 14 14), also known as Aéroport Marseille-Marignane, is 28km northwest of town in Marignane.

BOAT
Marseille's **passenger ferry terminal** (gare maritime; Map pp764-5; ☎ 04 91 56 38 63; fax 04 91 56 38 70) is 250m south of place de la Joliette (2e). It's modern and spacious, but facilities for foot passengers are fairly sparse. There is a poorly stocked snack bar, no ATMs and little to keep you amused while waiting for a boat.

The **Société Nationale Maritime Corse Méditerranée** (SNCM; Map pp764-5; ☎ 0 836 679 500; fax 04 91 56 35 86; 61 blvd des Dames, 2e; ♥ 8am-6pm Mon-Fri, 8.30am-noon & 2-5.30pm Sat) links Marseille with Corsica (see p865), Sardinia and Tunisia. It also serves the ports of Algiers, Annaba, Bejaia, Oran and Skikda in Algeria, although services are prone to disruption/cancellation because of the political troubles there.

There is an office for **Algérie Ferries** (Map pp764-5; ☎ 04 91 90 64 70; 29 blvd des Dames, 2e; ♥ 9-11.45am & 1-4.45pm Mon-Fri). Ticketing and reservations for the Tunisian and Moroccan ferry companies, **Compagnie Tunisienne de Navigation** (CTN) and **Compagnie Marocaine de Navigation** (COMANAV; ☎ 04 67 46 68 000), with departures from 4 quai d'Alger in Sète, are handled by SNCM.

For more information on ferry services to/from North Africa and Sardinia see p920.

BUS
The **bus station** (gare des autocars; Map p764-5; ☎ 04 91 08 16 40; 3 place Victor Hugo, 3e) is 150m to the right as you exit the train station. Tickets are sold at company ticket counters (closed most of the time) or on the bus.

Buses travel to Aix-en-Provence (€4.20, 35 minutes via the autoroute or one hour via the N8, every five to 10 minutes), Avignon (€17, two hours, one daily), Cannes (€21, two hours, four daily), Carpentras (€12, two hours), Cassis (€3.30, 1¼ hours), Cavaillon (€9.50, one hour), Nice (€22, 2¾ hours), Nice airport, Orange, Salon-de-Provence and other destinations. There is a service to Castellane on Saturday morning at 8.30am.

Eurolines (☎ 0 892 289 9091, 04 91 50 57 55; fax 04 91 08 30 01) has buses to Spain, Belgium, the Netherlands, Italy, Morocco, the UK and other countries. Its counter is in the bus station. **Intercars** (☎ 04 91 50 08 66; fax 04 91 08 72 34), with an office next to Eurolines in the bus station, has buses to the UK, Spain, Portugal, Morocco, Poland and Slovakia. There's also a joint **office** (Map p768; ☎ 04 91 50 57 55; 3 allées Léon Gambetta) for these two firms nearer the Vieux Port.

CAR
Rental agencies offering better rates include **Thrifty** (Map p768; ☎ 04 91 95 00 00; 8 blvd Voltaire, 1er), situated near the train station, and **Europcar** (Map p768; ☎ 04 91 99 40 90), inside the train station.

TRAIN
Marseille's passenger train station, served by both metro lines, is called Gare St-Charles. The **information and ticket reservation office** (♥ 9am-8pm Mon-Sat; ticket purchases 4am-1am) is one level below the tracks, next to the metro entrance. Luggage may be kept at the **left-luggage office** (small bag for 72hr €3.40; ♥ 7.15am to 10pm), next to platform A.

In town, tickets can be bought at the **SNCF Boutique** (Map p768; ♥ 9.30am-6.30pm Mon-Fri, 10am-6pm Sat), near place de la Préfecture.

From Marseille there are trains to more or less any destination in France and beyond. Some sample destinations include Paris' Gare de Lyon (€83.90, three hours, 17 daily), Nice (€25, 2½ hours, 21 daily), Avignon (€19.40, 30 minutes, 27 daily), Lyon (€39.40, 3¼ hours, 16 daily), Barcelona (€66.80, 8½ hours) and Geneva (€58, 6½ hours).

PROVENCE

Getting Around
TO/FROM THE AIRPORT

Navette (☎ Marseille 04 91 50 59 34, ☎ airport 04 42 14 31 27) shuttle buses link Marseille-Provence airport (€8.50, one hour) with Marseille's train station. Buses heading to the airport leave from outside the station's main entrance every 20 minutes between 5.30am and 9.50pm, and buses to the train station depart the airport between 6.10am and 10.50pm.

BUS & METRO

Marseille is served by two well-maintained, fast metro lines (Métro 1 and Métro 2), a tramline and an extensive bus network.

The metro and most buses run from 5am to 9pm. From 9.25pm to 12.30am, metro and tram routes are covered every 15 minutes by buses M1 and M2 and Tramway 68; stops are marked with fluorescent green signs reading *métro en bus* (metro by bus). Most of the 11 **Fluobus** (☎ information 04 91 91 92 10) night buses leave from in front of the **Espace Infos-RTM** (Map p768; ☎ 04 91 91 92 10; 6 rue des Fabres, 1er; ☒ 8.30am-6pm Mon-Fri, 9.30am-12.30pm & 2-5.30pm Sat). This office distributes route maps and sells tickets.

Bus/metro tickets (€1.50) can be used on any combination of metro and bus for one hour after they've been time-stamped (no return trips). A pass for one/three days costs €4/9.50.

TAXI

There's a taxi stand to the right as you exit the train station through the main entrance.

Marseille Taxi (☎ 04 91 02 20 20) and **Taxis France** (☎ 04 91 49 91 00) run taxis 24 hours a day.

AIX-EN-PROVENCE
pop 137,067

Aix-en-Provence, or just Aix (pronounced like the letter 'x'), is one of France's most graceful and popular cities. Its harmonious fusion of majestic public squares, shaded avenues and mossy fountains, many of which have gurgled since the 18th century, couldn't form a greater contrast to its rowdier, less-polished neighbour, Marseille, only 25km down the road.

There's something for everyone here: the art heritage of Cézanne who lived and painted here, a good choice of fine dining, a lively nightlife and plenty of charm. Cours Mirabeau, a graceful, plane tree–lined boulevard overlooked by the haughty stone lions guarding the large central fountain, is the perfect place to amble, shop and, most importantly, watch the world pass as you nurse a slow espresso in one of the many large cafés lining it.

Some 200 elegant mansions in the city centre date from the 17th and 18th centuries. Many are Italian baroque in style and coloured that distinctive Provençal yellow.

The city – its bars and cafés in particular – is enlivened by the presence of the University of Aix-Marseille, the forerunner of which was established in 1409. The university has 30,000 students, many of them foreigners undertaking intensive French-language courses.

TOP FIVE PROVENÇAL MARKETS

- **Aix** (p780) Lose track of time among colourful produce on place des Prêcheurs (Tuesday, Thursday and Saturday) and place Richelme (daily). Flowers are on sale at place de l'Hôtel de Ville (Tuesday, Thursday and Saturday morning) and place des Prêcheurs on Sunday morning.

- **Marseille** (p771) Mooch among the stalls at the tiny but captivating quayside fish market on the old port (daily) or the livelier, Middle Eastern–style bazaars (on weekends) further out of the city.

- **Apt** (p779) Go crazy at the huge Saturday market packed with scrumptious local fare, including the local speciality, crystallised fruit, then demolish your purchases on a picnic in the lovely Parc Naturel Régional du Lubéron.

- **Carpentras** (p797) Stock up on nougat, great local cheeses, lavender marmalade and the luscious local melons at the market (Friday) in this untouristy, down-to-earth town.

- **Arles** (p805) Head here for the large, varied Saturday market stretching the length of the main boulevard and selling great cheese, Camargue salt, olive oil, spices and gifts.

AIX-EN-PROVENCE

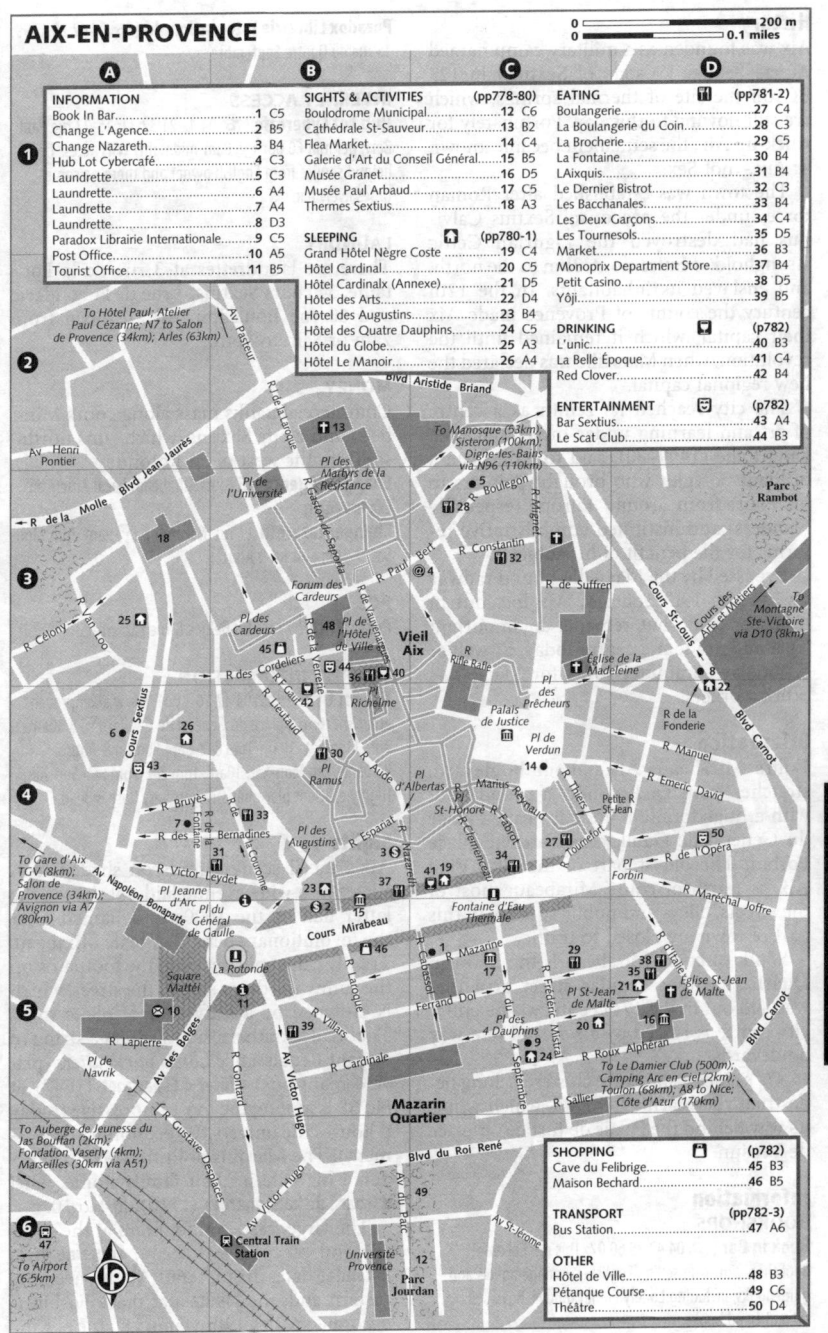

INFORMATION	
Book In Bar	1 C5
Change L'Agence	2 B5
Change Nazareth	3 B4
Hub Lot Cybercafé	4 C3
Laundrette	5 C3
Laundrette	6 A4
Laundrette	7 A4
Laundrette	8 D3
Paradox Librairie Internationale	9 C5
Post Office	10 A5
Tourist Office	11 B5

SIGHTS & ACTIVITIES	(pp778-80)
Boulodrome Municipal	12 C6
Cathédrale St-Sauveur	13 B2
Flea Market	14 C4
Galerie d'Art du Conseil Général	15 B5
Musée Granet	16 D5
Musée Paul Arbaud	17 C5
Thermes Sextius	18 A3

SLEEPING	(pp780-1)
Grand Hôtel Nègre Coste	19 C4
Hôtel Cardinal	20 C5
Hôtel Cardinalx (Annexe)	21 D5
Hôtel des Arts	22 D4
Hôtel des Augustins	23 B4
Hôtel des Quatre Dauphins	24 C5
Hôtel du Globe	25 A3
Hôtel Le Manoir	26 A4

EATING	(pp781-2)
Boulangerie	27 C4
La Boulangerie du Coin	28 C3
La Brocherie	29 C5
La Fontaine	30 B4
LAixquis	31 B4
Le Dernier Bistrot	32 C3
Les Bacchanales	33 B4
Les Deux Garçons	34 C4
Les Tournesols	35 D5
Market	36 B3
Monoprix Department Store	37 B4
Petit Casino	38 D5
Yôji	39 B5

DRINKING	(p782)
L'unic	40 B3
La Belle Époque	41 C4
Red Clover	42 B4

ENTERTAINMENT	(p782)
Bar Sextius	43 A4
Le Scat Club	44 B3

SHOPPING	(p782)
Cave du Felibrige	45 B3
Maison Bechard	46 B5

TRANSPORT	(p782-3)
Bus Station	47 A6

OTHER	
Hôtel de Ville	48 B3
Pétanque Course	49 C6
Théâtre	50 D4

PROVENCE

History

Aix was founded as a military camp named Aquae Sextiae (Waters of Sextius) in 123 BC on the site of thermal springs, which are still flowing to this day. Fortunately for stuck-up Aix, the settlement became known as Aix – not Sex.

The town was established after Roman forces under the proconsul Sextius Calvinus had destroyed the Ligurian Celtic stronghold of Entremont, 3km to the north, and enslaved its inhabitants. In the 12th century the counts of Provence made Aix their capital, which it remained until the revolution, when Marseille was declared the new regional capital.

The city reached its zenith as a centre of art and learning under the enlightened King René (1409–80), said to have been a brilliant polyglot who brought painters to his court from around Europe (especially Flanders) and instituted administrative reforms for the benefit of his subjects.

Bypassed by the Marseille-bound railway line in the 19th century, Aix lost out in terms of trade but remains an important legal and academic centre today, as well as a popular commuter town for Marseille's office workers.

Orientation

Cours Mirabeau, Aix's main boulevard, stretches from La Rotonde, a roundabout with a huge fountain and also called place du Général de Gaulle, eastwards to place Forbin. The oldest part of the city, Vieil Aix, is north of cours Mirabeau; most of the streets, alleys and public squares in this part of town are closed to traffic.

South of cours Mirabeau is the Mazarin Quartier, with a regular street grid that was laid out in the 17th century. The entire city centre is ringed by a series of one-way boulevards.

Aix's chicest shops are clustered along pedestrian rue Marius Reinaud, which winds its way behind the Palais de Justice on place de Verdun.

Information

BOOKSHOPS

Book in Bar (☎ 04 42 26 60 07; 1bis rue Cabassol) Bookshop-cum-café selling English-language novels and guidebooks, including Lonely Planet guides. Buys/sells second-hand books.

Paradox Librairie Internationale (☎ 04 42 26 47 99; 15 rue du Quatre Septembre)

INTERNET ACCESS

Hub Lot Cybercafé (☎ 04 42 21 37 31; 15-27 rue Paul Bert; per min €0.06; ☻ 8am-midnight) WiFi access here, helpful service from English owner and there's a sometimes lively bar.

LAUNDRY

There are laundrettes at 3 rue de la Fontaine, 34 cours Sextius, 3 rue de la Fonderie and 60 rue Boulegon. All are open from 7am or 8am to 8pm.

MONEY

Commercial banks mass along cours Mirabeau and cours Sextius, which runs north–south to the west of La Rotonde.
Change L'Agence (15 cours Mirabeau) Local American Express agent.
Change Nazareth (7 rue Nazareth; ☻ 9am-7pm Mon-Sat, 9-5pm Sun Jul & Aug)

POST

Post Office (cnr av des Belges & rue Lapierre)

TOURIST INFORMATION

Tourist Office (☎ 04 42 16 11 61; www.aixenprovenc etourism.com; 2 place du Général de Gaulle; ☻ 8.30am-7pm Mon-Sat, 10am-1pm & 2-6pm Sun Jul & Aug; 8.30am-7pm Mon-Sat, 10am-1pm & 2-7pm Sun Sep-Jun) Highly efficient place but still gets very busy indeed.

Sights

Aix's social scene centres on shaded **cours Mirabeau**, a wide avenue laid out during the latter half of the 1600s and named after the revolutionary hero Comte de Mirabeau. Trendy cafés spill out onto the footpaths on the sunny northern side of the street, which is crowned by a leafy roof of plane trees. The shady southern side shelters a string of elegant Renaissance *hôtels particuliers* (private mansions); **Hôtel d'Espargnet** (1647) at No 38 is among the most impressive (today it houses the university's economics department). The Marquis of Entrecasteaux murdered his wife in their family home, **Hôtel d'Isoard de Vauvenargues** (1710), at No 10.

The large, cast-iron fountain at the western end of cours Mirabeau, **Fontaine de la Rotonde**, dates from 1860. At the avenue's eastern end, the **fountain** at place Forbin is decorated with a 19th-century statue of King

René holding a bunch of Muscat grapes, a varietal he is credited with introducing to the region. Moss-covered **Fontaine d'Eau Thermale** at the intersection of cours Mirabeau and rue du Quatre Septembre spouts water at a temperature of 34°C.

Other streets and squares lined with *hôtels particuliers* include **rue Mazarine**, which is one block south of cours Mirabeau; **place des Quatre Dauphins**, two blocks further south with a fountain that dates from 1667; the eastern continuation of cours Mirabeau, **rue de l'Opéra** (at Nos 18, 24 and 26); and the pretty, fountain-clad **place d'Albertas**, just west of **place St-Honoré**, where live music is sometimes performed on balmy summer evenings.

South of Aix's historic centre is the very pleasant **parc Jourdan**, a spacious green park dominated by Aix's largest fountain and home to the town's **Boulodrome Municipal**. Old men gather here, or on the court on av du Parc, opposite the park entrance, beneath the shade of the trees, to play *pétanque*. Spectators are welcome.

MUSEUMS

The tourist office sells a Visa for Aix-en-Provence for €2 that offers reduced entry for many city and regional museums.

Sadly, Aix's finest museum, **Musée Granet**, housed in a 17th-century priory of the Knights of Malta, will be closed until at least 2006 while it undergoes massive works that will see it triple in size. Exhibits in the reopened museum will include Celtic statues from Entremont as well as Roman artefacts, 16th- to 19th-century Italian, Dutch and French paintings as well as some of Aix-born Cézanne's lesser-known pieces.

Musée Paul Arbaud (☎ 04 42 38 38 95; 2a rue du Quatre Septembre; adult/student €2.50/1.50; ☼ 2-5pm Mon-Sat) displays books, manuscripts and a collection of Provençal faïence – tin-glazed earthenware.

Galérie d'Art du Conseil Général (☎ 04 42 93 03 67; 21bis cours Mirabeau; ☼ 10.15am-12.45pm & 1.30-6.30pm Mon-Sat) also has exhibitions of photography and contemporary art.

CATHÉDRALE ST-SAUVEUR

Cathédrale St-Sauveur (rue J de Laroque; ☼ 8am-noon & 2-6pm) is a interesting ragtag of styles through the ages, incorporating architectural features of every major period from the 5th to 18th centuries stuck onto one another with some modern touches, such as the chunky, golden contemporary altar piece. The main Gothic structure, built between 1285 and 1350, includes the Romanesque nave of a 12th-century church as part of its southern aisle; the chapels were added in the 14th and 15th centuries, and there is a 5th-century sarcophagus in the apse.

Mass is held here at 8am (Saturday at 6.30pm, and Sunday at 9am, 10.30am and 7pm). Gregorian chants are often sung here at 4.30pm on Sunday – an experience not to be missed.

The 15th-century *Triptyque du Buisson Ardent* (Triptych of the Burning Bush) in the nave is by Nicolas Froment; it is usually only opened for groups. Near it is a triptych panel illustrating Christ's passion. The tapestries encircling the choir date from the 18th century and the fabulous gilt organ is baroque. There's a son-et-lumière (sound-and-light) show at 9.30pm most nights in summer.

CÉZANNE TRAIL

Paul Cézanne (1839–1906), Aix's most celebrated son (at least after his death), did much of his painting in and around the city. If you are interested in the minutiae of his day-to-day life – where he ate, drank, played and worked – just follow the **Circuit de Cézanne**, which is marked by round, bronze markers in the footpaths and begins at the tourist office. The markers correspond with an English-language guide called *Cézanne's Footsteps*, which is available free from the tourist office.

Cézanne's last studio, now opened to the public as **Atelier Paul Cézanne** (☎ 04 42 21 06 53; 9 av Paul Cézanne; adult/student €5.50/2; ☼ 10am-noon & 2-5pm), is atop a hill approximately 1.5km north of the tourist office. It has been left exactly as it was when he died and though none of his works hang here, his tools do. Take bus No 1 to the Cézanne stop.

THERMAL SPA

Thermes Sextius (☎ 04 42 23 81 82; 55 cours Sextius) is the place to do as the Romans did on the same spot: chill out and get pampered silly at the thermal spas. By no means cheap, it's the place for luxurious treats such as 'zen spray massage' and a range of beauty treatments. A day's access to the fitness centre or a massage both start at €32.

PROVENCE

MARKETS

Aix is the premier market town in Provence. A mass of fruit-and-vegetable stands are set up each morning on place Richelme, just as they have been for centuries. Depending on the season, you can buy olives, *chèvre* (goat's cheese), garlic, lavender, honey, peaches, melons and a whole host of other sun-kissed products.

Another **grocery market** (place des Prêcheurs) is set up on Tuesday, Thursday and Saturday morning.

A **flower market** is set up on place des Prêcheurs (Sunday morning) and on place de l'Hôtel de Ville (Tuesday, Thursday and Saturday mornings). There's also a **flea market** (place de Verdun).

Tours

Between April and October, the tourist office runs a packed schedule of guided bus tours around the region in English and in French. There's also the guided Émile Zola literary walk or a free, self-guided *Literary Walk* brochure. Ask for the free *Guide Map* at the tourist office for details of all tours or study the noticeboard outside. Prices start from around €35.

Festivals & Events

Aix has a sumptuous cultural calendar. The most sought-after tickets are for the month-long **Festival International d'Art Lyrique d'Aix-en-Provence** (International Festival of Lyrical Art; www.festival-aix.com) in July, which brings the most refined classical music, opera and ballet to such city venues as the Théâtre de l'Archevêché, outside the Cathédrale St-Sauveur. Meanwhile, buskers bring the festival spirit to cours Mirabeau.

Other festivals include **Rencontres du 9ème Art** (www.bd-aix.com in French), a brand-new annual comic book, animation and cartoon-art festival in March, the two-day **Festival du Tambourin** (Tambourine Festival) in mid-April and the **Fête Mistralienne**, marking the birthday of Provençal hero Frédéric Mistral on 13 September. For detailed information contact the tourist office.

Sleeping

Despite being a student town, Aix is not cheap. Even so, the centre can fill up fast in summer and during busy conference and law exam times, so booking ahead is always

a good idea. The tourist office has comprehensive details of *chambres d'hôtes* (B&Bs) and *gîtes ruraux* (country cottages) in and around Aix. The tourist office also has a list (which is updated weekly) of all types of accommodation – including farmhouses – to rent on a long-term basis. Hotel bookings are coordinated through one address (resaix@aixenprovencetourism.com).

BUDGET

Auberge de Jeunesse du Jas de Bouffan (☎ 04 42 20 15 99; fax 04 42 59 36 12; 3 av Marcel Pagnol; dm incl breakfast & sheets €15) This is a smart, modern place with great views of a distant Mont Ventoux. It's about 2km west of the centre. Rooms are locked between 9am and 5pm. Take bus No 4 from La Rotonde to the Vasarely stop.

Hôtel des Arts (☎ 04 42 38 11 77; fax 04 42 26 77 31; 69 blvd Carnot; s/d from €29/33) Laid-back and friendly, Hôtel des Arts has decent rooms at least partially soundproofed from street noise by double glazing. Although on the city centre's eastern fringe (second entrance at 5 rue de la Fonderie) it's still only a short stroll from the milling crowds of the centre.

Hôtel Paul (☎ 04 42 23 23 89; hotel.paul@wanadoo .fr; 10 av Pasteur; s/d/tr €35/45/55) Although less central than others, Hôtel Paul has simple but welcoming rooms and a pleasant courtyard garden, making it an appealing budget option. Just north of blvd Jean Jaurès, it's a 10-minute walk from the tourist office or take minibus No 2 from La Rotonde or the bus station.

Camping

Camping Arc-en-Ciel (☎ 04 42 26 14 28; route de Nice; camping €17.10; ⏰ Apr-Sep) There are peaceful wooded hills out the back of this place, but a busy motorway in front. It's 2km southeast of town, at Pont des Trois Sautets. Take bus No 3 to Les Trois Sautets stop.

MID-RANGE

Hôtel Le Manoir (☎ 04 42 26 27 20; www.hotelmanoir .com; 8 rue d'Entrecasteaux; d/tr with toilet & shower from €54/72, with bath & toilet from €66/82; **P**) Immaculately kept and occupying a quiet yet central corner of town, Le Manoir has 40 individually decorated rooms with modern comforts and dark-wood period furniture. Enjoy breakfast (€7) under the 14th-century cloister and gaze onto that pleasant garden.

Hôtel Cardinal (☎ 04 42 38 32 30; fax 04 42 26 39 05; 24 rue Cardinale; s/d €47/60, self-catering ste €76) This is a charming place with large (mostly) en suite rooms and a mix of modern and period furniture. The upper rooms offer pretty views across town. The small self-catering suites are in its annexe at 12 rue Cardinale.

Hôtel des Quatre Dauphins (☎ 04 42 38 16 39; fax 04 42 38 60 19; 54 rue Roux Alpheran; s with shower & toilet €45, d with shower & toilet €55-74) Another hotel in a period building near the Cardinal, this place has character, although the rooms lack extensive facilities.

Hôtel du Globe (☎ 04 42 26 03 58; hotel-du -globe@wanadoo.fr; 74 cours Sextius; s with toilet €36, d/ tw/tr with shower or bath €59/62/67; **P**) Just out of the pedestrianised area, Hôtel du Globe is comfortable and reasonable value. Garage parking costs €8 a night and air-con costs €4 extra in July and August.

TOP END

Aix is well endowed with three- and four-star hotels, though many are on the outskirts of town.

Hôtel des Augustins (☎ 04 42 27 28 59; www .hotel-augustins.com; 3 rue de la Masse; standard/superior r low season €95/110, high season €110/125; **✹**) An elegant and atmospheric 15th-century former convent, this place is very comfortable, central and tastefully furnished. All rooms have air-con, cable TV, minibars and telephones. If the weather's good, have breakfast on the roof terrace beneath the bell tower.

Grand Hôtel Nègre Coste (☎ 04 42 27 74 22; www.hotelnegrecoste.com; 33 cours Mirabeau; r €78-100; **P** **✹**) Right in the heart of the action, this was the hotel of choice for Louis XIV in 1660 and many businesspeople today. The large, comfortable three-star rooms are showing their age somewhat but all are well equipped. Garage parking is available.

Eating

Aix and the surrounding area is a rich hunting ground for fine dining if you've the budget for it. Ethnic cuisine in town is usually high quality and generally inexpensive and there are enough restaurants to satisfy most mouths. Aix's cheapest dining street is rue Van Loo, lined with restaurants offering Italian and various Asian cuisines.

Aix's sweet speciality is the *calisson*, a soft, lozenge-shaped chew made with almond paste and fruit syrup.

RESTAURANTS

Rue de la Verrerie and rue Félibre Gaut offer a good range of culinary options, including a number of Vietnamese and Chinese restaurants.

Numerous cafés, brasseries and restaurants can be found nearby, in the heart of the city on place des Cardeurs and place de l'Hôtel de Ville.

La Brocherie (☎ 04 42 38 33 21; 5 rue Fernand Dol; menus €15-33; ☽ closed Sat lunch & Sun) A decent, affordable lunch and dinner option, La Brocherie serves imaginative Provençal mains, good wine and desserts.

Les Tournesols (☎ 04 42 38 30 88; 1 rue Cardinale; menus €16-20; ☽ closed Sat & Mon dinner, Sun) Painted in sunflower yellow (*tournesols* is French for sunflowers), this tiny place serves up good-value salads and tarts as well as heartier regional dishes.

La Fontaine (☎ 04 42 27 53 35; 40 rue de la Verrerie; menus €17; ☽ 7pm-12.30am Tue-Sat) Named after the pretty little fountain that flows on its outside terrace, La Fontaine offers hearty, generous *menus* of Provençal food.

Le Dernier Bistrot (☎ 04 42 21 13 02; 15-19 rue Constantin; lunch menu €10, dinner menus €16-23; ☽ Mon-Sat) This bistro boasts a lovely terrace and dishes that mix traditional bistro recipes with Provençal culinary fodder such as beef daubes and *carpaccios*, *soupe au pistou* and courgette flan with a tomato and basil coulis.

Les Bacchanales (☎ 04 42 27 21 06; 10 rue de la Couronne; lunch menu €18, menu gourmand €63; ☽ closed Wed & Sat lunch, Tue) An upmarket spot offering a delectable Provençal menu that usually offers several fish choices (such as delicately fennel-scented *rouget*) as well as heavier, traditional meat fare, including a good daube.

Yôji (☎ 04 42 38 84 48; 7 av Victor Hugo; lunch menus from €9.50, dinner menus €16-20) Yôji is often packed even midweek in low season and you'll taste why if you can get in (book ahead). The sushi is first rate and there are some tasty occidental/oriental fusion twists (the sake martini is an unlikely hit, as is the toothsome green-tea *brulée*). For real theatre, choose the sizzling Korean barbeques brought to your table (oh, so that's what those fancy smoke hoods above the tables are for).

L'Aixquis (☎ 04 42 27 76 16; 22 rue Victor Leydet; menus €18 & €60; ☽ lunch & dinner Tue-Sat) Although small, L'Aixquis is celebrated for its use of fresh produce, tried-and-tested Provençal classics, a good wine list and elaborately presented

PROVENCE

desserts. The kitchen turns out a good, richly flavoured *pieds et paquets* (slow stewed tripe 'n' trotter) but be warned you'll need to be a fan of that unique glue-and-gristle texture.

CAFÉS

Les Deux Garçons (☎ 04 42 26 00 51; 53 cours Mirabeau) Aix's most renowned café, Les Deux Garçons is on the sunny side of the street. No visit to Aix is complete without a pose here behind your shades. Dating from 1792, this pricey brasserie is a former artist's and intellectual's hang-out – Cézanne and his novelist mate Zola were patrons here.

Not quite so conspicuous are the plentiful open-air cafés that sprawl across the squares, such as place des Cardeurs, forum des Cardeurs, place de Verdun and place de l'Hôtel de Ville.

SELF-CATERING

The next best thing to bread from the market is the fresh and often-warm loaves sold at **La Boulangerie du Coin** (4 rue Boulegon; ⏰ Tue-Sun). It is also one of the few *boulangeries* to bake on Sunday, along with the **boulangerie** (5 rue Tournefort) that never closes, making it ideal for post-pub or club snacks.

Groceries are available in the basement supermarket at **Monoprix Department Store** (cours Mirabeau; ⏰ 8.30am-8pm Mon-Sat) and at **Petit Casino** (rue Cardinale; ⏰ 9am-7pm Mon-Sat).

Drinking

Several lively pubs and clubs have sprung up on and around rue de la Verrerie.

Red Clover (☎ 04 42 23 44 61; 30 rue de la Verrerie) An Irish pub attracting a studenty crowd and occasionally screening live sport, as does the late-closing bar and Internet café Hub Lot.

La Belle Époque (☎ 04 42 27 65 66; 29 cours Mirabeau; ⏰ 6.30am-2.30am) This place buzzes during its two-hour-plus happy 'hour' and boasts large TV screens and DJs playing Latino, house and funk every evening.

L'unic (☎ 04 42 96 38 28; place Richelme) Good for laid-back drinks or brasserie-style fare.

Entertainment

Pick up a free copy of the monthly *In Aix* at the tourist office to find out what's on where and when. Ballet fans may want to check out **Le Ballet Preljocaj** (www.preljocaj.org), a company that made Aix its permanent base in 2005.

NIGHTCLUBS

Le Damier Club (☎ 04 42 27 03 23; 31 av Infirmeries) Providing a good mixture of musical dance styles – rap, pop, nostalgia – Le Damier Club is spread over three floors.

Le Scat Club (☎ 04 42 23 00 23; 11 rue de la Verrerie; ⏰ from 11pm Tue-Sat) An institution in Aix, Le Scat Club presents rock and jazz bands to a young, casual crowd.

Bar Sextius (☎ 04 42 26 07 21; 13 cours Sextius; ⏰ 7am-2am Mon-Sat) Another small, intimate venue, Bar Sextius has live music (Thursday) and DJs playing house (Saturday), reggae and raga (Tuesday).

Shopping

Cave du Felibrige (18 rue des Cordeliers) Sells a splendid array of local wines – some *very* expensive.

Maison Bechard (12 cours Mirabeau) A classy patisserie and *confiseur*. What sweeter way to end that sunny summer picnic than with a couple of Aix's traditional almond confections or some great pastries?

Aix's rue Fabrot is also one of the best places in Provence to seek out desirable designer threads, with several boutiques to choose from.

Getting There & Away

AIR

Marseille-Provence airport is 25km from Aix-en-Provence and is served by regular shuttle buses (see opposite).

BUS

Aix's **bus station** (☎ information office 04 42 91 26 80; av de l'Europe) is a 10-minute walk southwest from La Rotonde. It is served by numerous companies.

There are buses to Marseille (€4.20, 35 minutes via the autoroute or one hour via the N8, every five to 10 minutes), Arles (€11.30, 1¾ hours, five daily), Avignon via the autoroute (€13.90, one hour, six daily) or the national road (€11.70, 1½ hours, four daily) and Toulon (€13.40, one hour, four daily Monday to Saturday).

Sumian buses serve Apt (€8, two daily) and Castellane (Monday, Wednesday and Saturday).

CAR

Getting into Aix by car can be a headache: the one-way, three-lane orbital system ringing the old town is busy and street parking can be hard to find, although (pricier) covered parking just around the edges of old town is plentiful.

TRAIN

Aix's tiny **train station** (5am-9.15pm Mon-Fri, 6am-9.15pm Sat & Sun, information office 9am-7pm) is at the southern end of av Victor Hugo. There are frequent services to Briançon (€28.80, 3½ hours), Gap (€22.44, two hours) and, of course, Marseille (€4.10, 35 minutes, at least 18 daily), from where there are connections to just about everywhere.

Aix's new TGV station is 8km from the city centre, accessible by shuttle bus (see below).

Getting Around

TO/FROM THE AIRPORT & TGV STATION

Both the new TGV station and the airport are linked to Aix's bus station (€7.50, from around 5am to 11.30pm) by the half-hourly **Navette** (04 42 93 59 13).

BUS

The city's 14 bus and three minibus lines are operated by **Aix en Bus** (04 42 26 37 28; 8.30am-7pm Mon-Sat). The information desk is inside the tourist office.

La Rotonde is the main bus hub. Most of the services run until 8pm. A single/*carnet* (book) of 10 bus tickets costs €1.10/7.70. A day pass costs €3.50. Minibus No 1 links the bus station with La Rotonde and cours Mirabeau. Minibus 2, starting at the train station, follows much the same route.

TAXI

You can usually find taxis outside the bus station. To order one, call **Taxi Radio Aixois** (04 42 27 71 11) or **Taxi Mirabeau** (04 42 21 61 61).

THE VAUCLUSE

The Vaucluse is Provence at its most picturesque. Many of the towns date from Roman times and boast impressive Gallo-Roman structures. The villages, which spring to life on market days, are surrounded by some of France's most attractive countryside, brightened by the rich hues of wild herbs, lavender and vines. The Vaucluse is

watched over by Mont Ventoux, which, at 1909m, is Provence's highest peak.

The Vaucluse is shaped like a fan, with Avignon, the region's capital, at the hinge. Orange, famed for its Roman theatre, and the smaller Roman town of Vaison-la-Romaine are north of Avignon and west of Mont Ventoux. Carpentras, near the centre of the Vaucluse, also dates from Roman times but is better known for its ancient Jewish community. Just to the south is Fontaine de Vaucluse, to the east of which are Gordes and Roussillon, enticing Provençal villages overlooking a fertile valley. Further east still is Apt, one of the best bases for exploring the pretty Lubéron Range to the south.

Getting Around

If you don't have access to a car, it is possible to get from town to town by local bus, but the frequency and pace of services are very much in keeping with the relaxed tempo of Provençal life.

AVIGNON

pop 88,312

Avignon is synonymous in France with the annual performing arts festival held here each summer. There's also plenty to see during the rest of the year.

Inside the 4km ring of superbly preserved ramparts, towers and crenellations that fence in the old city's narrow streets and ancient tenements you'll find café-filled squares, a number of interesting museums, the famous Pont d'Avignon and the massive fortress and des res of the medieval popes, the Palais des Papes.

History

The city first acquired wealth and power, its mighty ramparts and its reputation as a city of art and culture during the 14th century, when Pope Clement V and his court fled political turmoil in Rome and established themselves near Avignon. From 1309 to 1377, the seven French-born popes based themselves here, and invested huge sums of money in building and decorating the papal palace. Under the popes' tolerant rule, Jews and political dissidents took shelter here.

Opponents of the move to Avignon – many of them Italians, such as the celebrated poet Petrarch, who lived in Fontaine de Vaucluse at the time – called Avignon

PROVENCE

AVIGNON

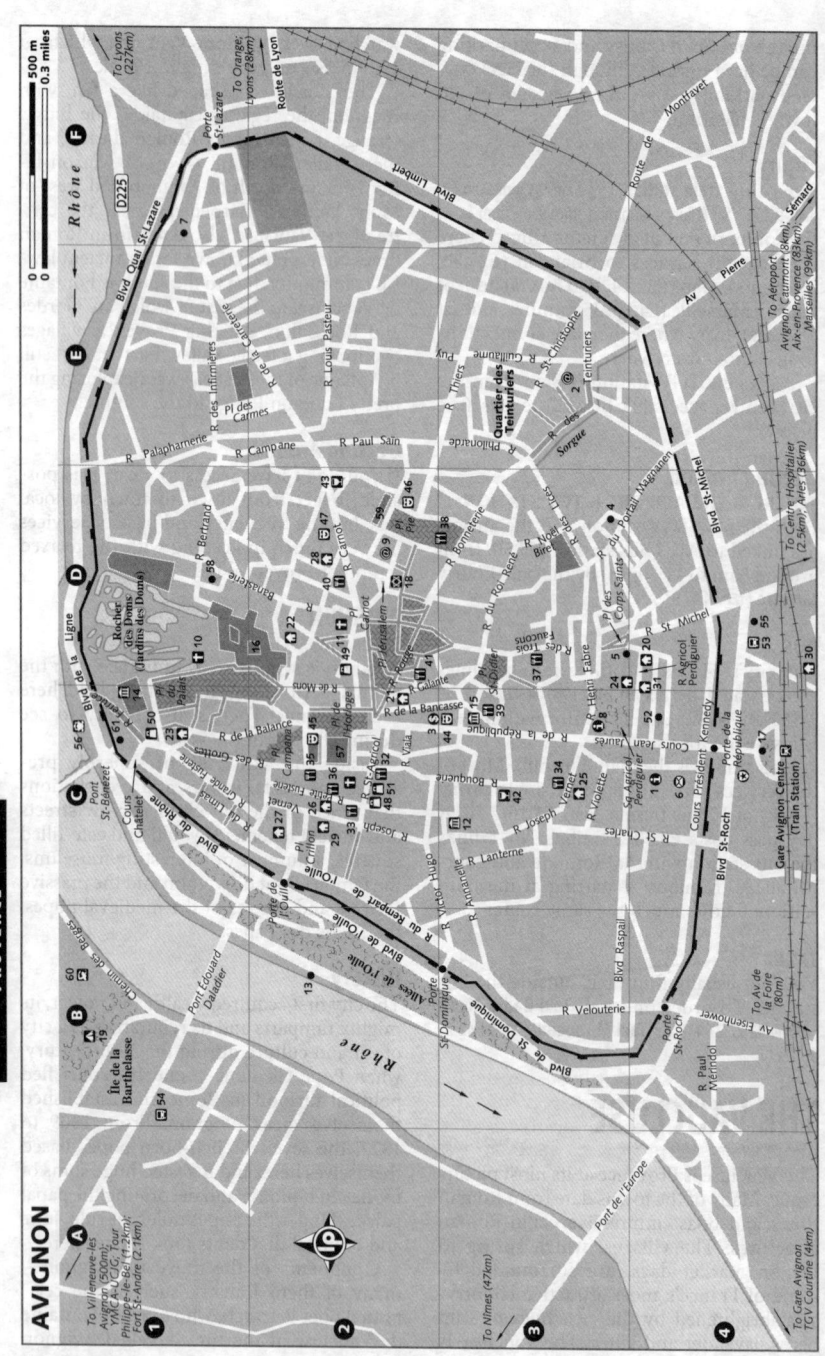

INFORMATION			Hôtel du Palais des Papes	23	C1	ENTERTAINMENT	⊡	(pp789-90)
Bureau du Festival	1	C4	Hôtel du Parc	24	D3	Cinéma Utopia		(see 58)
Chez Wam	2	E3	Hôtel Innova	25	C3	Fnac	44	C3
CIC	3	C2	Hôtel Le Provençal	26	C2	Opéra d'Avignon	45	C2
Laverie la Fontaine	4	D3	Hôtel L'Europe	27	C2	Red Lion	46	D2
Lavmatic	5	D3	Hôtel Médiéval	28	D3	Red Zone	47	D2
Main Post Office	6	C4	Hôtel Mignon	29	C2			
Shakespeare	7	F1	Hôtel Monclar	30	D4	SHOPPING	⊡	(p790)
Tourist Office	8	C3	Hôtel Splendid	31	D4	Comtesse du Barry	48	C2
Webzone	9	D2				Instant du Sud	49	D2
			EATING	⊞	(pp788-9)	Le Lavandin	50	C1
SIGHTS & ACTIVITIES		(pp786-7)	Boulangerie Pâtisserie	32	C3	Oliviers & Co	51	C2
Cathédrale Notre Dame des Doms	10	D1	Casino	33	C2			
Église St-Pierre	11	D2	La Compagnie des Comptoirs	34	C3	TRANSPORT		(pp790-1)
Hôtel de Villeneuve-Marrignan & Musée			La Fourchette	35	C2	Agence Commerciale TCRA	52	C4
Calvet	12	C3	La Marmiton		(see 22)	Bus No 10 Stop		(see 6)
Mireio Embarcadère	13	B2	La Tropézienne		(see 33)	Bus Station	53	D4
Musée du Petit Palais	14	C1	Le Bistrot d'Utopia		(see 58)	La Barthelasse Bus Stop	54	D1
Musée Lapidaire	15	C3	Le Brantes	36	C2	Provence Bike	55	D4
Palais des Papes	16	D2	Le Caveau du Théâtre	37	D3	Shuttle boat embarkment point	56	C1
Point d'Argent	17	C4	Les Halles & Food Market	38	D3	TGV Shuttle Bus Stop		(see 6)
Synagogue	18	C2	Maison Nani	39	C3			
			Restaurant Song Long	40	D2	OTHER		
SLEEPING	⊡ ⊡	(pp787-8)	Tapalocas	41	D2	Hôtel de Ville	57	C2
Auberge Bagatelle		(see 19)				La Manutention	58	D1
Camping Bagatelle	19	B1	DRINKING	⊡	(p789)	Palais de Justice	59	D2
Hôtel Colbert	20	D4	Bleu les Thés	42	C3	Pont St-Bénézet Entrance		(see 61)
Hôtel de Blauvac	21	C2	Le Café d'Utopia		(see 58)	Swimming Pool	60	B1
Hôtel de la Mirande	22	D2	LElectro	43	D2	Tour de Châtelet	61	C1

'the second Babylonian captivity' and a den of criminals and brothel-goers, unfit for papal habitation.

Pope Gregory XI left Avignon in 1376, but his death two years later led to the Great Schism (1378–1417), during which rival popes – up to three at one time – resided at Rome and Avignon and spent most of their energies denouncing and excommunicating one another.

Even after the schism was settled and a pope – Martin V – acceptable to all factions established himself in Rome, Avignon remained under papal rule and continued to serve as an important cultural centre. The city and the nearby Comtat Venaissin (now the *département* of Vaucluse) were ruled by papal legates until 1791, when they were annexed to France.

Orientation

The main avenue within the walled city (*intra-muros*) runs northwards from the train station to place de l'Horloge; it's called cours Jean Jaurès south of the tourist office and rue de la République north of it.

Place de l'Horloge is 300m south of place du Palais, which abuts the Palais des Papes. The city gate nearest the train station is Porte de la République, while the city gate next to Pont Édouard Daladier, which leads to Villeneuve-lès-Avignon, is Porte de l'Oulle. The rehabilitated Quartier des Teinturiers (old dyers' quarter), centred around rue des

Teinturiers, southeast of place Pie, is Avignon's bohemian part of town.

Information

BOOKSHOPS

The tourist office has a small boutique that sells maps and regional guides in both French and English.

Shakespeare (☎ 04 90 27 38 50; 155 rue Carreterie; ☽ 9.30am-12.30pm & 2-6.30pm Tue-Sat) English bookshop and *salon de thé* – enjoy scones with your tomes.

INTERNET ACCESS

Chez Wam (☎ 04 90 86 19 03; 68 rue Guillaume Puy; per 30 min/hr €3/5; ☽ 7am-1am Mon-Fri, noon-1am Sat & Sun)

Webzone (☎ 04 32 76 29 47; 3 rue St Jean le Vieux; per hr €4.57; ☽ 11am-10pm Mon-Sat, noon-5pm Sun)

LAUNDRY

Laverie La Fontaine (66 place des Corps Saints; ☽ 7am-8pm)

Lavmatic (27 rue du Portail Magnanen; ☽ 7am-7.30pm)

MEDICAL SERVICES

Centre Hospitalier (☎ 04 32 75 33 33; rue Raoul Follereau) 2.5km south of the train station, at the southern terminus of bus line Nos 1 and 3 (marked on bus maps as 'Hôpital Sud').

MONEY

CIC (13 rue de la République) In the train station forecourt with a 24-currency changing machine and ATM.

PROVENCE

POST

Main Post Office (cours Président Kennedy) Currency exchange and Cyberposte.

TOURIST INFORMATION

Tourist Office (☎ 04 32 74 32 74; www.ot-avignon.fr; 41 cours Jean Jaurès; ☺ 9am-6pm Mon-Sat, 9am-5pm Sun Apr-Jun & Aug-Oct, 9am-6pm Mon-Fri, 9am-5pm Sat, 10am-noon Sun Nov-Mar, 9am-7pm Mon-Sat, 10am-5pm Sun Jul) Around 300m north of the train station. During the Avignon Festival it opens 9am to 7pm (5pm on Sunday). On Tuesday, Thursday and Saturday between 1 April and 31 October, two-hour **city tours** (adult/child €10/7) in English and French depart from the tourist office at 10am.

AVIGNON PASSION

To encourage maximum sightseeing the tourist office has devised the Avignon Passion museum pass. Here's how it works: pay full price at the first monument or museum you enter and you receive a card entitling you to a reduced price in all other museums and discounts on the tourist office walking tours. The pass is good for 15 days in all the museums of Avignon as well as Villeneuve-lès-Avignon and covers a family of five. The discounted price is equal to the admission for students, so it's unnecessary for those with an ISIC card.

Sights & Activities

PONT ST-BÉNÉZET (LE PONT D'AVIGNON)

Pont St-Bénézet (St Bénézet's Bridge; ☎ 04 90 27 51 16; full price/pass €3.50/3; ☺ 9am-7pm Apr-Jun & Oct & Nov, 9am-8pm Jul-Sep, 9.30am-5.45pm Nov-Mar, to 9pm during theatre festival in Jul) was built between 1177 and 1185 to link Avignon with the settlement across the Rhône that later became Villeneuve-lès-Avignon. By tradition, the construction of the bridge is said to have begun when Bénézet (Benedict the Bridge Builder), a pastor from Ardèche, was told in three visions to get the Rhône spanned at any cost. Yes, this is also the Pont d'Avignon mentioned in the French nursery rhyme. In actual fact, people did not dance *sur le pont d'Avignon* (on the bridge of Avignon) but *sous* (under) it in between the arches.

The 900m-long wooden structure was repaired and rebuilt several times before all but four of its 22 spans were washed away once and for all in the mid-1600s.

Admission to the bridge is via cours Châtelet. Many people find a distant view of the bridge from the Rocher des Doms or Pont Édouard Daladier much more interesting. And it is, of course, free. Another pleasant alternative is to cross the river and take in the view with a stroll on the Île de la Barthelasse, on the promenade des Berges.

WALLED CITY

Avignon's most interesting bits are within the roughly oval walled city, which is surrounded by almost 4.5km of ramparts built between 1359 and 1370. The ramparts were restored during the 19th century, but the original moats were not, leaving the crenellated fortifications looking purposeless and certainly less imposing than they once did. Even in the 14th century this defence system was hardly state-of-the-art: the towers were left open on the side facing the city, and machicolations (openings in the parapets for dropping things such as boiling oil or for shooting arrows at attackers) are lacking in many sections.

Palais des Papes

The huge **Palais des Papes** (Palace of the Popes; ☎ 04 90 27 50 00; place du Palais; full price/pass €9.50/7.50; ☺ 9am or 9.30am-6.30pm or 7pm Oct-Jun, 9am-8pm Jul-Sep, to 9pm during theatre festival in Jul) was built during the 14th century as a fortified palace for the pontifical court. The cavernous stone halls and extensive grounds testify to the enormous wealth amassed by the papacy during the 'Babylonian Captivity'. The palace is an outstanding example of Gothic architecture but the undecorated rooms are nearly empty except for occasional art exhibits. The view of the palace complex is more impressive than the visit and the best view is from across the river along the chemin des Berges on the Île de la Barthelasse. The fabulous cours d'Honneur – the palace's main courtyard – has played host to the Avignon festival since 1947.

The admission price includes hire of a very user-friendly audioguide in English. Call for the schedule of guided tours in English given in July and August.

Musée du Petit Palais

During the 14th and 15th centuries **Musée du Petit Palais** (☎ 04 90 86 44 58; place du Palais; full price/pass €6/3; ☺ 10am-1pm & 2-6pm Wed-Mon Jun-Sep, 9.30am-1pm & 2-5.30pm Wed-Mon Oct-May) served as a bishops' and archbishops' palace. It now houses an outstanding collection of lavishly coloured 13th- to 16th-century Italian religious paintings from artists including Botticelli, Carpaccio and Giovanni di Paolo. There are accompanying information sheets in English in each room.

Rocher des Doms

Just up the hill from the cathedral is **Rocher des Doms**, a delightful bluff-top park that affords great views of the Rhône, Pont St-Bénézet, Villeneuve-lès-Avignon and the Alpilles. A semicircular viewpoint indicator tells you what you're looking at. There's shade, breeze and benches aplenty up here and it's a good spot for a picnic.

Musée Calvet

Housed in the elegant Hôtel de Ville-neuve-Martignan (1741–54), **Musée Calvet** (☎ 04 90 86 33 84; 65 rue Joseph Vernet; full price/pass €6/3; ☺ 10am-1pm & 2-6pm Wed-Mon) has an impressive collection of artefacts dating from prehistory to the Roman times, as well as paintings from between the 16th and the 20th centuries.

Musée Lapidaire

Not far from the tourist office, **Musée Lapidaire** (☎ 04 90 86 33 84; 27 rue de la République; full price/pass €2/1; ☺ 10am-1pm & 2-6pm Wed-Mon) is inexpensive and well worth a quick look for its somewhat random collection of Egyptian, Roman, Etruscan and early Christian bric-a-brac ranging from large sections of marble statuary and hieroglyphics to delicate vases and bronze figurines.

BOATING

Les Grands Bateaux de Provence (☎ 04 90 85 62 25; bateaugbp@aol.com; allées de l'Oulle), based at the Mireio Embarcadère opposite the Porte de l'Oulle, runs excursions from Avignon down the Rhône to Arles, vineyard towns and even the Camargue (€45 including a meal). There are also less-ambitious journeys to Villeneuve-lès-Avignon and Île de la Barthelasse from two to six times daily in July and August.

A free shuttle boat near Pont St-Bénézet connects the walled city with the **Île de la Barthelasse** (☺ 10am-12.30pm & 2-6.30pm Apr-Jun, 11am-9pm Jul & Aug, 2-5.30pm Wed, 10am-noon & 2-5.30pm Sat & Sun Oct-Dec).

Tours

Autocars Lieutaud (☎ 04 90 86 36 75; www.cars-lieutaud.fr in French), based at the bus station, offers a variety of thematic whole- and half-day bus tours between April and October, including the Pont du Gard (€15, 4½ hours), Nîmes, Arles and the Camargue (€48, seven hours), Vaison-la-Romaine and Orange (€29, 4½ hours), the Lubéron (€21, 4½ hours) and to the wine cellars at Châteauneuf-du-Pape (€14, three hours).

Festivals & Events

Avignon's streets buzz with life, buskers, street theatre, and leafleters enticing you into the hundreds of shows held during the city's now-world-famous **Festival d'Avignon**, founded in the late 1940s and held every year from early July to early August. It attracts many hundreds of performance artists (actors, dancers and musicians) who put on some 300 *spectacles* of all sorts each day in every imaginable venue. There are, in fact, two simultaneous events: the prestigious, government-subsidised and expensive official festival; and the fringe one, Festival Off.

Tickets for official festival performances in the Palais des Papes' cours d'Honneur cost around €30. A Carte Public Adhérent (€14) gives you a 30% discount on all Festival Off performances and can be obtained at the Conservatoire de Musique. Contact **Avignon Public Off** (☎ 01 48 05 01 19; www.avignon-off.org in French) for the schedule.

Information on the official festival can be obtained from the **Bureau du Festival** (☎ 04 90 27 66 50; www.festival-avignon.com; Espace St-Louis, 20 rue du Portail Boquier). Tickets can be reserved from mid-June.

Sleeping

During the festival, it's practically impossible to find a hotel room unless you've reserved months in advance. Hotel rooms are readily available in August, however, when places in the rest of the Vaucluse *département* are at a premium.

BUDGET

Auberge Bagatelle (☎ 04 90 85 78 45; auberge .bagatelle@wanadoo.fr; Île de la Barthelasse; dm €11-11.50, d with/without shower €34/26.50) Auberge Bagatelle has 210 beds and is part of a large, park-like area that includes Camping Bagatelle.

Rooms are for two, four, six or eight but are rather cramped.

YMCA-UCJG (☎ 04 90 25 46 20; www.ymca-avignon .com; 7bis Chemin de la Justice; s/d/tr/q with washbasin €22/28/33/44, s/d/tr with shower & toilet €33/42/51) This is a good hostel in Villeneuve-lès-Avignon with well-maintained rooms in a variety of sizes. Take bus No 10 to the Pont d'Avignon stop Monteau.

Camping

Camping Bagatelle (☎ 04 90 86 30 39; camping .bagatelle@wanadoo.fr; Île de la Barthelasse; sites s/d with tent & car high season €11/13; ☺ reception 8am-9pm) This attractive, shaded, three-star camping ground is just north of Pont Édouard Daladier, 850m from the walled city. Take bus No 10 from the main post office to the La Barthelasse stop. Follow the river to the camping ground.

MID-RANGE

Hôtel Innova (☎ 04 90 82 54 10; hotel.innova@wanadoo.fr; 100 rue Joseph Vernet; r with shower €32, with shower & TV €40, with shower, toilet & TV €44) This one-star place is always busy so book ahead. It has bright, comfortable and soundproofed rooms.

The following three hotels are close to each other on the same street. **Hôtel du Parc** (☎ 04 90 82 71 55; www.hotelduparc.fr.fm; 18 rue Agricol Perdiguier; s/d with shower €35/43, with shower & toilet €47/47; Ⓟ) has one-star rooms, **Hôtel Splendid** (☎ 04 90 86 14 46; www.avignon-splendid-hotel.com; 17 rue Agricol Perdiguier; s/d with shower €37/49, with shower & toilet €43/54; Ⓟ) is friendly with recently renovated rooms, and **Hôtel Colbert** (☎ 04 90 86 20 20; www.lecolbert-hotel.com; 7 rue Agricol Perdiguier; s with shower & toilet €35-55, d with shower & toilet €45-60; 🔲), which smells of disinfectant, is good value.

Hôtel Monclar (☎ 04 90 86 20 14; www.hotel -monclar.com; 13 av Monclar; s/d with washbasin €20/30, s/d with shower €26/45; Ⓟ) Occupying a handsome, peppermint-shuttered 18th-century building by the train station (next to the tracks, in fact, so noise can be a problem). This place has considerable charm. Rooms have washbasins and bidets, a couple have kitchenettes and there's a pretty back garden. Parking costs €4.50.

Hôtel de Blauvac (☎ 04 90 86 34 11; www.hotel -blauvac.com; 11 rue de la Bancasse; s/d/tr €48/51/65) Down a dark, scruffy side street just off the main square you'll find this hidden gem inside the lovely 17th-century former townhouse of the Marqui de Blauvac. The

hotel is friendly, comfortable and central; the rooms convivial and stylish.

Hôtel Médiéval (☎ 04 90 86 11 06; hotel.medieval@ wanadoo.fr; 15 rue Petite Saunerie; s/d €37/58) Hôtel Médiéval is another pretty good central bet. Also in a restored 17th-century house, it's down a quiet street not far from the Palais des Papes. It rents studios on a weekly or monthly basis.

Hôtel du Palais des Papes (☎ 04 90 86 04 13; www.hotel-avignon.com in French; 1 rue Gérard Philippe; s/d/q with shower, toilet & breakfast from €65/75/130) This is a sparsely appointed but nonetheless appealing old-world place with large rooms. The pricier rooms sport a view of the Palais des Papes.

Hôtel Mignon (☎ 04 90 82 17 30; www.hotel-mi gnon.com; 12 rue Joseph Vernet; s with shower €34, d/tr/tr with shower, toilet & breakfast €50/55/61; Ⓟ) Fairly central and reasonable value, Hôtel Mignon offers spotless, well-kept and soundproofed rooms with multichannel TV. The service is especially helpful and friendly.

Hôtel le Provençal (☎ 04 90 85 25 24; fax 04 90 82 75 81; 13 rue Joseph Vernet; s/d with shower & toilet €46/47) A comparable standard of accommodation to the Mignon opposite. It's popular so book ahead.

TOP END

Hôtel L'Europe (☎ 04 90 14 76 76; www.heurope.com; 12 place Crillon; r €129-410; Ⓟ ⊠ 🔲) This is a great four-star place with bags of charm. Napoleon Bonaparte is just one of the historic figures, artists and writers to have enjoyed its lovely plane tree–shaded courtyard and the large, graceful rooms. Garage parking costs €15.

Hôtel de la Mirande (☎ 04 90 14 20 20; www .la-mirande.fr; 4 place de la Mirande; r Nov-Mar from €280, Apr-Oct from €340; Ⓟ ⊠ 🔲) Avignon's most exclusive hotel, furnished in lavish but supremely tasteful period style. It occupies a former 14th-century cardinal's palace behind the Palais des Papes and has its own cooking school, Le Marmiton, which also runs an educational evening table d'hôte (see opposite).

Eating

From Easter until mid-November, half of place de l'Horloge is taken over by tourist restaurants and cafés. *Menus* start at about €14. Many restaurants open just for the festival; most have special (and more expensive) festival *menus*.

PROVENCE

Tapalocas (☎ 04 90 82 56 84; 15 rue Galante; dishes from €2; ⊗ 11.45am-1am) This is a down-to-earth Spanish tapas bar, selling cheap, beer-session ballast.

Le Brantes (☎ 04 90 86 35 14; 2 rue Petite Fusterie; menus €11-23) Serving above-average pizza and pasta that you can enjoy in the flowery courtyard out back.

Maison Nani (☎ 04 90 82 60 90; 29 rue Théodore Aubanel; plat du jour €9; ⊗ closed Sun, Mon-Thu dinner) A cheerful, popular bistro, Maison Nani serves Provençal salads, grilled meat and fresh fish.

Le Bistrot d'Utopia (☎ 04 90 27 04 96; 4 rue des escaliers Ste-Anne; mains from €13) Inside a high-ceilinged, elegantly distressed dining room in the Manutention cultural centre, the Utopia is great for atmosphere and simple, quality food. Peppery-leafed salads, mushroom tarts with buttery pastry, duck breasts done to a turn and ace desserts such as slender lemon curd tart topped with a sliver crystallised orange are typical fare.

La Fourchette (☎ 04 90 85 20 93; 17 rue Racine; menus from €24.40; ⊗ Mon-Fri) A classical French restaurant west of place de l'Horloge, La Fourchette offers a wide choice of dishes on its fixed-price *menu*. The *sauté d'agneau* is a house speciality. Book ahead.

Le Caveau du Théâtre (☎ 04 90 82 60 91; 16 rue des Trois Faucons; lunch/dinner menus €10/18; ⊗ closed Sat lunch & Sun) South of the square, this restaurant turns out rich, traditional French fare with some more adventurous items thrown in, such as butter fried fish in a curry paste with sun-dried tomatoes.

Heading east from place de l'Horloge, you come to rue Carnot, home to a handful of Vietnamese and Chinese places.

Restaurant Song Long (☎ 04 90 86 35 00; 1 rue Carnot; lunch/dinner menus from €5.35/6.90) Offers a wide variety of excellent Vietnamese dishes, including 16 *plats végétariens*.

La Compagnie des Comptoirs (☎ 04 90 85 99 04; 83 rue Joseph Vernet; mains €13-28, lunch formule €15) Opposite the Hôtel Innova, inside Le Cloître des Arts, this is a sophisticated restaurant wrapped around an enchanting 18th-century courtyard. The restaurant has an excellent selection of vegetarian and seafood dishes. Examples from the menu include raviolis of *queue de bœuf* (oxtail) and *daurade* (sea bream) fillets with fennel, *confit* tomatoes and basil. There are also lighter, Asian-flavoured dishes such as sushi.

Le Marmiton (☎ 04 90 85 93 93; 4 place de l'Amirande; table d'hôte €80; ⊗ dinner Tue-Sat) If you want to watch and learn how typical Provençal food should be prepared as well as eating it, consider the four-course feast cooked before you at a large scrubbed wood table in the intimate kitchen at the Hôtel de la Mirande (budget allowing of course).

SELF-CATERING
Les Halles has a great **food market** (place Pie; ⊗ 7am-1pm Tue-Sun).

Boulangerie Pâtisserie (17 rue St-Agricol; ⊗ 7.45am-7.30pm Mon-Sat), for breads and sandwiches, is near place de l'Horloge. For groceries there's **Casino** (22 rue St-Agricol; ⊗ 8am-12.45pm & 3-7.30pm Mon-Sat). After picking up healthy fruit at Casino, misbehave next door at **La Tropézienne** (☎ 04 90 86 24 72; 22 rue St-Agricol; ⊗ 8.30am-7.30pm Mon-Sat), with sinfully delicious pastries, pralines, candied fruit, jams and the creamy *tarte tropézienne*.

Drinking
You can't fail to find a decent café to sit and people watch on the main square around the Opéra.

L'Electro (☎ 06 99 48 97 49; 2 rue du Portail; ⊗ till late) This is a cosy, low-key but hip café-cum-bar that opens until the small hours most nights. At weekends, DJs get busy on the decks.

Le Café d'Utopia (☎ 04 90 27 04 96; 4 rue des escaliers Ste-Anne; ⊗ 11.30am-1am) Try this relaxed café/bar inside La Manutention, an entertainment and cultural centre where Avignon's resident artists and intellectuals chew over the cultural scene, including the latest films at the adjacent Cinéma Utopia, on plush banquettes.

Bleu les Thés (☎ 04 32 76 23 69; 26 rue Bouquerie; ⊗ salon de thé 2.30-6.30pm Mon-Fri) A smart, civilised place for an afternoon cuppa or the special house hot chocolate.

Entertainment
For information on the Festival d'Avignon and Festival Off, see p787. Tickets for many cultural events and performances are sold at the tourist office.

Events listings are included in the free *César* weekly magazine and in the tourist office's fortnightly newsletter, *Rendez-vous d'Avignon*. Tickets for most events are sold at **Fnac** (☎ 04 90 14 35 35; 19 rue de la République; ⊗ 10am-7pm Mon-Sat).

PROVENCE

Opéra d'Avignon (☎ 04 90 82 23 44; place de l'Horloge; ⊙ box office 11am-6pm Mon-Sat) Housed in an imposing structure built in 1847, Opéra d'Avignon stages operas, operettas, plays, symphonic concerts, chamber music concerts and ballet.

Cinéma Utopia (☎ 04 90 82 65 36; 4 rue des escaliers Ste-Anne; admission €3-5) In the cultural centre tucked behind the Palais des Papes, this cinema screens dubbed and subtitled films.

NIGHTCLUBS

Red Zone (☎ 04 90 27 02 44; 25 rue Carnot) Test drive those new dancing trousers at Red Zone, which rocks most nights. Monday is Afro, Tuesday is salsa, Wednesday there's a live concert and Thursday to Sunday there are DJs playing house, techno etc.

Red Lion (☎ 04 90 86 40 25; 21-23 rue St Jean le Vieux) Part ye-olde-English pub, part nightclub, the Red Lion is a lively spot with a different dance genre each night, including a Thursday disco.

Shopping

Instant du Sud (☎ 04 90 82 24 48; 1 place Nicolas Saboly) You can make your own perfume here.

Le Lavandin (☎ 04 90 85 90 01; 4 rue du puits de la Reille) Offers typically Provençal goods and presents such as elegantly patterned and coloured tablecloths.

Oliviers & Co (☎ 04 92 70 48 20; 19 rue St-Agricol) Sells the very finest olive oil and olive oil–based products such as soap, hand cream and biscuits.

Comtesse du Barry (☎ 04 90 82 62 92; 25 rue St-Agricol) Stock up on gourmet goodies such as fine wine and foie gras.

Getting There & Away

AIR

The **Aéroport Avignon-Caumont** (☎ 04 90 81 51 51) is 8km southeast of Avignon. There is no public transport into town; a taxi costs about €15.

BUS

The **bus station** (halte routière; ☎ 04 90 82 07 35; blvd St-Roch; ⊙ information window 10.15am-1pm & 2-6pm Mon-Fri) is in the basement of the building down the ramp to the right as you exit the train station. Tickets are sold on the buses, which are run by many different companies.

Places you can get to by bus include Aix-en-Provence (via the motorway €13.90, one hour; on secondary roads €11.70, 1½ hours, four to six daily), Arles (€8.50, 1½ hours, six daily), Carpentras (€3.80, 45 minutes, 27 daily), Marseille (€16.40, 35 minutes direct, one daily), Nice (€27, one daily), Nîmes (€8.10, 1¼ hours, five daily) and Orange (€5.10, 40 minutes, about 20 daily). Most lines operate on Sunday at reduced frequency.

Long-haul bus companies **Linebus** (☎ 04 90 85 30 48) and **Eurolines** (☎ 04 90 85 27 60; www .eurolines.fr) have offices at the far end of the bus platforms.

CAR

Most car-rental agencies are either inside the main train station complex or nearby (follow the signs). They include **Europcar** (Ibis Bldg ☎ 04 90 85 01 40; TGV station ☎ 04 32 74 63 40).

TRAIN

The **main train station** (⊙ information counter 9am-6.15pm Mon-Sat) is across blvd St-Roch from Porte de la République. The left-luggage room, to the left as you exit the station, opens from 6am to 10pm. Luggage left in the automatic lockers (security-controlled) costs €3 to €6.10 depending on size.

The TGV station, specially constructed to receive the super-fast trains from Paris and Lyon, is a few kilometres from town. A shuttle bus (€2) takes you from the TGV station to the bus stop just outside the main post office. It runs every 30 minutes from about 5.30am to 10.50pm.

There are trains to Arles (€5.70, 20 minutes, 14 to 18 daily), Marseille (€15.50, 40 minutes), Nice (€38.80, three hours), Nîmes (€7.40, 30 minutes, 15 daily), Orange (€4.70, 20 minutes, 17 daily) and, by TGV, Paris' Gare de Lyon (€67, 2½ hours) and Lyon (€29.60, one hour).

Getting Around

BIKE

There are several bike-hire places in town, including **Provence Bike** (☎ 04 90 27 92 61; www .provence-bike.com; 52 blvd St Roch), which also rents scooters and motorbikes.

BUS

Local TCRA bus tickets cost €1.05 each if bought from the driver; a *carnet* of 10 tickets costs €8 at TCRA offices. Buses run from 7am to about 7.40pm (8am to 6pm and less frequently on Sunday). The two most important bus transfer points are the Poste stop at the main post office and place Pie.

Carnets and free bus maps *(plan du réseau)* are available at the **Agence Commerciale TCRA** (☎ 04 32 74 18 32; av de Lattre de Tassigny; ⏲ 8.30am-12.30pm & 1.30-6pm Mon-Fri).

Villeneuve-lès-Avignon is linked with Avignon by bus No 10, which stops in front of the main post office and on the western side of the walled city near Porte de l'Oulle.

TAXI

Pick up a taxi outside the train station or call the **place Pie taxi stand** (☎ 04 90 82 20 20; ⏲ 24hr).

AROUND AVIGNON
Villeneuve-lès-Avignon

Villeneuve-lès-Avignon, across the Rhône from Avignon (and in a different *département*), was founded in the late 13th century. It became known as the City of Cardinals because many primates affiliated with the papal court built large residences in the town, despite the fact that it was in territory ruled by the French crown and not the pope.

Avignon's picturesque sister city, Villeneuve also has a few interesting sights, all of which are included in the Avignon Passion pass (p786). From Avignon, Villeneuve can be reached by foot or bus No 10 (from the main post office).

Chartreuse du Val de Bénédiction (☎ 04 90 15 24 24; 60 rue de la République; full price/pass €5.50/3.50; ⏲ 9am-6.30pm May-Aug, 9.30am-5.30pm Sep-Apr) is a well-preserved Carthusian monastery, once the largest and most important in France.

Musée Pierre de Luxembourg (☎ 04 90 27 49 66; rue de la République; full price/pass €3/1.90; ⏲ 10am-12.30pm & 2-6.30pm, closed Mon mid-Sep–mid-Jun) has a mostly middling collection of religious paintings, with one exception. If you're remotely interested in religious art it's well worth the visit for Enguerrand Quarton's lavish and dramatic 1453 painting *The Crowning of the Virgin*. It's worth asking for the accompanying notes, which give an interesting insight into the commissioning of the painting and the religious dogma that underpins its composition.

Tour Philippe-le-Bel (☎ 04 32 70 08 57; full price/pass €1.60/0.90; ⏲ 10am-12.30pm & 2-6.30pm, closed Mon mid-Sep–mid-Jun), a defensive tower built in the 14th century at what was then the northwestern end of Pont St-Bénézet, has great views of Avignon's walled city, the river and the surrounding countryside. The spiral stairs up are narrow and numerous, though. Another Provençal panorama can be enjoyed from 14th-century **Fort St-André** (☎ 04 90 25 45 35; full price/pass €4.60/3.10; ⏲ 10am-1pm & 2-6pm Apr-Sep, 10am-1pm & 2-5pm Oct-Mar).

Les Baux de Provence
pop 468

Twenty five kilometres south of Avignon, past the small town of St-Rémy de Provence (population 9340), is Les Baux de Provence, vividly immortalised on canvas by Van Gogh during his stay in an asylum in 1889–90. This breathtaking fortified village, named after the 245m-high *baou* (rocky spur) on which it is perched, pulls in some 2.5 million tourists a year (putting it on a par with Mont St-Michel in Normandy as one of France's biggest tourist attractions outside of Paris). The castle looms over a beautiful crescent of vineyards and olive groves set beneath dramatic limestone hills on one side and a picturesque valley on the other.

The most pleasant time to visit **Château des Baux** (☎ 04 90 54 55 56; adult/student €7/5.50; ⏲ 9am-7.30pm May & Jun, 9am-8.30pm Jul & Aug, 9am-5pm Sep-Apr), a former feudal home of Monaco's Grimaldi royal family, is early evening after the caterpillar of tourist coaches has evacuated the village. Audioguides in several languages give a thorough explanation of the history of the castle, village and region and there are demonstrations of medieval warfare in summer.

The **tourist office** (☎ 04 90 54 34 39; fax 04 90 54 51 51) has information on Les Baux's few accommodation options. Note, there is no free parking within 800m of the village. Park for free at the car park of the **Cathédrale d'Images** – a rather uninspiring and very overpriced sound and light show (€7) set in a former quarry cave just north of the village. From here, you can easily walk back to Les Baux.

ORANGE
pop 28,889

If it weren't for the Romans, Orange would be a rather workaday town, scarcely worth a visit. Fortunately, the Romans built a splendid theatre and triumphal arch, which have survived largely intact and are the pride of Provence. The town's network of plazas,

PROVENCE

fountains and pedestrian streets are agreeable to stroll along, but not hard to leave.

Through a 16th-century marriage with the German House of Nassau, the House of Orange (the princely dynasty that had ruled Orange since the 12th century) became active in the history of the Netherlands and later, through William III (William of Orange), also in England. Orange (Arenja in Provençal), which had earlier been a stronghold of the Reformation, was ceded to France in 1713 by the Treaty of Utrecht, but to this day many members of the royal house of the Netherlands are known as the princes and princesses of Orange–Nassau.

Orientation

Orange's train station is just over 1km east of place de la République, the city centre, along av Frédéric Mistral and rue de la République. Rue St-Martin links place de la République and nearby place Clemenceau with the tourist office, which is 250m to the west. Théâtre Antique, Orange's magnificent Roman theatre, is two blocks south of place de la République. The tiny River Meyne lies north of the centre. From the train station, bus No 2 from rue Jean Reboul (first left after exiting the station) goes to the Théâtre Antique or République stop.

Information

LAUNDRY
Laundrette (5 rue St-Florent; ⏰ 7am-8pm)

MONEY
There are lots of banks along the rue Aristide Briand.
Crédit Lyonnais (7 place de la République)

POST
Post Office (blvd Édouard Daladier) Has a Cyberposte.

TOURIST INFORMATION
Tourist Office (☎ 04 90 34 70 88; www.provence-orange .com; 5 cours Aristide Briand; ⏰ 9am-7pm Mon-Sat, 10am-6pm Sun Apr-Sep, 10am-1pm & 2-5pm Mon-Sat Oct-Mar)
Tourist Office Annexe (place des Frères Mounet; ⏰ 10am-1pm & 2.15-7pm Mon-Sat, 10am-12.30pm & 2.30-6pm Sun Apr-Sep) In front of the Roman theatre.

Sights
THÉÂTRE ANTIQUE
Orange's magnificent **Roman theatre** (☎ 04 90 51 17 60; adult/student €7.50/5.50; ⏰ 9am-6.30pm Apr-

early Oct, 9am-noon & 1.30-5pm early Oct-Mar), designed to seat 10,000 spectators, was probably built during the time of Augustus Caesar (who ruled from 27 BC to AD 14). Its stage wall *(mur de scène)*, the only such Roman structure still standing in its entirety (minus a few mosaics and the roof), is 103m wide and 37m high. Its plain exterior can be viewed from adjacent place des Frères Mounet to the north. Admission price includes an audio tour and entry to the attached museum across the road, worth a quick look for the friezes of Amazons and Centaurs that used to form part of the theatre's scenery.

For a panoramic view of the Roman masterpiece, follow montée Philbert de Chalons or montée Lambert to the top of **Colline St-Eutrope** (St-Eutrope Hill; elevation 97m), where a circular viewing table explains what's what. En route you pass the ruins of a 12th-century **chateau**, the former residence of the princes of Orange.

Those not into walking can always hop aboard the 54-seat **Orangeois tourist train** that departs every 30 minutes or so from outside the Théâtre Antique. The city tour (€5) lasts 30 minutes and takes in all the major sights.

ARC DE TRIOMPHE
Orange's Roman **triumphal arch**, one of the most remarkable of its kind in France, is at the northern end of plane tree–lined av de l'Arc de Triomphe, about 450m from the centre of town. Probably built around 20 BC, it is 19m in height and width, and 8m thick. The exceptional friezes commemorate Julius Caesar's victories over the Gauls in 49 BC, triumphs of which the Romans wished to remind every traveller approaching the city. The arch has been restored several times since 1825.

Festivals & Events
In June and August Théâtre Antique comes alive with all-night concerts, cinema screenings and musical events during **Les Nuits du Théâtre Antique**. During the last fortnight in July, it plays host to **Les Chorégies d'Orange**, a series of weekend operas, classical concerts and choral performances. Seats (€15 to €160) for the festival must be reserved months beforehand, although it is possible to catch a free glimpse of the action from the lookout atop Colline St-Eutrope. Orange also plays host to a week-long **jazz festival** in June.

Tickets for events held in the Théâtre Antique can be reserved at the **Location Théâtre Antique** (☎ 04 90 34 24 24; www.choregies.asso.fr; 14 place Silvain).

Sleeping

BUDGET

Camping Le Jonquier (☎ 04 90 34 49 48; www.avignon-et-provence.com/le-jonquier; 1321 rue Alexis Carrel; camping low/high season €18.50/24.40; ☒ Apr-Sep) A three-star place near the Arc de Triomphe. Take bus No 1 from the République stop (av Frédéric Mistral, 600m from the train station) to the Arc de Triomphe. From there, walk 100m back, turn right onto rue des Phocéens and right again onto rue des Étudiants. The camping ground, which has a pool, tennis courts and a golf course, is across the football field.

MID-RANGE

Hôtel Arcotel (☎ 04 90 34 09 23; fax 04 90 51 61 12; 8 place aux Herbes; s/d with washbasin €20/27, with shower & toilet €38/38) A friendly, basic establishment, Hôtel Arcotel has well-maintained, if bland rooms near the Théâtre Antique.

Hôtel St-Florent (☎ 04 90 34 18 53; fax 04 90 51 17 25; 4 rue du Mazeau; s/d from €27/55, f €70) Around the corner from Hôtel Arcotel, this place is atmospheric, with great rooms with giant murals painted on the walls and antique wooden beds adorned with crushed and studded velvet.

Le Glacier (☎ 04 90 34 06 26; www.le-glacier.com; 46 cours Aristide-Briand; d & tw €45-61, tr & q €61-70; P ⊠) Close to the Théâtre Antique, this is a welcoming place with well-equipped rooms and willing hosts who rent bikes and can recommend good touring itineraries of the nearby countryside and villages.

Eating

East of place Clemenceau, there are a number of moderately priced restaurants.

Le Marrakech (rue A Lacour; couscous €10) Cheap as chips, serving mounds of couscous.

La Sangria (☎ 04 90 34 31 96; 3 place de la République; lunch menu €8.50, dinner menus €11-19.50; ☒ closed Sun & Tue dinner) Tasty crepes and salads.

Chez Daniel (☎ 04 90 34 63 48; rue Second Weber; menu €24, pizzas €9.50; ☒ closed Tue dinner, Wed Sep-Jun & Jul & Aug) Near La Sangria, Chez Daniel has delicious Provençal dishes from Estouffade de Lotte Provençale for fish lovers and roast lamb with *chèvre* (goat's cheese) sauce for adventurous meat lovers.

Le Yaca (☎ 04 90 34 70 03; 24 place Silvain; menus €12-22; ☒ Thu-Tue) Highly recommended for its local fare, served up in a romantic little space marked by beams and stone walls.

Thursday is market day in Orange. Otherwise, self-caterers can pick up supplies at **Petit Casino** (35 rue St-Martin).

Getting There & Away

BUS

The **bus station** (☎ 04 90 34 15 59, 04 90 34 13 39; cours Pourtoules) is southeast of the city centre of the city. Buses from here go to Avignon (€5.10), Carpentras (€4.20), and Vaison-la-Romaine (€4.40), as well as Marseille.

TRAIN

Orange's tiny **train station** (☎ 04 90 11 88 64, 3635; av Frédéric Mistral) is 1.5km east of the tourist office.

Trains travel in two directions: south to Avignon (€4.70, 15 minutes, 17 daily), Marseille (€18.40, 1½ hours, 10 daily) and beyond and north to Lyon (€23, 2¼ hours, 13 daily) and Paris' Gare de Lyon (€75, two hours).

VAISON-LA-ROMAINE

pop 5986

Vaison-la-Romaine, 23km and 47km northeast of Orange and Avignon respectively, is endowed with extensive Roman ruins, a picturesque medieval city and plenty of tourists. However, it's not so overrun that you can't enjoy the sights and relax with a drink in the pretty tree-lined square.

In the 2nd century BC, the Romans conquered an important Celtic city on this site and renamed it Vasio Vocontiorum. The Roman city flourished, in part because it was granted considerable autonomy, but around the 6th century the Great Migrations forced the population to move to the hill across the river, which was easier to defend. The counts of Toulouse built a castle on top of the hill in the 12th century.

The resettlement of the original city site began in the 17th century.

The Roman remains discovered at Vaison include villas decorated with mosaics, colonnaded streets, public baths, a theatre and an aqueduct; the latter brought water down from Mont Ventoux.

The two-week Choralies, a choral festival held each year in August in the Roman

PROVENCE

theatre, is said to be the largest of its kind in Europe.

Vaison, like Malaucène and Carpentras 10km and 27km to the south, is a good base for exploring the Mont Ventoux region.

Orientation

Vaison is bisected by the ever-flooding River Ouvèze. The Roman city centre, on top of which the modern city centre has been built, is on the river's north bank; the medieval Haute Ville is on the south bank.

Pedestrianised Grand' rue heads northwest from the Pont Romain, changing its name near the Roman ruins to av du Général de Gaulle.

To get from the bus station to the tourist office, turn left as you leave the station then left again into rue Colonel Parazols, which leads past the Fouilles de Puymin excavations along rue Burrhus.

Information

Vaison's **tourist office** (☎ 04 90 36 02 11; www .vaison-la-romaine.com; place du Chanoine Sautel; ☿ 9am-noon & 2-5.45pm Mon-Sat, 9am-noon Sun Apr-Jun & Sep-Oct, 9am-noon & 2-6.45pm daily Jul & Aug) is inside the Maison du Tourisme et des Vins, just off av du Général de Gaulle.

The post office, opposite place du 11 Novembre, has an exchange service and Cyberposte.

Sights

GALLO-ROMAN RUINS

The Gallo-Roman ruins that have been unearthed in Vaison can be visited at two sites: **Fouilles de Puymin**, the excavations on the eastern side of av du Général de Gaulle, and (to the west of the same road) **Fouilles de la Villasse** (adult/student/child €7/3.50/3 for both; ☿ 10am-12.30pm & 2-6pm Mar-May, 9.30am-6.15pm Jun & Sep, 9.30am-6.45pm Jul & Aug, 10am-12.30pm & 2-5.30pm Feb & Oct; 10am-noon & 2-4.30pm Nov-Jan).

Fouilles de Puymin, with its entrance opposite Vaison's tourist office, is the more interesting of the pair. This site includes houses, mosaics and a theatre (designed to accommodate 6000 people) built around AD 20 under the reign of Tiberius. **Musée Archéologique** displays some of the artefacts. Its collection of statues includes the silver bust of a 3rd-century patrician and likenesses of Hadrian and his wife Sabina. At Fouilles de la Villasse, you can visit the mosaic-

and fresco-decorated house in which the silver bust was discovered.

From April to September, there are free guided tours in English; check the schedule at the tourist office.

MEDIEVAL QUARTER

Across the much-repaired **Pont Romain**, on the southern bank of the Ouvèze, lies the **Haute Ville**, which dates from the 13th and 14th centuries. Cobblestone alleyways lead up the hill past restored houses. At the summit, which affords a nice view, is an imposing 12th-century **chateau**, modernised in the 15th century only to be later abandoned.

Sleeping

The tourist office has comprehensive accommodation lists, including details on *chambres d'hôtes* and self-catering places in the surrounding region. The hotels are few and far between.

BUDGET

Escapade (☎ 04 90 36 00 78; fax 04 90 36 09 89; av César Geoffray; dm with obligatory half-board €39) Around 500m southeast of town along the river, Escapade is a modern place in large, quiet grounds with views of Mont Ventoux.

Camping du Théâtre Romain (☎ 04 90 28 78 66; info@camping-theatre.com; chemin de Brusquet; camping €18.50; ☿ 15 Mar-15 Nov; ☑) Located opposite Théâtre Antique in the northern section of the Fouilles de Puymin.

MID-RANGE

Hôtel Le Burrhus (☎ 04 90 36 00 11; www.burrhus .com; 1 place de Montfort; d €44-79; ☿ closed 12 Nov-20 Dec & Sun in Jan & Feb) Recently refitted superbly, this hotel is the pick in town. It's right on the square, near all the cafés, and boasts large, light, smart rooms decorated with considerable contemporary flair and modern fittings. Book ahead.

Shopping

Wine such as Gigondas, Châteauneuf-du-Pape and Villages des Côtes du Rhône, honey and honey nougat are all local specialities, but nothing can compare with the delectable black truffles harvested around Vaison-la-Romaine. They don't come cheap (€15 for 12.5g), but just a few shavings of the black fungus will turn the most prosaic plate of pasta into a bite-sized helping of heaven.

PROVENCE

Maison des Vins, in the basement of the Maison du Tourisme et des Vins, has local wines and local food products for tasting and purchase.

A vast and varied market snakes through the town centre every Tuesday from 6.30am to 1pm.

Getting There & Away

The bus station, where **Lieutard buses** (Vaison ☎ 04 90 36 05 22, Avignon ☎ 04 90 86 36 75; av des Choralies; ⏰ 9am-noon & 2-7pm Mon-Fri, Sat morning) has an office, is east of the modern town. There are limited services geared to the schedules of students from Vaison to Orange (€4.60, 45 minutes), Avignon (€7, 1¼ hours) and Carpentras (€3.90, 45 minutes).

MONT VENTOUX

Standing guard over the surrounding country and visible from as far away as Avignon, Mont Ventoux, is the most prominent geographical feature in northern Provence, thanks to its height (1909m) and its isolation. The radar- and antenna-studded summit, accessible by road, affords spectacular views of Provence, the southern Alps and – when it's especially clear – even the Pyrenees.

Mont Ventoux marks the boundary between the fauna and flora of northern France and that of southern France. Some species, including the snake eagle, numerous spiders and a variety of butterflies, are only found here. The mountain's forests were felled 400 years ago to build ships, but since 1860 some areas have been reforested with a variety of species, including the majestic cedar of Lebanon. The mix of deciduous trees makes the mountain especially colourful in autumn.

Since the summit is considerably cooler than the surrounding plains – there can be a difference of up to 20°C – and receives twice as much precipitation, bring warm clothes and rain gear at any time of the year. Areas above 1300m are usually covered in snow from December to April.

Mont Ventoux's mostly gradual but relentless gradients are regularly included in the route of the Tour de France, and it was here that British cyclist Tommy Simpson collapsed and died during the 1967 event. There is a memorial to him.

Just to the west of Mont Ventoux rise the sharp pinnacles of the limestone **Dentelles**

de Montmirail; the surrounding area makes great hiking terrain. Near the eastern end of the Mont Ventoux massif is the village of **Sault** (800m), surrounded in summer by a patchwork of purple lavender.

Malaucène, which is about 10km south of Vaison-la-Romaine and is the former summer residence of the Avignon popes, is where most people begin their forays into the surrounds of Mont Ventoux, about 21km to the east.

Come winter, **Mont Serein** (1445m), about 16km east of Malaucène and 5km from Mont Ventoux's summit on the D974, is transformed into a bustling ski station.

Information

Information Chalet (☎ 04 90 63 42 02; Mont Serein)

Malaucène Tourist Office (☎ 04 90 65 22 59; ot -malaucene@axit.fr; place de la Mairie; ⏰ 10am-noon & 2-4.30pm Apr-Jun, 9.30am-12.30pm & 2.30-6pm Jul & Aug, 10am-noon & 2-4.30pm Mon-Sat Sep-Mar)

Sault Tourist Office (☎ 04 90 64 01 21; ot-sault@axit .fr; av de la Promenade; ⏰ 10am-noon & 2-6pm Apr-Jun & Sep, 9am-1pm & 2-7pm Jul & Aug, 10am-noon & 2.30-4.30pm Tue-Sat Oct-Mar)

Walking

The GR4, running from the River Ardèche to the west, crosses the Dentelles de Montmirail before climbing up the northern face of Mont Ventoux. It then joins the GR9, and both trails follow the bare, white ridge before parting ways, with the GR4 winding eastwards to the Gorges du Verdon.

The GR9, which takes you across most of the area's ranges (including the Monts du Vaucluse and Lubéron Range), is arguably the most spectacular walking trail in all of Provence.

MAPS

Didier-Richard's 1:50,000 map No 27, *Massif du Ventoux*, includes Mont Ventoux, the Monts du Vaucluse and the Dentelles de Montmirail. It is available at some of the area's larger tourist offices, and many bookshops and newsagents. More detailed is IGN's Série Bleue 1:25,000 *Mont Ventoux* (No 3140ET).

Getting There & Around

If you've got a car, the summit of Mont Ventoux can be reached from Sault via the D164 or – in summer – from Malaucène

PROVENCE

or St-Estève via the switchback D974, built in the 1930s. This mountain road is often snow-blocked until as late as April. For information on bus services in the area, see opposite.

ACS (☎ 04 90 65 15 42) in Malaucène rents mountain bikes.

CARPENTRAS

pop 27,250

Drowsy Carpentras, equidistant from Avignon (25km) to the southwest and Orange to the northwest, is a small agricultural town, largely untouched by hordes of summer visitors and best known for its bustling Friday markets. The town hosts the eclectic Estivales de Carpentras, a two-week music, dance and theatre festival, in July.

History

Carpentras was an important trading centre in Greek times and later a Gallo-Roman city before becoming the capital of the papal territory of the Comtat Venaissin in 1320. It flourished in the 14th century, when it was visited frequently by Pope Clement V (who preferred it to Avignon) and numerous cardinals. During this time, Jews expelled from territory controlled by the French crown sought refuge in the Comtat Venaissin, where they lived – subject to certain restrictions – under the pope's protection. Today, Carpentras' 14th-century synagogue is the oldest such structure in France still in use.

Orientation

In the 19th century the city's fortifications and walls were replaced by a ring of boulevards: av Jean Jaurès, blvd Alfred Rogier, blvd du Nord, blvd Maréchal Leclerc, blvd Gambetta and blvd Albin Durand. The largely pedestrianised old city lies inside.

If you arrive by bus, walk northeastwards to place Aristide Briand, a major intersection at the southernmost point on the heart-shaped ring of boulevards. Avenue Jean Jaurès leads to the tourist office, while pedestrian-only rue de la République, which heads due north, takes you to the 17th-century Palais de Justice and the cathedral. The town hall is a few blocks northeast of the cathedral.

Information

There are commercial banks on central place Aristide Briand and blvd Albin Durand.

Banque de France (161 blvd Albin Durand; ⏰ 9am-noon & 1.30-3.30pm Mon-Fri)

Laundrette (118 rue Porte de Monteux; ⏰ 7am-8pm) On the road linking place du Général de Gaulle and blvd Albin Durand.

Post Office (65 rue d'Inguimbert)

Tourist Office (☎ 04 90 63 00 78; www.provenceguide .com; place Aristide Briand; ⏰ 9am-7pm Mon-Sat, 9.30am-1pm Sun mid-Jun–mid-Sep, 9.30am-12.30pm & 2-6pm Mon-Sat mid-Sep–mid-Jun) Sells a good range of regional maps and guides, and organises guided **city tours** (adult/child €4/2) from April to September. Ask for the free English-language brochure *Discover Carpentras Tour* if you prefer to do it yourself.

Sights

SYNAGOGUE

Carpentras' wonderful **synagogue** (☎ 04 90 63 39 97; place Juiverie; admission free; ⏰ 10am-noon & 3-5pm Mon-Thu, 10am-noon & 3-4pm Fri) was founded on this site in 1367, rebuilt between 1741 and 1743 and restored in 1929 and 1954. For centuries, it served as the focal point of the town's 1000-strong Jewish community. The sanctuary on the 1st floor is decorated with wood panelling and liturgical objects from the 18th century. You'll find the synagogue opposite the town hall (look for the stone plaque inscribed with Hebrew letters). About 100 Jewish families live in Carpentras today.

CATHEDRAL

Carpentras' one-time **cathedral** (⏰ 10am-noon & 2-4pm Wed-Mon, to 6pm in summer), now officially known as Église St-Siffrein, was built in the Méridional (southern French) Gothic style between 1405 and 1519. The 17th-century doorway is of classical design and in need of renovation. The bell tower is modern. **Trésor d'Art Sacré** (Treasury of Religious Art) displays various liturgical objects and reliquaries from the 14th to 19th centuries, including the St-Mors, the Holy Bridle bit supposedly made by St Helen for her son Constantine from a nail taken from the True Cross.

MUSEUMS

Carpentras' museums open 10am to noon and 2pm to 4pm (till 6pm April to September) Wednesday to Monday. Admission is €0.50. **Musée Comtadin** (243 blvd Albin Durand), which displays artefacts related to local history and folklore, and **Musée Duplessis** (243 blvd Albin Durand), with paintings from the personal collection of Monseigneur d'Inguimbert, are on the western side of the old city.

Musée Sobirats (112 rue du Collège), one block west of the cathedral, is an 18th-century private residence decorated and crammed with furniture, faïence and *objets d'art* in the Louis XV and Louis XVI styles.

The hospital in the 18th-century **Hôtel Dieu** (place Aristide Briand) has an old-time **pharmacy** and a **chapel**, but you must make arrangements with the tourist office to visit it. There are guided tours every Friday at 3pm year-round and an additional tour on Tuesday in July and August (€4).

MARKETS

Every Friday Carpentras hosts one of the most colourful and mouth-watering markets in Provence, which is saying something. Rue d'Inguimbert and most of av Jean Jaurès are laden with tables covered with nougat, strong local cheeses, orange and lavender marmalade, cauldrons of paella, buckets of olives and fresh fruit (especially the wonderful local melons). From November to the beginning of March, truffles are sold on **place Aristide Briand** (8-10am Fri). Carpentras' biggest fair is held on the Fête de St-Siffrein (Feast of St Siffrein) on 27 November. In July and August, there's a **wine market** in front of the tourist office.

Sleeping & Eating

Hôtel du Théâtre (☎ 04 90 63 02 90; hotel.dutheatre@wanadoo.fr; 7 blvd Albin Durand; d/tr from €56/76) A recently refurbished hotel overlooking place Aristide Briand. Rooms are large and quiet, with double-glazed windows and private bathrooms.

Hôtel La Lavande (☎ 04 90 63 13 49; 282 blvd Alfred Rogier; d with/without shower €38/28) A basic but comfortable eight-room hotel at the northern end of town. From the tourist office, follow blvd Jean Jaurès northeast into blvd Alfred Rogier; the hotel is on the left just past the intersection of rue Porte de Mazan.

Le Fin de Siècle (☎ 04 90 71 12 27; 46 place du Clos; lunch formule €13, lunch menus €20-27, dinner menus €20 & €27) A good, inexpensive lunch bet, Le Fin de Siècle offers things such as *moules frites* among *belle époque* surroundings. The tables spill onto the street in summer.

Le Marijo (☎ 04 90 60 42 65; 73 rue Raspail; menus €20; lunch & dinner Mon-Sat except Wed lunch) Regional fare rules here. Try the goat's cheese

marinated for 15 days in herbs and olive oil and sprinkled with *marc*, a local eau de vie.

Le Vert Galant (☎ 04 90 67 15 50; 12 rue de Clapiès; menus €28-46; closed Mon lunch & Sun May-Sep, Sun dinner & Mon Oct-Apr) Holds a prized Michelin star and serves extremely palatable truffles in season (January to March).

Chocolats Clavel (☎ 04 90 63 07 59; 30 Porte d'Orange; Mon-Sat) This shop appears to be selling cheese and olives but the displays are deceptive. Everything in this cosy place is made of sweets, including sculptured edifices carved from *berlingot*, a hard caramel candy and a local speciality.

Getting There & Away

The train station is served by goods trains only, so buses operated by Cars Comtadins and Cars Arnaud provide Carpentras' only intercity public transport. The **bus station** (place Terradou) is 150m southwest of place Aristide Briand.

Schedules are available from **Cars Comtadins** (☎ 04 90 67 20 25; 38 av Wilson) across the square and from **Cars Arnaud** (☎ 04 90 63 01 82; 8 av Victor Hugo). The tourist office can also help.

There are hourly services to Avignon (€3.80, 45 minutes) and infrequent runs to Vaison-la-Romaine (€3.90, 45 minutes) via Malaucène and Bédoin (€3.50, 40 minutes) at the southwestern foot of Mont Ventoux and Cavaillon (€4.60, 45 minutes), L'Isle-sur-Sorgue (€3.40, 20 minutes), 7km west of Fontaine de Vaucluse.

FONTAINE DE VAUCLUSE

pop 610

The mighty spring for which Fontaine de Vaucluse (Vau-Cluso La Font in Provençal) is named is actually the spot where the River Sorgue ends its subterranean course and gushes to the surface. Pretty Fontaine de Vaucluse lies about 1km downstream from the spring, the crystal waters of which flow animatedly and picturesquely through the village.

Up to 200 cu metres of water per second spill forth magnificently from the base of the cliff in late winter, forming one of the world's most powerful springs. During drier periods, the much reduced flow simply seeps through the rocks at various points downstream from the cliff, and the spring itself becomes little more than a still, very deep pond. Following numerous unsuccessful human and robotic

PROVENCE

attempts to reach the bottom, an unmanned submarine touched base – 315m down – in 1985.

Some 1.5 million visitors descend upon the village each year to stroll about its streets and throw pebbles into its deep, deep pond.

Information

If you come by car, you will have no choice but to fork out €3 for the privilege of parking. There is no free parking to be found *anywhere*.

Tourist office (☎ 04 90 20 32 22; officetourisme .vaucluse@wanadoo.fr; chemin de la Fontaine; ☯ 9am-7pm Tue-Sat) Southeast of central place de la Colonne on the way to the spring.

Sights
MUSEUMS

For its size, the attractive village has an inordinate number of small museums, dealing with many diverse subjects.

Musée d'Histoire 1939–1945 (☎ 04 90 20 24 00; admission €3.50; ☯ 10am-noon & 2-6pm Sat & Sun Mar, 10am-noon & 2-6pm Wed-Mon Apr-Jun, 10am-7pm Wed-Mon Jul & Aug, 10am-noon & 2-6pm Wed-Mon Sep & Oct, 10am-noon & 2-5pm Sat & Sun Nov & Dec), adjoining the tourist office, tells the story of the resistance movement during WWII.

Moulin à Papier (☯ 04 90 20 34 14; chemin de la Fontaine; admission free; ☯ 9am-12.30pm & 2-5pm Mon-Sat, 10.30am-12.30pm & 2-5pm Sun Sep-Jun, 9am-7pm Jul & Aug) is a reconstructed paper mill, built on the site of Fontaine de Vaucluse's old mill on the river banks opposite the tourist office. Beautiful, flower-encrusted paper, made as it was in the 16th century, is sold in the adjoining boutique and art gallery.

The Italian Renaissance poet Petrarch lived in Fontaine de Vaucluse from 1337 to 1353, immortalising his true love, Laura, wife of Hugues de Sade, in verse. **Musée Pétrarque** (☎ 04 90 20 37 20; admission €3.50; ☯ 10am-noon & 2-6pm Wed-Mon Apr-Sep, 10am-noon & 2-5pm Oct), on the left bank of the Sorgue, is devoted to his work, sojourn and broken heart.

Sleeping

Auberge de Jeunesse (☎ 04 90 20 31 65; fax 04 90 20 26 20; Chemin de la Vignasse; dm €8) This hostel is south of the Fontaine de Vaucluse in the direction of Lagnes (walk uphill from the bus stop).

The tourist office has a list of *chambres d'hôtes* in the village. Fontaine de Vaucluse

has three hotels. **Font de Lauro** (☎ /fax 04 90 20 31 49; plan de Saumane; d €27-37.50), a small, family-run, 16-room place is the best of the three. The rooms are pretty basic but they are decorated in an attractive Provençal style and there's a small pool.

Hôtel du Poète (☎ 90 20 34 05; www.hoteldupoete .com; r €115; Ⓟ Ⓧ Ⓡ) The pick of the places in town if the budget allows, this is a charming place surrounded by gurgling crystal waters and tall trees right in the heart of the village. The 23 rooms are comfortable and well equipped.

Camping

Camping Municipal Les Prés (☎ 04 90 20 32 38; route du Cavaillon) West of the village centre, this camping park is near the large public car park and the Sorgue.

Getting There & Away

Fontaine de Vaucluse is 21km southeast of Carpentras and 7km east of L'Isle-sur-Sorgue, the nearest 'real' town. From Avignon, Voyages Arnaud runs a bus (€4.50, one hour, two or three daily) with a stop at Fontaine de Vaucluse, from where it's a short walk to the spring. There are Arnaud buses from Carpentras to L'Isle-sur-Sorgue (20 minutes).

GORDES
pop 2127

On the white, rocky, southern face of the Vaucluse plateau, the tiered village of Gordes forms an amphitheatre that overlooks the Rivers Sorgue and Calavon. The top of the village is crowned by a sturdy chateau built between the 11th and 16th centuries. In summer this once-typical Provençal village is frighteningly overrun with tourists, but it's still worth a wander around if you've got the wheels to get you there.

The **tourist office** (☎ 04 90 72 02 75; www.gordes -village.com; place du Château; ☯ 9am-12.30pm & 2-6pm Jun-Sep, 9am-noon & 2-5pm Oct-May) is in the chateau's Salle des Gardes (Guards' Hall).

Gordes is about 20km west of Apt and 18km east of Fontaine de Vaucluse. The closest town is Cavaillon, 16km to the southwest, which is served by train and bus from many cities and towns in Provence. Buses run by **Les Express de la Durance** (☎ 04 90 71 03 00) link Gordes with Cavaillon twice a day except on Sunday.

PROVENCE

AROUND GORDES

The main reason people come to Gordes is to visit the walled **Village des Bories** (☎ 04 90 72 03 48; adult/under 17 €5.50/3; ☺ 9am-7.30pm), 4km southwest of Gordes, just off the D2 heading for Cavaillon. *Bories* are one- or two-storey beehive-shaped huts constructed without mortar using thin wedges of limestone. They were first built in the area in the Bronze Age and were continuously lived in, renovated and even built anew until as late as the 18th century. It is not known what purpose they first served, but over the centuries they have been used as workshops, wine cellars, shelters and storage sheds. The 'village' contains about 20 such structures, restored to their appearance of about 150 years ago. Some people say the *bories* remind them of Ireland's *clochán*.

ROUSSILLON

pop 1200

Roussillon lies in the valley between the Vaucluse plateau and the Lubéron Range. Two millennia ago, the Romans used its distinctive ochre earth to produce pottery glazes. These days the whole village – even the cemetery's gravestones – is built of the reddish local stone, making it a popular place for painters eager to try out the range of their palettes. The red and orange hues are especially striking given the yellow-white bareness of the surrounding area and the green conifers sprinkled around town.

Information

The **tourist office** (☎ /fax 04 90 05 60 25; place de la Poste; ☺ 10am-noon & 1.30-6.30pm Mon-Sat Apr-Sep, 9.30am-noon & 1.30-6pm Tue-Fri, 10am-noon & 2-5.30pm Mon & Sat Oct-Mar) is in the centre of Roussillon. A complete list of hotels, *chambres d'hôtes* and restaurants in and around Roussillon is pinned up outside the office.

Sights & Activities

Take a walk in nature's powder paint palette on the 1km **Sentier des Ocres** (Ochre Trail; admission €2; ☺ 9.30am-5.30pm Mar-11 Nov). It begins approximately 100m north of Roussillon's centre and will lead you through fairy-tale groves of chestnuts, maritime pines and scrub to the bizarre and beautiful ochre formations blushing the colours of a sunset and created by erosion and fierce winds over the centuries. Don't wear light colours or precious shoes; you'll return smudged in rust-coloured dust.

Getting There & Away

Roussillon, 9km east of Gordes in the direction of Apt (11km east again), is inaccessible by public transport. The GR6 walking trail passes through here.

APT & THE LUBÉRON

The beautiful Lubéron hills stretch from Cavaillon in the west to Manosque in the east, and from Apt southwards to the River Durance. The area is named after the main range, a compact massif with a gentle, 1100m-high summit. Its oak-covered northern face is a steep, striking natural rampart while its gentler southern face is drier and more Mediterranean in both climate and flora. Whichever side of the range you're on, the country around you will be enchantingly pretty.

Much of the Lubéron Range is within the boundaries of the Parc Naturel Régional du Lubéron. If you want to explore, the area has some great walking trails and is an excellent place for cycling.

The Lubéron area is dotted with *bories* (see left). The town of Apt, an ideal base for exploring the Lubéron, is largely unexceptional except for its grapes, cherries and *fleurions*, candied or crystallised fruits, which are sold everywhere. It celebrates its Cherry Festival each year in May and is renowned for its large and festive Saturday morning market.

Maps

The tourist office sells regional maps such as the Top 25 (3242OT) *Map of Apt and the Parc Naturel Régional du Lubéron*, or the *Cavaillon* map (3142OT). They cost €11.50 and €9 respectively.

Information

Maison du Parc (☎ 04 90 04 42 00; www.parcdu luberon.fr; 60 place Jean Jaurès; ☺ 8.30am-noon & 1.30-7pm Mon-Sat Apr-Sep, to 6pm Mon-Fri Oct-Mar) Has information on the Parc Naturel Régional du Lubéron, including details of the park's two dozen *gîtes d'étape* (hikers' accommodation). The centre has plenty of information on hiking and cycling in the park and sells an excellent range of guides, including the recommended topoguide *Le Parc Naturel Régional du Lubéron à Pied* (€11.90), which details 24 walks including the GR9, GR92 and GR97 trails (in French only).

PROVENCE

Tourist Office (☎ 04 90 74 03 18; www.ot-apt.fr; 20 av Philippe de Girard; ⊙ 9am-7pm Mon-Sat & 9.30am-12.30pm Sun Jul & Aug, 9am-noon & 2-6pm Mon-Sat & 9.30am-12.30pm Sun Jun-Sep, 9am-noon & 2-6pm Mon-Sat Oct-May) Over the bridge as you enter Apt from Cavaillon. Ask for the leaflet *Apt –à Découvrir*, which details, in English and French, two one-hour city tours signposted around town with colour-coded markers.

Parc Naturel Régional du Lubéron

The park's 1200 sq km encompass numerous villages, desolate forests, unexpected gorges and abandoned farmhouses well on the way to ruin – or perhaps restoration by fans of Peter Mayle. His purchase and renovation of a house just outside the pretty village of **Ménerbes** in the late 1980s formed the basis of his whimsical, best-selling books *A Year in Provence* and *Toujours Provence*.

Sleeping & Eating

Hôtel L'Aptois (☎ 04 90 74 02 02; fax 04 90 74 64 79; 289 cours Lauze de Perret; d with washbasin from €32, with shower & toilet from €46) A smartly refurbished place on the edge of the old town.

Auberge du Lubéron (☎ 04 90 74 12 50; www .auberge-luberon-peuzin.com; 8 place Faubourg du Ballet; r €52-73) On the opposite side of the river from Hôtel L'Aptois, Auberge du Lubéron is part of the Logis de France chain and offers a fine **restaurant** (menus €29-68). Rooms are cosy and contemporary Provençal in style.

Hostellerie le Paradou (☎ 04 90 08 54 94; www .laparadou-lacascade.com in French; route d'Apt, Lourmarin; r €55, half-board per person €77; P) About 15km out of Apt, this is a charming guesthouse in an idyllic country setting just on the edge of Lourmarin, one of the prettiest Lubéron villages. The rooms are comfortable, basic-farmhouse style and the friendly owners run an accomplished **restaurant** (menus from €22) that's good on the Provençal classics.

Camping

Camping Municipal Les Cèdres (☎ /fax 04 90 74 14 61; route de Rustrel; camping with electricity €12.70; ⊙ 25 Feb-14 Nov) This is a basic, no-frills camping ground by the river, just out of town.

Getting There & Away

Buses going to Aix-en-Provence (€12.35, 1½ hours, two daily) leave from the **bus station** (☎ 04 90 74 20 21; 250 av de la Libération) east of the centre. There are services to/from Avignon (€7.20, 1¼ hours, three or four daily),

Digne-les-Bains (€7.30, two hours, one or two daily), Cavaillon (€4.70, 40 minutes, two or three daily) and Marseille (€17.65, 2½ hours, two daily).

ARLES & THE CAMARGUE

ARLES

pop 51,614

Arles' most famous resident was Vincent Van Gogh (1853–90) and it's easy to see why the painter may have found Arles both soothing and visually exciting. Little has changed since Van Gogh immortalised the city's winding streets and shady squares. The baking sun casts a glow over the colourful old houses, keeping the tempo slow. The pace picks up quickly when the matadors come to town, for Arles is *corrida* (bullfighting) crazy and regularly presents bullfights in its Roman amphitheatre.

Arles sits on the northern tip of the Camargue alluvial plain on the Grand Rhône River, just south of where the Petit Rhône splits off from it.

The town began its ascent to prosperity and political importance in 49 BC, when the victorious Julius Caesar – to whom the city had given its support – captured and plundered Marseille, which had backed Caesar's rival, the general and statesman Pompey the Great.

Arles soon replaced Marseille as the region's major port and became the sort of Roman provincial centre that, within a century and a half, needed a 12,000-seat theatre and a 20,000-seat amphitheatre to entertain its citizens. These days, the two structures are still used to stage cultural events and bullfights.

Orientation

Arles is enclosed by the Grand Rhône River to the northwest, blvd Émile Combes to the east and, to the south, blvd des Lices and blvd Georges Clemenceau. It's shaped like a foot, with the train station, place de la Libération and place Lamartine (where Van Gogh once lived) at the ankle, les Arènes at the anklebone and the tourist office under the arch. Covering a relatively small area, it's easily explored on – what else? – foot.

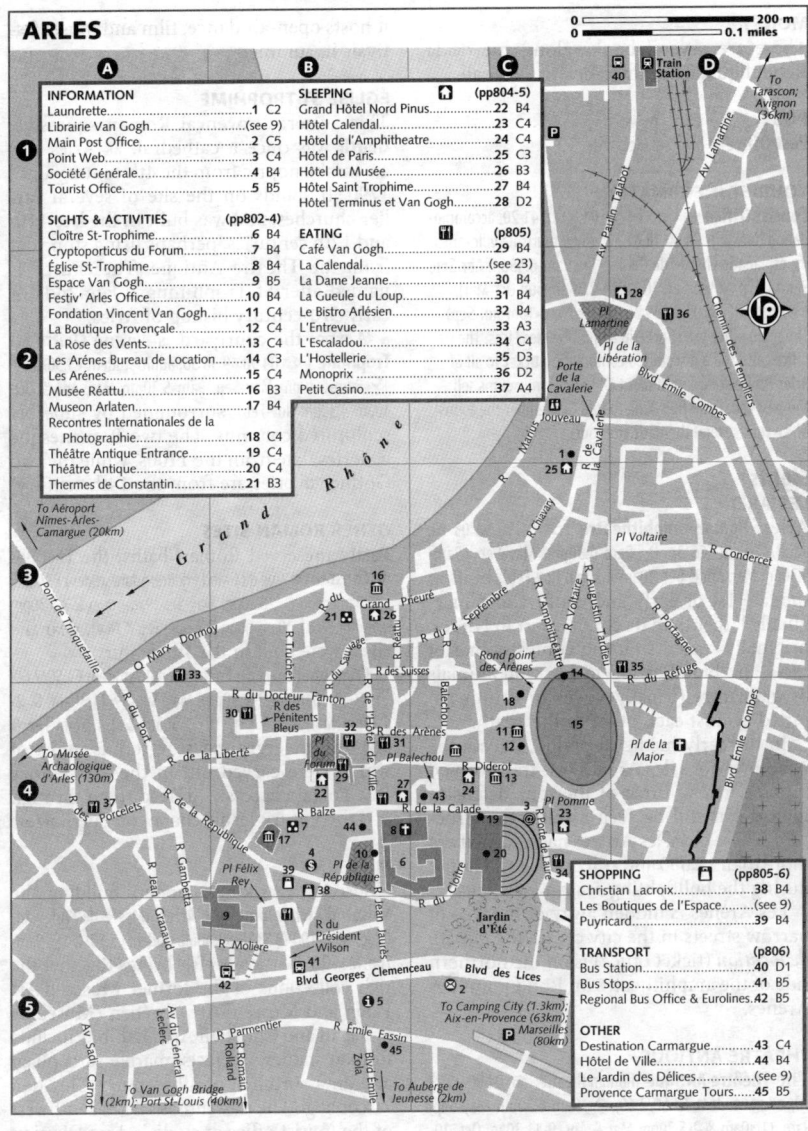

ARLES

INFORMATION	
Laundrette	1 C2
Librairie Van Gogh	(see 9)
Main Post Office	2 C5
Point Web	3 C4
Société Générale	4 B4
Tourist Office	5 B5

SIGHTS & ACTIVITIES	(pp802-4)
Cloître St-Trophime	6 B4
Cryptoporticus du Forum	7 B4
Église St-Trophime	8 B4
Espace Van Gogh	9 B5
Festiv' Arles Office	10 C4
Fondation Vincent Van Gogh	11 C4
La Boutique Provençale	12 C4
La Rose des Vents	13 C4
Les Arènes Bureau de Location	14 C3
Les Arènes	15 C4
Musée Réattu	16 B3
Museon Arlaten	17 B4
Recontres Internationales de la Photographie	18 C4
Théâtre Antique Entrance	19 C4
Théâtre Antique	20 C4
Thermes de Constantin	21 B3

SLEEPING	(pp804-5)
Grand Hôtel Nord Pinus	22 B4
Hôtel Calendal	23 C4
Hôtel de l'Amphithéatre	24 C4
Hôtel de Paris	25 C3
Hôtel du Musée	26 B3
Hôtel Saint Trophime	27 B4
Hôtel Terminus et Van Gogh	28 D2

EATING	(p805)
Café Van Gogh	29 B4
La Calendal	(see 23)
La Dame Jeanne	30 B4
La Gueule du Loup	31 B4
Le Bistro Arlésien	32 B4
L'Entrevue	33 A3
L'Escaladou	34 B4
L'Hostellerie	35 D3
Monoprix	36 D2
Petit Casino	37 A4

SHOPPING	(pp805-6)
Christian Lacroix	38 B4
Les Boutiques de l'Espace	(see 9)
Puyricard	39 B4

TRANSPORT	(p806)
Bus Station	40 D1
Bus Stops	41 B5
Regional Bus Office & Eurolines	42 B5

OTHER	
Destination Carmargue	43 C4
Hôtel de Ville	44 B4
Le Jardin des Délices	(see 9)
Provence Carmargue Tours	45 B5

PROVENCE

Information

BOOKSHOPS

Librairie Van Gogh (☎ 04 90 96 86 65; 1 place Félix Rey; ⏰ 10am-12.30pm & 2-6.30pm Tue-Sat) Wrapped around the courtyard of Espace Van Gogh, this is a fantastic bookshop with an extensive range of art and history books in French and English, as well as a good variety of regional travel guides.

INTERNET ACCESS

Point Web (☎ 04 90 18 91 54; 10 rue du 4 Septembre; per 10min €1; ⏰ 9am-7pm Mon-Sat) This is the best place to get on the Web. It is cheaper and the connection faster than other internet cafes in town.

LAUNDRY

Laundrette (6 rue de la Cavalerie; ⏰ 7am-7pm)

MONEY

There are several banks along rue de la République, including Société Générale.

POST

Post Office (5 blvd des Lices)

TOURIST INFORMATION

Tourist Office main office (☎ 04 90 18 41 20, accommodation bookings 04 90 18 41 22; www.tourisme.ville-arles .fr; esplanade Charles de Gaulle; ☺ 9am-6.45pm Apr-Sep, 9am-4.45pm Mon-Sat, 10.30am-2.30pm Sun Oct-Mar); train station (☎ 04 90 49 36 90; ☺ 9am-1pm Jun-Sep) The main office is a short trip along blvd des Lices. The offices also sell a discounted combination ticket to all of Arles' sights for adult/student €13.50/12; museums sell the pass too. From mid-June to mid-September the tourist office runs several thematic city tours.

Sights

LES ARÈNES

Arles' **Roman amphitheatre** (☎ 04 90 96 03 70; adult/student €6/3; ☺ 9am-6.30pm May-Sep, 9am-5.30pm Mar, Apr & Oct, 10am-4.30pm Nov-Feb), built in the late 1st or early 2nd century and marginally larger than its counterpart in Nîmes, originally staged sporting contests, chariot races and bloodier spectacles: wild animals or gladiators (usually slaves or criminals) pitted against each other to the death.

In the early medieval period, during the Arab invasions, les Arènes was transformed into a fortress; three of the four defensive towers can still be seen around the structure. These days, les Arènes has a capacity of more than 12,000 and still draws a full house during the bullfighting season (see p804).

Les Arènes is hidden away in the web of narrow streets in the city centre. Its *bureau de location* (ticket office) is on the northern side of the amphitheatre on Rond point des Arènes.

THÉÂTRE ANTIQUE

The **Théâtre Antique** (Roman theatre; ☎ 04 90 96 93 30; adult/student €3.50/2.60; ☺ 9am-6.30pm May-Sep, 9am-11.30am & 2-5.30pm Mar & Apr, 9-11.30am Oct, 10-11.30am & 2-4.30pm Nov-Feb), which dates from the end of the 1st century BC, was used for many hundreds of years as a convenient source of construction materials, so little of the original structure – measuring 102m in diameter – remains, except for two imposing columns. Entered through the Jardin d'Été (Summer Garden) on blvd des Lices,

it hosts open-air dance, film and music festivals in summer.

ÉGLISE ST-TROPHIME

This austere Provençal Romanesque-style **church** was once a cathedral, as Arles was an archbishopric from the 4th century until 1790. It stands on the site of several earlier churches, and was built in the late 11th and 12th centuries, perhaps using stone cut from the Théâtre Antique. The church is named after St Trophimus, a late-2nd- or early-3rd-century bishop of Arles.

Across the courtyard is serene **Cloître St-Trophime** (☎ 04 90 49 36 36; adult/student €3.50/2.60; ☺ 9am-6.30pm May-Sep, 9am-5.30pm Mar, Apr & Oct, 10am-4.30pm Nov-Feb), surrounded by superbly sculptured columns. The two Romanesque galleries date from the 1100s, while the two Gothic galleries are from the 14th century.

OTHER ROMAN SITES

Partly preserved Roman baths, the **Thermes de Constantin** (rue du Grand Prieuré; adult/student €3/2.20; ☺ 9am-noon & 2-6.30pm May-Sep, 9am-noon & 2-5.30pm Mar, Apr & Oct, 10am-noon & 2-5pm Feb & Nov), near the river, were built in the 4th century.

Cryptoporticus du Forum (adult/student €3.50/2.60; ☺ 9-11.30am & 2-6.30pm May-Sep, 9-11.30am & 2-4.30pm Mar, Apr & Oct, 10-11.30am & 2-4.30pm Feb & Nov) are underground storerooms, most of which were carved out in the 1st century BC. To gain access you need to go through a 17th-century Jesuit chapel on rue Balze.

MUSEUMS

Housed in a strikingly modern building, the **Musée d'Archéologique d'Arles** (Musée de l'Arles Antique; ☎ 04 90 18 88 88/89; adult/student €5.50/4; ☺ 9am-7pm Mar-Oct, 10am-5pm Nov-Feb) brings together the rich collections of the former Musée d'Art Païen and Musée d'Art Chrétien (Museums of Pagan and Christian Art). Exhibits include Roman statues, artefacts, marble sarcophagi and an assortment of 4th-century Christian sarcophagi. The museum is 1.5km southwest of the tourist office at av de la 1ère Division Française Libre on the Presqu'île du Cirque Romain.

Museon Arlaten (☎ 04 90 93 58 11; 29 rue de la République; adult/student €4/3; ☺ 9.30am-1pm & 2-6.30pm Jul & Aug, 9.30am-12.30pm & 2-6pm Tue-Sat Apr-Jun & Sep, 9.30am-12.30pm & 2-5pm Tue-Sat Oct-Mar), occupying a 16th-century townhouse, was founded by the Nobel Prize–winning poet

Frédéric Mistral (see p763). The museum is dedicated to preserving and displaying everyday objects related to traditional Provençal life: furniture, crafts, costumes, ceramics, wigs, a model of the Tarasque (a people-eating amphibious monster of Provençal legend) etc.

Musée Réattu (☎ 04 90 96 37 68; 10 rue du Grand Prieuré; adult/student €4/3; ♥ 10am-noon & 2-5pm Mar, Apr & Oct; 10am-noon & 2-6.30pm May-Sep, 1-5pm Nov-Feb) is housed in a former 15th-century priory. It exhibits works by some of the world's finest photographers, modern and contemporary works of art and paintings by 18th- and 19th-century Provençal artists. The museum also has 57 Picasso drawings, sketched by the artist between December 1970 and November 1971.

VAN GOGH TRAIL

The fact that Arles does not have a single painting from Van Gogh's amazingly productive stay in the area may be a huge disappointment for visitors today, but there's a certain poetic justice to it since the town was hardly kind to Van Gogh during his stay.

Far from treating him sympathetically while he was recovering from his first mental attack (the one that led him to threaten his housemate Paul Gauguin in place Victor Hugo with a cut-throat razor before using it slice off part of his left ear), a petition was raised, his house was sealed and he was locked up for a month on the mayor's orders.

There are fitting tributes to his art, however, at **Fondation Vincent van Gogh** (☎ 04 90 49 94 04; 24bis Rond Point des Arènes; adult/student €7/5; ♥ 10am-7pm Apr-15 Oct, 9.30am-noon & 2-5.30pm Tue-Sun 16 Oct-Mar), inside the Palais de Luppé, from some important modern-day artists, including David Hockney, Francis Bacon and Fernando Botero. It is well worth a visit.

Gallery **La Rose des Vents** (☎ 04 90 93 25 96; 18 rue Diderot; ♥ 10.30am-12.30pm Tue-Sat, 3-7pm Tue-Sun) displays various Van Gogh reproductions, as well as copies of letters written by the artist to his brother Theo.

Various art exhibitions take place at **Espace van Gogh** (☎ 04 90 49 39 39; place Félix Rey), housed in the old Hôtel Dieu and former hospital, where Van Gogh spent some time.

Tours

Jeep tours of the Camargue are organised by many companies, including **Provence Camargue Tours** (☎ 04 90 96 69 20; 1 rue Émile Fassin) and **Destination Camargue** (☎ /fax 04 90 96 94 44; 14bis rue de la Calade). The latter organises half-day trips (adult/child €30/15) departing daily from Arles at 3pm in summer. Reservations can also be made at **La Boutique Provençale** (☎ 04 90 49 84 31; 8 Rond Point des Arènes). For further operators see p808.

Festivals & Events

Arles' biggest event of the year is the **Feria Pascale**, which takes place around Easter and

---

VINCENT VAN GOGH

Vincent Van Gogh (1853–90) revelled in Provence's intense light and colours when he arrived here in 1888. During a highly productive year in Arles he worked with a burning fervour, unfazed even by howling mistrals, during which he would either kneel on his canvases and paint horizontally or lash his easel to iron stakes he had driven deep into the ground.

During his stay he painted, among many other locations, the Pont de Langlois, a little (rebuilt) bridge 3km south of Arles (from town, take bus No 1 to the Pont Van Gogh terminus). Some of Van Gogh's other best-known canvases – *Sunflowers*, *Van Gogh's Chair* and *Café at Night* – were painted in Arles.

In 1888 Van Gogh's friend and fellow artist Paul Gauguin came to stay with him for several months. But their different temperaments and approaches to art soon led to a quarrel and Van Gogh's first attack of mental illness. In May 1889, because of recurrent attacks, he voluntarily entered an asylum in St-Rémy de Provence (25km northeast of Arles over the Alpilles). During his year here he continued to be amazingly productive. In 1890, while staying in Auvers-sur-Oise (just north of Paris), Van Gogh – lonely, despairing and afraid his madness was incurable – shot and killed himself.

There are few tangible remains of Vincent Van Gogh's stay in Arles. All trace of his rented yellow house on place Lamartine was wiped out during WWII.

804 ARLES & THE CAMARGUE •• Arles

marks the beginning of the bullfight season. Bullfighting fans and a trail of pickpockets fill the town, creating traffic chaos and driving up hotel prices, but it is an exciting time.

In addition, Arles has a full calendar of summertime cultural events. In early July, **Les Rencontres Internationales de la Photographie** (International Photography Festival) attracts photographers and aficionados from around the world. The two-week **Fêtes d'Arles**, which usually kicks off at the end of June, brings dance, theatre, music and poetry readings to the city. For more information contact the **Festiv'Arles office** (☎ 04 90 96 47 00, 04 90 96 81 18; fax 04 90 96 81 17; 35 place de la République).

The **Fête des Gardians** in May features a procession of Camargue cowboys through the streets of town, the election of the Queen of Arles and Camargue games in the arena.

Other events include the **Festival Ame Gitane** in mid-August, which celebrates Gypsy (Romany) culture, and the 10-day-long **Fête des Prémices du Riz**, held in September, which marks the start of the rice harvest.

Sleeping

Except during festivals, bullfights and July and August, Arles has plenty of reasonably priced accommodation. There are lots of **gîtes ruraux** (for reservations ☎ 04 90 59 49 40) in the surrounding countryside, especially the Camargue. Ask the tourist office for the list.

BUDGET
Auberge de Jeunesse (☎ 04 90 96 18 25; arles@fuaj .org; 20 av Maréchal Foch; dm incl breakfast 1st night €13.50,

then €13.70; ☒ 5 Feb-20 Dec; ℗) This 100-bed place is 2km from the centre. Take bus No 3 or 8 from blvd Georges Clemenceau (No 8 from place Lamartine) to the Fournier stop. You must have an FUAJ card.

Hôtel Terminus et Van Gogh (☎ /fax 04 90 96 12 32; 5 place Lamartine; s/d with shower & toilet €36.60; ℗) Close to the station, this hotel is welcoming and has good-value rooms with private bathrooms.

Hôtel de Paris (☎ 04 90 96 05 88; 8 rue de la Cavalerie; r from €23) Above a cheap café, Hôtel de Paris provides cheap one-star rooms.

Camping
Camping City (☎ 04 90 93 08 86; www.camping-city .com; 67 route de Crau; camping €16; ☒ Apr-Sep) The closest camping ground to town, Camping City is 1km southeast of the city centre on the road to Marseille. Take bus No 2 to the Hermite stop.

MID-RANGE
Hôtel de l'Amphitheatre (☎ 04 90 96 10 30; www .hotelamphitheatre.fr; 5-7 rue Diderot; s/d €45/49; ☒) The wooden-beamed, 17th-century building this hotel occupies has been colourfully and tastefully decorated, as have most of the large, attractive rooms. There's also one room with wheelchair access. The fine breakfast (€6) served here is worth going for. This is one of the best all-round options in town.

Hôtel Calendal (☎ 04 90 96 11 89; www.lecalendal .com; 5 rue Porte de Laure; r €45-99; ℗ ☒ ☒ ▣) This is an attractive place next to the amphitheatre

---

In *mise à mort* bullfighting (*corrida*) a bull bred to be aggressive is killed in a colourful and bloody ceremony involving picadors, bandilleros, matadors and horses. For bullfighting aficionados in Spain, Latin America and parts of southern France, the *corrida* is not a sport as it does not involve a contest between the matador and the bull. The spectacle is a tragedy in three acts that centre on the inevitable death of the bull. When performed correctly (which is rarely the case) the matador and the bull execute a kind of dance in which each demonstrates heroism under pressure. Aside from the theatrical purpose, the bull must be killed because, after having been in a *corrida*, it is said to be too dangerous to be again placed in a ring with a matador. After the event, the bull is carved up and sold for meat. Because the growing bulls roam free and graze on grass, the meat has a different flavour than that of ordinary steers.

But not all bullfighting ends with a dead animal. In a *course Camarguaise* (Camargue-style bullfight), white-clad *razeteurs* try to remove ribbons tied to the bull's horns with hooks held between their fingers.

In Arles, the bullfighting season begins around Easter with a bullfighting festival known as the Feria (or Féria) Pascale and runs until the September rice harvest festival.

and overlooking the Théâtre Antique. Rooms are bright, airy and well equipped. There's a peaceful garden terrace at the back. Garage parking costs €10.

Hôtel Saint Trophime (☎ 04 90 96 88 38; fax 04 90 96 92 19; 16 rue de la Calade; s €40, d €55-65; P 🗙 📳) Occupying a fully renovated old building, Hôtel Saint Trophime is replete with antiques, high ceilings, a grand staircase (there's also an elevator) and stylish – if rather bare – rooms, which are of different sizes but all are beautifully maintained and have modern bathrooms.

Hôtel du Musée (☎ 04 90 93 88 88; www.hotel dumusee.com.fr; 11 rue du Grand Prieuré; r with shower €40-51, with bath €56-61) Another period hotel in a fine 12th- to 13th-century building. An appealing 20-room, two-star place with well-furnished rooms, it's spacious and has a rear terrace garden. The road-facing rooms can be noisy though.

TOP END

Grand Hôtel Nord Pinus (☎ 04 90 93 44 44; www.nord -pinus.com; place du Forum; r €137-275; P 📳) Models, circus performers, matadors, show people and artists have flocked here since 1927. The tastefully eccentric décor centres on bullfighting themes but also includes antiques and curios from Provence, Spain and North Africa. If the comfortable rooms are too steep for your budget, at least stop by the bar and check out the ever-changing photo exhibits.

Eating

Blvd Georges Clemenceau and blvd des Lices are lined with plane trees and brasseries with terraces. The latter are fine for a meal if you don't mind dining à la traffic fumes.

RESTAURANTS

Place du Forum, an intimate square shaded by eight large plane trees, turns into one big dining table at lunch and dinner time.

Le Bistrot Arlésien (☎ 04 90 96 07 22; place du Forum; salads €4-8, plats du jour €8) A no-frills place serving basic but decent staples at reasonable prices right in the heart of town.

La Dame Jeanne (☎ 04 90 96 37 09; 4 rue des Pénitents Bleus; menus €13-17) Unpretentious La Dame Jeanne offers three-course (and a four-course) *menus*.

L'Entrevue (☎ 04 90 93 37 28; 23 quai Max Dormoy; mains €7.70-15, menu €22.90; ✆ 9-12.30am) Occupies a calm, cool spot down by the riverfront, in

a cinema and bookshop complex. It doesn't offer a view of the water (it's blocked by high river ramparts) but is a stylish, laid-back place serving Asian and Caribbean-inspired cuisine, including a fantastic couscous royal and wonderfully refreshing mint and pine kernel tea.

L'Hostellerie (☎ 04 90 96 13 05; 62 rue du Refuge; menus €14.50-25.50; ✆ Wed-Mon) If you can, dine on the terrace at L'Hostellerie, which has an excellent view towards the amphitheatre. It offers a good selection of salads and a bargain lunch *formule*.

La Gueule du Loup (☎ 04 90 96 96 69; 39 rue des Arènes; meals €12; ✆ noon-4pm) A cosy, family-run place where you can watch your meal being prepared in the open kitchen. The food is typically regional and the standards are high. Try the herb-infused *crème brûlée*.

L'Escaladou (☎ 04 90 96 70 43; 23 rue Porte de Laure; menus €15-20) This place concentrates on fish. Try the *brandade* (€9), *bouillabaisse* (€20) or *aïoli* (€11).

CAFÉS

Café Van Gogh (☎ 04 90 96 44 56; place du Forum; menus €12-16) This very yellow café pays homage to the artist's Arles roots in its attempt to re-create the subject of his canvas *Café de Nuit*. Café Van Gogh is a busy bar by night.

La Calendal (☎ 04 90 96 11 89; 22 place Pomme; meals €12; ✆ noon-4pm) An endearing *salon de thé*–cum-restaurant-cum-hotel. Sip a cuppa between the dining room's cool, stone walls and beamed ceilings or in that quiet, shaded garden. There's also an all-you-can-eat daily buffet for €12.

SELF-CATERING

There is a **Petit Casino** (rue des Porcelets; ✆ 9am-7pm Mon-Sat) and a **Monoprix** (place Lamartine; ✆ 8.30am-7.25pm Mon-Sat).

On Wednesday, market stalls sprawl the length of blvd Émile Combes, along the outside of the city walls. The food section is at the northern end. On Saturday morning, the market moves to blvd des Lices and blvd Georges Clemenceau.

Shopping

Les Boutiques de l'Espace (Espace van Gogh, place Félix Rey) is a good place for gifts, postcards, souvenirs and art books. **Puyricard** (54 rue de la République) offers exquisite Provençal chocolates, while **Christian Lacroix** (52 rue de la République), next door, is the very first boutique of the famous Arlesienne clothes designer.

Getting There & Away

AIR

The **Aéroport Nîmes-Arles-Camargue airport** (Garons airport; ☎ 04 66 70 49 49) is 20km northwest of the city on the A54. There is no public transport into town.

BUS

The **bus station** (☎ information office 0 800 199 413, 0 810 000 816; av Paulin Talabot; ☼ 7.30am-4pm Mon-Sat) is about 1km north of les Arènes. Most intercity buses stop here. Some also stop at 24 blvd Georges Clemenceau. **Telleschi** (☎ 04 42 28 40 22) runs services to Aix-en-Provence (€11.30, 1¾ hours).

Buses also link Arles with various parts of the Camargue, including Les Stes-Maries de la Mer (€6, one hour, two daily in winter and six to nine daily in summer), Port St-Louis (€6.40, one hour five minutes, six daily) and many places en route, such as Mas du Pont de Rousty, Pioch Badet and Pont de Gau.

Eurolines (☎ 04 90 96 94 78), the long-haul bus company, sells tickets at 24 blvd Georges Clemenceau.

TRAIN

Arles' **train station** (☼ information office 9am-12.30pm & 2-6.30pm Mon-Sat) is just across from the bus station. Some major rail destinations include Nîmes (€6.60, 30 minutes), Montpellier (€12.20, one hour), Marseille (€11.60, 40 minutes) and Avignon (€5.70, 20 minutes).

Getting Around

BUS

Local buses are operated by **STAR** (☎ 04 90 96 87 47; information office 24 blvd Georges Clemenceau; ☼ 7.45am-12.45pm & 1.15-6pm Mon-Fri). This office, west of the tourist office, is the main bus hub, although most buses also stop at place Lamartine, a short walk south of the train station. In general, STAR buses run from 7am to 7pm (5pm on Sunday). A single ticket costs €0.80; a 10-ticket *carnet* €7. In addition to its 11 bus lines, STAR runs minibuses called Starlets that circle most of the old city every 30 minutes from 7.15am to 7.40pm Monday to Saturday. Best of all, they're free.

TAXI

If you need a taxi, the number to call is ☎ 04 90 49 69 59.

THE CAMARGUE

Utterly different from the rest of Provence, the haunting, sparsely populated Camargue, a 780-sq-km delta of the River Rhône, is famed for its desolate beauty and for the white horses and black bulls that graze among the rice fields and breeze-blown bull rushes.

The delta's extensive marshes and unique freshwater and saltwater habitats also support incredibly varied bird life: over 500 species of permanent and migratory land and water birds, including storks and bee-eaters. Huge flocks of pink flamingos nest here during spring and summer, many of them near the Étang de Vaccarès and Étang du Fangassier lakes.

The Camargue has been formed over the ages by sediment deposited by the Rhône as it flows into the Mediterranean. There are enormous salt-evaporation pools around Salin de Giraud on the Camargue's southeastern tip.

The northern part of the delta consists of dry land, and in the years following WWII huge tracts were desalinated as part of a drainage and irrigation programme designed to make the area suitable for large-scale agriculture, especially the cultivation of rice.

Most of the Camargue wetlands are within Parc Naturel Régional de Camargue, set up in 1970 to preserve the area's fragile ecosystems by maintaining a balance between its ecosystems and the region's economic mainstays of agriculture, salt production, hunting, grazing and tourism. Shaped like a croissant with the Étang de Vaccarès in the centre, the 850-sq-km park is enclosed by the Petit Rhône and Grand Rhône Rivers. The Étang de Vaccarès and nearby peninsulas and islands form the Réserve Nationale de Camargue, a 135-sq-km nature reserve.

Those black bulls are raised for bullfighting and roam free under the watchful eyes of a mounted *gardian* (or cowboy). But you're much more likely to see bulls grazing in fenced-in fields; and those white horses that are saddled and tethered, waiting in rows under the blazing sun for tourists willing to pay for a ride.

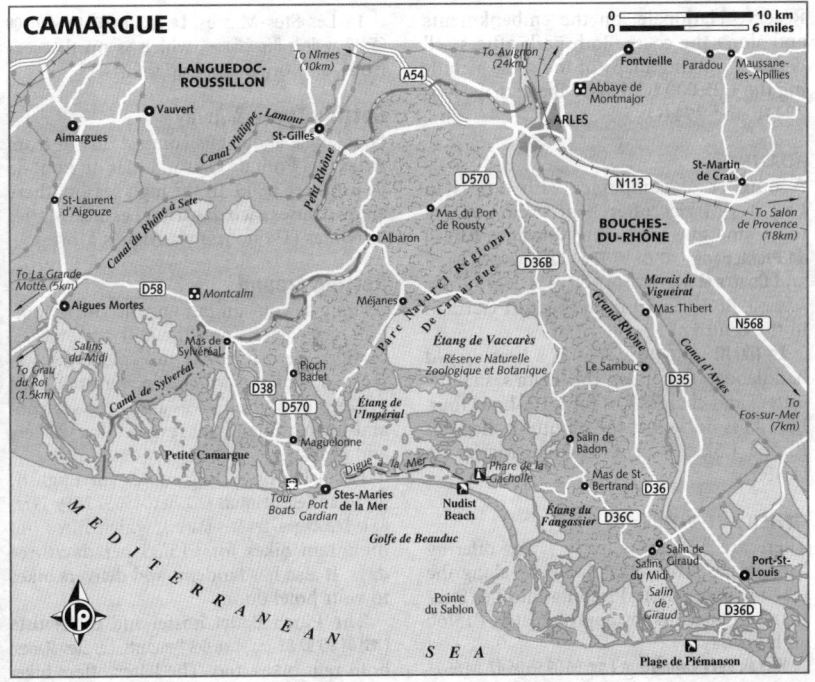

CAMARGUE

The Camargue is a wonderfully relaxing region to explore by bike, boat and horseback. Just beware of that other traditional Camargue phenomenon: the area's savage mosquitoes, which flourish on the blood of hapless passers-by. Pack *plenty* of insect repellent.

The two most important centres in the Camargue are the seaside resort of Les Stes-Maries de la Mer and the tiny, walled town of Aigues Mortes to the northwest. Both Aigues Mortes and Les Stes-Maries are larded with restaurants, usually offering good-value fare. Look for delicious *gardianne de taureau* (beef stew) and the delicate, thumbnail-sized clams that are called *tellines* on the menu.

Information

Parc Naturel Régional de Camargue information centre (☎ 04 90 97 86 32; www.parc-camargue .fr in French; Pont de Gau; admission free; ✆ 10am-6pm Apr-Sep, 10am-5pm Sat-Thu Oct-Mar) Four kilometres north of Les Stes-Maries, this centre's exhibits focus on environmental issues. From the glassed-in foyer you can watch birds through powerful binoculars. It also has plenty of information on walking and bird-watching.

Réserve Nationale de Camargue office (☎ 04 90 97 00 97; La Capelière; ✆ 9am-noon & 2-5pm Mon-Sat) Along the D36B, on the eastern side of Étang de Vaccarès. It also has exhibits on the Camargue's ecosystems, flora and fauna, and many trails and paths fan out from the area.

Sights & Activities
MUSÉE CAMARGUAIS

The **Camargue Museum** (Museon Camarguen in Provençal; ☎ 04 90 97 10 82; Mas du Pont de Rousty; adult/student €4.60/2.30; ✆ 9am-6pm Apr-Oct, 10am-5pm Wed-Mon Oct-Mar) is housed in a sheep shed built in 1812. Located 10km southwest of Arles on the D570 to Les Stes-Maries, it's an excellent introduction to the history, ecosystems, flora and fauna of the Camargue river delta. Much attention is given to traditional life in the Camargue (sheep and cattle raising, salt production at Salin de Giraud). A 3.5km nature trail, which ends at an observation tower, begins at the museum.

WALKING

There are numerous walking paths and trails in the Parc Naturel Régional and the

Réserve Nationale, on the embankments and along the coast. Both park offices sell detailed walking maps of the area, including the 1:25,000 IGN Série Bleue maps Nos 2944E and 2944O.

BOATING

A number of companies with offices in Les Stes-Maries offer boat excursions of the Camargue, including **Camargue Bateau de Promenade** (☎ 04 90 97 84 72; 5 rue des Launes) and **Quatre Maries** (☎ 04 90 97 70 10; 36 av Théodore Aubanel). Both depart from the Port Gardian in the centre of Les Stes-Maries.

Le Tiki III (☎ 04 90 97 81 68) is a beat-up old paddleboat that plies the delta's shallow waters and charges €10 for a 1½-hour tour. Le Tiki is docked at the mouth of the Petit Rhône 1.5km west of Les Stes-Maries de la Mer.

OTHER ACTIVITIES

There are numerous horse farms offering **horse riding** (*promenade à cheval*) along the D570 (Route d'Arles) leading into Les Stes-Maries. Expect to pay approximately €15/60 an hour/day.

Kayak Vert Camargue (☎ 06 09 56 06 47, 04 66 73 57 17; Mas de Sylvéréal), 14km north of Les Stes-Maries off the D38, arranges canoeing and kayaking on the Petit Rhône.

Tours

La Maison du Guide (☎ 06 12 44 73 52; www.maison duguide.camargue.fr in French) at Montcalm, between Aigues Mortes and Les Stes-Maries on the D58, organises a variety of guided tours with a variety of transport modes – on foot, by boat and by bike.

In Les Stes-Maries, **Le Gitan** (☎ 04 66 70 09 65; 17 av de la République), which is on the seafront, also organises jeep safaris.

Getting There & Away

For details about bus connections to/from Arles (via Pont de Gau and Mas du Pont de Rousty) see p806. In the high season, there are two buses each day from Les Stes-Maries to Nîmes (1¼ hours) via Aigues Mortes.

Getting Around

As long as you can put up with the ubiquitous insect pests and the stiff sea breezes, bicycles are a fine way to explore the Camargue, which is, of course, very flat. East of Les Stes-Maries, areas along the seafront and further inland are reserved for walkers and cyclists.

For a list of cycling routes (in English) go to **Le Vélo Saintois** (☎ /fax 04 90 97 74 56; 19 rue de la République, Les Stes-Maries), which hires out mountain bikes for €15/35 per day/three days. It also has tandems and delivers bikes to your hotel door.

The Pioch Badet hostel and **Le Vélociste** (☎ 04 90 97 83 26; place des Remparts, Les Stes-Maries) both rent bikes, too. The latter offers bike, horse and canoe packages.

Les Stes-Maries de la Mer
pop 2478

This coastal resort is known for its nearby beaches and fortified Romanesque church (12th to 15th century), a pilgrimage site for centuries. The neat, treeless rows of low houses are built to endure the three Camargue seasons: sun, wind and mosquitoes. Sandwiched between the sea and the

---

THE GITAN PILGRIMAGE

For two days at the end of each May, Gitans (Romany people, formerly called gypsies) from all over Europe gather at the Camargue fishing village of Les Stes-Maries de la Mer to honour their patron saint, Sarah. According to a Provençal legend, Sarah (along with Mary Magdalene, Mary Jacob, Mary Salome and other Biblical figures) fled the Holy Land in a small boat and landed near the River Rhône.

In 1448 skeletal remains said to belong to Sarah and the Marys were found in a crypt in Les Stes-Maries. Ever since, Gitans have been making the pilgrimage here, dancing and playing music in the streets or carrying a statue of Sarah through town, many of them in traditional dress. The Sunday in October closest to the 22nd is the date for another pilgrimage, dedicated to the Saintes Maries. *Courses Camarguaises* (nonlethal bullfights) are also held. The annual Festival Ame Gitane, a celebration of Gitan culture with theatre, music, film and dance, is held in Arles in mid-August.

marshes, either windswept or sunbaked, this bleached-out town blossoms each summer with pink-faced tourists, Gitans and bullfighters. There's a very Spanish flavour to this town, and not just because of the black bulls. On festival days, proud horse riders sporting traditional costume parade through the town and flamenco is danced in the squares.

INFORMATION

The modern **tourist office** (☎ 04 90 97 82 55; www.saintesmaries.com; 5 av Van Gogh; ☼ 9am-8pm Jul & Aug, 9am-7pm Apr-Jun & Sep, 9am-6pm Mar & Oct, 9am-5pm Nov-Feb) has an excellent website.

SIGHTS

Les Stes-Maries is most animated during the Gitan pilgrimage (opposite), held annually on 24-25 May.

There is a **Musée des Gitanes** (Panorama du Voyage; ☎ 04 90 97 52 85; Pioch Badet; admission €3; ☼ 10am-6pm Sep-Jun, 10am-8pm Jul & Aug), next to the Auberge de Jeunesse.

Tickets for bullfights at the **Méjanes arena** (☎ reservations 04 90 97 10 60; av Van Gogh), held in Les Stes-Maries' Arènes, are sold at the ticket office, tucked into its outer walls, between 3pm and 7pm Monday to Saturday.

The coast near Les Stes-Maries is lined with around 30km of uninterrupted finesand **beaches**. The area around **Phare de la Gacholle**, the lighthouse 11km east of town, is frequented by *naturalistes* (nudists).

SLEEPING & EATING

Auberge de Jeunesse (☎ 04 90 97 51 72; fax 04 90 97 54 88; Pioch Badet; ☼ reception 7.30-10.30am & 5-11pm, to midnight Jul & Aug) This hostel is 8km north of Les Stes-Maries on the D570 to Arles. Les Cars de Camargue buses from Arles drop you at the door (see p806 for details).

A number of old *mas* (farmhouses) surround Les Stes-Maries; many have rooms to let.

Mas de la Grenouillère (☎ 04 90 97 90 22; fax 04 90 97 70 94; d/tr incl breakfast from €60/80; P ⊠ ⊠) Small but comfortable rooms. They have a terrace overlooking open fields full of frogs, which sing guests to sleep each night. La Grenouillère (literally 'The Frog Farm') has stables and organises horse-riding trips. It's 1.5km down a dirt track signposted 1km north of Les Stes-Maries off the D570.

Étrier Camarguais (☎ 04 90 97 81 14; www.letrier .com; d low/high season from €85/105, high season half-board €133/171; P ⊠) This farmhouse-hotel built from 'a dream, flowers and the sun', is idyllic. The hotel is 500m before La Grenouillère along the same dirt track. The reception of the 'Camargue Stirrup' is in a traditional *cabane de gardian* (cowboy cabin). There's a large veranda with parasols to enjoy the food and a large swimming pool to cool off in. Note that half-board is mandatory in July and August.

Heaps of hotels – mostly three or four stars, in the low-rise 'farmhouse style' and generally costing €50 – line the D570, the main road from Arles into Les Stes-Maries. Most hotels in town are equally expensive.

Les Vagues (☎/fax 04 90 97 84 40; 12 av Théodore Aubanel; d without/with shower from €31/46) On the road that runs along the port west of the tourist office, Les Vagues has decent rooms with bathrooms and some have balconies with sea views.

Hôtel Méditerranée (☎ 04 90 97 82 09; fax 04 90 97 76 31; 4 av Frédéric Mistral; r €39-46) In the centre of town, this place is one of the cheapest options and also offers a homy, familial environment with a flower-decked terrace for breakfast.

Le Tamaris (☎ 04 90 97 93 29; 4 place des Remparts; menu from €11; ☼ closed Tue Oct-Mar) and **Le Delta** (1 place Mireille; menus €13-24) are both local favourites where you can dine well on little money.

Camping

Camping La Brise (☎ 04 90 97 84 67; fax 04 90 97 72 01; av Marcle Carrière; camping €13; ⊠) Three-star camping northeast of the centre of town.

Aigues Mortes

pop 6084

On the western edge of the Camargue, 28km northwest of Les Stes-Maries, is the curiously named, walled town of Aigues Mortes (which could be translated as 'Dead Waters'). Aigues Mortes was established on marshy flat land in the mid-13th century by Louis IX (St Louis) so the French crown would have a Mediterranean port under its direct control. (At the time, the area's other ports were controlled by various rival powers, including the counts of Provence.) In 1248, Louis IX's ships – all 1500 of them – gathered here before setting sail to the Holy Land for the Sixth Crusade.

Aigues Mortes' sturdy, rectangular ramparts, the tops affording great views over the marshlands, can be scaled from Tour de

Constance. Inside the walls, there's a fair bit of tourist hype, though the restored Église Notre Dame des Sablons is worth a look.

INFORMATION
Tourist office (☎ 04 66 53 73 00; www.ot-aigues mortes.fr; place St-Louis; ☼ 9am-noon & 1-6pm Sep-Jun, 9am-8pm Jul & Aug) Inside the walled city at Porte de la Gardette.

SLEEPING & EATING
L'Escale (☎ 04 66 53 71 14; av Tour Constance; s/d/tr €26/29/59) Just outside the walls, L'Escale is a central budget option, although aesthetics are not its strong point: the rooms are rather dark, very simple chalet-style affairs out the back of the old-school bar that fronts this place.

Le Victoria (☎ 04 66 51 14 20; fax 04 66 51 14 21; place Anatole-France; r from €46; menus €14-29) Just opposite the Tour Constance, this place is a cut above, as you'd expect from a Logis de France establishment. It also has a traditional restaurant serving all the local classics such as *soupe de poissons* and *gardienne de taureau*.

Camping Le Clos du Rhône (☎ 04 90 97 85 99; fax 04 90 97 78 85; route d'Aigues Mortes; camping €21.40; 🛋) At this park you can also rent four-person bungalows.

La Salicorne (☎ 04 66 53 62 67; 9 rue Alsace Lorraine; menus €25 & €31) Offers some imaginative culinary flourishes. It's especially strong on fish, for example *carpaccio de lotte* (fresh slivers of raw local fish marinated in lime juice).

NORTHEASTERN PROVENCE

DIGNE-LES-BAINS
pop 17,680 / elevation 608m

Provence hits the Alps, and the land of sun and olive trees meets the land of snow and melted cheese, around Digne-les-Bains, which is about 100km northeast of Aix-en-Provence and 152km northwest of Nice. This laid-back town is named after its thermal springs, visited annually by 11,000 people seeking to pamper themselves or ease rheumatism and respiratory ailments.

The area is also known for lavender production. The harvest is in August and honoured in Digne with a five-day festival, Corso

de la Lavande, starting on the first weekend of the month, and with Les Journées Lavande throughout the region in mid-August. In summer you'll smell the little purple flower everywhere.

Digne itself is unremarkable, although it makes a good base for walking and a wide range of adrenaline sports. The shale around Digne is rich in fossils.

The route Napoléon (now the N85), which Bonaparte followed in 1815 en route to Paris after escaping from Elba, passes through Digne and Castellane, the gateway to the Gorges du Verdon.

Orientation
Digne is built on the eastern bank of the shallow River Bléone. The major roads into town converge at the Point Rond du 11 Novembre 1918, a roundabout 400m northeast of the train station. The main street is blvd Gassendi, which heads northeastwards from the Point Rond and passes the large place du Général de Gaulle, the main square.

Information
INTERNET ACCESS
Cybercafé (☎ 04 92 30 87 17; 48 rue de l'Hubac; per hr €5; ☼ 10am-7pm Tue-Sat) In the centre of the town.

LAUNDRY
There are laundrettes at 4 place du Marché, in the old city (open 8am to 7pm Monday to Saturday), and 99 blvd Gassendi (open 9am to 7pm).

MONEY
BNP Paribas (5 blvd Gassendi)

POST
Post Office (4 rue André Honnorat) East of the tourist office.

TOURIST INFORMATION
Relais Départemental des Gîtes de France (☎ 04 92 31 30 40; www.gites-de-france.com; ☼ 9am-noon & 1-5pm Mon-Fri, 9am-noon Sat) Also in the Maison du Tourisme, it books accommodation at *gîtes* in the area. Bookings are only made between 9am and 11am and 1pm to 4pm.

Tourist Office (☎ 04 92 36 62 62; www.ot-dignelesbains .fr; place du Tampinet; ☼ 8.45am-noon & 2-6pm Mon-Sat, 10am-noon Sun Sep-Jun, 8.45am-12.30pm & 1.30-6.30pm Jul & Aug) Inside the Maison du Tourisme, with information on a variety of guided tours in the region, including lavender tours towards the end of August. The office also supplies some good walking and cycling maps of the area.

Sights & Activities

FONDATION ALEXANDRA DAVID-NÉEL

Paris-born writer and philosopher Alexandra David-Néel, made an incognito voyage in the 1900s to Tibet before settling in Digne. Her memory – and her interest in Tibet – are kept alive by the **Fondation Alexandra David-Néel** (☎ 04 92 31 32 38; 27 av Maréchal Juin), which also stages the annual Journées Tibétaines, a celebration of Tibetan culture, at the end of August. From October to June, free tours (with headphones for English speakers) start at 10.30am, 2pm and 4pm; and from April to September tours begin at 10.30am, 2pm, 3.30pm and 5pm. Drive out of town for 1km on the Nice road or take bus No 3 to the Stade Rolland stop.

MUSÉE GASSENDI

In the town centre, the eclectic **Musée Gassendi** (☎ 04 92 31 45 29; place des Récollets; adult/child €4/2; ☼ 11am-7pm Apr-Sep, 1.30-5.30pm Wed-Mon Oct-Mar) displays five centuries of art, history and natural history on its four floors. There are displays of traditional Provençal and contemporary art, including the landscapes and still-lifes of the 19th-century painter Etienne and a large and striking clay wall by modern artist Andy Goldsworthy. One floor is dedicated to the 16th-century philosopher/scientist/painter Pierre Gassendi, who revived Epicureanism, a Greek school of philosophy.

RÉSERVE NATURELLE GÉOLOGIQUE

Digne is in the middle of the **Réserve Naturelle Géologique**, with spectacular fossil deposits, including the footprints of prehistoric birds as well as ammonites, and ram's horn spiral shells. Ask for the detailed regional map to the Digne and Sisteron areas at the tourist office. You'll need your own transport (or a patient thumb) to get to the 18 sites, although there's an impressive limestone slab right next to the road to Barles 3km north of Digne with around 500 giant ammonites.

The Réserve Naturelle's impressive headquarters, the **Centre de Géologie** (☎ 04 92 36 70 70; www.resgeol04.org; adult/child €4.60/2.75; ☼ 9am-noon & 2-5.30pm Apr-Oct, Mon-Fri Nov-Mar) at St-Benoît, 2km north of town off the road to Barles, is well worth a visit. Artistically arranged outdoor

trails lead to a museum containing 10 aquariums, multimedia displays and plenty of fossils and plants. Take TUD bus No 2, get off at the Champourcin stop, then take the road to the left.

THERMAL SPA

Steep yourself in the healing warm waters, cover yourself in mud and seaweed treatments or luxuriate in herbal baths or massages at the **Établissement Thermal** (☎ 04 92 32 32 92; www.eurothermes.com in French; ☼ Feb-early Dec), 2km east of Digne's centre. The cost of a good soak starts at €10 and goes up to €38 for a spa bath and massage. There's also a gym.

Sleeping

In July and August you may be required to take half-board at many of Digne's hotels. The tourist office has a full list of *gîtes d'étape* in the surrounding countryside.

Hôtel L'Origan (☎ /fax 04 92 31 62 13; 6 rue Pied de Ville; s with washbasin from €15, d with shower from €25) This is a little place in the old city, with an upmarket **restaurant** (menus €19) and affordable accommodation in old-fashioned but comfortable rooms.

Hôtel Central (☎ 04 92 31 31 91; www.lhotel-central.com in French; 26 blvd Gassendi; s/d with washbasin €25/28, r with shower/shower & toilet €33/42) A good, central, two-star hotel. Avoid the traffic-noise-plagued road-facing rooms.

Hôtel Le Coin Fleuri (☎ 04 92 31 04 51; 9 blvd Victor Hugo; s/d with shower & toilet from €38/48) Two-star rooms and a great garden to relax in.

Tonic Hotel (☎ 04 92 32 20 31; www.eurothermes.com in French; 36 route des Thermes; r from €60; ⓟ ⌧ ⌧ ⌧) A couple of kilometres from town on the way to the Établissement Thermal, the Tonic is pretty good value for what you get. That includes large, modern rooms with satellite TV and hairdryers plus an attractive location at the foot of steep, wooded hills. It also offers a range of health and beauty packages with half-board and treatments at the thermal spa starting at €268 for two days and nights.

Camping

Camping du Bourg (☎ 04 92 31 04 87; route de Barcelonnette; camping €10.50; ☼ Apr-Oct) This park is 2km northeast of Digne (reduced to €10 if you're taking a cure). Take bus No 2 towards Barcelonnette and get off at Notre Dame du Bourg. From there it's a 600m walk.

Eating

Restaurant-Cafétéria Le Victor Hugo (☎ 04 92 31 57 23; 8-10 blvd Victor Hugo; plats du jour from €7; ☼ lunch Mon-Fri) One of the cheapest places for lunch.

Le Point Chaud (☎ 04 92 31 30 71; 95 blvd Gassendi; menu €12; ☼ Sat lunch & Sun) A local favourite for pizza, homemade pasta and a variety of fish and meat specialities.

La Braisière (☎ 04 92 31 59 63; 19 place de l'Évêché; lunch & dinner menus €10.80-24; ☼ closed Sat lunch) Away from the terraces on place du Général de Gaulle, La Braisière has good *menus* and a fine view over town. It does good *tartiflette* (€12) and *raclette* (€14).

SELF-CATERING

There's a **food market** (place du Général de Gaulle) on Wednesday and Saturday mornings.

There are a couple of good bread and pastry shops along blvd Gassendi plus the nearby **Boulangerie Pattisserie Andre Michel** (16 rue Pied de Ville), which sells tasty sweet and savoury treats.

Saveurs et Couleurs (7 blvd Gassendi) sells luxury local products.

There's also a **Casino Supermarket** (42 blvd Gassendi; ☼ 7.30am-12.30pm & 3.30-7.30pm).

Getting There & Away

BUS

The **bus station** (☎ 04 92 31 50 00; place du Tampinet; ☼ 9am-12.30pm & 3-6.30pm Mon-Sat) is behind the tourist office. Eleven regional companies operate buses to Nice (€14.60, 2¼ hours, two daily services Monday to Saturday) via Castellane (€10.50, 1¼ hours, one daily), Marseille (€14.10, 2½ hours, four daily) and Apt (€11.30, two hours, one daily).

There's also a shuttle bus linking Digne with the train station of Aix-en-Provence, timed to coincide with the TGV to and from Paris (€16.46, 1½ hours).

TRAIN

Digne's **train station** (☎ 04 92 31 00 67; av Pierre Sémard; ☼ ticket windows 8.15am-12.30pm & 1-8pm Mon-Fri, 8.15am-12.30pm & 1.45-4.45pm Sat) is a 10-minute walk westwards from the tourist office. There are four services daily to Marseille (€19.60, 2¼ hours) and three to Briançon (€21, 3½ hours) by bus to Chateau Arnoux and via St-Auban.

The two-car diesel trains operated by **Chemins de Fer de la Provence** (Digne ☎ 04 92 31 01 58, Nice ☎ 04 97 03 80 80) run along a scenic and winding narrow-gauge line to Nice's Gare de Nice CP via St-Martin du Var, 26km northeast of Nice. The entire trip takes about 3¼ hours. There are four runs in each direction daily.

THE PERFUME OF PROVENCE

Perhaps the most typical Provençal summer sight and smell is of lavender *(lavande)*, the sweet purple flower harvested between 15 July and 15 August for its fine perfume.

Lavender farms, distilleries and ornamental gardens open to visitors are listed in the English-language brochure *Les Routes de la Lavande* (free from tourist offices or online at www.routes-lavande.com). You can find lavender fields at the Abbaye de Sénanque near Gordes, the **Musée de la Lavande** (Lavender Museum; ☎ 04 90 76 91 23) in Coustellet and many more carpeting the arid Sault region, east of Mont Ventoux on the Vaucluse plateau. The tourist office at Digne-les-Bains also provides information on several lavender tours and festivals.

GORGES DU VERDON

The gorgeous 25km Gorges du Verdon (also known as the Grand Canyon du Verdon), the largest canyon in Europe, slices through the limestone plateau midway between Avignon and Nice. They begin at Rougon (near the confluence of the Verdon and the Jabron) and continue westwards until the river flows into Lac de Ste-Croix. The village of Castellane (population 1349) is east of Rougon and is the main gateway for the gorges.

Carved by the greenish waters of the Verdon River, the gorges are 250m to 700m deep. The bottom is 8m to 90m wide, while the rims are 200m to 1500m apart.

Information

The best information source for the Gorges du Verdon is the **Castellane tourist office** (☎ 04 92 83 61 14; www.castellane.org; rue Nationale; ☼ 9am-12.30pm & 1.30-7pm Mon-Sat, 10am-12.30pm Sun Jul & Aug, 9am-noon & 2-6pm Mon-Fri, 10am-noon & 3-6pm Sat Sep-Jun), or try the **Moustiers Ste-Marie tourist office** (☎ 04 92 74 67 84; fax 04 92 74 60 65; ☼ 10am-noon & 2-7pm).

There's a small **tourist office** (☎ /fax 04 92 77 32 02, 04 92 77 38 02) in the centre of La Palud-sur-Verdon and a **Syndicat d'Initiative** (☎ /fax 04 94 85 68 40) in Trigance.

Sights & Activities

The bottom of the gorges can be visited only on foot or by raft, but motorists and cyclists can enjoy spectacular (if dizzying) views from two cliff-side roads.

The D952 follows the northern rim and passes the **Point Sublime** viewpoint, offering a spectacular, almost fisheye lens–like panorama of riotous rock formations, that deep, deep gorge and the rushing river way, way below. The GR4 trail leads to the bottom of the gorge from here. The best view from the northern side is from **Belvédère de l'Escalès** along route de Crêtes (D23). Drive to the third bend and hold your breath since the drop-off into the gorge is quite stunning. Retrace your route to the D952.

Another stunning view is offered by **La Corniche Sublime** (the D19 to the D71), which goes along the southern rim and takes you to such landmarks as the **Balcons de la Mescla** (Mescla Terraces) and **Pont de l'Artuby** (Artuby Bridge), the highest bridge in Europe.

A complete circuit of the Gorges du Verdon via Moustiers Ste-Marie involves about 140km of driving; the tourist office in Castellane has the good English-language brochure *Driving Tours* with 11 itineraries. The only real village en route is **La Palud-sur-Verdon** (930m), 2km northeast of the northern bank of the gorges. In summer, heavy traffic often slows travel to a crawl.

The bottom of the canyon, first explored in its entirety in 1905, presents walkers and white-water rafters with an overwhelming series of cliffs and narrows. You can walk most of it along the often-difficult GR4, which is covered by Didier-Richard's 1:50,000 map No 19, *Haute Provence-Verdon*. It is also included in the excellent English-language book *Canyon du Verdon – The Most Beautiful Hikes* (€4.12), available at Castellane or Moustiers tourist offices, which lists 28 walks in the gorges. The full GR4 takes two days, though short descents into the canyon are possible from a number of points. Bring along a torch (flashlight) and drinking water. Camping in the rough on gravel beaches along the way is illegal, however people do it.

Castellane's tourist office has a complete list of companies offering rafting, canyon-

ing, horse riding, mountaineering, biking and other outdoor pursuits.

Aboard Rafting (☎ /fax 04 92 83 76 11; www .aboard-rafting.com; 8 place Marcel Sauvaire; ✆ Apr-Sep) runs white-water rafting trips (€30 to €75) as well as canyoning (€30 to €65), kayaking (€30) and hot-dogging (€45).

Sleeping & Eating

BUDGET

Gîte d'Étape de Fontaine Basse (☎ 04 94 85 68 36; fax 04 94 85 68 50; Trigance; dm incl breakfast €17) This place is 16km southeast of Castellane.

The tourist office has a full list of the area's many camping grounds. The river near Castellane is lined with seasonal camping areas that tend to be crowded and pricey in summer.

Domaine de Chasteuil Provence (☎ 04 92 83 61 21; www.chasteuil-provence.com; camping low/high season €14/20; ✆ May–mid-Sep; ⊠) Just south of Castellane.

MID-RANGE

If you're looking for something inexpensive, Castellane is the place for you. Numerous hotels line the central square, place Marcel Sauvaire and place de l'Église.

Grand Hôtel du Levant (☎ 04 92 83 60 05; www .touring-levant.com; place Marcel Sauvaire; r €35-65; ⓟ) Offers good-value rooms with bathrooms.

Ma Petite Auberge (☎ 04 92 83 62 06; fax 04 92 83 68 49; rue de la République; d from €43) Also has a restaurant.

Studi Hôtel (☎ 04 92 83 76 47; fax 04 94 84 63 36; d €43; ⊠) An excellent-value place, a 10-minute walk from town on the N85 out of Castellane (direction Digne-les-Bains). A week's stay in a two- to four-person studio costs €564.

La Bastide de Moustiers (☎ 04 92 70 47 47; www .bastide-moustiers.com; Moustiers-Ste Marie; d low/high season from €155/180; menus lunch/dinner €42/47; ⓟ ⊠ ⊠) This is the place for total indulgence, relaxation and especially for gourmet dining since this is part of the growing empire of French culinary legend Alain Ducasse. The rooms inside the thick stone-walled old farmhouse are elegant and, thank goodness, there's a place to park the helicopter. It's about 20km from Castellane.

Getting There & Away

Public transport to, from, and around the Gorges du Verdon is limited. **Autocars Sumian**

(☎ 04 42 67 60 34) runs buses from Marseille to Castellane via Aix-en-Provence (€19.90, 3½ hours), La Palud and Moustiers.

Getting Around

In July and August **Navettes Autocar** (☎ 04 92 83 40 27, 04 92 83 64 47) runs shuttle buses around the gorges daily except Sunday, linking Castellane with Point Sublime, La Palud and La Maline. Ask at the tourist office in Castellane for schedules and fares.

Aboard Rafting (see p813) rents mountain bikes for €10/20 per half/full day.

PRA-LOUP & LA FOUX D'ALLOS

The ski resort of Pra-Loup (elevation 1600m), 8.5km southwest of Barcelonnette and 70km southeast of Gap, is connected by a lift system across the Vallon des Agneliers with another ski resort called La Foux d'Allos. By road, Pra-Loup is 23.5km to the north, but there is no public transport available between the two resorts.

The majority of runs are for intermediate and advanced skiers and snowboarders. St-Paul-sur-Ubaye, in a valley below and to the northeast of Pra-Loup, has 25km of cross-country runs from 1400m to 1500m and Larche has 30km of runs from 1700m to 2000m.

Pra-Loup's 53 lifts are between 1600m and 2600m, with 160km of runs and a vertical drop of almost 1000m.

The Pra-Loup **tourist office** (☎ 04 92 84 10 04; www.praloup.com; ☺ 9am-noon & 2-6pm Jul & Aug, 9am-noon & 2-6pm Mon-Fri May, Jun & Sep-Nov, 9am-7pm Dec-Apr), **École de Ski Français** (ESF; ☎ 04 92 84 11 05) and post office, where you can also change money, are all inside the Maison de Pra-Loup. The La Foux d'Allos **tourist office** (☎ 04 92 83 80 70; www.valdallos.com in French) is in the Maison de la Foux on the main square.

Sleeping

Studios and apartments are usually the best option. The tourist offices have lists of all available establishments. Apartments are the main type of accommodation here and studios for two start at €165 per week during the low season and around €300 in the high season.

Getting There & Away

The nearest train station to Pra-Loup is Gap, from where there are a couple of buses daily travelling to Pra-Loup (€8.10, 1¾ hours) via Barcelonnette.

Buses link the village of La Foux d'Allos, which is 9km southeast of the resort, with Digne-les-Bains and Avignon.

It is possible to get to La Foux d'Allos from Nice by train departing Nice's Gare des Chemins de Fer de Provence to La Vœsubie-Plan-du-Var. The rest of the trip is by bus, with a change required at Thorame.

Côte d'Azur & Monaco

CONTENTS

A region of heart-palpitatingly dramatic ocean views, chic seaside towns, fine wine and great food, the beautiful Côte d'Azur (Azure Coast), also known as the French Riviera, stretches along the Mediterranean coast from Toulon to the Italian border.

Many towns on the coast – Nice, Monaco, Cannes, St-Tropez – are known as the playgrounds of the rich, famous and tanned. The reality is usually less glamorous and occasionally, at its worst, it can be a purgatory of traffic gridlock and overrun tourist attractions. Even so, the Côte d'Azur has much to entice visitors: sun, beach, warm sea water and all sorts of cultural activities.

The capital, Nice, is a good base for exploring the region. Following the coast west, you come to attractive Antibes, wealthy Cannes and, just west of the stunning red mountain range known as the Massif de l'Estérel, twin towns St-Raphaël and Fréjus. Inland, the hills over-looking the coast are dotted with villages such as Grasse, Vence and St-Paul de Vence.

Administratively part of Provence, Côte d'Azur also includes most of the *départements* of Alpes-Maritimes and Var. The forested Massif des Maures, and the tiny villages nestling inside it, stretches from St-Raphaël to Hyères. It's well worth a detour when you tire of the feel of sand between your toes.

West of fashionable St-Tropez you'll find the region's most unspoiled coastline, where capes and cliffs alternate with streams and beaches, many sheltered from the open sea by the Îles d'Hyères, three large islands (and a couple of tiny ones) some 10km offshore.

East of Nice, the foothills of the Alps plummet into the Mediterranean. Three coastal roads, known as corniches (and where you'll experience many of those dramatic views), pass villages overlooking the sea en route to Menton and the Italian border. The tiny principality of Monaco is roughly midway between Nice and Menton.

HIGHLIGHTS

- Savour the flavours of local **Niçois specialities** (p818) in old Nice
- Sample the liquid delights of **Maison des Vins Côtes de Provence** (p847)
- Admire the sculpture and artworks at **Fondation Maeght** (p833), St-Paul de Vence, or the **Musée d'Art Moderne et d'Art Contemporain** (p822)
- Make the most of the exuberance of **Nice's old-town nightlife** (p829)
- Be seen with the fashionable set in **St-Tropez** (p844)
- Spot the A-listers at the **Cannes Film Festival** (p836)
- Explore the wild and rocky coastline of the **corniches** (p851) east of Nice

 POPULATION: 1.100.000	 AREA: 4300 SQ KM

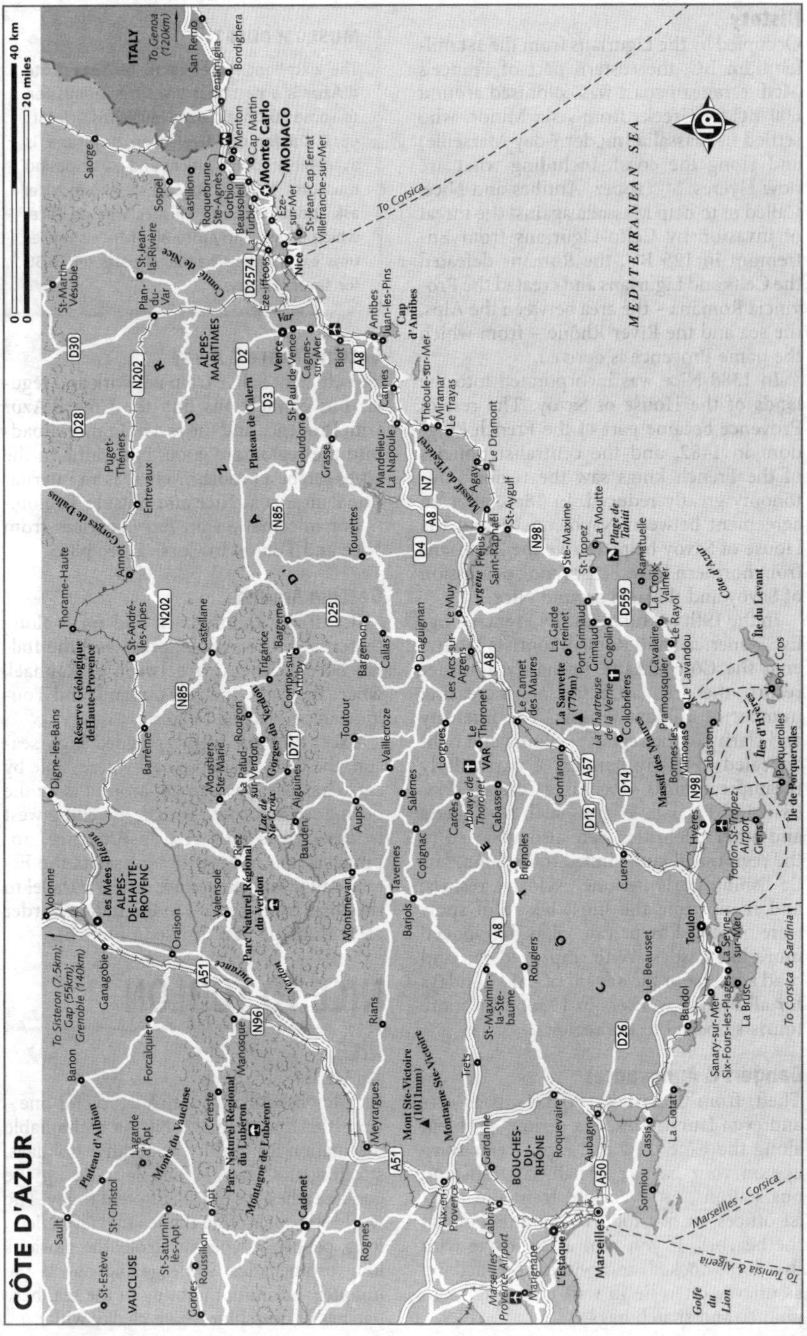

CÔTE D'AZUR & MONACO

History

Occupied by the Ligurians from the 1st millennium BC, the eastern part of France's Mediterranean coast was colonised around 600 BC by Greeks from Asia Minor, who settled in Massalia (modern-day Marseille) and along the coast, including what are now Hyères, St-Tropez, Antibes and Nice. Called in to help Massalia against the threat of invasion by Celto-Ligurians from Entremont in 125 BC, the Romans defeated the Celts and Ligurians and created the Provincia Romana – the area between the Alps, the sea and the River Rhône – from which the name Provence is derived.

In 1388 Nice was incorporated into the lands of the House of Savoy. The rest of Provence became part of the French kingdom in 1482, and the centralist policies of the French kings saw the region's autonomy greatly reduced. In 1860, after an agreement between Napoleon III and the House of Savoy helped drive the Austrians from northern Italy, France took possession of Savoy and the area around Nice.

In the 19th century wealthy French, English, American and Russian tourists discovered the Côte d'Azur. Primarily a winter resort, the area attracted an increasing number of affluent visitors. The intensity and clarity of the region's colours and light appealed to many painters – particularly the impressionists – including Cézanne, Matisse and Picasso. Writers such as Collette and other celebrities were also attracted to the region and contributed to its fame. Little fishing ports became exclusive resorts, and in no time the most beautiful spots were occupied by private villas that looked more like castles. With improved rail and road access and the advent of paid holidays for all French workers in 1936, even more tourists flocked to the region.

Dangers & Annoyances

Theft, from backpacks, pockets, bags cars and even laundrettes, is a serious problem along the Côte d'Azur. Keep a very sharp eye on your bags, especially at train and bus stations, on overnight trains, in tourist offices, in fast-food restaurants and on the beaches. If you rent a car, drive with the doors locked and windows rolled up as thieves often lie in wait at red lights to pounce and snatch bags.

MUSEUM BUFF?

The excellent-value **Carte Musées Côte d'Azur** is a pass that gives free admission to some 60 Côte d'Azur museums. It costs €8/15/25 for one/five/seven days and is available at tourist offices and participating museums. If you'll only be staying in Nice, ask about the Carte Musées Ville de Nice, which allows entry into all of Nice's museums except the Chagall. It costs €6/18.30 for seven/15 days.

Getting There & Away

The efficient SNCF train network and regular bus connections link the Côte d'Azur with Provence and the rest of France. Roads into the region are good, but traffic in the cities can be a problem. There is an international airport at Nice and outside Toulon.

For information on ferry services from Nice and Toulon to Corsica, see p865.

Getting Around

SNCF trains shuttle back and forth along the coast between St-Raphaël and the Italian border. The area between St-Raphaël, where the train line veers inland, and Toulon can be reached by bus.

Except for the traffic-plagued high season, the Côte d'Azur is easily accessible by car. The fastest way to get around is by the boring A8 autoroute which, travelling west to east, starts near Aix-en-Provence, approaches the coast at Fréjus, skirts the Estérel range and runs more or less parallel to the coast from Cannes to the Italian border at Ventimiglia (Vintimille in French).

NICE TO TOULON

NICE
pop 342,738

Rich English folk – Queen Victoria for one – were the first to make Nice a fashionable destination for healthy, restorative holidays, strolling the seafront and lapping up the good weather. It's not so different today. The world still cools off in the sea that laps Nice's long, pebbly beaches or strolls the glorious long promenades, while gazing out at the uniquely beautiful marbling of the sea: here patches of deep blue, there chalky white.

It remains a fashionable city (considered the capital of the Riviera), but it's relaxed and fun too. Nice also makes a great base from which to explore the rest of the Côte d'Azur, as it is only a short train or bus ride from Monaco, Cannes and other Riviera hot spots. The city is also blessed with museums as fine as you'll find anywhere in the south of France.

There's a lively nightlife in the old city's narrow warren of streets, an old harbour and hilltop gardens to explore and great markets to nose around in too. Unsurprisingly Nice is enormously popular with young travellers, so there are lots of budget places to stay. However, there's a profusion of good hotels and entertainment options for all budgets. In short, Nice has plenty to offer everyone.

History

Nice was founded around 350 BC by the Greek seafarers who had settled Marseille. They named the colony Nikaia, apparently to commemorate a victory (*nike* in Greek) over a nearby town. In 154 BC the Greeks were followed by the Romans, who settled further uphill around what is now Cimiez, site of a number of Roman ruins.

By the 10th century, Nice was ruled by the counts of Provence but turned to Amadeus VII of the House of Savoy in 1388. In the 18th and 19th centuries it was temporarily occupied several times by the French, but did not definitively become part of France until 1860, when Napoleon III struck a deal (known as the treaty of Turin) with the House of Savoy.

During the Victorian period Nice became popular with the English aristocracy, who came to enjoy the city's mild winter climate. European royalty soon followed.

Orientation

Avenue Jean Médecin runs south from near the Gare Nice Ville (the main train station) to place Masséna. The modern city centre, the area north and west of place Masséna, includes the upmarket pedestrianised streets of rue de France and rue Masséna. Station Centrale and intercity bus stations are located three blocks east of place Masséna.

The famous promenade des Anglais follows the gently curved beachfront from the city centre to the airport, 6km west. Vieux Nice (old Nice) is delineated by blvd Jean Jaurès, quai des États-Unis and, east, the hill known as Le Château. Place Garibaldi is at the northeastern tip of Vieux Nice.

The wealthy residential neighbourhood of Cimiez, home to several outstanding museums, is just north of the city centre.

Information
BOOKSHOPS

Cat's Whiskers (☎ /fax 04 93 80 02 66; 26 rue Lamartine) New and second-hand guides and English-language novels.

Magellan Librairie de Voyages (☎ 04 93 82 31 81; 3 rue d'Italie) An excellent selection of maps and travel guides, including Lonely Planet in English.

Maison de la Presse (place Masséna) Also has a wide selection of maps and guides, plus books and magazines in English.

NICE IN...

Two days
Breakfast by the flower and produce markets on **cours Saleya** (p828), meander or rollerblade along the **promenade des Anglais** (p824), head up to the lovely gardens of the **château** (p822) before grabbing a tapas-style lunch of fried nibbles and peppered-*socca* in **Vieux Nice** (p827), then hit the pebbly beach. Head back into old Nice for dinner and a bar-crawl around some of the many lively **bars and pubs** (p828) here. The next day visit the excellent **Musée Matisse** (p823) and **Musée Marc Chagall** (p823). Lunch in pretty **Villefranche-sur-Mer** (p851) and then take off to **Èze** (p852) for unforgettable sea views.

Four days
Head west along the coast for a day wandering the narrow streets of laid-back **Antibes** (p831) and visiting the **Musée Picasso** (p832). The next day drive the spectacular corniches on the way to the exclusive principality of **Monaco** (p854) or head inland for a feast of art at **Matisse's chapel** (p834) in Vence and the **Fondation Maeght** (p833) in St-Paul de Vence.

NICE

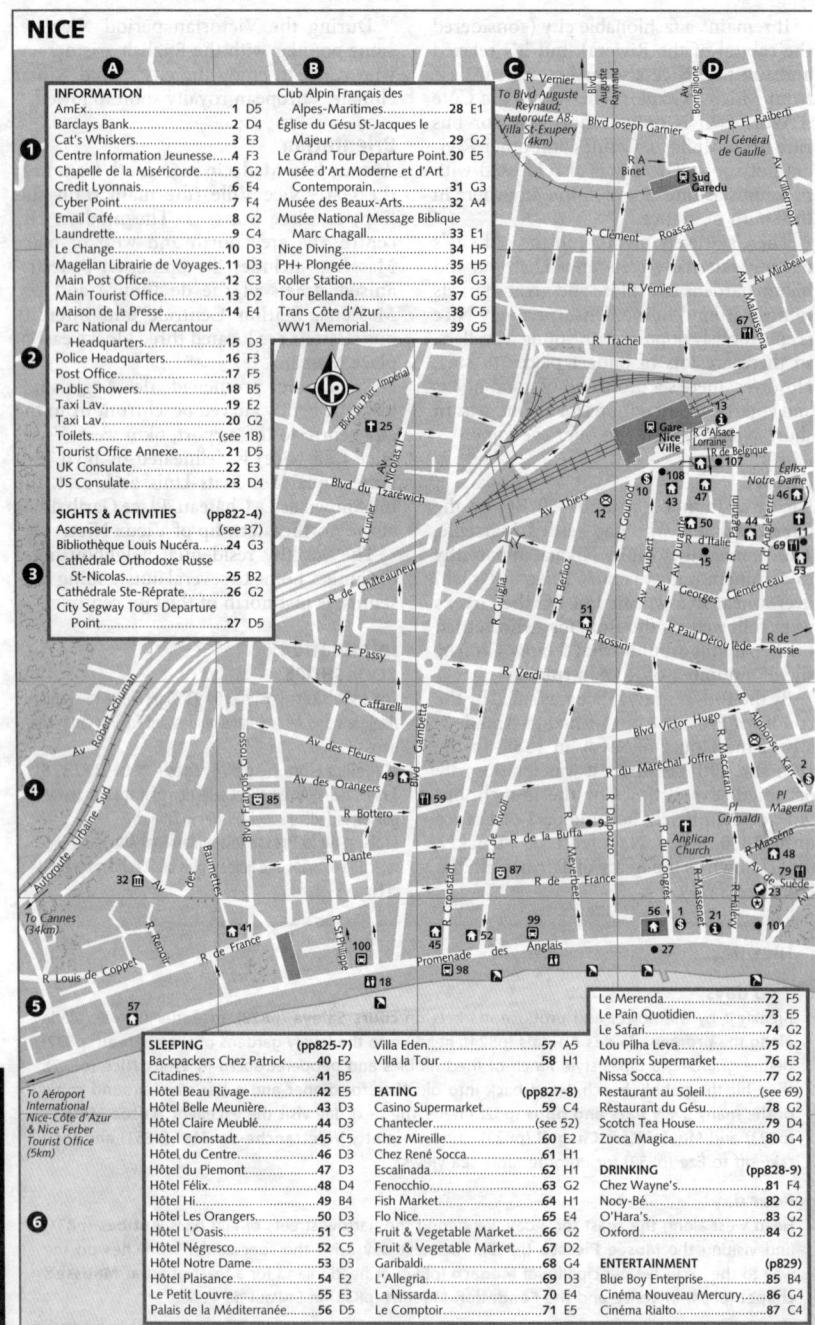

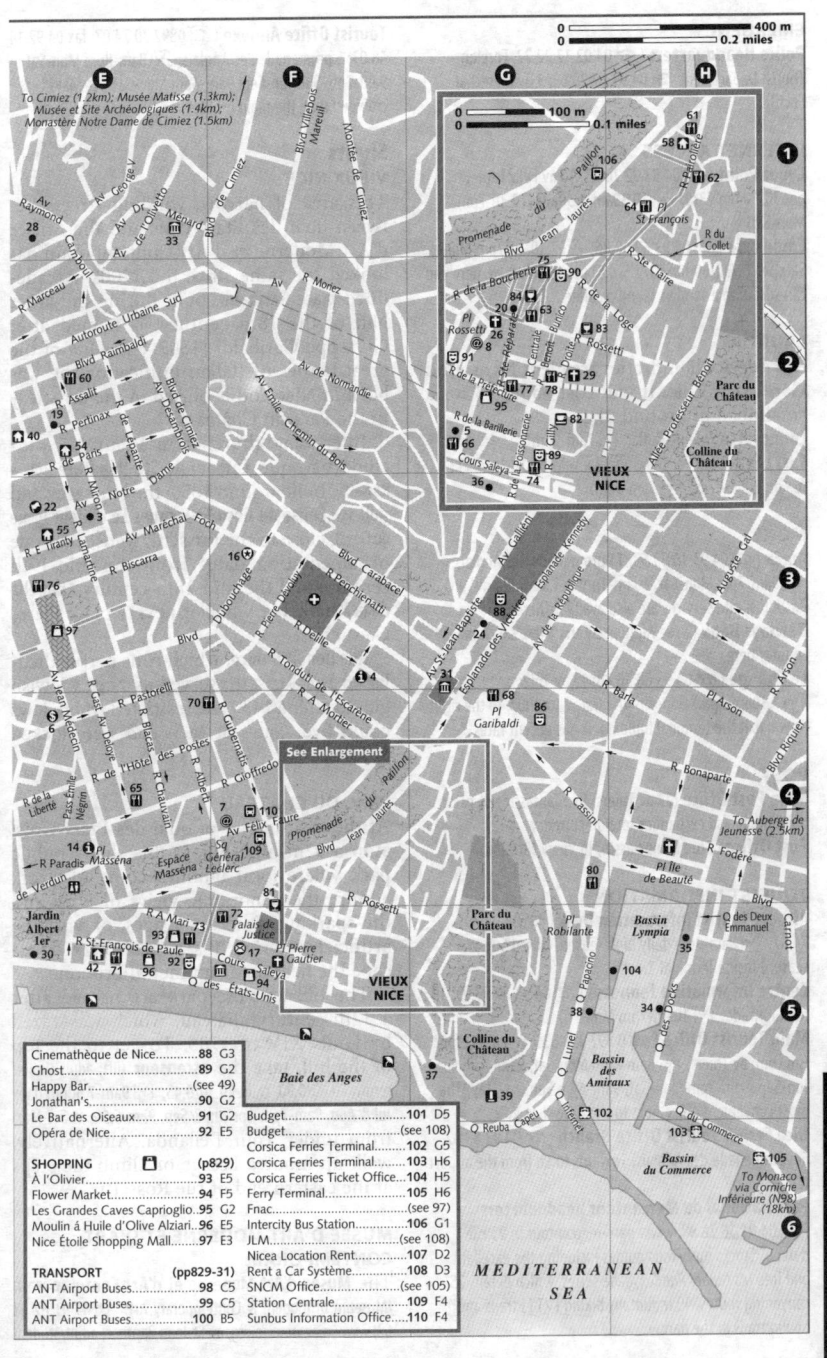

0 — 400 m
0 — 0.2 miles

To Cimiez (1.2km); Musée Matisse (1.3km);
Musée et Site Archéologiques (1.4km);
Monastère Notre Dame de Cimiez (1.5km)

0 — 100 m
0 — 0.1 miles

VIEUX NICE

Parc du Château

Colline du Château

See Enlargement

Parc du Château

VIEUX NICE

Colline du Château

To Auberge de Jeunesse (2.5km)

Pl Ile de Beauté

Bassin Lympia

Bassin des Amiraux

Bassin du Commerce

To Monaco via Corniche Inférieure (N98) (18km)

Baie des Anges

MEDITERRANEAN SEA

Jardin Albert 1er

Palais de Justice

Pl Pierre Gautier

Cinémathèque de Nice	88 G3
Ghost	89 G2
Happy Bar	(see 49)
Jonathan's	90 G2
Le Bar des Oiseaux	91 G2
Opéra de Nice	92 E5

SHOPPING	(p829)
À l'Olivier	93 E5
Flower Market	94 F5
Les Grandes Caves Caprioglio	95 G2
Moulin á Huile d'Olive Alziari	96 E5
Nice Étoile Shopping Mall	97 E3

TRANSPORT	(pp829-31)
ANT Airport Buses	98 C5
ANT Airport Buses	99 C5
ANT Airport Buses	100 B5

Budget	101 D5
Budget	(see 108)
Corsica Ferries Terminal	102 G5
Corsica Ferries Terminal	103 H6
Corsica Ferries Ticket Office	104 H5
Ferry Terminal	105 H6
Fnac	(see 97)
Intercity Bus Station	106 G1
JLM	(see 108)
Nicea Location Rent	107 D2
Rent a Car Système	108 D3
SNCM Office	(see 105)
Station Centrale	109 F4
Sunbus Information Office	110 F4

EMERGENCY
Police Headquarters (☎ 04 92 17 22 22, Foreign Tourist Department ☎ 04 92 17 20 63; 1 av Maréchal Foch)

INTERNET ACCESS
Cyber Point (☎ 04 93 92 70 63; 10 av Félix Faure; per 30/60min €3/5; ☼ 10.30am-1.30pm & 2.30-7pm Mon-Sat)
Email café (☎ 04 93 62 68 86; ☼ 7.30am-7pm Mon-Sat; per 10/30/60min €1/2.5/4.5) In the old town, here you can surf with a sandwich and a coffee.

LAUNDRY
Self-service laundrettes are plentiful around Gare Nice Ville. It will cost about €3 for a small load of around 5kg.
Laundrette (rue de Buffa; ☼ 7am-9pm)
Taxi Lav (22 rue Pertinax; ☼ 7am-9pm) Old Town (13 rue du Pont Vieux; ☼ 7am-9pm)

MONEY
AmEx (☎ 04 93 16 53 53; 11 promenade des Anglais; ☼ 9am-7pm Mon-Sat, 10am-1pm & 1.30-5.30pm Sun) Poste restante services are also available here.
Barclays Bank (2 rue Alphonse Karr) There's a change counter here.
Le Change (☎ 04 93 88 56 80; 17 av Thiers; ☼ 7.30am-8pm) Opposite the Gare Nice Ville, to the right as you exit the terminal building. It has decent rates.

POST
Main Post Office (23 av Thiers) In a fantastic red-brick building. It also exchanges foreign currency.
Post Office (2 rue Louis Gassin) In Vieux Nice.

TOURIST INFORMATION
Airport Tourist Information Desk (☎ 08 92 70 74 07; ☼ 8am-9pm daily high season, closed Sun low season) Inside Terminal 1.
Centre Information Jeunesse (☎ 04 93 80 93 93; 19 rue Gioffrédo; ☼ 10am-7pm Mon-Fri)
Main Tourist Office (☎ 0 892 353 535; www.nicetourism.com; av Thiers; ☼ 8am-8pm Mon-Sat, 9am-7pm Sun Jun-Sep, 8am-7pm Mon-Sat, 9am-6pm Sun Oct-May) The most convenient office next to the Gare Nice Ville.
Nice Ferber Tourist Office Branch (☎ 04 93 83 32 64; promenade des Anglais) Towards town from the airport terminal.
Parc National du Mercantour headquarters (☎ 04 93 16 78 88; www.parc-mercantour.fr; 23 rue d'Italie) Stocks numerous guides including the excellent and free *Les Guides Randoxygène* series, which details 25 canyoning routes, 40 mountain-biking (VTT) trails and hiking trails in the park.

Tourist Office Annexe (☎ 0892 70 74 07; fax 04 92 14 48 03; 5 promenade des Anglais; ☼ 8am-8pm Mon-Sat, 9am-7pm Sun Jun-Sep; 9am-6pm Mon-Sat Oct-May) Less crowded than the main office.

Sights
VIEUX NICE
This area of narrow, winding streets between quai des États-Unis and the Musée d'Art Moderne et d'Art Contemporain has looked the same since the 1700s. Arcaded-lined **place Garibaldi**, built during the latter half of the 18th century, is named after Giuseppe Garibaldi (1807–82). One of the great heroes of Italian unification, he was born in Nice and is buried in the cemetery in the Parc du Château.

Interesting churches in Vieux Nice include baroque **Cathédrale Ste-Réparate** (place Rossetti), built around 1650; the blue-grey and yellow **Église du Gésu St-Jacques Le Majeur** (place du Gésu), close to rue Rossetti, whose baroque ornamentation dates from the mid-17th century; and the mid-18th-century **Chapelle de la Miséricorde**, which is next to place Pierre Gautier.

Rue Benoît Bunico, which runs perpendicular to rue Rossetti, served as Nice's Jewish ghetto after a 1430 law restricted where Jews could live. Gates at each end were locked at sunset.

PARC DU CHÂTEAU
At the eastern end of quai des États-Unis, atop a 92m-high hill, is this shady public park where local families come to stroll, admire the panoramic views of Nice and the sparkling Baie des Anges, or visit the artificial waterfall. It's a great place to escape the heat on a summer afternoon.

The hill and the park are named after a 12th-century chateau, which was razed by Louis XIV in 1706. To get to the top of the hill, take the **ascenseur** (lift; adult single/return €0.60/0.90, child €0.30/0.45; ☼ 9am-7.50pm daily Jul & Aug, 9am-7pm Apr-Jun & Sep, 9am-5.50pm Oct-Mar) from under Tour Bellanda. Alternatively, walk up montée Lesage or climb the steps at the eastern end of rue Rossetti.

MUSÉE D'ART MODERNE ET D'ART CONTEMPORAIN
The **Musée d'Art Moderne et d'Art Contemporain** (Museum of Modern & Contemporary Art; ☎ 04 93 62 61 62; www.mamac-nice.org; av St-Jean Baptiste; adult/student

€4/2.50; ⊙ 10am-6pm Wed-Mon), Nice's pride and joy in the architectural as well as the art stakes, specialises in French and American avant-garde works from the 1960s to the present. The exhibits explode with colour in the fabulously light, large display spaces. Glass walkways connect the four marble-coated towers, on top of which is a must-see rooftop garden and gallery featuring pieces by Nice-born Yves Klein (1928–62). Other highlights include Andy Warhol's *Campbell's Soup Can* (1965), a shopping trolley wrapped by Christo, Armen's creepy *Venus aux Ongles Rouge,* and a pea-green Model-T Ford compressed into a 1.6m-high block by Marseille-born sculptor, César. The pop art sculptor Niki de St-Phalle (1930–2002) donated an impressive collection of her works to the museum before she died.

Next door is Nice's library, **Bibliothèque Louis Nucéra**, marked by a cubical 'head' of administrative offices over the underground reading rooms.

MUSÉE NATIONAL MESSAGE BIBLIQUE MARC CHAGALL

The **Musée National Message Biblique Marc Chagall** (Marc Chagall Biblical Message Museum; ☎ 04 93 53 87 20; adult/student Jul-Sep €5.80/4.25, rest of year €5.50/4; ⊙ 10am-6pm Wed-Mon Jul-Sep, to 5pm Oct-Jun), contains a series of large, impressive and colourful series of paintings of *Old Testament* scenes. Don't miss the mosaic of the rose window at Metz Cathedral, viewed through a plate-glass window across a small pond. Take bus No 15 from place Masséna to the front of the museum or walk.

MUSÉE MATISSE

Northeast of the Gare Nice Ville about 2.5km, in the bourgeois district of Cimiez, the **Musée Matisse** (Matisse Museum; ☎ 04 93 81 08 08; www.musee-matisse-nice.org; 164 av des Arènes de Cimiez; adult/student €4/2.50; ⊙ 10am-6pm Wed-Mon) houses a fine collection of works by Henri Matisse. Its permanent collection is displayed in a red-ochre, 17th-century Genoese mansion and the **Parc des Arènes**. Temporary exhibitions are hosted in the basement building that leads through to the stucco-decorated villa. Well-known pieces in the permanent collection include Matisse's blue paper cut-outs of *Blue Nude IV* and *Woman with Amphora.* The collection is striking for its variety: Matisse worked in a wide range of media, well represented here,

including cloth, paper, bronze, oil paint and pen and ink.

Matisse is buried in the cemetery of the **Monastère Notre Dame de Cimiez** (Cimiez Notre Dame Monastery; ☎ 04 93 81 00 04; ⊙ 8.30am-12.30pm & 2.30-6.30pm), which today houses a small **museum** (admission free; ⊙ 10am-noon & 3-6pm Mon-Sat) illustrating the everyday lives and activities of the monastery's monks. The artist's grave is signposted *sépulture Henri Matisse* from the cemetery's main entrance (next to the monastery church on av Bellanda). A flight of stairs leads from the eastern end of the olive grove to av Bellanda.

Take bus No 15, 17, 20, 22 or 25 from Station Centrale to the Arènes stop.

MUSÉE ET SITE ARCHÉOLOGIQUES

Behind the Musée Matisse, on the eastern side of the Parc des Arènes, lie the ruins of the Roman city of Cemenelum – the focus of the **Musée et Site Archéologiques** (Archaeology Museum; ☎ 04 93 81 59 57; 160 av des Arènes de Cimiez; adult/student €4/2.50; ⊙ 10am-noon & 2-6pm Wed-Mon Apr-Sep, 10am-1pm & 2-5pm Wed-Mon Oct-Mar). The public baths and amphitheatre – the venue for outdoor concerts during the Nice Jazz Festival (p825) – can both be visited.

To get here from Museé Matisse, turn left out of the main park entrance on av des Arènes de Cimiez, walk 100m, then turn left again onto av Monte Croce, where the main entrance to the archaeological site is located.

CATHÉDRALE ORTHODOXE RUSSE ST-NICOLAS

The multicoloured **Cathédrale Orthodoxe Russe St-Nicolas** (Russian Orthodox Cathedral of St-Nicolas; ☎ 04 93 96 88 02; av Nicolas II; ⊙ 9am-noon & 2.30-6pm, closed Sun morning), crowned by six onion domes, was built between 1902 and 1912 in early-17th-century style. It is opposite 17 blvd du Tzaréwich, an easy 15-minute walk from Gare Nice Ville. Step inside and you're transported to imperial Russia. Shorts, miniskirts and sleeveless shirts are forbidden.

MUSÉE DES BEAUX-ARTS

The **Musée des Beaux-Arts** (Fine Arts Museum; ☎ 04 92 15 28 28; 33 av des Baumettes; adult/student €4/2.50; ⊙ 10am-noon & 2-6pm Tue-Sun) is housed in a fantastic late-19th-century villa and displays works by Boudin, Dufy, Fragonard, Sisley and Rodin.

Activities

For information on the region's **walking** and **mountain-biking** trails, go to the headquarters of **Parc National du Mercantour** (see p822) or **Club Alpin Français** (CAF; ☎ 04 93 62 59 99; 14 av Mirabeau).

CITY WALKING

The palm-lined **promenade des Anglais** (English promenade), established by Nice's English colony in 1822 as a seaside walking path, provides a fine stage for a stroll along the beach and the Baie des Anges (Bay of Angels). Don't miss the magnificent façade of the Art Deco **Palais de la Méditerranée** (13-17 promenade des Anglais), formerly a lavish casino and theatre that fell into ruin after its owners experienced financial difficulties in the 1970s. Keeping the arcaded façade, the Palais has been restored to its former glory. It reopened in 2004 as a plush four-star hotel and casino (see p827).

Enjoy a stroll along **Quai des États-Unis**, the promenade leading east to Vieux Nice that honours the 1917 decision by President Wilson for the USA to enter WWI; a colossal **memorial** commemorating the 4000 people from Nice who died during the war is carved in the rock at the eastern end of the quay.

Other pleasant walking spots are **Jardin Albert 1er**, laid out in the late 19th century; **Espace Masséna**, a public square enlivened by fountains; **place Masséna**, with early-19th-century, neoclassical arcaded buildings in shades of ochre and red; **av Jean Médecin**, Nice's main commercial street; and **Cimiez**, the most exclusive quarter in Nice, just north of the city.

INLINE SKATING

Promenade des Anglais is *the* place to skate. **Roller Station** (☎ 04 93 62 99 05; 49 quai des États-Unis) rents skates and protective kneepads for €7 a day and bikes for €15 a day. A piece of identification is required as a deposit.

WATER SPORTS

If you don't like the feel of sand in your bathing suit, Nice's **beaches** are for you: they are covered with smooth, round pebbles. Free sections of beach alternate with 15 **plages concédées** (private beaches), for which you have to pay by renting a chair (around €11 a day) or mattress (around €9).

On the beach you can hire a catamaran, paddleboats, sailboards and jet skis, go parascending and water-skiing, or give paragliding a go.

There are outdoor showers on every beach, and indoor showers and toilets opposite 50 promenade des Anglais.

Dive companies **PH+ Plongée** (☎ 04 93 26 09 03; 3 quai des Deux Emmanuel) and **Nice Diving** (☎ 04 93 89 42 44; www.nicediving.com; 14 quai des Docks) offer courses, organise diving expeditions and rent equipment. An introductory dive costs around €33 with equipment.

Tours

The tourist office organises **guided walking tours** (€12; 9.30am Sat May-Oct) of Vieux Nice in English, starting at the tourist office annexe on promenade de Anglais.

See Nice aboard the buses of **Le Grand Tour** (☎ 04 92 29 17 00; adult/student/child €17/13/9; 1½hr) A headphone commentary in several languages is provided. Tours depart from the Jardin Albert 1er on the Promenade Anglais.

Trans Côte d'Azur (☎ 04 92 00 42 30; quai Lunel) organises glass-bottom boat trips around the Baie des Anges (adult/child €11/6) and runs cruises to the Îles de Lérins (€23; see p840), and transfers to St-Tropez (€42) and Monaco (€20).

EASY RIDERS

If walking the promenade des Anglais seems unthinkably hard work and skating its length seems a tad *passé* then climb aboard a Segway personal transporter (electronic, two-wheeled gyroscopic chariots) with **City Segway Tours** (☎ 01 56 58 10 54; www.citysegwaytours.com; 16 rue de la Buffa; €45). The three-hour tours, operating from March to November, take you effortlessly (but very conspicuously) along the seafront and into the old town. Day tours include shopping for a picnic on the cours Saleya, which you eat in the lovely gardens of the Château above town. Night tours include a whiz around Vieux Nice. It takes two minutes to master the controls (movement is controlled using your balance). It's a fun, if slightly silly, way to see the city.

Tours start in front of the Palais de la Méditerranée, but you have to book in advance online.

Festivals & Events

The colourful **Carnaval de Nice** (www.nicecarna val.com), held every spring around Mardi Gras (Shrove Tuesday), fills the streets with flower-bedecked floats and musicians.

The week-long **Nice Jazz Festival** (www.nice jazzfest.com) sets the town jiving in July, taking up the entire Arènes de Cimiez, Roman ruins and all. The music starts around 7pm and there can be up to 15 bands playing at three or four venues around the park throughout the evening. The programming is largely pop, rock and world with few jazz artists. Big-name performers in the past have included Peter Gabriel, Bryan Ferry, BB King, Dee Dee Bridgewater, Air, Cheb Mami and Dr John.

Sleeping

Nice has a surfeit of reasonably priced places to stay, particularly in the city centre and around the main railway station. Accommodation is scarcer in and around the old town but plentiful (and pricier) close to and on the seafront.

The tourist offices have information on Logis de France hotels, and Gîtes de France if you want a rural experience in the region.

BUDGET

Hostels

Hôtel Belle Meunière (☎ 04 93 88 66 15; fax 04 93 82 51 76; 21 av Durante; dm with shower & toilet under 26 yrs €15, d with shower/shower & toilet €47/51) A great and central option. The large four-bed dorm rooms are posh, panelled affairs and the place touts a great tree-studded garden to lounge in. Rates include breakfast.

Villa St Exupéry (☎ 04 93 84 42 83; www.villa saintexupery.com; 22 av Gravier; dm/s/d from €18/28/44; P 🖥) A fair trek out of town, this hostel in a lovely old former monastery with large grounds and gardens has been recommended by a number of readers. There's no curfew, a very friendly vibe and free Internet access, breakfast and station shuttle. It's also something of a party spot, so noise can be a problem. There are some new and wonderful private rooms, although some of the dorms, sharing too few bathrooms, are less appealing. From the town centre take bus No 1 or 2 along av Jean Médecin and get off at the Gravier stop.

Backpackers Chez Patrick (☎ 04 93 80 30 72; chezpatrick@voila.fr; 32 rue Pertinax; dm €18-21, r with 2 or 3 beds per person €20-25) A popular 24-bed spot. There's no curfew and Patrick, who runs the place, can direct party-mad backpackers to the hot spot of the moment.

Auberge de Jeunesse (☎ 04 93 89 23 64; fax 04 92 04 03 10; route Forestière de Mont Alban; dm incl breakfast €14; 🕒 curfew midnight) This is 4km east of Gare Nice Ville. Rooms are locked from noon to 5pm. Take bus No 14 (last one at 8.20pm) from the Station Centrale bus terminal on square Général Leclerc, which is linked to Gare Nice Ville by bus Nos 15 and 17, and get off at L'Auberge stop.

Hotels – Train Station Area

The quickest way to get to all these hotels is to walk straight down the steps opposite Gare Nice Ville onto av Durante.

Hôtel Les Orangers (☎ 04 93 87 51 41; fax 04 93 82 57 82; 10bis av Durante; dm in 6-bed r €16, s/d with shower €25/40) Occupying a turn-of-the-20th-century townhouse, Les Orangers is recommended for its large-windowed, sunlit rooms, although this scruffy old place could do with a refit. Rooms come with a fridge (and hotplate on request).

Rue d'Alsace-Lorraine is dotted with more upmarket two-star hotels: one of the cheapest is **Hôtel du Piemont** (☎ 04 93 88 25 15; hotel-du-piemont@wanadoo.fr; 19 rue d'Alsace-Lorraine; s/d with washbasin from €19/22, with shower from €22/27, with shower & toilet from €32/34).

Hotels – City Centre

Le Petit Louvre (☎ 04 93 80 15 54; petitlouvr@wanadoo .fr; 10 rue Emma Tiranty; s/d/tr with shower €37/43/57, s/d with shower & toilet €40/49; P) Midway between the sea and the station, this colourful place is run by friendly proprietors. A faceless *Mona Lisa* greets guests as they enter, and corridors are adorned with an eclectic bunch of paintings. There's no air-con but there are fans. Cheap parking is available locally for guests.

MID-RANGE

Near Gare Nice Ville there are several two- and three-star hotels on rue d'Angleterre, rue d'Alsace-Lorraine, rue de Suisse, rue de Russie and av Durante.

Villa Eden (☎ 04 93 86 53 70; hotelvilllaeden@caramail .com; 99bis promenade des Anglais; s/d/tr €50/75/90; P 🐾) Across the street from the beach and a good option for those who want to devote their stay to sunbathing. Some of the comfortable, old-fashioned rooms have terraces facing the sea.

Hôtel Claire Meublé (☎ 04 93 87 87 61; hotel _clair_meuble@hotmail.com; 6 rue d'Italie; 2-/3-/4-/5-person studio €42/50/64/70) A spotless place with compact, fully equipped studios well suited for self-catering families and couples.

Hôtel L'Oasis (☎ 04 93 88 12 29; www.hoteloasis -nice.com; 23 rue Gounod; s/d from 43/84; P ☒ ☒) An attractive period house where the playwright Chekhov wrote *The Three Sisters*. In a quiet close not far from the sea, the Oasis has a verdant, shady garden, appealing rooms and parking (€8).

Hôtel Cronstadt (☎ 04 93 82 00 30; www.hotelcron stadt.com; 3 rue Cronstadt; s €60-70, d €65-75). Near the sea and a welcoming, homely place. Rooms are quiet and graceful. The rates include breakfast.

Hôtel Félix (☎ 04 93 88 67 73; www.hotel-felix.com; 41 rue Masséna; r high/low season €70/50; ☒ ☐) This has considerable appeal, with small brightly coloured rooms equipped with hairdryers, air-con and satellite TV. Some of the soundproofed rooms have balconies overlooking rue Masséna and the telephones have modem plugs.

Citadines (☎ 08 25 01 03 62; www.citadines.com; 3-5 blvd François Grosso; d studio/4-person apt €125/176; P ☒) Near the seafront and well equipped with modern fittings and full self-catering facilities in smart studios and slightly larger one-bedroom apartments (which also come with a double sofa bed), this makes a good standby, although the somewhat bland décor is typical of this relentlessly uniform chain of 'aparthotels'.

The following places in the centre of town are also recommended for value, comfort and cleanliness:

Hôtel du Centre (☎ 04 93 88 83 85; hotel-centre@ webstore.fr; 2 rue de Suisse; d hall shower €28.50, s/d with shower & toilet €50/59) An attractively renovated place with very neat rooms.

Hôtel Notre Dame (☎ 04 93 88 70 44; fax 04 93 82 20 38; 22 rue de Russie; s/d/q with shower & toilet €39/42/60) A basic but popular place (so book ahead) offering spacious rooms.

Hôtel Plaisance (☎ 04 93 85 11 90; hotelplaisance@ wanadoo.fr; 20 rue de Paris; s/d from €46/56; P ☒) With soundproofed rooms with TVs and modern bathrooms.

TOP END

Hôtel Beau Rivage (☎ 04 92 47 82 82; www.nicebeau rivage.com; 24 rue St-François de Paule; r €140-300; ☒) Out went the *belle époque* chintz Matisse would have known when he stayed here in 1916 and in came cool minimalism in the 2004 refit: all cream marble and chocolate suede sofas. Rooms are smart and restful, although on the small side given the price.

Hôtel Négresco (☎ 04 93 16 64 00; www.hotel -negresco-nice.com; 37 promenade des Anglais; r €225-780) Still in the *belle époque* style, the Negresco is the four-star *grande dame* of the seafront who, dare we say it, is starting to show her age next to her brash young luxury rivals nearby. This pink-domed, green-shuttered monument is still strong on service though. And anyway, where else will you be able to relax on your own Louis Quatorze chair as you contemplate the original and valuable art hanging in your room or peruse the

---

AUTHOR'S CHOICE

Hôtel Hi (☎ 04 97 07 26 26; www.hotel-hi-nice.cote.azur.fr; 3 av des Fleurs; r €175-500; ☒ ☒ ☐ ☒) Step inside this modern, hi-tech place and you could be forgiven for thinking you've somehow boarded an ultrastylish, candy-coloured, interstellar spaceship. Philippe Starck had a hand in designing the functional, modular panelling in ice-cream limes and purples, all built around a large, light atrium, forming the space-age canteen-cum-restaurant-cum-bar and dance floor. There's also a modish rooftop plunge pool overlooking town and the Alps. Rooms are similarly striking with bright panels of colour and modern entertainment systems. A rather glam clientele, such as fashion designer Jean Paul Gaultier or rock stars like the band REM, may teleport in to join you.

If your budget doesn't quite stretch to the Hi consider **Villa la Tour** (☎ 04 93 80 08 15; www .villa-la-tour.com; 4 rue de la Tour; r from €56; ☒), a great new place in Vieux Nice set up by a former manager at the Negresco Hotel, so good service and charm are a given. The well-equipped rooms are individually decorated with contemporary flair, there's a cute roof patio, a good breakfast (continental/buffet €3.50/7) and, best of all, you're just a stumble from the bars and *socca* joints of the old town.

menu of the Négresco's Michelin-starred, fine-dining restaurant, Chantecler?

Palais de la Mediterranée (☎ 04 92 14 77 00; www .lepalaisdelamediterranee.com; r €280-680; P ✕ 🔄 🔄 🕽) The Negresco's latest rival has been rebuilt from the ruins of the old casino. The utter luxury of the original 1920s house of art and gambling was revived with the 2004 reopening of a four-star hotel and casino. Rooms are huge and the sea views from the rooms, the café and the restaurant are spectacularly framed by the massive pillars of that Art Deco façade, which also serves to cut out the sight (and noise) of the traffic below. There is disabled access at the Palais.

Eating

You won't have any problems finding good, interesting food in all price ranges in the city. Many of the local specialities are served by inexpensive, bustling places in the Vieux Nice (such as Chez Rene, right) and seafood is always a good bet, but a there's a wide range of options including some highly regarded, fine-dining restaurants.

RESTAURANTS – VIEUX NICE

The cours Saleya and the narrow streets of Vieux Nice are lined with restaurants, cafés and pizzerias of varying quality. Local specialities to watch out for include *socca* (a thin layer of chickpea flour and olive oil batter fried on a griddle and served with pepper), *salade niçoise, ratatouille* and *farcis* (stuffed vegetables, especially stuffed zucchini flowers).

Nissa Socca (☎ 04 93 80 18 35; 5 rue Ste-Réparate; menu €13, dishes from €6; ✓ closed Sun & lunch Mon) This is a good place to try many of those local specialities. It's a perennial favourite with locals, and specialises in Niçois dishes.

Lou Pilha Leva (place Centrale; dishes from €3; ✓ 11am-10pm) It won't win any prizes for ambience (you eat on outdoor wooden tables under an awning) but the *pissaladiére* (thin crust topped with onions and anchovies or olives), *soupe au pistou* (soup of vegetables, noodles, beans, basil and garlic) and other Niçois specialities are prepared the way *maman* would. Order at the counter, grab your plate and a waiter will come around for your drink order.

Restaurant du Gésu (☎ 04 93 62 26 46; 1 place du Gésu; plat du jour & pizzas from €7; ✓ lunch & dinner Mon-Sat) An exuberant place decorated with foot-

ball pennants with a terrace in front of Église du Gésu St-Jacques le Majeur. The pizzas and pastas are exceptionally well prepared.

Escalinada (☎ 04 93 62 11 71; 22 rue Pairolière; menu €20; ✓ lunch & dinner) Enchanting (smiling staff, candlelit terrace), you can get a decent bottle of wine and good, unpretentious fare such as *daube* (stew) and rouget fillets. The house speciality is *testicules de mouton panés* (sheep's testicles in batter).

Le Merenda (4 rue de la Terrasse; starters from €9, mains around €16; ✓ lunch & dinner Mon-Fri) Tiny and annoying (no phone, no credit cards, no phone reservations, as the blackboard menu proudly announces) but if you can manage a reservation (in person), you won't be disappointed by the first-rate food, which is hearty regional comfort food served to a mostly mature clientele. House specialities include *pâtes au pistou* (pasta with pesto sauce), stockfish and a range of French/Provençal dishes.

Le Safari (☎ 04 93 80 18 44; 1 cours Saleya; mains from €14, menu €28; ✓ lunch & dinner) Far and away the best of the lot on buzzing, touristy cours Saleya. Avoiding the heaviness of cheaper Provençal food, this local favourite brings a lighter touch to specialities such as *farcis* and stockfish. Good seafood choices might include octopus salad and langoustine pasta.

RESTAURANTS – CITY CENTRE

The rue Masséna pedestrian mall and nearby streets and squares, including rue de France and place Magenta, are crammed with touristy outdoor cafés and restaurants. Unfortunately most of them don't offer particularly good value.

Zucca Magica (☎ 04 93 56 25 27; 4bis quai Papacino; lunch/dinner menus €18/22; ☺ lunch & dinner Tue-Sat) Near the old port and always packed with regulars, along with the riot of pumpkins, squashes and gourd memorabilia that crowd the diners. The décor may be bizarre but the food is down-to-earth, homely, vegetarian Italian. Course after course of cheesy, vegie delicacies make dining here a veritable cheese assault course for your tummy. Book ahead.

La Nissarda (☎ 04 93 85 26 29; 17 rue Gubernatis; lunch menus €12 & €17, dinner menu €24; ☺ Mon-Sat) Fresh, well-prepared Provençal specialities plus a hearty *bœuf bourguignon* in the small, welcoming dining room are what to expect.

Flo Nice (☎ 04 93 13 38 39; 4 rue Sacha Guitry; menus €30; ☺ noon-3pm & 7pm-midnight) Housed in a converted theatre in which the glassed-in kitchen occupies centre stage, this is part of the Parisian Brasserie Flo chain. Like its cousins to the north, the restaurant turns out flawlessly executed dishes with an emphasis on fish and plentiful seafood platters.

Le Comptoir (☎ 04 93 92 08 80; 20 rue St-François de Paule; menu €30; ☺ closed Sat & Sun lunch) A smart place close to the seashore. The restaurant is decked out in Art Deco style and has a terrace too. The food has Italian and French flavours, such as *gnocchi* with *daube*.

Chantecler (☎ 04 93 16 64 00; 37 promenade des Anglais) Last seen trying to win back one of its two prized Michelin stars in 2004, but still the place for a mind-blowing traditional French meal in a luxurious setting inside Hôtel Négresco (p826). Expect impeccable service, tantalising cuisine and a hefty €100 per-head (at least) bill.

RESTAURANTS – TRAIN STATION AREA

There's plenty of value-for-money fare in this area, but head south if you're after finer dining.

L'Allegria (☎ 04 93 87 42 00; rue d'Italie; menus from €11; ☺ Tue-Sat) Corsican chants and energetic guitar duets are on hand to help the food go down. If it's a chilly day, ask for a filling, large bowl of *soupe corse* (with vegetables and beans), one of Corsica's staple soups.

Restaurant au Soleil (☎ 04 93 88 77 74; 9 rue d'Italie; menu €12; ☺ lunch & dinner, closed Sat year-round, Nov & Dec) Next door to L'Allegria, un-

pretentious and very friendly. It offers good local cuisine at unbeatable prices, including an all-day omelette breakfast for €5.50.

Chez Mireille (☎ 04 93 85 27 23; cnr blvd Raimbaldi & rue Miron; paella €20; ☺ lunch & dinner Wed-Sun) Specialises in paella, paella and more paella.

CAFÉS

Le Pain Quotidien (cnr rue Louis Gassin & Cours Saleya; breakfast from €6, brunch €18; ☺ 7am-7pm) *The* place in town to have breakfast or to tackle the mother of all brunches. Choose your breakfast formula, enjoy the excellent hot chocolate and take in the colour and fragrance of the adjacent flower market from the terrace or from inside through the large windows.

Scotch Tea House (☎ 04 93 87 75 62; 4 av de Suède; dishes €7.50-15; ☺ 9am-8pm Mon-Sat) Home-made cakes and hearty tarts – just like grandma bakes – make this a good, old-fashioned afternoon tea kind of place.

Fenocchio (☎ 04 93 80 72 52; 2 place Rossetti; ☺ 9am-midnight Feb-Oct) The mecca of ice cream and sorbet in town, with 86 flavours made on the premises, including tomato-basil and prune for the truly adventurous.

SELF-CATERING

There's a fantastic **fruit & vegetable market** (cours Saleya; ☺ 7am-1pm Tue-Sun) in front of the Palais de Justice selling every type of fresh, dried and preserved produce and another, cheaper and less touristy one that begins on av Malaussena, north of Gare Nice Ville. It's open the same hours. There's also a fresh **fish market** (place St-François; ☺ 6am-1pm Tue-Sun).

There are supermarkets across town.

Casino Supermarket (27 blvd Gambetta; ☺ 8.30am-8pm Mon-Sat) On the western side of the city.

Monoprix Supermarket (33 av Jean Médecin; ☺ 8.30am-8.30pm Mon-Sat); Garibaldi branch (place Garibaldi; ☺ 8.30am-8pm Mon-Sat)

Drinking

Terraced cafés and bars, perfect for quaffing beers and sipping pastis, abound in Nice. Almost all nightlife is in Vieux Nice, which throbs with activity on summer nights. The most popular pubs in Nice are run by Anglophones, with happy hours and live music.

Chez Wayne's (☎ 04 93 13 46 99; 15 rue de la Préfecture; ☺ 3pm-midnight) The best known place for liquor-fuelled carousing, hosts a quiz nightly except Tuesday, a ladies' night on Wednesday, karaoke on Sunday and live bands nightly. It opens later at weekends. Happy 'hour' is until 9pm.

Two fun British/Irish boozer-type places include **O'Haras** (☎ 04 93 80 43 22; 22 rue Droite; ☿ 11am-late), good for a pint of Guinness and **Oxford** (☎ 04 93 92 24 54; 4 rue Mascoïnat; ☿ until 4am), which offers a wide range of English and Irish draught beers.

Nocy-Bé (rue de la Préfecture; ☿ 10am-late) is a cool, dark Moroccan-style tea house where you can sit low on cushions and sip refreshing mint teas. **Le Pain Quotidien** (opposite) is a great place a coffee as well as breakfast.

Entertainment

The tourist office has detailed information on Nice's abundant cultural activities, many of which are listed in its free publications, *Nice Rendezvous* and *Côte d'Azur en Fêtes*. More useful is the weekly *Semaine des Spectacles* (€0.80), available from newsstands on Wednesday. Tickets to events of all sorts can be purchased at **Fnac** (☎ 04 92 17 77 77; 24 av Jean Médecin), inside the Nice Étoile shopping mall.

CINEMA

Nice has two cinemas offering nondubbed films, many of them in English: **Cinéma Nouveau Mercury** (recorded message in French ☎ 04 93 55 32 31; 16 place Garibaldi) and **Cinéma Rialto** (☎ 04 93 88 08 41; 4 rue de Rivoli). Art films (usually in the original version with French subtitles) are screened at **Cinémathèque de Nice** (☎ 04 92 04 06 66; 3 esplanade Kennedy), which is at the Acropolis conference centre and concert hall, Tuesday to Sunday.

LIVE MUSIC

Opéra de Nice (☎ 04 92 17 40 40; 4-6 rue St-François de Paule; box office ☿ 10am-5pm Mon-Sat) Built in 1885 and recently renovated this grand old place hosts operas and orchestral concerts. Tickets for operas, concerts and ballets cost €6 to €64; the opera house is closed between mid-June and September.

Le Bar des Oiseaux (☎ 04 93 80 27 33; 5 rue St-Vincent; ☿ 7am-midnight Mon-Sat) Attracts an assortment of artistic types and nonconformists for a programme of music, theatre and philosophical discussion sessions. Jazz is the strong point. You'll pay around €5 for admission when there's live music.

Jonathan's (☎ 04 93 62 57 62; 1 rue de la Loge; ☿ 8-11.30pm) Another live music venue where

(country, boogie-woogie, Irish folk etc) play every night in summer.

NIGHTCLUBS

Happy Bar (☎ 04 97 07 26 26; www.hi-hotel.com; 3 av des Fleurs; DJs Tue, Fri & Sat till late) A way from the centre or the old town, this is an ultracool bar in the space-age Hôtel Hi with a dance floor and DJs playing house and other bleep-bleep stuff three nights a week. It's a fairly quiet bar the rest of the week.

Ghost (☎ 04 93 92 93 37; 3 rue Barillerie; ☿ 8pm-2.30am Mon-Sat) A fun and relaxed club with comfortable *banquettes* (seating) and soft lighting. DJs lean towards world, trip-hop and house music.

Blue Boy Enterprise (☎ 04 93 44 68 24; 9 rue Spinetta; ☿ from 11pm) A trendy gay nightclub that also welcomes a straight crowd.

Shopping

Cours Saleya is divided between a wonderful flower market in the western half and a diverse food market on the eastern end, including stalls devoted to dried produce, mushrooms and *fruits glacés* (glazed or candied fruits), a regional speciality. The figs, ginger, tangerine slices and pears have to be tasted to be believed. Both markets open at 6am Tuesday to Sunday. The food market wraps up at 1pm and the flower market is open to 5.30pm (1pm Sunday).

The best-value place for wine-tasting and buying is a traditional wine cellar, and a good one is **Les Grandes Caves Caprioglio** (☎ 04 93 85 66 57; 16 rue de la Préfecture) sells wines from all over France, ranging from cheap, local tooth enamel stripper by the flagon to pricey Bandol and Burgundy by the bottle.

À l'Olivier (☎ 04 93 13 44 97; 7 rue St-François de Paule) and **Moulin à Huile d'Olive Alziari** (14 rue St-François de Paule), close to each other, both sell olive oil and its many and varied spin-offs.

Designer names abound above the beautiful fashion boutiques languishing along rue Paradis, av de Suède, rue Alphonse Karr and rue du Maréchal Joffre.

Nice Étoile shopping mall (av Jean Médecin) covers a large block of the city.

Getting There & Away

AIR

Nice's international airport, **Aéroport International Nice-Côte d'Azur** (☎ 08 20 42 33 33), is about 6km west of the city centre.

There are two terminals connected by a complementary **shuttle bus** (☺ at least every 10min btwn 6am-11pm).

BMIBaby (www.bmibaby.com) and **easyJet** (www.easyjet.com) have services to Nice from various UK airports.

BOAT

The fastest and least expensive SNCM ferries from mainland France to Corsica depart from Nice (see p865).

The **SNCM office** (☎ 04 93 13 66 66; ferry terminal, quai du Commerce) issues tickets (otherwise try a travel agency in town). From av Jean Médecin take bus No 1 or 2 to the Port stop. You can also try **Corsica Ferries** (☎ 08 25 09 50 95; www.corsicaférries.com; quai Lunel).

BUS

Lines operated by some two dozen bus companies stop at the **intercity bus station** (☎ 04 93 85 61 81; 5 blvd Jean Jaurès). There's a busy information counter at the station.

There are slow but frequent services until about 7.30pm daily to Antibes (€4.20, 1¼ hours), Cannes (€5.90, 1½ hours), Grasse (€6.30, 1¼ hours), Menton (€5.10, 1¼ hours) and Monaco (€3.90 return, 45 minutes). Hourly buses run to Vence (€4.70, 50 minutes) and St-Paul de Vence (€4.30, one hour). To Castellane, the gateway to the Gorges du Verdon, there's one bus a day at 7.30am (€17.20, 1½ hours). Buses run to the ski resort of Isola 2000 to the north two times a day (€17.10, 2¼ hours).

For long-haul travel, **Intercars** (☎ 04 93 80 08 70), at the bus station, takes you to various European destinations; it sells Eurolines tickets for buses to London, Brussels and Amsterdam.

TRAIN

Nice's main train station, **Gare Nice Ville** (Gare Thiers; av Thiers) is 1.2km north of the beach.

There are fast and frequent services (up to 40 trains a day in each direction) to towns up and down the coast from St-Raphaël to Ventimiglia (across the Italian border): Antibes (€3.50, 25 minutes), Cannes (€5.20, 40 minutes), Menton (€3.90, 35 minutes), Monaco (€3, 20 minutes) and St-Raphaël (€9.20, 45 minutes).

There are two or three TGVs that link Nice with Paris' Gare de Lyon (€81, 5½ hours), via Lyon (€55.50, 4½ hours).

Lost luggage and other problems are handled by **SOS Voyageurs** (☎ 04 93 16 02 61; ☺ 9am-noon & 3-6pm Mon-Fri).

The ever-popular, two-car diesel trains operated by **Les Chemins de Fer de la Provence** (in Nice ☎ 04 97 0 3 80 80, in Digne-les-Bains ☎ 04 92 31 01 58) make the scenic trip four times daily from Nice's **Gare du Sud** (☎ 04 93 82 10 17; 4bis rue Alfred Binet) to Digne-les-Bains (€17.40, 3¼ hours).

An equally scenic train trip run by the SNCF goes from Nice to Tende (€10, 1¾ hours) and on to Cuneo in Italy, stopping at a number of mountain villages. During summer you can break your journey a few times and qualify for reductions at local attractions, although this needs careful planning as there are not many services each day.

Getting Around
TO/FROM THE AIRPORT

Sunbus route No 23 (€1.30), which runs to the airport every 20 or 30 minutes from about 6am to 8pm, can be picked up at Gare Nice Ville or on blvd Gambetta, rue de France or av de la Californie. ANT's route 99 shuttles every half hour direct between Gare Nice Ville and both airport terminals daily from 8am to 9pm.

From the intercity bus station, you can also take the **ANT airport bus** (☎ 04 92 29 88 88; €3.50), which bears the symbol of an aeroplane (every 20 minutes; 30 minutes on Sunday). Bus No 99 also makes the airport run from the Gare Nice Ville.

A taxi from the airport to the centre of Nice will cost €25 to €30, depending on the time of day and whether you're at Terminal 1 or 2.

BUS

Local buses, run by Sunbus, cost €1.30/16 for a single/14 rides. After you time-stamp your ticket, it's valid for one hour and can be used for one transfer or return. The Nice by Bus pass, valid for one/five/seven days, costs €4/12.95/16.75 and includes a return trip to the airport. You can buy single trips, 14-trip cards and a day card on the bus. The other passes are sold in *tabacs* and kiosks as well as at the **Sunbus information office** (☎ 04 93 13 53 13; 10 av Félix Faure).

Station Centrale, Sunbus' main hub, takes up three sides of square Général Leclerc and contains a kiosk where you can get further information.

Bus No 12 links Gare Nice Ville with promenade des Anglais and the beach. To get from Gare Nice Ville to Vieux Nice and the intercity bus station, take bus No 2, 5 or 17. At night, four Noctambuses run north, east and west from place Masséna every half-hour from 9.10pm.

CAR & MOTORCYCLE
If you just want to tool around in the countryside for a day, your best bet is **Easycar** (in London ☎ 44-0906 33 33 33 3; www.easycar.com), which rents out subcompacts from Nice for as little as €27 per day, including 100km. Cars must be reserved either on the website or through its London call centre.

In Nice, try the following places, which offer subcompacts for around €37 a day, including 100km.

Budget (☎ 04 97 03 35 03; 1bis av Gustave V) Aubert branch (38 av Aubert)

JML (☎ 04 93 16 07 00; fax 04 93 16 07 48; 34 av Aubert)

Rent a Car Système (☎ 04 93 88 69 69; fax 04 93 88 43 36; 38 av Aubert)

Nicea Location Rent (☎ 04 93 16 10 30; fax 04 93 87 76 36; 12 rue de Belgique) rents 50cc scooters for €49 a day, and 125cc motorcycles for €73 a day.

TAXI
Some taxi drivers in Nice can be dishonest. Make sure the driver is using the meter and applying the right rate, clearly outlined in a laminated card, which the driver is required to display. There are taxi stands right outside the Gare Nice Ville and on av Félix Faure close to place Masséna; otherwise you can order one on ☎ 04 93 13 78 78.

ANTIBES–JUAN-LES-PINS
pop 73,383
Directly across the Baie des Anges from Nice, Antibes, Cap d'Antibes and neighbouring Juan-les-Pins have a surprising range of attractions packed into a relatively small space at the base of a peninsula. Antibes is the quintessential Mediterranean town where narrow cobblestone streets, festooned with plants and flowers, branch out from a central, covered marketplace. It boasts a fine Picasso museum and an extensive yacht-packed port. Cap d'Antibes is a favourite hideaway for the migrating rich

who own luxurious walled mansions amid the dense pines. Juan-les-Pins is popular for its 2km-long stretch of sandy beach and its sizzling nightlife.

Antibes was first settled around the 4th century BC by Greeks from Marseille, who named it Antipolis. It was later taken over by the Romans and then by the Grimaldi family, who ruled it from 1384 to 1608. Because of its position on the border of France and Savoy, it was fortified in the 17th and 18th centuries, but these fortifications were torn down in 1894 to allow the town to expand. Antibes has appealed to many artists over the years, most notably Picasso, Max Ernst and Nicolas de Staël.

Orientation
The centre of Antibes is place du Général de Gaulle linked to Juan-les-Pins by blvd du Président Wilson and to Cap d'Antibes by blvd Albert 1er. Avenue Robert Soleau links Antibes train station with place du Général de Gaulle. The bus station is just a few steps away, linked by rue de la République.

Information
BOOKSHOPS
Antibes Books-Heidi's English Bookshop (☎ 04 93 34 74 11; 24 rue Aubernon; ⏰ 10am-7pm) Near cours Masséna, this shop stocks new and used English-language books.

INTERNET ACCESS
The Office (☎ 04 93 34 09 96; 8 blvd d'Aguillon; per min €0.10; ⏰ 9.30am-9pm)

MONEY
Eurochange (4 rue Georges Clemenceau, Antibes; ⏰ 9am-7pm Mon-Sat, 10am-1pm Sat)
Exchange Office (17 blvd Albert 1er, Antibes; ⏰ 9am-7pm Mon-Sat, 10am-1pm Sat)

POST
Main Post Office (place des Martyrs de la Résistance, Antibes)

TOURIST INFORMATION
Antibes Tourist Office (☎ 04 92 90 53 00; www.antibesjuanlespins.com; 11 place de Gaulle; ⏰ 9am-7pm daily Jul & Aug, 9am-12.30pm & 1.30-6pm Mon-Fri, 9am-noon & 2-6pm Sat Sep-Jun) In the town centre.
Juan-les-Pins Tourist Office (☎ 04 92 90 53 05; fax 04 92 90 55 13; 55 blvd Charles Guillaumont) Has similar hours to the Antibes office.

Sights & Activities

Housed in the evocative, 12th-century Château Grimaldi overlooking a terrific stretch of coast, **Musée Picasso** (☎ 04 92 90 54 20; adult/student €4.60/2.30; ☻ 10am-6pm Tue-Sun Jun-Sep, 10am-noon & 2-6pm Tue-Sun Oct-May) is undoubtedly Antibes' star museum. Picasso used the chateau as a studio for six months in 1946, where he would paint late into the night in a kind of trance, his work lit by powerful arc-lights. Today it houses an excellent collection of his paintings, lithographs, drawings and ceramics. The museum also contains works by other artists, including Léger, Miró, Ernst and Calder.

Other worthwhile sights include **Musée Peynet** (☎ 04 92 90 54 30; admission €3; ☻ 10am-6pm Tue-Sun Jun-Sep, 10am-noon & 2-6pm Oct-May) interesting for its exhibits of pictures, cartoons, sculptures and costumes by Antibes-born cartoonist Peynet and some good temporary exhibitions from other illustrators and cartoonists.

Antibes has one small, sandy beach, **Plage de la Gravette**, but the best **beaches** are located in Juan-les-Pins, including some free ones on blvd Littoral and blvd Charles Guillaumont.

Festivals & Events

Antibes' premier occasion is **Jazz à Juan** or the Festival de Jazz d'Antibes Juan-les-Pins, which takes place for a week in mid-July in La Pinède, the park next to the casino. The line-up is always first-rate, the acoustics are superb and the outdoor setting under the stars can't be beaten. Tickets can be reserved through the tourist office but it's usually possible to find something at the gate an hour before show time.

Sleeping & Eating

Accommodation is generally costly in Antibes or Juan-les-Pins.

Relais International de la Jeunesse (☎ 04 93 61 34 40; 60 blvd de la Garoupe; dm incl breakfast €14, sheets €3) Beautifully located in Cap d'Antibes. It's possible to pitch a tent on site for €8, not including breakfast. Take bus No 2A from the bus station to L'Antiquité stop.

Le Relais du Postillon (☎ 04 93 34 20 77; www .relaisdupostillon.com; 8 rue Championnet; r €44-82; mains €11-27) A friendly establishment in a sprawling 17th-century coach house. Each different room is beautifully decorated. The hotel runs a smart, good-quality restaurant

with an accent on fish, such as langoustine risotto or crab and scampi. Book ahead for accommodation.

Hotel Savoy (☎ 04 93 61 13 82; hotelsavoysarl@aol .com; 144 blvd du Président Wilson; s/d high season €65/90, low season €52/58) The cheapest you'll find in Juan-les-Pins and right at the centre of the action. Rooms are soundproofed, have TV and a telephone, but the décor is a bit drab.

L'Étoile (☎ 04 93 34 26 30; www.hoteletoile.com; 2 av Gambetta; s/d €52/58; P ☒) Less central but offering good value for soundproofed rooms with TV and minibar.

Le Brulot (☎ 04 93 34 11 76; rue Frederick Isnard; menus €13; ☻ closed Sun & lunch Mon) A good bet for pizzas, seafood, pasta and *socca*.

Rice Bar (☎ 04 93 34 12 84; 1 rue des Bains; menus €10, €13 & €15; ☻ lunch & dinner Tue-Sun) The place to go for vegetarians, as many of the rice-based dishes are vegetable-adorned.

Marché Provençal (cours Masséna; ☻ mornings daily Jun-Aug, Tue-Sun Sep-May) One of the region's most colourful markets and a delightful place to pick up supplies. If you've missed the market, rue Sade is another good hunting ground for picnic goodies.

Getting There & Away

Antibes is an easy day trip by bus from Nice (€4.20, 1¼ hours) or Cannes (€2.20, 30 minutes).

AROUND ANTIBES
Biot
pop 7489

This charming *village perché* (perched village) was once a vital pottery-manufacturing centre specialising in large earthenware oil and wine containers. Although metal containers brought an end to this industry, Biot is still active in the production of handicrafts. The village streets are a pleasant place for a stroll, but you will have to get there early to beat the hordes.

The attractive **place des Arcades** dates from the 13th and 14th centuries. At the foot of the village is a **glass factory** where you can watch glass-blowers at work.

You can pick up information at the **tourist office** (☎ 04 93 65 78 00; www.biot-coteazur.com in French; 46 rue St-Sébastien; ☻ 10am-7pm Mon-Fri Jul & Aug, 2.30-7pm Sat & Sun, 9am-noon & 2-6pm Mon-Fri, 2-6pm Sat & Sun rest of year).

Musée National Fernand Léger (☎ 04 92 91 50 30; www.musee-fernandleger.fr in French; chemin du Val de Pôme; adult/child €4/2.60; 🕑 10.30am-6pm Wed-Mon Jul-Sep, 10am-12.30pm & 2-5pm Wed-Mon Oct-Jun) is dedicated to the artist Fernand Léger (1881–1955) and contains 360 of his works, including paintings, mosaics, ceramics and stained-glass windows. A huge, colourful mosaic decorates the museum's façade.

Bus 10a runs (€1, 20 minutes, hourly) from Antibes station to Biot. For detailed information contact **Antibes bus station** (🕑 04 93 34 37 60).

Cagnes-sur-Mer
pop 44,207
Cagnes-sur-Mer is made up of Le Haut de Cagnes, the old hill town; Le Cros de Cagnes, the former fishing village by the beach; and Cagnes Ville, a rapidly-growing modern quarter. The old city is dominated by the 14th-century **Château Grimaldi** (☎ 04 92 02 47 30; place Grimaldi; adult/child €3/1.50, combined ticket with Musée Renoir €4.50; 🕑 10am-noon & 2-6pm Wed-Mon), which houses a museum of contemporary Mediterranean art and stages an annual international art festival.

Near Cagnes Ville is **Musée Renoir** (☎ 04 93 20 61 07; chemin des Collettes; adult/child €3/1.50; 🕑 10am-noon & 2-6pm Wed-Mon), the home and studio of Renoir from 1907 to 1919. It has retained its original décor and has several of the artist's works on display. The villa is set within a magnificent olive grove. Guided tours in English are available.

The **tourist office** (☎ 04 93 20 61 64; www.cagnes-tourisme.com in French; 6 blvd Maréchal Juin, Cagnes Ville; 🕑 9am-7pm Mon-Sat, 9am-noon & 3-7pm Sun Jul & Aug, 9am-noon & 2-7pm Mon-Sat Jun & Sep, 9am-noon & 2-6pm rest of year) is just off the A8.

TAM (🕑 04 93 85 61 81; www.rca.tm.fr in French) runs regular buses between Cagnes and Nice.

ST-PAUL DE VENCE
pop 2900
Once upon a time, St-Paul de Vence was a modest village on a hill overlooking the coast, about 10km north of Cagnes-sur-Mer. Fortified in the 16th century, it remained beautifully intact and began to attract artists such as the Russian painter Marc Chagall, who moved to the village in 1966. St-Paul was also a favourite hang-out of singer/actor Yves Montand, who met and married his wife, actress Simone Signoret, here.

The cobblestones of the narrow streets, have been polished smooth by the cease-less flow of visitors and it can all get a bit wearing in summer. St-Paul may be looking weary from its annual onslaught but there is a hard nugget of fine art underneath it all. Braque, Chagall, Dufy and Picasso often dined at La Colombe d'Or and paid for their meals with their creations. The restaurant now houses one of France's most fascinating private art collections. The village is crammed with galleries of wildly varying quality,

Perhaps the most compelling reason for coming to town is to visit the nearby Fondation Maeght, the former home of a fabulously wealthy art dealer, which hosts an exceptional collection of 20th-century works featuring Braque, Bonnard, Chagall, Matisse, Miró and Léger.

Orientation & Information
The village is defined by one main street, rue Grande, which leads up to the cemetery containing the tomb of Marc Chagall. The **tourist office** (☎ 04 93 32 86 95; artdevivre@wanadoo.fr; 2 rue Grande; 🕑 10am-7pm Jun-Sep, 10am-6pm Oct-May) is on the right as you enter the walled village. The post office is outside the walled village across from the bus stop. There is a currency exchange and an ATM.

Fondation Maeght
Inaugurated in 1964, **Fondation Maeght** (Maeght Foundation; ☎ 04 93 32 81 63; adult/student €11/9.50; 🕑 10am-7pm Jul-Sep, 10am-12.30pm & 2.30-6pm Oct-Jun) is the finest museum in the region. Its extraordinary collection of painting and sculpture is exhibited on a rotating basis, and there are several temporary exhibitions a year. In the gardens behind the museum, visitors can stroll through **Miró Labyrinth**, an outdoor sculpture garden studded with reflecting pools and mosaics by the Spanish surrealist, Joan Miró.

The museum is about 1km uphill from the bus stop outside the old village. If you're arriving by bus, it's best to see the museum in the morning when the walk uphill will be cooler and visit the village after lunch when the tour buses leave.

Eating
La Colombe d'Or (The Golden Dove; ☎ 04 93 32 77 78; mains €17-40; 🕑 lunch & dinner) This is a top-end choice and tables must be reserved long in advance. The lovely outdoor terrace has a

view over the hills but the art collection is indoors. No, you may not take a peek at the art collection unless you book a table or stay in one of the upstairs rooms (€360).

Un Coeur en Provence (☎ 04 93 32 87 81; light meals from €9; ☺ 10am-9pm Thu-Tue) Dedicated to poetry and simple, light dishes this is a laid-back tea salon. There are books stacked in a corner, occasional poetry readings, soft music and an array of fresh soup, salads, pancakes and tarts and several vegetarian options.

There's a **grocery store** immediately to your right after entering to the village and plenty of benches for picnicking along the ramparts.

Getting There & Away
St-Paul is served by the Nice–Vence bus service (€4.30, one hour from Nice).

VENCE
pop 17,184
This pleasant but unremarkable town, 4km north of St-Paul de Vence, is noted for the exceptional **Chapelle du Rosaire** (☎ 04 93 58 03 26; 468 av Henri Matisse; admission €2.50; ☺ 2-5.30pm Mon, Wed & Sat, 10-11.30am & 2-5.30pm Tue & Thu). In 1943 an ailing Matisse moved to Vence and fell under the care of his former nurse and model, Monique Bourgeois, who had since become a Dominican nun. She persuaded the artist to design the chapel for her community, and the result is this treasure. Matisse, who regarded this as both his masterpiece and a summation of his artistic career, designed the entire interior including the chapel's stone altar, candlesticks, cross and even the priests' vestments displayed in an adjoining hall. The real impact comes from the colour of those huge stained-glass windows. A bright morning is the best time to come for the full, light-flooded effect.

The chapel is 800m north of Vence on route de St-Jeannet (the D2210). From place du Grand Jardin, head east along av de la Résistance, then turn right along av Tuby. At the next junction, bear right along av de Provence, then left onto av Henri Matisse.

Vence is served by frequent buses from Nice (€4.70, 50 minutes).

CANNES
pop 68,214
It's the money of the affluent, spent with the nonchalance of those for whom it is no object, that continues to keep Cannes' expensive hotels, fancy restaurants and exorbitant boutiques in business, and its yachts as big as ocean liners afloat. But the harbour, the bay, the hill west of the port called Le Suquet, the beachside promenade, the beaches and the people sunning themselves provide more than enough natural beauty to make at least a day trip here worth the effort.

Cannes hosts many festivals, the most renowned being the 10-day International Film Festival in mid-May, which sees the city's population treble overnight.

The film festival excepted, culture is hardly Cannes' strong point. It has just one museum and, since its speciality is ethnography, the only art you are likely to come across is in the many galleries scattered around town.

Perhaps the best way to spend time here is to wander along blvd de la Croisette, then sit and watch Cannes' human circus pass by in all its expensively but strangely dressed, permatanned, face-lifted, small-yappy-type-dog-carrying glory.

Cannes comes to life on a sunny day at any time of year and the view of town from Corniche de l'Estérel, with its background of the snowcapped Alpes-Maritimes in late winter, is a magnificent sight.

One big disappointment is the public beaches, which are small, crowded and often with rather murky water. You'll have to head out of town to the west to find good ones like Plages du Midi and Pages de la Bocca.

Orientation
Don't expect to be struck down by glitz the minute you set foot in Cannes: sex shops and peep shows abound near the train station on rue Jean Jaurès. Things improve along rue d'Antibes, the main shopping street a couple of blocks south. Several blocks further south is the huge Palais des Festivals et des Congrès, east of the Vieux Port (old port).

Cannes' most famous promenade, the magnificent, hotel-lined blvd de la Croisette, begins at the Palais des Festivals and continues east along the Baie de Cannes to Pointe de la Croisette. Place Bernard Cornut Gentille, where the bus station to Nice is located, is on the northwestern corner of Vieux Port.

Information
BOOKSHOPS
Cannes English Bookshop (☎ 04 93 99 40 08; 11 rue Bivouac Napoléon) For English-language novels.

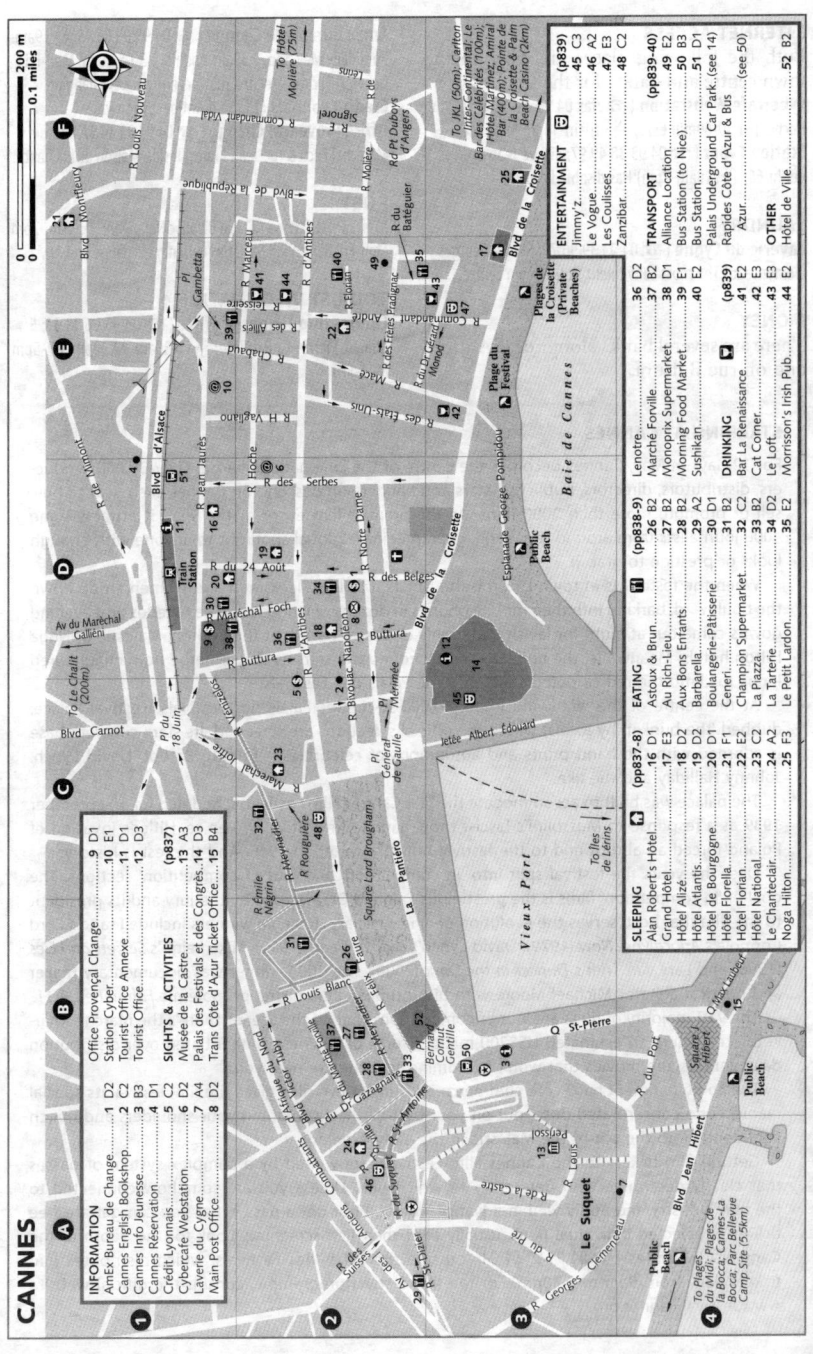

CANNES

INFORMATION	
AmEx Bureau de Change.............	1 D2
Office Provençal Change.............	9 D1
Cannes English Bookshop...........	2 C2
Station Cyber.............................	10 E1
Cannes Info Jeunesse.................	3 B3
Tourist Office Annexe.................	11 D1
Cannes Réservation....................	4 D1
Tourist Office............................	12 D3
Crédit Lyonnais..........................	5 C2	
Cybercafe Webstation................	6 D2	**SIGHTS & ACTIVITIES** (p837)
Laverie du Cygne.......................	7 A4	Musée de la Castre..................... 13 A3
Main Post Office........................	8 D2	Palais des Festivals et des Congrès.. 14 D3
	Trans Côte d'Azur Ticket Office.... 15 B4

SLEEPING 🛏	(pp837-8)
Alan Robert's Hôtel....................	16 D1
Grand Hôtel................................	17 E3
Hôtel Alizé.................................	18 D2
Hôtel Atlantis.............................	19 D2
Hôtel de Bourgogne....................	20 D1
Hôtel Florella.............................	21 F1
Hôtel Florian..............................	22 E2
La Piazza...................................	23 B2
Le Chanteclair............................	24 A2
Noga Hilton................................	25 E3

EATING 🍴	(pp838-9)
Astoux & Brun............................	16 D1
Aux Rich-Lieu.............................	17 E3
Aux Bons Enfants........................	18 D2
Barbarella..................................	19 D2
Boulangerie-Pâtisserie................	20 D1
Ceneri.......................................	21 F1
Champion Supermarket...............	22 E2
La Piazza...................................	23 B2
La Tarterie.................................	24 A2
Le Petit Lardon..........................	25 E3
Lenotre.....................................	26 B2
Marché Forville..........................	27 B2
Monoprix Supermarket................	28 D2
Morning Food Market..................	29 A2
Sushikan....................................	30 D1

DRINKING 🍷	(p839)
Bar La Renaissance.....................	31 B2
Cat Corner.................................	32 E2
Le Loft......................................	33 B2
Morrisson's Irish Pub..................	34 D2
	35 E2

ENTERTAINMENT 🎭	(p839)
Jimmy'z....................................	45 C3
Le Vogue...................................	46 A2
Les Coulisses.............................	47 E3
Zanzibar....................................	48 C2

TRANSPORT	(pp839-40)
Alliance Location........................	49 E2
Bus Station (to Nice)..................	50 B3
Bus Station................................	51 D1
Palais Underground Car Park.......	(see 14)
Rapides Côte d'Azur & Bus	
Azur...	(see 50)

OTHER	
Hôtel de Ville............................	52 B2

0 — 200 m
0 — 0.1 miles

CÔTE D'AZUR & MONACO

INTERNET ACCESS

Both the following places are close to the town centre and handy for the train station.

Cybercafé Webstation (☎ /fax 04 93 68 72 37; 26 rue Hoche; per 30/60min €3/6; ☻ 10am-11pm Mon-Sat)

Station Cyber (☎ 04 93 38 49 97; 32 rue Jean Jaurès; per hr €6; ☻ 10am-7pm) Has disabled access.

LAUNDRY

Laverie du Cygne (☎ 04 93 39 96 79; 58 rue Georges Clemenceau) The most convenient to the town centre.

MONEY

There are several banks along rue d'Antibes and on rue Buttura.

AmEx Bureau de Change (☎ 04 93 99 05 45; ☻ 9am-7pm daily May-Sep, 9.30am-noon & 1.30-5.30pm Mon-Fri Oct-Apr) For card-related matters and money changing.

Crédit Lyonnais (13 rue d'Antibes) In town.

Office Provençal Change (☎ 04 93 39 34 37; cnr rue Maréchal Foch & rue Jean Jaurès) Inside Maison de la Chance.

POST

Main Post Office (22 rue Bivouac Napoléon; ☻ 8am-7pm Mon-Fri, 8am-noon Sat). Has currency exchange and ATM.

TOURIST INFORMATION

Cannes Info Jeunesse office (☎ 04 93 06 31 31; 5 quai St-Pierre–La Pantiéro; ☻ 8.30am-12.30pm & 2-5pm Mon-Fri)

STARRING AT CANNES

For 12 days in May, Cannes becomes the centre of the cinematic universe. Over 30,000 producers, distributors, directors, publicists, stars and hangers-on descend on Cannes each year to buy, sell or promote more than 2000 films. As the premier film event of the year, it attracts some 4000 journalists from around the world, guaranteeing a global spotlight to anyone with enough looks or prestige to grab it.

When the festival is in town La Croisette bursts into life. Sleek men and women stride down the boulevard, barking into their mobile phones in dozens of languages. The tuxedos and evening gowns come out at night for lavish and highly exclusive parties at the Carlton, Majestic or Noga Hilton hotels. Meanwhile, the uninvited mass around the stars as they emerge from chauffeured limos to climb the red carpeted stairs into the Palais des Festivals.

At the centre of the whirlwind is the 60,000-sq-metres Palais des Festivals (Festival Palace; dubbed 'the bunker' by locals) where the official selections are screened. Its stark concrete base is adorned with the hand prints and autographs of celebrities – Brigitte Bardot, David Lynch, Johnny Halliday and the like.

The palace was built to accommodate the first Cannes Film Festival, scheduled for 1 September 1939 as a response to Mussolini's fascist propaganda film festival in Venice. Hitler's invasion of Poland forced an abrupt end to the festival but it restarted in 1946. And the rest is history.

Over the years the festival split into 'in competition' and 'out of competition' sections. The goal of 'in competition' films is the prestigious Palme d'Or, awarded by the jury and its president to the film that best 'serves the evolution of cinematic art'. Notable winners include Francis Ford Coppola's *Apocalypse Now* (1979), David Lynch's *Wild at Heart* (1990), Mike Leigh's *Secrets and Lies* (1996) and Lars van Trier's *Dancer in the Dark* (2000). The 2004 winner was documentary maker and political agitator Michael Moore with his anti-Bush administration polemic *Fahrenheit 9/11*.

The vast majority of films are 'out of competition'. Behind the scenes there's the Marché (marketplace), where an estimated US$200 million worth of business is negotiated over distribution deals for obscure movies that won't be coming to a theatre near you.

The combination of hard-core commerce and Tinseltown glitz gives the film festival its special magic. For a concentrated dose, put on your best clothes, straighten your shoulders and march confidently into the bar of the Majestic in the early evening.

Getting film tickets to the Cannes Film Festival is governed by a complex system of passes that clearly determine who gets entry to which film. Unless you are somehow connected to the film industry and apply well in advance, you will not get a pass. What you can get are free tickets to selected individual films, usually after their first screening. Look for the booth of the **Cannes Cinephiles** (☎ 04 93 99 04 04), outside the Palais des Festivals, which distributes film tickets daily from 9am to 5.30pm. For the film festival programme, consult the official website www.festival-cannes.org.

Tourist Office (☎ 04 92 99 84 22; www.cannes.com; ☯ 9am-8pm daily Jul & Aug, 9am-7pm Mon-Sat Sep-Jun) On the ground floor of the Palais des Festivals.

Tourist Office Annexe (☎ 04 93 99 19 77; ☯ 9am-7pm Mon-Sat) Next to the train station.

Musée de la Castre

Musée de la Castre (☎ 04 93 38 55 26; adult/concession €3/2; ☯ 10am-1pm & 3-7pm Tue-Sun Jun-Aug, 10am-1pm & 2-6pm Tue-Sun Apr, May & Sep, 10am-1pm & 2-5pm Wed-Mon Oct-Mar), housed in the chateau atop Le Suquet, has a diverse collection of Mediterranean and Middle Eastern antiquities, as well as objects of ethnographic interest from all over the world.

Beaches

Unlike Nice, Cannes is endowed with a beach of the sandy variety, most of which is sectioned off for guests of the fancy hotels lining blvd de la Croisette. Sun worshippers pay around €19 a day for the privilege of stretching out in a lounge chair and another €6 for a parasol. This arrangement leaves only a small strip of sand near the Palais des Festivals for the bathing pleasure of picnicking hoi polloi. Free public beaches, **Plages du Midi** and **Plages de la Bocca**, stretch for several kilometres westwards from the Vieux Port along blvd Jean Hibert and blvd du Midi.

Tours

Cannes makes a good base for boat trips up and down the coast. **Trans Côte d'Azur** (☎ 04 92 98 71 30; www.trans-cote-azur.com; quai St-Pierre) runs boats to St-Tropez or Monaco (adult/child €31/16 return), Île de Porquerolles (€46/21) and San Remo (Italy; €41/19.50).

Sleeping

Hotel prices in Cannes fluctuate wildly according to the season. Prices given are for the high season in July and August; rooms can be 50% cheaper in the low season. Don't even consider staying in Cannes during the May film festival unless you've booked months in advance. Most upmarket places only accept 12-day bookings during this time.

If you still want to try, get in touch with **Cannes Réservation** (☎ 08 26 00 06 06; www.cannes-reservation.com; 8 blvd d'Alsace; ☯ 7am-7pm Mon-Sat).

BUDGET

Le Chalit (☎ 04 93 99 22 11; www.le-chalit.com; 27 av du Maréchal Galliéni; dm Apr-Sep €20, Oct-Mar €18, film

festival €25-30, sheets €3; reception ☯ 8.30am-1pm & 5-8.30pm) Around 300m northwest of the station, this is a very pleasant private hostel. There is one kitchen with a food and drinks machine. There is no curfew. From July to September reservations are only accepted if you book three or more nights.

Hôtel Florella (☎ 04 93 38 48 11; fax 04 93 99 22 15; 55 blvd de la République; s/d with washbasin €40/45, with shower & toilet €60/64) A bit tatty but friendly, homely and good value.

Le Chanteclair (☎ /fax 04 93 39 68 88; 12 rue Forville; s/d with washbasin €33/36, with shower & toilet €40/42) This is a well-run hotel with functional whitewashed rooms in the colourful Le Suquet area, so it is close to many of the restaurants and the harbour.

Hôtel de Bourgogne (☎ 04 93 38 36 73; www.hotel-de-bourgogne.com; 11 rue du 24 Août; s/d with washbasin €33/40, d with shower/shower & toilet €55/65) The Bourgogne is a calm, orderly establishment with large, old-fashioned but rather dimly lit rooms.

Hôtel National (☎ 04 93 39 91 92; fax 04 92 98 44 06; 8 rue Maréchal Joffre; s/d 45/60; ☒) A friendly, well-kept establishment. The well-equipped, newly furnished rooms are soundproofed, have TVs and hairdryers. Reserve and try to get a room overlooking the courtyard.

Camping

Parc Bellevue (☎ 04 93 47 28 97; fax 04 93 48 66 25; 67 av Maurice Chevalier, Cannes-La Bocca; camping for 2 adults, tent & car €20; ☯ Apr-Sep) About 5.5km west of the centre. The No 9 bus from the bus station on place Bernard Cornut Gentille stops 400m away.

MID-RANGE

Hôtel Florian (☎ 04 93 39 24 82; fax 04 92 99 18 30; 31 rue Commandant André; s/d €62/72; ☒) Central, neat and modern. All rooms have private baths, TVs, telephones and hairdryers.

Hôtel Atlantis (☎ 04 93 39 18 72; www.cannes-hotel-atlantis.com; 4 rue de 24 Août; s/d with TV & minibar Jul & Aug €58/80, low season €42/50; ☒ ▢) This hotel has cheerful rooms with hairdryers, TVs and telephones. There's a spa and sauna for guests, plus cheaper use of a private beach (€7).

Alan Robert's Hôtel (☎ 04 93 38 05 07; www.cannes-hotels.com; 16 rue Jean Jaurès; s/d €54/65; ☒) Inside a handsome, classical building opposite the train station, you'll find large-ish, soundproofed rooms all with satellite TV and telephones.

Hôtel Alizé (☎ 04 93 39 62 17; www.alizecannes.com; 29 rue Bivouac Napoléon; s/d €49/56; 🕱 🖳) The rooms are not huge, you may recoil at the fake satin bedcovers and the early '90s décor but this remains a very central bet and, style aside, the rooms are well equipped (all have hairdryers, phones, satellite TV and a personal safe).

Hôtel Molière (☎ 04 93 38 16 16; www.hotel-moliere.com; 5 rue Molière; s/d from €79/97; 🕱) This is an immaculate, comfortable period place with a picture postcard garden and a pastel-pink, wedding-cake exterior. Some rooms have balconies.

TOP END

During the film festival, Cannes' stratospherically expensive hotels are abuzz with the frantic comings-and-goings of journalists, paparazzi and stars. All of the top-end hotels are along blvd de la Croisette.

Grand Hôtel (☎ 04 93 38 15 45; www.grand-hotel-cannes.com; 45 blvd de la Croisette; s/d high season €168/198, low season €100/122) The Grand has an appealing if perhaps somewhat 1960s ambience and, compared to its neighbours on La Croisette, offers affordable luxury.

Hôtel Martinez (☎ 04 92 98 73 00; www.hotel-martinez.com; 73 blvd de la Croisette; r high season from €490, low season €260) Arguably the loveliest luxury place in town is an ultrasmart Art Deco–styled place with huge, fabulous rooms and a posh Givenchy Spa (treatments €40 to €160).

Other luxury places along la Croisette:

Carlton Inter-Continental (☎ 04 93 06 40 06; www.intercontinental.com; 58 blvd de la Croisette)

Noga Hilton (☎ 04 92 99 70 00; www.cannes.hilton.com; 50 blvd de la Croisette)

Eating

Rue du Marché Forville is the area for the few less expensive restaurants. There are lots of little, though not necessarily cheap, restaurants along rue St-Antoine and rue du Suquet.

Barbarella (☎ 04 92 99 17 33; 14-16 rue St-Dizier; dishes €10-18; 🕑 7pm-1am) An eye-catching, gay-friendly establishment.

Le petit Lardon (☎ 04 93 39 06 28; 3 rue du Batéguier; menus €21; 🕑 lunch & dinner Tue-Sat) This place is small, intimate, friendly and reliable for reasonably priced local fare, such as *soupe de poisson* (fish soup) and *anchoiade* (anchovies, garlic and olive oil paste).

Astoux & Brun (☎ 04 93 39 21 87; 21 rue Félix Faure; menu €28; 🕑 10am-1am) *The* place for seafood.

Every type and size of oyster is available by the dozen here, as well as elaborate fish platters, scallops and mussels stuffed with garlic and parsley. In summer chefs draw the crowds by preparing the shellfish out front.

Aux Bons Enfants (80 rue Meynadier; menu €17; 🕑 closed Sun & dinner Sat low season) Another, popular choice, offers regional dishes like *aïoli garni* (garlic mayonnaise with a platter of fresh vegies) and *mesclun* (a rather bitter salad of dandelion greens and other greenery) in a convivial atmosphere. It's also strong on fish. Credit cards are not accepted.

There are several other small restaurants at this end of rue Meynadier.

La Piazza (☎ 04 92 98 60 80; 9 place Bernard Cornut Gentille; mains €12, menu €19; 🕑 lunch & dinner) A sprawling, friendly establishment that offers the best home-made pasta, risotto and pizza in town.

Au Rich-Lieu (☎ 04 93 39 98 75; 66 rue Meynadier; meals €15/20/24; 🕑 lunch & dinner) If you love mussels you get unlimited quantities here (with fries) for only €9.20. Fish dishes and pizza are also available.

Sushikan (☎ 04 93 39 86 13; 5 rue Florian; dishes €2.50-4.50; 🕑 lunch & dinner) This place is a smart sushi-on-a-conveyor-belt place that also does takeaways.

CAFÉS

Coffeehouses, cafés and *salons de thé* abound in upmarket Cannes.

Lenotre (☎ 04 92 92 56 00; 63 rue d'Antibes; breakfast around €7, lunch around €12; 🕑 8am-4.30pm) With a serene, classy dining room above the patisserie counter, the Lenotre is a great place to sip espresso, take breakfast or enjoy a light lunch of tarts and pastries among well-to-do ladies who lunch.

La Tarterie (☎ 04 93 39 67 43; 33 rue Bivouac Napoléon; 🕑 8.30am-4.30pm) The range of salads from €6 to €8 is good, but it's the house specialities – tarts and *clafoutis* (a kind of tart with fruit baked in a sweet batter) for €3 to €5 a slice – that bring in the crowds.

SELF-CATERING

The daily **food market** (place Gambetta; 🕑 closed Mon in winter) is one of Cannes' main markets. **Marché Forville** (rue du Marché Forville), a fruit and vegetable market two blocks north of place Bernard Cornut Gentille, is open every morning except Monday (when a flea market takes its place).

Square Lord Brougham, next to the Vieux Port, is a great place for a picnic – buy filled baguettes and other lunch-time snacks from **Boulangerie-Pâtisserie** (12 rue Maréchal Foch) or go upmarket at **Lenotre** (see opposite) nearby. Locals go to **Ceneri** (22 rue Meynadier) for its wondrous cheeses.

Large supermarkets:

Champion Supermarket (6 rue Meynadier).

Monoprix Supermarket (9 rue Maréchal Foch) Take the second entrance on the corner of rue Jean Jaurès and rue Buttura.

Drinking

Generally speaking the streets north of blvd de la Croisette between the Grand Hotel and the rue des États Unis offer the best night-time bar (and club) hopping potential. La Croisette is of course the best place for a posey coffee while you take in its strange parade.

Bar La Renaissance (☎ 04 93 38 38 20; cnr rue Teisseire & rue Marceau) Small and cosy Renaissance, overlooking the bustling place Gambetta market, is a very down-to-earth bar. Black-and-white photos of yesterday's stars line the walls – a pleasant contrast to the simple wooden tables and chairs.

Morrisson's Irish Pub (☎ 04 92 98 16 17; 10 rue Teisseire; ☺ 5pm-2am) is very Dublin, but French-style. Guinness flows freely weekend nights. There's live music on Wednesday, Thursday and Sunday and happy hour is between 5pm and 8pm.

Entertainment

Ask the tourist office for a copy of the free monthly *Le Mois à Cannes*, which lists what's on and where. Nondubbed films are screened from time to time at the cinemas along rue Félix Faure and rue d'Antibes.

NIGHTCLUBS & DISCOS

Cannes' nightlife becomes world class during the film festival. Autograph hunters and stalkers of the A-list can track down their stalkees at some classy places:

Amiral Bar (Hôtel Martinez; see opposite; ☺ 9am-2.30am) A swanky, upmarket place in the fabulous Hotel Martinez that enables you to rub shoulders with glamorous company, at a price.

Jimmy'z (☎ 04 92 98 78 00; Palais des Festivals, blvd de la Croisette; ☺ midnight-dawn daily Jun-Sep, Fri, Sat & Sun rest of year) The Cannes branch of the legendary Monaco club.

Le Bar des Célébrités (☎ 04 93 06 40 06; 58 blvd de la Croisette; ☺ 11am-at least 1am) At the Carlton Inter-Continental.

Le Loft (☎ 04 93 39 40 39; 13 rue du Dr Gérard; ☺ 10.30am-2.30am Mon-Sat) A more low-key place.

You may or may not see celebrities at the following places, but you'll certainly rub shoulders with local rich kids.

Cat Corner (☎ 04 93 39 31 31; 22 rue Macé; ☺ 11pm-5am) There's a sniffy door policy, so try to look fabulous. Inside you'll mingle with beautiful people from around the globe.

Les Coulisses (☎ 04 932 99 17 17; 29 rue Commandant André; ☺ 6pm-2.30am) A glam bar close to the seafront.

Le Vogue (☎ 04 93 39 99 18; 20 rue du Suquet; ☺ 7pm-2.30am Tue-Sat) Draws a young and trendy crowd up to Le Suquet.

Zanzibar (☎ 04 93 39 30 75; 85 rue Félix Faure; ☺ 6pm-4am) The oldest and most venerable gay bar on the coast. Pretty boys party to house music beneath erotically evocative ceiling frescoes.

Getting There & Away

BUS

The train is usually quicker and cheaper if you want to go up and down the coast, but for trips to the interior, you'll have to take a bus. Buses to Nice (€5.90, 1½ hours, every 20 minutes), Nice airport (€12.70 for the 40-minute trip via the autoroute, €2.20 for the 1½-hour trip via the regular road, hourly from 8am to 7pm) and other destinations leave from place Bernard Cornut Gentille, next to Hôtel de Ville in Cannes centre. Most are operated by **Rapides Côte d'Azur** (information office ☎ 04 93 39 11 39).

TRAIN

There's an **information desk** (rue Jean Jaurès) at the train station, but no left-luggage office.

Destinations within easy reach include St-Raphaël (€5.50, 20 minutes, two an hour), from where you can get buses to St-Tropez and Toulon. Other destinations include Nice (€5.20, 40 minutes, two per hour) and Marseille (€22.30, two hours).

Getting Around

BUS

Serving Cannes and destinations up to 7km away from town is **Bus Azur** (☎ 08 25 82 55 99, 04 93 45 20 08; place Bernard Cornut Gentille). Its office is in the same building as Rapides Côte d'Azur.

CÔTE D'AZUR & MONACO

Single/10 tickets cost €1.30/8.50. Bus No 8 runs along the coast from place Bernard Cornut Gentille to the port and Palm Beach Casino on Pointe de la Croisette.

CAR & MOTORCYCLE

Car-rental agency **JKL** (☎ 04 97 06 37 77; www.jkl -forrent.com; 59 Angle de la Croisette) offers cars fit for a star (if you absolutely, positively have to get noticed, how about a yellow Humvee for €1000 a day?). Even if you don't have a Hummer, street parking can be a nightmare in Cannes, but there are plenty of pay car parks, which charge at least €2 an hour. The easiest park to get to is the Palais underground car park right next to the tourist office. The easy-to-spot entry is off blvd de la Croisette.

Alliance Location (☎ 04 93 38 62 62; 19 rue des Frères Pradignac) rents motorcycles (from €53 a day) and scooters (€38), as well as mobile phones (€11 plus calls).

TAXI

Taxis (☎ 04 93 38 91 91, 04 93 49 59 20) can be ordered by phone.

ÎLES DE LÉRINS

Two islands make up the Lérins and they are just a 20-minute boat ride from Cannes. The tiny eucalyptus- and pine-covered **Île Ste-Marguerite** is 1km from the mainland. It's where the enigmatic Man in the Iron Mask – immortalised by Alexandre Dumas in his novel *Le Vicomte de Bragelonne* (The Viscount of Bragelonne) and in the more recent 1998 Hollywood release *The Man in the Iron Mask* – was held during the late 17th century.

The island, home to 20 families and measuring only 3.25km by 1km, is encircled and crisscrossed by trails and paths. **Musée de la Mer** (☎ 04 93 38 55 26; adult/child €3/2; museum & cells ❧ 10.30am-1.15pm & 2.15-5.45pm Wed-Mon Apr-Sep, to 4.45pm Wed-Mon Oct-Mar), in the Fort Royal, has interesting exhibits dealing with the fort's history and various ships that have been wrecked off the island's coast. The door to the left as you enter leads to the old state prisons, built under Louis XIV and the home in 1685 to Huguenots imprisoned for their refusal to renounce their Protestant faith. The inventor of the steam boat, Claude François Dorothée, is said to have come up with the idea while in prison here in 1773.

The smaller, forested **Île St-Honorat**, which is just 1.5km long and 400m wide, was once the site of a renowned and powerful monastery founded in the 5th century. Today it is home to Cistercian monks who own the island but welcome people to visit their monastery and seven small chapels dotted around the island.

Neither island has a fantastic beach; in some places, sunbathers lie on mounds of dried seaweed. Camping, cycling and smoking are forbidden on both islands. There are no hotels, *gîtes* or camping areas.

All boats leave from the same point on the quai des Îles (along from Quai Max Laubeuf) on the western side of the harbour. **Compagnie Maritime Cannoise** (CMC; ☎ 04 93 38 66 33) runs ferries to Île Ste-Marguerite (€9 return, 20 minutes), while **Compagnie Estérel Chanteclair** (☎ 04 93 39 11 82) operates boats to Île St-Honorat (€10 return, 20 minutes, almost hourly between 7.30am and 4pm).

Trans Côte d'Azur (see p837) charges €10 for trips to/from Ste-Marguerite. **Les Bateaux de St-Raphaël** (see p843) has daily excursions to the islands.

GRASSE

pop 44,790

For centuries Grasse, with its distinct red and orange tile roofs rising up the slopes of the pre-Alps, has been one of France's most important centres of perfume production, along with Paris and Montpellier. Perfume is a natural product of the highly prized flowers – lavender, jasmine, centifolia roses, mimosa, orange blossom and violets – you'll see growing profusely in the countryside.

Orientation & Information

While the town of Grasse and its suburbs sprawl over a wide area of hill and valley, the old city is a small area, densely packed into the hillside. The N85, better known as Route Napoléon, runs right through Grasse, where it becomes the town's main (and often very congested) thoroughfare, blvd du Jeu de Ballon.

The tourist office marked **Grasse Espace Accueil** (☎ 04 93 36 21 68; www.grasse-riviera.com; place de la Foux; ❧ 9am-7pm Mon-Sat, 9am-1pm & 2-6pm Sun Jul-Sep, 9am-12.30pm & 2-6pm Mon-Sat Oct-Jun) is close to the bus station.

In town, there's a tiny **tourist office** (☎ 04 93 36 66 66; 22 cours Honoré Cresp; ❧ 9am-7pm daily

Jul-Sep, 9am-12.30pm & 2-6pm Mon-Fri Oct-Jun) inside the Palais de Congrès.

Banks abound on blvd du Jeu de Ballon. You can also change money at the **Change du Casino** (☎ 04 93 36 48 48; Palais de Congrès).

Perfumeries

While more than 40 perfumeries exist in Grasse, only a few are open to the public, offering free visits to their showrooms and an introduction to the art of perfume making. During the tour you'll be taken through every stage of perfume production, from extraction and distillation to the work of the 'noses'. It's unlikely that you'll know any of the perfumeries by name, as the perfumes are sold only from their factories or by mail order. Naturally there is a boutique attached to each perfumery where you can buy the house scents in all their forms, from essences to talcum powder. The perfumes are bewitching and less expensive than store-bought fragrances, but the scent usually doesn't linger long.

Fragonard (☎ 04 93 36 44 65; 20 blvd Fragonard; 🕑 9am-6.30pm Jun-Sep, 9am-12.30pm & 2-6pm Oct-May) is the most convenient perfumery if you're on foot.

Galimard (☎ 04 93 09 20 00; 73 route de Cannes; 🕑 9am-6.30pm Jun-Sep, 9am-12.30pm & 2-6pm Oct-May) is not far from Fragonard's factory, about 3km out of town. Unless you have wheels, a visit is not a feasible option.

Close by is Galimard's **Studio des Fragrances** (☎ 04 93 09 20 00; 5 route de Pégomas), where you can create your own unique fragrance during a seminar under the guidance of a professional *nez* (€34, two hours).

Molinard (☎ 04 92 42 33 11, 04 93 36 01 62; 60 blvd Victor Hugo; 🕑 9am-6.30pm Mon-Sat Jul-Sep, 9am-12.30pm & 2-6pm Mon-Sat Oct-Jun) is a much ritzier affair, with 'create your own perfume' sessions (€40, 1¼ hours) that include a seminar about the history of perfume, after which participants walk away with a Molinard diploma.

Getting There & Away

There's a **ticket office** at the bus station (☎ 04 93 36 08 43; place de la Buanderie; 🕑 to 5.15pm). Several companies operate from here. **Rapides Côte d'Azur** (☎ 04 93 36 49 61) has buses to Nice (€6.30, 1¼ hours) via Cannes (€3.80, 45 minutes) every 30 minutes (hourly on Sunday).

MASSIF DE L'ESTÉREL

The most stunning natural feature of the entire Côte d'Azur (apart from the azure-blue sea) is the lump of red porphyry rock known as the Massif de l'Estérel. Covered by pine, oak and eucalyptus trees, this range is situated between St-Raphaël and Mandelieu-La Napoule, which is inland from Cannes.

A drive or walk along the Corniche de l'Estérel (also known as the Corniche d'Or and the N98), the coastal road that runs along the base of the range, is not to be missed as the views are spectacular. Along the way you will find many small summer resorts and inlets where you can swim. Some of the places worth visiting include **Le Dramont**, where the 36th US Division landed on 15 August 1944; **Agay**, a sheltered bay with an excellent beach; the resorts of **Le Trayas** and **Théoule-sur-Mer**; and **Mandelieu-La Napoule**, a pleasant resort with a large pleasure-boat harbour near a fabulously restored 14th-century castle. In summer when the Corniche de l'Estérel gets very crowded, choose the inland N7, which runs through the hills and feels like a whole different world.

There are all sorts of walks you can take in the Massif de l'Estérel, but for the more difficult trails you will need to come equipped with a good map, such as IGN's *Série Bleue* (1:25,000) No 3544ET. Many of the walks, such as those up to Pic de l'Ours (496m) and Pic du Cap Roux (452m), are signposted.

FRÉJUS & ST-RAPHAËL

pop 47,897 & pop 31,196

Fréjus, first settled by Massiliots (the Greeks who founded Marseille) and colonised by Julius Caesar around 49 BC as Forum Julii, is known for its Roman ruins. Once an important port, the town was sacked by various invaders, including the Saracens in the 10th century. Much of the town's commercial activity ceased after its harbour silted up in the 16th century. The ruins are often busy, but the lively town centre, with its rows of low, pastel buildings and shady plazas, is usually unclogged with tourists, leaving an appealing Provençal ambience.

At the foot of the Massif de l'Estérel is St-Raphaël, a beachside resort town southeast of Fréjus. St-Raphaël was one of the main landing bases of US and French troops in August 1944.

PROVENÇAL WINE AT A GLANCE

Long known for its rosé but little else, the region offers a wealth of great wines of all types and colours. There are more and more terrific little producers out there making excellent reds and whites. A good way to start planning tastings is with the free *Wine Routes of Provence* booklet and the excellent, unpretentious *100 Top Vineyards in Provence* (€10.50) by British resident and wine buff Ian Parkin, both available at the Maison des Vins Côtes de Provence (p847) and, if you're lucky, other tourist offices in the area.

Côtes de Provence

A large, geographically diverse appellation, with a variety of soils, altitudes and microclimates stretching roughly in the triangle between Aix-en-Provence, Toulon and St-Raphaël, means there's no such thing as a typical Côtes de Provence. Rosé makes up 75% of production.

Coteaux Varois

An island of vineyards around Brignoles (surrounded by Côtes de Provence vineyards), this appellation, which produces mostly rosé, is shaking off a reputation for mass-produced blandness. Quality is improving all the time.

Coteaux d'Aix

Half the wine made in this geographically broad appellation (stretching from Les Baux de Provence across to Aix-en-Provence and down to the salty Étang de Berre) is an usually fruity rosé but there are some well-regarded Bordeaux-style reds too.

There are a few smaller appellations well worth sampling including **Bandol** (especially for beefy, heavy, sometimes tanniny reds) **Cassis** (for delicate whites), **Muscat de Beaumes de Venise** (for sweet white) and **Bellet** (a tiny, obscure and expensive appellation better known for its whites and a good to name drop if you need to get the better of a sniffy *sommelier*).

Orientation

Although St-Raphaël is 2km from Fréjus, the suburbs of both have become so intertwined they seem almost to form a single town. Fréjus comprises the hillside Fréjus Ville, about 3km from the seafront, and Fréjus Plage, on the Golfe de Fréjus. The Roman remains are mostly in Fréjus Ville.

Information

MONEY
Banque National de Paris (BNP; rue Jean Jaurès) Just west of the Fréjus tourist office and there's an ATM.

POST
Fréjus Post Office (264 av Aristide Briand)
Post Office Branch (blvd de la Libération) Opposite the tourist office kiosk in Fréjus.
St-Raphaël Post Office (av Frédéric Mistral) East of the tourist office.

TOURIST INFORMATION
Fréjus Tourist Office (☎ 04 94 51 83 83; www.ville-frejus.fr in French; 325 rue Jean Jaurès; ꘖ 9am-noon &

2-6pm Mon-Sat year-round, plus 10am-noon & 2-6pm Sun Jul & Aug) Staff make hotel reservations and distribute an excellent map of Fréjus locating its archaeological treasures.
St-Raphaël Tourist Office (☎ 04 94 19 52 52; www.saint-raphael.com; rue Waldeck Rousseau; ꘖ 9am-7pm daily Jul & Aug, 9am-12.30pm & 2-6.30pm Mon-Sat Sep-Jun) Across the street from the train station.
Tourist Office Kiosk (☎ 04 94 51 48 42; ꘖ 10am-noon & 3-7pm daily Jun–mid-Sep) By the beach opposite 11 blvd de la Libération in Fréjus.

Roman Ruins

West of Fréjus' old city (past the Porte des Gaules) is the mostly rebuilt 1st- and 2nd-century **arènes** (amphitheatre; ☎ 04 94 51 34 31; rue Henri Vadon; ꘖ 10am-1pm & 2.30-6.30pm Mon-Sat Apr-Oct, 10am-noon & 1.30-5.30pm Mon-Fri, 9.30am-12.30pm & 1.30-5.30pm Sat Nov-Mar). The amphitheatre once seated an audience of 10,000 and is today used for rock concerts and bullfights.

At the southeastern end of rue des Moulins is **Porte d'Orée**, the only arcade of the thermal baths still standing. North of the old town are the remains of a **Roman theatre** (rue du Théâtre Romain; ☉ as for amphitheatre).

Le Groupe Épiscopal

On place Formigé, on the site of a Roman temple, is an episcopal ensemble, comprising an 11th- and 12th-century **cathedral** (☎ 04 94 51 26 30). One of the first Gothic buildings in the area, it retains certain Roman features. The carved wooden doors at the entrance were added during the Renaissance.

To the left of the cathedral is the octagonal 5th-century **baptistry**, with a Roman column on each of its eight corners. Stairs from the entrance porch lead up to the stunning 12th- and 13th-century **cloister**, which features some of the columns of the Roman temple and painted wooden ceilings from the 14th and 15th centuries. It looks onto a courtyard with a well-tended garden.

In the cathedral's cloister is the **Musée Archéologique** (Archaeological Museum; adult/student €3.80/2.50; ☉ 10am-1pm & 2.30-6.30pm Mon & Wed-Sat Apr-Oct, 10am-noon & 1.30-5.30pm Mon & Wed-Sat Nov-Mar), which has a marble statue of Hermes, a head of Jupiter, and a stunning 3rd-century mosaic depicting a leopard. Admission includes entry to the baptistry and cloister.

Activities

Fréjus Plage, lined with buildings from the 1950s, and St-Raphaël both have excellent sandy **beaches**.

St-Raphaël is a leading **diving** centre, thanks in part to the **WWII shipwrecks** off the coast. Most diving clubs in town organise dives to the wrecks, which range from a 42m-long US minesweeper to a landing craft destroyed by a rocket in 1944 during the Allied landings.

Plongée 83 (☎ 04 94 95 27 18; 29 av de la Gare, St-Raphaël) and **CIP** (☎ 04 94 52 34 99; Fréjus east port) organise night and day dives and courses for beginners.

Tours

Les Bateaux de St-Raphaël (☎ 04 94 95 17 46; fax 04 94 83 84 55; Gare Maritime, St-Raphaël) organises daily boat excursions from St-Raphaël to the Îles de Lérins (€16 return), and daily boats to St-Tropez and Port Grimaud (€13 return).

Sleeping & Eating

BUDGET

Auberge de Jeunesse Fréjus-St-Raphaël (☎ 04 94 53 18 75; fax 04 94 53 25 86; chemin du Counillier; dm incl break-

fast €14) Near Fréjus Ville, in a 7-hectare park. If you arrive by train, get off at St-Raphaël, take bus No 7 and walk up the hill. In July and August bus No 6 goes directly to the hostel. From Fréjus' train station or from place Paul Vernet, bus No 3 is the best option.

Hôtel Riviera (☎ 04 94 51 31 46; fax 04 94 17 18 34; 90 rue Grisolle, Fréjus; r with shower €32, with shower & toilet €34, with bath & toilet €36) A backpackers' hotel in the best sense of the word. The rambling old building and dark but neat rooms are kept in good shape by a friendly young couple who clearly enjoy their clientele. The hotel has a **restaurant** (main course & 0.25L wine €9).

Camping

Holiday Green (☎ 04 94 19 88 30; www.holiday-green .com; route de Bagnols, Fréjus; camping €30; ☉ Apr-end Sep) This is a four-star place and one of the best of the dozen or so camping grounds around Fréjus. It's 7km from the beach but has its own large pool.

MID-RANGE

L'Aréna (☎ 04 94 17 09 40; www.arena-hotel.com; 145 rue du Général de Gaulle, Fréjus; s €60-80, d €80-160; menus €35/45/55; P ⊠ ⌨ 🐾) The Arena is a simply delightful hotel with a flower-lined garden terrace, where you can eat wonderful breakfasts or lounge by the pool. The rooms are bright and summery, there's a decent **restaurant** serving refined and imaginative food and it's about 1km from the beaches. Highly recommended; with disabled access.

Hôtel L'Oasis (☎ 04 94 51 50 44; fax 04 94 53 01 04; www.hotel-oasis.net; impasse Jean-Baptiste Charcot, Fréjus Plage; r €38-65; ☉ mid-Feb–Oct; P ⊠) A 27-room place set amid pine trees, with comfortable rooms with TV. There is also disabled access.

Hôtel Le Flore (☎ 04 94 51 38 35; fax 04 94 55 59 89; 35 rue Grisolle; s/d €53/56) The Flore is a two-star hotel on a main street. A couple of the front rooms have balconies.

Getting There & Away

Bus No 5, run by **Forum Cars** (in Fréjus ☎ 04 94 95 16 71), links Fréjus train station and place Paul Vernet with St-Raphaël.

Fréjus and St-Raphaël are on the train line from Nice to Marseille. There's a frequent service (€9.20, 95 minutes) from Nice to **St-Raphaël-Valescure train station** (information office ☎ 08 92 35 35 35; 🕓 9.15am-1pm & 2.30-6pm), southeast of the centre.

ST-TROPEZ
pop 5542

A destination for the jet-set, the Eurotrashy and, in summer, too many visitors for comfort, St-Tropez has long since ceased to be the quiet, charming, isolated fishing village that attracted artists, writers and the glitterati here in the 20th century. The year things really changed for good was 1956 when *Et Dieu Créa la Femme* (And God Created Woman) starring Brigitte Bardot was shot here. Its stunning success brought about St-Tropez's rise to stardom – or destruction, depending on your point of view.

Attempts to keep St-Tropez small and exclusive have created at least one tangible result in the busiest summer months: you'll probably crawl into town behind huge traffic queues. Yachts, so out of proportion to the size of the old harbour that they block the view, chased away simple fishing boats a long time ago. And while painters and their easels jostle each other for space along the quay, in summer there's little of the intimate village air that artists (such as the pointillist Paul Signac) found so alluring.

But for all that it's still a place of interest and even, still, charm. Sitting in a café on place des Lices in late May, watching the locals engage in a game of *pétanque* (bowls) in the shade of the age-old plane trees, you could be in any little Provençal village (if you squint to ignore the exclusive boutiques and the expensive threads on display, that is).

St-Tropez is a fascinating place to watch the rich and famous at play, and a surprising proportion of the film, music and sporting A-list holiday here each summer. To get up close to them (apart from ogling them aboard their boats from the quayside cafés) it helps to be famous too – or rich at least. The clubs, restaurants, private beaches and hotels they patronise are seriously pricey and/or selective.

Orientation

St-Tropez lies at the end of a narrow peninsula on the southern side of the narrow Bay of St-Tropez, opposite the Massif des Maures. The old city, with its narrow streets, is packed between quai Jean Jaurès

(the main quay of Vieux Port), place des Lices (a lovely shady rectangular 'square' a few blocks inland) and a handsome 16th-century citadel overlooking the town from the northeast.

Information

Crédit Lyonnais (21 quai Suffren) At the port and there's an ATM.

Kreatik Café (☎ 04 94 97 40 61; 19 av Gal Lerclerc; 🕓 10am-1am) The best place to go online.

Laverie du Port (quai de l'Épi; 🕓 7am-10pm) Close to the town-facing edge of the car park near the port. A load will cost about €4.

Post Office (place Celli) One block from the port. There's also an exchange service.

Tourist Office (☎ 04 94 97 45 21; www.saint-tropez.st; quai Jean Jaurès; 🕓 9.30am-8.30pm Jul & Aug, 9.30am-12.30pm & 2-7pm Apr-Jun, Sep & Oct, 9.30am-12.30pm & 2-6pm Nov-Mar) It organises guided city tours (€6) every Thursday at 10.30am and distributes a wealth of informative brochures.

Sights

Musée de l'Annonciade (☎ 04 94 97 04 01; place Grammont, Vieux Port; adult/student €4.50/2.50; 🕓 10am-noon & 3-7pm Wed-Mon Jun-Sep, 10am-noon & 2-6pm Wed-Mon Oct-May, closed Nov), in a disused chapel, contains an impressive collection of modern art, including works by Matisse, Bonnard, Dufy, Derain and Rouault. Signac, who set up his home and studio in St-Tropez, is well represented.

If you're bored with watching the antics of the rich and (maybe not so) famous, **Citadelle de St Tropez** (☎ 04 94 97 59 43; adult/concession €4/2.50; 🕓 10am-12.30pm & 1.30-6.30pm Apr-Sep, 10am-12.30pm & 1.30-5.30pm Oct-Mar) is worth strolling to just for the views across the bay, a view you may share with the resident peacocks. Inside the citadel, which is just east of the town centre, there are displays recounting the town's maritime history and the Allied landings that took place here in 1944. The best photographs of St-Tropez can be taken from the citadel grounds.

Activities
BEACHES

About 4km southeast of the town is the start of a magnificent sandy beach, **Plage de Tahiti**, and its continuation, Plage de Pampelonne. It runs for about 9km between Cap du Pinet and the rocky Cap Camarat. To get there on foot, head out of town along av de la Résistance (south of place des Lices) to route de la Belle Isnarde and then route de Tahiti. Otherwise, the bus to Ramatuelle, a village south of St-Tropez, stops at various points along a road that runs about 1km inland from the beach.

The coastline east of Toulon, from Le Lavandou to the St-Tropez peninsula (including spots around the peninsula), is well endowed with *naturiste* (nudist) beaches. Naturism is also legal in some other places, mostly in secluded spots or along sheltered streams further inland.

On the southern side of Cap Camarat is a secluded nudist beach, **Plage de l'Escalet**. Several streams around here also attract bathers in the buff. To get there you can take the bus to Ramatuelle, but you'll have to walk or, if lucky, hitch the 4km southeast to the beach. Closer to St-Tropez is **La Moutte**, a *naturiste* beach 4.5km east of town – take route des Salins, which runs between two of the houses owned by BB (as Bardot is known in France).

WALKING

The **Sentier Littoral** (Coastal Path) goes all the way south from St-Tropez to the beach of Cavalaire along some 35km of splendid rocky outcrops and hidden bays. In parts, the setting is reminiscent of the tropics minus the coconut palms. If the distance is too great, you can walk as far as Ramatuelle and return on the bus.

If you can read French, invest in the pocket-sized *Promenez-vous à Pied – Le Golfe de St-Tropez*, which details 26 walks around St-Tropez; buy a copy from the **Librairie du Port** (11 rue des Commerçants).

Sleeping

BUDGET & MID-RANGE

Surprise, surprise! There's not a cheap hotel to be found in St-Tropez. However, to the southeast along Plage de Pampelonne there are plenty of multistar camping grounds.

Le Baron (☎ 04 94 97 06 57; fax 04 94 97 58 72; 23 rue de l'Aïoli; r €54-100; ❄) Well worth the cash, Le Baron is calm and quiet. Rooms – all with TV and bathrooms – overlook the citadel. Some have balconies. Book ahead.

Lou Cagnard (☎ 04 94 97 04 24; www.hotel-lou-cagnard.com; 18 av Paul Roussel; r €44-100; P ❄) A very pleasant option with attractive rooms containing TVs and telephones, and in a

traditional Provençal *mas* (farmhouse) surrounded by shrubs and plants.

Hôtel La Méditerranée (☎ 04 94 97 00 44; www .hotelmediterranee.org; 21 blvd Louis Blanc; r high/low season €150/50; ❄) The Méditerranée is an excellent place, as the DJs who play the local bars and clubs will confirm to since they stay here. This solid, period house has recently refurbished rooms, a cosy restaurant and courtyard garden and a proprietor who can tell you where to find all the St-Trop hot spots.

TOP END

St-Tropez' top-end hotels are mostly open from early April to mid-October.

Le Yaca (☎ 04 94 55 81 00; www.hotel-le-yaca.fr; 1 blvd d'Aumale; s/d high season from €300/380, low season from €250/300; P ❄ ❄) A former home of the writer Collette and a place where artists such as Signac and Hollywood legends including Clark Cable have stayed – and where bigwigs continue to stay. This is *the* hotel for unashamed, indulgent relaxation. Lounge by the pool or feed the peacocks *pain au chocolat* from your balcony window at dawn. All rooms are beautifully and individually decorated and the better rooms have splendid views over town and the bay. The concierge can get you into any club or restaurant in town, so be nice to him.

Eating

RESTAURANTS

Quai Jean Jaurès is lined with restaurants, most with mediocre *menus* from €17 to €26 and a strategic view of the silverware and crystal of those dining on the decks of their yachts.

La Table du Marché (☎ 04 94 97 85 20; 38 rue Georges Clemenceau; lunch or dinner formule €18, menu €25; ☯ lunch & dinner) A great and stylish place for savoury and sweet pastries in the café at the front (daytime only), for sushi upstairs (summer only) or excellent, simple and reasonably-priced brasserie-style food (like the house terrine with onion chutney, scallop raviolis in thyme butter or tomato and basil tart) at the back.

Le Petit Charron (☎ 04 94 97 73 78; 5 rue Charrons; dishes €16-23; ☯ dinner Tue-Sat) Off place des Lices, this restaurant serves a delicious Provençal menu.

Le Fregate (☎ 04 94 97 07 08; 52-54 rue Allard; menus €19-27; ☯ lunch & dinner Thu-Tue) The blue and white décor here heralds the excellent

CÔTE D'AZUR & MONACO

fish dishes. Try the *aïoli* at €15 if it's on the daily offerings.

Auberge des Maures (☎ 04 94 97 01 50; 8 rue du Docteur Boutin; menu €40; ☯ dinner only) Off rue Allard, this place is not far from the port. The food is good, rich and traditional (such as fresh barbequed fish, rice-stuffed squid and a tasty crème caramel). The portions are hearty. Book ahead.

Café Joseph (☎ 04 94 97 01 66; 1 place de l'Hôtel de Ville; dishes €22-42; ☯ lunch & dinner) The constant beat of house music accompanies reliably decent food (inventive pasta dishes, good beef tartare), served to a very wealthy, often fabulous, sometimes strange, crowd of loyal locals. It's a tad pricey for what you get and the service can be snooty but the people-watching here is strangely compelling.

CAFÉS

Several cafés with vast, open-air terraces line quai Jean Jaurès. You will spend *beaucoup* to nurse a drink and watch tourists watching you, but if you must, try **Sénéquier** or **Le Gorille**.

Le Café (☎ 04 94 97 44 69; place des Lices) St-Tropez' most historic café, Le Café was one of the former haunts of BB and her glam friends and foes. Formally called Le Café des Arts, it should not to be confused with the place of that name on the corner of place des Lices and av du Maréchal Foch.

SELF-CATERING

The **place des Lices market** is held on Tuesday and Saturday mornings. There's also a **market** on place aux Herbes behind quai Jean Jaurès, open until about noon daily.

La Tarte Tropézienne (36 rue Georges Clemenceau) is a good way to beat the high food prices of St-Tropez. Sandwiches are made from freshly baked bread and you can finish up with the local speciality, *tarte Tropézienne*, a sweet sandwich filled with custard.

There's also the **Prisunic Supermarket** (9 av du Général Leclerc; ☯ 8am-8pm Mon-Sat).

Entertainment

If you think the cafés in town are expensive, then arrange an overdraft for the clubs: €13 to €25 is standard for a drink and you'll be watched to make sure you drink. Even if money is not a problem, getting in may be, so try to look fabulous. It will also help if you can say your first name is Paris or Puff and

your second name is Hilton or Daddy. Your reward for convincing the door staff will likely be admittance to the strange world of massive affluence and celebrity. Most bars open from around 11pm to dawn.

Le Café de Paris (☎ 04 94 97 00 56; Quai Suffren) Smart, lively and good for late-night carousing if the clubs don't appeal to you (or you to them).

Cohiba Café (☎ 04 94 97 26 20; 23 rue du Portail Neuf) This is a cosy, low-key place away from the quayside brouhaha. Knock back a cocktail or chew on a cigar from the humidor.

There are four clubs in town to try, all of them *trés en vogue*. Broadly speaking **Papagayo** (☎ 04 94 54 82 89; Residence du Port) and the gay-friendly **L'Esquinade** (☎ 04 94 97 87 45; 2 rue du Four) are slightly less picky about who they let in (although during May Papagayo becomes the official nightclub of the Cannes Film Festival) than the ultraswanky **VIP Room** (☎ 04 94 97 14 70; Residence du Port) or **Les Caves du Roy** (☎ 04 94 97 16 02; av Foch), another A-list celeb haunt.

Getting There & Away

BOAT

In July and August **MMG** (in Ste-Maxime ☎ 04 94 96 51 00) operates a shuttle-boat service from St-Tropez to Ste-Maxime and Port Grimaud. Between April and October, **Transports Maritimes Raphaelois** (in St-Raphaël ☎ 04 94 95 17 46) runs two to six boats daily from St-Tropez to St-Raphaël (€10, 50 minutes).

A day trip by boat from Nice or Cannes can be a good way to avoid St-Tropez' notorious traffic jams and high hotel prices. Trans Côte d'Azur runs day trips from Nice (see p824) and Cannes (see p837) between Easter and September.

BUS

St-Tropez **bus station** (av Général de Gaulle) is on the southwestern edge of town on the main road. There's an **information office** (☎ 04 94 54 62 36; ☯ 8am-noon & 2-6pm Mon-Fri, 8am-noon Sat) at the station. Buses to Ramatuelle (€8.30, 1½ hours, five daily) leave from the here and run parallel to the coast about 1km inland. **Sodetrav** (in Hyères ☎ 04 94 12 55 12) has eight buses daily from St-Raphaël-Valescure train station to St-Tropez bus station, via Fréjus (€7.60, 1¼ hours). Eight daily buses from St-Tropez to Toulon go inland before joining the coast at Cavalaire; they also stop at Le Lavandou and Hyères.

CAR

If you go to St-Tropez by car be prepared for long delays, both getting in and out of town. Here is a tip to minimise the frustration of waiting: avoid the coastal roads. Instead approach from the Provençale Autoroute (the A8) and exit at Le Muy (exit 35). Take the D558 road across the Massif des Maures and via La Garde Freinet to Port Grimaud. Park your car (easily) here and take the regular shuttle boat that runs to St-Tropez from Easter to October. Exit the same way.

Getting Around

MAS (☎ /fax 04 94 97 00 60; 3-5 rue Joseph Quaranta) rents mountain bikes. There are several car-hire places lining av du Général Leclerc.

To order a taxi ring ☎ 04 94 97 05 27. To order a taxi boat call **Taxi de Mer** (☎ 06 09 53 15 47; 5 quartier Neuf).

THE VAR HINTERLAND

Inland from St-Tropez and Fréjus, the dark-green wooded hills, sleepy hilltop villages and vineyards of the Var hinterland (broadly speaking north of the A8 and south of the Gorges du Verdon) are well worth a day or two of exploration if you have your own car. It's a great area in which to sample Provençal wines and makes a welcome escape from the crowded summer coast.

Villages and attractions worth stopping for include **Cabasse**, a quiet, shady village near a large trout-filled lake; **Tourtour**, a pretty hilltop village with views over the area's forests; and **Cotignac** an enchanting, plane-tree shaded town sitting below a cliff face peppered with grottos. Pure, fountains gush clear around the attractive town square and there are a couple of decent restaurants including **Hôtel Restaurant du Cours** (☎ 04 94 04 78 50; 18 cours Gambetta; menus €21-28), which serves tasty Provençal food.

Well worth the visit also is **Abbaye du Thoronet** (☎ 04 94 60 43 90; adult/child €6.10/free; ☼ 10am-6pm Mon-Sat, 10am-noon & 2-6.30pm Sun Apr-Sep, 10am-1pm & 2-5pm Mon-Sat, 10am-noon & 2-5pm Sun Oct-Mar), a remote, partly restored Cistercian monastery near Le Thoronet. The guided tours are well worthwhile and your guide may sing beautiful plainsong. The acoustics are incredible.

The area is one of the best places in Provence to sample a good range of its wines and to get an overview of many different styles. At Les Arcs-sur-Argens, on the N7, the **Maison des Vins Côtes de Provence** (☎ 04 94 99 50 29; ☼ 10am-8pm daily Jul & Aug, 10am-1pm & 1.30-6pm Mon-Sat Oct-Apr) offers free wine tastings and explanations in English.

For free maps of the area and brochures offering other itinerary ideas ask at the Toulon (p850) and Fréjus (p842) tourist offices.

ST-TROPEZ TO TOULON
Massif des Maures

Stretching from Hyères to Fréjus, this arc-shaped massif is covered with pine, chestnut and cork oak trees. The vegetation makes it appear almost black and gives rise to its name, which comes from the Provençal word *mauro* (dark pine wood).

The Massif des Maures offers superb walking and cycling opportunities. There are four roads you can take through the hills, the northernmost being a ridge road, the 85km-long **route des Crêtes**, which runs close to La Sauvette (779m), the massif's highest peak. It continues east through the village of **La Garde Freinet**, a perfect getaway from the summer hordes. Within the massif are a number of places worth visiting.

If you like chestnuts, the place to go is **Collobrières**, a small town renowned for its chestnut purée and *marrons glacés* (candied chestnuts). If you like wine, the area is a good place to sniff out some excellent Provençal nectar.

There are some interesting cultural sites too, such as the partly restored Cistertian **Abbaye de Thoronet** and, east of Collobrières, the ruins of a 12th- to 13th-century monastery, called **La Chartreuse de la Verne**. Northeast of the monastery is the village of **Grimaud**, notable for its castle ruins, small Roman church, windmill and pretty streets.

The tourist office in St-Tropez distributes a map/guide called *Tours in the Gulf of St-Tropez – Pays des Maures*, which describes four driving, cycling or walking itineraries.

Le Lavandou
pop 5200

Once a fishing village, Le Lavandou, about 5km southeast of Bormes-les-Mimosas, has become a very popular destination, thanks mainly to its 12km-long sandy beach. Although the town itself may not have much to offer, it is a good base for exploring the nearby Massif des Maures, especially if you are interested in cycling. The resort is also close to the three idyllic Îles d'Hyères, which you can reach easily by boat.

For local information, Le Lavandou has a **tourist office** (☎ 04 94 00 40 50; www.lelavandou .com; quai Gabriel Péri; ☽ 9am-noon & 3-6pm, closed Sun low season).

Corniche des Maures

This 26km-long coastal road (part of the D559) stretches from Le Lavandou north-east to La Croix-Valmer. All along here you can enjoy breathtaking views. There are also lots of great beaches for swimming, sunbathing or windsurfing. Among the towns that the road passes through are Cavalaire, Pramousquier and Le Rayol.

Îles d'Hyères

The oldest and largest *naturiste* colony in the region is on Île du Levant, the easternmost of the three Hyères islands. Indeed, half of this 8km-long island is for naturists. Port-Cros is the smallest island and Porquerolles the largest.

PARC NATIONAL DE PORT-CROS

Created in 1963 to protect at least one small part of the Côte d'Azur from overdevelopment, Port-Cros is France's smallest national park, encompassing just 700 hectares of land – essentially the island of Port-Cros – as well as an 18-sq-km zone of water around it. The middle island of the Îles d'Hyères, Port-Cros is a marine reserve, but is also known for its rich variety of insects and butterflies. Keeping the water around it clean (compared with the rest of the coast) is one of the reserve's big challenges.

The park's **head office** (☎ 04 94 12 82 30; www .portcrosparcnational.fr in French; 50 rue St Claire, Hyères) is on the mainland. The island can be visited year-round, but walkers must stick to the marked paths. Fishing, camping and fires are not allowed.

GETTING THERE & AWAY

Boats to the Îles d'Hyères leave from various towns along the coast, including Le Lavandou and Hyères. **Vedettes Îles d'Or** (☎ 04 94 71 01 02; www.vedettesilesdor.fr in French), which has an office at the ferry terminal in Le Lavandou, operates boats to Île du Levant and Port Cros (adult/child return €22/17.50, 35

to 55 minutes). There is a supplement of €6.50 for visiting both islands. There are at least four boats a day in the warmer months (hourly in summer) but only four a week in winter. To Porquerolles there is a boat three times a week (daily in July and August) and the return adult/child fare is €27.70/21.30. Boats also sail from Hyères (one hour) in the high season.

Boats from Toulon run only from Easter to September (see p851).

TOULON

pop 166,442

Toulon is France's most important naval port: it's the base for the French navy's Mediterranean fleet. Partly as a result of heavy bombing in WWII, and partly due to the presence of dodgy bars and sex shops near the naval base, Toulon's run-down centre looks and feels grim (especially by night) compared to Nice, Cannes or even Marseille. Toulon is not a tourist magnet when pulsating Marseille, fine beaches and the tranquil Îles d'Hyères are so close, however a day trip is worthwhile.

Initially a Roman colony, Toulon only became part of France in 1481 – the city grew in importance after Henri IV founded an arsenal here. In the 17th century the port was enlarged by Vauban. The young Napoleon Bonaparte first made a name for himself in 1793 during a siege in which the English, who had taken over Toulon, were expelled.

By day the large, excellent market runs the length of Cours Lafayette. Perhaps the best way to see Toulon is from a distance, atop the giddying Mont Faron, where you will get a classic Côte d'Azur vista of cobalt sky, dazzling sea and pine-clad, resin-scented hills in one heady hit.

Orientation

Toulon is built around the *rade*, a sheltered bay lined with quays. To the west is the naval base and to the east the ferry terminal, from where boats set sail for Corsica. The city is at its liveliest along quai de la Sinse and quai Stalingrad (from where ferries depart for the Îles d'Hyères) and in the old city. The train station is northwest of the old city.

Separating the old city from the northern section is a multilane, multinamed thoroughfare (known as av du Maréchal Leclerc

TOULON

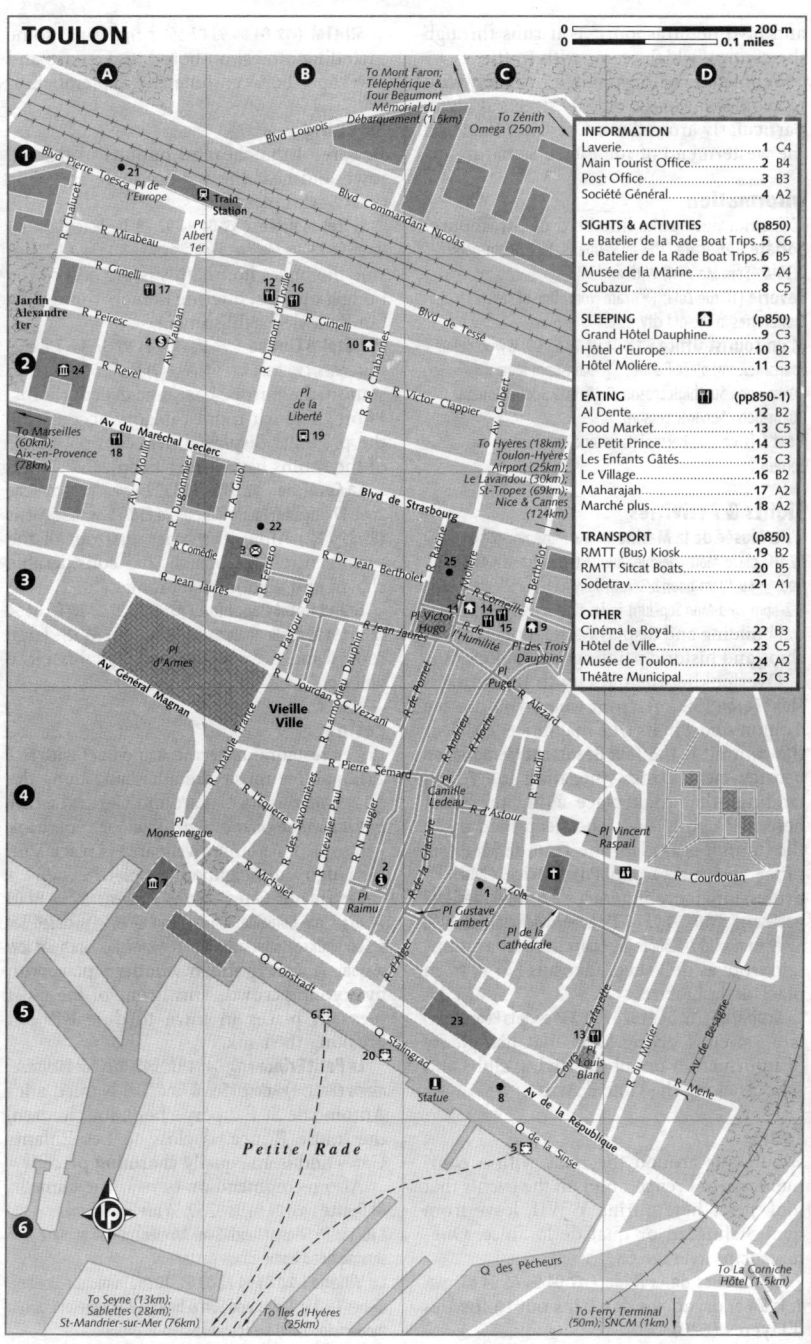

| 0 | 200 m |
| 0 | 0.1 miles |

INFORMATION
Laverie.....................................1 C4
Main Tourist Office....................2 B4
Post Office................................3 B3
Société Général.........................4 A2

SIGHTS & ACTIVITIES (p850)
Le Batelier de la Rade Boat Trips.5 C6
Le Batelier de la Rade Boat Trips.6 B5
Musée de la Marine....................7 A4
Scubazur...................................8 C5

SLEEPING (p850)
Grand Hôtel Dauphine................9 C3
Hôtel d'Europe.........................10 B2
Hôtel Molière...........................11 C3

EATING (pp850-1)
Al Dente..................................12 B2
Food Market............................13 C5
Le Petit Prince..........................14 C3
Les Enfants Gâtés.....................15 C3
Le Village.................................16 B2
Maharajah................................17 A2
Marché plus.............................18 A2

TRANSPORT (p850)
RMTT (Bus) Kiosk......................19 B2
RMTT Sitcat Boats....................20 B5
Sodetrav..................................21 A1

OTHER
Cinéma le Royal........................22 B3
Hôtel de Ville...........................23 C5
Musée de Toulon......................24 A2
Théâtre Municipal....................25 C3

CÔTE D'AZUR & MONACO

and blvd de Strasbourg as it runs through
the centre), which teems with traffic.

Women travelling on their own may wish
to avoid some of the old city streets at night,
particularly around rue Chevalier Paul and
the western end of rue Pierre Sémard.

Information

Commercial banks line blvd de Strasbourg.
Société Generale (1bis av Vauban; ☽ 8.30am-noon &
1.30-4.45pm Mon-Fri) With an ATM.
Laverie (10 rue Zola; ☽ 7am-9pm) One of several
laundrettes in the old city.
Main Tourist Office (☎ 04 94 18 53 00; www.toulon
tourisme.com; place Raimu; ☽ 9am-6pm Mon-Sat,
10am-noon Sun high season, 9.30am-5.30pm Mon-Sat,
10am-noon Sun low season).
Post Office (rue Bertholet) Second entrance on rue
Ferrero.

Sights & Activities

The **Musée de la Marine** (Naval Museum; ☎ 04 94 02
02 01; place Monsenergue; adult/student/child €4.60/2.30/
free; ☽ 9.30am-noon & 3-7pm daily Jul & Aug, 9.30am-noon
& 2-6pm Wed-Mon Sep-Jun) is in the lovely old arsenal building and displays scale models of old
ships and historic paintings of Toulon.

Overlooking the old city to the north is
Mont Faron (580m), from where you can see
Toulon's port in its true magnificence. Near
the summit is the **Tour Beaumont Mémorial du
Débarquement**, commemorating the Allied
landings that took place along the coast
here in August 1944. The steep road up to
the summit is used for the Tour de Méditerranée (February) and Paris–Nice (March)
professional cycling races. A **téléphérique**
(cableway; ☎ 04 94 92 68 25; adult/child return €5.80/4;
☽ 9am-noon & 2-5.30pm Tue-Sun) climbs the mountain from av de Vence. Take bus No 40 from
place de la Liberté.

Scubazur (☎ 04 94 92 19 29; 334 av de la République)
is a 1st-class diving shop that has plenty
of information on all the diving clubs and
schools along the Côte d'Azur.

Tours

Excursions around the *rade*, with a commentary (in French only) on the events that
took place here during WWII, leave from
quai Stalingrad or quai de la Sinse. One-
hour trips average €8.

Le Batelier de la Rade (☎ 04 94 46 24 65; quai
de la Sinse) organises day trips out to the Îles
d'Hyères (€20).

SNRTM (☎ 04 94 93 07 56) runs trips, some
including a meal on board, to Cannes and
St-Tropez between June and September.

Sleeping

Beware of the cheapest options in the old
town and near the station; there are some
pretty grim places.
Hôtel Molière (☎ 04 94 92 78 35; hotel.moliere@
tiscali.fr; 12 rue Molière; r with shower & toilet €35) Beside the opera house, this is the best of the
budget options, offering homely rooms in a
family-style establishment.
Hôtel d'Europe (☎/fax 04 94 92 37 44; 7 rue de
Chabannes; r with shower & toilet €47) East of the train
station, the Europe has some decent rooms.
Photos of each room category accompany
the price list displayed in reception. Some
of the rooms have little balconies.
La Corniche (☎ 04 94 41 35 12; www.hotel-corniche
.com; 17 littoral Frédéric Mistral; s/d €70/75, with sea views
€85/95; ✷) Along the coast, just out of the
town centre, La Corniche has considerable
charm and a good restaurant.
Grand Hôtel Dauphiné (☎ 04 94 92 20 28; fax 04 94
62 16 69; 10 rue Bertholet; s/d €44/50; [P]) With large
rooms and near secure parking, this place
will do.

Eating

Pricey restaurants, terraces and bars with occasional live music are abundant along the
quays; *menus* start at around €20 and a tiny
bouillabaisse or *aïoli garni* will set you back
€15 to €20. Another lively area is place Victor Hugo and neighbouring place Puget.
Les Enfants Gâtés ('Spoiled Children'; ☎ 04 94 09
14 67; 7 rue Corneille; lunch menu €7.60; ☽ closed Sat
& Sun high season, closed dinner Mon-Fri & lunch Sat low
season) A very popular, modern place run
by a young crowd. This is one of the most
pleasant places in town to dine without
breaking the bank.
Le Petit Prince (☎ 04 94 93 03 45; 10 rue de l'Humilité;
mains €8-11; ☽ closed Sun & lunch Sat) Named after
Antoine de St-Exupéry's book for children,
the 'Little Prince' is close to Les Enfants
Gâtés and is an equally charming place.

Also recommend on or near rue Gimelli:
Al Dente (☎ 04 94 93 02 50; 30 rue Gimelli; menu
€10/18; ☽ closed lunch Sun) An elegant Italian place
serving good home-made pasta.
Le Village (☎ 04 94 22 03 03; 10 rue Dumont d'Urville;
dishes €9-15; ☽ closed Sun & lunch Sat) Unpretentious,
modern food and jazz concerts.

Maharajah (☎ 04 94 91 93 46; 15 rue Gimelli; menus €10 & €20; ☺ lunch & dinner Tue-Sun) Known for its vegetarian *thalis* (trays with an assortment of dishes).

SELF-CATERING

The southern half of cours Lafayette is one long, excellent **open-air food market** (☺ 9am-early afternoon Tue-Sun) held, in typical Provençal style, under the plane trees. A few blocks south of the train station there is a small grocery shop, **Marché Plus** (av du Maréchal Leclerc).

Getting There & Away

BOAT

Ferries to Corsica and Sardinia are run by the **SNCM** (☎ 08 91 70 18 01), which has an **office** (49 av de l'Infanterie de Marine; ☺ 8.30am-noon & 2pm-5.45pm Mon-Fri, from 11.30am Sat) opposite the ferry terminal. For details, see the Getting There & Away section of the Corsica chapter.

Boats from Toulon to the Îles d'Hyères only run from Easter to September and are operated by several companies, such as **Trans Med 2000** (☎ 04 94 92 96 82). All depart from quai Stalingrad. The trip to Porquerolles (€18 return) takes one hour. It's another 40 minutes to Port Cros, from where it's a 20-minute hop to Île du Levant (€30 return to tour all three islands).

BUS

From the Toulon bus terminal **Sodetrav** (☎ 04 94 12 55 00; 4 blvd Pierre Toesca) operates buses along the coast. Bus No 103 to Hyères runs east along the coast via Le Lavandou to St-Tropez (€17, two hours, eight daily).

TRAIN

There are frequent connections to coastal cities including Marseilles (€9.20, 50 minutes, hourly), St-Raphaël, Cannes (€16.60, one hour 20 minutes, hourly), Monaco (€21.40, 2½ hours, frequent) and Menton.

Getting Around

Local buses are run by **RMTT** (☎ 04 94 03 87 03), which has an **information kiosk** (place de la Liberté; ☺ 7.30am-7pm Mon-Fri, 8am-12.30pm & 1.30-6.30pm Sat) at the main local bus hub. Single/10 tickets cost €1.30/8.60. Buses generally run until around 7.30pm or 8.30pm. Sunday service is limited. Bus No 7 and 13 link the train station with quai Stalingrad. One-day bus tickets cost €3.30 and combined one-day bus, boat and cable-car tickets cost €5.

Sitcat boats (☎ 04 94 46 35 46; ticket office ☺ 8am-12.15pm & 2-5.15pm) run by **RMTT** (☎ 04 94 03 87 03), the local transport company, link quai Stalingrad with the towns on the peninsula across the harbour, including La Seyne (line 8M), St-Mandrier-sur-Mer (line 28M) and Sablettes (line 18M). The 20-minute ride costs the same as a bus ticket: €1.30 (€1.70 if you buy your ticket onboard, or €5 for an all-day bus, boat and cable-car ticket). Boats run from around 6am to 8pm.

NICE TO MENTON

THE CORNICHES

Nice and Menton (and the 30km of towns in between) are linked by three corniches (coastal roads), each one higher up the hill than the last. If you're in a hurry and don't mind missing the scenery, you can drive a bit further inland and take the A8.

Corniche Inférieure

The Corniche Inférieure (also known as the Basse Corniche, the Lower Corniche and the N98) sticks pretty close to the villa-lined waterfront and the nearby train line, passing (as it goes from Nice eastwards to Menton) through Villefranche-sur-Mer, St-Jean-Cap Ferrat, Beaulieu-sur-Mer, Èze-sur-Mer, Cap d'Ail, where there's a very pleasant **seaside hostel** (☎ 04 93 78 18 58; clajpaca@cote-dazur.com) right by the sea and Monaco.

VILLEFRANCHE-SUR-MER

Set in one of the Côte d'Azur's most charming harbours, this little port (population 6877) overlooks the Cap Ferrat peninsula. It has a well-preserved 14th-century old city with a 16th-century citadel and a church dating from 100 years later. Steps break up the tiny streets that weave through the old city, the most interesting of which is rue Obscure. Keep a lookout for occasional glimpses of the sea as you wander through the streets that lead down to the fishing port. Villefranche was a particular favourite of Jean Cocteau, who painted the frescoes (1957) in the 17th-century **Chapelle St-Pierre**.

ST-JEAN-CAP FERRAT

Once a fishing village, the seaside resort of St-Jean-Cap Ferrat (population 1907) lies on the spectacular peninsula of Cap Ferrat, which conceals a bounty of millionaires' villas. On the narrow isthmus of Cap Ferrat is the extravagant **Musée de Béatrice Ephrussi de Rothschild** (☎ 04 93 01 33 09; adult/student €8/6; ☼ 10am-7pm daily), housed in the Villa Île de France, which was built in the style of the great houses of Tuscany for the Baroness de Rothschild in 1912. It abounds with antique furniture, paintings, tapestries and porcelain and is surrounded by beautiful gardens. Admission includes entry to the gardens and the collections on the **rez-de-chaussée** (ground floor). It costs an extra €2 to view those on the 1st floor.

BEAULIEU-SUR-MER

This upmarket resort (population 3700) boasts the wonderful **Villa Grecque Kérylos** (☎ 04 93 76 44 09; av Gustave Eiffel; adult/student €7.50/5.50; ☼ 10am-7pm), a wonderful reproduction of an Athenian villa built by archaeologist Théodore Reinach in 1902. After visiting the luxurious marble interior, take a walk on the botanical trail through the gardens, planted with vegetation typical to Greece and the French coast.

Moyenne Corniche

The Moyenne Corniche, the middle coastal road (the N7), clings to the hillside, affording great views if you can find a place to pull over. It takes you from Nice past the Col de Villefranche, Èze and Beausoleil, the French town up the hill from Monte Carlo.

ÈZE

Perched on a rocky peak at an altitude of 427m is the picturesque village of Èze (population 2526), once occupied by Ligurians and Phoenicians. Below is its coastal counterpart, Èze-sur-Mer.

Make your way to the **exotic garden** for fabulous views up and down the coast. The German philosopher Friedrich Nietzsche (1844–1900) spent some time here, during which he started *Thus Spoke Zarathustra*. The spectacular walking path that links Èze-sur-Mer and Èze is named after him. Allow an hour to complete the walk The bus between Èze and Nice costs €3. There's also a train between Èze-sur-Mer and Nice.

Grande Corniche

The Grande Corniche, whose panoramas are by far the most spectacular, leaves Nice

as the D2564. It passes the **Col d'Èze**, where there's a great view; **La Turbie**, which is on a promontory directly above Monaco and offers a stunning night-time vista of the principality; and **Le Vistaëro**.

ROQUEBRUNE

Dominating this appealing hilltop village (population 11,966), which lies just between Monaco and Menton, is a medieval dungeon that is complete with a re-created manor house. Roquebrune's tortuous little streets, which lead up to the castle, are lined with shops selling handicrafts and souvenirs and are overrun with tourists in the high season. Carved out of the rock is the impressive rue Moncollet, with arcaded passages and stairways.

For more information, contact the **tourist office** (☎ 04 93 35 62 87; fax 04 93 28 57 00; 218 av Aristide Briand; ☼ 9am-12.30pm & 2-6.30pm Mon-Sat), in nearby **Cap Martin**, an exclusive suburb of Menton known for its sumptuous villas and famous past residents (Winston Churchill and the architect Le Corbusier among them).

MENTON

pop 29,266

Menton, a confection of elegant historic buildings in sugared-almond pastels, is only a few kilometres from the Italian border and reputed to be the warmest spot on the Côte d'Azur (especially during winter). In part because of the weather, Menton is popular with older holiday-makers, whose way of life and preferences have made the town's after-dark entertainment a tad tranquil compared to other spots along the coast. Guy de Maupassant, Robert Louis Stevenson, Gustave Flaubert and Katherine Mansfield all found solace in Menton. Jean Cocteau lived here from 1956 to 1958 and made a number of important contributions to the town. Today, Menton draws Italians from across the border, and retains a sedate charm free of the airs and pretensions found in other areas of the Côte d'Azur.

Menton is famed for its cultivation of lemons. Giant, larger-than-life sculptures made from lemons, lemons and yet more lemons take over the town for two weeks during the fabulous **Fête des Citrons** (Lemon Festival) in February. The festival kicks off on Mardi Gras.

Orientation

Promenade du Soleil runs southwest to northeast along the beach; the train line runs approximately parallel about 500m inland. Avenue Édouard VII links the train station with the beach. Avenue Boyer, home to the tourist office, is 350m to the east. From the station, turn left and walk along av de la Gare, then take the second right onto what appears to be a two-way divided promenade. The tourist office is about halfway down av Boyer.

The old town is on and around the hill at the northeastern end of promenade du Soleil. Vieux Port lies just beyond it.

Information

BOOKSHOPS

Librairie de la Presse (25 av Félix Faure) Stocks a fine range of guides, travel books and foreign-language newspapers.

INTERNET ACCESS

Café des Arts (☎ 04 93 35 78 67; 16 rue de la République; ☽ 8am-10pm Mon-Sat; per 15min €2). Log-on, *pastis* in hand, from an elegant green leather banquette.

MONEY

There are plenty of banks with exchange facilities along rue Partouneaux.

Barclays Bank (☎ 04 93 28 60 00; 39 av Félix Faure) Has an automatic exchange machine outside.

Crédit Lyonnais (av Boyer) Two doors down from the tourist office. There's another 24-hour currency machine outside.

POST

Post Office (cours George V) With a Cyberposte.

TOURIST INFORMATION

Information Office (☎ 04 92 10 97 10; fax 04 93 28 46 85; 24 rue St-Michel) More central than the tourist office. Runs thematic organised tours (Menton and the *belle époque*, artists, gardens etc) arranged by the Service du Patrimoine for €5 per person.

Tourist Office (☎ 04 92 41 76 76; www.menton.fr; 8 av Boyer; ☽ 9am-7pm Mon-Sat, 10am-noon Sun Jul & Aug; 8.30am-12.30pm & 2-6pm Mon-Fri, 9am-noon & 2-6pm Sat low season) Inside the Palais de l'Europe.

Sights & Activities

The early-17th-century **Église St-Michel** (Church of St Michael; usually ☽ 10am-noon & 3-5.15pm, closed Sat morning) is the grandest and possibly the prettiest baroque church in this part of France. It is perched in the centre of the old town, which

has many narrow, winding passageways. The ornate interior is Italian in inspiration.

Musée Jean Cocteau (Jean Cocteau Museum; ☎ 04 93 57 72 30; quai Napoléon III; admission €3; ☽ 10am-noon & 2-6pm Wed-Mon), southwest of the Vieux Port, displays work by Jean Cocteau (1889–1963) – poet, dramatist, artist and film director – in a seafront bastion dating from 1636. Cocteau's work includes drawings, tapestries and mosaics. Do not miss Cocteau's frescoes in the **Salle des Mariages** (Marriage Hall; place Ardoïno; admission €1.50; ☽ 8.30am-noon & 1.30-5pm Mon-Fri) in the Hôtel de Ville.

The **beach** along promenade du Soleil is public but, like its counterpart in Nice, it's covered with smooth little rocks. There are more beaches directly north of the Vieux Port, including Plages des Sablettes with sand and clean water, and east of Port de Garavan, the main pleasure-boat harbour.

Base Nautique (☎ 04 93 35 49 70; promenade de la Mer) rents laser-class dinghies/catamarans/kayaks for €19/31/8 per hour. The **sailing school** also runs courses that cost €115 for five two-hour sessions.

Sleeping

BUDGET

Auberge de Jeunesse (☎ 04 93 35 93 14; fax 04 93 35 93 07; Plateau St-Michel; dm incl breakfast €14.40; ☽ reception closed noon-5pm, 10am to 5pm in winter; P) The hostel is in a lovely spot overlooking town and the bay. The walk from the train station is quite a hike uphill. Otherwise take a Line 6 bus and get off at Camping Saint Michel, 500m away. Curfew is midnight (10pm in winter).

Hôtel Le Terminus (☎ 04 92 10 49 80; fax 04 92 10 49 81; place de la Gare; s/d with washbasin €28/31, with shower & toilet €30/40; P) A no-star, but welcoming, clean place with a few rooms right next to the station. Hall showers are free. Reception is often closed but you can always find someone to help you in the bar-restaurant areas during opening times.

Camping

Camping Saint Michel (☎ 04 93 35 81 23; route des Ciappes de Castellar; camping €10.90; ☽ 1 Apr-15 Oct) One kilometre northeast of the train station up Plateau St-Michel, and close to the youth hostel.

MID-RANGE

Hôtel de Londres (☎ 04 93 35 74 62; www.hotel-de-londres.com; 15 av Carnot; s/d from €35/38, with bathroom from €53/58; (P) (X)) Close to the sea, central enough and exuding a certain charm, this appealing place with a leafy dining terrace and garden is our pick in town.

Saint Michel (☎ 04 93 57 46 33; fax 04 93 57 71 19; 1684 promenade du Soleil; s/d €60/70) This place has the best sea views in town.

Hôtel Claridges (☎ 04 93 35 72 53; www.claridges -menton.com; 39 av de Verdun; s/d from €43/62) A two-star place with comfortable rooms.

Hôtel des Arcades (☎ 04 93 35 70 62; fax 04 93 35 35 97; 41 av Félix Faure; s/d with washbasin €41/46, with shower & toilet €53/55) In town under the arches, this hotel is one of Menton's most pictur-esque, if no-frills, options.

Eating

There aren't any outstanding restaurants in town, so if you have wheels or a train timetable, consider breaking for the nearby Italian border. In town there are places to eat galore along av Félix Faure and its pe-destrianised continuation, rue St-Michel. Place Clemenceau and place aux Herbes in the Vieille Ville are equally popular. The pricier restaurants with terraces fanned by cool breezes are along promenade du Soleil. Slightly cheaper places, including pizzerias, line quai de Monléon in the Vieille Ville.

Le Chaudron (☎ 04 93 35 90 25; 28 rue St-Michel; menu €20; ⊙ closed Wed & dinner Tue) Offers filling salads (€8 to €12) and some fresh fish mains (€9 to €20).

Ulivo (☎ 04 93 35 45 65; place du Cap; menu €15; ⊙ Fri-Wed) Run by an Italian family and serv-ing home-made Mediterranean-style dishes.

SELF-CATERING

The **Marché Municipal** (Les Halles; quai de Monléon; ⊙ 5am-1pm Tue-Sun), in the old town, sells all kinds of food.

The **8 à Huit** (7 rue Amiral Courbet) is the place for groceries and the **Comtesse du Barry** (36 rue Partouneaux) sells luxury foie gras products.

Getting There & Away

BUS

The **bus station** (☎ 04 93 28 43 27, information office ☎ 04 93 35 93 60) is next to 12 promenade Maréchal Leclerc, the northern continua-tion of av Boyer.

There are buses to Monaco (€2.10 return, 30 minutes), Nice (€5.10 return, 1¼ hours), Ste-Agnès (€7.20 return, 45 minutes) and Sospel (€4.90 return, 45 minutes). There are

also buses to the Nice–Côte d'Azur airport (€16.10, 1½ hours) via Monaco run by **Bus RCA** (☎ 04 93 85 64 44).

TRAIN

Trains to Ventimiglia cost €2.10 and take 10 minutes. For more information on train services along the Côte d'Azur see p830.

Getting Around

TUM (Transports Urbains de Menton; ☎ 04 93 35 93 60) runs nine bus lines in the area. Lines 1 and 2 link the train station with the old town.

MONACO (PRINCIPAUTÉ DE MONACO)

pop 30,000

Tiny, glamorous Monaco (its territory only covers 1.95 sq km) is a fantasy land of per-fectly groomed streets, lush gardens, chic boutiques and extravagantly opulent 19th-century pleasure palaces.

With a photogenic royal family whose heritage stretches back to the 13th century and a stream of high-rollers filling its fa-mous casino or gathering for the annual Formula One Grand Prix race, Monaco never seems to go out of style.

The Principality of Monaco has been under the rule of the Grimaldi family for most of the period since 1297 and is a sov-ereign state with close ties to France. It has been ruled since 1949 by Prince Rainier III (b 1923). Rainier's rule has modernised Monaco and weaned it from its depend-ence on gambling revenue. His marriage to the much beloved Princess Grace (re-membered from her Hollywood days as the actress Grace Kelly) restored Monaco's glamour.

Tourism in all its permutations, from day-trippers to conventioneers, is now the backbone of Monaco's economy. Prince Al-bert is the heir to the throne but the tabloids have always been more fascinated with the ever-changing personal lives of his two sisters, Caroline and Stephanie. The 2003 marriage of Stephanie to a circus acrobat was just another episode in the princess' unconventional life.

The citizens of Monaco (known as Moné-gasques), of whom there are only about

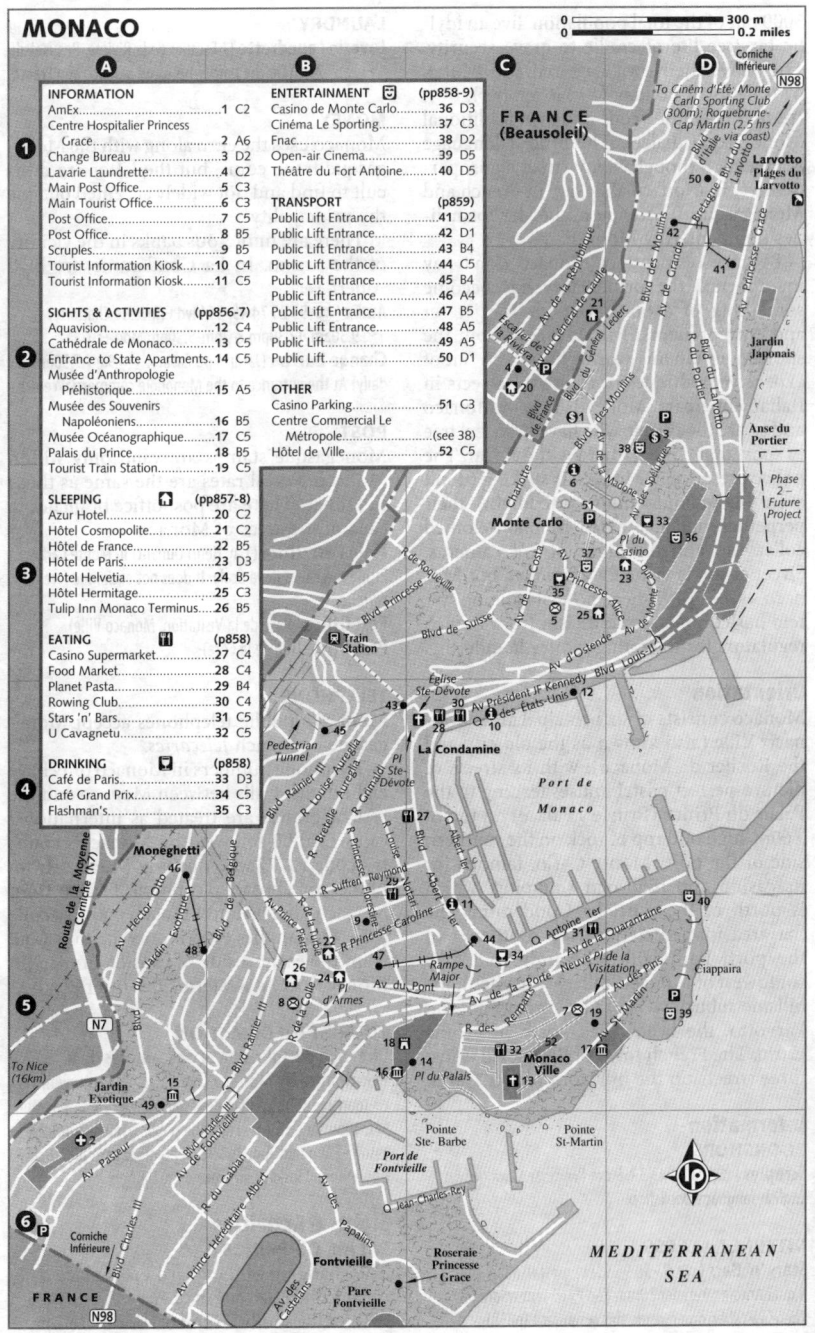

MONACO

0   300 m
0   0.2 miles

INFORMATION
AmEx....................................1 C2
Centre Hospitalier Princess
  Grace.................................2 A6
Change Bureau.....................3 D2
Lavarie Laundrette................4 C2
Main Post Office...................5 C3
Main Tourist Office...............6 C3
Post Office...........................7 C5
Post Office...........................8 B5
Scruples..............................9 B5
Tourist Information Kiosk.....10 C4
Tourist Information Kiosk.....11 C5

SIGHTS & ACTIVITIES (pp856-7)
Aquavision.........................12 C4
Cathédrale de Monaco........13 C5
Entrance to State Apartments..14 C5
Musée d'Anthropologie
  Préhistorique....................15 A5
Musée des Souvenirs
  Napoléoniens....................16 B5
Musée Océanographique.....17 C5
Palais du Prince..................18 B5
Tourist Train Station...........19 C5

SLEEPING (pp857-8)
Azur Hotel..........................20 C2
Hôtel Cosmopolite..............21 C2
Hôtel de France...................22 D2
Hôtel de Paris.....................23 D3
Hôtel Helvetia....................24 B5
Hôtel Hermitage.................25 C3
Tulip Inn Monaco Terminus..26 B5

EATING (p858)
Casino Supermarket.............27 C4
Food Market.......................28 C4
Planet Pasta.......................29 B4
Rowing Club.......................30 C4
Stars 'n' Bars......................31 C5
U Cavagnetu......................32 C5

DRINKING (p858)
Café de Paris......................33 D3
Café Grand Prix..................34 C5
Flashman's.........................35 C3

ENTERTAINMENT (pp858-9)
Casino de Monte Carlo........36 D3
Cinéma Le Sporting.............37 C3
Fnac..................................38 D2
Open-air Cinema................39 D5
Théâtre du Fort Antoine......40 D5

TRANSPORT (p859)
Public Lift Entrance.............41 D2
Public Lift Entrance.............42 D1
Public Lift Entrance.............43 B4
Public Lift Entrance.............44 C5
Public Lift Entrance.............45 B4
Public Lift Entrance.............46 A4
Public Lift Entrance.............47 B5
Public Lift Entrance.............48 A5
Public Lift..........................49 A5
Public Lift..........................50 D1

OTHER
Casino Parking....................51 C3
Centre Commercial Le
  Métropole.....................(see 38)
Hôtel de Ville....................52 C5

FRANCE
(Beausoleil)

To Ciném d'Été; Monte
Carlo Sporting Club
(300m); Roquebrune-
Cap Martin (2.5 hrs
via coast)

Corniche
Inférieure
N98

Larvotto
Plages du
Larvotto

Jardin
Japonais

Anse du
Portier

Phase
2
Future
Project

Monte Carlo

Pl du
Casino

Train
Station

Eglise
Ste-Dévote

La Condamine

Pedestrian
Tunnel

Monéghetti

Port de
Monaco

Monaco
Ville

Pl du Palais

Pointe
Ste-Barbe

Pointe
St-Martin

Port de
Fontvieille

Ciappaira

To Nice
(16km)

Jardin
Exotique

MEDITERRANEAN
SEA

Fontvieille

Roseraie
Princesse
Grace

Parc
Fontvieille

FRANCE
N98

Route de la Moyenne Corniche (N7)

N7

5000 out of the total population, live an idyllic tax-free life of cradle-to-grave security. They have their own flag (red and white), own national holiday (19 November), own country telephone code and own traditional Monégasque dialect. The official language is French, although many street signs, particularly in Monaco Ville, are in French and Monégasque. There are no border formalities upon entering Monaco.

Because residents of Monaco don't pay income tax, the principality has become something of a tax haven for the jet set and entrepreneurs. Famous faces from the sporting or cinema worlds flit in and out of expensive boutiques or cruise the streets in Italian supercars. Money is safe in Monaco and so are the people who have it, so feel free to sport that emerald tiara without fear. The police presence in Monaco is striking (don't even think about running a red light), their perpetual vigilance aided by plain-clothed colleagues and hundreds of TV cameras. Street crime is virtually unknown, but Monaco's see-no-evil-hear-no-evil banking system has come under criticism from French regulators for tolerating money laundering.

Orientation

Monaco consists of six principal areas: Monaco Ville (also known as the old city and the Rocher de Monaco), with its streets of picture-perfect pastel houses leading to the Palais du Prince (Prince's Palace) on top of a 60m-high outcrop of rock on the southern side of the port; Monte Carlo, famous for its casino and high-end shopping, which is north of the port; La Condamine, the flat area immediately to the southwest of the port; Fontvieille, the industrial area southwest of Monaco Ville; Moneghetti, the hillside suburb west of La Condamine; and Larvotto, the beach area north of Monte Carlo. The French town of Beausoleil is just three streets up the hill from Monte Carlo.

Information
BOOKSHOPS
Scruples (☎ 93 50 43 52; 9 rue Princesse Caroline) An English-language bookshop.

INTERNET ACCESS
Stars 'n' Bars (☎ 93 50 95 95; info@starsnbars.com; 6 quai Antoine 1er; per 30min €5; ⏰ 11am-midnight) There's a cybercorner inside this restaurant (p858).

LAUNDRY
Laverie Laundrette (1 Escalier de la Riviera, Beausoleil; ⏰ 7am-7pm) On the border between Monaco and France.

MONEY
Monaco uses the euro along with the Monégasque franc coins, but the latter are difficult to find and not widely accepted outside the principality.

There are numerous banks in the vicinity of the casino. In La Condamine, try blvd Albert 1er.
AmEx (☎ 93 25 74 45; 35 blvd Princesse Charlotte; ⏰ 9.30am-12.30pm & 2pm-5.30pm Mon-Fri)
Change Bureau (Jardins du Casino; ⏰ 9am-7.30pm daily) At the entrance to the Monopole commercial centre.

POST
Monégasque stamps are valid only within Monaco. Postal rates are the same as those in France. There are post office branches in each of the areas of Monaco.
Main Post Office (1 av Henri Dunant) In Monte Carlo inside the Palais de la Scala. It does not exchange foreign currency.
Post Office (place de la Visitation, Monaco Ville)
Post Office (rue de la Côte)

TELEPHONE
Monaco's public telephones accept Monégasque or French télécartes.

Telephone numbers in Monaco only have eight digits. Calls between Monaco and the rest of France are treated as international calls. Dial 00 followed by Monaco's country code (377) when calling Monaco from France or abroad. To phone France from Monaco, dial 00 and France's country code (33). This applies even if only making a call from the eastern side of blvd de France (in Monaco) to its western side (in France)!

TOURIST INFORMATION
Direction du Tourisme et des Congrès de la Principauté de Monaco (☎ 92 16 61 16; www.mona co-tourisme.com; 2a blvd des Moulins; ⏰ 9am-7pm Mon-Sat, 10am-noon Sun) Across the public gardens from the casino. From mid-June to late-September several tourist information kiosks open around the harbour.

Sights & Activities
PALAIS DU PRINCE
The changing of the guard takes place daily outside the **Palais du Prince** (Prince's Palace; ☎ 93 25 18 31), at the southern end of rue des Remparts

in Monaco Ville, at precisely 11.55am. The guards, who carry out their duties of state in spiffy dress uniform (white in summer, black in winter), are apparently resigned to the comic-opera nature of their duties. You can also visit the **state apartments** (adult/child €6/3; ⏰ 9.30am-6.30pm Jun-Sep, 10am-5pm Oct, closed Nov-May) with audioguide commentary.

A combined ticket including admission to the **Musée des Souvenirs Napoléoniens** – a display of Napoleon's personal effects in the southern wing of the palace – costs €8 (children €4).

MUSÉE OCÉANOGRAPHIQUE DE MONACO
If you're planning to see just one aquarium on your whole trip, the world-renowned **Musée Océanographique de Monaco** (☎ 93 15 36 00; av St-Martin, Monaco Ville; adult/student €11/6; ⏰ 9.30am-7pm Jul & Aug, to 6.30pm Apr-Jun & Sep) should be it. It has 90 tanks, and upstairs there are all sorts of exhibits on ocean exploration. Bus Nos 1 and 2 are the alternatives to a relatively long walk up the hill.

CATHÉDRALE DE MONACO
Albeit unspectacular, the 1875 Romanesque-Byzantine **Cathédrale de Monaco** (4 rue Colonel) has one major draw: the grave of former Hollywood film star Grace Kelly (1929–82), which lies on the western side of the cathedral choir. Her modest tombstone, inscribed with the Latin words *Gratia Patricia Principis Rainerii III*, is heavily adorned with flowers. Tourists usually do a quick march around the cathedral to see her grave. Grace Patricia Kelly wed Prince Rainier III in 1956 and died in a car crash in 1982. The remains of other members of the royal family, buried in the church crypt since 1885, today rest behind Princess Grace's grave.

Between September and June, Sunday Mass at 10am is sung by Monaco's boys choir, Les Petits Chanteurs de Monaco.

JARDIN EXOTIQUE
The steep slopes of the wonderful **Jardin Exotique** (☎ 93 15 29 80; 62 blvd du Jardin Exotique; adult/student €6.40/3.20; ⏰ 9am-7pm mid-May–mid-Sep, 9am-6pm mid-Sep–mid-May) are home to some 7000 varieties of cacti and succulents from all over the world. The spectacular view alone is worth at least half the admission fee, which also gets you into the **Musée d'Anthropologie Préhistorique** and includes a half-hour guided

visit to the **Observatory Caves**, a network of stalactite and stalagmite caves 279 steps down the hillside. From the tourist office, take bus No 2 to the Jardin Exotique terminus.

BEACHES
The nearest beaches, **Plages du Larvotto** and **Plage de Monte Carlo**, are a few kilometres east of Monte Carlo. In town sun worshippers lie their oiled bodies out to bake on giant concrete slabs on the eastern side of the jetty, at the northern end of quai des États-Unis.

Tours
You can explore the waters off Monaco in a glass-bottom boat (adult/student €11/8, 55 minutes) with **Aquavision** (☎ 92 16 15 15; www .aquavision-monaco.com; quai des États-Unis). Boats depart at 11am, 2.30pm and 4pm (2.30pm only May to October).

If the hills of Monaco are too much for you, the slightly tacky **Azur Express tourist train** (☎ 92 05 64 38) starts from opposite the Musée Océanographique. The 30-minute city tour costs €6 and it runs every day from 10.30am to 6pm (11am to 5pm in winter). Commentaries are in English, French, Italian and German.

Festivals & Events
GRAND PRIX AUTOMOBILE DE MONACO
In May of each year Monaco transforms itself into the giant racing circuit that is the Monaco Grand Prix, a unique arena in which the world's top Formula 1 drivers pit their skills against each other and against the city's narrow lanes, tortuous road layout and impossible hairpins. It's arguably the most thrilling and atmospheric of all the Formula 1 venues owing to the spectacular location and the fact that spectators can often get closer to the action than on more conventional circuits.

You can try to purchase tickets (from about €50) to get trackside from the **Automobile Club de Monaco** (www.amc.mc), but be warned it's a hugely popular event, so you'll need to get in early to stand a chance. Tickets for the better locations can be fiercely expensive.

Sleeping
BUDGET
Relais Internationale de la Jeunesse Thalassa (☎ 04 93 78 18 58; blvd de la Mer) Monaco has no

hostels. On Cap d'Ail, this is the closest to Monaco and is right by the sea.

MID-RANGE
Cheap hotels are nonexistent in Monaco. All is not lost though as the neighbouring town of Beausoleil is a better-value location for accommodation.

Azur Hotel (☎ 04 93 78 01 25; www.azurhotel.biz; 12 blvd de la Republique; s/d/tr from €42/52/62; **P** **⬚**) Probably the pick of places in the area for value, with appealing décor and location. It's also close to a couple of multistorey car parks.

Hôtel Cosmopolite (☎ 04 93 78 36 00; fax 04 93 41 84 22; 19 blvd du Général Leclerc; s/d €51/54) Comfortable rooms with TVs, telephones, minibars and hairdryers.

The above two hotels are three streets up from the casino and close to the Beausoleil market. When calling these hotels from Monaco (eg from the train station), dial 00 33, then the listed phone number (dropping the first 0). The following are in Monaco proper.

Hôtel de France (☎ 93 30 24 64; fax 92 16 13 34; 6 rue de la Turbie; s/d with shower & toilet €71/90) This two-star place has small rooms with showers, toilets and TVs; rates include breakfast.

Tulip Inn Monaco Terminus (☎ 92 05 63 00; www .terminus.monte-carlo.mc; 9 av Prince Pierre; s/d €130/170; **⬚**) A three-star hotel in a 1960s brick of a building, the Tulip Inn offers rooms with soundproofing, hairdryers, TVs and telephones. Some have sea views.

Hôtel Helvetia (☎ 93 30 21 71; www.monte-carlo .mc/hotels/helvetia; 1bis rue Grimaldi; s/d €62/71) While this is a more expensive two-star hotel, it doesn't necessarily offer more comfort.

TOP END
World-famous places to spend a luxury holiday:

Hôtel de Paris (☎ 92 16 30 00; www.montecarlo sort.com; place du Casino; r from high season €570, low season €385) Spectacularly plush; where the writer Colette spent the last years of her life.

Hôtel Hermitage (☎ 92 16 40 00; www.montecarlo resort.com; square Beaumarchais; r 490 high season, low season from €355) The entrance is lined with Bentleys and Maseratis.

Eating
Finding a place to eat in Monaco won't be hard. The trick is to do it at a price you can afford. For more choices grab the free *Monaco Shopping: Commerce and Restaurant Guide* booklet from the tourist office.

The lower end of the range restaurants tend to be in La Condamine along rue de la Turbie, and there are simple sandwich bars along quai Albert 1er. In Monte Carlo, there are a few sandwich and snack places inside the Centre Commercial Le Métropole.

Rowing Club (quai des États-Unis; mains €9-12; ☺ lunch Tue-Sat) The good food available in the quiet little bar and bolt hole above the where locals smoke and play cards is a closely kept local secret – until now.

Planet Pasta (☎ 93 50 80 14; 6 rue Imberty; pizza/ pasta €9-13, mains €17-22; ☺ lunch & dinner Tue-Sat) A reliable choice, serving filling portions of what its name advertises in a busy, often hot and stuffy dining room.

Stars 'n' Bars (☎ 93 50 95 95; 6 quai Antoine 1er; ☺ noon-3am Tue-Sun) On the south side of the port, this place has become a Monaco institution, despite being utterly American. It's a kind of huge country and western saloon where you can listen to live music and eat American-sized mains (€14 to €25) and huge salads (from €11) served by staff in starred-and-striped leather shorts and boots.

U Cavagnetu (☎ 93 30 35 80; 14 rue Comte Félix-Gastaldi; lunch menu €14.50, dinner menus €20 & €25) One of the few affordable restaurants specialising in Monégasque dishes.

SELF-CATERING
In La Condamine, there's a **food market** (place d'Armes; ☺ from 7am Mon-Sat) and a **Casino Supermarket** (blvd Albert 1er).

Drinking
Café de Paris (☎ 92 16 20 20; place du Casino). In Monte Carlo, this is the place to people-watch and spot the limo from the sprawling terrace. The action gets particularly intense after 10pm when the most exclusive rooms in the casino open.

Other drinking options:

Café Grand Prix (☎ 93 25 57 02; 1 quai Antoine 1er) Live music every night.

Flashman's (☎ 93 30 09 03; 7 av Princess Alice) An unreconstructed British boozer hosting a pot-bellied expat Brit crowd.

Entertainment
Monaco has a lively cultural scene of concerts, opera and ballet, held in the various

venues. Stop by the tourist office for a schedule of local events. Tickets for most cultural events are sold at **Fnac** (☎ 93 10 81 81; Centre Commercial le Métropole, 17 av Spélugues).

CASINO

The drama of watching people risk their money in Monte Carlo's spectacularly ornate **Casino de Monte Carlo** (☎ 92 16 20 00; www.casino -monte-carlo.com; European/Private Rooms ☒ from noon Sat & Sun, from 2pm Mon-Fri), built between 1878 and 1910, makes visiting the gaming rooms almost worth the stiff entry fees: €10 for admission to the European Rooms, which have slot machines, French roulette and *trente et quarante;* and €20 for the Private Rooms, which offer baccarat, blackjack, craps and American roulette. You'll need to show your passport or driving licence to enter the casino.

Gamblers can also head to the less glamorous gaming rooms adjoining the Café de Paris (see opposite), which are more casual and have lower minimum bets.

CINEMAS

Cinéma Le Sporting (☎ 0836 68 00 72; place du Casino; tickets €9) often has movies in their original language. An **open-air cinema** (parking des Pêcheurs) has nightly shows at 9.30pm in July and August, specialising in crowd-pleasing blockbusters (€10 to €15).

THEATRE

A charming spot to while away a summer evening is the 18th-century fortress, **Théâtre du Fort Antoine** (☎ 93 50 80 00; av de la Quarantaine), which is now used as an outside theatre. Plays are staged here at 9pm or 9.30pm on Monday in July and August.

Getting There & Away
BUS

There is no bus station in Monaco. Intercity buses leave from various stops around the city.

CAR

Parking facilities are good in Monaco, with some 25 official pay car parks scattered around the principality. One of the most convenient parks is the casino parking from where you exit directly to the door of the tourist office. It's cheaper to park in Beausoleil, if you can find a space.

Driving around Monaco is not recommended (or really necessary). If you are thinking of driving, be aware that you cannot take your car up into Monaco Ville unless you have either a Monaco or a 06 (Alpes-Maritimes) licence plate.

TRAIN

Trains to and from Monaco are run by the French SNCF. For more information visit the **information desk** (av Prince Pierre) at Monaco train station.

Taking the train along the coast is highly recommended – the Mediterranean Sea and the mountains provide a truly magnificent sight. There are frequent trains east to Menton (€1.70, 10 minutes), Nice (€2.90, 20 minutes) and the first town across the border in Italy, Ventimiglia (Vintimille in French; €3, 25 minutes).

Getting Around
BUS

Monaco's urban bus system has six lines, though in practice you are unlikely to ever need to use the bus since Monaco is so compact. The most useful bus is Line No 4, linking the train station with the tourist office and the casino. A ticket/*carnet* of eight costs €1.30/5.25.

Full bus route details can be found in the free Monaco map given out at the tourist office.

LIFTS

Some 15 public lifts *(ascenseurs publics)* run up and down the hillside, all marked on the free town brochure distributed by the tourist office. Most operate 24 hours, while others run between 6am and midnight or 1am only.

TAXI

To order a taxi, call ☎ 93 15 01 01.

Corsica

Though Corsica (Corse) has been governed by mainland France for over 200 years, the island remains a nation apart, with its own distinctive language, customs and character – not to mention an entirely unique landscape. In many ways, Corsica resembles a miniature continent, with 1000km of sea-swept coastline, mountain ranges that stay snowcapped until July, a world-renowned marine reservation (Reserve Naturelle de Scandola), an uninhabited desert (Désert des Agriates) and a 'continental divide' running down the island's centre.

Much of the island is covered with *maquis* – a typically Corsican vegetation with fragrant shrubs that provide the herbs and spices used in Corsican cooking – but a single day's travel can carry you through a kaleidoscopic landscape of secret coves, booming waterfalls, plunging canyons, sweeping bays, megalithic menhirs and dense forests of chestnut and pine. Though the annual influx of tourists outnumbers the island's residents by six to one, Corsica has remained fiercely protective of its heritage, and away from the main holiday resorts, you'll discover the quiet fishing villages, remote mountain towns and deserted beaches that died out in the rest of the Mediterranean long ago.

From the ramshackle harbourfront of Bastia to the bustling streets of Ajaccio, and from the glittering bays of the west coast to the soaring central mountains, nowhere could be more deserving of the title of *l'île de beâuté* – the island of beauty – than Corsica.

HIGHLIGHTS

- Sample the island's best at **Ajaccio's restaurants** (p883) and food markets
- Cruise the waters of the **Réserve Naturelle de Scandola** (p877)
- Explore Calvi's 15th-century **citadel** (p872)
- Meander along the clifftop road from **Calvi to Porto** (p866)
- Marvel at the **menhirs** (p885) of Filitosa
- Hike through the spectacular **Gorges de Spelunca** (p877)
- Explore isolated **Cap Corse** (p871), Corsica's unspoiled peninsula
- Ponder the permanence of the 'hanging buildings' of **Bonifacio** (p886)

- POPULATION: 260,150
- AREA: 8680 SQ KM

History

From the 11th to 13th centuries Corsica was ruled by the Italian city-state of Pisa, superseded in 1284 by its arch rival, Genoa. To prevent seaborne raids, mainly from North Africa, a massive defence system was constructed that included citadels and coastal watchtowers (many of which can still be seen around the coastline).

On several occasions, Corsican discontent with foreign rule led to open revolt. In 1755, after 25 years of sporadic warfare against the Genoese, Corsicans finally threw off the shackles and declared their independence, led by Pasquale Paoli (1725–1807), under whose rule they established a National Assembly and adopted the most democratic constitution in Europe.

The Corsicans made Corte their capital, outlawed blood vendettas, founded schools and established a university, but the island's independence was short-lived. In 1768 the Genoese ceded Corsica to the French king Louis XV, whose troops crushed Paoli's army in 1769.

The island has since been part of France, except for a period (1794–96) when it was under English domination, and during the German and Italian occupation of 1940–43. Corsica's most famous native son was Napoleon Bonaparte, emperor of France and, in the early 19th century, ruler of most of Europe.

Government & Politics

Despite having spent only 14 years as an autonomous country, the people of Corsica have retained a defiantly independent streak. Although Corsica is heavily subsidised by the French government, nationalists argue that the island should be an independent EU member. In fact, few Corsicans support the Front de Libération Nationale de la Corse (FLNC), whose slogans are spray-painted all over the island.

Since the assassination of Corsica's *préfet* (prefect), Claude Erignac, in Ajaccio in 1998, the French government has cracked down on the corruption that has dogged the island for decades. An undercover investigation into French bank Crédit Agricole in March 1998 uncovered US$150 million of unpaid agricultural loans. Shortly afterwards, a parliamentary report exposed organised gangs and continuing racketeering.

In 2001, the French parliament granted Corsica limited autonomy in exchange for an end to separatist violence, but the bill was overturned by France's high court because it breached the principle of national unity. The only victory for the autonomy movement was the right to have the Corsican language taught in schools.

Language

The Corsican language (Corsu) is more closely related to Italian than French. It's an important part of Corsican identity, and many people (especially at the university in Corte) are working to ensure its survival. Road signs are now bilingual or exclusively in Corsican. You'll see lots of French signs 'edited' with spray paint into their *nomi Corsi* (Corsican names).

THE MOOR'S HEAD

La Tête de Maure (Moor's Head) – a black head wearing a white bandanna and a hooped earring – is the emblem of Corsica. It has been a symbol of victory since the Crusades, but it first showed its face in Corsica in 1297.

Following the island's declaration of independence in 1755, Pasquale Paoli adopted the insignia as a national emblem. According to legend, the bandanna originally covered the Moor's eyes, and was raised to the forehead to symbolise the island's liberation.

When to Go

The best time to visit Corsica is in April and May, when the sun is shining, the olives are ripening, the wildflowers are blooming – and tourists are few. Many hotels, camping grounds and restaurants operate seasonally. Before Easter, there are practically no visitors, but in July and August, prices rocket and Corsica entertains an unending circus of holidaymakers.

Dangers & Annoyances

When Corsica makes the headlines, it's often because nationalist militants have turned nasty (previous acts include bombings, bank robberies and the murder of the prefect). But the violence is not targeted at tourists, and visitors have no need to worry about their safety.

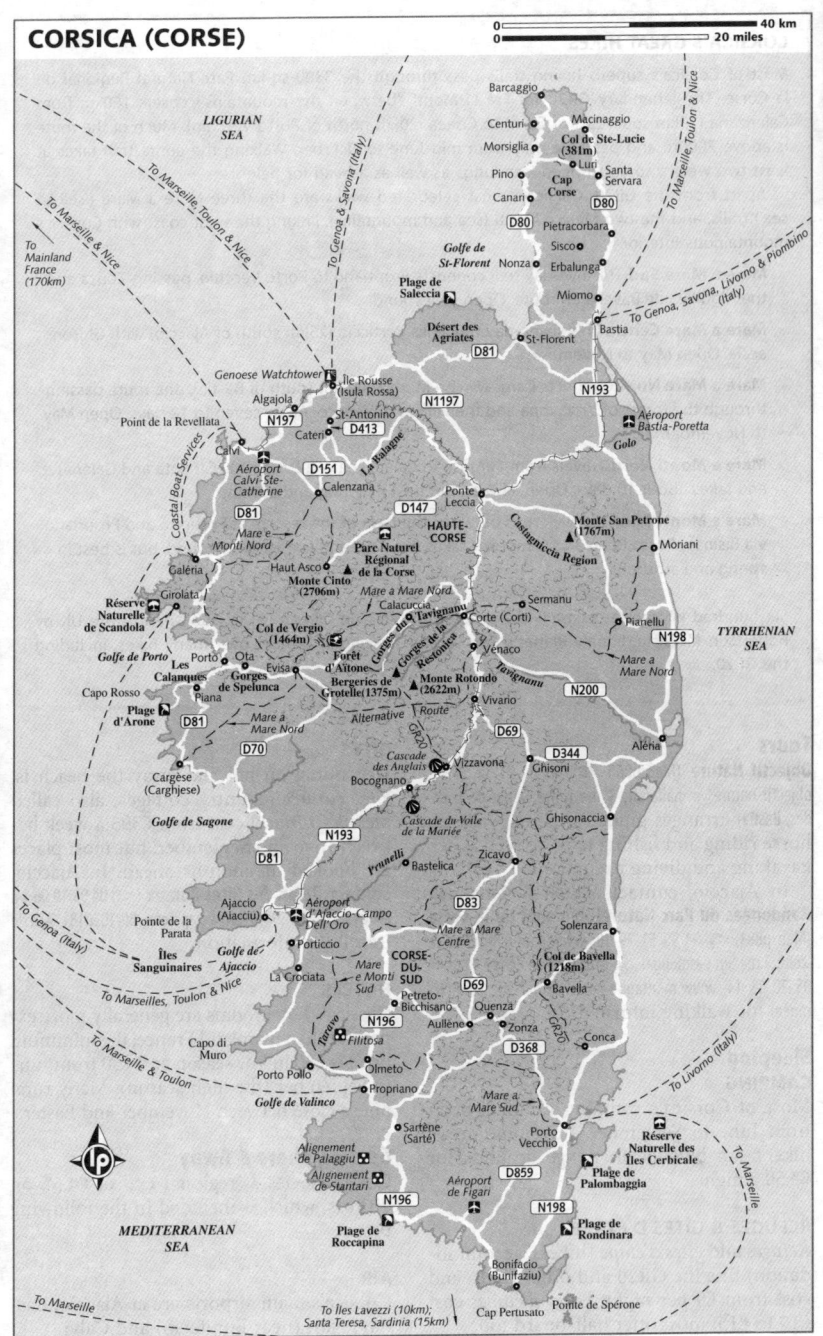

CORSICA (CORSE)

0   40 km
0   20 miles

*LIGURIAN
SEA*

To Marseille, Toulon & Nice

To Genoa & Savona (Italy)

To Marseille, Toulon & Nice

Barcaggio
Centuri
Macinaggio
Morsiglia
Col de Ste-Lucie
(381m)
Pino
Luri
Santa
Servara
Cap
Corse
Canari
Sisco
D80

To Mainland
France (170km)

To Marseille & Nice

Pietracorbara
*Golfe de
St-Florent* Nonza
Erbalunga
Miomo
D80

To Genoa, Savona, Livorno & Piombino (Italy)

Plage de
Saleccia
*Désert des
Agriates*
St-Florent
Bastia

Genoese Watchtower
Île Rousse
(Isula Rossa)
N1197
N193
Algajola
St-Antonino
*Aéroport
Bastia-Poretta*

Point de la Revellata
Caten
D413
Golo

Calvi
D151
Calenzana
D147
Ponte
Leccia
Castagniccia Region
Monte San Petrone
(1767m)
Moriani

*Aéroport Calvi-Ste-
Catherine*
D81
La Balagne
**HAUTE-
CORSE**

*Mare e
Monti Nord*
Galéria
Haut Asco
*Parc Naturel
Régional
de la Corse*
Calacuccia
Sermanu
Pianellu

**Réserve
Naturelle
de Scandola**
Girolata
Monte Cinto
(2706m)
Mare a Mare Nord
Tavignanu
Corte (Corti)
*TYRRHENIAN
SEA*

Col de Vergio
(1464m)
*Gorges de la
Restonica*
Vénaco
*Mare a
Mare Nord*

Golfe de Porto
Porto
Ota
Evisa
Forêt
d'Aïtone
Bergeries de
Grotelle(1375m)
Monte Rotondo
(2622m)
N200

Coastal Boat Services

Les
Calanques
Gorges
de Spelunca
Piana
Vivario

Capo Rosso
*Mare à
Mare Nord*
Alternative
Route
GR20
D69
Aléna

Plage
d'Arone
D81
D70
Cascade
des Anglais
Vizzavona
D344

Cargèse
(Carghjese)
Bocognano
Ghisoni

Golfe de Sagone
Cascade du Voile
de la Mariée
Ghisonaccia

N193
Zicavo

Prunelli
Bastelica
D83

D81
Ajaccio
(Aiacciu)
*Aéroport
d'Ajaccio-Campo
Dell'Oro*
Solenzara

Pointe de la
Parata
Porticcio
*Mare a Mare
Centre*
Col de Bavella
(1218m)

**Îles
Sanguinaires**
*Golfe de
Ajaccio*
La Crociata
**CORSE-
DU-
SUD**
D69
Bavella

To Genoa (Italy)
*Mare e Monti
Sud*
Petreto-
Bicchisano
Quenza
Conca

To Marseilles, Toulon & Nice
Capo di
Muro
Filitosa
N196
Aullène
Zonza
GR20

Tavaro
Olmeto
D368

To Marseille & Toulon
Porto Pollo
Propriano
*Mare a
Mare Sud*

Golfe de Valinco
Porto
Vecchio
**Réserve
Naturelle des
Îles Cerbicale**

Sartène
(Sartè)
Plage de
Palombaggia

**MEDITERRANEAN
SEA**
Alignement
de Palaggiu
Alignement
de Stantari
*Aéroport
de Figari*
D859
N198

To Marseille

N196
Plage de
Roccapina
Plage de
Rondinara

To Marseille

Bonifacio
(Bunifaziu)

To Marseille

To Îles Lavezzi (10km);
Santa Teresa, Sardinia (15km)
Cap Pertusato
Pointe de Spérone

CORSICA'S GREAT HIKES

Most of Corsica's superb hiking trails pass through the 3300-sq-km Parc Naturel Régional de la Corse. The legendary **GR20** (or Frá Li Monti, 'between the mountains') covers 160km from Calenzana (10km southeast of Calvi) to Conca (20km north of Porto Vecchio). Much of the route is above 2000m and passable only from mid-June to October. Walking the entire trail takes at least two weeks, so you'll need iron lungs as well as a head for heights.

Apart from the GR20, Corsica's most celebrated walks are the three Mare a Mare ('sea to sea') trails, and the two Mare e Monti (sea and mountains), linking the west coast with Corsica's mountainous interior.

■ **Mare a Mare Sud** This five-day trail connects Propriano to Porto Vecchio, passing Zonza and the Aiguilles de Bavella en route. Open year-round.

■ **Mare a Mare Centre** This seven-day trail links Porticcio (25km south of Ajaccio) with Ghisonaccia. Open May to November.

■ **Mare a Mare Nord** Connects Cargèse with Moriani (40km south of Bastia), one route passing through the forest of Vizzavona and the village of Vénaco. Allow seven to 12 days. Open May to November.

■ **Mare e Monti Nord** Travels from Cargèse to Calenzana (via Évisa, Ota, Girolata and Galéria) and takes about 10 days. Open all year, but best in spring and autumn.

■ **Mare e Monti Sud** This walk runs between the bays of the resorts of Porticcio and Propriano via Bisinao, Porto Pollo and Olmeto. It takes five days and is open year-round, but is best in spring and autumn.

Six hundred kilometres of trails are covered in *Walks in Corsica* (€18), published in the UK by Robertson McCarta. Lonely Planet's *Corsica* and *Walking in France* cover many hikes, including the GR20.

Tours

Objectif Nature (Map p868; ☎/fax 04 95 32 54 34; objectif-nature@wanadoo.fr; 3 rue Notre Dame de Lourdes, Bastia) arranges guided cycling, walking, horse riding and fishing trips, as well as sea kayaking and diving excursions.

In Ajaccio, contact **Maison d'Information Randonées du Parc Naturel Régional de la Corse** (Map p881; ☎ 04 95 51 79 10; www.parc-naturel-corse .com; 2 rue Sgt Casolonga) or **Muntagne Corse** (☎ 04 95 20 53 14; www.montagne-corse.com; 7 rue Méditerranée) for walking information.

Sleeping

CAMPING

Most of Corsica's camping grounds open from June to September. In remote areas, hikers can bivouac in *refuge* grounds for €3.50 a night.

REFUGES & GÎTES D'ÉTAPE

Refuges and *gîtes d'étape* (hikers' accommodation) line the GR20 and other trails, and cost from €9 per night. *Gîtes d'étapes* cost €10 to €15; most offer half-board too.

GÎTES

Depending on how far away the beach is, *gîtes ruraux* (country cottages, also called *meublés ruraux*) cost from €395 a week between June and September, but most places are booked up months ahead. In Ajaccio, contact **Relais des Gîtes Ruraux** (☎ 04 95 10 06 14; fax 04 95 10 54 39; 77 cours Napoléon, BP 1020181, Ajaccio Cedex 1) for information.

HOTELS

Corsica's hotel rooms are generally more expensive than mainland France; the minimum price is €30 in low season and €50 from June to September (the high season). Many rural hotels close between November and Easter.

Getting There & Away

Corsica levies a 'regional tax' of €4.57 on visitors, which is included in the following prices.

AIR

Corsica's main airports are at Ajaccio, Bastia, Figari (near Bonifacio) and Calvi.

Air France (☎ 0 820 820 820; www.airfrance.com) has year-round flights from Paris and Lyon to all airports except Figari. Seasonal flights operate from Bordeaux, Lille, Nantes, Mulhouse and Strasbourg to Bastia or Ajaccio. Air France also flies regularly from London to Corsica's main airports.

Compagnie Corse Méditeranée (☎ 0 820 820 820; www.ccm-airlines.com) flies from Bastia and Ajaccio to Marseille, Lyon and Nice year-round, and to Bordeaux, Lille, Lyon, Mulhouse Nantes and Strasbourg in summer.

Littoral Air (www.littoral-airlines.com in French) flies to Calvi, Bastia, Figari and Ajaccio.

BOAT
Mainland France
Most ferries between France (Nice, Marseille and Toulon) and Corsica (Ajaccio, Bastia, Calvi, Île Rousse, Porto Vecchio and Propriano) are handled by **Société Nationale Maritime Corse-Méditerranée** (SNCM; ☎ 0 891 701 801; online bookings www.sncm.fr).

Schedules and fares are listed in the SNCM timetable, available free from tourist and SNCM offices. In summer there are up to eight ferries daily; in winter there are as few as eight a week and fares are much cheaper. In high season, reservations are essential. Remember that ferries are dependent on weather conditions and boats can be cancelled at very short notice (often on the day of departure).

One-way tickets cost €30 (up to €42 for peak summer crossings) from Nice, €35 (€53 in peak periods) from Marseille or Toulon. Daytime crossings from Nice take around four hours. Most crossings from Marseille and Toulon are overnight: the cheapest couchette/most luxurious cabin costs €18/185 extra in summer.

For people under 25 and over 60, single fares are €27/15 in summer/winter from Nice, €40/20 from Marseille and Toulon. Children between four and 12 pay €17/13 in summer/winter from Nice, €19/7 from Marseille or Toulon. Under fours travel free.

Small cars cost €40 to €100 from Marseille or Toulon, or €40 to €108 from Nice, depending on the season. Motorcycles cost €21 to €59 and bicycles cost €10 to €14.

Corsica Ferries and SNCM also have 70km/h express NGV (Navire à Grande Vitesse) ferries from Nice to Calvi (three hours), Île Rousse (three hours), Ajaccio (four hours) and Bastia (four hours). Fares on these zippy NGVs are the same as on normal ferries, but there's a €5 to €8 supplement on peak-period crossings in summer.

In addition to basic fares, each port levies visitor taxes (€7.21 to €10.57 per passenger, €5.45 to €9.27 per vehicle), which vary according to the ports you use.

Italy
Between April and October, scheduled ferries link Corsica with the Italian mainland ports of Genoa, Livorno and Savona, and Porto Terres on neighbouring Sardinia. The season is shorter for smaller boats that cross between Bonifacio and Santa Teresa di Gallura on Sardinia.

Corsica Ferries and Moby Lines are the main operators on these routes. From Livorno (near Pisa and Florence) it's a two-hour voyage to Bastia. A Propriano–Porto Terres trip takes 3½ hours, Genoa–Bastia 6½ hours and Savona to Bastia/Calvi takes six/eight hours.

Fares from mainland Italy are lower than those from mainland France. Corsica Ferries charges €40 to €110 to transport a small car one way and upwards of €16/23 per person (up to €33/33 in high season) on a day/night crossing from Savona to Bastia, Calvi or Île Rousse. Passengers sailing with La Méridionale to Ajaccio or Propriano from Porto Terres pay €19, plus €35 for a car. For port taxes, add about €6 per passenger and €5 per car.

La Méridionale (CMN; France ☎ 08 10 20 13 20; www.cmn.fr), an SNCM subsidiary, has year-round sailings between Marseille and Ajaccio, Bastia and Propriano; and seasonal ferries (April to October) between Porto Terres (Sardinia) and Propriano and Ajaccio.

Corsica Ferries (France ☎ 08 25 09 50 95, Livorno ☎ 0586 88 13 80, Savona ☎ 019 215 62 47; www.corsicaferries.com) runs year-round from Nice to Ajaccio, Bastia, Calvi and Île Rousse, and from Toulon to Ajaccio and Bastia. It runs seasonal ferries from Livorno to Bastia (from April to early November) and from Savona to Bastia, Calvi and Île Rousse (from April to September).

Moby Lines (Corsica ☎ 04 95 34 84 94, Genoa ☎ 010 254 15 13, Livorno ☎ 0565 93 61; www.mobylines.it) has seasonal ferries (from May to September) from Genoa and Livorno to Bastia. Seasonal boats (from April to September) also

CORSICA

CORSICA'S TOP FIVE ROAD TRIPS

- **Cape Quest** (Cap Corse, four to six hours, D80) The roller-coaster road around Corsica's windswept peninsula snakes through the bays and fishing villages of the east coast, swings past Corsica's northernmost point, and shoots down the peninsula's windswept western clifftops.

- **West Coast Wonders** (Calvi to Porto, four to six hours, D81 and D81B) One of Corsica's most scenic drives, passing tiny inlets, vertical drops and thundering waves along the cliffs from Calvi to Porto. Take your time, savour the view – and look out for mountain goats.

- **Mountain Madness** (Porto to Vergio, three to four hours, D124 and D84) From Porto, this route climbs through Ota, Évisa and the Gorges de Spelunca to Col de Vergio (1464m), the highest road pass in Corsica. It's a spectacular journey through mountains, chestnut forests and canyons – bring plenty of spare film.

- **Peak Performance** (Zonza to Bavella, two to three hours, D268) The D268 connects Zonza with the Col de Bavella (1261m), a mountain landscape covered by flowers in spring and snow in winter. From the hilltop, you can drink in alpine views all the way to the hazy blue Mediterranean.

- **Hairpin High Jinks** (Vivario to Zicavo, two to four hours, D69) From Vivario, south of Corte, the D69 traverses peaks and valleys on its way through the Vizzavona Forest to Zicavo. Those without a head for heights should stay at home, but they'll be missing one of the island's classic drives.

operate between Santa Teresa di Gallura (Sardinia) and Bonifacio.

Getting Around
BUS
Corsica's buses are slow, infrequent and handled by several independent companies. On longer routes, mostly operated by **Eurocorse** (Ajaccio ☎ 04 95 21 06 30, Porto Vecchio ☎ 04 95 70 13 83), there are one, two or, at most, four runs daily. Except in high summer, buses rarely run on Sunday and holidays.

CAR & MOTORCYCLE
Travelling by road is the most convenient way to explore Corsica, but driving isn't easy. Most roads are spectacular but narrow, with hairpin curves and huge drops that demand nerves of steel. Count on averaging 50km/h (and look out for Corsican drivers). The speediest road is the east-coast N198 from Bastia to Bonifacio. A good road map (such as Michelin's yellow-jacketed 1:200,000 map No 90) is indispensable.

TRAIN
Corsica's single-track railway is at least a century behind the TGV, but it's a great (if bone-shattering) way to explore the island. In Corsica, trains are known as *U Trinighellu* ('the trembler'), and you only have to spend

five minutes on one to understand why. The tiny trains screech and judder their way through the mountains, stopping at tiny rural stations and, when necessary, for sheep, goats and cows.

The network's two lines meet at Ponte Leccia. Between September and July, the Ajaccio–Corte–Bastia line is served by four daily trains (two on Sunday and holidays). Two daily trains (coordinated with the Ajaccio–Corte–Bastia service) link Bastia with Ponte Leccia, Île Rousse and Calvi. Services are reduced in winter and increased in August.

Fares range from €9.70 (Bastia–Corte) to €24.50 (Ajaccio–Calvi). Children under 12 travel half-price; under fours travel free. Transporting a bicycle costs €18. For further details, contact **Chemins de Fer de Corse** (CFC; Bastia ☎ 04 95 32 80 61; www.ter-sncf.com/trains_touristiques/corse_anglais.htm).

Rail Passes
For return journeys of less than 200km within 48 hours, the *billet touristique* (tourist ticket) is 25% cheaper than a regular ticket, but is unavailable from July to September.

Holders of InterRail passes get 50% off normal fares. The CFC sells its own rail pass – the Carte Zoom – which costs €47 and buys unlimited train travel for seven days.

BASTIA AREA

BASTIA

pop 37,800

Bustling Bastia is Corsica's main centre of business and commerce. With its crumbling citadel, narrow streets, colourful tenement buildings and tree-lined squares, the city has a distinctly Italian atmosphere and was once the seat of the island's Genoese governors. Little effort has been made to smarten up the city for tourists, making it an authentic and atmospheric introduction to modern-day Corsica. You can easily spend a day exploring, the old port being Bastia's highlight – but most visitors move on pretty quickly.

Orientation

The focal point of the Bastia is place St-Nicolas. Bastia's main thoroughfares are the busy shopping street of boulevard Paoli and av Maréchal Sébastiani, which links the ferry port with the train station. The town's three older neighbourhoods are south of place St-Nicolas: Terra Vecchia (centred on place de l'Hôtel de Ville), the old port and the citadel.

Information

BOOKSHOPS

Librairie Album (☎ 04 95 31 08 59; 19 blvd Paoli; ❤ 8am-noon & 1.30-7.30pm Mon-Sat, 9am-12.30pm Sun) Big bookshop with an excellent travel section.

Librairie-Papeterie Papi (☎ 04 95 31 00 96; 5 rue César Campinchi; ❤ 7.30am-noon & 1.30-7pm Mon-Sat) Sells walking maps, topoguides and travel books.

EMERGENCY

Centre Hospitalier Général Paese Nuovo (☎ 04 95 59 11 11; Route Impériale)

Police National (☎ 04 95 54 50 22) Near the northern ferry terminal.

INTERNET ACCESS

Cyber Space (☎ 04 95 30 70 83; 3 blvd Paoli; per 15min/hr €1/3.80; ❤ 9am-midnight Mon-Sat, 4pm-midnight Sun) Mainly geared towards Internet gamers.

Oxy Cybercafé (☎ 04 95 58 27 96; rue Salvatore Viale; per hr €3.10; ❤ 9am-midnight Mon-Sat)

LAUNDRY

Le Lavoir du Port (❤ 7am-9pm) In the car park near the end of rue du Commandant Luce de Casabianca.

MONEY

Banks are dotted along place St-Nicolas, rue César Campinchi and rue du Conventionnel Salicetti. Most have ATMs. The exchange bureau in the southern ferry terminal is only open in summer.

POST

Post Office (av Maréchal Sébastiani; ❤ 8am-7pm Mon-Fri, 8am-noon Sat)

TOURIST OFFICES

Tourist Office (☎ 04 95 55 96 85; www.bastia-tourisme.com; place St-Nicolas; ❤ 8am-6pm Mon-Sat, 8am-1pm Sun)

Sights

Bastia can be covered in a half-day stroll starting with **place St-Nicolas**, a vast seafront esplanade laid out in the 19th century. The square is lined with trees and cafés, and at the southern end, a bizarre statue of **Napoleon Bonaparte** depicted as a muscle-bound Roman emperor stands guard, ringed by a phalanx of palm trees.

Between place St-Nicolas and the old port lies **Terra Vecchia**, a historic neighbourhood of old houses and tumbledown tenement blocks. Its centre is the shady **place de l'Hôtel de Ville**, now an open-air marketplace. On rue Napoléon, the baroque **Oratoire de l'Immaculée** once served as the seat of the Anglo-Corsican parliament.

The **old port** is an atmospheric jumble of boats, restaurants and crumbling buildings, dominated by the twin towers of the **Église St-Jean Baptiste**, which loom over the north side of the harbour. The best views are from **Jetée du Dragon** (Dragon Jetty) on the southern side of the harbour, where you can admire the luxury pleasure cruisers and watch the local blue-and-white fishing boats setting out to sea.

Bastia's most historic quarter juts out above the old port. The **citadel** in Terra Nova was built by the Genoese between the 15th and 17th centuries to protect Bastia's harbour. To reach it, climb the stairs through **Jardin Romieu**, the hillside park on the southern side of the harbour. Inside the citadel, winding streets lead to **Cathédrale Ste-Marie**, which contains one of the city's most precious relics, a mysterious black-oak crucifix hauled from the sea by fishermen in the 14th century.

BASTIA

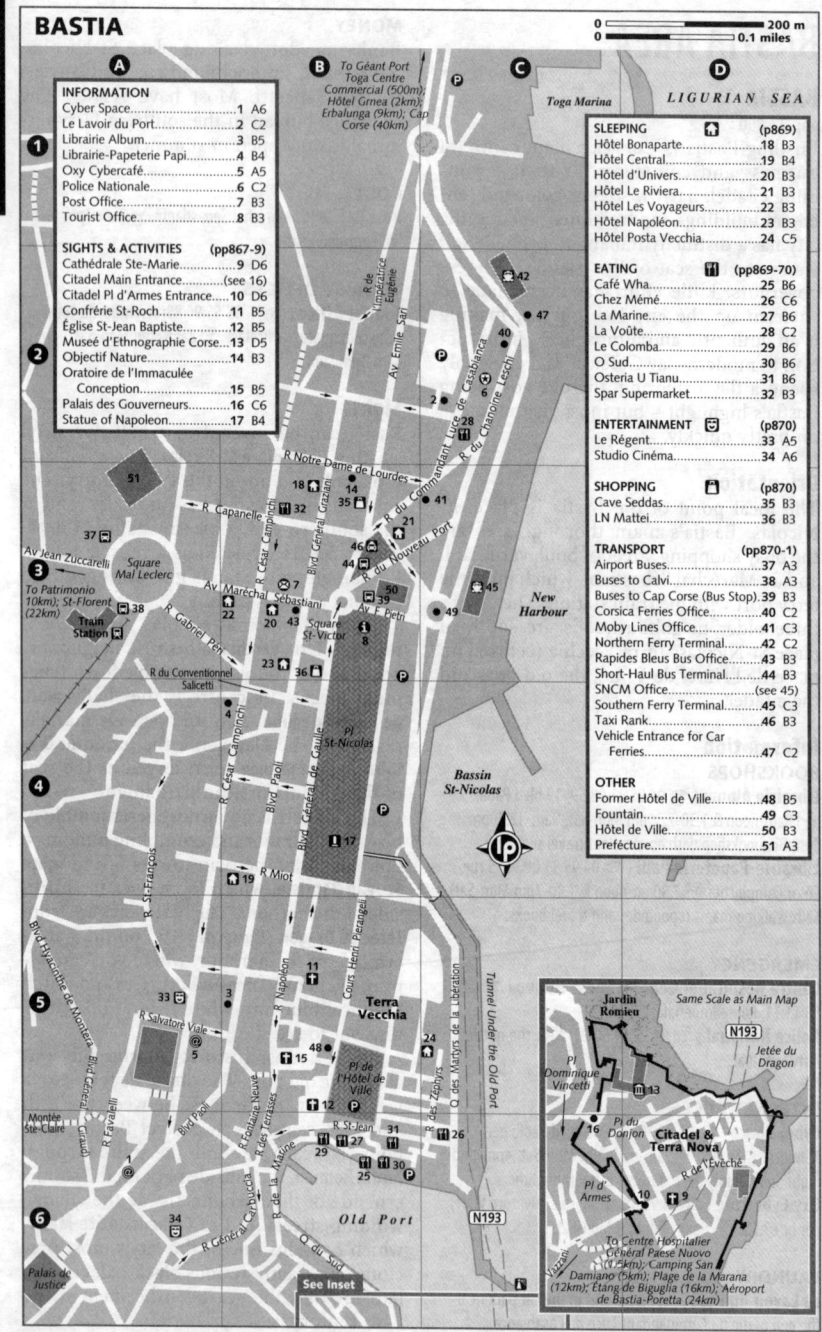

0 — 200 m
0 — 0.1 miles

INFORMATION
Cyber Space...................................1	A6
Le Lavoir du Port..........................2	C2
Librairie Album.............................3	B5
Librairie-Papeterie Papi.................4	B4
Oxy Cybercafé..............................5	A5
Police Nationale............................6	C2
Post Office....................................7	B3
Tourist Office...............................8	B3

SIGHTS & ACTIVITIES   (pp867-9)
Cathédrale Ste-Marie.....................9	D6
Citadel Main Entrance.............(see 16)	
Citadel Pl d'Armes Entrance..........10	D6
Confrérie St-Roch.........................11	B5
Église St-Jean Baptiste..................12	B5
Musée d'Ethnographie Corse.........13	D5
Objectif Nature............................14	B3
Oratoire de l'Immaculée	
Conception..............................15	B5
Palais des Gouverneurs.................16	C6
Statue of Napoleon.......................17	B4

SLEEPING   🛏   (p869)
Hôtel Bonaparte...........................18	B3
Hôtel Central................................19	B4
Hôtel d'Univers.............................20	B3
Hôtel Le Riviera............................21	B3
Hôtel Les Voyageurs.....................22	B3
Hôtel Napoléon............................23	B3
Hôtel Posta Vecchia......................24	C5

EATING   🍴   (pp869-70)
Café Wha....................................25	B6
Chez Mémé.................................26	C6
La Marine....................................27	B6
La Voûte.....................................28	C2
Le Colomba.................................29	B6
O Sud...30	B6
Osteria U Tianu............................31	B6
Spar Supermarket.........................32	B3

ENTERTAINMENT   🎭   (p870)
Le Régent....................................33	A5
Studio Cinéma..............................34	A6

SHOPPING   🛍   (p870)
Cave Seddas................................35	B3
LN Mattei....................................36	B3

TRANSPORT   (pp870-1)
Airport Buses...............................37	A3
Buses to Calvi..............................38	A3
Buses to Cap Corse (Bus Stop).39	B3
Corsica Ferries Office....................40	C2
Moby Lines Office.........................41	C3
Northern Ferry Terminal................42	C2
Rapides Bleus Bus Office...............43	B3
Short-Haul Bus Terminal...............44	B3
SNCM Office.........................(see 45)	
Southern Ferry Terminal................45	C3
Taxi Rank...................................46	B3
Vehicle Entrance for Car	
Ferries.....................................47	C2

OTHER
Former Hôtel de Ville....................48	B5
Fountain.....................................49	C3
Hôtel de Ville..............................50	B3
Préfecture...................................51	A3

To Géant Port
Toga Centre
Commercial (500m);
Hôtel Grnea (2km);
Erbalunga (9km); Cap
Corse (40km)

Toga Marina

LIGURIAN SEA

R de l'Impératrice Eugénie

Av Émile Sari

R du Commandant Luce de Casabianca

R du Chanoine Leschi

R Notre Dame de Lourdes

R Capanelle

R César Campinchi

Blvd Général Graziani

R du Nouveau Port

New Harbour

Square Mal Leclerc

Av Jean Zuccarelli

Av Maréchal Sebastiani

Square St-Victor

Av F Pietri

To Patrimonio
10km); St-Florent
(22km)

Train Station

R Gabriel Peri

R du Conventionnel Salicetti

Bassin St-Nicolas

Pl St-Nicolas

Blvd Général de Gaulle

Blvd Paoli

R César Campinchi

R St François

R Miot

R Napoléon

Terra Vecchia

Cours Henri Pinzarelli

Q des Martyrs de la Libération

Tunnel Under the Old Port

Blvd Hyacinthe de Montera

Blvd Général
Blvd Paoli

Montée Ste-Claire

R Cavalelli

R Salvatore Viale

R Fontaine Neuve

R des Terrasses

Pl de l'Hôtel de Ville

R St-Jean

Old Port

R Général Carbuccia

Q de la Marine

Q du Sud

Palais de Justice

N193

See Inset

Jardin Romieu

Same Scale as Main Map

N193

Jetée du Dragon

Pl Dominique Vincetti

Pl du Donjon

Citadel & Terra Nova

R de l'Evêché

Pl d'Armes

To Centre Hospitalier
Général Paese Nuovo
(1.5km); Camping San
Damiano (5km); Plage de la Marana
(12km); Étang de Biguglia (16km); Aéroport
de Bastia-Poretta (24km)

Close by, the fiery-orange **Palais des Gou-verneurs** (Governors' Palace; place du Donjon) is home to Bastia's anthropology museum, **Musée d'Ethnographie Corse**. Both are currently closed as part of a €6 million restoration project. There's also an old Clarissian convent, which became a **prison** in the 19th century.

Activities

Objectif Nature (☎ /fax 04 95 32 54 34; objectif-nature@ wanadoo.fr; 3 rue Notre Dame de Lourdes; ✆ 9am-6pm Mon-Sat) organises outdoor activities in the Bastia area, including kayaking, sea fishing, hiking, mountaineering and diving.

Sleeping

Like the rest of Corsica, Bastia's hotels hike up their prices in summer. Many have their reception desks on the 1st floor.

BUDGET

Hôtel Central (☎ 04 95 31 71 12; www.centralhotel.fr; 3 rue Miot; s €40-65, d €40-78 depending on season; ✆) As its name suggests, it's right in the city centre and the rooms have all been refurbished: the best have balconies and kitchenettes. You can also rent apartments (€50 to €65 per day, €305 to €420 per week).

Hôtel Le Riviera (☎ 04 95 31 07 16; www.corseho telriviera.com in French; 1bis rue du Nouveau Port; s €40-60, d €60-80 depending on season; ✆) Rather like the rest of town – in dire need of some tender-loving care. The rooms are about as cheap as they get in Bastia, if you don't mind the odd spot of peeling plasterwork.

Camping

Camping San Damiano (☎ 04 95 33 68 02; www.camp ingsandamiano.com; camping low/high season €5.50/6.50; ✆ Apr-Oct) A shady seaside camping ground 5km south of Bastia, with furnished bungalows available. Served by the airport bus.

MID-RANGE

Hôtel d'Univers (☎ 04 95 31 03 38; fax 04 95 31 19 91; 3 av Maréchal Sébastiani; s/d/tr low season €45/55/65, high season €60/70/80; ✆) The pick of Bastia's mid-range hotels, tucked between the old and new towns. The tasteful rooms have white walls, colourful bedspreads and wooden floors.

Hôtel Les Voyageurs (☎ 04 95 34 90 80; www.hotel -lesvoyageurs.com; 9 av Maréchal Sébastiani; d low season €52-80, high season €55-90; ✆) A smart three-star hotel with luxurious touches, up the street

from the Univers. Features include a lovely dining area behind a wrought-iron screen.

Hôtel Posta Vecchia (☎ 04 95 32 32 38; www.hotel -postavecchia.com; quai des Martyrs de la Libération; s/d with sea views €37/41, low season €54/60; ✆) One of the few hotels with sea views in Bastia. Don't be put off by the pebble-dash outside – inside the hotel is full of charm, and the old port is just around the corner.

Hôtel Napoléon (☎ 04 95 31 60 30; 43 blvd Paoli; d low season €49-75, high season €64-95) Another central option with small, comfortable doubles, though some of the décor is dated. Check out the colourful Corsican mural as you climb the stairs to reception.

Also recommended:

Hôtel Bonaparte (☎ 04 95 34 07 10; www.hotel-bona parte-bastia.com; 45 blvd Général Graziani; s/d/tr low season €58/60/75, high season €68/87/100) Plain, modern hotel close to the port.

Hôtel Cyrnea (☎ 04 95 31 41 71; route de Cap; d low season €45-83; P ✆) Purpose-built seafront hotel 2km north of Bastia.

Eating

For a quick *café créme* or ice cream, terraced cafés line place St-Nicolas. More restaurants are clustered around the old port, quai des Martyrs de la Libération and place de l'Hôtel de Ville.

La Voûte (☎ 04 95 32 47 11; 6 rue du Commandant Luce de Casabianca; lunch/dinner menu €12.95/20.70; ✆ Mon-Sat) Sophisticated French cuisine is served here under brick vaults or on a balcony with harbour view. The fish soup (€10) and *gambas à la provençale* (king prawns, €19) offer a true taste of the Mediterranean.

The old port is crammed with restaurants to suit all tastes: some are cosy and traditional, while others have packed terraces and lay on summer entertainment.

La Marine (☎ 06 12 21 38 09; 8 rue St-Jean; menus €12-21; ✆ Mon-Sat) An informal seafood restaurant that also offers pizzas and Corsican fare on its portside terrace; most of the fish literally comes straight off the boats.

Café Wha (☎ 04 95 34 25 79; Vieux Port; mains €7.80-14.90) A popular place on the old port, with a cheap Tex-Mex menu and regular theme nights. It serves generous *quesadillas* (€6 to €8) and fajitas (€8 to €10), and is nearly always chock-a-block with Bastiais and tourists alike.

Chez Mémé (☎ 04 95 31 44 12; quai des Martyrs de la Libération; menus €14-17) One of many seafront

---

COMIC BOOKS, CHECKMATE & CORSICAN BLUES

In April, Bastia hosts France's trendiest *bandes dessinées* (comics) festival, BD à Bastia. The graphic novel is a revered French art form, and the festival attracts big names from the pen-and-ink world – this is not the place to show off your second-rate Astérix collection.

In late summer, the tiny village of Patrimonio, about 10km west of Bastia, hosts **Nuits de la Guitare à Patrimonio** (☎ 04 95 37 12 15; www.festival-guitare-patrimonio.com), one of Europe's major guitar festivals. Jazz, blues, rock and classical guitar all find a home on the main outdoor stage.

Bastia's annual Italian Cinema Festival is held in February. There are British and Spanish film weeks later in the year. Other events include a Corsican music festival in October, and the island's hotly contested chess championships in November.

---

restaurants near the old port. It's a simple, unpretentious place that specialises in fish and shellfish: the €14 *menu corse* includes Corsican meats and cheeses.

Osteria U Tianu (☎ 04 95 31 36 67; 4 rue Rigo; menu €19; ⏲ 7pm-1am Mon-Sat) This small, homely restaurant, hidden away down a backstreet behind the old port, is one of the best places in Bastia to sample authentic Corsican cuisine. The €19 five-course *menu* includes a range of traditional dishes and includes wine, so it's usually packed to the gunnels.

Also recommended:

Le Colomba (☎ 04 95 32 79 14; Vieux Port; pizzas €7-10) The best pizzas in the old port.

O Sud (☎ 04 95 31 00 90; Vieux Port; menus from €12) Upbeat restaurant next door to Café Wha.

SELF-CATERING

There's a lively morning **food market** (place de l'Hôtel de Ville; ⏲ Tue-Sun). The large **Spar supermarket** (rue César Campinchi) is the most convenient place for supplies. Out of town, the huge Géant Port Toga Centre Commercial houses a Casino supermarket.

Entertainment

Le Régent (☎ 04 95 31 30 31; www.leregent.fr; rue César Campinchi) A large multi-screen cinema screening the latest releases (nearly always in French).

Studio Cinéma (☎ 04 95 31 12 94; www.studio -cinema.com; rue Miséricorde) A small arts cinema near the Palais de Justice that shows both French and international films, and also hosts several of Bastia's annual film weeks.

Shopping

Cave Seddas (3 av Emile Sari) is stocked with Corsican wines, while **LN Mattei** (15 blvd Général de Gaulle) is the place to buy the local liqueur, Cap Corse – Louis Napoléon Mattei invented

the liqueur in the late 19th century. Both of these shops sell Corsican jams, honeys and other delicacies.

Arrive at the Sunday **flea-market** (place St-Nicolas) before 9am for the best selection.

Getting There & Around

AIR

Aéroport Bastia-Poretta (☎ 04 95 54 54 54; www .bastia.aeroport.fr) is 24km south of the city. Buses (€8, seven to nine daily, fewer on Sunday) depart from outside the Préfecture building. The tourist office has schedules, and timetables are posted at the bus stop. A taxi to the airport costs €20 to €30.

BUS

The bus service in Bastia is bewildering – there is no central terminus and buses leave from several locations around town. The tourist office can provide timetables and show you where to catch your bus. Rue du Nouveau Port, north of the tourist office, is a makeshift terminus for buses serving villages south and west of Bastia.

Eurocorse (☎ 04 95 31 73 76) travels to Ajaccio (€18, three hours) via Corte (€10, two hours) twice daily except on Sundays.

Rapides Bleus (☎ 04 95 31 03 79; 1 av Maréchal Sébastiani) runs buses to Porto Vecchio (€18.50), with connections to Bonifacio and Sartène. It also sells tickets for the Eurocorse service to Corte and Ajaccio.

Les Beaux Voyages (☎ 04 95 65 11 35) travels to Calvi (€12.50, two hours) daily except Sunday. Buses leave at 4.30pm from outside the train station.

TRAIN

The **train station** (☎ 04 95 32 80 61; av Maréchal Sébastiani; ⏲ 6am-8.40pm Mon-Sat, 8.40am-12.40pm & 4.15-8.40pm Sun) is beside the large roundabout on Square Mal Leclerc. Main destinations include Ajaccio (€20.70, four hours, four daily) via Corte, and Calvi (€15.70, three hours, three or four daily) via L'Île Rousse.

BOAT

The southern ferry terminal is at the eastern end of av François Pietri. The vehicle entrance is 600m north.

There's an **SNCM** (☎ 04 95 54 66 81; www.sncm .com; ☒ 8-11.45am & 2-5.45pm Mon-Fri, 8am-noon Sat) office in the southern terminal. Tickets are sold two hours before departure in the Corsica Marittima section of the terminal building.

Moby Lines (☎ 04 95 34 84 94; www.mobylines.it; 4 rue du Commandant Luce de Casabianca; ☒ 8am-noon & 2-6pm Mon-Fri, 8am-noon Sat) has a bureau in the ferry terminal, open two hours before each sailing.

The **Corsica Ferries** (☎ 04 95 32 95 95; corsicafer ries.com; 15bis rue Chanoine Leschi; ☒ 8.30am-noon & 2-6pm Mon-Fri, 9am-noon Sat) office is across the road from the ferry terminal.

CAP CORSE

The narrow peninsula at Corsica's upper tip stretches 40km north from Bastia. It's a wild, ruggedly beautiful area, sliced down the centre by mountains and ringed by spectacular coastline dotted with crumbling Genoese watchtowers, sandy coves and rocky cliffs.

Cap Corse can be visited by bus from Bastia, but the trip is more fun if you have your own transport. With legs of steel and time to spare, the area can also be explored by bike. Less energetic types can cover it in a day by car, but be prepared for some adventurous driving – Cap Corse's clifftop roads are not for the faint-hearted.

North of Bastia, the road winds through gentle bays and quiet fishing villages, including **Erbalunga**, **Sisco** and **Pietracorbara**, where you'll find one of the coast's best beaches.

At Santa Servara, the road splits in two. The western branch climbs though the village of Luri to the hilltop tower at **Col de Ste-Lucie**, where the Roman poet-philosopher Seneca was exiled in the 1st century. The second branch continues north to **Macinaggio**, a small fishing port and tourist town, and **Barcaggio**, near Corsica's northernmost point.

The west coast is wilder, with villages perched high on the steep cliffs and jagged inlets cut into the coastline. From Barcaggio, the road swings south to **Centuri**, with its traditional Corsican houses clustered around a pretty harbour. Further south, past the villages of **Pino** and **Canari**, you'll arrive at **Nonza**, where the houses tumble down the cliff in steep terraces to a vast grey-sand bay. The historic village is famous for the fortified tower perched above the beach and the 11th century chapel of St Julia (who was martyred in Nonza in the 5th century).

The final stretch passes sweeping bays on the way to **St-Florent**, a busy harbour at the end of the Cap Corse peninsula.

Sleeping & Eating

Macchia e Mare (☎ 04 95 35 21 36; www.macchia-e -mare.com in French; d Oct-Mar €44-53, Apr-Aug €45-63; P) In the east-coast village of Pietracorbara. The best rooms have sea views and terraces, and the white, sandy beach is moments away.

Le Vieux Moulin (☎ 04 95 35 60 15; www.le-vieux -moulin.net in French; d Apr-May & Oct €47-65, Jun-Sep €50-75; P) A traditional cottage hotel near Centuri harbour. The attached seafood restaurant is one of the most popular on the peninsula.

Les Tamaris (☎ 04 95 37 81 91; www.lestamaris .com; d May & Sep-Oct €51-58, Jun-Aug €60-75; P) This modern hotel in Canari is close to the beach and organises activities such as horse riding and local walks. Self-catering apartments cost €305 to €615 per week.

CAMPING

Camping La Pietra (☎ 04 95 35 27 49; ☒ May-Oct) A large, family-oriented camping ground near Sisco, which has all the creature comforts, but gets crowded in summer.

Camping L'Isulottu (☎ 04 95 35 62 81; www.paradisu .com; ☒ Feb-Nov; ☒) A shady, secluded camping area near Morsiglia, south of Centuri, with swimming pool, restaurant and bar.

Getting There & Away

The main road around Cap Corse is the D80. **Société des Transports Interurbains Bastiais** (☎ 04 95 31 06 65) handles buses to Cap Corse. Destinations include Erbalunga (€2, six to eight daily), Pietracorbara (€2.60) and Macinaggio (€6.40, two daily except Sunday). Buses leave from av François Pietri, opposite the tourist office, in Bastia.

CORSICA

THE NORTH COAST

CALVI

pop 4800

The prosperous harbour town of Calvi sits at the edge of a sparkling crescent-shaped bay, backed by the snowy peaks of Monte Cinto (2706m) and its neighbours. Once a strategic military outpost, today Calvi is a thriving pleasure port that attracts sun seekers and weekend sailors from all over the Mediterranean, though the towers, bastions and clustered houses of its 15th-century citadel remain as relics of its martial past.

In 1794, a British expeditionary fleet assisting Pasquale Paoli's Corsican nationalist forces besieged and bombarded Calvi. In the course of the battle, a certain Captain Horatio Nelson was wounded by rock splinters and lost the use of his right eye.

Orientation

The citadel – also known as the Haute Ville (upper city) – is on a rocky promontory northeast of the Basse Ville (lower city). Blvd Wilson, the major thoroughfare through town, is uphill from the marina.

Information

BOOKSHOPS

Hall de la Presse (☎ 04 95 65 05 14; 13 blvd Wilson; ☺ 9am-noon & 2-6pm Mon-Sat) Sells topoguides and walking maps.

EMERGENCY

Antenne Médicale du SAMU (☎ 04 95 65 11 22; route du Stade)

INTERNET ACCESS

Café de l'Orient (☎ 04 95 65 00 16; quai Landry; connection/per min €1/0.10; ☺ 9am-late)

MONEY

Banks, including Crédit Lyonnais, can be found along blvd Wilson.

POST

Post Office (blvd Wilson)

TOURIST OFFICES

Tourist Office main office (☎ 04 95 65 16 67; omt .calvi@wanadoo.fr; ☺ 8.30am-1pm & 2.30-7pm Jun–mid-Sep, 9am-noon & 2-6pm Mon-Sat Oct-May); Citadel (☺ 9am-noon Mon-Sat, Jun-Sep) The main office is near the marina.

Sights & Activities

CITADEL

Set atop a granite promontory surrounded by massive Genoese fortifications, Calvi's 15th-century **citadel** dominates the harbour skyline. The town's loyalty to Genoa is recalled by the motto *Civitas Calvi Semper Fidelis* (the city of Calvi, forever faithful) carved over the citadel gateway. The majority of its buildings are closed to the public.

The **Palais des Gouverneurs** (Governors' Palace; place d'Armes) was once the seat of power for the Genoese administration and now serves (under the name Caserne Sampiero) as a base for the French Foreign Legion. Look out for soldiers wearing the regiment's distinctive white caps around town.

Up the hill from Caserne Sampiero is the 13th-century **Église St-Jean Baptiste**, rebuilt in 1570. The women of the local elite sat in the screened boxes, with grilles sheltering them from the rabble's inquisitive gaze. Near the altar is the *Christ des Miracles*, an ebony statue that was paraded around town in 1553 shortly before the besieging Turkish forces fell back. Credited with saving Calvi from the Saracens, the statue has become a much-revered relic.

CORSICAN POLYPHONY

Corsican band Les Nouvelles Polyphonies Corses won the heart of a nation with its magnetic polyphonic performance at the 1992 Winter Olympics in Albertville, France.

Corsican chants are traditionally sung a cappella (without musical accompaniment). *Paghjellas* feature three male voices – a tenor, baritone and bass – and mark the passage of life. Equally compelling are the church chants of the mountainous Castagniccia region, east of Corte. In Pigna, south of 'Île Rousse, summer polyphonic evenings are held in the **Casa Musicale** (☎ 04 95 61 77 31). Calvi hosts the five-day Rencontres Polyphoniques festival every September.

The recordings of the Sartène Male Voice Choir and contemporary bands I Muvrini, Canta U Populu Corsu and Les Nouvelles Polyphonies Corses are available on CD.

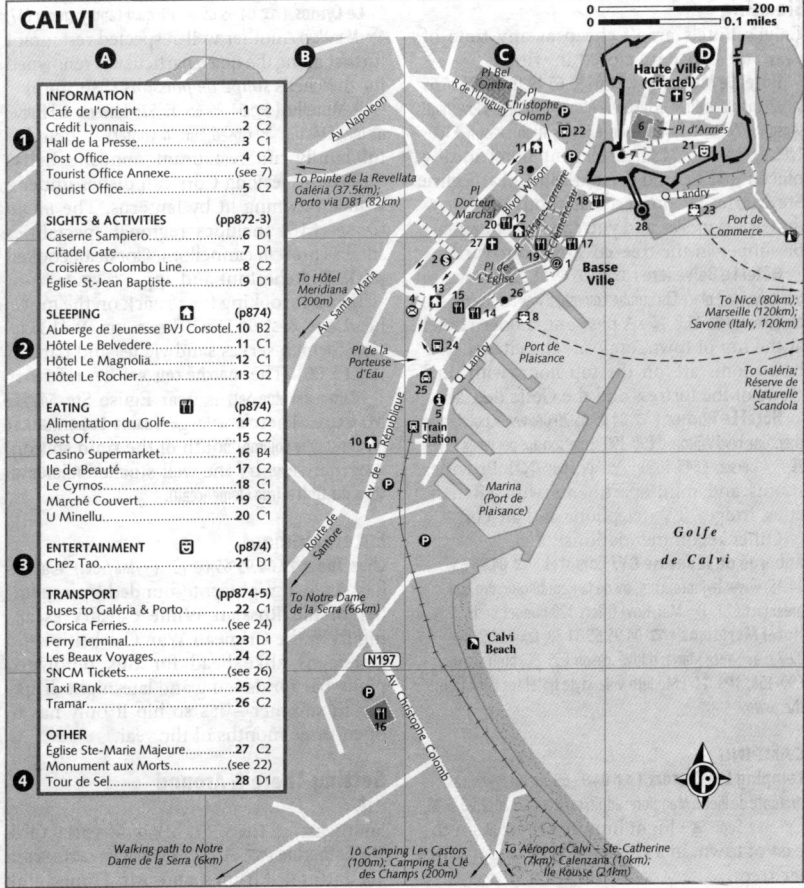

CALVI

INFORMATION	
Café de l'Orient	1 C2
Crédit Lyonnais	2 C2
Hall de la Presse	3 C1
Post Office	4 C2
Tourist Office Annexe	(see 7)
Tourist Office	5 C2

SIGHTS & ACTIVITIES	(pp872-3)
Caserne Sampiero	6 D1
Citadel Gate	7 D1
Croisières Colombo Line	8 C2
Église St-Jean Baptiste	9 D1

SLEEPING	(p874)
Auberge de Jeunesse BVJ Corsotel	10 B2
Hôtel Le Belvedere	11 C1
Hôtel Le Magnolia	12 C1
Hôtel Le Rocher	13 C2

EATING	(p874)
Alimentation du Golfe	14 C2
Best Of	15 C2
Casino Supermarket	16 B4
Ile de Beauté	17 C2
Le Cyrnos	18 C1
Marché Couvert	19 C1
U Minellu	20 C1

ENTERTAINMENT	(p874)
Chez Tao	21 D1

TRANSPORT	(pp874-5)
Buses to Galéria & Porto	22 C1
Corsica Ferries	(see 24)
Ferry Terminal	23 D1
Les Beaux Voyages	24 C2
SNCM Tickets	(see 26)
Taxi Rank	25 C2
Tramar	26 C2

OTHER	
Église Ste-Marie Majeure	27 C2
Monument aux Morts	(see 22)
Tour de Sel	28 D1

In the northern part of the citadel, a plaque marks the house where navigator Christopher Columbus was supposedly born – though the historical evidence is sketchy. The best views are from the citadel's ramparts, where you can gaze across the glittering Golfe du Calvi and the harbour.

BEACHES
Calvi's 4km of beach begins at the marina and runs east around the Golfe de Calvi.

Tours
Croisières Colombo Line (☎ 04 95 65 32 10; www .colombo-line.com in French; marina; ☼ Apr-Oct) offers glass-bottomed boat excursions (€45) to the seaside hamlets of Galéria and Girolata

(€50) via the Réserve Naturelle de Scandola nature reserve (see p877). Shorter trips just visit Scandola (€40).

Festivals & Events
Calvi's major events include **La Granitola** (an Easter penitential procession), a **fireworks festival** in May and Corsica's biggest **jazz festival** in June. More traditional tones can be heard at the **Rencontres Polyphoniques** music festival in September.

In autumn, **Le Festival du Vent** (☎ 04 95 65 16 67; www.le-festival-du-vent.com) celebrates wind in all its forms, with music, theatre and art exhibitions in town, sailing and windsurfing in the harbour and paragliding and air displays in the skies above Calvi.

Sleeping

Calvi's hotels aren't cheap at any time of year, and most are closed in winter.

Hôtel Le Magnolia (☎ 04 95 65 19 16; fax 04 95 65 08 02; cnr place du Marché & rue Alsace-Lorraine; s low/high season €65/85, d low season €77-97, high season €100-120; ☒ Apr-Jan; ☒) An elegant hotel ideally placed just behind the harbour, near Église Ste-Marie. The impeccable rooms have garden or sea views, and you can have breakfast or supper in the tree-covered courtyard.

Hôtel Le Belvedere (☎ 04 95 65 01 25; www.resa-hotels-calvi.com; place Christophe Colomb; d low season €45-54, high season €85-115; ☒) A pleasant, modern hotel at the top of town, opposite the citadel. The best rooms are on the top floor, with dual views of the fortress and the Golfe de Calvi.

Hôtel Le Rocher (☎ 04 95 65 20 04; www.hotel-le-rocher.com; blvd Wilson; d €90-190, 2-person apt per week €389-793, 4-person €645-1080; ☒ Apr-Sep; ☒) Provides rooms and mini-apartments with kitchenettes, fridges, TV, telephone and air-con.

Other recommendations:

Auberge de Jeunesse BVJ Corsotel (☎ 04 95 65 14 15; www.bvjhotel.com; av de la République; dm incl breakfast €22; ☒ Mar-Nov) Offers 120 budget beds.

Hotel Meridiana (☎ 04 95 65 31 38; fax 04 95 65 32 72; av Santa Maria; d low season €55-80, high season €90-158; ☒ ☒) Modern villa-style hotel set back from the town.

CAMPING

Camping Les Castors (☎ 04 95 65 13 30; www.castors.fr; route de Pietra Maggiore; adult/car/tent €8.20/2.90/3.20; ☒ May-Sep; ☒) Eight hundred metres southeast of town, in a sheltered spot under poplar trees.

Camping La Clé des Champs (☎ 04 95 65 00 86; camagni2@wanadoo.fr; route de Pietra Maggiore; per adult/car/tent €6/2/2.50; ☒ reception 9am-10.30pm Apr-Oct) South of Les Castors, but still only a short walk to the beach.

Eating

Calvi's restaurants are generally good, but you won't find many *menus* for under €12. From May to September, quai Landry and rue Clemenceau buzz with well-heeled visitors browsing for a place to eat.

Île de Beauté (☎ 04 95 65 00 46; quai Landry; menus €20) The best of the romantic cafés and restaurants along Calvi's waterfront. It specialises in fish and Corsican cuisine: delicacies include red mullet salad, sea bream in pesto sauce, and crab soup.

Le Cyrnos (☎ 04 95 65 06 10; quai Landry; menu €17; ☒ Mar-Nov) Another well-respected restaurant further along the quay, particularly renowned for the chef's *soupe de poissons* (fish soup).

U Minellu (☎ 04 95 65 05 52; Traverse à l'Église; menus €14-16; ☒ closed Sun in winter) A delightful family-run restaurant opposite Église Ste-Marie, serving Corsican dishes under a wooden awning lit by lanterns. The *menu Corse* (€16) includes regional specialities such as *brocciu* cannelloni, Corsican cooked pork, and chestnut and apple cake.

If you're looking for a snack on the move, head for **Best Of** (1 rue Clemenceau; ☒ 11.30am-10pm), which serves sandwiches and paninis (€4 to €6). The **marché couvert** (covered market; ☒ 8am-noon Mon-Sat) is near Église Ste-Marie Majeure. There's a large **Casino Supermarket** (av Christophe Colomb) south of the train station. Alternatively, try the well-stocked **Alimentation du Golfe** (rue Clemenceau).

Entertainment

Chez Tao (☎ 04 95 65 00 73; ☒ May-Oct) Calvi's best-known nightspot, founded by a member of the Russian White Cavalry escaping from the Crimean War. Celebrities and Corsicans alike head for this renowned piano bar for dancing and late-night drinking in summer – it's so hip it only has to open three months of the year.

Getting There & Around

AIR

Southeast of town (7km) is **Aéroport Calvi-Ste-Catherine** (☎ 04 95 65 88 88; www.calvi.aeroport.fr). Littoral Airlines and Air France link Calvi with Nice, Marseille, Lyon and other French cities. There is no bus service from Calvi to the airport. **Taxis** (☎ 04 95 65 03 10) can be picked up from place de la Porteuse d'Eau for around €15.

BOAT

The ferry terminal is below the southern side of the citadel. From Calvi there are express NGV ferries to Nice (2½ hours, five a week).

Ferry tickets can be bought at the port two hours before departure. At other times, SNCM tickets are handled by **Tramar** (☎ 04 95 65 01 38; quai Landry; ☒ 9am-noon & 2-6pm Mon-Fri, 9am-noon Sat). Tickets for Corsica Ferries are handled by **Les Beaux Voyages** (☎ 04 95 65 15 02; place de la Porteuse d'Eau).

BUS

The tourist office can provide bus information and can supply timetables. Buses to Bastia (€12.50, 2¼ hours) are run by **Les Beaux Voyages** (☎ 04 95 65 15 02; place de la Porteuse d'Eau).

From mid-May to mid-October, **Autocars SAIB** (☎ 04 95 22 41 99) runs buses from Calvi's Monument aux Morts (war memorial) to Galéria (1¼ hours) and Porto (three hours). There are no buses on Sunday.

TRAIN

Calvi's **train station** (☎ 04 95 65 00 61; ☼ until 7.30pm) is off av de la République. There are two departures daily to Ajaccio (€24.10), Bastia (€15.70) and the stations between.

From April to October, the single-car trains of CFC's Tramway de la Balagne (see p866) make 19 stops along the coast between Calvi and Île Rousse (45 minutes). The line is divided into three sectors – you need one ticket for each sector. *Carnets* (books) of six tickets (€8) are sold at stations.

LA BALAGNE

The Balagne is an area of low hills between the Monte Cinto massif and the sea. Its coastline stretches northeast from Galéria, all the way to **Désert des Agriates**, the maquis-covered desert east of Île Rousse. The coast between Calvi and Île Rousse is dotted with fine-sand beaches, including **Algajola**, **Aregno** and **Renalta**. Many are served by Le Tramway de la Balagne.

Inland, La Balagne is known as the 'Garden of Corsica', renowned for the fertility of its soil. The main town of **Calenzana** marks

the northern terminus of the GR20 and Mare e Monti trails.

After the village of Cateri, bear right along the D413 for 2.5km to **St-Antonino**, dramatically perched on a hilltop and offering stunning views.

ÎLE ROUSSE (ISULA ROSSA)
pop 2300

The port of Île Rousse was founded by Pasquale Paoli in 1758 to compete with pro-Genoese Calvi, 24km northeast. During the 18th and 19th centuries, it became an important commercial harbour, but these days it's a busy beach resort and the main trade is in tourists. Its name comes from the red granite of Île de la Pietra, a rocky island (now connected to the mainland) with a Genoese watchtower that presides over the present-day port.

Orientation

From the main square of place Paoli, the old city stretches 400m northwest to the train station. The ferry port is on a peninsula north of town. The **tourist office** (☎ 04 95 60 04 35; www.ot-ile-rousse.fr in French; place Paoli; ☼ 9am-7pm Jul & Aug, 9am-12.30pm & 2-6.30pm May, Jun & Sep, 9am-noon & 2-6pm Mon-Fri Oct-Apr) is on the southern side of place Paoli.

Sights

Promenade a Marinella runs along the seafront. There is more sandy coastline east of town, near the **Musée Océanographique** (☎ 04 95 60 27 81), which houses eels, rays, fish and octopuses, but nothing much more impressive.

CORSICA'S TOP FIVE BEACHES

- **Rondinara** (10km northeast of Bonifacio) A perfect ring of white sand enclosing a circular bay of crystal-clear water, with brilliant snorkelling and sheltered sunbathing.
- **Algajola** (8km west of Île Rousse) Fantastic white-sand beach within easy reach of Île Rousse, served by the Tramway de la Balagne in summer. As with all Corsica's beaches, it's at its very best when there's no-one else around.
- **Palombaggia** (3km southeast of Porto Vecchio) Like the other beaches near Porto Vecchio, this sandy cove ringed by pines and rocks is becoming well known – but arrive off-season and you might have the beach all to yourself.
- **Rocapina** (12km south of Sartène) For those who like their beaches wild and windswept, Rocapina is just the ticket. Look out for the 'Lion of Rocapina' rock above the cove.
- **Saleccia** (10km northwest of St-Florent) Corsica's most unspoiled beaches are hidden away in the Désert des Agriates. They can only be reached by sea or a long trek on foot or quad-bike, but you won't regret the effort – the island's beaches simply don't get any better.

CORSICA

Île de la Pietra, the island-turned-peninsula where the ferries dock, has a **Genoese watchtower** and a **lighthouse**.

The town's beaches are usually overflowing in summer, so if you're looking for empty sand, you might have better luck at nearby **Lozari** (7km east) or **Guardiola** (4km west).

Sleeping & Eating

Hôtel L'Isola Rossa (☎ 04 95 60 01 32; isolarossa@ absolucorse.com; promenade du Port; d €45-105 depending on season) One of a handful of pricey hotels lining the promenade. The seaside location is fantastic and the rooms have more character than other nearby hotels.

Splendid Hotel (☎ 04 95 60 00 24; www.le-splen did-hotel.com; s €45-62, d €50-92, tr €69-127 depending on season; P) Good value in a period building (which once served as a war hospital) near place Paoli. The rooms aren't grand but most have balconies and pleasant views.

Restaurant L'Île d'Or (☎ 04 95 60 12 05; place Paoli; menus €12-30) Salads, pizzas, pasta and fresh fish are the order of the day at this buzzy restaurant – and you can watch the nightly *boules* contests from the terrace.

Le Libecciu (☎ 04 95 60 13 82; rue Paoli; dishes €15-20; noon-2am) This respected restaurant is particularly popular for its giant king prawns and delicious mussels.

Chez Paco (☎ 04 95 60 03 76; rue Paoli; menus €22 & €28; Mon-Sat) An informal brasserie that does good simple seafood and light meals.

The daily **covered market** (place Paoli) sells fish, vegetables, fruit and Corsican goods.

Getting There & Away

On the Calvi–Bastia line, buses leave from av Paul Doumer. The **train station** (☎ 04 95 60 00 50) is between place Paoli and the ferry port. Île Rousse makes an easy day trip from Calvi.

Southeast of place Paoli, **Tramar** (☎ 04 95 60 09 56; av Joseph Calizi; 8.30am-noon & 2-5.30pm Mon-Fri, 8.30am-noon Sat) handles ferry tickets.

PORTO TO AJACCIO

Corsica's wildest and most beautiful coastline runs from Calvi to Ajaccio.

PORTO (PORTU)

pop 460

The seaside village of Porto, which nestles among huge outcrops of red granite and fragrant groves of eucalyptus, is renowned for its fiery sunsets and proximity to the Réserve Naturelle de Scandola (Scandola Nature Reserve). Hotel prices are reasonable, making it a good base for exploring Les Calanques (p879), Girolata and the mountain villages of Ota and Évisa (p878).

Orientation

Porto is split into three sections: the marina area, the Vaita quarter further uphill and the main road from Calvi. There are shops, hotels and restaurants in all three districts. From the Calvi road to the marina is a walk of about 1km.

Information

The **main tourist office** (☎ 04 95 26 10 55; www .porto-tourisme.com in French; 9am-noon & 2-6pm Mon-Sat Apr-Jun, Sep & Oct; 9am-6pm Jul & Aug) is built into the wall below the marina's upper car park. It publishes a good English brochure, *Hikes & Walks in the Area of Porto* (€2.50).

Crédit Agricole has the only ATM in town. There's a currency exchange bureau next to the Spar supermarket, open only in summer.

Sights & Activities

Porto's seafront is surrounded by hotels and restaurants. A short trail leads up the rocks

---

UNDERWATER ADVENTURES

The Golfe de Porto offers fantastic diving. Top spots include Capo Rosso and the outskirts of the Réserve Naturelle de Scandola, where you'll glimpse multicoloured coral forests and all kinds of Mediterranean marine life.

Porto's accredited diving operators include **École de Plongée Génération Bleue** (☎ 04 95 26 24 88; www.generation-bleue.com; Porto Marina; May-Oct) and **Centre de Plongée du Golfe de Porto** (☎ 04 95 26 10 29; www.plongeeporto.com in French; Porto Marina; Apr-Nov). Both companies run diving courses and trips into the bay.

Other excellent locations in Corsica include the protected coastal areas around Finocchiarola (Cap Corse), Îles Lavezzi (Bonifacio) and Cerbicale (Porto Vecchio), and the bays of Galéria, Valinco (near Propriano) and Calvi.

to a **Genoese tower** (admission €2.50; 🕙 10am-noon & 2-7pm Apr-Jun, Sep & Oct; 9am-9pm Jul & Aug). Nearby, the marina overlooks the estuary of the Porto River. On the far side, across a footbridge, there's a modest pebbly **beach** and one of Corsica's best-known **eucalyptus groves**.

You can rent a boat from **Les Bateaux du Soleil** (☎ 06 08 69 75 20; half-day/full day €75/115) to visit the Réserve Naturelle de Scandola and Girolata independently. You'll be missing out on the educational experience of one of the excursions (see below), but you'll have more freedom to explore and for a group it would be cheaper.

Tours

From April to October **Nave Va Promenades en Mer** (☎ 04 95 26 15 16; www.naveva.com) and **Porto Linéa** (☎ 04 95 26 11 50, 06 08 16 89 71) offer excursions (€35 to €40 depending on season) to the Réserve Naturelle de Scandola, listed by Unesco for its unique marine environment. The boats afford incredible views of the fire-coloured coastline, and stop at Girolata, a remote fishing village only accessible by sea. There are shorter trips to Les Calanques (from €20).

Sleeping

Le Colombo (☎ 04 95 26 10 14; www.hotelcolombo.com; route de Calvi; d low/high season incl breakfast €59/120; 🕙 Apr-Oct; 🅿 ✖) Charming little hotel on the Calvi road, with quirky décor and valley views. Get a balcony if you can.

Hôtel Calypso (☎ 04 95 26 11 54; www.hotel-la-calypso.com in French; marina; d low/high season €55/95; 🕙 Apr-Oct; 🅿 ✖ 🖳) One of the best hotels on the marina, in a pretty stone building decorated with awnings and window boxes. Small, smart and sophisticated.

Le Subrini (☎ 04 95 26 14 94; www.hotels-porto.com; marina; d low season €65-80, high season €90-110; 🕙 Apr-Oct; 🅿 ✖) A luxurious hotel in a fabulous seafront position opposite Tour de Genoise. The rooms are spacious and comfortable and the views just don't get any better.

Le Golfe (☎ 04 95 26 13 33; marina; r low season €35-50, high season €55-70) This cheap hotel above a café offers basic rooms, some with little balconies overlooking the bay.

Other recommendations:

Cala di Sole (☎ 04 95 26 10 96; www.hotel-caladisole.com; Vaita quarter; d low season €50-60, high season €75-85; 🅿 ✖) Modern motel with big rooms or apartments.

GORGES DE SPELUNCA

The partly paved trail linking Ota and Évisa was originally a mule track that carried supplies from Porto to the highland villages. These days, it's one of Corsica's great hikes. The trail winds along the plunging valley of the River Porto, past huge rock formations and soaring orange cliffs, some more than 1000m high. The trail passes the Genoese pont de Zaglia en route and takes about five hours return, but it's worth the effort (and the blisters). Aim to reach the gorge in late afternoon, when the fiery rocks are at their most vivid.

Other good walks near Évisa include the Sentier du Châtaigner (1½ hours), which travels through chestnut groves to a waterfall and mountain lake; and the 1½-hour hike uphill through the Forêt d'Aïtone to the Bocca a u Saltu (1391m) hilltop.

Le Riviera (☎ 04 95 26 10 15; www.hotel-restaurant-porto.com in French; marina; d low season €30-35, high season €38-48) Ultrabudget option with bay views.

CAMPING

Camping Les Oliviers (☎ 04 95 26 14 49; www.campinglesoliviers.com; per person/tent/car in summer €8.50/3.50/3.50, 4-person bungalow per week low/high season €367/640; 🕙 May-Nov; ✦) Located on an olive-treed hillside near the supermarkets.

Le Funtana al' Ora (☎ 04 95 26 11 65; fax 04 95 26 15 48; per person/tent/car €5.50/2.20/2.20, 4-person bungalow per week low/high season €300/540; 🕙 Apr-Oct) Two kilometres east of Porto on the road to Évisa.

Eating

Le Sud (☎ 04 95 26 14 11; menu €25; 🕙 Apr-Oct) A sophisticated restaurant near the Tour Genoise, serving Mediterranean-style seafood and Corsican cooking on a veranda overlooking the rocks.

La Tour Genoise (☎ 04 95 26 17 11; menus €15.60-20.20; 🕙 Apr-Oct) Serves up Corsican cuisine and seafood in a cosy indoor restaurant or on a portside terrace.

Self-caterers can find two supermarkets near the pharmacy on the road from Calvi.

Getting There & Around

BUS

Autocars SAIB (☎ 04 95 22 41 99) has two buses daily, linking Porto and Ota with Ajaccio

CORSICA

CHESTNUT BREAD & BEER

The Corsicans have been planting *châtaigniers* (chestnut trees) since the 16th century. The tree became known as *l'arbre à pain* (the bread tree) because of the many uses the Corsicans found for chestnut flour (*farine de châtaigne*). These days the flour is mainly used to make pastries.

The meat of pigs raised on chestnuts is famous for its flavour. Other chestnut delights include *falculelli* (pressed, frittered *brocciu* cheese served on a chestnut leaf), *beignets au brocciu à la farine de châtaigne* (*brocciu* cheese frittered in chestnut flour), *délice à la châtaigne* (chestnut cake) and, last but certainly not least, *bière à la châtaigne* (chestnut beer).

(€11, two hours, none on Sunday). From May to October a bus runs from Porto to Calvi (€16, three hours).

Transports Mordiconi (☎ 04 95 48 00 44) connects Porto with Corte (€19, 2½ hours, one daily) via Évisa and Ota.

CAR & MOTORCYCLE

From May to late September, two and four wheels can be hired from **Porto Locations** (☎ /fax 04 95 26 10 13), across the street from the supermarkets. Daily rates for a scooter/car/mountain bike are €60/46/15.

TAXI

For a taxi contact **Mr Ceccaldi Félix** (☎ 04 95 26 12 92).

ÉVISA

pop 250 / elevation 830m

Surrounded by chestnut groves (*châtaigneraies*), the highland village of Évisa sits above a deep valley between the Gorges de Spelunca and the Forêt d'Aïtone. It makes an excellent base for hiking – several trails leave near the village, including the path through the Spelunca gorge itself, which ends near the tiny village of Ota.

Sights

The **Forêt d'Aïtone** (Aïtone Forest) contains Corsica's most impressive stands of larício pines. These arrow-straight trees reach 60m in height and once provided beams and masts for Genoese ships. The forest begins

---

east of Évisa and stretches to the 1477m-high **Col de Vergio** (Vergio Hill). The **Cascades d'Aïtone** (Aïtone Falls) are 4km northeast of Évisa via the D84 and a short footpath.

Sleeping & Eating

Hôtel L'Aïtone (☎ 04 95 26 20 04; www.hotel-aitone .com; d low season €32-85, high season €56-100; ☺ Feb-Nov; P ☢) Évisa's main hotel has rustic rooms, a homely restaurant and a welcoming country atmosphere. The more expensive rooms have balconies with panoramic valley views.

La Châtaigneraie (☎ 04 95 26 24 47; hotellachatai gneraie@wanadoo.fr; d from €50) A traditional Corsican house offering simple, homely rooms on the western edge of the village, ideal after a long day's hike.

For cheap accommodation, dorm beds are available at **Gîte d'Étape Chez Marie** (☎ 04 95 26 11 37; dm €13) and **Gîte d'Étape Chez Félix** (☎ 04 95 26 12 92; dm €12, d €33.50-40) in Ota, further down the valley.

Village bars include Bar de la Poste and Modern Bar. Both are open daily and serve simple meals, cakes and good coffee.

Getting There & Away

There are two daily buses from Monday to Saturday from Évisa to Ajaccio (€10.70, two hours) via Ota and Porto.

PIANA

pop 500 / elevation 438m

The quiet hillside village of Piana affords breathtaking views of the Golfe de Porto and the soaring central mountains, and makes an excellent base for exploring Les Calanques. Good Friday is marked by La Granitola, a traditional festival during which

---

AUTHOR'S CHOICE

Hôtel des Roches Rouges (☎ 04 95 27 81 81; fax 04 95 27 81 76; d from €69; ☺ Apr–mid-Nov) A grand old 30-room hotel dating from 1912, and without doubt one of Corsica's most romantic places to stay. The elegant double rooms have views of Les Calanques, Ficajola and the deep-blue Mediterranean, and the panoramic windows, antique dining room and period furnishings conjure the air of a bygone age. There are lots of luxury hotels in Corsica, but not many of them can match the 'Red Rocks' for atmosphere.

hooded penitents parade through the village to Piana's Église Ste-Marie.

The **syndicat d'initiative** (tourist office; ☎ 04 95 27 84 42; www.sipiana.com; ☼ 8.30-11.30am, 1.30-4pm Mon-Fri, longer hours in summer) is next to the post office. It has lots of information on exploring Les Calanques, and distributes the free leaflet *Piana Randonnées*.

Nearby beaches include **Anse de Ficajola**, reached by a narrow 4km road from Piana, and **Plage d'Arone**, 11km southwest of town via the scenic D824. From the D824, a trail leads to the tower-topped **Capo Rosso**.

Hôtel Continental (☎ 04 95 27 83 12; www.conti nentalpiana.com; d low season €29-35, high season €32-38, ☼ Apr-Sep) is an old, converted townhouse 100m uphill from the church, which has 17 old-fashioned rooms and antique décor to match.

Hôtel Le Scandola (☎ 04 95 27 80 07; fax 04 95 27 83 88; balcony d/tr incl breakfast €90/120; ☼ Apr-Oct) is a modern hotel on the road towards Cargèse that offers comfort but not much character.

Buses between Porto and Ajaccio stop near the church and the post office.

LES CALANQUES

One of Corsica's most stunning natural sights is just outside Piana: Les Calanques de Piana (E Calanche in Corsican), a spectacular landscape of red granite cliffs and spiky outcrops, carved into bizarre shapes by the wind, water and weather. Less-rocky areas support pine and chestnut forests, the green foliage of which contrasts dramatically with the technicoloured granite.

Buses travelling from Ajaccio to Porto stop at the chalet.

CARGÈSE (CARGHJESE)
pop 900

Perched on cliffs between the Golfe de Sagone and Golfe de Pero, Cargèse feels more like a Greek village than a Corsican town – which is hardly surprising, as the town was founded by Greek settlers fleeing their Ottoman-controlled homeland in the 17th century. On Easter Monday and 15 August, a colourful religious procession, led by Cargèse's Greek-Catholic congregation, wends its way through the village.

Orientation & Information
The D81, Cargèse's main street, is called av de la République towards Ajaccio, and rue Colonel Fieschi towards Porto. The **tourist office** (☎ 04 95 26 41 31; www.cargese.net; rue du Docteur Dragacci; ☼ 8.30am-7pm Jul & Aug, 9am-12.30pm & 2.30-6pm Mon-Fri Sep-Jun) is a few streets up from the Latin Church.

Sights & Activities
Cargèse is best known for its **twin churches** – one Eastern (Orthodox), the other Western (Catholic) – which face each other across hillside vegetable plots, like boxers squaring up for a fight. Both have fine views of the town and the glittering Golfe de Sagone. The interior of the Greek church – constructed from 1852 to 1870 by the faithful, who worked on Sunday after attending Divine Liturgy – is adorned with icons

---

HIKING IN LES CALANQUES

Though the Calanques are impressive from the main road, you have to take to one of the clifftop walking trails to fully appreciate the views. Eight kilometres southwest of Porto on the D81 is Le Chalet des Roches Bleues, a souvenir shop that makes a useful landmark. Four trails begin nearby:

■ **Chemin des Muletiers** The steep, one-hour 'Mule-Drivers' Trail' begins 400m towards Piana from the chalet; the trailhead is 15m downhill from the sanctuary dedicated to the Virgin Mary. Trail markings are blue.

■ **Chemin du Château Fort** A one-hour trail to a fortress-shaped rock with stunning views of the Golfe de Porto. It begins 700m towards Porto from the chalet; the trailhead is on the D81 right of the Tête de Chien (Dog's Head) rock. Trail markings are blue.

■ **La Châtaigneraie** A three-hour circuit through chestnut groves, beginning 25m uphill from the chalet.

■ **La Corniche** A steep, forested, 40-minute walk to a fantastic view of Les Calanques. Begins on the bridge 50m towards Porto from the chalet. Trail markings are yellow.

brought from Greece in the 1670s by the original settlers.

Cargèse's **port**, where fishing boats dock beside luxury leisure cruisers, is downhill from the churches.

The Genoese **towers** atop Pointe d'Omigna and Pointe de Cargèse overlook **Plage de Pero**, a long beach of white sand 1km north of Cargèse. Take the road downhill from the top of rue Colonel Fieschi.

Tours

Croisières Grand Bleu (☎ 04 95 26 40 24; http://croisiere.grandbleu.free.fr in French; rue Marbeuf) offers boat excursions in the Golfe de Porto, including visits to Girolata and tours of the Réserve Naturelle de Scandola. Prices vary depending on season.

Sleeping & Eating

M'hôtel Punta e Mare (☎ 04 95 26 44 33; www.hotel-puntaemare.com in French; chemin de Paomia; d with sea views low season €40-60, high season €65-85; **P**) A cosy, welcoming motel set back from the main town. The smart rooms offer great year-round value and there's a lovely breakfast terrace shaded by trees and climbing plants.

Le Cyrnos (☎ /fax 04 95 26 49 47; www.torraccia.com; rue de le République; d with sea view low/high season €40/60) In the centre of the village, quaint, good-value rooms in a lemon-yellow townhouse. The rooms facing the road are cheaper.

Hôtel Le St-Jean (☎ 04 95 26 46 68; www.lesaintjean.com in French; place St-Jean; d with/without sea view €70/63; **P** **⊠**) Near the old *lavoir* (laundry) on the main road from Porto, the St-Jean is a large café-restaurant that offers modern, villa-style rooms upstairs. Most have balconies overlooking the bay.

A Volta (☎ 04 95 26 41 96; rue du Docteur Petrolacci; menu €22; ⊠ May-Sep) A simple seafood restaurant offering a varied local *menu* and a fabulous ocean view.

There are a few summer-only restaurants on Pero beach, including **A Piaghja** (☎ 04 95 26 47 49; Plage de Pero; mains €10-15; ⊠ Jun-Sep), which does pizzas and seafood and has weekly music nights.

Getting There & Away

Two daily buses from Ota (1½ hours) via Porto (one hour) to Ajaccio (one hour) stop in front of the post office.

AJACCIO (AJACCIU)
pop 60,000

The pastel-shaded port of Ajaccio (pronounced Ajaxio) is the most cosmopolitan city in Corsica. With its designer shops, fashionable restaurants and hectic traffic, it's one of the few Corsican towns that seems to have its feet in the 21st century; but inland from the harbour, the modern shopping streets lead into the alleyways and narrow lanes of the old city, where 18th-century townhouses stand side-by-side with tiny restaurants and brightly coloured tenement blocks. For educational value, there are several museums dedicated to Ajaccio's most famous native son, Napoleon Bonaparte.

Orientation

Ajaccio's main street is cours Napoléon, which stretches from place de Gaulle northwards to the train station and beyond. The old city is south of place Foch. The port is on the eastern side of town, from where a tree-lined promenade leads west along plage St-Francois.

Information
BOOKSHOPS
Album (2 place Foch; ⊠ 8.30am-noon & 2.30-7pm Mon-Sat, 8.30am-noon Sun Oct-May)

EMERGENCY
Centre Hospitalier de la Miséricorde (☎ 04 95 29 90 90; 27 av Impératrice Eugénie; ⊠ 24hr)
Police Station (☎ 04 95 29 21 47; rue Général Firoella)

INTERNET ACCESS
Absolut Game (☎ 04 95 21 56 60; av de Paris; per hr €3; ⊠ 9-2am)
Game Net (☎ 04 95 50 72 79; 2 av de Paris; per 15min/hr €2/5; ⊠ 9am-noon & 2-9pm Mon-Fri, 2-9pm Sat & Sun)

LAUNDRY
Lavomatique (rue Maréchal Ornano; ⊠ 8am-10pm)

MONEY
Banks are found along place de Gaulle and cours Napoléon.
Banque Populaire (place Foch) ATM.
BNP (33 cours Napoléon) ATM.

POST
Main Post Office (13 cours Napoléon; ⊠ 8am-6.45pm Mon-Fri, 8am-noon Sat)

AJACCIO (AJACCIU)

INFORMATION			
Absolut Game	1	B5	
Air France	2	C4	
Album	3	C5	
Assemblée Territoriale de la			
Corse	4	A5	
Banque Populaire	5	C5	
BNP	6	C3	
Centre Hospitalier de la			
Miséricorde	7	B3	
Game Net	8	B5	
Lavomatique	9	B5	
Maison d'Information Randonées du			
Parc Naturel Regional	10	B4	
Police Station	11	B5	
Post Office	12	B4	
Tourist Office	13	C4	
SIGHTS & ACTIVITIES		(p882)	
Cathédrale Ste-Marie	14	C5	
Chapelle Imperial	(see 15)		
Hôtel de Ville	(see 18)		
Musée Fesch	15	C4	
Musée National de la Maison			
Bonaparte	16	C5	
Nave Va Promenades en Mer			
Ticket	17	C5	
Salon Napoléonien	18	C5	
SLEEPING		(p883)	
Hôtel Fesch	19	C4	
Hôtel Kallisté	20	C3	
Hôtel Le Dauphin	21	C3	
Hôtel Napoléon	22	B4	
Hôtel San Carlu	23	C6	
EATING		(pp883-4)	
A La Funtana	24	C5	
Au Bec Fin	25	C4	
Café de Paris	26	B5	
Fresh Fish Market	27	C5	
Globo	(see 26)		
Le 20123	28	B5	
Le Bocaccio	29	C5	
Le Don Guichotte	30	C4	
Le Grand Café Napoléon	31	B4	
Monoprix Supermarket	32	C4	
Open-Air Food Market	33	C4	
Scampi	34	C5	
Spar Supermarket	35	B5	
Tropicana Beach	36	B5	

ENTERTAINMENT		(p884)	
Au Son des Guitares	37	C5	
Casino Municipal	38	B5	
Theatre Kallisté	39	C2	
TRANSPORT		(pp884-5)	
Budget	40	B5	
Bus Station	(see 47)		
Europcar	41	A5	
Hertz	42	B5	
Moto Corse Évasion	43	D1	
SNCM Ticket Office	44	C4	
Taxi Rank	45	B5	
TCA Boutique	46	C2	
Terminal Maritime et Routier	47	C4	
OTHER			
Complex Municipal Sportif	48	A5	
Palais de Justice	49	C2	
Préfecture	50	B4	
Vehicle Access to Ferry			
Terminal	51	D2	

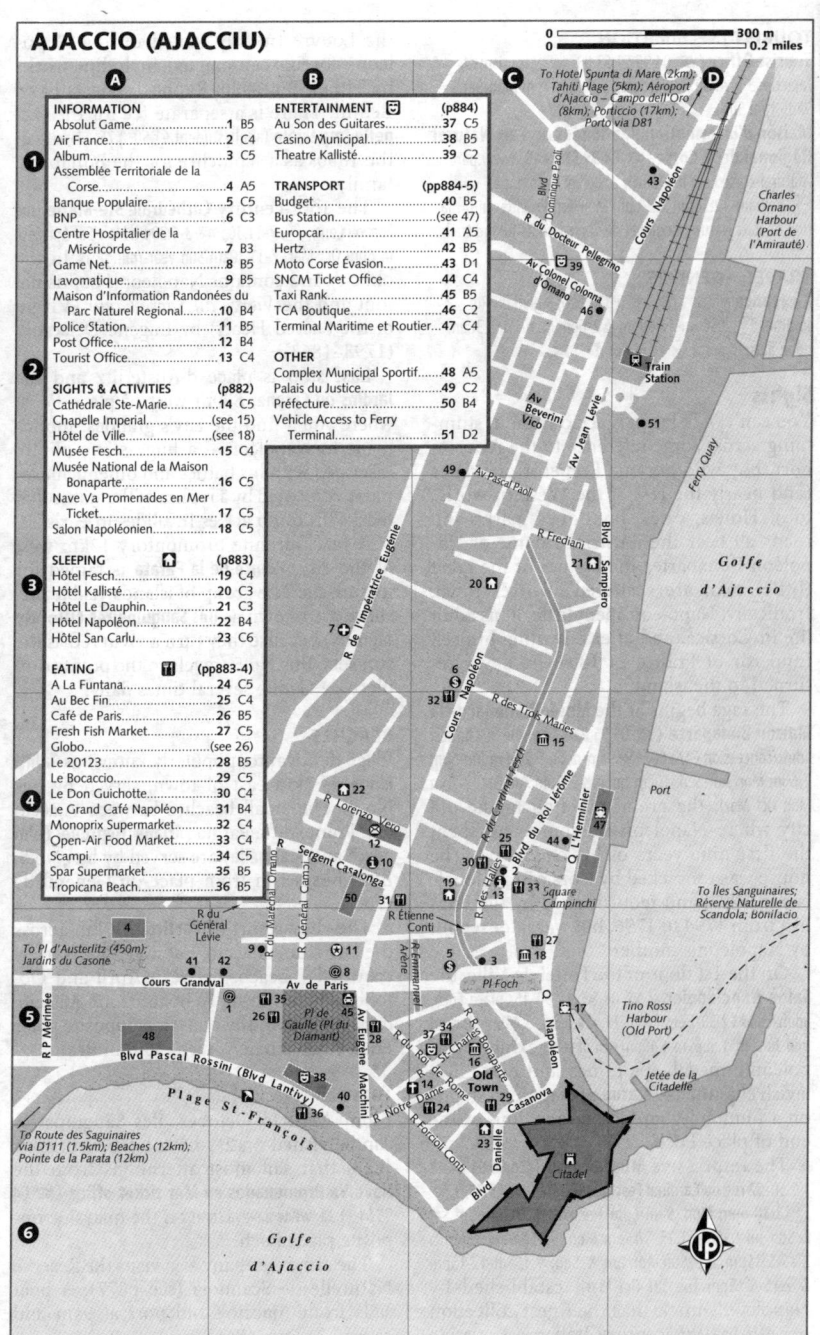

CORSICA

TOURIST INFORMATION

Tourist Office (☎ 04 95 51 53 03; www.tourisme.fr
/ajaccio; 3 blvd du Roi Jérôme; ◔ 8am-7pm Mon-Sat,
9am-1pm Sun)

**Maison d'Information Randonées du Parc Naturel
Régional de la Corse** (☎ 04 95 51 79 10; www.parc
-naturel-corse.com in French; 2 rue Sgt Casolonga;
◔ 8.30am-12.30pm & 2-6pm Mon-Fri) Provides information on Parc Naturel Régional de Corse and its hiking trails.

TRAVEL AGENCIES

Air France Ajaccio (☎ 0 820 820 820; 3 blvd du Roi
Jérôme; ◔ 8.30am-12.30pm & 2-6pm Mon-Fri, 8.30am-
noon Sat); Airport (◔ 6am-8pm)

Sights

You can't walk far in Ajaccio without stumbling across some reference to the Ajaccio-
born boy who became Emperor of France
(and nearly the rest of the Western world,
too). Hotels, cafés, boutiques, parks and
roads all bear the illustrious name of Napoléon Bonaparte, and statues of the great
(little) man are scattered all over town.
Ironically, Napoléon spent little of his adult
life in Corsica, and after crowning himself
Emperor of France in 1804, he never returned to the island.

The saga begins at the **Musée National de la
Maison Bonaparte** (☎ 04 95 21 43 89; rue St-Charles;
adult/concession €4/2.60; ◔ 9am-noon & 2-6pm Tue-Sun,
2-6pm Mon Apr-Sep, 10am-noon & 2-5pm Tue-Sat, 2-5pm
Mon Oct-Mar), the grand building in the old
city where Napoleon was born and spent
the first nine years of his childhood. The
house was ransacked by Corsican nationalists in 1793, and requisitioned by the English from 1794 to 1796, but was later rebuilt
by Napoléon's mother.

On the 1st floor of the Hôtel de Ville, the
Salon Napoléonien (☎ 04 95 21 90 15; place Foch;
adult/child €2.30/free; ◔ 9-11.45am & 2-5.45pm Mon-Fri
mid-Jun–mid-Sep, to 4.45pm rest of year) exhibits Napoleonic medals, paintings and busts in a
lavish chamber. A **statue** of Napoléon stands
on a fountain guarded by four lions at the
end of place Foch.

The impressive **Musée Fesch** (☎ 04 95 21 48
17; 50-52 rue du Cardinal Fesch; adult/student €5.35/3.80;
◔ 1.30-6pm Mon, 9am-6pm Tue-Fri, 10.30am-6pm Sat
& Sun Jul & Aug, 1.15-5.15pm Mon, 9.15am-12.15pm &
2.15-5.15pm Tue-Sun Apr-Jun & Sep, 9.15am-12.15pm
& 2.15-5.15pm Tue-Sat Oct-Mar), established by
Napoleon's uncle, has the finest collection
of 14th-to-19th-century Italian art outside

the Louvre (mostly looted during Napoléon's foreign campaigns), including works
by Titian, Botticelli, Raphael, Poussin and
Bellini. There is a separate fee for the **Chapelle Impériale** (adult/student €1.50/0.75), built in
the 1850s as a sepulchre for the Bonaparte
family.

The 16th-century **Cathédrale Ste-Marie** (rue
Forcioli Conti; ◔ 7-11.30am & 3-6.30pm Mon-Sat Apr-Sep,
to 6pm Oct-Mar, 7-11.30am Sun year-round) is in the
old city and contains Napoleon's baptismal
font and the *Vierge au Sacré-Cœur* (Virgin
of the Sacred Heart) by Eugène Delacroix
(1798–1863).

Last stop is place d'Austerlitz and the
Jardins du Casone, 800m west of place Foch,
where you'll find the city's grandest monument to Napoléon – a huge stone plinth,
inscribed with his battles and other achievements, crowned by a replica of the statue that
marks his tomb at Les Invalides in Paris.

A black-granite promontory 12km west
of the city, **Pointe de la Parata** is famed for
its sunsets. The group of islands visible offshore are known as **Îles Sanguinaires** (Bloody
Islands) because they turn a vivid red as the
sun sets. Bus No 5 travels to the point from
place de Gaulle several times daily.

BEACHES

Plage de Ricanto, popularly known as **Tahiti
Plage**, is 5km east of town, served by bus
No 1. The small beaches between Ajaccio
and Pointe de la Parata (**Ariane**, **Neptune**, **Palm
Beach** and **Marinella**) are served by bus No 5.
Both buses run from place du Général de
Gaulle.

The ritzy resort of **Porticcio**, 17km across
the bay from Ajaccio, has a great – if overcrowded – beach. Between April and October, there are daily boats from Ajaccio,
departing from the quayside opposite place
Foch (€5/8 single/return, 30 minutes).

Tours

From April to October, Îles Sanguinaires
can be visited on 2½-hour boat excursions
(€22) that sail most afternoons from the
Nave Va Promenades en Mer ticket office (☎ 04
95 51 31 31; www.naveva.com) on the quayside opposite place Foch.

The same company also visits the Réserve
Naturelle de Scandola (see p877). A boat
sails from Ajaccio's old port at 9am and
returns at 6pm (€46).

Sleeping

There are no budget options in Ajaccio, short of sleeping in your car – which you might have to do if you don't reserve ahead in summer.

Hôtel Napoléon (☎ 04 95 51 54 00; www.hotel-napoleon-ajaccio.com; 4 rue Lorenzo Vero; s/d low season €58/68, high season €85/100; P ✖) With elegant, tasteful rooms set back from the hustle of cours Napoléon, this is one of Ajaccio's most stylish hotels – and in Boney's birthplace, how could you stay anywhere else?

Hôtel Kallisté (☎ 04 95 51 34 45; www.hotel-kalliste-ajaccio.com in French; 51 cours Napoléon; s/d low season €51/56, high season €58/68; ✖ ✖ ▯) An excellent city hotel with clean lines and contemporary bedrooms. Stylish features such as the glass elevator, terracotta floors and exposed brickwork don't normally come this cheap.

Hôtel Fesch (☎ 04 95 51 62 62; www.hotel-fesch.com; 7 rue du Cardinal Fesch; s/d low season €54/63, high season €73/84; ✖) A traditional hotel on one of Ajaccio's oldest streets. The period building, grand rooms and old-fashioned service make this a favourite with regular visitors, so book ahead.

Hôtel San Carlu (☎ 04 95 21 13 84; fax 04 95 21 09 99; 8 blvd Danielle Casanova; s low season €62-76, s high season €76-86, d low season €76-84, d high season €85-99; ✖) One of the best hotels in the quiet old town, in a prime position overlooking the citadel. The top rooms have sea views with a price tag to match.

Also recommended:

Hôtel Le Dauphin (☎ 04 95 21 12 94; www.ledauphinhotel.com; 11 blvd Sampiero; s/d/tr low season €49/54/66, high season €54/60/69; P ✖) Local café opposite the ferry port with standard rooms.

Hôtel Spunta di Mare (☎ 04 95 23 74 40; hotelspuntadimare@wanadoo.fr; Quartier St Joseph; s/d low season €48/57, high season €64/74; P) Modern seafront hotel 2km north of the city.

Eating

RESTAURANTS

In the old city, rue St-Charles and rue Conventionnel Chiappe are lined with tiny terraced restaurants that are always crammed in summer. It's a great place for a night-time wander, even if you're not planning on eating.

Au Bec Fin (☎ 04 95 21 30 52; 3bis blvd du Roi-Jérôme; menu €13.90; ✖ closed Sun & dinner Mon) A relaxed restaurant near the market, decked out as a 1930s brasserie. The excellent-value menu includes grilled tuna, *carpaccio de boeuf* and salmon fillet.

Le 20123 (☎ 04 95 21 50 05; 2 rue du Roi de Rome; menu €26; ✖ 7.30-11pm, closed Mon) This Corsican bistro started life in the village of Pila Canale (postcode 20123); when the owner upped sticks to Ajaccio, he decided to re-create his old restaurant – village square, water-pump, washing lines and all.

Le Scampi (☎ 04 95 21 38 09; 11 rue Conventionnel Chiappe; menus from €12.95; ✖ closed dinner Fri & lunch Sat) Serves seafood and Corsican dishes (including sardines with *brocciu* cheese) on a flower-filled terrace.

Le Don Quichotte (☎ 04 95 21 27 30; rue des Halles; pizzas €7.60-10, menus from €12.50; ✖ Mon-Sat) A down-to-earth Italian restaurant near the quay that's often packed with a local crowd who come for the delicious seafood and wood-fired pizzas.

A La Funtana (☎ 04 95 21 78 04; 7 rue Notre Dame; lunch/dinner menu €25/55, à la carte dishes €24-30; ✖ lunch Tue-Sat, dinner in summer) One of Ajaccio's grandest *grandes tables*, regularly featured in the gourmet guides. The grilled lobster and *l'anima Corse* (a delicious pudding made with chestnut flour and *brocciu* cheese) are particularly renowned.

Other recommendations:

Le Boccaccio (☎ 04 95 21 16 77; 19 rue du Roi de Rome; dishes €18-30; ✖ closed Wed Nov-Mar) High-quality Italian cuisine in the old town.

Tropicana Beach (☎ 04 95 51 12 98; blvd Pascal Rossini; menus from €12.50; ✖ Mon-Sat) A seafront brasserie with a terrace above the waves.

CAFÉS

Ajaccio's thriving café culture centres on blvd du Roi Jérôme, quai Napoléon and place de Gaulle.

Le Grand Café Napoléon (☎ 04 95 21 42 54; 10 cours Napoléon; ✖ Mon-Sat) The queen of cours Napoléon's terrace cafés, founded in 1821 and still going strong. Whether it's for afternoon coffee or supper in the grand dining room, this graceful establishment will fit the bill.

Café de Paris (☎ 04 95 51 03 90; dishes €8-15; place de Gaulle) A traditional café and brasserie with a fine terrace overlooking place de Gaulle.

Globo (☎ 04 95 21 01 54; dishes €8-15; ✖ Mon-Sat) Next door to the Café de Paris, this hip café aims for a contemporary crowd, with modern fusion cooking and funky wooden furniture.

SELF-CATERING

Ajaccio's **open-air food market** (square Campinchi; to noon, closed Mon) fills the area with Corsican atmosphere every morning. There's a daily **fish market** in the building behind the food market. Get there *very* early if you want to beat the restaurants to the day's catch.

Spar Supermarket (cours Grandval; 8.30am-12.30pm & 3-7.30pm Mon-Sat) is close to place de Gaulle, while **Monoprix Supermarket** (8.30am-7.15pm Mon-Sat; cours Napoléon) is not far away from the port.

Entertainment

Théâtre Kallisté (04 95 22 78 54; 6 av Colonel Colonna d'Ornano) Ajaccio's municipal theatre hosts music, dance and dramas.

Au Son des Guitares (04 95 51 15 47; 7 rue du Roi de Rome) A good bet for traditional music. It hosts local guitar bands most evenings from around 10pm.

Casino Municipal (04 95 50 40 60; blvd Pascal Rossini; 1pm-3am) The place to go if you have money to burn. There are poker machines, roulette and blackjack to soak up your cash, or you can simply relax in the piano bar.

PARTYING WITH NAPOLÉON

Fêtes Napoliennes, Ajaccio's annual celebration of its most beloved son, kicks off in mid-August. The varied programme of events includes displays, outdoor shows processions, and exhibitions, but the highlight is a huge street parade in which the participants dress up as Napoleonic soldiers. Usually the festival coincides with the fireworks display that lights up the night sky on 15 August to mark Napoléon's birthday.

Getting There & Away

AIR

Aéroport d'Ajaccio-Campo dell'Oro (04 95 23 56 56) is 8km east of the city centre.

BOAT

The ferry terminal is in the bus station. The **SNCM ticket office** (04 95 29 66 99; 3 quai l'Herminier; 8am-8pm Tue-Fri, to 6pm Mon, to 1pm Sat) is across the street. The SNCM bureau in the ferry terminal sells tickets a few hours before departure for evening ferries; tickets for vehicles are available at the port's vehicle entrance.

BUS

Bus companies operate from **Terminal Maritime et Routier** (quai l'Herminier). Most have ticket kiosks on the right as you enter the station. The **information counter** (04 95 51 55 45; 7am-7pm) provides schedules.

Eurocorse (04 95 21 06 30) travels to Bastia (€18, three hours, two daily), Bonifacio (€19.50, four hours, two or three daily), Calvi (€19.85, change at Ponte Leccia), Corte (€10.50, 2¾ hours, two daily) and Sartène (€11.50, two hours, two daily). Services run daily except Sundays; some routes operate reduced services out of season.

Autocars SAIB (04 95 22 41 99) travels to Porto (€11, two hours, two daily).

Autocars Ricci (04 95 51 08 19) also travels to Sartène (€10.70, two hours, two daily).

CAR

The main car-rental companies have airport bureaus as well as being in town.

Budget (04 95 21 17 18; 1 blvd Lantivy)

Europcar (04 95 21 05 49; 16 cours Grandval)

Hertz (04 95 21 70 94; 8 cours Grandval)

Hôtel Kallisté (p883) rents cars cheaply. A three-door car costs €49/227 per day/week, including unlimited mileage. Prices rise in July and August.

TRAIN

The **train station** (04 95 23 11 03; place de la Gare) is staffed until 6.30pm (to 8pm May to September). Services include Bastia (€20.70, four hours, three to four daily), Corte (€11, two hours, three to four daily) and Calvi (€24.10, five hours, two daily; change at Ponte-Leccia).

Getting Around

TO/FROM THE AIRPORT

Transports Corse d'Ajaccio (TCA) bus No 8 links the airport with Ajaccio's train and bus stations (€4.50). Hourly buses run from around 8am to 7pm from the bus station, 9am to 11pm from the airport. A taxi from the airport to Ajaccio costs €25 to €35.

BUS

TCA Boutique (04 95 23 29 41; 75 cours Napoléon) distributes bus maps and timetables. A single ticket/carnet of 10 costs €1.15/9. Most buses operate from place Général de Gaulle and cours Napoléon.

MOPED
Hôtel Kallisté (p883) rents mopeds for €31/157 per day/week in summer.

About 500m north of the train station, **Moto Corse Évasion** (☎ 04 95 20 52 05; fax 04 95 22 48 11; montée St-Jean) rents mountain bikes for €7/13 per half-day/full day.

TAXI
There's a **taxi rank** (☎ 04 95 21 00 87; place de Gaulle) or you can call **Radio Taxis Ajacciens** (☎ 04 95 25 09 13).

SOUTH OF AJACCIO

FILITOSA
Corsica's most important prehistoric site is 25km northwest of Propriano. Inhabited from 5850 BC until Roman times, the **megaliths** and **menhirs** of Filitosa have been intensely studied since their accidental discovery in 1946. The atmospheric hilltop site, shaded by 1000-year-old olive trees, has a small **museum** (☎ 04 95 74 00 91; admission €5; ⏲ 8am-sunset) displaying major finds.

CORSICA BC (AND BEYOND)

For prehistory buffs, Corsica is a Mediterranean treasure trove. Other sites within driving distance of Filitosa include the figures and menhirs of the Alignement de Stantari and the Alignement de Palaggiu, and the eerie megaliths of Cauria, all southwest of Sartène near the D48. Theories abound regarding their purpose, ranging from magical armies to celestial communication centres, but the truth is no-one knows why they were made – which is half the fun.

SARTÈNE (SARTÈ)
pop 3500
The sombre hillside town of Sartène has long been suspicious of outsiders, and with good reason. In 1583 Barbary pirates raided the town and carried 400 people into slavery in North Africa; raids only ended in the 18th century. Sartène was notorious for its banditry and bloody vendettas. In the early 19th century a disagreement between rival landowners deteriorated into house-to-house fighting, forcing most of the population to flee.

Orientation & Information
From place de la Libération, Sartène's main square, cours Sœur Amélie leads south, while cours Général de Gaulle heads north. The old Santa Anna quarter is north of place de la Libération. The **tourist office** (☎ 04 95 77 15 40; 6 rue Borgo; ⏲ 9am-noon Mon-Fri) is 30m uphill from place de la Libération. **Crédit Lyonnais** (14 cours Général de Gaulle) has an ATM.

Sights
Near the **WWI memorial** on place de la Libération is the granite **Église Ste-Marie**. Inside hangs the 32kg cross and 14kg chain used in the Procession du Catenacciu (p886). The arch through the **town hall** (formerly the Governors' Palace), on the northern side of the square, leads to the **Santa Anna quarter**, a residential neighbourhood of austere grey houses and solemn alleyways.

Musée de la Préhistoire Corse (Museum of Corsican Prehistory; ☎ 04 95 77 01 09; rue Croce; admission free; ⏲ 10am-noon & 2-6pm Mon-Sat May-Sep), housed in a former 19th-century prison, displays exhibits on Corsica's prehistoric past.

Sleeping & Eating
Hôtel des Roches (☎ 04 95 77 07 61; hotel.des.roches@ wanadoo.fr; d €46-126 depending on season; ⏲ Apr-Oct) Sartène's only central hotel is in a sober grey-granite building typical of the village. Inside, it's more welcoming, with snug rooms and a good restaurant. Rooms with a valley view cost more.

Hôtel La Villa Piana (☎ 04 95 77 07 04; www.lavilla piana.com; d €55-95 depending on season; ⏲ Apr–mid-Oct; Ⓟ ☂) Situated 1.5km outside Sartène on the N196, this modern hotel offers private terraces and fabulous valley views.

Aux Gourmets (☎ 04 95 77 16 08; 10 cours Sœur Amélie; menus €10-15; ⏲ daily high season, closed Sun low season) Small, simple and Sartène's top eating spot, serving delicious Corsican specialities such as courgettes stuffed with *brocciu* (€9).

La Chaumière (☎ 04 95 77 07 13; 39 rue Médecin-Capitaine Louis Bénédetti; menu €15) This traditional restaurant serves Corsican food and Sartenaise specialities, including a delicious lamb-and-bean stew.

There's also a **Spar supermarket** (14 cours Général de Gaulle) for self-catering.

Getting There & Away
Sartène is on the **Eurocorse** (Ajaccio ☎ 04 95 21 06 30) bus line linking Ajaccio (€11.50, two

CORSICA

PROCESSION DU CATENACCIU

On Good Friday, the people of Sartène perform the Procession du Catenacciu, a colourful re-enactment of the Passion, in which the Catenacciu ('the chained one'), an anonymous, barefoot penitent covered in a red robe and cowl (to preserve his anonymity), carries a huge cross through the town while dragging a heavy chain shackled to the ankle. The Catenacciu is followed by a procession of penitents, clergy and local notables and, as the chain clatters by on the cobblestones, locals look on in great (if rather humourless) excitement. The penitent is chosen by the parish priest from applicants seeking to expiate a grave sin; hopefuls apply years in advance to fulfil the honoured role.

---

hours, two daily) with Bonifacio (€10, two hours, two daily). Buses stop at the **Ollandini travel agency** (☎ 04 95 77 18 41; cours Gabriel Péri), near the end of cours Sœur Amélie.

BONIFACIO (BUNIFAZIU)
pop 2700

The citadel of Bonifacio sits about 70m above the Mediterranean on a rock promontory sometimes called 'Corsica's Gibraltar'. On all sides, white limestone cliffs drop vertically into the sea, while the tall houses of the old city lean out precariously over the water. The northern side of the citadel overlooks Bonifacio Sound (Goulet de Bonifacio), while the southern ramparts afford views of Sardinia, 12km away across the Bouches de Bonifacio (Strait of Bonifacio).

With its dramatic clifftop location, fine architecture and lively marina, Bonifacio is one of Corsica's most appealing seaside towns – so it's hardly surprising that the town is overflowing with tourists in summer. From the geographical details in Homer's *Odyssey*, it's possible that Ulysses' encounter with the cannibalistic Laestrygonians was set in Bouches de Bonifacio.

Orientation

Bonifacio's marina lies at the southeastern corner of Bouches de Bonifacio. The citadel – also known as the Haute Ville (upper city) – occupies the promontory above the harbour, reached by car via av Charles de Gaulle, or on

foot by two sets of steps. The ferry terminal is further west along the marina.

Information

Boniboom (☎ 04 95 73 59 47; quai Jérôme Comparetti; per min/hr €0.15/8; ☼ 8–2am daily) Internet access.
Lavoir de la Marine (1 quai Jérôme Comparetti; €6.10; 7am-10pm) Laundrette.
Post Office (place Carrega; ☼ 8.30am-6pm Mon-Sat Jul–mid-Sep, 9am-noon & 2-5pm Mon-Fri, 9am-noon Sat mid-Sep–Jun).
Société Générale (38 rue St-Érasme; ☼ Mon-Fri) Exchanges currency and has the only ATM in town. In summer, there are exchange bureaus along the marina.
Tourist Office (☎ 04 95 73 11 88; www.bonifacio.com in French; 2 rue Fred Scamaroni; ☼ 9am-8pm daily Jul & Aug, 9am-noon & 2-6pm Mon-Fri, 9am-noon Sat Sep-Jun) In the citadel.

Sights & Activities
CITADEL

The steps linking rue St-Érasme with Porte de Gênes are known as Montée Rastello and Montée St-Roch further up. At the top of Montée St-Roch stands the **Porte de Gênes**, reached by a drawbridge dating from 1598. Just inside the gateway, you can visit the **Grand Bastion** (admission €2; ☼ 9am-6pm daily Jul & Aug, Mon-Sat Apr, May, Sep & Oct), above Porte de Gênes.

Close by, along the citadel's ramparts, there are great views from **place du Marché** and **place Manichella**. The two holes covered by glass pyramids in place Manichella were used to store grain, salted meats and other supplies to use during times of siege.

Crisscrossed by meandering alleyways lined with tall stone houses, the old city has a distinctly medieval feel. **Rue des Deux Empereurs** is so named because Charles V and Napoleon once slept in the houses at Nos 4 and 7. **Église Ste-Marie Majeure**, a 14th-century Romanesque church, is known for its loggia (roofed porch) and communal cistern, a vital asset in times of siege. The cistern is now used as a conference hall.

From the citadel, the **Escalier du Roi d'Aragon** (Staircase of the King of Aragon; admission €2; ☼ 9am-6pm daily Jul & Aug, Mon-Sat Apr, May, Sep & Oct) leads down the cliff. Its 187 steps were, according to legend, constructed by Aragonese troops in a single night during the siege of 1420. The staircase is closed if it's windy or stormy.

Outside the citadel, west along the limestone headland, stands **Église Ste-Dominique** – one of the only Gothic buildings in Corsica.

BONIFACIO (BUNIFAZIU)

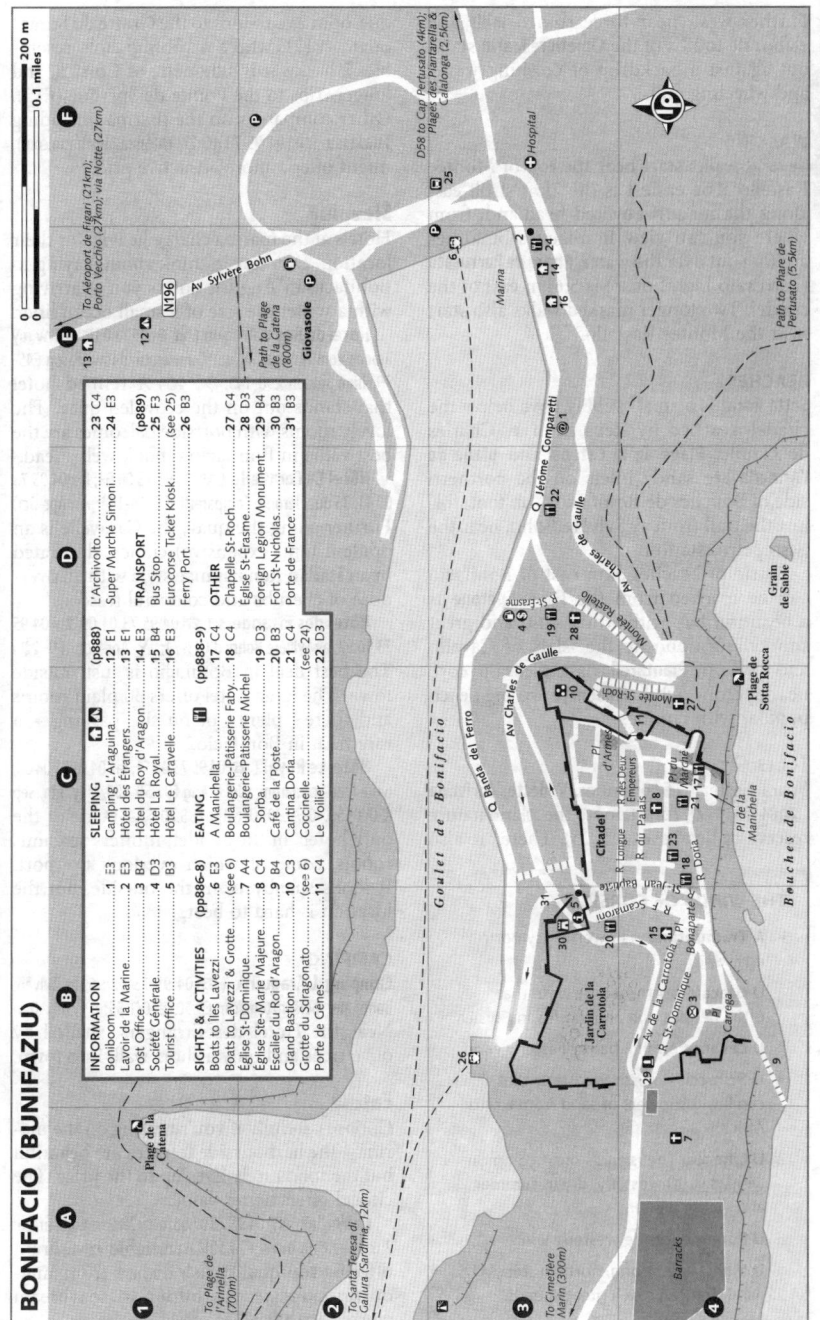

INFORMATION	
Boniboom......	**1** E3
Lavoir de la Marine....	**2** E3
Post Office....	**3** B4
Société Générale....	**4** D3
Tourist Office....	**5** B3

SIGHTS & ACTIVITIES	(pp886–8)
Boats to Îles Lavezzi....	**6** E3
Boats to Lavezzi & Grotte....	(see 6)
Église St-Dominique....	**7** A4
Église Ste-Marie Majeure....	**8** C4
Escalier du Roi d'Aragon....	**9** B4
Grand Bastion....	**10** C3
Grotte du Sdragonato....	(see 6)
Porte de Gênes....	**11** C4

SLEEPING	(p888)
Camping L'Araguina....	**12** E1
Hôtel des Étrangers....	**13** E1
Hôtel du Roy d'Aragon....	**14** E3
Hôtel La Royal....	**15** B4
Hôtel Le Caravelle....	**16** E3

EATING	(pp888–9)
A Manichella....	**17** C4
Boulangerie-Pâtisserie Faby....	**18** C4
Boulangerie-Pâtisserie Michel	
Sorba....	**19** D3
Café de la Poste....	**20** B3
Cantina Doria....	**21** C4
Coccinelle....	(see 24)
Le Voilier....	**22** D3

L'Archivolto....	**23** C4
Super Marché Simoni....	**24** E3

TRANSPORT	(p889)
Bus Stop....	**25** F3
Eurocorse Ticket Kiosk....	(see 25)
Ferry Port....	**26** B3

OTHER	
Chapelle St-Roch....	**27** C4
Église St-Érasme....	**28** D3
Foreign Legion Monument....	**29** B4
Fort St-Nicholas....	**30** B3
Porte de France....	**31** B3

Further west, near three ruined **mills**, the elaborate tombs of the **Cimetière Marin** stand out against a backdrop of crashing waves and wheeling gulls.

WALKING

Several walks start near the top of Montée Rastello. The easiest is the 2km stroll east along the maquis-covered headland, from where you can view Bonifacio's buildings arching out over the water. **Phare de Pertusato** (Pertusato Lighthouse) is 5.6km east of the citadel. Two longer marked walks also start near the Montée Rastello.

BEACHES

Sotta Rocca is a small pebbly cove below the citadel, reached by steps from av Charles de Gaulle. **Plage de la Catena** and **plage de l'Arinella** are sandy inlets on the northern side of Bouches de Bonifacio – on foot, follow the trail from av Sylvère Bohn, near the Esso petrol station.

A trio of beaches 3km east of Bonifacio can be reached from the D58. **Spérone** is a beautiful bay with white sand and great snorkelling opposite the islets of Cavallo and Lavezzi. **Piantarella** is a pleasant cove near Spérone, while **Calalonga** is a big beach popular with families.

Tours

From Easter to September, **Vedettes Christina** (☎ 04 95 73 09 77) runs trips to the island nature reserve of Îles Lavezzi (€25). There are also one-hour excursions to the Grotte du Sdragonato (€12), where a rooftop hole resembles a backwards silhouette of Corsica, and longer trips to the Pointe de Spérone (€15). Other companies on the marina, including **Thalassa** (☎ 04 95 73 10 17; thalassa@bonifacio.com), might offer a more attractive price.

Sleeping

Hotels at the marina charge heavily for their location. Don't even think about staying in Bonifacio in August, unless you're arriving with a wallet the size of a small ocean liner.

Hotel du Roy d'Aragon (☎ 04 95 73 03 99; www.roy aragon.com; 13 quai Jérôme Comparetti; d low season €45-79, high season €90-145; ✗ ✗) A refined hotel that stands out on the crowded quay. The lovely rooms with portside balconies are the best value in Bonifacio – book well ahead.

Hôtel La Caravelle (☎ 04 95 73 00 03; fax 04 95 73 00 41; 35 quai Jérôme Comparetti; d €114-144; ☾ Apr-Oct) Further along the quay, the Caravelle is an opulent (and expensive) choice, decorated in an Italian Renaissance style with an overdose of cherubs and colourful frescoes.

Hôtel des Étrangers (☎ 04 95 73 01 09; fax 04 95 73 16 97; av Sylvère Bohn; d €43-71; ☾ Apr-Oct; P ✗) The best deal in Bonifacio is just outside town. The large hotel offers 30 plain rooms and there's plenty of on-site parking – a rare treat in Bonifacio.

Hôtel Le Royal (☎ 04 95 73 00 51; fax 04 95 73 04 68; 6 rue Fred Scamaroni; r Jul & Aug €91.50-106, May, Jun, Sep & Oct €53.40-79.30, Oct-Apr €38.20-53.40) One of the only hotels in the citadel, it offers spacious rooms, some of which overlook the port. It looks shabby from the outside, but the location is hard to beat.

CAMPING

Camping L'Araguina (☎ 04 95 73 02 96; av Sylvère Bohn; per person/tent/car €5.50/1.70/1.85; ☾ Mar-Oct) Near the Hôtel des Étrangers, shaded by olive trees and only a short walk into town.

Eating

Choose carefully if you're eating on the marina – the harbourside terraces are beautiful but the food rarely lives up to the price. The citadel offers better value.

Le Voilier (☎ 04 95 73 07 06; quai Jérôme Comparetti; 2 courses €19, menu €24.50) A reliable restaurant offering top-quality fish dishes, from langoustines roasted in butter to sea bream cooked with basil sauce.

THE WINDS OF CORSICA

- **A Tramuntana** A powerful, icy northerly wind.

- **U Grecale** Northeasterly wind that often heralds rain and storms in Corsica.

- **U Levante** A mild, balmy easterly wind.

- **U Sciroccu** Hot, southeasterly that can bring showers of sand from North Africa.

- **U Libecciu** The island's most common wind is southwesterly, dry in summer and wet in winter.

- **U Punente** Gentle westerly wind.

- **U Maestrale** Strong, northwesterly wind that can reach great speeds.

BREAD OF THE DEAD & OTHER TREATS

Bonifacio's pastry speciality is *paides morts*, a nut and raisin bread, which delightfully translates as 'bread of the dead'. Other sweet Corsican delights include *fougazi* (flat, sugar-covered, aniseed-flavoured biscuits), *canistrelli* (sugar-crusted biscuits), *canistrone* (cheese tarts) and *moustachole* (bread with sugar crystals on top).

In the citadel, local specialities are baked at **Boulangerie-Pâtisserie Faby** (4 rue St-Jean Baptiste; 🕑 8am-8pm Jul & Aug, 8am-12.30pm & 4-7pm Sep-Jun). Try **Boulangerie-Pâtisserie Michel Sorba** (1-3 rue St-Érasme; 🕑 6am-8pm Jul & Aug, 8am-12.30pm & 4.30-7pm Tue-Sat, 8am-12.30pm Sun Sep-Jun) at the marina.

L'Archivolto (☎ 04 95 73 17 58; rue de l'Archivolto; plats du jour €7-14; 🕑 Mon-Sat) A wonderfully quirky restaurant-cum–antique shop in the citadel, serving imaginative food in a dining room filled with bric-a-brac. Try the chicken in Pietra beer and the fresh herb tart with *brocciu*.

Cantina Doria (☎ 04 95 73 50 49; 27 rue Doria; menus €10-16.50; 🕑 Apr-Oct) A classic Corsican eatery where diners sit on wooden benches, surrounded by farming tools, old photos and rusty signs. The *soupe Corse* (€6) is hearty enough for two, and the pork cooked in Pietra beer is a house speciality.

Café de la Poste (☎ 04 95 73 13 31; 5 rue Fred Scamaroni; menus €13.50-22) Housed in the town's former post office, this buzzy restaurant contains an informal café-bar, a good-value pizza-and-pasta joint, and a more sophisticated restaurant serving seafood and Corsican cuisine.

A Manichella (☎ 04 95 73 12 75; place du Marché; 🕑 9am-11pm Apr-Oct) A pleasant café offering light lunches, crepes and panoramic sea views near the city ramparts.

SELF CATERING
Super Marché Simoni (93 quai Jérôme Comparetti; 🕑 8am-12.30pm & 3.30-7.30pm Mon-Sat, 8am-12.30pm Sun) is on the marina. Next door, Coccinelle supermarket has a fresh bakery counter.

Getting There & Away
AIR
Bonifacio's airport, **Aéroport de Figari** (☎ 04 95 71 10 10), is 21km north of town. An airport bus runs from the town centre from the end of July to the beginning of September (€7 to €8).

BOAT
Ferries to Santa Teresa in Sardinia are offered by **Saremar** (☎ 04 95 73 00 96) and **Moby**

Lines (☎ 04 95 73 00 29) from Bonifacio's ferry port (50 minutes, two to seven daily).

Saremar charges €6.70/8.50 one way in low/high season, while Moby Lines charges €22/30 return. Cars cost between €21 and €43. Port taxes are €3.

BUS
Eurocorse (Porto Vecchio ☎ 04 95 70 13 83) runs two buses to Ajaccio (€19.50, four hours) via Sartène from Monday to Saturday. For Bastia, change at Porto Vecchio (€6.50, 45 minutes, two to four buses daily). Buses leave near the Eurocorse kiosk on the marina in summer only.

CORTE AREA

CORTE (CORTI)
pop 5700 / elevation 400m
When Pasquale Paoli led Corsica to independence in 1755, one of his first acts was to make this fortified town at the centre of the island the country's capital. To this day, Corte remains a potent symbol of Corsican independence and arguably the island's most authentic town. Paoli founded a national university here in 1765, but it was closed four years later when the short-lived Corsican republic foundered. Università di Corsica Pasquale Paoli was reopened in 1981 and now has about 3000 students.

Ringed with mountains and bordered in the east by the forest region of Castagniccia, it's also an excellent base for hiking. Some of the island's highest peaks are just west of town, and the city marks the midpoint on the Mare a Mare Nord trail.

Orientation
Corte's main street is cours Paoli, which is lined with shops and cafés. At its southern

CORSICA

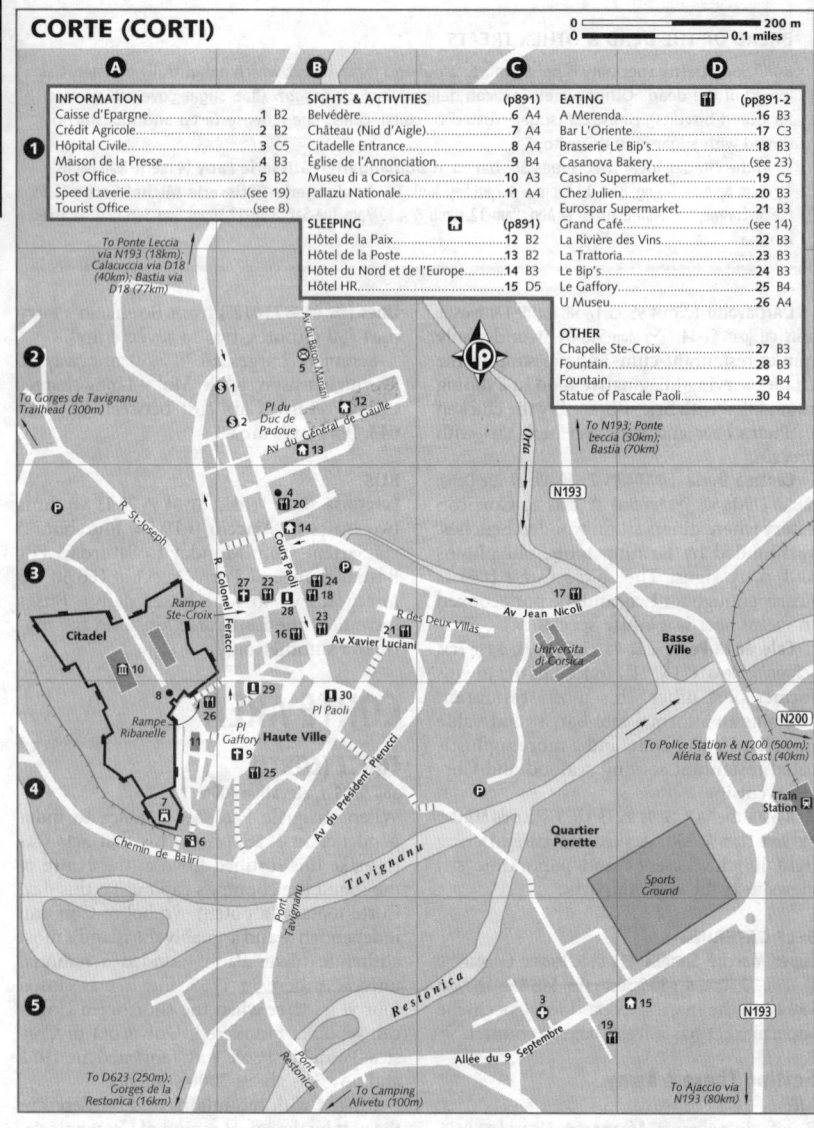

CORTE (CORTI)

INFORMATION		
Caisse d'Epargne	1	B2
Crédit Agricole	2	B2
Hôpital Civile	3	C5
Maison de la Presse	4	B3
Post Office	5	B2
Speed Laverie	(see 19)	
Tourist Office	(see 8)	

SIGHTS & ACTIVITIES		(p891)
Belvédère	6	A4
Château (Nid d'Aigle)	7	A4
Citadelle Entrance	8	A4
Église de l'Annonciation	9	B4
Museu di a Corsica	10	A3
Pallazu Nationale	11	A4

SLEEPING		(p891)
Hôtel de la Paix	12	B2
Hôtel de la Poste	13	B2
Hôtel du Nord et de l'Europe	14	B3
Hôtel HR	15	D5

EATING		(pp891-2)
A Merenda	16	B3
Bar L'Oriente	17	C3
Brasserie Le Bip's	18	B3
Casanova Bakery	(see 23)	
Casino Supermarket	19	C5
Chez Julien	20	B3
Eurospar Supermarket	21	B3
Grand Café	(see 14)	
La Rivière des Vins	22	B3
La Trattoria	23	B3
Le Bip's	24	B3
Le Gaffory	25	B4
U Museu	26	A4

OTHER		
Chapelle Ste-Croix	27	B3
Fountain	28	B3
Fountain	29	B4
Statue of Pascale Paoli	30	B4

---

end is place Paoli, from where the narrow streets of the Haute Ville lead uphill to the citadel. The train station is downhill from cours Paoli.

Information

Banks with ATMs are found along cours Paoli. The post office also has an ATM.

Grand Café (22 cours Paoli; per 15min/hr €1/3.50; 7-2am) Internet access while you eat.
Hôpital Civile (04 95 45 05 00; allée du 9 Septembre)
Maison de la Presse (24 cours Paoli; 8am-6pm) Sells maps and walking guides and has a good Corsican section.
Police Station (04 95 46 04 81) On the road to Aléria.

Post Office (av du Baron Mariani)

Speed Laverie (⏰ 8am-9pm) Laundrette in the same shopping complex as the Casino supermarket.

Tourist Office (☎ 04 95 46 26 70; corte.tourisme@ wanadoo.fr; La Citadelle; ⏰ 9am-noon & 2-6pm Mon-Sat Apr & May, 9am-1pm & 2-7pm Mon-Sat Jun & Sep, 9am-8pm daily Jul & Aug, 9am-noon & 2-6pm Mon-Fri Oct-Mar)

Sights

CITADEL

Corte's citadel juts from a rocky outcrop above the Rivers Tavignanu and Restonica and the cobbled alleyways of the Haute Ville. The highest point of the citadel is the **château** (known as the Nid d'Aigle, or Eagle's Nest), built in 1419 by a Corsican nobleman allied with the Aragonese. It was expanded during the 18th and 19th centuries and served as a Foreign Legion base from 1962 until 1983.

The **Museu di a Corsica** (Museum of Corsica; ☎ 04 95 45 25 45; museu@sitec.fr; adult/student €3/2.30; ⏰ 10am-6pm in summer, until 5pm Nov-Apr, closed Mon in low season) houses an outstanding exhibition on Corsican traditions, crafts, agriculture and anthropology. It has a small cinema and hosts art and music exhibitions on the ground floor. Captions are in French and Corsican.

Outside the ramparts, a path leads to **le belvédère** (viewing platform), which has views of the city and the Eagle's Nest. Close by, a precarious staircase leads down to the river.

OTHER SIGHTS

The Genoese-built **Palazzu Naziunale** (National Palace) was home to Corsica's government during the island's short-lived independence, but it is now occupied by a Corsican studies centre. The basement (once a prison) is used to display temporary exhibitions.

Further down the hill is the 15th-century **Église de l'Annonciation** (place Gaffory). The walls of nearby houses are pockmarked with bullet holes, reputedly from Corsica's war of independence.

Sleeping

Hôtel de la Paix (☎ 04 95 46 06 72; fax 04 95 46 23 84; av du Général de Gaulle; s/d/tr from €35/42/55; **P**) A big, comfortable hotel with 60 spic-and-span rooms on a quiet square off cours Paoli. The in-house **Corsican restaurant** (menu €13) is decent, too.

Hôtel de la Poste (☎ 04 95 46 01 37; 2 place du Duc de Padoue; r €33.50) On the same square as Hôtel de la Paix, but looking worse for wear, this is a typically Corsican no-frills hotel with mismatched décor and run-down charm.

Hôtel du Nord et de L'Europe (☎ 04 95 46 00 68; www.hoteldunord-corte.com in French; 22 cours Paoli; s/d/tr low season €45/50/70, high season €65/70/90) A family-run hotel offering 15 rooms with high ceilings and soundproofed windows; the best have mountain views.

Hôtel HR (☎ 04 95 45 11 11; 6 allée du 9 Septembre; s/d low season €21/35, high season €40/52; **P**) Clean and functional, this hotel is outside the town centre and has an on-site laundrette and sauna, but don't expect much charm.

CAMPING

Camping Alivetu (☎ 04 95 46 11 09; fax 04 95 46 12 34; faubourg de St-Antoine; per adult/car/tent €5/2/2; ⏰ Apr-Oct) Attractive and shaded by olive trees, this camping area is south of town.

Eating

RESTAURANTS

U Museu (☎ 04 95 61 08 36; rampe Ribanelle; menus €13-15; ⏰ closed Sun Oct-Jun) Corte's outstanding Corsican restaurant serves traditional cuisine on a gazebo-covered terrace. Its menus include *civet de sanglier aux myrtes sauvages* (wild boar with myrtle), *soissons Corses* (Corsican lima beans) and *truite au peveronata* (trout in red pepper sauce).

La Trattoria (☎ 04 95 46 00 76; 6 cours Paoli; menus €9-14; ⏰ closed Sun) A family-run restaurant held in high esteem by locals, serving up classic Corsican meat dishes and enormous salads. The next-door patisserie is the best in town, so the cakes are rather good, too.

Le Bip's (☎ 04 95 46 06 26; 14 cours Paoli; fish dishes €7.60-13; ⏰ Sun-Fri) This cellar restaurant is always packed with a boisterous crowd who come for the atmosphere and homely food. The restaurant is down a flight of stairs beside Brasserie Le Bip's.

Le Gaffory (☎ 04 95 61 05 58; place Gaffory; menus €11.50-16.50) Nestling in the shadow of Église de l'Annonciation, this restaurant offers pizzas, cheap Corsican food and multilanguage menus. The €16.50 menu includes wine.

Also recommended:

Bar L'Oriente (☎ 04 95 61 11 17; av Jean Nicoli; ⏰ 9am-midnight) Funky student hang-out opposite the university.

Chez Julien (☎ 04 95 46 02 90; 24 cours Paoli; menu €13; ⌚ Mon-Sat) Rustic restaurant offering meals with a Corsican twist.

La Rivière des Vins (☎ 04 95 46 37 04; 5 rampe Ste-Croix; menus €9.90-11; ⌚ closed Sun Oct-Mar) Cosy wine bar serving charcuterie and cheese.

CAFÉS

A Merenda (☎ 04 95 46 30 99; 3 cours Paoli; ⌚ 9am-midnight Mon-Sat) A café-bar and *salon du thé* with delicious coffee, ice cream and light meals, including *croques-monsieurs*.

Grand Café (☎ 04 95 46 00 33; 22 cours Paoli; ⌚ 7-2am) A cosy café in the Hotel du Nord where you can leave your backpacks for free.

SELF-CATERING

Corte's top *boulangerie* is Casanova, next door to La Trattoria (see p891) – practically the whole town comes here to buy its cakes. There's also a **Eurospar** (7 av Xavier Luciani) and a **Casino Supermarket** (allée du 9 Septembre).

Getting There & Away

BUS

Eurocorse travels through town twice daily from Ajaccio (€10.50, 2¾ hours) towards Bastia (€10, two hours) except Sunday.

TRAIN

The **train station** (☎ 04 95 46 00 97; ⌚ 6.30am-8.30pm Mon-Sat, 9.45am-noon & 4.45-8.35pm Sun) is east of the city centre. Destinations include Bastia (€9.70, two hours, three to four daily) and Ajaccio (€11.00, two hours, three to four daily).

AROUND CORTE

Southwest of Corte are the grey-granite **Gorges de la Restonica**. Some of the area's best walking trails begin 16km southwest of Corte at **Bergeries de Grotelle** (1375m), which is accessible via the D623. The **Lac de Mello** (Melu; 1711m) is a one-hour walk from the Bergeries (sheepfolds), while **Lac de Capitello** (Capitellu; 1930m) is 40 minutes further. Both lakes are ice-covered for much of the year.

West of Corte, there are walking trails around the **River Tavignanu Valley**. **Lac Nino** (Ninu; 1743m) is a 9½-hour walk from Corte. Twenty kilometres south, the 15-sq-km **Forêt de Vizzavona** has 43km of forest trails. Two waterfalls, the **Cascade des Anglais**, accessible from Vizzavona, and the **Cascade du Voile de la Mariée**, near Bocognano, are both worth the hike.

Directory

CONTENTS

ACCOMMODATION

Be it a luxurious castle, a quaint hotel room or a mountain *refuge,* France has accommodation of every sort and for every budget.

In general, hotels listed under 'budget' have doubles that cost less than two hostel beds, that is up to €40 (€50 in Paris). Most are equipped with a washbasin but lack private bath or toilet. Hall showers usually cost €2 or €3.

Hotels listed under 'mid-range' are usually in the range of €40 to €100 for a double room (up to €150 in Paris) and always have en-suite shower and toilet facilities. These places are comfortable and good value. Top-

PRACTICALITIES

- Use the metric system for weights and measures.

- Plugs will have two round pins, so you will need an international adapter; the electric current is 220V at 50Hz AC (you may need a transformer for 110V electrical appliances).

- Videos in France work on the PAL system while TV is Secam.

- Read the French *informations* in *Le Monde,* the righter-wing *Figaro* or the left-leaning *Libération.*

- Tune in to Radio France Info (105.5 FM) or the multilanguage RFI (738AM) for round-the-clock news; BBC World Service/Europe (648AM); Nova (101.5FM) for an eclectic blend of modern beats; Paris Jazz (98.1 FM) for jazz in the capital; Nostalgie, Skyrock and Fun Radio for commercial hits (see http://windowsmedia.com/radiotuner/My Radio.asp for local frequencies).

- Pick up *France USA Contacts* (Fusac) magazine (www.fusac.fr) in Anglophone haunts in Paris for classified ads about housing, babysitting, jobs and language exchanges.

- Switch on French TV: private stations TF1 and M6; and state-owned France 2, France 3 and Arte.

end accommodation will cost more than €100 (€150 in the capital). Of course, when it comes to the cream of French hotel opulence the price will skyrocket.

During periods of heavy domestic or foreign tourism (eg Easter, Christmas–New Year, the February–March school holidays, as well as July and August and most long weekends) popular destinations are packed out (reservations are a must) and hotels will charge peak rates.

Tourist offices will often make room reservations for you (sometimes there will be a small fee), though not over the phone – you have to stop by the office. While staff sometimes have information on vacancies, they rarely give recommendations.

Hotels almost always ask for a credit card number and written (faxed) confirmation, and some may require a deposit. Most places will hold a room only until a set hour, rarely later than 6pm or 7pm (and sometimes earlier).

Camping & Caravan Parks

Camping is immensely popular in France, and many of the thousands of camping areas are near rivers, lakes or oceans. Most close from October or November to March or April. Hostels sometimes let travellers pitch tents in the back garden.

In this book 'camping' refers to fixed-price deals for two or three people including a tent and a car. Otherwise the price is broken down per person/tent/car, but does not include extras. Rates are generally the same for campervan, plus an extra fee for electricity. Camping-ground offices are often closed for most of the day. Getting to and from most camping grounds without your own car or bike can often be slow and costly.

Gîtes de France (see below) coordinates farm camping and publishes an annual guide: *Camping à la Ferme*.

Camping in nondesignated spots (*camping sauvage*) is generally illegal, though sometimes tolerated (ask permission on private land). Except in Corsica, you probably won't have problems if you're at least 1500m from a camping area (or, in national parks, at least an hour's walk from the road). Camping on the beach is not a good idea in areas with high tidal variations. Always ask permission before camping on private land.

Gîtes Ruraux & B&Bs

Several types of accommodation – often in charming, traditional-style houses with gardens – are available through Gîtes de France for people who would like to spend time in rural areas and who have a vehicle.

A *gîte rural* is a self-contained holiday cottage (or part of a house) in a village or on a farm, and makes a great base from which to explore the surrounding area.

A *chambre d'hôte*, basically a bed and breakfast (B&B), is a room in a private house rented to travellers by the night. The website www.bbfrance.com is useful for arranging B&Bs and vacation rentals.

Ask about Gîtes de France offices and brochures and guides at local tourist offices, or contact directly the **Fédération Nationale des Gîtes de France** (☎ 01 49 70 75 75; www.gites-de -france.fr; 59 rue St-Lazare, 9e, Paris; metro Trinité).

Homestays

Under an arrangement known as *hôtes payants* or *hébergement chez l'habitant*, students, young people and tourists can stay with French families. In general you rent a room and have access (sometimes limited) to the family's kitchen and bathroom. Ask local tourist offices for details. Language schools such as Alliance Française can organise homestays.

Accueil Familial des Jeunes Étrangers (☎ 01 45 49 15 57; www.afje-paris.org; 23 rue du Cherche Midi, 6e, Paris; metro Sèvres Babylone) arranges welcoming homestays in carefully selected French families in central and greater Paris, from €550 per month, including breakfast.

France Lodge (☎ 01 56 33 85 80; 2 rue Meissonier, 17e, Paris; metro Wagram) arranges accommodation in private homes and apartments in Paris, for €22 to €40 per night per person.

Hostels & Foyers

Official hostels are known as *auberges de jeunesse*. A hostel bed generally costs around €20 including breakfast in Paris, and €8 to €13 in the provinces, where a sometimes-optional breakfast costs around €3.

France's major hostel associations, **Ligue Française pour les Auberges de la Jeunesse** (LFAJ; ☎ 01 44 16 78 78; www.auberges-de-jeunesse.com; 7 rue Vergniaud, 13e, Paris; metro Glacière) and **Fédération Unie des Auberges de Jeunesse** (FUAJ; ☎ 01 48 04 70 30; www.fuaj.org; 9 rue de Brantome, 3e, Paris; metro Rambuteau) will require you to have or purchase an Hostelling International card or a nightly Welcome Stamp. You can bring your own sleeping sheet or rent one for a small fee.

The nonprofit organisation **Union des Centres de Rencontres Internationales de France** (UCRIF; ☎ 01 40 26 57 64; www.ucrif.asso.fr) has 'international holiday centres' with bedrooms, dorm rooms and restaurant facilities.

In the university towns, *foyers d'étudiant* (student dormitories) are sometimes converted for use by travellers during summer. *Foyers de jeunes travailleurs* or *travailleuses* (workers' dormitories, usually mixed sex) often take passing visitors when they have room. Relatively unknown to travellers, these places frequently have space when other hostels are full.

Hotels

French hotels are rated with one to four stars, but these ratings are based on objective criteria (eg the size of the entry hall), not the quality of the service, the décor or the cleanliness. Prices often reflect these intangibles far more than they do the number of stars.

A double has one double bed, so specify if you prefer two twin beds *(deux lits séparés)*; triples and quads usually have two or three beds.

Look out for great weekend deals to 33 cities and towns in France, offering two nights' accommodation for the price of one and other discounts. See www.bon-week-end -en-villes.com for details.

Consortiums **Logis de France** (☎ 01 45 84 83 84; www.logis-de-france.fr), which publishes an annual guide with maps, and **Citotel** (☎ 04 73 746 590; www.citotel.com) group together affiliated hotels that meet strict standards of service and amenities while retaining their own identity and charm. They are usually reliable and good value. The **Best Western** (☎ 0800 91 40 01; www.bestwestern.com) group is increasingly muscling in on the upper end of mid-range accommodation.

Then you have the identical hotel chains. A remarkably cheap option for those travelling by car are the Accor group 'clones' in convenient (though uninspiring) locations on the outskirts of towns and cities, usually on the main access route.

Etap (☎ 0 836 68 89 00; www.etaphotel.com) Slightly more comfortable rooms for a few euros more, usually closer to the town centre.

Formule 1 (☎ 0 836 68 56 85; www.hotelformule1 .com) €22 to €28 for an efficient three-person room with hall shower and toilet.

Refuges & Gîtes d'Étape

A *refuge* (mountain hut or shelter) is a very basic dorm-room cabin established along trails in uninhabited mountainous areas and operated by national park authorities, Club Alpin Français (see p897) or other private organisations. *Refuges* are generally marked on hiking and climbing maps.

A bunk bed in the dorm usually costs between €10 and €16 per night. Meals are sometimes available. It's a good idea to make a reservation: you don't want to hike all the way there to find there's no room.

Gîtes d'étape, generally better equipped and more comfortable than *refuges* (some even have showers), are situated in less remote areas, often in villages. Contact Gîtes de France (see opposite) for information and an annual guide.

For more information about *gîtes d'étape* and *refuges* look on the website at www.gites -refuges.com, which has a France-wide directory. Otherwise contact a tourist office near where you'll be hiking. Regional guides with *refuge* listings are available.

Rental Accommodation

Finding an apartment for a long-term rental in France can be a gruelling ordeal for natives and foreigners alike. Landlords usually require substantial proof of financial responsibility and sufficient funds in France; many ask for a *caution* (guarantee) and a hefty deposit.

Classified ads appear in *De Particulier à Particulier* (www.pap.fr) and *La Centrale des Particuliers* (www.lacentrale.fr in French), both issued each Thursday. *Fusac* magazine (see p893) also has short- and long-term apartment ads by people who'll rent to foreigners at a price.

For the best selection of apartments outside Paris it's best to be on-site. Check places like bars and *tabacs* for free local newspapers (named after the number of the *département*) with classifieds listings. The ads can also be accessed on the Internet at www.maville.com (in French).

Self-Catering Apartments

Renting a studio or apartment can be an economical alternative for stays longer than a week, plus it gives you the opportunity to live as a native. The apartments are usually furnished and fully equipped, with kitchens. Watch out for hidden extra charges that can add up: cleaning fees, linen fees, electricity fees etc. Expect to pay from €70 to €120 per night or (at least) €270 per week, depending on the location.

B & W Apartment Hotels (☎ 800-755 8266; www .apartmenthotels.com; 140 East 56th St, NY, NY 10022) A variety of apartments throughout France.

DIRECTORY

Citadines (☎ 0 825 010 362; www.citadines.com)
A favourite with business travellers for its convenient
apartments.
Maeva (☎ 0 825 070 060, 01 53 61 62 00; www.orion
-vacances.com) Apartment hotels primarily in mountain
and sea resorts.

A small hotel that rents rooms with kitchenettes, generally by the week, is known as
a *hôtel meublé*. They are common on the
Côte d'Azur.

ACTIVITIES

France's varied geography and climate make
it a superb place for a wide range of outdoor
pursuits. From the snowy peaks, rivers,
lakes and canyons of the Alps to the striking
mountains and volcanic peaks of the Massif
Central – not to mention 3000km of coastline from the Mediterranean to the Straits
of Dover – France's stunning scenery lends
itself to adventure sports and exhilarating
outdoor activities of all kinds.

See the individual destinations for details and check with both local and regional
tourist offices and websites for information
on local activities, clubs and companies (see
p911).

Some hostels, for example those run
by the Fédération Unie des Auberges de
Jeunesse (FUAJ; see p894), offer week-long
sports *stages* (training courses).

Adventure Sports

France is a fantastic place for adventurous
activities. In large cities and picturesque
places – particularly the Côte d'Azur and
the Alps – local companies offer all kinds of
high adrenaline pursuits such as canyoning
and bungy jumping.

If you are interested in *alpinisme* (mountaineering) or *escalade* (rock climbing), you
can arrange climbs with guides – and other
alpine activities – through the Club Alpin
Français (see opposite).

Deltaplane (hang-gliding) and *parapente*
(paragliding) are all the rage in many parts
of France. See the Pyrenees, Brittany, Massif
Central and Languedoc-Roussillon chapters
for more information or contact **Fédération
Française de Vol Libre** (☎ 04 97 03 82 82; www.ffvl.fr
in French) in Nice.

Vol à voile (gliding) is most popular in
France's south, where the temperatures are
warmer and the thermals better. Causse

Méjean (eg near Florac; p746) in Languedoc
is one of the most popular spots. For the addresses and details of gliding clubs around
France, contact the **Fédération Française de Vol
à Voile** (FFVV; ☎ 01 45 44 04 78; www.ffvv.org; 29 rue
de Sèvres, 6e, Paris).

For details on *montgolfière* flights in the
Loire Valley, see p401 and in Burgundy,
see p428).

Speleology, the scientific study of caves,
was pioneered in France; there are still some
great places for cave exploration. Club Alpin
Français (see opposite) has information.

Cycling

The French take their cycling very seriously,
and whole parts of the country almost grind
to a halt during the annual Tour de France
(see p).

A *vélo tout-terrain* (VTT, or mountain
bike) is a fantastic tool for exploring the
countryside. Some GR and GRP trails (see
opposite) are open to mountain bikers, but
take care not to startle walkers. A *piste cyclable* is a bicycle path.

Some of the best areas for cycling (with
varying grades of difficulty) are around the
Alpine resorts of Annecy (p508) and Chambéry (p512) and through the Pyrenees. In
southwestern France, the Dordogne and
Quercy offer a vast network of scenic,
tranquil roads for cycle tourists, while the
beautiful Mont Aigoual region has a huge
network of paths (see p741). The Loire Valley and coastal regions such as Brittany,
Normandy and the Atlantic coast offer a
wealth of easier options.

For maps, see p908. Lonely Planet's *Cycling France* includes essential maps, advice,
directions, and technical tips. For information on transporting your bicycle and bike
rental, see p922. Details on places that rent
bikes appear at the end of each city or town
listing under Getting Around.

Skiing

France has more than 400 ski resorts in the
Alps, the Jura, the Pyrenees, the Vosges,
the Massif Central and even the mountains of Corsica. The ski season generally
lasts from December to March or April.
January and February tend to have the best
overall conditions, but the slopes can be
very crowded during the February–March
school holidays.

The Alps have some of Europe's finest –
and priciest – ski facilities. In a few places,
you can even ski on glaciers during the
summer (for details, see p493 and individual destinations).

Much cheaper and less glitzy, smaller,
low-altitude stations in the Pyrenees and
the Massif Central are more suited to beginners and intermediates. In the Alps, low-
altitude skiing is popular on the Vercors
massif (p528).

Ski de fond (cross-country skiing) is possible at high-altitude resorts but is usually
much better in the valleys. Undoubtedly
some of the best trails are in the Jura range
(p535).

One of the cheapest ways to ski in France
is to buy a package deal before leaving
home. Ask your travel agency for details.
Many hostels in the Alps offer reasonable
week-long packages in winter. Websites
for online bookings include www.discover
-france.info, www.ski-europe.com and www
.alpsweek.com.

Paris-based **Ski France** (Ski France; ☎ 01 47
42 23 32; www.skifrance.fr; 61 blvd Haussmann 8e, Paris;
metro Opéra) has information and an annual
brochure covering more than 50 ski resorts.
The Club Alpin Français office (see right)
may also be able to provide information on
alpine activities.

Walking

The French countryside is crisscrossed by
a staggering 120,000km of *sentiers balisés*
(marked walking paths), which pass through
every imaginable terrain in every region of
the country. No permits are needed for hiking, but there are restrictions on where you
can camp, especially in national parks.

Probably the best known trails are the
sentiers de grande randonnée, long-distance
footpaths marked by red-and-white-striped
track indicators. Some trails are many hundreds of kilometres long, such as the GR5,
which goes from the Netherlands through
the French Alps to Nice.

The *grandes randonnées de pays* (GRP)
trails, whose markings are yellow, are designed for intense exploration of one particular area. Other types of trails include
sentiers de promenade randonnée (PR),
walking paths marked in yellow; *drailles*,
paths used by cattle to get to high-altitude
summer pastures; and *chemins de halage*,
canal towpaths. Shorter day-hike trails are
often known as *sentiers de petites randonnées* or *sentiers de pays*.

Fédération Française de la Randonnée Pédestre
(FFRP; French Ramblers' Association) has an **information centre and bookshop** (Map pp96-8; ☎ 01 44 89
93 93; www.ffrp.asso.fr in French; 14 rue Riquet 19e, Paris;
metro Pernety) in Paris.

The **Club Alpin Français** (Map pp96-8; ☎ 01 53 72
87 00; www.clubalpin.com; 24 av de Laumière, 19e, Paris;
metro Laumière) has a centre in Paris with useful
information – joining is probably worthwhile
if you're doing a great deal of hiking.

Lonely Planet's *Walking in France* is full
of lively detail and essential practical information. For details on *refuges* (mountain
huts) and other overnight accommodation
for walkers, such as *gîtes d'étape,* (see p894).
For maps, see p908.

Water Sports

France has lovely beaches along all of its
coasts – the English Channel, the Atlantic
and the Mediterranean – as well as on lakes
such as Lac d'Annecy and Lake Geneva.
The fine, sandy beaches stretching along
the family-oriented Atlantic Coast (eg near
La Rochelle; p620) are much less crowded
than their rather pebbly counterparts on the
Côte d'Azur. Corsica has some magnificent
spots. Brittany and the north coast are also
popular (though cooler) beach destinations.

The general public is free to use any beach not marked as private.

The best surfing in France is on the Atlantic coast around Biarritz (p654), where waves can reach heights of 4m. Windsurfing is popular wherever there's water and a breeze, and renting equipment is often possible on lakes.

White-water rafting, canoeing and kayaking are practised on many French rivers, especially in the Massif Central and the Alps. The **Fédération Française de Canoë-Kayak** (FFCK; ☎ 01 45 11 08 50; www.ffck.org in French) can supply information on canoeing and kayaking clubs around the country.

BUSINESS HOURS

French business hours are regulated by the controversial 35hr week work limit. Shop hours are usually 9am or 9.30am to 7pm or 8pm, often with a midday break from noon or 1pm to 2pm or 3pm. The midday break is uncommon in Paris. French law requires that most businesses close on Sunday; exceptions include grocery stores, *boulangeries,* patisseries, florists and businesses catering exclusively to the tourist trade. Many will also close on one other weekday, usually Monday.

Restaurants are usually open for lunch between noon or 12.30pm and 2pm and for dinner from 7.30pm; they are often closed on one or two days of the week. Cafés open early morning until around midnight. Bars usually open early evening and close at 1am or 2am.

National museums are closed on Tuesday and local museums are closed on Monday, though in summer some open daily. Local or less famous regional museums may close at lunchtime.

Banks usually open from 8am or 9am to 11.30am or 1pm and then 1.30pm or 2pm to 4.30pm or 5pm, Monday to Friday or Tuesday to Saturday. Exchange services may end half an hour before closing time.

Post offices generally open from 8.30am or 9am to 5pm or 6pm on weekdays (perhaps with a midday break) and Saturday morning from 8am to noon.

Supermarkets open Monday to Saturday usually from about 9am or 9.30am to 7pm or 8pm (plus a midday break in smaller towns); some open on Sunday morning. Small food shops may shut on Monday also, so Saturday

morning may be your last chance to stock up on provisions until Tuesday. Open-air markets start at about 6am and finish at 1pm or 1.30pm. Many service stations have small groceries open 24 hours a day.

CHILDREN

Country France can be a great place for travel with children and, while big cities can be more difficult, lots of activities are on offer for *les enfants*, especially in Paris.

Practicalities

France is generally child-friendly but children are expected to behave themselves in public. French parents would not ordinarily take their children to a restaurant any more sophisticated than a corner café. Chain restaurants such as Hippopotamus and Bistro Romain are casual and serve the kind of food that most kids like. Take drinks with you on sightseeing days to avoid costly café stops. Picnics can be a great way to feed the troops and enjoy local produce.

The weekly entertainment magazine *L'Officiel des Spectacles* advertises babysitting services *(gardes d'enfants)* in Paris. It's out on Wednesday and is available at any newsstand.

Most car-rental firms in France have children's safety seats for hire at a nominal cost, but it is essential that you book them in advance. The same goes for high chairs and cots (cribs); they're standard in most restaurants and hotels but numbers are limited. The choice of baby food, infant formula, soy and cow's milk, disposable nappies (diapers) and the like is as great in French supermarkets as it is back home, but the opening hours may be quite different. Run out of nappies on Saturday afternoon and you could be facing a long and messy weekend.

As an alternative to hotels, you might prefer renting a self-contained apartment or *gîte* (cottage), which provides a comfortable base for exploring an area and makes you less reliant on eating out. The fancier camping grounds have pools and children's facilities.

Sights & Activities

Include the kids in the trip planning: if they've helped work out the itinerary and activities they will be much more interested when they get there. Lonely Planet's *Travel with Children* is a good source of information.

Paris' narrow streets and metro stairways can be a trial, but the capital has wonderful parks with amusements and activities like pony rides and puppet shows, as well as attractions like La Villette (p130) and Disneyland Resort (p184).

Beaches are always a child-pleaser, and the Atlantic coast is especially popular with families. The French Alps also have lots of outdoor activities year-round, like horse riding or snow-shoe walking. You might also get them into some light hiking or bike riding (see p896).

Try to find things that will capture their imagination: discovering volcanoes at Vulcania (p553); marvelling at how Airbus planes are put together in Toulouse (p800); exploring the lavish castles of the Loire Valley (p395); riding the 'Magic Carpet' at Futuroscope cinematic theme park (p619); or simply cavorting in lavender fields in Provence.

CLIMATE

In general, France has a temperate climate with mild winters, except in mountainous areas and Alsace. For climatic considerations concerning your trip, see p13.

COURSES

Art, cuisine, language, cinema – the best of France is there for the learning. The website www.edufrance.fr/en has information about higher education, while www.studyabroad links.com can help you find specific courses and summer programmes.

Cooking

For information on cooking short courses and specialised sessions, like pastry making, see p79.

RAIN, HAIL, SNOW OR SHINE

Discover what France's weather-forecasters are saying at www.meteo.fr (in French) or call:

National forecast	☎ 0 836 701 234
Regional forecasts	☎ 0 836 680 000
Département forecasts	☎ 0 836 6802 +
	2-digit *département* number
Mountain areas & snow forecasts	☎ 0 836 680 404
Marine forecast	☎ 0 836 680 808

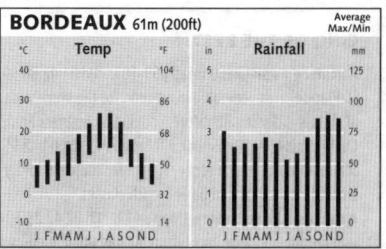

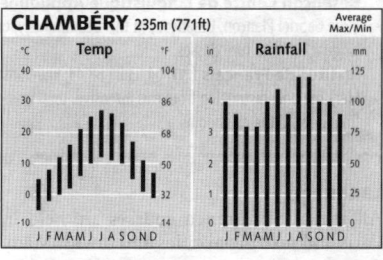

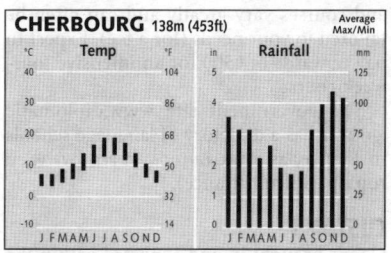

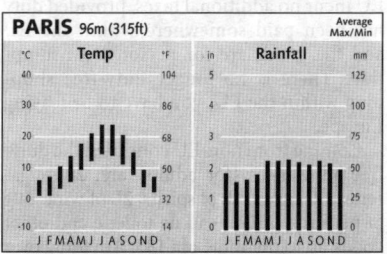

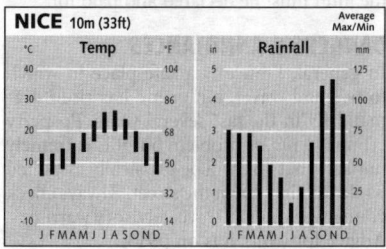

CINQ OF THE BEST

Alliance Française (Map p99-101; ☎ 01 42 84 90 00; www.alliancefr.org; 101 blvd Raspail, 6e Paris; metro St-Placide) This venerable institution for the worldwide promotion of French language and civilisation offers a variety of classes including literature, cooking or business French.

Université de Provence (Map p777; ☎ 04 42 95 32 17; www.up.univ-mrs.fr/wscefee in French; 29 av Robert Schumann, Aix-en-Provence) A popular choice in lovely Aix: academic language and methodology courses, as well as writing workshops and basic French classes.

Amboise Eurocentre (Map p413; ☎ 02 47 23 10 60; www.eurocentres.com; 9 Mail St-Thomas, Amboise) Dip into French language and culture at this small, well-organised school in the charming Loire Valley.

Besançon Centre de Linguistique Appliquée (Map p538; ☎ 03 81 66 52 00; http://cla.univ-fcomte.fr/; 6 rue Gabriel Plançon, Besançon) In this beautiful city, one of France's largest language schools with a variety of language and culture classes.

Institut de Français (☎ 04 93 01 88 44; www.institutdefrancais.com; 23 av Général Leclerc, Villefranche-sur-Mer) The only distraction from this intensive, total immersion course is the spectacular Mediterranean sea beckoning from beyond the classrooms.

Language

All manner of French courses are held in Paris and provincial cities and towns. Many can also arrange accommodation. Prices and courses vary greatly and can often be tailored to your needs (for a fee). Expect to pay upwards of €500 for an intensive four-week course.

The government site www.diplomatie.gouv.fr has a directory of language schools in France, as does *Europa Pages* (www.europa-pages.com/france).

CUSTOMS

Goods brought in and exported within the EU incur no additional taxes, provided duty has been paid somewhere within the EU and the goods are for personal consumption. There is no longer duty-free shopping within the EU; you have to be leaving Europe.

Coming from non-EU countries, the duty-free allowances (for adults) are: 200 cigarettes, 50 cigars, 1L of spirits, 2L of wine, 50g of perfume, 250ml eau de toilette and other goods up to the value of €183. Anything over the limit must be declared and paid for.

DANGERS & ANNOYANCES

In general, France is a safe place in which to live and travel, but crime has risen dramatically in the last several years. Property crime is a *major* problem but it is extremely unlikely that you will be physically assaulted while walking down the street. Always check your government's travel advisory warnings. Advice for women is on p913.

Hunters

The hunting season usually runs from the end of September to the end of February. If you see signs reading *'chasseurs'* or *'chasse gardée'* strung up or tacked to trees, you might want to think twice about wandering into the area. As well as millions of wild animals, fifty French hunters die each year after being shot by other hunters. Hunting is traditional and common place in all rural areas in France, especially Les Vosges, Sologne, the southwest and the Baie de Somme.

Natural Dangers

There are powerful tides and strong undertows along the Atlantic coast, Brittany and Normandy. Only swim in Zones de Baignade Surveillée (monitored beaches with life guards). Many people drown each year, especially on the Atlantic coast. Be aware of tide times, and if sleeping on a beach, always ensure you are above the high tidemark.

Thunderstorms in the mountains and hot southern plains can be extremely sudden and violent. So check the weather report before you set out on a long walk and be very well prepared if you're heading into the high country of the Alps or Pyrenees.

Smoking

By nature many French people dismiss laws they consider stupid or intrusive. Laws banning smoking in public places do exist, for example, but no-one pays much attention to them. In restaurants, diners will often smoke in the non-smoking sections – and the waiter will happily bring them an ashtray.

Strikes

France is the only European country in which public workers enjoy an unlimited right to strike and avail themselves of it with carefree abandon. An air traffic controllers strike in June 2002 disrupted air travel across Europe, and 2003 was the year of festival cancellations all over the country as arts workers protested. Aggrieved truck drivers have been known to block the autoroutes and farmers agitating for more government support occasionally dump tonnes of produce on major arteries.

Getting caught in one of the 'social dialogues' that characterise labour relations in France can put a serious crimp in your travel plans. It's best to leave some wriggle room in your schedule, particularly around the departure times.

Theft

The problems you're most likely to encounter are thefts (which can be aggressive), mainly pick-pocketing/bag snatching, especially in dense crowds and public places. A common ploy is for one person to distract you while another steals your wallet, camera or bag. Tired tourists on the train from the airport are a frequent target. Big cities – notably Paris, Marseille and Nice – have high crime levels. Particularly in Paris, museums are beset by organised gangs of seemingly innocuous children who are trained pickpockets.

Although there's no need whatsoever to travel in fear, a few simple precautions will minimise your chances of being ripped off.

- Photocopy your passport, credit cards, plane tickets, driver's licence, and other important documents – leave one copy at home and keep another one with you, separate from the originals.
- A hidden money belt remains the safest way to carry money and valuable documents.
- Take only what you need on busy sightseeing days: use the hotel/hostel safe.
- On trains, keep bags as close as possible: the luggage racks (if in use) at the ends of the carriage are an easy target for thieves; in sleeping compartments, lock the door carefully at night.
- Be especially vigilant at train stations, airports, fast-food outlets, cinemas, outdoor cafés, public transport and beaches.

TRAVELLING BY CAR

Car thefts and break-ins of parked cars are a frequent problem. Gangs cruise seemingly tranquil tourist areas for unattended vehicles. Foreign or out-of-town plates and rental stickers are a dead giveaway and will be targeted. Never, ever leave anything valuable (or otherwise) inside your car. Hiding your bags in the trunk is risky; in hatchbacks it is an open invitation to theft.

Aggressive theft from cars stopped at red lights is a problem, especially in the south at intersections and autoroute exits. Thieves are usually on motorcycle. Your car should have autolocking doors (and air-conditioning).

DISABLED TRAVELLERS

France is not well equipped for *handicapés* (disabled people): kerb ramps are few and far between; older public facilities and budget hotels often lack lifts; cobblestone streets are a nightmare to navigate in a wheelchair; and the Paris metro, most of it built decades ago, is hopeless. But disabled people who would like to visit France can overcome these difficulties.

The French government has increased efforts to improve conditions for disabled people, creating the national *Tourisme et Handicap* rating. This classification is given

---

SECURITY

The Plan Vigipirate is a set of ongoing security measures enacted by the French government in 1978 to protect the public from terrorist threats. There are two main phases, Simple and Renforcé. When Vigipirate Renforcé is announced, as was the case following September 11 or the Madrid attacks, heightened security measures are taken by police and armed forces, and surveillance is stepped up in public places such as stations and airports. Rubbish bins are sealed off (during the terrorist attacks in Paris in the 1980s and '90s bombs were placed in major department stores and in rubbish bins on the Metro and RER), security barriers are erected in front of embassies and other public buildings, some entrances to larger multi-entrance train stations are closed, and vehicles are not allowed to park in front of airports.

to sites, restaurants and hotels that meet strict requirements and standards: different symbols indicate whether establishments have access for people with physical, mental, hearing and/or seeing disabilities. Places marked *Accessible normes handicapés* subscribe to certain access standards, but the rating is not officially verified.

With the SNCF, a traveller in a wheelchair *(fauteuil roulant)* can travel in both TGV and regular trains (make a reservation at least a few hours before departure). Details are available in SNCF's booklet *Guide du Voyageur à Mobilité Réduite*. You can also contact **SNCF Accessibilité** (☎ 0 800 154 753) which has information (French only) for travellers with physical, sight and hearing disabilities.

Tourism for All (☎ 0845-124 9971; outside UK 44-208 760 0027; www.tourismforall.info) is a UK-based group that publishes an information guide to France which can be ordered online. **Access Project** (www.accessproject-phsp.org; 39 Bradley Gardens, West Ealing, London W13 8HE) publishes a fairly dated but useful guide, *Access in Paris*. The **Paris Tourist Office** (p111) also has information and brochures.

If you speak French, specialised guidebooks with comprehensive information for travellers with physical disabilities include Bernic's *Guide Rousseau* and the Petit Futé *Handiguide*. They are available at major bookshops. The portal www.jaccede.com (in French) has loads of information, reviews and links.

Michelin's *Guide Rouge* indicates those hotels with lifts and facilities for disabled people, while Gîtes de France (see p894) can provide a list of *gîtes ruraux* and *chambres d'hôtes* with disabled access.

Specialised travel agencies abroad include US-based **Wheels Up!** (☎ 1-888 38 4335; www.wheelsup.com) and UK-based **Access Travel** (☎ 01942 888 844; www.access-travel.co.uk).

Organisations
Association des Paralysées de France (AFP; ☎ 01 53 80 92 97; 13 Place de Rungis, 13e, Paris) This national organisation has branches throughout France with region-specific information.

Groupement pour l'Insertion des Personnes Handicapées Physiques (☎ 01 43 95 66 36; '10 rue Georges de Porto Riche, 14e, Paris; metro Porte d'Orléans) Provides vehicles outfitted for people in wheelchairs; the national office will put you in touch with local services.

DISCOUNT CARDS
Student, Youth & Teachers' Cards
These cards, available from student unions and travel agencies, can get fantastic discounts, but not all places will recognise them. An International Student Identity Card (ISIC; €12) can pay for itself through half-price admissions, discounted air and ferry tickets, and cheap meals in student cafeterias. Many places stipulate a maximum age, usually 24 or 25. For more details, check the International Student Travel Confederation (ISTC; www.istc.org) website.

If you're under 26 but not a student, you can apply for an International Youth Travel Card (ITYC or Go25, €12), also issued by ISTC, which entitles you to much the same discounts as an ISIC. The European Youth Card (Euro<26 card) offers similar discounts across 35 European countries for nonstudents under 26 (see www.euro26.org).

Teachers, professional artists, museum conservators and certain categories of students are admitted to some museums free. Bring along proof of affiliation, for example, an International Teacher Identity Card (ITIC).

Seniors Cards
Senior citizens are entitled to discounts in France on things like public transport, museum admission fees, public theatres and so on. The **Société Nationale des Chemins de Fer** (SNCF; www.sncf.fr) issues the Carte Senior (€45) to those aged over 60, which gives reductions of 25% to 50% on train tickets, valid for one year.

Camping Card International
The Camping Card International is a form of ID that can be used instead of a passport when checking into a camping ground and includes third-party insurance. As a result, many camping grounds offer a small discount if you sign in with one. CCIs are issued by automobile associations, camping federations and, sometimes, on the spot at camping grounds.

EMBASSIES & CONSULATES
French Embassies & Consulates
France's diplomatic and consular representatives abroad are listed on the website www.france.diplomatie.fr. For some of the following countries, additional consulates exist.

Australia Canberra (☎ 02-6216 0100; www.ambafrance
-au.org; 6 Perth Ave, Yarralumla, ACT 2600) Sydney Consulate
(☎ 02-9261 5779; www.consulfrance-sydney.org; 20th fl,
St Martin's Tower, 31 Market St, Sydney, NSW 2000)

Belgium Brussels (☎ 02-548 8711; www.ambafrance
-be.org; 65 rue Ducale, 1000) Brussels Consulate (☎ 02-
229 8500; www.consulfrance-bruxelles.org; 12a Place de
Louvain, 1000)

Canada Ottawa (☎ 613-789 1795; www.ambafrance
-ca.org; 42 Sussex Dr, Ottawa, Ont K1M 2C9) Toronto
Consulate (☎ 416-925 8041; www.consulfrance-toronto
.org; 130 Bloor West, Ste 400, Ont M5S 1N5)

Germany Berlin (☎ 030-590 039 000; www.botschaft
-frankreich.de; Parizer Platz 5, 10117) Munich Consulate
(☎ 089-419 4110; Möhlstrasse 5, 81675)

Ireland Dublin (☎ 01-217 5000; www.ambafrance
-ie.org; 36 Ailesbury Rd, Ballsbridge, 4)

Italy Rome (☎ 06-686 011; www.ambafrance-it.org;
Piazza Farnese 67, 00186)

Netherlands The Hague (☎ 070-312 5800; www
.ambafrance-nl.org; Smidsplein 1, 2514 BT) Amsterdam
Consulate (☎ 020-530 6969; www.consulfrance-amster
dam.org; Vijzelgracht 2, 1017 HR)

New Zealand Wellington (☎ 04-384 2555; www.am
bafrance-nz.org; Rural Bank Bldg, 34–42 Manners St)

South Africa Pretoria (☎ 012-42 51 6000; www.amba
france-rsa.org; 250 Melk St, New Muckleneuk, 0181)

Spain Madrid (☎ 91-423 8900; www.ambafrance-es.org;
Calle de Salustiano, Olozaga 9, 28001) Barcelona Consulate
(☎ 93-270 3000; www.consulfrance-barcelone.org;
Ronda Universitat 22, 08007)

Switzerland Berne (☎ 031-359 2111; www.amba
france-ch.org; Schosshaldenstrasse 46, 3006) Geneva
Consulate (☎ 022-319 0000; www.consulfrance-geneve
.org; 11 rue Imbert Galloix, 1205)

UK London (☎ 020-7073 1000; www.ambafrance-uk.org;
58 Knightsbridge, London SW1X 7JT) Consulate (☎ 020-
7073 1200; 21 Cromwell Rd, London SW7 2EN) Visa section
(☎ 020-7838 2051; 6A Cromwell Place SW7 2EW)

USA Washington (☎ 202-944 6000; www.ambafrance
-us.org; 4101 Reservoir Rd NW, DC 20007) New York Consulate (☎ 212-606 3600/89; www.consulfrance-newyork
.org; 934 Fifth Ave, NY 10021) San Francisco Consulate
(☎ 415-397 4330; www.consulfrance-sanfrancisco.org;
540 Bush St, CA 94108)

Embassies & Consulates in France

All foreign embassies are in Paris. Many
countries – including the UK, USA, Canada,
Japan and most European countries – also
have consulates in other major cities such as
Nice, Marseille and Lyon. To find an embassy
or consulate not listed here, look up 'Ambas-
sades et Consulats' in the *Yellow Pages* (Pages
Jaunes; www.pagesjaunes.fr) for Paris.

Australia Paris (Map pp99-101; ☎ 01 40 59 33 00; www
.austgov.fr; 4 rue Jean Rey, 15e; metro Bir Hakeim)

Belgium Paris (Map pp93-5; ☎ 01 44 09 39 39; 9 rue de
Tilsitt, 17e; metro Charles de Gaulle-Étoile)

Canada Paris (Map pp93-5; ☎ 01 44 43 29 00; www
.amb-canada.fr; 35 av Montaigne, 8e; metro Franklin
D Roosevelt) Nice Consulate (Map pp820-1; ☎ 04 93 92 93
22; 10 rue Lamartine)

Germany Paris (Map pp93-5; ☎ 01 53 83 45 00; www
.amb-allemagne.fr; 13-15 av Franklin D Roosevelt, 8e;
metro Franklin D Roosevelt)

Ireland Paris (Map pp93-5; ☎ 01 70 20 00 20; 33 rue
Miromesnil, 8e; metro Miromesnil)

Italy Paris (Map pp99-101; ☎ 01 49 54 03 00; www.amb
-italie.fr; 51 rue de Varenne, 7e; metro Rue du Bac)

Japan Paris (Map pp93-5; ☎ 01 48 88 62 00; www.amb
-japon.fr; 7 av Hoche, 8e; metro Courcelles)

Netherlands Paris (Map pp99-101; ☎ 01 40 62 33 00;
www.amb-pays-bas.fr; 7 rue Eblé, 7e; metro St-François
Xavier)

New Zealand Paris (Map pp93-5; ☎ 01 45 01 43 43;
www.nzembassy.com; 7ter rue Léonard de Vinci, 16e;
metro Victor Hugo)

South Africa Paris (Map pp99-101; ☎ 01 45 55 92 37;
59 quai d'Orsay, 7e; metro Invalides)

Spain Paris (Map pp93-5; ☎ 01 44 43 18 00; 22 av
Marceau, 8e; metro Alma Marceau)

Switzerland Paris (Map pp93-5; ☎ 01 49 55 67 00;
142 rue de Grenelle, 7e; metro Varenne)

UK Paris (Map pp93-5; ☎ 01 44 51 31 00; www.amb
-grandebretagne.fr; 35 rue du Faubourg St-Honoré, 8e;
metro Concorde) Consulate (Map pp93-5; ☎ 01 44 51 31
02; 16bis rue d'Anjou, 8e; metro Madeleine) Nice Consulate
(Map pp820-1; ☎ 04 93 62 13 56; 26 av Notre Dame)
Marseille Consulate (off Map pp764-5; ☎ 04 91 15 72 10;
24 av du Prado)

USA Paris (Map pp93 5; ☎ 01 43 12 22 22; www.amb
-usa.fr; 2 av Gabriel, 8e; metro Concorde) Consulate (Map
pp93-5; ☎ 01 43 12 47 08; 2 rue St-Florentin, 1er; metro
Concorde) Nice Consulate (Map pp820-1; ☎ 04 93 88 89
55; 7 av Gustav V, 06000) Marseille Consulate (Map pp764-5;
☎ 04 91 54 92 00; place Varian Fry)

FESTIVALS & EVENTS

Most French cities have at least one major
music, dance, theatre, cinema or art festival
each year. Villages hold *foires* (fairs) and
fêtes (festivals) to honour anything from
a local saint to the year's garlic crop. We
list these important annual events in city
and town sections; for precise details about
dates, contact the local tourist office. During big events towns get extremely busy and
accommodation is usually booked out in
advance.

MARCH & APRIL
Feria Pascale (p803; www.ville-ales.fr/feria in French)
In the ancient *arène* of Arles, this Feria kicks the bullfight
season with much cavorting and merriment (Easter).

MAY & JUNE
May Day Across France, the workers' day is celebrated
with trade union parades and diverse protests. People give
each other *muguet* (lilies of the valley) for good luck. No
one works – except waiters and *muguet* sellers (1 May).

International Film Festival (p836; www.festival-cannes
.com) The stars walk the red carpet at Cannes, the epitome
of see-and-be-seen cinema events in Europe (mid-May).

Fête de la Musique (www.fetedelamusique.culture.fr)
Bands, orchestras, crooners, buskers and spectators take to
the streets for this national celebration of music (21 June).

JULY
National Day Fireworks, parades and all-round hoo-ha to
commemorate the storming of the Bastille in 1789, symbol
of the French Revolution (14 July).

Gay Pride (www.gaypride.fr in French) Effervescent
street parades, performances and parties throughout Paris
(p136) and other major cities (July).

Festival International d'Art Lyrique (p780; www
.festival-aix.com) Attracting the world's best classical
music, opera, ballet and buskers, Aix-en-Provence is the
place to be for the discerning visitor (July).

Festival d'Avignon (p787; www.festival-avignon.com)
Actors, dancers and musicians flock to Avignon to perform
in the official and fringe art festivals (late July & early
August).

Fêtes de Bayonne (p651) Bullfighting, cow-chasing and
Basque music are the order of the day at Bayonne's biggest
event (July).

Nice Jazz Festival (p825; www.nicejazzfest.com) See
jazz cats and other pop, rock and world artists take over
public spaces and the Roman ruins of Nice (July).

AUGUST & SEPTEMBER
Festival Interceltique (p309; www.festival-intercelt
ique.com) This massive event pulls hundreds of thousands
of Celts to Lorient from all over Brittany and the UK for a
massive celebration of their shared Celtic culture (August).

American Film Festival (p255; www.festival-deauville
.com) The silver screen comes to the seaside at this celebration of Hollywood cinema in Deauville (September).

Braderie de Lille (p205) Three days of madness and
mussel-munching as this colossal flea market engulfs the city
with antiques, handicrafts and bric-a-brac (early September).

DECEMBER
Christmas Markets Alsace is the place to be for a
traditional-style festive season, with world-famous
Christmas markets, decorations and celebrations.

FOOD
Our special food and drinks chapter (p63) is
full of succulent information about French
gastronomy.

In this book, we usually indicate the price
of *menus* (two- or three-course set menus);
ordering à la carte (from the menu) is generally more expensive.

Budget eating options are usually more
casual places with simple meals under €10 or
set *menus* for around €8 to €13. Mid-range
restaurants will have more atmosphere and
offer seasonal specialities and fine local flavours, with *menus* from €15 to €25 (less at
lunchtime). In France, 'top-end' restaurants
are superb establishments with impeccable
quality and service and *menus* from €25.

GAY & LESBIAN TRAVELLERS
France is one of Europe's most liberal countries when it comes to homosexuality, in
part because of the long French tradition of
public tolerance towards people who choose
not to live by conventional social codes.
Paris has been a thriving gay and lesbian
centre since the late 1970s. Montpellier,
Lyon, Toulouse, Bordeaux and many other
towns also have significant active communities. Predictably, attitudes towards homosexuality tend to become more conservative
in the countryside and villages. France's lesbian scene is much less public than its gay
counterpart and is centred mainly around
women's cafés and bars, which are the best
place to find information.

Gay Pride marches are held in major
French cities each June.

There are a number of useful gay and
lesbian publications:
Action Act Up's free monthly publication with information
and issues.
Guide Gai Pied A French- and English-language travel
guide.
Lesbia A women's monthly with articles and useful listings.
Spartacus International Gay Guide An English-
language travel guide for men.

Têtu A glossy men's monthly with a France-wide directory of bars, clubs and hotels. There are also listings for lesbians.
Women's Traveller An English-language travel guide for lesbians, published by Damron.

Online, www.gayscape.com (in French) has hundreds of links, while www.france.qrd .org is a 'queer resources directory' for gay and lesbian travellers. Another good site for finding out about gay events is http://cite gay.fr (in French).

Organisations

Most of France's major gay and lesbian organisations are based in Paris:

Act Up-Paris (☎ 01 48 06 13 89; www.actupparis.org in French; 45 rue Sedaine, 11e; metro Voltaire) This organisation defends France's gay community and can provide advice and information. Advice by phone is available 2pm to 6pm on Wednesday.
AIDES (☎ 0 820 160 120; www.aides.org in French; 119 rue des Pyrénées, 20e; metro Jourdain) France-wide organisation fighting against HIV/AIDS and for the rights and wellbeing of those affected.
Association des Médecins Gais (☎ 01 48 05 81 71) The Association of Gay Doctors, based in the Centre Gai et Lesbien, deals with gay-related health issues.
Centre Gai et Lesbien (CGL; Map pp102-4; ☎ 01 43 57 21 47; www.cglparis.org in French; 3 rue Keller, 11e; metro Ledru Rollin) A welcome and support centre. Friday is women's (only) day, with meetings, debates, outings and workshops.
SIDA-info service (☎ 0 800 840 800; www.sida-info -service.org in French) HIV/AIDS information service that can help with anonymous testing and treatment. Advice is available in foreign languages between 2pm and 7pm.

HOLIDAYS

The following *jours fériés* (public holidays) are observed in France:
New Year's Day (Jour de l'An) 1 January – parties in larger cities; fireworks are subdued by international standards.
Easter Sunday and Monday (Pâques & lundi de Pâques) Late March/April.
May Day (Fête du Travail) 1 May – traditional parades
Victoire 1945 8 May – the Allied victory in Europe that ended WWII.
Ascension Thursday (L'Ascension) May – celebrated on the 40th day after Easter.
Pentecost/Whit Sunday & Whit Monday (Pentecôte & lundi de Pentecôte) Mid-May to mid-June – celebrated on the seventh Sunday after Easter.
Bastille Day/National Day (Fête Nationale) 14 July – *the* national holiday.
Assumption Day (L'Assomption) 15 August.

All Saints' Day (La Toussaint) 1 November.
Remembrance Day (L'onze novembre) 11 November – celebrates the WWI armistice.
Christmas *(Noël)* 25 December.

The following are *not* public holidays in France: Shrove Tuesday (Mardi Gras; the first day of Lent); Maundy (or Holy) Thursday and Good Friday just before Easter; and Boxing Day (26 December). Good Friday and Boxing Day, however, are holidays in Alsace.

INSURANCE
Travel Insurance

A travel-insurance policy to cover theft, loss and medical problems is a good idea. Some policies specifically exclude dangerous activities, which can include scuba diving, motorcycling, even trekking.

You may prefer a policy that pays doctors or hospitals directly rather than you having to pay on the spot and claim later. If you have to claim later ensure you keep all documentation. Check that the policy covers ambulances or an emergency flight home. Paying for your airline ticket with a credit card often provides limited travel accident insurance. Ask your credit card company what it's prepared to cover.

See p929 for health insurance and p924 for car insurance.

INTERNET ACCESS

After somewhat of a late start, Internet cafés have sprung up all over the country and are listed under Information in the regional chapters of this guide. You'll pay around €3 to €5 per hour. You may also come across Netanoo (http://www.netanoo.com in French) phonecard-operated Internet terminals. A 120-unit *télécarte* will get you two hours' surfing time.

Roughly 1000 post offices across France have been equipped with a Cyberposte, a card-operated Internet terminal for public use. Access cards cost €7.60 for the first hour and €4.60 for a recharge. There is a list of post offices with a Cyberposte at www .cyberposte.com (in French).

If you're using your laptop, check that it is compatible with the 220V current in France; if not you will need a converter. You'll also need a telephone plug adaptor. Having a reputable global modem will prevent access problems that can occur with PC-card modems brought from home.

If you do not go with a global Internet Service Provider (ISP; such as AOL) make sure your ISP has a dial-up number in France. Local ISPs Free (www.free.com), Tiscali (www.tiscali.fr) and Wanadoo (www.wanadoo.fr in French) have cheap or free short-term membership (look out for free trial membership CD-ROMs). For WiFi users things are improving rapidly: wireless access points are being installed in major airports, hotel chains and cafés. Check sites like www.wifinder.com for access points.

For useful travel websites, see p15.

LEGAL MATTERS
Drugs & Alcohol
Contrary to popular belief, French law does not officially distinguish between 'hard' and 'soft' drugs. The penalty for any personal use of *stupéfiants* (including cannabis, amphetamines, ecstasy, heroine etc) can be a one-year jail sentence and a €3750 fine, but depending on the circumstances it might be anything from a stern word to a compulsory rehab programme.

Importing, possessing, selling or buying drugs can get you up to 10 years' prison and massive fines. Police have been searching chartered coaches, cars and passengers getting off trains for drugs just because they are coming from Amsterdam.

Being drunk in public places is punishable with a €150 fine.

Police
French police have wide powers of search and seizure, and can ask you to prove your identity at any time – whether or not there is plausible cause. Foreigners must be able

---

LEGAL AGES

- Driving: 18
- Buying alcohol: 16
- Age of majority: 18
- Age of sexual consent for everyone: 15
- Age considered minor under anti-child-pornography and child-prostitution laws: 18
- Voting: 18

---

to prove their legal status in France (eg passport, visa, residency permit) without delay.

If the police stop you for any reason, be polite and remain calm. Verbally (and of course physically) abusing a police officer can carry a hefty fine, and even imprisonment. You may refuse to sign a police statement, and have the right to ask for a copy.

People who are arrested are considered innocent until proven guilty, but can be held in custody until trial. The website www.service-public.fr has information on legal rights.

French police are very strict about security. Do not leave baggage unattended at airports or train stations: suspicious objects will be summarily blown up.

LOCAL GOVERNMENT
Metropolitan France (the mainland and Corsica) is made up of 22 *régions* (regions) which are subdivided into 96 *départements* (departments), which are subdivided into 324 arrondissements, which are in turn subdivided into *cantons*, which are subdivided into 36,400 *communes* (communes).

Invariably named after a geographic feature, *départements* tout a two-digit code (see the map opposite) which make up the first two digits of the area's postcode.

MAPS
In Paris, the best place to find a full selection of maps is at the **Espace IGN** (Map pp93-5; ☎ 01 43 98 85 12; 107 rue La Boétie, 8e; metro Franklin D Roosevelt). The two major map producers are Michelin (www.michelin-travel.com) and Institut Géographique National (IGN; www.ign.fr in French): their websites list sales outlets. Road maps and city maps are available at Maisons de la Presse (large newsagencies found all over France), bookshops, tourist offices, and even some newspaper kiosks. IGN publishes themed maps about wine, museums and so on.

The book in your hand contains over 145 city and town maps. Lonely Planet publishes a laminated *Paris City Map*. Michelin has excellent road maps of cities and towns, which are coordinated with its travel guides. Plans-Guides Blay offers orange-jacketed street maps of 125 French cities and towns.

For road maps, *Environs de Paris* (Michelin) will help you with the very confusing drive out of Paris. Michelin's *Atlas Routier France*, which covers the whole country in

RÉGIONS & DÉPARTEMENTS

0 ————— 200 km
0 ————— 120 miles

ALSACE
67 Bas-Rhin
68 Haut-Rhin

AQUITANE
24 Dordogne
33 Gironde
40 Landes
47 Lot-et-Garonne
64 Pyrénées-Atlantiques

AUVERGNE
03 Allier
15 Cantal
43 Haute-Loire
63 Puy-de-Dôme

BASSE-NORMANDIE
14 Calvados
50 Manche
61 Orne

BRETAGNE
22 Côtes d'Armor
29 Finistère
35 Ille-et-Vilaine
56 Morbihan

BOURGOGNE
21 Côte d'Or
58 Nièvre
71 Saône-et-Loire
89 Yonne

CENTRE
18 Cher
28 Eure-et-Loir
36 Indre
37 Indre-et-Loire
41 Loir-et-Cher
45 Loiret

CHAMPAGNE-ARDENNE
08 Ardennes
10 Aube
51 Marne
52 Haute-Marne

CORSE
2A Corse-du-Sud
2B Haute-Corse

FRANCHE-COMTÉ
25 Doubs
39 Jura
70 Haute-Saône
90 Territoire de Belfort

HAUTE-NORMANDIE
27 Eure
76 Seine-Maritime

LAUGUEDOC-ROUSSILLON
11 Aude
30 Gard
34 Hérault
48 Lozère
66 Pyrénées-Orientales

LIMOUSIN
19 Corrèze
23 Creuse
87 Haute-Vienne

LORRAINE
54 Meurthe-et-Moselle
55 Meuse
57 Moselle
88 Vosges

MIDI-PYRÉNÉES
09 Ariège
12 Aveyron
31 Haute-Garonne
32 Gers
46 Lot
65 Hautes-Pyrénées
81 Tarn
82 Tarn-et-Garonne

NORD-PAS-DE-CALAIS
59 Nord
62 Pas-de-Calais

PAS DE LA LOIRE
44 Loire-Atlantique
49 Maine-et-Loire
53 Mayenne
72 Sarthe
85 Vendée

PICARDIE
02 Aisne
60 Oise
80 Somme

POITOU-CHARENTES
16 Charente
17 Charente-Maritime
79 Deux-Sèvres
86 Vienne

PROVENCE-ALPES-CÔTE D'AZUR
04 Alpes-de-Haute-Provence
05 Hautes-Alpes
06 Alpes-Maritimes
13 Bouches-du-Rhône
83 Var
84 Vaucluse

RÉGION PARISIENNE
75 Ville de Paris
77 Yvelines
91 Essonne
92 Haut-de-Seine
93 Seine-St-Denis
94 Val-de-Marne
95 Val-d'Oise

RHÔNE-ALPES
01 Ain
07 Ardèche
26 Drôme
38 Isère
42 Loire
69 Rhône
73 Savoie
74 Haute-Savoie

- - - International Boundary
- - - Région Boundary
———— Département Boundary

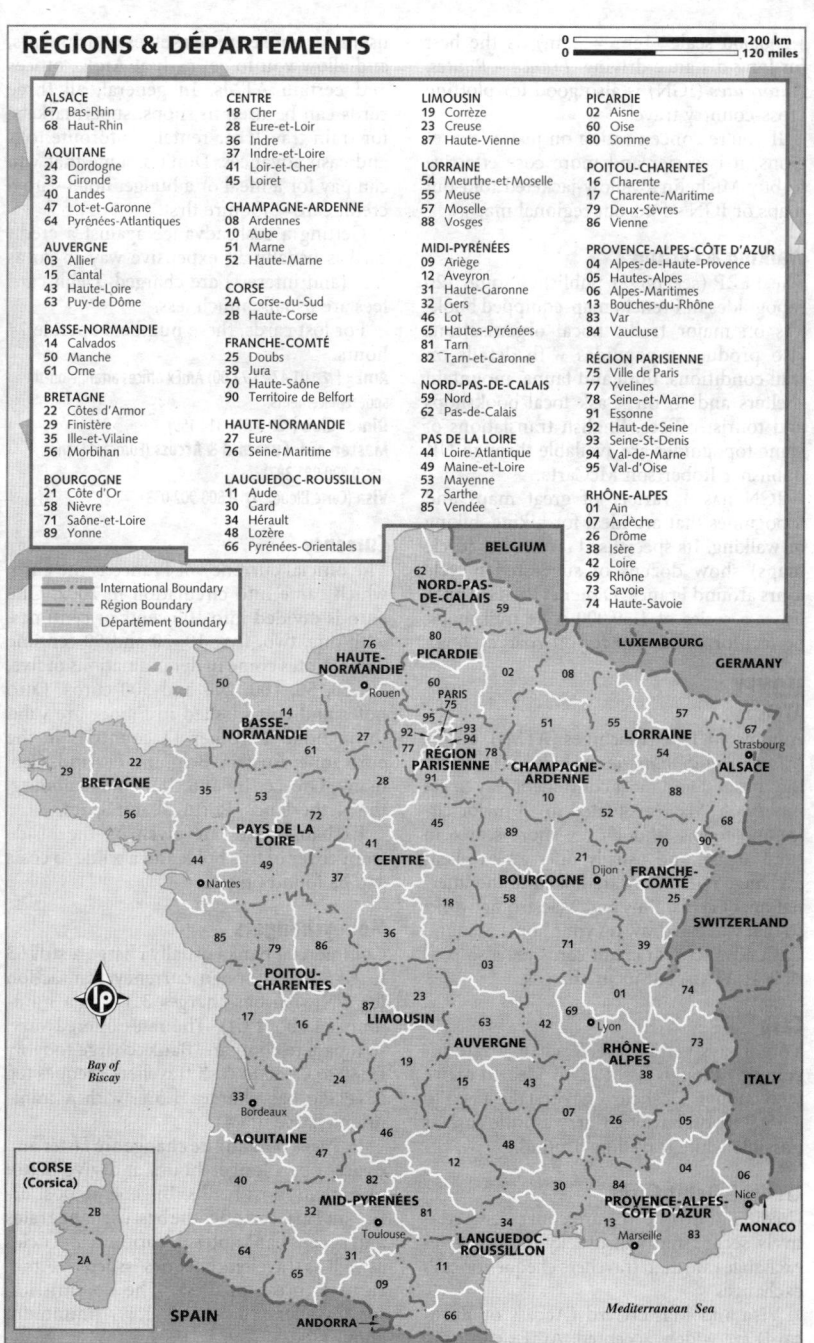

1:200,000 scale (1cm = 2km), is the best for long-distance driving. *France – Routes, Autoroutes* (IGN) is also good for plotting cross-country travel.

If you're concentrating on just a few regions, it is easier and more cose effective to buy Michelin's yellow-jacketed fold-out maps or IGN's fold-out regional maps.

Walking & Cycling

The FFRP (see p897) publishes some 120 topoguides in French, map-equipped booklets on major trails. Local organisations also produce topoguides with details on trail conditions, flora and fauna, mountain shelters and so on – ask local bookshops and tourist offices. English translations of some topoguides are available through UK publisher Robertson McCarta.

IGN has a variety of great maps and topoguides that are ideal for hiking, biking or walking. Its specialised *cyclocartes* (cycle maps) show dozens of suggested bicycle tours around France. Didier et Richard publishes a series of 1:50,000-scale trail maps, perfect for walking or for off-road cycling.

MONEY
ATMs

Automated Teller Machines (ATMs), or *distributeurs automatiques de billets* (DAB), are the cheapest and most convenient way to get money. ATMs are situated in all major cities and towns (though are more scarce in rural areas), and usually offer an excellent exchange rate. Many are linked to the international Cirrus, Plus and Maestro networks so that you can draw on your home account. Cash advances on credit cards are also possible at ATMs, but incur charges.

Cash

You always get a better exchange rate incountry, though it's a good idea to arrive with enough local currency to take a taxi to a hotel if you have to. Carry as little cash as possible while travelling around.

Credit & Debit Cards

Credit and debit cards are convenient, relatively secure and will usually offer a better exchange rate than travellers cheques or cash exchanges.

Visa and MasterCard (Access or Eurocard) are widely accepted; AmEx cards are useful at more upmarket establishments, and allow you to get cash at AmEx offices and certain ATMs. In general, all three cards can be used in shops, supermarkets, for train travel, car rentals, autoroute tolls and cash advances. Don't assume that you can pay for a meal or a budget hotel with a credit card – inquire first.

Getting a cash advance against a credit card is usually an expensive way to go as fees (and interest) are charged. Debit card fees are usually much less.

For lost cards, these numbers operate 24 hours:

AmEx (☎ 01 47 77 72 00) AmEx offices arrange on-the-spot replacements.
Diners Club (☎ 0 810 314 159)
MasterCard, Eurocard & Access (Eurocard France; ☎ 0 800 901 387)
Visa (Carte Bleue; ☎ 0 800 902 033)

Currency

The official currency of France is the euro, which came into circulation in 2002. One euro is divided into 100 cents or centimes, with one, two, five, 10, 20 and 50 centime coins. Notes come in denominations of five, 10, 20, 50, 100, 200 and 500 euros. Euro notes and coins issued in France are valid throughout the other 11 countries in the euro zone: Austria, Belgium, Finland, Germany, Greece, Ireland, Italy, Luxembourg, the Netherlands, Portugal and Spain.

Exchange rates are given on the inside front cover of this book and a guide to costs can be found on p13.

Moneychangers

Commercial banks usually charge a stiff €3 to €4.50 per foreign-currency transaction (eg BNP Paribas charges 3.3% or a minimum of about €4). The rates offered vary, so it pays to compare. Banks charge roughly €3.40 to €5.30 to cash travellers cheques (eg BNP Paribas charges 1.5%, with a minimum charge of €4).

In Paris, bureaux de change are faster and easier, open longer hours and give better rates than most banks. In general, post offices in Paris can offer the best exchange rates and accept banknotes in various currencies as well as travellers cheques issued by American Express or Visa. The commission for travellers cheques is 1.5% (minimum about €4).

It's best to familiarise yourself with rates offered by the post office and compare them with those at bureaux de change, which are not generally allowed to charge commissions. On small transactions, even exchange places with less-than-optimal rates may leave you with more euros in your pocket.

Travellers Cheques

The most flexible travellers cheques are those issued by AmEx (in US dollars or euros) and Visa (in euros) because they can be changed at many post offices as well as commercial banks and exchange bureaux. Note that you will not be able to pay most merchants with travellers cheques directly. AmEx offices don't charge commission on their own travellers cheques.

For lost travellers cheques call **AmEx** (☎ 0 800 908 600) and **Thomas Cook** (☎ 0 800 908 330) for replacements. For **Visa** and **Mastercard**, see opposite.

PHOTOGRAPHY & VIDEO

Colour-print film is widely available, but it's fairly expensive in France compared to a lot of other countries, so it pays to stock up ahead of time. Developing a 24-exposure film costs from €8 to €14. For slides (dia-positives), avoid Kodachrome: it's difficult to process quickly in France and may not be handled correctly. You can easily obtain video cartridges in large towns, but it's good to come with a few from home.

A good companion when on the road is *Travel Photography: A Guide to Taking Better Pictures*, by travel photographer Richard I'Anson.

POST

Each of France's post offices is marked with a yellow or brown sign reading 'La Poste'. Since La Poste also has banking, finance and bill-paying functions, queues can be long, but there are automatic machines for postage.

Postal Rates

Domestic letters of up to 20g cost €0.50. For international post, there are three different zones: a letter/package under 20g/2kg costs €0.50/12.50 to Zone A (EU, Switzerland, Iceland, Norway); €0.75/14 to Zone B (the rest of Europe and Africa); and €0.90/20.50 to Zone C (North and South America, Asia & Middle East, Australasia).

Rates are automatically given for *prioritaire* (somewhat fast post); specify if you want the cheaper *économique* (rather slow post).

Worldwide express-mail delivery, called **Chronopost** (☎ 0 825 801 801), costs a fortune and is not as rapid as advertised.

All mail to France *must* include the five-digit postcode, which begins with the two-digit number of the *département* (postcodes are listed under the main city or town headings in this book). The notation 'CEDEX' after a town name simply means that mail sent to that address is collected at the post office, rather than delivered to the door.

Receiving Mail

Picking up poste-restante mail costs €0.50; you must show your passport or national ID card. Mail will be kept 15 days. Poste-restante mail not addressed to a particular branch goes to the city's main post office.

AmEx has a poste-restante service (mail is held for 30 days or returned to sender). There's a €0.76 if you don't have an AmEx card or travellers cheques. AmEx addresses are given in the relevant city listings.

SHOPPING

France is renowned for its luxury goods, particularly *haute couture*, high-quality clothing accessories (eg Hermès scarves), lingerie, perfume and cosmetics. Such goods may not be any cheaper here than at home.

Sale periods *(soldes)* – held for three weeks in January and July – can be a gold mine for fashion finds. The fashion- and budget-conscious should also look out for the words *degriffés* (cut price; usually the labels have been cut out) or *dépôt-vente* (ex-showroom garments sold at steep mark-downs).

For local crafts and art it's best to go directly to the source. In Brittany, look for colourful Quimper faïence and in Normandy pick up unique Rouen faïence or some intricate lace from Alençon. Other good buys include crystal and glassware from Baccarat in southern Lorraine or enamel and porcelain from Limoges in Limousin.

Even though wines from Bordeaux, Burgundy, Alsace and Champagne are available everywhere, you'll get a better selection in a local wine shop. Local brandies make good souvenirs since they may not be available in your home country, such as cognacs (from Cognac!) and Calvados, Pommeau or

Fécamp Bénédictine (from Normandy). Corsicans sell unusual liqueurs in local markets and Charentes is the place to pick up Pineau de Charentes.

Goodies that travel well include macaroons from St-Émilion, *calissons* from Aix-en-Provence and candied fruit from Nice. For information on local shopping options, see the individual towns and cities.

Non-EU residents can get a rebate of some of the 19.6% value-added tax (VAT) for large purchases, including when several different purchases are made in the one department store. There are forms to fill out in-store which must be shown, with the purchases, upon departure.

SOLO TRAVELLERS

Travelling by yourself in France is easy and rewarding, and shouldn't pose any problems. Many hotels will charge the same price for single and double rooms, and if single prices are available, they tend not to be significantly cheaper. It is quite common to eat in restaurants alone in France, particularly at lunch, when *menus* are also considerably cheaper – you might want to make that the main meal of the day. Women shouldn't encounter any particular problems travelling alone in France, but may come across some minor hassles. See p913 for more information.

TELEPHONE

A quarter of a century ago, France had one of the worst telephone systems in Western Europe. But thanks to massive investment, the country now has one of the most modern and sophisticated telecommunications systems in the world.

Domestic Dialling

France has five telephone dialling areas. You dial the same 10-digit number no matter where you are, but it is cheaper to call locally.

For France Telecom's directory inquiries *(services des renseignements)*, dial ☎ 12 (around €0.45 per minute). Not all operators speak English.

Domestic rates are billed at about €0.15 for three minutes with a *télécarte*, but numbers starting with 08 are more expensive.

Emergency numbers (see inside the front cover) and 0 800 numbers can be dialled free from public and private telephones.

International Dialling

To call France from another country, dial your country's international access code, then dial ☎ 33 (France's country code), then omit the 0 at the beginning of the 10-digit local number.

To call someone outside France, dial the international access code (☎ 00), the country code, the area code (without the initial zero if there is one) and the local number. International Direct Dial (IDD) calls to almost anywhere in the world can be placed from public telephones.

To make a reverse-charges (collect) call *(en PCV)* or a person-to-person call *(avec préavis)*, dial ☎ 3123 or ☎ 0 800 990 011 (for the USA and Canada) and ☎ 0 800 990 061 for Australia. Expect to pay about €12 for a three-minute call.

For directory inquiries for numbers outside France, dial ☎ 3212. The cost is about €2.50.

Hotels, *gîtes*, hostels and pensions are free to meter their calls as they like. The surcharge is usually around €0.30 per minute but can be higher.

Phonecards (see below) offer much, much better international rates than Country Direct services (which allow you to be billed by the long-distance carrier you use at home).

Mobile Phones

France uses GSM 900/1800, which is compatible with the rest of Europe and Australia but not with the North American GSM 1900 or the totally different system in Japan (though some North Americans have GSM 1900/900 phones that do work here). If you have a GSM phone, check with your service provider about using it in France, and beware of calls being routed internationally (very expensive for a 'local' call).

The three major providers of mobile phone access are **SFR** (0 800 106 000; www.sfr.com), **Bouygues** (☎ 0 810 630 100; www.bouygtel.com) and France Telecom's **Orange** (☎ 0 800 830 800; www.orange.fr). If you already have a compatible phone, you can buy a 'prepay' phone kit which gives you a SIM-card with a mobile phone number and a set number of calls. When these run out you purchase a recharge card at most *tabacs*. You can also get similar 'prepay' deals that include the phone itself.

Mobile phone numbers in France always begin with 06. France has a 'caller pays' system which means that you do not pay to receive a call on your mobile phone unless it is an international call.

Public Phones & Telephone Cards

Almost all public telephones in France are card-operated – coin-operated phones are virtually nonexistent. Most public phones have a button displaying two flags which you push for explanations in English.

Cards can be purchased for €7.50 or €15 at post offices, *tabacs* (tobacconists) and anywhere that you see a blue sticker reading '*télécarte en vente ici*'. There are two kinds of phone cards, *cartes à puce* (cards with a magnetic chip, that are inserted chip-first into public phones) and *cartes à code* (that you can use from public or private phones by dialling the free access number and then punching in the card's scratch-off code).

Your choice of card will depend on your needs. France Telecom offers different cards suited to national and international dialling. For help in English on all France Telecom's services, dial ☎ 0 800 364 775.

A whole bevy of other cards are available for cheap international calls, especially in Paris, and most can be used elsewhere in Europe. Compare the rates on the posters, or ask which one is best for the place you're calling.

TIME

France uses the 24hr clock and is on Central European Time, which is one hour ahead of GMT/UTC. During daylight-saving time, which runs from the last Sunday in March to the last Sunday in October, France is two hours ahead of GMT/UTC.

Without taking daylight-saving time into account, when it's noon in Paris it's 3am in San Francisco, 6am in New York, 11am in London, 8pm in Tokyo, 9pm in Sydney and 11pm in Auckland. The Australian eastern coast is between eight and 10 hours ahead of France. Refer to the time-zone world map on p931 for additional data.

TOURIST INFORMATION
Local Tourist Offices

Every city, town, village and hamlet seems to have either an *office de tourisme* (a tourist office run by some unit of local government) or a *syndicat d'initiative* (a tourist office run by an organisation of local merchants). Both are

excellent resources for local maps, accommodation, restaurants and activities. Very few of their many, many brochures are on display. If you have a special interest, such as walking tours, cycling or wine sampling, ask about it. Some have limited currency-exchange services. Many tourist offices will make local hotel reservations, usually for a small fee.

Regional tourist offices (*Comité Régional de Tourisme*) and their websites are great for regionwide information, particularly concerning activities. The website www.fncrt.com (in French) links to the different CRTs.

Details on local tourist offices appear under Information at the beginning of each city, town or area listing.

Tourist Offices Abroad

French government tourist offices (usually called Maisons de la France) can provide every imaginable sort of tourist information on France, most of it in the form of brochures. The general website www.franceguide.com lets you access the site for your home country.

Australia (☎ 02-9231 5244; 25 Bligh St, 22nd floor, Sydney, NSW 2000)

Belgium (☎ 0902 88 025; 21 ave de la Toison d'Or, 1050 Brussels)

Canada (☎ 514-876 9881; 1981 McGill College Ave, Suite 490, Montreal, Que H3A 2W9)

Germany (☎ 0190 570 025; Westendstrasse 47, D-60325 Frankfurt)

Ireland (☎ 01560 235 235; 10 Suffolk St, Dublin 2)

Italy (☎ 166 116 216; Via Larga 7, 20122 Milan)

Netherlands (☎ 0900 112 2332; Prinsengracht 670, 1017 KX Amsterdam)

Spain Madrid (☎ 807 117 181; Plaza de España 18, 28008) Barcelona (☎ 807 117 181; Gran Via Corts Catalanes 656, 08010)

Switzerland Zurich (☎ 01-211 3085; Rennweg 42) Geneva (☎ 0900 900 699; 2 rue Thalberg, 1201)

UK (☎ 09068 244 123; 178 Piccadilly, London W1V 9AL)

USA New York (☎ 410-282 8310; 444 Madison Ave, 16th fl, NY 10022-6903) Los Angeles (☎ 310-271 6665; 9454 Wilshire Blvd, Ste 715, Beverly Hills, CA 90212-2967)

VISAS

For up-to-date information on visa requirements, see the Foreign Affairs Ministry site, www.diplomatie.gouv.fr under 'Entering France'.

EU nationals and citizens of Switzerland, Iceland and Norway need only a passport or national identity card to enter France and stay in the country. However, for nationals of the 10 new (in 2004) member countries, conditions for living and working in France vary from those for nationals of the original countries.

Citizens of Australia, the USA, Canada, New Zealand, Japan and Israel do not need visas to visit France as tourists for up to three months; the same goes for citizens of EU candidate countries (except Turkey).

As a practical matter, if you don't need a visa to visit France, no-one is likely to kick you out after three months. The unspoken policy seems to be that you can stay and spend your money in France as long as you don't try to work, apply for social services or commit a crime. Being in a *situation irrégulière* is nonetheless illegal, and without a *carte de séjour* you can face real problems renting an apartment, opening a bank account and so on.

Tourist (Schengen) Visa

Those not exempt will need a Schengen Visa, named after the Schengen agreement that abolished passport controls between Austria, Belgium, Denmark, Finland, France, Germany, Greece, Iceland, Italy, Luxembourg, the Netherlands, Norway, Portugal, Spain and Sweden. A Schengen visa allows unlimited travel throughout the entire zone within a 90-day period.

Applications are made with the consulate of the country you are entering first, or that will be your main destination. Among other things, you will need medical insurance and proof of sufficient funds to support yourself. See www.eurovisa.com for information.

If you enter France overland, it is unlikely that your visa will be checked at the border, but major problems can arise if you don't have one later on.

Tourist visas *cannot* be extended except in emergencies (such as medical problems); you'll need to leave and reapply from outside France when your visa expires.

Long-Stay & Student Visas

This is the first step if you'd like to work or study in France, or stay for over three months. Long-stay and student visas will allow you to enter France and apply for a *carte de séjour* (residency permit). Contact the French embassy or consulate nearest your residence, and begin your application

well in advance as it can take months. Tourist visas cannot be changed into student visas after arrival. However, short-term visas are available for students sitting university-entrance exams in France.

Working Holiday Visa

Citizens of Australia, Canada, Japan and New Zealand aged between 18 and 29 years (inclusive) are now eligible for a one-year, multiple-entry Working Holiday Visa, allowing combined tourism and employment in France. You have to apply to the embassy or consulate in your home country, and must prove you have a return ticket, insurance and sufficient funding to get through the start of your stay. Make sure you get in early with the application, as quotas apply.

Once you have arrived in France and have found a job, you must apply for a Temporary Work Permit (*autorisation provisoire de travail*), which will only be valid for the duration of the employment position offered. The permit can be renewed under the same conditions up to the limit of the authorised length of stay.

The idea is to supplement your funds with unskilled work. You can also study or do training programmes, but the visa can not be extended, nor turned into a student visa. After one year you *must* go home.

Once in France, the Centre d'Information et Documentation Jeunesse (CIDJ; see opposite) can help with information.

Carte de Séjour

Once issued with a long-stay visa, you can apply for a *carte de séjour* (residence permit), and are usually required to do so within eight days of arrival in France. Make sure you have all the necessary documents *before* you arrive. EU passport-holders and citizens of Switzerland, Iceland and Norway no longer need a *carte de séjour* to reside or work in France. Other foreign nationals must contact the local *préfecture* (prefecture), or *commissariat* (police station) for their permit.

Students of all nationalities must apply for a *carte de séjour* at the **Centre des Étudiants** (Map pp99-101; 13 rue Miollis, 15e, Paris; metro Cambronne or Ségur) in Paris. For more information (in French) see the Paris Préfecture website (www.prefecture-police-paris.interieur .gouv.fr), or the national migrations office website (www.omi.social.fr).

WOMEN TRAVELLERS

For information about health issues while travelling, see p930.

Safety Precautions

Women tend to attract more unwanted attention than men, but female travellers need not walk around France in fear; people are rarely assaulted on the street. Be aware of your surroundings and of situations that could be potentially dangerous: empty streets, lonely beaches, dark corners of large train stations. Using the metros late at night is generally OK, as stations are rarely deserted, but there are a few to avoid. See p112 for details.

In some places women may have to deal with what might be called low-intensity sexual harassment: 'playful' comments and invitations that can become overbearing or aggressive, and which some women find threatening or offensive. Remain polite and keep your distance. Hearing a foreign accent may provoke further unwanted attention.

Be alert to vibes in cheap hotels, sometimes staffed by apparently unattached men who may pay far more attention to your comings and goings than you would like. Change hotels if you feel uncomfortable, or allude to the imminent arrival of your husband (whether you have one or not).

On overnight trains, you may prefer to ask (when reserving) if there's a women's compartment available. If your compartment companions are overly attentive, don't hesitate to ask the conductor for a change of compartment. Second-class sleeping cars offer greater security than a *couchette*.

You can reach France's national **rape crisis hotline** (☎ 0 800 059 595) toll-free from any telephone without using a phonecard. It's run by a Paris women's organisation, **Viols Femmes Informations** (9 villa d'Este, 13e; metro Porte d'Ivry).

The **police** (☎ 17) will take you to the hospital if you have been attacked or injured. In Paris, medical, psychological and legal services are available to people referred by the police at the 24hr **Service Médico-Judiciaire** (☎ 01 42 34 84 46) of the Hôtel Dieu hospital (Map pp93–5).

Organisations

The women-only **Maison des Femmes** (Map pp102-4; ☎ 01 43 43 41 13; 163 rue Charenton, 12e; metro Reuilly Diderot) is the main meeting place for women of all ages and nationalities.

WORK

EU nationals have an automatic right to work in France. Non-EU citizens will need to apply for a work permit, for which they first need a *carte de séjour* or a Working Holiday Visa (see opposite), as well as a written promise of employment. Permits can be refused on the grounds of high local unemployment.

Working 'in the black' (that is, without documents) is difficult and risky for non-EU travellers. The only instance in which the government turns a blind eye to undocumented workers is during fruit harvests (mid-May to November) and the *vendange* grape harvest (mid-September to mid- or late October).

Even with a permit, employers generally must pay 'foreigner fees' for non-EU employees, and must prove that the job cannot be done by an EU-citizen (there are some exceptions for artists and computing and translation specialists). So getting qualified work is extremely difficult.

Summer and casual work is more flexible, and can be found in restaurants and hotels (particularly in the Alps). Teaching English is another option, either for a company or through private lessons.

Au-pair work is also very popular and can be done legally even by non-EU citizens, but they must contact the placement agency from their home country at least three months in advance.

The administration for freelance workers (*travailleurs indépendants*) is **URSSAF** (☎ 01 49 20 10 10; www.urssaf.fr in French; 3 rue Franklin 93100, Montreuil). Organising freelance work status is complicated; it is highly advisable to consult a local attorney experienced in immigration matters.

France's national employment service, the **Agence National pour l'Emploi** (ANPE; www.anpe .fr in French) has offices throughout France; the website has job listings.

The **Centre d'Information et de Documentation Jeunesse** (CIDJ; Map pp99-101; ☎ 01 44 49 12 00; www.cidj.com; 101 quai Branly, 15e; metro Champ de Mars) provides all sorts of information for young people on jobs, housing, education and more: in 2004 they advertised 20,000 summer jobs on their website.

In Paris, the magazine *Fusac* (see p893) advertises jobs for English speakers, including au-pair work, babysitting and language teaching.

Transport

GETTING THERE & AWAY

ENTERING THE COUNTRY

Thanks to European integration you can cross fluidly between France and neighbouring countries without passing through customs or border checkpoints. If you are arriving from a non-EU country, you will have to show your passport – and your visa permit if you need one (see p911) – or your identity card if you are an EU citizen, and clear customs.

AIR
Airports

Air France (www.airfrance.com), the national carrier, and scores of other airlines link Paris with every part of the globe. France has two major international airports: **Roissy-Charles de Gaulle** (CDG; ☎ 01 48 62 12 12) and **Orly** (ORY; ☎ 01 49 75 15 15), both run by **Aéroports de Paris** (☎ 01 43 35 70 00; www.adp.fr). For details on these airports see p170.

A number of other airports have significant international services (mainly within Europe):

Bordeaux (BOD; ☎ 05 56 34 50 50; www.bordeaux .aeroport.fr)

THINGS CHANGE...

The information in this chapter is particularly vulnerable to change. Check directly with the airline or a travel agent to make sure you understand how a fare (and ticket you may buy) works and be aware of the security requirements for international travel. Shop carefully. The details given in this chapter should be regarded as pointers and are not a substitute for your own careful, up-to-date research.

Lille (LIL; ☎ 03 20 49 68 68; www.lille.aeroport.fr in French)

Lyon (LYS; ☎ 0 826 800 826; www.lyon.aeroport.fr)

Marseille (MRS; ☎ 04 42 14 14 14; www.marseille -provence.aeroport.fr)

Nantes (NTE; ☎ 02 40 84 80 00; www.nantes.aeroport.fr)

Nice (NCE; ☎ 0 820 423 333; www.nice.aeroport.fr)

Strasbourg (SXB; ☎ 03 88 64 67 67 www.strasbourg .aeroport.fr)

Toulouse (TLS; ☎ 0 825 380 000; www.toulouse .aeroport.fr)

Some airlines and budget carriers use small provincial airports for flights to the UK, continental Europe and, sometimes, North Africa. Smaller airports with international flights include Biarritz, Caen, Deauville, Metz-Nancy-Lorraine, Montpellier, Morlaix, Mulhouse-Basel (EuroAirport), Nîmes, Rennes, St-Étienne, Tours and Quimper. Relevant local airports are listed relevant destination chapters.

Airlines

Most of the world's major carriers serve Paris at the very least.

Aer Lingus (☎ 01 70 20 00 72; www.aerlingus.com; airline code EI; hub Dublin)

Air Canada (☎ 0 825 880 881; www.aircanada.ca; airline code AC; hub Toronto)

Air France (☎ 0 820 820 820; www.airfrance.com; airline code AF; hub Paris)

Alitalia (☎ 0 820 315 315; www.alitalia.com; airline code AZ; hub Rome)

American Airlines (☎ 0 810 872 872; www.american airlines.com; airline code AA; hub Dallas)

Austrian Airlines (☎ 0 820 816 816; www.austrian airlines.com; airline code OS; hub Vienna)

Basiqair (☎ 0 821 231 214; www.basiqair.com; airline code HV; hub Amsterdam)

BMI BritishMidland (short haul ☎ 0870 6070 555, long haul ☎ 0870 6070 555; www.flybmi.com; airline code BD; hub London)

British Airways (☎ 0 825 825 400; www .british airways.com; airline code BA; hub London)

Cathay Pacific (☎ 01 41 43 75 75; www.cathaypacific .com; airline code CX; hub Hong Kong)

Continental Airlines (☎ 01 42 99 09 09; www .contin ental.com; airline code CO; hub Houstan)

easyJet (☎ 44-023-568 4880; www.easyjet.com; airline code EZY; hub London Luton)

Flybe (☎ 44-0871 700 0535; www.flybe.com; airline code BE; hub Southampton)

Iberia (☎ 0 820 075 075; www.iberia.com; airline code IB; hub Madrid)

KLM (☎ 0 890 710 710; www.klm.com; airline code KL; hub Amsterdam)

Lufthansa (☎ 0 820 020 030; www.lufthansa.com; airline code LH; hub Frankfurt)

Olympic Airlines (☎ 01 44 94 58 58; www .olympic airlines.com; airline code OA; hub Athens)

Qantas Airways (☎ 0 820 820 500; www.qantas.com; airline code QF; hub Sydney)

Ryanair (www.ryanair.com; airline code FR; hub London Stansted, Dublin)

Singapore Airlines (☎ 01 53 65 79 01; www .singa poreair.com; airline code SQ; hub Singapore)

South African Airways (☎ 01 55 61 94 55; www .flysaa.com; airline code SA; hub Johannesburg)

Thai Airways International (☎ 01 44 20 70 15; www.thaiair.com; airline code TG; hub Bangkok)

Tickets

A bit of research – calling around, checking Internet sites, comparing the airline and travel agent prices, scouring newspapers – can often result in real savings on your air ticket. Start early: some of the cheapest tickets have to be bought well in advance.

We mention well-known travel agents later in this chapter, under individual country headings. For cheap tickets from no-frill carriers, contact them directly or use online ticket searches. Good online agencies:

Anyway (www.anyway.com in French) French-based discount site.

Cheap Tickets (www.cheaptickets.com)

Expedia (www.expedia.com)

Last Minute (www.lastminute.com)

Priceline (www.priceline.com) With this US-based site you can bid for a ticket online.

Travel Cuts (www.travelcuts.com)

Travelocity (www.travelocity.co.uk)

Budget carriers such as Ryanair, BMI and easyJet have sprung up mushroom-like all over Europe. Usually tickets are bought directly from the airline, online or by phone. Bear in mind that budget-airlines are often changing their routes and going into liquidation, so check websites for up-to-date information.

INTERCONTINENTAL (RTW) TICKETS

Round-the-world (RTW) tickets can be a great way to combine destinations, and can be no more expensive than an ordinary return fare for residents of Australasia. The flight dates (but not the overall routing) are changeable en route. The departure date from your home country usually determines the fare (that is, whether you're charged high- or low-season rates). Validity usually lasts for a year.

Australia & New Zealand

From Melbourne or Sydney, many major airlines fly to Europe. Return tickets to Paris range from A$1900 to A$3000. Fares from Perth are about A$200 cheaper. A return flight from Auckland will cost from NZ$1900. A RTW ticket is worth considering, it might be better value than the return fare. Small agencies advertise in the *New Zealand Herald*, *Sydney Morning Herald* and the *Melbourne Age*. Other major dealers in cheap fares, with many branches:

Flight Centre (Australia-wide ☎ 131 131, in New Zealand ☎ 0800 24 35 44; www.flightcentre.com)

STA Travel (Australia-wide ☎ 1300 733 035, ☎ 0508 782 872; www.statravel.com)

Canada

From Toronto or Montreal, return flights on Air Canada to Paris are available from about C$820 in the low season; prices are C$200 or C$300 more from Vancouver. For lower fares, scan the travel-agency ads in the *Globe & Mail*, *Toronto Star* and *Vancouver Province*. **Travel CUTS** (☎ 1 888 359 2887; www .travelcuts.com) has branches across Canada.

Continental Europe

Most European airlines fly into Paris. Air France offers competitive fares on most of its routes as well as good discounts for young people, seniors and couples (married or legally cohabiting). Local travel agencies and online ticket sites follow.

DENMARK
Kilroy Travels (☎ 70 80 80 15; www.kilroytravels.com; Skindergade 28, Copenhagen)
STA Travel (☎ 33 14 15 01; www.statravel.dk; Fiolstraede 18, Copenhagen)

GERMANY
STA Travel (☎ 030-310 00 40; www.statravel.de; Hardenbergstrasse 9, Berlin)

ITALY
Viaggi Wasteels (☎ 091 34 96 86; Viale Piemonte, Palermo)
CTS Viaggi (☎ 06 462 043 116; www.cts.it; Via Genova, Rome) One of many branches throughout Italy.

THE NETHERLANDS
Kilroy Travels (☎ 020-524 51 00; wwww.kilroytravels .com; Singel 413, Amsterdam)
ISSTA (☎ 020-618 80 31; 226 Overtoom Straat, Amsterdam)

NORWAY
Kilroy Travels (☎ 81 55 96 33; wwww.kilroytravels .com; Nedre Slottsgate 23, Oslo)
STA Travel (☎ 81 55 99 05; www.statravel.no; Karl Johansgate 8, Oslo)

SWEDEN
Kilroy Travels (☎ 0771-545769; wwww.kilroytravels .com; Kungsgatan 4, Stockholm)
STA Travel (☎ 0771-611010; www.statravel.se; Kungsgatan 30, Stockholm)

SWITZERLAND
STA Travel (☎ 022-818 02 00; www.statravel.ch; rue de Rive 10, Geneva)

The UK & Ireland
Low-cost carriers now offer astounding rates from the UK and Ireland to destinations throughout France. Some of the best deals, especially to destinations other than Paris such as Lyon, Marseille Toulouse and La Rochelle, are offered by Ryanair, Flybe and easyJet. Prices vary wildly from a ridiculously low UK£17 between London and Paris. Aer Lingus flies from Dublin or Shannon to Paris' Charles de Gaulle for €115 return.

Air France and British Airways link cities throughout the UK and France, fares are often very reasonable. Other airlines that may have decent prices include British Midland and KLM (UK).

Look for special deals in the travel pages of the weekend broadsheet newspapers, as well as in *Time Out*, the *Evening Standard* and the free magazine *TNT*.

Recommended travel agencies and online ticket sites:
Cheap Flights (www.cheapflights.co.uk)
Cheapest Flights (www.cheapestflights.co.uk)
Online Travel (www.onlinetravel.com) Good deals on flights from more than a dozen British cities.
STA Travel (☎ 0870 1 600 599; www.statravel.co.uk) Caters especially to student and youth travel.
Usit Voyages (in Dublin ☎ 01-602 1600, in Paris ☎ 01 42 34 56 90; Irish Republic www.usitworld.com)

The USA
The flight options across the North Atlantic, the world's busiest long-haul air corridor, are bewildering. A return flight from New York to Paris costs around US$370 in the low season and US$800 in the high season; even lower promotional fares are sometimes on offer. Tickets from the west coast are US$150 to US$250 higher.

The *New York Times*, *LA Times*, *Chicago Tribune* and *San Francisco Chronicle* all have weekly travel sections in which you'll find any number of travel-agency ads. Independent periodicals such as the *San Francisco Guardian* and New York's *Village Voice* are other good places to check.

There are a number of local travel agencies and online ticket sites:
Expedia (www.expedia.com)
Flight Centre (www.flightcentre.com)
STA Travel (www.statravel.com)
Travelocity (www.travelocity.com)

STAND-BY & COURIER FLIGHTS
Other rock-bottom options for discounted – and even free – air travel include charter, stand-by and courier flights.
Airhitch (☎ 877-247-4482; www.airhitch.org) Specialises in stand-by flights.
Courier Travel (☎ 303 570 7586; www.couriertravel .org) A comprehensive search engine for courier and stand-by flights.
International Association of Air Travel Couriers (☎ 561-582 8320; www.courier.org)

LAND
If you are doing a lot of travel around Europe, look for discount bus and train passes, which can be conveniently combined with discount air fares.

Bus

Buses are slower and less comfortable than trains, but are cheaper, especially if you qualify for discount rates (people under 26, over 60, teachers and students) or get one of the reduced-price fares on offer at times.

BUSABOUT

From April to October, the UK-based **Busabout** (in London ☎ 207 950 1661; www.busabout.com), based in London, links 41 European cities in 11 countries, mostly in Western Europe, and offers a Europe-wide bus pass. Within France the buses stop at Bordeaux, Tours, Paris, Avignon and Nice. There are two types of pass available:

Flexipass Allows for a set number of travelling days within an certain number of days within the entire six-month operating season. Full/discount passes costs €419/379 for eight days and €729/649 for 16 days.

Unlimited Pass Allows for unlimited use of the bus system within a set period. Full/discount passes cost €359/329 for two weeks, €729/649 for six weeks or €1239/1109 for the six-month season.

You can hop on or off the buses as you like, and can pay extra for additional links to places like Croatia. On-board guides can take care of hostel reservations or you can book ahead online – in many places the pick-up/drop-off point is a central hostel. For information and bookings, check out its website.

EUROLINES

Eurolines (☎ 08 92 69 52 52, 01 43 54 11 99; www.euro lines .com) groups together more than 30 European coach operators and links points all across Europe as well as Morocco and Russia. Eurolines' all-Europe website has links to each national company's site and gives detailed information on fares, routes, bookings and special deals. You can usually book online. Return tickets cost about 20% less than two one-ways. In summer make reservations at least two working days in advance. The main hub is Paris. Sample one-way fares:

Route	Full Fare (€)	Duration (hr)
Paris–Prague	75	16
Paris–Amsterdam	46	8
Bordeaux–Barcelona	55	10¼
Nice–Rome	67	10
Lyon–Berlin	90	20

The Eurolines Travel Pass is a flexible ticket that allows for unlimited travel within a set period between 31 European cities, including several in France – but you are not able to visit other cities en route. A 15-/30-/60-day pass during high season (June to September) will cost €285/425/490 for adults and €240/345/380 for the discount (youth/senior) fares. The rest of the year the cost is €220/310/390 for adults and €185/250/310 for discount fares.

INTERCARS

French coach company **Intercars** (www.intercars .fr in French) links France with cities throughout in Europe, notably Eastern Europe and Russia. The office in **Paris** (☎ 01 42 19 99 35; 139bis rue de Vaugirard, 15e; metro Falguière) links with Berlin (€77, 13 hours), Moscow (€234, 50 hours) and many places in between. From **Lyon** (☎ 04 78 37 20 80; Perrache bus station) you can reach Venice, Naples, Porto, Minsk or Zagreb. From **Nice** (☎ 04 93 80 08 70; Nice bus station) you can reach San Sebastian, Casablanca and Warsaw.

You can reserve by emailing the agency closest to your place of departure.

Car & Motorcycle

Arriving in France by car is easy to do. At some border points you may be asked for passport or identity card (your driver's licence will not be sufficient ID). Police searches are not uncommon for vehicles entering France, particularly from Spain and Belgium (via which drugs from Morocco or the Netherlands can enter France). See p923 for details about driving in France.

EUROTUNNEL

The Channel Tunnel, inaugurated in 1994, is the first dry-land link between England and France since the Ice Age.

High-speed **Eurotunnel shuttle trains** (in the UK ☎ 0870 535 3535, in France ☎ 03 21 00 61 00; www .eurotunnel.com) whisk cars, motorcycles and coaches from Folkestone through the Channel Tunnel to Coquelles, 5km southwest of Calais, in air-conditioned and sound-proofed comfort. Shuttles run 24 hours a day, every day of the year, with up to five departures an hour during peak periods (one an hour from 1am to 5am). LPG and CNG tanks are not permitted, which eliminates many campers and caravans.

Prices vary with market demand, but the regular one-way fare for a passenger car, including all its passengers, costs from UK£150 (in February or March) to UK£250 (in July or August); return passage costs twice as much. Return fares valid for less than five days are much cheaper. The fee for a bicycle, including its rider, is UK£32 re-

turn; advance reservations are mandatory. To take advantage of promotional fares you must book at least one day ahead.

Train

Rail services link France with every country in Europe; schedules are available from major train stations in France and abroad.

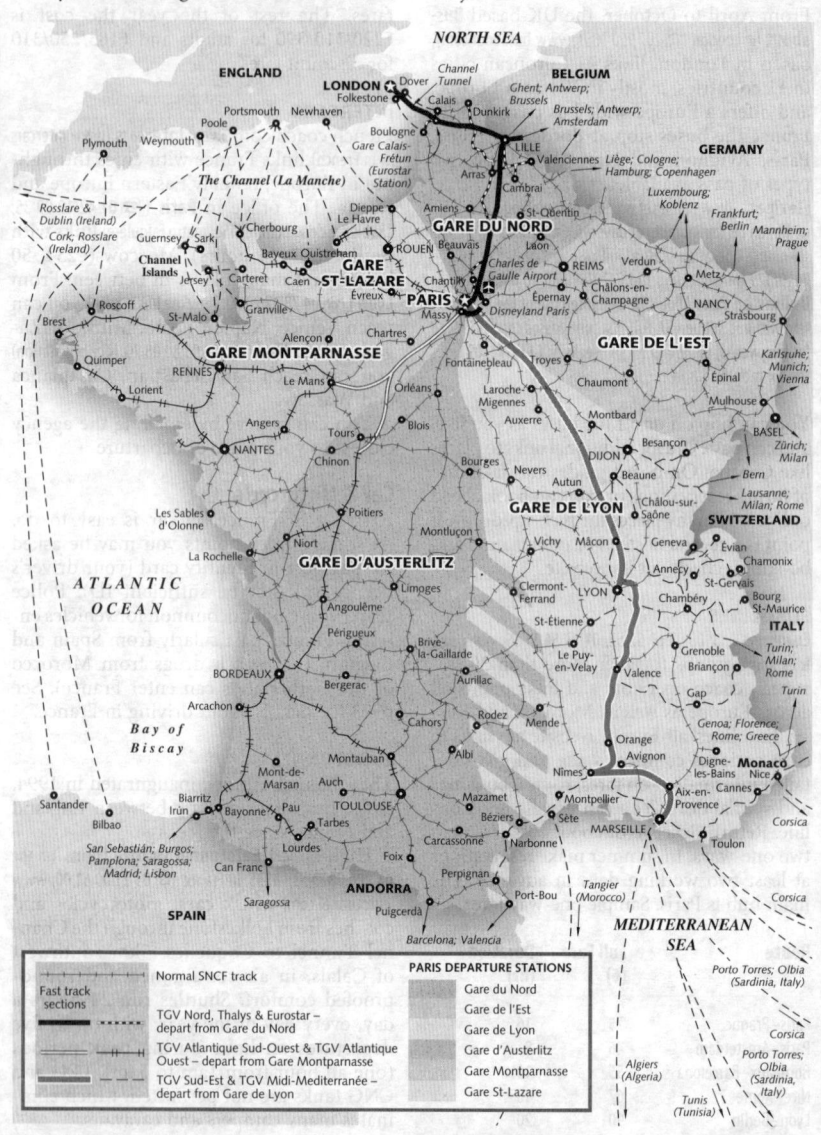

Because of different track gauges and electrification systems, you sometimes have to change trains at the border (eg when travelling to Spain). Many national rail companies are linked to Paris:

Austria (☎ 01-93 00 00; www.oebb.at)
Belgium (☎ 02-528 28.28; www.b-rail.be)
Germany (☎ 0800 1 50 70 90; www.bahn.de)
Italy (☎ 89 20 21; www.trenitalia.it)
The Netherlands (☎ 06 92 96; www.ns.nl)
Spain (☎ 902 24 02 02; www.renfe.es)
Switzerland (☎ 0900 300 300; www.sbb.ch)

The **Thalys** (www.thalys.com) service links Paris' Gare du Nord to Brussels-Midi (from €65, 1½ hours, 20 per day), Amsterdam CS (from €87, 4¼ hours, five per day) and Cologne's Hauptbahnhof (€78, four hours, seven per day).

You can book tickets and get information from **Rail Europe** (www.raileurope.com) up to two months ahead. In France ticketing is handled by the national train network **SNCF** (☎ 08 92 35 35 35; www.sncf.com). Telephone and Internet bookings are possible, but they won't post tickets outside France. See p928 for information about discounts.

EUROPEAN TRAIN PASSES

These discount passes are worthwhile only if you plan to travel extensively around France by train and other European countries.

Eurail Passes (www.eurail.com) A variety of passes are available to non-European residents for travel in 17 countries. For people over/under 26, 15 days' consecutive, unlimited travel costs €588/414; and five days' travel over a two-month period costs €356/249.

InterRail (www.raileurope.co.uk/inter-rail) and **Euro-Domino** passes are available to European residents. All are valid on the French national train network and allow unlimited travel for varying periods of time.

See p928 for discounts and passes from the SNCF and for travel within France. Eurail and some other train passes must be validated at a train station ticket window before you begin your first journey, in order to begin the period of validity.

EUROSTAR

On the highly civilised **Eurostar** (in France ☎ 08 92 35 35 39, in the UK ☎ 08705 186 186; www.eurostar .com), the trip from London to Paris takes just two hours and 35 minutes. There are direct daily services between London and Ashford (Kent) and Paris, Brussels, Lille, Parc Disneyland Paris and Calais-Fréthun. A direct seasonal service goes from London and Ashford to Avignon (May to October) and the French Alps (November to April).

A full-fare, 2nd-class ticket from London to Paris can be as low as UK£50 (and as high as £300). From Paris, the trip to London varies immensely from €60 to €525. You'll get the best deals if you stay over a Saturday night, if you book 14 or seven days ahead, if you're under 25 or if you're a student. Student travel agencies often have youth fares not available directly from Eurostar.

SEA

Tickets for ferry travel to/from the UK, the Channel Islands and Ireland are available from most travel agencies in France and the countries served. Except where noted, the prices given below are for standard one-way tickets; in some cases, return fares cost less than two one-way tickets. Prices vary greatly according to the season and the demand. There are discounts for children.

Note that if you're travelling with a vehicle you are usually denied access to it during the voyage.

The Channel Islands

Passenger-only catamarans operated by **Hugo Express** (in France ☎ 02 33 61 08 88) link the Channel Islands with two small ports on the western coast of Normandy: Granville (daily April to September, weekends only in March) and Carteret (daily April to September). The one-way pedestrian fare is UK£35.

Émeraude Lines (in the UK ☎ 01534 766 566, in France ☎ 0 825 165 180; www.emeraudelines.com) runs express car ferries between Jersey and St-Malo (foot passenger/car and two adults from UK£35/114, 1¼ hours).

Ireland

Eurail pass holders pay 50% of the adult pedestrian fare for crossings between Ireland and France on Irish Ferries (make sure you book ahead).

Irish Ferries (☎ 01-638 3333, in France ☎ 01 43 94 46 94; www.irishferries.ie) has overnight services from Rosslare to either Cherbourg (18½ hours) or Roscoff (16 hours) every other day (three times a week from mid-September

TRANSPORT

to October, with a possible break in service from November to February). A pedestrian/car with two adults costs around €90/389. There are special prices for five- and nine-day returns.

From April to September, **Brittany Ferries** (☎ 0870 366 5333, in France ☎ 0 825 828 828; www .brittany-ferries.com) runs a car ferry every Saturday from Cork (Ringaskiddy) to Roscoff (14 hours), and every Friday in the other direction. Foot passengers pay around €198 for a three-person couchette.

Freight ferries run by **P&O Irish Sea** (☎ 0870 242 4777; www.poirishsea.com) link Rosslare with Cherbourg (18 hours, three per week); cars with two passengers cost from €154. From April to September there is also a weekly Dublin–Cherbourg route (18 hours); cars with two adults cost €174. Foot passengers are not accepted on either service.

Italy

From late April to mid-October, the **Société Nationale Maritime Corse Méditerranée** (SNCM; ☎ 0 891 701 801; www.sncm.fr) has five or six car ferries per week from Marseille or Toulon to Porto Torres on the island of Sardinia (Sardaigne in French). The one-way adult pedestrian fare is around €100 and takes about 11 hours.

A variety of ferry companies ply the waters between Corsica and Italy. For details, see p865.

North Africa

SNCM and **Compagnie Tunisienne de Navigation** (CTN; www.ctn.com.tn) link Marseille with the Tunisian capital, Tunis (about 24 hours, three or four a week). The standard adult fare is €300 one way, with discounts for seniors and those under 25. In France, ticketing is handled by SNCM, which also links Marseille with Algiers (Alger in French; Algeria).

Compagnie Marocaine de Navigation (CoMaNav; ☎ 04 99 57 21 21) links Sète, 29km (20 minutes by train) southwest of Montpellier, with the Moroccan port of Tangier (Tanger; 36 hours, five to seven a month). The cheapest berth costs €168 (€228 in August and for some other summer sailings) one way; return tickets cost 15% to 20% less than two one-ways. Discounts are available if you're aged under 26 or in a group of four or more. In France ticketing is handled by SNCM.

Spain

If you would like to start your trip in southwestern France (or return to England from there), a couple of ferry services from northern Spain are worth considering.

P&O Ferries (in the UK ☎ 0870 598 0555, in France ☎ 0825013013; www.poferries.com) links Portsmouth with Bilbao (Santurtzi port, 35 hours and two nights *to* Bilbao, 29 hours and one night *from* Bilbao), which is only about 150km west of Biarritz, twice a week (once a week from late October to late March; no services from early January to early February). A one-way pedestrian ticket including a mandatory sleeping berth costs around €180.

From mid-March to mid-November, **Brittany Ferries** (☎ 0870 366 5333, in France ☎ 0 825 828 828; www.brittany-ferries.com) runs twice-weekly car-ferry services from Plymouth to Santander (24 hours), which is around 240km west of Biarritz. Foot passengers pay around €104; a couchette costs around €10 extra.

The UK

Fares vary widely according to demand, which depends on the season (July and August are especially popular) and the time of day (a Friday night ferry can cost much more than a Sunday morning one); the most expensive tickets can cost almost three times as much as the cheapest ones. Three- or five-day excursion (return) fares generally cost about the same as regular one-way tickets; special promotional return fares, often requiring advance booking, are sometimes cheaper than a standard one-way fare. On some overnight sailings you have to pay extra for a mandatory reclining seat (UK£5) or sleeping berth (UK£16 to UK£38).

Check out **Ferry Savers** (☎ 0870 990 8492; www .ferrysavers.com), which guarantees the lowest prices on Channel crossings. Ferry companies may try to make it hard for people who use supercheap, one-day return tickets for one-way passage – a huge backpack is a dead giveaway.

Eurail passes are *not* valid for ferry travel between the UK and France. Transporting bicycles is often (but not always) free.

TO BRITTANY

From mid-March to mid-November, Plymouth is linked to Roscoff (six hours for day crossings, one to three per day) by Brittany

Ferries. The one-way fare for foot passengers is around UK£35.

Brittany Ferries also links Portsmouth and Plymouth with St-Malo (8¾ hours for day crossing, one per day). Pedestrians pay from UK£27 one way.

From April to September, **Condor Ferries** (☎ 0845 345 2000, in France ☎ 02 99 20 03 00; www .condorferries.com) has at least one daily ferry linking Weymouth with St-Malo (UK£35) that can take anywhere from seven to 10 hours, including a stopover in Guernsey.

TO FAR NORTHERN FRANCE
The fastest way to cross the English Channel is between Dover and Calais, served by Hoverspeed's SeaCats (catamarans), which take 50 minutes. For foot passengers, a one-way trip (or a return completed within five days) costs UK£39. From Calais, there are five daily trains to Le Tréport, the northernmost town in Normandy (€19, five hours).

The Dover–Calais crossing is also handled by car ferries, run by **SeaFrance** (☎ 0870 571 1711, in France ☎ 0 804 044 045; www.seafrance .com; 1½hr; 15 daily) and **P&O Ferries** (☎ 0870 520 20 20; www.poferries .com; 1-1½hr; 29 daily) for about the same price.

Ferries run by **Norfolk Line** (☎ 03 28 59 01 01; www.norfolkline.com) link Loon Plage, about 25km west of Dunkirk, with Dover, while **Speed Ferries** (in the UK ☎ 01304-20 3000, in France ☎ 03 21 10 50 00; www.speedferries.com) offers an ultramodern, ultrafast catamaran service between Boulogne and Dover (50 minutes, five daily).

TO NORMANDY
The Newhaven–Dieppe route is handled by **Hoverspeed** (☎ 0870 240 8070, in France ☎ 00 800 1211 1211; www.hoverspeed.co.uk) and **Transmanche Ferries** (☎ 0800 917 1201; www.transmancheferries.com). The hovercraft trip (one to three daily) takes 2¼ hours, while the ferry trip (two daily) takes four hours. Pedestrians pay from UK£30 one way, with special deals available.

There's a 4¼-hour crossing (two or three per day) from Poole to Cherbourg with **Brittany Ferries** (☎ 0870 366 5333, in France ☎ 0 825 828 828; www.brittany-ferries.com). Foot passengers pay from UK£33 one way.

On the Portsmouth–Cherbourg route, Brittany Ferries, Condor Ferries and **P&O Portsmouth** (in the UK ☎ 0870 598 0555, in France ☎ 0 825 013 013; www.poferries.com) have two or three car ferries a day (five hours by day, eight hours overnight) and, from April to September, two faster catamarans a day. Foot passengers pay from UK£29 one way.

The Portsmouth–Le Havre crossing is handled by P&O Portsmouth (5½ hours by day, 7¾ hours overnight, three car ferries a day, fewer in winter). Passage costs somewhat more than Portsmouth–Cherbourg.

Brittany Ferries also has car-ferry services from Portsmouth to Caen (Ouistreham; six hours, three per day). Tickets cost the same as for Poole–Cherbourg.

The USA, Canada & Elsewhere
The days when you could earn your passage to Europe on a freighter have well and truly passed, but it's still possible to travel as a passenger on a cargo ship from North America (and ports further afield) to France's Atlantic coast. Such vessels typically carry five to 12 passengers (more than 12 would require a doctor on board). Good websites:

The Cruise People (www.cruisepeople.co.uk) In the UK.

Freighter World Cruises (www.freighterworld.com) In the USA.

Traveltips (www.traveltips.com)

GETTING AROUND

France's domestic transport network, much of it owned or subsidised by the government, tends to be monopolistic: the state-owned Société Nationale des Chemins de Fer Français (SNCF) takes care of most land transport between *départements*, and short-haul bus companies are either run by the *département* or grouped so each local company handles different destinations. In recent years domestic air travel has been partly deregulated, but local smaller carriers have struggled.

While the efficient train system can get you to major cities and towns, travel within rural regions on sparse public bus services can be slow and difficult – if not impossible. If you wish to see rural areas and visit small towns off the major train routes, you really need your own wheels.

AIR
All of France's major cities – as well as many minor ones – have airports, which we mention in the destination chapters. National carrier **Air France** (☎ 0 820 820 820; www .airfrance. com) continues to control the lion's share of

France's long-protected domestic airline industry, particularly since the demise of local carriers Aeris and Air Lib. Other local carriers have been bought by Air France. British budget carrier easyJet has begun flights linking Paris with Marseille, Nice and Toulouse. Other European budget carriers may soon try to muscle in on France's domestic market.

Until then, the stiffest competition in the transport price war comes from the *Train à Grande Vitesse* (TGV), which has made travel between some cities (eg Paris and Lyon or Marseille) faster and easier by train than by air.

Any French travel agency or Air France office can make bookings for domestic flights and supply details on the complicated fare options. Outside France, Air France representatives sell tickets for many domestic flights.

Up to 84% reduction is available if you fly during the week and buy your ticket three weeks in advance. Significant discounts are available to children, young people, families, seniors, and couples who are married or have proof of cohabitation. Special last-minute offers are posted on the Air France website every Wednesday.

BICYCLE

France is an eminently cyclable country, thanks in part to its extensive network of secondary and tertiary roads, many of which carry relatively light traffic. One pitfall: the roads rarely have proper shoulders (verges). Many French cities have a growing network of urban and suburban *pistes cyclables* (bicycle paths), and in some areas (eg around Bordeaux) such paths link one town to the next. *Never* leave your bicycle locked up outside overnight if you want to see it or most of its parts again.

French law dictates that bicycles must have two functioning brakes, a bell, a red reflector on the back and yellow reflectors on the pedals. After sunset and when visibility is poor, cyclists must turn on a white light in front and a red one in the rear. When being overtaken by a car or lorry, cyclists are required to ride in single file.

Bicycles are not allowed on most local or intercity buses or on trams. On some regional trains you can take a bicycle free of charge. On train timetables, a bicycle symbol

indicates that bicycles are allowed on particular trains. On some regional trains, bikes have to be covered and stored in the luggage van. The SNCF baggage service **Sernam** (☎ 0 825 84 58 45) will transport your bicycle (or any other luggage) door to door or station to station for €44.90.

European Bike Express (☎ 01642-251 440; www .bike-express.co.uk) transports cyclists and their bikes from the UK to places all over France.

More information of interest to cyclists can be found on p896. A useful source is the **Fédération Française de Cyclisme** (☎ 01 49 35 69 00; www.ffc.fr in French).

Hire & Purchase

Most towns have at least one shop that hires *vélos tout-terrains* (mountain bikes), popularly known as VTTs (€12 to €20 a day), or cheaper touring bikes. In general, they require a deposit of €150 or €300, which you forfeit if the bike is damaged or stolen. Some cities (eg Strasbourg, p356, and La Rochelle, p624) have remarkably inexpensive rental agencies run by the municipality. For details about rental shops, see the city and town listings throughout this book.

A VTT can be purchased for €250. Reselling your bike at the end of your trip (for around two-thirds of its purchase price) is possible at certain bike shops and pawnbrokers. French-language websites www .argusvtt.net and www.velo101.com have classified ads and advice.

BOAT

For information on ferry services linking towns along the coast of France see individual town and city sections. For information on ferry services from other countries, see p919.

Canal Boating

One of the most relaxing ways to see France is to rent a houseboat for a leisurely cruise along canals and navigable rivers, stopping at your whim along the way. Changes in altitude are taken care of by a system of *écluses* (locks).

Boats generally accommodate from four to 12 passengers and are fully outfitted with bedding and cooking facilities. Anyone over 18 can pilot a river boat without a special licence, but first-time skippers are given a short instruction session. The speed limit is 6km/h on canals and 10km/h on rivers.

Prices start at €1100 a week for a small boat. Reservations are a must if you're boating during a holiday period. Quercy (p598) and Burgundy (p428) chapters. For information on inland waterway rental:

Crown Travel (☎ 01603-630 513; 8 Ber St, Norwich NR1 3EJ, UK) For canal-boat rental in Brittany, Alsace, Languedoc and other areas.

French Nautical Industries Federation (☎ 01 44 37 04 00; www.france-nautic.com) Information about rental companies throughout France.

Syndicat National des Loueurs de Bateaux de Plaisance (☎ 01 44 37 04 00; Port de Javel, 75015 Paris; metro Javel) Publishes a booklet listing rental companies.

BUS

Within France, bus services are provided by numerous different companies, usually based within one *département*. For travel between regions, a train is your best bet since inter-regional bus services are limited. Buses are used quite extensively for short-distance travel within *départements*, especially in rural areas with relatively few train lines (eg Brittany and Normandy) – but services are often slow and few and far between.

Over the years, certain uneconomical train lines have been replaced by SNCF buses – unlike regional buses, these are free for people with train passes. City and town entries include bus connections with other destinations.

CAR & MOTORCYCLE

Having your own wheels gives you exceptional freedom and allows you to visit more remote parts of France. Unfortunately it can be expensive and, in cities parking and traffic are frequently a major headache. Motorcyclists will find France great for touring, with winding roads of good quality and lots of stunning scenery. Just make sure your wet-weather gear is up to scratch.

France (along with Belgium) has the densest highway network in Europe. There are four types of intercity roads, which have alphanumeric designations:

Autoroutes (eg A14) Multilane highways, usually with tolls (*péages*).

Routes Nationales (N, RN) National highways.

Routes Départementales (D) Local roads.

Routes Communales (C, V) Minor rural roads.

Information on tolls, rest areas, petrol (gas) stations and itineraries is available on www.france-nautic.com. The websites www.viamichelin.com and www.mappy.fr give suggested itineraries for getting from one place to another.

By autoroute, the drive from Paris to Nice (about 950km; eight hours of driving) costs at least €130 in petrol and autoroute tolls. By comparison, a regular, one-way, 2nd-class TGV ticket for the 5½-hour Paris–Nice run costs around €90 per person.

Roads throughout France block up during holiday periods and long weekends.

As insurance is compulsory for all cars in France, the number of the appropriate roadside assistance company is written on the insurance papers that will be in the car or stuck to the inside of the windscreen. Rental drivers should call their rental company for assistance.

Motorcycle and moped rental is popular in southern France, especially in the beach resorts, but accidents are all too common. Where relevant, details on rental options appear at the end of city and town listings. To rent a moped, scooter or motorcycle you usually have to leave a large *caution* (deposit), which you forfeit – up to the value of the damage – if you cause an accident or if the bike is in some way damaged or stolen.

Bring Your Own Vehicle

A right-hand drive vehicle brought to France from the UK or Ireland must have deflectors affixed to the headlights to avoid dazzling oncoming traffic. A motor vehicle entering a foreign country must display a sticker identifying its country of registration. In the UK information on driving in France is available from the **RAC** (☎ 0870 010 6382; www.rac.co.uk) and the **AA** (☎ 0870 600 0371; www.theaa.com).

Driving Licence & Documents

All drivers must carry at all times: a national ID card or passport; a valid driver's licence (*permis de conduire*; most foreign licences can be used in France for up to a year); car-ownership papers, known as a *carte grise* (grey card); and proof of third-party (liability) insurance. An International Driving Permit (IDP) is valid for a year and can be issued by your local automobile association before you leave home.

TRANSPORT

ROAD DISTANCES (KM)

	Bayonne	Bordeaux	Brest	Caen	Cahors	Calais	Chambéry	Cherbourg	Clermont-Ferrand	Dijon	Grenoble	Lille	Lyons	Marseille	Nantes	Nice	Paris	Perpignan	Strasbourg	Toulouse	Tours
Bayonne	---																				
Bordeaux	184	---																			
Brest	811	623	---																		
Caen	764	568	376	---																	
Cahors	307	218	788	661	---																
Calais	164	876	710	339	875	---															
Chambéry	860	651	120	800	523	834	---														
Cherbourg	835	647	399	124	743	461	923	---													
Clermont-Ferrand	564	358	805	566	269	717	295	689	---												
Dijon	807	619	867	548	378	572	273	671	279	---											
Grenoble	827	657	1126	806	501	863	56	929	300	302	---										
Lille	997	809	725	353	808	112	767	476	650	505	798	---									
Lyons	831	528	1018	698	439	755	103	820	171	194	110	687	---								
Marseille	700	651	1271	1010	521	1067	344	1132	477	506	273	999	314	---							
Nantes	513	326	298	292	491	593	780	317	462	656	787	609	618	975	---						
Nice	858	810	1429	1168	679	1225	410	1291	636	664	337	1157	473	190	1131	---					
Paris	771	583	596	232	582	289	565	355	424	313	571	222	462	775	384	932	---				
Perpignan	499	451	1070	998	320	1149	478	1094	441	640	445	1081	448	319	773	476	857	---			
Strasbourg	1254	1066	1079	730	847	621	496	853	584	335	551	522	488	803	867	804	490	935	---		
Toulouse	300	247	866	865	116	991	565	890	890	727	533	923	536	407	568	564	699	205	1022	---	
Tours	536	348	490	246	413	531	611	369	369	418	618	463	449	795	197	952	238	795	721	593	---

Fuel & Spare Parts

Essence (petrol or gasoline), also known as *carburant* (fuel), is considerably more expensive in France (€1.10/L for 95 unleaded) than Australia or North America. Filling up (*faire le plein*) is most expensive at the rest stops along the autoroutes and cheapest at small rural petrol stations and supermarkets.

Many small petrol stations close on Sunday afternoons. If you are out in the country you may have to drive to a self-service supermarket petrol station and pay by credit card.

If your car is *en panne* (breaks down), you'll have to find a garage that handles your *marque* (make of car). There are Peugeot, Renault and Citroën garages all over the place, but if you have a non-French car you may have trouble finding someone to service it in more remote areas.

Hire

To hire a car in France you'll generally need to be over 21 years old and in possession of a valid driver's licence and an international credit card. Arranging your car rental or fly/drive package before you leave home is often considerably cheaper. Major rental companies include:

ADA (☎ 0 825 169 169; www.ada.fr in French)
Avis (☎ 0 820 050 505; www.avis.com)
Budget (☎ 0 825 003 564; www.budget.com)
Easycar (☎ 0906 333 333 3; www.easycar.com) Cheap rates and offices in Paris and Nice.
Europcar (☎ 0 825 358 358; www.europcar.com)
Hertz (☎ 0 825 342 343; www.hertz.com)
National Citer (☎ 01 44 38 61 61, 0 800 202 121; www.citer.com)
OTU Voyages (☎ 01 40 29 12 12; www.otu.fr in French) For students.

Deals can be found on the Internet, with travel agencies and through companies like **Auto Europe** (☎ 1-888 223 5555; www.autoeurope .com) in the US, **Holiday Autos** (☎ 0870 5300 400; www.holidayautos.co.uk) in the UK. In this guide car-rental addresses are listed under large cities and towns.

Insurance

Unlimited third-party liability insurance is mandatory for all automobiles entering

France, whether the owner accompanies the vehicle or not. As proof of insurance, the owner must present an international motor insurance card showing that the vehicle is insured in France. A temporary insurance policy is available from the vehicle-insurance department of the **French Customs Office** (Direction Générale des Douanes et Droits Indirects; ☎ 01 40 04 04 04; 23bis rue de l'Université, 7e, Paris) with a validity of eight to 30 days. Third-party liability insurance is provided by car-rental companies, but things such as collision-damage waivers (CDW) vary greatly from company to company. When comparing rates, the most important thing to check is the *franchise* (excess/deductible), which is usually €350 for a small car. Your credit card may cover CDW (*assurance tout risqué*) if you use it to pay for the car rental.

Purchase-Repurchase Plans

If you'll be needing a car in Europe for 17 days to six months (one year if you're studying or teaching in France), by far your cheapest option is to 'purchase' a brand-new one from **Peugeot** (www.peugeot-openeurope.com) or **Renault** (www.eurodrive.renault.com) and then, at the end of your trip, 'sell' it back to them. In reality, you pay only for the number of days you use the vehicle. Eligibility is restricted to people who are not residents of the EU (citizens of EU countries are eligible if they live outside the EU).

Prices include unlimited kilometres, 24-hour towing and breakdown service, and comprehensive insurance with – incredibly – no excess (deductible), so returning a damaged car is totally hassle-free. Extending your contract is possible (using a credit card), but you'll end up paying about double the prepaid per-day rate.

Cars can be picked up in cities all over France and returned to any other purchase-repurchase centre, including other European capitals.

Road Rules

Enforcement of road safety rules has been stepped up in France over the last few years. French law requires that all passengers, including those in the back seat, wear seat belts, and children who weigh less than 18kg must travel in backward-facing child seats. A passenger car is permitted to carry a maximum of five people. North American drivers should remember that turning right on a red light is illegal in France.

You will be fined for going 10km over the speed limit. Unless otherwise posted, a limit of 50km/h applies in *all* areas designated as built-up, no matter how rural they may appear. Speed limits outside built-up areas:

- 90km/h (80km/h if it's raining) on undivided N and D highways
- 110km/h (100km/h if it's raining) on dual carriageways (divided highways) or short sections of highway with a divider strip
- 130km/h (110km/h in the rain, 60km/h in icy conditions) on autoroutes

Under the *priorité à droite* rule, any car entering an intersection (including a T-junction) from a road on your right has the right-of-way, unless the intersection is marked 'vous n'avez pas la priorité' (you do not have right of way) or 'cédez le passage' (give way). *Priorité à droite* is also suspended on priority roads, which are marked by an up-ended yellow square with a black square in the middle.

It is illegal to drive with a blood-alcohol concentration over 0.05% (0.5g per litre of blood) – the equivalent of two glasses of wine for a 75kg adult. There are periodic random breathalyser tests. Mobile phones may only be used when accompanied by a hands-free kit or speakerphone.

Motoring in Europe, published in the UK by the RAC, gives an excellent summary of road regulations in each European country, including parking rules. British drivers committing driving offences in France can receive on-the-spot fines and get penalty points added to their driving licence at home.

Riders of any type of two-wheeled vehicle with a motor (except motor-assisted bicycles) must wear a helmet. No special licence is required to ride a motorbike whose engine is smaller than 50cc, which is why you often find places renting scooters rated at 49.9cc.

HITCHING

Hitching is never entirely safe in any country in the world, and we don't recommend it. Travellers who decide to hitch should understand that they are taking a small but potentially serious risk. Remember that it's safer to travel in pairs and be sure to inform someone of where you are planning to go. Hitching is not really part of French culture, and is not recommended for women in France, even in pairs.

Hitching from city centres is pretty much hopeless: take public transport to the outskirts. It is illegal to hitch on autoroutes, but you can stand near the entrance ramps as long as you don't block traffic. Thumbing around the Côte d'Azur is nearly impossible. Remote rural areas are often a good bet, but once you get off the *routes nationales* there are few vehicles. If your itinerary includes a ferry crossing, it's worth trying to score a ride before the ferry goes, since vehicle tickets sometimes include a number of passengers free of charge. At dusk, give up and think about finding somewhere to stay.

Ride Share Organisations

A number of organisations around France put people looking for rides in touch with drivers going to the same destination. Usually you pay a per-kilometre fee to the driver, as well as a flat administration fee.

Allostop (☎ 0 825 803 666; www.allostop.net in French) The best known; based in Paris.

Autostop Bretagne (☎ 02 99 67 34 67; http://allostoprennes.com in French) Rennes.

La Clef de Contact (☎ 03 80 66 31 31) Dijon.

Stop Plus (☎ 04 76 43 14 14) Grenoble.

Voyage au Fil (☎ 02 51 72 94 60) Nantes.

LOCAL TRANSPORT

France's cities and larger towns generally have excellent public-transport systems. Remember that French cities are small and compact – most can be visited entirely on foot.

There are underground subway systems (metros) in Paris, Lyon, Marseille, Lille and Toulouse.

Ultramodern tramways exist in Paris, Grenoble, Nantes, Lille, Strasbourg, Lyon, Nancy and Bordeaux, and are being built in cities across the country. Bus systems tend to be less reliable.

Details on routes, fares, tourist passes etc, are available at tourist offices and from local bus companies. We list information in the individual destination sections.

See p896 and p922 for information on bicycles and bike hire.

Taxi

All large and medium-sized train stations – and many small ones – have a taxi stand out the front. For details on the tariffs and regulations applicable in major cities, see p176.

In small cities and towns, where taxi drivers are unlikely to find another fare anywhere near where they let you off, there are four kinds of per-kilometre tariffs, set locally by the *préfecture*. Rates are more expensive at night and on Sundays and holidays.

Travel under 20km/h (or thereabouts) is calculated by time (about €15 an hour) rather than distance. There may be a surcharge of €1 to get picked up at a train station or airport, a fee of €0.90 per bag and a charge of €2.45 for a fourth passenger.

TOURS

Local tourist offices, museums, wineries, chateaux and private minibus companies all over France offer a wide variety of guided tours that you arrange locally. Some tourist offices also offer tours to destinations outside of town. Details appear under Tours in city listings and at the beginning of regional chapters. Details on guided hikes, cycling tours and other organised outdoor activities appear under Activities. Some places are difficult to visit unless you have wheels, or are much more interesting with expert commentary.

An extensive list of UK-based companies offering trips to France is available from the website of the **Association of British Tour Operators to France** (www.holidayfrance.org.uk).

There is a surfeit of companies that run activities-based tours, usually including accommodation, meals and transport.

ATG Oxford (www.atg-oxford.co.uk) Cycling and rambling holidays for independent travellers.

Butterfield & Robinson (www.butterfield.com) Canada-based company with upmarket walking and biking holidays.

CBT Tours (www.biketrip.net) Cycling tours from the USA.

Cycling for Softies (www.cycling-for-softies.co.uk) Unescorted cycling trips through rural France.

French Wine Explorers (www.wine-tours-france.com) Small group wine tours of Beaujolais, Bordeaux, Burgundy and the Rhône Valley.

Old Ipswich Tours (www.ipswichtours.com) Specialising in wine tours (USA based).

Ramblers Holidays (www.ramblersholidays.co.uk) Tours based on outdoor activities like walking, trekking and cross-country skiing.

TRAIN

France's superb rail network reaches almost every part of the country. Many towns and villages not on the SNCF train and bus network are served by bus lines linking *départements*.

France's most important train lines radiate from Paris like the spokes of a wheel, making train travel between provincial towns situated on different spokes infrequent and rather slow. In some cases you have to transit through Paris. For details, see the map on p918.

The pride and joy of SNCF – and the French – generally is the world-renowned TGV (*Train à Grande Vitesse*, www.tgv.com. Pronounced 'teh-zheh-veh', it reaches speeds of over 300km/h (186mph) and was developed in the 1960s and 70s. The first service was in 1981. The French are really exceedingly proud of the TGV.

TGV Atlantique Sud-Ouest & TGV Atlantique Ouest
These link Paris' Gare Montparnasse with western and southwestern France, including Brittany (Rennes, Quimper, Brest), Nantes, Tours, Poitiers, La Rochelle, Bordeaux, Biarritz and Toulouse.

TGV Nord, Thalys & Eurostar
These link Paris' Gare du Nord with Arras, Lille, Calais, Brussels, Amsterdam, Cologne and, via the Channel Tunnel, Ashford and London Waterloo.

TGV Sud-Est & TGV Midi-Méditerranée
These link Paris' Gare de Lyon with the southeast, including Dijon, Lyon, Geneva, the Alps, Avignon, Marseille, Nice and Montpellier.

A line leading northeast to Strasbourg and Germany (called TGV Est) is planned for 2007. TGV lines are now connected to each other, making it possible to go directly from, say, Lyon to Nantes or Bordeaux to Lille, without switching trains in Paris. Stops on the link-up, which runs east and south of Paris, include Roissy Charles de Gaulle airport, Massy and Disneyland Paris.

A train that is not a TGV is often referred to as a *corail*, a *classique* or a TER *(train express régional)*. For details on Thalys and the Eurostar, see p919.

Classes & Sleeping Cars

Most French trains have both 1st- and 2nd-class sections. On overnight trains the 2nd-class couchette compartments have six berths, while those in 1st class have four. In addition to bed linen, you are issued a bottle of water and a little 'welcome kit'. Some couchette compartments are reserved for

---

---

women travelling alone or with children. On some overnight trains a 2nd-class *siège inclinable* (reclining seat) costs €1.50.

Many overnight trains have *voitures-lits* (sleeping cars), which provide private facilities, a continental breakfast and greater security. Second class holds up to three people. First-class compartments are somewhat larger and accommodate one or two people.

Costs

Significant discounts are available (see p928) on regular train fares. Full-price fares can be very expensive (eg TGV Paris–Lyon €73 one-way). Full-fare return (round-trip) passage costs twice as much as one-way. Travel in 1st class is 50% more expensive than 2nd class. Train tickets (including the TGV) are more expensive during the peak periods (commuting hours, weekends, holiday periods).

Fantastic deals are available exclusively on the website www.sncf.com: last-minute offers at up to 50% off, published on the site every Tuesday; and *Prem's* early bird deals (eg Paris–Nice €25) available only through online bookings made at least three weeks in advance.

Tickets & Reservations

You can buy a ticket with a credit card via the SNCF's website and either have it sent to you by post or collect it from any SNCF

TRANSPORT

SNCF DISCOUNT FARES

Discounted fares and passes are available at all SNCF stations. See earlier for discount European bus (p917) and train (p919) passes.

Children aged under four travel free of charge; those aged four to 11 travel for half-price. Discounted fares (25% reduction) automatically apply to: travellers aged 12 to 25, seniors aged over 60, one to four adults travelling with a child aged four to 11, two people taking a return journey together or anyone taking a return journey of at least 200km and spending a Saturday night away. Purchasing tickets well in advance will also usually get you a discounted fare. The **Découverte J30**, which must be purchased 30 to 60 days before the date of travel, offers savings of 45% to 55%. The **Découverte J8**, which you must buy eight days ahead, gets you 20% to 30% off.

Purchasing a one-year travel pass can yield a 50% discount (25% if the cheapest seats are sold): a **Carte 12-25** (€48) aimed at travellers aged 12 to 25; the **Carte Enfant Plus** (€63) for one to four adults travelling with a child aged four to 11; and a **Carte Sénior** (€49) for those aged over 60.

The **France Railpass** entitles nonresidents of France to unlimited travel on SNCF trains for four days over a one-month period. In 2nd class it costs US$218; each additional day of travel costs US$28. The **France Youthpass** entitles holders to four days of travel over a one-month period. In 2nd class it costs US$164, plus US$21 for each extra day. These two passes can be purchased from travel agencies or on www.eurorail.com.

---

ticket office. Nearly every SNCF station in the country has at least one *billeterie automatique* (automatic ticket machine) that accepts credit cards. Large stations often have separate ticket windows for *international, grandes lignes* (long-haul) and *banlieue* (suburban) lines, and *achat à l'avance* (advance purchase) and *départ du jour* (same-day departure).

Before boarding the train you must validate your ticket by time-stamping it in a *composteur*, one of those orange posts located at the start of the platform. If you forget, find a conductor on the train so they can punch it for you (otherwise you're likely to be fined). Tickets *can* be purchased on board the train (straight away from the conductor) with cash but there a surcharge is incurred.

Reserving in advance (€1.50) is optional unless: you're travelling by TGV, Eurostar or Thalys; you want a couchette (sleeping berth; €14) or a bed; or you'll be travelling during peak holiday periods when trains may be full. Reservations can be made by telephone or via the SNCF's website. Reservations can usually be changed before departure time by telephone.

Long-distance trains sometimes split at a station, that is, each half of the train leaves for a different destination. Verify the destination as you board the car, or you could wind up very, very far from where you want to go.

Health

CONTENTS

Travel health depends on your predeparture preparations, your daily health care while travelling and how you handle medical problems that do develop. France is a healthy place. Your main risks are likely to be sunburn, foot blisters, insect bites and mild stomach problems from eating and drinking too much.

BEFORE YOU GO

Prevention is the key to staying healthy. Planning before departure, particularly for pre-existing illnesses, will save trouble later. See your dentist before a long trip, carry a spare pair of contact lenses and glasses, and take your optical prescription. Bring medications in their original, clearly labelled, containers. A signed and dated letter from your physician describing your medical conditions and medications, including generic names, is also helpful. If carrying syringes or needles, be sure to have a physician's letter documenting their medical necessity.

Insurance

Citizens of the EU, Switzerland, Iceland, Norway or Liechtenstein, are coverd by the European Health Insurance Card for emergency health care or accidents while in France. It does not cover nonemergencies or emergency repatriation. This card is being phased in from mid-2004 to the end of 2005. Old documentation (such as the E111) will be available in the interim. Each family member will need a separate card. In the UK, get application forms from post offices or download them from the Department of Health website (www.dh.gov.uk).

Citizens from other countries will need to check if there is a reciprocal arrangement for free medical care between their country and the country visited. If you need health insurance, strongly consider a policy covering the worst possible scenario, such as an accident requiring an emergency flight home. Find out in advance if your insurance plan will make payments directly to providers or reimburse you later for overseas health expenditures.

Recommended Vaccinations

No vaccinations are required to travel to France. However, the WHO recommends that all travellers should be covered for diphtheria, tetanus, measles, mumps, rubella and polio, regardless of their destination.

IN TRANSIT

Deep Vein Thrombosis (DVT)

Blood clots may form in the legs during plane flights, chiefly because of prolonged immobility. The chief symptom of DVT is swelling or pain of the foot, ankle or calf, usually but not always on just one side. When a blood clot travels to the lungs, it may cause chest pain and breathing difficulties. Travellers with any of these symptoms should immediately seek medical attention.

To prevent the development of DVT on long flights walk about the cabin, contract the leg muscles while sitting, drink plenty of fluids and avoid alcohol and tobacco.

Jet Lag

To avoid jet lag (common when crossing more than five time zones) drink plenty of nonalchoholic fluids and eat light meals. Upon arrival, get exposure to natural sunlight and readjust your schedule (for meals, sleep and so on) as soon as possible.

IN FRANCE

Availability & Cost of Health Care

Excellent health care is readily available and for minor illnesses pharmacists can give valuable advice and sell medications. They can also advise on more specialised help and point you in the right direction. Dental care is usually good, however, it is sensible to have a dental check-up before a long trip.

Diarrhoea

If you develop diarrhoea, drink plenty of fluids, preferably an oral rehydration solution (eg Dioralyte). If diarrhoea is bloody, persists for more than 72 hours or is accompanied by fever, shaking, chills or severe abdominal pain seek immediate medical attention.

Environmental Hazards

ALTITUDE SICKNESS

Lack of oxygen at high altitudes (over 2500m) affects most people to some extent. Symptoms of Acute Mountain Sickness (AMS) usually develop in the first 24 hours at altitude but may be delayed up to three weeks. Mild symptoms are headache, lethargy, dizziness, difficulty sleeping and loss of appetite. Severe symptoms are breathlessness, a dry, irritative cough (followed by the production of pink, frothy sputum), severe headache, lack of coordination and balance, confusion, vomiting, irrational behaviour, drowsiness and unconsciousness. There's no rule as to what is too high: AMS can be fatal at 3000m, but 3500m to 4500m is the usual range.

Treat mild symptoms by resting at the same altitude until recovered, usually a day or two. Paracetamol or aspirin can be taken for headaches. If symptoms persist or grow worse, however, *immediate descent is necessary;* even 500m can help. Drug treatments should never be used to avoid descent or to enable further ascent. Diamox (acetazolamide) reduces the headache of AMS and helps the body acclimatise to the lack of oxygen. It is only available on prescription.

To prevent acute mountain sickness:

- Ascend slowly – have frequent rest days, spending two to three nights at each rise of 1000m. Acclimatisation takes place gradually.
- Sleep at a lower altitude than the greatest height reached during the day if possible. Also, once above 3000m, care should be taken not to increase the sleeping altitude by more than 300m per day.
- Drink extra fluids. Monitor hydration by ensuring that urine is clear and plentiful.
- Eat light, high-carbohydrate meals for more energy.
- Avoid alcohol, sedatives and tobacco.

HEAT EXHAUSTION

Heat exhaustion follows excessive fluid loss with inadequate replacement of fluids and salt. Symptoms include headache, dizziness and tiredness. Dehydration is already happening by the time you feel thirsty – aim to drink enough water to produce pale, diluted urine. To treat heat exhaustion, replace lost fluids by drinking water and/or fruit juice, and cool the body with cold water and fans.

HYPOTHERMIA

Even on a hot day in the mountains weather can change rapidly; carry waterproof garments and warm layers, and inform others of your route. Acute hypothermia follows a sudden drop of temperature over a short time. Chronic hypothermia is caused by a gradual loss of temperature over hours. Hypothermia starts with shivering, loss of judgment and clumsiness. Unless rewarming occurs, the sufferer deteriorates into apathy, confusion and coma. Prevent further heat loss by seeking shelter, warm dry clothing, hot sweet drinks and shared bodily warmth.

Sexual Health

Emergency contraception is available with a doctor's prescription in France. Condoms are readily available; when buying, look for a European CE mark, which means they've been rigorously tested. Keep them in a cool dry place or they may crack and perish.

Travelling with Children

All travellers with children should know how to treat minor ailments and when to seek medical advice. Be sure children are up to date with routine vaccinations, and discuss possible travel vaccines well before departure as some vaccines are not suitable for children under a year.

If your child has vomiting or diarrhoea, lost fluids and salts must be replaced. It may be helpful to take rehydration powders for reconstituting with boiled water.

Women's Health

Emotional stress, exhaustion and travelling across time zones can all contribute to an upset in the menstrual pattern. Some antibiotics, diarrhoea and vomiting can interfere with the effectiveness of oral contraceptives and lead to the risk of pregnancy – remember to take condoms just in case. Time zones, gastrointestinal upsets and antibiotics do not affect injectable contraception.

Travelling during pregnancy is usually possible but always consult your doctor before planning your trip. The most risky times for travel are during the first 12 weeks of pregnancy and after 30 weeks.

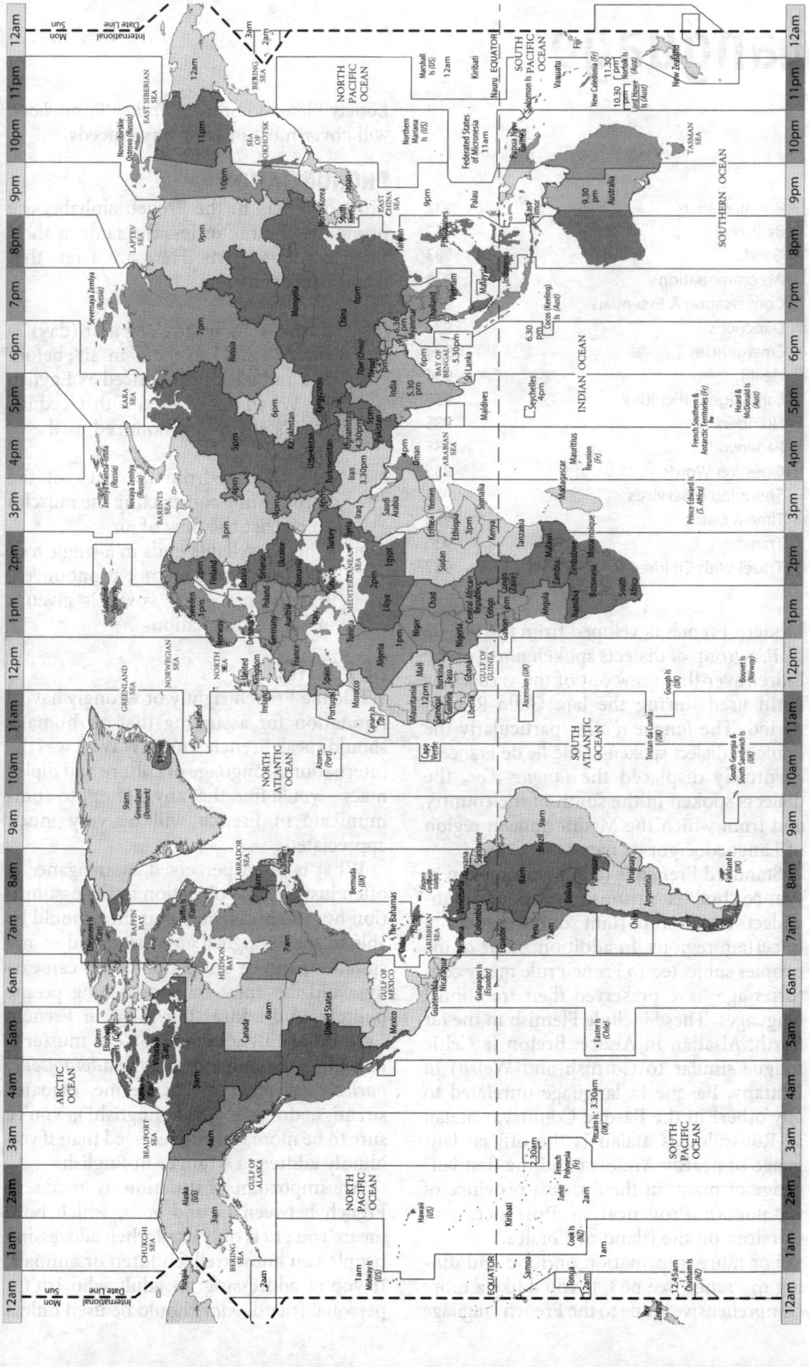
12am
1am
2am
3am
4am
5am
6am
7am
8am
9am
10am
11am
12pm
1pm
2pm
3pm
4pm
5pm
6pm
7pm
8pm
9pm
10pm
11pm
12am
International Date Line
Sun
Mon
ARCTIC OCEAN
CHUKCHI SEA
BEAUFORT SEA
BERING SEA
GULF OF ALASKA
NORTH PACIFIC OCEAN
SOUTH PACIFIC OCEAN
HUDSON BAY
BAFFIN BAY
LABRADOR SEA
GULF OF MEXICO
CARIBBEAN SEA
NORTH ATLANTIC OCEAN
SOUTH ATLANTIC OCEAN
GREENLAND SEA
NORWEGIAN SEA
NORTH SEA
BARENTS SEA
KARA SEA
LAPTEV SEA
EAST SIBERIAN SEA
SEA OF OKHOTSK
EAST CHINA SEA
MEDITERRANEAN SEA
ARABIAN SEA
BAY OF BENGAL
GULF OF GUINEA
INDIAN OCEAN
SOUTHERN OCEAN
TASMAN SEA
EQUATOR
Alaska (US)
Canada
United States
Mexico
Greenland (Denmark)
Iceland
Russia
China
Mongolia
India
Australia
New Zealand
Brazil
Argentina
Chile
Peru
Bolivia
Hawaii (US)
Midway Is (US)
Cook Is (NZ)
Samoa
Tonga
Chatham Is (NZ)
Kiribati
French Polynesia (Fr)
Pitcairn Is
Easter Is (Chile)
Galapagos Is (Ecuador)
Bermuda (UK)
The Bahamas
Azores (Port)
Cape Verde
Canary Is (Sp)
Falkland Is
Tristan da Cunha (UK)
Gough Is (UK)
Bouvet Is (Norway)
South Georgia & South Sandwich Is (UK)
Ascension (UK)
Prince Edward Is (S. Africa)
French Southern & Antarctic Territories (Fr)
Heard & McDonald Is (Aust)
Madagascar
Mauritius
Reunion (Fr)
Seychelles 4pm
Maldives
Sri Lanka 5.30pm
Cocos (Keeling) Is (Aust) 6.30 pm
India 5.30 pm
Nepal 5.45 pm
Myanmar 6.30 pm
Afghanistan 4.30pm
Iran 3.30pm
Australia 9.30 pm
New Caledonia (Fr)
Norfolk Is (Aust) 11.30 pm
Lord Howe Is (Aust) 10.30 pm
Vanuatu
Fiji
Solomon Is
Papua New Guinea
Nauru
Marshall Is (US) 12am
Federated States of Micronesia 11am
Northern Mariana Is (US)
Palau
Japan
North Korea
South Korea
Taiwan
Philippines
Vietnam
Thailand
Malaysia
Indonesia
East Timor
Novosibirskie Ostrovo (Russia)
Severnaya Zemlya (Russia)
Zemlya Frantsa-Iosifa (Russia)
Novaya Zemlya (Russia)
Svalbard (Norway)
Queen Elizabeth Is (Can)
Ellesmere Is (Can)
Baffin Is (Can)
Victoria Is (Can)
Banks Is (Can)
Guyana
Suriname
Venezuela
Colombia
Ecuador
Panama
Paraguay
Uruguay
Cuba
Haiti
Guatemala
Nicaragua
Portugal
Spain
France
Ireland
United Kingdom
Norway
Sweden
Finland
Denmark
Germany
Poland
Austria
Italy
Latvia
Belarus
Ukraine
Romania
Greece
Turkey
Syria
Iraq
Saudi Arabia
Yemen
Oman
Egypt
Libya
Tunisia
Algeria
Morocco
Mauritania
Mali
Senegal
Guinea
Liberia
Burkina Faso
Ghana
Niger
Nigeria
Chad
Sudan
Eritrea
Ethiopia
Somalia
Kenya
Tanzania
Central African Republic
Congo
Congo (Zaïre)
Gabon
Angola
Namibia
Botswana
Zambia
Zimbabwe
Malawi
Mozambique
South Africa
Kazakhstan
Uzbekistan
Turkmenistan
Kyrgyzstan
Pakistan
Tibet (China)

Language

CONTENTS

Modern French developed from the *langue d'oïl*, a group of dialects spoken north of the Loire River that grew out of the vernacular Latin used during the late Gallo-Roman period. The *langue d'oïl* – particularly the Francien dialect spoken in the Île de France – eventually displaced the *langue d'oc*, the dialects spoken in the south of the country and from which the Mediterranean region of Languedoc got its name.

Standard French is taught and spoken in France, but its various accents and sub-dialects are an important source of identity in certain regions. In addition, some of the peoples subjected to French rule many centuries ago have preserved their traditional languages. These include Flemish in the far north; Alsatian in Alsace; Breton (a Celtic tongue similar to Cornish and Welsh) in Brittany; Basque (a language unrelated to any other) in the Basque Country; Catalan in Roussillon (Catalan is the official language of nearby Andorra and the first language of many in the Spanish province of Catalonia); Provençal in Provence; and Corsican on the island of Corsica.

For more information on food and dining in France, see p63. If you'd like a more comprehensive guide to the French language Lonely Planet's compact *French Phrasebook* will cover most of your travel needs.

PRONUNCIATION

Most of letters in the French alphabet are pronounced more or less the same as their English counterparts. Here are a few that may cause confusion:

j	as the 's' in 'leisure', eg *jour* (day)
c	before **e** and **i**, as the 's' in 'sit'; before **a**, **o** and **u** it's pronounced as English 'k'. When undescored with a 'cedilla' (**ç**) it's always pronounced as the 's' in 'sit'.
r	pronounced from the back of the throat while constricting the muscles to restrict the flow of air
n, m	where a syllable ends in a single **n** or **m**, these letters are not pronounced, but the preceding vowel is given a nasal pronunciation

BE POLITE!

While the French rightly or wrongly have a reputation for assuming that all humans should speak French – until WWI it was the international language of culture and diplomacy – you'll find that any attempt to communicate in French will be very much appreciated.

What is often perceived as arrogance is often just a subtle objection to the assumption by many travellers that they should be able to speak English anywhere, and in any situation, and be understood. You can easily avoid the angst by approaching people politely, and addressing them in French. Even if the only sentence you can muster is *Pardon, madame/monsieur/mademoiselle, parlez-vous anglais?* (Excuse me, madam/sir/miss, do you speak English?), you're sure to be more warmly received than if you blindly address a stranger in English.

An important distinction is made in French between *tu* and *vous*, which both mean 'you'; *tu* is only used when addressing people you know well, children or animals. If you're addressing an adult who isn't a personal friend, *vous* should be used unless the person invites you to use *tu*. In general, younger people insist less on this distinction between polite and informal, and you will find that in many cases they use *tu* from the beginning of an acquaintance.

GENDER

All nouns in French are either masculine or feminine and adjectives reflect the gender of the noun they modify. The feminine form of many nouns and adjectives is indicated by a silent **e** added to the masculine form, as in *ami* and *amie* (the masculine and feminine for 'friend').

In the following phrases both masculine and feminine forms have been indicated where necessary. The masculine form comes first and is separated from the feminine by a slash. The gender of a noun is often indicated by a preceding article: 'the/a/some', l*e/un/du* (m), *la/une/de la* (f); or one of the possessive adjectives, 'my/your/his/her', *mon/ton/son* (m), *ma/ta/sa* (f). With French, unlike English, the possessive adjective agrees in number and gender with the thing in question: 'his/her mother', *sa mère*.

ACCOMMODATION

I'm looking for a ...	Je cherche ...	zher shersh ...
campground	un camping	un kom·peeng
guesthouse	une pension (de famille)	ewn pon·syon (der fa·mee·ler)
hotel	un hôtel	un o·tel
youth hostel	une auberge de jeunesse	ewn o·berzh der zher·nes

Where is a cheap hotel?
Où est-ce qu'on peut trouver un hôtel pas cher?
oo es·kon per troo·vay un o·tel pa shair

What is the address?
Quelle est l'adresse?
kel e la·dres

Could you write the address, please?
Est-ce que vous pourriez écrire l'adresse, s'il vous plaît?
e·sker voo poo·ryay ay·kreer la·dres seel voo play

Do you have any rooms available?
Est-ce que vous avez des chambres libres?
e·sker voo·za·vay day shom·brer lee·brer

I'd like (a) ...	Je voudrais ...	zher voo·dray ...
single room	une chambre à un lit	ewn shom·brer a un lee
double-bed	une chambre	ewn shom·brer
room	avec un grand lit	a·vek un gron lee
twin room with two beds	une chambre avec des lits jumeaux	ewn shom·brer a·vek day lee zhew·mo
room with a bathroom	une chambre avec une salle de bains	ewn shom·brer a·vek ewn sal der bun
to share a dorm	coucher dans un dortoir	koo·sher don zun dor·twa

MAKING A RESERVATION
(for phone or written requests)

To ...	A l'attention de ...
From ...	De la part de ...
Date	Date
I'd like to book ...	Je voudrais réserver ... (see the list under 'Accommodation' for bed and room options)
in the name of ...	au nom de ...
from ... (date) to ...	du ... au ...
credit card number	carte de crédit numéro
expiry date	date d'expiration
Please confirm availability and price.	Veuillez confirmer la disponibilité et le prix.

How much is it ...?	Quel est le prix ...?	kel e ler pree ...
per night	par nuit	par nwee
per person	par personne	par per·son

May I see it?
Est-ce que je peux voir la chambre?
es·ker zher per vwa la shom·brer

Where is the bathroom?
Où est la salle de bains? oo e la sal der bun

Where is the toilet?
Où sont les toilettes? oo·son lay twa·let

I'm leaving today.
Je pars aujourd'hui. zher par o·zhoor·dwee

We're leaving today.
Nous partons aujourd'hui.
noo par·ton o·zhoor·dwee

CONVERSATION & ESSENTIALS

Hello.	Bonjour.	bon·zhoor
Goodbye.	Au revoir.	o·rer·vwa
Yes.	Oui.	wee

SIGNS

Entrée	Entrance
Sortie	Exit
Renseignements	Information
Ouvert	Open
Fermé	Closed
Interdit	Prohibited
Chambres Libres	Rooms Available
Complet	Full/No Vacancies
(Commissariat de)	Police Station
Police	
Toilettes/WC	Toilets
Hommes	Men
Femmes	Women

No.	*Non.*	no
Please.	*S'il vous plaît.*	seel voo play
Thank you.	*Merci.*	mair-see
You're welcome.	*Je vous en prie.*	zher voo-zon pree
	De rien. (inf)	der ree-en
Excuse me.	*Excuse-moi.*	ek-skew-zay-mwa
Sorry. (forgive me)	*Pardon.*	par-don

What's your name?

Comment vous appelez-vous? (pol)	ko-mon voo-za-pay-lay voo
Comment tu t'appelles? (inf)	ko-mon tew ta-pel

My name is ...

Je m'appelle ...	zher ma-pel ...

Where are you from?

De quel pays êtes-vous?	der kel pay-ee et-voo
De quel pays es-tu? (inf)	der kel pay-ee e-tew

I'm from ...

Je viens de ...	zher vyen der ...

I like ...

J'aime ...	zhem ...

I don't like ...

Je n'aime pas ...	zher nem pa ...

Just a minute.

Une minute.	ewn mee-newt

DIRECTIONS

Where is ...?

Où est ...?	oo e ...

Go straight ahead.

Continuez tout droit.	kon-teen-way too drwa

Turn left.

Tournez à gauche.	toor-nay a gosh

Turn right.

Tournez à droite.	toor-nay a drwat

at the corner

au coin	o kwun

at the traffic lights

aux feux	o fer

behind	*derrière*	dair-ryair
in front of	*devant*	der-von
far (from)	*loin (de)*	lwun (der)
near (to)	*près (de)*	pray (der)
opposite	*en face de*	on fas der
beach	*la plage*	la plazh
bridge	*le pont*	ler pon
castle	*le château*	ler sha-to
cathedral	*la cathédrale*	la ka-tay-dral
church	*l'église*	lay-gleez
island	*l'île*	leel
lake	*le lac*	ler lak
main square	*la place centrale*	la plas son-tral
museum	*le musée*	ler mew-zay
old city (town)	*la vieille ville*	la vyay veel
palace	*le palais*	ler pa-lay
quay	*le quai*	ler kay
riverbank	*la rive*	la reev
ruins	*les ruines*	lay rween
sea	*la mer*	la mair
square	*la place*	la plas
tourist office	*l'office de tourisme*	lo-fees der too-rees-mer
tower	*la tour*	la toor

EMERGENCIES

Help!

Au secours!	o skoor

There's been an accident!

Il y a eu un accident!	eel ya ew un ak-see-don

I'm lost.

Je me suis égaré/e. (m/f)	zhe me swee-zay-ga-ray

Leave me alone!

Fichez-moi la paix!	fee-shay-mwa la pay

Call ...!

Appelez ...!		a-play ...
a doctor	*un médecin*	un mayd-sun
the police	*la police*	la po-lees

HEALTH

I'm ill.	*Je suis malade.*	zher swee ma-lad
It hurts here.	*J'ai une douleur ici.*	zhay ewn doo-ler ee-see
I'm ...	*Je suis ...*	zher swee ...
asthmatic	*asthmatique*	(z)as-ma-teek
diabetic	*diabétique*	dee-a-bay-teek
epileptic	*épileptique*	(z)ay-pee-lep-teek
I'm allergic to ...	*Je suis allergique ...*	zher swee za-lair-zheek ...
antibiotics	*aux antibiotiques*	o zon-tee-byo-teek

bees	*aux abeilles*	o za·bay·yer
nuts	*aux noix*	o nwa
peanuts	*aux cacahuètes*	o ka·ka·wet
penicillin	*à la pénicilline*	a la pay·nee·see·leen

antiseptic	*l'antiseptique*	lon·tee·sep·teek
aspirin	*l'aspirine*	las·pee·reen
condoms	*des préservatifs*	day pray·zair·va·teef
contraceptive	*le contraceptif*	ler kon·tra·sep·teef
diarrhoea	*la diarrhée*	la dya·ray
medicine	*le médicament*	ler may·dee·ka·mon
nausea	*la nausée*	la no·zay
sunblock cream	*la crème solaire*	la krem so·lair
tampons	*des tampons hygiéniques*	day tom·pon ee·zhen·eek

LANGUAGE DIFFICULTIES

Do you speak English?
Parlez-vous anglais? — par·lay·voo ong·lay
Does anyone here speak English?
Y a-t-il quelqu'un qui parle anglais? — ya·teel kel·kung kee par long·glay
How do you say ... in French?
Comment est-ce qu'on dit ... en français? — ko·mon es·kon dee ... on fron·say
What does ... mean?
Que veut dire ...? — ker ver deer ...
I understand.
Je comprends. — zher kom·pron
I don't understand.
Je ne comprends pas. — zher ner kom·pron pa
Could you write it down, please?
Est-ce que vous pourriez l'écrire, s'il vous plaît? — es·ker voo poo·ryay lay·kreer seel voo play
Can you show me (on the map)?
Pouvez-vous m'indiquer (sur la carte)? — poo·vay·voo mun·dee·kay (sewr la kart)

NUMBERS

0	*zero*	zay·ro
1	*un*	un
2	*deux*	der
3	*trois*	trwa
4	*quatre*	ka·trer
5	*cinq*	sungk
6	*six*	sees
7	*sept*	set
8	*huit*	weet
9	*neuf*	nerf
10	*dix*	dees
11	*onze*	onz
12	*douze*	dooz
13	*treize*	trez
14	*quatorze*	ka·torz

15	*quinze*	kunz
16	*seize*	sez
17	*dix-sept*	dee·set
18	*dix-huit*	dee·zweet
19	*dix-neuf*	deez·nerf
20	*vingt*	vung
21	*vingt et un*	vung tay un
22	*vingt-deux*	vung·der
30	*trente*	tront
40	*quarante*	ka·ront
50	*cinquante*	sung·kont
60	*soixante*	swa·sont
70	*soixante-dix*	swa·son·dees
80	*quatre-vingts*	ka·trer·vung
90	*quatre-vingt-dix*	ka·trer·vung·dees
100	*cent*	son
1000	*mille*	meel

PAPERWORK

name	*nom*	nom
nationality	*nationalité*	na·syo·na·lee·tay
date/place	*date/place*	dat/plas
of birth	*de naissance*	der nay·sons
sex/gender	*sexe*	seks
passport	*passeport*	pas·por
visa	*visa*	vee·za

QUESTION WORDS

Who?	*Qui?*	kee
What?	*Quoi?*	kwa
What is it?	*Qu'est-ce que c'est?*	kes·ker say
When?	*Quand?*	kon
Where?	*Où?*	oo
Which?	*Quel/Quelle?*	kel
Why?	*Pourquoi?*	poor·kwa
How?	*Comment?*	ko·mon

SHOPPING & SERVICES

I'd like to buy ...
Je voudrais acheter ... — zher voo·dray ash·tay ...
How much is it?
C'est combien? — say kom·byun
I don't like it.
Cela ne me plaît pas. — ser·la ner mer play pa
May I look at it?
Est-ce que je peux le voir? — es·ker zher per ler vwar
I'm just looking.
Je regarde. — zher rer·gard
It's cheap.
Ce n'est pas cher. — ser nay pa shair
It's too expensive.
C'est trop cher. — say tro shair
I'll take it.
Je le prends. — zher ler pron

Can I pay by ...?	*Est-ce que je peux*	es·ker zher per
	payer avec ...?	pay·yay a·vek ...
credit card	*ma carte de*	ma kart der
	crédit	kray·dee
travellers	*des chèques*	day shek
cheques	*de voyage*	der vwa·yazh
more	*plus*	plew
less	*moins*	mwa
smaller	*plus petit*	plew per·tee
bigger	*plus grand*	plew gron
I'm looking	*Je cherche ...*	zhe shersh ...
for ...		
a bank	*une banque*	ewn bonk
the ... embassy	*l'ambassade*	lam·ba·sahd
	de ...	der ...
the hospital	*l'hôpital*	lo·pee·tal
the market	*le marché*	ler mar·shay
the police	*la police*	la po·lees
the post office	*le bureau de*	ler bew·ro der
	poste	post
a public phone	*une cabine*	ewn ka·been
	téléphonique	tay·lay·fo·neek
a public toilet	*les toilettes*	lay twa·let
the telephone	*la centrale*	la san·tral
centre	*téléphonique*	tay·lay·fo·neek

TIME & DATES

What time is it?	*Quelle heure est-il?*	kel er e til
It's (8) o'clock.	*Il est (huit) heures.*	il e (weet) er
It's half past ...	*Il est (...) heures et*	il e (...) er e
	demie.	day·mee
in the morning	*du matin*	dew ma·tun
in the afternoon	*de l'après-midi*	der la·pray·mee·dee
in the evening	*du soir*	dew swar
today	*aujourd'hui*	o·zhoor·dwee
tomorrow	*demain*	der·mun
yesterday	*hier*	yair
Monday	*lundi*	lun·dee
Tuesday	*mardi*	mar·dee
Wednesday	*mercredi*	mair·krer·dee
Thursday	*jeudi*	zher·dee
Friday	*vendredi*	von·drer·dee
Saturday	*samedi*	sam·dee
Sunday	*dimanche*	dee·monsh
January	*janvier*	zhon·vyay
February	*février*	fayv·ryay
March	*mars*	mars
April	*avril*	a·vreel
May	*mai*	may
June	*juin*	zhwun
July	*juillet*	zhwee·yay

August	*août*	oot
September	*septembre*	sep·tom·brer
October	*octobre*	ok·to·brer
November	*novembre*	no·vom·brer
December	*décembre*	day·som·brer

TRANSPORT
Public Transport

What time does	*À quelle heure*	a kel er
... leave/arrive?	*part/arrive ...?*	par/a·reev ...
boat	*le bateau*	ler ba·to
bus	*le bus*	ler bews
plane	*l'avion*	la·vyon
train	*le train*	ler trun
I'd like a ...	*Je voudrais*	zher voo·dray
ticket.	*un billet ...*	un bee·yay ...
one-way	*simple*	sum·pler
return	*aller et retour*	a·lay ay rer·toor
1st class	*de première classe*	der prem·yair klas
2nd class	*de deuxième classe*	der der·zyem klas

I want to go to ...
Je voudrais aller à ...   zher voo·dray a·lay a ...
The train has been delayed.
Le train est en retard.   ler trun et on rer·tar
The train has been cancelled.
Le train a été annulé.   ler trun a ay·tay a·new·lay

the first	*le premier (m)*	ler prer·myay
	la première (f)	la prer·myair
the last	*le dernier (m)*	ler dair·nyay
	la dernière (f)	la dair·nyair
platform	*le numéro*	ler new·may·ro
number	*de quai*	der kay
ticket office	*le guichet*	ler gee·shay
timetable	*l'horaire*	lo·rair
train station	*la gare*	la gar

Private Transport

I'd like to hire	*Je voudrais*	zher voo·dray
a/an...	*louer ...*	loo·way ...
car	*une voiture*	ewn vwa·tewr
4WD	*un quatre-quatre*	un kat·kat
motorbike	*une moto*	ewn mo·to
bicycle	*un vélo*	un vay·lo

Is this the road to ...?
C'est la route pour ...?   say la root poor ...
Where's a service station?
Où est-ce qu'il y a   oo es·keel ya
une station-service?   ewn sta·syon·ser·vees
Please fill it up.
Le plein, s'il vous plaît.   ler plun seel voo play
I'd like ... litres.
Je voudrais ... litres.   zher voo·dray ... lee·trer

ROAD SIGNS

Cédez la Priorité	Give Way
Danger	Danger
Défense de Stationner	No Parking
Entrée	Entrance
Interdiction de Doubler	No Overtaking
Péage	Toll
Ralentissez	Slow Down
Sens Interdit	No Entry
Sens unique	One-way
Sortie	Exit

petrol/gas	*essence*	ay·sons
unleaded	*sans plomb*	son plom
leaded	*au plomb*	o plom
diesel	*diesel*	dyay·zel

(How long) Can I park here?
(Combien de temps) (kom·byun der tom)
Est-ce que je peux es·ker zher per
stationner ici? sta·syo·nay ee·see?
Where do I pay?
Où est-ce que je paie? oo es·ker zher pay?
I need a mechanic.
J'ai besoin d'un zhay ber·zwun dun
mécanicien. may·ka·nee·syun
The car/motorbike has broken down (at ...)
La voiture/moto est la vwa·tewr/mo·to ay
tombée en panne (à ...) tom·bay on pan (a ...)
The car/motorbike won't start.
La voiture/moto ne veut la vwa·tewr/mo·to ner ver
pas démarrer. pa day·ma·ray

I have a flat tyre.
Mon pneu est à plat. mom pner ay ta pla
I've run out of petrol.
Je suis en panne zher swee zon pan
d'essence. day·sons
I had an accident.
J'ai eu un accident. zhay ew un ak·see·don

TRAVEL WITH CHILDREN

Is there a/an ...?	*Y a-t-il ...?*	ya teel ...
I need a/an ...	*J'ai besoin ...*	zhay ber·zwun ...
baby change room	*d'un endroit pour changer le bébé*	dun on·drwa poor shon·zhay ler bay·bay
car baby seat	*d'un siège-enfant*	dun syezh·on·fon
child-minding service	*d'une garderie*	dewn gar·dree
children's menu	*d'un menu pour enfant*	dun mer·new poor on·fon
disposable nappies/diapers	*de couches-culottes*	der koosh·kew·lot
formula	*de lait maternisé*	de lay ma·ter·nee·zay
(English-speaking) babysitter	*d'une baby-sitter (qui parle anglais)*	dewn ba·bee·see·ter (kee parl ong·glay)
highchair	*d'une chaise haute*	dewn shay zot
potty	*d'un pot de bébé*	dun po der bay·bay
stroller	*d'une poussette*	dewn poo·set

Do you mind if I breastfeed here?
Cela vous dérange si ser·la voo day·ron·zhe see
j'allaite mon bébé ici? zha·lay·ter mon bay·bay ee·see
Are children allowed?
Les enfants sont permis? lay zon·fon son pair·mee

Glossary

For a glossary of food and drink terms, see the Food & Drink chapter (p80).

(m) indicates masculine gender, (f) feminine gender and (pl) plural

accueil (m) – reception

alignements (m pl) – a series of standing stones, or menhirs, in straight lines

alimentation (f) – grocery store

AOC – appellation d'origine contrôlée; system of French wine classification

arrondissement (m) – administrative division of large city; abbreviated on signs as 1er (1st *arrondissement*), 2e or 2ème (2nd) etc

auberge de jeunesse (f) – (youth) hostel

baie (f) – bay

bassin (m) – bay or basin

bastide (f) – medieval settlement in southwestern France, usually built on a grid plan and surrounding an arcaded square

belle époque (f) – literally 'beautiful age'; era of elegance and gaiety characterising fashionable Parisian life in the period preceding WWI

billet (m) – ticket

billetterie (f) – ticket office or counter

billet jumelé (m) – combination ticket, good for more than one site, museum etc

boulangerie (f) – bakery or bread shop

boules (f pl) – a game not unlike lawn bowls played with heavy metal balls on a sandy pitch; also called *pétanque*

BP – *boîte postale*; post office box

brasserie (f) – restaurant usually serving food all day (original meaning: brewery)

bureau de poste (m) or **poste** (f) – post office

bureau de change (m) – exchange bureau

CAF – Club Alpin Français

carnet (m) – a book of five or 10 bus, tram or metro tickets sold at a reduced rate

carrefour (m) – crossroad

carte (f) – card; menu; map

caserne (f) – military barracks

cave (f) – wine cellar

chambre (f) – room

chambre d'hôte (f) – B&B

charcuterie (f) – pork butcher's shop and delicatessen; the prepared meats it sells

cimetière (m) – cemetery

col (m) – mountain pass

consigne (f) – left-luggage office

consigne automatique (f) – left-luggage locker

consigne manuelle (f) – left-luggage office

correspondance (f) – linking tunnel or walkway, eg in the metro; rail or bus connection

couchette (f) – sleeping berth on a train or ferry

cour (f) – courtyard

crémerie (f) – dairy or cheese shop

cyclisme (m) – cycling

dégustation (f) – tasting

demi (m) – 330mL glass of beer

demi-pension (f) – half-board (B&B with either lunch or dinner)

département (m) – administrative division of France

douane (f) – customs

église (f) – church

embarcadère (m) – pier or jetty

épicerie (f) – small grocery store

ESF – École de Ski Français; France's leading ski school

fauteuil (m) – seat on trains, ferries or at the theatre

fest-noz or **festou-noz** (pl) – night festival

fête (f) – festival

FN – Front National; National Front

forêt (f) – forest

formule or **formule rapide** (f) – similar to a *menu* but allows choice of whichever two of three courses you want (eg starter and main course or main course and dessert)

fouilles (f pl) – excavations at an archaeological site

foyer (m) – workers or students hostel

fromagerie (f) – cheese shop

FUAJ – Fédération Unie des Auberges de Jeunesse; France's major hostel association

funiculaire (m) – funicular railway

galerie (f) – covered shopping centre or arcade

gare or **gare SNCF** (f) – railway station

gare maritime (f) – ferry terminal

gare routière (f) – bus station

gendarmerie (f) – police station; police force

gîte d'étape (m) – hikers accommodation, usually in a village

gîte rural (m) – country cottage

golfe (m) – gulf

GR – *grande randonnée;* long-distance hiking trail

grand cru (m) – wine of exceptional quality

halles (f pl) – covered market; central food market
halte routière (f) – bus stop
horaire (m) – timetable or schedule
hôte payant (m) – paying guest
hôtel de ville (m) – city or town hall
hôtel particulier (m) – private mansion
hôtes payants (m pl) – paying guest
l'habitant or **hébergement chez** (m) – homestay

intra-muros (m) – old city (literally 'within the walls')

jardin (m) – garden
jardin botanique (m) – botanic garden
jours fériés (m pl) – public holidays

laverie (f) or **lavomatique** (m) – laundrette

mairie (f) – city or town hall
maison de la presse (f) – newsagent
maison du parc (f) – a national park's headquarters and/or visitors centre
marché (m) – market
marché aux puces (m) – flea market
marché couvert (m) – covered market
mas (m) – farmhouse; tiny hamlet
menu (m) – fixed-price meal with two or more courses
mistral (m) – incessant north wind in southern France said to drive people crazy
musée (m) – museum

navette (f) – shuttle bus, train or boat

Occitan – a language also known as langue d'oc or sometimes Provençal, related to Catalan

palais de justice (m) – law courts
parapente – paragliding
pardon (m) – religious pilgrimage
parlement (m) – parliament
parvis (m) – square
pâtisserie (f) – cake and pastry shop
pensions de famille (f pl) – similar to B&Bs
pétanque (f) – a game not unlike lawn bowls played with heavy metal balls on a sandy pitch; also called *boules*
piste cyclable (f) – bicycle path
place (f) – square or plaza
plage (f) – beach
plan (m) – city map
plan du quartier (m) – map of nearby streets (hung on the wall near metro exits)
plat du jour (m) – daily special in a restaurant
pont (m) – bridge

port (m) – harbour or port
port de plaisance (m) – marina or pleasure-boat harbour
porte (f) – gate in a city wall
poste (f) or **bureau de poste** (m) – post office
préfecture (f) – prefecture (capital of a *département*)
presqu'île (f) – peninsula
pression (f) – draught beer
puy (m) – volcanic cone or peak

quai (m) – quay or railway platform
quartier (m) – quarter or district

refuge (m) – mountain hut, basic shelter for hikers
rez-de-chausée (m) – ground floor
rive (f) – bank of a river
rond point (m) – roundabout
routier (m) – trucker or truckers restaurant

sentier (m) – trail
service des urgences (f) – casualty ward
ski de fond – cross-country skiing
SNCF – Société Nationale des Chemins de Fer; state-owned railway company
SNCM – Société Nationale Maritime Corse-Méditerranée; state-owned ferry company linking Corsica and mainland France
sortie (f) – exit
spectacle (m) – performance, play or theatrical show
square (m) – public garden
supplément (m) – supplement or additional cost
syndicat d'initiative (m) – tourist office

tabac (m) – tobacconist (also selling bus tickets, phone-cards etc)
table d'orientation (f) – viewpoint indicator
taxe de séjour (f) – municipal tourist tax
télécarte (f) – phonecard
téléphérique (m) – cableway or cable car
télésiège (m) – chair lift
téléski (m) – ski lift or tow
TGV – *train à grande vitesse;* high-speed train or bullet train
tour (f) – tower
tour d'horloge (f) – clock tower

vallée (f) – valley
v.f. (f) – *version française;* a film dubbed in French
vieille ville (f) – old town or old city
ville neuve (f) – new town or new city
v.o. (f) – *version originale;* a nondubbed film with French subtitles
voie (f) – train platform
VTT – *vélo tout terrain;* mountain bike

Behind the Scenes

THIS BOOK

For this 6th edition of *France*, Nicola Williams co-ordinated a skilled team of authors comprising Oliver Berry, Steve Fallon, Annabel Hart, Jonathan Knight, Daniel Robinson, Miles Roddis and Andrew Stone. Nicola, Steve, Annabel, Daniel and Miles also made major contributions to previous editions, as did Teresa Fisher, Jeremy Gray, Leanne Logan, Paul Hellander, Oda O'Carroll and Jeanne Oliver. Dr Caroline Evans reviewed and contributed to the Health chapter.

THANKS from the Authors

Nicola Williams A big *grand merci* to my fellow authors for their good-humoured cooperation during what was, at times, a mind-boggling affair; to friends and acquaintances in Lyon for uncovering tasty places to eat, drink and enjoy over the years – and sharing them with me; and to my Frencher-than-German husband Matthias (not to mention Niko and Mischa) for being sweeter-than-Montélimar sweet.

Oliver Berry Lots of people helped during the writing of this book. Special thanks go to Susie Berry for love, support and lending me my wheels; to Laura Brammar for listening; to Carl and Si at o-region for keeping the show on the road; to the Hôtel L'Aïtone in Évisa for putting up with me; to Nicola Williams and Sam Trafford for patience, support and long-distance correspondence; and to all the staff of the many French tourist offices who helped along the way. I'd also like to thank the late Dorothy Carrington for writing the best book on Corsica anyone could hope to read.

Steve Fallon A number of people helped in the updating of the Paris chapter, but first and foremost stands resident Brenda Turnnidge, whose knowledge of all things Parisian – but especially fashion, transport and *les bonnes addresses* – never ceases to amaze and excite. Thanks, too, to Zahia Hafs, Olivier Cirendini, Caroline Guilleminot and Chew Terrière for assistance, ideas, hospitality and/or a few laughs during what was a very grey, very bleak winter in every way.

As always, I'd like to dedicate my efforts to my partner, Michael Rothschild, whose knowledge of menu French grows in direct proportion to... Well, *peu importe* (never mind).

Annabel Hart Special acknowledgment and thanks to Lonely Planet's Paris office and the wonderful people there, without whom none of this would have happened. Thanks especially to Didier, Olivier and, above all, *petite* Claire for her tactical and moral support. Thanks also to Georgia for being my 3am pen pal, Diana for cutting those last 200 words and Edouard for putting up with me. Thanks finally to editor Sam Trafford and co-ordinating author Nicola Williams for their hard work and understanding.

Jonathan Knight Thanks to hundreds of helpful tourist officials across southwestern France, particularly Séverine Michau, Samuel Buchwalder, Catherine Senand, Françoise Tetard, Séverine Pigeaud and David Morton. Thanks also to Sam and Nicola for assistance and deadline flexibility; to Grands Garages de Touraine for helping to get my trusty

THE LONELY PLANET STORY

The story begins with a classic travel adventure: Tony and Maureen Wheeler's 1972 journey across Europe and Asia to Australia. There was no useful information about the overland trail then, so Tony and Maureen published the first Lonely Planet guidebook to meet a growing need.

From a kitchen table, Lonely Planet has grown to become the largest independent travel publisher in the world, with offices in Melbourne (Australia), Oakland (USA) and London (UK). Today Lonely Planet guidebooks cover the globe. There is an ever-growing list of books and information in a variety of media. Some things haven't changed. The main aim is still to make it possible for adventurous travellers to get out there – to explore and better understand the world.

At Lonely Planet we believe travellers can make a positive contribution to the countries they visit – if they respect their host communities and spend their money wisely. Every year 5% of company profit is donated to charities around the world.

old four-wheeler back on the road; to Rose and Archie for company, wine, food and a bed in the tower; and most of all to Shellani for saying yes.

Daniel Robinson In Far Northern France, I am indebted to Jean-Christophe Le Goaër of Clairière de l'Armistice; Jocelyne Mitchell (PEI) and Laura Floyd (Ottowa) of the Vimy Canadian National Memorial; Alexandra Limousin of Boulogne's Nausicaä, and tourist office professionals Stéphanie Noël (Amiens), Stéphanie Seulin (Lille) and Madame Baudeuille (Boulogne). In Champagne, my research was nourished and lubricated by Jacqueline & Pascal Maillard and Jean-Paul Dzitko of Reim's Le Lion de Belfort and, in Troyes, Raquel & Elie Margen, Claude Margen, Olivier Galliot and my old friend Thierry Di Costanzo. In Lorraine, Jean-Pierre Collet of the Verdun municipality kindly provided up-to-the-minute mapping information. In Strasbourg, people who lent an enthusiastic hand include Claudine Lévy of the Agence de Développement Touristique du Bas-Rhin, Musica Schmidt of the Maison des Projets, Kiera Tchelistcheff of The Bookworm, Philippe Roth of Strasbourg's L'Assiette du Vin and the tourist office's Valérie Garnier. In Colmar, my special thanks go to Temple St-Mathieu organist Paul Florence, Cécile Lannoy of the tourist office and Aurélien, Adrien, Patricia & Jean-Michel Kempf. My travels around Alsace were considerably enlivened by the trans-Rhine visit of my Lonely Planet colleague Becca Blond.

Finally, I would like to thank Réka Kocsis of Sopron, Hungary and the 15e, for her warmth, enthusiasm and sense of adventure; and Kristy Marks of Sydney-based DriveAway Holidays, who arranged the purchase-repurchase Peugeot 206 that served me for 4250 problem-free kilometres.

Miles Roddis Thanks to so many cheerful tourist office staff. It was a pleasure to see once more Laurence Tapie and Myriam Blanchard (Bedous), Mathilde Lardat (Cauterets), Marie (Murat), Élodie Juillard (Le Mont-Dore) and Françoise Cros (Montpellier).

Thanks too to Myriam (Laruns), Stéphanie (Gavarnie), Fabrice Doucet (Lourdes), Mme Mouries (Millau), Xavier Brilhaut (Ste-Énimie), Benjamin Bonnet (Florac), Riccardo (Mende), Laurence Lescuyer and Virginie (St-Nectaire), Philippe (Clermont-Ferrand), Françoise Gioux (Vichy), Lise Gauthier (Orcival), Matthieu Aubignat-Fournet – good to meet another Durham graduate – (Thiers), Candice Taillandier (Ambert), Céline Charrat (Le Puy), Magani (Alès), Laurent Chateaux (Uzès), Armand Descombes (Nîmes), Francine (Agde), Véro-

nique (Narbonne), Laure (Carcassonne), Sylvette (Foix), Dominique Fabre (Collioure), Marie-Pierre (Perpignan) and Agnès Chassin (Parc Naturel Régional Livradois-Forez). And a special thank you to ebullient Eddy Delobel (Service Relations Presse, Pau), also to reader Jennifer Barclay for a detailed and most helpful updating letter about Montpellier and its environs.

Andrew Stone For all the visits over the years and all the hospitality, my main thanks go to the Foucault and Peyre de Fabrègues families and in particular to Evelyn, Xavier, Michael and Sharmion. Special thanks to Ruth and Paulo at the Hub Lot for the Aix tips, to Michel Caraisco in Toulon for the Var tour and to Jean-Jacques Benetti at the Maison des Vins Côtes de Provence for the whistlestop wine tour. Thanks also to all the helpful tourism offices in the south and in particular thanks to Fabienne Fertilati in Nice and Nathalie Steinberg in Marseille. Finally, thanks to Fabienne Dupuis for all the tips, insights and, most importantly, the pints of Guinness.

CREDITS

France 6 was commissioned and developed in Lonely Planet's London office by Sam Trafford, and assessed by Sam Trafford and Susie Ashworth. The book was coordinated by Yvonne Byron (editorial) and Helen Rowley (cartography). Andrew Bain, Cinzia Cavallaro, Charlotte Harrison, Margedd Heliosz, John Hinman, Maryanne Netto, Nina Rousseau, Diana Saad and Helen Yeates assisted with editing and proofing. Paul Bazalicki, Christopher Crook, Csanad Csutoros, Piotr Czajkowski, Daniel Fennessy, Tadhagh Knaggs, Joelene Kowalski, Kusnandar, Mandy Sierp, Chris Thomas and Simon Tillema assisted with cartography. Chris Lee Ack and Lachlan Ross provided invaluable technical assistance. Jacqueline McLeod and Wibowo Rusli laid out the book, Pablo Gastar designed the colour content. Pepi Bluck designed the cover with artwork by Wendy Wright. Kate Evans, Sally Darmody, Adrianna Mammarella and Kate McDonald assisted with layout checking. Quentin Frayne prepared the Language chapter. Overseeing production were Glenn van der Knijff (Project Manager), Bruce Evans (Managing Editor) and Mark Griffiths (Managing Cartographer), who was assisted by Daniel Fennessy. Alison Lyall helped with map checking. The series was designed by James Hardy, with mapping development by Paul Piaia.

Our thoughts have been with our beloved late friend, Shelley Muir, during production of this 6th edition – an inspirational friend and colleague.

BEHIND THE SCENES

THANKS from Lonely Planet

Many thanks to the following travellers who used the last edition and wrote to us with helpful hints, useful advice and interesting anecdotes.

A Susan Alexander, J Anderson, Helene Andersson, **B** Sue Baker, Simon Ball, James Barisic, CM Beattie, Paola Benini, Cindy Bestland, Gail Bishko, Kate Black, Paul Bloomfield, Monica & Richard Booth, Truman Bradley, John Buckley, Chris Burin, M Burness, Maria Bursey, Alison Butcher, Robert Button, **C** Belinda Catterall, Kam Champaneri, Nikitas Chondroyannos, Greta Cleghorn, Colin Coffey, Marco Conte, Pat & John Cooper, Ali Coton, Florence Counil, Philip Crosby, **D** Lynn Dawson, Daniel De Groot, Audrey Dean, Joanna Delaney, Laura & Ami Diner, Terry Dolman, Fred Dugenet, Benjamin Dyson, **E** Robert Edmunds, **F** Rachel Faggetter, Craig Falls, Lea Feng, John Fletcher, Ian Fulcher, **G** Jason Galea, John Gibson, Amelia Greenberg, Martijn Grimmius, Pallav Gupta, **H** Jacob Halpin, Frank Harker, Jim Hendrickson, Lennart Henriksson, Katherine Hickey, Francis Higbie, Helen Hofsted, Tina Hough, Robert Hubbard, KA Humphries, Geoff Hutcheison, **J** Barry Johnston, Eve Jones, Philip Jones, Ronaele Jones, Michl Joos, **K** R Karlmarx, Mark Kemper, Pete Kitching, Madame Mary Ellen Kitler, Henry Koster, Ann Kramer, **L** Bart Langerwerf, Rebekah Lawrence, Tram Anh Le, Oliver Lewis, Nana Lim, Phil Linz, Ynyr Lloyd, **M** Peter MacLean, Suzy Mangion, Mark & Jaime Manson, Alison Matthews, Marco Mazzocchi, Dr JS McLintock, GJ Mensink, Peter Millett, Peter & June Millett, Peter Monk, **N** Travis Kane Nairn, Mikael Nojd, **O** Ruth O'Connell, Paul Ozorak, **P** Emma Payne, Murray Pearce, Inga Pfannebecker, Monique Pierre, Lizzy Pike, Alan & Maree Porter, **R** Susan Reilly, Stephane Reynolds, Lita Roberts, Terry Rolleri, **S** RR Sanderson, Eivind Stene, Kimberly Stewart, **T** Elizabeth Thorpe, Edward Tsui, Peter Tudor, Liz Turner, **U** Christina Unterwurzacher, **V** Esther Van Den Reek, Monique Van Erp, **W** Bill Wagman, Andy Ward, Joanna Wilding, Matthew Wilner-Reid, **Y** Barbara Yoshida, Andrew Young, **Z** Jabi Zabala

ACKNOWLEDGMENTS

Many thanks to the following for the use of their content:

Globe on back cover © Mountain High Maps 1993 Digital Wisdom, Inc.

RATP for the use of its transit map © RATP – CML Agence Cartographique.

SEND US YOUR FEEDBACK

We love to hear from travellers – your comments keep us on our toes and help make our books better. Our well-travelled team reads every word on what you loved or loathed about this book. Although we cannot reply individually to postal submissions, we always guarantee that your feedback goes straight to the appropriate authors, in time for the next edition. Each person who sends us information is thanked in the next edition – and the most useful submissions are rewarded with a free book.

To send us your updates – and find out about Lonely Planet events, newsletters and travel news – visit our award-winning website: **www.lonelyplanet.com/feedback**.

Note: We may edit, reproduce and incorporate your comments in Lonely Planet products such as guidebooks, websites and digital products, so let us know if you don't want your comments reproduced or your name acknowledged. For a copy of our privacy policy visit www.lonelyplanet.com/privacy.

Index

INDEX

000 Map pages
000 Location of colour photographs

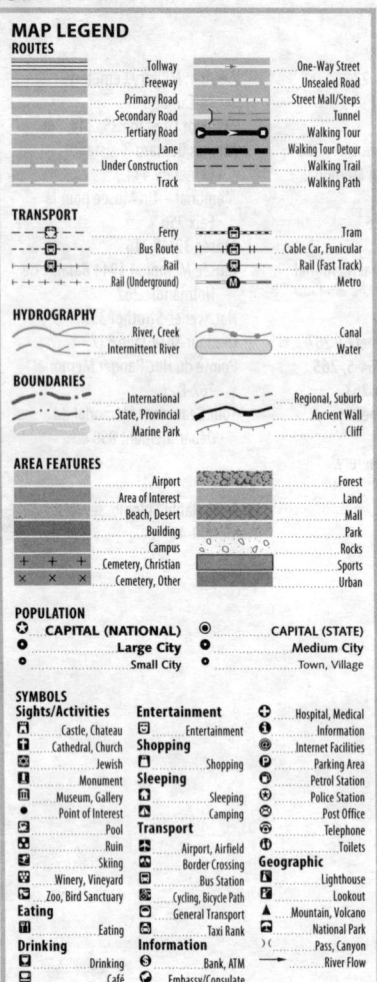

MAP LEGEND

ROUTES

Tollway	One-Way Street
Freeway	Unsealed Road
Primary Road	Street Mall/Steps
Secondary Road	Tunnel
Tertiary Road	Walking Tour
Lane	Walking Tour Detour
Under Construction	Walking Trail
Track	Walking Path

TRANSPORT

Ferry	Tram
Bus Route	Cable Car, Funicular
Rail	Rail (Fast Track)
Rail (Underground)	Metro

HYDROGRAPHY

River, Creek	Canal
Intermittent River	Water

BOUNDARIES

International	Regional, Suburb
State, Provincial	Ancient Wall
Marine Park	Cliff

AREA FEATURES

Airport	Forest
Area of Interest	Land
Beach, Desert	Mall
Building	Park
Campus	Rocks
Cemetery, Christian	Sports
Cemetery, Other	Urban

POPULATION

CAPITAL (NATIONAL)	CAPITAL (STATE)
Large City	Medium City
Small City	Town, Village

SYMBOLS

Sights/Activities
- Castle, Chateau
- Cathedral, Church
- Jewish
- Monument
- Museum, Gallery
- Point of Interest
- Pool
- Ruin
- Skiing
- Winery, Vineyard
- Zoo, Bird Sanctuary

Eating
- Eating

Drinking
- Drinking
- Café

Entertainment
- Entertainment

Shopping
- Shopping

Sleeping
- Sleeping
- Camping

Transport
- Airport, Airfield
- Border Crossing
- Bus Station
- Cycling, Bicycle Path
- General Transport
- Taxi Rank

Information
- Bank, ATM
- Embassy/Consulate

- Hospital, Medical
- Information
- Internet Facilities
- Parking Area
- Petrol Station
- Police Station
- Post Office
- Telephone
- Toilets

Geographic
- Lighthouse
- Lookout
- Mountain, Volcano
- National Park
- Pass, Canyon
- River Flow

LONELY PLANET OFFICES

Australia
Head Office
Locked Bag 1, Footscray, Victoria 3011
☎ 03 8379 8000, fax 03 8379 8111
talk2us@lonelyplanet.com.au

USA
150 Linden St, Oakland, CA 94607
☎ 510 893 8555, toll free 800 275 8555
fax 510 893 8572, info@lonelyplanet.com

UK
72–82 Rosebery Ave,
Clerkenwell, London EC1R 4RW
☎ 020 7841 9000, fax 020 7841 9001
go@lonelyplanet.co.uk

Published by Lonely Planet Publications Pty Ltd
ABN 36 005 607 983

© Lonely Planet 2005

© photographers as indicated 2005

Cover photographs: Eiffel Tower, Robert Landau/APL Corbis (front); Vineyards along the Route du Vin (winery route), Greg Elms/Lonely Planet Images (back). Many of the images in this guide are available for licensing from Lonely Planet Images: www.lonelyplanetimages.com

Printed through The Bookmaker International Ltd
Printed in China

USA

Lake Winnipeg

WINNIPEG

Ontario

Québec

NB

QUÉBEC

Maine

AUGUSTA

Thunder Bay

Lake Superior

Montréal

OTTAWA

MONTPELIER

N.H.

CONCORD

BOSTON

Minnesota

Wisconsin

ST PAUL

Green Bay

Michigan

TORONTO

Lake Ontario

New York

ALBANY

HARTFORD

PROVIDENCE

Newport

R.I.

C.T.

Minneapolis

Madison

Milwaukee

LANSING

Detroit

Cleveland

Pennsylvania

NEW YORK

TRENTON

New Jersey

40°N

Iowa

Chicago

Toledo

Pittsburgh

HARRISBURG

Philadelphia

DOVER

Delaware

Omaha

DES MOINES

Indiana

Ohio

COLUMBUS

Baltimore

ANNAPOLIS

WASHINGTON, DC

Maryland

LINCOLN

SPRINGFIELD

INDIANAPOLIS

Cincinnati

W.V.

RICHMOND

Illinois

FRANKFORT

CHARLESTON

Virginia

Kansas City

St Louis

Lexington

TOPEKA

JEFFERSON CITY

Ohio River

Kentucky

RALEIGH

Wichita

Missouri

NASHVILLE

Charlotte

North Carolina

Wilmington

Tulsa

Arkansas

Tennessee

Greenville

South Carolina

ATLANTIC OCEAN

OKLAHOMA CITY

LITTLE ROCK

Memphis

COLUMBIA

Birmingham

ATLANTA

Augusta

Charleston

Dallas

Fort Worth

Mississippi

Georgia

Savannah

30°N

JACKSON

Alabama

MONTGOMERY

Jacksonville

St Augustine

BATON ROUGE

TALLAHASSEE

AUSTIN

Louisiana

New Orleans

Gulf of Mexico

Tampa

Orlando

BAHAMAS

Houston

Florida

NASSAU

Corpus Christi

Miami

Key West

HAVANA

CUBA

20°N

80°W

HIGHLIGHTS

1. Yellowstone National Park—geothermal geysers and old-growth forest
2. Black Hills & Badlands—rugged landscapes and Native American history
3. San Francisco—architectural gems, outrageous festivities and a rich history
4. Yosemite National Park—amazing glacial valley with waterfalls and wildlife
5. Las Vegas—over-the-top, tack-o-rama Americana
6. Canyon Country—Grand, Bryce and Zion Canyons; stunning scenery
7. Rocky Mountains—sensational skiing and hiking
8. Santa Fe—Spanish and Native American history in a dramatic desert environment
9. Chicago—great, gritty city with art, architecture, jazz, blues, bars and restaurants
10. New York, New York—so good they named it twice
11. Washington, DC—Smithsonian museums and all-American monuments
12. Memphis—a mecca for blues buffs, Elvis fans and students of the civil-rights struggle
13. Savannah—restored city with Southern style
14. New Orleans—music, Mardi Gras and Creole cuisine; let the good times roll
15. Hawaii—volcanoes ooze molten lava to make tropical islands

Elevation

16,000ft
12,000ft
9000ft
5000ft
2000ft
1000ft
500ft
Sea Level
-500ft

USA
2nd edition – February 2002
First published – March 1999

Published by
Lonely Planet Publications Pty Ltd ABN 36 005 607 983
90 Maribyrnong St, Footscray, Victoria 3011, Australia

Lonely Planet Offices
Australia Locked Bag 1, Footscray, Victoria 3011
USA 150 Linden St, Oakland, CA 94607
UK 10a Spring Place, London NW5 3BH
France 1 rue du Dahomey, 75011 Paris

Photographs
Many of the images in this guide are available for licensing from
Lonely Planet Images.
email: lpi@lonelyplanet.com.au
Web site: www.lonelyplanetimages.com

Front cover photograph
1961 Cadillac fin, San Francisco (Richard Cummins)

Title page photographs
New York & the Mid-Atlantic States (Angus Oborn), New England
(Eoin Clarke Oldcastle), Washington, DC & the Capital Region
(Richard Cummins), Great Lakes (Richard Cummins), The South
(Greg Elms), Florida (Richard Cummins), Texas (Richard
Cummins), Great Plains (Matt Swinden), Rocky Mountains
(Andrew Brownbill), Southwest (Charlotte Hindle), California
(Richard Nebesky), Pacific Northwest (Richard Cummins), Alaska
(Kraig Lieb), Hawaii (Simon Foale)

ISBN 1 86450 308 4

text & maps © Lonely Planet Publications Pty Ltd 2002
photos © photographers as indicated 2002

Printed by SNP SPrint (M) Sdn Bhd
Printed in Malaysia

Contents

2   Contents

NEW ENGLAND   258

WASHINGTON, DC & THE CAPITAL REGION   332

GREAT LAKES   398

THE SOUTH

FLORIDA

TEXAS

GREAT PLAINS

ROCKY MOUNTAINS

SOUTHWEST

CALIFORNIA   918

PACIFIC NORTHWEST   1010

ALASKA   1058

HAWAII   1088

6   Contents

CHAPTERS

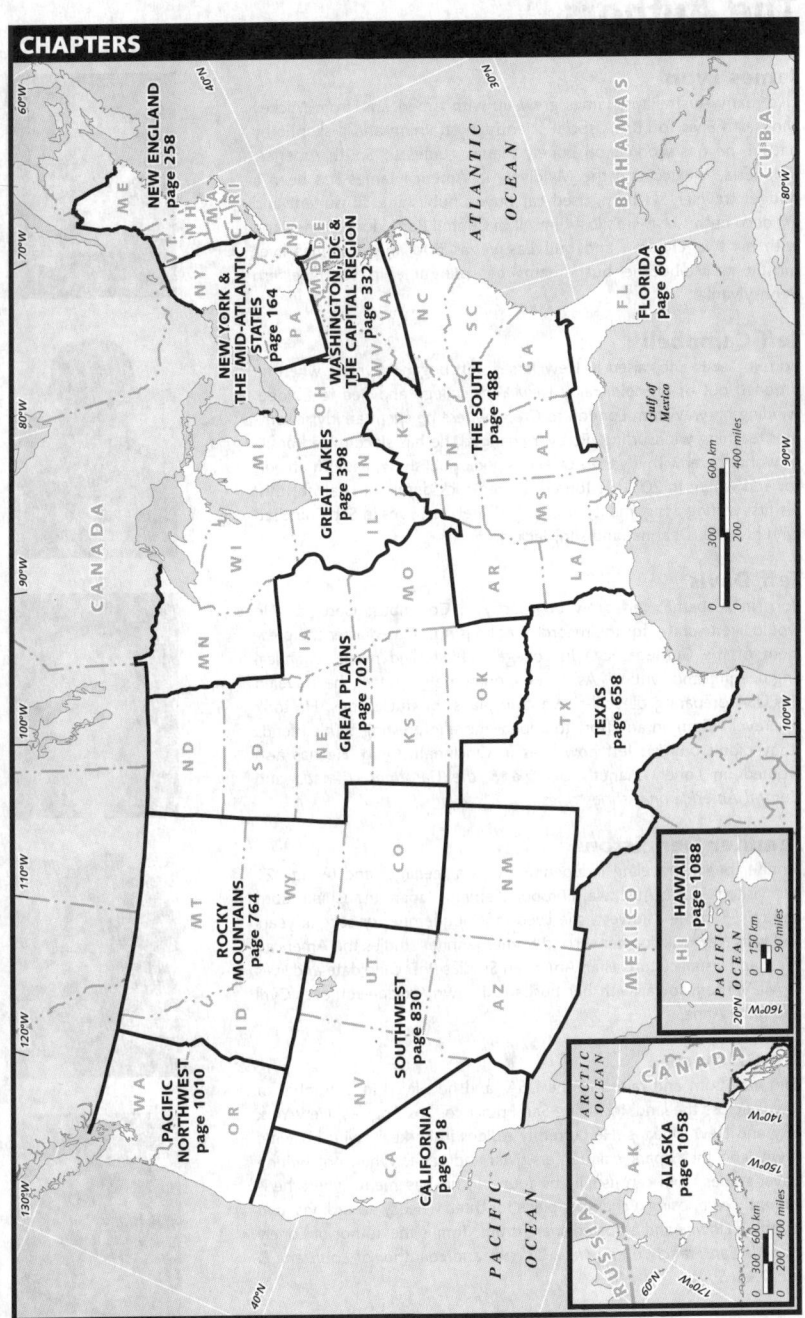

NEW ENGLAND
page 258

NEW YORK & THE MID-ATLANTIC STATES
page 164

WASHINGTON, DC & THE CAPITAL REGION
page 332

FLORIDA
page 606

THE SOUTH
page 488

GREAT LAKES
page 398

GREAT PLAINS
page 702

TEXAS
page 658

ROCKY MOUNTAINS
page 764

SOUTHWEST
page 830

HAWAII
page 1088

PACIFIC NORTHWEST
page 1010

CALIFORNIA
page 918

ALASKA
page 1058

ATLANTIC OCEAN

BAHAMAS

CUBA

Gulf of Mexico

CANADA

MEXICO

PACIFIC OCEAN

ARCTIC OCEAN

RUSSIA

ME
VT
NH
MA
CT
RI
NY
NJ
PA
MD
DE
WV
VA
NC
SC
GA
AL
FL
OH
IN
IL
KY
TN
MS
LA
AR
MO
MI
WI
MN
IA
ND
SD
NE
KS
OK
TX
CO
NM
WY
MT
ID
UT
AZ
NV
CA
OR
WA
HI
AK

0   300   600 km
0   200   400 miles

0   150 km
0   90 miles

0   300   600 km
0   200   400 miles

The Authors

James Lyon

Like many Australians, James grew up with Americans, from Mickey Mouse to Elvis to LBJ. A social scientist by training and a skeptic by nature, he has worked on Lonely Planet guides to South America, Indonesia, Mexico and the Maldives. In America James has been a budget traveler, ski bum, used-car buyer, publishing consultant and art deco enthusiast. He's lost himself in Central Park, done Disneyland with his two children and quit Las Vegas 50¢ ahead. James lives mostly in Melbourne but dreams of springtime in southwestern Pennsylvania.

Jeff Campbell

Born in Texas and raised in New Jersey, Jeff began traveling when he dropped out of his cold, rainy New York college and fled to Europe, winding his way from London to Crete, where he spent an idyllic summer teaching windsurfing. Forever changed, he has since mixed bouts of world travel with a varied career in book publishing, as both an editor and writer. In 2001 he toured the red-rock desert of Utah for this, his first writing assignment for Lonely Planet. Jeff lives in San Francisco with his wife, Deanna, and son, Jackson.

Jeff Davis

Born in Alabama, Jeff grew up mostly in Columbus, Georgia. (He would like to state, for the record, that he is *not* named after the president of the Confederacy.) In college, Jeff studied music, chemical engineering and writing. As an environmental engineer, he traveled the USA preparing oil-spill-prevention plans for truck stops. He took up travel writing in an effort to appear more interesting to his friends (they didn't buy it). Jeff now lives in Cincinnati, Ohio. He has also worked on Lonely Planet's *Georgia & the Carolinas, Canada* and *Central America on a shoestring.*

Jennifer Denniston

Jennifer began traveling independently as a teenager and by age 21 had visited Africa, Australia, Europe, Vietnam, Japan and China. Born and raised in the Midwest, she lived in Albuquerque for several years and calls New Mexico her second home. Jennifer studies the American West and visual culture as an American Studies PhD candidate and lives in Mt Vernon, Iowa, with her husband Rhawn, golden retriever Cyril and baby Anna.

Tom Downs

Tom was born and raised in the USA, and he's lived in a number of towns across the land, including San Francisco, Los Angeles, New York City and New Orleans. He currently resides in Berkeley with his wife, Fawn, and their sparkly daughters, Mai and Lana. When not writing travel guides, Tom can usually be found in his basement, where he is currently composing a chamber piece for three wheezy accordions, two laughing clowns and a busted snare drum. Tom is the author of Lonely Planet's *San Francisco* and *New Orleans* and coauthor of *Louisiana & the Deep South.*

Jim DuFresne

Except for a year covering the Texas religion of high school football as a sports writer, Jim has spent his entire life living in Michigan or Alaska. As a sports and outdoors editor for the *Juneau Empire*, he became the first Alaskan sportswriter in 1980 to win a national award from Associated Press. But his love of the mountains proved greater than football or basketball, and he began writing wilderness and travel guidebooks. Jim lives in Clarkston, Michigan, and is the author of 15 guidebooks, including Lonely Planet's *Alaska, Hiking in Alaska* and *Tramping in New Zealand*.

Mason Florence

A native New Yorker, Mason migrated west to Boulder, Colorado, to pursue a college degree while soaking up the great outdoors. When not skiing or mountain biking, he tried to realize his childhood dream of becoming a cowboy, joining the University of Colorado Rodeo team. After being flung from horseback one time too many, he graduated (barely), traded in his boots and spurs for a Nikon and a laptop and relocated to Japan. Now a Kyoto-based photojournalist, he spends half the year traveling and his free moments restoring a 300-year-old farmhouse. In addition to *Rocky Mountains*, Mason has coauthored Lonely Planet's *South-East Asia on a shoestring, Japan, Kyoto, Hanoi* and *Ho Chi Minh City (Saigon)*.

Ned Friary

Ned grew up near Boston, studied social thought and political economy at the University of Massachusetts in Amherst, and soon began to travel. He has taken the overland trail from Europe to Nepal, taught English in Japan and spent years traveling around the Pacific, with much of that time exploring the nooks and crannies of Hawaii. He now lives on Cape Cod in Massachusetts with his wife and traveling companion, Glenda Bendure. Together they are the authors of Lonely Planet's *Hawaii* and *Oahu*.

Marisa Gierlich

Marisa was born and raised in Hermosa Beach, California. Thanks to adventurous parents, she began traveling at age seven and hasn't stopped for more than eight months since. She did manage to earn an English degree at the University of California, Berkeley, where she began writing for the Berkeley Guides, an employ that took her to France, Sweden, Italy and Alaska. She has coauthored Lonely Planet's *Rocky Mountains, California & Nevada, Hiking in the USA, California Condensed* and *Cycling West Coast USA*. When not writing, Marisa leads hiking and biking tours for Backroads, and runs, skis and surfs with her husband, Paul.

Kim Grant

Although Kim has lived in the Boston area since age four, she's still not considered a New Englander. Before graduating from Mount Holyoke College in Massachusetts, she took a year off and drove around the USA on secondary roads. Between months spent living out of her car, she was a ranch hand at the Grand Tetons in Wyoming and a political canvasser for NOW in San Francisco. Kim now travels about 25,000 miles a year around New England, writing guidebooks and taking photos. She is the author of Lonely Planet's *Boston* and coauthor of *New England*. Kim also wrote *Cape Cod, Martha's Vineyard & Nantucket: An Explorer's Guide* and cowrote *The Best Places to Stay in New England*.

Jeremy Gray

A native of Shreveport, Louisiana, Jeremy studied literature at the University of Texas before moving to Germany on a scholarship. He stayed to write for wire services, TV and newspapers out of London, Frankfurt and Amsterdam, and since 1998 has contributed to or authored Lonely Planet's *France*, *Germany*, *The Netherlands* and *Montréal*. For this book he enjoyed a jaunt down memory lane through the Deep South. 'Home' nowadays is a coffee-stained desk in Amsterdam.

Judy Jewell

Judy researched her home town of Portland, Oregon, on bicycle, bus and light-rail train before heading up to Mt Hood (where she skied off a cliff and broke her ankle), the Columbia Gorge and central and eastern Oregon. (Many thanks to Paul for all his help behind the wheel and running for info.) When Judy is not writing about the out-doors and travel, she is lead technical writer at Camp Dusty Technical Services.

Mark Lightbody

Mark has been visiting the USA from his home in Toronto since early childhood and never tires of his neighbor to the south. (And they never seem to tire of his silly questions.) He holds an honors degree in journalism. Among a variety of jobs, he's worked in radio news and in the specialty-graphics industry. Mark also coauthored Lonely Planet's *Great Lakes*, *Canada*, *Papua New Guinea*, *Australia*, *Malaysia*, *Singapore & Brunei* and *South-East Asia on a shoestring*.

Maria Mack

Maria grew up on the northern coast of Massachusetts in the woodsy Boston suburb of Georgetown. Since her father took her to Soviet Russia at the age of nine, she has not been able to stop trav-eling and easily maintains her goal of leaving the country at least once a year. While at American University in Washington, DC, Maria fell in love with San Francisco on a senior year spring break. Swapping fall foliage for snow-free winters, she relocated to the West Coast right after graduation and has been in SF ever since. Maria is a five-year veteran of LP's Oakland office; this is her first (and hopefully not last) 'on the road' assignment.

Diane Marshall

Diane writes about travel for the 'perks' of the job, among them meeting friendly and grumpy people; seeing sites in rain, snow and sunshine; eating at no-star and four-star restaurants; and sleeping in scary and luxury hotels. It's a terrible job, but somebody has to do it! Diane has been traveling since she moved to Europe at age six and has visited more than 30 countries. She was a coauthor of Lonely Planet's *Deep South* guide.

Andrew Dean Nystrom

Born a mile high in Colorado, Andrew began traveling in the womb and hasn't slowed down since. He received a geography and education degree from the University of California, Berkeley, and when not out rambling, works for Lonely Planet's New Media unit in Oakland, California. He has also contributed to Lonely Planet's *Rocky Mountains, Out to Eat San Francisco, Mexico* and CitySync digital city guides.

Rob Rachowiecki

Rob was born in London and became an avid traveler as a teenager. He has visited places as diverse as Greenland and Thailand and is the author of Lonely Planet guides to Ecuador, Peru, Costa Rica and the Southwest. Rob is an active member of the Society of American Travel Writers. Since 1989, he has lived in Tucson, Arizona, with his wife, Cathy, and children, Julia, Alison and David. He finds Tucson to be an ideal base from which to explore what he considers the most beautiful region of the USA.

Robert Reid

Raised in Oklahoma and molded by its public schools, Robert and his journalism degree left the state in 1993 to see Keith Richards play New York City. Robert then spent three years crafting memos at *House Beautiful* magazine before moving to Ho Chi Minh City, where 'Mr Bob' taught English and wrote and edited for *Vietnam News*. These days he takes up space in LP's Oakland office, where he is a senior editor and proud part of LP Soccer. Robert sobbed in joy when the Oklahoma Sooners football squad trampled Texas 63 to 14 on its path to the 2000 championship – a welcome backdrop for his USA pre-research.

Don Root

On the long, strange trip to get here, Don has studied music, journalism, art and law; been a ski bum and a paralegal; played drums in a rock band, blues band and symphony orchestra; edited travel books and a rural weekly newspaper; published an underground literary 'zine; and frittered away untold years backpacking and mountaineering throughout the West. When not off on writing assignments, he holes up between the Golden Gate and the Wine Country in glorious Northern California.

Daniel C Schechter

Born in Manhattan, Daniel refused to heed his father's helpful advice: 'When you leave New York, you're going nowhere.' Daniel went 'nowhere' fast. His career as teacher of English as a foreign language took him from Bogotá to Lisbon to Barcelona to Mexico City. After earning a teaching degree in Puerto Rico, he promptly left the field for editorial stints at *The News,* Mexico City's English language daily, and the magazine *Business Mexico*. Daniel and wife, Myra, have recently transplanted themselves to the moist earth of the Pacific Northwest.

Andrea Schulte-Peevers

Andrea is a Los Angeles-based writer, editor and translator who caught the travel bug early in life, hitting all continents but Antarctica by the time she turned 18. After finishing high school in Germany, Andrea decided the world was too big to stay in one place and moved to London, then to Los Angeles, where she graduated from UCLA. Since joining Lonely Planet, Andrea has authored and/or contributed to *Los Angeles, San Diego & Tijuana, California & Nevada, Baja California, Berlin, Germany* and *Spain*.

Jennifer Snarski

Jennifer grew up in a small timber town on the southern Oregon coast and now lives in Portland with her cat. In college she traveled to India, Sri Lanka and Thailand, and the writing assignments that followed sealed her fate as a travel writer. Jennifer feels most at home exploring the wilderness areas of Oregon and Washington. She was a coauthor of Lonely Planet's *Pacific Northwest* and *Hiking in the USA*. When she's not puttering her Toyota up a dirt road, you'll find Jennifer teaching Irish dance to nervous adults and dancing in bars.

Ryan Ver Berkmoes

Ryan grew up in Santa Cruz, California, which he left at age 17 for college in the Midwest. There, he discovered the joys of Chicago (many of which involved words beginning with 'b,' such as beer). After a string of jobs in Chicago journalism, Ryan became an author for Lonely Planet, penning a string of books, including two editions of *Chicago* and *Moscow*, and coauthoring *Texas, Canada* and *Western Europe*. He acted as coordinating author for *Russia, Ukraine & Belarus; Great Lakes; Out to Eat – London; Netherlands; Britain* and *England*. Ryan now lives in San Francisco and works as a publisher in Lonely Planet's Oakland office.

China Williams

China grew up in Aiken, South Carolina, but high-tailed it up north to attend a small liberal arts college in Annapolis, Maryland. Next came a term in the nation's capital as an editor for an itty-bitty geology magazine, followed by a teaching job in northeast Thailand. She now works as an editor in Lonely Planet's Oakland office (but continues to scan the want ads for a job as Queen of the World) and lives in San Francisco with her husband, Matt. Traces of China's Southern upbringing can still be found in her love of sweet iced tea, talking to strangers and drawling when necessary.

Jeff Williams

Jeff is a Kiwi from Greymouth on New Zealand's wild west coast. He has written or contributed to nearly 30 Lonely Planet titles over the last 10 years and traveled to four continents in the process. He is currently writing novels and more personal accounts of his adventures overseas. It's likely that when you meet him on the road, he will be doing something completely different, but still looking for 42.

Kurt Wolff

Born and raised in Ohio, Kurt has traveled and lived all over the USA, from Maine to Alaska, and currently resides in San Francisco. When he's not scouring junk stores for old Johnny Paycheck and Merle Haggard records, he works as a freelance writer and editor. He wrote Rough Guide's *Country Music* and *Country Music: 100 Essential CDs,* and contributed to Lonely Planet's *Out to Eat – San Francisco.*

FROM THE AUTHORS

James Lyon For hospitality and/or ideas on the boundless possibilities of New York City, thanks to Margaret Nomentana, Jim Williams, Matthew Huffman, Dani Valent, Deborah Faine and the staff of NYC & Company. For professionalism and personal support, thanks to all my fellow authors, but particularly Mason, Danny, Kim, Robert, Mark and Jeff. In Oakland, Michele, Suki and Annette have been especially supportive. Special thanks to Kerry Hook for researching Philly and other burgs – a fine job when I really needed it. And to Pauline, Michael and Ben – at home or on the road, it's always a great trip with you.

Jeff Campbell Rangers and information bureaus were unfailingly helpful throughout Utah. Many thanks to Susan Stordahl, Theresa Hallerin, Michael Cawley, Naomi Silverstone, Gene Hansen and James Beebe for sharing your insights, tips and favorite places. For great steaks and a home away from home, a million thanks to Rachel Blackham, Brian Mischo and Morgan. Thanks to my wife, Deanna, for her infinite patience, love and support, and to wee Jackson, who was always ready for a hike.

Jennifer Denniston Thanks to Rob Rachowiecki, Jeff, David, James, Suki and the cartographers at Lonely Planet. And to Rhawn, for spending months on the road in New Mexico with me and our newborn baby so I could research.

Kim Grant Many thanks (in return) to my friend and colleague Tom Brosnahan who organized and wrote the first edition of *New England.*

Jeremy Gray Thanks especially to John T Edge for guidance in Mississippi, David Nelson for fun in Louisiana, and Petra for inspiration at home.

Mark Lightbody After the September 2001 terrorist attack on my southern neighbor, I, like thousands of others, donated blood for New York City medical use. This very small gesture is a thank you for the generosity shown me in my travels, and a token of what friends are all about.

Maria Mack Thanks to Carolyn Miller, Kate Hoffman, Michele Posner and James Lyon and my many co-authors. Thanks to Sean and Andy for the place to crash and the blackjack; Josh, George and Rosie in Palm Springs, Annie in San Diego; the Brit boys. Many thanks to Laura Kinsey, Moira Potter, Dave Moyse, Mr Glen, Christian Luxton, Steve Zweir, Cashel O'Boyle, Sarra Lederman, Florence Clutch, Katsie Jerinic, Leena Jayaswal, Chris Gillis, Aimee Panyard, Scott McNeely and Radiohead. Special thanks to Mom and Dad for everything.

Andrew Dean Nystrom In Idaho, thanks to Joyce, Auntie Rachel, Victor and the Scotts in Kellogg; the Smiths at Three Rivers Resort in Lowell; Dugout Dick; Noel and Betty Stone in North Fork; Julie Fanselow in Twin Falls; the Wights in Idaho Falls. In Wyoming, thanks to Joyce Speidel at Warren Peak Fire Lookout; Pinedale Online; Steve at Louis Lake Lodge; Eleanor Carrigen at Crimson Dawn; Gary Rolland in Cheyenne; Casey and Amy at the Sundance Inn in Jackson; and Monte and Maxine for teaching me the importance of establishing a rapport with the wildlife. Finally, much love to my family, and to Morgan for the shared laughs.

Rob Rachowiecki I thank the staffers at chambers of commerce throughout the Southwest who provided town maps and useful information. Rangers and officials at all federal and state parks were unfailingly helpful with updating. I especially thank my family for enabling me to travel for many weeks to update this book and for being unfailingly supportive of my work. I love you.

Robert Reid Thanks go to countless pals made along the 13,770-mile trail through the Great Plains, including Shannon Bryant, John Hackett, Randy Van Hosen and the visitor centers. At Lonely Planet, piles of thanks to Michele Posner for offering me the gig, Mariah Bear for parking my Nissan, Annette Olson for fielding 'what is map?' queries, Suki Gear for cheerfully editing the thing, Jeff Williams for the great text from the 1st edition and James Lyon for many grand tips. Also, thanks to part-time partners on the road Uncle David and Dad. Lastly, thanks to Mai for letting me paw the new computer.

Don Root Lone Star State hospitality is the stuff of legend. A hearty Texas-size thanks goes out to Bobby Byrd, David Romo, and Joe Nebhan and his crew in El Paso; Johnny Mack & the Mojo Cowboys in Fort Worth; Sheriff Marge, Jimmy Lee Jones and Tom in Luckenbach; Candace Kunz in Kerrville; Christine Hopkins in Galveston; Jim Glendinning in Alpine; and Jon 'Big Dog' Bohach in Terlingua. ¡Hasta la vista, amigos!

Daniel C Schechter These folks deserve mention for their hospitality and/or willingness to share their considerable knowledge of the Pacific Northwest: Surjit Chabra, Greg and Laurie Clayton, Carl Haarstad, Judy Jewell and Paul Levy, Deb Miller and John Schoppert. Special thanks to my wife, Myra Ingmanson, for her editorial and emotional support, and to her parents, Earl and Margaret Ingmanson, intrepid Northwest travelers.

China Williams Big thanks to Matt for heroically tolerating my absence (to research this book) following our wedding. Thanks to my family at the South Carolina homestead. Susan Fox, Stan Gray and the folks at Bed, No Breakfast extended the famous Charleston hospitality. Thanks to John Williams (my brother) and Gordon Williams (no relation) for recommending Columbia's best beef and beer joints. Thanks also to the talented folks of the USA production team led by Suki Gear.

Jeff Williams Jeff would like to thank Randy Peffer foremost, as he has been a great companion (even by Internet) on previous Capital Region projects. To all the people on the road who made my research easier, thanks. Heaps of praise is due to the staff at information centers and CVBs, especially those who put up with an inquisitive Kiwi who wanted to dissect their towns into Things to See & Do, etc. And to the great staff in Oakland – you fashion these guides into usable commodities, and you have been great to work with, thorough professionals. To Floyd County, Virginia, a special thanks for great mountain hospitality. And to West Virginia, 'thanks for all the fish.' Lastly, and most importantly, love and thanks to my son, Callum.

This Book

This 2nd edition of *USA* was written by a team of authors led by James Lyon, who also coordinated the 1st edition and drafted many of the book's chapters. This edition's text is based on the last edition but also draws from many recent Lonely Planet guides to US regions and cities.

The primary authors who contributed to this guide are as follows: James Lyon (introductory chapters and New York & the Mid-Atlantic States, with help from Kerry Hook), Jeff Campbell (Utah), Jeff Davis (Georgia), Jennifer Denniston (New Mexico), Tom Downs (San Francisco & the Bay Area), Jim DuFresne (Alaska and Michigan), Mason Florence (Colorado), Ned Friary (Hawaii), Marisa Gierlich (Montana), Kim Grant (New England), Jeremy Gray (the South), Judy Jewell (Portland and Central, Northeast and Southeast Oregon), Mark Lightbody (Great Lakes), Maria Mack (Southern California and Las Vegas), Diane Marshall (Florida), Andrew Dean Nystrom (Wyoming and Idaho), Rob Rachowiecki (Arizona and southwest New Mexico), Robert Reid (Great Plains), Don Root (Texas), Daniel Schechter (Washington State), Jennifer Snarski (Oregon Coast, Willamette Valley and Southern Oregon), Andrea Schulte-Peevers (Los Angeles), Ryan ver Berkmoes (Chicago), China Williams (South Carolina), Jeff Williams (Washington, DC & the Capital Region), Kurt Wolff (Northern California and Nevada).

FROM THE PUBLISHER

Just about the entire Oakland, California, office pitched in to map, edit, proofread and design this book. Suki Gear was the lead editor, who relied heavily on Michele Posner and Kate Hoffman for guidance and laughs during the project. Vivek Waglé heroically edited a large chunk of the book, as did Paul Sheridan. China Williams, Susan Shook Malloy, Jacqueline Volin and Don Root also helped edit. Vivek, China, Susan, Christine Lee, Emily Wolman, Pelin Thornhill, Wendy Taylor and Sarah Hawkins Hubbard proofread. Maria Donohoe, Robert Reid, David Zingarelli and Wade Fox also provided editorial support. Ken DellaPenta indexed the book.

On the mapping end, Graham 'Captain Canuck' Neale headed up the cartography team with guidance from Annette Olson, Tracey Croom and Alex Guilbert. Toiling over the maps were Buck Cantwell, Justin Colgan, John Culp, Lee Espinole, Ivy Feibelman, Gina Gillich, Molly Green, Christopher Howard, Patrick Huerta, Anneka Imkamp, Rachel Jereb, Brad Lodge, Tim Lohnes, Laurie Mikkelsen, Carole Nuttall, Don Patterson, Patrick Phelan, Andrew Rebold, Tessa Rottiers, Kat Smith, Herman So, John Spelman, Eric Thomsen, Ed Turley, Rudie Watzig and Bart Wright.

Up on the Designer Deck, Gerilyn Attebery, Beca Lafore and Lora Santiago laid out the book with panache, while Susan Rimerman kept the design process rolling along smoothly. Beca also designed the color pages and cover. Justin Donohoe Marler created many of the illustrations. Also contributing illustrations were Mark Butler, Trudi Canavan, Hugh D'Andrade, John Fadeff, Hayden Foell, Rini Keagy, Henia Miedzinski, Hannah Reineck, Lora Santiago, Jim Swanson and Jennifer Steffey.

'The team' would like to thank James Lyon and the other authors for all their incredible hard work.

Dedication This book is dedicated to Tim Roufael (May 14, 1969–October 4, 2001), a Lonely Planet employee who taught us the importance of living fearlessly, embracing love no matter the risk and finding self-realization through selfless service to others. Tim had an absolute dedication to discovering joy in every moment. We humbly thank the universe for sending Tim and his iridescent soul our way.

Foreword

ABOUT LONELY PLANET GUIDEBOOKS

The story begins with a classic travel adventure: Tony and Maureen Wheeler's 1972 journey across Europe and Asia to Australia. Useful information about the overland trail did not exist at that time, so Tony and Maureen published the first Lonely Planet guidebook to meet a growing need.

From a kitchen table, then from a tiny office in Melbourne (Australia), Lonely Planet has become the largest independent travel publisher in the world, an international company with offices in Melbourne, Oakland (USA), London (UK) and Paris (France).

Today Lonely Planet guidebooks cover the globe. There is an ever-growing list of books, and there's information in a variety of forms and media. Some things haven't changed. The main aim is still to help make it possible for adventurous travelers to get out there – to explore and better understand the world.

At Lonely Planet we believe travelers can make a positive contribution to the countries they visit – if they respect their host communities and spend their money wisely. Since 1986 a percentage of the income from each book has been donated to aid projects and human-rights campaigns.

Updates Lonely Planet thoroughly updates each guidebook as often as possible. This usually means there are around two years between editions, although for more unusual or more stable destinations the gap can be longer. Check the imprint page (usually following the color map at the beginning of the book) for publication dates.

Between editions up-to-date information is available in two free newsletters – the paper *Planet Talk* and email *Comet* (to subscribe, contact any Lonely Planet office) – and on our Web site at www.lonelyplanet.com. The *Upgrades* section of the Web site covers a number of important and volatile destinations and is regularly updated by Lonely Planet authors. *Scoop* covers news and current affairs relevant to travelers. And, lastly, the *Thorn Tree* bulletin board and *Postcards* section of the site carry unverified, but fascinating, reports from travelers.

Correspondence The process of creating new editions begins with the letters, postcards and emails received from travelers. This correspondence often includes suggestions, criticisms and comments about the current editions. Interesting excerpts are immediately passed on via newsletters and the Web site, and everything goes to our authors to be verified when they're researching on the road. We're keen to get more feedback from organizations or individuals who represent communities visited by travelers.

> Lonely Planet gathers information for everyone who's curious about the planet – and especially for those who explore it firsthand. Through guidebooks, phrasebooks, activity guides, maps, literature, newsletters, image library, TV series and Web site we act as an information exchange for a worldwide community of travelers.

16

Research Authors aim to gather sufficient practical information to enable travelers to make informed choices and to make the mechanics of a journey run smoothly. They also research historical and cultural background to help enrich the travel experience and allow travelers to understand and respond appropriately to cultural and environmental issues.

Authors don't stay in every hotel because that would mean spending a couple of months in each medium-size city and, no, they don't eat at every restaurant because that would mean stretching belts beyond capacity. They do visit hotels and restaurants to check standards and prices, but feedback based on readers' direct experiences can be very helpful.

Many of our authors work undercover; others aren't so secretive. None of them accept freebies in exchange for positive write-ups. And none of our guidebooks contain any advertising.

Production Authors submit their manuscripts and maps to offices in Australia, the USA, UK or France. Editors and cartographers – all experienced travelers themselves – then begin the process of assembling the pieces. When the book finally hits the shops, some things are already out of date, we start getting feedback from readers and the process begins again...

WARNING & REQUEST

Things change – prices go up, schedules change, good places go bad and bad places go bankrupt – nothing stays the same. So, if you find things better or worse, recently opened or long since closed, please tell us and help make the next edition even more accurate and useful. We genuinely value all the feedback we receive. A well-traveled team reads and acknowledges every letter, postcard and email and ensures that every morsel of information finds its way to the appropriate authors, editors and cartographers for verification.

Everyone who writes to us will find their name listed in the next edition of the appropriate guidebook. They will also receive the latest issue of *Planet Talk*, our quarterly printed newsletter, or *Comet*, our monthly email newsletter. Subscriptions to both newsletters are free. The very best contributions will be rewarded with a free guidebook.

We may edit, reproduce and incorporate your comments in all Lonely Planet products, such as guidebooks, Web sites and digital products, so let us know if you don't want your comments reproduced or your name acknowledged.

Send all correspondence to the Lonely Planet office closest to you:

Australia: Locked Bag 1, Footscray, Victoria 3011
USA: 150 Linden St, Oakland, CA 94607
UK: 10a Spring Place, London NW5 3BH
France: 1 rue du Dahomey, 75011 Paris

Or email us at: talk2us@lonelyplanet.com.au

For news, views and updates, see our Web site: www.lonelyplanet.com

HOW TO USE A LONELY PLANET GUIDEBOOK

The best way to use a Lonely Planet guidebook is any way you choose. At Lonely Planet, we believe the most memorable travel experiences are often those that are unexpected, and the finest discoveries are those that you make yourself. Guidebooks are not intended to be used as if they provided a detailed set of infallible instructions!

Contents All Lonely Planet guidebooks follow roughly the same format. The Facts about the Destination chapters or sections give background information ranging from history to weather. Facts for the Visitor gives practical information on issues like visas and health. Getting There & Away gives a brief starting point for researching travel to and from the destination. Getting Around gives an overview of the transport options when you arrive.

The peculiar demands of each destination determine how subsequent chapters are broken up, but some things remain constant. We always start with background, then proceed to sights, places to stay, places to eat, entertainment, getting there and away, and getting around information – in that order.

Heading Hierarchy Lonely Planet headings are used in a strict hierarchical structure that can be visualized as a set of Russian dolls. Each heading (and its following text) is encompassed by any preceding heading that is higher on the hierarchical ladder.

Entry Points We do not assume guidebooks will be read from beginning to end, but that people will dip into them. The traditional entry points are the list of contents and the index. In addition, however, some books have a complete list of maps and an index map illustrating map coverage.

There may also be a color map that shows highlights. These highlights are dealt with in greater detail in the Facts for the Visitor chapter, along with planning questions and suggested itineraries. Each chapter covering a geographical region usually begins with a locator map and another list of highlights. Once you find something of interest in a list of highlights, turn to the index.

Maps Maps play a crucial role in Lonely Planet guidebooks and include a huge amount of information. A legend is printed on the back page. We seek to have complete consistency between maps and text and to have every important place in the text captured on a map. Map key numbers usually start in the top left corner.

Although inclusion in a guidebook usually implies a recommendation, we cannot list every good place. Exclusion does not necessarily imply criticism. In fact there are a number of reasons why we might exclude a place – sometimes it is simply inappropriate to encourage an influx of travelers.

Introduction

The USA is a country that needs no introduction – it's so well known that even first-time visitors feel like they've been there before. It's just like on TV, only more so. There's something very satisfying about seeing all those fast-food franchises, Coca-Cola commercials and baseball caps in the place where they really belong. The biggest surprise is the scale and extent of all that Americana. You expect to see freeways, but the spaghettilike crisscrossing of a six-level interchange and the endlessness of the interstate highways are still astonishing.

Images of the USA's natural wonders have been promoted since the days of westward expansion. Parks like Yellowstone, Yosemite and the Grand Canyon were the foundations of the US tourist industry. From coral reefs to glaciers, rain forest to high desert, grasslands to wetlands, sand dunes to snowfields, the grandeur of the landscape surpasses even American superlatives. Wildlife, fish, birds and flowers await any naturalist who has ever dreamed of the American wilderness.

For those who like their nature laced with adrenaline, the beaches, forests, mountains, deserts and rivers cater to every conceivable outdoor pursuit, from ice climbing to boogie boarding, fly-fishing to triathlons. And because every pastime is an industry in America, this is the best place to see the very latest in snowboarding, mountain biking, in-line skating, hot-air ballooning or whatever else you're into.

American culture came into its own early in the 20th century, when European cultural traditions were abandoned in favor of jazz and ragtime music, modern art and architecture, new styles in literature and the great new medium of the motion picture. The USA's cities, especially New York, have been cultural capitals ever since, attracting artists, writers, composers and performers from around the world. Now, every region has its literature, every state its historical

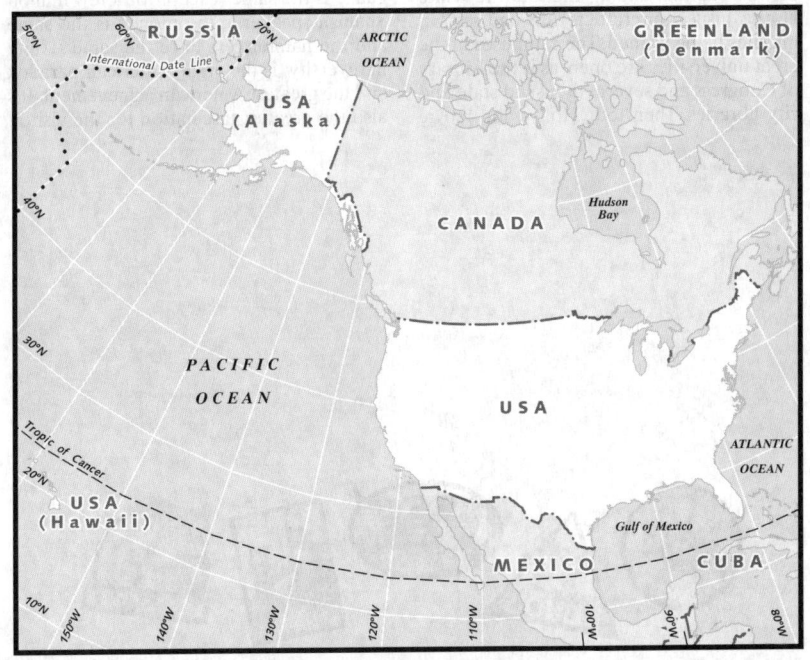

sites and museums, and every city has its galleries and theaters. In contrast, America's indigenous cultures are not as widely appreciated as they deserve to be – interest is growing, but some remarkable archaeological sites remain all but ignored.

On the level of popular culture, the USA is at its democratic best. Though gospel, blues, country, soul and rock are all commercialized now, it's not hard to find venues where local musicians play authentic American music. Authentic American TV is easily accessible, just by flipping through the 100-plus stations of shopping shows, talk shows, sports shows, soap operas, reruns, telethons and TV evangelists.

Of course, the USA is much more than a tourist destination. It's the richest, most powerful, most inventive country on earth. If you're out to discover what makes the USA mighty, your quest is made easier by the fact that it's also the most open of countries. This very openness has been exploited by fanatics, but even faced with such threats, the American way is to permit as much public access as possible. Unless there are exceptional security concerns, you can visit the US Capitol building and tour the White House, inspect aircraft carriers and see US marines being trained. The campuses of the great universities are open, as is the Library of Congress and several thousand state and city libraries. Then tour Hollywood movie studios and the CNN headquarters, see jumbo-jet factories and the New York Stock Exchange, visit Houston's space center and watch as million-dollar machines harvest 1000-acre wheat fields.

From a practical point of view, the USA has everything a traveler might need or want. Accommodations range from free campsites to luxury suites, and the eating options run from fast-food takeout to gourmet restaurants with celebrity chefs. The cities have nightclubs, comedy clubs and dance clubs and every luxury and frivolity that can be imagined. Suburban life centers on the shopping mall, where the business of buying and selling has been raised from a necessity to an art form, and where shopping is a major leisure activity.

Contradiction and paradox abound in America. You can be impressed by efficiency and dismayed by commercialism; enraptured by the natural beauty and appalled by urban ugliness; overwhelmed by kindness and offended by indifference; staggered by wealth and shocked by poverty. Alaska and Florida may be vastly different, but they are equally American. The language is the same (except for a few million Spanish speakers), the money is the same and the hamburgers taste the same. 'Unity in diversity' is the great American paradox and the greatest American achievement. It's also the greatest fascination for the visitor.

Facts about the USA

HISTORY
The First Immigrants

It's generally accepted that the first people in the Americas came from east Asia, over a land bridge to Alaska across what is now the Bering Strait. The land bridge, called Beringia, occurred when sea levels were lowered during an ice age between 25,000 and 10,000 years ago. The first immigrants were probably nomadic hunters following large game animals, moving south and east to all corners of the Americas. Impenetrable ice sheets would have made the land bridge impassable during the middle of the ice age (20,000 to 13,000 years ago), so it's thought that the first settlers came across either before the ice peaked, or they came afterward and migrated throughout the Americas with remarkable speed. Estimates of the timing of this epic migration vary from as recently as 12,500 years ago to as far back as 70,000 years, but the oldest estimates are largely speculative.

Human artifacts from a site in southern Chile, recently carbon dated to about 12,500 years old, are among the oldest undisputed evidence of human occupation in the Americas. Many sites in North and South America are claimed to be older than this, but there is no evidence at all of a progression in the age of artifacts from North to South America, which one would expect if the Americas were populated by a gradual land migration from Alaska to southern Patagonia.

There were probably several periods of prehistoric migration, the most recent being that of the Inuit people (also called Eskimos), who are thought to have arrived by boat, skirting the edge of the ice fields around 4000 years ago.

Among the earliest known inhabitants of North America were the makers of stone tools (probably butchering tools), found near Clovis, New Mexico. These 'Clovis points' have been dated to around 11,000 years ago. Numerous other sites all over the continent have yielded hunting implements almost as old, or possibly older.

After the ice age, many or the continent's large animals, like the mammoth, became extinct. Americans turned to hunting smaller game, fishing and gathering wild berries, seeds, roots and fruits. Agriculture developed, especially as the use of new crops spread north from cultures in the area of modern Mexico. Primitive corn (maize) was cultivated in the Southwest from about 3000 BC, and by 500 BC maize, squash and beans were widespread in the South, East and Midwest.

Moundbuilders The Hopewell culture arose in the Ohio and Mississippi Valleys from around 500 BC. Their settlements were characterized by earthen mounds, initially made for defense, but later used as burial sites and temples. These people had many towns, well-developed agriculture and extensive trading links north to Lake Huron, west to the Rocky Mountains and south to Mexico.

The lower Mississippi moundbuilders peaked somewhat later, but declined and disappeared by about AD 1200. Later, many new Native American groups came to occupy the forestlands in the East, South and Midwest. The remains of mounds can be seen at many sites across these regions, most notably at Poverty Point in northern Louisiana, the Cahokia Mounds in East St Louis, Illinois, and around Chillicothe, Ohio.

Ancestral Puebloans In the Southwest were three other early cultural groups, who lived in communities that the Spanish later called pueblos. The Hohokam, noted for their irrigation systems and pottery, thrived from 300 BC to about AD 1450. The Mogollon, who depended more on hunting, emerged around 200 BC and were apparently absorbed by the third group, the Ancestral Puebloans (previously known as Anasazi), who built the amazing cliff dwellings of Mesa Verde and Canyon de Chelly before moving south around AD 1300. All these groups started as hunter-gatherers, became more settled as their agriculture improved, but largely disappeared by the 15th century.

Indigenous Peoples Circa 1600 The indigenous population at the time of the first European contact is variously estimated

Chronology of US History

Before 10,000 BC – migration from Asia to North America across Bering Strait

900 BC – stone butchering tools made in Clovis, New Mexico

1000 BC – earliest rock art in California

500 BC – first moundbuilding cultures, Mississippi Valley

AD 300 – Hohokam people develop irrigation in the Southwest

450 – cliff dwellings built at Mesa Verde, Colorado

1000 – Norse seafarers land along northeast coasts; temporary settlements in Newfoundland area

1492 – Columbus 'discovers America,' making landfall in the Bahamas

1497 – John Cabot claims New England for his patron, Henry VII

1534 – Jacques Cartier sails up the St Lawrence River

1540 – Francisco Vásquez de Coronado expedition wanders through the Southwest

1542 – Juan Rodríguez de Cabrillo's ships enter San Diego harbor while charting the West Coast and the Channel Islands

1565 – Spanish settlement at Saint Augustine, Florida

1579 – Francis Drake lands on northern California coast and claims land for England

1584 – Walter Raleigh claims the Atlantic coast for England

1585 – Walter Raleigh founds the 'lost colony' of Roanoke

1607 – first permanent English settlement at Jamestown, Virginia

1608 – first French settlements in Quebec

1619 – first black slaves sold in Virginia

1620 – *Mayflower* lands in Cape Cod with 102 English 'Pilgrims'

1624 – first Dutch settlement along Hudson River

1664 – English take over Dutch colonies in the northeast; New Amsterdam renamed New York

1682 – La Salle travels the length of the Mississippi River; claims the region for France

1759 – British defeat French in Battle of Quebec; crucial victory in French & Indian War

1763 – Peace of Paris gives Britain control of Canada and all land east of the Mississippi

1769 – Padre Junípero Serra establishes California's first mission, in San Diego

1773 – Boston Tea Party protests against British taxation

1775 – Revolutionary War starts with battles at Lexington and Concord, near Boston

1776 – American colonies sign Declaration of Independence on July 4

1778 – France recognizes US independence; Captain James Cook lands in Hawaiian Islands

1781 – British surrender at Yorktown

1783 – Treaty of Paris; US independence from Britain

1787 – Constitutional Convention in Philadelphia draws up the US Constitution

1788 – Constitution ratified by nine states; George Washington elected first president of the USA

1791 – Bill of Rights adopted as constitutional amendments

1794 – Battle of Fallen Timbers ends Indian resistance in Ohio

1800 – Washington, DC, becomes national capital

1803 – Louisiana Purchase from France doubles the area of US territory

1804–6 – Lewis and Clark Expedition explores the new territory from the Mississippi to the Pacific Ocean

1810 – USA annexes West Florida (the Gulf Coast panhandle west to New Orleans)

1811 – Battle of Tippecanoe ends Indian resistance in Indiana

1812 – War of 1812 starts with battles against British and Indians around Great Lakes; Russians build Fort Ross, north of San Francisco Bay

1815 – War of 1812 ends without clear victory

1819 – Spain cedes Florida to the USA

1821 – Mexico becomes independent of Spain after 10-year struggle

1823 – Monroe Doctrine warns European countries against interference in the Americas

Chronology of US History

1827 – Jedediah Smith arrives in Southern California after overland journey from the Midwest

1830 – Indian Removal Act begins final forced exodus of Indians from Eastern states

1841 – first wagons follow new immigrant trails to California

1845 – annexation of Texas

1846 – Oregon territory acquired from Britain; USA declares war on Mexico

1848 – Treaty of Guadalupe Hidalgo cedes present-day California, Arizona, Nevada and New Mexico and parts of Wyoming, Utah and Colorado to the USA

1849 – California gold rush; 80,000 immigrants arrive

1856 – first railroad bridge over the Mississippi, at Moline, Illinois

1861 – Abraham Lincoln becomes president; Southern states secede; attack on Fort Sumter starts Civil War

1863 – emancipation of slaves

1865 – Southern forces surrender; Lincoln assassinated

1867 – Alaska purchased from Russia

1869 – completion of first transcontinental railway enables travel from New York to San Francisco in four days

1871 – Great Chicago Fire

1872 – Yellowstone becomes the first national park

1876 – Custer's Last Stand

1880 – New York City population exceeds one million

1881 – gunfight at OK Corral

1883 – USA adopts four standard time zones; Brooklyn Bridge opens

1886 – Statue of Liberty unveiled; Geronimo surrenders; American Federation of Labor formed

1889 – first movie made in New Jersey; Oklahoma land rush

1894 – Pullman Railroad strike

1897 – Klondike gold rush

1898 – victory in Spanish-American War gives USA control of Philippines, Puerto Rico and Guam; annexation of Hawaii

1906 – San Francisco earthquake and fire

1914 – Panama Canal opens

1917–18 – US involvement in WWI

1920 – 18th amendment bans alcohol, Prohibition starts; 19th amendment gives women the vote

1924 – Native Americans granted American citizenship

1929 – stock market crash starts the Great Depression

1932 – Olympic Games in Los Angeles

1933 – Franklin D Roosevelt introduces New Deal economic initiatives; Prohibition ends

1937 – Golden Gate Bridge opens in San Francisco

1941 – Pearl Harbor bombed; USA enters WWII

1945 – end of WWII

1950 – start of Korean War

1954 – US Supreme Court rules racial segregation unconstitutional

1955 – Disneyland opens

1957 – nine black students enroll in Little Rock Central High School under military protection

1961 – first US forces in Vietnam

1962 – Cuban missile crisis

1963 – President John F Kennedy assassinated in Dallas; California becomes the most populous state in the USA

1965 – race riots in Los Angeles leave 34 killed

1967 – 'Summer of Love,' San Francisco

1968 – Martin Luther King Jr assassinated in Memphis; Robert Kennedy assassinated in Los Angeles

1973 – last US forces leave Vietnam

1974 – Nixon resigns over Watergate

1979 – nuclear accident at Three Mile Island

1979–80 – US hostages held in Iran

1983 – Reagan announces 'Star Wars' strategic defense initiative

1984 – Olympic Games in Los Angeles

1987 – October stock market crash

1991 – USA leads Gulf War coalition against Iraq

1996 – Olympic Games in Atlanta

1998 – President Clinton survives impeachment over Monica Lewinsky scandal

2000 – George W Bush wins controversial election amid vote-counting fiasco

2001 – Terrorists hijack four planes and crash into the World Trade Center and Pentagon, killing thousands

from less than one million to more than 15 million – a range that indicates how little is really known about native North Americans. Archaeological evidence reveals much about the material basis of Native American life and generally identifies a broad cultural grouping associated with each of the major environmental regions of the continent.

The eastern woodland people, who occupied the northeast and eastern part of the continent, were probably not direct descendants of the moundbuilders, but they lived in permanent settlements, cultivated maize and other crops, and had a well-organized system of government. Further south, people also lived principally by agriculture, though the warmer climate entailed lifestyle differences, so these groups are sometimes categorized separately as Mississippi farmers.

Most of the Plains Indians lived in villages along the valleys, cultivated corn and organized buffalo hunts in which bison were herded into corrals or over cliffs. In the 18th century, some Plains Indians domesticated the wild horses that had descended from animals left by Spaniards 200 years before. This led to a brief but glorious period of Indians as mounted, nomadic hunters and warriors, using the plentiful buffalo for food, clothing and shelter.

The people of the Pacific Northwest lived mostly by fishing in coastal waters and rivers, and also gathering plant foods onshore. The fishing was so rich that these people were able to devote much of their time and energy to highly developed cultural pursuits, most notably the elaborate decoration of longhouses, canoes and totem poles. Farther north, forest dwellers were hunters and gatherers, while those in the arctic tundra and on the coasts lived solely by hunting and fishing. On the California coast, people gathered and stored acorns as a reliable staple, and also caught fish and collected shellfish.

Inland on the Columbian plateau, the main activities were fishing, hunting small game and foraging for plants. Further south, in the deserts of the Great Basin, game and fish were scarcer, and wild plants were the main food source. Pueblo farming communities were limited to a few areas of what is now New Mexico and Arizona.

Language Groups, Nations & Tribes

Within the broad cultural areas, archaeologists and anthropologists try to identify major language groups (language 'phyla' and 'families'), which usually embrace a number of disparate and largely independent communities called Indian Nations or tribes, speaking different dialects of the language. Two or more language groups may be interspersed with one another in the same area, but most Indian Nations occupied permanent settlements on their own territory and made seasonal use of other sites for hunting or gathering. The Nations were engaged in territorial conflicts, alliances, expansions and retreats before and after European settlement, and this makes it hard to say exactly who lived where (see the Indigenous Peoples map).

The New World

Norse seafarers landed in North America as early as the 10th century and founded a settlement called Vinland, which was probably in Newfoundland. This colony was soon abandoned, but it's likely that northern Europeans continued as regular visitors to the rich cod fisheries of the North Atlantic coast.

Columbus landed in the Caribbean in 1492 while in search of a route to the spice islands of Asia. Believing that he had landed in the East Indies, he called the native people Indians, creating a lasting linguistic confusion. The Spanish, who had sponsored his expedition, continued building their American Empire, most dramatically when Cortés conquered Mexico in 1519–20.

Spanish Juan Ponce de León explored the coasts of Florida in 1513, and Alonzo Alvarez de Pineda followed the perimeter of the Gulf of Mexico in 1519. Cabeza de Vaca became separated from another expedition in Florida, and between 1528 and 1536 he traveled right across the continent before finding his way back to Mexico. Pushing north from modern-day Mexico, Francisco de Coronado wandered for two years (1540–41) in what is now Arizona, New Mexico and Colorado, seeking cities of gold and islands of spice, but finding only arid land and hostile natives. Juan Rodríguez de Cabrillo sailed up the Pacific coast in 1542, reaching as far as Oregon but finding little of value to Spain.

For most of the 16th century, the Spanish devoted their attention to exploiting other

INDIGENOUS PEOPLES CIRCA 1600

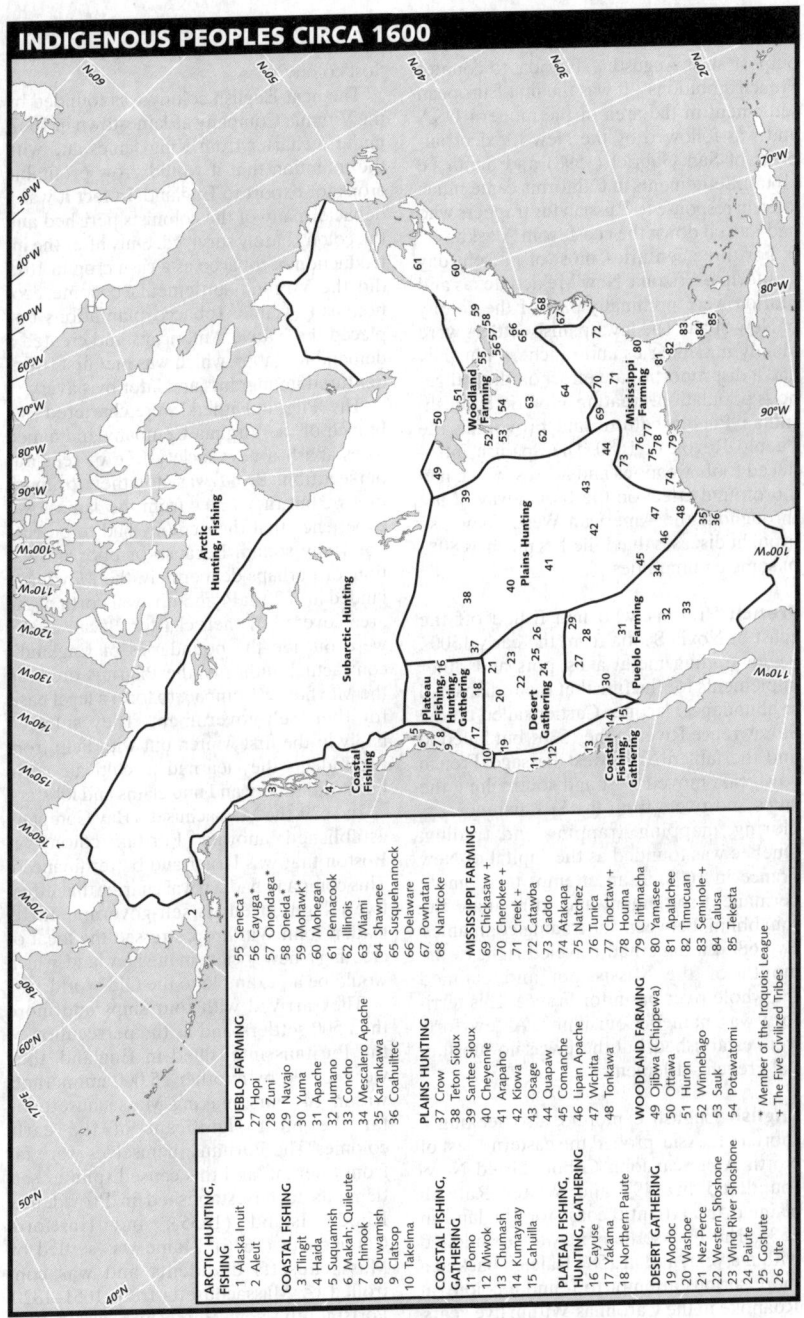

ARCTIC HUNTING, FISHING
1 Alaska Inuit
2 Aleut

COASTAL FISHING
3 Tlingit
4 Haida
5 Suquamish
6 Makah, Quileute
7 Chinook
8 Duwamish
9 Clatsop
10 Takelma

COASTAL FISHING, GATHERING
11 Pomo
12 Miwok
13 Chumash
14 Kumayaay
15 Cahuilla

PLATEAU FISHING, HUNTING, GATHERING
16 Cayuse
17 Yakama
18 Northern Paiute

DESERT GATHERING
19 Modoc
20 Washoe
21 Nez Perce
22 Western Shoshone
23 Wind River Shoshone
24 Paiute
25 Goshute
26 Ute

PUEBLO FARMING
27 Hopi
28 Zuni
29 Navajo
30 Yuma
31 Apache
32 Jumano
33 Concho
34 Mescalero Apache
35 Karankawa
36 Coahuiltec

PLAINS HUNTING
37 Crow
38 Teton Sioux
39 Santee Sioux
40 Cheyenne
41 Arapaho
42 Kiowa
43 Osage
44 Quapaw
45 Comanche
46 Lipan Apache
47 Wichita
48 Tonkawa

WOODLAND FARMING
49 Ojibwa (Chippewa)
50 Ottawa
51 Huron
52 Winnebago
53 Sauk
54 Potawatomi

55 Seneca*
56 Cayuga*
57 Onondaga*
58 Oneida*
59 Mohawk*
60 Mohegan
61 Pennacook
62 Illinois
63 Miami
64 Shawnee
65 Susquehannock
66 Delaware
67 Powhatan
68 Nanticoke

MISSISSIPPI FARMING
69 Chickasaw +
70 Cherokee +
71 Creek +
72 Catawba
73 Caddo
74 Atakapa
75 Natchez
76 Tunica
77 Choctaw +
78 Houma
79 Chitimacha
80 Yamasee
81 Apalachee
82 Timucuan
83 Seminole +
84 Calusa
85 Tekesta

* Member of the Iroquois League
+ The Five Civilized Tribes

parts of their empire and fending off rival European nations. In 1565, they founded an outpost at St Augustine, Florida, to counter French ambitions – it was the first European settlement in the area of the modern USA and was followed by the New Mexico outposts of San Gabriel (1598) and Santa Fe (1609). Settlements in California came much later, in response to Russian fur trappers who had moved down the coast from Alaska.

For three centuries, most of present-day California, Arizona, New Mexico, Texas and Florida were nominally part of the colony of New Spain. The few Spanish settlers were mainly missionaries and ranchers, but they had a disproportionate effect on the indigenous population, creating a hybrid Spanish-Indian Pueblo culture and provoking the Pueblo Revolt of 1680. The Spanish introduced tools, weapons and horses, which had a profound effect on the Indian way of life throughout the American West. They also brought diseases that killed as much as 80% of some communities.

French Bretons, who had fished off the coast of Novia Scotia from the early 1500s, began trading metal axes, pots and other implements for the furs that the Indians had in abundance. Jacques Cartier sailed up the St Lawrence River in the 1530s, but failed to find the fabled Northwest Passage. French *voyageurs* moved west and south along the lakes and rivers from the St Lawrence, exploring, mapping, trapping and trading. Quebec was founded as the capital of New France in 1608, in an attempt to promote permanent settlement and to regulate the squabbling between fur-trading companies. By 1682 La Salle had traveled right to the mouth of the Mississippi and claimed the whole river basin for France. This territory was named Louisianne. A few forts were established, but there was no substantial French settlement.

English English explorers, also seeking a shortcut to Asia, probed the eastern coast of North America; John Cabot skirted Newfoundland in 1497 and Walter Raleigh claimed the Atlantic coast for England in 1584. The first settlement was abandoned within a year, and in 1587 Raleigh backed a more serious attempt to found a colony at Roanoke in the Carolinas. Within five years,

the colony mysteriously disappeared, almost without a trace, earning it the name 'lost colony.'

The next English colony was founded by the Virginia Company at Jamestown in 1607, under a charter from King James and with the intention that it would grow profitable crops for export to England. In fact it was a debacle; many of the colonists perished and the colony barely survived. Only after the introduction of tobacco as a cash crop in 1615 did the Virginia settlements become economically viable. Tobacco plantations displaced the Native Americans and created a demand for labor, which was met first by indentured immigrants and later by slavery.

The 'Pilgrim Fathers' were chartered as a branch of the Virginia Company and aimed to establish a new society free of religious persecution. Profit was not their primary motive, but they knew from the Jamestown experience that their colony had to be economically sound. Because of poor navigation, or perhaps deliberately, the *Mayflower* landed in 1620 at Plymouth, well north of the area covered by their charter. Because they were outside the boundaries of England's contractual authority, the Pilgrims drew up the Mayflower Compact to form a legal basis for their self-government. They suffered badly in the first winter, but with help from the Indians they learned to cultivate corn, hunt wild turkey and find clams and lobsters.

In 1629, the Massachusetts Bay Company established another Puritan colony at Boston that was larger and better financed. This company had a royal charter that effectively legitimized its self-government. Its leader, John Winthrop, stressed the ideal of creating a new society in the new land, which would be an example to the Old World.

They arrived with four ships and more than 500 settlers, and as the persecution of the Puritans intensified in England, they were joined by another 25,000 immigrants within 10 years, making Massachusetts by far the most significant of the early colonies. The Puritans themselves were far from tolerant, and this caused splinter settlements to be established in Providence, Rhode Island (1635), and Hartford, Connecticut (1636). Maine was settled by Massachusetts dissidents and was controlled by Massachusetts from 1651–1820. Portsmouth, New Hampshire, was settled

PRE-19TH CENTURY EUROPEAN EXPLORATION & SETTLEMENT

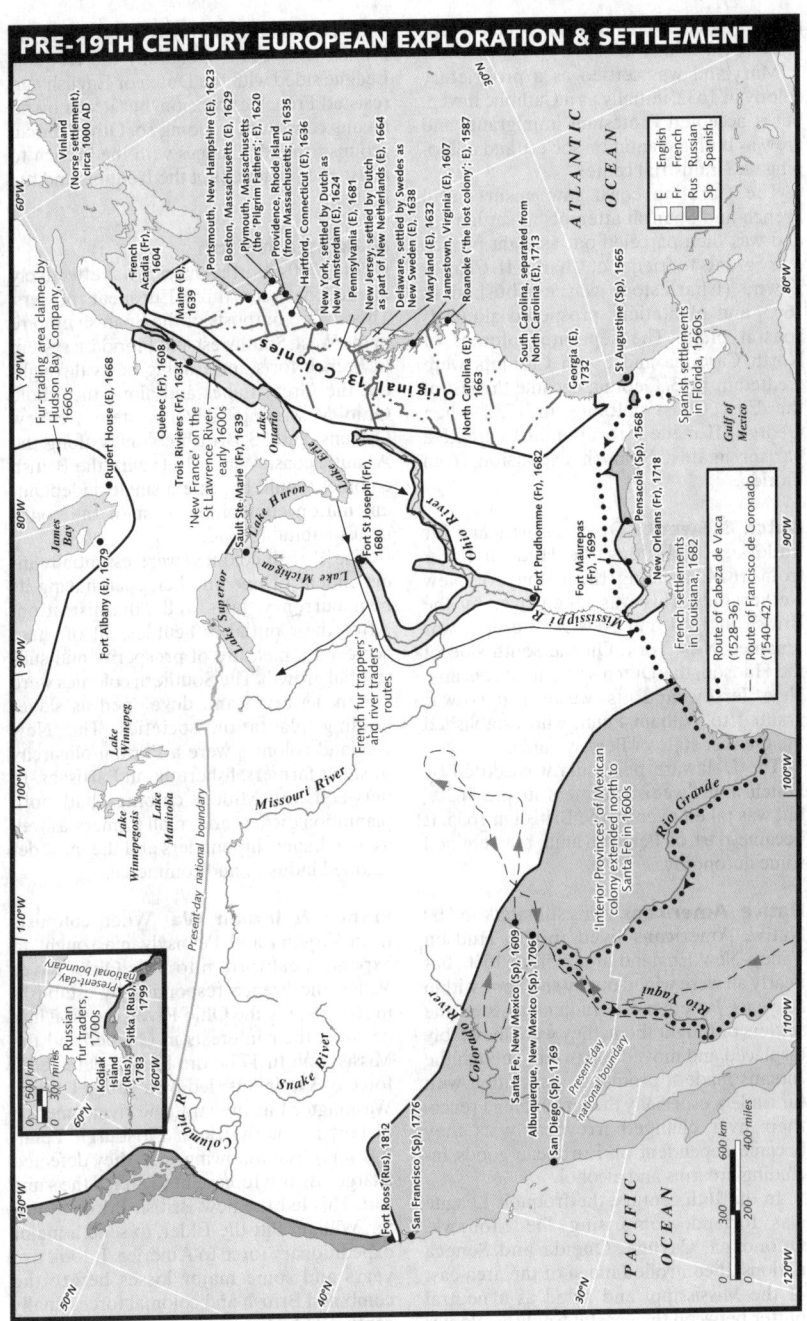

Vinland (Norse settlement), circa 1000 AD

Fur-trading area claimed by Hudson Bay Company, 1660s

French Acadia (Fr.), 1604

Rupert House (E), 1668

Fort Albany (E), 1679

Quebec (Fr.), 1608
Maine (E), 1639
Trois Rivières (Fr.), 1634
'New France' on the St Lawrence River, early 1600s
Sault Ste Marie (Fr.), 1639
Fort St Joseph (Fr.), 1680
French fur trappers' and river traders' routes

Portsmouth, New Hampshire (E), 1623
Boston, Massachusetts (E), 1629
Plymouth, Massachusetts (E), 1620 (the 'Pilgrim Fathers')
Providence, Rhode Island (from Massachusetts) (E), 1635
Hartford, Connecticut (E), 1636
New York, settled by Dutch as New Amsterdam (E), 1624
New Jersey, settled by Dutch as part of New Netherlands (E), 1664
Delaware, settled by Swedes as New Sweden, 1638
Maryland (E), 1632
Jamestown, Virginia (E), 1607
Roanoke ('the lost colony': E), 1587

Pennsylvania (E), 1681
North Carolina (E), 1663
South Carolina, separated from North Carolina, 1713
Georgia (E), 1732

St Augustine (Sp.), 1565

Spanish settlements in Florida, 1560s

Pensacola (Sp.), 1568
New Orleans (Fr.), 1718
Fort Maurepas (Fr.), 1699
French settlements in Louisiana, 1682
Fort Prudhomme (Fr.), 1682

Original 13 Colonies

ATLANTIC OCEAN

Gulf of Mexico

Lake Ontario
Lake Erie
Lake Huron
Lake Michigan
Lake Superior
Ohio River
Mississippi R.

James Bay

Lake Winnipeg
Lake Winnipegosis
Lake Manitoba

Missouri River

Present-day national boundary

'Interior Provinces' of Mexican colony extended north to Santa Fe in 1600s

Rio Grande
Rio Yaqui

Santa Fe, New Mexico (Sp), 1609
Albuquerque, New Mexico (Sp), 1706
Colorado River
Snake River
Columbia R.
San Diego (Sp) 1769
San Francisco (Sp) 1776
Present-day national boundary

Fort Ross (Rus), 1812

Route of Cabeza de Vaca (1528–36)
Route of Francisco de Coronado (1540–42)

PACIFIC OCEAN

Russian fur traders, 1700s
Sitka (Rus), 1799
Kodiak Island (Rus), 1783
Present-day national boundary

0 300 600 km
0 200 400 miles

English   E
French   Fr
Russian   Rus
Spanish   Sp

0 500 km
0 300 miles

in 1623, and New Hampshire became a separate royal colony in 1679.

Maryland was settled as a proprietary colony in 1632, initially as a Catholic haven, but it accepted Protestant immigrants and grew as both a plantation society and a shipping and industrial center.

The Carolina coast saw unsuccessful French and Spanish attempts at settlement and was then parceled out as eight proprietary grants to friends of Charles II. Charles Towne (Charleston) was established in 1663, and plantations prospered along its coastal plain. The separate colonies of North Carolina and South Carolina were created in 1713. Georgia became the last of the East Coast colonies in 1732 when George III made a royal grant to create a barrier against Spanish expansion from Florida.

Dutch & Swedes Dutch farmers and fur traders settled along the Hudson River from 1624, forming the colony of New Netherlands. This was taken over by the British in 1664 and New Amsterdam was renamed New York. On the south side of the Hudson, the Dutch settlements became New Jersey, and its western part was granted to William Penn, who established the Quaker state of Pennsylvania.

The Delaware peninsula was settled by Dutch and Swedish farmers in the 1630s, but was taken over by the British in 1655. It became part of Pennsylvania, but retained some autonomy.

Native Americans An estimated 75,000 Native Americans lived in the Hudson Valley–New England area before 1650, but nearly all were wiped out by smallpox within 50 years. Whether the Indians assisted the settlers or fought them, they were inevitably displaced and moved westward. Though the Indians made a profitable association with fur traders, especially the far-ranging French, their lives changed irrevocably as they became dependent on European goods, including firearms and alcohol.

In the 16th century, the Iroquois League was formed, comprising the Mohawk, Onondaga, Cayuga, Oneida and Seneca nations. It controlled much of the area east of the Mississippi and acted as a neutral buffer between the coastal English colonies and the isolated outposts protecting the French river trade. Generally the Iroquois League sided with the Dutch or English and resisted French expansion, but it was by no means consistent in doing so. Other Indian groups formed alliances with the French to resist encroachment of the Iroquois and the British.

Making a Nation

By the 1750s, North America was effectively divided between three European powers. There were outposts of the Spanish empire in the West, Southwest and Florida; a system of French forts and trading posts throughout the Great Lakes and along the whole Ohio–Mississippi River system to New Orleans; and 13 British colonies along the Atlantic coast. Within 100 years, the British colonies would become a single, independent nation controlling most of the continent's habitable land.

The British colonies were essentially independent of one another, each having its own currency, laws and administration. After their initial difficulties, all of them achieved a measure of prosperity and substantial growth. The Southern colonies were mainly agrarian and developed as slave-holding plantation societies. The New England colonies were a Puritan oligarchy of small farmers, fisherfolk and artisans. In between, the Middle colonies had both plantation owners and small farmers, as well as merchants, shipbuilders and the most developed industry and commerce.

French & Indian War When colonists from Virginia and Pennsylvania sought to expand westward into the Ohio River Valley, the French responded by establishing forts along the Ohio River, the vital link between their interests in Quebec and the Mississippi. In 1754, the French defeated a force of Virginians (led by a young George Washington) at the strategic river junction of Fort Duquesne (later Pittsburgh, Pennsylvania). The following year, they defeated a larger British force sent to attack the same fort. This led the new British Prime Minister, William Pitt the Elder, to send a major expeditionary force to America. It took five years and some major losses before the combined British and colonial forces finally captured Quebec in 1759.

The so-called French and Indian War was part of a larger conflict, the Seven Years War, which was also fought in Europe and India – one of the earliest 'world wars.' It was a major defeat for France, and in the 1763 Peace of Paris, all of Canada and the French territory east of the Mississippi, except New Orleans, was ceded to Britain. In a secret treaty, the French gave the land west of the Mississippi to Spain, to keep it out of British hands.

The removal of France opened up new lands for settlement, but this created a potential for conflict with the Indians and rivalry between the colonies. Without an army to control the situation, the British proclaimed in 1763 that the land west of the Appalachians would be a crown reserve for the Indians.

Discontent in the Colonies The French and Indian War had increased Britain's costs in America tremendously. Britain in turn raised the taxes levied on the colonies and introduced controls on colonial trade. In response to the Stamp Act of 1765, which imposed a tax on written documents, representatives of nine colonies met in New York. There they pledged allegiance to the king, but asserted that only the colonial legislatures had the right to tax the colonies and called for a boycott of British goods. After civil protests and demonstrations against tax collectors, the Stamp Act was soon repealed.

Two years later, the Townshend Acts placed taxes on glass, lead, tea and paper. These provoked another boycott and more protests, including the Boston Massacre, in which five Americans were killed. The Townshend Acts were also repealed, except for the tax on tea, which soon assumed a symbolic importance. In 1773, several colonies turned back cargoes of tea or refused to distribute them. At the celebrated Boston Tea Party, a shipment was dumped into the sea.

The British parliament responded with the Coercive Acts, which shut down the Massachusetts legislature and closed the Port of Boston. Four regiments were sent to garrison the city. These threats served to further unite the colonies, and 12 of them sent representatives to the First Continental Congress in Philadelphia (1774). This congress denounced the Coercive Acts, asserted the right of the colonies to defend themselves and planned another boycott of British goods.

Revolutionary War The shooting war started in April 1775 when British troops went to Concord, near Boston, looking for a colonial weapons cache. Colonial minutemen fired on them, then harried them all the way back to Boston. The Second Continental Congress, in May 1775, acted decisively to tackle the logistics of the war – taxing, borrowing, negotiating alliances and creating a continental army. Most importantly, it appointed Virginian George Washington as commander, thus committing the Southern and Middle colonies to a war that at first involved only the Northern ones.

In March 1776, the Revolutionaries had guns trained on Boston and the British moved their headquarters to New York. Washington lost badly in pitched battles for Long Island and Manhattan.

In the middle of the war, the Second Continental Congress began drafting the Articles of Confederation, which would unite the colonies. In July 1776, it adopted the Declaration of Independence, setting down the grievances against the crown and declaring that the colonies 'are and of right ought to be free and independent states.' The document was signed by representatives of the 13 colonies on July 4, which has ever since been celebrated as the nation's birthday.

Meanwhile, the British sent a major expeditionary force to quell the Revolution, comprising 32,000 British soldiers and 8000 mercenaries. In September 1777, the British took Philadelphia and the congress fled to the countryside. Washington's army spent the winter camped in Valley Forge, where more than half his men either perished or deserted.

The British suffered a major setback when they surrendered 5700 troops at Saratoga, in upstate New York (October 1777). Moving their attention to the South, they advanced successfully through Georgia and South Carolina. The French entry into the war (February 1778) was decisive, and when the main British force moved onto the York Peninsula in Virginia, they found themselves surrounded by French ships instead of the Royal Navy. Almost 7000 British troops surrendered at Yorktown in

October 1781, and the Revolutionary War was won.

The 1783 Treaty of Paris recognized American independence and set the western boundary of the new nation at the Mississippi River. Spain regained possession of Florida and kept most of the land west of the Mississippi.

The Constitution The Articles of Confederation nominally united the states during the war, but did not give the Congress of the Confederation powers to address postwar problems like the war debts, the regulation of interstate commerce, the enforcement of international agreements or relations with the Native Americans. In 1786, the Annapolis Convention called on the states to send delegates to a Constitutional Convention in Philadelphia, to 'revise' the Articles of Confederation.

The delegates, who later became known as the Founding Fathers, disregarded their instructions and proceeded to formulate a completely new constitution. The new constitution was remarkable for the balance it established between the powers of the central government (which were necessary to manage the new nation) and the interests of the individual states (which had their own traditions of self-government). Within a year, the United States Constitution was ratified by nine state legislatures and came into effect. The first US Congress met in March 1789, and its first act was to elect George Washington as president. It also resolved to impose heavy tariffs on North Carolina and Rhode Island unless they ratified the Constitution and joined the Union, which they soon did.

The Constitution provided for amendments, and several states only ratified it in the expectation that a Bill of Rights would be added. This took the form of 10 amendments adopted in 1791, including the right to free speech (the First Amendment), the right to bear arms and the right not to incriminate oneself (as in, 'You have the right to remain silent').

Manifest Destiny

Even before the Revolution, explorers, speculators and settlers had started moving west of the Appalachian Mountains. After 1783, the new federal government took several measures to regulate the expansion. Indians, many of whom had sided with the British in the Revolution, were not treated sympathetically. In a series of ad hoc treaties, individual chiefs were bribed to give away the lands of their people. Treaties that provided for Indian land rights were soon disregarded.

Rather than allow existing states to expand, the federal government divided the new land into territories, surveyed the land, divided it into 'sections' of 1 sq mile and sold it off cheaply to settlers (or speculators). A territory could become a new state when its population reached 60,000 and it had its own state constitution and legislature. The first of the new states was Kentucky (1792), followed by Tennessee (1796), Ohio (1803) and five more by 1819.

Louisiana Purchase In 1802, James Monroe was sent to France to negotiate for US shipping rights on the Mississippi River. The French, hard pressed by conflicts in Europe and the Caribbean, offered to sell all of Louisiana for $15 million. The purchase was beyond Monroe's authorization and beyond President Jefferson's constitutional powers, but they bought it anyway, doubling the area under US control.

Jefferson sent the famous Lewis and Clark Expedition to explore the new territory and in particular to find a trading route to the Pacific. The 4000-mile excursion, from 1804 to 1806, did not find an easy route to the Pacific, but did make clear the great extent of the new lands. Again, the new territories were administered as federal lands until they had sufficient population and internal administration to be admitted to the Union as new states.

War of 1812 Conflicts between France and Britain damaged US trade interests and led Britain to impose sanctions against US shipping. Britain also formed alliances with Native Americans to oppose US expansion. Ultimately the USA declared war on Britain and attempted to invade Canada. Despite important victories on Lake Erie and in New York State, the US troops were stalled near Detroit by Oneida Indians. The British navy blockaded US ports, and in 1814 they captured Washington, DC, and burned the Capitol and the White House.

US TERRITORIAL EXPANSION

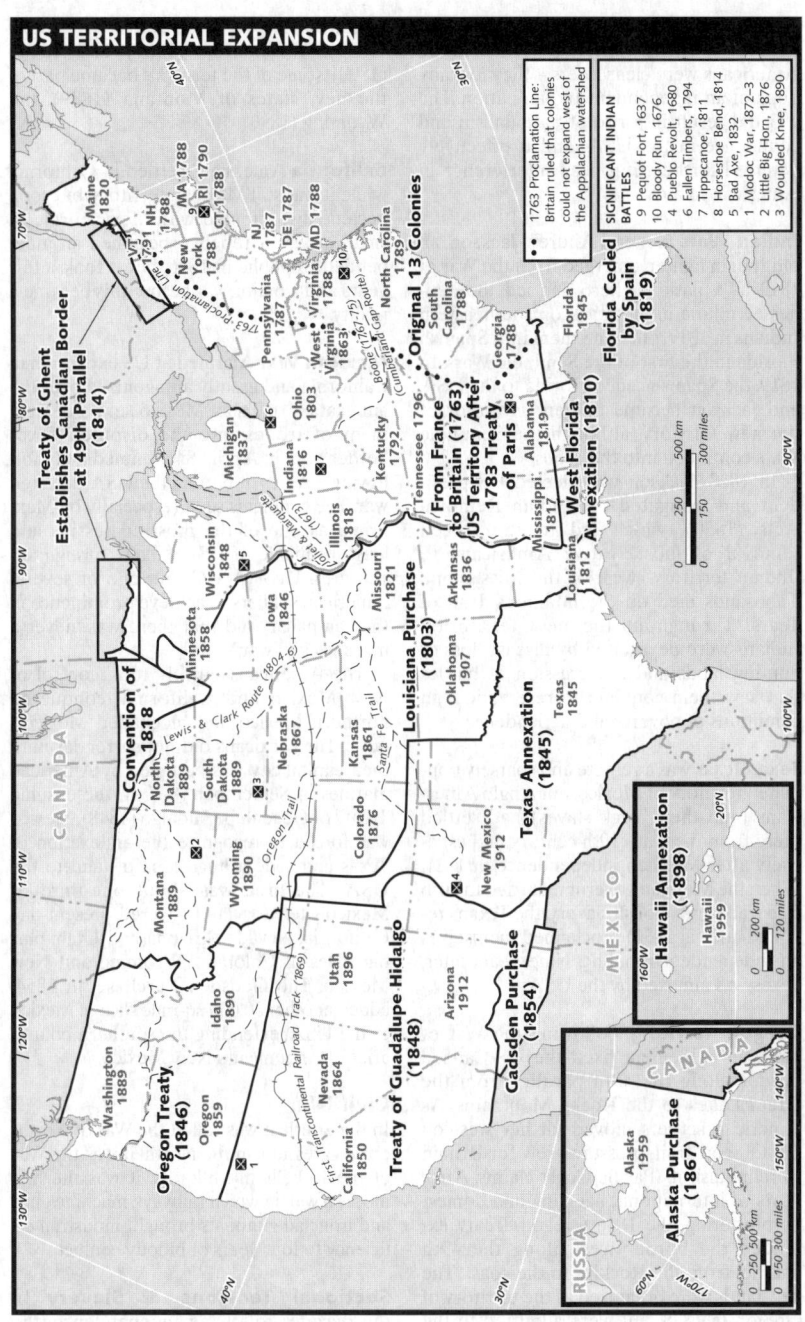

1763 Proclamation Line: Britain ruled that colonies could not expand west of the Appalachian watershed

SIGNIFICANT INDIAN BATTLES
9 Pequot Fort, 1637
10 Bloody Run, 1676
6 Pueblo Revolt, 1680
4 Fallen Timbers, 1794
7 Tippecanoe, 1811
8 Horseshoe Bend, 1814
5 Bad Axe, 1832
1 Modoc War, 1872–3
2 Little Big Horn, 1876
3 Wounded Knee, 1890

Treaty of Ghent Establishes Canadian Border at 49th Parallel (1814)

Maine 1820

Original 13 Colonies

Florida Ceded by Spain (1819)

From France to Britain (1763) US Territory After 1783 Treaty of Paris

Boone (1767–75) (Cumberland Gap Route)

West Florida Annexation (1810)

Convention of 1818

Louisiana Purchase (1803)

Texas Annexation (1845)

Oregon Treaty (1846)

Treaty of Guadalupe Hidalgo (1848)

Gadsden Purchase (1854)

First Transcontinental Railroad Track (1869)

Lewis & Clark Route (1804–6)

Oregon Trail

Santa Fe Trail

Joliet & Marquette (1673)

New Hampshire 1788
Vermont 1791
New York 1788
Massachusetts 1788
Rhode Island 1790
Connecticut 1788
New Jersey 1787
Pennsylvania 1787
Delaware 1787
Maryland 1788
Virginia 1788
West Virginia 1863
North Carolina 1789
South Carolina 1788
Georgia 1788

Michigan 1837
Ohio 1803
Indiana 1816
Illinois 1818
Kentucky 1792
Tennessee 1796
Wisconsin 1848
Minnesota 1858
Iowa 1846
Missouri 1821
Arkansas 1836
Mississippi 1817
Alabama 1819
Florida 1845

North Dakota 1889
South Dakota 1889
Nebraska 1867
Kansas 1861
Oklahoma 1907
Texas 1845

Montana 1889
Wyoming 1890
Colorado 1876
New Mexico 1912

Washington 1889
Idaho 1890
Utah 1896
Arizona 1912

Oregon 1859
Nevada 1864
California 1850

CANADA
MEXICO
RUSSIA

Hawaii Annexation (1898)
Hawaii 1959

Alaska Purchase (1867)
Alaska 1959

The Treaty of Ghent ended the war without a clear winner, but the Native Americans were clear losers – they lost any hope of an independent Indian nation. The war did result in a rise of nationalism and confidence in the USA, and it effectively deterred further European interference in American affairs.

Indian Wars General Andrew Jackson, an old Indian fighter, emerged from the War of 1812 as a national hero. He led the Tennessee militia in an attack on southeastern Indians in 1817, pursuing them into Spanish Florida in the first of the Seminole Wars. In 1819, the Spanish ceded Florida to the USA and Jackson became military governor of the new territory, although the Seminole Wars continued into the 1850s.

In 1828, Jackson was elected US president and instigated the Indian Removal Acts (1830), which led to the forced removal of most Native Americans to 'Indian territory' west of the Mississippi. Thousands died on the infamous Trail of Tears. Throughout the new territories, Indians were devastated by disease, loss of hunting lands and a succession of battles that saw them confined to reservations in conditions of poverty and dependence.

Texas Texas was a remote and sparsely populated territory of Mexico, but Anglo Americans (and their black slaves) had settled there from the early 19th century and especially after Mexican independence in 1821. When the Mexican government tried to curb free trade and abolish slavery, the Texans revolted and (in 1836) proclaimed themselves an independent republic. Nine years later, Texas was annexed by the USA.

Oregon Territory Following the War of 1812, an agreement fixed the US-Canada border along the 49th parallel from the Great Lakes to the Rocky Mountains. As American settlers moved farther west on the Oregon Trail, pressure grew for Britain to relinquish its Pacific Coast claims. After years of international haggling and domestic blustering, the 1846 Oregon Treaty extended the border west along the 49th parallel from the Rockies to the coast. The new lands were organized as the territory of Oregon in 1848, but were admitted to the Union as the separate states of Oregon (1859), Washington (1889) and Idaho (1890); some of the territory became part of the new states of Montana (1889) and Wyoming (1890).

California Americans settled in California while it was still Mexican territory, but soon became discontented with Mexican rule. A small group of rebels proclaimed an independent republic in 1846, but it took a few years and a major war before this became a reality.

Mexican War Alarmed at US expansion in California and greatly antagonized over the annexation of Texas, Mexico sent a detachment of troops into the disputed Texas border area in April 1846. Immediately following a series of battles, the USA declared war. The conflict is seen (especially by Mexicans) as one of the most aggressive and least justifiable of USA's many foreign adventures. Ulysses S Grant, one of several American soldiers to achieve prominence in the campaign, said that there was 'never a more wicked war.'

The Americans quickly took control of New Mexico and California, conquered northern Mexico and blockaded Mexico's ports. The Mexicans did not surrender until their capital city was occupied by American marines in September 1847. In the ensuing Treaty of Guadalupe Hidalgo (1848), Mexico was forced to recognize the annexation of Texas and cede a huge area of land to the USA. The area was about one-third of Mexico's territory and covered present-day California, Nevada, Arizona and Utah, plus big slices of Colorado, Wyoming and New Mexico. The Gadsden Purchase, in 1854, added another 30,000-sq-mile slice of Mexico to the USA, extending the southern boundaries of Arizona and New Mexico.

Civil War

In the South, it was called the War of Northern Aggression; in the North, it was the War of the Rebellion. Militarily, it was the first modern war, in which railways, machine guns and ironclad gunboats brought industrial efficiency to four years of bloody conflict.

Sectional Tensions & Slavery In the decades following independence, the

Northern economy became more diverse and industrialized, and public sentiment against slavery grew. All the Northern states had abolished slavery by 1804. In the South, the economy became increasingly dominated by cotton, more dependent on Northern financiers, traders and shippers, and ever more dependent on slavery.

As the USA expanded in the West and as the North grew richer and more powerful, Southerners feared that the national balance of power would move against them – that congress would abolish slavery and destroy their way of life. New states on the Western frontier did not want slavery, and by 1860 the Union had 18 free states and only 15 slave states.

Slaves who crossed into the North, as property or as fugitives, created a legal dilemma. This dilemma became acute as abolitionists helped slaves escape from the South through a clandestine network called the Underground Railroad. In the 1857 Dred Scott case, the pro-South supreme court ruled, in effect, that slaves were chattel, not citizens. Northern abolitionists became more militant. Abolitionist John Brown led a raid on the federal arsenal at Harpers Ferry to obtain weapons for a slave rebellion. The raid was a failure, but it inflamed the longstanding Southern fears of a slave revolt.

The US Constitution recognized the existence of slaves ('persons held to service') and gave congress the power to prohibit the importation of slaves after 1808 but otherwise allowed states to make their own laws about slavery. The Bill of Rights guaranteed certain rights 'of the people,' without defining who were 'people.' Many in the South believed that the Constitution guaranteed the right of people to keep slaves, but were afraid that a preponderance of anti-slave states would have the Constitution changed. Moreover, there was no provision in the Constitution for the Southern states to secede from the Union (an interesting omission in the constitution of a country that had unilaterally dissolved its bonds with Britain).

Secession & War In November 1860, Abraham Lincoln was elected president on an antislavery stance and South Carolina seceded from the Union. Within months it was joined by six other Southern states, united as the Confederate States of America, under Jefferson Davis as their president. Lincoln did not recognize the secession, and hostilities started when South Carolinians bombarded the Union's Fort Sumter in the Charleston Harbor. Lincoln called for troops to suppress the rebellion, and four more Southern states promptly joined the Confederacy. Four slave-holding states, on the boundary between North and South, remained with the Union.

For Lincoln, the main objective was to preserve the Union regardless of slavery. His Emancipation Proclamation, not made until 1863, was a calculated political tactic to appease the Northern states, recruit blacks to the Union army and alienate foreign support for the Confederacy. For the South, the only objective was survival and recognition as an independent nation.

The North's military strategy was to force a total surrender of the South by occupying its capital (Richmond, Virginia), blockading its ports, and taking control of the Mississippi River. The South had less than half the population of the North and far fewer industrial resources. Its sole hope for decisive victory was to capture the Union capital,

Abe at Antietam, Maryland (1862)

LIBRARY OF CONGRESS

Washington, DC. Failing that, the South could only fight a defensive war and try to outlast the North's determination.

Eastern Theater Most of the fighting took place in the Eastern Theater, with great armies struggling for strategic advantage in northern Virginia (Confederate territory) and southeastern Maryland (Union territory), where the opposing capital cities were only 100 miles apart. The South had the benefit of consistent and decisive leadership from Generals Robert E Lee and Thomas 'Stonewall' Jackson, but ultimately the numerical and material superiority of the North prevailed. There were more than 2300 engagements, including a dozen or so major battles in which both sides suffered appalling casualties. Some of the most historically interesting include the following:

First battle of Manassas (Bull Run; June 1861) – A Confederate victory, which halted the Union's initial invasion of Virginia.

Shenandoah Valley Campaign (March–June 1862) – Jackson's tactically brilliant campaign, which successfully diverted Union forces from Richmond.

Seven Days' battles (June–July 1862) – The Union's cautious General McClellan led the Peninsular Campaign against Richmond, but was beaten back in this series of battles.

Second battle of Manassas (Bull Run; August 1862) – A decisive Southern victory but with enormous casualties: 14,500 Union troops and 9500 Southerners.

Antietam (Sharpsburg; September 1862) – The bloodiest battle of the war (more than 23,000 men were killed in one day), when Union forces stalled General Lee's bold invasion of Maryland but failed to consolidate the victory.

Fredericksburg (December 1862) – Disastrous Union attack against strong defenses.

Chancellorsville (May 1863) – Lee's greatest victory, where a Southern force of 60,000 turned back an attack of 130,000 Union troops.

Gettysburg (July 1863) – General Lee's northern advance into Pennsylvania was halted by General George Meade's Union troops in this bloody battle (51,000 dead), a turning point in the war.

Spotsylvania Courthouse (May 1864) – This two-week battle was the largest in General Ulysses S Grant's protracted campaign to isolate Richmond.

Richmond and Petersburg (April 1865) – When General Grant finally cut the railroad supplying these cities, General Lee retreated west, but was cut off, and surrendered at Appomattox Court House.

Western Theater In the Western Theater, the Union was more consistently successful, first consolidating control in the border states of Kentucky and Missouri. This gave Union forces access to the Mississippi River, cutting the Confederacy in two and providing a corridor into the midst of Confederate territory. Admiral Farragut's fleet took New Orleans, and after two attempts and a six-week siege, General Grant occupied the strategic river port of Vicksburg, Mississippi, in mid-1863.

The next Union advance was across Tennessee. After several battles, the forces of General William Tecumseh Sherman fought their way down to Atlanta, Georgia, and took it after a protracted siege. Perhaps the first exponent of total warfare, Sherman had Atlanta evacuated and torched, then destroyed everything of strategic value between there and Savannah on his 250-mile 'March to the Sea.' Turning north, the Union army continued its rampage through the Carolinas, until the last Confederate forces surrendered in June 1865.

Naval Blockade The naval blockade of the South was very slow to take effect, but Southern ports were progressively closed by attacks from sea and land. Despite the daring blockade runners, supply became an increasing problem for the Confederacy.

Reconstruction The war left 620,000 dead, about one-fifth of whom were killed in battle but the vast majority died of disease or wounds. Another 300,000 were permanently maimed. Much of the South was in ruins, and without slaves, its once-prosperous plantation cotton industry was no longer viable. The North suffered little material damage, and its industrial capacity and know-how was greatly enhanced by the war effort. Lincoln wanted reconciliation and rebuilding of the South, but he was assassinated as the war was finishing, and a more punitive reconstruction policy was applied (see the South chapter).

Growth & Transformation
Throughout the 19th and early 20th century, and especially from the Civil War to the end

of WWI, the USA experienced phenomenal growth in its economy and population, a revolution in transport and technology, and a transformation of its industry and social structures.

Settling the Frontier By the 1850s, the continental USA had reached its maximum territorial extent, and the process of settling the newly acquired lands became one of the most romanticized episodes in American history. First there were the explorers, trailblazers and scouts, followed by the pioneers who crossed the country in wagon trains. Then there were the buffalo hunters, Indian fighters, prospectors, prostitutes, cowboys, cardsharps and gunfighters who were scattered across the 'Wild West' in its brief transition from a wilderness to a frontier to a region of productive farms and prosperous towns. Less romanticized, but more permanent, were the homesteader families, sodbusters, storekeepers, school mistresses and railway workers who really domesticated the wilderness.

Some prosaic but powerful new technology also helped to tame the West. Barbed wire enabled homesteaders to enclose their land and protect their crops. When rain was scarce or the ground was frozen, the new windmills pumped water from beneath the prairie. The land was cultivated with a new type of plow that cut the solid soil with disks of steel and made John Deere a byword for agricultural machinery. Most important of all was the railroad, which conquered the vast distances, moved cattle, grain and timber to distant markets, and brought essentials and luxuries to every town and city.

In the 1860s and 1870s, another series of Indian Wars raged across the new territories. The Plains Indians, with rifles and horses, put up strong resistance in many battles, but they were no match for the ruthless and battle-hardened units of US cavalry. Ultimately, the deliberate destruction of the buffalo (the Indians' main source of food and clothing) forced the Plains Indians onto reservations, where they were dependent on government handouts and their lands were freed for new settlers. The so-called 'Battle' of Wounded Knee, a massacre of several hundred men, women and children in 1890, was one of the final tragedies of the Indian Wars.

Industrial Transformation As the manufacturing industry moved from small workshops to huge factories, the USA was transformed from a rural, agrarian society into an urban, industrial power. Steel production increased from 13,000 tons per year in 1860 to 46 million tons in 1920, as the price of steel rails fell from $168 a ton to $12 a ton. The railroad expanded from 6000 miles of track in 1848 to 250,000 miles in 1920 – completion of the transcontinental railroad in 1869 was a national milestone. Land grants and tax breaks were essential for profitable railroad development, and corruption and cronyism between railroad companies and politicians became common.

The new industries required large-scale financing and organization, which led to incorporation and specialized management. Innovation, increasing scale and improving efficiency were the hallmarks of the period – 500,000 patents were granted between 1865 and 1900. Competition and innovation lowered prices but also created a tendency toward mergers, monopolies and pressure to reduce workers' wages.

Social Changes The so-called robber barons acquired enormous wealth in the period of unrestrained capitalism, gaining control of whole industries by the use of interlocking trusts. In 1901, for example, Carnegie Steel merged with eight of its main competitors to control two-thirds of the steel market. There were 4000 millionaires by 1900, and perhaps 20 of them had fortunes of $100 million or more. Along with Carnegie, some of the richest were Henry Clay Frick (coal and iron ore), John D Rockefeller (oil), EH Harriman (railroads), JP Morgan (banking) and the Vanderbilts (shipping). They sought status in conspicuous consumption, and built lavish mansions on New York's Fifth Ave and at Newport, Rhode Island. They also started a tradition of philanthropy that has endowed museums, hospitals, libraries, cultural centers and universities all over the country.

A new industrial working class grew up in the inner cities and the company towns, in appalling working and living conditions. Most of the skilled workers were American-born whites or immigrants from northern Europe. Unskilled workers were typically immigrants from eastern and southern

Europe. Blacks were mostly employed as cleaners, laborers, porters and servants. Despite blatant exploitation, there was some improvement in wages, especially for skilled workers, but periodic recessions created desperate insecurity – the worst years were 1876 and 1894.

Corporate clerks, bookkeepers, engineers, accountants and managers formed a new middle class, which benefited from the lower prices and greater variety of consumer goods. Domestic servants and labor-saving devices allowed more leisure time, and increasingly people looked to education to improve the lot of their children.

Urbanization In 1860, 20% of Americans lived in cities, and only 16 cities had more than 50,000 people; none exceeded a million. Industrialization led to the spectacular growth of existing cities, and new ones mushroomed around the Great Lakes and the Midwest. By 1920, half of Americans lived in towns and cities, New York had 5.6 million people; Chicago, 2.7 million; and 144 cities, populations of more than 50,000. City governments were notoriously corrupt and inefficient, and the poorest urban areas were overcrowded tenements with no sanitation and few services.

Iron- and steel-frame buildings enabled factories, warehouses and residential apartments to be built higher, faster and cheaper. Many of the 'historic districts' and 'heritage areas' that tourists see today date from the period of growth after the Civil War, when many inner urban areas were built or redeveloped.

Immigration Some five million immigrants arrived in the first half of the 19th century, and 15 million more arrived between 1850 and 1900. About 90% of the newcomers came from northern and western Europe (mainly Britain, Ireland and Germany). Many went to frontier areas; Minnesota and Wisconsin, for instance, were settled predominately by Scandinavians. There was also a migration of blacks from the agricultural South to the industrial North.

Another 15 million immigrants arrived between 1900 and 1920, but the majority of these, perhaps 80%, were from southern and eastern Europe, notably Italy and Russia. Most of them settled in the cities of the Midwest and Northeast, providing cheap labor for the new industries. A substantial number were Jewish refugees who found work in the clothing industries of New York City.

Immigrants often settled in neighborhoods with others from their home country, and though conditions were often crowded and unsanitary, they provided a basis for community life. Black neighborhoods were often totally segregated from the rest of the city, becoming almost permanent ghettos, where black churches and mutual-aid societies offered the only social support.

The Progressive Era The evils of the industrial age became more widely recognized toward the end of the 19th century, not least because popular magazines began publishing shocking photos and muckraking articles about the plight of the poor. Middle-class women led many campaigns for social reform, civic improvement, prohibition and women's suffrage. 'Settlement houses,' like Hull House in Chicago (1889), were established to provide education, child care, employment advice and other assistance for poor families.

Workers had formed craft unions since the mid-19th century, and the first national labor organization started in the 1860s. Labor agitation was often violently repressed by hired thugs, and major strikes in the railroads (1877, 1894), coal mines (1878), textile factories (1879) and steel mills (1892) were largely unsuccessful. The continuing supply of cheap immigrant labor helped keep wages down, and the courts, state governments and city authorities usually sided with the bosses.

Farmers organized the Granger movement in the 1860s and 1870s to break the power of the railroads, grain mills and cotton gins, which had kept farm prices low and freight charges high. State legislation was passed to regulate railroad rates and grain elevator charges, and reformist laws in various states mandated school attendance, prohibited trusts, banned alcohol, limited working hours and enfranchised women.

The 1887 Interstate Commerce Act began federal regulation of railroads, but there was little effective reformist action from the federal government until Theodore (Teddy) Roosevelt became president in 1901. He strengthened and enforced anti-trust legislation, increased the powers of the Interstate Commerce Commission, introduced the Pure Food & Drug Act and proposed other 'Square Deal' reforms, though many were not carried through congress. The National Association for the Advancement of Colored People (NAACP) was founded in 1909.

The American Century

Immigration, economic growth, industrialization and urbanization all continued and accelerated into the 20th century. Social struggles also continued, and important new legislation restricted monopoly trusts, protected labor rights, prohibited child labor, provided for workers' compensation and introduced income tax. There was one crucial new dimension – America was becoming inextricably involved with the rest of the world.

Becoming a World Power From the late 19th century, US commercial interests began extending into Central America, the Caribbean and the Pacific. US sugar producers in Hawaii led to a US naval base in 1887 and annexation in 1898. US support for Cuban independence precipitated the Spanish-American War, in which Spain was quickly defeated, and the Philippines, Puerto Rico and Guam became US territories. The idea of an American Empire never gained much support, but new overseas interests meant that isolationism became a difficult option.

Teddy Roosevelt's foreign policy formula was to 'speak softly and carry a big stick,' and he strengthened the US Navy and Marine Corps. He waved the stick in 1903 to support Panamanian secession from Colombia, and the USA took over the Panama Canal project.

As the self-appointed policeman of the Caribbean, US forces intervened in Cuba (1902–34), the Dominican Republic (1904, 1916–24), Haiti (1915–34), Guatemala (1906), Honduras (1907, 1924), Nicaragua (1906, 1909–10, 1912–33) and Mexico (1914, 1916–17). Speaking more softly, Roosevelt negotiated a treaty to end the Russian-Japanese War in 1905.

WWI President Woodrow Wilson wanted to keep trading with both sides of WWI, but early in 1917, after German U-boats had sunk

five American ships in two weeks, the USA declared war. The American involvement was decisive; its two million troops arrived at a time when both the German and Allied armies were depleted and nearly exhausted. In the USA, there was a massive propaganda campaign, conscription, a suppression of civil liberties and unprecedented government intervention in the economy. Some 80,000 Americans were killed in the war – a terrible number, but not huge by the awful standards of WWI (France, Germany, Russia and Austria/Hungary lost well over a million people each). Wilson argued for a treaty that would promote lasting peace, but other Allied powers insisted on reparations. The US senate didn't ratify the Treaty of Versailles, so America didn't join the League of Nations which its own president had proposed.

Roaring '20s Two constitutional amendments set the tone for the 1920s; the 18th Amendment banned the distribution and sale of alcohol and the 19th Amendment gave women the right to vote. Prohibition did not stop the use of alcohol, but it did encourage smuggling, illegal manufacture, speakeasies and a rise in organized crime. The vote did not give women equality, but it was associated with a greater freedom in style and manners, though educational and employment opportunities improved only marginally.

Many new products and amusements became available to a mass market – radio, movies, cars and phonograph records. Skyscrapers grew in the cities, and cultural innovations included a popularizing of jazz, modern dance, art deco architecture, new literature and abstract art. It was the beginning of modernism and the consumer age.

Great Depression Stock-market speculation became a fashion, then a mania, as millions bought stocks on credit at artificially high prices. In late October 1929, panic set in, prices crashed and people all over the country were instantly bankrupted. Demand fell, businesses closed, banks failed, mortgages foreclosed on homes and farms, and many lost their life savings.

A drought compounded the problems of farmers, and many left their lands in the 'dust bowl.' The Depression spread worldwide and trade slumped. By 1933, more than 13 million Americans were unemployed, and people stood in 'bread lines' for charity handouts. The homeless lived in shanty towns, called Hoovervilles after Herbert Hoover, who was president during the crash.

New Deal In 1932, Franklin D Roosevelt was elected on a platform to end the Depression and repeal Prohibition. Roosevelt's 'New Deal' policies acted immediately to set up relief and welfare agencies and to provide federal funds for local projects creating temporary jobs.

A new Federal Securities Act (1933) was passed to regulate financial markets, and the Securities and Exchange Commission supervised new issues of securities and protected investors from fraud. The Emergency Banking Relief Act (1933) empowered the government to manage insolvent banks and the Federal Deposit Insurance Corporation guaranteed bank deposits. The National Labor Relations Act (1935) protected workers, and the Social Security Act (1935 and 1939) provided for unemployment compensation, old-age benefits and welfare payments.

This was unprecedented government involvement in the economy, and the supreme court ultimately overturned a lot of New Deal legislation. Though the New Deal did much to alleviate the misery of the Depression, and to lift the economy from its lowest ebb, the USA did not return to full production until it began filling orders for the war in Europe.

WWII With war brewing, isolationist sentiment increased. As Germany and Japan became more aggressive, Roosevelt introduced a trade embargo against them, arguing that totalitarian regimes should be opposed by 'all means short of war.' When war started, the USA supplied war material to Britain and France, and began building its own defense forces. Later, Britain could no longer pay for US-made supplies but materials were made available under the Lend-Lease Act (1941).

After the attack on Pearl Harbor (December 7, 1941), congress declared war on Japan and, at last, on Germany. The war involved a total mobilization of US resources at home, a high degree of government control and an incredible output of ships, planes, trucks, food and everything else a

modern war requires. Fifteen million Americans served in the armed forces, including 340,000 women.

The USA spent $341 billion on the war; $50 billion of that on material supplied to other countries. More than 292,000 Americans were killed in battle and 115,000 died from other war causes. At the war's end, the USA and the USSR were the only major military powers left, but the USA's nuclear capability made it *the* world power.

Post War The USA launched the Marshall Plan in 1947 to provide funds for rebuilding industry and infrastructure in Europe. Not totally altruistic, the plan was aimed at curbing Soviet influence and developing markets for the US economy. As well as developing the economy and containing communism, postwar America has been challenged to live up to its pledge of liberty and justice for all.

The Abundant Society The postwar period has been, for most of the people most of the time, a period of tremendous economic growth and increasing affluence. This is clearly visible in the miles of new suburbs, the vast shopping malls, the network of freeways, and the continuous flow of late-model cars. (For some numbers, see Economy, later in this chapter.) America's scientific achievements, technological and social advances, and its much-loved popular culture are largely predicated on this material prosperity.

Economic growth has not been uniform, but has occurred in periods of prosperity interspersed with recessions. Nor have the benefits been uniformly distributed. Wage earners did well in the '50s and '60s, which were years of full employment, high union membership, and government spending on highways, defense and research. Employment was strong in traditional industries like car making, but there was also huge growth in services and white-collar employment.

In the 1970s, times got tougher as foreign competition challenged US manufacturers, and the 1973 OPEC oil price rise led to inflation and recession. Unemployment peaked in 1982. The response of the Reagan administration was 'Reaganomics' – less regulation, reduced taxes, reduced welfare, and record government deficits. Unemployment fell, but so did wages. The stock-market crash of 1987 led to recession in 1990, but recovery was aided by the 'peace dividend' of reduced defense spending. Growth was strong through most of the 1990s and into the new century – high-tech software companies experienced dramatic growth and spectacular collapse, but underneath these bubbles the economy has been a steadily rising tide.

Cold War & the Global Cop America's fear of communism dates back to the strikes and radicalism of 1919, which many associated with the Russian revolution. The spread of Soviet power in postwar Europe and the communist takeover in China convinced many Americans that there was a real threat of communist domination abroad and communist subversion at home. The fears were compounded by sensationalist media reports and opportunistic political posturing, not least by Senator Joseph McCarthy, who conducted an officially sanctioned witch-hunt for communists in the early 1950s.

The 1947 Truman Doctrine committed the US to support any country threatened 'by external pressure or internal subversion,' and for the next 45 years foreign policy aimed to contain communism and make the world safe for trade and investment. In 1949 the USA joined Canada and nine European nations in the NATO pact for defense against the Soviet block. The USSR exploded its first A-bomb that year, and America's strategic advantage became a nuclear stalemate, leaving the superpowers to struggle by proxy in 'limited' local wars and covert operations around the world.

In Korea in 1950, communist North Korea invaded US-backed South Korea, and the USA sent in air, sea and ground forces backed by UN allies. Chinese forces then joined in to support the north. The 1953 peace settlement restored the north-south border about where it had been at the start of the war. The Korean War cost 54,000 American lives and illustrated the difficulty of achieving a clear military victory in the nuclear age.

In the early 1950s, the US sent its first weapons and military advisors to support pro-French forces in Vietnam, and later it supported several dubious anticommunist military regimes in South Vietnam. The first US troops arrived in 1961, and their numbers peaked at 541,000 in 1969. Meanwhile, domestic opposition to the war kept mounting. There were massive bombings, peace negotiations and gradual troop withdrawals until 1973, when the last US forces left. South Vietnam surrendered in April 1975, and the country was reunited under a communist government. The war cost 58,000 American lives and left grave doubts about national leadership, foreign policy and military might. Vietnam veterans are now treated with honor, and the Vietnam Memorial in Washington is one of the most-visited sites in the country, but the memory looms whenever foreign military commitments are mooted – nobody wants another Vietnam.

Involvement in the Middle East started with moves to keep the USSR out of Iran and install a pro-American Shah. The USA backed Israel from its earliest days, thereby alienating the Arab world, while becoming increasingly dependent on its oil reserves. In a mixed record, the USA has brokered Israel-Egypt and Israel-Jordan peace agreements, lost 250 marines in Lebanon, had its embassy staff held hostage in Iran, and accidentally shot down an Iranian airliner. The quick victory of US-led forces in the 1991 Persian Gulf War got the Iraqis out of Kuwait, but the persistence of the Iraqi regime has been another reminder that even superpowers can't win them all.

The USA has regarded Latin America as its 'sphere of influence' since the 1823 Monroe Doctrine. Some of the major postwar interventions, more or less overt, have occurred in Guatemala (1954), Cuba (1961, 1963), Chile (1972), Honduras (1970s), El Salvador (1980s), Nicaragua (1980s), Panama (1989), Dominican Republic (1965–66), Grenada (1983) and Haiti (1994). The most alarming instance of Cold War brinkmanship occurred in 1962, when President Kennedy threatened nuclear war and ordered a blockade of Cuba to prevent the installation of Soviet missiles there.

Partly as a result of the Cuban crisis, the USSR increased its nuclear capability, and the arms race reached absurd degrees of overkill. The USSR gave up on the race in the mid-1980s when it couldn't match Reagan's spending, especially the extra billions for the fanciful Strategic Defense Initiative ('Star Wars'). The Cold War ended when the Soviet block disintegrated, but you can see some of its material legacies at the Strategic Air Command Museum in Omaha, Nebraska, or the graveyard of surplus aircraft near Tucson, Arizona.

After the Cold War, the USA could no longer define its role in the world as 'containment of communism.' US forces have been involved, with varying success, in peacekeeping roles in Africa and the Balkans. A continuing military involvement in the Middle East strives to keep potential conflicts in check, but the USA is in a difficult position. It is committed to supporting Israel but must also maintain good relations with the oil-rich Arab states. Inevitably US involvement has aroused resentment in some quarters – resentment expressed in terrorist attacks on US embassies in Tanzania and Kenya in August 1998, and most horribly on New York City and Washington, DC, in September 2001.

Civil-Rights Movement & Social Justice Disadvantaged and minority groups pressed for social justice throughout the postwar period, and great changes were achieved. Black and white students now study together on campuses that were racially segregated in the 1950s; openly gay congressmen get reelected; and even conservative president George W Bush has women in senior cabinet positions.

Racial segregation was the norm for African Americans until the 1950s, in the

King of the civil-rights movement

South by official policy under the 'separate but equal' doctrine, and in the North by economic circumstance and social custom. When the supreme court ruled that segregation was unconstitutional, many Southern states resisted the integration of schools and services (see the South chapter). In a series of nonviolent civil disobedience campaigns led by Martin Luther King Jr, blacks sat at segregated lunch counters, boycotted buses and enrolled in schools under federal protection. Some demonstrations were violently repressed, but TV coverage aroused great sympathy and respect for the black cause.

Civil Rights Acts of 1957, 1960 and 1964 outlawed discrimination in government services and employment. A black voter-registration campaign in 1964 saw 1000 arrests, 37 church bombings and three murders. The 1965 Voting Rights Act was the most successful legislation, resulting in a million new black voters. But by the early 1960s, many blacks had lost patience with nonviolent protests – persuaded by Nation of Islam leader Malcolm X, who espoused equality by 'any means necessary,' and by the Black Panther party, who called for black power. Violence and rioting erupted in New York and New Jersey in 1964, Los Angeles' Watts district in 1965 and other cities in 1966 and '67. Black votes became important and by the 1980s, black mayors had been elected in New York, Chicago, Detroit and Los Angeles.

Official policy for Native Americans declared the 1950s a 'termination period' in the name of assimilation; federal services were withdrawn and federally protected reservation lands were sold off. By the late 1960s, it was clear that Indians had fared badly under this policy, and protests grew. A new policy of self-determination stressed tribal administration of federal programs like health, housing, education and welfare. Native Americans also had some success in the courts, pursuing entitlements under long-ignored treaties. Native languages and traditional culture are encouraged on many reservations.

Mexicans and other Latinos from Central America, Cuba and Puerto Rico form large Spanish-speaking communities. Nationally, there are now as many Latinos as African Americans. Often employed in low-paying farm and factory jobs, Latinos began to organize and protest in the 1960s and '70s. The United Farm Workers union, led by César Chávez, achieved some success getting labor contracts in 1975. The many illegal immigrants, at least five million, are especially vulnerable to exploitation and have little protection from the law. The problems of international inequality and illegal immigration are painfully obvious in the border towns of Texas and California.

The political activism of American gays really started with the Stonewall Rebellion against police harassment of a gay bar in New York City in 1969. Groups like the National Gay and Lesbian Task Force actively promote gay rights, and many prominent people have made their sexual orientation public. AIDS, which emerged in 1981, has killed hundreds of thousands of gays in the USA and in its first decades served to unite the gay community as never before. A ban on gays in the military was lifted in 1993, but the new policy, dubbed 'don't ask, don't tell,' does not permit open admission of homosexual orientation. Homosexual acts, particularly by males, are still a criminal offense in some states, but more-progressive states outlaw discrimination and now recognize gay marriages.

During WWII, the work of women in many nontraditional occupations did much to demolish old stereotypes about gender roles. Women's movements had been active promoting women's voting rights in the early 20th century and mobilized again in the 1960s to demand equal rights in all fields; the National Organization of Women (NOW) was set up in 1966. An Equal Rights Amendment (ERA) to the Constitution was passed by congress in 1972 but was ratified by only 35 states, three short of the minimum required. The 1973 supreme court decision *Roe* v *Wade* legalized abortion and has been under attack by antiabortion/prolife forces ever since. By 1980, 50% of the workforce was female, but women's earnings were still on average less than men's. Sexual harassment, rape, domestic violence, child care and equal pay are ongoing national concerns.

Problems, Promise & Prosperity Scandals, failures and deceptions have periodically undermined confidence in the US government and its agencies. The bungled 1961 Bay of Pigs invasion of Cuba, the My Lai massacre in Vietnam, and the carpet bombing of Cambodia, raised real doubts about who the bad guys were. Political cynicism plunged to new depths when dirty tricks and cover-ups were revealed in the Watergate scandal of the 1970s. Bill Clinton's presidency was tainted with a different type of scandal, regarded variously with disgust, embarrassment or mild despair. At least there's some reassurance that the secrets come to light – it's time to get worried when scandals *stop* coming out.

The morality debate has swung from conformity and conservatism in the 1950s to liberalism and permissiveness in the 1960s and '70s, then back to conservatism and fundamentalism in the '80s and '90s. TV evangelists and the 'Moral Majority' bemoan family breakdown, drug use, sexual permissiveness and the decline of traditional values, but even these crusaders have been caught in moral lapses. This is a tiny reflection of the great American moral dilemma – it's a nation that espouses the highest standards, but it is not always able to live up to them.

Violence has been a recurring horror in postwar America, from the assassinations of President Kennedy (1963), Robert Kennedy and Martin Luther King Jr (1968), to the killing of demonstrators at Kent State University (1970). Fifty people died in Los Angeles riots following the Rodney King verdict (1992); 87 were killed in the siege of a cult headquarters in Waco, Texas (1993); a bomb in Oklahoma City took 168 lives (1995); and several high school shootings were especially disturbing. Despite such shocking events and the media fixation on them, violent crime rates stabilized in the 1990s and fell significantly in many cities.

Though many countries now share America's technological sophistication, none can come close in sheer size and capacity. Notwithstanding US military might, one of the USA's worst disasters was inflicted by a handful of terrorists who destroyed an American icon (the World Trade Center) and caused thousands of deaths, but failed to cause panic, economic collapse or the curtailment of American liberties.

GEOGRAPHY

The USA covers about 3,618,000 sq miles, made up of the 48 contiguous states of the continental USA ('the lower 48'), plus the huge state of Alaska, northwest of Canada, and the volcanic islands of Hawaii, 2000 miles southwest in the Pacific Ocean. In addition the USA has a number of external territories (not covered in this book) including Puerto Rico, Guam, American Samoa, Navassa Island, Northern Mariana Islands and the US Virgin Islands.

The continental USA stretches 2600 miles across North America, in a band 1250 miles wide, comprising a number of reasonably distinct physical regions.

The Atlantic Coastal Plain is narrow in the Northeast but broadens farther south, including the low-lying Florida peninsula. The Gulf Coastal Plain extends west of Florida and south into Mexico and includes the rich alluvial plains and wetlands of the Mississippi Delta. The eastern and southern coastlines are heavily indented, with many sand dunes, barrier islands, wetlands and shallow inlets.

The Appalachian Mountains parallel the East Coast, stretching from Alabama to the Canadian border. They include a number of subsidiary mountain ranges, including (from south to north) the Blue Ridge Mountains, the Allegheny Mountains, the Catskills and the Green Mountains.

West of the Appalachians, the Interior Plain is the area drained by the extensive Mississippi-Missouri-Ohio River system. This comprises the eastern-central lowland area (with the 'cotton belt' in the south and the 'corn belt' in the north) and the Great Plains, or prairies, which rise gradually westward to the Rocky Mountains. The Ozark Plateau lies at the southern edge of the Interior Plain.

To the north is the Canadian Shield, a wide area of mineral-rich Precambrian rock, which extends into the northern USA–Great Lakes area, forming the ranges of northern Minnesota, upper Michigan and the New York's Adirondacks.

The Rocky Mountains are part of the complex North American Cordillera, running roughly north-south from the Brooks Range in Alaska, through western Canada and the USA and down into Mexico's Sierra Madre Oriental. The Rockies have many subsidiary ranges in the western USA, like the Sangre de Cristo Mountains in New Mexico, Utah's Wasatch Range and Idaho's Bitterroot Mountains.

West of the Rocky Mountains are a series of Intermontane Plateaux, including Mexico's Altiplano, the Mojave Desert, Nevada's Great Basin, the Great Salt Lake of Utah, the Columbia Plateau in Oregon and Washington, the Plateau of British Columbia and the Yukon Plateau.

The Coastal Range comprises a series of smaller ranges following the full length of North America's West Coast, from the Baja California peninsula, through the coastal ranges of California, Oregon and British Columbia, to the St Elias and Alaska Ranges. Farther inland, the Sierra Nevada and volcanic Cascade Ranges extend from southern California to northern Washington State.

In the far Southwest, the low deserts of southern Arizona and California are on the edge of the Sonora Desert, which extends into Mexico.

GEOLOGY

The geology of the USA is a result of three basic processes: plate tectonics, changing sea levels and erosion. Over the past two billion years, tectonic plates, including those of Europe and Africa, pushed into the sides of North America, folding and uplifting the edges into mountain ranges and melting rocks that erupted as volcanoes. A prominent example is the Cascade Range, in the Pacific Northwest. Some smaller ranges, such as the Appalachians of West Virginia, the Adirondacks of New York and the Ozarks of Missouri and Arkansas, are the eroded remnants of ancient and much larger mountains.

North America adopted its present appearance about 50 million years ago when the last waters receded from the Cretaceous Seaway, a narrow strip of ocean that extended northward from New Mexico into Canada. The modern Rocky Mountains began to rise at this time (the ancestral Rockies existed in the same place but eroded away).

Superimposed on these tectonic forces were a series of sea-level rises that flooded North America, depositing thick sequences of limestone, sandstone and shale that make up the horizontal strata dominant across the Midwest. Much of the land west of the Adirondacks was flooded six times in the last 550 million years. Rocks deposited

PHYSICAL REGIONS OF NORTH AMERICA

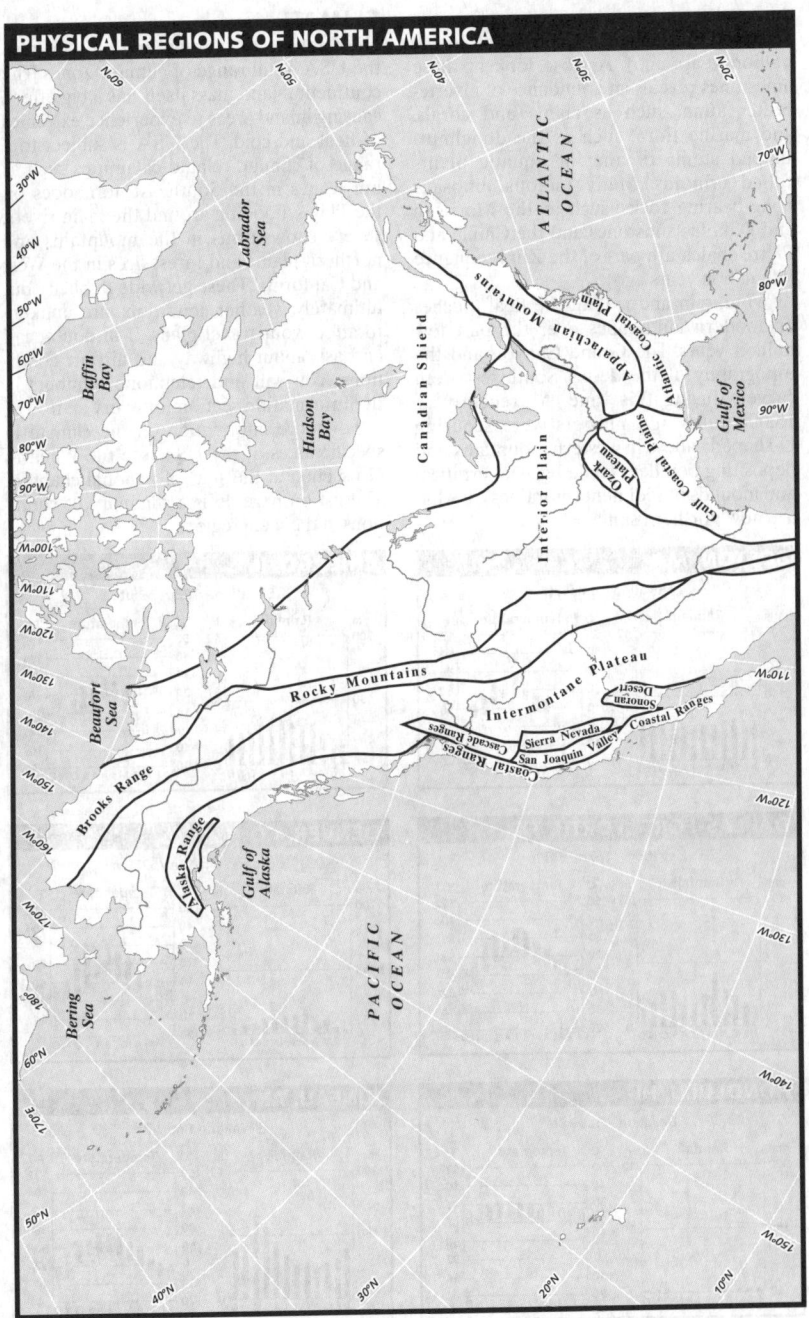

during these oceanic advances include the Sauk and Tippecanoe sequences (48 to 440 million years ago). A close look at these limestones reveals an abundance of invertebrate fauna, such as clams and corals, and marine flora, such as the doughnut-shaped stems of ancient aquatic plants called crinoids. Many famous dinosaur bone-bearing rocks, such as the Morrison and Dakota sandstones and the Chinle and Pierre shales, are part of the Zuni sequence (80 million years ago).

Wind, rain and ice put the final touches on modern landscapes over the past few million years. The Grand Canyon and the topography of the desert Southwest were carved during this time. As recently as 15,000 years ago, glaciers were scouring U-shaped valleys in western mountains, and depositing boulders (called glacial erratics) and mounds of sediment (moraines) in what are now northern states.

CLIMATE

Huge ranges of latitude and altitude give the USA a full range of climatic zones. The continental land mass itself has a big effect, causing inland areas to experience extremes of heat and cold. The USA is subject to a range of climate-related calamities such as hurricanes in the Southeast, tornadoes on the Plains, flooding around the main rivers, severe snowstorms in the mountains and northern plains and forest fires in the West and California. These get wide publicity but ultimately weather conditions are unlikely to affect your travel plans. If in doubt, call and ask about highway and airport conditions. You will find telephone numbers in the Information section for every state.

For more information on the climate in specific areas of the USA, see the When to Go section at the start of regional chapters. The list on page 46 is a summary of conditions in the main regions.

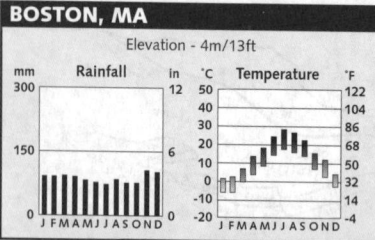

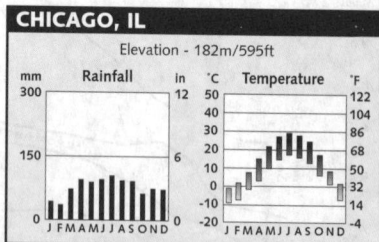

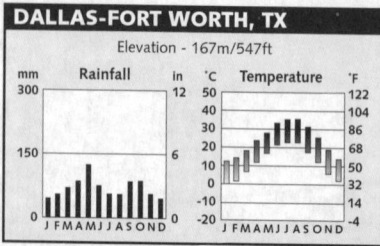

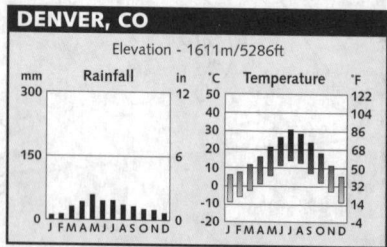

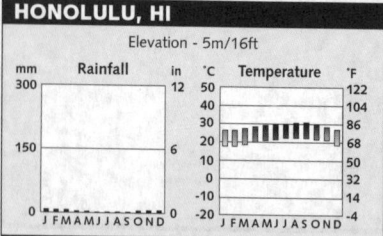

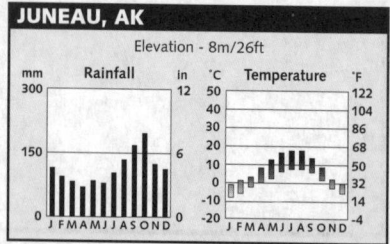

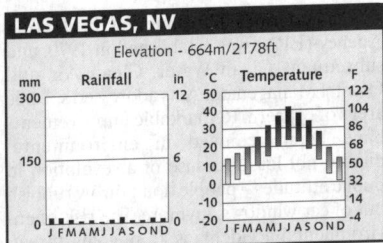

LAS VEGAS, NV
Elevation - 664m/2178ft

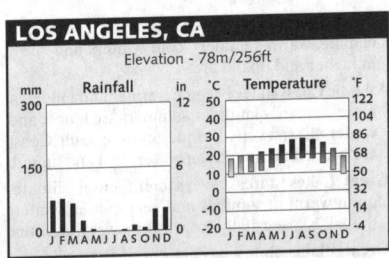

LOS ANGELES, CA
Elevation - 78m/256ft

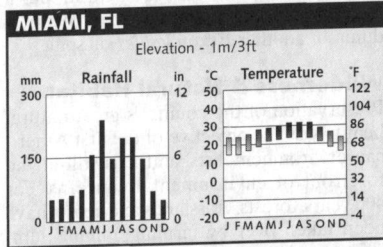

MIAMI, FL
Elevation - 1m/3ft

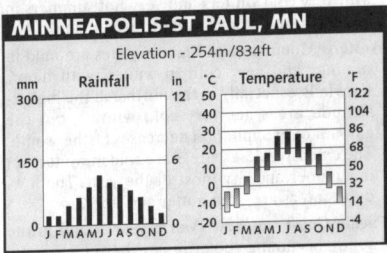

MINNEAPOLIS-ST PAUL, MN
Elevation - 254m/834ft

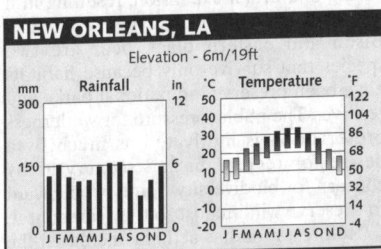

NEW ORLEANS, LA
Elevation - 6m/19ft

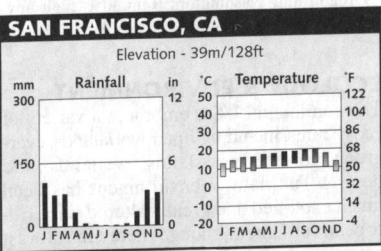

SAN FRANCISCO, CA
Elevation - 39m/128ft

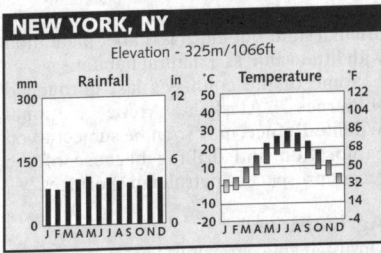

NEW YORK, NY
Elevation - 325m/1066ft

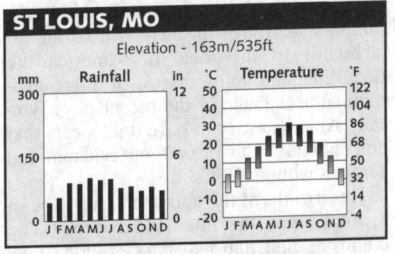

ST LOUIS, MO
Elevation - 163m/535ft

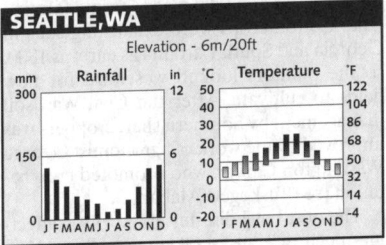

SEATTLE, WA
Elevation - 6m/20ft

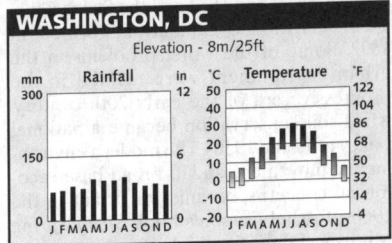

WASHINGTON, DC
Elevation - 8m/25ft

New England states have a cool, temperate climate, warm summers, cold winters and snow in higher and inland areas.

Atlantic Coast states become warmer and milder at more southerly latitudes, summers are longer and winters less severe. Florida and the Gulf Coast are warm all year and can be very wet and humid.

Great Lakes states have a continental climate, quite warm in summer and very cold in winter; the lakes are usually frozen for several months.

Great Plains states have a continental climate, with very cold winters and very hot summers in the north, and milder winters farther south.

Western Mountain and Plateau states are mild in summer and very cold in winter, with heavy snowfalls, especially in the north. All the higher-altitude areas get very cold winters, but the amount of precipitation decreases farther south. The extensive desert areas are cold in winter, hot in summer and dry most of the year. The low-desert areas are even hotter and drier.

Pacific Coast states are warm year round in the south, becoming cooler in Northern California, Oregon and Washington. Rainfall is high anywhere north of San Francisco.

ECOLOGY & ENVIRONMENT

The continental USA embraces a variety of ecosystems, including open woodlands, evergreen forests, grasslands, wetlands and deserts. The natural environment has been much exploited and greatly altered since European settlement, though there are still vast areas in a more or less natural state. While the USA remains absolutely committed to consumption and growth, there is a strong attachment to the ideal of 'America the Beautiful,' and an awareness of tragic environmental damage in the recent past. Typically, Americans try to have it all – cars that don't pollute, industries without acid rain, and aerosols without CFCs.

Environmental activism has been around since the late 19th century. The country's first national park, Yellowstone, was established in 1872 and the Sierra Club, a conservation organization, formed in 1892. Some of the worst problems in the urban environment were tackled in the progressive era of the early 20th century, while soil conservation became a national policy after the 1930s. The modern environmental movement, and its broad-based ecological concerns, became important in the 1960s; Rachel Carson's book *Silent Spring* was especially influential.

The federal Environmental Protection Agency (EPA) was established in 1970, and subsequent Clean Water, Clean Air and Coastal Management Acts addressed specific areas of concern. Remarkable improvements have been achieved in environmental quality, not least because of a revolution in public attitudes – people don't throw rubbish out of car windows anymore. The risk of environmental accidents is an ongoing threat, whether it's a wash of feedlot waste into a local river, leakage from a toxic chemical dump or another *Exxon Valdez* oil spill.

Wilderness & Natural Habitat

Preservation of the country's great natural beauty was the objective of the first American environmentalists, and it is still at the forefront of environmental concerns. For 400 years, forests, grasslands and coasts have been taken over by farming, mining, lumbering and urban expansion, resulting in a loss of habitat for many types of wildlife. Bison and eastern black bear are two species that survive only because habitats have been preserved in national parks and reserves. The public pressure for wilderness preservation is motivated as much by a desire for recreation and scenery as by concern for biodiversity. Some people want to preserve wildlife just so they can hunt it.

Reforestation has actually increased the area under forest in the last 20 years; some of this is eastern farmland returning to its original state, but much is timber plantation with little value as a natural habitat.

Some of the country's last untouched wilderness, Alaska's Arctic National Wildlife Refuge, may soon be subject to oil exploration and drilling because of the recent prospect of petroleum shortages.

Agriculture

Unsustainable agricultural practices have at times caused great damage to prime farming land. Cotton crops were exhausting soils in Georgia and South Carolina as early as 1800, so the planters looked westward for new fields to cultivate. After the Civil War, soil management by Southern sharecroppers was improved by the work of agronomist George Washington Carver, who promoted crop rotation (see Tuskegee, Alabama).

The dust bowl disaster in the 1930s, affecting much of Kansas, Oklahoma, Texas, New

Mexico and Colorado, was caused by a combination of drought and high winds on land that had recently been cultivated and grazed. Thousands of tons of topsoil were stripped away in giant dust clouds, farms were ruined and dust-bowl refugees went west. From 1935, state and federal governments helped farmers develop contour plowing, crop diversification and other techniques to conserve soil. Nevertheless, erosion remains a big problem.

The use of chemical fertilizers and pesticides has caused great damage to water and wildlife. The national bird, the bald eagle, almost became extinct because of pesticide build-up in its prey. Some of the most damaging chemicals, like DDT, are now banned, and integrated pest management has proved to be more economical and less toxic than overuse of pesticides. And bald eagles are now a common sight in many areas.

Water

The water supply is clean and plentiful in most of the country, but surface water is very limited in much of California and the rapidly growing Southwest. In the Southwest, water is drawn from natural underground reservoirs called aquifers, and there is some concern that these are being used up faster than rainfall is replenishing them.

After years of having waste products dumped into them, many rivers and lakes had become totally polluted, devoid of all fish and plant life. Since the 1970s, new laws and clean-up programs have greatly reduced water pollution, so that fishing now occurs in the once-lifeless Lake Erie and New York's Hudson River. Agricultural runoff and sewage has affected the coastal environment in Chesapeake and Delaware Bays, but active environmental groups have helped limit the damage.

Air Pollution

The USA uses a quarter of the world's energy and is the largest emitter of carbon dioxide from the burning of fossil fuels. It's therefore the greatest single contributor to the greenhouse effect and global warming, but as of 2001, the present administration has refused to endorse international protocols committing it to a reduction in greenhouse gas emissions.

Air pollution, caused mainly by motor vehicles, is a problem in many cities. It's especially bad in areas where the topography favors temperature inversions, as in Los Angeles and Denver. Stringent exhaust emission controls have reduced the problem to some extent.

Nitrogen oxide and sulfur dioxide emissions from US factories are a major cause of acid rain, which has killed aquatic life in many lakes in the northeastern USA and Canada and damaged large areas of forest. Federal regulations and international agreements are pegging back emission levels, and fish populations are now increasing in all the Great Lakes.

Domestic Waste

The USA is the world's leading producer of garbage. In the densely populated Northeast of the country, dump sites are becoming scarce, and big cities like New York incur increasing costs to take out the trash. Recycling glass, aluminum, paper products and some plastics is becoming more widespread, supported by public opinion and government regulation. New Yorkers, for instance, can be fined if they don't separate their garbage what is recyclable.

Toxic Waste & Chemicals

The high level of industrial development in the USA means a large volume of toxic and hazardous byproducts that have caused some hideous instances of environmental damage. The Cuyahoga River in Cleveland was so polluted with chemicals in the 1950s and '60s that it caught fire; leakage of chemical waste at Love Canal in upstate New York forced the evacuation of a neighborhood and caused national outrage. Numerous unsafe toxic waste dumps have been identified across the country. Decontaminating these sites and developing satisfactory methods of toxic waste disposal are major environmental problems.

Nuclear Industry

About 18.5% of the US energy supply is generated by nuclear power plants. The accident at the Three Mile Island plant in 1979 dispelled much complacency in the nuclear power industry and led to stricter standards. Compliance with new standards made nuclear power less profitable, but after being off the agenda for two decades, new plants are being considered again. There is no permanent nuclear waste storage facility in the country and no reprocessing plant, so for years all radioactive waste has been placed in 'temporary' storage. A site in Nevada has been chosen for nuclear waste storage, and another in New Mexico is under investigation.

NATIONAL PARKS

The world's first national park, Yellowstone, was created by congress in 1872, 'for the benefit and enjoyment of the people.' Other national parks were created in California, Colorado and Arizona, and in 1916 the National Park Service (NPS) was established within the Department of the Interior to 'promote and regulate their use' and to 'conserve the scenery…and the wildlife for the enjoyment of future generations.' When all the national monuments and battlefield sites were transferred to the national park system in 1933, the NPS became the all-purpose guardian of the nation's natural and historical treasures.

The following are the USA's national parks. See the National Parks map for locations.

Pacific Northwest

North Cascades – glaciated landscape, great backcountry hiking; few facilities

Olympic – hiking in dramatically varying ecosystems; waterfalls, lakes, alpine meadows, temperate rainforests; lots of rain

Mt Rainier – superb volcanic mountain with glaciers, alpine meadows and rainforest; backcountry skiing, hiking and climbing

Crater Lake – vast volcanic cone with incredibly blue lake; hiking and cross-country skiing trails, boats to rugged islands; very popular in summer

California

Redwood – 177 sq miles of virgin redwood forest

Lassen Volcanic – volcanic peak with lava tubes, fumaroles, hot springs and hiking trails

Yosemite – glacial valley with forested floor, sheer sides, waterfalls and alpine meadows; 800 miles of hiking trails provide escape from summer crowds; sublime ski trails in winter; serious rock climbing

Kings Canyon and Sequoia – the biggest and oldest trees; rugged Sierra scenery, hiking and ski-touring; an alternative to Yosemite

Death Valley – deep depression with dramatic desert vistas and unique ecology; wildflowers in spring, a sauna in summer

Joshua Tree – varied desert flora features the spiky Joshua tree; good rock climbing

Channel Islands – 'remote,' rocky islands within sight of LA; seals, sea lions, sea otters; primitive camping

Southwest

Great Basin – 13,000-foot Wheeler Peak, an island of ecological diversity surrounded by desert, with forests, lakes, ancient bristlecone pines and a limestone cave system; remote, uncrowded, few facilities

Zion – colorful canyon where oasis-like Virgin River cuts through desert; brilliant 16-mile hike through the Narrows; canyon road can be congested in summer

Bryce Canyon – natural amphitheater filled with brilliantly colored rock steeples; main viewpoints can be crowded, wonderful walking and horseback trails

Capital Reef – desert wilderness, petroglyphs and pioneer ruins; less crowded than nearby parks

Arches – 2000 natural sandstone arches; scenic drives

Canyonlands – archetype Southwestern scenery: rugged canyons, arches, bridges, craters, mesas, spires and buttes; hiking, white-water rafting; less accessible, developed and visited than other parks

Grand Canyon – spectacular canyon features a wide variety of 'life zones,' Native American history, hiking, mule trips and river running; South Rim is crowded in summer; higher, cooler North Rim is less so but closed by snow in winter

Petrified Forest – fossilized trees, petroglyphs and Painted Desert scenery

Saguaro – small park preserving large stands of giant saguaro cactus

Carlsbad Caverns – extensive cave system with vast underground chambers; a range of underground excursions

Rocky Mountains

Glacier – mountain goats, bighorn sheep and impressive glaciated landscapes; popular scenic drive on Going-to-the-Sun Rd; July-August hordes stick close to roads, but backcountry hikes are uncrowded

Yellowstone – world's first national park (est 1872); geysers and geothermal phenomena, impressive canyon and prolific wildlife; big summer crowds-go backcountry or visit in other seasons

Grand Teton – jagged granite spires mirrored in perfect lakes; spectacular hikes, classic climbs; less crowded than nearby Yellowstone

Rocky Mountain – stunning peaks and alpine tundra along the Continental Divide; elk, bighorn sheep, moose and beaver; Trail Ridge

Rd is a spectacular drive; crowds near the roads, but solitude on the trails

Mesa Verde – prominent mesa surrounded by sheer cliffs with extensive remains of ancient Pueblo dwellings

Texas

Guadalupe Mountains – desert high country with varied 'life zones' and fabulous fall colors; excellent hiking

Big Bend – diverse geography, varied wildlife (including mountain lions); scenic drives, spring wildflowers; fall river running

Great Plains

Theodore Roosevelt – prairie grasslands in north; badlands in south with a 36-mile scenic driving loop; hiking and horseback trails

Wind Cave – prairie grassland and forest home to elk, bison and prairie dogs; the cave 'breathes'; Mount Rushmore National Monument not far away

Badlands – desolate landscape with eroded cliffs, pinnacles and canyons; remnant prairie grasslands, golden eagles; hiking and mountain biking trails

Great Lakes

Voyageurs – lake and forest area with moose, black bear and timber wolf; limited access, usually explored by motorboat

Isle Royale – remote island with conifer forest and diverse wildlife; hiking and canoeing; ferry or light plane access

The South

Hot Springs – the 1915 Fordyce bathhouse and Hot Springs Mountain, with forest and hiking trails

Mammoth Cave – extensive cave system with NPS-led tours; delightful river and forests

Great Smoky Mountains – diverse forest flora, gorgeous in spring and fall; bears; 10 million visitors per year, but not too crowded in winter and spring, or in the backcountry

New England

Acadia – rugged coastal scenery, fir forests, granite cliffs; ideal cycling, rock climbing and sea kayaking

Capital Region

Shenandoah – highest part of the Blue Ridge Mountains; traversed by Skyline Drive and the Appalachian Trail; hiking, horse riding, hang gliding, bird-watching

Florida

Everglades – subtropical, wetland wilderness; hiking, biking, canoeing, airboat tours, birding and wildlife watching

Alaska

Denali – includes Mt McKinley, the USA's highest mountain; unspoiled wilderness, moose, caribou, wolves, brown bears-but scariest of all, crowds in July-August

Kenai Fjords – huge Harding Icefield, tidewater glaciers and fjords; boat trips and bluewater paddling amid marine wildlife

Wrangell-St Elias – three mountain ranges meet amid icefields and glaciers; plentiful wildlife; remote, limited facilities

Glacier Bay – icebergs calve from the tidewater glaciers ringing this remote bay; best seen by boat

Hawaii

Haleakala – vast volcanic crater, lunar landscape, superb at sunrise; hiking trails

Hawaii Volcanoes – two active volcanoes, tropical beaches, icy summit; lava tubes and flows; amazing scenic drives, rainforest hikes

Although the national parks were once called 'the best idea America ever had,' there are fears that the parks are being loved to death; as many as 10 million people a year visit some parks, mostly concentrated in the summer months. NPS policy is now to err on the side of preservation rather than public enjoyment, and parks are regulated, some quite restrictively, in the interests of conservation. In the 1970s, national recreation areas were created to help reduce the demand for activities in the most hard-pressed parks.

If you can't stand crowds when you're communing with nature, seek out the less popular parks and avoid the summer vacation period. Best of all, make an effort to walk away from the roads and parking lots – a half-hour walk will get you away from 90% of park visitors, and an overnight hike will usually get you a campsite all to yourself. Don't be put off altogether, though – the Grand Canyon isn't popular for nothing.

The NPS budget, allocated by congress, varies from stringent to miserly, and the service finds it difficult to maintain all the buildings, roads and trails for which it is responsible. On the other hand, the standard of the interpretive services and publications is extremely high, and staff are very dedicated, well informed and wonderfully helpful. The NPS Web site (ⓦ www.nps.gov) has information about all the national parks and areas.

The NPS manages some 367 federal sites in 20 different categories. The best known

NATIONAL PARKS

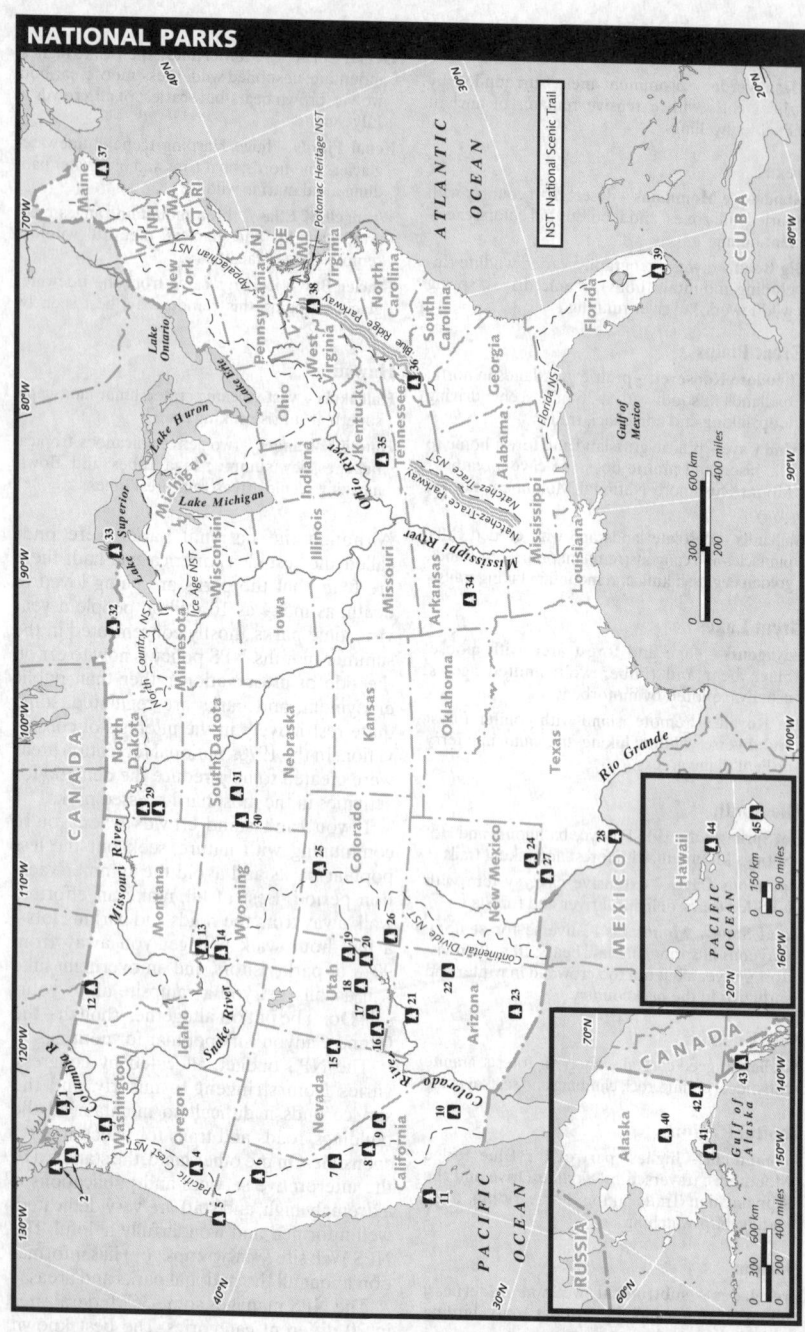

NATIONAL PARKS

1 North Cascades	16 Zion	31 Badlands
2 Olympic	17 Bryce Canyon	32 Voyageurs
3 Mt Rainier	18 Capital Reef	33 Isle Royale
4 Crater Lake	19 Arches	34 Hot Springs
5 Redwood	20 Canyonlands	35 Mammoth Cave
6 Lassen Volcanic	21 Grand Canyon	36 Great Smoky Mountains
7 Yosemite	22 Petrified Forest	37 Arcadia
8 Kings Canyon & Sequoias	23 Saguaro	38 Shenandoah
9 Death Valley	24 Carlsbad Caverns	39 Everglades
10 Joshua Tree	25 Rocky Mountain	40 Denali
11 Channel Islands	26 Mesa Verde	41 Kenai Fjords
12 Glacier	27 Guadalupe Mountains	42 Wrangell-St Elias
13 Yellowstone	28 Big Bend	43 Glacier Bay
14 Grand Teton	29 Theodore Roosevelt	44 Haleakala
15 Great Basin	30 Wind Cave	45 Hawaii Volcanoes

are the national parks, which protect areas of outstanding natural beauty and provide access and facilities for visitors. Some are as small as 40 sq miles; the largest is more than 13,000 sq miles. National preserves are created mainly for the protection of a natural area and may have few visitor facilities. Designated wilderness areas within some national parks do not allow any permanent improvements. National monuments are usually smaller in size and protect a specific natural or historic site, including both structures like the Statue of Liberty and natural areas like Cedar Breaks in Utah.

For the protection, preservation and restoration of historically significant sites, there are also historical parks, sites, military parks and battlefields. In many cases, the NPS undertakes archaeological excavations and presents interpretive displays.

National recreation areas are intended principally for outdoor recreation and enjoyment and often have extensive facilities or concessionaires. In this recreational category are national seashores, lakeshores and rivers. The NPS is also responsible for two scenic parkways and administers eight national scenic trails and nine historic trails. The NPS doesn't control all the land through which the trails pass, but it has a coordinating and advisory role for the various federal, state and private interests.

GOVERNMENT & POLITICS

The USA is governed according to the provisions of the Constitution, originally drawn up in 1787 and amended some 27 times. The Constitution provides for separate executive, legislative and judiciary arms of government, with various checks and balances between them. It also provides for a sharing of powers between federal and state governments.

The President

The US president is head of state, chief of the executive government and commander in chief of the armed forces. A presidential term is four years, and (since 1951) no person can be elected president for more than two consecutive terms. Presidential elections are held in early November and the successful candidate is inaugurated on January 10 of the

George 'Dubya,' 43rd US president

following year. The heads (called secretaries) of the 13 executive departments are political appointments of the president.

The president is not elected directly, but by an electoral college in which each state has a number of votes equal to the number of its representatives in congress (which relates to its population) plus the number of its senators (always two per state). California, the most populous state, has 54 electors, while the five least-populous states have three each. The people vote for their choice of presidential candidate, and the candidate with the most votes in a state gets all that state's electoral college votes – if 51% of Florida voters choose Bush, then he gets all 25 of Florida's electoral college votes, and his opponent, with 49% of the popular vote, gets nothing. The candidate with the majority of electoral college votes becomes president. One consequence of this has been to focus presidential campaigning on the most populous states.

Congress

The legislative arm of government is the congress, comprising the senate, with two senators from each state, and the house of representatives, with 435 members, in varying numbers from each state depending on population. All budget, tax and revenue laws must originate in the House of Representatives, while the senate has special powers in respect to foreign relations, senior government appointments and impeachment. The Speaker of the House is the leader of the majority party, not a neutral chairperson as in the British system. After a bill is passed by congress, it can be vetoed by the president, but the presidential veto can be overturned by a two-thirds majority in both houses, which allows it to become law.

House members serve two-year terms and senators serve six-year terms. Elections are held every two years for all representatives' seats and approximately one-third of the senators. Every four years, these coincide with presidential elections, when the turnout is around 50% of eligible voters. In non–presidential election years, voter turnout is about 35%.

Political Parties

Politics is dominated by the two main parties. The Republicans, nicknamed the Grand Old Party (or GOP) and symbolized by an elephant, are traditionally more conservative, opposed to big government and for states' rights. The Democrats, symbolized by a donkey, are generally more liberal and favor a more active role for the federal government. Smaller parties like the Green Party are insignificant in terms of their elected representation, but in a close election they may be important in diverting votes away from the major parties.

The parties are not as monolithic as in other political systems, and there are conservative Democrats and progressive Republicans. Members of congress do not vote strictly on party lines. It's common for the president to be from one party while both houses of congress have a majority from the other party. In this situation of 'divided government,' there is generally a limited output of new legislation and an increase in presidential vetoes.

Judiciary

The highest judicial authority is the US Supreme Court, whose nine justices are appointed for life by the president, with the advice and consent of the senate. The supreme court can overrule any federal or state law or executive action that violates the Constitution. Beneath it are 13 federal courts of appeal, 94 US district courts and various special courts.

State & Local Government

The USA is a federal system, and powers not delegated to the federal government by the Constitution are retained by the states. Nevertheless, the powers of the central government have increased over the years relative to those of state governments.

Each state has its own constitution and a government that generally mirrors that of the federal government. The governor is the state's chief executive, and a state senate and a house delegation enact state laws (Nebraska alone has a unicameral state government), and a state police and court system enforce them. Among other things, states are responsible for education, criminal justice, prisons, hospitals, administration of elections, regulation of commerce and maintenance of highways. Many of these things are now done in cooperation with federal government, especially for funding purposes.

The states are further divided into counties, boroughs, parishes, cities, towns, school districts and/or special districts that provide services like police, sanitation, schools and so on. Local government units often combine to administer a large urban area as a single unit, as in the five boroughs of New York City.

ECONOMY
Statistics
The USA has an extremely large, diverse economy, and the grossest domestic product in the world. Its total GDP in 1999 was $9255 billion, compared with $4800 billion for China, $2950 billion for Japan and $1864 billion for Germany. (The fact that international economic statistics are expressed in US dollars is significant.)

Whether it is the richest country per person depends on currency exchange rates, the price of oil and which set of figures you believe. If you believe the CIA, the USA was way in front in 1999 with a per-capita GDP 'purchasing power parity' at $33,900, compared with Switzerland at $27,100, Norway at $25,100, Japan at $23,400, Canada at $23,300, United Arab Emirates at $17,700, and Mexico at $8500. (Visit ⓦ www.odci.gov/cia/publications/factbook.) Is the average American really doing that well?

The USA does have extremes of wealth and poverty, but by most measures of equality it rates quite well, in part because of the large number of middle-income earners. The poorest 10% of households receive about 1.5% of the national income, while the top 10% receive 28.5%. Many advanced economies and most developing countries show more unequal distributions than this. Income distribution has become significantly more unequal over the last two decades. Figures for the distribution of wealth, as opposed to income, show much higher levels of inequality – one estimate is that the wealthiest 1% of the population owns more than 30% of the nation's wealth.

Poverty remains a persistent problem in the USA, and many visitors are shocked at the visible presence of destitute people in affluent cities and at slum-standard housing in some urban and rural areas. About 12.5% of Americans (35 million people) are estimated to be living 'below poverty level' – for a family of four, that's about $17,700 per

year. The incidence is widely variable. In the poorest state, it's around 20%. In terms of race, 10% of whites are below the poverty line, compared with 23% of blacks.

Unemployment figures for the USA are low by international standards, even during economic recessions (9.7% in 1982 is the highest level since WWII). This is partly for statistical reasons (a person who worked even one hour in the week of the survey is counted as employed), partly because of very low pay rates at the bottom end of the labor market, and partly because of a large number of part-time and temporary jobs in the economy. In the 2000 census, when the American economy was doing quite well, unemployment was about 5.4%.

Debt & Government Spending
Despite its enormous productive capacity and the 1990s economic upswing, the USA as a whole consumes more than it produces. In 1998, exports totaled $663 billion, but imports were $912 billion, leaving a trade deficit of $249 billion. The 1998 trade deficit was running at about $246 billion. Total external debt, estimated at $862 billion in 1995, is quite moderate as a proportion of GDP.

For years, successive federal governments spent more than they collected in taxes, and by the mid 1990s, the accumulated federal debt was some $4350 billion. In 1998, as the growing economy provided larger tax revenues, the Clinton administration produced the first budget surplus in 28 years, despite an interest bill that swallowed around 15% of the government's annual expenditures. In 1999, federal government revenues were $1828 billion and expenditures were $1703 billion, leaving a surplus of $125 billion. The potential surplus increased as the economy continued to grow, but the George W Bush administration promised that the surplus would be used to fund tax cuts rather than to pay off the accumulated federal debt.

Federal government spending totals about 20% of GDP; Social Security payments, mainly for the aged, are the largest single item. Military spending, though still huge (3.2% of GDP), has declined since the end of the Cold War.

Economic Structure
Structurally and technologically, the USA is a highly advanced economy. It is one of the

world's leading food producers, and vast amounts of minerals and other resources are extracted, but just 3% of the workforce is in primary industry. Manufacturing employs about 24% of the workforce and is much more diverse than the traditional 'steel belt' industries of the Northeast. The leading manufacturing sectors, in order, are food processing and packaging, transportation equipment (including cars and aircraft), chemicals (plastics, rubber, petroleum products), industrial machinery and electronic equipment. The services sector employs 73% of the workforce and contributes 80% of GDP; the largest single component is retailing, and transport, entertainment and tourism are all huge industries.

A so-called New Economy emerged in the 1990s, based on information technology and, in particular, the growth of the Internet. Investor interest ran hot for 'dot-com' companies that promised to leverage an internet presence into a major market and huge profits. In a classic speculative bubble, stock prices surged way ahead of actual profits, and in 2000 suffered the inevitable collapse. There was nothing new about this. The dot-com bubble diverted some resources from more productive sectors of the economy and its collapse cost some speculators a lot of money. Some workers lost their jobs, but it was by no means an economic disaster. After a sustained period of strong growth the US economy may be due for a slowdown, but its underlying strengths remain – diversity, flexibility, sound infrastructure, technological sophistication and sheer size.

POPULATION & PEOPLE

In the April 2000 national census, the US population was 281.4 million, an increase of 32.7 million from 1990 – a record increase for a 10-year inter-census period. The official estimate in August 2001 was 284,936,101. For census results and literally up-to-the-minute population estimates, check the US Census Bureau's Web site (W www.census.gov).

The population is about 77% white, 13% black, 4% Asian and 1% Native American. These figures include the 12.5% who identify as Hispanic, whether of white, Native American or other race. (Race and Hispanic-ness were separate questions on the 2000 census form.) The mix varies greatly between states and is changing over time, because a high proportion of new immigrants come from Asia and Latin America, and the black community has a higher-than-average birthrate.

The rate of natural population increase is low, but continued immigration maintains the overall population growth rate at about 0.9% per year. The number of illegal residents (also called 'undocumented workers' or 'illegal aliens') in the USA is variously estimated at six to 11 million, mostly Hispanic. Historically, America is a nation of immigrants, and currently about one million new immigrants arrive annually. Nevertheless, only 11% of the resident population was born outside the USA, which is considerably less than the proportion in Canada (16%) or Australia (19%), and comparable to that in many western European countries.

The median age of the population is 35.4 years, and increasing as a result of longer life expectancy and lower birth rates. About 12.4% of people are older than 65 years. This proportion has been steadily rising for years and will continue to do so. Providing services, especially medical care, for a growing aged population is an emerging problem for the country.

Geographically, the Northeast states have approximately 53.6 million people; the Midwest, 64.4 million; the South, 100.2 million; and the West, 63.2 million. In the past two decades, population growth has been above average in the West and the South, while the Northeast and Midwest states have grown more slowly. During the 1980s and 1990s, populations actually declined in some northern cities like Detroit and Philadelphia. Historically there has been a movement away from the countryside, and 80% of people now live in urban areas, defined as cities or towns with more than 2500 inhabitants.

EDUCATION

Education is basically a state responsibility; state boards of education determine policy, curriculum, teacher certification and so on. There is some federal and state funding, but the school system is actually run by local school districts at a city or county level and is funded by local property taxes. This means that there is some correlation between the price of real estate and the quality of primary and secondary education. Elementary (or primary) school runs from grades one to six (ages five to 11), junior high (or middle) school is grades seven to nine (ages 12 to 14), and senior high school is grades 10 to 12 (ages 15 to 17), although there are variations on this pattern. The school year is usually nine months, from September to May.

All public schools are coeducational, nonreligious and open to all races. Some schools reflect the racial make-up of the local community with a student body of virtually all one race (be it white, black or Latino). Some cities have a program of 'bussing' students to schools in distant neighborhoods to achieve more racially and socially integrated schools.

Apart from the free public schools, about 13.5% of students attend private schools that charge fees. The majority of these are church-run schools; more than two million students are in Roman Catholic schools. There was an upsurge in the popularity of private schools in the South when public schools became racially integrated in the late 1950s. Especially in the Northeast, private secondary schools have social cachet and are traditional for the New England upper crust. Imitative of English 'public' schools, they're called preparatory schools because they prepare students for prestigious colleges and careers – hence 'preppy,' meaning upper class in style or pretension.

Over 80% of Americans now complete high school, though the educational standards can vary considerably between high schools. Over half of high school graduates go on to some form of higher education.

Two-year community or junior colleges offer associate degrees, which prepare students for semiprofessional occupations or further study. Four-year colleges grant bachelors degrees, which are often a precursor to further professional or academic studies. State and private universities (commonly called colleges) usually comprise undergraduate colleges of arts and sciences, plus graduate schools for postgraduate training in the professions (law, medicine, architecture, etc), research and advanced degrees (masters and PhD). The standard of higher education varies greatly, from colleges that will admit and graduate almost anyone, to elite institutions that attract the world's best

scholars, do the world's most advanced research and win more Nobel prizes than anywhere else.

ARTS

Colonial Americans, understandably, followed their old European traditions in the arts. Even after the Revolutionary War, Americans adopted European styles in a deliberate attempt to continue the best of European culture in the New World. But at some stage every art form began to develop distinctively American styles, and a new American culture flourished. By the 20th century, Americans were setting new trends in literature, music, art and architecture, eagerly followed by Europe and the rest of the world.

Literature

Colonial & Revolutionary The first American writings were accounts of early exploration, notably Captain John Smith's *The Generall Historie of Virginia, New England and the Summer Isles* (1624), and descriptions of the new lands. The Puritan colonies produced sermons, pious poetry and theological works including the weighty *Magnalia Christi Americana* by Cotton Mather (1702), an ecclesiastical history of New England.

Early novels and poetry followed English fashions, but increasing discontent with colonial government saw the emergence of distinctly American political tracts, such as Thomas Paine's *Common Sense* (1776), Thomas Jefferson's *Notes on the State of Virginia* (1782) and *The Federalist* (1787–8) by John Jay, James Madison and Alexander Hamilton. *Poor Richard's Almanack* (1732), by Benjamin Franklin, was a collection of letters, political pamphlets and homespun aphorisms that was popular at the time.

Early & Mid-19th Century After Independence, some writers consciously attempted to develop an American style of writing, but nationalism did not become a real force until after the War of 1812. Washington Irving, poet, essayist, satirist and wit, was the creator of several enduring American characters. His *Sketch Book* (1819–20) included 'Rip Van Winkle' and 'The Legend of Sleepy Hollow,' which helped establish the short story as a popular literary form in the USA.

James Fenimore Cooper's Leatherstocking series of five novels form an epic of the conquest of America, with the pioneer Natty Bumppo as hero. *The Last of the Mohicans* (1826) is the best known of the series.

Another early success was Edgar Allan Poe (1809–49), who penned gloomy verse, literary criticism and timeless short stories, including 'The Fall of the House of Usher' (1839), 'The Pit and the Pendulum' (1842) and 'The Tell-Tale Heart' (1843). He is credited as the originator of two genres – the horror story and the detective story.

The mid-19th century, especially between 1850 and the Civil War, saw a great flowering of American literature. The national mood of expansion was reflected in larger-than-life heroes like Ahab in Herman Melville's *Moby-Dick* (1851), now seen as an epic on the nature of evil. The democratic ideal was articulated as individualism. A focus on 'the common man,' seen in the exuberant verse of Walt Whitman's unusual progressive autobiography, *Leaves of Grass* (initially 1855), sympathetically and perceptively depicts a diversity of ordinary Americans.

The transcendentalists followed an idealistic, romantic philosophy, believing that individuals could have a direct, personal experience of the divine; this was a reaction to orthodox religion and 18th-century rationalism. Essayist Ralph Waldo Emerson articulated transcendentalist philosophy in *Nature* (1836). Henry David Thoreau's *Walden* (1854) extolled a nonmaterialistic life, and his *Civil Disobedience* (1849) argued for individual freedom. The leading character of Nathaniel Hawthorne's *The Scarlet Letter* (1850) was a woman who defied a repressive, moralistic society.

Emily Dickinson was also writing at this time, but her exquisite poems were not published until after her death. Less literary, but more influential was the antislavery novel *Uncle Tom's Cabin* (1852) by Harriet Beecher Stowe, whom Lincoln described as 'the little woman who caused this big war.' Also influential was *Narrative of the Life of Frederick Douglass, an American Slave* (1845), the first of three autobiographies by Douglass and the most important work by a black writer at that time.

Late 19th Century After the Civil War, in the late 19th century, the great territorial expansion was probably a factor in the awakening of regionalist (or 'local colorist') interest in the country's various regions and their mores. Mark Twain tweaked California folklore in *The Celebrated Jumping Frog of Calaveras County and Other Stories* (1867), and he sketched Nevada silver-mining life in *Roughing It* (1872). His best-known works were *The Adventures of Tom Sawyer* (1876) and *The Adventures of Huckleberry Finn* (1884), both set on the Mississippi River. Robert Louis Stevenson's *Silverado Squatters* (1872) also described early California life, while Jack London's *The Call of the Wild* (1903) depicted Alaska in the gold-rush era.

Hamlin Garland was one of the writers who tried to realistically depict all sides of late-19th-century life – his *Main-Travelled Roads* (1891) is an unvarnished view of an Iowa farmer's struggles. Stephen Crane's gritty story of a young soldier in *The Red Badge of Courage* (1895) was one of the rare, memorable novels of the Civil War. Upton Sinclair's *The Jungle* (1906), an account of workers' hard times in the Chicago stockyards, is an American classic.

As an expatriate in England for much of his life, Henry James stood outside the main American literary trends. Many of his novels explore the differences between European and American societies. *The American* (1877) and *The Portrait of a Lady* (1881) are two examples. His literary analysis and critiques, starting with *Notes on Novelists* (1914) influenced many later American writers.

Between the Wars After the horrors of WWI, many writers felt a great disillusionment with society, and became known as the Lost Generation. Some congregated in New York's Greenwich Village, where playwright Eugene O'Neill and poet ee cummings contributed works to the neighborhood's magazines and journals. Also associated with this scene was F Scott Fitzgerald, author of *The Great Gatsby* (1925), whose main character is seemingly successful but inwardly discontent.

Another Lost Generation writer, Ernest Hemingway, lived in France and Florida among other places; *A Farewell to Arms* (1929) and *To Have and Have Not* (1937) were his best novels of the period. Also of the genre are Sinclair Lewis' classics *Babbitt* (1922) and *Arrowsmith* (1925), both cynical portraits of middle-class men.

Meanwhile, the Harlem Renaissance writers, including Langston Hughes and Claude McKay, produced vibrant works about black American life. Zora Neale Hurston penned evocative stories of rural black Florida life; *Their Eyes Were Watching God* (1937) is her best-known work.

Regional writing became less fashionable, but the South retained a great regionalist in William Faulkner, whose novels, set in fictional Yoknapatawpha County, Mississippi, were hilarious, mordant and deeply concerned with troubled Southern history. *The Sound and the Fury* (1929) is his best-known novel. Also continuing the regionalism and realism genres are John Steinbeck's Depression-era novels *The Grapes of Wrath* (1939) and *Cannery Row* (1945), which paint portraits of a California now hidden beneath subdivisions and shopping malls. Another grim reflection of the state is Nathanael West's apocalyptic *Day of the Locust* (1939).

Post WWII WWII itself was the subject of several successful books, including *The Naked and the Dead* (1948) by Norman Mailer, *Tales of the South Pacific* (1947) by James A Michener. Years later, the war was still the basis for fine works like Joseph Heller's *Catch 22* (1961) and Kurt Vonnegut Jr's *Slaughterhouse Five* (1969). The latter included sequences of science fiction, a genre that became increasingly popular in the 1950s and '60s.

A recurrent postwar theme was the questioning of American values and conventions. The Beatniks, notably Allen Ginsberg, Jack Kerouac and William S Burroughs, flouted literary conventions with free-form fiction and nonconformist poetry.

JD Salinger's *The Catcher in the Rye* (1951) touched a generation of disaffected young Americans, while John Updike chronicled middle-class disillusionment in his series of novels *Rabbit, Run* (1960), *Rabbit Redux* (1971), *Rabbit Is Rich* (1981) and *Rabbit at Rest* (1990).

Philip Roth is one of the most productive and enduring Jewish writers, with novels such as *Goodbye, Columbus* (1959), *Portnoy's Complaint* (1969), *The Counterlife*

(1987) and *American Pastoral* (1997), which won the 1998 Pulitzer Prize. Another important Jewish writer is Nobel laureate Saul Bellow, whose novels *The Adventures of Augie March* (1953) and *Herzog* (1964) are compelling portraits of modern life.

The South continues its own literary tradition with Kentucky writer Robert Penn Warren's novels of Southern politics; the classic *All the King's Men* (1946) is loosely based on former Louisiana Governor Huey Long. Georgia-born Flannery O'Connor crafted dark stories of the Southern grotesque, including *A Good Man Is Hard to Find* (1955). Alabama-writer Walker Percy explored the sorrows and struggles of modern Southerners in novels such as *The Moviegoer* (1961).

Western mythology owes much to the novels of pulp writers Zane Grey and Louis L'Amour. A darker side of the West is seen in Truman Capote's landmark 'nonfiction novel' *In Cold Blood* (1965), a story of murder in Kansas. Another modern Western classic is Texan Larry McMurtry's *The Last Picture Show* (1966). Also from Texas, Cormac McCarthy reshaped Western archetypes of cowboys, cattle ranching and south-of-the-line adventures in his Border Trilogy: *All the Pretty Horses* (1992), *The Crossing* (1994) and *Cities of the Plain* (1998).

The Southwest has produced several excellent Native American novelists, including N Scott Momaday, author of the Pulitzer-winning novel *House Made of Dawn* (1969), and Leslie Marmon Silko, whose sprawling *Almanac of the Dead* (1991) weaves Indian myth and history into a fierce narrative of modern life.

The postwar resurgence of African American writing began with *Black Boy* (1945), by Richard Wright, a gripping realist portrayal of racism, and Ralph Ellison's *Invisible Man* (1952). James Baldwin is perhaps the most acclaimed African American writer (though he lived most of his life in France). His first novel *Go Tell It on the Mountain* (1953) established his reputation. *Nobody Knows My Name* (1961) was based on his early life in Harlem, while *The Fire Next Time* (1963) explored the broader moral and psychological issues of race relations. He was also one of the first American writers to deal openly with gay sexuality in *Giovanni's Room* (1956).

Toni Morrison's rich novels delve deep into the world of African American women, but draw on broader sources too. Her works include *Song of Solomon* (1977) and *Beloved* (1987), a Pulitzer Prize winner. Alice Walker won the 1983 Pulitzer for *The Color Purple*. Other prominent women writers include Anne Tyler, who writes poignant novels about the lives of modern Baltimoreans; *Dinner at the Homesick Restaurant* (1982) is a good one. Californian Amy Tan explores the Asian American experience in *The Joy Luck Club* (1989).

Drama

Though many plays were written and performed in the USA before the 20th century, they were mostly for entertainment and very few achieved a lasting resonance, especially compared to the wealth of early novels and other writing. After WWI, some of the Lost Generation who'd traveled to Europe and experienced its progressive theater scene sought to emulate it at home, where theater had long been dominated by commercial performances following New York's Broadway. The Little Theater movement was founded to enable innovative, experimental drama to be produced in cities all over the USA.

In Provincetown, Massachusetts, the Provincetown Players provided an avenue for Eugene O'Neill to develop his talents as a dramatist and a theater company manager. His first play to achieve wider recognition was *The Emperor Jones* (1920), about a paranoid black dictator; it was successfully produced on Broadway. The tragedy *Beyond the Horizon* (1920) won a Pulitzer Prize, and was also a Broadway success. *Strange Interlude* (a 1928 Pulitzer Prize winner), was an innovative psychological drama that showed O'Neill's renowned versatility as a playwright. His *Mourning Becomes Electra* (1931) set a classical Greek tragedy in 19th-century New England. Other critically acclaimed dramas included *Anna Christie* (1922 Pulitzer Prize), *The Iceman Cometh* (1946) and *Long Day's Journey into Night* (1957 Pulitzer Prize).

Arthur Miller achieved critical recognition with *The Man Who Had All the Luck* (1944) and popular acclaim with *Death of a Salesman* (1949), a Pulitzer Prize winner

about the modern-day tragedy of an ordinary man. *The Crucible* (1953), ostensibly about the Salem witchcraft trials, was an allegory of the anticommunist witch-hunts led by Senator Joseph McCarthy; Arthur Miller was himself called before the House Un-American Activities Committee in 1956.

The great Southern playwright Tennessee Williams achieved success in 1945 when *The Glass Menagerie* was performed on Broadway to critical acclaim. *A Streetcar Named Desire* (1947) and *Cat on a Hot Tin Roof* (1955) both won the Pulitzer Prize. All these plays, and six others, were made into movies.

Master of absurdist theater Edward Albee had a hit with *Who's Afraid of Virginia Woolf?* (1962), which became a memorable movie. *A Delicate Balance* (1966) won the 1967 Pulitzer Prize and established him as one of the three leading postwar playwrights. Other successes included *Seascape* (1976 Pulitzer Prize), an adaptation of Nabokov's novel *Lolita* (1979), and *Three Tall Women* (1991), another Pulitzer Prize winner.

Many women have made their mark on the American stage, often by addressing social issues. Lillian Hellman's work provides insight into the changing culture of the mid-20th century. Both *The Little Foxes* (1939) and *Another Part of the Forest* (1946) deal with materialism and morality. Another sharp satire of the time is *The Women* (1936) by Clare Boothe Luce. Lorraine Hansberry's *A Raisin in the Sun* (1959) and Anna Deveare Smith's *Fires in the Mirror* (1992) delve into US race issues. Feminist themes are addressed by Wendy Wasserstein, who won a Pulitzer Prize for *The Heidi Chronicles* (1988).

Other prominent current playwrights include Tony Kushner, David Mamet, David Rabe, Sam Shepard, Neil Simon and August Wilson. Their latest works are most likely to be seen in off-Broadway productions in New York or the main theaters of other cities.

Music

Jazz I regard as an American folk music; not the only one but a very powerful one which is probably in the blood and feeling of the American people more than any other style.

– George Gershwin

Early colonists brought European musical traditions to the New World, notably hymns and psalms put to music. Identifiably American variants emerged as early as the 18th century. Some of this was written as 'shape note' music and, especially after the Revolutionary War, spread south where it was incorporated into the music of revival churches. American classical music, centered on New England, followed European, especially German, musical styles through the 19th century. The most distinctive American musical sounds all originated in the South, heavily influenced by African American traditions.

Gospel, Blues & Soul The work songs of black slaves drew on African rhythms and the 'call and response' pattern used in religious singing. A wholly oral tradition, the music was first published in 1867 as *Slave Songs of the United States.* Black Christian choral singing evolved as gospel and gained a wider audience when it was performed in post–Civil War concerts by Nashville's Fisk University Jubilee Singers. Gospel composer Thomas A Dorsey came to Chicago in the early 1920s, followed a few years later by gospel's greatest singer, Mahalia Jackson. Gospel sounds and spirituals were adopted as protest songs in the civil-rights movement of the 1960s and are still an essential feature of African American church services.

Blues also has its origins in African musical forms, slave music and the deep sadness and poverty of black life before and after the Civil War. The Mississippi River Delta was the home of such early blues masters as Charley Patton, Son House and Robert Johnson. Texas-native Leadbelly and Tennessee-daughter Bessie Smith were also blues pioneers. Chicago became the new base of the blues in the late 1940s and '50s when Muddy Waters, Willie Dixon, John Lee Hooker and other Southerners came north and went electric.

Later, the more individual singing of soul music was an outgrowth of gospel and R&B, popularized by performers such as James Brown, Ray Charles and Aretha Franklin, notably at Harlem's Apollo Theater in the 1950s and '60s. Stevie Wonder and other artists on Detroit's Motown label continued the soul tradition.

Jazz The origins of jazz were in Congo Square, New Orleans, where slaves gathered on Sunday to sing and dance as early as the 1830s. At first only drums were used, then banjos and violins were added, and brass band instruments after the 1880s. A leader-response pattern and a tendency to improvisation were adopted from the gospel tradition. The lively, syncopated style and improvised patterns led to the description 'ragged' rhythms, hence ragtime music, which was hugely popular as sheet music and on piano rolls by 1900.

The first true jazz is credited to Buddy Bolden in the 1890s, though jazz music was never written down, and no recordings exist before 1916. Jelly Roll Morton claimed to have invented jazz in the brothels of New Orleans; although this may overstate Morton's very significant role, the Storyville red-light district was certainly the center of jazz before 1920. New Orleans bandleader King Oliver went to Chicago in 1919 and in 1922 he was joined by his star second trumpet player, Louis Armstrong.

Within a few years Chicago was the new center of jazz, Armstrong had established the solo improvisation as an essential element in jazz performance, and his own band had a worldwide following. Also in Chicago was Paul Whiteman (whose band included trumpet legend Bix Beiderbecke) and clarinetist Benny Goodman.

In the 1920s came the Jazz Age – jazz music became popular in New York, where it was a key ingredient in the Harlem Renaissance of African American culture. Harlem bands led by Fletcher Henderson and Duke Ellington crafted a new, urbane, big-band jazz sound that grew in popularity in the 1930s and '40s. Kansas City, Missouri, was another jazz capital, where innovators included Count Basie, Charlie Christian and Lester Young. Notable jazz singers like Ella Fitzgerald and Billie Holiday combined blues with jazz, as did guitarist BB King.

Composers Irving Berlin, George Gershwin and Leonard Bernstein combined jazz and classical traditions, notably for the popular Broadway musicals of Tin Pan Alley (named for the music publishers' neighborhood in New York City). In the late 1940s and '50s Charlie Parker, Dizzy Gillespie and Thelonius Monk pioneered the new style known as bebop (also known

Billie Holiday sings the blues.

as bop or rebop). Numerous other jazz variants include cool jazz (Miles Davis, Stan Getz), free jazz (John Coltrane), avant-garde (Ornette Coleman) and fusion (with Latin and Caribbean influences).

Rock & Roll In the 1940s, a combination of African American swing music and the blues evolved as R&B (rhythm and blues), popularized by artists such as T-Bone Walker, Fats Domino, James Brown, Ray Charles and gospel singer Sam Cooke. R&B was categorized as 'race music' and almost exclusively followed by black audiences until Bill Haley's landmark 'Rock around the Clock' came out in 1954. Visionary producer Sam Phillips, of Memphis Sun Studios, recorded Elvis Presley that same year, and rock & roll was born. Chuck Berry, Little Richard, Jerry Lee Lewis and Buddy Holly were other original 1950s rock & rollers.

The 1960s saw a cross fertilization of US rock with British sounds, and with folk, Latin, soul and country music. On the West Coast, commercial bands like the Beach Boys were popular, but soon the hazy shadow of San Francisco's Haight-Ashbury district produced the acid-rock revolution with bands like the Grateful Dead and Jefferson Airplane. Other products (and victims) of the drug-fueled '60s included

Janis Joplin, Jimi Hendrix, the Doors and Frank Zappa. In New York, the Warhol-sponsored Velvet Underground was a largely underground phenomenon, but it launched rough-edged artists like Lou Reed and John Cale. Other hard rockers emerged from the depressed industrial areas of Detroit (Iggy Pop) and New Jersey (Bruce Springsteen).

Punk and new-wave groups like the Ramones, Patti Smith, Talking Heads and Blondie shook up the late '70s and '80s, and in Athens, Georgia, the B-52s and REM put the New South on the modern rock map. The San Francisco Bay Area has had its punks (Dead Kennedys) and punk revivalists (Green Day). Farther up the coast, Seattle's Nirvana sent grunge rock to the top of the charts in the early 1990s.

The Red Hot Chili Peppers, Smashing Pumpkins and Beck gave it their best in that decade, but the '90s could just as easily be remembered for the money-spinning factory pop of performers like Britney Spears and the ubiquitous boy (and girl) bands like 'N Sync and Backstreet Boys. In recent years, mainstream rock & roll has embraced Latin rhythms with a vengeance, courtesy of artists like Ricky Martin, Jennifer Lopez and Santana, who had a Grammy-winning comeback. The new millennium is experiencing other cross-over styles too, notably R&B- and hip-hop–influenced pop, with artists like Lauryn Hill and Macy Gray.

Rap & Hip-Hop Derived from black and Puerto Rican street culture in New York's South Bronx, the hip-hop beat thumped into prominence around 1976 from the turntables of DJs like Kool Herc, snatching breaks from records, punctuated with rhythmic scratching of the disc. Harlem's Sugar Hill Gang spearheaded the rap revolution with the first international rap hit 'Rapper's Delight' (1979). Rap soon became mainstream, and even Blondie did a successful rap-rock crossover. In the '80s rap lost a lot of its disco beats and became more lyrically driven by new stars like Public Enemy, De La Soul and the Beastie Boys.

Hip-hop came into its own in the '90s, splintering into several strains, including hardcore 'gangsta rap' – groups like NWA broke all the rules with songs about killing cops, prostitution and drug use – and other styles with wider appeal, as seen in acts like A Tribe Called Quest and Salt-N-Pepa. Hip-hop went on to become the highest-selling genre in popular music by the end of the '90s. A sampling of rap and hip-hop artists popular in the last decade are Snoop Dogg, Missy Elliott, DMX, Eminem and Lil' Kim.

Country Scottish, Irish and English folk music transplanted to the Appalachian Mountains became the foot stompin', thigh slappin' southern mountain dance music of fiddles, banjos and mandolins. When this old time string-band sound came out of the mountains, the record companies called it hillbilly music. Jimmie Rodgers and the Carter Family made their first records in Tennessee in the late 1920s and brought hillbilly music to a wider audience. Nashville became the mecca for country music (as it was later called), especially after 1939 when the Grand Ole Opry radio show began broadcasting nationwide.

Melded with jazz and blues in Kentucky, it became bluegrass, pioneered by Bill Monroe and his Blue Mountain Boys. Honky tonk (using piano and small electrified instruments) and western swing (using drums and saxophones) were other early variants on country music. Country had a natural affinity with early rock, and the resulting rockabilly sound was best exemplified by Conway Twitty. Later, country rock was made hugely popular by Linda Ronstadt and Emmylou Harris. Now mainstream country & western is a major industry, and is pervasive on radio stations throughout North America. Recent artists in the limelight include Garth Brooks, Billy Ray Cyrus, the Dixie Chicks and Shania Twain. Faith Hill, also very popular, straddles the country-pop line.

Folk If folk music is that which is passed down among common people by oral tradition, then hillbilly, blues and even jazz are true American folk traditions.

Recordings cut in the 1930s and '40s made Woody Guthrie America's best-known folk musician, his music rooted in the country & western tradition. Guthrie traveled throughout the USA during the Depression, singing of migrant workers, the urban poor and the dust-bowl refugees. In the 1940s he performed with Pete Seeger, the other definitive American folk figure.

Seeger, the son of an academic musicologist, had abandoned his Harvard University course to travel the country collecting folk songs, writing and singing.

A folk revival in the 1960s was largely instigated by Seeger and attracted performers like Joan Baez, Buffy Saint-Marie and Bob Dylan to the coffeehouses of New York's Greenwich Village. Woody Guthrie greatly influenced Dylan, who went further musically with a folk-rock fusion, and later took up blues and country influences. Folk music was at the fore of the 1960s protest movements, doing for whites what gospel and blues did for blacks.

Cajun & Zydeco Cajun and zydeco came out of a blend of African and French cultures in the Louisiana bayous. Cajun features a strong stomp rhythm with new influences from country & western; Clifton Chenier and Queen Ida give zydeco a lustier, syncopated sound from Caribbean influences.

Dance
Ballet The School of American Ballet was founded in 1934 by Russian-born choreographer George Balanchine (1904–83). He then became artistic director of the New York City Ballet when it was founded in 1948 and turned it into one of the best ballet companies in the world. He adapted traditional ballet to modern influences and set new standards in performance. Jerome Robbins (1918–98), who took over from Balanchine in 1983, had previously collaborated with Leonard Bernstein on several of Broadway's biggest musicals, including *West Side Story* (1957).

The New York City Ballet delights upstate visitors every summer in Saratoga Springs, its summer home away from home. Saratoga Springs is also the home of the fine National Museum of Dance. Boston, Philadelphia, Pittsburgh, Miami, Chicago, Denver, San Francisco and Seattle all have professional ballet companies.

Modern Dance The pioneer of modern dance, Isadora Duncan (1877–1927) spent four years in New York City before heading for Europe. Basing her ideas on ancient Greek concepts of beauty, she challenged the strictures of classical ballet and sought to make dance an intense form of self-expression.

In Los Angeles in 1915, Ted Shawn (1891–1972) and Ruth St Denis (1879–1968) formed Denishawn, a modern-dance company and school, which moved to New York in 1920 and remained the nation's leading company into the '30s.

Its most influential student was Pittsburgh's Martha Graham (1894–1991), who founded her Dance Repertory Theater in New York and a modern-dance school at Bennington College in Vermont. In her long career she choreographed more than 140 dances and developed a new dance technique, now taught worldwide, aimed at expressing inner emotion and dramatic narrative. Her two most famous works were *Appalachian* (1944), dealing with frontier life, and *Clytemnestra* (1957), based on Greek myths.

Paul Taylor (b 1930) and Twyla Tharp (b 1942), two students of Martha Graham, succeeded her as the leading exponents of modern dance, but differed from her in that they borrowed themes from popular culture. Tharp danced with her own company until 1987, when she became artistic associate of the American Ballet Theater. Another student of Martha Graham, Alvin Ailey (1931–89) set up the Alvin Ailey American Dance Theater in 1958. His most famous work is *Revelations* (1960), a dance suite set to gospel music. Mark Morris (b 1956) is a celebrated dancer and choreographer who formed his own dance group in 1988, which performs at the Brooklyn Academy of Music.

City Center in New York City is the main venue for the dance companies of Martha Graham, Paul Taylor and others, along with the Joyce Theater, which is in the Chelsea neighborhood.

Architecture

The only lasting indigenous influence on American architecture originated in the Southwest, where 17th- and 18th-century Spanish colonial and mission buildings incorporated elements of Pueblo Indian design and construction, notably the flat-roofed, thick-walled adobe building (see Taos, New Mexico). The hybrid Spanish-Indian influence reappeared in 20th-century architecture as mission-revival style in Southern California and Pueblo style in the Southwest.

Colonial The 17th-century East Coast colonists brought English, Dutch and German architectural influences, though the first buildings reflect necessity as much as style. In the New England colonies, abundant local timber was used in plain weatherboard farm buildings and meeting halls. Rectangular, with steep-pitched shingle roofs, they are similar to structures in southeastern England from the same period.

In Virginia and the Carolinas, the would-be gentry was able to ape a grander English style when the tobacco money started coming in. Williamsburg, Virginia, was built with imported bricks rather than local timber. The symmetrical design and the contrasting white cornice and window details were based on pictures of English houses. (The present Williamsburg is an accurate reconstruction; Philadelphia has several original examples.) The oldest urban areas, like central Boston and lower Manhattan, had haphazard street patterns following animal tracks and native walking trails, but it didn't take long for civic order to assert itself in the planned street grids of Philadelphia, Baltimore and other cities.

Neoclassic & Federal Toward the mid-18th century, buildings became more refined, adopting neoclassical details of Palladian and Georgian styles. Symmetry ruled, Doric columns framed doorways or supported pediments, and the fanciest buildings featured domes and porticoes. After the Revolutionary War, the leaders of the new nation, especially Thomas Jefferson, deliberately adopted neoclassicism as a style befitting the republic – it embodied the ideals of the Greek and Roman republics, and it wasn't English. The Virginia State Capitol, designed by the multitalented Jefferson, was modeled on a Roman temple, while his home, Monticello, and the University of Virginia both had Romanesque rotunda.

Professional architects, starting with Charles Bulfinch, used the basic geometrical elements of classicism (well-proportioned triangles, rectangles, cubes, arches, ellipses and domes) in what became known as Federal style, though in fact it paralleled the

English Georgian style of Robert Adam. The decoration was refined, displaying flat surfaces, slender columns and narrow cornices. The grandest example is the US Capitol in Washington, which became the model for many state legislative buildings, from Georgia to California.

In the early 19th century, tastes moved toward the heavier Greek-revival style, which had become a fashion in England since the acquisition of Athens' Elgin Marbles in 1806. Courthouses, churches, banks, libraries, colleges and mansions all over the country took the form of Greek and Roman temples or had a mini-Parthenon-shaped portico tacked on the front. Even today, mock Georgian houses are built with decorative Doric columns supporting the front porch. Around 1850, Gothic-revival style became popular for church and college buildings, again following English fashion, but the Civil War stalled most new building work.

Structural Developments In the mid-19th century, small-scale building was revolutionized by 'balloon-frame' construction: A light frame of standard-milled, 2-by-4-inch timber was joined by cheap, mass-produced nails. Developed in Chicago in the 1830s, it provided a fast and economical building form for the rapidly growing cities of the Midwest and the West Coast and is still used today. The simplest balloon-frame building was the two- or three-room 'shotgun shack' that housed poor farmers all over the South (the structure was supposedly named because a shotgun could be fired straight through the doors from front to back). Balloon-frame saloons, stores and stables were thrown up in mining and cattle towns all over the expanding Western frontier.

Well-to-do houses in San Francisco and other cities were also of balloon-frame construction but were larger and fancier, adding balconies, bay windows, towers, turrets and ornate, colorful trim. Commonly called Victorian houses (Victoria reigned from 1837–1901), these houses had decorative features that showed a variety of influences, including neoclassical, Queen Anne, Gothic and Italianate. The decorative woodwork, and sometimes the whole house, was prefabricated. Condemned as a fire hazard in the inner cities, free-standing timber frame houses proliferated in the suburbs, where home ownership came in reach of middle American salary earners, and new rail and trolley lines put them within reach of their downtown workplaces.

At the same time, the fast-developing iron industry began to turn out girders for iron frame buildings. Initially used for commercial buildings in the SoHo district of New York City in the 1850s, the internal iron frame allowed greater freedom of design. The external walls no longer supported the building, so many more windows were possible. Also, iron could be cheaply cast in decorative shapes, from Corinthian columns to art nouveau flourishes. Another innovation, the Otis elevator, made tall buildings usable.

Beaux Arts After the Civil War, communications with Europe improved, influential architects studied at the École des Beaux-Arts in Paris, and American buildings showed increasing refinement and confidence in decoration and detail. The epitome of confidence and decoration was reached by Richard Morris Hunt in the mansions of the super-rich at Newport, Rhode Island, and at the Biltmore Estate in North Carolina. Beaux arts style became democratic in major public buildings, like the railway station in Washington, DC, City Hall in San Francisco and the Great Hall of the Metropolitan Museum of Art in New York.

Beaux arts married the metal frame building in Chicago, after the fire of 1871. The Chicago School produced the first true skyscrapers and the first 'modern' architecture. Its leading exponent, Louis Sullivan, had studied at both MIT and the École des Beaux-Arts. His first skyscraper (actually in Buffalo, New York) was the 13-story Guaranty Building; it had strong vertical lines, which accentuated the height of the building, and an Italianate cornice capped it off. Another intriguing Sullivan survivor is the Carson Pirie Scott & Co department store in Chicago, featuring ornate metalwork at street level and numerous windows above. But it was New York that saw the skyscraper pushed ever higher by the irresistible pressures of profit and high-priced real estate. Beaux arts and neo-Gothic decorations were imposed on the early skyscrapers, but looked increasingly out of place in the new machine age.

Frank Lloyd Wright Initially an apprentice to Sullivan's firm, Frank Lloyd Wright created an architectural style all his own. Working mainly on private houses, he abandoned all the historical elements of architecture, making each building a unique sculptural form characterized by strong horizontal lines. Wright called them 'prairie houses,' though invariably they were built in the suburbs.

Interior spaces flowed from one to another, rather than being divided into rooms, and the inside was connected to the outside rather than separated by solid walls. Texture and color came from the materials themselves, not from applied decoration. Wright was innovative in his use of steel, glass and concrete, creating shapes and structures like nothing in the past, and he pioneered panel heating, indirect lighting, double glazing and air conditioning.

As well as visiting the revolutionary Guggenheim Museum in New York City, Wright fans should check out Buffalo, New York; southern Wisconsin; eastern Pennsylvania; and, of course, Chicago.

Skyscrapers & Art Deco After Wright had broken free of the traditional architectural forms, the new, tall city buildings could take on new appearances. The horizontals and verticals of the structural grid (especially the verticals), and the surfaces of concrete, glass and steel, were allowed to create the appearance of the building.

The profile of the mid-20th-century skyscraper was largely determined by New York 'air rights' ordinances, which required tall buildings to be stepped back from the street frontage as their height increased, allowing some sunlight down to the city streets. The effect was that of a tall, stepped pyramid, exemplified in the 1930 Chrysler Building and the 1931 Empire State Building. Both these buildings used the new art deco style, which burst into fashion from the 1925 Paris exposition. Instantly popular in the USA, art deco was also a feature of the 1932 Rockefeller Center and its Radio City Music Hall, and was adopted for other new skyscrapers as well as movie houses, gas stations, ocean liners and resort hotels, most notably in Miami.

International Style Wright's thinking had influenced modern architecture in Europe, and the influence bounced back when the Bauhaus School left Nazi Germany to set up in the USA. In America, Bauhaus became known as the International style, and its principles were taught at Harvard by Walter Gropius and practiced in Chicago by Ludwig Mies van der Rohe. By using glass 'curtain walls' over a steel frame, the best International style buildings became abstract, sculptured shapes and the worst of them became ugly glass boxes. The Seagram Building in New York and the North Lake Shore Dr Apartments in Chicago are two of the best.

One response to the starkness of the International style was to re-emphasize the structural form of the building and the spaces between its different parts, as in the heavy-duty concrete blocks of Louis Kahn's Salk Institute in La Jolla, California. Another response was postmodernism, which re-introduced decoration, often in whimsical or incongruent ways, like the Chippendale-style pediment atop the AT&T building in New York City.

Arguably the best American architect today is Canadian-born Frank Gehry, whose trademark curves and stainless steel finishes are inspired by the shapes and surfaces of fish. A truly 21st-century designer, he has been greatly influenced by installation art, and his firm has pioneered computer design techniques that allow the conception and construction of perfectly composed whole buildings out of irregular and unmatched shapes.

Mass Production & Urban Renewal Since WWII, there has been a growing demand for mass housing, as freeways and suburbs spread like cancer. City fringes are subdivided for 'tract housing,' where hundreds of near-identical, partly prefabricated houses make instant homes. Even more mass-produced are mobile homes, 40 feet long by 10 feet wide, made in factories and delivered like shipping containers. Dozens of these boxes are planted on sometimes barren and barely serviced lots called trailer parks, which have become a byword for lower-income, working-class life.

Suburban shopping centers and strip malls have sucked the commercial and communal life from neighborhoods and city centers, and the shopping mall has become a town in itself. Now many downtown areas have been redeveloped, creating new multi-function zones and restoring old commercial buildings as shops, galleries, restaurants and nightspots. Renovation, recycling and retrofitting are the buzzwords of urban renewal, from Baltimore to Pittsburgh to San Diego.

Painting & Sculpture

There are fine examples of American art in museums all over the country, but two of the best places to study its development are the Whitney Museum in New York City and the Corcoran Gallery in Washington, DC. For an excellent and well-illustrated overview of the subject, see *American Visions*, by Robert Hughes.

Native American Arts Most Native American arts and crafts were personal adornments and decoration of everyday tools and weapons, but several cultures produced work of exceptional interest. In the Pacific Northwest, the coastal societies had an abundant economy and developed unique styles of painting and carving to depict their gods and ancestors. Murals, masks and totem poles used distinctive, semi-abstract, black-and-red designs to show whales, fish, otters and 'thunderbirds.' In the Southwest, Pueblo people produced pottery that was skillfully made and painted in a variety of distinctive styles. Influenced by the Spanish missionaries, the Navajo learned to weave blankets using ancient designs and to make silver jewelry.

Spanish & Mexican Influences From the early 17th century, the artistic skills of the Pueblo were turned to making Christian icons and decorations for the churches of Spanish colonists. Often styled after European prints, these works are a strange combination of naive and baroque, and incorporate some indigenous elements in their design. The brightly colored decoration of whitewashed adobe walls and roughly hewn timber became an element of Santa Fe style decoration in the late 20th century.

Colonial Art The first colonists on the Atlantic seaboard had little time or resources for fine arts, but they soon began to decorate everyday household objects, perhaps as a response to the undomesticated wilderness around them. Religious art was prohibited by Puritans, and the first paintings (around 1660) were portraits intended to document the social position of prominent colonists (see the Worcester Art Museum in Massachusetts). The finest colonial arts were furniture and silverware, which not only had practical value, but could also be used to display the wealth and status of the owner.

The southern colonies of Virginia and the Carolinas were slow to achieve stability or prosperity. The planter elite invested mostly in grand houses, imported furnishings and a little second-rate portraiture.

In 1729, John Smibert arrived in Boston. A portraitist who had trained in London, he had a great influence on colonial artists, who had little direct access to the European art whose tradition they naturally sought to follow. John Singleton Copley (1738–1815) was influenced by Smibert's work and became very successful doing portraits of leading Bostonians like Paul Revere and Samuel Adams (both in the Boston Museum of Fine Arts).

Benjamin West (1738–1820), a self-taught artist from Pennsylvania, achieved limited success in America, then left for Europe and ultimately became a court painter to George III, an associate of Joshua Reynolds and president of the Royal Academy of the Arts. West made his name with a history painting, *The Death of General Wolfe*, considered revolutionary because the heroes of the Battle of Quebec were dressed in contemporary military uniforms, not Greco-Roman garb.

Neoclassicism West's studio became a center for American painters studying in London and did much to promote the standard of American painting. Portraits and history scenes achieved a high degree of realism and classical formality, sometimes highly romanticized. This paralleled the neoclassical movement in architecture, reflecting the new republic's ambition to build on the best traditions of Europe.

Copley came to West's studio in 1775 and spent the rest of his life in England. Charles Willson Peale (1741–1827) arrived in 1776, but returned to fight in the Revolution and to become a noted painter of history scenes and portraits. Gilbert Stuart (1755–1828) trained in West's studio at the same time, returning after independence to make a good living painting George Washington portraits. A Stuart portrait of Washington was used for the US $1 note and might be the most reproduced portrait in history. John Trumbull (1756–1843) spent five years in West's studio and became a leading historical painter. His *Declaration of Independence* is copied on the $2 note.

American Landscape From about 1825, landscape painting became the strongest current in American art. It reflected the trend of territorial expansion and took a romantic, sometimes allegorical view of a wilderness that was rapidly disappearing in the Eastern states. Asher Durand (1796–1886) and Thomas Cole (1801–48) were the leading figures of the Hudson River School, which initially concentrated on the Catskill Mountains near New York. Their 'luminist' emphasis on atmosphere and light was developed in the landscapes of Cole's student Frederick Church, who extended his subject matter to monumental paintings of Niagara Falls, the Andes and the tropics.

After the Civil War, landscapes and seascapes became more populated and were used as backdrops for human drama. The postwar work of Winslow Homer (1836–1910) emphasized rural renewal and often showed children playing in fields. From the 1880s, he turned his attention to the sea, often using storms to provide a setting for drama and impending doom.

Academic Art & Impressionism In the late 19th century, America's new wealth demanded European-style sophistication. The rich acquired European masterpieces and decorated their mansions in European style. Artists studied at the École des Beaux-Arts in Paris and the Academy in Munich, and sought commissions for society portraits. The most notable was John Singer Sargent, who lived in Europe nearly all his life.

Augustus Saint-Gaudens (1848–1907) brought European refinement and great sensitivity to monumental bronze sculpture. The statues of Admiral Farragut and General Sherman in New York and the monument to black soldiers on Boston Common are some of the best.

The most recognized American impressionists, James Whistler (1834–1903) and Mary Cassatt (1844–1926), both spent most of their working lives in Europe. Cassatt was influential in having impressionism accepted in the USA when it was still being ridiculed in Europe; American museums still hold many of the finest works by European impressionists.

Western Art The land west of the Mississippi, acquired in the 1803 Louisiana Purchase, offered not just new landscapes but also a new mythology. George Catlin (1796–1872) went west in 1832 to document Indian life, even as the 'Indian removals' were decimating the last of the Eastern tribes. His paintings (many are in the Smithsonian's National Gallery of Art) are none too professional, but they are a detailed, accurate and not unsympathetic record. Before long, Indians would be depicted as savage warriors threatening white settlers, but doomed to extinction by Manifest Destiny.

The first magnificent images of the West were the monumental landscapes of Albert Bierstadt (1830–1902), a German-born, European-trained artist who went west with surveyors in 1859. Some of his later work was sponsored by railroad companies and was used to publicize the scenic possibilities of train travel. Thomas Moran's paintings of the Yellowstone River gorge promoted the North Pacific Railroad and also helped persuade congress to proclaim the area a national park.

As railways and civilization conquered the West and as Indians were relegated to reservations, a cultural industry grew up perpetuating the myths of the frontier, the pioneer, the Indian fighter and the cowboy. Many of the images that would be endlessly recycled in Western movies were originally created by Western artists, whose work is still widely imitated and more sought after than ever.

The greatest romanticizer of the West, Frederic Remington (1861–1909), was an Easterner who became popular as an illustrator for magazines and pulp Western novels. He made regular trips out West but did most of his painting in a New York studio. Many of his paintings, like *The Last*

Stand (1890) and *Fight for the Waterhole* (1903), used the theme of white men surrounded by hostile Indians, facing certain death. Realistic, and often thought to be real, these images were fraudulently fictional – the last big 'battle' of the Indian Wars was in 1890 and it was white soldiers slaughtering Indians.

Charles Russell (1864–1926) was born in St Louis and actually worked as a wrangler on cattle drives and spent time in Indian camps. His depiction of Indians is based on his experience, but the images of shoot-'em-up cowboys are mostly imaginative inventions. Despite its historical inaccuracies and artistic limitations, Western art is as much fun as Western movies; the best places to see it include Dallas-Fort Worth, Texas, Oklahoma City, Oklahoma and Remington's birthplace, Ogdensburg, New York.

American Realism Thomas Eakins (1844–1916) was the first major artist to draw his inspiration from contemporary American urban life. He studied in Paris but spent his career in Philadelphia, painting surgeons, scientists, oarsmen and sailors in the context of their work or leisure.

In the early 20th century, a group of artists began to paint with the eye of the muckraking journalist – in New York, of course. They were later known as the Ashcan School. The best example is George Bellows (1882–1925) who portrayed the poor of lower Manhattan and the brutality of boxers and who was briefly popular among the better class of slumming voyeurs.

Despite the evolution of modernism (see below), the realist style continued. Artists depicting small-town and rural life were called regionalists and included Grant Wood (1892–1942), whose *American Gothic* (1930) became one of the most parodied pictures in history. Thomas Hart Benton (1889–1975) was the doyen of regionalists, doing popular paintings and murals of ordinary people in workplaces, bars and dance halls. Reminiscent of Soviet social-realist paintings, regionalism dominated the work of WPA artists during the 1930s.

The definitive American realist was Edward Hopper (1882–1967), whose bleak urban landscapes are a stage set for alienated actors. His visual and psychological images are echoed in films and widely recognized.

Anyone who has seen them will find much of America instantly familiar.

The illustrations of Norman Rockwell (1894–1978) are also realist images of American life, but usually in an idealized, old-fashioned, small-town setting. Rockwell's patriotic pictures appeared on the covers of family magazines from the 1920s to the 1960s, but you may search in vain for a reality to match them.

Modernism American artists had followed cubism, fauvism and the early moves toward abstract art, and New York's 291 Gallery displayed European modernist works from 1908. The 1913 Armory Show introduced a wider audience to modernism and caused a sensation. American artists Joseph Stella, Charles Demuth and Charles Sheeler began to 'abstract' colors and forms from US urban and industrial scenes, while Stuart Davis derived abstract forms from still-life objects. Georgia O'Keeffe (1887–1986) did the same using desert flowers and landscapes. Her brilliantly luminous colors, flowing shapes and subtle eroticism made her one of the USA's most popular artists.

After WWII, New York became a world center for the avant-garde, partly because of an influx of European artists during the war. The artists who took abstraction to its ultimate form, including Willem de Kooning and Jackson Pollock, became known as abstract expressionists or the New York School.

Even as abstract expressionism (AbEx) reached its peak, other artists began to appropriate images from advertising and popular culture, enlarging, coloring and combining them in the pop-art style made famous by Roy Lichtenstein and Andy Warhol (the best Warhol collection is in Pittsburgh, his birthplace). Accessible, enjoyable and popular, pop art was also identifiably American in its imagery, not least in Jasper Johns' pictures of the US flag.

The avant-garde art scene is now more international than American, though perhaps the faddishness and commercialism of contemporary art is American in itself. The Next Big Thing, for better or worse, is more likely to appear in the galleries of SoHo and Chelsea than anywhere else in the world.

Film

Thomas Edison's laboratory in New Jersey developed the first practical movie camera in the 1890s, using the sprocket system devised by Edison employee William Dickson. Edison's lab also produced the first real American movie, *The Great Train Robbery,* in 1903. The eight-minute Western was carefully edited and for a climax, it cut to a chase.

More than any other art form, the movies have represented the USA to the world. Most movies conform to a genre (if not a formula) that producers hope will strike a chord with the audience. Many feature a somewhat stereotypical central character whom the audience will recognize or identify with. If you start your pre-trip research at the video store, you will be well prepared for the big question – is America really like it is in the movies?

Charlie Chaplin, the first movie star

Westerns This definitively American genre turns the cowboy loose on the boundless, lawless frontier, with lots of action, great scenery, good guys and bad guys. Of the thousands of horse operas, quite a few go beyond the clichés and conventions. The silent epic *Covered Wagon* (1923) was a pioneering movie in more ways than one, with magnificent scenery and Indian action shots. *Stagecoach* (1939) also had wild action shots, but it is more noted for its intense depiction of the characters in the imperiled coach. John Wayne does the classic tough cowboy in *Red River* (1948), one of the few cowboy movies that actually has cattle in it. *Broken Arrow* (1950) was just about the first Western to take the Indian viewpoint, and in *Shane* (1953), Alan Ladd plays one of the first gunfighters to feel remorse. In the 1950s, the cowboy heroes became more cynical, and in the '60s they became more violent. In 1969, *Butch Cassidy & the Sundance Kid* introduced the feel-good Western, even if it didn't have a happy ending. *Unforgiven* (1992) won awards as a sort of antiviolence anti-Western.

Comedy Comedies have been a movie mainstay since the earliest days of the silent era, with Mack Sennett developing the fast-paced slapstick style out of the vaudeville stage tradition. Charlie Chaplin was the first true movie star, and his 'Little Tramp' character appeared in a string of movies including *The Tramp* (1915), *The Immigrant* (1917), *The Gold Rush* (1925) and *Modern Times* (1936; his first movie with sound). The recurring theme was of the common man struggling for survival, individuality and romance in the face of uncaring authorities and great social forces. When talkies came in, the Marx brothers added witty word play to madcap comedy; Groucho was an early master of the American one-liner and snappy comeback – *Duck Soup* (1933) is one of the funniest.

The 1930s social comedies of Frank Capra present an idealized America in films like *Mr Smith Goes to Washington* (1939). Other light comedies tried a satirical touch – *The Secret Life of Walter Mitty* (1947) has Danny Kaye as a suburbanite whose daydreams are more exciting than his daily life. With the depiction of sex restricted by the 1934 Hays Code, romantic comedies provided an amusing but often bland substitute.

After 1960, comedies became more perceptive and revealing of American life. *The Graduate* (1967) depicted 1960s middle-class California so accurately it now looks dated. *Manhattan* (1979) is Woody Allen's satirical, romantic but affectionate ode to the Big Apple. *National Lampoon's Summer Vacation* (1983) is a devastating warning to anyone planning a cross-country driving trip, especially with their kids. In *LA Story* (1991), Steve Martin parodies every aspect of LA life, from traffic to earthquakes to movie industry obsessions. Edgy black comedy *American Beauty* (2001) is an update on *The Graduate* for aging baby boomers – the now-familiar mid-life crisis theme is brilliantly played out in an all-too-convincing suburban environment.

Musicals After sound film became practical in the late 1920s, the musical and the song-and-dance film were natural developments. It's no coincidence that these exuberant, optimistic films were a hit during the Great Depression; *42nd St* (1933) is one of the classic musicals, starring a chorus girl who rises to stardom and every other showbiz cliché. *Top Hat* (1935) features fabulous Fred Astaire and Ginger Rogers and a great Irving Berlin score.

A much-loved variant on the standard musical, *The Wizard of Oz* (1939) has Judy Garland plucked by a tornado from her Kansas farm – a dust-bowl allegory, or good old escapism? *Cabaret* (1972) was a darker twist on the musical, while *The Blues Brothers* (1980) was a revolution, using soul-blues-R&B backing for Jake and Elroy's madcap dash for cash in Chicago. *Moulin Rouge* (2001) is a lavishly mounted musical spectacular. With a grab bag of great songs from the last five decades and the fast-paced cinematography of a music video, it's the first new twist on the musical in years.

Crime & Gangsters Inspired by the lawlessness of the Prohibition era, gangster movies provided high drama, action and violence. They thrived in the '30s, at the same time as the musicals, but offered a different type of escape. One of the first and best was *Little Caesar* (1930), set in New York, with Humphrey Bogart, Edward G Robinson and James Cagney all working up the Tough Guy stereotype. The focus on the seamy underside of city life, the dark images and the suspense were all developed further in melodramas and horror movies later described as *film noir*.

Gangsters became less relevant during WWII, but were revived in the '70s by *The Godfather* (1972) and *The Godfather Part II* (1974), which told the crime story from the gangsters' point of view. *Pulp Fiction* (1994) is a recent incarnation of the genre, with drugs, guns and graphic violence. A murder-for-money story billed as a comedy-drama, *Fargo* (1996) is not wholly successful as either, but its North Dakota setting and its cast of Midwestern characters are so realistically depicted you'll think you're there.

LA Confidential (1997) is a snapshot of the city in the crime-ridden '50s.

Drama Sharing the dark mood and moral ambiguity of the gangster movies, *Citizen Kane* (1941) introduced many of the cinematic techniques of film noir. A thinly disguised biography of William Randolph Hearst, the film's premise was that really rich people can be unhappy inside. This may be heresy in a land dedicated to self-improvement, but it was no doubt a comfort to many poor people.

Consistently cited as America's favorite movie, *Casablanca* (1942) is a claustrophobic, moody melodrama whose cynical tough-guy hero must recover his lost idealism and make a stand against the Nazis. The film was made at a time when the USA was divided about its entry into WWII.

On the Waterfront (1954) brought the familiar themes of corruption and despair to a labor union and longshoreman setting, starring Marlon Brando as a brooding, semi-articulate half-hero. A mixture of crime and historical drama, *Chinatown* (1974) is a chilling story of the early-20th-century water wars in southern California. Robert Altman's *Nashville* (1975) builds an epic around the country-music business.

Perhaps the first feminist road movie, *Thelma & Louise* (1991) follows two women who start on a weekend getaway and finish up in a wild-western car chase. Perhaps inspired by the Reagan years, *Forrest Gump* (1994) was a feel-good movie that advanced the dubious notion that simple-minded people could become very successful with a sufficiently positive attitude. One of the most popular movies ever, *Titanic* (1997) offers an epic setting for the archetypal American romance – poor-but-spirited boy wins rich girl despite family objections.

War Movies DW Griffith's silent Civil War epic, *Birth of a Nation* (1915), was one of the earliest full-length films (159 minutes). Technically and stylistically innovative, its sympathetic portrayal of the Ku Klux Klan did not stop it from becoming a box office smash. Despite a good number of jingoistic action movies, many of the most memorable American war movies have had an antiwar stance.

More a romance than a war movie, the perennially popular *Gone with the Wind* (1939) featured spectacular scenes of the burning of Atlanta and shocking depictions of Civil War suffering. It's famous as the first big Technicolor epic and, at 220 minutes, as one of the longest Hollywood hits.

WWII was well covered by newsreel cameras, which perhaps reduced the demand for movies about the war. *Sands of Iwo Jima* (1949), with John Wayne, was one of the better ones.

The brilliantly satirical *Dr Strangelove* (1964) is the definitive Cold War movie (even if it is British). *M*A*S*H* (1970) gave a farcical treatment to the Korean War at the same time that the Vietnam War was becoming a deadly farce, and *Apocalypse Now* (1979) advanced the plausible possibility that the US generals in Vietnam were out of their tree.

Made as a TV documentary, Ken Burns' *The Civil War* is a superb nine-part series using lots of original photographs and period music (available on video). *Glory* (1989) is the well-told story of a black infantry unit in the Civil War. *Saving Private Ryan* (1999), a WWII D-Day drama, employs all the usual clichés of the genre, but its gut-wrenching realism redefines the depiction of war in movies. *The Patriot* (2000) takes place during the Revolutionary War in the late 18th century.

Youth Movies Social problems like poverty, crime, corruption and racism were an element in many drama, gangster and comedy movies, but rebellious youth, alienation and the generation gap became influential themes starting in the 1950s. One of the first was *The Wild One* (1954), in which Marlon Brando and his motorcycle gang terrorizes a small town. *Blackboard Jungle* (1955), set in a tough New York high school, opens with the Bill Haley song 'Rock Around the Clock.'

Easy Rider (1969) captured the mood of the '60s, as two drug-dealing, motorcycle-riding rebels search for 'the real America.' George Lucas' tribute to small-town teenagers, *American Graffiti* (1973), was a popular piece of nostalgia with a golden-oldies soundtrack. A new realism came to the teen theme with *Boyz N the Hood* (1991), a disturbing drama about a black family in inner-city Los Angeles.

The last decade saw its share of light-hearted coming-of-age films, including *Clueless* (1995) and *American Pie* (1999).

Contemporary Movies The introduction of TV, home videos and cable created a challenge for the mainstream movie industry. In response, the studios have gone for more big-screen spectaculars employing special effects and big sound. Theaters have become smaller and more accessible, and many suburban malls now boast multiscreen cinemas. If the current trend for fantasy and action movies says anything about US society, it says that the desire for escapist entertainment is as strong as ever. They've got the bread, so give them *Gladiator*.

SOCIETY & CONDUCT
Traditional Culture

Native American communities are generally based on reservation lands, mostly west of the Mississippi River. Many of these reservations are engaged in commercial activities, including farming, tourism and especially casinos, and the people have a modern lifestyle while retaining traditional cultures to a greater or lesser extent. Traditional ceremonies are practiced most often in Alaska, the Northwest, the Southwest and at powwows in other parts of the country.

Reservations are governed by federal and tribal law. Each tribe is independent and what is permitted on one reservation may be banned on another. Language, customs and religious ceremonies differ from one reservation to the next. Many Native Americans prefer to speak their own language, and some don't speak English. Visitors to reservations are generally welcome, but should behave in an appropriately courteous and respectful manner. It is considered polite to listen without comment, particularly when an elder is speaking. Many reservations ban the sale or use of alcohol, and drugs are banned on all of them. Tribal rules are often posted at the entrance.

Many tribes ban all forms of recording – photography, videotaping, audiotaping or drawing. Others permit these activities in certain areas only if you pay a fee. Obtain permission before you photograph anyone on a reservation, including children – a tip is usually expected.

Some ceremonials and powwows are open to the public, but others are for tribal members only. Ceremonials are religious events and applauding or chatting is rude; taking photos or making recordings is rarely permitted. While powwows also hold spiritual significance, they are usually less formal. Modest dress is customary, so halter or tank tops and miniskirts or short shorts are inappropriate.

The rip-off of Native American arts has become a lucrative business, as cheap imported imitations are passed off as authentic. If you're considering purchasing Indian art, find a legitimate shop and look for authenticating labels.

Dos & Don'ts

The USA is not a social minefield, but everyone is expected to be polite and considerate, and to show respect for the country and its symbols.

The USA is a very well-ordered society and, generally speaking, people stand in line, obey the rules and follow the instructions. You should be punctual for any business or social occasion and be appropriately dressed – this could mean anything from a bikini to a dark suit, so ask first if you're not sure. People dress a little more formally in the East, especially in New England.

Both men and women shake hands, while family and friends embrace and kiss with varying degrees of visible affection. Straight men tend to avoid hugging or kissing each other. Unless you're introduced to someone as Mr or Ms So-and-So, it's usually OK to use first names. Police and other officials are an exception to this – they call people 'sir' and 'ma'am' in a very assertive fashion, and prefer to be addressed as 'Officer.'

Self-confidence and a positive outlook are highly valued in the USA, so if someone asks 'How are you?' the correct answer is 'Fine, thanks,' 'Very well' or something even better. Polite understatement is rarely called for and may be interpreted as a regrettable lack of enthusiasm. 'Have a nice day' is a common way of saying goodbye and is seldom meant to be irritating. Another social nicety is saying, 'You're welcome' after being thanked.

The level of overt patriotism in the USA is very high, and the culturally sensitive visitor will go along with it. The national flag, known as the Stars and Stripes or Old Glory, flies over schools, libraries and government offices, outside businesses and in front of many private homes. Americans swear allegiance to the flag and are taught never to let it touch the ground. Though the flag is often displayed on baseball caps and bumper stickers, it might be seen as disrespectful to have it on the seat of your pants.

The national anthem ('The Star-Spangled Banner') is played at public occasions. Everyone stands when it is played and many people place a hand on their heart (some reveal a poor grasp of anatomy). Those in uniform salute, while civilian men remove their hats (this may be the only time some baseball caps are removed). Most people join in the singing. There's usually a lot of mumbling during the difficult, high-pitched fourth and fifth lines (about the rocket's red glare), but everyone comes in strongly for the rousing chorus about the land of the free and the home of the brave.

Underneath all this is a very real sense of national pride, and it's well to be aware of it when discussing political and social issues. Freedom of speech is one thing, but critical comments, especially from a foreigner, might be interpreted as a slight to national honor and can provoke a negative reaction. Some other topics of conversation should also be avoided, at least until you're quite sure about who you're talking to. Gun control is a dodgy subject because some surprisingly mild-mannered people are gun owners and cherish their right to bear arms. Religion is risky because many people have fundamentalist beliefs and don't accept scientific notions of geological time or human evolution. The abortion/right-to-life issue is the touchiest subject of all, because many people hold very strong views.

The following are some other don'ts for foreign visitors:

- Don't assume that Americans know anything about your country, but allow for the possibility that some will be extremely well informed.
- Don't expect Americans to answer for US foreign policy in your part of the world.
- Don't smoke anywhere unless it's clearly permitted.
- Don't discard litter anywhere except in a trash can.

- Don't swim or sunbathe nude or (for women) topless – it's unacceptable at all but a few beaches and resorts.
- Don't forget to tip 15% to 20% in restaurants, bars and taxis.

RELIGION

Most Native American religions have been greatly modified since contact with Europeans, but traditional religious ceremonies are still practiced on some reservations. Religion was an element in most of the early colonies, from the Roman Catholic missions of the Spanish to the 'Pilgrim Fathers' of Massachusetts, and has been an important part of American life ever since.

The Constitution mandates separation of church and state, and the First Amendment says that congress 'will make no law respecting an establishment of religion.' Thus, prayers are not permitted in public schools, though students take the oath of allegiance to 'One nation under God.' The words 'In God We Trust' have been stamped on the currency since 1864 and were officially adopted by congress in 1956 as the national motto.

Numerically and culturally, the USA is predominantly a Christian country: 56% Protestant, 25% Roman Catholic, 2% Judaic, 6% other religion, 11% no religion (1994). Of the Protestants, the main sects are (in descending order of number of adherents) Baptist, Methodist, Lutheran, Presbyterian and Episcopalian.

The so-called Bible Belt stretches roughly through Oklahoma, Arkansas, Mississippi, Tennessee and Kentucky. It's the heartland of the fundamentalist Southern Baptist church, which has about 16 million followers and is known for its literal interpretation of the Bible, full-body baptisms and fire-and-brimstone sermons. Some Christian denominations have almost exclusively African American adherents, including the African Methodist Episcopal Church (about 3½ million members), the National Baptist Convention USA (eight million) and the National Baptist Convention of America (3½ million). Black churches have been enormously important in promoting the cultural identity and well-being of the black community.

The Nation of Islam, a black American Muslim sect, has at least 100,000 members who call themselves Bilalians and wear distinctive colored robes and caps. Other religions of interest include the Shakers, of whom only a few in Maine survive; the Amish in Pennsylvania and Ohio; Mormons, headquartered in Utah; and the Christian Scientists, Seventh-day Adventists and Jehovah's Witnesses (all founded in the USA). In addition, there are numerous sects, cults and confidence men who cater to congregations and TV audiences of varying sizes – some 1300 radio and TV stations are devoted exclusively to preaching and collecting donations. Members of the Religious Society of Friends, better known as Quakers, were among the first immigrants to the USA, and still number more than 100,000.

LANGUAGE

English is spoken throughout the USA, though it is not designated as the country's official language. Some believe that it should be, especially those concerned about the increasing use of Spanish. Other minority languages are French (in Louisiana and upstate New York near Quebec), Pennsylvania 'Dutch' (a German dialect), Chinese (mostly Cantonese, in the Chinatowns of several large cities), Yiddish (among Orthodox Jews in New York) and Gullah, an African American dialect (on sea islands off South Carolina). A few immigrant ethnic communities retain their own languages, but historically these have tended to dissipate within one or two generations (Spanish is the exception). A few Native American communities speak indigenous languages, of which about 200 survive. Some indigenous languages have fewer than a dozen native speakers.

There are regional differences in accent, idiom and vocabulary, but American English is relatively uniform when compared to, say, the varieties of English spoken in Britain. Most foreign visitors will be familiar with American English from the media, but may have difficulty following Deep South speech or African American idiom. On the other hand, many Americans are unfamiliar with foreign accents and may not understand the English of foreign visitors. Apart from speaking clearly and slowly, it may help to mimic an American accent, especially in the use of vowels – say *bath* with a short 'a,' as in 'mat', rather than a long 'a', as in 'cart.'

In the 18th century Benjamin Franklin, by trade a printer, sought to rationalize and standardize the disordered spelling of the English language. Although his plans weren't adopted at the time, he did influence Noah Webster, who published the *American Dictionary of the English Language* in 1828. It was Webster who popularized spelling changes of such words as *theatre* to *theater*, *colour* to *color* and *organise* to *organize*.

But it's not the spelling that makes American English so distinctive – it's the wealth of new words and expressions that it has brought to the language. Several Native American words have come into English, including *moccasin*, *moose*, *toboggan* and *kayak*. Many more words have come from European languages via immigrants to America: from German, there are words like *loafer*, *hoodlum* and *kindergarten*; from Dutch, *boss*, *stoop* (a front step) and *nitwit*; from Yiddish, *schmuck*, *schlock* and *schmaltz*; from French, *prairie*, *saloon* and

levee; and from Italian, *pasta*, *pizza* and other food words. Spanish has contributed *canyon*, *ranch*, *rodeo* and numerous place names in the Southwest and the West.

Nevertheless, the vast majority of Americanisms come from America itself. American inventiveness produces not only new products, but new words to describe them and a new vocabulary to market them. So there's not just *soda pop*, *root beer* and *sarsaparilla* (all American inventions), but the brand names *Coca-Cola*, *Coke* and *Pepsi* are also in the language, along with advertising slogans like 'the Pepsi Generation,' and imaginative new concepts like Coca-Colonization. American business, technology, cars, movies, military forces and especially sports have all contributed words that are so familiar that it's easy to forget they're American. For more on American language, see Bill Bryson's *Made in America*.

Facts for the Visitor

The USA is a very easy place to travel in, and no one with a few dollars or a credit card will have trouble finding a place to stay or eat. The biggest problem is deciding which of the many destinations and possibilities will interest you most. Each chapter of this book starts with a list of highlights – the very best the region has to offer. Remember that this is subjective, and one traveler's highlight is another's horror story. Also at the start of each chapter, there's a map of the region marked with some possible detours, many of them less-publicized places, so consider these when planning your route.

The text itself includes many more museums, parks, buildings, natural attractions and tourist traps, each with a brief description. Sometimes the description is very brief, but if it sounds appealing, go for it. If it doesn't, it's probably not for you. There's usually information about opening days, but not the exact times. Most attractions will be open around 9am-4pm or 5pm; if they are open on Sunday, it will usually be from around 11am or noon. Generally the regular adult admission price is given, with the children's price only if it's an attraction kids will like. Children are commonly defined as ages two through 12, but sometimes it's six to 14, and sometimes it's those 'under 48 inches tall.' Other discounts are often available for seniors (those older than 60, 62 or 65 years), students, AAA (American Automobile Association) members, war veterans and coupon clippers. These prices are often not advertised, so ask when buying your ticket. If you need more details about exact opening times, discounts, disabled access or whatever, phone numbers are given for all attractions.

The USA is a big place to cover in a single guidebook, so the information in this book is highly selective. Don't worry – an abundance of tourist information is freely available wherever you go. For planning your trip, contact one of the many state and local tourist offices listed, or visit their Web sites.

SUGGESTED ITINERARIES

In general terms, the best strategy is to select the places and activities that attract you most, do those thoroughly first, then move on to whatever other highlights are accessible, allowing enough time for diversions, distractions and dalliances along the way. This might involve an unhurried drive around one region and then some flights to see more distant cities. If you plan to visit someone, do a specific activity or pursue a special interest, do it first, before you go sightseeing.

Here are some itineraries for trips of about two weeks around various popular regions. They are all circuits, starting and finishing in a major city:

New York & Pennsylvania – New York City, Hudson Valley, Catskills, Finger Lakes, Rochester, Niagara Falls, Buffalo, Oil Creek, Pittsburgh, Pennsylvania Dutch Country, Philadelphia, New York City

New England – Boston, Portsmouth, White Mountains, Berkshires, Connecticut Valley, Newport, Cape Cod, Nantucket, Boston

Northeastern Cities – New York City, Newport, Boston, Québec, Montréal, Ottawa, Toronto, Niagara Falls, Buffalo, Albany, Hudson Valley, New York City (this popular circuit takes in some of the main cities in Canada; see Lonely Planet's *Canada* guide)

Historic East – Philadelphia, Valley Forge, Baltimore, Annapolis, Washington, DC, Mt Vernon, Yorktown, Williamsburg, Jamestown, Charlottesville, Monticello, Harpers Ferry, Gettysburg, Philadelphia

Civil War Sites – Washington, DC, Harpers Ferry, Antietam, Gettysburg, Winchester, Shenandoah Valley, Lexington, Appomattox, Richmond, Petersburg, Washington, DC

Great Lakes – Chicago, Ann Arbor, Detroit, Grand Rapids, Traverse City, Petoskey, Mackinac Island, Sault Ste Marie, Pictured Rocks National Lakeshore, Door County, Madison, Galena, Chicago

Old South – Atlanta, Savannah, Beaufort, Charleston, Asheville, Great Smoky Mountains, Lexington, Nashville, Chattanooga, Atlanta

Deep South – New Orleans, Baton Rouge, Natchez, Mississippi Delta, Memphis, Tupelo, Natchez Trace Parkway, Lafayette, New Orleans

Florida – Miami Beach, Cape Canaveral, St Augustine, Orlando, Walt Disney World, Tampa, Fort Myers, the Everglades, Florida Keys, Miami

Texas – Dallas, Fort Worth, Austin, Fredericks-burg, San Antonio, Corpus Christi, Houston, Dallas

Prairie & Mountain – Denver, Cheyenne, Rapid City, Mt Rushmore National Monument, Devils Tower National Monument, Buffalo, Cody, Yel-lowstone National Park, Grand Tetons, Jackson, Vernal, Denver

Central Rocky Mountains & Southwest – Denver, Rocky Mountain National Park, Vail, Colorado National Monument, Arches National Park, Moab, Mesa Verde, Durango, Black Canyon of the Gunnison, Colorado Springs, Pikes Peak, Denver

Southwest – Albuquerque, White Sands National Monument, Carlsbad Caverns, Roswell, Santa Fe, Taos, Durango, Mesa Verde, Monument Valley, Albuquerque

Canyon Country – Phoenix, Oak Creek Canyon, Grand Canyon National Park, Monument Valley, Lake Powell, Bryce Canyon National Park, Zion National Park, Las Vegas, Hoover Dam, Phoenix

Southern California Deserts – Los Angeles, San Diego, Anza-Borrego Desert State Park, Joshua Tree National Park, Death Valley National Park, Las Vegas, Los Angeles

Central California – San Francisco, Pacific Coast Hwy, Los Angeles, Sequoia National Park, Kings Canyon National Park, Yosemite, Lake Tahoe, Gold Country, San Francisco

Pacific Northwest – Seattle, Olympic National Park, Mt Rainier, Mt Hood, Columbia River, Hells Canyon, Coeur d'Alene Lake, North Cas-cades National Park, Seattle

PLANNING
When to Go

For outdoor activities, the weather is criti-cal, while many city-based cultural attrac-tions can be enjoyed year round, subject mainly to crowds and costs. For specific advice, see the When to Go sections at the start of the regional chapters. Generally, the USA is well set up for its extremes of climate. Most hotels, restaurants, trains, buses and attractions are appropriately equipped with heating and/or air-conditioning.

Summer is the main holiday season for Americans. For the tourist industry, summer means the period from Memorial Day (the last Monday in May) to Labor Day (the first Monday in September). With a few excep-tions, most destinations will be more crowded in these months, and prices will be higher. Many facilities and attractions, espe-

cially in the northern states, have longer hours in summer, and some close altogether outside this period. On the other hand, many states in the South are uncomfortably humid in summer, while much of the Midwest and Southwest are extremely, perhaps unpleasantly, hot.

Spring is a lovely season in most of the country, but in northern states and at higher altitudes, spring comes later and often lasts only a brief few weeks between a slushy, muddy snow thaw and a hot, sticky summer. Special attractions include forest and desert wildflowers and blossoms in many fruit-growing areas.

Fall (autumn) also brings pleasant weather in most states. The beautiful display of fall foliage is a major attraction. 'Leaf peeping' is a mania in New England, but fine fall colors can be seen in many areas south to Louisiana, often with fewer crowds. The peak of the fall color moves south as the season advances, starting in mid-Sep-tember near the Canadian border, progress-ing to Virginia in October and to the Deep South as late as November. Out west in the Rocky Mountains, aspens turn brilliant gold in fall, and towns all over the country display colorful deciduous trees.

Winter is the best time for snow sports in the northern states and Rocky Mountains (though spring skiing is popular) and is a de-lightful season in the desert states, the Deep South and Florida. Many cities run their music, dance and theater seasons over winter, and the great museums are less crowded. Small towns and rural areas can be particu-larly picturesque under a layer of snow.

If you're planning your trip around some special event, like Mardi Gras in New Orleans or Halloween in San Francisco, that will determine when you go (see Special Events, later). These events are popular, so be sure to make reservations well in advance. If you want to catch one of the many small, local events, any state tourist office will tell you what's on during your visit.

What Kind of Trip

City Hopping If your main interests are art, architecture and other city-based at-tractions, then it's easy to plan a trip that picks up several major cities. Arrange an airfare that includes stops in New York, Chicago, New Orleans, Los Angeles and/or

The Best

Natural Beauty
Fall colors in New England, the Adirondacks and the Appalachians
Maine coast
Michigan's Upper Peninsula
Great Smoky Mountains
Florida Keys coral reefs
Rocky Mountains
Badlands & Black Hills
Grand Canyon, Bryce Canyon, Zion Canyon
Monument Valley
Death Valley
Sierra Nevada
Redwood forests
Oregon coast
Olympic Peninsula
Alaska's Inside Passage
Hawaii's volcanoes

Big Cities
New York City
Boston
Washington, DC
Chicago
New Orleans
Los Angeles
San Francisco
Seattle

Smaller Cities
Ann Arbor, Michigan
Charleston, South Carolina
Savannah, Georgia
Memphis, Tennessee
Natchez, Mississippi
Austin, Texas
Santa Fe, New Mexico
Portland, Oregon

Americana
Graceland, Tennessee
Route 66 between Arizona and Oklahoma
Las Vegas, Nevada
Disneyland, California
Venice Beach, California
Mt Rushmore, South Dakota
Miami Beach, Florida
The National Mall, Washington, DC

Native America
National Museum of the American Indian, New York City
Mound City at Hopewell Culture National Historic Park, Ohio
Serpent Mound, Ohio
Cherokee, North Carolina
Poverty Point, Louisiana
Museum of the Great Plains, Lawton, Oklahoma
Indian Pueblo Cultural Center, Albuquerque, New Mexico
Canyon de Chelly National Monument, Arizona
Seattle Art Museum, Washington

Black America
Afro-American Historical & Cultural Museum, Philadelphia
Banneker-Douglass Museum, Annapolis, Maryland
Shaw district, Howard University, Frederick Douglass National Historic Site, Washington, DC
Museum of African American History, Detroit
DuSable Museum of African American History, Chicago
Martin Luther King Jr National Historic Site, Atlanta
National Civil Rights Museum, Memphis
Birmingham Civil Rights Institute, Alabama
Civil Rights Memorial, Rosa Parks Monument, Montgomery, Alabama
Central High School Museum, Little Rock, Arkansas
California Afro-American Museum, Los Angeles

San Francisco. Boston, Philadelphia and Washington, DC, are close enough to New York to connect by train or bus, while Las Vegas and San Diego are an easy detour from Los Angeles. You'll only need a car for excursions outside the cities (and in LA). When you're planning, remember that it's usually better (and less expensive) to spend more time in fewer places than to rush around to a dozen cities and have only a day or two in each.

On the Road Presented with vast distances, excellent roads and cheap gas

The Worst

Lines & Crowds

Many of the country's finest attractions are very popular, especially with Americans, who will wait for hours to get up the Statue of Liberty, the Washington Monument or Disneyland's Magic Mountain. The most accessible viewpoints at Yellowstone, the Grand Canyon and Yosemite can have tourists standing shoulder to shoulder, clicking cameras and expressing voluble opinions about what they're looking at.

The Sheep Treatment

Partly as a response to crowding and security concerns, many buildings and sites can only be visited as part of a guided tour. Some tours are wonderful, but others offer the sheep treatment: Groups of visitors are herded from room to room, given a canned commentary and allowed only minimal opportunities for questions, photos or a really good look at anything of particular interest.

Restorations, Re-Creations & Fakes

Improving things is an American trait, and many would prefer a completely reconstructed building to a totally authentic ruin. The boundary between the original and the imitation has become fuzzy, and no one is keen to point out the difference. It's only when you see the black and white photos of weathered ruins that you realize the 'old' church you're standing in has been rebuilt from the ground up, and possibly in a 'better' location. What's the most popular activity at the Grand Canyon? Watching the IMAX movie about the Grand Canyon!

'Have a Nice Day'

For many visitors, this phrase epitomizes the superficiality of much social interaction in the USA. Especially in the service industries, niceness is a prerequisite, and staff are expected, even required, to mouth vacuous corporate platitudes. Though this is sometimes grating for the visitor, it's often worse for the workers, who may have to answer every call with the words 'Crescent Hotel, the legend continues...'

Ugliness

Though many cities are well built, elegant and squeaky clean, much of the development on urban fringes and beside highways is excruciatingly ugly. This can be especially jarring near places of natural beauty, and some of the most appalling commercial strips are right outside superb national parks. Many visitors respond by acquiring a taste for tackiness and relishing the most hideous strip malls, trailer parks and billboard jungles.

(petrol), many travelers feel a compelling urge to hit the road and drive from sea to shining sea in search of 'the real America.' This can be an unsatisfying trip.

Firstly, it's a long way across the USA, and if your itinerary is too ambitious, you'll spend many long days on the interstates, leaving very little time to enjoy what you're driving through. Secondly, the most interesting and attractive places are off the interstates. If you're looking for engaging small towns, unassuming Americana or idyllic rural vistas, you're more likely to find them on a small state road or rural route, and this means more time and fewer miles. You might be better doing a loop out of LA and another out of Boston rather than driving through everything in between.

Outdoor Adventures The USA is a land of breathtaking natural beauty, and any effort to get deeper into the landscape will be richly rewarded. You can plan a whole trip around one or more outdoor adventures, whether it's diving in Florida, skiing in the Rockies, canoeing the lakes, rafting the rivers, hiking the canyons or biking the back roads. This takes some planning. You may need to book campsites, get wilderness permits, arrange transport, rent equipment, buy food and so on.

The easy way is to book a package with a tour operator who offers the activities you want. Otherwise, try to contact outfitters in areas that are popular for the activities you're interested in. These businesses provide equipment and commonly offer local transport, guides and general information.

Independent travelers should invest in some long-distance phone calls to park authorities, outfitters and tourist offices; on arrival, allow some time in a convenient town to organize the logistics. Don't begrudge this organizing time, as it's a great opportunity to see something of a US city and experience its working side. See the Activities section later in this chapter for more detailed information.

Special Interest The USA has specialists, enthusiasts and devotees of everything from art deco architecture to zydeco music, wheelchair design to organic farming. If you have a special interest – cultural, sporting, professional or personal – it can provide a wonderful focus for a trip, take you to places off the tourist track and introduce you to like-minded Americans. Some research should reveal the most promising sites and enable you to make contacts in advance. Allow some flexibility to explore the possibilities that arise on the way and be open to the broader experience of the USA as you go.

Visiting Friends & Relatives Nearly every foreigner knows someone in the USA, whether it's a long-lost cousin or a recent business associate. Americans can be amazingly hospitable, and a personal host can introduce you to family and community life that you'll rarely see as a tourist, as well as provide a reason to visit some places that may be well off the tourist trail. Most Americans lead busy lives, so if you'd like to visit, give your potential host as much warning as possible and let them suggest a convenient time and some things to see and do.

Try to do your visiting early in the trip, because your hosts may be able to help with planning or contacts for further exploration (be prepared for good-natured, parochial discouragement – 'Why would you want to go to New York when you could stay here in Hicksville for next week's Asparagus Festival?').

Connecting the Dots It's common for visitors to have a list of places they want to go, then try to make an itinerary that takes them all in – 'We want to see New York, New Orleans and Disneyland, trek the Grand Canyon and visit an old friend in

Seattle. Now if we rent a car in LA...' Time and distance are the big problems. A circuit around the places just mentioned is about 6500 miles, and to drive around all of them would take around three weeks of solid travel at 300 miles per day. A four-coupon air pass could make it possible, though it would still involve three or four days of internal air travel and a long (but memorable) driving detour to the Grand Canyon.

To make a more realistic itinerary, reconsider your motives. If New Orleans appeals because you like jazz, consider the alternative of staying a few extra days in New York City to hit the jazz clubs. If your Grand Canyon fantasy includes a trek to the canyon floor, can you allow three days to do it? Is it worth doing if you'll only have a couple of hours on the canyon rim?

Maps

The maps in this book are designed to give travelers a good overview of each region, and to locate attractions, accommodations, restaurants and services in the most-visited cities and localities. Note that key numbers read roughly from top left to bottom right.

Excellent and inexpensive USA road atlases are widely available overseas and may help to plan a driving trip. Good ones include the venerable, annually updated Rand McNally editions ($17), and the *National Geographic Road Atlas* ($15). The more expensive DeLorme Mapping series of atlases and gazetteers has detailed topographic and highway maps of individual states at a scale of 1:250,000, showing well detailed secondary and rural roads.

The American Automobile Association (AAA) issues comprehensive and dependable highway maps, which are available free to AAA members and associates (see Useful Organizations, later) and for sale to nonmembers. These range from national, regional and state maps to very detailed maps of cities, counties and even relatively small towns.

Most atlases and state maps will have inset city maps, which will help you find downtown and follow the highways. To find a specific address, you'll really need a detailed city map with an index of streets. The AAA also has good maps of most cities, but if you arrive without one, drop into a local convenience store or gas station and look for folded sheet maps published by Rand McNally, Gousha or USA Maps Inc (around $3).

The National Park Service (NPS) will usually give out a good park map at park entrances, and most parks have an information center and a wide range of maps. City bookstores and outdoor-equipment specialists carry a wide selection of topographic maps. The US Geological Survey (USGS), an agency of the federal Dept of the Interior, publishes very detailed topographic maps of the entire country at different scales, and the US Forest Service (USFS) produces good topographic maps of national forest areas (see Activities later in this chapter for more information).

What to Bring

It's always better to travel light. Anything you forget will be available in the USA at least as cheaply as at home, and you'll want to have room for things you buy on the way. The old travel adage applies: Bring half the things you think you'll need, and twice the money.

Bring some souvenirs of home as gifts for hosts and newfound friends. Scenic postcards, small flags, stamps, coins, pins, badges and T-shirts are easy to carry and fun to give away. A few photos of your home, friends and family will show something about where you come from.

Clothing You may need an assortment of clothing to deal with the wide range of weather conditions. Thick sweaters and coats can be difficult to travel with. It's better to bring thinner garments that can be worn in layers. Rainy, windy weather is a possibility anywhere, so a waterproof, windproof jacket is indispensable. Light, thin, breathable fabric is best. Wear sweaters and shirts underneath for warmth.

For very hot weather, you'll need a shady hat and light, loose clothing. Long pants and long sleeves aid in protection from sunburn and heat stroke and help retain moisture. For very hot cities like Houston or Phoenix, you may also need a warm sweater or jacket to wear in the arctic chill of over-air-conditioned buildings.

For very cold weather, bring gloves, a warm hat and sturdy, waterproof footwear. A down jacket has the best warmth-to-weight ratio, as long as it stays dry. Long underwear will provide more extra warmth than thick outer clothing. Of course, all this layering and long underwear is a hassle to remove when you enter an overheated building.

Casual dress is acceptable in most public places, especially in the West and the South. Men will only need a jacket and tie for the fanciest restaurants or if they're doing business. Pantsuits are acceptable business attire for women, except in conservative arenas such as banking and law, where skirt suits are the norm; but even in these industries, things are changing.

Equipment Budget travelers will find a sleeping bag useful for staying in hostels, camping out or sleeping on a friend's living-room floor. To save on hostel linen charges, a sheet sleeping bag might be sufficient. Bring a tent if you intend to stay in campgrounds, but if you plan just one hiking trip, it may be better to rent a tent locally or even buy one. Basic utensils like a cup, bowl, knife and spoon allow you to have cereal and a drink for a light breakfast or a sandwich for lunch. Some travelers bring a small immersion heater and cup to heat water for instant coffee or soup in their rooms or a camp stove, pots and cooking utensils for near self-sufficiency.

There are a zillion other travel aids, from inflatable coat hangers to electronic currency converters. Don't bring any of them. Whole stores in the USA specialize in these gadgets, and if you can hold off until after you arrive, you'll probably realize that you don't need them anyway.

TOURIST OFFICES

There is no national tourist office promoting US tourism in other countries, though some states may have an office or agent in a prime market.

Tourist promotion and information is done by states, cities and local areas, not by the federal government. Every state has a tourist office that will, on request, send out a swag of promotional materials, mostly aimed at domestic tourists and vacationers, and also has a Web site (see the introduction to each state section for state tourist office details). Many cities and tourist resort areas also send out information and promotional material and have Web sites with useful links.

Tourist information services in individual towns and cities vary in style and usefulness. A lot depends on the staff you talk to. The enthusiastic amateurs in small offices are often much more helpful than tourism professionals giving the official line. Tourist offices can tell you about any special events in town and what attractions are operating. They will all have self-service racks of brochures, pamphlets, tourist newsletters and advertising, and sometimes they have good maps and local histories on request or for sale. Look for discount coupons to local attractions.

Many cities have an official convention & visitors bureau (CVB) that provides tourist information services, but its main function is to promote the city and attract the convention trade. Most aren't really set up to assist low-budget independent travelers, but some are really helpful. CVBs distribute the usual tourist literature but don't usually give accommodations information or make referrals. Generally they keep standard business hours and close on weekends.

In smaller towns, the local chamber of commerce often runs a tourist information service. (A chamber of commerce is an organization of local businesses that promotes a town and the commercial interests of its members.) It will often maintain a list of hotels, motels, restaurants and services, but the list will mention only chamber members and may not include the cheapest options. Most chamber information centers are open on weekdays, some on Saturday and a few on Sunday, especially where tourism is a big local business.

You'll also come across tourist information offices, tourist centers, visitor centers or similarly named services that are specifically oriented to visitors' needs, especially in places keen to promote tourism. Some state governments maintain 'Welcome Centers,' found on the main highways as you enter a state or approach a city. They are usually open quite long hours and on weekends, especially during holiday times. Try to visit one to pick up the cheap-looking booklets that are filled with discount coupons for motels on the main highways.

Most of these official sources will give you a very positive, promotional picture of

the place they represent, but may be less than frank about the negatives. Try asking if there are any high-crime areas that should be avoided and see if you get a straight answer.

In major tourist traps, like Niagara Falls or Las Vegas, privately run tourist booking services often advertise 'as visitor centers, information offices or the like, but are really agents who book hotel rooms and tours on commission. They can offer excellent service and great deals, but don't expect much information about museums or nearby national parks.

The Travelers Aid Society often has a counter in airports, train stations or bus stations, providing information on basics like local transport, cheap accommodations and emergency services.

VISAS & ENTRY

All foreign visitors (other than Canadians) must bring their passports. Canadians must have proof of citizenship, such as a citizenship card with photo identification, or a passport.

Visas

Apart from Canadians and those entering under the Visa Waiver Program (see below), foreign visitors need to obtain a visa from a US consulate or embassy. In most countries the process can be done by mail or through a travel agent. The relevant authority is the US Immigration & Nationalization Service (INS), a body not noted for its easygoing attitude. For detailed information about visas, immigration etc, check the Web site of the US State Dept (Ⓦ www.travel.state.gov/visa_services.html).

Your passport must be valid for at least six months longer than your intended stay in the USA, and you'll need to submit a recent photo (37 x 37mm) with the application (plus a fee of about $45). Documents of financial stability, a roundtrip or onward ticket and/or guarantees from a US resident are sometimes required, particularly for those from developing countries.

Visa applicants may be required to 'demonstrate binding obligations' that will ensure their return back home. Because of this requirement, those planning to travel through other countries before arriving in the USA are generally better off applying for a US visa while they are still in their home country, rather than while on the road.

The most common visa is a Nonimmigrant Visitors Visa, type B1 for business purposes, B2 for tourism or visiting friends and relatives. A visitor's visa is good for multiple entries over one or five years, and specifically prohibits the visitor from taking paid employment in the USA. The validity period depends on what country you are from. The length of time you'll be allowed to stay in the USA is determined by the INS at the port of entry (see Entering the USA below).

If you're coming to the USA to work or study, you will probably need a different type of visa, and the company or institution to which you are going should make the arrangements. Other categories of nonimmigrant visas include an F1 visa for students undertaking a recognized course; an H1, H2 or H3 visa for temporary employment; a J1 visa for exchange visitors in approved programs; a K1 visa for the fiancé or fiancée of an American citizen; and an L1 visa for intracompany transfers. Allow six months for processing an application.

Visa Waiver Pilot Program Under the Visa Waiver Program, citizens of certain countries may enter the USA without a US visa for stays of 90 days or less. Currently these countries are Andorra, Argentina, Australia, Austria, Belgium, Brunei, Denmark, Finland, France, Germany, Iceland, Ireland, Italy, Japan, Liechtenstein, Luxembourg, Monaco, the Netherlands, New Zealand, Norway, Portugal, San Marino, Singapore, Slovenia, Spain, Sweden, Switzerland, the UK and Uruguay.

Under this program, you *must* have a roundtrip or onward ticket that is nonrefundable in the USA, and you may be required to show evidence of financial solvency. You will be asked many of the same questions as on the nonimmigrant visa application form, and the same 'grounds for exclusion' apply (see below), except that you will have no opportunity to appeal the grounds or apply for an exemption. If the INS doesn't admit you under the Visa Waiver Program, you will have to use your onward or return ticket on the next available flight.

Grounds for Exclusion & Deportation
The visa application form asks, among other things, if you are a drug trafficker, whether you seek to enter the USA to engage in terrorist activities or if you have ever participated in a genocide. If you admit to being a subversive, smuggler, prostitute, junkie or an ex-Nazi, you may be excluded. You can also be refused a visa or entry to the USA if you have a 'communicable disease of public health significance' or a criminal record (see below) or if you've ever made a false statement in connection with a US visa application.

In many cases, the INS will grant an exemption (a 'waiver of ineligibility') to a person who would normally be subject to exclusion, but this requires referral to a regional INS office and can take some time (allow at least two months). If you're tempted to conceal something, remember that the INS is strictest of all about false statements. It will often review favorably an applicant who admits to an old criminal charge or a communicable disease, but it is extremely harsh on anyone who has ever attempted to mislead it, even on minor points. After you're admitted to the USA, any evidence of a false statement to the INS is grounds for deportation.

Prospective visitors to whom grounds of exclusion may apply should consider their options *before* applying for a visa. For immigration law information and referrals to immigration advocates, contact the National Immigration Project of the National Lawyers Guild (☎ 617-227-9727, Ⓦ www.nlg.org/nip, 14 Beacon St, Suite 506, Boston, MA 02108).

Criminal Records The INS has a very broad definition of a criminal record. If you've ever been arrested or charged with an offense, that's a criminal record, even if you were acquitted or discharged without conviction. In these days of computer databases and high-security awareness, you should assume that US authorities can find out anything of which there is an official record.

HIV & AIDS Like tuberculosis and the Ebola virus, HIV (human immunodeficiency virus) is regarded as a communicable disease and is a ground for exclusion from the USA. The INS doesn't test people for HIV, but if you answer yes to the question 'Have you ever been afflicted with a communicable disease of public health significance?' you will probably not be granted a visa unless you apply for an exemption to the general exclusion of HIV-positive visitors.

INS officials at the point of entry may question anyone about his or her health. They can exclude anyone whom they believe has a communicable disease, perhaps because they are carrying medical documents, prescriptions or AIDS/HIV medicine. Being gay is not a ground for exclusion; being an IV drug user is. Visitors may be deported if the INS finds that they have HIV but did not declare it. Being HIV-positive is not a ground for deportation, but failing to provide accurate information on the visa application is. For more information, contact the Immigrant HIV Assistance Project, Bar Association of San Francisco (☎ 415-782-8995, ⓦ www.sfbar.org, 465 California St, Suite 1100, San Francisco, CA 94104).

Entering the USA

If you have a non-US passport, you must complete an Arrival/Departure Record (form I-94) before you reach the immigration desk. It's usually handed out on the plane along with the customs declaration. It's a rather badly designed form, and lots of people take more than one attempt to get it right. Answers should be written *below* the questions. For question 12, 'Address While in the United States,' give the address where you will spend the first night (a hotel address is fine). Complete the Departure Record (the lower part of the form) giving exactly the same answers for questions 14 to 17 as for questions 1 to 4.

INS officers have an absolute authority to refuse admission to the USA or to impose conditions on admission. Their main concern is to exclude those who are likely to work illegally or overstay, so visitors will be asked about their plans and perhaps about whether they have sufficient funds for their stay. INS officers can be less than welcoming, but it helps to be neatly dressed, polite and patient. If they think you're OK, a six-month entry is usually approved.

It's a good idea to be able to list an itinerary that will account for the period for which you ask to be admitted and to be able to show you have $350 or $400 for each week of your intended stay. An onward or roundtrip ticket helps, and a couple of major credit cards will go a long way toward establishing 'sufficient funds.' Don't make too much of having friends, relatives or business contacts in the USA. The INS official may decide that this will make you more likely to overstay.

Visa Extensions If you want, need or hope to stay in the USA longer than the date stamped on your passport, go to the local INS office (call ☎ 800-375-5283 or look in the local white pages telephone directory under 'US Government') to apply for an extension *before* the stamped date. Calling any time after that will usually lead to an unamusing conversation with an INS official who will assume you want to work illegally. If you find yourself in that situation, it's a good idea to bring a US citizen with you to vouch for your character. It's also a good idea to have some verification that you have enough money to support yourself.

Short-Term Departures & Reentry It's easy to make trips across the border to Canada or Mexico, but upon return to the USA, non-Americans can be subject to the full immigration bit. Always take your passport when you cross the border. If your immigration card still has plenty of time on it, you will probably be able to reenter using the same one, but if it has nearly expired, you will have to apply for a new card, and border control may want to see your onward air ticket, sufficient funds and so on.

A quick trip across the border is a way to extend your stay in the USA without applying for an extension at an INS office. In this case, make sure you hand in your old immigration card to the immigration authorities when you leave the USA. Be aware that the INS may be very suspicious of anyone who attempts to update their immigration status more than once by making quick trips to Canada or Mexico.

Citizens of most Western countries won't need a visa for Canada, so it's no problem to cross to the Canadian side of Niagara Falls, detour up to Québec or pass through on the way to Alaska. Travelers entering the USA by bus from Canada can be closely scrutinized. A roundtrip ticket that takes you back to Canada will make the INS feel less suspicious. Mexico has a visa-free zone along most of its border with the USA, including the Baja Peninsula and most of the border towns, like Tijuana and Ciudad Juárez. You'll only need a Mexican visa or tourist card if you want to go beyond the border zone.

DOCUMENTS

All visitors should bring their home driver's license and any health- or travel-insurance cards. You'll need a picture identification to show that you are over 21 to buy alcohol and gain admission to bars or clubs.

Photocopy all important documents (passport data page and visa page, credit cards, travel insurance policy, air/bus/train tickets, driving license etc) before you leave home. Leave one copy with someone at home and keep another with you, separate from the originals.

Details of important travel information such as passports, visas, health information, banking details etc can be securely stored in the encrypted Travel Vault section of Lonely Planet's eKno Web site, W www.ekno.com.

Onward Tickets

A roundtrip or onward ticket is a definite requirement only for the Visa Waiver Program. If you have a visitors visa, a ticket out of the country may help persuade the INS that you don't intend to stay permanently, but it's not obligatory.

Travel Insurance

No matter how you're traveling, make sure you take out travel insurance. This should cover you for medical expenses, hospital treatment and an emergency flight home if necessary. Coverage for luggage theft or loss, cancellations, delayed travel arrangements and ticket loss is also advisable. Coverage against civil liability is recommended. The USA is a very litigious society, and if you accidentally cause someone loss or damage, he or she may sue you for millions. Some policies specifically exclude 'dangerous activities,' which can include scuba diving, skiing and even trekking.

You may prefer a policy that pays doctors or hospitals directly rather than you having to pay on the spot and claim later. If you have to claim later make sure you keep all documentation. Some policies ask you to call back (reverse charges) to a center in your home country where an immediate assessment of your problem is made.

The delay and cancellation coverage you need depends on the type of ticket you have, so ask both your insurer and your ticket-issuing agency to explain the finer points. Any reputable travel agent will sell travel insurance policies, usually with lower and higher levels of approved medical expenses and other options. For travel to the USA, which has extremely high medical costs, top-level coverage is recommended. The cost depends on the period of coverage. One month can cost around $100 for a single traveler, or $200 for a couple or family (or the equivalent in the local currency of the country where you buy the policy). One year is usually the maximum period available, and will run to about $500 for an individual, $1000 for a couple or family.

Buy travel insurance as early as possible. If you buy it the week before you fly, you may find, for instance, that you're not covered for flight delays caused by strikes or other industrial actions that may have been in force before you took out the insurance.

Insurance may seem very expensive, but it's nowhere near the cost of a medical emergency in the USA.

Driver's License

Most visitors can legally drive in America for up to a year using their home driver's license. An International Driving Permit (IDP) is a very useful adjunct. See the Getting Around chapter for details.

Hostel Cards

Hostelling International-American Youth Hostel (HI-AYH) operates some 150 hostels in the USA, and is affiliated with the International Youth Hostel Federation (IYHF). Most hostels are open to non-members, but members get a discount of around $5 per night. If you're a member of an HI-affiliated organization in your home country, bring your membership card. Otherwise, you can join up in the USA. See the Accommodations section later in this chapter for more on HI-AYH.

Student & Youth Cards

If you are a student, bring your school identification or get the ISIC (International

Student Identity Card) to take advantage of any student discounts. A 'Youth Card' (also called a GO-25 card), issued to anyone under age 26, can also help you get discounts on airfares, car rental and other costs, but it's not as widely recognized as an ISIC card. Both the ISIC card and Youth Card are issued at many budget travel agencies. For the ISIC card, you'll need an application form endorsed by a school, college or university saying that you're a full-time student, plus a passport photo and a fee (about $10). For the Youth Card, you just need the photo, the fee and proof of age.

Seniors Cards

People over the age of about 60 often get discounts in the USA. All you need is identification with proof of age. Organizations such as the American Association of Retired Persons (AARP; see Senior Travelers later in this chapter) offer membership cards for further discounts and extend coverage to citizens of other countries.

Automobile Association Cards

If you're a member of a national or state motoring association that is affiliated with the American Automobile Association (AAA), bring your membership card and/or a letter of introduction. The AAA (see Useful Organizations in this chapter) has a great range of maps and travel information, and it's worth using them even if you don't plan to drive in the USA.

US EMBASSIES & CONSULATES

Australia
21 Moonah Place, Yarralumla ACT 2600 (☎ 2-6214-5600)
Level 59 MLC Center, 19-29 Martin Place, Sydney NSW 2000 (☎ 2-9373-9200)
553 St Kilda Rd, Melbourne, Victoria 3004 (☎ 3-9526-5900)

Austria
Boltzmanngasse 16, A-1091, Vienna (☎ 1-313-39)

Belgium
Blvd du Regent 27, B-1000, Brussels (☎ 2-508-21-11)

Canada
490 Sussex Dr, Ottawa, Ontario, K1N 1G8 (☎ 613-238-5335)
1095 W Pender St, Vancouver, BC, V6E 2M6 (☎ 604-685-4311)
1155 Rue St-Alexandre, Montréal, Québec, H2Z 1Z2 (☎ 514-398-9695)

Denmark
Dag Hammarskjolds Allé 24, Copenhagen (☎ 45-3555-3144)

Finland
Itainen Puistotie 14A, Helsinki (☎ 9-171-931)

France
2 Av Gabriel, 75382 Paris (☎ 1 4312 2222)

Germany
Neustaedtische Kirchstrasse 4-5, 10017 Berlin (☎ 30 238 5174)

Greece
91 Vasilissis Sophias Blvd, 10160 Athens (☎ 1-721-2951)

India
Shanti Path, Chanakyapuri 110021, New Delhi (☎ 11-419-8000)

Ireland
42 Elgin Rd, Ballsbridge, Dublin (☎ 1-668-8777)

Israel
71 Hayarkon St, Tel Aviv (☎ 3-519-7575)

Italy
Via Vittorio Veneto 119A-121, 00187 Rome (☎ 6-46-741)

Japan
1-10-5 Akasaka, Minato-ku, Tokyo (☎ 3-224-5000)

Kenya
Mombasa Rd, Unit 64100, Nairobi (E) (☎ 2-537-800)

Korea
82 Sejong-Ro, Chongro-ku, Seoul (☎ 2-397-4114)

Malaysia
376 Jalan Tun Razak, 50400 Kuala Lumpur (☎ 3-2168-5000)

Mexico
Paseo de la Reforma 305, Cuauhtémoc, 06500 Mexico City (☎ 5-209-9100)

Netherlands
Lange Voorhout 102, 2514 EJ The Hague (☎ 70-310-9209)
Museumplein 19, 1071 DJ Amsterdam (☎ 20-5755-309)

New Zealand
29 Fitzherbert Terrace, Thorndon, Wellington (☎ 4-472-2068)

Norway
Drammensvein 18, Oslo (☎ 22-44-85-50)

Russia
Bolshoy Devyatinckiy Pereulok No 8, 121099 Moscow (☎ 95-728-5000)

Singapore
27 Napier Rd, Singapore 258508 (☎ 476-9100)

South Africa
877 Pretorius St, Box 9536, Pretoria 0001 (☎ 12-342-1048)

Spain
Calle Serrano 75, 28006 Madrid
(☎ 1-91587-2200)

Sweden
Dag Hammarskjolds Vag 31, S-115 89 Stockholm (☎ 8-783-5300)

Switzerland
Jubilaumsstrasse 93, 3005 Berne (☎ 31-357-70 11)

Thailand
120 Wireless Rd, Bangkok (☎ 2-255-4365)

UK
24/31 Grosvenor Sq, London W1A 1AE
(☎ 20-7499-9000)
3 Regent Terrace, Edinburgh EH7 5BW
(☎ 131-556-8315)
Queens House, 14 Queens St, Belfast BT1 6EQ
(☎ 2890-328-239)

EMBASSIES & CONSULATES IN THE USA

Just about every country in the world has an embassy in Washington, DC. Call ☎ 202-555-1212 for embassy phone numbers. Many countries also have consulates in other large cities. Look under 'Consulates' in the yellow pages. Most countries have an embassy for the United Nations in New York City.

CUSTOMS

US Customs allows each person to bring 1 liter of liquor (provided you are 21 years old or older), 100 cigars and 200 cigarettes duty free into the USA. US citizens are allowed to import, duty free, $400 worth of gifts from abroad, while non-US citizens are allowed to bring in $100 worth.

US law permits you to bring in, or take out, as much as $10,000 in US or foreign currency, traveler's checks or letters of credit without formality. There's no maximum limit, but any larger amount of any or all of the above must be declared to customs.

There are heavy penalties for attempting to import illegal drugs. It's also forbidden to bring in to the USA chocolate liqueurs, pornography, lottery tickets, items with fake brand names and goods made in Cuba or Iraq. Any fruit, vegetables, or other food or plant material must be declared or left in the bins in the arrival area. Most food items are prohibited to prevent the introduction of pests or diseases.

The USA, like 140 other countries, is a signatory to CITES, the Convention on International Trade in Endangered Species. As such, it prohibits the import and export of products made from species that may be endangered in any part of the world, including ivory, tortoise shell, coral, and many fur, skin and feather products. If you want to bring a fur coat, snakeskin belt or bone carving with you, you may have to show a certificate that it was not made from an endangered species. The easiest option is not to bring anything even remotely suspect. CITES restrictions apply to what you take home, too. Alligator-skin cowboy boots might be a great souvenir, but be ready to convince customs authorities that they're not made from endangered 'gators.

MONEY
Currency

The US dollar is divided into 100 cents (¢). Coins come in denominations of 1¢ (penny), 5¢ (nickel), 10¢ (dime), 25¢ (quarter), the seldom-seen 50¢ (half-dollar)

Your Own Embassy

It's important to realize what your own embassy – the embassy of the country of which you are a citizen – can and can't do to help you if you get into trouble. Generally speaking, it won't be much help in emergencies if the trouble you're in is remotely your own fault. Remember that you are bound by the laws of the country you are in. Your embassy will not be sympathetic if you end up in jail after committing a crime locally, even if such actions are legal in your own country.

In genuine emergencies you might get some assistance, but only if other channels have been exhausted. For example, if you need to get home urgently, a free ticket home is exceedingly unlikely – the embassy would expect you to have insurance. If you have all your money and documents stolen, it might assist with getting a new passport, but a loan for onward travel is out of the question.

Some embassies used to keep letters for travelers or have a small reading room with home newspapers, but these days the mail holding service has usually been stopped and even newspapers tend to be out of date.

and the recently introduced $1 coin featuring Sacajawea, the Indian guide. Quarters are the coins most commonly used in vending machines and parking meters, so it's handy to have a stash of them. Notes, usually called bills, come in $1, $2, $5, $10, $20, $50 and $100 denominations; $2 bills are rare, but perfectly legal. All bills have a green, black and white color scheme, but two designs are in circulation. The newer design has a larger portrait and several innovations designed to make forgery more difficult.

Exchange Rates

Banks in cities will exchange cash or traveler's checks in major foreign currencies, though banks in outlying areas don't do so very often, and it may take them some time. Thomas Cook and American Express offices and exchange counters at airports and international borders will also exchange foreign currencies, though you'll probably get a better rate at a bank. At press time, exchange rates were as follows:

country	unit		US dollar
Australia	A$1	=	$0.52
Canada	C$1	=	$0.64
European Union	€1	=	$0.91
Hong Kong	HK$10	=	$1.28
Japan	¥100	=	$0.83
New Zealand	NZ$1	=	$0.43
UK	UK£1	=	$1.46

Cash

Though carrying cash is more risky, it's still a good idea to travel with some for the convenience. It's useful to pay all those tips, and some smaller, more remote places may not accept credit cards or traveler's checks.

ATMs

ATMs (automated teller machines) are available 24 hours a day at almost every bank, as well as at shopping centers, airports, grocery stores and casinos. You can withdraw cash from an ATM using a credit card (Visa, MasterCard etc), which will usually incur a fee. Alternatively, most ATMs are linked with one or more of the main ATM networks (Plus, Cirrus, Exchange, Accel), and you can use them to withdraw funds from an overseas bank account if you have a card affiliated with the appropriate network. This is usually cheaper than a credit card transaction. The exchange rate on ATM transactions is usually as good as you'll get.

Check with your bank or credit card company for exact information about using its cards at ATMs in the USA. If you will be relying on ATMs, bring more than one card and keep them separate. Don't forget your PIN (personal identification number), but don't write it on the card. Contact your bank if you lose your ATM card.

Traveler's Checks

Traveler's checks offer the possibility of a refund in the event of theft or loss, and traveler's checks in US dollars are almost as convenient as cash. American Express and Thomas Cook are widely accepted and have efficient replacement policies.

Keep a record of the check numbers you purchased and of those you have used, and keep the record separate from the checks themselves. The numbers are necessary for obtaining a refund of lost checks.

Bring traveler's checks in US dollars, which can be used at most restaurants, hotels, gas stations and big stores as if they were cash; get them in $50 and $100 denominations. Traveler's checks in a foreign currency can only be changed at a bank or at one of the few exchange counters. This can be inconvenient; you may not get a good exchange rate, and you may have to pay an exchange fee. If you're reluctant to buy US-dollar traveler's checks up front because you think that your currency might soon appreciate against the dollar, you're better off relying on credit cards and/or ATMs.

Credit & Debit Cards

Major credit cards are accepted at hotels, restaurants, gas stations, shops and car rental agencies throughout the USA. It's almost impossible to rent a car or make phone reservations without one. (Though, strangely, some US companies, such as airlines, require your credit card billing address to be in the USA – a hassle if you want to book a domestic flight once you're in the country. If you encounter this while buying online or over the phone, visit a travel agent in person.) Even if you prefer to rely on traveler's checks and ATMs, it's highly recommended that you carry a credit card for emergencies, rentals and reservations. If you're planning to rely primarily upon credit cards, bring more than one and include a Visa or MasterCard in your deck, since other cards aren't as widely accepted.

Places that accept Visa and MasterCard are also likely to accept debit cards. A debit card deducts payment directly from the user's bank account, and the user is charged a small fee for the transaction. Check with your bank to confirm that your debit card will be accepted in the USA.

Carry copies of your credit card numbers separately from the cards. If you lose your credit cards or they are stolen, contact the company immediately. Following are toll-free numbers for the main credit card companies:

American Express	☎ 800-528-4800
Diners Club	☎ 800-234-6377
Discover	☎ 800-347-2683
MasterCard	☎ 800-826-2181
Visa	☎ 800-336-8472

International Transfers

You can instruct your bank back home to send you a draft. Specify the city, bank and branch to which you want the money directed, or ask your home bank to tell you where a suitable one is and make sure you get the details right. The procedure is easier if you've authorized someone back home to access your account.

Money sent by telegraphic transfer should reach you within a week; by mail, allow at least two weeks. When it arrives, it will most likely be converted into local currency; you can take it as cash or buy traveler's checks.

You can also transfer money by American Express, Thomas Cook or Western Union, though the latter has fewer international offices. These services are more expensive.

Security

To be cautious, don't carry more cash than you need for the day. Carry it in an inside pocket, money belt or your socks, rather than in an outside pocket or a handbag. It's a good idea to divide your money and credit cards and stash them in several places. Most hotels and hostels provide safekeeping, so you can leave your valuables with them. Hide or don't wear any expensive jewelry. Using a safety pin or key ring to hold the zipper tags of a daypack together can help deter theft.

Costs

The cost of travel in the USA depends a great deal on the degree of comfort you require and the things you want to do. Generally, it's more expensive to travel alone than as a couple, a family or a small group. Moving around a lot costs more than staying longer in fewer places. Big cities, especially New York, are much more expensive than other places. The main expenses are transportation, accommodations, food, sightseeing and entertainment.

Low-budget travelers who stay in campgrounds and hostels, eat in cheap restaurants or prepare their own food may get by on as little as $50 a day each, not including transportation. For reasonably comfortable motel accommodations, good food, and some entertainment and sightseeing, a couple could budget maybe $150 per day for two, not including transportation. For luxury travel, allow $250 or more for two people per day – there's no upper limit.

Transportation Intercity transportation is inexpensive considering the distances involved. Buses are normally the cheapest way to get around (you can cross the country for under $150) while trains are usually a bit more expensive (coast to coast costs about $170). The cost of flying varies greatly, but discount tickets, air passes and other deals can get you across the country for $200. Car rental rates also vary widely, but can cost as little as $120 a week for a small car. For more information on US transportation costs, see the Getting Around chapter.

Accommodations It's free to sleep in your car or camp backcountry in a national forest. You wouldn't do it all the time, but the occasional rough night sure brings the average cost down. Campers usually stay in campgrounds, which start at $5 for a basic site on public land. Developed campgrounds, public or private, charge around

$12 for a tent site if there are hot showers and other facilities available. An RV site, with power and water hookups, will cost around $25. Camping isn't really a convenient option unless you have a car.

Youth hostels affiliated with HI-AYH usually cost around $12-17 for a bunk bed in a dorm room, but in expensive cities like New York, they're around $25. Independent hostels are becoming more common and charge about the same. For couples, a cheap and basic motel room will cost about $40 near an interstate highway, $55 or more near a big city. Single rooms are not much cheaper, and a room for a family or group won't cost much more.

Comfortable mid-range accommodations cost $70-100 a double in most places, while luxury hotels run from $120-200 and more. Any place near a beach, national park or major attraction will be more expensive in the tourist season and up to double price if there's a major event on.

Food & Drink Basic food items and prepackaged meals are cheap. With minimal cooking facilities or camping equipment, you could prepare your own meals for as little as $7 for two people. At the cheapest fast-food restaurants, you can get a large hamburger, soft drink and french fries for about $5. At better places, a good meal can be had for under $10. Tax and tips add to the cost of eating out, so budget a minimum of around $6 for breakfast, $10 for lunch and $15 for dinner. At better restaurants, you can eat very well for under $25 per person, including a beer or glass of wine.

A six-pack (six 12oz bottles) of domestic beer costs $4-7 in a supermarket. A bottle of the same beer in a bar or restaurant will range from $2.50-5. Soft drinks are cheap, and a cup of brewed coffee costs around $1.50.

Sightseeing Admission to museums and attractions runs from free to over $30. Children are usually charged one-half to three-quarters of the adult price, while seniors and students often get discounts of 10% or more. Other places give discounts to war veterans, AAA members and the physically challenged. Many public museums have a free day and/or half-price evening hours once a week or month.

Tipping

Tipping is expected in restaurants and better hotels and by taxi drivers, hairdressers and baggage carriers. People waiting tables in restaurants are paid minimal wages and rely upon tips for their livelihoods. Tip 15% unless the service is terrible (in which case a complaint to the manager is warranted) or up to 20% if the service is great. Don't tip in fast-food, takeout or buffet-style restaurants where you serve yourself.

Taxi drivers expect 10% and hairdressers 15% if their service is satisfactory. Baggage carriers (skycaps in airports and bellhops in hotels) should be tipped $1 for one bag and 50¢ for each additional bag. In budget hotels, tips are not expected, but at luxury places, tipping can reach irritating proportions. Bellhops, doormen, housekeepers and parking attendants are all tipped at least $1 for each service performed.

Special Deals & Bargaining

The USA is probably the most promotion-oriented society on earth. Though bargaining as such is not common, you can often save by asking for a discount. If you need a pretext, try asking for a AAA discount (if you have a card), student discount, foreign visitors discount or a discount for cash payment. At hotels in the off season, mentioning a competitor's rate may prompt a manager to lower the original price. Or politely ask if they have any rooms under $35 or whatever you're prepared to pay.

Discount coupons for local attractions, restaurants and accommodations are widely available. Check circulars in Sunday papers, at supermarkets, tourist offices and chambers of commerce. There's usually a catch with the coupons. 'Free Pizza' can mean something like a free version of their smallest, cheapest pizza for a party of four, with purchase of another pizza of equal or greater value; offer not valid after 5pm or on weekends; tax and gratuity not included. But $2 off the admission price of an attraction you wanted to see anyway is not to be sneezed at.

Taxes
Almost everything you pay for in the USA is taxed. The tax on restaurant meals and drinks, accommodations and most purchases is added to the advertised cost. Occasionally, the tax is included in the advertised price (eg, gas, drinks in a bar and admission to museums or theaters).

A few states have no sales tax, and in others it varies up to about 8% (see the introductory information about each state for rates). In addition, there may be local and city sales taxes (maybe an extra 5% to 8%) and sometimes other separate taxes, such as a 'bed tax' on lodging or a special tax on car rentals. When inquiring about hotel or motel rates, be sure to ask whether taxes are included. Unless otherwise stated, the prices given in this book don't include taxes.

POST & COMMUNICATIONS
Post
The US Postal Service (USPS), by a wide margin the busiest postal service in the world, handles astronomical numbers of letters and parcels every day. The service is inexpensive and reasonably reliable, but if you're sending something really important, it's probably better to use the more expensive door-to-door services of Federal Express (commonly called FedEx; ☎ 800-463-3339) or United Parcel Service (UPS; ☎ 800-782-7892).

Postal Rates As of July 2001, the postal rates for 1st-class mail within the USA were 34¢ for letters weighing up to one ounce (23¢ for each additional ounce) and 21¢ for postcards.

International airmail rates (except to Canada and Mexico) are 80¢ for a 1oz letter and 70¢ for a postcard. To Canada and Mexico it's 60¢ for a 1oz letter and 50¢ for a postcard. Aerograms are 70¢ to all countries.

The cost for parcels sent Priority Mail anywhere within the USA is $3.95 for 2lb or less, increasing according to the weight and the distance mailed. The maximum weight is 70lbs. Books, periodicals and computer disks can be sent for a cheaper (but slower) rate called book rate or media mail.

For 24-hour postal information, call ☎ 800-275-8777 or check ⓦ www.usps.com. You can get zip (postal) codes for a given address, the rules about parcel sizes and the location and phone number of any post office.

Sending & Receiving Mail If you have the correct postage, you can drop any mail weighing less than 16oz into any blue mailbox. To buy stamps, weigh your mail or send a package 16oz or heavier, go to a post office. There are branch post offices and post-office centers in many supermarkets and drugstores. Post offices in main towns are usually open 8am-5pm weekdays and 8am-3pm Saturday.

General delivery mail (ie, poste restante) can be sent to you c/o General Delivery at any post office that has its own zip code. Mail is usually held for 10 days before it's returned to the sender; you might request your correspondents to write 'Hold for Arrival' on their letters. You'll need picture identification to collect general delivery mail. In some big cities, general delivery mail is not held at the main post office, but at a postal facility away from downtown.

Alternatively, have mail sent to the local representative of American Express or Thomas Cook, which provide mail services for their customers. This is only for letters (no parcels or packets), which should be marked 'Client Mail.'

Telephone
The US phone system comprises numerous regional phone companies (many are Bell subsidiaries) plus competing long-distance carriers plus lots of smaller mobile-phone and pay-phone companies. Technically, the system is very efficient, but it's geared to the needs of local users, and for foreign visitors it can be inconvenient and expensive. Try to bring a telephone card from your home phone company. It may not be the cheapest option, but it will probably offer better

information and service than a US pay-phone company or a phone debit card.

Telephone Numbers If you're calling from abroad, the international country code for the USA is 1.

All phone numbers within the USA consist of a three-digit area code followed by a seven-digit local number. If you are calling a number within the same area code, just dial the seven-digit number. If you are calling long distance, dial ☎ 1 plus the area code plus the phone number.

Because of increasing demand for phone numbers, some cities and states are being subdivided into more telephone areas, and new codes are being added and changed in patches all over the country.

The 800, 888 and 877 prefixes are for toll-free numbers. These calls are free, though sometimes the toll-free number is not available either when calling from the same locality or state as the business or from outside the state. Some can be used in Canada, while a few can be used in other foreign countries. To find an organization's 800 number, call ☎ 800-555-1212.

The 550, 554, 900, 920, 940, 976 codes and some other prefixes are for calls charged at a premium rate – phone sex, horoscopes, jokes, etc. Be sure you understand the per-minute charge at the start of the call.

Many businesses use letters instead of digits for their telephone numbers in an attempt to make them snappy and memorable. Sometimes it works, but sometimes it is difficult to read the letters on the keyboard. If you can't read the letters, here they are: 1 – doesn't get a letter, 2 – ABC, 3 – DEF, 4 – GHI, 5 – JKL, 6 – MNO, 7 – PQRS, 8 – TUV, 9 – WXYZ, 0 – doesn't get a letter.

Directory Assistance For local directory assistance, dial ☎ 411. For directory assistance outside your area code, dial ☎ 1 plus the three-digit area code of the place you want to call plus 555-1212 – this is charged as a long-distance call to that area. All area codes are listed in telephone directories, but make sure you're looking at a recent edition.

To find a number in another country, call the international operator at ☎ 00. International directory assistance can be very expensive from a pay phone.

International Calls To make an international call direct, dial ☎ 011, then the country code (which you can find in the front of most phone directories), followed by the area code and the phone number. You may need to wait as long as 45 seconds for the ringing to start. International rates vary depending on the time of day and the destination. Call the operator for rates. The first minute is always more expensive than those that follow.

Call Charges Most local calls can be made for free from private phones and for a flat fee from a pay phone (usually 35¢). Calls made to numbers within the same area code but outside the local calling zone (typically about 15 miles) are charged by the minute. Long-distance charges vary depending on the destination and the telephone company you use. Call the operator (☎ 0) for rate information. Don't ask the operator to put your call through, however, because operator-assisted calls are much more expensive than direct-dial calls. Generally, nights (11pm-8am), all day Saturday and 8am-5pm Sunday are the cheapest times to call (about 60% discount). Evenings (5-11pm, Sun-Fri) are mid-priced (about 35% discount). Daytime calls (8am-5pm Mon-Fri) are full-price within the USA.

Phone Cards Phone cards are now almost essential for travelers using the US phone system. There are two basic types.

A phone credit card allows you to make calls that are billed to your home phone number. Some cards issued by foreign phone companies will work in the USA – inquire before you leave home. When using a phone credit card, be aware of people watching you, especially in public places like airports and bus stations. Thieves will memorize numbers and use them to make calls at your expense. Shield the telephone with your body when punching in your credit card number.

A prepaid phone card is a good alternative for travelers and widely available from vending machines in airports, bus stations, hotel lobbies and other locations. You purchase the card with a specified value, say $5, $10, $20 or $50 for 18, 38, 80 or 220 'units.' To call, you access the company through an 800 number and key in your

PIN, and a synthetic voice will tell you how many domestic or international minutes your card is good for. The cost of calls is debited from the value of the card. A unit is good for a call of one minute within the USA, half a minute or less to overseas. Rates vary among different brands of cards. The cheapest are competitive with rates charged by a US phone company on a domestic phone. Some phone debit cards allow you to add extra value by billing an additional amount to your regular credit card. If you use a phone debit card from a pay phone or a hotel, many systems will debit two or more units from your card for the initial connection. If you've several calls to make, use the card's follow-on option to save the connection fee and the hassle of repeating the PIN. (Also, see eKno Communication Service, later.)

Pay Phones Local calls usually cost 35¢ at pay phones, but sometimes more. You can use nickels, dimes or quarters, though phones don't give change. Local-call charges usually only apply to quite a small area. If you try to call a number outside the local calling zone or with a different area code, a synthetic voice will tell you to insert 75¢ (or whatever) for the first three minutes. Calling from pay phones can be very expensive. You can pump in coins, call collect or, on modern phones, use a phone card or credit card.

For long-distance calls from a pay phone, use the access lines of major carriers, such as AT&T (☎ 800-321-0288), MCI (☎ 800-888-8000) or use a prepaid phone card.

Mobile Phones In the USA cellphones use GSM 1900 or CDMA 800, operating on different frequencies from systems in other countries. The only foreign phones that will work in the USA are tri-band models, operating on GSM 1900 as well as other frequencies. If you have a GSM tri-band phone, check with your service provider about using it in the USA, but be aware that calls will be more expensive than using your home network (the US service provider's charges are added to the regular charges). Your mobile phone number stays the same, and callers at home will be connected to your phone automatically (they may not be aware you're in a different time zone, or that the call is costing way more than usual).

You may be able to take the SIM card from your home phone, install it in a rented mobile phone compatible with the US systems and use the rental phone as if it were your own phone – same number, same billing basis. Ask your mobile phone company about using your SIM card for global (or international) roaming. You can rent a phone for about $45 per week, but rates vary.

Phone shops in the USA will rent you a GSM 1900 compatible phone with a set amount of prepaid call time. Pricing plans are complex, but generally this is an expensive option – perhaps $45 per week for the phone, plus $60 for about 40 minutes of air time (making *and* receiving calls), plus a hefty deposit of about $300 held against your credit card. Voicestream (☑ www .voicestream.com) is one US company that provides rental phones with prepaid service minutes.

Another option is to sign up with a US mobile phone service. You'll need a local address, a credit card and a cash deposit if you don't have a credit rating in the USA. Buying the phone itself may not cost much more than renting one for a couple of months, but most mobile phone plans are for a 12-month period. Sprint PCS has 3-month plans that might suit a short-term visitor.

Hotel Phones Many hotels (especially the more expensive ones) add a service charge of 50¢ to $1 for each local call made from a room phone, and they have hefty surcharges for long-distance calls. They even charge you for calling 800 numbers. It's cheaper to use a pay phone in the hotel lobby.

On the other hand, many cheaper hotels and motels avoid the hassle of billing for phone calls altogether. They offer free local calls, and any other calls must be collect or billed to a phone card.

Fax & Telegram

Fax machines are easy to find in the USA at shipping companies like Mail Boxes Etc, copy services like Kinko's, and hotel business-service centers, but be prepared to pay high prices (more than $1 a page). Telegrams can be sent from Western Union (☎ 800-325-6000).

eKno Communication Service

Lonely Planet's eKno global communication service provides low-cost international calls. For local calls you're usually better off with a local phonecard. eKno also offers free messaging services, email, travel information and an online travel vault, where you can securely store details of all your important documents. Register online at ⓦ www.ekno.lonelyplanet.com, where you will find the local-access numbers for the 24-hour customer-service center. Once you have joined, always check the eKno Web site for the latest access numbers and updates on new features.

Email & Internet Access

If you want to surf the Net or send the occasional email message, most public libraries have a computer with Internet access. Other options are an Internet cafe, a copy center (like Kinko's, which charges about $10 per hour) or a hotel that caters to business travelers. An increasing number of hostels offer Internet access to their guests. The cheapest way to have email access while traveling is to get a free Web-based email account from eKno (ⓦ www.ekno .com), Hotmail (ⓦ www.hotmail.com), Yahoo! (ⓦ www.yahoo.com) or Netscape (ⓦ www.netscape.com) that you can access from any online computer with a browser.

If you're traveling with a computer, you'll need a suitable AC adapter and a plug adapter for US sockets. Often it's easiest to buy these before you leave home. You'll also need a global modem, and a phone line to plug it into. Be careful plugging into a phone jack connecting through a hotel or motel switchboard. If a hotel has a digital phone system, you may not be able to use it for a modem connection. Many hotels and motels now have special jacks for computers (sometimes labeled 'data'), and these are safe.

Then you have to program your computer to dial an Internet service provider (ISP). This can be difficult if the ISP is not a local or 800 number, because most cheap and mid-range accommodations won't let you direct-dial a long-distance number. If you're using a phone card, you (or the computer) will have to dial at least two numbers and supply a PIN. The different numbers to be dialed may need to be separated by pauses, such as between dialing the phone card's 800 access number and dialing in the PIN. Do this by putting commas between the numbers as you type them into the dial-up software.

If you can get access to a direct-dial long-distance phone connection, set your modem to make an international call to your ISP at home. You can upload/download a big bunch of email at your regular address within a minute or so, but if you want to stay online for a while, the phone call can get expensive.

The best solution is probably to sign up with a big US service provider that has a local access number in most major cities (eg, Earthlink, AOL, CompuServe). If you have a credit card, the ISP should have you up and running in a few days, with a user name, password and email address for about $30 for the first month.

With a little technical savvy, you can access your home email on the road from any online computer. Change the POP3 email settings on the computer to connect to your home ISP (before you leave, ask your ISP what settings to use). Just be sure to switch the settings back to the defaults, or the next person to use the computer will be able to download your email.

DIGITAL RESOURCES

CitySync is Lonely Planet's digital city guide for Palm OS hand-held devices. With CitySync you can quickly search, sort and bookmark hundreds of restaurants, hotels, attractions, clubs and more – all pinpointed on scrollable street maps. Sections on activities, transport and local events mean you get the big picture plus all the little details. At ⓦ www.citysync.com you can purchase or demo CitySync for Boston, Chicago, Las

Vegas, Los Angeles, Miami, New Orleans, New York and San Francisco.

The World Wide Web is a rich resource for travelers. You can research your trip, hunt down bargain airfares, book hotels, check on weather conditions or chat with locals and other travelers about the best places to visit (or avoid!).

There's no better place to start your Web explorations than the Lonely Planet Web site (W www.lonelyplanet.com). Here you'll find succinct summaries on traveling to most places on earth, postcards from other travelers and the Thorn Tree bulletin board, where you can ask questions before you go or dispense advice when you get back. You can also find travel news and updates to many of LP's most popular guidebooks, and the subWWWay section links you to the most useful travel resources elsewhere on the Web.

Web site addresses are given in this book for many state and city information services. For other travel information, the following sites are a good start and will quickly link you to more information than you'll ever need:

American Automobile Association (W www .aaa.com) – information from AAA tour books, reservations service and travel articles

Business Travel (W www.thetrip.com) – information for business and general travelers, and reservations for airline tickets, rental cars and accommodations

Citysearch (W www.citysearch.com) – travel and entertainment guide to 40 US cities, with links to event-booking agents

CNN's Travel Guide (W edition.cnn.com/ TRAVEL/) – travel section of CNN's news site, with online reservations services

Excite Travel on North America (W www.city.net/ regions/north_america) – detailed travel site with lots of information, Farefinder and online booking – now merged with Travelocity

History Travel (W www.historytravel.com/today) – TV's History Channel provides a guide to historic travel destinations in the USA

Hotels and Resorts in the US (W www .hotelstravel.com/us.html) – lists and links to lots of mid-range to top-end hotels and resorts

National Park Service (W www.nps.gov) – information on every national park, historic site, monument, trail, etc

Roadside America (W www.roadsideamerica .com) – the 'online guide to offbeat attractions' covers lots of stuff you won't see at the CVB

Route 66 (W route66.netvision.be) – 'Where the Mother Road meets the Information Superhighway,' in Belgium

Travel Organization's Directory (W www.travel.org/ na.html#usa) – comprehensive travel site with pages of lots of links

US Cities (W www.usacitylink.com) – detailed travel and relocation information

US Survival Tips for Aussies (W www.uq.edu.au/ ~zzdonsi/us_tips.html) – interesting information and observations on the USA for Aussies and others

Worldwide Hostel Guide (W www.hostels.com/ us.html) – state-by-state list of every hostel and backpackers' place

BOOKS

Most books are published in different editions by different publishers in different countries. As a result, a book might be a hardcover rarity in one country while it's readily available in paperback in another. Fortunately, bookstores and libraries search by title or author, so your local bookstore or library is best placed to advise you on the availability of the following recommendations.

Art, life and polyester collide in Sean Condon's off-beat *Sean & David's Drive Thru America,* as Sean and David sample coast-to-coast Motel-o-Ramas (published by Lonely Planet's travel literature series, Journeys). Outdoor enthusiasts should look for *Hiking in the USA* and *Hiking in Alaska.*

Guidebooks

The classic US travel series is the *WPA Guides to America,* published in the 1930s as part of the New Deal Federal Writers Project to employ writers. Out of print and out of date, they can still be found in many libraries and are still great reading for nostalgia buffs. Some have been republished as reproduction editions.

Living & Working in America, by David Hampshire, is a thorough and useful guide for anyone planning a long-term visit. For guides relating to specific interests and activities, see the Activities section, later.

Travel

There's a long history of foreigners and Americans traveling around the country and trying to make sense of it. They include Alexis de Tocqueville in 1835–40, with *Democracy in America*; Charles Dickens,

Lonely Planet US Guides

For more detailed information about specific regions of the USA, look for Lonely Planet's guides to the following destinations.

Travel Guides
Alaska
California & Nevada
California Condensed
Florida
Georgia & the Carolinas
Great Lakes
Hawaii
Louisiana & the Deep South
New England
New York, New Jersey & Pennsylvania
Oahu
Pacific Northwest
Rocky Mountains
Southwest
Texas
Virginia & the Capital Region

City Guides
Boston
Boston Condensed
Chicago
Chicago Condensed
Miami
Las Vegas
Los Angeles
New Orleans
New York City
New York City Condensed
San Francisco
San Diego & Tijuana
Seattle
Washington, DC

Phrasebooks
USA

Walking Guides
Hiking in Alaska
Hiking in the Sierra Nevada
Hiking in the USA

Diving & Snorkeling
California's Central Coast
Florida Keys
Hawaii
Monterey Peninsula & Northern California
Pacific Northwest
Southern California & the Channel Islands
Texas

who wrote *American Notes* in 1842; London *Times* journalist William Russell, who described his visit in *My Diary North and South* (1850); Oscar Wilde, who wrote *Impressions of America* (1883); and GK Chesterton, who described his visit in *What I Saw in America* (1923).

On the Road (1957), by Jack Kerouac, describes the Beat odyssey from New York to San Francisco in 'spontaneous prose,' but as description or travelogue it's pretty unsatisfying. In *Travels with Charley* (1962), John Steinbeck describes his three-month journey from New York to the West Coast in a truck with his wife's pet poodle.

The Lost Continent (1989), by Bill Bryson, is a wonderfully funny, personal and perceptive account of the author's search for the perfect American town. *Blue Highways: A Journey into America* (1991), by William Least Heat Moon, describes people and places the author encounters in his travels through side roads, rural areas and reservations. *How Can I Be Lost When I Don't Know Where I'm Going* (1996), by Barb Thacker, is the enjoyable story of the author and her dog traveling cross-country in an RV.

States of Desire: Travels in Gay America, by Edmund White, covers most of America, but especially New York and San Francisco.

Activities
There are quite a few good how-to and where-to books in outdoors stores or the sports/recreation or outdoors section of a good bookstore. Lonely Planet's walking guides outline hiking possibilities in all parts of the country (see 'Lonely Planet US Guides.') *The Backpacker's Handbook* (1996), by Chris Townsend, is one of the best introductory guides. *The Complete Walker III: The Joys and Techniques of Hiking and Backpacking* (1984), by Colin Fletcher, is regarded as a classic. *How to Shit in the Woods* is Kathleen Meyer's explicit, comical and useful manual on toilet training in the wilderness.

Also see 'Lonely Planet US Guides' for diving and snorkeling in the USA.

History
It's easier to find histories of specific periods, places and peoples than of the whole country. The *Penguin History of the*

USA (2001 ed), by Hugh Brogan, gives a good overview. More detailed are the three volumes of *The Americans* (1964–88), by Daniel J Boorstin. One of the most readable histories is *Alistair Cooke's America* (1973), a well-illustrated book, rich in feeling and thoughtful observation. *A People's History of the United States, 1492–Present,* by Howard Zinn, is a fascinating and respected history that describes the lifestyles of the poor and ignominious, often overlooked in more conventional works.

Native Americans For the history (or prehistory) of the earliest Americans, see *The American Indians: Their Archeology and Prehistory* (1976), by Dean Snow, or *Ancient North America,* by Brian Fagan. Serious students should look for the 20-volume *Handbook of North American Indians,* published by the Smithsonian Institution – different volumes cover various regions and nations.

Bury My Heart at Wounded Knee, by Dee Brown, is a revealing, heartbreaking account of the displacement of the Native American people as the USA expanded. For more accounts, see *Stolen Continents: The Americas Through Indian Eyes Since 1492* by Ronald Wright.

The West In *Undaunted Courage,* Stephen Ambrose tells the real-life adventure story of the Lewis and Clark expedition, which explored the Northwest in 1804–6. *The Legacy of Conquest,* by Patricia Nelson Limerick, presents a thorough, readable and non-Hollywood-focused history of the American West. *Cadillac Desert: The American West and its Disappearing Water,* by Marc Reisner, is an altogether fascinating environmental history of the West and its quest for water. Jonathan Raban's *Bad Land: An American Romance* describes the lives of homesteaders on the Montana prairie.

African Americans For an overall history, try *From Slavery to Freedom: A History of Negro America,* by JH Franklin and Alfred Moss. The Civil Rights era from 1954 to '65 is chronicled in Juan William's *Eyes on the Prize,* which was also a PBS TV series. For a very personal account of 20th-century African American life, see *I Know Why the Caged Bird Sings,* poet Maya Angelou's au-tobiography of her early years in Arkansas, the Midwest and California.

Civil War There are thousands of books on this most written-about period in US history. In three volumes, *The Civil War: A Narrative,* by Shelby Foote, is considered one of the most authoritative. A magnificent PBS TV series on the war included many poignant observations by Foote and has a superbly illustrated companion book, *The Civil War,* by Geoffrey Ward, Ric Burns and Ken Burns. Another noted Civil War scholar, Bruce Catton, gives more of a Northern perspective in his *Army of the Potomac* trilogy.

Confederates in the Attic: Dispatches from the Unfinished Civil War, by Tony Horwitz, documents the war's continuing fascination for battlefield tourists and battle re-enacters.

Society & Culture

Different books give different angles on understanding the USA. Those by Chicago radio man Studs Terkel consist almost entirely of interviews in which Americans from every class and culture talk about their lives. His books include *Division Street* (1967), about Chicagoans; *Working* (1972), in which 'people talk about how they feel about what they do;' *American Dreams: Lost and Found*; and *The Great Divide: Second Thoughts on the American Dream* (1988).

Caste Marks: Style & Status in the USA (1984), by Paul Fussell, is a pointed but perceptive look at the almost taboo subject of class in a supposedly classless society, deconstructing the status implications of speech, dress and interior decoration. *Hunting Mister Heartbreak: A Discovery of America* is Jonathan Raban's insightful but affectionate look at immigrants and how they've fared in the USA.

Made in America (1994), by Bill Bryson, analyzes American English in history, sport, technology, advertising and popular culture. It's an entertaining read, but very scholarly compared with Bryson's funny travelogues. *Cracking Jokes* (1987), by Allen Dundes, exposes America through its folktales, jokes and urban myths.

In Search of Gay America (1989), by Neil Miller, is a good book about gay and lesbian life across America in the 1980s, especially outside the major cities.

NEWSPAPERS & MAGAZINES

There are over 1500 daily newspapers published in the USA, for a combined circulation of about 60 million. The newspaper with the highest circulation is the populist *USA Today,* with lots of color and sports coverage. It's printed at centers across the country and sells 5 million copies per day. The *Wall Street Journal* is the preeminent financial and business paper, published daily in four regional editions. The well-respected *New York Times* and *Washington Post* are also available nationwide. Other quality regional papers include the *Los Angeles Times, Boston Globe, Chicago Tribune* and *San Francisco Chronicle.*

Sunday papers are several times larger than weekday editions and proportionally more expensive. The extra paper and money go to classified ads, color comic strips and supplements dealing with everything from arts and culture to travel, leisure and news analysis.

Most cities have a local daily newspaper, which covers local issues and some items of national and international news, usually just a few stories from the wire services. The big cities also have one or more free weekly newspapers, which have some good local and even national stories but specialize in current entertainment listings, restaurant reviews and critiques of film and theater.

National weekly tabloids include the incredibly trashy *National Enquirer, National Examiner* and *Star,* as well as quality news magazines like *Newsweek, Time* and the *US News & World Report.* Newsstands offer an incredible range of special interest publications on every conceivable sport, hobby and peccadillo.

RADIO

All rental cars have radios, and travelers can choose from hundreds of stations. Most radio stations have a range of less than 100 miles, and in and near major cities scores of stations crowd the airwaves with a wide variety of music and entertainment. In rural areas, there's a predominance of country & western music, Christian and evangelical programming, local news and 'talk radio.' The most aggressively opinionated talk-radio hosts are called 'shock jocks,' and whether they're arch-conservatives or irreverent iconoclasts, they target a specific audience and have little regard for objective reporting.

National Public Radio (NPR) features a more level-headed approach to news and discussion. NPR stations normally broadcast on the lower end of the FM band. Some public radio stations feature BBC and CBC news, and almost all produce shows on local music and culture.

TV & VIDEO

Even the cheapest motel rooms have a color TV, though sometimes the set doesn't work very well. TVs receive the local affiliates of the five networks that dominate American broadcast television – ABC, CBS, NBC, FOX and PBS. The commercial networks have all your favorite American shows and a surfeit of sports. Broadcast news is parochial, covering lots of local stories interspersed with patter between the presenters.

PBS, the Public Broadcasting System, is noncommercial and has a good news service and thoughtful current-affairs programming. Check the *Newshour with Jim Lehrer.* PBS special productions can be 1st-class, like the excellent series on the Civil War. Other PBS programs include educational shows, classical music and theater, and quite a few BBC productions.

Better motels boast TV with access to cable stations, usually ESPN (sports), CNN (news), HBO (movies) and the Weather Channel. Other channels are variously devoted to home shopping, talk shows, music videos, '60s and '70s sitcoms, cartoons or TV evangelists. Among the 50-plus programs to choose from, you'll probably find something worth watching. Any visiting TV junkie or sociologist can catch enough popular culture to stay entranced for days. Be sure that the TV is free before you go on a movie binge, as some motels charge you per movie watched (usually called 'pay per view').

Video Systems

The USA uses the NTSC color-TV standard, which is not compatible with other standards such as PAL, used in Africa, Europe, Asia and Australia, or SECAM, used in France. If you buy prerecorded videotapes in the USA or record US TV programs, you won't be able to play them at home on a PAL video player. The tapes can be converted, but it's usually not worth the trouble. Some modern video machines can play tapes using either PAL or NTSC.

PHOTOGRAPHY & VIDEO
Film & Equipment

Print film is available everywhere – at supermarkets, drugstores and (most expensively) in the souvenir shop at any tourist attraction. Slide film is not as widely available, and black-and-white film is rarely sold outside major cities. Specialized camera batteries may only be available in camera stores, so it's wise to carry spares.

Drugstores are a good place to get your film processed cheaply – around $6 for a roll of 24 exposures. One-hour processing services are more expensive, usually from around $11.

Film can be damaged by excessive heat, so don't leave your camera or film in the car on a hot day, especially not under the windshield.

Technical Tips

When the sun is high, photographs tend to emphasize shadows and wash out highlights. It's best to take photos during early morning and late afternoon hours, when the light is softer. This is especially true of landscape photography. Always protect camera lenses with a haze or ultraviolet (UV) filter. At high altitudes, the UV may not adequately prevent washed-out photos; a polarizing filter can correct this problem and dramatically emphasize cloud formations.

Video

Unlike still photography, video 'flows,' so scenes like a busy freeway will give an overall impression that isn't possible with ordinary photos. Try to film in long takes, and don't move the camera around too much. If you want to pan across the Grand Canyon, do it slowly and smoothly. The microphones are sensitive and will pick up any ambient noises, like the engine of a bus.

Make sure you keep the batteries charged and that you have the necessary charger, plugs and transformer. Video cartridges are widely available. You don't have to worry about whether the cartridge is compatible with your camera. If it fits, it will work, but you will only be able to play it back on a video player that is compatible with your camera.

Finally, remember people's sensitivities. Being tracked by a video camera is probably even more annoying than being the subject of a snapshot. Always ask permission first. Reciting a commentary into a video recorder can be an intrusion for other people trying to enjoy the scenery.

Restrictions

There don't seem to be any restrictions on photographing military hardware or bases. If you're allowed to see it, you're allowed to photograph it.

You're much more likely to encounter restrictions for commercial or PR reasons. Many galleries won't let you photograph artwork but will sell photos of it in the museum store. At some attractions, like Disneyland, it's a condition of entry that you won't take photos for commercial purposes. This might be to stop you breaching a mouse's copyright, or maybe to prevent negative publicity, like a shot of 850 people waiting in line for Splash Mountain.

Photographing People

This can be a very sensitive issue in the USA. There's usually no problem taking medium or long shots, but if you want a close-up, you should always ask. Pointing at the camera and smiling will usually get an affirmative nod. Street people and the destitute may refuse or ask for money.

Photography is commonly prohibited at Native American pueblos, ceremonies and reservations, but sometimes permitted upon payment of a fee. Native Americans usually expect to be tipped if you take their photo.

Airport Security

All airline passengers have to pass their luggage through X-ray machines. Technology as it is today doesn't jeopardize lower-speed film, so you shouldn't have to worry about cameras going through the machine. If you have high-speed film (1600 ASA and above), then you may want to carry your film and cameras with you and ask the X-ray inspector to visually check the film.

TIME, DATES & SEASONS

There are four one-hour time zones across the continental USA, and Alaska and Hawaii cover two more time zones. From east to west, they are as follows:

Eastern time zone – Greenwich Mean Time (GMT) minus five hours

Central time zone – GMT minus six hours

Mountain time zone – GMT minus seven hours

Pacific time zone – GMT minus eight hours

Alaska time zone – GMT minus nine hours

Hawaii-Aleutian time zone – GMT minus 10 hours

When it's 1pm in New York, Detroit, Atlanta and Miami, it's noon in Chicago, Kansas City and Dallas; 11am in Salt Lake City, Denver and Albuquerque; 10am in Seattle, San Francisco and Los Angeles; 9am in Anchorage; and 8am in Honolulu.

Daylight saving time, when clocks are moved forward one hour, runs from the first Sunday in April to the last Sunday in October in most states. Among the few exceptions are Arizona and Hawaii.

In the USA, dates are written with the month first, then the day, then the year. So 7/4 means July 4, not the seventh of April.

Americans reckon the seasons to start at the solstices and equinoxes, not the first of the month, so the first day of summer is June 22, not June 1. For the tourist industry, the most important season is the holiday season from Memorial Day to Labor Day.

ELECTRICITY

In the USA, voltage is 110V and plugs have two flat pins, or two flat pins plus a round one. Plugs with three pins don't fit into a two-hole socket, but adapters are easy to buy at hardware stores and drugstores. Two-pin plugs can easily slip out of the socket, so stretch the prongs apart a little for a tighter fit.

WEIGHTS & MEASURES

Distances are in feet, yards and miles. Three feet equal 1 yard (.914m); 1760 yards, or 5280 feet, are 1 mile (1.61km). Dry weights are in ounces (oz), pounds (lb) and tons – 16oz equal 1lb (.45kg) and 2000lbs equal 1 ton (907kg). Liquid measures differ from dry measures. One pint equals 16 fluid oz

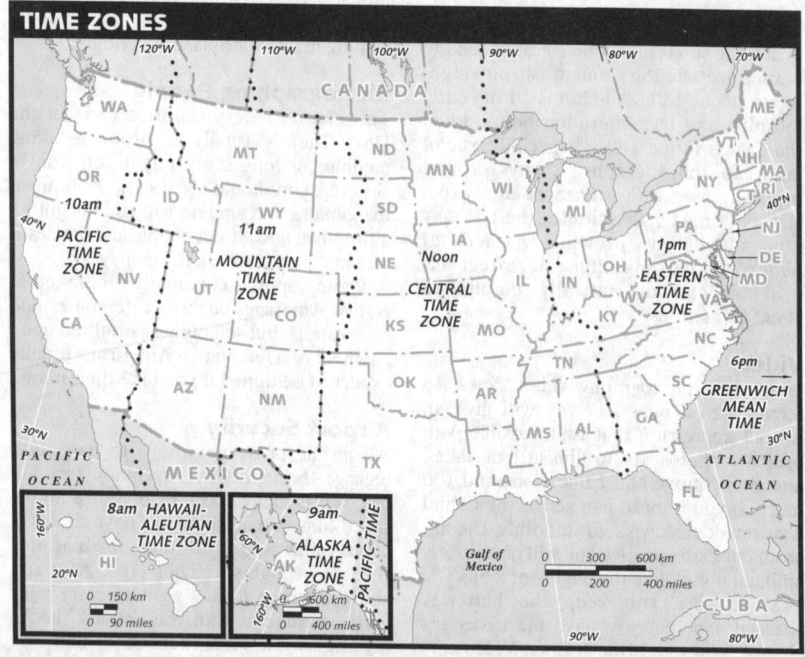

Comes a Time

For centuries, communities around the world set their own time by the sun – 12 midday was at high noon, when the sun was overhead. But when it was noon in Chicago, it was 12:18pm in Detroit and 11:50am in St Louis. In the late 19th century, as the telegraph and the railroad accelerated communication and transport to unprecedented speeds, this became a problem for railroad scheduling. The noon train from Chicago (the center of the world's biggest rail network) might take only seven hours to reach Detroit, but it never arrived before 7:15pm.

In 1883, the US railroad companies decided to standardize their times into four zones across the nation. Such was the importance of the railroads that cities and states soon adopted the railroad's time, as did the country as a whole. The system of time zones was eventually applied around the world, and though its zero point is at Greenwich, England (from where longitude is measured), its origin is in the USA.

and 2 pints equal 1 quart – a common measure for liquids like milk. Milk is also sold in half gallons (2 quarts) and gallons (4 quarts). US pints and quarts are 20% less than imperial ones. Gasoline is dispensed by the US gallon, which is also about 20% less than the imperial gallon. A conversion chart is at the back of this book.

LAUNDRY

There are self-service, coin-operated laundry facilities (Laundromats) in most towns of any size and at better campgrounds. Washing a load costs about $1.50 and drying it another $1.50. Some laundries have attendants who will wash, dry and fold your clothes for an additional charge. To find a laundry, look under 'Laundries' or 'Laundries – Self-Service' in the yellow pages of the telephone directory. Dry cleaners are listed under 'Laundries' or 'Cleaners.'

WASTE & RECYCLING

The consumer society generates vast amounts of packaging, but the waste disposal industry is very efficient. Littering is frowned upon by most Americans, and travelers should show respect for the places they are visiting. All states have antilittering laws and can impose hefty fines on offenders. Trash bins are everywhere you're likely to need them and are emptied regularly. There are a few dirty neighborhoods, but in general, highways, parks and urban areas in the USA are clean and free of rubbish.

You'll find recycling centers in many towns. Materials accepted are usually plastic and glass bottles, aluminum and tin cans, and newspapers. Some campgrounds and a few roadside rest areas also have recycling bins next to the trash bins. Perhaps better than recycling is to reduce your use of throwaway products. Many gas stations and convenience stores sell large, plastic insulated cups with lids, which are inexpensive and ideal for hot and cold drinks. You can usually save a few cents by using your own cup when buying drinks.

When hiking and camping in the wilderness, take out everything you bring in.

TOILETS

The standard of plumbing and sanitation is very high, but public toilets can be scarce on city streets. You'll find them at most highway rest stops, and it's generally possible to use the facilities at fast-food restaurants, bars or shopping centers, though in many establishments the facilities are often 'for customers only.' If you have to ask, it's a 'bathroom' or a 'restroom.'

HEALTH

Generally speaking, the USA is a healthy place to visit. There are no prevalent diseases, and the country is well served by hospitals and clinics. However, due to the high cost of health care, international visitors should definitely take out comprehensive travel insurance.

Hospitals and medical centers, walk-in clinics and referral services are easily found. Ask the staff of your hotel to recommend a local doctor or clinic. In an emergency, call ☎ 911 for an ambulance to take you to the nearest hospital emergency room (ER), but note that both the ambulance and the ER will be incredibly expensive. Many city hospitals have 'urgent care clinics,' which are designed to deal with less-than-catastrophic injuries and illnesses and are much cheaper.

Metrication in the USA

Despite the recommendations of the Metric Study Group in 1971, the USA has not generally adopted the metric system. To do so would require a concerted effort by federal authorities, and this is unlikely with the continuing cynicism about the role of 'big government.' Metrication is actually raised as a bogeyman by right-wing types who regard it as unwarranted government interference and an attempt to foist world government on freedom-loving Americans. The politicians are keeping well clear.

Nevertheless, substantial sections of US society have already adopted the metric system. The largest of these is the military, which had to go metric to be compatible with other NATO forces. Presumably most defense-related industries have to supply the military with goods in metric measures. The whole scientific community has for years been using SI (International System of Units) measurements, which are basically metric. Medicine is metric in the laboratories, but not in the clinics, where patients are weighed in pounds, measured in inches and have their temperatures taken in Fahrenheit. Blood pressure, however, is measured in millimeters of mercury (mmHg).

Most consumer goods are sold in imperial units, but the metric equivalent is usually marked somewhere on the packaging. This may be for the convenience of the large immigrant population or to facilitate export sales. One product that is always marketed in metric units is wine – the standard bottle of wine is 750ml.

Predeparture Preparations

Make sure you're healthy before you start traveling. If you are embarking on a long trip, make sure your teeth are in good condition. If you wear glasses, take a spare pair and your prescription. You can get new spectacles made up quickly and competently for under $100, depending on the prescription and frame you choose. If you require a particular medication, take an adequate supply and bring the prescription with you. Pharmaceuticals are expensive in the USA.

No immunizations are generally required for entry, though cholera and yellow fever vaccinations may be necessary for those coming from infected areas. Hepatitis and tetanus shots offer good protection for travelers and may be recommended for at-risk individuals.

Health Insurance

Travel health insurance is essential – some hospitals will refuse care without evidence that the patient is covered. If you have a choice between lower or higher medical expenses options, take the higher one for visiting the USA. See the Documents section, earlier, for more information on insurance.

Food & Drink

Stomach upsets are the most common health problems for travelers, but these will be minor in the USA, where places serving food and drink have very high standards of cleanliness. Tap water is usually OK to drink, though it may smell or taste of chlorine. It may also contain some bacteria to which your gut may not be quite accustomed, at least for the first few days. Bottled drinking water is widely available.

If you're hiking in the backcountry, avoid drinking water directly from streams or lakes, even if they look crystal clear. Organisms from wildlife droppings can contaminate the water and cause some quite serious illnesses. Vigorous boiling for 10 minutes should destroy all the germs.

If you cannot boil water, it should be treated chemically. Chlorine tablets (Puritabs, Steritabs or other brand names) will kill many but not all pathogens, including giardia and amebic cysts. Iodine is very effective in purifying water and is available in tablet form (such as Potable Aqua), but follow the directions carefully – too much iodine can be harmful. Tincture of iodine (2%) can also be used. Four drops of tincture of iodine per liter or quart of clear water is the recommended dosage; let the treated water stand for 20 to 30 minutes before drinking. Flavored powder will disguise the taste and is a good idea if traveling with children.

Motion Sickness

Eating lightly before and during a trip will reduce the chance of motion sickness. If you are prone to motion sickness, try to sit near the wing on an aircraft or near the center of a bus. Fresh air usually helps. Commercial antimotion sickness preparations, which can cause drowsiness, have to be taken before the trip commences; once you feel sick, it's too late.

Jet Lag

Jet lag is experienced when a person travels by air across more than three time zones (each time zone usually represents a one-hour time difference). When traveling rapidly over long distances, your body takes time to adjust to the 'new time' of the destination, and you may experience fatigue, disorientation, insomnia, anxiety, impaired concentration and loss of appetite. These effects will usually be gone within three days of arrival, but there are ways of minimizing the impact of jet lag:

- Rest for a couple of days prior to departure; try to avoid late nights and last-minute dashes.
- Try to select flight schedules that minimize sleep deprivation; arriving in the early evening means you can go to sleep soon after you arrive. For very long flights, try to organize a stopover.
- Avoid excessive eating and alcohol during the flight. Drink plenty of fruit juice or water.
- Make yourself comfortable by wearing loose-fitting clothes and perhaps bringing an eye mask and ear plugs to help you sleep.

Deep-Vein Thrombosis

Remaining seated for more than five or six hours, as on a long plane or bus journey, is conducive to the formation of blood clots in the legs. If a clot becomes detached from its original site, it may form a thromboembolism (an obstruction in a blood vessel) elsewhere in the body, which can be serious or even fatal. To minimize the chances of a clot forming, drink lots of water, regularly stretch and move your legs while seated, and get up and move around every couple of hours. Wearing supportive hosiery may also help.

Sunburn

In the desert or at high altitude, you can get sunburned surprisingly quickly, even through clouds. A shady hat is the most basic protection. Use a sunscreen with a high protection factor, especially on skin not normally exposed to sun. In extreme conditions, you should also use zinc cream or some other barrier cream for your nose and lips. Calamine or aloe-vera lotion can provide some relief from mild sunburn.

Heat Exhaustion

Dehydration or salt deficiency can cause heat exhaustion. Take time to acclimatize to high temperatures, drink sufficient liquids and do not do anything too physically demanding. Salt deficiency is characterized by fatigue, lethargy, headaches, giddiness and muscle cramps. Salt tablets may help, but adding extra salt to your food is better. Vomiting or diarrhea can also deplete your liquid and salt levels. Always carry a water bottle in hot weather and take frequent drinks.

Heatstroke

Insufficient fluids and long, continuous periods of exposure to high temperatures can leave you vulnerable to this serious, sometimes fatal, condition that occurs when the body's heat-regulating mechanism breaks down and body temperature rises to dangerous levels. Avoid excessive alcohol intake or strenuous activity when you first arrive in a hot climate.

Symptoms include feeling unwell, lack of perspiration and a high body temperature of 102°F to 105°F (39°C to 41°C). Hospitalization is essential for extreme cases, but meanwhile, get the victim out of the sun, remove clothing, cover with a wet sheet or towel and fan continuously.

Fungal Infections

Fungal infections, which occur with greater frequency in hot weather, are most likely to occur on the scalp, between the toes or fingers (athlete's foot), in the groin (jock itch) and on the body (ringworm).

To prevent fungal infections, wear loose, clean and comfortable clothes; avoid artificial fibers; wash frequently and dry carefully. If you do get an infection, wash the area daily with a disinfectant or medicated soap and water, and rinse and dry well. Apply an antifungal powder or cream and try to expose the infected area to air or sunlight. Wash all towels and underwear in hot water, and let them dry in the sun.

Hypothermia

Temperatures in the mountains or desert can drop quickly from balmy to below freezing. Even in temperatures above freezing, a combination of wind, wet clothing, fatigue and hunger can quite quickly cause hypothermia. For outdoor activities, it's best to dress in layers; silk, wool and some artificial fibers are all good insulating materials. Head covering and a strong, waterproof outer layer are essential. Carry water and snack foods like chocolate or dried fruit. People traveling alone are more at risk than those in groups. Always seek shelter when bad weather is unavoidable.

Hypothermia occurs when the body loses heat too fast, and its core temperature falls. Symptoms include exhaustion, numb skin (particularly toes and fingers), shivering, slurred speech, irrational behavior, lethargy and stumbling. To treat mild hypothermia, get the person out of the wind and rain and make sure they're in warm, dry clothing. Give them hot liquids (not alcohol) and some high-energy, easily digested food. Do not rub victims: instead, allow them to slowly warm themselves.

Altitude Sickness

Lack of oxygen at high altitudes (over about 7500 feet) affects most people to some extent. The effect may be mild or severe and occurs because less oxygen reaches the muscles and the brain at high altitude. Acute Mountain Sickness (AMS) usually develops during the first 24 hours at high altitude but may be delayed by several weeks. Mild symptoms include headache, lethargy, dizziness, difficulty sleeping and loss of appetite. Severe symptoms include breathlessness, a dry, irritative cough (which may progress to the production of pink, frothy sputum), severe headache, lack of coordination and balance, confusion, irrational behavior, vomiting, drowsiness and unconsciousness. Mild AMS may become more severe without warning and has been fatal at as low as 10,000 feet, although it is much more common above 11,500 feet.

If mild symptoms occur, don't ascend farther until acclimatized, which may take a day or more. Everyday painkillers such as aspirin will relieve symptoms until the body adapts. If the symptoms persist it is imperative to descend to lower elevations.

• Ascend slowly – take frequent rest days, spending two to three nights for each climb of 3000

feet. If you reach a high altitude by trekking, acclimatization takes place gradually, and you are less likely to be affected than if you fly direct.

• Try to sleep at a lower altitude than the greatest height reached during the day.

• Drink extra fluids. Mountain air is dry and cold, and you lose moisture as you breathe.

• Eat light, high-carbohydrate meals for more energy.

• Avoid alcohol (which may increase the risk of dehydration), sedatives and smoking.

Hepatitis

A general term for inflammation of the liver is hepatitis. The symptoms are fever, chills, headache, fatigue, a feeling of weakness and aches and pains, followed by loss of appetite, nausea, vomiting, abdominal pain, dark urine, light-colored feces and jaundiced skin. The whites of the eyes may also turn yellow.

Hepatitis A is transmitted by contaminated food or drinking water. **Hepatitis B** is spread through contact with infected blood, blood products or body fluids (by sexual contact, contaminated blood transfusions, contact with blood via small breaks in the skin, use of unsterilized needles or contaminated shaving, tattooing or body-piercing equipment).

Vaccination against hepatitis A and B is effective and recommended for anyone likely to be at risk. There are no vaccines against the comparatively rare strains of hepatitis C, D, E and G.

Tetanus

Also known as lockjaw, tetanus occurs when a wound becomes infected by a germ that lives in the feces of animals or people. To prevent it, thoroughly clean any cuts, punctures and animal bites. Tetanus is difficult to treat but is preventable with immunization, so consider getting a shot before leaving home.

HIV & AIDS

Infection with the human immunodeficiency virus (HIV) may lead to acquired immunodeficiency syndrome (AIDS) – a fatal disease. Any exposure to blood, blood products or body fluids may put an individual at risk. Infection can come from unprotected sex or sharing contaminated needles, including those used for acupuncture, tattooing or body-piercing. The blood supply in the USA is well screened, so blood transfusions are not a likely source of infection. The US Center of Disease Control has a helpful AIDS hotline (☎ 800-342-2437). AIDS support groups are listed in the front of phone books.

Snake Bites

There are several varieties of venomous snake in the USA, but they do not cause instantaneous death, and antivenins are available. First aid is to place a light constricting bandage above the bite, keep the wounded part below the level of the heart and move it as little as possible. Administer CPR if breathing stops. Stay calm and get to a medical facility as soon as possible. Bring the dead snake for identification if you can, but don't risk being bitten again.

Insect Bites & Stings

Bee and wasp stings and nonpoisonous spider bites are usually painful rather than dangerous. Calamine lotion will give relief, and ice packs will reduce the pain and swelling. Bites are best avoided by not using bare hands to turn over rocks or large pieces of wood. See Safety in the Activities section later for more on snakes and spiders.

Ticks

Ticks are parasitic arachnids that may be present in brush, forest and grasslands, where hikers often get them on their legs or in their boots. Adult ticks suck blood from hosts by burrowing into the skin and can carry infections such as Rocky Mountain spotted fever or Lyme disease.

Always check your body for ticks after walking through high grass or thickly forested area. If ticks are found unattached, they can simply be brushed off. If one has attached itself to you, pulling it off and leaving the head in the skin increases the likelihood of infection.

If a tick is found attached, press down around the tick's head with tweezers, grab the head and gently pull upwards – do not twist it. (If no tweezers are available, use your fingers, but protect them from contamination with a piece of tissue or paper.) Do not squeeze the tick or touch it with a hot object as this can make it regurgitate noxious gut substances into the wound. Do not rub oil, alcohol or petroleum jelly on it. If you get sick in the next couple of weeks, consult a doctor.

WOMEN TRAVELERS
Safety Precautions

Women, especially those traveling alone, need to develop an extra awareness of their surroundings. In towns and cities, be aware of 'bad,' or unsafe, neighborhoods, particularly after dark. If you must go into these areas, it's less risky in a private car or taxi. If you are unsure which areas are considered unsafe, ask at your hotel or telephone the tourist office or women's center for advice. While there is less crime in rural areas, women may still be harassed, and crimes can still happen in even the nicest neighborhoods.

Men may interpret a woman drinking alone in a bar as a bid for male company, whether it is intended that way or not. If you don't want the company, most men will respect a firm but polite 'no, thank you.' Be extra careful at night on public transit and remember to check the time of the last bus or train before you go out at night. If in doubt, call a taxi.

When driving, it's a good idea to have a sign requesting help, which you can display if you get stuck on a road. At night avoid getting out of your car to flag down help; turn on your hazard lights and wait for the police to arrive. A rented mobile phone is good insurance.

Hitchhiking is always risky and not recommended, *especially* hitchhiking alone. Don't pick up hitchhikers when driving.

Rape occurs mostly in cities, but also in rural areas to a lesser degree. Common

sense will help you avoid most problems. You're more vulnerable if you've been drinking or using drugs than if you're sober, and you're more vulnerable alone than if you're with your own companions.

If you are assaulted, call the police (☎ 911). In the few rural areas where 911 is not active, dial '0' for the operator. Cities and larger towns have rape crisis centers and women's shelters that provide help and support; they are listed in the telephone directory, and the police should also be able to refer you.

To deal with potential dangers, many women protect themselves with a whistle, mace, cayenne-pepper spray or some self-defense training. If you decide to purchase a spray, contact a police station to find out about regulations and training classes. Having a gun may actually increase the risk of being seriously hurt. Laws regarding guns and sprays vary from state to state, but federal law prohibits them being carried on planes.

Resources & Organizations

The National Organization for Women (NOW; ☎ 202-331-0066, ⓦ www.now.org, 1000 16th St NW, Suite 700, Washington, DC 20036), is a good resource for women-related information. NOW can refer you to state and local chapters. Planned Parenthood (☎ 212-541-7800, ⓦ www.plannedparenthood.org, 810 7th Ave, New York, NY 10019) also has offices nationwide and can offer advice on medical issues and referrals to clinics throughout the country.

The Web site ⓦ www.journeywoman.com has lots of information and links for women traveling in the USA and around the world. *A Journey of One's Own,* by Thalia Zepatos, contains travel tips, anecdotes and a long list of sources and resources for the independent female traveler. For local resources, check the yellow pages directory under 'Women's Organizations and Services.' Women's bookstores (look under 'Bookstores') are good places to find out about gatherings, readings and meetings, and often have bulletin boards where you can find or place travel and housing notices.

GAY & LESBIAN TRAVELERS

Gay communities are most visible in the major coastal cities, where it is easier for gay men and women to live their lives with a certain amount of openness. In the middle of the country it is much harder to be open. Gay travelers should be careful, *especially* in the rural areas where simply holding hands might attract very negative reactions. There are big gay scenes in New York, San Francisco, Los Angeles, New Orleans, Miami, Key West, Washington, DC, and Atlanta.

Resources & Organizations

There are a few well-known gay publications worth checking out. *The Women's Traveller,* with listings for lesbians; *Damron's Address Book* for men; and *Damron Accommodations* listing gay-owned and gay-friendly hotels, B&Bs and guesthouses nationwide, are published by Damron Company (☎ 415-255-0404, 800-462-6654, ⓦ www.damron.com). *Ferrari's Places for Women* is also useful. Gay guides to specific cities can be found in many bookstores.

Another good resource is the Gay & Lesbian Yellow Pages (☎ 212-674-0120, ⓦ www.glyp.com), which has a national edition plus regional editions. Also worth contacting are the National Gay/Lesbian Task Force (☎ 202-332-6483, ⓦ www.ngltf.org) and Lambda Legal Defense Fund (☎ 212-995-8585 in New York City, 213-937-2728 in Los Angeles).

DISABLED TRAVELERS

The USA is a world leader in providing facilities for the disabled. The Americans with Disabilities Act (ADA) requires that all public buildings (including hotels, restaurants, theaters and museums) and public transit be wheelchair accessible. The more populous areas have the best and most widespread facilities, but always call ahead to confirm what is available. Planning is particularly important for disabled travelers.

Buses and trains must have wheelchair lifts, and telephone companies are required to provide relay operators (available via TTY numbers) for the hearing impaired. Many banks now provide ATM instructions in Braille, and you will find audible crossing signals as well as dropped curbs at many intersections.

All major airlines, Greyhound buses and Amtrak trains will allow service animals like guide dogs to accompany passengers and will frequently sell discount or two-for-one packages when disabled passengers require an attendant. Airlines must accept wheelchairs as checked baggage and must have an onboard chair available, though some advance notice may be required on smaller aircraft. Airlines will also provide assistance for connecting, boarding and deplaning flights. Just ask for assistance when making your reservation.

Larger private and chain hotels have suites for disabled guests. Hilton, Hyatt, Embassy Suites, Red Roof Inns and Best Western are among the most reliable. Car rental agencies such as Budget, Hertz and Enterprise offer hand-controlled vehicles and vans with wheelchair lifts at no extra charge, but you must reserve them well in advance.

Resources & Organizations

A number of organizations and tour operators specialize in serving disabled travelers:

Access-Able Travel Source (☎ 303-232-2979, W www.access-able.com, PO Box 1796, Wheat Ridge, CO 80034) – an excellent Web site with many links

Mobility International USA (☎ 541-343-1284, fax 541-343-6812, W www.miusa.org, PO Box 10767, Eugene, OR 97440) – advises disabled travelers on mobility issues and runs an educational exchange program

Moss Rehabilitation Hospital's Travel Information Service (☎ 215-456-9600, TTY 456-9602, W www.mossresourcenet.org/travel.htm, 1200 W Tabor Rd, Philadelphia, PA 19141) – a concise list of useful contacts

Society for Accessible Travel & Hospitality (SATH; ☎ 212-447-7284, W www.sath.org, 347 Fifth Ave, No 610, New York, NY 10016) – lobbies for better facilities and publishes *Open World* magazine

Travelin' Talk Network (☎ 615-552-6670, W www.travelintalk.net, PO Box 3534, Clarksville, TN 37047) – offers a global network of people providing service to disabled people

Twin Peaks Press (☎ 360-694-2462, W home.pacifier.com/~twinpeak, PO Box 129, Vancouver, WA 98666) – publishes a quarterly newsletter plus directories and access guides

SENIOR TRAVELERS

Travelers aged 50 years and up can expect to receive discounts and benefits, though the applicable age varies. It's worth asking about a senior discount rate at hotels, museums and restaurants.

Visitors to national parks and campgrounds can cut costs greatly by using the Golden Age Passport, a card that allows US citizens age 62 and over (and those traveling in the same car) free admission nationwide and a 50% reduction on camping fees. You can apply in person for a Golden Age Passport at any national park or regional office of the USFS or NPS, or call ☎ 800-365-2267 for information.

Organizations

Some national advocacy groups that can help in planning your travels include the following:

American Association of Retired Persons (AARP; ☎ 800-424-3410, W www.aarp.org, 601 E St NW, Washington, DC 20049) – an advocacy group for Americans 50 years and older and a good resource for travel bargains. A one-year membership costs $10.

Elderhostel (☎ 877-426-8056, W www.elderhostel.org, 11 Avenue de Lafayette, Boston, MA 02111) – a nonprofit organization that offers seniors (55 years and older) the opportunity to attend academic college courses and study tours throughout the USA and Canada.

TRAVEL WITH CHILDREN

On a practical level, the USA is one of the easiest, safest and most convenient places to travel with kids. For example, just about any restaurant will have a high chair, children's menu and paper placemat printed with kids' puzzles. Food is served promptly, generally within the attention span of a five-year-old, and if the kids don't eat it, you can always get a box for the leftovers. For light, cheap meals, bring some cups, plates and utensils and buy cereals, soft drinks and sandwich makings from a supermarket.

Motels commonly have rooms with two double beds, which are ideal for a family of two adults and two small kids. An extra 'roll-away' bed is usually available at an extra charge (this is commonly called a 'cot,' but it's full size and big enough for most adults). Some motels have a 'kids stay free' policy, and others charge only a small amount extra for a family using two double beds, plus maybe $10 more for an extra bed in the same room. Most motels have swimming pools and cable TV, which will appeal to kids. If your family can stand camping together, campgrounds can be great places to stay and at holiday times are a good way to meet other kids and families.

With a rental car, a family can get around as cheaply as a solo traveler, though you might have to pay more to get a slightly bigger car. Appropriate child restraints are required in every state, and car rental agencies should be able to provide them – ask when you book a car. Domestic and international flights sometimes offer special family deals, including 'kids fly free' promotions. Though buses offer the cheapest intercity transport, trains are more comfortable for restless children. Inquire early with Amtrak to get the best deals.

Public toilets commonly have a baby change table, even in the men's toilet.

Many theme parks and amusements are aimed at children, and children love them. These attractions are highly commercialized and often expensive, as much as $35 for adult admission and $28 for children. Food, drinks and souvenirs can easily add another $50. Other suitable attractions for kids include interactive, hands-on science museums (in nearly every city); in-line skating, cycling and boating (equipment can be rented in many parks, lakes and beachfronts); movies, including big-screen IMAX shows; and outdoor activities like skiing,

white-water rafting, swimming, snorkeling, horseback riding and even walking. It's a good idea to alternate adult activities (museums, galleries, shopping, scenic drives) with things that kids will enjoy.

To get beyond the commercial hype, it's worth making an effort to make contact with a local family. Your kids will be pleased to play with others their own age, and you can experience some American home and community life. Try to arrange your visit well in advance.

For more information, advice and anecdotes, look at Lonely Planet's *Travel With Children* by Cathy Lanigan.

USEFUL ORGANIZATIONS

See also the organizations listed above for women, seniors, gays and lesbians, and disabled travelers.

American Automobile Association

AAA provides great travel information, distributes free road maps and guide books, and sells American Express traveler's checks without commission to its members. The AAA membership card will often get you discounts for accommodations, car rental and admission charges. All major cities and many smaller towns have an AAA office. Addresses and phone numbers are given in AAA publications and at Ⓦ www.aaa.com.

AAA also provides emergency roadside service to members in the event of an accident or breakdown or if you lock your keys in the car. The nationwide toll-free roadside assistance number is ☎ 800-222-4357 (800-AAA-HELP).

Members of other national and state motoring associations, like the AA in the UK or the NRMA in Australia, can use AAA services if they bring a membership card or a letter of introduction from their home organization. If you're not in an affiliated motoring association, it can still be worthwhile to join the AAA, especially if you plan to do a lot of driving.

National Park Service

The National Park Service (NPS), part of the Dept of the Interior, manages some 360 national parks, monuments, historic sites, battlefields, memorials and recreation areas throughout the USA and its territories. National park campground and reservations information can be obtained by calling ☎ 800-365-2267, by writing to National Park Service Public Inquiry, Dept of the Interior, 1849 C St NW, Washington, DC 20013, or by checking its comprehensive Web site, ⓦ www.nps.gov. Contact individual parks for specific information.

Most NPS areas charge entrance fees, valid for seven days, of $6-20 per vehicle (usually half-price for walk-in or biking visitors). A few are free, and some don't collect entrance fees during periods of low visitation (usually late fall to early spring). Additional fees are charged for camping and some other activities, depending on each park. See Accommodations (in this chapter) and National Park Service (in the Facts About the USA chapter) for more details on the NPS.

Golden Passports You can apply in person for any of the following passes at any national park or regional office of the USFS or NPS, or from the address above.

Golden Eagle Passports cost $50 annually and offer one-year entry into national parks to the holder and accompanying guests.

Golden Age Passports allow US residents 62 years and older unlimited entry to all NPS sites. They are issued at any NPS site entrance for $10 (proof of age and residence required) and offer discounts up to 50% on camping and other fees.

Golden Access Passports offer the same to US residents who are medically blind or permanently disabled. They are issued free at any NPS site entrance (proof of disability and residence required).

US Forest Service

The US Forest Service (USFS) is part of the Dept of Agriculture and manages national forests. National forests are less protected than parks, allowing commercial exploitation in some areas (usually logging or privately owned recreational facilities).

Entrance to national forests is generally free, although visitor fees of about $5 have been instituted in several areas. For national forest campground and reservations information, call ☎ 800-280-2267. For information about specific forests, contact the appropriate ranger stations.

Bureau of Land Management

The BLM, as it is commonly called, manages public use of federal lands other than national parks and forests, mostly in the desert Southwest. BLM lands are available for no-frills camping, often in untouched settings. Regional BLM offices are usually in the state capital. Look in the front of the white pages directory under 'US Government, Dept of the Interior,' or call the Federal Information Center (☎ 800-688-9889).

Fish & Wildlife Services

Each state has a Fish & Wildlife Service (variously called Fish & Game, Fishing & Hunting, Wildlife Resources etc). These issue fishing and hunting licenses and may provide information about viewing local wildlife as an alternative to killing it. Look in the phone book under US Government, Dept of the Interior, or call the Federal Information Center (☎ 800-688-9889). Licenses are often available at outfitters, tackle shops and post offices.

DANGERS & ANNOYANCES

The USA is not generally a dangerous place to travel, but there are some things to beware of. The most publicized problem is violent crime, but this is most common in areas where few visitors would go. Travel in desert and mountain areas can be hazardous, as can outdoor activities like skiing and canoeing (see Activities, later in this chapter). Wildlife presents some potential dangers, and there is the dramatic but unlikely possibility of a natural disaster. Road accidents probably pose the greatest single risk of injury.

Crime

Crime is most unlikely in well-trafficked, well-lit tourist and nightlife areas. The usual local advice is to avoid the 'bad neighborhoods,' especially after dark. Most locals know where not to go; if you're not sure, ask a police officer or hotel manager. If you find yourself in a neighborhood where you would rather not be, do your best to look confident and sure of yourself (don't stop every few minutes to look at a map), hail a taxi or go into the nearest store and call one, and get out of there. Don't abandon a bright street for a darker one.

Be aware of your surroundings and who may be watching you, especially if you are alone. Exercise particular caution in large parking lots or parking structures at night. Try to use ATM machines only in well-trafficked areas. Of course crimes also occur in the 'better neighborhoods,' notably burglaries and thefts from motor vehicles, but the fact remains that some areas pose a much greater risk of violent street crime than others.

If you are accosted by a mugger, there's no 100%-recommended policy, but handing over whatever he or she wants is much better than getting knifed or shot. Don't carry large amounts of cash or valuables. And don't carry all your money in the same pocket or wallet: Have about $60 separate, and hand it over fast. Muggers are not too happy to find their victims are penniless.

In hotels, don't leave your valuables lying about the room. Use safety deposit boxes or at least place valuables in a locked bag. Don't open your door to strangers – check the peephole or call the front desk if unexpected people try to enter.

Always lock your car and put valuables out of sight, even if you're leaving the car for only a few minutes. Vans and station wagons may be more at risk because the contents are more visible. Avoid displaying rental car insignia or anything else that makes a car look like it might be loaded with a tourist's valuables.

If your car is bumped by another car from behind, it is best to keep going to a well-lit area, gas station or even a police station. Faking such an accident is often used to lure victims out of their cars. Locking car doors when driving around town is a standard precaution.

Guns The USA has a widespread reputation as a dangerous place because of the availability of firearms. This is partly true, but the problem is exaggerated by the media. The incidence of shooting deaths is much higher than in other countries, but many of them are accidents or suicides, and many of the homicides are domestic incidents or related to street-gang conflicts. In cities, muggers and thieves are more likely to be armed with a knife than a gun.

Residents of more rural states often have guns, but they usually target animals or isolated traffic signs rather than humans. Do be careful in the woods during hunting season, when unsuccessful or drunken hunters may be less selective in their targets than one might hope. None of this sounds good, but the fact is that a visitor is extremely unlikely to be threatened with a firearm or hit by a stray bullet.

The 'right to bear arms' was originally conceived as a protection against invasion and tyranny, but it's not often seen in its constitutional context:

A well regulated Militia being necessary to the security of a free State, the right of the people to keep and bear Arms shall not be infringed.

– US Constitution, Amendment II

Many Americans keep a gun in their homes or cars, most commonly because it's seen as a defense against criminals. The freedom to do so is greatly cherished by a surprising number of people, even grandmothers and gentle middle-class suburbanites. In some rural areas, gun ownership is sacrosanct, and the greatest danger might be to suggest that the right to bear arms could be limited in the interests of public safety – this can engender heated arguments. In fact, most gun owners are quite proud of their weapons, look after them carefully and use them responsibly.

Cons & Scams It's probably as common for tourists to be tricked out of their money as to be robbed. Anything that looks like an easy way to make some quick bucks is likely to be a con. A big reward for a small service, a super cheap camera or a simple gambling game are all ploys to trick the gullible. A healthy skepticism is your best defense.

Panhandlers & Homeless People

You're likely to bump into beggars on the streets of many American cities. They are often called panhandlers, transients, indigents or bums and are generally harmless. Aggressive or threatening requests for money occur occasionally, but this 'panhassling' is more of an annoyance than a danger.

Many of these people are homeless, sleeping under freeways or in alleyways and abandoned buildings. Many suffer from medical or psychiatric problems, or the effects of alcohol or drug abuse, and their behavior can be decidedly weird. At least a proportion of the homeless resist any institutional help and may be genuinely free spirits in the American hobo tradition. The presence of beggars on the streets of wealthy communities is often rationalized by a belief that 'they choose to be there, and they could get a home if they wanted to,' though this often defies credibility.

There's an argument that giving to panhandlers will only encourage them to target tourists and to concentrate in tourist areas. It's really a matter of conscience. If you want to contribute toward a solution, consider a donation to a charity that cares for the urban poor.

Natural Disasters

With its varied geography and climate, the USA gets its share of fires, floods, tornadoes, snow storms, dust storms, volcanoes, avalanches and earthquakes. They make such good television that you might think that disasters are an everyday event, but it's very unlikely that you'll be caught in one on a short visit.

Authorities can usually give plenty of warning of an impending disaster, and evacuation may be obligatory, if not merely sensible. Emergency services are very efficient. If an area is prone to certain disasters, detailed precautions will be listed in the front of phone books.

EMERGENCIES

Throughout most of the USA, dial ☎ 911 for emergency service of any sort. This is a free call from any phone. A few rural phones might not have this service, in which case dial ☎ 0 for the operator and ask for emergency assistance.

Carry a photocopy of your passport separately from your passport, in case of theft or loss. Copy the pages with your photo and personal details, passport number and US visa. If it is lost or stolen, this will make replacement easier. Call your embassy or the nearest consulate.

Similarly, carry copies of your traveler's check numbers, airline ticket and credit-card numbers separately. If you lose your credit cards or they get stolen, contact the company immediately (see Credit & Debit Cards, earlier, for company phone numbers). Contact your bank if you lose your ATM card.

LEGAL MATTERS

If you are stopped by the police for any reason, bear in mind that there is no system of paying fines on the spot. Attempting to pay the fine to the officer is frowned upon at best and may result in a charge of bribery. For traffic offenses, the police officer or highway patroller will explain the options to you. There is usually a 30-day period to pay a fine, but the officer has the authority to take you directly to a magistrate to pay immediately.

If you are arrested for a more serious offense, you are allowed to remain silent. There is no legal reason to speak to a police officer if you don't wish, but never walk away from an officer until given permission. All persons who are arrested are legally allowed the right to make one phone call. If you don't have a lawyer, friend or family member to help you, call your embassy. The police will give you the number upon request.

Each state has its own civil and criminal laws, and what is legal in one state may be illegal in others. Federal laws are applicable to the postal service, US government property and many interstate activities.

Driving

In all states, driving under the influence of alcohol or drugs is a serious offense, subject to stiff fines and even imprisonment. For more information on driving and road rules, see the Getting Around chapter.

Drinking

The legal drinking age is 21, and you will often be asked for a photo identification to prove your age. Being 'carded' is standard practice in many places – it may be a pain if you're in your 20s, but it's nice to be carded after you turn 30. The sale of liquor is subject to local government regulations, and some counties ban liquor sales on Sunday, after midnight or before breakfast. In 'dry' counties, liquor sales are banned altogether.

Drugs

Recreational drugs are prohibited by federal and state laws. Some states, such as California and Alaska, treat possession of small quantities of marijuana as a misdemeanor, though it is still punishable with fines and/or imprisonment. In California you can be prescribed marijuana products for certain ailments, but the legalities of this are being argued in courts.

Possession of any other drug, including cocaine, ecstasy, LSD, heroin, hashish or more than an ounce of pot is a felony, punishable by lengthy jail sentences, depending on the circumstances. Conviction of any drug offense is grounds for deportation of a foreigner.

BUSINESS HOURS

Generally businesses open at 9 or 10am and close at 5 or 6pm, but there are no hard and fast rules. In large cities, there are a few supermarkets, restaurants and a post office that stay open 24 hours. Some stores are open until 9pm, especially those in shopping malls, and many open for shorter hours on Sunday (typically noon to 5pm).

In most areas, post offices are open 8am to 4 or 5:30pm Monday to Friday, and some are also open 8am to 3pm on Saturday. Banks usually open from either 9 or 10am to 5 or 6pm Monday to Friday. A few banks are open 9am to 2 or 4pm on Saturday. Hours are decided by individual branches.

PUBLIC HOLIDAYS

National public holidays are celebrated throughout the USA (though in fact they are mandated by state laws). Banks, schools and government offices (including post offices) are closed and transportation, museums and other services operate on a Sunday schedule. Many stores, however, maintain regular business hours. Holidays falling on a weekend are usually observed the following Monday.

January 1 – New Year's Day

3rd Monday in January – Martin Luther King Jr Day

3rd Monday in February – Presidents' Day

Last Monday in May – Memorial Day

July 4 – Independence Day (also called the Fourth of July)

1st Monday in September – Labor Day

2nd Monday in October – Columbus Day

November 11 – Veterans' Day

4th Thursday in November – Thanksgiving

December 25 – Christmas Day

CULTURAL EVENTS & HOLIDAYS

Besides the above holidays, the USA celebrates a number of other events. Here are some of the most widely observed ones:

January

Chinese New Year – begins at the end of January or beginning of February and lasts two weeks. The first day is celebrated with parades, firecrackers, fireworks and lots of food.

February

Valentine's Day – the 14th. No one knows why St Valentine is associated with romance, but this is the day to celebrate.

March

St Patrick's Day – the 17th. The patron saint of Ireland is honored by all those who feel the Irish in their blood as well as by those who want to feel Irish beer in their blood. Everyone wears green (if you don't, you can get pinched).

Easter – (sometimes April) secular rituals of painting eggs, eating chocolate and searching for eggs hidden by the 'Easter bunny.' (Good Friday is not a public holiday.)

May

Cinco de Mayo – the 5th. The day the Mexicans wiped out the French Army in 1862. Now it's the day all Americans get to eat lots of Mexican food and drink margaritas.

Mother's Day – the 2nd Sunday. Children send cards and flowers and call Mom. Restaurants are likely to be busy.

June

Father's Day – the 3rd Sunday. Same idea, different parent

October

Halloween – the 31st. Kids and adults dress in costumes. Children go 'trick-or-treating' for candy. Adults go to parties to act out their alter egos.

November

Day of the Dead – the 2nd. Observed in areas with Mexican communities, this is a day for families to honor deceased relatives and make breads and sweets resembling skeletons, skulls and such.

Election Day – the 2nd Tuesday

December

Chanukah – date determined by the Hebrew calendar. An eight-day Jewish holiday (also called Hanukkah or the Feast of Lights) commemorating the victory of the Maccabees over the armies of Syria.

Kwanzaa – starts on the 26th and lasts to the 31st. This African American celebration is a time to give thanks for the harvest.

New Year's Eve – the 31st. People celebrate with few traditions other than dressing up and drinking champagne or watching the festivities on TV. The following day people stay home to nurse their hangovers and watch college football.

SPECIAL EVENTS

Hundreds of state and county fairs, multicultural events, pioneer days and harvest celebrations fill the calendar. Contact a state tourist office to find out what's happening during your visit.

Most of the national public holidays and events listed above are celebrated everywhere, but with more fanfare in some places than others. On the Fourth of July, there are authentic and moving displays of patriotism in towns throughout the country, and these can be a fine experience for a foreign visitor.

The following are some of the really special events – the ones people plan a whole trip around. If you want to be there, you'll have to plan ahead, because accommodations can be booked up, and be prepared to pay more.

January

Tournament of Roses Parade – New Year's Day cavalcade of enormous flower-coated floats on Colorado Blvd in the Los Angeles suburb of Pasadena (☎ 818-795-4171).

Chinese New Year – in late January or early February, the biggest celebration is in San Francisco, where the Golden Dragon Parade is led by a 75-foot-long dragon. Contact the Chinatown Chamber of Commerce (☎ 415-982-3000).

February

Speed Weeks – early February is the start of a three-week auto-racing celebration leading up to the Daytona 500 at the Daytona International Speedway, Florida (☎ 904-253-7223).

Mardi Gras – in late February or early March, the day before Ash Wednesday, Mardi Gras ('Fat Tuesday') in New Orleans, Mobile, Alabama, and some other Deep South cities, is the culmination of Carnival, which starts on Twelfth Night (January 6). Parades of elaborate floats and marching bands get going three weeks before Mardi Gras, and the outrageous activity reaches a costumed climax in New Orleans' French Quarter at midnight.

March

St Patrick's Day – on the 17th, the St Patrick's Day Parade is huge in New York and Boston, which both now have rival events by gay Irish groups, and in Chicago, where the river is dyed green for the occasion.

April

Spring Break – usually the weeks surrounding Easter, this college vacation sees tens of thousands of students descend on various towns to drink, dance and engage in mating rituals. If you are of like mind and age, head for Palm Springs, California; Lake Havasu City, Arizona; Daytona and Panama City Beach, Florida; or Myrtle Beach, South Carolina – otherwise keep well away.

New Orleans Jazz Fest – over two weekends in late April and early May, the town reverberates with good sounds and fills up with great food (☎ 504-522-4786).

May

Carnaval – Memorial Day weekend (the last in May), San Francisco celebrates Carnaval a month or so after Rio; music and dancing in the streets of the Mission District (☎ 415-826-1401).

Indianapolis 500 – in late May, half a million people hit Indianapolis for the big race and associated celebrations. Book tickets 51 weeks ahead (☎ 317-248-6700).

June

Chicago Blues Festival – on the first weekend of June, this highly regarded musical festival runs for three days in Grant Park, Chicago.

Gay Pride Week – this wild week in San Francisco climaxes on the last weekend in June, with the Dyke March between Dolores Park and the Castro on Saturday evening, and Sunday's colorful Gay Freedom Day Parade, which brings up to a half a million people to Market St. It's followed by a huge party and fair at City Hall. Other cities also turn on big parades to celebrate gay pride.

July

Independence Day Concert & Fireworks – on the 3rd, Chicago pulls out the stops for a really long fireworks show and the '1812 Overture' played with gusto in Grant Park; other cities, especially New York and Washington, DC, set off their fireworks on the 4th.

September

US Open Tennis Tournament – the tournament runs over the first two weeks of the month at the National Tennis Center, Flushing Meadows Park, Queens, New York City (☎ 718-760-6200).

October

Halloween – the night of the 31st is a fun time for kids all over the country, but totally outrageous in San Francisco; hundreds of thousands of costumed revelers gather in the Civic Center and the Castro and at the Exotic Erotic Halloween Ball.

November

Thanksgiving Day Parade – on the fourth Thursday in November, Macy's sponsors this huge event on Broadway in New York City.

December

Christmas – a four-week festival of consumerism is observed in New York City, where the big tree is lit up in Rockefeller Center the Tuesday after Thanksgiving and the department store windows have amazing displays. Costumed carolers and the Radio City Music Rockettes perform their annual Christmas shows.

Orange Bowl Parade – on New Year's Eve, most of the population turns out for floats, clowns, folkloric dancers and fireworks in Miami.

ACTIVITIES

No matter what you're into – nude bungee jumping, organic ballooning, power fishing – you'll find a spot to do it and folks to do it with in the USA. You'll also find specialist shops, services, tours, organizations and publications, as American affluence and know-how go in pursuit of happiness.

Treading Lightly

Backcountry areas are fragile environments and cannot support insensitive or careless activity, especially with an increasing numbers of visitors. Conservation organizations, hikers' manuals and the NPS all promote backcountry codes that seek to minimize the impact of hikers on the environment. Make sure you are familiar with these before you set out. The following are the basic rules:

- Stay on the main trail, even if it means walking through mud or crossing a patch of snow.
- Camp at least 200 feet (70 steps) away from the nearest lake, river or stream.
- Bury human waste at least 300 feet from water, camp or trails; use toilets where available.
- Avoid using soap, detergents or toothpaste, and don't use them near watercourses.
- Carry a stove and use it instead of a campfire.
- Carry out all trash.

Safety

In the backcountry, you're always safer with others than alone, but in any case, always let someone know where you are going and how long you plan to be gone. Use sign-in boards at trailheads or ranger stations. Travelers looking for hiking companions can inquire or post notices at ranger stations, outdoors stores, campgrounds and youth hostels.

Fording rivers and streams is potentially the most dangerous part of a wilderness hike. In national parks most streams have foot bridges, but otherwise exercise extreme caution.

Weather Conditions can change suddenly in the mountains, so be prepared for cold weather and rain, even on a short hike. Carry a rain jacket and a light set of long underwear at all times. In the deserts, wear a shady hat and loose, long-sleeved clothing, and take plenty of water. In desert canyons, be ever watchful for sudden rains that can cause flash flooding.

Wildlife Bears are attracted to campgrounds where they may find accessible food in bags, tents, cars or (Yogi's favorite) picnic baskets. They may rip tents, break car windows and scratch, bite or maul people who obstruct them. Never feed bears (or any other wildlife) and ensure that food and nice-smelling stuff, like toothpaste and soap, is kept in a bear-resistant container well away from your tent. Note that many campgrounds supply these containers.

Puma (mountain lion) attacks on hikers are extremely rare, but they have happened in the West's Sierra Nevada. Seemingly placid beasts like bison and mule deer are capable of inflicting serious injury or even fatal wounds, so keep your distance from all wild animals. Some, including squirrels and prairie dogs, carry rabies.

There are snakes, spiders, scorpions and other venomous creatures in urban as well as rural areas, but fatalities are very rare. This is partly because these animals tend to avoid humans and partly because their venom is designed to kill small animals rather than big ones. When hiking, watch your step, particularly on hot afternoons and evenings when rattlesnakes like to bask in the middle of the trail. They are also often active at night. See the Health section, earlier, for more information on snakebites.

Maps

The US Geological Survey (USGS; ☎ 800-435-7627, W www.usgs.gov, PO Box 25286, Denver, CO 80225), an agency of the federal Dept of the Interior, publishes very detailed topographic maps of the entire country at different scales, up to 1:250,000. Maps at 1:62,500, approximately 1 inch = 1 mile, are ideal for backcountry hiking and backpacking. The USGS 1:62,500 map series has been discontinued, but some individual cartographers are producing updated versions of the old USGS 1:62,500 maps.

The US Forest Service (USFS) produces good topographic maps of National Forest areas at a scale of 1:126,720 (2 inches = 1 mile). Most NPS and USFS information centers at parks have a good range of topographical maps. In the absence of a ranger station, try the local stationery or hardware store.

The University of Texas maintains an extensive online library of maps. In its collection are maps of the national parks, monuments and battlefields (W www .lib.utexas.edu/Libs/PCL/Map_collection/ National_parks/National_parks.html).

Courses

For comprehensive instruction in a range of outdoor skills (including hiking, climbing, sailing and canoeing) contact the National Outdoor Leadership School (☎ 307-332-5300, W www.nols.edu, 288 Main St, Lander, WY 82520).

Hiking & Backpacking

In the USA, hiking means just about any walk in a natural area, while backpacking means a hike when you camp out overnight. Short hikes are highly recommended as a way to better appreciate the landscape and to escape the crowds that come by car. Overnight hikes offer a wonderful experience, but require a little more planning and preparation.

Most national and state parks have several easy, well-marked short trails, usually under 2 miles. They often have interpretive displays and are marked on maps as nature trails or self-guided interpretive trails. These trails are popular, but vastly less crowded than anyplace adjacent to a parking lot. Wilderness areas and forests are less likely to have fully developed self-guided interpretive trails, but usually have some paths suitable for easy walks.

Longer hikes, up to eight hours, are slightly more demanding, but trails are usually very well marked, so you won't need a topographic map or compass if you stick to the main routes. Ask at a ranger station or visitor center for suggestions about trails to suit your interest and ability. For any walk longer than an hour, take water, snack food, a sweater and a raincoat.

Overnight hiking may not guarantee solitude, but it should enable you to get away from most people, except on weekends and holidays in the most popular parks. Hikers seeking true wilderness should avoid the best-known national parks and try less-celebrated forests and mountain ranges. Most national parks require overnight hikers to carry backcountry permits, which must be obtained 24 hours in advance and require you to follow a specific itinerary. Always call the visitor center or ranger station before you plan to start an overnight hike.

The Rails-to-Trails Conservancy (W www .railtrails.org/content.html, 1400 16th St NW, Suite 300, Washington, DC 20036) is a nationwide movement to convert abandoned railroad corridors into public biking and hiking trails. Many of the routes have interesting historical features.

All the national parks offer excellent hiking trails. Some of the state parks and national forests are also excellent – check out the Adirondack Forest Preserve in New York State, Allegheny National Forest in Pennsylvania, Monongahela National Forest in West Virginia, Humboldt National Forest in Nevada and Anza-Borrego Desert State Park in California.

Perhaps the best-known hiking trail anywhere is the legendary **Appalachian Trail**, which runs some 2160 miles along Appalachian ridge lines from Maine in the north to Georgia in the south. Constructed and marked during the 1920s and '30s, the trail traverses state and federal lands along 96% of its course. Backpackers and day hikers cover short lengths of the trail by the thousands each year. For information, contact the Appalachian Trail Conference

(☎ 304-535-6331, ⓦ www.atconf.org, PO Box 807, Harpers Ferry, WV 25425). Bill Bryson's *A Walk in the Woods* is an entertaining and very informative account of the author's failure to walk the length of the Appalachian Trail.

Even longer is the **Pacific Crest Trail**, which goes 2640 miles across California, Oregon and Washington, through six state parks, seven national parks, 24 national forests and 33 designated wilderness areas, following the crest of the Sierra Nevada in California and the Cascade Range in Oregon and Washington. For detailed information and advice on wilderness permits, contact the Pacific Crest Trail Association (☎ 888-728-7245, ⓦ www.gorp.com/pcta, 5325 Elkhorn Blvd, Suite 256, Sacramento, CA 95842).

If that's not enough, the 3100-mile **Continental Divide Trail** is planned to run the length of the Rocky Mountains, from Canada to Mexico, though segments totaling nearly 1000 miles are not yet officially designated. For information contact the Continental Divide Trail Alliance (☎ 888-909-2382, ⓦ www.cdtrail.org, PO Box 628, Pine, CO 80470) or CDTS (☎ 410-235-9610, ⓦ www.gorp.com/cdts, 3704 N Charles St, Suite 601, Baltimore, MD 21218).

Bicycling & Mountain Biking

Biking options run from a cross-country marathon to an hour on a beachfront boardwalk. American cities are increasingly bike-friendly, and bicycling can be a great way to get around the sights (see the Getting Around chapter for more on traveling by bike). Rental bikes are widely available, from around $5 per hour, or $10-25 per day. Enthusiasts might be interested in the Pedaling History Bicycle Museum near Buffalo, New York, or the high-tech bicycles at the Technology Museum of Innovation in San Jose, California.

Bikes are often banned from designated wilderness areas and national park trails, but can generally be used on national forest and BLM single-track trails. Trail etiquette requires that cyclists yield to other users.

Many areas are ideal for cycle touring, including the forests of New England, the islands of the Atlantic coast (from Nantucket off Massachusetts to Amelia off Florida), Virginia's Shenandoah Valley,

southern Louisiana, the islands in the Great Lakes, Colorado's Summit County and California's Wine Country and coast. In most of these areas you will be able to rent bikes and equipment once you arrive.

Marin County, near San Francisco, and Crested Butte, Colorado, both claim to be the birthplace of mountain biking, which is now hugely popular across the country. In summer, many ski areas open their trails and chairlifts to mountain bikes. California's Mammoth Mountain, for example, has a mountain bike park, a slalom course and miles of steep dirt. It hosts the annual Kamikaze World Cup Downhill Race in early July.

Helmets should always be worn to reduce the risk of head injury and are a legal requirement in many states. National parks require that all riders under 18 years wear a helmet. A headlight and reflectors are requirements everywhere for riding at night, and reflective and/or bright clothing is a good idea. Carry water and a repair kit with you.

Using a heavy-duty bicycle lock is essential, as bicycle theft is a big business. Some locks, including Citadel and Kryptonite, come with insurance against bicycle theft. Etch your driver's license number or other identification onto the frame of your bike and register it with the police – though this is no guarantee that you'll ever see it again.

Skiing

The skiing season lasts from about mid-December to early April, though in some places you can ski as early as November and as late as May. From overseas, ski packages can be a good value and offer maximum ski time with minimum hassle. Within the USA, many packages offer transport, accommodations and lift tickets. Check the travel pages of major newspapers for special offers. The peak times, roughly Christmas through early February, are more expensive and crowded, and the conditions are no better. Many resorts are close to towns, so it's quite feasible to travel on your own and make a short daily commute to the slopes. Make sure your insurance covers you for winter sports.

Integrated resorts, where one developer owns everything, tend to be more expensive, whereas resorts built near a pre-existing town have more variety in facilities and prices. Equipment rental can be cheaper off the mountain, and discount lift tickets are sometimes sold at local gas stations and supermarkets. Combined lesson and equipment packages might be cheaper on the mountain. At major ski areas, lift tickets cost $40-65 for a full day, but many smaller ski areas have conditions just as good as the big-name resorts and are less expensive (under $30 per day). Children's ski schools include lessons, day-care and lunch from around $40 per child.

Skiing America, by Charles Leocha, has facts and figures about all of the USA and Canada's big ski resorts. *Ski* and *Skiing* are both year-round magazines. *Snow Country* magazine ranks ski areas throughout the USA. Virtually every ski area has a Web site, and state tourist office sites will have links to them.

To assess snow conditions, listen to the weather bureau. Ski industry reports are inclined to describe frozen trails as 'packed powder.'

Downhill Skiing There are ski resorts all over the USA, but the best downhill skiing is in the Rocky Mountains. Moist air from the Pacific Coast is lifted over the Rockies and dumps feet of dry, powdery snow on the western slopes. California also has excellent ski areas, though the snow tends to be heavier – the wet stuff is called 'Sierra cement.' There can be good skiing in the Pacific Northwest and in the traditional ski areas of the Northeast, though conditions are less reliable. Small ski areas in the Appalachians can have good snow but not much vertical, and you can also ski in Alaska. The following areas are considered the best in the country. See the regional chapters for more information about them.

Colorado is the most popular ski destination. Summit County, 80 miles west of Denver, has accessible resorts like Breckenridge, an old mining town known for nightlife, and Arapahoe Basin, where deep snow and a long season attract extreme skiers. Keystone and Copper Mountain are both popular with families. Winter Park is renowned for moguls (bumps) and easy access from Denver on the Ski Train. Vail is the mink-coat ski resort ($62 lift tickets), offering great skiing on a wide variety of terrain. Singles favor Aspen and Telluride, both 19th-century mining towns. Crested Butte is another scenic mining town surrounded by challenging terrain. Snowmass and Tiehack have plenty of beginner and intermediate slopes, while Steamboat Springs gets so much snow it always has a long season.

In Wyoming, Jackson Hole is the largest resort and offers world-class skiing. In Montana, Big Sky is the premier resort, while Idaho's Sun Valley has great powder, steep slopes and celebrity skiers.

Utah, on the western slopes of the Rockies, has some of the best powder skiing. The big Park City resort is the headquarters of the US Ski Team and the site for the 2002 Winter Olympic Games. Snowbird and Alta are also large resorts within commuting distance of Salt Lake City.

In California's Sierra Nevada, the Lake Tahoe area has several great ski areas, including Squaw Valley and Heavenly Valley. Farther south, Mammoth Mountain is another big ski resort and LA party scene.

New England's best skiing is in Vermont, at Killington, Mt Snow, Stratton and Stowe, and in New Hampshire's White Mountains at Waterville Valley. In upstate New York, Whiteface Mountain, near Lake Placid in the Adirondacks, has twice hosted the Winter Olympics.

Cross-Country Skiing Many downhill ski areas also have cross-country trails, and there are many more places for cross-country skiing (often called Nordic skiing). Many city parks and golf courses are given over to ski trails in the northern winters. Hiking trails in national parks and forests become cross-country trails, and there are specialized cross-country ski resorts where it costs $12-17 to use groomed tracks and trails. The truly adventurous can ski backcountry areas, especially where there are hut systems (see below). The Cross-Country Ski Areas Association (☎ 603-239-4341, Ⓦ www.xcski.org, 259 Bolton Rd, Winchester, NH 03460) provides information about all aspects of the sport in North America.

In California, Royal Gorge, near Lake Tahoe, is North America's largest cross-country ski resort and a mecca for enthusiasts. Yosemite and Kings Canyon National Parks offer superb, challenging ski touring.

In the East, there are wonderful cross-country skiing possibilities in the New England forests going from village to village or inn to inn. North Conway, New Hampshire, and Stowe, Vermont, have elaborate systems of well-groomed cross-country trails. New York's Finger Lakes region provides scenic cross-country touring, while Pennsylvania has the Allegheny National Forest and the Laurel Highlands.

The Great Lakes states of Wisconsin and Michigan have cross-country ski areas, while Minnesota's Grand Marais is noted for backcountry ski touring.

In the Rocky Mountains, there are some hut systems for backcountry touring. Huts are about 15 miles apart and provide beds, stoves and fireside camaraderie. Contact the Colorado Cross Country Ski Association (W www.coloado-xc.org, PO Box 8937 Keystone, CO 80435) for maps and guides to several cross-country ski centers in Rocky Mountain National Park, Mesa Verde National Park and Black Canyon of the Gunnison National Monument. The Grand Tetons, near Jackson, Wyoming, and Yellowstone National Park also provide excellent backcountry access.

Snowboarding

Boards are permitted at nearly all ski areas, and many mountains have half-pipes, snowboard lessons and rental equipment. Snowboarders who love powder snow and hate ice should head for the downhill resorts in the Rockies and avoid the Northeast. There's also serious shredding in fad-mad California and the grunge capital of Washington State. Check W www.snowboard.com for all sorts of snowboarding stuff.

Mountaineering

Rock climbing and mountaineering are especially popular pursuits in the Sierra Nevada and Rockies. El Capitan and Half Dome are both legendary climbs up the face of sheer granite walls in Yosemite National Park. Mt Whitney, in California's Sequoia and Kings Canyon National Parks, is the highest in the contiguous 48 states at 14,500 feet, and has a mountaineers' route that is both fun and challenging. With its high mountains, extreme weather and remote location, Alaska has the most challenging mountaineering possibilities.

Surfing

Invented by Pacific Islanders, made popular by Duke Kahanamoku in Hawaii in the 1920s, and brought to California in 1951, surfing is still a serious obsession in both places. *Surfer* magazine's travel reports (formerly the *Surf Report*) cover just about every inch of the US coastline. You can order copies by phone (☎ 949-661-5147) or on the net (W www.surfermag.com/travel).

Hawaii has good surfing throughout the year. The very biggest waves hit from November to February along the north shores of the islands. Summer swells, which break along the south shores, are usually not as frequent and nowhere near as large. Oahu's north shore has the legendary breaks of Waimea, Sunset Beach and the Banzai Pipeline. Competition for the main breaks is intense, and visitors should be aware that local Hawaiian surfers can be very territorial. Look for smaller, lesser-known breaks that are well within your capabilities, and show respect. Waikiki has the best south shore surf on Oahu. Maui and Kauai islands also have some excellent surfing spots.

In California, the 'big three' surf spots are Rincon, Malibu and Trestles, all of them point breaks and all very crowded. Huntington Beach, site of the state's biggest pro surfing contest (in June/July), is a popular left and right beach break. Farther south, San Clemente and San Diego's Blacks Beach are good. Northern California has its own surf scene, with colder water and bigger waves. The Santa Cruz coast is good, while Mavericks, near Half Moon Bay, is legendary for big waves. Learners should go for beach breaks like San Onofre and San Diego's Tourmaline.

Surfboard rentals cost around $10 per hour and lessons, which are much less common, cost about $20. Boogie boards are popular, but not in the serious surf, while soft Morey Doyle boards are good for beginners.

Crowding is a problem, especially on fine weekends. Any place with a parking lot facing the surf will be crowded, but breaks that require a long walk or paddle will be better. There's a possessive local scene at many places, notably Oxnard and San Diego's Windansea. Hook up with a local surfer for an introduction. International visitors may be less unwelcome because they won't be around every weekend. You'll need a car to chase the surf, and you can pick up information from many surf shops.

There's surf potential all the way up the Pacific coast, but it's cold and frequently closed out by huge swells. The Atlantic coast has surf too, but it's unreliable. You have to be lucky to get a good day. Cape Hatteras, North Carolina, may be the best bet.

Windsurfing

If you have your own equipment, you can windsurf on lakes and coasts throughout the country. There are many windsurfing shops, but few places rent windsurfing equipment outside resorts. Beaches in Hawaii and southern California are the most popular windsurfing areas because of the mild weather, but many places have excellent wind and water conditions. The Columbia Gorge in Oregon, near the town of Hood River, and Canadian Hole, in North Carolina's Outer Banks, are both noted windsurfing scenes.

Canoeing, Kayaking & Rafting

The best rivers for white-water canoeing and rafting are in the Appalachians, Rocky Mountains and Sierra Nevada. Commercial trips range from short, inexpensive morning or afternoon trips to three- or four-day expeditions. 'Tubing' in old inner tubes is popular on smaller streams. Outfitters using rivers in publicly managed parks and forests operate with permits from the appropriate agency. Individuals and groups with their own or rented equipment sometimes also need a permit.

Lakes throughout the Northeast and the Great Lakes states are ideal for summer canoeing. Canoes are also great for exploring the wetland areas of Georgia, Louisiana and Florida. Sea kayaking is excellent in the Pacific Northwest, the Maine coast

and Alaska's Inside Passage. Canoe rentals are widely available at popular paddling places.

Rivers and rapids are ranked on the international six-point scale:

Class I (easy) – very small rapids, safe for beginners

Class II (medium) – larger waves, easy chutes, ledges and falls, possible in open canoes; best route is easy to identify, and no great skill or maneuvering is required

Class III (difficult) – high, irregular waves and difficult chutes and falls, not suitable for open canoes; requires some skill to identify the best route and some maneuvering in rapids

Class IV (very difficult) – long stretches of high, irregular waves, powerful back eddies, 3- to 5-foot drops, and constricted spaces; requires inspection before shooting and considerable skill to identify the best route and to maneuver in rapids

Class V (extremely difficult) – continuous violent rapids, large drops, powerful rollers and high, unavoidable waves and haystacks; requires hard paddling, very skillful maneuvering in heavy water and proficiency in the Eskimo roll

Class VI (highest level of difficulty) – only for the most skilled paddlers, involving a definite risk to life

The American Whitewater Affiliation (☎ 866-262-8429, W www.americanwhitewater.org, 1430 Fenwick Lane, Silver Spring, MD 20910) is a national organization that promotes white-water activities. Another good source of information is the American Canoe Association (☎ 703-451-0141, W www.aca-paddler.org, 7432 Alban Station Blvd, Suite B226, Springfield, VA 22150), which publishes *Paddler* magazine.

Caving

Experienced spelunkers can explore caves in several areas, and a number of caves are open to the casual visitor for guided interpretive tours. Mammoth Cave, Kentucky, a national park, is one of the world's largest cave systems, with 335 miles of passages. Carlsbad Caverns National Park in New Mexico and Lehman Caves in Nevada's Great Basin National Park are other accessible underground highlights.

For general information, enthusiasts can get in touch with the National Speleological Society (☎ 256-852-1300, W www.caves.org, 2831 Cave Ave, Huntsville, AL 35810). Subterranean ecosystems are very delicate, and cavers should avoid contact with sensitive formations and not disturb bats or other animals.

Horseback Riding

Horses have a big place in American history and mythology, and equestrian activities are hugely popular, from Anglophile hunt clubs in the East to the contemporary cowboys out West. The heart of American horse country is in between, in the states of Kentucky and Tennessee, home of Thoroughbreds and quarter horses. Recreational riding is quite expensive, from around $15 per hour or $25 for two hours. Full-day trips can cost from around $75 with a guide.

For the cowboy experience, many guest ranch (or dude ranch) vacations include unlimited use of horses. Guided backcountry pack trips cost upward of $100 per person, per day.

Diving & Snorkeling

Diving is done all over the states, even in the Great Lakes, but the best locations are Florida, southern California and Hawaii. For detailed information about diving in these areas, see the appropriate edition of Lonely Planet's Pisces diving & snorkeling guide series (see 'Lonely Planet US Guides' near Books, earlier). Experienced divers go for the Carolina coast, where there's unlimited wreck diving in the 'Graveyard of the Atlantic.'

If you want to try diving for the first time, some dive operations offer a short beginner's course that includes a brief instruction, followed by a shallow beach or boat dive. The cost ranges from $60-90, depending upon the operation and whether a boat is used.

To dive with an operator, or to have tanks filled, the minimum qualification required is an open-water certificate from PADI, NAUI or another recognized organization like BSAC. An open-water certificate course will cost from $300-400, equipment included, and take three days to a week.

COURSES

Education is a huge industry in the USA, and foreigners can enroll in many regular colleges and universities, adult and general courses, and language-teaching institutions.

In most cases, tuition will be quite expensive, and living costs will be extra, though an F1 student visa does permit part-time and vacation work. Students at private colleges can apply to their institution for limited financial aid.

Applications must be made directly to the institution, and for most universities you should start inquiries at least 18 months ahead of your expected enrollment. You need to be admitted by the institution *before* you apply for a student visa.

Sources of information include the US Information Services at American embassies, the Institute of International Education (IIE; ☎ 212-984-5413, ⓦ www.iie.org, 809 United Nations Plaza, New York, NY 10017-3580) and some state tourist offices. Many overseas institutions have exchange programs with American colleges, which will simplify the arrangements.

If you're not a native English speaker, an English test may be a prerequisite for college/university admission, and many institutions offer preparatory English as a Foreign Language (EFL) classes. Many other colleges, adult education centers and language schools provide English classes, too. For more information, contact IIE (see above); TOEFL/TSE (☎ 609-951-1100, ⓦ www.toefl.org, PO Box 6151, Princeton, NJ 08541); or World Learning Inc (☎ 802-257-7751, ⓦ www.worldlearning.org, PO Box 676, Brattleboro, VT 05302).

Adult and general courses, including hobby and cultural courses as well as technical and further education, are mainly for locals. Generally, entry to these courses will not entitle you to a student visa.

WORK

If you are a foreigner in the USA with a standard nonimmigrant visitors visa, you are expressly forbidden to take paid work in the USA and will probably be deported if you're caught working illegally. Legislation passed in the 1980s makes it an offense to employ an illegal worker, so there is a requirement on employers to establish the bona fides of their employees. Thus, it's much tougher for a foreigner to get work than it used to be.

For foreigners to work legally, they need to apply for a work visa before leaving home, and they aren't easy to get. A J1 visa, for exchange visitors, is issued to young people (age limits vary) for study, student vacation employment, work in summer camps, and short-term traineeships with a specific employer. The following organizations will help arrange student exchanges, placements and J1 visas:

American Institute for Foreign Study (AIFS; Ⓦ www.aifs.com)

BUNAC (☎ 020-7251-3472, Ⓦ www.bunac.org, 16 Bowling Green Lane, London EC1R 0QH)

Camp America (☎ 020-7581-7377, Ⓦ www.campamerica.co.uk, 37A Queens Gate, London SW7 5HR)

Council on International Educational Exchange (CIEE; Ⓦ www.ciee.org)

International Exchange Programs (IEP) Australia: (☎ 1300-300-912, Ⓦ www.iep-australia.com, 196 Albert Road, South Melbourne, Vic 3205; Level 2, 333 George St, Sydney, NSW 2000). New Zealand: (☎ 09-366-6255, Ⓦ www.iepnz.co.nz, PO Box 1786, Shortland Street, Auckland)

For non-student jobs, temporary or permanent, you need to be sponsored by a US employer who will have to arrange one of the various H-category visas. These are not easy to obtain, since the employer has to prove that no US citizen or permanent resident is available to do the job. Seasonal work is possible in national parks, tourist sites and especially ski areas. Contact park concessionaires, local chambers of commerce and ski-resort management. Many menial jobs, like cleaning, fruit picking and dishwashing, are done by immigrant workers (legal and otherwise) from Latin America, and offer extremely poor pay and conditions.

ACCOMMODATIONS

For budget travelers, finding inexpensive accommodations can be a major problem, so this book has comprehensive coverage of hostels and other backpacker lodgings. At least one campground is suggested near most towns, but these can be closed in colder months (it's a good idea to call first). Inexpensive motels are plentiful around the highway exits on the outskirts of cities. The text gives details for some of the cheapest and best-value choices, but there are usually plenty of others of a similar standard and price. Top-end hotels are easy to find, and

only a few are included in this book, usually hotels of some historical or architectural significance.

Prices are given for most accommodations, but they are a general, indicative guide only, based on a standard room with single/double occupancy during high season, unless otherwise stated. Prices might be even higher during local special events (eg, in New Orleans during Mardi Gras), at times of exceptionally high demand (eg, in college towns at graduation time), or on the busiest holiday weekends. On the other hand, prices might be lower than those listed, especially outside holiday seasons or at other times of low demand (eg, on weekends at many downtown hotels). Discount coupons, an AAA discount or a little polite haggling may also get you a room for less than the price quoted here (especially for extended stays). Prices do not include tax, which can add anything up to 15% to a hotel bill.

Special events and conventions can fill up a town's hotels and campsites quickly, so you may want to call the tourist office to find out if you will be arriving at a busy time. Many of the cheaper places may not accept reservations, but you can at least phone ahead to see what's available; even if they don't take reservations they'll often hold a room for an hour or two. Outside of holiday times and local events, a reservation is usually unnecessary as most areas have plenty of rooms. In fact it might be better to wait until you can see for yourself what's available.

Camping

Visitors can camp on some public lands or use one of the thousands of public and private campgrounds. Campsites in this book are described as primitive (no facilities at all), basic (water and toilets available) or developed (with showers, shop, laundry etc).

Public Lands Most national forests, state and national parks and BLM lands have at least basic campgrounds, and 'dispersed' camping is usually permitted in the backcountry. Information is available from ranger stations or BLM offices, and regulations are generally posted on access roads. Sometimes a camping permit is required. In other places you can stop anywhere along a dirt road and camp near your car, especially in BLM and national forest areas, but obviously there will be no facilities.

For camping outside designated campgrounds, choose a tent site and wash place at least 200 feet (70 steps) away from the nearest lake, river or stream. Bury human waste at least 6 inches deep, and cover and camouflage it well when finished. Carry out all trash. Use a portable grill or camping stove rather than making a fire. If it's permitted, and you do make a fire, it is better to use an existing fire ring than to blacken a new area. Use only dead and downed wood or wood you have carried in yourself. Extinguish the fire completely and leave the campsite as you found it.

Basic campsites usually have toilets, fire pits, picnic benches and drinking water (but it's always a good idea to have a few gallons of water with you). In national forests or BLM areas, these will typically cost about $5-15 a night. Many are occupied on a first-come, first-served basis. Arrive early, especially on weekends.

More developed public campgrounds, typically in national or state parks, have more facilities, hot showers, and somewhat higher prices. Some have RV hookups and cost even more. Public campgrounds often have seven- or 14-night limits and may accept or require reservations. They usually allow up to six people and two vehicles per site.

Campsites at many national parks can be booked over the phone (☎ 800-365-2267, 301-722-1257 outside the USA) or online at Ⓦ reservations.nps.gov. For reservations at other national parks, call the park itself (see the numbers in this book) or go through the NPS Web site (Ⓦ www.nps.gov). You can reserve a park campsite up to five months prior to your visit.

The National Forest Service also has a reservation system (☎ 877-444-6777, 518-885-3639 outside the USA; Ⓦ reserveusa.com) allowing visitors to make camping reservations up to four months in advance. The cost is $10 per reservation.

Private Campgrounds These are usually close to a town or recreational area and are often designed mainly for RVs. Many are horrid and look like paved parking lots, but some are delightful and have grassy, shaded sites for tents. Tent sites run from around $15 for two people, plus $1-3 for each extra person, plus taxes. RV sites with electricity and water hookups usually cost around $15-25, but $30-40 is possible at peak times in popular locations. Facilities include hot showers, coin laundry and often a swimming pool, games area, playground and convenience store.

Kampgrounds of America (KOA) is a national network of private campgrounds, offering sites from $22 for tents to around $30 with hookups. Get the free annual directory from KOA (☎ 406-248-7444, Ⓦ koa.com, PO Box 30558, Billings, MT 59114).

Camping Cabins Some campgrounds have basic cabins, typically with screened windows and camp cots for four to eight people. 'Tent cabins' usually have a wooden floor, basic furnishings, and canvas roof and walls. Cabins cost from around $25 per night to well over $100, depending on location, size, comfort and season. Some excellent ones in state and national parks are booked months in advance. For a small group, they can be quite economical.

Hostels

The USA has both HI affiliated and independent hostels. Most are included in this book, and you can also get information about them on Ⓦ www.hostels.com. *The Hostel Handbook* has a comprehensive list of hostels; it's sold at many hostels ($4), or on the net (Ⓦ www.hostelhandbook.com).

HI-AYH About 150 hostels are affiliated with Hostelling International-American Youth Hostels (HI-AYH). They are scattered thinly across the country. The Northeast, Colorado and the West Coast have the most facilities, while many states have no hostel at all. Some are only open during the tourist season.

Prices for a dormitory bed vary greatly, from $10 in rural areas to $29 in New York City, plus $3 for nonmembers. Some have private rooms, from $25-30 for two up to $75 for a family ($140 in New York!). If you have to rent linen, they charge a few dollars more. Strictly, you must have a sheet sleeping bag, but many hostels accept use of a regular sleeping bag if they're convinced it doesn't harbor bugs. Dormitories are segregated by sex.

Some hostels have a curfew (around 10pm), most prohibit alcohol, and some require you to do a small housekeeping chore. Most also have kitchen and laundry facilities, information and advertising boards, a TV room and lounge area.

Some 'home hostels' have just a few beds in a private house and are not always available – call first. Other hostels are set up in university dormitories during the summer vacation and are only open for a couple of months.

Reservations are accepted and advised during the high season, when there may be a maximum stay of three nights. Get further information from HI-AYH (☎ 202-783-6161; ⓦ www.hiayh.org, 733 15th St NW, Suite 840, Washington, DC 20005). Reservations at some 60 hostels can be made through the central booking service (☎ 800-909-4776; you need the access code for the hostels to use this service, available from any HI-AYH office or listed in their handbook). For other hostels, call the number in this book.

Independent Hostels There is also a growing number of independent hostels, sometimes called backpackers hostels, offering inexpensive dormitory accommodations for low-budget, mostly young travelers. Most are in cities or near areas of interest to travelers, and many organize parties, local excursions and longer trips. Prices are similar to HI-AYH hostels ($12-30, depending on location), but they don't have curfews, housekeeping chores or petty restrictions. Standards are variable – the best ones are excellent, the worst are dives with overcrowded rooms and low standards of cleanliness. Dorms are often mixed, male and female (coed). Some hostels have a few private single/double rooms.

University Accommodations

During vacations, some universities and colleges offer accommodations in student dormitories. This generally seems to be a service for those doing summer courses on campus, and is not usually a popular option for independent travelers. Dorm accommodations are not well publicized, services are minimal, booking conditions can be restrictive (often with minimum stay requirements), campuses are often located away from areas of visitor interest and they are not very lively places during vacations.

YMCAs & YWCAs

Most cities have a 'Y' in or near downtown, sometimes in a less than pleasant neighborhood. Some are strictly exercise and recreation facilities, but many provide inexpensive accommodations for men and women. A single room with shared bath costs around $20-30 per night. Often it will be much cheaper by the week, as many YMCAs are oriented toward temporary residents rather than travelers in transit. They vary a lot in quality, with some being pretty seedy and others very good. Most have the bonus of a gym and/or swimming pool. YWCAs are much less common and are mostly for women only, though a few take couples.

B&Bs

In the USA, B&Bs are for people who want a comfortable, atmospheric alternative to impersonal motel rooms. Typically they are in restored old houses with floral wallpaper, antique or country-style furnishings and a cute, cozy ambience. They appeal more to romantic weekenders than budget travelers. In New England, inns are generally similar to B&Bs, though some are quite large.

Most B&Bs are in the $50-100 price range, some are way over $100, and very few are under $50. The cheapest places have plainer rooms and shared bathrooms, but they're still clean. Pricier places offer private bathrooms and feature fireplaces, balconies and private gardens. They should all have a substantial breakfast included in the price, but sometimes it's a self-serve continental.

B&B owners prefer advance reservations, though some will be happy to oblige the occasional drop-in. Many towns have a central agency listing approved B&Bs and handling bookings. Several specialist guidebooks list and evaluate B&Bs. Look for *Bed & Breakfast USA,* the *Complete Guide to American Bed & Breakfasts* or guides concentrating on the areas you fancy.

Motels & Hotels

Hotels differ from motels in that they do not surround a parking lot and usually have some sort of a lobby. Hotels may offer extra services such as laundry, but these can be very expensive. Long-distance phone calls can also be very expensive.

Prices vary tremendously from season to season. A hotel charging $80 for a double in high season may drop to $40 in the off-season or raise its rates to over $150 for a special event when the town is overflowing. Advertised prices (or 'rack rates') can be negotiable. Simply asking about any 'specials' can often save money. Booking through a travel agent can be cheaper, and retired people, students, AAA members and business travelers may get a discount, special or 'corporate' rate. You can often get a cheaper rate for a stay of several days, but you may have to pay it all in advance.

Many tourist publications, brochures, books and flyers have discount coupons for hotels and motels. Highway Welcome Centers and even gas stations will often stock a cheap-looking newsprint booklet offering excellent discounts on motels near the interstates. The best coupon deals can reduce a $55 room to $30. However, most discounts are unavailable at peak times.

Budget The cheapest motels, with rates as low as $25, are found in small towns along major highways and along motel strips on the outskirts of larger towns. These places are usually small, independent (ie, nonchain) establishments, often called 'mom-and-pop' motels. Some towns are unaccountably more expensive than others. The cheapest motel in one town might be $25, while 50 miles down the highway you can't get a room of the same standard for under $40.

Rooms are usually small, and beds may be soft or saggy, but the sheets should be clean. A minimal level of cleanliness is maintained, but expect scuffed walls, atrocious decor, old furniture and strange plumbing noises. Even the cheapest places normally have a private shower, toilet and a TV in each room, plus air-con and heating. Some motel rooms have 'kitchenettes,' which may be just a small burner, fridge and sink, but you can still make coffee and snacks. If you're particular about views, noise, pets, disabled access etc, call first.

Budget motels are very standardized, so don't expect detailed descriptions in the text. In many motel strips, competition is intense, and the cheapest rates are advertised on street signs. Ten minutes' cruising up and down will give you a good idea what's available.

When motels first appeared in the 1920s, many communities condemned them as locations for vice and immorality. Undoubtedly motels are used for a variety of purposes, but very few rent rooms by the hour. Those that do are noisy at best, dangerous at worst.

Downtown hotels tend to be either very expensive or very seedy, without much in between. Old hotels often double as transient rooming houses. They may be near the train and bus stations, often in less-than-desirable parts of town. The cheapest of them will have shared bath and toilet facilities and no car parking. In dubious places, insist on seeing the room before you take it. Even the worst dives may overcharge. Don't pay more than $30 for a scummy-looking hotel just because it's near the train station.

Chains Chain motels usually fall in the mid-range price category and maintain a consistent level of quality and style across the country, though prices can vary for identical rooms in different cities. The cheapest national chain is Motel 6, with rates as low as $30 for a single in smaller towns, but more commonly around $40-50, plus an extra $6 for each additional person. Most have a small pool, and rooms have cable TV and a phone. They are a pretty good value and a useful index of local prices. If the Motel 6 costs $35, there won't be anything decent under about $30. If the Motel 6 costs $55, then everything in town will be expensive.

Better motel chains will run from $40 in smaller towns to over $55 in larger or more popular places. The main difference is the size of the room and the extras: firmer beds, pictures on the walls, possibly a light breakfast. If these sorts of thing are worth an extra $10 or $15 a night to you, then you'll be happy with the Super 8 Motels, Days Inns and Econo Lodges.

Paying more ($50-90) will get you a noticeably nicer room, an on-site restaurant and/or bar, and perhaps an indoor swimming pool, spa or exercise room. The Best Western chain offers good rooms in this price range. Less widespread but also good are Comfort Inns and Sleep Inns.

Chain motels will all take reservations days or months ahead. Normally, you have to give a credit-card number to hold the room. If you don't show and don't call to cancel, you will be charged for the first night's rental. Cancellation policies vary, so find out when you book. Let them know if you plan to arrive late. Many motels will give your room away if you haven't arrived or called by 6pm. Chains have toll-free numbers, but their central reservation systems might not give you any special local discount price and won't know details about the rooms or facilities. For reservations, call the following:

Best Western	☎ 800-528-1234
Budget Host	☎ 800-283-4678
Comfort Inn	☎ 800-221-2222
Days Inn	☎ 800-329-7466
Econo Lodge	☎ 800-553-2666
Fairfield Inn	☎ 800-228-2800
Holiday Inn	☎ 800-465-4329
Howard Johnson	☎ 800-446-4656
Motel 6	☎ 800-466-8356
Quality Inn	☎ 800-228-5151
Red Roof Inn	☎ 800-843-7663
Rodeway Inn	☎ 800-424-4777
Sleep Inn	☎ 800-753-3746
Super 8 Motel	☎ 800-800-8000
Travelodge	☎ 800-578-7878

Some of the better hotel chains have in-house restaurants, bars, swimming pools, fitness centers, business centers and room service. Most offer central 24-hour reservation numbers (shown here). Prices at these places start at $100-150 per night for a double room, or even more in expensive cities like New York.

Hilton	☎ 800-445-8667
Hyatt	☎ 800-233-1234
Marriott	☎ 800-228-9290
Radisson	☎ 800-333-3333
Ramada	☎ 800-272-6232
Sheraton	☎ 800-325-3535
Westin	☎ 800-228-3000

Resorts & Lodges

Luxury resorts offer so many activities that often they are destinations in themselves.

They are very expensive, and only a few are mentioned in the text.

Ski resorts usually have a central reservations hotline to fill their full range of accommodations, from motel rooms to condos. They might charge up to $200 or so per night/per bed in midwinter and drop prices to less than half that in the snowless summer.

Lodges in attractive scenic areas typically affect a rusticated style (lots of logs and stonework) but are usually very comfortable inside. They often have restaurants and excellent services, but can be very expensive. In national parks, the only accommodations other than camping are park lodges. These are usually operated as a concession and are quite comfortable, but overpriced for the quality they offer – over $100 for a double during the high season, when you need to make a reservation months in advance.

FOOD

If you stick to the cheaper dishes at bars, grills and diners, the food is inexpensive, filling, fattening and somewhat monotonous. Americanized 'international' restaurants, Italian, Mexican or Asian, are good for variety, no more expensive and no less fattening.

This book includes a selection of places that are conveniently located, reasonably priced, well established and more interesting than the standard greasy spoon, fast-food franchise, pizza shop or Chinese takeout. Some are included because they're good places to try a local or regional specialty, others because they're open 24 hours or because they offer vegetarian dishes. Many are in areas with a big selection of restaurants, where you'll find plenty of excellent options apart from the ones listed here. Expensive, top-end restaurants are only suggested if they are really distinctive places where a visitor might want to splurge on a big night out. Phone numbers are included only for places where you should make a reservation.

You can save a lot by putting your own meals together. The ubiquitous supermarkets, commonly open 24 hours, have about the lowest food prices and a wide selection of meat, fruit and vegetables. They often have self-serve areas with ready-to-eat salads, pastas and baked goods. Farmer's markets offer even cheaper fruits and vegetables. Delis and health-food stores sell food by the pound and have premade foods like sandwiches, burritos and smoothies. You could easily get ingredients to make two meals for two people for around $10. With an inexpensive car cooler and some ice, anyone can be self-sufficient for breakfasts and picnic lunches.

Eating Out

Americans love eating out, for every meal of the day, and the earlier in the day you start, the better value you get. While the majority of restaurants offer à la carte dishes, some offer fixed-price meals of three or four courses. Others specialize in the all-you-can-eat buffet, which is a boon to a starving traveler, though it's more like feeding than dining. Buffet meals are a casino special – the best bet by far in Las Vegas.

When looking at menus, remember to add about 25% to advertised prices. Food and beverage taxes run up to about 10%, and you should tip about 15% to 20% unless the service is awful. A smaller tip is OK if you eat and eat at a counter, and no tip is expected in fast-food places. Some food items may be taxed if you eat them in a restaurant, but are tax-free if you take them away to eat.

Breakfast Big breakfasts are an affordable way to fill yourself up, provided you can stomach large quantities of greasy food before noon. A breakfast of pancakes, eggs and sausage or a hearty omelette costs around $5 and usually includes home fries (sliced potatoes fried with spices) or hash browns (shredded potatoes, often mixed

with onion and fried to a golden brown), toast and lots of coffee. You get a choice of how your eggs are cooked – scrambled, sunny-side up, over easy (flipped, but with a runny yolk) or over hard (flipped with a hard yolk). Typically the good-value breakfast special is served from about 6-11am. Some popular spots serve breakfast all day long. On weekends, many restaurants serve an all-you-can-eat brunch menu, featuring a mixture of breakfast and lunch dishes, from about 9am until 2pm.

Lunch Usually served from 11:30am to 2pm, lunch is often the best-value meal. Prices may be one-third less than the dinner menu, though the food and portions are identical. For a bustling, energetic lunch scene, head to the business district of any city, where the number of suit-clad businesspeople is an indication of the best or cheapest places to eat.

Dinner In large cities, many restaurants offer 'early-bird specials' that feature a complete meal (usually the menu is limited) for around $5 between 4pm and 6pm. Spending a few dollars on drinks during 'happy hour' (usually between 4pm and 7pm) will often get you free appetizers, which can be anything from a bowl of peanuts to a hot buffet; sports bars and bars in large hotel chains have the best deals. People tend to eat early, and many restaurants are closed or deserted by 10pm.

Vegetarian

If you're a vegetarian or just want to avoid a lot of red meat, you won't have too much trouble finding alternatives. Most restaurants are very service-oriented and will try hard to give customers what they want. Most restaurants will offer vegetarian choices, and in bigger cities and college towns you'll find vegetarian restaurants.

In any restaurant, salads are a standard offering, and are often big enough to be a complete meal. At roadside diners, you might be eating a lot of eggs or grilled-cheese sandwiches. Fast-food restaurants with fixed menus can be difficult, though some (like Wendy's) have all-you-can-eat salad bars. Mexican food and pizzas can usually be had in vegetarian variants. Soul food and Southern restaurants often serve

The All-American Meal

Standard American fare is served everywhere, at diners, cafeterias, bars, grills and inexpensive restaurants, for both lunch and 'supper' (dinner). The typical meal has all the ingredients of a healthy diet, but often in quantities way in excess of what a healthy person needs. Food is frequently flavored with salt and seasoning, served with sauce and deep fried in oil or fat.

Salad is usually served first, with a choice of dressings – French, Italian, Thousand Island, blue cheese, ranch etc. There's also soup, or 'starters' (also called appetizers), like fried potato skins with cheese, barbecued chicken wings or garlic bread. This will be enough for many people, and it's quite OK to order salad and/or an appetizer and nothing else.

An entrée is a main dish in the USA, and it's often one of a dozen variants on the hamburger or the sandwich. Common ways to customize your burger or sandwich include melted cheese (to make a cheeseburger); different types of bread (rye, whole wheat, sourdough); and various other vegetables (onion, mushroom, etc) as toppings. One of the most popular sandwiches is the BLT (bacon, lettuce and tomato). Other common entrées include a half-chicken, usually barbecued and served with barbecue sauce; pork ribs, also with barbecue sauce; fish, served with tartar sauce; steak, chicken or pork chops, served with gravy; and roast beef, turkey or pork, served with gravy and/or sauce. Usually the entrée will come with a pile of french-fried potatoes, but you can also have your potato baked, whipped (ie, mashed) or made into hash browns (grated and fried).

Then there's dessert. Try fudge cake, cheesecake, carrot cake, key lime pie, peach pie, apple pie, mud pie or death by chocolate. If you want it with ice cream, ask for it 'à la mode.' If you want the ice cream without the pie, try a sundae or a banana split. Don't expect homemade. Desserts are a profitable item if they can be delivered by truck, stored for months and served in seconds. They taste good, though.

Coffee comes regular or decaf. It's usually good, and the 'bottomless cup' means free refills. But you can't linger over it. As soon as you stop asking for refills, the server asks if there's anything else you want, and this is your cue to leave the table to the next customer. American restaurants rely on rapid turnover, and their staff rely on tips – the more customers, the more money. If you can't finish your dinner, ask for a take-out box or doggie bag for the leftovers.

a vegetable platter, but the vegetables may be cooked with pork fat. Strict vegetarians might have difficulty making sure that no animal products have been used in cooking.

Regional Specialties

Regional foods reflect local cultures and local ingredients. New England is known for seafoods like clam chowder and lobster; the Pennsylvania Dutch serve hearty family-style meals; Scandinavian 'fish boils' are a specialty around the Great Lakes; and Texans like a big steak. New American cuisine means the old 'comfort food' with a gourmet twist – chicken pot pie with organic seasonal vegetables, garlic mashed potatoes and shiitake mushroom gravy.

The Deep South has no less than four culinary styles – Cajun, Creole, Southern and soul. When California cuisine became fashionable, the tiny servings, high prices and arty presentation probably said something about 1980s obsessions with health, wealth and appearances. These days it's more about balance – the same healthy cooking, fresh ingredients and creative combinations, but more substance and better value. Pacific Rim cuisine features fresh seafood and a marked Asian influence.

Fast-Food Chains

Not particularly exciting or healthy, fast-food chains are cheap, reliable stand-bys for just about any meal and will usually have clean bathrooms. The decor is often hideous, to encourage fast eating and no lingering. The big names are all over the country, but other chains have a strong presence in just one region, while others have only a few outlets in their hometown. Generally, fast-food chains are not mentioned in this book, but you will rarely have trouble finding one.

For hamburgers, the choices include McDonald's, Burger King and Wendy's. Jack in the Box (mostly in the Western states) has tacos and burritos as well as burgers, while Dairy Queen is best known for ice cream. Taco Bell serves really cheap and perfectly edible quasi-Mexican food, though its outlets often lack a place to sit indoors. Pizza Hut and Round Table are the most common pizza places, and require a little more time and money than other fast foodstuffs. KFC is the most widespread fried-chicken chain. 'Family restaurants,' like Sizzler or Denny's, often have big servings of good quality but unspectacular food.

International Cuisine

Even small towns can have a Mexican restaurant, a Chinese restaurant and a pizza place (though pizza is commonly regarded as an American invention). Other offerings depend on where you are. Italian and Greek are common in northern cities, less so Polish and German. French (or 'continental') restaurants are usually expensive and mostly in big cities. There's more Asian food on the West Coast, where Japanese, Vietnamese, Thai and Indian are widely served. Korean and Indonesian restaurants are less common. Cuban cooking is easy to find in Florida.

Some traditions go back a long way, so you still find Basque food in Nevada and Portuguese food in New England. Other trends are much more recent, especially in the fashion-conscious cities, which can have sudden fads for sushi, Szechwan or Spanish tapas.

As you travel farther south, Mexican restaurants become better and more common. For the real thing, find a place with red-vinyl booths, Mexican music blaring on the radio and fake flowers hung on the wall. Here you will get authentic enchiladas (chicken, beef or cheese wrapped in corn tortillas and covered with red or green sauce and cheese), tacos (fried or soft corn tortillas filled with beef or chicken, cheese, lettuce and sauce), tamales (cornmeal patties stuffed with chicken or pork and wrapped in corn husks) and *huevos rancheros* (corn tortillas topped with fried eggs and red ranchero sauce), all accompanied by chips, salsa, rice and beans. Not for the calorie conscious, most Mexican food contains substantial amounts of cheese and lard. The milder Mexican food from the Taco Bell chain may be better for the faint of stomach.

Tex-Mex food features more beef, beans and wheat-flour tortillas. A burrito is a flour tortilla filled with beans, rice and meat or vegetables. New Mexican food (ie, from New Mexico) can include blue corn tortillas, whole beans (not refried) and chilies served as a vegetable, as in *chiles rellenos* (stuffed chilies). Southwestern food used to be like Tex-Mex – Mexican but with more steak. Nouvelle Southwestern, or Santa Fe–style food, has elements of Mexican, Californian and continental cuisine, which means fresh ingredients, imaginative combinations, tasteful presentation, smaller servings and higher prices.

DRINKS
Nonalcoholic

Tap water is fine to drink (though it can smell of chlorine), but trendy tipplers go for designer brands and imports like Vittel and Evian. For fizz without a fancy name, ask for club soda (ie, soda water) or a local mineral water.

All the usual soft drinks are available, but you may be asked if you'll drink Coke instead of Pepsi and vice versa. 'Lemonade' is a mixture of lemon, sugar and ice water. If you want the clear, fizzy stuff that the British call lemonade, ask for Sprite or 7-Up. Some US soft drinks may be unfamiliar – Dr Pepper is some sort of sarsaparilla; Mountain Dew is a yellow liquid very high in sugar and caffeine.

Many restaurants offer milk, including low-fat varieties. You can often get fresh-squeezed orange juice at better restaurants, but packaged juices are more common.

Coffee is served with a choice of regular or 'decaf' (decaffeinated). If you ask for milk or cream, expect 'non-dairy whitener' that has no relationship to a cow. In most cities and even some small towns, there's a wide choice of coffee drinks, from a single shot of espresso to a double decaf latte or a mocha made with soy milk. Even gas stations in Idaho now serve espresso drinks.

Tea is much less commonly offered – usually as a cup of hot water with a tea bag next to it. Milk is not normally added, but a slice of lemon often is. Iced tea, with sugar and lemon, is available in cans as a soft drink.

Alcoholic

If your identification says you're over 21 and you're not in a dry county, you can enjoy some of the best and cheapest booze in the world. Even in dry counties, some restaurants let you bring your own wine or beer.

Beer The big name brands of domestic beer are available everywhere, though many find them lacking in taste. To order beer, you must specify the type you want. If you just ask for a beer, you will get a rapid-fire list of every brand on the market.

Microbreweries, or brew pubs, offer beers brewed on the premises, and you can get a dozen different types on tap. Supermarkets and big liquor stores can stock a bewildering variety of imported beers, which are more expensive but may be more to your taste.

Beer sold in the USA has a lower alcohol content than the beer in most other countries, which may be why many visitors find it bland. Imported beers must conform to the same restriction on alcohol content and are often specially made for export to the USA. If you're particularly fond of Fosters, Heineken or Moosehead at home, you may be disappointed to find that it has been wimped down for the American market. Note that 'lite' beer means lower in calories (90 instead of 180), but not lower in alcohol.

Wine California is America's leading wine producer, but there are plenty of other wineries in New York, Pennsylvania, Washington, Oregon, Colorado, New Mexico and elsewhere. A reasonable bottle of California red or white can be bought for around $10 at a supermarket or liquor store, but will be much more expensive in restaurants.

Spirits All bars have a big range of 'hard liquor': gin, brandy, rum, vodka, whiskey etc, invariably served with lots of ice ('on the rocks') unless you ask for it 'straight up.' If you ask for whiskey, you'll get American whiskey, which is called bourbon if it's made in Kentucky (eg, Jim Beam) or whiskey if

it's not (eg, Jack Daniels). If you want Scotch whisky, ask for Scotch. The American taste for cocktails originated during Prohibition, when lots of flavorful mixers were used to disguise the taste of bathtub gin. These days there are thousands of named cocktail recipes, and many bars will have their own special concoction, usually with a fancy or a funny name.

ENTERTAINMENT

Many small and medium-size cities have a full range of entertainment, but generally the quality and variety increases with the size of the city. There's usually at least one free weekly newspaper that lists all the entertainment options in town. For hard-to-get tickets, contact an agency like Ticketmaster. For cheap entry, call the venue directly and ask if they have last-minute 'rush' tickets.

Cinemas

Despite videos and cable TV, just about every town still has a movie theater. A few old-style movie palaces remain, though there are probably less than a dozen drive-ins in the whole country. The main venues are now multiscreen complexes in suburban shopping malls. Admission is around $7 or $8, often with discounts on Monday and Tuesday and for matinees or the first show of the day. Larger cities have 'art house' theaters showing alternative, classic and foreign films.

Performing Arts

Some smaller cities surprise with their live theater scene, especially college towns. For really innovative theater, New York, Chicago and Los Angeles have the most to offer. Ballet, opera and classical music performances are typically concentrated during a 'season' in larger cities. Often the performing arts seasons are in winter or some other nontouristy time and are a good reason to visit off-peak. If you have a particular interest, it's worth calling ahead to the venue or the city's tourist office to find out what will be on when you visit.

A uniquely American art form, the outdoor historical drama is a combination stage show and history lesson for an amphitheater full of tourists, often staged outdoors.

Popular Music

Just about any sizable town will have live rock venues, but big-name touring acts appear mainly in huge stadiums in the main cities. Catch new bands and new sounds in the big music scenes of Seattle, Los Angeles and New York, but don't overlook less glamorous cities and student towns – Hoboken (New Jersey), Boston, Minneapolis-St Paul (Minnesota), Athens (Georgia), Austin (Texas) and Portland (Oregon). Cleveland, with the Rock & Roll Hall of Fame, and Memphis, with Elvis' Graceland, are also destinations for rockers on the road.

All the big towns have good jazz, but the biggest jazz scenes are in New Orleans (of course), Chicago, New York and Kansas City (Missouri). The same cities also have an abundance of blues bars, but the Mississippi Delta and the city of St Louis both claim to be the birthplace of the blues. Memphis also has a big blues heritage.

Anywhere between the coasts, country music is almost unavoidable, in honky-tonk bars and on a million radio stations. Nashville is the center of commercial country music, and Branson, Missouri, is its overcommercialized nadir. The authentic, folksy antecedents of country music can be found not far away in the mountain music of the Appalachians and the Ozarks, and in the bluegrass music of Kentucky and of Tennessee.

Though Cajun and zydeco music have some following in the big cities, these styles should be heard at the source in Louisiana (see the South chapter).

Bars

The mainstay of American nightlife is bars, which run from the sleaziest booze joints to the slickest cocktail lounges. Some classic variants are the neighborhood bar (as in *Cheers*), the sports bar (where vocal spectators cheer big-screen TVs), the gay bar, the pickup bar (in decline since the AIDS epidemic) and the Western bar (with the pickups outside). The best bars have friendly regulars, good conversation, cheap drinks, free snacks, your favorite music and long hours. The city with the best bars is either Baltimore, Boston, Chicago, New Orleans, New York, San Francisco or a good subject to argue about.

Clubs

Every big town has its discos, dance clubs, gay clubs, nightclubs and just plain clubs. The biggest party scenes are in New York, Chicago, Los Angeles, New Orleans and Miami. The most fashionable places change by the month, and you only get in if you're gorgeous, outrageous, famous or flashing money to the thug at the door. Note that strictly enforced drug laws inhibit any ecstasy-fueled rave scenes.

SPECTATOR SPORTS

To judge by the media coverage, professional sport is the most important activity in the country, and therefore the world. For visitors who want to explore this obsession, or even understand the blather of statistics and jargon that accompany every game and commentary, the following basics might help. To find out more, spend the next 10 years in a sports bar, then get cable TV. Information about professional teams is provided for most of the big cities covered in this book.

Not long ago, recreational, intercollegiate and professional sports were dominated by men, but in the last 25 years women's sports have been boosted by the passage of Title IX, a federal law prohibiting gender-based inequities in programs receiving federal funding. Each year more women and girls participate, but women's professional sport as a spectacle has been slower to develop.

Baseball

Though football and basketball may get higher TV ratings, baseball is still the 'national pastime,' steeped in tradition and a major contributor to the language and culture. Once your understanding gets past first base, it's an enjoyable game to watch, with many of the subtleties of cricket but a lot less tedium (cricket has been described as 'baseball on Valium').

Two teams of nine players compete on a 'diamond,' a 90-foot square with a 'base' in each corner. The pitcher, from a low mound in the center of the diamond, hurls the ball toward the batter over the home plate. The batter wallops the ball, drops the bat and runs for first base. If the fielding team gets the ball there first, the runner is out. If not, the runner is 'safe on first,' and the next batter faces the pitcher. If it's a big hit (or the fielders fumble) the player can try for second base or more; if he gets around all the bases that's a 'home run.' If he hits the ball over one of the outfield fences, that's also a home run. If the fielding team catches the ball 'on the fly' (before it bounces), the batter is out. Now for the complications.

If the batter swings and misses, that's a 'strike' – three strikes and you're out. If the batter hits the ball and it goes behind the base lines, that's also a strike. If the batter doesn't swing, and the pitch is in the strike zone, that's a strike, too. (A pitch is in the strike zone if it passes over the home plate between the knees and chest; an umpire behind home plate makes the often-controversial ruling.) If the batter doesn't swing, and the pitch is outside the 'strike zone,' it's a 'ball' – four balls and the batter can 'take a walk' to first base. When three batters have made outs, the first half of the inning is over and the opposing team goes to bat. Now for the excitement.

A runner can try to reach the next base anytime the pitcher is on the mound. If the runner makes it, that's 'stealing a base,' but if he's tagged by the ball between the bases, he's out. (This cat-and-mouse stuff is a compelling subplot to the main game.) After a batter hits, all the runners on base can go, but if it's a fly ball, they can't advance to the next base until after the ball is caught, and they may be tagged out before they get back. If the batter and a runner are both out on one hit, that's a double play. When a runner makes it all the way around to home plate, the team scores one run. If there are runners on first, second and third, the 'bases are loaded,' and a good hit can result in several runs; if the hitter sends the ball over the fence with the bases loaded, it's a 'grand slam.'

Each team bats in an inning and there are nine innings per game, but teams continue playing if the score is tied at the end of nine innings. Baseball can be quite a low-scoring game, but a big hit with the bases loaded, or an error in the outfield, can allow a badly losing team to score big in the last innings and win the game. There's always room for hope because, as baseball legend Yogi Berra said, 'it ain't over till it's over.'

Major Leagues The major obsessions are the American League (AL) and the National League (NL), which combined comprise 30 teams. The season runs from April to October, with each team playing 162 games, as many as five per week. In October the top four teams in each league compete in the 'playoffs,' and the winning team from each league contest the World Series in a best-of-seven series. With so many games in the regular season, seats are usually obtainable and inexpensive ($7-14).

Rituals include the playing of the national anthem at the start of every game, the 'seventh-inning stretch' when spectators can sing 'Take Me Out to the Ball Game' and get psyched for the end of the game. Other customary tunes accompany good, bad or exciting plays throughout, adding to the sense of occasion. The classic venues for big ballgames are Wrigley Field in Chicago, Camden Yards in Baltimore, Yankee Stadium in New York City and Boston's Fenway Park. It can be a great spectacle, but the high standard of play means low scores and infrequent upsets. A good pitcher will beat a good batter, and these guys don't make many mistakes.

During March, spring training games in Arizona (the Cactus League) and Florida (the Grapefruit League) are a great chance to see big league players in small, intimate parks. Tickets (about $6) are usually available before each game. For more information about professional baseball, check Ⓦ www.majorleaguebaseball.com.

Other Leagues Small cities across the country have minor league teams. Some are known as 'farm teams' because they grow players for a major league club. Minor league games may not have the spectacular scale and hype of the majors, but as a sporting event they can actually be more entertaining.

College baseball doesn't generate the same mania as college football, but games are still hugely popular. A high-school baseball game is a staple of suburban and small town life, while Little League baseball is where parents teach children about self-control and respect for rules.

Football

An American football field is 53 yards wide and 100 yards long, with a 10-yard 'end zone' and goal posts at each end. Teams have 11 players on the field, and an unlimited number of replacements are possible. The game starts with a kickoff to the offensive (attacking) team, which must then move the ball down the field to score a touchdown (worth six points) in the end zone, while the defensive team tries to stop them.

When an attacker with the ball is 'downed,' the game clock stops, and the teams go into a huddle to discuss the next 'play.' Teams take up formations on either side of the ball, and play begins again when the attacking team's center player 'snaps' the ball back between his legs to the quarterback. The quarterback, who leads the attack, can run with the ball himself, pass it to a running back or throw it to a receiver. There's a flurry of action as the offensive team uses a repertoire of well-rehearsed tactical plays and brute force to get past the defenders and advance the ball. Defenders try to down whoever has the ball, intercept any passes or forcibly obstruct any member of the offensive team.

When the attack is downed again, usually in a matter of seconds, the play is finished, and the process is repeated. If a pass is intercepted, or if the offensive team doesn't advance the ball 10 yards in four downs, possession passes to the other side. In professional games, the sides will then replace all their defensive players with offensive players and vice versa, and the game restarts with two new teams. Actually kicking the football ('punting') can score a field goal (three points), or add a bonus point to a touchdown, or improve a team's position as they head for the fourth down. The game ends after an hour of playing time, which usually stretches to three hours or more because of all of the timeouts and breaks for TV commercials.

The fascination of the game lies in the complexity of the attacking and defending strategies (often compared to chess), and in the tremendous athleticism of the players, who are usually huge and powerful but terrifically fast and agile. Football is often perceived as a violent sport, but games are usually very well ordered. Though the game does involve fearsome physical conflict, fistfights and foul play are unusual, especially compared with ice hockey.

High school football games are usually played on Friday afternoon, and can be a lot of fun despite being taken very seriously. 'Touch football,' played without tackles, is a popular variant for recreational players.

National Football League The National Football League (NFL) is divided into the National Conference and the American Conference, each with 16 teams. The professional season runs August to December, with teams almost every week. For popular teams, especially at their home fields, tickets cost from around $25-35 or more and are hard to get. In January the top teams from each Conference compete in the Super Bowl. For more information, see ⓦ www.nfl.com.

College Football Almost as popular as the NFL and almost as professional, NCAA college games are played from September until mid-December. The season culminates in the 'Bowl' games, between the best teams in the various college leagues. The Rose Bowl in Pasadena on New Years Day is the biggest; the Sugar Bowl (New Orleans), Orange Bowl (Miami) and Cotton Bowl (Dallas) are also major events; check ⓦ www.ncaafootball.net for the latest standings.

Basketball

Invented in the USA in 1891 (by a Canadian), basketball gained great popularity after the National Basketball Association (NBA) formed in 1949 and the sport became televised. A popular sport in schools and colleges, 'hoops' also rules in the streets, parks and driveways. Unlike other American sports, it has become well known internationally and is, along with baseball, an Olympic event.

Two teams run back and forth on a court, attempting to shoot the ball into a 10-foot-high hoop while preventing their opponents from doing the same. Each basket is worth two points. Players who have been fouled, as determined by a referee, get a free throw from the foul line, worth one point. A shot from 22 feet or more from the basket is worth three points.

The NBA has an Eastern Conference (15 teams) and a Western Conference (14 teams), each with two divisions, and teams play 80 or so games in a season from September to April, followed by playoffs between the top teams in May, and the world championship in June.

Women's professional basketball leapt into the national consciousness with the heavily sponsored Women's National Basketball Association (WNBA) in 1997. The success of the league is based partly on the rise of basketball as a popular participant sport for women. Fans who have tired of the antics of the starstruck men's NBA are turning to women's leagues to see real team play. For more information on the leagues, see ⓦ www.nba.com and ⓦ www.wnba.com.

There are some 270 college teams in the NCAA (National College Athletic Association) league. Its season culminates in the 'March Madness' tournament.

Hockey

This means ice hockey, the Canadian national game, which draws big crowds in the USA, too. Each team has six players armed with wooden sticks and heavily padded, competing on an ice rink 200 feet by 80 feet, desperately trying to hit a small rubber disk (the puck) into a 6-foot-wide goal. The action is extremely fast, and as the main defense tactic is to 'check' an opposing player by bumping or pushing him, there are plenty of opportunities for rough play – a big part of the attraction for many fans.

The National Hockey League (NHL) has eight Canadian teams and 16 US teams (with more than a few Canadian players), playing about 80 games in a season from October to April. Tickets cost $20 or more, and are often scarce. The top teams play for the Stanley Cup in May; see ⓦ www.nhl.com for more details.

Soccer

Soccer is enormously popular as a participant sport, enjoyed by over 16 million regular players, but it has been slow to develop as a professional spectacle in the USA. The 1994 World Cup attracted record numbers of spectators, but was ignored by most US sports fans. A new Major League Soccer (MLS) league started in 1996, with 12 teams playing from April to October, though attendance is not great and TV ratings are minuscule. One reason that networks are reluctant to promote soccer is the lack of convenient breaks in the game for TV commercials. It's also hard to imagine how the networks could fit in more sports programming than the existing saturation coverage.

Soccer is a popular participant sport for women, and the US team won the Women's World Cup in 1999. An eight-team professional women's league, the Women's United Soccer Association (WUSA), kicked off its first season in spring 2001, featuring many of the star players from the World Cup–winning team. For information on the men's league, see ⓦ www.mlsnet.com; for the women, see ⓦ www.wusa.com.

Motor Sports

Unlike Grand Prix races elsewhere in the world, US car racing takes place on an oval track with banked curves and plenty of overtaking space. It's more about speed and endurance than braking and cornering. American freeway drivers must identify with this, because half a million fans turn up in May to watch the Indianapolis 500, the world's biggest live sports spectacle.

In fact NASCAR (National Association for Stock Car Auto Racing) racing is the most popular motor sport, especially in the South. It is said to have originated with moonshiners on mountain back roads trying to outrun government agents. Modern stock cars are anything but stock, consisting of a race-car engine and chassis covered by a thin shell in the shape of a production car, then plastered with corporate logos. For schedules, see ⓦ www.nascar.com.

SHOPPING

The sheer variety and quantity of consumer goods in the USA is staggering to many visitors. Some things are just fantastic in their frivolity. If you come around Halloween, look at the huge selection of masks and costumes. At Christmas, be overwhelmed by decorations and Yuletide junk. At any time, you'll be impressed with the wit and cleverness in greeting cards, bumper stickers, refrigerator magnets and T-shirts.

Also interesting are the many highly specialized shops with incredible stocks of such esoteric items as high-performance kites, reproduction road

signs, hunting knives and Harley-Davidson belt buckles. Prices of most consumer goods are lower in the USA than just about anywhere else.

Handicrafts

Some traditional handcrafted items include quilts, duck decoys, Pueblo jewelry, Navajo blankets, Gullah sweetgrass baskets, tooled leather cowboy boots and engraved belt buckles. Good pieces are all very expensive. If a craftsperson spends 12 hours making a quality basket, it will have to sell for hundreds of dollars to provide a reasonable income. A similar basket might cost $5 in an Asian market.

Antiques

The browsing can be brilliant, but antique bargains are hard to find. Antique shops within a day's drive of a big city can be grossly overpriced, and far into the countryside there are junk shop owners who really believe an old toaster is worth $200. Anything that looks vaguely colonial, Victorian, Amish, Shaker, art deco or '50s moderne will have a hefty price tag.

Americana & Kitsch

Baseball caps and other sports merchandise, Bart Simpson shorts, stars-and-stripes T-shirts or a George W Bush rubber mask could be a great gift for that special someone. Look for stuff with puke-worthy sentimentality – odes to motherhood, patriotic slogans, mawkish religiosity – nobody does them better (or worse) than Americans. Don't forget the touristy stuff. You don't want to get home without a miniature Statue of Liberty, do you?

Museum Stores

All good museums have gift shops, selling some of the best quality, most interesting souvenirs in the country. As well as excellent prints and art books, many have tasteful T-shirts, high-brow fridge magnets and other small items with classy cultural associations. Even a paper bag from the Met is a high-status icon.

Factory Outlets

Usually clumped together near a freeway exit on the outskirts of a city, these places have designer clothes, shoes, housewares and so on at discounted prices. The stuff is often damaged, irregular or left over from the previous season and thus can't be sold in stores, although some manufacturers now make lines specifically for outlets. Some outlets (also called 'warehouses') cut costs by employing few workers and omitting things like dressing rooms, racks and mirrors; at these places you basically serve yourself. You can usually find some good deals at Levi's, Nike, Polo and J Crew outlets.

Thrift Shops & Garage Sales

One person's trash is another person's treasure. Old-fashioned thrift stores, run by churches, Goodwill or the Salvation Army, have everything from salt and pepper shakers to bicycles to record players. Grunge and retro fashions have made used-clothing stores so popular that the poor may not be able to afford them.

When people clean out their garage and can't bring themselves to throw out the junk, they put price tags on it, scatter it across the lawn and hope someone else will find a use for it. Some people spend every Saturday driving from sale to sale, starting at 7am to get the 'good stuff.' You can occasionally find a bargain, but the only guarantee in the garage sale business is good people-watching. Look in the newspaper classified ads and on local bulletin boards for times and locations.

Getting There & Away

AIR
Airports

The USA has a number of main 'gateway' airports, and most international flights will arrive at one of them. If you want to fly into a non-gateway city, you'll probably have to land first at one of the gateway airports, where you'll do the immigration and customs thing, then take another flight to your final destination. These are the main international gateway airports:

New York (John F Kennedy) – JFK

Newark – EWR

Boston (Logan International) – BOS

Washington, DC (Dulles International) – IAD

Chicago (O'Hare International) – ORD

Atlanta (Hartsfield International) – ATL

Miami – MIA

Dallas-Fort Worth – DFW

Houston (George Bush Intercontinental) – IAH

Los Angeles – LAX

San Francisco – SFO

Seattle (Seattle-Tacoma International) – SEA

Honolulu – HNL

Many other airports are called 'international' but have only a few flights from other countries – typically links to Mexico or Canada, or just facilities for incoming charter flights at seasonal destinations like Orlando or Denver. Even travel to an international gateway sometimes requires a connection in another gateway city. For example, many of the London–Los Angeles flights involve a transfer connection in Chicago.

Airlines

Major international airlines include US-based carriers with domestic and international services as well as foreign airlines that fly to the USA.

Calling the following airline 800 numbers is free within the USA and Canada, but you can dial the numbers from any other country as a regular international call:

Aer Lingus	☎ 800-474-7424
Aerolíneas Argentinas	☎ 800-333-0276
Air Canada	☎ 800-776-3000
Air France	☎ 800-237-2747
Air New Zealand	☎ 800-262-1234
Alitalia	☎ 800-223-5730
American Airlines	☎ 800-433-7300
British Airways	☎ 800-247-9297
Canadian Airlines	☎ 800-426-7000
Cathay Pacific	☎ 800-228-4297
Continental Airlines	☎ 800-525-0280
Delta Air Lines	☎ 800-221-1212
El Al	☎ 800-223-6700
Garuda Indonesia	☎ 800-342-7832
Iberia	☎ 800-772-4642
Icelandair	☎ 800-223-5500
Japan Airlines (JAL)	☎ 800-525-3663
KLM	☎ 800-374-7747
Korean Air	☎ 800-438-5000
Kuwait Airways	☎ 800-458-9248
Lufthansa	☎ 800-645-3880
Northwest Airlines	☎ 800-447-4747
Qantas	☎ 800-227-4500
Scandinavian Airlines (SAS)	☎ 800-221-2350
Singapore Airlines	☎ 800-742-3333
South African Airways	☎ 800-722-9675
Thai Airways International	☎ 800-426-5204
TWA	☎ 800-221-2000
United Airlines	☎ 800-241-6522
US Airways	☎ 800-428-4322
Virgin Atlantic	☎ 800-862-8621

Buying Tickets

Numerous airlines fly to the USA, and a variety of one-way, roundtrip and Round-the-World fares are available. Start your research by looking at travel sections of magazines like *Time Out* and *TNT* in the UK, or the Saturday editions of newspapers like the *Sydney Morning Herald* and *The Age* in Australia. Ads in these publications offer cheap fares, but don't be surprised if they happen to be unavailable or sold out when you contact the agents: They're usually low-season fares on obscure airlines with conditions attached.

Warning

The information in this chapter is particularly subject to change: Prices for international travel are volatile, routes are introduced and cancelled, schedules change, special deals come and go, and rules and visa requirements are amended. Airlines and governments seem to take a perverse pleasure in making price structures and regulations as complicated as possible. The travel industry is highly competitive and there are many hidden costs and benefits.

Get opinions, quotes and advice from as many airlines and travel agents as possible, and make sure you understand how a fare (and any ticket you may buy) works before you part with your cash. The details given in this chapter should be regarded as pointers and are not a substitute for your own careful, up-to-date research.

Start shopping for a ticket early. Some of the cheapest tickets must be bought months in advance, and some popular flights sell out early. Talk to recent travelers, contact a few travel agents and watch for special offers. Online travel agencies list some of the cheapest fares available (see below), but as with travel agent advertisements, the best fares often seem to be unavailable. Airlines themselves can supply information on routes and timetables, but unless there's a price war they won't offer the cheapest tickets.

High season for most of the USA is mid-June to mid-September (the northern summer). May and October are often 'shoulder' periods, with the low season November through March, except for the week before and the week after Christmas, which are peak.

The best fares often have complicated conditions and catches. Find out about the fare, the route, the duration of the journey and any restrictions on the ticket.

Discounted tickets are available in two distinct categories: official and unofficial. Official tickets have a variety of names including 'APEX,' 'excursion,' 'promotional' or 'advance-purchase' fares. Unofficial tickets are simply discounted tickets that the airlines release through selected travel agencies (not through airline offices). The cheapest tickets are often nonrefundable and require an extra fee for changing your flight (usually $25-50). Many insurance policies will cover this loss if you have to change your flight for emergency reasons. A roundtrip (return) ticket usually works out to be cheaper than two one-way fares – often *much* cheaper.

Use the fares quoted in this book as a guide only. They are approximate and based on the rates advertised by travel agencies and airlines at press time. Quoted airfares are not necessarily a recommendation for the carrier.

Once you have your ticket, make a copy of it, and keep the copy separate from the original ticket. This will help you get a replacement if your ticket is lost or stolen. Remember to buy travel insurance as early as possible to protect yourself against any penalties for an unavoidable cancellation (see Documents in the Facts for the Visitor chapter for details).

Online Purchase Most airlines have their own Web sites with online ticket sales, often discounted for online customers. To buy a ticket via the Web, you'll need to use a credit card; this should be straightforward and secure, as card details are encrypted. Commercial reservation networks offer airline ticketing as well as information and bookings for hotels, car rental and other services. Networks include the following:

Atevo Travel (W www.atevo.com)
Biztravel.com Inc (W www.biztravel.com)
Cheap Tickets (W www.cheaptickets.com)
Excite Travel by City.Net (W www.city.net)
Internet Travel Network (W www.itn.net)
LowestFare.com (W www.lowestfare.com)
Microsoft Expedia (W www.expedia.com)
Priceline (W www.priceline.com)
Travelocity (W www.travelocity.com)
Yahoo! Travel Last-Minute Special
   (W travel.yahoo.com/destinations/bargains/)

Round-the-World Tickets Round-the-World (RTW) tickets can be great if you want to visit other regions as well as the USA. They're usually a bit more expensive than a simple roundtrip ticket to the USA, but the extra stops come pretty cheap. They're of most value for trips that combine the USA with another two continents – Europe, Asia or Australasia. RTW itineraries that include South America or Africa as well as North America are substantially more expensive.

Official airline RTW tickets are usually put together by a combination of airlines, or a whole alliance, and they permit you to fly to a specified number of stops and/or a maximum mileage on their routes, so long as you don't backtrack. Other restrictions are that you must usually book the first sector in advance and cancellation penalties apply. The tickets are valid for a fixed period, usually one year. An alternative type of RTW ticket is one put together by a travel agent using a combination of discounted tickets.

Most RTW fares restrict the number of stops within the USA and Canada. The cheapest fares permit only one stop; others allow two, three or more. Some airlines 'black out' a few heavily traveled routes (like Honolulu to Tokyo). In most cases a 14-day advance purchase is required. After the ticket is purchased, dates can usually be changed without penalty, and tickets can be rewritten to add or delete stops for an extra charge.

From the UK, an interesting RTW fare goes to New York, with cross-country travel to Los Angeles, then stops in New Zealand, Australia and Asia and back to London – advertised from £651. In Australia, STA advertises a RTW ticket with stops in New York and Los Angeles (plus London and Bangkok) for A$1929 from mainland capitals (A$300 less for students). Another RTW fare, using the One-World Alliance (including American Airlines), offers stops in three continents, including three stops in North America, for A$2059. RTW fares including North and South America start around A$2500, and those including Africa and North America are from about A$2800.

Courier Flights Some firms provide very cheap fares to travelers who will act as couriers, hand-delivering documents or packages. Courier opportunities are not easy to come by, and they are unlikely to be available on other than principal routes. The traveler is usually allowed only one piece of carry-on baggage, with the checked-baggage allowance being taken by the item to be delivered. In the UK, try British Airways Travel Shop (☎ 0870-606-1133) or ACP (☎ 0208-897-5130). Also try the International Association of Air Travel Couriers (W www.courier.org), but remember that joining the organization does not guarantee that you'll get a courier flight.

Travel Passes & Add-On Fares Some deals for travel within the USA can only be purchased overseas in conjunction with an international air ticket. These include various air passes, Greyhound bus line's International Ameripass, and some Amtrak rail passes. Also, you can often get domestic flights within the USA as an inexpensive add-on to your international airfare. It pays to think about your travel connections within the USA when you're shopping for your air ticket (see the Getting Around chapter for details).

Baggage

On flights to or from the USA, the weight limit is commonly higher than the usual allowance of 20kg (44lb), though there may be a limit on the number of items – check with the airline to be sure. On most domestic flights you are limited to two checked bags, or three if you don't have a carry-on bag. There could be a charge if you bring more, or if the size of a bag exceeds the airline's limits. A ski bag, snowboard or a packed bicycle is usually OK, but a surfboard or a Windsurfer may cost extra. Again, check with the airline.

If your baggage is delayed upon arrival (which is rare), some airlines will provide you with cash to purchase necessities. If sporting equipment is misplaced, the airline may pay for rentals. Should the baggage be lost, it is important that you submit a claim. The airline doesn't have to pay the full amount of the claim; instead they can estimate the value of your lost items and reimburse you accordingly. It may take them anywhere from six weeks to three months to process the claim and pay you.

Flight Restrictions

During check-in, you may be asked questions about whether you packed your own bags, whether anyone else has had access to them since you packed them and whether you have received any parcels to carry. These questions are asked for security reasons. As a result of recent terrorist activity on US flights, more restrictions may be imposed in the near future.

Items that are illegal to take on a plane, either as checked or carry-on baggage, include aerosols of polishes, waxes etc; tear gas and pepper spray; camp stoves with fuel; and divers' tanks that are full. Matches should not be packed in checked baggage. Note that airlines may implement more restrictions. At press time, airlines would not allow *anything* on board that could potentially be used as a weapon (scissors, razors, knitting needles, metal nail files, etc).

Smoking is prohibited on all domestic flights and on most international flights to and from the USA.

Travelers with Special Needs

If you have special needs of any sort – a broken leg, dietary restrictions, use of a wheelchair, responsibility for a baby, fear of flying – let the airline know as soon as possible. It may also be worth calling around the airlines before buying your ticket to find out how they can handle your needs. Remind the airline when you reconfirm your reservation (at least 72 hours before departure) and again when you check in at the airport.

Airports and airlines can be very helpful, but they do need some warning. Most international airports can provide escorts from check-in desk to plane where needed, and there should be ramps, elevators, accessible toilets and reachable phones. Aircraft toilets, on the other hand, may present a problem; travelers should discuss this with

Air Travel Glossary

Alliances Many of the world's leading airlines are now intimately involved with each other, sharing everything from reservations systems and check-in to aircraft and frequent-flyer programs. Opponents say that alliances restrict competition. Whatever the arguments, there is no doubt that big alliances are the way of the future.

Fares Airlines traditionally offer 1st class (coded F), business class (coded J) and economy class (coded Y) tickets. These days there are so many promotional and discounted fares available that few passengers pay full fare.

Lost Tickets If you lose your airline ticket, an airline will usually treat it like a travelers check and, after inquiries, issue you another one. Legally, however, an airline is entitled to treat it like cash, and if you lose it then it's gone forever. Take very good care of your tickets.

Onward Tickets An entry requirement for many countries is that you have a ticket out of the country. If you're unsure of your next move, the easiest solution is to buy the cheapest onward ticket to a neighboring country or a ticket from a reliable airline which can later be refunded if you do not use it.

Open-Jaw Tickets These are tickets where you fly out to one place but return from another. If available, this can save you backtracking to your arrival point.

Overbooking Since every flight has some passengers who fail to show up, airlines often book more passengers than they have seats. Usually excess passengers make up for the no-shows, but occasionally somebody gets 'bumped' onto the next available flight. Guess who it is most likely to be? The passengers who check in late. If you do get 'bumped,' you are normally offered some form of compensation.

Reconfirmation Some airlines require you to reconfirm your flight at least 72 hours prior to departure. Check your travel documents to see if this is the case.

Restrictions Discounted tickets often have various restrictions on them, such as needing to be paid for in advance and incurring a penalty to be altered or cancelled. Others have restrictions on the minimum and maximum period you can be away.

Ticketless Travel On simple one-way or roundtrip flights, reservations details can be held on computer and passengers merely show photo IDs to claim their seats – paper tickets are not issued.

Transferred Tickets Airline tickets cannot be transferred from one person to another. Travelers sometimes try to sell the return half of their ticket, but officials ask you to prove that you are the person named on the ticket. On an international flight, tickets are compared with passports.

the airline at an early stage and, if necessary, with their doctors.

Guide dogs for the blind often have to travel in a specially pressurized baggage compartment with other animals, away from their owners, though smaller guide dogs may be admitted to the cabin. Guide dogs are not subject to quarantine as long as they have proof of being vaccinated against rabies.

Deaf travelers can ask that airport and in-flight announcements be written down for them.

Children Kids younger than two years old travel for 10% of the standard fare (or free on some airlines) as long as they don't occupy a seat. (They don't get a baggage allowance, either.) 'Skycots' should be provided by the airline if requested in advance; these will take a child weighing up to about 22lb. Strollers can often be taken on as hand baggage. Children between two and 12 can usually occupy a seat for one-half to two-thirds of the full fare and do not get a baggage allowance. Sometimes there is a child's rate on a discounted fare, sometimes not – it can be cheaper for a child to fly on an adult discounted fare than on a child's fare at two-thirds the full adult fare. For pricing purposes, the child's age is reckoned at the time of departure on the first leg of the flight.

Arriving in the USA

Even if you are continuing immediately to another city, the first airport that you land in is where you must go through immigration and customs procedures. If your baggage is checked from, say, London to Phoenix, you will still have to take it through customs if you first land in Chicago. Passengers from Asia will go through immigration and customs in Honolulu if their flights stop there on the way to California.

Passengers aboard the airplane are given standard immigration and customs forms to fill out. After the plane lands, you'll first go through immigration. There are two lines: One is for US citizens and residents, and the other is for nonresidents. After immigration, you collect your baggage and then pass through customs. If you have nothing to declare, you'll probably clear

customs quickly and without a baggage search, but don't count on it. For details on customs and entrance requirements, see the Facts for the Visitor chapter.

If your flight is continuing to another city, or you have a connecting flight, it is your responsibility to get your bags to the right place. Normally, there are airline representatives at counters just outside the customs area who will help you. Most airports will have pay phones and car rentals, but other facilities may be minimal. Don't count on a foreign exchange office, tourist information desk or luggage-storage service – some US airports are not very user-friendly.

Departure Tax

Taxes for US airports and an arrivals tax are included in the cost of tickets bought in the USA or abroad. Taxes may not be included in an advertised fare, but they will always be added on at some stage – be ready for a few dollars in extra charges.

Canada

Travel CUTS has offices in Toronto (☎ 416-979-2406, 187 College St), Montréal (☎ 514-284-1368, 2085 Ave Union) and other major cities. The *Toronto Globe & Mail* and *Vancouver Sun* carry travel agencies' ads; the magazine *Great Expeditions* (PO Box 8000-411, Abbotsford, BC V2S 6H1) is also useful.

Daily flights go from Vancouver, Toronto and many smaller cities to all the big US centers. Commuter flights to cities like New York and Chicago can be very expensive. Some of the best deals are charter and package fares to sunny destinations like Florida, California and Hawaii, with higher prices in the winter peak season.

It may be much cheaper to travel by land to the nearest US city, then take a discounted domestic flight. For example, roundtrip fares to New York are much cheaper from Seattle, Washington, than from Vancouver, BC, only 130 miles away.

Central & South America

The main gateway from Central and South America is Miami, but there are also many direct flights to Los Angeles and Houston. Check the international flag-carrier airlines of the countries you want to connect to

(Aerolíneas Argentinas, LANChile, Varig etc) as well as US airlines like United and American.

Regular flights link the major cities of Mexico and the USA. At times, depending on prices and exchange rates, it can be substantially cheaper to fly to a Mexican border town than to the adjacent town on the US side. A flight from Mexico City to Tijuana can cost quite a bit less than a flight to San Diego, just a few miles north on the US side.

The UK & Ireland

One of the busiest, most competitive air sectors in the world is the UK to the USA, with hundreds of scheduled flights by British Airways, American Airlines, United, Delta, Northwest, Continental, Kuwait, Air India, TWA and discount specialist Virgin Atlantic.

Discount air travel is big business in London. Advertisements for many travel agencies appear in the travel pages of the weekend broadsheet newspapers, in *Time Out,* the *Evening Standard* and in the free magazine *TNT.* For online bookings, try W www.travelocity.co.uk.

Most British travel agents are registered with ABTA (the Association of British Travel Agents), which will guarantee a refund or an alternative if you've paid money to an agent who goes out of business. Using an unregistered agent is not recommended.

Popular discount travel agencies in the UK include STA Travel (☎ 020-7361-6262, W www.statravel.co.uk, 86 Old Brompton Rd, London SW7) and usit Campus (☎ 0870-240-1010, W www.usitcampus.co.uk, 52 Grosvenor Gardens, London SW1). Both of these agencies have branches throughout the UK and sell tickets to all travelers, but they cater especially to young people and students. Trailfinders (☎ 020-7937-5400, W www.trailfinders.co.uk, 215 Kensington High St, London W8 6BD) is another good agency, with branches in Manchester (☎ 0161-839-6969), Glasgow (☎ 0141-353-2224) and Dublin (☎ 01-677-7888). Also check Flightbookers (☎ 020-7757-2000, W www.ebookers.com, 177 Tottenham Court Rd, London W1) and Bridge the World (☎ 020-7916-0990, W www.b-t-w.co.uk, 47 Chalk Farm Road, Camden NW1 8AJ).

Discounted fares are highly variable, volatile and subject to various conditions and restrictions, but as an indication, here are some sample roundtrip fares from various discount agencies on a variety of carriers (fares include tax):

London to	low season/high season
New York	£199/412
Boston	£214/432
Chicago	£238/422
Charlotte	£245/444
Miami	£277/475
Los Angeles	£282/488
San Francisco	£282/488
Las Vegas	£282/499
Denver	£283/522

Manchester to	low season/high season
New York	£248/436
Boston	£248/456
Los Angeles	£294/500

Glasgow to	low season/high season
New York	£251/425
Boston	£262/456
Los Angeles	£298/500

Dublin to	low season/high season
New York	£275/577
Boston	£275/540
Los Angeles	£319/561

From UK regional airports, discounted flights may be routed via London, Paris or Amsterdam, and will probably not fly direct to smaller US cities like Las Vegas or Denver.

For these fares, high season is at various times between April and October, and most of the rest of the year is low season. Note that there's also a 'super peak' season from December 12 to 24, when fares are even higher than in high season.

Virgin Atlantic (☎ 01293-747-747, W www .virgin-atlantic.com) is an airline with consistently low fares, but all prices are based on availability. Fares are published 11 months in advance so the sooner you purchase the tickets the cheaper they will be. The occasional special offers are usually in January, February and November.

Continental Europe

There are nonstop flights to many US cities, but the discounted fares often involve indirect routes and changing planes. The main airlines between Europe and the USA are Air France, Alitalia, British Airways, KLM, Continental, TWA, United, American, Delta, Scandinavian Airlines and Lufthansa. Sometimes an Asian or Middle Eastern carrier will have cheap deals on flights in transit to the USA, if you can actually get a seat. Also try Icelandair connections via London.

The newsletter *Farang* (La Rue 12, 4261 Braives, Belgium) covers exotic destinations, as does Globe-Trotters *Aventure du Bout du Monde* (W www.abm.fr, 11 Rue de Coulmiers, 75014 Paris, France).

Netherlands Amsterdam is one of the best places to get cheap airfares, and its Schiphol airport is excellent. Look along Rokin for discount travel agencies such as Budget Air (☎ 020-627-1251, W www.nbbs.nl, 34 Rokin). The official student agency, NBBS Reizen (☎ 020-620-5071, W www.nbbs.nl, 66 Rokin, Amsterdam), has branches in most cities, as does Holland International (☎ 070-307-6307). Some of the recommended online agents include W www.budgettravel.com and W www.airfair.nl.

Some of the cheapest advertised fares for low-season roundtrips start around €272 to New York, €318 to Miami and €386 to Los Angeles.

Germany For discount fares, STA Travel (☎ 030 3110950, Goethestrasse 73, 10625 Berlin) has branches in major cities across the country. Usit Campus (☎ 01805 788336, W www.usitcampus.de) has several offices in Germany, including one in Cologne (☎ 0221 923990, 2a Zuelpicher Strasse).

Some online agencies include W www.justtravel.de (the English-language site of a Munich-based travel agent), W www.lastminute.de (useful for last-minute deals) and W www.expedia.de (the German version of Expedia). The cheapest advertised fares, low-season roundtrip from Frankfurt, start around €290 to New York, €363 to Orlando and €470 to Los Angeles.

France In Paris, Council Travel (☎ 01 44 55 55 44) is at 22 Rue des Pyramides, 1er. Nouvelles Frontières (☎ 08 03 33 33 33,

W www.nouvelles-frontieres.fr) and Havas Voyages (☎ 01 53 29 40 00) both have branches throughout Paris. Also worth trying in Paris are Charters Plus (☎ 01 44 09 06 24, 6 Rue Troyon, 75017), Voyageurs du Monde (☎ 01 42 86 16 00, 55 Rue Ste-Anne, 75002) and, especially for students, Usit Connections (☎ 01 42 44 14 00, W www.usitconnect.fr, 14 Rue Vivienne, 75002) and OTU Voyages (☎ 01 40 29 12 12, W www.otu.fr, 39 Ave Georges-Bernanos, 75005).

Recommended online agencies and useful Web sites include W www.snav.org/recherche/decoup/form6.htm, and W www.anyway.fr, both auction sites for air tickets. Also try W www.lastminute.fr for last-minute deals from France.

Some of the cheapest advertised fares, low-season roundtrip from Paris, start around €350 to New York, €427 to Miami and €457 to Los Angeles.

Belgium Recommended agencies in Brussels include Airstop (☎ 07 023 31 88, W www.airstop.be, 28 Wolvengracht) and Connections (☎ 02 550 01 00, W www.connections.be, 19-21 Rue du Midi), with branches in other Belgian cities. Nouvelles Frontières (☎ 02 547 44 44, W www.nouvelles-frontieres.be, 2 Blvd Maurice Lemmonier) is in Brussels and also has branches in Anvers, Bruges, Liège and Gand.

Switzerland SSR has branches throughout the country, including Geneva (☎ 022 818 02 02, W www.ssr.ch, 8 Rue de la Rive) and Lausanne (☎ 021 617 56 27, 20 Bd de Grancy). It specializes in student, youth and budget fares. In Geneva, there are also Nouvelles Frontières (☎ 022 906 80 80, 10 Rue Chante Poulet) and Jerrycan (☎ 022 346 92 82, fax 022 789 43 63, 11 Rue Sauter).

Scandinavia STA and Kilroy Travels are reliable discount agencies. In Sweden, try STA Travel (☎ 046 13 72 05, Kiliansgatan 17, S-223 51 Lund) and Kilroy Travels (☎ 08 23 45 15, W www.kilroytravels.com, Kungsgatan 4, Stockholm) and the online agency W www.se.lastminute.com/se. In Denmark, there's STA Travel (☎ 33 14 15 01, Fiolstraede 18, Copenhagen 1171) or Kilroy Travels (☎ 33 11 00 44, Skindergarde 28, Copenhagen). In Norway, contact STA

Travel (☎ 23 01 02 90, Karl Johans Gt. 33, Vika 0121, Oslo) or Kilroy Travels (☎ 23 10 23 10, Nedre Spottsgate 23, Oslo).

Australia

Some flights go from Sydney and Melbourne direct to Los Angeles and San Francisco, and quite a few more go via Auckland. Flights to other US cities will usually involve a stop in Los Angeles, or possibly San Francisco or Honolulu. Qantas, Air New Zealand and United are the main airlines on the route. Fares from Melbourne, Sydney, Brisbane and sometimes Adelaide and Canberra are 'common rated' (the same for all cities). From Hobart and Perth, there'll be an add-on fare.

The main discount travel agencies, STA Travel (☎ 1300-360-960, W www .statravel.com.au) and Flight Centre (☎ 133-133, W www.flightcentre.com.au) have offices in all main cities. They usually have rates to the USA within a few dollars of each other and will often match a lower fare offered by the other agency. British discount agency Trailfinders (☎ 03-9600-3022, W www.trailfinders.com.au) now has offices in major Australian cities. It's also worth checking the online agency W www .travel.com.au. Low season is roughly February, March, October and November. High season is mid-June to mid-July and mid-December to mid-January. The rest of the year is considered shoulder season.

Some sample discount low-season roundtrip fares from Sydney/Melbourne include Los Angeles for A$1450 and New York for A$1600. High-season fares will be more like Los Angeles for A$1800 and New York for A$2200. Discounted tickets have minimum- and maximum-stay provisions. The cheapest fares are for a maximum stay of 30 days. Full-time students can get an extra discount of A$80 to A$140 on some roundtrip fares to the USA.

Another inexpensive deal is with Japan Airlines, involving an indirect route and a night layover in Tokyo, but the savings really aren't worth it if your time is limited.

New Zealand

Air New Zealand has regular flights from Auckland direct to Los Angeles. Flights from Christchurch and Wellington require a plane change in Auckland or one of the Pacific islands. For discount fares in Auckland, try STA Travel (☎ 09-309-0458, W www .statravel.co.nz, 10 High St), or Flight Centre (☎ 09-309-6171, W www.flightcentre.co.nz, National Bank Tower, 205–225 Queens St); both also have offices in other main cities. Low, shoulder and peak seasons are roughly the same as for Australia. Low season discount fares to Los Angeles start around NZ$1400.

Africa

Only a few cities in West and North Africa have direct flights to the USA – Abidjan (Côte d'Ivoire), Accra (Ghana), Cairo (Egypt), Casablanca (Morocco) and Dakar (Senegal). Apart from South African Airways flights from Johannesburg to New York, most flights from Africa to the USA go via a European hub, most commonly London, or sometimes Cairo.

In South Africa, Rennies Travel has offices in Johannesburg (☎ 011-833-1441, W www.renniestravel.co.za, 42 Marshall St) and several other locations – it offers the most comprehensive range of travel services. STA Travel has offices in Cape Town (☎ 021-418-6570, W www.statravel.co.za, 31 Riebeeck St) and throughout the country. Advertised low season fares to the USA are about R5000 to New York, R6000 to Los Angeles. High season is mid-June to mid-September, and December through mid-January.

In Kenya, two good agencies in Nairobi for budget travelers are Flight Centres (☎ 02-210-024, @ fcswwat@arcc.or.ke, Lakhamshi House, Biashara St) and Let's Go Travel (☎ 02-340-331, W www.letsgosafari.com), on Standard St, close to the intersection with Koinange St.

Asia

Bangkok, Singapore, Kuala Lumpur, Hong Kong, Seoul and Tokyo all have good connections to the US West Coast on high-quality national airlines. Many flights to the USA go via Honolulu and allow a stopover. Bangkok is the discounted fare capital of the region, though its cheapest agents can be unreliable. Hong Kong, Kuala Lumpur and Singapore are also very competitive. STA Travel has branches in Hong Kong, Tokyo, Singapore, Bangkok and Kuala Lumpur.

Pacific Islands

Hawaii and the US territories of American Samoa and Guam (Micronesia) are the main gateways to the USA from the islands of the vast Pacific Ocean. From some islands, you may have to go via New Zealand, Australia, Papua New Guinea or Japan. To see what connections are available, contact airlines like Air New Zealand (☎ 64-9-488-3700, ⓦ www.airnz.co.nz), Air Tahiti Nui (☎ 1-310-662-1860), Aloha (☎ 1-808-484-1111, ⓦ www.alohaair.com), AOM French Airlines (☎ 1-310-338-9613), Continental (ⓦ www.continental.com), Hawaiian Airlines (ⓦ www.hawaiianair.com), Japan Airlines (ⓦ www.japanair.com) and Polynesian Airlines (ⓦ www.polynesianairlines.co.nz). There's not much competition on Pacific Islands routes, so don't expect bargain prices.

LAND

If you're driving into the USA from Canada or Mexico, don't forget the vehicle's registration papers, liability insurance and your home driver's license. Canadian and Mexican driver's licenses are valid; an international driver's permit is a good supplement. A vehicle rented in the US can usually be driven into Canada and back, but very few car rental companies will let you take a car into Mexico.

Canada

Bus Greyhound has direct connections between main cities in Canada and the northern USA, but you may have to transfer to a different bus at the border. Note that Greyhound US and Greyhound Canada are two different companies. Greyhound's Ameripass is not valid for travel within Canada, but you can use it to get into Canada via certain routes (from Boston or New York to Montréal, from Detroit to Toronto or from Seattle to Vancouver) and back to the USA by the same routes. See the Bus section of the Getting Around chapter for more on Greyhound bus passes.

Train Amtrak and Canada's VIA run daily services from Montréal to New York, Toronto to New York via Niagara Falls, Toronto to Chicago, and Vancouver to Seattle. Amtrak rail passes get you to/from Vancouver and Montréal only.

Car & Motorcycle If your papers are in order, taking your own car across the US-Canadian border is usually quick and easy, but occasionally the authorities of either country decide to search a car *thoroughly*. Canadian auto insurance is valid in the USA. Make sure your policy is current before you cross the border. On weekends and holidays, and especially during holiday weekends in summer, traffic at the main border crossings can be very heavy and there will be a long wait. Avoid crossing at these times, or try to cross at a smaller, less-trafficked border post.

Mexico

Bus There are direct buses between main towns in Mexico and the USA, but northbound buses can take some time to cross the US border. Sometimes the whole bus is delayed as the Immigration & Naturalization Service (INS) checks everyone on board.

Train Amtrak gets close to the Mexican border at San Diego, California, and El Paso, Texas, but there are currently no cross-border services (a new rail connection between Monterrey, in northeastern Mexico, and San Antonio, Texas, is being considered). All Mexican train services to towns on the US border have been closed.

Car & Motorcycle US auto insurance is not valid in Mexico, so even a short trip into Mexico's border region requires you to buy Mexican car insurance, available for about $6 per day at most border crossings. At some border towns, like Tijuana or Ciudad Juárez, there can be very long lines of vehicles waiting to re-enter the USA. For a short visit, it's usually more convenient to leave your car in a lot on the US side and walk or bus across the border. For a longer trip into Mexico, beyond the border zone or Baja California, you'll need a Mexican *permiso de importación temporal de vehículos*. See Lonely Planet's *Mexico* guide for the tedious details.

SEA

From about May to October, Cunard's *QE2* sails between Southampton (UK) and New York in about six days. The cheapest standard fare, with a bunk bed in an inside cabin, is around US$1900; in peak season (June-August) it's about US$2400. For better accommodations, the prices are higher – some are *much* higher. Occasional special deals are as low as US$1225. For details, contact Cunard's Florida office (☎ 305-463-3000, 800-728-6273, W www .cunardline.com).

Most other passenger liners in US ports are cruise ships doing all sorts of interesting circuits around the Caribbean, Canada's Maritime provinces, the Pacific Northwest, the Mediterranean and the Pacific. To find out more, contact a specialized agency like the Cruise Web (☎ 800-377-9383, W www .cruiseweb.com).

It is possible to travel to and from the USA on a freighter, though it will be slower and the comfort and facilities will not be up to cruise ship standards. Prices vary hugely, but start at about US$1200 a double for a one-way, 14-day crossing from Europe to the USA; US$3500 for a 55-day trip round the Pacific from Australia to Los Angeles with many stops. An excellent source of information is Cruise & Freighter Travel Association (☎ 800-872-8584, W www.travltips .com/freighterdirectory, PO Box 580188, Flushing, NY 11358).

ORGANIZED TOURS

Travel agents offer a huge selection of organized tours, with the basic options being bus tours, holiday packages and fly-drive packages. Fly-drive packages are an alternative to arranging a rental car yourself, and prices are comparable (see the Getting Around chapter for car rental options). Most tours can be combined with flexible airfare arrangements, so that you can have some time for independent travel before or after the tour.

Bus Tours

Very few bus tours attempt to cover the whole country. Most are for one to three weeks, and concentrate on one region; a few of the longer trips take various routes across the country in three to four weeks. If you want to see more, you can take two or more consecutive tours and probably get a discount.

The price of tours varies greatly with the number of meals included, the standard of

accommodations (from tent camping to four-star standard), what extras you'll want to pay for (adventure activities, special attractions, party nights), the dates (July to September are most expensive), whether you're traveling alone or with a companion, and so on. Be sure that you understand these details when you book, and budget enough for meals and activities that aren't included. Package-tour rates are usually quoted per person, but are based on double occupancy. A person traveling alone usually has to pay a single-room supplement.

Of the tour companies, Contiki (W www .contiki.com) caters especially to 18- to 35-year-olds. For single travelers (a large proportion of their clients), Contiki will arrange a roommate, saving the traveler the cost of the single supplement. Other tour companies, like Globus (W www .globusandcosmos.com), are more suited to older travelers and have a generally higher standard of comfort. Trek America (W www.trekamerica.com) offers more activity-oriented tours, traveling in 12- or 14-seat vans rather than full-size buses. Most nights are spent camping in tents, and everyone helps with the camping chores. Stops are often for two or three nights to permit hiking and individual sightseeing. The standard Trek America trips are for the 18- to 38-year-old age group, but the 'Footloose' trips are designed for older travelers.

Obviously, you'll enjoy these tours most if you're a sociable type and you get on well with the rest of the group. Try to pick one that will suit you in terms of age, gender and interests. Tours usually include a mix of nationalities, but very few Americans, and this might be a drawback. You'll have a great time with everyone in the tour group, but you might not meet many locals.

Holiday Packages

These include the 'one week in Waikiki,' 'six days in Disneyland' or 'ski Steamboat Springs' type of trips, with airfares, transfers, some meals and attractions included. With lots of guests, standardized services and efficient organization, these packages can be a good value for the money. If you want to see more of the USA, arrange some time for independent travel after your holiday.

Getting Around

AIR

Flying is the only practical way to get around the USA if your time is limited. The domestic air system is extensive, with dozens of competing airlines, hundreds of airports and thousands of scheduled flights every day. Flying is usually more expensive than traveling by bus, train or car, but a special airfare deal can make the cost very competitive. The availability of discount deals varies, depending on when you're travelling, how far in advance you buy your ticket, the route, and a few other factors.

For good airfare deals, you need to shop around. A good travel agent will have all the up-to-the-minute details on fares, routes, discounts and so on. Visit several agents if you have time. The Internet is a useful way to check the range of fares on offer, but a good travel agent will have access to pretty much any deal that's offered on the Web. Flights are most frequent, most direct and least expensive between main 'hub' airports. These include all of the international gateways listed in the Getting There & Away chapter, plus quite a few other cities, especially those that serve as the home base for a big airline. Most cities and towns have a local airport, some bigger and busier than others, but you might have to travel via a hub airport to reach them. This can make flying less convenient and more expensive.

A number of routes have especially frequent and convenient service. Flights are scheduled every few minutes between Los Angeles and New York. It's possible to just show up at the airport, buy your ticket and hop on, but this is much more expensive than buying a ticket in advance. Airlines recommend that you make reservations to guarantee yourself a seat.

Domestic Air Services

Many US airlines offer both domestic and international services, but some are purely domestic, and the small airlines only cover one region or a few states. Domestic airlines include the following:

Air Tran	☎ 800-825-8538
Alaska Airlines	☎ 800-426-0333
America West	☎ 800-235-9292
American Airlines	☎ 800-433-7300
American Trans Air	☎ 800-435-9282
Continental Airlines	☎ 800-523-3273
Delta Air Lines	☎ 800-241-4141
Hawaiian Airlines	☎ 800-367-5320
Jet Blue	☎ 800-538-2583
Midwest Express	☎ 800-452-2022
Northwest Airlines	☎ 800-225-2525
Reno Air	☎ 800-736-6247
Shuttle America	☎ 800-999-3273
Skywest	☎ 800-453-9417
Southwest Airlines	☎ 800-435-9792
Spirit Airlines	☎ 800-772-7117
TWA	☎ 800-892-4141
United Airlines	☎ 800-241-6522
US Airways	☎ 800-428-4322

Tickets & Fares

Two reputable discount travel agents are STA Travel (☎ 800-777-0112, ⓦ www.statravel.com) and Council Travel (☎ 800-226-8624, ⓦ www.counciltravel.com), with offices nationwide (call for the nearest location). Both companies sell the International Student Identity Card (ISIC), offer discounted tickets for students and those under 26 and provide competitive airfares for nonstudents of all ages.

Special fares are sometimes available through other discount travel agents. Check the ads in the Sunday travel sections of the larger newspapers such as the *Los Angeles Times, San Francisco Chronicle, New York Times* and *Chicago Tribune.* Browsing the Internet for cheap airfares is another option (see Online Purchase under Buying Tickets in the Getting There & Away chapter).

Advance-purchase options often give a series of graduated discounts for purchasing your ticket seven, 14 or 21 days in advance, with the biggest savings on a 21-day advance purchase (this system varies for different airlines and routes). A common variant is that a certain number of seats are made available at a big discount, and when they are sold another block of seats becomes available at a smaller discount, and so on until the last seats are sold at full price. It might cost much less to fly at night, or on a weekend rather than a weekday. Some airlines offer companion fares that are practically a two-for-the-price-of-one discount from the full coach fare. Discount tickets may be subject to a minimum or maximum stay, and often require that you stay over a Saturday night at your destination.

Fares are usually lower on the major 'air highways.' Flying between the East and West Coasts, check charter flights in addition to the regular airlines; travel agents will have information on both. Often you can get good deals on flights to/from New York and Chicago from both San Francisco and Los Angeles, and between Los Angeles and Miami. Bargain fares get as low as $300 roundtrip for New York-San Francisco or Los Angeles-Miami.

Airlines often have 'price wars,' lowering their prices drastically to compete when one airline declares a special promotion. Price wars don't usually last long – often only a few days – so if you hear of a price war and want to take advantage of the low fares, don't delay.

Thinking Ahead

Reasonably priced airfares usually have 'advance-purchase' requirements, and last-minute purchases are nearly always the most expensive – sometimes as much as five times the price of tickets paid for two weeks in advance. When planning your trip, you'll reap considerable savings by purchasing air tickets as far ahead as possible. The advance-purchase system is common among US airlines, and with bus and rail carriers as well. Don't expect to find bargains for last-minute travel – except on the Web.

If you do find yourself looking for last-minute airfares and are very flexible about travel dates and times, try the Internet. Web sites like W www.priceline.com and www.hotwire.com can offer excellent bargains, but read the rules and regulations carefully before committing to these tickets.

Package tours – in which an airfare is combined with accommodations, sightseeing tours or a rental car – are sometimes a good deal. Packages typically involve travel to major tourist destinations like Disneyland or Las Vegas, beach resorts or winter sports areas, or to major events.

International Fares & Domestic Flights

Domestic flights are often cheaper when bought in conjunction with an international airfare, so foreign visitors should consider their plans for air travel within the USA while shopping for their international ticket.

Generally, it's cheaper to get the international ticket to your farthest destination and make a stopover on the way than it is to get the international ticket to the nearest gateway airport, and buy a separate domestic flight from there. For example, a roundtrip flight from Sydney to New York might cost only A$100 more than a roundtrip flight from Sydney to Los Angeles, and the New York ticket might permit a free (or inexpensive) stopover in Los Angeles. If you took the international flight only as far as LA, you'd never be able to get a domestic roundtrip fare to New York for less than A$100.

If you can't get a through flight to your final destination with stopovers where you want, it might still be cheaper to buy the domestic flights as 'add-on' fares in conjunction with your international ticket, especially if the domestic legs use airlines that have an alliance with your international carrier. Add-on fares can be quite flexible, permitting a choice of several destinations within the US, and 'open-jaw' options allowing for land transport between cities. For example, you might get a roundtrip fare to New York, use an add-on fare to fly to Las Vegas, travel around by land, then fly from San Francisco back to New York, and take your return flight from there. There will likely be an extra charge (US$25-50) for changes to your travel date.

Air Passes

Most US airlines offer some sort of air pass to overseas visitors. They are only sold to foreigners (non-US or Canadian residents) in conjunction with an international airfare, and to get the best deal you have to buy the pass and the international flight from the same airline, or from a 'partner' airline. An airpass with one airline will cost more if you make your international flight with another, non-partner airline. The passes are actually a book of coupons. Each coupon equals a flight, good for 60 days from the use of the first coupon. One catch is that if a connection is not a direct flight (ie, if it involves a change of flight number), that counts as two coupons. It's therefore worth getting your pass with an airline that offers direct flights between the cities you want to visit. The following are representative of the kind of deals available. Ask your travel agent about the options before you decide on your international ticket.

In the UK, for example, a Continental Airlines Airpass costs from £269 for a minimum of three coupons, with slightly lower rates for more coupons up to a maximum of 10. In Australia, US air passes are commonly priced in US dollars, and you pay the Australian dollar equivalent when you book. They must be bought in conjunction with a roundtrip or Round-the-World fare. Air passes cost from US$489-641 for three coupons, US$729-941 for six coupons, depending on the season and whether or not you fly with a partner airline.

The conditions and cost structures are quite complicated, so you really have to work out your itinerary and schedule and get a travel agent to provide cost estimates for the options. Alaska and Hawaii are usually excluded, but if these places are on your itinerary, ask if there is a special deal for air-pass holders. Some deals let you leave the flight times open. You reserve your seat at least one day in advance (if seats are available!). Even if you book specific flights when you buy the pass, you can change the dates later without penalty, as long as the last flight is scheduled within the 60-day period. If you decide to change destinations once in the USA, you will generally be charged US$50-75 per change.

Getting Bumped

Airlines try to guarantee themselves consistently full planes by overbooking and

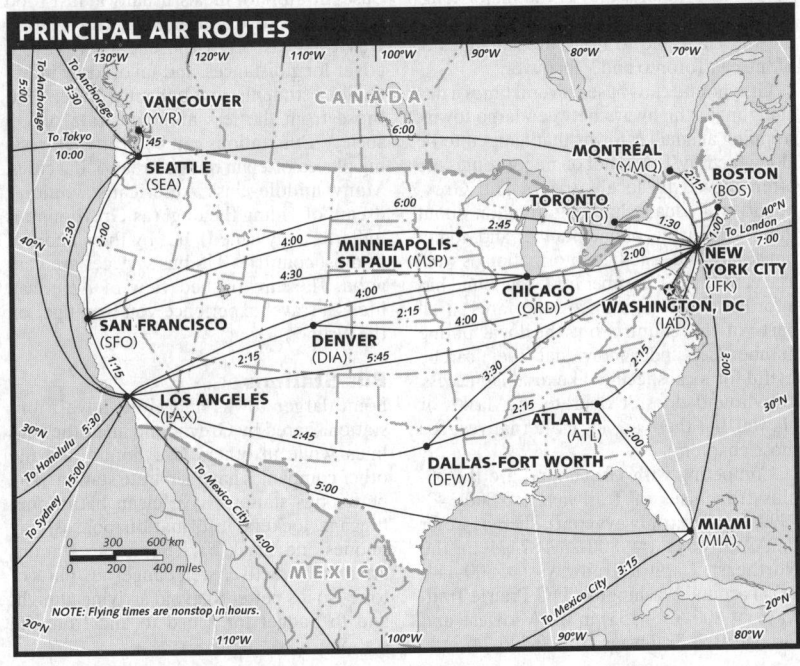

PRINCIPAL AIR ROUTES

NOTE: Flying times are nonstop in hours.

counting on some passengers not showing up. If everyone does show up, passengers can get 'bumped' off, which usually entails some compensation. Getting bumped can be a nuisance because you have to wait around for the next flight, but if you have a day's leeway, the compensation can make it worthwhile. When you check in at the airline counter, ask if they will need volunteers to be bumped, and ask what the compensation will be. It can range from a $200 voucher toward your next flight to a fully paid roundtrip ticket. Be sure to try to confirm a later flight so you don't get stuck in the airport on standby. If you have to spend the night, airlines frequently foot the hotel bill for their 'bumpees.'

Getting bumped can be a great deal, and some people plan their travel with a day to spare so they can try for a free ticket. Be aware, however, that being just a little late for your flight can get you bumped with none of these benefits.

BUS

Greyhound (☎ 800-231-2222 for fares and schedules, 800-822-2662 for customer service, W www.greyhound.com) is the major long-distance bus company, with routes throughout the USA and to the Canadian cities of Montréal, Toronto and Vancouver.

Greyhound runs buses several times a day along major highways between large towns, stopping at smaller towns that happen to be along the way. Towns not on major routes are often served by local carriers, and Greyhound will usually have information about them – the name, phone number and, sometimes, fare and schedule information as well. The central '800' number for Greyhound has information about services and fares in all parts of the country, but the local phone number (see under individual cities) can be useful for local specifics like disabled access. Greyhound doesn't operate in Alaska or Hawaii, but there are local alternatives (see those chapters).

Competing with Greyhound are the 50-plus franchises of Trailways (☎ 800-343-9999, W www.trailways.com), such as Peter Pan Trailways (☎ 800-237-8747) in the Northeast, Capitol Trailways (☎ 800-444-2877) around Washington, DC, Prairie Trailways (☎ 800-621-4153) in the Midwest, and Orange Belt Trailways (☎ 800-226-7433) in

California. Trailways may not be as useful as Greyhound for very long trips, but fares are generally a little lower.

Most baggage has to be checked in and should be properly labeled. Larger items, like skis and bicycles, can be transported, but there may be an extra charge. Call first to be sure. Don't leave hand baggage on the bus during rest stops.

The frequency of bus service varies, but even the least popular routes will have one bus per day. Main routes will have buses every hour or so, sometimes around the clock. Buses are reasonably fast, traveling mostly on the interstate highways, but bus trips can still be very long because of the great distances. Nonexpress buses will stop every 50 to 100 miles to pick up passengers, and long-distance buses stop for meal breaks and driver changes. A cross-country trip from New York to Los Angeles will take at least 60 hours.

Generally, buses operated by Greyhound and its main competitors are clean, comfortable and reliable. Buses have air-conditioning, onboard lavatories and reclining seats. Smoking is not permitted. The buses do stop for meals, usually at fast-food restaurants or cafeteria-style truck stops. Bus travel is often the cheapest way to cover long distances, and favored by impecunious students, low-budget travelers and those from the less affluent strata of US society. Bus stations can be pretty depressing places, often in unsafe areas of big cities. Many middle-class Americans wouldn't dream of 'riding the dog' (as Greyhound is unflatteringly called), but by the standards of most countries, US bus services are very good. The unvarnished view of American life is a travel experience you won't get on the airlines.

Bus Stations

Some larger towns and cities have a bus station shared by Greyhound and other bus lines, while in others Greyhound and the other companies have separate stations. The better bus stations have clean bathrooms, luggage lockers, information boards, pay phones and snack bars. Some bus stations are in unattractive, even dangerous, parts of town, so it's better to avoid arriving at night and to budget for a taxi to and from the station.

In small towns with no bus station, Greyhound and other buses stop at a given location, such as a McDonald's, a post office or the Amtrak train station. To board at these stops, know exactly where and when the bus arrives, be emphatic when you flag it down and be prepared to pay the driver with exact change.

Green Tortoise

The 'alternative' bus line, Green Tortoise (☎ 415-956-7500, 800-867-8647, W www .greentortoise.com), offers 12-day trips across the USA between San Francisco, New York and Boston (from May to September), as well as a range of sightseeing trips in the western part of the country, and other trips either north to Alaska or south through Baja California and as far as Costa Rica. Green Tortoise provides more than transport: Its well-used buses are fitted out as homes-on-wheels, with foam-mattress bunks and cooking facilities. The group-oriented trips feature communal cooking and eating, and stops for hiking, swimming, white-water rafting, park visits and cookouts. A 12-day Green Tortoise trip from its base in San Francisco to New York will cost around $469-499, plus $121-131 for the food fund, depending on when you travel. A quick weekend trip to Yosemite costs $99 (plus $31 for food) while the full 16-day loop through western national parks costs $629 (plus $191). It's worth calling Green Tortoise to discuss your plans – they're very helpful and flexible.

Tickets & Fares

Tickets for some Trailways and other buses can only be purchased immediately prior to departure. Greyhound bus tickets can be bought over the phone (☎ 800-229-9424) or on the Internet with a major credit card; they will be mailed to you if purchased 10 days in advance, or you can pick them up at the terminal with proper identification. Greyhound terminals also accept American Express, traveler's checks and cash. Note that only by purchasing a ticket can you reserve a seat. You can buy a ticket as late as 15 minutes before departure, but they will only fill the number of seats on the bus – no standing allowed. Buy your ticket in advance, if possible, to ensure that you get a seat.

You can usually get a substantial discount on tickets purchased seven days in advance. A roundtrip ticket is generally cheaper than two one-ways, but not always. Special promotional fares are regularly offered (eg, 'Anywhere that Greyhound goes for $109,' or 'Anywhere in California for $55'). If you're traveling with a friend, ask about Greyhound's companion fares, where two can travel for the price of one on a roundtrip journey.

There are many discounts available: Tickets for children ages two to 11 are half the standard fare. People over 62 can get a 5% discount, or join the Greyhound Seniors Club and get 10% off. A disabled passenger and a companion can travel together for the price of one. Student discounts are available occasionally on specific routes during certain times of the year – call Greyhound.

Here are some examples of Greyhound's long-distance services (route – standard fare; 7-day advance purchase fare; distance in miles; duration of quickest service):

New York to Chicago – $99; $49; 878; 16½ hours
New York to Miami – $116; $59; 1426; 27 hours
New York to New Orleans – $93; $59; 1415; 29 hours
New York to Los Angeles – $138; $99; 3083; 60 hours
Los Angeles to New Orleans – $90; $75; 2131; 41 hours
Los Angeles to Seattle – $119; $59; 1237; 24½ hours

Bus Passes

Greyhound 'Discovery Passes' can be economical if you want to travel a lot in a short period, but they also can be an inducement to cover too much ground in an attempt to get value out of the pass. The passes are for unlimited travel on seven, 15, 30, or 60 consecutive days (for options, see below), not for a number of days spread out over a longer period. Greyhound stamps your pass the first time you use it, and the days start from then. Two short-term passes cost more per day, but may better suit your itinerary.

The pass is valid on dozens of regional bus lines as well as on Greyhound and allows short side trips to Montréal, Toronto and Vancouver. For longer journeys inside Canada, a combined pass is available. Passholders can call ☎ 888-454-7277 in the USA for information, but seat reservations must be made in person at a bus station.

Domestic Discovery Pass This pass can be purchased in the USA and costs $209 for seven days of travel, $319 for 15 days, $429 for 30 days or $599 for 60 days. Buy one by phone or at any Greyhound station.

International Discovery Pass Also called an Ameripass, this pass is not available to US or Canadian citizens/residents. International visitors can buy the pass through their home travel agent, or on the Internet, or from the Greyhound International Office in New York City (☎ 212-971-0492, 800-246-8572). Passes are priced in US dollars, and you pay the current equivalent in the country where you buy it. Prices are $185 for seven days of travel, $285 for 15 days, $385 for 30 days or $509 for 60 days.

TRAIN

Amtrak (☎ 800-872-7245, Ⓦ www.amtrak .com) has an extensive rail system throughout the USA, with Amtrak Thruway buses providing convenient connections to and from the rail network to some smaller centers and national parks. The advantages of train travel include comfort, sociability and great scenery. Besides that, American railroads have a great tradition, and train travel still has a special romance, especially for rail enthusiasts, who will also enjoy many historic rail routes, restored steam trains and railroad museums. Some cities, including Chicago, Boston, Washington, DC, and San Diego, retain an elegant train station in the heart of town. Others, unfortunately, have replaced handsome, historic old stations with soulless, modern, no-frills facilities.

Train travel is quicker than bus travel, but the time saved may be offset by less convenient departure and/or arrival times. Traveling by train is usually more expensive than by bus on the same route, but special deals may make train travel competitive. On a busy, long-distance connection, it's often possible to get an airfare cheaper than a train ticket. In short, trains are rarely the quickest, cheapest or most convenient option, but they can be close on all counts, and people enjoy them for the travel experience.

Services & Facilities

Long-distance services are on named trains that run most routes daily, though some routes are covered only three to five days per week. See the Principal Railroad Routes map. Details are in the introductory section of each regional chapter; you can also check the Amtrak Web site. Principal long-distance routes are listed here:

Cascades – Eugene-Portland-Seattle-Vancouver

Empire Builder – Portland-Seattle-Chicago via Spokane, Glacier National Park and Minneapolis-St Paul

Maple Leaf – New York City-Toronto via Albany, Syracuse, Buffalo and Niagara Falls (*Acela Regional* does the same route)

Adirondack – New York-Montréal via Albany, Saratoga Springs and Westport

Acela Express – Boston-New York-Philadelphia-Baltimore-Washington

Twilight Shoreliner – Boston-New York-Philadelphia-Baltimore-Washington-Richmond-Newport News

Three Rivers – New York-Philadelphia-Pittsburgh-Cleveland-Chicago (the *Pennsylvanian* does the Philadelphia-Chicago sector)

The Crescent – New York-New Orleans via Washington, Charlotte, Atlanta and Birmingham

Silver Service – New York-Miami via Philadelphia, Washington, Richmond, Charleston, Jacksonville and Orlando (side connections to Raleigh and Charlotte)

Lake Shore Limited – Chicago-New York (or Boston) via Cleveland, Buffalo and Albany

Capitol Limited – Chicago-Washington via Cleveland and Pittsburgh

Cardinal – Chicago-Washington via Indianapolis, Cincinnati and Charleston (the *Kentucky Cardinal* runs Chicago-Indianapolis-Louisville)

Vermonter – Washington-St Albans via New York

City of New Orleans – Chicago-New Orleans via Memphis

California Zephyr – Chicago-San Francisco/Oakland via Omaha, Denver, Salt Lake City, Reno, Sacramento and Emeryville

Southwest Chief – Chicago-Los Angeles via Kansas City, Albuquerque and Flagstaff

Coast Starlight – Los Angeles-Seattle via Oakland/Emeryville, Sacramento and Portland

Pacific Surfliner – San Luis Obispo-Los Angeles-San Diego

Sunset Limited – Los Angeles-Orlando via Tucson, El Paso, San Antonio, Houston, New Orleans and Jacksonville (with connections to Miami)

Texas Eagle – Chicago-San Antonio via St Louis, Little Rock, Dallas and Austin

Heartland Flyer – Fort Worth-Oklahoma City

Commuter trains provide very fast and frequent services on shorter routes, especially along the Northeast corridor – Boston,

PRINCIPAL RAILROAD ROUTES

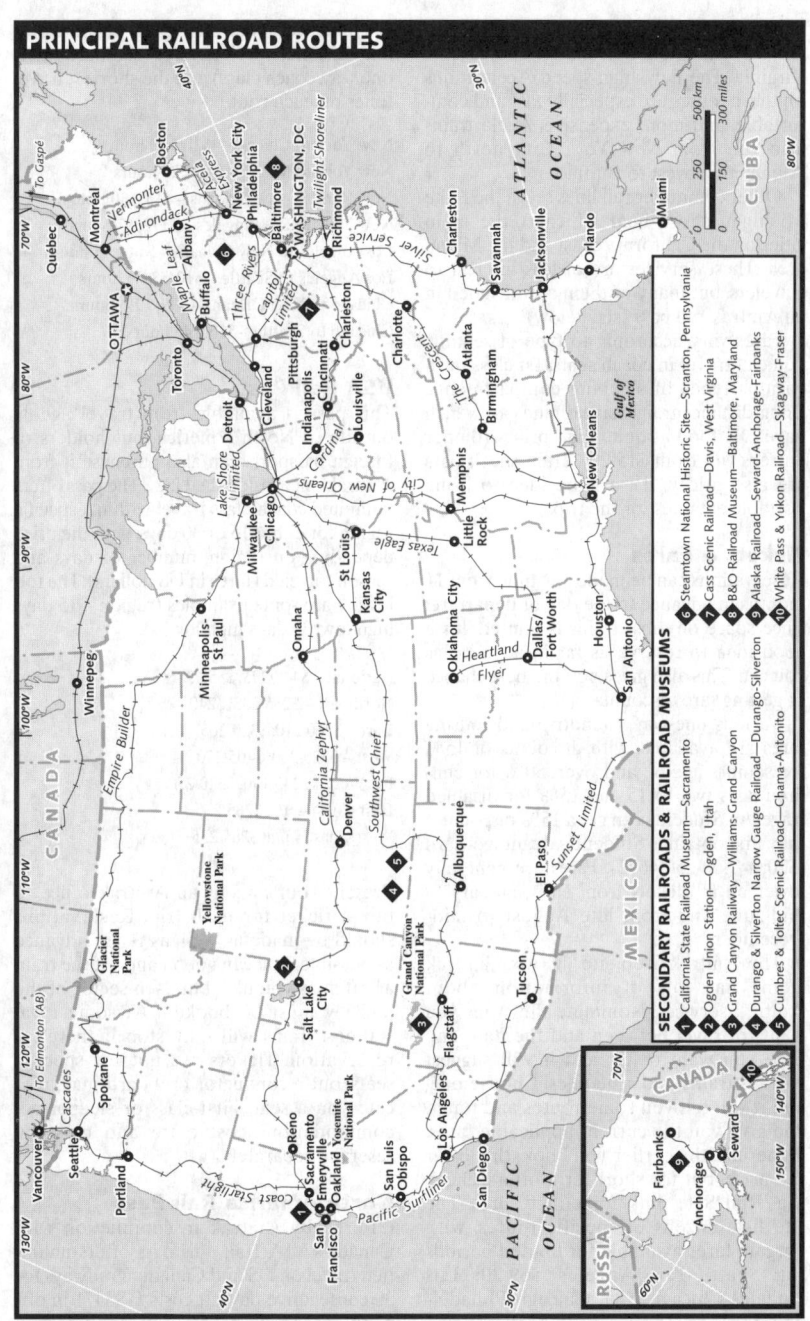

SECONDARY RAILROADS & RAILROAD MUSEUMS

1 California State Railroad Museum—Sacramento
2 Ogden Union Station—Ogden, Utah
3 Grand Canyon Railway—Williams–Grand Canyon
4 Durango & Silverton Narrow Gauge Railroad—Durango–Silverton
5 Cumbres & Toltec Scenic Railroad—Chama–Antonito
6 Steamtown National Historic Site—Scranton, Pennsylvania
7 Cass Scenic Railroad—Davis, West Virginia
8 B&O Railroad Museum—Baltimore, Maryland
9 Alaska Railroad—Seward–Anchorage–Fairbanks
10 White Pass & Yukon Railroad—Skagway–Fraser

Hartford, New York, Philadelphia, Baltimore, Washington, DC, and Newport News, Virginia. The new, high-speed Acela trains on these routes are especially fast and comfortable, and more expensive. Acela trains also run from New York City north to Albany then west to Buffalo.

Other commuter rail lines serve the Lake Michigan shore near Chicago, the main cities on the California coast and the Miami area. These services are of less interest to travelers, but many of them are included in an Amtrak rail pass (see below).

Fares vary according to type of seating; you can travel in coach seats, 1st class or in various types of sleeping compartments. Long-distance trains have dining cars, which have OK food at quite high prices (dinner entrées run from $15-20). Train snack bars are also pricey. It's a good idea to bring portable eatables for the trip.

Tickets & Fares

Reservations can be made any time from 11 months in advance to the day of departure; since space on most trains is limited, it's a good idea to reserve as far in advance as you can. This also gives you the best chance of getting fare discounts.

Various one-way, roundtrip and touring fares are available, with discounts of 15% for seniors age 62 and over, 50% for children ages two to 15 and 15% for disabled travelers. Students can get a 15% discount if they first obtain a 'Student Advantage' card ($20; ☎ 800-256-4672). Fares are generally lower on all tickets from early January to mid-June and from late August to mid-December.

The Amtrak Web site (Ⓦ www.amtrak.com) has lots of information about Amtrak services. Nominate the cities you want to travel between and the date and time you want to go, and it will suggest various trains and schedules. Choose one, and it will tell you some routes and times, and give you the current applicable fares. Generally, the earlier you book, the lower the price, but for short-term offers, check the 'Rail Sale' link for online fares. The site lists dozens of specific routes, with bargain fares available for limited periods (eg Seattle-Los Angeles $69.20; Los Angeles-Chicago, $85; Chicago-Philadelphia $16).

Here are some examples of Amtrak's long-distance services, fares (standard price, one way, coach class) and the shortest travel times on each route:

New York to Chicago – $106; 19 hours
New York to Miami – $153; 26 hours
New York to New Orleans – $133; 30 hours
New York to Los Angeles – $172; 67 hours
Los Angeles to New Orleans – $144; 43 hours
Los Angeles to Seattle – $104; 34½ hours
Chicago to New Orleans – $99; 19½ hours
Chicago to Seattle – $155; 46 hours

USA Rail Pass

This pass is available from travel agents outside of North America, but holders of foreign passports can also purchase it from Amtrak once inside the USA. The pass offers unlimited coach-class travel within a specific region for either 15 or 30 days, with the price depending on region, number of days and season traveled (fares in US dollars). The following are some examples (region – 15 days high/low; 30 days high/low):

National – $440/295; $550/385
Northeast – $285/235; $240/225
East – $260/210; $320/265
West – $325/200; $405/270
Far West – $245/190; $320/250
East Coast – n/a; $285/235
West Coast – n/a; $285/235

Present your pass at an Amtrak office to buy a ticket for each trip. Reservations should be made as well, as far in advance as possible. You can get on and off the train as often as you like, but each sector of the journey must be booked. At some rural stations, trains will only stop if there's a reservation. Tickets are not for specific seats, but a conductor on board may allocate you a seat. First-class or sleeper accommodations cost extra and must be reserved separately.

North America Rail Pass

Offered by Amtrak in conjunction with Canada's VIA Rail, this pass offers unlimited travel on US and Canadian railways for 30 consecutive days. It costs US$471 in off-peak season, or US$674 in peak season

(June 1 to October 15). It's available to American and Canadian residents as well as foreign visitors.

Package Deals

Amtrak offers a variety of vacation packages, with options for rental cars, hotels, tours and tickets for theme parks or other attractions. Air-Rail packages offer train travel in one direction and a plane trip going the other way. Check to see if any packages suit your plans. They'll be cheaper than booking the same services and attractions yourself.

Other Railroads

The only non-Amtrak long-distance passenger railroad in the US is the wonderful Alaska Railroad from Seward to Fairbanks via Denali and Anchorage. See the Alaska chapter for details.

Dozens of historic, scenic and narrow-gauge railroads operate more as attractions than viable transport options. Most only run in the warmer months, and the most popular ones can be booked solid. Some of the most interesting are listed below.

The Cass Scenic Railroad (☎ 304-456-4300) was once used to haul timber from the Appalachians. Today, this scenic narrow-gauge railroad in West Virginia hauls tourists 10 miles up into a historic park (see the Washington, DC & the Capital Region chapter).

The Grand Canyon Railway (☎ 520-773-1976, 800-843-8724) is a restored steam train that makes a daily roundtrip from the town of Williams, 30 miles west of Flagstaff, to the south rim of the Grand Canyon, with period play-acting on the way. Overnight stays at the canyon are possible (see the Southwest chapter).

Railroad Museums

Despite the declining importance of railroads, or perhaps because of it, there are railroad museums across the country. What else can you do with an old steam engine, or an old railroader for that matter? Rail buffs will find the following worth a detour:

B&O Railroad Museum (☎ 410-752-2490) – Baltimore, Maryland (see the Washington, DC & the Capital Region chapter)

California State Railroad Museum (☎ 916-324-0539) – Sacramento, California (see the California chapter)

Ogden Union Station (☎ 801-629-8444) – Ogden, Utah (see the Southwest chapter)

Steamtown National Historic Site (☎ 717-340-5200) – Scranton, Pennsylvania (see the New York & Mid-Atlantic States chapter)

The Cumbres & Toltec Scenic Railroad (☎ 719-376-5483) is the longest and highest narrow-gauge service in the country. It starts in Chama, New Mexico, and makes a 64-mile trip over the 10,015-foot-high Cumbres Pass and into Colorado. Hikers get on and off along the way (see the Southwest and Rocky Mountains chapters).

The Durango & Silverton Narrow Gauge Railroad (☎ 970-247-2733, 888-872-4607) is another Colorado Rocky Mountain favorite, traveling 45 miles north from Durango to the old mining town of Silverton (see the Rocky Mountains chapter).

The White Pass & Yukon Railroad (☎ 907-983-2217) is a narrow-gauge gold-rush relic; it runs from Skagway, Alaska, to Fraser, British Columbia (see the Alaska chapter).

CAR

Driving yourself is undoubtedly the most convenient way to get around the countryside, see small towns, cross sprawling suburbs and explore wide-open spaces. Driving in the USA is a cultural and sensual experience in itself, as you go with the flow on the endless interstates, tune in to local radio stations and develop a taste for tacky roadside architecture and highway hamburgers.

It's easy to list the circumstances in which you *won't* want a car. In some of the bigger, older cities, traffic is terrible, parking impossible and public transport is perfectly adequate. This is especially true in New York and also in the central areas of Boston, Chicago, New Orleans and San Francisco. For very long trips, driving may be too time-consuming for your itinerary. It's about 2800 miles from New York to Los Angeles – about eight to 10 days driving at 300 to 350 miles per day (don't plan on doing any more than this over a long trip). If your time is limited, plan to do the long stretches by plane or train, and rent a car where you need it.

Another problem is car addiction – a common affliction in America. If you can't drag yourself away from the car, your experience of many natural attractions will be greatly impaired. It's hard to leave a $50-a-day rental car in a lot for two days while you go hiking, but it's the best thing you can do at popular national parks like Yellowstone, Yosemite and the Grand Canyon.

For young travelers, car rental may not be a viable option. Drivers under 25 must pay a surcharge, and those under 21 are not permitted to rent at all from many car rental companies. Young travelers buying a car might find insurance prohibitively expensive.

The main advantages of a car are convenience, independence and flexibility. Driving can also be very cheap, especially with two or more people to share the cost. With a car it's feasible to carry camping and cooking gear and a cooler, and some of the cost of the car can be offset by savings in accommodations and food.

Road Rules

The use of seat belts and child safety seats is required in almost every state.

The speed limit is generally 55 or 65mph on highways, 25mph in cities and towns and as low as 15mph in school zones (strictly enforced during school hours). On interstate highways in designated rural areas, the speed limit is 65, 70, 75 or even 80mph – always watch for posted speed limits. It's forbidden to pass a school bus when its lights are flashing.

Drivers should watch for livestock on highways, especially in the deserts and range country. High-risk areas are signed as Open Range or with the silhouette of a steer. Hitting a steer at 55mph will total your car, kill the animal and might kill you as well.

Most states have laws against littering. If you are seen throwing anything from a vehicle, you can be fined $1000 and be forced to pick up what you discarded.

In winter conditions, you may have to carry snow chains and fit them if there is snow on the road. Many cars are fitted with steel-studded snow tires for winter driving.

Penalties are very severe for 'DUI' – driving under the influence of alcohol and/or drugs. Police can give roadside sobriety checks ('touch your nose, walk along this line' etc) to assess if you've been drinking or using drugs. If you fail, they'll require you take a breath test, urine test or blood test to determine the level of alcohol or drugs in your body. Refusing to be tested is treated as if you'd taken the test and failed. The maximum legal blood alcohol concentration is 0.08%. During holidays and special events, roadblocks are sometimes set up to deter drunk drivers.

In some states it is illegal to carry 'open containers' of alcohol in a vehicle, even if they are empty. Containers that are full and sealed may be carried, but if they have ever been opened, they must be carried in the trunk.

Insurance

Every owner or driver of a motor vehicle must 'maintain financial responsibility' to protect the health and property of others in case of an accident. The easiest way to do this is to have auto liability insurance, and most states specify a minimum level of coverage. For rental cars, the company will arrange insurance if you're not already covered. Ask what level of liability coverage is included in the standard rental deal.

If you buy a car, you must take out liability insurance, and this can be difficult if you don't have a local license (see below). A car dealer or the AAA may be able to suggest an insurer. Even with a local license, insurance can be expensive and difficult to obtain if you don't have evidence of a good driving record. Bring copies of your home auto insurance policies if they can help establish that you are a good risk. Drivers under 25, and especially those under 21, will have big problems getting insurance.

Driver's License

Visitors can legally drive in the USA for up to 12 months with their home driver's license. An International Driving Permit (IDP) is a very useful adjunct and may have more credibility with US traffic police, especially if your home license doesn't have a photo or is in a foreign language. Your automobile association at home can issue an IDP, valid for one year, for a small fee. You must carry your home license together with the IDP.

It's much easier and less expensive to get car insurance if you have a local driver's license. In most states it is not difficult or expensive to get one. Call the state Department of Motor Vehicles for details. It usually involves a simple multiple-choice test of the highway code and an undemanding driving test. You'll need a birth certificate or passport and proof of residence (an address) in the state. You may also need to get a Social Security card, which can involve some Social Security Department bureaucracy – the card is stamped 'not valid for employment.' Getting a license can be an educational experience of US public administration.

AAA Membership

If you'll be doing much driving, whether in your own vehicle, someone else's or a rental, membership in the American Automobile Association (AAA; called 'triple A') is highly recommended. Having a AAA card entitles you to free 24-hour emergency roadside service anywhere in the USA in the event of an accident, breakdown or locking your keys in the car. Members are entitled to free service within a given radius of the nearest service center, and service providers will tow your car to a mechanic if they can't fix it. The nationwide toll-free roadside assistance number is ☎ 800-222-4357.

AAA also offers free road maps, tour books and other travel literature, gives advice on how to buy a used car and provides travel agency services. It also sells car insurance and issues traveler's checks without commission.

If you're considering buying a used car, some AAA offices have diagnostic centers where they can perform vehicle inspections on site for its members and those of foreign affiliates.

The AAA membership card will often get you discounts for accommodations, car rental and admission charges. AAA offices are found in major cities and in many smaller towns throughout the USA. For addresses, see the appropriate AAA publications or check the AAA Web site at Ⓦ www.aaa.com. The cost of AAA membership varies by region, ranging from $50-65 for the first year and $35-45 per year thereafter – call for information (☎ 800-874-7532).

If you are a member of an automobile association in another country, this will probably entitle you to reciprocal rights in the USA. Bring a letter of introduction and proof of membership.

Parking

Parking is scarce and expensive in many inner-city areas. Metered street parking is geared toward short-term use, with time limits usually from 10 minutes to three hours. Put in enough dimes and quarters to prepay the whole time you'll be parked. You can't extend the time by putting more money in later. That's 'meter-feeding,' and you can be fined for it. Metered parking spaces are usually free on Sundays and public holidays and outside business hours (8am-6pm).

Commercial parking lots charge around $6-15 per day – more in big city downtown areas. Many are unattended and require prepayment, either by credit card or by stuffing cash into a paybox. Attended parking garages are the most secure places to park, but also the most expensive. Some parking garages offer 'validated parking,' which is free or discounted for customers who spend money at certain stores. Get your parking stub 'validated' with a stamp or a sticker when you make a purchase. Many hotels charge $12-20 for parking, on top of the room rate. Ask about parking charges when you book.

Penalties for unauthorized parking might be $10 for parking in a no-parking zone, $20 for parking at an expired meter, and as high as $300 for parking in a zone reserved for the disabled. Pay parking fines promptly or you'll be charged even more. Rental car companies can bill fines to your credit card.

Rental

Car rental is a huge business in the USA, and rates are very competitive. The following are the major nationwide car rental companies:

Alamo
☎ 800-327-9633, W www.alamo.com

Avis
☎ 800-831-2847, W www.avis.com

Budget
☎ 800-527-0700, W www.drivebudget.com

Dollar
☎ 800-800-4000, W www.dollar.com

Enterprise
☎ 800-325-8007, W www.enterprise.com

Hertz
☎ 800-654-3131, W www.hertz.com

National
☎ 800-328-4567, W www.nationalcar.com

Rent-a-Wreck
☎ 800-535-1391, W www.rent-a-wreck.com

Thrifty
☎ 800-367-2277, W www.thrifty.com

To check the smaller local companies, look in the yellow pages section of the phone book under 'Automobiles.'

Most rental companies require that you have a major credit card, that you be at least 25 years old and that you have a valid driver's license (your home license will do).

Alamo, Thrifty, Enterprise and Rent-A-Wreck may rent to drivers between the ages of 21 and 24 for an additional charge (around $20 per day).

Rental Rates, Deals & Discounts Car rental prices vary widely from city to city, company to company, car to car and day to day. Florida and California are generally the cheapest places to rent, and New York and Illinois among the most expensive. As a very rough indication, renting the cheapest subcompact economy car for one week with unlimited mileage might cost around $120 in Florida or California, and over $300 in New York City. Rates in other parts of the USA will fall between these extremes.

If you're arranging a rental before you get to the USA, check all the options with your travel agent. If you get a fly-drive package (car rental booked together with an air ticket), local taxes may be an extra charge when you collect the car. Several online travel reservation networks have up-to-the-minute information on car rental rates at all the main airports and let you make online reservations. Compare their rates with any fly-drive package you're considering. Rates are usually lower in main cities with lots of competing companies, but if there's a big conference or sports event in town, rental cars will cost more for a few days before and after.

Once you're in a city, shop around. Use toll-free numbers to check the big national companies, but try the local operators too. Many airports have a board with advertisements for local car rental agencies as well as the big names, and a courtesy phone which lets you call them for free. You can spend 30 minutes calling a dozen of them, select the most suitable, and they'll pick you up and take you to their lot. Lower prices may apply for renting on weekends, for three days or more, for renting by the week or month, or even for renting a car in one place and returning it to another if the company needs to move cars in that direction.

Compare the total cost, including insurance, tax and mileage; one company may charge a little less for the car, but a little more for the insurance. Tax on car rentals varies from state to state, so check that too. Estimate the distance you'll be driving. 'Unlimited mileage' plans usually work out

DRIVING DISTANCES & TIMES (MILES/HOURS)

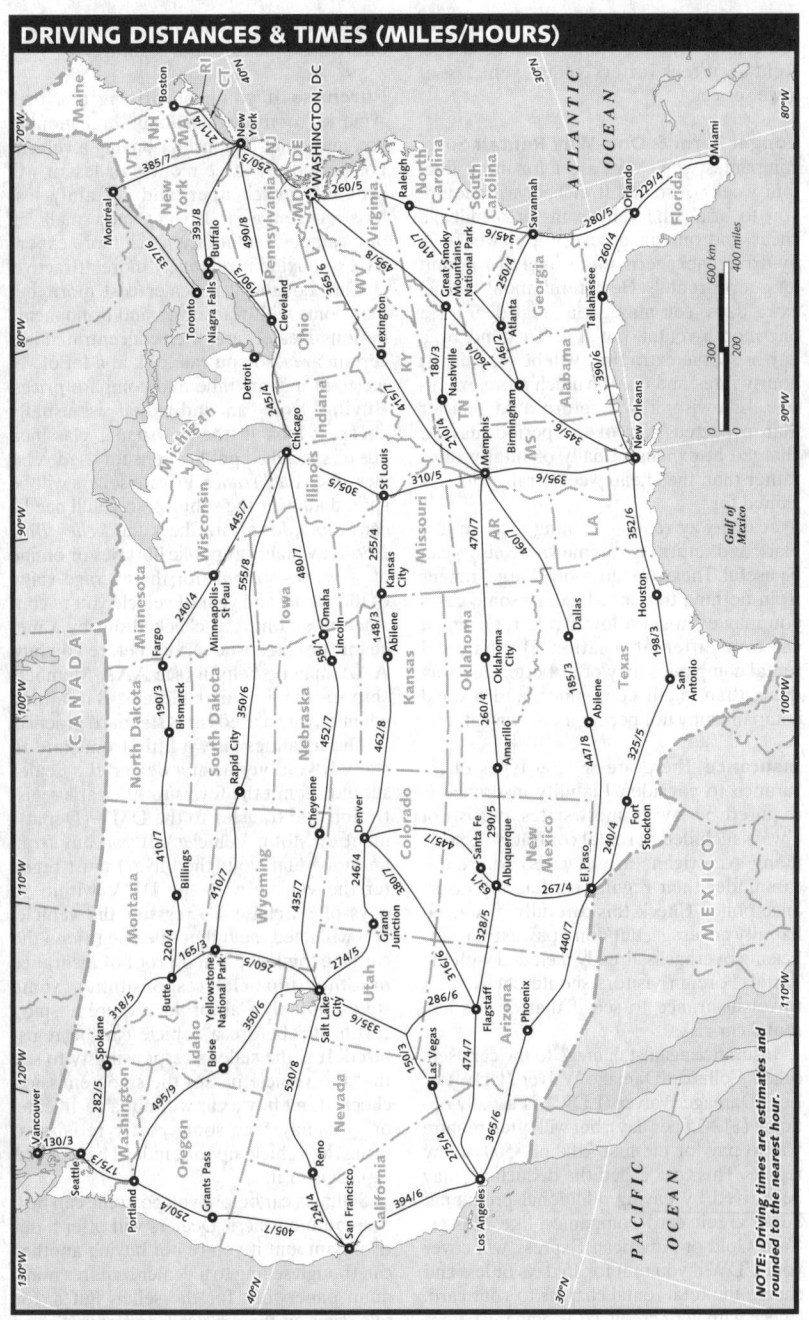

NOTE: Driving times are estimates and rounded to the nearest hour.

cheaper than 'cost-per-mile' deals, but sometimes not for short-distance usage. Rent-A-Wreck offers older vehicles at lower prices.

Longer Term & One-Way Rentals Some companies won't rent a car for more than four weeks or so at a stretch, or will require you to bring the vehicle in for a mileage check and oil change every four weeks. A fly-drive package is more likely to permit long-term rentals. Be careful about adding extra days. You may get a great deal for a one-month rental, but if you extend by a day or so, the extra time will be on daily or hourly rates, and may be much more expensive. Likewise, if you return a car earlier than expected, part of the period may be charged at expensive daily or hourly rates rather than the cheap weekly rate you bargained for.

A one-way rental – renting a car in one place and returning it somewhere else – can be useful. The extra 'drop-off charge' ranges from nothing to over $1000. In some cases you may even get a lower rate returning a car to a different location. Big national rental companies may offer better one-way deals than small companies, and a local company may not permit a one-way at all.

Insurance There are several types of insurance to consider. Liability insurance is required by law in most states, but is not always included in rental contracts because many Americans are covered for rental cars under their regular car liability insurance policy. Check this carefully. You need liability coverage, but don't pay extra if sufficient coverage is already included with the rental. Foreign visitors should check their travel insurance to see if that covers any rental car risks.

Insurance against damage to the car itself, called Collision Damage Waiver (CDW) or Loss Damage Waiver (LDW), is usually optional ($12-15 per day), but will often require you to pay for the first $100 or $500 of any repairs. This cost, called the deductible, may be waived by paying additional premiums. Some credit card companies, like Master-Card Gold or American Express, will cover your CDW if you rent for 15 days or less and charge the total rental charges to your card. Check with your credit card company before

you leave home to determine if this service is offered and the extent of coverage.

Purchase If you'll be driving in North America for more than about three months, you may want to consider buying a vehicle. For periods of three months or less, it will probably be cheaper, and certainly less hassle, to rent a car. If you want a small van or a camper, rentals are much more expensive, so buying is relatively more attractive.

Cars bought at a dealer cost more, but may come with warranties and/or financing options. Dealers are often concentrated in a certain area, so you can look at a lot of vehicles in a short time and compare prices. Buying from an individual is usually cheaper; look in the newspaper classified ads or special ad publications for used vehicles, like *Auto Trader*. Private sellers will be spread all over the suburbs, so you'll need a car to look for a car. Check the *Kelley Blue Book* (available at public libraries or online at W www.kbb.com) for the average value of the model and year of vehicle you're considering and have it checked out by a mechanic or diagnostic service before you buy. AAA may be helpful (see AAA Membership earlier in this chapter). Bargaining when buying a used car is standard practice.

The legalities vary a little from state to state. If you buy from a dealer, the dealer should submit the forms for the car's registration and transfer to the DMV (Department of Motor Vehicles). If you buy from an individual, you (the buyer) must register the vehicle with the DMV within 10 days of purchase. To register the vehicle, you will need the bill of sale, the title to the car (the 'pink slip') and proof of insurance or other financial responsibility. Some states, notably California, require a 'smog certificate' before a vehicle can be registered. It is the seller's responsibility to see that the vehicle passes the smog emission check; don't buy a car without a certificate, or you may face some costly repairs to bring the vehicle up to standard before you can register it.

Selling a car before you go home can be a desperate business. Dealers will offer a derisory amount if you're not buying another car, though selling to a dealer requires minimum paperwork for the seller. Put a 'for sale' sign on the car itself, and advertise as

Driving by Numbers

Most roads in the USA are identified by numbers. To navigate, you need to know the numbers of the highways to your destination. Don't expect signs saying 'To San Jose' – you need to know the way is via I-880, US 101, Hwy 82 or Hwy 87.

On the main system of interstate highways, even numbers indicate the east-west routes and odd numbers are for north-south routes: I-80 connects New York to San Francisco; I-95 goes from Maine to Miami. I-80 heads north out of San Francisco, but the freeway entrance will be marked I-80 East, because that's where the highway is going. Where an interstate skirts a city, it has an even digit added to the front – I-295 is the bit of I-95 that goes around Washington, DC. Where an interstate goes into or through the middle of a city, an odd number is added to the front – I-395 is the bit of I-95 that goes through central Washington, DC. Where two interstate routes merge, the same stretch of highway can have two numbers, like I-70/ I-76 between Pittsburgh and Chicago.

The national numbering system was introduced in the 1920s, and old highway names were dropped from use – 'National Old Trails Hwy' became US Route 66. The classic 'US' highways used the system of odds and evens, but the old routes were often buried under new interstates in the 1950s and '60s. Leaving San Francisco, US 50 is the same road as I-80, but it becomes US 50 itself east of Sacramento, and there's an alternate route, Alt 50, going through Reno.

State highways, secondary state highways and country highways all have two- or three-digit numbers. Often three or more highway numbers apply to the same stretch of road. It's all very logical, but it can be confusing.

widely as possible, especially in hostels, colleges and local papers. Have a phone number where buyers can call you, and be prepared to drop your price for a quick sale. Be sure to officially notify the DMV that you've sold the vehicle, or you may have to pay someone else's parking tickets.

There are often advertisements for vans and cars for sale at youth hostels and traveler's haunts, especially in California, but there doesn't seem to be any established marketplace where there are dozens of vehicles with 'for sale' signs.

Where to Buy Cars Generally, California, Nevada, Arizona and Texas are good places to buy, because cars last longer in dry conditions. Many states salt the roads to reduce ice in winter, and this causes corrosion. Seattle might be a good place, because insurance is easier to obtain. You could even buy in Vancouver, Canada, where there's government liability insurance at fixed rates. Canadian cars can be driven in the USA without additional documentation, but used cars are more costly, and the tax is significantly higher.

Buying a car or van is vastly easier if you can do it in a place where you can stay with friends or relatives. You'll have an address for the registration and license papers, a private phone to call prospective sellers and you won't go broke paying hotel bills while you're looking. Just be sure you buy your wheels before you wear out your welcome.

Out-of-State Vehicles If you buy a car with out-of-state plates, it has to be re-registered in the state where you bought it, which will involve fees, new plates and possibly roadworthiness and smog checks. Selling a car outside the state of purchase is also problematic, and buyers will want to pay considerably less.

RVs, Vans & Campers

A recreational vehicle, or RV, is a vehicle fitted out for sleeping and eating – anything from a Volkswagen van to a luxury motor home as big as a Greyhound bus. The word 'camper' often refers to a small pickup truck with a shell on the back, fitted out with bunks, tables etc. RVs are more expensive than cars to rent, buy and run, but they solve all your transport, accommodations and cooking needs in one go. Campgrounds with 'hookups' for electricity, water and even cable TV connections are found almost everywhere in the countryside. If you want to visit a big city, the nearest campground may be a long way out of town.

Some tour packages include RV rental, with cooking gear, maps and everything you need. RVs can also be rented in the USA;

look in the yellow pages under 'Recreational Vehicles – Renting & Leasing,' or try Grand Travel Systems (☎ 800-849-9959), Cruise America (☎ 800-327-7799, W www .cruiseamerica.com), Adventures on Wheels (☎ 732-583-8714, W wheels9.com), and Happy Travel Camper Rental & Sales (☎ 800-370-1262, W www.camperUSA.com). The latter two companies advertise guaranteed buy-back or repurchase schemes. Auto Tour (☎ 206-999-4686) in Seattle, Washington, has been helping visitors buy and sell cars for several years.

As with rental cars, the cost of renting an RV is variable and is often based on season. As a very rough indication, a mini-camper suitable for a couple might cost $385 per week in Florida during low season or $752 per week in California during high season, with additional charges for mileage, insurance and servicing. At these prices it may be cheaper to stay in motels, or use a tent.

Ride-Sharing

If you're looking for someone to ride along to share the cost of fuel, ask around, put a notice up in hostels, check the ride boards at universities and even look at the newspaper classified ads. Hostels can be especially good places to find riders, not only for long trips but also for sharing the cost of a rental car for local day trips.

Drive-Away Cars

One option for longer trips is a 'drive-away car' from a vehicle transport company that needs drivers to move cars from one place to another.

To be a driver you must be over 21 and be able to present a valid driver's license, personal references and a $200-400 cash deposit that is refunded upon safe delivery of the car. Some companies also require a printout of your driving record, a major credit card or three forms of identification. You pay nothing for the use of the car, but you do pay for the fuel you use. The company pays you nothing to drive the car, but they do pay the insurance. Check the car carefully for damage before you start.

You must deliver the car to its destination at a specified time; the time allotted for a trip usually works out to about six hours of driving per day. Maximum mileage is also stipulated, so you have to follow the shortest route. Be clear about the conditions for deposit refund and how you can cash the refund check.

There may or may not be cars available when and to where you want to go, so it helps to be flexible, plan ahead and contact several companies. Availability depends on demand, with coast-to-coast routes the most easily available. Some demand is determined by holiday movements. Lots of cars need drivers from the Northeast to Florida at the start of winter.

Drive-away car companies are listed in the yellow pages under 'Automotive Transport & Drive-Away Companies.' (Phone a week or two ahead of when you want to travel.) They include the following:

A-A Auto Transport & Driveaway
☎ 800-466-6935

A Anthony Driveaway Truckaway
☎ 800-606-2006

Across America Driveaway
☎ 800-964-7874
W www.shultz-international.com

Auto Driveaway Co
☎ 800-346-2277
W www.schultz-international.com/ aadriveaway.htm

National Auto Transport
☎ 800-225-9611

MOTORCYCLE

Riding a bike in America is an almost mythic experience, with a heritage going back beyond *Easy Rider* and *The Wild One*. The biker on the road descends from the cowboy on the range and endures many of the same discomforts, as well as enjoying the same sense of freedom and the wide-open spaces.

You'll need a US state motorcycle license or an International Driving Permit endorsed for motorcycles. A state DMV can give you the rules relating to motorcycle use. Helmets are required in almost every state.

Motorcycle rental and insurance is expensive, especially if you want to ride a Harley-Davidson. EagleRider motorcycle rentals (☎ 800-910-1520, W www.eaglerider .com), with offices in major cities nationwide, charges $75-150 per day for a Harley, including helmet and liability insurance, but collision insurance (CDW) is extra. Buying

Biker Highlights

The Harley-Davidson motorcycle company headquarters is in Milwaukee, Wisconsin, where they make the hog engines. It's more interesting, however, to visit the **Harley-Davidson assembly plant** in York, Pennsylvania (☎ 717-848-1177; see the New York & Mid-Atlantic States chapter). A motorcycle museum there displays a bike from every production year since 1906, and a gift shop sells Harley-Davidson merchandise.

Springfield, Massachusetts, claims to be the home of gasoline-powered motorcycles, and its **Indian Motorcycle Museum** (☎ 413-737-2624; see the New England chapter) has nostalgia appeal.

Sturgis, South Dakota, has an annual hog fest in early August and a classic collection at the **Sturgis Motorcycle Museum & Hall of Fame** (☎ 605-347-2556; see the Great Plains chapter).

The first week in March is **Bike Week** in Daytona, Florida, when lawyers, accountants, Hell's Angels and speed heads get together for a wild party that's based around motorcycle races at the Daytona International Speedway (☎ 904-254-2700; see the Florida chapter).

Dubbing itself 'the world's largest multi-brand motorcycle touring rally,' **Americade** goes on for one week in summer every year in Lake George, New York. For information and registration, call ☎ 518-798-7888, or visit W www.tourexpo.com.

Alabama's most famous motorcycle route is the **Trail of Tears corridor**, which stretches 200 miles from Ross Landing in Chattanooga, Tennessee, to Waterloo, Alabama, tracing the official Indian Removal Act of 1830 route. The corridor is open year round, and an annual motorcycle ride is held in September to honor the Native Americans who suffered and died en route. There are historic markers and signs along the way that follow much of what is now Hwy 72.

For more on biking in the USA, check the links from W www.lets-ride.com, or contact the American Motorcyclist Association (☎ 614-856-1900, W www.ama-cycle.org).

a bike would be cheaper if you're staying a few months and if you can take a loss to sell it in a hurry.

Bike Tours Amerika (☎ 61-3-5473-4469 in Australia, 49 2764 7824 in Germany, W www.biketours.com.au) offers a selection of escorted group tours on Yamaha XT 600s, BMWs and other bikes, including a three-week trip from San Francisco to Vancouver via the Grand Canyon and the Rocky Mountains, from US$2650. Other trips go from Vancouver to Alaska and back via two different routes. They also do rentals and buybacks for Yamaha XT 600 motorcycles.

BICYCLE

The country is so big that cycling around it would take a long time, though it's entirely feasible. Bicycles are not permitted on freeways, and you wouldn't want to ride on them anyway. Even long-distance trips can be done entirely on quiet backroads.

Adventure Cycling Association (☎ 406-721-1776, 800-755-2453, W www.adv-cycling.org, PO Box 8308P, Missoula, MT 59807) is a nationwide bicyclists' club that organizes tours. Alternatively, arrange a cycle tour with a bike tour specialist like Backroads (☎ 510-527-1555, 800-245-3874, W www.backroads.com, 1516 5th St, Berkeley, CA 94710). Members of the national League of American Bicyclists (LAB; ☎ 410-539-3399, 800-288-2453, 190 W Ostend St, Suite 120, Baltimore, MD 21230) can obtain a list of hospitality homes in each state offering simple accommodations to touring cyclists. LAB also publishes an annual *Almanac* listing contacts in each state along with information about bicycle routes and special events.

For transporting your own bike, most international and domestic airlines will carry bikes as checked baggage if they're in a box without extra charge. Many carriers impose an oversize-baggage charge (for domestic carriers up to $50) for bikes that aren't disassembled first – check before you buy the ticket. Amtrak trains and Greyhound buses will transport bikes within the USA, sometimes with an extra handling charge of about $10. Ask about packaging and boxing requirements and extra charges.

If you want to buy a bike in the USA, you'll find the best range at specialist bike shops. Check the yellow pages, or refer to one of the above organizations for specific suggestions. General sporting goods stores will have a more limited range of bikes and accessories, while warehouse stores will have the lowest prices on a range of basic models and can't offer specialized advice. Used bicycles are sold at flea markets and garage sales and advertised in newspapers and on notice boards at hostels and colleges.

HITCHHIKING

Hitchhiking in the USA is potentially dangerous and definitely not recommended. There have been so many nasty incidents and lurid reports that drivers are very reluctant to pick up hitchhikers anyway. This may be less so in rural parts, but traffic can be sparse, and you might get stranded. Hitchhiking on freeways is prohibited; there's usually a white sign at the on-ramp stating 'no pedestrians beyond this point,' and anyone caught hitching past there can be arrested.

Even hitching to and from a hiking trailhead should be avoided. Try to arrange something at a ranger station or with other hikers. If you're flat broke, there are still alternatives to standing by a roadside with your thumb out. Look for ride shares at hostels, or ask at campgrounds.

BOAT

Coastal ferry services, often state-run, provide economical, efficient and scenic links to the many islands off the US coasts. Most larger ferries will transport private cars, motorcycles and bicycles. Some of the most interesting boat connections are to the Cape Hatteras National Seashore in North Carolina, Catalina Island off Southern California

and through Puget Sound in the Pacific Northwest. Windjammer cruises off the coast of Maine are another option. The most spectacular coastal cruises, however, are on the south coast of Alaska, and along the Inside Passage.

The Great Lakes have a number of attractive islands that can only be visited by boat. In many cases, the lack of cars is a great part of the islands' attraction. Popular boat trips go to historic Mackinac Island, Michigan; the Apostle Islands, off Wisconsin; Kelleys Island and the Bass Islands, Ohio; and the remote Isle Royale National Park, most easily reached from Michigan.

Rivers and canals were enormously important transport routes before the advent of railways. There are a couple of ways to relive the era of Mark Twain and the Mississippi. If you can afford it, try the luxury steamboat cruises organized by the Delta Queen Steamboat Co (☎ 504-586-0631, 800-543-1949, ⓦ www.deltaqueen.com). From New Orleans, it offers three luxurious old-style steamboats making two- to 14-day excursions on the Mississippi, Missouri, Tennessee and Ohio Rivers, calling at river ports like Natchez, Vicksburg, Memphis, Louisville, Cincinnati, Pittsburgh, Nashville, Chattanooga, St Louis and St Paul. The least expensive accommodations cost around $165 per night, and the most expensive are about $685 per night.

For something shorter, cheaper but less atmospheric, try one of the casino cruises on the Mississippi from Wisconsin or Illinois.

LOCAL TRANSPORTATION

Getting around US cities can be difficult without a car, especially in the sprawling suburbs of newer cities. Larger, older cities like New York, San Francisco and Chicago have adequate public transport and limited parking, so a car is more trouble than it's worth. Public transportation options for main cities are outlined in the regional chapters.

To/From Airports

Most airports offer a choice of transport, from stretch limos to public buses. Airport shuttle buses are usually a reliable, inexpensive and convenient compromise. These are minibuses (about 12 seats) that pick up from several locations, including the main hotels, on their way to the airport, and deliver incoming passengers to their doors within their service area. Shuttle phone numbers for most main airports are provided in the regional chapters.

Bus

Most cities and larger towns have local bus systems, but many are designed for commuter service and provide limited service in the evening, sometimes none at all on weekends.

Subway

A few cities have underground or elevated metropolitan rail systems, which provide the best local transport. These include the subway in New York; the Metro in Washington, DC; the El in Chicago; and the Bay Area Rapid Transit (BART) in and around San Francisco.

Taxi

Taxis are metered, with charges from $1 or $2 to start, plus at least $1.20 per mile. They charge extra for handling baggage, and drivers expect a minimum 10%-15% tip. If you don't spot a taxi cruising, you can phone for one; look under 'Taxi' in the yellow pages.

ORGANIZED TOURS

Apart from tours sold as part of an international package (see the Getting There & Away chapter), there are many tours available within the USA. Some of these can be excellent, even for the most die-hard independent traveler. One advantage of tours run for the local market is that they offer a chance to meet like-minded Americans.

City Tours

Most cities will have local tours around the main attractions. These can help orient you and identify attractions that you can explore later in more depth. City tours are advertised everywhere a tourist is likely to draw breath.

Gray Line Tours is the generic operator, with tours in almost every urban area. A half-day tour will cost from around $25/12 for adults/children. In bigger cities, they offer a variety of different tours. Check the yellow pages for a local Gray Line office.

Another company offers city tours in imitation old-style streetcars, usually under a local name like the Old Town Trolley, Waikiki Trolley or Philadelphia Trolley. These do a circuit of local attractions, and passengers can get off at whichever ones they like and board a later trolley. They're a good blend of organized tours and independent sightseeing (usually around $20 for a day-long ticket).

Local specialty tours can be the most fun. They're commonly offered by local companies and feature commentary with lots of local color. They might focus on homes of the stars (Beverly Hills, California), political scandals (Washington, DC), architectural highlights (Chicago), or ghost and vampire tours (New Orleans).

Special Interest Tours

Many tours are designed for specialized interests and activities, and can be cheaper and less trouble than arranging your own trip. For example, ski/snowboard trips to Rocky Mountain resorts are available from most US cities throughout the winter, sometimes at heavily discounted prices if there are a lot of unfilled rooms in the resorts. Even at the regular prices, a ski package may be cheaper than the combined cost of airfares, accommodations, rentals and lift passes.

Other offerings include white-water rafting trips, tours and tastings in wine-producing areas, gambling trips to Las Vegas or Atlantic City, African American heritage tours in the South, leaf-peeping rambles in New England, and scuba diving courses on the Great Lakes. So many options are available that it's impossible to list them all here, or to generalize about the range of possibilities and prices.

To find out what's available, contact some of the organizations listed in the Activities section of the Facts for the Visitor chapter, find a travel agent that specializes in the activities that interest you (check the yellow pages, or at an appropriate sports store), and look in the travel sections of Sunday newspapers in the main cities.

New York & the Mid-Atlantic States

New York
& the Mid-Atlantic States

New York, New Jersey and Pennsylvania are the country's most densely populated states, the focus of early US history and the engine of US industrial development. For travelers, New York City is a major gateway and a compelling destination in itself. One of the most visited cities in the world, it has the USA's largest collection of museums and galleries, excellent eateries, endless shopping and unlimited entertainment.

Other cities in the region offer many of the same attractions in more manageable doses. Visitors may be surprised at the natural beauty of these states – the picturesque farmlands, the Adirondack lakes and mountains, Niagara Falls and the New Jersey Shore.

History

Native American settlement was sparse when Europeans first arrived here. The area was probably home to fewer than 100,000 people, comprising two major cultural groups.

The Algonquians included the Lenni-Lanape (called the 'Delaware Indians' by the British), Shawnee, Mohegan (or Mohican), and Munsee. They occupied the Hudson Valley, Long Island, New Jersey, the Delaware River Valley and parts of Pennsylvania.

The Iroquois included the Cayuga, Mohawk, Oneida, Onondaga and Seneca peoples, who in 1570 formed the powerful Iroquois Confederacy (also called the 'Iroquois League' or 'Five Nations'). The Iroquois Confederacy controlled central and western New York and most of western Pennsylvania. The Susquehannock were also Iroquois and occupied the Susquehanna River Valley in central Pennsylvania.

French fur trappers and traders on the St Lawrence River reached the region by the mid-16th century. In 1609, Henry Hudson found, named and sailed up the Hudson River, claiming the land for the Dutch, who started several settlements in 'New Netherlands.' The Iroquois soon controlled the booming fur trade, selling to Dutch, English and French agents.

Highlights

- New York, New York – king of the hill, top of the heap
- Metropolitan Museum of Art – the world's best museum?
- Statue of Liberty & Ellis Island – icons and immigrants
- The Adirondacks – lovely lakes and mountains, in all four seasons
- Independence National Historic Park – 'America's most historic square mile,' in Philadelphia
- Pennsylvania Dutch Country – where the Amish still travel by horse-drawn buggy
- Celebrity spotting – seasonal sightings at Saratoga and the Hamptons; resident and migratory species in New York City

OTHER MAPS
New York & the Mid-Atlantic States
pages 166-167
NEW YORK CITY MAPS
Lower Manhattan pages 176-178
Midtown & Chelsea pages 188-189
Upper Manhattan & Harlem pages 194-195

CANADA

Lake Ontario

Lake Erie

ME

VT NH

NY MA

CT

New York City
(see New York City maps)
page 174

PA NJ

Philadelphia
pages 238-239

Pittsburgh
page 250

MD DE

ATLANTIC OCEAN

The tiny Dutch settlement on Manhattan Island surrendered to a Royal Navy warship in 1664, in the midst of a series of Anglo-Dutch wars. Locally, there was little resistance to the English takeover, which was ratified by the 1667 Treaty of Breda. The new colonial power created two territories, called 'New York' and 'New Jersey.' In 1676, New Jersey was divided into East and West. West Jersey (actually the *southern* portion) became America's first Quaker settlement, and in 1681 East Jersey was purchased by a group of Quakers led by William Penn. In the prolonged French and Indian War (1754–63) the British defeated the French to secure control of northeast America. The shift of Indian allegiances away from the French was a crucial factor in the British victory. The new British territory, extending to the Mississippi, was made an Indian reserve, but this was short-lived.

Pennsylvania played a leading role in the Revolutionary War (1775–83). New York and New Jersey loyalties were split, but important battles still occurred in all three states. Many Iroquois allied themselves with the British, and they suffered badly from military defeats, disease, European encroachment and reprisals. Entire communities were wiped out, and much of their land was deeded to Revolutionary War veterans. Farmers displaced the Algonquians from coastal areas and river valleys.

Railways linked the area's major cities as early as the 1840s. The population grew with waves of immigration, starting with the Irish in the 1840s and 1850s. Natural resources, abundant labor and unfettered capitalism transformed the region into a powerhouse of industry and commerce. During the Civil War (1861–65), the Mid-Atlantic states supplied men and material for Union forces. A Confederate thrust into Pennsylvania was halted at Gettysburg in one of the war's bloodiest battles.

After the Civil War, the West was opened by steel railroad tracks made in Pittsburgh, the engines of growth used Pennsylvania coal and oil, and the profits went back to the 'robber barons' (the super-rich industrialists and financiers) in New York. All the region's cities were swollen with immigrants – blacks from the South, Chinese from California, and over 12 million Europeans who arrived at Ellis Island, in the middle of New York harbor. The growth, the industry, the wealth, the cultural diversity and the constant flow of people continues in the Mid-Atlantic states to this day.

Geography

Most big cities are on the main rivers of the eastern coastal plain, including the Hudson, Delaware, Susquehanna and Ohio Rivers. Low mountain ranges extend across the region's heavily forested interior. Farther inland, the waterways of the Great Lakes and the Ohio River link many smaller industrial cities.

Flora & Fauna

Much of the original forest was cleared for timber. But with regrowth, forest now covers much of the region, notably the Adirondacks, New Jersey's Pine Barrens and western and northern Pennsylvania. The area's many tree species include white pine, red spruce, maple, oak, ash and birch. Wildlife includes deer, black bear, raccoon and moose.

This is a transitional zone for plants and animals: Several northern species end their range here and many southern ones begin. It's also on the Atlantic flyway, so many migratory waterfowl are present, as well as the raptors that prey on them. Acid rain is a serious environmental problem.

When to Go

New York City is a year-round attraction, but it's hot and humid in the summer, when locals flock to the beaches on Long Island and the Jersey Shore. Spring is a beautiful time in the cities and the countryside, and it's not nearly as touristy as summer. Fall, with its pleasant weather and vivid colors, is peak time in places like the Adirondacks, Catskills and Pennsylvania woodlands. Winter is cold and days are short, but it's high season for the performing arts and for winter sports.

Activities

Hiking and backpacking information can be obtained from the following sources: Adirondack Mountain Club (☎ 518-668-4447, Ⓦ www.adk.org, RR 3, Box 3055, Lake George, NY 12845), Appalachian Mountain Club Manhattan Resource

NEW YORK & THE MID-ATLANTIC STATES

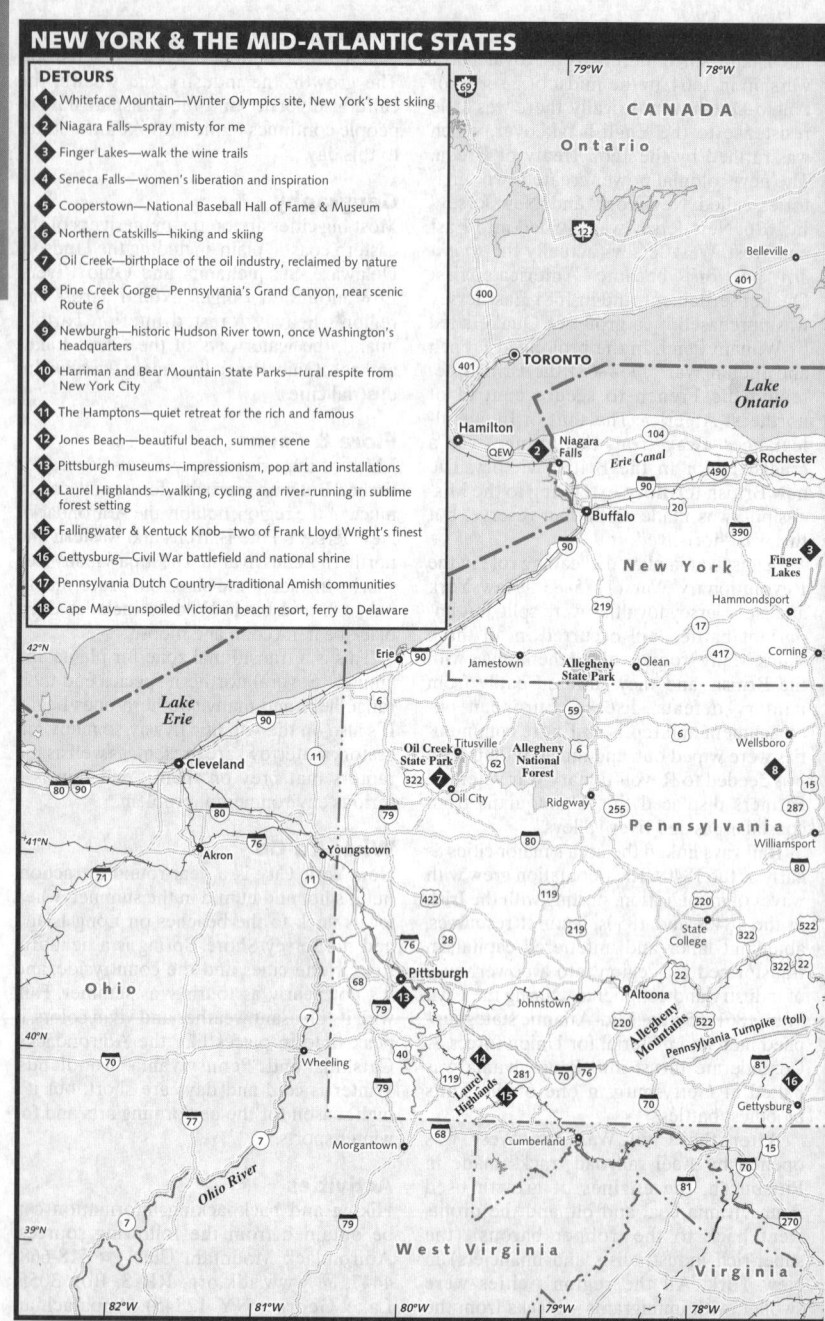

DETOURS

1. Whiteface Mountain—Winter Olympics site, New York's best skiing
2. Niagara Falls—spray misty for me
3. Finger Lakes—walk the wine trails
4. Seneca Falls—women's liberation and inspiration
5. Cooperstown—National Baseball Hall of Fame & Museum
6. Northern Catskills—hiking and skiing
7. Oil Creek—birthplace of the oil industry, reclaimed by nature
8. Pine Creek Gorge—Pennsylvania's Grand Canyon, near scenic Route 6
9. Newburgh—historic Hudson River town, once Washington's headquarters
10. Harriman and Bear Mountain State Parks—rural respite from New York City
11. The Hamptons—quiet retreat for the rich and famous
12. Jones Beach—beautiful beach, summer scene
13. Pittsburgh museums—impressionism, pop art and installations
14. Laurel Highlands—walking, cycling and river-running in sublime forest setting
15. Fallingwater & Kentuck Knob—two of Frank Lloyd Wright's finest
16. Gettysburg—Civil War battlefield and national shrine
17. Pennsylvania Dutch Country—traditional Amish communities
18. Cape May—unspoiled Victorian beach resort, ferry to Delaware

NEW YORK & THE MID-ATLANTIC STATES

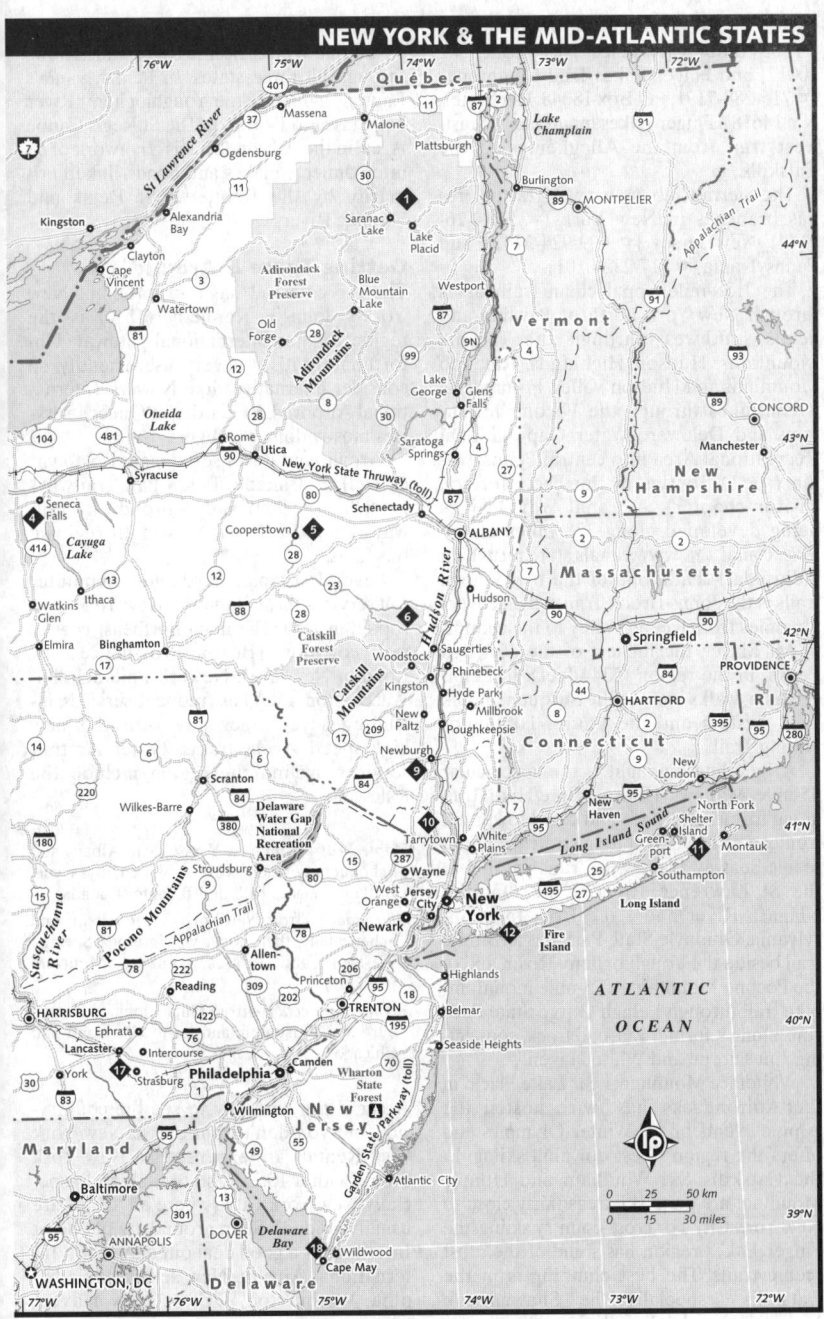

Center (☎ 212-986-1430, ⓦ www.outdoors
.org, 5 Tudor City Place, New York, NY
10017) and Finger Lakes Trail Conference
(☎ 716-288-7191, PO Box 18048, Rochester,
NY 14618). Finger Lakes maintains an east-
west trail from the Alleghenies to the
Catskills.

The Sierra Club (ⓦ www.sierraclub.org)
has branches in New York (☎ 518-426-
9144), New Jersey (☎ 609-924-3141), and
Pennsylvania (☎ 717-232-0101).

The 2158-mile Appalachian Trail passes
through New York north of Pawling and
heads southwest through the Taconic
Mountains, Hudson Highlands, Ramapo
Mountains and Hudson Valley. From there,
it continues through the Pocono Mountains and Delaware Water Gap National
Recreational Area into central Pennsylvania (see Activities in the Facts for the
Visitor chapter). A Canal Way Trail is
being developed along 338 miles of the
Erie Canal (ⓦ www.canals.state.ny.us). In
Adirondack Park, one of the best-known
trails is the Johns Brook Trail, which covers
9½ miles from Keene Valley to the summit
of Mt Marcy, the highest of the 46 'High
Peaks' in the region (5344 feet). In Pennsylvania, walks include the Susquehannock
Trail System and the Laurel Highlands
Hiking Trail.

A bicycling highlight is the spectacular
35-mile Mohawk-Hudson Bike/Hike Trail
along former railroads and canal towpaths.
You can also cycle on long stretches of the
scenic Seaway Trail, which runs parallel to
the St Lawrence River, Lake Ontario,
Niagara River and Lake Erie. In Pennsylvania, Ohiopyle State Park has a 25-mile
trail beside the Youghiogheny River, and in
the Pocono Mountains a 25-mile mountain-
bike trail through Lehigh Gorge State Park
runs along a former railroad track, connecting Jim Thorpe and White Haven.

Whiteface Mountain, near Lake Placid in
the Adirondacks, has twice hosted the
Alpine events of the Winter Olympics and
offers the region's best downhill skiing. In
the Catskills, Ski Windham and Hunter
Mountain are good ski areas fairly close to
New York City. For cross-country skiing, the
Finger Lakes region has some of the most
scenic trails. The best climbing is in the
Catskills (especially the Shawangunk
Mountains) and Adirondacks.

Rafts and canoes go down the Delaware,
a National Wild & Scenic River, which flows
through all three states. In Pennsylvania's
Laurel Highlands, the Youghiogheny River
has Class I to IV rapids. The St Regis Canoe
Area, in the Adirondacks, is a network of 58
interconnected lakes and ponds, linked primarily by the Raquette, St Regis and
Saranac Rivers.

Getting There & Around

The big cities all have airports, but New
York's John F Kennedy (JFK) is the
region's major international gateway. Unfortunately it's not very user-friendly, so
consider alternatives like Newark International Airport. La Guardia, in Queens, services mostly domestic flights.

Greyhound buses serve main US towns
as well as Canada. Peter Pan Trailways
(☎ 800-343-9999) and Adirondack Trailways (☎ 800-225-6815) are both regional
bus lines.

Several companies provide commuter
rail services throughout the New York metropolitan area. The main northeast coastal
rail corridor (Boston-Providence-New
London-New York-Newark-Philadelphia-
Washington, DC) has frequent services, including several per day with the new
high-speed Acela trains. Other Amtrak
services around the region include the
following:

Maple Leaf – from New York City to Albany and
Schenectady, then west to Utica, Syracuse,
Buffalo, Niagara Falls and Toronto (Canada)

Adirondack – from New York City to Albany and
Schenectady, then north via Saratoga Springs,
Westport and Rouses Point to Montreal
(Canada)

Skyline Connection – from Philadelphia to Harrisburg and Pittsburgh, and on to Cleveland and
Chicago

A car is the best way to see the countryside, but you don't want one in New York
City. Rentals are expensive in New York
State (with a 13.25% state tax), and especially New York City (where all 'deals' are
usually voided). Shop around, by phone or
Internet, for a good deal out of Newark International Airport, New Jersey; Philadelphia; Washington, DC; or New Haven,
Connecticut.

New York State

History

New York State's history is linked largely to its inland waterways. The first settlements were along the Hudson River, including tiny Newburgh, where George Washington made his headquarters during the Revolutionary War. Completed in 1825, the Erie Canal, between Albany and Buffalo, connected New York and the Hudson River with the Great Lakes and Midwest. The canal system helped open the continent's interior, promoted industrial development in cities like Buffalo, Rochester and Syracuse, and established New York City as the USA's major shipping port.

Geography

The Greater New York megalopolis surrounds the mouth of the Hudson River and the western end of Long Island. The Hudson flows south from the Adirondack Mountains, from where the St Lawrence River system drains west into the Great Lakes. The Catskills drain into the Delaware River. Just about every part of the state north of New York City can be loosely called 'upstate' New York.

New York

Nicknames: Empire State, Excelsior State

Population: 18,976,500 (3rd)

Area: 54,471 sq miles (27th)

Admitted to Union: July 26, 1788 (11th)

Capital city: Albany (population 95,700)

Other cities: New York City (8,008,300), Buffalo (292,700), Rochester (219,800)

Birthplace of: Teddy Roosevelt (1858–1919), the US women's suffrage movement (1872), Franklin D Roosevelt (1882–1945), Eleanor Roosevelt (1884–1962), Humphrey Bogart (1899–1957), Woody Allen (b 1935), *Catch 22* author Joseph Heller (b 1923)

Home of: United Nations headquarters, Wall Street, perfect pizza and blemish-free bagels

Government & Economy

With 31 US Congressional representatives, the state is the country's second-largest voting block. New York City is generally Democratic, while other parts lean Republican. That reflects statewide political tensions – downstate versus upstate. The state's politics received wide attention in the 2000 election for the US Senate, when the high-profile Republican mayor of New York City, Rudolph Giuliani, took on high-profile Democrat First Lady Hillary Rodham Clinton. Giuliani dropped out of the contest for health reasons, and Senator Clinton now represents the state in Washington, DC.

New York State still has several manufacturing centers, despite layoffs and shutdowns. Agriculture and forestry are also major industries, and tourism is a growth area. New York City commerce, retailing and service industries are all huge.

Arts

New York City is an international center for TV and film production, music recording, publishing, and the visual and performing arts. It has been an important center for new music styles such as ragtime, jazz, R&B, folk, rock, rap and hip-hop. All the modern art movements – from cubism and Dada to abstract expressionism and pop art – have a strong New York influence. And writers Henry James, Edith Wharton, F Scott Fitzgerald and Tom Wolfe, among many others, have featured New York City in their books.

Outside the city, painters of the 19th-century Hudson River school (like Thomas Cole, Asher Durand and Frederick Church) produced the first distinctly American art, abandoning European-style portraiture for romantic depictions of the American landscape. Author Washington Irving also immortalized the Hudson's rural charms in *The Legend of Sleepy Hollow*.

Information

The New York State tourist bureau (☎ 518-474-4116, 800-225-5697, ⓦ www.iloveny.com) is at PO Box 2603, Albany, NY 12220-0603. For fishing licenses, contact the Department of Environment Conservation (☎ 518-457-3521). The basic state sales tax is 4%, but varying local taxes increase the bite – up to 13.25% in New York City.

New York City

More than eight million residents of every color and culture are packed into New York City's 309 sq miles, and almost 40 million visitors come to the city each year. All of them expect something big, brash and energetic, and nobody is disappointed.

New York City is a crowded, demanding destination where you need to clearly define your sightseeing priorities and get to them early. You'll feel a rush when you emerge from a hotel doorway or a subway station – you're about to experience a dysfunctional miracle.

History

The area now known as New York City was occupied by Native Americans for more than 11,000 years – the name 'Manhattan' was derived from local Munsee Indian words meaning 'island of hills.' The first recorded European visitor was Giovanni da Verrazano (1524), but Henry Hudson was the first to claim the land for his sponsors, the Dutch East India Company, in 1609. He reported it to be 'as beautiful a land as one can hope to tread upon.'

Colonial Era The Dutch established their first trading post, Nieuw Amsterdam, in 1624. The story goes that they purchased Manhattan Island for goods worth about 60 guilders, and it may well be true. Governor Peter Stuyvesant was sent to impose order on the unruly colony, but his ban on alcohol and curtailment of religious freedoms caused unrest among the settlers, and after a struggle the colony was taken over by the British in 1664.

Renamed 'New York,' the town retained much of its Dutch character well into the mid-18th century. Opposition to British colonial rule eventually developed and was expressed in newspapers and in protest marches on New York's Commons, where City Hall stands today. But many New Yorkers, with family ties back in Britain, resisted a war for independence. In fact, New York was a British stronghold, and George III's troops controlled the city for most of the Revolutionary War.

Boom Years George Washington was sworn in here as the republic's first president in 1789, but the founding fathers disliked New York City; Thomas Jefferson described the city as 'a cloacina of all the depravities of human nature.' The city was then a bustling and dirty seaport of 33,000 people. The Erie Canal, opened in 1825, linked New York to the Great Lakes and made it the main port for the whole country,

What They Said about New York

'Never have I experienced so much in one week as here. I feel as if I'm in a film. Life here is very different than in Europe. Only the moment counts; no one seems to care what he'll do tomorrow.'

– Photographer Robert Frank

'New York is a work of art – a complete work of art….A real bohemia. Delightful. Why, Greenwich Village was full of people doing absolutely *nothing*.'

– Artist Marcel Duchamp

'A third-rate Babylon.'

– Writer HL Mencken

'I spent my childhood in New York, riding on the subways and buses. And you know what you learn if you're a New Yorker? The world doesn't owe you a damn thing.'

– Actress Lauren Bacall

'I support a very specific type of immigration control. I think we should only let people born in other countries get into New York.'

– Humorist Fran Lebowitz

as well as the major center for trade and finance. By 1830, New York had grown eightfold, to a metropolis of 250,000.

The following decades were occupied with commerce and the building of infrastructure. Manhattan's distinctive street grid was imposed by the Planning Commission in 1811 – the simple system of numbered streets and avenues was intended to help unlettered immigrants find their way around. The Croton Aqueduct, completed in 1842, brought 72 million gallons of freshwater daily into the city, greatly improving public health.

From the earliest days there were tensions among ethnic groups and between the rich and poor. In 1863 poor Irish immigrants launched the 'draft riots,' protesting a law that allowed wealthy men to pay $300 to avoid conscription into the Civil War. Within days the rioters turned their anger on black citizens, whom they considered the reason for the war and competitors for jobs.

Growing Pains New York's explosive growth continued in the late 19th century, from 515,000 residents in 1850 to 1.1 million in 1880. Corrupt politicians milked millions from public works projects, while industrial barons amassed tax-free fortunes. The poorest New Yorkers worked in dangerous factories and lived in squalid apartment blocks, where a tenement culture developed. Journalist Jacob Riis chronicled their miseries, and his reports shocked the city and led to the establishment of an independent health board and a series of workplace reforms. Another newspaperman, William Cullen Bryant, championed the establishment of Central Park, which opened on the swampy northern outskirts of the city in 1876. Meanwhile, multimillionaire philanthropists began pouring money into public institutions like the New York Public Library and Carnegie Hall.

The severely limited space in the downtown business district left no room for growth. The only way to go was up, and by the late 19th century Manhattan had a cluster of new multistory office buildings called 'skyscrapers.' A growing network of subways and elevated trains ('els') made the city's outer reaches accessible. Growth beyond the official borders led to the 'consolidation movement,' and in 1898 the independent districts of Manhattan, Queens, Staten Island, the Bronx and Brooklyn became the five 'boroughs' of a consolidated New York City.

With another wave of European immigrants, the population leapt from three million in 1900 to seven million in 1930. The Depression caused residents enormous distress, but Mayor Fiorello La Guardia fought municipal corruption and expanded the social service network, and autocratic civic planner Robert Moses remade the city's landscape – whole working-class neighborhoods were destroyed to make room for new parks, roads and bridges.

Decline & Renewal After WWII, New York was the premier city in the world, but it suffered from a new phenomenon: the middle-class flight to the suburbs. Television production, manufacturing jobs and even the fabled Brooklyn Dodgers baseball team moved to the West Coast. By the 1970s the unreliable, graffiti-ridden subway system had become a symbol of New York's civic and economic decline. Only a massive federal loan program saved the city from bankruptcy.

New York regained much of its swagger in the 1980s, led by colorful three-term mayor Ed Koch. The city elected its first African American mayor, David Dinkins, in 1989. After his largely ineffectual single term, the city's overwhelmingly Democratic voters ousted Dinkins in favor of liberal Republican Rudolph Giuliani. The economic boom of the 1990s saw billions made on Wall St, soaring real-estate prices, gentrification of older neighborhoods, and renewed pride in a city that had never really lacked self-confidence.

Giuliani, a strong and colorful character to match the city's style, introduced 'zero tolerance' policing, which has seen the virtual disappearance of panhandlers, prostitutes, and drug dealers from the streets. Serious crime rates have also fallen dramatically, and former no-go areas now attract new-money residents. As Mayor Giuliani approached his legislated two-term limit, old-timers complained that the city was losing its gritty character, and Giuliani went through a very public divorce and a court case on whether his girlfriend could move into the mayoral mansion. New York will elect a new mayor in late 2001, and for the first time a Latino, Fernando Ferrer, is the front-runner.

Catastrophe On September 11, 2001, terrorist attacks destroyed the World Trade Center in Manhattan's Financial District, killing more than 5000 people. The 110-story twin towers of the Trade Center were icons of New York City, the US and world capitalism, and were almost certainly targeted for just that reason. The impact of the collapsing towers wrecked other buildings in the surrounding blocks, which will be a construction zone for years to come. The vast and spectacular disaster was matched by the city's reactions. Emergency services responded efficiently, and tens of thousands of office workers escaped the stricken buildings in a way that was as quick and orderly as could be hoped for, resulting in far fewer casualties than at first expected. Hundreds of rescue workers died as heroes, fearlessly entering the doomed towers, which then collapsed on top of them. Mayor Giuliani was conspicuous throughout as a compassionate, cool and effective leader.

There's no doubt that New York will recover physically and economically from the attack, though the blow to business and consumer confidence is a big damper on the economy. Will the attack do lasting damage to the city's psyche? Not judging by the words of one firefighter, commenting on the sheer scale of the disaster: 'Wadda ya expect? This is New York.'

Orientation

New York City lies near the mouth of the Hudson River, at the west end of Long Island Sound, linked to the Atlantic Ocean through the Verrazano Narrows. The metropolitan area sprawls east into the neighboring state of Connecticut and is linked to urban areas of New Jersey, on the west side of the Hudson. The whole conurbation, known as the 'Tri-State Area,' is home to over 17 million people.

The City of New York proper comprises five boroughs: Manhattan, Staten Island, Brooklyn, Queens and the Bronx. The island of Manhattan (especially its southern half) is the densely packed heart of New York and the epicenter of its attractions.

New York is the principal transport hub of the northeast US, served by three major airports, two train terminals and a massive bus depot. Several interstate highways converge on the city, including I-95, I-87, I-80 and I-78.

Manhattan The oldest section of New York City, the southern tip of Manhattan Island, has a haphazard layout, with streets that perhaps began as cow paths and Indian walking trails. Farther north, Manhattan has a regular street grid with avenues running north-south and streets running east-west. Along the avenues, nearly every block is about 90 yards (20 blocks equal approximately 1 mile); along the streets the blocks are longer, typically about 350 yards. Most streets and avenues have a number rather than a name, but a few have both. For example, Sixth Ave is also known as Avenue of the Americas.

North of Washington Square Park, Fifth Ave is the dividing line between the East Side and the West Side. Buildings on the cross streets are numbered east and west from Fifth Ave, so the Hard Rock Cafe (221 W 57th St) is just over two blocks west of Fifth Ave.

New Yorkers give street addresses in shorthand with the street number first and the avenue second, eg, 'We're at 33rd and Third.' For an address on an avenue – such as '1271 Sixth Ave' – be sure to ask for the nearest cross street.

Broadway is the only major avenue that cuts diagonally across Manhattan. It was originally a woodland path used by Native Americans, and its route runs all the way to Albany.

The many neighborhoods and districts of Manhattan are named according to various geographical, ethnic or historical associations, and their boundaries may not be precisely defined. The southern tip of the island is Lower Manhattan, with the area up to Houston (**how**-sten) St divided into the Lower East Side (which includes Little Italy and Chinatown), SoHo and Tribeca. North of Houston St are the East Village on one side and Greenwich Village on the other. Chelsea is the area west of Broadway between 14th and 28th Sts, just east of which is the Flatiron District. Generally, Midtown refers to the largely commercial district from 34th St north to 59th St, an area that includes Rockefeller Center, Times Square, the Empire State Building, the Broadway theater district, Grand Central Terminal, Madison Square Garden, Port Authority Bus Terminal and many of the major hotels.

North of 59th St, Uptown comprises the Upper East Side and the Upper West Side, with the 2½-mile strip of Central Park between them. Harlem is roughly north and northeast of Central Park.

Outer Boroughs The grid plan is fitfully repeated in the other boroughs, typically with numbered streets running east-west and numbered avenues running north-south, though some winding thoroughfares follow the routes of old country roads.

Maps Good Midtown street plans are provided free by most hotels. Lonely Planet publishes a laminated pocket-size map of New York City. 'Streetwise' also does a pocket map, available at most newsstands ($7.75). Most comprehensive are the street atlases. Geographia, Hagstrom and Van Dam all publish compact editions for around $13. Subway stations have a 'Passenger Information Center' next to the ticket booth, with a wonderfully detailed map of the surrounding neighborhood. Free maps of bus and subway routes are available at any station.

Information

Tourist Offices New York City & Company (☎ 212-484-1222, fax 212-245-5943, Ⓦ www.nycvisit.com, 810 Seventh Ave), at 53rd St, is the official information service of the Convention and Visitors Bureau (open 8:30am-6pm Mon-Fri, 9am-5pm Sat-Sun). It has helpful multilingual staff and plentiful brochures. The 24-hour toll-free line (☎ 800-692-8474) provides information on special events and reservations.

Money Thousands of ATMs are linked to Cirrus, Plus and other networks. Withdrawal fees are as much as $5 at ATMs in convenience stores. Banks are normally open 9am-3:30pm weekdays. Many of the Chase Manhattan Bank branches offer commission-free currency-exchange services; the one in Chinatown at Mott and Canal Sts is open daily.

Post & Communications The general post office (421 Eighth Ave), at 33rd St, is open 24 hours. However, its general delivery (poste restante) service is unreliable and not recommended.

Thousands of pay telephones line the streets, but those maintained by Verizon are usually the most reliable. Many pay phones accept credit cards, but some will bill you an outrageous amount for a long-distance call.

For many years Manhattan's telephone numbers carried the area code 212, the quickest digits for fast-living New Yorkers to dial on a rotary phone. In 1998, Manhattan got a new area code, 646, to cope with the huge demand for new lines. The four other boroughs carry the 718 and 347 area codes. You do not need to dial the area code if you are calling from a borough with the same area code.

The New York Public Library (☎ 212-930-0800), on Fifth Ave at 42nd St and at various branch locations, offers 30 minutes of free Internet access, but all terminals may be busy. For 24-hour access from as little as $1, try easyEverything (☎ 212-398-0775, 234 W 42nd St), at 7th Ave, which has over 800 PCs available, or one of the Kinko's copy centers.

Travel Agencies Apart from regular and discount agencies, such as Council Travel and STA Travel (which have several offices), there are consolidators selling last-minute flights. Most are in Midtown office buildings and advertise weekly in the *Village Voice* and the Sunday *New York Times*. The more reliable agencies take credit cards and can book tickets on scheduled carriers.

Bookstores & Libraries Manhattan bookstores include St Marks Bookshop (31 Third Ave), Coliseum Books (1775 Broadway), Gotham Book Mart (41 W 47th St), Complete Traveller (199 Madison Ave) and huge Barnes & Noble stores, including those at 33 E 17th St and at Rockefeller Plaza. For used books, visit the Strand Bookstore (828 Broadway).

The superbly elegant main branch of the New York Public Library (☎ 212-930-0800), on Fifth Ave at 42nd St, is worth a visit for its famous 3rd-floor reading room and its temporary exhibitions (open 10am-6pm

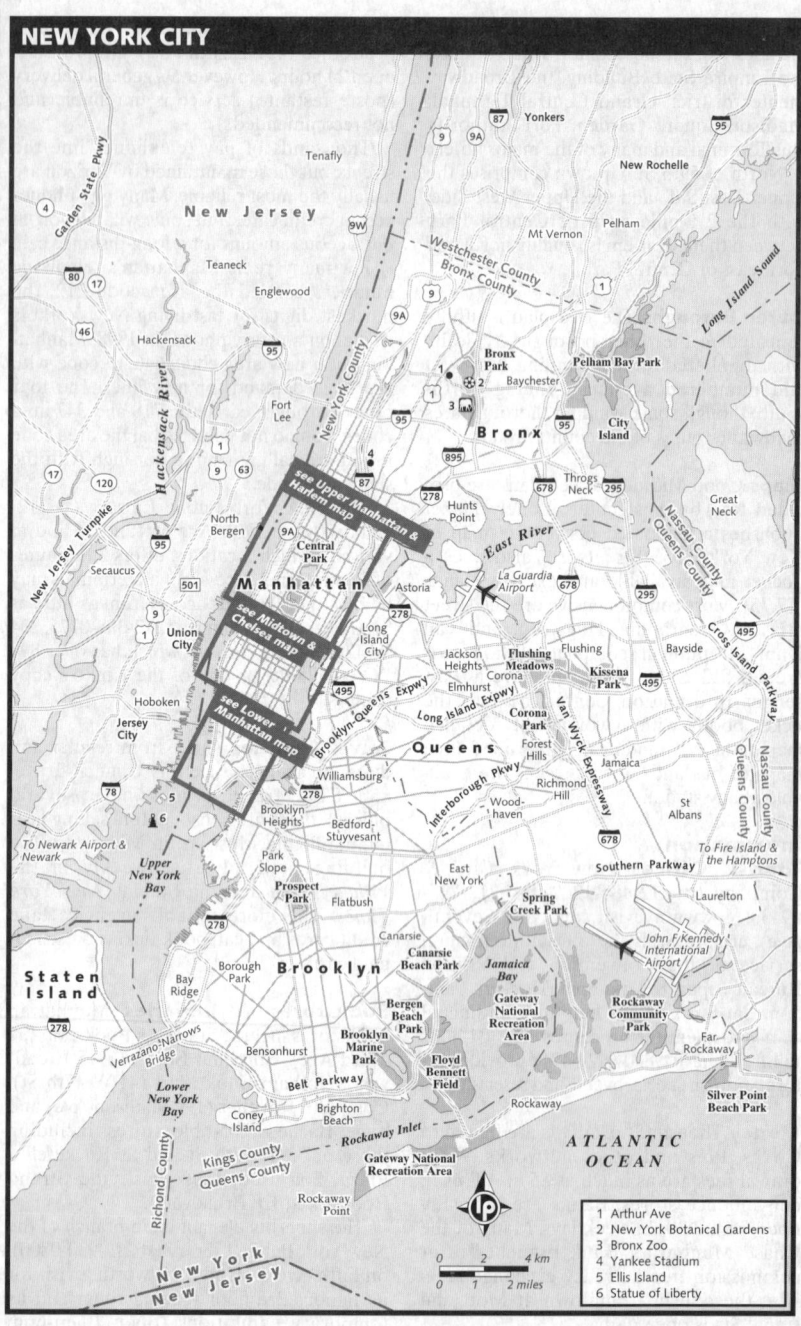

NEW YORK CITY

New Jersey

Yonkers

New Rochelle

Tenafly

Pelham

Mt Vernon

Westchester County

Bronx County

Teaneck

Englewood

Hackensack

Fort Lee

Bronx Park

Pelham Bay Park

Baychester

Bronx

City Island

Throgs Neck

North Bergen

Hunts Point

East River

Great Neck

Secaucus

La Guardia Airport

Central Park

see Upper Manhattan & Harlem map

Manhattan

Astoria

Union City

Long Island City

Jackson Heights

Flushing Meadows Corona

Flushing

Bayside

see Midtown & Chelsea map

Hoboken

Elmhurst

Kissena Park

Jersey City

see Lower Manhattan map

Corona Park

Forest Hills

Jamaica

Queens

St Albans

Williamsburg

Richmond Hill

Wood-haven

Brooklyn Heights

Bedford-Stuyvesant

East New York

Laurelton

Park Slope

Prospect Park

Flatbush

Spring Creek Park

John F Kennedy International Airport

Canarsie

Canarsie Beach Park

Staten Island

Brooklyn

Bay Ridge

Borough Park

Jamaica Bay

Gateway National Recreation Area

Rockaway Community Park

Bensonhurst

Bergen Beach Park

Brooklyn Marine Park

Floyd Bennett Field

Far Rockaway

Silver Point Beach Park

Belt Parkway

Coney Island

Brighton Beach

Rockaway

ATLANTIC OCEAN

Kings County

Queens County

Gateway National Recreation Area

Rockaway Inlet

Rockaway Point

New York

New Jersey

0   2   4 km
0   1   2 miles

1 Arthur Ave
2 New York Botanical Gardens
3 Bronx Zoo
4 Yankee Stadium
5 Ellis Island
6 Statue of Liberty

Thurs-Mon, 11am-7:30pm Tue-Wed). Other branches are less crowded for casual reading (check the phone book yellow pages under 'Libraries – Public').

Newspapers & Magazines The *New York Times* (Ⓦ www.nytimes.com) is still the nation's premier newspaper (75¢, $3 on Sun). Friday's 'Weekend Section' is an invaluable guide to cultural events. The *Wall Street Journal* is essential financial reading, with excellent coverage from Washington, DC, and a conservative editorial position. The *Daily News* and *New York Post* compete for the tabloid market, with a heavy emphasis on media gossip and sports.

The venerable *New Yorker* magazine ($4) publishes news, fiction and critical reviews, and its 'Goings on about Town' section lists major art, cinema and music events. *New York* magazine ($3) does the same for younger, more restaurant-oriented readers. The *Village Voice* ($1), published each Wednesday, is well known for listings of clubs and music venues and is the best source for rental apartments and roommate listings. The weekly *New York Observer* specializes in local media and politics.

Time Out New York ($3), published every Wednesday, has comprehensive listings, including gay and lesbian events. Gay clubs and bars are also listed in *HX/Homo Xtra* and *Next,* free at most restaurants and bars. *Where New York,* available at most hotels, is the best free monthly guide to mainstream city events and museums.

Toilets Public toilets are almost nonexistent, and those in commercial establishments are for customers only. It's sometimes possible to slip into the bathroom of a busy bar or restaurant if you are discreet and well dressed. If you're in distress, head to a major department store.

Medical Services & Emergencies All hospital emergency rooms are obligated to receive sick or distressed visitors regardless of ability to pay. But if you show up without any insurance or money, you will have to wait a long time unless you're a really serious case. The New York University Medical Center (☎ 212-263-5550, 462 First Ave), at 32nd St, is easily reached by taxi.

Apart from the usual 911 emergency number, there are federal, state and city government offices and community organizations listed in the front of every phone book. The important ones are the police (☎ 212-374-5000), crime victims services (☎ 212-577-7777) and Legal Aid Society (☎ 212-577-3300).

Dangers & Annoyances Statistically, New York has become a very safe city by US standards, but some caution is still warranted. You're most unlikely to be assaulted or robbed in any of the areas frequented by tourists, especially during daylight hours, though you should take precautions against pickpockets. At night avoid places that are largely deserted or badly lit. Central Park should generally be avoided at night, but it's quite safe when there are lots of people around for a concert, a play at Delacorte Theater, or a free event. Security is good in the subway system, but before you leave a station you should be aware of the neighborhood you're entering. Don't flaunt money or valuables, especially in poor areas.

Drug dealing has virtually disappeared from Manhattan streets, especially in areas frequented by visitors. A few panhandlers and hustlers remain; some give a very polished presentation to the captive audience in subway cars. If you really want to help those in need and avoid supporting a drug habit, get in touch with Citymeals-on-Wheels (☎ 212-687-1234).

Financial District & Around

For most visitors, Manhattan *is* New York City. Lower Manhattan, the southern end of Manhattan Island, is a good place to start exploring. It has important historical sites dating back to the Dutch period and includes the fabled Financial District. It's also the place from which to access two of New York's greatest tourist attractions – the Statue of Liberty and the Brooklyn Bridge.

At the time of writing, the area around the World Trade Center site is off-limits and will be for some time; it's not known at this stage what other effects the September 2001 disaster will have on the attractions and accessibility of Lower Manhattan.

Financial District Walking Tour This area is a center for business, politics and the

LOWER MANHATTAN

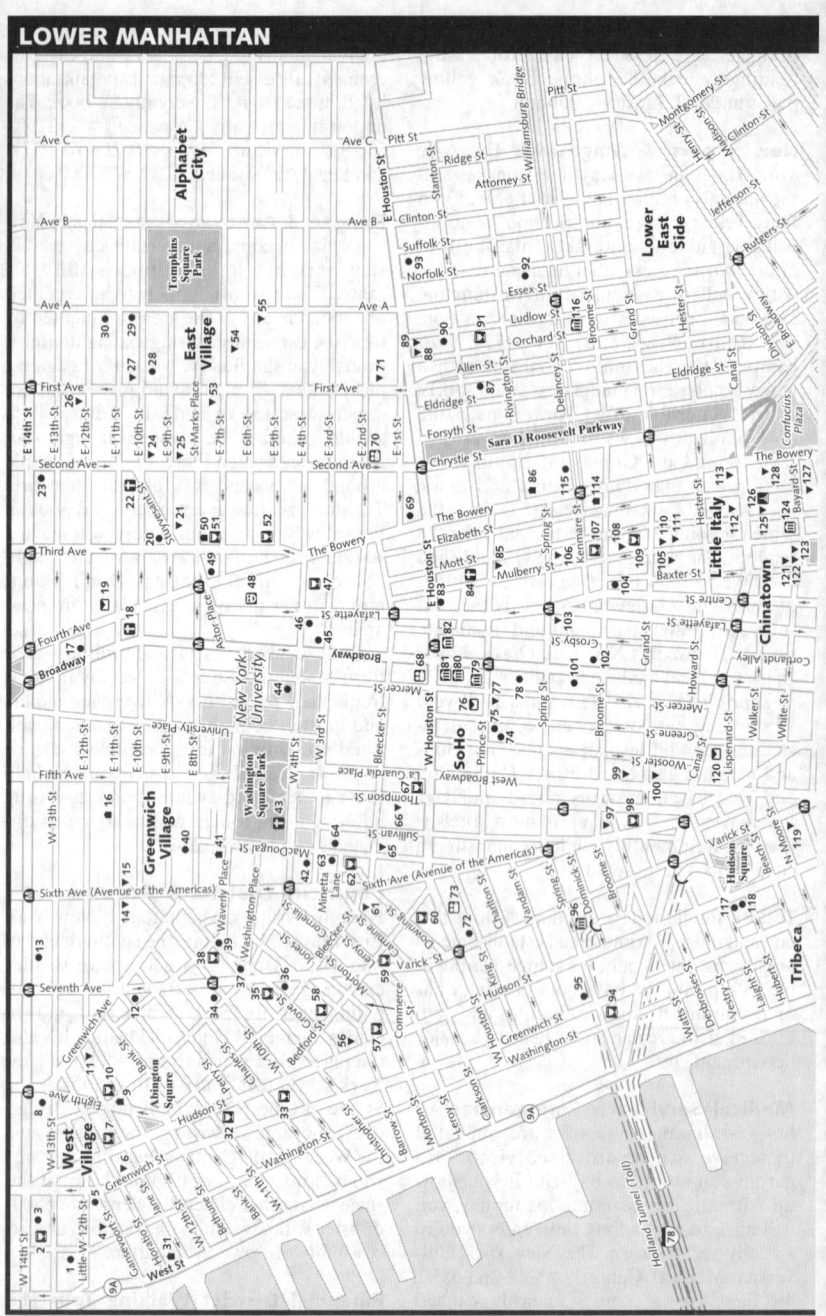

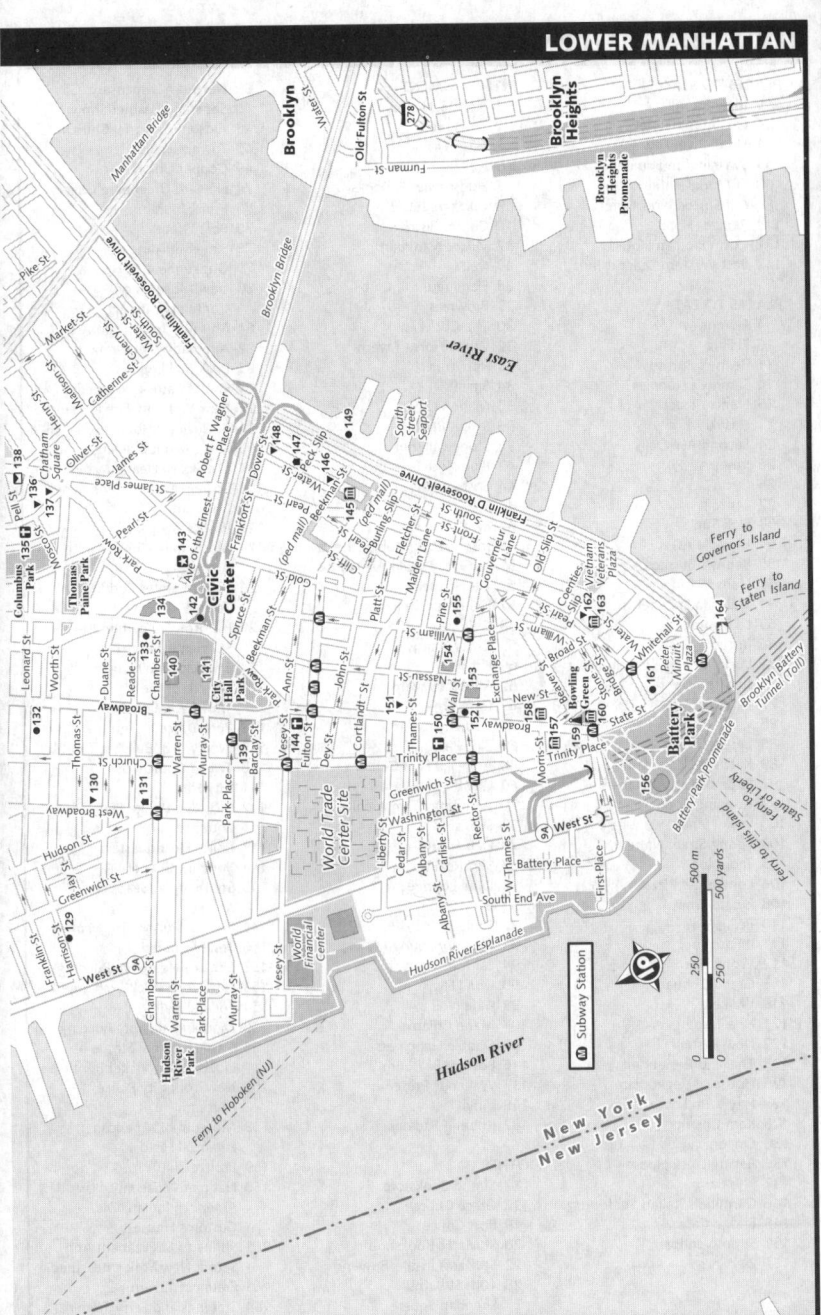

LOWER MANHATTAN

LOWER MANHATTAN

PLACES TO STAY
9 Incentra Village
16 Larchmont Hotel
31 Hotel Riverview
41 Washington Square Hotel
50 St Marks Hotel
86 Off SoHo Suites Hotel
114 Pioneer Hotel
131 Cosmopolitan Hotel
147 Best Western Seaport Inn

PLACES TO EAT
4 Florent
6 El Faro
11 Benny's Burritos
14 Sammy's Noodles
15 French Roast
21 Hasaki
24 Second Ave Deli
25 Veselka
26 Cyclo
27 Lanza's
53 Dok Suni's
54 Roetelle AG
55 Benny's Burritos
56 Hudson Diner
61 Trattoria Spaghetto
65 Le Figaro
66 Rocco
71 Lucky Cheng's; La Nouvelle
   Justine
77 Fanelli's Cafe
85 Kitchen Club
88 Bereket
89 Katz's Delicatessen
97 Lupe's East LA Kitchen
99 Cupping Room
100 Lucky Strike
103 Spring Street Natural
105 Taormina
106 Lombardi's Pizza
108 Benito One
110 Pelligrino's
111 Il Fornaio
112 Wong Kee
113 Grand Sichuan
119 Walkers
121 Nha Trang
122 New Pasteur
123 Thailand Restaurant
125 House of Vegetarian
127 Hay Wun Loy
128 Kam Chueh
130 Odeon
136 Peking Duck House
137 Pho Bang
146 Carmine's Italian Seafood
148 Bridge Cafe
151 Street Vendors
162 Zigolini's

ENTERTAINMENT
1 Hogs & Heifers
2 The Lure
3 Filter 14
5 Hell
7 Hudson Bar & Books
8 Chicago BLUES
10 Corner Bistro
12 Village Vanguard
13 Nell's
23 Flamingo; Clit Club
29 Brownies
30 The Cock
32 White Horse Tavern
33 Rubyfruit
34 Small's
35 Marie's Crisis
36 Sweet Basil
38 Stonewall Inn
42 Blue Note
44 Bottom Line
46 Fez
47 Swift
48 Joseph Papp Public Theater
51 McSorley's Old Ale House
52 The Scratcher
57 Henrietta Hudson's
58 Chumley's
59 Crazy Nanny's
60 Bar d'O
62 Minetta Tavern
63 Cafe Wha?
64 Comedy Cellar
67 Zinc Bar
68 Angelika Film Center
69 CBGB
70 Anthology Film Archives
72 SOB's
73 Film Forum
87 Surf Reality
90 Luna Lounge
91 Barramundi
92 Tonic
93 Mercury Lounge
94 Ear Inn
95 Don Hills
98 Cafe Noir
107 Marie Chiaro
109 Double Happiness
115 Bowery Ballroom
117 Wetlands Preserve
118 Vinyl
132 Knitting Factory

OTHER
17 Strand Bookstore
18 Grace Church
19 Post Office
20 St Marks Bookshop
22 St Marks-in-the-Bowery
28 10th St Baths
37 Sheridan Square
39 Northern Dispensary; Gay St
40 Shoe and Leather Shops
43 Judson Memorial Church
45 Tower Records
49 Cooper Union
74 Howard Greenberg Gallery
75 Haas' Mural
76 Post Office
78 Singer Building
79 Guggenheim SoHo
80 New Museum of
   Contemporary Art
81 Museum for African Art
82 Alternative Museum
83 Puck Building
84 Old St Patrick's Cathedral
96 New York City Fire Museum
101 St Nicholas Hotel
102 Haughwout Building
104 Old Police Headquarters
116 Lower East Side Tenement
   Museum
120 Post Office
124 Museum of Chinese in the
   Americas
126 Eastern States Buddhist
   Temple
129 Harrison St Townhouses
133 Surrogate's Court
134 Municipal Building
135 Church of the
   Transfiguration
138 Post Office
139 Woolworth Building
140 Tweed Courthouse
141 City Hall
142 Brooklyn Bridge Pedestrian
   Entrance
143 Police Headquarters
144 St Paul's Chapel
145 South Street Seaport
   Museum
149 Pier 17; Fulton Fish Market
150 Trinity Church
152 Bank of New York Building
153 New York Stock Exchange
154 Federal Hall
155 Morgan Guaranty Building
156 Castle Clinton; Statue of
   Liberty Ferry Ticket Booth
157 New York City Police
   Museum
158 Museum of American
   Financial History
159 Bronze Bull
160 National Museum of the
   American Indian; Old
   Customs House
161 Shrine to St Elizabeth Ann
   Seton; New York Unearthed
163 Fraunces Tavern
164 Staten Island Ferry Terminal

law, so it's best to explore it on a weekday. The walk is just over 2 miles, but if you stop to shop, eat and look at the sights in detail, it will make a very full day.

Start at **City Hall**, in the Civic Center precinct, home to New York City's government since 1812. The front steps are a popular site for demonstrations and press conferences by grandstanding politicians. It's worth looking inside – the building is open weekdays (despite the discouraging security presence at the front door). Just behind (north of) City Hall, the 1872 County Courthouse building is commonly called **Tweed Courthouse**, after the notoriously corrupt 'Boss' Tweed, the Tammany Hall political organizer who embezzled $10 million of the $14 million construction cost. The opulent structure is undergoing extensive renovation. Nearby, at the intersection of Chambers and Centre Sts, the former **Surrogate's Court**, completed in 1914, has an interior in the French beaux arts style.

Turn south and go down past the **Woolworth Building** (233 Broadway). It was the world's tallest building when it opened in 1913, and the lobby has a relief of proprietor Frank Woolworth counting his change. Farther down Broadway, **St Paul's Chapel**, built in 1766, is the oldest church in the city. (The blocks west of Broadway from Barclay St south to about Cedar St were extensively damaged in the attack of September 11, 2001.) Continue south on Broadway for six blocks to **Trinity Church**. Back when it was built in 1846, it was the tallest building in the city. Old gravestones behind these churches are worth contemplating.

Turn east off Broadway onto narrow **Wall Street**, the metaphorical home of US commerce, named for the wooden barrier built by Dutch settlers in 1653 to protect Nieuw Amsterdam from Native Americans and the British. The **Bank of New York Building** (1 Wall St), with its blazing art deco lobby, is one of many monuments to money. Farther east is **Federal Hall**, distinguished by a huge statue of George Washington on the steps. This is where the first US Congress convened and Washington was sworn in as the first president, though it is not the original building. A small museum is dedicated to postcolonial New York (open Mon-Fri).

On the corner opposite, tycoon JP Morgan displayed his wealth by building a bank of only two stories on the enormously expensive Wall St real estate. Across the street, the **New York Stock Exchange** (NYSE; 8 Broad St) has a facade like a Roman temple. A visitor gallery overlooks the frenetic trading floor and includes an exhibit describing the exchange's history. Free tickets to view the NYSE are available from a booth at 20 Broad St (open 8:45am-4pm Mon-Fri), but they're usually snapped up before noon.

Go down Broad St and turn right on Beaver St, recalling that New York's first fortunes were founded on the fur trade. At the tiny Bowling Green park, British residents relaxed with quiet games in the late 17th century. The large bronze bull here is an obligatory tourist photo stop. Nearby, the old Standard Oil Building was built in 1922 by John D Rockefeller and now houses the **Museum of American Financial History** (☎ 212-908-4519, 26 Broadway), worth checking for its special exhibits ($2; open 10am-4pm Tue-Sat). Across the street, the **New York City Police Museum** (☎ 212-301-4440, 25 Broadway) covers cops, Capone and killers (free admission; open 9am-3pm Mon-Fri).

The elegant 1907 beaux arts building south of the Bowling Green was designed by Cass Gilbert as the Customs House, with elaborate decorations on a mercantile theme. It's now the **National Museum of the American Indian** (NMAI; ☎ 212-668-6624, 1 Bowling Green), housing an extensive collection of Native American arts, crafts, exhibits, a library and a gift shop (free admission; open 10am-5pm daily). An affiliate of the Smithsonian Institution, the NMAI is planned to relocate to Washington, DC, in 2002.

Follow Whitehall St southeast and turn left on Pearl St, which has some of the few remaining examples of colonial-era buildings in New York. The **Fraunces Tavern** (☎ 212-425-1778, 54 Pearl St), on the corner of Broad St, is a 1907 restoration of the Queen's Head Tavern, where Washington gave his farewell address to Continental Army officers in 1783. There is a restaurant and a small museum ($4; open 10am-4pm Mon-Fri, noon-4pm Sat-Sun). Just across Pearl St, the windows in the sidewalk let you see down onto the excavated remains of the old Dutch **Stadt Huys**, which served as Nieuw Amsterdam's administrative center, courthouse and jail from 1641 to '64. The next block is the historical **Coenties Slip**, a former Dutch docking station that became a street as the city extended south on reclaimed land. Farther up, at the sharply angled corner of Beaver St, the J & R Cigar Bar has a huge humidor and a club-like ambience. Crossing Wall St again, look left at the sleek, slick Morgan Guaranty Building – very 1980s.

Continue up Pearl St and turn right at Fulton St to **South Street Seaport**, a much-visited 11-block enclave of new shops and historic sights. One small block south, Schermerhorn Row has old warehouses with novelty shops, seafood restaurants and a pub. **South Street Seaport Museum** (☎ 212-748-8600) includes three galleries, a children's center and the three historic ships just south of the pier ($6/3 adults/kids; open 10am-5pm daily). A booth on Pier 16 sells tickets for an hourlong riverboat excursion from the Seaport Cruise Line (☎ 212-630-8888) highlighting Manhattan's maritime history. One-hour tours ($13/7 adults/kids) run three times daily March to November.

Pier 17 is also the site of the **Fulton Fish Market**, busiest from midnight to 8am. The fish market will soon move to a new site in the Bronx. The waterfront feel and a few fish warehouses survive around Peck Slip, but renovation and redevelopment can't be far off. If you finish your walking tour as night falls, you can watch the Brooklyn Bridge light up while you enjoy an (expensive) drink at a South Street Seaport bar. Walk west on Fulton St for the nearest subway stations.

Statue of Liberty This great statue, *Liberty Enlightening the World,* is an American icon and New York's best-known landmark. As early as 1865, French intellectual Edouard Laboulaye conceived a great monument to the republican ideal in France and the USA. French sculptor Frédéric-Auguste Bartholdi traveled to New York in 1871 to select the site, then spent over 10 years in Paris designing and making the 151-foot figure, which was then shipped to New York, erected on a small island in the harbor and unveiled in 1886. Structurally, it consists of an iron skeleton (designed by Gustave Eiffel) with a copper skin attached to it by stiff but flexible metal bars that can accommodate thermal expansion and movement in strong winds. Corrosion of the copper became a serious problem, and over $100 million was spent restoring Liberty for her centennial in 1986.

The Statue of Liberty National Monument (☎ 212-363-3200) is a major attraction and can be overcrowded. It's usually visited in conjunction with nearby Ellis Island, and the trip involves pleasant ferry rides with spectacular views of downtown Manhattan. You can climb 354 steps (22 stories) to the statue's crown, though this

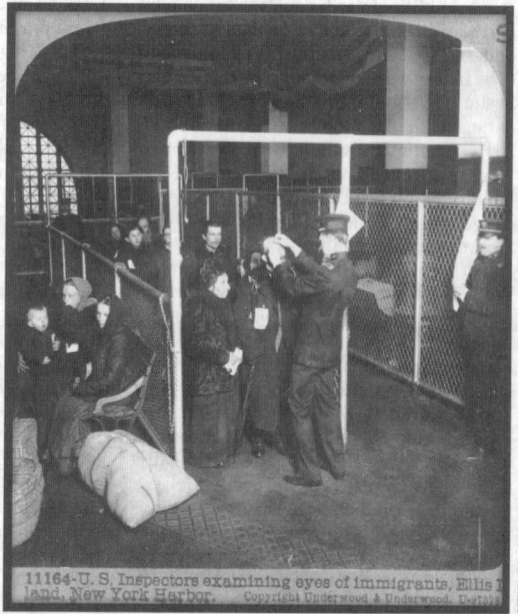

11164-U.S. Inspectors examining eyes of immigrants, Ellis Island, New York Harbor.   Copyright Underwood & Underwood, Uni[...]

Immigrants hoping to pass the eye test on Ellis Island (1913)

may involve hours of waiting for a very brief moment at the top. But it's wonderful to see the statue from the inside and close up, and to share the experience in a confined space with a few thousand other pilgrims – and you'll never forget your glimpse of New York Harbor as Liberty sees it. The National Park Service (which runs the site) will usually allow only early arrivals to go to the top, so get on a boat by 9am to guarantee a climb to the crown, and be prepared to wait two hours or longer before you even get inside the base of the statue. If you can't handle that, you can enjoy great views of Manhattan and a great angle on the lady from the balconies around the base of the statue with a lot less waiting. The fine museum in the base is well worth seeing for its fascinating exhibits on the statue's structure, restoration and cultural significance.

Ferries (☎ 212-269-5755) from Battery Park leave every 30 minutes 8:30am-3.30pm, with extended hours during the summer ($8 roundtrip). South Ferry and Bowling Green are handy subway stations.

Ellis Island Ferries to the Statue of Liberty make a second stop at Ellis Island, the country's main immigration station from 1892 to 1954, where over 12 million immigrants first set foot in the New World. The handsome main building is now restored as an **Immigration Museum** (☎ 212-363-7772), with exhibits and a film on immigrant experiences, the processing of immigrants, and how the influx changed the USA. You can listen to fascinating narratives with actors reading from immigrants' letters, or take a 50-minute audio guided tour ($3.50). It's open daily until about 5pm, when the last ferry heads back to Battery Park. Try to leave the Statue of Liberty before 2pm to allow enough time at Ellis Island, or make a separate trip here – it's worth it.

Brooklyn Bridge This was the world's first steel suspension bridge, with an unprecedented span of 1596 feet. It remains a compelling symbol of US achievement and a superbly graceful structure, although its construction was plagued by budget overruns and the deaths of 20 workers. Among the casualties was designer John Roebling,

who was knocked off a pier in 1869 while scouting a site for the western bridge tower and died of tetanus poisoning. At the bridge's opening in 1883 there was a sudden fear of imminent collapse, and 12 pedestrians were trampled to death in the ensuing panic.

The bridge was extensively renovated in the early 1980s, and the pedestrian walkway, beginning just east of City Hall, affords a wonderful view of Lower Manhattan. Observation points under the two stone support towers have illustrations showing panoramas of the waterfront at various points in New York's history.

World Trade Center Site The World Trade Center was a complex of seven main buildings occupying several blocks between West and Church Sts. Its two 110-story towers, each 1350 feet high, were a fixture in the New York skyline. Built between 1966 and '73, the towers housed more than 50,000 people. The federal and state government offices made it a target for terrorists, who set off a truck bomb in the underground parking garage in 1993, killing six people. On September 11, 2001, terrorists flew two of four hijacked passenger planes into the towers, causing them and several surrounding buildings to collapse, and killing more than 5000 people.

Battery Park Area The southwestern tip of Manhattan Island has been extended with landfill to form Battery Park. **Castle Clinton**, a fortification built in 1811 to protect Manhattan from the British, was originally 900 feet offshore but is now at the edge of Battery Park, with only its walls remaining.

West of the park, the **Museum of Jewish Heritage** (☎ 212-786-0820, 18 1st Place, Battery Park City) depicts many aspects of New York Jewish history and culture and incorporates a holocaust memorial ($7; open Sun-Fri).

On the eastern edge of Battery Park, near Pearl St and Broadway, the **Shrine to St Elizabeth Seton** is dedicated to the country's first Roman Catholic saint. Just behind the shrine, 'New York Unearthed' is an interesting exhibit of artifacts discovered by archaeologists and construction workers (open noon-6pm Mon-Fri). Farther southeast,

Peter Minuit Plaza is where Manhattan was reputedly purchased for 60 guilders.

Chinatown & Little Italy

These two long-standing ethnic enclaves are just north of the Financial District. Chinatown proper sprawls largely south of Canal St but is now spreading north and east as well – you can now find Chinese businesses in the area above Canal St, particularly Grand St, which has busy fruit stands and fish stores open until 8pm. Chinatown is a thriving community of more than 120,000 residents, many living and working in their minisociety without using a word of English. Throughout the 1990s, Chinatown saw an influx of Vietnamese immigrants, who set up their own shops and some incredibly cheap restaurants.

Traditionally, Little Italy was a narrow strip around Mulberry St north of Canal St, but in the last few decades it has lost much of its ethnic character. Mulberry St is a tourist-trap enclave of cheap (not necessarily good) pasta restaurants and overpriced tobacco shops. Off Mulberry St, on Elizabeth and Lafayette Sts, the feeling is more cosmopolitan, as the overflow of SoHo-style shops, cafes and restaurants takes over storefronts that once served the local Italian community. Real-estate hype runs hot in the area dubbed 'NoLIta' (North of Little Italy), which is getting trendier every month.

Chinatown Walking Tour Start on Canal St, west of Lafayette St, a somewhat seedy area of street vendors. The Chinese shopping district begins east of Baxter St. Turn south down Mott St, past the Eastern States Buddhist Temple (64B Mott St), a busy shrine with dozens of Buddhas on display. Detour along Bayard St to the **Museum of Chinese in the Americas** (☎ 212-619-4785, 70 Mulberry St), which has exhibits and sponsors walking tours and workshops on Chinese crafts ($3; open noon-5pm Tue-Sun).

Back on Mott St, go down to the Church of the Transfiguration (29 Mott St), which began as an Episcopal church in 1801, later became a Roman Catholic church for Irish and Italian communities, and today holds services in Chinese. Go back up Mott St and turn onto Pell St, then make a right on Doyers St, where Chinatown began in the

1870s. The first Chinese settlers were former railway workers, fed up with discrimination in the US West. South of Doyers St are reminders of earlier ethnic associations, like **Chatham Square**, where the goods of Irish debtors were auctioned in the early 19th century. It now houses a monument to Chinese Americans killed in war.

Little Italy Walking Tour Confined largely to Mulberry St, north of Canal St, Little Italy is famous for Italian restaurants. A block west of Mulberry, the imposing **Old Police Headquarters** (240 Centre St) overwhelms its neighbors, but it is hard to appreciate its grandeur from street level. Three blocks north, **Old St Patrick's Cathedral** (263 Mulberry St) became the city's first Roman Catholic cathedral in 1809 and remained so until 1878, when its more famous uptown successor was completed. The stunning red-brick **Puck Building**, on Mulberry St near Houston St, was home to the late-18th-century humor magazine. The building has two gold-leaf statues of the portly Puck.

Tribeca

The 'TRIangle BElow CAnal' St, bordered roughly by Broadway to the east and Chambers St to the south, has old warehouses, loft apartments and funky restaurants. It's not as established or as architecturally significant as SoHo, but its retro-industrial look and (relatively) cheap real estate have made it an up-and-coming area, and several celebrity residents add to the trendiness. Fashion photographers come here for the desolation chic.

The eight **townhouses** on Harrison St west of Greenwich St were built between 1804 and '28 and are New York's largest remaining collection of Federal architecture. Only those at Nos 31 and 33 were actually built here, though; the others were relocated from a nearby development site.

SoHo

This neighborhood, 'SOuth of HOuston St' down to Canal St, is a paradigm of inadvertent urban renewal. The many blocks of cast-iron industrial buildings originally housed textile and clothing factories, but retail businesses relocated uptown, and manufacturing moved out of the city. In the 1950s the huge lofts and low rents attracted artists and other members of the avant-garde, whose influence and political lobbying saved the neighborhood from destruction. The 26-block area was declared a 'protected historic district' in 1973, and today SoHo is a center for clothing stores, boutiques and established art galleries (though several big-name galleries have relocated to Chelsea or farther uptown). On weekday mornings you can see the gallery set in their sleek black outfits and adventurous eyewear. On weekends W Broadway and nearby Prince St are packed with tourists and street artists.

Start at the Broadway–Lafayette St subway station and walk south down Broadway. On the first block are several galleries and four art museums:

Alternative Museum (☎ 212-966-4444, 594 Broadway, 4th floor) – more a noncommercial gallery than a museum; there are several galleries in the building ($3 suggested; open Tue-Sat Sept-July)

Guggenheim SoHo (☎ 212-423-3500, 575 Broadway) – the SoHo branch of the Guggenheim Museum (free admission; open Wed-Sun)

Museum for African Art (☎ 212-966-1313, 593 Broadway) – features African religious works, tribal crafts and traditional musical instruments ($5; open Tue-Sun)

New Museum of Contemporary Art (☎ 212-219-1222, 583 Broadway) – displays works fewer than 10 years old ($6; open Wed-Sun)

As you walk, look up at the buildings to see decorative flourishes that have been obscured or destroyed at street level – the use of cast iron allowed elaborate decoration to be inexpensively incorporated into the structure. A fine example is the **Singer Building** (561–563 Broadway), the main warehouse for the famous sewing-machine company, built in 1904. From an earlier era, the marble-faced **St Nicholas Hotel** (521–523 Broadway) was *the* place to stay in 1854. During the Civil War it was the headquarters of Abraham Lincoln's War Department.

The 1857 **Haughwout Building** (488 Broadway) was the first building to use the exotic steam 'elevator' developed by Elisha Otis. One block farther south, the parking lot at Grand St has a Sunday antique market.

Turn right on Grand St and walk four blocks west to W Broadway – the corner has several late-night restaurants and bars. Backtrack a block to Wooster St and go north past numerous galleries, including the long-standing Howard Greenberg Gallery. Head east on Prince St and look up to see the fantastic (but slightly faded) mural on the Greene St corner, where artist Richard Haas created a cast-iron facade on a plain brick wall. Walk down Greene St to see more fine (and genuine) cast-iron architecture.

Southwest of central SoHo, the **New York City Fire Museum** (☎ 212-691-1303, 278 Spring St) is a grand old firehouse dating back to 1904. Gleaming gold horse-drawn fire-fighting carriages, modern-day fire engines, pictures and documents tell the story of New York's fire-fighting history ($4 open 10am-4pm Tue-Sun).

Greenwich Village

One of New York's most popular neighborhoods, Greenwich Village is bounded by 14th St, Lafayette St/Fourth Ave, Houston St and the Hudson River. The center of 'the Village' is dominated by New York University (NYU), which owns most of the property surrounding Washington Square Park. Southwest of the park is a lively, crowded collection of cafes, shops and restaurants; west of Seventh Ave, the West Village is a delightful neighborhood of quaint, crooked streets and restored townhouses.

After the Civil War, Greenwich Village became New York's most prominent black neighborhood, but in the early 1920s many of these residents moved to Harlem. The early 20th century also saw artists and writers move in, and from the 1940s the neighborhood was known as a gathering place for gays, beats, artists and musicians.

Washington Square Park & Around This park began as a 'potter's field' – a burial ground for the penniless – and its status as a cemetery protected it from development. It is now an incredibly well-used park, especially on the weekends. The landmark arch on the park's northern edge was designed in 1889 by society architect Stanford White. The row of townhouses along Washington Square North was the inspiration for Henry James' novel of late 19th-century mores, *Washington Square*, though James never actually lived here. In the blocks east and south of the park, many of the buildings are NYU classrooms, dorms, libraries and other facilities.

Under the arch and around the dry central 'fountain,' street comedians and musicians do their thing and food carts cater to the snack-needy. People and dogs enjoy fresh air and exercise; the dog park on the southwest corner is an especially lively location.

One block east of the park, at 245 Greene St, is the building where the Triangle Shirtwaist Fire took place in 1911. This sweatshop had locked its doors to prevent the seamstresses from taking unauthorized breaks. The inferno killed 146 young women and prompted a much-needed review and regulation of working conditions and fire safety.

Greenwich Village Walking Tour From the middle of Washington Square Park, head south to Thompson St, where **Judson Memorial Church** stands on the corner. Designed by Stanford White, it's a national historic site with notable stained-glass windows and a marble facade. Go down Thompson, past a series of chess shops where Village denizens meet to play the game ($1.50 per hour). Turn right at Bleecker St (spelled 'Bleeker' on some city signs) and go two blocks to Le Figaro, one of the coffeehouses associated with the beatniks of the 1950s – it still does a jazz brunch on weekends, and it's busy but touristy.

Turn right on MacDougal St and go up to Minetta Tavern, an old Village hangout with a decent restaurant and fabulous wooden bar. On the opposite corner is **Cafe Wha?**, where Jimi Hendrix played – it's still a popular, unpretentious place. Head west down Minetta Lane and turn left onto Minetta St past a block of 18th-century slums, now preserved and improved. The old Minetta Brook still runs under some of the row houses.

Crossing Sixth Ave and walking west on Bleecker St brings you past a three-block stretch of record stores, leather shops, restaurants and Italian pastry shops. Turn right on Seventh Ave, with the famous jazz club Sweet Basil on the left. Head north to Grove St, where a right turn puts you in **Sheridan Square** (also called 'Stonewall

Place'), a small, triangular park where life-size white statues honor the gay community and the gay pride movement that began in the nearby Stonewall Inn. East of the 'square,' the triangular brick building is the Northern Dispensary, built in the cholera epidemic of the 1830s. A block farther east, a bent street is officially named Gay St.

Cross Seventh Ave and go southwest down **Christopher Street**, the center of gay life in the Village. At Bedford St, turn left and look for the quirky, early-19th-century home called **Twin Peaks** (102 Bedford St). Take a short detour south on Grove St – its houses are featured in several Woody Allen movies. Back on Bedford St, there's a wonderful 1894 horse stable that has been turned into a brewery at No 95, and Chumley's (86 Bedford St), a onetime speakeasy enjoyed by socialists and writers in the late 1920s. Turn left up Barrow St and pass the ivy-covered Federal row houses at Nos 49 and 51, and the six perfectly preserved red-brick residences on the west side of the street.

At Seventh Ave, go northwest up Bleecker St and follow it to W 10th St. Turn left here, past a handsome, block-long brick

Woody Allen, a New York fixture

The Stonewall Rebellion

On June 27, 1969, police raided the Stonewall Inn, a Christopher St men's bar. Its patrons were mourning the death of Judy Garland, an icon for the gay community, who had been buried earlier that day. Many men angrily resisted the bust, and three nights of riots followed. The 'Stonewall Rebellion' and other protests led to the introduction in 1971 of the first bill designed to ban discrimination on the basis of sexual orientation. The controversial measure was finally passed by the city council in 1986.

building, and go down to busy Hudson St, a lively stretch of cafes, curio shops and bars.

If you want to walk farther into the West Village, go three blocks north on Hudson St to the White Horse Tavern (567 Hudson St), where Dylan Thomas reputedly drank himself to death in 1953 (he actually died in the hospital). Continue north about four blocks, past Abington Square, and turn left on Jane or Horatio Sts; both have lovely old stone row houses heading down to the Hudson River running path. To glimpse an as-yet-ungentrified part of town, go a block north of Horatio St, where the Gansevoort-Little W 12th St meatpacking district is still active and odorous on weekday mornings. At night and on weekends it has some of the city's roughest gay bars, as well as a few newer, straighter places. To get out of there, the closest subway stations are along W 14th St.

East Village

Bordered roughly by 14th St, Lafayette St, E Houston St and the East River, the East Village has gentrified rapidly in the last decade. Old tenements, especially those in the blocks bordering Greenwich Village, have been taken over by artists, restaurateurs and real-estate developers. It's not as trendy as Greenwich Village yet – the ambience is more fashionable grunge, and its restaurants cater to a rich ethnic mix. Poorer residents have moved farther toward the East River into **Alphabet City** (Aves A, B, C and D), where Latino culture prevails – note the murals around Ave B.

Despite the general upmarket movement, the areas east of about Ave C can still be a bit threatening at night.

Tompkins Square Park is an unofficial border between the East Village (to the west) and Alphabet City (to the east). Once an Eastern European immigrant area, it still features old Ukrainians and Poles in the park and the odd Slavic restaurant, alongside punks, students, panhandlers and dog-walking yuppies. On E 10th St, **Grace Church** was designed by James Renwick and built mostly in the 1840s. The steeple was added in 1888, and the church's white marble exterior glows beautifully when it's floodlit at night, among the dance clubs, record stores and pizza parlors. Renwick is also credited with the perfect group of brownstone Italianate houses at 112–128 E 10th St, one block east.

The historic **10th St Baths** (☎ 212-674-9250, 268 E 10th St) still offer a traditional Russian-style massage followed by an ice-cold bath ($20, from $42 with massage; open 9am-10pm daily, ladies only 9am-2pm Wed, men only 7:30am-2pm Sun).

To explore the recently reinvented East Village, walk along First, Second or Third Ave between 14th and Houston Sts. They're lined with laundries, bars, coffee shops, delis and multiethnic restaurants. The blocks around E 9th St are popular with Japanese expatriates and visitors for their shops and sushi restaurants, while St Mark's Place is an eclectic and lively mix. Lots of shops around E 7th, 9th and St Mark's Sts sell high-end secondhand name-brand clothing and new stuff from pre-famous cutting-edge designers.

At the west end of St Mark's Place, **Astor Place** was once an elite neighborhood, and some of its impressive original Greek Revival residences remain. Across the street, in the public library built by John Jacob Astor, is the Joseph Papp Public Theater, home to the New York Shakespeare Festival. The large brownstone Cooper Union is a public college founded by glue millionaire Peter Cooper in 1859. Abraham Lincoln gave his 'Right Makes Might' speech condemning slavery before his election to the White House in the college's Great Hall. The Astor Place subway station is decorated with beaver mosaics, a reminder that John Jacob Astor's first fortune came from the fur trade.

Lower East Side

In the early 20th century, about half a million Jews from Eastern Europe lived in tenements and worked in the factories of the Lower East Side. The neighborhood had 400 synagogues then, but only a few of them still stand, serving the few remaining Jewish residents. Those living behind the crumbling doorways are now as likely to be young people in their first city apartment as long-term residents holding onto a place with rent control. The four-block area on and around **Ludlow Street** is packed Saturday nights with grunge rockers, dance-club addicts, late eaters and drinkers who should be carded.

The **Orchard St Bargain District**, the market area around Orchard, Ludlow and Essex Sts north of Delancey St, is where Eastern European merchants sold their wares from pushcarts when this was a largely Jewish neighborhood. Today shops sell sporting goods, belts, hats and off-brand 'designer fashions.' While the businesses are not exclusively owned by Orthodox Jews, they still close early Friday afternoon and remain shuttered Saturday. Shop owners may offer a discount to their first customer of the day (usually 10%), so arrive at 10am. Paying cash may also attract a discount. The local specialty is kosher food products, and the pastrami sandwiches at Katz's Delicatessen, on the corner of Ludlow and Houston Sts.

For a fascinating glimpse into tenement life, take a tour of an authentically restored tenement building conducted by the **Lower East Side Tenement Museum** (☎ 212-431-0233, 90 Orchard St). The museum itself shows an interesting video and sells some good social-history books, but the real highlight is the tenement house tour, which must be booked in advance ($9; Tue-Sun). Guides, exhibits, old documents and the apartments themselves tell about a few of the 7000 or more people who lived here during the slow improvement from the insalubrious slum conditions of the 1860s to the cleaner but still crowded community of the 1930s.

Chelsea

West of Broadway between 14th and 28th Sts, this neighborhood was an upscale retail area during the late 19th century, served by warehouses and factories extending west to the Hudson River. Many of the fancy emporiums are now office buildings, while Eighth and Ninth Aves are dominated by public housing projects and recycled warehouses. Chelsea is also home to a large gay population as well as much of New York's nightlife, especially from Seventh Ave to the West Side piers.

On noisy 23rd St, the red-brick **Chelsea Hotel** has long been notorious as a hangout for writers and musicians, including Mark Twain, Dylan Thomas, Arthur Miller, Jack Kerouac, Andy Warhol and Sid Vicious. Chelsea's burgeoning art-gallery scene is mostly between Tenth and Eleventh Aves, from 22nd through 26th Sts.

In Chelsea's southeast corner, where Broadway meets 14th St, **Union Square** was the site of many 19th-century workers' rallies – hence the name. Now a pleasant garden square, it has the city's largest open-air produce market, the **Greenmarket** (open Wed, Fri and Sat), and the surrounding streets are thick with bars and restaurants.

At the intersection of Broadway, Fifth Ave and 23rd St, the famous 1902 **Flatiron Building** has a distinctive triangular shape to match its site. It was New York's first iron-frame high-rise and the world's tallest building until 1909. The surrounding Flatiron District is a fashionable area of boutiques and loft apartments.

Midtown

Teeming Midtown is archetypical New York, with many of the best-known buildings and most popular attractions as well as some old industrial and ethnic neighborhoods. The Port Authority Bus Terminal, on Eighth Ave at 41st St, is one of the city's main gateways. The stretch of 42nd St east of the terminal was once a sleazy strip, but is now cleaned up and leads directly to New York's best-known junction, Times Square.

Times Square & Theater District Actually a triangle at the junction of 42nd St, Seventh Ave and Broadway, Times Square is a showplace for spectacular outdoor advertising, crowded with visitors late at night bathing in the flashy electric glow of giant screens, corporate logos and nonstop banner headlines. Up to a million people gather here every New Year's Eve to see the same thing with added fireworks. The blocks to the north, up to 53rd St, are home to New York theater – Broadway, off-Broadway, and off-off-Broadway (see Entertainment, later).

If you come during the day, look for the variety of architectural styles, from the art deco McGraw Hill Building (330 W 42nd St) to the Greek Revival Town Hall (113 W 43rd St). Note the more recent and garish office blocks on Broadway itself, like the Morgan Stanley Building (1589 Broadway). Times Square Visitors' Center (☎ 212-869-1890, 1560 Broadway) does a free two-hour walking tour at noon every Friday and is a useful source of information (open 8am-8pm daily).

Empire State Building A long-standing symbol of New York's skyline, the classic Empire State Building (☎ 212-736-3100, 350 Fifth Ave), at 34th St, 1454 feet high (including antennae), was the world's tallest from 1931 to 1977. Built in 410 days during the depths of the Depression at a cost of $41 million, it features a stepped shape that was primarily a response to the 'air rights' planning regulations, which required tall buildings to be set back from street frontages in proportion to their height.

Observatories on the 86th and 102nd floors of the Empire State Building are a major attraction – there may be a long wait, so come very early or very late ($9; open 9:30am-midnight daily). Check out the art deco medallions around the lobby.

Grand Central Terminal Built in 1913 as a prestigious terminal by New York Central and Hudson River Railroad, Grand Central Station is no longer a romantic place to begin a cross-country journey – it's the terminus for Metro North commuter trains to the northern suburbs and Connecticut. The huge Romanesque south facade is marred by an ugly car ramp, but it's worth looking inside at the vast, vaulted main concourse. The ceiling is decorated with a star map that is actually a 'God's eye' image of the sky. Balconies give a fine overview of the concourse, while the lower-level Oyster Bar is a famous seafood restaurant and raw bar. The Municipal Art Society (☎ 212-935-3960) conducts guided walks through Grand Central ($6 donation; 12:30pm Wed). Towering over the terminal, the 60-story

MetLife Building was a controversial but innovative structure in 1963, when it was built as the Pan Am headquarters.

Chrysler Building Just east of Grand Central Terminal, the Chrysler Building (405 Lexington Ave), an art deco masterpiece adorned with motorcar motifs, was designed by William Van Alen and completed in 1930. Unfortunately, visitors can't go up the building, and some details are barely visible from the ground. In the lobby, admire the African marble, onyx lights and other decorative elements.

New York Public Library The superb beaux arts–style New York Public Library (☎ 212-930-0800), at Fifth Ave and 42nd St, is a wonderful retreat from the Midtown bustle. The elegant lobby, marble stairs, and impressive halls lead to the brilliant 3rd-floor reading room with its natural light and magnificent ceiling. This, the main branch of the library, has galleries of manuscripts on display, as well as fascinating temporary exhibits (open 10am-6pm Mon and Thurs-Sat, 11am-7:30pm Tue-Wed).

Rockefeller Center Known for its ice rink, Christmas tree, statuary and decorated facades, this art deco complex was started in 1931 and took nine years to complete. Some 200 dwellings were removed to make way for the project, but at the time that was less controversial than the lobby mural by Mexican artist Diego Rivera, which depicted Lenin; it was covered up during the opening ceremonies and later destroyed. Its replacement, painted by José María Sert, features the more acceptable figure of Abraham Lincoln.

Look for the tile work above the Sixth Ave entrance to the GE Building, the entrance to the East River Savings Bank building at 41 Rockefeller Plaza, the triptych above the entrance to 30 Rockefeller Plaza and the famous statues of Prometheus and Atlas.

The 1932 **Radio City Music Hall** (☎ 212-247-4777, 1260 Sixth Ave), a 6000-seat theater, is a protected landmark perfectly restored in all its art deco grandeur. Guided tours leave the lobby every half hour (☎ 212-247-4777). The cost is $15 (open 10am-5pm daily).

MIDTOWN & CHELSEA

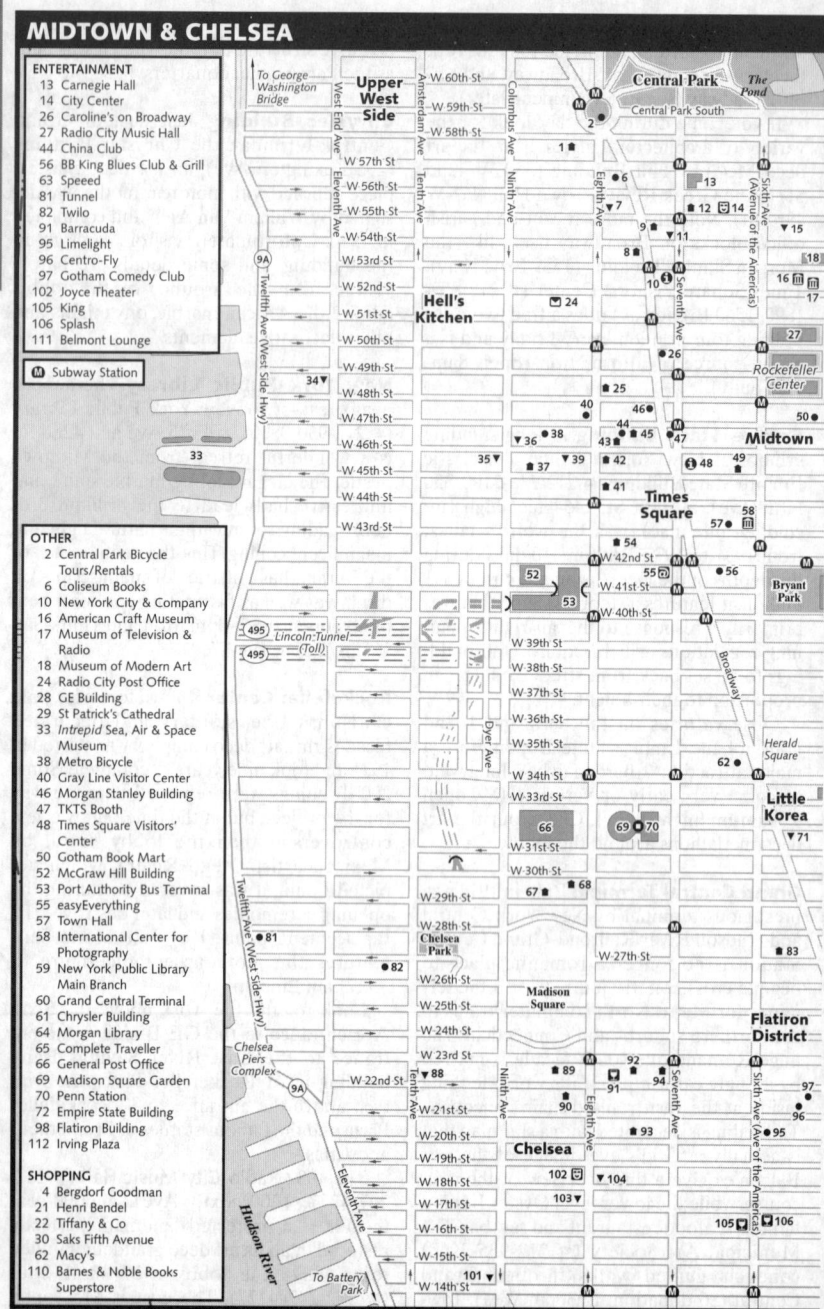

ENTERTAINMENT
13 Carnegie Hall
14 City Center
26 Caroline's on Broadway
27 Radio City Music Hall
44 China Club
56 BB King Blues Club & Grill
63 Speed
81 Tunnel
82 Twilo
91 Barracuda
95 Limelight
96 Centro-Fly
97 Gotham Comedy Club
102 Joyce Theater
105 King
106 Splash
111 Belmont Lounge

Ⓜ Subway Station

OTHER
2 Central Park Bicycle Tours/Rentals
6 Coliseum Books
10 New York City & Company
16 American Craft Museum
17 Museum of Television & Radio
18 Museum of Modern Art
24 Radio City Post Office
28 GE Building
29 St Patrick's Cathedral
33 Intrepid Sea, Air & Space Museum
38 Metro Bicycle
40 Gray Line Visitor Center
46 Morgan Stanley Building
47 TKTS Booth
48 Times Square Visitors' Center
50 Gotham Book Mart
52 McGraw Hill Building
55 Port Authority Bus Terminal
55 easyEverything
57 Town Hall
58 International Center for Photography
59 New York Public Library Main Branch
60 Grand Central Terminal
61 Chrysler Building
64 Morgan Library
65 Complete Traveller
66 General Post Office
69 Madison Square Garden
70 Penn Station
72 Empire State Building
98 Flatiron Building
112 Irving Plaza

SHOPPING
4 Bergdorf Goodman
21 Henri Bendel
22 Tiffany & Co
30 Saks Fifth Avenue
62 Macy's
110 Barnes & Noble Books Superstore

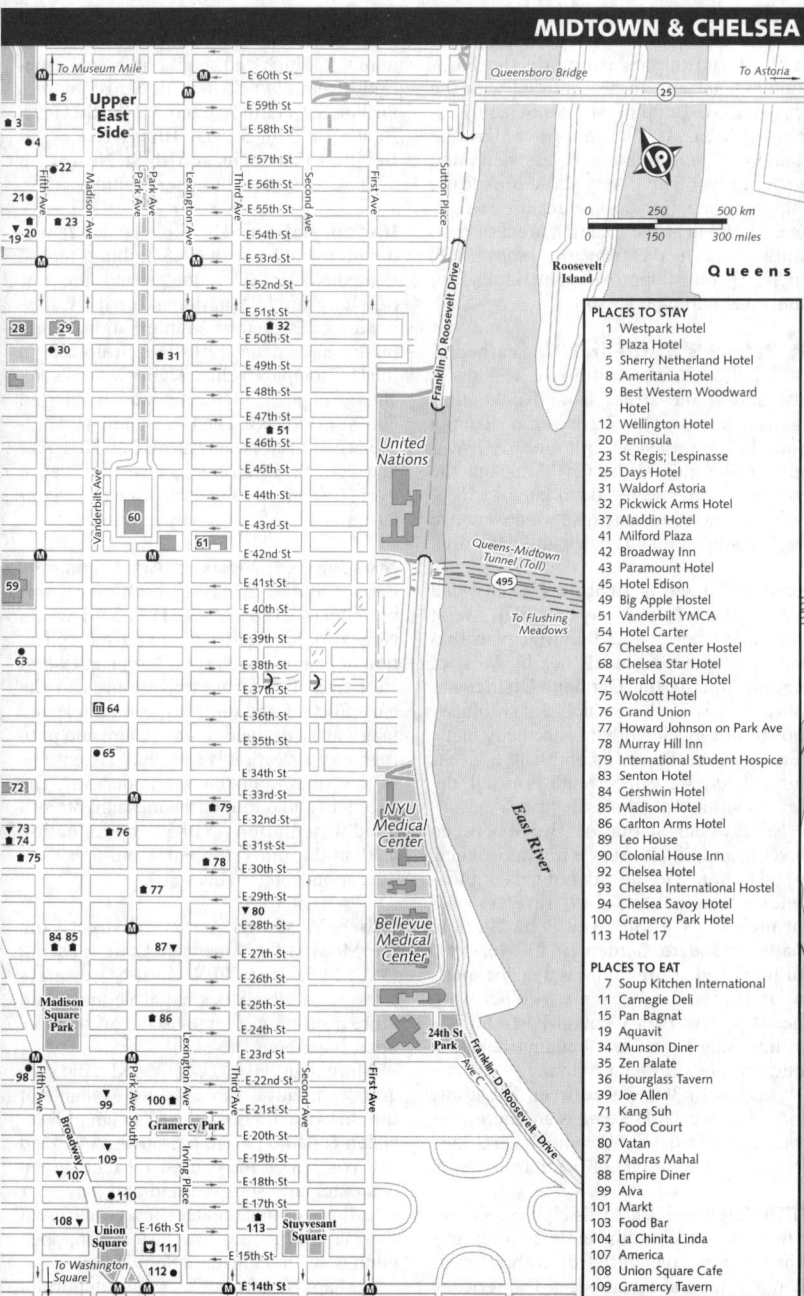

MIDTOWN & CHELSEA

To Museum Mile

Upper East Side

To Astoria

Queensboro Bridge

Roosevelt Island

Queens

0   250   500 km
0   150   300 miles

United Nations

Queens-Midtown Tunnel (Toll)

To Flushing Meadows

East River

NYU Medical Center

Bellevue Medical Center

24th St Park

Madison Square Park

Gramercy Park

Union Square

Stuyvesant Square

To Washington Square

Franklin D Roosevelt Drive

PLACES TO STAY
1 Westpark Hotel
3 Plaza Hotel
5 Sherry Netherland Hotel
8 Ameritania Hotel
9 Best Western Woodward Hotel
12 Wellington Hotel
20 Peninsula
23 St Regis; Lespinasse
25 Days Hotel
31 Waldorf Astoria
32 Pickwick Arms Hotel
37 Aladdin Hotel
41 Milford Plaza
42 Broadway Inn
43 Paramount Hotel
45 Hotel Edison
49 Big Apple Hostel
51 Vanderbilt YMCA
54 Hotel Carter
67 Chelsea Center Hostel
68 Chelsea Star Hotel
74 Herald Square Hotel
75 Wolcott Hotel
76 Grand Union
77 Howard Johnson on Park Ave
78 Murray Hill Inn
79 International Student Hospice
83 Senton Hotel
84 Gershwin Hotel
85 Madison Hotel
86 Carlton Arms Hotel
89 Leo House
90 Colonial House Inn
92 Chelsea Hotel
93 Chelsea International Hostel
94 Chelsea Savoy Hotel
100 Gramercy Park Hotel
113 Hotel 17

PLACES TO EAT
7 Soup Kitchen International
11 Carnegie Deli
15 Pan Bagnat
19 Aquavit
34 Munson Diner
35 Zen Palate
36 Hourglass Tavern
39 Joe Allen
71 Kang Suh
73 Food Court
80 Vatan
87 Madras Mahal
88 Empire Diner
99 Alva
101 Markt
103 Food Bar
104 La Chinita Linda
107 America
108 Union Square Cafe
109 Gramercy Tavern

NBC Studios and the NBC television network headquarters are on the 70th floor of the GE Building (formerly the RCA Building, and not to be confused with the art deco GE Building at 50th St and Lexington Ave), at the top of which the Rainbow Room offers priceless views and pricey drinks. The *Today* show broadcasts 7am-9am daily from a glass-enclosed street-level studio near the fountain area/ice rink. Studio tours leave from the lobby ($18; open 8:30am-5:30pm Mon-Sat, 11am-5pm Sun; no children under six).

St Patrick's Cathedral This cathedral (☎ 212-753-2261), on Fifth Ave at 50th St, just across the street from Rockefeller Center, serves the 2.2 million Roman Catholics in the New York diocese. It was built mostly during the Civil War, but the two front spires were added later, in 1888. Look for the handsome rose window above the 7000-pipe organ (open 6am-9pm daily).

Herald Square & Around This crowded convergence of Broadway and Sixth Ave at 34th St is where you'll find Macy's, with a couple of shopping malls nearby. West of Herald Square, the **Garment District** has most of New York's fashion design offices, though not much clothing is actually made here anymore. Stores on 36th and 37th Sts immediately west of Seventh Ave sell 'designer clothing' at wholesale prices.

Nearby Penn Station, on 33rd St between Seventh and Eighth Aves, is not the original, grand entrance to the city, but tens of thousands of commuters and travelers pass through daily. Built over Penn Station, **Madison Square Garden** (☎ 212-465-5800 for tours and information) is a major sporting and entertainment venue. A block west, the 1913 New York General Post Office is an imposing beaux arts building behind a long row of Corinthian columns.

On 31st to 36th Sts between Broadway and Fifth Ave, **Little Korea** is an interesting, lively neighborhood. Look on 31st and 32nd Sts for a proliferation of Korean restaurants.

Fifth Avenue Fifth Ave's high-class reputation dates back to the early 20th century, when it was considered desirable for its 'country' air and open spaces. The series of mansions called **Millionaire's Row** extended right up to 130th St. Today, midtown Fifth Ave is the site of airline offices and a number of high-end shops and hotels, especially from 49th St to 57th St. Big names include Saks Fifth Avenue, at 50th St; Henri Bendel, at 55th St; and Tiffany & Co and Bergdorf Goodman, at 57th St. Nearby on 57th St are several designer boutiques.

United Nations The Rockefeller family donated land worth $8.5 million to the United Nations (UN); the grounds are now officially an international territory. The building, designed by an international committee, has a dated 1950s feel. Sculptures in the UN complex include Henry Moore's *Reclining Figure* and Reutersward's knotted gun *Non-Violence*. The UN Building (☎ 212-963-8687) visitors entrance is at First Ave and 46th St. English-language tours leave every 30 minutes ($7.50; open 9:15am-4:45pm daily, Mon-Fri only in winter).

Museum of Modern Art Commonly known as the 'MoMA' (**moh**-mah), this museum (☎ 212-708-9480, 11 W 53rd St) is a New York highlight, with an all-star collection of painting, sculpture, design and weird stuff from the early impressionists to the early 2000s. Exhibitions focus on a selected major artist or theme, and the film and photography collection is excellent. Extensions to the MoMa building are under way. The excellent audio tour of the museum offers a good orientation ($10.50, by donation 4:30pm-8:15pm Fri; open 11am-6pm Sat-Tue, noon-8:30pm Thurs-Fri).

Other Museums Across the street from the MoMA, the **American Craft Museum** (☎ 212-956-3535, 40 W 53rd St) displays crafts in wood, textiles, metal, ceramics and more from colonial times to the present ($5; open 10am-6pm Tue-Sun).

More than 100,000 US TV and radio programs and advertisements are available at the click of a mouse in the **Museum of Television & Radio** (☎ 212-621-6600, 25 W 52nd St). You search the extensive catalogue on computer, and staff will find and play your selection. A small theater shows some great specials on broadcasting history ($6; open noon-6pm Tue-Sun, until 8pm Thurs).

Perhaps New York City's most important photography showplace, the **International**

Center for Photography (☎ 212-860-1777, 1133 Sixth Ave), at 43rd St, has regularly rotating exhibitions by major photographers – always interesting, sometimes stunning ($8; open 11am-8pm Tue, 11am-6pm Wed-Sun).

Once banker, financier, railroad and steel magnate JP Morgan's lavish mansion, the three-tiered **Morgan Library** (☎ 212-685-0008, 29 E 36th St), off Madison Ave, features JP Morgan's collection of Italian Renaissance artwork, manuscripts, tapestries and books, including three Gutenberg Bibles. The rooms themselves are magnificent ($8; open 10:30am-5pm Tue-Thurs, 10:30am-8pm Fri, 10:30am-6pm Sat, noon-6pm Sun).

Most of the exhibits in the *Intrepid* **Sea-Air-Space Museum** (☎ 212-245-0072, Pier 86, W 46th St) are in or on a WWII aircraft carrier, including fighter planes, helicopters, a space capsule and other artifacts from the military-industrial complex. The museum also includes a submarine and a destroyer ($10; open 10am-5pm Mon-Sat, until 6pm Sun).

Central Park

This enormous rectangular park, right in the middle of Manhattan, is for many what makes New York livable and lovable. On weekends it's packed with joggers, skaters, musicians and tourists. Though it's heavily used and quite safe during the day, New Yorkers avoid walking in the park after dark.

The park's 843 acres were set aside in 1856 on the marshy northern fringe of the city. The landscaping (the first in a US public park), by Frederick Law Olmsted and Calvert Vaux, was innovative in its naturalistic style, with forested groves, meandering paths and informal ponds.

One of the prettiest parts is the **Ramble**, a lush wooden expanse that's a meeting place for dog owners. At the W 72nd St entrance, **Strawberry Fields**, with plants from 100 nations, is dedicated to John Lennon, who lived (and was murdered) at the nearby Dakota apartment building. Other highlights are the zoo (particularly the polar bears and feeding times; $3.50/50¢ for adults/kids), Shakespeare in the Park performances in the Delacorte Theater and the formal promenade called The Mall, which culminates at elegant **Bethesda Terrace** – a fun place on weekends. The Central Park roadway is regularly closed to traffic and is

popular for running, cycling and skating. The most touristy activity is to rent a horse-drawn carriage on 59th St (Central Park South). It costs from $40 for 30 minutes, and drivers expect a generous tip. A better option is to rent a bike at **Loeb Boathouse** (☎ 212-517-2233), for about $10 per hour.

The park features various concerts and performances in the summer. For information, go to the park visitor information center in the Dairy building (☎ 212-794-6564), in the middle of the park along the 65th St pathway (open 11am-4pm Tue-Sun).

Upper West Side

Many celebrities live in the massive apartment buildings that line Central Park West all the way up to 96th St.

A complex of performance spaces built in the 1960s, **Lincoln Center** (☎ 212-875-5400), at Columbus Ave and Broadway, is uninspiring during the day, but its chandeliered interiors look simply beautiful at night. See Entertainment, later, for information about the various theater, film, opera, music and dance performances. Tours of the complex leave from the concourse level daily and explore at least three of the theaters ($9.50). Call ahead (☎ 212-875-5350) for times and bookings.

The antiquated, hyphenated **New-York Historical Society** (☎ 212-873-3400, 2 W 77th St) is the city's oldest museum, founded in 1804. The original watercolors for John James Audubon's *Birds of America* are displayed in a 2nd-floor gallery. The quirky permanent collection is like New York City's attic – George Washington's old army cot is in here somewhere ($5; open 11am-5pm Tue-Sun).

There are over 30 million artifacts in the **American Museum of Natural History** (☎ 212-769-5100), on Central Park West at 79th St, but the three dinosaur halls are by far the most popular. Knowledgeable guides are ready to answer questions, and 'please touch' displays will captivate kids ($10/6 adults/kids donation; open 10am-5:45pm Sun-Thurs, 10am-8:45pm Fri-Sat). The recently rebuilt Hayden Planetarium is the amazing sphere-in-a-cube structure beside the museum on 79th St; at night it's illuminated in an eerie blue and looks extraterrestrial. The planetarium is part of the Rose Space Center, and most of its exhibits are included in the normal museum entry ($10), but the shows inside the spherical Space Theater cost $9 extra. Free guided tours run several times daily.

The **Children's Museum of Manhattan** (☎ 212-721-1234, 212 W 83rd St) features hands-on exhibits, discovery centers for toddlers, a 'Brainatarium' and a postmodern Media Center for older children ($6; open 1:30pm-5:30pm Mon and Wed-Thurs, 10am-5pm Fri-Sun).

Columbia University's gated campus is on upper Broadway between 114th and 121st Sts. The spacious central quadrangle is dominated by the 1895 Low Library, one of several neoclassical campus buildings by McKim, Mead & White. Hamilton Hall, in the southeast corner of the main square, is periodically a place for protests and parties. Free campus tours (☎ 212-854-4900) are available weekdays. The surrounding neighborhood is filled with inexpensive restaurants, good bookstores and cafes.

Dark and massive, the Episcopal **Cathedral of St John the Divine** (☎ 212-316-7540, 1047 Amsterdam Ave), at 112th St, is the largest place of worship in the USA. Though the cornerstone was laid in 1892, the cathedral is nowhere near completed. Yet it's an active place of worship and the site of holiday concerts, lectures and memorial services for famous New Yorkers. The cathedral is open 8am-6pm daily. High Mass at 11am Sunday often features sermons by well-known intellectuals.

A 1930 Gothic marvel, **Riverside Church** (490 Riverside Dr), at 122nd St, is famous for its 74 carillon bells, rung every Sunday at noon and 3pm. The church's observation deck affords a superb view of the Hudson River ($2; open 11am-4pm Tue-Sat, 12:30pm-4pm Sun).

Upper East Side

The area east of Central Park is home to New York's greatest concentration of cultural centers: Fifth Ave above 57th St is called 'Museum Mile.' The neighborhood also has many of the city's most exclusive hotels and residential blocks. Look on the side streets from Fifth Ave east to Third Ave between 57th and 86th Sts for elegant brownstones, especially at nightfall, when you can peer into grand libraries and luxurious living rooms.

Metropolitan Museum of Art Commonly called 'The Met,' this vast museum (☎ 212-879-5500, ⓦ www.metmuseum.org, 1000 Fifth Ave), at 82nd St and surrounded by Central Park, is New York's most popular single-site attraction – and deservedly so. It receives about five million annual visitors, and crowds can be impossible, but on a Friday evening in winter the place might be nearly deserted. It always helps to arrive early (open 9:30am-5:15pm Tue-Thurs, 9:30am-8:45pm Fri-Sat, 9:30am-5:15pm Sun). The suggested donation is $10 and includes same-day admission to the Cloisters (see Washington Heights, later).

Other Museums On the east side of Fifth Ave, the **Museum of the City of New York** (☎ 212-534-1672, 1220 Fifth Ave), at 123rd St, is the most northern of the Museum Mile institutions. It traces the city's history from beaver trading to futures trading. A 2nd-floor gallery has entire rooms from demolished homes of New York grandees and an excellent collection of antique dollhouses, teddy bears and toys ($7, families $12; open 10am-5pm Wed-Sat, noon-5pm Sun).

The **Jewish Museum** (☎ 212-423-3200, 1109 Fifth Ave), at 92nd St, examines 4000 years of Jewish history, ceremony and art ($8, free Tue; open 11am-5:45pm Sun-Thurs, 5pm-8pm Tue).

Billionaire Andrew Carnegie built a sumptuous 64-room mansion in 1901, just off Fifth Ave and far from the downtown bustle, but it was soon surrounded by other homes of the super-rich. Now the **Cooper-Hewitt National Museum of Design** (☎ 212-849-8400, 2 E 91st St), Carnegie's home is a branch of the Smithsonian Institution and a must for anyone interested in architecture, engineering, jewelry, textiles or even domestic design ($8, free 5pm-9pm Tue; open 10am-9pm Tue, 10am-5pm Wed-Sat, noon-5pm Sun).

The opulent 1914 mansion housing the **Frick Collection** (☎ 212-288-0700, 1 E 70th St), off Fifth Ave, was part of the Fifth Ave Millionaires Row in the age of the robber barons, of whom Henry Clay Frick was among the most ruthless. Outstanding European paintings include works by Holbein, Titian, Vermeer, Gainsborough and Constable. A useful little guide ($1) explains the significance of the paintings ($7; open 10am-6pm Tue-Sat).

Still going....Battle-worn subway train; Brooklyn, New York City

If you've got it, flaunt it. New York City

Empire State Building, New York City

'Taxiiii!' Yellow jam in New York City

Green and pleasant countryside rolls across southwestern Pennsylvania.

Portland Head Light, the oldest of Maine's functioning lighthouses; Cape Elizabeth, Portland, Maine

Swanning about on the lake; Boston, Massachusetts

Exploring the Met

Visitors enter via the Great Hall (designed after the Roman baths of Caracalla), pick up a floor plan and head to the ticket booths, where there's a list of special exhibitions, installations and museum talks. An information desk to the right offers guidance in several languages (depending on the volunteers) and audio tours of special exhibits ($10). Ask about the free volunteer-led tours of museum highlights and specific galleries, available Tuesday to Friday.

To get an overview of this stupendous collection, start at the **Egyptian Art** section in the north wing, where you find the tomb of Pernebi (c. 2415 BC), several mummies and some incredibly well-preserved wall paintings. In a magnificent glassed gallery is the entire Temple of Dendur, saved from submersion in the waters behind the Aswan Dam.

Exit behind the temple and head to the **American Wing**, starting with a valuable collection of baseball cards. Continue to the left through exhibits of furniture and architecture, including a complete room from a Frank Lloyd Wright prairie house. Along an enclosed garden are displays of Tiffany stained-glass works and the entire two-story facade of the Branch Bank of the US.

Detour to **Arms & Armor**, where swords, shields and complete suits of armor are displayed as artworks as much as historical artifacts, then look through several large galleries of **European Sculpture & Decorative Arts**, including the darkened medieval collection, with jewelry and religious art. Turn right to the pyramid-like addition that houses the Lehman Collection of Italian, impressionist and modern art. An unexpected bonus in this gallery is an entire facade from the original 1880 Met building.

Continue to the southwest corner, with the large collection of **20th-Century Art**, then back toward Fifth Ave through the Rockefeller collection of **Africa & Pacific Island Arts**. At the museum cafe, turn left through the long rows of fine classical pieces in the **Greek & Roman Art** section and back to the Great Hall.

After resting your feet a bit, take the stairs to the 2nd-floor collection of **European Paintings**, with works by every major artist and an especially fine selection of Flemish and Dutch paintings. There's more of the fine American art collection here, and a series of galleries of **Asian** art – Japanese, Chinese, Korean, Indian and Southeast Asian – and some more with **Islamic and Near East** art. Finally, the **19th-Century European** galleries feature sculpture and impressionist/postimpressionist painting and the upper levels of the **20th-Century Art collection**. In good weather, finish your visit at the rooftop **Sculpture Garden**, with great views over Central Park (and a bar!).

One of the few museums that concentrates on American works of art, the **Whitney Museum of American Art** (☎ 212-570-3676, 945 Madison Ave), at 75th St, is actually a block east of Fifth Ave. The distinctive concrete and stone building, designed by Marcel Breuer in the late 1950s, has been variously described as 'odd,' 'brutal' and 'extraordinarily ugly.' The collection specializes in 20th-century and contemporary art, with works by Hopper, Pollock, de Kooning, O'Keeffe, Rothko, Johns and others, as well as brilliant temporary shows. The Whitney's important biennial exhibitions serve as a status report on contemporary American art ($12.50, free 6pm-8pm Thurs; open 11am-6pm Fri-Sun and Tue-Wed, 1pm-8pm Thurs).

The inspired work of Frank Lloyd Wright, the sweeping spiral of the **Solomon R Guggenheim Museum** (☎ 212-423-3500, 1071 Fifth Ave) is a superb sculpture in which the excellent collection of 20th-century paintings is almost an afterthought. The museum's permanent collection includes work by Picasso, Pollock, Chagall, Cézanne and (especially) Kandinsky. A controversial 1993 extension allows for more works to be displayed, and for special exhibitions in the spiral ($12, 'pay what you can' 6pm-8pm Fri; open 9am-6pm Sun-Wed, 9am-8pm Fri-Sat).

Roosevelt Island

This narrow island lies in the East River between Manhattan and Queens. Most

MID-ATLANTIC STATES

UPPER MANHATTAN & HARLEM

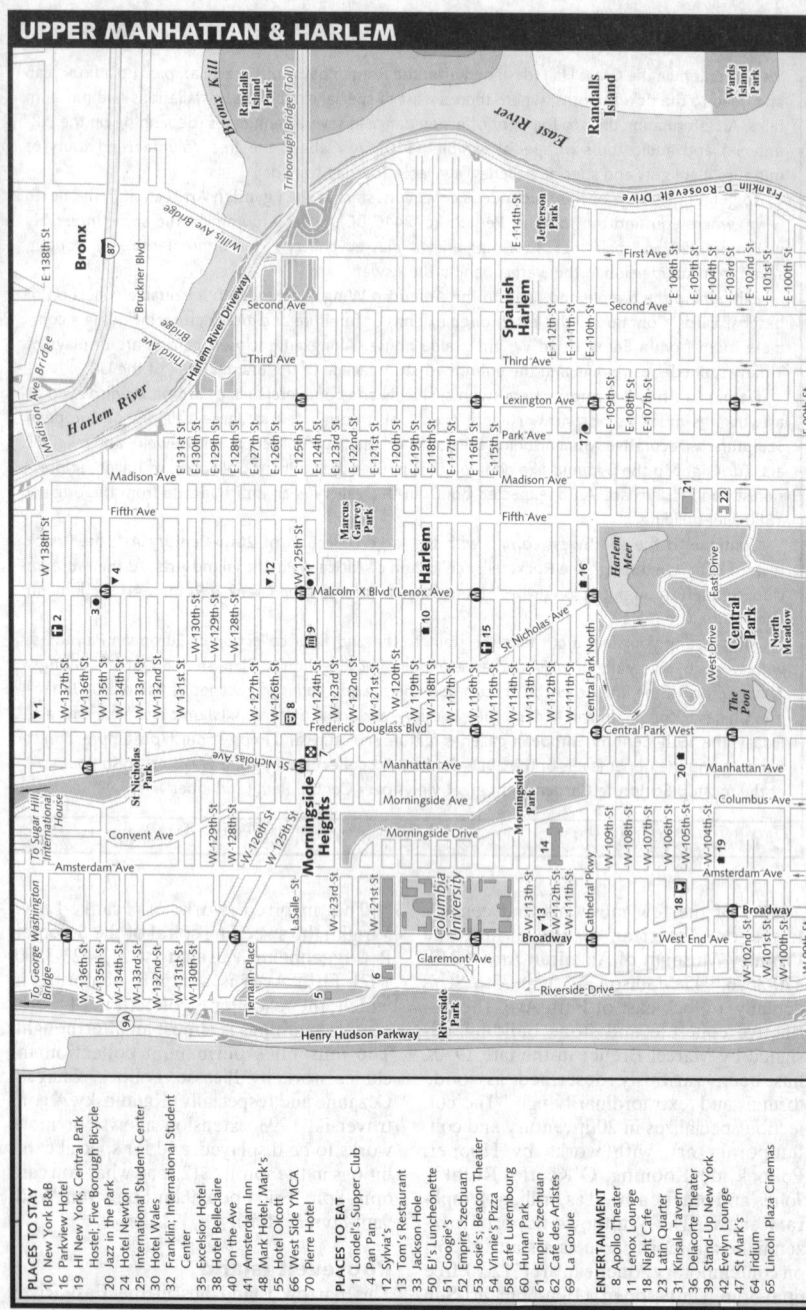

PLACES TO STAY
10 New York B&B
16 Parkview Hotel
19 HI New York; Central Park
   Hostel; Five Borough Bicycle
20 Jazz in the Park
24 Hotel Newton
25 International Student Center
30 Hotel Wales
32 Franklin; International Student
   Center
35 Excelsior Hotel
38 Hotel Belleclaire
40 On the Ave
41 Amsterdam Inn
48 Mark Hotel; Mark's
55 Hotel Olcott
66 West Side YMCA
70 Pierre Hotel

PLACES TO EAT
1 Londel's Supper Club
4 Pan Pan
12 Sylvia's
13 Tom's Restaurant
33 Jackson Hole
50 EJ's Luncheonette
51 Googie's
52 Empire Szechuan
53 Josie's; Beacon Theater
54 Vinnie's Pizza
58 Cafe Luxembourg
60 Human Park
61 Empire Szechuan
62 Cafe des Artistes
69 La Goulue

ENTERTAINMENT
8 Apollo Theater
11 Lenox Lounge
18 Night Cafe
23 Latin Quarter
31 Kinsale Tavern
36 Delacorte Theater
39 Stand-Up New York
42 Evelyn Lounge
47 St Mark's
64 Iridium
65 Lincoln Plaza Cinemas

MID-ATLANTIC STATES

UPPER MANHATTAN & HARLEM

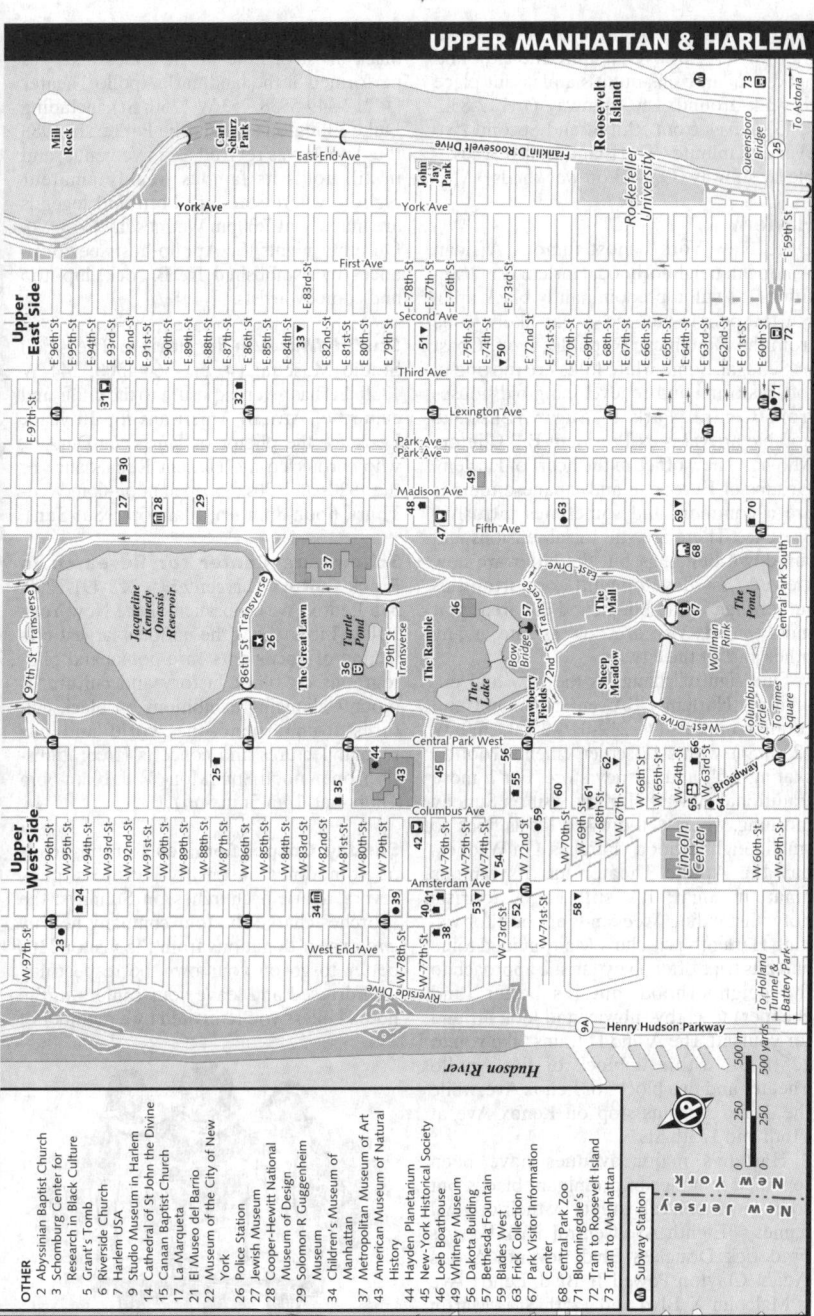

Mill Rock

Carl Schurz Park

Roosevelt Island

East End Ave

John Jay Park

Franklin D Roosevelt Drive

Rockefeller University

Queensboro Bridge

To Astoria

73

York Ave

York Ave

E 59th St

Upper East Side

First Ave

Second Ave

Third Ave

Lexington Ave

Park Ave
Park Ave

Madison Ave

Fifth Ave

E 96th St
E 95th St
E 94th St
E 93rd St
E 92nd St
E 91st St
E 90th St
E 89th St
E 88th St
E 87th St
E 86th St
E 85th St
E 84th St
E 83rd St
E 82nd St
E 81st St
E 80th St
E 79th St
E 78th St
E 77th St
E 76th St
E 75th St
E 74th St
E 73rd St
E 72nd St
E 71st St
E 70th St
E 69th St
E 68th St
E 67th St
E 66th St
E 65th St
E 64th St
E 63rd St
E 62nd St
E 61st St
E 60th St

E 97th St

31
32
33 ▼
51 ▼
50
30
27
28
29
49
48
47
63
69 ▼
70
68
71
72

Jacqueline Kennedy Onassis Reservoir

86th St Transverse

The Great Lawn

79th St Transverse

Turtle Pond

The Ramble

The Lake

Bow Bridge

Strawberry Fields

Sheep Meadow

The Mall

Wollman Rink

The Pond

East Drive

West Drive

Central Park South

Columbus Circle

To Times Square

97th St Transverse

37
26
36
46
57
67

Upper West Side

Central Park West

Columbus Ave

Amsterdam Ave

West End Ave

W 97th St
W 96th St
W 95th St
W 94th St
W 93rd St
W 92nd St
W 91st St
W 90th St
W 89th St
W 88th St
W 87th St
W 86th St
W 85th St
W 84th St
W 83rd St
W 82nd St
W 81st St
W 80th St
W 79th St
W 78th St
W 77th St
W 76th St
W 75th St
W 74th St
W 73rd St
W 72nd St
W 71st St
W 70th St
W 69th St
W 68th St
W 67th St
W 66th St
W 65th St
W 64th St
W 63rd St
W 60th St
W 59th St

23
24
25
35
44
43
45
56
55
54
53 ▼
52
39
40 41
38
42
34
59
60
61
62
58 ▼
65
66
64

Lincoln Center

Broadway

To Holland Tunnel & Battery Park

9A Henry Hudson Parkway

Riverside Drive

Hudson River

New Jersey **New York**

500 m
500 yards
250
250
0

Subway Station Ⓜ

visitors take the three-minute aerial tramway ($1.50) over, admire the view and head straight back, but it's a pleasant place to walk around. The tramway (☎ 212-832-4543) leaves from 59th St and Second Ave every 15 minutes. The island is also accessible by subway (Q, or B on weekends).

Harlem

Once New York's most famous African American neighborhood, Harlem is in transition. It's still a predominantly black area, but the people you see are as likely to be from the Dominican Republic, Ivory Coast or Senegal. Some white folks are moving in too, restoring and redeveloping old houses from Central Park to Sugar Hill. One notable arrival is ex-President Bill Clinton, who has a new office in the heart of Harlem. Groups of European and Japanese tourists are a common, and sometimes intrusive, presence. There are still racial tensions and run-down buildings, but the latter are now viewed as development opportunities rather than urban blight, and the areas that most tourists visit are now as safe as any other part of the city.

One sign of change is the new and uninviting 'Harlem USA' entertainment and retail complex (☎ 212-316-2500, 300 W 125th St), with a 12-screen cinema, rooftop skating rink and Disney store. For a more traditional view of Harlem, visit on Sunday morning, when well-dressed locals flock to small neighborhood churches. On Wednesday the Apollo Theater has its famous amateur night; it's still good, tourists notwithstanding. Weekends are best for visiting Harlem's jazz clubs. Many guided tours and bus trips offer a voyeuristic approach to the neighborhood, but it's better (and cheaper) to go by subway and look around for yourself. The A and D trains take you to 125th St, within a block of the Apollo Theater and two blocks of Lenox Ave, while the 2 and 3 trains stop on Lenox Ave at 116th and 125th Sts.

Harlem's major avenues have been renamed in honor of prominent blacks, but some locals still call streets by their original names – Eighth Ave/Central Park West is Frederick Douglass Blvd, Seventh Ave is Adam Clayton Powell Jr Blvd, Lenox Ave is Malcolm X Blvd and 125th St is Martin Luther King Jr Blvd.

Apollo Theater Virtually every major black artist of note in the 1930s and '40s performed at the landmark Apollo Theater (☎ 212-749-5838, 253 W 125th St), including Duke Ellington and Charlie Parker. In 1983 the Apollo was revived as a live venue, and it still holds its famous weekly amateur night – 'where stars are born and legends are made' – at 7:30pm Wednesday ($15-23). On other nights the Apollo hosts performances by established R&B, rock, hip-hop and comedy artists.

Studio Museum in Harlem The small Studio Museum (☎ 212-864-4500, 144 W 125th St) has given exposure to the crafts and culture of African Americans for 30 years. Look for the photos of James VanDerZee, who chronicled the Harlem Renaissance of the 1920s and '30s ($5; open noon-6pm Wed-Thurs, noon-8pm Fri, 10am-6pm Sat-Sun).

Schomburg Center for Research in Black Culture This center (☎ 212-491-2200, 515 Lenox Ave), a branch of the New York Public Library, has the nation's largest collection of documents, rare books and photographs on black history and culture. It mounts changing exhibitions on black cultures from around the world and has regular lectures and concerts (free admission; open noon-8pm Mon-Wed, 10am-6pm Thurs-Sat, 1pm-5pm Sun).

Sunday Gospel Services Tour-bus loads of sometimes insensitive visitors pack several Harlem churches on Sundays; the churches charge the tour company heavily *and* expect donations from the visitors. It's better to go on your own, be respectfully well dressed and leave your camera in the hotel. Unless you're invited by a member of

the congregation, stick to the bigger churches like those mentioned here, which are accustomed to visitors. **Abyssinian Baptist Church** (☎ 212-862-7474, 132 W 138th St), with its superb choir and charismatic pastor, Calvin O Butts, welcomes tourists and prays for them. Sunday services start at 9am and 11am – the later one is *very* well attended. **Canaan Baptist Church** (☎ 212-866-0301, 132 W 116th St) also welcomes visitors, but it's best to arrive early and introduce yourself before the Sunday service (10:45am, 10am in summer).

Spanish Harlem Spanish Harlem, also called 'El Barrio' (the Neighborhood), is a formerly Italian area that now contains one of the biggest Latino communities, predominantly Puerto Rican, in the city. It runs from Lenox Ave (Malcolm X Blvd) east to the river, and from around 122nd St in the north (where it merges with Harlem's prominently black areas) to around 96th St in the south (not including the swanky Upper East Side blocks between Fifth Ave and Park Ave – there are some abrupt transitions here). On Park Ave just north of 110th St, **La Marqueta** is a colorful ad hoc collection of produce stalls.

In an unprepossessing old school building, **El Museo del Barrio** (☎ 212-831-7272, 1230 Fifth Ave) began in 1969 as a celebration of Puerto Rican art and culture and has since expanded to include the folk art of Latin America, the Caribbean and Spain. It also features pre-Columbian artifacts, hand-carved wooden *santos* (saints) and temporary exhibitions of work by local artists ($5; open 11am-5pm Wed-Sun, until 7pm Thurs).

Washington Heights

The north end of Manhattan has some surprisingly rural landscapes, especially around Fort Tryon Park and Inwood Hill. The Washington Heights residential area has large and unremarkable apartment buildings and an increasingly Latino population. Visitors come mainly to see the Cloisters and a few other attractions, which are linked by free shuttle buses on Sundays (call the Cloisters for details at ☎ 212-923-3700).

The Cloisters A branch of the Metropolitan Museum of Art, the Cloisters (☎ 212-923-3700), in Fort Tryon Park (Ⓜ 190th St),

was constructed in the 1930s using stones and fragments from several French and Spanish medieval monasteries. It looks remarkably authentic, and the courtyards and herb gardens are delightful. Inside, the Met's fine collection of medieval frescoes, tapestries and paintings is on display ($10 donation, includes same-day admission to the Met; open 9:30am-5pm Tue-Sun).

Audubon Terrace The former home of naturalist John James Audubon, on Broadway between 153rd and 155th Sts (Ⓜ 157th St–Broadway), is home to three little-known free museums.

The **American Numismatic Society** (☎ 212-234-3130), on Broadway at 155th St, displays a large permanent collection of coins, medals and paper money (open 9am-4:30pm Tue-Sat, 1pm-4pm Sun).

The little-visited **Hispanic Society of America** (☎ 212-926-2234, 613 W 155th St) has a collection of Spanish and Portuguese furniture and artifacts, including significant artworks by El Greco (open 10am-4:30pm Tue-Sat, 1pm-4pm Sun).

The **American Academy & Institute of Arts and Letters** (☎ 212-368-5900, 633 W 155th St) opens to the public several times a year for temporary exhibitions.

Dyckman House Museum This house (☎ 212-304-9422, 4881 Broadway) was built in 1783 and is the last Dutch farmhouse in Manhattan. Take the subway to the 207th St station *(not Dyckman St)* and walk one block south (free admission; open 11am-5pm Tue-Sun).

The Bronx

This borough includes both the run-down South Bronx, home of hip-hop and rap and site of a massive low-income housing project, and suburban Fieldston in the north, with its posh pseudo-Tudor homes.

The Bronx Tourism Council (☎ 718-590-3518, Ⓦ www.ilovethebronx.com) has a visitor guide, and the Bronx County Historical Society (☎ 718-881-8900, 3266 Bainbridge Ave) sponsors weekend walking tours.

Don't pass up a pilgrimage to baseball's mecca, **Yankee Stadium** (☎ 718-293-6000), on 161st St at River Ave, 15 minutes from downtown Manhattan via the 4 and D trains. Fans arrive when the gates open, 90 minutes before game time. **Memorial Park** has plaques dedicated to baseball greats, and shops across the street sell all kinds of memorabilia.

The 250-acre **New York Botanical Gardens** (☎ 718-817-8705), at 200th St and Kazimiroff Blvd, feature the restored Victorian-era Enid A Haupt Conservatory and glasshouses full of tropical and desert plants. There's 40 acres of original forest and a garden of 2700 roses. Take the D train to Bedford Park Blvd and walk east seven blocks to the gate, or catch a Metro North train from Grand Central Terminal ($3, free Sat morning and Wed; open 10am-6pm Tue-Sun).

It's officially been renamed the Bronx Wildlife Conservation Park, but almost everyone still calls it the **Bronx Zoo** (☎ 718-367-1010). On Bronx River Pkwy at Fordham Rd, this is one of the biggest, best and most progressive zoos anywhere. Monorail and aerial tram rides take you through naturalistic settings that are home to some 6000 animals ($9/5 adults/kids, free Wed; open 10am-5pm daily Apr-Oct). Prices are lower, hours are shorter and some attractions are closed in the colder months. Take the No 2 or 5 subway train to the Pelham Pkwy station or catch a Liberty Lines Express bus (☎ 718-652-8400) on Madison Ave.

Just south of Fordham University, the Belmont section of the Bronx is New York City's most authentic Italian neighborhood and is great for gastronomic exploration, especially along **Arthur Ave**. Get to the Fordham Rd station on the No 4 subway or the Metro North train from Grand Central, then walk east 11 blocks and turn right at Arthur Ave.

Queens

Queens is the largest (282 sq miles), most ethnically diverse, and fastest-growing borough in the city, with over two million people speaking 120 different languages. The Queens Tourism Council (☎ 718-286-2741) has information on attractions, special events, and accommodations.

Astoria The largest Greek community in the USA, Astoria also has a smattering of Eastern Europeans. It is still proudly working-class, with brick-and-concrete apartment blocks and two-story wooden homes. One of the best-known factories, the **Steinway Piano Company** (☎ 718-721-2600) offers free tours once a month (call ahead).

Moviemaking started in Astoria in the 1920s, and the **American Museum of the Moving Image** (☎ 718-784-0077), at 35th Ave and 36th St, exposes some of the mysteries of filmmaking. There are galleries and interactive displays that let you create your own video backdrop or redub dialogue from famous films ($8.50; open noon-5pm Tue-Fri, 11am-6pm Sat-Sun). Take the subway to Steinway St.

Enjoy Greek food, cafes, pastries and atmosphere on Astoria's Broadway.

Flushing This now-bustling neighborhood (Ⓜ Main St–Flushing) was a secluded forest that 17th-century Quakers used for secret meetings. It was later used for junkyards and a huge commercial ash heap before being redeveloped for the 1939 World's Fair. With many Asian immigrants, most recently from Korea and China, it's a wonderful area for restaurants.

Site of Shea Stadium, the National Tennis Center and the new Arthur Ashe Stadium (now home to the US Open), **Flushing Meadows–Corona Park** was also used for the 1939 and 1964 World's Fairs, of which there are a few faded leftovers. The park was also the site of the first New York City sessions of the United Nations (Ⓜ Willets Point–Shea Stadium). The **Queens Museum of Art** (☎ 718-592-9700) contains displays on both fairs and the UN. The Panorama of New York City is a detailed and up-to-date model of the metropolis, with 835,000 tiny buildings and a lovely sunset every 15 minutes ($5; open 10am-5pm Wed-Fri, noon-5pm Sat-Sun).

Brooklyn

With 2.3 million people, Brooklyn is the most populous of the outer boroughs, and it would be a significant destination city but for the overwhelming attractions of adjacent Manhattan. A walk across the Brooklyn Bridge is an experience in itself. For information, especially about the numerous special events, contact Brooklyn Information & Culture (☎ 718-855-7882, Ⓦ www.brooklynX.org, 647 Fulton St).

New York's Best Bargains

After paying for food and lodging, budget travelers will be wilting at the expense of visiting New York City. However, many of the finest attractions are free or cost only a few dollars. It costs nothing to walk across the iconic Brooklyn Bridge, offering breathtaking views of Manhattan, or to stroll through picture-perfect Central Park. For fantastic, free people-watching, visit Washington Square Park (on weekends), Wall St (weekday lunchtime), Fifth Ave, Harlem, Chinatown and the Chelsea/SoHo gallery scene. Some of the city's finest buildings are free too, such as Tweed Courthouse, the old Customs House, the New York Public Library and Grand Central Terminal.

To access much of New York's best, you need chutzpah and presentable appearance more than money. Why not browse in Cartier or Tiffany's, admire the fashions in Saks Fifth Ave, or check exquisite antiques on E 12th, W 32nd or E 59th Sts? You can sit in the lobbies of the swankiest hotels, and hang out in an opulent bar for the price of a drink.

For a free harbor cruise past the Statue of Liberty, just catch a Staten Island Ferry. The statue itself, and intriguing Ellis Island, are both free, but you need to buy a boat ticket – a full day of sightseeing for $8. Many of the great cultural institutions offer admission by donation, free days or pay-what-you-can entry times (eg, Friday evening at the MoMA and the Guggenheim, Thursday evening at the Whitney, Tuesday evening at Cooper-Hewitt). Some attractions are always free, like the National Museum of the American Indian, Guggenheim Museum SoHo, New York City Police Museum or a tour of the New York Stock Exchange. The New York CityPass gets you into five big attractions (the Empire State Building, Guggenheim, MoMA, American Museum of Natural History and *Intrepid* Sea-Air-Space Museum) for $28.

One of the best bargains of all is the $17 weekly MetroCard. It lets you use the whole subway and the bus system over all five boroughs, 24 hours a day. Creative advertising, outstanding people-watching and impromptu entertainment are included, and the ticket can get you to the airport at the end of your stay.

Brooklyn Heights When Robert Fulton's steam ferries started regular service across the East River in the early 19th century, well-to-do Manhattanites began building comfortable houses on Brooklyn Heights. Begin a tour of 'The Heights' at the 1848 beaux arts **Brooklyn Borough Hall** – take the subway to Jay St–Borough Hall or make the 20-minute walk across the bridge from Manhattan and continue south along Adams St.

Two blocks south of Borough Hall, the **New York Transit Museum** (☎ 718-243-8601), at Boerum Place and Schermerhorn Row, has a collection of original subway cars and transit memorabilia dating back 100 years ($3; open Tue-Sun).

Northwest of the hall, Montague St is the main avenue for cafes and bars; follow it down to the waterfront. Turn right along the promenade and continue north to Fulton Landing, the old ferry dock at the base of the Brooklyn Bridge, where several places offer food and drink with stunning sunset views of Lower Manhattan.

Head back up the hill along Henry St past Middagh St, with its old wooden frame houses and Middle Eastern restaurants. The **Brooklyn Historical Society Museum** (☎ 718-254-9830, 128 Pierpoint St) is due to reopen in late 2001 after major renovation.

Prospect Park Area Created in 1866, 526-acre Prospect Park (☎ 718-965-8999) is considered the greatest achievement of all landscape designers Olmsted and Vaux, who also designed Central Park. Attractions include ice skating, boating, strolling, a small zoo, the Children's Museum and the immense art deco Brooklyn Public Library (Ⓜ Grand Army Plaza or Prospect Park). The excellent 52-acre **Brooklyn Botanic Garden** (☎ 718-622-4433, 1000 Washington Ave) is on the east side of Prospect Park ($3 Wed-Sun, free Tue). Take the subway to Eastern Parkway–Brooklyn Museum.

Beside the Botanic Gardens, the **Brooklyn Museum of Art** (☎ 718-638-5000, 200 Eastern Pkwy) has some comprehensive collections of African, Islamic and Asian art, Egyptian mummy casings and classical antiquities. There are also over 20 reconstructed rooms, from a 17th-century Dutch kitchen to a 1920s gentleman's study, 58 Rodin sculptures and reliably good temporary shows ($4; open 10am-5pm Wed-Fri, 10am-6pm Sat-Sun).

Immediately west of Prospect Park, the **Park Slope** neighborhood has classic brownstones and a literary atmosphere. Bookstores, cafes and restaurants are interspersed along 18 blocks of Seventh Ave.

Extending east from Prospect Park, the Eastern Pkwy crosses through Prospect Heights and Crown Heights, home to the Lubavitch sect of Orthodox Jews and a large Caribbean community.

Coney Island Now a ghostly shadow of its former summer-playground self, the home of the old Dreamworld amusement park retains a certain skanky fascination. You emerge from the colorfully decrepit Coney Island subway station (check out the all-night diner inside) onto Surf Ave, with flea-market stalls, Nathan's historic hot dog stand and the tacky Coney Island Sideshow. Along the **boardwalk**, the bright red 1930s 'parachute jump' and the ivy-covered Thunderbolt roller coaster are now defunct, but the famous 1927 Cyclone roller coaster, in Astroland Amusement Park (☎ 718-265-2100), still offers a $3 thrill from mid-June to Labor Day.

Farther along the boardwalk, the New York Aquarium, pretentiously renamed the **Aquarium for Wildlife Research** (☎ 718-265-3474), on W 8th St at Surf Ave, has a touch pool, dolphin shows and 10,000 specimens of sea life ($9/5 adults/kids; open 10am-5pm daily). A five-minute walk north of the beach, **Brighton Beach Ave** ('Little Odessa') is lined with Russian shops, bakeries and restaurants (Ⓜ Brighton Beach).

Williamsburg Cross the Williamsburg Bridge from Manhattan and you land in the middle of an Orthodox Jewish community. The northern part of Williamsburg has an aging community of Central European immigrants, now augmented by artists and writers seeking low rents and large lofts. Cafes, restaurants and arty ambience prevail on and around **Bedford Avenue**. Get

a sunset view of Manhattan from Kent Ave along the waterfront.

Staten Island

The 'forgotten borough' was mostly farmland until the 1960s, when the Verrazano Narrows Bridge provided a land link with the rest of the city. Population grew by 15% in the 1990s, to around 450,000. The Staten Island Chamber of Commerce (☎ 718-727-1900) has information on events and attractions.

The free **Staten Island Ferry** (☎ 718-727-2508) provides a wonderful 6-mile ride, passing close to the Statue of Liberty and offering breathtaking views of Manhattan and Brooklyn Heights. It departs from Lower Manhattan every half hour, 24 hours a day, and arrives at the St George Ferry Terminal (one of the island's least attractive areas), from where local buses radiate to the major sights. There's a cluster of cheap restaurants near the terminal, so avoid eating on the ferry (Ⓜ South Ferry).

Originally a home for retired sailors, the **Snug Harbor Cultural Center** (☎ 718-448-2500) has some fine Greek Revival structures, and you can explore the Botanical Garden, Children's Museum and the Newhouse Center for Contemporary Art.

The **Jacques Marchais Center of Tibetan Art** (☎ 718-987-3478, 338 Lighthouse Ave) has a large collection of Buddha statues, clothing and religious objects in a Tibetan-temple-style building ($3; open 1pm-5pm Wed-Sun Apr-Nov). Just across from the museum, the low-slung, cliff-side residence at 48 Manor Court is the only Frank Lloyd Wright house in New York City.

Once the county seat of Staten Island, **Historic Richmond Town** (☎ 718-351-1611, 441 Clarke Ave) has 22 restored original buildings. Volunteers in period garb explain 17th-century colonial life ($4; open 10am-5pm Wed-Fri, 1pm-5pm Sat-Sun).

In the middle of Staten Island, the 2500-acre **Greenbelt** environmental preserve (☎ 718-667-2165) is one of New York City's natural treasures, with miles of walking trails and 60 bird species.

Activities

The Chelsea Piers Complex (☎ 212-336-6666), on the Hudson River at 23rd St, has a four-level driving range, indoor ice-skating rink, running track, swimming pool, workout center, a rock-climbing wall and even sand volleyball courts (day pass $40; open 6am-11pm Mon-Fri, 8am-8pm Sat-Sun). Gyms charge at least $20 for day use (check the *Village Voice*). YMCAs are about $25, while many fancy gyms require subscriptions.

Central Park's 6-mile roadway is closed to cars 10am-3pm weekdays and all weekend, perfect for **running**. Also in Central Park, the Jacqueline Kennedy Onassis Reservoir is encircled by a soft 1½-mile path. Another runner's pathway goes along the Hudson River from 23rd St down to Battery Park City. New York Road Runner's Club (☎ 212-860-4455, 9 E 89th St) organizes weekend runs and the October New York Marathon.

Bicycling on the streets can be a high-risk activity in Manhattan, but Central Park has lovely cycling paths. For cycling tips and weekend trips, contact Five Borough Bicycle Club (☎ 212-932-2300 ext 115) at the HI New York (891 Amsterdam Ave), by W 103rd St. For bike rentals, try Metro Bicycle (☎ 212-581-4500), on W 47th St at Ninth Ave and other locations, or Central Park Bicycle Tours/Rentals (☎ 212-541-8759, 2 Columbus Circle), at Broadway and 59th St.

In-line skating is also popular in Central Park. For rentals try Blades West (☎ 212-787-3911, 120 W 72nd St), two blocks from the park.

Organized Tours
Though bus tours may offer a quick introduction to the city, many have nonnative guides who aren't well informed. This is especially true of some foreign-language tours. Gray Line (☎ 212-397-2620) has nearly 30 different tours from its main terminal at the Port Authority and from the visitor center (777 Eighth Ave) at 48th St, including a hop-on, hop-off loop of Manhattan. Short loop tours cost from $26, while the comprehensive 'Essential New York' tour is $60/44. Other bus tours focus on specific districts or special interests.

Many companies and organizations conduct urban treks. Big Onion Walking Tours (☎ 212-439-1090) operates year-round guided tours specializing in ethnic New York ($12). The Municipal Art Society (☎ 212-935-3960) also has various scheduled tours focusing on architecture and history ($10).

Kenny Kramer (☎ 212-268-5525, 800-572-6377), the real-life inspiration for the *Seinfeld* character, offers fun three-hour tours past major sites from the TV series ($38; noon Sat-Sun; reservation required).

The Big Apple Greeters Program (☎ 212-669-8198) has free volunteer-led tours of lesser-known neighborhoods. Some greeters are multilingual and specialize in helping the disabled (book at least two days ahead).

The three-hour, 35-mile boat cruise around Manhattan with Circle Line (☎ 212-563-3200) leaves from Pier 83, at W 42nd St on the Hudson River ($24; Mar-Dec). This is a very popular and informative tour, especially attractive when the weather is good, though it's still OK if it's not – boats are covered and heated. Shorter tours are offered, but go the whole way if you can. On-board drinks and snacks are pricey. For a 30-minute rush, *The Beast* (☎ 212-630-8855) will take you around the Statue of Liberty at 45mph ($16). For a cheaper, slower ride, take the Staten Island Ferry (free).

Special Events
Some 50 officially recognized annual parades honor various causes or ethnic groups. There are also several hundred annual street fairs, mostly in summer. Fifth Ave shuts down for the major parades. Here's a sample:

New Year's Eve – festivities in Times Square, 5-mile midnight run in Central Park, fireworks at South Street Seaport, family day at Grand Central Terminal

Chinese New Year (☎ 212-619-4785) – fireworks and parades in and around Chinatown

St Patrick's Day Parade – Mar 17; huge Irish parade from St Patrick's Cathedral and up Fifth Ave

Easter Sunday – New Yorkers in Easter bonnets parading on Fifth Ave

Fleet Week (☎ 212-245-2533) – late May; annual convocation of sailors, naval ships and air rescue teams

Carnaval – Memorial Day weekend; celebration of Hispanic culture

Comedy Festival (☎ 888-338-6968) – early June; comedians on stage at Carnegie Hall and a host of clubs

Jazz Festival (☎ 212-501-1390) – mid- to late June; all the concert halls in town jumping with the top names in jazz

Lesbian & Gay Pride Week – last weekend in June; huge parade down Fifth Ave, happenings in Greenwich Village

Independence Day – July 4; huge celebration, special events, East River fireworks

Harlem Week – most of Aug; celebration of Harlem's history and culture

US Open Tennis Tournament – Sept; Grand Slam event in Flushing Meadows

New York Film Festival – late Sept; major event at Lincoln Center

Halloween Parade – Oct 31; wild and colorful march down Sixth Ave to Christopher St, Greenwich Village street party

New York Marathon – first weekend in Nov; road race through all five boroughs

Macy's Thanksgiving Day Parade – fourth Thurs in Nov; huge balloons and floats paraded down Broadway from W 72nd St to Herald Square

Rockefeller Center Christmas Tree Lighting – Tue after Thanksgiving; marking the start of the Christmas season, celebrity performances and the Radio City Music Hall Rockettes

Places to Stay

It's harder than ever to find a good, affordable place to stay in New York City. Make a reservation as far in advance as possible and confirm the booking just before you arrive. If you come with no reservation and a limited budget, start with a night in a pricier hotel (or in a hostel), then phone around for somewhere cheaper (or more comfortable). Note that prices are flexible – often more on Friday and Saturday night, and more in spring and fall than summer or winter. Tax is 13.25% plus $2 per night, in addition to the prices quoted here.

Several companies handle B&B reservations, some offering spots in 'outlaw' B&Bs not registered with the city. B&Bs are not a cheap alternative in New York City, as rooms cost about the same as budget hotels ($100-180), with a two-night minimum in summer. Because B&Bs are small, with flexible prices and opening dates, it's best to book through an agency, which should give a detailed description of the accommodations, the neighborhood and the level of contact with the host. B&B agencies include Bed and Breakfast Network of New York (☎ 212-645-8134, 800-900-8134), with a good selection in Greenwich Village; Urban Ventures (☎ 212-594-5650, Ⓦ www.nyurbanventures.com); and Bed &

Breakfast in Manhattan (☎ 212-472-2528, fax 212-988-9818).

For stays of a week or more, an apartment rental or sublet can be the best option (there's no tax on rentals, so you're already 13.5% ahead). Some agencies include Gamut Realty (☎ 212-879-4229, Ⓦ www.gamutnyc.com), Manhattan East Side Suites Hotels (☎ 800-637-8483), Hart Parker Agency (☎ 212-752-7433) and The Hospitality Company (☎ 212-965-1102).

Places to Stay – Budget

Most hostels require guests to have a passport, hostel card, international air ticket or other proof that they're genuine travelers. Some limit the length of stay to a couple of weeks. Most are nonsmoking, and the better ones have a laundry, Internet access, kitchen facilities and a sociable common room.

Some of the basic budget hotels listed resemble backpacker hostels, but with private rooms (sometimes with shared bath) and a few dorm beds, if any. A double under about $100 is a budget room in Manhattan.

Lower Manhattan, Chelsea & Midtown

The nice **Pioneer Hotel** (☎ 212-226-1482, Ⓦ www.xprss.com/pioneer, 341 Broome St) is near Little Italy, with rooms from $60 with shared bath to $120 for a large double with private facilities. In the West Village, **Hotel Riverview** (☎ 212-929-0060, 113 Jane St) has cheap, closetlike single rooms from $36, but it really is a dive.

In Chelsea is **Chelsea International Hostel** (☎ 212-627-0010, 251 W 20th St), with a spartan party atmosphere and beds/rooms for $25/60. Quieter **Chelsea Center Hostel** (☎ 212-643-0214, 313 W 29th St) has 22 beds ($30). **Chelsea Star Hotel** (☎ 212-244-7827, 300 W 30th St) is a theme hostel of sorts, with dorm beds from $30. Across town, small, funky **International Student Hospice** (☎ 212-228-7470, 154 E 33rd St) fits in 15 bunk beds among the stacks of old books and dusty decor. It takes only students under 30, charges about $25 per person and is more like a private boarding house than a hostel.

In Midtown, the basic, clean and very friendly **Big Apple Hostel** (☎ 212-302-2603, Ⓦ www.bigapplehostel.com, 119 W 45th St), just off Times Square, is open all day and has $33 beds, $85 rooms and a laundry. The large **Vanderbilt YMCA** (☎ *212-756-9600, 224 E 47th St*) offers small but adequate singles/doubles from $85/95 with shared bath, suites with private bath at $150 and an inexpensive restaurant. Guests can use the gym and pool free of charge.

As for hotels, Christian-run **Leo House** (☎ *212-929-1010, 800-732-2438, 332 W 23rd St*) is a quiet, respectable place with rooms from $62/70 with shared bath, $72/78 with private bath (family room $140). Reservations are essential. One of the weirdest places is **Carlton Arms Hotel** (☎ *212-684-8337, 160 E 25th St*), where each room is a floor-to-ceiling walk-in artwork. Singles/doubles/triples go for $70/90/110 with shared bath, $85/100/120 with private bath. **Hotel 17** (☎ *212-475-2845, 225 E 17th St*) is clean, reliable and economical (singles/doubles $80/110).

Long-popular **Gershwin Hotel** (☎ *212-545-8000,* W *www.gershwinhotel.com, 3 E 27th St*) features a funky lobby and eclectic international clientele. It has moved upscale a little, with private doubles starting at $89 with shared bath, superior rooms at $189. There are a few dorm beds at $30. At peak times rates may be higher and reservations are a must. Cheap **Madison Hotel** (☎ *212-532-7373, 21 E 27th St*) is an alternative for those without reservations. Very basic singles/doubles with bath cost $99/121. **Senton Hotel** (☎ *212-684-5800, 39–41 W 27th St*) looks a bit dicey from the outside, but rooms are reasonably clean and well priced ($70 with shared bath, $73-100 with private bath).

Murray Hill Inn (☎ *212-683-6900, 888-996-6376, 143 E 30th St*) grudgingly offers small, clean, well-equipped rooms for $75/95 with shared bath, $115/125 with private bath. **Aladdin Hotel** (☎ *212-246-8580, 317 W 45th St*) has dorm beds for $31 and tiny rooms from $75/85, all with shared bath. It's clean, fun and popular with young travelers.

Upper West Side Near Lincoln Center, **West Side YMCA** (☎ *212-875-4100, 5 W 63rd St*) has the usual YMCA facilities, and rooms from $85/95. Several other places on the Upper West Side are close to the subway and park. **International Student Center** (☎ *212-787-7706, 38 W 88th St*) has dorm beds for non-US students (age 18-35)

for only $20. It's more strictly run than some of the hostels, and thus probably more peaceful. The renovated and well-run **Central Park Hostel** (☎ *212-678-0491,* W *www.centralparkhostel.com, 19 W 103rd St*) is a good deal in a good location – dorm beds from $25, private rooms $75.

Popular **HI New York** (☎ *212-932-2300,* W *www.HInewyork.org, 891 Amsterdam Ave*) fills its 624 beds quickly during summer, from $29/32 members/nonmembers. It also has some private accommodations, up to around $135 for a four-bed room (no tax!). It's open for check-in 24 hours a day and has a cafeteria, laundry, Internet access, tours, guest speakers and a busy, sociable atmosphere despite its large size (Ⓜ 103rd St).

Slick **Jazz on the Park** (☎ *212-932-1600,* W *www.jazzhostel.com, 36 W 106th St*) has dorm and double rooms for $30-44 per person – food, coffee, Internet, music and fun are all available.

Parkview Hotel (☎ *212-369-3340, 55 Central Park North*) is brightly painted, lies close to Central Park and offers dorm beds (from $25) and small private rooms with shared bath (from $75/82). Take the subway to 110th St.

Harlem & Outer Boroughs Farther up in Harlem, **New York Bed & Breakfast** (☎ *212-666-0559, 134 W 119th St*) is a small hostel-guesthouse, where clean dorm beds or rooms with shared bath cost $25-33 per person. It's best to call ahead and talk to the helpful owner. Even farther north, **Sugar Hill International House** (☎ *212-926-7030, 722 St Nicholas Ave*) is a basic but well-run place in Harlem's historic Sugar Hill area. A dorm bed is $25, and double rooms with shared bathroom are $30 per person (Ⓜ 145th St).

If you want to stay in the outer boroughs, try **Flushing YMCA** (☎ *718-961-6880, 138–46 Northern Blvd*) in Queens ($50/70) or **Greenpoint YMCA** (☎ *718-389-3700, 99 Meserole Ave*) in Brooklyn ($46/56).

Places to Stay – Mid-Range & Top End

Hotel discounters or consolidators can be helpful. Try Hotel Reservations Network (☎ *800-964-6835,* W *www.180096hotel.com*), which covers many inexpensive Manhattan hotels. You must pay in advance, though the room can be canceled upon 24-hour notice. Accommodations Express (☎ 800-444-7666) offers smaller discounts (around 15%) but deals with a larger number of rooms in every price category. Quikbook (☎ 800-789-9887) discounts moderate Midtown hotels, including many of those listed below. Few Manhattan hotels offer parking – and parking at a Midtown hotel can cost over $35 a day.

Lower Manhattan Hotels below Houston St cater to businesspeople, so most offer good deals on weekends. But the neighborhood is dead once the office workers go home – even the restaurants are closed. *Best Western Seaport Inn* (☎ 212-766-6600, 33 Peck Slip), in the shadow of the Brooklyn Bridge, has pleasant rooms ($184-269).

On the Lower East Side, *Off SoHo Suites Hotel* (☎ 212-979-9808, 800-633-7646, Ⓦ www.offsoho.com, 11 Rivington St) offers a variety of 'efficiency units' ($119-209, $129-259 at peak times).

In Tribeca, the economical, clean, convenient *Cosmopolitan Hotel* (☎ 212-566-1900, 888-895-9400, Ⓦ www.cosmohotel .com, 95 W Broadway), at Chambers St, has quite good rooms ($99-159).

Greenwich Village and the East Village offer a couple of options. Though the block is a bit noisy, *St Marks Hotel* (☎ 212-674-2192, 2 St Marks Place) has a great East Village location. It's a pretty good value, with small rooms at $110 and larger rooms at $140. *Incentra Village* (☎ 212-206-0007, 32 Eighth Ave) is quiet and charming, caters to gays and lesbians, and is usually booked solid on weekends (singles/doubles $119/169 for smaller rooms, $149/199 for suites).

The well-regarded *Washington Square Hotel* (☎ 212-777-9515, ⓔ wshotel@ ix.netcom.com, 103 Waverly Place) has a good location and a variety of rooms ($125-142 for singles, $142-160 for doubles); book well ahead. Another good choice is nearby *Larchmont Hotel* (☎ 212-989-9333, 27 W 11th St), on a quiet block just off Fifth Ave, with single/double/queen rooms at around $80/99/109 (less with shared bath, more on weekends).

Chelsea & Around The *Chelsea Hotel* (☎ 212-243-3700, 222 W 23rd St) is cashing in on its notoriety (the Sid Vicious room

has been redone – don't ask). The decor is lively, and single/double rates run from about $225/250. A much better value is the nearby *Chelsea Savoy Hotel* (☎ 212-929-9353, 204 W 23rd St), with singles/doubles from $115/185.

The well-recommended and gay-oriented *Colonial House Inn* (☎ 212-633-1612, Ⓦ www.colonialhouseinn.com, 318 W 22nd St) has clean rooms for $99-140 – book at least a month ahead. *Gramercy Park Hotel* (☎ 212-475-4320, 2 Lexington Ave), at E 21st St, has a fine lobby and a perfect location overlooking Gramercy Park, but the rooms are nothing special ($180/190).

Midtown There are several good places just south of Herald Square. *Wolcott Hotel* (☎ 212-268-2900, 4 W 31st St) is a 280-room beaux arts building with a classy lobby and nice (small) singles/doubles at around $140/150. The no-frills *Herald Square Hotel* (☎ 212-279-4017, 800-727-1888, Ⓦ www .heraldsquarehotel.com, 19 W 31st St) is recommended for its choice of rooms and reasonable rates. Small singles with shared bath are about $70, while a double with private bath will run $125-140. The well-located *Grand Union* (☎ 212-683-5890, 34 E 32nd St) has very clean, small air-conditioned rooms for $116, $132/158 for three/four people.

The busy stretch of Park Ave south of Grand Central Terminal has a number of reasonably priced hotels. *Howard Johnson on Park Ave* (☎ 212-532-4860, 429 Park Ave St) has standard double rooms from $149 weekdays, $179 weekends. Larger rooms with two double beds are $209. The popular 400-room *Pickwick Arms Hotel* (☎ 212-355-0300, 250 E 51st St) offers a variety of rooms at reasonable prices: Singles with shared bath are only $85, while nice doubles with private facilities start at about $150. *Ameritania Hotel* (☎ 212-247-5000, 230 W 54th St), used by European bus tours, has comfortable doubles from $165.

Close to Central Park South, *Best Western Woodward Hotel* (☎ 212-247-2000, 210 W 55th St) is quiet and efficient (from $190). *Wellington Hotel* (☎ 212-247-3900, 871 Seventh Ave), at 55th St, has a glitzy lobby and 700 unremarkable rooms from $175, family suites at $220. Just south of Columbus Circle, *Westpark Hotel* (☎ 212-

246-6440, 308 W 58th St) is popular with European travelers (from $130/150).

For something fancy in Midtown you'll pay at least $250, with prices fluctuating greatly according to demand. The legendary *Waldorf Astoria* (☎ 212-355-3000, 301 Park Ave), where British royals host fund-raising dinners, has rooms for around $305-675 depending on the season. Ask about weekend package specials.

Peninsula (☎ 212-247-2200, 700 Fifth Ave), at 55th St, is one of Midtown's oldest surviving grand hotels, with its famous spa and athletic club sprawling over three floors. Rooms are $399-690; the Peninsula Suite is $8500. Across the street, *St Regis* (☎ 212-753-4500, 800-759-7550, 2 E 55th St) has rooms from $590 and a Presidential Suite for $11,500.

The historic *Plaza Hotel* (☎ 212-759-3000, 768 Fifth Ave) has a brilliant location across from Central Park. It does a big line in B&B and Romance Packages, from $469. Around the corner, *Sherry Netherland Hotel* (☎ 212-355-2800, 781 Fifth Ave) is an elegantly understated alternative, from $345 and up.

As Times Square continues its rejuvenation, formerly budget places are raising their prices, if not their standards. *Hotel Carter* (☎ 212-944-6000, 250 W 43rd St) still has rooms for $90-121, but it's far from 1st class. *Broadway Inn* (☎ 212-997-9200, 264 W 46th St) is well located, with singles/doubles from $99/135 in low season to around $190 in high season.

Mammoth *Milford Plaza* (☎ 212-869-3600, 800-221-2690, 270 W 45th St) has 1300 standard rooms from $129/134 to $225/240, often used by bus tours and airline crews. *Days Hotel* (☎ 212-581-7000, 790 Eighth Ave) is a bland chain hotel, but an OK value at $179-209 for a room with two double beds.

For more character, try the art deco *Hotel Edison* (☎ 212-840-5000, 228 W 47th St), from $150/170. And for ultramodern, edgy designer ambience, head for the *Paramount Hotel* (☎ 212-764-5500, 235 W 46th St), which charges $265/325.

Upper West Side Close to Central Park, and a short subway ride from Midtown, the Upper West Side has some of Manhattan's best values. *Amsterdam Inn* (☎ 212-579-

7500, ⓦ www.amsterdaminn.com, 340 Amsterdam Ave) has small, sparse, spotless singles/doubles with shared bath for $75/95, or $145 with private bath. Renovated *Hotel Belleclaire* (☎ 212 362-7700, 250 W 77th St) has a few rooms with shared bath for $99, and stylish doubles for $169-219 depending on season. Nearby *On the Ave* (☎ 212-362-1100, 2178 Broadway), at 77th St, is also recently renovated and has double rooms for $240 in high season, $165 in low.

The *Excelsior Hotel* (☎ 212-362-9200, ⓦ www.excelsiorhotelny.com, 45 W 81st St) is a classy old hotel in a classic location, reasonably priced in low season from $189, but over $300 in high season. The 96-room *Hotel Newton* (☎ 212-678-6500, 2528 Broadway) has clean but characterless rooms from $95/115, with family rooms and suites for $140-175. The pleasantly old-fashioned *Hotel Olcott* (☎ 212-877-4200, 27 W 72nd St) is a well-known bargain near the Dakota building, with studio rooms from $130, spacious two-room suites from $150, and substantially discounted weekly rates – book early.

Upper East Side Close to Central Park and Museum Mile, the Upper East Side has some of New York's most elegant and expensive hotels.

A reasonably priced option is the *Franklin* (☎ 212-369-1000, 164 E 87th St), with tastefully furnished singles/doubles for $179/199 to $249/269. At the top end, you can enjoy the quiet elegance of the *Pierre Hotel* (☎ 212-838-8000, 2 E 61st St) or the *Mark Hotel* (☎ 212-744-4300, 25 E 77th St), for at least $500. *Hotel Wales* (☎ 212-876-6000, 1295 Madison Ave), at 92nd St, is a restored century-old hotel with special rates from around $220.

Places to Eat

Eating in a different place every night, you'd need over 60 years to try all New York's restaurants. The variety is overwhelming and the quality generally very high – New Yorkers are demanding, and second-rate restaurants don't last long. As well as the ethnic diversity – everything from Argentine to Ukrainian – New York can offer every culinary style and ingredient imaginable. Vegetarians are well catered for, and the seafood is superb.

The *Zagat Survey* is the best source of dining information, available at bookstores all over town. Restaurant reviews appear in *Time Out*, the *New York* magazine and the Wednesday and Friday *New York Times*.

Apart from the many fine top-end restaurants, there's an incredible selection of reasonably priced eateries (bring cash, because many bargain places don't take plastic). Beware of paying a lot for ambience: Many mid-range bistros are overpriced. Don't be shy about checking prices, especially off-menu 'specials' or recommended wines. If you want to enjoy a few drinks, do it at a bar, not a restaurant, where specialty drinks can be especially expensive.

Financial District Many places here are open only for lunch. Proper restaurants are expensive, so stick with a light snack or a sandwich to get you through the day. Get a bargain after 5pm, when sandwiches, sushi and other snacks are sold at half price. *Zigolini's (66 Pearl St)* does a fine focaccia for under $10. Broadway is packed with street vendors south of Liberty St. Near touristy South Street Seaport, *Carmine's Italian Seafood*, at Front and Beekman Sts, is among the best of a mediocre bunch. *Bridge Cafe (279 Water St)*, in a 1794 building beneath the Brooklyn Bridge, serves well-prepared mid-priced American cuisine.

Chinatown Every New Yorker has a favorite Chinatown restaurant. The definitive Peking duck is still done at *Peking Duck House* (☎ *212-227-1810, 28 Mott St*) – proudly patronized by former mayor Ed Koch, and now in new, more opulent premises. The following are suggested for taste and price, not for decor. *Hay Wun Loy* (☎ *212-285-8686, 28–30 Pell St*) specializes in dim sum and fish fresh from the tank. For Cantonese, try *Wong Kee (113 Mott St)*; for Szechuan, *Grand Sichuan (125 Canal St)*; for seafood, *Kam Chueh (40 The Bowery)*. Vegans should check out *House of Vegetarian (68 Mott St)*. Get a filling Vietnamese meal for under $15 at *Nha Trang (87 Baxter St)*, where jurors and lawyers share crowded tables with tourists and total strangers. Next door, *New Pasteur* has a virtually identical menu (mostly under $10). *Pho Bang (6 Chatham Square)*, at Mott St, is a favorite –

order shrimp salad and extra rice paper and make your own spring rolls. *Thailand Restaurant (106 Bayard St)* serves superbly authentic Thai dishes ($5-12).

Little Italy In summer the two blocks of Mulberry St north of Canal St close to traffic, allowing more space for outdoor dining. It's not a cheap-eats street, but *Il Fornaio* (☎ *212-226-8306, 132A Mulberry St*) comes close, with substantial servings of Italian standards. *Benito One (174 Mulberry St)* is also good, with entrées from $15. *Pelligrino's* (☎ *212-226-3177, 138 Mulberry St*) is even better (and slightly pricier). *Taormina (147 Mulberry St)* is consistently good, moderately expensive and full of Italian character. Around the corner, between Mott and Mulberry Sts, legendary *Lombardi's Pizza* (☎ *212-941-7994, 32 Spring St*) is the oldest, and some say the best, pizza place in town.

SoHo & Tribeca Once the center of nouveau dining, SoHo restaurants are typically trendy and pricey, imaginative but sometimes inconsistent. Many don't accept reservations, and 'a 20-minute wait' is SoHo-speak for one hour. Pre-nouveau *Lupe's East LA Kitchen (110 Sixth Ave)* has long been popular among locals for a cheap Mexican lunch. *Fanelli's Cafe (94 Prince St)* is a gritty, dark, smoky old-style bar serving inexpensive grilled dishes. *Lucky Strike (59 Grand St)* is an updated, upscale version of the same, offering French bistro fare – it's crowded Friday and Saturday evenings. *Cupping Room* (☎ *212-925-2898, 359 W Broadway)* has an eclectic menu, moderate prices, regular entertainment and sometimes slow service.

Spring Street Natural (62 Spring St) is inexpensive, busy and bustling, with a large vegetarian menu and fish and chicken dishes (under $20). *Kitchen Club* (☎ *212-274-0025, 30 Prince St)*, an intimate, eccentric place, uses organic ingredients, mushroom dumplings and pumpkin ice cream; the Japanese-French fusion cuisine doesn't come cheap.

Trendy Tribeca still has a healthy selection of moderately priced places. The art deco *Odeon (145 W Broadway)* serves bistro fare for under $24 (open until 2am daily). *Walkers (16 N Moore St)* is a dark watering hole selling sandwiches, beer and burgers (meals around $12).

Greenwich Village & East Village There are lots of restaurants to choose from around Bleecker St between Broadway and Seventh; some are much better than others. A reliable, inexpensive Italian restaurant is *Trattoria Spaghetto* (☎ 212-255-6752, 232 Bleecker St), where pastas cost $12. Venerable *Rocco* (☎ 212-677-0590, 181 Thompson St) is rather more colorful and slightly more expensive, and features authentic, exquisite Italian home cooking. At the north edge of the Village, *Sammy's Noodles* (453–461 Sixth Ave) serves substantial noodle dishes ($6-8), dumplings ($7) and other Chinese standards ($10); lunch specials start at $5. Nearby *French Roast* (78 W 11th St) is a 24-hour cafe serving light sandwiches and desserts at reasonable prices.

In the West Village, *El Faro* (☎ 212-929-8210, 823 Greenwich St) is a classic Spanish restaurant with large servings and lashings of garlic (around $20). Nearby *Florent* (☎ 212-989-5779, 69 Gansevoort St), a nouvelle diner, attracts all sorts with its excellent French food, hip ambience and all-night hours. For a more traditional version, try *Hudson Diner* (468 Hudson St), an unpretentious place with late hours and meals under $10.

For value and choice, the East Village is the best area in the city. *Benny's Burritos* (93 Ave A) features minimalist-Mex decor, filling Cal-Mex food and lethal margaritas. A big burrito costs about $10. Another Benny's branch is at 113 Greenwich Ave, in the West Village. The quintessentially Jewish *Second Ave Deli* (156 Second Ave) serves up delicious dishes like matzo-ball soup. *Veselka* (144 Second Ave), a Ukrainian diner popular with local artists, serves hearty breakfasts 24 hours a day. *Dok Suni's* (119 First Ave) attracts crowds with its cheap, delicious Korean dishes.

South and east of the Union Square subway station, many delis and diners offer cheap, filling meals. *Bereket* (187 E Houston St) is a 24-hour kebab cafeteria for cabbies and cops, with a great selection of Turkish and vegetarian dishes. East-side institution *Katz's Delicatessen* (205 E Houston St) makes mountainous pastrami sandwiches

($10) – you can have what Meg Ryan had in *When Harry Met Sally*.

Mid-range places include *Roettelle AG* (☎ 212-674-4140, 126 E 7th St), a Swiss-German restaurant on a Polish block, with healthy portions for $10-20. *Lanza's* (☎ 212-674-7014, 168 First Ave), near E 10th St, has old East Village character and serves a five-course Italian dinner ($14). *Cyclo* (203 First Ave) is trendy Vietnamese with tasty food and moderate prices.

For an East Village tourist experience, try *Lucky Cheng's* (☎ 212-473-0516, 24 First Ave), an Asian restaurant with drag-queen 'waitresses' (come for the scene, not for the food). Below Lucky Chen's, *La Nouvelle Justine* is billed as an S&M cafe. Excellent sushi restaurants line E 9th St. *Hasaki* (210 E 9th St) has the best reputation and the longest lines.

Chelsea & Around Chelsea has an excellent variety of eateries, but you have to book early and spend a lot for the trendy places. The currently fashionable Meatpacking District straddles the West Village and southwest Chelsea, where the barn-size Belgian brasserie *Markt* (☎ 212-727-3314, 401 W 14th St) features fine seafood, a big beer list and lots of beautiful people.

For cheap, untrendy Chelsea eats, try the Cuban-Chinese food at *La Chinita Linda* (166 Eighth Ave), where you can fill up for under $10. Late-night clubbers hit the 24-hour *Empire Diner* (210 Tenth Ave). For something better, *Food Bar* (☎ 212-243-2020, 149 Eighth Ave) has an imaginative menu, consistent quality and comfortable surroundings. Main courses are around $15, fresh salads $5-8.

Farther east in the Flatiron District, *America* (9 E 18th St) is a huge, noisy place with an inexpensive multipage menu and large servings – popular with families. *Alva* (☎ 212-228-6808, 36 E 22nd St) is a sleek bistro with New American entrees around $18 and a snazzy bar in front.

Arguably the city's finest food is served at *Union Square Cafe* (☎ 212-243-4020, 21 E 16th St), where the imaginative gourmet fare and fine wines are enhanced by an unpretentious atmosphere. Elegant, excellent and slightly more expensive, *Gramercy Tavern* (☎ 212-477-0777, 42 E 20th St) is also at the very top of the culinary totem pole. For both these places, book ahead and budget at least $60 per person, or come at lunchtime and enjoy the same quality for less money.

Midtown More than two dozen delis, pubs and moderately priced restaurants on 55th and 56th Sts between Sixth and Fifth Aves serve Midtown office workers. *Pan Bagnat* (*54 W 55th St*) does divine baguettes and pastries for under $8. *Soup Kitchen International* (*259A W 55th St*), near Eighth Ave, will be familiar to *Seinfeld* fans: The owner demands that you choose one of his superb soups within seven seconds. A filling meal with soup, salad, bread and fruit costs around $12 (closed May-Sept). *Carnegie Deli* (*854 Seventh Ave*) is another institution, with small tables, *huge* pastrami sandwiches, and full Manhattan prices.

Lespinasse (☎ 212-339-4100, 2 E 55th St), in the St Regis, is perhaps the finest, fanciest and priciest restaurant in New York. Slightly less expensive and also acclaimed *Aquavit* (☎ 212-307-7311, 13 W 54th St) serves classic Scandinavian seafood in a stunning six-story atrium.

In Little Korea, try *Food Court* (*12 W 32nd St*) for an extensive point-and-choose selection of very inexpensive noodle dishes, soups, stews and specials. For sensational Korean barbecue, go around the corner to *Kang Suh* (☎ 212-564-6845, 1250 Broadway).

On the east side of Midtown, in the Hell's Kitchen neighborhood, classic *Munson Diner* (*600 W 49th St*), at Eleventh Ave, is an authentic New York experience, where cops and cab drivers get greasy burgers in stainless-steel surroundings.

In Little India, Indian restaurants abound along Third Ave and Lexington between 27th and 29th Sts. The well-recommended *Madras Mahal* (☎ 212-684-4010, 104 Lexington Ave) has kosher vegetarian food and a $7 lunch buffet. *Vatan* (☎ 212-689-5666, 409 Third Ave) is another Indian vegetarian joint with an enjoyable atmosphere.

The side streets off Times Square are filled with hamburger joints and mid-range ethnic restaurants of varying quality – stick to basic menu items. 'Restaurant Row' is the block of W 46th St between Eighth and Ninth Aves, featuring many mediocre and overpriced eateries providing pre-theater sustenance. Tiny *Hourglass Tavern*

Street Eats

Apart from its many restaurants, the city has hundreds of street food vendors. They sell the quintessential hot dog ($1) or hot dog with onions ($2) as well as hot pretzels ($1), and they also offer soups, sandwiches, falafel, focaccia, noodles, knishes, kebabs, gyros, souvlaki, chicken, chips and Philly cheesesteaks (all around $2-5). You'll find lots of stands on side streets in Midtown. A filling meal costs $3-5, more near museums and tourist sites.

(☎ 212-265-2060, 373 W 46th St) makes a novelty of the pretheater rush, guaranteeing quick service with its tasty, reasonably priced stews and fish. *Zen Palate* (☎ 212-582-1669, 663 Ninth Ave) is exclusively and imaginatively vegetarian. *Joe Allen* (☎ 212-581-6464, 326 W 46th St) is a reliable provider of standard American fare at off-Broadway prices.

Upper West Side You can grab cheap eats at dozens of Chinese restaurants, pubs and coffee shops. Reliable *Empire Szechuan* has branches at 251 W 72nd St, 193 Columbus Ave above 68th St, and five other locations. All serve sushi and $6 lunch specials. *Hunan Park* (*235 Columbus Ave*), at W 71st St, serves Chinese favorites for under $10, even cheaper at lunchtime (another location is at 721 Columbus Ave and 96th St). *Vinnie's Pizza* (*285 Amsterdam Ave*) looks like a dive but dishes up fantastic, gooey pizzas for a few bucks a slice. For healthier fare go to *Josie's* (☎ 212-769-1212, 300 Amsterdam Ave), where creative and satisfying vegetarian dishes are served to a cheerful, bustling crowd. Farther north, *Tom's Restaurant* (*2880 Broadway*), at W 112th St, attracts students and *Seinfeld* fans with typical American fare and low prices.

If you're looking to splurge, try either **Cafe Luxembourg** (☎ 212-873-7411, 200 W 70th St), which attracts occasional celebrities, or romantic **Cafe des Artistes** (☎ 212-877-3500, 1 W 67th St), known for its naked-nymph murals as much as its classic French cooking.

Upper East Side Dozens of moderately priced American restaurants on Second and Third Aves between 60th and 86th Sts, offer lunch specials for under $10 and are packed for weekend brunches. **EJ's Luncheonette** (1271 Third Ave), at 73rd St, features classic diner food in a 1950s retro setting. **Googie's** (1491 Second Ave), at 78th St, is a popular, inexpensive Italian diner. Kids and cowboy wannabes fill up for few bucks at **Jackson Hole** (1611 Second Ave), between 83rd and 84th Sts.

Closer to Central Park, intimate, expensive wood-paneled restaurants are discretely dotted around Madison Ave and side streets north of 60th St. Two fine places with chic clientele are **La Goulue** (☎ 212-988-8169, 746 Madison Ave), close to 64th St, and **Mark's** (☎ 212-879-1864, 25 E 77th St), at the Mark Hotel.

Harlem Surprisingly few restaurants serve up soul food in Harlem, and even fewer represent the growing West African influence. Harlem's most famous soul-food restaurant is **Sylvia's** (☎ 212-996-0660, 328 Lenox Ave), known for its Sunday gospel brunch (reservations required). The food's authentic, but the ambience suffers when the tour buses turn up – and it ain't cheap (entrées around $11). Nearby **Pan Pan** (500 Lenox Ave) offers spicy Jamaican meat patties and coffee-and-roll breakfasts for just a couple of dollars.

Londel's Supper Club (☎ 212-234-6114, 2620 Frederick Douglass Blvd) does delicious, satisfying Southern food in a friendly atmosphere (live music weekends). **Copeland's** (☎ 212-234-2357, 547 W 145th St) has a weeknight buffet ($15) and Sunday gospel brunch ($17); à la carte entrées cost $12-27. For identical food at lower prices, go next door to the cafeteria section. **Charles' Southern-Style Kitchen** (2839 Eighth Ave), between 151st and 152nd Sts, does a bargain all-you-can-eat buffet of sensational Southern food.

Outer Boroughs Arthur Ave, in Belmont, the Bronx, is renowned for old Italian neighborhood restaurants like **Mario's** (☎ 718-584-1188, 2342 Arthur Ave) and **Dominick's** (☎ 718-733-2807, 2335 Arthur Ave).

At the east end of the Brooklyn Bridge, you'll need a reservation and at least $70 for a window seat at sunset in the justly famous **River Cafe** (☎ 718-522-5200, 1 Water St). Lunch is less expensive and less in demand. Much cheaper is nearby **Grimaldi's** (☎ 718-858-4300, 19 Old Fulton St), a shrine to Frank Sinatra that serves the perfect pizza.

Go Greek on Astoria's Broadway in Queens, where **Uncle George's** (33-19 Broadway) serves spicy dips and cheap specials 24 hours a day. **Omonia** (32-20 Broadway), just across the street, is a sleek Greek espresso bar. The best place in the city for fresh fish is inelegant, inexpensive and exquisite **Elias Corner** (☎ 718-932-1510, 24-02 31st St); take the N train to Ditmas Blvd.

Entertainment

Time Out is the best guide to the city's nightlife. High culture is well covered in the Sunday and Friday editions of the *New York Times* and *New Yorker*. Dance clubs, smaller music venues and alternative happenings advertise in the *Village Voice*.

NYC On Stage (☎ 212-768-1818) is a 24-hour information line for music and dance, and is connected to TKTS, which sells same-day tickets to Broadway and off-Broadway musicals and drama from a conspicuous booth in Times Square. Tickets are up to 75% off regular prices, and evening tickets go on sale at 3pm. A line starts forming at 2pm, but the best seats become available at 7pm (no credit cards).

Ticketmaster (☎ 212-307-7171, W www.ticketmaster.com) and Telecharge (☎ 212-239-6200, W www.telecharge.com) handle tickets for most performances, major concerts and sporting events. Ticket Central (☎ 212-279-4200, 416 W 42nd St) does Broadway and off-Broadway theater tickets. Broadway Ticket Center, at the Times Square Visitors' Center (1560 Broadway) has Broadway tickets for sale and information, as does the Broadway Line (☎ 212-302-4111, W www.broadway.org/league.html). CenterCharge (☎ 212-721-6500) books Lincoln Center events.

Major concerts are usually held at **Madison Square Garden** (☎ 212-465-5800), on Seventh Ave between 31st and 33rd Sts;

Radio City Music Hall (☎ 212-247-4777), on Sixth Ave at 50th St; or **Beacon Theater** (☎ 212-496-7070, 2124 Broadway), at 74th St.

Theater The center of the New York theater district, Times Square, is dominated by big-budget spectaculars. The so-called Broadway shows are those in the large theaters around Times Square (tickets $40-100). 'Off-Broadway' refers to dramas in smaller spaces (200 seats or fewer) elsewhere in town – still big business ($20-50). 'Off-off-Broadway' events are readings, experimental performances and improvisations in spaces with fewer than 100 seats ($12-30).

The Lincoln Center Theater group (☎ 212-239-6200) runs the 1000-seat **Vivian Beaumont Theater** and the smaller, more intimate **Mitzi Newhouse Theater**.

Cinemas New Yorkers take film seriously, and first-run films (around $9) sell out early Friday and Saturday nights. Save some waiting by calling ☎ 212-777-3456 and prepaying for the ticket ($1 extra).

Angelika Film Center (☎ 212-777-3456, 18 W Houston St), at Mercer St, and the **Lincoln Plaza Cinemas** (☎ 212-757-2280, 1886 Broadway), opposite Lincoln Center, specialize in foreign films and are always crowded on weekends. **Film Forum** (☎ 212-727-8110, 209 W Houston St) shows revivals and independent and classic movies.

Independent films and career retrospectives are shown at Lincoln Center's **Walter Reade Theater** (☎ 212-875-5600, 70 Lincoln Center Plaza), which hosts the New York Film Festival every September. For far-out fringe works and otherwise unreleased fare, go to **Anthology Film Archives** (☎ 212-505-5181, 32 Second Ave), at 2nd St.

Classical Music & Opera The **New York Philharmonic** (☎ 212-721-6500) performs at Lincoln Center's Avery Fisher Hall (tickets $19-80). Visiting orchestras and the New York Pops play at **Carnegie Hall** (☎ 212-247-7800, 881 Seventh Ave), at 57th St (tickets $15-90).

The American Symphony Orchestra, the Chamber Music Society of Lincoln Center and the Little Orchestra Society hold their seasons at Lincoln Center's **Alice Tully Hall** (☎ 212-875-5050).

The **Metropolitan Opera** (☎ 212-362-6000) season is September to April at the Lincoln Center theater. It's extremely difficult to get tickets for the big-name performances, but it might be possible later in the season ($18-250).

The more daring and affordable **New York City Opera** (☎ 212-870-5630) performs at the New York State Theater (☎ 212-870-5570) in Lincoln Center for a few weeks in early autumn and again in late spring.

Dance & Ballet The **New York City Ballet** (☎ 212-870-5570) performs in winter at the New York State Theater in Lincoln Center (tickets $16-85). In spring the **American Ballet Theater** (☎ 212-477-3030) takes over at the Metropolitan Opera House for a short season.

City Center (☎ 212-581-1212, 131 W 55th St), between Sixth and Seventh Aves, is home to the Alvin Ailey American Dance Theater every December and hosts visiting foreign companies. The most offbeat dance venue is **Joyce Theater** (☎ 212-242-0800, 175 Eighth Ave), at 19th St, a renovated cinema in Chelsea.

Jazz Cover charges at jazz venues vary with the popularity of the performer; late-night sets can be cheaper. 'Music charges' may be added to your bill, but you're not obliged to pay tips on them. The famous **Village Vanguard** (☎ 212-255-4037, 178 Seventh Ave), at 11th St, has featured major stars for 50 years. By far the most expensive club is the **Blue Note** (☎ 212-475-8592, 131 W 3rd St), where big stars play short sets.

Sweet Basil (☎ 212-242-1785, 88 Seventh Ave), between Grove and Bleecker Sts, has a jazz brunch Sunday. **Small's** (☎ 212-929-7565, 183 W 10th St), a unique place without a liquor license, hosts a $10, 10-hour jazz marathon every night from 10pm that attracts top talent. **Zinc Bar** (☎ 212-477-8337, 90 W Houston St) hosts new and established jazz acts and definitely serves liquor.

You can hear acid jazz and other fringe music at **Knitting Factory** (☎ 212-219-3055, 74 Leonard St), in Tribeca. **Fez** (☎ 212-533-2680, 380 Lafayette St) has experimental music, while **Iridium** (☎ 212-582-2121, 44 W 63rd St) features new jazz acts.

Harlem's Cotton Club era is long gone, but several places still present modern and traditional jazz, mostly on weekends; call ahead to check times and prices. The old

Lenox Lounge (☎ *212-427-0253, 288 Lenox Ave*), at 125th St, is worth visiting anytime for its art deco interior. *St Nick's Pub* (☎ *212-769-8275, 773 St Nicholas Ave*), at 149th St, is a cramped, smoky Harlem hangout with great jazz acts and atmosphere.

Rock, Blues & World Music In the Village, *Bottom Line* (☎ *212-228-6300, 15 W 4th St*) is a rock cabaret–style music hall for mainly name acts. The prototypical punk club *CBGB* (☎ *212-982-4052, 315 The Bowery*), is still going strong after 25 years. The Deadhead tradition continues on at *Wetlands Preserve* (☎ *212-966-4225, 161 Hudson St*), offering everything from classic 1960s rock to reggae, ska and hip-hop.

Big names play the small *Mercury Lounge* (☎ *212-260-4700, 217 E Houston St*) and *Irving Plaza* (☎ *212-777-6800, 17 Irving Place*). New clubs open frequently on the Lower East Side, but *Brownies* (☎ *212-420-8392, 169 Ave A*) is a long-time indie incubator. *Luna Lounge* (☎ *212-260-2323, 171 Ludlow St*), on the Lower East Side, has a small room in back for garage bands, local musicians and new indie talent. *Bowery Ballroom* (☎ *212-533-2111, 6 Delancey St*), between The Bowery and Chrystie St, hosts popular touring acts and top local talent in a big, atmospheric venue. *Tonic* (☎ *212-358-7503, 107 Norfolk St*) is the place to hear the latest in electronic, underground and inventive rock.

Visiting blues masters play at *Chicago BLUES* (☎ *212-924-9755, 73 Eighth Ave*), at 13th St, and the Monday-night blues jam is good. *BB King Blues Club & Grill* (☎ *212-997-4144, 237 W 42nd St*), a flash new 500-seat venue, hosts top-quality blues, jazz and rock acts – drinks are expensive and cover is high, but it's sometimes free after 11pm. There's a Sunday gospel brunch from 1pm.

SOB's (☎ *212-243-4940, 204 Varick St*) specializes in Afro-Cuban and salsa music. Uptown, check out *Latin Quarter* (☎ *212-864-7600, 2551 Broadway*), at 95th St.

Bars Here's a highly selective list of assorted and well-established Manhattan bars. Most stay open until 2am, sometimes until 4am Friday and Saturday.

Cabana (*89 South St*) is the coolest bar at South St Seaport; chow down on Latino snacks with your ice-cold Corona.

North of Chinatown proper, *Double Happiness* (*173 Mott St*), between Broome and Grand Sts, is a cavernous, crowded onetime speakeasy. For classic Little Italy, *Mare Chiaro* (*176½ Mulberry St*) is a solid drinking place with a movie-Mafia feel. Convivial *Barramundi* (*147 Ludlow St*) serves reasonably priced drinks and is a good place to start a Lower East Side bar crawl.

On the edge of SoHo, the old and cozy *Ear Inn* (*326 Spring St*) attracts a mixed clientele with old-fashioned pub atmosphere and inexpensive food. Somewhat trendy *Cafe Noir* (*32 Grand St*) has North African appetizers and a bar overlooking the passing parade.

Hard-to-find *Chumley's* (*86 Bedford St*), in Greenwich Village, is a former speakeasy serving decent pub grub and US microbrews. The famous *Corner Bistro* (*331 W 4th St*) has carved tables and serves charred hamburgers.

The East Village specializes in Irish pubs like *The Scratcher* (*209 E Fifth St*), pleasantly quiet by day and suitably raucous at night. *Swift* (*34 E 4th St*) has live music and the best pint of Guinness in town. *McSorley's Old Ale House* (*15 E 7th St*) is a storied, stodgy old bar that now admits women (and tourists). In the Meatpacking District, *Hogs & Heifers* (*8859 Washington St*) is an animal act selling cheap booze to a rowdy crowd.

On the Upper West Side, Columbia students support a few bars like *Night Cafe* (*938 Amsterdam Ave*), at 106th St. On the Upper East Side, look for Irish pubs such as *Kinsale Tavern* (*1672 Third Ave*), which has 20 beers on tap and live satellite broadcasts of European rugby and soccer.

Lounges Lounges are classier than bars and often provide entertainment. Downtown and Midtown lounges offer cigars and bourbon to the after-work crowd and may require a jacket and tie. Chelsea lounges are almost exclusively gay.

Hudson Bar and Books (*636 Hudson St*), in Greenwich Village, is a narrow faux library with free jazz on weekends. Slick *Bar d'O* (*29 Bedford St*) has drag acts and a chic, mixed crowd. *Belmont Lounge* (*117 E 15th St*) has space and style, with cozy nooks for schmoozing or making out.

On the Upper West Side, *Evelyn Lounge* (*380 Columbus Ave*), at 78th St, is a clubby multiroom cellar with a classy cigar lounge and a long martini list. The green-velvet lounge at **St Mark's** *(22 E 77th St)* epitomizes Upper East Side elegance.

Dance Clubs The monthly magazine *Paper* is the best source for the ever-changing club scene ($3.50 at newsstands, or online at W www.papermag.com), but watch for flyers in the East Village, on walls and in cool record shops. It ain't easy to sneak into of-the-moment clubs unless you're famous or fabulous; find flyers and ads with phone numbers and email addresses, then get in touch ahead of time to request a spot on the guest list.

Tough drug laws keep the real rave scene under wraps. Two long-standing clubs are periodically closed down by authorities: **Tunnel** *(☎ 212-695-4682, 220 Twelfth Ave)*, at W 28th St, a massive three-floor club with different DJs on each level; and **Limelight** *(☎ 212-807-7780, 47 W 20th St)*, at Sixth Ave, reinventing itself again as a multimusic venue, variously offering deep house, tech house, soul, funk, hip-hop etc.

Vinyl *(☎ 212-343-1379, 6 Hubert St)*, between Hudson and Greenwich Sts, pulls a mixed older crowd with classic house, old-time soul and big-name DJs (no alcohol). Friendly **Filter 14** *(☎ 212-366-5680, 432 W 14th St)* is for dancing, especially Tuesday and Saturday party nights and Thursday '80s night. **Nell's** *(☎ 212-675-1567, 246 W 14th St)* is the original European velvet lounge.

Centro-Fly *(☎ 212-627-7770, 45 W 21st St)* attracts island groovers midweek and assorted dance bunnies on weekends – it's big, cool and popular. **Speeed** *(☎ 212-719-9867, 20 W 39th St)* surprises with different sounds every night – salsa to hip-hop, tribal to merengue. **China Club** *(☎ 212-398-3800, 268 W 47th St)* gets a classy clientele, some celebs and quite a few tourists, playing house, hip-hop and Latin sounds.

Gay & Lesbian Venues Generally, gay drinking places cater only to men, but many gay dance clubs welcome women. *Time Out* and the *Village Voice* have special sections for gay party-hunters. *Blade, Homo Xtra, LGNY* and *Next* are free gay newspapers available in bars, clubs and bookshops. Also see W www.nyblade.com and www.hx.com for listings.

For dancing, go to a gay night at a mainstream club or try **Twilo** *(☎ 212-268-1600, 530 W 27th St)*, popular for its hot DJs, high-tech lighting and hi-NRG dance scene ($20 cover). **The Lure** *(☎ 212-741-3919, 409 W 13th St)* is a full-on gay leather fetish bar with a strict dress code – you have to look the part. **Splash** *(☎ 212-691-0073, 50 W 17th St)* has a water show featuring well-toned boys. It's a big place with a big crowd of cute guys, guppies and out-of-towners. **Barracuda** *(275 W 22nd St)* is a fun lounge with a retro feel and the odd drag show. **King** *(☎ 212-366-5464, 579 Sixth Ave)*, at 16th St, features a male-only grope room on top of a three-level bar and dance club.

In the Meatpacking District, **Hell** *(☎ 212-727-1666, 59 Gansevoort St)* is a smallish lounge with devilish decor and a comely crowd. Greenwich Village is the home of gay pride and has many popular restaurants and bars in the Christopher St area. Bars catering to older gays include **Marie's Crisis** *(☎ 212-243-9323, 59 Grove St)*.

The Cock *(☎ 212-777-6254, 188 Ave A)*, at 12th St, is a boozy, cruisy club with cabaret nights, DJs, dancing and drag. Varied, vibing **Don Hills** *(☎ 212-334-1390, 511 Greenwich St)* gets gays and straights going with lesbian rock, pole dancers and a mix of soul, Brit pop and dance.

Crazy Nanny's *(☎ 212-366-6312, 21 Seventh Ave)* calls itself a 'place for gay women – biological or otherwise,' while **Henrietta Hudson's** *(☎ 212-924-3347, 438 Hudson St)* offers its all-female crowd a fun time till 4am nightly. **Rubyfruit** *(☎ 212-929-3343, 531 Hudson St)* is an old favorite with older women. The famous, fabulous **Clit Club** is now meeting Fridays at **Flamingo** *(☎ 212-533-2860, 219 Second Ave)*, between 13th and 14th Sts.

Comedy See gig guides for comedy nights and performances at many bars, lounges and clubs. For guaranteed laughs, go to one of the big-name stand-up comedy clubs. With cover charges and two-drink minimums, these clubs can make for an expensive night. **Caroline's on Broadway** *(☎ 212-757-4100, 1626 Broadway)* is the best known ($10-20 cover). The **Comedy Cellar** *(☎ 212-254-3480, 117 Macdougal St)*, between 3rd and Bleecker Sts, has high-profile comics and surprise guests.

Make a reservation for **Stand-Up New York** (☎ 212-595-0850, 236 W 78th St), which features funny theme nights like Southern-Fried Humor and also gets surprise appearances from star comedians ($5-12).

For more innovative acts, try **Gotham Comedy Club** (☎ 212-367-9000, 34 W 22nd St). **Surf Reality** (☎ 212-673-4182, 172 Allen St), on the Lower East Side, presents eclectic, alternative, cutting-edge comedy, especially on Sunday's open-mike night.

Spectator Sports

The National League New York Mets (☎ 718-507-8499) play baseball at the windswept Shea Stadium in Flushing Meadows, Queens (Ⓜ Willets Point–Shea Stadium). The American League New York Yankees (☎ 718-293-6000) play at Yankee Stadium in the Bronx (Ⓜ 161st St–Yankee Stadium). Tickets are generally available ($8-45).

The NBA New York Knicks (☎ 212-465-6741) play basketball at Madison Square Garden, but seats are more than scarce ($35-1500); try Ticketmaster. The WNBA New York Liberty also play at Madison Square Garden. The NBA New Jersey Nets (☎ 800-765-6387) play at the Meadowlands sports complex in Rutherford, New Jersey.

The NHL New York Rangers (☎ 212-465-6000) hit the ice at Madison Square Garden, and New York Islanders play at Nassau Coliseum (☎ 516-794-4100).

New York City's NFL (pro football) teams, the Giants (☎ 201-935-8222) and the Jets (☎ 516-560-8200), share Giants Stadium in the Meadowlands, Rutherford, New Jersey.

Shopping

New York's two department stores are Bloomingdale's ('Bloomie's'; ☎ 212-705-2000), at 59th St and Lexington Ave, and Macy's (☎ 212-695-4400), on Broadway at 34th St.

Dozens of shops sell wholesale off-brand clothing in the Garment District, mainly on W 37th St between Eighth and Ninth Aves. The funkiest boutiques are in SoHo, but Madison Ave above 42nd St, on the Upper East Side, has the big-name designer stores.

Low-cost leather goods are available along Broadway just above Houston St, on Bleecker St and on W 4th St immediately off Sixth Ave. A dozen stores sell sturdy footwear on W 8th St between Fifth and Sixth Aves. For competitively priced diamonds and pearls, visit the Diamond District on W 47th St off Fifth Ave (closed Sat-Sun). Tower Records (☎ 212-505-1500, 692 Broadway) has the best selection of music.

Getting There & Away

Air Most airlines have an office downtown or at one of the three airports that serve New York City.

In southeastern Queens, 15 miles from Midtown Manhattan, John F Kennedy International Airport (JFK) is where most international flights land. A few airlines have their own terminals, but most use the crowded International Arrivals Building. The airport information line (☎ 718-244-4444) is not especially helpful.

In northern Queens, La Guardia Airport (☎ 718-533-3400) has mostly domestic flights, including shuttles to Boston and Washington, DC. It's more convenient than JFK.

Though it's in New Jersey, about 10 miles west of Manhattan, Newark International Airport (☎ 973-961-6000) is just as accessible as JFK or La Guardia, has a large, new international terminal, and is making further improvements. It's the hub for Continental Airlines and is used by many major carriers.

Bus All suburban and long-haul buses arrive and depart from the modern Port Authority Bus Terminal (☎ 212-564-8484), at 41st St and Eighth Ave; you may still be confronted by beggars here.

Greyhound (☎ 212-971-6300) links New York with major cities across the country. Regular buses go to Albany ($30; 2½ hours); Buffalo ($65; 9 hours); Boston, Massachusetts ($42; 4½ hours); Philadelphia, Pennsylvania ($21; 2 hours); and Washington, DC ($42; 4½ hours).

Peter Pan Trailways (☎ 800-343-9999) runs buses to the nearest major cities, including a daily express to Boston ($42).

Short Line (☎ 212-736-4700) offers numerous departures to towns in northern New Jersey and upstate New York. New

Jersey Transit (☎ 973-762-5100) serves all of that state.

Train Pennsylvania Station (Penn Station), on 33rd St between Seventh and Eighth Aves, is the departure point for all Amtrak trains (☎ 212-582-6875). There are regular services to Albany ($41; 2½ hours); Buffalo ($60; 7½ hours); Boston, Massachusetts ($58; 4¼ hours); Philadelphia, Pennsylvania ($45; 1¼ hours); and Washington, DC ($69; 3½ hours). Acela high-speed trains, with all business- or 1st-class seating, are available on some routes. Destinations include Boston ($120; 3½ hours), Philadelphia ($92; 1 hour) and Washington, DC ($144; 2¾ hours).

The Long Island Rail Road (LIRR; ☎ 718-217-5477) has its own platform at Penn Station for commuters to Brooklyn, Queens and the suburbs of Long Island. NJ Transit trains (☎ 973-762-5100) go from Penn Station to the Jersey suburbs and Jersey Shore.

Metro North Rail Road (☎ 212-532-4900), which serves northern suburbs and Connecticut, is the only commuter train company using Grand Central station.

PATH (☎ 800-234-7284) has a separate subway system that runs up Sixth Ave to 33rd St and on to Hoboken, Jersey City and Newark. These reliable trains run every 15 minutes ($1).

Getting Around
Manhattan's street grid system carries a lot of traffic, but outside rush hours it is rarely gridlocked. The worst traffic jams are on the roads leading in and out of the city. Cyclists will find wide wheels are best for the city's pockmarked streets. Wear a helmet and watch for taxi doors.

To/From the Airports The Air Ride line (☎ 800-247-7433) has information on transportation to and from all three airports. *Do not* accept transport from or entrust your baggage to anyone except uniformed airport staff.

At JFK, staff at Ground Transportation desks, near the baggage claim areas, sell taxi vouchers and shuttle bus tickets, and can explain how to get into town on the subway. An official yellow taxi from JFK into Midtown charges a fixed rate of $30; bridge and tunnel tolls and tip are extra. From Midtown to JFK a taxi costs about $45-55, plus tolls and tip (allow at least 1½ hours). Airport shuttle bus services with Gray Line (☎ 212-315-3006, 800-451-0455) or Super Shuttle (☎ 212-209-7000, 800-258-3826) cost about $18 per person and take a circuitous route around Manhattan to drop off passengers at their various destinations. Going *to* the airport, you might have to leave more than two hours before check-in time. New York Airport Service (☎ 212-944-2391) buses run every 15 to 30 minutes between JFK and a handful of Midtown locations ($13).

The cheapest way to JFK is to take the A train to Howard Beach–JFK (at least an hour), then a free yellow-and-blue bus to the terminals (another 15 minutes). It's a hassle with luggage.

Taxis to and from La Guardia are metered, so the cost depends on time and distance – about $45 from Midtown in light traffic, plus tolls and tip. Gray Line or Super Shuttle airport shuttle bus services cost about $15. New York Airport Service buses run every 15 to 30 minutes to and from Midtown ($10).

To get to La Guardia via public transportation, take an A, B, C, D, 2 or 3 subway to 125th St in Harlem, then an M60 bus right to the terminals. Alternatively, an E, F, G, R or 7 subway to Roosevelt Ave–Jackson Heights or 74th St–Broadway stops in Queens, then a Q33 bus takes you to the main terminals. It takes well over an hour, and it's difficult with luggage.

A taxi from Midtown to Newark International Airport will run about $55 plus tolls and tip. Allow 40 minutes to an hour. Gray Line or Super Shuttle airport shuttle bus services cost about $18. Alternatively, take a bus from the Port Authority Airport Bus Center ($11).

Subway Generally, the subway is the cheapest, most reliable way to get around Manhattan and the adjacent boroughs, 24 hours a day – four million people a day can't be wrong. Run by the MTA – New York City Transit Authority (☎ 718-330-1234), New York's subway system began as privately operated lines designed to compete with rather than complement each other. The city wound up owning all

SUBWAY
SARDINES
Packed in Stagnant Air

the lines (depicted in different colors on the subway map), which form 26 different subway routes, designated by letters and numbers. A funding boost in the 1980s resulted in quieter, more reliable, graffiti-free trains. Much-needed renovation of subway stations is under way.

Note that as a result of the destruction of the World Trade Center, there may be disruption to the subway system, especially the A, C, 2 and 3 lines, for some time.

Almost every subway booth offers a good bus and subway map, and the subway clerks are generally helpful. A common mistake is boarding an express train that doesn't stop at the station you want – on subway maps, local stops are solid black dots, while express stops are white dots.

A subway ride costs, basically, $1.50 for any distance. The $1.50 subway tokens are being phased out in favor of plastic Metro-Cards – a $15 MetroCard gets you 11 rides (one free ride!). A MetroCard ride includes free transfers from subway to a city bus within two hours. Even better value are the $4 MetroCard, good for a day of unlimited travel on subways and city buses, and the $17 MetroCard, good for seven days' unlimited travel.

For safety, wait in the middle of the platform so you can board near the conductor's car. Don't leave a wallet in your back pocket on a crowded subway, and secure your daypack with a safety pin.

Bus Blue-and-white city buses operate 24 hours a day, generally along avenues in a south or north direction, and crosstown along the major thoroughfares. You need exact change of $1.50 (no pennies or bills), a MetroCard or a subway token to board the bus. If you intend to take a connecting bus, ask for a 'transfer' when boarding – a transfer ticket is good for two hours. Drivers can tell you if their bus stops near a specific site. Bus maps are available at subway and train stations.

Some 'limited stop' buses pull over only every 10 blocks or so, but at night you can ask to be left off at any point along a bus route. 'Express' buses are for outer-borough commuters.

Car & Motorcycle Parking in Manhattan is difficult or very expensive. Street-cleaning rules require you to move your car several times a week. Parking garages in Midtown charge at least $35 during daylight hours. Cheaper lots can be found along West St in Chelsea (around $18). Hotel parking lots charge $35-45 a day for guests' cars.

Car rentals are expensive in New York City and at the airports, though you might get an OK deal out of Newark airport. Returning a rental car to a Manhattan location is fine outside rush hours – the traffic isn't *that* bad.

Taxi Taxi flagfall is $2, plus 30¢ for every fifth of a mile and 20¢ a minute while stuck in traffic; 8pm-6am, a 50¢ nighttime surcharge is tacked on to your fare. The passenger must pay any bridge or tunnels tolls and tip 10% to 15% (minimum 50¢), and don't expect many thanks for it.

For trips of 50 blocks or more, ask the driver to take a road well away from Midtown traffic – it will be quicker and cheaper. Any taxi with its rooftop license number lit is available for hire, though it's hard to see it from a distance. Taxi drivers are required to take you anywhere in the city and to all airports. The city's Taxi & Limousine Commission (☎ 212-302-8294) is a strong regulator, and the threat of a complaint should deter any abuses.

Long Island

The crowded boroughs of Brooklyn and Queens occupy the western tip of Long Island, which extends about 120 miles east from the mouth of the Hudson River. The next county east, Nassau, is mostly suburban housing and strip malls, built as commuter trains linked the area to Manhattan. Partly rural Suffolk County covers the eastern two-thirds of the island; its tip splits into the North and South Forks.

The first European settlements on the island were whaling and fishing ports, established as early as 1640. In the late 19th and early 20th centuries, the ultrarich built big estates along the secluded coves and cliff tops of the north shore.

For most visitors, Long Island means a trip to the beach – crowded Jones Beach, frenetic Fire Island, quiet Shelter Island or the posh Hamptons, all accessible by train or bus. To explore the rural areas, it's best to have a car, though traffic to and from the city can be hellish in summer.

The Long Island Convention and Visitors Bureau (☎ 631-951-3440, 877-386-6654, W www.licvb.com) publishes an annual free travel guide. Local chambers of commerce provide maps, restaurant listings and lodging guides.

Activities

For bicycling, try Route 25 on the North Fork, side roads in the Hamptons and the 7-mile Route 114 from East Hampton to Sag Harbor. There's pleasant hiking October and April on Fire Island, Shelter Island and along the shoreline from East Hampton to Montauk. Georgica Jetties, Montauk and Shinnecock Inlet are the main surfing spots; call ☎ 631-283-7873 for information.

Getting There & Around

From Manhattan, Hampton Jitney buses (☎ 800-936-0440) leave several times daily for the South Fork ($48 roundtrip). Sunrise Coach Lines (☎ 800-527-7709) services the North Fork (around $22 one way).

Long Island Rail Road (LIRR; ☎ 631-217-5477) trains run from New York City's Penn Station to 134 stations throughout Long Island, as far as Greenport on the

North Fork and Montauk on the South Fork. Fares are similar to the buses'.

In summer, LIRR offers roundtrip deals to the south-shore beaches (buy tickets the day before to avoid long lines just before departure).

ATLANTIC SHORE

Long, narrow rows of sand dunes form a stretch of islands with remarkably clean and pleasant beaches. The ones closest to New York get very crowded.

On summer weekends, it's a mob scene on the 6-mile stretch of **Jones Beach**, the *least* exclusive area on Long Island. There are boardwalk concessions, miniature golf courses and parking lots for 25,000 cars. LIRR makes a bus connection to Jones Beach.

The stretch of dunes forming **Fire Island** includes Fire Island National Seashore (☎ 631-289-4810) and a few summer-only villages accessible by ferry from Long Island. It's *the* major local gay summer scene. Ferry terminals to Fire Island beaches and the national seashore are close to LIRR stations at Bayshore, Sayville and Patchogue ($12 roundtrip, May-Nov). At the western end of Fire Island, **Robert Moses State Park** is the only spot accessible by car and can get very crowded. There are not many places to stay, and you must book ahead in summer.

South Fork & the Hamptons

Artists, musicians and writers have long been attracted to the beautiful beaches and rustic Cape Cod–style homes of the South Fork. Celebrities like Steven Spielberg, Uma Thurman and Robert De Niro have homes here.

Restaurants and hotels are generally expensive and open only June to October. Most B&Bs and smaller inns charge well over $200 in high season. Prices drop and traffic jams disappear about two weeks after Labor Day.

Though not quite as flashy as its neighbors, the village of **Southampton** is still pretty upscale and a nice place to spend an afternoon seeking history and art. The town's historic Halsey Homestead, on Main St, is a simple saltbox house built in 1648. The Parrish Art Museum (☎ 631-283-2111, 25 Jobs Lane) has quality exhibitions ($4).

Seven miles north of Bridgehampton on Peconic Bay is the old whaling town of **Sag Harbor**. Its Whaling Museum (☎ 631-725-0770) is open daily ($3; open May-Oct).

Long Island's trendiest town is **East Hampton**, where you can catch readings and art exhibitions at Guild Hall (☎ 631-324-0806, 158 Main St) and dine at *Maidstone Arms (☎ 631-324-5006, 207 Main St)*, the most elegant and expensive restaurant in town. You may get glimpses of estates on Main Beach and Ocean Ave and grand houses behind shrubbery on Lilly Pond Lane.

The eastern extension of East Hampton is **Amagansett**, marked by a huge flagpole in the middle of Montauk Hwy. *Stephen Talkhouse (☎ 631-267-3117, 161 Main St)* is a concert venue and bar where many significant artists, such as Billy Joel and James Taylor, have played. *Sea Breeze Inn (☎ 631-267-3159, 30 Atlantic Ave)*, has 12 rooms from $140, $60 off-season. In summer, cheap seafood stands near Napeague Beach (east of Amagansett) serve fish sandwiches, fresh steamers, fried clams and other sea fare for $10 and up. Try *Lobster Roll*, *Clam Bar* or *Cyril's*.

More honky-tonk than the rest of the Hamptons, **Montauk** has relatively reasonable restaurants and a louder bar scene, largely because all the service personnel – mainly students – live here in communal housing. *Shagwong Restaurant*, on Main St, serves good tavern-style meals year round. Motel rooms cost about $125 a night in summer, but many are booked solid.

Covering the eastern tip of the South Fork is **Montauk Point State Park**, where the Montauk Lighthouse looks impressive, but the museum inside isn't. Camp nearby at windswept *Hither Hills State Park (☎ 631-668-2461)*, right by the ocean ($16).

NORTH FORK

The main North Fork town and the place for ferries to Shelter Island, **Greenport** is friendly and more affordable than South Fork villages, though the restaurants around the marina are still pretty pricey. The Long Island Wine Council (☎ 631-369-5887) provides details of the local wine trail, along Route 25 (Long Island makes some nice whites).

At the tip of the North Fork, **Orient Point** is where Cross Sound Ferries (☎ 631-323-2525) leave for New London, Connecticut (cars $32 one way, plus $9 per person; reservations recommended). On the way there, visit **Orient**, a cute 17th-century hamlet with well-preserved white-clapboard houses.

SHELTER ISLAND

Between the North and South Forks, Shelter Island is occupied mainly by the **Mashomack Nature Preserve**. Shelter Island Heights is a cluster of Victorian buildings on the island's north side.

B&Bs include *Azalea House (☎ 631-749-4252, 1 Thomas Ave)*, with five rooms ($50-125). *Ram's Head Inn (☎ 631-749-0811)*, on Ram Island Dr, is a large, columned place overlooking the water (from $200 in summertime, $70 off-season).

Dory, near the Shelter Island Heights Bridge, is a smoky bar that serves simple fare on a waterfront patio. *Shelter Island Pizza*, on Route 114, is about the only place open year round.

The North Ferry Company (☎ 631-749-0139) runs boats every 10 minutes or so to Shelter Island from Greenport ($6.50 for car and driver, $1 per additional passenger, $1 per pedestrian or cyclist). South Ferry Inc (☎ 631-749-1200) leaves from a dock 3 miles north of Sag Harbor and costs about the same. The ferries shut down about midnight.

Piccozzi's Bike Shop (☎ 631-749-0045), on Bridge St, rents bikes for $20 a day.

Upstate New York

New York State has some magnificent wilderness and surprisingly rural areas, with a rich history preserved in many pretty towns and grand estates. You can reach the main towns by bus or train, but to explore the countryside, you need a car. Take a train to a town like Albany and rent one there – you'll avoid driving in the metropolis. Many museums and historic sites are open only from May to October or keep shorter hours off-season – call for details. Most campgrounds close in the winter.

HUDSON VALLEY

Winding roads along the Hudson River take you by picturesque farms, Victorian cottages, apple orchards and old-money mansions built by New York's elite. Hudson Valley Tourism (☎ 800-232-4782) has regional information about sites and events. Painters of the Hudson River school romanticized these landscapes – you can see their work at museums in Albany, Poughkeepsie and New York City.

Lower Hudson Valley

On the west side, 40 miles north of New York City, **Harriman State Park** covers 72 sq miles and offers swimming, hiking, camping and a visitor center (☎ 845-786-5003). Adjacent **Bear Mountain State Park** (☎ 845-786-2701) offers great views from its 1306-foot peak. The Manhattan skyline looms beyond the river and surrounding greenery. You can enjoy hiking in summer, wildflowers in spring, gold foliage in fall and cross-country skiing in winter.

During the Revolutionary War, colonial troops stretched a massive iron chain across the Hudson River at **West Point** to blockade British ships. The strategic fort became the US Military Academy in 1802. West Point's graduates include Generals Ulysses S Grant, Douglas MacArthur and H Norman Schwarzkopf; military buffs will enjoy the museum and the well-manicured Gothic campus. The visitor center (☎ 845-938-2638) in Highland Falls has exhibits and maps and can tell you when cadets will parade in their finery.

West of Route 9W, the **Storm King Art Center** (☎ 845-534-3115), on Old Pleasant Hill Rd in Mountainville, showcases stunning avant-garde sculpture by Calder, Moore and Noguchi, among others. Tucked among rolling hills, this outdoor park occupies 400 acres and combines art and nature. Enjoy a picnic here – it's worth a visit ($9; open Apr-Nov).

Once an important whaling village, nearby **Newburgh** (population 24,100) was George Washington's longest lasting wartime headquarters during the Revolutionary War. Washington's Headquarters State Historic Site (☎ 845-562-1195) has a museum, galleries and maps.

About 20 miles north, **New Paltz** (population 11,000) is an outdoorsy college town. Founded by French Huguenots in 1677, it still has old stone houses on Huguenot St (☎ 845-255-1660 for tours). There's excellent rock climbing and hiking at Min-

newaska State Park Preserve and Mohonk Preserve. The walkable Main St has plenty of restaurants and bars and a friendly student atmosphere.

On the east side, picturesque, upscale **Tarrytown** (population 10,700) is a good base for exploring the many historic 18th-century houses nearby. In 1996, North Tarrytown changed its name to **Sleepy Hollow** to attract nostalgic tourists and honor Washington Irving's romantic prose. Historic Hudson Valley (☎ 800-448-4007) maintains six regional buildings, including Sunnyside, which was Irving's quaint cottage ($8); the Union Church at Pocantico Hills, with stained-glass windows by Matisse and Chagall ($3); and Kykuit, the Rockefeller family mansion ($20).

The closest mid-range motels are in Elmsford, east on Route 287. Metro North (☎ 212-532-4900) offers train and bus packages to Tarrytown and the area. Alternatively, take a boat ride up the Hudson from New York City. New York Waterway (☎ 800-533-3779) runs boats from Pier 78 in Manhattan.

Middle Hudson Valley

The largest town on the Hudson's east bank, **Poughkeepsie** (pooh-**kip**-see; population 28,800) is famous for **Vassar**, a private liberal-arts college that admitted only women until 1969. Its modern **Francis Lehman Loeb Art Center** (☎ 845-437-5632) features Hudson River–school paintings and contemporary work. Dutchess County Tourism Office (☎ 800-445-3131, 3 Neptune Rd) has regional information. Motels in Poughkeepsie along Route 9, south of the Mid-Hudson Bridge, include *Econo Lodge* (☎ 914-452-6600), at $75-100, and *Holiday Inn Express* (☎ 845-473-1151), at $119-139. Motels to the north in Hyde Park are closer to the historical sites.

Between the Hudson River and Connecticut, **Millbrook** is an old getaway for old-money New Yorkers. Garden lovers will enjoy the **Institute of Ecosystem Studies** (☎ 845-677-5343) and the beautiful 200-acre **Innisfree Garden** (☎ 845-677-8000).

Hyde Park (population 21,200) has long been associated with the Roosevelts, a prominent family since the 19th century. The **Franklin D Roosevelt Library and Museum** (511 Albany Post Rd/Route 9) features exhibits on the man who created the New Deal and led the USA into WWII. You can hear recordings of FDR's 'fireside chats' and see his Ford Phaeton with custom hand-controls ($10; open daily). It's the only US presidential library that a sitting president has used.

Eleanor Roosevelt's cottage, **Val-Kill**, was her retreat from Hyde Park, FDR's mother and FDR himself ($5). You can learn about her humanitarianism and work on the United Nations' Universal Declaration of Human Rights. The **Vanderbilt Mansion**, a national historic site 2 miles north on Route 9, is a spectacle of lavish beaux arts and eclectic architecture ($8). A combination ticket to all three sites costs $18; reservations (☎ 800-967-2283) are recommended.

A nearby country inn, *The Village Square* (☎ *914-229-7141, 4159 Albany Post Rd)*, has exceptional rooms ($40 midweek to $100 weekends). Two miles south, basic *Golden Manor* (☎ *845-229-2157)* charges $50-65 nightly.

The well-regarded Culinary Institute of America trains future chefs and can satisfy anyone's gastronomic cravings. Its four student-staffed restaurants are formal, but *St Andrew's Cafe* (☎ *914-471-6608)* is more casual and the least expensive. Dinner averages $30 per person (reservations required). For value, selection and American atmosphere, try *Eveready Diner*, also on Route 9.

The pretty village of **Rhinebeck** was once a stagecoach stop – rustic *Beekman Arms* (☎ *845-876-7077)*, opened in 1766, still rents rooms ($95-145) and is the USA's oldest operating inn. On summer weekends, see WWI planes and air shows at the **Old Rhinebeck Aerodrome** (☎ 845-758-8610), an aviation museum ($6/12 Mon-Fri/Sat-Sun).

Upper Hudson Valley
Once an old whaling station, **Hudson** now has a variety of antique shops. About 5 miles south, **Olana** (☎ 518-828-0135) was the home of painter Frederic Edwin Church (1826–1900). The idiosyncratic Persian-esque house has lovely gardens (tours $3; open Apr-Oct).

CATSKILLS
This scenic region of small towns, farms, resorts and forests offers great hiking, river rafting and skiing. Adirondack Trailways

(☎ 800-858-8555) operates daily buses to Kingston, the Catskills' gateway town, as well as to Saugerties, Catskill, Hunter and Woodstock.

Woodstock
Ten miles northwest of Kingston, Woodstock (population 6200) symbolizes the tumultuous 1960s, when US youth questioned authority, experimented with freedom and redefined popular culture. Today it's a combination of quaint and hip. The town has been an artists' colony since the 1900s, and it's a good place to people-watch. The 1969 Woodstock music festival (see 'Woodstock I, II & III') actually occurred in Bethel, a town over 40 miles southwest, about 10 miles from the Pennsylvania border, where a simple plaque marks the famous spot. For information, call the chamber of commerce (☎ 845-679-6234).

Saugerties-Woodstock KOA (☎ *845-246-4089)* charges $25-28 per site. From I-87 exit 20, take Route 212 west 2¼ miles. Nearby, *Rip Van Winkle Campground* (☎ *845-246-8334)* costs $24-28. *Twin Gables Guesthouse* (☎ *845-679-9479, 73 Tinker St)* is central, with nicely furnished singles/doubles at $59/69 with shared bath. *Woodstock Inn* (☎ *800-697-8211, 38 Tannery Brook Rd)* is attractive and quiet ($99-139). Tinker St restaurants offer vegetarian, Asian, New Age and hip country gourmet. At downtown *F-Stop Cafe*, listen to local musicians jam in a photography gallery.

Southern Catskills
In the Southern Catskills, the 'Borscht Belt' resorts were once enormous, if not especially graceful, holiday spots for New York's Jewish families. The glory days, exemplified in the 1990 movie *Dirty Dancing,* are long gone, but a few resorts remain. They attract visitors with special-interest promotions, conference facilities and big-name entertainers from comedy and music circuits. *Kutscher's* (☎ *800-431-1273)*, off Route 17 on Kutscher's Road (exit 105B), retains the decadent spirit with nightly entertainment, golf, a spa and an indoor ice-skating rink ($92-159).

Northern Catskills
Route 28 crosses the Catskills west of Woodstock, then winds past the Ashokan

Woodstock I, II & III

Billed as 'Three Days of Peace & Music' in August 1969, the Woodstock Festival included performances by greats such as Joan Baez, Joe Cocker & the Grease Band, Country Joe & the Fish, Jimi Hendrix, Santana, Sly & the Family Stone, The Who and Crosby, Stills & Nash. Some 500,000 people converged on Max Yasgur's farm, near the quiet town of Bethel, New York, for the three-day extravaganza. Tickets cost $18, but only about 125,000 people paid.

Overall, the event went smoothly, despite broken toilets and a downpour, which created a serious mud problem. The festival was, for the most part, violence-free, though Pete Townsend did smash a guitar on Abbie Hoffman's head. It was probably the greatest hippie gathering ever.

The 1994 Woodstock II Festival, in nearby Saugerties, New York (where organizers wanted to hold the 1969 event), failed to live up to its predecessor's reputation. Still, the concert featured Aerosmith, Peter Gabriel, the Red Hot Chili Peppers, and (again) Crosby, Stills & Nash. This time tickets cost $135 and the concert was broadcast on pay-per-view cable TV.

In July 1999, a 30th-anniversary 'Woodstock' was held at Griffiss Air Force Base, near Rome, New York, 100 miles northwest of the original site. Over 180,000 tickets were sold at around $150 each. This time the ambience was 'rage rock' rather than peace and love, with bands like Limp Bizkit rapping angst, anger and obscenities calculated to shock the establishment and achieve commercial success. On the last night, the venue erupted in flames and the event ended in chaos with reports of violence and rape – some publicist's dream.

Reservoir and through the 'French Catskills.' Along it are excellent restaurants, camping and inexpensive lodging. In Mt Tremper is the **Kaatskill Kaleidoscope** (☎ 888-303-3936), the world's largest ($5). The 60-foot tube, an old farm silo, is touristy, but the 10-minute presentation is worthwhile, featuring US history, psychedelic colors and even images of marijuana leaves. Inner-tubing and **white-water rafting** enthusiasts will enjoy Esopus Creek and the town of Phoenicia. In Arkville, the Catskill Center for Conservation & Development (☎ 845-586-2611) has a gallery and hiking information.

Belleayre Hostel (☎ 845-245-4200), off Main St in quaint Pine Hill, has $15 bunks. In Margaretville, the major commercial town, picturesque *Margaretville Mountain Inn* (☎ 845-586-3933), on Margaretville Mountain Rd, has pristine rooms from $65. *Merritt's Motel* (☎ 914-586-4464), on Route 28, is cheaper.

Farther north, Routes 23 and 23A lead to **ski areas**: Hunter Mountain Ski Bowl (☎ 518-263-4223), a year-round resort with challenging runs and a 1600-foot vertical drop, and Ski Windham (☎ 518-734-4300), with more intermediate runs. From Haines Falls there are several hikes, including the

walk to **Kaaterskill Falls**, which was immortalized in a Thomas Cole painting and the novel *Kaaterskill Falls*, by Allegra Goodman. A trail leads to the site of the old Catskill Mountain House in the North/South Lake Area. *North/South Lake Campground* (☎ 518-589-5058), 3 miles northeast of Route 23A, has 200 sites ($16; open May-Oct) and canoe rentals.

ALBANY

The state capital (population 101,100) has revived its northeastern charm in several neighborhoods. Lark St has many restaurants and 'alternative' establishments; at night, strings of lights illuminate the area. The main visitor center (☎ 518-434-1217, 25 Quackenbush Square) has information about the city's mansions and churches. It's easy to get around on foot or by car. However, the downtown empties after business hours.

The **Empire State Plaza** houses legislative offices, state agencies, modern art and a performing-arts center dubbed 'the Egg' for its oval architecture. The **New York State Museum** (☎ 518-474-5877) documents the state's political, cultural and natural history (donation requested; open daily). East of the plaza, **Albany Institute of History & Art**

(☎ 518-463-4478), founded in 1791, houses local furnishings, decorative arts and works by Hudson River–school painters, including Thomas Cole and Asher Durand.

Motels along Central Ave, west of I-87 exit 2, are some distance from downtown, but prices are low. A nice downtown option is *Pine Haven B&B* (☎ *518-482-1574, 531 Western Ave)*, which offers hostel beds for $25. East of Empire State Plaza, *State Street Mansion* (☎ *518-462-6780, 281 State St)*, a former seminary, has rooms from $79. Try *Grandma's Country Restaurant* (☎ *518-459-4585, 1273 Central Ave)*, west of downtown, for home-cooked American fare.

From the bus terminal (34 Hamilton St), Trailways (☎ 518-436-9651) and Greyhound (☎ 518-434-8095) head to/from New York City ($33; 3 hours), Long Island, the Catskills, the Adirondacks, Buffalo ($53; 6 hours) and Montreal, Canada ($53; 5 hours). The Amtrak station (☎ 518-462-5763, 555 East St) is 2 miles from downtown and has regular trains to New York ($41; 2½ hours), Buffalo ($56; 5 hours) and north to the Adirondacks and Montreal. Local CDTA (☎ 518-482-8822) buses run to/from the airport with various stops throughout the city.

AROUND ALBANY
Cooperstown
Fifty miles west of Albany, Cooperstown (population 2200) sits on the banks of Lake Otsego. The town's brick buildings and baseball institution give it an all-American feel. The chamber of commerce (☎ 607-547-9983) is at 31 Chestnut St.

The **National Baseball Hall of Fame & Museum** (☎ 607-547-7200), a shrine to the national sport, has exhibits on players, uniforms and equipment; a theater; a library; and an interactive statistical database ($9.50). The **Farmer's Museum & Village Crossroads** (☎ 607-547-1450) consists of a dozen relocated 19th-century buildings, including a store, printing office and barn ($9). The old stone **Fenimore Art Museum** (☎ 607-547-1420) has an outstanding collection of Americana, James Fenimore Cooper memorabilia and Thomas Cole's painting *Last of the Mohicans* ($9).

Cooperstown Beaver Valley Campground (☎ *800-726-7314)*, on Route 28 about 4 miles south of town, has full facili-

ties ($28-31). Motels are somewhat pricey, though lakeside accommodations may be cheaper off-season. *Baseballtown Motel* (☎ *607-547-2161, 61–63 Main St)* has large but ordinary rooms from $69. The quaint *Chestnut St Guest House* (☎ *607-547-5624, 79 Chestnut St)* offers rooms for $85-120 including breakfast.

Several restaurants along Main St serve inexpensive 'family style' food. Plush *Otesaga Hotel* (☎ *607-547-9931, 60 Lake St)* has a lunch buffet and set dinners.

Pine Hills Trailways and Adirondack Trailways (☎ 800-858-8555) stop in front of the Chestnut St Deli. By car from I-88, take exit 16 and then Route 28 north for 18 miles to town. From I-90, take exit 30 to Route 28 south for 28 miles to town.

Saratoga Springs
This gracious Victorian town (population 25,000) is famous for mineral springs, performing arts and horse racing.

Most of the springs are in **Saratoga Spa State Park**, open daily until dusk ($4 per car), which offers soothing mineral baths and massages (☎ 518-584-2011). The visitor center (☎ 518-587-3241) is in a former trolley station across from Congress Park. The **Saratoga Performing Arts Center** (☎ 518-587-3330) is the summer home of the New York City Ballet and Philadelphia Orchestra, offering world-class cultural performances ($15-53). The **National Museum of Dance** (☎ 518-584-2225) is next to the Lincoln Baths ($5).

From late July through September, fans of horse racing flock to the **Saratoga Race Course** (☎ 518-584-6200), the country's oldest active thoroughbred racetrack. The **National Museum of Racing & Hall of Fame** (☎ 518-584-0400) is located across from the track ($7).

The nearest campground is *Cold Brook Campsites* (☎ *518-584-8038)*, about 10 miles north in Gansevoort ($20). Independent motels along Route 9/S Broadway (exit 13N) are the cheapest. *Saratoga Motel* (☎ *518-584-0920, 440 Church St)*, 2 miles west of town, costs $65/85 for singles/doubles, $120 during racing season. There is a good selection of B&Bs, especially *Brunswick Bed & Breakfast* (☎ *518-584-6751, 143 Union Ave)*, where rooms with TVs, VCRs and telephones start at $79.

Greyhound and Adirondack Trailways stop at 133 S Broadway. Amtrak has daily trains from Montreal and New York City.

Saratoga National Historical Park

The 1777 British defeat at the Battle of Saratoga was a major turning point in the Revolutionary War, demonstrating that the colonists could win against a European army. Following the battle France entered the war supporting the Americans – a decisive alliance. The battlefield (☎ 518-664-9821) is 14 miles to the east of Saratoga Springs via Route 29.

THE ADIRONDACKS

Adirondack Parks' 6 million acres include towns, mountains, lakes, rivers and over 2000 miles of hiking trails. The Adirondack Forest Preserve covers 40% of the park; the state constitution designates it as 'forever wild.' There's good trout, salmon and pike fishing. Insects, especially black flies, are a summer nuisance. In colonial times, settlers exploited the forests for beaver fur, timber and hemlock bark. In the 19th century, wilderness retreats became fashionable, and large hotels and millionaires' estates adopted the rusticated Adirondack style: log cabins on a grand scale.

Local tourist offices are plentiful. The Adirondack Mountain Club (ADK; ☎ 518-668-4447, Ⓦ www.adk.org, 814 Goggins Rd, Lake George) publishes excellent maps and guides.

Adirondack Trailways (☎ 800-858-8555) runs throughout the region, with limited winter service. Amtrak stops at Westport (☎ 518-962-8730), 37 miles east of Lake Placid.

Lake George

At the park's southeastern entrance, 32-mile-long Lake George has clear blue water and wild shorelines. The village of Lake George (population 900) is a bit tacky; still, it's a gateway to the Adirondacks. The **Great Escape Fun Park** (☎ 518-798-1084) features raft rides, roller coasters, shows and a beautiful Adirondack backdrop ($29/15 adults/kids). At Glens Falls, a few miles south of the village, the remarkable **Hyde Collection** (☎ 518-792-1761) includes works by Rembrandt, Rubens and Matisse (free admission).

The state maintains campgrounds on Lake George's islands; call ☎ 800-456-2267 for reservations. *Lake George Battleground Public Campground* (☎ 518-668-3348), at the town's south end, has 50 shady sites ($10-16). Canada St/Route 9 is lined with motels. Rates are highest in summer. Friendly *Balmoral Motel* (☎ 518-668-2673) has nicely furnished rooms (from $55 in summer, $30 in winter) and a big pool.

Along Route 9N

This scenic road follows the western shore of Lake George through little towns like **Bolton Landing** that have B&Bs and eateries. At Lake George's northern tip, strategic and historic **Fort Ticonderoga** (☎ 518-585-2821) was attacked six times between 1758 and 1775 ($8). *Brookwood Park Campsites* (☎ 518-585-2158), south of town, charges $15 (open May-Oct). Motels are on the main road. Farther north, in the picturesque hamlet of **Essex**, the 1810 *Essex Inn* (☎ 518-963-8821) has rooms for $85-115.

Lake Placid

This mountain resort (population 2500) hosted the Winter Olympics in 1932 and 1980, and elite athletes still train here. The visitor center (☎ 518-523-2445, 216 Main St) has maps, brochures and information about skiing, fishing, cycling, hiking and canoeing.

On Main St, the **Olympic Center** (☎ 518-523-1655) has four ice rinks now used for training, hockey and ice shows (tours available). You can drive up **Whiteface Mountain** (☎ 518-946-2223) in the warmer months for an $8 toll plus $4 per passenger; a chairlift ($10) goes up another 3600 feet to the summit.

Ski jumpers train year round at the **Olympic Ski Jumping Complex**, southeast of town on Route 73. The **Mt Van Hoevenberg** complex (☎ 518-523-4436) is for bobsled, luge and cross-country-skiing events. If you need an adrenaline fix, shoot through the bobsled run with a professional driver, or try the Olympic luge run for $30 ($125 in winter, on real ice).

The **John Brown Farm & Grave** (☎ 518-523-3900), in North Elba outside Lake Placid, was the home of the American abolitionist. Brown was hanged for his part in the 1859 raid on Harpers Ferry, West Virginia.

Lake Placid has expensive accommodations, especially in summer and in ski season. Wilmington, 15 miles east, may be cheaper. South of town, ADK's *Adirondack Loj* (☎ 518-523-3441) is a large house beside a small lake – it's a lovely, rustic retreat with great atmosphere, but it's not cheap. Bunk beds cost $25-32 per person, $32-41 weekends (including a good breakfast); a few doubles with shared bath are also available. Campsites cost about $15, lean-to shelters about $18. Call first for details and directions. *Whispering Pines Campground* (☎ 518-523-9322), 6 miles south of Lake Placid, has 80 sites for $15-22 (open May-Oct).

Motels extend along Saranac Ave west of town. For a place with character, check *Hotel St Moritz* (☎ 518-523-9240, 31 Saranac Ave), from $45-55. *Alpine Air Motel* (☎ 518-523-9261, 99 Saranac Ave) has a pool and convivial atmosphere ($44-85, more on weekends). *Econo Lodge* (☎ 518-523-2817), on Cascade Rd, offers singles/doubles at $65/70, $45/50 off-season. Mid-range places include *Adirondack Inn* (☎ 518-523-2424, 217 Main St) and *Interlaken Inn* (☎ 518-523-3180, 15 Interlaken Ave), both with rooms from around $60.

Saranac Ave, the main street, has mainly American eateries. *Cameron's* (☎ 518-523-7872, 57 Saranac Ave) offers hearty food and a fun atmosphere.

Saranac Lake
In the middle of several lakes, the village of Saranac Lake (population 5400) offers canoeing, skiing, hiking and camping. The chamber of commerce (☎ 518-891-1990, 800-347-1992, 30 Main St) has information on wilderness areas. The **Robert Louis Stevenson Cottage** (☎ 518-891-1462) contains a large selection of memorabilia ($5). Rooms at *Adirondack Motel* (☎ 518-891-2116), on the lake, are $60-115, $45-80 off-season. *Hotel Saranac* (☎ 518-891-2200, 101 Main St), has comfortable singles/doubles at $99/119, $69/81 off-season. The restaurant is reasonably priced; try Sunday brunch.

About 14 miles north of town, the fascinating **Six Nations Indian Museum** (☎ 518-891-2299) preserves the culture of the Iroquois Confederation ($2; open in summer only – call first).

Blue Mountain Lake
In the park's center, this tiny town is a gateway for canoeing the Fulton Chain of Lakes and hiking the Blue Mountain Trail. Blue Mountain Outfitters (☎ 518-352-7306, 144 Main St) provides information and equipment. The excellent **Adirondack Museum** (☎ 518-352-7311) includes an exhibit on boat building ($10; open June-Oct). Lodgings are available here; alternatively, go 11 miles north to Long Lake, where *Adirondack Hotel* (☎ 518-624-4700) has clean doubles for $45-50 ($55-60 with bath).

Old Forge
Adirondack Park's southwest corner offers snowmobiling, canoeing and hiking, as well as an information office (☎ 315-369-6983). The classic 90-mile Adirondack Canoe Route follows the Racquette River from Old Forge up to the Saranac Lakes. A good outfitter is Tickner's (☎ 315-369-6286). Basic motels abound between Blue Mountain Lake and Old Forge. *Old Forge KOA* (☎ 315-369-6011) is open year round. *Limekiln Lake Campground* (☎ 315-357-4401), about 3 miles southeast, has tent sites ($11; open May-Nov). B&Bs start around $65.

ST LAWRENCE RIVER
East of Lake Ontario, over 1890 tiny islands dot the wide St Lawrence River in what's called the **Thousand Islands** region. Once a summer playground for the very rich, it's now a popular area for boating, camping and even scuba diving, promoted by the 1000 Islands International Tourism Council (☎ 800-847-5263, Ⓦ www.visit1000islands.com).

The relaxing village of **Cape Vincent** (population 700) is at the western end of the St Lawrence River, where it meets Lake Ontario. The 1854 Tibbetts Point Lighthouse is wonderful place to view spectacular sunsets. Friendly *HI Tibbetts Point Hostel* (☎ 315-654-3450) is right on the lighthouse grounds, open mid-May to October ($10/15 members/nonmembers).

Farther east, Clayton has an **Antique Boat Museum** (☎ 315-686-4104), which appeals to lovers of fine woodwork. For a great panorama of the river, take the Thousand Islands International Bridge across to Canada ($2). Nearby Alexandria Bay (Alex Bay), an early-20th-century resort town, has lost its charm but remains the departure point for ferries to Heart Island, where **Boldt Castle** (☎ 800-847-5263) marks the sad love story of a rags-to-riches New York hotelier who built the castle for his beloved wife, who died before its completion (open mid-May to Sept). The same hotelier once asked his chef to create a new salad dressing, which was popularized as 'Thousand Island.'

Since 1959 the 15 locks of the **St Lawrence Seaway** have allowed oceangoing cargo vessels to travel from the Atlantic to the Great Lakes. At the Eisenhower Lock Visitor Center (☎ 315-769-2049), near Massena, gaze at 700-foot ships passing through the canal. A 3200-foot dam spans the river as part of the **St Lawrence–Franklin D Roosevelt Power Project**. The visitor center (☎ 315-764-0226) has an observation deck and interactive displays on electricity (free admission). *Hillside Motel & Kampground* (☎ 315-769-5403, 15 Smith Rd) has efficiencies from $50, tent sites and a pool.

About 30 miles west of Massena, the town of Ogdensburg is the unlikely birthplace of artist Frederic Remington (1861–1909), chronic romanticizer of the American West. The **Frederic Remington Art Museum** (☎ 315-393-2425) displays his sculptures, paintings and personal effects ($4; open Tue-Sat).

FINGER LAKES REGION

Eleven long, narrow lakes stretch north to south and form the fingers of this western New York region. It's an ideal place for boating, fishing, bicycling, hiking and cross-country skiing, and the rolling hills are the state's best wine-growing region. At more than 65 vineyards you can sample an array of palate-pleasing whites and reds. The **New York Wine & Grape Foundation** (☎ 315-536-7442, Ⓦ www.uncork@nywine.com), in Penn Yan, distributes free brochures on wine trails.

Seneca Falls

This tiny town (population 7400) is where the USA's organized women's rights movement was born. After being excluded from an antislavery meeting, Elizabeth Cady Stanton and her friends drafted an 1848 declaration asserting that 'all men and women are created equal.' The inspirational

Women's Rights National Historical Park (☎ 315-568-2991) has a visitor center offering tours of Cady Stanton's house. At the **National Women's Hall of Fame** (☎ 315-568-8060) you can honor a woman on the Wall of Fame – ask for details.

Ithaca & Around

This handsome college town (population 29,500) has pedestrian-friendly streets lined with bookstores, eateries, art cinemas and a summertime farmers' market. The visitor bureau (☎ 800-284-8422) is at 904 E Shore Dr.

Ithaca's suburbs and surrounding countryside are interspersed with waterfalls, gorges and gorgeous parks, popular with hikers and rock climbers. Eight miles north on Route 89, the spectacular **Taughannock Falls** spill 215 feet into the steep gorge below; Taughannock Falls State Park has two major hiking trails. In tiny Trumansburg, 15 miles north, the friendly Podunk Cross Country Ski Shop & Ski Center (☎ 607-387-6716) rents skis and has cross-country-trail information.

Founded in 1865, **Cornell University** boasts a lovely campus that mixes traditional and contemporary architecture. The striking, modern **Johnson Museum of Art** (☎ 607-255-6464), designed by IM Pei, has a major Asian collection; pre-Columbian, American and European exhibits; and a nice view from its top floor (free admission; closed Mon).

Three state parks provide excellent *camping* (☎ 800-456-2267) – call two days ahead for reservations. *Meadow Court Inn* (☎ 607-273-3885, 529 S Meadow St) offers the best value, with economy rooms starting at $50, including continental breakfast. There are also chain motels in downtown Ithaca and reasonably priced B&Bs throughout the area. For summer B&B info call ☎ 607-272-7344.

Ithaca has a great variety of international, gourmet and vegetarian restaurants. For lighter fare, *Collegetown Bagels* has three locations serving fresh bagels and soups. *Just a Taste Wine & Tapas Bar* (116 N Aurora St) incorporates food and wines from local merchants into its daily changing menu. Popular *Moosehead Restaurant* (215 N Cayuga St) is famous for its vegetarian dishes and its recipe books.

LEE FOSTER

Vietnam Veterans Memorial; Washington, DC

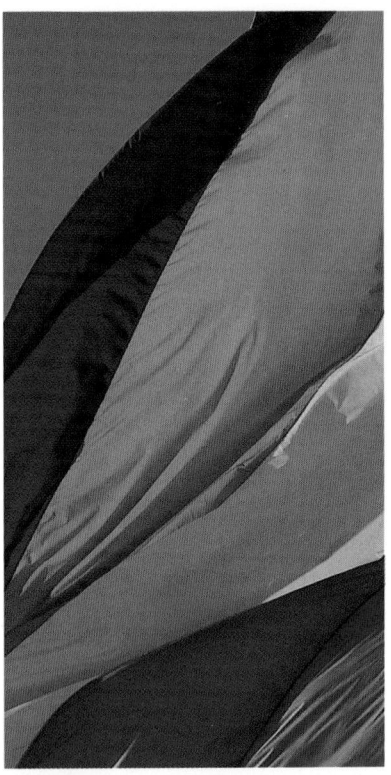

KIM GRANT

Gay rights march; Washington, DC

DENNIS JOHNSON

Jefferson Memorial; Washington, DC

LEE FOSTER

Arlington National Cemetery, Virginia

RICHARD I'ANSON

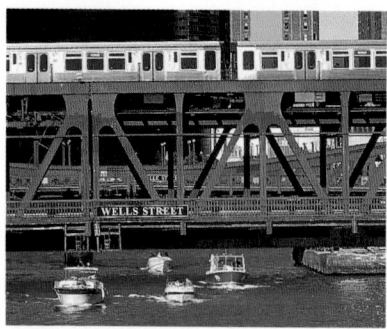

The El; Chicago, Illinois

RICHARD CUMMINS

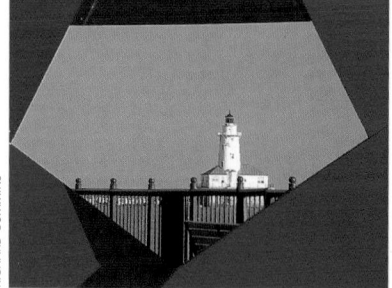

Lighthouse through sculpture; Navy Pier, Chicago

RICHARD CUMMINS

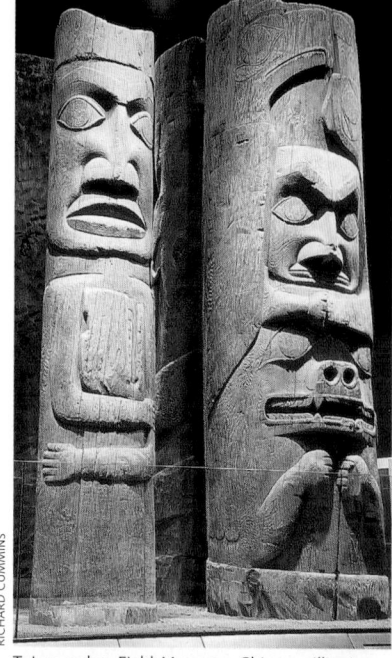

Totem poles; Field Museum, Chicago, Illinois

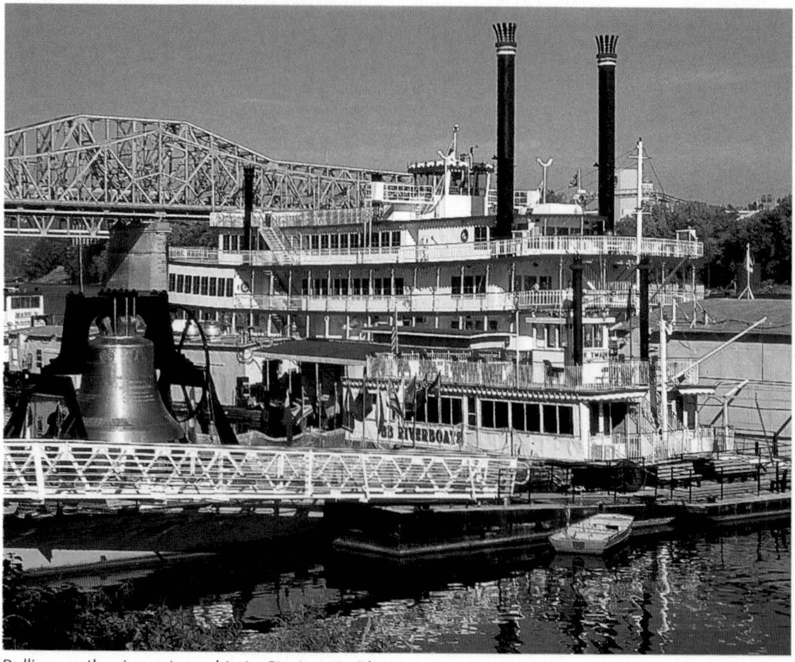
THOMAS HUHTI

Rolling on the river; steamship in Cincinnati, Ohio

Watkins Glen

This modest town (population 2200) is famous for its motor-racing track (☎ 607-535-2481) and for **Watkins Glen State Park** (☎ 607-535-4511), where superb walking trails follow a spectacular gorge and behind cascading waterfalls ($6 per vehicle, $17-20 for campsites). The chamber of commerce (☎ 607-535-4300) is at 1000 N Franklin St.

Corning

This historic glass-blowing town is home to Corning Inc, manufacturers of objets d'art, fiber optics and space-shuttle windows. In the Corning Glass Center the newly renovated **Corning Museum of Glass** (☎ 607-937-5371) has 26,000 glass objects (from 1400 BC to the present) and an impressive Steuben glassmaking demonstration ($11).

Rockwell Museum (☎ 607-937-5386) showcases American Western art, with works by Remington, Russell and the 1830s 'explorer artists' ($6.50). Visit the **National Soaring Museum** (☎ 607-734-3128), for $5 admission, then try the sky yourself on a glider ride ($55-65).

Clean but noisy *Lando's Hotel* (☎ 607-936-3612), at William and Bridge Sts, has rooms from $49. It's within walking distance of historic Market St and its coffee shops, restaurants and boutiques. Try the local hangout *Glory Hole* (☎ 607-962-1474) for filling pub grub ($5-8).

WESTERN NEW YORK

The Erie Canal spawned a number of early industrial centers along its route between Albany and Buffalo. Tracing the canal is an alternative to the I-90 toll route, and a more interesting way to get to Niagara Falls, 430 miles northwest of New York City. Rome and Syracuse have canal museums, and there are surviving sections of the canal itself. The canal's towpaths are ideal for easygoing cycling trips.

Syracuse

At the southern end of Onondaga Lake, Syracuse (population 163,900) is a college town that makes a pleasant stop. The visitor center (☎ 800-234-4797, 572 S Salina St) has information on the surrounding region. The **Erie Canal Museum** (☎ 315-471-0593, 318 Erie Blvd E) displays an old canal boat in an original 'weighlock.' Also take a look at the Niagara Mohawk building (300 Erie Boulevard W), an art deco classic.

HI Downing Hostel (☎ 315-472-5788, 535 Oak St), a mile northeast of downtown, has dorm beds for $12. *Motel 6* (☎ 315-433-1300, 6577 Baptist Way) is near I-90 exit 35; singles/doubles cost $34/40 on slow weekdays, $40/46 on summer weekends. *Dinosaur Bar* (☎ 315-476-4937, 246 W Willow St) is a busy, bustling bar and restaurant serving great-value ribs, burgers and barbecue.

Rochester

A few miles south of Lake Ontario, Rochester (population 231,600) used its waterfalls as a power source as early as 1790. In 1824 the Erie Canal arrived and the flour-milling industry boomed. Later, Rochester became famous as the home of abolitionists, suffragettes and the Eastman Kodak film and photography company. The visitor center (☎ 716-546-3070, 45 East Ave) is very helpful.

The **George Eastman House & International Museum of Photography & Film** (☎ 716-271-3361, 900 East Ave) has an enormous collection of historic films, cameras and books about photography, as well as examples of work by well-known photographers, interactive displays and exciting special exhibits ($6.50; open Tue-Sun). The house and gardens are well worth seeing.

The **Rochester Museum & Science Center** (☎ 716-271-4552, 657 East Ave) contains a first-rate exhibit about Seneca Indians and colonial Europeans ($6; open daily). The **Strong Museum** (☎ 716-263-2700, 1 Manhattan Square) has lots of exhibits for kids under 10, as well as a vast collection of toys, dolls, furniture, household appliances and assorted Americana ($6; open daily).

The **Susan B Anthony House** (☎ 716-235-6124, 17 Madison St) was home to the Rochester suffragette who voted in 1872, when it was still illegal for women to do so (Anthony was arrested for the offence). Admission is $6.

Days Inn Downtown (☎ 716-325-5010, 384 East Ave) has singles/doubles for $69/79 and is close to the museums. Cheaper motels are outside town near the freeway exits. *Dorkat Motel* (☎ 716-334-7000, 3990 W Henrietta Rd) has clean, spacious rooms for about $41.

Niagara Falls

Misty sprays and the majestic scale of this roaring cascade make it a marvelous spectacle. Long before tourism invaded, Seneca Indians populated the area. In 1678 they led the French priest Louis Hennepin to the falls. His description was widely read in Europe: 'The universe does not afford its parallel.'

The falls have attracted daredevils who used various barrels and contraptions to plunge to the bottom; some of them survived. Honeymooners arrive in the thousands, despite jokes that the falls will be the first (or second) disappointment of married life. To keep tourists and their dollars for longer than it takes to see the falls, the US side has nice parks and assorted attractions (some unrelated to waterfalls), and casinos are being contemplated. The Canadian side has gone even farther: As well as the best views of the falls, it offers a whole street full of tacky attractions and already has a casino.

Orientation & Information Two separate towns, Niagara Falls, New York (USA), with 61,800 people, and Niagara Falls, Ontario (Canada), with 75,400 people, face each other across the Niagara River, which is spanned by the Rainbow Bridge.

On the US side, the convention and visitor bureau (☎ 716-285-2400) is at 4th and Niagara Sts, next to the NFTA bus terminal. The Orin Lehman State Park Visitors Center (☎ 716-278-1796), in Prospect Park adjacent to the falls, stays open later and shows a good film on the falls ($2).

Things to See & Do On the US side you can see side views of the **American Falls** and their western portion, the Bridal Veil Falls, dropping 180 feet. Take the Prospect Point Observation Tower elevator up for a vista (50¢). Cross the bridge to **Goat Island** for other viewpoints, including Terrapin Point, which has a fine view of Horseshoe Falls and pedestrian bridges to Three Sisters Islands in the upper rapids. From the north corner of Goat Island, an elevator descends to the **Cave of the Winds** (☎ 716-278-1730), where walkways go within 25 feet of the cataracts ($6.50; raincoat provided).

Crossing the river to Canada, you get a great panorama of the falls from Rainbow Bridge. Canada's **Horseshoe Falls** are wider, and the curved shape makes them especially photogenic from Queen Victoria Park. The **Journey Behind the Falls** gives access to a spray-soaked viewing area beneath the falls (US$4). The observation towers offer another angle on the falls, as well as high-end dining: Skylon Tower (525 feet) is higher and has a revolving restaurant (US$5.50 admission); Minolta Tower (325 feet) is closer to the falls and has better meal deals (US$4.50 admission). The Canadian side is lovely at night, when colored lights illuminate the falls and the clouds of spray.

The *Maid of the Mist* boat trip around the bottom of the falls has been a major attraction since 1846 and is highly recommended. Boats leave every 15 minutes from the base of the Prospect Park Observation Tower on the US side (☎ 716-284-8897; $8.50) or from the waterside at the end of Clifton Hill St on the Canadian side (☎ 905-358-5781; US$7).

On the US side, **Schoellkopf Geological Museum** (☎ 716-278-1780), in Niagara Reservation State Park, explains the region's geology ($1). The New York State Park Interpretive Office (☎ 716-278-1728) gives walking tours of the area ($1).

On the Canadian side, Clifton Hill St has kitschy attractions and a carnival atmosphere – it's fun in the evening. The Niagara Falls IMAX Theater (☎ 905-374-4629, 6170 Buchanan Ave) shows a Niagara Falls feature (US$5). At Casino Niagara (☎ 905-374-3598, 5705 Falls Ave), you can gamble in two currencies.

Organized Tours Many tours stop at major sights on both sides and include a *Maid of the Mist* ride. Bedore Tours (☎ 716-285-7550) is an established operator ($40-50). Rainbow Helicopters (☎ 716-284-2800) does 10-minute sightseeing flights over the falls ($50); Niagara Helicopters does similar trips from Canada (☎ 905-357-5672). Whirlpool Jetboat Tours (☎ 905-468-4800, 888-438-4444, 61 Melville St, Niagara-on-the-Lake, Ontario) does an exciting one-hour roundtrip from Lake Ontario to the Whirlpool, downstream from the falls (US$34).

Places to Stay & Eat The US side tends to be the more expensive. On Grand Island, a few miles south of Niagara Falls on I-190,

MID-ATLANTIC STATES

Niagara Falls KOA (☎ 716-773-7583) is next to the Fantasy Island amusement park (sites $20-28). *HI Niagara Falls Hostel* (☎ 716-282-3700, 1101 Ferry Ave) has 46 beds in an old house ($14/16 members/non-members). *YMCA* (☎ 716-285-8491, 1317 Portage Rd) has basic rooms for men only at $25. Route 62 (Niagara Falls Blvd) has numerous cheap motels ($45-60, $30-45 off-season) but is some distance from the falls. Try *Red Carpet Inn* (☎ 716-283-2010, 6625 Niagara Falls Blvd), for $40-70.

In Canada, *HI Niagara Falls Hostel* (☎ 905-357-0770, 4549 Cataract Ave) has 69 beds (US$11.50), Internet access, a kitchen and bikes for rent. *Niagara Falls Backpackers Hostel* (☎ 905-357-4266, 800-891-7022, 4219 Huron St) charges US$10.50 for basic dorm accommodations. West of the falls, motels on Murray and Ferry Sts advertise heart-shaped Jacuzzis and vibrating waterbeds for honeymooners and dirty-weekenders. Farther west, Ferry St becomes Lundy's Lane and has less stimulating, less expensive options, from around US$35.

There's more fast food than fine dining. *George's (420 Niagara St)* is a simple neighborhood restaurant, good for a big breakfast, sandwich lunch or meatloaf dinner. *Tommy Ryan's (1 Prospect Point)* is a 1950s-style diner. Clifton Hill Ave, on the Canadian side, has plenty of eateries. *Victoria Park Dining Room & Cafeteria*, near the falls, has moderately priced set menus and bargain buffets.

Getting There & Around From the NFTA terminal, at 4th and Niagara Sts, frequent No 40 buses go to Buffalo ($1.85; 1 hour) for air and bus connections. The Amtrak station (☎ 716-285-4224) is 2 miles northeast of downtown. From Niagara Falls, daily trains go to Buffalo, Toronto and New York City ($60; 8 hours). The Canadian-side Greyhound/Trailways terminal (☎ 905-357-2133, 4555 Erie Ave) has buses to Toronto (US$15.50, 1½ hours).

Avoid driving around on either side. You can park free at the downtown Rainbow Mall and walk around. Parking near the falls costs $5 on the US side, US$6.50 on the Canadian side. The Viewmobile trolley (☎ 716-282-0028) does a loop around the US side ($5 per day), and the People Mover shuttles up and down the riverfront on the Canadian side of the falls (US$3.50 per day).

Crossing the Rainbow Bridge to Canada costs US$2.50/50¢ for cars/pedestrians and includes a magnificent view. There are customs and immigration stations at each end – carry proper papers (see Visas and Entry in the Facts for the Visitor chapter).

Around Niagara Falls

Four miles north, **Lewiston** is the home of the Niagara Power Authority (☎ 716-285-3211), one of the world's first and largest hydropower generators. Its visitor center is open daily (free admission). The **Earl W Bridges Artpark** (☎ 716-754-4375, 800-659-7275) combines the natural attractions of the Niagara River Gorge with a summer program of music and theater performances.

About 15 miles north of Niagara Falls, **Old Fort Niagara** (☎ 716-745-7611) was built by the French in 1726, captured by the British in 1759 and taken over by the USA in 1796 ($7; open daily).

Buffalo

This area was settled by the French in 1758 – its name is believed to derive from *beau fleuve* (beautiful river). When the Erie Canal was opened in 1825, Buffalo became a shipping nexus between the Great Lakes and the eastern US. Railroads boosted the area further, and the city thrived as an industrial center, acquiring fine buildings, parks and well-endowed museums (the Albright-Knox Art Gallery is a must for modern-art enthusiasts).

Post-WWII decline in its traditional industries hit the city hard, the population fell, and much of the inner city became badly run-down. Recent urban renewal has improved the downtown area (though it's not exactly vibrant), and the huge student population adds another dimension to a city still known for its working-class roots and football fanatics.

The helpful visitor center (☎ 716-852-0511, 617 Main St) has some good walking-tour pamphlets. Despite cold, snowy winters, the city is dubbed 'the Miami of the North' for its pleasant, sunny weather May to September.

Architectural Highlights Louis Sullivan designed the 1895 Guaranty Building at

28 Church St, now the **Prudential Building,** using an innovative steel-frame construction to create the first modern skyscraper – it's elaborately decorated with terra-cotta tiles. Other notable downtown buildings are the art deco **city hall** (65 Niagara Square), built in 1931; the neo-Gothic **Old Post Office** (121 Ellicot St), built in 1894; and the gold-domed **M&T Bank** (545 Main St), which was Buffalo Savings Bank when it was built back in 1901.

Northeast of downtown, **Kleinhans Music Hall,** by Finnish American architects Eliel and Eero Saarinen, is famous for its curving lines and excellent acoustics.

North of downtown, beautiful **Delaware Park** was designed by Frederick Law Olmsted. The nearby Elmwood neighborhood has four **Frank Lloyd Wright houses;** most are privately occupied, but the 1904 Darwin Martin House (125 Jewett Pkwy) and neighboring Barton House (118 Summit Ave) are being restored and may be accessible by appointment (☎ 716-856-3858). The Theodore Roosevelt Inaugural National Historic Site (☎ 716-884-0095, 641 Delaware Ave) offers architectural walking tours ($5).

Other Attractions The excellent collection of 20th-century artwork at the **Albright-Knox Art Gallery** (☎ 716-882-8700, 1285 Elmwood Ave) includes some of the best French impressionists, as well as American works by Pollock, O'Keefe, Lichtenstein, Ernst, Warhol and others ($4; open Tue-Sat). Buffalo also has good science, history and children's museums, a fine zoo, and QRS Music Inc (☎ 716-885-4600), which still produces rolls for player pianos ($2) – weekday tours are offered. Three full-size navy ships, aircraft and military models are featured at **Naval & Military Park** (☎ 716-847-1773), on Lake Erie at Main St ($6).

Places to Stay & Eat The *HI Buffalo Hostel* (☎ 716-852-5222, 667 Main St) is right in the middle of downtown ($17/19 members/nonmembers). Old-style *Hotel Lenox* (☎ 716-884-1700, 140 North St), in the historic Allentown district, has some character (around $60/70 for singles/doubles, with discounts for students). Cheap motels are found east of town around Williamsville and I-90 – call around to places like *Microtel-Inn* (☎ 716-633-6200,

50 Freeman Rd), with rates from $45, and *Econo Lodge* (☎ 716-634-1500, 7200 Transit Rd), at $50. There's also an economical selection on Grand Island Blvd, en route to Niagara Falls.

The local specialty is Buffalo wings – deep-fried chicken wings covered in a spicy sauce and served with blue-cheese dressing and celery. *Anchor Bar* (1047 Main St) claims credit for this innovation and still serves them up – 10 wings for $5.80. *La Nova* (☎ 716-881-3303, 371 W Ferry St) is a new-looking diner, well regarded for its inexpensive wings and pizzas. *Rendezvous* (520 Niagara St), a former speakeasy, is another local favorite. *Amy's Place* (☎ 716-832-6666, 3234 Main St) is popular with students for its healthy, economical and tasty sandwiches, vegetarian dishes and Middle East–style food.

Elmwood Ave is lined with bars, cafes and restaurants. Check *Artvoice,* a free local paper, for lotsa listings. Chippewa St, west of Main St, is the burgeoning nightlife area, and a mob scene on a warm Saturday night. *Calumet Cafe* (54 W Chippewa St) or *Zoo Bar* (75 W Chippewa St) are good places to start.

Spectator Sports Locals worship the NFL Buffalo Bills football team (☎ 716-648-1800), which plays at Ralph Wilson Stadium (☎ 716-648-1800, ⓦ www.buffalobills.com, 1 Bills Dr, Orchard Park). Other franchises include the Buffalo Sabres ice-hockey team (☎ 716-855-4100), Buffalo Bisons minor-league baseball team (☎ 716-846-2000), Buffalo Bandits lacrosse team (☎ 716-855-4100) and Buffalo Blizzard indoor soccer team (☎ 716-855-4151).

Getting There & Around Buffalo Niagara International Airport (☎ 716-630-6000), about 16 miles east of downtown, is a regional hub. The Greyhound station (☎ 716-855-7531) is at 181 Ellicott St. NFTA (☎ 716-285-9319) local bus No 40 goes to Niagara Falls ($1.85). The downtown Amtrak station (☎ 716-856-2075) is at 75 Exchange St, where you can catch trains to New York City ($60; 7½ hours).

Around Buffalo

Just south of Buffalo, off I-90 exit 55 in Orchard Park, the **Pedaling History Bicycle**

Museum (☎ 716-662-3853, 3943 N Buffalo Rd) has 300 bicycles, mainly antique US models. At Derby, beside Lake Erie, **Graycliff** (☎ 716-947-9217, 6472 Old Lakeshore Rd) is a fine Frank Lloyd Wright house ($10; open Apr-Nov); call first.

East Aurora, 20 miles southeast of Buffalo, was the site of the Roycroft Campus and (from around 1900) the center of the American Arts & Crafts style of furniture and decoration. The diminutive **Roycroft Museum** (☎ 716-652-4735, 363 Oakwood Ave) is a cottage with a small collection ($3; open Wed and Sat-Sun June-Oct). *Roycroft Inn (☎ 716-652-5552, 40 S Grove St)* offers accommodations (from $120) and fine dining in an Arts & Crafts ambience.

Kids might prefer a stop at Darien Center, about 20 miles east of Buffalo, where **Six Flags Darien Lake** (☎ 716-599-2211) has thrilling rides (day pass $30/15 adults/kids; open June-Oct).

In Jamestown, 70 miles south of Buffalo, fans of the USA's first lady of comedy, Lucille Ball, can reminisce about the famed redhead and view her belongings at the **Lucy-Desi Museum** (☎ 716-484-7070, 212 Pine St). Admission is $5.

At the north end of Chautauqua Lake, the **Chautauqua Institution** (☎ 800-836-2787) is a perfectly preserved Victorian town offering an excellent summer program of symphonies, concerts and plays; call for information. The area's delightful backroads are dotted with Amish communities – watch for their horse-drawn buggies.

New Jersey

New Jersey is the most urbanized, most densely populated state in the USA. About two-thirds of the population live within 30 miles of New York City, and much of the state can be regarded as part of the great metropolis: Most of New York's port facilities are in New Jersey, along with its second international airport, the bulk of its industry and many of its workers. Two of New York's greatest icons, the Statue of Liberty and Ellis Island, are actually in New Jersey, as is the home stadium for New York's two pro football teams, the Giants and the Jets. But there's another side of New Jersey – 40% of

the state is forest, and a quarter is farmland. It has 127 miles of beaches, extensive parkland, and beautiful Victorian buildings.

Culturally, the state runs the gamut from waterfront workers to Ivy League intellectuals. The state has been home to two US presidents (Woodrow Wilson and Grover Cleveland), physicist Albert Einstein, inventor Thomas Edison and hard rocker Bruce Springsteen. New Jersey has America's diversity in a concentrated form.

History

The state's original residents were called *lenni lenape* (original people), a group of Delaware speakers probably numbering less than 20,000 when European settlers arrived in the early 17th century. Dutch settlers built a trading post at Bergen (now Jersey City) in 1618 and another at Camden in 1623. When the British took over New Netherlands in 1664, the new colony of New Jersey offered generous terms and religious freedom to attract new settlers. The surviving Native Americans were placed in the Brotherton reservation and later moved to the states of New York and Wisconsin.

New Jersey saw many Revolutionary War battles, and George Washington placed his Continental Army headquarters at

---

New Jersey

Nicknames: Garden State, Clam State

Population: 8,414,000 (9th)

Area: 8722 sq miles (47th)

Admitted to Union: December 18, 1787 (3rd)

Capital city: Trenton (population 88,700)

Other cities: Newark (275,200), Jersey City (228,500)

Birthplace of: 22nd *and* 24th US president Grover Cleveland (1837–1908); athlete, entertainer and social activist Paul Robeson (1898–1976); jazz musician Count Basie (1904–84); Frank Sinatra (1915–98); astronaut Buzz Aldrin (b 1930); Meryl Streep (b 1949); Bruce Springsteen (b 1949)

Home of: the first movie (1889), professional basketball game (1896), drive-in theater (1933)

Morristown in the winters of 1776–77 and 1779–80. New Jersey's population grew from 15,000 in 1700 to more than 185,000 by 1795, and industry boomed. Post–Civil War industrial expansion also spawned a movement to improve working conditions. One of its leaders, Democratic Governor Woodrow Wilson, a former Princeton University president, later served as US president (1913–21). After WWII, Newark and Jersey City saw influxes of immigrants. By the mid-1980s, New Jersey had some of the country's fastest-growing urban areas. Decline in traditional industries has been offset by new activities like chemicals and services, and by the benefits of being part of the thriving New York conurbation.

Geography

Most of New Jersey is low-lying Atlantic coastal plain, but the Kittatinny Mountains, in the northwest, reach up to 1803 feet. The population is nearly 90% urban, with most living in the Newark–Jersey City conurbation adjoining New York City.

Government & Economy

In presidential politics, New Jersey is a bellwether state, tending to support the winner. In 1993, Republican Christine Todd Whitman became the state's first female governor; she survived a close race to be reelected in 1997. In 2000 she ran as a senate candidate, but pulled out and was later appointed Administrator of the Environmental Protection Agency by George W Bush. Republican Donald T DiFrancesco is now acting governor.

The busy Port of New York and New Jersey and the Delaware River Port are both major container ports. Heavy industry has declined in importance, but manufacturing still employs 17% of the workforce. Pharmaceuticals, petrochemicals, high-tech industry, tourism, trade and services constitute big employers. The state's per-capita income is among the country's highest.

Arts

Frank Sinatra was born in Hoboken, jazz great Count Basie hailed from Red Bank and singers Frankie Valli and Whitney Houston are from Newark. Bruce Springsteen will be forever associated with the Jersey Shore. Edison invented the motion-

picture camera in northern New Jersey, and one of the first films with a distinguishable narrative, *The Great Train Robbery*, was filmed here in 1903. The movie *On the Waterfront* is a memorable depiction of New Jersey's tougher side.

Information

The New Jersey Division of Travel & Tourism (☎ 609-292-2470, 800-537-7397, Ⓦ www.state.nj.us/travel) has a tough job but is a good source of information.

The State Park Service (☎ 800-843-6420) lists campgrounds. For fishing licenses, call the Fish, Game and Wildlife Commission (☎ 609-292-2965). The New Jersey Hotel & Motel Association (☎ 800-365-6965) runs a reservation service. For B&Bs, call the Bed & Breakfast Innkeepers Association of New Jersey (☎ 732-449-3535).

State sales tax is 6%, and local hotel occupancy tax can add another 6%.

Getting There & Around

Newark International Airport's proximity to Manhattan makes it a worthwhile option (see Getting There & Away in New York City, earlier). New Jersey Transit trains service western New Jersey suburbs and Hoboken. Trains from New York City's Penn Station service the Jersey Shore as far as Bay Head. For NJ Transit bus and train information, call ☎ 973-762-5100 or ☎ 800-772-2222.

Amtrak trains to Washington, DC, stop in Princeton Junction and Philadelphia.

NORTHERN NEW JERSEY

Northern New Jersey is packed with history and people. Along the Hudson River are Hoboken and Jersey City, old industrial towns that once had large ethnic populations. The state's northwest, known as the Skylands region, includes the Great Swamp National Wildlife Refuge and the Delaware Water Gap National Recreation Area, ideal for hiking, bird-watching and fishing.

Hoboken & Jersey City

Hoboken (population 33,400) is a longtime respectable community to which many younger people have moved in the last few years – it now has a reputation as a weekend party town. Directly across from New York City, Hoboken developed as a railroad terminal and seaport. The city has an important place in US popular culture: The first organized baseball game was probably played nearby in 1846, Frank Sinatra was born here and got his start in local clubs, and *On the Waterfront* was filmed here.

Schnackenberg's Luncheonette *(1110 Washington St)* dates from the 1940s and has old-fashioned prices. **Cafe Louis** *(505 Washington St)* was one of Hoboken's first gay-friendly establishments. The back room at **Maxwell's** *(1039 Washington St)* has featured up-and-coming rock bands since 1978 (Bruce Springsteen's 'Glory Days' video was filmed here). To get there from Manhattan, take the PATH train or a New York Waterway ferry (☎ 800-533-3779).

Jersey City (population 228,500) is worth visiting only to see the 1114-acre **Liberty State Park** (☎ 201-915-3403), which offers Manhattan views, walking trails, horseback riding and water activities, and is an alternative departure point for Statue of Liberty and Ellis Island Ferries ($7).

Newark

With its growing international airport and proximity to New York City, Newark (population 275,200) is the starting or finishing point for many visits, but there's no need to linger here. The city-hall information office (☎ 973-733-8165) is helpful. The **Newark Museum** (☎ 973-596-6550, 49 Washington St) has a renowned Tibetan Collection (free admission; open Wed-Sun). The **New Jersey Performing Arts Center** (☎ 973-642-0404) is home to the New Jersey Symphony – tickets start around $15.

In the Ironbound district surrounding Penn Station, try the Portuguese and Spanish eateries, like **Iberia** *(82–4 Ferry St)*. Lunch is a real bargain, with excellent specials for $6-10. Visit Newark via Amtrak, PATH train ($1) or NJ Transit, since most attractions are near Newark's Penn Station.

West Orange

Hell, there ain't no rules around here. We're trying to accomplish something.

– Thomas Edison

History students may want to take a guided tour of **Edison National Historic Site** (☎ 973-736-0550), on Lakeside Ave, where Thomas Alva Edison invented the phonograph, complete with wax recording cylinders. His company developed many more products in this custom-built laboratory, including the incandescent lamp, telephone transmitter, storage battery and motion picture. The site includes Glenmont, the Edisons' mansion. Take the NJ Turnpike to I-280 west (exit 15W), then exit 10 at West Orange.

Delaware Water Gap NRA

The Delaware River meanders through 40 miles of this national recreation area, carving the 1400-foot-deep Kittatinny Ridge chasm at the southern end. Activities include canoeing, swimming, rock climbing, horseback riding and hiking – the Appalachian Trail passes through the area. The park straddles the New Jersey–Pennsylvania border – from New Jersey, exit I-80 at the Kittatinny Point Visitor Center (☎ 973-496-4458).

CENTRAL NEW JERSEY
Princeton

This tony town and its Ivy League university have lovely architecture and noteworthy historic sites. Nassau and Witherspoon Sts are the main streets. The Historical Society of Princeton (☎ 609-921-6748, 158 Nassau St) has maps and brochures. Orange Key Guide Service & Campus Information Office (☎ 609-258-3603) arranges free university tours.

In 1756, Princeton became the home of the College of New Jersey – now Princeton University. The 1777 Battle of Princeton proved a decisive victory for General Washington's troops during the Revolutionary War – it's commemorated at Princeton Battlefield State Park. Einstein's old house (112 Mercer St) is closed to the public, but you can visit several historic houses in town. The McCormick Art Museum (☎ 609-452-3787) has a varied collection, from pre-Columbian art to Andy Warhol.

Accommodations are expensive and hard to find during graduation time in May and June. The most affordable motels are along Route 1 and include **Red Roof Inn** *(☎ 609-896-3388, 3203 Brunswick Pike),* at $70. Pricey but atmospheric, **Peacock Inn** *(☎ 609-924-1707, 20 Baynard Lane)* charges $145-165.

On Nassau St, *The Annex Restaurant & Bar* is a formal throwback serving pub grub, popular with the university crowd. Modern *Triumph Brewing Co* offers moderately priced food, fresh beer and brewery tours Saturday. For homemade soup in a sourdough bread bowl, go to *Panera Bread* ($5). Around the corner, *Lahiere's* (☎ 609-921-2798, 11 Witherspoon St) is the town's poshest place ($16-34).

Suburban Transit buses (☎ 800-222-0492) run from New York City ($9), and NJ Transit and Amtrak trains stop at Princeton Junction. Take the 'Dinky' line to campus.

Trenton

The state capital (population 85,403) offers colonial history and a few museums; attractions can be seen quickly. The visitor bureau (☎ 609-777-1770), at Lafayette and Barrack Sts, provides maps and brochures. The main sights are along State St. History buffs can visit the **Old Barracks Museum** (☎ 609-396-1776), built in 1758, the state's last remaining barracks from the French and Indian War ($6). In the Revolutionary War it housed British troops and Hessian mercenaries, attacked by George Washington's forces on Christmas night in 1776.

The **New Jersey State Museum** (☎ 609-292-6464, 205 W State St) is home to the first dinosaur found in North America (free admission). Washington Crossing Historic Park (☎ 609-737-0623), 8 miles north on Route 29, is great for picnicking and biking (see Around Philadelphia later). The closest motels are 15 minutes north off Route 1. *McIntosh Inn* (☎ 609-896-3700) is on Route 1 in Lawrenceville (about $90).

JERSEY SHORE

The shore stretches 127 miles from Sandy Hook to Cape May, with holiday towns from seedy to beautiful and architecture from tacky to spectacular. During summer weekends, some towns see up to 100,000 visitors; weekdays are almost as busy, and reservations are highly recommended. Many New Yorkers rent a house for the whole summer. In September crowds diminish, and lots of places close after Labor Day.

In the north, beaches are narrow, while farther south they are wider and whiter. Most towns make you buy a 'beach badge' ($3-5) to use the beach during the day in summer, and there are extensive regulations about where you can surf, when you can have a picnic, and what you can't do with your dog. Parking regulations are strictly enforced.

North Jersey Shore

NJ Transit trains service beaches from Long Branch to Bay Head, and NJ Transit buses ply points farther south to Cape May. A combination roundtrip train ticket to various shore points plus a one-day beach pass costs $15 from New York's Penn Station. Seastreak ferries (☎ 800-262-8743) go from Pier 11 and E 34th St in Manhattan to Highlands, near Sandy Hook, several times a day ($17 one way) – a good option for cyclists.

At the north tip of the Jersey Shore, **Sandy Hook National Recreation Area** (☎ 732-872-5970) is an appropriately sandy, 6-mile-long peninsula at the entrance to New York Harbor. Most of the area is undeveloped, and the ocean side of the peninsula has lovely beaches. At the northern end is the Coastguard station and Fort Hancock – an amazing, disused defense complex, with empty army buildings and huge gun emplacements. Its 'disappearing guns' and Nike missiles have never fired a shot in anger. The NRA visitor center, halfway up the peninsula, has an exhibit on the US Lifesaving Service. The area is open daily until dusk ($10 per car in summer). Camping is not permitted – the closest accommodations are farther south in Sea Bright, where *Fairbanks Motel & Marina* (☎ 732-842-8450, 344 Ocean Ave) has singles/doubles from $74/99 in summer.

Going south on Route 36, it's mile after mile of run-down coastal resorts interspersed with occasional, unattractive redevelopments. Once a dowdy middle-class resort, **Asbury Park** experienced passing prominence in the 1970s, when Bruce Springsteen 'arrived' at the Stone Pony nightclub. The *Stone Pony*, at 2nd and Ocean Aves, still has loud live music some weekends, but the area is depressingly skanky.

Farther south are some nicer communities like **Ocean Grove** (population 8000), founded by Methodists in the 19th century and keeping itself nice ever since. The town retains its Victorian architecture and a 6500-

seat wooden auditorium, which featured in Woody Allen's *Stardust Memories* and now hosts concerts and religious events. Ocean Grove's chamber of commerce (☎ 732-774-1391, 800-388-4768) has tourist information and lists accommodations. Most are B&Bs and small 'inns'; many are booked solid in summer and close in winter. Less pricey than most, *Ocean Park Inn* (☎ 732-988-5283, 38 Surf Ave) has singles/doubles from $45/65.

Not-so-straightlaced **Belmar** (population 7340) attracts a younger crowd, but it's not rowdy. The chamber of commerce (☎ 732-681-2900, 1005½ Main St) has event information. Eastern Lines Surf Shop (1603 Ocean Ave) rents bikes and surfboards. *Carol's Guest House* (☎ 732-681-4422, 201 11th Ave) is friendly, fun and inexpensive (from $30 per person). Facing the beach, *Mayfair Hotel* (☎ 732-681-2620, 1000 Ocean Ave) has a touch of class ($75 in summer, cheaper off-season and by the week). *Havens & Hampton* (☎ 732-681-1231, 618 5th Ave) serves up fresh seafood from $14.

The next town south is **Spring Lake**, a very classy community once called the 'Irish Riviera.' The lush gardens and Victorian houses are lovely to look at, but accommodations are limited and expensive. More popular with young visitors is nearby **Manasquan**, which can get good surf but is otherwise unappealing.

Across the inlet, the **Barnegat Peninsula** is a narrow barrier island/sand spit extending some 22 miles south from Point Pleasant. Half of it is densely developed with beach resorts. In the center of the peninsula, **Seaside Heights** sucks in the twentysomething summer crowds with beaches, boardwalks, bars and two amusement piers. It's very colorful and fun – call ☎ 732-793-1510 for information. On the boardwalk, *Sand & Surf Motel* (☎ 732-793-7311, 1201 Ocean Terrace) has a variety of room types (around $55 weekdays, $75 weekends in summer). A block inland, *Hershey Motel* (☎ 732-973-5000, 1415 Atlantic Blvd) looks classic 1960s; double rooms run $111 in summer, $40 in December. Atlantic Blvd is thick with eateries, bars and clubs from Sumner to Dupont Aves.

Occupying the southern third of Barnegat Peninsula is **Island Beach State Park** (☎ 732-793-0506), a flat 3000-acre stretch of dunes and wetlands. The attractions are unspoiled beaches, swimming, surf fishing and bird-watching. Entry is $7 per car ($4 off-season). Near the park entrance, *Island Beach Motor Lodge* (☎ 732-793-5400), at 24th and Central Aves, is a good place to stay (from $90 in summer, under $40 most of the year).

Connected by causeway to the mainland, **Long Beach Island** is a low-lying barrier island developed end to end with beach cottages and summer accommodations. The only reason to come is for ocean activities like sailing, fishing or scuba diving. A pleasant alternative to the overdeveloped and overpriced seashore are the quiet inland areas along Route 9, where *Sea Pirate Campground* (☎ 609-296-7400) and *Baker's Acres* (☎ 609-296-2664) have tent sites from around $25.

Atlantic City

When the railway arrived on Absecon Island in the 1850s, city dwellers came here for the wide white beach and the seaside atmosphere. The resort was a hot spot by 1900, where exclusive hotels and economical guesthouses catered to affluent summer residents and short-term visitors. In the 1920s it was a hotbed of vice, with smuggled liquor, speakeasies and illegal gambling. After WWII, faster transportation made other destinations more accessible, and Atlantic City went into steep decline. In 1977 the state approved casinos to revitalize the place, and the city has reemerged as a high-profile destination.

Now a dozen huge casinos dot the once-busy beachfront boardwalk, but behind them are vacant lots, derelict buildings and mean streets. Thousands of visitors bus in every day from New York, Philadelphia and Washington, DC, but most of them leave by nightfall and never set foot outside the casino that paid for their bus fare. The city's current strategy involves new convention centers, sports stadiums and an international airport – as well as more casinos.

If you come by car, you'll see the visitor center under the giant teepee in the middle of the Atlantic City Expressway. Call before you come to obtain the best deals on transportation and accommodation (☎ 609-449-7130, 888-228-4748).

As in Las Vegas, the casinos have themes, from Wild West to Mardi Gras, but they're very superficially done. Inside they're all the same, with clanging slot machines, flashing lights and chaotic colored carpets. Note that you must be 21 to be on the gambling floor. There's talk of more family-oriented entertainment, but it doesn't seem likely while day-trippers keep coming by the busload.

Built in 1870, the **Boardwalk** was the first in the world. Enjoy a walk and drop in on the informative Atlantic City Historical Museum (free admission), the Tivoli Pier family amusement center, and the Ripley's Believe It or Not Museum ($10). The Miss America Pageant – held every September in the city's Convention Hall – remains a very popular draw.

For lodging, contact the city's reservations service (☎ 800-447-6667) or Ameri-Room Reservations (☎ 800-888-5825). Room rates vary by season: $50 for a top hotel in winter, much more in summer, especially during Miss America week. If you plan to gamble and want a mid-range hotel, book a casino hotel package.

Some cheap motels off the Boardwalk are known for prostitution, but others are quite OK. *Burgundy Motor Inn (☎ 609-345-5665, 116 S North Carolina Ave)* looks dodgy from the front but has clean singles/doubles for as low as $40/45. Several chain motels are on side streets near the Boardwalk. The cheapest motels are in nearby Abescon (Garden State Pkwy exit 40).

Food bargains include the Boardwalk's sandwich and pizza shops and nearby pubs. Some casinos do all-you-can-eat buffets for lunch (about $8) or dinner (about $14) – try *Claridge's* or *Bally*. *Le Palais (☎ 609-340-6400)*, in Resorts Casino, serves the city's finest French cuisine in an elegant environment (about $50 per person).

The free weekly *Whoot* has local entertainment listings. Tickets for big-name performers at the casinos start at $20-40, but some of the smaller lounge shows are free. *Tropicana (☎ 609-340-4020)* has the Comedy Spot for a laugh. The *Irish Pub (☎ 609-344-9063, 164 S St James Place)* turns on Irish music as well as pub food and good Guinness.

Atlantic City 'International' Airport (☎ 800-645-7895) is a 20-minute drive away. Greyhound and NJ Transit buses run from New York ($20 roundtrip; 3 hours one way); Greyhound, Capitol Trailways and NJ Transit run from Philadelphia (about $14 roundtrip; 1½ hours one way). A casino will often refund the fare (in chips, coins or coupons) if you get a bus directly to its door, so inquire before you book. NJ Transit trains from Philadelphia cost $10/11.50 one-way/roundtrip. Casino parking garages cost about $2, but they waive the fee if you have a receipt showing you spent money inside.

Around Atlantic City

In Brigantine, the **Marine Mammal Center** (☎ 609-266-0538) rehabilitates stranded sea mammals and sea turtles (donation requested; open Sat-Sun, daily in summer). Twelve miles north on Route 9, the town of Historic Smithville dates from 1787. Cozy *Smithville Inn (☎ 609-652-7777)* was the town's first building and is now a restaurant. Other old buildings have been brought here and restored. The *Renault Winery (☎ 609-965-2111)*, off Route 30, is the country's oldest continuously operating winery.

Five miles south on Abescon Island, Lucy (☎ 609-823-6473), a six-story wooden elephant, stands tall in **Margate**. The elephant is open daily in the summer and weekends in spring and fall ($3). Margate has popular bars, gaudy motels and a great beach.

Pine Barrens

This million-acre pine forest is a haven for bird-watchers and wildlife enthusiasts. For camping and canoeing, call the information office (☎ 609-894-9342). *Wharton State Forest (☎ 609-561-3262)* rents cabins in the forest ($28/56 for four/eight people). Bring utensils, linen and food. **Batsto Village** (☎ 609-561-3262), a well-restored 19th-century settlement in Wharton, is open daily; take Route 542 off Route 9.

The Wildwoods

Just north of Cape May, the three towns of North Wildwood, Wildwood and Wildwood Crest are an archaeological find, with whitewashed motels and their flashing neon signs, turquoise curtains and pink doors. Wildwood Crest is an especially kitschy slice of 1950s Americana. Wildwood (population 4500) is the main focus, a party town popular with teens and young overseas visitors. The Wildwood tourist office (☎ 609-729-4000, W www.gwcoc.com) hands out

MID-ATLANTIC STATES

information on self-guided tours about the 'doo-wop' motels. The beach is free, and there are rides on the pier. About 250 motels offer rooms for $50-200, making it a good alternative if Cape May is booked.

Cape May

Founded in 1620, Cape May is on the state's southern end and is the country's oldest seashore resort. Its sweeping beaches get crowded in summer, but the stunning Victorian architecture is attractive year round. In addition to 600 gingerbread-style houses, the city boasts a 157-foot lighthouse, the Cape May County Park & Zoo, antique shops, whale-watching and bird-watching. It's also the only place in the state where the sun rises and sets over the water. It can be expensive, and accommodations reservations are recommended.

The downtown welcome center (☎ 609-884-9562) provides maps and information. Pick up *This Week*, which lists town activities. Cape May Beach costs $4/8/11 for a day/three-day/week pass. On Washington St are the renovated Italian-style villa, Southern Mansion, and the Victorian, 18-room Emlen Physick House & Estate ($8). The latter houses the Mid-Atlantic Center for the Arts (☎ 609-884-5404), which runs architectural and sightseeing tours. The New Jersey Audubon Society's **Cape May Bird Observatory** (☎ 609-884-2736) is open daily in the summer, as is the **Cape May Lighthouse** (☎ 609-884-5404), built in 1859 ($4). Cape May Whale Watcher (☎ 609-884-5445) 'guarantees' sighting a marine mammal on its ocean tour ($17-26). Farias, on Beach Ave, rents bodyboards/surfboards ($6/20 a day).

NJ Transit buses come from New York City and Philadelphia. The daily ferries between Cape May and Lewes, Delaware, cost $20 for cars plus $6.50 each for drivers and passengers ($2 less Nov-Apr). Make reservations in summer (☎ 800-643-3779).

Cape May's B&Bs are pricey, and many places have a two- to three-night minimum stay summer weekends. The best budget options ($35-45) remain *Hotel Clinton* (☎ 609-884-3993, 516-799-8889 off-season, 202 Perry St) and *Parris Inn* (☎ 609-884-8015, 204 Perry St). The basic *Cape Winds Motel* (☎ 609-884-4884, 810 Lafayette St) charges $100, $15 extra on weekends. Opulent *Mainstay Inn* (☎ 609-884-8690, 635

Columbia St) charges $200-300; their $3 self-guided tours may suit your budget better.

Akroteria is a collection of fast-food shacks on Beach Dr. *Sunset Beach Grill* is great for a sandwich and ocean view. For nightlife, *Cabanas*, on Beach Ave, offers an upscale menu upstairs and a pub menu downstairs; it also has nightly live music during summer. Locals head to *The Ugly Mug* for pub grub and spirits.

Pennsylvania

Though often bypassed between New York and Washington, Pennsylvania is worth a stop for Philadelphia's historical attractions, the quaint Pennsylvania Dutch communities and Gettysburg, the Civil War battlefield. Those heading west should allow time to visit Pittsburgh and to appreciate the glorious, four-seasons scenery of Western Pennsylvania – the Allegheny Forest and the Laurel Highlands are just gorgeous.

History

In 1681, King Charles II gave William Penn a charter for land west of the Delaware River. Penn, a Quaker, founded his colony as a 'holy experiment' that respected religious freedom and liberal government. William Penn also showed some respect for indigenous people and purchased land, rather than seizing it. Ultimately,

---

Pennsylvania

Nicknames: Keystone State, Quaker State

Population: 12,300,000 (5th)

Area: 46,058 sq miles (33rd)

Admitted to Union: December 12, 1787 (2nd)

Capital city: Harrisburg (population 53,500)

Other cities: Philadelphia (1,586,600), Pittsburgh (369,900), Erie (108,700)

Birthplace of: the US Constitution (b 1787), writer Louisa May Alcott (1832–88), comedian WC Fields (1880–1946), Andy Warhol (1928–87), actress Grace Kelly (1929–82), Bill Cosby (b 1937)

European settlers displaced these indigenous communities.

The 1701 Charter of Privilege was the colony's constitution, giving its elected assembly more power than any equivalent British body. Pennsylvania became the richest and most populous British colony in North America and played a major role in the independence movement. The First and Second Continental Congresses met in Philadelphia, and colonists adopted the Declaration of Independence in its State House in July 1776.

Philadelphia became the new nation's capital. But in one of the Revolutionary War's first battles, British troops defeated Washington's forces at Brandywine Creek. In September 1777 they occupied Philadelphia, forcing Washington to withdraw to Valley Forge. After the war, state representatives met again in Philadelphia for the 1787 federal constitutional convention. Pennsylvania accepted the new national constitution and adopted a new state constitution in 1790.

Development of canals, turnpikes and, later, railroads enabled the residents to relocate to the west and north. Pennsylvania became the country's main supplier of coal, iron and timber, while Philadelphia and Pittsburgh became important industrial centers. Slavery was not deeply entrenched in Pennsylvania because of Quaker opposition. Border towns close to Maryland became havens on the Underground Railroad, which helped slaves escape from the South. About 350,000 Pennsylvanians, including 8600 blacks, served in the Union army during the Civil War, and the state's industries were vital to the North's war effort. Southern forces attacked along Pennsylvania's Cumberland Valley. In July 1863, the North halted the biggest invasion at the bloody three-day battle of Gettysburg.

After the Civil War, Pennsylvania's political influence waned, but its industrial importance expanded. European immigration provided factory fodder for the booming industries, and Pennsylvania saw the emergence of national labor unions. During WWI and WWII, Pennsylvania supplied massive raw material and labor. In the postwar period its industrial importance gradually declined. Urban renewal programs and the growth of service and high-tech industries have boosted the economy, most notably in Philadelphia and Pittsburgh.

Geography

The Appalachian Plateau (or Allegheny Plateau) occupies most of western and northern Pennsylvania. A series of ridges and valleys curves northeast through the state's central part. Fertile lowlands cover the southeastern segment, with the Atlantic Coastal Plain extending into New Jersey and Delaware. Most people live around Philadelphia in the southeast and around Pittsburgh in the southwest. Once severely polluted, Pennsylvania's environment has improved with state and federal legislation and the decline of old industries.

Government & Economy

Opposition to slavery turned many Pennsylvanians to the Republican Party, which dominated state politics into the 1930s. With urbanization and the growth of organized labor, Philadelphia and Pittsburgh became Democratic strongholds. The state legislature is generally split evenly between the two parties. The current governor, Tom Ridge, is a moderate Republican.

Coal is still mined, along with oil, natural gas, building stone, clay and sand. Manufacturing is important, as are forest products. Some 30% of the state is productive farmland, used mostly for poultry and dairy farming. Other crops include hay, corn, mushrooms, fruits and Christmas trees.

Arts

Philadelphia is important in the early history of American painting. Benjamin West (1738–1820) and Charles Willson Peale (1741–1827) both produced portraits and scenes of early American life. Thomas Eakins (1844–1916) specialized in water scenes around Philadelphia and contemporary portraits. Some Pennsylvanian artists achieved fame outside their home state, including impressionist Mary Cassatt (1845–1926), who lived in Europe, and Andy Warhol (1928–87), who lived in New York (the Warhol museum is in Pittsburgh). In their self-imposed isolation from mainstream America, the Amish produce crafts of striking simplicity and quilts of transcendental beauty.

Religion

Quakers founded Pennsylvania on the principle of religious tolerance, and that tolerance attracted other minority religious sects. Many Quakers still live here, along with the well-known communities of Mennonites and Amish in the Pennsylvania Dutch Country.

Information

The state information office (☎ 717-787-5453, 800-847-4872, W www.state.pa.us/visit, 453 Forum Building, Harrisburg, PA 17120) oversees the state's tourist offices. The Welcome Centers on state highways provide information.

Contact the Private Campground Owners Association (PCOA, ☎ 610-767-5026, W www.pacamping.com) for a list of campgrounds. Hotels are expensive in the main cities – look for hostels. The Pennsylvania Travel Council (☎ 717-232-8880, W www.patravel.org) publishes an annual B&B directory.

State sales tax is 6% (clothing is exempt). Accommodations taxes are 9% in Pittsburgh and 12% in Philadelphia. Packaged liquor is sold only in state-government-run liquor stores, called Wine & Spirits Shoppes.

Activities

Pennsylvania has 114 state parks, which offer hiking, bicycling, swimming, boating, fishing, white-water rafting, and downhill and cross-country skiing. Contact the Bureau of State Parks (☎ 888-727-2757, W www.dcnr.state.pa.us) in Harrisburg. The Bureau of Forestry (☎ 717-783-7941), in Harrisburg, has information about activities in the state forests. For fishing licenses, call the Pennsylvania Fish and Boat Commission (☎ 717-657-4518).

PHILADELPHIA

Famous for historic sites such as the Liberty Bell and Independence Hall (as well as for cheesesteaks and hoagies), Philly also has world-class museums and performing-arts centers, as well as terrific restaurants.

William Penn made Philadelphia his capital in 1682, basing its plan on a grid with wide streets and public squares – a layout copied by many US cities. For a time the second-largest city in the British Empire (after London), Philadelphia became a center for opposition to British colonial policy. It was the new nation's capital at the start of the Revolutionary War and again after the war until 1790, when Washington, DC, took over. By the 1800s, New York had superseded Philadelphia as the nation's cultural, commercial and industrial center. Philly never regained its early preeminent status. In the 1970s, the nation's bicentennial prompted an urban renewal program that still continues.

Orientation

Philadelphia is easy to get around. Most sights and accommodations are within walking distance of each other, or a short bus ride away. East-west streets are named; north-south streets are numbered, except Broad and Front Sts.

Historic Philadelphia includes Independence National Historic Park and Old City, which extends east to the waterfront. West of the historic district is Center City, home to Penn Square and City Hall. The Delaware and Schuylkill Rivers border South Philadelphia, which features the colorful Italian Market, restaurants and bars. West of the Schuylkill, University City has two important campuses and a major museum. Northwest Philadelphia includes Chestnut Hill, Manayunk, and Germantown – all genteel suburbs. The South St area, between S 2nd, 10th, Pine and Fitzwater Sts, has bohemian boutiques, bars, eateries, and music venues.

Information

The main visitor center (☎ 215-636-1666, W www.gophila.com), in JFK Plaza, distributes the useful 'Philadelphia Official Visitors Guide' and a map of downtown.

The main post office (2970 Market St), in University City, is open 24 hours daily. The branch in the federal building (900 Market St), at 9th St, is more central. The Free Library of Philadelphia (☎ 215-686-5322), at Logan Circle, has free Internet access.

Pennsylvania Hospital (☎ 215-829-3000, 800 Spruce St) at S 8th St, was founded by Ben Franklin and was the country's first hospital.

Downtown, the Walnut and S 13th Sts area can be sleazy at night, particularly on weekends. Avoid West Philadelphia, west of University City, and North Philadelphia.

PHILADELPHIA

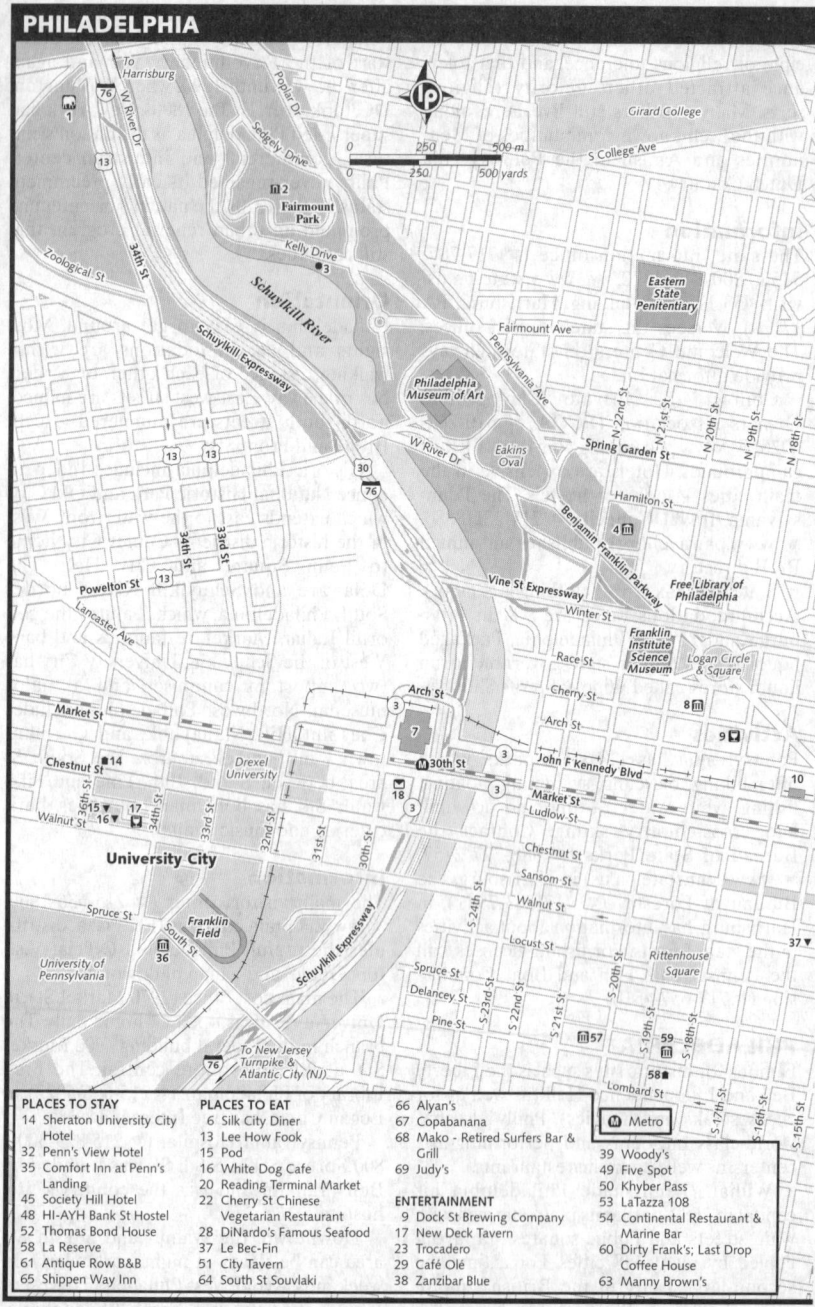

PLACES TO STAY
14 Sheraton University City Hotel
32 Penn's View Hotel
35 Comfort Inn at Penn's Landing
45 Society Hill Hotel
48 HI-AYH Bank St Hostel
52 Thomas Bond House
58 La Reserve
61 Antique Row B&B
65 Shippen Way Inn

PLACES TO EAT
6 Silk City Diner
13 Lee How Fook
15 Pod
16 White Dog Cafe
20 Reading Terminal Market
22 Cherry St Chinese Vegetarian Restaurant
28 DiNardo's Famous Seafood
37 Le Bec-Fin
51 City Tavern
64 South St Souvlaki

66 Alyan's
67 Copabanana
68 Mako - Retired Surfers Bar & Grill
69 Judy's

ENTERTAINMENT
9 Dock St Brewing Company
17 New Deck Tavern
23 Trocadero
29 Café Olé
38 Zanzibar Blue

Ⓜ Metro

39 Woody's
49 Five Spot
50 Khyber Pass
53 LaTazza 108
54 Continental Restaurant & Marine Bar
60 Dirty Frank's; Last Drop Coffee House
63 Manny Brown's

PHILADELPHIA

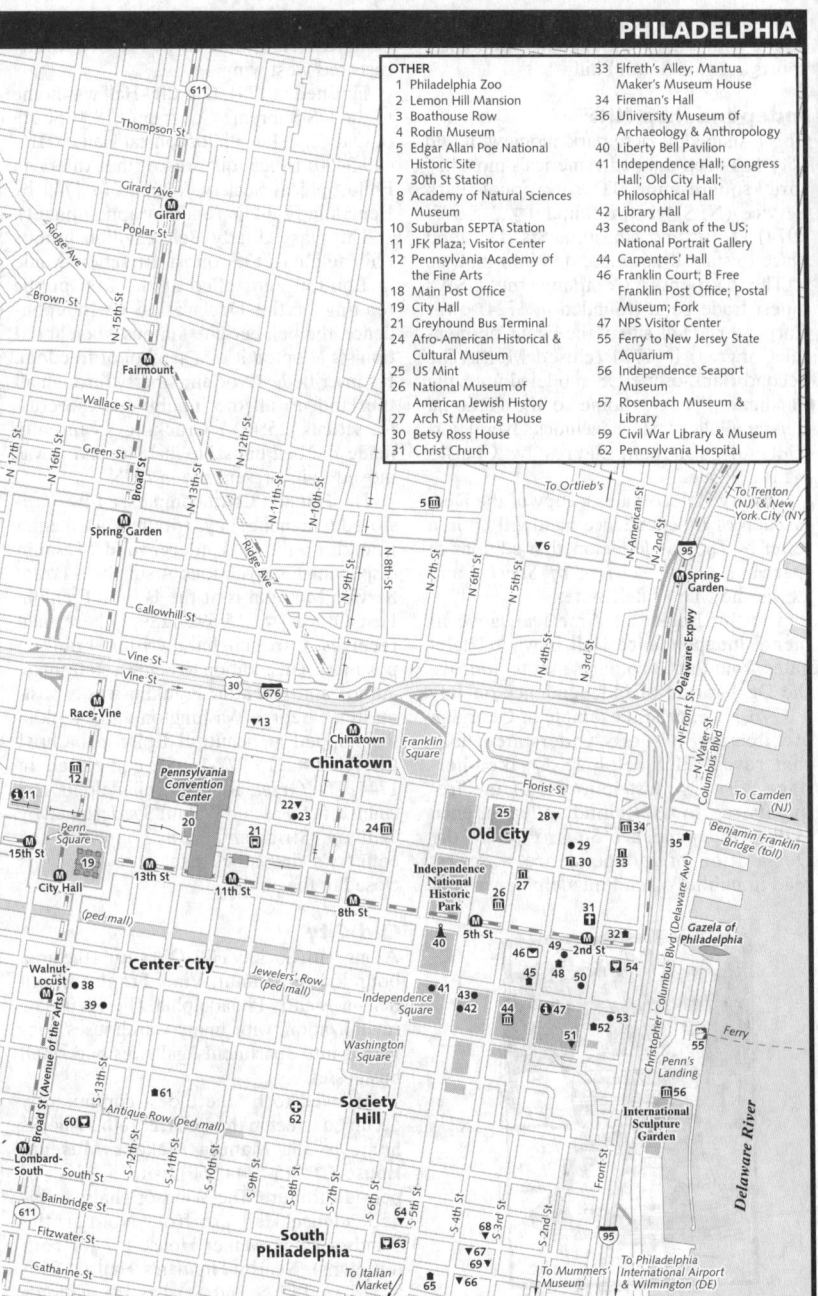

OTHER
1 Philadelphia Zoo
2 Lemon Hill Mansion
3 Boathouse Row
4 Rodin Museum
5 Edgar Allan Poe National Historic Site
7 30th St Station
8 Academy of Natural Sciences Museum
10 Suburban SEPTA Station
11 JFK Plaza; Visitor Center
12 Pennsylvania Academy of the Fine Arts
18 Main Post Office
19 City Hall
21 Greyhound Bus Terminal
24 Afro-American Historical & Cultural Museum
25 US Mint
26 National Museum of American Jewish History
27 Arch St Meeting House
30 Betsy Ross House
31 Christ Church
33 Elfreth's Alley; Mantua Maker's Museum House
34 Fireman's Hall
36 University Museum of Archaeology & Anthropology
40 Liberty Bell Pavilion
41 Independence Hall; Congress Hall; Old City Hall; Philosophical Hall
42 Library Hall
43 Second Bank of the US; National Portrait Gallery
44 Carpenters' Hall
46 Franklin Court; B Free Franklin Post Office; Postal Museum; Fork
47 NPS Visitor Center
55 Ferry to New Jersey State Aquarium
56 Independence Seaport Museum
57 Rosenbach Museum & Library
59 Civil War Library & Museum
62 Pennsylvania Hospital

Also avoid the subway at night, unless you're with a few thousand fans attending a sports event in South Philly.

Independence NHP

This L-shaped 45-acre park, along with Old City, has been dubbed 'America's most historic square mile.' The National Park Service (NPS) visitor center (☎ 215-597-8974) at 3rd and Chestnut Sts is a good place to start; it has maps and information.

The Carpenter Company, the USA's oldest trade guild (founded in 1724) owns Carpenters' Hall, site of the First Continental Congress in 1774 (closed Mon). The Second Bank of the US, modeled after the Parthenon, is now home to the National Portrait Gallery, which includes several portraits of prominent figures by Charles Willson Peale.

Library Hall contains a copy of the Declaration of Independence handwritten in a letter by Thomas Jefferson, first editions of Darwin's *On the Origin of Species* and Lewis and Clark's field notes.

The 'birthplace of American government,' **Independence Hall** is where delegates from the 13 colonies met to approve the Declaration of Independence on July 4, 1776. An excellent example of Georgian architecture, it sports understated lines that reveal Philadelphia's Quaker heritage. Visitors must join one of the frequent free tours. Behind Independence Hall is Independence Square, where the Declaration of Independence was first read in public. When Philadelphia was the nation's capital, the US Congress met in Congress Hall, housed in the beautifully restored west wing.

Finished in 1791, **Old City Hall** was home to the US Supreme Court until 1800. South of Old City Hall, **Philosophical Hall** (☎ 215-440-3400) is headquarters of the American Philosophical Society, founded in 1743 by Benjamin Franklin (open by appointment).

The glass **Liberty Bell Pavilion** houses Philadelphia's top tourist attraction. Made in London and tolled at the first public reading of the Declaration of Independence, the bell became famous when abolitionists adopted it as a symbol of freedom. It's inscribed, '"Proclaim liberty through all the land, to all the inhabitants thereof." (Leviticus 25:10).' Cracking eventually made the bell unusable in 1846, and it was moved to its present site in 1976.

The **Franklin Court** complex, a row of restored tenements, pays tribute to Benjamin Franklin with an Underground Museum displaying his inventions. A small US Postal Service Museum is at the B Free Franklin Post Office (☎ 215-592-1289), where mail receives a special handwritten Franklin postmark. (In addition to being a statesman, author and inventor, Franklin was a postmaster.) George Washington and Franklin worshipped at beautiful Episcopal **Christ Church** (☎ 215-922-1695), completed in 1744. The Greek Revival Philadelphia Exchange, at S 3rd and Walnut Sts, designed by William Strickland and home of the country's first stock exchange (1834), is closed to the public.

Old City

Along with Society Hill, Old City – the area bounded by Walnut, Vine, Front and 6th Sts – *was* early Philadelphia. The 1970s saw revitalization, with many warehouses converted into apartments, galleries and small businesses.

Believed to be the oldest continuously occupied street in the USA, **Elfreth's Alley** is home to the **Mantua Maker's Museum House** (☎ 215-574-0560), with displays of period furniture. The Windsor chairs in Independence Hall are from No 124, the Windsor Chair Maker House ($2 for both museums). Nearby **Fireman's Hall** (☎ 215-923-1438, 147 N 2nd St) has the nation's oldest fire engine and an exhibit on the rise

Liberty Bell

Benjamin Franklin

This colonial Renaissance man with the bald spot and long, flowing hair is best known for flying his kite during a storm, but he left an unequaled legacy of other inventions, ideas and achievements.

After serving as an apprentice in his brother's print shop, Franklin (1707–90) started the *Pennsylvania Gazette,* which became the colonies' top newspaper. He pushed for cleaner city streets in Philadelphia, started the country's first circulating library, and founded the American Philosophical Society and the University of Pennsylvania. After representing the colonies in Britain, Franklin came to resent the corruption in colonial administrations. Upon his return to America in 1775, he broke with London, opposed British taxes and openly supported independence.

Franklin eventually helped write the Declaration of Independence with Thomas Jefferson, and his intellect and noted oratory helped secure France's support for the Revolutionary War. After his return from France in 1784, he worked on the final version of the US Constitution, of which he was a signatory. Franklin's final public act was a petition to congress calling for an end to slavery. In addition to contributing to the country's political birth, Franklin also helped start the post office and the country's first hospital and fire company, as well as a local militia.

of organized volunteers led by Ben Franklin (donation requested; open Tue-Sat). Betsy Griscom Ross (1752–1836), upholsterer and seamstress, may have sewn the first US flag in the **Betsy Ross House** (☎ 215-686-1252, 239 Arch St). A donation is requested (closed Mon).

The **National Museum of American Jewish History** (☎ 215-923-3811, 55 N 5th St) examines the historical role of Jews in the USA ($4). At the **US Mint** (☎ 215-408-0114), on Arch St between 6th and 7th Sts, watch coins being made and learn about counterfeits (free admission; closed Sat-Sun Sept-May). **Arch St Meeting House** (320 Arch St) is the USA's largest Quaker meeting house (donation requested; closed Sun). The **Afro-American Historical & Cultural Museum** (☎ 215-574-0380, 701 Arch St) has excellent collections on black history and culture ($6).

Waterfront

The 1.8-mile Benjamin Franklin Bridge, the world's largest suspension bridge when completed in 1926, spans the Delaware River. Its lights dominate the night skyline.

The Penn's Landing riverfront area, between Vine and South Sts, contains the **Independence Seaport Museum** (☎ 215-925-5439, 211 S Columbia Blvd), with displays that highlight Philadelphia's role as an immigration hub and its shipyard, which closed in 1995 after 200 years ($8). The huge **New Jersey State Aquarium** (☎ 800-616-

5297) is in nearby Camden, New Jersey ($13). RiverLink Ferry (☎ 215-925-5465) runs hourly from Penn's Landing ($5 roundtrip).

Society Hill & South Philadelphia

Eighteenth- and 19th-century architecture dominates the lovely residential neighborhood of Society Hill. An interesting mix of colonial and contemporary homes can be seen upon Delancey, American, Cypress and Philip Sts. **Washington Square**, from William Penn's original city plan, offers a peaceful respite from sightseeing.

Succeeding waves of immigrants settled in South Philadelphia, and its museums and restaurants reflect this diversity. One highlight is the **Italian Market**, the country's largest outdoor market (open Tue-Sat). The **Mummers' Museum** (☎ 215-336-3050, 1100 S 2nd St) celebrates the tradition of disguise and masquerade ($2.50; open Tue-Sun Sept-June, Tue-Sat other months). The famed Mummers parade takes place here every New Year's Day.

Center City & Around

The best known of William Penn's city squares is **Rittenhouse Square**, with its wading pool, trees and fine statues. In nearby Penn Square, **City Hall** (☎ 215-686-1776), at Broad and Market Sts, was completed in 1901. It's probably Philadelphia's architectural highlight, at 548 feet high and topped by a bronze statue of William Penn (tours 12:30pm-2pm; donations requested).

The prestigious **Pennsylvania Academy of the Fine Arts** (☎ 215-972-7600, 118 N Broad St) has a museum with works by American painters, including Charles Willson Peale and Thomas Eakins ($5; closed Mon). Highly recommended for Civil War buffs, the comprehensive **Civil War Library & Museum** (☎ 215-735-8196, 1805 Pine St) boasts artifacts and exhibitions ($5; open Thurs-Sat). **Rosenbach Museum & Library** (☎ 215-732-1600, 2010 Delancey St) has rare books and manuscripts, including James Joyce's *Ulysses* manuscript and pages from Bram Stoker's *Dracula* ($5; closed Mon).

At the slightly spooky **Edgar Allan Poe National Historic Site** (☎ 215-597-8780, 532 N 7th St), Poe wrote 'The Black Cat' (free admission; open daily June-Oct, Wed-Sun Nov-May).

Benjamin Franklin Parkway

Modeled after the Champs-Elysées in Paris, the parkway is a center of museums and other landmarks. There's a terrific dinosaur exhibition at the **Academy of Natural Sciences Museum** (☎ 215-299-1000, 1900 Benjamin Franklin Pkwy) where you can dig for fossils on weekends ($9).

The exciting **Franklin Institute Science Museum** (☎ 215-448-1200), at 20th St, pioneered hands-on science displays and also has exhibits on Ben Franklin. Downstairs in Fels Planetarium, laser shows feature rock music, including Pink Floyd. The Mandell Futures Center highlights computers, health issues and environmental problems (tickets $10-15). The extensive collection at the **Rodin Museum** (☎ 215-763-8100), at Benjamin Franklin Pkwy and 22nd St, includes Rodin's great works *The Thinker* and *The Burghers of Calais* ($3 donation; closed Mon).

A few blocks north of the parkway, the old **Eastern State Penitentiary** (☎ 215-236-3300), on the block of 22nd St and Fairmount Ave features Al Capone's cell and death row ($7). It opened in 1829 and was so effective that 300 other prisons were modeled after it.

University City

Commonly called 'Penn,' the **University of Pennsylvania** was founded in 1740 and is an Ivy League school. With nearby Drexel University, the area has 30,000 students. Definitely worth a look is the neoclassical 30th St Station, beautifully lit at night and a romantic spot. Penn's magical **University Museum of Archaeology & Anthropology** (☎ 215-898-4000), at 33rd and Spruce Sts, contains archaeological treasures from ancient Egypt, Mesopotamia, the Mayan peninsula, Greece, Rome and North America. Its fragments of Sumerian script are among the oldest examples of writing ever found ($5; open Tue-Sat).

Fairmount Park

The **Schuylkill River** (**skoo**-kill) divides this expansive park into east and west. On the east bank is **Boathouse Row**, Victorian-era rowing-club buildings that are illuminated at night.

The **Philadelphia Museum of Art** (☎ 215-763-8100), at the end of Benjamin Franklin Pkwy, has superb European and Asian art, but may be better known for its steps, which featured in the movie *Rocky*. Highlights include the 19th-century European & Impressionist Galleries, featuring Renoir, Manet and van Gogh, the 1832 Diana statue by Augustus St Gaudens, and complete Hindu and Japanese Buddhist temples. The building itself is modeled on Greek temples ($8, free Sun morning; closed Mon).

The **Philadelphia Zoo** (☎ 215-243-1100, 3400 W Girard Ave), the country's oldest, has been modernized with naturalistic habitats ($11/8 adults/kids). In Fairmount Park, early American houses open to the public include **Lemon Hill Mansion** (☎ 215-232-4337), 'the most elegant seat in Pennsylvania'; **Mount Pleasant** (☎ 215-763-8100); **Woodford** (☎ 215-229-6115), a Georgian mansion; **Laurel Hill** (☎ 215-235-1776); and the largest, **Strawberry Mansion** (☎ 215-228-8364), offering an antique-toy exhibit. Most are open Tuesday to Sunday ($2.50).

Beyond Fairmount Park, 6 miles northwest of downtown, the **Barnes Foundation Gallery** (☎ 610-667-0290, 300 N Lodges Lane) houses an exceptionally fine collection of impressionist, postimpressionist and early French modern paintings, including works by Cézanne, Degas, Matisse, Monet, Picasso, Renoir and van Gogh ($5). The grounds are an arboretum. Take Septa's R5 train to Merion or bus No 44 from downtown.

Organized Tours

You can explore downtown on foot, and Independence National Historical Park (see earlier) offers free maps. Centipede Tours (☎ 215-735-3123) has summer walking tours ($5) of Society Hill on Friday and Saturday evening with guides in period costume. Contact the Preservation Alliance for Greater Philadelphia (☎ 215-546-1146) for architectural tours ($15; not available summer months).

Both American Trolley Tours (☎ 215-333-2119) and Philadelphia Trolley Works & 76 Co (☎ 215-925-8687) offer guided 'trolley' tours of the historic, business and cultural districts. Passengers can get off at any designated stop to sightsee and reboard another trolley at their convenience. American's tour ($14) lasts 1½ hours, as does Philadelphia's ($18), which also goes to Fairmount Park.

Places to Stay

Avoid graduation week (late May), when the city is crowded. Downtown hotels are expensive, but some do offer discounted weekend packages (ask about parking). Some hotels advertise 'cheap accommodations and friendly service' at the Greyhound station and around town – these cannot be recommended.

The closest campground is *Timberlane Campground* (☎ 856-423-6677, 117 Timber Lane), 15 miles southwest across the Delaware River in Clarksboro, New Jersey (tent sites $24, cabins $46). *West Chester KOA* (☎ 610-486-0447, Route 162) is 3 miles north of Unionville on Route 162 beside the Brandywine River ($25-27; closed in winter).

The excellent *HI-AYH Bank St Hostel* (☎ 215-922-0222, 32 S Bank St) is in a safe neighborhood, a short walk from 2nd St Station and major sights ($18/21 members/nonmembers) and has Internet access for $8 an hour. *HI-AYH Chamounix Mansion Hostel* (☎ 215-878-3676), on Chamounix Dr in West Fairmount Park, is a 19th-century mansion away from downtown ($13/16; closed Dec 15-Jan 15).

On the waterfront, *Comfort Inn at Penn's Landing* (☎ 215-627-7900, 100 N Columbus Blvd) has rooms starting at $99. *Penn's View Hotel* (☎ 215-922-7600), at Front and Market Sts, also overlooks the water (standard rooms $165). Friendly *Society Hill Hotel* (☎ 215-925-1919, 301 Chestnut St) has a European atmosphere, is in a central location near Independence Park and offers small but quaint rooms ($85-150). *Sheraton University City Hotel* (☎ 215-387-8000), at S 36th and Chestnut Sts, is near the universities ($149-169).

The city has some great B&Bs, but book ahead, especially for weekends and during graduation week in late May. The B&B Reservation Line (☎ 800-448-3619) is open weekdays.

Try *Antique Row B&B* (☎ 215-592-7802, 341 S 12th St) or *La Reserve* (☎ 215-735-1137, 1804 Pine St). Both charge $65-110. If they're full, the owners will suggest alternatives. Friendly *Shippen Way Inn* (☎ 215-627-7266, 416–418 Bainbridge St) is a B&B in a lovely 1750s building with afternoon wine and tea and rooms (with bath) for $80. The beautifully restored *Thomas Bond House* (☎ 215-923-8523, 129 S 2nd St) is on the National Register of Historic Places ($95-175).

Places to Eat

At the budget end, you'll find great pretzels, hoagies and groceries at the lively indoor *Reading Terminal Market*. Chinatown, especially near the corner of Race and N 10th Sts, has many options – try *Lee How Fook* or *Cherry St Chinese Vegetarian Restaurant*.

The *Silk City Diner* (☎ 215-592-8838, 425 Spring Garden St), at N 5th St, is a 1940s classic open 24 hours, with entertainment some nights. *DiNardo's Famous Seafood* (312 Race St) offers main courses from $10 and its specialty, Baltimore-style steamed crabs ($20). In 1774, Paul Revere arrived at *City Tavern* (☎ 215-413-1443), at S 2nd and Walnut Sts, with news that the British had

Philly Cheesesteak

A stack of tender, juicy, thinly sliced beef, topped with lashings of freshly fried onion rings, covered with gorgeous, gooey melted cheese, served in a soft, warm, white bread roll – that's the city's namesake taste sensation. Among Philadelphia's contributions to American civilization, it ranks right up there with the Declaration of Independence.

closed Boston Harbor. Try the mushroom bisque or turkey pie (dinner entrées $20-30; reservations recommended). The east end of Market St has many trendy places with summer sidewalk dining.

Mako – Retired Surfer's Bar & Grill (301 South St) has great decor and unmissable mussels. *Copabanana (344 South St)* serves dangerously delicious margaritas and gourmet burgers. For terrific, inexpensive Greek food, head to *South St Souvlaki (509 South St)*. *Alyan's (603 S 4th St)* serves Middle Eastern dishes. *Judy's*, at S 3rd and Bainbridge Sts, is an institution for brunch or dinner.

On the high end, many gourmets rate *Le Bec-Fin (☎ 215-567-1000, 1523 Walnut St)* as the country's best restaurant for its setting, service and superb French food. It's expensive, of course, but the fixed-price lunch ($38) or dinner ($120) are comparative bargains.

In south Philadelphia, the Italian Market is the best option. Two of Philadelphia's most popular cheesesteak places, *Geno's* and *Pat's King of Steaks*, are both at S 9th St and Passyunk Ave and are open 24 hours. *Dmitri's (795 S 3rd St)* has Greek- and Middle Eastern–style dishes. A South Philly classic, *Victor Cafe (☎ 215-468-3040, 1303 Victor St)* is renowned for its Italian cuisine and opera-singing staff ($13-21).

Food carts lining University City streets are bargains, and the food court on the Market St side of 30th St Station offers good choices. The cluster of diverse restaurants on Sansom St is worth the journey. The socially active *White Dog Cafe (3420 Sansom St)* stages political lectures and seminars with eclectic American cuisine. *Pod (3636 Sansom St)* serves psychedelic sushi in a retro-futuristic setting ($6-30).

Entertainment

Philadelphia has something for everyone: a rich theater scene, the acclaimed *Pennsylvania Ballet (☎ 215-551-7000)*, the *Opera Company of Philadelphia (☎ 215-928-2100)*, and the renowned *Philadelphia Orchestra (☎ 215-893-1999)*. The latter holds summer concerts at Mann Center in Fairmount Park; prices range $23-58, $5-8 for lawn seats. The premier cultural destination is Broad St south of City Hall, called the 'Avenue of the Arts.'

Jazz, blues and music clubs abound. Try upmarket *Zanzibar Blue (200 S Broad St)* or casual *Ortlieb's (847 N 3rd St)* for jazz. Listen to live tunes at *Khyber Pass (56 S 2nd St)*, *Trocadero (1003 Arch St)* and *LaTazza 108 (108 Chestnut St)* – cover charges vary. *Woody's (202 S 13th St)* is a popular gay bar and club. The waterfront north of Benjamin Franklin Bridge is the summer nightlife center. A water taxi between clubs is safer than negotiating Christopher Columbus Blvd on foot.

For weekend events, check Friday's *Philadelphia Inquirer* or the weekly *City Paper* and *Philadelphia Weekly*. Tower Records, on South St, has music and dance club information. Ticketmaster (☎ 215-336-2000) sells tickets for most entertainment, as does Upstages (☎ 215-569-9700), which offers half-price same-day tickets.

Most bars stay open until 2am. *Five Spot*, on Bank St near the youth hostel, is a fun dance club. For the lounge life, try *Continental Restaurant & Martini Bar (138 Market St)*. On Antique Row at Pine and S 13th Sts, *Dirty Frank's* is a dive that's a local institution, with cheap booze and artsy patrons. In University City, students enjoy a choice of 18 draft beers at *New Deck Tavern (3408 Sansom St)*. More draft lines flow at *Dock St Brewing Company (2 Logan Square)*. South St also has a good selection, including *Manny Brown's (512 South St)*. Take Septa bus No 61 from the city center to Manayunk's cute, trendy Main St.

For mellowing out, the new *Café Olé (147 N 3rd St)* has a funky vibe and potent java. *Last Drop Coffee House*, at Pine and S 13th Sts, receive thumbs-up reviews. In South Philadelphia, *Anthony's Italian Coffee House (903 S 9th St)* serves good cakes and coffee.

Spectator Sports

Philadelphia's two major sporting venues are in South Philadelphia on S Broad St. The major-league Philadelphia Phillies baseball team (☎ 215-463-1000) and NFL Philadelphia Eagles football team (☎ 215-463-5500) both call Veterans Stadium home. At the indoor CoreStates Complex (☎ 215-336-3600), you can usually get game-day tickets ($12-68) for the NBA Philadelphia 76ers basketball games and NHL Philadelphia Flyers hockey games; or call Ticketmaster (☎ 215-336-2000).

Getting There & Around

Air Philadelphia International Airport (☎ 215-937-6937) has direct flights from Europe, the Caribbean, Canada and more than 100 US cities. The Septa (☎ 215-580-7800) R1 airport rail line ($5.50) and door-to-door shuttle-bus services ($8-10) run there. One-way cab fare to Center City is about $20.

Bus The Greyhound bus terminal (☎ 215-931-4014) is at 1001 Filbert St; NJ Transit (☎ 215-569-3752) and Capitol Trailways (☎ 800-444-2877) buses also stop there. Daily buses run to New York ($21; 2 hours); Atlantic City, New Jersey ($7; 1½ hours); and Washington, DC ($21; 3½ hours). To reach Jersey City, catch a bus to Newark, then take NJ Transit.

Train Amtrak trains stop at 30th St Station, in University City. Philadelphia is on Amtrak's *Northeast Corridor* route between Richmond, Virginia, and Boston, Massachusetts, via Washington, DC, and New York City. There are also trains west to Lancaster, Harrisburg, Altoona, Pittsburgh and Chicago, and south to Florida. One-way fares include New York (from $45; 1¼ hours); Washington, DC ($48; 2 hours); and Pittsburgh ($89; 8 hours). NJ Transit (☎ 800-228-8246) has a frequent rail service to Atlantic City ($10/11.50 one way/roundtrip).

Car & Motorcycle Parking in central Philadelphia is difficult, and regulations are enforced. Hostel and hotel validation can reduce fees at some garages. The Vine St Expressway, under the city streets, is the quickest east-west route across downtown.

Philly is an inexpensive place to rent cars. Typical daily rates for a compact are $30-50 with unlimited mileage, less on weekends or by the week. Check the rental companies' offices at the airport or call Alamo (☎ 215-492-3960) or Budget (☎ 215-492-9400).

Local Transportation Septa (☎ 215-580-7800) operates the subways and buses. Its three subway routes are the Market-Frankford line, the Broad St line (servicing Veterans and CoreStates Spectrum stadiums) and the Subway-Surface line along Market St (one-way peak fares $3-6; 50-75¢ less off-peak). Most Septa bus trips cost $2 (plus 60¢

a transfer); a DayPass ($5.50) and weekly pass ($19) allow unlimited rides on city transit vehicles. Bus No 76 runs from Penn's Landing through Society Hill/South St, along Market St to City Hall and the Benjamin Franklin Pkwy to the Philadelphia Museum of Art, Fairmount Park and zoo. Bus No 42 connects Old City with the Civic Center and University City.

The Phlash (☎ 215-474-5274) shuttle bus loops downtown from Logan Circle through Center City to the waterfront and South St ($2/4 one-way/all day). The Patco (☎ 215-922-4600) subway line to Camden, New Jersey, crosses downtown ($1).

Taxi fares are $1.80 for the first sixth of a mile, then 30¢ per additional sixth of a mile, plus 20¢ per minute of waiting time. Drivers serve major hotels. Call Quaker City Cab (☎ 215-728-8000) or Olde City Taxi (☎ 215-338-0838).

AROUND PHILADELPHIA
Valley Forge NHP

In 1777 the British defeated the colonists at the Battle of Brandywine Creek and occupied Philadelphia. In December, General Washington and 12,000 Continental troops withdrew to Valley Forge, 20 miles northwest, where 2000 lost their lives in a bitter winter of cold, hunger and disease, and many others returned home. The rest were trained, drilled and organized into a disciplined force. Today, Valley Forge symbolizes Washington's endurance and leadership. The visitor center (☎ 610-783-1077) has information and a film on the winter encampment. The **Valley Forge Historical Society Museum** (☎ 610-783-0535) features exhibits on George Washington ($2). Septa bus No 125 runs from Philly weekdays.

Brandywine Valley

Straddling the Pennsylvania-Delaware border, the Brandywine Valley is a patchwork of rolling, wooded countryside, historic villages, gardens, mansions and museums. The spectacular **Longwood Gardens** (☎ 800-737-5500), on Route 1 near Kennett Square, has 1050 acres, 20 indoor gardens and 11,000 kinds of plants, with something always in bloom ($12). There's also a Children's Garden with a maze, illuminated fountains in summer and festive lights at Christmas.

A showcase of American artwork, the **Brandywine River Museum** (☎ 610-388-2700), on Hwy 1 and Route 100 at Chadd's Ford, includes the work of the 'Brandywine School' – Pyle, several Wyeths and Maxfield Parrish ($5).

On Hwy 1 just north of the Chadds Ford Bridge, **Brandywine Battlefield Park** (☎ 610-459-3342) has exhibits on the battle (free admission; closed Mon) and tours ($3.50) of historic buildings.

For more information on local attractions, see the Brandywine Valley section in the Washington, DC & the Capital Region chapter.

Washington Crossing HP

On Christmas night 1776, Washington crossed the Delaware and led his army in a successful attack on Hessian mercenaries at Trenton, New Jersey. The Historic Park visitor center (☎ 215-493-4076) on the Pennsylvania side shows a short film. A 45-minute tour costs $4. There's no public transportation to the park.

PENNSYLVANIA DUTCH COUNTRY

The Amish (**ah**-mish) Mennonite and Brethren religious communities are collectively known as the 'Plain People.' The Old Order Amish, with their dark, plain clothing, live a simple, Bible-centered life but have managed to become a major tourist attraction. Anabaptist sects, persecuted in their native Switzerland, settled in tolerant Pennsylvania starting in the early 1700s. Speaking German dialects, they became known as 'Dutch' (from 'Deutsch'). Most Pennsylvania Dutch live on farms, and their beliefs vary from sect to sect. Many do not use electricity, and most opt for horse-drawn buggies – a delightful sight, and sound, in the area.

The charmingly rural 'Dutch Country' is actually a very small area, perhaps 20 miles square, east of the town of Lancaster, and it attracts a *lot* of tourists. The visitor center (☎ 717-299-8901, W www.paduntchcountry .com), off Route 30 in Lancaster, offers comprehensive information, an excellent map and discount coupons for accommodations. East of Lancaster, both Route 30 (through Ronks and Paradise) and Route 340 (through Bird-in-Hand and Intercourse) are heavily visited. To escape the crowds and learn about the region, rent a bike, pack some food and explore the numerous backroads. Or consider hiring a guide for a private tour. Some farm homes rent rooms for $50-100 – they welcome kids and offer a unique opportunity to experience farm life.

Craft shops sell quilts, wooden furniture and faceless dolls. Farmers' markets are popular for pies, preserves, fresh fruit and vegetables. For mainstream shopping, Route 30 has factory-outlet malls. The Amish don't like being photographed – they consider photos a 'graven image.' While some photographers have befriended and photographed Amish people, it's best to respect their wishes. Most Amish businesses close Sunday.

RRTA (☎ 717-397-4246) local buses link the main towns, but a car is better for sightseeing. Amish Country Tours (☎ 717-768-3600) runs 2½-hour bus tours that take backroads and visit farms (from $20). Lancaster County Bicycle Tours (☎ 717-768-8366) rents bikes and leads intimate tours that visit an Amish home and grocery store ($50 per half day).

Lancaster

On the western edge of the Amish country, this pleasant town (population 58,000) was briefly the US capital in September 1777, when Congress stopped here overnight. The downtown chamber of commerce (☎ 717-397-3531, 100 Queen St) is open daily. Historic Lancaster Walking Tours (☎ 717-392-1776) depart from there daily April to October ($5).

The touristy **Central Market**, held on Penn Square from 6am Tuesday, Friday and Saturday, offers good food and crafts. Nearby, the **Heritage Center Museum** (☎ 717-299-6440) has a collection of 18th- and 19th-century paintings, period furniture and local craftwork (free admission; open Tue-Sat). **Wheatland** (☎ 717-392-8721), President James Buchanan's former home, is a restored 1828 Federal mansion northwest of town ($5.50; open Mar-Dec).

90 Greenfield Tourist Home (☎ 717-299-5964, 90 Greenfield St) has singles/doubles for $25/30. Cheaper motels are southeast on Route 462/Route 30. *O'Flaherty's Dingeldein House* (☎ 717-293-1723), 2 miles east of town, is a small, comfortable B&B

($85-95). *Garden Spot Motel* (☎ *717-394-4736)*, 5 miles east on Route 30, has clean, bright rooms ($66/77). *Lancaster Dispensing Co (33 Market St)* offers food, drink and weekend music.

The Capitol Trailways/Greyhound terminal (☎ 717-397-4861), at the train station, has buses to Philadelphia ($15; 2 hours) and Pittsburgh ($38; 5 hours). The Amtrak station (☎ 717-291-5080, 53 McGovern Ave) has trains to and from Philadelphia ($14; 80 minutes) and Pittsburgh ($85; 6 hours). Hertz (☎ 717-396-0000, 625 E Orange St) rents cars.

Intercourse, Bird-in-Hand & Around

Probably named for its crossroads location, Intercourse (population 1200) has shops selling clothing, quilts, candles, furniture, fudge and souvenirs with Intercourse jokes. Browse along Route 340 or 772 northwest of Intercourse. Friendly **People's Place** (☎ 800-390-8436) gives a sensitive overview of Amish and Mennonite life with a *Who Are the Amish?* documentary ($5; closed Sun).

Bird-in-Hand (population 500) has craft stores, restaurants and a farmers' market. Country Barn Quilts & Crafts, east of town, has a good selection. Abe's Buggy Rides (☎ 717-392-1794) does a 2-mile tour ($10). The **Amish Farm & House** (☎ 717-394-6185) is an original farmhouse with a tour describing Amish culture ($6.50).

Country Haven Campground (☎ *717-354-7926)*, about 7 miles northeast in New Holland, overlooks farmland ($22-26). At *Old Road Guest House* (☎ *717-393-8182, 2501 Route 340)* rooms with private bath start at $46. The 1814 brick farmhouse at *Eby's Pequea Farm* (☎ *717-768-3615, 459 Queen Rd)* has singles/doubles from $50/60 with breakfast. At *Harvest Drive Family Motel* (☎ *717-768-7186, 800-233-0176, 3370 Harvest Dr)* rooms are $85 in peak season; the restaurant offers buffet and menu options.

The main-street shops sell pretzels and sandwiches. Kitchen Kettle Village in Intercourse offers inexpensive lunches at *Kettle House* and an all-day sit-down menu at *Kling House*. For Pennsylvania Dutch family-style eating (see 'Going Dutch'), try the less touristy *Stoltzfus Farm Restaurant*, one block east of Intercourse on Route 772

($14; open May-Oct, closed Sun). Go hungry to *Miller's Smorgasbord*, on Route 30 near Ronks, for a seemingly endless buffet of hot and cold dishes.

Strasburg & Around

The picturesque town of Strasburg (population 2600) has escaped much commercialization, but does have a visitor center (☎ 717-687-7922).

Mill Bridge Village (☎ 717-687-6521), northeast of Strasburg on S Ronks Rd, is a colonial re-creation, with an Amish house, school, bridge, barnyard and buggy tour ($8). Campsites here cost $26-39, including 'village' admission. The **Strasburg Railroad** (☎ 717-687-7522) does a scenic 45-minute roundtrip to Paradise from the station east of town ($9.50). The **Railroad Museum of Pennsylvania** (☎ 717-687-8628), opposite the station, features steam locomotives and railcars going back 150 years ($6; open daily).

White Oak Campground (☎ *717-687-6207)*, south of town, has sites for $18-21. *Rayba Acres Farm* (☎ *717-687-6729, 183 Black Horse Rd)* has single rooms with some cooking facilities starting at $47. *Sycamore Haven* (☎ *717-442-4901, 35 S Kinzer Rd)* offers lodging in a farm home ($35). Train lovers will like *Red Caboose*

Going Dutch

Famous not only for its plainly clad Amish folk, the Dutch Country is also home to hearty Pennsylvania Dutch food. In Amish style, you sit at a long table beside other diners sharing friendly conversation and oven-baked bread with melting butter. These fresh, home-cooked, all-you-can-eat meals are not for the faint of stomach. From applesauce and pepper cabbage appetizers to homemade sausage, candied sweet potatoes and farm-grown vegetables, the food keeps coming until you can't contemplate another bite. Save room for the local favorite, shoofly pie – a sticky, sweet dessert topped with molasses and cinnamon that has been known to capture pesky critters in the kitchen. Authentic Amish meals cost around $14 per person; go with an appetite.

Motel (☎ 717-687-5000, 312 Paradise Lane), where you can sleep in a train caboose (from $69). The inside is basic, but the surrounding countryside is quiet.

Lititz & Ephrata

Moravians fleeing persecution in Europe arrived in Lititz in 1756. Now visitors come for the **Sturgis Pretzel House** (☎ 717-626-4354), the USA's first pretzel factory (tour $2), and the **Wilbur Candy Americana Museum** (☎ 717-626-1131).

Ephrata (population 8300) was founded in 1732 as a community of ascetic religious celibates. At the **Ephrata Cloister** (☎ 717-733-6600), a collection of medieval-style buildings, the Pietists lived and worked under rigorous conditions ($6). Ephrata is also renowned for *frakturschriften* calligraphy and a cappella singing.

Reading & Around

In Reading (**red**-ing; population 78,400), 45 miles northwest of Philadelphia, the visitor center (☎ 610-375-4085) has information about area attractions. The reconstructed **Daniel Boone Homestead** (☎ 610-582-4900), 9 miles east, is supposedly on the site of Boone's birthplace ($4; closed Mon).

Sill's Family Campground (☎ 717-484-4806), southeast in Adamstown, has tent sites for $19.50-23.50. Motels are near Route 422 in West Reading – try *Wellesley Inn (☎ 610-374-1500, 910 Woodland Ave)*, for $69-79.

HARRISBURG

The state capital (population 53,500), on the Susquehanna River, has century-old buildings near the center and along Front St. The chamber of commerce (☎ 717-232-4099, 3211 N Front St) gives out maps. The impressive **capitol dome** was modeled after St Peter's Basilica in Rome; its staircase was styled after the one in the Paris Opera House. The **State Museum of Pennsylvania** (☎ 717-787-4978) exhibits Civil War artifacts and the huge *Battle of Gettysburg* painting (free admission; closed Mon).

Highmeadow Campground (☎ 717-566-0902), between Harrisburg and Hershey, has sites for $25, $30 with hookup. Opposite the Transportation Center, basic *Alva Restaurant & Hotel (☎ 717-238-7553, 19 S 4th St)* has singles/doubles for $35/55. Many

motels in the $50 range, like *Red Roof Inn South (☎ 717-939-1331, 950 Eisenhower Blvd)*, are on or around Eisenhower Blvd off I-83.

Both buses and trains use the Harrisburg Transportation Center (☎ 717-232-4251). Several Greyhound and Capital Trailways buses go to Philadelphia ($16.50; 2½ hours). Trains run to Philly ($19; 1 hour) and Pittsburgh ($68; 5¾ hours).

AROUND HARRISBURG

The infamous **Three Mile Island** nuclear power plant is about 10 miles south of Harrisburg. Unit 2 experienced a partial meltdown in 1979 and is permanently closed; unit 1 is back in action. The visitor center (☎ 717-948-8829), on Route 441, opens erratically in the afternoon Thursday to Saturday or Sunday. Call for tour information.

Twelve miles east of Harrisburg, **Hershey** (population 11,900) is the home of Milton S Hershey's chocolate empire. Chocolate World (☎ 717-534-4900) is a disappointing mock factory/giant candy store; kids might like it (free admission). Hersheypark (☎ 800-437-7439) is an amusement park with over 50 rides ($34/19 adults/kids). The adjacent ZooAmerica wildlife park (☎ 717-534-3860) features North American animals ($6.50). Motels are along Chocolate Ave.

Twenty miles southeast of Harrisburg, **York** (population 42,200) dates from 1741 and is famous for the Harley-Davidson motorcycle – the pop-culture classic. After fleeing Philadelphia in 1777, the First Continental Congress met at York's courthouse to draft the Articles of Confederation, the country's first constitution. The historical society (☎ 717-848-1587) offers tours ($5). At the **Harley-Davidson plant** (☎ 717-848-1177), watch tattooed workers assemble the two-wheeled legends. The plant features historic Harleys – including an Elvis Presley bike – a free tour and a gift shop.

GETTYSBURG

Gettysburg (population 9000), 145 miles west of Philadelphia, saw one of the Civil War's most decisive and bloody battles. Much of the battlefield became a National Cemetery soon afterward; Lincoln delivered his famous Gettysburg Address at its dedication:

Four score and seven years ago our fathers brought forth on this continent, a new nation, conceived in Liberty, and dedicated to the proposition that all men are created equal…. We here highly resolve that these dead shall not have died in vain – that this nation, under God, shall have a new birth of freedom – and that government of the people, by the people, for the people, shall not perish from the earth.

Gettysburg is compact, surrounded by the Gettysburg National Military Park, memorials and monuments. Lincoln Square is the town center. The Gettysburg Convention & Visitors Bureau (☎ 717-334-6274, Ⓦ www .gettysburg.com, 35 Carlisle St) distributes a comprehensive list of attractions. Free Internet access is available at the Adams County Library (140 Baltimore St). There's no public transportation to or around Gettysburg.

Gettysburg National Military Park
This 8-sq-mile park encompasses most of the area of the three-day battle. Gettysburg Tour Center (☎ 717-334-6296) packages include a battlefield bus tour and various attractions ($19). At the visitor center (☎ 717-334-1124), get a free 'Official Map & Guide' for a self-driving tour, purchase an audiotape for your vehicle ($20), or hire a licensed battlefield guide for $40 per carload for a two-hour personal tour. South of the visitor center along the High Water Mark Trail, **Cemetery Ridge** is the site of Pickett's Charge, where the Confederates suffered 80% casualties. Other hikes include the mile-long **Big Round Top Loop Trail**. There's also **Devil's Den**, a mass of boulders Confederate snipers used as a hideout. The **Cyclorama Center** is a 360-degree painting of the battle ($2.50).

Other Attractions
The **Eisenhower National Historic Site** (☎ 717-338-9114), Ike's former home, can be visited only on a $5.25 tour departing from the National Military Park visitor center. The house that served as **General Lee's Headquarters** (☎ 717-334-3141), on Buford Ave, exhibits assorted memorabilia ($3). Lincoln prepared his Gettysburg Address in the **Wills House** (☎ 717-334-8188), now a museum, on Lincoln Square ($3.50).

The battle's only civilian fatality was a woman killed in her sister's home. The **Jennie Wade House Museum** (☎ 717-334-4100) tells the story ($6). Uniforms, guns and detailed dioramas are at the **Soldiers National Museum** (☎ 717-334-4890); admission is $5.25. The **Gettysburg Railroad** (☎ 717-334-2411) steam train makes a 1½-hour excursion April to October ($7.50).

In the evening, mingle with the spirits on the **Ghosts of Gettysburg Candlelight Walking Tours** (☎ 717-337-0445) for $6.50 or attend the free nightly campfire lectures at the park's amphitheater.

Places to Stay & Eat
Accommodations are crowded in summer, especially on weekends and during Civil War Heritage Days (late June and early July). Several large, full-facility campgrounds are nearby, most open May to October. Try **Battlefield Heritage Resort** (☎ 717-334-1577), southwest on Business Route 15 (sites $17-24), or **Round Top Campground** (☎ 717-334-9565), off Taneytown Rd (tents/RVs $13/19).

HI Ironmaster's Mansion (☎ 717-486-7575, 1212 Pine Grove Rd, Gardners) sits amid a picturesque landscape right on the Appalachian Trail, 20 miles northwest of town ($14/17 for members/nonmembers). Immerse yourself in Civil War ambience at **Homestead Guest Home** (☎ 717-334-2037, 785 Baltimore St), a former orphanage ($35/40 for singles/doubles). Some cheaper motels are along Business Route 15 south or Route 34 north. **Blue Sky Motel** (☎ 717-677-7736, 2585 Biglerville Rd) is quiet and has a pool ($49-58). Call Inns of Gettysburg Area (☎ 800-587-2216) for their 20 listings.

Step back into the 1800s at the **Historic Farnsworth House Tavern** (401 Baltimore St), where staff in period clothing serve tasty early-American cuisine ($3-7). The authentic **Lincoln Diner** (32 Carlisle St) is cheap and never closes. **Jo's Corner Delicatessen** (48 Baltimore St) has an all-you-can-eat salad bar ($4). Steinwehr Ave, opposite the park entrance, has fast-food franchises.

PITTSBURGH
Built on iron and steel, Pittsburgh was once so polluted that people called it the 'Smoky City.' It's now reinventing itself as a corporate, financial and educational center, with several museums (including the Andy

MID-ATLANTIC STATES

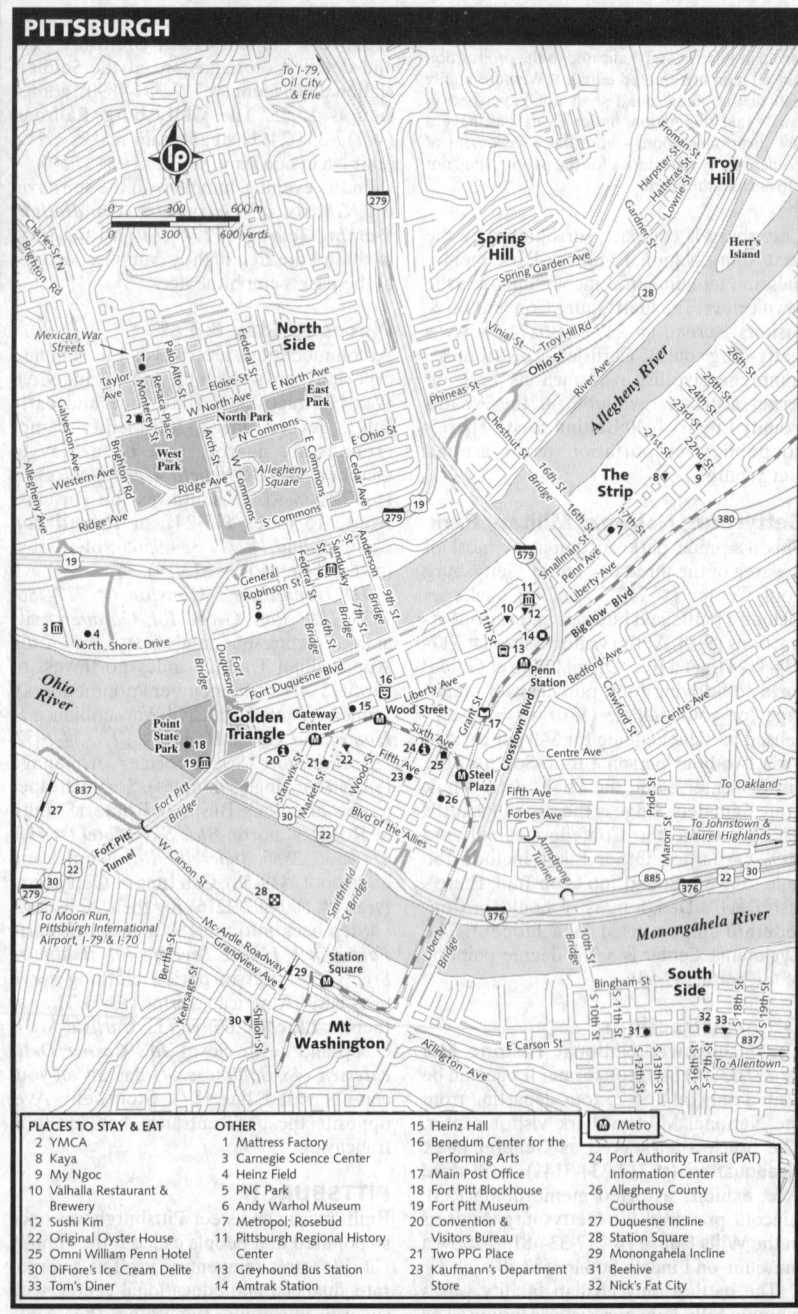

PITTSBURGH

Warhol Museum), fun nightlife and a substantial student population.

Pittsburgh's location at a major river junction made it a colonial-era trading center and a focus of French-British rivalry. In 1758 the British took possession of 'the Point' – the land at the river junction – and proceeded to build Fort Pitt (named for Prime Minister William Pitt the Elder). Nearby coal and iron ore deposits enabled Pittsburgh to produce 50% of the country's iron and steel by the Civil War's end, and it also became a center for glass and textile production.

Andrew Carnegie introduced the Bessemer steelmaking process and greatly expanded production. Pittsburgh became Steel City, and Carnegie became the world's richest man and a famous philanthropist (Pittsburgh is endowed with four excellent Carnegie museums). The steel industry's harsh conditions produced labor unions and bitter strikes in 1892 and 1919. In the 1960s and 1970s, competition from newer, more efficient steelworks overseas devastated Pittsburgh's heavy industries. Factories closed, and the population fell over several decades.

Today, a scrappy blue-collar element remains, as do distinct, closely knit neighborhoods, a growing white-collar workforce and marked ethnic diversity. Air quality and civic amenity have improved greatly from the closure of many old industrial plants, with much of the city now pleasantly clean and green. Proud locals focus on the city's economic future, but the powerful Pittsburgh Steelers football team is a constant reminder of its great industrial past.

Orientation & Information
The Golden Triangle, between the converging Monongahela and Allegheny Rivers, is Pittsburgh's downtown, now comprehensively (if soullessly) renovated. Just northeast of downtown, the Strip offers warehouses, food stores, cheap restaurants and clubs along Penn Ave and Smallman Ave. Across the Allegheny River, the North Side has the big new sports stadiums, several museums and appealing neighborhoods around Allegheny Square.

Across the Monongahela River, the South Side slopes up Mt Washington; incline railways give access to the views

from the top. E Carson St has numerous clubs, galleries and restaurants – it's the fun part of town. East of downtown is Oakland, the university area, with student life and some imposing neo-Gothic architecture. Shadyside Business District, a white-collar neighborhood with upscale boutiques, is farther east.

The Pittsburgh Convention & Visitors Bureau (☎ 412-281-7711, 800-366-0093, Ⓦ www.visitpittsburgh.com) has a downtown branch on Liberty Ave (open 9am-5pm Mon-Fri, 9am-3pm Sat-Sun), a branch at the Station Square and two desks at the airport. The Pittsburgh Council for International Visitors (☎ 412-624-7800) can also help.

Golden Triangle
The renovated downtown has a few fine older buildings, such as Kaufmann's department store, and some distinctive modern architecture, including the Disneyesque castle of PPG Place. At the triangle's tip, Point State Park is popular during summer, though you can't swim in the big fountain. The **Fort Pitt Museum** (☎ 412-281-9284), undergoing renovation in 2001, displays material on Native Americans and the French-British conflicts ($4; open Tue-Sun). Nearby Fort Pitt Blockhouse is the fort's only remaining portion. The 19th-century **Allegheny County Courthouse** (☎ 412-350-5410), at Forbes Ave and Grant St, is a Romanesque stone building designed by Henry Hobson Richardson (free admission; open Mon-Fri).

For a good take on Pittsburgh's past, visit the **Pittsburgh Regional History Center** (☎ 412-454-6000, 1212 Smallman Ave). The nicely remodeled brick warehouse has audiovisuals and exhibits giving varied perspectives on the French & Indian War, early settlers, immigrants, steel, the glass industry, and of course the HJ Heinz company ($6). Senator John Heinz was a major supporter of the center.

North Side
The **Andy Warhol Museum** (☎ 412-237-8300, 117 Sandusky St), just over the 7th St Bridge, is one of the town's Carnegie museums. A Pittsburgh native, Warhol became famous for his pop art, avant-garde movies, celebrity connections and Velvet Underground spectaculars (see 'Andy Warhol'). Warhol's work

Andy Warhol

Andy Warhol (1928–87) was one of the most influential US artists of the 20th century. Born in the Oakland district of Pittsburgh, Warhol was the son of Polish immigrants. At his mother's suggestion, he studied art at the Carnegie Institute (now Carnegie Mellon University).

After graduation in 1949 he moved to New York City, where he became a leading freelance commercial artist. He developed an interest in pop art and by the early 1960s was exhibiting some of his now famous works, including the large, multi-image silkscreen paintings of Marilyn Monroe, Mao Tse-tung, Campbell's soup cans and Coca-Cola bottles. In addition to painting, Warhol produced experimental, underground movies. *Sleep* (1963) was one of his first and most memorable: The silent movie showed a man sleeping for eight hours.

Warhol eventually opened the Factory, a studio known for innovative work and a meeting place for avant-garde artists. In 1968 he was shot by Valerie Solanis, once part of his artistic circle. A year later, he started *Interview* magazine, featuring articles on fashion, movies and glamorous celebrities. In the 1970s and '80s he continued to produce portraits and some of his most famous paintings.

After his death (following a gallbladder operation), it was decided to devote a museum to the man and his work. He had lived most of his life and achieved fame in New York City, but, despite some controversy, the museum is now firmly established in his hometown of Pittsburgh.

mimicked mechanization, industrialization and mass production. Exhibits include the classic Campbell's soup cans (for 20 years, he reportedly drank the soup every day), celebrity portraits and frequent film screenings ($8; open Tue-Sun). Take bus No 13A, 13B or 13C from downtown.

Modern-art enthusiasts should definitely see the installations at the **Mattress Factory** (☎ 412-231-3169, 500 Sampsonia Way), northwest of the Warhol museum ($4).

The **Carnegie Science Center** (☎ 412-237-3400, One Allegheny Ave) is a cut above the average hands-on science museum. The 'try your hand at surgery' exhibition simulates high-tech medical treatments (one of Pittsburgh's cutting-edge industries). A planetarium and a submarine are among many other great permanent exhibits ($10; open 10am-5pm Sun-Fri, 10am-9pm Sat).

South Side & Mt Washington

The Monongahela Incline (☎ 412-442-2000) and Duquesne (doo-**kane**) Incline (☎ 412-381-1665) funicular railroads run up and down Mt Washington's steep slopes. Last century, 15 incline railroads opened the South Side to suburban development. The Monongahela Incline starts near **Station Square** (☎ 412-261-9911), a group of railway buildings recycled as a shopping and entertainment complex. Take the Incline up to the aptly named Grandview Ave ($1.60) and walk northwest to the Duquesne Incline, which has historical railcar photos. You can ride that down and walk back to Station Square, but it's more scenic to go back the way you came.

Oakland Area

The University of Pittsburgh and Carnegie Mellon University are here, along with mansions and cultural attractions. From downtown, take bus No 61A to 61C, or 71A to 71D along 5th Ave.

Two Carnegie institutions share a site at 4400 Forbes Ave. The terrific **Carnegie Art Museum** (☎ 412-622-3131) has a collection of impressionist, postimpressionist and modern American paintings, plus a fine architecture exhibit. **Carnegie Museum of Natural History** (same ☎) features a complete tyrannosaurus skeleton, Pennsylvania geology and Inuit prehistory. Admission covers both museums ($6; open Tue-Sun), and the complex includes the Carnegie Library of Pittsburgh and the Carnegie Music Hall.

The 42-story **Cathedral of Learning** (☎ 412-624-6000), on the University of Pittsburgh campus, is a Gothic tower that houses the Nationality Classrooms, each representing a different style and period (call ahead to book a $2 guided tour).

The **Frick Art & Historical Center** (☎ 412-371-0600, 7227 Reynolds St) is in Point Breeze, east of Oakland. The highlight is Clayton, the restored 1872 mansion of industrialist Henry Clay Frick (tours $8; call first). The free Frick Art Museum displays some of Frick's Flemish, French and Italian paintings. The Car & Carriage Museum includes assorted Frickmobiles like a 1914 Rolls Royce (free admission; open Tue-Sun).

Places to Stay

Accommodations are expensive, especially near the city center. *Raccoon Creek State Park* (☎ 412-899-2200), 25 miles west, has attractive campsites open year round ($18). In South Side's Allentown neighborhood, *HI Pittsburgh Hostel* (☎ 412-431-1267, 830 E Warrington Ave) is in a still-splendid early-20th-century bank ($19/22 members/nonmembers); call first for reservations and directions. The YMCA (☎ 412-321-8594, 600 W North Ave) has basic rooms for men only ($28).

The best area for inexpensive lodgings is 10 miles west of town at Moon Run, off I-79 at Exit 16, Steubenville Pike, where there's a choice of chains. *Econo Lodge* (☎ 412-922-6900, 4800 Steubenville Pike) is a pretty good value (singles/doubles $40/50). Nearby *Days Inn* (☎ 412-922-0120, 100 Kisow Dr) has doubles for around $45, and *Motel 6* (☎ 412-922-9400, 211 Beecham Dr) charges $40/46 weekdays, $46/51 weekends.

Pittsburgh's best is the downtown *Omni William Penn Hotel* (☎ 412-281-7100, 530 William Penn Place), a renovated national historic landmark where rooms start at $169, but promotional specials might be as low as $109.

Places to Eat

Downtown has the usual office-worker lunchtime options. The *food court* at Two PPG Place sells Chinese, Greek and Italian dishes. *Original Oyster House*, on Market Square, serves fresh oysters, fish and fries. *Sushi Kim* (☎ 412-281-9956, 1241 Penn Ave) is an inexpensive Korean-Japanese place with fresh sushi and lunch specials. The high-ceilinged *Valhalla Restaurant & Brewery* (☎ 412-434-1440, 1150 Smallman St) serves wild boar and charred salmon as well as the usual steaks, salads and pizza (entrées $10-20).

There's a livelier choice in the evenings along the Strip, where ethnic eateries include *My Ngoc (1120 Penn Ave)*, at 22nd St, with Asian dishes ($7-10), and *Kaya* (☎ 412-261-6565, 2000 Smallman Ave), a cool Caribbean place with vegetarian paella for around $13.

On the South Side, Station Square has numerous eateries. Near the top of Monongahela Incline, walk down Shiloh St to find some very economical options, including *DiFiore's Ice Cream Delite (120 Shiloh St)*. Near the top of Duquesne Incline, classy restaurants on Grandview Ave offer suitably grand views.

South Side's E Carson St is thick with coffee bars, pubs and interesting eateries. *Tom's Diner (1715 E Carson St)* serves up the all-American favorites in a nifty 1950s setting. *Mallorca* (☎ 412-488-1818, 2228 E Carson St) is an upscale Spanish restaurant boasting 'the best paella in town.'

In Oakland, cheap places on and around Forbes Ave cater to local students. About the cheapest is the *Original Hot Dog Shop (3901 Forbes Ave)*, at Bouquet St, with get-it-yourself greasy pizzas, burgers, fries, hot dogs and draft beer in plastic cups.

Entertainment

Downtown, the *Benedum Center for the Performing Arts* (☎ 412-456-6666, 719 Liberty Ave) hosts dance, ballet, opera and Broadway shows (tickets from $15). The Pittsburgh Symphony Orchestra plays October to May at *Heinz Hall* (☎ 412-392-4800, 600 Penn Ave). The free weeklies *City Paper* and *In Pittsburgh* have detailed listings of Pittsburgh's active nightlife.

E Carson St, South Side, is the place for rock, R&B and all-around funk. *Nick's Fat City* (☎ 412-481-6880, 1601 E Carson St) is a local favorite. *Lava Lounge* (☎ 412-431-5282, 2204 E Carson St) offers a variety of shows. *Beehive (1327 E Carson St)* is a fun and funky coffee lounge.

In Oakland, *Beehive Coffee House & Theater* (☎ 412-683-4483, 3807 Forbes Ave) turns on entertainment and weekend live music for an artsy crowd of caffeine freaks.

The Strip has enough bars for a regular pub crawl, but the dance clubbers head for *Metropol* (☎ 412-261-2232, 1600 Smallman Ave) and adjacent *Rosebud* (☎ 412-261-2221). Metropol spins hip-hop, house, trance, acid jazz etc, depending on the night. Rosebud does mostly house and has live acts too.

Spectator Sports

The old Three Rivers Stadium is mourned by real Pittsburghers, while the Pittsburgh promotion industry hypes the replacements. The Pittsburgh Pirates major-league baseball team now plays at PNC Park (☎ 412-321-2827), and the NFL Pittsburgh Steelers play football at Heinz Field (☎ 412-323-1200). Both venues are on the North Side, by the Allegheny River. The NHL Pittsburgh Penguins play hockey at Civic Arena (☎ 412-642-1800), just east of downtown.

Getting There & Around

Pittsburgh International Airport (☎ 412-472-3500), 18 miles from downtown, has direct connections to Europe, Canada and major US cities. Airport buses (☎ 412-321-4990) run downtown every hour ($14).

Greyhound (☎ 412-392-6513), at 11th St and Liberty Ave, has frequent buses to Philadelphia ($40; 7 hours); New York ($52; 11 hours); and Chicago, Illinois ($60; 8-12 hours). Amtrak (☎ 412-471-6171, 1100 Liberty Ave) is behind the magnificent original railroad station. Trains head to Philadelphia ($48; 8 hours); New York ($65; 10 hours); and Chicago, Illinois ($57; 10 hours).

Port Authority Transit (PAT) operates buses and a light-rail system called the 'T.' The information center (☎ 412-442-2000, 534 Smithfield St) is open weekdays. Most bus and T fares are $1.25 or less; transfers cost 25¢. For taxis, call Yellow Cab (☎ 412-665-8100) or People's Cab (☎ 412-681-3131) – unmarked cabs may be uninsured or unsafe.

Car rental companies include Budget (☎ 412-261-1628), Enterprise (☎ 412-505-5000) and National (☎ 412-472-5094). There are several rental companies at the airport.

AROUND PITTSBURGH
Johnstown

A Swiss Mennonite founded this town, 70 miles east of Pittsburgh, in the early 19th century. It thrived as a substantial industrial town, until a devastating deluge in 1889 cost 2209 lives – the country's worst flood. But its inhabitants survived and rebuilt the town. The friendly visitor center (☎ 814-536-7993) is at 111 Market St.

The **Johnstown Flood Museum** (☎ 814-539-1889, 304 Washington St) shows an excellent 3D documentary using contemporary stereo photos ($4). The Inclined Plane cable car rises 896 feet up Yoder Hill from central Johnstown ($3).

The **Johnstown Heritage Discovery Center** (☎ 814-539-1889), in the Cambria City Historic District, has a multimedia role-playing exhibit on Johnstown's immigrant workers ($5.50).

In nearby Windber, 12 miles southeast, the **Windber Coal Heritage Center** (☎ 814-467-6680) documents the area's once rich and labor-intensive coal industry ($4).

Woodland Park Campground (☎ *814-472-9857, 220 Campground Rd)*, about 18 miles north of town, has tent/RV sites ($12/14; open Apr-Oct). The *Holiday Inn Express* (☎ *814-266-8789, 250 Market St)* charges $65. Go south to Somerset for a bigger choice of budget accommodations.

Ohiopyle State Park

The picturesque wooded hills of Laurel Highlands are just 40 miles southeast of Pittsburgh, making for a popular weekend destination.

The little riverfront village of Ohiopyle (oh-**hi**-oh-pile), on Route 381 in the middle of the park, is a base for rafting and canoeing on the Youghiogheny River ('Yough,' pronounced yock) and a focus for visitors to this lovely area. The park office (☎ 724-329-8591) and visitor center is at the end of the old steel railway bridge.

Several companies arrange guided river trips: Laurel Highlands River Tours (☎ 800-473-3846), Wilderness Voyageurs (☎ 800-272-4141), Mountain Streams (☎ 800-723-8669) and Whitewater Adventurers (☎ 800-992-7238). Easy, guided trips on the Middle Yough (Class I and II rapids) cost around $22/29 per person on weekdays/weekends; more exciting trips on the Lower Yough (Class III and IV rapids) are $32/58. Even more demanding trips can be arranged on other rivers in the area. Experienced boaters can rent equipment for unguided trips ($15-20 per person per day). There are also canoeing and kayaking courses, trails for hiking and cross-country skiing, and 27 miles of cycling trails along disused rail lines (bike rentals from $3/12 per hour/day).

Ohiopyle State Park Campground (☎ 724-329-8591), on Campground Rd, has 234 sites, hot showers and toilets ($13/16 weekdays/weekends; open Mar-Dec). The appealing 25-bed *HI-AYH Ohiopyle Hostel* (☎ 724-329-4476), just north of the village, has beds at $12/15 for members/nonmembers. *Falls Market Inn & Restaurant* (☎ 724-329-4973), on the main road, has five singles/doubles with shared bathroom ($35/50) and serves inexpensive eats. *Yough Plaza Motel* (☎ 800-992-7238), half a block east of the visitor center, charges $82 for a double. Somerset, a scenic 25 miles northeast, has several budget motels.

Fallingwater & Kentuck Knob
A Frank Lloyd Wright masterpiece, Fallingwater (☎ 724-329-8501) is 3 miles north of the park on Route 381. Completed in 1939 as a weekend retreat for the Kaufmanns, owners of the Pittsburgh department store, the buildings sports a design acclaimed for integrating it with its natural setting. Walls and floors of local sandstone seem to grow out of the steep hillside, while balconies are cantilevered dramatically over the waterfall for which the house is named. Most of the interior furniture and fittings are just as Wright designed them.

To see inside, you must take one of the guided tours ($10/15 Mon-Fri/Sat-Sun; 10am-

Frank Lloyd Wright's Fallingwater

4pm Tue-Sun Apr-Nov, Sat-Sun only in winter). Reservations are recommended. A more intensive two-hour tour, with photography permitted, is offered at 8:30am ($50). The attractive, forested grounds open at 8:30am.

Much less visited is Kentuck Knob (☎ 724-329-1901), another Frank Lloyd Wright house (designed in 1953), built into the side of a rolling hill. It's noted for its natural materials, hexagonal design and honeycomb skylights. House tours last about an hour ($10 Tue-Fri, $15 Sat-Sun).

NORTHERN PENNSYLVANIA
Along Route 6
Called the Grand Army of the Republic Hwy, Route 6 traverses some beautiful greenery and mountains. Heading east from the Alleghanies, **Wellsboro** is a picturesque town with old gas lamps. The tourist office (☎ 570-724-0635) has information about sites like the superb 47-mile-long Pine Creek Gorge (sometimes called 'Pennsylvania's Grand Canyon').

Just south of Route 6, **Scranton** was an important 19th-century coal-mining area. The Steamtown National Historic Site (☎ 570-340-5204) has railroad exhibits and operating steam locomotives (train rides $8). Southeast of Scranton, *HI Poconos Hostel* (☎ 570-676-9076) is north of the small town of La Anna ($14).

The road then passes through the Pocono Mountains, a popular forested area with rivers, waterfalls and wildlife. It's busy during peak season. The Pocono Mountains Vacation Bureau (☎ 570-424-6050, Ⓦ www.poconos.org) has information.

Route 6 ends at the **Delaware Water Gap NRA**, on the New Jersey border (see New Jersey, earlier).

Allegheny National Forest
Northwestern Pennsylvania was stripped of its timber in the late 19th and early 20th century. Now the 797-sq-mile Allegheny National Forest has hemlock, maple, white ash and the valuable Allegheny black cherry. Encompassing several state parks, it's also a habitat for black bear, elk, deer, fox, beaver, muskrat and turkey. Various lakes and dams form part of a flood-control system. It's a good place for outdoor activities.

Warren (population 11,100), on the forest's northwest edge, is the region's main town. Its tourist office (☎ 814-726-1222) has information, as does the USFS (☎ 814-723-5150). Several roads cross the forest – Route 6 goes from Kane in the east, via Sheffield to Warren.

Oil Creek Area

Natural petroleum had long been collected from Oil Creek by Native Americans and used for medicine. Later it was used as a lubricant and refined into kerosene for lamps. In 1859, Edwin Drake, trying to improve the output of a natural oil spring, had a pipe drilled into the ground. Soon he was pumping 20 barrels a day from the world's first commercially successful oil well, fueling a new industrial age.

Most of the Oil Creek valley was stripped of timber, towns and railways were built, and the oil reserves were pretty near sucked dry within 20 years. Now nature has reclaimed much of the valley, protected as **Oil Creek State Park** (☎ 814-676-5915) – a delightful combination of forest, stream and history.

At the park's northern end, in Titusville, **Drake Well Museum** (☎ 814-827-2797) displays rickety old oil rigs and shows an informative film ($4). *Oil Creek Campground* (☎ 814-827-1023), south off Route 8, has large sites for $15 ($19 with hookup).

The **Oil Creek & Titusville Railroad** (☎ 814-676-1733) runs a restored steam train through the park on 13 miles of very scenic railroad. Oil City is the place where

John D Rockefeller made his first million. Nearby, the attractive 19th-century town of **Franklin** has good food and lodgings.

Erie

Lake Erie is named for the Eriez Indians whom the Seneca killed in the 17th century. The city of Erie (population 108,700) is an industrial center and a stop for travelers skirting the lake. The visitor bureau (☎ 814-454-7191) is at State and W 7th Sts. During the War of 1812, Lieutenant Oliver Perry was sent here, had six ships built and went to confront the British on Lake Erie. After the battle, Perry reported 'We have met the enemy and they are ours.' A working replica of Perry's flagship, US Brig *Niagara,* is at the **Erie Maritime Museum** (☎ 814-452-2744, 150 E Front St), which has various exhibits on Great Lakes' history ($6; open daily). **Presque Isle State Park** (☎ 814-833-7424) is an attractive, curving, sandy peninsula, great for biking, hiking, boating and watching migrating waterfowl.

Sara's Beachcomber Campground (☎ 814-833-4560), just outside the park, has tent/RV sites ($15/20). *Super 8 Downtowner Inn* (☎ 814-456-6251, 205 W 10th St) has a pool ($50-60). Many motels are near the intersection of Route 5 and Peninsula Dr (Route 832). The 1960s-style *Peninsula Motel* (☎ 814-838-1938, 1002 Peninsula Dr) charges $50-85, depending on demand.

New England

While cruising the rugged northeastern coast of North America in 1614, English explorer Captain John Smith christened the land 'New England.' The area's six states – Massachusetts, Rhode Island, Connecticut, Vermont, New Hampshire and Maine – have preserved their character as a unique region, with graceful towns of colonial and Federal architecture, thousands of miles of beautiful coastline, and cities stuffed with museums, libraries, universities and high-tech businesses. Besides culture and history, New England offers outstanding opportunities for hiking, biking, rafting, kayaking and sailing. The heavily forested region is scattered with granite mountain ranges and glacial lakes and ponds.

Americans from other regions of the country come to New England for its history, culture and cuisine, and to feel as though they're 'almost in Europe.' Europeans and other visitors from abroad come to beautiful, refined, stable New England to experience the contrast to the brash energy of New York City, the machismo of Texas, and the good-natured but bewildering trendiness of California.

History

Algonquian peoples inhabited present-day New England when the first European settlers arrived. They lived in small, semi-agrarian tribes, raising corn, beans and other foodstuffs while hunting plentiful game and harvesting the rich coastal waters. Intertribal warfare was common in New England, rendering a united defense against the encroachments of European settlers impossible.

Though the Norse explored New England around AD 1000, their colonies failed. The famous explorers – Columbus, John Cabot and others – followed in the late 15th century, but it was the second wave of mariners, including Bartholomew Gosnold, that successfully explored the New England coast from Maine to Rhode Island in 1602 and opened the area to colonization. John Smith arrived in the area in 1614. He coined the name for the region and, upon his return to London, praised its possibilities for settlement. With the landing of the Pilgrims at Plymouth in the summer of 1620, European settlement of New

Highlights

- Boston – an appealing city with rich culture and colonial history, plus some amazing clam chowder
- Cape Cod – a popular summer vacation destination, with Nantucket and Martha's Vineyard
- Newport – palatial mansions of the late-19th- and early-20th-century super-rich
- Maine coast – 3500 miles of rugged granite, pine-cloaked Atlantic beauty
- Fall foliage – spectacular colors in the Berkshires, White Mountains, Green Mountains, interior Maine and Litchfield Hills

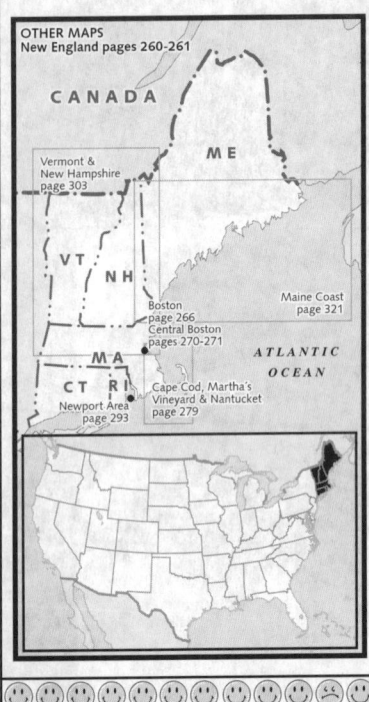

OTHER MAPS
New England pages 260-261

CANADA

Vermont & New Hampshire page 303

ME

VT

NH

Boston page 266
Central Boston pages 270-271

Maine Coast page 321

MA

ATLANTIC OCEAN

CT RI
Newport Area page 293

Cape Cod, Martha's Vineyard & Nantucket page 279

England began in earnest, almost always on the model of the self-governing colony.

From the 1650s to 1750s there was rapid growth of the European population and the wealth of the New England colonies. Ship-building thrived all along the coast, particularly in Maine, where vast stands of virgin pine were reserved as masts for royal vessels. The native peoples of the region, however, were reduced to small, relatively powerless groups of survivors.

Though independent-minded New Englanders still considered themselves subjects of the British crown, they had no representation in Parliament and felt put upon when the crown imposed taxes. When these taxes – particularly those on the colonies' burgeoning maritime economy – became oppressive, as with the Stamp Act (1765) and the Townshend Acts (1767), revolution followed, beginning with the battles of Lexington and Concord, Massachusetts, on April 18, 1775. On May 4, 1776 – two months before the Declaration of Independence was signed in Philadelphia – the colony of Rhode Island and Providence Plantations formally renounced allegiance to King George III, which provoked the British to occupy Rhode Island.

When the Revolutionary War was over, New England's mariners and merchants were free from the restrictions imposed by Great Britain. They quickly built up the young nation's trade in fishing and commerce. The designs for textile machinery powered by river flow were smuggled out of England, and the first water-powered cotton-spinning mill in North America was established at Pawtucket, Rhode Island, in 1793. Soon afterward, New England's many short, swift rivers were bordered by vast mills turning out a wealth of clothing, shoes and machinery.

But no boom lasts forever. The settlement and cultivation of the Great Plains made farming New England's rocky soil even less profitable, and the Civil War encouraged industrialization of other areas. With the emancipation of slaves and the invention of steam power, many New England industries moved south to take advantage of cheaper labor. Steel vessels replaced New England's renowned wooden clipper ships, and petroleum, gas and electricity superseded whale oil for illumination.

New England suffered greatly during the 1930s Depression, but its factories and shipyards boomed during WWII, and its traditional strengths in education, commerce, medicine and manufacturing served it well during the following recession. In recent decades, finance, insurance, high-tech and biotech industries, and tourism have also become mainstays of the economy.

Geography

The Appalachian Mountains partly isolate New England from states to the west. The Atlantic Ocean defines its eastern boundary. A scant million years ago, glaciers covered New England. When they retreated (10,000 to 20,000 years ago) they left glacial deposits, such as oblong hills called 'drumlins' (Bunker Hill is one), scooped-out holes that became glacial ponds (Thoreau's Walden Pond) and huge granite boulders (glacial erratics) in fields and streams.

The resulting landscape has appealing variety: verdant, winding valleys, abundant forests and a rocky coastline sculpted into many coves and sprinkled with sandy beaches. The mountains lack dramatic height, which makes them all the more accessible.

Flora & Fauna

Thick forests of oak, maple, hemlock, beech, pine and spruce blanket the region, covering as much as 85% of the land in the northern states, and New England's fall-foliage color extravaganza is world famous. The area's sugar bushes (groves of sugar maple trees) are busy with moose, white-tailed deer, wild turkeys, raccoons, woodchucks, squirrels and, in summer, swarms of mosquitoes. Seagulls throng the coasts, and graceful great blue herons stalk the many glacial ponds, while hawks favor the mountain areas. The coastal waters, once rich with sea life, have been badly overfished by domestic and foreign craft, though seafood is still available.

When to Go

Late May to early July and September are the best times to visit. Everything's open, prices are moderate, days are warm, nights are cool. The busiest, most expensive times are high summer (mid-July and Aug) and foliage season (late Sept to mid-Oct). The winters are often quite severe, more so than in the southern and western states.

NEW ENGLAND

NEW ENGLAND

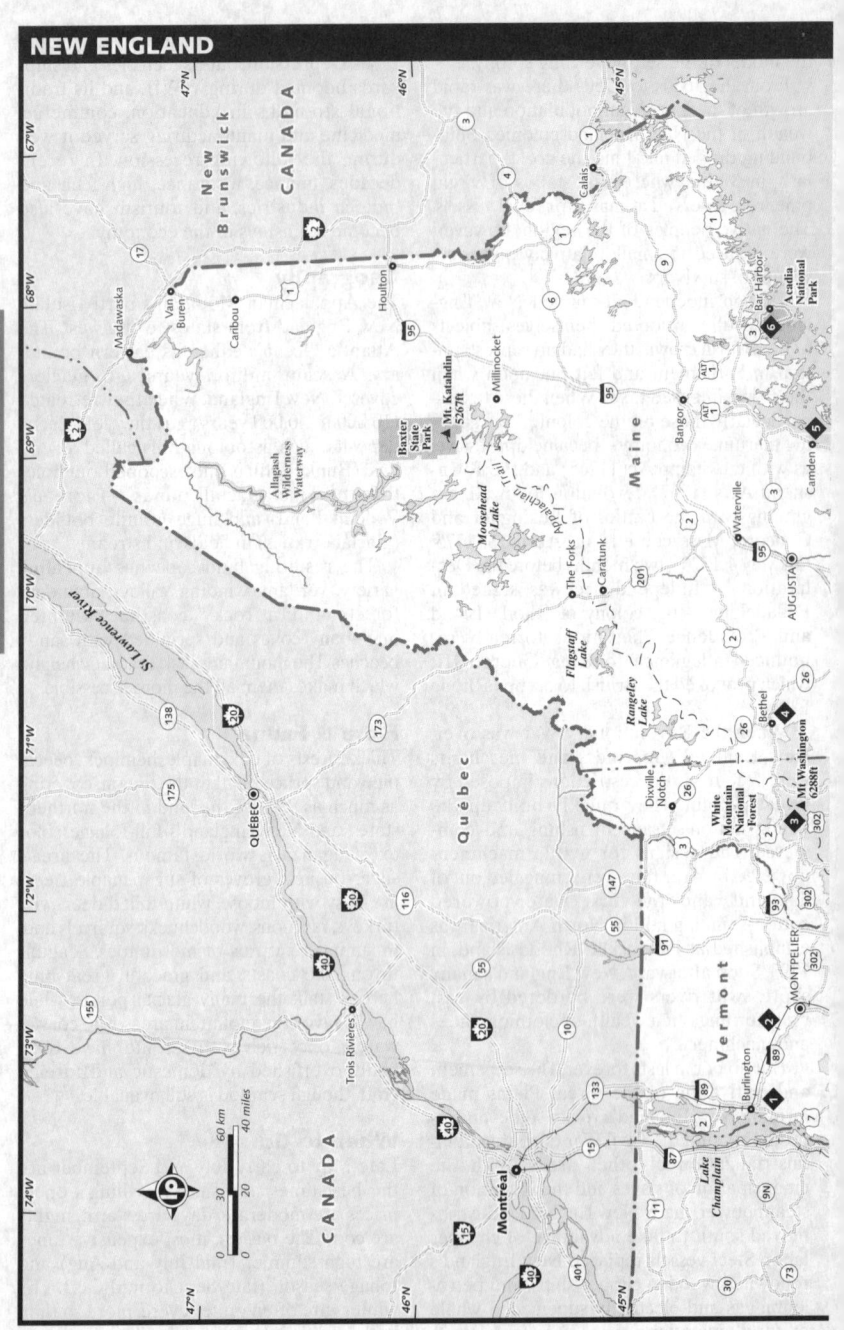

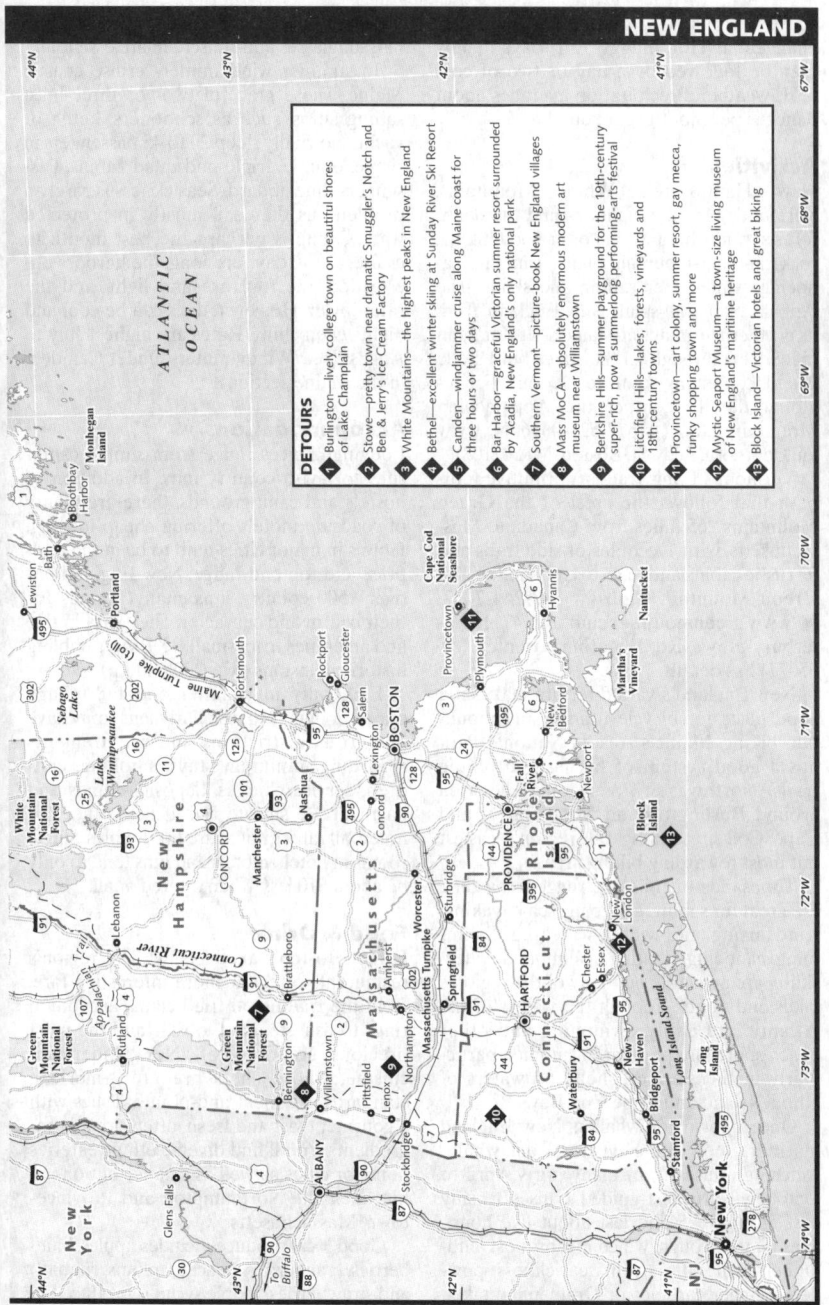

DETOURS

1. Burlington—lively college town on beautiful shores of Lake Champlain
2. Stowe—pretty town near dramatic Smuggler's Notch and Ben & Jerry's Ice Cream Factory
3. White Mountains—the highest peaks in New England
4. Bethel—excellent winter skiing at Sunday River Ski Resort
5. Camden—windjammer cruise along Maine coast for three hours or two days
6. Bar Harbor—graceful Victorian summer resort surrounded by Acadia, New England's only national park
7. Southern Vermont—picture-book New England villages
8. Mass MoCA—absolutely enormous modern art museum near Williamstown
9. Berkshire Hills—summer playground for the 19th-century super-rich, now a summerlong performing-arts festival
10. Litchfield Hills—lakes, forests, vineyards and 18th-century towns
11. Provincetown—art colony, summer resort, gay mecca, funky shopping town and more
12. Mystic Seaport Museum—a town-size living museum of New England's maritime heritage
13. Block Island—Victorian hotels and great biking

New England's weather is famously changeable. Hot, muggy 90°F days in July may be followed by a day or two of cool 65°F weather. Precipitation averages about 3 inches per month year round.

Activities

New Hampshire's White Mountains, Vermont's Green Mountains and the dense forests of northern Maine offer good hiking, rock climbing, mountain biking, camping, canoeing, white-water rafting and skiing. The Appalachian Trail spans New England, from its northern terminus at Maine's Mt Katahdin (5268 feet) through all the states but Rhode Island, continuing south to Georgia. For regional details, contact the Appalachian Mountain Club (☎ 617-523-0636, W www .outdoors.org, 5 Joy St, Boston, MA 02108).

Vermont's Long Trail is a primitive footpath that follows the crest of the Green Mountains 265 miles from Canada to Massachusetts, with 175 miles of side trails and 62 rustic cabins and lean-tos for shelter. The Green Mountain Club (☎ 802-244-7037, W www.greenmountainclub.org, 4711 Waterbury-Stowe Rd, Waterbury Center, VT 05677) has details.

New England's varied terrain makes it a good place for bicycle touring and mountain biking. Maine's Acadia National Park has a good system of hiking and biking trails. Northwestern Vermont (the area around Burlington and Middlebury) and Cape Cod are among the region's easiest but most rewarding biking areas.

Thousands of miles of rugged coastline are great for sailing, canoeing, sea kayaking, windsurfing and whale-watching. Swimming, canoeing, boating, fishing and water-skiing are available on many of the region's lakes and ponds. Though the waters of the Atlantic are chilly, swimming and other beach sports are popular in summer, particularly in the warmer, sheltered waters of Rhode Island and Cape Cod Bay.

Once known for whaling, New England mariners now take visitors on whale-watching cruises from many ports April to October. Naturalist-guided cruises usually cost around $25 and last about five hours. Seas may be rough, which means most land-lubbers will suffer from seasickness; powdered ginger capsules or Dramamine taken before boarding can help. A warm sweater or jacket (a lined windbreaker is perfect), sun hat, sunglasses and sunscreen are essential.

In summer windjammers cruise coastal Maine. These graceful two- or three-mast sailing ships, such as schooners, ketch or yachts, normally sleep 20 to 45 passengers in single, double, triple and quad cabins. Passengers dine aboard. Seasickness is rarely a problem, as they sail mostly in protected waters. June is perhaps the best month to cruise, as the days are long, the harbors uncrowded, the fog rare and light, and the rates lower. However, days can be cool and nights even chilly. Rates are highest July to August (see 'Windjammers' under Camden, in the Maine section).

Accommodations

Lodging choices range from simple campsites to lavish country inns. In addition to hostels and campgrounds, there are plenty of roadside motels offering cheap lodging. Hotels in major cities tend to be in the mid-price and top-end range. New England has over 1500 country inns, many famous for their charm and character. They vary in size and amenities from small B&Bs to rambling historic mansions ($75-200 and up).

Especially in summer and fall-foliage season, lodgings (particularly inns) may have numerous restrictions and requirements regarding minimum stays, smoking, children, service charges, deposit refunds and payment. Be sure to ask. Unless otherwise noted, all rates quoted are for doubles. Single rooms in hotels, motels and inns tend to only be about $10 less, when offered at all.

Food & Drink

Forget Boston baked beans! The region's restaurants offer far more interesting fare, from the traditional fried clams and onion rings to fish, steamed lobster and the most precious creations of 'New American' cuisine, whose chefs prepare American standards like meat-and-potato dishes with a gourmet twist and fresh, often organic, ingredients. You'll find diverse ethnic eateries in major cities as well as smaller but oh-so-hip ones like Northampton and Provincetown, Massachusetts.

Good local produce includes apples, blueberries, cranberries, peaches, plums, rhubarb and strawberries. Maple syrup is produced in all New England states. Local vintners

New England Chow

Some culinary terms you might encounter in New England include the following:

boiled dinner a one-dish meal of boiled beef, cabbage, carrots and potatoes

bread pudding baked pudding made with bread, milk, eggs, vanilla, nutmeg and diced fruit such as dates, nuts or raisins

clam chowder a New England staple, made with chopped sea clams (quahogs), potatoes and perhaps corn in a base of milk and cream

clambake a meal of lobster, clams and corn on the cob, usually steamed

cranberries very tart, sour berries from Massachusetts and Rhode Island, sweetened and used in juice, sauces, muffins, etc

frappe whipped milk and ice cream, pronounced 'frap'; called a 'milkshake' in other regions

fried dough deep-fried pastry dough sprinkled with powdered sugar, served at snack stands and fairs

grinder a large sandwich of sliced meat, sausage, meatballs, cheese, etc, on a long bread roll, called an 'oven grinder' if the sandwich is heated; known as a 'hoagie,' 'sub(marine),' 'po'boy' or 'Cuban' in other regions

Indian pudding baked pudding made of milk, cornmeal, molasses, butter, ginger, cinnamon and raisins

onion rings onion slices dipped in batter and deep-fried.

raw bar place to eat fresh-shucked live (raw) oysters and clams

tonic a sweet and carbonated beverage; known as 'soda' or 'pop' in other regions

produce respectable wines, and brewers concoct award-winning beers. Vermont dairy products – milk, cream, yogurt and cheese – are less renowned than that state's most famous edible: Ben & Jerry's ice cream.

Getting There & Around

Driving around New England is your best bet for ease and accessibility, but buses will get you almost anywhere you want to go (eventually). It's difficult to reach all but a few cities via train. Boston is the region's hub, so you'll no doubt pass through on your way to somewhere else.

Air Boston's Logan International Airport is New England's air hub. Bigger cities, like Worcester, Massachusetts; Providence, Rhode Island; Windsor Locks (near Hartford), Connecticut; Burlington, Vermont; Manchester, New Hampshire; and Portland, Maine, have airports with regional and some national flights. Many smaller towns accommodate regional and commuter flights. Albany, New York, is the closest airport to the Massachusetts Berkshires.

Bus Bonanza Bus Lines (☎ 212-564-8484, 800-556-3815) operates routes from New York to Albany, New York, via the Berkshires (Great Barrington, Stockbridge, Lee, Lenox and Pittsfield); and from New York to Cape Cod (Falmouth, Woods Hole and Hyannis) via Providence. Bonanza also operates buses to Hartford, Connecticut; Bennington, Vermont; and other cities.

Greyhound (☎ 800-231-2222) operates buses from New York to Hartford, New Haven, Springfield, Worcester, and Providence. There are several daily buses between New York and Boston. Other routes run from Boston to Portsmouth and then along the Maine coast. Peter Pan Trailways Bus Lines (☎ 413-781-3320, 800-343-9999) connects Boston with New York; Philadelphia, Pennsylvania; Baltimore, Maryland; and Washington, DC. Regional routes are fairly extensive, with service to Amherst, Northampton, Lenox, New Haven and Hartford.

Vermont Transit Lines (☎ 802-864-6811, 800-451-3292), based in Burlington, serves Boston, Vermont, New Hampshire and Maine from New York and Albany, with connections to Montréal, Canada. Concord Trailways (☎ 603-228-3300, 800-639-3317), based in Concord, New Hampshire, operates buses between Boston and the New Hampshire towns of Manchester, Concord, Laconia, Meredith, Conway, Jackson and Gorham. There's also a route through Plymouth, Lincoln, Franconia and Littleton. From Boston, buses also travel along the Maine coast and to Bangor.

Train The Northeast Corridor is served by 10 to 15 daily Amtrak (☎ 800-872-7245) trains connecting Boston with New York's Penn Station ($58-73; from 4 hours) and Union Station in Washington, DC ($103; from 6½ hours). Some trains are cellphone-free. The new Acela Express isn't as fast (yet) as it's supposed to be, but it is more expensive: The three-hour Boston–New York route costs $120. Boston-Portland service is expected by late 2001.

Northeast Direct Shore Route – runs from Washington, DC, to Boston, stopping in New York; New Haven, Old Saybrook and Mystic, in Connecticut; and Westerly and Providence, Rhode Island, among other places

Northeast Direct Inland Route – follows the main line from Washington, DC, through New York as far as New Haven, Connecticut, then runs west up the Connecticut River Valley. It stops at Wallingford, Meriden, Berlin and Hartford, in Connecticut, then Windsor and Springfield, Massachusetts. One or two trains daily continue past Springfield to Worcester, Framingham and Boston. This route takes much longer than the Northeast Direct Shore Route

Vermonter – offers daily service between Washington, DC, via New York to Stamford, New Haven and Hartford, in Connecticut; Springfield and Amherst, in Massachusetts; and Brattleboro, Montpelier Essex Junction (Burlington) and St Albans, in Vermont

Ethan Allen Express – runs daily from New York via Albany, New York, to Rutland, Vermont

Massachusetts

Massachusetts, the most populous state in New England, has many of the places visitors want to see: Boston, Plymouth, Salem, Marblehead, Cape Cod, Nantucket and Martha's Vineyard, the Five College Area and the Berkshire hills. Since colonial times, Boston has been the hub of the state and indeed of all New England.

History

From the earliest days of colonial settlement, Massachusetts has been the heart of New England. As shipbuilding and maritime trade developed in the 18th century, making many coastal towns wealthy, Massachusetts felt acutely the trade restrictions imposed from London. The Stamp Act (1765) and Townshend Acts (1767) preceded the Boston Massacre (1770), in which British sentries fired into a rowdy mob, killing five.

The 1773 Boston Tea Party – when colonists thinly disguised as Native Americans or blacks dumped chests of taxable British tea into Boston harbor – set the stage for the 1775 battles between British troops and colonial militia at Lexington and Concord, which began the Revolutionary War.

Following the war, speedy clippers brought rich cargoes to Massachusetts ports from the Pacific Northwest, China and the Mediterranean. Ship captains and merchants in Boston, Salem and Marblehead built fine mansions with the proceeds. Fishing craft brought in huge hauls of cod from the Grand Banks, while whaling vessels out of Gloucester, New Bedford and Nantucket caught and rendered the leviathans for their precious oil, bone and ambergris.

Before the Civil War, the Great Potato Famine sent thousands of Irish immigrants to Boston. They were later joined by waves of immigrants from French Canada, Italy and Portugal, with some staying in the port towns and others moving inland to work

Massachusetts

Nicknames: Bay State, Old Colony, Taxachusetts

Population: 6,349,000 (13th)

Area: 10,555 sq miles (44th)

Admitted to Union: February 6, 1788 (6th)

Capital city: Boston (population 589,000; metro area 3 million)

Other cities: Worcester (173,000), Springfield (152,000)

State cliché: Why botha?

State insect: ladybug

Birthplace of: Ben Franklin (1706–90), Paul Revere (1735–1818), John Hancock (1737–93), Ralph Waldo Emerson (1803–82), Emily Dickinson (1830–86), Dr Seuss (1904–91), cotton-gin inventor Eli Whitney (1765–1825), Samuel Morse (1791–1872), heavyweight boxer Rocky Marciano (1924–69), Presidents John Adams (1735–1826), John Quincy Adams (1767–1848), John F Kennedy (1917–63) and George Bush (b 1924)

in the mills and factories of Fall River, Fitchburg, Northampton, Springfield and Worcester.

Government & Economy

With a gaggle of Kennedys elected to high offices over the last 50 years, and Tip O'Neil reigning as speaker of the House of Representatives for so many years, Massachusetts has always been a stalwart liberal bastion. Nonetheless, since 1992 voters have put Republicans in the governor's office. In 2001, Acting Governor Jane Swift became the first head of a state to give birth while in office (and twins at that). With 10 of 10 Democratic US representatives and two US Democratic senators (including liberal giant Ted Kennedy), the state leans left of center.

Massachusetts' shipyards were kept busy during WWII, but they stand idle today. The state's population continued to grow into the 21st century, thanks to a boom in the computer and electronics industries.

Arts

If New England is the birthplace of US culture, then Massachusetts represents the center of the center. Scrimshaw, carved from ivory and whalebone by sailors on long voyages in the mid-19th century, remains a treasured art. Shakers (in communities in western Massachusetts, New Hampshire and Maine) were the finest furniture makers in the 19th century; their simple but artful designs still reign. Even Paul Revere, remembered for his midnight ride to warn that redcoats were coming, was a master silversmith.

Abbott McNeill Whistler (1834–1903), of Lowell, blurred the lines of representational painting and emphasized the play of light. In the 20th century John Singer Sargent (1856–1925) painted telling portraits of Boston's upper class, while Norman Rockwell (1894–1978) painted common men for *Saturday Evening Post* covers. Daniel Chester French (1850–1931) sculpted the seated Lincoln in Washington's Lincoln Memorial; his studio is in Lenox. In Boston, modern architect IM Pei's radical JFK Library and John Hancock Tower stand in stark contrast to traditional European works by Henry Hobson Richardson (1838–86), including Trinity Church, and Charles Bulfinch (1763–1844), such as the State House. Cape

Cod cottages, town greens with steepled churches and Georgian brick campuses are well known around the country.

New Englanders' passion for literature was evident as early as 1828, when Noah Webster (1758–1843) published his *American Dictionary of the English Language*. Concordian Ralph Waldo Emerson (1803–82) gained a nationwide – even worldwide – audience for his philosophical and ethical teachings, as did Henry David Thoreau (1817–62), who was among the first Americans to advocate living simply in harmony with nature. *Little Women* author Louisa May Alcott (1832–88) resided and wrote down the street from her colleagues in Concord. Poet Henry Wadsworth Longfellow (1807–82) lived and worked in Cambridge for 45 years, while Henry James (1843–1916) wrote about Boston parlor society in *The Bostonians* (1886). Pulitzer prize–winning novelist Edith Wharton (1862–1937) wrote *Ethan Frome* while summering in Lenox. Sold from a slave ship in Boston, Phyllis Wheatley (1753–84) was the first African American female poet of note. Reclusive poet Emily Dickinson (1830–86) lived quietly in Amherst.

Information

Contact the Massachusetts Office of Travel & Tourism (☎ 617-973-8500, 800-447-6277, Ⓦ www.massvacation.com, Transportation Building, 10 Park Plaza, Suite 4510, Boston, MA 02116) for information on the state's many attractions. The state sales tax is 5%; restaurant tax is also 5%. The combined state and local lodging tax varies from 9.7% in most towns to 14.15% in Boston and major cities.

BOSTON

Once called 'the hub of the solar system' by proud resident Oliver Wendell Holmes, Boston is at least the hub (and largest city) of New England. Historic, attractive and with strong neighborhoods of manageable size, it's also young at heart because of the 35 colleges and universities in the greater Boston area.

History

Called 'Trimountain' (for its three hills) when it was settled in 1624, Boston later took its permanent name from the English town. As capital and chief port of the Massachusetts

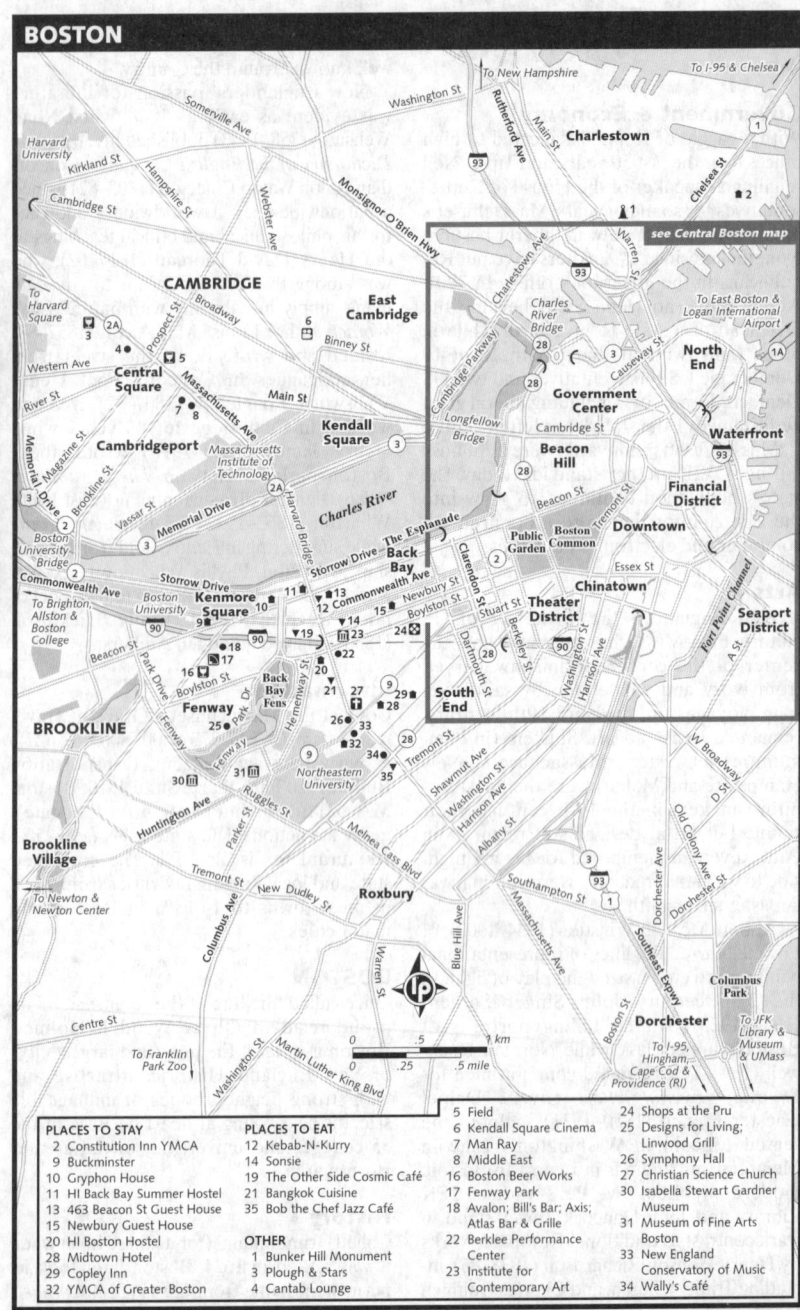

BOSTON

NEW ENGLAND

PLACES TO STAY
2 Constitution Inn YMCA
9 Buckminster
10 Gryphon House
11 HI Back Bay Summer Hostel
13 463 Beacon St Guest House
15 Newbury Guest House
20 HI Boston Hostel
28 Midtown Hotel
29 Copley Inn
32 YMCA of Greater Boston

PLACES TO EAT
12 Kebab-N-Kurry
14 Sonsie
19 The Other Side Cosmic Café
21 Bangkok Cuisine
35 Bob the Chef Jazz Café

OTHER
1 Bunker Hill Monument
3 Plough & Stars
4 Cantab Lounge
5 Field
6 Kendall Square Cinema
7 Man Ray
8 Middle East
16 Boston Beer Works
17 Fenway Park
18 Avalon; Bill's Bar; Axis;
   Atlas Bar & Grille
22 Berklee Performance
   Center
23 Institute for
   Contemporary Art
24 Shops at the Pru
25 Designs for Living;
   Linwood Grill
26 Symphony Hall
27 Christian Science Church
30 Isabella Stewart Gardner
   Museum
31 Museum of Fine Arts
   Boston
33 New England
   Conservatory of Music
34 Wally's Café

Bay Colony (established in 1630), it was the center of Puritan New England. The Boston Public Latin School was founded in 1635, followed by Harvard College a year later and a public library in 1653. The first newspaper in the 13 original colonies was founded here in 1704. Boston was also the center of resistance to British rule during the Revolutionary War. The Boston Massacre (1770), Boston Tea Party (1773) and Battle of Bunker Hill (1775) were significant events in the colonies' fight for freedom. Prominent Bostonians such as John Hancock, Samuel Adams, James Otis and Paul Revere were among the founders of the American republic.

Today, greater Boston remains at the forefront of American education. Its education resources have spawned important industries in electronics, biotechnology, medicine and finance. The city has always been a leader in US intellectual life.

Orientation
The Boston Common is the nucleus of the city. The Park St station, the hub of the Massachusetts Bay Transportation Authority (MBTA) subway system (the 'T') is beneath the Common's northeast corner. Boston is eminently walkable: The most interesting area for travelers is only about 1 mile wide by 3 miles long. Harvard Square, the heart of neighboring Cambridge (on the other side of the Charles River) is about 5 miles west of the Common. Red Line trains from Park St whisk you there in minutes.

Information
Tourist Offices The visitor information center (☎ 617-426-3115, Ⓦ www.bostonusa .com), on the Boston Common near Tremont and West Sts, is open daily. The Boston National Historical Park Visitor Center (☎ 617-242-5642, 15 State St), across from the Old State House, has more information about the Freedom Trail (open daily). The Cambridge Office for Tourism (☎ 617-441-2884, 800-862-5678) has an information kiosk in Harvard Square.

The volunteer Traveler's Aid Society (☎ 617-542-7286, 17 East St), across from South Station, helps with problems 8:30am-5pm weekdays. Their desk inside South Station is open on weekends. The booth at Logan Airport's Terminal E (☎ 617-567-5385) is open noon-9pm daily.

Post & Communications Boston's main post office (☎ 617-654-5326, 25 Dorchester Ave) is one block southeast of South Station. Remarkably, it never closes. Go here for general delivery (poste restante) mail. You can access the Internet (free for 15 minutes) at the Boston Public Library (☎ 617-536-5400, 666 Boylston St), at Exeter St. Alternatively, get a visitor courtesy card at the circulation desk and sign up for one hour of free terminal time (arrive at 9am, when the library opens). Designs for Living (☎ 617-536-6150, 52 Queensberry St) also offers Internet access.

Travel Agencies Budget travel specialists include Council Travel (☎ 617-266-1926, 800-226-8624, 273 Newbury St). The Vacation Outlet at Filene's Basement (☎ 617-267-8100, 426 Washington St) offers lots of last-minute travel bargains, as does Last Minute Travel Services (☎ 617-267-9800, 800-527-8646).

Bookstores The Globe Corner Bookstore (500 Boylston St), in Back Bay, sells travel books and maps. It has another location in Harvard Square (49 Palmer St), behind the Harvard Coop. Harvard Square, a book lover's paradise, boasts more than 30 bookstores; pick up a pamphlet at the information kiosk. Among the best are the Harvard Book Store (1256 Massachusetts Ave), Wordsworth (30 Brattle St) and the specialty Grolier Poetry Book Shop. Back in Boston, seek out Avenue Victor Hugo Bookshop (339 Newbury St) for used books, and We Think the World of You (540 Tremont St) for gay titles.

Boston Common & Public Garden
Established in 1634, the 50-acre Boston Common is the city's heart and the country's oldest public park. In the park's northeast corner is the **Robert Gould Shaw Memorial**, dedicated to the leader and troops of the first African American regiment to fight for the Union in the Civil War. Sculptor Augustus Saint-Gaudens (1848–1907) created the bas-relief of the white colonel.

Adjacent to the Common is the Public Garden, a 24-acre botanical oasis of cultivated flower beds, clipped grass, ancient trees, a tranquil lagoon and pedal-powered swan boats, which children enjoy. Historic buildings, top-end hotels, shopping and entertainment surround both parks.

Freedom Trail

The 2½-mile Freedom Trail (☎ 617-242-5642) links 16 important colonial and revolutionary history sites. Follow the double row of red sidewalk bricks (or painted red line) beginning near the Park Street T station, winding through downtown and the North End, and terminating at the USS *Constitution* in Charlestown. Maps are available from both visitor information centers (see Information). National Park Service rangers lead free tours daily. Unless otherwise noted, all the sites listed in the Beacon Hill & Downtown and North End & Charlestown sections are on the trail and free.

Beacon Hill & Downtown

North of Boston Common is Beacon Hill, Boston's most historic and affluent residential neighborhood. It's crowned by the 1798 golden-domed **State House** (☎ 617-727-3676), where free tours are available. Seek out Louisburg Square, an elegant cluster of million-dollar homes facing a private park. The nearby **African Meeting House** (☎ 617-723-8863, 8 Smith Court) is the country's oldest African American meeting house, a stirring place where Frederick Douglass and William Lloyd Garrison delivered passionate speeches. Next door is the **Museum of Afro American History** (☎ 617-725-0022).

Next to the historic **Park Street Church** on Tremont St, southeast of the State House, is the wonderful **Old Granary Burying Ground**, dating to 1660. Continue north to **King's Chapel** (58 Tremont St), at School St, which houses the largest bell made by Paul Revere. Head south on School St to the traditional **Old South Meeting House** (☎ 617-482-6439, 310 Washington St), where colonists met before throwing the Boston Tea Party ($3). South along Washington St, Downtown Crossing is a bustling pedestrian-only shopping area that's home to pushcart vendors and street musicians.

Two blocks northeast, the 1713 **Old State House** (☎ 617-720-3290, 206 Washington St), now a museum of revolutionary memorabilia, was once the colonial government house ($3). The Declaration of Independence was first read to Bostonians from its balcony in 1776. Due east of City Hall, **Faneuil Hall** (**fan**-yool hall) is the brick building with the grasshopper weather vane on top. Constructed in 1740 as a market and public meeting place, it has been a venue for inspired speeches since the mid-18th century. Today, with the granite Quincy Market and North and South Market buildings, it is part of Faneuil Hall Marketplace, a shopping and dining complex.

North End & Charlestown

The North End has been Boston's Italian quarter since the 1920s. Follow the Freedom Trail north on Hanover St to the **Paul Revere House** (☎ 617-523-1676, 19 N Square). Built in 1680, it's the oldest house in Boston and former home of the patriot who carried advance warning of British maneuvers to Lexington and Concord on the night of April 18, 1775 ($2.50). **Old North Church** (☎ 617-523-6676, 193 Salem St) is Boston's oldest church (1723). On the night of April 18, 1775, two lanterns were hung in its lofty steeple, signaling Revere and two other messengers waiting across the river that the British force would set out by sea ('one if by land, two if by sea').

Cross Charlestown Bridge from Commercial St to reach the **USS *Constitution*** (☎ 617-242-5670), in Charlestown Navy Yard. Cannonballs bounced off the sturdy oaken sides of what is now the US Navy's oldest commissioned ship afloat (built in 1797), thus its nickname, 'Old Ironsides.' Walk northwest along narrow streets lined with colonial houses and gas lanterns to the **Bunker Hill Monument** (☎ 617-242-5641), in Monument Square. This 220-foot granite obelisk commemorates the battle of June 17, 1775, when a small US force entrenched on the hill inflicted huge casualties on a much larger British force. Running low on ammunition, the Americans were told, 'Don't fire until you see the whites of their eyes.'

Back Bay

Once a tidal flat, this chic neighborhood west of Boston Common was filled in during the population boom of the 1850s. Its grid of streets boasts fine Victorian houses, churches, boutiques and restaurants. **Gibson House** (☎ 617-267-6338, 137 Beacon St) is a splendid six-story Victorian brownstone ($5).

Copley Square is surrounded by historic buildings, including the 1877 French-Romanesque **Trinity Church** (☎ 617-536-0944) and the venerable **Boston Public Library** (☎ 617-536-5400). Chic boutiques, galleries and cafes are on Newbury St. More are indoors at Copley Place and the Shops at the Pru, a few blocks farther west.

The **Institute for Contemporary Art** (☎ 617-266-5152, 955 Boylston St) raises an eyebrow or two every now and then with its exhibits ($6, free after 5pm Thurs). The **Christian Science Church** (☎ 617-450-3790, 175 Huntington Ave), a few blocks south along Massachusetts Ave, is the international home of the...guess what...Christian Science Church.

Cambridge

Founded in 1638, Cambridge is synonymous with Harvard University and the Massachusetts Institute of Technology (MIT). With a combined enrollment of almost 25,000 students from 100 countries, the schools keep Cambridge lively, smart and young. **Harvard Square** overflows with cafes, bookstores, restaurants and street performers. The 'square' is in fact a triangle of brick above the Harvard T station. The epicenter is Out of Town News, the place for foreign newspapers and magazines. The gates to famed **Harvard Yard** (1636), a quadrangle of ivy-covered brick buildings, are just across Massachusetts Ave. Harvard campus tours (☎ 617-495-1573, 1350 Massachusetts Ave) start from the modern Holyoke Center.

Harvard's museums are outstanding. The **Harvard Museums of Natural History** (☎ 617-495-3045, 24 Oxford St) have good exhibits on Central American ethnology and archaeology and an amazing collection of glass flowers ($6.50). The **Fogg Art Museum** (☎ 617-495-9400, 32 Quincy St) presents exquisite exhibits of Western art from the Middle Ages to the present ($5). The **Busch-Reisinger Museum**, entered through the Fogg, specializes in Northern European art. The **Arthur Sackler Museum** (☎ 617-495-9400, 485 Broadway) is devoted to Asian and Islamic art ($5). The **Massachusetts Institute of Technology** is 2 miles southeast of Harvard Square along Massachusetts Ave. Walking tours begin at the information center (☎ 617-253-4795, 77 Massachusetts Ave).

Other Attractions

At most of the following attractions and the Boston Common visitor information center, you should purchase a discount visitor pass ($28.25) if you plan on visiting at least half of them.

The **Museum of Fine Arts Boston** (☎ 617-267-9300, 465 Huntington Ave) is among the country's finest art museums, especially strong in American painting, decorative arts, Asian treasures and European painting, including French impressionists ($12, 'voluntary contribution' Wed evening). A few blocks west, the **Isabella Stewart Gardner Museum** (☎ 617-566-1401, 280 The Fenway) is a magnificent Venetian-style palazzo filled with almost 2000 priceless art objects, primarily European. The palazzo itself, with a four-story greenhouse courtyard, is worth the admission ($11; closed Mon).

The excellent **Museum of Science** (☎ 617-723-2500), on the Charles River Dam, is an educational feast of fun, especially for kids ($11/8 adults/kids). Check what's playing at its exciting Omni Theater.

On the waterfront at Atlantic Ave, the three-story-high tank in the **New England Aquarium** (☎ 617-973-5200) holds over 700 sea creatures ($13). The **Children's Museum** (☎ 617-426-8855, 300 Congress St) entertains preschoolers to teenagers for an entire day with interactive educational exhibits ($7/6 adults/kids, Fri evenings $1). The nearby *Beaver II* and **Boston Tea Party Museum** (☎ 617-338-1773) commemorate the colonial protest against the tea tax imposed from London in 1773, when locals dumped tea into the harbor ($8).

The **John F Kennedy Library & Museum** (☎ 617-929-4500), at Columbia Point, Dorchester, is the repository for memorabilia related to the 35th US president ($8). Take the T's Red Line to JFK/UMass, then hop on a free shuttle bus.

Boston Harbor Islands State Park is a refuge on hot summer days. A kiosk on Long Wharf (☎ 617-223-8666) dispenses all the details. Boston Harbor Cruises (☎ 617-227-4320) offers daily ferries from Long Wharf off Atlantic Ave ($8 roundtrip).

Organized Tours

Boston Duck Tours (☎ 617-723-3825), at the Boylston St side of the Prudential Center, offers touristy but popular land-and-water

CENTRAL BOSTON

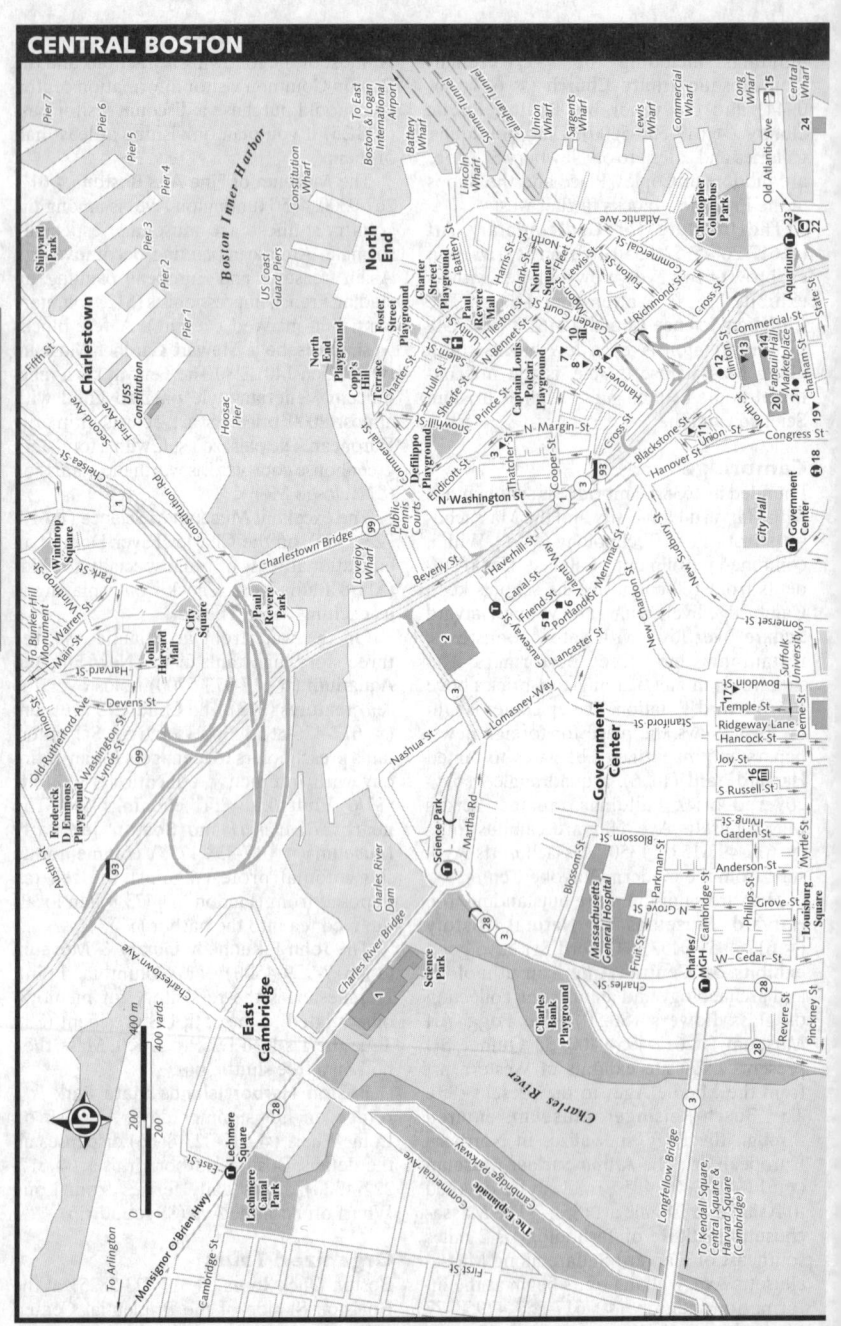

CENTRAL BOSTON

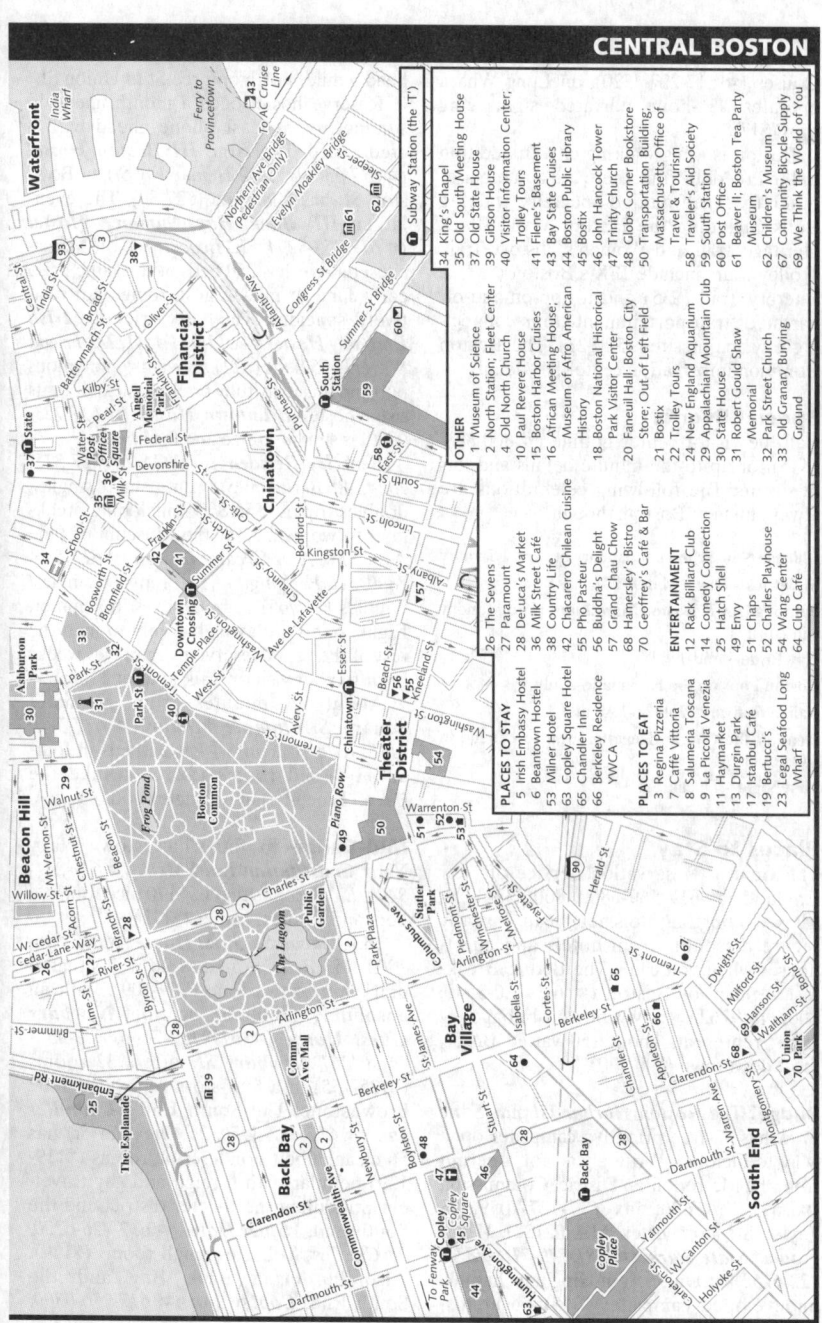

Subway Station (the 'T')

OTHER
1 Museum of Science
2 North Station; Fleet Center
4 Old North Church
10 Paul Revere House
15 Boston Harbor Cruises
16 African Meeting House;
   Museum of Afro American
   History
18 Boston National Historical
   Park Visitor Center
20 Faneuil Hall; Boston City
   Store; Out of Left Field
21 Bostix
22 Trolley Tours
24 New England Aquarium
29 Appalachian Mountain Club
30 State House
31 Robert Gould Shaw
   Memorial
32 Park Street Church
33 Old Granary Burying
   Ground

34 King's Chapel
35 Old South Meeting House
37 Old State House
39 Gibson House
40 Visitor Information Center;
   Trolley Tours
41 Filene's Basement
43 Bay State Cruises
44 Boston Public Library
45 Bostix
46 John Hancock Tower
47 Trinity Church
48 Globe Corner Bookstore
50 Transportation Building;
   Massachusetts Office of
   Travel & Tourism
58 Traveler's Aid Society
59 South Station
60 Post Office
61 Beaver II; Boston Tea Party
   Museum
62 Children's Museum
67 Community Bicycle Supply
69 We Think the World of You

PLACES TO STAY
5 Irish Embassy Hostel
6 Beantown Hostel
53 Milner Hotel
63 Copley Square Hotel
65 Chandler Inn
66 Berkeley Residence
   YWCA

PLACES TO EAT
3 Regina Pizzeria
7 Caffè Vittoria
8 Salumeria Toscana
9 La Piccola Venezia
11 Haymarket
13 Durgin Park
17 Istanbul Café
19 Bertucci's
23 Legal Seafood Long
   Wharf

26 The Sevens
27 Paramount
28 DeLuca's Market
36 Milk Street Café
38 Country Life
42 Chacarero Chilean Cuisine
55 Pho Pasteur
56 Buddha's Delight
57 Grand Chau Chow
68 Hamersley's Bistro
70 Geoffrey's Café & Bar

ENTERTAINMENT
12 Rack Billiard Club
14 Comedy Connection
49 Hatch Shell
51 Envy
52 Chaps
52 Charles Playhouse
54 Wang Center
64 Club Café

NEW ENGLAND

tours using WWII amphibious vehicles known as 'ducks' ($22). Boston Harbor Cruises (☎ 617-227-4320), on Long Wharf, operates 1½-hour narrated sightseeing trips ($17).

Boston is a big walking city. In addition to the Freedom Trail, there are a number of other free, self-guided specialty walking trails, including the Harbor Walk, Black Heritage Trail and Women's History Trail. Trolley tours include JFK's Boston ($27), a Literary Trail ($35) and a hop-on-and-off narrated 'transportainment' tour connecting city major sites ($20-23). The Boston Common information center has details.

Special Events

Call the visitor center hotline (☎ 800-888-5515) for up-to-the-minute details and lots of events. The following celebrations are always huge in Boston, though:

Chinese New Year – late January or early February

St Patrick's Day – March 17

Patriot's Day & Boston Marathon – third Monday in April

Gay Pride – mid-June

Boston Pops on the Esplanade – July 4

Italian festivals – July and August

Head of the Charles Regatta – third weekend in October

First Night – December 31

Places to Stay

The Central Reservation Service of New England (☎ 617-569-3800, 800-332-3026, Ⓦ www.bostonhotels.net) can usually secure discounts from hotels and guest-houses when you can't. The Bed & Breakfast Agency of Boston (☎ 617-720-3540, 800-248-9262, Ⓦ www.boston-bnbagency .com) represents about 150 varied B&Bs, most downtown ($90-140).

Budget The *Boston Harbor Islands State Park* has 42 free primitive campsites open May to October. Write ahead for a permit from the Metropolitan District Commission (☎ 617-727-7676, fax 617-727-7059, 98 Taylor St, Dorchester, MA 02122). *Wompatuck State Park* (☎ 781-749-7160, 877-422-6762), at Union St in Hingham, has 400 undeveloped campsites ($15) on almost 4000 acres 30 minutes south of Boston by

car (open May-Oct). Take I-93 south to MA 3, continue south to MA 228 exit 14, then head 5 miles north on Free St to Union St.

Reserve hostel beds a month ahead in summer, or at least phone ahead with a credit card. The large *HI Boston Hostel* (☎ 617-536-9455, 12 Hemenway St), at Boylston St, has 208 beds ($27-30). The even-larger *HI Back Bay Summer Hostel* (☎ 617-353-3294, 512 Beacon St), off Massachusetts Ave, has 250 beds at the same price early June to mid-August; rooms are relatively spacious. The very friendly *Irish Embassy Hostel* (☎ 617-973-4841, 232 Friend St) rents 55 beds ($22) above its eponymous pub and is usually fully booked. Next door its sister hostel, *Beantown Hostel* (☎ 617-723-0800) is similar in size and facilities.

Berkeley Residence YWCA (☎ 617-375-2524, 40 Berkeley St) rents small singles/doubles/triples ($56/86/99, including breakfast) to women. Near the Museum of Fine Arts, *YMCA of Greater Boston* (☎ 617-536-7800, 316 Huntington Ave) rents 95 singles/doubles ($45/65) to both sexes in summer. Eight rooms are available only to men the rest of the year. Reserve by mail two weeks prior to your visit or walk in after 11am.

About 20 minutes from Kenmore Square, *Strathmore Manor* (☎ 617-730-4118, 1876 Beacon St) has 32 beds in four- and two-bed rooms ($25-30). Take the Green Line C train to Englewood.

Mid-Range In the Charlestown Navy Yard, *Constitution Inn YMCA* (☎ 617-241-8400, 150 Second Ave) has 170 nice rooms, a pool and a fitness center ($115).

463 Beacon St Guest House (☎ 617-536-1302, 463 Beacon St) has 20 well-situated units in a brownstone ($89-109). With an absolutely fabulous location, *Newbury Guest House* (☎ 617-437-7666, 800-437-7668, 261 Newbury St) offers 32 rooms ($125-155) in a four-story renovated 1882 brownstone. The South End's *Chandler Inn* (☎ 617-482-3450, 26 Chandler St) has 56 clean, albeit nondescript, rooms ($119-139) popular with foreign and gay travelers. Straddling the theater district and the South End, *Milner Hotel* (☎ 617-426-6220, 78 Charles St) has 67 small rooms ($129). Also bordering Back Bay and the South End, *Copley Inn* (☎ 617-236-0300, 800-232-0306, 19 Garrison St) has 21 comfortable studios ($125) in a residential neighborhood.

Considering the 17 rooms of *A Friendly Inn* (☎ *617-547-7851, 1673 Cambridge St)* are just a 10-minute walk to Harvard Square, you can't beat the price: $137, including private bath.

Five miles south in Dorchester, immediately off I-93, you'll find two *Ramada Inns* (☎ *617-287-9100, 800 and 900 Morrissey Blvd)* with standard issue rooms ($149-159); take the T to JFK, then a free shuttle.

Top End Near Fenway Park, *Buckminster* (☎ *617-236-7050, 645 Beacon St)* has 94 standard rooms with private bath ($139-169). Built in 1891, *Copley Square Hotel* (☎ *617-536-9000, 800-225-7062, 47 Huntington Ave)* attracts a low-key European crowd to its 134 refurbished rooms, which vary in size ($169-229). At *Midtown Hotel* (☎ *617-262-1000, 800-343-1177, 220 Huntington Ave)* the 159 rooms fill up with families, businesspeople and tour groups; a pool and parking are included ($119-259). A very nice five-story brownstone near Kenmore Square, *Gryphon House* (☎ *617-375-9003, 9 Bay State Rd)* offers eight 19th-century period rooms, modern amenities, and parking ($185-245).

Places to Eat

Offering far more than old-time New England fare, 'Beantown' (a reference to Boston's baked beans) provides a cornucopia of options for the food connoisseur.

Beacon Hill & Downtown In Faneuil Hall Marketplace, Quincy Market offers a wide variety of food shops under one roof, with decent prices. The king of open-air produce markets, *Haymarket*, on Blackstone St near Faneuil Hall, offers cheap goods Friday and Saturday. Adjacent to the Common and Public Garden, *DeLuca's Market (11 Charles St)* has convenient if pricey picnic supplies.

On Beacon Hill, *The Sevens (77 Charles St)* is a friendly pub that's crowded 11:30am-1am. Get a sandwich and a beer for about $10. A neighborhood hangout, *Paramount (44 Charles St)* has cafeteria-style breakfasts and lunches, but more upscale dinners ($8-16). *Istanbul Café (37 Bowdoin St)* features some of the best Turkish cuisine this side of

the Izmir Peninsula; portions are large and it's moderately priced, too.

If you're walking the Freedom Trail, detour to tranquil Post Office Square's *Milk Street Café (50 Milk St)*, serving above-average pastas, salads, soups and sandwiches ($6-8). Nearby, *Chacarero Chilean Cuisine (426 Washington St)* dispenses enormous hot takeout sandwiches ($4-6). Many restaurants feature vegetarian dishes, but the financial district's *Country Life (200 High St)* boasts a meat- and dairy-free all-you-can-eat lunch buffet ($7).

Durgin Park, in Faneuil Hall Marketplace, has been serving market workers and shoppers since 1827 and is aggressively unfancy. It serves huge slabs of prime rib, chowder, chicken potpie, Boston baked beans and Indian pudding for lunch and dinner ($8 and up). *Bertucci's (22 Merchants Row)*, next to the marketplace, has very good wood-fired brick-oven pizza.

How to Eat a Lobster

Lobsters molt (shed their shells) in mid-summer. Before that, the shells are bone-hard and a chore to crack. The new, soft shells of late summer and fall make them easier to eat, but – purists say – not as tasty.

Eating lobster is a messy pleasure. The best place to go is an informal eatery called a lobster 'pound' or 'pool,' where you can tear them apart with your fingers. You'll get a plastic bib, metal cracker for the claws, melted butter with lemon juice for dipping the meat, a dish for the shells and lots of napkins. Suck the meat out of the legs and back flippers, crack and eat the claws, then twist off the tail and fork out the meat in one piece.

Lobsters are cheapest during the summer harvest season; part of the catch is kept alive in saltwater pools for winter sale. Lobster pounds sell them cooked for about $10 apiece, restaurants for $12-40.

On the waterfront, a few blocks from Faneuil Hall, *Legal Seafood Long Wharf (255 State St)* has built its prime seafood reputation on the motto 'If it's not fresh, it's not Legal.' Lunch costs about $15; dinner will be double that if you're not careful.

In Chinatown, crowds throng *Pho Pasteur (682 Washington St)* for hearty, hot, cheap and filling meal-in-a-bowl noodle soups ($6 for extra large). *Grand Chau Chow (45 Beach St)* has excellent seafood specials and ample portions ($5-10). *Buddha's Delight (5 Beach St)* will thrill vegetarians with noodle soups and tasty tofu (lunch $5, dinner $10).

North End Of the more than 50 Italian eateries here, *La Piccola Venezia (263 Hanover St)* consistently provides a great value with huge portions of old-fashioned dishes ($10-14). *Salumeria Toscana (151 Richmond St)* is an atmospheric place for prosciutto, salami, cheese, bread and olives. *Regina Pizzeria (11½ Thatcher St)* serves Boston's best thin-crust pizza ($13 for a large pepperoni) with pitchers of beer ($10-15). *Caffè Vittoria (296 Hanover St)* is a nice spot for old-world charm and coffee.

Back Bay & Around Near the Boston International Hostel, *Bangkok Cuisine (177A Massachusetts Ave)* has good pad Thai ($7 lunch, $10 dinner). For neighborhood Indian food, *Kebab-N-Kurry (30 Massachusetts Ave)* can't be beat ($6 lunch, $10-14 dinner). *The Other Side Cosmic Café (407 Newbury St)* has a funky, Seattle-inspired style. *Sonsie* (☎ 617-351-2500, 327 Newbury St), near Massachusetts Ave, is one of the trendiest place to sip a cappuccino; the creative French-Asian fusion cuisine is excellent, if pricey, so try their lighter dishes.

In the South End, cruise Columbus Ave for a varied selection of hip restaurants. Sunday brunch is fashionable with the gay crowd, and *Geoffrey's Café & Bar (578 Tremont St)* is one of the more popular places. *Bob the Chef Jazz Cafe (604 Columbus Ave)* serves up Boston's best down-home soul food; we're talking barbecue ribs or fried chicken with a side of black-eyed peas ($5-12). For fantastic upscale dining, *Hamersley's Bistro* (☎ 617-423-2700, 553 Tremont St), among Boston's best bistros, will cost you about $100 for two (make reservations).

Cambridge Near Harvard Square, *The Garage (36 John F Kennedy St)* contains a dozen fast food eateries, including the highly regarded Pho Pasteur (their main location is in Chinatown – see Beacon Hill & Downtown, earlier). Three short blocks east of the square, *Bartley's Burger Cottage (1246 Massachusetts Ave)* is the primo hamburger joint. For old-world ambience, try *Cafe Pamplona (12 Bow St)* for a coffee. *Sabra Grill (20 Eliot St)* serves great Middle Eastern cuisine for vegetarians and their contrarian friends.

Entertainment

Boston boasts an impressive variety of cultural attractions. For up-to-the-minute listings, buy Thursday's *Boston Globe,* Friday's *Boston Herald* or the weekly *Boston Phoenix.* Pick up the sassy biweekly competitors, *Improper Bostonian* and *Stuff @ Night.* Gay and lesbian travelers might want to pick up *Bay Windows* for up-to-the-minute information (especially for women's clubs), since nights devoted to one sex or the other frequently change. Most bars close at 1am, clubs around 2am. Subway service is infrequent after 11pm and stops altogether at 12:30am.

Half-price tickets to same-day theater, dance, music, comedy and sporting events are sold for cash only (beginning at 10am or 11am) at the Bostix kiosks on the south side of Faneuil Hall (☎ 617-723-5181) and in Copley Square at Dartmouth and Boylston Sts.

Bars & Pubs The *Rack Billiard Club (20 Clinton St)*, on the edge of Faneuil Hall Marketplace, is an upscale pool hall and bar. Prior to hitting the strip of nearby clubs on Lansdowne St, hit *Atlas Bar & Grille (145 Ipswich St)* for a round or two. The neighborhood *Linwood Grill (81 Kilmarnock St)* is a Fenway mainstay, as is *Boston Beer Works (61 Brookline Ave)*, which brews its own seasonal concoctions. *Club Café (209 Columbus Ave)*, a convivial bar and restaurant, caters to gays and lesbians.

Cambridge is swarming with good places. In Harvard Square, subterranean *John Harvard's Brew House (33 Dunster St)* smells and feels like an English pub. Between Harvard and Central Squares, *Plough & Stars (912 Massachusetts Ave)* is but one of the city's friendly Irish bars. Funky *Field (20 Prospect St)* represents Central Square's unpretentious roots. In trendy Davis Square, *Burren (247 Elm St)* bucks trends with traditional Irish music nightly.

Live Music Again, head to Cambridge. In Central Square, look for the diverse and highly regarded *Middle East (☎ 617-354-8238, 472 Massachusetts Ave)*, hosting three different gigs nightly; *Man Ray (☎ 617-864-0400, 21 Brookline St)*, the city's most 'underground' club; and *Cantab Lounge (☎ 617-354-2685, 738 Massachusetts Ave)*, grungy and laid-back, with good blues and bluegrass. In Harvard Square, *House of Blues (☎ 617-491-2583, 96 Winthrop St)* is a major force on the national blues scene, while venerable *Club Passim (☎ 617-492-7679, 47 Palmer St)* is renowned for supporting the early careers of many notable artists such as Patty Larkin, Tracy Chapman and Jackson Browne. Upscale *Regattabar (☎617-661-5000)*, in the Charles Hotel, has a yacht-club atmosphere and hosts big-name acts. Near Davis Square in Somerville, *Johnny D's Uptown (☎ 617-776-2004, 17 Holland St)* is one of the best and most eclectic rock venues.

Back in Boston, stop by gritty and smoky *Wally's Café (☎ 617-424-1408, 427 Massachusetts Ave)* for traditional jazz, R&B, Latin and Cuban. *Berklee Performance Center (☎ 617-747-2261, 136 Massachusetts Ave)* hosts impressive (and inexpensive) student and faculty jazz concerts.

Dance Clubs Many clubs are along Lansdowne St near Kenmore Square and the Fenway, but the Theater District (on tiny Boylston Place, between Tremont and Charles Sts, and on Tremont St near Stuart St) has some too. Cover varies widely, from free (if you arrive early) to $15. Most clubs are open 10pm-2am Friday and Saturday; call about other days.

Avalon (☎ 617-262-2424, 15 Lansdowne St) is a huge club featuring house, techno, international and industrial dance music. Sunday night is popular with the gay crowd. Everyone from the transgender community to drag queens converges on *Axis (☎617-262-2437, 13 Lansdowne St)* on Monday night.

The smaller *Bill's Bar (☎ 617-421-9678, 5½ Lansdowne St)* is usually packed with students. The Theater District's *Envy (☎ 617-542-3689, 25 Boylston Place)* is an envious place to see and be seen, featuring Top 40, dance and house music.

Chaps (☎ 617-695-9500, 100 Warrenton St) has a little something for all the guys.

Cinema In Harvard Square run to the *Brattle Theater (☎ 617-876-6837, 40 Brattle St)*, which shows art and foreign films, and the *Harvard Film Archive (☎ 617-495-4700, 24 Quincy St)*, at the Carpenter Center for the Visual Arts, which screens at least two films daily. Call the *Kendall Square Cinema (☎ 617-494-9800, 1 Kendall Square)* to see what artsy films are showing. The City of Boston shows free movies under the stars at the *Hatch Shell (☎ 617-727-9547)*, on Charles River Esplanade, on Friday at dusk July to August; bring a blanket and picnic.

Performing Arts The cavernous *Wang Center (☎617-482-9393, 270 Tremont St)* hosts the Boston Ballet and modern dance, opera and theater. The two-stage *Charles Playhouse (74 Warrenton St)* hosts the long-running comical whodunit mystery *Shear Madness* (☎ 617-426-5225) and the Blue Man Group (☎ 617-426-6912), mixed media performance art. The prestigious *American Repertory Theater (A-R-T; ☎ 617-547-8300, 64 Brattle St)* produces serious and experimental plays in Harvard Square. *Comedy Connection (☎ 617-248-9700)*, in Quincy Market, is the city's oldest and biggest comedy venue; tickets are cheaper on weekdays.

Boston boasts both one of the world's best symphony orchestras and the beloved Boston Pops. Both perform at *Symphony Hall (☎ 617-266-1492, 266-1200 for tickets, 301 Massachusetts Ave)*. Many free summer concerts take place at the *Hatch Shell* (see Cinema), of which the Boston Pops' July 4th concert, complete with fireworks and brass cannons, is the most lavish and crowded. The *New England Conservatory of Music (☎ 617-585-1122, Jordan Hall, 30 Gainsborough St)* hosts free classical concerts by professors and students.

Spectator Sports

The Boston Red Sox (☎ 617-267-1700, 4 Yawkey Way) play major-league baseball in Fenway Park from early April to late September (tickets $14-32). See the fabled park and 'Green Monster' while you can; the team continues to talk about moving to new Boston digs. Maybe some day they'll win the World Series, too. For sold-out games (most of the time these days), there are often first-come, first-served standing-room-only tickets available 1½ hours before game time.

The NBA Boston Celtics (☎ 617-523-3030) play basketball at the Fleet Center (150 Causeway St) mid-October to mid-April (tickets $85). The NHL Boston Bruins (☎ 617-624-1000) play ice hockey at the center October to April (tickets from $20). The NFL New England Patriots (☎ 800-543-1776) and MLS New England Revolution (☎ 877-438-7387) play football and soccer, respectively, in Foxboro Stadium, about 50 minutes south of Boston.

Shopping

Newbury St is chock-full of chic boutiques, upscale merchants and art galleries. But the renegade western end has used CDs and clothing stores, condom shops and retro home goods. Charles St is lined with blue-blood antique stores and a smattering of intriguing newcomers. Shops in Downtown Crossing, a pedestrian zone enlivened with street performers and pushcart vendors, are geared to everyday needs like shoes and music.

Faneuil Hall Marketplace is tourist central, with two very good memento and souvenir shops dominating the historic Faneuil Hall: Boston City Store and Out of Left Field. Copley Place (100 Huntington Ave) and the Shops at the Pru (800 Boylston St), both in Back Bay, are luxe indoor malls.

Most independent Harvard Square shops have been supplanted by the likes of the Gap and HMV, but it's still fun to walk around. Where have all the cool shops gone? Follow their migration north on Massachusetts Ave toward Porter Square. Lastly (perhaps firstly), don't overlook hip Davis Square, on the Red Line in neighboring Somerville.

Getting There & Away

Since Boston is the region's hub, getting in and out of town is easy. The train and bus stations are adjacent, and the airport is a short subway or bus ride away.

The Big Dig

The depression of Boston's central artery and creation of a third harbor tunnel connecting downtown to the airport is the country's biggest public works project – $12 billion and continually rising. Slated for completion in 2004, the project has been likened to performing open-heart surgery on someone while she is running a marathon. When it's done, developers plan on creating parklands where the raised highway currently stands. In the meantime, roads and ramps near the waterfront are moved almost daily, making traffic a nightmare even for Bostonians. Peer into stories-deep caverns near North Station, the North End, South Station, Fort Point Channel and South Boston.

Air Logan International Airport (☎ 800-235-6426) is in East Boston, just across Boston Harbor from the city center. The airport is served by all US airlines and many foreign ones. It has currency-exchange booths, as well as a traveler's aid booth.

Bus Boston's main bus station is in South Station (700 Atlantic Ave), at Summer St. Bonanza (☎ 617-720-4110) serves western Massachusetts; Hyannis and Falmouth on Cape Cod; Providence, Rhode Island; and New York and Albany, New York. Greyhound (☎ 617-526-1808) departs for New York throughout the day ($42; from 4½ hours), as well as New Haven ($29; from 3½ hours) and Hartford ($21; from 2¼ hours), Connecticut; Albany, New York ($28; from 3½ hours); and Newark, New Jersey ($42; from 5½ hours).

Plymouth & Brockton (☎ 508-746-0378) provides frequent service to most Cape Cod towns, including Hyannis ($14; 1½ hours) and Provincetown ($23; 3 hours). Peter Pan Trailways (☎ 617-946-0960) serves Amherst, the Berkshires, Springfield, Hartford, New Haven and New York. Concord Trailways (☎ 800-639-3317) has routes from Boston to New Hampshire, as well as Portland and Bangor, Maine. Vermont Transit (☎ 800-451-3292) links Boston with White River Junction and Keene in New Hampshire,

Portland and Bar Harbor in Maine, and many destinations in Vermont.

Train The Amtrak (☎ 617-345-7460) terminus is South Station at Atlantic Ave and Summer St; most Amtrak trains also stop at the Back Bay Station on Dartmouth St. Trains to New York cost $58-73 and take from 4 hours. Acela express service costs $120 and takes about 3 hours. MBTA Commuter Rail (☎ 617-722-3200) trains from Boston's North Station serve cities west and north of Boston.

Boat Bay State Cruises (☎ 617-723-7800) operates boats from Commonwealth Pier in South Boston to Provincetown at the tip of Cape Cod (see Provincetown, later, for details). AC Cruise Line (☎ 617-261-6633, 290 Northern Ave), across Fort Point Channel in South Boston, operates boats to Gloucester on the North Shore.

Getting Around

Logan Airport is reachable via the T Blue Line to the Airport station ($1). Free shuttle buses (Nos 22 and 33) connect the subway with all terminals. A water shuttle ($10) also runs between the airport and Rowes Wharf, near the Boston Harbor Hotel. There is direct bus service ($5) to South Station (bay No 25). A taxi to/from the city costs $17-25.

Most major car rental companies have offices at the airport. Bear in mind, however, that driving in Boston is confusing, and parking is difficult and expensive. It's almost always better to stick to public transportation.

The MBTA (☎ 617-722-3200) operates the USA's oldest subway (the 'T'), begun in 1897. Four color-coded lines – Red, Blue, Green and Orange – radiate from the system hub at Park St and neighboring Downtown Crossing and Government Center stations. They operate 5:30am-12:30am. 'Inbound' trains are headed for these three stations, 'outbound' trains away from them. The fare is $1 for adults. Tourist passes ($5 per day, $9 for three days, $18 per week) for unlimited travel are sold at Airport, North Station, South Station, Alewife, Back Bay, Government Center and Hynes, as well as Bostix booths in Faneuil Hall and Copley Square.

Taxis are plentiful but also expensive; expect to pay about $6-8 for a short ride downtown, $13-18 from Back Bay to Harvard Square. Find taxis at major hotels or call Metro Cab (☎ 617-242-8000) or Checker Taxi (☎ 617-497-9000).

Biking on Charles River bike paths is fine, but be careful in the city. The Community Bicycle Supply (☎ 617-542-8623, 496 Tremont St), in the South End, rents mountain and hybrid bikes.

AROUND BOSTON

Boston is surrounded with historic, beautiful and interesting towns. MBTA Commuter Rail (☎ 617-722-3200) trains from North Station serve Concord, Salem, Gloucester and Rockport.

Just northwest of Boston, the colonial town of **Lexington** is where the first battle of the Revolutionary War took place. After the battle, the British redcoats marched to **Concord**, 22 miles northwest, where they encountered, and were pushed back by, the minutemen at the town's North Bridge – the first American victory. Next to the bridge is Nathaniel Hawthorne's former home, Old Manse.

Within a mile northeast of Concord's Monument Square, the center of town, are the Ralph Waldo Emerson house, Concord Museum, Louisa May Alcott's Orchard House and The Wayside, where Alcott's *Little Women* was set. Emerson, Alcott and Thoreau are buried on Author's Ridge in Sleepy Hollow Cemetery. Legendary Walden Pond is 3 miles south of Monument Square.

Concord's little woman, Louisa May Alcott

Salem, 14 miles northeast of Boston, is most famous for its witch trials, when 19 people – the majority women – were put to death for witchcraft (see 'Salem Witch Trials'). Salem also has grand and historic houses, the fabulous Peabody Essex Museum and the Salem Maritime National Historic Site. A few miles southeast, **Marblehead** is a charming, historic seaport and yachting town. View *The Spirit of '76* in Abbott Hall, on Washington St.

Farther north along the coast is the fishing port of **Gloucester**, founded in 1623.

Salem Witch Trials

In the late 17th century it was widely believed that one could make a pact with the devil to gain evil powers. In fact, the colony's fiery Reverend Cotton Mather wrote a book on the subject of witchcraft. When a number of local girls began behaving strangely in March of 1682, their parents believed that the devil had come to their village. (The girls had probably gotten hold of Mather's book, complete with descriptions of witch behavior, and begun playacting.)

Partly as a prank, the girls accused a slave named Tituba of being a witch. Tituba 'confessed' under torture and then accused two others to save her own life. Soon accusations flew thick and fast, as the accused confessed to riding broomsticks, having sex with the devil and participating in witches' sabbaths. They implicated others in attempts to save themselves.

When a special court convened to deal with the accusations, its justices accepted 'spectral evidence,' evidence of 'spirits' seen only by witnesses. With imaginations and religious passions inflamed, the situation careened out of control. By September 1692, 156 people stood accused, 55 people had pled guilty, and 14 women and five men who would not 'confess' to witchcraft had been hanged. Giles Corey, who refused to plead either way, was pressed to death.

The frenzy died down when the accusers began pointing at prominent merchants, clergy and the governor's wife. With the powers-that-be in jeopardy, the trials were called off and the remaining accused were released.

Follow the Maritime Trail around town, visit the Rock Neck Artists' Colony and drop in for tea at Beauport Mansion. Two miles southwest of the town center, Hammond Castle Museum, on MA 127, was the former palatial home of an eccentric but brilliant inventor. Several companies offer good whale-watching cruises. There's daily summer ferry service to Boston.

Just north, **Rockport** is a beautiful, historic seaport much favored by 19th-century painters and 20th-century tourists. Walk out onto Bearskin Neck for quaint shops or around Halibut Point State Park for dramatic views of the sea.

About 40 miles south of Boston, **Plymouth** is where the small *Mayflower* ended up in 1620. Having set sail from Plymouth, England, in late summer, the ship was bound for the New York harbor. Carrying 102 passengers, some animals, tools, seed, household effects and foodstuffs, it was blown onto Cape Cod instead. By December the Pilgrims had found their way here and decided to stay. This first toehold at Plymouth was followed by the foundation of the Massachusetts Bay Colony in 1628. Soon the region boasted several thousand English settlers, with more coming every year. Today, travelers make the pilgrimage to Plymouth Rock, the *Mayflower II* (a replica of the ship) and Plimoth Plantation, a re-created 1627 village. Cranberry World shows you everything about the native New England fruit. Plymouth & Brockton buses (☎ 508-746-0378) travel to Plymouth from Boston's South Station.

Farther south, **New Bedford** was once New England's major whaling port and now boasts the great Whaling Museum. Also visit the nearby Seamen's Bethel, immortalized in Melville's *Moby-Dick*. The Steamship Authority (☎ 508-997-1688) runs passenger boats to Martha's Vineyard. To the west, on the Rhode Island border, **Fall River** is famous for hundreds of cheap factory outlet stores and the grand WWII warcraft at Battleship Cove.

CAPE COD

This 65-mile-long peninsula and the neighboring islands of Nantucket and Martha's Vineyard are among the region's top vacation destinations. Attractions include well-preserved historic towns, fresh seafood, long beaches and good walking and biking. The

CAPE COD, MARTHA'S VINEYARD & NANTUCKET

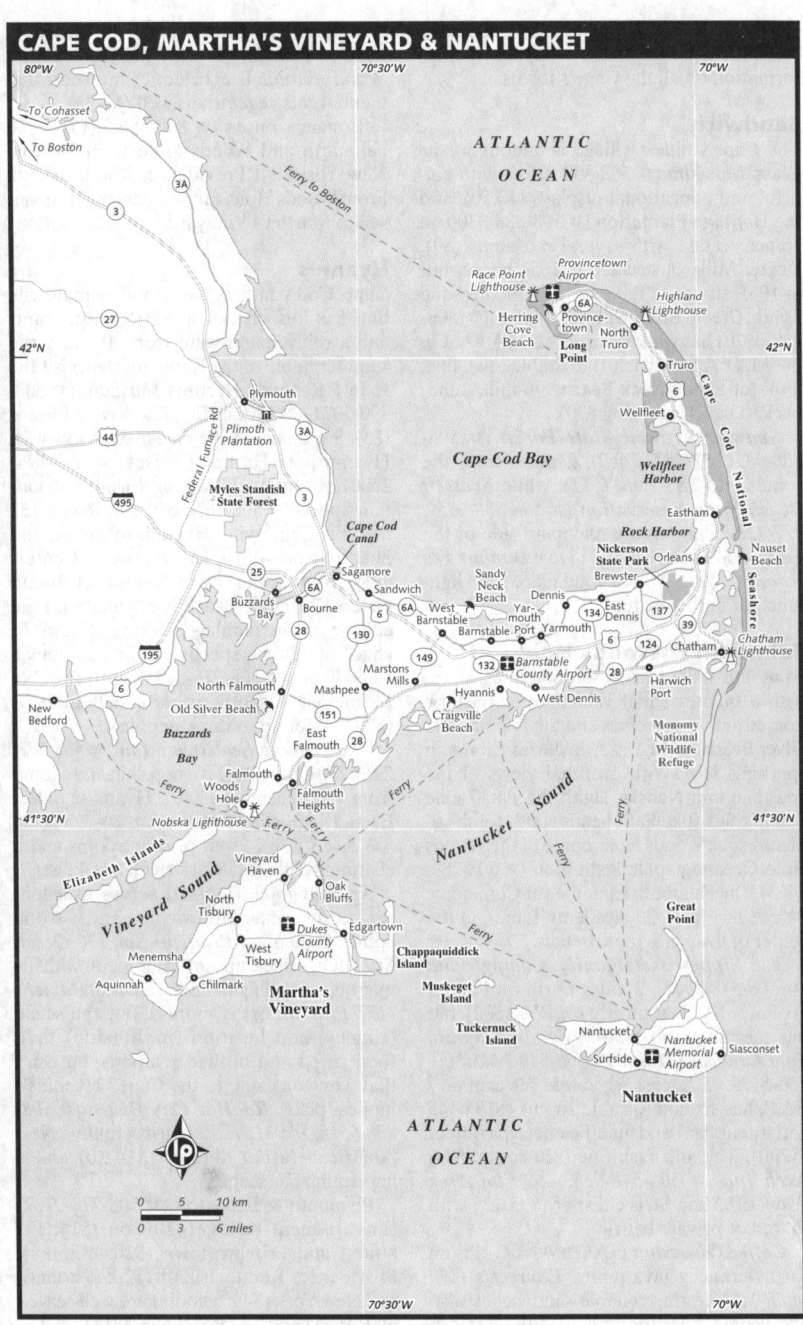

Cape Cod Regional Chamber of Commerce (☎ 508-759-3814, 888-332-2732) provides information on all the Cape's towns.

Sandwich

The Cape's oldest village is famous for its **Glass Museum** (☎ 508-888-0251), with colorful and educational displays ($3.50), and the **Heritage Plantation** (☎ 508-888-3300), a 76-acre estate with several museums ($9). **Dexter Mill**, constructed in 1654 but rebuilt in 1961, stands at the edge of a picturesque pond. **Green Briar Nature Center** (☎ 508-888-6870) has walking trails off MA 6A. On the MA 6A Sandwich-Barnstable town line, look for **Sandy Neck Beach**, a 6-mile dune-backed beach (parking $10).

Shawme Crowell State Forest (☎ 508-888-0351, 877-422-7662), 2 miles from the center, has 185 sites ($12), while *Scussett Beach State Reservation* (☎ 508-888-0859, 877-422-7662), on the mainland side of the Cape Cod canal, has 103 ($15). *Dunbar Tea Room* (1 Water St) is a good place for a light lunch or authentic tea.

Falmouth & Woods Hole

Falmouth is the Cape's second-largest town, with a quintessential village green, historic homes, nature preserves and the popular **Old Silver Beach** off MA 28A in North Falmouth (parking $10). With eventual views of the coastline and **Nobska Light**, the flat, 7-mile **Shining Sea Bike Path** heads south to oh-so-picturesque Woods Hole, home of the **Woods Hole Oceanographic Institution** (☎ 508-289-2663). The Falmouth Chamber of Commerce (☎ 508-548-8500, 20 Academy Lane), in the center of town, has more details.

The *Sippewisset Family Campground* (☎ 508-548-2542), 2 miles north on Palmer Ave off MA 28, is mostly for RVs ($32), but has tent sites too ($30). Friendly *Captain Tom Lawrence House* (☎ 508-540-1445, 800-266-8139, 75 Locust St), an old sea captain's B&B, has six comfortable rooms ($135-145 with breakfast) and an efficiency apartment ($200). The old-fashioned 20-room *Elm Arch Inn* (☎ 508-548-0133, 26 Elm Arch Way), off Main St, is cheaper ($95-125 with shared or private bath).

Coffee Obsession (110 Palmer Ave) is an earthy-crunchy java joint. *Laureen's* (170 Main St), offering reliable sandwiches, also has veggie burritos and Middle Eastern

samplers. For great waterfront seafood, head to *Fishmonger Café* (56 Water St), in Woods Hole. The eclectic, international menu treats vegetarians well ($7-23).

Bonanza buses (☎ 800-556-3815) serve Falmouth and Woods Hole from Boston, New York and Providence, Rhode Island. From Woods Hole, car and passenger ferries sail to Martha's Vineyard.

Hyannis

Cape Cod's largest town and commercial hub has lots of motels, varied restaurants and a rejuvenated waterfront. It's also the summer home of the Kennedy clan; visit the **John F Kennedy Hyannis Museum** (☎ 508-790-3077, 397 Main St), filled with photos ($3). Set sail from the Ocean St docks with Hyannisport Harbor Cruises (☎ 508-778-2600) or rent a kayak from Eastern Mountain Sports (☎ 508-362-8690), on Route 132 near the Centerville-Hyannis town line, and head out on your own. Nearby in Centerville, fronting the warm Nantucket Sound waters, **Craigville Beach** is popular with the college set and families (parking $15-20). To check out the perspective from high above, Cape Flight (☎ 508-775-8171), at Barnstable Municipal Airport, offers excellent trips ($79-220 for up to three people).

The 14-room *Sea Breeze Inn* (☎ 508-771-7213, 270 Ocean Ave) is a hop, skip and a jump from the beach ($80-140). Hyannis' oldest B&B, *The Inn on Sea Street* (☎ 508-775-8030, 358 Sea St), has seven pristine rooms and a charming cottage ($85-150 with breakfast).

Spiritus (500 Main St) serves excellent pizza, focaccia sandwiches and strong coffee. Bohemian *Prodigal Son* (10 Ocean St) often dishes up entertainment with its microbrews and light, limited menu. *Baxter's* (177 Pleasant St) is more about the scene (singles) and location (harborside) than food (fried and broiled seafood), but isn't that why you came to the Cape? Hyannis's hippest place, *RooBar City Bistro* (☎ 508-778-6515, 586 Main St) boasts creative New American fusion dinners ($14-20) and a happening bar scene.

Plymouth & Brockton (☎ 508-778-9767) runs frequent buses to Boston ($14; 1¾ hours) and Provincetown ($20; 2 hours). Providence, Rhode Island ($20; 2 hours), and New York ($49; 6 hours) are well served by Bonanza buses (☎ 800-556-3815).

Brewster

This little town boasts the old-fashioned **Brewster Store** (1935 MA 6A) and **Old Grist Mill and Herring Run**, at Setucket and Stony Brook Rds, one of the Cape's most tranquil spots. The **Cape Cod Museum of Natural History** (☎ 508-896-3867, 869 MA 6A) has pleasant nature trails ($5). The 2000-acre oasis of **Nickerson State Park** (☎ 508-896-3491), on MA 6A, has it all: beaches, biking and walking trails.

Nickerson (☎ 877-422-6762) has 418 wooded, popular campsites; reserve early ($12). If you have no luck, try the 100 sites at *Shady Knoll Campground (☎ 508-896-3002)*, on MA 6A at MA 137 ($30/34 tents/RVs). Once a girls' school, spic-and-span *Old Sea Pines Inn (☎ 508-896-6114, 2553 MA 6A)* now rents 24 smallish rooms ($95-150).

Cobie's (3260 MA 6A), just off the Cape Cod Rail Trail, has good seafood platters ($4-13) and outdoor picnic tables. *Brewster Fish House (2208 MA 6A)* has excellent, highly creative seafood at relatively moderate prices (lunch $8-12, dinner $14-26).

Chatham

Chatham is among the Cape's prettiest towns, lined with sea captain's houses, manicured lawns and lots of shoreline. Lodgings and Main St shops are commensurately tony. Visit **Chatham Light** (1878), on Shore Rd, and **Monomoy Island** (☎ 508-349-2615), an offshore bird sanctuary accessible only by boat. Contact the Monomoy Island Ferry *Rip Ryder* (☎ 508-945-5450) to take you to the island and secluded beach. Heading toward Harwich, Monomoy Theatre (☎ 508-945-1589), on MA 28, is among the Cape's best-known playhouses. Friday-night summertime concerts in Kate Gould Park, off Main St, are nostalgia-in-the-making (free admission).

A short walk to the center of town, *Chatham Highlander (☎ 508-945-9038, 946 MA 28),* with 28 spotless rooms and two pools, is a great bargain ($115-125). Across from the lighthouse and beach, *Port Fortune (☎ 508-945-0792, 201 Main St),* with 13 renovated rooms, is also a bargain considering the prime location ($135-190).

In summer, try the alfresco *Beach House Grill*, on Shore Rd opposite its regal parent Chatham Bars Inn, for buffet breakfasts ($15) and casual lunchtime seafood ($7-16). Townsfolk appreciate low-key *Chatham*

Squire (487 Main St) for its varied menu ($5-25), which will suit everyone. After dark the tavern gets boisterous.

Orleans

This quiet town, with lots of coastline and inlets, has one particularly big claim to fame: **Nauset Beach**, a 9-mile-long beach with facilities (parking $10). The Goose Hummock Outdoor Center (☎ 508-255-2620), off MA 6A on Town Cove, rents canoes and kayaks, gives beginner lessons and leads guided trips. On the bay side of MA 6A, for some postbeach perfection, *Cap't Cass Rock Harbor Seafood*, at Rock Harbor, serves simple but delectable lobster and seafood inside a colorful little shack (lunch $6-11, dinner $10-30).

Eastham

In 1620 the Pilgrims first encountered Native Americans upon Eastham's First Encounter Beach. The meeting was less than friendly, so the Pilgrims didn't return for 24 years. Most modern-day pilgrims zoom through Eastham, but a few stop to see the cape's **oldest windmill** and the set of huge whalebones in front of the **Edward Penniman House** (☎ 508-255-3421), on Fort Hill. Peer inside this sea captain's house if it's not open (free admission).

Rent bikes ($13 per half day) at Little Capistrano Bike Shop (☎ 508-255-6515), opposite the Salt Pond Visitor Center (see Cape Cod National Seashore), and follow the bike path across a tranquil salt marsh and through a pretty forest to Coast Guard Beach. Here you can hop onto the Cape Cod Rail Trail, a 26-mile dedicated bike trail carved from a former railroad bed. Farther north, **Nauset Light Beach** is prime ($7 parking).

Atlantic Oaks Campground (☎ 508-255-1437), on MA 6, has 100 shady tent/RV sites ($30/42). *HI Mid-Cape Hostel (☎ 508-255-2785, 617-531-0459 off-season, 75 Goody Hallet Dr)* rents 50 beds ($19-22); reservations are essential. *Midway Motel & Cottages (☎ 508-255-3117),* on MA 6, has nice, quiet rooms ($88-94). *First Encounter Coffee House (☎ 508-255-5438),* on Samoset Rd, holds folksy concerts ($10-15) twice a month; maybe you'll score with timing.

Cape Cod National Seashore

Covering more than 42 sq miles, the Cape Cod National Seashore (CCNS) includes the whole eastern shoreline from Chatham to Provincetown. It's known for beaches, crashing waves, dunes, nature trails, ponds, salt marshes and forests. Everything of interest is on or barely off MA 6, the only highway from the Orleans rotary (traffic circle) to Provincetown. Salt Pond Visitor Center (☎ 508-255-3421), in Eastham, has exhibits, films and nature walks explaining the cape's geology, history and landscape. The Province Lands Visitor Center (☎ 508-487-1256), on Race Point Rd in Provincetown (see that section), has similar services and exhibits, as well as local trail and bike maps.

Wellfleet

Visitors dine on famous Wellfleet oysters, enjoy fine beaches and hike in the **Wellfleet Bay Wildlife Sanctuary** (☎ 508-349-2615), 1000 acres of tidal creeks, salt marshes, forest and beach ($3). Completing the **Great Island Trail**, off Chequessett Neck Rd (free parking), entails four hours of walking on shifting sand around Wellfleet Bay; take sunscreen and water, and stop for a swim. Parking is $7 at broad and unending **Marconi Beach**, within the National Seashore on the Atlantic Ocean.

More than 20 Wellfleet art galleries host receptions on summer Saturday evenings. The **Wellfleet Flea Market** (☎ 508-349-2520) is the Cape's biggest trading fest ($2 per car; open Wed, Thurs, Sat and Sun in summer, Sat and Sun only in spring and fall). At dusk, park at *Wellfleet Drive-In* (☎ 508-349-7176), on MA 6, one of a dwindling number of drive-in cinemas left in the USA ($6.50 per person).

Maurice's Tent & Trailer Park (☎ 508-349-2029), on MA 6 just north of the Eastham-Wellfleet line, allots about half of its 180 sites to tents ($24); they also have a few cabins and cottages. *Inn at Duck Creeke* (☎ 508-349-9333, 70 Main St) has 25 simple rooms with shared ($75-90) and private ($90-100) bath within walking distance of town. *Holden Inn* (☎ 508-349-3450), on Commercial St, hasn't changed much since the 1920s; spartan rooms in this period piece cost $76-87.

Melville would have enjoyed seafood at *Moby Dick's*, on MA 6, with deservedly popular fried clams, scallops, fish and chips, and chowder ($8-20). For excellent Wellfleet oysters, try *Captain Higgins Seafood Restaurant* (☎ 508-349-6027), opposite the Town Pier. *Painter's* (☎ 508-349-3003, 50 Main St) is the hippest place, serving creative

New American dishes ($16-26); they're also open for morning coffee and pastries. When all else fails, *Box Lunch (50 Briar Lane)* will probably be open, selling very good 'rollwiches' (rolled sandwiches on pita).

In its present incarnation on Cahoon Hollow Beach, *Beachcomber* (☎ 508-349-6055), on Ocean View Dr, a former lifesaving station, currently serves as a cool bar, club and eatery ($6-16) for bronzed twentysomethings. *Wellfleet Harbor Actors Theater* (☎ 508-349-6835, 1 Kendrick Ave), known locally as WHAT, produces raucous and thoughtful experimental theater ($18).

Truro

There are good bayside and Atlantic beaches here, as well as two noteworthy small sites. In North Truro, **Cape Cod Light** (or 'Highland Light'), off South Highland Rd, shines the brightest light on the New England coastline (tours $3). Next door, the old **Highland House Museum** (☎ 508-487-3397) is dedicated to the area's maritime and agrarian roots ($3).

In North Truro, *HI Truro* (☎ 508-349-3889, 617-531-0459 off-season), on North Pamet Rd, is a former Coast Guard Station dramatically sited amid dunes and marshes. The 42 dorm beds cost $19-22; reservations are essential. Pop into *Jam's*, off MA 6 in Truro, for your daily hit of espresso, not to mention upscale picnic fixings. For more substantial fare, *Adrian's*, on MA 6, excels at fine Italian ($8-23), brick-oven pizzas and breakfast dishes ($4-9) like *huevos rancheros*.

Provincetown

The Pilgrims first set foot on American soil in 1620 at Provincetown, anchoring here for five weeks in search of abundant freshwater and fertile ground. Finding neither, they sailed on to Plymouth. Today, Provincetown is the funky end of the Cape – a mecca for tourists and artists, with an active gay scene. Your first impression is likely to be of the carnival atmosphere along Commercial St, but your memories may be of a walk across the dunes or a bike ride through ocean-edged forest.

The town's main drag (where you'll undoubtedly see a queen or two), Commercial St, runs parallel to the shoreline. MacMillan Wharf sits in the center, where you'll find the chamber of commerce (☎ 508-487-3424, 305 Commercial St).

Things to See & Do Climb the 116 stairs and 60 ramps of the **Pilgrim Monument & Provincetown Museum** (☎ 508-487-1310), on High Pole Rd, for a panoramic view of town and sea ($6) – on a clear day you can see Boston. Provincetown is famous for artists and galleries; openings are generally held Friday evenings. Dating from 1914, the **Provincetown Art Association & Museum** (☎ 508-487-1750, 460 Commercial St) ranks among the country's best small museums ($5). **Expedition** *Whydah* (☎ 508-487-8899, 16 MacMillan Wharf) tells the story of the only pirate ship ever salvaged, and off Marconi Beach at that ($6). **Race Point Beach** is known for pounding surf; **Herring Cove Beach** is calmer, with spectacular sunsets; **Long Point Beach** is reached by Flyer's Water Shuttle (131A Commercial St), which charges $10 roundtrip, or a two-hour walk across the jetty at the western end of Commercial St (bring water, food and sunscreen).

Rent a bike ($14-19 a day) from Arnold's (☎ 508-487-0844, 329 Commercial St) or Galeforce Beach Market (☎ 508-487-4849, 144 Bradford St Extension) to explore the 7 miles of paved CCNS **bicycling** trails. A half dozen companies offer **whale-watching cruises** from Macmillan Wharf. Try the 3½-hour cruise ($20) by Dolphin Fleet Whale Watch (☎ 508-349-1900, 800-826-9300). Art's Dune Tours (☎ 508-487-1950), at Commercial and Standish Sts, takes folks on hour-long 4WD tours along the beach ($12); reservations are required for the sunset trip ($15).

Places to Stay Provincetown has nearly 100 inns and guesthouses. In summer most will require minimum stays and be booked well in advance. If you don't have a reservation, arrive early and ask the chamber of commerce for help. Most lodgings offer steep discounts off-season and close for the winter; call for exact rates and dates.

Dune's Edge Campground (☎ 508-487-9815), off MA 6, has about 100 pine-shaded campsites for tents/RVs ($28/34). *Coastal Acres Camping Court* (☎ 508-487-1700), on West Vine St Extension at the western edge of town, has more sites for about the same price; it's open later into the season. The non-HI *Outermost Hostel* (☎ 508-487-4378, 28 Winslow St), off Bradford St, has 30 well-worn bunk beds ($18.50) in five depressing cabins.

Value-laden *Bill White's Motel* (☎ 508-487-1042, 29 Bradford St Extension), perched at dune's edge, is a family-run place with 12 units ($80). *Cape Colony Inn* (☎ 508-487-1755, 280 Bradford St) has 60 rooms ($98-107). Though made of charmless concrete, the 87-room *Surfside Beach Club & Inn* (☎ 508-487-1726, 800-421-1726, 543 Commercial St) offers family-friendly motel rooms ($175-249).

As for guesthouses, the historic and convenient *Fairbanks Inn* (☎ 508-487-0386, 90 Bradford St) offers 14 renovated rooms amid authentic 1770s details ($145-165). Bohemian *White Horse Inn* (☎ 508-487-1790, 500 Commercial St) rents simple rooms, many with shared bath ($75-80), and artsy studio apartments ($125-140). Friendly *Windamar House* (☎ 508-487-0599, 568 Commercial St) offers six modest rooms ($85-140) and two apartments ($850-950 a week).

The gated, ultra-luxe *Brass Key* (☎ 508-487-9005, 800-842-9858, 67 Bradford St) is mostly full of buff, tanned men gathered around the pool; the 33 rooms can't be beat for amenities ($230-425). *The Masthead* (☎ 508-487-0523, 31-41 Commercial St), which offers a huge variety of charming and eccentric cottages and apartments at the far end of town, is a good off-season option, when rates are $63-134 for rooms and cottages.

Places to Eat Whether it's fast food or cuisine-as-high-art, Provincetown has the best dining on Cape Cod. In fact, many people drive more than an hour to eat here. Try a favorite local snack from authentic *Portuguese Bakery* (299 Commercial St) – a big wad of hot, sugar-dusted fried dough ($2). *Angel Foods* (467 Commercial St) is the town's best gourmet delicatessen. *Joe* (148A Commercial St and 353 Commercial St) boasts the finest cappuccino at both its locations. *Mojo's*, on Ryder St at MacMillan Wharf, is a classic clam shack with large portions of fried clams, onion rings and other traditional New England fare at moderate prices. *Spiritus* (190 Commercial St) is the late night pizza hangout for those who'll be nursing hangovers.

Cafe Heaven (199 Commercial St) offers all-around good food from breakfast ($5-8) through dinner ($12-20). Tourists form lines outside venerable *Lobster Pot*

NEW ENGLAND

(321 Commercial St), which serves seafood, fish and chowder at tables overlooking the harbor (lunch $7-13, dinner $13-19); service is hurried.

The second floor *Café Edwige* (☎ 508-487-2008, 333 Commercial St) is very popular for breakfast ($4-8). It also serves sophisticated, creative and pricey dinners (entrées $18-24). As you're wandering Commercial St, check out the following exceptional places and make reservations: *Lorraine's* (☎ 508-487-6074, 463 Commercial St)*, for waterfront Mexican; *Mews Restaurant and Cafe* (☎ 508-487-1500, 429 Commercial St)*, for romantic waterfront dining; *Chester* (☎ 508-487-8200, 404 Commercial St)*, for chi-chi bistro food; *Front Street* (☎ 508-487-9715, 230 Commercial St)*, for fine Italian; *Gallerani's Cafe* (☎ 508-487-4433, 133 Commercial St)*, a neighborhoody bistro; *Sal's Place* (☎ 508-487-1279, 99 Commercial St)*, for outdoor waterfront Italian; and *Napi's* (☎ 508-487-1145, 7 Freeman St)*, at Bradford St, with an eclectic menu for veggies served year round.

Entertainment People-watching is prime. *Post Office Cabaret* (☎ 508-487-2234, 303 Commercial St) hosts impersonators and comedians. *Governor Bradford* (☎ 508-487-9618, 312 Commercial St)*, a dark bar with big windows, is a throwback to a different era.

As prime as the people-watching is Provincetown's gay life. *Crown & Anchor* (☎ 508-487-1430, 247 Commercial St)*, offers something for everyone – a disco, four bars, cabaret and female impersonators. *Boatslip Beach Club* (☎ 508-487-1669, 161 Commercial St)* hosts wildly popular afternoon tea dances. Waterfront *Pied Piper* (☎ 508-487-1527, 193A Commercial St)* is the town's women's bar. *Atlantic House* (☎ 508-487-3821, 4 Masonic Place)*, more commonly referred to as 'the A-House,' is the men's equivalent.

Shopping Along Commercial St you'll find everything from leather implements of torture to rubber stamps, from edgy women's clothing to artsy T-shirts, from sculpture to handcrafted jewelry. Don't miss Marine Specialties (235 Commercial St), a cavernous store filled to the rafters with random, surplus army and navy stuff and other odd items, all priced to sell.

Getting There & Away Cape Air (☎ 508-487-0241, 800-352-0714) flies from Boston for about $115. Plymouth & Brockton buses (☎ 508-778-9767) leave MacMillan Wharf four times daily for Boston in summer ($23; 3 hours). Also in summer, Bay State Cruise Company (☎ 508-487-9284, 617-457-1428) runs a fast ferry ($49 roundtrip; three times a day; 1½ hours) and a weekend-only slow ferry ($30 roundtrip; 3 hours) between Boston's Commonwealth Pier and MacMillan Wharf.

MARTHA'S VINEYARD

Thought to be named after the daughter of mariner Bartholomew Gosnold, who found wild grapes on the island when exploring the coast in the 16th century, Martha's Vineyard was a prosperous haven for whaling vessels and merchant fleets in the early 20th century. After the Age of Steam, it became a popular vacation resort known for its beaches, sea breeze, bike paths and charming towns.

The main ports of entry are the year-round commercial center Vineyard Haven and the honky-tonk, more seasonal, more diverse Oak Bluffs. The other major town, Edgartown, is the pricey grande dame, filled with whaling captains' houses separated by white picket fences. The island's other towns – West Tisbury, Chilmark, Menemsha and Aquinnah (formerly Gay Head) – are relatively undeveloped and collectively referred to as 'Up-Island.'

Departures of Gay Head Sightseeing buses (☎ 508-693-1555) coincide with incoming ferries at the terminals in Vineyard Haven and Oak Bluffs May to October ($15; 2½ hours). The Martha's Vineyard Chamber of Commerce (☎ 508-693-0085, W www.mvy.com) is on Beach Rd just off Main St in Vineyard Haven.

Vineyard Haven

This island's hub is an appealing year-round town with as many shops catering to tourists as to locals. **West Chop Lighthouse**, a few miles from the center of town at the western end of Main St, is worth a look if you have a bicycle. A vineyard on the Vineyard? But of course: About 3½ miles southwest of town off State Rd, **Chicama Vineyards** (☎ 508-693-0309) offers free tours daily. Contact Wind's Up (☎ 508-693-4252), on Beach Rd, for sailboard, canoe and kayak rentals and instruction.

Martha's Vineyard Family Camping (☎ 508-693-3772), on Edgartown Rd, offers the island's only camping ($34/38 tents/ RVs). *Vineyard Harbor Motel* (☎ 508-693-3334, 60 Beach Rd) has about 40 modern doubles ($120-140), some with small kitchens. Within walking distance of town, *Crocker House Inn* (☎ 508-693-1151, 12 Crocker Ave) takes one-night reservations for its eight very nice rooms ($205-345 with breakfast). A bit farther out, *Kinsman Guest House* (☎ 508-693-2311, 278 Main St) has three homey rooms for $125.

Vineyard Haven is 'dry,' meaning that no alcoholic beverages are sold in restaurants or shops. You're allowed to bring your own bottle (BYOB) to most restaurants, however, which will uncork it for a small fee. *Black Dog Tavern*, on Beach St Extension, is decent but always crowded, with dinner entrées at $13-26; lunch is a better value. Next door, *Black Dog Bakery* has good coffee and pastries. A good all-around eatery, *Zephrus* (☎ 508-693-3416, 9 Main St) is a casual bistro with contemporary food at lunch ($10-14) and dinner ($18-32).

Oak Bluffs

In 1835 the Methodist Campmeeting Association began holding summer revival meetings in Oak Bluffs (OB). Participants pitched tents, but after a few years they began constructing more substantial shelters. The result was a village of some 300 Carpenter Gothic cottages surrounding the Trinity Park Tabernacle (1879), where the association still holds its meetings. Ever since this time, OB has had a very strong African American community. For a close look, find the **Cottage Museum** (☎ 508-693-0525, 1 Trinity Park), stocked with memorabilia ($1.50). The **Flying Horses Carousel**, at Circuit and Lake Aves, is over 125 years old and still going strong ($1). There are nice ocean views from the **East Chop Lighthouse** (c. 1850), on Telegraph Hill off the Vineyard Haven–Oak Bluffs Rd.

Generally speaking, lodging and dining is cheaper here than in other towns. Gingerbread-style *Attleboro House* (☎ 508-693-4346, 42 Lake Ave) has 11 basic rooms with shared bath ($85-95). Newly renovated *Nashua House* (☎ 508-693-0043), on Ken-

nebec Ave smack in the middle of the action, has 16 rooms with shared bath ($99-109). Open year round, rooms at *Surfside Motel* (☎ 508-693-2500, 800-537-3007), on Oak Bluffs Ave, tend to be noisy in summer because of the central location ($150-160).

Linda Jean's (25 Circuit Ave) is the town's best all-around inexpensive restaurant, and everyone knows it. Established in 1930, *Giordano's*, at Circuit and Lake Aves, serves large portions of home-style Italian American fare ($8-16) – try the excellent fried clams from the takeout window. Between OB and Edgartown on Beach Rd, *Lola's Southern Seafood* dishes up absolutely huge dinnertime portions of good down-home cookin'. The pub menu is cheaper ($6-13) and the bar is bouncing; there's live music weekends.

After the sun sets on the beach, OB is the Vineyard's playground. *Atlantic Connection* (☎ 508-693-7129, 19 Circuit Ave), or 'AC,' has live music nightly. *Ritz Cafe* (☎ 508-693-9851, 4 Circuit Ave) features mostly blues. The second-floor *Lamppost* (☎ 508-693-9847), also on Circuit Ave, has dancing. Beautiful people gather around the bar at *Balance* (57 Circuit Ave).

Edgartown

The island's most graceful town has a patrician air and many grand 17th-, 18th- and 19th-century **historic buildings**. Visit the Dr Daniel Fisher House (☎ 508-627-8619, 99 Main St); the Old Whaling Church, next door; and the island's oldest house, the Vincent House Museum, all of which you can tour with a combination ticket ($8). The **Martha's Vineyard Historical Society** (☎ 508-627-4441), at Cooke and School Sts, has whaling and maritime displays ($7).

Once you've strolled through the town and walked out to **Edgartown Lighthouse** at the end of North Water St at sunset, take the ferry ($6 car and driver) over to **Chappaquiddick Island**, which has good beaches. On the way to Vineyard Haven, the **Felix Neck Wildlife Sanctuary** has five short walking trails ($3), and the **Manuel E Correllus State Forest** has miles and miles, plus bike trails. **Katama Beach** (or 'South Beach'), off Katama Rd, stretches for 3 miles facing moderate surf. Get onto the water aboard *Vela* Daysails (☎ 508-627-1963), on Memorial Pier (two-hour sails $55).

Central *Edgartown Inn* (☎ 508-627-4794, *56 N Water St*) has 20 doubles ($100, $140-220 with private bath). The 34 units at *Shire-town Inn* (☎ 508-627-3353, 800-541-0090, 44 *N Water St*) are of extremely varying quality ($149-299). *Edgartown Commons* (☎ 508-627-4671), on Pease's Point Way, has 36 efficiencies near the center of town ($160-185).

Friendly but small *Among the Flowers*, on Mayhew Lane off N Water St, serves omelettes, soups, salads and quiches ($6-12). *The Newes from America* (23 Kelley St) offers traditional pub grub and modern variations (like tomato-basil focaccia) for around $10. Try the 'rack of beer,' five small samples of unusual beers. *Alchemy* (☎ 508-627-9999, 71 Main St), a boisterous bistro with sidewalk tables, offers innovative variations of old standbys like a 'soft shell crab BLT' (lunch $9-15, dinner $28-34).

Up-Island

Outside the busy towns, Martha's Vineyard is rolling fields dotted with sheep and framed by stone walls. The main 'sight,' 21 miles from Edgartown, is the colorful 150-foot **Clay Cliffs of Aquinnah**, formerly known as 'Gay Head Cliffs.' Formed by glaciers 100 million years ago, the cliffs are on lands owned by the Wampanoag Indians. To the south is the 5-mile **Aquinnah Beach**, where clothes seem optional in some stretches (parking $15). At **Menemsha Harbor**, an authentic fishing village where you can pick up a quick bite (preferably at sunset), you'll notice **Menemsha Beach** – pebbly, but with calm waters.

The **Cedar Tree Neck Sanctuary**, off Indian Hill Rd in West Tisbury, covers over 300 acres of bogs, fields and forests, and has a few trails. The 600-acre **Long Point Wildlife Refuge** (☎ 508-693-7662), off the Edgartown–West Tisbury Rd, has just a few short trails, one of which leads to a deserted stretch of South Beach (parking $7, people $3).

In West Tisbury, *HI Manter Memorial Hostel* (☎ 508-693-2665, 800-909-4776), on the Edgartown–West Tisbury Rd, is open April to early November ($19-22). Although they have 80 beds, make reservations as early as possible.

Getting There & Around

Cape Air (☎ 800-352-0714) flies frequently from Boston; Nantucket; Hyannis; New Bedford; and Providence, Rhode Island.

Car and passenger ferries operated by the Woods Hole, Martha's Vineyard & Nantucket Steamship Authority (☎ 508-477-8600) run from Woods Hole to Vineyard Haven (about 15 per day) and to Oak Bluffs (about half that), a 45-minute voyage. Cars cost $104 roundtrip, people $11 and bikes $10. The Steamship Authority (☎ 508-997-1688) also runs three boats daily from New Bedford to Oak Bluffs May to September ($20 roundtrip; 1½ hours).

Two summertime passenger-only ferries operate out of Falmouth. The *Island Queen* (☎ 508-548-4800), on Falmouth Heights Rd, has frequent service to Oak Bluffs ($10 roundtrip). The Falmouth-Edgartown Ferry (☎ 508-548-9400, 278 Scranton Ave) docks in Edgartown five times daily ($24 roundtrip). From Hyannis, Hy-Line Cruises (☎ 508-778-2600) runs four boats daily from the Ocean St Dock to Oak Bluffs ($27 roundtrip; 2 hours). Hy-Line Cruises (☎ 508-693-0112, 508-228-3949) also operates four boats between Martha's Vineyard (Oak Bluffs) and Nantucket (June to mid-Sept) for $13.50; the trip takes just over two hours.

The year-round Martha's Vineyard Regional Transit Authority (☎ 508-627-7448) operates a good network of buses that travel frequently between all towns. Pick up the ubiquitous VTA map for details (day pass $5, weekly pass $15).

Thrifty & Adventure Rentals (☎ 508-693-1959), on Beach Rd in Vineyard Haven, has convertibles, mopeds, 4WDs and regular cars. Budget (☎ 508-693-1911) is opposite the Oak Bluffs ferry terminal, while All-Island Rent-a-Car (☎ 508-693-6868) is based at the airport. Expect to shell out about $75 daily for car rental, $135 for 4WD.

Vineyarders disdain mopeds, but you can still rent them for $36-53 a day from Adventure Rentals. All three main towns have plenty of bicycle rental shops ($20 a day).

NANTUCKET

Thirty miles south of the Cape Cod coast, Nantucket is a beautiful island of grassy moors, salt bogs, blueberry fields and warm-water beaches. Its one real town, also called Nantucket, is filled with graceful old houses shaded by lofty elms.

There are two ferry terminals, Steamboat Wharf and Straight Wharf, both about a block off Main St in the town center and within walking distance of most lodgings. The visitor office (☎ 508-228-0925, 25 Federal St) has room-availability information, bus schedules and a helpful, glossy booklet.

Things to See & Do
The Nantucket Historical Association (☎ 508-228-1894, 2 Whaler's Lane) oversees the island's most important **historic buildings**, including the excellent Whaling Museum (13 Broad St) and the 1686 Jethro Coffin House, the island's oldest, on Sunset Hill Rd. A combination ticket ($12) covers all houses and includes a walking tour. The wonderful **Atheneum** (☎ 508-228-1110), on Lower India St, isn't just for rainy days (free admission).

The island's pace, terrain and dedicated paths are well suited to **bicycling**. All rental shops have good, free island maps with routes highlighted. The island's only real destination is Siasconset ('Sconset), 7 miles away. On the way, stop at the **Lifesaving Museum** (☎ 508-228-1885, 158 Polpis Rd) to appreciate the heroic rescue efforts made on nearby shoals ($5). The prime beaches are reached via bus, but for a quick fix head to the popular **Jetties Beach**, off Bathing Beach Rd from N Beach Rd.

Sea Nantucket (☎ 508-228-7499), on Washington St Extension, offers kayak rentals ($35 per half day). Nantucket Community Sailing (☎ 508-228-5358), at Jetties Beach, rents Sunfish and sailboards. The Friendship Sloop *Endeavor* (☎ 508-228-5585, Slip 1015, Straight Wharf) offers 1½-hour daily harbor sails ($25) and sunset cruises ($35). Alternatively, board Barrett's Tours (☎ 508-228-0174, 20 Federal St) for a 1½-hour narrated island tour ($12).

Places to Stay & Eat
Lodging is expensive; minimum stays and advance reservations are de rigueur. As such, you might consider a long day trip from Hyannis. Camping (or sleeping under the stars or in your car) is strictly prohibited.

Three miles from town at Surfside Beach, the 49-bed *HI Nantucket Youth Hostel* (☎ 508-228-0433, 617-531-0459 off-season, 31 Western Ave) is open late April to mid-October ($19-22). Reservations are essential. Central, delightfully old-fashioned *Nesbitt Inn* (☎ 508-228-0156, 21 Broad St) has 12 rooms with shared bath ($85-95). *Accommodations et al* (☎ 508-228-9267) is a consortium of three guesthouses ($125-325).

There are hordes of good restaurants in the center of Nantucket. *Espresso Cafe (40 Main St)* serves strong coffee, vegetarian dishes, hearty soups and cold salads ($5-10) year round and has a quiet patio. *Provisions*, on Straight Wharf, makes great takeout sandwiches ($5). Friendly *Brotherhood of Thieves (23 Broad St)*, a dark tavern frequented by locals, has chowder and burgers ($9-15). You can always count on *Arno's 41 Main (41 Main St)* for reliable, varied and moderately priced dishes. For a splurge, creative *American Seasons (☎ 508-228-7111, 80 Centre St)* never disappoints; entrées roam the USA ($23-30). *Cambridge Street Victuals (12 Cambridge St)* has microbrews, including the local Cisco.

Getting There & Around
Cape Air and Nantucket Airlines (☎ 800-352-0714) offer many daily flights between Nantucket and Boston, Hyannis, New Bedford, and Martha's Vineyard, as well as Providence, Rhode Island.

The Steamship Authority (☎ 508-771-4000, 477-8600 for car reservations), at South St Dock, carries people and autos year round from Hyannis (1 or 2 hours). At least 10 ferries run daily in summer, three in winter. In summer roundtrip tickets cost $26 for passengers ($48 for the faster ferry), $320 for cars. Hy-Line (☎ 508-778-2600), on Ocean St Dock, has plenty of boats in summer too; fast ones take less than an hour and cost $58 roundtrip. Slower ones take twice as long but cost only $27.

Freedom Cruise Line (☎ 508-432-8999), on Route 28 at Saquatucket Harbor in Harwichport, is far from Hyannis' traffic. Morning, 'noonish' and evening ferries depart mid-May to mid-October ($43 roundtrip; 1½ hours). Hy-Line Cruises (☎ 508-693-0112, 228-3949) operates four interisland boats to the Vineyard June to September ($22 roundtrip; 2¼ hours).

The NRTA Shuttle (☎ 508-228-7025) operates buses to popular beaches and 'Sconset. Some buses have bike racks. Pick up a full schedule and pass information at visitor services (25 Federal St). Bicycling is the best way to get away from the summertime crowds, savor the island's natural beauty and reach much of the protected conservation land. Besides, the generally flat island has honest-to-goodness bike paths, a rarity on the mainland. There are hundreds of bikes to rent from at least half a dozen shops. Try Young's Bicycle Shop (☎ 508-228-1151), on Broad St near Steamboat Wharf ($25 for 24 hours).

CENTRAL MASSACHUSETTS

One of New England's least touristed regions, this area of Massachusetts features several industrial centers.

Worcester

This small city, 40 miles west of Boston, grew rich on industry and innovation during the 19th century, but had largely been eclipsed by Boston by the 20th. Worcester (**woos**-ta) preserves several monuments from its golden age, including the fine **Worcester Art Museum** (☎ 508-799-4406, 55 Salisbury St), off Park and Main Sts ($8); the nearby **American Antiquarian Society Library** (☎ 508-755-5221, 185 Salisbury St); and the **Higgins Armory Museum** (☎ 508-853-6015, 100 Barber Ave), with over 100 suits of armor ($7).

Most accommodations are near I-290 exit 20, including *Hampton Inn (☎ 508-757-0400, 110 Summer St)*, with $90 rooms, and *Worcester Inn (☎ 508-852-2800, 50 Oriol Dr)*, with $79-89 rooms. Central *Regency Suites (☎ 508-753-3512, 70 Southbridge St)* has doubles (from $115) and suites with kitchens (from $125).

Sturbridge

Brimming with summer travelers, Sturbridge, 65 miles west of Boston, has reclaimed its past by hosting one of the country's first 'living museums.' **Old Sturbridge Village** (OSV; ☎ 508-347-3362) is an authentically re-created 1830s New England town, with 40 restored, antique-filled structures and 'interpreters' dressed in period style (two-day pass $20). The town's tourist office (☎ 508-347-7594, 800-628-8379), on US 20 opposite OSV, doubles as the bus station.

The closest campground is mega *Yogi Bear's Sturbridge Jellystone Park (☎ 508-347-9570)*, with over 400 tent/RV sites ($41/45), pools, a hot tub and a water slide; take I-84 exit 2 and follow signs. At the op-

posite end of the spectrum, *Wells State Park (☎ 508-347-9257, 877-422-6762)*, on MA 49 north of I-90, has wooded sites ($12). US 20 is lined with many motels, among them family-owned *Green Acres Motel (☎ 508-347-3496)*, with a pool and 16 rooms ($72-78), and *Rodeway Inn (☎ 508-347-9673)*, with more expensive doubles ($95). The grande dame option is the 1771 *Publick House Inn (☎ 508-347-3313, 800-782-5425)*, on MA 131, with inn, motel and B&B rooms ($104-160) and traditional dining on the Common.

Springfield

In the 19th century, Springfield and other valley towns became important industrial centers. Today, Springfield is often bypassed. **Court Square** is ground zero, where you'll find the visitor center (☎ 413-787-1548, 1441 Main St). Two blocks northeast, the **Museum Quadrangle** (☎ 413-263-6800) is formed by the Smith Art Museum, the Museum of Fine Arts, the Springfield Science Museum and the Connecticut Valley Historical Museum ($6 for all museums). Basketball, invented here, is enshrined at the **Basketball Hall of Fame** (☎ 413-781-6500, 1150 W Columbus Ave), south of I-91 exit 7 ($10). Springfield also claims that gasoline-powered motorcycles were invented in this town. Find out more at the funky **Indian Motorcycle Museum** (☎ 413-737-2624), on Hendee St off Page Blvd from I-291 exit 4 ($3).

If you need to stay overnight, try *Red Roof Inn (☎ 413-731-1010, 1254 US 5)*, with 111 rooms ($59-99); *Quality Inn (☎ 413-739-7261, 1150 US 5)* boasts a pool ($75).

The bus station (☎ 413-781-2900, 1776 Main St), at Liberty St, and train station (☎ 800-872-7245, 66 Lyman St) are a 10-minute walk north of Court Square. Six daily trains connect Springfield and New York ($42; 3 hours); there are two trains to Boston ($24; 3 hours).

FIVE COLLEGE AREA

A few years after the Pilgrims landed at Plymouth in 1620, fur traders and settlers began making their way up the great Connecticut River, earning this region the name 'Pioneer Valley.' Today, Hampshire County (north of Springfield) is more often called the Five College area because it's home to Amherst, Hampshire, Mount

Holyoke and Smith Colleges and the University of Massachusetts.

Northampton

Northampton, a lesbian mecca, is the region's most sophisticated town, with a surprising number and variety of ethnic restaurants, cafes and funky stores. Smith College makes its presence felt here, but 10 miles south in quiet South Hadley is Mount Holyoke College (☎ 413-538-2222), the oldest women's college in the USA (1837). The Greater Northampton Chamber of Commerce (☎ 413-584-1900, 99 Pleasant St) offers lots of information.

In the town center, *Haymarket Café & Juice Joint (185 Main St)* brews java and mixes juices for the literary set. Nearby *Java Net Café* adds a cyber component to its caffeine offerings. *Bakery Normand (192 Main St)* serves rich pastries, while *Pizzeria Paradiso (12 Crafts Ave)* is a wine bar masquerading as a brick-oven pizza place. For vegetarian food, try *Paul and Elizabeth's (150 Main St),* inside Thorne's Market. For Mexican, head for down-home *La Veracruzana (31 Main St)* or hipper *La Taqueria Cha Cha Cha! (134 Main St). Northampton Brewery (11 Brewster Court)* serves pub fare with its excellent pints. Upscale *Spoleto (☎ 413-586-6313, 50 Main St)* has classic dishes with modern accents.

Amherst

Nearby Amherst boasts three colleges and the home of poet Emily Dickinson (1830–86), the 'belle of Amherst.' The **Dickinson Homestead** (☎ 413-542-8161, 280 Main St) is now a museum ($5), toured by reservation. Contact Amherst College (☎ 413-542-2000), Hampshire College (☎ 413-549-4600) and the University of Massachusetts (☎ 413-545-0111) for campus tours and event information. For more information, visit the chamber of commerce (☎ 413-253-0700, 409 Main St).

The nearest camping is in Whatley, 8 miles away off MA 116. *White Birch Campground (☎ 413-665-4941, 122 North St)* has 60 tent/RV sites ($22/24). Motels are strung out along MA 9, including *Amherst Motel (☎ 413-256-8122),* for $58-68, and *Howard Johnson (☎ 413-586-0114),* for $89-149. *Allen House B&B (☎ 413-253-5000, 599 Main St)* charges $105-150 with breakfast.

Deerfield

Sixteen miles northwest of Amherst on MA 5, Deerfield was settled in the 1660s. The noble main street of Historic Deerfield Village (☎ 413-774-5581) presents a dozen well-preserved houses dating from the 18th and 19th centuries open to the public ($12).

THE BERKSHIRES

The hills of western Massachusetts have been a summer retreat for wealthy families from Boston, Hartford and New York for more than a century. And as such, the hill towns boast surprising cultural riches. Peter Pan Trailways buses run to the Berkshires from Boston and Bennington. Bonanza Bus Lines connects the Berkshire towns with New York.

Stockbridge & Around

This postcard-perfect New England town is straight out of a Norman Rockwell illustration. In fact, the artist lived and worked here, and the Norman Rockwell Museum (☎ 413-298-4100), on MA 183 south of MA 102, holds mementos and much of his art ($10). The Chesterwood estate and museum (☎ 413-298-3579), off MA 183, was the summer home of Daniel Chester French ($8).

For lodging, try central *Red Lion Inn (☎ 413-298-5545),* on Main St, a historic wood-frame hotel ($91-189, some with shared bath). Or ask the Stockbridge Lodging Association (☎ 413-298-5327) to assist you; expect to spend at least $125 for an area B&B.

On your way to Williamstown, stop at Hancock Shaker Village (☎ 413-443-0188), on US 20 southwest of Pittsfield's center, near the intersection with MA 41 ($13.50). The Shakers, a religious sect founded in England in 1747, believed in communal ownership, pacifism, celibacy, gender equality and the sanctity of work. The products of their hands – including the buildings and artifacts in this community – are of a very high order.

Lenox

Gracious Lenox hosts one of the country's premier music series, the Tanglewood Music Festival (☎ 617-266-1492, 413-637-5165 in summer), June to September. Featuring the Boston Symphony Orchestra, the festival costs from $14 for lawn seats to $78 for the best seats in the house. Formerly the home of novelist Edith Wharton, **The Mount** (☎ 413-637-1899), at Plunkett St and US 7, has hour-long guided tours ($8). Memorable summer theater performances are given at The Mount by Shakespeare & Company (☎ 413-637-3353). The Jacob's Pillow Dance Festival (☎ 413-243-0745), 10 miles east of Lenox in Becket, stages renowned dance events ($20-50). The Lenox Chamber of Commerce (☎ 413-637-3646, 5 Walker St) helps with accommodations and other information.

Lenox lodgings consist primarily of charming, pricey inns charging $300-500 on summer weekends (when vacancies are rare), with 20% to 35% weekday reductions. Try **Walker House** (☎ *413-637-1271, 74 Walker St)*, **Hampton Terrace** (☎ *413-637-1773, 91 Walker St)* or **The Village Inn** *(☎ 413-637-0020, 16 Church St)*. You'll find rooms here in the $125-200 range.

The centrally situated Church St has good eateries. **Church Street Deli** has decent daytime sandwiches, while **Church Street Café** offers lovely lunches (under $10) and inventive dinners ($17-27).

Williamstown & Around

Williamstown, 145 miles northwest of Boston, is the pastoral seat of Williams College and the **Clark Art Institute** (☎ 413-458-9545, 225 South St), a gem of a museum particularly strong in the impressionists, their French academic contemporaries and mid-19th-century Barbizon artists (free admission).

In nearby North Adams, don't miss **MassMoCA** (☎ 413-662-2111), on Marshall St, a sprawling, truly enormous modern art museum that's powering the local economic engine ($8). After exercising your mind and arousing your spirit, move your body around the 45 miles of hiking trails at Mt Greylock State Reservation (☎ 413-499-4262).

There are scenic campsites, hiking and biking trails at Mt Greylock and the extensive **Savoy Mountain State Forest** *(☎ 877-422-6762)*, on Central Shaft Rd off US 2 in Florida. Savoy has canoeing ponds, too; camping costs $12 at both. Head to US 7 N for **Northside Motel** (☎ *413-458-8107, 45 North St)*, charging $78-90, or **Cozy Corner Motel** *(☎ 413-458-8006, 284 Sand Springs Rd)*, for $75-125. Just off US 7 N, **River Bend Farm** *(☎ 413-458-3121, 643 Simonds Rd)* dates from 1770, with period antiques and shared baths ($90).

Spring St is loaded with eateries, but look for **Cold Spring Coffee Roasters** *(47 Spring St)* for java and sweet fixes. Grilled specialties ($13-20) are the way to go at **Hobson's Choice** *(159 Water St)*.

Rhode Island

The Ocean State is the smallest of the United States, but it has its own special character and charm. Providence, the state capital and third-largest New England city, has recently undergone an ambitious facelift. Newport, the famed 19th-century summer playground of the colossally wealthy, is the region's yachting capital and the summer home of the merely inordinately wealthy. Block Island is a junior version of Nantucket or Martha's Vineyard, perfect for a day or overnight trip. Southwestern Rhode Island has good beaches.

In 1636 Reverend Roger Williams (1603–83) founded Providence as a haven for freedom of conscience and separation between religion and civil government. A mere 140 years later, the Colony of Rhode Island and Providence Plantations was the first American colony to declare independence from England. Relatively unscathed

---

Rhode Island

Nicknames: Ocean State, Little Rhody

Population: 1,048,000 (43rd)

Area: 1545 sq miles (50th)

Admitted to Union: May 29, 1790 (13th)

Capital city: Providence (population 174,000)

Other cities: Newport (26,000)

Birthplace of: Broadway composer George M Cohan (1878–1942)

Famous for: the Rhode Island Red, a chicken that revolutionized the poultry industry

First state to: declare independence from Britain (1776), abolish slavery (1784), use steam-powered mills (1848)

☺ ☺ ☺ ☺ ☺ ☺ ☺ ☺ ☹ ☺

after the Revolutionary War, Providence surpassed Newport, which had been heavily damaged by the British, as the state's most important city.

Rhode Island built its wealth on maritime commerce, first in slaves and then in the China trade. Despite economic decline in the early 20th century, Rhode Island now prospers through government, higher education, publishing, insurance, light manufacturing and tourism.

State governor Lincoln Almond hails from the Republican party, but Rhode Islanders have elected two Democratic US representatives (including Patrick Kennedy) and split the senate seats between the two parties (Republican senator Chafee is a moderate, though).

Information

Contact the Rhode Island Tourism Division (☎ 401-222-2601, 800-556-2484, Ⓦ www.visitrhodeisland.com, 1 W Exchange Pl, Providence, RI 02903). Bed & Breakfast of Rhode Island (☎ 401-849-1298, 800-828-0000, 175 Spring St, PO Box 3291, Newport, RI 02840) has statewide listings. The state sales and meals taxes are both 7%; lodging tax is 13%.

PROVIDENCE

Rhode Island's capital is small, pleasant, pretty, walkable and well endowed with cultural and academic institutions. Forty-five miles southwest of Boston, Providence makes a good day trip. Since the city recently completed its $1 billion revitalization project, and reclaimed its curvaceous riverway waterfront, it has been a place to linger.

Kennedy Plaza, anchored by the Providence Biltmore Hotel, constitutes the city center. North of the plaza and Waterpark Place are the train station and, perched atop a hill, the capitol. Grab a map at the Providence-Warwick Convention & Visitors Bureau (☎ 401-274-1636, 800-233-1636, 1 W Exchange St).

Looming above the skyline and Kennedy Plaza, the marble **State Capitol** (☎ 401-222-2357) is modeled in part on St Peter's Basilica in the Vatican City. There are free guided weekday tours (reservations necessary). Downhill from the capitol, follow the cobblestone walkways along the Woonasquatucket River to Waterplace Park, lively

in summer. It's also fun to tour **Brown University** (☎ 401-863-2378) and the artsy **Rhode Island School of Design** (RISD; ☎ 401-454-6300). Near RISD, colonial Benefit St skirts the lovely College Hill neighborhood, while the colorful Italian enclave of Federal Hill lies on (and off) Atwells Ave just west of the city center.

South of the city, visit spacious **Roger Williams Park** (☎ 401-785-3510), at I-95 exit 17, Elmwood Ave, with its lakes, woods, lawns, boathouse, carousel and greenhouses. The park also has a planetarium, natural-history museum ($2) and an excellent zoo ($6).

Places to Stay & Eat

In nearby West Gloucester, *George Washington Management Area (☎ 401-568-2248)*, on US 44, has 45 simple wooded tent and RV sites ($12). Neighboring *Bowdish Lake Camping Area (☎ 401-568-8890)* has 340 sites costing $19-45 for a waterfront locale. Back in town, *Providence Biltmore (☎ 401-421-0700)*, in Kennedy Plaza, is a classic grand hotel of the 1920s ($159-180).

Downtown *Arcade (65 Weybosset St)* offers an array of inexpensive first-floor lunchtime eateries. For modestly priced, hearty Italian fare, family-run *Casa Christine (145 Spruce St)* is the locals' top choice (entrées $14-17). Afterward, have coffee and dessert at *Pastiche (92 Spruce St)*. *L'Epicureo (238 Atwells Ave)* features wood-grilled meats (as high as $27) and inventive pasta (as low as $13). Trendy *XO Café (☎ 401-273-9090, 125 N Main St)* offers pricey New American dishes ($15-28) and fancy pizzas for dinner.

Entertainment

Legendary *Lupo's Heartbreak Hotel (☎ 401-272-5876, 239 Westminster St)* hosts cool national bands in an intimate club. For brew pubs, try *Union Station Brewery (36 Exchange Terrace)*, on Kennedy Plaza, serving American-style beers, and *Trinity Brew House (186 Fountain St)*, across from the Civic Center, with hop-heavy Irish- and British-style brews.

The *Providence Civic Center (☎ 401-331-6700, 1 LaSalle Square)* welcomes rock groups and sporting events. The excellent *Trinity Repertory Company (☎ 401-351-4242, 201 Washington St)* performs classic

NEW ENGLAND

and contemporary plays downtown. The popular *Providence Performing Arts Center* (☎ *401-421-2787, 220 Weybosset St)* hosts touring Broadway shows.

Getting There & Away

TF Green State Airport (☎ 401-737-8222), in Warwick about 20 minutes south of Providence, handles regional and national flights. The Rhode Island Public Transit Authority (Ripta; ☎ 401-781-9400, 800-244-0444) links Providence with other state localities. Bonanza Bus Lines (☎ 401-751-8800) connects Providence with Boston, Cape Cod and New York. Eleven daily Amtrak (☎ 800-872-7245) trains connect Providence with Boston ($21; 1 hour) and New York ($50; from 3 hours).

NEWPORT AREA

Perfectly situated for access by sea, Newport was an important commercial port, a conquered war prize and a wealthy summer resort before becoming one of New England's busiest tourist destinations. Most people visit the town to ogle sumptuous Bellevue Ave mansions, admire colonial architecture or attend a famous music festival.

Downtown Newport's main north-south commercial streets are America's Cup Ave and the harborside Thames (that's thaymz, not temz) St. The Newport County Convention & Visitors Bureau (23 America's Cup Ave) hosts an information center (☎ 401-849-8048, 800-976-5122), a bus station and a great parking facility.

Mansions

During the 19th century, the wealthiest New York bankers and business families chose Newport as their summer resort. Many mansions are now managed by the Preservation Society of Newport County (☎ 401-847-1000, 424 Bellevue Ave), which offers combination tickets. It costs $15 to visit The Breakers, but only $6 more for an additional mansion, or $29 to visit five. Don't miss **The Breakers** (1895), a 70-room Italian Renaissance palace built for Cornelius Vanderbilt II, which is Newport's most splendid 'cottage.' **Rosecliff** looks like the Grand Trianon at Versailles but is even grander, with Newport's largest ballroom. The palace of Versailles was the inspiration for **Marble House** (1892), filled with Louis

XIV–style furnishings. Elizabethan-style **Kingscote** (1841) was Newport's first 'cottage' strictly for summer use. **The Elms**, nearly identical to the Chateau d'Asnières near Paris, was built in 1901 for a coal magnate. Victorian Gothic **Chateau-sur-Mer** (1852) has a decidedly more lived-in feel to it than the others. **Ochre Court** (1892) is now the administration building of Salve Regina University (free tours).

At the 1856 **Beechwood** (☎ 401-846-3772, 580 Bellevue Ave), actors portray a typical summer's house full of family, staff and visitors ($10). **Belcourt Castle** (☎ 401-846-0669, 657 Bellevue Ave) was designed according to the 17th-century tastes of France's King Louis XIII ($10).

Other Attractions

You can walk the walk – the **Cliff Walk**, that is, a footpath hugging the eastern edge of the peninsula, with sweeping seaside and mansion views. The hour-long trek starts at the Cliff Walk Manor inn, just west of Easton's Beach, and ends at Bailey's Beach. Built in 1763, **Touro Synagogue** (☎ 401-847-4794), on Touro St, is North America's oldest Jewish house of worship. Look for the **International Tennis Hall of Fame** (☎ 401-849-3990, 194 Bellevue Ave) inside the historic Newport Casino building (1880), once the wealthy Newporters' summer club ($8).

Fort Adams, built between 1824 and 1857, crowns a rise at the peninsula's end. Like many American coastal fortresses, it had a short practical life as a garrison but has a long life as a tourist attraction. A fine place to picnic, fish or sunbathe, it's the centerpiece of **Fort Adams State Park** (☎ 401-847-2400), the staging ground for the Newport Jazz and Folk Festivals and other special events. For decades Newport was the home port for America's Cup races, which explains the park's **Museum of Yachting** (☎ 401-847-1018).

Easton's Beach, also called 'First Beach,' is the largest sweep of sand, with bathhouses, showers and a snack bar. East along Purgatory Rd is Sachuest (Second) Beach, with showers and a snack bar. Continuing east, Third Beach is a favorite with windsurfers. Parking costs $8-15. **Gooseberry Beach**, on Ocean Ave, charges $10 weekdays, $15 weekends, to park.

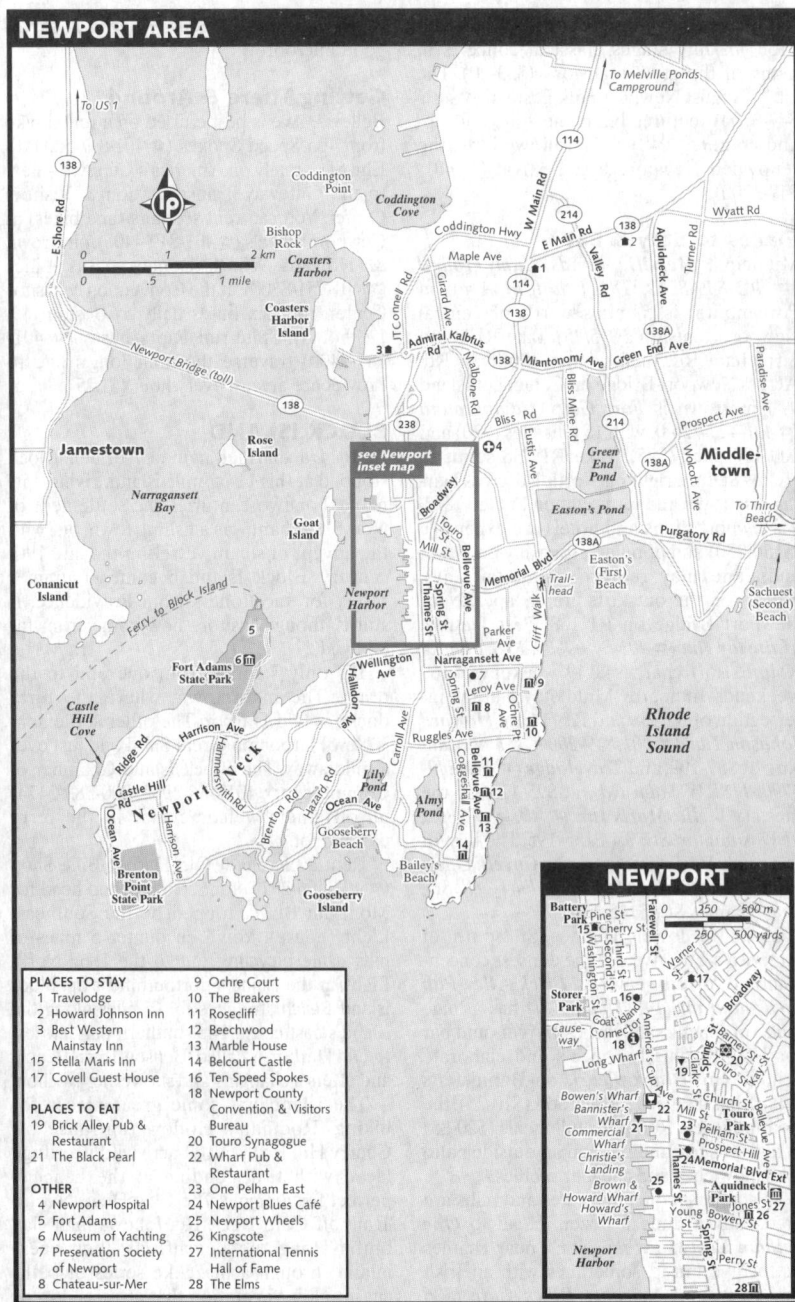

NEWPORT AREA

To US 1
138
E Shore Rd
Coddington
Point
**Coddington
Cove**
Bishop
Rock
**Coasters
Harbor**
To Melville Ponds
Campground
114
214
Wyatt Rd
Coddington Hwy
W Main Rd
E Main Rd
138
Maple Ave
114
Valley Rd
Aquidneck Ave
Turner Rd
2
1
Girard Ave
138
JT Connell Rd
Admiral Kalbfus Rd
138
3
Mahone Rd
138
Miantonomi Ave
Green End Ave
Paradise Ave
**Coasters
Harbor
Island**
Newport Bridge (toll)
138
238
Bliss Rd
Bliss Mine Rd
214
Prospect Ave
138A
Jamestown
**Rose
Island**
4
Eustis Ave
**Green
End
Pond**
138A
Wolcott Ave
**Middle-
town**
**Narragansett
Bay**
*see Newport
inset map*
Broadway
Touro St
Mill St
Bellevue Ave
Easton's Pond
To Third
Beach
Purgatory Rd
138A
**Goat
Island**
Spring St
Thames St
Memorial Blvd
Easton's
(First)
Beach
Sachuest
(Second)
Beach
**Conanicut
Island**
Ferry to Block Island
**Newport
Harbor**
Trail-
head
Cliff Walk
**Rhode
Island
Sound**
Parker
Ave
5
Narragansett Ave
Wellington
Ave
7
Spring St
Leroy Ave
Ochre Pt Ave
9
**Fort Adams
State Park**
6
Halidon Ave
8
10
Ruggles Ave
Bellevue Ave
Ochre Pt Ave
11
**Castle
Hill
Cove**
Ridge Rd
Harrison Ave
Hammersmith Rd
Newport Neck
Carroll Ave
Coggeshall Ave
12
13
**Castle Hill
Rd**
Harrison Ave
Ocean Ave
Brenton Rd
Hazard Rd
**Lily
Pond**
Ocean Ave
**Almy
Pond**
14
**Brenton
Point
State Park**
**Gooseberry
Beach**
Bailey's
Beach
**Gooseberry
Island**

NEWPORT

Battery
Park
15
Farewell St
Pine St
Cherry St
Third St
Second St
Wash ington St
250   500 m
250   500 yards
Warner St
17
**Storer
Park**
16
Goat Island
Connector
Broadway
Cause-
way
18
America's Cup Ave
Spud's Alley
19
Mill St
Clarke St
Church St
Touro
St
20
Barney St
**Bowen's
Wharf**
**Bannister's
Wharf**
**Commercial
Wharf**
21
22
23
Pelham St
**Touro
Park**
24
Prospect Hill Ave
Memorial Blvd Ext
Bellevue Ave
**Christie's
Landing**
**Brown &
Howard Wharf**
**Howard's
Wharf**
25
Thames St
Young St
Bowery St
**Aquidneck
Park**
Jones St
26
27
Spring St
**Newport
Harbor**
Perry St
28

PLACES TO STAY
1 Travelodge
2 Howard Johnson Inn
3 Best Western
   Mainstay Inn
15 Stella Maris Inn
17 Covell Guest House

PLACES TO EAT
19 Brick Alley Pub &
   Restaurant
21 The Black Pearl

OTHER
4 Newport Hospital
5 Fort Adams
6 Museum of Yachting
7 Preservation Society
   of Newport
8 Chateau-sur-Mer

9 Ochre Court
10 The Breakers
11 Rosecliff
12 Beechwood
13 Marble House
14 Belcourt Castle
16 Ten Speed Spokes
18 Newport County
   Convention & Visitors
   Bureau
20 Touro Synagogue
22 Wharf Pub &
   Restaurant
23 One Pelham East
24 Newport Blues Café
25 Newport Wheels
26 Kingscote
27 International Tennis
   Hall of Fame
28 The Elms

NEW ENGLAND

The Newport Music Festival (☎ 401-846-1133) in July stages classical concerts in many of the great mansions ($33-40). The early-August Newport Folk Festival (☎ 401-847-3700) features big-name stars and up-and-comers ($48). It's followed by the renowned Newport Jazz Festival (☎ 401-847-3700).

Places to Stay & Eat

Municipal *Melville Ponds Campground* (☎ *401-849-8212, 181 Bradford Ave)*, in Portsmouth, is 5 miles north of central Newport (tents/RVs $15/25). Take RI 114 to Stringham Rd, then head to Sullivan Rd. Across Newport Bridge on Conanicut Island in Jamestown is *Fort Getty Campground* (☎ *401-423-7264)*, with 15 tent sites ($20) and 100 RV sites ($25). Take RI 138 south to Helms St, turn right on North Rd, cross Narragansett Ave and turn right on Ft Getty Rd.

Newport's inns and hotels are expensive ($150-250) and popular, especially on weekends, and may require minimum stays. Motels on the outskirts are cheaper. Near Newport Bridge on RI 138, *Best Western Mainstay Inn* (☎ *401-849-9880, 151 Admiral Kalbfus Rd)* charges $119 weekdays, $169 weekends. In nearby Middletown at the intersection of RI 138 and RI 114 are *Howard Johnson Inn* (☎ *401-849-2000, 351 N Main Rd)*, at $89-199, and *Travelodge* (☎ *401-849-4700, 1185 W Main Rd)*, at $95-175. Of the inns, try *Stella Maris Inn* (☎ *401-849-2862, 91 Washington St)*, for $155-195. The best of the small B&Bs is five-room *Covell Guest House* (☎ *401-847-8872, 43 Farewell St)*, near Thames St ($115-170).

Head to lower Thames St, south of America's Cup Ave, for the densest concentration of diverse eateries. *Brick Alley Pub & Restaurant (140 Thames St)* has a huge menu of snacks, sandwiches, burgers and bar food ($6-8) plus full meals and elaborate drinks. *The Black Pearl*, on Bannister's Wharf, has a tavern for seafood ($10-25), the Commodore's Room for full meals ($20-35) in fancier surroundings and an outside patio for sandwiches and cheaper nibbles.

In summer, congenial cafes and pubs are practically a dime a dozen. Head to *One Pelham East (1 Pelham St E)*, near Thames St, for live music, sometimes with an Irish ring to it, and *Newport Blues Café (286 Thames St)* for…take a guess. *Wharf Pub & Restaurant (37 Bowen's Wharf)* serves good microbrews.

Getting There & Around

Bellevue Ave is best cruised on a rental bike from Ten Speed Spokes (☎ 401-847-5609, 18 Elm St) – really on America's Cup Ave – next to the Gateway Transportation & Visitors Center. You can rent scooters (and bikes) at Newport Wheels (☎ 401-849-4400), on Brown & Howard Wharf. Bonanza Bus Lines (☎ 401-751-8800), at the Convention & Visitor Center, runs six buses daily to Boston ($9; 1½ hours). State-run Ripta buses (☎ 401-781-9400) traverse the hour long route to Providence at least every hour ($1.25).

BLOCK ISLAND

In 1614 a mariner named Adriaen Block stopped at this 11-sq-mile island, giving it its name. For two centuries the settlement of New Shoreham was a fishing town, but with the advent of steam vessels in the late 19th century, Block Island became a summer resort for vacationers from Providence. It still is, though visitors now come from far and wide.

It's only 7 miles from one end to the other. The main town, where the ferry docks, is Old Harbor. The other settlement is New Harbor, on Great Salt Pond just over a mile away. The Block Island Chamber of Commerce (☎ 401-466-2982, 800-383-2474) unrolls their welcome mat in the ferry parking lot.

Rent a bicycle at Old Harbor Bike Shop (☎ 401-466-2029) for $20 a day, and head for Mohegan Bluffs, topped by the Southeast Light (house). You'll encounter 5 miles of hills while **bicycling** out to the 1867 North Light, at the island's northernmost tip. **Block Island Beach** stretches for 2 miles along the island's east coast. The southern part, closest to Old Harbor, is called 'Benson Town Beach' and offers a changing and showering pavilion.

The island has some great places for **hiking**. Rodman's Hollow (entrance off Cherry Hill Rd) is a 100-acre wildlife refuge laced with trails ending at the beach – perfect for a picnic. The Clay Head Nature Trail, off Corn Neck Rd, follows high clay bluffs along the beachfront, then veers inland through a mazelike series of paths cut into low vegetation that attracts dozens of bird species.

Places to Stay & Eat

Camping isn't allowed and rooms ain't cheap. There are some 35 B&Bs and guesthouses, many of which require summertime minimum stays. Advance reservations are imperative. The 17-room *Rose Farm Inn* (☎ *401-466-2034*), on Roslyn Rd, is convenient to Old Harbor and the beach ($155-235). *Blue Dory Inn & Adrian Inn* (☎ *401-466-2254, 800-992-7290*), on Dodge St, charges around $165-225. The 1879 *Atlantic Inn* (☎ *401-466-5883, 800-224-7422*), on High St, overlooks Old Harbor from a lofty hill ($150-245). The fanciest inn is the *1661 Inn & Hotel Manisses* (☎ *401-466-2063, 800-626-4773*), on Spring St, with small guest rooms for $175-300, including a buffet breakfast, wine and cheese, and an island tour.

The *1661 Inn*, on Spring St, serves an excellent – if somewhat pricey – outdoor champagne buffet brunch ($13). For lunch, *Harborside Inn*, on Water St, is a good choice ($8-15); dinner entrées costs a lot more ($20-30). Near the ferry, *Ballard's Inn*, offering everything from sandwiches to lobster, is popular with twentysomethings and the boating crowd.

Getting There & Away

New England Airlines (☎ 401-596-2460, 800-243-2460) makes the 12-minute flight from Westerly State Airport, on Airport Rd off RI 78, to Block Island ($69 roundtrip). Make reservations.

Interstate Navigation Co and Nelseco Navigation Co (☎ 401-783-4613) operate ferries. Interstate runs car-and-passenger ferries from Galilee State Pier, Point Judith, to Old Harbor (passengers $14 roundtrip; 1 hour) and summertime passenger boats from Newport's Fort Adams Dock to Old Harbor ($12 roundtrip; 2 hours). Nelseco runs a daily car-and-passenger ferry from early June to mid-September, departing from New London, Connecticut, during the morning, returning from Old Harbor in the late afternoon (passengers $30 roundtrip; 2 hours).

SOUTH COUNTY BEACHES

'South County' refers to the southwestern coastline towns from Narragansett to Watch Hill in Westerly. For more information, contact the South County Tourism Council (☎ 401-789-4422, 800-548-4662, 4808 Tower Hill Rd), in Wakefield.

South Kingstown Town Beach is among the best, as is family-friendly Roger Wheeler State Beach (also called 'Sand Hill Cove'), just south of Galilee. Misquamicut State Beach, just south of Westerly, is one of the busiest. It's close to a charmingly old-fashioned amusement area, Atlantic Beach Park, and has convenient facilities. Beaches charge daily parking fees of $8-15 from mid-June to early September.

Home to waterfowl and shellfish, South County's salt ponds and tidal rivers are ideal for **kayaking** and **canoeing**. Area outfitters include Quaker Lane Bait & Tackle (☎ 401-294-9642, 4019 Quaker Lane), in North Kingstown. To the east, Narragansett Town Beach is considered among the top East Coast spots for **surfing**. Rent surfboards, sailboards and any other watersport gear you need at The Watershed (☎ 401-789-3399, 396 Main St), in Wakefield.

Burlingame State Park Campsites (☎ *401-322-7994*), off US 1 in Charlestown, has more than 755 wooded sites ($12, no hookups) near crystal-clear Watchaug Pond. First-come, first-served is the rule, but call ahead to check on availability. *Worden's Pond Family Campground* (☎ *401-789-9113, 416A Worden's Pond Rd*), off RI 110 in South Kingstown, has several tent/RV sites ($20/25).

A Rhode Island landmark since the mid-1920s, *Aunt Carrie's* at Point Judith, RI 108 and Ocean Rd, offers noteworthy traditional shore dinners ($40 for steamed clams, corn on the cob and lobster), clam cakes and chowder. At the port in Galilee, look for *Champlin's Seafood*, similarly casual, with an outdoor deck overlooking all the activity, and *George's of Galilee*, with a takeout window where hordes of sandy summer people line up for clam cakes ($4.50 per dozen).

Connecticut

Connecticut has a surprising variety of landscapes and cityscapes. The southeastern region looks to New York. The coast is an ever-changing mix of historic towns and villages and booming high-tech cities. Hartford, the capital, is an oasis of skyscrapers amid miles of farmers' fields. The northwestern corner is a more sedate, low-key version of the Massachusetts Berkshires.

Connecticut

Nicknames: Constitution State, Nutmeg State

Population: 3,406,000 (28th)

Area: 5544 sq miles (48th)

Capital city: Hartford (population 122,000)

Admitted to Union: January 9, 1788 (5th)

Other cities: New Haven (124,000)

Home of: the first written US constitution (1639), Webster's dictionary (1806), Colt revolver (1835), pay telephone (1889)

Birthplace of: abolitionist John Brown (1800–59), Harriet Beecher Stowe (1811–96), traitor Benedict Arnold (1741–1801), circus man PT Barnum (1810–91), Katharine Hepburn (b 1909), Ralph Nader (b 1934)

History

In 1633, Dutch settlers built a small settlement at what is now Hartford, but it was the English who settled Connecticut in numbers. Many came from Massachusetts, such as Thomas Hooker, who founded Hartford in 1636. A year later a separate colony was set up at New Haven. Both joined the New England Confederation in 1643, and Connecticut received a royal charter in 1662.

These early colonists set up their own government and did not appreciate it when, in 1687, British governor general Sir Edmund Andros demanded that they surrender their charter and submit to his rule. Legend has it that the charter was hidden in the hollow of an oak tree, the Charter Oak, and thus saved from forfeiture. Overall, few Revolutionary War battles took place in Connecticut, but the colony was an important source of military supplies for the Continental Army.

Because of the industrial inventiveness of the state's citizens, the Connecticut Yankee peddler became a fixture in early American society, traveling by wagon from town to town selling clocks, buttons and other manufactured goods. In 1798, Eli Whitney established a factory at New Haven that made firearms with interchangeable parts – the beginnings of modern mass production.

Government & Economy

The state generally votes Democratic, although Governor John Rowland is a Republican and the state sent three Democrats and three Republicans to the US House of Representatives. Of the two Democratic senators, Joe Lieberman was the vice presidential candidate during the 2000 election and remains a strong liberal voice.

Connecticut is known for its submarine bases in New London and Groton, Yale University in New Haven, and Hartford's many insurance companies.

Arts

Among Connecticut's most famous artistic residents, Alexander Calder (1898–1976) made many of his world-famous mobiles and stabiles at his studio in Roxbury. Harriet Beecher Stowe (1811–96), who penned the enormously popular and influential tale of the abuses of slavery, *Uncle Tom's Cabin*, and Mark Twain (1835–1910), who wrote *The Adventures of Tom Sawyer,* were Hartford neighbors for 17 years.

Information

The Connecticut Tourism Department (☎ 860-270-8081, 800-282-6863, ☒ www.ctbound.org, 505 Hudson St, Hartford, CT 06106) sends guides and maps and makes lodging reservations. The state sales tax is 8%, with an additional 8% tax on meals and lodging.

HARTFORD

It's a rare person who vacations in Hartford – it's a workaday city – but if you're here, you'll enjoy it. Need insurance? Connecticut's capital is also a world-class insurance center, boasting the headquarters of 35 companies. The Greater Hartford Tourism District (☎ 860-244-8181, 800-793-4480, 234 Murphy Rd) provides information and a good walking-tour pamphlet. More convenient visitor centers are in the Old State House and the State Capitol.

The former homes of authors **Mark Twain** (☎ 860-493-6411, 351 Farmington Ave) and **Harriet Beecher Stowe** (☎ 860-525-9317, 73 Forest St) share spacious lawns in an area once called Nook Farm, a mile west of the city center along CT 4. Admission fees are $9 and $6.50, respectively. Samuel Langhorne Clemens penned some of his most famous works while living in his striking orange-and-black brick Victorian house. Harriet Beecher Stowe's 1871 home reflects the author's strong ideas about decorating. Her book on the subject was nearly as popular as *Uncle Tom's Cabin*, making her the Martha Stewart of her time.

The **State Capitol** (☎ 860-240-0222), at Capitol Ave and Trinity St, is an imposing white marble and granite building (1879) with neo-Gothic details and a gold-leaf dome. Hartford's 37-acre **Bushnell Park**, adjoining the capitol grounds, features a working 1914 carousel and the Pump House Gallery, scene of art exhibits and summer concerts. Housed in a castlelike Gothic Revival building, the **Wadsworth Atheneum** (☎ 860-278-2670, 600 Main St) is an excellent small art museum, especially strong in Hudson River school paintings ($7). Pacifists should ignore the **Museum of Connecticut History** (☎ 860-757-6500, 231 Capitol Ave), in the State Library & Supreme Court Building, which holds a prime collection of Colt firearms manufactured in Hartford (free admission).

The *HI Mark Twain Hostel* (☎ 860-523-7255, 131 Tremont St), off Farmington Ave, has dorm beds ($15-18) and a few private rooms ($45); reservations are advised. Off I-91, *Motel 6* (☎ 860-563-5900, 1341 Silas Deane Hwy) is 10 miles south of the city ($50-54). The city's fancy and historic *Goodwin Hotel* (☎ 860-246-7500, 1 Haynes St), across from the Civic Center, was built in 1881 ($200-269).

Inside the Wadsworth Atheneum, the *Museum Cafe (600 Main St)* serves lunch Tuesday to Sunday (main courses $9-14). For upscale, creatively prepared New England dishes in an airy locale, try *Max Downtown* (☎ 860-522-2530, 185 Asylum St), across from the Civic Center (lunches $9-17, dinners $16-25).

Greyhound, Peter Pan Trailways and Bonanza buses link Hartford's Union Station to other northeast cities. Amtrak trains connect Hartford to New York ($31; 2½ hours) and Boston ($32; 3½ hours).

LOWER CONNECTICUT RIVER VALLEY

The Lower Connecticut River Valley has many charming, unspoiled towns dating from the colonial era, best explored by car.

Essex

Established in 1635, Essex makes a good starting point for poking around the valley. It's genteel and well endowed with Federal-period houses, the legacy of 19th-century rum and tobacco fortunes. The **Connecticut River Museum** (☎ 860-767-8269), at Steamboat Dock, depicts the area's history with exhibits including a reproduction 1776 *Turtle*, the world's first submarine ($4). A good way to see some of the countryside is aboard the Valley Railroad's **Essex Steam Train and Riverboat** (☎ 860-767-0103), on Railroad Ave. A coal-fired steam locomotive hauls the train 12 miles (1 hour) to Deep River, where you may board a cruising riverboat before heading back by train ($10.50; $18.50 with cruise).

Revolutionary War–era *Griswold Inn* (☎ 860-767-1776, 36 Main St) has been a hostelry since 1776, but Sunday-morning 'hunt breakfasts' at the Griz have been a tradition only since 1812. The 31 rooms ($95-125) feature colonial decor and modern conveniences.

Old Lyme

Some 60 sea captains lived here in the 19th century, but since the early 1900s it has been better known as a center for American impressionist painters. Many stayed in the mansion of local art patron Florence Griswold, decorating its walls with murals in lieu of rent. The house has been converted into the **Griswold Museum** (☎ 860-434-5542, 96 Lyme St), open for touring ($5). *Bee & Thistle Inn* (☎ 860-434-1667, 100 Lyme St) is a 1756 Dutch Colonial farmhouse with 11 rooms ($150-189) and very fine dining.

Chester

Cupped in the valley of Pattaconk Brook, this village has a general store, post office, library, and a few antique shops and boutiques. Stop by **Connecticut River Artisans** (☎ 860-526-5575), on CT 149, a nonprofit artist cooperative featuring paintings, photographs, jewelry, pottery, prints, wearable art and more (closed Mon-Tue).

Off CT 148, *Inn at Chester* (☎ 860-526-9541, 800-949-7829, 318 W Main St) is yet another exemplary 1776 building transformed into a modern inn ($105-115), with good food. *Fiddler's (4 Water St)* specializes in seafood, with lunch from $7 and dinner entrées from $14. *Restaurant du Village* (☎ *860-526-5301, 59 Main St*) is a little corner of Provence (dinner entrées $26-31).

Hadlyme

An eight-car ferry (☎ 860-443-3856) makes the five-minute trip from Chester across the river to Hadlyme from April to November ($2.25 for car and driver). Looming above the crossing is the **Gillette Castle** (☎ 860-526-2336, 67 River Rd), a 24-room, stone-turreted 1919 mansion set in a 117-acre state park ($4).

Haddam & East Haddam

Riverside in Haddam, the 1876 **Goodspeed Opera House** (☎ 860-873-8668) is an American Gothic–style confection known as 'the birthplace of the American musical'; check it out. The 860-acre **Devil's Hopyard State Park** boasts great hiking trails and the 60-foot Chapman Falls. *Devil's Hopyard State Park* (☎ *860-873-8566, 877-668-2267*) has 21 primitive campsites ($9), but there are better facilities at *Wolf's Den Campground* (☎ *860-873-9681*), in East Haddam ($28.50) and *Little City Campground* (☎ *860-345-4886*), in Haddam ($30).

CONNECTICUT COAST

The southwestern coast is crowded with industrial and commercial cities, along with suburban bedroom communities within the magnetic influence of New York. The central coast, from New Haven east to the mouth of the Connecticut River, is less urban, with historic towns and villages. The southeastern coast includes New London and Groton, both important in naval history, and Mystic, where the Mystic Seaport Museum brings maritime history to life. The charming town of Stonington lives it for real.

Connecticut Commuter Rail Service's Shore Line East (☎ 203-777-7433) travels along this shoreline. At New Haven, trains connect with Metro North and Amtrak routes.

New London & Groton

In the mid-19th century, New London, 46 miles east of New Haven, was home port to some 200 whaling vessels. Today this city of 30,000 preserves its links to the sea. Across the river, the country's largest submarine base resides in Groton.

Amistad

On July 2, 1839, the slave ship *Amistad* was sailing along the Cuban coast with its 'cargo' of 55 abducted Africans. During the voyage one captive managed to remove his shackles and lead a rebellion to seize control of the ship. The US Coast Guard eventually towed the ship to New London, Connecticut, where the Africans were accused of rebellion and sent to New Haven to await trial.

The case became a *cause célèbre* among abolitionists and made its way to the US Supreme Court, where former president John Quincy Adams was persuaded to emerge from retirement to plead their case. The court found that since the abductees had been taken illegally, they couldn't be held liable for mutiny. The victory was a powerful moral and legal victory for the anti-slavery forces, and the *Amistad* abductees were repatriated to Africa. The compelling tale was made into a movie by Steven Spielberg.

New London has a well-laid-out walking tour, starting along the restored pedestrian mall, called the **Captain's Walk** (State St). The boyhood home of playwright Eugene O'Neill, **Monte Cristo Cottage** (☎ 860-443-0051, 325 Pequot Ave) can also be toured ($5). The **Lyman Allyn Art Museum** (☎ 860-443-2545, 625 Williams St) is a neoclassical building with exhibits that include early-American silver; Far Eastern, Greco-Roman and European art; and ethnic art of many other cultures ($4). In Groton, non-claustrophobic visitors board the world's first nuclear-powered submarine at the **Historic Ship Nautilus & Submarine Force Museum** (☎ 860-694-3174, 800-343-0079).

Off I-95, omnipresent chains include *Red Roof Inn* (☎ *860-444-0001, 707 Colman St*), for $66-89, and *Holiday Inn* (☎ *860-442-0631*), for $109-164. The high-Victorian 1903 *Queen Anne Inne* (☎ *860-447-2600, 800-347-8818, 265 Williams St*) features eight spiffy guest rooms ($95-175 with breakfast). On a private beach, *Lighthouse Inn* (☎ *860-443-8411, 6 Guthrie Place*) occupies a restored 1902 mansion ($100-190). For more options, head to Mystic. For great, inexpensive pizza,

New London has **Recovery Room** *(445 Ocean Ave)*, a family-run place near the beach.

Cross Sound Ferry (☎ 860-443-5281, 631-323-2525, 2 Ferry St) operates ferries between New London and Orient Point on Long Island year round (car and driver $34, extra passengers $10; 1½ hours).

Mystic & Around

Long before its popular museum was built and the movie *Mystic Pizza* (starring Julia Roberts) was released, Mystic was a lovely, centuries-old seaport town. Contact the Mystic Chamber of Commerce (☎ 860-572-9578, 28 Cottrell St) for information.

Mystic Seaport Museum (☎ 860-572-5315), on CT 27, encompasses 17 acres, more than 60 historic buildings, three ships and many smaller vessels ($17). Seaport buildings are staffed by costumed interpreters who talk with visitors about their crafts and trades. Visitors can board the *Charles W Morgan* (1841), the last surviving wooden whaling ship in the USA; the *LA Dunton,* a three-masted fishing schooner; and the *Joseph Conrad,* a square-rigged training ship. The *Sabino* (☎ 860-572-5315), a 1908 steamboat, takes visitors on half-hour excursion trips up the Mystic River ($5).

The **Mystic Aquarium** (☎ 860-572-5955, 55 Coogan Blvd) has more than 6000 species of sea creatures on view ($16). The **Denison Homestead** (☎ 860-536-9248), on Pequotsepos Rd, contains memorabilia from 11 generations of the Denison family, from the colonial period through the 1940s ($4; open Thurs-Mon).

In nearby Ledyard, **Foxwoods Resort & Casino** (☎ 800-752-9244), on CT 2, is run by the Mashantucket Pequot Indian tribe. It's open day and night, with the standard lineup of entertainment, sports events, hotels, restaurants, shops and, of course, gambling. Bring money and plan to leave without it. You can lose money just as easily at **Monhegan Sun** (☎ 888-226-7711, I-395 exit 79A), a smaller version of Foxwoods. **Mashanucket Pequot Museum & Research Center** (☎ 860-396-6800, 800-411-9671), on CT 214, is a beautiful, ultramodern museum paying homage to an ancient people ($12).

Many hotels and motels are clustered at I-95 exit 90. A few more are on US 1 to Stonington, a 10-minute drive from Mystic. **Whaler's Inn** (☎ 860-536-1506, 800-243-2588, 20 E Main St) is centrally located ($129-209). **Seaport Motor Inn** (☎ 860-536-2621), on CT 27, has clean, simple rooms ($118-139), while the smaller, family-friendly **Taber Motel & Townhouse** (☎ 860-536-4904, 29 William St) offers beds from $165. **The Inn at Mystic** (☎ 860-536-9604, 800-237-2415), at US 1 and CT 27, has a variety of accommodations ($95-295) and many amenities.

Next to the drawbridge with excellent views, **S&P Oyster Co** (1 Holmes St) features lunchtime fish and chips and sandwiches (about $9) and more 'real' dinnertime dishes ($11-29). **Captain Daniel Packer Inne** (32 Water Ave), in a historic 1754 building, is big into beef. You'll spend $15-24 for dinner entrées, less at lunch. **Abbott's Lobster in the Rough**, on the waterfront in neighboring Noank, serves traditional summer shore dinners of lobsters and clams at picnic tables ($18-24, depending on the lobster's girth).

Stonington

This was once an important whaling and sealing port. On August 9, 1814, four British ships used 158 Royal Navy guns to batter the town, which was suspected of harboring rebel torpedoes. The **Old Lighthouse Museum** (☎ 860-535-1440, 7 Water St), at the tip of the point, boasts an octagonal-towered granite lighthouse, built in 1823. It was moved to its present location in 1840 ($4).

Campers head to **Highland Orchards Resort Park** (☎ 860-599-5101, 800-624-0829), in North Stonington, with 270 sites ($30). The least expensive motels are along US 1 between Stonington and Mystic. Try **Stonington Motel** (☎ 860-599-2330), on US 1, or **Sea Breeze Motel** (☎ 860-535-2843, 812 Stonington Rd), both with rooms for $79-99. Upscale **Randall's Ordinary** (☎ 860-599-4540), on CT 2 in North Stonington, rents rooms ($99-229) and serves hearth-cooked, authentic colonial dinners ($39); reservations are required.

For casual seafood lunches ($11-15) and dinners (entrées $18-24) tucked away on the harbor, **Skipper's Dock** (66 Water St) reels 'em in with a waterside deck. If you're not that hungry, get picnic fixins at **Water St Market & Deli** (142 Water St).

New Haven

Shipping, manufacturing, health care and the local telephone company power New Haven's economy, which also feels the influence of mighty New York, 75 miles southwest. But this city, established in 1637, is best known for Yale University, founded 80 years later. New Haven has urban pleasures and problems, including street crime. Avoid run-down neighborhoods and empty streets after dark, and don't leave *anything* visible in your parked car.

The city's chamber of commerce (☎ 203-777-8550, 800-332-7829, 59 Elm St) is near the town green. For campus tours, contact Yale University's visitor center (☎ 203-432-2302, 149 Elm St), on the north side of the green.

New Haven's traditional **town green**, the city's spiritual center, is spacious and framed by beautiful churches. Crowded with university Gothic buildings, the historic campus of **Yale University**, to the north and west, is marked by Harkness Tower, from which a carillon peals at appropriate moments throughout the day. West of the green, the **Yale Center for British Art** (☎ 203-432-2800, 1080 Chapel St) holds the most comprehensive collection of British art outside the UK. Just opposite, the **Yale University Art Gallery** (☎ 203-432-0600, 1111 Chapel St) boasts masterworks by Frans Hals, Peter Paul Rubens, Manet, Picasso and van Gogh, as well as other art from Africa, Asia, Europe and the Americas. Both are free and closed Monday. Yale's **Peabody Museum of Natural History** (☎ 203-432-5050, 170 Whitney Ave), five blocks northeast of the green along Temple St, has dinosaur fossils, wildlife dioramas, meteorites and minerals ($5).

Places to Stay & Eat The *Hammonasset Beach State Park* (☎ 860-424-3200, 877-668-2267), 20 miles east of New Haven, between Madison and Clinton (I-95 exit 62), has 558 sites ($12) and, despite its size, is crowded in high summer. *Riverdale Farm Campsites* (☎ 860-669-5388), on River Rd in Clinton, is one-quarter the size ($28).

The 58-room *Motel 6 New Haven North* (☎ 203-469-0343, 270 Foxon Blvd), north of the city at I-91 exit 8, charges $62. At *Hotel Duncan* (☎ 203-787-1273, 1151 Chapel St), the decor, facilities and price ($60) of fin de siècle New Haven have been preserved.

Nearby, *The Colony* (☎ 203-776-1234, 800-458-8810, 1157 Chapel St) is modernish, with modern prices ($109).

Louis' Lunch (261–263 Crown St), between College and High Sts, is the self-proclaimed birthplace of the hamburger – almost. Around the late 18th century, when the vertically grilled ground-beef sandwich was first introduced at Louis', the restaurant was in a different location. It still uses the historic vertical grills, though, and serves the patties on white toast, as it always has, for around $4 (open Tue-Sat). Don't even think of asking for ketchup.

Between High and York Sts, *Atticus Bookstore Café* (1082 Chapel St) serves coffee, scones, soups, sandwiches and good books. *Claire's Cornucopia* (1000 Chapel St) attracts health-conscious students with its veggie dishes (averaging $6.50). *Frank Pepe's* (157 Wooster St), located six blocks east of the green, is the old reliable pizza joint, but many New Havenites prefer nearby *Sally's Pizza* (237 Wooster St). Near the green, *Tibwin Grill* (☎ 203-624-1883, 220 College St) is an upscale New American bistro featuring exotic appetizers, grilled main courses and select wines (lunch $7-11, dinner entrées $16-22).

Toad's Place (☎ 203-624-8623, 300 York St) is the hot nightclub, but in this college town, theater, music and dance offerings are many and varied. The Yale visitor center has details on current happenings.

Getting There & Away Peter Pan Trailways buses connect New Haven to New York ($20; from 2½ hours) and other cities. Amtrak and Metro North trains (☎ 212-532-4900, 800-638-7646) run to New York City's Grand Central Terminal ($31; 1½-hours).

LITCHFIELD HILLS

Sprinkled with lakes and dotted with state parks and forests, this beautiful, tranquil area of northwestern Connecticut offers an excess of natural beauty but few accommodations. The historic town of Litchfield is at the region's center. The Litchfield Hills Visitors Bureau (☎ 860-567-4506) can send you a booklet with maps.

Litchfield

Founded in 1719, Litchfield prospered thanks to the commerce brought by stagecoaches traveling between Hartford (34 miles away) and Albany. In the mid-19th century railroads superseded coaches, and industrial machinery drove Litchfield's artisans bankrupt. But the town's grand 18th-century houses survive.

Stroll along North and South Sts to see the fine houses, including the 1773 **Tapping Reeve House** (☎ 860-567-4501, 82 South St), beside which the tiny shed once housed the USA's first law school (1775). John C Calhoun and 130 members of Congress were trained here ($5). The **Litchfield Historical Society** (☎ 860-567-4501, 7 South St) has a museum ($5). One mile southeast of town off CT 118, **Haight Vineyards** (☎ 860-567-4045, 29 Chestnut Hill Rd) offers tours and wine tastings. The **White Memorial Conservation Center** (☎ 860-567-0857), 2½ miles west of town along US 202, has 35 miles of hiking trails. Also, visit the hilltop **Topsmead State Forest**, 2 miles east of the town green along CT 118.

Along US 202 you'll find the simple *Looking Glass Hill Campground* (☎ 860-567-2050), 5 miles west of Litchfield in Bantam, and the elaborate *Hemlock Hill Camp Resort* (☎ 860-567-2267), on Hemlock Hill Rd off Milton Rd. To reach year-round *Valley in the Pines* (☎ 860-491-2032), go west on US 202 (almost to Bantam), turn north on Maple St and go 5½ miles to the quiet campground (tents/RVs $26/29). At the other end of the spectrum, elegant *Litchfield Inn* (☎ 860-567-4503, 800-499-3444), on US 202, 2 miles west of the town green, has 32 rooms ($125-200).

Barnidge & McEnroe, on West St, serves coffee and pastries and sells books. *West Street Grill* (☎ 860-567-3885), also facing the green, offers excellent, creative New American cuisine ($5-20 lunch, $18-34 dinner entrées).

Lake Waramaug
Of the dozens of lakes and ponds in the Litchfield Hills, Lake Waramaug, north of New Preston, is the most beautiful. As you make your way around the northern shore on North Shore Rd, stop at Hopkins Vineyard (☎ 860-868-7954), on Hopkins Rd, for tastings. It's next to country-style *Hopkins Inn* (☎ 860-868-7295), with 11 rooms ($77-87). The wines, made mostly from French-American hybrid grapes, are eminently drinkable.

Around the bend in the lake is *Lake Waramaug State Park* (☎ 860-868-0220, 30 Lake Waramaug Rd). With 77 beautiful lakeside campsites ($10), it's usually booked well in advance in summer. Flanking US 7 north of Cornwall Bridge, **Housatonic Meadows State Park** (☎ 860-927-3238) is famous for its 2-mile stretch of Carse Brook that's set aside for fly-fishing. The *campground* (☎ 860-672-6772, 877-668-2267) has 95 sites ($10).

Vermont

Vermont is mountainous and green, with far more trees than people. There's only one city worthy of the title: Burlington. To enjoy Vermont properly, you must drive slowly, hike in the forests or canoe down a rushing stream.

History
The French explorer Samuel de Champlain gave his name to Vermont's largest lake in 1609, but the French did not settle here until 1666. Though their settlements didn't survive, the English settlement at Fort Dummer (1724), close to present-day Brattleboro, did. Even so, Vermont was something of a wilderness for years, important only in the eyes of New York and New Hampshire, which disputed its ownership.

Ethan Allen organized his Green Mountain Boys to push the claim of New Hampshire against New York. But when the

---

Vermont

Nickname: Green Mountain State

Population: 609,000 (49th)

Area: 9615 sq miles (45th)

Admitted to Union: March 4, 1791 (14th)

Capital city: Montpelier (population 8000)

Other cities: Burlington (39,000), Bennington (16,000), Brattleboro (12,000)

Birthplace of: Calvin Coolidge (1872–1933), Mormon church founder Joseph Smith (1805–44), Mormon leader Brigham Young (1801–77), farm-equipment manufacturer John Deere (1804–86)

Revolutionary War broke out, Allen turned his efforts against the British, capturing Ticonderoga. In 1777 Vermont proclaimed itself a free and independent nation, and it stayed that way until 1791, when it was admitted to the USA.

Lacking a wealthy landowning class, Vermont was among the most egalitarian and democratic of the early states and remains so today. It supported the Union strongly in the Civil War, voting overwhelmingly for Lincoln in 1860 even though his opponent, Stephen Douglas, was a Vermonter.

Government & Politics

The state's independent streak is as long and deep as a vein of Vermont marble. Senator Jim Jeffords turned the US Senate and country upside down in 2001 when he switched from Republican to Independent because of the rightward swing Republicans were taking after Bush was elected in 2000. With the defection, the scales of an evenly divided senate tipped back to the Democrats by one. Senator Patrick Leahy is a staunch Democrat. Vermont's singular representative, Independent Bernie Sanders, is a registered Socialist.

In 2000 the Supreme Court of Vermont declared that gay couples have the same rights and privileges as heterosexual ones; it is the only US state to acknowledge these civil unions.

Economy

Long a land of self-sufficient farmers, Vermont turned to sheep raising when, in the mid-19th century, the new Western farms began producing agricultural goods more cheaply. But the Western farms, as well as Australia, were soon also supplying New England's textile mills with wool cheaper than Vermont could, and the state went into decline. Today the state is still mostly rural, with the lowest population of any New England state. Dairy farming and tourism drive the economy.

Arts

In summer the Vermont hills are alive with the sound of music – in the form of music festivals, that is. New England's signature poet is Robert Frost (1874–1963), long associated with Vermont and New Hampshire. Anna Mary Moses (1860–1961), known as 'Grandma Moses,' painted lively, natural depictions of farm life around Bennington until she was 100 years old. Illustrator Norman Rockwell (1894–1978) lived and worked in Arlington in addition to Lenox, Massachusetts. These days, E Annie Proulx, the award-winning author of *The Shipping News,* describes rural Vermont in her novel *Postcards.*

Information

VT 100 is the state's scenic highway, winding its way right through the center of Vermont. Call or write to Vermont Travel & Tourism (☎ 802-828-3236, 800-837-6668, W www.travel-vermont.com, 6 Baldwin St, Montpelier, VT 05633). The Vermont Chamber of Commerce (☎ 802-223-3443, PO Box 37, Montpelier, VT 05601) can also help. Vermont's sales tax is 5%; its meals and lodging taxes are 9% each. For highway information, call ☎ 802-828-2648.

SOUTHERN VERMONT

Vermont's southern part has some of the state's most beautiful small villages and one of its two funkiest towns.

Brattleboro

Founded in 1724, Brattleboro is a pleasant, workaday place. It's where the USA's 1960s alternative lifestyle settled down to live: lots of bookstores, coffee shops and facial hair. Rudyard Kipling married a Brattleboro woman in 1892 and lived for a time in a big Brattleboro house he named 'Naulaukha,' where he wrote *The Jungle Book.*

Town Meetings

The traditional form of local New England government is the famous 'town meeting,' an annual convocation at which an entire town's citizenry is invited to comment, complain and vote on ordinances and budgets for the coming year. Meetings can be contentious, fiery, unpolished, absurdly mundane or passionately profound. They're grassroots democracy in action, where every person can have his or her say in local matters. Keep your eyes peeled for posted flyers.

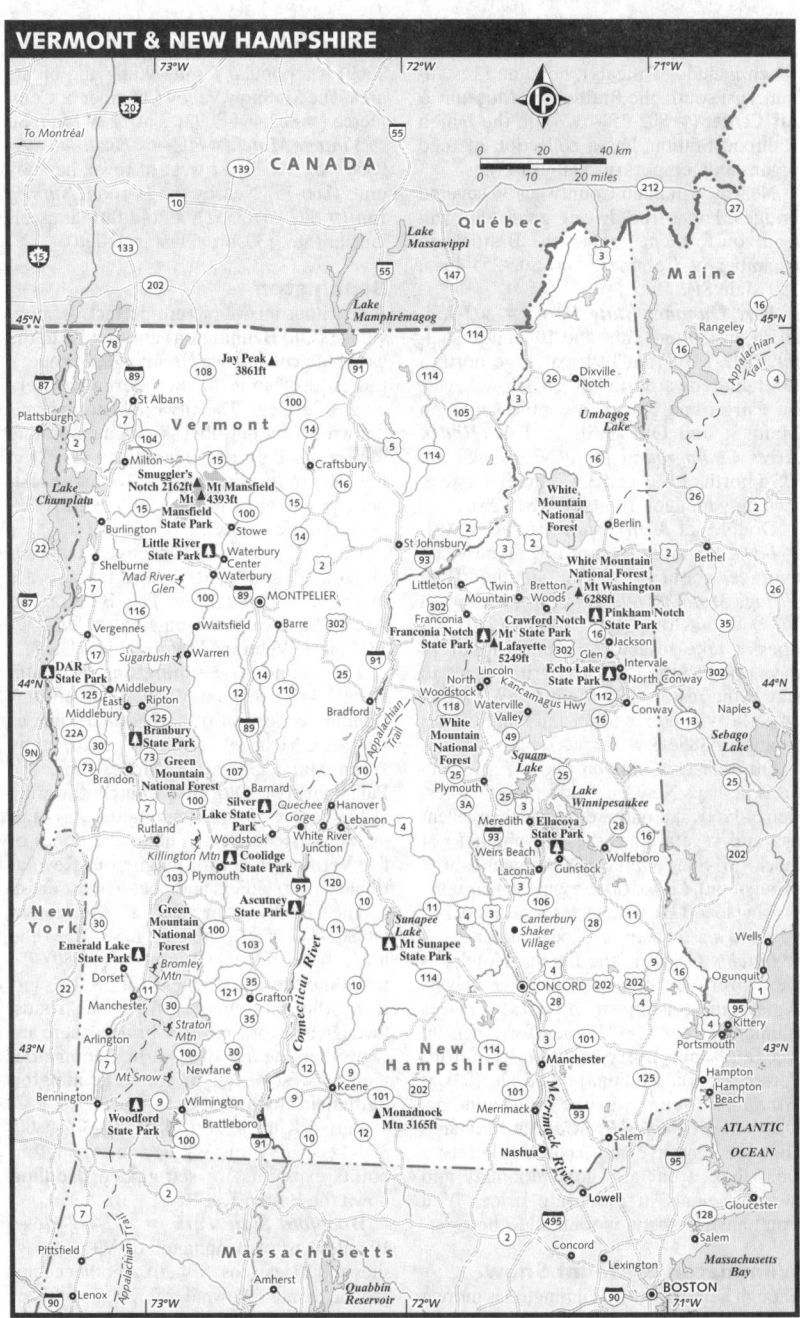

VERMONT & NEW HAMPSHIRE

At the center of the town's commercial district is the art deco Latchis Building, which includes a theater, hotel and restaurant. Just south, the **Brattleboro Museum & Art Center** (☎ 802-257-0124), in the Union Railroad Station, has a collection of reed organs and temporary exhibits ($3).

Nearby Windham County has 30 **covered bridges**. For a free driving guide that will lead you to them, contact the Brattleboro Chamber of Commerce (☎ 802-254-4565, 180 Main St).

Fort Dummer State Park (☎ *802-254-2610)* has 50 tent sites and 10 lean-to shelters ($12-18). From I-91 exit 1, go north a few hundred yards on US 5, a half-mile east on Fairground Rd, then a mile south on Main St and Old Guilford Rd. *Hidden Acres Campground* (☎ *802-254-2098)*, on US 5 north of I-91 exit 3, has many services, including minigolf (tents/RVs $19/23).

Doubles at *Molly Stark Motel* (☎ *802-254-2440)*, 3 miles west of I-91 along VT 9, average about $70. The simpler *West Village Motel* (☎ *802-254-5610)*, nearby on VT 9 W, has only eight rooms ($50) but doesn't take reservations until about 10 days prior to the date. The prime place to stay is the restored 30-room *Latchis Hotel* (☎ *802-254-6300)*, at Main and Flat Sts, with rooms for $85-95.

Off Main St, *Common Ground* (25 Elliot St) is perhaps New England's purest expression of 1960s alternative dining, with excellent fish and vegetarian dishes for about $6 at lunch (Fri-Sun). Dinner is a bargain as well (Thurs-Sun). *Coffee Country*, in the Harmony parking lot off High St, serves java and baked goods to hipster teens and local farmers.

Latchis Grille, in the Latchis Hotel, has views over Whetstone Brook and good New American cuisine at moderate prices (dinner entrées $18-22; open for lunch on weekends only). Try the Olde Guilford Porter, a dark, medium-bodied ale ($3) at *Windham Brewery*, in the same building. Oak-paneled *Moles Eye Cafe*, at Main and High Sts, has live music on weekends, a well-stocked bar and good noonday and evening meals at moderate prices. You won't have to spend more than $7 here.

Wilmington & Mount Snow

Though a pretty town, Wilmington is more a crossroads where people traveling between Massachusetts and Vermont stop for a rest or meal. **Mt Snow** (☎ 802-464-3333, 800-245-7669) is a popular family skiing and biking area. The Mt Snow Valley Chamber of Commerce (☎ 802-464-8092) is at 21 W Main St.

Vintage Motel (☎ *802-464-8824, 800-899-9660)*, on VT 9 just west of town, has tidy units ($60-75). Nearby, the 14-room *Nutmeg Inn* (☎ *802-464-3351)*, an old farmhouse, is fancier ($89-139, breakfast included).

Bennington

A felicitous mix of picture-perfect Vermont village (Old Bennington) and, a mile to the east, blue-collar town (Bennington proper), this is also home to the alternative Bennington College. The city is a historic place, known for its tall obelisk commemorating the crucial Battle of Bennington (1777) in the Revolutionary War. Robert Frost, perhaps the most famous 20th-century US poet, is buried here.

US 7, VT 7A and VT 9 converge in Bennington. Most lodgings and restaurants are in the downtown area. The Bennington Area Chamber of Commerce (☎ 802-447-3311) is on Veterans Memorial Dr (US 7).

The famous **Bennington Museum** (☎ 802-447-1571), on VT 9, holds an outstanding collection of early Americana, as well as a rich collection of paintings by Anna Mary 'Grandma' Moses ($6). The Palladian-style **Old First Church**, towering at the center of Old Bennington, was built in 1806. Its churchyard holds the bones of five Vermont governors, numerous Revolutionary War soldiers and poet Robert Frost.

The **Bennington Battle Monument** (☎ 802-447-0550), built in 1887–91, is the loftiest structure in Vermont ($1.50). To reach the actual battlefield, follow the signs from the monument along backroads, through a historic covered bridge (there are two others nearby) to North Bennington, then go west on VT 67 to the **Bennington Battlefield Historic Site**.

Batten Kill Canoe Ltd (☎ 802-362-2800, 800-421-5268), on VT 7A in Arlington, outfits explorers for self-guided **paddling** down the Batten Kill River.

Woodford State Park (☎ *802-447-7169)*, 10 miles east of Bennington on VT 9, has 80 sites and 20 lean-tos ($14-20). Another campground is near Pownal, off US 7 south of Bennington: *Shady Acres* (☎ *802-442-4960)*, on Jackson Cross Rd, with 25 sites ($15). *HI Greenwood Lodge Hostel & Campsites* (☎ 802-442-2547), 8 miles east of Bennington, on VT 9 at Prospect Mountain in Woodford, has dorm beds ($18-21), guest rooms ($40-44) and tent sites ($17) with free hot showers.

Vermonter Motor Lodge (☎ 802-442-2529), on VT 9 about 2 miles west of Old Bennington, offers quiet doubles ($55-80). Also on VT 9, *Mid-Town Motel* (☎ 802-447-0189, 107 W Main St) rents doubles ($65-75). *Paradise Motor Inn* (☎ 802-442-8351) is the big, fancy place with a heated pool in the town center ($61-86).

Create your own lunchtime sandwich at *Alldays & Onions* (519 Main St), or splurge on rack of lamb and the like at dinner (entrées $13-23). *Blue Benn Diner*, on US 7 at North St, supplements standard diner fare with vegetarian and Middle Eastern dishes ($6-11) throughout the day. Pair a margarita at *Rattlesnake Café* (230 North St) with a hefty burrito ($8) and leave feeling sassy.

Manchester

For almost two centuries, Manchester has been a popular summer resort. The mountain scenery, the equable summer climate and the Batten Kill River – one of Vermont's best trout streams – continue to draw crowds. Now there's also skiing, golfing and shopping.

Manchester Village is the southern part of town, a dignified, historic Vermont village centered on the posh Equinox Hotel. Manchester Center, a few miles north along VT 7A, is devoted mostly to upscale outlet stores, inns and restaurants. The Manchester Regional Chamber of Commerce (☎ 802-362-2100) is on the green in Manchester Center.

Things to See & Do A 24-room Georgian Revival mansion, **Hildene** (☎ 802-362-1788), on VT 7A just south of Manchester, was the country estate of Robert Todd Lincoln, son of President Abraham Lincoln ($8). The **American Museum of Fly Fishing** (☎ 802-362-3300), on VT 7A at Seminary Ave, just north of Manchester Village, has a fine display of fly-fishing equipment ($3).

Drive to the summit of **Mt Equinox** (3835 feet), departing from VT 7A south of Manchester via Sky Line Dr (☎ 802-362-1114), a private 5-mile toll road ($8 for car and two passengers). For **bicycling**, rent a road, mountain or hybrid bike from Batten Kill Sports Bicycle Shop (☎ 802-362-2734), on VT 11 and VT 30, between VT 7A and US 7 (from $20 a day).

Bromley Mountain (☎ 802-824-5522, 800-865-4786), a small family ski resort, switches gears in the summer. Chairlifts take hikers up the summit and kids swoosh down the Alpine Slide. **Stratton Mountain** (☎ 802-297-2200, 800-843-6867), 16 miles east of Manchester on VT 30, is a larger ski area, with a vertical drop of more than 2000 feet, 90 downhill trails and almost 20 miles of cross-country trails.

The **Appalachian Trail**, which overlaps the **Long Trail** in Vermont, passes just east of Manchester. There are shelters about every 10 miles; some have caretakers. For details and maps of good area hikes, contact the USFS Green Mountain National Forest (☎ 802-362-2307), 3 miles northeast of VT 11 and VT 30 in Manchester.

Places to Stay & Eat The *Emerald Lake State Park* (☎ 802-362-1655), on US 7 just north of the village of East Dorset, has 69 tent sites ($14) and 32 lean-tos ($20).

The chamber of commerce can usually help you find a room. *Chalet Motel* (☎ 802-362-1622, 800-343-9900), on VT 11 and VT 30 east of the center, costs $70-90, while cottages at *Wedgewood Motel* (☎ 802-362-2145), on VT 7A, rent for $68. *Stamford Motel* (☎ 802-362-2342), on VT 7A N, has 14 tidy doubles ($65-70). Nearby *Aspen Motel* (☎ 802-362-2450) tops out at $95. Central *Barnstead Innstead* (☎ 802-362-1619, 800-331-1619) is among the town's best motels, with rooms ($130-210) in a renovated 1830s hay barn.

Manchester's top place to stay dominates the town: The 183-room *Equinox* (☎ 802-362-4700, 800-362-4747), on VT 7A, boasts its own 18-hole golf course, indoor and outdoor pools, multiple tennis courts and a multitude of other resort services ($199-359). At least sit in the front-porch rocking chairs and act like you belong.

4940 (4940 Main St) was the setting for Normal Rockwell's painting *War News*. These days, you can get a burger all day ($7) or something nicer for dinner ($13-22). *The Little Rooster Cafe*, on VT 7A, makes fancy

NEW ENGLAND

soups like mango gazpacho and constructs flatbread sandwiches with goat cheese for $7-8. *Mrs Murphy's Donuts & Coffee Shop*, at VT 30 and VT 11, is a few blocks to the east of VT 7A on the right (look for the pickup trucks). *The Restaurant at Willow Pond* (☎ *802-362-4733)*, on VT 7A N, serves northern Italian cuisine (dinner entrées $13-25).

Newfane & Grafton

A short stroll through Newfane allows you to take in all of its 'attractions' – the stately Congregational Church (1839), the Greek Revival–style Windham County Courthouse (1825) and a few antique shops. *Townshend State Park (☎ 802-365-7500)*, 3 miles north of Newfane off VT 30, has 34 tent sites and lean-tos ($12-18) and a challenging path to the summit of Bald Mountain (1680 feet). *Four Columns Inn (☎ 802-365-7713)*, on West St, has a very good dining room and doubles from $125. The eight-room *West River Lodge (☎ 802-365-7745)*, just outside town, features farmhouse accommodations ($85-100, breakfast included).

Graceful Grafton is virtually an open-air museum, the classic Vermont village. At the Grafton Village Cheese Company (☎ 802-843-2221), a half-mile south of the village, you can watch Covered Bridge Cheddar being made. *The Old Tavern at Grafton (☎ 802-843-2231, 800-843-1801)*, at VT 35 and Townshend Rd, is quite formal, while its cafe (offering lots of sandwiches) in the adjoining barn is less so. The 59 guest rooms, scattered throughout the village, cost $135-195.

CENTRAL VERMONT

Vermont's midsection, bisecting the Green Mountains, features ski villages, a college town and a rarified postcard-perfect village.

Plymouth

The small farming village of Plymouth is known for the **President Calvin Coolidge State Historic Site** (☎ 802-672-3773), birthplace of the 30th US president ($6). At the **Plymouth Cheese Company** (☎ 802-672-3650) you can watch delicious granular-curd cheddar being made from Vermont milk and taste free samples.

Coolidge State Park (☎ 802-672-3612), on VT 100A, 3 miles northeast of Plymouth, has 25 campsites ($12) and 35 lean-tos ($18). *HI Trojan Horse Hostel (☎ 802-228-5244,*

800-547-7475, 44 Andover St) is on VT 100 in Ludlow, 11 miles south of Plymouth. The 18 beds cost $15.

Killington

Killington is Vermont's prime ski resort (☎ 802-422-3333), with 200 runs on seven mountains, a vertical drop of more than 3000 feet, and 32 lifts, including the Skyeship and K1 Express gondolas. From Killington Base Lodge, the Mountain Bike Center (☎ 802-422-6232) rents mountain bikes for $45 a day (helmet and trail map included). You and your bike can take the gondola ($9) to the 4215-foot summit of Killington Mountain and ride down, finding your way among 45 miles of trails. All-day access costs $30.

There are well over a hundred lodging places in the Killington area. The best way to find a bed is to call the Killington Travel & Lodging Bureau (☎ 800-372-2007). *Gifford Woods State Park (☎ 802-775-5354)* has campsites/lean-tos ($12/18) on 114 acres just a half-mile north of the intersection of US 4 and VT 100.

Woodstock

This Vermont town is the antithesis of Woodstock, New York, that symbol of 1960s hippie living. Vermont's version, chartered in 1761, has been the highly dignified shire town of Windsor County since 1766 and has a lovely village green. The Woodstock Chamber of Commerce (☎ 802-457-3555, 18 Central St) has more information.

Marsh-Billings-Rockefeller National Historical Park (☎ 802-457-3368), on VT 12, emphasizes the conservation and stewardship of open spaces (mansion and garden tours $4). Life at the **Billings Farm & Museum** (☎ 802-457-2355), less than a mile north of the Woodstock green along VT 12 at River Rd, is a mix of 19th- and 20th-century farming techniques ($8). The **Vermont Institute of Natural Sciences** (☎ 802-457-2779), 1½ miles southwest of the green on Church Hill Rd, has a raptor center, nature trails and a collection of rare herbs ($7).

Eight miles east of Woodstock along US 4, the highway passes over the 170-foot **Quechee Gorge** (**kwee**-chee), a craggy chasm cut by the Ottauquechee River. Quechee Gorge State Park has hiking trails, campsites and picnic facilities.

About 10 miles west of Woodstock, visit the brewery at **Long Trail Brewing Company** (☎ 802-672-5011), in the Marketplace on US 4. They produce 'Vermont's No 1 selling amber.'

Places to Stay & Eat The *Quechee Gorge State Park* (☎ *802-295-2990*) has 52 pine-shaded sites ($12) and seven lean-tos ($18). Ten miles north of town off VT 12 in Barnard, *Silver Lake State Park* (☎ *802-234-9451*) has 40 sites ($14) and seven lean-tos ($20). For the same price, *Ascutney State Park* (☎ *802-674-2060*), about 22 miles southeast of Woodstock, has 49 sites, 10 of which are lean-tos, at a 3144-foot elevation. Historic *HI Hotel Coolidge* (☎ *800-909-4776 ext 68, 17 S Main St*), in nearby White River Junction, has 36 beds ($19-20) in double and triple rooms.

Five miles from Woodstock, *Quality Inn* (☎ *802-295-7600*), on US 4 east of Quechee Gorge, rents doubles for $79-115. *Pleasant View Motel* (☎ *802-295-3485*) is cheaper ($49-79) because it's 13 miles from Woodstock. *Rosewood Inn B&B* (☎ *802-457-4485*), on Wood Rd 4 miles north of town in South Pomfret, has rooms with shared and private bath ($75-125 with breakfast).

For coffees, pastries and light lunches, try *Pane e Salute* (*61 Central St*). Roast turkey dinner with all the trimmings is a great value ($18) at *Village Inn of Woodstock* (*41 Pleasant St*). *The Prince & the Pauper* (☎ *802-457-1818, 24 Elm St*), an elegant New American bistro, serves a three-course prix fixe menu for $38. *Simon Pearce Restaurant* (☎ *802-295-1470*), on Main St in Quechee, overlooks a waterfall and covered bridge; luckily, the New American dishes (lunch dishes $12-15, dinner entrées $19-28) rival the scenery.

Middlebury

Prosperity lives at the crossroads, and Middlebury, at the nexus of eight highways and home of Middlebury College, obviously has its share. The Addison County Chamber of Commerce (☎ 802-388-7951, 2 Court St) can help with local information. For information about and tours of Middlebury College, contact the Admissions Offices (☎ 802-443-3000), on S Main St. On the same street, the **Middlebury College Museum of Art** (☎ 802-443-5007) is worth a look since it's free.

Bring some cash to the **Vermont State Craft Center at Frog Hollow** (☎ 802-388-3177, 1 Mill St), which showcases and sells fine works by Vermont artisans.

Morgan horses, America's first unique breed, all derive from a Thoroughbred-Arabian colt bred by Justin Morgan in the late 18th century. You can see 70 registered Morgans at the University of Vermont's **Morgan Horse Farm** (☎ 802-388-2011), about 3 miles from Middlebury; take VT 125 west and go north (right) on VT 23. Vermont's flattest region offers fine countryside bicycling. The Bike Center (☎ 802-388-6666, 74 Main St), at Frog Hollow Alley, rents hybrid bikes.

About 10 miles south of Middlebury, *Branbury State Park* (☎ *802-247-5925*), on VT 53 in Brandon, has sites/lean-tos ($14/20) dotted around 69 acres. On Lake Champlain, *DAR State Park* (☎ *802-759-2354*), on VT 17 in Vergennes about 17 miles west of Middlebury, has 45 campsites ($12) and 24 lean-tos ($18). *Blue Spruce Motel* (☎ *802-388-4091*), on US 7 S, rents rooms and cottages for $65-85. *Sugarhouse Motel* (☎ *802-388-2770, US 7*), 2 miles north of town, is competitively priced ($69-79). In Ripton, *Chipman Inn* (☎ *802-388-2390*), on VT 125, 8 miles east of Middlebury, is close to the farm where poet Robert Frost spent 23 years. The inn ($115-125 with breakfast), a beautiful Federal house built in 1828, is thick with Frostiana.

Frequented by faculty and students alike, *Steve's Park Diner* (*66 Merchants Row*) provides the best cheap eats for breakfast and lunch. *Storm Cafe*, in the basement of the stone Frog Hollow Mill, is popular with artists and artisans. Lunchtime soups, salads, sandwiches and organic dishes cost $7-8. *Otter Creek Bakery* (*14 College St*) excels in takeout pastries and coffee. *Mister Up's* (*4 Bakery Lane*) features a vibrant American menu of steaks and seafood ($6-14).

Sugarbush, Warren & Waitsfield

The towns of Warren and Waitsfield, though small, boast three significant ski areas: Sugarbush, Sugarbush North and Mad River Glen, all in the mountains west of VT 100. There are hordes of opportunities for bicycling, canoeing, horseback riding, kayaking, gliding and other activities. Stop at the Sugarbush Chamber of Commerce (☎ 802-496-3409,

NEW ENGLAND

800-828-4748 for lodging only), on VT 100 in Waitsfield, for a mountain of current details.

NORTHERN VERMONT

Northern Vermont's draws are diverse: a remarkably tiny state capitol, a groovy university town dramatically sited on the edge of Lake Champlain and a ski mecca.

Montpelier & Barre

Montpelier (mont-**peel**-yer) would qualify as a large village in some countries. But in sparsely populated Vermont it's the capital, complete with a gold-domed **State House** (☎ 802-828-2228), built in 1836 of granite quarried in nearby Barre. The Vermont Chamber of Commerce (☎ 802-223-3443) can answer questions. You'll probably visit Montpelier only if you're intensely interested in Vermont history and affairs or a gourmand. First-year New England Culinary Institute (NECI) students gain prowess at *Main Street Grill & Bar (118 Main St)*, open for all meals. Finesse and flair are more evident upstairs at *Chef's Table (☎ 802-229-9202)*, where creative dinner entrées run $14-18 (lunch less).

Montpelier's smaller neighbor, Barre (**ba**-ree), boasts the world's largest granite quarries. Visit the **Rock of Ages** quarries (☎ 802-476-3119), 4 miles southeast of Barre off VT 302, which mine a vein that's 6 miles long, 4 miles wide and 10 miles deep. **Hope Cemetery**, a mile north of US 302 on VT 14, answers the age-old riddle about where granite carvers end up when they die. The tombstones here are works of art!

Stowe & Around

Founded in 1794, Stowe was a simple, pretty backwoods farming town until 1859, when the Summit House was built as a summer resort atop Mt Mansfield (4393 feet), Vermont's highest peak. Skiing was introduced around 1912, and in the late 1930s the longest and highest chairlift in the USA at the time was installed, and skiing really took off. Today the charming town draws visitors for its great ski trails and famous nearby attractions, including the Ben & Jerry's factory and the Trapp Family Lodge. Set in a cozy valley, the town has Central European–style architecture and weather.

Most lodgings and restaurants are along VT 108, the Mountain Rd. The Stowe Area Association (☎ 802-253-7321, 800-247-8693), on Main St in Stowe village at the VT 100 and VT 108 intersection, helps with rental cars and accommodations.

Things to See & Do The 5¼-mile **Stowe Recreation Path** is the obvious choice for a short walk away from the village. The Green Mountain Club (☎ 802-244-7037), on VT 100 a few miles south of Stowe, maintains the **Long Trail** (see Activities at the beginning of this chapter) and is an excellent resource for long and short hikes. **Bicycling** is allowed on the Stowe Recreation Path; the Mountain Bike Shop (☎ 802-253-7919), on Mountain Rd, rents them for $11 per two hours, $25 per day. AJ's Mountain Bikes (☎ 802-253-4593) rents in-line skates. Be sure to drive through dramatic **Smuggler's Notch**, northwest of Stowe on VT 108.

The two-peak **Stowe Mountain Resort** (☎ 800-253-4754) boasts a vertical drop of 2360 feet, 11 lifts (including a gondola) and 48 ski trails, the longest of which is 3¾ miles. **Cross-country skiing** is available at several places near Stowe, most prominently at the Stowe Mountain Resort Touring Center (☎ 802-253-3688), on Mountain Rd. The Catamount Trail is a ski trail following forest paths and old logging roads from northern to southern Vermont. For information, contact the Catamount Trail Association (☎ 802-864-5794).

For **canoeing** and **kayaking**, Umiak Outdoor Outfitters (☎ 802-253-2317, 849 S Main St) has rentals for $38 a day and offers river shuttle trips ($25) and instruction for all levels. Heritage Flights (☎ 802-888-7845, 800-898-7845), at Morrisville-Stowe State Airport on VT 100, will take two people on a **glider ride** for 20 minutes ($64) or an hour

Ben & Jerry, worshipped by the lactose-tolerant

($174). Worked up an appetite and deserve a treat? Head 10 miles south to the **Ben & Jerry's Ice Cream Factory** (☎ 802-882-1260), in Waterbury just north of I-89, and find out how their super-premium ice creams are made (tours $2, free sample included).

Places to Stay & Eat North of I-89, *Little River State Park* (☎ *802-244-7103)* has campsites ($14) and some lean-tos ($20); go 1½ miles west of Waterbury on US 2, then 3½ miles north on Little River Rd. With 35 quiet sites, small *Smugglers Notch State Park* (☎ *802-253-4014)*, 8 miles northwest of Stowe on the Mountain Rd, has the same rates high up the mountain. *Gold Brook Campground* (☎ *802-253-7683)*, on VT 100, 7½ miles north of I-89, has 77 sites (half with hookups), free hot showers and many services ($18).

Stowe-Bound Lodge (☎ *802-253-4515, 645 S Main St)*, about a half-mile from the center, has 10 beds (some of which are private rooms) in an old farmhouse ($20). *Die Alpenrose Motel* (☎ *802-253-7277, 800-962-7002, 2619 Mountain Rd)* has two rooms and three efficiency units ($50-60), while the 25-room *Innsbruck Inn* (☎ *802-253-8582, 4361 Mountain Rd)* is fancier ($84-109). *Stowe Motel* (☎ *802-253-7629, 800-829-7629, 2043 Mountain Rd)* has both rooms and efficiencies ($89-94). *Auberge de Stowe* (☎ *802-253-7787)*, on VT 100 just southwest of the town center, is a homey eight-room B&B with a swimming pool and hot tub ($70). *Fiddler's Green Inn* (☎ *802-253-8124, 800-882-5346, 4859 Mountain Rd)* has six rustic but comfortable rooms ($60). South of the center, *Nichol's Lodge* (☎ *802-253-7683)*, on VT 100, has eight basic rooms ($45-55).

Locals breakfast at *McCarthy's*, on Mountain Rd, feasting on French toast, apple pancakes and omelettes ($3-7). For the town's best takeout sandwiches, head to *Brown Bag Deli and Donuts*, in the Baggy Knees Shopping Center on Mountain Rd. Moderately priced pizzas and pastas reign at *Pie in the Sky (492 Mountain Rd)*. *Gracie's Restaurant*, on Main St behind Carlson Real Estate, offers light lunches (about $10) and eclectic dinners ($9-17) until midnight. *Trattoria La Festa (4080 Mountain Rd)* has great regional Italian dinner classics ($15-19).

Burlington

With the University of Vermont's student population and a vibrant cultural and social life, Burlington has a spirited, youthful ambience. The Lake Champlain Regional Chamber of Commerce (☎ 802-863-3489, 60 Main St) provides city information.

Set on a 45-acre estate, the **Shelburne Museum** (☎ 802-985-3346), 7 miles south of Burlington off US 7, holds 100,000 works of American arts and crafts in 39 exhibition buildings ($18 for two consecutive days). There's a classic round barn (1901), a railroad station complete with locomotive (1915), a circus building, a sawmill (1786), a lighthouse (1871) and even the 1906 side-wheeler SS *Ticonderoga*. The Champlain Flyer train ($1), departing from the waterfront off Main Street, runs along Lake Champlain to the museum.

Shelburne Farms (☎ 802-985-8686), a 1000-acre working farm with a 24-bedroom English country manor (1899), was the Vermont hideaway of the wealthy Webb family. The mansion is now a fine inn (☎ 802-985-8498), and the farm still produces good cheese, maple syrup, mustard and other comestibles you can buy (tours $6). Kids will like the Children's Farm. The **Fleming Museum** (☎ 802-656-2090, 61 Colchester Ave) is the University of Vermont's art museum, boasting more than 17,000 objects ($3).

Places to Stay The *North Beach Campground* (☎ *802-862-0942, 60 Institute Rd)* has tent/RV sites ($20/24) on 45 acres near the city center; go north along the lakeshore on Battery St and North Ave (VT 127) and turn left on Institute Rd. *Shelburne Camping Area* (☎ *802-985-2540, 2056 Shelburne Rd)*, near the prominent Dutch Mill Motel, has sites in a pine grove ($19). *HI Mrs Farrell's Home Hostel* (☎ *802-865-3730)* has six beds ($15-18); call for reservations and directions.

Many of the chain motels are grouped on Williston Rd east of I-89 exit 14. At exit 12, *Susse Chalet* (☎ *802-879-8999)* offers doubles for about $89. Perhaps the best selection of budget and mid-range places is along Shelburne Rd (US 7) in South Burlington on the way to Shelburne. Near central Burlington, *Colonial Motor Inn* (☎ *802-862-5754, 462 Shelburne Rd)* charges

$58. *Econo Lodge* (☎ *802-985-8004)*, 1 mile north of Shelburne Museum, costs about $75, while doubles at *Countryside Motel* (☎ *802-985-2839, US 7)*, just south of Shelburne Museum, are $82. *Town & Country Motel* (☎ *802-862-5786)* and the wonderfully named *Ho Hum Motel* (☎ *802-658-1314)* are nearby on US7.

Places to Eat The good-coffee mecca *Uncommon Grounds* (*482 Church St)* has prime sidewalk tables. You'll rarely find more innovative breakfasts (eg, polenta with eggs) than those at *Penny Cluse Cafe* (*169 Cherry St)*, for about $4-10. *Stonesoup* (*211 College St)* is a godsend for vegetarians, with soups, sandwiches ($5) and a salad bar (about $10 for a hefty salad); it's open until 7pm.

A Burlington fixture since 1925, *Henry's Diner* (*115 Bank St)* serves a daily special, including soup, main course, dessert and beverage ($5-7). In fact, nothing is more than $8. Another old-time place, the stainless steel *Oasis Diner* (*189 Bank St)* serves breakfast and lunch (usually 6am-2pm).

Daily Planet (*915 Center St)* offers eclectic, world-influenced dinner entrées ($12-16). *Sweetwaters* (*120 Church St)*, with nouveau-Victorian decor, is a local watering hole for the upwardly mobile. Impress your companion by ordering the bison burger, medium-rare ($7).

Entertainment Grab Thursday's *Burlington Free Press* for up-to-the-minute party-scene information. *Vermont Pub & Brewery* (*144 College St)* has pints for $3.50 (made on the premises). And just to reinforce the idea that beer is big here, *Three Needs* (*207 College St)* wins local microbrewery awards. The college hangout *Rasputin's* (☎ *802-864-9324)*, on Church St, has a DJ mixing loud dance tunes. Stylish *Red Square* (☎ *802-859-8909, 136 Church St)* mixes mean martinis and roadhouse music. *135 Pearl* (☎ *802-863-2343, 135 Pearl St)* is the center of northern Vermont's gay scene.

Getting There & Away Vermont Transit (☎ *802-864-6811, 800-451-3292)* is based in Burlington, with its terminal at 345 Pine St. Greyhound operates one bus daily between Burlington and Montréal ($20; 2½ hours). The Lake Champlain Transportation Co

(☎ *802-864-9804)*, at King St Dock, runs car ferries late May to mid-October across the lake to Port Kent, New York (car and driver $13, extra passengers $4; 1 hour).

New Hampshire

Mountainous, politically conservative and naturally beautiful, New Hampshire is appropriately symbolized by the Old Man in the Mountain (or Great Stone Face), a natural 'profile' of a man formed by a granite hillside at Franconia Notch. Make a beeline (via Portsmouth, the state's coolest small city) for the White Mountain National Forest, which covers much of the state.

History
In 1629, Captain John Mason laid claim to the area between the Piscataqua and Merrimack Rivers, coining the name 'New Hampshire.' In 1679 the region became a royal colony, governed jointly with Massachusetts by Boston's royal governor-general. Only in 1741 did New Hampshire get its own royal governor. By the mid-1750s, the indigenous peoples had been subdued by the colonists, and Europeans poured into the area. Lum-

---

New Hampshire

Nicknames: Granite State, White Mountain State

Population: 1,200,000 (42nd)

Area: 9351 sq miles (46th)

Admitted to Union: June 21, 1788 (9th)

Capital city: Concord (population 38,000)

Other cities: Manchester (106,000), Portsmouth (23,000)

State motto: Live Free or Die

Birthplace of: astronaut Alan Shepard (1923–98), teacher and *Challenger* space-shuttle astronaut Christa McAuliffe (1948–86), *New York Tribune* founder and editor Horace Greeley (1811–72), Tupperware inventor Earl Tupper (1907–83)

Famous for: the 1944 Bretton Woods conference establishing the postwar economic order

bering, flax and linen production kept the inhabitants busy. In 1788 New Hampshire ratified the new US Constitution, providing the necessary vote to inaugurate the new form of government.

Government & Economy

This conservative state currently has two Republican US senators and two Republican US representatives, one of which is John Sununu, former president Reagan's former chief of staff. Moderate Democrat Jeanne Shaheen is the state governor.

During the 19th-century industrialization boom, Manchester became a manufacturing powerhouse, with the great Amoskeag Mills stretching for more than a mile along the Merrimack River banks. Today agriculture, some manufacturing and tourism are the state's economic mainstays.

Information

The New Hampshire Division of Travel & Tourism (☎ 603-271-2665, 800-386-4664, Ⓦ www.visitnh.gov) is at 172 Pembroke Rd (PO Box 1856), Concord, NH 03302. For highway conditions, call ☎ 603-271-6900. There is no state sales tax, but there's a 9% tax on lodging and meals.

HAMPTON BEACH AREA

New Hampshire's short stretch of seacoast (which is only 18 miles long) begins just north of the Merrimack River and traces the shoreline northward for 24 miles to Portsmouth. A cool breeze blows off the fine sands at **Hampton Beach State Park**, just north of Salisbury Beach in Massachusetts.

Nine miles north is Hampton Beach, honky-tonk New England beachfront at its best (or worst). Clam shacks, motels, fast-food eateries, arcades, nightly entertainment and weekly fireworks, all spiced with sun-bronzed bodies and lots of neon, keep the young sun-seeking swarms happy in summer. For more information, the Hampton Beach Chamber of Commerce (☎ 603-926-8717, 800-438-2826) maintains a visitor center at 180 Ocean Blvd (US 1A). Beach parking fees fluctuate according to the weather and volume of visitors; expect to shell out about $10 a day. Drive north beyond the commercial district to find easier, cheaper beachside parking.

Smaller public beaches backed by quiet residential areas extend northward, including North Hampton State Beach, Jenness State Beach and Rye Harbor State Park. Wallis Sands State Park has a beach that rivals Hampton's in size, not that size matters.

PORTSMOUTH

In 1623 a band of intrepid settlers sailed to the mouth of the Piscataqua River and scrambled up a bank covered with wild strawberries. Deciding to stay, they originally named the place 'Strawbery Banke' but changed it to 'Portsmouth' 30 years later. The town grew wealthy on fishing and maritime trade. Today the city center is filled with many good restaurants housed in old brick buildings. The Greater Portsmouth Chamber of Commerce (☎ 603-436-1118) dispenses information at 500 Market St and from a kiosk at Market and Congress Sts.

Set in a 10-acre park, the **Strawbery Banke Museum** (☎ 603-433-1100), on Marcy St, is a living-history enclave encompassing 40 buildings, and a gem for those who enjoy living in the past (two-day pass $12). Several of Portsmouth's grand **historic houses** have been beautifully preserved, including the

---

Nuclear Seabrook

In 1976 construction began on a controversial nuclear electricity plant on the coast at Seabrook. Despite vociferous protests from local and regional groups and charges of inappropriate use of governmental powers, construction progressed. In 1989 the Nuclear Regulatory Commission approved dubious emergency evacuation procedures for the plant despite the strenuous objections of many citizens' groups and the governor of nearby Massachusetts.

The plant began generating electricity commercially in 1990, after 14 years of construction and testing. Today, New Hampshirites pay some of the highest electricity rates in the USA, due largely to the folly of Seabrook. Meanwhile, the plant contains tons of high-level radioactive waste that will be a danger to the environment for thousands of years, with no plan for permanent storage, no permanent storage facility available and no budget to build one.

NEW ENGLAND

1758 John Paul Jones House (43 Middle St), at State St, and the 1760 Wentworth Gardner House (50 Mechanic St). Most are open mid-June to mid-October and cost $5. The 205-foot-by-27-foot **USS Albacore** submarine (☎ 603-436-3680), on Market St near I-95 exit 7, was launched from the Portsmouth Naval Shipyard in 1953 and has been converted into a museum for the nonclaustrophobic ($5). The **Children's Museum of Portsmouth** (☎ 603-436-3853, 280 Marcy St) delights kids ($4).

Portsmouth Harbor Cruises (☎ 603-436-8084, 800-776-0915), on Ceres St Dock, runs 2½-hour trips that ply neighboring waters, including a trip to the Isles of Shoals ($16). Oceanic Expeditions Whale Watch (☎ 603-431-5500, 800-441-4620, 315 Market St), at Barker Wharf, runs an impressive variety of whale-watching, harbor and music cruises ($12-27).

Places to Stay & Eat

Portsmouth's motels are clustered at exits 5 and 6 off I-95. Try *Fairfield Inn* (☎ 603-436-6363), *Anchorage Inn* (☎ 603-431-8111, 800-370-8111) or *Meadowbrook Inn* (☎ 603-436-2700, 800-370-2727), offering doubles for $99-129. You'll spend more for the same at *Port Motor Inn* (☎ 603-436-4378, 800-282-7678). *The Inn at Strawbery Banke* (☎ 603-436-7242, 800-428-3933, 314 Court St) has seven rooms ($145-150, breakfast included).

Cafe Brioche (14 Market Square) serves upscale coffee, pastry, light meals and takeout sandwiches ($5). *Breaking New Grounds* (16 Market St) is a coffee purist's spot, but your sweet tooth will be satisfied too. *Portsmouth Brewery* (56 Market St) is a brew pub with a long menu of appetizers ($5-8) and main dishes ($11-16). In a historic building, *Portsmouth Gas Light Company* (64 Market St) specializes in brick-oven pizza.

The Stockpot (53 Bow St) advertises 'good food cheap' and delivers. Nothing on the menu is over $15. *Harpoon Willy's* (67 Bow St) has fine water views, 'lobster in the rough' (simple steamed lobster), large plates of fish and chips ($9), fried clams and peel-and-eat shrimp. Next to the tugboats, the *Old Ferry Landing* (10 Ceres St) serves seafood plates for lunch ($10-15) and dinner (under $20).

The Press Room (☎ 603-431-5186, 77 Daniel St) offers nightly music of some sort and jazz most Sunday and Monday nights. Their long menu of reasonable bar food will prevent you from drinking on an empty stomach. For jazz, head to *The Metro* (☎ 603-436-0521, 20 High St) Friday and Saturday.

Getting There & Away

The Coach Company (☎ 800-874-3377) runs coastal commuter shuttles between Portsmouth, Boston and Boston's Logan Airport, as does the Hampton Shuttle (☎ 603-659-9893, 800-883-6663). Reserve the day before departure. The Federal Cigar Store (☎ 603-436-0163, 10 Ladd St), just off Market Square, doubles as Portsmouth's Greyhound/Vermont Transit bus station. (Smoke your stogie before boarding.) Service connects Boston and Portsmouth with the Maine cities of Portland, Bangor and Bar Harbor.

MANCHESTER

Exploiting the abundant waterpower of the Merrimack River, Manchester became the state's manufacturing and commercial center in the 19th century. Today students crowd the campuses of New Hampshire Technical College, Notre Dame College and the University of New Hampshire.

The Greater Manchester Chamber of Commerce (☎ 603-666-6600, 889 Elm St) has more information than you'll need. There's little reason to tarry in Manchester except to view the mighty brick **Amoskeag Mills** (1838), which stretch along the Commercial St riverbanks for almost 1½ miles, and to visit the **Currier Gallery of Art** (☎ 603-669-6144, 201 Myrtle Way), off Orange St, an excellent small museum ($5).

Why you'd go out of your way to sip a free Budweiser is beyond us. Nonetheless, the large **Anheuser-Busch Brewery** (☎ 603-595-1202, 221 Daniel Webster Hwy), in nearby Merrimack, offers free tours, tastings and sightings of Bud's hallmark Clydesdale horses; take I-293 to the Everett Turnpike (US 3) exit 10 (Industrial Dr). They don't make beer like this in Belgium or Germany, that's for sure.

If you need to sleep it off after imbibing, try *Fairfield Inn* (☎ 603-625-2020, 860 Porter St), off I-293 exit 1 and S Willow St, 2 miles from the city center ($99).

CONCORD & AROUND

The state capital is a well-rounded place but will not captivate or detain you very long. The Greater Concord Chamber of Commerce (☎ 603-224-2508, 40 Commercial St) can address every inquiry.

The handsome 1819 **State House** (☎ 603-271-2154, 107 N Main St) is open weekdays for free self-guided tours. The **Museum of New Hampshire History** (☎ 603-226-3189), in Eagle Square, chronicles the 'live free or die' ethic and history of the Granite State ($5). The **Christa McAuliffe Planetarium** (☎ 603-271-7827), northeast of I-93 exit 15, honors the New Hampshire schoolteacher-astronaut who died in the tragic *Challenger* explosion on January 28, 1986 ($7).

Well worth a visit, **Canterbury Shaker Village** (☎ 603-783-9511), 15 miles north of Concord on NH 106 (or I-93 exit 18), founded in 1792 and actively occupied for two centuries, has been preserved as a non-profit trust. Interpreters in period dress present Shaker history ($10).

Overnighters in Concord should try *Comfort Inn* (☎ *603-226-4100, 71 Hall St)*, with rooms for $109-139, or *Holiday Inn* (☎ *603-224-9534, 172 N Main St)*, for $129-139.

LAKE WINNIPESAUKEE

The euphonious Indian name of New Hampshire's largest lake means 'smile of the Great Spirit.' Winnipesaukee has 183 miles of coastline, more than 300 islands and, despite being landlocked, excellent salmon fishing.

Laconia & Around

The largest population center of the lakes region, this regional gateway offers lots of services. The Greater Laconia & Weirs Beach Chamber of Commerce (☎ 603-524-5531, 11 Veterans Square) maintains an information office in the old railroad station.

Ellacoya State Beach (☎ 603-293-7821), off NH 11 just southeast of Glendale, has a 600-foot-wide beach ($3), as well as a picnic area and a campground with 35 unshaded RV sites ($25). A few miles south of West Alton on NH 11, a sign points right for the **Mt Major Trail**. Park just off the road and make the 2-mile trek up Mt Major (1780 feet) in Belknap Mountain State Forest.

Gunstock (☎ 800-486-7862), on NH 11A in Gilford, has an active summer sports center and a winter ski area with a vertical drop of 1400 feet and lots of cross-country trails. The campground (tents/RVs $24/30) also has two sleeping cabins ($55, $330 a week in summer).

The cheapest area motel is *Super 8 Motel* (☎ *603-286-8882)*, at I-93 exit 20 in Tilton ($75-85). On NH 11, friendly *Belknap Point Motel* (☎ *603-293-7511, 107 Belknap Point Rd)* has rooms and efficiencies ($88-98). *Ellacoya Resort & Cottages* (☎ *603-293-7792)*, a bit farther south, is similar but costs $10-20 more.

Concord Trailways (☎ 603-228-3300), departing from the Greater Laconia & Weirs Beach Chamber of Commerce, runs three buses daily to and from Boston via Concord and Manchester.

Weirs Beach

Called 'Aquedoctan' by its Native American inhabitants, Weirs Beach takes its English name from the Indian fishing weirs found here by the first white settlers. The Greater Laconia & Weirs Beach Chamber of Commerce (☎ 603-524-5531) has an information booth on US 3 a mile south of Weirs Beach. They can help with same-day accommodations.

The heart of Lake Winnipesaukee's childhood amusements, Weirs Beach is famous for video arcades and junk food. But there is also a nice lakefront promenade, a small state park and beach, and the **Winnipesaukee Scenic Railroad** (☎ 603-745-2135). You can take any of several cruises (☎ 603-366-2628), including a 2½-hour trip ($18) aboard the MS *Mount Washington*, a 2-hour cruise on the US mailboat MV *Sophie C* ($14) and a one-hour cruise ($10) on the MV *Doris E.*

Look for *Weirs Beach Tent & Trailer Park* (☎ *603-366-4747)* on US 3 south of town ($22-25). Several more campgrounds north of town on US 3 cater mostly to vans and pop-up tent trailers, including *Pine Hollow Camping World* (☎ *603-366-2222)*, a mile north ($22); *Hack-Ma-Tack Campground* (☎ *603-366-5977)*, 1½ miles north (tents/RVs $21/24); and *Paugus Bay Campground* (☎ *603-366-4757)*, on Hilliard Rd off US 3 ($31).

Near the beach and docks, with a heated pool, *Birch Knoll Motel* (☎ *603-366-4958, 867 Weirs Blvd)* is among the better places

($72-99). *Half Moon Motel* (☎ 603-366-4494), just up the hill off the main street in Weirs Beach, has 15 cottages and 16 motel rooms ($82-92). *Bay Top Motel* (☎ 603-366-2225), off US3, is similar.

Weirs Beach is all about eating: burgers, hot dogs, fried dough, lobsters, ice cream, doughnuts – anything sweet and anything fatty. Stroll the main street for the snack shops. Try *Weirs Beach Lobster Pound*, on US 3, for more substantial chicken, steak and seafood. Kids' meals cost 5¢ per pound of child (that's $1.75 for a 35lb kid).

Meredith

More sedate and upscale than Weirs Beach, Meredith is still a real Lakes Region town with a long lakeside commercial strip of restaurants, shops and places to stay. Get more information from the centrally located Meredith Chamber of Commerce (☎ 603-279-6121), on US3.

Just east of Meredith, *Harbor Hill Camping Area* (☎ 603-279-6910), on NH 25, has mostly wooded tent/RV sites ($24/28). *Long Island Bridge Campground* (☎ 603-253-6053), 13 miles northeast near Moultonboro, has a private beach and very popular sites ($21/23). Follow NH 25 east from Center Harbor 1½ miles, then head south on Moultonboro Neck Rd 6½ miles. Popular *White Lake State Park* (☎ 603-323-7350, 271-3628 for reservations) has 150 sites about 22 miles northeast of Meredith at White Lake ($16).

Tuckernuck Inn (☎ 603-279-5521, 25 Red Gate Lane), off Water St from Main St, has five cozy doubles ($95-125, including breakfast). North of Meredith, *Red Hill Inn* (☎ 603-279-7001), off NH 25B in Center Harbor, commands a fine view from its hilltop perch and has rooms in cottages and a farmhouse ($115-185, including breakfast). The dining room is excellent.

Wolfeboro

Named for General Wolfe, who died vanquishing Montcalm on the Plains of Abraham in Quebec, Wolfeboro claims to be 'the oldest summer resort in America.' It is certainly the state's most pleasant lakeside resort town, with good examples of New England's architectural styles, from Georgian through Federal, Greek Revival and Second Empire. You will find the Wolfeboro

Chamber of Commerce (☎ 603-569-2200, 32 Central Ave) in the old railroad building.

The **Clark House Museum Complex** (☎ 603-569-4997), located on S Main St, is Wolfeboro's eclectic historical museum ($4). If you're still itching for something to do, head three miles north to Winter Harbor for the **Libby Museum** (☎ 603-569-1035), on NH 109, which contains the lifework of Dr Henry Forrest Libby, a local dentist and avid amateur naturalist ($2). The Wolfeboro Inn (☎ 603-569-3016) has a quaint excursion boat taking inn guests and others on the lake daily during summer.

Off NH 28 north of town, *Wolfeboro Campground* (☎ 603-569-9881), on Haines Hill Rd, has tent/RV sites ($18/19). The 44-room *Wolfeboro Inn* (☎ 603-569-3016, 800-451-2389, 90 N Main St) has been the town's principal lodging since 1812 ($129-159). A few hundred yards north is *Tuc' Me Inn* (☎ 603-569-5702, 118 N Main St), a nice B&B with 7 rooms ($95-105).

Farther north along N Main St (NH 28) are several good motels, including *Lakeview Inn & Motor Lodge* (☎ 603-569-1335), less than a mile north of central Wolfeboro ($85-95); its dining room is a local favorite. *Clearwater Lodges* (☎ 603-569-2370), 3 miles north of Wolfeboro, is a collection of 14 dark-wood cottages on the shore beneath tall trees. They're rented weekly ($505-600) in summer.

For breakfast or a light lunch, try *Strawberry Patch* (50 N Main St). Pancakes, eggs and sandwiches run $4-8. *Maddie's*, just off Main St in the center of town by the docks for the MS *Mount Washington*, serves good seaside fare such as clam rolls and seafood combo plates ($9-16). Within Wolfeboro Inn, *Wolfe's Tavern* (90 N Main St) has substantial but traditional offerings ($8-20); on good-weather days its terrace is prime.

WHITE MOUNTAINS

New England's greatest range is one of its prime outdoor playgrounds, and the White Mountain National Forest is action central for hiking, camping, canoeing, kayaking and skiing. The main White Mountain National Forest Headquarters (☎ 603-528-8721, 719 Main St) is in Laconia.

Waterville Valley

There was an incorporated town here in the shadow of Mt Tecumseh, on the banks of the Mad River, as early as 1829, but the valley shaped up during the latter 20th century, when the town was developed as a resort community. Hotels, condominiums, golf courses, ski trails and services were all laid out according to plan.

The town's sports facilities include downhill and cross-country ski trails, hiking trails, tennis and golf, road and mountain-bike routes, in-line skating routes and lots of other organized fun for the whole family. The Waterville Valley Regional Chamber of Commerce (☎ 603-726-3804), on NH 49 off I-93 exit 28, has details.

Make resort lodgings reservations through the central service (☎ 800-468-2553). In nearby Plymouth, *Waterville Campground* (☎ *800-280-2267*) has 26 basic, wooded sites ($14), and *Campton Campground* (☎ *800-280-2267*) has rudimentary sites near the Mad River ($16).

Kancamagus Highway

The stretch of NH 112 between Lincoln and Conway, through White Mountain National Forest and over Kancamagus Pass (2868 feet), is an absolutely beautiful paved road. It remains unspoiled by commercial development, with many USFS campgrounds along it. Parking anywhere along the highway costs $3 per trailhead (honor system), $5 per week or $20 per season. Passes may be purchased at the Kancamagus Country Store on NH 112 in Lincoln (open 24 hours). To avoid having 1200lbs of warm meat come hurtling through your windshield, beware of moose crossing the road at dawn and dusk. There are hundreds of accidents each year.

About 1684, Kancamagus (Fearless One) assumed the powers of *sagamon* (leader) of the region's Pennacook Confederacy of Native American peoples. He was the third and final sagamon, succeeding his grandfather, the great Passaconaway, and his uncle, Wonalancet. Kancamagus worked to keep the peace between indigenous peoples and European explorers and settlers, but provocation by whites finally pushed his patience to the breaking point. He resorted to battle to rid the region of the whites, but by 1691 he and his followers were fleeing north.

White Mountain National Forest is laced with excellent **hiking** trails. Stop at the Lincoln-Woodstock Chamber of Commerce

(☎ 603-745-6621) at Laconia Savings Bank in Lincoln, just east of I-93 exit 32, for details. Alternatively, purchase the excellent *AMC White Mountain Guide* from the Appalachian Mountain Club (5 Joy St, Boston, MA 02108) or from an outfitter or local bookshop.

Most of the heavily wooded national-forest campgrounds along the Kancamagus Hwy east of Lincoln have pit toilets and charge $14; a few have flush toilets ($16). Arrive in the morning to secure a site and on Thursday or Friday morning to pin one down for the weekend – they fill up early.

The campgrounds, from west to east (Lincoln to Conway) are as follows:

Big Rock Campground (☎ 603-744-9165) – 6 miles east of Lincoln; 28 sites

Hancock Campground (☎ 603-744-9165) – 27 miles east of Lincoln; 56 sites

Passaconaway Campground (☎ 603-447-5448) – 15 miles west of Conway; 33 sites

Jigger Johnson Campground (☎ 603-447-5448) – 12 miles west of Conway; 76 sites

Covered Bridge Campground (☎ 603-447-5448, 877-444-6777 for reservations) – 6 miles west of Conway; 49 sites ($9 reservation fee)

Blackberry Crossing Campground (☎ 603-447-5448) – 6 miles west of Conway; 26 sites

North Woodstock & Lincoln

These towns straddle the Pemigewasset River, just south of Franconia Notch. The Kancamagus Hwy comes into Lincoln from Conway, about 18 miles east of Kancamagus Pass (2860 feet). The Lincoln-Woodstock Chamber of Commerce (☎ 603-745-6621, 800-227-4191 for lodging reservations) has a big information center in Lincoln just east of I-93 exit 32.

For the USFS campgrounds, see the Kancamagus Hwy section. For camping in Franconia Notch State Park, see that section, later. *Maple Haven Camping* (☎ *603-745-3350*), a mile west of North Woodstock on NH 112, charges $20/25 for its 36 tent/RV sites. *Lost River Valley Campground* (☎ *603-745-8321, 800-370-5678*), 3 miles farther west, has lots more sites ($22/27). *Country Bumpkins* (☎ *603-745-8837*) has 45 sites (from $17) near the Pemigewasset River and Bog Brook; take I-93 to exit 33, then go south on US 3 for half a mile.

At NH 112, convenient *Lincoln Motel* (☎ *603-745-2780, 5 Church St*) offers seven rooms for $60. Just east, **Kancamagus Motor Lodge** (☎ 603-745-3365, 800-346-4205) boasts rooms with steam baths ($69-79). Going north along US 3 brings you to **Riverbank Motel & Cabins** (☎ 603-745-3374, 800-633-5624), at $42-67; **Cozy Cabins** (☎ 603-745-8713), with or without kitchens ($49-56); and **Red Doors Motel** (☎ 603-745-2267), with 30 rooms from $65. **Woodstock Inn** (☎ 603-745-3951, 800-321-3985, Main St, North Woodstock) is comprised of three restored houses with a good dining room ($105-155, including breakfast).

The best food is west of the highway on Main St (US 3) in North Woodstock. Authentic **Sunny Day Diner**, on US 3, dishes up classic, inexpensive diner fare. Touristy **Chalet Restaurant**, on US 3 at NH 112, specializes in lobster ($11-15) – aren't we in the mountains? Next door, locals head to **Peg's Breakfast & Lunch** for early breakfasts ($1-6) and cheap late lunches (open 5:30am-4pm). **Woodstock Inn Station & Brewery**, on Main St, satisfies most food cravings with fish, pasta, steaks, Mexican food and sandwiches. With over 100 items for $10 or less, it should please your wallet, too. **Govoni's Italian Restaurant**, 1½ miles west of North Woodstock along NH 112, presents excellent Italian summer dinners ($9-18).

Franconia Notch State Park
Among the most dramatic of the state's several notches, Franconia Notch is a narrow gorge shaped over the eons by a wild stream cutting through craggy granite. The symbol of the Granite State, the natural rock formation called the 'Great Stone Face,' or more commonly, 'Old Man of the Mountain,' gazes across Franconia Notch from its lofty perch high on the west wall of the gorge. The visitor center (☎ 603-745-8391) is conveniently located at The Flume.

Four miles north of North Woodstock, **The Flume** is a natural cleft in the granite bedrock. A 2-mile self-guided nature walk takes you to and through the dramatic cleft – 12 feet to 20 feet wide – along an 800-foot boardwalk ($7). **The Basin**, a huge glacial pothole 20 feet in diameter, was carved deep into the granite 15,000 years ago by the action of falling water and swirling stones.

Two hundred million years in the making, the **Old Man of the Mountain**, a 40-foot-tall,

25-foot-wide rock outcrop high up on the west wall of Franconia Notch, was 'discovered' by white settlers passing through Franconia Notch in the early 19th century. The striking profile of a man's face (à la Picasso, perhaps) can be seen from the north (follow 'Old Man Viewing' signs). Just north of the Old Man, the **Cannon Mountain Aerial Tramway** (☎ 603-823-5563) offers a truly breathtaking view of Franconia Notch and the surrounding mountains ($9 roundtrip).

Franconia Notch State Park has a good system of **hiking** trails; most are relatively short, some are steep. Trail maps are available at the visitor center. Along the Kancamagus Hwy east of Lincoln, **Loon Mountain** (☎ 603-745-8111) offers winter skiing (vertical drop over 2000 feet) and many summer activities.

The **campground** at Lafayette Place in Franconia Notch State Park (☎ 603-823-9513, 603-271-3628 for reservations) has 97 wooded tent sites ($16), but they fill up early in summer.

Franconia
This pleasant village, a few miles north of Franconia Notch along I-93, features a poetic attraction: Robert Frost's farm. You'll find the Franconia Notch Chamber of Commerce (☎ 603-823-5661, 800-237-9007) on Main St in the middle of town.

Robert Frost (1874–1963) was America's most renowned and best-loved poet in the middle of the 20th century. Born in San Francisco, Frost moved to Massachusetts with his mother after his father's death. After a sojourn of several years in England, Frost lived near Franconia on what is now referred to as the **Frost Place** (☎ 603-823-5510). He wrote many of his best poems to describe life on this farm and the scenery surrounding it, including 'The Road Not Taken' and 'Stopping by Woods on a Snowy Evening.' Follow NH 116 south from Franconia for a mile, then turn right onto Bickford Hill Rd and left onto unpaved Ridge Rd. Look for the farm on the right ($3).

Mt Washington Valley & North Conway
The Mt Washington valley, stretching north from the eastern terminus of the Kancamagus Hwy, includes the towns of Bartlett, Conway, Glen, Intervale, Jackson and North Conway. Every conceivable outdoor activity

is available here. The outfitter EMS (☎ 603-356-5433), on Main St in North Conway, sells maps and operates a year-round climbing school.

Two miles west of North Conway off US 302, placid **Echo Lake State Park** (☎ 603-356-2672) rests at the foot of a sheer rock wall called **White Horse Ledge**. There's a scenic road up to the 700-foot-high **Cathedral Ledge** and panoramic views of the White Mountain Range ($2.50).

The touristy **Conway Scenic Railroad** (☎ 603-356-5251, 800-232-5251), on Main St in the center of North Conway, takes passengers on a one-hour, 11-mile antique steam train ride through the Mt Washington Valley ($10).

The Mt Washington Valley Chamber of Commerce (☎ 603-356-3171, 800-367-3364), has an office on North Conway's main street. The state maintains an office in the rest area at Intervale, on NH 16/US 302, 2 miles north of North Conway.

Concord Trailways (☎ 603-228-3300, 800-639-3317) runs a daily route between Boston and Berlin, stopping at Manchester, Concord, points near Lake Winnipesaukee, Conway, Jackson and Pinkham Notch. The trip between Boston and the Mt Washington Valley takes about 3½ hours ($27).

Activities Areas for **skiing** include Attitash/Bear Peak (☎ 603-374-2368, 800-223-7669 for lodging reservations), on US 302 west of Glen; Cranmore Mountain Resort (☎ 603-356-5543, 800-786-6754), right on the outskirts of North Conway; and Black Mountain Ski Area (☎ 603-383-4490, 800-677-5737 for lodging reservations), on NH 16B in Jackson. Jackson, 7 miles north of North Conway, is famous for its 93 miles of cross-country ski trails.

The ski lifts keep working in summer at Attitash to take you to the top of the Alpine Slide (☎ 603-374-2368), on Route 302, a long track that you schuss down on a little cart – an exhilarating ride safe for all ages ($10 per ride).

For **canoeing** and **kayaking**, Saco Bound Inc (☎ 603-447-2177), 2 miles east of Center Conway on US 302, has rentals ($26 a day). Shuttle service costs $11 per canoe or kayak. Kayak Jack Fun Yak Rentals (☎ 603-447-5571), on NH 16 next to Eastern Slope Campground in Conway, also rents canoes

and kayaks ($25-30 including upstream transportation).

Places to Stay & Eat In Conway, look for the aptly named *Cove Camping Area* *(☎ 603-447-6734)*, off Stark Rd on Conway Lake. *Eastern Slope Camping Area* *(☎ 603-447-5092)*, on NH 16, has over 200 tent/RV sites ($24/32) and long beaches on the Saco River. In North Conway, try *Saco River Camping Area* *(☎ 603-356-3360)*, on the river off NH 16. In Conway, *HI Albert B Lester Memorial Hostel, White Mountains* *(☎ 603-447-1001, 36 Washington St)*, off Main St/NH 16, is perched on the edge of the White Mountain National Forest. This 'sustainable living center' focuses on environmentally friendly practices and conservation (dorm beds $19, rooms $48).

Most of North Conway's motels are south of town along NH 16/US 302. *Yankee Clipper Motel* *(☎ 603-356-5736)* has standard rooms ($59-99). *Briarcliff Motel* *(☎ 603-356-5584, 800-338-4291)* is well positioned, with rooms ($84-94) featuring sun porches and mountain views. *Maple Leaf Motel* *(☎ 603-356-5388)* is most reasonably priced ($55-84).

Cranmore Mountain Lodge *(☎ 603-356-2044, 800-356-3596)* charges $17 for a dorm bed, $99-115 for a double, breakfast included. One block east of Main St, you'll find quiet *Sunny Side Inn* *(☎ 603-356-6239)*, on Seavey St, with doubles for $75-99, including breakfast, and *Cranmore Inn* *(☎ 603-356-5502, 800-526-5502)*, on Kearsarge St, with nine rooms and five cottages ($88-116 including breakfast).

Call the Jackson Area Chamber of Commerce (☎ 603-383-9356, 800-866-3334, PO Box 304, Jackson, NH 03846) for reservation assistance.

In the center of town, *Horsefeathers*, on Main St, has a long, jokey menu featuring lots of bar food, sandwiches, snacks and light meals ($6-17). *Elvio's Pizzeria & Restaurant*, on Main St at Kearsarge St, has indoor and outdoor dining, pizza and Italian American dishes for $8-18 at lunch and dinner.

Pinkham Notch & Crawford Notch

From Pinkham Notch (2032 feet), an excellent system of trails provides access to the natural beauties of the Presidential Range,

NEW ENGLAND

especially **Mt Washington** (6288 feet), the highest mountain in the northeastern USA. For the less athletically inclined, the **Mt Washington Auto Road** (☎ 603-466-2222) provides easy summit access (car and driver $16, extra passengers $6). If your engine and brakes aren't in peak condition, take the van ($22). Mt Washington's weather is notoriously severe and can turn on a dime. The average temperature at the summit is 45°F in summer, and the wind is always blowing. Dress accordingly.

The Appalachian Mountain Club's **Pinkham Notch Visitor Center** (☎ 603-466-2725, 800-262-4455) is the area's informational nexus and meeting ground for like-minded adventurers. The main office (☎ 617-523-0636) is at 5 Joy St, Boston, MA 02108. Pick up the *AMC White Mountain Guide*, with detailed maps and vital trail stats. *Joe Dodge Lodge* has 100 beds for $33, $51 with breakfast and dinner. Reserve well in advance. *Dolly Copp Campground* (☎ 603-466-3984), a USFS campground 6 miles north of the AMC camp, has 173 simple sites ($15). About 12 miles north of the Notch in Gorham, *Hikers Paradise* (☎ 603-466-2732, 370 Main St) has converted three apartments into spaces for 30 beds ($12). In addition to serving unlimited breakfast pancakes, the hosts pick up Appalachian Trail hikers and others on foot.

US 302 heads west from Glen, then north to Crawford Notch (1773 feet) through some beautiful mountain scenery. Crawford Notch State Park maintains a system of shorter hiking trails as well as trailheads for longer hikes to the Mt Washington summit.

Bretton Woods

Before 1944, Bretton Woods was known only among locals and wealthy summer visitors who patronized the grand Mt Washington Hotel. When President Roosevelt chose the hotel for the historic conference to establish a new post-WWII economic order, the whole world became aware of it. The Twin Mountain–Bretton Woods Chamber of Commerce (☎ 800-245-8946) maintains a booth in the center of Twin Mountain, several miles northwest of Bretton Woods at the intersection of US 302 and US 3.

The quaintest way to the summit of Mt Washington is aboard the **Mt Washington Cog Railway** (☎ 603-846-5404, 800-922-8825), 6 miles east of US 302. A coal-fired, steam-powered locomotive follows a 3½-mile track along a steep trestle up the mountainside ($44; 3 hours roundtrip). Make reservations. Upon seeing the dizzying degree of incline, visitors will hear echoes in their heads: 'I think I can. I think I can.'

The 70 sites at *Twin Mountain KOA* (☎ 603-846-5559, 800-743-5819), north off US 302 along US 3 to NH 115, enjoy lots of facilities (from $25). *Bretton Woods Motor Inn* (☎ 603-278-1000, 800-258-0330) is the cheapest of Mt Washington Resort's four lodgings ($99-149). There are numerous motels nearby. The grand *Mt Washington Hotel* (☎ 603-278-1000, 800-258-0330), on US 302, boasts more than 200 rooms and thousands of acres of grounds, 27 holes of golf, 12 clay tennis courts, an equestrian center, indoor and outdoor heated pools etc (doubles $269-329, breakfast and dinner included). Stop by and wander around; they don't make 'em like this anymore.

HANOVER

Hanover, settled in 1765, is defined by Dartmouth College, which was chartered in 1769 primarily 'for the education and instruction of Youth of the Indian Tribes.' Smart people of all colors are admitted today. Bring questions to the Hanover Area Chamber of Commerce (☎ 603-643-3115, 216 Nugget Building), on Main St.

North of the town green, the basement reading room at **Baker Memorial Library** (☎ 603-646-2560) has a series of murals by José Clemente Orozco (1883–1949), the renowned Mexican muralist who taught and painted at Dartmouth from 1932 to 1934. Check posted notices for offerings at the **Hopkins Center for the Arts** (☎ 603-646-2422), Dartmouth's outstanding performing-arts venue. To the south, the **Hood Museum of Art** (☎ 603-646-2808) has fine collections, ranging from ancient Greece and Rome through the European Renaissance to modern times (free admission).

Storrs Pond Recreation Area (☎ 603-643-2134) has 30 tent/RV sites ($15/25); from I-89 exit 18, follow NH 10 north and look for signs. On NH 10 N, *Chieftain Motor Inn* (☎ 603-643-2550, 800-845-3557, 84 Lyme Rd)* offers large doubles for $101. But the 56 rooms at *Airport Econo Inn* (☎ 603-298-

8888, 7 Airport Rd), in West Lebanon, cost less ($75). ***Days Inn*** *(☎ 603-448-5070)*, at I-89 exit 18 in Lebanon, charges the most ($99-109).

Murphy's Tavern *(11 S Main St)*, opposite the Hanover Inn, hosts students and faculty discussing weighty matters over pints of Catamount amber ale ($4.50) and hearty bar food. ***Mai Phai*** *(44 S Main St)* sticks to pad Thai ($8-13) for lunch and dinner. Student hangout ***Patrick Henry's*** *(39 S Main St)* serves lots of sandwiches ($5-7) and a few dinner specials in the vicinity of $12. Have a luncheon 'gourmet burger' at ***Molly's Bar & Grill*** *(43 S Main St)*, and return for a fancier dinner ($10-19).

Vermont Transit (☎ 603-643-2128, 800-552-8737 in New England) has direct buses from Boston and Boston's Logan Airport; many stop in Hanover. They also serve Springfield, Massachusetts, and have connecting service from New York, Hartford and Montréal to White River Junction, Vermont, from which it is a 6-mile taxi ride to Hanover. Dartmouth Mini Coach (☎ 603-448-2800) operates seven shuttles daily from Hanover via Manchester's airport to Logan Airport ($35). Commuter airlines link Lebanon Municipal Airport, 6 miles south of Hanover, with Boston, Montréal, New York and Hartford.

Maine

Maine has the largest land area of the six New England states but the most sparse population of any state east of the Mississippi River. The 'rockbound coast of Maine' is about 225 miles long as the crow flies, but a tall-masted schooner sailing its tortuous course would cover almost 3500 miles.

Southern coastal Maine is thickly populated. The villages vary from beautiful, well-preserved historic towns to miles of shopping malls and factory outlet stores. You'll find both genteel summer resorts and blue-collar beach resorts. Northern, inland Maine is wilderness, with vast (for New England) areas of dense forest and thousands of glacial lakes inhabited only by fish and fowl.

Though a car is by far the best means of getting around Maine, several bus companies serve the coastal resorts, Portland and Bar Harbor. Amtrak currently does not serve the state, though some plans are now afoot to restore service between Boston and Portland.

History

French and English colonists vied to establish the first European colony in Maine in the early 17th century. In 1639, King Charles I issued a royal charter 'for the province and countie of Maine,' and settlement began, but in 1659 the province was subsumed in the colony of Massachusetts Bay. Conflict between the Wabanaki tribal confederation and colonists was savage at times in this frontier province, with the colonists usually getting the worst of it, but by the mid-18th century the power of the indigenous peoples was broken.

During the Revolutionary War, Portland (then called 'Falmouth') was devastated by a British fleet. In the War of 1812, Maine suffered again due to inadequate defense measures, which strengthened the faction that wanted statehood apart from Massachusetts. In the Missouri Compromise of 1820, Maine was admitted to the Union as a free state, and Missouri as a slave state, preserving the political balance between North and South.

Government & Economy

Since the 2000 presidential election, Maine's US senators, moderate Republican women Olympia Snow and Susan Collins, have seen their stature rise as they broker deals trying to bring their party to the center. The state's two US representatives

---

Maine

Nickname: Pine Tree State

Population: 1,200,000 (39th)

Area: 35,387 sq miles (39th)

Admitted to Union: March 15, 1820 (23rd)

Capital city: Augusta (population 20,000)

Other cities: Portland (64,000), Bangor (33,000)

State cliché: Ayuh!

Birthplace of: Henry Wadsworth Longfellow (1807–82), LL Bean (1872–1967), Stephen King (b 1947)

are Democrats, revealing its independent streak. Indeed, Governor Angus King is an Independent.

Though its great stands of virgin pine forest are now gone, the 'Pine Tree State' still harvests a living out of lumbering, in addition to shipbuilding, agriculture and tourism.

Arts

Winslow Homer (1836–1910), though a Bostonian, is most famous for his accurate depictions of the Maine coast. Edna St Vincent Millay (1892–1950) wrote poetry that reflected her native Maine, while horror writer Stephen King sets many novels and stories, notably *Dolores Claiborne*, in his home state.

Information

The Maine Office of Tourism (☎ 800-533-9595, W www.visitmaine.com, 111 Sewall St, 3rd floor, Augusta, ME 04333) can send information. For highway conditions, call ☎ 207-287-3427. Maine has a sales tax of 5%, as well as a 7% tax on meals and lodging.

SOUTHERN MAINE COAST

The most accessible and touristed part of Maine has developed beaches, outlet shopping and resort villages that are packed in the summer The southernmost town of any size is Kittery, famous for shopping malls and outlet stores along US 1.

Ogunquit

Ogunquit ('Beautiful Place by the Sea' in the Abenaki tongue), 35 miles south of Portland, is a small town famous for its 3-mile sand beach. The unique beach affords swimmers the choice of chilly, pounding surf or warm, peaceful back-cove waters. Main St (US 1), Shore Rd and Beach St intersect at Ogunquit Square, the center of town. 'Trolleys' (disguised buses), circulate through Ogunquit every 15 minutes 8am-9pm in summer to take you from the center of town to the beach or to Perkins Cove ($1). The information bureau (☎ 207-646-2939) is on US 1, 600 yards south of the town's center.

The mile-long **Marginal Way** footpath hugs the coastline from Shore Rd, southeast of Beach St, south almost to Perkins Cove. Little Beach is near the lighthouse on Marginal Way, best reached on foot. The **Ogunquit Playhouse** (☎ 207-646-2402), on US 1, offers three musicals and two plays each summer. **Ogunquit Beach** ('Main Beach' to the locals) is only a five-minute walk east from US 1 along Beach St; this proximity saves beach parking fees. (The lot is often full anyway.) Services include toilets, changing rooms, restaurants and snack shops. The *Finestkind* lobster boat (☎ 207-646-5227) takes clients on a 50-minute voyage to pull up lobster traps ($9). You can also cruise ($20; 1½-hours) out of Perkins Cove aboard the *Cricket,* a locally built catboat.

The nearby **Wells Auto Museum** (☎ 207-646-9064), on US 1, has 80 cars of 45 different makes and models, from luxurious Rolls-Royce and Cadillac cruisers to rare Knox and Pierce-Arrow machines ($5).

Elmere Campground & Guest House (☎ 207-646-5538), on US 1 between Ogunquit and Wells, has tent/RV sites ($15/22) and 10 simple guest rooms ($42-45). South of town in Cape Neddick, *Dixon's Campground* (☎ 207-363-3626), on US 1, has 100 sites ($24/28). *Pinederosa Camping Area* (☎ 207-646-2492), is on Captain Thomas Rd, off US 1 just a mile north of Ogunquit's center (turn just south of The Falls at Ogunquit Motel). Tent sites cost $20 here. Wells has several other campgrounds, mostly on US 1.

The 40-room *Bourne's Motel* (☎ 207-646-2823), on Ocean St at US 1, isn't far from Footbridge Beach ($68-105). Friendly and quiet, the 34-room *Studio East Motor Inn* (☎ 207-646-7297), on US 1, is similar.

In the middle of town, *Fancy That*, on Shore Rd, serves light fare and sandwiches on the terrace, including wonderful pastries and coffee. *Gypsy Sweethearts (30 Shore Rd)* serves seafood at moderate prices ($15 to as much as $24 for lobster). In Perkins Cove try *Barnacle Billy's*, a lobster house where a full meal costs $20-30 with a beer, or *Lobster Shack*, on Oarweed Ave. Bar none, the area's finest creative dining is done by *Arrows* (☎ 207-361-1100), on Berwick Rd; reservations are essential.

Kennebunks

The Kennebunks are comprised of Kennebunk, Kennebunkport and Kennebunk Beach, 29 miles southwest of Augusta. Kennebunkport, the most famous village, is beautiful, historical and absolutely packed

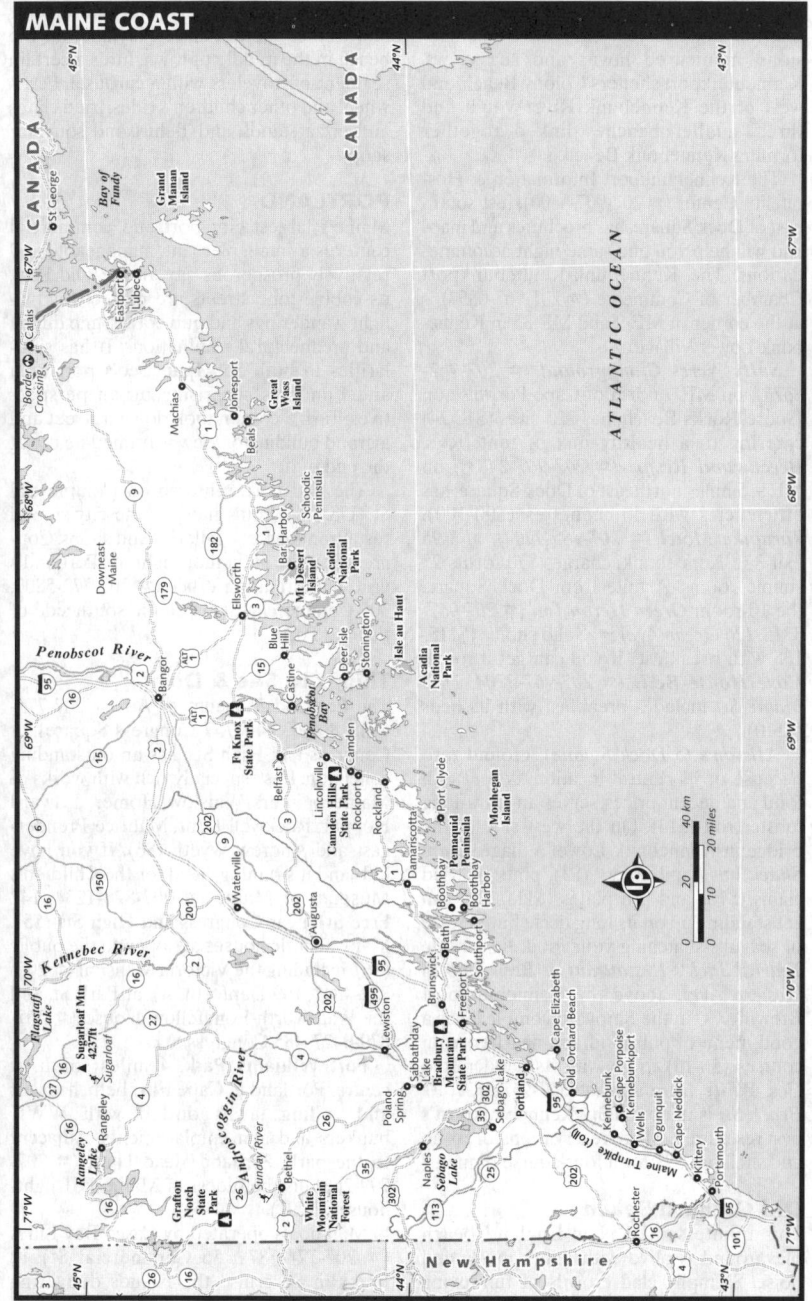

MAINE COAST

NEW ENGLAND

in the summer. Walk anywhere to see pristine 100- and 200-year-old houses and mansions, manicured lawns and sea views. Kennebunkport shelters Colony Beach, and west of the Kennebunk River you'll find three smaller beaches linked together forming Kennebunk Beach.

The Kennebunkport Information & Hospitality Center (☎ 207-967-8600), just southeast of Dock Square, has brochures and maps and will help you find same-night accommodations. The Kennebunk-Kennebunkport Chamber of Commerce (☎ 207-967-0857) is at the corner of ME 9 and ME 35 in Kennebunk Lower Village.

Salty Acres Campground (☎ 207-967-8623), on ME 9 north of Cape Porpoise on Goose Rocks Beach, has 225 sites ($18/24) catering to a healthy mix of tents/RVs. *Beechwood Resort* (☎ 207-967-2483), on ME 9, 5 miles northeast of Dock Square, has efficiencies with kitchenettes ($90-100). *Turnpike Motel* (☎ 207-985-4404), at I-95 exit 3 in Kennebunk, charges $70 for its 25 simple rooms. A mile from Dock Square, the 10-room *Green Heron Inn* (☎ 207-967-3315, 126 Ocean Ave) is a solid choice ($115-135 with breakfast) if you can get a room. *Cove House B&B* (☎ 207-967-3704, 11 S Maine St) includes breakfast with its beds ($110).

Alisson's (5 Dock Square), ground zero because of its central location, decent pub food and decent prices, serves an extra-long lobster roll ($14). On the west side of the bridge in Kennebunk Lower Village, *Clam Shack* has hamburgers ($3), pints of fried clams ($10) and fish plates ($11). You can eat standing up on its long deck, but beware of seagulls snatching your food. Just south, *Federal Jack's Restaurant & Brew Pub (8 Western Ave)*, above the Kennebunkport Brewing Co in the Shipyard complex, has a good menu of pub food and heartier main courses ($6-16) to go with its handcrafted ales. *White Barn Inn* (☎ 207-967-2321, 37 Beach St) is undoubtedly Kennebunkport's best restaurant. Make reservations, dress up and shell out $77 for a four-course dinner.

Old Orchard Beach

This quintessential New England beach playground is alive with lights, music and noise. Skimpily clad crowds of fun-loving sun worshippers make the rounds of fast-food emporiums, mechanical amusements and trinket shops. Palace Playland, on the beach in the middle of town, lures a certain segment of travelers with a carousel, Ferris wheel and other children's rides, fried clams and pizza stands, and T-shirt and souvenir shops.

PORTLAND

Maine's largest city, port and commercial center is a small, pleasant, manageable and relatively prosperous city. In the Old Port, its cobblestone streets are perfect for twilight wanderings and pub crawls, fine dining and architectural ruminations. It has similarities to both San Francisco's port area and London's surprising urban perspectives: Turn a corner, look down a street and a grand building or view is framed neatly at the end of it.

The Old Port, centered on Commercial St (US 1A), holds most of the city's good restaurants, hotels, galleries and shops. Congress St is the main thoroughfare. Portland's visitor information office (☎ 207-772-5800, 305 Commercial St) is on the south side of the Old Port.

Things to See & Do

The **Portland Museum of Art** (☎ 207-775-6148, 800-639-4067, 7 Congress Square), at Congress and High Sts, has an outstanding collection. It is especially rich with works of Maine painters Winslow Homer, Edward Hopper, Rockwell Kent, Maurice Prendergast and Andrew Wyeth ($6). If you have kids and it's raining, head for the **Children's Museum of Maine** (☎ 207-828-1234, 142 Free St), near Congress and High Sts ($5). Many **historic houses** are open to the public ($6), including the Victoria Mansion (☎ 207-772-4841, 109 Danforth St), at Park St, and the Wadsworth-Longfellow House (☎ 207-879-0427, 485 Congress St).

Fort Williams Park, 4 miles south of central Portland in Cape Elizabeth, has vast and rolling lawns dotted with WWII bunkers and gun emplacements. Adjacent to the park, **Portland Head Light** (☎ 207-799-2661) is the oldest of Maine's 61 lighthouses (1791).

Mail boats operated by Casco Bay Lines (☎ 207-774-7871, 56 Commercial St), at Franklin St, cruise the islands delivering letters, freight and visitors ($11; 3 hours).

The *Palawan* (☎ 207-773-2163), a 58-foot racing yacht, offers cruises under full sail ($20-35; 3 hours). The Olde Port Mariner Fleet (☎ 207-775-0727, 800-437-3270), on Commercial St, departs Long Wharf on deep-sea fishing, whale-watching and lobstering trips, plus one-hour harbor cruises.

Places to Stay
You'll find the closest camping 16 miles to the northeast near Freeport. Off Congress St in the center of town, *Oak Leaf Inn (☎ 207-773-7882, 51 Oak St)*, open only during the summer, has 40 bunk beds in 10 rooms, two kitchens and laundry facilities ($22/25 for HI members/nonmembers). The *Inn at St John (☎ 207-773-6481, 939 Congress St)*, diagonally across from the bus station, has some shared-bath quarters for $59-99; otherwise it's $114-154. *Fairfield Inn (☎ 207-871-0611, 340 Park Ave)* charges $80, while its competitor, *Travelodge (☎ 207-774-6101)*, at I-95 exit 8, offers similar rooms for $89. Also off I-95 exit 8 you'll find *Howard Johnson's (☎ 207-774-5861, 155 Riverside St)* and *Holiday Inn West (☎ 207-774-5601, 81 Riverside St)*, both for $125-153.

Places to Eat & Drink
The main Old Port restaurant streets are Exchange St between Fore and Federal Sts, and Wharf St between Union and Dana Sts. *Portland Public Market (25 Preble St)*, an excellent open food hall, features Maine products and fresh picnic supplies. *Becky's Diner (390 Commercial St)* fills the bellies of working fishermen 4am-9pm for very little of their hard-earned cash. *Breaking New Grounds (13 Exchange St)* is just one of Portland's good coffee outlets. *Bintliff's American Café (98 Portland St)* boasts the best brunches (try the salmon Benedict or banana-pecan pancakes), for about $8. *Gilbert's Chowder House (92 Commercial St)*, at Pearl St, is a simple diner with a lunch counter and tables, good for fish and chips ($8) or a big bowl of clam chowder ($6).

This is a town for serious eating, but most nicer restaurants don't take reservations. *Street & Company (33 Wharf St)* is a fantastic area bistro, featuring fresh ingredients and seafood (entrées $14-28). *The Pepperclub (78 Middle St)* specializes in exotic international fish and vegetarian dishes and is packed after 6pm (entrées $9-15).

The most popular spot for locally made pints (under $4) is *Gritty McDuff's Brew Pub (396 Fore St)*. *Brian Ború*, on Center St, is a fun Irish pub. *Una (505 Fore St)* is for hip martini drinkers, while *Wharf St Café and Wine Bar (38 Wharf St)* is for lesser spirits.

Getting There & Around
Portland International Jetport is the state's largest airport, served by many domestic carriers. Those on long-distance international flights must connect through Boston or New York.

Vermont Transit (☎ 207-772-6587, 950 Congress St), inside the Greyhound Terminal at St John St, is near I-295 exit 5. It runs six buses daily to Boston ($15; 2½ hours), connecting with buses to Hartford, Connecticut, and New York. Vermont Transit also runs three buses northeast to Brunswick and four up the Maine Turnpike to Lewiston, Augusta, Waterville and Bangor ($20; 3¼ hours). One bus continues to Bar Harbor ($29; 4 hours), with connections to Canada's Atlantic provinces.

Concord Trailways (☎ 207-828-1151, 161 Sewall St), off I-295, runs 11 buses daily between Portland, Boston and Boston's Logan Airport. There's also local service (three buses daily) from Portland along the coast, stopping at Brunswick, Bath, Damariscotta, Waldoboro, Rockland, Camden/Rockport, Lincolnville, Belfast and Bangor. On this route, the Portland-Bangor trip takes around four hours. From Portland, four buses go northeast to Bangor; one bus connects at Bangor with Cyr Bus Lines (☎ 207-942-3354), which has routes headed north. In mid-2001, Amtrak was set to begin Boston-Portland service, but state and local politics were holding things up. Call Amtrak for up-to-the-minute status.

Prince of Fundy Cruises' MF *Scotia Prince* (☎ 207-775-5616, 800-341-7540) takes cars ($105) and passengers overnight to Yarmouth, Nova Scotia ($66-86, $47-100 more for a four-person sleeping cabin). Roundtrip prices are always about 20% lower; cars are half-price Tuesday and Wednesday. Bay Ferries (☎ 888-249-7245) also operates this route.

The local bus line, Metro (☎ 207-774-0351), has its main terminus (Metro Pulse) at the parking garage on the corner of Elm and Congress Sts. For a good, cheap look at the city, hop aboard bus No 1 ($1) and ride until you've had enough.

CENTRAL MAINE COAST

Midcoast Maine features long, scraggy peninsulas jutting deep into the Atlantic, friendly seaside villages, thick pine forests and lots of opportunities for biking, hiking, sailing and kayaking.

Freeport

The fame and fortune of Freeport, 16 miles northeast of Portland, began a century ago, when Leon Leonwood Bean opened a shop to sell equipment and provisions to hunters and fishers heading north into the Maine woods. LL Bean's good values earned him loyal customers, and over the years the **LL Bean** store (☎ 800-341-4341), on Main St, added lots of other no-nonsense, good-quality outdoor gear. The store became so popular that now it *never* closes.

Ironically, this former stopover for hearty outdoor types amid the natural beauty of Maine's rockbound coast is now devoted entirely to city-style shopping, with more than 100 shops selling tony luggage, perfumed soaps, trendy clothes etc. Freeport's mile-long Main St (US 1) is a perpetual traffic jam of cars from all over the country and Canada, their occupants coming with nature in their hearts but discounted urban luxuries on their shopping lists.

The Freeport Merchants Association (☎ 207-865-1212) maintains information centers on Main St at Mallet St and on Mill St a block south of Main St. The State of Maine has a large information center at exit 17 off I-95 in Yarmouth, covering Freeport and indeed all of Maine.

Bradbury Mountain State Park, 6 miles west of Freeport on ME 9, just north of Pownal, has several miles of forested trails for **hiking**. For a quickie, try the instant-gratification 10-minute hike from the picnic area uphill to the summit for a spectacular view all the way to the ocean. Follow ME 125 and ME 136 north from Freeport, but turn left just after crossing I-95, following the state-park signs.

The choicest campground is *Winslow Memorial Park* (☎ 207-865-4198), on Staples Point Rd, with tent/RV sites for $17/19. Go south from Freeport along US 1,

turn left at the towering Indian statue, then right onto Staples Point Rd. Next best, *Bradbury Mountain State Park* (☎ 207-688-4712), on ME 9, has 41 forested sites ($11) north of Pownal. Closest to Freeport is *Cedar Haven Campground* (☎ 207-865-6254, 39 Baker Rd), on ME 125 N, with 58 mostly wooded sites ($18).

Motels are mostly south of town on US 1 near I-95 exit 19. At exit 17 off US 1, the handsome and classic *Eagle Motel* (☎ 207-865-4088, 800-334-4088, 291 US 1 S) charges $87 per night.

Several Main St B&Bs are just north of fancy *Harraseeket Inn* (☎ 207-865-9377, 800-342-6423, 162 Main St), which has cookie-cutter rooms for $180-275. Others are within an easy walk of the town center, like *Country at Heart B&B* (☎ 207-865-0512, 37 Bow St), which charges $115-125 for its three rooms with breakfast.

There are plenty of places on Main St, but most serve uninteresting tourist fare. Try *Lobster Cooker* (39 Main St), a fast-food place with excellent clam chowder ($5), good coleslaw and steamed lobster lunches ($16). *Harraseeket Lunch*, near the Town Dock in South Freeport, has bayside picnic tables, lobsters and lobster rolls ($13). Despite the name, they're also open for dinner.

Bath

In colonial times, the forested Maine coasts were thick with tall trees – just right for making masts for the king's navy. Today Bath continues the tradition by building steel frigates, cruisers and other navy craft at the **Bath Iron Works** (BIW), one of the largest and most active shipyards in the USA. The **Maine Maritime Museum** (☎ 207-443-1316, 243 Washington St), south of the ironworks, is Bath's biggest attraction ($9). The Bath-Brunswick Chamber of Commerce office (☎ 207-725-8797, 59 Pleasant St) is in nearby Brunswick.

Boothbay Harbor

A beautiful little seafarers' town on a broad fjordlike harbor – that's Boothbay Harbor. The Boothbay Chamber of Commerce (☎ 207-633-4743) is on ME 27 in Boothbay. Just south is the Boothbay Harbor Region Chamber of Commerce (☎ 207-633-2353), in Boothbay Harbor.

From Pier 8, Balmy Days Cruises (☎ 207-633-2284, 800-298-2284) takes folks out to Monhegan Island for one day ($30) or a one-hour harbor tour ($9). Cap'n Fish's Boat Trips (☎ 207-633-3244), on Pier 1, sails in search of whales ($28; 3½ hours), puffins, seals and other wildlife ($20; 3 hours). And yes, there really is a Cap'n Bob Fish and a Cap'n John Fish.

Of the several large campgrounds north of Boothbay Harbor along ME 27, check out *Little Ponderosa Campground* (☎ 207-633-2700), 6 miles north of Boothbay Harbor (tents/RVs $18/27), with some waterfront sites, and *Gray Homestead* (☎ 207-633-4612), 4 miles south of Boothbay Harbor in Southport with 40 sites ($19/21).

Boothbay and Boothbay Harbor also have lots of comfortable motels. Those on Townsend Ave (ME 27) north of town are less expensive than the elaborate places on Atlantic Ave on the east side of the harbor. *Mid-Town Motel* (☎ 207-633-2751), in the very center of town close to the intersection of Todd Ave and McKown St, charges $74 for its 11 rooms. *Seagate Motel* (☎ 207-633-3900, 800-633-1707, 138 Townsend Ave), on ME 27 at the entrance to Boothbay Harbor coming from the north, has good rooms with refrigerators ($95).

Atop McKown Hill, *Topside Inn* (☎ 207-633-5404) has nearly unparalleled views, and its 23 motel and inn rooms rent for $72-95 with a light breakfast. Nearby, the nice *Welch House Inn* (☎ 207-633-3431, 56 McKown St) has 16 rooms that also have water views ($80-155 with breakfast).

Walk down the hill and toward the footbridge, but before reaching the bridge bear left through the parking lot to find the rough-board *Chowder House*, where a simple chowder-based lunch costs $8-12. On the east side of the bay, *Lobstermen's Co-Op*, on Atlantic Ave, serves informal lobster dinners (from $15). For a full sit-down restaurant in East Boothbay away from the tourists, try *Lobsterman's Wharf*, on ME 96. Boothbay's most innovative bistro, *Christopher's Boat House* (☎ 207-633-6565, 25 Union St) serves wood-fired dishes like pistachio-batttered haddock ($17-26, less at lunch). For a special treat, reserve a *Clambake at Cabbage Island* (☎ 207-633-7200), on Pier 6, Fisherman's Wharf ($40 per person, including boat trip).

Pemaquid Peninsula

ME 130 goes south from Damariscotta to Pemaquid Neck, the southernmost part of the peninsula. On the west side of Pemaquid Neck are Pemaquid Beach and **Fort William Henry** ($1), a relic of the colonial period. At the southern tip of Pemaquid Neck is **Pemaquid Point**, one of the most beautiful places in Maine because of its tortured, grainy igneous rock formations pounded by restless, treacherous seas. Perched atop the rocks in **Lighthouse Park** ($2) is the 11,000-candlepower Pemaquid Light, built in 1827. It's one of the 61 surviving lighthouses along the Maine coast. The keeper's house is now the **Fishermen's Museum** at Pemaquid Point.

Monhegan Island

This small island (1½ miles long by a half-mile wide), off the Maine coast due south of Port Clyde, is a popular goal for summer excursions. It's also a favorite of artists, who admire its dramatic views and agreeable isolation. Practically everyone appreciates the 17 miles of walking trails.

Virtually all island rooms are booked months in advance, so unless you have reservations, take a day excursion from Port Clyde or Boothbay Harbor, and allow four hours or more to walk the trails. Stop at the 1824 **lighthouse** for a look at the little museum set up in the former keeper's house.

Start dialing for reservations (and good luck). *Island Inn* (☎ 207-596-0371) is a typical Victorian mansard-roofed summer hotel with small, simple rooms ($120-200, breakfast included). *Tribler Cottage* (☎ 207-594-2445) has five doubles with kitchen for $70-125. You might also get one of the 33 rooms at *Monhegan House* (☎ 207-594-7983) for $105 with breakfast; the 35 rooms at *Trailing Yew* (☎ 207-596-0440) for $62 per person with dinner; the two rooms and five apartments at *Shining Sails* (☎ 207-596-0041) for $80-135; or the five rooms at *Hitchcock House* (☎ 207-594-8137) for $65 or $95 (with bath and kitchen).

From Port Clyde, the Monhegan Boat Company (☎ 207-372-8848) runs three daily boats ($27); make reservations. The MV *Hardy III* (☎ 207-677-2026) departs from New Harbor, on the east side of the Pemaquid Peninsula ($27.50).

Camden

Home to Maine's large and justly famed fleet of windjammers (sailing ships), Camden continues its historic close links with the sea. Its harbor is stunning when the fleet is in port. **Camden Hills State Park**, just over 1½ miles northeast of central Camden, has good hiking trails and camping ($2). The chamber of commerce (☎ 207-236-4404) runs an information office on the waterfront at the public landing, behind Cappy's Chowder House.

Camden Hills State Park (☎ 207-236-3109, 287-3824 for reservations) has hot showers and forested sites (no hookups) for $17; make summer reservations. Also try *Megunticook by the Sea* (☎ 207-594-2428, 800-884-2428), 3 miles south of Camden off US 1 ($26-31), with a quarter of its 100 sites reserved for tents, and *Camden Rockport Campground* (☎ 207-236-2498), with 60 tent/RV sites ($25/32). The latter campground is 2 miles west of Rockport on ME 90.

If you want help with last-minute lodging availability, call the chamber of commerce

---

Windjammers

Camden is the center of windjammer-cruise country, but many boats dock at Rockport and Rockland, too. Day sails take passengers out for two-hour cruises in Penobscot Bay May to October ($25-28). Usually you can book your place the same day, even the same hour. On the Camden waterfront, look for *Surprise* (☎ 207-236-4687), which doesn't take children under 12; *Appledore* (☎ 207-236-8353); and *Olad* (☎ 207-236-2323).

Some overnighters, such as Rockland's schooner *Wendameen* (☎ 207-594-1751), take passengers cruising for a day and a night ($170, all meals included). Other schooners make three- and six-day cruises, which may include stops at Stonington, Castine, various small islands offshore and points in and around Acadia National Park ($350-750 per person, accommodations and all meals included). Reservations are a must. Contact the Maine Windjammer Association (☎ 800-807-9463, W www.sailmainecoast .com) for details.

☺☺☺☺☺☺☺☺☺☺☺☹☺

(☎ 207-236-4404). There's a large concentration of motels in Lincolnville Beach, north of Camden on US 1. *Birchwood Motel & Cottages* (☎ 207-236-4204), on Belfast Rd/US 1 north of Camden, has 16 rooms ($77). The mom-and-pop-style *Towne Motel* (☎ 207-236-3377, 68 Elm St) has 18 rooms ($85-95). *Goodspeed's Guest House* (☎ 207-236-8077, 60 Mountain St), a half-mile uphill from town on ME 52, has nine nicely decorated rooms ($65-95). *Blue Harbor House* (☎ 207-236-3196, 800-248-3196, 67 Elm St) is a cozy 1810 house with 10 rooms ($95-125).

The town's old reliable is *Cappy's Chowder House* (1 Main St), with chowder ($4-10) and fish-plate specialties ($9-15). Just down the street is *Marriner's* (35 Main St), an old-fashioned inexpensive breakfast nook and lunchroom serving a big fish-and-chips plate ($11), garden burger ($7) or grilled tuna sandwich ($9). Inside Knox Mill, *Sea Dog Brewing Company* (43 Mechanic St) is a spacious restaurant, pub and nightspot serving sophisticated, light bar food ($8-12) and seasonal namesake beers.

Castine

The quiet, pretty town of Castine hosts the **Maine Maritime Academy** and its big training ship, the *State of Maine* (1952), which you can board when it's in port. *Castine Inn* (☎ 207-326-4365), on Main St, is a 19-room Victorian summer hotel ($90-215, breakfast included) that offers outstanding gourmet dinners. *The Pentagset Inn* (☎ 207-326-8616, 800-845-1701), across the street, has 16 rooms ($89-129 with breakfast).

Blue Hill

Charming and upscale, this dignified small Maine coastal town is brimming with tall trees, old houses and lots of culture. *Gatherings Family Campground* (☎ 207-667-8826), on ME 172, 4 miles southwest of Ellsworth, has 100 sites ($15, $25-35 with hookups). Especially good for tents, *Balsam Cove Campground* (☎ 207-469-7771, 800-469-7771), off ME 15 south of East Orland, is a mile south of US 1, then another mile east along an unpaved road. The most fortunate will capture a waterfront tent/RV site ($17/19). In the center of town, the 11 homey rooms at *Captain Isaac Merrill Inn* (☎ 207-374-2555, 1 Union St) go for $115-135. Central *Jonathan's Restaurant*, on

Main St, offers creatively prepared local seafood (dinner entrées $14-21).

Deer Isle

This 'isle' is really a collection of islands joined by causeways and connected to the mainland by a suspension bridge near Sargentville. In summer, the Deer Isle–Stonington Chamber of Commerce (☎ 207-348-6124) maintains a booth just south of the suspension bridge. Small **Deer Isle Village** is simply a collection of shops and services near Pilgrim Inn. Seven miles east of the village is the **Haystack Mountain School of Crafts** (☎ 207-348-2306), from which many area artisans refined their arts.

At the southern tip of Deer Isle, **Stonington** is a granite-quarrying, fishing and tourist town, proud that it is 'a real place, with a real working harbor,' rather than a fantasy tourist village. Make the effort to get here if you're in the neighborhood.

Sunshine Campground (☎ 207-348-2663), with 22 nice wooded tent/RV sites, is nearly 6 miles east off ME 15 ($17/20). *Deer Isle Village Inn* (☎ 207-348-2564) offers four simple shared-bath rooms for $80 with breakfast. In Stonington, *Boyce's Motel* (☎ 207-367-2421, 800-224-2421), on Main St, rents six simple but suitable rooms ($40-55) and five apartments ($65-85). Just up the hill on Main St, *Près du Port B&B* (☎ 207-367-5007) has three harbor-view rooms ($85).

ACADIA NATIONAL PARK

Established in 1919, Acadia National Park boasts a large variety of plant and animal species as well as 50 miles of one-lane 'carriage roads,' excellent for hiking and biking. Dramatic scenery and a plethora of outdoor sports possibilities make it a popular summer destination. The park covers over 62 sq miles, including most of mountainous Mt Desert Island and large tracts of land on the Schoodic Peninsula, across the Frenchman Bay to the east, and on Isle au Haut, far to the southwest.

The park's main entrance and visitor center (☎ 207-288-3338) are at Hulls Cove, northwest of Bar Harbor off ME 3 ($10 per vehicle, good for seven days). From here, the 20-mile Park Loop Rd, most of which is one way, circumnavigates the northeastern section of the island. See the Bar Harbor section for outfitters offering guided park tours as well as lessons and equipment rental. The Schoodic Peninsula and Isle au Haut areas are not easily accessible from Mt Desert Island.

Start your explorations with a drive along Park Loop Rd. On the portion called Ocean Dr, stop at Thunder Hole, south of the Overlook Entrance, for a look at the surf crashing into a granite cleft (the effect is best during a strong incoming tide). Otter Cliffs, not far south of Thunder Hole, is a wall of pink granite rising right from the sea. At Jordan Pond there's a self-guided nature trail. You should really stop for lunch, or classic tea and popovers, at *Jordan House*. For swimming, try Sand Beach or Seal Harbor (chilly salt water) or Echo Lake (barely less chilly freshwater). Finish your first exploration with a stop at the windy summit of Cadillac Mountain (1530 feet), the park's highest point. Insomniacs can drive to the summit for a stunning sunrise; they won't be alone.

There are two park campgrounds. *Blackwoods Campground* (☎ 800-365-2267), open all year, requires reservations in summer. *Seawall Campground*, open May to September, rents sites on a first-come, first-served basis. No backcountry camping is allowed. Commercial campgrounds are along ME 3 from Ellsworth and clustered near the entrances to Acadia National Park. This stretch is also dotted with cheap motels, some with doubles for as little as $75 in summer.

The best place for a lobster picnic is at one of the lobster pounds. A bunch are clustered north of Trenton Bridge on ME 3, about 6½ miles south of Ellsworth, including *Trenton Bridge Lobster Pound*. In beautiful Southwest Harbor, *Beal's* is the best bet, and in affluent Northeast Harbor, save your appetite for *Docksider*, on Sea St. A lobster dinner with steamed clams and corn or coleslaw costs about $15-17.

BAR HARBOR

Bar Harbor, which once rivaled Newport, Rhode Island, for the stature of its summer-colony residents, is a pleasant town of big old houses, many of which are now inns, and a good base for exploring Acadia National Park. The Bar Harbor Chamber of Commerce (☎ 207-288-5103, 800-345-4617, 93 Cottage St) is centrally located.

Bar Harbor Whale Watch (☎ 207-288-3322, 800-508-1499, 1 West St), at Main St next to the town pier, offers whale- and puffin-sighting cruises ($43), lobster and seal trips ($19) and nature cruises ($22). Downeast Windjammer Cruises (☎ 207-288-4585, 27 Main St) departs from the Bar Harbor Inn Pier on two-hour cruises ($27.50) aboard the 51-foot, four-mast schooner *Margaret Todd*.

Numerous outfitters provide guide service, equipment for rent or sale, and lessons on hiking, rock climbing, mountain biking, canoeing and sea kayaking. Head to the west end of Cottage St, near ME 3, to find Acadia Bike & Coastal Kayak (☎ 207-288-9605, 800-526-8615, 48 Cottage St); Acadia Outfitters (☎ 207-288-8118, 106 Cottage St); Bar Harbor Bicycle Shop & Island Adventures (☎ 207-288-3886, 141 Cottage St); National Park Kayak Tours (☎ 207-288-0342, 39 Cottage St); and Acadia Mountain Guides (☎ 207-288-8186), on Main St opposite the village green.

Places to Stay

The *Mt Desert Island YWCA* (☎ 207-288-5008, 36 Mt Desert St) offers lodging to women only for $21/32/52 in a dorm/single/double; it's cheaper by the week. It's usually booked by late April for the entire summer. The highly rated *Bar Harbor Youth Hostel* (☎ 207-288-5587, 27 Kennebec St) has 20 beds and very good facilities but doesn't take reservations – so it's likely to have rooms when you think it might not. Beds cost $12-15 (open mid-June through Aug). Centrally located with 52 rooms and a pool, the *Villager Motel* (☎ 207-288-3211, 207 Main St) charges $118-128. *Anchorage Motel* (☎ 207-288-3959, 51 Mt Desert St) has 50 modern rooms ($89), while nearby *Aurora Motel* (☎ 207-288-3771, 51 Holland Ave) is much smaller, simpler and about the same price ($80-96).

Of the huge old 'summer cottage' inns, try *Acadia Hotel* (☎ 207-288-5721, 20 Mt Desert St), for $135-150. South of the green, *McKay Lodging* (☎ 207-288-5226, 243 Main St) has 23 rooms ($85-105). *Stratford House Inn* (☎ 207-288-5189, 45 Mt Desert St) is a Tudor fantasy ($75-150) with only 10 rooms; the two cheapest rooms have a shared bath. The grandest downtown inn is the *Ledgelawn Inn* (☎ 207-288-4596, 800-274-

5334, 66 Mt Desert St), a vast Colonial Revival summer cottage that reeks of grandeur ($150-250).

Places to Eat

Within the Alternative Market, *Benbow's Coffee Roasters* (16 Mt Desert St) has the best coffee in town. For consistency and affordability, you can't beat *Café This Way* (14½ Main St), a favorite among locals for breakfast and dinner ($13-20). Sandwiches, salads and burgers are the thing at *Village Green Bakery Café* (195 Main St).

Head to Rodick and Cottage Sts for Bar Harbor's best eats. South of Cottage St, *Lompoc Cafe & Brewpub* (36 Rodick St) serves international lunch and dinner fare ($13-18) and creative pizzas ($9-10), plus excellent Bar Harbor Real Ale ($4). *Cafe Bluefish* (122 Cottage St), an intimate storefront bistro, offers great seafood (and some vegetarian dishes) for about $16-22 per dinner entrée.

Wanna grab a pizza and movie? Do it at *Reel Pizza* (33B Kennebec St), which slings pizza pies ($6.50-18) as you lounge on its couches catching a flick ($5).

Getting There & Away

US Airways (☎ 207-667-7171, 800-428-4322) connects Bar Harbor and Boston with several flights every day. The Hancock County–Bar Harbor Airport is at Trenton off ME 3 just north of the Trenton Bridge. Vermont Transit/Greyhound (☎ 800-451-3292) runs an early-morning bus daily from Bar Harbor, via Bangor and Portland, to Boston and New York. Buses depart from the Village Motel (☎ 207-288-3211, 207 Main St). Bay Ferries' fast car ferry *Cat* (☎ 207-288-3395) provides a maritime link between Bar Harbor and Yarmouth, Nova Scotia (cars $95, passengers $58; 3 hours).

DOWNEAST MAINE

The 900-plus miles of coastline east of Bar Harbor are sparsely populated, slower-paced, foggier and more traditional than the Maine to the south and west. Highlights include the **Schoodic Peninsula** territory of Acadia National Park; **Jonesport** and **Beals Island**, with Maine's largest lobster-boat fleet; and **Great Wass Island**, a large nature preserve with walking paths and good bird-watching opportunities (including puffins).

The county seat of Washington County, **Machias** shelters a branch of the University of Maine, thereby making it the center of commerce, culture and art along this stretch of coast. **Lubec**, a fish-processing center, is just across the bridge from Canada and Roosevelt Campobello International Park. Franklin Roosevelt's father James bought land here in 1883 and built a palatial summer 'cottage.' The future US president spent many boyhood summers here, and was later given the 34-room cottage. He and Eleanor made brief but well-publicized visits during his long presidential tenure.

Calais (**ka**-lus), at the northern end of US 1, is a twin town to St Stephen, in New Brunswick, Canada. St Stephen is the gateway to Atlantic Canada, covered in Lonely Planet's *Canada* guide.

INTERIOR MAINE

Northern and western Maine are far less visited than coastal Maine. The fine old town of Bethel and the outdoor pleasures of the Rangeley Lakes are popular getaways for outdoorsy Bostonians and New Yorkers.

Augusta & Bangor

There's no doubt about it, Augusta, Maine's capital, is small. Founded as a trading post in 1628, it was later abandoned, then resettled in 1724 at Fort Western (later Hallowell). Augusta became the capital in 1827. Take a gander at the granite **State House** (1832), but make time to stop at the adjacent **Maine State Museum** (☎ 207-287-2301), by far New England's best state museum (free admission). The Kennebec Valley Chamber of Commerce (☎ 207-623-4559), on University Dr, provides detailed information.

A boomtown during Maine's 19th-century lumbering prosperity, Bangor was largely destroyed by a disastrous fire in 1911. Today it's a modern, workaday town, perhaps most famous as the hometown of best-selling novelist Stephen King (look for his appropriately spooky mansion – complete with bat-and-cobweb fence – among the grand houses along Broadway).

Sabbathday Lake

Take Maine Turnpike exit 11, then ME 26 to reach the town of Sabbathday Lake, 30 miles north of Portland, near the lake of the same name. Sabbathday shelters the nation's only active Shaker community. It was founded in the early 18th century, and a handful of devotees keeps the Shaker tradition of prayer, simple living, hard work and fine artistry alive.

Sebago Lake

Sebago Lake, a mere 15 miles northwest of Portland, is among Maine's largest and most accessible lakes. At its northern end, southeast of Naples, is Sebago Lake State Park (☎ 207-693-6613), with camping, swimming, boating and fishing.

Bethel

For a small town nested in the Maine woods, Bethel, 63 miles northwest of Portland on ME 26, is surprisingly refined. Part of its backwoods sophistication comes from being the home of Gould Academy, a well-regarded prep school founded in 1836. The Bethel Area Chamber of Commerce (☎ 800-442-5826, 30 Cross St), in the Bethel train station, has more information.

As for **outdoor activities**, the knowledgeable folks at Bethel Outdoor Adventures (☎ 207-824-4224, 800-533-3607), on US 2, rent canoes and kayaks and arrange guided trips, lessons and shuttles to and from the Androscoggin River. There's golf at the Bethel Inn, hiking in nearby forests and scenic drives all around. **Grafton Notch State Park**, north of Bethel along ME 26, has hiking trails and pretty waterfalls, but no camping. In winter, visitors come to ski at **Sunday River Ski Area** (☎ 207-824-3000, 800-430-0771), 6 miles north of Bethel along ME 26. It's one of the best family-oriented ski centers in the eastern USA, with a 2011-foot vertical drop.

White Mountains National Forest (☎ 207-824-2134, 877-444-6777 for reservations), near Bethel has four basic campgrounds (tents/RVs $12/14); head to the Evan's Notch Visitor Center (18 Mayville Rd/US 2) for details. With only about 25 sites, *Bethel Outdoor Adventure Campground* (☎ 207-824-4224, 800-533-3607), on US 2, is one of a few private area campgrounds ($14/18).

Simple *Bethel Spa Motel* (☎ 207-824-2989, 800-882-0293), on Main St, has 10 doubles ($48). *Norseman Inn & Motel* (☎ 207-824-2002), on US 2 at ME 26, has 30 rooms ($58-78). The *Chapman Inn* (☎ 207-824-2657), at Main and Broad Sts, has 10 doubles for $65 with breakfast ($75 with private bath). ***River View*** *(☎ 207-824-2808, 357 Mayville Rd)*, at US 2 and ME 26, has 30 two-bedroom suites with kitchen ($80).

Caratunk & The Forks

The **Kennebec River** below the Harris Hydroelectric Station passes through a dramatic 12-mile gorge that's among the country's prime rafting places. The Kennebec Valley Chamber of Commerce (☎ 207-623-4559) will help with information. Campers should head to ***Loon Echo Campground*** *(☎ 207-668-4829)*, in Jackman on US 201, about 14 miles north of The Forks. The 20 sites cost $16; no electricity is available.

The villages of Caratunk and The Forks, on US 201 south of Jackman, are at the center of the Kennebec rafting area. Trips ($85-122 per person) are suitable for everyone from children eight and older to seniors. Some of the operators include Crab Apple Whitewater (☎ 207-663-4491, 800-553-7238), New England Outdoor Center Caratunk (☎ 207-672-5506, 800-766-7238) and Northern Outdoors (☎ 800-765-7238), which offers rafting, rock climbing, fishing and sea kayaking trips.

Baxter State Park

Mt Katahdin (5267 feet), Maine's tallest mountain and the northern terminus of the 2160-mile Appalachian Trail, is the centerpiece of Baxter State Park, which has 46 other mountain peaks, 1200 campsites and 180 miles of hiking trails.

To enjoy the park, you must arrive at the entrance early (ie, at the crack of dawn: only a certain number of visitors are allowed in per day) and should be well equipped. Campsites within the park's 10 campgrounds must be reserved well in advance by mail (preferably in Jan or Feb) by contacting Baxter State Park (☎ 207-723-5140, 64 Balsam Dr, Millinocket, ME 04462). You might also want to get information from the Millinocket Chamber of Commerce (☎ 207-723-4443, 1029 Central St).

If you are unable to get a reservation at one of the park's campsites, you can usually find a site at one of the ***private campgrounds*** just outside the Togue Ponds and Matagamon gates into the park. There are several campgrounds in Medway (just off I-95 exit 56), Millinocket and Greenville.

Washington, DC & the Capital Region

Washington, DC & the Capital Region

Home to such national symbols as the White House and the Capitol, along with memorials honoring the country's great leaders and defining events, Washington, DC, is a living monument to the USA itself as well as the nation's capital. The district's first-class museums and attractions draw visitors from around the globe.

Much of the country's formative history was played out in this region, and visitors can retrace the colonial past and movements of the Revolutionary and Civil Wars here. The cherished maritime heritage of the Chesapeake Bay is evident in attractions such as Baltimore's Inner Harbor, the yachting center at Annapolis, huge naval installations around Hampton Roads, and traditional 'watermen' communities on the Eastern Shore. In the summer, many visitors come to Atlantic beaches and islands for salt-water vacations.

Farther inland are the bucolic Shenandoah Valley and beautiful Blue Ridge Mountains, where forests, trails and rivers provide opportunities for outdoor activities. Deeper into the Appalachian and Allegheny mountain ranges, especially in West Virginia, are even more rugged adventures.

History

Artifacts found in southern Maryland indicate that hunter-gatherers inhabited the region some 12,000 years ago. By the 16th century, the Algonquian groups that populated coastal areas, cultivating corn, squash, beans and potatoes, came into contact with English settlers. Iroquois nations occupied inland areas and traded most actively with the French.

Early European settlements were variously assisted and resisted by Native Americans. The Powhatan initially helped the English when they arrived at Jamestown Island in 1607, but hostility contributed to the woes of the fledgling settlement as relations deteriorated. While the tale of how a chieftain's daughter named Pocahontas saved the life of English captain John Smith is now a treasured American legend, the

Highlights

- Washington, DC – national monuments, Smithsonian museums and Arlington National Cemetery
- Mt Vernon – George Washington's imposing country estate
- Williamsburg – living-history park, with Jamestown and Yorktown nearby
- Battlefields – evocative memories of the US Civil War
- Shenandoah Valley & Blue Ridge Mountains – Virginia's scenic blockbusters
- Baltimore – all-American city around the Inner Harbor
- Annapolis – Maryland's capital, with 18th-century buildings and a huge sailing scene
- New River Gorge – white-water rafting and mountain recreation in West Virginia.

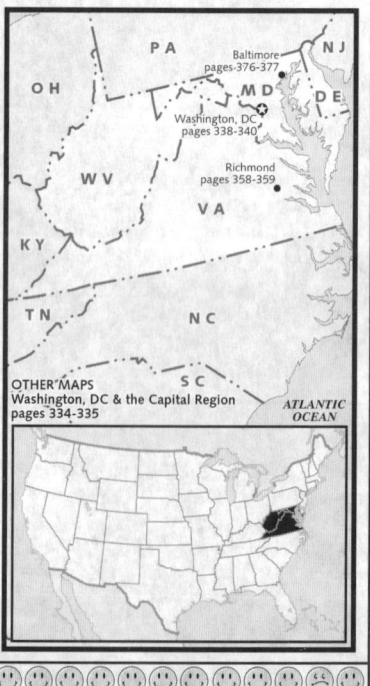

bulk of Native American history in the region is far less romantic.

Inhabitants of many European and Native American settlements engaged in 'Indian Wars,' though European-borne diseases proved more devastating than warfare, wiping out whole tribes. A handful of Native American communities remain on isolated reservations in Virginia today.

The successful cultivation of tobacco in 1615 gave the Jamestown colony a cash crop to ensure its survival, but the resulting expansion of cropland further encroached on Native American land and fueled a demand for cheap labor, which was met with the importation of African slaves starting in 1619. As across the USA, the region is only beginning to fully interpret the legacy of African Americans.

In 1624 the British founded the royal colony of Virginia in honor of the 'Virgin Queen' Elizabeth, liberally claiming all territory in a wide strip from the Atlantic Coast to the west. The English soon absorbed Dutch and Swedish settlements on the Delaware coast, established in 1631 and 1638, respectively. In 1634 a royal grant enabled Lord Baltimore to establish an independent Catholic colony, which he named 'Maryland.' To resolve early territorial disputes among Maryland, Delaware and Pennsylvania, a pair of English astronomers mapped out their namesake 'Mason-Dixon line,' which was later to represent the boundary between the industrial North and the slaveholding South.

The colonies were largely self-governing, but their legislatures were elected by a propertied elite. Economic development was retarded by British restrictions on trade and commerce, and resentment grew with increased British taxes. Virginians, including Patrick Henry, George Washington and Thomas Jefferson, were prominent in the Continental Congresses, which laid the groundwork for independence.

During the Revolutionary War, the region saw both the initial defeat of the Continental Army at the Battle of Brandywine Creek (1777) and the final surrender of the British at Yorktown (1781). Virginians were again influential in the 1787 Constitutional Convention, and four of the new republic's first five presidents came from that state.

After a search for a permanent capital for the newly independent nation, the site of Washington was selected as a convenient point between Northern and Southern states after a post–Revolutionary War compromise. The new capital's position proved particularly strategic during the Civil War. While Maryland and Delaware were technically 'slave states,' they chose to remain in the Union. Virginia seceded and established the capital of the Confederacy in Richmond. The 100 miles between the warring cities became heavily contested battlegrounds as each side sought to take control of its opponent's capital. The mountainous western part of Virginia – culturally separate from the plantation plain – was admitted to the Union as a separate state in 1863 to grant Lincoln the votes needed to advance Emancipation.

After the Civil War, the region slowly recovered on the strength of new industrial growth, and the coastal urban corridor became increasingly developed. The mountain regions, particularly West Virginia, remain much less developed; boom-to-bust coal production peaked here in the early 20th century. The growth of Washington, DC, particularly after WWII, has been a major source of employment and wealth in the central region.

Geography

The region's coastal areas include a low, flat, 100-mile-wide coastal plain as well as the 'Delmarva' (Delaware-Maryland-Virginia) Peninsula between the Chesapeake and Delaware Bays. The Chesapeake Bay is an estuary, where some 48 navigable rivers join the sea in a geographically and culturally distinct region called the 'Tidewater.'

Farther inland, the undulating Piedmont Plateau holds the region's farmlands and many of its cities and towns. The Appalachian range, forming a barrier to the northwest, has a number of subsidiary ranges, including the Allegheny Mountains and the Blue Ridge Mountains; the fabled Shenandoah Valley lies between them. On the west side of the Alleghenies, the principal rivers of heavily forested

WASHINGTON, DC & THE CAPITAL REGION

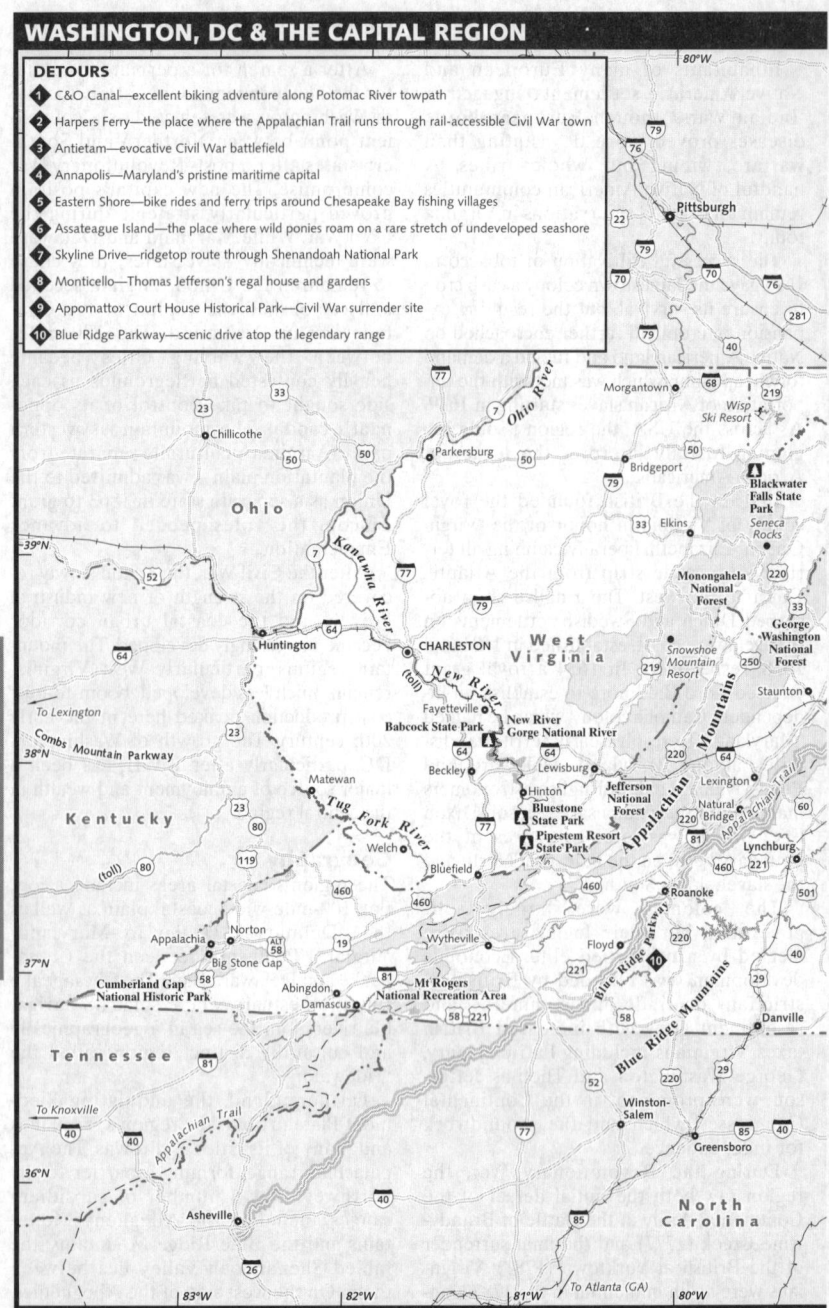

DETOURS

1. C&O Canal—excellent biking adventure along Potomac River towpath
2. Harpers Ferry—the place where the Appalachian Trail runs through rail-accessible Civil War town
3. Antietam—evocative Civil War battlefield
4. Annapolis—Maryland's pristine maritime capital
5. Eastern Shore—bike rides and ferry trips around Chesapeake Bay fishing villages
6. Assateague Island—the place where wild ponies roam on a rare stretch of undeveloped seashore
7. Skyline Drive—ridgetop route through Shenandoah National Park
8. Monticello—Thomas Jefferson's regal house and gardens
9. Appomattox Court House Historical Park—Civil War surrender site
10. Blue Ridge Parkway—scenic drive atop the legendary range

CAPITAL REGION

WASHINGTON, DC & THE CAPITAL REGION

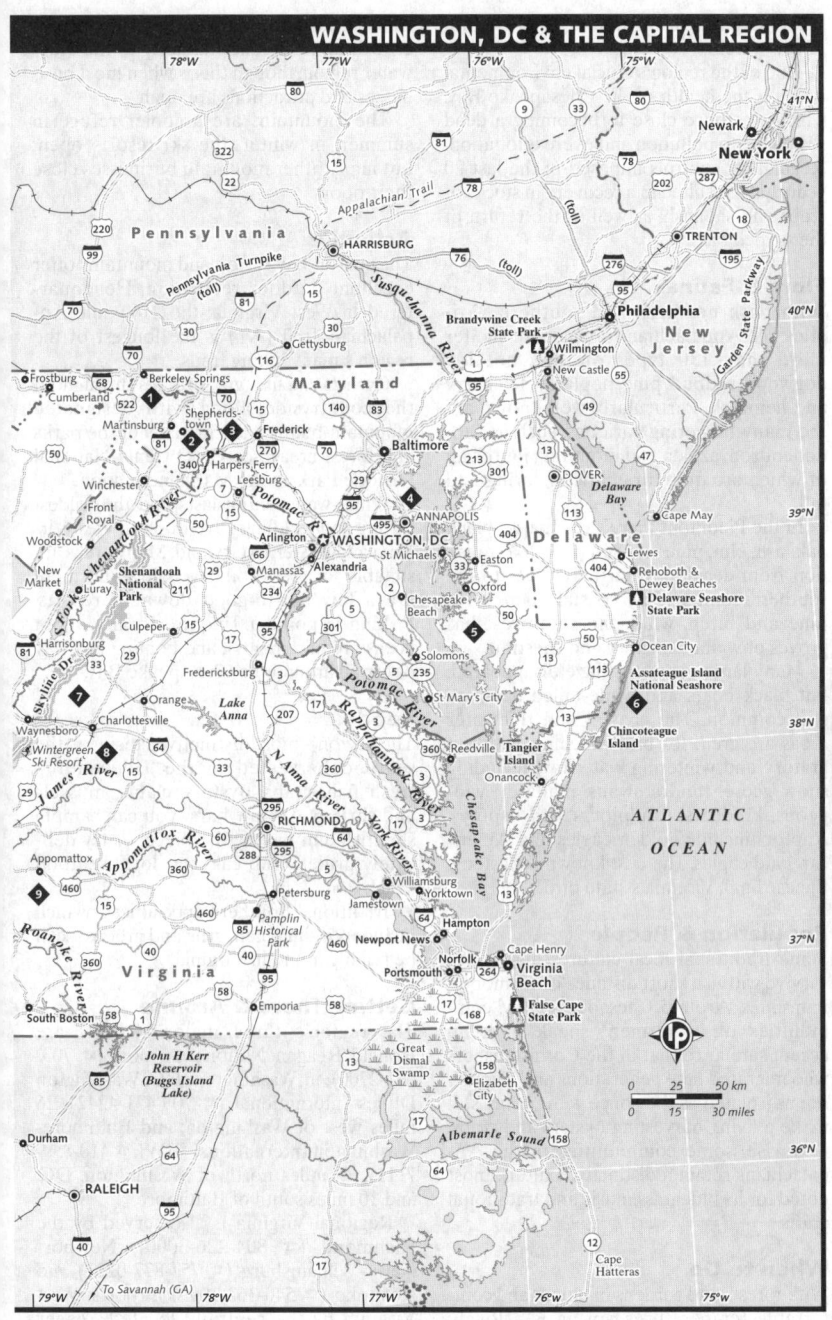

West Virginia drain inland to the Ohio River system.

One of the region's crucial environmental issues is the health of the Chesapeake Bay, which was once close to becoming a dead sea owing to pollution and overexploitation. Regulatory controls imposed in the last 20 years have resulted in a recovery in stocks of crabs and shellfish, as well as the return of the striped bass.

Flora & Fauna

With both northern and southern varieties, the Appalachian forests here shelter more than 130 types of tree, notably dogwood, redbud, pine, poplar, wild cherry and hemlock. Particularly well known are the many flowering varieties, such as rhododendron, azalea and mountain laurel, all of which are quite dramatic in spring and fall.

In the Piedmont there's red maple, black oak, ash, elm, pine and cedar, with a transition from deciduous northern trees to the southern conifers. The coastal plains have pine and birch, while the southwest has groves of walnut, hickory and chestnut.

Many large mammals have disappeared, but black bears and white-tailed deer are still common. The coastal and tidewater areas are great for bird-watching, with migratory and wintering waterfowl including snow geese, tundra swans, mallards, widgeons, killdeers, sandpipers and ospreys. Raptors include golden eagles and American bald eagles. The best known songster is the cardinal, Virginia's state bird.

Population & People

Some traditional local cultures manage to survive within a short distance of cosmopolitan cities. Around Chesapeake Bay, communities of 'watermen' speak with an accent similar to that of the Cornish fishers who migrated here generations ago. Though not as isolated as they once were, many still make a living harvesting oysters and crabs. Likewise, some communities in the Appalachians retain a distinctive culture most noted for its bluegrass music and traditional crafts.

When to Go

With forests and gardens in bloom and comfortable temperatures, spring is a lovely time to visit the region. Summer brings crowds and heat and humidity to the Tidewater region, though this is when most businesses and attractions are open.

The mountains are a cooler refuge in summer; in winter, the ski resorts open, but many other mountain businesses close their doors.

Activities

The coastal-bay region and mountains offer excellent outdoor recreation. Headquartered in West Virginia, the 2160-mile Appalachian Trail (AT) is the longest of the region's many hiking trails.

Cyclists can find great routes throughout the countryside along with designated mountain-biking trails in many of the parks and forest areas; see C&O Canal National Historic Park, in the Maryland section.

White-water enthusiasts find the wildest rafting and paddling adventures in West Virginia and western Maryland. Many areas are suitable for cross-country skiing, and there are a few fair-to-good downhill resorts. Fishing is popular (inquire locally about license requirements), and boating is a way of life all around the Chesapeake Bay.

Food

The region's most distinctive cuisine is the seafood harvested in the Tidewater – fresh fish, crabs, oysters, clams, mussels and shrimp. At 'raw bars' you can sample shellfish and pay by the piece, or try delicately grilled crab cakes at local seafood shacks.

Traditional Southern specialties – which include Virginia ham, grits and greens – can be readily found in Virginia.

Getting There & Around

The region's three major airports are Ronald Reagan National Airport (☎ 703-661-2700), in Washington, DC; Washington Dulles International (☎ 703-471-4242), 26 miles west of Washington; and Baltimore-Washington International (BWI; ☎ 410-859-7111), 35 miles north of Washington, DC, and 10 miles south of Baltimore.

Regional Virginia is also served by the Richmond (☎ 804-226-3000), Newport News–Williamsburg (☎ 757-877-0221) and Roanoke (☎ 540-362-1999) airports; West Virginia by the centrally located Yeager

Charleston Airport (☎ 304-344-8033); and Delaware by Philadelphia International Airport (PIA; ☎ 215-492-3181), a 30-minute drive north of Wilmington.

Buses are the budget alternative for reaching many smaller cities not served by air or rail (though travelers should check car rental rates and packages to compare costs). Nearly every city has a Greyhound (Ⓦ www.greyhound.com) bus station or stop; Trailways (Ⓦ www.trailways.com) is another bus line that often uses the same terminals. See individual city sections for more on local and regional bus transit.

Amtrak (Ⓦ www.amtrak.com for fares and schedules) and the regional MARC system (Ⓦ www.mtamaryland.com) provide rail transit to Washington, DC, and other regional destinations. See the Washington, DC, section for fares from that city to other East Coast destinations.

It's best to have your own transport for extensive exploring outside major cities. Skyline Dr and the Blue Ridge Pkwy are two famous scenic drives in Virginia.

Washington, DC

If the country keeps united, she will produce a capital city of such magnitude, inferior to none in Europe.

– prediction by George Washington, 1792

Apart from its well-known attractions, Washington is a pleasant city to visit, with good transport, bars, restaurants and cosmopolitan atmosphere. The peak visitor season is April to September.

History

Various capitals were considered for the fledgling US republic before Congress decided upon the Potomac River as a spot acceptable to North and South. The site was also across the river from George Washington's home at Mt Vernon. People started calling it 'the city of Washington,' and the name stuck.

Maryland and Virginia ceded land for the '10 miles square' District of Columbia, and French engineer Pierre Charles L'Enfant prepared the city plan. He was later fired from the task, but DC – often referred to

locally as 'the District' – was completed largely as he had planned.

The brand-new Capitol was torched in the War of 1812, and a dispirited proposal to abandon the capital failed by only nine votes. Washington was eventually rebuilt, and its ailing infrastructure was overhauled in the 1870s by territorial governor Alexander 'Boss' Shepherd. A late-19th-century beautification plan contributed landscaping, parks and monuments, but as late as the 1960s John F Kennedy derided it as 'a city of Southern efficiency and Northern charm.'

Modern-day DC is famous for its international community, with representatives from every country, and notorious for poverty and crime. Racial and economic divisions, typical of most US cities, are sharper here: Of DC's 575,000 residents, two-thirds are African American, and a similar proportion earn less than $32,000 annually. While aspiring to be a model of the country's grand ideals, DC represents a microcosm of its realities.

Government & Politics

The seat of the US government is within the federal enclave of the District of Columbia. As a federal protectorate, DC has a political life that resembles that of a colony more closely than of a state. The municipal government must operate under the imposing oversight of the federal government, and District residents won the right to vote in presidential elections only in 1961. DC's hard-fought struggle for congressional representation has so far earned it only non-voting representatives.

Architecture

Pierre L'Enfant's plan declared that no building should reach higher than the Capitol, and so today Washington's skyline is free of skyscrapers, and the 555-foot Washington Monument remains the tallest building. The many Roman- and Greek-style buildings and ornamentation reflect ambitions for a classical capital. The Victorian era contributed many lavish churches and houses, while post-WWII government monoliths overwhelm their surroundings. The National Building Museum (see Downtown, later) examines the District's architecture.

CAPITAL REGION

WASHINGTON, DC

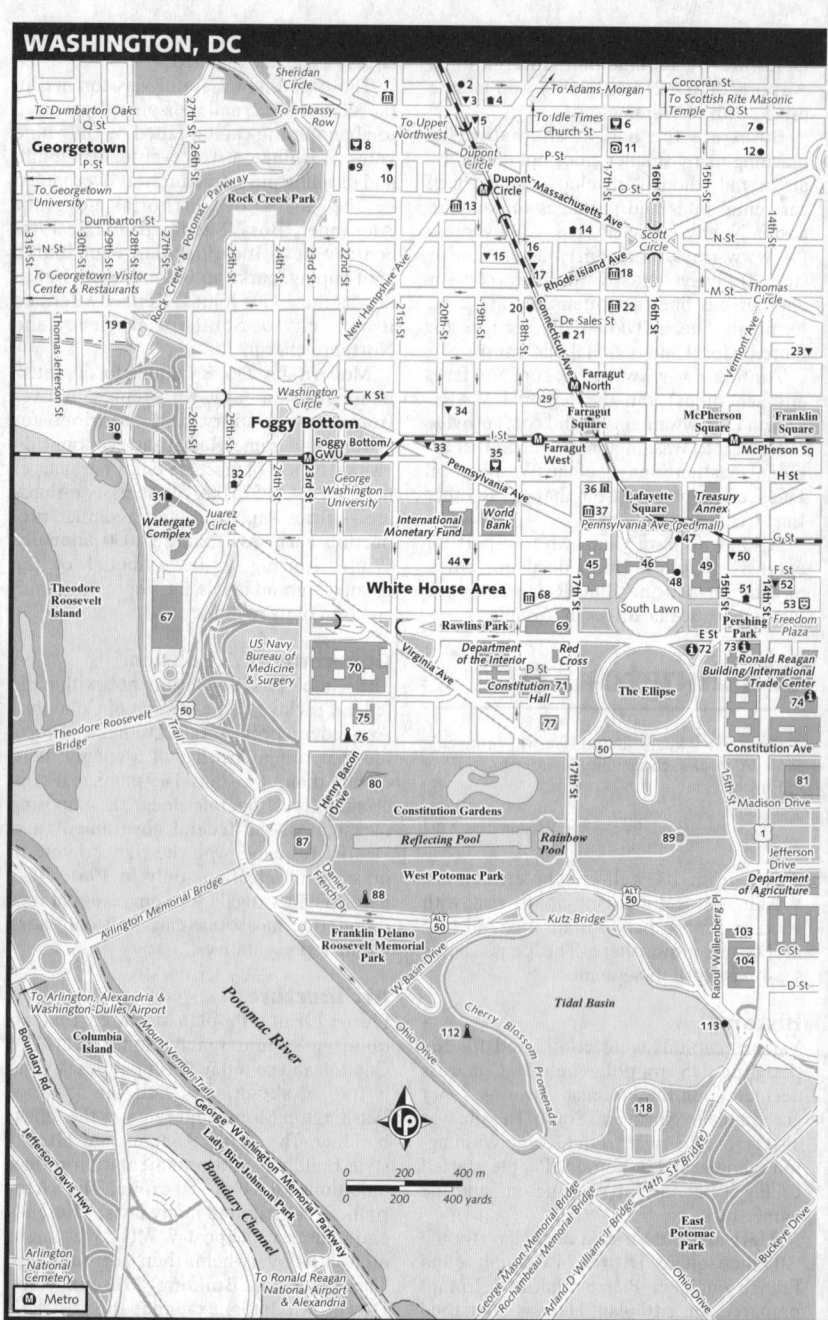

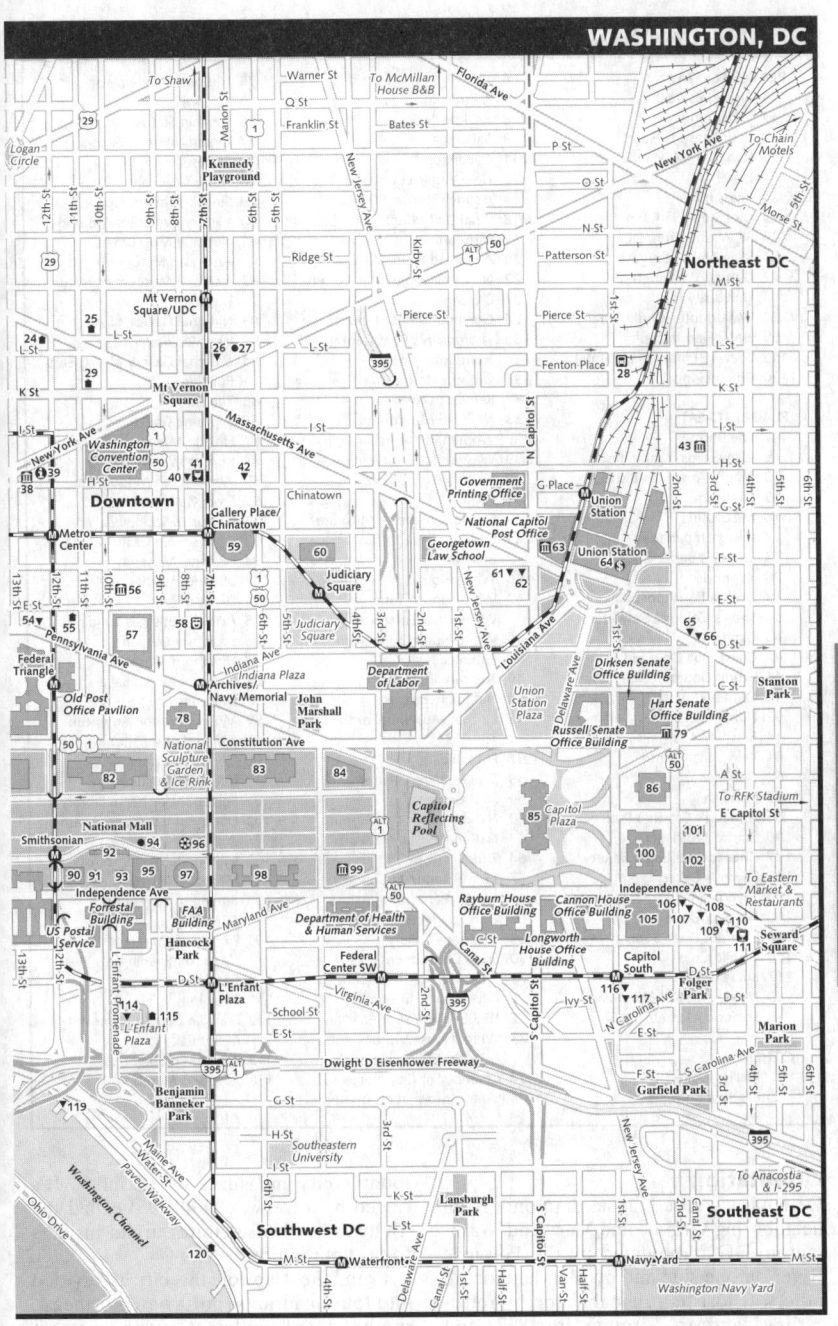

WASHINGTON, DC

WASHINGTON, DC

Orientation

Originally carved as a diamond from neighboring Virginia and Maryland, Washington, DC, is bounded by the Potomac River on one side and by Maryland on all others. It lost its original shape by retroceding land to Virginia in 1837, and today's city measures 69 sq miles. It's ringed by a freeway (I-495/95) called the 'Beltway,' which separates urban insiders from suburbanites.

From the Capitol, the city is divided into four quadrants (northwest, northeast, southeast and southwest) along axes that follow N Capitol St, E Capitol St, S Capitol St and the National Mall. Identical addresses appear in each quadrant. Most visitor attractions are in the northwest quadrant.

North-south streets are referred to by numbers, while the east-west streets are ordered alphabetically (with no B, J, X, Y or Z Sts; I St sometimes appears as 'Eye' St). Broad diagonal avenues, named after states, overlay the grid and are often interrupted by circular parks and plazas.

Capitol Hill, Downtown, the National Mall, Foggy Bottom, Dupont Circle, Adams-Morgan, Shaw and Georgetown are the capital's distinctive neighborhoods.

Information

Tourist Offices The Washington Convention & Visitors Association (☎ 202-789-7000, 1212 New York Ave NW, Suite 600, Washington, DC 20005) provides information and a disabled visitor service.

The Chamber of Commerce Visitor Information Center (☎ 202-328-4748, 1300 Pennsylvania Ave NW), in the Ronald Reagan Building, has a plethora of advice and information.

The useful National Park Service (NPS) and White House visitor centers are described later, in the White House Area section. The NPS operates most federal sites (W www.nps.gov/nama).

The International Visitors Information Service (☎ 202-536-4911) is at the Arrivals Terminal at Washington-Dulles Airport; its 'language bank' (☎ 202-939-5538) answers questions in over fifty languages (open weekdays only).

Online visitor information is available at W www.washington.org, www.dcvisit.com and www.washingtonpost.com.

Money Currency exchange is available at the three major airports, during weekday business hours at many banks, at American Express (☎ 202-457-1300, 1150 Connecticut Ave NW) and at Thomas Cook (☎ 202-237-2229), which provides daily service at its Gate G booth in Union Station.

Post & Communications General-delivery mail goes to the main post office (☎ 202-635-5300, 900 Brentwood Rd NE). Local telephone calls are 35¢. A popular

cybercafe is Cyberstop (☎ 202-234-2470, 153 17th St NW) in Dupont Circle.

Bookstores For good used books, try Idle Times (☎ 202-232-4774, 2410 18th St NW). Kramerbooks (☎ 202-387-1400, 1517 Connecticut Ave NW), in Dupont Circle, with its lively cafe-bar, is a good choice. (In 1998 Kramerbooks refused to turn over details of Monica Lewinsky's book purchases to special prosecutor Kenneth Starr.) Other stores to visit include Politics & Prose (☎ 202-364-1919, 5015 Connecticut Avenue NW) and Travel Books & Language Center (☎ 202-237-1322, 4437 Wisconsin Ave NW).

Newspapers The *Washington Post* is one of the nation's best newspapers. Also of interest are the *Washington Afro-American* and the free entertainment weekly *Washington City Paper*.

Dangers & Annoyances Although DC has bleak inner-city areas and one of the nation's highest murder rates, most violent crime occurs outside touristed areas. Almost all major sights are in relatively safe areas.

Note that many attractions get very crowded; prepare for long, standing waits in sun or rain. Thorough security checks are common.

Capitol Hill

Washington's most prominent landmark, the Capitol, sits atop Capitol Hill across a plaza from the equally regal Supreme Court and Library of Congress. Congressional office buildings surround the plaza. Popular lunch counters string out along Massachusetts Ave NW and Pennsylvania Ave SE. A pleasant residential district stretches from E Capitol St over to Lincoln Park, but beyond these areas the neighborhood starts to decline. The principal Metro stations servicing this area are Union Station, Capitol South and Eastern Market.

Capitol The cornerstone for the Capitol (☎ 202-225-6827) was laid by George Washington in 1793, and Congress moved in seven years later. Nearly destroyed in the 1814 British invasion, it was rebuilt within five years. The House (south) and Senate (north) wings were added in 1857, and the massive iron dome in 1863. A flag raised above either wing indicates that that body is in session.

Enter from the east (not the Mall side) into the dramatic central **Rotunda**; note the Constantino Brumidi fresco (inside the dome) and the hallway murals and ceilings.

To watch Congress in action, call ☎ 202-225-6827 for session dates. US citizens can request visitor gallery passes from their representatives or senators; foreign visitors show their passports at the House gallery. Committee hearings (often fascinating) are open to the public; check the *Washington Post*'s 'Today in Congress' notice. Special tours for the disabled are available (☎ 202-224-4048).

Library of Congress The world's largest library (☎ 202-707-4604 for exhibitions, Ⓦ www.loc.gov) fills three buildings with over 26 million books, 36 million manuscripts, and maps, photographs, sheet music and musical instruments.

The 1897 Jefferson Building features an impressive Main Reading Room and an ornate Great Hall with vaulted ceilings (open 10am-5:30pm Mon-Sat). The Madison Building houses the visitor center and cafeteria.

The library screens classic films (free), stages concerts and has four free tours daily.

Supreme Court This imposing 1935 marble building is home of the highest court in the land (sitting on various weekdays Oct-June, no sittings July-Sept); for dates, check the *Washington Post* or call ☎ 202-479-3211 ext 4. Arrive by 8am to get a seat.

Union Station Washington's most impressive gateway (☎ 202-371-9441) is a massive, beautifully restored 1908 beaux arts building; its great hall was modeled on the Roman Baths of Diocletian. It hosts Amtrak, Metro and commuter rail stations, as well as shops, restaurants, cinemas and traveler resources.

Museums The **National Postal Museum** (☎ 202-357-2700) across from Union Station features the world's largest stamp collection and kid-friendly exhibits, from the Pony Express to Cliff Clavin's uniform worn in TV's *Cheers* (free admis-

sion). Three floors of inviting interactive exhibits at the **Capital Children's Museum** (☎ 202-543-8600, 800 3rd St NE) include a TV studio, animation laboratory, Japanese schoolroom and Cityscapes fire-pole slide ($6).

Other Attractions The **Folger Shakespeare Library** (☎ 202-544-7077) has the world's largest collection of Shakespearean works (free admission; closed Sun). **Sewall-Belmont House** (☎ 202-546-1210) honors heroines of the women's rights movement and has a vast feminist library (admission by donation; closed Sun-Mon).

National Mall

I have a dream that one day this nation will rise up and live out the true meaning of its creed: 'We hold these truths to be self-evident, that all men are created equal.'

– Martin Luther King Jr, from the steps of the Lincoln Memorial, 1963

This 400-foot-wide green expanse stretching from the Potomac River to Capitol Hill is home to DC's most famous monuments and museums. It's also renowned for mass gatherings designed to influence public policy, such as anti–Vietnam War protests in the 1960s and Martin Luther King Jr's 'I Have a Dream' speech.

Pierre L'Enfant envisioned the Mall as a grand promenade lined with mansions and embassies, but it evolved in a more American way, into a national lawn lined with family-friendly museums and filled with joggers and picnickers.

Smithsonian Institution In 1826 Englishman James Smithson, without ever visiting the USA, willed £4,100,000 to the country to found an 'establishment for the increase and diffusion of knowledge.' Today's Smithsonian Institution is a world-class research center that administers more than a dozen Washington museums and galleries plus the National Zoo. Its collection is so large that only 1% is on display at any given point.

Admission to all museums is free; museums are open daily 10am-5:30pm. Call ☎ 202-357-2700 for general information on *all* museums or check Ⓦ www.si.edu.

The **Smithsonian Castle**, a turreted red-brick building on the south side of the Mall, the original Smithsonian museum, is now the information center.

The **National Museum of American History** is a celebration of US culture. The museum's eclectic collection includes the original American flag, first ladies' inauguration ball gowns, Archie Bunker's armchair (from TV's *All in the Family*), a whites-only Woolworth's lunch counter, and touching memorabilia left at the Vietnam Memorial; major African American and Native American exhibits are also featured.

The **National Museum of Natural History** has such highlights as a towering 13-foot elephant, the 45-carat Hope Diamond, a life-size model of a blue whale, dinosaur skeletons, a live insect zoo, and a state-of-the-art gem and mineral exhibit; get timed admission passes as soon as it opens.

The cavernous halls of the world's most popular museum, the **National Air & Space Museum**, hold full-size air- and spacecraft, from the Wright brothers' *Flyer* and Charles Lindbergh's *Spirit of St Louis* to the *Apollo 11* command module. There is an IMAX theater screening several movies ($5.50), plus a planetarium ($3.75), shops and a restaurant.

The **Hirshhorn Museum**, a modern doughnut-shaped building, houses a huge collection of 20th-century sculptures, including works by Rodin, Brancusi, Calder and Henry Moore, as well as paintings by Dubuffet, O'Keeffe, Warhol, Pollock and de Kooning. There's a sculpture garden outside and a patio cafe in summer. The **Arts & Industries Building**, an odd little structure, displays mainly Victorian-era inventions from the 1876 Philadelphia Centennial Exposition, in a ghostly, carnival-type ambience. There's an antique carousel outside ($1).

The **National Museum of African Art** and **Arthur M Sackler Gallery** are the 'bookends' behind the Castle; they deliver visitors to vast, interconnected underground galleries. The first gallery includes masks, textiles and ceramics from the sub-Sahara, and the Sackler exhibits Asian arts, including Chinese ritual bronzes and jade ornaments. The **Freer Gallery of Art** features American art, including an extensive collection of Whistler paintings, and evocative Asian exhibits.

The **National Museum of the American Indian** is due to open in 2002.

National Gallery of Art This famous gallery (☎ 202-737-4215, ⓦ www.nga.gov) consists of two buildings connected by an underground passage. The original, neo-classical West Wing exhibits primarily European art from the Middle Ages to the early 20th century, including works by Rembrandt, Vermeer, El Greco, Renoir, Monet and Cézanne, plus a lone da Vinci. The East Wing features a four-story atrium with a Calder mobile, plus various abstract and modern works. The sculpture garden outside has an ice-skating rink ($5).

US Holocaust Memorial Museum Opened in 1993, this haunting memorial (☎ 202-488-0400, ⓦ www.ushmm.org) to WWII Holocaust victims portrays in grim detail the events of Nazi Germany. Although the museum recommends that only those over 11 view the main exhibit, and provides a separate children's exhibit (no ticket required) for over-eight-year-olds, parental caution is advised.

Admission is free, but crowds necessitate tickets (limit four per person), distributed from 10am for admission at a specific time that day. Call ☎ 800-400-9373 for advance passes.

Bureau of Engraving & Printing The bureau (☎ 202-874-2330) designs and prints US paper currency. Lines are long for what is, essentially, a print-shop tour. In peak tourist season you'll need tickets (free) from the kiosk on 15th St.

Washington Monument This 555-foot-tall white obelisk (☎ 202-426-6841) rises above the Mall, offering wonderful views, especially at night. Construction began in 1848 but was not completed until 37 years later; the two phases are evident in the slightly different colors of the stone. Go at night to avoid long lines (free admission; open 8am-11:45pm daily Apr-Aug, 9am-5pm Sept-Mar). Ticketmaster (☎ 800-505-5040) advance tickets cost $1.25.

Lincoln Memorial This imposing monument (☎ 202-426-6895) to the 16th US president resembles a Greek temple, with its 36 columns representing the 36 states in Lincoln's Union. The Lincoln statue's hands read 'A' and 'L' in American Sign Language. Open 24 hours, the monument provides stunning nighttime views.

War Memorials The **Vietnam Veterans Memorial** features two black marble walls meeting in a V shape, on which are the names of more than 58,000 Americans who were killed or disappeared during the Vietnam War. Designed by Maya Lin, a 21-year-old student, in a national competition, it's now DC's most-visited memorial (☎ 202-462-6842, open 24 hours). Names are inscribed chronologically from date of death; registers and volunteers aid name searches.

Across the Mall, the **Korean War Memorial** consists of an eerie troop of 19 stone soldiers. Plans are afoot to build a **World War II Memorial** between the two; opponents hold that a new memorial there would ruin the landscape.

Tidal Basin

The scenic Tidal Basin, southwest of the Mall, is lined with cherry trees, a gift from Japan; their spring blossoming marks the beginning of DC's peak tourism season. Paddleboat rentals are available at the boathouse ($7 per hour for two).

Designed to mimic the Monticello home of the third president, the domed **Jefferson Memorial** (☎ 202-426-6822) was derided as the 'Jefferson muffin' when it was built by the basin. Inside, the walls are etched with Jefferson's writings.

Although Franklin Delano Roosevelt entreated that no memorial 'larger than his desk' be built in his honor, the 1997 **FDR Memorial** covers a 7.5-acre plaza of water sculpture with stone-etched quotes and a seated statue of the 32nd president (the only president elected for four terms).

Downtown

Downtown Washington began in what is now called Federal Triangle, but it has since spread north and east. It now encompasses the area east of the White House to Judiciary Square at 4th St, and from the Mall north to K or M St. Avoid the rough borderlands between Judiciary Square and

Capitol Hill, including 2nd, 3rd and 4th Sts NW. All the following sites are in the Federal Triangle (Ⓜ Federal Triangle).

Extremely popular 45-minute tours of the J Edgar Hoover building (☎ 202-324-3447), **FBI headquarters**, include crime laboratories, DNA testing, confiscated items and machine guns. Reserve early for the free tours, offered weekdays.

On April 14, 1865, John Wilkes Booth assassinated Abraham Lincoln in his box seat, now lovingly preserved in the still-operating **Ford's Theatre** (☎ 202-638-2941). The basement Lincoln Museum is devoted to the assassination. Across the street, **Peterson House** is where Lincoln died – another poignant memorial.

Within the grand neoclassical building housing the **National Archives** (☎ 202-501-5000, Ⓦ www.nara.gov) a small gallery displays blockbuster originals: the Declaration of Independence, the Constitution and the Bill of Rights. Also here is one of four remaining versions of the 1297 Magna Carta.

Handsomely restored, the **Old Post Office** (☎ 202-298-4224) is a 1899 Romanesque Revival landmark that's now the convenient Pavilion food and shopping complex. The 400-foot observation tower affords great downtown panoramas (free admission).

The **National Museum of Women in the Arts** (☎ 202-783-5000) is housed in a Renaissance Revival building that houses art by women from many countries, including Judy Chicago, Mary Cassatt and Georgia O'Keeffe (by donation). The stylish Old Pension Building houses the **National Building Museum** (☎ 202-272-2448), which occupies an entire city block. In its Great Hall, rows of pink marble Corinthian columns rise 75 feet. The dramatic interior courtyard, banked by four stories of ornate balconies, makes a grand setting for inaugural balls and concerts. One exhibit examines the symbolism of DC's architecture (free admission).

White House Area

An expansive park called the Ellipse borders the Mall; look for the well-stocked NPS Ellipse Visitor Pavilion (☎ 202-485-9880) in the northeast corner; it offers the free 'Welcome to Washington' map. On the Ellipse's east side is a power-broker block of Pennsylvania Ave, and Pershing Park, with an outdoor cafe in summer and fast-food vendors. Around Lafayette Square, modern offices loom behind Victorian row houses and presidential St John's Church. Federal Triangle Metro station is nearest the visitor center.

White House Since 1800 every US president has lived at 1600 Pennsylvania Ave. Torched by the British in 1814, the White House reopened in 1818. Jacqueline Kennedy redecorated extensively in the 1960s. Additions include Franklin Roosevelt's pool, Truman's 2nd-story porch, (daddy) George Bush's horseshoe-throwing lane and Clinton's jogging track.

Free guided tours (mornings Tue-Sat) cover eight rooms; get tickets at the nearby White House Visitor Center (☎ 800-717-1450, W www.whitehouse.gov; wheelchairs available), at 15th and E Sts, during peak times.

Executive Buildings The 1883 Greek Revival **Treasury Building** (☎ 202-622-0896), next to the White House, is decorated with golden eagles, ornate balustrades and a two-story marble Cash Room. (Free guided tours Sat morning; call for reservations – photo ID required.) On the White House's other side is the **Old Executive Office Building**. Designed by Alfred Mullet, this elaborate French Second Empire building (☎ 202-395-5895) contains the offices of White House staff. Call Tuesday to Friday mornings to arrange a free tour.

Renwick & Corcoran Galleries The regal entrance and the very dignified Grand Salon of the Smithsonian's Renwick Gallery (☎ 202-357-2700) are a startling contrast to the wild craftwork, whimsy and abstraction found within (free admission).

The Corcoran Gallery (☎ 202-639-1700) houses a superb collection of American art (Hudson River school, Ashcan, pop, abstract expressionism). These are exhibited in a beautiful beaux arts building (admission by donation; open 9am-5pm Mon-Wed, to 9pm Thurs).

Historic Buildings The Federal-style **Octagon House** (☎ 202-638-3221) houses the American Institute of Architects and its museum of architecture and interior arts ($3;

closed Mon). The **Daughters of the American Revolution Museum** (☎ 202-879-3241) contains more than 30 period rooms (free admission; open weekdays, Sun afternoon).

The **Organization of American States** (☎ 202-458-3751), housed in a 1910 beaux arts building, features an Aztec Garden and the Museum of Modern Art of Latin America (free admission; closed Mon). **Decatur House** (☎ 202-842-0920), on Lafayette Square, offers mannerly tours ($3; open Tue-Fri, weekend afternoons).

Foggy Bottom

DC's 'West End district' falls roughly between 17th St NW and Rock Creek Park, the Mall, and K or M St. Foggy Bottom got its name from a smelly gasworks once sited here. George Washington University was built here in 1912. The neighborhood is now a mix of workers, professionals and students (Ⓜ Foggy Bottom).

Tours of the **State Department** (2201 C St NW) diplomatic reception rooms are by appointment only (☎ 202-641-3241). The **National Academy of Sciences** (☎ 202-334-2000), facing the Mall, features interior exhibits and a climbable statue of Albert Einstein outside to the west of the building.

The **John F Kennedy Center for the Performing Arts** (☎ 202-467-4600, W www .kennedy-center.org, 2700 F St NW) is a 'living memorial,' with three theaters, a concert hall, opera house and movie theater. It was long considered an oasis in DC's cultural desert. The waterfront center offers frequent free performances, festivals and other events (see Entertainment, later, for details).

The posh riverfront **Watergate** complex (2650 Virginia Ave NW) encompasses apartments, boutiques, the deluxe Swissôtel Watergate, and the office towers that made 'Watergate' a byword for political scandal after President Nixon's plumbers broke into Democratic National Committee headquarters in 1972.

Dupont Circle

Once a marshland, the Dupont Circle area, north of the White House, became a fashionable residential district at the end of the 19th century and remains so today. Many mansions were later converted to elegant embassies along a stretch of Massachusetts

Ave known as 'Embassy Row' and nearby Sheridan Circle – now the center of Washington's diplomatic community. Scenic Dupont Circle itself is at Connecticut and Massachusetts Aves, though the term generally refers to the entire neighborhood, which offers restaurants, cafes, clubs and boutiques (Ⓜ Dupont Circle).

The first modern-art museum in the USA, the **Phillips Collection** (☎ 202-387-2151, Ⓦ www.phillipscollection.org, 1600 21st St NW) exhibits an outstanding collection (Renoir, Cézanne, Monet, Degas, van Gogh, Klee, Rothko and O'Keeffe) in an intimate setting ($7.50 weekends, donation weekdays; closed Mon).

Exhibits including a moon rock, short film and computer quizzes in the **National Geographic Society's Explorers Hall** (☎ 202-857-7588, Ⓦ www.nationalgeographic.com, 1145 17th St NW) are free, but less exciting than the magazines.

The **B'nai B'rith Klutznick Museum** (☎ 202-857-6583, 1640 Rhode Island Ave NW) maintains a vast Judaica collection (admission by donation; closed Sat). The **Textile Museum** (☎ 202-667-0441, 2320 S St NW) has 15,000 textiles from around the world, dating from 3000 BC to the present (admission by donation).

The artist-run **Fondo del Sol Visual Arts Center** (☎ 202-483-2777, 2112 R St NW) promotes the cultural heritage of the Americas. Exhibits include pre-Columbian artifacts and folk art (admission by donation; open Wed-Sat afternoons).

The Historical Society of Washington, DC (☎ 202-785-2068), operates medieval-looking **Heurich House** (1307 New Hampshire Ave NW), at 20th St, with intricate Victorian detailing ($3; closed Sun). Hour-long tours of the 1915 **Woodrow Wilson House** (☎ 202-387-4062, 2340 S St NW) include a 15-minute newsreel ($5; closed Mon). Patterned after the Mausoleum of Halicarnassus, the elaborate **Scottish Rite Masonic Temple** (☎ 202-232-3579, 1733 16th St NW) offers weekday tours of its J Edgar Hoover Room downstairs (free admission; open 8am-2pm weekdays).

Adams-Morgan & Shaw
The heart of ethnic, bohemian Adams-Morgan is 18th St between Florida Ave and Columbia Rd, and along Columbia Rd itself. Restaurants, cafes, bookstores, bars, clubs, and boutiques abound. Parking is difficult, and it's not convenient by Metro; cabs are best at night.

To the east, Shaw is a largely African American neighborhood stretching from around Thomas Circle to Meridian Hill Park and from N Capitol St to 15th St NW. Back in the 1930s, Shaw's **Lincoln Theater** (1215 U St NW) was a high point on the 'chitlin' circuit' of African American entertainment, hosting such celebrities as DC native Duke Ellington. Riots following the 1968 assassination of Martin Luther King Jr devastated the commercial district. Shaw's recent renaissance has followed the reopening of the historic theater, and new cafes, shops and clubs have popped up along U St around 14th St alongside neighborhood institutions. (Ⓜ U St–Cardozo).

Among the nation's most distinguished universities, **Howard University** (2400 6th St NW) was founded in 1867 to educate African Americans. Call ☎ 202-806-2900 for campus tours.

Georgetown
Predating the capital, Georgetown was the Native American settlement of Tohoga when British fur trader Henry Fleet arrived in 1632. In 1789 Georgetown University was founded, and it continues to dominate the district today. Many 18th-century buildings have been converted to fashionable restaurants, clubs and boutiques, surrounded by lovely historic residential districts (the Kennedys lived here in the 1950s). The nearest Metro station, Foggy Bottom, is almost a mile away – a pleasant walk in decent weather and preferable to Georgetown's parking congestion.

The Georgetown visitor center (☎ 202-653-5190) is at 1057 Thomas Jefferson St NW (open Apr-Oct); costumed guides relive history by running mule-driven barges along the towpath ($7.50).

Georgetown University (☎ 202-687-5055), the USA's oldest Roman Catholic college, sits atop a hill overlooking the Potomac and retains many stately historic buildings. The inaugural director of the university was the country's first black Jesuit, and Bill Clinton is among the university's distinguished alumni. Nearby, beautiful **Dumbarton Oaks** (☎ 202-339-6401), at R and 31st Sts NW, includes an intimate modern gallery of Byzantine tapestries and pre-Columbian gold (free admission) alongside a historic mansion with 10 acres of outstanding formal gardens ($5 afternoons Apr-Oct, free admission other times).

Big Wheel Bikes (☎ 202-337-0254, 1034 33rd St), between M St and the C&O Canal towpath, is a good bike rental/outfitter.

The **Potomac Heritage National Scenic Trail** has been planned to connect Chesapeake Bay to the Allegheny Highlands in a 700-mile corridor. It includes the C&O Canal towpath, the 17-mile Mt Vernon Trail (Virginia), and the 75-mile Laurel Highlands Trail (Pennsylvania).

Upper Northwest

The comfortable residential area northwest of Adams-Morgan has three major sights. The massive high-Gothic **Washington National Cathedral** (☎ 202-537-6200) is a venue for state funerals and other high-profile events. An Episcopal church, it covers all politically correct bases with weekly prayers devoted to different state and religious traditions. Check out the *Apollo 11* stained-glass window and tower views (tours daily; services open to all).

The Smithsonian's **National Zoological Park** (☎ 202-357-2700, 🖳 www.natzoo.si.edu, 3000 Connecticut Ave NW) was beautifully designed by Frederick Law Olmsted to follow the contour of its woodland canyon setting, with some 5000 animals in natural habitats. Parking is extremely limited (🚇 Woodley Park/Zoo).

Rock Creek Park starts at the Potomac River, extends north through DC along the narrow corridor of Rock Creek, then expands to wide parkland in the Upper Northwest district. It boasts terrific biking and hiking. Historic sights include the remains of two Civil War forts and the 1820 Pierce Mill (☎ 202-426-6908, open Wed-Sun). The western Soapstone Valley Park preserves Algonquian quarries.

Waterfront & Anacostia

The confluence of the Potomac and Anacostia Rivers was originally intended to be the national capital site. At the Southwestern Waterfront, a nice promenade along the Washington Channel has great sunsets and overrated seafood restaurants.

Stretching along the Anacostia River, the Washington Navy Yard features the **Marine Corps Museum** (☎ 202-433-3840) and **Navy Museum** (☎ 202-433-6897).

Across the river in hard-luck Anacostia, the **Frederick Douglass National Historic Site** (☎ 202-426-5960, 1411 West St SE) opens the hilltop home of the abolitionist and former slave; the visitor center screens a biographical film (free admission). The Smithsonian's **Anacostia Museum** (☎ 202-287-3369, 1901 Fort Place SE) operates as a cultural center and gallery.

Anacostia has a well-earned reputation for violent crime; take a cab from Anacostia Metro.

Activities

Outdoor enthusiasts head northwest to Rock Creek Park, with miles of trails for biking, hiking and horseback riding, and to the C&O Canal for biking along the towpath and many hiking trails in canal-side parks (see the Maryland section, later). Thompson Boat Center (☎ 202-333-9543), at the Potomac River end of Rock Creek Park, down from the Kennedy Center, rents tandem kayaks (from $10) and bikes ($8 an hour).

Organized Tours

Tourmobile Sightseeing (☎ 202-554-5100, 🖳 www.tourmobile.com) runs its convenient trams daily between all the major sights (from $16).

Gray Line (☎ 800-862-1400) offers a variety of city excursions, including bilingual tours ($28-38). Bike the Sites (☎ 202-966-8662) organizes an 8-mile, 55-landmark bike tour ($35 including all gear and snack; 3 hours). Scandal Tours (☎ 202-783-7212) gives you all the gossip about DC's infamous spots (expanding daily), covering George Washington to George 'Dubya.'

Special Events

DC is famous for its National Cherry Blossom Festival (☎ 202-547-1500), held late March to early April when the trees bloom. The Smithsonian's Folklife Festival (☎ 202-357-2700), held over two weekends in June and July, features distinctive regional folk art, crafts, food and music. Independence Day is also big here, celebrated on July 4 with parades, concerts and fireworks.

Places to Stay

DC is a business town, so hotel rates can drop as much as 50% on weekends and in summer; tourist season is April to September, with a heat-related August lull. Professional associations, veteran status, government or nongovernmental organization (NGO) affiliation and even museum membership can also earn discounts. Accommodation tax is 13% plus $1.50 per night.

Washington DC Accommodations (☎ 800-554-2220) provides assistance with lodging. For B&Bs citywide, call Bed & Breakfast Accommodations (☎ 202-328-3510) or the Bed & Breakfast League (☎ 202-363-7767).

Budget The year-round *Cherry Hill Park* (☎ 301-937-7116), northeast of town in College Park, Maryland, is the nearest campground. It features 400 sites and a pool ($30/40 tent/RV sites for two people); reserve for summer. *Greenbelt Park* (☎ 301-344-3948, 655 Greenbelt Rd), 12 miles northeast of DC, costs $10 (no hookups).

HI Washington, DC (☎ 202-737-2333, W www.hiwashingtondc.org, 1009 11th St NW), at K St, is a 300-bed place open 24 hours. It's a gathering spot for budget travelers (members/nonmembers $19/21 off-peak, $22/24 peak; reservations and photo ID required). *Washington International Backpackers* (☎ 202-667-7681, 2451 18th St NW) is in the more casual Adams-Morgan, upstairs from one of DC's liveliest blocks ($16); inquire about free pickup from the train or bus station, bike rentals and Internet access.

International Guest House (☎ 202-726-5808, 1441 Kennedy St NW), at 16th St NW, is in the Upper Northwest district. This tidy place has clean rooms with two or three twin beds ($25 adults, including breakfast). Note the 11pm curfew.

Adams Inn (☎ 202-745-3600, 1744 Lanier Place NW), in Adams-Morgan, is a comfortable guesthouse (from $55/70 shared/private bath). *Kalorama Guest House* (☎ 202-667-6369, 1854 Mintwood Place NW), nearby, has rooms with Victorian frills. *Kalorama Guest House at Woodley Park* (☎ 202-328-0860, 2700 Cathedral Ave NW) is a companion property. Both cost $55-105, continental breakfast included. *Connecticut-Woodley Guest House* (☎ 202-667-0218, 2647 Woodley Rd), not flash but comfortable nonetheless, is nearby ($50/90 shared/private bath).

Simpkin's B&B (☎ 202-387-1328, 1601 19th St NW), an 1888 townhouse, offers international-travelers discounts (from $25/$30 singles/doubles). *McMillan House B&B* (☎ 202-986-8989, 2417 1st St NW) is a newly renovated late-19th-century place with good-value rooms from $60.

Two miles northeast of the Capitol, Hwy 50/New York Ave NE has a strip of cheap motels in a so-so district convenient for drivers; among these, *Super 8 Motel* (☎ 202-543-7400, 501 New York Ave NE) charges from $55/70 for a standard room/suite.

Mid-Range Rooms with private baths in mid-range DC hotels start around $100.

Tabard Inn (☎ 202-785-1277, 1739 N St NW), a destination in itself, is comfortable and has idiosyncratic rooms in a Victorian house in Dupont Circle; ask about the $67 single shared-bath bargain (private-bath rooms from $105). It has an excellent restaurant with 'Scottish surprises.'

Hotel Harrington (☎ 202-628-8140), at 11th and E Sts NW, is a mid-range favorite, with basic singles/doubles with bath from $70/80. *Swiss Inn* (☎ 202-371-1816, 1204 Massachusetts Ave NW), in a modest brownstone downtown, charges $89/99 with kitchenettes. *Morrison-Clark Inn* (☎ 202-898-1200, 1015 L St NW) offers small rooms in an 1864 mansion ($145/165), with an elegant Southern dining room; it's in a bland area downtown.

George Washington University Inn (☎ 202-337-6620, 824 New Hampshire Ave NW), in a better location with good suites, costs $150. *Channel Inn* (☎ 202-554-2400, 650 Water St SW), away from the hubbub on the waterfront, has spacious modern rooms from $88/125 low/peak season. It's convenient for drivers.

Top End Washington's many top-end hotels start over $200, but prices drop summer and weekends.

Willard Inter-Continental (☎ 202-628-9100, 1401 Pennsylvania Ave NW) is a classic 1904 building with a colorful history. It houses the buzzing Round Robin Bar and the Nest Lounge jazz venue (rooms from $210 in summer).

CAPITAL REGION

Renaissance Mayflower Hotel (☎ 202-347-3000, 1127 Connecticut Ave NW) offers similar ambience in Dupont Circle.

Four Seasons Hotel (☎ 202-342-0444, 2800 Pennsylvania Ave NW), in Georgetown, is a deluxe modern hotel that is particularly family-friendly (but pricey – $270 minimum).

One of the world's most infamous hotels, *Swissôtel Watergate* (☎ 202-965-2300, 2650 Virginia Ave NW) has, among other things, hosted a famous 'plumbing' convention (it was here that Nixon aides broke in to spy on the Democrats). Rooms start at $150.

Washington DC also has exclusive hotels (priced above $300 a night), beyond the scope of most vacationers. *Loew's L'Enfant Plaza Hotel* (☎ 202-484-1000, 480 L'Enfant Plaza SW), above the eponymous Metro station, creeps into this category. It's a good place to bring children.

Places to Eat

Food is relatively expensive in DC; fortunately, many ethnic eateries serve hearty low-priced meals, including vegetarian options. Shopping at farmers' markets also minimizes expenses (see listings later in this section).

The Maine Ave SW *open-air seafood market* sells fresh seafood (crab cakes $5, seafood sandwiches from $3, fish platters $6). Some of the museums have inexpensive cafeterias for lunch, such as the *Hirshhorn's patio cafe* (summer only).

Capitol Hill On Capitol Hill, *Eastern Market*, on 7th St SE, has many food stalls selling inexpensive food. *Dubliner* (520 N Capitol St) is DC's premier Irish pub, serving classic corned beef and cabbage or potato soup ($4). *Kelley's Irish Times*, next door, is similar.

Armand's Chicago Pizzeria (226 Massachusetts Ave NE) offers Chicago-style pizzas from $7. *Neil's Deli* (208 Massachusetts Ave NE) has a good selection of sandwiches from $3.50.

Bullfeathers (410 1st St SE) has some inexpensive entrées for around $10. *Tortilla Coast* (400 1st St SE), next door, has spicy Tex-Mex dishes (burritos $8).

Cheaper still is Pennsylvania Ave from 2nd St SE over to Eastern Market; try *Burrito Brothers* (205 Pennsylvania Ave SE)

Fabulous Food Courts

Food courts in DC are attractive, lively places with a good selection of inexpensive food, but they're crowded weekdays.

At **Union Station**, look for the fabulous bargain food court downstairs, with two dozen fast-food vendors. Food courts at the **Old Post Office Pavilion and National Place** (in the Press Club Building at 14th and F Sts) offer an excellent variety of inexpensive choices; alternatively, follow office-worker throngs to bargain buffets and cafeterias in large government buildings. **L'Enfant Plaza Subway Mall** has subterranean delis and markets.

The Library of Congress' **Madison Building** has a 6th-floor cafeteria catered by different DC restaurants.

---

for Mexican, *Hawk & Dove* (329 Pennsylvania Ave SE) for Reuben sandwiches ($7), *Sherrill's Bakery* (233 Pennsylvania Ave SE) and *Chesapeake Bagel Bakery* (215 Pennsylvania Ave SE) for baked delights, and *Taverna* (307 Pennsylvania Ave SE) for tasty Greek dishes such as stuffed peppers ($8).

Farther down are *Anatolia's* (633 Pennsylvania Ave SE) for Turkish (excellent *kofte*), and *Bread & Chocolate* (666 Pennsylvania Ave SE) for breakfasts such as goulash in a bowl. *Las Placitas* (517 8th St SE) has *chiles rellenos* (cheese-stuffed chilies) and pitchers of delicious sangria.

White House Area & Downtown A cultural icon, *Sholl's Colonial Cafeteria* (1990 K St NW) sells regional rock-bottom cafeteria fare such as baked chicken and mashed potatoes. *Old Ebbitt Grill* (675 15th St NW), an American classic across from the White House, serves local grill favorites (entrées from $8) and weekend brunches.

Stoney's Bar & Grill (1307 L St NW), one of the few choices near the youth hostel, is a cozy dive for burgers ($6) or chicken and cornbread ($7.50). *Lindy's Bon Appetit* (2040 I St NW), in Foggy Bottom, has over 20 burgers to choose from (from $3). *World Gourmet Deli*, at 19th and F Sts NW, has Middle Eastern fare and good coffee.

CAPITAL REGION

Brasserie Les Halles (1201 Pennsylvania Ave NW) is a lively, casual place with reputedly the best *pommes frites* in town (and great crêpes). *Capital Q (707 H St NW)*, near Chinatown, gets raves for its inexpensive Texas barbecue, ribs, sausages and baked potatoes. *China Doll Gourmet (627 H St NW)* serves dim sum lunches (about $8). *Rupperts (1017 7th St NW)*, near Vernon Square, has dishes based on fresh market produce.

Dupont Circle Connecticut Ave NW on either side of Dupont Circle is the city's upscale restaurant district, with many cafes. *Afterwords (1517 Connecticut Ave NW)*, at Kramerbooks, is a good choice for meals, drinks or snacks from sunup to late night. *MCCXXIII (1223 Connecticut Ave NW)* is a hip 'place-to-be-seen' cafe with strict dress standards. *Julia's Empanadas*, next door, caters for the less well heeled (chilena empanadas $3).

The Burro (1621 Connecticut Ave NW) has hearty burritos and good frittatas ($3). *Mimi's American Bistro (2120 P St NW)*, an extremely chic theatrical bistro, serves delicious gourmet burgers for $7.

Quirky *Restaurant Nora (☎ 202-462-5143, 2132 Florida Ave NW)* specializes in New American cuisine, all of it certified organic with vegetarian and meat options (from $25; open dinner only Mon-Sat).

A power-center steakhouse, *The Palm (☎ 202-293-9091, 1225 19th St NW)* is great for people-watching and carving into a juicy sirloin (from $35; open lunch and dinner weekdays, dinner weekends).

Adams-Morgan & Shaw Choose from an international smorgasbord in DC's ethnic and bohemian restaurant district along 18th St NW, Adams-Morgan. *La Fourchette (2429 18th St NW)* gets many good reviews for its French bistro food; *I Matti (2436 18th St NW)* has excellent pizza; *Meskerem (2434 18th St NW)* serves classic Ethiopian fare; *Caravan Grill (1825 18th St NW)* is an inexpensive Persian place with great kabobs and cubed chicken; and *Canvas Tapas Cafe (1836 18th St NW)* is casual and comfortable, with good tapas and excellent wines.

Soul-food landmarks next to avant-garde cafes can be found in the emerging New U district in Shaw. Two cultural institutions are

Ben's Chili Bowl (1213 U St NW), at the U St Metro, and *Florida Avenue Grill (1100 Florida Ave NW)*, for Southern country cooking (tasty Cajun catfish), a short walk north.

U-topia (1418 U St NW) has an arty ambience and entrées from $9; it has a fun bar. The *18th & U Duplex Diner (2004 18th St NW)* is an upscale place, a great spot for burgers, desserts and cocktails; and *Jolt N' Bolt (1918 18th St NW)*, nearby, is a pleasant spot to sip coffee.

Georgetown Despite some wonderful choices lining this area's clogged arteries, M St and Wisconsin Ave NW, crowds and traffic make it an overrated restaurant district.

Booeymongers (3265 Prospect St NW) is a handy deli and sandwich shop (the 'Scheherazade' is a good value). *Ching Ching Cha (1063 Wisconsin Ave NW)* is the place for tea with a snack. *Heritage India (2400 Wisconsin Ave NW)* is a tad expensive but serves tandoori and other subcontinental delights. *Peacock Café (3251 Prospect St NW)*, a laid-back place, has contemporary American cuisine and hearty burgers and sandwiches. *DC Coast (☎ 202-216-5988, 1401 K St NW)* is a little pricey but simply worth it for its innovative fusion menu (eg, Thai calamari, Peking-style chicken with noodles).

Entertainment

The *Washington Post*'s 'Weekend' section and the free weekly *Washington City Paper* are useful for planning your time out. The Convention and Visitors Association issues a quarterly events calendar.

Conveniently located at the Old Post Office Pavilion, Ticketplace (☎ 202-842-5387, 1100 Pennsylvania Ave NW) sells same-day concert/show tickets at half price (cash only; closed Sun-Mon).

Performing Arts The *National Theater (☎ 202-628-6161, 1321 Pennsylvania Ave NW)* is Washington's oldest continuously operating theater (since 1835), though the *Shakespeare Theater (☎ 202-547-1122, 450 7th St NW)* is a more evocative venue. DC's theater district (such as it is) is east of Dupont Circle around 14th St, P and Q Sts NW.

CAPITAL REGION

The National Symphony and Washington Chamber Symphony perform at the *Kennedy Center* (see Foggy Bottom, earlier). The center is also currently home to the Washington Opera (W www.dc-opera.org), of which Placido Domingo is artistic director.

The symphony also performs summer concerts at *Wolf Trap Farm Park for the Performing Arts* (W www.wolftrap.org), a 40-minute drive away in Vienna, Virginia.

Live Music DC, birthplace of Duke Ellington (in Shaw), really excels in jazz and blues.

Blues Alley (☎ 202-337-4141, 1073 Rear Wisconsin Ave), in the alley south of M St, Georgetown, attracts well-known artists, but tickets are steep ($14-40). *Saloun* (3239 M St NW), nearby, is casual and much cheaper (blues Sat, live jazz other nights).

Cafe Lautrec (2431 18th St NW), in Adams-Morgan, features jazz and a tap-dancing bartender (on the bar). *City Blues* (☎ 202-232-2300, 2651 Connecticut Ave NW), in Woodley Park, is another popular jazz venue.

Another Adams-Morgan staple venue, *Madam's Organ* (☎ 202-667-5370, 2461 18th St NW) rocks out every day with nightly blues, bluegrass or jazz sessions. Redheaded women – natural or dyed – get half-price Rolling Rocks.

Chi-Cha Lounge (☎ 202-234-8400, 1624 U St NW), in Shaw, is Middle East comes to DC with Latin American fare and flair; enjoy jazz along with the low cushioned seats and hookahs ($15).

Metro Cafe (☎ 202-518-7900, 1522 14th St NW) is a 170-plus seat live venue, also in the U St precinct. The *9:30 Club* (☎ 202-265-0930, 815 V St NW) features alternative music (cover varies).

State of the Union (1357 U St NW) and *Black Cat* (1831 14th St) are other 'U' alternative music venues. *Kaffa House* (1212 U St NW) is a popular hip-hop club, but beer is expensive (cover on weekends). *New Vegas Lounge* (1415 P St NW) features blues Tuesday and Wednesday. *Chief Ike's Mambo Room* (1725 Columbia Rd NW), in Adams-Morgan, has mambo Monday, blues Thursday, and disco and hip-hop on weekends.

Bars & Clubs DC has great bars, many with live music. The greatest concentration is in Adams-Morgan; walk down 18th St NW between Florida Ave and Columbia Rd. Another good area is along Georgetown's M St between 29th and 33rd Sts NW.

Tune Inn (331 Pennsylvania Ave SE), on Capitol Hill, is a popular Southern-style pub that stays open late. *Fadó* (808 7th St NW) is an Irish pub in Chinatown that caters for sports fans visiting the MCI Center.

In Georgetown, *Billy Martin's Tavern* (1264 Wisconsin Ave NW) is a cozy, popular tavern with great prime rib, pasta and seafood. *Clyde's* (3236 M St NW) has been around longer than most care to remember. It lacks its old character, but its clientele have evolved upmarket with it.

Near the P St Bridge, *Brickskeller* (1523 22nd St NW) is an underground beer paradise with 1100 varieties from around the world.

In Dupont Circle, *Atomic Billiards* (3427 Connecticut Ave NW) is a good

---

Gay & Lesbian DC

DC is one of the most gay-friendly cities in the USA; more than 30 national gay and lesbian organizations are headquartered here. Additionally, there are about 300 miscellaneous support groups and nearly 40 bars catering predominantly to gay and lesbian clientele. Washington is often the scene of huge gay-rights marches, and gay pride is an integral part of DC's character.

Lambda Rising (1625 Connecticut Ave NW), in Dupont Circle, specializes in gay and lesbian titles. *La Cage aux Folles* (18 O St SE) is a happening dance club; *DC Eagle* (639 New York Ave NW), near Vernon Square, is 'leather and latex'; *Badlands* (1415 22nd St NW), at P St, is a popular, steamy club ($8); *Hung Jury* (1819 H St NW) is still the best-known lesbian bar in the city; and **JR's** (1519 17th St NW) is a friendly Dupont Circle gay bar.

For more information on the gay scene, check W www.gaybazaar.com or get the weekly *Washington Blade*.

place to 'bust 'em up'; dine here while you wait to play.

Spectator Sports The three-time NFL champion *Washington Redskins (☎ 301-276-6060)* play at Jack Kent Cooke stadium, east of DC in Maryland. Without a professional baseball team, locals tend to follow the Baltimore Orioles.

Robert F Kennedy Memorial Stadium (RFK; ☎ 202-547-9077) is home to the MLS *DC United (☎ 703-478-6600),* winners of the inaugural US soccer championship (1996). RFK is also home to the WUSA *Washington Freedom (☎ 202-547-3137)* women's soccer team, featuring Mia Hamm.

The Michael Jordan–run NBA *Washington Wizards* (formerly the Bullets), the WNBA *Washington Mystics,* the NHL *Washington Capitals* ice hockey team and the *Washington Power* lacrosse team all play at the downtown MCI Center megastadium (☎ 202-628-3200 for information, 202-432-7328 for tickets).

Shopping
Georgetown is the principal shopping district. Souvenirs can be bought at museum gift stores and vendors at the Mall. Keen shoppers head to Potomac Mills (☎ 703-643-1770), 12 miles south of the Beltway in Prince William, Virginia, to wade through its 220 discount stores. (Also see Williamsburg, Virginia, later in this chapter.)

Getting There & Away
For air connections, see Getting There & Around, earlier in this chapter.

Bus The Greyhound (☎ 800-231-2222) station is at 1005 1st St NE; Peter Pan Trailways (☎ 800-343-9999) buses stop opposite. Take a cab through this rough neighborhood to the nearest Metro station (Ⓜ Union Station), eight blocks away.

Sample one-way coach fares and travel times from Washington, DC, include the following:

Baltimore, Maryland – $10; 1 hour
Richmond, Virginia – $19; 2¼ hours
Wilmington, Delaware – $19; 3 hours
Philadelphia, Pennsylvania – $20; 3½ hours
New York – $40; 4½ hours
Charleston, West Virginia – $56; 10 hours

Train Passenger trains arrive at Union Station (☎ 202-371-9441), which connects directly to DC's Metro. Weekday MARC commuter trains (☎ 800-325-7245) run to many regional cities, including Baltimore and Harpers Ferry, West Virginia.

Amtrak services to and around the region include the *Metroliner* express service between DC and New York City; the *Cardinal* and *Capitol Limited* between DC and Chicago; the *Carolinian,* which stops in Baltimore, DC and Richmond; and *Crescent,* from New York to New Orleans with stops in DC and Charlottesville, Virginia. Sample one-way fares (which vary widely) and times from DC are as follows:

Baltimore – $22; 40 minutes
Harpers Ferry, West Virginia – $12; 1¼ hours
Richmond – $32; 2 hours
Charlottesville, Virginia – $44; 2½ hours
Philadelphia – $63; 3 hours
New York – $68; 3½ hours

Getting Around
SuperShuttle (☎ 800-258-3826) runs door-to-door van service between all three airports and downtown DC. Fares are $10 to Reagan National, $22 to Dulles and $28 to BWI (return fares vary by destination). Washington Flyer (☎ 888-927-4359) has a handy service from Dulles to West Falls Church, Virginia ($8), connecting to the Metro. Their bus service from Dulles to National Airport or downtown DC is $16/26 one way/roundtrip.

Amtrak and regional MARC commuter trains run between DC's Union Station and a rail terminal near BWI ($5/9 one way/roundtrip; a 10-minute free shuttle is provided to BWI proper).

Metrorail ('Metro'; ☎ 202-637-7000) runs to most sights, hotel and business districts, and to the Maryland and Virginia suburbs. Trains operate 5:30am-midnight weekdays, 8am-1am weekends. Machines inside stations sell computerized fare cards; fares (from $1.10) depend on distance traveled and time of day. All-day excursion passes cost $5. Metrobus (☎ 202-637-7000) operates buses throughout the city and suburbs (from $1.10). The L2, along 18th St through Adams-Morgan (connecting to Woodley Park and Foggy Bottom Metro stations) and the D5, from Union Station to Georgetown's central M St strip, are handy routes.

Drivers beware: Middle lanes of some streets change direction during rush hour. Street parking is often scarce, especially around Georgetown and the Mall. Most national car rental agencies in DC won't rent to those under 25. Taxis are plentiful in the central city and relatively inexpensive. Try Diamond (☎ 202-387-6200), Yellow Cab (☎ 202-544-1212) or Capitol (☎ 202-546-2400).

AROUND WASHINGTON, DC

Washington's suburbs sprawl into neighboring Maryland and Virginia. Some of the capital's most popular sights are in northern Virginia, but they are usually visited as excursions from DC.

A key attraction for kids is **Six Flags America**. This theme park (☎ 301-249-1500), east of Largo, Maryland, has huge roller coasters, including the Wild One and Batwing, and other diversions. It's open daily ($35/17.50 adults/kids).

For more on Maryland and Virginia, see those sections later in this chapter.

Arlington

Arlington, just across the Potomac River from the heart of DC, has several attractions. The Arlington Convention & Visitors Service (☎ 800-296-7996) is at 2100 Clarendon Ave. Chain accommodations in Arlington, close to DC, are less expensive than the capital. The suburb is easily reached from DC via several bridges, traffic permitting, or by Metro.

Arlington National Cemetery Just across the Potomac in Virginia, the 612-acre national cemetery (☎ 703-692-0931) is the burial ground for over 225,000 military personnel and their dependents, with veterans from every US war since the Revolution (open 8am-5pm, 8am-7pm in summer; Ⓜ Arlington Cemetery). Tourmobiles (☎ 202-554-5100, 888-868-7707) are a handy way to visit the cemetery's notable memorials; trams leave every 15 minutes from the visitor center.

Robert E Lee's 1100-acre property, and his home, **Arlington House**, were confiscated when Lee left to command northern Virginia's army. Union soldiers were buried around the house so he could never use it again. After the Civil War, the site became the national cemetery, and now the house is open to the public. The **Tomb of the Unknowns** represents unknown soldiers killed in action; military guards retain a round-the-clock vigil. One of Arlington's most impressive sights is the ritual changing of the guard (every hour or half hour). Arlington's newest sight is a memorial to women in military service, at the main gate. Don't miss the famous Iwo Jima monument nearby, depicting marines raising the Stars and Stripes. An eternal flame marks the **grave of John F Kennedy**, next to those of Jacqueline Kennedy Onassis and two of her infant children. The grave of Robert Kennedy is marked with a cross nearby.

Pentagon Home of the US Department of Defense, the Pentagon (☎ 703-695-1776; Ⓜ Pentagon) is reputedly the world's largest office building. In September of 2001, part of the building was destroyed by a Boeing 767 during the same attack that leveled the World Trade Center (see New York & the Mid-Atlantic States). Whether or not tours of the building will resume is unclear.

Newseum This museum (☎ 703-284-3544, Ⓦ www.newseum.org, 1101 Wilson Blvd) celebrates the 'Fourth Estate' with masses of press exhibits, including a TV news studio, historical press clips, and a monument to war correspondents killed in

---

WWWhere Did It Begin?

The idea of connecting computers together, the precursor to the modern Web, started off in Arlington, Virginia. Sometime in the late 1960s the US Advanced Research Projects Agency (ARPA), a think tank with heaps of government funds, came up with the idea of linking scientists in remote locations together. The brainpower of several universities throughout the country was eventually utilized to develop the TCP/IP protocol (Transmission Control Protocol/Internetworking Protocol) – the means by which the computers 'talked' to each other.

CAPITAL REGION

action (free admission; closed Mon-Tue; Ⓜ Rosslyn).

Places to Stay & Eat While often a day trip for DC visitors, Arlington offers plenty of modern chain motels at interstate exits.

Econo Lodge Metro Arlington (☎ 800-638-0006), off I-66, is from $65-89. *Inns of Virginia* (☎ 800-677-4797, 3335 Lee Hwy) has comfortable rooms from $65.

There's a gulch of inexpensive ethnic restaurants within walking distance of the Clarendon Metro. *Saigon Crystal (536 S 23rd St)*, at Jefferson Davis Hwy, is typical of many good Vietnamese eateries in the DC region.

Alexandria

Along with Georgetown, Alexandria preceded the founding of the nation's capital. As in Georgetown, walkable blocks of attractive brick row houses in the historic district find modern uses as restaurants, taverns and shops. The visitor bureau (☎ 800-387-9119, 221 King St) issues discount tickets to historic sights and free parking permits (know your license-plate number).

The **Torpedo Factory Art Center** (☎ 703-838-4565) heads up the waterfront and displays the work of local artists. At **Alexandria Archaeology** (☎ 703-838-4399), also in the converted WWI torpedo plant, archaeologists clean and catalog artifacts from local urban digs ($3; closed Mon). **The Lyceum** (☎ 703-838-4994, 201 S Washington St) relates Alexandria's history (free admission).

Northwest of town, **Fort Ward Museum & Historic Site** (☎ 703-838-4848, 4301 W Braddock Rd) preserves one of the largest of the 162 Civil War fortifications known as the 'Defenses of Washington' (free admission; closed Mon).

Warehouse Bar & Grill (214 King St), across from the visitor center, has simply superb seafood meals, featuring both Cajun and traditional cuisine.

DC's Metro and Amtrak service the King St station; local buses cover the mile to the visitor center.

Mt Vernon & Around

One of the most visited historic sites in the nation, George Washington's country

The original George W

estate of **Mt Vernon** (☎ 703-780-2000, Ⓦ www.mountvernon.org) has been meticulously restored and affords a glimpse of 18th-century farm life and of the first president as a country squire. Beautifully situated on the banks of the Potomac in Virginia, the estate holds a 19-room country house, immaculate gardens, slaves' quarters, a working farm and Washington's tomb.

The Washingtons lived here from 1759 to 1775, when George assumed command of the Continental Army. After the Revolutionary War and eight years as president, he retired to Mt Vernon, living here from 1797 until his death two years later ($9; open 8am-5pm daily Apr-Aug, 9am-4pm otherwise).

Mount Vernon Inn (☎ 703-780-0011), at the main gate, is a casual place serving hearty colonial fare (turkey pie for $6); there's an adjacent *snack bar*.

Mt Vernon is only 16 miles south of DC by road; you can take the Metro to Huntington, then bus No 11P to the estate.

Gunston Hall Six miles south of Mt Vernon off Route 1, Gunston Hall (☎ 703-550-9220), opens the elegant 1755 home and formal gardens of George Mason, one of the principal framers of the Constitution and the Virginia Declaration of Rights, upon which the US Bill of Rights is based ($5).

Woodlawn Plantation The centerpiece of this plantation (☎ 703-780-4000), 3 miles west of Mt Vernon, is the 19th-century plantation home Woodlawn, with its rose garden ($6). The nearby **Pope-Leighey House**, designed by Frank Lloyd Wright, was built in the 1940s. It was relocated here from Falls Church in 1964 to save it from demolition (daily guided tours $6; closed Jan-Feb).

Virginia

Travelers to Virginia will be overwhelmed by the state's rich historic past. The Revolutionary period is nowhere better represented than in the 'historic triangle' of Williamsburg, Jamestown and Yorktown, and the James River plantations. The bulk of the Civil War battles were fought on Virginian soil, and reminders of that cataclysm are everywhere. Jefferson, Washington, and many other founders of the nation also had long associations with Virginia – the 'mother of presidents.'

Virginia is more than a vast museum, and there is much scope for outdoor activities, especially in the rugged Blue Ridge Mountains and Shenandoah National Park, and along the coastline of Chesapeake Bay and the Eastern Shore.

History

In 1607 Jamestown Island became the site of the first permanent English settlement in Virginia. The settlement was short-lived, however, as the original 100 colonists were mostly gentry, hoping for easy profit, along with their personal servants, and they lacked the skills necessary for self-sufficiency in the New World. Two-thirds perished in the first year alone; between 1607 and 1625, 8500 settlers arrived but only 1200 survived.

Virginia grew on the tobacco trade under the strong governorship of Sir William Berkeley, who administered the colony from 1642. A slaveholding planter elite came to control most of the land and the colony's government. Expansionism led to conflict with the Native Americans, and Nathaniel Bacon's ragtag army took them on, then turned on the colonial elite in an abortive rebellion that destroyed much of Jamestown.

In 1699 the colony's capital moved to nearby Williamsburg, where stately public

---

Virginia

Nicknames: The Old Dominion State, Mother of Presidents

Population: 7,078,500 (12th)

Area: 42,777 sq miles (35th)

Admitted to Union: June 25, 1788 (10th); seceded April 1861; readmitted January 1870

Capital city: Richmond (population 207,000)

Other cities: Virginia Beach (435,000), Norfolk (263,500)

State motto: Thus Always to Tyrants

Birthplace of: Presidents George Washington (1732–99, first), Thomas Jefferson (1743–1826, third), James Madison (1751–1836, fourth), James Monroe (1758–1831, fifth), William Henry Harrison (1773–1841, ninth), John Tyler (1790–1862, 10th), Zachary Taylor (1784–1850, 12th) and Woodrow Wilson (1856–1924, 28th); Booker T Washington (1856–1915); Pocahontas (c. 1596–1617); Robert E Lee (1807–70); Ella Fitzgerald (1917–96); Bill Robinson (1878–1949, 'Mr Bojangles'); Arthur Ashe (1943–92)

Famous for: Presidents, ham, Southern aristocracy, battlefields

---

buildings echoed the English style (300 years later, the restored town is a big tourist attraction). Nearby at Yorktown, George Washington's 1781 victory over the British effectively brought an end to the Revolutionary War.

Despite high-sounding ideals about all men being created free and equal, the great contribution of Virginia to the new American nation was the 'Virginia Plan,' which provided a bicameral national legislature to balance the powers of a central government with the rights of individual states to manage their own affairs. Under this system the Union held together, 'half slave and half free,' for nearly 100 years, but fundamental differences between the North and South grew to be too great. In 1861 Virginia seceded from the Union.

During the Civil War, the brilliant general Robert E Lee of Arlington was offered command of the Northern armies, yet he elected to lead opposing Virginia's forces instead. The sense of defending a homeland gave Southern troops a grim determination but made their ultimate defeat more bitter, especially in Virginia, where so many battles were fought and so much damage suffered. After Emancipation the black population remained poor and disenfranchised, and many left for northern industrial cities. Others headed west.

Industrial growth – railways, ports and shipbuilding – revitalized the economy, along with expansion of the national capital and WWII naval and military bases. As in most Southern states, civil rights for blacks and school desegregation were a long time coming, but in 1989 Virginia elected the first black governor in the country. In 1997 the Virginia legislature voted to retire the state anthem, 'Carry Me Back to Old Virginia,' after critics charged it glorified slavery.

Virginia's colonial and plantation past is now a nostalgic memory, revived as the basis for a tourist industry that threatens to turn many parts of the state into a theme park of US history. Nevertheless, Virginia's many incomparable historical sites make an enduring impression.

Information

Virginia's Division of Tourism (☎ 800-321-3244, ☒ www.virginia.org, 901 E Byrd St, Richmond, VA 23219) produces a comprehensive state guide. There are 10 'welcome centers' throughout the state on the interstates. State sales tax is 4.5%.

NORTHERN VIRGINIA

Across the Potomac from Washington, many of northern Virginia's sights are so closely linked with the nation's capital that they're covered in the earlier Around Washington, DC section. Rural retreats provide weekend refuge for stressed-out Washingtonians.

Great Falls National Park

The Potomac crashes downstream in a spectacular series of rapids and falls 12 miles upriver from DC. On Virginia's side, this excellent park (☎ 703-285-2966), off Hwy 193, offers overlooks and trails ($4/2 per vehicle/cyclist).

Manassas Battlefield

South of where Dulles airport now stands, major Civil War battles known collectively as the Battles of Bull Run (by the North) or Battles of Manassas (by the South) were fought in July 1861 and August 1862. The Manassas National Battlefield Park visitor center (☎ 703-361-1339) is the start of a good self-guided tour ($2).

Horse Country

West of Dulles airport, Horse Country, in Fauquier and Loudoun Counties, is laced with many scenic drives past grand country estates, thoroughbred pasturelands and tiny historic villages.

Red Fox Inn (☎ 540-687-6301, 2 E Washington St), an elegant historic inn in the lovely town of Middleburg, attracts weekenders (from $150).

Leesburg

This charming town, at the Maryland border, retains many colonial-era buildings. The tourist office (☎ 703-777-2420, 108-D South St) is inside Market Station.

HI Bears Den (☎ 540-554-8708), on the Appalachian Trail at Bluemont (west of Leesburg), has dorm bunks ($12/14 members/nonmembers). *Laurel Brigade Inn (☎ 703-777-1010, 20 W Market St)*, in the historic district, offers colonial fare and the least expensive B&B rooms in town (from $70).

Fredericksburg

On the Rappahannock River, Fredericksburg prides itself on its illustrious history. Captain John Smith visited the site as early as 1608, George Washington grew up here, and James Monroe practiced law here. During the Civil War, many bloody battles were fought in the area.

Today the attractive 40-block historic district is fun to stroll through, taking in museums, shops, restaurants and B&Bs – an inviting weekend retreat, easily accessible by rail. The visitor center (☎ 800-678-4748, ☒ www.fredericksburgva.com, 706 Caroline St) offers parking passes and 'hospitality passes' for seven local sights ($20; 'pickfour' $14).

The **Fredericksburg Area Museum** (☎ 540-371-3037, 907 Princess St), in the 1816 town hall, covers local history ($4).

The **James Monroe Museum** (☎ 540-654-1043, 908 Charles St) honors the native son and author of the Monroe Doctrine ($4).

Mary Washington House (☎ 540-373-1569, 1200 Charles St) was the home of George Washington's mother for her last 17 years ($4).

Rising Sun Tavern (☎ 540-371-1494, 1304 Caroline St), once patronized by the town's luminaries, is now a museum, as is the nearby **Hugh Mercer Apothecary Shop** (☎ 540-373-3362). Admission is $4 for each.

The **Fredericksburg & Spotsylvania National Battlefield Parks**, maintained by the National Park Service, preserve the sites of some of the Civil War's bloodiest battles. The main visitor center (☎ 540-373-6122, 1013 Lafayette Blvd) offers informative exhibits, 75-mile driving-tour maps and week passes ($3). **Chatham Manor** (☎ 540-373-4461), across the river, is included in the NPS pass.

The *Fredericksburg DC South KOA (☎ 540-898-7252)*, off I-95 and 12 miles south in Massaponax, is open year round (sites from $25 for two).

Many budget motels are clustered at I-95 exits west of Fredericksburg. *Fredericksburg Colonial Inn (☎ 540-371-5666, 1707 Princess Anne St)* has 32-rooms exuding antebellum atmosphere (from $65 double). *Richard Johnston Inn (☎ 540-899-7606, 711 Caroline St)* is another of several historic-district B&Bs (from $95-145).

Goolrick's (901 Caroline St), the oldest continually operating soda fountain in the US, serves inexpensive lunches and milkshakes. *Virginia Deli (101 William St)* is another inexpensive alternative for breakfast and lunch (Brunswick stew $2.50).

Several daily Amtrak trains operate between DC and the train station on Caroline St. Weekday commuter trains (☎ 800-742-3873, Ⓦ www.vre.org) are cheaper ($6.70).

The Greyhound/Trailways depot (☎ 540-373-2103) is at 1400 Jefferson Davis Hwy.

Northern Neck & Middle Peninsula

The Northern 'Neck' peninsula extends east from Fredericksburg. Off its tip is **Tangier Island**, an isolated fishing community that retains it own unique dialect. Tangier & Chesapeake Cruises (☎ 804-453-2628) makes the six-hour roundtrip to the island daily ($20; May-Oct). Overnight lodging is available on the island or at B&Bs in Reedsville.

The **George Washington Birthplace National Monument** (☎ 804-224-1732) is along the way to the tip of the Northern Neck at Pope's Creek Plantation ($2). **Stratford Hall Plantation** (☎ 804-493-8038), to the east, is the birthplace of Robert E Lee. The impressive mansion is open for tours ($7); its log cabin *restaurant* serves Southern lunches from $10.

On the Middle Peninsula, outside West Point, the 100-member, 125-acre Mattaponi Indian Reservation offers a **tribal museum** (☎ 804-769-2194) that is open 2pm-5pm weekends in summer. In 1997 the Mattaponi successfully defended their opposition to a local reservoir project by citing their 1677 treaty with the British to retain a buffer zone surrounding their community.

Historic waterfront **Urbanna** offers several restaurants and places to stay. *HI Sangraal-by-the-Sea (☎ 804-776-6500)* is the nearest budget option to Williamsburg ($15/17 members/nonmembers). Call for directions.

RICHMOND

Richmond was the linchpin of the Confederacy during the Civil War, and many of its historic sites relate to that time of division. Today it still exudes an air of the antebellum Old South, with wide tree-lined boulevards, gracious houses and restaurants offering home-style Southern cooking.

The diminutive outpost of Richmond was founded in 1637 at the fall line of the James River. The town became Virginia's capital in 1779. During the Revolutionary War, British troops attacked Richmond three times. During the Civil War, Richmond was named the Confederate capital (1861–65), and again the city became a military target: In 1862 federal troops were repulsed in the Seven Days Battles. At war's end in April 1865, Richmond was evacuated, and fires destroyed much of the old city.

By the 1890s, iron and tobacco had revived the city's fortunes. Today Richmond is a pleasant city of monuments and state museums, and it even boasts a white-water run through town.

RICHMOND

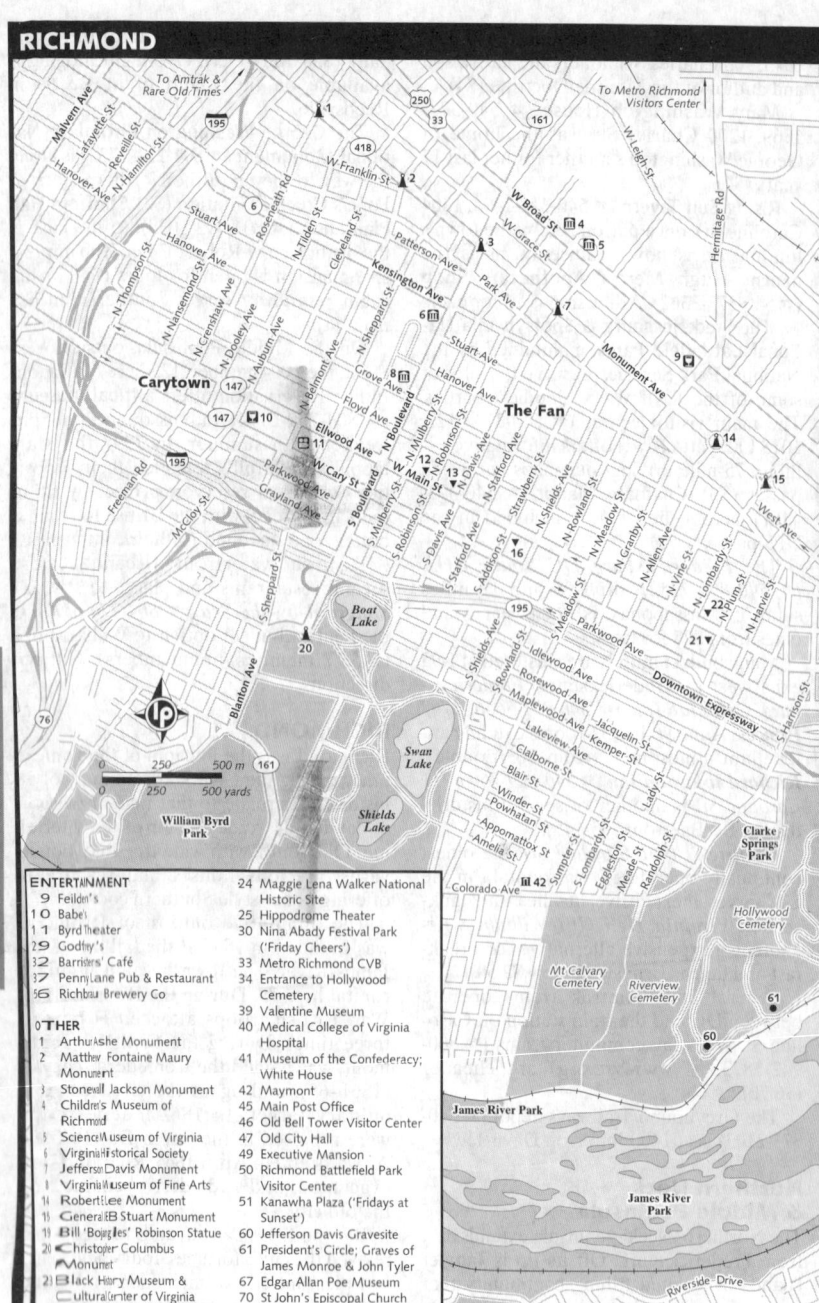

RICHMOND

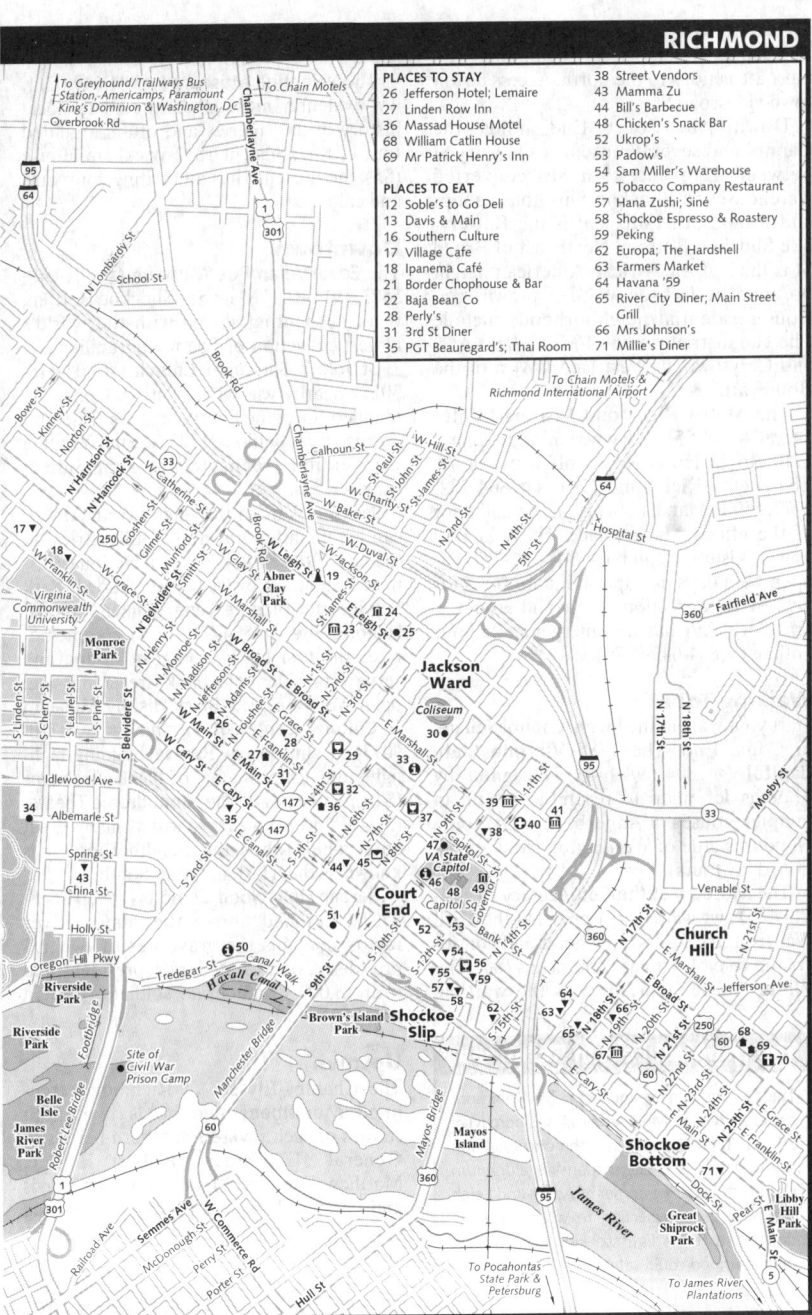

PLACES TO STAY
26 Jefferson Hotel; Lemaire
27 Linden Row Inn
36 Massad House Motel
68 William Catlin House
69 Mr Patrick Henry's Inn

PLACES TO EAT
12 Soble's to Go Deli
13 Davis & Main
16 Southern Culture
17 Village Cafe
18 Ipanema Café
21 Border Chophouse & Bar
22 Baja Bean Co
29 Perly's
31 3rd St Diner
35 PGT Beauregard's; Thai Room

38 Street Vendors
43 Mamma Zu
44 Bill's Barbecue
48 Chicken's Snack Bar
52 Ukrop's
53 Padow's
54 Sam Miller's Warehouse
55 Tobacco Company Restaurant
57 Hana Zushi; Siné
58 Shockoe Espresso & Roastery
59 Peking
62 Europa; The Hardshell
63 Farmers Market
64 Havana '59
65 River City Diner; Main Street Grill
66 Mrs Johnson's
71 Millie's Diner

CAPITAL REGION

Orientation & Information

The James River bisects Richmond, with most attractions to the north. Access downtown via Broad St.

Downtown, Court End holds the Capitol and several museums. On Cary St between 12th and 15th Sts, converted warehouses in Shockoe Slip house shops and restaurants. Adjacent is the Bowery-like Shockoe Bottom. Northeast of Broad St is the historic African American neighborhood of Jackson Ward. Uptown, gracious residential neighborhoods include The Fan district, south of Monument Ave, and Carytown, in West End ('West of the Boulevard').

The Metro Richmond Visitors Center (☎ 804-358-5511, www.richmondva.org, 1710 Robin Hood Rd) is off I-95 exit 78. The Metro Richmond CVB (☎ 804-782-2777, 550 E Marshall St) is on the 2nd floor of the 6th St Marketplace. The Old Bell Tower Visitor Center (☎ 804-782-2777) is open weekdays in Capitol Square (pass for 'five of 15' attractions $15, valid 30 days). Traveler's Aid has an emergency 24-hour hotline (☎ 804-643-0279).

Walking Tour

Start your walk at the lovely **Capitol Square**, in Court End. The 1785 **Virginia State Capitol** (☎ 804-698-1788), designed by Thomas Jefferson to resemble a Roman temple, houses a superb Jean Antoine Houdon statue of Washington (free admission; daily tours).

The **Museum of the Confederacy** (☎ 804-649-1861, www.moc.org) presents the Civil War from the losers' viewpoint and considers the role of African Americans ($6). The **White House**, adjacent, was the wartime

The Happiest Feet in Richmond

The famous dancer and actor Bill Robinson, better known as 'Mr Bojangles,' was born May 25, 1878, on N 3rd St in Richmond's Jackson Ward. There is a larger-than-life aluminum statue of him at the corner of Adam and Leigh Sts, near the intersection to which he once donated a traffic light so kids from his old neighborhood could safely cross the street.

residence of Confederate president Jefferson Davis ($7; combo pass to both $9).

The **Valentine Museum** (☎ 804-649-0711, www.valentinemuseum.com) explains local history in its galleries and offers a guided tour of the adjacent 1812 Wickham House ($5); the museum has an inviting courtyard and cafe.

Downtown

The **Edgar Allan Poe Museum** (☎ 804-648-5523, 1914–16 E Main St), Shockoe Bottom, is an enchanting shrine with the world's largest collection of Poe memorabilia ($6).

St John's Episcopal Church (☎ 804-648-5015), nearby, was where Patrick Henry demanded, 'Give me liberty or give me death!' during the rebellious 1775 Second Virginia Convention (reenacted at 2pm Sun in summer; $3).

Jackson Ward, a thriving African American community known as 'Little Africa' in the late 19th century, is now a National Historic Landmark district. The National Park Service–run **Maggie Lena Walker National Historic Site** (☎ 804-771-2017) commemorates the first black woman to found and serve as president of a bank (free admission; open Wed-Sun). The **Black History Museum & Cultural Center of Virginia** (☎ 804-780-9093), in a fine Greek Revival building, highlights the achievements of black Virginians ($4; open Tue-Sat). The **Hippodrome Theater** (528 N 2nd St), nearby, hosted many great entertainers when this neighborhood was known as the 'Harlem of the South.'

Serene **Hollywood Cemetery** (☎ 804-648-8501), perched above the James River rapids, contains the gravesites of two US presidents, one Confederate president and over 18,000 Confederate soldiers (printed guide $1).

Uptown

The Champs-Elysées of Richmond, tree-lined **Monument Ave** holds mammoth statues of such revered Southern heroes as General JEB Stuart, Robert E Lee, Matthew Fontaine Maury, Jefferson Davis and 'Stonewall' Jackson along a mile-long stretch east of I-95. A statue of tennis star Arthur Ashe was added in 1996 after much controversy.

The **Virginia Museum of Fine Arts** (☎ 804-367-0844, W www.vmfa.state.va.us)

displays its superb collection of European works (Monet, Goya, Picasso), sacred Himalayan art and the largest Fabergé egg collection on display outside Russia (free admission; closed Mon). The museum also has a sculpture garden and cafe.

The **Virginia Historical Society** museum (☎ 804-358-4901), next door, offers an excellent, aristocratic introduction to state history and Southern heritage, with many treasured artifacts ($4).

The **Science Museum of Virginia** (☎ 804-367-0000, W www.smv.org), in the gargantuan 1919 Broad St Station, holds three floors of entertaining hands-on exhibits covering aerospace, architecture, astronomy, chemistry, computers, electricity and more ($5). The **Children's Museum of Richmond** (☎ 804-474-2667) is adjacent ($5).

In the West End, **Maymont** (☎ 804-358-7166, 1700 Hampton St) offers a historic house tour, Japanese and Italian gardens, and children's farm within a 100-acre park on the north bank of the James River (free admission).

Canal Walk

The 1¼-mile Canal Walk along the James River is an ambitious redevelopment along the waterfront. There are many points of interest along the walk, and the city's history is carefully highlighted.

The Tredegar Iron Works houses the Richmond Battlefield Park Visitor Center (☎ 804-226-1981), at 5th and Tredegar Sts.

Activities

The James River boasts one of the country's only 'urban' white-water rapids (up to Class V), running through the heart of downtown Richmond. Richmond Raft Co (☎ 800-540-7238) runs raft trips from $32.

For hiking, the surrounding battlefield parks have miles of historic trails.

Organized Tours

The Historic Richmond Foundation (☎ 804-780-0107) organizes half-day bus and walking tours ($16).

Places to Stay

The *Pocahontas State Park* (☎ 804-796-4255, 10300 Beach Rd), 10 miles south on I-95 exit 61, is the closest campground ($11; no hookups). *Americamps* (☎ 804-798-5298,

11322 Air Park Rd), 20 minutes north of town off I-95 at exit 89, has a pool and year-round tent/RV sites from $18.50/23 for two. There are several modern chains on Williamsburg Rd near the airport (off I-64 exit 31B), the Midlothian Turnpike/Hwy 60 south of the river, and Chamberlayne Rd (off I-95) in the north.

Massad House Motel (☎ 804-648-2893, *11 N 4th St)*, downtown, charges $40/46 for spacious singles/doubles year round. *Linden Row Inn* (☎ 804-783-7000, *100 E Franklin St)*, downtown, occupies antebellum row houses set around a balcony-lined courtyard (from $100). *Jefferson Hotel* (☎ 804-788-8000, *101 W Franklin St)*, a grand old building, is the city's premier historic hotel (from $120 weekdays, rising considerably on weekends). Sunday brunch is served in The Rotunda. *William Catlin House* (☎ 804-780-3746, *2304 E Broad St)*, a B&B in Church Hill, charges from $85/95. *Mr Patrick Henry's Inn* (☎ 804-644-1322, *2300 E Broad St)*, nearby, is similar.

Places to Eat

Downtown There are *street vendors* along 10th St, some operated by popular Richmond restaurants. *Ukrop's*, at 10th and Main Sts, is a Richmond grocery chain with a great reputation for takeout. *Padow's (1110 E Main St)* is equally good for a snack.

3rd St Diner (218 E Main St) has breakfast specials, root beer floats and a laid-back bohemian crowd (open 24 hours). *Perly's (111 E Grace St)*, around the corner, is a more mainstream local favorite, with breakfasts from $1.75 and lunches from $5. *Bill's Barbecue (700 E Main St)* serves great pulled pork 'cue,' a local favorite.

Thai Room (103 E Cary St), upstairs at *PGT Beauregard's*, offers upscale Thai cuisine; at PGT's itself expect good ol' Southern fare.

Lemaire, at the Jefferson Hotel (see Places to Stay), is top-notch and fastidious about dress codes; it features Virginia-inspired dishes.

In the basement of the Capitol is *Chicken's Snack Bar*, known for limeade.

Shockoe Bottom & Church Hill Good restaurants can be found close to the *farmers' market* at 17th and Main Sts, including *Havana '59 (16 N 17th St)*, with advanced American diner meals (and palls of cigar smoke at night); *Main Street Grill (1700 E Main St),* for vegetarian; *River City Diner (1712 E Main St),* for hunger-busting burgers; *Millie's Diner (2603 E Main St),* for 'fusion' cuisine and yummy desserts; and *Mrs Johnson's (1802 E Franklin St),* a no-frills breakfast and lunch place specializing in 'down home cooking' (closed Sun).

Shockoe Slip Along E Cary St you'll find several great eateries. *Tobacco Company Restaurant (1201 E Cary St)* is a glam place with contemporary cuisine. *Hana Zushi (1309 E Cary St)* has inexpensive Japanese takeaway *bento* (lunch boxes), sushi and sashimi plates. *Sam Miller's Warehouse (1210 E Cary St),* here for over 20 years, is still popular for steaks and seafood. *Europa (1409 E Cary St)* is a trendy Mediterranean place. *The Hardshell (1411 E Cary St)* is a seafood place where you can get 'bottom feeders.' *Peking (1302 E Cary St)* serves inexpensive Chinese. *Shockoe Espresso & Roastery (104 Shockoe Slip)* is a quaint, reliable coffeehouse.

The Fan Along W Main St there is plenty to choose. *Border Chophouse & Bar (1501 W Main St)* has an eclectic menu (lunches from $6, dinner from $7.50). *Davis & Main (2501 W Main St)* is a grill that offers grilled vegetable sides. *Baja Bean Co (1520 W Main St)* has California-style meals in a cantina setting. *Southern Culture (2229 W Main St)* is still popular, with an eclectic menu (Cajun, Caribbean, Tex-Mex) and lively atmosphere. *Soble's to Go Deli (2600 W Main St)* has a well-stocked raw bar.

Ipanema Café (917 W Grace St), near Virginia Commonwealth University, is a great lunch spot with inexpensive entrées. *Village Cafe (1001 W Grace St),* nearby, is a funky little eatery serving cheese boards, among other things. It's been referred to as 'a counter with a culture behind it.' *Mamma Zu (501 S Pine St)* exudes the distinctive odor of garlic, but this Italian family business offers excellent meals and tasty desserts.

Entertainment

The free publication *Style Weekly* covers Richmond entertainment. At Nina Abady Festival Park, Kanawha Plaza and 14th St, free concerts are held Wednesday and Friday starting at dusk. A useful Web site is W www.shotfaces.com.

Rare Old Times (10602 Patterson Ave), in the city's north, is a bouncing Irish pub (live music Thurs). *Siné (1327 E Cary St),* in Shockoe Slip, is an Irish pub with an upmarket feel and good selection of beers. *Richbrau Brewing Co (1214 E Cary St)* has boutique ales, including raspberry and blackberry flavors.

Penny Lane Pub & Restaurant (207 N 7th St), in the business district, serves inexpensive English fare; it's Liverpool in the South. *Barristers' Café (101 N 5th St),* in the Hotel John Marshall, features jazz and blues.

Feilden's (2033 W Broad St) and *Babe's (3166 W Cary St)* are well-known gay clubs. There is a circle of gay bars along Grace St, affectionately known as the 'fruit loop,' including *Godfrey's (308 E Grace St).* For more on the gay/lesbian scene, see W www.gayrichmond.com.

At the fabulous old *Byrd Theater* (☎ 804-353-9911, 2908 W Cary St), Wurlitzer organ concerts precede movies ($2/1 weekdays/weekends).

Getting There & Around

The Greyhound/Trailways bus terminal (☎ 804-254-5938) is at 2910 N Blvd. Greater Richmond Transit Company (GRTC; ☎ 804-358-4782) runs local buses ($1.25 base fare, exact change only). Amtrak (☎ 800-872-7245) stops off way north of town at 7519 Staples Mill Rd. The local GRTC bus No 27 runs to/from downtown; cab fare is about $15.

AROUND RICHMOND

The many Civil War battlefields relating to the battles for Richmond are the main attractions in this area, but there are several other points of interest.

Paramount King's Dominion

This theme park (☎ 804-876-5000, W www .kingsdominion.com), 22 miles north of Richmond on I-95 (Doswell exit), includes roller-coaster rides, simulated white-water rafting, KidZville, and music and dance reviews ($36/26 adults/kids under 6).

Petersburg

At a vital junction on the Appomattox River, Petersburg fell to the British in 1781 and saw the Civil War's last great battle in April 1865. Old Towne Visitors Center (☎ 804-733-2400, 425 Cockade Alley) sells block tickets for city-run sites (all five $11, 'pick-three' $7).

The **Siege Museum** poignantly relates the plight of civilians during the 10-month siege of 1864–65. **Blandford Church**, a Confederate memorial with Tiffany windows, is also home to a cemetery that inspired the first Memorial Day.

Petersburg National Battlefield is site of the siege and the huge crater ($5). The visitor center (☎ 804-732-3531), off Route 36 via I-95 exit 52, features daily living-history programs in summer.

Budget *chain motels* are found off I-95 at exit 52/50D. The landmark *Virginia Diner* *(☎ 804-899-3106)*, 22 miles southeast in Wakefield, serves home-style Southern meals in the 'peanut capital of the world'; take I-95's Route 460 exit.

Pamplin Historical Park
The **Museum of the Civil War Soldier** (☎ 804-861-2408, W www.pamplinpark.org), southwest of Petersburg, is part of this developing historical park. The museum has an exceptional audio tour illustrating the privations faced by soldiers on both sides of the conflict ($10).

HISTORIC TRIANGLE
Set on the peninsula between the York and James Rivers, colonial Williamsburg, Jamestown and Yorktown constitute the 'historic triangle,' collectively one of the state's most popular tourist destinations. The National Park Service–maintained **Colonial Parkway** links all three sites. Williamsburg is accessible by train or bus, but the other sites require a car or bicycle.

Williamsburg
First settled as Middle Plantation in 1632, Williamsburg was from 1699 to 1780 the capital of England's largest, richest and most populous colony and the seat of power in the new nation's most influential state. Named to honor King William III and designed by Royal Governor Francis Nicholson, Williamsburg lives intimately with its distinguished past.

After Virginia's capital moved to Richmond in 1780, Williamsburg was nearly forgotten, but it became embroiled in the Civil War. Starting in the mid-1920s, John D Rockefeller contributed some $70 million to local restoration efforts, and endowments ensured continuing restoration of the historic district now known as Colonial Williamsburg. This 220-acre restoration is now surrounded by the city of Williamsburg, which is full of visitor services and home to the College of William & Mary.

Historic Precinct The nonprofit Colonial Williamsburg Foundation (☎ 757-220-7645, 800-447-8679, W www.cwf.org) opens dozens of authentic 17th- and 18th-century buildings to ticket-holders in the 173-acre restored historic district. Walking around the historic district and patronizing the shops and taverns is free, but entry to the gardens and participation in historic building tours are restricted to ticket-holders. Expect crowds, lines and a certain unavoidable theme-park quality, particularly in summer.

To park and purchase tickets, follow signs to the main visitor center, north of the historic district and sandwiched between Route 132 and the Colonial Pkwy. Parking here is free; shuttle buses run frequently to and from the historic district. Parking anywhere around the district is severely restricted. Exhibitions are open 9:30am-5:30pm daily.

The small Merchants Square information booth, within the district at the west end of Duke of Gloucester St (about four blocks from the bus/train station), also sells tickets.

A 'Basic Admission' ticket covers most exhibition buildings, not including the palace, along with two museums and is good for one day ($32/16 adults/kids, $5 each extra consecutive day). The Freedom Pass includes all exhibition buildings and museums and is good for 12 months ($38/19); the Liberty Pass ($55/23) includes year-round access and admission to special events. Museum-only passes are also available ($11). Disabled visitors should call ahead to arrange special vehicles (☎ 757-220-7644).

Places to Stay There are nearly 100 places to stay around town, including well-kept older motels and modern chains. For no extra charge, the Williamsburg Hotel/Motel Association (☎ 800-446-9244) finds accommodations.

CAPITAL REGION

Walking Williamsburg

Merchants Square is a good starting point. At the head of the beautiful Palace Green, the **Governor's Palace** is one highlight, with its lavish interiors, formal gardens and boxwood maze. The **Capitol**, where the legislature reenacts the topics of the day (it might be one of four historical days 1774–76), is the highlight at the opposite end of the main thoroughfare – Duke of Gloucester St. This street also holds colonial souvenir shops and taverns as well as the landmark **Bruton Parish Church**, home to an Episcopalian congregation since 1715.

In central **Market Square**, surrounding the 1770 courthouse, the magazine holds the town arsenal, stalls sell food, and a pillory and stocks provide irresistible photo opportunities. Around town, house tours tell stories of colonial home life and notable families, and craft shops demonstrate coopering, smithing, wheelmaking and other trades.

Chartered in 1693, the **College of William & Mary** (☎ 757-221-1540) retains the oldest college building in the USA (the Sir Christopher Wren Building) and the Muscarelle Museum of Art (☎ 757-221-2703; free admission). The school's esteemed alumni include Thomas Jefferson and James Monroe.

Reach *Williamsburg KOA* (☎ 757-565-2907, 5210 Newman Rd) via I-64 exit 234 (around $25 for tent sites); there's a pool. *Colonial Central KOA* (☎ 757-565-2734, 4000 Newman Rd) has sites for four ($20-25).

Johnson's Guest Home (☎ 757-229-3909, 101 Thomas Nelson Lane) is one of a dozen similar local guesthouses ($45/60 singles/doubles). *Liberty Rose B&B* (☎ 757-253-1260, 1022 Jamestown Rd), delightfully furnished, is from $135.

There are other guesthouses a short walk from the historic district behind Richmond St (from $60 for two), and several budget motels in a tourist gulch along Richmond Rd/Hwy 60 (from $40).

The central reservation line for Colonial Williamsburg Foundation (CWF) lodging is ☎ 800-447-8679; prices are given for one night's accommodation off-peak, breakfast, dinner and an attractions pass included (minimum two-night stay). *Governor's Inn* (506 N Henry St) is the most affordable (from $106). *Williamsburg Woodlands* (30 S England St) is around the same but more suitable for families (from $106), casual *Williamsburg Lodge* (310 S England St) adds a little more Southern graciousness (from $121), and *Williamsburg Inn* (136 E Francis St) is the CWF's premier property (from $193).

Places to Eat Several local promotional publications include tear-out discount coupons, offering savings on meals.

Williamsburg Shopping Center (157 Monticello Ave) is the place for campers to stock up with supplies.

A Good Place to Eat, Merchants Square, serves inexpensive snacks and lunches. *Paul's Deli* (761 Scotland St) has good pizza and pasta. *Green Leafe Cafe*, two doors away, has sandwiches, subs and beer. *College Delly* (336 Richmond Rd) has Greek and Italian fare, including vegetarian main courses (open until 2am). *Cary St Bistro & Tavern* (500 Jamestown Rd) has good food (delicious stuffed flounder), often live music, and plenty of ales on tap.

Trellis Cafe (☎ 757-229-8610), in Merchant Square, is expensive ($25 main dishes) but simply exquisite; reserve early. In four historic district taverns – *Chowning's*, *Christiana Campbell*, *King's Arms* and *James Shield's* – costumed waitstaff serve colonial food and drink (dinners from $15), with entertainment most evenings. Call ☎ 800-828-3767 for reservations (suggested for peak times).

Entertainment At night the crowds thin out and the historic district is particularly evocative as folks stroll to evening performances – choral concerts, 18th-century dances and even witch trials are just a sample of many interesting diversions sponsored by the CWF for around $10 per ticket (see event listings in the free program available to ticket-holders and at ticket booths).

Shopping Prime Outlets (☎ 757-565-0702, 5715 Richmond Rd) has 50 top designer outlet stores; Williamsburg Outlet Mall (☎ 757-565-0732), Hwy 60, has over 50 outlets specializing in clothing and gifts; and the Williamsburg Pottery Factory (☎ 757-564-3326), Hwy 60, has 32 buildings spread over 200 acres. Some three million people visit the pottery factory annually (open 8am-dusk).

Getting There & Around Amtrak (☎ 757-229-8750) runs to Richmond and Washington, DC, from the transportation center at the corner of Lafayette and N Boundary Sts. The center also houses a Greyhound/Trailways station (☎ 757-229-1460), with buses to the same major cities and smaller towns.

Bike rentals are available from Bikes Unlimited (☎ 757-229-4620) and Bikesmith (☎ 757-229-9858).

Around Williamsburg

Taking advantage of the local tourist trade, outlet shopping centers (see Shopping, above) and seasonal theme parks surround Williamsburg.

Busch Gardens (☎ 800-772-8886), 3 miles east of Williamsburg on Hwy 60, is a mega-theme park with many roller-coaster rides ($37/30 adults/kids three to six; open Mar-Oct). **Water Country USA** (☎ 800-343-7346), just off Route 199 east of Williamsburg, has a wave pool and water rides ($28/21; open May-Sept).

Carter's Grove James River plantation (☎ 757-220-7453), 8 miles east of Williamsburg, displays intricate carvings in its Colonial Revival mansion ($18; closed Mon).

Jamestown

Jamestown was founded in May 1607, but the first permanent English settlement on the continent survived less than a century before succumbing to starvation, disease and Native American attacks. In 1619 the first representative assembly met, and Jamestown served as Virginia's capital until 1699, when the colonists moved inland to what is now Williamsburg. By the end of the 19th century, only an overgrown churchyard and church tower remained, and the original Jamestown is now a collection of ruins and archaeological digs.

Jamestown Island National Historic Site is nevertheless an evocative place, a grassy park overlooking the James River. Paths lead to 'James Cittie,' where you'll find the 1640s church tower and several statues and monuments ($5). The visitor center (☎ 757-229-1733) offers living-history tours.

The state-run **Jamestown Settlement** (☎ 757-229-1733) features a reconstruction of the 1607 James Fort, a Native American village and full-scale replicas of the first ships to bring settlers to Jamestown, along with living-history fun ($10.25; $15.25 combo with Yorktown Victory Center).

Yorktown

Founded in 1691, the busy tobacco port of Yorktown became famous in 1781 as the site of the last major Revolutionary War battle – thousands of Cornwallis' troops surrendered to George Washington after the British defeat. Today many Revolutionary and Civil War fortifications remain intact.

Yorktown National Historic Park preserves the bluff site of the British defeat. The National Park Service visitor center (☎ 757-898-3400) has intriguing displays explaining the battle ($4) and rents audiotape tours ($2) of a 7-mile battlefield drive and a 10¼-mile encampment route. The **Yorktown Victory Center** (☎ 757-887-1776) features a reconstruction of the encampment and battle scene along with full-size toy soldiers come to life ($7.75). See Jamestown, earlier, for combination ticket prices.

Yorktown Pub, on Water St, is a friendly place with great daily specials.

James River Plantations

Many of the former homes of Virginia's slaveholding aristocracy lie near scenic Route 5 on the north side of the James River. It's best to see a couple in detail. Block tickets (Ⓦ www.jamesriverplantations.org; $28) sold at each cover the following four homes.

Berkeley (☎ 804-829-2947) was ravaged by British troops in 1781, and Union general George McClellan used the buildings as his 1862 headquarters in the Civil War ($8.50). **Shirley** (☎ 800-232-1613) is Virginia's oldest plantation (1660s). Its 'hanging' staircase ascends three stories without any apparent support ($9). **Evelynton** (☎ 800-473-5075) has antique furnishings and gardens filled with flowers ($7.50). **Sherwood Forest** (☎ 804-829-5377) was the home of the 10th US president, John Tyler ($8.50).

HAMPTON ROADS

The waterway called 'Hampton Roads' empties the James, Nansemond and Elizabeth Rivers into the Chesapeake Bay. Europeans settled the surrounding region in the 17th century. During the Revolutionary War, Norfolk was torched by the British, but it later prospered as an international port. The Civil War battle of the ironclad ships *Monitor* and *Merrimack* was fought near here.

Norfolk later boomed as an industrial and shipbuilding area, especially during WWI and WWII. Today the region bustles with maritime activity, from its huge naval bases and seafood industry to pleasure boating. Note that I-64 can get very congested through the region, particularly at the bridge-tunnel bottleneck.

Hampton

The city of Hampton, home of the historically African American Hampton University, was razed by retreating Confederates during the Civil War. Today a modern harborside waterfront off I-64 exit 267 holds a visitor center (☎ 800-800-2202, 710 Settlers Landing Rd); ask them about the landmark 1820s **Fort Monroe** (the USA's largest stone fort). The **Virginia Air & Space Center** (☎ 757-727-0900, W www.vasc.org, 600 Settlers Landing Rd), at the NASA Langley Research Center, holds 110,000 sq feet of air- and spacecraft, including an *Apollo* command module and lunar lander ($6, plus $3 each IMAX film). The **Hampton University Museum** (☎ 757-727-5308) displays traditional African, Asian, Pacific and Native American art, as well as contemporary works by African American artists (free admission).

Gosnold's Hope Park (☎ 757-850-5116, 901 Little Back River Rd), north of the junction of Route 258 via Route 278, has tent sites ($7). *Arrow Inn* (☎ 757-865-0300, 7 Semple Farm Rd), off I-64 exit 261B eastbound, exit 262B westbound, has singles/doubles from $46/62. *Second St Restaurant & Tavern* (132 E Queen St) will satisfy your eating and drinking urges. *Buckroe's Island*

Grill, at Salt Ponds Marina, has delicious crab dip and other seafood specialties.

Newport News

This city, 10 miles from Williamsburg, holds a few attractions along its James River waterfront. The tourist office (☎ 888-222-8072) is at 13560 Jefferson Ave.

The fascinating **Mariner's Museum** (☎ 757-596-2222, W www.mariner.org), one of the largest maritime museums in the world, features carved figureheads, scrimshaw and more than 50 full-size vessels ($5). The **Virginia Living Museum** (☎ 757-595-1900), nearby, guides you around a lakeside boardwalk to see wildlife in local habitats ($6).

Newport News Park (☎ 757-888-3333) offers year-round camping (tent/RV sites for $16/18) and boat and bike rentals. *Mulberry Inn* (☎ 757-887-3000, 16890 Warwick Blvd) has good rooms (doubles from $90). There are several reasonable chain accommodations off I-64 at exit 255A.

Norfolk

Dominating the Hampton Roads area, Norfolk features several attractions clustered downtown at the south end of the city along Waterside Dr. Here the Waterside Festival Marketplace includes shops, restaurants and nightclubs. The downtown visitor desk (☎ 757-664-6620) is nearby at 232 E Main St. An interstate visitor center (☎ 757-441-1852) is at Ocean View (I-64 exit 273), near the bridge-tunnel.

The **Nauticus** (National Maritime Center; ☎ 757-664-1000), on the waterfront, has ingenious exhibits and entertaining shows, including submarine rides, multimedia naval battles and flight simulators ($7.50; closed Mon). Within the complex, **Hampton Roads Naval Museum** (☎ 757-444-8971) is open daily (free admission).

The **Douglas MacArthur Memorial** (☎ 757-441-2965), in MacArthur Square, houses the WWII general's military and personal artifacts (free admission). The **Chrysler Museum of Art** (☎ 757-664-6200, 245 W Olney Rd) is a grand place with a superb collection and well worth a detour. Exhibits include paintings by Gainsborough, Renoir, Picasso, Pollock and Warhol, and glass ranging from ancient Roman to Tiffany pieces ($5; closed Mon).

The magnificent 135-foot schooner *American Rover* (☎ 757-627-7245) cruises Hampton Roads April to October ($14; 2 hours). The *Spirit of Norfolk* (☎ 757-625-1748) operates narrated cruises ($29-43).

Cheap motels can be found in the modest bay beach community of Ocean View, 4 miles north of downtown (the first exit south of the tunnel). *Econo Lodge W Ocean View Beach* (☎ 757-480-9611) and *Super 8* (☎ 757-588-7888) are both around $50.

Page House Inn (☎ 757-625-5033, 323 Fairfax Ave), uptown opposite the Chrysler Museum, is a glamorous place. They also operate the excellent *Bianca Boat & Breakfast* at the waterfront.

Doumar's (919 Monticello Ave) is the home of the world's original ice-cream-cone machine. The tour ($2) includes an ice cream. *Elliott's* (☎ 757-625-0259, 1421 Colley St), a local favorite in Ghent, has built its reputation on its great hamburgers. *The Dumbwaiter (117 Tazewell St)* has Mississippi-influenced meals (entrées start at $10).

The Greyhound/Trailways terminal (☎ 757-627-7500) is several blocks from the downtown waterfront at Monticello and Bramblet Aves.

The Amtrak terminal in Newport News (☎ 800-872-7245) runs a free Thruway shuttle to downtown Norfolk.

Tidewater Regional Transit (TRT; ☎ 757-623-7433) has buses serving Virginia Beach and Norfolk. TRT's Norfolk trolley tour runs downtown and into the shopping district of Ghent on its one-hour circuit ($3.50).

The Elizabeth River Ferry (☎ 757-222-6100) links Norfolk and Portsmouth (75¢).

COASTAL VIRGINIA

With the exception of glitzy Virginia Beach, the Virginia coastline is uncluttered, with many hidden-away places to fish, walk and relax. On the Delmarva peninsula are many remote wild refuges, including Assateague Island National Seashore. South of the 'Beach' are the equally remote Back Bay National Wildlife Refuge and False Cape State Park.

Virginia Beach

Burgeoning Virginia Beach (VB) started with the 1791 Cape Henry Lighthouse. The first oceanfront hotel went up in 1883 and the beach developed as a holiday retreat. Now it attracts young revelers to its crowded 6-mile beach. The visitor center (☎ 800-822-3224, W www.vbfun.com, 2100 Parks Ave) is off I-64 exit 284.

Virginia Marine Science Museum (VMSM; ☎ 757-425-3474, W www.vmsm.org) has hands-on exhibits, an otter habitat and an aviary ($9). The VMSM also runs dolphin-watching trips June-Sept ($12). The **Old Coast Guard Station** (☎ 757-422-1587), near the water at 24th St, has displays on local shipwrecks ($3). The area's central attraction is of course the beach, with its boardwalk–bike path and occasional markets and exhibitions.

Surfing is permitted at the beach's southern end, near Rudee Inlet, and alongside the 14th St pier. For scuba diving, contact Lynnhaven Dive Center (☎ 757-481-7949); for summer cruises, contact the Virginia Beach Fishing Center/Cruise (☎ 757-422-5700; $12); and for kayaking, contact Tidewater Adventures (☎ 757-480-1999).

The *First Landing/Seashore State Park (☎ 757-481-2131)*, Cape Henry, has standard sites ($11) and two-bedroom cabins amid sand dunes ($80). *Angie's Guest Cottage–B&B (☎ 757-428-4690, 302 24th St)* has an HI section ($13/15 members/nonmembers); B&B singles/doubles cost from $40/50. There are scores of budget motels west of Pacific Ave between 24th and 30th Sts and chains all along Atlantic Ave. *The Cavalier* (☎ 757-425-8555), at 42nd St and Atlantic Ave, has just about every style of accommodations available except budget (from $115 in summer).

Jewish Mother (3108 Pacific Ave) is a local institution with blintzes, hearty sandwiches and other deli fare. It turns into a pumpkin after midnight. *Virginia Beach Farmers' Market (3640 Dam Neck Rd)* suits those on a tight budget, as do *Farm Fresh Supermarket (521 Laskin Rd)* and *Heritage Natural Foods Deli (314 Laskin Rd)*. *Harpoon Larry's (216 24th St)*, in a converted railway carriage, is a popular raw bar.

Tacky clubs and bars abound between 17th and 23rd Sts around Pacific and Atlantic Aves. *Ocean Eddie's*, on the 14th St pier, has wild Friday-night bashes to the strains of a country/R&B band. *GTE Virginia Beach*

Amphitheater (☎ 757-671-8100) features headliners.

The Greyhound/Trailways bus station (☎ 757-422-2998) is at 1017 Laskin Rd; make sure when booking tickets that Virginia Beach is specified as the Greyhound terminus. Virginia Beach Trolley (☎ 757-428-3388) runs along Atlantic Ave in summer.

Around Virginia Beach

Many natural areas are within easy reach. **Back Bay National Wildlife Refuge** (☎ 757-498-2473) is a wildlife and migratory bird habitat. The 6-mile beach of **False Cape State Park** can be accessed only by bicycle, boat or foot. Primitive *camping* ($7) requires a permit (☎ 757-498-2473); bring drinking water. The fascinating **Great Dismal Swamp National Wildlife Refuge** (☎ 757-986-3705), 30 miles southwest of VB, is rich in flora and fauna (more than 200 bird species).

Eastern Shore

Across the impressive 17-mile Chesapeake Bay Bridge-Tunnel ($10) from VB, Virginia's isolated Eastern Shore offers bayside fishing villages and many natural areas on both the marshy bay and Atlantic shore.

Tucked behind windswept Assateague Island (see the Maryland section later), the town of Chincoteague (**shink**-o-teeg), on the island of the same name, is Virginia's principal Eastern Shore destination. A Virginia Welcome Center (☎ 757-824-5000) is nearby on US 13, south of the Maryland border. Legendary **Chincoteague Island** is famous for its July roundup, when the wild ponies that inhabit the Assateague Island refuge are led across the channel for annual herd-thinning foal auctions. Follow signs to the chamber of commerce (☎ 757-336-6161) for lodging and recreation directories (open daily during summer). The **Chincoteague National Wildlife Refuge** (☎ 757-336-6122) protects migratory waterfowl ($5 per vehicle).

Chincoteague has abundant accommodations. *Beach Road Motel* (☎ 757-336-6562, 6151 Maddox Blvd) is well kept, with doubles· from $50. At *Mariner Motel* (☎ 800-221-7490, 6273 Maddox Blvd), another good place, doubles cost from $47. Seafood eateries abound along Main St.

Muller's Ice Cream Parlor (4034 Main St) has soda-fountain treats, splits and malts.

THE PIEDMONT

The Virginia 'plain' is perhaps the least interesting part of an attraction-filled state. But if you are prepared to drive you will find several gems, especially examples of the architectural genius of Thomas Jefferson.

Charlottesville

Virginia's Cambridge, Charlottesville is a smart university town in a beautiful setting. As the home of Thomas Jefferson and the University of Virginia, 'C-ville' draws visitors to its impressive architecture and magnolia-lined streets set against a Blue Ridge Mountain backdrop. The helpful Charlottesville/Albemarle CVB (☎ 877-386-1102, ⓦ www.charlottesvilletourism.org), on Route 20S near I-64 exit 121A, features a 'Thomas Jefferson at Monticello' exhibit (free admission). The CVB sells block passes to area attractions ($22).

Monticello & Around East of town, Thomas Jefferson's magnificent home (☎ 804-984-9822), featured on the nickel coin, embodies its resident designer: Jefferson's quirky inventions and French-inspired innovations are scattered throughout. Jefferson's tomb is downhill; its inscription, noting the author of the Declaration of Independence and Virginia's religious freedom statute, and founder of the University of Virginia, was chosen by the man himself.

Daily specialty tours include a Plantation Community tour exposing the complicated past of the slave owner who declared all men to be equal.

Keep in mind that Monticello (mon-ta-**chel**-o) is one of Virginia's premier historic attractions ($9); arrive early to avoid long lines. Frequent shuttles run from the parking lot up the hill. Tours are offered of the 1784 Michie Tavern (☎ 804-977-1234), nearby, but the Jefferson-era tavern is best known for providing luncheon buffets in *The Ordinary* (around $10).

Ash Lawn-Highland (☎ 804-293-9539), James Monroe's 535-acre estate, 2½ miles east of Monticello, includes Monroe's house, boxwood gardens and farm craft demonstrations ($8).

University of Virginia At the west end of town, the *grounds* (never 'campus') of the university founded by Thomas Jefferson revolve around the stately Rotunda, a scale replica of Rome's Pantheon. UVA's **Bayly Art Museum** (☎ 804-924-3592) hosts traveling exhibits featuring works by the likes of Rodin.

Places to Stay & Eat The *Charlottesville KOA* (☎ 804-296-9881, 3825 Red Hill Rd) is southwest on County Rd 708; sites are from $19 and Kamping Kabins $33. *Budget Inn* (☎ 804-293-5141, 140 Emmet St) has reasonable rooms from $45. *Econo Lodge University* (☎ 804-296-2104, 400 Emmet St) is also convenient to downtown (from $49). Most budget chain motels are at interstate exits miles from downtown, and inbound traffic can be fierce. *English Inn* (☎ 804-971-9900, 2000 Morton Dr), a tidy motel near the Route 29 and 250 Bypass, charges from $67. Guesthouses Bed & Breakfast (☎ 804-979-7264) arranges exclusive B&B accommodations.

Inexpensive student eateries crowd 'the Corner,' the busy commercial district adjacent to UVA grounds. *Baja Bean Co* (1327 W Main St) has delicious, inexpensive Mexican food. *Greenskeeper* (1517 University Ave) has salads, sandwiches and plenty of beer. *Blue Ridge Brewing Co* (709 W Main St) has seafood, steak, pasta and desserts. *Miller's* (109 W Main St) is an unpretentious dive with smoke, junk food and character. *C&O Restaurant* (☎ 804-971-7044, 515 E Water St) serves excellent French bistro cuisine in a funky dive that was once a train workers' boardinghouse. The *Hardware Store* (316 E Main St) is a city landmark, with a great menu and heaps of memorabilia. The *farmers' market*, nearby, is held in the public parking lot behind the mall (Wed and Sat).

There's varied and lively nightlife and performing arts in town; check the free *C-ville Weekly* for exhaustive listings. Many bars and clubs along the downtown pedestrian mall feature local bands.

Getting There & Away The train station (☎ 804-296-4559) and Greyhound/Trailways terminal (☎ 804-295-5131) are conveniently located on Main St.

Around Charlottesville
Scenic Routes 20 and 231 lead east past pasturelands and wineries to Orange County, scene of the Battle of the Wilderness. The county visitor bureau (☎ 540-672-1653, 122 E Main St), in Orange, advises on winery tours, the **James Madison Museum** (☎ 540-672-1776; $4) and **Montpelier** (☎ 540-672-2728), where Madison lived ($7.50).

Lynchburg
Founded along the James River by an enterprising Quaker ferryman in 1757, Lynchburg is a pleasant enough city with a comfortably gritty downtown and refined hilltop historic districts. It's a convenient base from which to visit Appomattox. The visitor center (☎ 800-732-5821, 216 12th St) is near the Community Market.

Up 139 steep steps from downtown, landmark **Monument Terrace** holds a war memorial to the city's Confederate soldiers. Many historic buildings line Court House Hill, one of the city's seven noted hills. **Poplar Forest** (☎ 804-525-1806), a few miles southwest of downtown, preserves Thomas Jefferson's summer retreat – a mini-Monticello ($7).

Holliday Lake State Park (☎ 804-248-6308), near Appomattox, has $15 tent sites. A cluster of chain motels surrounds the intersection of Hwys 29 and 501. *Community Market*, at Main and 12th Sts, offers a variety of food stalls, including the excellent *Philippine Delight*. The *Farm Basket* (2008 Langhorne Rd) has a small, always-packed restaurant, and prepares lunch boxes.

Greyhound/Trailways (☎ 804-846-6614) buses stop south of downtown at Wildflower Dr and Odd Fellows Rd. Amtrak stops west of downtown.

Appomattox & Around
Robert E Lee surrendered the Army of Northern Virginia to Ulysses S Grant at Appomattox. Today the compact village is preserved within a 1300-acre park as **Appomattox Court House National Historic Park** (☎ 804-352-8987). The National Park Service visitor center (☎ 804-352-2621), within the evocative pedestrian-only village, provides maps of 27 surrounding restored buildings, including McLean House ($4). See 'Surrender at Appomattox,' later.

CAPITAL REGION

Around 25 miles east of Appomattox in Farmville, the **Robert Russa Moton Museum** (W www.moton.org) tells the story of the beginnings of the civil-rights movement within the high school that first pressed for desegregation in 1951. The Farmville Chamber of Commerce (☎ 804-392-3939, 116 N Main St) provides directions.

SHENANDOAH VALLEY

The beautiful Shenandoah Valley lies between the Blue Ridge and Allegheny Mountains. The Shenandoah River starts near Lexington, flowing northeast to the Potomac. The area was settled in the early 18th century by Scotch-Irish and German families. A vital Confederate troop corridor and food source, the fertile valley saw much Civil War action and is studded with historic sites.

Valley towns are accessible from I-81, and the Blue Ridge Pkwy provides a scenic alternative. But the true flavor of the region lies in the wilder mountain areas, beyond the towns and the beaten-path parkway.

Washington & Jefferson National Forests

The US Forest Service (USFS) oversees more than 1562 sq miles of mountainous terrain bordering the Shenandoah Valley. Trail networks include 300 miles of the **Appalachian Trail** (AT) and mountain-biking routes. Hundreds of developed campgrounds are scattered throughout ($8-12, few hookups, primitive camping free). Virgin forest is preserved in **Ramsey's Draft Wilderness Area**. USFS headquarters (☎ 540-265-5100, W www.southernregion.fs.fed.us/gwj), off the Blue Ridge Pkwy in Roanoke, oversees a dozen ranger stations along the ranges.

Shenandoah National Park

The centerpiece of this famously beautiful park (☎ 540-999-2243, W www.nps.gov/shen) is Skyline Drive, which crosses the spine of the Blue Ridge Mountains 105 miles from Front Royal in the north to Rockfish Gap in the south. It's spectacular in spring and fall particularly, but expensive ($10/5 vehicles/cyclists) and slow (35mph limit, congested in peak seasons).

Dickey's Ridge Visitors Center (☎ 540-635-3566), close to the park's northern entrance, distributes maps and information on hiking (the AT frequently crosses Skyline), horseback riding, hang gliding, biking (only on public roads) and other recreation. Within the park, Byrd Visitor Center (☎ 540-999-3283) is open seasonally.

Tent sites at four *NPS campgrounds* (☎ 800-999-3500) cost $14, with showers and laundry available. *Skyline Lodge* (☎ 703-242-0315), at Mile 41.7, has single units from $79, and *Lewis Mountain*, at Mile 57.5, has single-room cabins from $60/85 weekdays/weekends. Food service is available at convenient intervals.

Winchester

The first settlement west of the Blue Ridge Mountains, Winchester changed hands 72 times during the Civil War. The visitor

Surrender at Appomattox

On April 9, 1865 (Palm Sunday), in the modest house of Wilmer McLean at Appomattox Court House, Lee, resplendent in his best uniform with his sword by his side, sat down to talk with Grant, who was dressed in a private's tunic with lieutenant general's stars pinned to its shoulders. Traveller, Lee's horse, munched on the grass outside.

After a pause, Grant opened his notebook and in straightforward fashion spelled out the terms. These were generous and included the lines that would make it impossible for acts of vengeance to be taken against former Confederate soldiers. After an exchange of military salutes, Lee returned to Traveller and rode away.

Grant sat down in front of his tent and reminisced about the Mexican War, not outwardly savoring the moment of victory. Lee rode past his troops, many of whom had tears streaming down their faces. In the following days the once-proud Army of Northern Virginia stacked up its arms, formally surrendered, and wandered away to recommence their shattered lives.

center (☎ 800-662-1360, 1360 S Pleasant Valley Rd) directs you to such Old Town sights as the Civil War headquarters of 'Stonewall' Jackson and Robert E Lee. In the quiet historic district, the **Kurtz Cultural Center** explains the town's Civil War history (free admission).

Many low-cost motels string along Hwy 11 a couple of miles south of Old Town. *Cork Street Tavern (8 W Cork St)* serves sizable barbecue dinners from $12. The adjacent pedestrian mall shelters cafes, bagel shops and other choices. *Tucano's (☎ 540-722-4557, 12 S Braddock St)* is a really popular Brazilian place.

Front Royal

Once a raucous 18th-century packhorse stopover, Front Royal retains a certain roughness in its run-down downtown and clusters of cheap motels bordering town. Now it's a Shenandoah National Park gateway. The helpful visitor center (☎ 800-338-9758, 414 E Main St) has information on outdoor recreation, such as canoeing to the south near Bentonville.

Front Royal/Washington DC West KOA (☎ 540-635-2741), near Skyline Dr (I-81 exit 6), has good shady campsites ($28 for two) and Kamping Kabins ($39). *Main St Mill & Tavern (500 E Main St)* serves inexpensive dinners ($10).

Luray

Nestled in mountains between the national forest and national park, Luray is home to **Luray Caverns** (☎ 540-743-6551), on Hwy 211, which feature a stalactite organ recital ($14). The visitor center (☎ 540-743-3915) is at 46 E Main St; also downtown is a National Park Service office. The Shenandoah Natural History Association (☎ 540-999-3582) offers copious park information.

Luray Caverns Motel East (☎ 540-743-4531, 831 W Main St), downtown, or *Luray Caverns Motel West (☎ 540-743-4536)*, Hwy 211 Bypass, are both good budget accommodations (from $60).

New Market

Right off I-64 exit 264, the **New Market Battlefield Historical Park** (☎ 540-740-3101) has a Hall of Valor commemorating the part cadets from the Virginia Military Academy played in the battle. The Shenandoah Valley Travel Association (☎ 540-740-3132, Ⓦ www.shenandoah.org), Route 211 W (I-81 exit 264), highlights valley attractions.

Staunton & Around

At the junction of I-81 and I-64, near the junction of Blue Ridge Pkwy and Skyline Dr, Staunton (**stan**-tun) is a convenient stop.

The **Museum of American Frontier Culture** (☎ 800-332-7850, Ⓦ www.frontier-museum.org), overlooking I-81 exit 222, is a unique living-history farm. Authentic historic farm buildings from Germany, Ireland and England have been transported here to compare and contrast with an American frontier farm that's also on the sprawling grounds ($8). The **Woodrow Wilson Birthplace & Museum** (☎ 540-885-0897, 18–24 N Coalter St) reveals the stately 1846 Greek Revival house and garden of the 28th president ($6.50). **The Statler Brothers Museum** (☎ 540-885-7297, 501 Thornrose Ave) is a mecca for fans of these country singers (featured on the *Pulp Fiction* soundtrack).

Walnut Hills Campground (☎ 540-337-3920, 391 Walnut Hills Rd), in Mint Spring, is an excellent, well-equipped setup with sites from $17-23 for two. *Frederick House (☎ 540-885-4420, 28 N New St)*, a walk from Amtrak, is one of several romantic old B&Bs, with large rooms and suites (from $85). *Belle Grae Inn (☎ 540-886-5151, 515 W Frederick St)* is another of these gracious B&Bs ($95).

Rowe's Family Restaurant, I-81 exit 222, is a Staunton institution known for its Southern home-cooking. *Wrights Dairy Rite (☎ 540-886-0435, 346 Greenville Ave)*, another Staunton original, is a curb service drive-in operating since 1952.

Amtrak (☎ 800-872-7245) is downtown on Middlebrook Ave. Greyhound/Trailways (☎ 540-886-2424, 1211 Richmond Rd) has daily buses.

Ten miles north of Staunton, near Mt Solon, **Natural Chimneys Regional Park** (☎ 540-350-2510) features a remarkable rock formation and camping ($9/19 tent/RV hookups). **Wintergreen** (☎ 800-325-2200), 16 miles southeast, offers skiing (1000-foot drop) and snowboarding in winter.

Lexington & Around

The last resting place of 'Stonewall' Jackson and Robert E Lee, this graceful historic town is also renowned for two academies

CAPITAL REGION

accounting for nearly half of the town's population. The convenient visitor center (☎ 540-463-3777) is at 106 E Washington St.

The **Virginia Military Institute** (☎ 540-464-7207), founded in 1839, houses a free museum on the school's history. The **George C Marshall Museum** (☎ 540-463-7103), on campus, honors the creator of the Marshall Plan for post-WWII European reconstruction ($3). A full-dress parade takes place most Fridays at 4:30pm during the school year.

Colonnaded **Washington & Lee University**, founded in 1749, contains Lee Chapel and Museum (☎ 540-463-8768), with Lee interred downstairs and his horse Traveller buried outside (free admission). **Stonewall Jackson House** (☎ 540-463-2552, 8 E Washington St), a restored 1801 building, houses the general's possessions and period pieces ($5). Jackson is buried in Lexington Cemetery.

Natural Bridge/Lexington KOA (☎ 540-291-2770), 10 miles south of Lexington, has sites from $19. *Overnight Guests* (☎ 540-463-3075, 216 W Washington St) is Virginia's best lodging bargain, at $10 per bed. Chain motels are found at I-81 exit 195 and I-64 exit 55. *Historic Country Inns* (☎ 540-463-2044, 11 N Main St) operates two inns downtown ($55-180) and one outside town. *Blue Heron Cafe* (4 E Washington St) has creative vegetarian entrées (from $8).

Outside Lexington, horse shows and the Virginia Horse Festival (Apr) are held at the **Virginia Horse Center** (☎ 540-463-4300). Scenic Route 39 retraces an old stagecoach trail along a stream and over **Goshen Pass** to mineral-spring resorts in Bath County, including the preeminent *Homestead* (☎ 800-838-1766) resort in Hot Springs (from $230); contact the Hwy 220 visitor center (☎ 540-839-5409) for some affordable alternatives.

Natural Bridge

A limestone cave collapsed to expose this 215-foot-high natural arch, which must have been awesome to first chance upon; it's less so when accompanied by pavement, shuttles, wax museums and an $8 ticket. The **Natural Bridge Caverns** (☎ 540-291-2121) are some 34 stories down ($7; open Mar-Dec). Both attractions are operated by the relatively plush modern *Natural Bridge Resort* (☎ 540-291-2121, W www.naturalbridgeva.com); cottage/

hotel rooms are from $39/59. Lower-priced alternatives can be found off I-81 exit 180/180A.

A National Forest Service ranger station (☎ 540-291-2189), across from the resort, provides information about recreation and camping in nearby forest service areas, including $10 sites at Cave Mountain Lake, 8 miles south.

BLUE RIDGE HIGHLANDS & SOUTHWEST

The southwestern tip of Virginia is the most rugged part of the state and still retains a frontier feel. It has many natural attractions, including the stunning drive along the Blue Ridge Pkwy and the outdoor adventure playground of Mt Rogers National Recreation Area.

Blue Ridge Parkway

The Blue Ridge Pkwy traverses the southern Appalachian ridge from Shenandoah National Park at Mile 0 to North Carolina's Great Smoky Mountains National Park at Mile 469. Wildflowers bloom in spring, and fall colors are spectacular. High-quality National Park Service campgrounds and visitor centers are open May to October. To break up the scenery, detour often.

Check out **Floyd**, with free Friday-night jamborees at Floyd (also known as Cockram's) Country Store. Craftspeople and counterculturalists live in the surrounding hills. **Mabry Mill** (☎ 540-952-2947), at Meadows of Dan, is one of the most photogenic objects in the state. Galax hosts the Old Fiddlers' Convention (☎ 540-238-8130), the oldest and largest event of its kind in the nation, each August.

The parkway has nine campgrounds (☎ 800-933-7275), four in Virginia: the year-round *Otter Creek* (Mile 61), seasonal *Peaks of Otter* (Mile 86), *Roanoke Mountain* (Mile 120) and *Rocky Knob* (Mile 167). All sites are $9. *Peaks of Otter Lodge* (☎ 540-586-4357), a very scenic spot, has year-round lakeside accommodations and buffet dining. *HI Blue Ridge Country* (☎ 540-236-4962), at Mile 214.5 on the parkway, offers hostel-style dorm lodging with a view ($14/15 members/nonmembers).

Mabry Mill at Mile 176 provides food service; alternatively, search out options at several small towns just off the parkway.

Roanoke & Around

Illuminated by its giant star (the local equivalent of the 'Hollywood' sign), Roanoke is the big city in these parts, with a compact set of attractions based around the great farmers market downtown. Across the way is the visitor center (☎ 800-635-5535, W www.visitroanokeva.com, 114 Market St). The USFS headquarters (☎ 540-265-5100), north of the parkway, has regional recreation and camping information.

The **Center in the Square** (☎ 540-342-5700) has three levels of exhibits, including a science museum, planetarium, local-history museum, free art museum showcasing the work of folk and local artists, and **Mills Mountain Theater** (☎ 540-342-5740), the city's premier performing-arts venue ($2-6). Also inquire about the Virginia Museum of Transportation ($4) and Harrison Museum of African American Culture (free admission), both a short drive away.

Out at Blue Ridge Pkwy is a hilltop zoo ($5) with a wildflower garden, and **Virginia's Explore Park** (☎ 540-427-1800), a seasonal living-history frontier farm ($8).

Roanoke Appalachian Trail Club organizes hikes, Blue Ridge Bicycle Club has year-round rides and there's cross-country skiing at Mountain Lake (☎ 540-626-7121); the visitor center has a contact list.

Roanoke Mountain Campground (☎ 540-982-9242), maintained by the National Park Service, is on Blue Ridge Pkwy at Mile 120.4 (sites $9; open May-Oct). *Sleep Inn Tanglewood* (☎ 540-772-1500), near the parkway on Hwy 419 off Hwy 220, charges from $60 year round. Dozens more chains are farther north off I-58 exits. *Hotel Roanoke* (☎ 540-985-5900, 110 Shenandoah Ave NE), downtown, has faithfully integrated 1882 features into an ultramodern convention hotel (around $135).

City Market houses local vendors offering pizza, sushi, burritos and more, with counter seating. Surrounding restaurants and cafes offer more choices, including seafood, Brazilian and vegetarian cuisine, within a block. *Texas Tavern (114 W Church Ave)*, also known as 'Roanoke Millionaires Club,' is a must if you can nab one of the few seats; the chili bowls ($3) are great. *The Homeplace*, on Route 311N (near I-81 exit 141), offers heaps of old-fashioned country cooking.

About 20 miles southeast of Roanoke, the **Booker T Washington National Monument** (☎ 540-721-2094) has been restored to convey some idea of the circumstances into which the noted African American leader was born as a slave in 1856 (free admission).

Mt Rogers National Recreation Area

There's ample hiking, fishing and cross-country skiing in these ancient hardwood forests surrounding Virginia's highest peaks. The park headquarters (☎ 540-783-5196), on Route 16 in Marion, offers maps and recreation directories. The National Park Service operates five *campgrounds* in the area; contact park headquarters.

The **Virginia Creeper Trail** (W www.vacreeper.org), named for the railroad that once ran this route, travels 33 miles between Whitetop Station (3576 feet), near the North Carolina border, and downtown Abingdon – an enchanting excursion. Several outfitters rent bikes, organize outings and run uphill shuttles, including Blue Blaze (☎ 800-475-5095) and Adventure Damascus (☎ 888-595-2453), in Damascus.

Abingdon

A lovely theater and inn are the centerpieces of this cultural oasis in southwestern Virginia. Abingdon retains fine Federal and Victorian architecture in its 20-block historic district. The visitor center (☎ 800-435-3440) is at 335 Cummings St/Hwy 75.

The **Barter Theater** (☎ 540-628-3991, W www.bartertheatre.com), founded during the Depression, earned its name from audiences trading food for performances – 'ham for *Hamlet*.' Since that time, such well-known actors as Gregory Peck and Ernest Borgnine have cut their teeth on Barter's stage (tickets from $20; performances Wed-Sun Mar-Dec). Call for a schedule.

Abingdon hosts the Virginia Highlands Festival the first two weeks in August. Bluegrass lovers gather at the fairgrounds Saturday nights.

The *Alpine Motel* (☎ 540-628-3178, 882 E Main St), off I-81 exit 19, is a well-kept older motel (from $47). *Camberley's Martha Washington Inn* (☎ 540-628-3161, 150 W Main St), opposite the Barter, is the region's premier historic hotel and worth a splurge (from $159/169 standard/B&B). *The Tavern*

Booker T Washington

Booker Talioferro Washington was born on a plantation in Franklin County on April 5, 1856, the son of a slave. He lived on the plantation for nine years, and at the end of the Civil War his family moved to West Virginia. From 1872 to 1875 he went to a new school for blacks, today called the Hampton Institute, and paid his tuition by working as a janitor. He taught for two years in Malden after graduation. He returned to the Hampton Institute in 1879 and was selected in 1881 as organizer of the Tuskegee Normal School (now Institute) in Alabama.

He developed into a competent public speaker and an important and controversial race leader at a time when racism in the USA made it necessary for African Americans to adjust to a new era of oppression. Washington died in 1915, probably the most important spokesperson for African Americans at the time.

(222 E Main St), in Abingdon's oldest building, has an innovative menu (trout dishes for $14). *Hardware Company (260 W Main St)*, in a renovated store, is a popular meeting place with entrées from $12.

Coal Country

Far beyond the interstate world, Virginia's southwest tip is rugged Appalachian territory. Big Stone Gap is a no-frills mountain town, despite some nicer homes left from its entrepreneurial coal-hauling and railroading heyday. A vintage railway car houses a visitor center (☎ 888-798-2386) on Hwy 23 (open weekdays). The Virginia Coalfield Tourism Authority (☎ 888-798-2386, 311 Wood Ave) distributes information about the 125-mile 'Heart of Appalachia' bike route through the backcountry (office open weekdays only).

Cave Springs Recreation Area (☎ 540-328-2931), 2½ miles west on Route 58, then 6 miles south on County Rd 621, has sites for $8.

Outside Big Stone Gap, a drive north on Business 23 passes rugged downtown **Appalachia** and coal-hauling hollows on to **Norton**, where the downtown theater hosts the Virginia-Kentucky Opry (Sat nights).

Cumberland Gap National Historic Park

This break in the Appalachian mountains is where Virginia, Tennessee and Kentucky meet. In the late 18th century some 200,000 pioneers crossed this gap along the Wilderness Rd. The visitor center (☎ 606-248-2817) is across the border. The 20,000-acre park contains 70 miles of hiking trails (backpacking permits required). The year-round *Wilderness Road Campground* has sites for $8.

Maryland

Maryland is a state of three parts. The central portion almost surrounds the nation's capital and acts as a dormitory and service center for DC's workforce. The west offers all forms of outdoor activities and much for history buffs to explore, such as the Chesapeake & Ohio Canal and the Civil War battlefield of Antietam. It is the Chesapeake Bay region for which the state is most famous – this water playground includes the revitalized seafaring city of Baltimore, the world-renowned sailing center of Annapolis, 'watermen' communities along the bay's fringe, fishing, crabbing and just about every water-based pursuit imaginable.

History

A loyal servant of King Charles I of England, George Calvert (Lord Baltimore) was a Catholic. When Baltimore's religion became problematic in the court, he received a royal grant to establish a Catholic colony in what was then northern Virginia. Baltimore believed in religious tolerance, and his colony was founded in 1634 with a mixed group of 200 Catholics, Protestants and 'religious idealists.' They negotiated with the area's native inhabitants and occupied a site on the west side of Chesapeake Bay, where they planted corn and tobacco. The settlement was named St Mary's City, and it prospered as the capital of the new Maryland colony until 1695, when the colony's capital was moved to the superior port of Annapolis.

In 1729 the settlement of Baltimore was founded as a tobacco and flour-milling center, with a fine harbor and access to first-rate shipbuilding timber. Baltimore developed rapidly as colonial America's shipping center, and its ships and sailors dominated the American privateer fleet during the Revolutionary War. Bombarded by British ships in the War of 1812, Baltimore's soldiers kept the flag flying at Fort McHenry and resisted the attack. The event inspired a Maryland lawyer, Francis Scott Key, to write a poem called 'The Star-Spangled Banner,' which would provide the words for the national anthem.

South of the Mason-Dixon line, Maryland prospered in the early 19th century as a result of tobacco and wheat plantations worked by slaves, and also from Chesapeake Bay fisheries, Baltimore's thriving seaport, and railroads pushing west to the Ohio River. In the Civil War, Maryland stayed in the Union, but Lincoln imposed martial law as a precaution. An 1862 Confederate invasion of Maryland was halted at the bloody battle of Antietam. Maryland abolished slavery in 1864.

After the war Maryland continued its Baltimore-based industrial development. European immigration swelled the workforce, but African Americans continued to experience discrimination. The exponential growth of the nearby national capital, pushing its suburban population and development deep into Maryland, factors largely in the state's present-day economy.

Maryland is the only state with an official state sport – jousting. Nowadays, the jousters aim for rings, not other riders.

Information
Maryland's Office of Tourism Development (☎ 410-767-3400, 800-543-1036; Ⓦ www.mdisfun.org, 217 E Redwood St,

---

Maryland

Nicknames: Old Line State, Pine Tree State

Population: 5,296,500 (19th)

Area: 12,407 sq miles (42nd)

Admitted to Union: April 28, 1788 (7th)

Capital city: Annapolis (population 35,500)

Other cities: Baltimore (761,000), Frederick (53,000)

State motto: Manly Deeds, Womanly Words

Birthplace of: Frederick Douglass (1817–95), Babe Ruth (1895–1948), Billie Holiday (1915–59), John Wilkes Booth (1838–65), Frank Zappa (1940–93), 'Pope of Trash' John Waters (b 1946)

Famous for: Baltimore Orioles, crab cakes

Baltimore, MD 21202) has several information centers and provides maps and guides. State sales tax is 5%.

BALTIMORE
Baltimore is a great hardworking, ball-playing, no-nonsense US city. Plenty of interesting attractions in its compact downtown, its comfortable neighborhoods and ethnic enclaves, and convenient transit on light rail and water taxis are some of the city's highlights.

After the Revolutionary War, Baltimore's shipyards became famous for a new breed of ship – fast, two-masted schooners called Baltimore Clippers. Baltimore became the second-largest city in the USA, its ships plying trade routes to Europe, the Caribbean and South America.

Baltimore suffered no damage in the Civil War, but in 1904 a warehouse fire engulfed its business district, destroying 1500 buildings. Undaunted, Baltimore's wealthy financed a recovery that continued until the Great Depression. Thereafter Baltimore struggled with growing social problems, and following the 1968 murder of civil-rights leader Martin Luther King Jr, mobs burned and looted the city. Baltimore's transformation since then into a lively, attraction-filled destination is an urban-renewal success story.

CAPITAL REGION

BALTIMORE

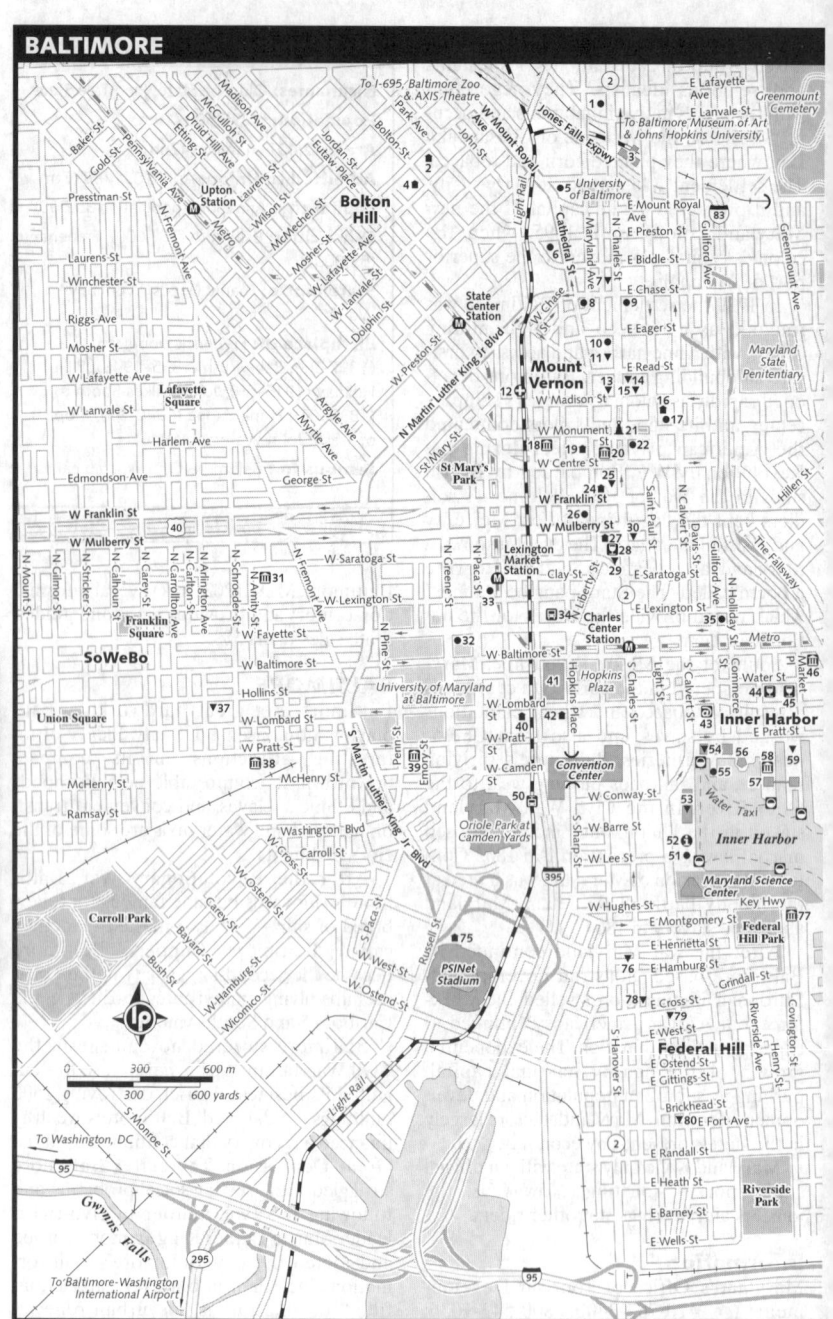

BALTIMORE

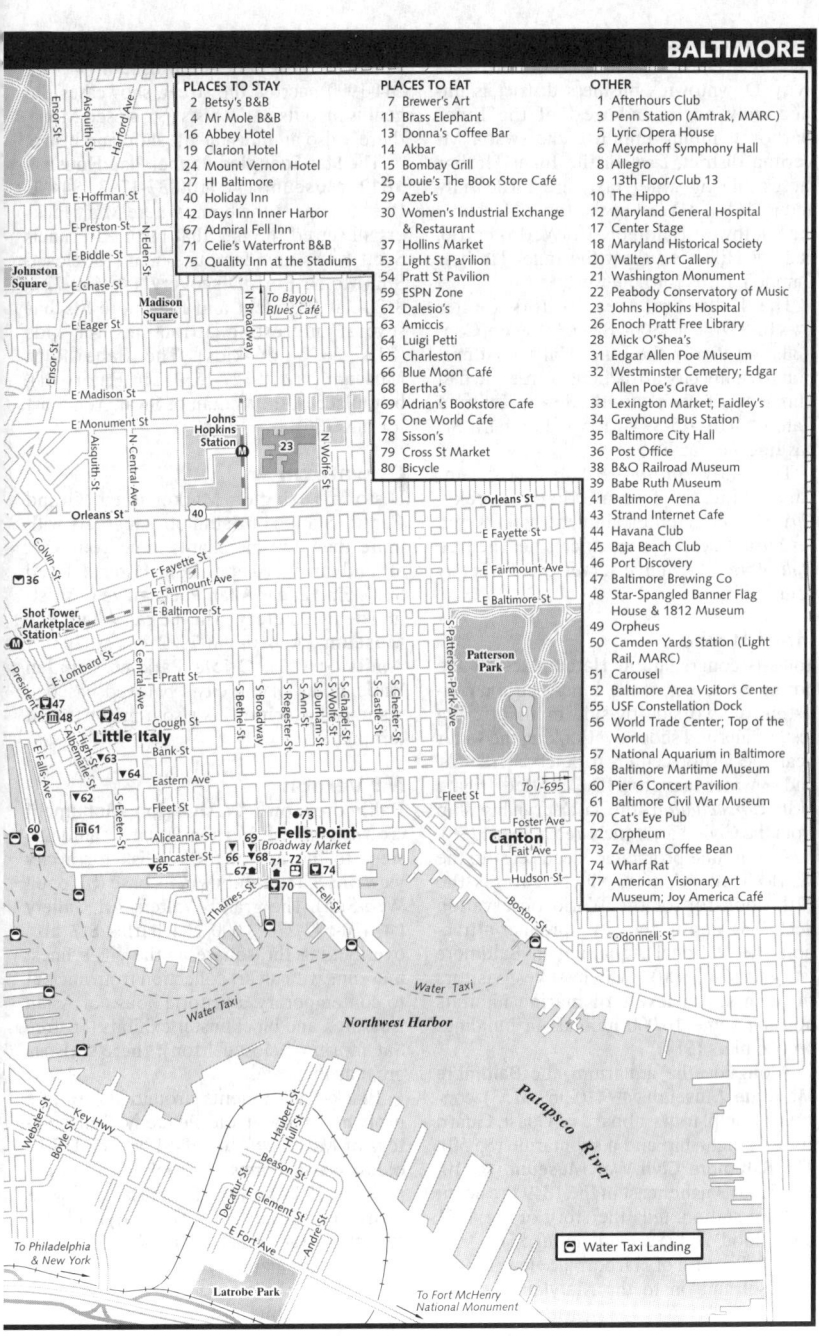

PLACES TO STAY
2   Betsy's B&B
4   Mr Mole B&B
16 Abbey Hotel
19 Clarion Hotel
24 Mount Vernon Hotel
27 HI Baltimore
40 Holiday Inn
42 Days Inn Inner Harbor
67 Admiral Fell Inn
71 Celie's Waterfront B&B
75 Quality Inn at the Stadiums

PLACES TO EAT
7   Brewer's Art
11 Brass Elephant
13 Donna's Coffee Bar
14 Akbar
15 Bombay Grill
25 Louie's The Book Store Café
29 Azeb's
30 Women's Industrial Exchange
    & Restaurant
37 Hollins Market
53 Light St Pavilion
54 Pratt St Pavilion
59 ESPN Zone
62 Dalesio's
63 Amiccis
64 Luigi Petti
65 Charleston
66 Blue Moon Café
68 Bertha's
69 Adrian's Bookstore Cafe
76 One World Cafe
78 Sisson's
79 Cross St Market
80 Bicycle

OTHER
1   Afterhours Club
3   Penn Station (Amtrak, MARC)
5   Lyric Opera House
6   Meyerhoff Symphony Hall
8   Allegro
9   13th Floor/Club 13
10 The Hippo
12 Maryland General Hospital
17 Center Stage
18 Maryland Historical Society
20 Walters Art Gallery
21 Washington Monument
22 Peabody Conservatory of Music
23 Johns Hopkins Hospital
26 Enoch Pratt Free Library
28 Mick O'Shea's
31 Edgar Allen Poe Museum
32 Westminster Cemetery; Edgar
    Allen Poe's Grave
33 Lexington Market; Faidley's
34 Greyhound Bus Station
35 Baltimore City Hall
36 Post Office
38 B&O Railroad Museum
39 Babe Ruth Museum
41 Baltimore Arena
43 Strand Internet Cafe
44 Havana Club
45 Baja Beach Club
46 Port Discovery
47 Baltimore Brewing Co
48 Star-Spangled Banner Flag
    House & 1812 Museum
49 Orpheus
50 Camden Yards Station (Light
    Rail, MARC)
51 Carousel
52 Baltimore Area Visitors Center
55 USF Constellation Dock
56 World Trade Center; Top of the
    World
57 National Aquarium in Baltimore
58 Baltimore Maritime Museum
60 Pier 6 Concert Pavilion
61 Baltimore Civil War Museum
70 Cat's Eye Pub
72 Orpheum
73 Ze Mean Coffee Bean
74 Wharf Rat
77 American Visionary Art
    Museum; Joy America Café

CAPITAL REGION

Orientation & Information

The Inner Harbor is the heart of tourist activity. Downtown's business district is immediately north and west of the Inner Harbor, climbing uphill to the swank Mt Vernon district. East of the Inner Harbor (accessible by water taxi) are Little Italy and Fells Point. West of the Inner Harbor is the Southwest Baltimore (SoWeBo) barrio. Federal Hill is south of the Inner Harbor; Camden Yards is to the west.

The Baltimore Area Visitors Center (☎ 410-837-4636, 800-282-6632) is on Constellation Pier in the Inner Harbor. Admission to many city attractions is free the first Thursday of each month. Strand Internet Cafe (☎ 410-625-8944, 105 E Lombard St) has Internet facilities.

The daily *Baltimore Sun* is a decent paper. Find the free alternative weekly *City Paper* for entertainment listings and restaurant descriptions by cuisine. The free *Baltimore Alternative* serves the city's gay community.

Inner Harbor

Tourists congregate at **Harborplace**, at the northwest corner of the Inner Harbor, consisting of two side-by-side malls offering restaurants and shops overlooking the water near the visitor center, paddleboat rentals, and a water-taxi stop. The refitted frigate USF *Constellation,* the last surviving ship from the Civil War, is anchored at Pier 1 ($6).

A shoreline promenade leads east to the World Trade Center, which features the 27th-floor Top of the World observation deck ($3), and to the city's premier attraction, the **National Aquarium in Baltimore** (☎ 410-576-3800), which takes visitors through seven levels of marine habitats housing some 10,000 animals in buildings on two piers ($14).

Alongside the aquarium, the **Baltimore Maritime Museum** (☎ 410-369-3153) consists of ship tours aboard a Coast Guard cutter, a lightship and a submarine ($5.50). The **Baltimore Civil War Museum** (☎ 410-385-5188), farther east in the 1849 President St train station, tells the story of the 1861 'first blood' riot ($2, guided tour $5).

A walk south of Harborplace leads past a carousel and on to the **Maryland Science Center** (☎ 410-685-5225), with interactive exhibits, a Hubble telescope and an IMAX

theater ($10, films extra). The avant-garde **American Visionary Art Museum** (☎ 410-244-1900), across the street, showcases the genius of 'outsider' artists ($6; closed Mon); there's also an unusual gift shop and bistro.

The **Star-Spangled Banner Flag House & 1812 Museum** (☎ 410-837-1793, 844 E Pratt St) opens the home where Mary Pickersgill sewed the flag that inspired Francis Scott Key's now-famous poem ($4; closed Sun-Mon). **Port Discovery** (☎ 410-727-8120), at President and Baltimore Sts, has several interesting attractions for kids ($10/7.50 adults/kids). The **Babe Ruth Museum** (☎ 410-727-1539, 216 Emory St), birthplace of the 'Sultan of Swat,' is a must for fans ($6).

Downtown

Historic Lexington Market is the Grand Central Station of Baltimore's markets, with more than 140 merchants; time your visit around lunch or happy hour Friday (closed Sun). Find **Edgar Allan Poe's grave** in Westminster Cemetery. The **Edgar Allan Poe Museum** (☎ 410-396-7932) is at 203 N Amity St ($3). **Oriole Park at Camden Yards**, home of the city's beloved baseball team, is due south (it's also a major transit terminal).

Mt Vernon

Baltimore's own **Washington Monument** crowns regal Mt Vernon Square; climb 228 steps to the top of the obelisk for a city view or see the exhibits in its base ($1; open Wed-Sun). The grand **Walters Art Gallery** (☎ 410-547-2787, 600 N Charles St), also overlooking the square, is the city's finest museum, with an art collection from ancient to contemporary, a historic house of Asian treasures, and blockbuster exhibits ($6, free Sat morning; closed Mon); there's also a great atrium cafe.

Black-clad students around the square probably study at the **Peabody Conservatory of Music** (☎ 410-659-8124), the USA's oldest classical-music school; note the impressive 1878 library. 'Restaurant Row' is nearby up N Charles St. The **Maryland Historical Society** museum (☎ 410-685-3750, 210 W Monument St) relates state history with period rooms and many inviting, kid-friendly exhibits ($4, free Sat morning; closed Mon).

Federal Hill & Around

On a bluff overlooking the harbor, **Federal Hill Park** lends its name to the comfortable neighborhood set around the Cross St Market. **Fort McHenry National Monument** (☎ 410-962-4290), southeast, is where the star-spangled banner still waved following the British attack on Baltimore during the War of 1812 ($5).

Southwest Baltimore & Around

'SoWeBo,' as locals like to call this area, is a low-rent district with a few bohemian hangouts set around Hollins Market. The **B&O Railroad Museum** (☎ 410-752-2490), in Mt Clare station, will impress even non–train buffs with its collection of 22 walk-aboard train cars and engines in a restored 1884 roundhouse with a 123-foot-high skylight ($7, extra for train rides, which operate weekends only).

Fells Point & Little Italy

Cobblestones fill Market Square (scene of many street festivals) between the **Broadway Market** and the harbor in the historic maritime neighborhood of Fells Point. A number of 18th-century homes now house restaurants, bars and shops that range from funky to upscale. Ethnic enclaves dot the area, most notably Little Italy, due west.

North Baltimore

Beyond North Ave, **Johns Hopkins University** (☎ 410-516-8171) and a few attractions are found within this largely residential district. The **Baltimore Museum of Art** (☎ 410-396-7100, W www.artbma.org), at N Charles and 31st Sts, houses the state's largest art collection ($6; open Wed-Sun). The **Baltimore Zoo** (☎ 410-366-5466), within Druid Park, has an exceptional children's section ($8.50/5).

Organized Tours

The Harbor Shuttle (☎ 410-675-2900) lands at many of the harborside attractions ($3-5). Nightly harbor cruises on the *Nighthawk* (☎ 410-327-7245) include a buffet meal ($33), and a two-hour sail aboard the *Clipper City* (☎ 410-931-6777) starts at $16.

Places to Stay

Baltimore, Quick Guide (☎ 410-783-7520), at tourist offices, has discount coupons and advertisements. Because of its proximity to the city and ample transit, Baltimore's airport does not have the gulch of motels typical of major airports.

HI Baltimore is currently closed for much-needed renovations; contact HI Washington, DC (☎ 202-737-2333) for updates. *Abbey Hotel* (☎ 410-332-0405, 723 St Paul St), run-down but still serviceable, charges from $28/49 with shared/private bath.

Budget motels can be found farther west on Washington Blvd in Elkridge, 8 miles from downtown. It is better to stick to a chain motel. *Super 8* (☎ 410-796-0400), off I-95 exit 41A in Jessup, 9 miles north of the airport, costs about $60 for a single.

Quality Inn at the Stadiums (☎ 410-727-3400) has standard singles/doubles at $70/75 (less in winter). *Holiday Inn* (☎ 410-685-3500, 301 W Lombard St), a mere block from Camden Yards, has a huge indoor pool (from $130). *Mount Vernon Hotel* (☎ 410-727-2000, 24 W Franklin St) has nine floors of functional rooms (from $95) and free shuttles. *Betsy's B&B* (☎ 410-383-1274, 1428 Park Ave), in Bolton Hill, has tidy singles/ doubles from $65/90. *Mr Mole B&B* (☎ 410-728-1179, 1601 Bolton St), nearby and more upmarket, charges from $110.

Days Inn Inner Harbor (☎ 410-576-1000, 100 Hopkins Place) has standard two-bed rooms from $135. *Clarion Hotel* (☎ 410-727-7101, 612 Cathedral St), a historic old building, overlooks Mt Vernon Square (from $160). *Admiral Fell Inn* (☎ 410-522-7377, 888 S Broadway), a guesthouse in Fells Point, overlooks Market Square (from $165, including continental breakfast). *Celie's Waterfront B&B* (☎ 401-522-2323, 1714 Thames St), a block away, charges from $135 for rooms with private baths. Large high-priced convention hotels line the Inner Harbor.

Places to Eat

Since the neighborhood markets cover the need for quick, inexpensive meals so well (most stay open until 5pm), the city's restaurants tend to be more formal and expensive than you might think.

Inner Harbor & Downtown There are many restaurants and food stalls in the popular Harborplace complex. *Light St*

Pavilion has bargain food with some stands representing the town's best restaurants, and **Pratt St Pavilion** has traditional sit-down restaurants.

The *ESPN Zone* mega-sports-bar is among many choices in Pier 5's Power Plant complex. *Joy America Café*, at the American Visionary Art Museum, a walk or water-taxi ride away, serves Latin American and Asian fare. *Charleston (1000 Lancaster St)* is known for its Southern cuisine, and the **Blue Moon Café** *(1621 Aliceanna St)* is a neat coffeehouse nearby (with hash browns to die for).

Downtown, Lexington Market offers a wide array of cheap stand-up food stalls. *Faidley's*, inside and seatless, has a popular raw bar known for $1 oysters and crab cakes ($4.50 regular to $12 'all lump'). *Women's Industrial Exchange & Restaurant (333 N Charles St)*, a place with character, has an old-fashioned menu and waitstaff (open for breakfast and lunch daily).

Mt Vernon There are many wonderful and exotic choices along nicely strollable blocks of N Charles St (watch for weekday all-you-can-eat lunches).

Louie's The Book Store Café (518 N Charles St) has bistro meals (from $6). *Akbar (823 N Charles St)* has Indian lunch buffets ($8). *Brass Elephant (924 N Charles St)* serves modern American cuisine ($20 pasta lunches). *Brewer's Art (1106 N Charles St)* is equally popular and has a similar menu. *Azeb's (322 N Charles St)* serves delicious Ethiopian meals and has a bar. *Donna's Coffee Bar (800 N Charles St)* started here and has spread all over the city; it's a reliable coffeehouse with Mediterranean cuisine. *Bombay Grill (2 E Madison St)* is another Indian place similar to Akbar's.

Federal Hill The *Cross St Market* has several places to sit down and eat, including a sushi bar, and weekend happy hours at the raw bar until 8pm. *Sisson's (36 E Cross St)*, among the many restaurants nearby, serves good Cajun/Creole food. *One World Cafe (904 S Charles St)*, a trendy vegan/vegetarian eatery (dishes under $5) displays the work of local artists. It's within walking distance of Camden Yards through a light in-dustrial area. *Bicycle (1444 Light St)* is a buzzing place serving Cuban roast pork and contemporary cuisine.

Fells Point & Little Italy The *Broadway Market*, in two buildings, has a health food/herb shop and several places to sit down and eat; the water taxi stops nearby. Restaurants and bars line both sides of Broadway for blocks. *Bertha's (7345 S Broadway)* has great mussels ($9 a bowl), salads and sandwiches. *Adrian's Bookstore Cafe (714 S Broadway)* serves coffee and focaccia and features couches and a 2nd-story view of the busy street below.

To the west, Little Italy's relatively pricey restaurants are concentrated along three hard-to-park blocks of S High St at Eastern Ave. *Amiccis (231 S High St)* has more of a fast-food setting, with a great appetizer of six jumbo shrimp in a hollowed-out loaf of Italian bread; *Luigi Petti (1002 Eastern Ave)* has outdoor seating; and *Dalesio's (829 Eastern Ave)* has traditional pasta meals from $15.

Other Locales In SoWeBo, *Hollins Market* has food stalls selling bean soup for $1.50 and chitterling platters along with fresh produce and seafood (closed Mon). *Bayou Blues Café (8133 Honeyglo Blvd)*, north of the city in White Marsh, is a really popular Louisiana-style place known for delicious Cajun/Creole food.

Entertainment

With the famous Peabody Conservatory of Music as a central reservoir for musical talent, there is no shortage of all forms of live entertainment in this town. The theater scene is particularly rich, and most spectator sports attract lively, vocal crowds.

Bars & Clubs For local live entertainment, head to the many bars and clubs in Fells Point, such as the popular *Wharf Rat (801 S Ann St)* or *Orpheus (1003 E Pratt St)*, which attracts a clientele of gays and Goths, among others.

Buzzing *Baja Beach Club (55 Market Place)* brings the sun to Baltimore, and *Havana Club (600 Water St)* is a very popular cigar bar. *Cat's Eye Pub (1730 Thames St)* and *Baltimore Brewing Co (104 Albemarle St)* are two popular watering holes. *Mick O'Shea's* (328 N Charles St) features Irish music.

Ze Mean Coffee Bean (1739 Fleet St) is a storefront coffeehouse that features live jazz on Sunday. *13th Floor/Club 13* (1 E Chase St), in Mt Vernon, has live music each night from 9:30pm.

Mt Vernon has been described as the 'gay ghetto'; for information on events and venues, get the *Baltimore Gay Paper* or *Baltimore Alternative*. *The Hippo* (1 W Eager St) is the city's largest gay club. *Afterhours Club* (1722 Charles St) is a mixed crowd these days, and *Allegro* (1101 Cathedral St) is a good meeting place on Friday night.

Performing Arts For classical arts, check for performances of the *Baltimore Symphony Orchestra* (☎ 410-783-8000) at Meyerhoff Symphony Hall, the *Baltimore Opera* (☎ 410-685-5086), at the Lyric Opera House, and student recitals at the *Peabody Conservatory of Music* (☎ 410-659-8124, 1 E Mount Vernon Place).

Theater companies include *Center Stage* (☎ 410-332-0033, 700 N Calvert St) for Shakespearean productions, and *AXIS Theatre* (☎ 410-243-5237, 3600 Clipper Mill Rd) for exciting new works. For movies, the *Orpheum* (☎ 410-732-4614), in Fells Point, screens revivals and art films. Huge concerts are held at the *Pier 6 Concert Pavilion* (☎ 410-625-3100).

Spectator Sports

The Baltimore Orioles (☎ 888-484-2473) play baseball in Oriole Park at Camden Yards during the April-to-October season. Attending a game is a sure way to experience the spirit of the city. The 2000 NFL champion Baltimore Ravens (☎ 800-551-7328) play football in PSINet Stadium at Camden Yards. The Baltimore Thunder (☎ 410-321-1908), the lacrosse team, plays at the Baltimore Arena, west of the Inner Harbor.

Getting There & Around

Most major airlines serve Baltimore-Washington International (BWI) Airport, 10 miles south of downtown via Route 295. The cheapest way downtown is by MTA light rail (☎ 410-539-5000) directly from BWI to Lexington Market and Penn Station. Weekday hourly MARC trains (☎ 800-325-7245 local) make the 16-minute trip between Penn Station and a rail station near BWI. Check ⓦ www .mtamaryland.com for all schedules and fares. SuperShuttle (☎ 800-258-3826) runs an airport-van service to the Inner Harbor for $12 one way; buy tickets at the ground transportation desk at C Pier. The taxi fare is around $20.

The Greyhound terminal (☎ 410-752-1393, 210 W Fayette St) is near Lexington Market. Buses run to Philadelphia, Pennsylvania ($18; 2½ hours); New York ($37; 4 hours); and Washington, DC ($10; 1 hour). Trains stop at Baltimore's Penn Station (1515 N Charles St), in a fine area bordering North Baltimore. Amtrak runs to Philadelphia, Pennsylvania ($60; 1½ hours); New York ($70; 2¼ hours); and Washington, DC ($22; 40 minutes). MARC operates weekday commuter trains to/from Washington, DC ($5.75/11.50 one way/roundtrip) – the cheapest, most convenient way to travel between these cities.

The congested one-way streets and parking that is either high-priced (particularly around the Inner Harbor) or difficult to find (around many restaurant districts) present challenges to out-of-town drivers. Fortunately, the compact downtown and ample transit (particularly the appealing water taxis) make Baltimore easy to see without a car. The Mass Transit Administration (MTA; ☎ 410-539-5000) has information on Baltimore's bus, light rail and metro systems. Travel anywhere within the city costs $1.35 (correct change required). Ed Kane's (☎ 410-563-3901) operates water taxis to a dozen convenient stops around the Inner Harbor, including Little Italy and Fells Point (day tickets $4.50) – a cheap harbor tour.

AROUND BALTIMORE

In the 100 sq miles of Piedmont fields and forests north of Baltimore lies the renowned **Horse Country**. The scenic Worthington and Greenspring Valleys here (which make for nice country drives off I-83) breed Olympic riders and champion horses – Sagamore Farms (between Worthington and Shawan), the birthplace of Secretariat, is the world's highest-earning thoroughbred stud farm.

The region's premier social event is Glyndon's Maryland Hunt Cup Race, in

April (☎ 410-429-4231); also watch for the 10-day Timonium State Fair, in August.

City folk like to go antiquing weekends in historic **Ellicott City**, a scenic old mill town that hugs steep hillsides 10 miles west of Baltimore via I-695 exit 13. The 1830 depot is now a rail museum (☎ 410-461-1944). There are plenty of cafes and shops, and the local business association (☎ 410-465-1449) has a historic-walking-tour map.

ANNAPOLIS

Maryland's capital since colonial times, Annapolis retains its colonial appearance with much original 18th-century architecture and design. Narrow lanes lined with brick row houses radiate from traffic circles drawn around the primary church and State House. From its perch on the highest hill, the State House overlooks the harbor that established Annapolis as an important port after the area was first settled by Puritans in 1649. The US Naval Academy was established here in 1845. Today the town is also well known as the USA's sailing capital; it has 17 miles of waterfront and is home dock to more than 2500 craft.

There's a visitor bureau (☎ 410-280-0445, W visit-annapolis.org, 26 West St) and a seasonal information booth at City Dock. The Maryland Visitors Center (☎ 410-974-3400) is in the State House.

Things To See & Do

The prestigious **US Naval Academy** is the undergraduate college of the US Navy. There's a visitor center (☎ 410-293-2293) at the City Dock entrance and a naval museum on the 338-acre 'yard' (never 'campus'). Most visitors come to see the **formation** daily at 12:05pm sharp. This is when the 4000 midshipmen or -women carry on a 20-minute military marching display in the plaza around their massive dormitory – a memorable spectacle (free admission).

The country's oldest state capitol in continuous legislative use, the stately 1772 **State House** (☎ 410-974-3400) also served as the fledgling national capitol for a short time in 1733–34, when it housed the Continental Congress. The Senate is in action here January to April (free tours Mon-Sat).

The **Maritime Museum** (☎ 410-268-5576), on the western side of City Dock, celebrates Annapolis' maritime and trading

history (free admission). There are several other historic buildings. Established in 1696, **St John's College**, at College Ave and King George St, is one of the USA's three oldest colleges. The 1735 **Old Treasury Building**, alongside the State House, is Maryland's oldest official building.

The city's premier historic houses are the 1774 colonial **Hammond Harwood House** (☎ 410-269-1714; $5) and 1765 Georgian **William Paca House & Garden** (☎ 410-263-5553; $5/7 house only/house and gardens).

The **Banneker-Douglass Museum** (☎ 410-974-2893, 84 Franklin St), long ago a church, relates Maryland's African American history (free admission; open Tue-Sat).

Annapolis abounds with **sailing** schools, cruises and bareboat (sail-it-yourself) charters. Among these, Chesapeake Marine Tours (☎ 410-268-7601) operates 40-minute harbor cruises for $6 – a great deal. Two-hour cruises on the 74-foot schooner *Woodwind* (☎ 410-263-7837) cost $25 (closed Nov-Apr); or stay aboard overnight – see Places to Stay & Eat. The 19-mile **Baltimore & Annapolis Trail** (☎ 410-222-6244) is a popular recreational route that follows the old B&A Short Line Railroad. Downtown Cycles (☎ 410-268-5794) rents bicycles. Historic Annapolis walking tours leave daily from their museum store (☎ 410-267-7619, 77 Main St), at City Dock.

Places to Stay & Eat

Unfortunately, there is no budget lodging downtown. *Capitol KOA Campground* (☎ *410-923-2771, 768 Cecil Ave)*, in Millersville, 12 miles away, has sites for $27 without hookups. Drivers can find motel rooms for around $60 clustered at Hwy 50 exit 22. *Econo Lodge* (☎ *410-224-4317)* and *Days Inn* (☎ *410-224-2800)* are here. For free accommodation referrals, call ☎ 800-848-4748.

Gibson's Lodgings (☎ *410-268-5555, 110 Prince George St)* has the least expensive rooms in the historic district (B&B-style from $75). *ScotLaur Inn* (☎ *410-268-5665)*, run by the folks from Chick & Ruth's Delly (see below) charge from $75 for B&B rooms upstairs. *Flag House* (☎ *410-280-2721, 26 Randall St)* is an upmarket B&B (from $120). *Historic Inns of Annapolis* (☎ *410-263-2641)* has three impressive historic inns in and around State Circle (from

$180 in summer). **Woodwind** (☎ 410-263-7837), a 74-foot schooner, costs $200 per couple for a night aboard.

All stand for the Pledge of Allegiance at **Chick & Ruth's Delly** (165 Main St) a 24-hour diner, at 8:30am (9:30am weekends). **La Rose de Saigon** (860 Bay Ridge Rd) dishes up tantalizing Vietnamese fare. **Market House**, at the city dock, offers many wonderful and inexpensive choices, including good muffins, brie-and-prosciutto sandwiches ($5) and a raw bar. **Middleton Tavern**, City Dock at Randall St, is a historic waterfront place, offering $1 'oyster shooters' and seafood feasts. **Buddy's Crabs & Ribs** (100 Main St) has rib-and-seafood plates from $15. Near Church Circle **49 West** (49 West St) serves traditional breakfasts and continental sandwiches and has live entertainment Tuesday to Saturday.

As the T-shirts proclaim, 'Annapolis is a drinking town with a sailing problem' – so there's no shortage of bars. **Rams Head Tavern & Fordham Brewing Co** (33 West St) attracts out-of-towners for well-known acts, and it's among a dozen such places in the historic district. **Galway Pub** (61 Maryland Ave) is a popular Irish bar with live entertainment and food (Irish stew $10).

Getting There & Around
Baltimore's MTA (☎ 800-543-9809) bus 210 travels between Baltimore and Annapolis. Greyhound runs buses to Washington, DC ($11.50; 1 hour). Annapolis Transit (☎ 410-263-7964) buses and trolleys provide local transport.

SOUTHERN MARYLAND
The shores of Chesapeake Bay south of Annapolis draw weekenders to convenient sailing and sunbathing spots nestled among forests, farms and marshland that get progressively quieter (sometimes deathly quiet) farther south.

Chesapeake Beach
This small-time clapboard resort peaked in the Roaring Twenties, but after the 1980s boaters rediscovered its sheltered and sandy shore, townhouse condos and espresso cafes followed. The inviting mile-long boardwalk is downtown, and a **railway museum** (☎ 410-257-3892) is sheltered in the small 1900 depot (free admission).

Breezy Point Beach & Campground (☎ 410-535-0259) is south of town ($20/25 tent/RV sites); there are cabins nearby. **Wesley Stinnetts** (8617 Bayside Rd), a seaside restaurant with home cooking, attracts 'CB' residents. **Lagoons Island Grille** (8416 Bayside Rd) has good daily specials (half a pound of shrimp for $7). **Rod N Reel**, at Mears Ave and Route 261, is also popular (jumbo crab cakes are $15).

Southern Calvert County
In Prince Frederick, Calvert County Tourism (☎ 410-535-6355) guides you to attractions, including Chesapeake Beach and popular parks farther south such as seasonal **Flag Ponds Nature Park** (☎ 410-586-1477; $6 per car; swimming permitted) and **Calvert Cliffs State Park** (☎ 301-872-5688; $3; no swimming), great for fossil hunting. **Lickedly Splits** (825 Solomons Island Rd), near Prince Frederick, is a good roadside stop for ice cream and deli food.

Jefferson Patterson State Park (☎ 410-586-8500), along the Patuxent River, charts 12,000 years of Native American culture through its archaeological sites and museum (free admission).

Solomons
Once a sleepy waterfolk town, Solomons Island has been transformed to a crisp New England–like sailing center. The visitor center (☎ 410-326-6027) is off Route 2.

Calvert Marine Museum (☎ 410-326-2042), across the way at the octagonal lighthouse, holds exhibits on estuarine biology and local maritime history ($5).

Small, outboard-motor boat rentals cost around $45 for half a day.

Patuxent River Campsites (☎ 410-586-9880, 4770 Williams Wharf Rd), on Broomes Island, is 15 miles north of Solomons; sites are $18-25 (open May-Oct). **Solomons Victorian Inn** (☎ 410-326-4811, 125 Charles St) has good rooms from $90. **By-The-Bay** (☎ 410-326-3428, 14374 Calvert St) is a tidy B&B. **Lighthouse Inn** (14636 Solomons Island Rd) has all-you-can-eat banquets for $25.

St Mary's City
Historic St Mary's City (☎ 301-862-0990) is a living-history park with costumed interpreters occupying original and re-created buildings on the site of Maryland's original

CAPITAL REGION

waterfront settlement, which dates back to 1634 – sort of a mini-Williamsburg in a now nearly deserted corner of the state ($7.50; open Mar-Nov).

Point Lookout State Park

At Maryland's southern tip, this breezy state park (☎ 301-872-5688) was once the site of a Civil War prison. Today it offers swimming, canoe rentals and an excursion ferry to Smith Island in summer ($20). *Campsites* are $15/21 per tent/RV site (reservations required; check ⓦ www.dnr.state.md.us).

EASTERN SHORE

On the Delmarva Peninsula, the Eastern Shore was settled 300 years ago by shorepeople (farmers) and waterfolk from England's west coast. Explore the backroads and Chesapeake waterways to discover the area's charm. The knot of villages west of Easton offer a particularly scenic bike tour, including a ferry ride and seafood stops.

Easton

Established around a 17th-century Quaker meeting house and an 18th-century courthouse still in use, Easton still has many 18th- and 19th-century buildings in its tidy historical district downtown. Handy local maps can be found at the Talbot County Office of Tourism (☎ 410-822-4606, ⓦ www.talbotcounty.md, 210 Marlboro Rd), off the Route 322 Bypass.

The **Historical Society of Talbot County** (☎ 410-822-0773, 25 S Washington St) runs a museum and offers house-museum tours (museum or three-house tour $3, combo $5). Three miles south of town, the hexagonal **No Corner for the Devil Church** dates back to 1881.

Budget motels charging around $80 are along Ocean Gateway/Hwy 50 just east of downtown. *Econo Lodge* (☎ *410-822-6330)* is one of these. *Chaffinch House* (☎ *410-822-5074, 132 S Harrison St)*, a Queen Anne building in town, has B&B rooms from $95. *Inn at Easton* (☎ *410-822-4910, 28 S Harris St)* is similar. *Tidewater Inn* (☎ *410-822-1300, 101 E Dover St)* is the town's premier inn.

Cafe 25 (5 Goldsborough St), an Italian deli, does a great seared-shrimp Caesar salad and pizza ($10). *Time Out Tap & Grill* (219 Marlboro Rd) is an atmospheric watering hole with good steaks. *Eagle*

Spirits (7590 Oxford St), in the Easton golf club, serves hearty lunches and dinners.

Trailways (☎ 410-822-3333) stops at the Texaco station on Hwy 50 N.

St Michaels

Standing beside the octagonal lighthouse that has become a symbol of Chesapeake Bay, St Michaels dates back to the 18th century. It's famous as 'the town that fooled the British': During the War of 1812, the inhabitants rigged up a system of lanterns in a nearby forest and blacked out the town. British naval gunners mistook the lanterns for the town and shelled the forest instead, allowing St Michaels to escape destruction. More notoriety followed the publication of James Michener's novel *Chesapeake*. Today this precious waterfront village attracts sailors from around the Chesapeake Bay to its marina, restaurants, B&Bs and 'shoppes.'

In the landmark lighthouse, the **Chesapeake Bay Maritime Museum** (☎ 410-745-2916) also features a boat shop, sailboats and historic houses at its base ($7.50). **St Mary's Square Museum** occupies an 1800 gristmill.

Rent bikes and motorboats at the town dock marina. One-hour narrated historic cruises aboard the *Patriot* (☎ 410-745-3100) leave from the Crab Claw dock ($9).

Best Western St Michaels Motor Inn (☎ *410-745-3333)*, a mile east on Route 33, charges from $85. In town, half a dozen exclusive B&Bs charge upward of $100 (or try a 'bed & boat' – ☎ 410-745-9701). *Carpenter St Saloon*, on Talbot St at Carpenter St, is a good old corner bar with meals. Though expensive *208 Talbot* (☎ *410-745-3838, 208 N Talbot St)* is expensive but has simply superb meals; try the rack of New Zealand lamb or oysters in champagne sauce.

Bay Hundred

The term 'Bay Hundred' comes from the English division of Maryland into 'hundreds' for administrative and military purposes. Anglo Saxon hundreds were 10 families, 10 estates, or 100 fighting men. Colonists used the distinction of 'hundreds' in Maryland until after the American Revolution.

– Randy Peffer

Tilghman Island

At the end of the road over the Hwy 33 drawbridge, the town of Tilghman Island retains its traditional waterfolk roots – traces of Cornish coastal dialects still distinguish islander accents. Local captains take visitors out on working boats from Dogwood Harbor. If you're interested, try the HM *Krentz* (☎ 410-745-6080) or the *Rebecca T Ruark* (☎ 410-886-2176), the oldest skipjack on the Chesapeake. There are tours with Tilghman Island Cruises (☎ 410-886-2513).

Harrison's Chesapeake House (☎ 410-886-2121), on Route 33, charges from $95 for rooms with two beds and has a restaurant; inquire about fishing charters. *Black Walnut Point Inn* (☎ 410-886-2452), on Black Walnut Rd, has excellent B&B rooms ($120-150 for one to two people). *Bay Hundred Restaurant* (6178 Tilghman Island Rd) serves steaks, seafood, and tasty cream-of-crab soup.

Oxford

Europeans settled here in the early 1660s, and English gentry thrived through the tobacco and slave markets. Oxford boomed again as a late-19th-century oyster-trading center.

Robert Morris Inn (☎ 410-226-5111), at the ferry dock, is a venerable 1710-era place with fine dining and rooms from $100. *Oxford Inn & Pope's Tavern* (☎ 410-226-5220, 506 S Morris St) has great rooms from $70/90 weekdays/weekends.

The Oxford-Bellevue Ferry (☎ 410-745-9023), the nation's oldest ferry (started in 1683) crosses the Tred Avon River to Bellevue in about 10 minutes (cars $6.50 roundtrip; closed in winter). From Bellevue you can drive or cycle 7 miles to St Michaels. Find bike rentals and picnic supplies at the Oxford Mews general store (☎ 410-820-8222).

Blackwater National Wildlife Refuge

Twenty miles south of Easton, 17,000 acres of tidal marshes protect migrating waterfowl; also here are the Delmarva fox squirrel and eagles. There are trails, drives and a visitor center (☎ 410-228-2677). Birdwatching is best mid-Oct to mid-Mar ($3/1 cars/cyclists).

Ocean City

Known as 'OC,' Maryland's mammoth Atlantic coast resort swells from a year-round population of 7500 to a summer throng of 300,000, when Coppertone-slicked beachgoers crowd the boardwalk corn-dog stands and Skee-Ball arcades and cruise along the Coastal Hwy, lined with budget motels.

The visitor bureau (☎ 410-289-8181) and local hotel-motel-restaurant association (☎ 410-289-5645, W www.ocvisitor.com), in the swank convention center on the Coastal Hwy at 40th St, can help you find lodging and more.

Extending 2½ miles from the inlet to 27th St, the **boardwalk** is the center of the action. At the southern end, a museum at the Coast Guard station has exhibits on lifesaving (☎ 410-289-4991; $2), but OC is all about the beach.

Many establishments are only open during temperate months; prices plummet in the off-season. Traffic is jammed and parking scarce in summer.

Carolina Trailways (☎ 410-289-9307), 2nd St and Philadelphia Ave, has regular buses to major regional cities. The Ocean City Municipal Bus Service (☎ 410-723-1607) runs the length of the beach daily (day pass $1).

Places to Stay & Eat The *Ocean City Travel Park* (☎ 410-524-7601), on Coastal Hwy at 70th St, has tent sites for $32 (for more camping options see Assateague Island, later). *Summer Place Youth Hostel* (☎ 410-289-4542, 104 Dorchester St), not an HI affiliate, fills quickly in high season ($25 per day, $90 per week).

Of the 9500 guest rooms in town, the cheapest are found around the inlet at the south end and throughout town on the bay side. *Thunderbird Beach Motel* (☎ 410-289-8136), 32nd St and Baltimore Ave, has good rooms from $35/65 weekdays/weekends. *Surf Villa* (☎ 410-289-9434, 705 N Baltimore Ave) costs from $45 but leaps to $74 in summer. *Buckingham Motel* (☎ 410-289-6246), at 14th St and Baltimore Ave, has remodeled rooms from $44 and lots of package deals. *Admiral* (☎ 410-289-4805), at 9th St and Baltimore Ave, has average rooms from $75. *Commander Hotel* (☎ 410-289-6166), at 14th St and the boardwalk, has comfortable cabanas from $69/92

CAPITAL REGION

on weekdays/weekends. *Hotel Monte Carlo* (☎ 877-375-6537), at 3rd St and Baltimore Ave, charges $45-120 for rooms with two double beds, depending on the season.

Restaurants are as plentiful as motels, and plenty of cheap eats line the boardwalk and Coastal Hwy (watch for many all-you-can-eat and early-bird deals, particularly on seafood). The *Hobbit*, on 81st St, is one of OC's best seafood restaurants (entrées from $20). *Fager's Island* (☎ 410-524-5500), on 60th St at the bay, is well known for prime rib and as the place where the *1812 Overture* precedes every sunset, followed by applause.

Seacrets, Bayside at 49th St, is a great place with festive atmosphere, Jamaican food and live entertainment. *Macky's Bayside Bar & Grill*, at 53rd St overlooking Assawoman Bay, has Creole food and great views. *Shenanigans*, at 4th St and Boardwalk, is a popular bar, and *Paddock/Big Kahuna*, at 17th St and Coastal Hwy, combines nightspots.

Assateague Island

This beautiful 37-mile-long barrier island preserves a rare stretch of undeveloped seashore. Legendary herds of wild horses roam free on the island. Its lower third is in Virginia (see Chincoteague Island under Virginia, earlier). Get maps and information at the Barrier Island visitor center (☎ 410-641-1441), on Route 611 (entry $5 per vehicle, $2 per cyclist or pedestrian).

Two *campgrounds* (☎ 800-365-2267) maintained by the National Park Service (NPS) are near the access road and cost $10 ($14 peak season). There is *backcountry camping*, a great alternative ($5 permit plus $5 NPS entry fee). *Assateague State Park* (☎ 410-641-2120) offers 350 campsites with bathrooms and hot showers for $20/30 without/with hookups.

WESTERN MARYLAND

This obscure region offers mountain recreation set against scenic Appalachian landscapes and significant Civil War sites, most notably Antietam. Note that many attractions in this area may close in winter (check Ⓦ www.mdmountainside.com).

Frederick

Halfway between the blockbuster battlefields of Gettysburg and Antietam, Frederick is a popular stop on the Civil War trail. Its quiet 50-square-block historic district retains many 18th- and 19th-century buildings in various states of renovation. The visitor center (☎ 301-663-8687, 19 E Church St), at Market St, conducts weekend walking tours ($4.50); there's parking next door.

The **National Museum of Civil War Medicine** (☎ 301-695-1864, 48 E Patrick St), Frederick's premier attraction, guides visitors through a personal look at the health conditions soldiers faced on battlefields and beyond ($5). The **Historical Society of Frederick** (☎ 301-663-1188), across from the visitor center, opens its historic mansion furnished with period antiques and local artwork ($2); inquire about other historic house museums in town.

Gambrill State Park (☎ 301-271-7574), 5 miles northwest on Route 40, charges campers $10/14 weekdays/weekends for sites. Chain-motel rooms at around $65 are south of town off I-270. *Comfort Inn* (☎ 301-695-6200) is at the Jefferson St exit, and *Days Inn* (☎ 301-694-6600) is at the Route 85 exit.

Taverns, a deli and an Irish pub can be found along Market St from the creek promenade north through the historic district. *Mudd Puddle (124 S Carroll St)* prepares tasty, inexpensive Italian sandwiches. The *Common Market (5813 Buckeystown Pike)* sells quality natural foods.

The Greyhound station (☎ 301-663-3311) is on E All Saints St. Weekdays, MARC trains stop 15 miles southwest at Point of Rocks; the extension to Frederick has not yet been completed.

Antietam National Battlefield

Called 'Sharpsburg' by Southerners, the Battle of Antietam (ann-**tee**-tum) was the bloodiest day of the Civil War and in US history. On September 17, 1862, General Lee's first invasion of the North was stalled in a tactical stalemate that left 23,000 dead, wounded or missing. The battlefield and surrounding area are solemn and haunting, uncluttered save for plaques and statues. Living-history demonstrations are held monthly June to December.

The visitor center (☎ 301-432-5124), on State Rd 65, offers driving-tour pamphlets and audiotapes ($5) to guide you past 8 miles of evocative landmarks; free summer talks and walks are also offered (admission $2).

The neighboring town of Sharpsburg has few services; it's better to continue across the river to eat (see Shepherdstown under West Virginia, later) or stay in a chain in Hagerstown to the north.

Cumberland

At the Potomac River, the frontier outpost of Fort Cumberland was the pioneer gateway across the rugged Alleghenies to Pittsburgh and the Ohio River (not to be confused with the famous Cumberland Gap between Virginia and Kentucky). It also was a vital base during the French and Indian War.

At the western end of the C&O Canal and the first national pike (Alt 40 these days), Cumberland boomed in 19th-century transport and later as an industrial center serving local coalfields. Today Cumberland remains largely industrial but has begun to expand an outdoor-recreation trade to guide visitors to the region's rivers, forests, mountains and ski areas.

The **Transportation & Industrial Museum** (☎ 301-724-4398, 13 Canal St) is in the 1913 Western Maryland Station Center, along with Allegheny County visitor bureau (☎ 301-777-5132). The terminus National Park Service visitor center (☎ 301-722-8226) for the C&O Canal National Historic Park is in the depot on Canal St.

Outside, passengers catch steam locomotive rides aboard the **Western Maryland Scenic Railroad** (☎ 800-872-4650, W www .wmsr.com), traversing forests and steep ravines to Frostburg ($16-18; 3 hours roundtrip). Nearby, Allegheny Adventures (☎ 301-729-9708) rents bikes seasonally; inquire about tours. Another local outfitter is Allegheny Expeditions (☎ 301-722-5170), on Route 2.

C&O Canal National Historic Park

The Chesapeake & Ohio (C&O) Canal was designed to stretch alongside the Potomac River from Chesapeake Bay to the Ohio River – linking commercial centers in the East with the frontier resources of the West. Construction on the canal began in 1828 but was halted in 1850 in Cumberland by the rugged Appalachian Mountains. By then the first railroad had made its way to Cumberland, in time rendering the canal obsolete.

The canal was considered a marvel of engineering technology. Studded with 74 lift locks, seven dams, 11 aqueducts and a 3000-foot tunnel, the canal diverted traffic around the rapids and waterfalls that had made the river unnavigable beyond Georgetown.

The C&O Canal National Historic Park (☎ 301-739-4200) commemorates the importance of river trade in eastern-seaboard history and provides recreational opportunities within its historic setting (see also Georgetown under Washington, DC, earlier). Along its protected 185-mile corridor, the park preserves the 12-foot-wide towpath as a hiking and biking trail. There are six visitor centers along the trail's length (Georgetown, Great Falls Tavern, Brunswick, Williamsport, Hancock and Western Maryland Station).

One of the best adventures the canal provides is a leisurely, near-level **mountain-biking** excursion from Cumberland to Georgetown, camping and stopping at locks, waterfalls and towns along the way (three days; bike it independently or with local groups and outfitters). Rentals are readily available along the trail.

Frostburg

In Frostburg, Cumberland's steam train stops at the depot center, where there's a restaurant and The Thrasher Carriage Museum (☎ 301-689-2010, 19 Depot St), a vintage horse-drawn carriage display. *Charlie's Motel (☎ 301-689-6557, 220 W Main St)* charges $30/36 for singles/doubles. *Gandalf's (16 W Main St),* a culinary oasis in these parts, has sizable vegetarian meals at reasonable prices.

Rocky Gap State Park

This park (☎ 301-777-2139), 15 miles east of Cumberland in Flintstone, has hiking, boating, swimming and campsites ($16/21 tents/RV hookups). The Rocky Gap Music Festival – the Woodstock of traditional bluegrass – is held the first week in August near the state park (contact the park office for details).

Green Ridge State Forest

This forest, southeast of Rocky Gap, shelters turkey, deer and black bear among its rugged woods and pristine streams; obtain

CAPITAL REGION

camping, hiking and fishing information at the visitor center (☎ 301-478-3124) within Rocky Gap State Park via I-68 exit 64.

Western Highlands

West of Cumberland lies mountain wilderness readily traversed on I-68 or the more scenic Route 40. A useful site is W www.visitwesternmaryland.com.

Ski areas include **New Germany State Park** (☎ 301-895-5453), best for Nordic skiing, and **Wisp Resort** (☎ 301-387-4911), for downhill. There's much mountain-biking activity in summer.

The Youghiogheny River (simply 'yock') is known for its top-notch Class V-plus rapids. Outfitters are centered in Ohiopyle, Pennsylvania.

Delaware

Despite some industrialist-backed grand homes and endowed museums in the northern part of the state, this region holds few attractions compelling enough for USA travelers to prolong a detour here. Some backroad wanderers consider stopping in New Castle or Dover for lunch on the way to seaside resorts. Beware: Sandwiched between Delaware Bay and the Atlantic, the state is often battered by foul weather.

Delaware is well known for the homespun 'Brandywine School' of artists of the early 20th century – Howard Pyle, NC Wyeth, Andrew Wyeth and Maxfield Parrish are highly regarded as illustrators and painters.

History

The first European settlement, by the Dutch in 1631, was wiped out by the local Nanticoke Indians. Swedes arrived in 1638 and began trading for furs and cultivating grain. In 1655 the flourishing settlement was claimed by the Dutch, and then later taken over by the English. The Swedes and Dutch continued to farm the north, while English settlers established tobacco plantations and slavery farther south.

Initially aligned with the Pennsylvania colony, largely autonomous Delaware became recognized as a separate colony when the Mason-Dixon line defined its boundaries, and by the mid-18th century it was a booming center for exports to the West Indies.

When Delaware joined the Revolutionary War, English frigates blockaded Wilmington's port and 18,000 British troops landed nearby. George Washington brought 11,000 soldiers to protect the Brandywine Valley and the port, but he was outflanked and withdrew to Valley Forge while the British occupied Wilmington. Dover Green was the site of the Delaware convention that ratified the Federal Constitution. Delaware was the first state to sign the Constitution and is thus the 'first state' of the Union, giving it precedence in national ceremonial occasions.

In 1802 a French immigrant named du Pont started a gunpowder factory on the Brandywine Creek, which profited greatly in the War of 1812. Despite its slave-owning farms, Delaware, like Maryland, sided with the Union in the Civil War.

In the 20th century, industrial growth in general, and du Pont's booming chemical businesses in particular, contributed to the state's prosperity. The state's low taxes (no sales tax) and liberal incorporation laws have made it a center for commerce. About 200,000 companies are incorporated here, including half of the nation's Fortune 500.

Information

The Delaware Tourism Office (☎ 302-739-4271, 866-284-7489, W www.visitdelaware.net)

Delaware

Nicknames: Diamond State, First State

Population: 783,600 (46th)

Area: 2489 sq miles (49th)

Admitted to Union: December 7, 1787 (1st)

Capital city: Dover (population 33,000)

Other cities: Wilmington/Newark (72,500)

Birthplace of: nylon, Miss USA pageant (1880)

Famous for: low taxes, liberal corporate regulations

Home of: half the nation's Fortune 500 companies

is at 99 King's Hwy, Dover, DE 19903. A useful visitor center (☎ 302-737-4059) is on I-95 between exits 1 and 3. There's an 8% lodging tax but no sales tax on other goods or services.

NORTHERN & CENTRAL DELAWARE

Northern Delaware, known as 'castle country,' includes the great du Pont mansion Winterthur. The state capital, Wilmington, lies at the gateway to the scenic Brandywine Valley. Central Delaware, the region south of the Chesapeake & Delaware Canal, is a mosaic of neatly tended farms and marshes and home to Dover, the state capital.

Wilmington

Delaware's largest city sits at the confluence of Brandywine Creek and Christina River. The central commercial district is along Market St. The visitor center (☎ 302-652-4088, W www.wilmcvb.org) is at 1300 Market St, and the local historical society and city history museum are in the 500 block. A mile from downtown, the **Delaware Art Museum** (☎ 302-571-9590, 2301 Kentmere Pkwy) exhibits examples of the local Brandywine School ($5).

Hotel du Pont (☎ 302-594-3100), in the commercial district at Market and 11th Sts, is the city's premier hotel (doubles from $180). *Deep Blue (111 W 11th St)* is an American fish house with live entertainment, and *Govato's (800 N Market St)* is an old-fashioned candy store and restaurant.

Greyhound/Carolina Trailways (☎ 302-655-6111) stops at 318 Market St. Amtrak (☎ 302-658-1515) stops at the foot of Market St.

Brandywine Valley

The rural Brandywine Valley, straddling the Delaware-Pennsylvania border, is accessible from Wilmington or Philadelphia. The Brandywine Valley Tourist Information Center (☎ 610-388-2900), outside Longwood Gardens in Kennett Square, Pennsylvania, distributes information on the region's châteaus and museums.

Winterthur (☎ 302-888-4600, W www.winterthur.org), the valley's highlight, includes the 175-room country estate of industrialist Henry Francis du Pont, along with a decorative arts museum and gardens that can be viewed by tram. It's a monument to American excess ($8).

See the Around Philadelphia section of the New York & Mid-Atlantic States chapter for more on the Brandywine Valley's attractions.

New Castle

Seven miles south of Wilmington, historic New Castle retains cobblestone streets and attractive blocks of 18th-century buildings. It was originally founded by the Dutch in 1651; later the English gained control, and the colony established its legislature here in 1704.

The Historic New Castle Visitors Bureau (☎ 302-322-8411) arranges walking tours, or you can wander the compact old town on your own. The district is laid out in an easy grid around a small park called 'The Green' and along Delaware St to the riverside Strand. Sights include the Old Court House (closed Sun-Mon), the arsenal on the Green, churches and cemeteries dating back to the 17th century, and historic houses, which can be toured.

Contact the visitor bureau about several *B&Bs* in town. *Jessop's Tavern (114 Delaware St)* is a 1724 English tavern serving inexpensive pub food, and *Arsenal on the Green* has regional and continental dishes ($30 for dinner).

Dover

Since William Penn laid out The Green on State St in 1722, the square remains the historical center of the state capital. The 1792 Old State House and 1874 Court House here are tucked beside attractive brick row houses shaded by tall trees.

Walk beside the State House to find the Delaware State Visitors Center (☎ 302-739-4266, 406 Federal St) and history exhibits at the foot of a long plaza from the new capitol. A few blocks away (look for signs), the **Johnson Victrola Museum** honors native son and 'talking machine' pioneer Eldridge Johnson with exhibits including the RCA trademark 'His Master's Voice' dog (free admission; open 10am-3:30pm Tue-Sat).

Dover Air Force Base, used by giant C-5 Galaxy aircraft, is also the US military morgue (shown on TV whenever the government brings home a dead American).

The **museum** (☎ 302-677-5938) has an expanding collection of vintage planes and other artifacts (free admission; open 9am-4pm daily).

There are budget motels along the tacky Hwy 13 strip. *Relax Inn* (☎ *302-734-8120*), south of the Hwy 113 split, has tidy rooms for $57/67. *Dover Inn* (☎ *302-674-4011*) and *Budget Host* (☎ *302-678-0161*) are similar.

Barking Frog (*33 Loockerman St*) is a good coffeehouse that features entertainment on weekends. *WT Smithers* (*140 S State St*) is an inviting downtown tavern good for a drink and food (jazz brunch on Sun). *La Tolteca* (*245 S Du Pont Hwy*) provides Tex-Mex well north of that border. *Hollywood Diner*, out on Hwy 13, is a 1950s-style diner with cheap fare (open 24 hours).

DELAWARE SEASHORE

Delaware has 28 miles of sandy Atlantic Ocean beaches, some preserved as state parks. Many businesses, campgrounds and services are open only for an extended summer season when prices are highest; off-season bargains abound.

Lewes

Anchoring Cape Henlopen, Lewes (**loo**-iss) has more history than your ordinary beach town. The Dutch founded a whaling settlement here in 1631, and though the whalers were massacred by Native Americans, more Europeans were soon attracted to its natural harbor. Today the rugged cape beachscapes are the town's biggest draw.

The visitor bureau (☎ 302-645-8073, 120 Kings Hwy) directs you to sights such as the small **Zwaanendael Museum** (☎ 302-645-1148), which houses 18th-century shipwreck treasures inside a distinctive 1931 replica of a Dutch town hall (free admission; closed Mon). Kids particularly enjoy hourlong steam-train excursions offered by **Queen Anne's Railroad** (☎ 302-644-1720) twice a week in summer ($11/7). Rent bikes at Lewes Cycle Sports (☎ 302-645-4544).

Savannah Inn (☎ *302-645-5592, 330 Savannah Rd*), in a house in tiny downtown, charges from $70 for twin rooms, with a vegetarian breakfast provided. *Zwaanendael Inn* (☎ *302-645-6466*), at 2nd and Market St, is a continental-style hotel with twins from $55 on weekdays. *Grist Mill Inn* (☎ *302-645-*

6968), on Robinsville Rd, is typical of excellent B&Bs (from $100 a double). *Aurora Grill* (*329 Savannah Rd*) serves good sandwiches under $5 and breakfast all day.

The Lewes–Cape May ferry (☎ 800-643-3779 for reservations, ☎ 302-426-1155 for schedule), across Delaware Bay to New Jersey, runs daily 70-minute ferries to and from the terminal a mile from downtown Lewes ($7.50 for pedestrians over age six, $20 and up for vehicles according to length).

Cape Henlopen State Park

East of Lewes, more than 3000 acres of tall dune bluffs, pine forests and wetlands are preserved in an attractive state park (☎ 302-645-8983) that's popular with bird-watchers and beachgoers ($5 per out-of-state car). You can see clear to Cape May, New Jersey. There's a nature center, well-kept bath-houses and paved bike paths. 'North Beach' draws many gay and lesbian couples. The *campground* (☎ *302-645-2103*) is a half-mile walk from the beach ($27 with hookups); there are also comfortable 'yurts' available.

Rehoboth & Dewey Beaches

Downtown Rehoboth Beach is an appealing old seaside town tucked behind a very congested and tacky stretch of Hwy 1 (follow signs to 'Resort Area'). The main drag, Rehoboth Ave, is lined with restaurants, food stalls and souvenir shops, from the easy-to-miss visitor center (☎ 302-227-2233) at the old depot (501 Rehoboth Ave) to the mile-long beach boardwalk.

It's overwhelmed by 50,000 visitors each summer, a blithe mix of families, gay couples, students and yuppies. 'Poodle Beach' is a favorite gay hot spot; under-30s tend to congregate farther south at **Dewey Beach**, among the condos, motels, restaurants and bars lining Hwy 1.

Greyhound/Carolina Trailways (☎ 919-833-3601) buses stop on Rehoboth Ave; buses run to/from Wilmington ($15) and Dover ($10).

The *Big Oaks Campground* (☎ *302-645-6838*), a largely residential RV park 3 miles from the boardwalk off Hwy 1, charges $20; pool and beach shuttles are available.

Homey guesthouses within two shady blocks of the beach are preferable to highway motels, though somewhat pricey in season for aging accommodations without pools. Most include continental breakfast (the visitor center has a list).

Summer Place Hotel (☎ *302-227-0766, 30 Olive Ave)* has condos and hotel rooms for $40-95 depending on room size (add $30 at peak times). *Dinner Bell Inn* (☎ *302-227-2561, 2 Christian St)* charges $55-95 for garden rooms midweek (more on weekends and in peak season). *Mallard Guest House* (☎ *302-226-3448, 60 Baltimore Ave),* close to the beach, is also highly recommended. *Rehoboth Guest House* (☎ *302-227-4117, 40 Maryland Ave)* is gay-owned and -operated. It is popular, and reservations are recommended.

The beach boardwalk and Rehoboth Ave have dozens of food stalls and bars. *Brew Ha Ha (70 Rehoboth Ave)* is an excellent coffeehouse, and the nearby *TCBY (60 Rehoboth Ave)* dispenses cups and cones for around $2. Good restaurants are on Wilmington Ave from the boardwalk to 2nd St; among these are *La La Land* and *Planet X*. *Obie's by the Sea* (☎ *302-227-6261),* at Olive Ave and the boardwalk, has a great outside deck and serves sumptuous dishes of seafood, chicken and ribs.

At *Sydney's Blues & Jazz (25 Christian St),* a good selection of visiting acts supplements tasty Creole dishes on the menu. *Sir Guy's (243 Rehoboth Ave)* offers reggae, rock and delicious crabcakes to a 20s-plus crowd. *Irish Eyes at the Anglers (213 Anglers Ave)* also has live music. Out on Route 1, *Renegade* (☎ *302-227-4713)* is the town's premier gay venue, with live music every night in season. *Cloud 9* (☎ *302-226-1999, 234 Rehoboth Ave)* gets a mix of gay, lesbian and straight folk.

Delaware Seashore State Park

On the narrow peninsula south of Dewey Beach, this state park (☎ 302-227-2800) offers a pristine beach and bayside trails ($5 per out-of-state vehicle). The *campground* (☎ *302-539-7202)* charges $18/25 for tents/ RV hookups.

West Virginia

Travelers to West Virginia will find rugged terrain, vast stretches of Appalachian topography and wild white-water rivers. It is one of the least developed states but has its own distinctive culture.

West Virginia

Nicknames: Mountain State, Switzerland of America

Population: 1,808,350 (35th)

Area: 24,231 sq miles (41st)

Admitted to Union: June 20, 1863 (35th)

Capital city: Charleston (population 57,300)

Other cities: Huntington (55,500), Wheeling (36,000)

State motto: Mountaineers Are Always Free

Birthplace of: General 'Stonewall' Jackson (1824–63), aviator Charles E 'Chuck' Yeager (b 1923), gymnast Mary Lou Retton (b 1968), actor Don Knotts (b 1924), Mother's Day (1908)

Famous for: Appalachian highland culture, mountain recreation

The Appalachian highlands are known for outstanding handicrafts, including woodworking, quilts, basketry and glassmaking, and for 'mountain' music. Outstanding recreational opportunities include whitewater rafting and paddling adventures along the New, Gauley and Cheat Rivers, hiking excursions, mountain biking, rock climbing, spelunking and skiing.

History

Originally part of Virginia, the land west of the Appalachians was settled in the mid-17th century by pioneering small farmers of a different stripe than the large tobacco plantation owners in the Tidewater. This rift grew with the Civil War and the secession of old Virginia's slave owners, and the mountain region that remained aligned with the Union was declared a separate state in 1863.

After the war, timber and coal companies arrived to exploit the natural resources – and the mountaineers – of West Virginia. Despite the early development of labor unions, West Virginia was economically depressed for many years, and it remains among the nation's poorest states. The effects of strip mining on the landscape can be most readily seen in the region south of the capital, around Madison. West Virginia's cities continue to serve largely as industrial centers, though as the seat of government, Charleston has more to offer.

Though coal, mineral and timber processed through West Virginia's industrial cities remain important to the state's economy, growing numbers of recreationists drawn to the natural beauty support a tourism industry that strives to disturb the environment less.

Information

The West Virginia Division of Tourism (☎ 304-348-2200, 800-225-5982, W www .state.wv.us, 2101 Washington St E, Charleston, WV 25305) operates Welcome Centers at interstate borders and in Harpers Ferry (☎ 304-535-2482).

The State Parks Office (W www .wvparks.com, State Capitol Complex, Charleston, WV 25305) operates a toll-free reservations line (☎ 800-225-5982). State sales tax is 6%.

EASTERN PANHANDLE

I, John Brown, am now quite certain that the crimes of this guilty land will never be purged away, but with blood....

– abolitionist John Brown,
on the way to the scaffold, 1859

The northeast of this rugged state is best known for the historic village of Harpers Ferry, but there are also quaint old towns where you can lose yourself in the past.

Harpers Ferry

This town packs a rich history and tremendous recreation onto a scenic spit of land where the Shenandoah and Potomac Rivers meet to form the boundaries of three states. The federal armory here was the target of abolitionist John Brown's raid in 1859, and though Brown's ambition to arm slaves and spark a national rebellion against slavery died once he was caught and hanged, the incident incited slaveholders' worst fears and helped precipitate the Civil War. Union and Confederate forces soon fought for control of the armory and town.

With little development altering the antebellum appearance of the tiny downtown, the district was declared a national historic

park in 1986. Today visitors and residents alike may walk the steep cobblestone lanes and wander among the shops without charge, but staffed museum buildings are accessible to pass holders only. Passes, parking and shuttles are available above town at the National Park Services visitor center off Hwy 340 (☎ 304-535-6298) for $5/3 per vehicle/pedestrian.

Things to See & Do Among a score of sites in the historic district, the 1858 **Master Armorer's House** explains how rifle technology developed here revolutionized the firearms industry; the **Storer College building**, long ago a teachers' college for freed slaves, now traces the town's African American history. The **John Brown Museum** tells the story of his raid in wax ($4).

Passing through town, the 2160-mile **Appalachian Trail** (AT) is headquartered at the Appalachian Trail Conference (☎ 304-535-6331, W www.atconf.org), at Washington and Jackson Sts, a tremendous resource for local hikers as well as backpackers (open Apr-Oct). Day hikers also scale the Maryland Heights Trail past Civil War fortifications or the Loudoun Heights Trail for scenic river views.

You can rent bikes to explore the **C&O Canal** towpath (also see C&O Canal National Historic Park, under Western Maryland, earlier); the visitor center has a list of outfitters. To arrange raft/float excursions, contact Rivers & Trails (☎ 301-695-5177) or River Riders (☎ 800-326-7238).

Places to Stay & Eat The *Harpers Ferry KOA* (☎ 304-535-6895), 2 miles southwest on Hwy 340, is open year round and boasts a pool ($26/32 tent/RV sites, $42 cabins).

In town are several higher-priced motels and B&Bs within walking distance of the AT or train station. *Hilltop House* (☎ 304-535-2132, 400 E Ridge St) has good views ($50/65 weekdays/weekends). *Cliffside Inn* (☎ 304-535-6302), on Route 340, is also a good choice ($60/75 weekdays/weekends). *Comfort Inn* (☎ 301-535-6391), on Route 340 across from the National Park Service visitor center, is a rare chain in these parts (rooms from $65).

HI Harpers Ferry Lodge (☎ 301-834-7652, 19123 Sandy Hook Rd), 2½ miles from the train station in Knoxville, Maryland, charges members/nonmembers $15/17 for dormitory lodging; inquire about camping or shuttles (closed Nov to mid-Mar). *HI Bears Den* is a 20-mile hike south of Harpers Ferry (see Leesburg, Northern Virginia, earlier).

The Anvil (1270 Washington St) has seafood and steak entrées and fun happy hours. *Country Cafe*, on Washington St near the West Virginia visitor center, is a local alternative to higher-priced cafe food in the park district. *Mudfort Crest* serves pub food a few doors down.

Getting There & Around Harpers Ferry is a rarity: a rural destination well served by rail. Daily Amtrak (☎ 800-872-7245) and MARC (☎ 800-325-7245) trains run between the historic-district station and Washington's Union Station (bikes permitted if disassembled and boxed).

Shepherdstown

An unexpected little jewel, Shepherdstown dates back to 1762 and is the oldest town in the state. Home of Shepherd College, the sophisticated town boasts several restaurants, cafes and arty shops along a short length of German St. It hosted the Israeli-Syrian Peace Talks in 2000. The visitor center (☎ 304-876-2786) is across from the courthouse. Shepherdstown makes a great biking destination along the C&O Canal towpath 12 miles north of Harpers Ferry (see C&O Canal National Historic Park, under Western Maryland, earlier).

Bavarian Inn (☎ 304-876-2551) has garden-view rooms for $85-135. *Old Pharmacy Cafe*, on E German St, offers gourmet sandwiches, salads and pasta plates, along with soda-fountain treats and espresso.

For entertainment, see movies at the restored 1909 *Opera House (☎ 304-876-3704)*, check out local musicians at the *Mecklenberg Inn (☎ 304-876-2126)* or call Sherpherd College (☎ 304-876-5497) for its performing-arts schedule.

Amtrak and MARC trains stop at a whistle-stop 4 miles from town.

Berkeley Springs

Off scenic Hwy 9, quirkily quaint Berkeley Springs was visited by George Washington and other founding fathers for its thermal springs. Today **Berkeley Springs State Park**

(☎ 304-258-2711) features Roman-style baths along with saunas and massage; it's open daily year round ($10 for 30 minutes' bathing).

Country Inn (☎ 800-822-6630), next door, offers its own 'Renaissance' spa with mineral whirlpools for two (more expensive than the state park); there are good weekend accommodation packages which include spa. Most B&Bs start at around $80 a double. *Lot 12 Public House (302 Warren St)* has a good selection of entrées ($17-25).

MONONGAHELA NATIONAL FOREST

This vast expanse of rugged terrain in the Allegheny Mountains is the kind that earned West Virginia the nickname 'the Colorado of the East.' Within its 1400 sq miles, the forest encompasses wild rivers, caves and the highest peak in the state (Spruce Knob). More than 850 miles of trails include the 124-mile **Allegheny Trail**, for hiking and backpacking, and the scenic 75-mile 'rails-to-trails' **Greenbrier River Trail**, popular with cyclists.

Elkins, at the forest's western boundary, is a good base of operations. Here the National Forest Service office (☎ 304-636-1800, 200 Sycamore St) distributes recreation directories for hiking, biking and camping (campsites from $5, primitive sites free; few hookups).

The **Augusta Heritage Center** (☎ 304-637-1209, 800-624-3157), on the Davis & Elkins College campus, hosts a folk music and dance summer camp for adults that culminates in a weeklong city festival in Aug.

Elkins Bikeworks (218 Randolph St) rents gear and sponsors excursions.

For city information, the visitor center (☎ 304-636-2717) is at the south end of town near McDonald's. The Forest Service (ⓦ www.fs.fed.us) has detailed information on Monongahela.

An 8-mile portion of the Allegheny Trail links two full-service state parks 30 miles northeast of Elkins: **Canaan Valley Resort State Park** (☎ 304-866-4121), a downhill ski resort, and **Blackwater Falls State Park** (☎ 304-259-5216), with backcountry ski touring (restaurants, lodge rooms, cabins and campgrounds available at both). Farther south, the **Snowshoe Mountain Resort** (☎ 877-441-4386, ⓦ www.snowshoemtn.com) is the state's

CAPITAL REGION

largest downhill resort and has also become a mountain-biking center from spring to fall (rentals and excursions available).

Nearby, the **Cass Scenic Railroad State Park** (☎ 304-456-4300) runs steam trains from an old logging town to mountaintop overlooks daily in summer and for peak fall foliage (from $10). Accommodations include *cottages* for six (from $85). Other highlights include the surreal landscapes at **Seneca Rocks**, 35 miles southeast of Elkins, which attract rock climbers to demanding challenges up 900-foot-tall sandstone strata. *Seneca Shadows Campground* (☎ 877-444-6777) is handy to the rocks (basic single/double sites for $8/10).

SOUTHERN WEST VIRGINIA
This is one of the true getaway places close to the eastern seaboard, truly representative of the 'Mountain' state. It is a mecca for white-water rafting, hiking, mountain biking and cross-country skiing. Check the Southern West Virginia Web site (W www.visitwv.com).

New River Gorge National River
A 1000-foot-deep gorge is the dramatic setting for the best white-water rafting adventures in the eastern USA. The National Park Service (NPS) protects a stretch of the New River that falls 750 feet in 50 miles, with a compact set of rapids up to Class V concentrated at the northernmost end.

The **Canyon Rim Visitor Center** (☎ 304-574-2115), in Lansing north of the impressive gorge bridge, is the only one of five NPS visitor centers along the river that is open daily year round to provide information on river outfitters, gorge climbing, hiking and mountain biking, as well as rafting on rougher white water to the north in the Gauley River National Recreation Area. Rim and gorge trails offer beautiful views. There are four free basic *camping areas*.

Nearby **Hawk's Nest State Park** (☎ 304-658-5212) offers views from its rim-top lodge (doubles from $67/71 for forest/gorge views); in summer it operates an aerial tram down to the river, where you can catch a cruising boat ride (tram closed Mon). **Babcock State Park** (☎ 304-438-3004) offers camping from $13, rental cabins ($65 double) and boats, and 15 miles of trails.

Fayetteville
Among the many state-licensed rafting outfitters in the area, Driftabit (☎ 800-633-7232, W www.driftabit.com) and USA Raft (☎ 800-872-7232, W www.usaraft.com) operate out of Fayetteville. A typical adventure costs $50-60.

Matewan

The Tug Fork River region in West Virginia's southwest, already infamous because of the feud between the Hatfields and the McCoys, was the scene of a tense standoff between coal miners and mine owners in the early 1920s.

The operators decided to evict coal miners' families from company houses and brought in armed Baldwin-Felts security agents to assist. On a gray, drizzly day in May 1920 the Felts, led by their president Thomas Felts (and his brothers Albert and Lee), commenced evictions at Stone Mountain Mining Camp near Matewan.

The miners were incensed and armed themselves in response. Matewan sheriff Sid Hatfield, not satisfied that the evictions were legal, went to stop them, but the Baldwin-Felts persisted. When the Felts returned to Matewan, Hatfield tried to arrest Albert Felts. A shot was fired, and after a minute of volleying Albert and Lee Felts, seven other agents, Matewan mayor C Testerman and two miners were killed.

Fifteen months later, now folk-hero Hatfield and a witness were gunned down by Felts agents on the steps of the McDowell County Courthouse in nearby Welch. More than 10,000 outraged miners armed themselves in response. The US Army was called in on four occasions to quell subsequent disturbances – the biggest armed insurrection on US soil since the Civil War.

Mountain Laurel RV Park/Campground *(☎ 304-574-0188)* is a cheap camping option in town. ***Elliot's Whitewater Grill***, at Laurel Crescent and Route 19, is a good place to replenish after rafting.

Farther south off of Hwy 19, a poignant coal-miner memorial stands outside the county tourist office (☎ 304-465-5617), where lodging/camping directories can be found.

Beckley

At the I-64/I-77 gateway (exit 45) to the New River in Beckley, the state-operated **Tamarack** arts center (☎ 304-256-6843) offers some authentic but pricey handicrafts and surprisingly good and inexpensive meals; try the 'taste of WVa' special Tuesdays ($9).

Budget motels are found at interstate exits. Note that I-64/I-77 is a toll road northwest of Beckley. ***King Tut Drive-In***, on Eisenhower Dr, has been serving car-bound clientele for years.

Hinton

An anachronistic riverside railroad town, Hinton marks the southern upriver National Park Service (NPS) New River boundary. The seasonal NPS office distributes rafting information. The visitor center (☎ 304-466-5420, 206 Temple St) is downtown. The Amtrak station is downhill on 2nd St.

Here the river is more placid, with a few Class III rapids. Local outfitters include Cantreel Ultimate Rafting (☎ 304-466-0595) and Appalachian Backcountry Expeditions (☎ 304-466-5546). More water recreation and trails are found at nearby state parks.

An 8-mile trail running along the **Bluestone National Scenic River** goes from the base of the 1000-foot aerial tram at Pipestem Resort State Park (☎ 304-466-1800) on to Bluestone State Park (☎ 304-466-1922); you'll cross a small stream.

Camping and cabins are available at both state parks. ***Sandman*** *(☎ 304-466-1700)* and ***Coast-to-Coast*** *(☎ 304-466-2040)*, on Route 3/20 near the NPS office, are well-worn riverside motels that cater to the rafting trade (both charge around $38/49 singles/doubles). ***Rivertowne Inn*** *(☎ 304-466-6166, 315 2nd St)*, downtown, offers rooms from $50; it's a steep walk up from the train station.

Charleston

Situated along the Kanawha (ka-**naw**) River, the state capital is pleasant enough, though most travelers do not come to West Virginia to see its cities. The visitor bureau (☎ 304-344-5075, W www.charlestonwv.com) is at 200 Civic Center Dr.

The gold-domed **capitol** is worth a look. Within the plaza, a cultural center features state-history and mountain-heritage exhibits, and the *Mountain Stage* radio program broadcasts mountain music statewide to public broadcasting stations from the State Theater every Sunday.

Budget lodging is available off I-77. At the foot of Capitol St, a ***farmers' market*** at the old depot offers quick eats along with fresh flowers and produce. The city's true cultural oasis, ***Taylor Books*** *(226 Capitol St)*, two blocks from the river, has a bookstore and espresso bar with live weekend entertainment. ***Allie's*** *(200 Lee St)*, in the Marriott, is a popular local watering hole.

Amtrak trains, running daily between Chicago, Illinois, and Washington, DC, stop at the station across the river.

Great Lakes

Great Lakes

The Great Lakes area – part of the Midwest – is known as the USA's heartland. With its blend of old and new, city and farm, the region represents and reveals American life and culture. It doesn't have the glitz of New York, the profile of Florida or the sex appeal of California, but this is where political pollsters and product marketers come to find out what the nation is thinking and feeling. Places such as Kalamazoo, Peoria and Muncie have come to stand for small-town USA. Writers, too, have used the area to explore what makes the country tick. This largely unsung region of the country is not high on the list for most foreign visitors, yet Americans know the area as a holiday destination, and intrepid international travelers can unearth much of interest here.

Most of the Great Lakes' larger cities, founded as trading outposts or farm towns, began developing into transport, processing and industrial centers almost 200 years ago. Many became very wealthy, and as tides of European immigrants arrived, these cities also became centers of culture, with excellent art galleries, museums, orchestras and universities. They have been at the forefront of innovation in everything from transportation technology to architecture and modern music.

Beginning in the 1970s, the decline of traditional manufacturing industries hit the region hard, causing urban decay and the so-called Rust Belt desolation. A few visible reminders of this time remain, but visitors today might be surprised by the area's revitalized downtown areas, recycled buildings, vibrant nightlife, friendly people and positive, confident attitude. You'll find more than enough attractions here to make an extended visit both interesting and well worthwhile.

The Great Lakes themselves are huge, like inland seas. Though some parts of their shores are given over to industry and docklands, other areas offer beaches, islands, dunes, resort towns and lots of fine scenery. In addition, many thousands of smaller lakes in the region provide virtually unlimited potential for camping, canoeing and fishing. Fall brings gorgeous colors, and

Highlights

- Art Institute of Chicago – world-class collection of impressionist and American artwork

- Chicago jazz and blues – long a nurturing home and still a progressive hotbed of great music

- Frank Lloyd Wright architecture – masterpieces scattered in Chicago and southern Wisconsin

- Henry Ford Museum and Greenfield Village – shrines to car culture and US inventiveness in Dearborn

- Rock & Roll Hall of Fame & Museum – Cleveland's homage to the music the world lives by

- Wilderness walking and canoeing – peace, wildlife and adventure in Minnesota and Michigan's Upper Peninsula

OTHER MAPS
Great Lakes pages 400–401
Minneapolis–St Paul page 474

Great Lakes Warning

Relentless and evidently starving blackflies (spring) and mosquitoes (summer) can be an unfortunate reality in the northern woods. Protect yourself with a repellent, such as Muskol (not recommended for kids). Widely available hats with pull-down netting are another option. Tenters, make sure your tent has a fine mesh screening. Light-colored clothing also helps (sort of), as does a smoky fire.

Ask rangers about deer ticks and how to prevent bites. By late summer most bugs are gone, making this an ideal time to wet a paddle or hike a trail.

In winter, thin ice is a deadly hazard for skiers and especially snowmobilers. Always err on the side of caution, and don't trust the ice-safety opinion of anyone other than police, park or forestry officials. Every year people die after crashing through supposedly frozen lake ice.

winter (if you dare to go then) features skiing, snowmobiling and ice-fishing.

History

Humans have lived in this region for 5000 to 7000 years. Early inhabitants included the Hopewell culture, which emerged around 300 BC, and the Mississippi River moundbuilders, who flourished from around AD 600. These peoples cultivated the three 'sisters' (corn, squash and beans) and traded along established routes with other indigenous cultures as far away as Ontario, the Rockies and the Gulf of Mexico. They also built distinctive and mysterious mounds that were tombs for their leaders and possibly also symbolic expressions of homage to their deities. Many of these mounds can still be seen, notably near Chillicothe, Ohio, and you can visit the remains of a full-blown Mississippian city in East St Louis, Illinois. The mound-building cultures began to decline around AD 1000, and when the first Europeans arrived in the early 17th century, the area was home to various groups of farmers and hunter-gatherers, including the Miami, Shawnee and Winnebago.

The first Europeans were French voyageurs, who explored, traded for furs with the indigenous people and established missions and forts. But the French soon had rivals: The Ohio Company, a group of British entrepreneurs from England and Virginia, formed in 1748 to develop trade and control the Ohio Valley. Its explorations helped precipitate the French and Indian Wars (1754–61), after which Britain gained all the lands east of the Mississippi.

Following the Revolutionary War, the area south of the Great Lakes first became the new USA's Northwest Territories, but it was soon divvied up into states.

New settlers moved rapidly westward into Ohio, Indiana, Michigan and Illinois in the late 18th century, causing conflicts as the Native Americans were progressively displaced. After the 1803 Louisiana Purchase, the region became the gateway to further expansion west of the Mississippi, and the War of 1812 consolidated the US border with Canada. Initially, waterways were the region's vital transport routes, and canals were built linking the Great Lakes to the area's river systems. Fueled by resources of coal, iron and copper, industries sprang up and grew quickly thanks to railroad development and Civil War demands. Initial white settlement was mostly from East Coast states. But the growth of the region involved huge influxes – often described as 'waves' – of European immigrants from Ireland (in the early and mid-19th century), Germany (in the mid- to late 19th century), Scandinavia (in the late 19th century), Italy and Russia (around the turn of the 20th century), and southern and eastern Europe (in the early 20th century). In addition, for decades after the Civil War a huge number of African Americans migrated to the region's urban centers from the South. The legacy of these movements is still seen here in the cosmopolitan nature of the industrial cities and the northern European heritage visible in many rural areas.

The region prospered during WWII and through the 1950s. Then came 20 years of

GREAT LAKES

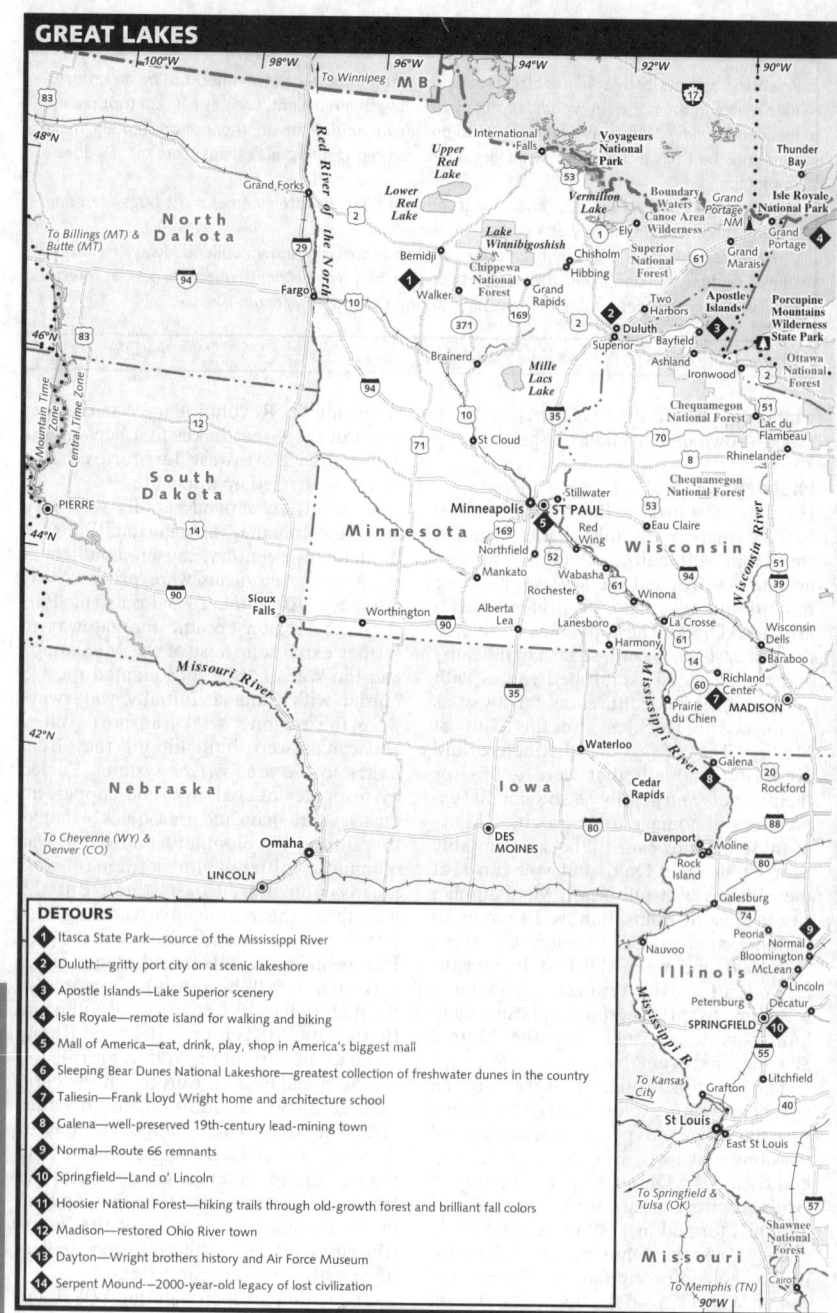

GREAT LAKES

DETOURS

1. Itasca State Park—source of the Mississippi River
2. Duluth—gritty port city on a scenic lakeshore
3. Apostle Islands—Lake Superior scenery
4. Isle Royale—remote island for walking and biking
5. Mall of America—eat, drink, play, shop in America's biggest mall
6. Sleeping Bear Dunes National Lakeshore—greatest collection of freshwater dunes in the country
7. Taliesin—Frank Lloyd Wright home and architecture school
8. Galena—well-preserved 19th-century lead-mining town
9. Normal—Route 66 remnants
10. Springfield—Land o' Lincoln
11. Hoosier National Forest—hiking trails through old-growth forest and brilliant fall colors
12. Madison—restored Ohio River town
13. Dayton—Wright brothers history and Air Force Museum
14. Serpent Mound—2000-year-old legacy of lost civilization

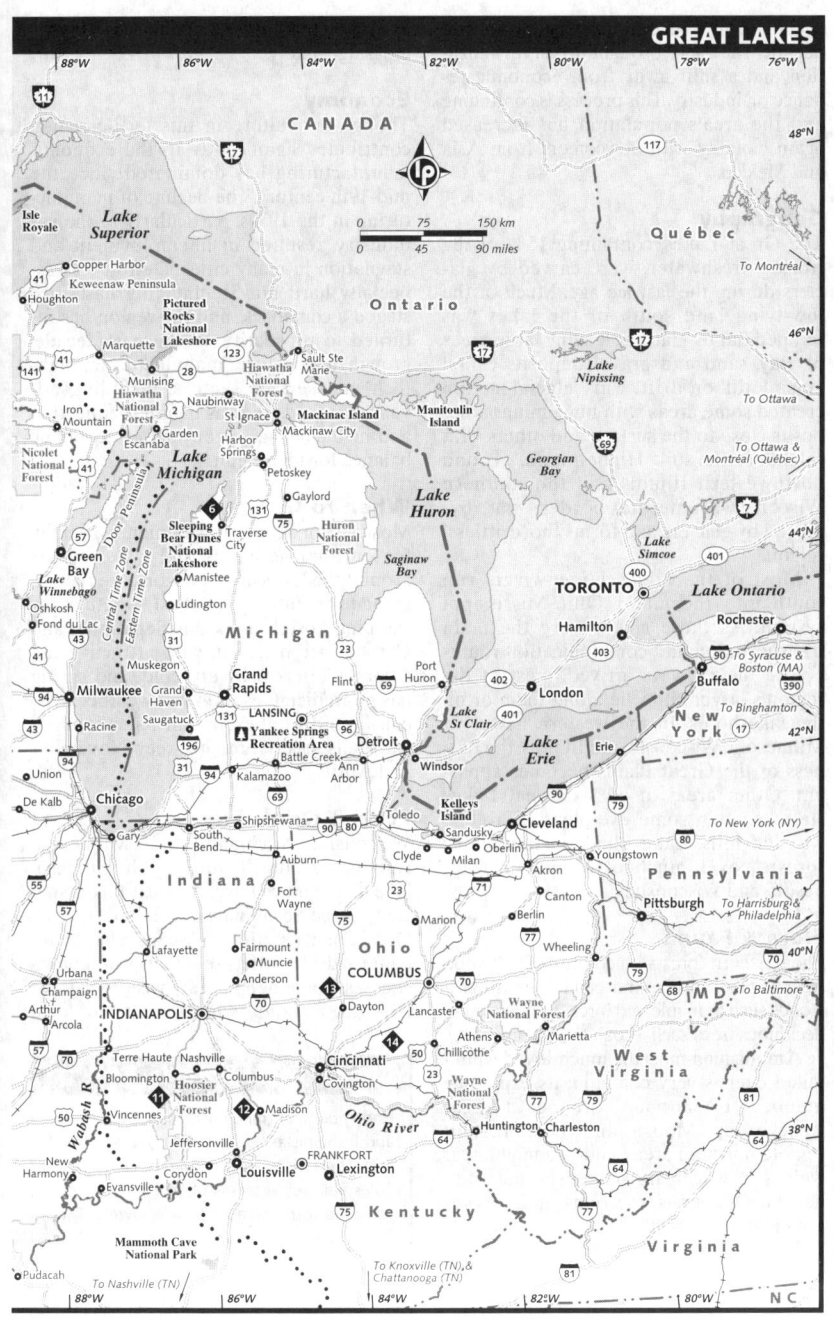

GREAT LAKES

social turmoil, economic stagnation and decline. The 1980s brought urban revitalization and a shift away from economic reliance on industry. This process is continuing and the area's population has increased again, notably with newcomers from Asia and Mexico.

Geography
The Great Lakes, containing 15% of the world's freshwater, were carved by glaciers during the last ice age. Much of the low-lying land south of the lakes was scraped flat by glaciers, leaving large areas of clay, sand and gravel deposits called glacial till or drift. This glacial action created some areas with huge mineral deposits close to the surface and others with thick, fertile soil. Higher land, around northwestern Illinois and the southern Wisconsin-Minnesota border, was bypassed by glaciers and forms the 'driftless' region.

Most of the area's larger rivers run south into the major Ohio-Mississippi system. As these rivers were the main transportation and communication routes before the railways arrived, most of the region's larger cities lie along them or on the lakeshores. In the western halves of Minnesota, Wisconsin and Illinois, the flatness of the Great Plains becomes apparent. Other areas of all six Great Lakes states contain some eye-pleasing, rolling wooded hills. Lake-filled north-country forests cover much of Michigan, Minnesota and Wisconsin.

Flora & Fauna
The northern forests hold a mix of softwood trees – pine, spruce and cedar – and hardwoods such as maple and birch. Farther south, deciduous trees such as oak are dominant.

Among mammals the much-loved white-tailed deer is very common; its exploding numbers often make driving at night treacherous. Moose and bear inhabit remote northern areas, and you might hear wolves in Michigan, Wisconsin and Minnesota. Opossums, raccoons and coyotes are plentiful.

Major sport fish include bass, lake trout, muskellunge, walleye and whitefish. Among birds, the loon charms visitors with its wonderful, varied cries, and bald eagle populations continue to rise, making a sighting increasingly likely.

Economy
Though agriculture in this fertile region contributes significantly to the economy, manufacturing has dominated since the mid-19th century. The decline of manufacturing in the 1970s, particularly in the car industry, resulted in unemployment and stagnation in many cities; Detroit was especially hard hit. Steelmaking has since staged a comeback, and the region has returned to prosperity. In the past decade, growth in the light manufacturing, high-tech and service sectors, including advances in fields such as banking, education and medicine, has meant better economic balance for the region.

When to Go
Most visitors come in summer, especially for outdoor activities and water sports around the lakes. Reservations are recommended in July and August, whether for camping, hostels or motels. September and October are pleasant, with attractive fall colors. Winters are very cold, and spring has unpredictable, often wet weather. Wisconsin and Minnesota can receive major snowfalls at any time between November and April.

Food & Drink
Wisconsin, Michigan and Minnesota restaurants often feature fresh whitefish, lake trout and walleye. A Great Lakes specialty is the Scandinavian fish boil (see the Door County section). Wisconsin has abundant roadside outlets selling its well-known cheeses. Some people may wish to sample the wines, mainly whites, made by local

Cheap, Local & Real
Had enough of trendy bistros, boutique beer and fashionistas? Grab a cold one at a VFW Hall. These visitor-welcoming, basic watering holes built for Veterans of Foreign Wars can be found scattered across the Midwest. They are tourist- and yuppie-free zones full of genuine Great Lakes character.

cottage industries, notably in Ohio and Michigan. If not, the cherry and grape ciders are certainly worth a try. Michigan's pasties are a specialty. The Midwest, notably Milwaukee, has long been known for beer, and several microbreweries maintain this tradition.

Activities

Hiking and backpacking opportunities abound in the area's numerous state and national parks and forests. Michigan's Upper Peninsula holds a long stretch of the 3000-mile North Country Trail, which extends from North Dakota to New York. Isle Royale National Park, Pictured Rocks National Lakeshore and Porcupine Mountains Wilderness State Park are also popular destinations. Minnesota's Lake Superior Hiking Trail is a beauty above the shoreline.

In northern Minnesota, the Boundary Waters Canoe Area Wilderness is renowned canoe country. Rivers in less wild areas throughout the Great Lakes states are suitable for canoeing – along many of them you'll find outfitters or 'canoe liveries' for rentals. Voyageurs National Park and Wisconsin's Apostle Islands provide challenging sea kayaking.

Bicycle touring opportunities are abundant as well. Excellent resurfaced 'rail trails' traverse converted old railroad grades in numerous areas, especially in Michigan and Wisconsin. Excellent cycling can also be found on many islands, including Mackinac in Lake Huron and Kelleys in Lake Erie. The area's forests are laced with trails for wintertime cross-country skiing. Snowmobiling is huge in northern Michigan, Wisconsin and Minnesota, which also offer downhill skiing.

Getting There & Around

Air Chicago's O'Hare International Airport is the main air hub for the region. Detroit, Cleveland and Minneapolis also have busy airports.

Bus Greyhound (☎ 800-231-2222), which originated in Minnesota, is the principal long-distance carrier and connects all major cities and towns. Secondary bus lines cover some areas. Some rural regions, particularly in northern Wisconsin and Minnesota, don't have any public transportation.

Train The national railroad network centers on Chicago, from where Amtrak (☎ 800-872-7245) runs trains regularly to major regional cities including Milwaukee, Detroit, Indianapolis, Cincinnati, Springfield and St Louis. Note that train stations are often closed except at arrival or departure times. Trains from Chicago to other parts of the country include the following:

Capitol Limited – to/from Washington, DC, via Toledo, Ohio; Cleveland, Ohio; and Pittsburgh, Pennsylvania

Cardinal – to/from Washington, DC, via Indianapolis, Indiana; Cincinnati, Ohio; and Charleston, West Virginia

Lake Shore Limited – to/from New York via Toledo, Ohio; Cleveland, Ohio; Buffalo, New York; and Albany, New York

International – to/from Toronto, Ontario (Canada), via Flint, Michigan; and Port Huron, Michigan

Empire Builder – to/from Seattle, Washington, via Minneapolis, Minnesota; Glacier National Park, Montana; and Spokane, Washington

California Zephyr – to/from San Francisco, California, via Omaha, Nebraska; Denver, Colorado; Salt Lake City, Utah; Reno, Nevada; and Sacramento, California

Southwest Chief – to/from Los Angeles, California, via Kansas City, Missouri; Albuquerque, New Mexico; and Flagstaff, Arizona

Texas Eagle – to/from San Antonio, Texas, via St Louis, Missouri; and Dallas, Texas

City of New Orleans – to/from New Orleans, Louisiana, via Memphis, Tennessee

Car & Motorcycle Southeast Michigan (including Detroit) is about the least expensive place in the region to rent cars. If you're traveling on major interstates (eg, the Ohio Turnpike), piles of change are useful for the tolls.

In winter, check conditions on the 24-hour weather station available on TVs with cable in most areas; heavy snow and road closings are not unusual. Carry a few candles to use for warmth in case you get stuck in the snow or suffer a breakdown; don't rely on your car heater, as leaving your car idling with the windows up could make you vulnerable to carbon monoxide poisoning.

Illinois

With its great museums, restaurants and jazz and blues clubs, Chicago (the 'City of Big Shoulders') can't help but dominate the state. But small, quiet, downstate towns, Abraham Lincoln history, Route 66 vestiges and prehistoric archaeological sites are among the many lesser-known treats Illinois offers its visitors.

History

Scattered prehistoric mounds across Illinois are evidence of early civilizations that not only used tools and pottery but had developed religious beliefs. When Europeans first arrived in the early 17th century, the southern and western parts of the region were inhabited by Algonquian-speaking peoples who had been displaced by Iroquois and other groups expanding from the north. French missionaries and traders explored the area via the Mississippi and Illinois Rivers and moved on to Lake Michigan, where they founded forts and villages in the late 17th century. After periods under the control of France, Britain and Virginia, Illinois became part of the Indiana Territory, allowing new settlers to acquire public land. Illinois Territory was proclaimed in 1809, and Illinois became a state in 1818.

In the state's first years, pioneer farming settlements spread rapidly. In the 1820s the completion of canals linking Lake Michigan with the eastern states stimulated growth in the north, especially in and around Chicago. New roads, steamboats and railroads facilitated further settlement of the western plains. This led to conflict with the Native Americans, culminating in the 1832 Black Hawk War and the forced removal of the indigenous people to areas west of the Mississippi.

Many early settlers were from the South and favored slavery, but there were abolitionists, too. The state's internal conflict on the issue was articulated in 1858 during the historic debates between senatorial candidates Abraham Lincoln and Stephen A Douglas. Despite divided loyalties, Illinois contributed greatly to the Union in the Civil War and in the process emerged as an industrial state, developing steelmaking, meatpacking, distilling and heavy manufac-

Illinois

Nicknames: Land of Lincoln, Prairie State
Population: 12,419,300 (5th)
Area: 57,900 sq miles (25th)
Admitted to Union: December 3, 1818 (21st)
Capital city: Springfield (population 105,200)
Other cities: Chicago (2,783,700), Rockford (139,400), Peoria (113,500)
Birthplace of: gunfighter Wyatt Earp (1848–1920); president Ronald Reagan (b 1911); author Betty Friedan (b 1921); former first lady and senator Hillary Rodham Clinton (b 1947); Rotary International
Famous for: the 'Chicago Schools' of architecture, poetry, sociology and economics

turing, including the production of farm machinery and railcars. This growth created great private wealth but also led to labor strife as workers struggled against low wages and poor conditions. Unions began forming in the mid-19th century, and violent strikes took place between 1877 and 1919.

The Prohibition era of the 1920s created a lucrative illegal alcohol trade that funded gangsterism and the wholesale corruption of the state's political system. Then the Great Depression hit hard – up to half of Illinois' workers were unemployed. In the 1930s, Democratic governor Henry Horner was able to rebuild state finances and restore honest and efficient government. WWII enabled the state economy to recover.

Today the state maintains one of the country's highest agricultural outputs: pork, corn and soybeans are most significant. Coal and oil are also major contributors to the economy. Chicago, despite battling social inequities and problems of serious poverty and crime, is a world center for trade and commerce and a major industrial center.

Geography

Most of Illinois is flat or undulating, with fertile soils of glacial till. The northwest corner has the most hills, while the scenic south encompasses sections of the Mississippi Alluvial Plain and the East Gulf

Coastal Plain. The state has hundreds of rivers and seven separate drainage basins.

Government & Politics

Illinois is predominantly Republican, although its representatives do not always enjoy a large margin over the Democrats. Chicago is a Democrat stronghold.

Information

The Illinois Bureau of Tourism (☎ 800-226-6632, W www.enjoyillinois.com) is at 620 E Adams St, Springfield, IL 62701. For highway conditions, call ☎ 800-452-4368. For state park information, call ☎ 217-782-7454 or individual parks. Some accept reservations. State parks are free to visit.

Sales tax in Illinois is 8.75% but may vary slightly depending on city and county.

CHICAGO

Chicago is, quite simply, a great city. It has great art, great architecture, great music, great shopping and great food. Its short history has seen it emerge as a leader in fields as diverse as trade unionism, blues music, nuclear physics and commodity trading. It's the prototypical modern city – the first place in the USA to develop a high-rise center surrounded by suburbs. Above all, Chicago has a gritty, hardworking realism about it. However in recent years Chicago has been going to great lengths to pretty itself up for its increasing numbers of visitors. It's a mecca for Midwesterners looking for culture and entertainment.

History

Native Americans in the region can be traced back to AD 1000. In the late 17th century, the region was dominated by the Potawatomi, who gave the name 'Checaugou' to the area around the Chicago River mouth. In 1779 Quebec trader Jean Baptiste Point du Sable established a fur-trading store on the north bank of the river. After the Louisiana Purchase, in 1803, the US government built Fort Dearborn here as a wilderness outpost.

The last Indian resistance was crushed in the 1832 Black Hawk War, and all the remaining Indian lands in Illinois were requisitioned, including the lands of the Potawatomi in Chicago. Five years later, Chicago incorporated as a town, with 4170 residents. When new canals opened in the 1840s, shipping between the Caribbean and New York began to flow through Chicago, traveling via the Mississippi River, Great Lakes and the St Lawrence Seaway. In 1851 the Illinois Central Railroad was given land to establish freight yards, and Chicago was soon the railroad hub of the USA.

The first steel mill opened in 1857, and immigrants flooded in to take jobs in industry and with the railroads – the population reached 100,000 by 1860. In 1871, the Illinois & Michigan Canal was deepened so that the Chicago River began to flow south, taking the city's sewage down the river instead of into the lake. On October 8, 1871, legend has it that Mrs O'Leary's cow kicked over a lantern and started the great Chicago Fire, which destroyed the whole inner city and left 90,000 homeless. This disaster enabled the city to replace wide areas of substandard housing and create space for modern industrial and commercial buildings.

The city's industrial workers had begun to organize as early as the 1860s, and for the next 50 years there were strikes and protests, many of them violent and brutally suppressed by police. The 1894 Pullman strike was put down by legal injunctions that effectively made strikes illegal in the USA for the next 30 years.

The Union Loop Elevated rail system was completed in 1897, defining the boundaries of the city center and making it feasible to commute from outer suburbs. Despite corruption and exploitation, more civic improvements were made in the early 20th century, and immigration swelled the population to more than 2 million by 1910.

In the 1920s, Prohibition led almost immediately to the infamous period of gangsterism and to even more widespread corruption. In the middle of the devastating Depression, after the murder of Mayor Anton Cermak, the Democratic Party machine gained control of city politics and maintained it for the next 50 years.

The city grew strongly during WWII; its population peaked in 1950, then started to decline as residents moved to outer suburbs and other states. Despite some improvements, the postwar period was dominated by corruption scandals, civil-rights

CHICAGO – LOOP AREA

GREAT LAKES

PLACES TO STAY
3   Howard Johnson Inn
7   Hotel Wacker
19 Ohio House Motel
23 Hilton Garden Inn
25 Cass Hotel
28 Motel 6
29 Best Western Inn of Chicago
37 Courtyard by Marriott
    Chicago Downtown
72 Hotel Burnham
100 HI Chicago
109 Chicago Hilton & Towers
111 Essex Inn
112 Best Western Grant Park Inn

PLACES TO EAT
1   Mr Beef
4   Cafe Iberico
6   Mike's Rainbow Restaurant
8   Whole Foods
9   Thai Star
10 Blackhawk Lodge
11 Giordano's
12 Rosebud on Rush
15 Treasure Island
16 Cyrano's Bistrot
17 Carson's – The Place for Ribs
18 Gino's East
20 Rock & Roll McDonald's
24 Pizzeria Uno
26 Big Bowl
27 O'Neil's Bar & Grill
30 Boston Blackies
31 Gene and Georgetti
34 Frontera Grill; Topolobampo
36 Gold Coast Dogs
39 Shaw's Crab House; Blue
    Crab Lounge
58 Corner Bakery; Peterino's
67 Heaven on Seven
71 Sopafrina
77 Italian Village
78 Miller's Pub
85 Berghoff; Stand Up Bar
88 Parthenon
89 Lou Mitchell's

90 Pockets
91 Burrito Buggy
92 European Sunny Cafe
97 Artist's Snack Shop
104 Edwardo's
117 Firehouse

M   Metro
T   Transfer
    Station

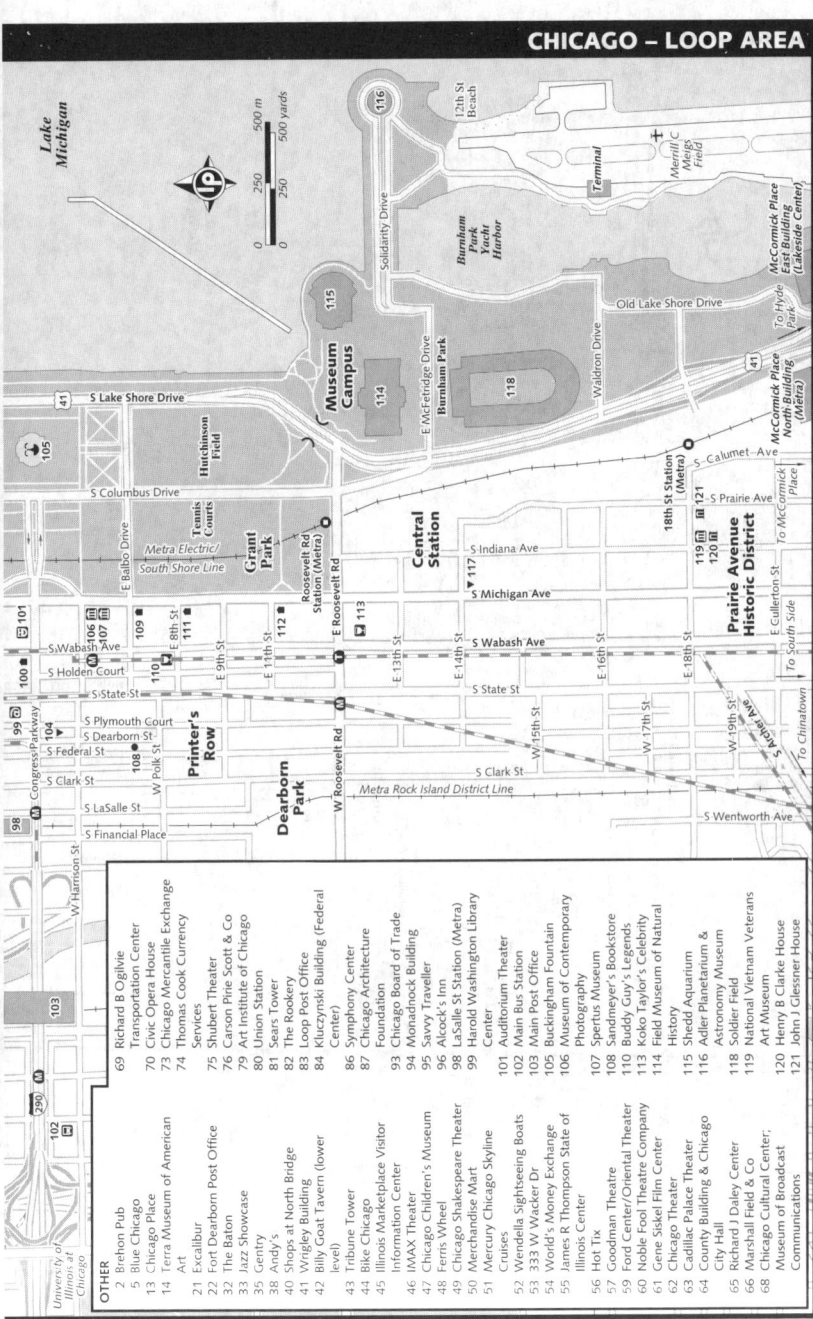

CHICAGO – LOOP AREA

OTHER
2 Brehon Pub
5 Blue Chicago
13 Chicago Place
14 Terra Museum of American Art
21 Excalibur
22 Fort Dearborn Post Office
32 The Baton
33 Jazz Showcase
35 Gentry
38 Andy's
40 Shops at North Bridge
41 Wrigley Building
42 Billy Goat Tavern (lower level)
43 Tribune Tower
44 Bike Chicago
45 Illinois Marketplace Visitor Information Center
46 IMAX Theater
47 Chicago Children's Museum
48 Ferris Wheel
49 Chicago Shakespeare Theater
50 Merchandise Mart
51 Mercury Chicago Skyline Cruises
52 Wendella Sightseeing Boats
53 333 W Wacker Dr
54 World's Money Exchange
55 James R Thompson State of Illinois Center
56 Hot Tix
57 Goodman Theatre
59 Ford Center/Oriental Theater
60 Noble Fool Theatre Company
61 Gene Siskel Film Center
62 Chicago Theater
63 Cadillac Palace Theater
64 County Building & Chicago City Hall
65 Richard J Daley Center
66 Marshall Field & Co
68 Chicago Cultural Center; Museum of Broadcast Communications
69 Richard B Ogilvie Transportation Center
70 Civic Opera House
73 Chicago Mercantile Exchange
74 Thomas Cook Currency Services
75 Shubert Theater
76 Carson Pirie Scott & Co
79 Art Institute of Chicago
80 Union Station
81 Sears Tower
82 The Rookery
83 Loop Post Office
84 Kluczynski Building (Federal Center)
86 Symphony Center
87 Chicago Architecture Foundation
93 Chicago Board of Trade
94 Monadnock Building
95 Savvy Traveller
96 Alcock's Inn
98 LaSalle St Station (Metra)
99 Harold Washington Library Center
101 Auditorium Theater
102 Main Bus Station
103 Main Post Office
105 Buckingham Fountain
106 Museum of Contemporary Photography
107 Spertus Museum
108 Sandmeyer's Bookstore
110 Buddy Guy's Legends
113 Koko Taylor's Celebrity
114 Field Museum of Natural History
115 Shedd Aquarium
116 Adler Planetarium & Astronomy Museum
118 Soldier Field
119 National Vietnam Veterans Art Museum
120 Henry B Clarke House
121 John J Glessner House

GREAT LAKES

CHICAGO – NORTH SIDE

500 m
500 yards

Lake
Michigan

North Ave
Beach

North Ave
Beach

Fullerton
Beach

Lake Shore Drive

41

N Cannon Drive

South
Pond

Lincoln
Park

Diversey
Harbor

Lincoln
Park

41

N Cannon Drive

18 🏛

23

30

32

33

N Stockton Drive

N Lincoln Park West

N Clark St

29 ▶

9

North
Pond

N Lakeview Ave

22

N Orleans St

N Sedgwick St

N Hudson Ave

N Cleveland Ave

N Mohawk St

N Lincoln Ave

N Diversey Parkway

N Hampden Ct

N Deming Pl

N Clark St

17 ▶

21

Lincoln
Park

N Geneva Ave

W Dickens Ave

To Wrigleyville &
Andersonville

W Surf St

1

W Diversey Parkway

5 🏠

🏠 4

▶ 8

16

W Arlington Pl

W Fullerton Ave

20

19 ▶

26 ▶

Ox
Park

N Howe St

N Orchard St

N Burling St

N Halsted St

To Majestic
Hotel

2

▶ 3

N Wrightwood Ave

N Orchard St

N Burling St

N Dayton St

W Schubert Ave

13

N Halsted St

27 ▶

28 ▶

31 ▶

N Dayton St

N Fremont St

N Bissell St

W Lill Ave 12

10 11

15

14

De Paul
University

N Belden Ave

W Webster Ave

25

N Sheffield Ave

N Dayton St

N Mildred Ave

N Wilton Ave

N Sheffield Ave

N Kenmore Ave

N Seminary Ave

N Clifton Ave

N Racine Ave

To City
Suites Hotel

6 ▶

7

N Kenmore Ave

W Diversey Parkway

N Lincoln Ave

W Altgeld St

W Montana St

24 ▶

N Magnolia Ave

W Wellington Ave

W Oakdale Ave

W George St

W Wolfram St

N Racine Ave

N Magnolia Ave

N Lakewood Ave

N Surrey Court

W Dickens Ave

N Dickens Ave

N Armitage Ave

N Maud Ave

N Clybourn Ave

W Cortland St

CHICAGO – NORTH SIDE

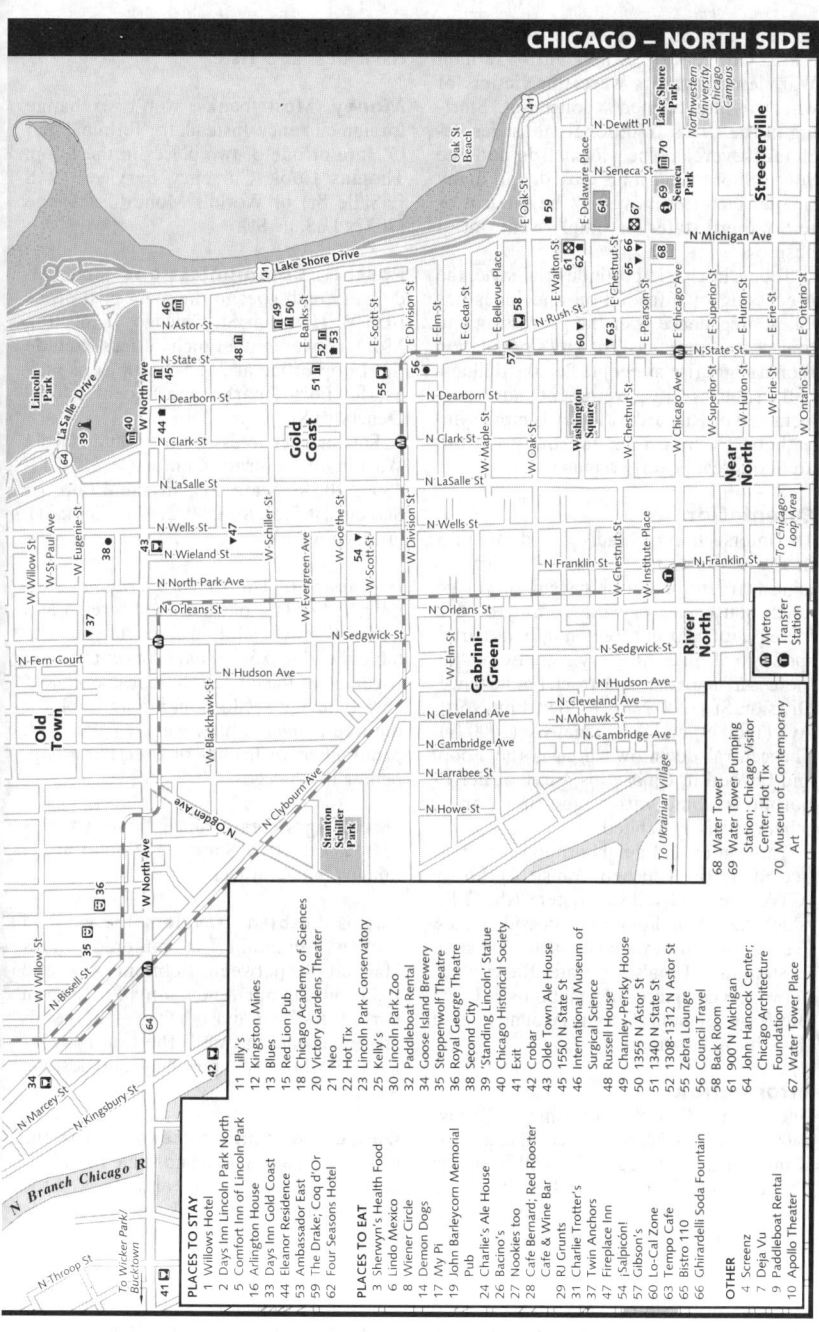

PLACES TO STAY
1 Willows Hotel
2 Days Inn Lincoln Park North
5 Comfort Inn of Lincoln Park
16 Arlington House
33 Days Inn Gold Coast
44 Eleanor Residence
53 Ambassador East
59 The Drake; Coq d'Or
62 Four Seasons Hotel

PLACES TO EAT
3 Sherwyn's Health Food
6 Lindo Mexico
8 Wiener Circle
14 Demon Dogs
17 My Pi
19 John Barleycorn Memorial
   Pub
24 Charlie's Ale House
26 Bacino's
27 Nookies too
28 Cafe Bernard; Red Rooster
   Cafe & Wine Bar
29 RJ Grunts
31 Charlie Trotter's
37 Twin Anchors
47 Fireplace Inn
54 ¡Salpicón!
60 Lo-Cal Zone
63 Tempo Cafe
66 Ghirardelli Soda Fountain

11 Lilly's
12 Kingston Mines
13 Blues
15 Red Lion Pub
18 Chicago Academy of Sciences
20 Victory Gardens Theater
21 Neo
22 Hot Tix
23 Lincoln Park Conservatory
25 Kelly's
30 Lincoln Park Zoo
32 Paddleboat Rental
34 Goose Island Brewery
35 Steppenwolf Theatre
36 Royal George Theatre
38 Second City
39 'Standing Lincoln' Statue
40 Chicago Historical Society
41 Exit
42 Crobar
43 Olde Town Ale House
45 1550 N State St
46 International Museum of
   Surgical Science
48 Russell House
49 Charnley-Persky House
50 1355 N Astor St
51 1340 N State St
52 1308-1312 N Astor St
55 Zebra Lounge
56 Council Travel
58 Back Room

OTHER
4 Screenz
7 Deja Vu
9 Paddleboat Rental
10 Apollo Theater

61 900 N Michigan
64 John Hancock Center;
   Chicago Architecture
   Foundation
67 Water Tower Place

68 Water Tower
69 Water Tower Pumping
   Station; Chicago Visitor
   Center; Hot Tix
70 Museum of Contemporary
   Art

GREAT LAKES

protests and the fiasco of the 1968 Democratic Convention, when anti–Vietnam War demonstrators were the victims of what was later termed a 'police riot.' Starting in the 1970s, traditional industries declined severely: The stockyards and the South Shore steel mills closed, and many smaller factories moved to the suburbs or to Southern states, or simply went out of business.

Today, in classic postindustrial style, the processing of information and ideas has taken precedence over the processing and transport of products. The city's population is on a slight rise as people flee the dullness of the suburbs. City government under long-term mayor Richard M Daley is more sympathetic to minorities and the poor, but areas of great poverty remain.

Orientation

The intersection of Madison and State Sts in the Loop is the center of Chicago's logical street-numbering system. As you go north, south, east or west from here, each increase of 800 in street numbers corresponds to 1 mile. At every increase of 400, there is a major arterial street. For instance, Division St (1200 N) is followed by North Ave (1600 N) and Armitage Ave (2000 N). The central downtown area is the Loop, and beyond it, Chicago is a city of neighborhoods, some with vague boundaries, others precisely defined.

The center and neighborhoods are connected by the Chicago Transit Authority (CTA) elevated railway system (the 'El'), which has seven different color-coded lines. Free maps of the system are available at all El stations. CTA also operates the city bus network. (For more information see Local Bus & the El under Getting Around later in this Chicago section.)

Information

The Chicago Office of Tourism (☎ 312-744-2400, 800-226-6632, Ⓦ www.ci.chi.il.us, 77 E Randolph St, Chicago, IL 60602), in the Chicago Cultural Center, will mail you information on request. Its visitor information center is open daily. A second visitor center is up N Michigan Ave in the Water Tower Pumping Station (163 E Pearson St). It's also open daily. They're both good places to shelter on a rainy day. Also look for information booths near the baggage claim areas at O'Hare.

Money Most banks won't exchange foreign currency. Instead, try Terminal 5 at O'Hare or one of two places in the Loop: Thomas Cook Currency Services (9 S LaSalle St) or World's Money Exchange (203 N LaSalle St).

Post & Communications General-delivery mail goes to the main post office (433 W Harrison St, Chicago, IL 60607). More convenient branch offices include the Loop office at 211 S Clark St as well as the Fort Dearborn office at 540 N Dearborn St.

For Internet access, try the grand Harold Washington Library Center (☎ 312-747-4300, 400 S State St), in the Loop; or Screenz (☎ 773-388-8300, 2717 N Clark St), in Lincoln Park.

Newspapers The *Chicago Tribune* is diminished of late but has good foreign and national news and arts coverage. The tabloid *Chicago Sun-Times* concentrates on coverage of the city. Both publish excellent entertainment sections on Friday. Look for the free *Reader,* a huge weekly paper with comprehensive listings of everything happening in Chicago.

Travel Agencies Council Travel (☎ 312-951-0585, 1160 N State St) is good at arranging budget travel.

Gay & Lesbian Travelers The gay and lesbian community is centered on N Halsted St between Belmont Ave and Addison St, but Andersonville, Lincoln Park, Bucktown and other neighborhoods are gay-friendly as well. The *Chicago Free Press* is the city's best gay and lesbian weekly.

Dangers & Annoyances At night, the lakefront, major parks and some neighborhoods, especially south and west of the Loop, can become bleak and forbidding places. Neighborhoods can change completely in just a few blocks, so be aware of your surroundings.

Most of Chicago's violent crime is by street gangs battling over drug turf. The most common crimes against tourists are pickpocketing, bag and jewelry snatching, vehicle break-ins and bike theft.

The Loop

The center of the city is named for the elevated tracks that circle its streets. It's busy all day and has a burgeoning nightlife, thanks in part to the newly named 'Theater District' – an area of new and refurbished theaters clustered near the intersection of N State and W Randolph Sts.

The **Chicago Cultural Center** (☎ 312-744-6630) occupies a whole block on N Michigan Ave between E Washington Blvd and E Randolph St. The former library has a beautiful interior with grand staircases and three floors of changing exhibitions (free admission; open daily). Located near the Washington entrance, the **Museum of Broadcast Communications** (☎ 312-629-6000) holds fascinating radio and TV nostalgia (free admission; open daily).

Sears Tower (☎ 312-875-9696, 233 S Wacker Dr), among the world's tallest buildings, attracts 1.5 million people a year to its Skydeck observation level. Check the visibility and waiting times at the Jackson Blvd entrance, then endure a series of waiting rooms, a film and more lines before the 70-second elevator ride to the top ($9.50; open daily). The John Hancock Center (see Gold Coast later) may be a better choice.

Chicago is the world center for commodities, futures and options trading. The two main trading organizations have free viewing areas overlooking their trading floors. **Chicago Board of Trade** (☎ 312-435-3500, 141 W Jackson Blvd) has a beautiful four-story lobby in marble, brass and platinum (open 8am-2pm Mon-Fri). **Chicago Mercantile Exchange** (☎ 312-930-8249, 10–30 S Wacker Dr) is in a modern building with a good view of the river (open 7:30am-3:15pm Mon-Fri).

Art Institute of Chicago

A legacy of Chicago's wealthy, this world-class museum (☎ 312-443-3600) houses masterpieces from around the globe, including a fabulous selection of both impressionist and postimpressionist paintings. Grant Wood's *American Gothic* and Edward Hopper's *The Nighthawks* are here. The primary entrance, where Adams St meets Michigan Ave, is flanked by bronze lions that have become true Chicago icons.

The primary collections, distributed throughout numerous numbered rooms, include African and ancient American art; American art from the 17th century to 1955; antiquities from Egypt, Greece, Rome and elsewhere; Chinese, Japanese and Korean art since around 3000 BC; European decorative arts since the 12th century; European painting and sculpture from 1400 to 1800; 19th-century European painting; photography; prints and drawings; textiles; 20th-century painting and sculpture; and exhibits on architecture.

The Institute provides excellent color maps of the museum and quality documentation alongside the artworks ($10, free Tue; open daily to 4:40pm, to 8pm Tue).

Grant Park

Department store magnate Aaron Montgomery Ward fought to save the lakeshore from development in the 1890s, and a plan by the Olmsted Brothers architectural firm turned a marshy wasteland into a park that has the formal lines of Versailles. Its centerpiece is **Buckingham Fountain**, modeled on (but bigger than) a fountain at Versailles. The fountain squirts from 10am-11pm daily May 1-Oct 1, with multicolored illumination on summer evenings.

Just north of the park along Michigan Ave, the new **Millennium Park** is slowly being completed (some would say in time for the next millennium). It will have a Frank Gehry–designed band shell.

Walking in a windy wonderland

South Loop

The gentrification of Printer's Row and the construction of several new neighborhoods such as Printer's Square and Central Station have revived the South Loop. Stroll S Dearborn St to see the scores of great old buildings that are now luxury lofts.

In one of the buildings of Columbia College, the **Museum of Contemporary Photography** (☎ 312-663-5554, 600 S Michigan Ave) shows US photography since 1959 (free admission; closed Sun).

A little farther south, the excellent **Spertus Museum** (☎ 312-922-9012, 618 S Michigan Ave) covers 5000 years of Jewish faith and culture ($5, free Fri; closed Sat).

Museum Campus

This lakefront area south of Grant Park has several great attractions, especially the **Field Museum of Natural History** (☎ 312-922-9410, 1400 S Lake Shore Dr). Among the highlights here: 'Africa' is a walk-through exhibit that moves from city streets to Saharan sand dunes, culminating in the hold of a slave ship; 'Inside Ancient Egypt' recreates an Egyptian burial chamber and has 23 actual mummies; and Dinosaur Hall is filled with skeletons, including Sue, the most complete *Tyrannosaurus rex* yet discovered ($8, free Wed; open daily).

Just east of the Field, **Shedd Aquarium** (☎ 312-939-2438) houses some 8000 marine species. Highlights include the Coral Reef, with 500 types of tropical fish; the Oceanarium, which replicates North America's northwest coast; and Amazon Rising, which traces that river's 2000-mile course ($15; open daily).

On the Lake Michigan promontory, the revitalized **Adler Planetarium & Astronomy Museum** (☎ 312-922-7827, 300 S Lake Shore Dr) has a digital sky show, multimedia display and introductions to space phenomena ($5, free Tue; open daily).

Near North

The area north of the river to Chicago Ave encompasses several points of interest, including the upscale shopping strip of N Michigan Ave known as the **Magnificent Mile**. This is the heart of the city for most visitors. **Art galleries** in renovated warehouses are concentrated in the neighborhood of W Superior and W Huron Sts around N Wells St.

Half-mile-long **Navy Pier** was once the city's municipal wharf. It's now massively rebuilt into a combination amusement park and meeting center, with fun fountains, a Ferris wheel, an IMAX theater and numerous shops and eateries (mostly fast-food and gimmicky chains). Near the pier entry, the **Chicago Children's Museum** (☎ 312-527-1000) has politically correct exhibits that cover garbage recycling, family-tree-building and inventing ($6.50; closed Mon). Nearby is the useful Illinois Marketplace Visitor Information Center, which provides regional information.

The modest **Terra Museum of American Art** (☎ 312-664-3939, 666 N Michigan Ave) gives an overview of American art since 1800, including works by Winslow Homer, James Whistler, John Singer Sargent, Mary Cassatt and a passel of Wyeths ($7, free Tue; closed Mon).

Gold Coast

Starting in 1882, Chicago's wealthy flocked to this neighborhood flanking the lake between Chicago and North Aves. Within 40 years, most of the Gold Coast was covered with grand mansions. After WWII, hideous high-rises sprouted along Lake Shore Dr, but preservationists managed to save most of the inland blocks. Today the Gold Coast's former grandeur can still be seen on **N Astor St**, where gems include the 1887 mansions at 1308–1312 N Astor, by architect John Wellborn Root; the Georgian Revival house at 1355 N Astor; Frank Lloyd Wright's Charnley-Persky House at 1365 N Astor, which he proclaimed the 'first modern building'; and the 1929 art deco Russell House at 1444 N Astor. On N State St, check out the flamboyant French apartment building at No 1550 and the former Playboy Mansion at No 1340.

The 154-foot-tall **Water Tower**, at the corner of Chicago and Michigan Aves, once dwarfed the surrounding buildings. It has survived the 1871 fire, obsolescence and several threats of demolition; across Michigan Ave, the tower's pumping station houses a visitor information center. Today the neighborhood giant is the 1127-foot-tall **John Hancock Center** (☎ 312-751-3681, 875 N Michigan Ave), which has a great 94th-floor observatory that's less crowded than the one at Sears Tower and has better views – you can see all the Loop from here ($8.50; open daily).

Though brutally boxy on the outside, the **Museum of Contemporary Art** (☎ 312-280-2660, 220 E Chicago Ave) seems much brighter inside, with works by Franz Kline, René Magritte, Cindy Sherman and Andy Warhol ($8, free Tue; closed Mon). At the **International Museum of Surgical Science** (☎ 312-642-6502, 1524 N Lake Shore Dr) you'll find an odd assortment of exhibits, including fascinating displays on bloodletting (free admission; closed Mon).

The area west of Clark St was once a slum called Little Hell, and the city's Cabrini-Green housing project, west of Orleans St, became a warehouse of social problems – it's now being progressively demolished. Just to the east, a huge middle-class development known as Sandburg Village has mixed townhouses and high-rises, luring young, educated professionals.

Old Town

North and west of Gold Coast, this once-simple neighborhood of wooden houses was one of the first in the city to gentrify, starting as a hippy haven in the late 1960s. Old houses now have been renovated or replaced, and Wells St is lined with swank restaurants. The narrow streets north of North Ave and west of Wells are wonderful to walk around.

Lincoln Park

The lakefront parks are among Chicago's most democratic institutions, with miles of beaches for every taste. Lincoln Park covers 1200 acres of shoreline between North Ave and Diversey Pkwy. The park and its surrounds are alive day and night with people skating, walking dogs, pushing strollers and driving in circles looking for a place to park.

The **Chicago Historical Society** (☎ 312-642-4600, 1601 N Clark St), in the park's southwest corner, focuses on Chicago's history as seen through the lives of ordinary citizens ($5, free Mon; open daily). It has good special exhibitions. Farther north, the **Standing Lincoln** sculpture is by the illustrious Augustus Saint-Gaudens.

The popular **Lincoln Park Zoo** (☎ 312-742-2000, 2200 N Cannon Dr) keeps 1600 animals in a range of renovated and new displays. It's renowned for its gorillas (free admission; open daily). Near the zoo's north entrance, the 1891 **Conservatory** (☎ 312-742-7736) has year-round blooms under 3 acres of glass (free admission; open daily). The **Chicago Academy of Sciences** (☎ 773-528-4500, 2430 N Cannon Dr) is in a new building and has good displays on Chicago's urban environment ($6, free Tue; open daily). For a duck's-eye view of the area, try **paddleboating**; rentals are available at either of two small ponds in the park.

Wrigleyville

North of Lincoln Park, this neighborhood can be enjoyed by strolling along Halsted St, Clark St, Belmont Ave or Southport Ave, which are well supplied with restaurants and bars. Beloved **Wrigley Field**, 1060 W Addison St at Clark, is named for the chewing-gum guy and is home to the much-loved but usually unsuccessful Chicago Cubs (see Spectator Sports later in this Chicago section).

Andersonville

Artists, creative types, lesbians, gays and yuppies occupy most of this walkable neighborhood, which was once heavily Swedish. The small **Swedish-American Museum Center** (☎ 773-728-8111; 5211 N Clark St) tells their story ($4; closed Mon). Take the CTA Red Line to the Berwyn stop and walk west.

Wicker Park/Bucktown

West of Lincoln Park, these two neighborhoods were once havens for working-class, central European immigrants. Bucktown was yuppified in the 1980s, but Wicker Park still has a polyglot character. Look for 19th-century houses scattered between new upscale palaces. The area's 1980s creative incarnation produced rock acts like Liz Phair and the Smashing Pumpkins, but recent creativity centers on procreation. It's an interesting place to wander around; take the CTA Blue Line to the Damen stop.

West Side

West of the Loop is a patchwork of ethnic neighborhoods, urban renewal, blight and gentrification. Old neighborhood names, like Greek Town and Little Italy, may not typify the current residents.

On S Desplaines St near W Adams St, the 1852 **Old St Patrick's Church** is the city's oldest – a Chicago Fire survivor. Farther out, the huge **United Center** (1901 W Madison St) is home to the Bulls and Blackhawks, and is a venue for various special events. Note the statue of an airborne Michael Jordan in front, and avoid the area at night.

Little Italy, between Eisenhower Expressway (I-290) and Roosevelt Rd, was a thriving community until the 1950s, when the expressway was rammed through and the commercial area demolished for the University of Illinois campus. Taylor St preserves many Italian family businesses. Blocks near the university have been gentrified, but blighted housing projects have created many grim areas.

In 1889 the neighborhood around S Halsted St was packed with recent European immigrants who worked for menial wages and lived in horrific tenements. At age 29, Jane Addams founded Hull House here, providing a kindergarten, employment bureau and space where burgeoning unions could meet. She fought for child labor regulations and public education, and won the Nobel Peace Prize in 1931. **Jane Addams Hull House** (800 S Halsted St) documents the struggle for social justice (free admission; closed Sat).

Pilsen

Long a first stop for immigrants, this neighborhood southwest of Little Italy is now predominantly Latino – 18th St has scores of taquerías, bakeries and small shops selling everything from devotional candles to Mexican CDs. The CTA Blue Line 18th St station is covered with Mexican murals.

The **Mexican Fine Arts Center Museum** (☎ 312-738-1503, 1852 W 19th St) exhibits work by Mexican artists (free admission; closed Mon).

Near South Side

A century ago, the best and worst of Chicago lived side by side south of the Loop. Prairie Ave between 16th and 20th Sts was Millionaire's Row, while the Levee District, four blocks to the west, was packed with saloons, brothels and opium dens. When the millionaires moved north, the neighborhood declined, and mansions were demolished for industry. Now trendy businesses are moving in, and once-derelict warehouses are loft apartments.

The **Prairie Ave Historic District** has preserved a few old mansions. The John J Glessner House (1800 S Prairie Ave) was designed in the 1880s by noted architect Henry Hobson Richardson. Nearby, the Greek Revival Henry B Clarke House (1855 S Indiana Ave) was built in 1836 and has been moved twice to escape demolition. You can tour both (☎ 312-326-1480; $11, free Wed; open Wed-Sun). In the same area, the National Vietnam Veterans Art Museum (☎ 312-326-0270, 1801 S Indiana Ave) exhibits artworks by veterans ($5; closed Mon).

In a humble building on Michigan Ave, the Chess brothers started a recording studio in 1957. Muddy Waters, Bo Diddley and Chuck Berry cut tracks here. Now incarnated as **Willie Dixon's Blues Heaven** (☎ 312-808-1286, 2120 S Michigan Ave), it holds a collection of memorabilia (call for hours and prices).

Vast **McCormick Place** (☎ 312-791-7000), the 'Mistake on the Lake,' is Chicago's convention center, with 2.2 million sq feet of meeting space.

Chinatown

The charm of Chinatown can best be enjoyed by wandering its streets and browsing in the many small shops and restaurants. Wentworth Ave south of Cermak is the retail heart of the neighborhood – the fanciful **On Leong Building** is at 2216 S Wentworth. Take the CTA Red Line to Cermak-Chinatown.

South Side

The South Side has had a tough time since WWII. Housing projects created impoverished neighborhoods where community ties were broken and gangs held sway. Whole neighborhoods vanished as crime and blight drove residents away. Some areas survived the damage, and redevelopment here now aims to promote mixed-income communities.

The **Illinois Institute of Technology** is noted for its 22 campus buildings, many of them designed by Mies van der Rohe. Crown Hall (3360 S State St) is the classic suspended black-glass box.

The neighborhoods radiating from 35th St and Martin Luther King Jr Dr are unofficially named **Bronzeville** and were the center of Chicago's black culture from 1920 until 1950, comparable to Harlem in New York. Shifting populations, urban decay and public housing led to its decline, and visitors should be cautious here. Some of the area's grand houses are being restored, especially on Calumet Ave between 31st and 33rd Sts. Note the Frank Lloyd Wright row houses at 3213–19 S Calumet. The Pilgrim Baptist Church (3301 S Indiana Ave) was an early home of gospel music and has a vast, opulent interior. To reach the area, take the CTA Green Line to 35th St-Bronzeville-IIT.

Hyde Park

At the prestigious University of Chicago, the heart of the Hyde Park enclave, graduate students outnumber undergrads, and some 73 Nobel prizes have been won. The bookish residents give the place an insulated, pleasant, small-town air. The area is easily reached via Metra Electric trains from the Randolph St station to the 55th-56th-57th St station.

The university's small **Oriental Institute Museum** (☎ 773-702-9507, 1155 E 58th St) displays artifacts from ancient Egypt, Mesopotamia and the Near East (free admission; open daily). The **David & Alfred Smart Museum** (☎ 773-702-0200, 5550 S Greenwood Ave) has the university's fine-arts collection, with works by Henry Moore and Rodin (free admission; closed Mon). Frank Lloyd Wright's Prairie style is epitomized in the **Robie House** (☎ 773-834-1847, 5757 S Woodlawn Ave), with its long, low lines and leaded-glass doors and windows. Much-needed restoration is underway and tours are worthwhile ($9; open 11am-3pm daily).

The **DuSable Museum of African American History** (☎ 773-947-0600, 740 E 56th Place), in Washington Park, has artworks and exhibits on black Americans from the time of slavery to the civil-rights era ($3; free Sun; open daily).

The **Kenwood** neighborhood, just north of Hyde Park and best toured by car, has many large and imposing mansions; it's a mixed neighborhood of middle-class and wealthy whites and blacks.

The **Museum of Science & Industry** (☎ 773-684-1414, 57 S Lake Shore Dr), on the lakefront, is a vast and confusing place that was the Palace of Fine Arts at the 1893 Columbian Exposition. Highlights include a WWII German submarine, a replica coal mine, an excellent exhibit on scientific imaging and a fun new multimedia feature called 'The Farm' ($7, free Thurs; open daily).

Pullman

Millionaire railcar manufacturer George M Pullman started a model factory town here in 1880, but his dream died with a violent strike in 1894. The factory finally closed in 1981, and the southern part of Pullman (where craftsmen and managers lived) was bought up by people determined to preserve it. North Pullman, with simpler housing for laborers, is only now being appreciated. Metra Electric trains go to 111th St station, in the heart of Pullman, 13 miles south of the Loop. The visitor center (☎ 773-785-8901, 11141 S Cottage Grove Ave) offers detailed maps and walking tours (call for hours).

Organized Tours

American Sightseeing (☎ 312-251-3100) offers standard two-hour bus tours ($16). Chicago Trolley Co (☎ 773-648-5000) operates silly imitation streetcars that let you hop on and off at the main attractions ($18).

Mercury Chicago Skyline Cruises (☎ 312-332-1353) and Wendella Sightseeing Boats (☎ 312-337-1446) offer identical 90-minute tours of the river and lake ($15). Both companies are below the Michigan Ave bridge. Various other lake cruises leave seasonally from Navy Pier.

For a choice of excellent architectural tours by foot, bus or boat, contact the Chicago Architecture Foundation (☎ 312-922-3432), which has two locations: 875 N Michigan Ave (in the John Hancock Center) and 224 S Michigan Ave. The tours are highly recommended, especially those by boat.

Special Events

Chicago has a full events calendar, but the two biggies are the St Patrick's Day Parade on March 17 and the Independence Day Concert occurring July 3 (which features Tchaikovsky's '1812 Overture' and big-time fireworks). Running concurrently with the Fourth of July celebrations is Taste of Chicago, a 10-day food fest in Grant Park.

GREAT LAKES

The park is also home to numerous free city-sponsored summer music events, including the following:

Blues Festival – first June weekend
Gospel Festival – second June weekend
Country Music Festival – last June weekend
Latin Music Festival – last July weekend
Jazz Festival – first September weekend

For more information on any of these festivals call the city's Office of Special Events (☎ 312-744-3315). Also in summer, watch for free classical concerts by the Grant Park Symphony Orchestra (☎ 312-742-7638), as well as a myriad of neighborhood festivals.

Places to Stay

Big conventions attract thousands of visitors, who fill up even the most remote locations. But when conventions aren't in town, Chicago's growing popularity means that deals may be hard to find. The rates listed below are normal midweek rates. Taxes add 14.9% to hotel bills. The closest decent campgrounds are at least an hour away in any direction.

Hostels The pick of Chicago hostels is the new *HI Chicago* (☎ 312-360-0300, 800-909-4776, e *reserve@hichicago.org, 24 E Congress Pkwy*). It's centrally located in a restored classic building. Rates are $19-23 for beds in six- to 10-person rooms.

Near Loyola University, the *Chicago International Hostel* (☎ 773-262-1011, e *chicagohostel@hotmail.com, 6318 N Winthrop Ave*), three blocks south of the CTA Red Line Loyola stop, is 35 minutes north of the Loop. Dorm beds cost $15, doubles with baths $40.

In the heart of Lincoln Park, the barebones *Arlington House* (☎ 773-929-5380, 800-467-8355, e *mitch@arlingtonhouse.com, 616 W Arlington Place*) has dorm beds for $20 and private rooms from $48.

The women-only *Eleanor Residence* (☎ 312-664-8245, 888-393-1898, e *information@eleanorresidence.com, 1550 N Dearborn St*), just south of Lincoln Park, is tightly regulated. Single rooms are $65, including breakfast and dinner.

B&Bs The company *Bed & Breakfast Chicago* (☎ 773-248-0005, 800-375-7084,

e *stays@chicago-bed-breakfast.com, PO Box 14088, Chicago, IL 60614*) represents rooms at more than 100 places throughout the city, mostly in the upscale Gold Coast, Old Town and Lincoln Park areas. Minimum stay is two nights, and rates for a single or double room run about $85-250. At the higher end you get an entire apartment.

The Loop Hotels here are convenient to Grant Park, the museums and the business and financial districts, but they're well away from the best nightlife. *Essex Inn* (☎ 312-939-2800, 800-621-6909, 800 S Michigan Ave) is a tatty choice with doubles from $89. *Best Western Grant Park Inn* (☎ 312-922-2900, 1100 S Michigan Ave) has adequate rooms for $159-189, but ask about special deals.

Hotel Burnham (☎ 312-782-1111, 877-294-9712, w *www.burnhamhotel.com, 1 W Washington Blvd*) is a favorite of architecture buffs. It's housed in the landmark 1890s Reliance Building and opened in 2000. The lavish rooms start at $170.

The *Chicago Hilton & Towers* (☎ 312-922-4400, 720 S Michigan Ave) was the largest hotel in the world in 1927, with nearly 2000 rooms. Renovated in the mid-1980s, it now has *only* 1543 rooms, but the public spaces and gilded ballroom are exquisitely grand. The lobby bar overlooking Michigan Ave is where Chicago police tossed protesters through plate-glass windows in 1968. Singles/doubles start at $120/145 but are usually much higher.

Near North Popular with visitors, this neighborhood has a plethora of places for eating, drinking, shopping and entertainment. The well-located *Cass Hotel* (☎ 312-787-4030, 800-227-7850, 640 N Wabash Ave) is not much to look at, but it has small, simple rooms from only $74/79 singles/doubles. *Hotel Wacker* (☎ 312-787-1386, 111 W Huron St) has clean rooms with TVs and air-con for $55/60, plus a $5 deposit. (Those who snicker at the name should know that Charles H Wacker was a great local brewer and preserver of the lakefront, and therefore deserves respect.)

Howard Johnson Inn (☎ 312-664-8100, 720 N LaSalle St), a block south of Chicago Ave, has free parking in a lot surrounded by classic American motel rooms ($88-115).

Ohio House Motel (☎ 312-943-6000, 600 N LaSalle St) is another 1960s classic. Basic rooms start at $85.

Best Western Inn of Chicago (☎ 312-787-3100, 162 E Ohio St) has an unbeatable location just east of Michigan Ave – it gets a lot of tour groups. Plain rooms run $89-189. *Motel 6* (☎ 312-787-3580, 162 E Ontario St) occupies a handsome 1930s building but has the usual utilitarian rooms, from $99/109.

One of a crop of new chain hotels in the area, *Hilton Garden Inn* (☎ 312-595-0000, 10 E Grand Ave) has comfy rooms and a small pool. Rooms start at $120 but are usually more. Try for the early-booking rate of $99. *Courtyard by Marriott Chicago Downtown* (☎ 312-329-2500, 30 E Hubbard St) is aimed at business travelers and has large rooms from $189.

Gold Coast *Ambassador East* (☎ 312-787-7200, 800-843-6664, 1301 N State St) is a period classic and was Cary Grant's hostelry in *North by Northwest*. Rooms cost from $165. The grand 1920s *Drake Hotel* (☎ 312-787-2200, 800-553-7253, 140 E Walton St) is an ageless dowager that has hosted the likes of Gloria Swanson and Queen Elizabeth II. The quiet rooms have heavy doors and marble baths and cost from $275. Its Coq d'Or is one of the classiest bars around. The *Four Seasons Hotel* (☎ 312-280-8800, 800-332-3442, 120 E Delaware Place) is regularly rated as the best in town, with rooms from $375.

Lincoln Park & North Hotels here are often cheaper than the big ones downtown and are near a lot of the best nightlife. Museums, the Loop and Near North are a short El ride away. *Days Inn Gold Coast* (☎ 312-664-3040, 1816 N Clark St) across from the zoo and in the midst of Old Town, is a good value, starting at $89/119 for singles/doubles.

Comfort Inn of Lincoln Park (☎ 773-348-2810, 601 W Diversey Pkwy) is right on enjoyable Diversey and about five minutes' walk from Lincoln Park and the lake; rooms start at $85/90. *Days Inn Lincoln Park North* (☎ 773-525-7010, 646 W Diversey Pkwy) is well located but not the most charming place; rooms start at $96/126.

City Suites Hotel (☎ 773-404-3400, 800-248-9108, W www.cityinns.com, 933 W Belmont Ave), near the CTA Red Line Belmont station, is a stylish little place with bright rooms from $140. The same company charges similar prices at *Willows Hotel* (☎ 773-528-8400, 800-787-3108, 555 W Surf St), near Lincoln Park, and at *Majestic Hotel* (☎ 773-404-3499, 800-727-5108, 528 W Brompton Ave), close to Wrigley Field and the Halsted St gay scene.

Places to Eat

Some of the USA's most innovative chefs work in Chicago kitchens. The range, quality and value are good at all prices, although the city tacks on an extra 9.75% tax that pays for things like those fancy planters in the middle of the roads. The restaurants listed here are just a sample, in areas with plenty more to choose from.

The Loop Most Loop eateries are geared for lunch crowds of office workers, but many now cater to evening diners as well. Fast-food franchises dot every block.

By Sears Tower are some good cheap lunch places, including *European Sunny Cafe* (304 S Wells St), with hearty Polish fare; *Pockets* (329 S Franklin St), with veggie sandwiches; and *Burrito Buggy* (206 W Van Buren St), serving fresh Mexican food.

Near HI Chicago, *Edwardo's* (521 S Dearborn St) has stuffed spinach pizza, sandwiches and salads, all fresh and cheap. *Artist's Snack Shop* (410 S Michigan Ave), in the Fine Arts Building, is an updated diner with a fine selection of coffees and beers. If you pay a bit more, you can have innovative Italian fare for lunch in a casual setting at *Sopraffina* (10 N Dearborn St).

Historic *Berghoff* (17 W Adams St) mixes old-world classics, like sauerbraten and schnitzel, with modern treats like swordfish Caesar salad. Next door, its *Stand Up Bar* serves sandwiches and excellent house-brand beer. *Miller's Pub* (134 S Wabash Ave) is another Loop classic. *Heaven on Seven* (111 N Wabash Ave) has spicy New Orleans fare in a 7th-floor diner setting.

A new Loop hot spot to go with the new Theater District, *Petterino's* (☎ 312-422-0150, 150 N Dearborn St) caters to the theater crowd. It's adjacent to a *Corner Bakery*, the local chain of gourmet sandwich and pastry shops. *Italian Village*

(☎ 312-332-7005, 71 W Monroe St) combines a moderately priced family restaurant with an upscale eatery in one building.

South of the Loop, *Firehouse* (☎ 312-786-1401, 1401 S Michigan Ave) serves great steaks to the residents of this fast-growing neighborhood.

Near North Hundreds of restaurants dot the area from the river to the Gold Coast, from family-run snackeries to famous restaurants and high-concept cafes. Budget-priced *Boston Blackies (164 E Grand Ave)* is an excellent Greek coffee shop, while *Rock & Roll McDonald's (600 N Clark St)* serves the schlock with rock. Strictly local, *Gold Coast Dogs (418 N State St)* is a great place to try a Chicago-style hot dog with its myriad of toppings. For good burgers and beer try *O'Neil's Bar & Grill (152 E Ontario St)*.

Mr Beef (660 N Orleans St) is famous for its Italian beef sandwiches, a Chicago institution. Another local invention, deep dish pizza, began at *Pizzeria Uno (29 E Ohio St)* in 1943. *Gino's East (633 N Wells St)* is another renowned pizza purveyor. *Giordano's (730 N Rush St)* is a popular local pizza chain.

Thai Star (660 N State St) makes excellent, inexpensive Thai dishes in a charmless corner location. Big portions and small prices are the hallmark at *Mike's Rainbow Restaurant (708 N Clark St)*, a classic Midwestern diner open 24/7 and catering to cops and cabbies craving big breakfasts.

The wildly popular *Big Bowl (60 E Ohio St)* serves big bowls of fairly cheap Asian noodles in any variety. *Cyrano's Bistrot (546 N Wells St)* is a good, casual French place. For more Mediterranean fare, try *Cafe Iberico (737 N LaSalle St)*, which has good, moderately priced Spanish tapas. Back home in the culinary sense, *Carson's – The Place for Ribs (612 N Wells St)* serves classic Chicago-style ribs: very tender pork ribs in a tangy sauce.

A favorite fish place is *Shaw's Crab House* (☎ 312-527-2722, 21 E Hubbard St), vaguely modeled on a Maryland seafood restaurant. Its adjoining *Blue Crab Lounge* is a good place for a drink and a seafood snack. *Frontera Grill* (☎ 312-661-1434, 445 N Clark St) serves innovative Mexican-inspired fare. The adjoining high-end

Topolobampo (same phone number as Frontera Grill) will provide a meal to remember.

The following are expensive but worth it for the food and atmosphere. *Gene and Georgetti* (☎ 312-527-3718, 500 N Franklin St) is a traditional steak house; *Rosebud on Rush* (☎ 312-266-6444, 720 N Rush St) offers huge portions of great Italian food; and *Blackhawk Lodge* (☎ 312-280-4080, 41 E Superior St) specializes in innovative takes on Midwestern fare.

If you're shopping for a picnic or need something to take to one of the Grant Park festivals, try *Whole Foods (50 W Huron St)* or *Treasure Island (680 N Lake Shore Dr)* – both large supermarkets with lots of organic and deli items.

Gold Coast Loads of restaurants crowd the streets of this affluent neighborhood. *Lo-Cal Zone (912 N Rush St)* is a budget vegetarian haven with calzones, veggie burgers, burritos and creamy frozen yogurt. For all-night diner fare, there's none better than *Tempo Cafe (6 E Chestnut St)*. Never has a $7 hot fudge sundae tasted better than one from *Ghirardelli Soda Fountain (118 E Pearson St)*.

Bistro 110 (110 E Pearson St) is a bright and bustling brasserie across from the Water Tower. To see Chicago's elite in action, join the well-coifed throng at *Gibson's* (☎ 312-266-8999, 1028 N Rush St). The steaks and prices are tops.

Old Town Wells St north of Division St has an assortment of eateries. *¡Salpicón! (1252 N Wells St)* has top-flight and off-beat Mexican fare at moderate prices. The *Fireplace Inn (1448 N Wells St)* has been serving up Chicago-style baby back ribs for almost 35 years. More baby back ribs, with fries, onion rings and baked potatoes on the side, appear at *Twin Anchors (1655 N Sedgwick St)*, a neon-lit 1950s bar. It's hugely popular, so expect a long wait on weekends.

Lincoln Park This pleasant and popular neighborhood teems with restaurants, clubs and bars. Parking is frightful, but the streets are generally safe, and it's handy to the CTA Fullerton El stop.

RJ Grunts (2056 N Lincoln Park W) is a '70s-era burger joint with a huge salad bar.

The **John Barleycorn Memorial Pub** *(658 W Belden Ave)* dates from the 1890s but is now more an eatery than a bar. The vast menu features comfort food favorites like burgers, tuna melts and potato skins.

Demon Dogs *(944 W Fullerton Ave)*, directly under the El stop, features Chicago-style hot dogs – the poppy-seed bun is steamed and the condiments are piled on high. It doubles as a shrine to the band Chicago. Late-night munchies are dealt with in raucous style at **Weiner Circle** *(2622 N Clark St)*, an all-night burger joint. Have the cheese fries.

My π *(2417 N Clark St)* has cheap pizza and a good salad bar. Spinach deep-dish pizza is the specialty at **Bacino's** *(2204 N Lincoln Ave)*. For yummy all-day breakfasts, head to **Nookies Too** *(2114 N Halsted St)*. Bustling **Lindo Mexico** *(2642 N Lincoln Ave)* serves up platters of cheap and cheerful Mexican fare.

The BMW set gets its burgers at **Charlie's Ale House** *(1224 W Webster Ave)*, a genteel bar and grill. For fun French, try **Cafe Bernard** *(2100 N Halsted St)*; the **Red Rooster Cafe & Wine Bar** out back has simple meals and live music.

At the very top end, **Charlie Trotter's** *(☎ 773-248-6228, 816 W Armitage Ave)* is a famous gourmet mecca that customers book months ahead of time and remember years afterward – around $150 per person with wine.

Sherwin's Health Food *(645 W Diversey Pkwy)* is good for picnics and for those desperate for a tofu fix.

Lake View/Wrigleyville This area offers a huge variety of eateries at generally moderate prices. The Belmont and Addison CTA El stops will get you close to the action.

Young professionals flock to **Ann Sather's Restaurant** *(929 W Belmont Ave)* for reasonably priced chow in stylish surrounds. Specialties include Swedish potato sausages for dinner and cinnamon rolls for breakfast. Legendary **Leona's** *(3215 N Sheffield Ave)* started here and now has outlets all over town serving excellent pizza, sandwiches, salads etc. **Moti Mahal** *(1031 W Belmont Ave)* makes excellent cheap Indian dishes and you can bring your own booze.

The heart of Chicago's gay community is N Halsted St. **Chicago Diner** *(3411 N Halsted)* serves large portions of fresh vegetarian food, such as tofu omelets for breakfast (lunch and dinner are also served). **Erwin** *(2925 N Halsted)* offers inexpensive, imaginative and filling food. The well-recommended **Yoshi's Cafe** *(☎ 773-248-6160, 3257 N Halsted)* serves low-fat dishes with Japanese style (typically about $25). **Arcos de Cuchilleros** *(3445 N Halsted)* is a popular, no-nonsense Spanish tapas place.

From Belmont Ave to Wrigley Field, N Clark St has scores of moderate- and budget-priced eateries. It's almost becoming a Chicago theme park with popular local eateries and bars opening outlets here to cash in on the nighttime mobs. **Mia Francesca** *(3311 N Clark)* is a small, popular, family-run Italian bistro with entrées around $15. The well-regarded **PS Bangkok** *(3345 N Clark)* has the usual Thai dishes for around $8 and a long list of elaborate seafood for considerably more. **Matsuya** *(3469 N Clark)* is one of the best-value Japanese restaurants in town; the menu highlights include sushi, octopus and teriyaki-marinated grilled fish. Try Ethiopian eating at **Addis Ababa** *(3521 N Clark)*, where legumes, grains, spices and vegetables on *injera* bread cost under $10 a head. Beware of **Billy Goat**, **Goose Island Brewery** et al in the 3500 block; the original locations of these places elsewhere in town (see Bars under Entertainment) are far better.

One of the hottest neighborhoods for nightlife is N Southport Ave from Belmont to Irving Park. Take the CTA Brown Line to Southport. Restaurants like **Chinalite** *(3457 N Southport)* and **Still Lite Cafe** *(3647 N Southport)* offer healthy food. **Hi Ricky** *(3730 N Southport)* has a long, cheap menu that covers most of Asia for under $7. **Cullen's** *(3741 N Southport)* is an upscale bar and grill connected to the adjoining Mercury Theater.

Near West Side Good restaurants are scattered throughout the west, but you need a cab to reach most of them easily. The ethnic areas are the main draw, but **Lou Mitchell's** *(565 W Jackson Blvd)*, near Union Station, has a top breakfast menu and premium coffee.

In Greek Town, authentic, cheap and lively restaurants abound on Halsted St.

Parthenon (314 S Halsted) is a long-standing favorite with Greeks visiting the city from their suburban refuges.

To the southwest in Pilsen, the signs are in Spanish, the mariachis make music and the Mexican restaurants are innumerable. The CTA Blue Line stops right at 18th St. *Playa Azul (1514 W 18th)* serves classic Mexican coastal cuisine, with entrées around $7. *Nuevo Leon (1515 W 18th)* has tacos, tamales and enchiladas for peso-size prices.

Chinatown Take the CTA Red Line to Cermak-Chinatown and walk one block west to Wentworth Ave, the traditional heart of the neighborhood. At *Three Happiness (2130 Wentworth)*, dim sum is served 10am-3pm, and you'll be hard-pressed to eat more than $10 worth. The enduring Cantonese-style *Emperor's Choice (2238 Wentworth)* is known for excellent seafood and has a special menu for more adventurous diners. *Seven Treasures (2312 Wentworth)* is quite a steamy, bustling family restaurant.

Entertainment

The free weekly *Reader* has comprehensive entertainment listings, while the hipper *New City* is for younger and more alternative readers. Before you pay full price for tickets to any performance in town, call the box office for possible discount deals. Hot Tix booths sell same-day tickets at half-price. Locations include 78 W Randolph St, 163 E Pearson St and 2301 N Clark St.

Gene Siskel Film Center (164 N State St) screens a fine selection of unusual and offbeat films.

Performing Arts Chicago's excellent reputation for stage drama is well deserved. The main theater companies are *Goodman Theatre* (☎ 312-443-3800, 170 N Dearborn St), known for its new and classic works; renowned *Steppenwolf Theatre* (☎ 312-335-1650, 1650 N Halsted St); *Court Theatre* (☎ 773-753-4472) at the University of Chicago, concentrating on classics; *Victory Gardens* (☎ 773-871-3000, 2257 N Lincoln Ave), specializing in plays by Chicago authors; and *Chicago Shakespeare Theater* (☎ 312-595-5600), at Navy Pier. Among dozens of smaller companies is the farcical

Noble Fool Theatre Company (☎ 773-202-8843, 16 W Randolph St). Major venues include the following:

Apollo Theater (☎ 773-935-6100, 2540 N Lincoln Ave)

Auditorium Theater (☎ 312-902-1500, 50 E Congress Pkwy)

Cadillac Palace Theater (☎ 312-902-1500, 151 W Randolph St)

Chicago Theater (☎ 312-443-1130, 175 N State St)

Ford Center/Oriental Theater (☎ 312-902-1400, 24 W Randolph St)

Royal George Theatre (☎ 312-988-9000, 1641 N Halsted St)

Shubert Theater (☎ 312-977-1700, 22 W Monroe St)

The Chicago Symphony Orchestra, directed by Daniel Barenboim, is headquartered in the superb *Symphony Center* (☎ 312-435-8122, 220 S Michigan). The Lyric Opera of Chicago, one of the country's best, performs in the grand old *Civic Opera House* (☎ 312-332-2244, 20 N Wacker Dr).

There are two local dance companies of great renown: *Joffrey Ballet of Chicago* (☎ 312-739-0120) and *Hubbard St Dance Chicago* (☎ 312-850-9744). Both perform at a variety of venues.

For something a bit more offbeat, try *The Baton (436 N Clark St)*, presenting nightly shows by female impersonators.

Comedy Clubs In Old Town, *Second City (1616 N Wells St)* is a must-see – the place where John Belushi, Bill Murray, Rick Moranis and many others first emerged from the suburbs. In the same building, *Second City ETC* is often more daring.

Jazz & Blues Blues and jazz both have deep roots in Chicago, and world-class performers appear at myriad venues any night of the week. In Near North, *Andy's (11 E Hubbard St)* is one of the bars featuring both styles, while the *Back Room (1007 N Rush St)* is strictly a jazz joint, so tiny it's like having a band in your bedroom. *Jazz Showcase (59 W Grand Ave)* is an upscale club. *Blue Chicago (736 N Clark St)* is a mainstream blues bar – look for Pabst signs in the window.

In Lincoln Park, try the venerable *Blues (2519 N Halsted St)*. *Kingston Mines (2548 N Halsted St)* is authentically noisy, hot and sweaty, and it gets big-name performers. *Lilly's (2513 N Lincoln Ave)* has excellent local blues.

In the South Loop, *Buddy Guy's Legends (754 S Wabash Ave)* is a cavernous space for top national and local groups. *Koko Taylor's Celebrity (1233 S Wabash Ave)* is owned by local blues legend Koko Taylor. On the South Side, the *New Checkerboard Lounge (423 E 43rd St)* is in a rough neighborhood and is one of the best-known blues clubs in town.

Rock In Wrigleyville, *Metro (3730 N Clark St)* has local bands and big names; the *Smart Bar* in the basement hosts dancing until dawn. *Double Door (1572 N Milwaukee Ave)* and *Empty Bottle (1035 N Western Ave)* epitomize the hard-edge Chicago music scene in Bucktown, Wicker Park and Ukrainian Village.

Bars During the long winters, Chicagoans seek social life indoors, and the city's many bars cater to every mood and personality. Usual closing time is 2am, but many places stay open until 4am weekdays and 5am Saturday. In summer many boast beer gardens and outdoor seating.

In the Loop, try *Berghoff (17 W Adams St; see The Loop under Places to Eat)* or *Alcock's Inn (411 S Wells St)*, where rowdy traders lament the day's losses or celebrate their winnings. Right under the Wrigley Building, *Billy Goat Tavern* is the real goods: a classic Chicago saloon. In Near North, *Brehon Pub (731 N Wells St)* is a fine example of the corner saloons that once dotted Chicago. *Gentry (440 N State St)* is a gay bar with a piano and a fireplace.

Zebra Lounge (1220 N State St) is a small smoky joint with a piano. Farther up in Old Town are neighborhood bars like *Olde Towne Ale House (219 W North Ave)*. *Goose Island Brewery (1800 N Clybourn Ave)* is the home of the widely sold local beer. *Kelly's (949 W Webster Ave)* is a classic Chicago Irish bar.

For a bar crawl, N Lincoln Ave is great. *Red Lion Pub (2446 N Lincoln)* has British brews and great onion rings, while *Deja Vu (2624 N Lincoln)* is open very late.

In Wrigleyville, N Clark St near Wrigley Field is chockablock with bars. Unpretentious *Bernie's Tavern (3664 N Clark)* is thronged with fans before, during and after Cubs games, but unexciting at other times. The *Ginger Man (3740 N Clark)* attracts theater types and has pool tables and good beer.

Among the myriad of gay bars on N Halsted St, the friendly *Roscoes (3354 N Halsted)* is an excellent place to start the night. A few blocks east, *Closet (3325 N Broadway)* attracts a lively gay and lesbian crowd.

Other bar-rich neighborhoods include Andersonville, Wicker Park and Bucktown.

Dance Clubs The club scene ranges from hip snooty places to casual joints where all you do is dance. Covers range from nix to $20.

In Near North, the multiroom *Excalibur (632 N Dearborn St)* packs in suburbanites – the Dome Room has the edgier rock bands. North and west, *Exit (1315 W North Ave)* is a punk club, and *Crobar (1543 N Kingsbury St)* is a huge and stylish club with a mixed crowd. In Lincoln Park, *Neo (2350 N Clark St)* is a gritty dance place.

North in Wrigleyville, *Berlin (954 W Belmont Ave)*, near the CTA Belmont station, caters to a crowd as mixed as the music. *Manhole (3458 N Halsted St)* is a hard-core gay club with heavy doses of disco.

Spectator Sports

The Chicago Cubs last won the World Series in 1908, but their fans still pack Wrigley Field (☎ 773-404-2827), known as 'The Friendly Confines.' Baseball's most charming and intimate stadium dates from 1916 and is known for its ivy-walled field and classic neon sign. The Cubs actually did well in 2001, so the always-scarce tickets may now be even harder to get. Wrigley Field is a block west of the CTA Red Line Addison stop.

The Chicago White Sox (1917 World Series winners) play in the big, antiseptic bowl of Comiskey Park (☎ 312-674-1000), near the CTA Sox-35th and 35-Bronzeville-IIT stations. Tickets are obtainable.

The once-successful Chicago Bulls play basketball in the huge United Center (☎ 312-559-1212, 1901 W Madison St). Since Michael Jordan moved on the team has just plain sucked. The mediocre Chicago Blackhawks play hockey at United Center, too. Tickets are usually available (☎ 312-455-7000). CTA runs special buses on game days; it's not safe to walk here.

Michael Jordan, former Bulls MVP

The Chicago Bears NFL football team (☎ 312-559-1212) plays at Soldier Field, and tickets will be available until they improve. The Chicago Fire soccer team (☎ 312-705-7200) competes for local loyalties at Soldier Field. (Note that the stadium may be rebuilt from 2002 to 2003, so games may move elsewhere.)

Shopping

For mainstream stores, head to N Michigan Ave. Large vertical malls include Shops at North Bridge, Chicago Place, Water Tower Place and 900 N Michigan. In the Loop, Marshall Field's, N State St at E Randolph Dr, covers a city block and is Chicago's premier department store. For smaller shops and edgier items, try Halsted and Clark Sts in Lincoln Park as well as Milwaukee and Damen Aves in Bucktown.

Two travel bookstores stand out: Savvy Traveller (310 S Michigan Ave) and Sand-meyer's Bookstore (714 S Dearborn St).

Getting There & Away

Air O'Hare International Airport (ORD; ☎ 800-832-6352), 17 miles northwest of the Loop, is the world's second busiest airport, fostering Chicago's historic and continuing role as a major transportation hub. O'Hare is huge but user-friendly, with good signs and maps. Most non-US airlines and international flights use Terminal 5 (except Lufthansa and flights from Canada). The terminals and the main long-term parking lot are linked by a people mover.

The cheapest, and often the quickest, way to/from O'Hare is by the CTA Blue Line ($1.50; see Local Bus & the El under Getting Around below), but the station is a long walk from the flight terminals, and the El is difficult if you have lots of luggage. At the airport, signs point variously to 'CTA,' 'Rapid Transit' and 'Trains to City.' Airport Express shuttles run between the airport and downtown ($17.50 per person). By taxi, the fare to/from downtown is $28-35, or a flat $19 per person using Share-a-Ride.

The smaller Midway Airport (MDW; ☎ 312-767-0500), 11 miles southwest of the Loop, has a new terminal and is used by domestic carriers like Southwest, which may have cheaper flights than airlines serving O'Hare. The CTA Orange Line goes from the Loop to Midway station ($1.50). Other options to and from downtown are airport shuttles ($12.50 per person), taxis ($18-25) and Share-a-Ride ($14 per person).

Bus The main bus station (☎ 312-408-5980, 630 W Harrison St) is two blocks from the Clinton stop on the CTA Blue Line. Greyhound has frequent buses to Cleveland ($39; 7 hours), Detroit ($28; 7 hours), Indianapolis ($30; 4 hours), Milwaukee ($14; 2 hours) and Minneapolis ($61; 9 hours). Also using the station is Indian Trails, a regional bus line serving Michigan; its fares are similar to Greyhound's.

Train Chicago's classic Union Station (225 S Canal St) is the hub for Amtrak's national and regional service. Three trains a day go to Detroit ($35-45 and up; 6½ hours), and six trains per day go to Milwaukee ($16; 1½ hours). Connections to other cities include the following:

Cleveland – $50; 7 hours; 3 trains daily

Minneapolis/-St Paul – $101; 9 hours; 1 train daily

New York – $131; 19 hours; 2 trains daily

St Louis – $27; 5 hours; 3 trains daily

San Francisco (Emeryville) – $195; 51 hours; 1 train daily

Getting Around

Local Bus & the El CTA (☎ 888-968-7282) operates the city bus network and the El (officially called Chicago Rapid Transit). CTA buses go almost everywhere, on erratic schedules from early morning until late evening. Two of the seven El lines – the Red Line and the Blue Line to O'Hare – operate 24 hours a day. The other lines run from about 5am to 11pm daily. During the day, you shouldn't have to wait more than 15 minutes for an El train. Get free maps from El stations.

The standard fare on a bus or the El is $1.50, but transfers involving buses cost 30¢. On buses, you can use a fare card (called a Transit Card) or pay with exact change. On the El, you must use a Transit Card. The cards are sold from vending machines at El stations for any value between $3 and $100.

Metra commuter trains (☎ 312-836-7000 for information) have 12 routes serving the surrounding suburbs from four terminals ringing the Loop. Some lines run daily, while others operate only during weekday rush hours. The Metra information line can tell you the best combination of CTA, Metra and bus services to use to reach your destination. Metra fares run from $1.75 to $5 or more. An all-weekend ticket costs $5.

The terminals for Metra trains are LaSalle St Station, Randolph St Station (trains also stop at Van Buren St Station), Richard B Ogilvie Transportation Center and Union Station.

Chicago is not very accommodating for people with reduced mobility. Much of the El is inaccessible to the disabled; however most CTA buses are now accessible.

Car & Motorcycle City parking is difficult or expensive, and rush hour traffic is awful. City taxes add 30¢ or more a gallon to gas prices. Car rental is subject to taxes of 18%.

Taxi Cabs are plentiful in the Loop and north to Wrigleyville. In other areas, call Yellow Cab (☎ 312-829-4222) or Flash Cab (☎ 773-561-1444). Fares are $1.90 to start, plus $1.60 per mile; extra passengers cost 50¢, and a 15% tip is expected.

Bicycle There are bike lanes on some major roads, but they aren't well marked or respected. A popular path runs 18½ miles along the lakefront. For rentals, try Bike Chicago (☎ 800-915-2453), at Navy Pier and other locations ($8.75/34 an hour/day, with map, lock and helmet). Lock it or lose it.

AROUND CHICAGO
Evanston

A pleasant place 14 miles north of the Loop, Evanston combines sprawling old houses with a compact and walkable downtown. It's home to Northwestern University and the small **Mitchell Indian Museum** (☎ 847-475-1030, 2600 Central Park Ave), which documents the lives of Native Americans past and present ($3; closed Mon). Evanston can be reached on the CTA Purple Line.

North Shore

Chicago's northern lakeshore suburbs became popular with the carriage set in the late 19th century. A classic 30-mile drive follows Sheridan Rd through various tony towns to the socioeconomic apex of Lake Forest. Attractions include the glistening white Baha'i temple in Wilmette and the Chicago Botanic Garden in Glencoe (☎ 847-835-5440, 1000 Lake Cook Rd).

Oak Park

From 1898 to 1908, Frank Lloyd Wright worked and lived in Oak Park, west of the Loop. The Oak Park Visitor Center (☎ 708-848-1500, 158 Forest Ave) has an architectural walking-tour map. The **Frank Lloyd Wright Home & Studio** (☎ 708-848-1976, 951 Chicago Ave) offers tours of the home itself and other Wright-designed homes ($8; open 11am-3pm daily). The town is easily reached on the CTA Green Line.

NORTHERN ILLINOIS

The highlight of northern Illinois is the hilly northwest, which was untouched by the last ice age and is bordered by the Mississippi River. It's an easy and popular excursion from Chicago. En route (on US 20) is Union, where the Illinois Railway Museum (☎ 815-923-4000) is a good stop for rail buffs. Farther along US 20, the industrial city of **Rockford** features the Time Museum, with an oddball assortment of clocks, and a time-warp 1950s downtown.

Galena

Though just a speck on the map, Galena is the area's main attraction. Much visited for quick stress reduction, the beautiful town spreads across wooded hillsides and is perfectly preserved, despite a slew of tourist-oriented antique shops, art galleries and restaurants.

Lead was mined in the upper Mississippi area as early as 1700, but industrial demands in the mid-19th century resulted in a boom. Galena (named for the lead sulfide ore) became a center for the industry, a major river port and the most important regional town, with solid businesses, hotels and mansions in Federal and Italianate styles. The boom ended abruptly after the Civil War, and Galena was all but deserted until restoration began in the 1960s.

The visitor center (☎ 815-777-3557, 101 Bouthillier St) is on the eastern side of the Galena River, in the 1857 train depot. A second office is at the Old Market House on Commerce St downtown. Get a walking guide, leave your car and explore on foot.

Elegant old Main St curves around the hillside and the historic heart of town. Among numerous sites is the **Ulysses S Grant Home** (☎ 815-777-0248, 500 Bouthillier St), which was a gift from local Republicans to the victorious general at the end of the Civil War ($2). When the war started, Grant had only lived in the town for a few years and was a not-very-successful store clerk. But thanks to his West Point background and Mexican War experience he was chosen to be colonel of the town's regiment.

The elaborate Italianate **Belvedere Mansion** (☎ 815-777-0747, 1008 Park St) and the 1826 **Dowling House** (☎ 815-777-1250, 220 Diagonal St) are both open to the public.

Galena Historical Museum (☎ 815-777-9129, 211 S Bench St) provides a comprehensive town background. Six miles north is **Vinegar Hill Lead Mine**, with tours and a museum; open in summer.

Good sleeps and eats are plentiful here. Most accommodations are B&Bs, guesthouses and inns, many of which are pricey – minimum $85. Except in winter, many places are full, especially on weekends.

The cozy *Grant Hills Motel* (☎ 815-777-2116), 1½ miles east of town on US 20, has singles/doubles for $50/65, fine views included. *Triangle Motel* (☎ 815-777-2897), west of town on US 20, is a second choice; $45/60. The historic 1855 *DeSoto House Hotel* (☎ 815-777-0090, 230 S Main St) was good enough for Grant and Lincoln. It offers spacious, well-furnished rooms for $120.

Galena Café, at the south end of Main St, is ideal for breakfast. The **Log Cabin** (*201 N Main St*) serves huge dinner portions amid Americana ambience. Homey, low-priced **Nelson Bakery** (*18 S Main*) had a bit part in the film *Field of Dreams*. The pricey, dressy **Perry St Brasserie** (*124 N Commerce St*) boasts a renowned European chef. For a little grit with some local people, have a beer at the **VFW Hall**, on Main St at Hill St.

Quad Cities

South of Galena along a pretty stretch of the Great River Road is scenic Mississippi Palisades State Park. Farther downstream, the Quad Cities (Moline and Rock Island in Illinois, and Davenport and Bettendorf across the river in Iowa), known as the Q-C, make a surprisingly good stop. The Quad Cities Convention & Visitors Bureau (☎ 309-788-7800) is at 2021 River Dr in Moline.

Moline is the home of John Deere, the international farm machinery manufacturer. The company has a museum/showroom in town.

Rock Island has a funky appealing downtown (based at 3rd Ave and 18th St) with a couple of cafes, restaurants, a lively pub and music scene and one of the paddle-wheeler casinos. **Black Hawk State Historic Site** (☎ 309-788-0177), on the edge of town, is a huge park with trails by the Rock River. Its Hauberg Indian Museum, on Watch Tower Hill, outlines well the sorry story of Sauk leader Black Hawk and his people, and has displays of Indian artifacts (free admission; open daily).

Out in the Mississippi River, the actual island of **Rock Island** once held a Civil War–era arsenal and POW camp; the old arsenal is still in use by the military. The island also has a visitor center, two military museums and a Civil War cemetery.

Around Quad Cities

East of the Quad Cities, serious political hounds could visit tiny Tampico, the birth-

GREAT LAKES

Casinos a Good Bet

Great Lakes residents *love* gambling. It's huge. Casinos are ubiquitous. And the region's governments love the dough they're raking in. But this is the Midwest, land of good, upright, God-fearing folk and, of course, responsible legislators. So the many games of chance are veiled in (diaphanous) cloaks of decency, responsibility and quirky regulations suggesting a hint of guilt. In Michigan, Minnesota and Wisconsin all the casinos are operated by Native American groups (except in Detroit, where the success of the nearby casino in Windsor, Canada, was too glaring to ignore). In Indiana and Illinois, casinos orbit Chicago, which has none. Other Indiana casinos are on riverboats along the Ohio River. These 'off-shore' casinos bypass land-based prohibitions. In Ohio, casinos have been disallowed, but with heavy advertising from nearby states (eg, Indiana) luring residents to bet, the pressure is on to reverse the anticasino votes on the issue, ostensibly because 'the lost revenue is hurting the children' as school funds are drawn from gambling income.

place of former US president Ronald Reagan, or Dixon, where he grew up. His boyhood homes are open to the public. **Bishop Hill**, southeast of the Quad Cities, is the heart of the local Swedish community. A historic site outlines their first communal society, founded in 1850. Many original structures remain.

Southward in pleasant **Galesburg**, a quiet college town, is the Carl Sandburg Historic Site, which outlines the life of this well-known poet, writer and socialist. Stroll revitalized Seminary St to satiate thirst or hunger.

On the Mississippi southwest of Galesburg, **Nauvoo** is a restored 19th-century Mormon settlement. The history of Joseph Smith and his Church of Latter-Day Saints is detailed through a historic center and some 25 preserved homes and shops.

CENTRAL ILLINOIS

The bulk of central Illinois is farmland plain, with just a few interesting sites for the traveler, most of them Lincoln-related. East of Decatur, Arthur and Arcola are centers for the Amish.

Peoria

During the 20th century's first decades, Peoria was a thriving, wealthy town built on whiskey. The phrase 'But will it play in Peoria?' originated in the '20s, when the local well-to-do spawned a vibrant vaudeville/theater scene and brought in big-name performers from New York and Europe. (The phrase is still heard today, but often in a political context.)

The town's tastefully reinvented riverfront along Water St makes a good pit stop for a meal or beer, but you could bypass Peoria without regret.

Springfield

The small state capital has fine architecture and a serious obsession with Abraham Lincoln, who practiced law and politics here from 1837 to 1861. Its Abe-related sites offer an in-depth look – which only some cynics find overdone – at the man and his turbulent times. The central Springfield Visitors Bureau (☎ 217-789-2360) is at 109 N 7th St. Many of the attractions in the friendly downtown are walkable.

Things to See & Do Abraham and Mary Lincoln lived at the **Lincoln Home**, at 8th and Jackson Sts, from 1844 to 1861, then moved to the White House. For a free tour, obtain a ticket at the visitor center (☎ 217-492-4150), where you can view a 19-minute film while you wait – in summer it's crowded. The site is considerably more than just the house: The whole block has been preserved, and several structures are open to visitors daily.

Walk northwest to the **Lincoln-Herndon Law Offices** (☎ 217-785-7289), at 6th St and Adams, then continue (as Lincoln did) to the **Old State Capitol** (☎ 217-785-7691), at 5th and Adams Sts. Here detailed tours outline Lincoln's early political life, including his dramatic pre–Civil War debates with Stephen Douglas.

In 1861 the newly elected Lincoln departed for Washington at the **train depot**,

10th and Monroe Sts, which has an exhibit on his journey. After his assassination, Lincoln's body was returned to Springfield, where it lies today – the impressive **Lincoln's Tomb** sits in Oak Ridge Cemetery, north of downtown. The gleam on the nose of Lincoln's bust, created by visitors' light touches, indicates the numbers of those who pay their respects here.

Lincoln-free attractions include the colossal **State Capitol** (☎ 217-782-2099), at 2nd and Capitol Sts, offering free tours around the sumptuous interior (Mon-Sat); the pristine 1904 **Dana-Thomas House** (☎ 217-782-6776, 301 E Lawrence St), one of Frank Lloyd Wright's first 'Prairie style' houses, which contains original Wright furniture and fittings ($3 with insightful tour; open Wed-Sun); and the **Illinois State Museum** (☎ 217-782-7386), at Spring and Edwards Sts, which features Illinois cultural and natural exhibits, including displays on Native American history (free admission; open daily).

Places to Stay & Eat *Springfield KOA* (☎ 217-498-7002) is near town; call for directions. The central *YWCA Hostel* (☎ 217-522-8828, 421 E Jackson St) welcomes travelers and even has a pool. Reliable *Motel 6* (☎ 217-529-1633, 6010 S 6th St), about 5 miles from town, charges $40/46 for singles/doubles. Downtown, *Lincoln Plaza* (☎ 217-523-5661, 101 E Adams St) has rooms from $60. For historic ambience, splurge on the *Inn at 835* (☎ 217-523-4466, 835 S 2nd St), a fine B&B in a 1909 landmark.

Cruise S 6th St between Monroe and Adams Sts for a tasty array of meal choices. A local specialty is the 'horseshoe,' a filling, artery-clogging fried meat sandwich covered with melted cheese; *Brewhaus (617 E Washington)*, a popular pub, serves them. The immaculate *Coney Island Restaurant (210 S 5th St)* is a classic from the '40s that serves all three meals simply and well. *Cozy Dog Drive In (2935 S 6th St)*, on the southern outskirts, has been operating since 1948 and is a Rte 66 legend. It's a friendly, funky place with all sorts of memorabilia (some for sale), but don't arrive hungry – this place could give junk food a bad name.

Getting There & Around The Greyhound station (☎ 217-544-8466, 2351 S Dirkson Pkwy), southeast of downtown, has frequent connections to St Louis ($25; 2 hours), Indianapolis ($47; 8 hours) and Chicago ($38; 5 hours).

The Amtrak station (☎ 217-753-2013) is at 3rd and Washington Sts. Amtrak offers about three daily trains to/from St Louis ($31; 2½ hours) and Chicago ($45; 4 hours).

Petersburg

When Lincoln first arrived in Illinois in 1831, he worked variously as a clerk, store-keeper and postmaster in the frontier village of New Salem before studying law and moving to Springfield. In Petersburg, northwest of Springfield, **Lincoln's New Salem State Historic Site** (☎ 217-632-4000) is a reconstruction of the frontier village where Lincoln spent his early adult years. The building replicas, historical displays and costumed performances make a pretty informative and entertaining package. Camping is available.

Route 66

The classic highway from Chicago to Los Angeles, known through legend, song and television, once cut diagonally across Illinois to St Louis and beyond. Though now almost totally superseded by I-55, the old route – affectionately called Main St, USA – still exists in scattered sections, and its associated Americana survives in towns bypassed by the interstate.

The original Steak 'n' Shake Main St restaurant is still in **Normal**. Off to the southwest in **McLean**, the modest Route 66 Hall of Fame display at Dixie Truckers Home, a gas station/restaurant complex, is a kick for 66ers.

Southwest of McLean, unremarkable **Lincoln**, formerly Postville, was renamed in 1853 in honor of a circuit judge of such integrity that he was called 'honest Abe.' Then little known, Lincoln christened the town by spitting watermelon seeds on the ground. Dedicated Lincoln followers can visit the courthouse, now a state historic site.

A nostalgic stretch of old Rte 66 runs south of Springfield toward Carlinville. The Virden segment has some of the highway's first narrow, paved sections, and in Nilwood (don't blink) some of the original road, made of brick, is visible.

Farther south, a good section of old Rte 66 parallels I-55 through Litchfield, with its unchanged ***Route 66 Motel Court*** (☎ 217-324-2179) on N Old Rte 66. Also in Litchfield, eat at time-defiant ***Ariston Café*** on S Old Rte 66. Mount Olive has Soulsby's, a classic old gas station from the 1920s.

SOUTHERN ILLINOIS
By all accounts, **East St Louis**, an extension of St Louis, Missouri, across the Mississippi, is one badass place, best avoided. Even asking about it raises eyebrows. To the north, **Grafton** lies at the confluence of the Illinois and Mississippi Rivers. The Great River Road in this area is edged with cliffs and especially scenic.

East of East St Louis about 10 miles in Collinsville, don't miss **Cahokia Mounds State Historic Site** (☎ 618-346-5160), which protects the remnants of North America's largest prehistoric city (dating from AD 1200). While the 65 earthen mounds, including enormous Monk's Mound and the 'Woodhenge' sun calendar, are not overwhelmingly impressive in themselves, this Unesco World Heritage Site is well worth seeing. After checking out the excellent interpretive center, take a captivating walk around this once-thriving Mississippian Indian city of 20,000 (it even had suburbs!). It's open daily and admission is by donation. Nearby, Hwy 157 is lined with motels and chain restaurants.

An exception to the state's flat farmland is the green southernmost section, punctuated by rolling **Shawnee National Forest** and rocky outcroppings. The area has numerous state parks and recreation areas good for outdoor activities. Union County, near the state's southern tip, has wineries and orchards. At little Cairo, on the Kentucky border, the Mississippi and Ohio Rivers converge.

Ohio

As a major industrial state, Ohio is associated with both the rise and fall of US manufacturing and with the resurgence and renewal of Rust Belt cities. Surprisingly, much of the Buckeye State (a buckeye is a type of horse chestnut) is farmland.

Cleveland's Rock & Roll Hall of Fame & Museum is a top-drawer attraction. Lake Erie summer resorts and the state's Amish communities also lure visitors. Columbus and Cincinnati have major universities and intriguing old neighborhoods, while southern Ohio cradles rolling countryside and prehistoric archaeological sites.

History
After the Revolutionary War and subsequent westward expansion, Ohio was among the first areas settled; the town of Marietta was established in 1788. Following clashes with the settlers, the local Indians were decisively beaten at the 1794 Battle of Fallen Timbers. Immigrants – from Ireland, Switzerland and particularly Germany – began arriving in the early 19th century. In 1832 the completion of the Erie-Ohio Canal between the Ohio River and Lake Erie provided excellent transport connections that, combined with abundant local resources, enabled Ohio cities to become early centers of industry. By 1850 Ohio was the third most populous state in the nation.

Many Ohio soldiers – including Union generals Sherman and Grant – fought in the Civil War, though many in the state's south pledged allegiance to the Confederacy. Ohio's industry grew as part of the Union war machine, and after the war, many

---

Ohio

Nickname: Buckeye State

Population: 11,353,100 (7th)

Area: 44,830 sq miles (34th)

Admitted to Union: February 19, 1803 (17th)

Capital city: Columbus (population 632,900)

Other cities: Cleveland (505,600; metro area 1,831,100), Cincinnati (364,000; metro area 1,452,600), Toledo (332,900), Akron (223,000)

Birthplace of: General George Armstrong Custer (1839–76), inventor Thomas Edison (1847–1931), markswoman Annie Oakley (1860–1926), flight pioneers Orville Wright (1871–1948) and Wilbur Wright (1867–1912), golfer Jack Nicklaus (b 1940)

Famous for: the first airplane and traffic lights

GREAT LAKES

Southern blacks migrated to Cleveland, Cincinnati and Toledo.

Ohio became a center for huge industrial plants and organized labor, experiencing several significant strikes and disputes. Growth in the 20th century was well below the national average, and the state was hit hard by the recessions of the 1930s and 1970s. The '90s brought recovery to the north's massive steel industry and more economic diversity, including oil extraction.

Environmental concerns are a major issue. The infamous Ohio Valley industrial area produces serious air pollution, and shallow Lake Erie is particularly vulnerable to contamination.

Geography
The north and west are primarily flat farmland. The Lake Erie shoreline dominates the northern edge. To the east, particularly in the southeast, undulating green hills reflect the adjacent Appalachians. The often picturesque Ohio River meanders along the southern boundary.

Government & Politics
Ohio is evenly split between Democrats and Republicans. Seven US presidents were born in Ohio, leading to the state's sometimes-heard moniker, 'Mother of Presidents.'

Information
The Ohio Division of Travel and Tourism (☎ 614-466-8844, 800-282-5393, Ⓦ www .OhioTourism.com) is at 77 S High St, Columbus, OH 43215. For road conditions, call ☎ 888-264-7623. State sales tax is 5.5%, and accommodation tax varies up to 8%.

For state park information, call individual parks; no campground reservations are accepted.

CLEVELAND
Long the butt of jokes about its urban decay, its river so polluted it caught fire and its lack of positive personality, Cleveland is now really turning things around.

Surveyed in 1796, the city boomed after the Civil War by using iron from the upper Great Lakes and coal transported along the river to become one of the biggest US steel producers. It diversified into machinery production, textiles, clothing and chemicals and became a center of trade unionism and socially progressive policies. Industrial wealth bankrolled cultural aspirations, and the city still surprises with its world-class museums and performing arts.

Cleveland reached its nadir in 1969 when the Cuyahoga River burned (again) and the demise of the city's traditional industries led to urban blight and severe social problems. Ongoing renewal started in the 1980s, as derelict waterfronts became bustling restaurant, bar and entertainment precincts. Three 1990s developments had major impacts – new baseball and football stadiums became the focus of local civic pride, and the Rock & Roll Hall of Fame & Museum brought international attention. Today Cleveland is a unique blend of early architecture and gentrified neighborhoods, with enough residual urban grit and grime to add an edgy ambience.

Orientation & Information
Cleveland's main attractions cluster around downtown or the spacious Case Western Reserve University. Superior, Prospect and Euclid Aves are the main streets. East and west street designations begin at Ontario St.

The downtown visitor information center (☎ 216-621-7981, 800-321-1004, Ⓦ www.travelcleveland.com, 3100 Terminal Tower, 50 Public Square) is closed weekends. Another center is in the Flats on Old River Rd; open daily in summer. Massive Cleveland Public Library (☎ 216-623-2800, 325 Superior Ave NE) has Internet access and a unique chess set collection.

Parking is scarce and expensive downtown. Visitors beware after dark in most areas other than the Flats and waterfront.

Things to See & Do
Downtown Cleveland's center is Public Square, dominated by the conspicuous Terminal Tower and Tower City Center office and shopping complex. The 42nd-floor observation deck is open weekends ($2). On downtown's west side, **The Flats**, once a riverfront industrial area, has been reborn as a nightlife zone. Factories and warehouses have been recycled with an emphasis on catering to the young. The riverside patios are pleasant, set around and beneath the old iron bridges.

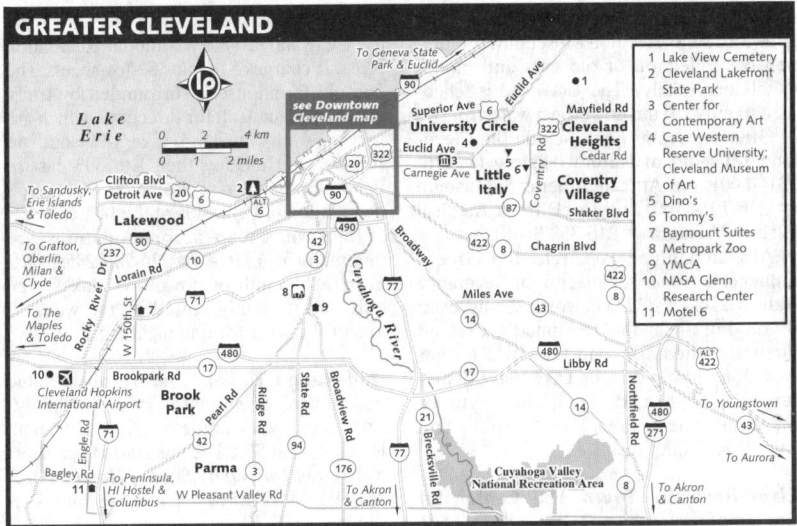

GREATER CLEVELAND

1 Lake View Cemetery
2 Cleveland Lakefront State Park
3 Center for Contemporary Art
4 Case Western Reserve University; Cleveland Museum of Art
5 Dino's
6 Tommy's
7 Baymount Suites
8 Metropark Zoo
9 YMCA
10 NASA Glenn Research Center
11 Motel 6

North of downtown on the overhauled Erie lakeshore is the renowned **Rock & Roll Hall of Fame & Museum** (☎ 216-781-7625, 888-764-7625, 1 Key Plaza), which is much more than a collection of rock star memorabilia, though it does have Janis Joplin's psychedelic Porsche and Ray Charles' sunglasses. Look for the insightful handwritten lyric notes and personal letters. Innovative, interactive multimedia exhibits trace the history and social context of rock music and the many performers who created it. Changing displays begin with rock's roots and originators and carry through to Seattle grunge and contemporary artists, simultaneously creating a historical record and fan nostalgia. IM Pei's architecture features towers, a pyramid and a phonograph-style entrance. Why is the museum in Cleveland? Because this is the hometown of Alan Freed, the disk jockey who popularized the term 'rock & roll' in the early 1950s, and because the city lobbied hard and paid big. The Hall of Fame, with its film showcasing members, is actually less interesting than the museum's ground floor artifacts and excellent thematic exhibits. The complex, open daily, is hugely popular (deservedly so), making weekends and holidays best avoided. Tickets are $15, with parking discounts for the adjacent Science Center lot.

Next door, the **Great Lakes Science Center** (☎ 216-694-2000) gives a good account of the lakes' environmental problems, with hands-on exhibits and an Omnimax theater ($8 for the exhibits or the theater; $11 for both). To the west is **Cleveland Browns Stadium**, the new home of the Browns NFL football team, which offers tours, a souvenir/merchandise shop and a free Browns Hall of Fame.

Nearby on the waterfront eastward is the storied submarine **USS Cod** (☎ 216-566-8770), a National Historic Landmark berthed alongside N Marginal Rd ($4; open daily May-Oct). Close by at the foot of E 9th St is the ***William G Mather*** (☎ 216-574-6262), a freighter incarnated as a steamship museum ($5; open daily May-Oct).

For a closer look at the lake and river, take a cruise (with meal) on the *Nautica Queen* (☎ 216-696-8888), which departs from the west side of the Flats.

University Circle Five miles east of downtown at Case Western Reserve University are eight museums. Star of the lot is the **Cleveland Museum of Art** (☎ 216-421-7340), which houses an excellent collection of European paintings, as well as African, Asian and American art (free admission; closed Mon). US history is revealed at the **Western Reserve Historical Society** (☎ 216-721-5722), which includes both a history museum and the Crawford Auto-Aviation Museum, a comprehensive collection of old cars and planes ($7.50; open daily). The Crawford is scheduled to move to the downtown waterfront.

Other museums here include the **Cleveland Museum of Natural History** (☎ 216-231-4600), the **African American Museum** (☎ 216-791-1700) and the **Dittrick Medical History Museum** (☎ 216-368-3648).

Also at University Circle, the Greek-influenced, art deco interior of **Severance Hall** (☎ 216-231-1111) is worth seeing, even if you don't hear the acclaimed Cleveland Orchestra there. Beyond the circle farther east, don't forget eclectic **Lake View Cemetery** (12316 Euclid Ave), the 'outdoor museum' where President Garfield and John Rockefeller rest.

Elsewhere in Town The **Center for Contemporary Art** (☎ 216-421-8671, 8501 Carnegie Ave) presents challenging exhibitions. **Metropark Zoo** (☎ 216-661-6500, 3900 Brookside Dr), about 5 miles south, features a rainforest environment with thunderstorms, waterfalls and tropical insects. The **NASA Glenn Research Center** (☎ 216-433-2000, 21000 Brookpark Rd), by the airport, has thorough exhibits on aerospace but is kid-friendly (free admission; open daily). **Coventry Village**, which is based on Coventry Rd at Mayfield Rd, is a small, relaxed neighborhood of alternative shops, restaurants, etc. The Big Fun store (1827 Coventry Rd) is sure to bring a smile. For a beach and picnicking, there is **Cleveland Lakefront State Park** (☎ 216-881-8141), just 3 miles east of downtown. Take Rte 2 east to exit 177, turn left on Martin Luther King Jr Blvd then right on Lakeshore Rd.

Places to Stay

Budget The closest campground (30 minutes southwest) is *The Maples* (☎ 216-926-3700), on Rte 83, a quarter-mile south of Rte 303, outside of Grafton. It offers tent and RV sites and a beach. Much better is *Geneva State Park* (☎ 216-466-8400), 50 miles northeast of Cleveland on Lake Erie. Sites ($20) are allocated on a first-come, first-served basis, but reservations are accepted for the RV rentals ($65).

In Peninsula, about 22 miles south of Cleveland, *HI Stanford House* (☎ 330- 467-

8711, 6093 Stanford Rd) sits peacefully in the leafy Cuyahoga Valley National Recreation Area. It charges $14, plus $2 for sheets. The fine old farmhouse is surrounded by trails; watch for deer. Call for directions, which are tricky: From Cleveland, take I-71 south to the exit at Hinckley, then Rte 303 east to Peninsula, then you're close. Note that there's no mention of Peninsula at the I-71 exit.

In town, cheap accommodations are minimal. The *YMCA* (☎ 216-749-2355, 3881 Pearl Rd), south of downtown, takes men only and is mainly rented by the week or longer. The cost for one night is $36.

Mid-Range & Top End The best value downtown is *Comfort Inn* (☎ 216-861-0001, 1800 Euclid Ave), at the corner of E 18th St. Rates start at $90. The bus station is a short walk away. *University Square Hotel* (☎ 216-361-8969, 3614 Euclid Ave), at E 36th St, is similar.

The best area for modest motels is southwest of Cleveland's center, near the airport in the Brook Park neighborhood, off I-71 or I-480. *Motel 6* (☎ 440-234-0990, 7219 Engle Rd), at the corner of Bagley Rd, charges about $52 for singles or doubles; *Baymount Suites* (☎ 216-251-8500, 4222 W 150th St) charges $75. Others (some a little dubious and maybe renting hourly) are found nearby along Brookpark Rd.

The brand-new *Hyatt Regency at Cleveland The Arcade* (☎ 216-575-1234, 420 Superior Ave) has opened in the Old Arcade building (1890) after a $60-million historical restoration. The central National Historic Landmark Building is a real beauty, and the expansive interior skylight and detailing are worth some effort to see. Well-appointed rooms run from $150-225, depending on scheduling and availability.

Places to Eat

Downtown, you'll find *Café 56* (340 Euclid Ave) serving fresh, quality juices, muffins, salads and sandwiches to area workers weekdays. Nearby, *Winking Lizard Tavern* (811 Huron Rd), at Prospect Ave, is a huge, popular branch of the local pub-grub outlet, complete with caged iguana. Countless beer varieties wash down salads and barbecued meats. *John Q's* (☎ 216-861-0900, 55 Public Square), right downtown, is a classic steak house (entrée $26).

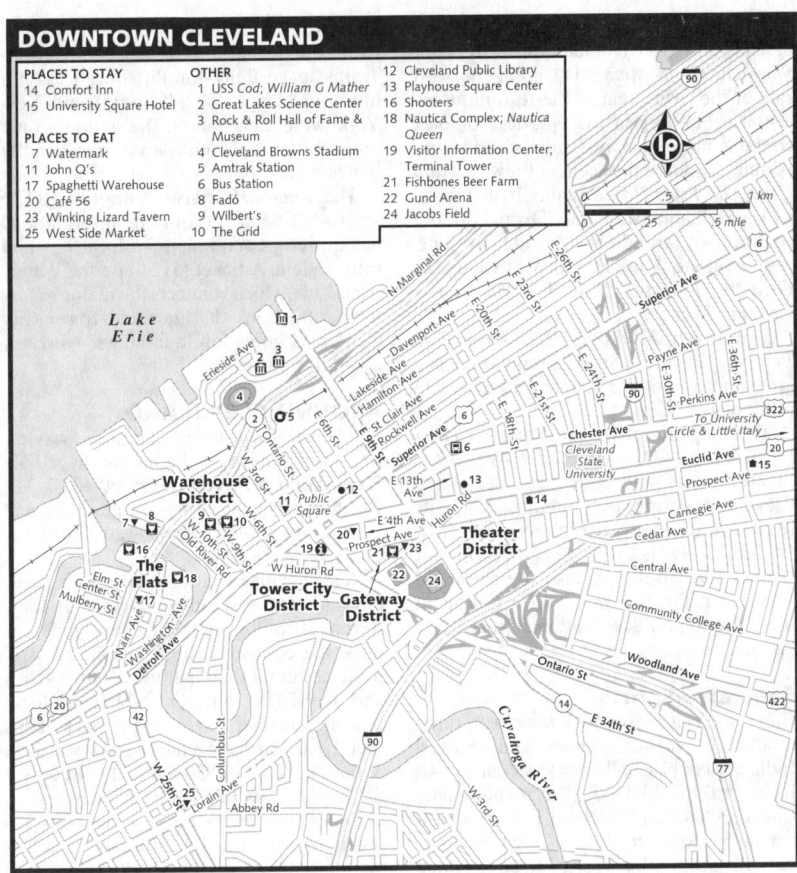

DOWNTOWN CLEVELAND

PLACES TO STAY
14 Comfort Inn
15 University Square Hotel

PLACES TO EAT
7 Watermark
11 John Q's
17 Spaghetti Warehouse
20 Café 56
23 Winking Lizard Tavern
25 West Side Market

OTHER
1 USS Cod; William G Mather
2 Great Lakes Science Center
3 Rock & Roll Hall of Fame & Museum
4 Cleveland Browns Stadium
5 Amtrak Station
6 Bus Station
8 Fadó
9 Wilbert's
10 The Grid

12 Cleveland Public Library
13 Playhouse Square Center
16 Shooters
18 Nautica Complex; Nautica Queen
19 Visitor Information Center; Terminal Tower
21 Fishbones Beer Farm
22 Gund Arena
24 Jacobs Field

In The Flats and Warehouse District, the area straddling the Cuyahoga River at the west edge of downtown has numerous places for a meal and even more for a drink. More upmarket than most is *Watermark (1250 Old River Rd)*, specializing in seafood and featuring a fine waterfront location. Across the river, the *Spaghetti Warehouse (1231 Main Ave)* serves low- to moderately priced pasta dishes in a colorful atmosphere. To the east a couple of blocks, around W 6th St in the dressier Warehouse District, you'll find a smorgasbord of quality choices.

In the University Circle area, Little Italy holds restaurants, cafes, a bakery and several pleasant blocks for strolling. It's along Mayfield Rd, a few blocks east of Euclid Ave from University Circle (look for the Rte 322 sign). Friendly *Dino's (12018 Mayfield)* serves authentic fresh entrées and sandwiches at good-value prices. Farther east, off Mayfield in food-abundant Coventry Village, casual *Tommy's (1820 Coventry Rd)* has a broad menu including vegetarian choices such as the outstanding Mary Lynn spinach pie.

The stalls at the *West Side Market*, under the clock tower at the corner of W 25th St and Lorain Ave, overflow with fresh produce and prepared foods, especially on elbow-rubbing Saturday mornings.

Entertainment

The best entertainment listings are in *Scene*, a free weekly. The *Plain Dealer* has a good Friday entertainment section.

GREAT LAKES

The Flats is a prime area for clubs, dancing and lively (sometimes rowdy) bars. **Shooters** *(1148 Main Ave)* is on the west side of the river. Nearby, the restored Powerhouse building in the Nautica complex contains more bars, restaurants and shops. A quieter spot with excellent brews is **Fadó** *(1058 Old River Rd),* a quality Irish pub.

The walkable Warehouse District offers a cocktail of trendier drinking options; wander along W 6th St and W St Clair. **The Grid** *(☎ 216-623-0113, 1281 W 9th St)* is a gay dance venue.

Downtown, **Fishbones Beer Farm** *(746 Prospect Ave)* has earned a reputation as a great spot to down a couple, and there are other places nearby.

The elegant **Playhouse Square Center** *(☎ 216-771-4444, 1501 Euclid Ave)* hosts theater, opera and ballet. The acclaimed Cleveland Symphony Orchestra holds its season (Aug–May) at **Severance Hall** *(☎ 216-231-1111, 11001 Euclid Ave),* near University Circle. It also performs in summer at the **Blossom Music Centre**, in the Cuyahoga Valley National Recreation Area.

Spectator Sports

Cleveland is a serious jock town with three modern downtown venues. The beloved Indians play baseball (Apr–Oct) at Jacobs Field (☎ 216-420-4200). The men's-league Cavaliers (☎ 216-420-2000) and women's-league Rockers (☎ 216-263-7625) play basketball at nearby Gund Arena, which doubles as an entertainment venue. In 1999, NFL football returned with the new Browns (☎ 440-891-5000) playing in the just built, open-roofed, split-sided Cleveland Browns Stadium by the lake.

Getting There & Around

Cleveland Hopkins International Airport (☎ 216-265-6030) is 11 miles southwest of town and linked to the city by the local Regional Transit Authority Red Line train ($1.50).

Greyhound offers frequent buses from the downtown bus station (☎ 216-781-0520, 1465 Chester Ave) to Pittsburgh ($23; 3 hours), Chicago ($39; 7 hours) and New York ($75; 9½ hours).

The Amtrak station (☎ 216-696-5115, 800-872-7245, 200 Cleveland Memorial Shoreway) is near the waterfront, across from the Great Lakes Science Center. Trains leave daily for Pittsburgh ($40; 3 hours), Chicago ($92; 7 hours) and New York ($128; 11½ hours). The station is only open for arrivals and departures, usually late at night.

The Regional Transit Authority (RTA; ☎ 216-621-9500 for 24-hour information) has a pretty comprehensive local bus and train system. A ticket ($1.50) on the Waterfront Line, which connects the major waterfront attractions, the Flats and Tower City Center, is good for four hours. Also ask about day passes.

AROUND CLEVELAND

Southeast of Cleveland (25 miles away off Rte 43 in Aurora) is the heavily hyped **Six Flags World of Adventure** (☎ 330-562-7131), which features thrill rides, a water park and a major marine-life park ($39/20 adults/children; $8 for parking).

A small village until Dr BF Goodrich established the first rubber factory in 1869, **Akron**, 30 miles south of Cleveland, was once the country's rubber capital. It still produces more than half the country's tires and over 50,000 different rubber products. Another rubber baron spent part of his Goodyear fortune on the Stan Hywet Hall & Gardens (☎ 330-836-5533, 714 N Portage St), noted for its Tudor Revival architecture, antiques and flowers. For an insight into US ingenuity, visit the Inventure Place & Inventors Hall of Fame (☎ 330-762-4463, 221 S Broadway), which holds lots of exhibits to inspire inventiveness.

Farther south in **Canton**, birthplace of the NFL, the popular Pro Football Hall of Fame (☎ 330-456-8207), off I-77, is a shrine for the gridiron-obsessed. Look for the football-shaped tower.

West of Cleveland, attractive **Oberlin** is an old-fashioned college town with noteworthy architecture by Cass Gilbert, Frank Lloyd Wright and Robert Venturi, and many fine preserved old houses. Farther west, just south of I-90, the tiny town of **Milan** is the birthplace of Thomas Edison. His home, restored to its 1847 likeness, is a small museum (☎ 419-499-2135) outlining many of his world-changing inventions, such as the lightbulb and phonograph ($5; closed Mon, except holidays).

Still farther west, on Hwy 20 and surrounded by farmland, is **Clyde**, which bills itself as the USA's most famous small town. It got that way when *Winesburg, Ohio* by native son Sherwood Anderson was published in 1919. It didn't take long for the unimpressed residents to figure out where the fictitious town really was. Stop at the Clyde Museum (☎ 419-547-9330, 124 W Buckeye St), in the old church, for more Anderson tidbits and details on a local Civil War officer James McPherson (open Thurs). A few doors down is the library, with several memorabilia/information-packed binders and an extensive Anderson book collection.

In **Toledo**, on the Michigan border, is the Toledo Museum of Art (☎ 419-255-8000, 2445 Monroe St), widely considered one of the country's best.

ERIE LAKESHORE & ISLANDS

In summer this good-time resort area is one of the busiest (and the most expensive) places in Ohio. Accommodations should be prebooked.

Sandusky, long a port, now mainly serves the Bass Islands and Kelleys Island, the major holiday destinations. The visitor center (☎ 419-625-2984, 231 Washington Rd) is on the parklike central square (closed weekends). Amid the 19th-century architecture is Follet House, at the corner of E Adams and Wayne Sts, once a stop for escaping slaves on the Underground Railroad. It's now a museum (free admission). Scads of chain motels line the roads heading into town.

Nearby, the **Cedar Point Amusement Park** (☎ 419-627-2350) features 14 roller coasters and live shows ($39/15 adults/kids; open daily May-Sept). To get there, just follow the signs from Sandusky. The surrounding area has a nice beach, a water park and a slew of tacky, old-fashioned attractions.

Lake Erie Islands

The islands in Lake Erie were inhabited by hostile Iroquois when the French first arrived. In the War of 1812's Battle of Lake Erie, Admiral Perry met the enemy English fleet near South Bass Island. His victory ensured that all the lands south of the Great Lakes became US, not Canadian. The islands were exploited for timber and later planted with grapevines. Today, while the nearby mainland gets very congested and isn't particularly attractive, the islands remain largely unspoiled, despite tourism's importance.

Access to the islands is from Sandusky, Marblehead, Catawba or the relatively sedate Port Clinton. One boat connects Sandusky to **Pelee Island**, Canada. Pelee, the largest Erie island, is a quiet, wine-producing and bird-watching destination connected by ferry to the Ontario mainland.

Kelleys Island Quiet and green, Kelleys is a popular weekend getaway. It has pretty 19th-century buildings, Native American pictographs, a good beach, glacial grooves…even its old limestone quarries are scenic. The Chamber of Commerce (☎ 419-746-2360) has accommodations information.

Sherwood: A Writer's Writer

Though hardly a household name even in literary circles, Sherwood Anderson (1876–1941) is considered a revolutionary force in US fiction. *Winesburg, Ohio*, his collection of connected short stories based on events and characters in Clyde, startled both critics and the public with its form and subject matter, ushering in a new era of realism. It's called his most important work.

Action and plot do not fuel his stories; instead, they are based on the emotions of the characters. Anderson became a major influence on Wolfe, Steinbeck, Saroyan, Henry Miller, Mailer, Terkel, Faulkner and Hemingway (he helped Faulkner and Hemingway get published for the first time). His unconventional life (leaving a successful business and wife and children) made him a symbol of those who reject materialism and middle-class values in favor of loyalty and devotion to the principles of art.

Other Anderson books include *Many Marriages*, *Dark Laughter* and his memoirs. His Virginia gravestone reads 'Life, not Death, is the Great Adventure.'

GREAT LAKES

Kelleys Island State Park (☎ 419-797-4530) quickly gets full, and it doesn't take campsite reservations. The Village, the small commercial center of the island, has places to eat, drink and shop. Bicycles, a good way to sightsee, can be rented.

The cheapest ferry is Neuman's (☎ 419-798-5800), which departs from Marblehead dock ($9.50/16.50 per person/car).

Bass Islands Forget the history and scenery – on a summer weekend, packed Put In Bay on **South Bass Island** is about drinking and carousing. But away from this party town full of restaurants and shops, you'll find a winery and opportunities for camping, fishing, walking and swimming. A singular attraction is the 352-foot Doric column commemorating Perry's victory in the Battle of Lake Erie – you can climb up to the observation deck for views of the battle site and, on a good day, Canada.

The Chamber of Commerce (☎ 419-285-2832) has information on lodging, which starts at $65 in summer and is often booked up. *South Bass Island State Park* fills up early, but you can reserve a campsite at *Bass Isle Resort* (☎ 419-285-6121, 800-837-5211). Taxis and tour buses serve the island, but bicycling is a fine way to get around. Most ferries to South Bass Island leave Port Clinton on the mainland, but Miller Ferries (☎ 800-500-2421) from Catawba is cheapest ($5/12 per person/car).

Middle Bass Island, a good day trip by ferry from South Bass, offers nature and quiet.

AMISH COUNTRY

The farming villages halfway between Cleveland and Columbus are home to a large proportion of Ohio's Amish community. Wayne and Holmes Counties have the USA's densest Amish concentration, followed by areas in Pennsylvania and Indiana. Around Millersburg and Apple Creek, horse-drawn buggies carry traditionally clothed families, and shops sell homemade crafts and foods. Near **Berlin**, east of Millersburg, is the Mennonite Information Center, which offers concise explanations of the history and life of these independent, religious people. Many places are closed Sunday.

COLUMBUS

Columbus, the state capital, is also a major center for education, research and commerce. Clean, spacious streets give it a prosperous air, while the 60,000 students of Ohio State University (OSU), plus those of five other colleges, lend the city a youthful vitality. Miles of sprawling suburbs surround the high-rise buildings of downtown.

The visitor center (☎ 614-221-6623, 800-345-4386, 90 N High St) offers a specialized African American attractions booklet. A second, smaller office is downtown, on the 2nd floor of City Center Mall (111 S 3rd St).

Things to See & Do

It's a short walk south from City Center Mall to the Greek Revival **state capitol**, which is notable for *not* having a dome.

Although little promoted, the **Ohio Historical Center** (☎ 614-297-2300), well north of downtown at E 17th Ave, is a highly recommended, excellent museum that could take three hours to see (open daily). For those planning to tour the state's southern Hopewell Indian sites, a visit is invaluable. Also on-site is a reconstructed 19th-century village (open Wed-Sun Mar-Dec). Back downtown, **COSI Columbus** (☎ 614-228-2674, 333 W Broad St), the new center for science and industry, is an interactive museum great for kids ($12/7 adult/child; open daily).

Wexner Center for the Arts (☎ 614-292-3535, 1871 N High St), on the OSU campus, offers cutting-edge art exhibits, films and performances.

Several distinct districts of the city are worth exploring. A half dozen blocks south of downtown is the remarkably large, all-brick **German Village**, a restored 19th-century neighborhood. The German Village Society (☎ 614-221-8888, 588 S 3rd St) has information. The adjacent **Brewery District**, now consuming more brew than it produces, has several buildings converted to restaurants and bars. About six blocks north of downtown, **Short North** is a redeveloped strip of High St running from Goodale St to 5th Ave; it holds contemporary art galleries, restaurants and clothing shops. North again, the university area has many casual storefronts.

Places to Stay

Surrounded by students, the convenient and central **HI Columbus Hostel** (☎ 614-294-7157, 95 E 12th St) is a friendly, well-run hostel in a house rumored to have been designed by Frank Lloyd Wright, but even the manager isn't sure. Dorm beds cost $13/15 members/nonmembers, and there is a family room.

Cheap chain motels are bunched near the I-270 ring road, where the main highways intersect. **Motel 6** (☎ 614-846-9860, 1289 E Dublin-Granville Rd) is 15 minutes north of downtown and offers singles/doubles for $40/46 (more on weekends); this is the most central and costly of the chain's four Columbus-area locations. Rooms at **Best Western Claremont** (☎ 614-228-6511, 650 S High St), in German Village, start at $80. Much more expensive is the classiest place in town: the restored, century-old **Westin Hotel** (☎ 614-228-3800, 310 S High St), formerly the Great Southern Hotel, with rates in the $100 range.

German Village has several B&Bs, including **German Village B&B** (☎ 614-444-7421, 908 City Park Ave), recommended for its warm, well-traveled owner, its garden and its excellent prices ($50/70 singles/doubles).

Places to Eat & Drink

The downtown **Wendy's** (257 E Broad St), at the corner of 55th St, was the first link in that hamburger chain and looks as it did in 1969. E Gay St has several restaurants.

German Village eateries run the gamut from overflowing-with-patrons **Katzinger's Deli** (475 S 3rd St) to top-end **Lindley's** (☎ 614-228-4343, 169 E Beck St). **Hoster Brew Pub**, open daily, is located in the Brewery District at the corner of S High St and E Hoster St.

Toward the university, **Buca di Beppo** (343 N Front St) offers heaping plates of classic southern Italian fare for about $10. The North Market, on Spruce St by the Short North area, has all manner of fresh foods and numerous prepared meals – from Middle Eastern to a decent $4 lunch at **Flavors of India**.

Around OSU and beyond along N High St you'll find everything from Mexican to Ethiopian, plus numerous quality coffee and bagel cafes. The area also has many bars, some with live music. The weekly *Alive* has full club listings.

Spectator Sports

The Ohio State Buckeyes football team (☎ 614-292-9908) attracts a rabid following to legendary horseshoe-shaped Ohio Stadium for its games, held on Saturdays in fall. The NHL Columbus Blue Jackets (☎ 614-540-4625) play hockey at the downtown Nationwide Arena. The popular Columbus Crew (☎ 614-447-2739), Ohio's professional soccer team, play in their own stadium of the same name Mar–Oct.

Getting There & Around

From the Greyhound station (☎ 614-221-2389, 111 E Town St), at 3rd St, buses run frequently to Cincinnati ($16; 2 hours), Cleveland ($19; 2½ hours) and Chicago ($51; from 7 hours). There is no Amtrak train service.

The Central Ohio Transit Authority (COTA; ☎ 614-228-1776) runs the local buses ($1.10).

SOUTHEASTERN OHIO

Ohio's southeastern corner offers visitors a pastoral respite from the state's many urban centers. Here you'll find most of Ohio's forested areas, many of them protected, as well as rolling hills and scattered farms.

Around Lancaster, southeast of Columbus, the hills begin gently leading into wonderful **Hocking County**, which contains more than half a dozen state parks. This region of streams and waterfalls, sandstone cliffs and cavelike formations is an excellent area to explore in any season. It has miles of trails for hiking and rivers for canoeing, as well as abundant campgrounds and rental cabins. One highlight is **Old Man's Cave State Park** (☎ 740-385-6841), which offers great scenery and camping in a mixed forest with abundant wildlife. This is a busy area in summer, especially on weekends. The historic Hocking Valley Railway offers short return trips from Nelsonville on to Logan on weekends – a popular excursion with autumn leaf-peepers ($11).

With a population of 21,000, plus 19,000 students, **Athens** makes a lovely stop and a good base for seeing the region. Situated where US 50 crosses US 33, it's set among wooded hills, built

GREAT LAKES

around the Ohio University campus (which comprises half the town) and features solid, unpretentious early-19th-century architecture. The visitor center (☎ 614-592-1819) is at 667 E State St. Inexpensive motels – including *Budget Host (☎ 740-594-2294)*, on Rte 50 W – dot the outskirts, and numerous student cafes and pubs line Court St, the main street. *Court Street Diner (18 N Court St)* is a '50s-style diner; try the potato soup. Around the corner, *Casa Nueva (4 W State St)* has Mexian-inspired dishes.

Farther south, the Ohio River marks the state boundary and flows through many scenic stretches. It's a surprisingly quiet, undeveloped area.

The area south of Columbus was a center for the fascinating prehistoric Hopewell moundbuilding culture from around 300 BC to AD 550, and there are a number of the 2000-year-old earthworks sites. For a fine introduction visit intriguing **Hopewell Culture National Historic Park** (☎ 740-774-1125), 3 miles north of Chillicothe. The visitor center ($2) has a film and exhibit; then you can wander about the variously shaped burial mounds spread over 13-acre **Mound City**, a mysterious city of the dead. The site is on Rte 104 north of Rte 35, right beside two scary-looking prisons...er, correctional facilities. Visit the Ohio Historical Center in Columbus to learn more about the Hopewell.

In 1802 **Chillicothe** became the capital of the USA's new Northwest Territory, and later it became the first capital of Ohio. Today it has some well-restored buildings and a big paper mill. The visitor center (☎ 740-702-7677) is central at the corner of Main and Paint Sts. A fair selection of moderate motels is available, along with a range of eating options, especially on Rte 159. The clean *Chillicothe Inn (☎ 740-774-2512)*, in town at the corner of N Bridge and Main Sts, is a good deal at $33/37 singles/doubles.

At an amphitheater (☎ 740-775-0700) on Delano Rd, 10 miles northeast of town, a theatrical rendition of the life and struggles of Tecumseh, the Shawnee chief, is performed ($14-16; nightly except Sun, mid-June to early Sept). This ersatz history is much more popular than the genuine, static Hopewell archaeological site.

West of Chillicothe, US 50 bobs pleasantly between hills, farms and woodlands.

Other **Hopewell sites** are in the area. Fort Hill State Memorial, off Rte 41 south in a pretty Amish district, preserves a Hopewell ceremonial site in a natural area with hiking trails and a gorge. It's one of the best-preserved Hopewell hilltop enclosures. Farther southwest, Serpent Mound National Historic Landmark, on Rte 73, 4 miles northwest of Locust Grove, is perhaps the most captivating of all. It's the largest effigy mound in the USA and one of the most finely represented of all the zoomorphic mounds. Over 450 yards long, it has a beautifully serpentine shape ($5).

DAYTON

Dayton is a nondescript city of interest primarily to aviation enthusiasts, who know it as the home of the Wright brothers. This is the place where they developed the world's first engine-powered plane.

The visitor center (☎ 937-226-8211) is on the ground floor of the convention center, downtown at E 5th and S Main Sts. The Greyhound bus station (☎ 937-224-1608) is close by at the corner of E 5th and Jefferson Sts.

Things to See & Do

The huge **USAF Museum** (☎ 937-255-3286), at the Air Force base 6 miles northeast of town, displays about 300 aircraft. It's got everything from a Wright exhibit, a Sopwith Camel and a Stealth bomber to astronaut ice cream, military propaganda, the world's largest aerial camera and an Aviation Hall of Fame. Admission price is a smile and it's open daily until 5pm. Expect a visit to take three or more hours (some food is available). And don't miss the annex, with its collection of presidential planes – a free shuttle bus takes you over to the hangar.

There are numerous Wright sites. Among them, **Carillon Historical Park** (☎ 937-293-2841, 2001 S Patterson Blvd) has the 1905 Wright Flyer III biplane and a replica of the Wright workshop. South of town, the **Dayton-Wright Brothers Airport** (☎ 937-885-2327, 10550 Rte 741, Miamisburg) has the world's only flying 'B' plane (free admission; open Tue, Thurs, Sat). Rides can be arranged by appointment. Back in town, the **Wright Cycle Company** (☎ 937-225-7705, 22 S Williams St) is the shop where the brothers developed bikes and aviation ideas (free admission; open daily Memorial Day to

The Hopewell & Their Enduring Mysteries

The Hopewell Indian culture, which flourished in the Ohio Valley region between about 300 BC and AD 550, was named after the farmer's field where its remnants were first unearthed. Although relatively unknown today, the Hopewell developed a sophisticated, village-based society where successful agriculture and management allowed for complex spiritual and artistic pursuits. The Indians' most intriguing traits were their internment rites and elaborate burial mounds, many of which remain. Finely worked artifacts indicate that they had far-flung trading relationships and influence. The causes of the Hopewells' decline and the later emergence of the Mississippi mound-building culture are not known.

Labor Day, then Wed-Sun). Also south of town is **Sunwatch** (☎ 937-268-8199, 2301 W River Rd), a replica/interpretation center of a 12th-century Fort Ancient Indian village ($5; open Apr-Nov, closed Mon).

Another aerospace attraction lies 50 miles north of Dayton in **Wapakoneta**, the birthplace of moon-walking astronaut Neil Armstrong. The always evolving and growing Neil Armstrong Air & Space Museum (☎ 419-738-8811, S Apollo Drive), at I-75 exit 111, outlines aviation and aerospace history ($5; open daily).

Places to Stay & Eat

Near the air museum, ***Days Inn*** (☎ *937-236-8083, 1891 Harshman Rd*) has rooms for $60. North of town off I-75, ***Motel 6*** (☎ *937-898-3606, 7130 Miller Lane*) charges $40.

Downtown at the corner of S St Clair and E 4th St, find timeless ***Roxy's Diner*** by the sun glinting off its chrome. It offers all the standards daily, and it's open all night on Friday and Saturday. The nearby Oregon District, along E 5th St east of Jefferson St, has a small, concentrated and eclectic mix of stores, bars and restaurants. South of town in Ketterling, ***L'Auberge*** (☎ *937-299-5536, 4120 Far Hills Ave*) is considered one of Ohio's best restaurants; entrées are from $20.

CINCINNATI

Stretching along the Ohio River, Cincinnati physically and culturally straddles the historic North and South division of the country. It's a significant industrial and commercial center lacking major visitor attractions, but it does have some well-preserved 19th-century neighborhoods, significant cultural sites and a major university, and it overlooks the attractive riverfront in Kentucky.

Cincinnati garnered bad press in 2001 for outbreaks in simmering racial tension resulting from young blacks being killed by white police. City hall has vowed to improve relations and upgrade the central low-income neighborhoods.

History

Founded in 1788, soon after the Revolutionary War, Cincinnati was one of the first US cities west of the Alleghenies. With the Ohio River as a principal transport route, Cincinnati became a base for wars against the Native Americans and a center of the rich agricultural hinterland. The introduction of steamboats and the completion of the Miami–Erie Canal made it even more important as a gateway to the expanding frontier. It soon became Ohio's largest city, and a huge influx of German and Irish immigrants pushed the population above 160,000 by 1860. The many meatpacking plants earned Cincinnati the nickname 'Porkopolis' and provided enough leftover lard for Messrs Procter & Gamble to become one of the world's largest soap makers.

Though in many respects a northern industrial city, Cincinnati had plenty of Southern sympathizers in the mid-19th century because of its proximity and connections to the South. Nevertheless, it became a center for the antislavery movement, an important station on the Underground Railroad and a home of abolitionist writing and publishing. The Civil War was a boost to Cincinnati's industries, but later the city suffered from corruption, maladministration and a decline in its river commerce as the railways expanded. Cincinnati is now

Meet Me at the Corner, Smiling

The corner of Grinn and Barret has been voted the funniest intersection name in the USA. Grinn Drive and Barret Road meet in West Chester, Ohio, just north of Cincinnati. 'Grin and bear it' means to tolerate something unpleasant.

the third-largest city in the state and maintains a wide manufacturing base. It's also a major coal port and cultural center working hard to stem downtown decay with new sports and art venues.

Orientation & Information

The flat grid of downtown is surrounded by welcome green hills on three sides and the snaking Ohio River to the south. The tucked-away visitor center (☎ 513-621-2142, 800-543-2613, ⓦ www.cincyusa.com, 300 W 6th St), at the corner of Plum St, has free walking-tour brochures; it's closed weekends. In summer there are information booths in Fountain Square and the Museum Center. The Cincinnati Public Library (800 Vine St) provides Internet access. The area between the train station and downtown is best avoided on foot, and caution should be used at night in the Over-the-Rhine neighborhood.

Things to See & Do

The center of downtown is **Fountain Square**, where people congregate around the fancy old 'Spirit of the Waters' fountain. At the corner of the square, Carew Tower has a great view from its 49th-floor observation deck ($2; open daily) and a fine art deco interior – its ceramics are from the celebrated local Rookwood pottery. West of the square, the Skywalk system of elevated walkways links hotels and shops in a 20-block area.

East of the square are the big postmodern Procter & Gamble building, with its attractive gardens, and the push-the-envelope **Contemporary Arts Center** (☎ 513-721-0390, 115 E 5th St, 2nd floor), which shows all manner of modern art ($3.50; open daily but only afternoons Sun). In 2002 it will be replaced by the stunning Rosenthal Center for Contemporary Arts, whose avant-garde

jigsaw design by Zaha Hadid has already shaken up the architectural world. A few blocks farther east, have a look in Lytle Park at the statue of Lincoln bearing the burdens of office, then continue to the **Taft Museum** (☎ 513-241-0343, 316 Pike St). The handsome 1820 mansion holds a notable collection of Chinese porcelain and European paintings ($4, free Wed; open daily).

East of downtown, **Mt Adams** (known as 'the hill') is a 19th-century neighborhood of narrow, winding streets sporting galleries, bars, restaurants and views. You can walk from the Taft Museum to hilly Mt Adams, though a lot of busy streets and highways are in between. The best route is to follow E 6th St, cross the bridge, then look for the stairs. It takes about 30 minutes, but walking's not a bad idea because driving is awkward, too; go via Eden Park Dr. On the way, in Eden Park, the **Cincinnati Art Museum** (☎ 513-721-5204) has the city's best collection, with an emphasis on Middle Eastern and European arts ($5; closed Mon). The **Krohn Conservatory** (☎ 513-421-4086), also in the park, is a vast greenhouse with rainforest and desert flora and superb seasonal flower shows (free admission), as well as a butterfly conservatory ($5).

Two miles northwest of downtown, the **Cincinnati Museum Center** (☎ 513-287-7000, 1301 Western Ave) occupies the classic 1933 Union Terminal, an art deco train station still used by Amtrak. The building looks a little like Darth Vader's helmet, and its interior has magnificent murals made of Rookwood tiles. Inside, the Cincinnati History Museum features a river steamboat and exhibits on the city and region ($6.50). More geared to kids is the Museum of Natural History, with an excellent exhibit on the ice age that shaped the Great Lakes region, and a limestone cave with real bats ($6.50). An Omnimax theater and the Cinergy Children's Museum round out the sites. Bargain combination tickets are offered, and the museums are free for the last half hour each day; parking costs $3.50.

South of the city center, the elegant 1876 **Roebling Suspension Bridge** was a forerunner of John Roebling's famous Brooklyn Bridge in New York. To the west, the Freedom Center, a national Underground Railway museum, opens in 2003. To the east you will find Cinergy

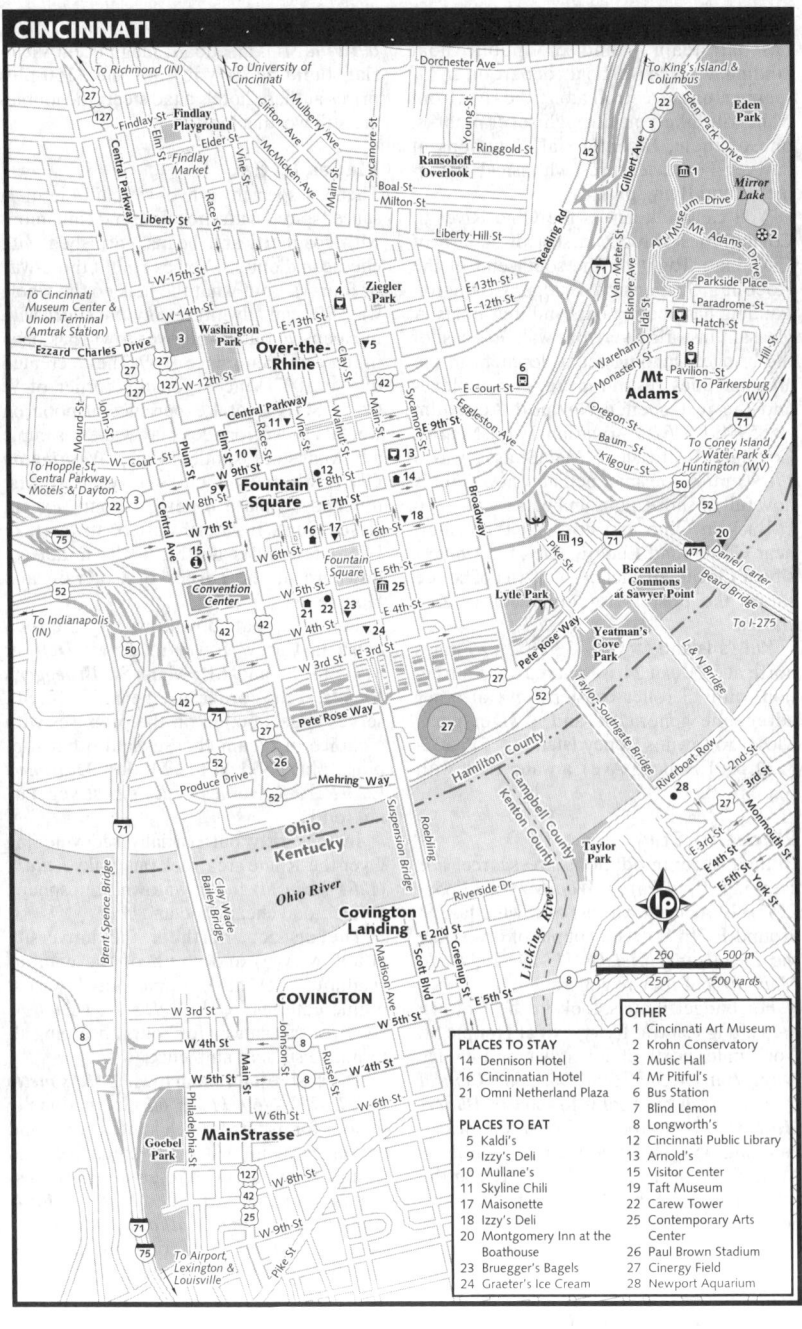

CINCINNATI

PLACES TO STAY
14 Dennison Hotel
16 Cincinnatian Hotel
21 Omni Netherland Plaza

PLACES TO EAT
5 Kaldi's
9 Izzy's Deli
10 Mullane's
11 Skyline Chili
17 Maisonette
18 Izzy's Deli
20 Montgomery Inn at the Boathouse
23 Bruegger's Bagels
24 Graeter's Ice Cream

OTHER
1 Cincinnati Art Museum
2 Krohn Conservatory
3 Music Hall
4 Mr Pitiful's
6 Bus Station
7 Blind Lemon
8 Longworth's
12 Cincinnati Public Library
13 Arnold's
15 Visitor Center
19 Taft Museum
22 Carew Tower
25 Contemporary Arts Center
26 Paul Brown Stadium
27 Cinergy Field
28 Newport Aquarium

Field – home of the Cincinnati Reds pro baseball team – and the public boat landing, where riverboats depart on sightseeing cruises. A stroll along the riverfront walk will take you through several parks; one of them, Bicentennial Commons at Sawyer Point, features whimsical monuments and flying pigs.

You can walk across the Ohio River to **Covington**, Kentucky, a sort of suburb of Cincinnati. Right by the south end of the Roebling Suspension Bridge, Covington Landing has floating bars and tour boats. A pleasant historic riverfront walk lies east of the bridge. Ongoing redevelopment in the area includes restaurant/retail complexes and the just-opened **Newport Aquarium** (☎ 859-491-3467, 1 Aquarium Way). Nearby, Covington's attractive **MainStrasse** was a 19th-century German neighborhood and is now full of shops, pubs and eats.

Back in Ohio and north of the center, near Clifton and Ludlow Aves, the **University of Cincinnati** anchors a district of coffee shops and posters for introductory Zen classes.

King's Island (☎ 800-433-1072), 25 miles north at I-71 exit 24, is the area's top attraction, with 13 roller coasters, several other adrenaline generators and a water park. Closer to town is **Coney Island** (☎ 513-232-8230, 6201 Kellogg Ave), a water park with some rides.

Places to Stay

Budget accommodations are scarce. For camping, try **Winton Woods** (☎ 513-851-2267), 12 miles northwest of town. Main St around E 7th St has a couple of dives, like the **Dennison Hotel** (☎ 513-241-7035, 716 Main St), but they're generally full.

For budget motels, look in the Uptown area along Central Pkwy; exit at Hopple St, 2 or 3 miles north of downtown on I-75. Try **Days Inn** (☎ 513-559-0400, 2880 Central Pkwy), which has rooms for $65, or **Budget Host** (☎ 513-559-1600, 3356 Central Pkwy), charging $55. Other less costly options – Motel 6 and the like – can be found near the interstates on the outskirts of town and across the river in Covington.

The central downtown hotels are gorgeous but pricey. The 1920s-era **Omni Netherland Plaza** (☎ 513-421-9100, 35 W 5th St) is an art deco monument, while the 1882 **Cincinnatian Hotel** (☎ 513-381-3000, 601 Vine St) is an equally magnificent Victorian building. If you find the $150-plus prices at these hotels a tad steep, the lobbies are still worth a look.

Places to Eat

The local specialty is five-way chili – ie, meat sauce (spiced with chocolate and cinnamon) with spaghetti and beans, garnished with cheese and onions. You can get it three-way or four-way, but what the hell, go the whole way; life's an adventure. **Skyline Chili**, with inexpensive outlets all over town, has been in the chili game since 1949. The re-created one at 1007 Vine St, on the corner of W Court St, is a total experience at noon on weekdays. Aficionados may want to sample a bowl at sleek, spotless **Camp Washington Chili**, where the city's fave food first touched a palate (open 24 hours, except closed Sun). It's northwest of town (take I-75 a few miles north), in the middle of nowhere at the corner of Colerain and Hopple Sts.

For cheap eats downtown, try the **food court** in Carew Tower or **Izzy's Deli**, at 819 Elm St and 610 Main St. **Bruegger's Bagels**, at the corner of Vine and E 4th Sts, serves bagels boiled on the premises with a choice of cream cheeses and other toppings, plus good coffee. Modest **Mullane's** (723 Race St) serves Cincy's best vegetarian food.

In the gritty but partially redeveloping Over-the-Rhine area, seek out funky **Kaldi's** (1204 Main St) for downtown atmosphere, coffee, good cheap food and beer.

The districts north of the university (Ludlow Ave) and south of the campus (Calhoun St) have numerous low-cost ethnic eateries. At **Sitwell's** (404 Ludlow Ave) you can sit well for hours absorbing alternative/student ambience.

The best restaurant in town is **Maisonette** (☎ 513-721-2260, 114 E 6th St), nationally famous for its fine French haute cuisine and extensive wine list. It's expensive and formal, and you'll need reservations. No less famous are the barbecued ribs at **Montgomery Inn at the Boathouse** (☎ 513-721-7427, 925 Eastern Ave), right by the river. Another celebrated Cincinnati experience is **Graeter's Ice Cream**, at 41 E 4th St and elsewhere.

Entertainment
In Mt Adams, look for **Blind Lemon** *(936 Hatch St),* a gem of a bar with lots of history, atmosphere and good live music. **Longworth's** *(1108 St Gregory St)* is also very comfortable, with pleasant outdoor tables.

Downtown, **Arnold's** *(☎ 513-421-6234, 210 E 8th St)* is a tavern dating from 1861, with food, drink and live jazz. Nightlife is happening in Over-the-Rhine, as new bars of all types continue to open; take care on the side streets. **Mr Pitiful's** *(☎ 513-369-0202, 1393 Main St)* is good for many kinds of live music including blues, R&B and rockabilly.

At Covington Landing, just across the Roebling Suspension Bridge, a couple of places literally on the Ohio attract young crowds. These places are especially good on a hot night when there's a breeze off the river.

The acoustically excellent **Music Hall** *(☎ 513-721-8222, 1241 Elm St)* is the city's classical music venue, where the symphony orchestra, pops orchestra, opera and ballet hold their seasons. This is not a very good neighborhood, so be cautious and park nearby.

Spectator Sports
The Cincinnati Reds (☎ 513-421-4510), direct descendants of the Cincinnati Red Stockings, the country's first professional baseball team, play at Cinergy Field. The Cincinnati Bengals pro football team (☎ 513-621-3550) scrimmage nearby at new Paul Brown Stadium.

Getting There & Around
The Greyhound station (☎ 513-352-6012, 1005 Gilbert Ave) is within a mile of Fountain Square. Buses run regularly to Louisville, Kentucky ($20; 2 hours), Indianapolis ($20; 2½ hours) and Columbus ($16; 3 hours).

The beautiful Amtrak station (☎ 513-651-3337, 1301 Western Ave), at the Cincinnati Museum Center, is served by three trains a week to Indianapolis ($35; 3½ hours), Chicago ($75; 8 hours) and Washington, DC ($117; 14 hours).

Metro (☎ 513-621-4455) runs local commuter buses daily, including the handy, cheap Downtowner (25¢).

Michigan

The Great Lakes are in the heart of the Midwest, and in the heart of the Great Lakes lies Michigan. Surrounded by four of the five lakes (Superior, Michigan, Huron and Erie), Michigan is a pair of peninsulas featuring 3200 miles of shoreline (second only to Alaska), the most extensive freshwater sand dunes in the country and 11,000 inland lakes. Stand anywhere in the state and you are never more than 6 miles from one of the Great Lakes, an inland lake or a blue-ribbon trout stream.

Thanks in part to three national park units (Isle Royale, Sleeping Bear Dunes and Pictured Rocks), Lake Michigan's golden beaches and the Great Lakes, Michigan is a major tourist destination, especially for outdoor enthusiasts. Michigan's state park system holds more than 14,000 campsites. Add almost 5000 more sites in its national and state forests, and it's easy to understand why camping holidays are a time-honored tradition in Michigan. If you have transportation and a tent, Michigan can be an extremely scenic and affordable place to visit from May through October.

History
Easy travel on the Great Lakes has led to a long and colorful history in Michigan. There is evidence of prehistoric copper mining in the Upper Peninsula and on Isle Royale. And when the first European explorers arrived in the mid-17th century, the state was already settled by five major indigenous tribes: the Ojibwa, Ottawa, Miami, Potawatomi and Huron (or Wyandot).

The state's first European settlement, Sault Ste Marie, was founded by French Jesuit Père Jacques Marquette in 1668, making it the third-oldest city in the USA. Père Marquette then founded St Ignace in 1671. In 1701 the French explorer Antoine de La Mothe, Sieur de Cadillac, established Detroit in a strategic position between Lake Erie and Lake Huron.

In 1763 the French settlements were taken over by the British, who used Michigan as a base for instigating Indian raids against the Americans during the Revolutionary War. They also built a fort on Mackinac Island in 1780. Its location in the straits

Michigan

Nickname: Great Lakes State

Population: 9,295,300 (8th)

Area: 96,705 sq miles (11th)

Admitted to Union: January 26, 1837 (26th)

Capital city: Lansing (population 127,300)

Other cities: Detroit (1,028,000), Grand Rapids (189,100), Flint (140,800), Ann Arbor (109,600)

State motto: If you seek a pleasant peninsula, look around you.

Birthplace of: industrialists Henry Ford I (1863–1947) and II (1917–87), aviator Charles Lindbergh (1902–74), Motown singers Diana Ross (b 1944) and Stevie Wonder (b 1950)

Famous for: cars, cornflakes, the Motown sound, the typewriter, the Model T Ford

between Lake Michigan, Lake Huron and the St Marys River, which flows from Lake Superior, made it one of the most important ports in the North American fur trade. The small island was also the site of one of the most infamous moments in Michigan's history. After the Americans took over Fort Mackinac diplomatically, the British recaptured it during the War of 1812 by secretly landing in the middle of the night and dragging a cannon up a bluff overlooking the stockade. When the US garrison awoke the next morning and saw what was aimed at them, they gave up without firing a single shot.

After the Erie Canal was completed in 1825, Michigan experienced its first major wave of settlers. Thanks to the newly cut Detroit-Chicago Rd and the federal government's sale of Michigan land for $1.25 an acre, the state endured an era of 'Michigan Fever' – its population jumped from 9000 in the early 19th century to more than 200,000 by 1840. During this period, many of the state's major cities – Kalamazoo, Battle Creek, Jackson, Grand Rapids and Lansing – were founded.

By 1835 Michigan had become populated enough to qualify for statehood, but congress delayed the admission due to a boundary controversy with Ohio over a sliver of land that included Toledo. Both sides eventually called out their militias in the so-called Toledo War, but, fortunately, there was no bloodshed. When Michigan gave up claims to the city, it was awarded both the Upper Peninsula and statehood, becoming the 26th state in 1837.

Geography

Passing through the middle of Michigan is the 45th Parallel, the halfway point between the Equator and the North Pole. The Lower Peninsula is shaped like a mitten and is 285 miles from north to south and 195 miles from east to west. This half of the state features a topography of low rolling hills in the south, a northern 1200- to 1500-foot plateau and wonderful sand dunes along the shore of Lake Michigan. Detroit is a bit of a geographical oddity; it actually lies north of Ontario, and it's the only US city that looks south to Canada.

The rugged and lightly populated Upper Peninsula (UP) stretches 325 miles from east to west. It's linked to the Lower Peninsula by the Mackinac Bridge, which spans the Straits of Mackinac (**mac**-in-aw).

Flora & Fauna

The southern half of the Lower Peninsula is predominantly agricultural land surrounding the urban sprawl of the state's largest cities. The rest of Michigan is well forested: The northern half of the Lower Peninsula features hardwoods with a mix of pine, while red and white pine are more dominant in the UP. On the whole, about three-quarters of the state's trees are hardwoods, resulting in spectacular October colors that rival those in New England.

A great variety of wildlife can be easily spotted, especially white-tailed deer, which inhabit every corner of the state. Elk roam the Pigeon River Country State Forest, north of Gaylord, and moose, wolves and black bears can be found in the UP. Michigan is renowned for its brown, brook and rainbow trout; the Ausable River is often called the finest trout stream east of the Mississippi River. Due to the Great Lakes, Michigan is a major flyway for migrating birds, and birding is excellent in both spring and fall.

Government & Economy

Prior to the mid-1970s, the car industry dominated Michigan, but the state has since worked hard to diversify its economy. Still, manufacture of passenger cars and transportation equipment accounts for 27% of the annual gross state product; General Motors (GM), Ford and the Chrysler Group of DaimlerChrysler all maintain their headquarters in or near Detroit. Agriculture is also very important, and Michigan is a leader in a variety of commodities, including navy beans, apples and cherries.

Michigan has had many Republican governors, but due in part to its long history of unionization, the state often votes Democratic in regional and national elections.

Information

The Michigan Travel Bureau (☎ 800-543-2937, Ⓦ www.michigan.org, 4225 Miller Rd, Suite 4, Flint, MI 48507-9821) will send you a free travel guide to Michigan along with a road map. The West Michigan Tourist Association (☎ 616-456-8557, 800-442-2084, Ⓦ wmta.org, 1253 Front Ave, Grand Rapids, MI 49504) publishes a free guide for the western half of the Lower Peninsula. The Upper Peninsula Travel and Recreation Association (☎ 906-774-5480, 800-562-7134, PO Box 400, Iron Mountain, MI 49801) publishes a similar one for the UP.

For a guide to the Michigan state park system, contact the Michigan Department of Natural Resources (DNR), Parks & Recreation Division (☎ 517-373-9900, Ⓦ www.michigandnr.com, PO Box 30257, Lansing, MI 48909). If you plan on camping at any of the state parks in summer, you'd be well advised to reserve a campsite in advance; reservations can be made on the DNR Web site or by calling ☎ 800-447-2757.

DETROIT

Since its 1950s heyday, when Detroit was home to more than 2 million residents, the city has suffered through some hard times. It's been considered a national symbol of urban decay – the center of the so-called Rust Belt – and its population has slipped to below 1 million.

But thanks to the car industry boom of the mid-1990s, Detroit is now staging a steady comeback. It's not a Chicago or even a Cleveland, but the Motor City is still a cul-turally rich region. Detroit's population is 80% black, and it is a national center for African American culture.

History

At the turn of the 20th century, Detroit was a medium-size city of 285,000 known as a manufacturing center for horse-drawn carriages and bicycles. Thanks in part to the massive iron and copper mines in the UP, cheap transport on the Great Lakes and such enterprising souls as Henry Ford, the Dodge brothers and the Fisher brothers, Detroit quickly became the motor capital of the world. Ford in particular changed the fabric of US society. He didn't invent the automobile, as so many mistakenly believe, but he did perfect the assembly line manufacturing method and became one of the first industrialists to use mass production. The result was the Model T, the first car that the USA's middle class could afford to own.

The car industry was crippled by the Great Depression, but WWII restored prosperity as Michigan led the nation in the production of military equipment. Among other things, war work in Detroit's converted car factories attracted black migrants from the South to a city that was already ethnically diverse. Racial tensions in Detroit led to a riot in 1943 that took 34 lives, and in 1967, during the height of the civil-rights struggle, a second riot left 43 dead and blocks of the city smoldering. The election of Detroit's first two black mayors (Coleman Young in 1974 and Dennis Archer in 1993), coupled with the prosperity of the car industry in the 1990s, has done much to heal the city's wounds. In 2001, Detroiters celebrated the 300th anniversary of their city.

Orientation

The heart of Detroit is Hart Plaza, at the foot of Woodward Ave, where in 1701 Cadillac built Fort Pontchartrain. Woodward Ave, the city's main boulevard, heads north from the plaza all the way to Pontiac.

Just east of Hart Plaza is the massive Renaissance Center, GM's world headquarters, which dominates the Detroit skyline. Ten blocks north along Woodward Ave is Detroit's Theater District, anchored on one side by new Comerica Park – where the Detroit Tigers baseball team plays – and on

GREAT LAKES

DETROIT

To Motown Museum
To Pontiac
To Hamtramck
To Port Huron

1
W Grand Blvd
Milwaukee Ave
Baltimore Ave
Piquette Ave
Harper Ave
Ferry Ave
Kirby Ave

Amtrak Station

To Oak Park, Royal Oak & Lansing
Amsterdam St
Palmer Ave
Ferry Ave
Frederick Douglass Ave

York Ave
94
Cultural Center
Kirby Ave
Frederick Douglass Ave
Farnsworth St
Theodore Ave
Warren Ave
Hancock Ave
Forest Ave
Garfield Ave

Wayne State University
■ 3
4 ▥
2 ■
Farnsworth St
Theodore Ave
Brush St
Beaubien St
John R St
St Antoine St
Orleans St
Russell St
Riopelle St

To Detroit Metro Airport & Ann Arbor
Warren Ave
Prentis Ave
Canfield Ave
Willis Ave
Woodward Ave
Cass Ave
2nd Ave
4th Ave
3rd Ave

75
▼5
1

To Lansing
Lodge Freeway
Trumbull Ave
Gibson Ave
Lincoln Ave
Commonwealth Ave
Alexandrine Ave
Selden Ave
Brainard St
ML King Jr Blvd
Peterboro St
Charlotte Ave
Mack Ave
Eliot St
Erskine St
Watson St
Edmund Place
Alfred St
Adelaide St
Henry St
Beaubien St
St Antoine St

To Port Huron
Alfred St
Division St
Adelaide St
Vernor Hwy

Eastern Market
3
Greektown Ave
St Aubin Ave
Orleans St

10
Grand River Ave
5
Sycamore St
Elm St
Temple Ave
Spruce St
Pine St
Wabash Ave

Cass Park
Ledyard St
Pine St
Park Ave
Montcalm St
Comerica Park
Adams Ave
Madison St

Future Detroit Lions Stadium

Lafayette Park
Lafayette Blvd

To Belle Isle & Comfort Inn

To Toledo (OH)
75
Plum St
Elizabeth St
Beech St
Plaza Drive
Bagley Ave
7
6
8
Columbia St
Grand Circus Park
9
Clinton St
Macomb St
Monroe
375
Larned St
Russell St
Rowland St

13
Woodbridge St
▼14
● 15
Riopelle St

Michigan Ave
12
To Dearborn
Leverette St
Bagley Ave
Labrosse St
Porter St
Abbott St
Howard St
Lafayette Blvd
Fort St
8th Ave
6th Ave
Brooklyn St
Trumbull Ave
Vermont Ave
2nd Ave
3rd Ave

▼16
10
17
20 ✉
Cobo Hall
● 18
● 19
Washington Blvd
Shelby St
Griswold St
Cass Ave
Randolph St
Beaubien St
Congress St
Jefferson Ave
Franklin Ave
10
11
Greektown
12
Renaissance Center
Hart Plaza
Atwater St
Rivertown

To Mexicantown
16th St
14th St
18th St
Jefferson Ave
3
People Mover
Detroit-Windsor Tunnel
(toll)

MICHIGAN (USA)
Ontario (CANADA)
Detroit River

Dieppe Park
Riverside Drive
McDougall St

Ambassador Bridge
(toll)

Centennial Park
LP
WINDSOR
Pitt St
Chatham St
University Ave W
Ouellette Ave
Goyeau Ave
Victoria St
Glengarry Ave
Wyandotte St
38

0   400   800 m
0   400   800 yards

PLACES TO STAY
1　Hotel St Regis
6　Park Avenue Hostel
13　Shorecrest Motor Inn

PLACES TO EAT
5　Traffic Jam & Snug
10　New Hellas Cafe
12　Jacoby's
14　Franklin East
16　Lafayette Coney Island

OTHER
2　Main Library
3　Detroit Institute of Arts
4　Wright Museum of African American History
7　Fox Theater
8　Second City Detroit
9　Pure Bar Room
11　Greektown Casino
15　Rhinoceros
17　Greyhound Terminal
18　Joe Louis Arena
19　Diamond Jack River Tours
20　Post Office

the other by the ornate Fox Theatre, where audiences have been entertained since 1928. Another lively area is Greektown, around Monroe St (just off I-375), which is lined with Greek restaurants, bakeries and one of the city's three casinos. Head south via the Detroit-Windsor Tunnel or Ambassador Bridge to reach the Canadian city of Windsor, another good spot for nightlife.

There are some areas in Detroit, such as 12th St where the 1967 riots began, that travelers should not go. Generally the main streets (Woodward Ave, Jefferson Ave, Lafayette Blvd etc) with office buildings, restaurants, nightclubs and attractions are as safe as any other large city in the USA.

Information

The Detroit Convention & Visitors Bureau (☎ 313-202-1800, Ⓦ www.visitdetroit.com) no longer has a tourist center in the downtown area, but it does maintain a 24-hour events hotline (☎ 800-338-7648) that lists upcoming festivals and activities in the city. The *Metro Times*, distributed free throughout southeast Michigan, is the best guide to Detroit's arts, music and nightclub scene. Free Internet access is available at the Detroit main public library (☎ 313-833-1000, 5201 Woodward Ave).

Things to See & Do

The People Mover (☎ 800-541-7245), Detroit's 2.9-mile elevated rail system, was more political pork than viable mass transportation. But it's cheap (50¢) and provides great views of the city, the riverfront and the Windsor skyline. Each of the loop's 13 stations, which include Greektown and Renaissance Center, features a distinctive work of art.

If the day is nice, you can enjoy the lively riverfront scene at Hart Plaza. On summer weekends, the plaza hosts ethnic festivals and free concerts. Diamond Jack River Tours (☎ 313-843-7676) offers two-hour cruises on the Detroit River ($12) departing from Hart Plaza. Or head to Belle Isle, 2½ miles northeast of the downtown area at E Jefferson Ave and E Grand Blvd. Among the attractions at this 981-acre island park are a nature center, a kids' zoo, the interesting Dossin Great Lakes Museum (☎ 313-852-4051; $2) and the Belle Isle Aquarium (☎ 313-852-4141; $2).

One place the People Mover doesn't go is Detroit's Cultural Center, clustered around Woodward Ave and Kirby Ave. Diego Rivera's mural, *Detroit Industry*, fills a room at the **Detroit Institute of Arts** (☎ 313-833-7900, 5200 Woodward Ave) and reflects the city's blue-collar labor history ($4; open Wed-Sun). At the **Wright Museum of African American History** (☎ 313-494-5800, 315 E Warren Ave), the full-scale model of slaves chained up on an 18th-century slave ship will leave you chilled ($5; open 9:30am-5pm Tue-Sun).

Motown Museum (☎ 313-875-2264, 2648 W Grand Blvd) is a string of large homes that became known as 'Hitsville USA' after Berry Gordy launched Motown Records here in 1959 ($6; open daily). Stars that rose from the Motown label include Stevie Wonder, Diana Ross, Marvin Gaye, Gladys Knight and Michael Jackson. Gordy and Motown split for the glitz of Los Angeles in 1972, but you can still step into Studio 4 and see where the Four Tops and Smokey Robinson recorded their first hits.

Detroit's cultural melting pot is best experienced at **Eastern Market**, said to be the oldest farmers' market in the country; on Tuesday and Saturday, the large halls at Gratiot Ave and Russell St are filled with bartering shoppers and vendors. Surrounding the open market are specialty shops, delis and restaurants.

Special Events

Windsor and Detroit team up in late June for the Freedom Festival, which includes a huge fireworks display over the Detroit River. The free four-day Montreux-Detroit Jazz Festival, held on Labor Day weekend in Hart Plaza, attracts local and international jazz artists and more than half a million fans.

Places to Stay

For the closest public campground, head west of Pontiac on M-59 to *Pontiac Lake Recreation Area* (☎ 248-666-1020, 7800 Gale Rd) in Waterford, where a site costs $11 per night plus a daily $4 vehicle entry permit.

There are only two hostels in southeast Michigan. In Detroit, the *Park Avenue Hostel* (☎ 313-961-8310, 2305 Park Ave) is not HI affiliated, but you need either a

GREAT LAKES

Classic Cars in Michigan

More than sand dunes, Mackinac Island fudge or even the Great Lakes, Michigan is synonymous with cars the world over. You don't have to drive far to see classic cars, particularly around Detroit:

Woodward Dream Cruise (☎ 248-433-3550) – In the 1950s and '60s 'cruisin' Woodward' in a souped-up Dodge or Chevrolet was how summer was spent in the Motor City. Now it's the largest single-day car event in the world. The Woodward Dream Cruise is held on the third Saturday of August, when more than 1.2 million people line the historic avenue to watch 6,000 classic cars cruise from Ferndale to Pontiac (free admission).

Henry Ford Museum (☎ 313-271-1620, 20900 Oakwood Blvd) – This Dearborn museum is loaded with vintage cars, including the first one Henry Ford ever built. In adjacent Greenfield Village you can get a ride in a Model T that rolled off the assembly line in 1923 ($14).

Automotive Hall of Fame (☎ 313-240-4000, 1400 Oakwood Blvd) – Also in Dearborn, this museum is loaded with classic cars as well as a replica of the first gasoline automobile ($6).

Motorsports Hall of Fame (☎ 800-250-7223, Novi Rd) – In the Novi Expo Center just off I-96 in Novi, this hall has three dozen vehicles that were driven by legendary racers ($3).

Walter P Chrysler Museum (☎ 888-456-1924, 1 Chrysler Dr) – Michigan's newest car museum is in the DaimlerChrysler Technical Center in Auburn Hills and has 70 vehicles on display, including rare models of Dodge, DeSoto, Nash, Hudson and Willys ($6).

Sloan Museum (☎ 810-237-3450, 1221 E Kearsley St) – This Flint museum has two buildings housing more than 60 cars, including the oldest production-model Chevrolet in existence and a 1910 Buick 'Bug' raced by Louis Chevrolet ($5).

Gilmore-Classic Car Club of America Museum (☎ 616-671-5089, Hickory Rd at M-43) – North of Kalamazoo along M-43 in Hickory Corners, this museum complex is 22 barns filled with 120 vintage automobiles, including 15 Rolls Royces dating back to a 1910 Silver Ghost ($6).

RE Olds Transportation Museum (☎ 517-372-0422, 240 Museum Dr) – In the old Lansing City Bus Garage are 20 vintage cars, from the first Oldsmobile, built in 1897, to an Indy 500 pace car ($4).

hostel card or a passport to stay there ($12). Southwest of Detroit in New Boston, 10 miles from Metro Airport, is *HI Country Grandma's Home Hostel* (☎ 734-753-4901, 22330 Bell Rd). Call in advance to secure a bed ($15/18 for members/nonmembers).

Accommodations, other than glitzy hotels and questionable flophouses, are scarce in the downtown area. *Shorecrest Motor Inn* (☎ 313-568-3000, 800-992-9616, 1316 E Jefferson Ave) is six blocks northeast of Hart Plaza and has singles/doubles for $69/89. A little farther away is *Comfort Inn* (☎ 313-567-8888, 1999 E Jefferson Ave), with free parking and singles or doubles for $119. *Hotel St Regis* (☎ 313-873-3000, 800-848-4810, 3071 W Grand Blvd) has large, comfortable rooms from $95 a night on the weekends, single or double.

Affordable motels abound in the Detroit suburbs. If you're arriving from Metro Airport, follow the signs for Merriman Rd when leaving the airport and take your pick. Among the dozen motels here is a new *Motel 6* (☎ 734-595-7400, 9095 Wickham Rd) with rooms from $48. Nearby and a step up is *Clarion Barcelo Hotel* (☎ 734-728-7900, 8600 Merriman Rd), with rooms from $70. Another *Motel 6* (☎ 248-583-0500, 32700 Barrington Rd) is close to downtown, near the 14 Mile Rd exit on I-75, across from Oakland Mall ($40/46 singles/doubles).

Places to Eat

Restaurants in Detroit and throughout southeast Michigan reward their ethnically diverse patrons with authentic dishes served in large portions at very reasonable prices. Great soul food, from fried catfish and collard greens to sweet potato pie, is at *Franklin East* (1440 Franklin St), while the best ribs are in Southfield at *Dap's Smoke*

& Grill (25832 W 9 Mile Rd). A half slap dinner is $11, a full slap is $16.

Middle-of-the-night appetites can be taken care of downtown at the legendary *Lafayette Coney Island (118 Lafayette Blvd)*, where hot dogs smothered with chili and onions are $2 and loose burgers with chili cost $2.50. A few blocks over is lively Greektown, where you'll find a dozen restaurants and Greek bakeries line Monroe St. The best of the bunch is *New Hellas Café (583 Monroe St)*, where flaming cheese and the cry of *'Opa!'* are a Detroit tradition. Dinners are $8-13. Mexicantown is along Bagley St, where you'll find inexpensive, authentic Mich-Mex food at *Xochimilco (3409 Bagley)* and *El Zocala (3400 Bagley)*. Sauerbraten, Wiener schnitzel and German beer are found at *Jacoby's (624 Brush St)*, while Detroit's best brew pub is *Traffic Jam & Snug (511 W Canfield Ave)*, not far from the Detroit Institute of Art.

Detroit's Polish community is centered in the city of Hamtramck, where Pope John Paul II once performed Mass. At *Polish Village Café (2990 Yehmans St)*, at the corner of Jos Campau Ave, you can dig into stuffed cabbage, pork goulash and pierogi for less than $8.

Keep heading north on the Lodge Freeway to reach Oak Park, the heart of Detroit's Jewish district. Among the many delis and bagel shops is *Bread Basket Deli (26052 Greenfield Rd)*, in a shopping center between 10 Mile and 11 Mile Rds. You'll have to wait for a table, but the corned-beef sandwiches, salads and matzo-ball soup are outstanding. Nearby, Main St in Royal Oak is a lively spot with outdoor cafes, coffee shops and offbeat nightclubs. Practically next door to each other are *BD's Mongolian Barbecue (310 S Main St)*, where you watch a chef cook your meal on an open grill ($14), and *Memphis Smokehouse (100 S Main St)*, for ribs. The best vegetarian cuisine in the area is a few blocks over at *Inn Season Café (500 E 4th St)*.

Entertainment
Nightlife in Detroit centers around the revived Theater District along Woodward Ave, anchored by the *Fox Theatre (☎ 313-596-3200, 2211 Woodward Ave)*. Built in 1928 and gloriously restored in 1988, the art deco icon attracts some of the best acts passing through the city. Next door is *Second City Detroit (☎ 313-965-2222, 2301 Woodward Ave)*, modeled after Chicago's famous comedy club. Detroit now has three casinos scattered throughout the downtown area. The best of the bunch is *Greektown Casino (555 E Lafayette Blvd)*, which can be reached via the People Mover.

Detroit may be Motown, but in recent years it's been rap and techno that have pushed the city to the forefront of the music scene; homegrown stars include Kid Rock and Eminem. The hottest dance club in Detroit is *Pure Bar Room (1500 Woodward Ave)*, which reenergized clubbing downtown when it opened in 1999. If that's too crowded, try *Clutch Cargo's (65 E Huron St)* in Pontiac, which features four dance floors, or *Motor Lounge (3515 Caniff St)* in Hamtramck, which pumps out electronic dance music. For dancing in gay-friendly Ferndale, try *Temple (344 W 9 Mile Rd)*.

Clubs for local blues and jazz include *Rhinoceros (265 Riopelle St)*; *Baker's Keyboard Lounge (20510 Livernois Ave)*; and *Attic Bar (11667 Jos Campau Ave)* in Hamtramck, a true blues bar where customers take over the piano when a band isn't around.

Spectator Sports
The Palace of Auburn Hills (☎ 248-377-0100) hosts pro basketball – the Detroit Pistons men's team and the Detroit Shock women's team. The Detroit Red Wings – 1998 and '99 Stanley Cup winners – play pro hockey at Joe Louis Arena (☎ 313-396-7444), though it is almost impossible to get tickets. The Detroit Lions pro-football team currently plays in the Pontiac Silverdome (☎ 248-335-4131), but they're scheduled to move to a new stadium in downtown Detroit in 2003. The Detroit Tigers (☎ 313-471-2555) pro baseball team just moved downtown into impressive Comerica Park.

Getting There & Around
Air Metro Airport, 15 miles southwest of Detroit, is the primary regional air center, offering direct flights to most major cities in the country. Northwest Airlines (☎ 800-225-2525) uses Detroit as a major hub and routes many of its European flights through Metro Airport, making it easy for overseas

travelers to spend some time in Michigan before moving onward.

Bus The Greyhound bus terminal (☎ 313-961-8562, 1001 Howard St) is near the Lodge Freeway. Greyhound provides service to more than 40 cities throughout Michigan, including Grand Rapids ($25; 3 hours), Grayling ($33; 4 hours), Traverse City ($39; 5 hours), Marquette ($90; 10 hours) and Ironwood, on the Wisconsin border ($100; 12 hours).

Train From the Amtrak station (☎ 313-873-3442, 800-872-7245, 11 W Baltimore Ave), at Woodward Ave, trains run daily to Kalamazoo ($35; 3 hours), Niles ($39; 4 hours) and Chicago ($43; 6 hours). You can also head east on Amtrak – to New York ($97; 16 hours) or destinations en route – but you'll first be bused to Toledo.

Local Transportation Commuter Express (☎ 313-292-2000, 888-854-6700) is among the many airport shuttle companies at Metro Airport's terminals and has a counter in the baggage claim area. It charges $21 per person to downtown Detroit.

Local bus service in Detroit is handled by the Detroit Department of Transportation (DOT; ☎ 313-933-1300, 888-336-8287). Service to the suburbs is limited. Fare is $1.25, transfers 25¢. Suburban Mobility Authority for Regional Transportation (Smart; ☎ 313-962-5515) handles bus service in southeast Michigan, with connections to Detroit. The fare is $1.50; transfers cost 25¢.

AROUND DETROIT
Dearborn
This is the city that Henry Ford built, and today Dearborn (10 miles west of downtown Detroit) is home to the world headquarters of the Ford Motor Company. You can learn all about the Ford story at the extensive **Henry Ford Museum** (☎ 313-271-1620, 20900 Oakwood Blvd). Then head over to the adjacent **Greenfield Village** (same phone), an outdoor museum featuring historic old buildings shipped in from all over the country, reconstructed and restored. Here you'll find Thomas Edison's laboratory from Menlo Park, Henry Ford's birthplace and the Wright brothers' old cycle workshop. Most of the buildings

contain exhibits and are staffed by period-dressed guides. The museum and the village are separate attractions. Entry to either one costs $14; for $24, you can get a combination ticket good for two days. Seriously consider the two-day ticket, as this is one of the finest museum complexes in the country, and anything short of a full day would be a rush job.

After spending all day immersing yourself in the car culture of the USA, head to the **Ford Wyoming Drive-In** (☎ 313-846-6910, 582-2200, Ford Rd), the largest drive-in theater in the Midwest with eight screens ($7). From I-94 in Dearborn, take exit 210 and head north on Wyoming Ave to reach the drive-in.

Ann Arbor
Trendy Ann Arbor, home to the University of Michigan (the 'Harvard of the Midwest'), is regarded by many as the cultural capital of the state. The university dominates the city with its campus and outbuildings. It also provides many of the town's top attractions, including the fine **Kelsey Museum of Archaeology** (☎ 734-764-9304, 434 S State St), with its nearly 100,000 artifacts from ancient Egypt, Greece and Rome (donation); the **University of Michigan Museum of Art** (☎ 734-764-0395, 525 S State St), with a $5 admission; and the **Exhibit Museum of Natural History** (☎ 734-764-0478, 1109 Geddes Ave), home to the most popular dinosaur collection in Michigan ($3).

Ann Arbor's biggest events are the University of Michigan football games, a fall tradition attracting 115,000 fans to each game. Tickets are nearly impossible to purchase (unless you're willing to pay scalpers' inflated prices), especially when nemesis Ohio State is in town. But it's possible to obtain tickets for other sporting events, from women's rugby to men's ice hockey, by calling the U of M Ticket Office (☎ 734-764-0247). The university also offers a variety of theater, drama, music and dance events throughout the year. For a schedule of upcoming events call the Campus Information Center (☎ 734-764-4636).

Just as you would expect, Ann Arbor abounds with great restaurants and nightclubs. In fact, the city's first tavern was built in 1824, a year before residents built their first school. Grab a streetside table at *Prickly Pear Southwest Café (328 Main St)*, or enjoy Ethiopian cuisine at the *Blue Nile (221 Washington St)*. Live music, brewery tours and handcrafted beer are found at *Arbor Brewing Co (300 Detroit St)*, while nearby *Zingerman's Delicatessen (422 Detroit St)* is often regarded as one of the finest delis in Michigan. Looking for a latte? There's a coffeehouse on every corner in Ann Arbor. At night, head to *Bird of Paradise (312 S Main St)* for Cajun cuisine and live jazz or to *The Ark (316 S Main St)*, an acoustic music club featuring folk, bluegrass, jazz and blues by local and nationally known performers.

HEARTLAND

Michigan's heartland is a 20-county region that lies at the center of the Lower Peninsula, south of US 10 and away from the Great Lakes shorelines. It includes agricultural and urban areas, farm fields and suburbs, connected by a network of interstates (I-94, I-96, I-69 and I-196) and US highways. Among the large cities, the most interesting to visit are Lansing (the state capital) and Grand Rapids.

Lansing

When Lansing was chosen as Michigan's capital in 1847, it was little more than a wilderness hamlet. In the 20th century, as the home of GM's Oldsmobile division, Lansing experienced the same economic roller-coaster ride that affected the automotive industry in Detroit and Flint. But due to its status as the seat of state government, the city had an easier time reviving itself after the hard times of the 1980s, and it now makes an interesting stop for visitors.

Attractions in Lansing are concentrated downtown and at Michigan State University (MSU; east of downtown, south of Grand River Ave). MSU, like Ohio State an archrival of Ann Arbor's University of Michigan, has an interesting campus that holds **MSU Museum** (☎ 517-355-2370), offering natural and historic displays, and **Kresge Art Museum** (☎ 517-355-7631). Both museums are free. North of the campus, East Lansing is a college town with great restaurants, pubs and nightclubs.

At the head of Michigan Ave, the **State Capitol** (☎ 517-373-2353) dominates the downtown area. Free tours are offered Mon-Sat. Far more interesting and also free

is the nearby **Michigan Historical Museum** (☎ 517-373-3559, 717 W Allegan St). This state museum features 26 permanent galleries, including a replica UP copper mine you can walk through, a 1920s street scene and a three-story relief map of the state.

Linking the MSU campus with downtown is Lansing's **River Trail**, which extends 7 miles along the shores of Michigan's longest river, the Grand. The paved path, popular with cyclists, joggers and in-line skaters, links a number of attractions, including a children's museum, zoo and salmon ladder. During the summer head to Oldsmobile Park on Michigan Ave, where the **Lansing Lugnuts** (☎ 517-485-4500), the city's minor league baseball team, make for an entertaining afternoon even when they don't win. Some seats are only $5.

The best selection of motels is found around Cedar St, exit 104 off I-96. In this area are *Days Inn* (☎ 517-393-1650, 6501 Pennsylvania Ave), with rates of $59/69 for singles/doubles, and *Econo Lodge* (☎ 517-394-7200, 1100 Ramada Dr), charging $50 single or double. The downtown hotels feed off politicians and lobbyists and are considerably more expensive. One option is to head north 10 miles on US 27 and then west on Price Rd to *Sleepy Hollow State Park* (☎ 517-651-6217, 7835 Price Rd), which has campsites for $12 a night.

Most of the city's best restaurants are clustered around the head of Michigan Ave. Try *Clara's (637 E Michigan Ave)*, in Lansing's historic railroad depot (dinners $10-20), or *Parthenon (227 S Washington Square)*, offering good Greek food. For a cheap breakfast in an authentic diner, head to *Great Lakes Diner (2211 S Cedar St)*.

Grand Rapids

The second-largest city in Michigan, Grand Rapids is known for office-furniture manufacturing, a conservative Dutch Reform attitude and the fact that it's only 30 miles from Lake Michigan's Gold Coast. Downtown Grand Rapids is a bustling, lively area split by the Grand River (thus the city's name) and features two outstanding museums, both on the river's west bank. The Grand Rapids Visitor Information Center (☎ 800-678-9859) is downtown at 134 Monroe Center, diagonal across from the Amway Grand Plaza Hotel.

GREAT LAKES

The **Gerald R Ford Museum** (☎ 616-451-9263, 303 Pearl St NW) is dedicated to the country's only Michigander president, who was also the USA's only nonelected president. Ford stepped into the Oval Office after Richard Nixon and his vice president, Spiro Agnew, resigned in disgrace. It's an intriguing period in US history, and the museum does an excellent job of covering it ($4). Nearby is the striking **Van Andel Museum Center** (☎ 616-456-3977, 272 Pearl St NW), dedicated to the history of Grand Rapids and west Michigan ($6). Great Rapids' newest attraction is **Frederik Meijer Gardens** (☎ 616-957-1580, 1000 E Beltline NE). The 118-acre gardens feature the state's largest tropical conservatory, more than 100 sculptures and three indoor theme gardens ($6).

For camping, head south 15 miles on US 131 and follow the signs to **Yankee Springs Recreation Area** (☎ 616-795-9081), which also features the most popular mountain-biking trails on the west side of the state (campsites $6-14 a night). Affordable motels, along 28th St on the south side of the city, include **Days Inn** (☎ 616-949-8400, 5500 28th St), offering singles/doubles for $79/89, and **Grand Rapids Inn** (☎ 616-452-2131, 250 28th St), a bit less expensive at $59/69. At night, head to **Grand Rapids Brewing Company** (3689 28th St SE) or **Cottage Bar** (18 LaGrave St SE), a hip place downtown that has outdoor dining when it's warm and the best hamburgers ($5.50) in Grand Rapids.

LAKE MICHIGAN SHORE

Michigan's west coast is its Gold Coast – a 300-mile shoreline featuring sand, surf and incredible sunsets best watched while sitting atop a towering sand dune. It's lined with endless stretches of beach, and dotted with shoreline parks and small towns that boom during the summer tourist season.

Saugatuck

This Lake Michigan resort town is a popular destination for gays and is known for its strong arts community and numerous B&Bs.

The best thing to do in Saugatuck is also the most affordable. Jump aboard the **Saugatuck Chain Ferry** ($1), and the operator will pull you across the Kalamazoo

River. On the other side you can climb the stairs to the grand views atop Mt Baldhead, a 200-foot-high sand dune. Then race down the north side to beautiful **Oval Beach**, where MTV once filmed a summer beach party show.

Most of the town's B&Bs are in century-old Victorian homes and range from $90-170 a night per couple. Try the charming **Bayside Inn** (☎ 616-857-4321, W www.baysideinn.net, 618 Water St), a former boathouse with an outdoor hot tub and doubles for $105-185, or **Twin Gables Inn** (☎ 616-857-4346, 800-231-2185, W www.twingablesinn.com, 900 Lake St), which overlooks Lake Michigan. Its 14 rooms range from $100-175. Mom-and-pop motels on the edge of the city, like **Pines Motel** (☎ 616-857-5211, 56 Blue Star Hwy), have rooms for under $100, while **Saugatuck RV Resort** (☎ 616-857-3315, 800-336-9724, 6473 Washington Rd), a half-mile north of the city, has tent sites for $25 a night.

Grand Haven & Muskegon

Clustered around these two cities are three state parks, all offering an opportunity to camp on or near Lake Michigan beaches. In touristy Grand Haven is **Grand Haven State Park** (☎ 231-798-3711, 1001 Harbor Ave), with 174 sites along the beach. It's connected to the downtown restaurants, bars and shops by a scenic boardwalk along the Grand River. Between Grand Haven and Muskegon is **PJ Hoffmaster State Park** (☎ 231-798-3711, 6585 Lake Harbor Rd), offering 293 sites, the interesting Gillette Nature Center and a 10-mile trail system that includes several miles along Lake Michigan. North of Muskegon is **Muskegon State Park** (☎ 231-766-3480, 3560 Memorial Dr), with 284 sites in two campgrounds and 12 miles of trails through rugged, wooded dunes.

Camping is $15 a night. It's best to reserve a site in advance during the summer (☎ 800-447-2757, W www.michigandnr.com).

Ludington & Manistee

The largest state park and one of the most popular along Lake Michigan is **Ludington State Park** (☎ 231-843-8671), on M-116. It has 342 campsites, an excellent trail system, a renovated lighthouse to visit and miles of beach. To its north is **Nordhouse Dunes**, a 3000-acre federally designated wilderness with its own trail system. You enter Nordhouse Dunes through the Lake Michigan Recreation Area, a US Forest Service campground several miles south of Manistee.

One of the most unusual backpacking trips in the Lower Peninsula is the 20-mile hike from Manistee to Ludington along the undeveloped beaches of these large parks, overnighting in Nordhouse Dunes. Stop at the Manistee Ranger Station (☎ 231-723-2211, 412 Red Apple Rd), just south of Manistee off US 31, for maps and information.

Sleeping Bear Dunes National Lakeshore

This national park stretches from north of Frankfort nearly to Leland, on the Leelanau Peninsula. Stop at the park visitor center (☎ 231-326-5134, W www.nps.gov/slbe, 9922 Front St) in Empire for information and trail maps and to purchase vehicle entry permits ($7/15 for a week/year).

Attractions here include **Sleeping Bear Point Coast Guard Station**, an interesting maritime museum in Glen Haven; **Pierce Stocking Scenic Dr**, a 7-mile, one-lane road that passes stunning Lake Michigan views; and the **Dune Climb** along M-109, where you trudge up the 200-foot-high dune and then run or roll down. Sleeping Bear Dunes also offers the best day hiking in the Lower Peninsula. Backpackers should head to Leland and catch the ferry (☎ 231-256-9061; $22 roundtrip) over to **North Manitou Island** for an overnight wilderness hiking adventure.

The park maintains two large campgrounds: *Platte River Campground*, south of Empire, and *DH Day*, near Glen Haven. Sites cost $10-19 per night. These campgrounds are very popular; either reserve a site in advance through the National Park Reservation Service (☎ 800-365-2267, W reservations.nps.gov) or get there early to stake out a site! If they are full, head east toward Traverse City along US 31 and try one of the half dozen state forest campgrounds signposted along the road.

Traverse City

Michigan's Cherry Capital is the largest city in the northern half of the Lower Peninsula. In recent years the urban sprawl has alarmed residents, but visitors find Traverse City safe, beautiful and fun, with lots to see and do.

Two blocks from the downtown area along US 31 is Clinch Park, with a beautiful beach, while nearby on the East Arm of Grand Traverse Bay is **Traverse City State Park** (☎ 231-922-5270, 1132 US 31 N), with 343 campsites ($15) and 700 feet of sugary sand on the water. Between the two are dozens of resorts, motels, Jet Ski rental shops and parasail operators. For a relaxing day on the bay, take an afternoon or sunset sail on the tall ship *Manitou* (☎ 231-941-2000), docked off M-22 in the West Arm of Grand Traverse Bay. The cruises last two to three hours, often include a meal and cost $30-38 per person.

Winding through the city and along the bay is the **Traverse Area Recreation Trail** (TART for short), an 11-mile paved path. At Brick Wheels (☎ 231-947-4274, 736 E 8th St) you can rent a road bike, mountain bike or in-line skates and then jump on the trail outside.

The most popular drive is to head north from Traverse City on M-37 for 20 miles to the end of **Mission Peninsula**. Along the way, stop at the Chateau Grand Traverse or Chateau Chantel wineries and sample their chardonnay or pinot noir. If you purchase a bottle, you can take it out to Lighthouse Park beach, on the end of the peninsula, and enjoy it with the waves licking your toes. Hungry? On the way back stop at *Old Mission Tavern (17015 Center Rd),* which doubles as a neighborhood pub and art gallery.

If you arrive mid-July you can feast on the state's sweet cherry harvest. Head north of Traverse City on US 31 to the village of Elk Rapids and beyond for roadside stands selling cherries and cherry pies, as well as farms where you can pick your own.

Traverse City has plentiful lodgings, but they are often full on weekends. Stop at the Traverse City Visitor Center (☎ 800-872-8377, W www.tcvisitor.com, 101 W Grandview Pkwy) downtown for a complete list of lodgings. *Northwestern Michigan College (☎ 231-995-1400, 1701 E Front St)* rents rooms in summer for $30 a night with shared bath. Motels on the other side of US 31 are more moderately priced. *Motel 6 (☎ 231-938-3002, 1582 US 31 N)* has rooms starting at $69. *Mitchell Creek Inn (☎ 231-947-9330, 894 Munson Ave),* near the state park, charges $59 and up. Resorts overlooking the bay range from $100-170 per night.

GREAT LAKES

Head north along US 31 for more affordable mom-and-pop motels, like **Crestwood Motel** (☎ *231-938-2670, 5200 US 31 N*) in Acme, where rooms range from $49-99.

Petoskey & Harbor Springs

Tucked away inside Little Traverse Bay, Petoskey and Harbor Springs are where Michigan's upper crusters maintain summer homes. The downtown areas of both cities have gourmet restaurants and high-class shops, and the marinas are filled with yachts. Between the two cities along M-119 is **Petoskey State Park** (☎ *616-347-2311, 2475 M-119*), with a beautiful beach and 170 campsites ($15 a night; reserve in advance at ☎ 800-447-2757 or Ⓦ www.michigandnr.com).

STRAITS OF MACKINAC

This region between the Upper and Lower Peninsulas features a long history, miles of beach and lots of attractions. Spanning the Straits of Mackinac is the 5-mile-long **Mackinac Bridge**, known locally as 'Big Mac.' The $1.50 toll is worth every penny, as the views from the bridge, which include two Great Lakes, two peninsulas and hundreds of islands, are second to none in Michigan.

Mackinaw City

At the south end of Mackinac Bridge, bordering I-75, is Mackinaw City, a tacky tourist town with a gift shop and fudge kitchen (fudge is Northern Michigan's most famous product) on every corner. Mackinaw City is best known as one of two departure points for Mackinac Island, but it does have a couple of interesting attractions of its own.

Right next to the bridge (its visitor center is actually beneath the bridge) is **Colonial**

Michigan's Hemingway Tour

A number of writers have ties to northwest Michigan, but none are as famous as Ernest Hemingway, who spent the summers of his youth at his family's cottage on Walloon Lake. Hemingway buffs often tour the area to view artifacts and places that made their way into his writing.

They begin in Petoskey at **Little Traverse Historical Museum** (☎ 231-347-2620, 100 Depot Court), housed in the town's historic railroad depot. Among the items on display are some rare first-edition books that Hemingway autographed for a friend when he visited Petoskey in 1947. Summer hours for the museum are 10am-4pm Mon-Sat and 1pm-4pm Sun ($1).

Continue the Hemingway tour by heading south on US 31 toward Charlevoix. Just before entering that town, turn east onto Boyne City Rd, which skirts beautiful Lake Charlevoix and eventually arrives at the **Horton Bay General Store**. Built in 1876 with a high false front, the store's most prominent feature is its large front porch, with benches and stairs at either end. Hemingway idled away some youthful summers on that porch and fished nearby Horton Creek for trout. He was married in Horton Bay's Congregational Church, and the general store appeared in the opening of his short story 'Up in Michigan.'

From Horton Bay, continue the tour by heading to Boyne City, and follow the Lake Charlevoix shoreline on Ferry Rd. Just before reaching the south arm of the lake, turn north onto Sanderson Rd to reach **Hemingway Point**, originally owned by Hemingway's uncle. It's said that the young author once fled across the lake to elude a conservation officer in Horton Bay.

The tour is completed by crossing the south arm on the **Ironton ferry**, a cable-guided ferry built in 1876. Although it's now powered by a diesel engine instead of the horses used a century ago, and though cars have replaced buggies as its cargo, the ferry still makes the 100-yard crossing. It's not documented whether Hemingway himself ever took the five-minute ride, but locals, perhaps using a touch of poetic license, say he must have. It's too pleasant a crossing to pass up.

Michilimackinac (☎ 231-436-5563), a National Historic Landmark that features a reconstructed stockade first built in 1715 by the French ($8). Some 3 miles southeast of the city on US 23 is **Historic Mill Creek** (☎ 231-436-4226), which has an 18th-century sawmill, historic displays and nature trails ($6.75).

The only things that outnumber fudge shops in Mackinaw City are motels, which line I-75 and US 23. Thanks to the popularity of Mackinac Island and a recently opened casino, it's almost impossible to find a room in Mackinaw City for less than $100 during the summer. Even *Motel 6* *(☎ 231-436-8961, 206 N Nicolet St)* charges $92 for a single or double. The one exception is *Rainbow Motel (☎ 231-426-5518, 800-888-6077, 602 S Huron St)*, with singles or doubles for $73. If you have a tent, skip the high-price accommodations in favor of a scenic campsite at *Wilderness State Park (☎ 616-436-5381, 898 Wilderness Park Dr)*, 8 miles west of town via County Rd 81 ($15).

St Ignace

At the north end of Mackinac Bridge is St Ignace, the second-oldest settlement in Michigan – Père Jacques Marquette founded a mission here in 1671. As soon as you've paid your bridge toll you'll pass a huge Michigan Welcome Center (☎ 906-643-6979) with racks of brochures.

In St Ignace, check out the **Museum of Ojibwa Culture** ($2; open daily in summer) inside the **Marquette Mission Park** (☎ 906-643-9161, 566 N State St), where the famous Jesuit priest is buried. Good camping is available 2 miles north of St Ignace at *Foley Creek Campground (no phone)*, on Mackinac Trail ($6).

Mackinac Island

From either St Ignace or Mackinaw City, you can catch a ferry to Mackinac Island, Michigan's first tourist destination and today its best-known one. The British built a fort on top of the famous limestone cliffs in 1780 and then fought with the Americans for control of it during the War of 1812. In 1875 (three years after Yellowstone was dedicated) the federal government preserved Mackinac Island as the country's second national park. But that status was short-lived; the feds handed the park back to Michigan in 1895.

The most important date on this 2000-acre island was 1898 – the year cars were banned to encourage tourism. Today all travel on the island is by horses or bicycles; even the police use bikes to patrol the town. The crowds of tourists (called Fudgies by the islanders) can be crushing at times, particularly on summer weekends. If at all possible and if funds allow it, spend a night on Mackinac Island; the real charm of this historic place emerges after the last ferry leaves at 6pm.

Things to See & Do Overlooking the downtown area is **Fort Mackinac** (☎ 906-847-3328), one of the best-preserved military forts in the country. The $8 ticket is also good for six other museums in town, including Indian Dormitory, Beaumont Memorial and Benjamin Blacksmith Shop. Skirting the shoreline of the island is M-185, the only state highway in Michigan that doesn't permit cars. The best way to view the incredible scenery along this 8-mile road is by bicycle; bring your bike on the ferry or rent one in town at any of almost a dozen bike shops ($16 per half day). The two best attractions – **Arch Rock** (a huge limestone arch that sits 150 feet above Lake Huron) and **Fort Holmes** (the island's 'other fort') – are both free. You can also ride past the **Grand Hotel**, which boasts a veranda stretching halfway to Detroit. The hotel was used to film several movies, the most recent being *Somewhere In Time*, with Christopher Reeve. Unfortunately if you're not staying at the Grand Hotel ($250 per night per person), then it's $10 to stroll its long porch and step inside the lobby. Not worth it.

Places to Stay & Eat Rooms are booked far in advance on summer weekends. Call the Mackinac Island Chamber of Commerce (☎ 906-847-6418) for help reserving lodging before you arrive.

Camping is not permitted anywhere on Mackinac Island. That means you have to spend a wad to spend the night. Most hotels and B&Bs charge at least $150 a night for two people. Exceptions include *Pontiac Lodge (☎ 906-847-3364)*, Main and Hoban Sts, which has rooms starting at $70 (though most are $130), and the nearby *Bogan Lane*

Inn (☎ *906-847-3439*), on Bogan Lane, which offers four rooms beginning at $75 for two people. Also check *La Chance Cottage* (☎ *906-847-3526*), on Huron St, a 30-room tourist home a short walk from downtown, with doubles for $80 per night.

The best-known eateries on Mackinac Island are the dozen *fudge shops*, which use fans to blow the tempting aroma of the freshly made confection out onto Huron St. Taste it, but don't gorge; Mackinac Island fudge is heavy and rich. Hamburger and sandwich shops abound downtown, but for a quieter spot, head toward the Grand Hotel and stop at *French Outpost*, on Cadotte Ave, where you can enjoy salads or sandwiches for under $8, along with a pint of beer. *Horn's Bar*, on Huron St, has good food, with dinners ranging $10-16 and live entertainment nightly. If you purchase a ticket to the fort, you can eat lunch at *Fort Mackinac Tea Room*, whose outdoor tables feature a million-dollar view of the downtown area and the Straits of Mackinac.

Getting There & Around Three ferry companies – Arnold Line (☎ 800-542-8528), Shepler's (☎ 800-828-6157) and Star Line (☎ 800-638-9892) – operate out of both Mackinaw City and St Ignace and charge the same rates: $16 roundtrip per adult and another $7 per bicycle. Once you're on the island, horse-drawn taxis will take you anywhere, even on a private tour ($17 per person per hour).

UPPER PENINSULA

A third of the state lies in this rugged, wooded and isolated region. The UP has only 45 miles of interstate highway and just a handful of cities, of which Marquette is the largest and most interesting. Between the cities are miles of undeveloped shoreline (on Lakes Huron, Michigan and Superior), scenic two-lane roads, small rural towns and lots of rustic campsites, many of them in the Hiawatha and Ottawa National Forests and three state forests.

Michigan's two best wilderness areas are both at the west end of the UP. Isle Royale National Park – famous for its populations of moose and wolves – is a 210-sq-mile island in Lake Superior. Porcupine Mountains Wilderness State Park, better known simply as 'the Porkies,' is a rugged 94-sq-mile park 20 miles west of Ontonagon via M-64.

Lake Michigan Shoreline

From the north end of Mackinac Bridge, you can head 6 miles west on US 2 and stop at the St Ignace Ranger District office of the Hiawatha National Forest (☎ 906-643-7900, 1798 US 2). This visitor center provides a wealth of information about camping, hiking, waterfalls and scenic drives along Lake Michigan and in the eastern half of the UP.

The drive continuing west along US 2 is one of the most scenic in the state, passing numerous campgrounds along Lake Michigan. *Lake Michigan National Forest Campground*, 18 miles west of St Ignace, has 35 wooded sites ($12) right above a beautiful beach. *Big Knob State Forest Campground*, off US 2 west of Naubinway, has 18 beautiful campsites ($8), plus interesting hiking.

Head 15 miles south of US 2 on County Rd 183, through the Garden Peninsula, to reach Fayette State Park (☎ 906-644-2603, 1700 13.25 Lane), which has a campground ($9), a beach and a preserved ghost town that was an iron-smelting center in the 19th century. North of the Garden Peninsula, via M-149, is Kitchi-iti-kipi (Big Spring), in Palms Brook State Park, where visitors pull themselves across the state's largest spring on a wooden raft ($4 per vehicle).

Iron Mountain, 52 miles to the west of Escanaba via US 2, is an interesting place to visit, with lots of affordable motels and good restaurants. Here you can climb the Pine Mountain Ski Jump, where skiers set a US record of 400 feet; go white-water rafting at Piers Gorge with Kosir's Rapid Rafts (☎ 715-757-3431, Ⓦ www.kosirs.com; $42 per person); or ride an underground train ($7) into an iron-ore mine at Iron Mountain Iron Mine (☎ 906-563-8077). *Woodlands Motel* (☎ *906-774-6106, 800-394-5505, 3957 US 2*) charges $30 for a single or double, or rent a cabin ($70-120 per night) on the Menominee River at *Edgewater Resort* (☎ *906-774-6244, 800-236-6244, 4128 US 2*).

Sault Ste Marie & Around

Founded in 1668, Sault Ste Marie (Sault is pronounced soo), near the eastern end of the UP, is the oldest city in Michigan and the third-oldest in the USA. The town is a popular tourist destination with loads of attractions; some are tacky, many are interesting and the best two are free. **Soo Lock Park** is at the end of Water St in the heart of downtown. It features an interpretive center and observation decks from which you can watch 1000-foot-long freighters being raised and lowered between the different lake levels. Heading south from the park is **Locks Park Walkway**, which features displays that cover the city's 350-year history. Among the handful of museums in town, check out the **SS Valley Camp** (☎ 906-632-3658), a 550-foot freighter you can walk through ($7).

An hour's drive west of Sault Ste Marie, via M-28 and M-123, is the top attraction in the eastern UP, **Tahquamenon Falls**. The Upper Falls in Tahquamenon Falls State Park (☎ 906-492-3415) are 200 feet across with a 50-foot drop, making them the third-largest falls east of the Mississippi River. The Lower Falls are a series of smaller cascades best viewed by renting a boat and rowing across the river to an island. The large state park also has 176 campsites ($14) and great hiking, and there's a brew pub in the middle of it. North of the park beyond Paradise is the fascinating **Great Lakes Shipwreck Museum** (☎ 906-635-1742) at Whitefish Point, dedicated to the 'Graveyard of the Great Lakes' and well worth the $7.50 admission.

Most of Sault Ste Marie's motels are along the I-75 Business Loop and Asmund St. *Super 8 (☎ 906-632-8882, 3826 I-75 Business)* has doubles for $64, while the nearby *Skyline Motel (☎ 906-632-3393, 800-531-6868, 2601 I-75 Business)* and the *Lockview Motel (☎ 906-632-2491, 800-854-0745, 327 Portage St)*, downtown across from Soo Locks, both charge $60 for a double. *Cup of the Day (406 Ashmun St)* is a coffee shop that serves breakfast and lunch and has Internet access. For dinner, head to the *Antlers (804 E Portage Ave)* to feast on giant hamburgers ($7) and ribs ($12) and to take in the hundreds of stuffed animals on the walls. This is no place for animal-rights enthusiasts.

Munising

Sitting roughly midpeninsula on the Lake Superior shoreline, Munising is the gateway to **Pictured Rocks National Lakeshore**, a 110-sq-mile national park just to the east that holds the namesake colored sandstone bluffs. Most people view the 200-foot-high cliffs on a two-hour boat tour with Pictured Rock Boat Cruises (☎ 906-387-2379); cruises depart from downtown Munising on the hour in summer ($24 per person). The most scenic backpacking adventure in the state is the **Lakeshore Trail**, a four- to five-day, 43-mile trek from Grand Marais to Munising through the heart of the park. Stop in at the Hiawatha National Forest/Pictured Rocks Visitor Center (☎ 906-387-3700, 400 E Munising Ave), at the corner of M-28 and H-58, for maps, backcountry permits and other details.

Just off Munising in the middle of Grand Island Harbor is **Grand Island**, now part of the Hiawatha National Forest. The best way to see the island is to hop aboard the Grand Island Ferry (☎ 906-387-3503; $14 roundtrip) and rent a mountain bike ($15) from the ferry company.

Camping is available on the mainland at *Bay Furnace Campground*, west of the Grand Island Ferry dock on M-28 ($8). Munising has lots of motels; try *Hillcrest Motel (☎ 906-387-2595)*, on M-28 E, where a room or a little cabin is $50 for two, or *Alger Falls Motel (☎ 906-387-3536)*, across the street, where a double is $63.

Marquette

From Munising, M-28 heads west and skirts Lake Superior. This beautiful stretch of highway has lots of beaches, roadside parks and rest areas where you can pull over and enjoy the scenery. Within 45 miles you'll reach Marquette, a city that abounds with outdoor-recreation opportunities. Stop at the Michigan Welcome Center (☎ 906-249-9066), an impressive log lodge on US 41/M-28 as it enters the city, and pick up brochures on area hiking trails and waterfalls.

Panoramic views of the city are enjoyed on the easy **Sugarloaf Mountain Trail** or the harder, wilderness-like **Hogsback Mountain Trail**. Both trails are reached from County Rd 550, just north of the city. Catch the sunset from the high bluffs at **Presque Isle Park** in the city, or head 15 miles south on County Rd 577 to **Anderson Lake State Forest Campground** in Gwinn, where you can camp ($8), hike and fish.

GREAT LAKES

Of the handful of museums in the Marquette area, the most interesting are in the neighboring towns of Negaunee and Ishpeming. The **Michigan Iron Industry Museum** (☎ 906-475-7857, 73 Forge Rd), off County Rd 492, 3 miles east of Negaunee, includes a reconstructed mine shaft (free admission; open daily 9:30am-4:30pm May-Nov). The **National Ski Hall of Fame** (☎ 906-485-6323), on US 41/M-28 in Ishpeming, is dedicated to the history of skiing ($3; open 10am-5pm daily). Ishpeming was the birthplace of US ski jumping.

Marquette is the perfect place to stay put for a few days to explore the central UP. The city-operated *Tourist Park (☎ 906-228-0465)*, on County Rd 550, has tent sites overlooking Dead River Basin ($9). Affordable motels include *Value Host Motor Inn (☎ 906-225-5000, 1101 US 41 W)*, where doubles cost $47 a night, and *Birchmont Motel (☎ 906-228-7538, 2090 US 41/M-28)*, three miles south of downtown, where singles or doubles are $45.

Jean Kay's Pasties & Subs (1639 Presque Isle St) makes the best pasties (meat pies) in town. *Sweet Water Café (517 N Third St)* serves espresso and vegetarian dishes. *Third Street Bagel Company (429 N Third St)* offers freshly baked bagels, delicious bagel sandwiches ($3-6) and gourmet coffee. *Vierling Saloon (119 S Front St)* serves good food and handcrafted beer.

Isle Royale National Park

The National Park Service headquarters servicing Isle Royale (☎ 906-482-0984, Ⓦ www.nps.gov/isro, 800 E Lakeshore Dr) is in Houghton. The park charges a backcountry fee of $4 per person per night to hike and camp on the island.

From the dock outside the headquarters, the *Ranger III* departs twice a week on the six-hour trip to Rock Harbor, at the east end of the island. Fare is $96 roundtrip. Near the dock is Isle Royale Seaplane Service (☎ 906-482-8850), which can fly you to the island in 20 minutes for $221 roundtrip. Or head 50 miles up the Keweenaw Peninsula to Copper Harbor (a beautiful drive) and jump on the *Isle Royale Queen* (☎ 906-289-4437), which charges $84 roundtrip.

Isle Royale is totally free of vehicles, roads, McDonald's, rush-hour traffic – you get the picture. It is laced with 165 miles of hiking trails that connect dozens of campgrounds along Lake Superior and on inland lakes. You must be totally prepared for this wilderness adventure, with a tent, camping stove, sleeping bags, food and water filter. Pick up a copy of *Isle Royale National Park: Foot Trails & Water Routes,* written by Jim DuFresne, for trail descriptions. In recent years the park has become a destination for kayakers and canoers, who bring their boats over on the ferry for an additional $20 fee.

Porcupine Mountains

Michigan's largest state park is another popular place for overnight backpacking and is a lot easier to reach than Isle Royale. The Porkies are so rugged that loggers bypassed most of the range in the early 19th century, leaving the park with the largest tract of virgin forest between the Rocky Mountains and Adirondacks.

From Silver City, head west on M-107 to reach the park headquarters (☎ 906-885-5275, 412 S Boundary Rd) and the Porcupine Mountains Visitor Center. Continue to the end of M-107 to scramble up the Escarpment for the stunning view of **Lake of the Clouds**. Along the way you pass *Union Bay Campground*, on M-107, a huge, 99-site facility on Lake Superior ($14 a night). Bypass it if you can and camp at the much more scenic *Presque Isle Campground*, on County Rd 519 ($9).

The Porkies feature a 90-mile trail system linking the walk-in cabins and backcountry camping areas. Pick up a copy of *Michigan's Porcupine Mountains Wilderness State Park,* by Jim DuFresne, for trail descriptions. A backcountry permit costs $6 per night for a party of four. You also need a vehicle entry permit ($4 a day, $20 for an annual pass).

Indiana

Though not considered much of a destination in itself, the state's position as the 'crossroads of America' means that many travelers pass through heading east and west or north and south. Perhaps surprisingly, there are worthwhile stops across the state. The capital, Indianapolis, is home of the world's oldest and most famous car race, but it has much more. Columbus is a living architectural museum.

The green, rolling lands of the central southern region, and the historic valley of the Ohio River, free of mass commercialism, make for choice, relaxed touring.

History

Prehistoric moundbuilding cultures once occupied much of Indiana; the state's central and southern regions hold fascinating preserved sites. But by the time the first Europeans arrived, the moundbuilders had been succeeded by Algonquian tribes.

French fur traders used the state's waterways by the mid-17th century, and by 1679 had charted a water route between the Great Lakes and the Mississippi River, forging a tenuous link across their North American empire. The French established several forts to protect this route. Vincennes, on the lower Wabash River, is the era's only surviving permanent settlement.

The British acquired the area in 1763, following the French and Indian War. But in the Revolutionary War, rebels from Kentucky overcame the British and their Native American allies, ensuring that the lands northwest of the Ohio River became part of the new USA.

Indiana was first settled by farmers from Kentucky (including Abraham Lincoln's family). Expanding settlement and resulting conflicts displaced the Native Americans, with the final battle fought in 1811 at Tippecanoe. The Kentucky connection meant that Indiana had many Southern sympathizers in the Civil War, but as elsewhere around the Great Lakes, the war's main impact on the state was the growth of the northern industrial towns. In 1906, steelmaking started in Gary, using coal from Illinois and Indiana and iron ore shipped from Minnesota. Today, Indiana is the country's number-one steel producer. The state also has oil refineries and is a major rail and trucking center.

Geography

The north of Indiana is generally flat, while glaciers left much of the south blessed with pretty, verdant hills, valleys and limestone caves punctuated with streams and lakes. The Ohio River marks the state's southern boundary.

Indiana

Nicknames: Hoosier State, Crossroads of America

Population: 6,080,500 (14th)

Area: 36,420 sq miles (38th)

Admitted to Union: December 11, 1816 (19th)

Capital city: Indianapolis (population 752,300)

Other cities: Fort Wayne (173,100), Evansville (126,300), Gary (116,600), South Bend (105,500)

Famous Hoosiers: Vice President Dan Quayle (b 1947), author Kurt Vonnegut (b 1922), TV host David Letterman (b 1947)

Government & Politics

Indiana is a politically moderate state. Republicans and Democrats find equal support, with both sides regularly winning state and federal elections.

Information

Indiana Tourism (☎ 317-232-8800, 800-289-6646, W www.enjoyindiana.com) is at 1 N Capitol Ave, Suite 700, Indianapolis, IN 46201.

For highway information call ☎ 800-261-7623. State sales tax is 5%, and some cities charge an accommodations tax of up to 5%.

For state park information call ☎ 317-232-4124 or 800-622-4931. Park entry permits are $2/18 a day/year for residents or $5/25 for nonresidents.

INDIANAPOLIS

The location of Indiana's capital, on flat cornfields in the geographical center of the state, was the result of a legislative compromise in 1820 between agricultural and industrial regions. The city became a natural hub for road and rail transport, but the lack of navigable waterways limited development of heavy industry. The city had many early carmakers but they were eclipsed by the Detroit giants. Their legacy was a 2½-mile rectangular test track that was used in 1911 for the first Indianapolis 500 race (won at an average speed of 75mph).

Indianapolis' considerable and ongoing downtown redevelopment began in the

GREAT LAKES

1980s. Many downtown commercial buildings around the Circle Centre retail/entertainment complex thoughtfully retained their original facades. Today the growing, prosperous city continues positive change. Public spending – remember that? – is everywhere. The spacious, clean center offers abundant museums, memorable architecture, various war memorials and major sports venues, collectively making a stopover worth planning.

Orientation & Information

Indianapolis is geometrically laid out, not unlike Washington, DC, with diagonal avenues superimposed on a grid layout. Everything radiates out from the massively impressive Monument Circle. Most places mentioned below are within walking distance of one another. Meridian St divides the east-west designations. The old Broad Ripple neighborhood, at 62nd Ave and College St, 6 miles northeast of the center, contains several blocks of restaurants, bars and interesting shops.

The visitor center (☎ 317-237-5206) is at 201 S Capitol Ave on the corner of Georgia St. There is also an information desk in the convention center, across the street beside the RCA Dome. The Marion County Public Library (☎ 317-269-1700, 40 E St Clair St) has Internet access.

Things to See & Do

At Monument Circle, the city center is marked by the jaw-dropping 284-foot **Soldiers and Sailors Monument**. Beneath is the **Civil War Museum**, which neatly outlines the conflict and Indiana's abolition position. Also on the circle are the 1916 Circle Theatre and the 1857 Christ Church Cathedral, with its Tiffany glass windows. From the same era, the cast-iron City Market houses food stalls and restaurants – a good place to stop for lunch. On the other side of Monument Circle are some much more modern developments, such as the glassy **Artsgarden**, over the intersection of Washington and Illinois Sts, a venue for performances and exhibitions. Nearby is the Circle Centre complex, with major department stores.

A block west is the gorgeous, restored 1880 **Indiana Statehouse**, and two blocks west is unique, sprawling White River State Park, containing several worthwhile sites. **Eiteljorg Museum of American Indian and Western Art** (☎ 317-636-9378, 500 W Washington St) features Native American artifacts, including basketry, pots and masks, as well as a fabulous realistic/romantic Western painting collection with works by Frederic Remington and Georgia O'Keeffe ($6; closed Mon except in summer). The building itself is noteworthy, constructed of stone, wood and adobe. The new **NCAA Hall of Champions** (☎ 800-735-6222, 700 W Washington St) reveals to outsiders and residents alike something of the country's fascination with college sports ($7; open daily). Other park highlights include gardens, a zoo, a canal walk and a military Medal of Honor Memorial.

The **Indiana State Museum** (☎ 317-232-1637, 202 N Alabama St), scheduled to move to White River State Park in 2002, includes displays on prehistory, early city storefronts and black settlement (free admission; open daily).

North of downtown, the **Scottish Rite cathedral** (650 N Meridian St) is a 1929 Tudor-Gothic Masonic wonder. Farther north, **Children's Museum** (☎ 317-334-3322, 3000 N Meridian St) offers the usual big-screen cinema and interactive exhibits as well as dinosaur displays and Egyptian tombs ($8/3.50 adults/children; open daily except Mon Sept-May). In the vicinity, the **Indianapolis Museum of Art** (☎ 317-923-1331, 1200 W 38th St) has an excellent collection of European art (especially Turner and some postimpressionists), African tribal art, Chinese works and some modern US pieces (free admission; closed Mon). The landscaped grounds are also attractive.

To join the 450,000 spectators at the annual **Indianapolis 500**, on Memorial Day weekend in May, book about 51 weeks in

Indy 500, going strong since 1911

Who's a Hoosier?

Since the 1830s, Indianans have been known by the odd moniker 'Hoosiers.' Everyone wants to know what the heck the nickname means. Well, here's the definitive explanation – sort of, maybe.

One theory is that early settlers knocking on a door were met with 'Who's yere?' which soon became 'Hoosier.' Another notion is that the early rivermen were so good at pummeling or 'hushing' their adversaries that they got reputations as 'hushers.' Then there's the one about a foreman on the Louisville and Portland canal whose name was Hoosier and who preferred workers from Indiana. They became known as Hoosier's men. More likely, others say, pioneers walking into a tavern on a fight-filled Saturday night would find a torn, displaced body part and say 'Whose ear?'

In a more academic vein, the word *hoozer*, from an early dialect in England's Cumberland District, was evidently used in the 19th-century South to describe woodsmen or hillbilly types. In any case, the word is now well entrenched and thought to have only honorable attributes.

advance (☎ 317-484-6700). Tickets cost $20-150. Cheap tickets for prerace trials and activities are usually available. Hotel rooms should be reserved and prices will be high; call ☎ 800-556-4639 for packages.

The rest of the year it's worth checking out the **Indi Hall of Fame Museum** (☎ 317-484-6747, 4790 W 16th St), which features 75 racing cars (including former Indy winners) and a bus tour of the track…at a very sedate 37mph.

Places to Stay

Everything is full and costs more in May and August, when the big races are held.

Budget accommodations are few, especially close to downtown. The closest camping is *Indiana State Fairgrounds Campground* (☎ 317-927-7500, 1202 E 38th St), where bleak sites cost $16, $19 with hookups. There's a *KOA* (☎ 317-894-1397) about 20 miles east of town in Greenfield.

Fall Creek YMCA (☎ 317-634-2478, 860 W 10th St) is a short city bus ride from downtown and has good facilities and simple rooms from $25, plus a very few with private bath at $35. There is one floor for women, but couples cannot share a room. The place is usually full of long-term tenants except in summer, when the lack of air-con makes the rooms hot!

Look for cheap motels off I-465, the freeway that circles Indianapolis. The basic *Dollar Inn* (☎ 317-248-8500, 6331 Crawfordsville Rd) charges $26/35 for singles/doubles; other Dollar Inns are numerous in all directions off I-465. Better is *Motel 6* (☎ 317-248-1231), 6 miles west of town center

off I-75 at Airport Expressway. Its singles/doubles are $40/46. Two other Motel 6 locations cost a few dollars less; one is at I-465 exit 16A (☎ 317-293-3220), just west of the speedway. *Days Inn East* (☎ 317-359-5500, 7314 E 21st St) has rooms starting at $55.

By the old train station, ***Crown Plaza Union Station*** (☎ 317-631-2221, 123 W Louisiana St) offers some accommodations in restored Pullman railroad cars. Rooms are $179. The classiest place is the ***Canterbury*** (☎ 317-634-3000, 123 S Illinois St), where renovated rooms with antique furnishings start at $175.

Places to Eat

At lunch it's hard to beat the incredible range of cheap eats at *City Market*, two blocks east of Monument Circle on Market St. Central Massachusetts Ave ('Mass Ave' to locals) is also bounteous when the stomach growls; try the downtown location of the popular pizza place *Bazbeaux (334 Massachusetts Ave)*, or head down the street to arty *Abbey Coffeehouse (771 Massachusetts Ave)*, which has good sandwiches and vegetarian items. *St Elmo's* (☎ 317-635-0636, 127 S Illinois St) has been *the* place for steak since 1902. The Broad Ripple dining and drinking area, 6 miles north of downtown at College Ave and 62nd St, has pubs and eateries representing numerous nationalities. *India Garden (830 Broad Ripple Ave)* is a local fave for curries and the like.

Entertainment

Slippery Noodle (372 S Meridian St), at South St, behind Union Station, was once a whorehouse and is the oldest bar in the state, not to mention one of the best blues bars in the country. There's live music nightly, and it's cheap – great stuff. Also very comfortable and with a varied clientele is the *Chatterbox* (☎ *317-636-0584, 435 Massachusetts Ave)*, just northeast of the center, which features some local jazz players. *Rathskeller (401 E Michigan St)*, in the Athenaeum building, is a long-established German haunt with traditional and modern fare and a *biergarten* pouring imported beers. Gay-oriented *Club Cabaret* (☎ *317-951-8569, 151 W 14th St)* features bombshell female impersonators on weekends.

Broad Ripple has numerous watering holes. *Patio* (☎ *317-353-0799, 6308 Guilford Ave)* gets a young crowd for local alternative bands. *Crackers Comedy Club* (☎ *317-255-4211, 6281 N College St)* is good for a laugh.

The *Madame Walker Urban Theatre Center* (☎ *317-236-2099, 617 Indiana Ave)* is a long-established venue for African American performing arts – jazz, dance, theater etc. It's worth visiting just to see the unusual African-Egyptian decor. Indianapolis also boasts the *Indianapolis Symphony Orchestra* (☎ *317-639-4300)*, *Indiana Repertory Theatre* (☎ *317-635-5252)* and *Indianapolis Opera* (☎ *317-940-6444)* seasons. The free weekly entertainment paper, *NUVO*, has complete listings.

Spectator Sports

You can't miss the RCA Dome (☎ 317-262-3452, 100 S Capitol Ave), where 63,000 fans can watch the NFL's Indianapolis Colts play football under a vast fiberglass dome. The beloved NBA Pacers play basketball at the new central Conseco Fieldhouse (☎ 317-917-2500, 125 S Pennsylvania St). Besides the Indianapolis 500, the other big car race in town is NASCAR's Brickyard 400, held in August at the Speedway.

Getting There & Around

The Greyhound station (☎ 800-231-2222, 350 S Illinois St), at South St, beside the old Union Station building, has frequent buses to Bloomington ($15; 1 hour), Cincinnati ($20; 2 hours) and Chicago ($32; 4 hours).

The Amtrak terminal (☎ 317-263-0550, 800-872-7245) is in the bus station and has three trains weekly to Chicago ($34; 4 hours), Cincinnati ($35; 3½ hours) and Washington, DC ($129; 18 hours). Late at night, the train desk is closed except at arrival/departure times.

IndyGo (☎ 317-635-3344) runs the local buses; service is minimal on weekends.

AROUND INDIANAPOLIS

Old Hwy 40 east of the city from Knightstown to Richmond is lined with shops selling antiques and collectibles.

Anderson

This town, on I-69, 50 miles northeast of Indianapolis, is worth a stop for archaeology buffs. Mounds State Park (☎ 765-642-6627) includes several prehistoric Hopewell mounds and an attractive campground.

Fairmount

Continuing north up Hwy 9 is the birthplace of James Dean, one of the original icons of cool. Fans should visit the Historical Museum, the Dean Memorial Gallery and his grave site.

Columbus

Forty miles south of Indianapolis on I-65, Columbus is remarkable for its outstanding architecture. It's a virtual art gallery of physical design. Since the 1940s, the city and its leading corporations have commissioned some of the world's best architects, includ-

---

Indiana Idiosyncratics

Despite a low-key image, the state has produced some noteworthy iconoclasts. Pop genius Michael Jackson, among the most derided of superstars for his often weird behavior, not to mention appearance, is from Gary. One of the country's best-known bad guys, local boy John Dillinger (from Mooresville), a public enemy number one, was wanted for robbery, murder and escaping prison, and killed by law officers in 1934. He was turned in by Anne Sage, the original 'woman in red.' James Dean, the rebel without a cause, is from Fairmont, and Axl Rose, hard-livin' Guns N' Roses band member is also a Hoosier. Are these the kids next door?

ing Eero Saarinen, Richard Meier and IM Pei, to design both public and private buildings. Impressive central historic buildings have also been preserved. For a good introductory display, or to join a guided walking or bus tour, stop at the visitor center (☎ 812-378-2622, 506 5th St), at the corner of Washington St (the town's main street); open daily. Over 60 notable buildings – most post-1960 – are spread over a wide area (car required), but about 15 diverse, interesting works can be seen on foot downtown. Motels are found on the city's outskirts, on Hwy 46, for example. For a really good bargain meal head to *Riviera*, west on Hwy 46 near I-65.

Nashville

Restored and gentrified, this 19th-century town west of Columbus on Rte 46 is now a bustling tourist center. Several streets are lined with the usual antique and souvenir shops, but there are also craft outlets, some of which feature work from the local arts community. The County Museum has a log jail.

Camping is available at nearby *Brown County State Park*, Indiana's largest, where trails give hikers and horseback riders access to the area's lovely green hill country.

Among several B&Bs, central *Artist's Colony Inn* (☎ 812-988-0600), on the corner of Van Buren and Franklin Sts, stands out for its wonderful rooms and rooftop hot tub. Prices start at $70 for a double with light breakfast. The inexpensive dining room offers traditional Hoosier fare, such as catfish. *Hobnob Corner*, on Main St, combines tasty food with good value; the Cuban black bean soup is excellent. Top country-music bands are featured regularly at several venues.

Bloomington

Lively and attractive Bloomington, 45 miles south of Indianapolis on Hwy 37, is the home of Indiana University. The town centers on Courthouse Square, surrounded by restaurants, bars, bookshops and the historic facade of Fountain Square Mall. The visitor center (☎ 812-334-8900, 2855 N Walnut St) is a few miles north of the center. Nearly everything else is walkable. On the lovely, expansive campus, the **Art Museum** (☎ 812-855-5445), designed by IM Pei, has an excellent collection of African art as well as European and US paintings. A significant Tibetan presence in town is indicated by a temple, retreat, cultural center and more.

Ten miles south of town, Lake Monroe makes an attractive outing. There, quiet *Paynetown Recreation Center* (☎ 812-837-9546) has campsites for $7, or $15 with electricity. In town, look for cheap lodgings along N Walnut St near Rte 46. The Midwest's most attractive *Motel 6* (☎ 812-332-0820, 1800 N Walnut St) charges $37/43 for singles/doubles and has a pool.

For a town its size, Bloomington offers a decision-cramping array of ethnic restaurants – everything from Eritrean to Mexican. Browse Kirkwood Ave and E 4th St. Charming *Little Tibet* (415 E 4th St) offers specialties from the Himalayan homeland, as well as Thai, vegetarian and various curries. *The Bakehouse*, corner of College and W 6th St, on the square, is excellent for coffee, bread and snacks. Pubs on Kirkwood Ave close to the university cater to the student crowd.

SOUTHERN INDIANA

The scenery and history of southern Indiana mark it as a completely different region than the flat, modern, industrialized north.

Ohio River

The Indiana segment of the historic 981-mile-long Ohio River marks the state's southern border. From tiny Aurora, in the southeastern corner of the state, Rtes 56, 156, 62 and 66, known collectively as the **Ohio River Scenic Route**, wind through a varied landscape that includes sections of the Hoosier Hills and the Hoosier National Forest. Towns like Rising Sun and Patriot were once on the US frontier. Riverboat casinos now dot the river that pioneers once followed.

Coming from the east, a perfect place to stop is little **Madison**, a well-preserved river settlement from the mid-19th century. This clean, attractive town lined with architectural gems is one of too few in the USA still unsullied by ugly commercial strips and rows of interchangeable franchises. And it works – it's busy (not overrun) with travelers. The visitor center (☎ 812-265-2956, 301 E Main St) is open daily. Pick up a pamphlet on the walking tour, which include the

James Lanier Mansion, a designated landmark site overlooking the river. Call Kate's Canoes (☎ 812-273-5915) to organize inexpensive Ohio River camping and canoeing trips from one to five days long.

Madison has motels around its edges, as well as several B&Bs. Large, wooded *Clifty Falls State Park (☎ 812-265-4135)*, a couple of miles west of town on Rte 56, has camping, hiking trails, views and waterfalls. Main St, with numerous antique stores and various other browser-enticing shops, also has several places for a bite. *Café Camille (149 E Main)* is ideal for breakfast or lunch.

In **Jeffersonville**, Falls of the Ohio State Park (☎ 812-280-9970, 201 W Riverside Dr) has only rapids, no falls, but is of interest for its Lewis and Clark expedition history and the 386-million-year-old fossil beds visitors are free to explore. The rest of town and adjacent New Albany, the only Indiana town of any size in the region, aren't much. Bypass them by skirting into Kentucky and catching I-64 west. It returns to Indiana with more of historical interest farther west along the river. The village of **Corydon** was once the capital of Indiana, and the Federal-style capitol building (☎ 812-738-4890) is now the town's main attraction.

From Corydon, scenic Rte 62, lined with historic plaques, leads to the Lincoln Hills and southern Indiana's fascinating **limestone caves**. A visit to Wyandotte Caves State Recreation Area (☎ 812-738-2782), near Leavenworth, is highly recommended. Tours, ranging anywhere from one hour to all day, are an excellent value at $5-15. They take you through caves featuring ancient formations, bats and more. Another cave that stands out is Marengo Cave (☎ 812-365-2705), north on Rte 66, in a park with various outdoor activities. Nearby in Milltown, Cave Country Canoes (☎ 812-365-2705) runs several good day-long or longer trips (some perfect for the inexperienced) on the scenic Blue River.

To the west, **Hoosier National Forest** provides opportunities for walking, swimming, camping and other outdoor recreation. Pick up a guide at a local Chamber of Commerce.

Four miles south of Dale, off I-64, is the **Lincoln Boyhood National Memorial**, where young Abe lived from age seven to 21. The isolated but good site includes a visitor center (open all year) and a working pioneer farm (open Apr–Oct). The adjacent, wooded **Lincoln State Park** has a dramatization of the president's early life ($14) and camping. Farther west, on the Ohio River, **Evansville** is one of the state's largest cities. The Riverside Historic District retains many early-19th-century mansions, but the riverboat *Casino Aztar* and the adjacent entertainment-retail-hotel complex get more attention. Well-preserved Angel Mounds State Historic Site contains the remains of a prehistoric Native American town (AD 1100–1450) and some reconstructed buildings. An interpretive center is under construction.

Wabash River

'His earthly race is over, now the curtains 'round
  him fall;
We'll carry him home to victory on the Wabash
  Cannon Ball.'

– from a traditional song about any train a hobo
could catch to something better, though there was a
train called the *Wabash Cannon Ball* between
Detroit and St Louis

In southwest Indiana, the Wabash River forms the border with Illinois. The river was an important route for the early French colonists, who established a fort at Vincennes in the late 17th century, although no evidence of this French period remains.

Near the Wabash, south of I-64, captivating **New Harmony** is the site of two early communal-living experiments and well worth a visit. In the early 19th century, a German Christian sect, the Harmonists, developed a sophisticated town here while awaiting the Second Coming. Later it was acquired by the British utopian Robert Owen. You can learn more at the angular Atheneum Visitor Center (☎ 812-682-4488), open daily. Today New Harmony retains an air of contemplation, if not otherworldliness, which you can experience at its newer sites, such as the templelike Church With No Roof and the Labyrinth, a sort of maze symbolizing the spirit's quest. The town has a couple of guesthouses, some pleasant eateries, and camping at *Harmonie State Park (☎ 812-682-4821)*.

NORTHERN INDIANA

The truck-laden I-80/I-90 tollways cut quickly across the north of the state. Parallel

US 20 is slower and cheaper but not much more attractive. Connoisseurs of classic cars might detour south on I-69 to the town of **Auburn**, where the Cord Company produced the USA's favorite cars in the 1920s and '30s. The Auburn Cord Duesenberg Museum (☎ 219-925-1444, 1600 S Wayne St) has a wonderful display of early roadsters in a beautiful art deco setting ($7; open daily). Almost next door is the National Automotive and Truck Museum.

Farther west, around the villages of Shipshewana, Middlebury and Elkhart, is one of the USA's largest **Amish communities**. The excellent Menno-Hof Visitors Center (☎ 219-768- 4117), in Shipshewana, provides a thorough and comprehensive background. The area holds numerous Amish and Mennonite craft outlets, bakeries and restaurants – most complete with hitching posts.

The city of **South Bend** is another ex-carmaker. Stop at the Studebaker National Museum (☎ 219-235-9714, 525 S Main St), with its gorgeous 1956 Packard and many other classic beauties ($5.50; open daily). South Bend is better known as the home of the University of Notre Dame, famous for its 'Fighting Irish' football team. To tour the legendary, pretty campus with its gold-domed administration building, Lourdes Grotto Replica and *Touchdown Jesus* painting, start at the Eck Center Visitor's Center (☎ 219-631-5726). US residents especially will be interested in seeing the downtown College Football Hall of Fame (☎ 219-235-9999, 111 S St Joseph St).

A good outdoor respite, with camping, is the popular **Indiana Dunes National Lakeshore** (☎ 219-926-7561), which stretches along 20 miles of Lake Michigan shoreline. Sandy beaches, dunes and woodlands are crisscrossed with hiking trails, which often afford glimpses of nearby steel mills and stark, industrial structures. The lakeshore is noted for its incredible variety of plant life – everything from cactus to grasslands to hardwood forests and pine trees. Mt Baldy has spectacular sunsets and views of Chicago on a clear day. Just avoid looking to the right (east). The beaches are open daily, usually 9am to sunset. Schedules for the visitor centers, other sites and activities vary widely with the season.

Adjacent *Indiana Dunes State Park* (☎ 219-926-1952), near Chesterton, has year-round camping and takes reservations. Two good budget motels lie between the park and Michigan City on Rte 12.

Near Illinois, the steel cities of **Gary** (population 110,000) and East Chicago present some of the bleakest, most desolate urban landscapes anywhere.

Wisconsin

Wisconsin's landscapes range from bucolic farmlands to the untouched Apostle Islands. Top draws include gentle Door County, the wooded lakelands and the architectural legacy of local genius Frank Lloyd Wright. Wisconsin Dells and Milwaukee's events generate festive crowds.

History

When Europeans arrived, Sioux-speaking Winnebago inhabited the Green Bay area, but most of the land was occupied by Algonquian peoples, who lived mainly by hunting, fishing and an annual harvest of wild rice.

In 1634 Frenchman Jean Nicolet landed near Green Bay, where a trading post opened in 1648. Others followed on the Mississippi, though it was 25 years before the inland routes between these outposts were explored. Jesuit missions were established in the 1660s, but French territorial claims passed first to the British and then to the new USA.

Development was spurred by a lead-mining boom in the 1820s. The many miners who came from nearby states were called 'badgers' for their subterranean activities. The elimination of local Native Americans, culminating in the brutal Black Hawk War of 1832, opened up new land for settlement.

Following statehood and the Civil War, immigrants poured in – from Germany and Scandinavia most notably. Wisconsin was soon known for its beer, butter, cheese and paper. In the past century, production of agricultural equipment has grown into a major and diverse specialized machinery-manufacturing industry. Tourism is increasingly important.

Geography

Wisconsin's northern upland plateau is mostly forested land less than 1500 feet

Wisconsin

Nicknames: Badger State, Dairyland

Population: 5,363,700 (18th)

Area: 65,500 sq miles (23rd)

Admitted to Union: May 29, 1848 (30th)

Capital city: Madison (population 191,300)

Other cities: Milwaukee (628,100), Green Bay (96,500), Racine (84,300)

Birthplace of: Frank Lloyd Wright (1869–1959), Senator Joseph McCarthy (1908–57), Liberace (1919–87), the Republican party

Famous for: first state to legislate gay rights

above sea level, but it's the source of the state's main rivers, which flow south. The southeast, covered in fertile glacial drift, has many lakes and the state's main cities. The southwest escaped the ice-age glaciers and has more rugged terrain, including scenic gorges cut by the rivers. The north and east are crowned with Lake Superior and Lake Michigan.

Government & Politics

The state is hard to figure. It leans slightly right, especially in federal politics, yet it's been a consistent leader in socially progressive reforms. On the state level, Wisconsin flips back and forth between Democrat and Republican, the party affiliation of the governor changing with almost every election.

Information

The Wisconsin Department of Tourism (☎ 608-266-2161, 800-432-8747, W www .travelwisconsin.com) is at 201 W Washington St, Madison, WI 53707-7976. For highway information, call ☎ 800-762-3947. State sales tax is 5%. Many counties tack on a small percentage, and some cities charge an extra hotel tax. In Milwaukee the total adds up to 15.5%!

For state park information and reservations call ☎ 888-947-2757. Park entry requires a vehicle permit ($5/18 per day/year resident, $7/25 nonresident).

MILWAUKEE

Somewhat veiled in obscurity, mid-size Milwaukee is nonetheless a city of charm and character smiling quietly in the shadow of Chicago. It enjoys a fine lakeside location where three rivers flow into Lake Michigan. The compact central downtown is vibrant night and day, and the city offers sports and arts in equal measure. An excursion here is a worthy proposition.

First settled by Germans in the 1840s, Milwaukee has a German character that's still evident in its architecture (the Germanic City Hall and beer-bankrolled Pabst Theater, for example) and restaurants. Later waves of Italians, Poles, Irish, African Americans, Mexicans and others have added to the varied culture. In summer there's a different ethnic festival almost weekly.

German settlers started small breweries here in the mid-19th century, but the introduction of bulk brewing technology in the 1890s turned beer into a major Milwaukee industry. Schlitz ('the beer that made Milwaukee famous'), Pabst and Miller were all based here at one time, but among the majors, only Miller remains. Light manufacturing, notably medical equipment, is now the principal industry.

Information

The visitor center (☎ 414-908-6205, 800-554-1448, 400 Wisconsin Ave) is in Midwest Express Center, at the corner of 4th St. It's open daily Memorial Day to Labor Day, then weekdays only. The beautiful Milwaukee Public Library (☎ 414-286-3000, 814 Wisconsin Ave) has Internet access.

Things to See & Do

The inspired Riverwalk is a system of redeveloped walking paths along both sides of the Milwaukee River. With pubs and restaurants wedged beside the city's central buildings and passing boats it makes for a distinctive downtown core. Nearby, browsing down N Old World 3rd St between W Wisconsin St and W Highland Ave reveals some fine older buildings. The Grand Ave shopping mall, incorporating early architecture, runs for several blocks along central E Wisconsin St.

The parks of the people-oriented lakefront are alluring. Right by the lake is the first-rate **Milwaukee Art Museum** (☎ 414-224-3200, 750 N Lincoln Memorial Dr), featuring a stunning winglike new addition by Calatrava (built into the just-upgraded original concept by Eero Saarinen). The museum's all-encompassing collection includes paintings from the 15th century onward (all major schools represented), a permanent display on Frank Lloyd Wright, a fabulous photo gallery and folk art ($6; closed Monday).

A few blocks west, **Milwaukee Museum Center** (800 W Wells St) houses the substantial Public Museum (☎ 414-278-2700), with popular exhibits focusing on dinosaurs and Native American life ($6.50; open daily). Also here is Discovery World (☎ 414-765-9966), a museum of science, economics and technology featuring hands-on exhibits ($5.50; open daily). Combination tickets are offered. There is also an IMAX cinema.

The 1893 **Pabst Mansion** (☎ 414-931-0808, 2000 W Wisconsin Ave) is the well-appointed home of a former local brewmaster ($7; closed Monday).

America's Black Holocaust Museum (☎ 414-264-2500, 2233 N 4th St) poignantly outlines the consequences of racism from slavery onwards ($5; closed Sunday).

Italian-based **Brady St**, between Astor and Cambridge Aves, is lined with bakeries, cafes, restaurants and some interesting stores. The historic **Third Ward**, anchored along N Milwaukee St south of I-94, features old warehouses redone as art galleries, antique outlets, graphic arts houses and a few tony shops.

Free, kind-of-technical, one-hour tours are offered at the **Harley-Davidson** powertrain plant (☎ 414-535-3666, 11700 W Capitol Dr), about 20 minutes from the center. No open-toed shoes permitted; call for schedule. Bike painting and assembly are done in Pennsylvania.

The Wisconsin State Fair, held each August, is one of the country's biggest and best.

Connoisseurs might dismiss the bland beers churned out by the big-name national companies, but lots of drinkers line up at mega **Miller Brewing** (☎ 414-931-2337, 4251 W State St), the company responsible for such popular brands as Miller High Life and Miller Genuine Draft (MGD). The free tour includes a slick slide show followed by visits to bottling and distribution areas that give some idea of just how much brew is swilled. The generous tasting session often adds a Leinenkugel brand from the former small brewery. Tours run 10am-3:30pm Mon-Sat.

Two of the newer microbreweries invite similar tours. Five miles north, **Sprecher Brewing** (☎ 414-964-2739, 701 W Glendale Ave) offers tours at 4pm Friday and at various hours Saturday afternoon. **Lakefront Brewery** (☎ 414-372-8800, 818A E Chambers St) gives tours Friday night and Saturday afternoon.

Places to Stay

The **HI Red Barn Hostel** (☎ 262-529-3299, 6750 W Loomis Rd), in Greendale, is 12 miles southwest of town but accessible by city bus plus a 10-minute walk. It's open May–Oct ($13/16 members/nonmembers). Another HI hostel is north of town in Newburg (see the Eastern Wisconsin section). A summer HI hostel is planned for Marquette University.

In summer, the University of Wisconsin's **Sandburg Halls** (☎ 414-229-4065, 3400 N Maryland Ave) offer simple singles/doubles at $33/45 that get booked up, so reserve if possible.

For cheap motels, try Howell Ave, south near the airport. **Motel 6** (☎ 414-482-4414, 5037 S Howell) costs $44/50. Another **Motel 6** (☎ 262-786-7337, 20300 W Bluemound Rd) is in Brookfield, 15 minutes west of Milwaukee.

The downtown **Hotel Wisconsin** (☎ 414-271-4900, 720 N 3rd St) is a delightful 1950s throwback. In summer rooms are $89 for one or two people; rates are lower in the off-season. The traditional 1918 **Astor Hotel** (☎ 414-271-4220, 24 E Juneau Ave) has doubles from $89 including continental breakfast.

The **Pfister Hotel** (☎ 414-273-8222, 424 E Wisconsin Ave) is a grand old hotel in a class, 1st class, of its own. Built in the 19th century, it has been meticulously restored and lost not a bit of its charm. A stroll through the lobby and a peek at the Victorian painting collection emphatically declare that this ain't no chain hotel. Rooms start at $265.

Places to Eat

With a New Orleans slant and a great location by the lake, **Nolas**, at the foot of E

Wisconsin Ave, is a good place to go for a po'boy sandwich, an ostrich burger ($9) or a seafood dinner (under $15).

Downtown, clever **Safehouse** *(779 N Front St)* is marked simply with a door indicating an import-export business. It's an inexpensive sandwich-burger restaurant like no other. Opening the door leads diners into the world of espionage. Take a look over your shoulder and slip inside; most diners are visitors. *African Hut (1107 Old World 3rd St)* has inexpensive and authentic African meat and vegetarian dishes.

South of town a few blocks (over the bridge and too far to walk), around S 5th and 6th Sts, the Latin enclave of Walker's Point holds about 10 Mexican restaurants. The good, inexpensive food draws crowds weekend nights; *Pedrano's (600 S 6th St)* is homey and cheap. Brady St has numerous Italian places, and N Falwell offers various ethnic options. The corner of Jefferson and Wells Sts is becoming trendy and is worth a look.

Moving upscale, German fare is readily available. **Mader's German Restaurant** *(☎ 414-271-3377, 1037 N 3rd St)* has been satisfying since 1902. The competition, **Karl Ratzsch's Restaurant** *(☎ 414-276-2720, 320 E Mason St)*, is two years younger and has an excellent wine list. Both have lots of heavy wood decor, rows of beer steins and attentive service. Main courses are about $24.

A Milwaukee specialty is frozen custard, available from small stands. See Entertainment below for pub grub.

Entertainment

The beer legacy ensures you don't go thirsty in this town – a thirst-quenching array of golden nectar is available. Over a dozen bars and restaurants lie around N Water St at E State St. Try some of the fine housemade beer at **Water Street Brewery** *(1101 N Water St)*. Across the street, **Brew City BBQ** is popular for its barbecue meals and beer selection. Down the river in the bank building is the more sedate **John Hawk's** *(100 E Wisconsin Ave)*, a 'British' pub with fish fries, sandwiches, a big choice of beers and live Saturday jazz.

Elsewhere, the very German **Von Trier** *(2235 N Farwell Ave)* has 20 draft beers, a *biergarten* and good German snacks. More bars can be found in Walker's Point on 1st and 2nd Sts. The **Dubliner** *(922 S 2nd St)* has Irish beers, whiskeys and often Celtic music.

Up and Under Pub (1216 E Brady St) is a well-established place for a range of good music, including frequent blues bands, with varying cover charges.

To complement the brew, the city has a full cultural slate. The **Marcus Center** *(☎ 414-273-7206, 929 Water St)* showcases theater, opera and ballet. The **Pabst Theater** *(☎ 414-286-3663, 144 E Wells St)* presents dance, opera, jazz and more. The **Riverside Theater** *(☎ 414-290-6800, 116 W Wisconsin Ave)*, Wisconsin's largest, offers stagings of Broadway shows.

The weekly *Shepherd Express* is a good source for events and club information.

Spectator Sports

The National League's Milwaukee Brewers *(☎ 414-902-4000)* play baseball in brand new Miller Park on S 46th St; the stadium features a retractable roof and real grass. The NBA Bucks *(☎ 414-227-0400)* dribble at the Bradley Center (1001 N 4th St).

Getting There & Around

Greyhound *(☎ 414-272-2156, 606 N 7th St)*, at Michigan Ave, is conveniently central and has frequent buses to Chicago ($14; 2 hours) and Minneapolis ($50; from 6 hours). Across the street, Badger Bus *(☎ 414-276-7490, 635 N 7th St)* goes to Madison ($12; 1½ hours).

The downtown Amtrak station *(☎ 414-271-0840, 433 W St Paul Ave)* is served by six trains a day to/from Chicago ($20; 1½ hours) as well as the daily *Empire Builder* between Chicago and Seattle.

The Milwaukee County Transit System *(☎ 414-344-6711)* provides efficient local bus service.

SOUTHERN WISCONSIN

Even though most of the state's population resides here, this part of Wisconsin has some of the prettiest landscapes. The hilly southwest missed the flattening of the last ice age and is particularly beautiful.

Highlights of the region include Kettle Moraine State Forest, around 40 miles southwest of Milwaukee, which offers good walking trails; and Madison, which is its own universe. In addition, there are must-sees here for Frank Lloyd Wright fans.

Racine

On the Lake Michigan shore 30 miles south of Milwaukee, Racine is an unremarkable industrial town, though Main St is quite agreeable. Dover Maps (323 Main St) has a huge selection. The key visitor attractions are two **Frank Lloyd Wright sites**. The first, Johnson Wax Company, at 14th and Franklin Sts, dates from 1939 and is a magnificent space with tall, flared columns. A free tour is offered on Friday and must be booked in advance (☎ 262-260-2154). The other is the lakeside Wingspread (☎ 262-681-3353, 33 E Four Mile Rd), the last and largest of Wright's Prairie houses. It's open to the public on a limited basis, ie when it's not being used for a function, so call first.

Madison

Wonderfully ensconced on a narrow isthmus between two lakes, Madison is an irresistible combination of small state capital and lively college town.

The Madison visitor center (☎ 608-255-2537, 615 E Washington Ave) is six blocks from Capitol Square and open weekdays. In the other direction, near the square, is the Wisconsin Tourist Department (☎ 608-266-2161, 201 W Washington St), which offers statewide information and is also open weekdays.

The central Greyhound station (☎ 608-257-3050, 800-231-2222, 2 S Bedford St) is also used by the Badger Bus to Milwaukee.

Things to See & Do At the town heart, surrounded by Capitol Square, is the grand **State Capitol**, which features an imposing white granite dome. The interior, which also houses the Wisconsin Supreme Court, features impressive murals. Free guided tours are available on the hour most days from the capitol foyer (☎ 608-266-0382).

Beside the square, the **State Historical Museum** (☎ 608-264-6555, 30 N Carroll St) offers solid coverage of Wisconsin's Native Americans ($3 suggested donation; closed Mon). Across the street, the **Veterans Museum** (☎ 608-264-6086) holds thoughtful displays that outline all the country's war involvements. It even has a piece of the Berlin Wall (free admission; open daily). The nearby **Civic Center** (211 State St) is a performance venue that also houses the Madison Art Center (☎ 608-257-0158), where local and visiting exhibitions are presented (free admission; closed Mon).

The impeccable **Monona Terrace Community and Convention Center** (☎ 608-261-4000, 1 John Nolen Dr), two blocks from the square, has arched windows overlooking Lake Monona and a fabulous rooftop garden. It finally opened in 1997, 59 years after Frank Lloyd Wright designed it. Tours are offered; check out the Wright display in the gift shop. The **First Unitarian Meeting House** (☎ 608-233-9774, 900 University Bay Dr) is a striking triangular structure designed by Wright in 1946. The church is open most days ($3 donation), and visitors are welcome at Sunday services. Call for meeting house or tour information.

State St, the lengthy pedestrians- and cyclists-only strip of student stores, bars and cafes, runs from the capitol west to the University of Wisconsin. The campus has its own attractions, including the **Elvehjem Art Museum** (☎ 608-263-2246), a geology museum, botanical gardens and a conservatory.

Places to Stay & Eat The convenient *HI Madison Hostel (☎ 608-441-0144, 141 S Butler St)* is a short walk from the capitol. It's open all year and has 28 dorm beds ($14/17 members/nonmembers) and four private rooms ($27/30). Downtown, *University Inn (☎ 608-285-8040, 441 N Frances St)* is a small, handy hotel charging $80, less in winter and for students, businesspeople, seniors etc so ask for a discount. Moderately priced motels can be found off I-90/I-94, Hwy 12/18 and along Washington Ave. North of town off the interstate, *Select Inn (☎ 608-249-1815, 4858 Hayes Rd)* has rooms starting at $42.

State St holds an outstanding range of eating options and cafes, many with inviting patios. Cheap and cheerful *Himal Chuli (318 State)* serves up homemade Nepali fare, including some vegetarian dishes. For nicely done Afghani food, head to *Kabul (521 State)*. For coffee and sweets try *Michelangelo's (114 State)*.

On Capitol Square, *L'Étoile (☎ 608-251-0500, 25 N Pinckney St)* is a sedate, upscale dining room with a contemporary menu featuring local produce. Entrées average $25. Cruising Williamson St, known as Willy St, will also turn up several good eateries.

For a beer, definitely join the multifaceted crowd and fun atmosphere at *Memorial Union (800 Langdon St)*, by the lake at the university. State St near the university also has numerous bars.

Around Madison

Northwest of Madison along Hwy 12, **Baraboo** was once the winter home of the Ringling Brothers Circus. Circus World Museum (☎ 608-356-8341) preserves a nostalgic collection of wagons, posters and equipment from the touring big-top heydays ($3.50; open daily). In summer, admission includes clowns, animals and acrobats doing the three-ring thing ($15). Among numerous motels, sprawling *Spinning Wheel (☎ 608-356-3933, 809 8th St)* is decent and reasonable at $60 in summer and less in other seasons.

Farther north, **Wisconsin Dells** is likely the state's best-known site. Despite the unspoiled natural appeal of the scenic limestone formations carved by the Wisconsin River, the Dells is a megacenter of artificial, touristy diversions, including family theme parks, super-minigolf courses and water slides. (Part of town is actually called Lake Delton but you can't tell where one designation ends and the other begins.) To appreciate the original attraction, take a boat tour or walk the trails at Mirror Lake or Devil's Lake State Parks. Devil's Lake has lakeside bluffs, and both parks have camping. Mirror Lake also has *Seth Peterson Cottage (☎ 608-254-6551, E9982 Fern Dell Rd, Lake Delton, WI 53940)*, a 1958 Frank Lloyd Wright cottage available for rent if you can book far enough ahead – and have deep enough pockets. Cheap tours are offered on the second Sunday of each month. There are countless garish (costly) motels and commercial campgrounds around town. Look for modest restaurants on Broadway Ave.

Cave of the Mounds National Natural Landmark (☎ 608-437-3038) is west of Madison on Hwy 18 at Blue Mounds (open daily, except weekends Nov 15-Mar 15). Beyond that, 40 miles from Madison and 3 miles south of Spring Green, **Taliesin** was the home of Frank Lloyd Wright for most of his life and is the site of his architectural school. It's now a major pilgrimage destination for fans and followers. The house was built in 1903, the Hillside Home School in 1932, and the Frank Lloyd Wright Visitor Center (☎ 608-588-7900), designed as a restaurant, in 1953. From May to October, a wide range of guided tours covers various parts of the complex ($10-65). The site is also open with diminished service in April and November. Call for information and reservations, which are required for the more lengthy detailed tours. The two-hour walking tour ($15; no reservation needed) is a good introduction. Aficionados should pick up the Wisconsin Wright tour pamphlet, also available at tourist offices.

Spring Green has a B&B in town and half a dozen motels strung along Rte 14, north of town. *Usonian Inn (☎ 608-588-2323)* and *Prairie House (☎ 608-588-2088)* both charge around $60 a double in summer. South of town on Rte 23, *Tower Hill State Park* (☎ 608-588-2116) offers good, basic camping ($10-14) and walking trails.

Wright was born 27 miles northwest of Spring Green in **Richland Center**. The AD German Warehouse (☎ 608-647-6205, 300 S Church St) was designed by Wright in 1915 and is the only remaining example of his work from that decade. It's notable for its geometric concrete decorations ($6; open May–Nov by appointment only).

South of Taliesin, the **House on the Rock** (☎ 608-935-3639), on Rte 23, is one of Wisconsin's busiest attractions. The strange 'house,' one man's obsession, was built atop a rock column and sprawled to become a monument of the imagination. The vast collection of objects and wonderments overwhelm. It's kitsch with class – whimsy extraordinaire for kids of all ages. The price is high at $20, but it takes three to five hours to see it all!

Along the Mississippi River

The Mississippi forms most of Wisconsin's western border, and alongside it run some of the most scenic sections of the Great River Road – the designated route that follows the river from Minnesota to the Gulf of Mexico. At numerous ports, such as Dubuque, Marquette and La Crosse, casinos housed in replica paddle wheelers offer cheap or free (if you can resist the gambling temptation) summer river cruises.

Named for the area's prevalent prairie dogs, **Prairie du Chien** was founded in 1673 as a French fur-trading post. The sumptuous Villa Louis mansion (☎ 608-326-2721, 521 N Villa Louis Rd) was built for a successful fur-trader in 1870 and houses an excellent collection of Victorian furnishings ($8.50; open daily May-Nov). For insight into the business, stop at the nearby Astor Fur Trade Museum, a walk across the parkland from the Villa (same phone number as the Villa).

The hilly riverside, once the scene of the final battle in the bloody Black Hawk War, is eye-pleasing heading north. Historic markers tell part of the story of the war, which finished at the Battle of Bad Ax when Native American men, women and children were massacred trying to flee across the Mississippi.

Upstream, **La Crosse** is a fine riverside town with a pleasant historic downtown nestling restaurants and pubs. It also has the world's largest six-pack of beer at the Heileman Brewery (111 S 3rd St); tours of the brewery are available. Grandad Bluff offers grand views of the river. It's east of town along Main St (which becomes Bliss Rd); follow Bliss Rd up the hill and then turn right on Grandad Bluff Rd. The town's visitor center (☎ 608-782-2366) is in Riverside Park. To bed down, try *Rode Star Inn (☎ 608-781-3070, 2622 Rose St)*, a deal at $40 with breakfast. For more on upriver attractions, see the Southeastern Minnesota section.

EASTERN WISCONSIN
North of Milwaukee

The 20-some **Lizard Mounds**, constructed by indigenous people between AD 500 and 1000, are now part of the Washington County Parks System (☎ 262-335-4445). Laid out in geometric and zoomorphic shapes, the mounds are about 2 miles north of West Bend, off Rte 33. In nearby Newburg, the peaceful *HI Wellspring Center (☎ 262-675-6755)* is a rustic hostel often used for retreats. It's open all year, but call ahead.

North of West Bend, **Kettle Moraine State Forest** offers good walking and cross-country skiing opportunities. Farther north, on the west side of Lake Winnebago, **Oshkosh** inspired the brand name of Oshkosh B'gosh, the cute country-look kids' clothing. The company has a shop, along with over 50 other retailers, in Prime

Outlets, south of town on US 41. Across the highway, the Experimental Aircraft Association AirVenture Museum (☎ 920-426-4810) shows its extensive collection of weird and wonderful winged things year round ($8; open daily). In late July the huge Oshkosh Air Show, featuring hundreds of historic planes and experimental aircraft, attracts some 300,000 aeronautical enthusiasts.

Green Bay

Founded in the 1660s as a fur-trading post, Green Bay boomed as a Lake Michigan port and later a terminus for Midwest railroads. Processing and packing agricultural products became a major industry and gave name to the city's legendary pro football team: the Green Bay Packers. One of the founding NFL teams, the Packers won the league's first two Super Bowls, in 1967 and 1968.

The Green Bay Area Visitor & Convention Bureau (☎ 920-494-9507, 888-867-3342, 1901 S Oneida St) is behind and beside the football stadium, just off Lombardi Ave, south of downtown. The town core is on the east side of the Fox River around Walnut St.

Green Bay is not a place most visitors linger, but it houses a few special-interest attractions. The **Green Bay Packer Hall of Fame** (☎ 920-499-4281), appropriately located on Lombardi Ave, is packed with memorabilia and has football movies and interactive exhibits ($8; open daily). Tours are given of the stadium next door. The **National Railroad Museum** (☎ 920-437-7623, 2285 S Broadway) features some of the biggest steam and diesel locomotives ever to haul freight into Green Bay's vast yards ($7; open daily). The **Oneida Nation Museum** (☎ 920-869-2768) outlines the tribe's past and present. It's 7 miles west of town; call for directions and hours.

Motel 6 (☎ 920-494-6730, 1614 Shawano Ave) is accessible and cheap at $38/44 singles/doubles.

Door County

Extending some 60 miles into Lake Michigan, the Door Peninsula narrows as it goes north and ends decorated by a string of islands off the tip. With its picturesque coastline, orchards and small 19th-century villages, Door County is often compared to New England. Despite considerable crowds in summer and increasing numbers of wealthy newcomers, development has remained essentially low-key and the atmosphere retains a certain highbrow gentility. Accommodations are expensive (and sometimes scarce) in high summer, but campgrounds are available. Spring and fall are good times to visit – the cherry and apple trees blossom in May. Ask at any tourist office about the summer theater programs.

Visitors usually make a loop up and down the peninsula on Hwys 57 and 42, stopping at some of the towns and county and state parks, and perhaps taking a ferry to the smaller islands. Many people enjoy making the rounds of the lighthouses. No public buses serve the peninsula.

The most attractive part of the loop begins at **Sturgeon Bay**, the peninsula's main town. Here the knowledgeable Chamber of Commerce (☎ 920-743-4456), on Green Bay Rd as you enter town, has bicycling maps, rental information and a free phone to county lodgings. The Door County Historical Museum (☎ 920-743-5809, 18 N 4th St) outlines all aspects of the peninsula's past, and the Maritime Museum (☎ 920-743-5958, 120 N Madison Ave) emphasizes boatbuilding and fishing.

Most activity is along the Green Bay shoreline, where you'll also find the best choice of accommodations. A regional specialty is the flaring Scandinavian 'fish boil,' which involves boiling whitefish, potatoes and onions in a cauldron. The Chamber of Commerce in Sturgeon Bay has a listing and schedule. Finish with cherry pie.

At easily found *Shipwrecked* in Egg Harbor you can wash down a good meal with the house-made brew. In Fish Creek, *Julie's Park Café and Motel* (☎ 920-869-2999) is a reasonably priced, well-run establishment offering a meal or bed. Excellent camping ($8-15) is available at *Peninsula State Park* (☎ 920-868-3258). More expensive private campgrounds include *Path of Pines* (☎ 920-868-3332), near Fish Creek, and *Camp-Tel* (☎ 920-868-3278), near Egg Harbor. When you're hungry, go to Sister Bay to choose among its varied offerings. Also, sample the smoked fish available around Gills Rock. From the tip of the peninsula, daily ferries go to **Washington Island**, which has 600 Scandinavian descendants, a couple of museums, beaches, bike rentals and carefree roads for cycling. Accommodations and camping are available. More remote is lovely **Rock Island**, a state park with no cars at all. It's a wonderful place for walking, swimming and camping.

Returning on the peninsula's quiet **east side**, secluded Newport State Park offers trails, camping and solitude. Whitefish Dunes State Park has sandscapes and a wide beach (beware of riptides). At adjacent Cave Point Park, watch the waves explode into the caves beneath the shoreline cliffs.

NORTHERN WISCONSIN

The north is a thinly populated region of forests and lakes, appreciated for camping and fishing in summer, skiing and snowmobiling in winter. Scenic Hwy 70 cuts east-west. The entire region has abundant mom-and-pop motels, resorts and rental cottages.

Northwoods & Lakelands

Nicolet National Forest is a vast, wooded district ideal for outdoor activities.

The simple crossroads of **Langlade** is a center for white-water river adventures. Bear Paw Outdoor Resort (☎ 715-882-3502) provides trips and accommodations. Tiny **Laona**, on Hwy 8 in the middle of the forest, has a *hostel (☎ 715-674-2615)* that makes a good base for exploring (canoes rented); beds cost $15.

In **Lac du Flambeau**, stop at the Ojibwe Museum & Cultural Center (☎ 715-588-3333), or, out of town on the reservation, visit Waswagoning (☎ 715-588-3560), a recreation of a traditional Ojibwe village ($7; open in summer only, closed Sun and Mon).

Lake Superior & the Apostle Islands

Wisconsin ends at the rugged, glaciated littoral of awesome Lake Superior, fringed by a sprinkling of unspoiled islands. **Ashland** has a large iron-ore loading dock and a good little museum explaining the town's transport terminal history. The substantial and quite impressively restored *Hotel Chequamegon (☎ 715-682-9095, 101 Lake Shore Drive W)* is fairly priced from $90. Cheaper motels lie along the town's north edge. See if the recently burned *Depot*, which has a restaurant and is in the historic train station, has yet reopened.

GREAT LAKES

Access to the emerald Apostle Islands is from **Bayfield**, a humming (and growing) resort town with narrow, hilly streets, Victorian-era buildings, and lake and island vistas. The Chamber of Commerce (☎ 715-779-3335) is on Manypenny Ave at Broad St. Storefront outfitters renting kayaks and bikes are easily found. *Dalrymple Park Campground (no ☎)*, just north of town on Hwy 13, has basic lakeside campsites from $12. *Kinney's Guest Rooms (☎ 715-779-3980)*, on Military Rd about eight blocks from the center, is cheap – rates start at $30. Delightful *Tree Top House (☎ 715-779-3293, 225 N 4th St)* is a B&B with rooms starting at $40. *Seagull Bay Motel (☎ 715-779-5558)*, on the corner of Hwy 13 and 7th St, charges $35/80 low/high season. By far the classiest and most expensive accommodations are at *Old Rittenhouse Inn (☎ 715-779-5111, 301 Rittenhouse Ave);* rates are $100-250.

The Big Top Chautauqua (☎ 888-244-8368) is a major regional summer event with big-name concerts and musical theater.

Before exploring the 21 islands of **Apostle Islands National Lakeshore**, drop by the visitor center (☎ 715-779-3397, 410 Washington Ave). Campers can pick up the required camping permit here (the permit is $15 no matter how long you stay). The islands have no facilities, and walking is the only way to get around. Various companies offer seasonal charter, sailing and ferry trips to and around the islands, and kayaking is very popular. Apostle Islands Cruise Service (☎ 715-779-3925), departing Bayfield's City Dock, offers a three-hour narrated trip ($25). Other trips call at islands to drop off/pick up campers *and* their kayaks, which avoids the long, possibly rough paddle.

Inhabited **Madeline Island**, a fine day trip, is also reached by ferry from Bayfield ($4; 20 minutes). Its walkable village of La Pointe has some mid-priced places to stay and varying places for a nosh. There's also a visitor center (☎ 715-747-2801) and a fur-trade museum ($4; open daily late May-Oct). Bus tours are available, and bikes and mopeds can be rented. Big Bay State Park has camping, a beach and trails.

Along Highway 13

This is a fine drive around the Lake Superior shore, past the Ojibwa community of Red Cliff and the mainland segment of the Apostle Islands National Lakeshore, which has a beach. Tiny Cornucopia, looking like a seaside village, has great sunsets. The road runs on through a timeless countryside of forest and farm reaching US 2 for the final miles into Superior.

Minnesota

It's a swell state, Minnesota.

– Judy Garland

Multifaceted Minnesota offers visitors a wealth of possibilities, from world-class wilderness canoeing to high culture in the Twin Cities of Minneapolis–St Paul. Following the Mississippi River from its source provides scenery and history. The central and northern areas boast superlative fishing and the unique Iron Range landscape. Duluth is a great stop, and the spectacular north shore parks are crossed with trails.

Note that in 'Minnesnowta' (as residents sometimes call it), the white stuff can fall into May.

Minnesota

Nicknames: North Star State, Gopher State

Population: 4,919,500 (21st)

Area: 86,943 sq miles (12th)

Admitted to Union: May 11, 1858 (32nd)

Capital city: St Paul (population 262,100)

Other cities: Minneapolis (354,600; Twin Cities metro area 2.3 million), Duluth (85,500)

State bird: common loon

State flower: pink lady's slipper

Birthplace of: actress Judy Garland (1922–69), Bob Dylan, (b 1941), Prince (b 1958), 3M Corporation

Famous for: the Greyhound bus line, whelped in Hibbing in the 1930s

Inspiration for: Garrison Keillor's engaging stories of Lake Wobegon

GREAT LAKES

History

The area was inhabited primarily by eastern Sioux bands when the first French trappers arrived in the 17th century. Starting in the early 18th century, Ojibwa bands (also called Chippewa) moved into northeast Minnesota and, armed with guns traded by the French, pushed the Sioux southwest onto the prairie.

The area east of the Mississippi became part of the US Northwest Territories in 1787, and the area west of the Mississippi was acquired from France in the 1803 Louisiana Purchase. Timber was the territory's first boom industry, and soon water-powered sawmills arose at Minneapolis, St Paul and Stillwater.

Shortly after admission to the Union, Minnesota became the first state to send volunteers to fight the Civil War, but in 1862 an uprising of the displaced Sioux meant a series of bloody battles at home.

The population boomed in the 1880s, with mass immigration (especially from Scandinavia), development of the iron mines and expansion of the railroads. Since the 1920s, depleted forests and larger farms have meant a declining rural population, but industry and urban areas have grown steadily.

Today Minnesota has a diverse economic base, including agriculture, forestry, mining, manufacturing and a strong information and services sector.

Geography

Minnesota is known as the land of 10,000 lakes (some say 15,000) for good reason. Glacial gouging created these waterways and also exposed the ore bodies of central-north Minnesota's Iron Range area. Northern Minnesota was covered with pine trees until the 19th-century timber boom, but many areas have now regrown and are managed as national forests. The western and southern portions of the state hold rich farmland on the edge of the Great Plains, but most state residents live in the undulating country that lies in Minnesota's southeast corner.

Government & Politics

Perhaps reflecting its Scandinavian heritage, Minnesota is mostly liberal and progressive, the home of noted Democrats like Eugene

McCarthy, Hubert H Humphrey and Walter Mondale.

Information

The Minnesota Office of Tourism (☎ 651-296-5029, 800-657-3700, ⓦ www.exploreminnesota .com) is at 121 E 7th Place, St Paul, MN 55101-5029. For highway information, call ☎ 800-542-0220. State sales tax is 6.5%, and a 3% lodging tax is added in major towns.

For state park information and reservations, call ☎ 800-246-2267. Note that state park entry requires a vehicle permit ($4/20 a day/year).

MINNEAPOLIS–ST PAUL

Commonly known as the Twin Cities, the sprawling Minneapolis–St Paul metropolitan area has around 2.3 million people. Known more as a congenial place to live than a compelling tourist destination, it's pure US heartland – industrious, prosperous and heavily into sports and shopping. The Twin Cities also have more theaters, dance companies and concert venues per person than anywhere outside New York. Another draw is the quality museums.

History

French trappers and fur traders were the first Europeans in the area, and Belgian missionary Louis Hennepin preached to local Native Americans in 1680. Fort d'Huillier was established in 1700 in Mankato, about an hour's drive to the southwest. Zebulon Pike explored the upper reaches of the Mississippi in 1804, a year after the USA acquired the region in the Louisiana Purchase. Fort Snelling, the most remote outpost of the USA's Northwest Territories, was built in 1820.

The first riverside flour mills appeared in the 1820s, using power from St Anthony waterfall. From the mid-19th century, Minneapolis grew as a processing center for wheat from the prairies and timber from the north. For a time the falls were the highest navigable point on the Mississippi and a natural terminus for river traffic. In the late 19th century an important railroad bridge at the falls contributed to rapid industrial growth, which was fueled by immigration. Today St Paul's German-Irish-Catholic heritage is evident, whereas Minneapolis is more Nordic.

Three-Dimensional Action Figure

Jesse Ventura, governor of Minnesota, is as hard to pin down now as he was as a WWF pro wrestler. Though often lampooned and labeled a buffoon, nobody should try to dismiss the imposing (6 feet 4 inches, 250lb), fast-talking, no-holds-barred politician.

He won the state in 1998 with a clever, street-smart campaign that consisted essentially of an 'I am not one of them' policy, referring to other politicians and their parties. His wrestling bad-boy persona and heavy-on-the-testosterone, politically incorrect style blew minds and blew across the state like a fresh Minnesota wind. He rants frankly, tossing insults and ideas and for the most part charming voters sometimes despite themselves.

Though he has no real party and seems like a one-man show, he has surrounded himself with good people and has a respected cabinet. His views vary widely, making him difficult to pigeon-hole. He is neither Republican nor Democrat. He supports gay rights and medicinal marijuana, opposes gun control and, after railing against spending, has given students and child-care programs heaps of cash. Despite supposed gaffes, his popularity remains incredibly high.

His book *I Ain't Got Time to Bleed*, complete with sex exploits, made the *New York Times* best-seller list, and he can be heard on a weekly phone-in radio show across Minnesota called 'Lunch with the Governor.'

Orientation

The Twin Cities form a metropolis on both sides of the generally hidden Mississippi River. On the west side, downtown Minneapolis – the heart of the two cities – is a modern grid of high-rise buildings, many linked by a series of enclosed overhead walkways called 'Skyways' (most welcome in winter). Downtown St Paul is 10 miles to the east on I-94. These two central areas include many attractions and are well served by local buses.

Suburbs sprawl in every direction, interspersed with lakes and parks; to explore the outlying areas you really need a car. (Beware: The locals drive very fast.) Downtown parking is costly – and scarce.

Note that in 'Minny,' the directional street designations come after the street name (eg, 7th St S). In St Paul, they come before (eg, W 5th St).

Information

The Greater Minneapolis Convention & Visitors Association (☎ 612-661-4700, 888-676-6757, Ⓦ www.minneapolis.org) is at 400 Multifoods Tower, 33 6th St S. Easier to access is the visitor center (☎ 612-335-5827) at street level in the City Center Complex, corner of Nicollet Mall and 7th St S. The St Paul Convention and Visitors Bureau (☎ 651-265-4900, 800-627-6101) is

at 175 W Kellogg Blvd, suite 502, in the RiverCentre.

General-delivery mail goes to the main post office in Minneapolis, 1st St S and Marquette Ave, by the river. The Minneapolis Public Library (☎ 612-630-6000, 300 Nicollet Mall) has Internet access.

Greater Minneapolis–St Paul has multiple telephone area codes. To call from one area code to another, dial the area code and the seven-digit telephone number, *not* preceded by 1.

Things to See & Do

Nearly every site in both cities is closed Monday.

Minneapolis Nicollet Mall is the main shopping street in the very modern downtown. The Skyways focus on Crystal Court in the eye-catching IDS Building. Other prominent downtown buildings include the Norwest Center and the Planetarium (☎ 612-630-6150), on Nicollet Mall, and the Hubert H Humphrey Metrodome, a few blocks southeast, with an air-supported rooftop.

Attractive Loring Park is a few blocks west of the south end of Nicollet Mall. From the park, a very sculptural pedestrian bridge crosses I-94 to the 1st-class **Walker Art Center** (☎ 612-375-7622), on Vineland Place.

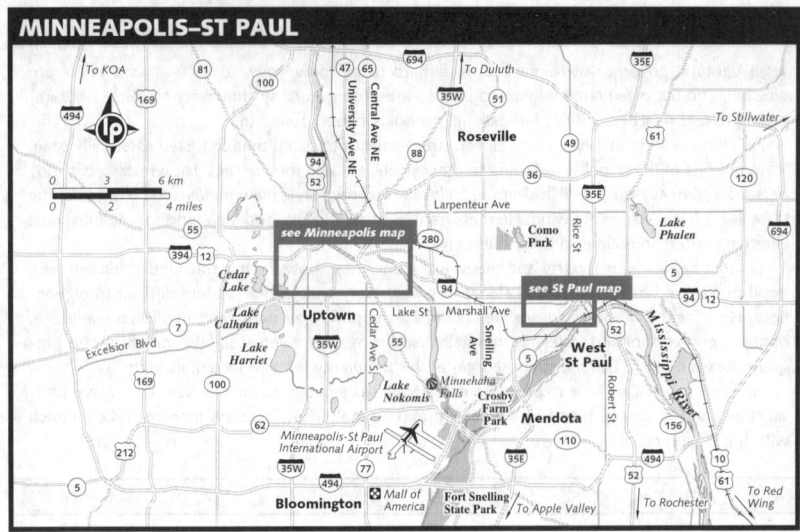

MINNEAPOLIS–ST PAUL

It has a strong permanent collection of 20th-century art and photography (including big-name US painters and some great US pop art), performance spaces and temporary exhibitions ($6, free Thurs; closed Mon). Beside the Walker is a free 7-acre sculpture garden studded with imaginative contemporary works.

To the south is **Minneapolis Institute of Arts** (☎ 612-870-3131, 2400 3rd Ave S), housing a veritable history of art, especially European (free admission; closed Mon). From here, go east on 24th St E to Park Ave. The **American Swedish Institute** (☎ 612-871-4907, 2600 Park Ave S) is a superb Romanesque mansion with artifacts and antiques from the time when Minneapolis had a bigger Swedish population than most cities in Sweden ($5; closed Mon).

On the north edge of downtown at the foot of Portland St, **Mississippi Mile** is a recommended 2-mile recreation trail that provides both interesting history and the city's best access to both banks of Old Man River. St Anthony Falls was the power source for the area's early mills and was later fitted with locks so river traffic could continue upstream. The car-free Stone Arch Bridge gives a good view of this much-modified watercourse. On the north side of the river, Main St SE has a stretch of re-developed buildings housing restaurants and bars. Don't miss the aptly named **Museum of Questionable Medical Devices** (☎ 612-379-4046, 201 Main St SE), displaying stacks of wacky quackery (free admission; closed Mon). And don't be too smug – some of this stuff is from the 1980s and '90s! Nearby on Prince St, behind Main St's Riverplace building, Our Lady of Lourdes church is the oldest in town and is still used by the French Catholic community – *tortieres* (meat pies) are available daily.

Downstream, the University of Minnesota, by the river, is one of the USA's largest campuses, with over 50,000 students. Most of the campus is in the **East Bank** neighborhood. A highlight is the Weisman Art Museum (☎ 612-625-9494, 333 E River Rd), occupying an angular, irregular, stainless-steel structure by architect Frank Gehry. Works inside include early 20th-century American painting (free admission; closed Mon and holidays). Also on campus, the Bell Museum of Natural History (☎ 612-624-7083) displays dioramas of Minnesota's wildlife ($3, closed Mon). Around the intersection of Washington Ave SE and Oak St SE is **Stadium Village**, a growing and very active commercial area with coffee shops and restaurants.

Dinkytown, a nearby area dense with student cafes as well as a few bookshops and cheap places to eat, is based at 14th Ave

SE and 4th St SE. A small part of the university is on the west side of the river amid the **West Bank** theater district, at the intersection of 4th St S and Riverside Ave. This generally unimpressive area has a few restaurants, student hangouts and a burgeoning Somali community.

Uptown, a busy area of shops and restaurants south of downtown Minneapolis, based around the intersection of Hennepin Ave S and Lake St, stays lively late.

Within a mile or two of downtown, a ring of lakes circles the inner-city area. Cedar Lake, Lake of the Isles, Lake Calhoun and Lake Harriet are surrounded by parks and comfortable suburbs. Cycling paths (cross-country ski trails in winter) meander around the lakes, where you can go boating in summer or ice-skating in winter – **Wirth Park**, just west of downtown, has the full gamut. Thomas Beach, on Lake Calhoun, is popular for swimming. Also visit **Minnehaha Park**, south of downtown, to see the falls made famous by Longfellow's epic poem *Hiawatha*, though Longfellow never actually visited. Call the Parks Board (☎ 612-661-4875) for recreation information.

St Paul Smaller and quieter than Minneapolis, St Paul has retained more of its historic character, although construction continues to modernize it. The turreted 1902 Landmark Center, facing Rice Park, is a former federal court building that now houses the **Minnesota Museum of American Art** (☎ 651-292-4355, 75 W 5th St). The museum features works from the 19th and 20th centuries, good changing exhibits and the Schubert Club Museum, which holds a vast collection of keyboard instruments (admission to both museums is free; closed Mon).

The **City Hall & Courthouse** is the 20-story art-deco-ish building at Wabasha St and W 4th St. The 30-foot sculpture out front claims a qualified superlative as the world's largest carved onyx figure. Nearby, the huge new **Science Museum of Minnesota** (☎ 651-221-9444, 120 W Kellogg Blvd) has some very good hands-on exhibits, a Mississippi display, a laser show and the usual Omnimax theater. Exhibits-only tickets are $7/5 adults/children; combination tickets are offered. Kids also like the interactive **Children's Museum** (☎ 651-225-6000), at Wabasha and W 7th Sts ($6/4).

On a hill northwest of downtown, the Cass Gilbert–designed **State Capitol** (free tours) has golden horses on its giant dome. From here, you can walk southwest across parkland to the **Minnesota History Center** (☎ 651-296-6126), which caters to serious researchers but has very good public exhibits on native peoples and state history (free admission; open daily in summer, closed Mon Sept-May).

Nearby, also on a hilltop, the dominating Cathedral of St Paul marks the very attractive **Summit-Selby neighborhood**. This wealthy 19th-century district, now ethnically mixed, is well worth a stroll. Follow Summit Ave, which has a fine string of Victorian houses, including the palatial James J Hill House (☎ 651-297-2555, 240 Summit), a railroad magnate's mansion open for tours ($6; Wed-Sat; call first). Writer F Scott Fitzgerald once lived at 599 Summit, and authors Garrison Keillor and Sinclair Lewis have also called the area home. Restaurants and shops are found along amenable Selby and Grand Aves. The architecturally interesting Lowertown area around Mears Park has some of the city's oldest buildings. Many of them have been converted to galleries and offices.

Revitalized Harriet Island, although still not an island, includes a park, river walk and boat tours. It runs off Wabasha St S.

Southern Suburbs In the southern suburb of Bloomington, the **Mall of America** (☎ 952-883-8800) is the USA's largest shopping center, with theaters, restaurants, bars, Knott's Camp Snoopy amusement park, the Underwater World aquarium and over 400 shops, all under one enormous roof. The mall, open daily, is off I-494 at 24th Ave and is well served by local buses.

Just east of the mall, **Fort Snelling** (☎ 612-726-1171), at the confluence of the Mississippi and Minnesota Rivers, is the state's oldest structure, established in the early 19th century as a frontier outpost in the remote Northwest Territories. Guides in period dress show restored buildings and displays of pioneer life ($6; open Wed-Sun May-Oct).

The respected **Minnesota Zoo** (☎ 952-431-9500), in suburban Apple Valley, 20 miles south of town, has naturalistic habitats for its 400-plus species, with an emphasis on

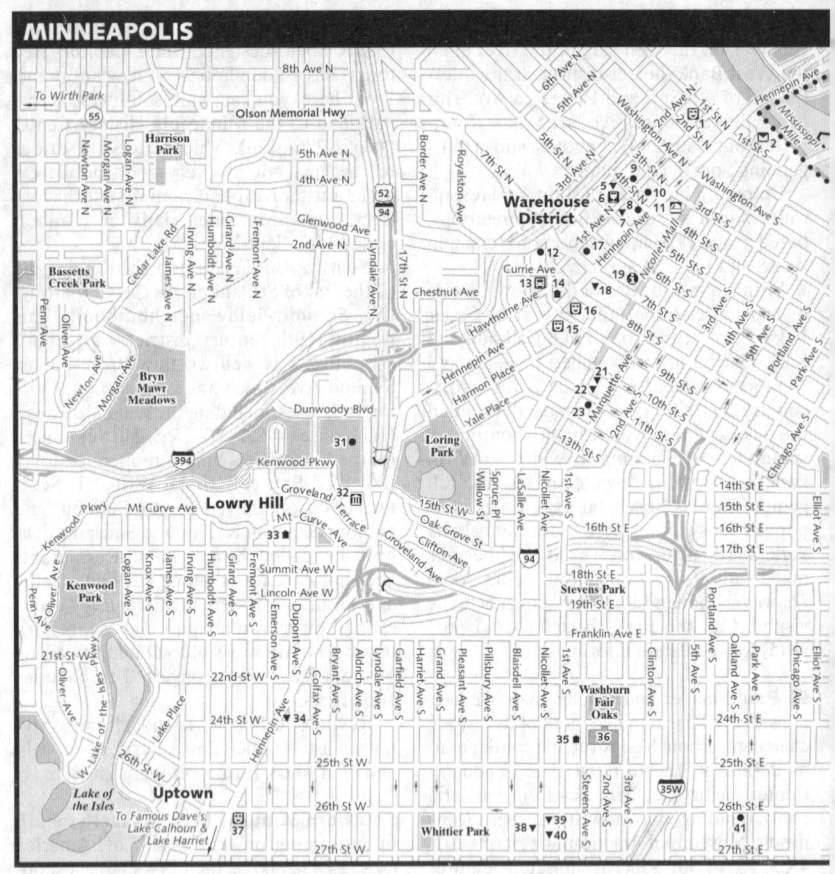

MINNEAPOLIS

cold-climate creatures. It's open daily year round ($10).

Places to Stay

The closest campground is *Northwest KOA* (☎ 763-420-2255), 15 miles northwest at I-94 exit 213, with tent sites ($24), hookups ($27) and cabins ($38).

Minneapolis The *City of Lakes International House* (☎ 612-871-3210, 2400 Stevens Ave S), off 24th St W, south of downtown Minneapolis beside the Institute of Arts, is a friendly backpackers' hostel with dorm beds ($20) and some private rooms ($28). Reservations are recommended. *Kaz's Home Hostel* (☎ 612-822-8286) is in a residential area 5 miles

south of Minneapolis on a bus route. Call for reservations and directions. The two beds are just $10 each, and guests have kitchen privileges.

The busy *Hotel Amsterdam* (☎ 612-288-0459, 830 Hennepin Ave) is a small, European-style gay-friendly downtown hotel (singles/doubles $33/44 and up).

The university area is good for moderately priced lodgings. *Econo Lodge* (☎ 612-331-6000, 2500 University Ave SE) is more than decent at $75 for doubles in summer. It has a pool and coffee shop. Nearby, the *Days Inn* (☎ 612-623-3999, 2407 University Ave SE) includes breakfast in its rates of $80/90.

1900 Dupont (☎ 612-374-1973, 1900 Dupont) is a B&B in an old, well-to-do

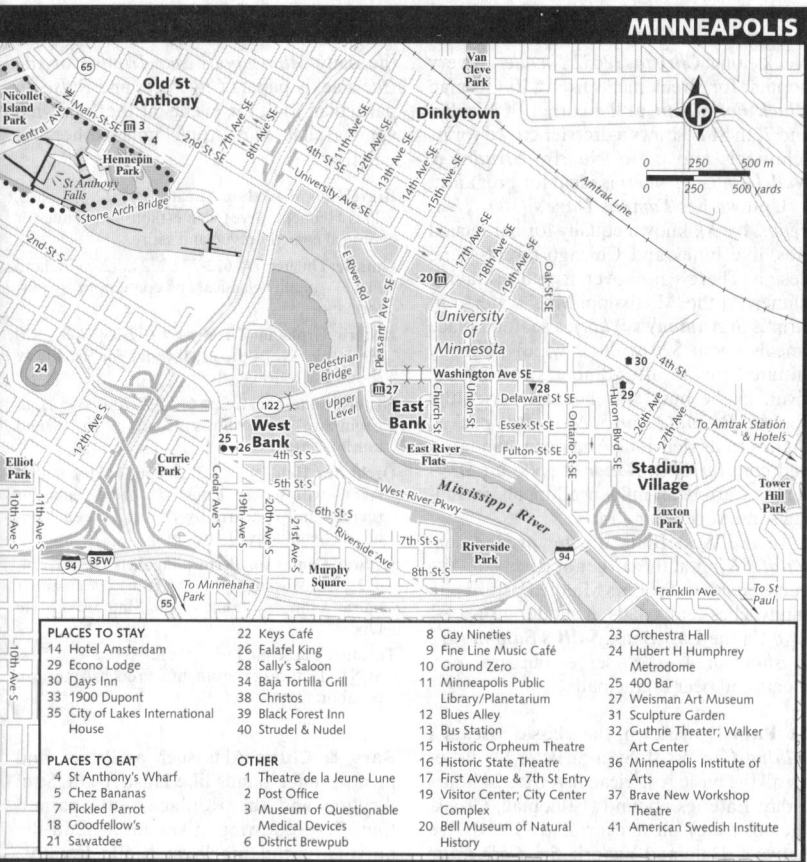

MINNEAPOLIS

PLACES TO STAY	22 Keys Café	8 Gay Nineties	23 Orchestra Hall
14 Hotel Amsterdam	26 Falafel King	9 Fine Line Music Café	24 Hubert H Humphrey
29 Econo Lodge	28 Sally's Saloon	10 Ground Zero	Metrodome
30 Days Inn	34 Baja Tortilla Grill	11 Minneapolis Public	25 400 Bar
33 1900 Dupont	38 Christos	Library/Planetarium	27 Weisman Art Museum
35 City of Lakes International	39 Black Forest Inn	12 Blues Alley	31 Sculpture Garden
House	40 Strudel & Nudel	13 Bus Station	32 Guthrie Theater; Walker
		15 Historic Orpheum Theatre	Art Center
PLACES TO EAT	OTHER	16 Historic State Theatre	36 Minneapolis Institute of
4 St Anthony's Wharf	1 Theatre de la Jeune Lune	17 First Avenue & 7th St Entry	Arts
5 Chez Bananas	2 Post Office	19 Visitor Center; City Center	37 Brave New Workshop
7 Pickled Parrot	3 Museum of Questionable	Complex	Theatre
18 Goodfellow's	Medical Devices	20 Bell Museum of Natural	41 American Swedish Institute
21 Sawatdee	6 District Brewpub	History	

neighborhood that's walkable from downtown ($120-150 double).

Lots of motels lie south of town, around I-494 near the airport. **Super 8 Motel** (☎ *952-888-8800, 7800 2nd Ave S*) costs $70/80. Farther south, 40 minutes from downtown, is **Motel 6** (☎ *952-469-1900*), off I-35 at Rte 70 ($44/50).

St Paul The brand new **Holiday Inn** (☎ *651-225-1515, 174 W 7th St*) has a great location adjacent to the RiverCentre. Rates are $99-129.

North of the center, the **Best Western Kelly Inn** (☎ *651-227-8711, 161 St Anthony Ave*) has rooms from $100. The **St Paul Hotel** (☎ *651-292-9292, 350 Market St*) is a classy five-star business hotel.

Victorian **Chatsworth B&B** (☎ *651-227-4288, 984 Ashland Ave*), in the Summit area, charges $70-130 including full breakfast.

Places to Eat

Minneapolis Nicollet Mall caters to thousands of shoppers and workers. Bustling **Keys Café** (*1007 Nicollet Mall*) serves breakfasts and sandwiches ($4-8) all day. Next door is **Sawatdee**, a local fave for Thai meals from $10. Also central, art deco **Goodfellow's** (☎ *612-332-1274, 40 7th St S*) is one of the best restaurants in the Midwest. It features expensive American regional specialties.

Baja Tortilla Grill, on Hennepin Ave S at 24th St W, serves an amazing vegetable burrito ($5) and a range of Mexican dishes.

Nicollet Ave S is a gold mine for the hungry, offering an international buffet blocks long. *Christos (2632 Nicollet)* is very popular for Greek meals from $10. German *Black Forest Inn*, at the corner of Nicollet and 26th St E, draws a dressier crowd for its schnitzels and patio. Nearby, *Strudel & Nudel (2605 Nicollet)* is ideal for breakfast.

Uptown has *Famous Dave's (3001 Hennepin Ave S)*, known equally for barbecued ribs, live blues and Chicago street-scene design. There's no cover if you're having dinner. At the 'Mississippi Mile' waterfront strip is *St Anthony's Wharf*, a seafood place (meals about $20 without wine) perfectly situated for an after-dinner stroll by the river. In the busy Warehouse District, the *Pickled Parrot (26 5th St N)* is often packed thanks to its delicious American standards, and colorful *Chez Bananas (119 4th St N)* serves Caribbean-influenced meals, including some vegetarian fare.

In the West Bank theater area, casual *Falafel King*, at the corner of Riverside Ave and Cedar Ave S, offers Middle Eastern pita sandwiches and salads at moderate prices. Over in the East Bank, *Sally's Saloon (712 Washington Ave SE)* serves burgers, spicy meats and beer on the patio.

St Paul Downtown, the classic *Mickey's Dining Car*, W 7th St at St Peter St, dishes up all the basic American favorites 24 hours a day. Eateries abound (Ethiopian, Greek, Mexican etc) on and around Grand Ave between Dale and Victoria Sts. *Café Latte (850 Grand Ave)* is popular for soups, sandwiches, pastries and coffees. The unpretentious *Tavern on Grand (656 Grand Ave)* is famous for its good-value walleye meals (lunch $10, dinner $15).

Expensive *St Paul Grill (☎ 651-224-7455, 350 Market St)*, in the St Paul Hotel, features great views and steaks, and the gracious setting is perfect for a cocktail, too.

Entertainment

With 100,000 students and a sizable gay community as well as excellent performing arts, the Twin Cities offer an active nightlife.

Performing Arts The Twin Cities are applauded for their range of performing arts companies, including dozens of fine theater troupes, dance companies and classical music groups. Ticketmaster (☎ 612-989-5151) books most events. For listings, see the daily *Minneapolis Star Tribune* or the free weekly papers *City Pages* and *Pulse*. In particular, look for events at the following venues (all in 'Mini-Apple' unless otherwise noted):

Brave New Workshop Theatre (☎ 612-332-6620, 2605 Hennepin Ave) – an established venue for musical comedy, revue and satire

Guthrie Theater (☎ 612-377-2224, 725 Vineland Place) – quality classical and contemporary performances

Historic Orpheum Theatre (☎ 612-339-7007, 910 Hennepin Ave) – the usual venue for Broadway shows and touring acts

Historic State Theatre (☎ 612-339-7007, 805 Hennepin Ave) – also hosts Broadway shows and touring acts

Orchestra Hall (☎ 612-371-5656, 1111 Nicollet Ave) – with superb acoustics, a great venue for recitals and concerts by the acclaimed Minnesota Symphony Orchestra

Ordway Center for Performing Arts (☎ 651-224-4222, 345 Washington St, St Paul) – a chamber music venue and home of the Minnesota State Opera

Theatre de la Jeune Lune (☎ 612-333-6200, 105 1st St N) – features experimental French-American collaborations

Bars & Clubs Acts such as Prince and proto-grunge bands like Hüsker Dü, Soul Asylum and the Replacements gained their first following in venues around the university and the West Bank. For live rock, funk and alternative, check out *400 Bar (☎ 612-332-2903)*, on 4th St S at Cedar Ave.

The Warehouse District in Minneapolis, with many drinking and dancing spots, is jammed weekend nights. *First Avenue & 7th St Entry (☎ 612-338-8388, 701 1st Ave N)* once featured the Purple Rain band and still get top bands and big crowds. *Fine Line Music Café (☎ 612-338-8100, 318 1st Ave N)* is a small venue featuring local pop, rock and alternative music. *District Brewpub*, on 1st Ave N near 5th St N, is popular. *Gay Nineties (☎ 612-333-7755, 408 Hennepin Ave)* has dancing, dining, drag shows and both gay and straight clientele. There's good blues at *Blues Alley (☎ 612-333-1327, 15 Glenwood Ave)*. Long-standing *Ground Zero (☎ 612-378-5115, 15 4th St N)* gets a

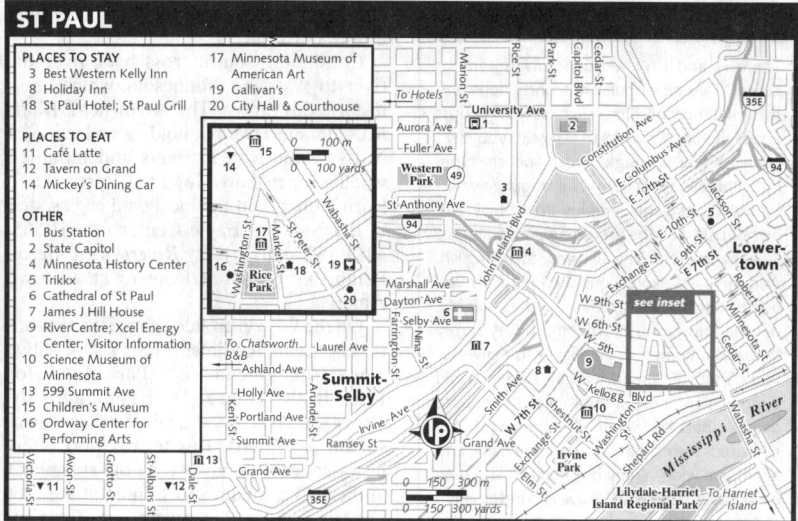

ST PAUL

PLACES TO STAY
3 Best Western Kelly Inn
8 Holiday Inn
18 St Paul Hotel; St Paul Grill

PLACES TO EAT
11 Café Latte
12 Tavern on Grand
14 Mickey's Dining Car

OTHER
1 Bus Station
2 State Capitol
4 Minnesota History Center
5 Trikkx
6 Cathedral of St Paul
7 James J Hill House
9 RiverCentre; Xcel Energy Center; Visitor Information
10 Science Museum of Minnesota
13 599 Summit Ave
15 Children's Museum
16 Ordway Center for Performing Arts
17 Minnesota Museum of American Art
19 Gallivan's
20 City Hall & Courthouse

mixed gay and straight dance crowd for recorded music.

Over in St Paul, downtown *Gallivan's* (☎ 651-227-6688, 354 Wabasha St) is a friendly, popular piano pub, while *Trikkx* (☎ 651-224-0703, 490 N Robert St) is a gay hot spot. Local musicians like the *Minnesota Music Café* (☎ 651-776-4699, 499 Payne Ave) for music and dancing. *Dakota Bar & Grill* (☎ 651-642-1442, 1021 E Bandana Blvd), on Bandana Square, is a well-established jazz and dinner club on the outskirts of St Paul that regularly gets name acts.

South of town, the top floor at *Mall of America* has assorted bars.

Spectator Sports
The Hubert H Humphrey Metrodome, in sports-mad Minneapolis, is home to the Vikings pro football team (☎ 612-333-8828) and the Twins major-league baseball team (☎ 612-375-7450). Both teams are whining about the stadium, threatening to leave town and seeking their own parks – at someone else's expense.

The Timberwolves pro basketball team plays at Target Center (☎ 612-337-3865, 600 1st Ave N). NHL hockey has returned with the Wild (☎ 651-222-9453) skating in the new Xcel Energy Center sport and entertainment venue adjacent to RiverCentre in downtown St Paul. Football and hockey are usually sold out, but scalpers offer tickets (illegally).

Getting There & Away
Minneapolis–St Paul International Airport is a major regional hub and home of Northwest Airlines, which operates several direct flights to/from various European cities.

Greyhound has stations at the corner of Hawthorne Ave and 9th St N in Minneapolis (☎ 612-371-3323) and at 166 W University Ave in St Paul (☎ 651-222-0509). There are frequent buses to Milwaukee ($38; 6 hours) and Chicago ($50; 8 hours).

The Amtrak station (☎ 612-644-1127, 730 Transfer Rd), off University Ave SE, is between the Twin Cities. Trains go east and west daily.

Getting Around
Airport Express Shuttles (☎ 612-827-7777) link the airport with downtown Minneapolis ($13) and St Paul ($11).

Metropolitan Council Transit Operations (MCTO; ☎ 612-373-3333) runs local buses throughout the metropolitan area ($1.50). Express bus No 94 connects the Twin Cities. Both cities' downtowns have limited trolley systems.

Auto-Delivery (☎ 612-323-3311) is a drive-away company based in Anoka, a northern suburb.

Talking Minnesotan

There is and isn't a Minnesota accent or dialect. Despite popular misconceptions and the influence of films such as *Fargo* (just across the border in North Dakota), you can't really define a single local speech type. But…there is a sort of in-joke language variation that residents employ for effect and humor based on the preceding generations of Swedes and Norwegians and *their* English. And there are expressions used regularly you don't hear much elsewhere such as alrighty, doncha know, you betcha and hokey dokey that add a homey, casual flavor to conversation. 'That's different' is often said to avoid disagreement, hurt or insult over an opposite opinion. Best known of all is the wonderful, all-purpose 'uff da,' a Scandinavian term heard in a wide variety of situations and seen on bumper stickers. It conveys consternation and disgruntlement…but politely, sort of like oops or oy vey. Start employing it and you'll soon find all sorts of funny applications.

SOUTHEASTERN MINNESOTA

Some of the scenic southeast can be seen on short drives from the Twin Cities. Better is a loop of a few days' duration, following the rivers and stopping in some of the historic towns and state parks.

A few miles east of St Paul, the **St Croix River** forms the border with Wisconsin. Northeast of the city along US 61, then east on US 8, attractive Taylors Falls marks the upper limit of navigation. Take a walk along the gorge in Interstate Park. Due east of St Paul, on Rte 36, touristy Stillwater, on the lower St Croix, is an old logging town with restored 19th-century buildings and river cruises. Larger Red Wing to the south on US 61, is a similar but less interesting restored town.

The best part of the **Mississippi Valley** area begins south of here, but on the Wisconsin side – cross the river on US 63. Maiden Rock, on Wisconsin Rte 35 downstream from Red Wing, offers views from its 400-foot Indian-legend namesake. A bit farther south, a great stretch of Rte 35 edges beside the bluffs around Stockholm (population 90); the village has a few craft outlets

and camping. To the south, Pepin has a busy little waterfront.

Continuing south, cross back over the river to Wabasha, Minnesota, which has a historic downtown. The Arrowhead Bluffs Museum, on Hwy 60, holds a collection of Native American artifacts and mounted wildlife (open daily May 1 to Christmas). To learn more about the local bald eagles, stop at the National Eagle Center (☎ 651-565-4989, 152 Main St). Try *Rivertown Café*, on Pembroke St, for a taste of small-town America.

On the Wisconsin side again, Rte 35 south is very scenic to **Alma**, offering superlative views from Buena Vista Park. Look for Rock in the House (!) at Fountain City. Cross the river once again farther downstream at **Winona**. This former port offers historical exhibits aboard an old steamboat at the Wilkie Steamboat Center, at the foot of Main St, as well as river cruises from adjacent Levee Park. Landlubbers can enjoy river views from Garvin Heights Park.

Inland and south, the Bluff Country is dotted with limestone bluffs, the southeast corner's main geological feature. **Lansboro** is a gem and acts as an activity center. Cycling and canoeing are popular. Seven miles westward on County Rd 8 (call for directions), *Old Barn Resort* (☎ 507-467-2512) is a pastoral hostel/campground/restaurant/outfitter. **Harmony**, the center of an Amish community, is another welcoming town. Unique *Slim's Woodshed* (☎ 507-886-3114, 160 1st St NW) has rooms at $35/45 singles/doubles. Nearby Forestville State Park has one of the area's caves to visit, and there is good walking in the stream valleys.

Head north on US 52 to **Rochester**, home of the famed Mayo Clinic, which attracts medical patients and practitioners from around the USA and the world. Free morning tours and a film outline the Mayo brothers' story and describe how the clinic developed its cutting-edge reputation. The extensive art collection, found throughout the complex, ranges from pre-Columbian pottery to Miró and Warhol paintings.

Tiny, tourist-oriented Mantorville, several miles west of Rochester, was once a stagecoach stop and retains several 1850s-era buildings and its old Opera House. Toward Minneapolis, **Northfield**, a pleasant college town with a well-restored late-19th-century downtown, makes a good lunch stop. The Jesse James gang was foiled in a bank robbery here in 1876.

NORTHEASTERN MINNESOTA
Duluth

At the westernmost end of the Great Lakes, Duluth (with its neighbor, Superior, Wisconsin) is one of the busiest ports in the country, sporting over 40 miles of wharf and waterfront. Daniel Du Lhut brokered a peace agreement here in 1679 with the Ojibwa and Sioux nations, which enabled French adventurers to develop the fur trade. Duluth grew as a shipping point for timber and, later, for Minnesota's iron ore. It now handles huge quantities of grain as well.

Duluth's heavy industries have downsized, and numerous former factories and freight depots now house restaurants and entertainment venues. The combination of gritty industrial history, dramatic lakeside location, working port and revitalized city center makes this a surprisingly absorbing place to linger.

The Endion Station Convention & Visitors Bureau (☎ 218-722-4011, 100 Lake Place Dr), near the clock tower, is open weekdays year round. The Summer Visitors Center (☎ 218-722-6024, 350 Harbor Dr), open daily, is in the Duluth Entertainment Convention Center (DECC) opposite the Vista dock.

Things to See & Do In addition to its distinctive atmosphere and lakeside views, Duluth has numerous attractions. Take in the waterfront area along the Lakewalk trail and the Canal Park/Lake St District. Look for the Aerial Lift Bridge, which rises to let ships through to the port area. The first-rate **Maritime Visitors Center** (☎ 218-727-2497) has a good view of the bridge and exhibits on Great Lakes shipping (free admission; open daily in summer, closed Mon spring and fall, open Fri-Sun Dec-May). Check the center's freighter schedule or call the boat-watchers' hotline (☎ 218-722-6489) to learn when the big ones come and go; 1000 ships a year pass here.

To continue the nautical theme, walk the *William A Irvin* (☎ 218-722-7876, 350 Harbor Dr), a 610-foot Great Lakes freighter. The interesting hourlong tour ($6.50) includes a look aboard a tug as well. The tug alone is $3.

Farther west along the shore, the impressive **Great Lakes Aquarium** (☎ 218-740-3474) is actually an all-encompassing testament to Lake Superior ($11; open daily, but call to confirm in winter). If you're grumpy, go look at the otters. Next door is new Bayfront Festival Park, used for concerts.

Back toward the city, in the fine old train station, is **The Depot** (☎ 218-727-8025, 506 Michigan St). It houses three museums: one for children, one on history and, perhaps of most interest, the Railroad Museum, which holds a good collection of old locomotives. Admission for all three is $8. The Art Institute and performance venues are also here.

Other sights include **Stora Enso Paper Mills** (☎ 218-726-8910), which offers free tours, and **Glensheen** (☎ 218-724-8863, 3300 London Rd), a grand 39-room Jacobean mansion on the National Historic register ($10). Lastly, follow Lake Ave south across the Aerial Lift Bridge to Minnesota Point – there are 5 miles of public beach on the north side, stretching all the way to Park Point Recreation Area.

Local tour excursions include a lakeside rail trip departing The Depot (☎ 218-722-1273) and lake cruises from Vista Fleet (☎ 218-722-6218). For a spectacular view (when it's not foggy!) of the city and harbor get to First United Methodist Church, at the corner of Skyline and Mesaba Aves.

Places to Stay This is a busy place in summer, and lodgings are often full (if so, try Superior). Camping at *Spirit Mountain* (☎ 218-628-2891), a ski area 10 miles south at I-35 exit 244, costs $18-25. It's geared to RVs, but there are a few tent sites; the best are the walk-ins. *Jay Cooke State Park* (☎ 218-384-4610), 20 miles south off I-35 exit 242, is a lovely forested area where campsites cost $12-15.

The small, year-round home hostel, *Hillside Hostel International* (☎ 218-726-0610, 1223 W 4th St) has room for just a few people. Call Greg, the congenial owner, to check on availability before walking up the hill. *College of St Scholastica* (☎ 218-723-6000, 1200 Kenwood Ave) has college dorm rooms in summer ($30) and two guest rooms all year at $55 singles or doubles.

GREAT LAKES

Right downtown with rooftop views, *Voyageur Lakewalk Inn* (☎ *218-722-3911, 333 E Superior St)* is a real find with rooms starting at $45 (more on weekends). London Rd, east of downtown, has a couple of inexpensive motels. More interesting and plush is *Fitgers Inn* (☎ *218-722-8826, 600 E Superior St)*, which occupies a former brewery. Rooms start at $100 (costlier for the lakeside).

Places to Eat & Drink The Canal Park waterfront area has eateries of all price ranges in restored commercial spaces. *Grandma's Saloon & Deli* offers filling down-home favorites, while *Taste of Saigon*, in the DeWitt-Seitz Marketplace, creates inexpensive Vietnamese meals, including vegetarian dishes. In the same complex, *Amazing Grace* is a comfortable cafe with excellent sandwiches, and folk music at night. Downtown, *Jitters (102 W Superior St)* serves up bagels and coffees. *Fitgers Brewhouse & Grill (600 E Superior St)* makes its own beer and has the usual pub fare.

Getting There & Away From the Greyhound station (☎ 218-722-5591, 4426 Grand Ave), several buses head over to Minneapolis–St Paul ($21; 3 hours) and Milwaukee ($74; 11 hours).

North Shore

Heading northeast, Hwy 61 (a continuation of Skyline Dr) is a wonderfully scenic strip of pavement along Lake Superior's shore. On its way to the Canadian border, the route passes numerous spectacular state parks, hiking trails (notably the long-distance Superior Hiking Trail) and low-key towns. Lots of weekend and summer traffic makes reservations essential.

Two Harbors has a museum and lighthouse. Just beyond town is the Houle Information Center (☎ 218-834-4005).

Route highlights are Spit Rock Lighthouse and Palisade Head. About 110 miles from Duluth, agreeable little **Grand Marais** is a good base for exploring Superior National Forest, Boundary Waters Canoe Area Wilderness (BWCAW) and the rest of the region. For information on Boundary Waters, visit the Gunflint Ranger Station (☎ 218-387-1750), just south of town. Outfitters rent equipment and organize trips. The Grand Marais visitor center (☎ 218-387-2524) is at 13 N Broadway St.

Lodging options include camping, motels and the friendly, rambling and

---

Bob Dylan's Boyhood

Robert Zimmerman was born in Duluth in 1941, but his family moved to Hibbing, in the Iron Range area, when he was seven. It was an area known more for its narrow-mindedness than for its folkloric or musical traditions, and Bob never fit in. He spent much time in the music shop, and at night tuned to black radio stations from Chicago and Little Rock that nobody listened to in Hibbing. His first group, the Golden Chords, wowed the kids in a local talent quest, but the Chamber of Commerce judges gave them second prize.

He was soon making frequent trips to more cosmopolitan Minneapolis, where he hung around the student area, going to jazz joints and coffeehouses and meeting musicians. In 1959 he started college in Minneapolis, but dropped out within a year. He adopted the name Bob Dylan and told many fanciful stories about himself, typically that he was an orphan from Oklahoma, that he'd been on the road for years, and that he knew Woody Guthrie and other folk musicians. These stories were none too credible, but they were Dylan's way of disowning his mundane, middle-class origins and creating a worldly image.

Dylan hit New York's Greenwich Village folk scene in early 1961 and never looked back, though a few songs do mention 'the North Country.' His 1965 album *Highway 61 Revisited* makes obscure references to northern Minnesota's most scenic road, though it doesn't suggest happy childhood memories. God tells Abraham to kill his son, out on Hwy 61; and a promoter suggests that the next world war could be easily done: 'We'll just put some bleachers out in the sun and have it on Highway 61.'

resorty *East Bay Hotel* (☎ 800-414-2807), with rooms from $26 to way up. Doors away are good eating choices such as the *Gunflint Tavern*.

Hwy 61 continues to **Grand Portage National Monument**, beside Canada, where the early voyageurs had to carry their canoes around the Pigeon River rapids. This was the center of a far-flung trading empire, and the reconstructed 1788 trading post is well worth seeing. May to October, daily ferries (☎ 715-392-2100) run to Isle Royale National Park in Lake Superior (see the Michigan section).

Boundary Waters
From Two Harbors, the Gunflint Trail runs inland through wilderness (watch for moose and bears), with lodges and outfitters providing access to the legendary Boundary Waters. At the north end of the trail, *HI Spirit of the Land Hostel* (☎ 218-388-2241), on an island in Sea Gull Lake, rents canoes. Call from Grand Marais before arriving.

Many argue the best BWCAW access is via the engaging town of **Ely**, northeast of the Iron Range area, which has accommodations, restaurants and scores of outfitters. The Chamber of Commerce (☎ 218-365-6123, 800-777-7281), on Sheridan St, has general information and accommodations assistance. Don't miss the International Wolf Center (☎ 218-365-4695), which offers intriguing exhibits and wolf-viewing trips. Also in the Wolf Center is Kawishiwi Wilderness Station (☎ 218-365-7600), which offers camping and canoeing details, trip suggestions, advice on 'no-trace' environmental camping and required permits. Camping is free in forest areas, except at established campgrounds.

NORTH-CENTRAL MINNESOTA
Wooded and lake-filled, this area is synonymous with outdoor activities and summer fun. Campsites and cottages abound, and almost everybody is fishing-crazy. The lakeland begins at large, circular Mille Lacs Lake, where an Indian museum outlines local Ojibwa culture.

Nearby *Kathio State Park* (☎ 320-532-3523) is excellent, offering camping, cabins, hiking trails, canoe rentals and small lakes to explore.

Chippewa National Forest Area
The original pine forests were almost eliminated by logging in the late 19th and early 20th centuries, but natural regrowth and commercial replanting now cover a third of the state. The 1036-sq-mile Chippewa National Forest is a mixed-use area with managed forests, water catchments, Indian reservations and recreational opportunities.

Attractive **Walker**, with a beach, makes a good break – drop in at the Walker Drug Store on Main St and get a wooden postcard. For information on hiking, canoeing and camping, check in at the Chippewa National Forest office either here (☎ 218-547-1044), at the south end of Main St, or in the town of Cass Lake, to the north.

Northwest of Walker, **Itasca State Park** (☎ 218-266-2100) is an area highlight. You can walk across the official headwaters of the mighty Mississippi, rent canoes or bikes, and hike trails. Other features include a stand of virgin pine forest, a good interpretive center and Native American sites. Camping is available (☎ 800-246-2267), or stay at the log *HI Mississippi Headwaters Hostel* (☎ 218-266-3415), which has dorm beds ($14/16 for members/nonmembers) and family rooms. Or if you want a little rustic luxury, try the venerable *Douglas Lodge* (☎ 800-246-2267), run by the park, which offers accommodations from $52 for doubles. The lodge has various cabins and two good dining rooms.

On the western edge of the forest, neat and tidy **Bemidji** is an old lumber town with a well-preserved downtown and a giant statue of legendary logger Paul Bunyan and his faithful blue ox, Babe. The visitor center (☎ 218-751-3541) display includes Paul's toothbrush. Morrell's Trading Post, across the street, has some genuine Native American crafts. There are campgrounds nearby. Among modest motels south of town, simple *Midway Motel* (☎ 218-751-1180, 1000 Paul Bunyan Drive NE) charges $45 in summer. *Cyber Bugs Paradise Café (311 3rd St NW)* has fine light lunches, coffees and computers.

The Greyhound bus stops at the south end of town behind the Midway Motel. North of Bemidji, the population thins, the land flattens and the vegetation becomes less lush.

On the east side of the forest, **Grand Rapids** is another old lumber town, with the

GREAT LAKES

enormous Blandin paper mill and some defunct open-pit mines nearby. A few attractions make it OK for a brief visit. The Chamber of Commerce (☎ 218-326-6619, 1 NW 3rd St), in the old railroad depot, has 24-hour accommodations information. Judy Garland was born here in 1922, and the Itasca Heritage Center (☎ 218-326-6431) has a collection of artifacts, including her ruby slippers and photos tracing her life. Also see the Judy Garland Birthplace Historic House and Museum, just south of town on Hwy 169, which has more fun Wizard of Oz memorabilia. Three miles southwest of town, the Forest History Center (☎ 218-327-4482) is a reconstructed logging camp, complete with lumberjacks ($5). Hwy 2 west of town has inexpensive local motels. For a much, don't miss central *Pasties Plus (22 NW 4th St),* where you can write your name on the wall.

Iron Range District

An area of red-tinged scrubby hills rather than mountains, Minnesota's Iron Range District consists of the Mesabi and Vermilion Ranges, running north and south of US 169 from roughly Grand Rapids northeast to Ely. Iron was discovered here in the 1850s, and at one time 70% of the nation's iron ore was extracted from these vast open-pit mines. When the high-quality ore was almost exhausted, the region developed techniques to use low-grade ore and taconite. The fascinating history is supplemented by the terrain's sparse, raw beauty. Visitors can see working mines and numerous related sites all along US 169. In Calumet, Hill Annex Mine State Park (☎ 218-247-7215) is a perfect introduction. It has an exhibit center (free) and offers an open-pit tour ($6). There's an even bigger pit in Hibbing, where a must-see viewpoint (☎ 218-262-4166) north of town overlooks the 3-mile-long Hull-Rust Mahoning Mine. The Greyhound bus company got its start in Hibbing, carrying miners to the pit. The Greyhound Bus Origin Center (☎ 218-263-5814, 1201 Greyhound Blvd) tells the story with models, posters and antique buses ($3). Bob Dylan lived at 2425 E 7th Ave as a boy and teenager; the Hibbing Public Library (2020 E 5th St) has two well-done Dylan displays. For a meal or bed, try

Hibbing Park Hotel (☎ 218-262-3481, 1402 E Howard St).

Chisholm has the engaging, hodgepodge Minnesota Museum of Mining (☎ 218-254-5543). At Hwy 169 is Ironworld Discovery Center (☎ 218-254-3321), a theme park featuring tours of an open-pit mine, displays on the wide ethnic array of the area's immigrants, as well as ethnic music and foods ($8). The Chamber of Commerce is at 10 NW 2nd St.

Farther east there are more mine sites in Mountain Iron and Virginia. In Virginia, *New China Buffet (322 Chestnut St)* is a bargain all-you-can-eat, and the dirt cheap *Ski View Motel (☎ 218-741-8918, 903 N 17th St)* could be the cleanest motel in the state.

Soudan has the area's only underground mine to visit ($6).

International Falls & Canadian Border

North up Hwy 53, the nondescript border town of International Falls is busy in summer due to its location. Grand Mound Center (☎ 218-285-3332), 17 miles west on Hwy 11, is the site of large prehistoric burial mounds and interpretive exhibits. Beyond, Hwy 11 leads through forest to Lake of the Woods, bordering Ontario. See the Facts for the Visitor chapter for information on border crossings.

Voyageurs National Park

In the 17th century, French Canadian fur traders, or voyageurs, began exploring the Great Lakes and northern rivers by canoe. Voyageurs National Park covers part of their customary waterway, which became the border between the USA and Canada.

Twelve miles east of International Falls on Hwy 11 is Rainy Lake (☎ 218-286- 5258), the main park office. There is a campground here, and ranger-guided walks and boat tours are available. Generally, however, park access by land is limited; the park is best and most commonly explored by motorboat (the waters are mostly too wide and too rough for canoeing, though kayaks are becoming popular). A few access roads lead to campgrounds and lodges on or near Lake Superior, but these are mostly used by those putting in their own boats.

Some seasonal visitor centers can be found at Ash River (☎ 218-374-3221) and

Kabetogama Lake (☎ 218-875-2111), and there's a ranger station at Crane Lake (☎ 218-993-2481). These areas have outfitters, rentals and services, plus some smaller lakes for canoeing. A long hiking trail on the Kabetogama Peninsula is accessible by water taxi. Also at Kabetogama, *Watson's Harmony Beach* (☎ *218-875-2811*) is a friendly reasonably priced resort with camping, rooms and cabins.

For those seeking wildlife and canoeing or forest camping, the Boundary Waters Canoe Area Wilderness is where you want to be (see Boundary Waters, earlier in this chapter).

The South

This complex and diverse region covers most of the southeast corner of the country, with nine states south of the old Mason-Dixon line. Travelers are attracted by cities that run the gamut from dynamic, modern Atlanta to old New Orleans and superbly restored Savannah, and by the natural beauty of coastal islands, primeval swamps and the Great Smoky Mountains. Civil War history is still a big draw, but the more recent history of the civil-rights struggle is both compelling and continuing.

Many come as culinary tourists, their palates primed for heaping helpings of Southern barbecue, Cajun crawfish, Creole gumbo, soul food, seafood and deep-fried chicken. Others come to see the source of the music they love. Blues, bluegrass, jazz, country, gospel, R&B, zydeco and rock & roll all have their origins in the South, and all are alive and playing at venues large and small.

Both town and country have their disturbing downsides – run-down neighborhoods, deserted downtowns and crass mass tourism. Plagued to this day by poverty and de facto racial inequality, the South has often been depicted in US literature, movies and TV as a backward region. Although most Southerners of all races acknowledge the problems facing their states, the majority are heartily sick of the nation's stereotyping them as hicks, hillbillies or racists. One stereotype that generally holds is Southern hospitality; there is a warmth and gentleness here that can be hard to find in the brash self-confidence and energy of the North and West.

History

Near Tuscaloosa (Alabama) and Poverty Point (Louisiana) and at numerous other sites in the South, earthen mounds are the legacy of the ancient 'Mississippian' culture, which built riverside settlements through much of the South from around 700 BC. It was probably related to the Hopewell culture that left mounds farther north (see Ohio and Illinois), but the Mississippian culture seems to have endured longer, perhaps until about AD 1200, though time estimates vary widely. There were no mound-building peoples when Europeans arrived;

Highlights

- Memphis – where King Cotton ruled, the King lived and Martin Luther King Jr died
- New Orleans – great eating, architecture and music
- Charleston & Savannah – two of the USA's loveliest towns
- Music – Nashville country, New Orleans jazz, Delta blues, bluegrass, zydeco and the roots of rock & roll
- Mardi Gras – party time in Mobile, Biloxi and New Orleans
- Southern cooking – barbecue, soul, Cajun and Creole: comfort food…mmmmm
- Civil War & civil rights – unforgotten history, unfinished story
- Alligators – up close and personal (watch your back)

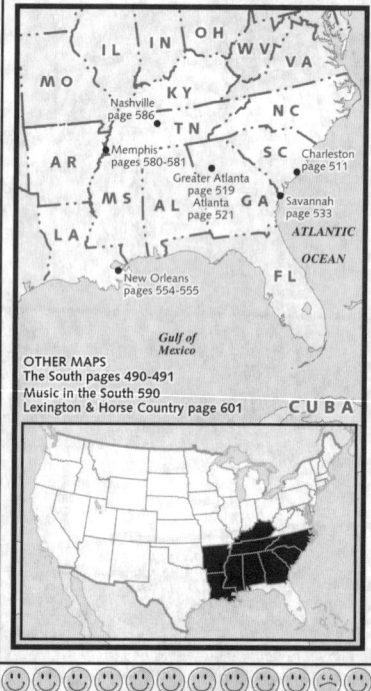

the Native Americans throughout the region were village dwellers who cultivated squash, beans and corn, hunted deer and fished.

Colonization European settlement came from several directions. Spanish explorers wandered through much of the Southeast in the 16th century but established no settlements outside of Florida. French explorers claimed the Mississippi River in the 17th century and established forts to protect a fur trade that extended from the Gulf of Mexico to the Great Lakes. After the 'Lost Colony' of Roanoke was abandoned in 1587, the coast of the Carolinas became a crown colony in 1663, and the Georgia coast was settled from 1733.

Where Indians were hostile to European settlers, they were usually removed by force of arms. Where Indians cooperated with European settlement, they often became dependent on European goods, then were forced to sell their land to pay debts. As elsewhere, European diseases did the most to wipe out the Native Americans. The 'Five Civilized Tribes' – the Cherokee, Choctaw, Chickasaw, Creek and Seminole – adapted to European encroachment and survived for a time in inland areas.

Expansion After the French and Indian War and the Revolutionary War, the new republic was in control of the fertile lands west of the Appalachian Mountains, though pioneers and speculators like Daniel Boone had already claimed land there and negotiated private 'treaties.' The 1803 Louisiana Purchase brought the land west of the Mississippi under US control. The new territory attracted settlers, both would-be planters seeking suitable lands and poor workers seeking their own farms. In 1830 the Indian Removal Act required the Five Civilized Tribes to relocate to 'Indian Territory' west of the Mississippi, and some 50,000 Indians were 'removed' in the following decades. In the winter of 1838, over 15,000 Cherokee were forced to trek west on the infamous Trail of Tears – 4000 died en route. A few isolated groups remained, but most of the South was 'cleared' for settlement.

In the 1790s Eli Whitney's cotton gin mechanized the process of removing seeds from raw cotton, which made large-scale cotton growing profitable. Cotton set the pattern for Southern society, with the dominant planters dependent not only on slave labor, but also on Northern financiers, agents, ships and merchants. The South produced valuable crops, but everything else was imported, and despite the grand mansions of the Southern elite, much of the wealth went north. Increasingly, the Northern states were regarded with resentment and mistrust.

Secession The majority of Southerners owned no slaves, but they were part of a slave-based society, fearful of slave rebellion on the one hand and Northern interference on the other. When Lincoln was elected US president on an antislavery platform, secession seemed the only option. In the upland areas of the South there were few plantations, and small farmers and workers opposed slavery. Though North Carolina, Georgia, Tennessee and Arkansas all seceded, their

Street in Sherman, Atlanta (1864)

THE SOUTH

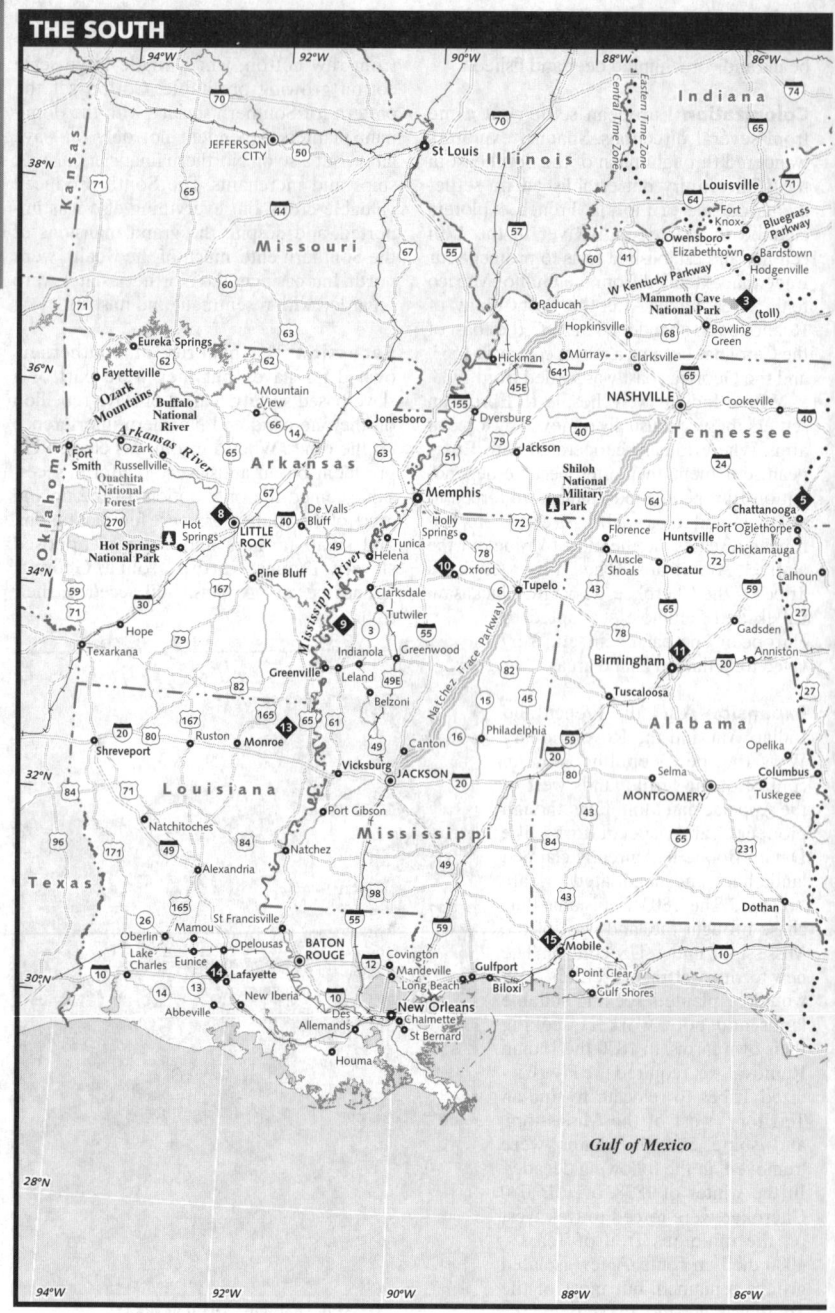

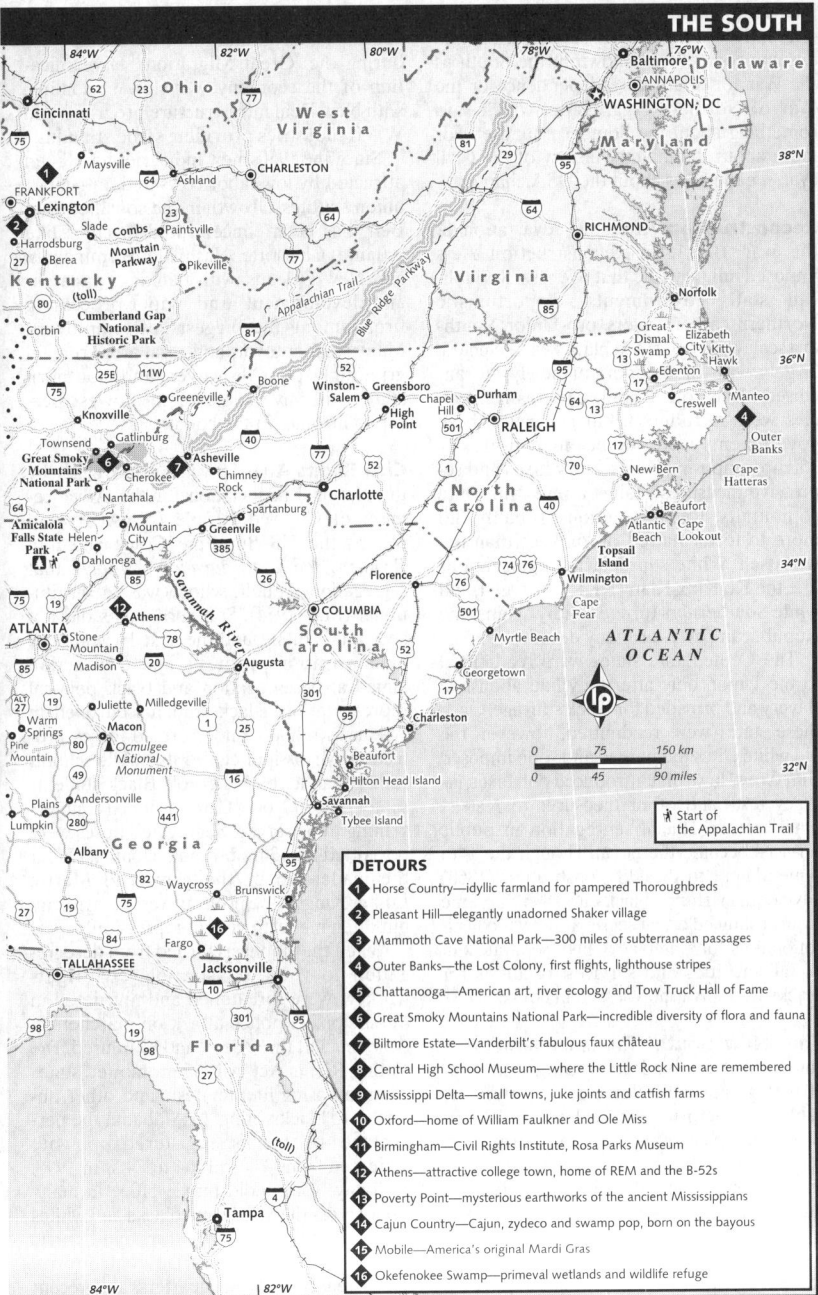

THE SOUTH

THE SOUTH

DETOURS

1 Horse Country—idyllic farmland for pampered Thoroughbreds

2 Pleasant Hill—elegantly unadorned Shaker village

3 Mammoth Cave National Park—300 miles of subterranean passages

4 Outer Banks—the Lost Colony, first flights, lighthouse stripes

5 Chattanooga—American art, river ecology and Tow Truck Hall of Fame

6 Great Smoky Mountains National Park—incredible diversity of flora and fauna

7 Biltmore Estate—Vanderbilt's fabulous faux château

8 Central High School Museum—where the Little Rock Nine are remembered

9 Mississippi Delta—small towns, juke joints and catfish farms

10 Oxford—home of William Faulkner and Ole Miss

11 Birmingham—Civil Rights Institute, Rosa Parks Museum

12 Athens—attractive college town, home of REM and the B-52s

13 Poverty Point—mysterious earthworks of the ancient Mississippians

14 Cajun Country—Cajun, zydeco and swamp pop, born on the bayous

15 Mobile—America's original Mardi Gras

16 Okefenokee Swamp—primeval wetlands and wildlife refuge

inland and mountain areas were largely pro-Union. Kentucky did not secede at all. The ensuing conflict was known in the South as the War for Southern Independence or the War of Northern Aggression, which says something about the Southern mindset. For more about the military history of the Civil War, see the Facts about the USA chapter.

Reconstruction After the devastation of the war, the 1867 Reconstruction Acts imposed military rule that oversaw Republican state governments. Opportunistic Northern carpetbaggers, pro-Union Southern scalawags and freed blacks were elected, largely with the support of newly enfranchised black voters. Some progressive policies were introduced, but generally these governments were inefficient and grossly corrupt, imposing confiscatory taxes and repressive measures against a resentful white community. Reconstruction probably did more to foster hatred of Yankees than the war itself. White supremacist organizations like the Ku Klux Klan (KKK) emerged, and white Southerners turned solidly against the Republican party for many decades.

The Confederate states were readmitted to the Union only after they had abolished slavery and provided for black suffrage. Once these states were readmitted, however, the old white elites reemerged and soon imposed 'Jim Crow' laws that introduced poll taxes, literacy tests and other measures to restrict black voting. Racial segregation in public services became the norm. Though the 14th Amendment to the US Constitution (1868) gave equal rights to blacks, an 1896 Supreme Court ruling held that segregation was constitutional as long as blacks had 'separate but equal' facilities and services. Facilities for blacks were invariably less than equal.

The 'New South' The modernization of the South involved rebuilding and constructing railroads. Northern investors established factories where land and labor were cheap. Mining and lumbering exploited the natural resources, but much of the region continued to be dependent on agriculture. The sharecropping system used black (and poor white) tenant farmers to work land in return for a share of the crop, though constant debt kept them in poverty. The 1914 boll weevil infestation ravaged the cotton crops and forced many blacks to Chicago, Detroit and other industrial cities during the 'Great Migration.' Diversification of the economy was slow in coming, with New Deal infrastructure programs and WWII industries providing some stimulus.

Since the 1950s, new industries have been attracted by low labor costs and anti–labor union statutes. Growth in the so-called 'Sun Belt' has been concentrated in cities like Atlanta, Charlotte, Nashville, Birmingham and New Orleans, with banking, research-and-development and paper-processing firms among the biggest new employers. Many smaller towns and rural areas remain grindingly poor, however, and Southern states still have some of the lowest per-capita incomes in the country.

Civil Rights After 20 years of advocacy by the National Association for the Advancement of Colored People (NAACP) and others, the US Supreme Court ruled in *Brown v Board of Education of Topeka* that segregation of public schools was unconstitutional (May 1954). Southern states did not accept this ruling, and the next 10 years saw demonstrations, protests and civil action aimed at desegregation and black political representation. Black students enrolled in Arkansas schools under armed-forces protection. Mississippi closed its public schools rather than let blacks enroll. Black students sat for days at North Carolina lunch counters waiting to be served. Segregated buses were boycotted for 13 months in Alabama. Under the leadership of the Reverend Martin Luther King Jr, the protests were nonviolent, but often met with violent repression.

When the emphasis turned from desegregation to voter registration, civil-rights workers were threatened and murdered in Mississippi. A police attack on marchers in Alabama left three dead and 87 injured. The Voting Rights Act in 1965 prohibited states from imposing literacy tests and other obstacles to black voting. In Alabama the percentage of blacks registered to vote increased from 7% in 1964 to 74% in 1998.

Today blacks hold public office in many cities across the South, and blacks and whites mix peacefully in schools, stores and public places. Yet racism and racial inequality are still a reality in some quarters, and recent controversy over the state and Confederate flags in Georgia, Mississippi and South Carolina show that the wounds of the past have not completely healed.

Educated Southerners, black and white, are quite open about these issues. They often see the rest of the country as somewhat hypocritical in its belief that racial problems are something peculiar to the South.

Geography

The coast of Georgia and the Carolinas is indented with estuaries and shielded by barrier islands. In the low-lying coastal areas, many swamps and marshes are preserved as wildlife refuges and state parks, though much has been drained for agriculture. Inland, the Piedmont is an undulating plateau with the best farmland and most of the main cities. Farther inland are the southern branches of the Appalachian Mountains, beyond which rich bluegrass country drains west into the Mississippi. South of the Appalachians, the land is mostly flat and fertile, with rivers meandering to the Gulf of Mexico. West of the Mississippi, the low ranges of Arkansas' Ozark and Ouachita Mountains mark the edge of the Great Plains.

Flora & Fauna

As a meeting place of northern and southern varieties, the Southern Appalachian forest has over 130 tree types. Flowering shrubs like rhododendron, azalea and mountain laurel, and blossoming trees like dogwood and redbud make gorgeous spring displays. In fall, oak, poplar, wild cherry, ash and elm turn on the colors. At higher altitudes are forests of northern fir and spruce.

On the Piedmont plateau, varieties such as ash, black locust and American elm thin as you go south, and the forest makes a transition from the deciduous northern varieties to southern conifers, pine and cedar. In coastal areas, bald cypress, black gum and sweet gum trees give way to maritime forests of oak, cedar and holly, with salt marsh and palmetto palms growing in the subtropical latitudes. The storied bayous of the Gulf Coast have a huge variety of plants – chinquapin, pawpaw, sassafras, holly, cypress, pine and oak.

The land south and west of the mountains was once covered in forest but was cleared for agriculture, bluegrass pastures in the hills of Kentucky and Tennessee, and cotton plantations in the bottomlands.

Other plants associated with the South are magnolia, live oak (an evergreen hardwood) and Spanish moss (the wispy gray epiphyte draped from trees and old buildings). The unstoppable kudzu (**kud**-zoo) vine was imported from Japan in the late 19th century for erosion control, and it now envelops whole forests.

Widespread clearing of forest for farmland has greatly reduced wildlife habitats. Large animals, including white-tailed deer and black bear, have reestablished themselves in protected areas. Small mammals like opossums, raccoons, squirrels, rabbits and bats are common throughout the region, but red foxes are endangered. In wetlands there are alligators, snapping turtles, and many varieties of frog, toad and newt. There are venomous snakes, too – water moccasins in low-lying lakes and swamps, rattlesnakes and copperheads in drier habitats.

Wild turkeys, bobwhites (quails), ducks and geese are among many game birds. Waterbirds include herons, egrets, ibis and anhingas, as well as migratory visitors. In the woodlands you'll hear songbirds like cardinals, warblers, sparrows, mockingbirds and thrashers. Owls, hawks and golden eagles are the main raptors, with the once-endangered American bald eagle making a comeback.

The lakes and streams shelter pike, bass, catfish, bream and carp, while saltwater anglers go for striped bass, menhaden, bluefish, weakfish, butterfish, herring and shad. Catfish farms are now common in the Mississippi Delta, as are oyster and shrimp farms on the Gulf. The crawfish is a crustacean found in swamps and marshes and a staple of Cajun cooking.

Insects are a feature of the subtropical southern wetlands, with dragonflies, katydids, crickets, many mosquitoes and cockroaches up to 3 inches long.

When to Go

The main tourist season is June to September, and some attractions are closed outside these months. Spring and autumn bring very pleasant weather to most of the region, with seasonal blossoms and colors a highlight of the mountain regions. In the Deep South, July and August can be quite hot and very humid, but winter is mild. Carnival and Mardi Gras are in February (in Biloxi, Mobile and the Cajun Country as well as

New Orleans). The Blue Ridge Pkwy is closed December to April.

Activities

Along the East Coast and Outer Banks, sea kayaking in the sounds is catching on, the surfing is OK sometimes, and the windsurfing can be excellent. Hang gliding is an attraction in the Kitty Hawk dunes, where the Wright brothers first flew. The 'Graveyard of the Atlantic' has great wreck diving, best accessed from Morehead City.

Hiking trails abound in the mountains, with the southern end of the Appalachian Trail starting in Georgia and winding north across North Carolina and Tennessee. The Natchez Trace and Blue Ridge Pkwys are suitable for bicycle touring. Arkansas, Tennessee and especially Kentucky have great possibilities for caving. None of the Appalachian ski areas, however, is very exciting.

The best white water is in the headwaters of rivers around the Southern Appalachians – the Nantahala in North Carolina, the Chattooga in Georgia (featured in the movie *Deliverance)* and the Ocoee in Tennessee (used for 1996 Olympic events).

Food

Don't expect to lose weight in the South. The food is rich and the servings large. Southerners have a sweet tooth; meats and vegetables are often flavored with sugar or honey, and there are tempting desserts like pecan pie, banana pudding and peach cobbler.

A Southern country meal is typically heaps of fried chicken, some ham, pork or ribs, with several vegetables and cornbread or 'biscuits' (soft bread rolls, like scones). Staple vegetables include okra, corn on the cob, black-eyed peas and collard greens. A 'meat-and-three plate' includes your choice of three vegetables. Grits (ground white corn, also called 'hominy') is a common breakfast offering, often served with butter. Buffet meals and cafeterias are common, and some places are 'family-style,' with unrelated groups seated together and passing plates around. Many Southerners say a prayer before eating.

The famous barbecue is usually pork (chopped, sliced, 'pulled' or in ribs), but sometimes beef or chicken. It's cooked long and slow on a smoking hickory fire, basted and served with special barbecue sauce (usually a secret recipe). In the southeast, sauces are primarily vinegar- or tomato-based; as you go west the sauce becomes sweeter.

African American cuisine, 'soul food,' includes the usual Southern vegetables, with meats such as chitterlings (or 'chitlins,' fried pig's tripe), hogsjaw (from pigs' heads) and pigs' trotters. Catfish was part of the black diet long before whites got the taste.

In Louisiana, Creole cuisine developed from French, Spanish and African styles with Caribbean influences. It tends to use butter and cream heavily, plus chopped celery, onion, green peppers and *filé* (ground sassafras). Gumbo, a soup of chicken, seafood and vegetables thickened with filé and okra, is the classic Creole dish. Cajun cooking is similar, but it derives from the poorer rural Acadian people and is more influenced by Southern country cooking. It uses a *roux* of flour and lard (usually pork fat) for thickening and is highly spiced. The classic Cajun dish is jambalaya, a big pan of spicy rice fried up with onions, peppers, celery, shrimp, sausage and whatever else is at hand. *Étouffée* means 'smothered' – in a rich, spicy tomato sauce. Both styles use lots of seafood, including crawfish (the 'poor man's lobster').

Getting There & Around

Atlanta, Georgia, is the main air gateway to the region. Charlotte and Raleigh, both in North Carolina, Memphis, in Tennessee, and New Orleans, Louisiana, have the region's largest airports.

A number of Amtrak routes traverse the South, several converging on New Orleans:

The Crescent – between New York and New Orleans, with stops including Washington, DC; Greensboro and Charlotte, North Carolina; Greenville, South Carolina; Atlanta, Georgia; Birmingham, Alabama; and Meridian, Mississippi.

City of New Orleans – between New Orleans and Chicago, with stops at Jackson, Mississippi; Memphis, Tennessee; and Fulton, in the western corner of Kentucky.

Sunset Limited – crosses the south of the country between Los Angeles and Jacksonville, Florida, with stops including Houston, Texas; Lafayette and New Orleans, Louisiana; Biloxi, Mississippi; Mobile, Alabama; and Pensacola and Tallahassee, Florida.

Other services parallel the East Coast going to and from Florida. They all follow a

common route between New York and
Richmond, Virginia, but at Rocky Mount,
North Carolina (near Raleigh), the services
separate:

Silver Palm and *Silver Meteor* – go closer to the
coast, with stops at Fayetteville, North Carolina;
Charleston, South Carolina; Savannah, Georgia;
and Jacksonville, Florida.

Silver Star – veers inland, with stops including
Raleigh, North Carolina; Columbia, South Carolina; then Savannah and Jacksonville.

Carolinian and *Piedmont* – go farther inland, to
and from Charlotte via Raleigh, Durham and
Winston-Salem, all in North Carolina.

The Blue Ridge Pkwy, the Natchez Trace
Pkwy and Hwy 12 along the Outer Banks
are three of the South's most scenic drives.

The Promised Land

Chuck Berry gave a cross section of the South
in the rock & roll classic 'The Promised Land,'
which describes how he left his home in
'Norfo'k, Virginny,' with California on his
mind. This echoed the aspirations of many
blacks to leave the discrimination and depression of the South and seek opportunity elsewhere in the country. Chuck's journey takes
him by Greyhound bus, in rollicking time,
through Raleigh (and all across 'Caroline'),
Charlotte and Atlanta. The 'hound breaks
down and leaves him stranded in downtown
Birmingham, but, after a short guitar solo, he
catches a midnight train to New Orleans. The
song might be longer if some folks in
Houston hadn't put him on a plane to Los
Angeles.

Today, this itinerary would take you from
the almost Northern navy town of Norfolk,
Virginia, through the progressive 'Research
Triangle' centered on Raleigh, North Carolina,
and two of the New South boomtowns, Charlotte and Atlanta. Birmingham, Alabama, was
the scene of a bloody civil-rights confronta-
tion. Despite much progress and a shift from
the steel industry to services, research and education, it's still definitely Deep South. You'll
want to stay longer in New Orleans than
Chuck did, but as soon as you get out of
Louisiana and across to Houston town, you'll
know you've left the South.

☺ ☺ ☺ ☺ ☺ ☺ ☺ ☺ ☺ ☺ ☺ ☺ ☺

I-10 runs along the Gulf coast from Florida
to Louisiana; I-20 links South Carolina with
Louisiana via Georgia, Alabama and
Mississippi; and I-40 goes from North Carolina to Arkansas via Tennessee. The chief
north-south routes include I-95, I-75, I-65
and I-55.

North Carolina

Mountain folk, New South workaholics and
beach bums all find solace in North Carolina, and its landscape – plains sandwiched
between mountains and shore – is that of
the US, but in miniature. Travelers can pass
quickly through the central Piedmont, but
the more scenic routes are along the coast
(via the islands of the Outer Banks) and
through the Appalachian Mountains, especially along the Blue Ridge Pkwy.

History

Iroquoian groups, including Cherokees and
Creeks, inhabited much of the coastal plains
and mountains, coexisting with Algonquians
along the coasts and islands. In the 16th
century, Algonquians met the New World's
first English settlers and were probably responsible for the disappearance of the 'Lost
Colony' of Roanoke (see the Outer Banks
section, later).

The first enduring English settlements
were established in the mid-17th century in
the Albermarle region, though initial problems led to the formation of separate colonial charters for North and South Carolina
in 1712. In the Tuscarora Wars (1711–13), a
series of battles defeated and displaced the
Indians, making way for European colonists.
Inland settlement was mostly by Scots, Irish
and Germans migrating from northern
colonies on the Great Wagon Road. The first
industry was the extraction of 'naval stores'
like tar, pitch and turpentine from coastal
forests, followed by cultivation of tobacco
and cotton.

The town of Edenton, on the Albermarle
Sound, was one of the first places to protest
British taxes on tea and was at the forefront
of the American independence movement.
Pro-British troops suffered an early defeat at
Moore's Creek Bridge, near Wilmington, in
1776, which secured North Carolina and
much of the South for the revolutionaries.

North Carolina

Nickname: Tar Heel State

Population: 8,049,000 (11th)

Area: 53,820 sq miles (28th)

Admitted to the Union: November 21, 1789 (12th); seceded 1861; readmitted 1868

Capital city: Raleigh (population 276,000)

Other cities: Charlotte (541,000; metro area 1.3 million), Greensboro (224,000), Winston-Salem (185,000), Durham (187,000)

State motto: To be rather than to seem

Birthplace of: President James Polk (1795–1849), John Coltrane (1926–67), evangelist Billy Graham (b 1918), senator Jesse Helms (b 1921)

Home of: the first English colony in America, powered airplane flight

Though well represented in the constitutional conventions, North Carolina languished as an agrarian backwater in the early years of the republic.

The North Carolinians were divided on slavery, between the plantation society of the coast and the small landholders and workers of the Piedmont. The state seceded reluctantly in 1861 and went on to provide more Confederate soldiers than any other state; it lost over 40,000 men.

WWII brought some new industries and large military bases, and the economy has boomed with the growth of finance in Charlotte and of research and development in the Raleigh-Durham Research Triangle. Still, poverty remains a problem in many rural and mountain areas.

Information

The North Carolina Division of Tourism (☎ 919-733-4147, 800-847-4862, Ⓦ www .visitnc.com, 301N N Wilmington St, Raleigh, NC 27601) sends out good maps and information. For highway information, call ☎ 919-733-3109. State sales tax is 6%, with bed taxes generally 3% to 6%.

Note that a 'members only' law applies at many entertainment venues, although it's usually easy to get 'invited in' on the spot.

RESEARCH TRIANGLE

The towns of Raleigh, Durham and Chapel Hill each have a university, and the area has been successfully promoted as the Research Triangle, a center for research and high-tech industry.

Raleigh

North Carolina's quiet, provincial state capital has a few good museums, some old buildings and pretty parks. Urban renewal has converted four blocks south of the handsome old state capitol into a trendy-looking pedestrian mall, but most of downtown is pretty dead, day or night. City Market and Moore Square, redeveloped with shops, restaurants and galleries, is a more interesting area two blocks south and east of the Capitol.

The visitor bureau (☎ 919-834-5900, 225 Hillsborough St) gives out a list of hotels with discounts. The Capital Area Visitors Center (☎ 919-733-3456, 301 N Blount St) has a walking-tour map of the government buildings and the old Oakwood district. The public library (334 Fayetteville Mall) has 16 terminals for free Web access.

The **North Carolina Museum of History** (☎ 919-715-0200, 5 E Edenton St) has good exhibits, including a dugout canoe from 700 BC, Civil War flags, a Wright Brothers plane model and a Sports Hall of Fame (free admission; closed Mon). Nearby, the fancy **North Carolina Museum of Natural Sciences** (☎ 919-733-7450, 11 W Jones St) has scary dinosaurs, habitat dioramas and lots of convincing taxidermy. The **Exploris** (☎ 919-857-1010) is a flashy hands-on museum that gives a fascinating look at cultures around the world ($7/5 adults/kids).

The **North Carolina Museum of Art** (☎ 919-839-6262, 2110 Blue Ridge Rd) is inconveniently located northwest of town off I-440 exit 5, but it's worthwhile for its fine collection of antiquities, baroque and Renaissance paintings, and a representative selection of the best-known American artists (free admission; open daily). **Mordicae Historic Park** (☎ 919-834-4844, 1 Mimosa St), north of town, features an old plantation house and several other old buildings that give a feel for antebellum life ($4; open daily).

Places to Stay & Eat The nearest camping is at **Umstead State Park** (☎ 919-787-3033), north off Hwy 70, 2 miles west of town, where woodland tent sites cost $9. *Regency Inn* (☎ 919-828-9101, *300 N Dawson St*) is the cheapest downtown option ($46 doubles).

Capital Blvd, north of town, has plenty of motels starting at $45. Off I-440 in Cary, southwest of town, *Motel 6* (☎ 919-467-6171, *1401 Buck Jones Rd*) charges $38/43 for singles/doubles. *Microtel Inn* (☎ 919-462-0061), at I-40 exit 284B, west of town, is quite good and often discounted ($48/54).

Brownstone Hotel (☎ 919-828-0811, *1707 Hillsborough St*) is a renovated place in a nicer location ($79-99, with weekend discounts).

The Glenwood Ave area northwest of downtown has an array of good restaurants and clubs. Popular *42nd St Oyster Bar*, at West and Jones Sts, has music, dancing, a raw bar and seafood restaurant. Lunch is $6-9, dinner $11-17.

Hillsborough St along the NCSU campus is lively at night, with the inexpensive *Rathskeller* eatery at No 2412. *Irregardless (901 W Morgan St)* is just south, with more upscale fare. *Time* (☎ 919-831-9222, *901 Tryon St)*, a dance temple with laser shows, is a block away.

Getting There & Around Raleigh-Durham International Airport (☎ 919-840-2123) is a 25-minute drive northwest of downtown Raleigh. The Greyhound/Trailways station (☎ 919-834-8410, 314 W Jones Rd) is just west of downtown. Sample fares include Winston-Salem ($20; from 3 hours), Charlotte ($30; from 4¼ hours) and Wilmington ($29; from 6¼ hours). Amtrak (☎ 919-828-3399, 302 W Cabarrus St) runs to Washington, DC (from $66; 7½ hours), and Savannah, Georgia ($66; 7 hours).

The Triangle Transit Authority (☎ 919-549-9999) operates buses linking Raleigh, Durham and Chapel Hill, and all three to the airport ($1.50).

Durham

At the northeast corner of the Triangle, Durham has an active black community and a helpful Visitor Information Center (☎ 919-687-0288, 101 E Morgan St). **Duke University**, generously endowed by the Duke family's cigarette fortune, has a Georgian-style East Campus and a West Campus with an impressive 1930s **neo-Gothic chapel**, best reached by a walk through the pleasant Sara P Duke Gardens. See the humble origins of the Duke family and have an uncritical look at the tobacco industry at **Duke Homestead** (☎ 919-477-5498, 2828 Duke Homestead Rd), on the north side of town (free admission).

Carolina Duke Motor Inn (☎ 919-286-0771, 2517 Guess Rd), off I-85, is a good value ($40/45 singles/doubles). Across the road, *Holiday Inn Express* (☎ 929-313-3244) has rack rates of $59/69.

For dining, seek out the Brightleaf complex downtown and Ninth St alongside the university campus. Good eateries include *Taverna Nikos (905 West Main St)* and *Fishmongers (806 W Main St)*. *Magnolia Grill* (☎ 919-286-3609, 1002 9th St) does imaginative dishes like brandy chicken in cranberry-apple chutney ($20). Ask at the visitor center about local blues clubs.

Chapel Hill

An attractive university town, Chapel Hill is conspicuously more affluent than the other corners of the Triangle. The University of North Carolina (UNC), founded in 1789, was one of the nation's first state universities. **Morehead Planetarium** (☎ 919-549-6863, 250 E Franklin St) features science exhibits and celestial shows in its big dome ($4.50). The visitor center (☎ 919-962-1630), at the planetarium's west entrance, offers walking tours of the campus.

Affordable accommodations are scarce. *Red Roof Inn* (☎ 919-489-9421, 5623 Chapel Hill Blvd) is comfortable ($48/53 singles/doubles). The classiest place is historic *Carolina Inn* (☎ 919-933-2001, 211 Pittborough St) downtown, with plush rooms and an elegant restaurant ($139-169).

Most restaurants and nightspots are along Franklin St. *Spanky's (101 E Franklin St)* is a popular cafe with good, cheap meals and a great upstairs view of the action. *Rathskeller (159 E Franklin St)*, down a flight of stairs, is a more student-oriented place. At *Carrburrito's (711 W Rosemary St)*, half a mile west in Carrboro, a bulging burrito and Mexican beer cost $8.

Popular alternative bands (Superchunk, Squirrel Nut Zippers) started out at venues like *Local 506* (☎ 919-942-5506, 506 W Franklin St), which hosts local and visiting bands. In Carrboro, the renowned *Cat's Cradle* (☎ 919-968-4345, 300 E Main St) has

THE SOUTH

His Royal Airness

Widely considered the greatest basketball player of all time, Michael Jeffrey Jordan enrolled at UNC at Chapel Hill in 1981. After his junior year, the Wilmington native was drafted by the Chicago Bulls and went on to become the top NBA scorer for seven years running, averaging 32 points per game. Known for his extraordinary leaps on court, 'Air' Jordan was only the second player in NBA history ever to score 3000 points in a single season, after Wilt ('the Stilt') Chamberlain. Jordan retired in 1998 (rumors of a comeback occasionally surface), but you can relive some of his glories at UNC's Blue Heaven Basketball Museum (☎ 919-929-5877, 1840 Airport Rd).

live rock, reggae and big visiting acts. Other venues worth checking are *Skylight Exchange* and *The Cave*.

THE TRIAD

The cities of Winston-Salem, Greensboro and High Point are known collectively as 'the Triad,' an echo of the bigger, more prosperous Triangle to the southeast. Winston-Salem takes special pride in its Moravian roots, Greensboro in its civil-rights history, and High Point (the least captivating of the trio) in its role as a furniture-making mecca.

Greensboro

Greensboro, the state's third-largest city, is noted for its early colleges for African Americans and women, and for the first civil-rights sit-in (1960). The friendly visitor bureau (☎ 336-274-2282) is at 317 S Green St. The **Greensboro Historical Museum** (☎ 336-373-2043) has a replica of the famous Woolworth's lunch counter and displays on short-story master O Henry (free admission). The **Mattye Reed African Heritage Center** (☎ 336-334-3209) houses an extensive collection of African art and artifacts. Downtown, *Pastiche (223 S Elm St)* has an eclectic menu and a wonderful pressed-tin ceiling.

Winston-Salem

Tobacco baron RJ Reynolds built his first factory here in 1875 and later named two cigarette brands after his adopted home. The visitor center (☎ 336-777-3796, 601 N Cherry St) has good maps – useful, as the sights are scattered.

An 18th-century Moravian settlement has been restored as **Old Salem**, a pretty if somewhat contrived 'living history museum' a few blocks from the skyscrapers of downtown. For about $4 each, you can tour seven homes guided by docents in period costume, or buy a combination ticket ($20; open daily). **Diggs Gallery** (☎ 336-750-2458, 601 Martin Luther King Dr), on the university campus, houses a good collection of African American art (free admission).

Northwest of downtown, the 64-room **Reynolds House Museum of American Art** (☎ 336-725-5325) was the home of the Reynolds family. Aside from works by Georgia O'Keefe, Grant Wood, Frederic Church and other American masters, there are splendid antiques, an old bowling alley and a massive Aeolian organ ($6; closed Mon).

Budget motels are clustered on 1-40 south of town. *Motel 6 (☎ 336-661-1588, 3810 Patterson Ave)*, on Hwy 52, 6 miles north, charges from $38. Downtown, refurbished *Salem Inn (☎ 336-725-8561, 127 S Cherry St)* has nicely appointed doubles ($61-65). Prices skyrocket during the annual furniture markets in High Point, a half hour's drive south.

Rainbow News & Cafe (712 Brookstown Ave) specializes in vegan dishes and salads, and doubles as a bookshop (closed Sun). The fine *Noble's Grill (☎ 336-777-8477, 380 Knollwood St)* serves pecan-crusted trout and other fancy dishes ($20-30).

Piedmont Triad International Airport (☎ 336-721-0088), 22 miles east of downtown, offers mainly regional flights. The Greyhound Station (☎ 336-724-1429, 250 Greyhound Court) has two or three buses daily to Asheville ($33; 3¼ hours); Columbia, South Carolina ($41; from 4¼ hours); and Atlanta, Georgia ($59; from 6¼ hours). The Winston-Salem Transit Authority (☎ 336-727-2000) runs buses from its transit center at 100 W 5th St ($1).

CHARLOTTE

Founded at the junction of two old Indian trails, Charlotte was described as a 'hornet's nest of rebellion' against British rule in the 1770s. Miners burrowed under the town in the early 1800s, and banks were founded to handle the gold. Today, Charlotte is a beehive of banking activity and a center for commerce and transport. The downtown area, called 'Uptown,' features futuristic high-rise buildings and overhead walkways, but it's not exactly engaging. The Fourth Ward Historic District, the northwest corner of Uptown, has a few streets of restored 19th-century houses.

The helpful Info!Charlotte visitor bureau (☎ 704-331-2700, 800-231-4636) is at 330 Tryon St, with free parking behind, off W 2nd St. The public library (301 N College St) has terminals for free Internet use.

Things to See & Do

The innovative **Museum of the New South** (☎ 704-333-1887, 324 N College St), Uptown, focuses on Southern life since the Civil War, from sharecropping to NASCAR racing. Headsets let you listen to contemporary radio programs ($2; open Tue-Sat). The **Mint Museum of Craft & Design** (☎ 704-337-2000), on N Tryon St, has imaginative jewelry and artwork of glass, metal, wood and more ($6; closed Mon). The **Afro-American Cultural Center** (☎ 704-374-1565), six blocks east on E 7th St at Myers, has temporary exhibits, performances and films.

Discovery Place (☎ 704-372-6261, 301 N Tryon St) is an OK hands-on science museum with an Omnimax cinema and planetarium ($6.50, $8.50 with cinema; open daily). The pricey **Carowinds Theme Park** (☎ 704-588-2600), 10 miles south off I-77, offers thrill rides themed around Carolinian history and Paramount movies ($39/27 adults/kids; open daily in summer, weekends Mar-Apr and Sept).

Places to Stay & Eat

Budget motels cluster around I-77 and I-85. Coming from the south, try **Cricket Inn** (☎ 704-527-8500), I-77 exit 7, from $40 with breakfast. Off I-85, there are many places to stay and eat near exit 41. **Red Roof Inn** (☎ 704-596-8222) usually charges around $48.

Uptown hotels cater mainly to business travelers. **Days Inn Central** (☎ 704-333-4733, 601 N Tryon St) is the most economical (from $59). Eight blocks west of downtown, **Doubletree Inn** (☎ 704-347-0070, 895 W Trade St) has a marble-and-wood lobby, comfy rooms and rack rates from $69.

Uptown eating is mostly upmarket. Cozy **Alexander Michael's** (☎ 704-332-6798, 401 W 9th St) serves New South dishes ($11-14) like blackened chicken in a former general store. The menu at **Crawford's Bistro** (☎ 704-375-5990, 322 S Church St) is Cajun and soul food, with excellent live jazz.

The Dilworth district, just south of Uptown, is good for eating and nightlife, with the **Southend Brewery & Smokehouse** (2100 S Blvd) serving boutique beers, smoked ribs and music. Go north on Davidson St to 35th St to find the small art district, with several galleries and earthy eateries like **Kelly's Café**.

Entertainment

For theater and classical concerts, check **Spirit Square Arts Center** (☎ 704-372-7469, 345 N College St). **Mythos** (☎ 704-375-8765, 300 N College St) is a high-energy dance locale in a strip of college bars downtown. Stevie Ray Vaughan and Eric Clapton played at the clapboard **Double Door Inn** (☎ 704-376-1446, 218 E Independence Blvd), the place for live blues, rock and zydeco. **300 E Stonewall** (☎ 704-347-4200), at that Uptown address, is a huge and popular gay club. For entertainment listings, see the free weekly **Creative Loafing**.

The NBA **Charlotte Hornets** (☎ 704-424-9622) and WNBA **Charlotte Sting** (☎ 704-357-0252) play professional basketball at Charlotte Coliseum (☎ 704-357-0489), off the Billy Graham Pkwy. The NFL **Carolina Panthers** football team plays at Ericsson Stadium (☎ 704-358-7800), on S Mint St. Insanely popular NASCAR races are held at **Charlotte Motor Speedway** (☎ 704-455-3200), 12 miles northeast of town.

Getting There & Around

Charlotte-Douglas International Airport (☎ 704-359-4000) has some direct flights to and from Europe. Taxis ($14), shuttle buses ($8) and infrequent city buses ($1) will get you into town.

The Greyhound station (☎ 704-372-0456, 601 W Trade St), handy to Uptown, has regular connections to Atlanta, Georgia ($42; from 4 hours); Charleston, South Carolina ($43; from 5 hours); and Washington, DC ($66; from 7½ hours). Amtrak (☎ 704-376-4416, 1914 N Tryon St) is farther out, with daily express services to New York ($134; 2 hours) and New Orleans ($170; 4½ hours).

Charlotte Area Transit (☎ 704-336-3366) provides local bus services throughout the metro area 5am-midnight ($1 with free local transfers, $1.40 for express buses). The transit depot is at 310 E Trade St.

NORTH CAROLINA MOUNTAINS

The western mountains of North Carolina provide an attractive route from the Northeast to the Deep South. Contrived attractions are all too common, but natural beauty and options for outdoor activities also abound: The Appalachian Trail roughly follows the state's western border, there's great white water around Nantahala, and the Great Smoky Mountains National Park is a huge destination. Of the three ski areas south of Boone, Sugar Mountain (☎ 800-784-2768) has the longest runs and steepest drop (1200-foot vertical).

Blue Ridge Parkway

This celebrated scenic drive follows the Blue Ridge Mountains from Virginia's Shenandoah National Park (Mile 0) to North Carolina's Great Smoky Mountains National Park (Mile 469). The parkway (see also Virginia in the Washington, DC & the Capital Region chapter) is closed by snow in winter and can take some time to clear. National Park Service (NPS) campgrounds and visitor centers close November to April. May and June are the best months for rhododendrons and wildflowers, October for the fall colors; the variation in altitude and latitude means that some place will always be at its peak of prettiness. Allow time for photo stops, short walks and detours off the parkway. Possible stops include the following:

Cumberland Knob (Mile 217.5) – NPS visitor center, easy walk to the knob

Doughton Park (Mile 241.1) – gas, food, trails, camping and small Bluffs Lodge (☎ 336-372-4499). Walk to the old Brinegar Cabin to feel the isolation of the old mountain life.

Blowing Rock (Mile 291.8) – small tourist town, named for a craggy, commercialized cliff that offers great views, occasional updrafts and an Indian love story ($4)

Moses H Cone Memorial Park (Mile 294.1) – a lovely old estate with pleasant walks and a craft shop

Linn Cove Viaduct (Mile 304.4) – graceful curves of concrete skirting the sheer domes of Grandfather Mountain

Grandfather Mountain (Mile 305.1) – a picturesque, privately run park (☎ 800-468-7325) with hiking trails ($10, $5 more for overnight camping)

Linville Falls (Mile 316.4) – lovely hiking trails to the falls

Little Switzerland (Mile 334) – old-style mountain resort

Mt Mitchell State Park (Mile 355.5) – highest mountain east of the Mississippi (6684 feet), hiking trails and tent camping

Folk Art Center (Mile 382) – traditional and contemporary local craft work (☎ 828-298-7903)

Boone

A 6-mile detour west of the Blue Ridge Pkwy, Boone offers good access to the surrounding area, and the Appalachian State University (ASU) is a bonus. The visitor bureau (☎ 704-262-3516, 888-251-9867, 208 Howard St) has information about canoeing outfitters, ski areas and parks.

The **Appalachian Cultural Museum** (☎ 704-262-3117), on University Hall Dr off Blowing Rock Rd, is a serious attempt to present mountain life and history beyond the hillbilly stereotypes. It has first-class exhibits and thoughtful interpretive material ($2; closed Mon). *The Horn in the West* (☎ 704-264-2120) is a musical drama that lets you 'relive the frontier days with Daniel Boone' at an amphitheater off Blowing Rock Rd ($12; June-Aug). Hwy 321 from Blowing Rock to Boone is studded with tourist traps. The cutesy **Tweetsie Railroad** (☎ 828-264-9061) is the best of them ($16/13 adults/kids; open summer only).

Boone KOA (☎ 704-264-7250) is 4 miles north, off Hwy 194. The cheapest accommodations are at *Boone Trail Motel* (☎ 704-264-8839, 820 E King St), where singles/doubles cost from $25/30. The ASU-run *Broyhill Inn* (☎ 828-262-2204), overlooking Boone, has nice rooms for $120.

Harvest Café, on Blowing Rock Rd opposite ASU, is an inexpensive, student-oriented place with vegetarian dishes. Other congenial eateries include *Mellow Mushroom* and *Macado's*, on W King St.

Asheville

Since the late 19th century, Asheville has been a summer retreat from the hot and humid lowland. Downtown retains a certain 1920s charm, with a dash of the bohemian. The tourist office (☎ 828-258-6101, 800-257-1300, 151 Haywood St) is at I-240 exit 4C (open daily). Malaprop's Bookstore & Café (☎ 828-254-6734, 55 Haywood St) is an excellent place for regional maps, travel books and cappuccino-sipping bohemians. The public library (67 Haywood Ave) offers free Internet access.

Billed as America's largest private house, the 250-room **Biltmore Estate** (☎ 828-255-1700, 800-543-2961), just south of downtown, is Asheville's largest tourist attraction. Built for the filthy-rich Vanderbilt family as a holiday home, the 1895 mansion is styled after a French château and is overwhelmingly sumptuous in scale and decoration. Contents include Chippendale furniture, Meissen porcelain, Flemish tapestries and artwork by Dürer, Renoir, Sargent and Whistler. The superb 70-acre gardens were laid out by Frederick Law Olmsted. The estate's winery offers tastings and sales. You need to spend quite a few hours here to see everything and to justify hefty admission charges ($32); guided tours cost extra. Mid-price meals are available at several venues, and the gift shop is the size of a small supermarket.

The **Thomas Wolfe Memorial** (52 N Market St) is the local literary landmark, an early-1900s boardinghouse that was the model for 'Dixieland' in Wolfe's novel *Look Homeward Angel*. The house has been closed since a 1998 arson attack, but the adjacent visitor center (☎ 828-253-8304) shows a video on the writer's life.

Places to Stay & Eat The *Bear Creek Campground* (☎ 828-253-0798), southwest of town at I-40 exit 47, has full facilities and tent/RV sites for $18/20. *Days Inn Downtown* (☎ 828-254-9661, 120 Patton Ave) is the cheapest downtown option, from about $53.

Chain motels cluster north of downtown on Merrimon Ave. East on Tunnel Rd are some independent places like *Skyway Motel* (☎ 828-253-2631) and *Townhouse Motel* (☎ 828-253-8753), both in the $35-45 range. *Budget Motel* (☎ 828-665-2100), at I-40 exit 44, has modern, spacious rooms for $35. For something different, try *Log Cabin Motor Court* (☎ 828-645-6546, 330 Weaverville Hwy) north of town, where rustic singles/doubles start at $32/35.

The top-end choice is *Grove Park Inn Resort* (☎ 828-252-2711, 290 Macon Ave), with 510 rooms in a classic Arts and Crafts building (1913). Rates start at $135 off season, with summer suites from $375. The sparkling new *Inn on Biltmore Estate* (☎ 828-274-9600) offers rooms from $179.

Downtown has many interesting eateries, like *Blue Moon Bakery & café* (60 Biltmore Ave), a good stop for breakfast and sandwiches. *Beanstreets* (3 Broadway Ave) has great coffee and light meals in a fun atmosphere. The veggie haunt *Laughing Seed Café* (40 Wall St) offers tofu, tempeh and organic Green Man beer. *Zambra's* (85A Walnut St) is a laid-back tapas bar with tasty mains for $12-15.

Entertainment The *Asheville Music Zone* (☎ 828-255-8811), on N Lexington Ave at Hiawassee St, has an eclectic concert agenda of folk, soul, rock and jazz. Other good venues include *Tressa's* (☎ 828-245-7072, 28 Broadway Ave), a bar with blues, jazz and swing dancing, and *Scandals* (☎ 828-252-2838, 11 Grove St), a gay club with a techno-fed dance floor.

Getting There & Around Greyhound (☎ 828-253-2222, 2 Tunnel Rd) has several buses daily to Knoxville, Tennessee ($23; from 2 hours), and Raleigh ($47; 7½ hours), and one to Atlanta, Georgia ($32; from 5½ hours). Asheville Transit provides a limited local bus service.

Chimney Rock Park

The photogenic 'chimney,' complete with US flag, is a widely publicized rock spire a pleasant 20-mile drive southeast of Asheville. An elevator takes visitors 258 feet up to the chimney, but the real draw is the exciting hike around the cliffs to a 404-foot waterfall. Allow at least two hours here. Entrance to this private park (☎ 828-625-9611) costs $11 in summer, $7 in winter.

Cherokee

Some of the Cherokee people escaped removal on the Trail of Tears by hiding here in the Great Smoky Mountains. Their descendants, some 11,600 members of the Eastern Band of the Cherokee, now occupy a 56,000-acre reservation at the edge of the national park. The small town of Cherokee caters to the lowest common denominator of the tourist trade, with ersatz Indian souvenir shops, tacky attractions, fast-food joints and Harrah's Cherokee Casino (☎ 800-427-7247) on Hwy 19.

The best thing here is the **Museum of the Cherokee Indian** (☎ 828-497-3481), on Drama Rd/US 441N, which has a special interpretive exhibit on the Trail of Tears ($6). Across the road, Qualla Arts & Crafts sells authentic (and expensive) Indian handicrafts. **Oconaluftee Indian Village** (☎ 828-497-2111) is a replica of an 18th-century Cherokee village where Cherokees demonstrate traditional crafts ($12; open mid-May to late Oct). The outdoor show *Unto These Hills* dramatizes the history of the Cherokee from the first European contact up to the Trail of Tears. Seats cost $14-16 and can be reserved by phone (☎ 828-497-2111). The show runs mid-June to late August.

The town has more than 40 *motels*, some charging $40 in low season. In summer prices rise above $50 and you may need to call the Visitor Center (☎ 800-438-1601) to find a room. The nicest *campgrounds* are out of town, especially in the national park.

Great Smoky Mountains NP

This park straddles the border with Tennessee and is noted for its biodiversity and its more than 10 million annual visitors. Near Cherokee, Oconaluftee Visitor Center (☎ 423-436-1200), on Hwy 441, is the main access point on the southeast side of the park; the re-created pioneer farm there is worth a look (free admission). The park can be accessed at four other points on the southeast side, which may not be as crowded. For more information about the park, see the Tennessee section, later.

Nantahala

About 25 miles southwest of Cherokee, the Appalachian Trail crosses the fast-flowing Nantahala River, creating a natural focus for outdoor activities. Nantahala Outdoor Center (☎ 828-488-2175, 800-232-7238), on Hwy 19/74 near Bryson City, provides equipment as well as services for **hiking**, **mountain biking**, **canoeing** and **white-water rafting**. In particular, it offers a great range of rafting trips on a selection of nearby rivers. Accommodations include several cabins, simple motel-style units ($55-65) and

dormitory beds ($14). There's also a good little riverside restaurant, a laundry and an outfitter store, as well as congenial, outdoorsy guests.

NORTH CAROLINA COAST

Barrier islands run the whole length of North Carolina's coast, with miles of sandy beaches facing the Atlantic and a series of estuaries, sounds and enclosed tidal lagoons. Many of the beaches are heavily developed as holiday resorts, but some areas are protected as national seashore.

The Albermarle

The wild, swampy region around Albermarle Sound was the site of the state's first European settlement, and from the 18th century it became a focus for canals that provided protected transport routes north to the Chesapeake and south to Wilmington. Today it's popular for boating, fishing and retirement.

Edenton Founded in 1712, this small town at the west end of Albermarle Sound was the center of economic, social and political life in early colonial times. In the 1774 'Edenton tea party,' 50 local-society ladies swore off tea in protest at British taxes. The town provided signatories to the Declaration of Independence and the Constitution, as well as two state governors and one of the first Supreme Court justices. Within 50 years, development bypassed Edenton, leaving pretty streets of 18th-century buildings. See the Visitor Center (☎ 252-482-2637, 108 N Broad St) for a guided walking tour ($6) or a self-guided-tour map. Ask about regional sites like the Newbold-White House (1730) and Hope Plantation (1803). *Coach House Motel* (☎ 252-482-2107, 919 N Broad St) has rooms from $36. The visitor center also carries a list of *B&Bs* in town ($65-175).

Elizabeth City At the Pasquotank River narrows, Elizabeth City became a shipping and transportation center after the Dismal Swamp Canal was completed in 1803. The Museum of the Albermarle (☎ 252-335-1453) gives a good account of the canals and the area's history (free admission; closed Mon). It's 2 miles southeast on Hwy 17, but will move downtown in 2002. The town center is pleasantly old-fashioned; the chamber of commerce (☎ 252-335-4365, 502 E Ehringhaus St) has a walking-tour map. Motels are on the North Road St/US 17 bypass road. *Travelers Motel* (☎ 252-338-5451), at the north end, has clean singles/doubles from $40/45.

Along US 64 The low-lying peninsula south of Albermarle Sound is crossed quickly on US 64 to the Outer Banks. **Somerset Place** (☎ 252-797-4171), 7 miles south of tiny Creswell, is a historic site with a detailed depiction of the slave community on a Southern plantation (free admission; open daily). At nearby Lake Phelps, **Pettigrew State Park** (☎ 252-797-4475) is a wildlife sanctuary and features some Indian artifacts, fishing and a campground ($12).

Outer Banks

Hwy 12 runs along this chain of barrier islands, curving east of Albermarle and Pamlico Sounds in a 100-mile arc that's like a road across the sea. From north to south, Bodie Island, Roanoke Island, Hatteras Island and Ocracoke Island are linked by bridges and ferries. The islands are low sand dunes, with long, sandy beaches on the ocean side and lagoons and marshes on the inland side. The northern islands are heavily developed, with holiday homes, beach resorts and hordes of summer visitors. Out of season, things are very quiet and many businesses close. Much of the central islands is protected as national seashore, with a few small towns and a wild, windswept beauty.

Orientation & Information Most of the tourist attractions and facilities are along a 16-mile strip of Bodie Island, in the virtually contiguous towns of Kitty Hawk, Kill Devil Hills and Nags Head. Hwy 12, also called Virginia Dare Trail, or 'the coast road,' is a two-lane road running close to the beach for the length of the strip. US 158, usually called 'the Bypass,' is a four-lane road running parallel but farther inland. Locations are often given in terms of 'Mile Posts,' starting from Mile Post 1 at the north end of the tourist strip, where US 158 crosses to the mainland on the Wright Memorial Bridge. At the south end of the strip, just past Mile Post 16, US 64/264 connects to the mainland via Roanoke Island. Roanoke Island has

Sunday afternoon in the making

two communities: upscale, tourist-oriented Manteo and the functional fishing town of Wanchese.

The best sources of information are the visitor centers at Mile Post 1½ in Kitty Hawk (☎ 252-441-8144) and on US 64/264 in Manteo (☎ 252-473-2138, 800-446-6262), both open year round. Other visitor centers in Nags Head are open April to October.

Wright Brothers NM The dunes of Kill Devil Hills are unspectacular, but the site carries some of the excitement of the Wright brothers' historic achievement. The memorial is near Mile Post 8, where there's a heavy-looking, art deco–style granite monument atop a sand dune, inscribed:

In commemoration of the conquest of the air by the brothers Wilbur and Orville Wright. Conceived by genius, achieved by dauntless resolution and unconquerable faith.

Exhibits at the visitor center (☎ 252-441-7430) trace the painstaking development work in Dayton, Ohio, and the experiments conducted at summer camps here over several years. Replicas of their 1902 glider and 1903 powered *Flyer* are displayed, with informative hourly talks. The distances of the first powered flights on December 17, 1903, are marked, from the first tentative 120-foot hop to the fourth flight of the day, which reached an impressive 852 feet. The center opens daily ($2 per person or $4 per car).

Fort Raleigh NHS This Roanoke Island site saw the first English colonies in North America meet with total failure. The first settlers, sponsored by Walter Raleigh, arrived in 1585 but returned to England after only a year. The next group landed in 1587 and within three years had disappeared, leaving nothing but the word 'Croatan' carved into a tree. This might refer to a place or the name of a Native American tribe – no one knows. The fate of the 'Lost Colony' remains a mystery, but the Visitor Center (☎ 252-473-5772) has exhibits, artifacts and a film that will fuel your imagination (free admission). Look for the prints based on 1585 illustrations by John White, some of the best-known depictions of pre-European North America. A small mound nearby is meant to re-create the earthwork of the original fort. Also nearby, the **Elizabethan Gardens** make a pretty association with the England of 400 years ago ($3).

The **Lost Colony Outdoor Drama** is an immensely popular and long-running show that dramatizes the debacle. It plays at 8:30pm June to August in the Waterside Theater (☎ 252-473-3414 for reservations; $16).

Another piece of re-created history is *Elizabeth II*, a 69-foot sailing ship built in the style of an old English vessel. It gives a good feel for 16th-century sea travel, as do exhibits and a film in the Visitor Center (☎ 252-473-1144). It's open daily April to October, closed Monday otherwise ($4).

Cape Hatteras National Seashore Saving much of the Outer Banks area from overdevelopment, this national seashore (☎ 252-473-2111) extends some 70 miles, encompassing the southern end of Bodie Island and nearly all of Hatteras and Ocracoke Islands. Visitor centers at the north and south ends of the seashore open only in the summer season, but the Hatteras Island Visitor Center, near Cape Hatteras itself, is open year round.

Natural attractions include local and migratory waterbirds, marshes, woodlands, dunes and miles of empty beaches. One of the best places for watching wildlife is **Pea Island National Wildlife Refuge** (☎ 252-473-1131), at the northern end of Hatteras Island, where there's an informative Visitor Center, nature trails and observation points.

Lighthouses are spaced all along the Outer Banks, including the horizontally striped Bodie Island Lighthouse, where the keepers' quarters are open March to September. The spirally striped Cape Hatteras Lighthouse is open for climbing (268 steps) April to October, and its visitor center

(☎ 252-995-4474) is open year round, with interesting displays on the area's checkered maritime heritage. **Chicamacomico Lifesaving Station**, in the village of Rodanthe, shows the heroic side, while the village of Ocracoke revels in its pirate past: Edward Teach, also known as Blackbeard, used to hide out in the area.

Other things to look for include the old village of Avon and the privately owned Native American Museum (☎ 252-995-4440) in Frisco, with an extensive, ill-sorted, but engaging collection ($2; closed Mon).

Activities Popular outdoor activities include kayaking on the sounds, fishing, sailing, windsurfing, hang gliding and cycling. Kitty Hawk Kites Outdoors (☎ 800-334-4777), at Jockey's Ridge State Park, offers beginners hang-gliding lessons from $65 and training to USHGA Hang One standard from $399; it also offers area tours. Ocean Atlantic Rentals (☎ 800-635-9559), at Mile Post 10, rents kayaks ($30 per day), bikes ($10) and surfboards ($15). Other such outfits include Adventure Bound Kayak & Camping Center (☎ 252-255-1130), which caters to beginners, campers and ecotourists.

Surfing on the beach breaks is best August to October, with the East Coast championships in early September and the hurricane season starting in October, bringing the really big waves. Whalebone Surf Shop (☎ 252-261-8737, 4900A N Croatan Hwy) offers equipment and advice. Canadian Hole, in Pamlico Sound just south of Avon, is a serious windsurfing site. There's pleasant walking on the beaches and dunes and over 400 bird species in the protected areas.

Places to Stay National Park Service (NPS) and private campgrounds are spread all along the Outer Banks. *NPS campgrounds* (summer only) have no hot showers and little shade. The *Ocracoke campground* (☎ 800-365-2267) can be reserved, but the others are on a first-come, first-served basis. Many private campgrounds are open only in summer, some mainly for RVs. *Colington Park* (☎ 252-441-6128), Kill Devil Hills; *Camp Hatteras* (☎ 252-987-2777), Waves; and *Frisco Woods* (☎ 252-995-5208), Frisco, open year round and have tent sites for $14-22.

The lodging tax is 4%. *HI Outer Banks Hostel* (☎ 252-261-2294, Ⓦ *www .talking-pages.com/obhostel, 1004 W Kitty Hawk Rd)* is in a pleasant but out-of-the-way location; call for directions. It has a communal kitchen, air-con, camping area and 24-hour access. The friendly management arranges kayak trips, bicycle rentals and summer campfires. Dorm beds are $15/18 for members/nonmembers, and private rooms start at $28/35.

The area has hundreds of motels, efficiencies and B&Bs, but many close in winter and most are booked up in summer. The chamber of commerce (☎ 252-441-8144) offers referrals. *Budget Host Inn* (☎ 252-441-2503), at Mile Post 9 on the Bypass Rd in Kill Devil Hills, starts at $35. The oceanfront *Days Inn Mariner* (☎ 252-441-2021), Mile Post 7 on the Beach Rd in Kill Devil Hills, has a variety of singles/doubles for up to $115/140 in high season. Rodanthe, Buxton and Ocracoke are less busy areas, with some smaller inns and B&Bs. Grand old *Island Inn* (☎ 877-456-3466), at Point Rd in Ocracoke, charges $75 per room with breakfast.

Places to Eat The main tourist strip on Bodie Island has the most restaurants to choose from and the nightlife, but only in season. The following are all nonchain places open year round on Beach Rd. *Black Pelican*, at Mile Post 4, does good seafood and excellent wood-fired pizzas. The building is an old lifesaving station. *Jolly Roger*, at Mile Post 6¾, is a small family place, good for breakfast, lunch or an inexpensive dinner. As well as being a friendly bar, *Goombays*, at Mile Post 7½, serves seafood and good sandwiches. *Kelly's Tavern*, at Mile Post 10½ on the Hwy 158 bypass, has great snow-crab legs and live music nightly.

Getting There & Away No public transport exists to or on the Outer Banks. Free car ferries between the Hatteras and Ocracoke Islands run at least hourly 5am-10pm (more frequently in the summer); bookings aren't necessary. Ferries between Ocracoke and Cedar Island run every two hours or so ($10 per car; 2¼ hours) and should be reserved, especially in summer (☎ 800-293-3779). Ferries also link Ocracoke and Swan

Quarter, on the mainland ($10; twice daily; 2½ hours); for Swan Quarter reservations, call ☎ 800-773-1094.

Crystal Coast
The southern Outer Banks, comprising several coastal towns, sounds, islands, inlets and barrier islands, are collectively called the 'Crystal Coast,' at least for tourist offices' promotion purposes.

Cape Lookout National Seashore This 55-mile-long barrier-island system, mostly dunes and shifting sands, has virtually no visitor facilities and can be reached only by boat. The visitor center (☎ 252-728-2250) is on Harkers Island, accessible by bridge from the mainland. The national seashore has seasonal nesting sites for turtles and shorebirds, and the picturesque abandoned village of Portsmouth is at its northern tip. With its striking diamond pattern, the **Cape Lookout Lighthouse** is arguably the most photogenic on the Atlantic coast. Primitive camping is permitted, but you'll have to bring in all your supplies, including food, water, insect repellent and long tent pegs. Day trips are possible by ferry (about $20 roundtrip) from Harkers Island and the coastal towns of Atlantic (☎ 252-225-4261), Davis (☎ 252-729-2791) and Beaufort (☎ 252-728-6888).

Beaufort One of the oldest towns in the state, Beaufort (**bow**-fort) was originally called 'Fish Town' and still trades off its maritime heritage. The Welcome Center (☎ 252-728-5225, 138 Turner St) is in the Beaufort Historic Site with several 18th-century buildings; it offers 1½-hour history tours ($6). The highlight is the **North Carolina Maritime Museum** (☎ 252-728-7317, 315 Front St),with diverse displays on lifesaving, outboard motors and local fishing, all very well done (free admission).

B&Bs are abundant and expensive in season. *Innlet Inn* (☎ 252-728-3600, 601 Front St) has big, comfy rooms with fireplaces for $110 ($65 in winter). On Front St are bars and eateries that can be lively on a warm evening, as well as boats and excursions to the islands.

Morehead City A rather unappealing industrial-commercial stretch of US 70 goes through Morehead City, but it's worth a short detour to the waterfront. The well-stocked Crystal Coast Visitors Bureau (☎ 252-726-8148) is at 3407 Arendell St/Hwy 70. So many ships have sunk along this coast that it's called the 'Graveyard of the Atlantic,' and some wrecks are superb for serious divers, especially June to September, when the water is warm and clear. Olympus Dive Center (☎ 252-726-9432, 713 Shepard St) runs dive charters ($55/100 for half-/full-day trips); drop in to see its fascinating artifacts.

Econo Lodge *(☎ 252-247-2940, 3410 Bridges St)*, near Hwy 70, has singles/doubles from $69/89 but offers frequent discounts. Closer to the water, ***Charter Motel*** *(☎ 252-726-3256, 404 Evans St)* is a little cheaper. ***Sanitary Fish Market*** *(501 Evans St)*, on the waterfront, has been serving seafood to appreciative locals since 1938.

Bogue Island A bridge from Morehead City crosses to Atlantic City on Bogue Island, which is a mass-market seaside resort. At the east end of the island, **Fort Macon** (☎ 252-726-3775) will interest Civil War buffs with its old fortifications and exhibits on army life.

Hammocks Beach State Park Accessible by ferries from Swansboro ($2), this state park (☎ 910-326-4881) features sand dunes, primitive camping, and some of the best (yet undervisited) beaches on the Atlantic coast.

Topsail Island Despite enticing place names like Surf City and Topsail Beach, this island is mostly a mass-market holiday destination, without the natural attractions of the Outer Banks seashores or the tacky appeal of South Carolina's Myrtle Beach.

Wilmington

The Cape Fear area was explored by Giovanni da Verrazano in 1524, but it was 200 years before the first European settlement was established here on the Cape Fear River. The area prospered as a provider of naval stores (turpentine, pitch and tar) for the Royal Navy, and Wilmington grew as a port and a trading center for goods brought downriver on flatboats. The town was an early leader in the American independence movement, and one of the first decisive battles of the Revolution was fought nearby at Moore's Creek. In the Civil War it was an important Confederate port, supplied by blockade-runners that sped in under the protection of the guns around the mouth of Cape Fear River. Federal forces did not take the city until 1865, after a massive naval bombardment of Fort Fisher.

Today, Wilmington is still a busy little port, with a university, film studios, and a neat old downtown and waterfront area. The Cape Fear Visitors Center (☎ 910-341-4030), in the 1892 Courthouse building at 3rd and Princes Sts, has a walking-tour map and details of several historic houses. You can surf the Web free at the public library (301 Chestnut St).

Greyhound's station (☎ 910-762-6073, 201 Hartnett St), north of downtown, sends daily buses to Raleigh ($29; 6¼ hours) and Charleston, South Carolina ($38; 5 hours).

Things to See & Do The St Johns Museum of Art (☎ 910-763-0281, 114 Orange St) exhibits work by local artists, plus an excellent collection of Mary Cassatt prints ($3; closed Mon). For local history, Cape Fear Museum (☎ 910-341-4350, 814 Market St) includes a model of Wilmington in the blockade-running 1860s, and a small display on local legend Michael Jordan ($4; closed Mon).

Take a river taxi ($2 roundtrip) or cross the Cape Fear Bridge to reach the **Battleship *North Carolina*** (☎ 910-251-5797). This 44,000-ton monster was the epitome of sea power when she was launched. Self-guided tours take in the crew quarters, captain's cabin, gun turrets, galleys and more. It's just old enough to be enjoyed as a technological relic ($8/4 adults/kids; open daily).

Screen Gems Studios (☎ 910-343-3433, 1223 N 23rd St), near the airport, offers a good behind-the-scenes tour. There are no Hollywood-style special effects, but the guides know their stuff and are full of anecdotes (eg, about actor Brandon Lee's fatal accident). The two-hour tours are at noon and 2pm weekends ($10).

Organized Tours Walking tours abound. Try Wilmington Adventure Walking Tours (☎ 910-763-1785), or, for a more historic view, Walk and Talk Tours (☎ 910-762-0492). Wilmington Trolley Co (☎ 910-763-4483) runs a loop around TV and movie locations in town, with slick commentary. The stern-wheeler *Henrietta III* (☎ 910-343-1611) does popular river cruises. Each attraction costs $10.

Places to Stay & Eat The closest camping is at *Carolina Beach State Park* (☎ *910-458-8206*), 18 miles south on US 421, with tent sites for $12. The cheapest accommodations are along Hwy 17/Market St, east of downtown. *Travel Inn* (☎ *910-763-8217, 4401 Market St*) charges $35-55. Much nicer is *Best Western Carolinian* (☎ *910-763-4653, 2916 Market St*), at $52-75. Comfy *Coastline Inn* (☎ *910-763-2800, 503 Nutt St*) has harbor views (from $99). For a list of the many historic B&Bs, contact the visitor bureau.

On the riverfront, *Water St Cafe* has good sandwiches, soups and salads and live music evenings. *Cedars* (*128 S Front St*) offers Lebanese fare for $8-10. *Café Deluxe* (☎ *910-251-0333, 114 Market St*) serves American fusion cuisine in intimate lighting (main dishes $14-25). Chandlers Wharf, at the south end of Water St, also has nice restaurants. N Front St has several good bars with live music, including *Bessie's* (*133 N Front St*) and *Firebelly Lounge* (*265 N Front St*).

Cape Fear
For a good day's detour, go south of Wilmington to the tip of Cape Fear, with possible stops at Carolina Beach, Kure Beach and **Fort Fisher State Historic Site** (☎ 910-458-5538), where earthwork and exhibits explain the fort's vital Civil War role. There's a big aquarium here, too. Catch a ferry across the mouth of the Cape Fear River ($3 per car) to the old fishing village of Southport, and return via **Orton Plantation**, with its exceptionally colorful gardens.

South Carolina

Although Charleston is South Carolina's gem, a place with real style and character, the mass-tourism ghetto of Myrtle Beach attracts more visitors. The north coast has some historical and environmental interest, while the south-coast sea islands are an intriguing detour for those with time to appreciate the unique Gullah culture. The central Piedmont area is more rural and hardscrabble; the highland area around

South Carolina	
Nickname: Palmetto State	
Population: 4,012,000 (26th)	
Area: 31,000 sq miles (40th)	
Admitted to the Union: May 23, 1788 (8th); seceded 1860; readmitted 1868	
Capital city: Columbia (population 100,000)	
Other cities: Charleston (80,000), Greenville (58,000)	
State dance: the shag	
Birthplace of: activist Mary Mcleod Bethune (1875–1955), James Brown (b 1933), Dizzy Gillespie (1917–93), Jesse Jackson (b 1941), songstress Eartha Kitt (b 1927), senator Strom Thurmond (b 1902)	
Home of: the first US public library (1698), museum (1773), steam railroad (1833)	

Greenville is more picturesque and worth a stop.

History
Both the Spanish and French made early attempts at settling the Carolina coast, which prompted King Charles I to issue land grants for British settlements in 1629. It wasn't until 1670 that Charles Towne was established, and by the early 1700s it sheltered nearly 15,000 people. Of the Native American inhabitants, the Yemasee made war on the British in 1715 and were driven out, the Catawba were decimated by disease over the next 80 years, and the Cherokee were expelled after the Revolutionary War.

In the 18th century the coastal colony prospered on the expanding rice and indigo trade. Charleston was the fifth-largest city on the Atlantic coast, with more black slaves than white colonists. The upcountry areas were settled later by small farmers migrating down the Great Valley from Northeastern colonies. Despite some loyalist sympathies, South Carolina took a leading role in the Revolution, and many battles were fought in the state; Kings Mountain (1780) and Cowpens (1781) were major victories for the Americans.

South Carolina was the first state to secede when Lincoln was elected, and the

Gullah Carolina

During plantation times, African slaves working the rice and cotton fields along coastal South Carolina and Georgia often outnumbered their white overseers. This isolation and their common origin from West Africa allowed for the continuation of many African traditions, including sweetgrass basketry, burial customs, net fishing and oral storytelling. A unique language, called Gullah, merged the many African languages (mainly Bantu) into English.

After the fall of the planter monarchy, many freed people remained on the plantations, cut off from the mainland. As a result, the Gullah culture survived and the language is still spoken by 500,000 people in the South Carolina Lowcountry and Sea Islands. Some Gullah words have slipped into the Southern lexicon: 'cooter' ('turtle') and 'bubba' ('brother').

Gullah storytellers relate the exploits of Buh Rabbit, more famously known as Brer Rabbit from the Uncle Remus books. This cunning character is common in the trickster tales of West Africa. He often outwits bigger and stronger animals and lives in constant danger of retribution.

Civil War started when South Carolinians fired on Fort Sumter in Charleston Harbor. No major battles were fought here, but General Sherman's forces destroyed everything in a wide strip across the state. Reconstruction was very difficult, with the once-wealthy plantations unworkable without slave labor. Attention turned to processing cotton, and textile mills using low-paid white workers became the main industry.

There was a boom during WWI, when cotton prices soared, but the Great Depression hit hard, and only New Deal programs saved South Carolina from bankruptcy. Agricultural diversification and increased manufacturing have bolstered the economy, and tourism has become significant, often at the expense of the coastal environment. In 1989 the barrier islands were devastated by Hurricane Hugo, which caused billions of dollars in damage.

Information

The state department of tourism (☎ 803-734-7000, 800-255-2059, 🖳 www.travelsc.com) is at 1205 Pendleton St, Suite 106, Columbia, SC 29201. For road conditions, call ☎ 803-896-9621. State sales tax is 6%, but local taxes can apply for lodging and meals. Tax on a room in Charleston totals around 12%.

NORTH COAST

The northern part of the South Carolina coast is dominated by the all-purpose resort town of Myrtle Beach. Farther south, sleepy villages and parks set a slower pace. A few minutes outside Charleston, grand houses remain as testaments to the state's plantation past.

Myrtle Beach

Myrtle Beach proper is the central area in the 25-mile strip of overdeveloped oceanfront called 'The Grand Strand,' which is smeared from North Myrtle Beach to Pawleys Island. College students swarm here for spring break and summer vacation, and holidaymakers come for the plethora of amusements and the more than 100 golf courses. Turn off the highway at US 17 Business (also called Kings Hwy) to go through the middle of it. The main Chamber of Commerce Visitor Center (☎ 843-626-7444) is at 1200 N Oak St, with offices on US 17 north and south and on US 501 west of town.

The beach is quite pretty for a resort town, with remnants of the Carolina's signature beach dunes, but is backed by a near-continuous row of high-rises. Along Ocean Blvd are parking lots, neon signs, tourist shops, bars and restaurants. The heart of the resort, historically and geographically, is the **Myrtle Beach Pavilion** amusement park (☎ 843-448-6456), at 9th Ave and Ocean Blvd, but the **Family Kingdom** (☎ 843-626-3447), close by at 3rd and Ocean Blvd, might be a better value (an all-ride pass costs about $19).

Places to Stay & Eat Most campgrounds are for RVs, but *Myrtle Beach State Park* (☎ *843-238-5325*), 3 miles south of central Myrtle Beach, has unshaded tent sites ($22) and its own beach and cabins ($200 per weekend).

Hundreds of hotels have prices that vary by the season and day; a room might cost $29 in January and over $150 in July. In summer, many will be all booked up, so it might be best to contact the chamber of commerce. In low season you'd do just as well driving on and around Ocean Blvd, looking at the signs for special prices. The big beachfront hotels may be no more expensive than a cheap-looking motel. Away from the beach, *Grand Strand Motel* (☎ 843-448-1461, 800-433-1461, 1804 S Ocean Blvd) has rooms for $50-100. For beachfront accommodations in the $150 range, try the small *Firebird Motor Inn* (☎ 843-448-7032, 800-852-7032, 2007 S Ocean Blvd) or the large *Compass Cove* (☎ 843-448-8373, 800-326-0234, 2311 S Ocean Blvd).

The 1700 or so restaurants are mostly mid-range and high volume, but competition keeps prices reasonable. For Americana ambience, hit the burger bars on Ocean Blvd near the amusement parks. Seafood, ironically, is not a specialty; locals go to the fishing village of Murrells Inlet. Theme restaurants such as *Planet Hollywood* and *Hard Rock Café* are in Broadway at the Beach, US 17 and 21st Ave. *Cagney's Old Place Restaurant* (☎ 843-449-3824), at N Kings Hwy and 71st Ave, is a dinner favorite for surf and turf. *Croissants Bakery & Café (504A 27th Ave N)* has sweets, coffee and lunch sandwiches ($6).

Entertainment Music variety shows are a Myrtle Beach standard, combining rock, country and bluegrass music with a dose of comedy, Christianity and patriotism. Some include a fixed-menu meal for around $35; reservations are recommended. Bars and clubs catering to the college crowd include *Studebakers* (☎ 843-626-3855, 2000 N Kings Hwy). *Dead Dog Saloon* (☎ 843-445-6700, 404 26th Ave N) hosts Saturday cookouts. *Bummz Beach Café* (☎ 843-916-9111, 2002 N Ocean Blvd) has an ocean view and a swimsuit-clad crowd.

Getting There & Around The airport (☎ 843-448-1589) is within the city limits, and travel from New York can be less than $100. Greyhound (☎ 843-448-2471, 511 7th Ave N) services New York ($110; from 16 hours); Atlanta, Georgia ($85; from 11 hours) and Charleston ($45; from 3 hours). Coastal Rapid Public Transport (☎ 843-488-0865)

has infrequent service up and down the resort area.

Around Myrtle Beach

At the south end of the Grand Strand, Murrells Inlet is a small village with charter boats for fishing trips and a choice of seafood restaurants. *Nance's Creekfront Restaurant and Oyster Roast (4583 Hwy 17)* is popular for steamed oysters ($15) and sunset views (open daily for dinner).

Farther south on US 17, **Brookgreen Gardens** (☎ 800-849-1931) is a former plantation now beautifully landscaped with moss-draped oaks, fragrant magnolias and azaleas. Over 500 works by noted American sculptors are displayed throughout the gardens ($9; open daily). Across the road, *Huntington Beach State Park* (☎ 843-237-4440) has a great beach, nature trails and pleasant RV and tent campsites for $11-25.

Georgetown

The Spanish tried to settle here in 1526 but soon retreated to St Augustine, Florida. In colonial times Georgetown became a center for rice plantations on the estuarine land around the Pee Dee and Sampit Rivers. West African slaves, experienced in rice cultivation, provided the expertise and labor. The small **Rice Museum**, on Front and Screven Sts, has explanatory models and maps ($5; closed Sun). The chamber of commerce (☎ 800-777-7705, 1001 Front St), at King St, has a map showing the town's 18th-century houses. The old downtown contrasts with the big steelworks and paper factory across the Sampit River.

Plantations

Between Georgetown and Charleston, some old plantation homes give a feel for antebellum life. Hopsewee (☎ 843-546-7891), off US 17, 12 miles south of Georgetown, was a rice plantation from about 1740 and has antique furnishings and atmospheric grounds ($6; open 10am-4pm Tue-Fri). From the same era, Hampton Plantation State Park (☎ 843-546-9361), off US 17 about 15 miles from Georgetown, is an imposing white building, but it's unfurnished and unrestored, with overgrown surroundings and big old trees ($2; open 1pm-4pm Thurs-Mon).

Eight miles from Charleston, Boone Hall Plantation (☎ 843-884-4371, 1235 Long

Point Rd) is a 1935 reconstruction, with costumed guides and tours ($10; open daily).

CHARLESTON

Charleston's historic district is one of the
most appealing urban areas in America,
with handsome old houses, charming little
streets, gorgeous gardens, good restaurants
and lively bars. Everyone loves it, though it
can be a bit snooty.

History

Even well before the Revolutionary War,
Charles Towne (named for Charles II) was
one of the busiest ports on the eastern
seaboard and the center of a prosperous
rice-growing and trading colony. With influences from the West Indies, Africa, France
and other European countries, it became a
cosmopolitan city often compared to New
Orleans. It saw some of the first battles of
the American Revolution, when British
ships attacked Fort Moultrie, at the entrance
to the harbor.

The Charleston & Hamburg Railroad
began operations in 1833, transporting
cotton 136 miles from the inland area to
Charleston's ports. At the time it was an engineering wonder, and it secured Charleston's
position as a principal East Coast port over
rival Savannah.

The first shots of the Civil War were fired
at Fort Sumter, in Charleston's harbor, but
after the war the city's importance declined,
as the labor-intensive rice plantations
became uneconomical without slave labor.
Natural disasters wrought more damage,
with a major earthquake in 1886, several
fires and storms, and devastating Hurricane
Hugo in 1989. It's remarkable that so much
of the town's historic fabric has survived –
and fortunate too, because tourism is now a
major money-spinner, with close to four
million visitors arriving each year.

Orientation & Information

The Charleston metropolitan area sprawls
over a broad stretch of coastal plains and
islands, but the historic heart is very compact,
about 4 sq miles at the southern tip of a
peninsula between the Cooper and Ashley
Rivers. I-26 goes to North Charleston and
the airport. Hwy 17, the main coastal road,
cuts across the Charleston peninsula as the
Crosstown Expressway, with soaring bridges

connecting west to James Island and West
Ashley, and east to Mount Pleasant.

The Visitor Information Center (☎ 843-
853-8000, 375 Meeting St) is about eight
blocks south of the Crosstown Expressway
and should be your first stop, if only to park
your car for the day ($12). The center can
help with accommodations and tours, but if
the lines are too long, just grab a map and
the free 'Official Visitors Guide.' The 23-
minute *Charleston Forever* audiovisual is
worth seeing ($2). Nearby, the chamber of
commerce (☎ 800-868-8000, W www
.charlestonsvb.com, 81 Mary St) is also
helpful. Buses or a tour will take you into
town. To walk downtown, take the most
pleasant route by going a block west from the
visitor center, then turning left (south) down
King St. The Charleston Preservation Society
(☎ 843-722-4630, 147 King St) has history and
architecture books, as does the Historic
Charleston Foundation Preservation Center
(☎ 843-724-8484, 108 Meeting St).

The main post office (☎ 843-577-0690) is
at 83 Broad St, and the library, which offers
Internet access, is at 68 Calhoun St. Banks
are around Market and Meeting Sts.

Things to See & Do

Charleston's main tourist activities are
visiting historic houses, shopping for sweetgrass baskets in the Market and imagining
what it must have been like during the 'Last,
Great Unpleasantness.'

Market Street & Around The main attraction is the city itself, especially the
quarter south of Beaufain St and east of
King St, where you can wander along
elegant thoroughfares and quaint, bending
backstreets. There are maps with walking
tours, but an aimless stroll is just as good –
Tradd, Meeting and Church Sts have some
of the best buildings. The old **Market Street**
now has some touristy shops, craft stalls,
eateries and bars, and is a good place to be
at lunch or dinnertime.

Overlooking the Cooper River, **Waterfront Park** is a shady retreat; farther south,
White Point Park & Gardens, at the tip of
the peninsula, is superb at sunset, when the
South Battery mansions are beautifully illuminated. Around the bottom end of Church
St, the area called Cabbage Row was the
model for Catfish Row in *Porgy & Bess*.

CHARLESTON

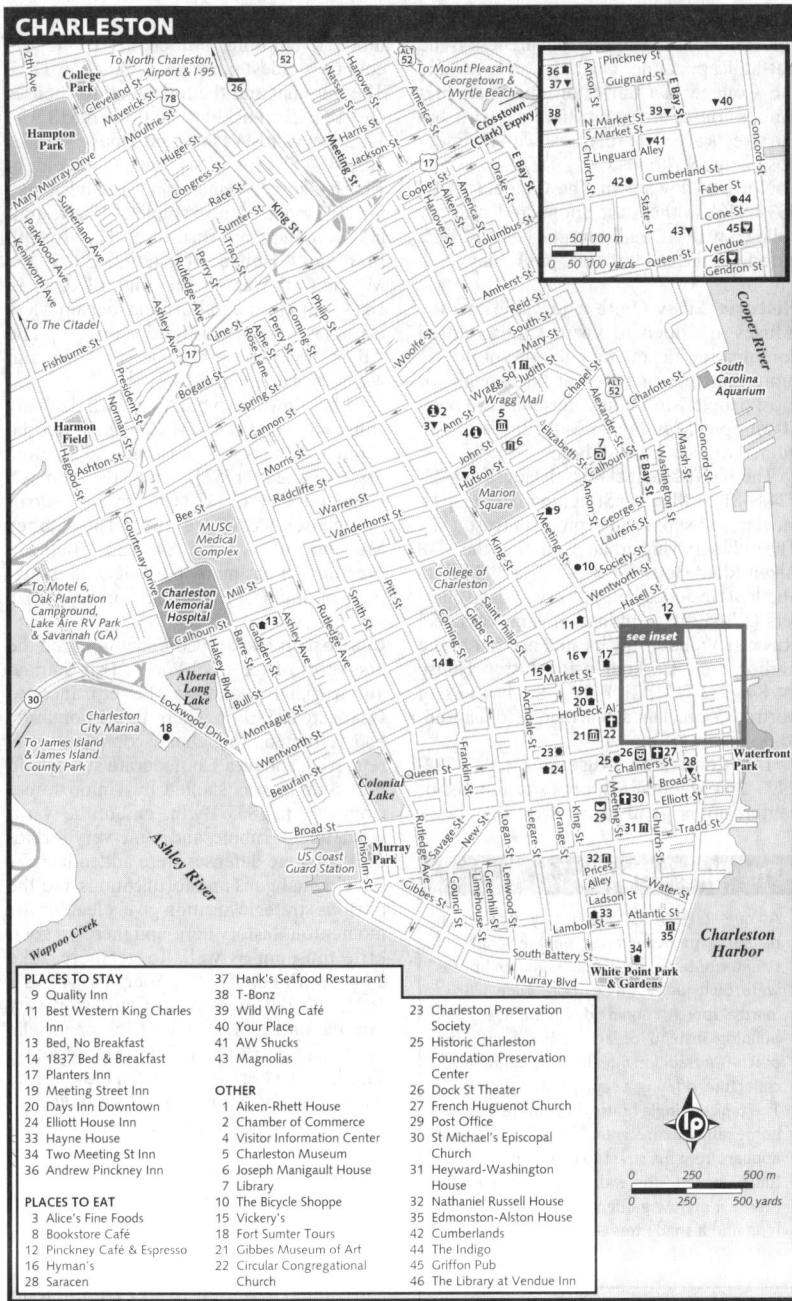

PLACES TO STAY
9 Quality Inn
11 Best Western King Charles Inn
13 Bed, No Breakfast
14 1837 Bed & Breakfast
17 Planters Inn
19 Meeting Street Inn
20 Days Inn Downtown
24 Elliott House Inn
33 Hayne House
34 Two Meeting St Inn
36 Andrew Pinckney Inn

PLACES TO EAT
3 Alice's Fine Foods
8 Bookstore Café
12 Pinckney Café & Espresso
16 Hyman's
28 Saracen

37 Hank's Seafood Restaurant
38 T-Bonz
39 Wild Wing Café
40 Your Place
41 AW Shucks
43 Magnolias

OTHER
1 Aiken-Rhett House
2 Chamber of Commerce
4 Visitor Information Center
5 Charleston Museum
6 Joseph Manigault House
7 Library
10 The Bicycle Shoppe
15 Vickery's
18 Fort Sumter Tours
21 Gibbes Museum of Art
22 Circular Congregational Church

23 Charleston Preservation Society
25 Historic Charleston Foundation Preservation Center
26 Dock St Theater
27 French Huguenot Church
29 Post Office
30 St Michael's Episcopal Church
31 Heyward-Washington House
32 Nathaniel Russell House
35 Edmonston-Alston House
42 Cumberlands
44 The Indigo
45 Griffon Pub
46 The Library at Vendue Inn

West of King St are residential blocks with colorfully painted houses that are less grand but still appealing. Farther north, around the College of Charleston, many smaller timber houses are somewhat timeworn, but the streets are a nice contrast with the more posh neighborhoods.

North of downtown, **The Citadel** (☎ 843-953-6846) is the state-sponsored military college, with a small museum and a dress parade of the cadets at 3:45pm Friday.

Historic Sites Quite a few fine historic houses are open to visitors. Discounted combination tickets may tempt you to see more, but one or two will be enough for most people. Most house museums are open 10am-5pm Monday to Saturday and run guided tours every half hour.

The 1808 **Nathaniel Russell House** (☎ 843-724-8481, 51 Meeting St) is noted for its spectacular, self-supporting spiral staircase ($7). The only surviving urban plantation, the 1818 **Aiken-Rhett House** (☎ 843-723-1159, 48 Elizabeth St) includes well-preserved slave quarters ($7, $12 in combination with Nathaniel Russell). Wonderfully located in front of the harbor, the 1828 **Edmonston-Alston House** (☎ 843-722-7171, 21 E Bay St) has lots of portraits, porcelain and artifacts from a well-to-do family ($8).

The **Charleston Museum** (☎ 843-722-2996, 360 Meeting St), opposite the visitor center, offers good exhibits on the state's history, but see Charleston first. It's in a modern building, but claims to be the country's oldest museum, founded in 1773. The museum and the following two houses cost $8 each; a ticket to all three is $18. The 1772 **Heyward-Washington House** (☎ 843-722-0354, 87 Church St) is one of the oldest, where George Washington was entertained in 1791, and has fine example of Charleston-made mahogany furniture. The **Joseph Manigault House** (☎ 843-723-2926, 350 Meeting St) was on the edge of town in 1803, but the neighborhood became less classy when the railroad came in. The Adams-style house became run-down and was nearly demolished.

Other downtown buildings include many churches, notably St Michael's Episcopal Church, at the corner of Broad and Meeting Sts (opened 1752), and the French Huguenot Church (136 Church St), a site of French services since 1681. The **Gibbes Museum of Art** (☎ 843-722-2706, 135 Meeting St) has many portraits and miniatures of South Carolina's aristocracy ($7).

Charleston Harbor Confederates fired the first shots of the Civil War at **Fort Sumter**, an artificial island at the entrance to Charleston Harbor, where the Union army had retreated. The Union contingent surrendered, and as a Confederate stronghold Fort Sumter was shelled by Union forces from 1863 to 1865. By the end of the war it was a pile of rubble, and some very forbidding concrete defenses were added later. A few original guns and fortifications and the obvious strategic location give a feel for the momentous history here, and there's a good little museum as well. To get here, take a boat with Fort Sumter Tours (☎ 843-722-1691, 800-789-3678) from Charleston City Marina, on the west side of the peninsula, or from Patriot's Point (see *Around Charleston*, later). A tour from either place takes about 2¼ hours and is first-come, first-served ($11; call for times).

Organized Tours

Bus tours from the visitor center start at $14 for a useful 75-minute introduction to the town. Carriage tours are very pleasant and start at $15 for a one-hour tour. Walking and ghost tours (☎ 843-723-1670), Civil War tours (☎ 843-722-7033) and black-history tours

---

The Single House

At one stage in its long history, Charleston based its property taxes on the length of street frontage. As a result, many houses were built just a single room wide with a 'piazza' (porch) running down the side of the building instead of across the front. The porch is a traditional feature of Southern architecture, offering a cool, private place to sit. The typical 'single house' is a smallish timber home rather than a grand mansion, and what appears from the street to be a front door actually opens to the end of the piazza. Often there's a narrow garden alongside, with wisteria and a shade tree – an essential ingredient of Charleston's unique charm.

☺ ☺ ☺ ☺ ☺ ☺ ☺ ☺ ☺ ☹ ☺

(☎ 843-763-7551) are all available. Nature and swamp tours are available through Barrier Island Ecotour (☎ 843-886-5000).

Places to Stay

Staying in the historic downtown is the most attractive option, but it's expensive, especially on weekends and during special events.

Three campgrounds southwest of Charleston offer shuttle services downtown. *Oak Plantation Campground* (☎ 843-766-5936, 3540 Savannah Hwy) has tent and RV sites for $14-18. *Lake Aire RV Park & Campground* (☎ 843-571-1271), at Hwy 17 and Hwy 162, also has sites for $11-18. Perhaps nicest is the campground at *James Island County Park* (☎ 843-795-9884, 800-743-7275, 871 Riverland Dr), with tent/RV sites ($18/24) and cabins ($100).

Most affordable motels are charmless highway jobs on the edge of town. A few miles west on US 17 (Savannah Hwy), near the I-526 junction, a trusty *Motel 6* (☎ 843-556-5144) has singles/doubles for $45/50. There are plenty more motels north of town around I-26 exits 199A and 203.

A small, friendly *pensione*-style place is *Bed, No Breakfast* (☎ 843-723-4450, 16 Halsey St), with just two rooms and a shared bathroom ($70-95; cash or checks only).

Downtown chain hotels are pretty standard. *Days Inn Downtown* (☎ 843-722-8411, 155 Meeting St) has a good location and motel-style rooms for $120-160. Prices are similar at *Best Western King Charles Inn* (☎ 843-723-7451, 237 Meeting St) and *Quality Inn* (☎ 843-722-3391, 125 Calhoun St).

Larger places with old-style ambience are usually called 'inns,' and most will cost at least $150 for a double. *Andrew Pinckney Inn* (☎ 843-937-8800, 800-505-8983, 199 Church St) has a good location near the market, a rooftop garden and 32 rooms from $120/190 on weekdays/weekends. *Meeting Street Inn* (☎ 843-723-1882, 173 Meeting St) has 56 small, nicely decorated rooms from $200. You'll find similar rates at *Planters Inn* (☎ 843-722-2345, fax 577-2125), at Meeting and Market Sts. Tucked behind a narrow courtyard, cozy *Elliott House Inn* (☎ 843-723-1855, 800-729-1855, 78 Queen St) charges $135 for doubles.

The best B&Bs are well-located historic homes like *Hayne House* (☎ 843-577-2633, 30 King St), with six rooms, private baths, antique furnishings and a Southern breakfast. Rates vary, but expect to pay about $200. A Queen Anne mansion on the Battery, *Two Meeting St Inn* (☎ 843-723-7322, 2 Meeting St) is the premier Charleston fantasy ($165-250). *1837 Bed & Breakfast* (☎ 843-723-7166, 126 Wentworth St) has five rooms ($120-145). Other small places start at around $100 for doubles with breakfast, but many have only one or two rooms, so it helps to use an agency like Historic Charleston B&B (☎ 843-722-6606).

Places to Eat

The highest concentration of restaurants and bars is on and around Market St. *T-Bonz (80 N Market St)* does steak and seafood entrées for around $11, with a good selection of burgers and sides. Nearby *Wild Wing Café (36 N Market St)* threatens meltdown with its Chernobyl wings. The well-promoted *AW Shucks (35 S Market St)* and *Hyman's (215 Meeting St)* are passable seafood restaurants, but not worth waiting in line. Locals go to *Hank's Seafood Restaurant* (☎ 834-723-3474, 10 Hayne St) for crab soup and other Lowcountry dishes ($15; dinner only).

Just north of Market St, *Pinckney Café & Espresso (18 Pinckney St)* is a moderately priced place that does fresh variations on Southern cuisine. Smack dab at the end of Market St is *Your Place (6 Market St)*, the best burger joint in town. South of Market St, there are fashionable places along E Bay St, such as *Magnolias* (☎ 843-577-7771, 185 E Bay St), which offers 'Down South dishes with uptown presentation' ($10-20) – try shrimp and grits. For an unusual architectural ambience, try *Saracen* (☎ 843-723-6242, 141 E Bay St), a Moorish-Gothic former bank building. It has an original menu (main dishes up to $20) and a comfortable little bar upstairs.

Up King St a long block west of the visitor center, several good-value places attract more students than tourists. *Alice's Fine Foods (470 King St)* is a Southern and soul-food buffet where you can fill up for well under $7. *Bookstore Café* (☎ 843-720-8843, 412 King St) offers an affordable breakfast of eggs and such.

Entertainment

The balmy evenings are conducive to late-night dining, drinking and dancing at the various venues around Market and E Bay Sts. *Griffon Pub (18 Vendue Range)* is a popular Celtic-style place with good bar food. Later on, try *The Indigo (5 Faber St)*, a late-night party place with dance, alternative, reggae and cabaret nights. A good place to catch the sunset is the rooftop bar at *The Library at Vendue Inn (23 Vendue Range)*. The Charleston outpost of an Atlanta gay landmark, *Vickery's (15 Beaufain St)* attracts a mixed crowd of gays and straights.

Check out the free weekly *Charleston City Paper* for cultural and live-music events. *Cumberlands (☎ 843-577-9469, 26 Cumberland St)* has mostly blues and regional acts. The historic *Dock St Theater (☎ 843-723-5648)*, at Church and Queen Sts, presents classical and contemporary works (Oct-May).

Getting There & Around

The airport (☎ 843-767-7009) is 12 miles outside town just off I-26 exit 212B. Fares to New York are about $250. The Greyhound station (☎ 843-747-5341, 3610 Dorchester Rd) has regular buses to New York ($140; 18 hours); Atlanta ($100; 6 hours) and Savannah, Georgia ($45; 3 hours); and Columbia ($45; 3 hours).

The Amtrak station (☎ 843-744-8263, 4565 Gaynor Ave) is an inconvenient 8 miles north of downtown. The *Silver Meteor* and *Silver Palm* travel the coast with stops at New York ($260; 14 hours) and Savannah ($45; 1½ hours). A city bus on Dorchester Rd goes into town from near the bus and train stations. At night, call a North Area Taxi (☎ 843-554-7575).

To reach Charleston by car from the north or south coast, use Hwy 17. From I-95, take I-26 west for about an hour to Charleston.

The Downtown Area Shuttle (DASH; ☎ 843-724-7420), has faux streetcars doing four loop routes from the visitor center (75¢, or $2 day pass). The Bicycle Shoppe (☎ 843-722-8168, 283 Meeting St) rents single-speed bikes from $4/15 per hour/day.

AROUND CHARLESTON

There's plenty to see in the surrounding area, ranging from fine old plantations and historic forts to retired superpower technology. The **Patriot's Point Naval & Maritime Museum** (☎ 843-884-2727), on the east side of the Cooper River, features the aircraft carrier USS *Yorktown*, a WWII veteran. You can also tour a submarine, a destroyer, a Coast Guard cutter and a re-created 'fire base' from Vietnam. It takes hours to see it all ($11). Restaurants on Shem Creek in Mt Pleasant attract a lot of tourists for seafood, but locals opt a more hidden spot, *The Wreck (☎ 843-884-0052)*. Call for directions and opening hours.

Popular beaches are Folly Island, only a 15-minute drive from downtown via Hwy 17 south to Hwy 171, and Isle of Palms, 12 miles from Charleston via Hwy 17 north to Hwy 517.

Drive south on US 17 and Hwy 703 to reach **Fort Moultrie** (☎ 843-883-3123), where a stockade of spongy palmetto logs absorbed the shells of the British navy in one of the first American victories of the Revolutionary War.

Heading up the Ashley River on Hwy 61, **Drayton Hall** (☎ 843-766-0188) is a fine brick mansion (c. 1738) still in very original condition ($10). The magnificent **Magnolia Plantation** (☎ 843-571-1266) has a 50-acre garden with azaleas and camellias, and the Audubon Swamp Garden, with alligators and cypresses ($16). The well-furnished Reconstruction-era house is $6 extra.

More educational is **Middleton Place** (☎ 843-556-6020), which features a terraced formal garden (1741) as well as working stables, a slave house and the 1755 mansion, with interesting items from the illustrious Middleton family ($15 for garden and stables, $23 for a house tour).

SOUTH COAST

South of Charleston, the land is fractured into a multitude of islands separated by tidal creeks and marshes. Picturesque Beaufort is the gateway to secluded beaches and Gullah communities, where descendents of African slaves maintain ancestral traditions and speak a hybridization of English and African languages. Farther south is Hilton Head Island, the world-famous golf capital.

Edisto Island

Only 45 miles from Charleston, but largely uncommercialized, Edisto (**ed**-is-tow) has luxuriant vegetation, a beautiful beach and rental houses for family holidays. *Edisto*

Beach State Park (☎ 843-869-2156) has tent spaces ($11), RV sites ($22) and marshfront cabins ($180/350 per weekend/week). Contact Edisto Island Vacation Rentals (☎ 800-868-5398) for short-term beach cottages.

Beaufort
Both French and Spanish settlements were attempted in this area in the 1560s, but Beaufort began as a British colony in 1711 and became wealthy with the boom in sea-island cotton. (It's pronounced **bew**-fort, not to be confused with **bow**-fort, North Carolina.) Today the town is a tidy grid on a small peninsula, with fine 18th-century houses facing the estuary. The chamber of commerce (☎ 843-524-3163, 1006 Cateret St) has a map with many old houses marked and can tell you where scenes from *Forrest Gump* and *The Big Chill* were shot. History buffs can see the museum at 713 Craven St ($2; open 10am-5pm daily except Wed and Sun). The Gullah Cultural Festival is held in late May.

The **Marine Corps Recruit Depot**, 3 miles south at Parris Island, has a museum covering local history from the time of the Spanish as well as the story of the marines from the Civil War to the Gulf War, with weapons, models and hardware (free admission; open 10am-4:30pm daily). You can also see some of this boot camp, which has trained over a million marines.

Beaufort's lodgings are relatively expensive, but *Red Carpet Inn* (☎ 843-521-1121, 301 Carteret St) is the cheapest place in the historic downtown ($50/60 weekdays/weekends). The visitor center has a list of historic B&Bs (from $120). *Plums* (☎ 843-525-1946, 904½ Bay St) serves innovative Lowcountry food in a casual atmosphere (main dishes around $20).

St Helena Island
Crossed by the Sea Island Pkwy (US 21), this island is serene, with fields, woods and expanses of salt marsh interlaced with salt-water creeks. Union forces captured St Helena early in the Civil War, freeing the slaves and allocating land to them. Missionaries set up a school for freed slaves in 1862, the first such school in the South. This school became Penn Center, which was used by civil-rights leaders up through the

1960s. Now it houses a community center and museum (☎ 843-838-2432) with exhibits and pictures of island life. For a taste of Gullah cuisine, stop at *Ultimate Eating – Gullah Style* (☎ 843-838-1314, 761 Sea Island Pkwy), or the *Shrimp Shack*, toward the east end of Sea Island Pkwy.

On the east side of St Helena, a bridge crosses to **Hunting Island State Park** (☎ 843-838-2011), which has a fine sandy beach, marshes and a forest of pine and palmetto. The lighthouse here was built in 1875 but moved to its present position in 1889. Camping costs $22, cabins $200/500 per weekend/week.

Hilton Head Island
Like St Helena, Hilton Head was occupied by Native Americans and contested by French, Spanish and English colonists, prospered as a plantation island, and was allocated to freed slaves after the Civil War. Unlike St Helena, it has been totally developed into a holiday and retirement resort, and now has upscale accommodations, recreation facilities and 25 golf courses. The chamber of commerce (☎ 800-523-3373) tells and sells.

COLUMBIA
South Carolina's capital was destroyed by General Sherman's troops in 1865 and rebuilt with cotton-mill money. The helpful visitor center (☎ 803-254-0479, 801 Lady St) has information about four historic houses open for tours, including Woodrow Wilson's boyhood home. The University of South Carolina (USC) student population gives the city some liveliness.

Columbia's focal point is the **State House**; look for bronze stars on its west side, where Northern troops' cannonballs hit.

The Confederate flag, still highly controversial

Around the capitol, assorted memorials attest to the state's military history, as does the **Confederate Relic Room & Museum** (☎ 803-898-8095), two blocks southeast at Sumter and Pendleton, where Carolinians come to check the Confederate credentials of their ancestors (free admission; open Mon-Fri). Nearby, the 'Horseshoe' is a parklike space surrounded by the refined old buildings of USC.

The interesting **South Carolina State Museum** (☎ 803-898-4921, 301 Gervais St), on the west side of downtown, is housed in an 1894 textile factory building, one of the world's first electrically powered mills. Excellent exhibits over three floors cover science, technology and the state's cultural and natural history ($5; open daily).

The ***Dreher Island State Park*** (☎ 803-364-4152), on Hwy 1, and ***Sesquicentennial State Park*** (☎ 803-788-2706, 9564 Two Notch Rd) have campsites for $16.

Close to the State House, ***Governor's House Hotel*** (☎ 803-779-7790, 1301 Main St) has standard rooms for $70. ***Chestnut Cottage B&B*** (☎ 803-256-1718, 1718 Hampton St) is where Confederate President Jefferson Davis was once entertained; rooms start at $170. Cheap chains include ***Fairground Plaza Motel*** (☎ 803-252-2000, 621 S Assembly St), at $45, and ***Motel 6*** (☎ 803-798-9210), on I-26 exit 106, at $37/44 for singles/doubles.

For eating and entertainment, head to the Five Points area in the southeast corner of downtown, where Harden, Greene and Devine Sts meet Saluda Ave.

The Greyhound station (☎ 803-256-6465, 2015 Gervais St) has buses to Charleston ($45; 2½ hours); Atlanta, Georgia ($85; 4 hours); and New York ($115; 14 hours). From the Amtrak station (☎ 803-252-8246, 850 Pulaski St), the *Silver Star* goes south to Savannah ($80; 2½ hours) and north to Washington, DC ($200; 11 hours).

GREENVILLE

It's not on many itineraries, but aptly named Greenville is a nice little city with lots of parks and a pleasantly planned downtown. Conservative Bob Jones University, the academy of fundamentalism, has a big collection of primarily Catholic religious art. The Greenville County Museum of Art has a good American collection, especially of Southern art. Contact the visitor center (☎ 864-421-0000) for accommodations and restaurants.

Georgia

Georgia is the largest state east of the Mississippi River. Its hub is Atlanta, the state capital and a nexus of business, culture and nightlife. But Atlanta is a far cry from the rest of Georgia. Savannah, like its larger cousin Charleston, South Carolina, is a finely preserved paean to the antebellum world and is one of the best walking cities in the nation. Northern Georgia's mountains offer wonderful hiking, mountain biking, canoeing and rafting, while the center of the state presents a vast landscape of gently rolling farms and forests, gradually flattening as one moves farther south.

History

The Spanish were the first Europeans to visit the area. Explorer Juan Ponce de León may have come to the state's coast in 1513, and other Spanish expeditions certainly visited the area over the next two decades.

Permanent English settlement dates from 1733, when James Edward Oglethorpe founded Savannah. Though the town was initially intended as a refuge for the penniless released from debtors' prison, this noble goal was subverted by the practical

---

Georgia

Nickname: Peach State

Population: 8,186,000 million (10th)

Area: 59,441 sq miles (24th)

Admitted to Union: January 2, 1778 (4th); seceded 1861; readmitted 1870

Capital city: Atlanta (population 426,600; metro area 3.6 million)

Other cites: Augusta (186,000), Columbus (182,000), Savannah (130,000), Macon (111,000)

Birthplace of: Martin Luther King Jr (1929–68), president Jimmy Carter (b 1924), Girl Scouts of America, Coca-Cola

Famous for: CNN, *Gone with the Wind*

need for soldiers, farmers and merchants. The settlement was a buffer between the Spanish in Florida and the English colony of South Carolina.

After some initial struggles the state grew rapidly. A lowland planter society was complemented by smaller-scale farming and industry in the more mountainous north. In 1828 gold was discovered near Dahlonega. This sped up the dispossession of northern Georgia's Cherokee population during the first half of the 19th century, culminating in their forced removal to Oklahoma along the 1838 Trail of Tears. Atlanta began as a railroad settlement in 1837, and by the time of the Civil War it was already one of the state's largest cities and one of the South's most important transport hubs.

Though far removed from the Civil War's early phases, Georgia was one of the most important battlefronts in the latter part of the war. Union forces moving down from Tennessee fought important battles at Chickamauga in 1863 and Kennesaw Mountain in 1864 on their way to Atlanta, where they occupied the city for 10 weeks. Much of the city was destroyed in the siege, and still more was destroyed when retreating Confederates blew up their own ammunition and explosives. When the Union army left, General William Tecumseh Sherman ordered the city burned lest its rail yards fall back into Confederate hands. By the time they were done, more than 90% of Atlanta's buildings lay in ruins.

Sherman then began his infamous march to the sea, during which his troops cut a 50-mile-wide swath of destruction to Savannah. As part of his effort to cripple the Confederacy, Sherman ordered that everything of any conceivable military value be destroyed. Though Savannah itself was spared, Sherman's name remains anathema to many Southerners to this day.

Atlanta was rebuilt with startling speed. By the beginning of the 20th century it was once again the most important industrial and transportation center in the South. The city and state continued to grow through the early part of the century. Georgia's passage through the civil-rights era was less traumatic than that of some other Southern states, and in the 1970s it became one of the fastest-growing areas of the country – a distinction that it retains today.

In recent decades the state has vaulted to national prominence on the back of an eclectic group of events and images: *Gone With the Wind;* Martin Luther King Jr; Jimmy Carter; and Atlanta's rise as a global media and business center, culminating in the 1996 Summer Olympics.

Geography

Like other East Coast states, Georgia has a coastal plain, an upland plateau and a portion of the Appalachian Range farther inland. The mountains, though they can provide some lovely views, are not particularly high. The state's highest point is Brasstown Bald, in northeast Georgia, 4784 feet above sea level. The primeval Okefenokee Swamp covers a large portion of the state's southeast corner.

Government & Economy

Like many Southern states, Georgia was solidly Democratic from shortly after the Civil War until the mid-1960s. Since then its politics have drifted to the right. As is so often the case in the South, race remains a major political fault line: After the 1998 elections, all of Georgia's Republican congresspeople were white and all of its Democrats black.

Though Atlanta tends to hog the spotlight with its corporate headquarters (Coca-Cola, UPS, Holiday Inn and CNN are all based here) and huge airport, much of the rest of Georgia still has an economy based on agriculture. The state has long been known for its cotton, peaches, peanuts and pecans.

Information

The Georgia Department of Industry, Trade & Tourism (☎ 404-656-3590, 800-847-4842, ⬛ www.georgia.org, PO Box 1776, Atlanta, GA 30301) will send you a very thick travel guide. They also run visitor centers throughout the state.

Georgia has a very extensive network of state parks and recreation areas (see ⬛ www.gastateparks.org). Most offer camping, and several offer cabins or lodges that tend to be very good values. In summer most cabin accommodations must be booked in advance, and the minimum stay is seven nights (waived if you call within 30 days of your visit). The central reservation number is ☎ 770-389-7275 or ☎ 800-864-7275.

Parking at most state parks is $2 per car. For $25 you can buy an annual park pass, a particularly good value if you plan to do a lot of hiking, fishing, mountain biking and more. The pass is available at any state park.

Georgia's sales tax varies from 5% to 7%.

ATLANTA

The 'Capital of the New South,' Atlanta is one of the nation's fastest-growing metropolitan areas. Internationally known as the host of the 1996 Olympics and the home of CNN, Atlanta was created as a railroad junction in 1837. Within a generation it was one of the region's main cities, and during the Civil War it became a major Confederate industrial, transportation and munitions center (see History, earlier).

After the war, Atlanta became the epitome of the New South, a concept that entailed reconciliation with the North, the promotion of industrialized agriculture, and a progressive business outlook. Its railroads were rebuilt within a year after the Civil War ended. Atlanta's relentless boosterism led to civil improvements and energetic business partnerships.

Today, freeways slice through the city, high-rises abound and the suburbs spill ever farther north and east. But Atlanta is appealing for its diverse and progressive population and its widely varied neighborhoods.

Musical Georgia

An astonishing amount of musical talent has originated in Georgia. In addition to musicians born here, clubs and recording studios in Atlanta, Athens and Macon have brought many acts to national attention. Ray Charles hit his stride in Atlanta; Athens introduced REM, the B-52s and Widespread Panic to the record shelves; and Otis Redding, 'Little Richard' Penniman, James Brown and the Allman Brothers got their start in Macon. Other Georgia music greats include Johnny Mercer, Lena Horne, Dr Thomas Dorsey (father of gospel music), blues great Gertrude 'Ma' Rainey, Trisha Yearwood, the Indigo Girls, Gladys Knight and opera diva Jessye Norman.

It has lots of young people and students, an active gay community and a prosperous black middle class.

Orientation

The sprawling Atlanta metropolitan area is crisscrossed by I-20, I-75 and I-85. I-75 and I-85 become a single road – 'the downtown connector' – as they pass through the city center. I-285 forms 'the perimeter.' In the center, Peachtree St is the main north-south artery, but be aware that a hundred other streets, avenues, roads etc are also called Peachtree. Addresses specify NE, SE, SW or NW, with W Peachtree St dividing east from west and Martin Luther King Jr Dr/Edgewood Ave dividing north from south.

East of downtown, 'Sweet Auburn' was a progressive black district in the 1920s. Auburn Ave is now being revived around sites associated with Martin Luther King Jr and the civil-rights movement. Northeast of Auburn is Little Five Points (L5P), with bars, bookstores, cafes and clubs for Atlanta's students and grunge set. Farther out, and further upmarket, is Virginia Highlands. Also to the east is Decatur – an independent city but still well inside the perimeter – home of several good nightspots. Turner Field (formerly Olympic Stadium) and Grant Park are south and southeast of downtown.

North of downtown, Midtown is another upmarket entertainment and nightlife area, with the posh suburb of Buckhead farther out. The West End, west of downtown, is Atlanta's oldest neighborhood and has a lively black community.

Many free maps are available at tourist centers, hotels and the like, usually with a detailed map of downtown and a usable map of surrounding areas. Be aware that new construction and constant neighborhood renewal make many maps out of date. As in the rest of Georgia, maps may retain older interstate exit numbers, which were changed in 2000.

Information

The Atlanta Convention and Visitors Bureau (☎ 404-222-6688, Ⓦ www.atlanta .com, 233 Peachtree St) mails out comprehensive visitor brochures. The bureau also runs information centers at the airport, Lenox Square (in Buckhead) and

GREATER ATLANTA

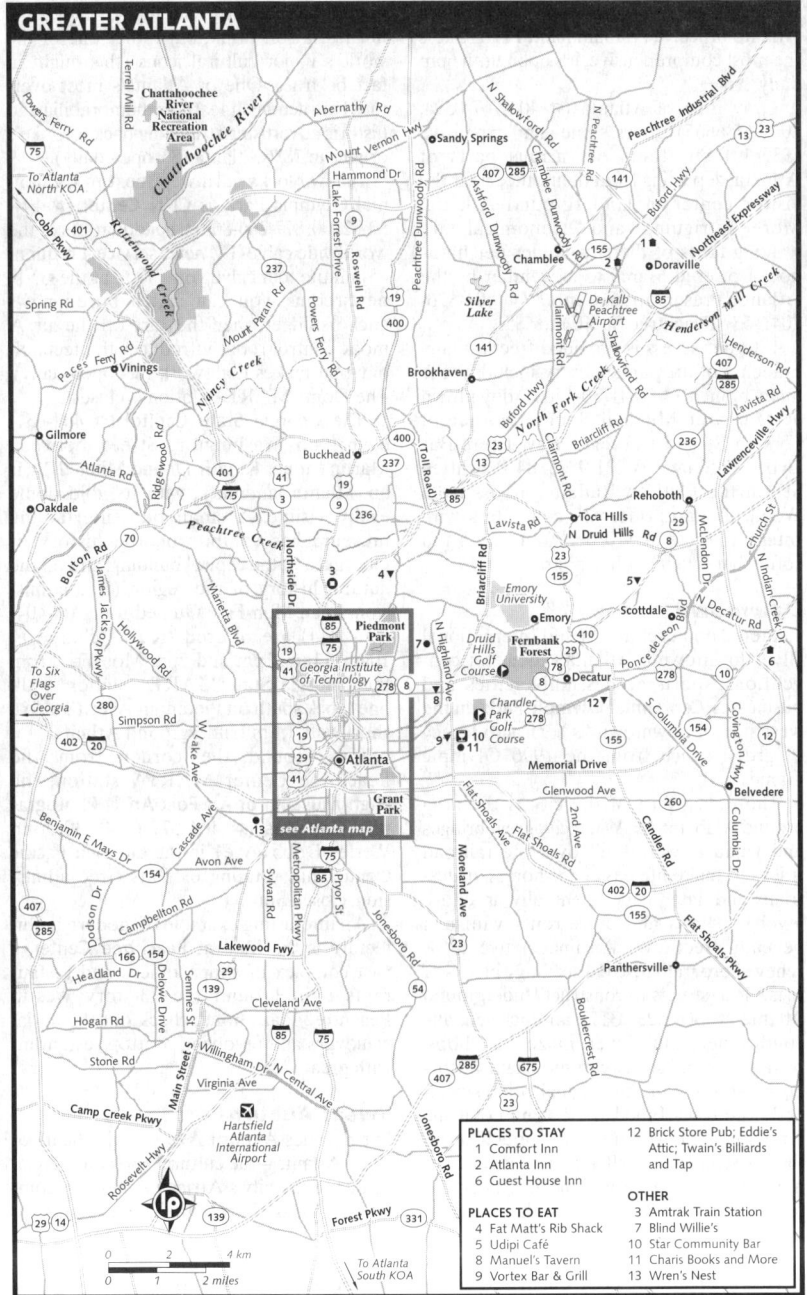

PLACES TO STAY
1 Comfort Inn
2 Atlanta Inn
6 Guest House Inn

PLACES TO EAT
4 Fat Matt's Rib Shack
5 Udipi Café
8 Manuel's Tavern
9 Vortex Bar & Grill

12 Brick Store Pub; Eddie's
   Attic; Twain's Billiards
   and Tap

OTHER
3 Amtrak Train Station
7 Blind Willie's
10 Star Community Bar
11 Charis Books and More
13 Wren's Nest

Underground Atlanta. The Underground Atlanta office, at Alabama and Pryor Sts, is the most comprehensive; it's open until 6pm daily.

Gray Line of Atlanta (☎ 404-767-0594, 800-965-6665) offers somewhat expensive ($35-40) bus tours of various parts of Atlanta, departing from their office near the visitor center in Underground Atlanta. More intriguing and economical are walking tours of the city's older neighborhoods, offered March to November by the Atlanta Preservation Center (☎ 404-876-2041, 537 Peachtree St NE) for $5.

Internet access is provided free at many branches of the public library, including the main branch (☎ 404-730-1700), downtown at Margaret Mitchell Square, corner of Forsyth St and Carnegie Way. The e-Bar Cyber Café (☎ 404-221-9825, 84 Peachtree St), in the Flatiron Building across from Woodruff Park, offers 10 computers with Internet access at $10 per hour and a full coffee bar in a hip atmosphere.

Downtown

Centered on Peachtree St and International Blvd, downtown is Atlanta's focus for conventions, sports arenas, universities and businesses. **Centennial Olympic Park**, on the west side of downtown, is a 21-acre legacy of green space from the 1996 Olympic Games.

The oldest part of the city is the area around Alabama St. As the city grew, bridges and viaducts were built over the railroad tracks to make life easier for horses, pedestrians and, later, cars. Eventually an entire level of shops and storefronts vanished beneath street level. An imaginative 1960s renewal program rescued six dingy blocks of these 'lost' streets to construct **Underground Atlanta** (☎ 404-523-2311), an enclosed, air-conditioned multilevel maze of shops, restaurants and street-cart merchants incorporating a few of the original brick streets and storefronts. Billed as the 'center of it all,' Underground Atlanta is not much more than a struggling mall set in a historic atmosphere. The information desk near the food court has a free guide to the historical markers scattered around the complex. Enter from the Five Points MARTA station.

Nearby, **World of Coca-Cola** (☎ 404-676-5151, 55 Martin Luther King Jr Dr) strives mightily to convince you that Coca-Cola is not just a soft drink, but rather one of the world's major cultural icons (this might in fact be true). One of Atlanta's most over-rated attractions, it features memorabilia and historic advertising stretching back to Coke's origins in 1886 Atlanta ($6; open daily).

A few blocks northwest, next to Centennial Olympic Park, is **CNN Center** (☎ 404-827-2300, 877-266-8687), headquarters of the worldwide cable-TV news service. Frequent 45-minute tours give you a look at the CNN newsrooms; you can watch bored news anchors fidget when they are off the air. A mock control room introduces the technology that makes it all work ($8; open daily). The Dome MARTA station is closest.

The **Georgia State Capitol** (☎ 404-651-6996), on Washington Street between Martin Luther King Jr Dr and Mitchell St, is an Atlanta landmark, with its gold dome easily visible. A small but entertaining museum has exhibits on the history of Georgia and the capitol building, and on the natural history of the region (free admission; open Mon-Fri). Guided tours (☎ 404-656-2844) are offered free of charge at 10am, 11am, 1pm and 2pm Mon-Fri. From the Georgia State MARTA station, walk one block south on Piedmont Ave; it's also a short walk from Underground Atlanta.

Just around the corner from the Peachtree Center MARTA station, the **High Museum of Art Folk Art & Photography Galleries** (☎ 404-577-6940, 30 John Wesley Dobbs Ave), in the Georgia-Pacific Center, has rotating exhibits (free admission; closed Sun).

An interesting example of modern architecture is the **Mall at Peachtree Center**, a vast complex of shops, offices and restaurants built around the 73-story Westin Peachtree Plaza hotel; check out the aerial walkways and revolving rooftop restaurant with great views.

Sweet Auburn

For decades Auburn Ave was the heart of black Atlanta – the cultural and commercial center of the city's African American community. Today many of the street's sights are associated with its most famous son: Martin Luther King Jr, who was born on Auburn and preached on Auburn and whose grave now looks out onto the street.

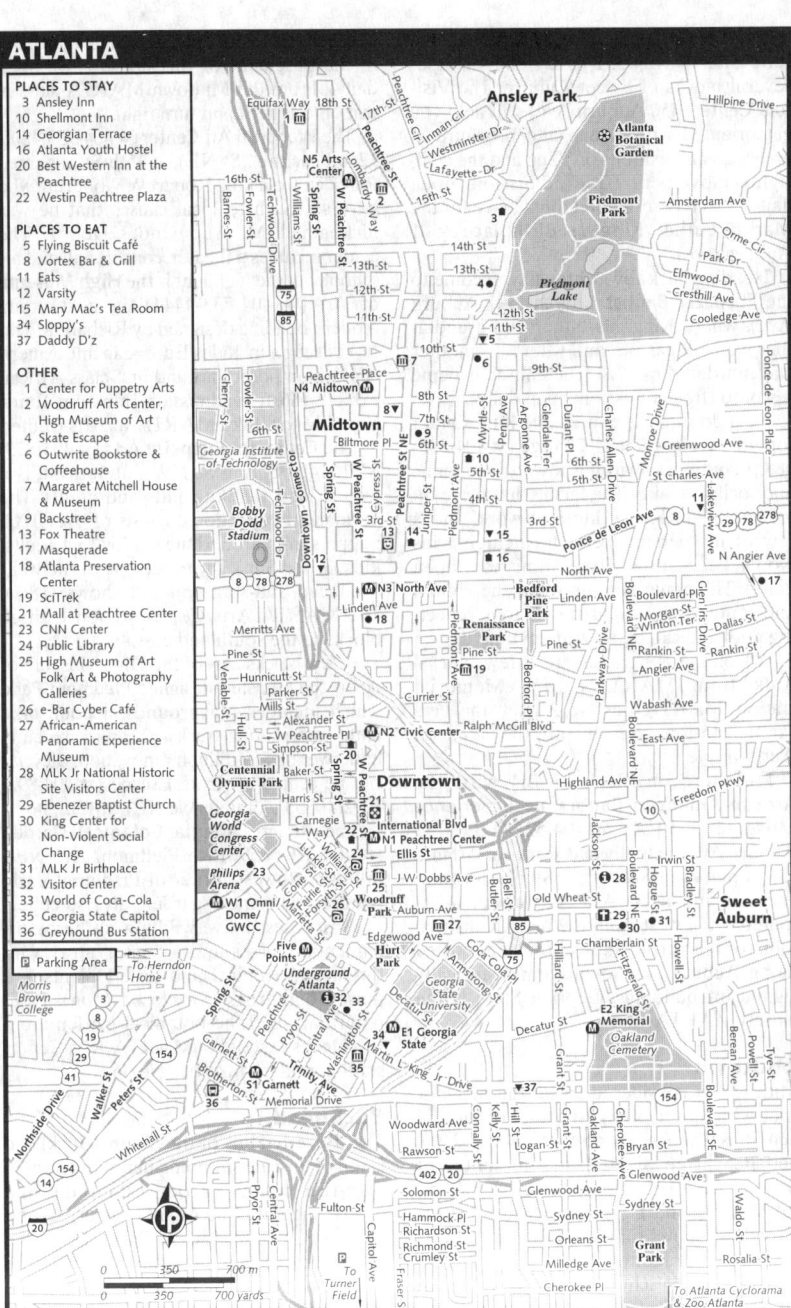

ATLANTA

PLACES TO STAY
3 Ansley Inn
10 Shellmont Inn
14 Georgian Terrace
16 Atlanta Youth Hostel
20 Best Western Inn at the Peachtree
22 Westin Peachtree Plaza

PLACES TO EAT
5 Flying Biscuit Café
9 Vortex Bar & Grill
11 Eats
12 Varsity
15 Mary Mac's Tea Room
34 Sloppy's
37 Daddy D'z

OTHER
1 Center for Puppetry Arts
2 Woodruff Arts Center; High Museum of Art
4 Skate Escape
6 Outwrite Bookstore & Coffeehouse
7 Margaret Mitchell House & Museum
8 Backstreet
13 Fox Theatre
17 Masquerade
18 Atlanta Preservation Center
19 SciTrek
21 Mall at Peachtree Center
23 CNN Center
24 Public Library
25 High Museum of Art Folk Art & Photography Galleries
26 e-Bar Cyber Café
27 African-American Panoramic Experience Museum
28 MLK Jr National Historic Site Visitors Center
29 Ebenezer Baptist Church
30 King Center for Non-Violent Social Change
31 MLK Jr Birthplace
32 Visitor Center
33 World of Coca-Cola
35 Georgia State Capitol
36 Greyhound Bus Station

P Parking Area

The **Martin Luther King Jr National Historic Site** (☎ 404-331-6922) encompasses several blocks of Sweet Auburn. The **Visitors Center** (450 Auburn Ave) will help you get oriented with a map and brochure of area sites and exhibits on King and the civil-rights movement (free admission; open daily). From here, guided tours leave for the **Martin Luther King Jr Birthplace** (501 Auburn Ave).

Heading back toward town, you come to the **Ebenezer Baptist Church** (407 Auburn Ave), where King, his father and grandfather were all pastors, and where his mother was murdered in 1974. The church is being restored (free admission; open daily).

Next door to the church, the **King Center for Non-Violent Social Change** (☎ 404-893-9882) continues working toward economic and social equality. The facility has more information on King's life and work, and a few of his personal effects, including his Nobel Peace Prize (free admission; open daily). His **grave site**, between the church and center, is surrounded by a long reflecting pool and can be viewed anytime.

All of the King sites are a few blocks' walk from MARTA's King Memorial station. MARTA bus No 3 from the Five Points station goes by all the sites on Auburn Ave.

For more on black history, visit the **African-American Panoramic Experience Museum** (APEX; ☎ 404-523-2739, 135 Auburn Ave), actually in downtown Atlanta ($3; open Tue-Sat, plus Sun afternoon summer and Feb). APEX is about a 15-minute walk west from the historic district; look for the purple-and-yellow signs posted along Auburn Ave identifying historically significant buildings. Georgia State is the closest MARTA stop.

Midtown

Midtown is considered to be the arts district, with the city's largest choice of cultural activities. The **Fox Theatre** (☎ 404-881-2100, 660 Peachtree St NE), in the center of Midtown, is a 1929 movie palace with fanciful Moorish and Egyptian designs. It hosts Broadway shows, film festivals and concerts in a 5000-seat auditorium.

Margaret Mitchell House & Museum (☎ 404-249-7015), 10th and Peachtree Sts, is a shrine to the author of *Gone With the Wind*.

Mitchell wrote her epic in a small apartment in the basement of this house ($10; open daily). From the Midtown MARTA station, exit onto 10th St and turn right.

The **Woodruff Art Center** (☎ 404-733-4200, 1280 Peachtree St NE), at 15th St, is named for Coca-Cola king Robert W Woodruff, who gave so much to local causes that he was nicknamed 'Mr Anonymous Donor.' The center includes a theater, concert hall and art school, but the highlight is the **High Museum of Art** (☎ 404-733-4444), in a stunning modern building designed by Richard Meier. Its collection includes European and American contemporary art and first-class African exhibits ($6; free admission 1pm-5pm Thurs; closed Mon). Take MARTA to Arts Center.

The **Center for Puppetry Arts** (☎ 404-873-3391, 1404 Spring St NW), at 18th St, is a wonderland for both kids and adults. The permanent collection consists of over 1000 puppets from around the world ($5/4 adults/kids; closed Sun). Try to see one of the well-produced, full-stage puppet shows ($8/7). The MARTA Arts Center station is three blocks to the south and east.

A few blocks east of the High Museum of Art is the Olmsted-designed **Piedmont Park**, which includes playgrounds, a pool, bike paths and skating tracks. The park recently underwent a $66-million renovation. Bicycles can be rented at Skate Escape (☎ 404-892-1292, 1086 Piedmont Ave NE), at 12th St.

The 30-acre **Atlanta Botanical Garden** (☎ 404-876-5859, 1345 Piedmont Ave NE), in the northwest corner of Piedmont Park, features a Japanese garden, diverse collections of roses, native wildflowers, herbs, ornamental grasses and a conservatory with threatened tropical and desert plants and poison dart frogs ($7; closed Mon). Piedmont Park and the botanical garden are a few blocks east of the MARTA Arts Center station; walk or take bus No 36.

Buckhead

The 'Beverly Hills of the South,' Buckhead is full of upscale shopping malls and homes, high-rise condos, good restaurants and diverse nightlife. The **Atlanta History Center** (☎ 404-814-4000, 130 W Paces Ferry Rd NW) is an excellent museum that covers the history of Atlanta from railroad junction to modern suburban metropolis ($10/8 adults/kids; open daily).

To reach the museum by MARTA, take bus No 40 from the Lindbergh Center station. By car, take I-75 to exit 255, W Paces Ferry Rd, and follow signs east. Free parking is available.

The nearby **Governor's Mansion** (☎ 404-261-1776, 391 W Paces Ferry Rd NE), completed in 1968, is a Greek Revival–style house, rich with 19th-century furniture, paintings and porcelain (free admission; open 10am-11:30am Tue-Thurs).

West End

Older than the city of Atlanta itself and a long-established African American community, West End was home to Alonzo Herndon, who was born a slave but who went on to found Atlanta Life Insurance and become one of the country's first black millionaires. The **Herndon Home** (☎ 404-581-9813, 587 University Place NW) is an impressive beaux arts mansion, built and decorated by black workers in 1910 (donation requested; hourly tours 10am-4pm Tue-Sat). The house sits on the edge of the campus of **Morris Brown College**, a three-block walk from the Vine City MARTA station.

South of I-20, the **Wren's Nest** (☎ 404-753-7735, 1050 Ralph David Abernathy Blvd SW) was the 1881–1908 home of Joel Chandler Harris, the white Atlanta journalist (born in Eatonton, Georgia) whose newspaper columns and Uncle Remus books retold and popularized African American folktales of Br'er Rabbit, Br'er Fox and Br'er Bear ($7; open 10am-4pm Tue-Sat and 1pm-4pm Sun). The Wren's Nest is about half a mile west of the MARTA West End station; bus No 71 passes the house.

Grant Park & Oakland Cemetery

Grant Park, like its northern neighbor Piedmont Park, is a large oasis of green on the edge of the city center. The park is home to the **Atlanta Cyclorama** (☎ 404-658-7625), one of Atlanta's most famous attractions. The Cyclorama is a circular painting 358 feet around and 42 feet high, depicting the Battle of Atlanta in July 1864. Painted in 1886, the interesting painting is the largest in the world and one of only three such Victorian-era circular paintings remaining in the USA. Even folks tired of the whole Civil War thing will enjoy the historic diorama. There's an ac-

companying Civil War museum as well ($5; open daily).

Next door, Zoo Atlanta (☎ 404-624-5600) provides natural environments for many African and Asian animals ($15/10 adults/kids; open daily).

From the Five Points MARTA station, take bus No 31. You can also reach Grant Park by walking south from Sweet Auburn or the King Memorial MARTA station. The route under the MARTA tracks on Boulevard is seedy; take Hillard/Grant St instead.

Gone With the Wind author Margaret Mitchell and golf great Bobby Jones are buried in the Oakland Cemetery (☎ 404-688-2107, 248 Oakland Ave), at Martin Luther King Jr Dr (free admission; open daily). Many interesting Victorian and neoclassical monuments and mausoleums are scattered throughout the site. Stop at the Visitors Center (open 9am-5pm Mon-Fri) for information and a walking brochure ($1). Guided tours ($3) are offered at 10am and 2pm Saturday and 2pm Sunday, March to October. Enter at Martin Luther King Jr Dr and Oakland Ave. From the MARTA King Memorial station, turn left, left again on Hillard/Grant St, go under the tracks, and take another left on Martin Luther King Jr Dr. Bus No 18 will also take you there from either the Five Points or King Memorial stations.

Places to Stay

Rates at downtown hotels tend to fluctuate wildly depending on whether there is a large convention in town (Atlanta is one of the country's most popular convention locations). Weekends are often cheaper, as are hotels away from the center of the action.

Budget The *Stone Mountain Family Campground* (☎ 770-498-5710, 800-385-9807) is Georgia's largest campground and the best camping option near Atlanta. Rates are $20 to $26 for tents. See the Stone Mountain Park section, later, for directions.

Atlanta South KOA (☎ 770-957-2610), a good 25 miles south of downtown at I-75 exit 222, charges $23/28 for tent/RV sites (two people). *Atlanta North KOA* (☎ 770-427-2406), about 25 miles north of the city at I-75 exit 269, charges $28 for tent or RV sites.

The *Atlanta Youth Hostel* (☎ 404-872-1042, Ⓦ *www.hostel-atlanta.com, 223 Ponce*

THE SOUTH

de Leon Ave), at Myrtle St, is in a Victorian house in Midtown. This lively hostel has 80 beds in dorm rooms with three to five bunk beds each. A kitchen, laundry, lockers, free morning coffee and donuts, and Internet access ($1 for 10 minutes) are available. The hostel's office is closed from noon-5pm. Beds cost $17 for members of Hostels America and $19 for nonmembers. The hostel is four long blocks east of the MARTA North Avenue station.

A cheap option is to stay somewhere along the perimeter and take MARTA into the city for sightseeing. You can park at the stations. The trip by train to downtown should take 30 to 40 minutes. One of the best values in this category, **Guest House Inn** (☎ *404-836-8100, 4649 Memorial Dr)* offers singles/doubles from $41/46 and has weekly rates from $197. The hotel is along an unattractive strip of Hwy 10 (Memorial Dr), a third of a mile east of I-285 exit 32 and about one mile from the Kensington MARTA station. MARTA bus No 121 passes the hotel and goes to the station.

A mile south of the MARTA Doraville station, **Atlanta Inn** (☎ *770-452-8500, 5114 Buford Hwy)* has worn, moderately clean singles/doubles for $45/50. Bus No 39 runs in front of the hotel to the station. Nearby, **Comfort Inn** (☎ *770-455-3700)* offers standard chain rooms for $69/74, including breakfast. Shuttle service is provided to the MARTA Doraville station. The hotel is at I-285 exit 32; follow the signs to a side road.

Mid-Range & Top End Near the northern edge of downtown and within striking distance of Midtown, **Best Western Inn at the Peachtree** (☎ *404-577-6970, 330 W Peachtree St)* has 110 nice, cozy rooms in a well-done renovation of an older hotel. Rates start at $80, including breakfast.

Ansley Inn (☎ *404-872-9000, 800-446-5416, 253 15th St)* is on a quiet residential street near Piedmont Park. This restored 1907 yellow-brick English Tudor mansion has 22 rooms featuring four-poster beds, period furnishings and Jacuzzis. Rooms start at $109 with breakfast.

Atlanta has plenty of expensive hotels, including the towering **Westin Peachtree Plaza** (☎ *404-659-1400, 210 Peachtree St NW)*, the tallest hotel in the Western Hemisphere (from $209), and **Georgian Terrace**

(☎ *404-897-1991, 659 Peachtree St)*, which is on the National Register of Historic Places. Many of the *Gone With the Wind* stars stayed here during the film's debut in 1939. Rates start at $129 for the tiny standard rooms. **Shellmont Inn** (☎ *404-872-9290, 821 Piedmont Ave NE)*, at 6th St, is a comfortable retreat in an 1891 classic Victorian home (from $135).

Places to Eat

The largest choice of downtown restaurants is at Underground Atlanta, Peachtree Center and CNN Center, all of which offer shopping-mall-style food courts as well as a few more expensive eateries.

Eats *(600 Ponce de Leon Ave NE)*, at Lakeview Ave (across from City Hall East), is one of the most popular cheap eateries in the city, offering home-cooked food at fast-food prices. Eats offers mix-and-match pasta, chicken and vegetables and little else, but a full meal can be had for under $5.

Another cheap choice is the huge cafeteria nicknamed **Sloppy's** in the basement of the James H 'Sloppy' Floyd Veterans Memorial Building (2 Martin Luther King Dr), catercorner from the state capitol. There's no atmosphere to speak of, but the Southern specialties are decent, and everything is cheap. Full meals cost about $5. It's open weekdays for breakfast and lunch.

Varsity, on the northwest corner of Spring St and North Ave, is hectic, crowded, dirty, loud and rude, yet it's *still* an Atlanta tradition. Nearly everyone who eats here has the chili dog ($1.50), and the onion rings are good and greasy.

Mary Mac's Tea Room *(224 Ponce de Leon Ave)*, three blocks east of the Fox Theatre, serves tasty Southern food in a bright, cheery, grandmotherly atmosphere. Prices are moderate ($9 lunch, $10 dinner).

Atlanta's barbecue aficionados will direct you to **Fat Matt's Rib Shack** *(1811 Piedmont Rd NE)*, less than a mile north of Piedmont Park. **Daddy D'z** *(264 Memorial Dr SE)*, at Hill St, also has great barbecue.

Flying Biscuit Café, in Midtown at Piedmont Ave and 10th St, serves all-day breakfasts of omelets, organic oatmeal pancakes, fried green tomatoes and tasty grits, all accompanied by their justifiably famous huge, fluffy biscuits. Ah, heaven. A diverse, happy crowd enjoys the rest of the vegetarian-friendly menu of black bean quesadillas and veggie burgers. Meals are about $6-8.

Bohemian-student types go for inexpensive health-food places around Little Five Points. This area is also well supplied with bars, many of which also serve decent food. *Vortex Bar & Grill* (☎ 404-688-1828, 438 Moreland Ave) offers some of the city's best burgers. Look for the huge skull. There's also a branch in Midtown.

In nearby Virginia Highland, *Manuel's Tavern* (602 N Highland Ave) is a longtime political hangout. It has a good range of salads and sandwiches ($6-10) and a friendly pub atmosphere.

There are several good dining options in Decatur, just east of Atlanta. On the town square, *Brick Store Pub* has great food, atmosphere and a large selection of beer and single-malt scotch. *Udipi Café* (1850 Lawrenceville Hwy), north of downtown Decatur, is somewhat out of the way but worth the trip for those seeking authentic vegetarian South Indian cuisine. Huge dishes cost about $7, combo dinners $12-15.

Entertainment
Atlanta has big-city nightlife, with most venues concentrated in several areas. The free weekly *Creative Loafing* has the best listings.

Buckhead has a concentrated strip of bars and dance clubs in an area bounded by Peachtree, E Paces Ferry and Pharr Rds.

Little Five Points has a young/college/punk scene. Start around the intersection of Euclid and Moreland Aves to explore the options. *Star Community Bar* (☎ 404-681-9018, 437 Moreland Ave) draws a funky crowd to its live acts four nights a week.

Virginia Highland draws a more affluent yuppie crowd. Bars and restaurants are concentrated on N Highland Ave. For serious blues, try *Blind Willie's* (☎ 404-873-2583, 828 N Highland Ave), a well-established blues bar with local and occasional big-name acts.

Decatur is another place to explore, with a few pubs near the courthouse square and MARTA station. *Twain's Billiards & Tap* (211 E Trinity Place), a popular pool hall, has a huge selection of beer and a limited menu. *Eddie's Attic* (☎ 404-377-4976, 515B N McDonough St), on the main square, is one of the city's best places to hear folk and

acoustic music, in a nonsmoking atmosphere seven nights a week.

Around Midtown, *Masquerade* (☎ 404-577-8178, 695 North Ave) is a mammoth dance place. *Fat Matt's Rib Shack* (see Places to Eat earlier) has up-and-coming blues acts nightly.

Backstreet (☎ 404-873-1986, 845 Peachtree St NE), in Midtown at 6th St, is Atlanta's top gay club, but it gets a good mix of everyone else as well. *My Sister's Room* (☎ 404-370-1990, 222 E Howard St), next to the railroad tracks in Decatur, is a popular lesbian hangout.

Midtown is the center of Atlanta's active gay life. Piedmont Park is a popular hangout, and there are several gay bars here. Start your explorations at *Outwrite Bookstore & Coffeehouse* (☎ 404-607-0082, 991 Piedmont Ave), at 10th St in Midtown, a cheerful gay and lesbian bookstore with a full coffee bar and wonderful desserts. In the Little Five Points neighborhood, *Charis Books & More* (☎ 404-524-0304, 1189 Euclid Ave NE) is a crowded, well-stocked feminist and lesbian bookstore.

Atlanta for Children

Atlanta has plenty of activities to keep the little ones occupied. In Midtown, **SciTrek** (☎ 404-522-5500, 395 Piedmont Ave) is a child-oriented science and technology museum with 150 interactive, hands-on exhibits ($7.50/5 adults/kids; open daily). It's about five blocks from the MARTA Civic Center station; you could also take bus No 16 from Five Points. The Center for Puppetry Arts, Zoo Atlanta and Atlanta Botanical Garden are other good options (see the Midtown and Grant Park sections).

Six Flags over Georgia (☎ 770-948-9290), 12 miles west of downtown Atlanta off I-20, is a huge theme park with roller coasters, white-water rafting, a 10-story free-fall ride and musical shows ($33/20 adults/kids; open daily in summer). The Six Flags shuttle (bus No 201) leaves from the Hamilton E Holmes MARTA station every 36 minutes when the park is open. In a similar vein, **White Water Theme Park** (☎ 770-424-9283, 250 Cobb Pkwy N) has 50 ways to get wet on 50 acres ($27/17). Take I-75 to exit 265.

Spectator Sports

The Atlanta Braves major-league baseball team plays at Turner Field (☎ 404-577-9100), formerly Olympic Stadium (after the games, the stadium was reconfigured into a baseball-only facility). Tickets cost $5-40; a few $1 seats are available only on game days. Turner Field is not near MARTA, but you can get there by taking buses No 17, 55, 90 or 97 from the Five Points station. Dedicated shuttle buses run between the stadium and the Five Points station during games.

The Atlanta Falcons NFL team (☎ 404-223-8000) plays in the Georgia Dome. Tickets start at $25. The Atlanta Hawks NBA team (☎ 404-827-3800) plays at the Philips Arena, next to the Georgia Dome. Regular ticket prices cost $10-65. A new ice-hockey team, the Atlanta Thrashers (☎ 404-584-7825) also plays in the Philips Arena. Tickets are $10-55.

Tickets can be ordered through Ticketmaster (☎ 800-326-4000, 404-249-6400, Ⓦ www.ticketmaster.com).

Getting There & Away

Hartsfield Atlanta International Airport, 12 miles south of downtown, is a major regional hub and an international gateway.

The Greyhound terminal (☎ 404-584-1731, 232 Forsyth St) is conveniently located next to the MARTA Garnett station. Sample fares with service frequency and travel time include the following (destination – distance in miles; cost; duration; frequency):

Chattanooga, Tennessee – 126; $17; from 2 hours; 7 daily

New Orleans, Louisiana – 533; $71; from 9 hours; 7 daily

New York – 956; $98; from 18 hours; 11 daily

Miami, Florida – 721; $94; from 16 hours; 9 daily

Savannah – 285; $47; 5½ hours; 5 daily

Washington, DC – 718; $77; from 13 hours; 10 daily

Atlanta's Amtrak station (☎ 404-881-3062, 1688 Peachtree St NW) is 3 miles north of downtown. Take bus No 23 from the MARTA Arts Center station. The *Crescent* runs daily to Charlotte, North Carolina (from $51; 5½ hours); New Orleans, Louisiana (from $61; 11 hours); New York (from $131; 19 hours); Philadelphia, Pennsylvania (from $112; 17 hours); and Washington, DC (from $105; 14 hours).

Getting Around

A MARTA rail line goes from the airport downtown ($1.75; 20 minutes). Atlanta Airport Shuttle (☎ 404-524-3400, 800-842-2770) transports passengers to hotels all over the city in a minibus ($12-18).

The Metropolitan Atlanta Rapid Transit Authority (MARTA; ☎ 404-848-4711) operates a small but efficient rail system and a very extensive bus network in Atlanta and some of the surrounding communities. The rail system has only two major lines (with a couple of branches), but manages to get close to many of the major sites. Use the white courtesy phones at the rail stations to find out which train or bus will take you to your destination.

All fares are $1.75. Exact change or a token is required on the buses, but the token machines in the stations make change. Free transfers are available between bus routes and between the rail and the bus. Weekly passes, accepted on all buses and trains, cost $13. Weekend passes, good for travel Friday to Sunday, are $9. Passes can be purchased only at the RideStores in the Five Points, Lenox, Lindburgh Center, Georgia State and Airport stations. The trains run about 5am-1am weekdays, 5am-12:30am weekends. Most buses start early in the morning, around 5am, and run until midnight or 1am.

The major car rental companies have offices at the airport and scattered around the downtown area.

AROUND ATLANTA

When you're tired of navigating the endless Peachtree Sts, Atlanta has plenty of interesting excursions beyond the perimeter.

Stone Mountain Park

This 3200-acre park (☎ 770-498-5690), 16 miles east of downtown, is home to 825-foot-high Stone Mountain, the world's largest outcropping of exposed granite. It is best known for the huge bas-relief carving of Confederate heroes Jefferson Davis, 'Stonewall' Jackson and Robert E Lee – the largest such sculpture in the world. The park also has a skylift (funicular), hiking trails, an antebellum plantation, a railroad, a laser show and many other attractions. The park is open daily and makes a good day trip ($7 per car, $17 for a pass to all attractions).

The park is located off Hwy 78 (I-285 exit 39). Bus No 120 can take you from the MARTA Avondale station to the village of Stone Mountain, where some buses continue into the park. There's also an 18-mile bike path that winds its way from downtown Atlanta through Decatur, ending at the park's west gate.

Lake Lanier
About 45 miles northeast of Atlanta's urban sprawl, off I-985, is Lake Lanier, site of Olympic rowing competitions in 1996. The **Lake Lanier Islands Resort** offers a bit of everything, including a water park and campground complex (☎ 770-932-7200 for information) that is very popular in summer. Admission is $6 per car.

NORTHERN MOUNTAINS
The southern end of the great Appalachian Range extends some 40 miles into Georgia's far north, providing some superb mountain scenery and wild white-water rivers. The fall colors emerge late here, peaking in October. Free brochures with directions for self-guided driving tours are available at most of the region's visitor centers.

A few days are warranted to see sites like the 1200-foot-deep **Tallulah Gorge**, the scenery and hiking trails at **Vogel State Park** and the small but interesting collection of Appalachian folk arts at the **Foxfire Museum** (☎ 706-746-5828), near Mountain City.

The extreme northeast corner of the state also offers Georgia's lone ski area, the **Sky Valley Resort** (☎ 800-437-2416), which has one lift, five trails and a *very* short season.

Dahlonega
In 1828 Dahlonega was the site of the first gold rush in the USA. The boom these days, though, is in tourism. It's an easy excursion from Atlanta and offers intriguing history surrounded by beautiful mountain scenery.

Walking around the historic main square is a major event itself. Many offbeat shops compete for tourist dollars. The visitor center (☎ 706-864-3711) has plenty of information on area sites and activities (including hiking, canoeing, kayaking, rafting and mountain biking). In the center of the square you'll find the **Dahlonega Gold Museum** (☎ 706-864-2257), which tells the fascinating story of gold mining in the region ($2.50; open daily).

Just off the square, *Smith House* (☎ 706-867-7000, 800-852-9577, 84 S Chestatee St) offers unlimited home-cooked Southern food served family-style for a steep $15. Smith House also operates a remodeled classic country inn decorated in 19th-century style. Its 16 rooms cost $60-178, depending on the room and season.

Amicalola Falls State Park
This 2050-acre park (☎ 706-265-4703) is one of the most popular destinations in northern Georgia, and it's easy to see why. The park offers spectacular scenery, in addition to excellent **hiking** and **mountain-biking** trails. There is a lodge, cottages and camping (☎ 770-389-7275 or 800-864-7275 for reservations). Lodge rates are $79-199; tent sites are $15 per day. A 4.9-mile trail leads to the *Len Foote Hike Inn* (same reservation number; three-day advance notice required), a rustic lodge with tiny rooms but marvelous public areas and decks with wonderful views; single/double rates are $89/$130. Entrance to the park is $2. An 8-mile hiking trail connects the park to Springer Mountain, the southern terminus of the Appalachian Trail.

Helen
Helen is the sort of town you can only find in the USA: a faux Swiss-German mountain village where the shops have names like 'Das Ist Leather.' Somehow this place has become one of northern Georgia's more popular tourist destinations. Oktoberfest, in mid-September to early November is a popular event, with plenty of oompah bands and bratwurst.

A good reason to come here is to get to nearby **Unicoi State Park** (☎ 706-878-3982), with its **hiking** trails and attractive mountain scenery.

Lodging is available in the park (☎ 770-389-7275, 800-864-7275). Hotel rooms cost $69-134 depending on the time of year and the day of week. Cabins are also available ($95-160). During the summer the park can be very crowded, and the cabins have a minimum rental period of one week (waived if you reserve within 30 days of your visit).

If you must stay in Helen itself, avoid the German-looking places. You'll get a modern hotel room for the same (or lower) price at **Best Western** (☎ 706-878-2111), a bit south of town, with rates starting at $35, zooming up to $119 during festival time. For food, get into the Bavarian spirit at **Hofer's Bakery**, on the north side of town, where you can choose between bratwurst, *spaetzle*, and *schweinebraten*, washed down with an imported Spaten Franziskaner Weisse (that's a beer). Sorry vegetarians, not much hope here. Prices are moderate.

New Echota State Historic Site

The independent Cherokee tribe established a short-lived capital here in 1825. The historic site (☎ 706-624-1321) contains a museum and reconstructed buildings similar to those that populated the Cherokee town ($3; closed Mon). From Atlanta, take I-75 north to exit 317 (GA Hwy 225) and go east three-quarters of a mile, just east of Calhoun.

Chickamauga Battlefield

In September 1863, Confederates defeated Union forces at the Battle of Chickamauga. This delayed the invasion of Georgia by a few months, but the battle claimed 34,000 casualties.

The battlefield, adjacent to the town of Fort Oglethorpe, is now part of the **Chickamauga & Chattanooga National Military Park** (☎ 706-866-9241), the nation's first military park. A 7-mile self-guided auto tour takes you by all the major sites, monuments and plaques, and over 60 miles of walking trails allow off-road exploration. The visitor center and museum are open 8am-4:45pm daily (free admission). The former has a half-hour multimedia show on the battle ($3).

CENTRAL GEORGIA

Between the northern Georgian mountains and the coastal plains lie the gently rolling hills of the Piedmont region. It is populated by most of Georgia's cities, as well as dozens of small towns and farming communities.

Athens

This attractive college town, 61 miles east of Atlanta, is characterized by a vibrant nightlife and world-renowned music scene. Local pop music stars catapulted to national fame include the B-52s, REM and Wide-spread Panic. The University of Georgia has almost 30,000 students. The downtown area is well supplied with music shops, bookstores, cafes, bars and clubs.

The Athens Welcome Center (☎ 706-353-1820), housed in a historic antebellum house at the corner of Thomas and Dougherty Sts, provides good information and maps, and offers tours of historic houses and sites ($10). Several houses, including the **Taylor-Grady House** (☎ 706-549-8688, 634 Prince St), can be visited individually.

College Ave between Clayton and Broad Sts is where the college crowd hangs out; it's a good place for people watching.

The **State Botanical Garden of Georgia** (☎ 706-542-1244), a mile south of the Athens loop road on S Milledge Ave, is a tranquil preserve (free admission; open daily). The **Georgia Museum of Art** (☎ 706-542-4662), on the university campus, has an impressive array of art exhibits (free admission; open daily).

The city also has a few odd sights: A double-barreled cannon in front of City Hall represents a spectacularly unsuccessful Civil War–era experiment in weapons technology.

The **Sandy Creek Park** (☎ 706-613-3631) has a walk-in campground with 23 tent-only spots. The cost is $5 per campsite, plus $1 per person park entry (closed Sun-Mon). **Hawkes-Nest Hostel** (☎ 706-769-0563, e eagltavern@aol.com) is a small, family-run hostel on 7 acres of land near Watkinsville, about 11 miles south of downtown Athens (singles/doubles $10/18; reservations required).

Hotel rates increase significantly during football weekends, and reservations can be hard to get. **Bulldog Inn** (☎ 706-543-3611, 1225 Commerce Rd) is a budget choice just north of the city (about $40). **Best Western Colonial Inn** (☎ 706-546-7311, 170 N Milledge Ave) has modern hotel rooms on the edge of a pretty, older residential district (from $49). **Holiday Inn Express** (☎ 706-546-8122, 513 W Broad St), a quarter-mile from downtown, starts at $69. **Magnolia Terrace** (☎ 706-548-3860, 277 Hill St) is a historic home with eight rooms; it enjoys a quiet residential spot with good walking. Rates are $95-135.

As you might expect in a college town, there's lots of affordable food and many coffeehouses. **Blue Sky Coffee** (128 College

Ave) has your basic coffee, cappuccino and muffins. *Five Star Day Café (229 E Broad St)*, just across from the campus, is an unpretentious cafe serving hot buttered soul chicken with Jamaican seasoning and other 'gourmet soul food dishes' for $4-6.

Vegetarians (or anyone who likes Indian food) will want to try *Bluebird Café (493 E Clayton)*. *The Grit (199 Prince Ave)* is another popular, good and inexpensive vegetarian restaurant.

The famous *40 Watt Club (☎ 706-549-7871, 285 W Washington St)*, where REM got its first exposure, is still one of the best places in the South to catch up-and-coming bands. *Georgia Theatre (☎ 706-549-9918, 215 N Lumpkin St)* is another of the South's premiere live music halls.

Southeastern Stages (☎ 706-549-2255, 220 W Broad St), a Greyhound connection service, has 11 buses daily to Atlanta ($14; 1¾ hours), five to Augusta ($48; from 5 hours), five to Columbia, South Carolina ($61; from 6 hours), and two to Savannah ($35; 3½ hours).

Augusta

Georgia's second-oldest and -largest city, best known for the annual Masters golf tournament, is relatively tranquil the rest of the year.

The city's Welcome Center (☎ 706-724-4067, 32 Eighth St), in the 1886 Historic Cotton Exchange building, has many helpful maps and walking tours (open daily).

Two blocks away is the **Riverwalk** along the banks of the Savannah River, linking restaurants, shops and museums. It's a good place to sit and watch the river. At one end you'll find Augusta's pride and joy, the **Morris Museum of Art** (☎ 706-724-7501), dedicated to artists of the South ($3; open daily). At the other end is the National Science Center's child-oriented **Fort Discovery** (☎ 706-821-0200), with more than 270 interactive science exhibits ($8/6 adults/kids; open daily).

The Masters golf tournament is played in early April, but if you think you can actually get tickets, we pity you. During the tournament the city is flooded with visitors and hotels prices skyrocket. If you don't have a reservation, *don't come.*

Cheapie motels sit around I-20 exit 199 (Washington Rd), west of downtown. Further upscale, *Partridge Inn (☎ 706-737-8888, 2110 Walton Way)*, in the historic area of Summerville, quotes rates starting at $153, but you can usually get something less expensive with advance reservations or coupons. For food, try *Hot Foods by Calvin (2027 Broad St)*, an unassuming restaurant with great Southern down-home cooking ($6-10).

Madison & Milledgeville

Off I-20, 65 miles east of Atlanta and 30 miles south of Athens, Madison was one of the few towns that Sherman spared on his path of destruction. Part of this picturesque town is a National Historic Site; you can walk a 1½-mile route through the historic district with a map from the Welcome Center (☎ 800-709-7406), on Madison's main square.

Tiny Milledgeville was the state capital from 1803 to '68, and it retains some stately buildings from the period.

Macon

Macon is a pleasant, though often overlooked, little city, with a few interesting sights. It features more structures on the National Register of Historic Places than any other Georgian city. The town was laid out in the 1820s and prospered as a cotton port on the Ocmulgee River. It is especially attractive in March, when thousands of cherry trees blossom.

The visitor center (☎ 912-743-3401; closed Sun) is in the 1916 railroad Terminal Station at the corner of 5th and Cherry Sts, just off Martin Luther King Jr Blvd.

The **Georgia Music Hall of Fame** (☎ 912-750-8555, 888-427-6257, 200 Martin Luther King Jr Blvd) showcases the multitude of musical talent that has bloomed in Georgia, from native sons and daughters to groups that got their start in the state, including REM, James Brown, Little Richard and Ray Charles (see 'Musical Georgia,' earlier). The museum is a collection of nostalgia-inducing artifacts, listening stations, hands-on exhibits and even a video theater where the audience chooses the video by yelling and clapping ($8; open daily). Inductee Duane Allman died in Macon while working on the Allman Brothers album *Eat a Peach*. He and fellow band member Berry Oakley are buried in the **Rose Hill Cemetery**. The **Georgia Sports Hall of Fame** (☎ 912-752-1585, 301 Cherry St) is nearby ($6).

Other notable sites include the **Tubman African-American Museum** (☎ 912-743-8544, 340 Walnut St), with a well-displayed collection of African art, work by contemporary black artists and a display on African American inventors ($3; open daily). The **Hay House** (☎ 912-742-8155, 934 Georgia Ave) is an amazing Italian Renaissance Revival mansion built in the 1850s ($7).

The **Ocmulgee National Monument** (☎ 912-752-8257), just east of town, is an archaeological site with Indian burial mounds, artifacts and an ancient earth lodge.

Macon has minor league baseball and hockey teams. The latter, the Macon Whoopee, may have the best name in sports.

Greyhound (☎ 912-743-2868, 65 Spring St) runs 11 buses daily to Atlanta ($14; 2 hours), two to Savannah ($37; 3½ hours), eight to Jacksonville, Florida ($51; from 5½ hours) and three to Tallahassee, Florida ($37; from 5 hours).

Warm Springs

In 1928, eight years before he was elected US president, polio-stricken Franklin D Roosevelt took a curative trip to Warm Springs. Later he built a home, founded a polio treatment center and ultimately died from a stroke here in April 1945. The **Little White House State Historic Site** (☎ 706-655-5870) is just south of the hamlet. The site also has a small museum with some of FDR's personal effects and other memorabilia ($5; open daily).

Nearby, **FDR State Park** (☎ 706-663-4858) offers 40 miles of hiking trails. Many of the 140 camping sites are located on a pretty lake ($15).

Pine Mountain

The tiny town of Pine Mountain serves as the gateway for **Callaway Gardens** (☎ 706-663-2281), one of Georgia's most popular and beautiful attractions. The gardens encompass more than 14,000 acres of artificial 'nature' and attractions, including a butterfly center, a horticultural center, a famous vegetable garden, a beach, and acres upon acres of azaleas that bloom March to May ($12; open daily).

Columbus

Georgia's third-largest city, 100 miles southwest of Atlanta, was established at the highest navigable point on the Chattahoochee River. Waterfalls powered Columbus' early industries, and the city produced Confederate armaments in the Civil War. Shortly after the South surrendered at Appomattox, Union General James H Wilson launched a mistaken attack that badly damaged the city. Modern Columbus is still mostly industrial. Fort Benning, a huge army base that is the home of the US infantry, is just south of town.

The Columbus Convention & Visitors Bureau (☎ 706-322-1613, 800-999-1613, 1000 Bay Ave), downtown at 10th St, has plenty of brochures and maps, and is open daily.

The downtown **historic district** covers 24 square blocks. Historic Columbus Foundation (☎ 706-322-0756, 700 Broadway) offers tours of several houses. The downtown **Riverwalk** is a pretty, peaceful stroll on a 12-mile paved path along the edges of the Chattahoochee River. The path is suitable for walking, jogging, skating or bicycling.

The **Port Columbus Civil War Naval Center** (☎ 706-327-9798, 1002 Victory Dr), in South Commons, contains two old ironclad warships built at the Columbus Naval Iron Works ($4.50; open daily). The **Columbus Museum** (☎ 706-649-0713, 1251 Wynnton Rd), close to downtown, is a combination regional-history and American-art museum. A film and exhibits give a good account of local history (free admission).

There are plenty of cheap motels along the sleazy expanse of Victory Dr south of town. Your best bets are the chain motels around I-185 exits 6 and 7, a couple of miles east of downtown. *La Quinta Inn* (☎ 706-568-1740, 3201 Macon Rd), at exit 6, is decent value from $49. *Courtyard by Marriott* (☎ 706-323-2323, 3501 Courtyard Way), near Peachtree Mall off Manchester Expressway (I-185 exit 7), has standard business rooms starting at $82/69 weekdays/weekends. *Columbus Hilton* (☎ 706-324-1800, 800-524-4020, 800 Front Ave) is the only worthwhile hotel downtown, located in the 1861 Empire Woodruff Grist Mill. Doubles start at $79/110 weekends/weekdays.

Columbus takes its barbecue seriously, and there's none better than *Country's Barbecue*, with locations off Macon Rd at 3137 Mercury Dr and downtown on Broadway between 13th and 14th Sts. The barbecue rib platter costs $8, including two sides (try the Brunswick stew). *Dinglewood Pharmacy (1939 Wynnton Rd)* serves the delicious scrambled dog – a Columbus tradition consisting of a hot dog buried in chili, mustard, pickles and onion, topped with oyster crackers and eaten with a spoon.

The Greyhound station (☎ 706-322-7393, 818 Veteran's Pkwy), near 9th St, has five buses a day to Atlanta ($17; 2 hours), among other destinations.

SOUTH GEORGIA

Georgia's agricultural heritage lives on in South Georgia. This area was once at the bottom of the sea. Its predominantly sandy soil is overlain in some spots by richer soils good for growing cotton. For the true South Georgia experience, be sure to visit in summer, when the high heat and humidity make you want to sit still, but the gnats swarming up your nose make you want to run for cover.

Westville & Around

A mile southeast of Lumpkin, Westville (☎ 912-838-6310) is an authentically re-created 1850s-era village containing over 30 buildings ($8; closed Mon). The 1,109-acre **Providence Canyon State Conservation Park** (☎ 229-838-6202), 7 miles west of Lumpkin on Georgia Hwy 39C, is an impressive and beautiful environmental disaster. The park is host to 16 canyons, the deepest 150 feet, that were created because of poor farming practices in the 19th century.

Plains

This tiny town is best known as the birthplace and current residence of Jimmy Carter, the 39th US president. Many Carter-related buildings are now part of the **Jimmy Carter National Historic Site** (☎ 912-824-4104). The main tourist attraction is the **Plains High School Museum and Visitor Center**, on N Bond St, featuring exhibits on the former president's life and career (free admission; open daily). The **Carter Boyhood Home**, 2½ miles west of downtown Plains, was renovated and opened to the public in 2000; the Carter family grew cotton, peanuts and corn here. Jimmy and Rosalynn still live in the **Carter Home**, west of downtown on Hwy 280, but it is closed to the public.

Andersonville National Historic Site

The site of the Civil War's most infamous prison lies 10 miles northeast of Americus on Georgia Hwy 49. The Andersonville prison camp was in operation only 14 months (1864–65), but in that time 12,919 of its 45,000 Union prisoners died from disease, poor sanitation, overcrowding and exposure.

Now a national historic site, Andersonville has been expanded to include the **National Prisoner of War Museum** (☎ 912-924-0343), honoring American prisoners of war throughout the country's history (free admission; open daily).

Okefenokee National Wildlife Refuge

The Okefenokee Swamp is a national gem, encompassing 650 sq miles and home to 234 species of reptile, including an estimated 9000 to 15,000 alligators; 234 species of bird; 49 types of mammal; and 60 species of amphibian.

The swamp has three main entrances. The entrance to the western side of the swamp is at **Stephen C Foster State Park** (☎ 912-637-5274), an 18-mile drive from the tiny town of Fargo along State Route 177, where you can canoe and take guided boat tours. There's a *campground* here. Northern access to the swamp is at the **Okefenokee Swamp Park** (☎ 912-283-0583), a private concession and wildlife park 8 miles south of Waycross. The park's main attraction is a zoo of live swamp creatures, including alligators (many unfenced), black bears, otters, turtles and deer. Guided boat tours are available.

At the eastern entrance, the **Suwannee Canal Recreation Area** (☎ 912-496-7836), 11 miles southwest of Folkston, is the most convenient for visitors exploring the Georgia coast, and it has some of the most comprehensive facilities. Gator sightings are a near certainty. Okefenokee Adventures (☎ 912-496-7156) rents canoes and boats.

The ultimate Okefenokee experience is a multiday canoe trip on the 120 miles of waterways through the swamp. Space is limited. Call for the US Fish & Wildlife Service's *Okefenokee National Wildlife Refuge Wilderness Canoe Guide* (☎ 912-496-7836, ⓦ okefenokee.fws.gov) if you're considering a trip.

SAVANNAH & THE COAST

The Georgia coast has a great variety of activities for travelers, from the historic city of Savannah to some of the state's most remote scenery, set amid a flat land of startling beauty – omnipresent live oak trees; small streams cutting through tidal marshlands, with hundreds of fiddler crabs scurrying for their hiding places and great egrets looking for their next meal; and mile after mile of cordgrass swaying with the wind.

The coast is dotted with 13 large and small barrier islands. Many of these are nature preserves with abundant wildlife. At the coast's southern end, several islands have been playgrounds for the wealthy throughout much of their history. These islands – St Simons, Jekyll, Sea, and Little St Simons – are referred to as the Golden Isles. Some islands are linked to the mainland by causeways.

Historically, this coast was important strategically in the colonization of Georgia and America, in the Revolutionary War and in the slave trade.

Savannah

Founded in 1733, Savannah was the first English settlement in the colony of Georgia. It became a wealthy shipping center, handling the export of cotton and import of slaves. In the 19th century, the railroads added to the city's wealth, bringing in ever greater volumes of plantation produce.

Savannah was the goal of General Sherman's devastating March to the Sea, and the city surrendered to him on December 21, 1864. Instead of burning the city, Sherman rested his troops there for six weeks before turning north to cut another path of destruction through South Carolina.

The collapse of cotton prices in the late 1800s sent Savannah into a severe economic decline. In the long run, this may have been a good thing; had it prospered, the elegant streets may well have been demolished in the name of development.

In 1955 the beautiful Davenport House nearly became a parking lot, but was saved by a local campaign that went on to protect and restore all of the historic downtown. The 2½-sq-mile district now has over 1000 restored Federal and Regency buildings, ranging from churches and private homes to the ornate US Customs House on Bay St.

The historic district offers wide, tree-lined streets, shady squares and a serene, Old South ambience.

More recently, John Berendt's hugely successful 1994 murder mystery-travelogue *Midnight in the Garden of Good and Evil* made Savannah a huge tourist destination. The book portrays the city as a bizarre remnant of the Old South, where tradition battles with debauchery. Some of the hoopla is finally beginning to die down, and tourism operators are looking for the next big hit.

Orientation & Information Savannah's historic district is a rectangle bounded by the Savannah River, Forsyth Park, E Broad St and Martin Luther King Jr Blvd. Almost everything of interest lies within or just outside this area.

The Savannah Visitors Center (☎ 912-944-0455, 301 Martin Luther King Jr Blvd, W www.savcvb.com) is in an impressive old train station. It is open daily and has good maps, walking-tour guides and discount coupons for local accommodations. It also sells parking passes for the historic district and is the starting point for a number of popular, privately operated city tours.

Many free maps of the city are available at hotels and tourist attractions around town. Free Internet access is available at public libraries.

Things to See & Do Savannah is a *great* walking city, and the best thing to do is just walk the squares. The **Savannah History Museum** (☎ 912-944-0455, 303 Martin Luther King Jr Blvd), next to the visitor center, is a good place to start, with exhibits that give a feel for the city's past ($3; open daily).

Just a short distance north is the **Ships of the Sea Maritime Museum** (☎ 912-232-1511, 41 Martin Luther King Jr Blvd). The well-done exhibits focus on models of ships and nautical memorabilia ($5; closed Mon).

Along the waterfront, **River Street** is home to touristy shops and restaurants of all price ranges. The brick-and-cobblestone waterside promenade is one of the city's highlights. The **Cotton Exchange**, once one of the world's busiest, and gold-domed city hall both stand nearby.

Davenport House (☎ 912-236-8097), on Columbia Square, was the first of Savannah's historic homes to be restored, and its tour is

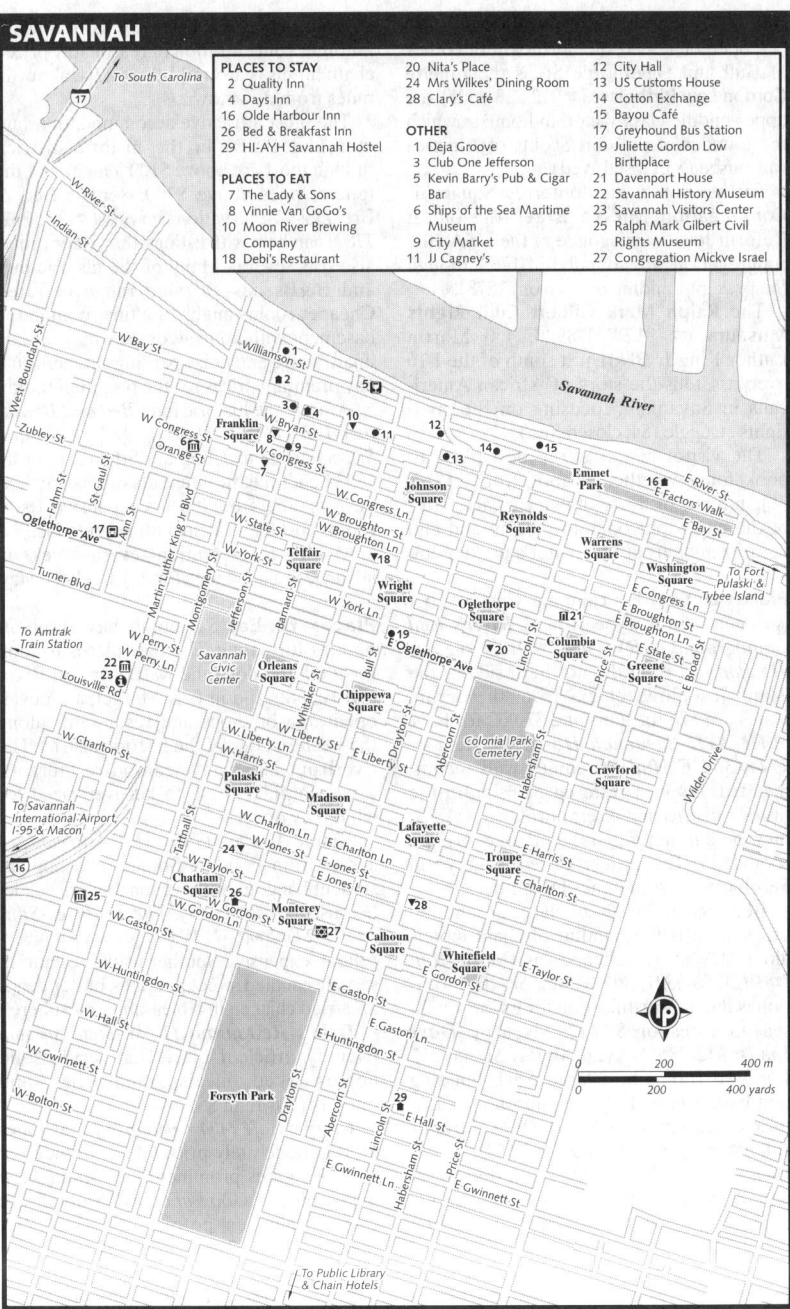

SAVANNAH

PLACES TO STAY
2 Quality Inn
4 Days Inn
16 Olde Harbour Inn
26 Bed & Breakfast Inn
29 HI-AYH Savannah Hostel

PLACES TO EAT
7 The Lady & Sons
8 Vinnie Van GoGo's
10 Moon River Brewing
   Company
18 Debi's Restaurant

20 Nita's Place
24 Mrs Wilkes' Dining Room
28 Clary's Café

OTHER
1 Deja Groove
3 Club One Jefferson
5 Kevin Barry's Pub & Cigar
   Bar
6 Ships of the Sea Maritime
   Museum
9 City Market
11 JJ Cagney's

12 City Hall
13 US Customs House
14 Cotton Exchange
15 Bayou Café
17 Greyhound Bus Station
19 Juliette Gordon Low
   Birthplace
21 Davenport House
22 Savannah History Museum
23 Savannah Visitors Center
25 Ralph Mark Gilbert Civil
   Rights Museum
27 Congregation Mickve Israel

still one of the most worthwhile in the city ($7; open daily). At the northeastern corner of Bull and Oglethorpe Sts is the **Juliette Gordon Low Birthplace** (☎ 912-233-4501), the upper-middle-class Victorian home in which the founder of the Girl Scouts of America was raised ($5; closed Wed).

Farther south, at Monterrey Square, is **Congregation Mickve Israel**, the oldest Reform Jewish synagogue in the USA (the congregation was founded in 1733, though the present building dates from 1878).

The **Ralph Mark Gilbert Civil Rights Museum** (☎ 912-231-8900, 460 Martin Luther King Jr Blvd), just south of the I-16 overpass, tells the story of African Americans in Savannah, focusing on the civil-rights struggle ($4; closed Sun).

The visitor center is the best place to book tours, whether by foot, trolley ($17-21), minibus or horse-drawn carriage. Most of the city's tour operators begin and end their excursions at the center's parking lot.

Places to Stay For camping, your best bet is to head out to Tybee Island. ***River's End Campground & RV Park*** (☎ 912-786-5518, 915 Polk St) is on the northern side of the island just three blocks from the ocean. Rates are $26 for tents and $30-32 for RVs.

HI-AYH Savannah Hostel (☎ 912-236-7744, 304 E Hall St) comes well recommended. It's in a restored mansion in the historic district and offers dorm beds ($18/20 members/nonmembers) and one private room ($36). The hostel is closed January and February, and sometimes December.

Better than the sleazy places around the bus station is the handful of chain motels along Bay St. The cheapest is ***Quality Inn*** (☎ 912-236-6321, 300 W Bay St). The location is the only justification for its low-/high-season rates of $89/129. Nearby ***Days Inn*** (☎ 912-236-4440, 201 W Bay St) has 253 standard rooms in a large brick building that blends in with the neighborhood's historic character (from $130). ***Olde Harbour Inn*** (☎ 912-234-4100, 800-553-6533, 508 E Factors Walk), in an 1892 converted warehouse on the riverfront, rents 24 comfortable suites, each with a full kitchen ($129-229).

For standard, decent budget and mid-range chain hotels, you have to travel 5 miles south of Forsyth Park on Abercorn St,

an area of Savannah known as Southside. Another concentration of reasonably priced chain hotels is around I-95 exit 94, about 15 miles from downtown.

The most attractive accommodations are inns and B&Bs in the historic district, though most are above $100 a night and the fancier ones above $200. Sonja's Bed & Breakfast Reservation Service (☎ 912-232-7787) can help with listings; the visitor center also lists several. Many of the historic inns and B&Bs have a wide range of rates. Cheaper rooms might be a tiny room in the basement with no view, or they may face an unattractive and noisy parking garage. You'll pay premium prices for the premium rooms.

Among the historic inns, ***Bed and Breakfast Inn*** (☎ 912-238-0518, 117 W Gordon St), adjacent to Chatham Square, is in an 1853 Federal Row house. Its rooms aren't as posh as others, but it's less expensive. Its 16 rooms cost $79-150, including breakfast.

Making a reservation several weeks in advance is a good idea for any weekend stay.

Places to Eat Savannah has excellent options for eating. The best places to look for food are along the waterfront on River and Bay Sts and in City Market, a redeveloped area of shops and restaurants along the western edge of the historic district. The riverfront has many seafood restaurants; locals consider these to be overpriced for what they offer.

Vinnie Van GoGo's (317 W Bryan St), across from Franklin Square, is a popular student hangout, with reasonably priced, delicious pizzas. Nearby, ***The Lady & Sons*** (☎ 912-233-2600, 311 W Congress St) is an excellent, expensive Southern-style restaurant serving candied sweet potatoes, butter beans and fried chicken in a pleasant atmosphere.

Debi's Restaurant (10 W State St) is a friendly, efficient place that serves solid home-cooked meals, sandwiches and burgers (less than $5).

Clary's Café (404 Abercorn St), at Jones St, is a moderately priced diner founded in 1903. It figures prominently in *Midnight in the Garden of Good and Evil*. Main dishes such as chicken potpie cost $9-16, but sandwiches ($4-7) and soups ($4) are also available.

Moon River Brewing Company (21 W Bay St), in an 1821 building a block from the riverfront, attracts a young crowd with its homemade brews and local artwork on the walls.

For soul food, try **Nita's Place** *(140 Abercorn St)*, just south of Oglethorpe Square. Meals are delicious but a bit pricey ($10-12); you get your choice of main dishes such as stewed beef or baked chicken, two vegetables (choose from okra, squash casserole, collards, black-eyed peas, candied yams) and cornbread.

Mrs Wilkes' Dining Room *(107 W Jones St)* is a longtime favorite for sociable Southern-style breakfasts and lunches. Breakfast is 8am-9am ($6); lunch is served 11am-3pm ($12). They accept cash only.

Entertainment There's plenty happening at night. Thursday's *Savannah Morning News* lists weekend activities, as does the free weekly *Creative Loafing*.

There are lots of bars and pubs along River St and in City Market. **Kevin Barry's Pub & Cigar Bar** *(117 W River St)* has live Irish music Wednesday to Sunday. *JJ Cagney's (17 W Bay St)* is an excellent place to spot up-and-coming local bands and singer-songwriter types. **Bayou Café** *(14 N Abercorn St)*, between Bay and River Sts, is a grittier place, popular with partying students. It also has music every night, mostly rock and country rock. **Deja Groove**, on Williamson St behind Quality Inn, is the hottest new singles dance club.

Club One Jefferson *(☎ 912-232-0200, 1 Jefferson St)* is Savannah's premier gay club.

Getting There & Around You don't need a car to enjoy Savannah. If you have one, it's best to park it and walk or take tours around town. The visitor center sells a 48-hour parking pass ($5) that covers all city-run parking garages and all metered spaces where parking is allowed for one hour or more.

Savannah International Airport (☎ 912-964-0514) is about 18 miles west of downtown off I-16. A taxi downtown costs $18 plus $5 per additional passenger.

The Greyhound station (☎ 912-232-2135, 610 W Oglethorpe Ave) is just north of downtown. There are 13 connections daily to Atlanta ($42; from 5½ hours), 13 to Jacksonville, Florida ($22; 2½ hours), two to Charleston, South Carolina ($24; 3¼ hours),

and four to Columbia, South Carolina ($31, 4 hours).

The Amtrak station (☎ 912-234-2611) is 4 miles from City Hall and is served only by taxis ($7). Three *Silver Service* trains per day go south to Jacksonville, Florida (from $40; 2½ hours), continuing on to Miami (from $66; 11½ hours). Northbound, there are two trains per day to Charleston, South Carolina (from $18; 2 hours).

Chatham Area Transit (CAT; ☎ 912-233-5767) operates local buses, including a shuttle that makes its way around the historic district (75¢).

Around Savannah

About 10 miles east of Savannah off US Hwy 80, **Fort Pulaski National Monument** (☎ 912-786-5787) occupies all of Cockspur Island and some of the adjacent mainland. The fort was built in 1829 and used during the Civil War. In addition to the fort, the 5000-acre site includes nature trails and picnic areas ($2; open daily).

About 18 miles east of Savannah at the end of US 80, **Tybee Island** is a small beach community sitting on a lot of history. The island has a small visitor center (☎ 912-786-5444, 802 1st St/Hwy 80), open daily.

The island's main attraction is the 3 miles of wide, sandy beach, good for swimming and castle building. The 154-foot-tall **Tybee Island Lighthouse** (☎ 912-786-5801) is the oldest in Georgia and still in use ($4; closed Tue). A nearby museum has exhibits and photographs on the island's history.

Brunswick

Used mainly as a jumping-off point for the nearby islands, Brunswick does have a pleasant downtown historic district. The Brunswick–Golden Isles Visitors Bureau (☎ 912-265-0620, ⓦ www.bgivb.com), at the southeast corner of Hwy 17 and the St Simons Causeway, has information on Brunswick and all the Golden Isles, including accommodations and dining.

For free spirits who appreciate communal living, **Hostel in the Forest** *(☎ 912-264-9738)* is a brilliant place to stay. Set on 105 acres in the middle of the forest, private accommodations are provided in nine rustic tree houses. Rates are $15 per person. The hostel is 9 miles west of town and 2 miles west of I-95, on US 82.

Greyhound (☎ 912-265-2800) has six buses daily to Savannah ($15; 1½ hours) and four to Jacksonville, Florida ($16, 1½ hours).

Golden Isles

With about 14,000 residents, **St Simons Island** is the largest and most developed of the Golden Isles. It's famous for its golf courses, resorts and landscape of majestic live oaks. 'The Village' is a bustling center of good restaurants and shops on the southern end of the island. The visitor center, tucked away in the library complex east of the fishing pier, has useful maps of the island and bike routes, and information on lodging. The **St Simons Island Lighthouse & Museum of Coastal History** (☎ 912-638-4666) has a wonderful view from the top ($3; open daily).

The rest of the island is fringed with sandy white beaches (the best are on the east side) and dotted with bright green salt marshes. In the middle is **Fort Frederica National Monument** (☎ 912-638-3639), the evocative ruins of an 18th-century English fort. Flat bike paths wind throughout the island.

An exclusive refuge for millionaires in the late 19th and early 20th centuries, **Jekyll Island** is a 4000-year-old barrier island 7 miles long and 2 miles wide, with 10 miles of beaches. The Welcome Center (☎ 912-635-3636), on the causeway to the island, has maps and good brochures on activities and lodging. The 240-acre **historic area** is a good place to just wander among the oaks and fancy cottages, although you cannot go inside the houses except on a tour. Jekyll Island has 20 miles of dedicated, paved **bicycle paths** around the entire island, including the historic district, the beach and some of the natural areas.

Cumberland Island

Most of this southernmost barrier island is occupied by the **Cumberland Island National Seashore** (☎ 912-882-4335). Almost half of its 36,415 acres are marsh, mudflats and tidal creeks. On the ocean side are 16 miles of wide, sandy beach that you might have all to yourself. The island interior is characterized by a maritime forest. Animals include deer, raccoons, feral pigs and armadillos (a recent arrival). Freshwater ponds harbor alligators.

Feral horses roam the island and are a common sight around the mansion ruins, in the interdune meadows and occasionally on the beach. The rich human history of the island includes Indians, Spanish soldiers, missionaries and fort-building Brits.

This is the perfect place to spend a day walking, meandering around the crumbling walls of mansions, along the beach and marshes, and through maritime forests and interdune meadows. The only public access to the island is via the *Cumberland Queen* ferry (☎ 912-882-4335 10am-4pm Mon-Fri), which leaves the St Mary's dock ($13.50). Reservations are strongly recommended.

Camping is available on the island at *Sea Camp Beach* ($4 per person per night), and in four backcountry campgrounds.

Alabama

Alabama has a surprising diversity of landscapes, from the Appalachian foothills to the central farmlands to the subtropical Gulf Coast. Visitors come to see the heritage of antebellum architecture, to celebrate the country's oldest Mardi Gras in Mobile, and to learn about the struggle for black civil rights.

Alabama

Nicknames: Camellia State, Heart of Dixie

Population: 4,447,000 (23rd)

Area: 52,423 sq miles (30th)

Admitted to the Union: December 14, 1819 (22nd); seceded 1861; readmitted 1868

Capital city: Montgomery (population 322,400)

Other cities: Birmingham (933,000), Mobile (200,200), Huntsville (177,900)

Birthplace of: Nat King Cole (1919–65), Helen Keller (1880–1968), boxer Joe Louis (1914–81), Olympic athlete Jesse Owens (1913–80), musicians Lionel Ritchie (b 1949) and Hank Williams (1923–53)

Home of: the first electric streetcars (1866), 300 uses for the peanut (1880s)

History

Alabama was occupied by Choctaws, Cherokees, Chickasaws and especially Creeks until the early 1800s, when white settlers began arriving from the Carolinas, Virginia and Tennessee. The Creeks were defeated in a series of conflicts that culminated in the Battle of Horseshoe Bend, and they ceded most of the state to the newcomers. All the surviving Indians were removed to Oklahoma by 1839.

Small-scale farming dominated the early economy, and though only a third of the farmers owned slaves, Alabama was among the first states to secede when Lincoln was elected. In the Civil War, Montgomery was the first Confederate capital, Mobile was a major Confederate port and Selma was a munitions center. Alabama lost around 25,000 men in the war, and Reconstruction was painful. Widespread rural poverty was partly alleviated by black agriculturist George Washington Carver, who promoted the rotation of crops and developed numerous new products that could be made from peanuts and sweet potatoes.

The boll weevil devastated cotton crops after 1914, destroying the livelihood of the sharecroppers, and many blacks left the state for good. New iron and steel factories made Birmingham the most industrialized city in the New South.

Racial segregation and Jim Crow laws survived well into the 1950s, when the civil-rights movement campaigned for desegregation of everything from public buses to private universities. Alabama saw brutal repression and hostility from governor George Wallace, but federal civil-rights and voting laws eventually prevailed. At a political level, reform has seen the election of dozens of black mayors and representatives, and even George Wallace became an integrationist. Economically, Alabama is one of the USA's poorest states, with many blacks among its poorest citizens, and there is abundant evidence of social inequality.

Information

The helpful Alabama Bureau of Tourism & Travel (☎ 334-242-4169, 800-252-2262, W www.touralabama.org, PO Box 4927, Montgomery, AL 36103) will send out a vacation guide and the publication *Alabama's Black Heritage*. The welcome centers at the state borders are staffed 8am-5pm. For road conditions, call ☎ 334-242-4378. State sales tax is around 8%, and hotels collect an additional 4% occupancy tax.

CENTRAL ALABAMA

Called the 'Black Belt,' central Alabama was named for the swath of fertile soil perfect for growing cotton. The region's treasures include seven state parks, numerous Civil War sights and a most formidable rivalry in football.

Tuskegee

In 1881 Booker T Washington founded the Tuskegee Normal & Industrial Institute, which became the country's most prestigious school for blacks. George Washington Carver (1864–1943), who headed the school's agriculture department, pioneered innovations that assisted small farmers and sharecroppers, including developing more than 300 uses for peanuts. Tuskegee Army Air Field trained black pilots in WWII, and the institute is now **Tuskegee University**, a National Historic Site. The visitor center (☎ 334-727-3200, 1212 Old Montgomery Rd) offers tours and a video.

Accommodations in town are limited; try *Days Inn (☎ 334-727-6034)*, I-85 exit 22, 16 miles west in Shorter ($45-58).

Montgomery

Alabama's capital sits on a bend in the Alabama River, where an Alibamu Indian village existed for hundreds of years. Montgomery was founded in 1817 and soon became an important port for shipping cotton. It became the state capital in 1846 and the first capital of the Confederacy in 1861. In March 1910, Orville and Wilbur Wright opened a school of aviation here and built an airfield that is now part of Maxwell Air Force Base.

In the mid-1950s, black anger over segregation and Jim Crow laws came to a boil when Rosa Parks was arrested for not giving up her bus seat to a white man. For 381 days, Martin Luther King Jr led a boycott of city buses, until the US Supreme Court ordered their desegregation. In 1961 Freedom Riders arriving at the Greyhound bus station were beaten by Ku Klux Klansmen. George Wallace was elected governor on a segregation platform as recently as 1963. Civil-rights history is now a tourist attraction, though de facto segregation endures in Montgomery's suburbs.

Montgomery sprawls across seven hills overlooking the Alabama River, but many attractions are downtown and can be reached on foot. The visitor center (☎ 334-262-0013, 800-240-9452) is in the Thompson Mansion, on Madison Ave at N Hull St downtown.

The Southern Poverty Law Center grew out of Montgomery's racial strife. It teaches tolerance and protects the rights of the poor and minorities. Outside the center, the **Civil Rights Memorial** (400 Washington Ave), designed by Maya Lin, honors 40 martyrs of the civil-rights movement. The **Rosa Parks Museum** (☎ 334-241-8615, 252 Montgomery St) features a bronze bust of Rosa and a sophisticated video re-creation of the bus-seat protest ($5/3 adults/kids).

Tours are available around the **Alabama State Capitol** (☎ 334-242-3935), where Jefferson Davis took the oath of office as the president of the Confederacy. The **First White House of the Confederacy** (☎ 334-242-1861) was moved to its current site opposite the capitol in 1919. It hosts a small Confederate museum (free admission).

A tour around the reconstructed Old Alabama Town (☎ 334-240-4500) gives a good take on the city's history ($7). The **Montgomery Museum of Fine Arts** (☎ 334-244-5700, 1 Museum Dr) focuses on 19th- and 20th-century American (especially southeastern) art (free admission).

Country-music star Hank Williams, born in nearby Mt Olive, is remembered with a life-size bronze statue in Lister Hill Plaza and an oversize hat in the Oakwood Cemetery Annex. The other celebrity attraction is the **Scott & Zelda Fitzgerald Museum** (☎ 334-264-4222, 919 Felder Ave), where the writers lived from 1931 to 1932. Zelda was born in Montgomery and spent most of her life here (free admission).

The *Montgomery KOA* (☎ 334-288-0728) is 4 miles south of town, at I-65 exit 164; tent/RV sites cost $19/28. Motel options include *Super 8* (☎ 334-284-1900, 1288 W South Blvd), with singles/doubles for $35/39, and *Econo Lodge* (☎ 334-284-3400, 4135 Troy Hwy), for $45/50.

Downtown, *Chris' Hot Dog (138 Dexter Ave)*, has been a Montgomery institution

since 1917. *Farmer's Market Cafeteria (315 N McDonough St)* is good for a Southern breakfast ($4). *Lek's Railroad Thai*, in Union Station, serves up tasty Thai lunches for about $5. *Wesley's Original Neighborhood Grill & Bar* (☎ 334-834-2500, 1061 Woodley Rd) is one of several choices in Cloverdale, and hosts rock and R&B acts.

Greyhound (☎ 334-286-0658, 950 W South Blvd) has regular buses to destinations including Atlanta, Georgia ($32; 4 hours); Memphis, Tennessee ($69; from 8 hours); and New Orleans, Louisiana ($53; 6 hours).

Selma

Selma thrived as a center for shipping cotton on the Alabama River and the railways. It was also a major slave-trading post. Confederate munitions were manufactured at the Selma Navy Yard and Ordnance Works, but Confederates suffered a serious defeat at the Battle of Selma in 1865. Federal troops torched the town, though scores of grand antebellum homes survive.

On Bloody Sunday, March 7, 1965, African Americans and white sympathizers were walking to the state capital to demonstrate for voting rights. State troopers and mounted deputies stopped them on Edmund Pettus Bridge, and the beatings and gassings were caught on film and televised around the world. This was the culmination of two years of violence, which ended when President Johnson signed the Voting Rights Act of 1965 and sent federal registrars and observers to Alabama.

Selma has a Welcome Center (☎ 334-875-7485) at 2207 Broad St, as well as a chamber of commerce (☎ 334-875-7241) at 513 Lauderdale St. Segregation and Bloody Sunday are remembered at the small National Voting Rights Museum (☎ 334-418-0800, 1012 Water Ave), near the Edmund Pettus Bridge ($4). The Old Depot Museum (☎ 334-874-2197, 4 Martin Luther King Jr St) houses Native American arrowheads, a large Civil War collection and the Works Progress Administration murals painted by black artist Felix Gaines ($4).

Campsites cost $8 at *Paul M Grist State Park* (☎ 334-872-5846), 15 miles north on Hwy 22. *Best Western* (☎ 334-872-1900, 1915 W Highland Ave) is clean and comfortable (singles/doubles from $45/49). *Jameson Inn*

(☎ 334-874-8600, 2420 N Broad St/Hwy 22) has a pool and spacious rooms ($59/63). Historic *St James Hotel (☎ 334-872-3234, 1200 Water Ave)* overlooks the river ($85/95).

Major Grumbles (☎ 334-872-2006, 1 Grumbles Alley), in a restored riverfront warehouse, offers red beans, rice and chicken gumbo. *Tally Ho (☎ 332-872-1390)*, on Mangum St, is Selma's best restaurant, with steaks and seafood ($11-17).

Greyhound (☎ 334-874-4503, 434 Broad St) has buses to and from Birmingham ($22; 2¼ hours), Mobile ($28; 3¾ hours) and Montgomery ($12; 1 hour).

SOUTHERN ALABAMA

Wedged like a doorstop between Mississippi and Florida, southern Alabama pays tribute to the forces of water, with beaches, rivers, estuaries, bays, a delta and pine-covered barrier islands. The coastline is all of 52 miles long, but the port of Mobile was such a strategic prize that it lured the French, the Spanish and the ill-fated Confederate government.

Mobile

In 1702 Jean Baptiste Le Moyne, Sieur de Bienville, constructed Fort Louis de la Mobile, naming it after the Maubila ('paddling') Indians of the area. In 1711 the French capital of Louisiana was moved to the site of modern-day Mobile, south of the original fort. Over the next 100 years Mobile passed from French to British to Spanish and finally to American control. In the 19th century cotton and timber from all over the state were shipped from the deep bay – a strategic Confederate port until the last days of the Civil War.

Still a major seaport and shipbuilding center, Mobile has green spaces, shady boulevards and four whole districts of historic houses. It's ablaze with azaleas in early spring, and Mardi Gras has been a big celebration for nearly 300 years. Pick up information and discount coupons weekdays at Fort Condé (150 S Royal St) or call ☎ 334-208-7658, 800-566-2453.

Reconstructed **Fort Condé** (☎ 334-208-7304) now serves as a museum, and it's replete with 'French soldiers' (free admission). You can get a good view of the city and maps with walking and driving tours of the historic districts here.

Guides in period costume lead visitors around **Oakleigh** (☎ 334-432-1281), an 1833 Greek Revival mansion with a modest Creole cottage on the grounds ($5). Other fine examples of antebellum architecture are the Bragg-Mitchell Mansion, west of downtown ($5), the beautiful Condé-Charlotte House (104 Theatre St), downtown ($4), and the Italianate Richards-DAR House (256 N Joachim St), downtown ($4). Ask about combination tickets.

The **Museum of the City of Mobile** (☎ 334-208-7569, 111 S Royal St) has maritime and military antiques, Civil War stuff and lavish Mardi Gras costumes (free admission). Moored near Fort Condé, the **USS Alabama** (☎ 334-433-2703, 800-426-4929) is a WWII battleship that you can tour to the tunes of the 1940s before climbing aboard a submarine ($8).

The *Olsson Motel (☎ 334-661-5331, 800-332-1004, 4137 Government Blvd/Hwy 90 W)*, 7 miles west of downtown, is spacious, friendly and cheap (singles/doubles $30/35). South of town off I-10 at Tillman's Corner are *Red Roof Inn South (☎ 334-666-1044, 5450 Coca-Cola Rd)*, for $38/44, and *Days Inn West (☎ 334-661-8181, 5480 Inn Rd)*, for $43/47.

Wintzell's Oyster House (605 Dauphin St) serves mouthwatering lunches for about $7, while *The Brick Pit (5456 Old Shell Rd)* offers the best barbecue for miles around.

Around Mobile

Mobile Bay was the scene of a decisive Civil War naval battle in 1864, when 18 Union ships under Admiral Farragut captured the port from a much smaller Confederate force. On the west side of the bay, the 65-acre **Bellingrath Gardens** (☎ 334-973-2217) feature 250,000 azaleas, with 'trail maids' in period costume every spring ($8.50).

On the east side of Mobile Bay, the charming Meaher State Park (☎ 334-626-5529) features wetlands with a boardwalk for wildlife viewing and primitive camping (just $1). Scenic Alt Hwy 98 goes through Fairhope and Point Clear, and you can continue to the Gulf Coast, where **Pleasure Island** has some great beaches and 32 miles of beachfront houses, condominiums and hotels. Gulf State Park (☎ 334-948-7275) preserves 2½ miles of beach and dunes in a more or less natural state, and has an enormous *campground* (tent/RV sites $12/18).

NORTHERN ALABAMA

During the 1930s, the Tennessee Valley Authority brought jobs to this poorest part of the state by building dams, which created numerous lakes. Not surprisingly, the northern third of Alabama, nestled in the Appalachian foothills, has became exceedingly popular with outdoor enthusiasts. Birmingham provides big-town culture and nightlife; Huntsville offers fantasies of space travel.

Tuscaloosa

Choctaw and Creek Indians lived here until settlers arrived in the early 1800s. Tuscaloosa became the state capital from 1826 to 1846, and the University of Alabama was established in 1831. Its successful Crimson Tide football team is a local obsession. The visitor bureau (☎ 205-391-9200, 800-538-8696, 1305 Greensboro Ave) is in the historic Jemison-Van de Graaf House.

At Gulf States Paper Corporation, the **Warner Collection** (☎ 205-562-5000) has works by American artists and artists from the Pacific Islands, Africa and Asia in a building like a Japanese temple (open weekends and weeknights only).

Fifteen miles south of Tuscaloosa, **Moundville Archaeological Park** (☎ 205-371-2234) has 26 archaeologically important Mississippian-era Indian mounds. A reconstructed mound shows dioramas of Indian life, and the **Jones Archaeological Museum** (☎ 205-371-2752) displays excavated artifacts and a replica of an Indian village ($4).

Many hotels line McFarland Blvd (Hwy 82) from I-59 north to the university. Cheaper ones include *Executive Inn* (☎ 205-759-2511), with singles/doubles at $35/40, and *Super 8* (☎ 205-758-8878), at $40/45. At University Blvd and 12th Ave, *Buffalo Phil's* is a popular student stop for wings, burgers and pasta. *Dreamland Barbecue (12 Jerusalem Heights Rd)*, off Hwy 82 in south Tuscaloosa, has legendary pork ribs ($8).

Birmingham

With the discovery of coal, iron ore and limestone in the late 19th century, Birmingham, once a small farming town, grew into the South's foremost industrial center, 'the Pittsburgh of the South.' It is now the largest and most cosmopolitan city in Alabama. Its Jim Crow legislation peaked in 1915, at a time when the Ku Klux Klan (KKK) dominated local politics. By the 1950s Birmingham became America's most segregated city. Racial tension erupted in 1963 when police attacked students marching for civil rights and turned a blind eye to more than 50 racially motivated bombings.

Orientation & Information The primary attractions are downtown, and the best dining and nightlife are in Southside off 20th St, the main north-south thoroughfare. The tourist office (☎ 205-458-8000, 800-458-8085) is at 2200 9th Ave N. The Historical 4th Ave Visitors Center (☎ 205-328-1850, 319 17th St N) conducts walking tours around the historic black business district (free).

Things to See & Do Audio, video, photography, art and artifacts tell the story of the civil-rights movement at the **Birmingham Civil Rights Institute** (☎ 205-328-9696, 520 16th St N), downtown ($5; closed Mon). Across the street at Kelly Ingram Park, civil-rights marches are recalled in sculptures of Martin Luther King Jr and of police dogs attacking children.

The Face in the Window

In 1876 a certain Henry Wells was accused of burning down the county courthouse in Carrollton, about 34 miles northwest of Tuscaloosa. Two years later the young black man was arrested on flimsy evidence and imprisoned in the garret of the newly rebuilt courthouse. An angry mob of townspeople saw Wells in the window, and as they approached he swore to haunt them if he were lynched. An instant later, a flash of lightning illuminated Wells' face and his anguished look was imprinted on the windowpane. What then happened to Wells is unclear, but to this day his terror-stricken face is visible on the window, despite repeated scrubbing of the glass.

B-a-ad Birmingham

During Birmingham's wild frontier days, there were more licenses issued for 'sin' businesses – pool halls, liquor outlets and tobacco shops – than regular businesses. Things got so bad in 1907 that a newspaper reported that more people were murdered in this town of 30,000 residents than 'in all of Great Britain with its forty millions.' The number of arrests peaked at 11,814 that year.

The **Alabama Jazz Hall of Fame** (☎ 205-254-2731, 1631 4th Ave N), downtown, celebrates jazz musicians with Alabama associations, like the fabulous Dinah Washington, Nat King Cole and Duke Ellington (donation; closed Mon). The **16th St Baptist Church** was a community gathering place during the protests and was bombed in 1963. The rebuilt church is a memorial and a house of worship.

The **Alabama Sports Hall of Fame** (☎ 205-323-6665, 2150 Civic Center Blvd) commemorates stars such as Jesse Owens, Joe Namath, Hank Aaron and Joe Louis ($5). The **Birmingham Museum of Art** (☎ 205-254-2565, 2000 8th Ave N) specializes in European decorative arts (especially Wedgwood) and has works from Africa and North America (free admission; closed Mon). Just east of downtown, **Sloss Furnaces National Historic Landmark** (☎ 205-324-1911, 20 32nd St N) is a museum of industry and a venue for concerts and special events.

Art deco buildings in Five Points South house shops, restaurants, breweries and nightclubs. **Vulcan Park** has a newly cleaned 55-foot iron statue of Vulcan, and its observation tower has fantastic views. Twelve miles south of town, **Oak Mountain** (☎ 205-620-2524) is Alabama's largest state park.

Places to Stay & Eat The *Birmingham South KOA Kampground* (☎ 205-664-8832, 222 Hwy 33) has a heated pool, bathhouse and cabins, and charges $20/25 for tents/RVs. *Birmingham Motor Court* (☎ 205-786-4397, 1625 3rd Ave W), west of downtown, has basic, inexpensive singles/doubles ($35/40). A notch up from the average, *Super 8 Eastwood Inn* (☎ 205-956-

3650, 1813 Crestwood Blvd) has a restaurant and pool ($49/55). The art deco *Pickwick Hotel* (☎ 205-933-9555, 800-255-7304, 1023 20th St S) is in Five Points South (from $94).

Rib-It-Up (830 1st Ave N), downtown, does Southern barbecue beef, pork and chicken ($2.50-8). In the historic black district, *La Vase* (328 16th St N) serves cheap home-style soul food. *Bombay Cafe* (☎ 205-322-1930, 2839 7th Ave S) is one of the best-value places in town, with entrées from $6.

Entertainment Check the monthly *black & white* for listings. Most popular nightclubs are in Southside. *The Garage Cafe* (☎ 205-322-3220, 2304 10th Terrace S) is a local favorite. *The Nick* (☎ 205-252-3831, 2514 10th Ave S) has the latest bands, both local and touring, while *22nd St Jazz Cafe* (☎ 205-252-0407, 710 22nd St S) is the place for live jazz and blues. *Club 21* (☎ 205-322-0469, 117 21st St N) has a mixed straight and gay clientele.

Getting There & Around Greyhound (☎ 205-251-3210, 618 19th St N), north of downtown, serves cities including Atlanta, Georgia ($20; 3 hours); Huntsville ($15; 2 hours); Memphis, Tennessee ($40; 6 hours); Montgomery ($18; 2 hours); Nashville, Tennessee ($26; 5½ hours); and New Orleans, Louisiana ($64; 8½ hours). Amtrak (☎ 205-324-3033, 1819 Morris Ave), downtown, has trains daily to New York at 2:07pm (from $109) and New Orleans at 1:06pm (from $29). Metro Area Express (☎ 205-322-7701) runs local buses on weekdays ($1).

Huntsville

Pioneer John Hunt settled in this area in 1805, following the removal of Creek and Chickasaw Indians. Wealthy merchants and planters built lavish houses in the Twickenham area, many of which survive today. Developed as an aerospace center after WWII, Huntsville now has 177,000 residents and a lively club scene. The visitor bureau (☎ 256-551-2230, 800-772-2348, 700 Monroe St) is in the Von Braun Civic Center.

The city's **US Space & Rocket Center** (☎ 256-837-3400), I-565 exit 15, has IMAX films, space demonstrations, simulators and the Space Shot ride, which takes you from four g's to weightlessness ($15/11 adults/kids). The old railroad passenger terminal served as a prison and hospital during the Civil War and now houses the **Huntsville Depot Museum** (☎ 256-564-8100, 320 Church St), in the Early Works complex, focusing on Huntsville history and transportation ($6). Costumed guides take visitors around the reconstructed buildings of the **Alabama Constitution Village** (☎ 205-535-6565, 404 Madison St) for $6.

Fourteen miles west of town is **Mooresville**, a town so old-style, picket-fence picturesque that Disney used it for Huck Finn movies.

The attractive *Monte Sano State Park* (☎ 256-534-3757, 5105 Nolen Ave) has a Japanese garden, 15 miles of trails and a campground with tent/RV sites ($10/15) and rustic cabins ($70). On University Dr NW, look for *Economy Inn* (☎ 256-534-7061), with singles/doubles from $26/34, or the nice *Baymont Inn* (☎ 256-830-8999), at $59/64; both have pools.

Jamo's Juice & Java & More (413 Jordan Lane), near the university, does good vegetarian dishes from $3.50. The little, laid-back *Caribbean House Restaurant* (2612 Jordan Lane) features authentic, inexpensive island-style foods. For Southern biscuits, gravy, ham, grits and eggs, try *Eunice's Country Kitchen* (1006 Andrew Jackson Way), downtown, where a full breakfast costs $6 tops. *Mollie Teal's* (2003 Whitesburg Dr), at Governors Dr, combines a bakery, eatery and brewery.

The hot *Crossroads Cafe* (☎ 256-533-3393, Market Square Mall) has live local and national rock acts ($3-6 cover). *Kaffeeklatsch Bar* (☎ 256-536-7993, 103 Jefferson St N) is where serious music fans catch rock, blues and pizzas.

Greyhound (☎ 256-534-1681, 601 Monroe St NW) has two or three buses daily to Atlanta, Georgia ($31; 8½ hours); Birmingham ($18; 2½ hours); Nashville, Tennessee ($18; 2½ hours); and New Orleans, Louisiana ($82; 11 hours). Huntsville Shuttle System (☎ 256-532-7433) runs 11 routes and an hourly tourist bus to most hotels ($2).

The Shoals

Four cities on the Tennessee River make up the area known as 'the Shoals': Florence, Sheffield, Tuscumbia and Muscle Shoals. The Wilson Dam, completed in 1924, improved navigation on the 37-mile Muscle Shoals rapids and brought inexpensive elec-

tricity to the area. The Shoals made a name for itself in the music industry from 1966, when Fame Recording Studios and Quinvy Studio got Atlantic Records to release hits from Percy Sledge, Wilson Pickett, Aretha Franklin, Paul Simon and many others.

In Florence, the **University of North Alabama** has a beautiful campus designed by Frederick Law Olmsted. The 1940 **Rosenbaum House** (☎ 256-764-5274, 601 Riverview Dr) is one of Frank Lloyd Wright's do-it-yourself 'Usonian' houses.

Blind and deaf from the age of 19 months, Helen Keller learned to speak, read and write with the help of teacher Anne Sullivan and later became a world-famous writer. She spent her early life in **Ivy Green** (☎ 256-383-4066), a white clapboard house at 300 W North Commons, Tuscumbia ($5). The **Alabama Music Hall of Fame** (☎ 256-381-4417, 800-239-2643), on Hwy 72, Tuscumbia, has Toni Tenille's self-embroidered bell-bottom jeans, Jim Nabors' Gomer Pyle uniform and stage clothes from Emmylou Harris and Jimmy Buffett ($6).

Florence has the most budget options. *McFarland Park Campground* (☎ 256-760-6416), on Hwy 20 just west of Hwy 157, is a city park on the Tennessee River (tents/RVs $11/14; open Apr-Nov). *Budget Inn* (☎ 256-764-7621, 1238 Florence Blvd) is basic but clean and cheap (singles/doubles $28/40). *Knights Inn* (☎ 256-764-5421, 1241 Florence Blvd) is similar ($35/40). *Howard Johnson* (☎ 256-760-8888, 400 S Court St) is friendly and a notch above the others ($52/58).

Mississippi

While Mississippi's Gulf Coast has some wonderful coastal environments and the famous history and scenery of Natchez Trace Pkwy, the state's principal attraction is a glimpse of the real South. It lies somewhere amid the Confederate defeat at Vicksburg, the literary legacy of William Faulkner at Oxford, the birthplace of the blues in the Mississippi Delta, and the humble origins of Elvis Presley in Tupelo.

History

There are several remnants from the ancient Mississippi culture in modern-day

Mississippi

Nickname: Magnolia State

Population: 2,845,000 (31st)

Area: 48,434 sq miles (32nd)

Admitted to Union: December 10, 1817 (20th); seceded 1861; readmitted 1870

Capital city: Jackson (population 184,000)

Other cities: Biloxi (51,000), Greenville (42,000)

Birthplace of: the blues, William Faulkner (1897–1962), Tennessee Williams (1911–83), Elvis Presley (1935–77), Kermit the Frog

Mississippi; three Indian nations were here when Hernando de Soto arrived in 1540, but only one Choctaw community survives. The Natchez were eliminated from their fertile lands by the first settlers, and most of the others were displaced by a series of sham treaties and ultimate removal to Oklahoma in the 1830s.

The French, Spanish and British contested the area, but it was all in American hands by 1816, with enough American occupants to qualify for statehood. Cotton dominated the economy, and by 1860 Mississippi was the country's leading cotton producer and one of the 10 wealthiest states. Cotton required slave labor, but the vast majority of slaves were owned by a few very big plantations. Most whites held no slaves at all. Nevertheless, the institution of slavery was entrenched and there was a great fear of slave rebellion. Mississippi was the second state to secede in the Civil War, which cost the state more than 60,000 lives. Vicksburg was the last Confederate stronghold on the Mississippi, and its fall to General Grant after a long siege was a turning point in the conflict.

The war ruined Mississippi's economy, and Reconstruction was traumatic. The discriminatory 'Black Code' laws made racial segregation a way of life, with most blacks and many whites doomed to wretched poverty. It was not until the late 1960s that the state's schools and colleges were integrated, and the civil-rights struggle was marked by violence, murder and federal intervention. Despite some economic diversification and the growth of oil and natural-gas industries, Mississippi has the lowest per-capita income in the country.

Information

The Mississippi Division of Tourism (☎ 601-875-0705, 800-927-6378, W www.visitmississippi.org, PO Box 1705, Ocean City, MS 39566) has Welcome Centers at the state line on most interstates. For road conditions, call ☎ 601-987-1212. State sales tax is 7%, plus lodging taxes in many areas.

NORTHEASTERN MISSISSIPPI

The Appalachian foothills begin in this lovely corner of the state – a gently rolling terrain of well-watered forests and cropland. Many visitors sensibly base themselves in Oxford, a literary and intellectual hub of the South and home to the University of Mississippi campus.

Tupelo & Around

Incorporated in 1870 and named after a native gum tree, Tupelo was once a railroad hub and today mass produces upholstered furniture. It's famous around the world as the birthplace of Elvis Presley, the King of Rock 'n' Roll, and everyone in town has their own story of who cut the King's hair or who taught him his first chord.

The Natchez Trace Pkwy and Hwy 78 intersect northeast of downtown. Gloster St has motels, restaurants and other services, especially at the intersection with McCullough Blvd. The older downtown area is about a mile east at 'Crosstown,' the intersection of Gloster and Main Sts, marked by an old blue-and-yellow neon arrow. The visitor center (☎ 662-841-6521, 800-533-0611) is at 399 E Main St, and the Natchez Trace Pkwy visitor center (☎ 601-680-4025, 800-305-7417) is on the parkway north of Hwy 78.

The **Elvis Presley birthplace** (☎ 601-841-1245, 306 Elvis Presley Blvd) is east of downtown off Hwy 78. The 15-acre park complex contains the actual house ($2), a museum displaying personal items ($5) and a tiny chapel that contains Elvis' own Bible.

The **Tupelo Museum** (☎ 662-841-6438), half a mile west of Natchez Trace Pkwy off Hwy 6, has a rambling collection of Indian dioramas and exhibits on the 1936

The King's Humble Origins

Elvis and his stillborn twin, Jesse, were born in Tupelo in the front room of a 450-sq-foot shotgun shack at 4:35am on January 8, 1935. The Presleys lived there until Elvis was three, when the house was repossessed.

Elvis bought his first guitar at Tupelo Hardware (114 W Main St) for $12; attended grades one to five at Lawhon School, down the road from his birthplace; won second prize in a talent quest at the fairgrounds west of town; earned A grades in music at Milam Junior High School, Gloster and Jefferson Sts; and attended the First Assembly of God church (909 Berry St).

When Elvis was 13, he and his family left Tupelo for Memphis. He returned at 21 to play the Mississippi-Alabama Fair, and the National Guard was called in to contain the crowds. The following year, Elvis came back for a benefit concert, with proceeds going to help the city purchase and restore his birthplace, which now attracts nearly 100,000 visitors each year.

HLR

'tornador' that killed 210 people ($1). Twelve miles northwest, **Brices Cross Roads** has a small cemetery and a monument to the Confederate victory here in 1864. More Civil War sites are farther north in Corinth, where you should lunch at old-style *Borroum's* drugstore. Twenty miles up Hwy 78, **New Albany** was the birthplace of William Faulkner. For a brochure on 'Faulkner Country' and the author's local travels, call ☎ 662-534-5354.

The *Tombigbee State Park*, southeast of town, and *Trace State Park*, to the west, have primitive campsites for $13. At the overpass rise there's a cluster of motels, including plain *Scottish Inn* (☎ 662-842-1961, 401 N Gloster St), at $35; and *Ramada Inn* (☎ 662-844-4111, 854 N Gloster St), with a nightclub, pool and singles/doubles for $47/57.

Commodore Motel (☎ 662-840-0285), on Business 78, a half-mile east of Elvis' birthplace, charges $30/35 (cash only).

A block northwest of the Crosstown arrow, *Jefferson Place*, off Gloster St, is a popular bar and grill serving steaks and sandwiches. *Rib Cage* (206 Troy St) downtown does good barbecue sandwiches and even a quail plate ($5.25).

The Greyhound station (☎ 662-842-4557, 201 Commerce St), downtown, has four buses daily to Memphis, Tennessee ($22; 3 hours), and one to Oxford ($12; 1½ hours).

Oxford

Cultivated, bustling and prosperous Oxford is home to the University of Mississippi (commonly called Ole Miss), which opened in 1848. During the Civil War, Oxford was captured and torched by Union soldiers, and only a few treasured buildings survived. Later, William Faulkner mythologized the area in his famous stories of Yoknapatawpha County:

I discovered my little postage stamp of native soil was worth writing about, and…I would never live long enough to exhaust it.

In 1962 ugly riots accompanied the enrollment of James Meredith, the first black student at Ole Miss. Troops were called in, and two people died. The university and town are now quietly integrated, with galleries, bookstores, cafes and the visitor center (☎ 662-234-4680, 800-758-9177) grouped around Courthouse Square.

The University of Mississippi, a mile or so west of the square, has an attractive 2500-acre campus shaded by magnolias and dogwoods. Its **Center for the Study of Southern Culture** (☎ 662-915-5993) covers everything from corn pone to Elvis cults, and has the largest collection of blues recordings and publications in the world. On University Ave at 5th Ave, the **University Museums** (☎ 662-915-7073) contain several collections

TOM DOWNS

Tuba Fats ponders a performance. New Orleans

JON DAVISON

Bonita Beach; Naples, Florida

RICHARD I'ANSON

Cherokee beadwork, South Carolina

'Uh-huh, thank you very much.' The King lives on; Beale St, Memphis, Tennessee

GREG ELMS

Pumping the pride of Texas, Galveston

Veggie burger? Stuffed cow at Texas restaurant

Des Moines, Iowa

Rural Kansas gets a burst of energy.

of ancient, decorative, fine and folk arts (free admission).

The 1840 house at **Rowan Oak** (☎ 662-234-3284), on Old Taylor Rd, was bought by William Faulkner in 1930, and he lived and worked here until his death in 1962. The sparsely furnished house, set in grounds behind an arcade of oak and cedar, attracts literary pilgrims and aspiring writers (free admission; closed Mon).

The USFS **Puskus Lake** campground, northeast off Hwy 30, has primitive sites for $5, and there are several campgrounds around **Sardis Lake**, northwest off Hwy 314. **Ole Miss Motel** (☎ 662-234-2424, 1517 University Ave), a few blocks away from the square, has modest singles/doubles for $30/35. Several budget motels cluster around exits off the Hwy 6 bypass. On campus, **Alumni Center Hotel** (☎ 662-232-7047, ✉ hotel@olemiss.edu, 172 Grove Loop) provides rooms with private baths for $55/63. **Oliver-Britt House** (☎ 662-234-8043, 512 Van Buren Ave) is comfortably worn and only three blocks from the square (from $45/55).

City Grocery (152 Courthouse Square) has nouveau Southern specialties like shrimp and cheese grits and 'angels on horseback' (a smoked oyster dish). Lunch costs $9-12, dinner up to $20. **Ajax** (118 Courthouse Square) does an amazing sweet-potato side and good cheese meatloaf ($9). For a cheap meal of chicken or catfish with flavors of the Dominican Republic, try **Don Pancho's** (512 Jackson Ave), a tiny five-table place.

Blues, bluegrass and roots rock can be heard most nights; check the free weekly **Oxford Town** for what's on at **Proud Larry's**, **Murff's** or **The Gin**.

Greyhound (☎ 662-234-0094) runs daily to Memphis, Tennessee ($20), from 2625 W Oxford Loop (off W Jackson Ave). Rent a bike from Base Camp (☎ 662-234-5882), near the square at 302 S Lamar Blvd.

Holly Springs

Elvis-obsessed Paul MacLeod has turned his Holly Springs house into **Graceland Too** (☎ 662-252-7954, 200 Ghoulson Ave) a shrine wallpapered with Elvis posters and crammed with Elvisania. He sells tiny swatches of Graceland carpet ($10) and does Elvis impersonations with little encouragement. Graceland Too is open just about any hour, day or night ($5).

The Blues & Gospel Folk Festival is held the second Saturday in September; call the chamber of commerce (☎ 601-252-2943) for details. Famous **Phillips Grocery** (541 Van Dorn Ave) serves acclaimed burgers and fried okra; it's close to the downtown square but tricky to find. To get there, follow Van Dorn Ave half a mile east from the square; at the traffic light near the gas station, veer left up the hill, and Phillips is a block up on the right.

MISSISSIPPI DELTA

The area called the Delta stretches for 250 miles along the Mississippi River from Memphis to Vicksburg. Technically it's an alluvial plain rather than a river delta, and flooding was a perennial problem until the levee system was completed, shortly before the Civil War.

The levees were destroyed in the conflict, then rebuilt after 1884. With flooding under control, the railroads moved in, trees were clear-cut for timber, and cotton fields were established using black sharecroppers instead of black slaves. Towns grew rapidly until boll weevils devastated the cotton in 1914, after which many sharecroppers joined the Great Migration to cities in the north and west. Later, cotton-picker machines and agribusiness displaced thousands more laborers. Now casinos, catfish farms, soybeans, rice and peanuts diversify the economy, but most Delta residents remain poor, and some shantytown communities look positively Third World.

The harsh lives of sharecroppers were reflected in their music – work chants based on African rhythms, old slave songs and spirituals. This evolved into the bittersweet sound known as the blues, and this heritage is the main attraction for visitors. Regular blues festivals occur in towns throughout the Delta, and local performers play small 'juke joints' every weekend. Steve Cheseborough's *Blues Traveling: The Holy Sites of Delta Blues* is an essential guide to blues history and places.

Don't flaunt valuables here, and don't stop for strangers on the road. Guns are prevalent in the region, and encounters with local law enforcement are best avoided; tent camping is not a good option. There are plenty of cheap chain motels, and even cheaper independent places, but book ahead during festivals. There's virtually no public transport, and visitors on foot or bike stand out like Martians. US 61 is the legendary Blues Route, but Hwy 1 is an often scenic alternative; small backroads between the two provide numerous diversions. There are also points of interest on the Louisiana and Arkansas side of the Delta.

Northern Delta
Coming south from Memphis, you'll see cotton fields stretching out to the horizon, dotted with gins, cabins and cypress swamps. You'll also see many Vegas-style casinos that were supposed to bring prosperity to Tunica County. On Hwy 61, stop for grits or steaks at the *Blue & White* cafe. About the only shade is at **Moon Lake**, where the Moon Lake Club once provided family-style drinking and gambling during Prohibition; it was a venue for several plays by Tennessee Williams. It's now *Uncle Henry's* (☎ 662-337-2757), where a good Southern meal costs around $12 and a room is $70.

Clarksdale
Clarksdale is a convenient base for exploring the Delta and also the site of the Sunflower River Blues and Gospel Festival the first weekend in August. 'Downtown' is the few blocks where the railroad tracks meet the Sunflower River. Across the tracks, in a rough-looking part of town along Martin Luther King Jr Blvd, are several eateries and juke joints, with lots of people hanging out in front of boarded-up stores. The chamber of commerce (☎ 662-627-7337, 1540 DeSoto Ave/Hwy 49) has some information, but knows little about the other side of the tracks.

The **Delta Blues Museum** (☎ 601-627-6820, 1 Blues Alley) has maps and charts that plot musical milestones, a re-created section of WC Handy's home, and a modest collection of artifacts (free admission; closed Sun). Specialist recordings and books are available.

Tennessee Williams spent much of his childhood in Clarksdale. The Tennessee Williams Festival, in the second weekend of October, features scholarly presentations and popular performances.

Greyhound buses (☎ 662-627-7893, 1604 State St) run to several cities including Memphis, Tennessee ($17; 1½ hours), and New Orleans, Louisiana ($68; from 5½ hours).

The niftiest option is *Shack Up Inn* (☎ 662-624-8329, ⓔ shackup@shackupinn.com), at Hopson Plantation, 2 miles south on the west side of Hwy 49. Comfortable, refurbished sharecropper shacks cost $35-50 (no air-con). *Up Town Motel* (☎ 662-627-3251, 305 E 2nd St) is an OK cheapie at $30/40 for singles/doubles. Friendly *Comfort Inn* (☎ 662-627-5122, 818 S State St) has lots of amenities, homemade waffles and rooms for $60.

Abe's (616 State St) has been serving the tenderest barbecue for 75 years. *Sarah's Kitchen* (208 Sunflower St) does dinners from $6, with live entertainment some weekends. *Chamoun's Rest Haven* (419 State St) is a Lebanese alternative, with combo plates for $8.50. Co-owned by actor Morgan Freeman, *Madidi* (☎ 662-627-7724, 164 Delta Ave) serves fancy nouveau Southern cuisine to a prosperous clientele for $17-35.

Musical events are often publicized by word of mouth and on last-minute posters around town. Usually only one juke joint features live entertainment on any given night; try *Red's* (395 Sunflower Ave) or *Smitty's* (377 Yazoo Ave). *Ground Zero* (☎ 662-621-0990), in Blues Alley, is the hottest new music club – another Morgan Freeman venture. *Commissary* (☎ 662-624-5756), at Hopson Plantation, hosts occasional gigs.

South of Clarksdale
Seventeen miles south, Stovall Farms is a former plantation where Muddy Waters lived and worked. In Tutwiler, an outdoor mural illustrates WC Handy's first exposure to the blues in 1903. Farther south on Hwy 49, Parchman Penitentiary has been a temporary home for many bluesmen and the subject of several songs – the 'Midnight Special' was the weekend train bringing prison visitors. On Hwy 61 in Shelby, *Do-Drop Inn* is a locally famed juke joint.

Barely a Podunk, Merigold has three draws: McCarty's Pottery Store (☎ 662-748-2293), with a wonderfully eccentric garden out back; *Crawdad's* (☎ 662-748-2254), a barn-sized restaurant with walls of animal heads and generous portions; and *Poor Monkey's Lounge* (☎ 662-748-2254), an old-time juke joint that's welcoming to strangers.

Greenville
The Delta's largest city has a more liberal reputation than its neighbors. The local

paper was urging racial moderation in 1946 (a mere 80 years after the Civil War!). The Mississippi Delta Blues Festival is held off Hwy 454, south of town, on the third Saturday in September. *Perry's Flowing Fountain* (*928 Nelson St*) anchors a rough strip of downtown blues clubs.

Around the junction of Hwy 82 and Hwy 1, miles of eyesore neon advertise inexpensive lodgings. The budget *Levee Inn* (☎ *601-332-1511*), Hwy 82 east of Hwy 1, has rooms for $30. *Budget Inn* (☎ *601-334-4591*), on Hwy 1, has better singles/doubles for $25/30. A culinary landmark, *Doe's Eat* (*502 Nelson St*), at Hinds St, has been serving generous steaks and skillet-fried potatoes since 1941.

North of town off Hwy 1, **Winterville Mounds State Historic Site** has a museum ($1) and 15 ancient Indian mounds.

Leland & Indianola

If you've been singing the blues as long as I have, it's kind of like being black twice.

– Riley (BB) King

A tiny visitor center in Leland displays photographs of Muppet man Jim Henson, his Delta childhood and early Kermit-like characters.

Indianola is home to bluesman BB King, civil-rights heroine Fannie Lou Hamer and the Citizens Council, a white-collar Ku Klux Klan. On the first weekend in June, BB returns to play an outdoor festival with local musicians, then retreats to sleek *Club Ebony* (☎ *601-887-9915, 404 Hannah Ave*).

Greenwood & Belzoni

Greenwood Le Flore negotiated the treaty of Dancing Creek, which banished the Choctaw to Oklahoma and gave Le Flore a 15,000-acre estate with hundreds of slaves. Greenwood is now the country's second-largest cotton market.

The visitor bureau (☎ 800-748-9064) is at 1902 Leflore Ave. The Mississippi Crossroads Festival is held on the last Saturday in May. **Cottonlandia** (☎ 662-453-0925), out on Hwy 82 west of town, is a quirky museum with cotton exhibits and a large collection of Indian crafts ($4; open daily). *Lusco's*

(☎ *662-453-5365, 722 Carrollton Ave*) serves steaks and seafood in booths that provided privacy during the Prohibition era.

The self-styled catfish capital of the world, Belzoni is surrounded by ponds where New Age catfish are bred and fed. The Catfish Visitor Center (☎ 800-408-4838, 111 Magnolia St) will reveal all. *Alison's* (*107 E Jackson St*) serves catfish and fries for $6.

Vicksburg

The high bluffs overlooking the Mississippi made this place a strategic location in the Civil War. General Ulysses S Grant besieged the city for 47 days, until its surrender on July 4, 1863. The major sights are readily accessible from I-20 exit 4B (Clay St). The visitor bureau (☎ 601-636-9421, 800-221-3536) is at the corner of Clay and Washington Sts, and there's a visitor center opposite the national park. The old, slow downtown stretches along several cobblestone blocks of Washington St, and casinos glitter beside the river.

Vicksburg's **National Military Park & Cemetery** (☎ 601-636-0583) is north of I-20 on Clay St. A 16-mile driving tour ($4 per car) passes historic markers explaining gun emplacements and key events. Rent an audiotape tour for the whole story ($5). The cemetery contains some 17,000 Union graves, and a museum houses the ironclad gunboat USS *Cairo*. Excellent personal guided tours start at $25 per car. Civil War reenactments are held in May and July.

Historic-house museums cluster in the Garden District, on Oak St south of Clay St, and also between 1st St E and Clay St ($5). The small **Museum of Coca-Cola Memorabilia** (☎ 601-638-6514, 1107 Washington St) is housed in an 1890 bottling building ($2.25). The **Gray & Blue Naval Museum** (☎ 601-638-6500) across the road has a diorama of the Vicksburg battlefield and a flotilla of modern ships ($2.50).

Downtown, the no-frills *Relax Inn* (☎ *601-631-0097, 1313 Walnut St*) offers singles/doubles for $25/30. *Battlefield Inn* (☎ *601-638-5811, 800-359-9363*), at I-20 exit 4B, is an incongruously comfortable road motel, from $40/45 including breakfast. *Cedar Grove B&B* (☎ *601-636-1000, 2300 Washington St*), an 1840 Greek Revival mansion, has gardens overlooking the river and rooms for $95-185.

Walnut Hills (1214 Adams St) does a feast of Southern favorites. The soul-food equivalent is *LD's Kitchen (1111 Mulberry St)*. *Burger Village (1220 Washington St)* provides an alternative to fast-food chains and casino buffets.

CENTRAL MISSISSIPPI

The rolling midlands of central Mississippi are largely agricultural, with Jackson the only sizable urban center. One of the most scenic ways to see the region is along the Natchez Trace Pkwy, which is ablaze in wildflowers in springtime. Detours along Hwys 15 and 16 to Philadelphia reveal an area rich in Choctaw mythology and civil-rights history.

Jackson

Earlier known as 'LeFleur's Bluff,' Jackson became state capital in 1821 and was renamed after the national hero of the time, General Andrew Jackson. During the Civil War the city was burned on three separate occasions by Sherman's troops, though the capitol, governor's mansion and city hall were spared. It's now Mississippi's largest city, with suburbs sprawling to the north. The downtown area is a short stretch of Capitol St, from the Amtrak station to the old capitol.

The visitor bureau (☎ 601-960-1891, 800-354-7695, Ⓦ www.visitjackson.com) has an information desk at the **Agriculture & Forestry Museum** (☎ 601-713-3365, 1150 Lakeland Dr), east of I-55 exit 98B. The 'Ag Museum' incorporates cultural and ecological history in displays of farm machinery, crop-dusting planes, a re-created 1920s town and an 1860s farmstead ($4/2 adults/kids). Next door, the **Mississippi Sports Hall of Fame** (☎ 601-982-8264) comprises 21,500 sq feet of sports statistics and athletic idolatry ($5; open daily).

The **Old Capitol Museum of Mississippi History** (☎ 601-359-6920), in the beautifully restored 1833 capitol building, has a good 20th-century exhibit with vintage footage of civil-rights clashes (free admission). The new capitol, styled after the one in Washington, DC, was completed in 1903.

Nearby, the **Mississippi Museum of Natural Science** (☎ 601-354-7303) examines cypress swamps, Delta bottomlands and abandoned farms ($4). The **Mississippi**

Museum of Art (☎ 601-960-1515, 201 E Pascagoula St) displays a small, bright collection of contemporary works, including pieces by Georgia O'Keeffe, Andy Warhol and several New Orleans surrealists ($5; open daily). A small room in the city's **Eudora Welty Library** (☎ 601-968-5811, 300 N State St) is dedicated to Mississippi literati.

African American heritage sites include the excellent **Smith Robertson Museum** (☎ 601-960-1457, 528 Bloom St), a cultural center and museum with photographs and contemporary art ($1). Since the 1900s, Farish St north of Capitol St has been the hub of black political, economic, social, religious and cultural development.

Greyhound buses (☎ 601-353-6342) leave from a modern station at Jefferson and Pearl Sts, bound for New Orleans, Louisiana ($27; 4 hours), and Memphis, Tennessee ($30; 4 hours). Amtrak's *City of New Orleans* stops at the run-down station (☎ 601-355-6350) on Capitol St at Mill St.

A nicely wooded lakeside campground, *LeFleur's Bluff State Park (☎ 601-987-3985, I-55 exit 98B)* offers tent and RV sites at $12. A 1950s relic, *Sun-n-Sand Motel (☎ 601-354-2501, 401 N Lamar St)*, near the capitol, is orange and turquoise, with a trapezoidal pool and singles/doubles at $35/40. *Edison-Walthall Hotel (☎ 601-948-6161, 800-932-6161, 225 E Capitol St)* has a dark wood lobby, atrium pool and comfortable, motel-like rooms from $72. Chain motels line the freeway exits.

Mayflower Cafe (123 Capitol St), behind the giant flashing neon sign, is a local institution serving Southern plates and Greek salads. Tricky to find, *Hal & Mal's (200 S Commerce St)* has autographed glossy photos of recording stars who came for burgers, catfish, quiche and occasional live music (closed Sun). *Kiefers (705 Poplar St)* serves cheap souvlaki, falafel and salads to a mixed crowd on its comfy patio.

Downstairs at *Sun-n-Sand Motel* is a retro lounge with vinyl bar stools, big-haired divorcées and good old boys. *Subway Lounge (619 W Pearl St)* hosts live lowdown blues in an intimate basement. *Da Groove (☎ 601-353-5357, 444 Mill St)* is a recycled warehouse offering R&B, soul and Top 40 on weekends (cover $10 after 10pm; no jeans or sneakers).

Around Jackson

A shabby exit road from I-55, 25 miles north of Jackson, leads to **Canton**, a classic Southern town and movie set, with Victorian homes and a tidy square with a Greek Revival centerpiece.

Around 30 miles north in Vaughan, the **Casey Jones Museum** (☎ 662-673-9864) occupies a restored railroad station near the site of the 1900 train crash that killed Luther 'Casey' Jones ($1).

Northeast of Jackson, the landscape fills with croplands, chicken farms, trailers, shacks and cinder-block churches. A triangular detour off Natchez Trace Pkwy, via Hwys 16 and 15, takes you through **Philadelphia**, with memorials to the three civil-rights workers murdered here in 1964. Nearby, the Mississippi Band of Choctaw, who managed to avoid removal, still work their ancestral lands, which now support an industrial park and casino.

West of Jackson on I-20, you can stop at Chunky, where a Rhythm & Blues Festival is held the third Saturday in July. Meridian is a more common stop, with the Jimmie Rodgers Museum (☎ 601-485-1808) dedicated to the father of country music ($2).

NATCHEZ & NATCHEZ TRACE

Natchez Indians gave their name to this area on the lower Mississippi and also to the path they regularly 'traced' between their homeland and the game-rich Cumberland River valley.

Natchez

Perched on a bluff overlooking the Mississippi, this antebellum town attracts tourists with its opulent architecture, especially during the 'pilgrimage' season, when local mansions are opened to visitors. The large, modern Natchez Vistor Reception Center (☎ 601-446-6345, 800-647-6724, Ⓦ www .natchez.com) is on S Canal St at Hwy 84.

Over a dozen fine **historic houses** are open for tours year round. Some of the best include the House on Ellicott's Hill (☎ 601-442-2011), Longwood (☎ 601-442-5193), Melrose (☎ 601-446-5790), Rosalie (☎ 601-445-4555) and Stanton Hall (☎ 601-442-6282). Most charge about $6 and are open daily.

Natchez-under-the-Hill was once the commercial center of town. When the legitimate businesses moved higher up to the bluff, this cove beside the Mississippi retained its lusty riverboat activities. The present reconstruction features picturesque cafes, saloons and a number of popular family restaurants.

The **Natchez Museum of African-American History & Culture** (☎ 601-445-0728, 307A Market St), on the 2nd floor, recounts local black history from the 1880s to the 1950s (donation requested; Wed-Sat afternoons). The **Grand Village of the Natchez** archaeological park and museum (☎ 601-446-6502, 400 Jefferson Davis Blvd) contains a set of small mounds and a reconstructed hut or two. The museum describes the traditions of the Natchez Indians.

Places to Stay & Eat The shady, 50-site *Natchez State Park* (☎ 601-442-2658) is 10 miles north at the start of the Natchez Trace. Motels dot the highways north and south of town. The budget *Natchez Inn* (☎ 601-442-0221, 218 John R Junkin Dr) offers basic rooms starting at $35.

Within walking distance of downtown, *Radisson Eola* (☎ 601-445-6000, 110 Pearl St) was once the town's preeminent hotel. Renovated rooms start at $99.

The inns and B&Bs in grand old houses start at around $90 a night. They feature antique furnishings, elaborate breakfasts and Southern hospitality, but most won't take children. The tourist board (☎ 800-647-6742) lists over 40 properties, and you reserve through Historic Inns of Natchez, at the visitor center.

Several eateries around the old depot on Canal St offer reasonably priced, family-friendly meals in cute settings. At the bluff, *Cock of the Walk* (200 N Broadway) is a casual Southern restaurant serving fried catfish and skillet cornbread. Downtown, *Pearl St Pasta* (105 S Pearl St) does fresh pasta and vegetables, which you can enjoy on a 2nd-story balcony. *Biscuits & Blues* (☎ 601-446-9922, 315 Main St) has blues music every weekend.

Getting There & Around Delta Bus Lines (☎ 601-445-5291, 103 Lower Woodville Rd), a Greyhound affiliate, offers daily bus service to Jackson ($22; 2¾ hours). Downtown attractions are easily seen on foot, but you can rent bikes at the Natchez Bicycle Center (☎ 601-446-7794, 334 Main St) at

$15/20 per half-/full day. Tours can be done by pseudotrolley (☎ 601-442-5082) – a bus done up to look like a streetcard – or carriage (inquire at the depot downtown).

Natchez Trace Parkway

Early European explorers followed this Indian route, and French explorers set up trading posts at its northern and southern ends. In the late 18th century, traders coming downriver would sell their cargo, boats and timber rafts, and return north on foot. The route became a US post road and was later widened to serve as a military road. When steamboats arrived the road was supplanted by river traffic, and the trace fell into disuse until it was revived as a national historic route in the 1930s.

Today the Natchez Trace Pkwy is a scenic two-lane road through woodlands and pasture from Natchez to Nashville. The parkway headquarters and a visitor center (☎ 662-680-4025, 800-305-7417) are in Tupelo, and several other centers also distribute maps and information. Commercial vehicles are banned, and there are no businesses or advertising on the roadside. The parkway is popular for bicycle touring, and driving it is pleasant but slow. Some stops and detours include the following:

Emerald Mound – A turnoff about 10 miles from Natchez, this is one of the largest Indian mounds in the Southeast, constructed around AD 1400.

Port Gibson – The town General Grant thought 'too pretty to burn' retains an attractive residential district and a small exhibit on the town's civilrights movement.

Sunken Trace – This is a deeply worn stretch of the original route.

Rocky Springs – This ghost town has a nicely wooded National Park Service free campground and hiking trails along the original trace.

Woodville – This is a little town with an attractive courthouse square; detour west to Clark Creek Nature Area, with winding trails, waterfalls and hardwood forest.

GULF COAST

More cosmopolitan than the rest of Mississippi, the Gulf Coast retains some of the character of old French and Spanish settlements. The economy is traditionally based on the seafood industry, with most schooners and canneries based in Biloxi. Since 1992 a dozen huge casinos have appeared in sleepy fishing villages along the coast. Ocean Springs is the nicest residential community and has great beaches, while industrial Gulfport is being developed as a casino resort. The Mississippi Gulf Coast Convention & Visitors Bureau (☎ 228-896-6699, 800-237-9493, W www.gulf-coast.org, 135 Courthouse Rd) is in Gulfport.

Biloxi

The French landed here in 1699 and also established settlements on the Gulf Islands. Biloxi was the capital of French Louisiana from 1699 to 1702, and again from 1719 to 1722, when the village of New Orleans took over the role. Now Biloxi is the center of vacation action, with a visitor center (☎ 228-374-3105, 710 Beach Blvd/Hwy 90) next to the town green.

The last home of Confederate President Jefferson Davis, **Beauvoir** (☎ 228-388-1313, 2244 Beach Blvd) is a 52-acre seaside estate offering public tours ($7.50). The **Seafood Industry Museum** (☎ 228-435-6320) is at Point Cadet, with old photos, nets, crab pots and cannery equipment ($3).

For camping, *Cajun RV Park* (☎ 228-388-5590, 1860 Beach Blvd) has comfortable worn tent and RV sites for $18.50. Motels line the coast around Biloxi, mostly modest budget places such as *Ocean Manor* (☎ 228-388-2529, 2484 Beach Blvd), from $33. Fancy new casino hotels are reasonably priced, if you can stand the decor and resist the gambling. *Ole Biloxi Schooner*, two blocks north of the beach on Myrtle St at Howard Ave, is an old diner with fishermen's breakfasts (from $4), po'boy lunches (from $5.50) and seafood plates at dinner ($13).

Gulfport & the Islands

Besides having two casinos and a busy industrial port, Gulfport is also the jumping-off point for ferry rides out to West Ship Island. Pan Isles Ferries (☎ 228-864-1014) makes the short trip once or twice a day ($18 roundtrip).

The **Gulf Islands National Seashore** comprises four barrier islands 12 miles off the Mississippi coast: West and East Ship Islands, Horn Island and Petit Bois Island. In 1965 Ship Island was split in two by Hurricane Camille, and though the two islands are now officially named West Ship and East Ship, folks still refer to a singular 'Ship Island.'

It's a great place to sunbathe, swim and hike, and West Ship is also home to the Civil War–era **Fort Massachusetts**. A shop there sells snacks and drinks. *Camping* is permitted on all islands except West Ship. Boats to the other islands can also be arranged via the Gulf Islands ranger station (☎ 228-875-3962) at Davis Bayou, on Hwy 90 just east of Ocean Springs. Horn Island is remarkable for pristine wilderness with pine and palmetto forests, lagoons and 13 miles of deserted beach.

ALONG US 90

Going west on US 90, the town of **Long Beach** has historic buildings and tall old trees. Pass Christian is a favorite resort for families from New Orleans, and many attractive houses and shady old oaks have survived through centuries of hurricanes. **Buccaneer State Park** (☎ 228-467-3822) features water slides, a *campground*, a pier and a nice stretch of beach. Tent/RV sites cost $8, $13 with full hookups.

East of Gulfport, US 90 passes Sandhill Crane National Wildlife Refuge and **Shepard State Park** (☎ 228-497-2244), which has hiking trails and a wooded campground ($8). At the mouth of the Pascagoula River, La Pointe–Krebs House (☎ 228-769-1505) was built around 1721 as a carpenter's shop. A museum displays pre-Columbian artifacts and memorabilia from the early 19th century and the Civil War ($4).

Louisiana

Truly a highlight of the USA, Louisiana is best known for the frenetic Mardi Gras festival in New Orleans, but there's much more than that here. The food alone is worth the trip, from Creole haute cuisine to a down-home crawfish boil. The music is another major attraction, running the gamut from sophisticated jazz clubs to impromptu swamp-pop jams. Ecotourists enjoy the unusual swamp and bayou environment, while the house-and-garden set drools over picturesque antebellum plantations and New Orleans' French and Spanish colonial architecture.

History

The lower Mississippi River area was dominated by the Mississippian moundbuilding culture until around AD 1000. But when Europeans arrived there were perhaps 15,000 Indians divided into six cultural groups: the Caddo, Tunica, Atakapa, Muskogee, Natchez and Chitimacha. The Indians were dispossessed with the usual combination of disease, unfavorable treaties and outright hostility, though it seems that under the French influence there was more intermarriage with immigrant Acadian, black and Creole groups.

Spanish explorers passed through in the 16th century, but the French explorer La Salle claimed the land for France in 1682, naming it in honor of Louis XIV. The town of Natchitoches was settled in 1714, and New Orleans was founded four years later, becoming the capital of French Louisiana in 1722. The colony was not an economic success, and to reduce the drain on the treasury, French officials passed the territory west of the Mississippi to Spain in 1762. The territory east of the Mississippi (except New Orleans) went to England in 1763 after the French and Indian War. After the American Revolution and some more colonial double-dealing, the whole area passed to the USA in the 1803 Louisiana Purchase, and Louisiana became a state in 1812.

The first steamboats reached New Orleans at about the same time, and the

---

Louisiana

Nicknames: Bayou State, Pelican State

Population: 4,469,000 (22nd)

Area: 51,843 sq miles (31st)

Admitted to the Union: April 30, 1812 (18th); seceded 1861; readmitted 1868

Capital city: Baton Rouge (population 228,000)

Other cities: New Orleans (485,000; metro area 1.3 million), Shreveport (200,000), Lafayette (110,000)

Birthplace of: jazz, Louis 'Satchmo' Armstrong (1901–71), Antoine 'Fats' Domino (b 1928), Huddie 'Leadbelly' Ledbetter (1885–1949), author Truman Capote (1924–84)

Famous for: Creole and Cajun cooking, Mardi Gras, Tabasco sauce

river system became a vital trade network across the whole interior of the continent. New Orleans became a major port, and Louisiana developed a slave-based plantation economy exporting rice, livestock, tobacco, indigo, sugarcane and especially cotton. Alarmed by Abraham Lincoln's election as president, Louisiana seceded from the Union and was an independent republic for about two months before joining the Confederacy. The Mississippi River was a crucial strategic objective, and Union forces seized control of New Orleans in 1862, occupying the city and the central and northern part of the state for most of the war. Some 24,000 Louisiana blacks joined Union forces, though quite a few 'free people of color' volunteered to fight for the Confederacy.

Louisiana was readmitted to the Union in 1868, after a new state constitution granted suffrage to blacks. The next 30 years were marked by political wrangling and economic stagnation, and in 1898 most blacks were effectively disenfranchised by the imposition of literacy tests and other impediments. In the early 20th century the discovery of oil was a big economic boost, while the devastation of cotton crops by boll weevils forced some agricultural diversification. From the 1920s, autocratic governor Huey Long was able to modernize much of the state's infrastructure. Industry developed further after WWII, particularly petrochemical, timber and paper processing based on the state's natural resources. Tourism cashed in on the state's cultural heritage, but the tradition of unorthodox, volatile and sometimes ruthless politics continues to the present.

Information

The Louisiana Department of Culture, Recreation & Tourism (☎ 225-342-8119, 800-633-6970, ⒲ www.louisianatravel.com, PO Box 94291, Baton Rouge, LA 70804-9291) has Welcome Centers in Baton Rouge and New Orleans and on freeways at state borders. State and parish sales taxes amount to about 8%.

NEW ORLEANS

Naturally languid from the subtropical heat and humidity, New Orleans is a town where nothing ever goes too fast or grows too worrisome. The town's unofficial motto is *Laissez les bons temps rouler* (let the good

The Genesis of Jazz

From their first unwilling arrival in Louisiana, Africans met in Congo Square to dance and sing to African drums – the only place in the South where this was permitted. Later they added violins, banjos and instruments won as souvenirs from the Spanish-American War. A syncopated fusion of ragtime, blues and marching music was developed at picnics, parades and funerals. Self-taught black musicians improvised the first jazz sounds in the bars and brothels of early-20th-century Storyville.

The first jazz record, At the Darktown Strutters' Ball, was not cut until 1917, and it was done by white musicians who merely copied the style. The real origins of the jazz genre remain very much a mystery.

times roll). African, Spanish, French, Italian and Caribbean culinary influences make New Orleans one of the country's best places to eat, and the music is equally exciting, with hot brass bands, jazz performers, and Cajun and zydeco groups, as well as rock, blues and R&B.

It's a great city to walk around, with the French Quarter and the adjoining faubourgs ('false towns') full of colorful Spanish architecture. But above all, New Orleans is famous for its Mardi Gras, a raucous celebration that climaxes a month of Carnival balls and festivities.

History

When French explorers sailed up the Mississippi River in 1699, they noticed a small portage that led across a narrow spit of land to a large lake. The town of Nouvelle Orléans was founded on the spit in 1718. Early immigrants arrived from France, Canada and Germany, and the French also imported thousands of African slaves. Many Africans earned their freedom and had an established place in the community as *les gens de couleur libres* (free people of color), regulated by the Code Noir. Unsuccessful as a mercantile economy, the colony came to rely on barter, smuggling and local trade, and the city developed a reputation for extralegal enterprises.

The essential French character of New Orleans was little affected by the change from French to Spanish rule in 1764. After the French and Indian War, French-speaking refugees from Canada arrived, but these Acadians were shunted off to westward swamplands. The 1791 slave revolt in the French colony of St Domingue (now Haiti) caused thousands of former slaves to move to New Orleans as free people of color. Fires in 1788 and 1794 wiped out most of the French architecture, and the Spanish Cabildo ruled that new buildings would be of brick with tile or slate roofs.

The French resumed control in 1803, but within days Napoleon sold the city to the US, along with the rest of Louisiana, and soon the French Creoles and Africans were joined by Anglo Americans. The Americans developed slave-based plantations similar to those that operated in Georgia and the Carolinas. In the War of 1812 (actually, just *after* the war), a motley crew of free blacks, Acadians, Choctaws and pirates defeated the Brits in the Battle of New Orleans, making a national hero of General Andrew Jackson. By 1840 New Orleans was the nation's fourth-largest city, with over 100,000 people.

Threatened by the Americans' Protestant beliefs and English legal system, the territorial legislature sought to preserve Creole culture by adopting elements of Spanish and French laws. The city became divided between the French Quarter's Creole community and the distinctly American residential section farther upriver. Americans took control of the municipal government in 1852, eroding the Creole influence in New Orleans, diminishing the rights of free people of color and marginalizing their economic position. At the time, New Orleans was the South's largest slave-trading center, with some 25 markets.

Pressing the Union strategy to control the Mississippi during the Civil War, Admiral David Farragut led a Union squadron up the river in 1862. In a daring action, it bombarded Confederate forts, ran the river blockade and captured New Orleans in only two days.

New Orleans survived the war as the South's largest city, while new federal laws required that voting and civil rights be extended to black males. White supremacists formed the White League, which ousted the government elected by newly enfranchised black voters, and introduced the Jim Crow laws. The end of the plantation economy and the declining importance of river traffic hit New Orleans hard, and its economy languished until oil and petrochemical industries developed in the 1950s.

Though now eclipsed by Atlanta as the South's largest city, metropolitan New Orleans has over 1.3 million people, with a growing African American population (67%), Anglo Americans (28%) and Latinos (3%), including an established Cuban community. Despite the Civil War and the gains of the civil-rights movement, many blacks remain impoverished, and the gap between wealthy whites and poor blacks seems as wide as ever.

Orientation

New Orleans is bounded by the Mississippi River to the south and Lake Pontchartrain to the north. Places are referred to as either 'lakeside' or 'riverside,' 'upriver' or 'downriver.' For example, the Lower Garden District is downriver from the central Garden District, so it's called 'lower,' even though it appears higher on maps. Street numbering between the river and lake typically starts at the river. For routes that run parallel to the river, street numbers begin at Canal St.

The historic French Quarter (the Vieux Carré) consists of 80 blocks around Jackson Square. Southwest of the French Quarter, the Central Business District (CBD) extends from Canal St to around Lee Circle. Upriver (ie, south) from the French Quarter, the old Warehouse District is becoming an appealing arts precinct, south of which is the Lower Garden District, a ramshackle neighborhood with budget guesthouses and a bohemian enclave. This adjoins the lovely Garden District, well known for its walking tours past historic homes. Uptown is farther west, accessed by the venerable St Charles Ave streetcar. Farther upriver, 3 miles west of the French Quarter, the Riverbend area is populated by many university students.

The Tremé district, centered on Louis Armstrong Park, west of the French Quarter, is a predominantly black residential district. Faubourg Marigny, a lively and predominantly gay district, is centered on Frenchmen St, downriver from the French Quarter. The rugged Bywater district of the city is located even farther downriver.

THE SOUTH

NEW ORLEANS

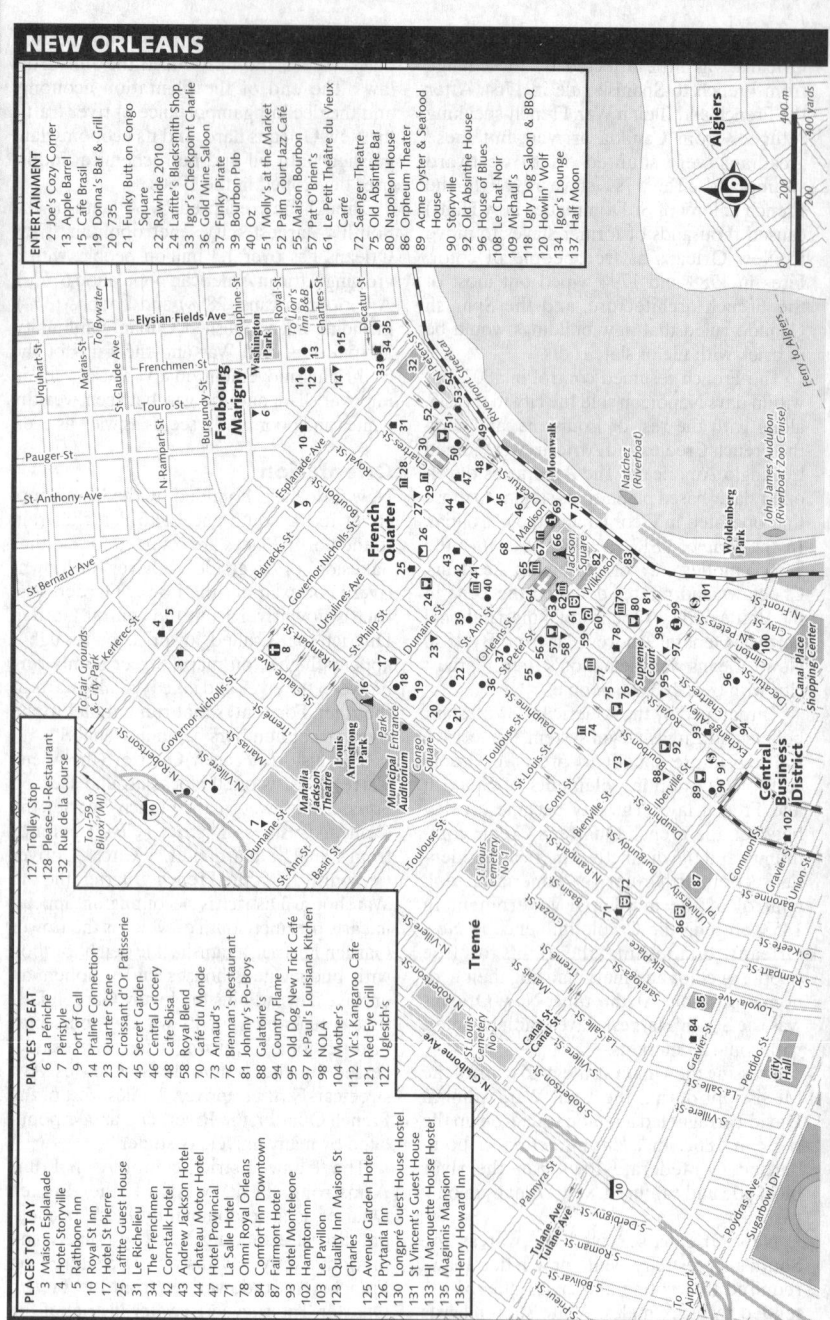

ENTERTAINMENT
2   Joe's Cozy Corner
13   Apple Barrel
15   Café Brasil
19   Donna's Bar & Grill
21   Funky Butt on Congo
    Square
20   Rawhide 2010
22   Lafitte's Blacksmith Shop
24   Igor's Checkpoint Charlie
36   Gold Mine Saloon
37   Funky Pirate
39   Bourbon Pub
40   Oz
51   Molly's at the Market
52   Palm Court Jazz Café
55   Maison Bourbon
57   Pat O'Brien's
61   Le Petit Théâtre du Vieux
    Carré
72   Saenger Theatre
75   Old Absinthe Bar
80   Napoleon House
86   Orpheum Theater
89   Acme Oyster & Seafood
    House
90   Storyville
92   Old Absinthe House
96   House of Blues
108   Le Chat Noir
109   Michaul's
118   Ugly Dog Saloon & BBQ
120   Howlin' Wolf
134   Igor's Lounge
137   Half Moon

PLACES TO STAY
3   Maison Esplanade
4   Hotel Storyville
5   Rathbone Inn
10   Royal St Inn
17   Hotel St Pierre
25   Lafitte Guest House
31   Le Richelieu
34   The Frenchmen
42   Cornstalk Hotel
43   Andrew Jackson Hotel
44   Chateau Motor Hotel
47   Hotel Provincial
71   La Salle Hotel
78   Omni Royal Orleans
84   Comfort Inn Downtown
87   Fairmont Hotel
93   Hotel Monteleone
102   Hampton Inn
103   Le Pavillon
123   Quality Inn Maison St
    Charles
125   Avenue Garden Hotel
126   Prytania Inn
130   Longpré Guest House Hostel
131   St Vincent's Guest House
133   HI Marquette House Hostel
135   Maginnis Mansion
136   Henry Howard Inn

PLACES TO EAT
6   La Peniche
7   Peristyle
9   Port of Call
14   Praline Connection
23   Quarter Scene
27   Croissant d'Or Patisserie
45   Secret Garden
46   Central Grocery
48   Cafe Sbisa
58   Royal Blend
70   Café du Monde
73   Arnaud's
76   Brennan's Restaurant
81   Johnny's Po-Boys
88   Galatoire's
94   Country Flame
95   Old Dog New Trick Café
97   K-Paul's Louisiana Kitchen
98   NOLA
104   Mother's
112   Vic's Kangaroo Cafe
121   Red Eye Grill
122   Uglesich's

127   Trolley Stop
128   Please-U-Restaurant
132   Rue de la Course

Algiers

NEW ORLEANS

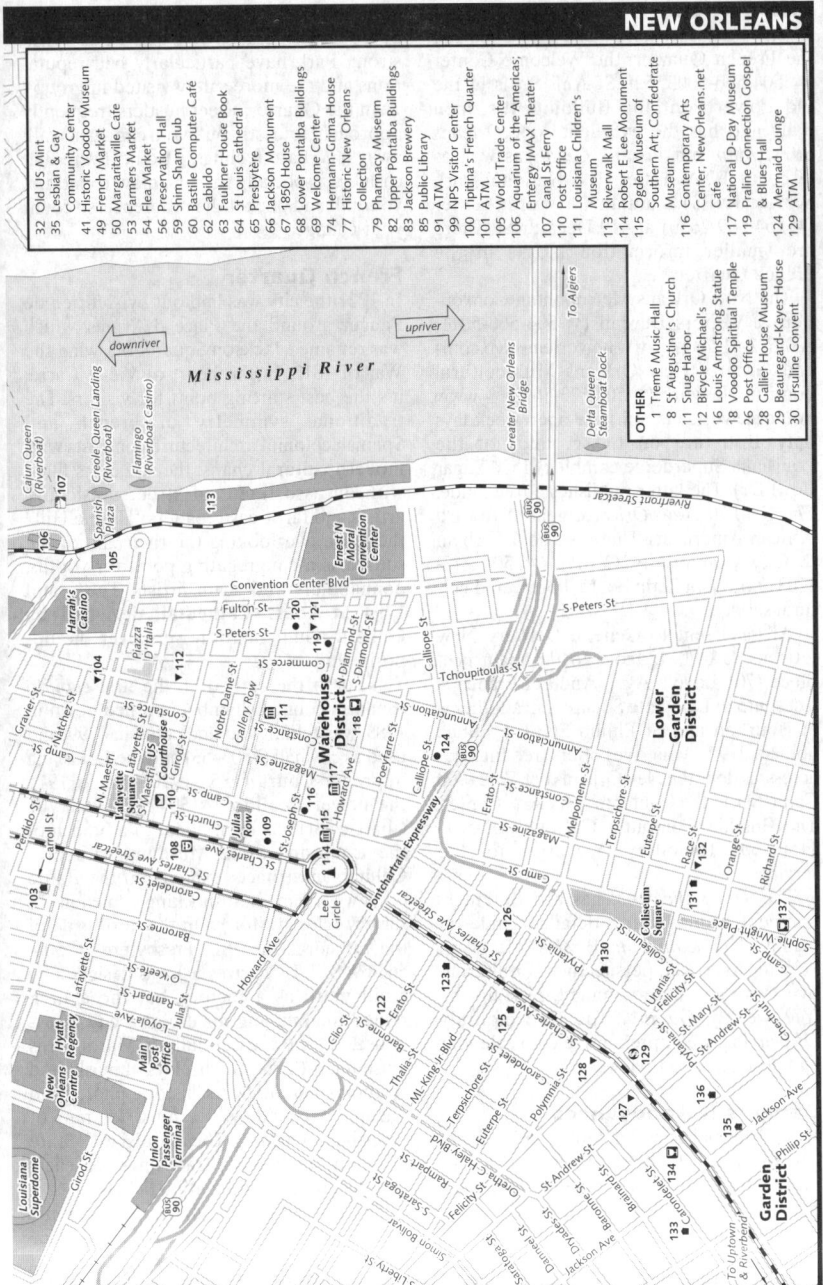

32 Old US Mint
35 Lesbian & Gay
     Community Center
41 Historic Voodoo Museum
49 French Market
50 Margaritaville Cafe
53 Farmers Market
54 Flea Market
56 Preservation Hall
59 Shim Sham Club
60 Cabildo
62 Bastille Computer Café
63 Faulkner House Book
64 St Louis Cathedral
65 Presbytère
66 Jackson Monument
67 1850 House
68 Lower Pontalba Buildings
69 Welcome Center
74 Hermann-Grima House
77 Historic New Orleans
     Collection
79 Pharmacy Museum
82 Upper Pontalba Buildings
83 Jackson Brewery
85 Public Library
91 ATM
99 NPS Visitor Center
100 Tipitina's French Quarter
101 ATM
105 World Trade Center
106 Aquarium of the Americas;
     Entergy IMAX Theater
107 Canal St Ferry
110 Post Office
111 Louisiana Children's
     Museum
113 Riverwalk Mall
114 Robert E Lee Monument
115 Ogden Museum of
     Southern Art; Confederate
     Museum
116 Contemporary Arts
     Center; NewOrleans.net
     Cafe
117 National D-Day Museum
119 Praline Connection Gospel
     & Blues Hall
124 Mermaid Lounge
129 ATM

OTHER
1   Tremé Music Hall
8   St Augustine's Church
11 Snug Harbor
12 Bicycle Michael's
16 Louis Armstrong Statue
18 Voodoo Spiritual Temple
26 Post Office
28 Gallier House Museum
29 Beauregard-Keyes House
30 Ursuline Convent

Information

Overlooking Jackson Square in the heart of the French Quarter, the Welcome Center (☎ 504-566-5003, 529 St Ann St) is in the old Lower Pontalba Building. It's open daily and has the excellent *New Orleans Street Map* and *Visitors Guide,* as well as discount RTA passes. The National Park Service (NPS) maintains a visitor center (☎ 504-589-2636) at 419 Decatur St. There are smaller information kiosks in the French Quarter.

The New Orleans Metropolitan Convention & Visitors Bureau (☎ 504-566-5011, 800-672-6124, Ⓦ www.neworleanscvb.com) and Greater New Orleans Multicultural Tourism Network (☎ 504-523-5652, Ⓦ www .soulofneworleans.com) are open weekdays only. Both are on the grounds of the Louisiana Superdome complex (1520 Sugar Bowl Dr). The latter publishes a free guide, *The Soul of New Orleans,* geared toward African Americans. There is also a Lesbian & Gay Community Center (☎ 504-945-1103), with a bulletin board, library and cultural services.

All mail sent to General Delivery, New Orleans, LA 70112, goes to the main post office (701 Loyola Ave). Another branch is just south of Lafayette Square; still another is at Bourbon and St Phillip Sts. The public library (219 Loyola Ave) offers free Internet access, as does the NewOrleans.net Cafe (900 Camp St), in the Contemporary Arts Center. The Bastille Computer Café (☎ 502-581-1150, 605 Toulouse St) charges for the service.

The *Times-Picayune* has a daily entertainment listing, with a detailed guide on Friday. The *Louisiana Weekly* offers an African American perspective. For alternative news and entertainment, pick up the free weekly *Gambit.* The free monthly *Offbeat* has a comprehensive club calendar and performance reviews.

Dangers & Annoyances

New Orleans has a high violent-crime rate; it's not a city to be careless in. Stick to places that are well traveled and well peopled, particularly at night, and budget for a taxi fare to avoid dark walks, even on the edge of the Quarter. There may be an abrupt transition from a relatively safe neighborhood to a dangerous one. Make it a habit to ask the locals which areas are OK. St Louis Cemetery No 1 and Louis Armstrong Park have particularly bad reputations and are more safely visited in groups.

In the Quarter, street hustlers frequently approach tourists, but you can just walk away – no hard feelings. Also be aware that cashiers, especially in bars, may 'round up' your bill and pocket the difference, so count your change.

French Quarter

In 1721 the city was laid out by Audrien de Pauger around the Place d'Armes, which was renamed **Jackson Square** following the War of 1812. In the heart of Vieux Carré, it's the best starting point for visitors. The traditional symmetry of French and Spanish colonial architecture contrasts with modern cultural chaos; the square is filled with an assortment of street musicians, artists and tarot-card readers. 'Hippie Hill,' the levee overlooking the river end of the square, is a congregating point for youths, panhandlers and scam artists. The grand 1794 **St Louis Cathedral**, designed by Gilberto Guillemard, towers over the opposite end.

Next to the cathedral, the first *cabildo* (Spanish council chamber) burned down in 1788, was rebuilt and dedicated in 1799, and used as city hall (1803–53) and the Louisiana Supreme Court (1853-1910). Since 1911 the newer **Cabildo** (☎ 504-568-6968, 701 Chartres St) has been home to a branch of the Louisiana State Museum, with pre-Columbian artifacts, exhibits on the Battle of New Orleans, and shocking depictions of slavery (closed Mon). On the north side of the cathedral, the 1813 **Presbytère** (☎ 504-568-6968, 751 Chartres St) was designed by Guillemard as a rectory, but the church rented the building for use as a city courthouse. It's now essentially a Mardi Gras museum, with vibrant displays of masks and costumes, parade floats, historic photos and documentary videos – a must for fans of Louisiana culture. The Louisiana State Museum has four separate units ($5 each, 20% less with a combination ticket).

The whole French Quarter is a National Historic District. The National Park Service oversees architectural preservation, and rangers offer free walking tours. Stroll through the residential lower Quarter, with lacy ironwork balconies, brightly colored rows of shops, and fragrances wafting from flowerpots and lush pocket gardens. Then hit the upper Quarter, with bright lights and noisy bars along Bourbon St and the tony antique shops and galleries on Royal St. Both streets have fine old Creole restaurants. To the southeast, the riverfront Woldenberg Park has a grass-lined promenade where concerts and other events are staged.

US coinage was struck at the **Old US Mint** (☎ 504-568-6968, 400 Esplanade Ave) in two periods between 1838 and 1910. Now a unit of the Louisiana State Museum, it has great exhibits on New Orleans jazz from its African roots in Congo Square, an intelligent assemblage of memorabilia and photographs, as well as dented horns played by Crescent City artists. There's also a display of contemporary folk art by Houma Indians ($5; closed Mon).

The **Historic New Orleans Collection** (☎ 504-523-4662, 533 Royal St) is a complex of historic buildings anchored by Merieult House. A survivor of the 1794 fire, the house displays the original transfer documents of the Louisiana Purchase, as well as early maps and artifacts. It's an excellent short introduction to New Orleans' past, and the house itself is an interesting mélange ($4; tours Tue-Sat). The collection also includes the Williams Gallery, with rotating exhibits on local history.

In 1823 the nation's first licensed pharmacist, Louis J Dufilho, dispensed gold-coated pills, opium, alcohol and cannabis from a shop at 514 Chartres St. Now it's the **Pharmacy Museum** (☎ 504-565-8027), with intriguing exhibits but nothing for sale ($3; closed Mon). The African American alternative was voodoo, described in the **Historic Voodoo Museum** (☎ 504-523-7685, 724 Dumaine St), behind a storefront, where two rooms are packed with voodoo charms, potions, powders and mojos ($7).

In 1728, 12 Ursuline nuns arrived in New Orleans to care for the French garrison's 'miserable little hospital' and to educate the young girls of the colony. Between 1745 and 1752, the French colonial army built a convent and girls' school that is now the oldest structure in the French Quarter. The **Ursuline Convent** (☎ 504-529-3040, 1114 Chartres St) is open for guided tours ($5; closed Mon).

Historic Houses A wide array of houses is open for tours, mostly Monday to Saturday, for $5 or $6.

Madame Micaëla Pontalba commissioned the long rows of red-brick apartments flanking the upper and lower portions of Jackson Square, with the initial plans by noted architect James Gallier Sr. The **1850 House** (☎ 504-568-6968, 523 St Ann St) is one of the apartments in the Lower Pontalba Buildings; tours take in the attractive central court and the servants' quarters with period furnishings ($3; closed Mon).

An 1826 Greek Revival structure, the **Beauregard-Keyes House** (☎ 504-523-7257, 1113 Chartres St) was home to Southern hero PGT Beauregard, who was quite a heartthrob in the 1850s. Tours run on the hour.

James Gallier Sr and James Gallier Jr were both architects who popularized Greek Revival in New Orleans; the 1857 **Gallier House Museum** (☎ 504-525-5661, 1118 Royal St) was one of Junior's jobs. In 1831 the **Hermann-Grima House** (☎ 504-525-5661, 820 St Louis St) was how Samuel Hermann introduced the American-style Federal design to the French Quarter.

Not your usual historic restoration, **Faulkner House** (☎ 504-524-2940, 624 Pirates Alley) is now a bookstore, Faulkner House Books (open to 6pm daily). One of America's greatest novelists, William Faulkner (1897–1962), stayed here during a sojourn in bohemian New Orleans in 1935.

French Market A trading site since pre-Columbian times, this area now has three different markets; the most recent part is a bevy of air-conditioned stores. The open-air **Farmers Market**, on Ursulines Ave, was built in 1937 by the Works Projects Administration (WPA), and has a good stock of fresh fruit, vegetables, kitchen supplies, hot sauces, garlic strings and cookbooks. It's open 24 hours, as is the enjoyable Café du Monde, the market's oldest tenant (see Places to Eat, later).

A great place for souvenirs, the **Flea Market** sells inexpensive Mardi Gras masks and dolls, preserved alligator heads and CDs of dubious origin.

Tremé

On the western edge of the French Quarter, the Tremé district was New Orleans' first suburb, traditionally populated by black

Creoles. The celebrated architect JNB DePouilly designed the 1824 **St Augustine's Church** (1210 Governor Nicholls St). One of its stained-glass panels depicts the Sisters of the Holy Family, the order of black Creole nuns founded in 1842.

One of New Orleans' more macabre attractions, **St Louis Cemetery No 1** received the remains of most early Creoles. The shallow water table necessitated above-ground burials, with bodies placed in family tombs or long rows of 'oven' vaults. A few steps from the entrance gate and to the left is the purported resting site of voodoo queen Marie Laveau, a well-visited tomb covered with chalked Xs. Don't enter the cemetery alone; if the ghosts don't get you, the muggers might.

CBD & Warehouse District

On the upriver side of Canal St, the CBD (Central Business District) and Warehouse District comprise the American commercial section that was established after the Louisiana Purchase in 1803. Artists moved into the Warehouse District following the 1984 Louisiana World Exposition, galleries appeared on Julia St, and bistros blossomed along the surrounding streets.

Most sights in the CBD and Warehouse District are a considerable walk from the French Quarter; take the streetcar lines or No 11 Magazine bus. The **Canal St Ferry** from the foot of Canal St is the best way to admire the city from the traditional river approach (free admission; ferries 6am-midnight).

Nearby, the **Aquarium of the Americas** (☎ 504-378-2695) simulates a selection of watery habitats – the Amazon Basin, Caribbean coral reefs, Mississippi River and Delta wetlands ($13.50/6.50 adults/kids; open daily). Combination tickets include admission to the Entergy IMAX theater next door and excellent Audubon Zoo in Uptown (boats from the aquarium will take you there).

The 33-story **World Trade Center** (2 Canal St) has a revolving observation deck where the Top of the Mart Lounge (☎ 504-522-9795) offers spectacular views for the price of a drink (about $6). Relax and enjoy the view.

In a renovated warehouse, the **Contemporary Arts Center** (☎ 504-528-3805, 900 Camp St) has galleries ($5) and two performance spaces for plays, dance and concerts.

Extending nearly half a mile along the Mississippi, the shop-till-you-drop **Riverwalk Mall** includes an uncrowded walkway to watch the paddle wheelers and freighters plying the Mississippi. When Bienville founded New Orleans in 1718, this site was underwater, but shifts in the river's course enabled land reclamation east of the old warehouses that were once on the waterfront.

The **Confederate Museum** (☎ 504-523-4522, 929 Camp St), humanizes the Civil War without overdoing the Southern angle, with strangely moving personal effects, guns, and artifacts of the industrial age. It's Louisiana's oldest museum, opened in 1891 ($5; closed Sun).

In spring 2002, a new, expanded **Ogden Museum of Southern Art** (☎ 504-539-9600, 900 Camp St) will open five floors of paintings – including Dominico Canova's allegorical masterpiece *Mother Louisiana* – as well as sculpture, photography, ceramics and multimedia exhibits. The main entrance will be via the neo-Romanesque Taylor Library (615 Andrew Higgins Ave), with a short introductory film. Until the move, the collection can be viewed at its old location at 603 Julia St ($3).

Half a world away from Normandy, the **National D-Day Museum** (☎ 504-527-6012, 923 Magazine St) is a worthwhile stop for its eyewitness accounts of the Allied invasion, planes, weaponry and landing craft ($7; open daily).

Garden District & Uptown

Following the Louisiana Purchase in 1803, new American arrivals settled the area upriver from the Warehouse District, while Creoles remained in the French Quarter. Subdivision of former plantation lands began in the Lower Garden District, and extended Uptown following the steam railway on St Charles Ave, where the St Charles Ave streetcar now runs. Many elegant mansions line the route, surrounded by live oaks and palms, lawns and lush, fragrant floral gardens. In the 1850s and 1860s, the Greek Revival style was a symbol of staunch classical tastes.

Farther west, Tulane and Loyola Universities occupy adjacent campuses in a more diverse area. Modest shotgun shacks sit next

Carnival & Mardi Gras, New Orleans–Style

Mardi Gras, or 'Fat Tuesday,' began as a pagan rite of spring and evolved into bacchanalia. Under the Roman Catholic influence, it became a pre-Lenten celebration, on the day before Ash Wednesday. In Europe it was an opportunity to mock the aristocracy with ridiculously regal antics, and Creoles in New Orleans and the Caribbean maintained that tradition. Americans used the occasion to satirize Creole pretensions, and began to institutionalize Carnival in the late 19th century by establishing 'krewes' (men-only social clubs). In the 1950s, drag queens and gay masquerade balls became a popular mode of parody, and they are still a vital component of Mardi Gras.

Carnival While most krewe balls held during Carnival season are exclusive events open only to members and guests, public celebrations, parades and partying start around two weeks before Mardi Gras, with nonstop frivolity from the Thursday before. Most parades are held Uptown, along St Charles Ave to Canal St. The only krewe to parade through the French Quarter is the Krewe du Vieux, whose procession is three weeks before Mardi Gras. From the last weekend before Mardi Gras, the Quarter is jammed with people; it's difficult to walk around and can be frightening for youngsters.

Krewe parades usually feature a dozen or more tractor-drawn floats and marching bands. Crowds scramble for the souvenir 'throws' of beads, doubloons, condoms or candy. Dramatic nighttime parades feature flambeaux carriers wielding flaming torches. Following the Orpheus parade on Lundi Gras (Fat Monday), head for Woldenberg Park with your mask to the city-sponsored bash and fireworks display.

TOM DOWNS

Mardi Gras Before sunrise on the big day, the entire parade corridor along St Charles Ave is staked out with chairs, ladders and coolers. The Zulu Krewe parade moves out at dawn to its starting point at the statue of Martin Luther King Jr. At 8:30am, more than 30 floats and 30 marching bands begin rolling down Jackson Ave toward St Charles Ave before continuing past Lee Circle to Canal St and through the Tremé district along N Galvez St and Orleans Ave.

Rex Krewe begins its elaborate procession at about 10am farther up S Claiborne Ave at Napoleon Ave, then continues along St Charles Ave from Jackson Ave to Canal St. Trucks and throws follow the parade, and by midafternoon it's beer and beads on Bourbon St. By the evening, a besotted mass of humanity is tightly wedged on the street. Celebrations in the lower Quarter vary from block to block. Check out the ribald costume contest in front of the Rawhide 2010 bar on Burgundy St and the festivities across from the Quarter on Esplanade Ave at Dauphine St or at Chartres and Frenchmen Sts.

to multistory Arts and Crafts bungalows; Greek Revival mansions next to neo-Gothic campus buildings. Tulane was founded in 1834 as a medical college in an attempt to control repeated cholera and yellow-fever epidemics. Its **Amistad Research Center** (☎ 504-865-5535) is one of the nation's largest repositories of African

American history (open Mon-Fri). The **Hogan Jazz Archive** (☎ 504-865-5688) is a must for jazz scholars.

Established in 1833, **Lafayette Cemetery No 1** has German and Irish names on its aboveground tombs. Fraternal organizations (like Jefferson Fire Company No 22) buried members and their families in large shared crypts. The gates are closed at 2:30pm – don't get locked in. Volunteers from Save Our Cemeteries (☎ 504-525-3377) run tours ($6).

Among the country's best zoos, the **Audubon Zoological Gardens** (☎ 504-581-4629) are also the headquarters of the Audubon Institute. Its Louisiana Swamp exhibit displays flora and fauna in a Cajun cultural setting, with alligators, bobcats, red foxes, black bears and snapping turtles. The Reptile Encounter, Butterflies in Flight and Audubon Flight exhibits are well worth seeing. The nicest way to get there is a zoo cruise from Woldenberg Park, downtown. Get a combined ticket for the aquarium, riverboat and zoo ($26/13 adults/kids), or just check out the zoo ($9/4.75; open daily).

City Park & Fair Grounds

Besides hosting the regular horse-racing season, the Fair Grounds are also the site of the huge springtime New Orleans Jazz & Heritage Festival. Acquired in 1850, the 1500-acre City Park is famous for its huge moss-draped live oaks and scenic bayou lagoons, especially along the narrow strip fronting City Park Ave. Unfortunately, I-610 slices through the park, so most visitors stick to the southern third of the area, where the **Botanical Garden** features an art deco pool and fountain ($3; closed Mon). You'll also find a vintage carousel, other rides and canoes for rent. In the 19th century, Creoles settled affairs of honor at the **Dueling Oaks**, one of which is still standing.

Also in City Park, the **New Orleans Museum of Art** (☎ 504-488-2631) was founded in 1910. It hosts traveling exhibits and has a permanent collection featuring pre-Columbian and African art ($6).

On the banks of Bayou St John, the 1799 **Pitot House** (☎ 504-482-0312) is done in French-colonial plantation style. James Pitot (pee-**toh**), the first mayor of the incorporated city of New Orleans, acquired it in 1810, and it was used later as an orphanage ($3).

Lakeshore Park

This park stretches nearly 10 miles along a narrow shoreline strip fronting Lake Pontchartrain. It's where locals come to jog, bike, skate or check each other out – but not to swim in the polluted water.

Organized Tours

There are many tours available; check the *New Orleans Official Visitors Guide* for a full selection. The NPS visitor center (see Information earlier) offers free walking tours of the French Quarter daily at 9:30am (show up at 9am).

Friends of the Cabildo (☎ 504-523-3939) offers volunteer-led walking tours of the French Quarter daily. Two-hour tours emphasize history, folklore and architecture. The cost ($10) includes admission to any two of the four Louisiana State Museums (see French Quarter earlier).

Of the many voodoo tours available, the one run by Historic New Orleans Walking Tours (☎ 504-947-2120) offers the most authenticity and humor. The two-hour guided walk includes St Louis Cemetery No 1 and the Voodoo Spiritual Temple ($15). The company also excellent tours of the French Quarter and Garden District.

The tourist cliché, a carriage ride through the French Quarter, is actually a great way to see the narrow streets at a gentle pace. The drivers are entertaining, if not always historically precise. Carriages depart all day and evenings until midnight. Half-hour tours for up to four people cost around $40, plus tip.

Take a paddle-wheel riverboat cruise on the Mississippi aboard the *Creole Queen* to visit the 1815 Battle of New Orleans site at Chalmette. A brief walking tour of the battlegrounds and Beauregard-Keyes House is included. Cruises depart at 10:30am and 2pm daily from Spanish Plaza at the foot of Canal St ($16; 2½ hours). The less regal *Cajun Queen* does one-hour cruises from Canal St wharf at 11:30am, 1pm, 2:30pm and 4pm ($12). Reserve on both boats at ☎ 800-445-4109. The *Natchez* does two-hour cruises from a dock behind the Jackson Brewery at 11:30am and 2:30pm daily ($14.75).

Special Events

Just after New Year's Eve (which is no slouch celebration here), New Orleans residents break out the king cakes and spirits to begin celebrating Carnival, which culminates in the Mardi Gras madness. *Arthur Hardy's Mardi Gras Guide* contains a good history along with detailed descriptions and maps of all parades. Visitors should make an effort to get into a costume – a goofy hat or a simple mask at the very least. It really adds to the fun.

Other excuses to celebrate include St Patrick's Day, Jazz Fest in late April and early May, and Halloween.

Places to Stay

Most visitors want to stay within easy reach of the French Quarter; it's more expensive, but the ambience and convenience are usually worth it. Better deals are available in the lower Quarter or Faubourg Marigny, where you'll find charming small Creole-style hotels and guesthouses, some with secluded courtyards and fountains. Budget travelers go for backpacker hostels and guesthouses in the Lower Garden District or the Bywater.

Room rates peak during Mardi Gras and Jazz Fest, but in the hot, sticky summer months, prices fall by as much as 50%. The prices below are mid- to low-season rates. Book as soon as you know you'll be going; even four months ahead may be too late for some places. Sales and lodging tax amounts to 11%, plus $1 per room per night.

Budget Four state parks within a half hour's drive of New Orleans offer shady, well-maintained sites with toilets, hot showers and hookups. Most convenient is *St Bernard Parish State Park* (☎ 504-682-2101), about 13 miles south near the Mississippi, with lagoons, nature trails and a swimming pool ($12). Take Hwy 46 along the east bank to Bayou Rd and turn right on Hwy 39.

The closest privately operated RV parks and campgrounds are along the Chef Menteur Hwy/Hwy 90) in eastern New Orleans. *Jude Travel & Trailer Park* (☎ 504-241-0632, 7400 Chef Menteur Hwy) offers a pool, laundry and both tent and RV sites for $22. Out near the international airport, *New Orleans West KOA* (☎ 504-467-1792, 11129 Jefferson Hwy) offers tent/RV sites for $22/29 per night.

A mile or so northwest of the French Quarter, *India House Hostel* (☎ 504-821-1904, W www.indiahousehostel.com, 124 S Lopez St), off Canal St, is two adjoining houses with a swimming pool. Dorm beds cost $14, and Cajun shacks out back (with pet alligators) are $35.

La Salle Hotel (☎ 504-525-4188, 1113 Canal St), on the edge of the Quarter, has decent singles/doubles with TV and phone – $33/39 with shared bath, $65/69 with private bath.

In the Garden District, the 176-bed *HI Marquette House Hostel* (☎ 504-523-3014, e hineworleans@aol.com, 2253 Carondelet St) has dorm beds at $15/18 members/non-members, and doubles from $43.

Longpré Guest House Hostel (☎ 504-581-4540, 1726 Prytania St), an 1850s Italianate-style home, has 24 bunk beds at $12 and a great front porch. *Prytania Inn* (☎ 504-566-1515, 1415 Prytania St) has well-worn singles/doubles from $29/39 with private baths. *Henry Howard Inn* (☎ 504-568-0858, 2041 Prytania St) offers similar rates and quality; the same people own the more upscale *Maginnis Mansion* (2127 Prytania St), from $49/69.

In Uptown, *Loyola University* (☎ 504-865-3622) rents out the dormitory rooms on its Uptown campus for $37/52 mid-May to mid-August.

Out in the Bywater district, bargain hunters should try homey *Mazant Guest House* (☎ 504-944-2662, 906 Mazant St), a two-story former plantation house. Rooms with shared baths and kitchen facilities cost $30-40.

Mid-Range Of many wonderful places in the Quarter, *Chateau Motor Hotel* (☎ 504-524-9636, 1001 Chartres St) enjoys a quiet location. Singles/doubles including continental breakfast and parking cost from $79/99. Elegant *Le Richelieu* (☎ 504-529-2492, 1234 Chartres St) has a bar, pool and parking (from $85/95). *Cornstalk Hotel* (☎ 504-523-1515, 915 Royal St) is an old house with high ceilings and antique furnishings. Rooms run to $185, but drop as low as $75 off-season.

Hotel St Pierre (☎ 504-524-4401, 911 Burgundy St) is a group of historic Creole cottages with modern furnishings and a pool ($119-139). *Andrew Jackson Hotel* (☎ 504-561-5881, 800-654-0224, 919 Royal St) has similar rates and a more central location.

Lafitte Guest House (☎ 504-581-2678, *1003 Bourbon St)*, an elegant, three-story French manor house, offers 14 rooms from $119. The finely restored *Hotel Provincial* (☎ 504-581-4995, 800-535-7922, 1024 Chartres St)* costs $79-225, depending on season.

Esplanade Ave has several good options close to the Quarter. *Maison Esplanade* (☎ 504-523-8080, 1244 Esplanade Ave)* has 9 modest, antique-furnished rooms with private baths starting at $79. *Rathbone Inn* (☎ 504-947-2101, 1227 Esplanade Ave)* is an 1850s mansion offering 11 rooms with private baths and kitchenettes from $109. Farther north, *Hotel Storyville* (☎ 504-548-4800, 1261 Esplanade Ave)* is a modern place with spotless two- to four-person suites for $80-300.

In Faubourg Marigny, an easy walk to Bourbon St, *Royal St Inn* (☎ 504-948-7499)* operates a 'bed and beverage' out of the R Bar at the corner of Royal and Kerlerec Sts. Comfortable small rooms are $90, and four-person rooms cost $130. *The Frenchmen* (☎ 504-948-2166, 417 Frenchmen St)* is a refurbished 1850s Creole townhouse with a courtyard and pool (from $89). Six blocks from the Quarter, *Lion's Inn B&B* (☎ 504-945-2339, 2517 Chartres St)* 'welcomes all sexual persuasions' and has four nice rooms for $45-100.

The CBD contains the bulk of chain and convention hotels. The high-rise *Comfort Inn Downtown* (☎ 504-586-0100, 1315 Gravier St)* has basic rooms from $59 on weekdays, $90 on weekends. A step up, *Hampton Inn* (☎ 504-529-9990, 226 Carondelet St)* has modern rooms with continental breakfast for $79-129.

In the Garden District, *St Vincent's Guest House* (☎ 504-566-1515, 1507 Magazine St)* is a former orphanage with charmless but remodeled rooms for $59-89, including breakfast. The somewhat chaotic but endearing *Avenue Garden Hotel* (☎ 504-521-8000, 1509 St Charles Ave)* has nice refurbished rooms for $79-159, including continental breakfast in the inner courtyard. *Quality Inn Maison St Charles* (☎ 504-522-0187, 1319 St Charles Ave)* offers modern rooms for $69-119 and shuttle service to the French Quarter.

Top End In the Quarter, *Hotel Monteleone* (☎ 504-523-3341, 800-535-9595, 214 Royal St)* offers glamorous singles/doubles from $155/175 ($95 in summer).

In the CBD, *Omni Royal Orleans* (☎ 504-529-5333, 800-843-6664, 621 St Louis St)*, in the CBD, is the best-furnished hotel in town ($99-259). Elegant *Le Pavillon* (☎ 504-581-3111, 800-535-9095, 833 Poydras Ave)*, built in 1907, offers a lovely marble lobby and plush updated rooms for $105-230. *Fairmont Hotel* (☎ 504-529-7111, 800-527-4727, 123 Baronne St)*, among the city's best since the 1920s, charges from $229 in peak season.

Places to Eat

Eating is a major activity in New Orleans, with the indigenous Creole and Cajun cooking, plus flavors from Italy, Mexico and the Caribbean and a mouthwatering selection of snack foods. With its strong French influences and a taste for liquid refreshment, this is a city that enjoys its food.

French Quarter The classic choice for inexpensive eats is *Café du Monde*, at the French Market, for café au lait and beignets (sweet pastries dusted with powdered sugar; $2). A New Orleans institution, it's open 24 hours. *Royal Blend* (621 Royal St)* makes another easy coffeehouse stop, with a pleasant garden courtyard. Tucked in the lower Quarter, *Croissant d'Or Patisserie* (617 Ursulines Ave)*, offers filled croissants, fluffy quiches and cakes in a small courtyard.

Louisiana's signature sandwich, the muffuletta, was created by a Sicilian immigrant in 1906. It's a round, seeded loaf of bread filled with ham, salami and provolone and drizzled with oily olive relish. The mother church of muffulettas is *Central Grocery* (923 Decatur St);* don't wait till Sunday. *Johnny's Po-Boys* (511 St Louis St)* is good for sandwiches and budget hot plates for breakfast and lunch.

For cheap and tasty Cuban and Mexican dishes, try *Country Flame* (620 Iberville St)*, where a vegetarian fajita costs just $5. A good late-night menu is at *Quarter Scene* (900 Dumaine St)*, where a spicy grilled vegetable plate with rice and salad costs $7, $9 with chicken or shrimp. Ex-meat-eaters dig into stuffed polenta and grilled tofu at *Old Dog New Trick Café* (307 Exchange Alley).

For fine dining at mid-range prices, *NOLA* (☎ 504-522-6652, 534 St Louis St) features trendy veggies, meat and seafood for $13-25. Spicy Creole sauces on pasta and seafood are specialties at *Secret Garden (538 St Philip St);* it's a good fallback option, at around $15.

At the top end, Paul Prudhomme, a big name among New Orleans chefs, runs *K-Paul's Louisiana Kitchen (☎ 504-596-2530, 416 Chartres St),* with convivial communal seating. Outrageously rich Cajun and Creole dishes cost $26-39. The venerable *Café Sbisa (☎ 504-522-5565, 1011 Decatur St),* with an exposed-brick dining room, has a reputation for innovative Creole cuisine.

A meal at elegant, clubby *Galatoire's (209 Bourbon St)* costs around $30 per person (no reservations). Start with oysters Rockefeller ($16). Men will need a jacket at *Arnaud's (☎ 504-523-5433, 813 Bienville St),* an institution serving classic Creole cuisine, with à la carte main dishes for $19-38. A long-standing tradition is breakfast at swanky *Brennan's Restaurant (417 Royal St),* where great Creole meals cost around $35.

Peristyle (☎ 504-593-9535, 1041 Dumaine St) is one of the more romantic spots for dinner. The menu blends American and French Provençal palates (entrées $22-25; closed Mon).

Faubourg Marigny Classic dives on Esplanade Ave include *Port of Call (838 Esplanade Ave),* which serves some of New Orleans' best burgers ($7). *Praline Connection (542 Frenchmen St)* does good but pricey Creole and soul food. Walk up Frenchmen St for more eating options. *La Péniche (1940 Dauphine St)* is a popular late-night dinner spot (open 24 hours, *except* from 2pm Tue to 9am Thurs).

CBD & Warehouse District At *Vic's Kangaroo Cafe (636 Tchoupitoulas St),* a transplanted Aussie pub, $6 pies are washed down with Fosters until 2am. *Mother's (401 Poydras Ave)* serves up a classic 'pile of debris' (shredded beef with pan drippings; $7) and red beans with rice and andouille sausage. *Red Eye Grill (852 S Peters St)* is perfect for a late-night burger or fish stew.

Garden District & Uptown Restaurants conveniently near local guesthouses open for breakfast, lunch and late-night snacks. *St Vincent's Guest House* (see Places to Stay) does a $5 home-style breakfast with coffee, juice and Southern hospitality, and a $6 set tea noon-4pm. Across the street, *Rue de la Course* is a comfortable coffee-shop hangout. The 24-hour *Trolley Stop (1923 St Charles Ave),* in a former gas station, draws a mixed crowd for basic diner fare.

Open weekdays only, *Uglesich's (1238 Baronne St)* is a funky lunchtime institution serving top-notch oysters (six for $6) and seafood specials such as crawfish bisque ($7). *Please-U-Restaurant (1751 St Charles Ave)* is a frayed counter-and-booths place with cheap, satisfying meals (under $6).

The boiled crawfish is legendary at *Franky & Johnny's (321 Arabella St),* at Tchoupitoulas St. For an appetizer, try alligator pie. *Juan's Flying Burrito (2018 Magazine St)* does enormous burritos ($5) and quesadillas ($8) for an alternative crowd, lunch and dinner.

Commander's Palace (☎ 504-899-8221, 1403 Washington Ave) offers outstanding old-style Creole cuisine with fresh, local ingredients (lunches from $15; four-course dinners from $44). You'll need a reservation and a tie.

Riverbend There's a cluster of restaurants, bars and shops where the St Charles streetcar turns onto Carrollton Ave. The immensely popular counter in *Camellia Grill (626 S Carrollton Ave)* serves up rich milkshakes, pecan waffles and standard short-order items until late at night.

Entertainment

Generations of New Orleans club owners have thrived by promoting a combination of music and booze. Look out for shows by top performers like the Iguanas, Dr John and Terence Blanchard, and the musical dynasties of Marsalises and Neville Brothers. Also watch for brass bands like Kermit Ruffins or the Dirty Dozen Brass Band.

The free monthly *Offbeat* and weekly *Gambit* are your best sources for reviews and performances. Tune into WWOZ (90.7 FM) for Louisiana music, or call the station's events hotline (☎ 504-840-4040). TicketMaster (☎ 504-522-5555) has several outlets.

Live Music In the French Quarter, live jazz, blues, Dixieland, zydeco and Cajun music emanate from clubs along upper Bourbon St between Bienville and St Ann Sts. Below St Ann St, disco throbs in clubs with gay and lesbian crowds. Clubs on the Quarter's riverfront margin are more for mainstream crowds seeking headline acts, while smaller venues toward the Quarter's periphery offer live brass bands, Irish folk music and disco. 'Kitty' clubs provide musicians with an opportunity to jam and pass the hat, especially in the Tremé district.

The institutionalized *Preservation Hall* (☎ 504-522-2841, 726 St Peter St) attracts mostly veteran jazz musicians, but it's a class act ($5). At *Maison Bourbon* (☎ 504-522-8818, 641 Bourbon St) or *Palm Court Jazz Café* (☎ 504-525-0200, 1204 Decatur St) you can enjoy a great Dixieland set for the price of drink. *Funky Pirate* (☎ 504-523-1960, 727 Bourbon St) regularly features Big Al Carson & the Blues Masters.

Some hot music spots are clustered on N Rampart St. Check out *Donna's Bar & Grill* (☎ 504-596-6914, 800 N Rampart St) and *Funky Butt on Congo Square* (☎ 504-558-0872, 714 N Rampart St).

Quint Davis' *Storyville* (☎ 504-410-1000, 125 Bourbon St) is a breath of fresh air in the Quarter, featuring outstanding local music day and night on two stages with New Orleans bar food. Dan Aykroyd's *House of Blues* (☎ 504-529-2583, 255 Decatur St) fills

Jazz pioneer Louis 'Satchmo' Armstrong

its calendar with fine musical talent – the Sunday Gospel Brunch will fortify your soul. Jimmy Buffett's *Margaritaville Cafe* (☎ 504-592-2565, 1104 Decatur St) has first-rate blues, jazz and zydeco. *Tipitina's French Quarter* (☎ 504-895-8477, 233 N Peters St) doesn't match the original Uptown 'Tips' but still has great music. *Shim Sham Club* (☎ 504-565-5400, 615 Toulouse St) features punk and acid jazz in dark, theaterlike decor.

The Faubourg Marigny has the city's premier contemporary jazz venue, *Snug Harbor* (☎ 504-949-0696, 626 Frenchmen St), and hopping *Vaughan's* (☎ 504-947-5562, 800 Lesseps St), featuring Kermit Ruffins' traditional Barbecue Swingers. *Cafe Brasil* (☎ 504-949-0851, 2100 Chartres St) appeals to an alternative-lifestyle crowd that dances to bands from brass to reggae. Loud rock and R&B groups perform at *Igor's Checkpoint Charlie* (☎ 504-947-0979, 501 Esplanade Ave), where you can do your laundry and play pool with no cover.

In down-at-heel Tremé, *Joe's Cozy Corner* (1030 N Robertson St) is a local kitty club, popular for brass, soul and R&B. Well-known groups play at *Tremé Music Hall*, across the street. Run by a local trumpet legend, the clapboard *Kermit Ruffins Jazz & Blues Hall* (☎ 504-299-0790, 1533 St Phillip St) has rich offerings throughout the week.

The Warehouse District has a first-rate club: *Howlin' Wolf* (☎ 504-523-2551, 828 S Peters St), which hosts blues groups, rock bands and other local acts. *Michaul's* (☎ 504-522-5517, 840 St Charles Ave) offers Cajun music and dance lessons as well as pricey Cajun cooking. *Praline Connection Gospel & Blues Hall* (☎ 504-523-3973, 907 S Peters St) offers a fine gospel brunch Sunday ($24). Grunge, alternative and occasional jazz bands raise the roof at *Mermaid Lounge* (☎ 504-524-5740, 1100 Constance St).

Perhaps the best music club in New Orleans is *Tipitina's* (☎ 504-895-8477, 501 Napoleon Ave), marked by a bust of Henry Roland Byrd (1918–80), also known as 'Professor Longhair.' Cover is $15-20.

Bars Most bars serve a 'hurricane,' with dark rum, white rum, orange juice, pineapple juice and grenadine in a hurricane-lantern shaped glass. Get the classic version

($6) at *Pat O'Brien's* (☎ *504-525-4823, 718 St Peter St)*, which has a labyrinthine series of alcoves linking Bourbon St and St Peter St in a continuous party. *Molly's at the Market (1107 Decatur St)* is the Irish cultural center of the French Quarter, serving Guinness and pub grub to a diverse mix of local characters. *Lafitte's Blacksmith Shop (941 Bourbon St)* is a well-worn corner bar with sing-along piano in the rear. Another old bar is *Napoleon House (500 Chartres St)*.

Absinthe, 'the spirit of New Orleans,' was outlawed in 1914 because of its potential for brain damage. Pernod, a safe liqueur flavored with anise, is now the poison of choice at the original *Old Absinthe House (240 Bourbon St)* and *Old Absinthe Bar (400 Bourbon St)*.

Most oyster bars now feature food rather than drink, but *Acme Oyster & Seafood House (724 Iberville St)* still has a busy bar where you drink beer and watch a crew shuck oysters.

The place to chill with a brew and pulled pork is *Ugly Dog Saloon & BBQ (401 Andrew Higgins Ave)*.

The budget bars in the Garden District and Uptown attract a local crowd plus visitors from nearby hostels. A dive that never closes, *Igor's Lounge* (☎ *504-522-2145, 2133 St Charles Ave)* has a greasy grill, pool tables and washing machines. *Half Moon (1125 St Mary St)* is a draw for bar-hopping trendsetters.

Gay & Lesbian Venues The best dance clubs are the large gay venues on lower Bourbon St. *Oz* (☎ *504-593-9491, 800 Bourbon St)* and *Bourbon Pub* (☎ *504-529-2107, 801 Bourbon St)* are both fine for straights who want to dance nonstop and don't mind guys in G-strings. Flashy new *735* (☎ *504-581-6740, 735 Bourbon St)* spins industrial/house for glow-stick groupies. *Rawhide 2010* (☎ *504-525-8106, 740 Burgundy St)* is – surprise! – a leather bar. A young, mixed crowd packs the dance floor at *Gold Mine Saloon* (☎ *504-586-0745, 705 Dauphine St)*. Ask around here about high-energy nightspots and unadvertised rave parties.

The Faubourg Marigny has some cool gay venues, including *Apple Barrel (609 Frenchmen St)*, a cozy bar that hums after the pride parades.

New Orleans for Children

Apart from the **Audubon Zoo** and **Aquarium of the Americas**, most children's activities are set apart from the city's major attractions for grown-ups. Check out the 'kid stuff' listings in the *Times-Picayune*'s Living section on Monday.

The **Louisiana Children's Museum** (☎ 504-523-1357, 420 Julia St) has the usual hands-on exhibits ($5; open daily in summer, closed Mon other months). Children under 16 must be accompanied by an adult.

Accent on Children's Arrangements (☎ 504-524-1227, 938 Lafayette St) is a service that will take the kids off your hands for organized activities.

Theater & Cinemas Major touring troupes perform at *Saenger Theatre* (☎ *504-524-2490, 143 N Rampart St)*, an ornate and finely restored 1927 theater. Old *Le Petit Théâtre du Vieux Carré* (☎ *504-522-2081, 616 St Peter St)* and the *Southern Repertory Theatre* (☎ *504-861-8163, 333 Canal Place)*, on the 3rd floor of the Canal Place Shopping Center, both present classic Southern plays. New Orleans politics become drama fodder at *Le Chat Noir* (☎ *504-581-5812, 715 St Charles Ave)*.

The *Entergy IMAX Theatre* (☎ *504-581-4620)*, next to the Aquarium of the Americas at the foot of Canal St, charges $7.75/5 adults/kids.

Classical Music The *Louisiana Philharmonic Orchestra* (☎ *504-523-6530)* is one of the few musician-owned symphonies in the country. It presents concerts at the richly ornamented Orpheum Theater (129 University Place) September to May.

Spectator Sports

The 60,000-seat Louisiana Superdome (☎ 504-733-0255, 1500 Poydras Ave) is home to the New Orleans Saints NFL football team and the minor-league baseball team, the New Orleans Zephyrs (☎ 504-282-6777). Seats are available for most games ($22-50).

Horse racing is a New Orleans tradition at the Fair Grounds Race Track (☎ 504-944-5515, 1751 Gentilly Blvd).

The most exciting college games occur when local Tulane University plays long-standing rival Louisiana State University (LSU), from Baton Rouge.

Getting There & Away

New Orleans International Airport (☎ 504-464-0831), 11 miles west of the city, handles mostly domestic flights.

Greyhound (☎ 800-231-2222, 800-531-5332) runs from the Union Passenger Terminal (1001 Loyola Ave), west of the Warehouse District. Regular services go to Baton Rouge ($11.50; 1½ hours); Memphis and ($38; 9 hours) Nashville ($41; 15 hours), Tennessee; and Atlanta, Georgia ($71; from 9 hours). To get to the French Quarter from the Union Passenger Terminal, search for the sheltered stop east of the station across broad Loyola Ave at Howard Ave and take the RTA No 17 S Claiborne Ave bus to the corner of Canal and Rampart Sts. It's not far to walk, but be wary of going through the CBD at night. A cab to the corner of Bourbon and Canal Sts costs about $5.

Amtrak (☎ 504-528-1610) trains also operate from the Union Passenger Terminal. The *City of New Orleans* runs to Jackson, Mississippi; Memphis, Tennessee; and Chicago, Illinois. The *Crescent* serves Birmingham, Alabama; Atlanta, Georgia; Washington, DC; and New York. New Orleans is also on the *Sunset Limited* route between Los Angeles, California, and Miami, Florida.

The Delta Queen Steamboat Co (☎ 504-586-8777) does expensive package tours upriver to Natchez and beyond (see the Getting Around chapter). The cheapest way to cruise the Mississippi is aboard the state-run ferries between Canal St and the west bank community of Algiers (free).

Getting Around

To/From the Airport There's an information booth at the airport's A & B concourse. Airport shuttles (☎ 504-522-3500) go to downtown hotels ($10 per passenger). Jefferson Transit Airport Express (☎ 504-737-7433), route E2, goes into town with stops along Airline Hwy (Hwy 61) and Tulane Ave ($1.10).

Taxis downtown cost $24 for one or two people, $30 for three, $40 for four.

Car & Motorcycle In downtown New Orleans, narrow one-way streets and crowds in the French Quarter will hamper your progress. During daytime, street parking has a two-hour limit. Parking garages in the upper (southern) part of the Quarter charge about $4 for the first hour, from $12 for 24 hours.

Most national car rental companies are in the airport, but you pay a $50 airport charge, and rates may be better in town. Econo-Cars (☎ 504-827-0187) has cheap older cars for local travel, but you need proof of insurance ($69 for three days, $139 for a week).

Local Transportation The Regional Transit Authority (RTA; ☎ 504-248-3900) runs the local bus service. Fares are $1.50, plus 25¢ for transfers; express buses cost $1.50. Exact change is required. RTA Visitor Passes cost $5/12 for one/three days.

The RTA also operates two streetcar lines. The St Charles Ave Line (opened 1835) extends all the way from the French Quarter to Riverbend, passing through Uptown and the Garden District en route. The 6½-mile trip costs $1.50 each way, with frequent services during peak hours, hourly midnight-4am. The Riverfront Line has vintage red streetcars running 2 miles from the Old US Mint, past Canal St, to the upriver convention center and back ($1.50), 6am-midnight.

For a taxi, call White Fleet Cabs (☎ 504-948-6605) or United Cabs (☎ 504-522-9771).

Rent a bicycle from $15 a day at Bicycle Michael's (☎ 504-945-9505, 618 Frenchmen St), in Faubourg Marigny.

AROUND NEW ORLEANS

South of New Orleans, the Mississippi River flows 90 miles to the swampy environment of the 'bird's foot' delta. At **Chalmette Battlefield** on January 8, 1815, General Andrew Jackson's polyglot troops whipped the British attackers in the Battle of New Orleans. The National Park Service (NPS) Visitor Center (☎ 504-281-0510) has an excellent half-hour film. On Hwy 90 farther west, **Westwego** has a huge open-air fish market ringed by earthy shacks, plus the intimate Chacahoula Swamp Tours (☎ 504-436-2640), at $22 per person.

The **Barataria Preserve**, part of Jean Lafitte National Historic Park, isn't pristine wilderness but teems with wild animals and plants. The NPS Visitor Center (☎ 504-589-2330) has maps, a film, ranger-led walks and a guided canoe trek. *Bayou Barn* (☎ *504-689-2663),* just outside the park, rents canoes and has Cajun or zydeco bands every Sunday afternoon.

Just south, the quaint town of **Lafitte** is home to hardy commercial fishers; although it has scant tourist sights it does boast an abundance of waterside funk worth a few hours' wandering. *Cochiara's Marina* (☎ *504-689-3701),* at Goose Bayou Bridge, offers scruffy motel rooms with nice views from $55.

Some 30 miles west of New Orleans you run into the Cajun wetlands around Des Allemands. Turn north off Hwy 90 to Kraemer on Hwy 307, a scenic road that barely skims the swamp surface. Zam's Swamp Tours (☎ 504-633-7881) are offered in small motorboats guided by Cajun locals ($15), including a half-hour walking tour on shore.

On Lake Pontchartrain's North Shore, **Fontainebleau State Park** (☎ 504-624-4443) is a 2700-acre gem on the lakeshore near Mandeville, with nature trails, plantation ruins, a sandy beach, a swimming pool, picnic areas and campsites for $10-12. North of Mandeville, the bucolic burg of **Abita Springs** has an eponymous *brewery* (☎ 504-893-3143), with free tours at 1pm and 3pm Saturday, 3pm Sunday.

In Covington, *Mt Vernon Motel* (☎ *504-892-1041, 1110 N Hwy 190)* is a spiffy little 10-room place at $40/50 for singles/doubles. Dine at popular *Rags Too*, on Hwy 190 at Hwy 433, for po'boys, boiled seafood or a cheap lunch buffet.

PLANTATION COUNTRY

First indigo, then cotton, rice and sugarcane brought great wealth to the plantations along the banks of the Mississippi River between New Orleans and Baton Rouge.

About 25 miles north of Baton Rouge, off US 61, **St Francisville** makes a pleasant day trip if you like quaint towns, 18th- and 19th-century architecture, antique shops and cozy B&Bs.

Mississippi River Plantations

More than a dozen plantations are open to the public as historic sites, usually with costumed guides leading 45- to 60-minute tours ($6-8). Many present a romantic picture of plantation life, and most ignore the story of plantation slaves.

It's easy enough to explore the region by car, and organized tours are widely available in both New Orleans and Baton Rouge. A full-day trip, including visits to two or three plantations and lunch, will cost you around $75. Try Le Ob's Tours (☎ 504-288-3478), in New Orleans.

In Burnside, the **Tezcuco Plantation** (☎ 504-562-3929, 3138 Hwy 44), on the east bank, is a Greek Revival mansion in a complex that includes a garden, restaurant, antique shop and attractive guest cottages ($8, $5 for the grounds only). The modest **River Road African-American Museum** has photos, recipes, documents and other items that relate the history of slavery ($4). The mansion's B&B accommodations cost $65-160. Nearby **Houmas House Plantation** (☎ 504-473-7841) is one of the state's oldest buildings, started in the late 1700s.

Farther downriver, **Laura Plantation** (☎ 225-265-7690, 2247 Hwy 18), on the west bank, doesn't gloss over the role of slaves and also covers the indigenous people of the region.

A bit closer to Baton Rouge, **Nottoway Plantation** (☎ 504-545-2730), on Hwy 1 (west bank), is the largest plantation house in the South, with 64 rooms and 53,000 sq feet. It retains its original furnishings, and tours are rich in personal history.

Baton Rouge

Native Americans painted a cypress pole with blood, and planted it here on the east bank of the Mississippi to mark the boundaries of their hunting grounds. French explorers named the area *baton rouge* (red stick). Now Louisiana's capital, Baton Rouge has two universities, two state capitol buildings, a few casinos and a riverfront entertainment complex.

Highland Rd is the main thoroughfare, while Perkins Rd has many restaurants, bookstores and shops north and south of I-10. The convention and visitor bureau (☎ 225-383-1825, 800-527-6843, 730 North Blvd), downtown, is open weekdays. The Backpacker (☎ 225-925-2667, 7656 Jefferson Hwy/Hwy 73), opposite Bocage Mall, is a great source of information on outdoor activities and rents tents, canoes and other equipment.

Things to See & Do The 'new' **Louisiana State Capitol** building (☎ 225-342-7317), on State Capitol Dr, is a somewhat brutal art deco pile completed in 1932 at the behest of populist state governor Huey Long. A tour is worthwhile, and the 27th-floor observation deck has a great view (free). The **Old State Capitol** (☎ 225-342-0500, 100 N Blvd) is a neo-Gothic structure overlooking the river, with exhibits and multimedia presentations on Huey Long and the state's colorful political history ($4; closed Mon).

In the middle of urban Baton Rouge, the **Rural Life Museum** (☎ 225-765-2437, 4600 Essen Lane), just south of I-10, has 20 buildings that depict life in 18th- to early-20th-century Louisiana, covering folk art, vernacular architecture and plantation life ($5; open daily). The Creole-style **Magnolia Mound Plantation** (☎ 225-343-4955, 2161 Nicholson Dr) was built around 1791 and features period furnishings and guides in costumes ($5; closed Mon).

The **Bluebonnet Swamp Nature Center** (☎ 225-757-8905, 10503 N Oak Hills Pkwy), off Bluebonnet Blvd, has a mile-long boardwalk with two observation decks. Inside are wildlife, ecology and folk-art displays and exhibits on insects, alligators and mammals ($3; closed Mon).

Places to Stay & Eat The *Greenwood Park Campground* (☎ 225-775-3877, 3601 Thomas Rd) is north of downtown. Tent/RV sites are $2/7.

Many moderate-to-expensive chain hotels are just off I-10 around the College Rd and Acadian Thruway exits. Cheaper chains cluster along the north side of I-12, within a mile of I-10. *Budget Inn* (☎ 225-291-6600, 10555 Rieger Rd), off I-10, charges $47/51 for singles/doubles. *Shoney's Inn* (☎ 225-925-8399, 9919 Gwenadale Dr) is moderately priced and conveniently located, with small but attractive rooms from $49/57. Posh *Embassy Suites* (☎ 225-924-6566, 4914 Constitution Ave) has two-room suites with a galley kitchen ($129), an indoor pool and a sauna.

Around the LSU campus – College Dr, W Chimes Rd and Highland Rd – you'll find affordable eateries with lots of atmosphere. *Louie's Cafe* (209 W State St) is a locally popular 24-hour place with 1950s ambience. For seafood, po'boys and Louisiana specialties, try *The Caterie* (3617 Perkins Rd), at Acadian Thruway, or *The Chimes* (3357 Highland Rd).

Two downtown favorites are the cafeteria-style *Louisiana House of Representatives Dining Hall*, in the basement of the new capitol, for weekday breakfast and lunch; and *Phil's Oyster Bar* (5162 Government St), with $6 lunch specials, seafood and Italian fare till 9:30pm. *DeAngelo's* (7955 Bluebonnet Rd), 6 miles south off I-10, does rich pizzas (from $8), focaccia, calzones and salads.

Entertainment *Sex, Lies and Videotape* was filmed at *The Bayou* (☎ 225-346-1765, 124 W Chimes Rd), which still hosts high-quality live music acts. *The Varsity Theatre* (☎ 225-343-5267, 3353 Highland Rd) is another top live venue. For blues, check out either *Phil Brady's* (☎ 225-927-3786, 4848 Government St) or *Tabby's Blues Box & Heritage Hall* (☎ 225-387-9715, 244 Lafayette St).

Getting There & Around The Baton Rouge Metropolitan Airport (☎ 225-355-0333), north of the city off I-110, is served by flights from US air hubs.

Greyhound (☎ 225-383-3811, 1253 Florida Blvd), at N 12th St, has regular buses to Atlanta, Georgia ($82; from 10½ hours); Birmingham, Alabama ($72; from 10 hours); Lafayette ($10; 1 hour); and New Orleans ($10; from 1½ hours). Capital Transportation City Bus (☎ 225-389-8920) provides local transport 6am-6pm Monday to Saturday from the transfer station (2222 Florida St).

CAJUN COUNTRY

Officially called 'Acadiana,' this region covers southwest Louisiana from the Mississippi to the Texas border. The logical starting point is Lafayette, 130 miles west of New Orleans, but the real Cajun experience is to be found in small towns, bayous and rural backroads. Cajun and zydeco music is played at many restaurants, Cajun dances *(fais-do-do)* are mostly held on weekends, and Cajun food is available everywhere. Jean Lafitte National Historic Park, with three units in Cajun Country, focuses on Acadian heritage.

Note that the remote Cajun Coast area near the Texas border is mostly wildlife refuge. (The unattractive coast near Holly

Beach has accommodations that are subpar and overpriced.)

History The French settlers exiled from L'Acadie (now Nova Scotia, Canada) sought refuge in Louisiana from the mid-18th century, but were shunted off to the western swamplands. Houma and Chitimacha Indians taught their new neighbors to trap, fish, hunt and eat crawfish. These Indians corrupted 'Acadian' to 'Cagian,' and hence 'Cajun.'

The Acadians, with their own language and traditions, soon became the dominant culture in southern Louisiana, absorbing Indians, French Creoles, Spanish, Germans, Anglos and Afro-Haitians. Their isolation started to diminish in the Civil War, when Union forces occupied the area, and many Acadians joined the Confederate army.

From 1916 to 1956 the state banned French in schools, during a period called the *Heure de la Honte* (Time of Shame). In WWII, Acadian soldiers in France became valuable interpreters, and GIs returned with the seeds of renewed cultural pride. In a complete reversal of earlier policies, the Council for the Development of French in Louisiana (Codofil) began fostering the local language and culture. The I-10 bridge over the Atchafalaya Basin, completed in 1973, made the area readily accessible for the first time, and interest in Cajun music and cuisine has attracted an increasing number of visitors, many from French-speaking countries. The Acadian French dialect differs considerably from Parisian French but is quite understandable. Schools now teach a more standard form of the language.

For many years the Acadian economy was largely self-sufficient, but agriculture and fishing are now commercialized. The oil boom in the 1970s, and the oil bust in the 1980s, have had dramatic effects.

Lafayette

This small city isn't exceptionally attractive, with the old downtown somewhere between decline and renewal, and suburban sprawl along the main roads. The University of Louisiana at Lafayette (ULL), with 17,000 'Ragin' Cajuns,' gives Lafayette some college-town vitality. From I-10 exit 103A, the Evangeline Thruway (Hwy 167) goes to the center of town via the visitor center

(☎ 337-232-3808, 800-346-1958). The *Times of Acadiana* is a free weekly of local news and events. Pack & Paddle (☎ 337-232-5854, 601 E Pinhook Rd) outfits kayaking, canoeing and hiking trips throughout the region.

Things to See & Do Operated by the National Park Service, the **Acadian Cultural Center** (☎ 337-232-0789, 501 Fisher Rd) has thoughtful, well-presented exhibits, artifacts and interpretive captions (free admission; open daily).

Vermilionville (☎ 337-233-4077, 1600 Surrey St), a 23-acre park and 'living history museum,' has landscaped walkways going past craft shops, cabins and Acadian village–style houses. Cajun bands perform, and Cajun cooking demonstrations include sample tastings ($8/5 adults/kids; open daily). The Natural History Museum (☎ 337-291-5544, 433 Jefferson St), in modern new digs, features changing exhibits on southern Louisiana's natural environment.

The ULL Art Museum (☎ 337-482-5326) has primarily 19th- and 20th-century paintings by American (especially Louisianan) artists. Cypress Lake is a civilized swamp in the center of campus. Visitor parking is on McKinley St, off University Ave.

On St John St, look for the 500-year-old live oak next to the cathedral. **Lafayette Museum/Mouton House** (☎ 337-234-2208, 1122 Lafayette St) is a historic house with exhibits, including a collection of Mardi Gras costumes ($3; open daily).

Places to Stay & Eat Woodsy, unserviced *Acadiana Park* (☎ 337-291-8448, 1201 E Alexander St) has 75 sites ($9). Refurbished *Blue Moon Hostel* (☎ 337-654-1444, Ⓦ www .bluemoonhostel.com, 215 E Convent St), south of I-10 exit 103A, offers dorm beds for $15-17 and private rooms from $45. The usual motel chains are found here, including *Super 8* (☎ 337-232-8826, 2224 NE Evangeline Thruway), south of I-10 (singles/doubles $32/39). Friendly *Maison Mouton* (☎ 337-234-4661, 402 Garfield St), near the Greyhound station, is a 100-year-old inn with nice rooms from $59 ($89 with private bath).

Many places offer one-stop entertainment, dancing and regional cuisine. *Prejean's* (☎ 337-896-3247, 3480 Hwy 167N), pronounced **pray**-jhonz, is next to

Evangeline Downs and has the most creative kitchen (entrées from around $15). **Randol's** (☎ 337-981-7080, 2320 Kaliste Saloom Rd), on the south side of town, offers plenty of Cajun seafood and a big dance floor. **Deano's** (305 Bertrand Dr), near the west side of campus, is famous for its Cajun pizzas. Markets, convenience stores and even gas stations keep a pot of hot boudin (pork-and-rice-filled sausage) by the cash register, a sure sign you're in Cajun country.

Entertainment A free 'Downtown Alive' block party is held on Jefferson Blvd 6pm-8pm Friday from April to June and September to October. For zydeco, **El Sido's** (☎ 337-237-1959, 1523 Martin Luther King Dr), at St Antoine St, is a big welcoming cinder-block joint. **Hamilton Club** (☎ 337-984-5583, 1808 Verot School Rd) is an old clapboard place farther out past the airport. The cavernous **Grant St Dance Hall** (☎ 337-237-2255, 113 W Grant St) books a variety of bigger acts, including blues, reggae, classic rock and lots of zydeco. **Bob's Pub** (☎ 337-984-9540, 104 Republic St) is a comfortable place to hear live blues.

Getting There & Around Greyhound buses (☎ 337-235-1541) operate from a hub beside the central commercial district, making 11 runs daily to New Orleans ($17; 3½ hours) and Baton Rouge ($10; 1 hour). The decrepit Amtrak station is served by the *Sunset Limited*, which goes to New Orleans three times a week. For car rentals, try Thrifty (☎ 337-237-1282), Enterprise (☎ 337-237-2864) or Budget (☎ 337-233-8888).

Cajun Wetlands

Southwest of Lafayette, historic **Abbeville** has great seafood (try **Dupuy's** or **Blacks**), and the surrounding communities are well known for small-town festivals. Southeast of Lafayette, along US 90 beside the Atchafalaya Basin, the heart of the Cajun wetlands is a lowland area of dense vegetation, swamps, lakes and bayous.

Nine miles east of Lafayette, **Breaux Bridge**, 'the Crawfish Capital of the World,' has a Crawfish Festival in early May and good times all year. **Bayou Cabins** (☎ 337-332-6258, 100 Mills Hwy) have porches over the bayou (from $60). Barnlike **Mulate's** (325 Mills Hwy/Hwy 94) has Cajun food, music and dancing nightly. Off I-10, Henderson is popular for swamp tours, but smaller, more personal tours ($20) are run by Champagne's Swamp Tours (☎ 337-845-5567) on **Lake Martin**, just south of Breaux Bridge. The Cypress Island Preserve here has the largest white-ibis rookery in the world.

Established around 1765, **St Martinville** is home of the famed Evangeline Oak from Longfellow's 1847 poem *Evangeline*. The town has wooden storefronts, a manicured square and a nice old church. Nearby Lake Fausse Pointe State Park (☎ 337-229-4764) is a good swampside stop.

Near US 90, **New Iberia** was settled by the Spanish in 1779 and prospered on the sugar crop; plantation homes can still be seen. **Teche Motel** (☎ 337-369-3756, 1830 Main St) has simple rooms ($35). On Avery Island, the McIlhenny Tabasco factory (☎ 337-365-8173) offers free tours daily.

In **Thibodaux** (**ti**-ba-doh), at the confluence of two bayous, the Wetlands Acadian Cultural Center (☎ 504-448-1375) has an impressive museum and a gallery of Acadian history. Local musicians jam here Monday nights. Renovated **Economy Inn** (☎ 504-446-3667, 1113 St Mary St) has comfy singles/doubles for $35/45.

There's not much in **Houma**, but it's a good base for swamp tours (from $15). The 1960s-era **Sugar Bowl Motel** (☎ 504-872-4521), Hwy 90 east, has OK rooms ($38). At the end of Hwy 1, Grand Isle is a grimy beach resort with shabby, overpriced motels.

Cajun Prairie

North and west of Lafayette, prairie towns have a heritage of Cajun and zydeco music, rice cultivation, fishing camps and crawfish boils. **Opelousas** has a historic city center and a museum covering Indian, Acadian and Creole cultures. **Palace Cafe** does great crawfish étoufée and bisque ($10). Top zydeco venues include **Slim's Y-Ki-Ki** (☎ 337-942-9980), a few miles up Washington St, and **Richard's** (☎ 337-543-8223), 8 miles west in Lawtell. **Plaisance**, northwest of Opelousas, hosts the Southwest Louisiana Zydeco Festival (☎ 337-942-2392) around Labor Day weekend.

North of Opelousas, Washington retains its character as a historic steamboat port. To the southwest, Church Point is known for Cajun music.

In **Eunice**, the Prairie Acadian Cultural Center (☎ 337-457-8499) explains the influence of Caribbean immigrants and cattle ranches on local culture. The restored 1924 Liberty Theater (☎ 337-457-7389) hosts *Rendez-Vous Des Cajuns* Saturday nights. *Cajun Campground* (☎ 337-457-5753), 5 miles east on Hwy 190, has tent/RV sites for $12/16. The best budget motel is refurbished *La Parisienne* (☎ 337-457-4274, *Hwy 190*), just east of downtown (singles/doubles $28/40).

The self-styled 'Cajun Music Capital,' **Mamou** has a big bash starting at around 8*am* every Saturday morning at *Fred's Lounge*. The party kicks on to *Diana's* and several other bars.

Off I-10 between Lafayette and Lake Charles, the Rice Belt sports 19th-century railroad towns like Rayne, 'Frog Capital of the World,' and Crowley, the 'Rice Capital of Louisiana.'

CENTRAL LOUISIANA
The central part of the state draw on cultures from all directions. You'll find French heritage in Nachitoches, Tunica Indian traditions in Marksville, and Franco-African people along the Cane River. This is also the region where bilingual French Catholic Louisiana shades into the monolingual, chiefly Protestant parishes of the north.

Natchitoches
In 1714 French explorers established the first European settlement here as Fort St Jean-Baptiste. A river town, its commerce dried up after 1825 when the river changed course. The river is now a tranquil lake, and the economy depends upon Northwestern State University and a tourist trade that was kick-started by the movie *Steel Magnolias*, filmed here in 1988.

The attractive 33-block National Historic District lies along the west bank of Cane River Lake and is best seen on foot. Start your exploration at the Tourist Commission (☎ 318-352-8072, 781 Front St).

Fort St Jean Baptiste (☎ 318-357-3101) is a 1979 reconstruction based on original 1733 plans. The 5-acre compound features eight wood-and-mud buildings surrounded by a pointy wooden fence (open daily). At the university, the **Folklife Center** (☎ 318-357-6361) has cultural documents, audio- and videotapes, a library and 5000 photographs.

Lakeview Inn (☎ *318-352-9561, 1316 Washington St)*, on the north side near the Hwy 1 bypass, is the best value ($40). The down-at-heel *Louisiane Motel* (☎ *318-352-6401, 340 Hwy 1 S)* charges $33. Chain motels west of town off I-49 are overpriced ($45 and up). Thirty-some B&Bs cost $65-120 or more.

Authentic Natchitoches meat pies are crusty, crescent-shaped little turnovers, stuffed with spicy ground beef, pork and onions and fried. Try them at *Lasyone's Meat Pie Kitchen (229 2nd St)*. *Almost Home (729 3rd St)* does home-style breakfasts and lunch buffets. It's worth a trip to nearby Clarence to eat at *Grayson's Bar-b-q (5849 Hwy 71)*; start with the mixed plate ($7).

Around Natchitoches
South on Hwy 119, **Melrose Plantation** (☎ 318-379-0055) is a whole complex of buildings with an interesting history. In the early 20th century, hostess Cammy Henry offered lodging in the 'Yucca House' to artists and writers like William Faulkner and John Steinbeck. Africa House is done in Congo style and looks like a squat brick mushroom. Inside is a vivid 50-foot mural depicting plantation life by folk artist Clementine Hunter ($6; open noon-4pm daily).

Five separate units of **Kisatchie National Forest** cover 937 sq miles of northern and central Louisiana. Most have free campgrounds and extensive hiking trails.

A forgettable crossroads town, Alexandria is worth a stop for *Hotel Bentley* (☎ *318-448-9600, 200 Desoto St)*, dubbed the 'Biltmore of the Bayous.' The imposing neoclassical building contains a lobby with a marble fountain and stained-glass ceiling, and standard rooms from $89.

On the cusp of Cajun Country, Marksville has a proud French heritage and Native American connections. The **Marksville State Commemorative Area** (☎ 318-253-8954) is a series of mounds used for burial ceremonies 1000 years ago ($2; open daily). The **Tunica-Biloxi Museum** (☎ 318-253-8174), on Hwy 1 just south of town, has a mound for the reinternment of 200,000 artifacts looted from

Tunica graves. Many restored objects are displayed, most from the 18th-century Tunica trade with French settlers ($2; open Mon-Fri). *Terrace Inn (☎ 318-253-5274, 915 Tunica Dr W)* is a nice, inviting little motel with singles/doubles for $40/50. *Grand Casino Avoyelles (☎ 318-253-1946)* is run by the local Tunica tribe.

NORTHERN LOUISIANA

The Baptist Bible Belt of northern Louisiana runs from rural backwaters to the oil-industry center of Shreveport – it's a world away from the Cajun and Creole south.

Shreveport

Captain Henry Shreve cleared a 165-mile logjam on the Red River so this town could be founded as a river port in 1839. The city boomed with oil discoveries in the early 1900s, but the port declined after WWII. Many downtown businesses were closed, but there has been an attempt to revitalize the area with Vegas-size casinos and a riverfront entertainment complex.

The city is bisected by I-49 and I-20 and encircled by I-220. The visitor center (☎ 318-222-9391, 629 Spring St) is downtown. Nearby are some attractive old buildings, including the opulent 1925 **Strand Theater** (619 Louisiana Ave). An eight-story New Age mural graces the AT&T building (725 McNeil St).

The **Norton Art Gallery** (☎ 318-865-4201, 4747 Creswell Ave) has a good collection of Fred Remington's 'Old West' sculptures, paintings and ornate handguns (free admission; closed Mon). The **American Rose Society** (☎ 318-938-5402) has a 118-acre plot on the west side of town with over 20,000 rose bushes.

A cluster of cheap motels is around Airline Dr just across the river in Bossier City, including a good *Days Inn (☎ 318-742-9200)*, with singles/doubles for $32/38. In west Shreveport, *Travelodge (☎ 318-425-7467, 2134 Greenwood Rd)*, off Texas Ave, is convenient to downtown but nothing opulent ($36/46). The *Best Western Chateau Suite Hotel (☎ 318-222-7620, 201 Lake St)* is a nice place with a pool ($89).

Fertitta's Deli (1124 Fairfield Ave) is revered for its 'Muffy' sandwiches at lunch ($3.50-8). For something unique, hit *Herby*

K's (1833 Pierre Ave) for its legendary 'Shrimp Buster' ($9) and cold fishbowls of beer. *Olive St Bistro (1027 Olive St)* has an outdoor deck ideal for a glass of wine and penne Amalfi ($9).

Downtown, *Noble Savage Tavern (☎ 318-221-1781, 417 Texas St)* features bluegrass, blues and other roots music, as well as excellent food. Run by Elvis' lead guitarist, *James Burton's Rock-n-Roll Café (☎ 318-424-5000, 616 Commerce St)* books some great live bands on weekends.

Along US 80

A not-too-scenic alternative to I-20 is old US 80, which follows the railroad route through sleepy small towns. Bonnie and Clyde met their sticky end near **Gibsland**, where a small museum has gruesome pictures (reception is at town hall). The biggest town in the area is **Ruston**, to the east, where leafy Lincoln Parish Park (☎ 318-251-5156) is a mecca for mountain bikers, campers and anglers.

Monroe

Monroe traces its origins to a French soldier who wrangled a land grant from the Spanish king in 1785. In the early 20th century the town boomed with the discovery of oil and natural gas, but those prosperous times are long gone. The **Biedenharn Museum & Garden** (☎ 318-387-5281, 2006 Riverside Dr) has handmade Bibles, a hothouse and a pretty garden filled with plants mentioned in the good book (free admission).

Poverty Point National Monument

In the northeast of the state, this archeological site (☎ 318-926-5492), 50 miles northeast of Monroe on Hwy 577, has a remarkable series of earthwork and mounds along what was once the Mississippi River. Around 1000 BC it was the hub of a civilization comprising hundreds of communities, with trading links as far north as the Great Lakes. There's a good introductory film, and a two-story observation tower gives a view of the site's six concentric ridges. A shuttle bus does a complete tour; alternatively, you can walk to the spectacular bird-shaped mound ($2; open daily).

Arkansas

Once a jumping-off point for frontier expeditions to the west and south, Arkansas later attracted visitors with its natural hot springs. Today it promotes itself as 'the Natural State,' with camping, fishing and hunting in the Ozark and Ouachita Mountains. Unnatural attractions include sites associated with Bill Clinton, civil-rights history and the Mississippi Delta blues.

History

Mounds of the ancient Mississippi culture can be seen at several sites in Arkansas. Caddo, Osage and Quapaw Indians had permanent villages here when the first French explorers arrived, though they were often erroneously called 'Cherokee.' After the 1803 Louisiana Purchase, Arkansas became a US territory, and slaveholding planters moved into the Delta to grow cotton. Poorer immigrants from the Appalachians settled in the poorer lands of the Ozark and Ouachita plateaus, bringing their music and craft traditions.

Arkansas was on the edge of the frontier, and problems of lawlessness persisted until the Civil War. Reconstruction was difficult, and development did not take off until after 1870, when the expansion of railroads permitted strong growth in farming. Oil and gas added to the state's wealth, but the industrial sector did not become substantial until the 1950s. Racial tension peaked in 1957, when the federal government intervened to enforce the integration of Arkansas schools.

The state has one of the lowest per-capita incomes in the US, with many poor blacks in the Delta area and poor whites in the Ozarks. The Ku Klux Klan (KKK) is rumored to have a following in some rural areas, but race relations seem quite harmonious in the larger towns, and black and white students mix freely at schools that were once segregated.

Information

The Department of Parks & Tourism (☎ 501-682-7777, 800-628-8725, Ⓦ www.1800natural.com, 1 Capitol Mall, Little Rock, AR 72201) sends out a vacation plan kit on request. For highway information, call ☎ 501-569-2000. State sales tax is 4.6%,

---

Arkansas

Nickname: Natural State

Population: 2,673,000 (33rd)

Area: 53,187 sq miles (27th)

Admitted to Union: June 15, 1836 (25th); seceded May 1861; readmitted 1868

Capital city: Little Rock (population 183,000)

Other cities: Fort Smith (80,000), North Little Rock (60,000), Pine Bluff (55,000)

Birthplace of: General Douglas MacArthur (1880–1964), musician Glen Campbell (b 1936), Helen Gurley Brown (b 1922), Bill Clinton (b 1946), Wal-Mart

Famous for: electing the first female US senator, Hattie Caraway (1931)

---

but many places have a local innkeeper tax, food tax and/or liquor tax.

LITTLE ROCK

Established in 1814 as an outpost on the Arkansas River, Little Rock became the capital of the Arkansas territory in 1821 and state capital in 1836, though federal troops controlled the city in the Civil War. Little Rock boomed in the late 19th century as the commercial and administrative center of a growing state, and some fine homes and public buildings went up. Development was sporadic in the 20th century, dogged by political corruption and official policies of racial segregation.

Today, downtown Little Rock is an uninspiring grid of undistinguished 19th- and 20th-century architecture on the south bank of the Arkansas River. City Hall, the Old State House and some big hotels sit on Markham St, parallel to the riverfront. The Statehouse Convention Center, adjoining the Excelsior Hotel, has a visitor information desk (☎ 501-376-4781). Check email at the public library (100 Rock St).

Things to See & Do

The **Old State House** (☎ 501-324-9685, 300 W Markham St) was the state capitol from 1836 to 1911, with impressively restored legislative chambers, period furnishings and displays on

Arkansas history (free admission). Visits begin with a Clinton video next to his old gubernatorial desk and running shoes.

Behind Markham St, Riverfront Park provides a pleasant, walkable area along the riverbank. At the park's eastern end you might discern the little rock for which the city is named. Nearby, the River Market has a good food court and outdoor spaces overlooking the water. The museum building at 500 E Markham houses a good bar and the interesting Pyramid Bookshop, which specializes in African American titles. The **Museum of Discovery** (☎ 501-396-7050) is mainly for kids but has good exhibits on local Native American cultures ($5/4.50 adults/kids). The official **Children's Museum** (☎ 501-374-6655, 1400 W Markham St) is in the old Union Station ($4).

Two blocks inland, the **Arkansas Territorial Restoration** (☎ 501-324-9351, 200 E 3rd St) offers a guided tour through several old buildings reconstructed on site and has some good exhibits on Arkansas crafts, like making Bowie knives ($2). Seven blocks south, in MacArthur Park, the surprisingly good **Arkansas Arts Center** (☎ 501-372-4000) mounts a variety of temporary exhibits (free admission).

The most moving attraction is the National Park Service's **Central High Museum & Visitor Center** (☎ 501-374-1957, 2125 W 14th St), west of downtown (take bus No 3). It's in a restored 1950s-era Mobil gas station, opposite the school where, in 1957, nine black teenagers defied the state's policy of racially segregated schooling. Despite a US Supreme Court ruling that Arkansas must integrate its schools, the state militia was deployed to prevent the black students from enrolling. After three weeks of court battles and racial tension, President Eisenhower sent in the 101st Airborne Division, and the students were able to enroll under armed protection. Scenes of emotional, sometimes violent, confrontations were televised around the world, rendering the facade of Little Rock Central High School a familiar image of the times.

Newspaper reprints, old photos and TV footage outline the history of segregation and the integration movement, and show what happened to the 'Little Rock Nine' after they enrolled – a story of great moral courage (free admission; open daily). The school itself, now thoroughly integrated, is closed to visitors.

East of Little Rock off US 165, **Toltec Mounds Archeological Park** (☎ 501-961-9442) is a complex of some 18 earthen mounds that were a ceremonial center of the Mississippi culture between AD 600 and 1050. There's an interpretive center, walking trail and exhibits ($2.50; closed Mon).

Places to Stay & Eat

The **KOA Kampground** (☎ 501-758-4598, 800-562-4598), 6 miles northwest of I-40 exit 148, has tent/RV sites for $20/27. There's nothing cheap downtown, but **Masters Economy Inn** (☎ 501-372-4392) is just to the east, at I-30's 9th St exit, from $28/32 for spacious singles/doubles. The classiest place is Victorian-era **Capital Hotel** (☎ 501-374-7474, 111 W Markham St), from $143/168 ($115 weekends).

Cheap motels are off the interstates, including three **Motel 6**s: north (☎ 501-758-5100) at I-40 exit 153A ($37/43); west (☎ 501-225-7366) at I-430 exit 6 ($39/45); and southeast (☎ 501-568-8888) at I-30 exit 134 ($33/39).

The food court at **River Market** is an economical place for lunch – Greek, Lebanese, burgers, barbecue, you name it. **Great Wall** (418 W 7th St) serves up Chinese standards ($7-9) till 9:30pm, which is late for Little Rock. **Fat Tuesday's** (☎ 501-375-3287, 801 W Markham St) serves upscale Cajun fare for $15-20. The snazziest restaurant is **Ashley's**

Romance in a Bottle

Who says you can't buy love? In Little Rock, lovelorn women are buying it by the case. Niagara is a fizzy Swedish tonic that contains an herbal recipe that reportedly makes women's – and some men's – libidos turn from a trickle into a rush. Its sole American distributor is Lari Williams, who runs **Wycoff Coffeehouse** (☎ 501-228-4448, 10700 N Rodney Parham Rd). Order ahead, as mega-shipments of the 6oz bottles of blue ($4.50) can sell out in a few days, if not hours. If you get that tingly feeling, remember that this 'aphrodisiac energy drink' is loaded with caffeine.

(☎ 501-374-7474, 1112 W Markham St), inside the Capital Hotel, where dinner will set you back around $30.

Pleasant and popular **Juanita's Cafe & Bar** (☎ 501-372-1228, 1300 S Main St) has authentic Mexican food from about $8 and live music nightly (rock, reggae, jazz, whatever). **Midtown Billiards** (1316 Main St) offers meals, entertainment and a well-tended bar ($7 'membership').

Getting There & Around
Little Rock National Airport (☎ 501-372-3430), just east of downtown, is strictly domestic.

The Greyhound station (☎ 501-372-3007, 118 E Washington St) is over the river, in North Little Rock. Regular buses go to Memphis, Tennessee ($19; 2¼ hours); New Orleans ($74; from 12½ hours); Dallas, Texas ($50; from 6 hours); and St Louis, Missouri ($43; 8½ hours). Local buses are run by CAT (☎ 501-375-1163), more for commuters than visitors.

Amtrak occupies the old Union Station (☎ 501-372-6841, 1400 W Markham St). The *Texas Eagle* runs daily to Dallas (from $57; 6½ hours) and San Antonio (from $91; 16½ hours), Texas; St Louis, Missouri (from $50; 7½ hours); and Chicago, Illinois (from $91; 13 hours).

ARKANSAS RIVER VALLEY
The Arkansas River cuts right across the state from the Oklahoma border to the Mississippi. Downstream from Little Rock on US 65 is **Pine Bluff**, an early river trading post, now a city of 55,000. Arkansas Post, near the confluence with the Mississippi, was set up in 1686 and also became an important river port, yet it was all but abandoned by 1900. Arkansas Post National Memorial (☎ 501-548-2207) has exhibits about French, Spanish and American life on the river.

Upstream from Little Rock, I-40 is the fast route, but **US 64** is studded with small-town Americana: Atkins, the 'Pickle Capital of Arkansas' (try fried dill pickle); Russellville, home of Jimmy Lile Custom Knives, as used in Rambo movies; Clarksville, a college town and capital of 'Arkansas Peach Country'; Ozark, where the bridge across the river is rated by the Institute of Steel Construction as 'one of the 16 most beautiful long spans in the US'; Altus,

the center of Arkansas' Germanic wine-growing region; and Alma, 'Spinach Capital of the World,' with a giant can of spinach and a statue of Popeye.

In **Van Buren**, have a look at the six-block historic district, a sometime movie set left over from the town's heyday as a river port and trading outpost. The Ozark Scenic Railway (☎ 800-687-8600) offers a three-hour, 70-mile trip through the Ozarks in antique railroad carriages ($20-28; Wed and Sat).

Across the river, **Fort Smith** was set up in 1817 and became a base for anti-Indian operations and the last outpost of law and order on the edge of the Oklahoma frontier. Get information at Miss Laura's Visitors Center (☎ 501-783-8888m 2 North B St), a century-old brothel. The Fort Smith National Historic Site (☎ 501-783-3961), at 3rd and Rogers Sts, includes the courtroom, jail and gallows used by Judge Isaac C Parker, 'the hanging judge,' from 1875 to 1896.

SOUTHWESTERN ARKANSAS
The **Ouachita Mountains** are part of a hilly plateau south of the Arkansas River. Largely national forest, the area is studded with artificial lakes and popular for hunting, fishing and boating. Hwy 7 is a pretty drive between Hot Springs and the Arkansas River. **Petit Jean State Park** (☎ 501-727-5441), a detour east off Route 7, has particularly attractive scenery, walking trails, campgrounds, and rustic lodges built by the Civilian Conservation Corps (CCC).

Hot Springs National Park, 55 miles southwest of Little Rock, is almost surrounded by the city of **Hot Springs**. A few people still come for the waters, but these days there's more interest in the Victorian architecture, the horse racing at Oaklawn and scenes from Bill Clinton's boyhood. The elaborate old bathhouses line up on Bathhouse Row, behind shady magnolias on the east side of Central Ave. Opposite is a row of restored 19th-century commercial buildings.

The National Park Visitor Center (☎ 501-624-3383) is in the 1915 Fordyce bathhouse, in the middle of Bathhouse Row. A short film tells of Hot Springs' history as a Native American free-trade zone, a quack-cure capital, and its early 20th-century zenith imitating a European spa. The Gatsby-era marble and mosaic, hydrotherapy apparata and chrome-plated plumbing can be viewed on a free tour.

Just south of Bathhouse Row, the visitor bureau (☎ 800-772-2489) has information about the surrounding area. Its map of Clinton-related sites includes his church, hamburger joint, bowling alley and Masonic Temple.

The only operating bathhouse is the Buckstaff (☎ 501-623-2308), just south of the Fordyce, where a thermal bath costs $15, and a Swedish massage $18 (closed Sun). Resort spa/hotels like the Arlington, the Majestic and the Downtowner have private bathhouses. If you want to take the waters, bring some containers; there are several fountains where you can fill them.

A promenade runs around the hillside behind Bathhouse Row, where some springs survive in a more or less natural state. Arlington Lawn, at the north end of the Row, is a gathering place in the evening, with its own hot spring. A network of trails covers Hot Springs Mountain, and a scenic drive goes to the top, where the 216-foot Hot Springs Mountain Tower lets you see a long way ($5, 50¢ with a visitor-bureau coupon).

The surrounding mountains are covered with dogwood, hickory, oak and pine – lovely in the spring and fall. A popular excursion is the Duck Tours in amphibious vehicles. National Park Duck Tours (☎ 501-321-2911, 318 Central Ave) and Duck Tours (☎ 501-321-2911, 418 Central Ave) charge $11/7 adults/kids for a 1¼-hour trip. The *Belle of Hot Springs* (☎ 501-525-4438) does cruises on Lake Hamilton ($10-28).

The National Park Service's attractive *Gulpha Gorge Campground*, 2 miles northeast of downtown, costs $10 (no showers, hookups or reservations). The cheap motels are on the highways around town. *Alpine Inn* (☎ 501-624-9164, 741 Park Ave/Hwy 7 N) offers decent rooms from $30. *Quality Inn* (☎ 501-624-3321, 1125 Grand Ave) has more comfortable singles/doubles ($64/69).

Imposing *Arlington Resort Hotel & Spa* (☎ 501-623-7771, 800-643-1502, 239 Central Ave), at the top end of Bathhouse Row, has spa packages and rooms starting at $58/68 and snazzier quarters like the Al Capone Suite ($295). The lobby is more impressive than the rooms. There are other old hotels

in town and newer resorts around nearby lakes; ask at the visitor bureau.

Two good eateries on the Central Ave tourist strip are *Granny's Kitchen (332 Central Ave)*, where a down-home breakfast, lunch or dinner will cost $4-10; and *Faded Rose (210 Central Ave)*, serving inexpensive New Orleans cuisine. There's a good choice farther south on Central Ave, including *Brick House Grill (801 Central Ave)*, with well-prepared seafood, steaks and chicken dishes (mostly $8-12). Bill Clinton's favorite boyhood barbecue was *McClard's (☎ 501-624-9586, 505 Albert Pike)*, southwest of the center, where you can fill up on sweet, succulent ribs, pork, beef and slaw for under $6.

From the Greyhound station (☎ 501-623-5574, 222 W Grand Ave) buses go regularly to Memphis, Tennessee ($37; 4 hours); Dallas, Texas ($51; 6 hours); St Louis, Missouri ($74; 10 hours); and New Orleans, Louisiana ($84; 16½ hours).

I-30 makes a pretty straight run from Little Rock to the Texas border. Clinton buffs might stop at **Hope**, where the ex-pres spent his first seven years. Check the Hope Visitor Center & Museum (☎ 870-722-2580, 800-233-4673), at S Main and Division Sts. The biggest attraction in **Texarkana** is straddling the state line in the middle of town.

OZARK MOUNTAINS

The Ozarks still bring to mind the Al Capp comic strip *Li'l Abner*, which depicts a ramshackle town where the men were too lazy to work and the women were desperate enough to chase them. Although locals tend to milk the hillbilly angle, the region is also blessed with gorgeous scenery, clear river waters and some good outdoor sports outfitters.

Mountain View & Around

Heading north from Little Rock, detour east of US 65 to this perfectly ordinary Ozark town, known for its tradition of informal weekend music making on Courthouse Square. Creeping commercialism is taking its toll, as the chamber of commerce (☎ 870-269-8068) promotes the place as the 'Folk Music Capital of the World.' Cash's White River Hoe-Down (☎ 870-269-8042) is a heavily hyped country-music and comedy show ($14). A calendar of annual events also pulls in the punters, from the Folk Festival

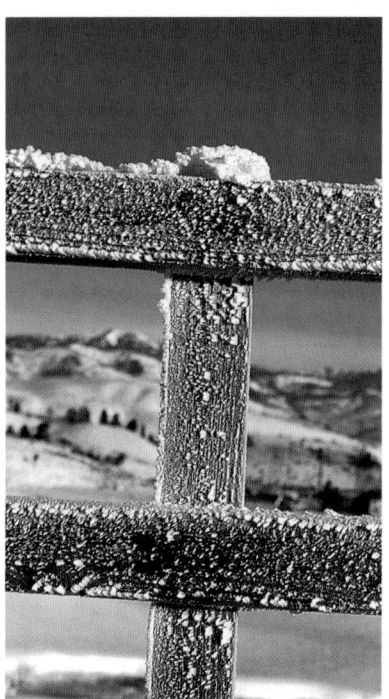

LEE FOSTER
Winter wonderland, Yellowstone National Park

CLEM LINDENMAYER
Mesa Verde National Park, Colorado

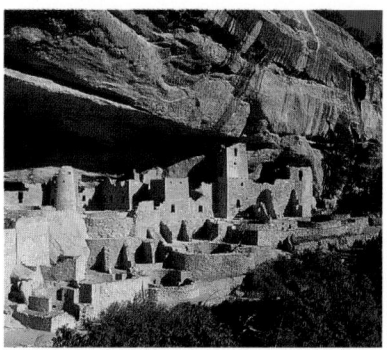

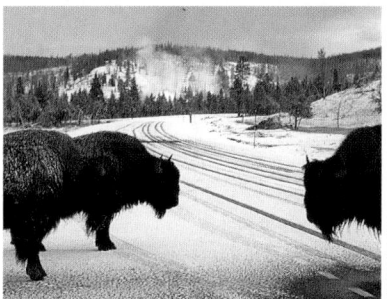

MATT SWINDEN
Bison hitching south, Yellowstone National Park

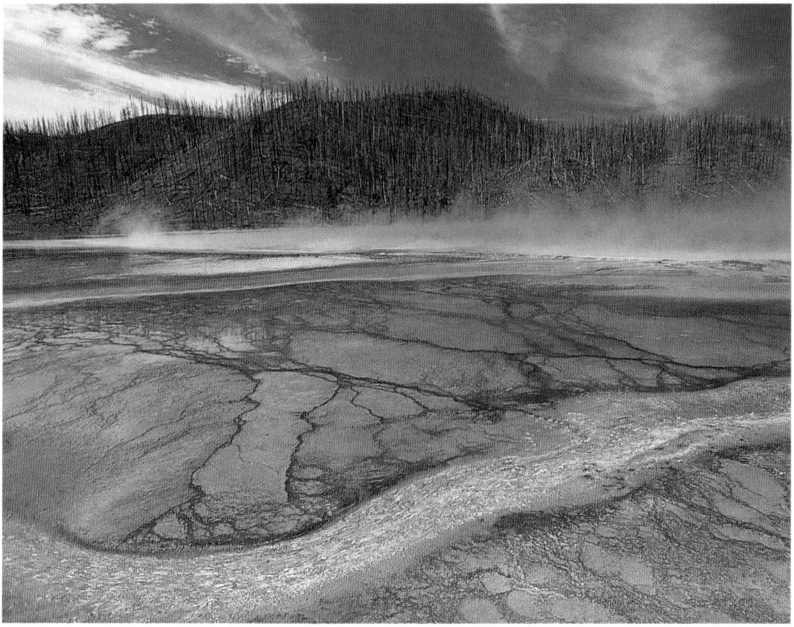
JOHN ELK III
Yellowstone National Park's Grand Prismatic Spring, Wyoming

JOHN HAY

Santa Fe souvenirs, New Mexico

NEIL SETCHFIELD

Bring lots of quarters to Las Vegas, Nevada.

LEE FOSTER

One cowgirl who never gets the blues, Las Vegas

IZZET KERIBAR

Mission to Mars, or at least Arches National Park, Utah

and Auto Show (Apr) to the Bean Fest (Oct) and Ozark Christmas (early Dec).

The **Ozark Folk Center State Park** (☎ 870-269-3851, 800-264-3655), just north of town, is a sanitized but sincere attempt to preserve the crafts, traditions and music of the Ozarks. Demonstrations cover basket weaving, gunsmithing, country cooking, quilting and so on ($8; Apr-Oct). The theater features traditional mountain music, square dancing, clogging and jigs ($8). About 10 miles north of town, **Blanchard Springs Recreation Area** (☎ 870-757-2211) has a cave system with spectacular formations ($9).

At Ozark Folk Center, try home-style Southern food in *Skillet Restaurant*, or stay in a forest setting at *Dry Creek Lodge* (☎ *870-269-3871*) for $45-80. There's a very nice *campground* at Blanchard Springs, with an inviting swimming hole. The old-fashioned, family-run *Riverview Hotel* (☎ *870-297-8208*) in nearby Calico Rock is a homey place to stay (from $45).

Accommodations in town include *Mountain View Motel* (☎ *870-269-3209, E Main St*), from $35, and chain motels like *Days Inn* (☎ *870-269-3287*) and *Econo Lodge* (☎ *870-269-3775*). The chamber of commerce has details on RV parks, cabins and B&Bs. *The Inn at Mountain View* (☎ *870-269-4200, 307 W Washington St*) is a nice old B&B (singles/doubles $50/60 including seven-course breakfast).

Woods Soda Fountain, on W Main St, has faux-'50s decor, ice cream, sodas and lunch specials. A local favorite, *Tommy's Famous*, is just west off Hwy 66, with sensational pizza, calzones, ribs and nonalcoholic beer (it's a dry county). *Puttin' on the Ritz* (☎ *870-269-4311*), on E Main St, does swanky steak and seafood dinners ($12-16). Apart from the musicians in Courtyard Square (just pickin' and grinnin'), *Jimmy Driftwood Barn* (☎ *870-269-8042*), north of town on Hwy 5, hosts country/mountain music at 7:30pm Friday and Sunday (free admission).

Buffalo National River

It mightn't look like the Colorado or the Columbia, but the Buffalo River sure is purty, flowing beneath dramatic bluffs through unspoiled Ozark forest. The Buffalo National River (☎ 870-741-5443), administered by the National Park Service, covers about 130 miles of river in a 60-mile swath of land from the Boston Mountains to the White River. The most interesting canoeing is from Ponca down to Pruitt, with Class I and II white water. The stretch from Ponca to Kyle's Landing is a leisurely day trip.

Outfitters such as Lost Valley (☎ 870-861-5522) and Buffalo Outdoor Center (☎ 800-221-5514) in Ponca can arrange canoes for around $36 plus $20 for transport. The usual access is from scenic Hwy 7.

Eureka Springs

Near the northwest corner of the state, Eureka Springs could easily be mistaken for an old mining village, but tourists are the only things ever mined here. It's pretty enough, with Victorian buildings lining crooked streets in a steep valley, but the combination of commercialized country music, honeymoon romance and Bible-themed attractions is a touch much.

The chamber of commerce (☎ 501-253-8737, 137 W Van Buren/Hwy 62) has information about lodging, tours and attractions. The best things to do are walk the streets, shop for tacky souvenirs and ride on the old **ES & NR Railway** (☎ 501-253-9623), which puffs through the hills on an hourlong tour ($9; closed Sun). Do the mineral-spring thing at the Palace Hotel & Bathhouse (☎ 501-253-7474, 135 Spring St).

The inspirational attractions are east of town on Statue Rd, off of US 62, where the oddly proportioned 70-foot *Christ of the Ozarks* looms over the town. Nearby is the amphitheater for *The Great Passion Play*, which has been reliving the death of Christ for 30 years, employing 250 actors in 'authentic Bible-time attire' (☎ 800-882-7529 for reservations; $18). The Bible Museum has 6000 editions of the same book, and the New Holy Land Tour takes you past life-size tableaux of famous biblical scenes. And there's more – a piece of the Berlin Wall, 1000 pictures in the Sacred Art Center and lunch at the Mission Buffet. Most attractions close November to April.

The cheapest accommodations are out of town on US 62E. Prices vary greatly with the season. *Timberline Inn* (☎ *501-253-9815)* is a '60s-style motel (from $30). *Travelers Inn* (☎ *501-253-8386)* charges $34/42 for singles/doubles in summer. Some of the grand old hotels are worn but still ooze character, including the 1905 *Basin Park*

Hotel (☎ *501-253-7837, 12 Spring St)*, downtown, from $55 in the off-season, or the 1886-era **Crescent Hotel** (☎ *501-253-9766, 75 Prospect St)* overlooking town, from $65. **Bed & Breakfast Connection** (☎ *800-243-8218)* has a long list.

The town is full of restaurants. Some good ones include **De Vitos** *(5 Center St)*, with fresh Italian dishes; the alternative **Mud Street Espresso Cafe** *(22G Main St)*, open all day with music at night; and **Bubba's Barbecue** *(60 King's Hwy)*.

The main entertainment is the 'Music Theaters,' offering a combination of corny comedy, gospel, bluegrass and country music. **Pine Mountain Jamboree** and **Ozark Mountain Hoe-Down** are out on US 62, and both charge about $17. For those who really like this stuff, Branson, Missouri, is not far away (see the Great Plains chapter).

Fayetteville

One of Arkansas' oldest towns, dating from the 1820s, Fayetteville is home to the University of Arkansas (UA). Bill Clinton taught constitutional law at UA from 1973 to 1976, and he and Hillary were hitched here in 1975. The campus is moderately attractive, and there's a posh Victorian residential district. The Arkansas Air Museum (☎ 501-521-4947), 5 miles south of town, specializes in pre-WWII aircraft, especially racing and aerobatic biplanes.

MISSISSIPPI DELTA

The Great River Rd goes through the Delta in eastern Arkansas. With cotton and rice fields and juke joints, the Arkansas Delta is less interesting than the Mississippi side. If you're on I-40 east of Little Rock, detour to Devalls Bluff, where **Craig's Barbecue** is a small shack serving the definitive article.

A few fine old houses remain, but **Helena**, 120 miles from Little Rock on Hwy 49, has declined somewhat since its heyday as a river port. It's been a center for blues since the 1940s, when the radio program 'King Biscuit Time' was hosted here by Sonny Boy Williamson, sponsored by the distributors of King Biscuit Flour. There's an information center (☎ 870-338-9831) near the Mississippi Bridge, with maps and material for the whole state. The **King Biscuit Blues Festival**,

in the second weekend of October, is a major blues event. The *King Biscuit Times* reports on the blues scene.

The **Delta Cultural Center** (☎ 870-338-4350, 95 Missouri St)*, in a renovated railway station, has a comprehensive exhibit on the geography and history of the Delta (free admission; open daily). Its 'Delta Sounds' exhibit nearby (141 Cherry St) features musical excerpts and an interactive blues display. The King Biscuit Time is broadcast live on KFFA 1360 AM, 12:15pm-12:45pm weekdays.

Chain motels are on US 49B in West Helena. **Edwardian Inn** (☎ *870-338-9155, 317 Biscoe St)* is a great old house with antique singles/doubles from $55/69 including breakfast. **Pasqualino's Tamales**, on Missouri St, is a local institution.

Tennessee

Geographically, Tennessee comprises three regions – the Great Smoky Mountains in the east, the central plateau around Nashville, and the Mississippi bottomlands in the west around Memphis. These regions embody the musical heritage of the state. This is where the mountain music from the East became the country music of the West and fused with the blues of the Mississippi Delta. It's also the place where a white boy adapted black rhythms and became the King of Rock & Roll.

History

European encroachment on this Cherokee territory began when de Soto wandered through in 1540. Though the British crown colony of Carolina nominally extended to the Mississippi, the French were actively trading on the rivers from the late 17th century. After the French and Indian War, Virginian pioneers soon established a settlement west of the Appalachians, creating their own treaty of purchase with the Cherokee. They drafted a written constitution that asserted their independence from British Carolina and were soon active participants in the American Revolution. After independence, Tennessee alternated between North Carolina and the US government, then acquired territorial status and eventually statehood.

Tennessee

Nickname: Volunteer State

Population: 5,689,000 (16th)

Area: 42,146 sq miles (36th)

Admitted to the Union: June 1, 1796 (16th); seceded 1861; readmitted 1866

Capital city: Nashville (population 545,000)

Other cities: Memphis (614,300), Knoxville (173,000), Chattanooga (156,000)

Birthplace of: Davy Crockett (1786–1836), Bessie Smith (1894–1937), Carl Perkins (1932–98), Aretha Franklin (b 1942), Dolly Parton (b 1946), rock & roll (arguably)

Famous for: Tennessee walking horses, the Tennessee Waltz, country music

Home of: the world's biggest cotton market; the world's first supermarket, Piggly Wiggly (1916)

Treaties in 1818 displaced the Chickasaw from west Tennessee, and President Andrew Jackson (himself an early Tennessee settler) imposed treaties that removed the last Native Americans from the state in the 1830s. While immigrants from Scotland, Ireland and the Eastern states established small farms in east Tennessee, the west was settled by planters from the Deep South, and the state became increasingly divided between the proslavery west and abolitionist east. Tennessee was the last state to secede in the Civil War, contributing 115,000 soldiers to the Confederacy, as well as 30,000 to the Union, and many battles were fought here.

Tennessee actually abolished slavery itself by popular vote in 1865 (the only state to do so), and it was the first Confederate state readmitted to the Union, thereby avoiding the worst of military occupation and Reconstruction. Nevertheless, there was a hostile reaction to Emancipation. The Ku Klux Klan (KKK), originally a social club, became influential in 'protecting whites' and disenfranchising the state's blacks by restrictive poll-tax laws.

In the early 20th century, 'New South' industries like timber, paper, iron and textiles overtook agriculture, while many farmers and sharecroppers suffered badly. The Depression hit hard, and drought added to farmers' woes. The Tennessee Valley Authority (TVA) was created as a New Deal project to provide flood control and hydroelectricity, and it became both a symbol and an engine of Tennessee's industrial growth. WWII munitions and manufacturing were a big boost, and the state is now the country's largest producer of aluminum and a major auto manufacturer. It was not until the 1960s that electoral reform and the civil-rights movement brought representative politics.

Information

The Tennessee Department of Tourist Development (☎ 615-741-8299, 800-462-8366, Ⓦ www.tnvacation.com, Rachel Jackson Bldg, 320 6th Ave N, Nashville, TN 37243) runs welcome centers at the state borders, with toll-free phones for accommodations bookings. For highway conditions, call ☎ 800-342-3258. State sales tax is 6%, and additional accommodations taxes run from around 3% to 5%.

MEMPHIS

Named for the ancient Egyptian capital on the Nile, Memphis on the Mississippi is best known as the capital of Elvis Presley idolatry and a musical heritage going back to the birth of the blues. Memphis is also a landmark of the civil-rights struggle, where Martin Luther King Jr was martyred in 1968. Today the city retains a certain soulful grittiness from its history of cotton, riverboats and black culture.

History

Bluffs on the eastern shore of the Mississippi River were occupied by a community of the sophisticated Mississippian civilization, who built mounds here over 1000 years ago. There was a Native American village here in 1541, when Hernando de Soto arrived. The French established Fort Assumption on the bluffs in 1739 to protect their river trade. After the US took control, a treaty in 1818 edged the Chickasaw nation out of western Tennessee, and Andrew Jackson helped found the settlement of Memphis. The city was incorporated in 1826 and prospered on

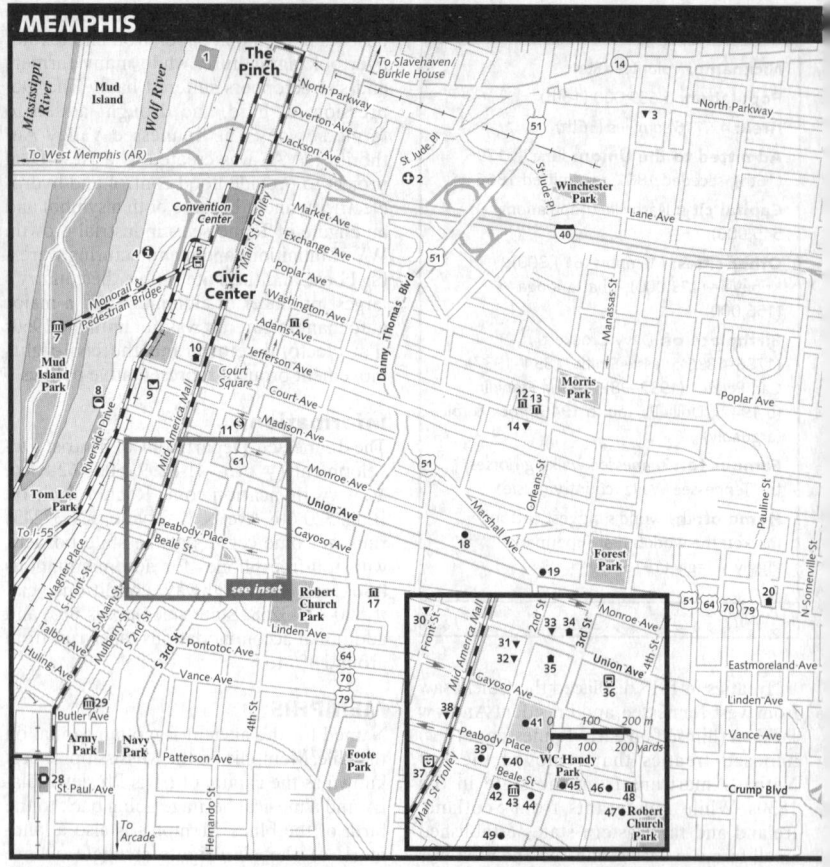

the expanding cotton trade of the Mississippi Delta.

Early in the Civil War a Union fleet defeated the Confederates and occupied the city, but the postwar collapse of the cotton trade was much more devastating. A yellow-fever epidemic in 1878 claimed more than 5000 lives, and the city was abandoned by many white residents. Memphis declared bankruptcy and its city charter was revoked until 1893. The black community revived the town. A former slave named Robert Church became a prominent landowner, civic leader and millionaire, and by the 1920s Beale St was the hub of social, civic and business activity, but it was equally well known as a place of gambling, drinking and prostitution.

WC Handy's 'Beale Street Blues' established Memphis as an early center of blues music, and in the 1950s local recording company Sun Records cut tracks for blues, soul, R&B and rockabilly artists, both white and black.

The old downtown was largely abandoned by the 1970s, and Beale St was nearly demolished to make way for 'redevelopment.' Instead, a restoration program was implemented, and a new entertainment district was created on the strip of old commercial buildings.

Orientation & Information

Downtown Memphis runs along the east bank of the Mississippi, with Riverside Dr and a promenade parallel to the river. The

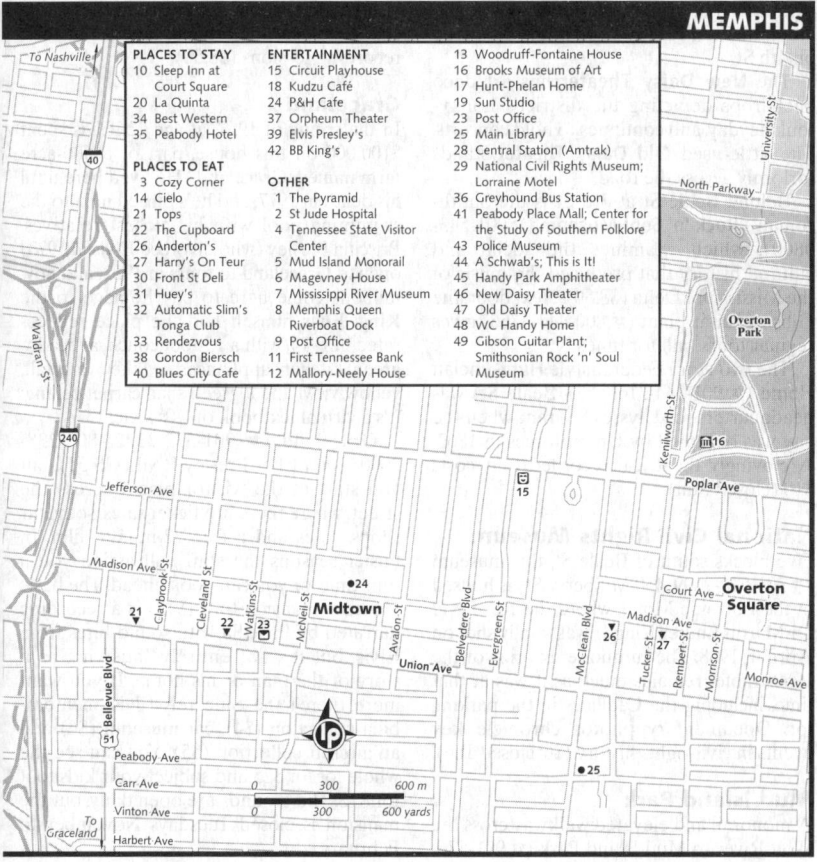

MEMPHIS

PLACES TO STAY
10 Sleep Inn at Court Square
20 La Quinta
34 Best Western
35 Peabody Hotel

PLACES TO EAT
3   Cozy Corner
14 Cielo
21 Tops
22 The Cupboard
26 Anderton's
27 Harry's On Teur
30 Front St Deli
31 Huey's
32 Automatic Slim's Tonga Club
33 Rendezvous
38 Gordon Biersch
40 Blues City Cafe

ENTERTAINMENT
15 Circuit Playhouse
18 Kudzu Café
24 P&H Cafe
37 Orpheum Theater
39 Elvis Presley's
42 BB King's

OTHER
1   The Pyramid
2   St Jude Hospital
4   Tennessee State Visitor Center
5   Mud Island Monorail
6   Magevney House
7   Mississippi River Museum
8   Memphis Queen Riverboat Dock
9   Post Office
11 First Tennessee Bank
12 Mallory-Neely House

13 Woodruff-Fontaine House
16 Brooks Museum of Art
17 Hunt-Phelan Home
19 Sun Studio
23 Post Office
25 Main Library
28 Central Station (Amtrak)
29 National Civil Rights Museum; Lorraine Motel
36 Greyhound Bus Station
41 Peabody Place Mall; Center for the Study of Southern Folklore
43 Police Museum
44 A Schwab's; This is It!
45 Handy Park Amphitheater
46 New Daisy Theater
47 Old Daisy Theater
48 WC Handy Home
49 Gibson Guitar Plant; Smithsonian Rock 'n' Soul Museum

THE SOUTH

principal tourist district is a bit inland, roughly the area bounded by Union Ave and 2nd, Beale and 4th Sts. Farther east, Union Ave and Overton Square have shops, bars and restaurants. Graceland is 3 miles south of town on US 51, also called 'Elvis Presley Blvd.'

The excellent Tennessee State Visitor Center (☎ 901-543-5333, 119 Riverside Dr) is open 24 hours. For news or entertainment listings, pick up the free weekly *Memphis Flyer*. The *Triangle Journal News* is a resource for the gay community. The public library (3030 Poplar Ave) has free Internet access.

Beale Street

The strip from 2nd to 4th Sts is filled with clubs, restaurants, souvenir shops and neon signs – a veritable theme park of the blues – though only one of the stores is an original from Beale St's heyday in the early 1900s.

The **Orpheum Theater**, at Main St, is restored to its 1928 glory, and an Elvis statue stands at the corner of 2nd Ave in front of a nightclub and restaurant called 'Elvis Presley's.'

Between 2nd and 3rd Sts, the **Walk of Fame** features musical notes embedded in the sidewalk with the names of well-known blues artists.

The Beale St substation **Police Museum** exhibits assorted criminalia, and the original **A Schwab's** dry-goods store has three floors of voodoo powders, 99¢ neckties, clerical collars and a big selection of hats. Between 3rd and 4th Sts, a statue of songwriter and composer WC Handy overlooks a park and amphitheater; Handy's old home is nearby on 4th St.

The **New Daisy Theater** has art deco backdrops depicting the district's honky-tonk heyday, and continues to hold concerts. The little-used **Old Daisy Theater** stands forlornly across the road.

Behind Beale St at 3rd St is the Smithsonian's **Rock 'n' Soul Museum** (☎ 901-543-0800), which examines the social and cultural history that produced the music of the Mississippi Delta ($8.50). Next door, the Gibson guitar plant (☎ 800-444-4766) gives regular tours; call for times.

The two-story Federal-style **Hunt-Phelan Home** (☎ 901-344-3166, 533 Beale St) was headquarters for Ulysses S Grant when the city was occupied by Union forces in 1862. A cloyingly theatrical recorded tour costs $10 (closed Sun).

National Civil Rights Museum

Five blocks south of Beale St, this museum (☎ 901-521-9699, 450 Mulberry St) is housed in the Lorraine Motel, where the Reverend Dr Martin Luther King Jr was fatally shot on April 4, 1968. The turquoise exterior of the 1950s motel remains much as it was at that time, including the Cadillacs in the parking lot. Documentary photos chronicle key events in civil-rights history ($6; closed Tue).

Mud Island Park

A monorail and elevated walkway cross the Wolf River to Mud Island Park (☎ 901-576-7241), where there's a model of the lower Mississippi River and the Gulf, and various exhibits in the Mississippi River Museum ($8; open mid-Apr to Oct, closed Mon in spring and fall).

Sun Studio

Starting in the early 1950s, Sam Phillips recorded blues artists like Howlin' Wolf, BB King and Ike Turner, followed by the Sun rockabilly dynasty of Jerry Lee Lewis, Carl Perkins, Johnny Cash, Roy Orbison and, of course, Elvis Presley (who started here in 1955 with 'Don't Be Cruel'). Sun Records moved on in 1959, but the studio reopened in 1987, and Ringo Starr, U2 and Def Leppard have all come here to record. Today the studio (☎ 901-521-0664, 706 Union Ave) offers a 30-minute narrated visit to a tiny room with warped tiles and a chance to hear the original tapes of historic recording sessions ($8.50).

Graceland

In the spring of 1957, at age 22, Elvis spent $100,000 on this house, part of a 500-acre farm named 'Graceland.' He lived here until his death in 1977, and he's buried next to the swimming pool with his closest relatives. Priscilla Presley (who divorced Elvis in 1973) opened Graceland to tours in 1982, and now millions come here to pay homage to the King. Elvis himself had the place redecorated in 1974, with a 15-foot couch, avocado-green kitchen appliances, a fake waterfall, yellow vinyl and a green shag carpet ceiling; it's a virtual textbook of '70s style.

Graceland (☎ 901-332-3322, 800-238-2000) is on Elvis Presley Blvd (US 51), but you start at the 'visitor plaza' across the street, where there are ticket sales, souvenir shops, cafes and a free 22-minute film. In busier seasons the staff will assign you a tour time, or you can book ahead. The basic 1½-hour mansion tour ($12) is a recording narrated by Priscilla with sound bites from Elvis, but it's not entirely satisfying as a story of the man or his home. If you want more, there's the 'Sincerely Elvis' memorabilia collection ($4), car museum ($6) and an aircraft collection ($5). You can see the whole lot for $25 and subject your kids to it for $12. The grounds are open daily, but the mansion is closed Tuesdays November to February.

Historic Houses

In the 'Victorian Village' district on Adams Ave, east of downtown, two grand houses are open for public tours: the 1870 Woodruff-Fontaine House (☎ 901-526-1469, 680 Adams Ave) and the 1852 Mallory-Neely House (☎ 901-523-1484, 652 Adams Ave), both for $5. The smaller Magevney House (☎ 901-526-4464, 198 Adams Ave) reflects the lifestyle of a 19th-century Irish immigrant family (free admission).

The **Slavehaven/Burkle House** (☎ 901-527-3427, 826 N 2nd St) is thought to have been a way station for runaway slaves on the Underground Railroad; check out the trapdoors and tunnels ($5/3 adults/kids; tours Thurs-Sat and Mon).

Reverend Green's Gospel

Some of Memphis' most soulful music isn't heard in the Beale St clubs, but rather at the Full Gospel Tabernacle presided over by '70s recording star Al Green. Reverend Green's powerful oratory is backed by electric guitar and a formidable choir. Visitors are welcome to attend the 2½-hour service (11am Sun). The church (☎ 901-396-9192, 787 Hale Rd) is in Whitehaven, four traffic lights south of Graceland off Elvis Presley Blvd.

Museums

Within Overton Park (a greenway that's surrounded by stately homes), the **Brooks Museum of Art** (☎ 901-544-6200) has a varied collection from Peruvian effigy vessels to spray-paint art ($5; closed Mon).

The **Pink Palace Museum & Planetarium** (☎ 901-320-6362, 3050 Central Ave), east of town off US 72, was built here in 1923 as a residence for Piggly Wiggly founder Clarence Saunders and reopened in 1996 as a natural- and cultural-history museum. It mixes fossils, Civil War exhibits, restored Works Projects Administration (WPA) murals and an exact replica of the original Piggly Wiggly, the world's first self-service grocery store ($6, free Thurs evening).

Also east of town, the **Dixon Gallery** (☎ 901-761-5250, 4339 Park Ave) houses an impressive collection of impressionist and postimpressionist paintings, including works by Monet, Degas, Renoir and Cézanne ($5; closed Mon).

The **Center for the Study of Southern Folklore** (☎ 901-525-3655, 119 S Main St), in the Peabody Place Mall, exhibits arts and crafts and holds music performances, local tours and film screenings.

On a bluff south of downtown Memphis, **Chucalissa Archaeological Site & Museum** (☎ 901-785-3160) has a reconstructed 15th-century Native American village, with exhibits and demonstrations about the sophisticated Mississippian civilization that once dominated much of the Mississippi River valley. It's built on the site of ancient earthwork, with a revealing cutaway trench ($5; closed Mon).

Organized Tours

Riverboat rides aboard the *Memphis Queen* (☎ 901-527-5694) depart from the foot of Monroe Ave at Riverside Dr, starting at $12 for a 1½-hour sightseeing tour. Gray Line (☎ 901-346-8687) does bus tours, or try a horse-drawn carriage tour (☎ 901-527-7542) departing from Beale St or outside the Peabody Hotel (30-minute ride for two passengers around $25). The Center for the Study of Southern Folklore (see Museums) offers cultural-heritage walking tours of the neighborhood.

Places to Stay

The **KOA Kampground** (☎ 901-396-7125, 3691 Elvis Presley Blvd), practically across the street from Graceland, has campsites from $21 (hookups extra) and cabins ($36). South of town off Hwy 61, **TO Fuller State Park** (☎ 901-543-7581) has 53 tent sites on a remote bluff ($13).

Total tax on accommodations is a stiff 15%. **La Quinta** (☎ 901-526-1050, 42 S Camilla St), at Union Ave a half-mile east of downtown, charges $45/55 for singles/doubles. **Best Western** (☎ 901-527-4100, 164 Union Ave) is only three blocks from Beale St; OK rooms are $65. **Sleep Inn at Court Square** (☎ 901-522-9700, 40 N Front St) has a great location near the river (from $79). Better-value budget motels are across the river in West Memphis, where chain places cluster at I-40 exit 279.

Half a block from Graceland, **Days Inn** (☎ 901-346-5500, 3839 Elvis Presley Blvd) features a guitar-shaped swimming pool and 24-hour in-room Elvis movies (from $89). Behind Graceland's parking lot, **Heartbreak Hotel** (☎ 901-332-1000, 800-945-7667, 3677 Elvis Presley Blvd) has a Gracelandish lobby and Elvis movies in the rooms (from $97).

The landmark **Peabody Hotel** (☎ 901-529-4000, 800-732-2639, 149 Union Ave) is the classiest place to stay, with rooms starting at $195/225. It's a social center in Memphis, and it boasts its own quirky (quacky?) tradition: At 11am sharp, the hotel's ducks file from the elevator across the red-carpeted lobby to cavort in the fountain until 5pm, when they return to their penthouse.

The small and tidy **Skyport Inn** (☎ 901-345-3220), in the airport's terminal A, has bargain rooms from $40, not far from Graceland.

Places to Eat

The Memphis specialty is barbecue, specifically chopped pork shoulder, often served in a sandwich. The famous *Cozy Corner* (745 North Pkwy) serves its trademark dry-rub pulled pork under multicolored lights, with Aretha Franklin on the jukebox. *Rendezvous*, tucked in an alleyway off Union Ave, sells 5 tons of barbecue ribs weekly (closed Sun-Mon). *Front St Deli* (77 S Front St), featured in the movie *The Firm*, makes great sandwiches.

For lunch or dinner on the strip, *Blues City Cafe* (138 Beale St) is a good choice, though it's often packed. *Huey's* (77 S 2nd St), at Union Ave, is a casual pub with burgers, beer and live entertainment. *Automatic Slim's Tonga Club* (☎ 901-525-7948, 83 S 2nd St) serves slow-roasted yellowfin tuna, jerk duck and voodoo stew in an artsy interior. Entrées are about $15 at dinner, less at lunchtime (closed Sun). *Gordon Biersch* (145 S Main St) is a handsome brewery/bar with hearty food and sports TV. Completely different is *Cielo* (☎ 901-524-1886, 679 Adams Ave), where creative cuisine is served in a Victorian manor (entrées around $20).

In Midtown, assorted eateries include *Tops* (1286 Union Ave), a link in a local chain of decent barbecue joints. *The Cupboard* (1400 Union Ave) serves Southern gems like fresh buttered squash and catfish fillet. A Memphis institution since 1945, *Anderton's* (1901 Madison Ave) serves steaks and seafood. *Harry's On Teur* (2015 Madison Ave) is an old favorite for veggie dishes and pecan-smoked sausages.

Entertainment

Beale St features lots of live blues at clubs, saloons and theaters, mostly on weekend nights, when the two-block strip is closed to traffic. Cover for most clubs is only a few dollars. The fancy *Elvis Presley's* (☎ 901-527-9036, 126 Beale St) and *BB King's* (☎ 901-524-5464, 143 Beale St) both aim for a swank, supper-club atmosphere. Farther east, *This is It!* (☎ 901-527-8200, 167 Beale St) is another lively option. Near downtown, *Kudzu Café* (☎ 901-525-4924, 603 Monroe Ave) has comedy and regular pickin' contests.

In Midtown, check out *P&H Cafe* (☎ 901-726-0906, 1532 Madison Ave). Run by colorful matriarch Wanda Wilson, it hosts an annual Dead Elvis Ball each August.

The *Orpheum Theater* (☎ 901-525-7800, 203 S Main St) is a 1928-era vaudeville palace, recently restored as a venue for Broadway shows and major concerts. *Circuit Playhouse* (☎ 901-726-4656, 1705 Poplar Ave), in Overton Square, offers alternative drama.

Sports fans can check out the *Memphis Redbirds* (☎ 901-721-6000), a AAA minor-league baseball team that plays at the 15,000-seat Autozone Park. For basketball, the NBA's *Memphis Grizzlies* (☎ 901-678-2331), formerly in Vancouver, play at The Pyramid.

Getting There & Around

Memphis International Airport (☎ 901-922-8000) is 20 miles southeast of downtown via I-55; a taxi to or from downtown will run about $28.

Greyhound (☎ 901-523-1184, 203 Union Ave) runs frequent buses to Nashville ($27; 4 hours); Little Rock, Arkansas ($19; 2½ hours); and New Orleans, Louisiana ($40; 8 to 10 hours).

Central Station (☎ 901-526-0052, 545 S Main St), the Amtrak terminal, has been restored to its original 1914 splendor. The *City of New Orleans* goes to Chicago, Illinois (from $84; 10½ hours), and New Orleans, Louisiana (from $44; 8 hours).

Local buses run by the Memphis Area Transit Authority (MATA; ☎ 901-722-7100) are of little use to visitors. The Main St trolley (☎ 901-274-6282) runs vintage trolley cars on a loop from the Amtrak station to the Pyramid via Main St and Riverside Dr ($1).

AROUND MEMPHIS

Near the Mississippi border, 100 miles east of Memphis, **Shiloh National Military Park** (☎ 901-689-5275) commemorates the famous Civil War battle of Shiloh. The visitor center shows a film describing military strategy and distributes an self-guided-tour map of the monuments and battlefields ($2/4 per person/family).

In the northwestern corner of the state, 110 miles north of Memphis, **Reelfoot National Wildlife Refuge** is a good place to see the bald eagles who take up winter residence here December to March. Reelfoot Lake is also noted for its water lilies, large cypress trees, rampant vines and other bizarre vegetation. It was created when the 1811–12 New Madrid earthquakes lowered the ground level and the Mississippi flooded into the depression. The visitor center (☎ 901-253-7756) is a few miles east of Tiptonville, which has food and lodging.

NASHVILLE

The country-music capital of the world, Nashville (nash-vul) offers a musical experience for everyone, from rough blues bars to the Grand Ole Opry House. It also has friendly people, cheap food and an unrivaled assortment of tacky souvenirs. Once a mainstay of the city, the kitschy Opryland theme park has been replaced by an upscale shopping mall and is scarcely missed.

History

Ancient moundbuilders and the wandering Shawnee occupied the Cumberland River bluffs for centuries before Europeans established Fort Nashborough, in 1779. The legendary Daniel Boone brought emigrants on his Wilderness Road over the Appalachians from Virginia, the Carolinas and Northeastern states.

Renamed 'Nashville' around 1784, the town was an important railroad junction with a riverboat connection to the Mississippi, and a strategic point during the Civil War. It surrendered to federal troops in 1862, and Andrew Johnson (then a US senator) was appointed military governor, imposing martial law until 1865. In the 1864 Battle of Nashville, south of the city, Confederate General Thomas Hood's troops were destroyed. Nashville survived the war intact, though its postwar recovery was hampered by two major cholera epidemics. The Tennessee Centennial Exposition in 1897 signaled the city's eventual recovery.

From 1925, Nashville became known for its live-broadcast Barn Dance, later nicknamed the 'Grand Ole Opry.' Its popularity soared, the city proclaimed itself the 'country-music capital of the world,' and recording studios and production companies established themselves along Music Row, just west of downtown. The Fisk Jubilee Singers built on another musical tradition in the 1870s, popularizing black spirituals with benefit tours for Fisk University, a struggling black college. Ninety years later, Fisk students led sit-in demonstrations at downtown lunch counters, supported economic boycotts and marched on city hall to demand desegregated facilities.

Orientation & Information

Nashville sits on a rise beside the Cumberland River, with the capitol at the highest point. The compact downtown slopes south to Broadway, the city's central artery. Historic commercial buildings along 2nd Ave and Broadway have been renovated as an entertainment area called 'the District,' where old-favorite dives and rib joints sit alongside slick new places like the Hard Rock Cafe. Elliston Place is a stretch of alternative culture a mile or so west of downtown, with restaurants along Broadway and West End Ave near Vanderbilt University. Off the Briley Pkwy northeast of town, Music Valley is a tourist ghetto of budget motels, franchise restaurants and outlet stores built around the Grand Old Opry.

The central visitor center (☎ 615-259-4747) is in the space-age tower adjacent to the new arena at Broadway and 5th Ave. The convention center (☎ 615-259-4700, 800-657-6910, 211 Commerce St) maintains a 24-hour hotline (☎ 615-244-9393). The free alternative weeklies *Nashville Scene* and *The Rage* cover local entertainment and news. The public library at Church and 7th Sts allows free Web access.

Downtown

It's pleasant to walk around downtown, where tall office buildings and modern halls don't overwhelm the city's historic structures. The 1845 Greek Revival **state capitol** is the principal landmark, with steep stairs leading down the northern side to the Farmers Market and the Tennessee Bicentennial Mall.

To the south of the capitol, government buildings surround Legislative Plaza, where the cherry trees blossom in the spring. The Performing Arts Center covers an adjacent block and houses the **Tennessee State Museum** (☎ 615-741-2692), which traces the state's history from effigy pots of ancient tribes to pioneer daguerreotypes and Confederate dollars. Exhibits cover the abolitionist movement from as early as 1797, as well as the KKK, which began here in 1868 (free admission; closed Mon).

THE SOUTH

NASHVILLE

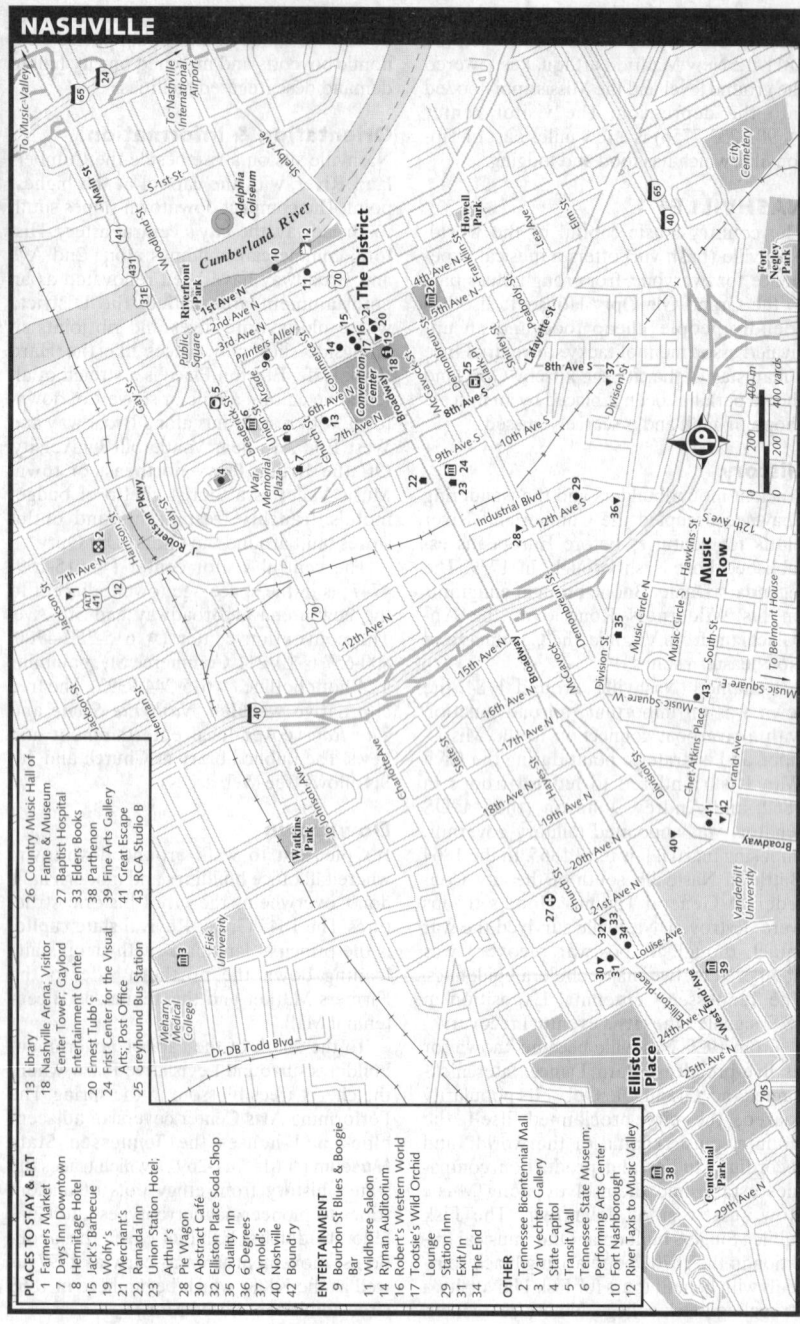

The historic 2nd Ave N business area was the center of the cotton trade in the 1870s and '80s, when most of the Victorian warehouses were built; note the cast-iron and masonry facades. Today it's the heart of **the District**, with shops, restaurants, underground saloons and nightclubs. Two blocks west, Printers Alley is a narrow cobblestone lane known for its nightlife since the 1940s.

The monumental **Country Music Hall of Fame & Museum** (☎ 615-416-2001, 222 5th Ave) is a great introduction to Nashville and country music. It's chock-full of artifacts like Elvis' gold Cadillac, Gene Autry's string tie and the handwritten lyrics to 'Mamas Don't Let Your Babies Grow Up to Be Cowboys' ($15/8 adults/kids; open daily). Everything's state-of-the-art, and touch screens allow access to recordings and photos from the Country Music Foundation's enormous archives.

Along the Cumberland River, Riverfront Park is a shady, landscaped promenade featuring **Fort Nashborough**, a 1930s replica of the city's original outpost, and a dock from which river taxis cruise out to Music Valley.

The **Ryman Auditorium** (116 5th Ave N) was built in 1890 by a former riverboat captain. Thomas Ryman 'got the call' late in life and dedicated this huge, gabled, brick tabernacle to spiritual music. It has been used for various performances, including the Saturday-night Barn Dance, later dubbed the 'Grand Ole Opry.' The Opry stayed here for 31 years, until it moved out to the Opryland complex in 1974. The Ryman reopened in 1994, and it's a great place to see a show, or just to view the fine interior: You can do a self-guided tour of the empty theater ($5.50; open daily).

Behind the glamorous Ryman, there's a seedy cowboy strip on 'Lower Broad' between 4th and 5th Aves, with barbecue joints, country bars and adult bookstores.

The new **Frist Center for the Visual Arts** (☎ 615-244-3340, 919 Broadway) hosts traveling exhibitions of anything and everything from American folk art to the European masters. It's in a grand, refurbished post office building.

West End

Nashville's West End consists of Music Row, home of the production companies, agents, managers and promoters who run Nashville's country-music industry, and Elliston Place, home to a tiny bohemia anchored by the ancient Elliston Place Soda Shop and Elders Books.

RCA Studio B (30 Music Square E) is the 1950s studio credited with producing the original 'Nashville Sound.' It's a working studio again, but group tours are by appointment only (☎ 615-514-2200).

The Centennial Exposition of Tennessee was held in **Centennial Park** in 1897; its centerpiece is a full-scale plaster reproduction of the Parthenon, symbolizing Nashville as the 'Athens of the South.' The Parthenon proved so popular that a second, more permanent replacement was built in the 1930s. Inside is an art museum with a good American collection ($3.50) and a 42-foot statue of Athena.

South of Centennial Park, the campus of Vanderbilt University maintains a **Fine Arts Gallery** (☎ 615-322-0605) at 23rd and West End Aves (free admission; open afternoons only). North of Centennial Park, at Fisk University, the small **Van Vechten Gallery** (☎ 615-329-8720) has works by Alfred Stieglitz, Georgia O'Keeffe, Picasso, Renoir and Cézanne (donations appreciated; closed Mon and university holidays). The Fisk's fine African art collection is in the Aaron Douglas Gallery.

Music Valley

This suburban tourist zone is about 10 miles northeast of downtown at Hwy 155 (Briley Pkwy) exits 11 and 12B, and also reachable by riverboat. Shuttle buses ($3) run around the zone from the Grand Ole Opry House at the south to the KOA Kampground in the north.

The **Grand Ole Opry House** (☎ 615-889-3060) seats 4400 fans for the Grand Ole

---

Rocky Top & Roll

Tennessee may be the only member of the US to boast a state song celebrating casual sex and illegal alcohol consumption. Rocky Top warbles wistfully for a girl 'wild as a mink but sweet as soda pop' and folk who 'get their corn from a jar' (in other words, moonshine).

☺ ☺ ☺ ☺ ☺ ☺ ☺ ☺ ☺ ☺ ☹ ☺

Opry Friday and Saturday night year round (see Entertainment, later). Guided backstage tours are offered daily by reservation ($9). The museum across the plaza tells the story of the Opry with wax characters, colorful costumes and artifacts (free admission). Don't miss the Patsy Cline classic – a 1950s rec-room diorama.

Next door, on the former site of Opryland, the Opry Mills mall houses an IMAX cinema, theme restaurants and the **Gibson Bluegrass Showcase** (☎ 615-514-2200), a working factory and concert venue where you can see banjos, mandolins and resonator guitars being made through the glass.

Exit 12B goes to the Opryland Hotel as well as several other **museums**: The Music Valley Car Museum (☎ 615-885-7400), with an Elvis limo; Music City Wax Museum (☎ 615-883-3612), with stacks of wax statues of costumed country stars; and the Willie Nelson Museum (☎ 615-885-1515), with guitars and gold records. They all charge about $3.50.

Historic Houses

Andrew Jackson's former home, **The Hermitage** (☎ 615-889-2941) is northeast of town off Lebanon Pike at Old Hickory Blvd. A museum and monument to the state's most famous political figure and the seventh US president, it was once the hub of a cotton plantation with 150 slaves. The elegant 1821 house is in Federal style, with Palladian flourishes and Grecian columns added in the 1830s ($10).

Other antebellum delights are the 1853 Greek Revival **Belle Meade Plantation** (☎ 615-356-0501, 5025 Harding Place), 10 miles southwest of town ($10), and the 1850 **Belmont Mansion** (☎ 615-460-5459, 1900 Belmont Blvd), where they let you in for $7.

Places to Stay

At the north end of Music Valley, *Opryland KOA Kampground* (☎ 615-889-0282, 800-562-7789, 2626 Music Valley Dr) has a pool, every convenience and tent/RV sites for $22/35. At J Percy Priest Lake, about 12 miles east of downtown at I-40 exit 221, *Seven Points* (☎ 615-889-5198) has tent and RV sites ($17-21) and nice swimming.

There's a cluster of budget motels north of downtown, at I-65 exit 87B, including *Knights Inn* (☎ 615-226-4500, 1360 Brick Church Pike), *Hallmark Inn* (☎ 615-228-2624, 309 W Trinity Lane) and *Motel 6* (☎ 615-227-9696) next door. They all charge from around $34/40 for singles/doubles.

Days Inn Downtown (☎ 615-242-4311, 711 Union St) is near the capitol (singles/doubles $80/88). The new 284-room *Ramada Inn* (☎ 244-0150, 920 Broadway) is convenient to the District (from $89). At Music Row, *Quality Inn* (☎ 615-242-1631, 1407 Division St) charges from $49/59. Much classier, the 1900 *Union Station Hotel* (☎ 615-726-1001, 800-331-2123, 1001 Broadway) is grandly restored and costs $124-139; elegant *Hermitage Hotel* (☎ 615-244-3121, 231 6th Ave N) starts at $109.

In Music Valley, family-oriented tourist motels include *Fiddlers Inn North* (☎ 615-885-1440, 2410 Music Valley Dr), at $70 in peak season; it has a pool. Sprawling *Opryland Hotel* (☎ 615-889-1000, 2800 Opryland Dr) features a self-contained 'Oprysphere' with waterfalls, boat rides, magnolia trees and an elevated walkway above the rainforest. Rates start at $200.

Places to Eat

The *Farmers Market*, along 8th Ave N at Jefferson St, holds a great variety of cheap food, with stands selling gyros, empanadas, muffulettas, Reubens and more. Two blocks north, *Mad Platter* (☎ 615-242-2563, 1239 6th Ave N) has an innovative, upscale eclectic menu (entrées around $20).

In the District, *Jack's Barbecue (416A Broadway)* packs 'em in for cheap brisket, ribs and smoked turkey. *Wolfy's (425 Broadway)* does good burgers and a fine veggie Reuben, with live music. It's best to reserve at *Merchant's (☎ 615-254-1892, 401 Broadway)* for pricey seafood, steaks, pastas and great window seats. *Arthur's (☎ 615-254-1494)*, in the Union Station Hotel, serves $60 fixed-price dinners to the *Southern Living* set.

The true taste of Nashville can best be found in cinder-block cabins in the industrial zone south of Broadway, where meat-and-threes come in heaping portions. Look for the line outside *Arnold's (605 8th Ave S)* or *Pie Wagon (118 12th Ave S)*. Both are open weekdays for breakfast and lunch. *6 Degrees (☎ 615-244-3888, 601 12th Ave S)* serves sophisticated dishes in a recycled warehouse for $15-30, with live noncountry music.

Elliston Place Soda Shop (2111 Elliston Place) serves soda fountain treats along with meat-and-three plates 6am-7:45pm (closed Sun). Panini, artwork and grunge rock go hand in hand at *Abstract Cafe* (☎ 615-321-9033, 205 22nd Ave N).

Near Music Row, *Bound'ry (911 20th Ave S)* has a lengthy nouveau Southern menu and classy to kitschy decor, while *Noshville (1918 Broadway)* offers New York deli specialties (lox, borscht, pickles) in a crisp chrome interior.

Entertainment

Apart from the big venues, many talented country, folk, bluegrass, Southern-rock and blues performers play smoky honky-tonks, blues bars, seedy storefronts and organic cafes for tips. Check what's on at the *Ryman Auditorium (☎ 615-254-1445)*. The *Grand Ole Opry (☎ 615-889-3060)* always has a lavish production Friday and Saturday evenings (from $23).

Catch 'New Country' dance music at *Wildhorse Saloon (120 2nd Ave N)*, which offers free dance lessons 4pm-9pm. The 'Lower Broad' cowboy gulch has clubs ranging from raunchy to respectable. The best is *Robert's Western World (☎ 615-256-7937, 417 Broadway)*, while *Tootsie's Wild Orchid Lounge (☎ 615-726-7937, 422 Broadway)* is a venerated dive.

The classic bluegrass venue is *Station Inn (☎ 615-255-3307, 402 12th Ave S)*. Unassuming *Bluebird Cafe (☎ 615-383-1461, 4104 Hillsboro Rd)*, in a strip mall in suburban Green Hills (2½ miles south of I-440 exit 3), attracts some of the city's most talented musicians.

Try *Exit/In (☎ 615-321-4400)*, at Elliston Place and 23rd Ave N, or *The End (☎ 615-321-4400, 2219 Elliston Place)* for rock and alternative music. *Bourbon St Blues & Boogie Bar (☎ 615-242-5837, 220 Printers Alley)* is the city's premier blues venue.

Spectator Sports

The NFL Tennessee Titans (☎ 615-565-4000), veterans of the 1999 Super Bowl, play in Adelphia Coliseum, across the river from downtown. The Nashville Sounds (☎ 615-242-4371), a minor-league AAA baseball team for the Pittsburgh Pirates, play at Greer Stadium, south of town. For NHL professional hockey, catch the Nashville Predators (☎ 615-770-7825) at Gaylord Entertainment Center.

Shopping

Nashville's music stores are numerous and well stocked. Try Great Escape (☎ 615-327-0646, 1925 Broadway) for new and used CDs or records of all genres, comic books and videos. Ernest Tubb's (☎ 615-255-7503, 417 Broadway) has a great selection of country and bluegrass.

Getting There & Around

Nashville International Airport (☎ 615-275-1662), 8 miles east of town, is not a major air hub. MTA bus No 18 links the airport and downtown ($1.45); the Gray Line Airport Express (☎ 615-883-5555) serves major downtown and West End hotels ($11, roundtrip $17).

The busy Greyhound station (☎ 615-255-3556, 200 8th Ave S) has frequent buses to Memphis ($27; 4 hours); Atlanta, Georgia ($37; 6 hours); Birmingham, Alabama ($26; from 3½ hours); and New Orleans, Louisiana ($43; from 13 hours).

You can get around downtown and Music Valley without a car. Between the two, take a river taxi (☎ 615-871-5701) along the Cumberland River ($13 roundtrip). The Metropolitan Transit Authority (MTA; ☎ 615-862-5950) operates city bus services ($1.45) based at the downtown transit mall at Deaderick St and 4th Ave N. A trolleylike shuttle also goes between major tourist sites at the riverfront and out to Music Row ($1).

AROUND NASHVILLE

About 25 miles southwest of Nashville off Hwy 100, drivers pick up the Natchez Trace Pkwy, which leads 450 miles southwest to Natchez, Mississippi. This northern section is one of the most attractive stretches of the entire route. Near the parkway entrance, look for the landmark *Loveless Cafe (☎ 615-646-9700, 8400 Hwy 100)*. It's a 1940s roadhouse serving ample portions of Southern country cooking (reserve on weekends).

EASTERN TENNESSEE

Probably the least 'Southern' place in this chapter, eastern Tennessee is a largely rural region with unhurried towns dotting the

THE SOUTH

MUSIC IN THE SOUTH

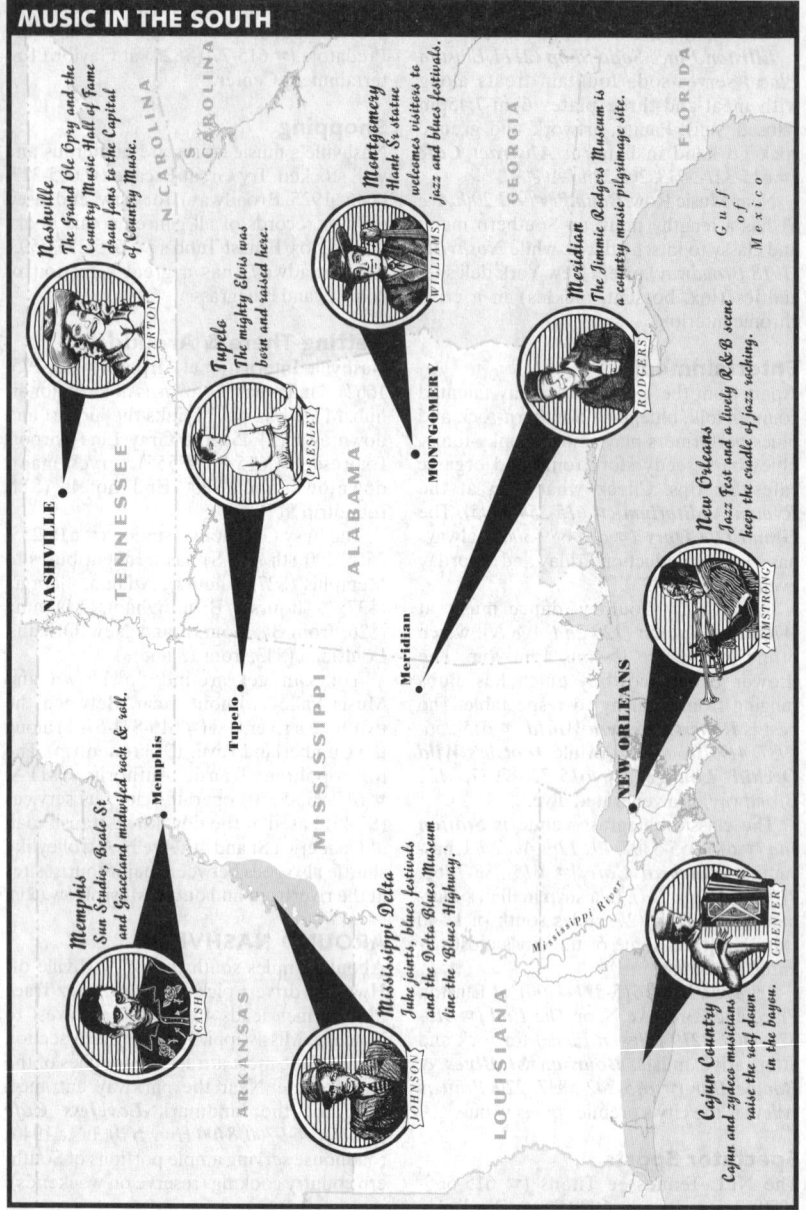

Nashville
The Grand Ole Opry and the Country Music Hall of Fame draw fans to the Capital of Country Music. (PARTON)

Tupelo
The mighty Elvis was born and raised here. (PRESLEY)

Montgomery
Hank St statue welcomes visitors to jazz and blues festivals. (WILLIAMS)

Meridian
The Jimmie Rodgers Museum is a country music pilgrimage site. (RODGERS)

Memphis
Sun Studios, Beale St and Graceland midwifed rock & roll. (CASH)

Mississippi Delta
Juke joints, blues festivals and the Delta Blues Museum line the Blues Highway. (JOHNSON)

New Orleans
Jazz Fest and a lively R&B scene keep the cradle of jazz rocking. (ARMSTRONG)

Cajun Country
Cajun and zydeco musicians raise the roof down in the bayou. (CHENIER)

N CAROLINA
S CAROLINA
GEORGIA
FLORIDA
Gulf of Mexico
TENNESSEE
ALABAMA
MISSISSIPPI
LOUISIANA
ARKANSAS

NASHVILLE
MONTGOMERY
Tupelo
Meridian
Memphis
NEW ORLEANS

Mississippi River

hills and river valleys. Nature is the biggest draw, with the Great Smoky Mountains for bear spotting, hiking and camping, the white waters of the Ocoee River for rafting, and a portion of the Appalachian Trail.

Chattanooga

Chattanooga was born of one of the great injustices of the early USA: the removal of the Cherokee along what became known as the Trail of Tears. One of the trail's two starting points was Ross's Landing in what is now downtown Chattanooga.

Once the Indians were gone, the city grew quickly. It was a key strategic point during the Civil War, and several important battles were fought nearby at Lookout Mountain and Chickamauga. After the war it became a major transport hub, hence the 'Chattanooga Choo-Choo,' originally a reference to the Cincinnati Southern Railroad's passenger service from Cincinnati to Chattanooga and later the title of a Glenn Miller song.

Today, Chattanooga is one of the most interesting – and most often overlooked – small cities in the South. The local tourist industry plays quite heavily on the song 'The Most Famous Train in the World Returns to Track 29,' but those with sharp memories will remember that the musical train was going *to* Tennessee, and the famous Track 29 is actually at Penn Station in New York.

Orientation & Information Downtown Chattanooga occupies a relatively small area between the Tennessee River and ML King Jr Blvd along Chestnut, Broad and Market Sts. Lookout Mountain, site of a major Civil War battle and home to a number of the city's attractions, is a few miles southwest of the center.

Most of Chattanooga's main sites are within a few blocks of the visitor center (☎ 423-856-8687, 800-322-3344) at the corner of 2nd and Broad Sts (open daily). It's a good spot for maps, lodging and dining information, and sells tickets to most local attractions. Check your email at Greyfriar's (see Places to Stay & Eat, later).

Things to See & Do Downtown, the architectural centerpiece is the **Tennessee Aquarium** (☎ 800-262-0695). It is set up to mirror a large river system and is often visited by school groups from around the region ($13/7 adults/kids; open 10am-6pm daily, until 8pm Fri-Sun in summer). Nearby, Ross's Landing is a good place for a riverfront stroll. A bit farther afield, the Bluff View Art District has a few upscale shops and restaurants overlooking the river and is the location of the **Hunter Museum of American Art** (☎ 423-267-0968), with works by Ansel Adams and Willem de Kooning ($5; closed Mon).

The **Chattanooga Regional History Museum** (☎ 423-265-3247, 400 Chestnut St) is also well regarded ($4). Also worth a visit is the **Chattanooga African-American Museum** (☎ 423-266-8658, 200 ML King Jr Blvd), especially for the exhibit on Chattanooga native Bessie Smith ($5; closed Sun). More bizarre is the **International Towing & Recovery Hall of Fame and Museum** (☎ 423-267-3132, 401 Broad St). Yes, it's a tow-truck museum (celebrating a Chattanoogan invention) and well worth the $3.50 admission just for the curiosity value.

Some of Chattanooga's oldest and best-known attractions are outside the city at nearby **Lookout Mountain**. These include the Incline Railway, underground caverns called 'Ruby Falls' and Rock City – a garden with a dramatic clifftop overlook that is just inside Georgia. All of these cost $9-12 each, though combination tickets are available. **Point Park**, at the mountain's summit, is part of the National Park Service's Chickamauga and Chattanooga National Military Park complex. Entry to the visitor center (☎ 423-866-9241) is free, but admission to the park costs $2.

Next door, **The Battles for Chattanooga Electric Map & Museum** (☎ 423-821-2812) is a private museum laying out Chattanooga's role in the Civil War ($5). See the Georgia chapter for details of the main Chickamauga battlefield.

Places to Stay & Eat There are many, many campgrounds around Chattanooga. The *KOA Chattanooga North* (☎ 423-472-8928) is 15 miles north at I-75 exit 20. To the west, try *Raccoon Mountain RV Park & Campground* (☎ 423-821-9403), at I-24 exit 174 ($12/20 for tent/RV sites).

Total tax on accommodations is 13%. The closest cheapies to downtown are in the less than wonderful area around I-24 exit

178. *Motel 6* (☎ 423-265-7300) charges $35/40 for singles/doubles, while nicer *Comfort Suites* (☎ 423-265-0008) charges $69/79. *King's Lodge* (☎ 423-698-8944), exit 181A, charges $30/35 year round for spacious rooms with fridges.

If you're going to splurge, there are really only two choices. *Chattanooga Choo-Choo Holiday Inn* (☎ 423-266-5000, 1400 Market St) is in the old railway terminal. Basic rates are $99 (nothing special) and $125 for neat rooms in converted railcars. Downtown, *Radisson Read House* (☎ 423-266-4121, 827 Broad St) is a meticulously restored early-20th-century hotel, parts of which date from the Civil War era. Rooms in the charming old section cost $110-120, less with discounts.

In the center, locals agree that *Sticky Fingers* (420 Broad St) has the best rib dinners in town ($10-15). Try the sampler, which gives you a taste of all four varieties. Another good bet is *Big River Grill & Brewing Works* (222 Broad St), with an extensive menu of sandwiches, pasta, steaks and Mexican food. For breakfast, a quiet cup of coffee or Web access, try *Greyfriar's* (406B Broad St).

Getting There & Around Chattanooga's modest airport is just east of the city. The Greyhound station (☎ 423-892-1277, 960 Airport Rd) is nearby, opposite Shepherd St. There are eight buses daily to Atlanta, Georgia ($17; 2 hours), and three per day to Nashville ($18; from 2½ hours). Change at Nashville for Memphis ($38; from 9 hours). There are also four buses per day to Knoxville ($14; 2 hours).

Proving that it has no sense of nostalgia, Amtrak does not serve Chattanooga.

For access to most downtown sites, ride the free electric shuttle buses that ply the center. The visitor center has a route map.

Knoxville & Around

Knoxville was once Tennessee's territorial capital and is now the seat of the state university. It's a good base for exploring the region, but not much of an attraction itself. The Gateway visitor center (☎ 865-523-7263, 800-727-8045) is on the riverfront off I-40 exit 388A.

The city's visual centerpiece is the **Sun-sphere**, the main remnant of the 1982 World Fair, with a fun free elevator ride to the top.

Until early 2002 the tower will remain closed owing to construction of a new convention center. The **Knoxville Museum of Art** (☎ 865-525-6101), on 10th St, is worth a visit for its rotating exhibits focusing on American artists ($7; closed Mon).

On the edge of downtown are two noteworthy historical sites. The 1792 **Blount Mansion** (☎ 865-525-2375), at W Hill and S Gay Sts, was the governor's residence when Knoxville served as the capital of all US territories south of the Ohio River ($5; open Tue-Fri). A few blocks up W Hill St is a replica of **James White's Fort** (☎ 865-525-6514). The original, built in 1786, was the town's first house ($4; closed Sun).

Just south of the city is the **Sam Houston Schoolhouse** (☎ 865-983-1550). Houston taught here for five months in 1812 before joining the army. He later achieved fame as governor of Tennessee, president of the Republic of Texas and US senator once Texas became a state. The one-room schoolhouse was built in 1794. It is set in a beautiful rural area off Route 33 (50¢; closed Mon). Go south for 10 miles from the center of Knoxville, turn left, then left again; it's well signposted.

The sleek **Women's Basketball Hall of Fame** (☎ 865-633-9000, 700 Hall of Fame Dr) features memorabilia, a touring wagon owned by the All-American Redheads, and practice courts downstairs ($8/6 adults/kids).

The *KOA Kampground* (☎ 865-933-6369), at I-40/I-75 exit 117, is your best bet for camping close to the city. You'll also find a lot of RV parks about an hour south of the city heading toward Pigeon Forge and Gatlinburg. There are no cheap motels in the center. Your best bets are north of downtown on I-40 at exits 394 and 398, and south of the center at exits 378A and 378B. *Gateway Inn* (☎ 865-525-8001), at exit 394, is OK at $35. Note that on fall weekends when the university's football team is playing at home, motel rates skyrocket.

Tomato Head, in Market Square downtown, is a popular lunchtime hangout with pizza and good $5 sandwiches. *Calhoun's*, a Tennessee-based chain of rib and barbecue restaurants, has a location on the river between downtown and the University of Tennessee campus. Close to the visitor center, the patio-rich *Riverside Tavern by Regas* (☎ 865-637-0303) serves tasty fish and steak meals for up to $22 (cheaper at lunch). *11th Street Expresso House*, in a row of Victorian homes near the art museum, is good for coffee or a snack.

Knoxville is one of Greyhound's smaller hubs. The station (☎ 865-522-5144, 100 Magnolia Ave) has four daily buses to Chattanooga ($14; 2 hours), with continuing service to Atlanta, Georgia ($25; 4¼ hours). A direct service goes five times a day to Nashville ($23; 3½ hours) and Memphis ($43; 8 hours). There are three direct buses daily to both Washington, DC ($60; from 12 hours), and Chicago, Illinois ($64; from 11 hours).

Great Smoky Mountains National Park

Eastern Tennessee's most famous attractions are its mountains, centered on the Great Smoky Mountain National Park, the most visited park in the country. The 810-sq-mile park, which spreads into North Carolina, was established in 1934 and now draws 10 million visitors a year. The park rises from an elevation of 840 feet to over 6600 feet. This, and its position at the point where northern and southern foliage and climate patterns meet, gives the park a large variety of flora and fauna – about 100,000 species, of which only around 15% have been identified. Wildflowers are a particular delight, and there are more than 125 species of tree – more than in all of Europe. There are also some 60 species of mammal, including the bears for which the park is famous. Elk have been reintroduced recently.

The best-known sites are **Clingman's Dome**, the highest point in the park (6643 feet), and the dramatic twin summits of **Chimney Tops**. These and the popular hiking trails around Mt LeConte are all fairly close to Gatlinburg. The **Cades Cove** area features an 11-mile, one-way driving loop that's very popular with cyclists.

Summer is peak season, and you can expect the park to be extremely crowded at any time May to September. The least crowded area of the park (in relative terms) is Cades Cove, which is reached via the small town of Townsend.

On the Tennessee side, the Sugarlands Visitor Center (☎ 865-436-1291) is on the main access road from Gatlinburg. This road, US 441, crosses the park for 35 scenic miles to Cherokee, North Carolina, where there's another visitor center at Oconaluftee (see Great Smoky Mountains NP in the North Carolina section, earlier). Entrance to the park is free.

Backcountry hiking and camping are probably your best bet for avoiding the worst of the crowds (permit required; call ☎ 865-436-1231).

Gatlinburg Several gateway communities provide access to the park. The best known, and most crowded, is Gatlinburg. Because the **Ober Gatlinburg Ski Area** (☎ 865-436-5423) is just outside town you'll find more services here in winter, when many of the shops, restaurants and motels at other park gateways may be closed. The ski area itself is small (three lifts, eight trails), and its season is short. There are visitor centers (☎ 865-436-0504, 865-436-0520) at the third stoplight in town and just north of town on US 441. They have separate information desks run by the local chamber of commerce (for restaurant and motel information) and by the park service (for campsite reservations, hiking routes etc), all open 8am-6pm daily (Fri-Sat to 8pm, to 10pm in summer).

Pigeon Forge Ten miles north of Gatlinburg, Pigeon Forge is an impossibly tacky complex of motels, outlet malls and country-music theaters and restaurants, all of which have grown up in the shadow of **Dollywood** (☎ 865-428-9488), Dolly Parton's personal theme park ($32/23 adults/kids). It's open only April to December, but many of the town's entertainment venues operate year round.

Places to Stay & Eat There are over 1000 campsites in the park, but it can still be tough going in summer. Sites at the 10 developed campgrounds may be reserved from five months in advance (☎ 301-722-1257, 800-365-2267, Ⓦ reservations.nps.gov). Otherwise it's first-come, first-served. Camping fees are $17-20 per night, except for the five horse camps, which cost $30-35 per site. There are no showers or hookups. Of the park's 10 campgrounds only Cades Cove, Elkmont and Smokemont are open year round.

The rest are open from spring (usually March or April) through October. Cataloochee, in the southwest, is usually the least crowded. A permit is required for backcountry camping; call ☎ 865-436-1297 or drop into the Oconaluftee Visitor Center (see Great Smoky Mountains NP in the North Carolina section, earlier).

Prices in the gateway towns vary greatly with the season. Spring is cheapest, with rooms under $40 fairly easy to find. Summer and the brief fall-foliage season are the most expensive, when hotel rooms can easily hit $100. Because of the ski area, Gatlinburg is also expensive in winter, though places that remain open in Townsend or Cherokee are likely to be fairly cheap.

Campers should seek out the **KOA** (☎ 865-453-7903, 2849 Middle Creek Rd), in Pigeon Forge (open Apr-Nov). Cottage rentals are available at **Wa-Floy's Mountain Village** (☎ 865-436-7700, 3610 E Pkwy), about 10 miles east of Pigeon Forge. Prices start around $40 per night for two people (cheaper by the week). **Tennessee Mountain Lodge** (☎ 854-453-4784, 800-446-1674, 3571 Pkwy) charges similar rates and even has waterbeds.

Close to the park, just about the only pleasant eatery is **Old Mill** (160 Old Mill Ave), in Pigeon Forge. It's housed in the town's oldest building. **Mel's Diner** is a fake 1950s railroad joint, but open 24 hours with OK food. Turn south at Wears Valley Rd (third traffic light) and it's on the left.

Panther Creek State Park

Just outside the small, nondescript city of Morristown, Panther Creek is one of the better state parks in eastern Tennessee. There are (shortish) hiking and mountain-biking trails, good picnic spots and a scenic overlook above Cherokee Lake. Camping costs $10.

Greeneville & Around

The pleasant town of Greeneville (about 55 miles to the northeast of Knoxville) is where Andrew Johnson, Abraham Lincoln's hapless successor, got his start in politics. Johnson has the dubious distinction of being the first US president to be impeached.

The National Park Service now preserves Johnson's tailor shop, two residences, his gravesite and a statue as historical monuments. The visitor center (☎ 423-638-3551) is adjacent to the tailor shop right at the corner of E Depot and S College Sts. It includes a small museum outlining Johnson's life and career (free admission). The homestead (one of the residences), a few blocks away, can be seen only as part of a tour ($2; open daily).

One block away on College St is a small wooden cabin. This is a reproduction of the capitol of the short-lived 'State of Franklin,' which occupied the same site from 1784 to '88. Franklin was an attempt by some early settlers to secede from North Carolina, which later claimed the region. Congress never granted it statehood, however, and the territory was included in Tennessee when that state was formed a few years later.

Just outside the town of Limestone, **Davy Crockett State Park** (☎ 423-257-2167) has a reproduction of the cabin where the famous frontiersman was born in 1786.

Kentucky

Kentucky is a wonderful combination of the South and North, the East and West. It combines mountains and forests with some of the most beautifully manicured rural landscapes imaginable. The cities are small but somehow appealing, and even the industries are engaging – a state that produces bourbon, baseball bats and Corvettes can't be all bad.

Kentucky

Nickname: Bluegrass State

Population: 4,042,000 (25th)

Area: 40,395 sq miles (37th)

Admitted to Union: June 1, 1792 (15th)

Capital city: Frankfort (population 28,000)

Other cities: Louisville (256,000), Lexington (261,000), Owensboro (54,000)

Birthplace of: bourbon, folk heroes James Bowie (1796–1836) and Kit Carson (1809–68), Confederate president Jefferson Davis (1808–89), Abraham Lincoln (1809–65), Muhammad Ali (b 1942)

Famous for: Kentucky bluegrass, the Kentucky Derby, the Kentucky long rifle, the Louisville Slugger

History
The fertile lands to the west of the Appalachians were inhabited by Cherokee, Shawnee and Iroquois, who resisted the encroachment of whites. In 1775 a treaty with the Cherokee opened the way for settlers from the eastern colonies, and Daniel Boone marked a trail through the Cumberland Gap. Within 20 years, 100,000 people had migrated into the 'wilderness' that was Virginia's western territory. Kentucky became the first non-seaboard state admitted to the Union.

Kentucky, like the country as a whole, became divided between its slaveholding plantation class and the small farmers, traders and craft workers who opposed slavery. Both the Union and Confederate presidents were Kentucky-born, but when the Civil War began, 25,000 Kentuckians fought for the Confederacy, while 75,000 others fought for the Union. It is estimated that some 10,000 soldiers were killed in battle, and that another 20,000 died of exposure and disease.

Because Kentucky did not secede, it avoided the trauma of Reconstruction, but the state became strongly pro-South after the war. Coal, discovered in the Appalachians, became a source of wealth and of the state's first labor movements.

Information
Kentucky Travel (☎ 502-564-4930, 800-225-8747, Ⓦ www.kytravel.com, Box 2011, Frankfort, KY 40602) sends out a detailed booklet on the state's attractions. For road conditions, call ☎ 800-459-7623. State sales tax is 6%, but local bed taxes can add another 5% or so.

The boundary between Eastern and Central time goes through the middle of Kentucky. If you go from Mammoth Cave to Lincoln's birthplace, you'll arrive an hour later than you thought.

LOUISVILLE
Call it Looeyville, Lewisville or Louahvul; the locals don't mind – it's an easygoing kind of place. The world-famous Kentucky Derby is the big annual event, on the first Saturday in May. For the rest of the year, Louisville is a nice place to stop, a cultural and industrial center with some classic Americana and more sights worth seeing farther south.

Early river traffic had to portage around the falls of the Ohio, which made the area a strategic location for pioneering settlement as early as 1778. It was named 'Louisville' in recognition of French help in the Revolutionary War. As river traffic grew in importance, trading, warehousing and cargo transshipment made it a thriving center and a jumping-off point for westward migration. In 1830 the Portland Canal bypassed the falls, and Louisville's business slumped. It revived again when railroads arrived in 1850. Industry expanded after the Civil War, and Louisville competed with Cincinnati, Ohio, as the prime port on the busy Ohio River.

Orientation & Information
Louisville's old downtown is a compact grid beside the Ohio River – actually, it's now beside the I-64 freeway. The main restaurant and nightlife strip is Bardstown Rd, running southeast from downtown. A series of pretty parks (laid out by Frederick Law Olmsted in the 1890s) encircle the city, along with an inner (I-264) and outer (I-265) ring road. The visitor bureau (☎ 502-582-3732, 800-792-5595) runs an outlet (221 S 4th St) in the convention center. It has maps, lodging referrals and transport information, as well as the good *African American Historic Guide*. Surf the Web free at the public library (301 York St) downtown.

Things to See & Do
On Kentucky Derby day, the **Churchill Downs** racetrack, 3 miles south of downtown, is the most important place in the country. The surprisingly interesting **Kentucky Derby Museum** (☎ 502-637-7097), at Gate 1 on Central Ave, has displays on horses, jockeys and mint juleps, a 360-degree audiovisual on the race and a tour ($7/3 adults/kids; open daily). For details of spring and fall race meetings, as well as Derby Week events, call ☎ 502-636-4400 or 800-283-3729. On Derby Day, $40 gets you into the Paddock party scene if you arrive by 6am, but it's so crowded you won't see much of the race. Most seats are reserved years in advance.

The handsome neoclassical **JB Speed Art Museum** (☎ 502-634-2700, 2035 S 3rd St) has Renaissance paintings, some American art and a good selection of sculpture (free admission; closed Mon). Children enjoy the interactive exhibits at the **Louisville Science**

Kentucky Bluegrass

Kentucky 'bluegrass' isn't native to Kentucky, and it isn't really blue, though it sports a small blue flower in spring that can give the fields a bluish tinge. Mostly, however, grazing animals eat the flowers and new growth, so the Bluegrass State is brilliantly green. Seeds of the bluegrass, *poa pratensis* (also called smooth-stalked meadow grass), were actually brought from England via Virginia. The bluegrass thrived on Kentucky's limestone soils and proved ideal for grazing horses, which also became emblematic of the state.

Center (☎ 502-561-6100, 727 W Main St), an interesting warehouse conversion ($6.50/5.50 adults/kids).

It's hard to miss the **Louisville Slugger Museum** (☎ 502-588-7228, 800 W Main St) – look for the 120-foot baseball bat leaning against the building. The plant here makes regulation wooden baseball bats for all major- and minor-league players. Entry ($6/3.50) includes a video, baseball exhibits, a plant tour, enthusiastic guides and a collection of baseball memorabilia. For more Americana, check out the **Colonel Harland Sanders Museum** (☎ 502-456-8353), west of town off I-264 exit 1441, documenting the Kentucky Fried empire.

Across the river in Indiana, the **Falls of the Ohio State Park** (☎ 812-280-9970, 201 W Riverside Dr) describes the impact of human development on the natural environment; it's a good place to look for fossils. The **Howard Steamboat Museum** (☎ 812-283-3728, 1101 E Market St) has models and artifacts of the riverboat era ($4; closed Mon).

There are four **historic homes** open for tours (all $4): Farmington (☎ 502-452-9920) is an 1810-era house designed by Thomas Jefferson; Locust Grove (☎ 502-897-9845) was a 1790 Georgian mansion owned by the city's founder, with a guest list of 19th-century presidents and explorers; Whitehall (☎ 502-897-2944) is an 1855 house remodeled in Classic Revival style; and Thomas Edison House (☎ 502-585-5247) is a shotgun cottage where Edison rented a room in the 1860s while working as a telegrapher for

Western Union. The latter features examples of inventions and humble furnishings, but not much that Edison actually used.

Organized Tours

Joe & Mikes' Pretty Good Tours (☎ 502-459-1247) offers good 2½ tours ($20) with lots of local flavor. The *Star of Louisville* (☎ 502-589-7827) does scenic three-hour sightseeing cruises on the Ohio River, departing from the wharf near the 2nd St bridge (lunch/dinner cruises $25/46).

Belle of Louisville (☎ 502-574-2992), a 1914-era stern-wheeler, offers sightseeing cruises ($10; 2 hours) and Saturday-night dance cruises ($25; 2½ hours) from the end of 4th Ave (summer only).

Places to Stay & Eat

The closest camping is at **Louisville Metro KOA** (☎ 812-282-4474, 900 Marriott Dr), across the river in Clarksville, Indiana. It features tent/RV sites ($23/28) and some cabins. Friendly **Emily Boone Home Hostel** (☎ 502-585-3430, 102 Pope St) provides a few futon beds with kitchen facilities in a private home. Space is limited, so call first.

The cheapest motels are on the outskirts, especially around I-65 near the airport. Look for **Economy Inn** (☎ 502-456-2861, 3304 Bardstown Rd), which charges $30/33 for singles/doubles. **Red Roof Inn** (☎ 502-968-0151, 4704 Preston Hwy) starts at $40/44.

Downtown, **Travelodge** (☎ 502-583-2629, 401 S 2nd St) is nothing special (doubles $63). Much nicer is **Doubletree Club** (☎ 502-585-2200, 101 E Jefferson St), with an indoor pool and business-traveler facilities (from $119). **Galt House** (☎ 502-589-5200, 140 N 4th Ave) is a big convention hotel with rack rates from $109, specials from $69. Some rooms have great river views.

Downtown eateries are mainly for office workers' lunches. **Luigi's** (702 W Main St) is a good choice for pizza and pasta in the old part of town. One of the best restaurants is **Timothy's** (☎ 502-561-0880, 826 E Broadway), with original American/Latino dishes from around $15.

For a larger choice of places to eat and drink, head out to Baxter Ave/Bardstown Rd. **Lilly's** (☎ 502-451-0447, 1147 Bardstown Rd) features fresh ingredients and a varied menu with entrées for $15-28, and

Judge Roy Bean's Tavern & Grill has Southwestern favorites from $11. Retro *Lynn's Paradise Café* (*984 Barret Ave*) serves creative Southern meals from about $15 and cooks a mean breakfast. Frankfort Rd is another restaurant row, where *The Irish Rover* is popular for pub grub and a choice of beers.

Entertainment
The free weekly *Leo* lists gigs and entertainment. The prime performance venue, *Kentucky Center for the Arts* (☎ *502-562-0100, 5 Riverfront Plaza*) has theater, ballet, opera, orchestra, modern dance and popular music. It's worth checking what's on or looking around the center, with its unusual design and sculptures. The 1928 *Palace Theater* (☎ *502-583-4555, 625 4th Ave*) is a wonderfully ornate venue for theater and concerts.

Toy Tiger (☎ *502-458-1137, 3300 Bardstown Rd*) is a party place with dance music, DJs and live rock. *O'Malley's Corner* (☎ *502-589-3866*), downtown at 2nd and Liberty Sts, offers separate spaces for country, rock, disco and a piano bar, attracting an older crowd (cover about $4). *The Connection* (☎ *502-585-5752, 130 Floyd St*) is a wildly popular gay dance club.

The *Louisville Riverbats* (☎ *502-367-9121*) play AAA minor-league baseball at Cardinal Stadium in the Fairgrounds.

Getting There & Around
Standiford Field Airport (☎ *502-367-4636*), 5 miles south of town on I-65, has good domestic connections. Get there by cab ($15) or local bus No 2.

The Greyhound station (☎ *502-585-3331, 720 W Muhammad Ali Blvd*), just west of downtown, has buses to Chicago, Illinois ($44; 5¾ hours); Lexington ($17; 1¾ hours); and Memphis ($56; from 6½ hours) and Nashville ($25; from 3 hours), Tennessee.

Local buses are run by TARC (☎ *502-585-1234, 1000 W Broadway*), based at the Union Station depot.

CENTRAL KENTUCKY
This region holds several big cultural attractions, including a real-life Shaker Village and the boyhood home of Abraham Lincoln. It's also home to an extensive cave system and an icon of American sports-car culture, the Corvette, not to mention bourbon whiskey.

Fort Knox
About 30 miles south of Louisville on US 31W, Fort Knox is the proverbially safe depository of the USA's gold bullion and has also held other valuables at times of crisis, including the Magna Carta and the British Crown Jewels. There's a visitor bureau in the Challenger Learning Center (☎ 800-334-7540), nearby in Radcliff, on Hwy 31W at Hwy 313. You can see the outside of the bombproof Bullion Depository, but there are no tours or free samples. The Patton Museum of Cavalry & Armor (☎ 502-624-3812, 4554 Fayette Ave) has a big collection of US, German and Japanese military vehicles and mementos from the career of General George S 'Blood 'n Guts' Patton (free admission; open daily).

Bardstown
A sleepy town with a gaggle of distilleries, Bardstown comes alive in mid-September for the Kentucky Bourbon Festival. The visitor bureau (☎ 502-348-4877, 800-638-4877), just east of the square, has a walking-tour map of other historic sites.

The most hyped attraction is **My Old Kentucky Home State Park** (☎ 502-348-3502, 501 E Stephen Foster Ave), supposedly the place where, in 1852, Stephen Foster wrote the song 'My Old Kentucky Home.' The mansion appears on the back of the US Mint's special-edition quarter for Kentucky (2001). In fact, Foster was from Pittsburgh and spent his whole life in the North, though he may have visited his cousin's plantation here once. The state's official and much-loved song, which originally said that 'the darkies are gay,' is today rendered as 'the people.' Later verses, now rarely heard, elaborate on the not-so-gay life of the slaves. Costumed guides take tours of the house and garden ($4.50; open daily). *Stephen Foster, The Musical* (☎ 502-348-5971) features Foster favorites like 'Camptown Races' and 'Oh, Susannah' ($15/7 adults/kids; performances nightly except Mon, June-Sept).

The **Old Bardstown Village Civil War Museum** (☎ 502-349-0291, 310 E Broadway) features authentic uniforms, weapons,

The Bourbon State

Named after the French royal family, bourbon whiskey was first distilled in Bourbon County, north of Lexington, in 1789. Today 90% of all bourbon is produced in Kentucky (no other state is allowed to put its own name on the bottle). The mint julep, the archetypical Southern drink made by adding sugar syrup and crushed mint, is a familiar sight on Derby Day. Legal versions of Kentucky moonshine, distilled from fermented corn mash, are available in some liquor stores: guaranteed less than one month old, cheap as spit, highly flammable.

The **Oscar Getz Museum of Whiskey History** (☎ 502-348-2999, 114 N 5th St), in Bardstown, tells the story pretty well. Most of Kentucky's distilleries now are in the central part of the state, but several in the Bardstown area are open for tours, including Heaven Hill Distillery (☎ 502-348-3921, 1064 Loretto Rd) and Jim Beam's American Outpost (☎ 502-543-9877), I-65 exit 112, at Clermont. Perhaps the most attractive is **Maker's Mark Distillery** (☎ 502-865-2099, 3350 Burks Spring Rd), near Loretto in very pretty countryside 15 miles southeast of Bardstown. It's a National Historic Landmark where the Samuels family has been making whiskey since 1840. Samples are limited to free bourbon chocolates and full-price takeout bottles.

maps, documents and more ($5; open Tue-Sun, closed in winter).

Camping is available at the state park ($8.50-12.50). Motels include pleasant *Bardstown Inn* (☎ 502-349-0776, 510 E Stephen Foster Ave), at about $50, and the family-run *Wilson Motel* (☎ 502-348-3364, 530 N 3rd St), north of Court Square in the historic district ($40). The most interesting B&B is *Jailer's Inn* (☎ 502-348-5551, 111 W Stephen Foster Ave), a thoroughly renovated jailhouse ($70-125).

An unusual eatery is *My Old Kentucky Dinner Train* (☎ 502-348-7300), which starts at 602 N 3rd St and runs 35 miles through the Kentucky countryside while guests enjoy lunch ($43) or dinner ($60) in vintage 1940s dining cars. *Tom Pig's* (732 N 3rd St) serves cheap breakfasts and down-home chicken and steak dishes to locals in padded booths.

Elizabethtown

Settled in 1779, Elizabethtown was once home to Abe Lincoln's father. The visitor center (☎ 800-437-0092) has details of walking tours and the historic Brown-Pusey house. It also houses Schmidt's Museum of Coca-Cola Memorabilia (☎ 270-765-2175), with a 100,000-piece collection highlighting 'the real thing' in American life ($2; closed Sun).

Hodgenville & Around

Three miles to the south of Hodgenville, the **Abraham Lincoln Birthplace National Historic Site** (☎ 270-358-3137) features a replica of a Greek temple constructed around an old log cabin. Research has established that Lincoln was not actually born in the cabin, so it's referred to as his 'symbolic birthplace.' In front are 56 steps, one for every year of Lincoln's life, and the visitor center features a film and diorama. When Abe was 2½, his family moved to Knob Creek, 10 miles away on US 31E, where his first memory was of slaves being driven down a public road. The **Lincoln Boyhood Home** (☎ 270-549-3741) is a reproduction of the cabin where he lived ($1; open Apr-Oct).

In the town of Hodgenville itself, the **Lincoln Museum** (☎ 270-358-3163, 66 Lincoln St) has life-size dioramas of key events in Lincoln's life ($3). Outside the museum is a bronze statue of a seated and thoughtful Lincoln, with the chamber of commerce (☎ 270-358-3411) nearby.

Mammoth Cave National Park

If you like caves, this is a good one. Even if you don't, the aboveground attractions of the Green River, the hiking trails and the natural forest are alluring. Mammoth Cave National Park (☎ 270-758-2328) is usually accessed from I-65 exit 53 or 48. The visitor center shows a film on the caves, books cave tours, issues permits for backcountry camping (free) and has the usual excellent publications. The caves are in the central time zone, an hour earlier than Louisville.

The caves have been used for prehistoric mineral gathering, as a source of saltpeter for gunpowder and as a tuberculosis hospital.

Tourists started visiting around 1810 and guided tours have been offered since the 1830s. The area became a national park in 1926 and now brings millions of visitors each year. To see the caves, you must take a **ranger-guided tour** (☎ 800-967-2283), and it's wise to book ahead, especially in summer. Here's a partial list of the offerings:

Frozen Niagara Tour – The prettiest trip, with lots of decorative formations; strenuous ($8; four tours daily; 2 hours)

Grand Avenue Tour – Covers a wide variety of features, with steep ascents, many stairs and a lunch break; very strenuous ($16; 11:30am daily; 4½ hours)

Historic Tour – Includes a few Native American artifacts, some mining remnants and large chambers; strenuous ($8; three tours daily; 2 hours)

Travertine Tour – Very little climbing, pretty formations, pits and chambers; easy ($7; three tours daily; 1¼ hours)

Wild Cave Tour – In-depth exploration of side caves by climbing, crawling, squeezing and scrambling; lights and helmets provided, but bring lunch, water, gloves and boots; extremely strenuous ($35; 10am daily, weekends only in winter; 6½ hours)

'Strenuous' usually means climbing up and down a lot of steps. There's also a moderate half-hour Discovery Tour ($3.50) offered on demand, an Introduction to Caving course ($18; weekends only) and a one-hour Mobility-Impaired Tour ($7; 9:45am and 1:50pm). On some longer tours, there's a restroom stop in the Great Relief Hall. Ranger-led surface walks are free. Enjoyable one-hour launch cruises on the Green River cost $6.

Mammoth Cave Hotel (☎ 270-758-2225), near the visitor center, has an inexpensive restaurant and singles/doubles for $62/68. Even nicer are the cottages that open in the warmer months (from $36/45). Three developed campgrounds have tent sites on a first-come, first-served basis ($10-25). Cave City has downmarket eateries and inexpensive motels like *Scottish Inn* (☎ 270-773-3118) and *Quality Inn* (☎ 270-773-2181).

Greyhound buses go to nearby Cave City, I-65 exit 53, which has touristy attractions and facilities. A few miles northeast, Horse Cave also has tourist facilities and the attraction of **Kentucky Down Under** (☎ 800-762-2869), for those who really need to ogle an emu or cuddle a koala.

Bowling Green

Corvettes and a college combine to make Bowling Green worth a stop. It's also the only place to buy booze between Louisville and Nashville. The tourist office (☎ 270-782-0800, 352 Three Springs Rd), off I-65 exit 22, has a driving tour of Civil War sites.

All GM's Corvette sports cars are now produced at the Bowling Green plant (☎ 270-745-8419), I-65 exit 28, which offers a one-hour guided tour (9am and 1pm Mon-Fri). Opposite, the **National Corvette Museum** (☎ 270-781-7973, 800-538-3883) has over 50 examples of this classic American car. Exhibits span half a century and cover racing, advertising and motorcar culture. The cars are sexy for sure, but the written displays are overly technical ($8/6 adults/kids; open daily).

At Western Kentucky University, the **Kentucky Museum & Library** (☎ 270-745-2592) has an impressive collection on the state's history, with books, maps, photographs and documents (free admission; closed Mon and university holidays). The university has 15,000 students and some interesting buildings on its hilltop site.

There's a *KOA* (☎ 270-843-1919, 1960 Three Springs Rd) at I-65 exit 22, and a cluster of budget chain motels near the same exit, including *Motel 6* (☎ 270-843-0140), from $32/38 for singles/doubles; *Days Inn* (☎ 270-781-6470), from $40/45; and *Econolodge* (☎ 270-842-6730), from $43. Exit 22 leads to Scottsville Rd, which has good restaurants like *Hops* (2945 Scottsville Rd), which brews its own beers.

For drinking and music with a friendly student crowd, try *Kelly Green's* (☎ 270-781-8888, Fountain Square) and *Baker Boys Cafe* (☎ 270-843-0851, 1265 College St), which also does a good line of light lunches.

WESTERN KENTUCKY

The most direct route through western Kentucky is the Purchase Pkwy, confusingly signposted with a blue 'P' that looks like a 'parking' sign. It's not a scenic route, and about the only thing worth stopping for is a dose of re-created history at the **Adsmore Living History Museum** (☎ 270-365-3114), with seasonal theme decor and costumed interpreters.

Along US 68

About 15 miles west of Bowling Green, at South Union, the **Shaker Museum** (☎ 270-542-4167) is not as extensive as the settlement near Lexington, but the 1824 Centre House is a fine Shaker building with many excellent examples of Shaker crafts and furnishings ($4; open Mar-Dec).

At Fairview, the imposing, newly renovated **Jefferson Davis Monument** is a 351-foot obelisk marking the birthplace of the first and only president of the Confederacy. The visitor center (☎ 270-886-1765) makes a good case that Davis (1808–89) was an honorable man reluctantly caught up in a series of tragic events. The obelisk elevator runs May to October ($2).

Farther to the west, US 68 passes through the **Land Between the Lakes National Recreation Area** (☎ 270-924-2000), with many hiking and camping spots and two lakes that are popular for boating and fishing.

Along the Ohio River

No road follows the river very closely. The towns here grew on the strength of river transport. Owensboro has an International Bar-B-Q Festival in May, a bluegrass festival in October and the **International Bluegrass Music Museum** (☎ 270-926-7891). Henderson was for several years home to renowned ornithologist and artist John James Audubon. **John James Audubon State Park** includes a nature reserve and a museum (☎ 270-827-1893) featuring over 400 original engravings from Audubon's definitive 1839 *Birds of America*.

At the meeting of the Ohio and Tennessee Rivers, Paducah was the scene of important Civil War battles. The tourist office (☎ 800-723-8224) has tour maps of Civil War sites and the historic downtown. The **Museum of the American Quilter's Society** (☎ 270-442-8856) has three galleries of antique and modern quilts ($5) and the National Quilt Show in April. Across the river in Illinois, the small town of Metropolis gets mileage from its Superman associations.

Great River Road

Sixty miles of the Great River Rd (GRR) cut across the western end of Kentucky, though the great river is mostly hidden by levee banks. Near the confluence of the Ohio and Mississippi, Wickliffe Mounds (☎ 270-335-3681) have archaeological excavations of 1000-year-old Mississippi-culture settlements. Other small, declining towns include Bardwell and Hickman.

BLUEGRASS COUNTRY

The Bluegrass region once supported oak-ash woodlands interlaced with canebrakes and clover meadows. Today its defining features are genteel pastures, white picket fences and cavernous barns in a concerted attempt at landscape aesthetics.

Frankfort

Kentucky's diminutive capital, 26 miles west of Lexington, was a locational compromise with rival city Louisville. It's a small country town with some imposing buildings, notably the neoclassical 1910 **capitol building** (open for tours) and the nearby governor's mansion.

The older part of town is across the Kentucky River, where the old state capitol functioned from 1827 to 1910 (tours daily). Nearby is the handsome **Kentucky History Center** (☎ 502-564-3016), for those interested in state history, and the **Kentucky Military History Museum** (☎ 502-564-3265), with lots of weapons dating back to the famous Kentucky long rifle (closed Mon).

On the east bank of the river, Frankfort Cemetery has the grave of Daniel Boone and a big war memorial. Farther south, the oft-visited Kentucky Vietnam Veterans Memorial is a giant sundial engraved with 1000 names.

Lexington

With a distinctly small-town feel, Lexington is saved from parochialism by University of Kentucky (UK) students and the international jet-setting Thoroughbred racehorse industry. The top attractions and superb surrounding countryside are all horse-related. Get good maps from the convention and visitor bureau (☎ 859-233-7299, 800-845-3959, 301 E Vine St). The public library offers free Internet access.

Downtown Lexington has a pleasant mix of old and new buildings and historic houses. The 1803 **Mary Todd-Lincoln House** (☎ 859-233-9999, 578 W Main St) has articles from Mary's childhood and her years as Abe's wife. The **Hunt-Morgan House**

LEXINGTON & HORSE COUNTRY

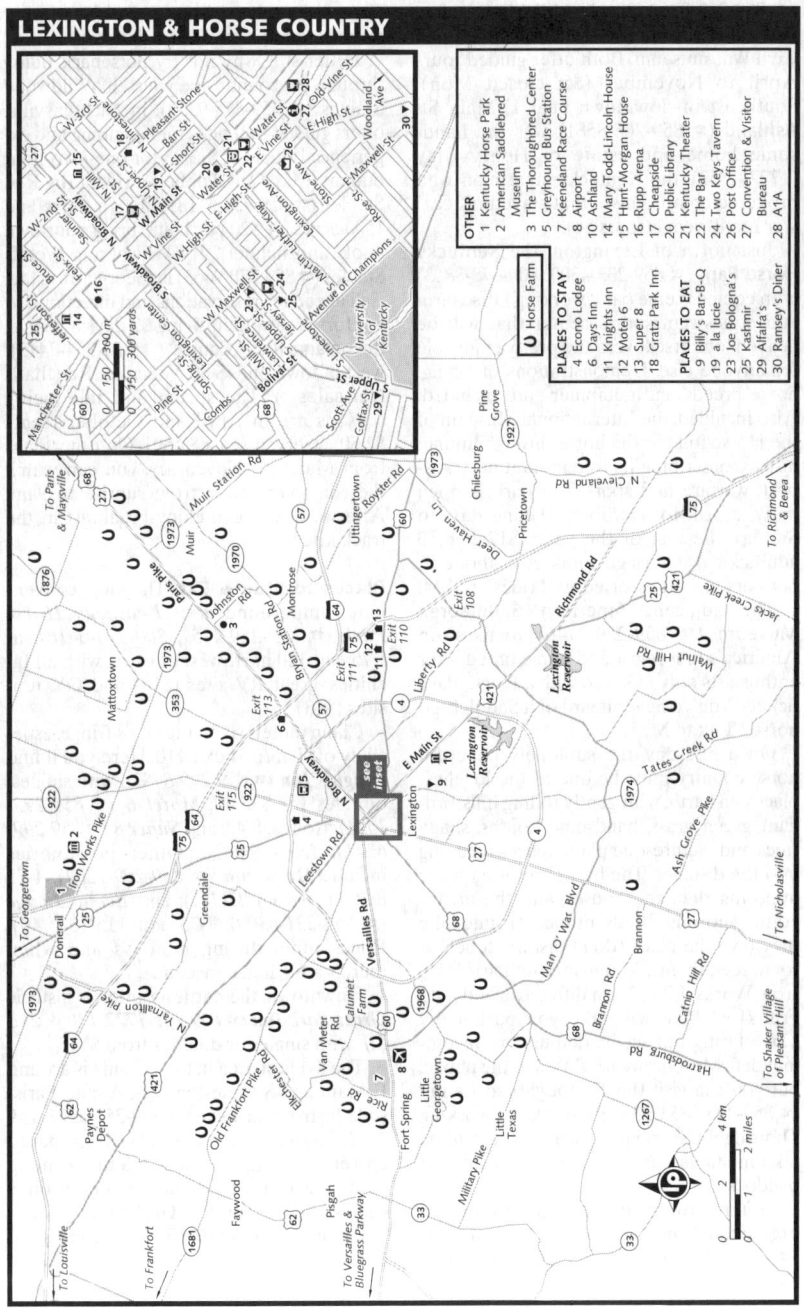

OTHER
1 Kentucky Horse Park
2 American Saddlebred Museum
3 The Thoroughbred Center
5 Greyhound Bus Station
7 Keeneland Race Course
8 Airport
10 Ashland
14 Mary Todd-Lincoln House
15 Hunt-Morgan House
16 Rupp Arena
17 Cheapside
20 Public Library
21 Kentucky Theater
22 The Bar
24 Two Keys Tavern
26 Post Office
27 Convention & Visitor Bureau
28 A1A

☺ Horse Farm

PLACES TO STAY
4 Econo Lodge
6 Days Inn
11 Knights Inn
12 Motel 6
13 Super 8
18 Gratz Park Inn

PLACES TO EAT
9 Billy's Bar-B-Q
19 a la lucie
23 Joe Bologna's
25 Kashmir
29 Alfalfa's
30 Ramsey's Diner

(☎ 859-253-0362, 201 N Mill St) is a fine Federal-style mansion (c. 1814) with a small Civil War museum. Both offer guided tours April to November ($5; closed Mon). Southeast of downtown near E Main St, **Ashland** (☎ 859-266-8581) was the handsome home and estate of Henry Clay (1777–1852), the Kentucky statesman who brokered compromises that staved off civil war for 40 years (tours $6).

Just north of Lexington, the **Kentucky Horse Park** (☎ 859-233-4303, 800-678-8813) is an equine theme park, working horse farm and equestrian sports center that will be heaven for horse lovers and pretty enjoyable for anyone else. Demonstrations of riding, horse breeds and equipment are included. Also included, the International Museum of the Horse follows the horse through human history, describing its role in hunting, transport, warfare and sport. The park is open daily April to October, Wednesday to Sunday the rest of the year ($12.20/6.50 adults/kids). Carriage tours cost about $5 per person, and escorted trail rides are $14.

The adjacent **American Saddlebred Museum** (☎ 859-259-2746) focuses on America's first registered horse breed – for enthusiasts only ($3, free with a Horse Park ticket). You've never heard of a Saddlebred horse? Talk to Mr Ed.

On a fine day, the sublimely beautiful horse country must be one of the loveliest places on earth, with gently rolling hills, brilliant green grass, handsome houses, shady trees and picturesque plank fences receding into the distance. The barns are often more imposing than the houses, and the aristocratic Thoroughbreds prance around like they own the place (don't disturb, touch or try to feed them). A loop around Paris Pike, Iron Works Pike, Yarnallton Rd and Old Frankfort Pike will take you past many horse farms, but scenic detours are recommended. Most farms are closed to the public, but you can visit the **Thoroughbred Center** (☎ 859-293-1853, 3380 Paris Pike), a working Thoroughbred training facility where tours take in stables, practice tracks and turnout paddocks.

Other farms may welcome visitors on **organized tours**. Horse Farm Tours Inc (☎ 859-268-2906) offers visits to Calumet Farm on some tours; Blue Grass Tours (☎ 859-252-5744) also visits a private horse farm. Ask at the visitor bureau about other tours (around $20-25 for a half-day).

Better still, why not try **horseback riding** through the countryside yourself? Wildwood Stables (☎ 859-885-9359), in Nicholasville, offers guided trail rides for beginning and experienced riders at $13/23 for one-/two-hour outings (May-Oct). For better riders, Big Red Stables (☎ 859-734-3118) offers a horse and 1500 acres for $20 per hour (bring your own boots and helmet). Try Whispering Woods Stables (☎ 859-570-9663) in Georgetown, too. Call ahead for reservations and directions.

Horses earn their living 32 days a year at **Keeneland Race Course** (☎ 859-254-3412), west of town on US 60, Versailles Rd (that's 'ver-**sales** '). The spring and fall racing seasons are in April and October (seats $2.50, reserved seats $7.50). On other days from March to November, you can watch the champions train from sunrise to 9am. Afterward, you can enjoy breakfast in the track kitchen.

Places to Stay & Eat The most convenient campground is at *Kentucky Horse Park* (☎ 859-259-4257, 800-370-6416), at I-75 exit 120 northwest of town, with all facilities, great RV sites ($18) and OK tent sites ($13).

Chain motels sit on the city's fringe, especially off I-75/I-64 exit 110. Here you'll find *Knights Inn* (☎ 859-299-8481), with singles/doubles for $35/40; *Motel 6* (☎ 859-293-1431), from $38/42; and *Super 8* (☎ 859-299-6241), from $40/50. Other possibilities include *Days Inn* (☎ 859-299-1202), I-75 exit 113 (from $36/41); and *Econo Lodge* (☎ 859-231-6300), I-75 exit 115 ($35/40). Prices jump during holidays and when there's a big horse race on.

Downtown, the nattiest option is historic *Gratz Park Inn* (☎ 859-231-1777, 120 W 2nd St), with singles or doubles from $145.

The liveliest area in the evening is around E Main and S Limestone Sts. A cute Parisstyle bistro, *a la lucie* (☎ 859-252-5277, 159 N Limestone St) serves well-prepared entrées for $13-22 (closed Sun). Among several eateries on S Limestone St, look for *Alfalfa's*, a vegetarian place, and *Kashmir*, for economical Indian food ($5 lunch buffets). Around the corner in a recycled church on Maxwell St, *Joe Bologna's* is popular for pizza and pasta.

Farther out, *Ramsey's Diner (496 E High St)* does standard American plates ($8-10). *Billy's Bar-B-Q (101 Cochran Rd)* does inexpensive hickory-smoked pork, beef and mutton. Look out for 'burgoo,' which is a satisfying Kentucky beef stew.

Entertainment For beer, bourbon and bar food, try friendly watering holes like *Cheapside* (☎ 859-254-0046, *131 Cheapside St)*, *Two Keys Tavern* (☎ 859-254-5000, *333 S Limestone St)* and *A1A* (☎ 859-231-7263, *367 E Main St)*, which all have live music. *The Bar* (☎ 859-255-1551, *224 E Main St)* is a poorly marked but popular gay venue.

The 23,000-seat *Rupp Arena* (☎ 859-233-4567), on Patterson St, is the home court for the UK Wildcats and also hosts any big-name rock and country acts in town. The restored 1927 *Kentucky Theater* (☎ 859-231-6997, *214 E Main St)* shows movies and is an intimate venue for occasional live music.

Getting There & Around Greyhound (☎ 859-299-8804) stops at 477 New Circle Rd, 2 miles from downtown. Regular buses go to Louisville, some by very indirect routes ($17; 1¾ hours). There's one bus to Nashville, Tennessee ($51; 7½ hours) and four to Washington, DC ($79; from 14 hours). Lex-Tran (☎ 859-253-4636) runs local buses (No 6 goes to the Greyhound stop).

Georgetown
About 10 miles north of Lexington, Georgetown was settled in 1776 and named after George Washington. The town's claims to fame include a historic downtown, the first bourbon whiskey (1789; see 'The Bourbon State,' earlier), a gaggle of antique shops and a Toyota plant (☎ 502-868-3027), which offers tours by appointment.

Maysville
About 60 miles northeast of Lexington, Maysville is a late-18th-century river town. The visitor center (☎ 859-564-6986) has information about covered bridges in the area, and houses the small Underground Railway Museum, which tells how thousands of slaves escaped to the North.

Harrodsburg & Around
Set in bucolic farmland 16 scenic miles southwest of Lexington, the old **Shaker**

Village of Pleasant Hill (☎ 800-734-5411) is truly delightful. Founded by Shakers from New England in 1805, it became a farming and craft-based community. Its population peaked at about 500 in the 1830s and declined as strict celibacy took its toll. The village officially closed in 1910, but the 33 original buildings survive intact because of sound construction and recent restoration. Fine Shaker craftwork abounds, and there's a full program of events, demonstrations and craft workshops. A *communal dining room* serves traditional Shaker country cooking (around $8 for lunch, $18 for dinner), and you can stay overnight in old *village buildings* (from $70/80 for singles/doubles). Entry is $10/5.50 adults/kids, or $14/7.50 with a one-hour riverboat excursion. For accommodations and meals, call ☎ 800-734-5611.

In 1774, James Harrod settled on land that is now **Old Fort Harrod State Park** (☎ 606-734-3314), founding the first English-speaking colony west of the Appalachians. Now costumed craftspeople act out pioneer fantasies in a facsimile of the first fort ($3.50). On summer evenings, an outdoor drama does a Daniel Boone show ($12). The Harrodsburg Tourist Commission (☎ 859-734-2364) has historic tour maps.

Farther southwest, **Perryville** was the site of a major Civil War battle. In 1862, Confederate troops were stalemated by a larger Union force, which managed to secure most of the state for the North. Many of the casualties ended up in a mass grave, 22 miles west at Lebanon National Cemetery. It's a pleasant drive west to the Hodgenville and Bardstown areas (see Central Kentucky, earlier).

Berea
About 35 miles south of Lexington off I-75, Berea (buh-**re**-ah) is on the edge of the Appalachians and big on folk arts and crafts. Berea College has a long tradition of employing its own students in lieu of charging tuition fees. You might find students working at the Berea Welcome Center (☎ 859-986-2540, 800-598-5263) or at the college's **Appalachian Gallery** (☎ 859-985-3140), with artifacts, pictures and displays on mountain life. Shops stock some excellent craft items among lotsa schlock.

Boone Tavern Hotel (☎ *859-985-3700, 800-366-9358, 100 Main St)* is a handsome 1909-era building with singles/doubles from

$65/70, and its dining room specializes in hearty regional fare (meals around $17). It's all staffed by the college's hospitality students and has a lot more character than your average motel.

EASTERN HIGHLANDS

Extending down the east side of Kentucky in the shadow of the Appalachians, US 23 is nicknamed the 'Country Music Hwy.' At its north end, **Ashland** was settled in 1786 and boasts a Highlands Museum. Fifty-five miles south, through some depressed rural areas, is **Paintsville**, where country music star Loretta Lynn was born. Farther south, **Pikeville** was the scene of the legendary 30-year feud between the Hatfields and the McCoys in the late 1800s. Continuing to the Virginian border, **Breaks Interstate Park** has a 1600-foot-deep gorge in superb forested country.

Daniel Boone National Forest

This vast area in the east of the state is noted for its rich variety of plants and wildlife and an extensive trail system. The north end, around Morehead, is popular for boating in Cave Run Lake and for the Zilpo Rd Scenic Byway. The central area, around Stanton and Slade, features the dramatically symmetrical **Natural Bridge**. The nearby Red River Gorge has excellent hiking trails as well as Class I to III white water.

The south end of the national forest, easily accessed from I-75, has some depressed communities and old coal-mining areas around Stearns, on US 27. Within the forest, **Cumberland Falls State Resort Park** (☎ 859-528-4121) has a rustic lodge, a swimming pool and *campgrounds* ($12). Nearby Corbin is the site of the original outlet of *Kentucky Fried Chicken*. The chicken tastes extra good, and some exhibits are appealingly nostalgic.

Cumberland Gap National Historic Park

In the southeast corner of the state, where Kentucky, Virginia and Tennessee come together, the Cumberland Gap has long been a crucial link across the mountains. Indians followed buffalo, Daniel Boone followed the Indians and the pioneers followed Boone. Now a four-lane highway and a railway both tunnel under the gap. A drive and a walk to Pinnacle Overlook ou see three states. The visitor center (☎ 859-248-2817) is at the Kentucky end of the road tunnel, while the 100-site *Wilderness Road Campground* is off Hwy 58 in Virginia, with wooded spots for tents/RVs ($10/15).

Florida

Historians say that when Florida was admitted to the Union, residents handed the new governor a proposed state flag that read 'Let Us Alone.' The flag was scrapped, and Florida became one of the world's most popular vacation places.

What attracts visitors to the long, narrow peninsula is a 1350-mile coastline that features silky white-sand beaches in the Panhandle, hard-packed sand beaches that you can drive your car on and surf from on the east coast, seashell-rich beaches along the west coast, and mangrove-studded beaches leading to brilliant coral reefs in the Keys. In addition, a score of rivers crisscrosses the state, making it ideal for canoeing. There are forests, lakes and state and national parks galore, with camping, hiking, biking, canoeing and an incredible diversity of wildlife. Warm weather year round – save for an occasional Canadian cold front in winter – lets you sample the natural wonders anytime.

What the heavens didn't create naturally, visionaries built from the ground up. Floridian innovators include Walt Disney (Disney World, MGM Studios, EPCOT Center and the Animal Kingdom), Henry Flagler (St Augustine and Palm Beach), Julia Tuttle (Miami and Miami Beach), Vincente Martinez Ybor (Ybor City) and President John F Kennedy (NASA's Kennedy Space Center).

History

Hunter-gatherer communities appeared here around 9000 BC. Early settlements along the coasts left large seashell mounds in the northeast and Panhandle. Evidence of permanent villages, corn cultivation, fishing and burial mounds dates from 600 BC. When the Europeans arrived, the principal groups were the Apalachee in the Panhandle, Timucuan in the north and Calusa in the southwest, probably numbering around 60,000 total.

Spanish explorer Juan Ponce de León arrived near present-day Cape Canaveral in 1513 and was soon driven off by attacks from the Calusa. In honor of Pascua Florida, the Easter Feast of Flowers, he named this new land 'Florida.' Attempted settlements by the French encouraged the Spanish to consolidate their hold on the region. In 1565, St Augustine (the USA's oldest European

Highlights

- Everglades National Park – one of nature's rarest ecosystems, a combination 'river of grass,' mangrove swamps and bay
- Miami's Art Deco District – biking and walking tours through the pride of Miami Beach
- Key Largo coral reefs – snorkeling and diving among brilliantly colored fish
- Kennedy Space Center – the sensation of the *Apollo 8* liftoff in a reassembled control room
- Walt Disney World's Animal Kingdom – get close enough to a free-roaming giraffe to see its eyelashes

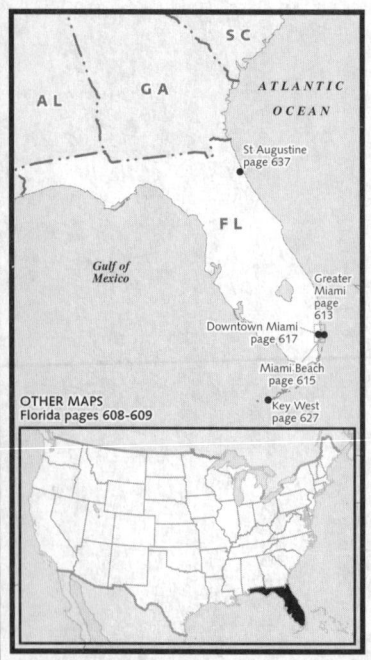

settlement) was founded by Pedro Menéndez de Avilés. Over the next 300 years Florida found itself at the epicenter of a struggle for control of the New World between the British and French. In the French and Indian War, Spain sided with the French, and the British responded by taking the Spanish port of Havana, Cuba. Under the First Treaty of Paris (1763), Spain forfeited Florida to the British to regain this vital port. The Second Treaty of Paris (1783) ended the Revolutionary War and returned Florida to Spain.

In 1814, Andrew Jackson, a US general and notorious hunter of Native Americans, embarked on a bloody march. With the help of Creek warriors from farther north, he massacred the southern Creeks and appropriated their land. The Seminole group was formed by a combination of defeated Creeks, escaped slaves and other refugee Indians. Spain ceded its territories to the USA in 1819, with Jackson as governor. Jackson was elected US president in 1828 and passed the Indian Removal Act in 1830. After three Seminole Wars, from 1817 to 1853, most of the indigenous people were removed to reservations west of the Mississippi, with a few surviving Seminoles taking refuge in the Everglades.

Florida was admitted to the Union on March 3, 1845, only to secede 16 years later at the onset of the Civil War. It was readmitted in 1868, and the new Florida government began what continues to this day: an agenda of probusiness, prodevelopment activities.

Post–Civil War construction of railroads, notably by Henry Flagler (1830–1913) on the east coast and Henry Plant (1819–99) on the west coast, connected the main towns on the coasts, eventually linking Tampa and Key West to the northern states. This unlocked the state's tourism potential and led to the first real-estate boom. The 1898 Spanish-American War and WWI both contributed to Florida's development with the construction of naval stations and the influx of thousands of new residents. During Prohibition, Florida's unguarded coastline made it a smuggler's haven. Illicit drinking and gambling flourished, along with land speculation and instant fortunes. Hurricanes in the late 1920s wiped out new construction, killed hundreds and resulted in plummeting land prices. Banks folded, businesses failed, developers went bust and the Great Depression hit Florida harder than most states.

WWII turned Florida into a huge war factory and training ground, and created enormous demand for its produce. Postwar Florida thrived with new immigrants, a new aerospace industry, gambling, gangsters and connections to Batista's Cuba. After the 1959 Cuban revolution, South Florida was flooded with anti-Castro immigrants, and a permanent Cuban community was established in Miami. A second wave of less affluent, less educated Cubans arrived in Miami in the 1980s.

In the 1970s, Walt Disney World created hundreds of thousands of tourist-related jobs and impelled a theme-park boom. However, Florida is not the Disney happy-ever-after fairy tale it appears at first glance. Racial tension arises periodically, and Miami's Caribbean location makes it a port of entry for drugs. Heightened security and the creation of a tourist police force have significantly reduced attacks on tourists, which occurred systematically in the early 1990s.

FLORIDA

Florida

Nickname: Sunshine State

Population: 15,982,400 (4th)

Area: 65,755 sq miles (22nd)

Capital city: Tallahassee (population 135,000)

Other cities: Jacksonville (735,600), Miami (362,500), Orlando (186,000)

Admitted to Union: March 3, 1845 (27th); seceded January 10, 1861; readmitted July 4, 1868

State symbols: Florida panther (animal), manatee (tropical marine mammal), porpoise (saltwater mammal), alligator (reptile)

Birthplace of: Zora Neale Hurston (1891–1960), Sydney Poitier (b 1927), Pat Boone (b 1934), Janet Reno (b 1938), Faye Dunaway (b 1941), Jim Morrison (1943–71), Tom Petty (b 1950), Chris Evert (b 1954), Wesley Snipes (b 1962)

Unusual headstone: Jackie Gleason's – 'And away we go!'

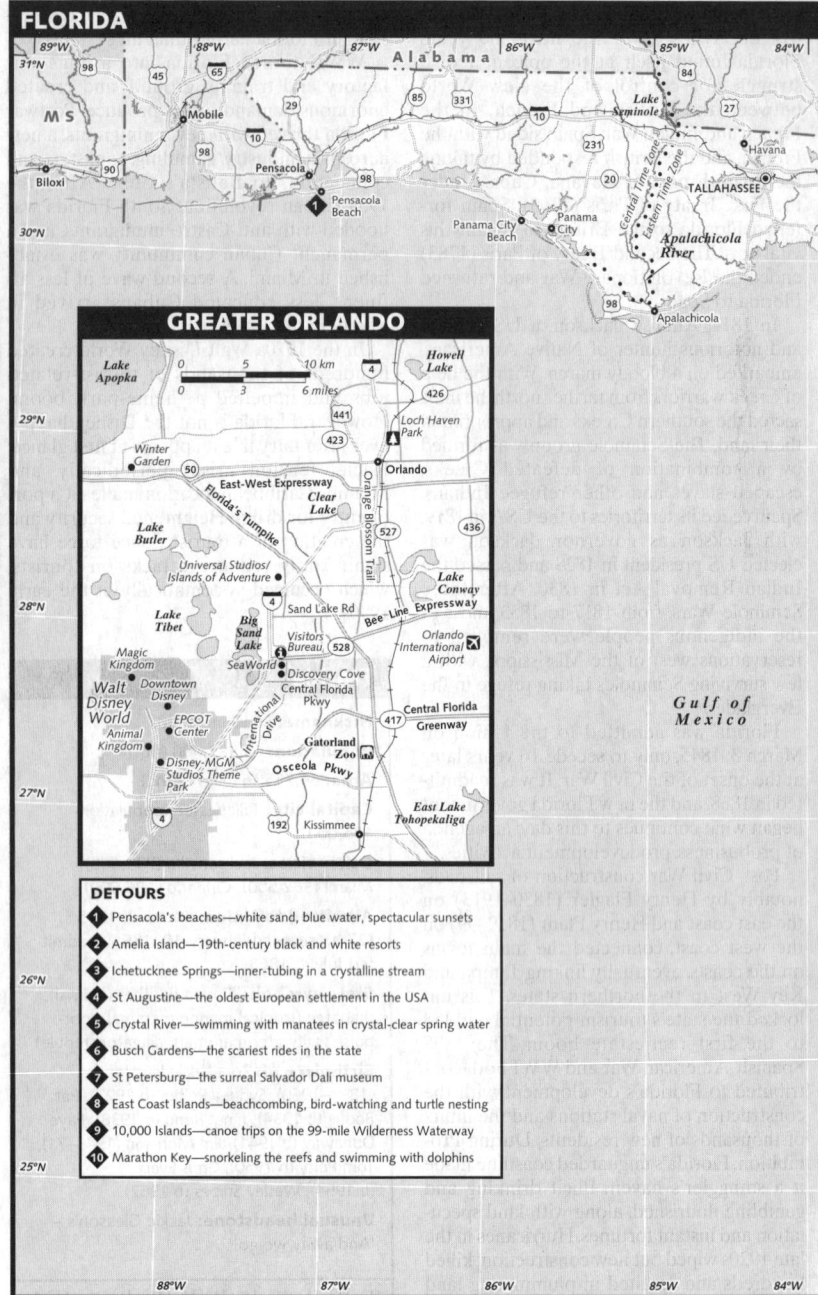

FLORIDA

GREATER ORLANDO

DETOURS

1 Pensacola's beaches—white sand, blue water, spectacular sunsets

2 Amelia Island—19th-century black and white resorts

3 Ichetucknee Springs—inner-tubing in a crystalline stream

4 St Augustine—the oldest European settlement in the USA

5 Crystal River—swimming with manatees in crystal-clear spring water

6 Busch Gardens—the scariest rides in the state

7 St Petersburg—the surreal Salvador Dali museum

8 East Coast Islands—beachcombing, bird-watching and turtle nesting

9 10,000 Islands—canoe trips on the 99-mile Wilderness Waterway

10 Marathon Key—snorkeling the reefs and swimming with dolphins

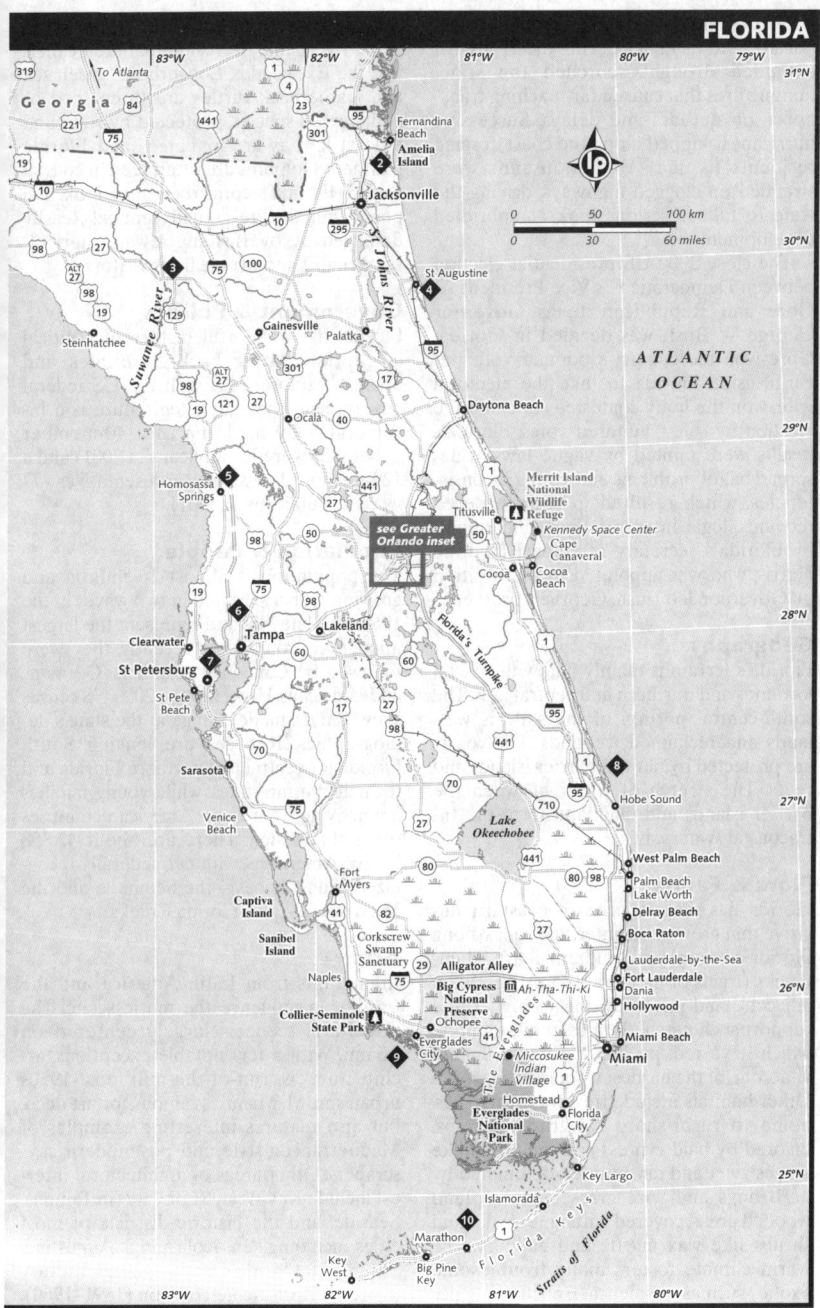

Nature and development brought transportation to its knees during the 1990s. An extended drought scorched the state, fanning fires that caused far-reaching transportation detours and delays. Successive hurricanes skipped along the coast, forcing residents to flee – but thousands were stranded on clogged highways, driving the state to take a serious look at unbridled development.

The close 2000 US presidential election between Democratic US Vice President Al Gore and Republican Texas Governor George W Bush was decided in Florida. Gore won the country's popular vote, but Bush, using Florida to take the electoral vote, won the hotly contested state and the election by a few hundred votes. Florida's results were tainted by vague laws, widespread ballot problems and voting inconsistencies, which resulted in court-ordered recounts, legal interpretations, and rulings by Florida's secretary of state, Katherine Harris, who was appointed to the position by Governor Jeb Bush, George's brother.

Geography

Florida's terrain is mainly flat, with coastal lowlands and northern and central hills. The south-central portion of the state is wetlands and reclaimed wetlands. The coasts are protected by natural barrier islands and reefs. The stretch of water between the barrier islands and mainland form the Intracoastal Waterway.

Flora & Fauna

Florida has three species of coastal mangrove that grow in the intertidal zones along Florida's central and southern coasts. Hammocks (tracts of hardwood forest) grow on adjacent land just a few inches higher and support such native flora as gumbo limbos, which have red, peeling bark, and lignum vitae, one of the hardest woods in the world. Other habitats include freshwater marshes, home to razor-sharp sawgrass; swamps, favored by bald cypress and their alienlike 'knees'; wet and dry prairies, dominated by herb bogs and wire grasses; and upland wooded areas, covered with pines, oaks, and shrubs like wax myrtle and gallberry. The warm climate fosters many troublesome exotics such as melaleuca, Brazilian pepper and Australian pine.

Alligators frequently sun themselves along riverbanks, in residential-area canals and the Everglades. Loggerhead, green sea and leatherback turtles are threatened or endangered species, protected by state and federal law, as are manatees and Florida panthers. Dolphins are often seen in coastal waters. Florida's coral reefs may look like plants, but they're actually animals, easily damaged by overfishing, sewage, agricultural runoff and overzealous visitors.

Government & Politics

Florida has a colorful history of political corruption dating back to pirates and Spanish explorers. As with the US federal government, the state's legislature is a bicameral body made up of a 40-member Senate (23 were Republicans in 2001) and a 120-member House of Representatives (77 were Republicans in 2001).

Population & People

The population is almost 16 million and growing. Cubans arrived in two waves in the 1960s and late '80s and represent the largest immigrant group. Until recently, they were followed by Canadians, Haitians, Germans and Jamaicans. However, the 2000 US census showed a dramatic change in the state's demographics. Retirees are leaving South Florida for central and northern Florida and for neighboring states, while young families are arriving from Latin American countries other than Cuba. There are about 42,358 Native Americans, with two federally recognized Indian tribes – the Seminole and the Miccosukee – plus Florida Creeks.

Arts

Immigrants from Latin America and the Caribbean influence the music scene. The visual-arts scene is largely centered on Miami. With a few notable exceptions, architecture is run-of-the-mill post-1950s urban sprawl. Miami is famous for art deco, but also features interesting examples of Mediterranean-style and postmodern skyscrapers. Other areas of architectural interest include Key West, Ybor City (in Tampa), Seaside, and the historic districts of most cities, including Pensacola and St Augustine.

One of Florida's most famous literary figures is Zora Neale Hurston (1891–1960), whose depictions of growing up black in

Florida include the internationally acclaimed works *Mules and Men* and *Their Eyes Were Watching God*.

Information
Visit Florida (☎ 850-488-5607, 888-735-2872, fax 850-224-2938, ⓦ www.flausa.com, 126 W Van Buren St, Tallahassee, FL 32399) has information at the Welcome Center, New Capitol, Plaza Level, Duval St side, Tallahassee. The Division of Recreation and Parks (☎ 850-488-9872, 3900 Commonwealth Blvd, MS 536, Tallahassee, FL 32399) manages the state's park system.

Many museums and cultural venues are closed Monday. Call in advance.

When to Go
In Miami and South Florida, the peak season is December through March, with warm, dry weather, big crowds and high prices. The hottest and wettest time is June through October, but it's still quite OK. Orlando and central Florida are hot and wet in summer but remain popular year-round. Jacksonville and Panhandle cities can be cold in winter, and summer is the main tourist season.

Activities
Five hundred miles of the 880-mile Florida National Scenic Trail (which runs almost the length of the state) is maintained by the Florida Trail Association (☎ 352-378-8823, 800-343-1882, 5415 SW 13th St, Gainesville) as a hiking trail. There's another 1700 miles of hiking, nature and multipurpose trails primarily on state and federal lands. Florida Greenways and Trails System (☎ 850-488-3701, 3900 Commonwealth Blvd, 8th floor, Tallahassee) provides information on outfitters and canoe liveries, bicycle touring, stables and other greenways.

The best opportunities for canoeing and kayaking are in the Everglades (the 99-mile Wilderness Waterway and the Ten Thousand Islands) and on the rivers and coast between Naples and Crystal River. Canoe rentals average $20 a day. If you plan to visit several state parks, which charge $3.25-4 car admission, consider a seven-day ($10 for up to four people) or annual ($30-60) pass. Entrance fees are waived for campers.

The best places for diving and snorkeling are the reefs of the Florida Keys.

> ### Sparks & Sharks
>
> Not to alarm you, but keep in mind that Florida offers its share of natural perils. For one thing, more people are struck by lightning in the Sunshine State than in any other. Even scarier, perhaps, is the fact that Floridian waters hosted more than half of reported shark attacks in the *world* for the first seven months of 2001.
>
> If you're caught in the open during a thunderstorm, stay as low as possible to avoid attracting Zeus' wrath. And when swimming, make sure that there are lifeguards present (or at least a swimming companion) and heed shark-attack warnings. Come to think of it, the safest place to spend your vacation may just be in your hotel room with your favorite Danielle Steel novel.
>
>

Getting There & Around
Miami International Airport is an international gateway. Orlando and Fort Lauderdale get significant numbers of US and international flights. Fort Lauderdale and Miami airports are about 30 minutes apart, and it's almost always cheaper to fly into or out of Fort Lauderdale.

Greyhound has widespread service throughout the state. Walk-up fares cost more than passes and advance-purchase tickets (see the Getting Around chapter). From Miami, buses run to Atlanta, Georgia ($109; 16 hours); New York ($109; 31 hours); and Los Angeles, California ($130; 59 hours).

Amtrak's *Silver Meteor, Silver Star* and *Silver Palm* run daily between New York and Miami. The *Sunset Limited* crosses the south between Los Angeles, California, and Orlando three times weekly. Unless you have a special deal or a rail pass, it's probably better to take a bus or fly within the state.

The Tri-Rail (☎ 800-874-7245, ⓦ www.tri-rail.com) commuter system is the cheapest mode of transportation among Miami, Fort Lauderdale and Palm Beach, with stops at the three airports and bus connections to beaches, downtowns and neighboring cities. It's slow but cheap (see city sections for rates).

Car rental rates in Florida tend to be relatively low: A small car might cost $24/125 a day/week. Liability insurance is not included in rates. Auto drive-aways to Florida are common. Contact Auto Driveaway Company of Chicago (☎ 800-346-2277), which has locations throughout the country, or National Driveaway (☎ 888-333-2353), in Jacksonville, to transfer cars back and forth across the USA.

South Florida

Most visitors to this region seek the glamour, culture and hip lifestyle of Miami's South Beach. Beyond that glittery realm lies the lure of the laid-back Florida Keys, made famous by Jimmy Buffett, Zane Grey and Ernest Hemingway, among others. Natural diversions rank high on the must-do list, from snorkeling and diving the coral reefs of the Keys to birding, hiking and canoeing through Everglades National Park.

MIAMI & MIAMI BEACH

In just over 100 years, Miami (population 362,500) has developed a burgeoning financial and tourist economy, and its multiethnic and multicultural metropolitan population numbers over 2.2 million. It's blessed with natural areas and tropical beaches and has cultivated six major sports teams, a 20th-century district on the National Register of Historic Places, and an image as a 'New World Center.' Across the Intracoastal Waterway lies Miami Beach (population 87,900). Since the restoration of Miami Beach's Deco District in the 1980s, South Beach (SoBe) has become the Fabulous Spot, perhaps the world's hippest photo backdrop and a playground for the rich and beautiful, the youthful and the retired. South Beach is also a major gay and lesbian destination.

History

The first passenger train to Miami, in 1896, encouraged thousands of people whose livelihoods had been wiped out by the previous year's freeze in north Florida to flock to the region's warmer climes. Blacks were among the first settlers, coming from the Bahamas as farm laborers and railroad workers. The establishment of military training facilities during WWI and WWII encouraged many trainees to return permanently. The 1930s saw a boom and the construction of Miami Beach's art deco buildings. In the 1950s blacks were relegated to federal housing projects in Liberty City, and Miami's Cuban population swelled following the 1959 Castro coup. In 1968, blacks – displaced and disillusioned by the American Dream – rioted in Liberty City.

The early 1970s brought more integration and advances in arts and education, before the 1975 recession halted yet another boom. As Miami found solutions by transforming itself into an international tourism and business center, Barbara Capitman led the revival of Miami Beach's Deco District. The 1980s brought a second wave of Cuban refugees, race riots, a burgeoning drug trade and skyrocketing crime. The 1990s unfolded with violence directed at tourists and Hurricane Andrew, one of the country's worst natural disasters. It took two years, bad northern winters and a city committed to protecting visitors to revive the tourism industry.

In 2000, cultures clashed over Elián González, whose mother died while fleeing Cuba on a raft en route to the USA. Cuban expatriate relatives in Miami refused to return the boy to his father, still in Cuba. The city, state and country were divided. The standoff ended when US Attorney General Janet Reno sent in commando-style forces to seize the boy. He was returned to Cuba.

Orientation

Greater Miami is a sprawling metropolis that includes suburbs like Coral Gables and Coconut Grove and neighborhoods like Little Havana and Little Haiti. Miami is on the mainland, while the City of Miami Beach lies 4 miles east on a stretch of white sand crowded with buildings.

Downtown Miami is divided by the Miami River. The north-south divider is Flagler St; the east-west divider is Miami Ave. It's laid out in a numerical grid, with numbers

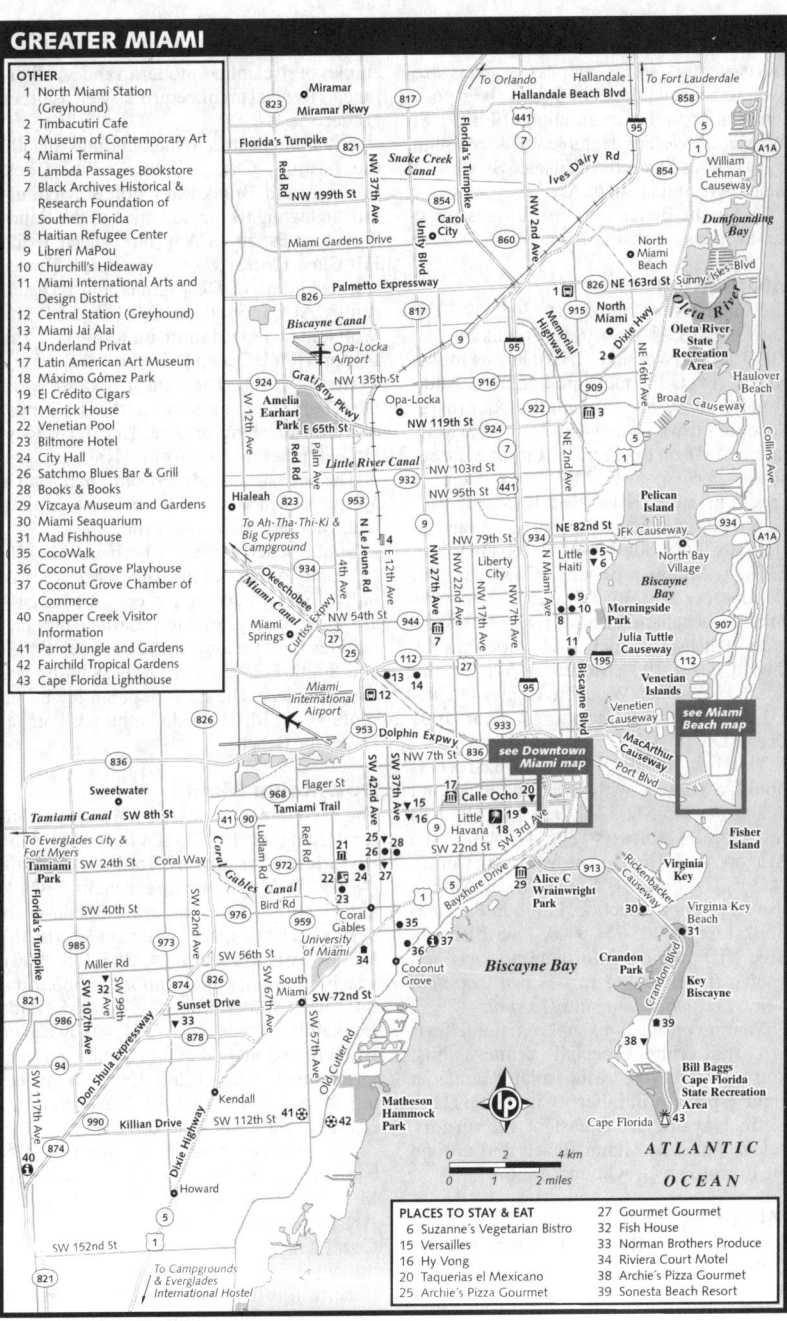

GREATER MIAMI

OTHER
1 North Miami Station (Greyhound)
2 Timbacutiri Cafe
3 Museum of Contemporary Art
4 Miami Terminal
5 Lambda Passages Bookstore
7 Black Archives Historical & Research Foundation of Southern Florida
8 Haitian Refugee Center
9 Librerí MaPou
10 Churchill's Hideaway
11 Miami International Arts and Design District
12 Central Station (Greyhound)
13 Miami Jai Alai
14 Underland Privat
17 Latin American Art Museum
18 Máximo Gómez Park
19 El Crédito Cigars
21 Merrick House
22 Venetian Pool
23 Biltmore Hotel
24 City Hall
26 Satchmo Blues Bar & Grill
28 Books & Books
29 Vizcaya Museum and Gardens
30 Miami Seaquarium
31 Mad Fishhouse
35 CocoWalk
36 Coconut Grove Playhouse
37 Coconut Grove Chamber of Commerce
40 Snapper Creek Visitor Information
41 Parrot Jungle and Gardens
42 Fairchild Tropical Gardens
43 Cape Florida Lighthouse

PLACES TO STAY & EAT
6 Suzanne's Vegetarian Bistro
15 Versailles
16 Hy Vong
20 Taquerias el Mexicano
25 Archie's Pizza Gourmet
27 Gourmet Gourmet
32 Fish House
33 Norman Brothers Produce
34 Riviera Court Motel
38 Archie's Pizza Gourmet
39 Sonesta Beach Resort

FLORIDA

see Downtown Miami map

see Miami Beach map

To Orlando
Hallandale
To Fort Lauderdale
Hallandale Beach Blvd

Miramar
Miramar Pkwy

Florida's Turnpike

Snake Creek Canal

Ives Dairy Rd

William Lehman Causeway

NW 199th St

Carol City

Dumfounding Bay

Miami Gardens Drive

Palmetto Expressway

North Miami Beach

Oleta River

Sunny Isles Blvd

Oleta River State Recreation Area

Biscayne Canal

North Miami

Opa-Locka Airport

NW 135th St

Haulover Beach

Grat-igny Pkwy

Amelia Earhart Park

Opa-Locka

Broad Causeway

Little River Canal

NW 103rd St

NW 95th St

Pelican Island

Hialeah

NE 82nd St

JFK Causeway

To Ah-Tha-Thi-Ki & Big Cypress Campground

NW 79th St

Little Haiti

North Bay Village

Liberty City

Biscayne Bay

Morningside Park

Miami Springs

NW 54th St

Julia Tuttle Causeway

Miami International Airport

Dolphin Expwy

Venetian Islands

Venetien Causeway

MacArthur Causeway

Port Blvd

Sweetwater

Flager St

Calle Ocho

Tamiami Trail

Little Havana

Fisher Island

Tamiami Canal   SW 8th St

To Everglades City & Fort Myers

Coral Way

Alice C Wrainwright Park

Virginia Key

Coral Gables

Bird Rd

University of Miami

Bayshore Drive

Rickenbacker Causeway

Virginia Key Beach

SW 40th St

Coconut Grove

Biscayne Bay

Crandon Park

Key Biscayne

Miller Rd

Sunset Drive

South Miami

SW 72nd St

Don Shula Expressway

Killian Drive

Kendall

Matheson Hammock Park

Bill Baggs Cape Florida State Recreation Area

Cape Florida

ATLANTIC OCEAN

To Campgrounds & Everglades International Hostel

0   2   4 km
0   1   2 miles

increasing away from the two dividing thoroughfares. Streets run east-west, avenues and courts north-south. Compass prefixes are given to thoroughfares based on their position relative to the intersection of Flagler St and Miami Ave. For example, 10786 SW 40th St is on 40th St south of Flagler St, west of Miami Ave and at 107th Ave.

In Miami Beach, streets run east-west and avenues north-south.

Information

The main visitor bureau (☎ 305-539-3000, 800-933-8448, W www.tropicoolmiami.com, 701 Brickell Ave, suite 2700), in downtown Miami, covers the metropolitan area. Additionally, there are information booths in Coconut Grove (☎ 305-444-7270, 2820 MacFarlane Rd); on the Florida Turnpike Extension (☎ 305-969-5927, MM 19) at Snapper Creek; in Sunny Isles Beach (☎ 305-947-5826, 17100 Collins Ave, suite 208); and in Florida City (☎ 305-245-9180, 160 Hwy 1).

The Miami Beach Chamber of Commerce (☎ 305-672-1270, W www.miamibeachchamber.com) is at 333 41st St, suite 402; by October 2001, though, they should be at 1920 Meridian Ave. Miami Beach's Art Deco Welcome Center (☎ 305-531-3484, W www.mdpl.org) is at 1001 Ocean Dr.

The best locally owned bookstore is Books & Books, with locations in Miami Beach (☎ 305-532-3222, 933 Lincoln Rd) and Coral Gables (☎ 305-442-4408, 265 Aragon Ave). The Downtown Book Center (☎ 305-377-9941, 247 SE 1st St), in Miami, also has a good selection. Lambda Passages Bookstore (☎ 305-754-6900, 7545 Biscayne Blvd NE) provides information to gay and lesbian travelers and carries *twn, Fountain News, Lesbian Nation* and *Hotspots*.

Miami continues to make major efforts to curtail crime, especially crime against tourists. However, avoid isolated areas at night, especially in Liberty City, Little Haiti, Little Havana, areas east of the airport, below 5th St in Miami Beach and around the downtown Greyhound station.

Miami Beach

In 1979, Miami Beach's **Art Deco Historic District** was placed on the National Register of Historic Places. The district lies between the Atlantic Ocean and Lenox Ave on the east and west, and 6th St and 23rd St–Dade Blvd on the south and north. It includes examples of streamline, moderne and Mediterranean Revival architecture, as well as other art deco styles.

Examples of streamline buildings include the Avalon, Chesterfield, Leslie, Tides, Cardozo and Breakwater hotels. Mediterranean highlights include most of the buildings along **Española Way**, but especially the HI Clay Hotel & International Hostel (former home of Desi Arnaz and a casino run by Al Capone), the Old City Hall, the Wolfsonian Foundation building and the Edison Hotel. **Ocean Drive** boasts the Park Central Hotel. The finest example of Depression-era moderne is the 1937 post office on **Washington Ave**. The Betsy Ross Hotel typifies neoclassical revival.

The pedestrian-only **Lincoln Road Mall** is Miami Beach's cultural epicenter, replete with galleries, restaurants and cafes.

South Beach is the most crowded beach, especially on weekends. The beaches north of 21st St – especially the one at 53rd St – are more family-oriented. Latin American families tend to congregate between 5th St and South Pointe, where topless bathing is commonplace. The most popular gay beach centers on 12th St. Nude bathing is legal at Haulover Beach.

Downtown Miami

The Mediterranean-style Metro-Dade Cultural Center (101 W Flagler St) includes the **Historical Museum of Southern Florida** (☎ 305-375-1492), with an excellent series of kid-friendly exhibits covering 10,000 years of Florida history ($5/2 adults/kids), and the **Miami Art Museum** (☎ 305-375-3000), which showcases international contemporary art ($5, free admission Sun). **Bayside Marketplace** (☎ 305-577-3344, 401 Biscayne Blvd) is a popular shopping, dining and entertainment center. Island Queen Sightseeing Tours (☎ 305-379-5119) leaves here for cruises around Biscayne Bay ($14).

The **Latin American Art Museum** (☎ 305-644-1127, 2206 SW 8th St), formerly the Museum of Hispanic and Latin American Art, has changed its name and moved from Coral Gables, but it hasn't changed its mission to showcase contemporary Latin American artists with special emphasis on women (free admission).

MIAMI BEACH

PLACES TO STAY
2   The Governor
4   Fairfax
16 Tropics Hotel & Hostel
19 HI Clay Hotel &
    International Hostel
21 Brigham Gardens
    Guesthouse
24 Cavalier
27 Leslie
31 Kent
33 Jefferson House
34 Kenmore Hotel; Park
    Washington Hotel; Taft
    Hotel & Belaire Hotel
42 Royal Hotel
43 Miami Beach International
    Travelers Hostel
52 Century Hotel

PLACES TO EAT
5   Epicure Market
8   Van Dyke Hotel Cafe; Van
    Dyke
9   Noodles of Asia
11 World Resources Café
32 Biga Bakery
36 11th St Diner
38 Clarke's
48 Tap Tap

ENTERTAINMENT
3   Jackie Gleason Theater
7   Finnegan's 2
10 Score
12 Lincoln Theatre
15 Shadow Lounge
17 Samba Room
18 Starfish
20 Crobar
22 Jazid
37 Twist
44 Pump
50 Fabrik After Hours
53 Nikki Beach Club

OTHER
1   Miami Beach Chamber of
    Commerce
6   Books & Books
13 Tourist Information Kiosk
14 Citibank
23 Post Office
25 Cardozo
26 Miami Design Preservation
    League
28 Tides
29 Old City Hall
30 Police Station
35 Wolfsonian Foundation
39 Edison Hotel
40 Breakwater
41 Art Deco Welcome Center
45 Chesterfield
46 Avalon
47 South Shore Hospital
49 Miami Beach Bicycle Center
51 Park Central Hotel

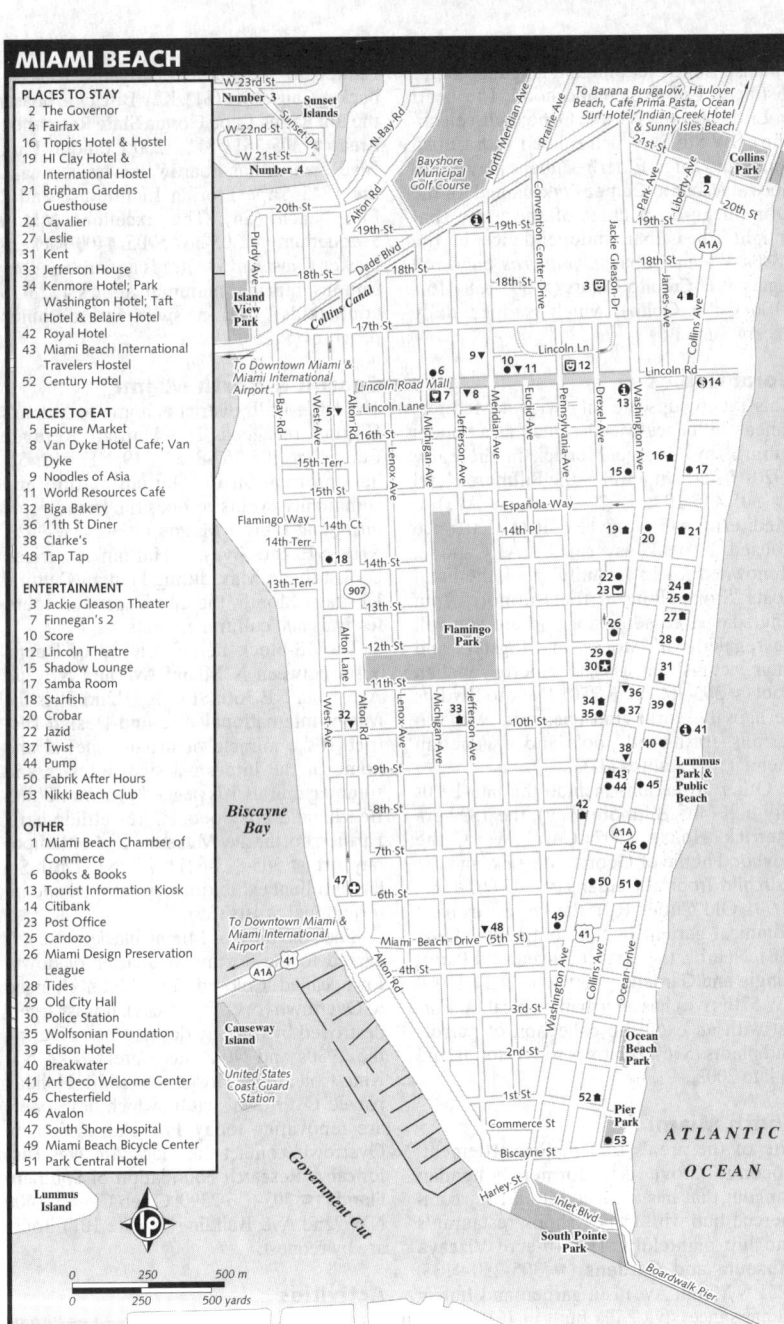

FLORIDA

Little Havana

Spanish is the predominant language in this distinctly Cuban neighborhood. The heart of Little Havana is Calle Ocho (kah-yeh oh-cho), SW 8th St, which is lined with Cuban shops and cafes. Elderly Cubans play dominoes at **Máximo Gómez Park**, named for the Dominican-born chief of the army that fought for Cuban independence in the 1890s. Watch Cuban *tabaqueros* hand-roll cigars at **El Crédito Cigars** (☎ 305-858-4162, 1106 Calle Ocho), which is open daily except Sunday.

Coral Gables

This lovely, upscale city with a Mediterranean influence was designed as a 'model suburb' by George Merrick in the early 1920s. Its crown jewel is the **Biltmore Hotel** (☎ 305-445-1926, 1200 Anastasia Ave), a Mediterranean Revival edifice that once housed a speakeasy run by Al Capone. Renowned for its beautiful pool, the hotel hosts 'Storytelling at the Biltmore' 7pm Thursday (free admission), where you will be regaled with stories of gangsters and their victims' ghosts. The superb **Venetian Pool** (☎ 305-460-5356, 2701 DeSoto Blvd) is perhaps the world's most beautiful, with waterfalls, spring-fed pools and a Venetian theme ($8/4 adults/kids).

Other attractions include the late-1920s city hall (405 Biltmore Way); the 1899-era **Merrick House** (907 Coral Way), the boyhood home of George Merrick; and the **Fairchild Tropical Gardens** (☎ 305-667-1651, 10901 Old Cutler Rd), the largest tropical botanical garden in the continental USA ($8). Nearby, the almost 70-year-old **Parrot Jungle and Gardens** (☎ 305-666-7834, 11000 SW 57th Ave) has an urban tropical rainforest with an exquisite collection of parrots and plants ($16). It moves to Watson Island in late 2002.

South Miami

Site of the area's first major settlement, **Coconut Grove** is a former bohemian hangout that has evolved into a ritzy commercial hub with trendy shops, restaurants and hip nightclubs. The 10-acre **Vizcaya Museum and Gardens** (☎ 305-250-9133, 3251 S Miami Ave) is a garden and Italian Renaissance–style villa built in 1916 by industrialist James Deering ($10).

Key Biscayne

Linked to the mainland by the Rickenbacker Causeway ($1), Key Biscayne boasts the **Bill Baggs Cape Florida State Recreation Area** (☎ 305-361-5811, 1200 Crandon Park Blvd), which has boardwalks, trails, a cafe, the 1845 Cape Florida Lighthouse and a fine beach ($4). The excellent **Miami Seaquarium** (☎ 305-361-5705, 4400 Rickenbacker Causeway) features aquariums, continuous marine mammal shows ($23/18 adults/kids) and a swim-with-dolphins program ($125).

Central & North Miami

The **Little Haiti** district is home to Miami's Haitian refugees. The Haitian Refugee Center (☎ 305-757-8538, 119 NE 54th St) has information on Haitian culture and community events, as does the friendly and intriguing Libreri MaPou (☎ 305-757-9922, 5919 NE 2nd Ave), a Haitian American bookstore. In May, during Haitian Cultural Heritage Month, the city stages bus tours, festivals and cultural exhibits.

The 18-block neighborhood of Buena Vista between N Miami Ave and NE 2nd Ave, from NE 36th St to NE 42nd St, is the **Miami International Arts and Design District**. It's a miracle of urban renewal and home of the interior-design industry and stunning murals. It's pegged as a 'new South Beach,' and artsy people are settling here. Farther north, the **Museum of Contemporary Art** (☎ 305-893-6211, 770 NE 125th St) has excellent exhibitions by national and international artists ($5).

Since the birth of Miami, blacks were relegated to the northwest quarter of downtown, called 'Colored Town,' later changed to **Overtown** (over the tracks). It was largely destroyed by freeway development. During the 1930s and '40s, music greats like Nat King Cole, Lena Horne and Billie Holiday played Overtown's clubs, which developers are renovating today. For information on Overtown, contact the **Black Archives Historical & Research Foundation of Southern Florida** (☎ 305-636-2390, Caleb Center, 5400 NW 22nd Ave, Building C, suite 101). Tours are by request.

Activities

Bicycle rental rates start at $5/20 per hour/day at Miami Beach Bicycle Center

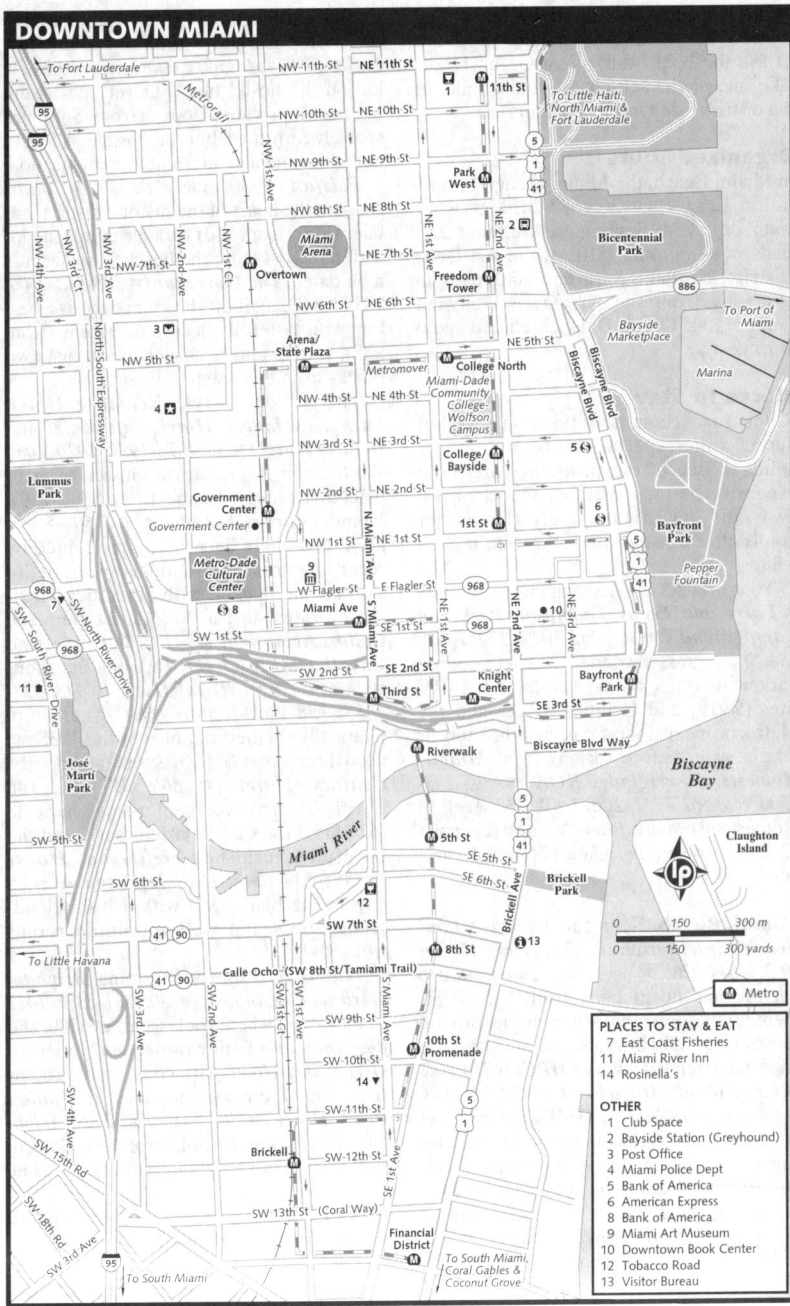

DOWNTOWN MIAMI

FLORIDA

PLACES TO STAY & EAT
7 East Coast Fisheries
11 Miami River Inn
14 Rosinella's

OTHER
1 Club Space
2 Bayside Station (Greyhound)
3 Post Office
4 Miami Police Dept
5 Bank of America
6 American Express
8 Bank of America
9 Miami Art Museum
10 Downtown Book Center
12 Tobacco Road
13 Visitor Bureau

Ⓜ Metro

(☎ 305-674-0150, 601 5th St). In-line skating ($10/25 per hour/day) is also popular. Cruise the boardwalk along Ocean Dr, or take one of the self-guided audio tours of the district (see Organized Tours).

Organized Tours

In Miami Beach, the Miami Design Preservation League (☎ 305-672-2014, W www .mdpl.org, 1234 Washington Ave, suite 207) leads walking tours ($10) of the Art Deco District 10:30am Saturday and 6:30pm Thursday from the Art Deco Welcome Center (1001 Ocean Dr). Self-guided audio tours cost $5.

Places to Stay

Rates for accommodations are higher during winter, special events and summer holidays. Beachfront properties are more expensive; try for something a block or two away for big savings. Only the pricier hotels offer free parking; otherwise it's $10 a day.

Your best bet for sleeping under the stars is *Larry and Penny Thompson Park and Campground* (☎ 305-232-1049, 12451 SW 184 St), a grassy, wooded 270-acre county park with trails, paths, well-kept tent/RV sites ($8/19) and facilities, a lake and the Metrozoo next door. Soak in a hot tub or take a swim before turning in at *Miami-Homestead-Everglades KOA* (☎ 305-233-5300, 800-562-7732, 20675 SW 162 Ave), in Homestead, where tent/RV sites run from $24/28. Also see Everglades National Park, later.

Miami Beach Near the beach, *Miami Beach International Travelers Hostel* (☎ 305-534-0268, W www.sobehostel.com, 236 9th St) has dorm beds from $15/17 HI members/nonmembers and basic private rooms from $38. In a historic Spanish-style villa, the perennial favorite *HI Clay Hotel & International Hostel* (☎ 305-534-2988, W www.clayhotel.com, 1438 Washington Ave) has clean, comfortable dorm rooms with a refrigerator ($14/15 members/nonmembers) and stylish private hotel rooms (from $42). It's a happening place. One block from the beach, cool *Tropics Hotel & Hostel* (☎ 305-531-0361, W www.tropicshotel.com, 1550 Collins Ave) also has dorm beds ($20) and private rooms (from $75). Tropics has a full

kitchen and huge pool, and requires a passport for dorm stays. *Banana Bungalow* (☎ 305-538-1951, 2360 Collins Ave) is the new kid on the hostel block. Dorm beds (from $17) and private rooms (from $68) are sparsely furnished, but the hostel has lots of amenities and activities, and a great location.

Fairfax (☎ 305-538-7082, 1776 Collins Ave), in the heart of the historic district, has beer rates (from $80) with a champagne location (across from the beach); the decor is a bit dated. *The Governor* (☎ 305-532-2100, 435 21st St), a bit off the main drag, is a best buy with tastefully decorated rooms (from $85), a cafe and a garden pool, just two blocks from the beach.

The art deco–style *Kenmore Hotel*, *Park Washington Hotel*, *Taft Hotel* and *Belaire Hotel* (☎ 305-674-1930, 1020–1050 Washington Ave) form a cluster of well-priced art deco properties ($109-159). Island Outpost hotels (☎ 305-604-5000) are individually decorated, frequented by recording artists and models, in prime locations and packed with amenities. High-season rates start at $175 at *Leslie* (1200 Collins Ave), *Kent* (1131 Collins Ave) and *Cavalier* (1320 Ocean Dr). It's all about style at the new *Royal Hotel* (☎ 800-337-4685, 758 Washington Ave), where hip, nautically themed doubles in the 1938 art deco hotel cost $150. Its sister property, *Century Hotel* (☎ 800-337-4685, 140 Ocean Dr), puts you center stage in SoBe for $115. Gates and gardens surround the tastefully furnished *Jefferson House* (☎ 305-534-5247, 1018 Jefferson Ave), a gay and lesbian B&B with a lushly landscaped pool and well-appointed rooms from $140.

Collins Ave sports charming *Brigham Gardens Guesthouse* (☎ 305-531-1331, 1411 Collins Ave), where rooms start at $100, and the oceanfront family-owned and -oriented *Ocean Surf Hotel*, with comfortable rooms from $99. The cozy, deco-dazzling *Indian Creek Hotel* (☎ 305-531-2727, 2727 Indian Creek Dr) has a pool, lovely gardens, a superb staff, and rooms and suites from $140.

Miami The nice, clean 1950s-era *Riviera Court Motel* (☎ 305-665-3528, 5100 Riviera Dr), at US 1, has pool- and water-view rooms from $75. Charming *Miami River Inn* (☎ 305-325-0045, 118 SW South River Dr) offers tasteful rooms from $99. For those who require pampering, **Sonesta Beach Resort** (☎ 305-361-2021, 350 Ocean Dr), on Key Biscayne, is very smart and has excellent beaches. All rooms overlook the water (from $295).

Places to Eat

In Miami Beach, Alton Rd features **Epicure Market** (1656 Alton Rd), with great deli items and pastas from $5, and **Biga Bakery** (1080 Alton Rd), with earthy breads. Argentines and Italians team up for fab food at **Cafe Prima Pasta** (414 71st St). **11th St Diner** (1065 Washington Ave) is open 24 hours. On Lincoln Rd, the indoor/outdoor **Van Dyke Hotel Cafe** (846 Lincoln Ave) always has great salads and crowds. **World Resources Café** (719 Lincoln Ave) has an eclectic menu; and **Noodles of Asia** (805 Lincoln Rd) is highly regarded for bargain pan-Asian dishes. **Tap Tap** (☎ 305-672-2898, 819 5th St) is a feast of Haitian fare for all the senses.

Downtown Miami eateries cater to nine-to-fivers and close Sunday. **East Coast Fisheries** (330 W Flagler St), on the Miami River, is Miami's oldest seafood restaurant (lunch/dinner $15/19). **Rosinella's** (1040 S Miami Ave) prides itself on homemade pasta and attractive prices. **Suzanne's Vegetarian Bistro** (7251 Biscayne Blvd) has it all – good, healthy food, good service, a pleasant setting and bargain prices. At the **Fish House** (☎ 305-595-8453, 10000 SW 56th St) you'll have to overindulge to spend more than $7 on well-prepared seafood. En route to the Metrozoo, Everglades or Keys, don't miss **Norman Brothers Produce** (☎ 305-274-9363, 7621 SW 87th Ave) for an appealing farmers' market and delicious takeout lunches and dinners like $4 rotisserie chicken and meatloaf Tuesday and Wednesday.

Little Havana's Calle Ocho is home to yummy, inexpensive Mexican food at **Taquerías El Mexicano** (521 SW 8th St). **Versailles** (3555 SW 8th St) has slightly more expensive Cuban fare, and tiny **Hy Vong** (3458 SW 8th St) is worth the wait for its Vietnamese dinners (under $12).

In Coral Gables, the moderately priced 'restaurant row' on Giralda Ave runs from Ponce de León Blvd to Miller Ave. **Archie's Pizza Gourmet** (166 Giralda Ave) serves deliciously inspired pizzas and Italian dishes under $10. It also has a Key Biscayne location (600 Crandon Blvd, No 130). **Gourmet** (210 Valencia Ave), a Gables fixture, has Chinese lunch for $6, dinner for $8-10.

Entertainment

The free *Miami New Times* and the *Miami Herald*'s 'Friday Weekend' supplement have the best entertainment (and dining) listings. The acclaimed **Coconut Grove Playhouse** (☎ 305-442-4000, 3500 Main Hwy), in Coconut Grove, stages major shows in an intimate setting. The **Jackie Gleason Theater** (☎ 305-673-7300, 1700 Washington Ave) is Miami Beach's premier showcase for Broadway shows, headliners and the Miami City Ballet. Miami Beach's **Lincoln Theatre** (☎ 305-673-3331, 555 Lincoln Rd) hosts the New World Symphony (☎ 305-673-3331) and major shows.

The **Museum of Contemporary** Art (see Central & North Miami earlier) marries art and jazz at free concerts at 8pm the last Friday of each month. There's always a hip crowd to enjoy the free entertainment at **CocoWalk** (☎ 305-444-0777, 3015 Grand Ave), in Coconut Grove.

Miami Beach has the liveliest nightspots. Look to Euro-hip **Shadow Lounge** (1532 Washington Ave), where the world's best DJs spin. To party all night, start at **Nikki Beach Club** (1 Ocean Dr) or **Crobar** (1445 Washington Ave) before ending the night – starting the day – at **Pump** (841 Washington Ave) and **Fabrik After Hours** (627 Washington Ave), where the hip-hop starts at 4am. Go Irish at **Finnegan's 2** (942 Lincoln Rd), Latin at **Samba Room** (1501 Collins Ave) or **Starfish** (1427 West Ave).

The beach gay scene heats up the dance floor at **Twist** (1057 Washington Ave) and **Score** (727 Lincoln Rd), home to theme nights.

For the latest underground, cross over to the mainland's **Underland Privat** (3835 NW 32nd Ave) or **Club Space** (142 NE 11th St), two converted warehouses. Listen to local live rock and big acts at **Churchill's Hideaway** (5501 NE 2nd Ave), live Afro-Caribbean tunes at **Timbacutiri Cafe** (14080 W Dixie Hwy), in North Miami, and live reggae at **Mad Fishhouse** (3301 Rickenbacker Causeway), on Key Biscayne.

For excellent jazz on the beach, check out **Jazid** (1342 Washington Ave) and **Van Dyke** (846 Lincoln Rd). The mainland boasts **Satchmo Blues Bar and Grill** (60 Merrick

Looking for Love in All the Right Places

Looking for love? Come to Miami, where girls – and boys – just wanna have fun, at least according to Forbes.com's guide to the best places to be single. In a list of 40 metropolitan areas, Miami stood out at number two, right behind...Washington, DC?

To come up with the rankings, Forbes.com took statistical data on everything from census figures to job growth to the number of nightspots and singles. How expensive it is to live in a city was a factor, too. Along with the cost of renting an apartment, they calculated the cost of a pizza, movie tickets and a six-pack of beer. Not exactly Miami fare – Miamians prefer to think of themselves as more of a mango-salsa-covered mahimahi and martini set – but what the heck.

The guide made special note of Miami's physical attractions (gorgeous bodies covered by little clothing), its international flavor (English is almost a second language) and its intense nightlife.

Incidentally, Orlando came in at number 20 and Tampa at number 23, making the Sunshine State one of the best places to find love.

Way), in Coral Gables, and downtown Miami's institution, **Tobacco Road** *(626 S Miami Ave)*.

Spectator Sports

The NFL Miami Dolphins (☎ 305-620-2578) play football September to December; the Florida Marlins (☎ 305-626-7400) play major-league baseball April to September. Both teams call ProPlayer Stadium (2269 Dan Marino Blvd) home.

American Airlines Arena (601 Biscayne Blvd) hosts the NBA Miami Heat (☎ 305-577-4328) and WNBA Miami Sol (☎ 786-777-4765) basketball teams. The NHL Florida Panthers (☎ 954-835-7000) play hockey October to April at the Florida Panthers Hockey Club (One Panther Parkway, Sunrise). Major-league soccer's Miami Fusion (☎ 888-387-4664) competes March to September at Lockhart Stadium (5201 NW 12th Ave, Fort Lauderdale). Watch and bet on jai alai at Miami Jai Alai (☎ 305-633-6400, 3500 NW 37th Ave).

Getting There & Around

Miami International Airport (MIA; ☎ 305-876-7000, flight information ☎ 305-876-7770) is 12 miles west of downtown and accessible by SuperShuttle (☎ 305-871-2000). Prices are $10 to downtown, $12 to Miami Beach.

Greyhound stops at MIA (across from baggage claim in Concourse E) and three Miami stations: downtown's Bayside (☎ 305-379-7403, 100 NW 6th St), Central (☎ 305-871-1810, 4111 NW 27th St) and North Miami (☎ 305-945-0801, 16560 NE 6th Ave). Frequent buses go to Fort Lauderdale ($6; 45 minutes), Jacksonville ($45; 7 hours), Key West ($32; 4 hours), Orlando ($37; 5 hours), Tallahassee ($67; 11 hours) and Tampa ($39; 8 hours).

Miami Terminal (☎ 305-835-1222, 8303 NW 37th Ave) hosts Amtrak. Tri-Rail (☎ 800-874-7245) commuter system serves Miami (free transfer to Miami's transit system) and MIA, Fort Lauderdale ($3) and its airport ($3), and West Palm Beach and its airport ($5.50).

Major and minor car rental companies have booths or phones at MIA.

Metro-Dade Transit (☎ 305-770-3131) runs the local Metrobus, Metromover (downtown) and Metrorail services. Metromovers are monorails that run on loops over the downtown region – great for orientation (25¢). The Metrorail line runs from Hialeah through downtown Miami and then south to Kendall ($1.25).

THE EVERGLADES

Called Pa-hay-okee (Grassy Water) by the Calusa Indians, the Everglades is the largest subtropical wilderness in the continental USA. It's part of a sheet-flow ecosystem beginning at the Kissimmee River, which empties into Lake Okeechobee. In times past the lake overflowed, sending sheets of water through the region and creating an ecosystem that became home to thousands of animal, bird and plant species. Since the late 19th century the waters have been redirected through canals to reclaim land for agricultural, residential and commercial development, and drinking water, causing substantial ecological damage.

More than 3125 sq miles of land were designated the Everglades National Park in 1947, but the threat to this biologically diverse region is far from over. Industry and conservationists continue to battle over millions of dollars earmarked to combat the ecological crisis. That said, this visitor-friendly park still offers excellent opportunities for hiking, biking, canoeing, kayaking, boating, camping, fishing and wildlife observation. The area features museums, land and water tours and lectures.

Everglades National Park

There are three entrances to Everglades National Park: the main or east entrance near Homestead, the north entrance at Shark Valley on US 41, and the west or Gulf entrance at Everglades City. No roads within the park connect the entrances. Admission – good for seven days at all three entrances – is $10 per car, $5 per pedestrian or bike. If you enter at Shark Valley ($8 per car, $4 per pedestrian or bike) you must pay the extra $2 per car, $1 per pedestrian or bike to enter the other areas. For information, contact Everglades National Park (☎ 305-242-7700, 40001 State Rd 9336, Homestead, FL 33034). The park's five visitor centers are open daily 8am-5pm.

Mosquitoes are the summer visitor's bane – bring strong repellent. Never provoke or feed alligators, which are common except around Ten Thousand Islands. Poisonous snakes, which you're not likely to see, include rattlesnakes, water moccasins and coral snakes. Wear long, thick socks and lace-up boots on hikes.

The main entrance, open 24 hours, leads to the **Ernest F Coe Visitor Center** (☎ 305-242-7700, 40001 State Rd 9336), a 45-minute drive from downtown Miami. It has interesting interactive exhibits, films, a bookstore and fun ranger-led activities such as slough slogs (see 'A Walk on the Squishy Side'), hikes, talks and canoe trips. A few miles beyond is the **Royal Palm Visitor Center** (same ☎), the entryway to the short Gumbo-Limbo and Anhinga trails – favorites for wildlife viewing, especially in winter.

The road continues 38 miles to Florida Bay and the **Flamingo Visitor Center** (☎ 941-695-3101), at the southernmost point in the park. En route and at Flamingo are some of the park's best birding areas (Eco Pond, Mrazek Pond and Snake Bight), as well as short walking trails. The **Flamingo Lodge, Marina & Outpost Resort** (☎ 941-695-3101) offers boat tours ($10-32) and fishing trips into the mangroves and Florida Bay; rents canoes ($22/32 per half/full day), kayaks ($27/43), bikes ($8/14) and power-boats ($65/90); and has accommodations and dining.

You'll come face-to-face with nature at **Shark Valley** (☎ 305-221-8776), on US 41, 25 miles west of Florida Turnpike, when you walk or cycle ($4.50 per hour) the alligator-strewn, 15-mile paved loop road. Those with less energy or interest in getting that close to nature can take a narrated two-hour tram tour (☎ 305-221-8455), which costs $10.50.

The **Gulf Coast Visitor Center** (☎ 941-695-3311), on Route 29 in Everglades City, is at the park's west entrance. It sits at the edge of a terrific canoe and kayak region called Ten Thousand Islands. You can take short trips to sandy beaches and shallow, brackish lagoons, or you can be really adventurous and tackle the mangrove- and island-studded 99-mile **Wilderness Waterway**, which runs along the park's southern edge from here to the Flamingo Visitor Center. Rangers lead canoe trips and walks. A concessionaire (☎ 941-695-2591) offers 90-minute boat tours ($16) and canoe rentals ($20 per day).

Miccosukee Indian Village

At this cultural center (☎ 305-223-8380) are a museum, educational alligator shows, 30-minute airboat rides ($10), craft and food demonstrations and a restaurant. The center is on US 41 just west of Shark Valley, 25 miles west of the Florida Turnpike. Admission is $5.

Organized Tours

The best outfitter for outings and rentals is Everglades Rentals & Eco Adventures (☎ 941-695-3299, 107 Camellia St), at the Ivey House B&B in Everglades City. They provide rental canoes ($25 a day) and kayaks ($35), plus single/multiday tours (from $40/250). The Gulf Coast Visitor Center has a few canoes, too. For Flamingo area trips, use the concessionaire at the

FLORIDA

FLORIDA

A Walk on the Squishy Side

Most people don't voluntarily get knee-deep in muck, but for the truly intrepid and totally unsqueamish, there are slough slogs – ranger-led knee- to waist-high immersions in the swamps of the Everglades and Big Cypress. Slough slogs are wet, muddy, messy and lots of fun. Beware: Rangers recommend that those who don't shave their legs wear long pants. It seems the floating leg hairs look a lot like mosquito larvae to the gambusia minnows, who nip at them.

Flamingo Lodge, Marina & Outpost Resort (see Everglades National Park, earlier).

Several companies along Hwy 41 offer airboat tours into the River of Grass surrounding Everglades National Park (airboats are prohibited in the park). Most make day trips, but Ray Cramer's Everglades Airboat Tours (☎ 305-852-5339) depart at sundown, when the animals are most active ($40).

Places to Stay & Eat

Camping on the park's west side includes beach sites, ground sites and 'chickees' (covered wooden platforms above the water) in the backcountry along the Wilderness Waterway, all of which require a permit ($10) from the Gulf Coast Visitor Center (☎ 941-695-3311) and a boat for access. In Everglades City, *Glades Haven* (☎ 941-695-2746, 800 SE Copeland Ave) has camping ($20), boating and marina facilities. The east side of the park (☎ 305-242-7700, 305-251-0371, 800-365-2267) has two developed campgrounds: Long Pine Key, near the park entrance, and Flamingo, near boating, tours and restaurants. Pets are welcome. Reservations are recommended November to April; the rest of the year is first-come, first-served. Developed sites are free June to August, $14 during other times. The decor might be described as 'old Mexico meets hippie '60s' at *Everglades International Hostel* (☎ 305-248-1122, 20 SW 2nd Ave) in Florida City, where the friendly owners live on site. There are dorm (from $13), semiprivate (from $26) and private (from $33) rooms as well as winter-only campsites ($10).

On the west side, *Ivey House* (☎ 941-695-3299, W www.iveyhouse.com, 107 Camellia St), a remodeled 1928 boardinghouse in Everglades City, is now a year-round inn (from $60). Near Shark Valley, *Miccosukee Resort* (☎ 305-925-2555, 877-242-6464, 500 SW 177th Ave), on US 41 at Krome Ave, is loaded with modern conveniences, entertainment and a casino (from $105). The resort boasts three attractively priced restaurants and a deli. The park's only hotel is the *Flamingo Lodge, Marina & Outpost Resort* (☎ 941-695-3101), with water-view rooms for $95. Clean, basic properties near the east park entrance include bright *Coral Roc Motel* (☎ 305-246-2888, 1100 N Krome Ave), with a small pool (from $45), and *Everglades Motel* (☎ 305-247-4117, 605 S Krome Ave) and *Rodeway Inn* (☎ 305-248-2741, 815 N Krome Ave), both with rooms from $39.

West-side eateries are limited unless you go into Naples. Otherwise, try *Seafood Depot* (102 Collier Ave), in Everglades City, for inexpensive riverfront seafood dining. In between park entrances is *Joanie's Blue Crab Cafe* (39395 Tamiami Trail), in Ochopee 50 miles west of Florida's Turnpike. It's a funky, quintessential 1950s-style swamp cafe that serves blue crabs, burgers and chicken.

On the east side, try the inexpensive local favorite, *El Toro Taco* (1 S Krome Ave), for authentic Mexican food, and *Farmers' Market Restaurant* (300 N Krome Ave) for great, cheap breakfasts, and seafood and veggies for lunch and dinner. Both are in Homestead. From Friday to Sunday, dine with locals at *Taco Loco* (941 Palm Dr), a fenced, roof-covered mobile kitchen that serves authentic, inexpensive Mexican dishes.

AROUND THE EVERGLADES

State and national parks occupy most of the land around Everglades National Park. In between is the Miccosukee Reservation, with Native American cultural attractions, gaming and accommodations.

Big Cypress National Preserve

On the Tamiami Trail (Hwy 41), which crosses swamp, prairie, hammock and other ecosystems between Miami and Naples, this preserve is a 1139-sq-mile federally protected area on the north edge of Everglades National Park. It came about as a compromise among environmentalists, cattle ranchers and oil and gas explorers.

The preserve is a major player in the Everglades' ecosystem, as the rains that flood the prairies and wetlands here slowly filter down through the 'Glades. The preserve's name comes from its sheer acreage, not the height of the occupying dwarf pond cypress trees. Try to spot alligators, snakes, wading birds, the endangered Florida panther, wild turkeys and red-cockaded woodpeckers.

At the **Oasis Visitor Center** (☎ 941-695-4111), 20 miles west of Shark Valley, you can watch a film, then sign up for ranger-led activities including bike and canoe tours, exciting swamp hikes and lectures. The preserve's Turner River is excellent for canoeing and kayaking (for rentals, see Organized Tours earlier).

Within the preserve lie 31 miles of the **Florida National Scenic Trail**, accessible by car from the Monroe or Tamiami ranger stations. There's also the short **Tree Snail Hammock Nature Trail**, off Loop Rd.

The preserve's four no-fee primitive campgrounds (☎ 941-695-4111) are along the Tamiami Trail and Loop Road. *Monument Lake Campground* ($14) has facilities. *Dona Drive Campground* ($4) has a dump station and potable water. They're all very buggy in summer.

Ah-Tha-Thi-Ki

This Seminole museum (☎ 863-902-1113) showcases Seminole culture from ancient to modern times through interesting exhibits, films, a mile-long boardwalk and high-tech interactive videos ($6). In Seminole, the name means 'A Place to Remember.' It's in the Seminole Big Cypress Reservation on Hwy 833, 17 miles north of I-75 exit 14 and 40 miles west of Fort Lauderdale. It's closed Monday. The reservation's *Big Cypress Campground* (☎ 800-437-4102) has primitive sites ($15), improved tent/RV sites ($20/22) and cabins ($35).

Big Cypress Gallery

Clyde Butcher's award-winning B&W photography captures nature in the Big Cypress Swamp and the Everglades in elaborate detail. His studio (☎ 941-695-2428) is at 52388 US 41, Ochopee (open Wed-Sat).

Collier-Seminole State Park

Freshwater and salt water meet in this 6423-acre state park (☎ 941-394-3397, 20200 US 41), 17 miles southeast of Naples, home to manatees (in winter), white ibis, snowy egrets and alligators ($3.25). There's a 13½-mile canoe trail along the Blackwater River; canoes cost $3/15 per hour/day. Ranger-led canoe trips ($10) on Sunday are limited to four canoes, so call in advance. You'll need reservations to canoe to the primitive *campsites* ($3) at Grocery Place. Picturesque developed sites start at $8. There's also a 6-mile hiking trail and an interpretive center near the main campsites. Mosquitoes are ferocious in summer.

FLORIDA KEYS

In 1513 Juan Ponce de León sailed around the string of islands known as the Florida Keys (current population 79,600). Former home of Hemingway and other modern literary types, Key West (population 25,500) is the end of the 126-mile string. The Keys are connected by US 1, with mile markers (indicated as 'MM') showing distances between Key West (MM 0) and the mainland at Florida City (MM 126). The string is divided into the Upper, Middle and Lower Keys. The Florida Keys & Key West Visitors Bureau (☎ 800-352-5397, Ⓦ www.fla-keys.com, 402 Wall St), in Key West, has information on

---

Key Lime Pie

Many places say they serve the original key lime pie, but who actually made the first is questionable. Types of crust vary, and whether a pie has meringue or not is equally often left to the discretion of the preparer. However, what is not debatable is the color. Beware of establishments that serve green key lime pie: Key limes are yellow, not green. Restaurants that add green food coloring say that tourists expect it to be green. Steer clear. Always on the shortlist of 'Best Key Lime Pie' is *Manny & Isa's Restaurant* on Islamorada, where for over 30 years Manny has picked key limes from his backyard trees to make an original-style pie with a short-crust pastry, luscious sweet-tart filling and thick meringue on top.

the entire area. The multilingual Keys Hotline (☎ 800-771-5397) provides information and emergency assistance.

Key Largo

Key Largo leapt to the public eye after the eponymously named 1948 film starring Humphrey Bogart and Lauren Bacall. It's best known as an absolutely fabulous place to snorkel, dive and, more recently, kayak. It appears tacky from the road, but from the water it looks like paradise. The Chamber of Commerce (☎ 305-451-1414, 800-822-1088) is at MM 106.

You'll find good beaches at **John Penne-kamp Coral Reef State Park** (☎ 305-451-1202, MM 102.5), which also has a small but interesting museum and aquarium, and excellent ranger-led programs in winter ($4). The park is the most user-friendly way to get out onto the Florida reef. Snorkel trips cost $26, plus $5 for gear; dive trips are $39, plus $29 for gear. There are also reasonably priced rentals on canoes, kayaks, powerboats and personal glass-bottom boats. Glass-bottom-boat tours depart regularly to **Molasses Reef** ($18).

Other good dive options are American Diving Headquarters (☎ 305-451-0037, MM 105.5), which has predive reef and marine-life orientations, and Quiescence Diving Service (☎ 305-451-2440, MM 103.5), which specializes in small groups and twilight dives. Rates are around $60 for a two-tank dive with tank and weight rental, $85-90 if you need everything.

The best way to enjoy the Keys is by water. Florida Bay Outfitters (☎ 305-451-3018, MM 104) makes it happen up close and personal in kayaks and canoes from $20/35 for a half/full day. It leads kayak tours from $45, including a full-moon paddle, and will deliver the kayak to your hotel. It also rents camping equipment.

Places to Stay & Eat Sites at *John Pennekamp Coral Reef State Park* (☎ 305-451-1202, MM 102.5) cost $19. There are amenities galore, including free modem hookup, at beachfront *America Outdoors* (☎ 305-852-8054, MM 97.5), where tent/RV sites start at $40/55.

Key Largo has lots of clean, cheerful mom-and-pop resorts. At the top of the charm list are the bayfront *Largo Lodge*

(☎ 305-451-0424, 800-468-4378, MM 101.5), with adult-only efficiencies (from $115) set in a tropical hardwood forest, and family-run *Popp's Motel* (☎ 305-852-5201, MM 95.5), with a nice beach and hammocks (from $89). If you live to dive, *Frank's Key Haven Resort* (☎ 305-852-3017, 800-765-5397, MM 92, 198 Harborview Dr), in Tavernier, is a good choice (from $112). If you want to go upscale but don't want a large chain, there's the relaxed *Kona Kai Resort* (☎ 305-852-7200, 800-365-7829, MM 97.8), with an art gallery, water toys, tropical gardens and a tennis court (from $196).

The Fish House (MM 102.4) delivers great service and large portions (from $14). There's inexpensive Mexican food at *Señor Frijoles* (MM 104). *Chad's Deli & Bakery* (MM 92.3) sells gigantic sandwiches ($6-7) made with freshly baked bread (no dinner, closed Sun).

Harriette's Restaurant (MM 95.7) has good, fast, entertaining breakfasts from $4.25. Casual, screened, Keys-funky *Mrs Mac's Kitchen* (MM 99.4) serves barbecue, seafood and burgers ($7-12). The very Keys-ey waterfront *Calypso* (MM 99.5, 1 Seagate Blvd) features innovative dishes like seafood-and-black-bean burritos (from $9). There are two Italian choices: upscale *Cafe Largo* (MM 99.5), with dishes from $15, and neighborhood-style *Anthony's Italian Restaurant & Lounge* (MM 97.6). *The Frog and The Fly Cafe* (MM 91), in Tavernier Towne Center, serves up healthful smoothies, veggie wraps, and panini sandwiches for breakfast and lunch (from $6).

Islamorada

This area boasts some of the world's most diverse sea life, making for wonderful fishing and diving, as well as lots of good restaurants and an active nightlife. The Chamber of Commerce (☎ 305-664-4503, 800-322-5397, MM 82.5) distributes visitor information from an old caboose.

Locals like to kayak out to **Indian Key State Historic Site**, a little island where only foundations, an observation tower and trails remain, and to **Lignumvitae Key State Botanical Site**, site of the Matheson House, former private retreat of chemical magnate William Matheson. There are ranger-led tours on both keys. Rent kayaks from **Robbie's Marina** (☎ 305-664-9814, MM

77.5), which also offers powerboat shuttle service twice daily ($15 one island, $25 both). Get information on both keys from nearby **Long Key State Recreation Area** (☎ 305-664-4815, MM 67.5), a park offering canoeing (rentals $4 an hour), hiking trails, a not-very-sandy beach and a breezy beach-front campground ($17).

Theater of the Sea (☎ 305-664-2431, MM 84.5) has exhibits, continuous marine mammal shows and opportunities to swim with dolphins, stingrays and sea lions ($35-110). Admission is $17.25. Visit the Environmental Center at **Windley Key Fossil Reef State Geologic Site** (☎ 305-664-2540, MM 85.5), then take a guided or self-guided tour to see the fossil-rich quarry walls. The village of Islamorada has good sun and sand at **Anne's Beach** (MM 73.5); **Library Beach** (MM 81.5), behind Islamorada Public Library; and **Islamorada Founder's Park** (MM 87). The latter, which also has a dog park, Olympic-size pool and tennis courts, charges $10 per car.

Places to Stay & Eat The *Long Key State Recreation Area* (☎ 305-664-4815, MM 68) has shady oceanfront campsites ($17). *KOA* (☎ 305-664-4922, MM 70) tent/RV sites, on Fiesta Key, start at $43/68.

Simple rooms at *Key Lantern & Blue Fin Inn* (☎ 305-664-4572, MM 82) start at $45. *Drop Anchor Motel* (☎ 305-664-4863, MM 85) has doubles from $79. Small, basic and friendly, *Star of the Sea* (☎ 306-664-2961, 800-664-2961, MM 77.5) has a beach and pool (from $70). Kick back and relax at the laid-back, rough-around-the-edges *Ragged Edge Resort* (☎ 305-852-5389, MM 86.5, 243 Treasure Harbor Rd) from $79 a night. *Lime Tree Bay Resort Motel* (☎ 305-664-4740, 800-723-4519, MM 68.5) is a cozy 2½-acre waterfront hideaway with rooms from $107, cottages and an on-site water-sports concessionaire.

Top-of-the line places include lovely cottages and townhouses at *The Moorings* (☎ 305-664-4708, MM 81.5, 123 Beach Rd), from $185 per night with a two-night minimum; and the ecofriendly 27-acre *Cheeca Lodge* (☎ 305-664-4651, 800-327-2888, MM 82), with lagoons, gardens, two pools, a nice beach and a new spa (from $295). There are accommodations (from $90) and restaurants at *Holiday Isle Resort* (☎ 305-664-2321, 800-327-7070, MM 84), the

area's hottest nightspot among the 20- to 40-year-old crowd.

For good eatin', inexpensive perennial favorites include *Manny & Isa's (MM 81.6)*, for great Cuban food and award-winning key lime pie; *Rain Barrel Garden Cafe (MM 86.7)*, for generously sized, healthy sandwiches and salads in a garden setting; rowdy *Hog Heaven (MM 85.3)*, for waterfront beer, hanging out and 16oz steaks under $12; and *Little Italy (MM 68.5)*, for flavorful pasta and low prices. Good moderately priced options include *Squid Row (MM 81.9)*, for fresh seafood; *Lazy Days (MM 79.9)*, for waterfront yellowtail sandwiches; and the more upscale bayfront *Morada Bay (MM 81.5)*, for the setting, trendy Floribbean (Floridian-Caribbean) cuisine and full-moon parties.

Marathon

Midway down the chain is Marathon, doorway to the scenic Seven Mile Bridge and historic Pigeon Key. The visitor center (☎ 305-743-5417) is at MM 53.5.

The graceful **Seven Mile Bridge** is the longest of the 40-plus bridges that link the island chain. On its north side stand remnants of the original Seven Mile Bridge, built in the early 1900s by Henry Flagler.

Park at the north/east end of the Seven Mile Bridge (MM 45) and walk (or take the tram) across a 2¼-mile stretch of the Old Seven Mile Bridge (you saw it in the movie *True Lies*) to **Pigeon Key National Historic District** (☎ 305-289-0025), a restored 5-acre railroad work camp that dates from 1908. Its museum and video chronicle the railroad and its baron, Henry M Flagler ($7.50). You can swim and picnic here. Recently, the district opened two of its historic buildings as *guesthouses*, with prices less than $100 for four people. The **Museums and Nature Center of Crane Point Hammock** (☎ 305-743-9100, MM 50.5) includes the Museum of Natural History, Florida Keys Children's Museum, restored George Adderly House ($7.50) – one of the state's only remaining examples of tabby construction – and a nature trail.

A sandy beach, clean bathhouse, picnic tables and kayak trails where you can see manatees and birds constitute the worthwhile **Curry Hammock State Park** (☎ 305-664-4815, MM 57), on Crawl Key. The **Dolphin Research Center** (☎ 305-289-1121,

MM 59), on Grassy Key, is a not-for-profit educational facility where you can study and swim with dolphins ($70-110; 30-day advance reservations recommended). Admission is $12.50.

Knight Key Campground (☎ *305-743-4343, MM 47*) has shaded, grassy tent/RV sites ($39/47). *Sea Cove* (☎ *305-289-0800, MM 54.5*) is a friendly, family-owned place with rooms on houseboats, efficiencies and a floating motel (from $99). *Siesta Motel* (☎ *305-743-5671, MM 51*) has basic, comfortable doubles ($70). Pleasantly landscaped *Coral Lagoon* (☎ *305-289-0121, MM 53.5*) has pastel-colored canalfront duplex cottages loaded with amenities (from $75). Art-filled *Seascape Ocean Resort* (☎ *305-743-6455, 800-332-7327, MM 50.5, 1075 75th St*) is an upscale option (from $125, breakfast and afternoon hors d'oeuvres included).

Folks have been pulling up a chair for three squares at the weatherworn, open-air *7 Mile Grill* (*MM 47*) for almost 50 years. On weekdays local workers gather for breakfast and lunch (burgers, sandwiches and pasta) at friendly *Village Cafe* (*MM 50.5*), in Gulfside Village Plaza. *The Hurricane* (*MM 49.5*) isn't much on atmosphere (except at night, when there's always entertainment), but the servings are generous and there's lots of fresh seafood, including a raw bar.

Lower Keys

The Lower Keys (MM 46–MM 0) are the least developed area of the island chain. The chamber of commerce (☎ 305-872-2411, 800-872-3722) is at MM 31, Big Pine Key.

Some not-to-be-missed sights include the **National Key Deer Refuge** on Big Pine Key, where you can see the endangered dog-size deer; and the largest body of freshwater in the Keys, the **Blue Hole**, a former quarry that's home to alligators, turtles and fish along with wading birds (free admission). **Watson's Nature Trail** is a short self-guided walk through the key deer's natural habitat. On weekends November to March, there are volunteer-led guided walks of **Watson's Hammock**, a prime key deer fawning area (closed Apr-May). Refuge headquarters (☎ 305-872-2239, MM 30.5), in the Big Pine Shopping Center (open Mon-Fri), also provides information on the **Great White Heron National Wildlife Refuge**, a large wading-bird nesting area. Guided kayak

nature tours are offered to both refuges through Big Pine Kayak Adventures (☎ 305-872-2896, 305-395-0930, 877-595-2925), run by award-winning nature photographer Bill Keogh and naturalist Emily Graves. Both run memorable three- to four-hour trips from $49.

Looe Key is a grove reef off Ramrod Key teeming with colorful tropical fish, coral and other sea life. Looe Key Dive Center (☎ 305-872-2215 ext 2, 800-942-5397, MM 27.5), on Ramrod Key, provides snorkeling ($30, plus $9 for gear) and dive trips (from $45, plus $40).

The Keys' best beach is **Bahia Honda State Park** (☎ 305-872-2353, MM 37), which is also the chain's only large natural beach. The 524-acre park ($4) has nature trails, ranger-led programs, bike and kayak rentals ($10 an hour), snorkeling ($26, plus $5 for gear), camping ($19) and waterfront cabins ($110).

See Bahia Honda State Park for *camping* options. Repeat business allows *Big Pine Key Fishing Lodge* (☎ *305-872-2351, MM 33*) to thrive year round. It has tent sites ($29-39) and spotless furnished trailers and rooms (from $79). Big Pine Key has three lovely oceanside B&Bs: *Casa Grande* (☎ *305-872-2878, 1619 Long Beach Dr*); *The Barnacle* (☎ *305-872-3298, 1557 Long Beach Dr*); and *Deer Run B&B* (☎ *305-872-2015, 1985 Long Beach Dr*), for $95-110.

Big Pine Shopping Center (*MM 30.5*) has pizza and sandwich joints. *No Name Pub* (*MM 30*), on N Watson Blvd, serves up lots of local color as well as the best pizza for miles. Ultracasual *Montes Restaurant & Fish Market* (*MM 25*), on Summerland Key, specializes in the Keys staple – fish sandwiches – and other bounty from the sea.

Key West

While Key West still exudes charm and eccentricity, overdevelopment is straining the resources and patience of old-timers. Since the Great Depression, artists and craftspeople have converged on the area. Like Fort Lauderdale and South Beach, Key West is a major gay destination. The town is divided into the historic Old Town and the New Town, occupied by businesses, residences, the airport and the US Navy.

The Chamber of Commerce (☎ 305-294-2587, 800-527-8539, 402 Wall St), off Mallory Square, provides an accommodations

FLORIDA

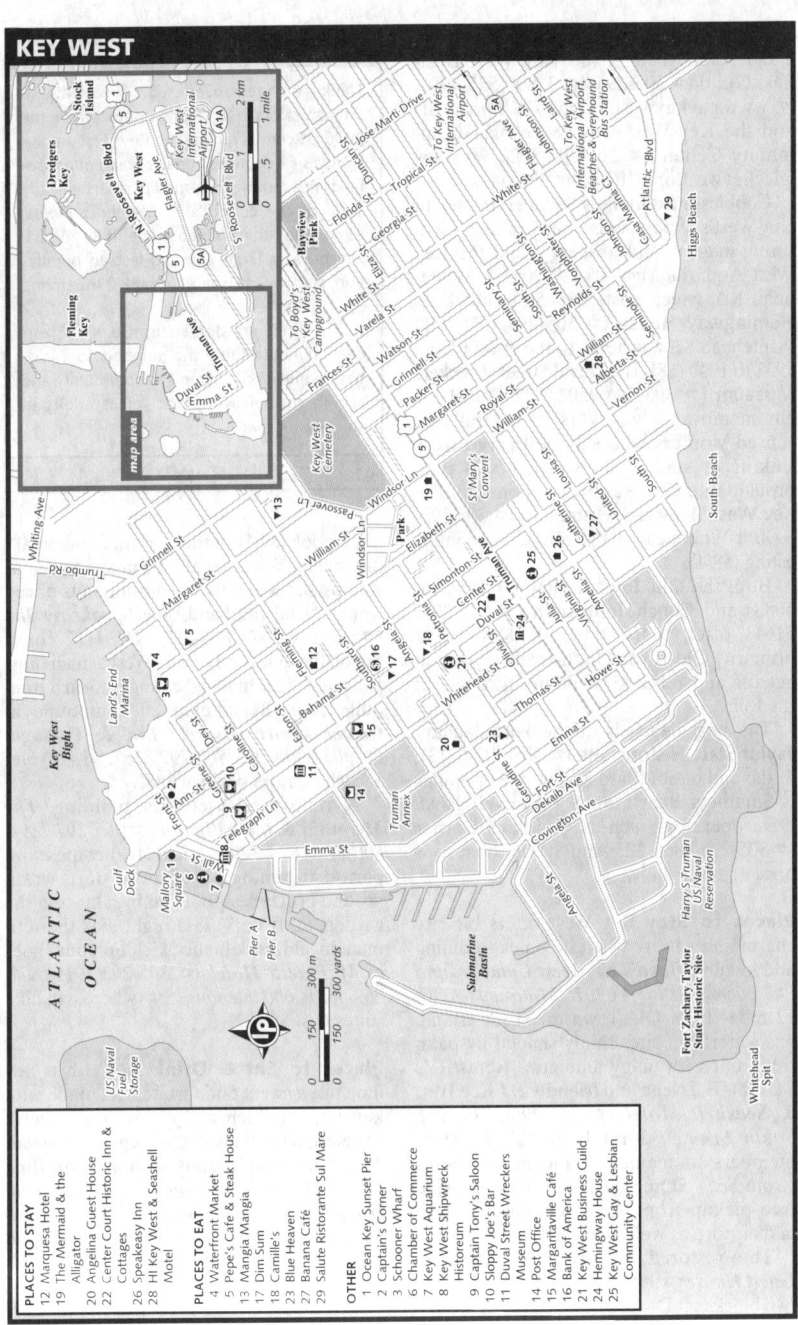

KEY WEST

PLACES TO STAY
12 Marquesa Hotel
19 The Mermaid & the
    Alligator
20 Angelina Guest House
22 Center Court Historic Inn &
    Cottages
26 Speakeasy Inn
28 HI Key West & Seashell
    Motel

PLACES TO EAT
4   Waterfront Market
5   Pepe's Cafe & Steak House
13 Mangia Mangia
17 Dim Sum
18 Camille's
23 Blue Heaven
27 Banana Café
29 Salute Ristorante Sul Mare

OTHER
1   Ocean Key Sunset Pier
2   Captain's Corner
3   Schooner Wharf
6   Chamber of Commerce
7   Key West Aquarium
8   Key West Shipwreck
    Historeum
9   Captain Tony's Saloon
10 Sloppy Joe's Bar
11 Duval Street Wreckers
    Museum
14 Post Office
15 Margaritaville Café
16 Bank of America
21 Key West Business Guild
24 Hemingway House
25 Key West Gay & Lesbian
    Community Center

booking service. Two groups cater to gay and lesbian visitors: the Key West Business Guild (☎ 305-294-4603, 800-535-7797, Ⓦ www.gaykeywestfl.com, 728 Duval St) and the Key West Gay & Lesbian Community Center (☎ 305-292-3223, Ⓦ www .glcckeywest.org, 1075 Duval St).

Cobblestoned **Mallory Square** is the site of Key West's famous sunset celebrations – featuring jugglers and buskers – and the Key West Aquarium (☎ 305-296-2051, 1 Whitehead St), which costs $8/4.50 adults/kids. **Hemingway House** (☎ 305-294-1575, 907 Whitehead St) was home to the author from 1931 to 1940 ($8). The **Duval Street Wreckers Museum** (☎ 305-294-9502, 322 Duval St) commemorates 'wreckers' – federally licensed workers who salvaged cargo from sinking or sunken ships, which was then brought into Key West for auction ($5). The **Key West Shipwreck Historeum** (☎ 305-292-8990, 1 Whitehead St) is a little more interesting ($8/4).

Both the **Old Town Trolley** (☎ 305-296-6688) and **Conch Tour Train** (☎ 305-294-5161) offer tours ($19) of Key West, primarily Old Town. On the trolley you can get off and reboard at points throughout the tour.

The best beach is at the **Fort Zachary Taylor State Historic Site** (☎ 305-292-6713), at the end of Southard St; the most popular is **Smathers Beach**, on S Roosevelt Blvd. Dive operators such as Captain's Corner (☎ 305-296-8865, 125 Ann St) run boat trips once or twice daily.

Places to Stay Key West offers big-city charm and variety when it comes to dining and lodging. *Boyd's Key West Campground* (☎ 305-294-1465, 6401 Maloney Ave), 12 miles from Old Town on Stock Island, has waterfront sites thinly shaded by palm trees, but with many amenities (tents/RVs $41/51). The clean and friendly *HI Key West & Seashell Motel* (☎ 305-296-5719, 718 South St) has dorm beds ($18.50/21.50 members/nonmembers) and motel rooms (from $65). Dinner costs $3. They provide free pickup from the Greyhound station and airport, as well as excursion discounts.

The restored Victorian-era *Angelina Guest House* (☎ 305-294-4480, 302 Angela St), two blocks off Duval St, is one step up from a hostel in price, hospitality and ambience, and

has a pool, lovely garden, continental breakfast and high-season rates from $95. Spacious studios, suites and two-bedroom units priced from $85 fill the handsome *Speakeasy Inn* (☎ 305-296-2680, 800-217-4884, 1117 Duval St), on the quiet end of Key West's main drag. Restored cigar makers' cottages form a tranquil, tropically landscaped compound at *Center Court Historic Inn & Cottages* (☎ 305-296-9292, 800-797-8787, 915 Center St), where rates begin at $88.

A renovated Victorian building, *The Mermaid & the Alligator* (☎ 305-294-1894, 800-773-1894, 729 Truman Ave) comes with period trimmings, a friendly staff, wraparound porches, a pool and breakfast in the garden, all from $178 a night. For the ultimate in laid-back luxury, kick off your shoes at *Marquesa Hotel* (☎ 305-292-1919, 800-869-4631, 600 Fleming St), where villalike suites cost $260.

Places to Eat & Drink Don't miss key lime pie, a sweet and tart dessert made with key limes (which are yellow, not green), sweetened condensed milk, eggs and sugar.

Breakfast with locals at funky *Camille's* (703½ Duval St) or *Pepe's Cafe and Steak House* (806 Caroline St), which oozes character. Both serve three meals. *Waterfront Market* (201 William St) is great for sandwiches, organic produce, baked goods and health foods. Casual French *Banana Café* (1211 Duval St) serves lunches ($4) and dinners ($14-20). Moderately priced *Dim Sum* *(613½ Duval St)* successfully combines French and Asian cuisine with many vegetarian entrées.

Dine inside or outdoors on natural, Caribbean-influenced food at artsy, popular *Blue Heaven* *(729 Thomas St)*. For fresh, homemade pasta – and great wines – there's no place better than *Mangia Mangia* *(900 Southard St)*. At lunch and dinner, you can watch or listen to the surf from *Salute Ristorante Sul Mare* *(1000 Atlantic Blvd)*, on Higgs Beach, a funky wooden beachfront indoor and open-air Italian restaurant.

Duval St is the entertainment center, with most places offering nightly live music. Key West is a gay hot spot, and all venues are gay-friendly – they'd be run out of town if they weren't. Old-time favorites of the party-hard crowd include *Sloppy Joe's Bar* *(201 Duval St)* and *Captain Tony's Saloon* *(428 Greene St)*, both with Hemingway connections and live entertainment. Jimmy Buffett's *Margaritaville Café* *(500 Duval St)* appeals to die-hard fans and a college-age crowd. And for the crowd that wants to gaze out across the sea, don't miss *Ocean Key Sunset Pier* *(Zero Duval St)*. If variety is the spice of life, the funky waterfront *Schooner Wharf* *(202 William St)* is one of the spiciest.

Getting There & Around

There's service between Key West International Airport (☎ 305-296-5439, 3535 S Roosevelt Blvd) and Miami, Tampa, Naples, Fort Lauderdale and Orlando.

Greyhound (☎ 305-296-9072, 800-410-5397, 800-231-2222) runs four buses daily between Miami and the Keys, stopping en route at Miami International Airport. There are designated stops, but the driver also stops on request. The Key West station ($32; 4 hours) is at the airport. Along the way you can get off in the Upper, Middle and Lower Keys with tickets priced $12-29. The new Dade-Monroe Express (☎ 305-770-3131) runs daily buses ($1.25) from Key Largo (MM 98) to Florida City.

The best way to get around the Keys is by rental car or Greyhound. Key West is best navigated on foot, especially in Old Town, and by moped, with rates from $12 per three hours. Try Keys Moped & Scooter (☎ 305-294-0399, 523 Truman Ave).

East Coast

This section of land and barrier islands comprises the Gold Coast and Treasure Coast, so named for the affluent communities that dot it and the treasures that went down with a Spanish fleet in the early 1700s.

FORT LAUDERDALE

Until the late 1980s, Fort Lauderdale (population 152,400) was *the* college spring-break destination. Today it is known more as an international yachting center, although there's still plenty of partying in its clubs, bars and pubs. It's also a major destination for gay visitors. As well, Fort Lauderdale has a surprising number of cultural and historical sites. Many are near the river and thus accessible by the very entertaining Water Taxi.

The visitor bureau (☎ 954-765-4466, 800-227-8669, W www.sunny.org, 1850 Eller Dr), in Port Everglades, also has an activities and African-Caribbean information line (☎ 954-527-5600), and there's also a Gay & Lesbian Community Center of South Florida (☎ 954-463-9005, W www.glccftl.org, 1717 N Andrews Ave).

The best features of the **Museum of Art** (☎ 954-525-5500, 1 E Las Olas Blvd) are works from the post-WWII Cobra art movement (from Copenhagen, Brussels and Amsterdam), as well as collections of Cuban and ethnographic African and South American art ($10). Blockbuster exhibits at the **Museum of Discovery & Science** (☎ 954-467-6637, 401 SW 2nd St) make it a must-stop, not to mention its IMAX theater, which shows 3D films (admission and movie $12.50).

The **Old Fort Lauderdale Museum of History** (☎ 954-463-4431, 231 SW 2nd Ave) covers the history of Fort Lauderdale and Broward County, Seminole folk art and baseball ($5). Built in 1901, **Stranahan House** (☎ 954-524-4736, 1 Stranahan Place), on SE 6th Ave, is one of Florida's oldest residences ($5). **Bonnet House** (☎ 954-563-5393, 900 N Birch Rd), near Hwy A1A and Sunrise Blvd, is a beautiful historic estate near the beach with a nature trail, native and imported tropical plants and tours ($9). Stranahan and Bonnet are closed Monday and Tuesday.

FLORIDA

Florida's Top Two

Zero points if you guess that Disney World is Florida's number-one tourist destination; everybody knows that. Ten points if you guess what ranks just behind the home of the big-eared mouse.

No, it isn't a theme park. Nor is it the Panhandle's pristine beaches. And no, it isn't Everglades National Park. The number-two tourist destination is Sawgrass Mills Mall in Sunrise, 10 miles west of Fort Lauderdale (☎ 954-846-2300, 800-356-4557, 12801 W Sunrise Blvd). Visitors flock to shop more than 2 miles of outlets for such stores as Saks Fifth Avenue, Neiman Marcus, Disney, Kenneth Cole, Tommy Hilfiger, Gap and Polo Ralph Lauren (open daily to 9:30pm). When not shopping they're munching at more than 30 eateries.

Boredom is not an option. Nonshopping and dieting partners can play at GameWorks or watch the silver screen at Regal 23 Cinemas.

Foreign visitors can pick up a $1,500-discount coupon book at area hotels or print out the VIP Card from [W] www .sawgrassmillsmall.com, then exchange it for a coupon book at the mall.

Daily roundtrip shuttle service ($10) is available from many Miami, Miami Beach, Fort Lauderdale and Hollywood hotels. Step off the bus and you're handed the coupon book and a shopping bag.

The *Carrie B* (☎ 954-768-9920) riverboat departs daily at 11am, 1pm and 3pm from Riverwalk, SE 5th Ave and W Las Olas Blvd for harbor tours ($12). The glass-bottom *Pro Diver II* (☎ 954-467-6030) charges $27 including gear, $20 for nondiving companions. The *Jungle Queen* (☎ 954-462-5596, Bahia Mar Yacht Center, 801 Sea Breeze), a Fort Lauderdale tradition, has afternoon ($13) and dinner/show cruises ($28). Water Taxi drivers give a lively narration of riverfront homes, attractions and history as they ply the New River (see Getting There & Around later).

Places to Stay

The highest concentration of hotels, motels and B&Bs is on the beach, in the '-mars' area – from Rio Mar St at the south to Vistamar St at the north, and from Hwy A1A at the east to Bayshore Dr. Rates are highest in winter.

The closest campground to Las Olas Blvd's action is 4 miles away at quiet, woodsy **John D Easterlin County Park** (☎ 954-938-0610, 1000 NW 38th St), in Oakland Park. The 47-acre park has nature trails, a fishing lake and clean facilities, and allows pets. The 10 tent sites cost $17-18. Just beyond the city limits in Deerfield Beach (12 miles from Las Olas) is **Quiet Waters County Park** (☎ 954-360-1315, 4015 N Powerline Rd), between Hillsborough and SW 10th St. It's a 430-acre tent-only park where you can reserve sites with permanent tents on a platform or bring your own equipment (all sites $25). The park has quality facilities, bike and boat rentals, mountain biking, hiking trails and an aquatic park.

The best deal on a cheap bed – **Floyd's Hostel & Crew House** (☎ 954-462-0631) – has lots of freebies, including Internet service and laundry. It's tucked away in the Port Everglades section of town, close to most of the crew placement agencies and a short bus ride to the beach. Dorm beds start at $15. Several 'crew houses' provide accommodations for people seeking work on yachts. **Joanne's Crew House** (☎ 954-527-1636, 916 SE 12th St), a really clean five-bedroom, four-bath house, is the best established crew house, charging $125 a week (crew workers only).

The price for hotels is right, but if you have serious design sensibilities, yikes! The decor in many of the less expensive properties warrants a 911 to the design police. That said, the following have clean, comfortable rooms close to the beach, and most have a heated pool. Rates at the 11-unit **Estoril Paradise Inn** (☎ 954-563-3840, 888-385-2322, 2648 NE 32nd St) and **By-Eddy Apartment Motel** (☎ 954-764-7555, 1021 NE 13th Ave), which has laundry facilities, start at $65. For real basic lodgings, try **Birch Patio Motel** (☎ 954-563-9540, 617 N Birch Rd), on a quiet street (from $50). The garden-ensconced **Tropi Rock Resort** (☎ 954-564-0523, 2900 Belmar St) oozes artistic charm (from $65).

The three-story (no elevator) **Caribbean Quarters Bed & Breakfast** (☎ 954-523-3226, 3012 Granada St) is one notch up, with island furnishings, a lush courtyard and spacious rooms from $110. History, old-world charm and location make *Riverside Inn* (☎ 954-467-0671, 620 E Las Olas Blvd) one of the best places to stay (from $169). *The Pillars* (☎ 954-467-9639, 111 N Birch Rd) has reinvented itself as a stylish boutique hotel overlooking the New River (from $119).

There are many gay-friendly options, including the *Royal Palms Resort* (☎ 954-564-6444, 800-237-7256, 2901 Terramar St), which caters to men and has a pool and spa (from $189); the *Worthington Guest House* (☎ 954-563-6819, 800-445-7036, 543 N Birch Rd), a more intimate 13-room resort (from $90); and *The Grand Resort* (☎ 954-630-3000, 800-818-1211, 539 N Birch Rd), the largest exclusively gay resort in Fort Lauderdale (from $145).

Places to Eat

On the mainland, locals frequent *Franco & Vinny's Pizza Shack* (2884 E Sunrise Blvd) for lasagna and baked ziti just like Mama made. Delicious smells (and low prices) greet you at *Vila's Mexican-Cuban Restaurant* (2027 S State Rd 7), with another location at 1417 E Commercial Blvd. It's East Coast meets West Coast at *Topanga* (5001 N Federal Hwy), offering price-sensitive vegetarian fare and California-cool grilled fish, roasted meatloaf dishes and salads. Downhome Southern barbecue doesn't get much better than *Tom Jenkins' Bar-B-Q* (1236 S Federal Hwy), which also serves greens, baked beans and sweet-potato pie. East meets hip at *Red Thai Room* (☎ 954-925-2080, 2039 Hollywood Blvd), in Hollywood, a trendsetter serving acclaimed Thai food at attractive prices. There's more stellar Asian influence at *Sushi Blues* (236 S Young Circle), in Hollywood. It's a little pricier, but worth the splurge.

In the hip Las Olas Blvd zone, 'Real food for real people' is the motto at *Pink Big* (300 SW 1st Ave), at Las Olas Riverfront. It's an inexpensive, fun diner with a huge menu, from granola to meatloaf. Tuna stars at *Ugly Tuna Saloon* (300 SW 1st Ave), also at Las Olas Riverfront, but there's also shrimp, burgers and other fish at attractive prices. For upscale dining without the price tag, try swank *Brasserie Las Olas* (333 E Las Olas Blvd), open late. Love fish? Then you'll love *Tarpon Bend Food & Tackle* (200 SW 2nd St) for its fresh catch of the day, raw bar and live entertainment. South Florida's hottest chefs are at *Himmarshee Bar & Grille* (210 SW 2nd St), *Mark's Las Olas* (1032 E Las Olas Blvd) and *Max's Grille* (300 SW 1st Ave), at Las Olas Riverfront.

Entertainment

There's a 24-hour hotline (☎ 954-357-5700, 800-249-2787) for events and same-day discount tickets. Foremost are programs at the *Broward Center for the Performing Arts* (☎ 954-462-0222, 201 SW 5th Ave), at the Riverwalk, which hosts everything from Broadway musicals to pop and classical concerts. *Suntrust Sunday Jazz Brunch* (☎ 954-828-5985, SW 2nd St), Riverwalk, is a free outdoor jazz concert the first Sunday of the month.

On the club scene, there's live blues and classic rock at *Cheers* (941 E Cypress Creek Rd) and blues and jazz nightly at *O'Hara's Pub & Jazz Cafe* (722 E Las Olas Blvd). *Beach Place* (17 S Atlantic Blvd) offers an all-in-one experience, with clubs, restaurants and shops. *Club Cathode Ray* (1105 E Las Olas Blvd) remains a hip gay dance spot, as does *Copa* (2800 S Federal Hwy).

Getting There & Around

Fort Lauderdale/Hollywood International Airport (☎ 954-359-1200) is about 20 minutes from Las Olas Blvd. BCT Bus No 1 goes from the airport to the Broward Central Terminal. Airport Express (☎ 954-561-8888) runs shuttles ($8 shared, $30 private).

The Greyhound station (☎ 954-764-6551, 515 NE 3rd St), at Federal Hwy, is five blocks from Broward Central Terminal. Frequent buses go to Miami ($6; 45 minutes), Orlando ($37; 5 hours) and Tampa ($39; 6 hours).

The train station (☎ 954-587-6692, 200 SW 21st Terrace) serves Amtrak and Tri-Rail service to Miami and Palm Beach.

BCT buses (☎ 954-357-8400) operate between downtown and the beach, Port Everglades and surrounding towns and beaches ($1, day pass $2.50). The Central Bus Terminal (101 NW 1st Ave) is one block west of S Andrews Blvd. TMAX, BCT's free downtown minibus (☎ 954-761-3543), loops downtown every 15 minutes (Mon-Fri) and Las Olas Blvd every 30 minutes (weekends). The very cool, narrated Water Taxis (☎ 954-467-0008) run between Oakland

FLORIDA

Park Blvd to Las Olas Riverfront and the New River ($7.50/14/16 one-way/roundtrip/day pass).

PALM BEACH

Palm Beach (population 10,500), one of the world's most elite enclaves, is populated during the winter 'social season' by the rich, famous and powerful, plus lots of elderly snowbirds. Condos obstruct the skyline, attractions are limited and it's expensive (though the beaches are pretty decent). The Chamber of Commerce (☎ 561-655-3282) is at 45 Cocoanut Row.

While Worth Ave grabs most of the fame and glamour, **Ocean Blvd** (Hwy A1A) has some of the country's most grandiose houses. Whitehall Mansion, at Cocoanut Row and Whitehall Way, was built by wealthy railroad baron Henry Flagler in 1901 for $2.5 million. It now houses the **Henry Morrison Flagler Museum** (☎ 561-655-2833); admission is $8 (closed Mon). Get an eyeful on a tour ($10) through Flagler's elegant Italian Renaissance–style **Breakers Hotel** (☎ 561-655-6611, 1 S County Rd), offered at 3pm Wednesday.

For economical accommodations, see West Palm Beach below. Winter is high season. If you're looking for budget, clean and no-frills, try *Beachcomber Apartment Motel* (☎ 561-585-4646), starting at $95. The central *Heart of Palm Beach Hotel* (☎ 561-655-5600, 160 Royal Palm Way) has rooms from $169. Charming and well-located *Palm Beach Historic Inn* (☎ 561-832-4009, 365 S County Rd) has rooms from $150. For sheer opulence, try *The Breakers* (☎ 561-655-6611), from $465.

Mizner's Cafe (14 Via Mizner) has salads, sandwiches and pastas. European-style *Chuck & Harold's* (207 Royal Poinciana Way), a popular local haunt (especially at breakfast) usually has a waiting list to dine alfresco or inside on salads, polenta and pasta. 'New York deli goes hip' best describes *Toojay's* (313 Royal Poinciana Way).

The *Society of the Four Arts* (☎ 561-655-7226), in Four Arts Plaza, throws its arms open to the public with concerts, films, lectures, recitals and documentaries December to May.

There is no direct public transportation to Palm Beach. However, from West Palm Beach you can take PalmTran buses (☎ 561-841-4200).

WEST PALM BEACH

This town (population 82,100) is on the west side of the Intracoastal Waterway, which separates it from its wealthier cousin, Palm Beach. The visitor bureau (☎ 561-471-3995, 800-833-5733, W www.palmbeachfl.com) is at 1555 Palm Beach Lakes Blvd, suite 204.

The **Norton Museum of Art** (☎ 561-832-5196, 1451 S Olive Ave) displays a small but superb collection of American and European art as well as notable temporary exhibits ($6, free admission 1pm-5pm Wed). Duane Hanson's *Young Worker* is eerily realistic, and don't miss James Chapen's *Ruby Green Singing.* Looking for something other than a bar or club at night? **South Florida Science Museum** (☎ 561-832-1988, 4801 Dreher Trail N) is open until 10pm Friday ($6). Its Aldrin Planetarium has comfy high-back chairs to watch the sky shows ($2).

Cool off at **Mid-Town Beach** (400 S Ocean Blvd) and **Phipps Ocean Park Beach** (2145 S Ocean Blvd). Watch the sport of kings at **Palm Beach Polo** (☎ 561-793-1440), Wellington, and **Royal Palm Polo** (☎ 561-994-1876), Boca Raton, from January to April.

Places to Stay & Eat

The *KOA* (☎ 561-793-9797) has camping ($24.50) with a pool at Lion Country Safari. Old Northwood Historic District, an attractive community north of downtown, has two homey B&Bs: *Hibiscus House* (☎ 561-863-5633, 800-203-4927, 501 30th St), from $95, and *Royal Palm House* (☎ 561-863-9836, 3215 Spruce Ave), from $75.

Red Roof Inn West Palm Beach (☎ 561-697-7710, 2421 Metro Center Blvd E) offers one of the best buys ($40). Other cheap motels and places to eat are at the south end of town along the 4200 to 7800 block of S Dixie Hwy. Among the options are *Apollo Motor Lodge* (☎ 561-833-1222, 4201 S Dixie Hwy), with friendly management and simply furnished rooms from $50; and the slightly pricier but super clean *Parkview Motor Lodge* (☎ 561-833-4644, 7000 S Dixie Hwy), for $70.

Along S Dixie Hwy is *Oriental Food Market & Takeout* (4919 S Dixie Hwy), which offers great Thai food until 8pm, and *Havana* (6801 S Dixie Hwy) for flavorful, decently priced Cuban dishes (24-hour takeout window). *Derby (5926 Okeechobee Blvd)* has nil to do with hats or horses, just inexpensive breakfast and lunch. Clematis St has restaurants as well as nightlife: try *Sforza Ristorante (223 Clematis St)* for moderately priced Italian food, the very cool *Pizza Girls (114 Clematis St)* for fun, creative pizzas, simple salads and late hours, and *Rooney's Pub (213 Clematis St)* for traditional Irish fare and entertainment.

Vying with Clematis for your dining and entertainment dollars is the new *CityPlace* (☎ *561-366-1000)*, on Rosemary Ave at Okeechobee Blvd, a Tuscan-style complex with apartments, clubs, stores and restaurants (among them *Legal Sea Foods*, Italian *Mezzanote*, Latin *Tamayo* and *Mark's* – as in ace chef Mark Militello).

Entertainment
Check out the schedule at the *Raymond F Kravis Center for the Performing Arts* (☎ *561-832-7469, 800-572-8471, 701 Okeechobee Blvd)* for cultural performances and headline acts. Clematis Street and CityPlace are the best options for nightlife. A free trolley links the two venues. *Clematis by Night* (☎ *561-659-8007, 100 Clematis St)* lights up the streets with free live outdoor concerts at 5pm Thursday. *CityPlace* has theaters, movies and live entertainment nightly. Off the beaten track is the sleek *Bamboo Room Blues (25 South J St)*, Lake Worth, named for its decor. Here regional artists play weekdays and international names come out on weekends.

Getting There & Around
Greyhound (☎ 561-833-8536, 205 S Tamarind Ave) operates buses to Miami ($9; 2 hours) and Orlando ($33; 4 hours). The downtown Tri-Rail station (☎ 800-874-7245, 201 S Tamarind Ave), which also serves as the Amtrak station (☎ 561-832-6169), is near Okeechobee Blvd. PalmTran (☎ 561-841-4200) provides local buses ($1.25, day pass $3).

SPACE COAST
On the Space Coast, high technology and nature comfortably coexist. The highlight of the area is the Kennedy Space Center (KSC), one of only two places in the world (Russia is the other) from which people have been hurtled into space. Night launches of the space shuttle are visible throughout the region, but with advance notice visitors can watch the launch from within the KSC.

A large buffer of natural wilderness and gorgeous beaches – most of which is protected national parkland – surrounds the KSC. Birding, canoeing and kayaking opportunities abound. There is splendid camping on both beach and land, and hotel accommodations are inexpensive.

Visitor information is available through Florida's Space Coast Office of Tourism (☎ 321-868-1126, [W] www.space-coast.com, 8810 Astronaut Blvd, No 102).

Kennedy Space Center
This place is awesome, even if you're not a techie. Plan to spend an entire day at the **Kennedy Space Center Visitor Complex** watching fascinating films like the *Apollo/Saturn V Center,* where the sensation of the *Apollo 8* liftoff is so real that the windows in the theater shake; touching moon and Mars rocks; climbing through a full-scale mock-up of the International Space Station; and walking through the Rocket Garden of vehicles that launched astronauts into space. Two new programs let you meet and dine with an astronaut, and a new special-effects show takes you to Mars. You can see the spacecraft and space exhibits at the center at no cost, but the $24/15 adults/kids admission buys entrance to the visitor center exhibits, IMAX films and a bus tour that stops at the Apollo/Saturn V Center, International Space Station Center and the LC 39 Observation Gantry. From the latter you get a bird's-eye view of launchpads at the KSC and nearby Cape Canaveral. Tickets for launch viewings within 4 to 6 miles of the pad are sold separately ($15) or with KSC admission ($34.50/22.50).

The KSC has three restaurants, gift stores, a post office and pet kennels. The KSC Visitor Center (☎ 321-452-2121, [W] www.kennedyspacecenter .com) is at the east end of the NASA Causeway, which begins at the junction of Hwy 405 and US 1. For launch tickets call ☎ 321-449-4444 or log on to the Web site.

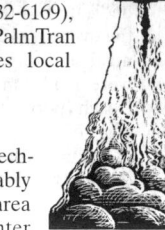

Space shuttle

FLORIDA

Merritt Island National Wildlife Refuge

This refuge (☎ 321-861-0667, SR Hwy 402), in Titusville, contains in its mangrove swamps, marshes and hardwood hammocks more endangered and threatened species than any other refuge in the continental USA. It is also one of the best birding spots, as it's on the migration path between North and South America. The best time to visit is October to May; the best viewing times are early morning and after 4pm. Be sure to cruise the 6-mile Black Point Wildlife Dr. The refuge is closed two days prior to shuttle launches. The visitor center is closed Sunday from April to October.

Two outfitters offer water excursions. A Day Away (☎ 321-268-2655) takes the quiet approach, by kayak, and Space Coast Nature Tours (☎ 321-267-4551) uses a pontoon boat for a 90-minute narrated tour ($14).

Canaveral National Seashore & Cocoa Beach

These 25 miles of windswept and mainly pristine beach are favored by surfers (at the south end), vacationing families (at the north end) and campers and nature lovers (on Klondike Beach, in the center). The seashore has a ranger station at the south end (☎ 321-867-4077), near Playalinda Beach ($5) at the end of Hwy 406/402; and a visitor center (☎ 904-428-3384) at the north end at Apollo Beach, on Hwy A1A east of New Smyrna Beach. The visitor center offers activities every month, including beach walks, cast-netting demonstrations, studies of Timucuan Indian culture and lectures on wildlife.

Greyhound has service only as close as Cocoa and Titusville. A taxi costs $13-17 from Cocoa to the Kennedy Space Center.

Places to Stay & Eat

Camping is free by permit at *Canaveral National Seashore* (☎ 904-428-3384), on Klondike Beach (Nov 1 to Apr 30 only) or on the islands that fill the north end of Mosquito Lagoon. The beach is closed to campers the night before shuttle launches. *Jetty Park Campground* (☎ 321-783-7111, 400 E Jetty Park Rd), in Port Canaveral's South Cruise Terminal, has tent/RV sites from $16/23 (two-night minimum). The jetty is a good spot for watching shuttle launches.

Mangroves (6615 N Atlantic Ave), in Cape Canaveral, makes to-die-for black-bean burritos, fish and grilled portobello sandwiches. The ambience at *Yen Yen Chinese Restaurant* (☎ 321-783-9512, 2 N Atlantic Ave) is elegant yet comfortable; the food is well above average Chinese takeout.

You can go vegetarian or ethnic at two local favorites: *Rita's Vegetarian Restaurant* (1637 N Cocoa Blvd), Cocoa, where they focus on healthy Indian fare, and *Thai Dixie* (24 N Orlando Ave), Cocoa Beach, which serves aromatic, flavorful Thai food. For a quick, healthy lunch, try *Living Greens* (205 McLeod St), Merritt Island, which closes at 3pm.

The 37-acre *Riverbreeze Park* (☎ 904-345-5525, 250 HH Burch Rd), in Oak Hill, 18 miles north of Titusville off US 1, is a gem. It has 17 wooded sites ($15) with grills, fire pits and tables. The park is immaculately maintained and has excellent facilities, a boardwalk and pier, pay phones and kayak rentals. You can get a clean, no-frills room for $45 at *Smyrna Motel* (☎ 904-428-2495, 1050 N Dixie Freeway). For more upscale lodgings, check into either of two historic B&Bs overlooking the Indian River in New Smyrna Beach – *Little River Inn B&B* (☎ 904-424-0100, 532 N Riverside Dr) and *Night Swan Intracoastal B&B* (☎ 904-423-4940, 512 S Riverside Dr). Rates start at $80-85.

Locals consistently vote the seafood gumbo ($5) at *JB's Fish Camp & Restaurant* (859 Pompano Ave), New Smyrna Beach, No 1 in the county. The rustic structure overlooks the Indian River just north of the Canaveral National Seashore's north entrance.

DAYTONA BEACH

What began with men and their expensive, fast cars racing along the hard-packed sand here in 1902 has culminated in an entire city dedicated to the pursuit of speed. By 1904 the event was called the Winter Speed Carnival, and this was the place where records were made and smashed. Today Daytona Beach (population 62,400) thrives on racing and young, party-based tourism. It has one of the last Atlantic Coast spring breaks, and during Bike Week (early March), hordes of Harleys roar into town. The visitor bureau (☎ 386-255-0415, 800-854-1234, W www .daytonabeach.com, 126 E Orange Ave) has a booth in Daytona USA (1801 W International Speedway Blvd). The Greater Daytona Beach Business Guild (☎ 386-252-5180) can assist gay and lesbian travelers with information.

Things to See & Do

The beach is hard, flat and wide. You can drive your car ($5), jog, walk or bike on it. It's well lit by the scores of small motels, so you can walk at night. There's good swimming and great waves for boogie boarding and surfing. Some areas are reserved for nesting turtles.

The **Daytona International Speedway** (☎ 386-254-2700, 1801 W International Speedway Blvd) hosts Winston, NASCAR, stock- and sports-car, go-cart, monster truck and motorcycle races; daily tours are available. The place goes crazy in February for the Daytona 500. Take an interesting behind-the-scenes track tour at the adjoining **Daytona USA** (☎ 386-947-6800) museum complex, with exhibits, cars, high-tech interactive displays and two new motion simulator rides ($6). The **Museum of Arts & Science** (☎ 386-255-0285, 1040 Museum Blvd) collects American, African and Cuban art, and has planetarium shows ($5). Downtown's renovated **Beach Street**, with shops, restaurants and brew pubs, is less frenetic than the beach, especially during spring break. Bus No 17A runs hourly to the **Ponce de León Inlet Lighthouse & Museum** (☎ 386-761-1821, 4931 S Peninsula Dr). Climb the stairs for a terrific view.

Places to Stay & Eat

There's no shortage of inexpensive and moderately priced accommodations – except during holidays, Bike Week and spring break, when prices soar. Unless you're into huge crowds, traffic jams and nonstop partying, consider staying in New Smyrna Beach or west of Daytona Beach (see Around Daytona Beach, later) for quieter lodging. However, even these areas raise rates during Daytona Beach's special events. Summer is high season.

Dream Inn (☎ *386-767-2821, 800-767-9738, 3217 S Atlantic Ave)*, a small property with big-hotel conveniences, is a bargain at $50, especially considering all the extras. At the pet-friendly *Manatee Suites* (☎ *386-761-1121, 800-378-6826, 3167 S Atlantic Ave)*, renovated rooms (from $59) have full

kitchens, and the property has a pool, laundry and free newspapers. *Royal Arms* (☎ *386-253-0558, 801 S Atlantic Ave)* is recommended for nicely appointed, clean and inexpensive doubles (from $45). Sterile *Beachside Budget Inn* (☎ *386-258-6238, 1717 N Atlantic Ave)* has rooms from $35. The very hospitable *Buccaneer Motel* (☎ *386-253-9678, 2301 N Atlantic Ave)* rents rooms, apartments, studios and efficiencies (from $40-140), complete with refrigerators, and it's gay-friendly.

At the high end are *Daytona Beach Hilton* (☎ *386-767-7350, 2637 S Atlantic Ave)*, starting at $149 (ask about lower rates), and *Adam's Mark Beach Resort* (☎ *386-254-8200, 100 N Atlantic Ave)*, from $95.

Historic *Coquina Inn B&B* (☎ *386-254-4969, 544 S Palmetto Ave)* has four pleasant rooms from $80. *The Villa B&B* (☎ *386-248-2020, 801 N Peninsula Dr)*, a Spanish-style manse in a garden setting, features smoke-free rooms from $125.

Veggie and meat burgers at the funky waterfront *Lighthouse Landing* (*4940 S Peninsula Dr)* cost $4-5. *Starlite Diner* (*401 N Atlantic Ave)* serves up hearty American fare from $4. *Steak & Shake* (*1000 International Speedway Blvd)*, open 24 hours, has double hamburgers for $3. Friendly *Anna's Italian Trattoria* (*304 Seabreeze Blvd)* has early-bird pasta specials (5pm-6:30pm) from $6. After drooling over the bikes at Daytona Harley Davidson, head into the adjoining *Daytona Diner* (*290½ N Beach St)* for lunch and affordable breakfasts.

Check out *Razzles* and *Oyster Pub* on Seabreeze Blvd, *Steamers Oyster & Ale House* for everything from blues to acoustic guitar on S Atlantic Ave, and *Bank & Blues Club* for blues and *Dirty Harry's* for classic rock on Main St.

Getting There & Around

The Greyhound station (☎ 386-255-7076) is at 138 S Ridgewood Ave. The nearest Amtrak station (☎ 386-734-2322) is in DeLand, where there is a connecting Amtrak bus. Votran buses (☎ 386-761-7700) run landside and beachside from Ponce Inlet (south end of Daytona Beach) to Ormond Beach ($1). Scooters Cycles (☎ 386-253-4141, 2020 S Atlantic Ave) rents scooters for cruising the beach and streets.

FLORIDA

AROUND DAYTONA BEACH

About 25 miles west of Daytona Beach you'll find three superb state parks within 5 miles of one another. They offer a rare opportunity to experience Florida 'BD' (before developers).

Blue Spring State Park (☎ 386-775-3663, 2100 W French Ave), in Orange City, is one of the two best places to see manatees in Florida (the other is Homosassa Springs Wildlife State Park on the west coast), especially November to March. Warm, spring-fed waters for swimming, fishing and canoeing are another attraction. Book ahead for the excellent campsites ($16-18) and air-conditioned cabins ($56). Admission is $4.

The free pontoon ferry to **Hontoon Island State Park** (☎ 386-736-5309, 2309 River Ridge Rd), in DeLand, leads to 1650 pristine acres with 12 tent sites ($8), primitive cabins ($25), canoe and pontoon docks and trails, all visible from an 80-foot tower ($2).

The spring-fed pool at **DeLeon Springs State Recreation Area** (☎ 386-985-4212, 601 Ponce de León Spring Blvd), DeLeon Springs, never gets below 72°F ($4). After a swim, hike the trails or rent a paddleboat, canoe or kayak, then stop at the park's *Old Spanish Sugar Mill and Griddle House* for lunch.

DeLand has the most accommodations and eateries in the area. *Quality Inn* (☎ 386-736-3440, 2801 E NY Ave) starts at $50. Rooms are slightly less ($40) at *Chimney Corner Motel* (☎ 386-734-3146, 1941 S Woodland Blvd). Next to the park's ferry landing is the pleasant *Hontoon Landing Resort & Marina* (☎ 386-734-2474, 2317 River Ridge Rd), in a garden/waterfront setting with amenity-full rooms from $70. *Brian's Bar-B-Q* (☎ 386-736-8851, 795 SR 15A), between Hontoon and DeLeon Parks, serves award-winning barbecue. Locally grown edible flowers and homemade pasta make *Pondo's Restaurant* (☎ 386-734-1995, 1915 Old New York Ave), off SR 44, a good dinner choice ($10-15).

Greyhound (☎ 386-734-2747, 224 East Ohio Ave) buses connect DeLand to Daytona ($7; 45 minutes) and Orlando ($9; 45 minutes), among other cities. Amtrak (☎ 386-734-2322, 2491 Old New York Ave), in DeLand, is less than 2 miles from Blue Spring State Park. It has connecting bus service to Daytona Beach. Taxis serve all three parks.

ST AUGUSTINE

The nation's oldest city, St Augustine (population 11,600) was settled in 1565 by Spanish explorer Don Pedro Menéndez de Avilés. After being twice attacked by the British, St Augustine built the Castillo de San Marcos in 1672. Over the next nearly 150 years, the city traded hands three times among the Spanish, British and finally the USA. In the late 1880s, Henry Flagler brought his railroad through town, creating a building boom.

Today St Augustine's historic district is a charming mix of narrow cobblestone streets, European architecture and Spanish colonial flair. Across the Intracoastal Waterway is 18-mile Anastasia Island, with a state park, pier and dunes and beaches. The main visitor center (☎ 904-825-1000, 800-653-2489, ☒ www.visitoldcity.com) is at 10 Castillo Dr. Another useful site is ☒ www.oldcity.com. Note that St George St is a pedestrian-only zone.

Things to See & Do

The state-operated **Spanish Quarter Living History Museum** (☎ 904-825-6830, 53 St George St) is a re-creation of Spanish colonial St Augustine in 1740 ($6.50). St Augustine's City Hall Complex (75 King St), the former luxury Hotel Alcazar (1888), is home to the **Lightner Museum** (☎ 904-824-2874), with 19th-century fine and decorative arts, early Americana and European art ($6). **Government House Museum** (☎ 904-825-5033, 48 King St) houses historical exhibits as well as archaeological artifacts ($3).

The **Oldest Wooden School House** (☎ 904-824-0192, 14 St George St) was built from 1750 to 1763 out of cypress and red cedar with handmade nails and joists ($2.75). The restored **González-Alvarez House** (☎ 904-824-2872, 14 St Francis St) is alleged to be the oldest house in America ($5). Built in 1887, Henry Flagler's **Hotel Ponce de León** (☎ 904-819-6383), at King and Cordova Sts, is now Flagler College but was once an exclusive winter resort. Tours ($4) are given May to August.

The Spanish began the fort that is now called **Castillo de San Marcos National**

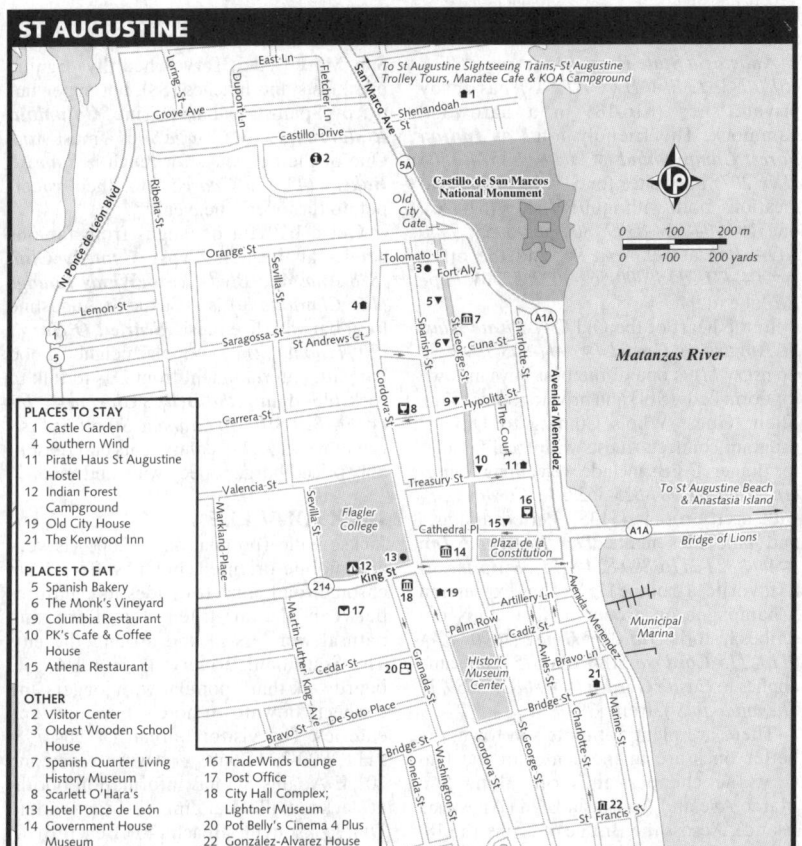

ST AUGUSTINE

PLACES TO STAY
1 Castle Garden
4 Southern Wind
11 Pirate Haus St Augustine Hostel
12 Indian Forest Campground
19 Old City House
21 The Kenwood Inn

PLACES TO EAT
5 Spanish Bakery
6 The Monk's Vineyard
9 Columbia Restaurant
10 PK's Cafe & Coffee House
15 Athena Restaurant

OTHER
2 Visitor Center
3 Oldest Wooden School House
7 Spanish Quarter Living History Museum
8 Scarlett O'Hara's
13 Hotel Ponce de León
14 Government House Museum
16 TradeWinds Lounge
17 Post Office
18 City Hall Complex; Lightner Museum
20 Pot Belly's Cinema 4 Plus
22 González-Alvarez House

FLORIDA

Matanzas River

Monument (☎ 904-829-6506) in 1627, making it the country's oldest masonry fort. It is under renovation until early 2002, with reduced admission. One of the city's most distinctive features, the **Bridge of Lions** – known for its trademark Mediterranean Revival–style towers – was built in 1926 to connect the city with Anastasia Island, which leads to St Augustine Beach and **Anastasia State Recreation Area** (☎ 904-461-2033, 1340A Hwy A1A S). The park has a terrific beach, campground, trail, bird-watching and rentals (☎ 904-460-9111) for windsurfing ($20 an hour), kayaking and canoeing ($15 an hour) and sailing ($30 an hour).

Two companies provide interesting, convenient tours on open-air trams ($12): St Augustine Sightseeing Trains (☎ 904-829-6545, 800-226-6545, 170 San Marco Ave) and St Augustine Trolley Tours (☎ 904-829-3800, 167 San Marco Ave). For a little evening fun, take the 90-minute 'Ghostly Walking Tour' (☎ 904-461-1009, 888-461-1009) to learn about St Augustine's spirited past ($8).

The nearest airport is Jacksonville International (☎ 904-741-4902), 50 miles north. Greyhound (☎ 904-829-6401, 100 Malaga St) has easy connections to Jacksonville ($9.50, 45 minutes). The closest Amtrak is off US 17 in Palatka, 25 miles west.

Places to Stay

Weekend getaways to St Augustine are popular, so rates can differ as much by weekday and weekend as by season. The least expensive high-season weekend rate is quoted here.

Anastasia State Recreation Area (☎ 904-461-2033, 1340A Hwy A1A S) has shady private sites ($16-18) in a hardwood hammock. The friendly folks at *Indian Forest Campground* (☎ 904-824-3574, 1505 Hwy 207) have sites for $19. *KOA* has two locations, both with tent/RV sites ($20/26): one (☎ 904-824-8309, 800-562-3433, 9950 KOA Rd) at I-95 exit 96, and the other (☎ 904-471-3113, 800-562-4022, 525 W Pope Rd) at exit 94.

In the heart of the Old City, *Pirate Haus St Augustine Hostel* (☎ 904-808-1999, 32 Treasury St) is one of the best buys in town for dorm beds ($14) and private rooms ($31). Their 'Guess Who's Coming to Dinner' program connects guests with local families for dinner. B&Bs include welcoming *Southern Wind* (☎ 904-825-3623, 18 Cordova St), with pretty rooms ($135). Period antiques and balconies make *The Kenwood Inn* (☎ 904-824-2116, 800-824-8151, 38 Marine St) a favorite (from $115). The expression 'Champagne on a beer budget' aptly describes historic *Old City House* (☎ 904-826-0113, 115 Cordova St), from $75. The same applies to *Castle Garden* (☎ 904-829-3839, 15 Shenandoah St), from $79.

There are plenty of motels in town; the better ones are in the center of the Old City, the cheaper ones run along San Marco Ave and Anastasia Blvd (Anastasia Island). Across the Bridge of Lions, the 18-room *Edgewater Inn* (☎ 904-825-2697, 2 St Augustine Blvd) has good views and spotless rooms ($82). Built in 1998 to mimic a historic building, *Anastasia Inn* (☎ 904-825-2879, 888-226-6181, 218 Anastasia Blvd) has comfy rooms with furnishings typical of a moderately good chain hotel (from $50).

Places to Eat & Drink

Go Greek at *Athena Restaurant* (14 Cathedral Place), a classic Greek diner. A few tables at *PK's Cafe & Coffee House* (136 St George St) spill out onto the street, where diners enjoy breakfast, sandwiches and baked potatoes. *The Monk's Vineyard* (56 St George St) has good pub food. *Gypsy Cab Co* (828 Anastasia Blvd), on Anastasia Island, is a longtime, attractively priced favorite that kicked it up a notch by adding a

comedy club and a late-night bar and grill with live music. *The Manatee Cafe* (179A San Marco Ave) serves healthy organic breakfasts and lunches ($8). For super but pricey Spanish-Cuban cuisine, *Columbia Restaurant* (98 St George St) is a must-stop. One of the best buys for lunch is *Spanish Bakery* (42½ St George St) – their sweet-potato turnover is heavenly.

Get a bellyful of laughs from famous comics at the new *Gypsy Comedy Club* (828 Anastasia Blvd). *TradeWinds Lounge* (124 Charlotte St) is a classic St Augustine local bar with live music. *Scarlett O'Hara's* (70 Hypolita St) is a popular neighborhood bar with entertainment from DJs to folk to rock, plus dining. *Pot Belly's Cinema 4 Plus* (☎ 904-829-3101, 36 Granada St) offers first-run movies ($3.75), comfy seats and reasonably priced burgers, beer, wine and soda.

JACKSONVILLE

Jacksonville (population 735,600) is very automobile-oriented, but it suffers from chronic road jams. It divides its pleasures between the art-filled downtown and natural wonders in and around the city. The Southbank Riverwalk is a 1¼-mile boardwalk that's popular with joggers and connects downtown hotels, museums and eateries. The visitor bureau (☎ 904-798-9111, 800-733-2668, Ⓦ www.jaxcvb.com, 201 E Adams St) has information booths at Jacksonville Landing (2 Independent Dr), Jacksonville Beach (403 Beach Blvd) and Jacksonville Airport (2400 Yankee Clipper Dr).

Spend an idyllic afternoon viewing European artwork and beautiful riverfront Italian-style gardens ($5; free 4pm-9pm Tue) at the **Cummer Museum of Art & Gardens** (☎ 904-356-6857, 829 Riverside Ave). Then get to know the city through the trio of museums on the Southbank Riverwalk (1015 Museum Circle): the **Museum of Science & History and Alexander Brest Planetarium** (☎ 904-396-6674), with Florida history and local marine and wildlife exhibits ($6/4 adults/kids); **Jacksonville Maritime Museum** (☎ 904-398-9011), with model ships and local maritime photos ($2); and the **Jacksonville Historical Center** (☎ 904-398-4301), which chronicles the city's colorful history (a donation is requested).

Miles of beaches are another reason to come to Jacksonville. They're toasty late spring through fall, then cool to cold but uncrowded in winter. Take your pick of **Little Talbot Island State Park** (☎ 904-251-2320, 12157 Heckscher Dr); **Kathryn Abbey Hanna Park** (☎ 904-249-4700, 500 Wonderwood Dr), with exceptional hiking, biking, fishing and beaches; and three community locales – **Atlantic Beach** for surfing, **Neptune Beach** for quiet beaches and **Jacksonville Beach** for swimming, biking, skating and nightlife.

Places to Stay & Eat

Jacksonville's hotels are not affected by seasonal travelers, except for beach properties, where B&Bs and mom-and-pop motels charge $10-25 more during summer, weekends and special events.

The three closest campgrounds are 27 miles east of downtown on the beach at *Little Talbot Island State Park* (see above), where rates are $14-16; *Huguenot Memorial Park* (☎ 904-251-3335, 10980 Heckscher Dr/Hwy 105), with sandy sites ($6, $8 on the river); and *Kathryn Abbey Hanna Park*, with shady sites from $12.

Downtown, your best option is the riverfront *Hilton* (☎ 904-398-8800, 1201 Riverplace Blvd), which has good views (from $75; ask for weekend specials). In the neighboring historic Riverside district, antiques and fresh flowers fill the *House on Cherry St* (☎ 904-384-1999, 1844 Cherry St), a quiet B&B ($85).

On the beaches, try the oceanfront *Atlantis of Jacksonville Beach* (☎ 904-249-5006, 731 N 1st St), a casual inn with a pool that's near good restaurants ($70). The larger, more motelish *Surfside* (☎ 904-246-1583, 1236 N 1st St) has bright, clean rooms (from $69), a big pool and free breakfast. Get that home-away-from-home feeling at the wide-porched *Fig Tree Inn* (☎ 904-246-8855, 185 4th Ave S) and cedar-shingled *Ruby Inn by the Sea* (☎ 904-241-5551, 802 2nd St S), two relaxing B&Bs with lots of beach toys (from $95).

In the downtown and Riverwalk areas, try *Coney Island Joe's Deli*, Southbank Riverwalk; *Da Real Ting Cafe* (45 W Monroe St), for inexpensive Jamaican and Caribbean fare (weekday lunch and Fri-Sun dinner); *River City Brewing Company* (835 Museum Circle Dr), a local hangout, for tours, light lunches, seafood dinners and weekend music; and *Crawdaddy's* (1643 Prudential Dr), for a rustic setting with Cajun and Creole specialties.

At Jacksonville Beach, go for fancy at *First Street Grille* (807 N 1st St) or super casual at *Harry's Seafood Bar & Grille* (1018 N 3rd St). On Atlantic Beach it's all laid-back at the Memphis-style rib joint *Sticky Fingers* (363 Atlantic Blvd), and at Jacksonville's first brew pub, *Ragtime Tavern* (207 Atlantic Blvd), with local bands Wednesday to Sunday.

Entertainment

Jacksonville boasts a fine performing-arts venue, *Times-Union Center* (300 Water St), where the Jacksonville Symphony Orchestra (☎ 904-354-5547) and other groups perform. The smaller *Florida Theatre* (☎ 904-355-2787, 128 E Forsyth St) features headline artists as well.

For an acid trip without the drugs, check out the *Museum of Science & History* planetarium's 18,000-watt Cosmic Concert Laser Light Show, with mega-sounds like Pink Floyd's *Dark Side of the Moon* Friday and Saturday nights ($6). *Bo's Coral Reef* (☎ 904-246-9874, 201 5th Ave) is a long-standing gay bar, with a DJ and weekend drag shows.

The NFL *Jacksonville Jaguars* (☎ 904-633-2000) play professional football at Alltell Stadium September to December.

Getting There & Around

Jacksonville International Airport (☎ 904-741-4902) has rental cars, taxis and buses. Greyhound (☎ 904-356-9976, 10 Pearl St) operates buses to Miami ($45; 7 hours), Orlando ($25; 3 hours) and Tallahassee ($28; 3 hours), among other towns. Jacksonville is a hub for Amtrak (☎ 904-766-5110, 3570 Clifford Lane). Jacksonville Transit (☎ 904-630-3100) runs horribly inconvenient buses (75¢, week pass $10, no transfers).

AMELIA ISLAND

The French landed on this island, 30 miles northeast of Jacksonville, in 1562. It was eventually to be controlled by Spanish, British, Confederates, the Union and various renegade groups. The island has been a slave market, pirate's lair and

FLORIDA

general den of iniquity. After the Civil War, hotels popped up, and resorts (separate ones for whites and blacks) rose on the beach. The main town and restored historic district is Fernandina Beach, where you'll find the chamber of commerce (☎ 904-261-3248, 800-226-3542, 102 Centre St).

Displays of Spanish artifacts are found at the **Amelia Island Museum of History** (☎ 904-261-7378, 233 S 3rd St), which conducts 90-minute walking tours through the historic district at 3pm Thursday and Friday ($4 admission, $8 tours; closed Sun). **Fort Clinch** (☎ 904-277-7274, 2601 Atlantic Ave), begun in 1847 but never completed, is now a super state park with 19th-century military stuff, reenactments, good facilities and lots for nature lovers and active outdoor types ($3.25). Head east on Atlantic Ave for the beaches.

American Beach was founded in the 1930s for African American beachgoers at a time when beaches were segregated. It remains an interesting – but run-down – area and a popular vacation spot, especially (but not exclusively) for middle-class African Americans. It's easily the most tranquil spot on the island. For information, contact American Beach Villas (☎ 904-261-0840).

Shaded riverfront and sandy beachfront campsites at *Fort Clinch State Park (☎ 904-277-7274, 2601 Atlantic Ave)* cost $17. *Ocean View Inn (☎ 904-261-0193, 2801 Atlantic Ave)* has rooms from $55. *Florida House Inn (☎ 904-261-3300, 22 S 3rd St)*, Florida's oldest hotel (1857), is wonderfully restored (from $79).

The very upscale *Ritz-Carlton Resort (☎ 904-277-1100, 4750 Amelia Island Pkwy)* starts around $250 in summer. In quiet American Beach, *American Beach Villas (☎ 904-261-0840, 5553 Gregg St)* is a nicely furnished one-story motel in an unpolished neighborhood that offers the island's best buy ($50).

Resembling a longshoreman's bar, *Crab Trap (31 N 2nd St)* serves tourist families seafood and burgers. There's innovative cooking at the *Beech Street Grill (801 Beech St)*, located in a historic house. Enjoy traditional Southern family fare at *Florida House Inn (22 S 3rd St)*.

Hwy A1A links the island to the mainland, but there's no public transportation. Rent bikes ($7/15 per hour/day) to cruise the island

at Pipeline Surf Shop (☎ 904-277-3717), on Sadler St at 1st Ave in Fernandina Beach.

West Coast

From culture to stature to nature, the Gulf Coast's diversity offers visitors an almost endless palette of opportunity. It has the biggest, baddest roller coaster at Busch Gardens, world-class arts in Sarasota and St Petersburg, a party-hearty nightlife with a Latin beat in Tampa's Ybor City, clear springs that attract manatees, and parks with canoe trails that meander through miles of unspoiled landscape.

FORT MYERS

Home at one time to Thomas Edison and Henry Ford, sprawling Fort Myers (population 48,200) is best known for its beach and excellent parks. The city is on the Gulf Coast and is divided by the Caloosahatchee River, which is lined with stately homes.

Get information from the visitor bureau (☎ 941-338-3500, 2180 W 1st St) and Chamber of Commerce (☎ 941-332-3624, 2310 Edwards Dr).

Things to See & Do

Visitors are drawn to the **Edison Estate, Laboratory & Museum** (☎ 941-334-3614, 2350 McGregor Blvd) to see the great inventor's winter home, a museum housing hundreds of his inventions and possessions, and the gardens. Guided tours of the estate ($12) include a visit to **Henry Ford's winter home**, across the street.

The **Fort Myers Historical Museum** (☎ 941-332-5955, 2300 Peck St) has exhibits on southwest Florida and the city's history, including Calusa and Seminole artifacts ($6; closed Sun-Mon).

Two state parks are worth a visit. **Koreshan State Historic Site** (☎ 941-992-0311), on Corkscrew Rd at US 41, is the intact former community of a 19th-century religious sect; the site boasts furnished historical structures. The park also has canoe rentals ($4/20 per hour/day) and an attractive campground ($3.25). **Delnor–Wiggins Pass State Recreation Area** (☎ 941-597-6196, 11100 Gulf Shore Dr) is a quiet, long, narrow beach park with great facilities ($2-4). The **Lee County Regional Park Program**

Office (☎ 941-432-2004, Lakes Park, 7330 Gladiolus Dr) offers fishing, swimming, hiking, paddling, beaches, equipment rentals and access to Manatee Park, a winter home for manatees.

You'll find wet and dry outdoor experiences with Southwest Florida Yachts (☎ 941-656-1339, 800-262-7939, 3444 Marinatown Lane NW), in North Fort Myers, offering sailing rentals, lessons and charters; and Babcock Wilderness Adventure (☎ 941-489-3911), providing swamp buggy excursions through a variety of ecosystems.

Fort Myers Beach is on Estero Island, about 40 minutes southwest of downtown. It manages to be both a party town (at Times Square) and a quiet beach resort (at the south end). Many people make this their base for exploring the area. Look for blue, white and yellow flags marking beach access between houses. There are loads of hotels and condos and a few energetic bars. To get around, try Fun Rentals (☎ 941-463-8844, 1901 Estero Blvd) for bikes ($10), scooters ($40) and skates ($10).

In March, major-league baseball's Boston Red Sox play exhibition games at their spring training camp (☎ 941-334-4700), as do the Minnesota Twins (☎ 800-338-9467).

Places to Stay & Eat

In Fort Myers Beach you can bed down under the stars at the beachfront *Red Coconut RV Resort & Campground* (☎ 941-463-7200, 3001 Estero Blvd), with tent and RV sites from $45, and at *San Carlos RV Park* (☎ 941-466-3133, 18701 San Carlos Blvd), where tent and RV sites cost $32.50. There's a cluster of downtown motels, including *Ta Ki-Ki Motel* (☎ 941-334-2135, 2631 1st St), with rooms from $70.

Fort Myers Beach has scores of small motels in the $85-95 range. Among them is the family-operated *Lighthouse Island Resort* (☎ 941-463-9392, 1051 5th St), where the focus is on family fun ($95). The small beachfront *Silver Sands Villas* (☎ 941-463-6554, 1207 Estero Blvd) has rooms with water views (from $90).

Join locals in the nightly pilgrimage to *Mel's Diner* (4820 Cleveland Ave), a throwback to *Happy Days* of meat, mashed potatoes, fruit pies and economical prices. Equally sensitive to your dollars and tastes

---

It's the Water

The Sunshine State's water is what attracts many tourists – so why not vacation on it? Two cost-effective ways to enjoy the water are houseboats and sailboats. On both you can spend your days island-hopping or anchored looking ashore rather than out to sea.

No boating skills? Few are needed with the houseboats, which chug along slowly. However, you are given some basics before you're given the keys. Two options are Houseboat Vacations of the Florida Keys (☎ 305-664-4009) and Everglades National Park's Flamingo Lodge, Marina & Outpost Resort (☎ 941-695-3101). Two to three days with a fully equipped boat will run about $495-595 per boat.

Lack of boating skills shouldn't stop you from chartering a sailboat, at least not at Southwest Florida Yachts, which offers live-aboard sailing classes. By day you sail and learn to work the lines; by night you relax, cook dinner, watch the stars and sleep on board. For details, contact Southwest Florida Yachts (☎ 941-656-1339, 800-262-7939). Two days of lessons, accommodations and food run $395 per person.

---

is *Munch Box* (6101 Estero Blvd). *The Veranda* (2122 2nd St) and *Peter's La Cuisine* (2224 Bay St) are extravagances well worth your indulgence. Just landside of Fort Myers Beach, *Sunrise Family Restaurant* (17633 San Carlos Blvd) has good lunches and dinners for $6-8, with daily specials a buck less. On Fort Myers Beach, *Snug Harbor* (645 San Carlos Blvd) is a popular seafood spot with picturesque views (most dinners under $16). The same goes for *The Bridge* (708 Gulf Star Marina), across the Matanzas Bridge, which also has live music on weekends.

Getting There & Around

Southwest Florida International Airport (☎ 941-768-1000) has regional, national and international service and car rentals. Greyhound (☎ 941-334-1011, 2250 Peck St) goes to Miami ($25; 4 hours), Tampa ($25; 4 hours) and Orlando ($31; 4 hours). Lee Trans' (☎ 941-275-8726) Orange bus No 50 leaves downtown at Daniels Rd and Hwy 41 for Fort Myers Beach every hour on the hour ($1). The Beach Connection runs from pickup points on the mainland in Fort Myers to Bonita Beach all day for just 25¢.

AROUND FORT MYERS

Within minutes north of urban Fort Myers lie charming Sanibel and Captiva Islands. They offer restaurants, hotels and shops along a maze of tree-lined streets that lead to beaches – where shell collecting is nonpareil – and natural areas teem with wildlife and ideal spots for kayaking and canoeing. A little farther south is one of the most idyllic spots in Florida, Audubon's Corkscrew Swamp Sanctuary.

Sanibel & Captiva Islands

Despite residential and commercial development, Sanibel and Captiva retain much natural appeal. They're ideally suited for biking and hiking, with trails all over the islands. The chamber of commerce (☎ 941-472-1080, ☒ www.sanibel-captiva.org) is at 1159 Causeway Rd.

The islands' best feature is the 6000-acre **JN 'Ding' Darling National Wildlife Refuge** (☎ 941-472-1100, 1 Wildlife Dr), which has a marvelous 5-mile wildlife drive that's as popular with drivers ($5) as it is with hikers ($1) and bikers ($1). When it's closed on Friday, other trails are open. Tarpon Bay Recreation (☎ 941-472-8900), the refuge's concessionaire in Tarpon Bay Marina, supplies canoes, kayaks and bikes and gives darn good guided paddle tours ($25) at 10:30am daily through the refuge waters. Wildside Adventures/Captiva Kayak Co (☎ 941-395-2925, McCarthy's Marina, 15041 Captiva Dr) has attractive rates on kayak rentals ($15/35 per hour/half day). 'Tween Waters (☎ 941-472-5161, 15951 Captiva Dr) rents canoes ($30/55 half/full day).

The **Sanibel-Captiva Conservation Foundation** (☎ 941-472-2329, 3333 Sanibel-Captiva Rd) is another good place to hike. You can identify beach shells you pick up by visiting the **Bailey-Matthews Shell Museum** (☎ 941-395-2233, 3075 Sanibel-Captiva Rd). Admission costs $5. Finnimore's Cycle Shop (☎ 941-472-5577, 2353 Periwinkle Way) rents bikes ($4 a day) and skates ($20 a day).

Even among the more affordable hotels, Christmas and February-to-April rates are

over $100. Visit outside that period for big savings. *Periwinkle Park (☎ 941-472-1433, 1119 Periwinkle Way)* is the island's only campground. It's rich with facilities and has shady tent/RV sites ($27/35) about half a mile from the beach. The folks are helpful and friendly at both **Kona Kai Motel** *(☎ 941-472-1001, 1539 Periwinkle Way)*, where high-season rates are $100, and **Anchorage Inn** *(☎ 941-395-9688, 1245 Periwinkle Way)*, where they start at $109. The rooms are bright with cool tile floors at the adult-only **Seahorse Cottages** *(☎ 941-472-4262, 1223 Buttonwood Lane)*, in a quiet residential area with a small garden and rates from $135.

Stop for light meals like bagel and panini sandwiches, salads, coffees and desserts at **The Bean** *(☎ 941-395-1919, 2240 Periwinkle Way)*; good black or red beans and rice ($3.50-4.75) at **East End Deli** *(359 Periwinkle Way)*; and scrumptious hummus, made-to-order pizza (two slices $4) and sandwiches at **The Canoe and the Kayak Waterfront Deli** *(☎ 941-472-5161, 15951 Captiva Dr)*, in Captiva behind 'Tween Waters Marina (open 11am-6pm, 7pm on weekends). With its old-fashioned bubbling Christmas lights and antiques, the moderately priced **Bubble Room** *(☎ 941-472-5558, 15001 Captiva Dr)* has become something of an attraction as well as a place that serves steaks, seafood and incredible desserts.

Corkscrew Swamp Sanctuary

This 11,000-acre National Audubon Society preserve (☎ 941-348-9151, 375 Sanctuary Rd), off Hwy 846 in Naples, is one of the most idyllic places in the state. Start at the visitor center ($8), pick up a wildlife guide and rent binoculars ($4), then head toward the 2-mile boardwalk, which passes under the canopy of the world's largest subtropical old-growth bald-cypress forest. You'll see lots of wildlife. Knowledgeable trail volunteers answer questions and point out wildlife your untrained eyes miss. It's open until sunset in summer. The new Blair Audubon Center features exhibits, theater and interactive productions.

SARASOTA

The largest city between Fort Myers and Tampa–St Petersburg, Sarasota (population 52,700) is an affluent but welcoming place.

The visitor bureau (☎ 941-957-1877, 800-522-9799) is at 655 N Tamiami Trail.

The former winter retreat of railroad, real-estate and circus baron John Ringling, the **Ringling Museum Complex** (☎ 941-359-5700, 5401 Bayshore Rd) encompasses museums, tropical gardens, a cafe and a 30-room mansion. The Ringlings were avid art collectors, and the John and Mable Ringling Museum of Art has a first-rate collection. Ca' d'Zan was the Ringling's lavish winter home, a combination of architectural styles. The fascinating **Museum of the Circus** has circus wagons, costumes, paraphernalia and memorabilia ($9).

Towles Court (☎ 941-362-0960, 1945 Morrill St) is a cozy complex of art galleries, studios and restaurants (free admission). Equally refreshing is the **Marie Selby Botanical Gardens** (☎ 941-366-5731, 811 S Palm Ave), a green respite in an urban landscape ($8).

The **Pelican Man's Bird Sanctuary** (☎ 941-388-4444, 1708 Ken Thompson Pkwy), on City Island, rehabilitates injured wildlife ($4). View sea life next door at the **Mote Marine Aquarium** (☎ 941-388-4441), a research center and marine rehabilitation facility ($10/7 adults/kids). Avoid crowds by going when everyone else is at the beach. It's packed on rainy days.

Beaches abound on the barrier islands. Local favorites are South Lido Beach, at the end of Ben Franklin Dr on Lido Key; Turtle and Siesta Key Beaches, on Siesta Key; and Coquina Beach, on Longboat Key.

Greyhound (☎ 941-955-5735, 575 N Washington Blvd) runs to Miami ($38; 6 hours), Tampa ($11; 2 hours) and Fort Myers ($13; 2 hours). Sarasota County Area Transit (☎ 941-316-1234) buses cost 50¢ (no transfers).

Places to Stay & Eat

Sarasota has some of the priciest hotels around. If you like the beach and don't mind tight spaces, try the **Gulf Beach Campground** (☎ 941-349-3839, 8862 Midnight Pass Rd), on Siesta Key ($37).

Halfway between the airport and downtown Sarasota on N Tamiami Trail is a slew of small, economical motels. Weekly rates are considerably better. **Sunset Terrace Resort** (☎ 941-355-8489, 4644 N Tamiami Trail) has rooms from $69. A good option is **Cadillac Motel** (☎ 941-355-7108, 4021 N Tamiami Trail), with a pool (from $39). Friendly, family-run **Sundial Motor Inn** (☎ 941-351-4919, 4801 N Tamiami Trail) has rooms from $60.

On Siesta Key, **Crescent House B&B** (☎ 941-346-0857, 459 Beach Rd) charges from $110. Enormous **Harrington House** (☎ 941-778-5444, 5626 Gulf Dr), on Anna Maria Island, is an excellent beachside B&B with large rooms from $179. From a five-course breakfast to turndown service with fresh-baked cookies, **Cypress B&B Inn** (☎ 941-955-4683, 621 S Gulfstream Ave) is a wonderfully elegant getaway (from $150).

Burns Lane Cafe (516 Burns Lane) serves contemporary fare in a chic indoor/outdoor bistro setting. **Yoshino** (417 Burns Court) serves haute Japanese cuisine, and **Kismet** (1938 Adams Lane) offers a light, healthy menu. Hidden away in a ramshackle garden is the rustic yet romantic **Alley Cat Cafe** (1558 Fourth St), offering a sophisticated menu and live music. Good service, lots of vegetarian selections and flavorful dishes sets **Tropical Thai** (1420 Main St) apart. Amish families run two popular family-style eateries: **Yoder's** (3434 Bahia Vista St) and **Sugar & Spice** (4000 Cattlemen Rd). For more than 40 years, the **Original Oyster Bar** (7250 S Tamiami Trail) has packed in folks looking for good buys on seafood.

Entertainment

The **Sarasota County Arts Council** (☎ 941-365-5118, 506 Burns Court) has schedules for theater and ballet performances, jazz clubs, orchestras and film groups. The Sarasota Film Society's **Burns Court Cinema** (☎ 941-955-3456) shows foreign and independent films. **Patrick's** (1400 Main St), a popular sports bar, attracts large crowds for drinks, games and breaking bread. **Gator Club** (1490 Main St) has live rock, blues or alternative music nightly.

ST PETERSBURG

Across the bay from Tampa, St Petersburg (population 248,200) is a cultural mecca, and most of the attractions are centered downtown. The visitor bureau (☎ 727-464-7200, 877-352-3224, Ⓦ www.floridasbeach.com, 14450 46th St N No 108), in Clearwater, has satellite offices at 2001 Ulmberton Rd, I-275 exit 18, and on the St Petersburg Pier (☎ 727-821-4715, 800 2nd Ave N).

The **Salvador Dalí Museum** (☎ 727-823-3767, 1000 3rd St S) houses the largest collection of works by the artist outside Spain ($10, $5 Thurs evening). **St Petersburg Museum of Fine Arts** (☎ 727-896-2667, 255 Beach Dr NE) includes Asian, Indian and African art and pre-Columbian sculpture ($6). The **Florida International Museum** (☎ 727-822-3693, 800-777-9882, 100 2nd St N) features blockbuster exhibitions ($14). At the foot of the pier, the **St Petersburg Museum of History** (☎ 727-894-1052, 335 2nd Ave NE) covers the city, Pinellas Peninsula and early days of commercial aviation ($5). The **Florida Holocaust Museum** (☎ 727-820-0100, 55 5th St S) has permanent and changing exhibits on Europe's Holocaust ($6).

The **Pinellas Trail** (☎ 727-464-4751) is an awesome 33¾-mile urban biking, skating and walking trail that's oh so popular. It starts north of downtown at 34th St and Fairfield Ave (bus No 19 stops there) and ends at US 19 in Tarpon Springs. The free *Guidebook to the Pinellas Trail,* with mile-by-mile details, is available at visitor centers. The crown jewel of the county park system, **Fort DeSoto Park** (☎ 727-582-2267, 866-2484, 3500 Pinellas Bayway S) has a fort, a historic trail, concessions, camping and one of Florida's best beaches.

The area's major-league baseball franchise is the Tampa Bay Devil Rays (☎ 727-825-3250), who play at Tropicana Field. Spring training games at Al Lang Stadium (230 1st St S) cost $3-12.

Places to Stay & Eat

One of the very best views of the elegant Sunshine Skyway Bridge is from waterfront *Fort DeSoto Park Campground* (☎ 727-582-2267, 866-2484, 3500 Pinellas Bayway S), where amenity-rich sites cost $30. The area's best hostel, 25 miles northwest of downtown in Clearwater, is the *HI Clearwater Beach International Youth Hostel* (☎ 727-443-1211, 606 Bay Esplanade Ave), with dorm beds ($12/13 members/nonmembers), rooms ($35), a pool and gardens; it's a three-minute walk from the beach. There are lots of accommodations near downtown St Pete attractions. Popular with snowbirds for their clean rooms are *Grant Motel* (☎ 727-576-1369, 9046 4th St N) and *Tops Motel* (☎ 727-526-9071, 7141 4th St N), both from $40.

For those who want to do the resort thing, the beachfront *Sheraton Sand Key Resort* (☎ 727-595-1611, 1160 Gulf Blvd), at Clearwater Beach, has enough activities and amenities to keep you busy, yet relaxed, during your stay (from $150). The fun-filled *Suncoast Resort Hotel* (☎ 727-867-1111, 3000 34th St S) is the region's largest gay hotel ($49).

B&Bs abound, with options like *Bayboro Inn B&B* (☎ 727-823-0498, 357 3rd St S), at $75; *Claiborne House* (☎ 727-822-8855, 340 Rowland Circle NE), another serene historic house (from $95); and the pampering *Mansion House B&B* (☎ 727-821-9391, 105 5th Ave NE), from $115.

Lots of low-priced rustic restaurants serve good seafood. Among them are the longtime favorite *Fourth Street Shrimp Store* (1006 4th St N), *Casual Clam* (3336 9th St N) and *Crab Shack* (11400 Gandy Blvd). *Fred's Famous Barbecue and Brewery* (4351 4th St N) smokes up lunch and dinner. Moderately priced, tasty curries, jerks and vegetarian dishes ($5-20) are offered at Caribbean-style *Saffron's* (1700 Park St N). For the ultimate in grazing and trendy dining, try *Ovo Cafe* (515 Central Ave), surprisingly well priced (from $10) for the quality.

Getting There & Around

St Petersburg–Clearwater International Airport (☎ 727-535-7600) has car rentals. Greyhound (☎ 727-898-1496, 180 9th St N) goes to Miami ($39; 8 hours), Tampa ($7; 30 minutes) and Orlando ($18; 3 hours). Amtrak has a bus link from Tampa's station to St Petersburg, where it stops at the Pinellas Square Mall (7200 Hwy 19 N).

Pinellas Suncoast Transit Authority (☎ 727-530-9911) operates buses ($1, $2.50 day pass, no transfers). The Looper trolley (50¢, day pass $2.50) links the museums and pier on a 30-minute narrated loop 11am-5pm, at the St Petersburg Pier.

TAMPA

Tampa (population 303,500) is a city on the rise. At the center of its revitalization is Ybor City, the historic heart of the old cigar industry. Another draw is Busch Gardens, which combines an excellent zoo with great roller coasters. Most attractions are downtown.

Fort Brooke was established in Tampa in 1855. From the late 19th century until the mid-20th century, Cuban cigar makers established factories in Ybor City. An influx of foreign workers descended on the region. Importing high-quality tobacco from Cuba, Ybor City remained the USA's cigar-making capital until the Cuban Revolution in 1959 and the resulting US embargo on Cuban products. Now renovated, historic Ybor City is Tampa's prime tourist destination.

The visitor bureau (☎ 813-223-1111, 800-448-2672, W www.visittampabay.com) is at 400 N Tampa St, suite 2800. The Ybor City Chamber of Commerce (☎ 813-248-3712, W www.ybor.org) is at 1600 E 8th Ave, suite 104. Tampa Bay Business Guild (☎ 813-237-3751, W www.tbbg.org) provides information for gay and lesbian visitors.

Downtown
The **Tampa Museum of Art** (☎ 813-274-8130, 600 N Ashley St) has exhibits from avant-garde to old masters, sculpture, photography and works by emerging Florida artists ($5, free 10am-1pm Sat and 5pm-8pm Thurs). At the **Florida Aquarium** (☎ 813-273-4000, 701 Channelside Dr), explore the state's five ecosystems, including the coral reefs, marshes, bays, wetlands and beaches, and the animals that thrive within them ($14/9 adults/kids).

Would-be scientists explore the heavens, hurricanes and hearts at the **Museum of Science & Industry** (☎ 813-987-6000, 4801 E Fowler Ave) before sitting down to view a feature in the IMAX Dome theater ($13/9 adults/kids, including film).

Ybor City
A national historic district in the northeast of Tampa, Ybor (**ee**-bore) City began as a community of Cuban and Spanish cigar makers and Italian immigrants. It's now a lively area for day and evening historic tours, entertainment, shopping and dining.

The **Ybor City State Museum** (☎ 813-247-6323, 1818 E 9th Ave), in the former Ferlita Bakery building, chronicles the history of cigar making ($2). Historic walking tours depart at 10:30am Saturday ($4, including museum admission). Dramatic, actor-led one-hour **Ybor City Ghost Walk** tours (☎ 813-242-9255, 813-242-4660) lend a spicy touch to history and architecture ($10). Tours depart at 7pm Thursday and 4pm weekends from Centro Ybor (1600 E 8th

Ave), where you also can pick up free self-guided audio tours.

The **Ybor City Brewing Company** (☎ 813-242-9222, 2205 N 20th St) has tours ($3) and tastings at 11am, noon and 1pm weekdays.

Busch Gardens & Adventure Island
Thrills, spills and exotic animals await you at Busch Gardens (☎ 813-987-5082, W www.buschgardens.com, 3000 E Busch Blvd), an African-themed amusement park and world-class zoo that features two of the country's most thrilling roller coasters ($48/39 adults/kids, plus $6 parking). Next door is **Adventure Island** (☎ 813-987-5600), a 25-acre water park with rides, slides and pools ($28/26). A combination ticket for one day at each park costs $60/50.

Activities
Tampa is deep in the heart of **canoeing** country. Owners Jean and Joe Faulk are the reasons canoeists and kayakers return to Canoe Escape (☎ 813-986-2067, 9335 E Fowler Ave), in Thonotosassa west of I-75 exit 54, for any of seven trips ($14.50-24, including shuttle) on the Hillsborough River, which offers outstanding scenery. You can do the trips individually or combine them into an all-day affair. Hillsborough River State Park (☎ 813-987-6771, 15402 Hwy 301 N) is an outdoor jewel with canoeing, **hiking** trails and a spring-fed pool.

Places to Stay
Camping doesn't get any better than at *Hillsborough River State Park* (see Activities), where shady sites ($13) are grouped in separate loops to create a feeling of privacy. *KOA Tampa East* (☎ 813-659-2202, 12870 Hwy 92), 12 miles east, features RV sites (from $22) and separate tent sites ($20). *Florida Sawmill Campground* (☎ 352-583-0664, 21710 Hwy 98), in Dade City 39 miles northeast of Tampa, is a private 80-acre campground catering to gay and lesbian campers. It's loaded with amenities and has tent/RV rates from $10/27, as well as $59 cabins.

Economical choices abound near Busch Gardens, along Fowler Ave/Morris Bridge Rd (Hwy 582) and Busch Blvd (Hwy 580). You get a lot of bang for $50-60 at *Shoney's Inn* (☎ 813-985-8525, 8602 Hwy 582). Ditto for $50 at *Red Roof Inn* (☎ 813-932-0073,

FLORIDA

2307 E Busch Blvd) and *Value Inn* (☎ *813-933-6760, 2523 E Busch Blvd).*

There are two interesting B&Bs: cozy *Behind the Fence*(☎ *813-685-8201, 1400 Viola Dr),* 15 miles east in Brandon ($60-89), which caters to canoeists, and *Gram's Place B&B, Guesthouses and Youth Hostel* (☎ *813-221-0596, 3109 N Ola Ave),* a music buff's haven named after '60s singer-songwriter Gram Parsons. It features a new recording studio. Dorm beds are $25; rooms are $65 with shared bath, $95 with private bath.

Want to be close to nightlife? Stay at the new *Hilton Garden Inn* (☎ *813-769-9267, 1700 E 9th Ave),* the only hotel in Ybor City ($159). Less than 20 minutes away, the rates go down to $45 at the plain-Jane but clean and comfy *East Lake Inn* (☎ *813-622-8339, 6529 E Hillsborough Ave).* Get away from it all at the 480-acre *Saddlebrook Resort Tampa* (☎ *813-973-1111, 5700 Saddlebrook Way),* in Wesley Chapel, with a golf course, spa, restaurants and activities galore (rates start at $170).

Places to Eat

Oenophiles (wine connoisseurs) and steak lovers come from around the country to *Bern's Steak House* (☎ *813-251-2421, 1208 S Howard Ave),* a Tampa landmark. Reservations are recommended. Its budget-conscious sister *SideBern's (2208 W Morrison Ave)* features world cuisine and indoor/outdoor seating.

Hyde Park Historic District has two excellent, surprisingly inexpensive choices – *Cactus Club (1601 Snow Ave),* for fine Southwestern fare, and *Mis En Place (2616 MacDill Ave),* one of Tampa's best restaurants, serving Floribbean cuisine.

In Ybor City grab a traditional Cuban breakfast of toast and gear-revving coffee at *La Tropicana (1822 E 7th Ave)* or *La Segunda Central Bakery (2512 N 15th St);* a Cuban sandwich at *Carmine's (1802 E 7th Ave);* a flavorful calzone at *Little Sicily (1724 E 8th Ave);* moderately priced gumbos, crawfish and andouille at *Café Creole & Oyster Bar (1330 E 9th Ave);* or sushi and sashimi at *Sushi on 7th (1919 E 7th Ave).*

Entertainment

Find out what's happening from the *Weekly Planet, Tampa Tribune's* 'Friday Extra,' the *Times's* 'Friday Weekend,' or the arts hotline (☎ 813-229-2787). Gay and lesbian publications include the monthly *Gazette.*

The *Tampa Bay Performing Arts Center* (☎ *813-229-7827, 1010 N MacInnes Place)* has four stages for concerts and theatrical productions. The artsy crowd flocks to the renovated 1926 *Tampa Theater (*☎ *813-274-8286, 711 N Franklin St)* to sit in red fabric chairs and watch independent and classic films and special events ($6.25).

When it comes to nightlife, head for Ybor City's 7th Ave and pick your pleasure.

Spectator Sports

The NFL Tampa Bay Buccaneers (☎ 813-879-2827) play football at Raymond James Stadium (4201 Dale Mabry Hwy) August to December. The MLS Tampa Bay Mutiny (v 813-289-6811) kick soccer balls there April to September. The NHL Tampa Bay Lightning (☎ 813-229-2658) play hockey October to April at the Ice Palace (401 Channelside Dr). And there's no charge to watch the New York Yankees (☎ 813-875-7753) practice at Legends Field (Dale Mabry Hwy at Martin Luther King Jr Blvd).

Getting There & Around

There's commuter, national and international service into Tampa International Airport (☎ 813-870-8700). Major car rental agencies have counters inside. Greyhound (☎ 813-229-2174, 610 E Polk St) has buses to Miami ($39; 8 hours), Orlando ($18; 2 hours) and St Petersburg ($7; 30 minutes). Amtrak (☎ 813-221-7600) is at 601 Nebraska Ave N. HARTline (☎ 813-254-4278) buses ($1.15 or $2.50 all day) have bike racks. Electric streetcars debut in spring 2002 and run between downtown Tampa and Ybor City.

CITRUS COUNTY

The Citrus County area remains unspoiled because almost half of it is state or federal land. Canoeing, hiking and horseback-riding trails abound. The region is 70 miles north of Tampa and 60 miles northwest of Orlando. The headwaters of the Homosassa and Crystal Rivers are freshwater springs that remain at 72°F year round, attracting manatees and divers October to March to the only place in Florida where humans can legally interact with manatees. Strict rules regulate activities.

Citrus County offers a natural and inexpensive Florida vacation. The visitor center (☎ 352-527-5223, 800-587-6667, Ⓦ www .visitcitrus.com) is at 801 SE US 19, Crystal River, FL 34429.

Things to See & Do

The **Homosassa Springs Wildlife State Park** (☎ 352-628-5343, 4150 S Suncoast Blvd), in Homosassa, is a unique 166-acre park showcasing native Floridian wildlife and endangered species in a zoolike setting. The Fishbowl Underwater Observatory takes you beneath the surface to view fish and manatees. Trails, pontoon boats and trams take you around the park ($8/5 adults/kids).

The **Crystal River Archaeological State Park** and **Yulee Sugar Mill Ruins State Historic Site Park** (☎ 352-795-3817, 3400 N Museum Pt), in Old Homosassa, chronicle Native American and pioneer history ($2). Next door is the **Olde Mill House Gallery & Printing Museum** (☎ 888-248-6672, 10466 W Yulee Dr).

You can go **diving** or **snorkeling** in spring-fed rivers, shallow gulf coastal waters and underwater caverns. Weekdays are best, as weekends are crowded. Bird's Underwater Manatee Snorkel Tour (☎ 352-563-2763, 320 NW Hwy 19), in Crystal River, takes visitors on tours ($28) and videotapes the experience ($30). Homosassa Riverside Resort (☎ 352-628-2474, 5300 S Cherokee Way) offers

FLORIDA

Mad about Manatees

A cute little nose barely breaks the surface of the water, with a 'pfft' and spray of water and air. Below that nose stretches a 15-foot, nearly 2000lb gray mass with a walruslike body that tapers to a beaverlike tail. That's a big manatee, about as big as they get.

For all their size and weight, West Indian manatees (Trichechus manatus), which are related to the elephant, are shy and elusive. So shy, in fact, that early explorers who glimpsed them thought they were mermaids. Later, as they watched them graze on underwater vegetation, they called them 'sea cows.'

These slow, nearly blind mammals are an endangered species, protected by federal and state laws. They have no natural enemies, but their numbers are threatened by loss of habitat, careless anglers and increasing boat traffic. When they come to the water's surface to breathe they are vulnerable to being hit by boats. It's not uncommon to see pink propeller scars across their backs. Frequently they are also injured or killed by fishing lines, which strangle them or tangle their fins.

The best places to see manatees are Blue Springs State Park and Homosassa Springs State Wildlife Park, and along the Crystal River. They winter (Nov-Mar) in the parks' 72°F springs. If you're in a boat, you can catch them warming themselves in the heated water discharged by electric power plants, near Sanibel Island and Fort Myers and in the canals, marinas and nearshore areas of the Florida Keys. In warmer periods, they also swim in St Johns River.

kayaks ($20/30 half/full day), bikes and eco-tours (from $50). Grab your bicycle and skates and head to the paved 46-mile **With-lacoochee State Trail** (☎ 352-394-2280, 12549 State Park Dr), in Clermont, which stretches over a former railroad right-of-way.

River Safaris & Gulf Charters (☎ 352-628-5222, 800-758-3474, 10823 Yulee Dr), in Homosassa, leads 90-minute tours ($15-25) on pontoon boats for an eyeful of birds, rare white pelicans, dolphins and manatees.

Places to Stay & Eat
In Inverness, *Fort Cooper State Park* (☎ 352-726-0315, 3100 S Old Floral City Rd) has deeply wooded primitive tent campsites ($3 per person) with tables, grills, a fire ring and portable restrooms. *Trail's End Camp* (☎ 352-726-3699, 12900 Trails End Rd), in Floral City, has wooded sites ($8), good facilities, canoeing and fishing. About 10 miles away in Brooksville, *Withlacoochee State Forest* (☎ 352-754-6896, 15003 Broad St) has hiking, fishing and canoeing, and nine full-feature campgrounds (from $9) and primitive sites (free).

On the banks of Lake Tsala Apopka, sprawling, family-owned *Moonrise Resort* (☎ 352-726-2553, 800-665-6701, 8801 E Moonrise Lane), in Floral City, has clean and fully equipped one- and two-bedroom cabins ($50-70). *Best Western* (☎ 352-795-3171, 614 NW US 19), in Crystal River, has nicely appointed rooms from $85. Step back in time at *The Last Resort* (☎ 352-628-7117, 800-968-7117, 10738 W Halls River Rd), in Homosassa, where six stilt cabins stand over the Homosassa River ($90).

In Homosassa, *Misty River Seafood House* (4135 S Suncoast Blvd) features an eclectic seafood menu ($5-18). *KC Crump* (11210 W Halls River Rd), in a beautiful old house on the Homosassa River, serves seafood, steaks and chicken dinners ($10-16). *Fat Fred's Famous Bar-B-Q* (734 SE US 19), in Crystal River, has won more than 76 national barbecue cook-offs.

Getting There & Around
Greyhound has stations in Crystal River (☎ 352-795-4445, 640 SE 8th Terrace) and Inverness (☎ 352-726-3772, 1010 N US 41) with service to Miami ($65; 11 hours) and Tampa ($14; 2 hours). There's no local transportation, but Enterprise (☎ 352-563-5511,

622 NE First Terrace), in Crystal River, delivers rental cars. Enterprise also has an office (☎ 352-637-6632, 3730 E Gulf to Lake Hwy) in Inverness.

Central Florida

As the story goes, in 1964 Walt Disney flew over central Florida looking for a site for his new theme park. He looked out the window, saw the vacant land near the confluence of two major highways and said, 'This is it.' Within 10 years, what had been thousands of acres of citrus groves became the theme-park capital of the world and the businesses, communities and infrastructure that support it. Beyond Disney are charming small towns, lakes, rivers and cool, clear swimming springs.

ORLANDO
Orlando (population 186,000) has been, successively, a railroad, real-estate, citrus and space-technology boomtown. The 1971 opening of Walt Disney World, 20 miles southwest, placed the city firmly on the tourist map as a theme-park paradise as well as home of first-rate museums. The visitor bureau (☎ 407-363-5872, 800-551-0181, W www.orlandoinfo.com, 8723 International Dr) publishes multilingual guides and maps. Gay visitors should also check the Gay, Lesbian and Bisexual Community Center (☎ 407-228-8272, W www.glbcc.org, 946 N Mills Ave).

SeaWorld & Discovery Cove
Water is a theme for the Anheuser-Busch parks in Orlando. SeaWorld (☎ 407-351-3600, W www.seaworld.com, 7007 SeaWorld Dr) has entertaining and educational marine-theme exhibits, including Kraken, the tallest and fastest roller coaster in Orlando; Journey to Atlantis, a thrilling water-coaster ride; killer-whale and sea-lion shows; and polar bears. There are interaction programs such as swims with dolphins and touch tanks ($48/39 adults/kids, plus $6 parking).

The new **Discovery Cove** (☎ 877-434-7268, W www.discoverycove.com, 6000 Discovery Cove Way) is a tropical island where you can snorkel on a heated saltwater coral reef face to face with denizens of the deep –

separated by a Plexiglas window, of course. You can swim and interact with dolphins, inner-tube on a river and walk through an aviary. Admission ($109, $199 with dolphin program) is limited to 800 to 1000 guests a day, so it's not crowded.

Universal Studios & Islands of Adventure

This combination working movie studio and theme park features film-related rides and shows. Get the *Official Studio Guide* map and information packet from Universal Studios Florida (☎ 407-363-8000, W www .universalstudios.com, 1000 Universal Studios Plaza).

Islands of Adventure, the newest sister park, features five themed island rides and shows based on the fictional and mythical characters of *Jurassic Park, The Incredible Hulk,* Marvel Super Heroes and *The Cat in the Hat.*

Admission to Universal Studios or Islands of Adventure is $48/39 adults/kids for one day plus $6 parking. Multipark and multiday passes are available. Pick up a free Express Pass, which gives you a confirmed one-hour window for certain rides. VIP Tours (☎ 407-363-8295; advance reservations required) of the studios last five hours and get you into rides and shows without waiting in line ($120).

Other Attractions

Leave the thrills and make-believe behind to find cultural sustenance at Loch Haven Park, home to three museums. The **Orlando Science Center & John Young Planetarium** (☎ 407-514-2000, 777 E Princeton St) is the largest science center in the southeast, with exhibits, large-format films and planetarium and laser-light shows ($12.50/9.25 adults/kids). The **Orlando Museum of Art** (☎ 407-896-4231, 2416 N Mills Ave) presents blockbuster touring exhibits and American, pre-Columbian and African art ($6). The **Mennello Museum of American Folk** (☎ 407-246-4278, 900 E Princeton St) houses works of Earl Cunningham and features traveling shows ($2).

To learn about Orlando before Disney, check out the new **Orange County Regional History Center** (☎ 407-836-8500, 65 E Central Blvd), in the 1927 courthouse ($7/3.50).

Places to Stay

There are hundreds of accommodations options. The Central Reservation Service (☎ 800-548-3311) works with the visitor bureau to assist in making hotel reservations. The service is free.

KOA Orlando (☎ 407-277-5075, 12345 Narcoossee Rd) has tent sites, some shaded by pines, with full hookup (from $20). *Raccoon Lake Camp Resort* (☎ 800-776-9644, 8555 Hwy 192) has tent sites from $18 as well as furnished trailers and cabins. There are dozens of chain lodgings along International Dr ('I-Drive') – *Best Western, Holiday Inn* etc, many priced in the $35-75 range.

Neighboring Kissimmee offers low-priced options, many within a few miles of Disney World's main gate and providing free scheduled shuttles to the parks. The family-oriented *Tropical Palms Resort* (☎ 407-396-4595, 800-647-2567, 2650 Holiday Trail) has a theme-park shuttle, a pool, lots of extras, and palm- and pine-shaded sites ($24-29). It also has a friendly staff and furnished cabins ($49-69). *HI Orlando/Kissimmee Resort* (☎ 407-396-8282, 4840 W Hwy 192) has dorm beds ($16/19 members/nonmembers), private rooms (from $35/41) and cheap shuttles to Disney World and other attractions.

Dozens of reasonably priced chains and simple, clean budget motels line Hwy 192, including *Apollo Inn* (670 E Hwy 192) and *Flamingo Inn* (801 E Hwy 192), for $30-40. For a little bit more ($40-60) you get more amenities and bigger rooms at *Travelodge Hotel* (8600 W Hwy 192) and *Sleep Inn Maingate* (8536 W Hwy 192). Intimate *Wonderland Inn* (3601 S Orange Blossom Trail) has pretty rooms from $60.

Places to Eat

Prices tend to be higher at theme parks than at restaurants outside, but good options include Emeril Lagasse's *Emeril's Orlando,* in Universal's CityWalk complex, and *California Grill,* in Disney's Contemporary Resort. Sand Lake Rd, near Universal, has been dubbed 'Restaurant Row' for its many eateries. For attractively priced options outside the parks, consider the fun, multi-ethnic *Cafe Tu Tu Tango* (8625 International Dr) and *Little Saigon* (1106 E Colonial Dr), for excellent Vietnamese food. For haute cuisine at bistro prices, try *Le Coq au Vin*

FLORIDA

Her Eyes Were Watching Them

How special it must have been to be born in a town created just for you. Not the 'colored' section of an otherwise white town, but a town plotted just for African Americans. Writer and folklorist Zora Neale Hurston was born in 1891 in just such a special place – Eatonville, the nation's oldest African American incorporated municipality, established in 1886, a few miles from Orlando.

One of eight children of Lucy Ann Potts and the Reverend John Hurston, Zora vividly captured life in an African American town and what it was like to be African American in the South.

Zora's 'Mama' exhorted her children to 'jump at de sun.' Zora did just that. While working as a maid for a writer in New York, she attended and graduated from Barnard College. In the 1930s and '40s she reached the pinnacle of her writing career by gaining international recognition for such works as *Mules and Men, Their Eyes Were Watching God* and numerous short stories, including 'How It Feels to Be Colored Me.' Her book *Dust Tracks on A Road* is an autobiographical account of growing up in Eatonville. She was also instrumental in the Harlem Renaissance.

But fame was fleeting. Zora died in 1960 poor and again working as a maid. Today, the **Zora Neale Hurston National Museum of Fine Arts** (☎ 407-647-3307, 227 E Kennedy Blvd), in Eatonville, honors her work and the works of midcareer and critically acclaimed African American artists (open 9am-4pm Mon-Fri, by appointment Sat-Sun). A self-guided walking tour through the community visits Hurston's school, church and other sites that influenced her life and writings.

(4800 S Orange Ave). The authentic racing memorabilia captures your attention at **Race Rock** (8986 International Dr). Though it's a bit pricey, **Del Frisco's** (729 Lee Rd) does steak just right.

If you like fun with your food, don't miss **Mad-Lyn's Cafe** (932 N Mills Ave), a gay-friendly eatery near Out and About Books and the Gay, Lesbian and Bisexual Community Center. The mood is decidedly bohemian at equally gay-friendly **White Wolf Cafe** (1829 N Orange Ave).

In neighboring Kissimmee, consider one of the theme dinner buffets, especially if you have kids. **Medieval Times** (☎ 407-396-1518, 4510 W Hwy 192) offers dinner shows ($42/36 adults/kids), including jousting. One of the funniest buffets is **Capone's** (☎ 407-397-2378, 4740 W Hwy 192), with a gangland revue and buffet dinner ($40/24).

Entertainment

The theme parks win it for entertainment. Universal Studio's **CityWalk** features movies, clubs and restaurants. Downtown Disney and Disney's Pleasure Island are very similar (see Walt Disney World, below). **Parliament House** (☎ 407-425-7571, 410 N Orange Blossom Trail), with six clubs and bars, is the biggest, baddest gay hangout in town. The daily *Orlando Sentinel* is the best source for entertainment options.

Getting There & Around

Orlando International Airport (☎ 407-825-2001) has easy connections to the major tourist areas via the Lynx Bus system. Taxis cost about $25-30, shuttle vans $15-20.

Greyhound (☎ 407-292-3440, 555 N John Young Pkwy) serves Miami ($37; 6 hours), Jacksonville ($25; 3 hours), Tampa ($18; 2 hours) and other cities. Amtrak (☎ 407-843-7611, 1400 Sligh Blvd) offers daily service to Orlando.

City buses ($1, transfers 10¢, week pass $10) are operated by Lynx System (☎ 407-841-8240).

WALT DISNEY WORLD

The mother of all theme parks, Walt Disney World (WDW) covers nearly 43 square miles. It's a conglomeration of four parks, the Magic Kingdom, Disney-MGM Studios, Animal Kingdom and EPCOT, plus several water parks, a sports complex and an evening entertainment park, Downtown Disney. It's an amazing place with something for everyone.

WDW is least crowded in January, February (except President's Day weekend), September (after Labor Day), October and early December. Weekends are less busy than early in the week. For inexpensive accommodations, the best time is August to December; holidays are expensive. June.

July and August are *very* hot and humid, with frequent downpours. Weather-wise, autumn tends to be best. The immensely popular annual Gay Day at Disney World (W www.gayday.com) kicks off the first weekend in June.

From Orlando's Lynx Bus Center, bus No 50 leaves hourly for WDW. Many hotels provide scheduled shuttles to the parks.

Orientation & Information

WDW is 20 miles southwest of downtown Orlando, 4 miles northwest of Kissimmee. The four main parks are the Magic Kingdom, EPCOT Center, Disney-MGM Studios Theme Park and Animal Kingdom. Also on the grounds is Downtown Disney, an entertainment, shopping and dining complex. For reservations at Disney resorts and WDW information, call ☎ 407-934-7639.

Ticket lines can be long, so buy your tickets in advance from a Disney store, online at W www.waltdisneyworld.com, through AAA (multiday only) or by mail from WDW Guest Communications, PO Box 10000, Lake Buena Vista, FL 32830. There are numerous ticket options, ranging from the One-Day One-Park ticket ($48/38 adults/kids) to the Four-Day Park-Hopper for unlimited admission to the four parks ($192/152). Parking costs $6.

Crowds are horrific in summer, but entertainment in the lines makes waiting less painful. Pick up a free FastPass to get confirmed times on certain rides. Bring drinking water (refills free at Disney restaurants) and sunscreen. Food from outside is not permitted.

Things to See & Do

The centerpiece of WDW is the **Magic Kingdom**, home of Cinderella's Castle; Splash Mountain, a thrilling 50-foot drop; and the wild Big Thunder Mountain Railroad ride. New stuff includes Buzz Lightyear's Space Ranger Spin, which spins you into outer space and lets you defend the galaxy, and The Many Adventures of Winnie the Pooh, a kids' ride through the characters' storybook pages.

The rides and attractions at the **Disney-MGM Studios Theme Park** are absolutely first-rate. You can go for a wild ride on the new Rock 'n' Roller Coaster (starring Aerosmith) or chill at Jim Henson's Muppet Vision 3D, so real that kids reach for the characters.

EPCOT Center is broken into two main sections. Future World offers corporate-sponsored journeys through the history of technology, with bold predictions about the future. The park's longest, fastest ride, the new Test Track, mimics an automotive testing ground. At the other end of the park, the World Showcase re-creates a permanent world exposition.

At Disney's 500-acre **Animal Kingdom** (☎ 407-824-4321), visitors go on safaris, riverboat rides and trails to see wild animals up close in re-created 'natural' environments. There are shows like *Tarzan Rocks!* with stunts, and live music and rides like Kali River Rapids.

Disney also has several **water parks**, including Blizzard Beach ($30/24 adults/kids), where you can free-fall down a 100-foot slide, and Typhoon Lagoon ($30/24), with a huge wave pool and a fish observatory.

Places to Stay

Disney-owned lodging is designed with families in mind, so rooms usually accommodate four or more. Guests at Disney-owned properties can enter the parks 1½ hours early and whiz through all the best rides and shows before the crowds arrive.

The Disney-owned *Fort Wilderness Resort & Campground* (☎ 407-824-2900) has great sites (from $34) and air-conditioned cabins with full kitchens ($224 for up to six guests). Don't confuse the above with rustic *Wilderness Lodge* (from $219), which oozes elegant pioneer atmosphere. Two campgrounds in nearby Davenport are *Mouse Mountain RV Camping Resort* (☎ 863-424-2791, 800-347-6388, 7500 Osceola Polk Line Rd), with above-standard facilities and sites from $24; and *Fort Summit KOA* (☎ 863-424-1880, 800-424-1880, 2525 Frontage Rd), with small grassy tent/RV sites ($27/34), many amenities, car rentals and free shuttles to WDW.

All Star Sports Resort (☎ 407-939-5000) and *All Star Music Resort* (☎ 407-939-6000) are the least expensive Disney-owned hotels (from $99). *Dixie Landings* (☎ 407-934-6000) exudes a rural South theme, while *Port Orleans* (☎ 407-934-5000)

FLORIDA

reproduces New Orleans' French Quarter; both start at $149. Some top-of-the-line resorts include *Grand Floridian Resort & Spa* (from $359) and *Polynesian Resort* (from $324).

Places to Eat & Drink

To dine at a restaurant inside WDW, you'll need a ticket for whichever park the restaurant's in. Call ☎ 407-939-3463 for information and reservations at WDW restaurants. Character restaurants, where you dine with Mickey or his colleagues, require reservations (especially for breakfast) up to 60 days in advance. They offer buffet meals at fixed prices.

In the Magic Kingdom, *Columbia Harbour House* offers economically priced chowder and sandwiches. A pretty good buffet and salad, pasta and dessert bars at *Crystal Palace* are enlivened with Disney characters ($16-20.) *Tony's Town Square* serves generous portions of Italian fare with a *Lady and the Tramp* motif.

The international food at the EPCOT Center is somewhat pricey, but you usually get your money's worth. *Coral Reef* derives its name from the dining room's giant aquarium as well as the bounty found on it (from $17). *Bistro de Paris* serves excellent French fare at Paris prices. Prices in Japan's *Yakitori House* are more reasonable. The excellent Moroccan *Marrakesh Restaurant* serves up couscous and similar dishes (from $11/19 lunch/dinner) in a re-created palace.

Go retro at Disney-MGM's *Prime Time Cafe*, where diner foods are served (from $14); and grab a quick lunch from the international menu at *The Commissary* (from $6). In the Animal Kingdom, you don't have to go fancy – or expensive – for good food at *Tuskar House*, which sports an African theme (from $6).

Disney offers late-night fun at Downtown Disney, an entertainment, dining and shopping complex that features *Pleasure Island* (☎ 407-934-7781), where one ticket ($21) admits you into more than half a dozen cool themed nightclubs and an outdoor stage show.

You will also find the *House of Blues* (☎ 407-934-2583), where big-name artists perform just about everything from blues to gospel ($10-20).

ICHETUCKNEE SPRINGS STATE PARK

The stunningly clear and refreshing waters of the Ichetucknee (Pond of the Beaver) River draw hordes of visitors to this park (☎ 904-497-4690, 497-2511). It's a fine place to float lazily downstream in an inner tube, rubber raft or canoe. Look for otters, alligators, turtles, beaver, birds, spectacular flora and fish. Rangers assure inner tubers that alligators pose no threat. Alcohol, tobacco, *anything* disposable, pets, bottles and cans are prohibited on the river. The park is 4 miles northwest of Fort White, off Hwys 47 and 238 in High Springs.

Concessionaires along both highways rent inner tubes ($4) and rafts ($6-17). The longest ride (3½ hours) begins at the north entrance ($4.25), off Hwy 238. It's open for tubing from Memorial Day weekend to Labor Day. There are three options, ranging from 30 to 90 minutes, at the south entrance ($3.25; open year round).

Canoes ($20 a day) can be launched at the north entrance year round. Wildlife abounds on two-hour ranger-led canoe trips ($10). There's great swimming ($3.25 per car) and snorkeling through the north entrance along the river in summer and through the south entrance all year. There's also hiking on two trails and spelunking (explorers must be cave- and cavern-certified).

Fort Ichetucknee Resort (☎ 904-497-1928), on Hwy 47 at Hwy 238, has campsites ($6 per person). The *Ichetucknee Springs Campground* (☎ 904-497-2285), on CR 238 next to the north entrance, is a small, private tent/RV campground ($10/15) with extras like a tavern, game rooms and ball courts.

There's no public transportation to or near the park, which is about 40 miles northwest of Gainesville.

The Panhandle

When people talk about Florida's great beaches, they're usually referring to the miles and miles of fine, white sandy shoreline here. Yet except for the coastal area, the Panhandle is the least-traveled region, although it boasts some of the most beautiful natural areas. It's also home to the state capital, Tallahassee.

TALLAHASSEE

This city (population 150,600) was made the capital of the Florida territories in 1824 because it was midway between St Augustine and Pensacola. It's home to the state legislature, Florida State University (FSU) and the Florida Agricultural and Mechanical University (FAMU), but offers little of real interest to visitors. If you're driving between Pensacola and St Augustine, it's worth a stop, but given the state's other attractions, it's not worth a special trip. The visitor bureau (☎ 850-413-9200, 106 E Jefferson St) is off Monroe St.

Spend part of the day in the beautiful **Old Capitol** (☎ 850-487-1902, 400 S Monroe St), now a museum of Floridian political and social history (free admission). An architectural tour is offered at 11am Saturday. Also see the **New Capitol** (☎ 850-413-9200), at Pensacola and Duval Sts, where the Florida legislature meets 60 days a year, starting in March, and an observation deck affords a panoramic view (free admission).

The **Black Archives Research Center & Museum** (☎ 850-599-3020), in Carnegie Library on the FAMU campus, and also in the historic Union Bank Building (☎ 850-561-2603, 219 S Calhoun St), showcases African American and African artifacts (free admission). The **Museum of Florida History** (☎ 850-488-1484, 500 S Bronough St) chronicles Florida through its art, artifacts, weapons and clothing.

The 16-mile **Tallahassee–St Marks Historic Railroad State Trail** (☎ 850-922-6007), on Woodville Hwy near Hwy 319, follows the abandoned historic rail line of the same name. Rent bikes or skates ($5 an hour) from About Bikes (☎ 850-656-0001, 4780 Woodville Hwy), at the northern terminus.

Places to Stay & Eat

Note that accommodations rates go up for football games and the busy March through May legislative session.

Deep in the Apalachicola National Forest on the Ochlockonee River are two campgrounds, *Whitehead Landing* and *Mack Landing* (☎ 850-926-3561, Wakulla Ranger Station, 57 Taff Dr), in Crawfordville. Sites feature pit toilets, hand-pumped potable water and picnic tables ($3). It's about 30 minutes from the Tallahassee–St Marks Historic Railroad State Trail.

Most accommodations are uninspiring and are clumped at exits along I-10 and along Monroe St between I-10 and downtown. One of the exceptions is *Calhoun Street Inn* (☎ 850-425-5095, 525 N Calhoun St), a B&B in a quiet residential neighborhood (from $65). *Quality Inn & Suites* (☎ 850-877-4437, 2020 Apalachee Pkwy) gives you a lot of room and extras for the money (from $61). A little south of the capital, in Wakulla Springs State Park, you can stay in the refreshing *Wakulla Springs Lodge* (☎ 850-224-5950, 550 Wakulla Park Dr), a small, rustic historic hotel surrounded by nature ($65-75). It has a decent restaurant that offers a menu of Southern dishes.

Most restaurants are closed Sunday. If fish is your thing, try two local standbys: *Po' Boys Creole Cafe*, with locations at 224 E College Ave and 1944 W Pensacola St, for shrimp pie, and *Catfish Pad (1108 S Magnolia Dr)*, where salt- and freshwater seafood (mostly fried) is served with the usual Southern suspects: cheese grits, fries, beans and applesauce. There are more good Southern bites at family-priced *Coosh Bayou Rouge (2910 Kerry Forest Pkwy)*, where half a muffuletta (huge) costs $7 and a Cajun sampler of three dishes runs $6. *Bahn Thai (1319 S Monroe St)*, has a generous weekday lunch buffet for $7.

¡Cuba libre! is the cry at *Gordo's (111 W College Ave)*, downtown, where you can order a dozen tapas ($1.25-2) to make dinner for two. The hipsters hang at mid-priced *Mozaik (1410D Market St)*, in The Pavilions, for trendy goods like goat-cheese and fried-eggplant-with-mozzarella sandwiches.

For a special treat, colorful *Kool Beanz Cafe (921 Thomasville Rd)* serves delicious New Age salads and New World cuisine, with dinner and wine averaging $25. *Chez Pierre (☎ 850-222-0936, 1215 Thomasville Rd)* is a top-rated, cozy French place in a historic house.

Getting There & Around

Greyhound (☎ 850-222-4249, 112 W Tennessee St) serves Pensacola ($24; 4 hours), Jacksonville ($28; 3 hours), Miami ($67; 11 hours) and other locales. Amtrak (☎ 850-224-2779) is at 918½ Railroad Ave. TalTran (☎ 850-891-5200) bus fare is $1, $2.50 for a day pass. Take the free downtown Old Town Trolley weekdays.

FLORIDA

FLORIDA

Sand & Sun Fun

It's official: Dr Beach's list of the USA's best beaches puts seven of Florida's in the top 20. Since 1991, Dr Beach (Stephen Leatherman) has annually ranked the country's beaches, taking into consideration 50 criteria, from sand softness and water temperature to rip currents and vistas. The following are the Florida winners:

2	St Joseph Peninsula State Park in Port St Joe
5	Caladesi Island State Park in Dunedin
6	Fort DeSoto Park in St Petersburg
9	Bill Baggs Cape Florida State Park on Key Biscayne (Miami)
13	Siesta Beach on Siesta Key (Sarasota)
16	St George Island State Park on St George Island
17	Perdido Key State Park in Pensacola

Excluded from the running were the past number-one-ranked beaches, including Bahia Honda State Park in the Florida Keys, Grayton Beach State Park in Santa Rosa and St Andrews State Park in Panama City.

Incidentally, South Beach (Miami) and Panama City Beach came in second and fourth in the 'best beaches with nightlife' category.

You can check out Dr Beach's Web site at �W www.drbeach.org or pick up the book *America's Best Beaches*.

PANAMA CITY BEACH

During spring break, students flock to the white, Appalachian-quartz sand beaches of Panama City Beach (population 7700), a 27-mile-long gulf barrier island almost due west of the separate municipality of Panama City. It extends east from St Andrews State Recreation Area, one of the finest beaches in the country, to the Philips Inlet Bridge at the west. Front Beach Rd is garishly lined with fast-food joints, motels, hotels, condos and minigolf and amusement parks that seem to scream, 'Give me your money!' The visitor bureau (☎ 850-233-6503, 800-722-3224, 17001 Panama City Beach Pkwy) is at the intersection of Hwys 98 and 79.

The **Glass Bottom Boat** (☎ 850-234-8944, 3605 Thomas Dr), in Treasure Island Marina, affords a fantastic view of sea life through the clear water ($15/8 adults/kids) as well as snorkeling, shelling and swimming-with-dolphins trips. Ask for a $3 discount coupon. Thankfully, the state created **St Andrews State Recreation Area** (☎ 850-233-5140, 4607 Thomas Dr), or this region too would be overbuilt ($4). Instead, it has dunes with tall grasses, a jetty, a lagoon safe for small kids to swim in, nature trails, swimming, hiking, snorkeling ($17.50 including gear) and lots of wildlife. Take a kayak tour ($35) or rent kayaks ($12 per half day) to explore the shore or visit Shell Island from Shell Island Kayaks (☎ 850-235-4004).

Places to Stay & Eat

The *St Andrews State Recreation Area* (☎ 850-233-5140) has both waterfront and wooded campsites ($17). If you can't get in there, then pine woods, a lake, and a beautiful beach make *Grayton Beach State Recreation Area* (☎ 850-231-4210, 357 Main Park Rd) worth the short drive to Santa Rosa. Campsites cost $14-17; new, fully furnished two-bedroom cabins are $160 in spring and summer, half that in fall and winter. Bask in the sun on the deck of the family-oriented *Sunset Inn* (☎ 850-234-7370, 8109 Surf Dr), featuring a pool and beachfront (from $65). At *The Palmetto Motel* (☎ 850-234-2121, 17255 Front Beach Rd), beachfront rooms start at $96, landside rooms from $70. At the top end, the fancy *Marriott Bay Point Resort Village* (☎ 850-236-6000, 4200 Marriott Dr) charges from $189.

Family-run *Plaza Mexico* (☎ 850-230-9588, 13312 Front Beach Rd), in a flamboyant pink-and-green house, has delicious, light lunch specials and attractively priced dinners (closed for siesta 2pm-5:30pm). *Capt Anderson's* (☎ 850-234-2225, 5551 N Lagoon Dr) is probably the area's best restaurant, serving steaks, seafood and pasta ($11-35, closed Sun). *Scampy's on the Beach* (☎ 850-235-4209, 4933 Thomas Dr) is a top seafood eatery ($10-19).

Entertainment is geared to the MTV crowd at beachfront nightclubs like *Club La Vela* (8813 Thomas Dr), *Harpoon Harry's* (12627 Front Beach Rd) and *Sharky's* (15201 Front Beach Rd), which serve up food, fun and nightly entertainment, including national touring acts.

Getting There & Around

Panama City Bay County International Airport (☎ 850-763-6751) is served by major airlines and regional commuters. Car rentals and taxis are available, but there is no local bus service. Greyhound (☎ 850-785-6111, 917 Harrison Ave) runs buses to Tallahassee ($14; 2 hours), Pensacola ($21; 3 hours) and Miami ($79; 14 hours). The closest Amtrak service is in Chipley, 57 miles away. There are bike racks on the Bay Town Trolley (☎ 850-769-0557), which runs weekdays along the beach to St Andrews State Recreation Area and into Panama City for 50¢.

PENSACOLA

This city (population 56,300) became a permanent settlement in 1568, and much of the downtown area today dates from the 19th century, though there are remnants of British and Spanish buildings from the late 18th century. Pensacola's three historic districts have undergone extensive reconstruction and renovation. Gently curving Pensacola Beach features white sand, clear gulf water and spectacular sunsets.

The city is a typical Florida sprawler – it's difficult to get around without a car. The visitor center (☎ 850-434-1234, 800-874-1234) is at 1401 E Gregory St.

Things to See & Do

The **Historic Pensacola Village** (☎ 850-595-5985, Tivoli House, 205 E Zaragoza St) is an interesting collection of early homes and museums through which costumed guides give entertaining walking tours Tuesday to Saturday ($6). The enormous **Pensacola Naval Air Station** (☎ 850-452-0111), on Navy Blvd, is home to the Blue Angels, the navy's amazing precision-flying outfit, and one of the best air museums in the world, the **National Museum of Naval Aviation** (☎ 850-452-3604). Don't miss it, even if you're antiestablishment. Exhibits such as the prisoner-of-war artifacts are enlightening (free admission). The museum's IMAX theater shows thrilling, G-pulling aviation films ($6).

Gulf Islands National Seashore (☎ 850-934-2600) covers many of the barrier islands for 150 miles between West Ship Island, Mississippi, and Santa Rosa Island, Florida ($6, valid seven days). Within the park is Fort Pickens (☎ 850-934-2635), built between 1829 and 1834, the site of Geronimo's 1886–7 incarceration. There's swimming, nature and bike trails. The park's other fort, **Fort Barrancas** (☎ 850-934-2600), has been built, destroyed and remodeled, and occupied by Spanish, French, British, Confederate and US forces (free admission).

Places to Stay & Eat

Campsites at *Big Lagoon State Recreation Area* (☎ 850-492-1595, 12301 Gulf Beach Hwy, Alt Hwy 292) are from $12. *Fort Pickens National Park* (☎ 850-934-2622, reservations ☎ 800-365-2267) has sites for $15 and up.

The very simple *Civic Inn* (☎ 850-432-3441, 200 N Palafox St), downtown, has rooms from $44 in the summer. *The Yacht House B&B* (☎ 850-433-3634, 1820 Cypress St), with rooms tastefully furnished in African, Asian and marine themes, costs from $75. On Pensacola Beach is the two-story beachfront *Five Flags Inn* (☎ 850-932-3586, 299 Fort Pickens Rd), where all rooms face the Gulf and cost from $75 in summer. From circa 1880s box factory to cozy inn in the downtown historic district, *New World Landing* (☎ 850-434-7736, 600 S Palafox St) has come a long way with well-appointed rooms and rates are $75.

In the historic district, there are numerous eateries along Zaragoza and Alcaniz Sts such as *Jamie's Wine Bar & Restaurant* (424 E Zaragoza) whose reputation was built on fine wine and finer food. Beer, wine and burgers – plus some Irish specialties – keep them coming back to *McGuire's Irish Pub* (600 E Gregory St, Pensacola). Highly regarded *Boy on a Dolphin* (400 Pensacola Beach Blvd, Pensacola Beach) serves steaks, chicken and seafood dinners from $12 (dinner only). The enormously popular indoor/outdoor *Peg Leg Pete's* (1010 Fort Pickens Rd, Pensacola Beach) features oysters any way you like them, plus seafood dishes with a Louisiana flavor, like jambalaya ($8.50).

Getting There & Around

Pensacola Regional Airport (☎ 850-436-5000) has commuter and jet service, taxis, rental cars and local bus service. Greyhound (☎ 850-476-4800, 505 W Burgess Rd) has buses to New Orleans ($28;

FLORIDA

4 hours), Panama City ($21; 3 hours) and Miami ($79; 15 hours), among others. Amtrak's *Sunset Limited* (☎ 850-433-4966, 980 E Heinburg St), at 15th Ave, stops on its way from Los Angeles, California, to Jacksonville.

Escambia County Area Transit (☎ 850-436-9383) has a very efficient system of trolleys (25¢) and buses ($1, 10¢ transfers, $9 weekly pass) that run to major attractions, the airport, the visitor center, downtown and the beaches.

Texas

Much of the American West's exported image comes from this immense Southern state. But Texas is more than cactus, cowboys and Cadillacs. From Austin's blues bars to Big Bend's natural splendor, Texas is full of surprises. It's a film capital and a music powerhouse. It offers great rock climbing, kayaking, river running and backpacking. And the country's booming wine industry didn't start in California but right here in the Lone Star State.

The Texas border with Mexico has created an entire Tex-Mex subculture, blending the best from each side of the Rio Grande into a uniquely Texan stew. Down in laid-back San Antonio, for example, you can listen to Dixieland jazz on Saturday night and go to mariachi Mass Sunday morning.

More surprising is the legacy left by early European settlers in Central Texas. When you see a region of Czech bakeries, German breweries and French bistros, where else could you be but the Texas Hill Country – a polyglot place where *Wilkommen* appears on as many signs as Welcome.

History

Pre-Colonial & Colonial Eras The area's earliest-known human society lived on the Panhandle's plains and hunted bison. When the Spanish arrived in 1519, the area was inhabited by many distinct Indian groups. The Spaniards named 'their' new territory *tejas* (**tay**-has), a corruption of the Caddo Indian word for 'friend.' Soon thereafter, the French arrived, and over the ensuing 200 years the two powers tried to claim the region.

In 1803 France sold its claim to the US as part of the Louisiana Purchase. That left Spain and the US to posture for control. In a face-saving deal, both sides agreed to call the Texas territory 'neutral.' In 1821 Texas became a state of the newly independent country of Mexico.

War for Independence & Mexican War Mexican rule was tough and hindered business activities in Texas, something Texans never liked. Additionally, Texans began to resent being ruled from a capital

almost 1000 miles south. By 1830 the situation was becoming, well, revolting.

A Mexican decree banning any more US immigrants created an 'us-against-them' atmosphere and set the stage for fighting. The

Texas War for Independence (1835–6) started when William B Travis led a group of armed, hotheaded Texans against Mexican troops defending a customs office.

At the outbreak, Texan troops (comprising Americans, Mexicans and a fair number of English, Irish, Scots, Germans and other Europeans) captured San Antonio and the Alamo. After Mexicans sacked the Alamo, Texans trounced Mexican troops at San Jacinto, and independence was theirs.

Although Texans wanted to join the US right away, American politics prevented admission until nine years later. The admission of Texas to the Union led directly to the Mexican War (1846–8, also known as the Mexican-American War), which the US won with ease. At war's end, Mexico ceded modern-day Texas, California, Utah, Colorado and most of New Mexico and Arizona – fully a third of its territory – to the US. In 1853 the US paid Mexico $10 million for the remaining bits of New Mexico and Arizona.

Boom & Bust The Civil War hardly touched Texas, as the state's main role was providing beef and soldiers to the Confederacy. In 1870 Texas was readmitted to the Union, and the US Cavalry began raiding Comanche settlements. In just three years, most Indians had been 'removed.'

Texas' early boom came from free-range cattle ranching. But this cowboy way of life mostly disappeared after the invention of barbed wire led to the fencing off of Texas.

Everything changed on January 10, 1901, when the Spindletop drilling site struck oil – a gusher so powerful it took crews days to control it. As the automobile and railroads turned to the oil industry for fuel, an oil boom developed that financed the construction of much of modern East Texas.

WWII brought more prosperity to Texas, in the form of military bases, and the energy crisis of the 1970s brought the state unadulterated Sultan-of-Bruneian wealth. Petroleum prices tripled, gasoline prices quadrupled, and Texans – the biggest domestic oil suppliers – laughed all the way to the bank.

The bubble burst in the 1980s, when a glut devastated the Texas oil industry. The result was a refocusing of state resources, mainly to education and space.

Texas

Nickname: The Lone Star State

Population: 20,851,820 (2nd)

Area: 268,600 sq miles (2nd)

Admitted to Union: December 29, 1845 (28th); seceded 1861; readmitted 1870

Capital city: Austin (population 656,562)

Other cities: Houston (1.9 million), Dallas-Fort Worth (1.7 million), San Antonio (1.1 million)

State small mammal: armadillo

State large mammal: longhorn steer

State flying mammal: Mexican free-tailed bat

Birthplace of: Buddy Holly (1936–59), Howard Hughes (1905–76), Ima Hogg (1882–1975), Janis Joplin (1943–1970), Dwight D Eisenhower (1890–1969), Lyndon B Johnson (1908–73), Steve Martin (b 1945), Renee Zellweger (b 1969)

Famous for: the Alamo; the Bushes; the 'Six Flags' – French, Spanish, Mexican, Texas Republic, USA and Confederate States – that have flown over Texas

1990s to the Present The early 1990s saw an explosion of technology businesses, turning South-Central Texas into a high-tech corridor that rivals Silicon Valley. The 1994 North American Free Trade Agreement (NAFTA), loosening trade restrictions between the US, Mexico and Canada, was a huge economic shot in the arm for Texas, which does a booming business with Mexico.

In 2001 former Texas oilman and Republican governor George W Bush followed in his daddy's footsteps to become the 43rd president of the United States.

Geography

Texas, as any Texan will say, is big. Though less than half the size of Alaska, it's larger than Germany, England, Scotland, Ireland, Northern Ireland, Belgium and the Netherlands combined.

Most of the state is relatively flat, so any hills are a welcome highlight. West Texas has the state's high point – Guadalupe Peak

TEXAS

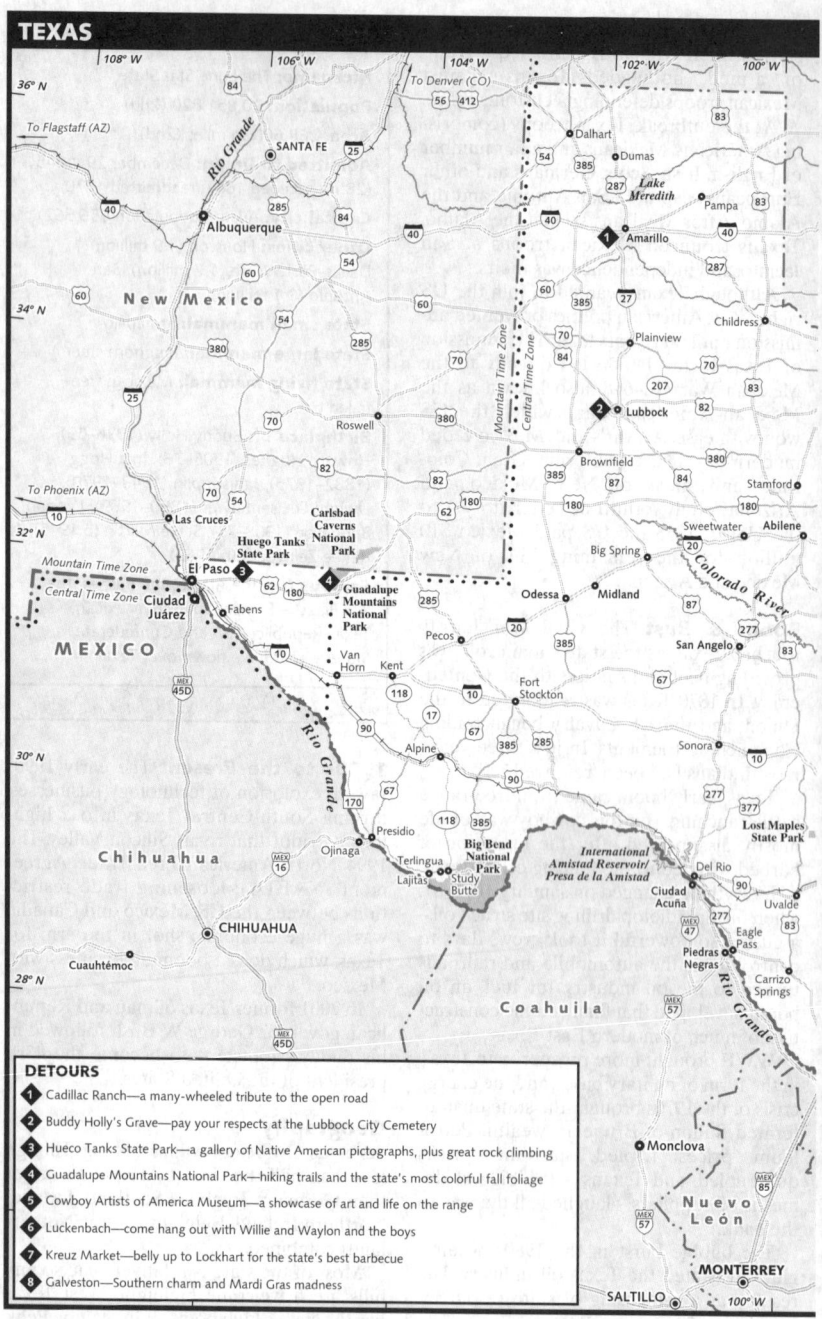

DETOURS

1 Cadillac Ranch—a many-wheeled tribute to the open road

2 Buddy Holly's Grave—pay your respects at the Lubbock City Cemetery

3 Hueco Tanks State Park—a gallery of Native American pictographs, plus great rock climbing

4 Guadalupe Mountains National Park—hiking trails and the state's most colorful fall foliage

5 Cowboy Artists of America Museum—a showcase of art and life on the range

6 Luckenbach—come hang out with Willie and Waylon and the boys

7 Kreuz Market—belly up to Lockhart for the state's best barbecue

8 Galveston—Southern charm and Mardi Gras madness

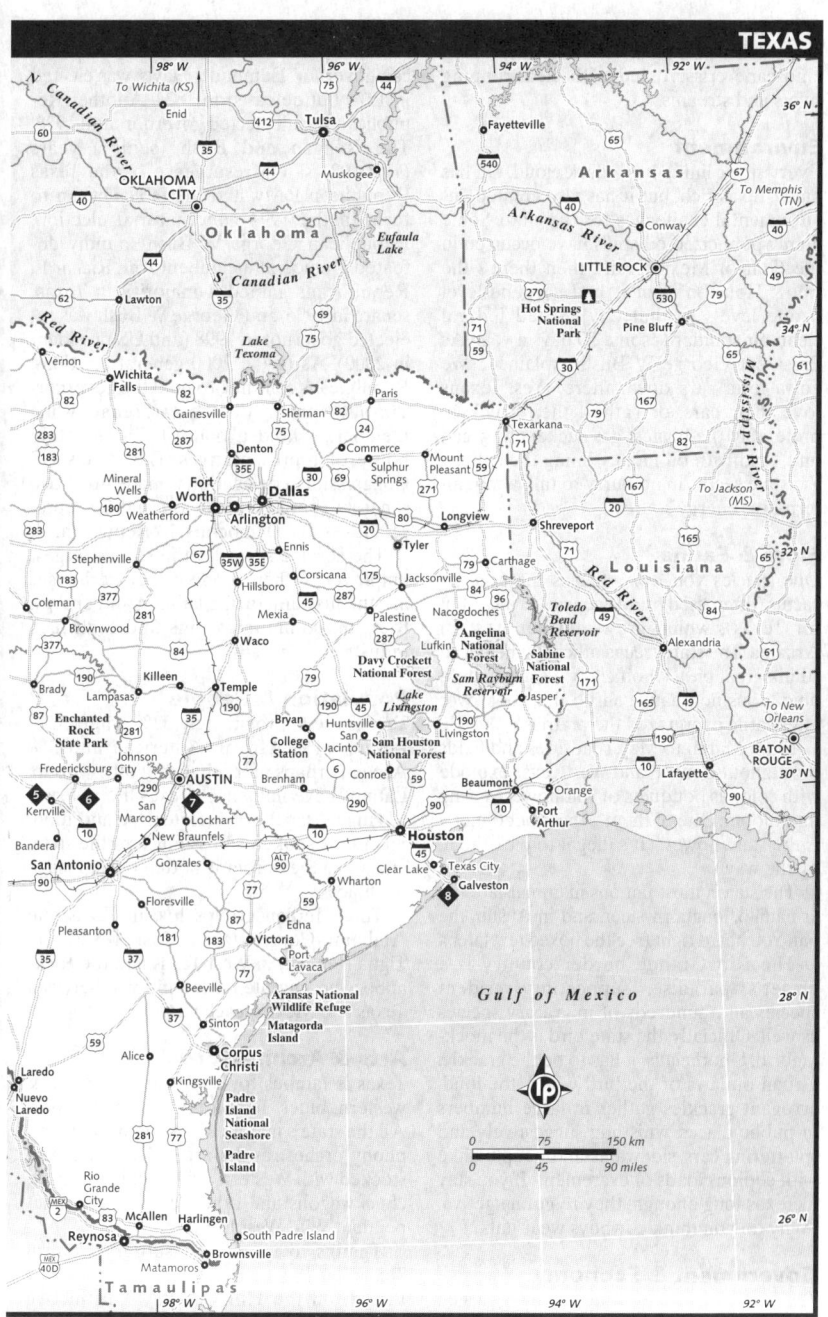

TEXAS

(8749 feet) – while the beautiful Central Texas Hill Country offers a gently rolling landscape crisscrossed with clear-running rivers and streams.

Environment

Every silver lining has a dark cloud. Oil has made Texas rich, but it has also created environmental challenges for the state. Some highly publicized oil spills have occurred in the Gulf of Mexico. And then there's the smog: Houston's got it bad. Ground-level ozone levels in that city exceed federal clean-air standards some 50 days a year. As President George W Bush explained, 'We gotta lotta cars down there.' Yes, Texans love their cars, or rather, their trucks – preferably the biggest gas suckers they can find. And with oil money lining the coffers, the state seems in no hurry to talk about alternative energy sources.

Flora & Fauna

One species you *won't* find is the saguaro cactus (often used by ad agencies as a symbol for Texas), which grows farther west in Arizona. The state tree is officially the pecan (think great pie). Unofficially it's mesquite, a ubiquitous non-native shrub that took over after cattle overgrazed the prairies.

From March to May, roadsides and fields throughout Central and West Texas explode with color as bouquets of wildflowers spring into bloom. One of them – the bluebonnet – is the state flower. (It's illegal to pick them, by the way.)

The state's most famous mammals are the armadillo, longhorn steer, and in Austin, the bat. You heard right (see the boxed text later).

The Rio Grande border country is a birder's paradise, supporting resident species and hundreds of migratory species as well. Officially, the state bird is the mockingbird. Unofficially, it has to be the grackle. Urban outlaws of the bird world, the loud, arrogant grackles gather in large numbers in public places, whistling suggestively and splattering cars, sidewalks and people alike with copious loads of excrement. If you stay in Texas long enough, they're gonna get ya. (Why do you think cowboys wear hats?)

Government & Economy

Texas (like many Southern states) turned solidly Democrat following the Civil War, largely due to resentment of Republican Abraham Lincoln. The state's first Republican governor, Edmund J Davis, was elected in 1870 but defeated in 1874. Another Republican wasn't elected governor until 1978. The Reagan and Bush (senior) years (1980–92) saw a resurgence of the Texas Republican Party, and the tables began to turn. In the 1994 gubernatorial election, Republican George W Bush soundly defeated Democrat incumbent Ann Richards. Republicans gained a majority in Texas' senate in 1996, and George W Bush was reelected governor in 1998 (and US president in 2000). As of the 2000 general elections, Republicans continue to hold the governorship and a majority in the state senate, while Democrats hold a majority in the state house of representatives. The state's US Congressional delegation is made up of two senators (both Republican) and 30 representatives (17 Democrats, 13 Republicans).

The service sector is the state's largest employer. Other economic powerhouses are the manufacturing, mining and energy, tourism, communications and high-tech industries.

Population & People

Texans are approximately 52% white, 32% Latino, 11% African American and 3% Asian. Perhaps more than any other group, Latinos have influenced Texas life in terms of language, culture, architecture and food. Spanish is spoken across much of the state, and along the border it's often the language of choice.

Three Indian groups live in Texas: the Alabama-Coushatta in East Texas, the Tigua (**tee**-wa) in West Texas and the Kickapoo, who migrate back and forth between Texas and Mexico each year.

Arts & Architecture

Texas is famous for its music – country & western, blues, Tejano and especially rock. All the state's major cities support fine symphony orchestras. Its art galleries are well stocked with Western art – buckin' broncos, chuckwagons and other icons of the independent Wild West lifestyle.

Thanks to its earliest settlers, Central Texas has lots of European-style architecture, from the Hill Country's distinctive German *fachtwerk* (beam-and-masonry)

'...An' Ah Crush Mah Beer Cayans'

One of the most wonderful qualities of Texas is the language. Regardless of accent, Texans have the darnedest way of speaking. Their sentences are peppered with folksy expressions like 'wise as a tree full o' owls.' They have lots of ways to describe stupidity ('If dumb was dirt, he'd cover an acre').

Two of the biggest Texisms you'll come across – affected as they may be – are 'I reckon' and 'I'm fixin' to.' One great Texan named Tim once said, in all seriousness, 'I'm pretty much yer avridge Texan. Ah don't eat quiche, Ah *don't* cross mah laygz an' Ah crush mah beer cayans.'

The following are other gems collected in travels throughout the Lone Star State:

Ahtellyawhut – I tell you what; the start of many a sentence in Texas

awl – oil

big ol' – big, as in 'Dallas is a big ol' city'

howdy; hidey – fewer and fewer people use this to say hello; mainly it's a tourist thing

little bitty, itty bitty, bitty – small, as in 'Ah couldn't drahv me one uh them itty bitty Nissans.'

Meskin – Mexican

sheeyit – shit, drawn out to as many syllables as possible: two is fine, three is better (shhh-eee-yit)

shucks – golly, gosh, as in 'aw, shucks, ma'am'

yassir – Yes sir, a catch-all response

y'all – contraction of you all, as in 'y'all come back now, ya hear?,' though more and more frequently used as singular – 'where y'all goin'?' spoken to one person is not uncommon

buildings to the Spanish Colonial missions near El Paso and San Antonio.

Information

The free *Texas State Travel Guide* lists information offices and attractions for almost every city and town. It's available at all 12 Texas Travel Information Centers (☎ 800-452-9292, ⓦ www.traveltex.com) or by writing the Texas Department of Transportation, Travel Division, PO Box 149249, Austin, TX 78714. The *Texas Triangle* (☎ 877-903-8407) is a statewide gay-and-lesbian newspaper with club listings for most major Texas cities.

The state sales tax is 6.25%. Local taxes usually add another 2%.

When to Go

Summer is the state's peak travel season, which can be stiflingly hot – dry in some places, humid in others. Spring and fall are better; most attractions are fully operating, but crowds are thinner and temperatures more moderate. Winter can be chilly and wet across Texas; the Panhandle can see snow and ice storms, but the state's southern reaches usually stay warm, if not sunny.

Activities

Most cities maintain hiking and biking trails, and hiking is a highlight at Big Bend and Guadalupe Mountains National Parks. Horseback riding is hugely popular; guests pay to play cowboy at the many Central Texas dude ranches. Texas water sports include windsurfing, sea kayaking and even some lame surfing along the Gulf Coast; canoeing and river kayaking in Central Texas; and white-water rafting around Big Bend.

Texas has more than 100 state parks. For general information call ☎ 800-792-1112. Day-use fees are $1-5 per person, and most parks have campgrounds ($4-16, depending on facilities). Ten parks also rent cabins ($40-75); for campsite reservations or cabin information, call ☎ 512-389-8900.

Getting There & Around

The busiest international gateways to the state are Dallas–Fort Worth International Airport (DFW) and Houston's George Bush Intercontinental Airport (IAH). Austin, San Antonio and El Paso also have major airports.

Amtrak (☎ 800-872-7245) offers two routes through Texas. The *Sunset Limited* runs between Orlando, Florida, and Los

TEXAS

Angeles three times a week, with stops in Houston, San Antonio, Del Rio, Alpine (near Big Bend National Park) and El Paso. The *Texas Eagle* runs between Chicago and San Antonio daily, with stops in Texarkana, Dallas-Fort Worth, Austin and San Marcos.

Dallas-Fort Worth

Just 30 miles apart, Dallas and Fort Worth anchor a gigantic megalopolis known as the Metroplex. The two cities offer distinct takes on the Texas experience. Dallas lives up to the state's exported image: big and flashy, rich and prosperous. It's driven, a city preoccupied with growth and status. Fort Worth is going places, too, but doesn't seem as concerned with how its image plays outside the city limits. Combining lots to see and do with an easy-to-manage layout, Fort Worth might be the state's best-kept secret.

DALLAS

The 'Big D' is famous for its contributions to popular culture – everything from the Dallas Cowboys football team and its balloon-breasted cheerleaders to *Dallas*, the long-running TV series that became a worldwide symbol for the US. It's a city known for its business acumen, especially in banking, along with its restaurants and shopping. In the materially minded US, Dallas stands tall as a paragon of conspicuous consumption. The city's biggest event is the annual Texas State Fair in October.

History

Dallas was founded in 1839 and became a major railroad junction in the 1870s, sparking a boom that ensured the city's preeminence as a trade center. When the nearby East Texas Oil Field struck black gold in 1930, Dallas became the oil industry's financial center.

The city's image took a dive after President Kennedy was assassinated here in November 1963. It reclaimed its Texas swagger through Larry Hagman's portrayal of scheming oil tycoon JR Ewing on *Dallas* and the Dallas Cowboys, who won the Super Bowl five times.

Orientation

Downtown Dallas is just east of the junction of I-30 and I-35 E; take the Commerce St exit off I-35. The West End of downtown is a developed tourist area with restaurants, shops and nightclubs. The Arts District, on downtown's north edge, holds the city's art museum, symphony center and other cultural-arts venues. North up McKinney Ave is Uptown, with a concentration of art galleries, clubs and posh restaurants.

Northeast of downtown, Greenville Ave is lined with hip restaurants and nightclubs. It's one of the city's two premier entertainment districts, the other being Deep Ellum, at the east end of Elm St – a former warehouse district and now the nucleus of Dallas' energized live-music scene.

Information

The Dallas CVB Visitor Center (☎ 214-571-1300, 100 S Houston St) occupies the 1890s Romanesque Old Red Courthouse and offers public Internet access. The Dallas Gay & Lesbian Alliance (☎ 214-528-4233) is at 2701 Reagan Ave. The *Dallas Observer* is the city's alternative free weekly, and the *Dallas Voice* is the city's excellent gay-and-lesbian newspaper.

Dallas can be dangerous. Park your car in well-lit, secure areas and never leave valuables in sight. Better yet, take a cab and head home by about 1:30am. Always keep your wits – and maybe a few level-headed buddies – about you, especially in such party-hearty areas as Deep Ellum and Lower Greenville. The West End ranks among the city's safest areas after dark, with visible police patrols.

JFK Sites

Dallas will forever be known as the city where President John F Kennedy was shot. Visitors congregate at Dealey Plaza to stare up at the former Texas School Book Depository, swap conspiracy theories and survey the infamous grassy knoll.

The **Sixth Floor Museum** (☎ 214-747-6660, 411 Elm St), in the old Book Depository, explains in minute-by-minute detail the events of Nov 22, 1963 ($10; open daily). The most evocative exhibit is the corner window that supposedly gave Lee Harvey Oswald his sniper's-eye view.

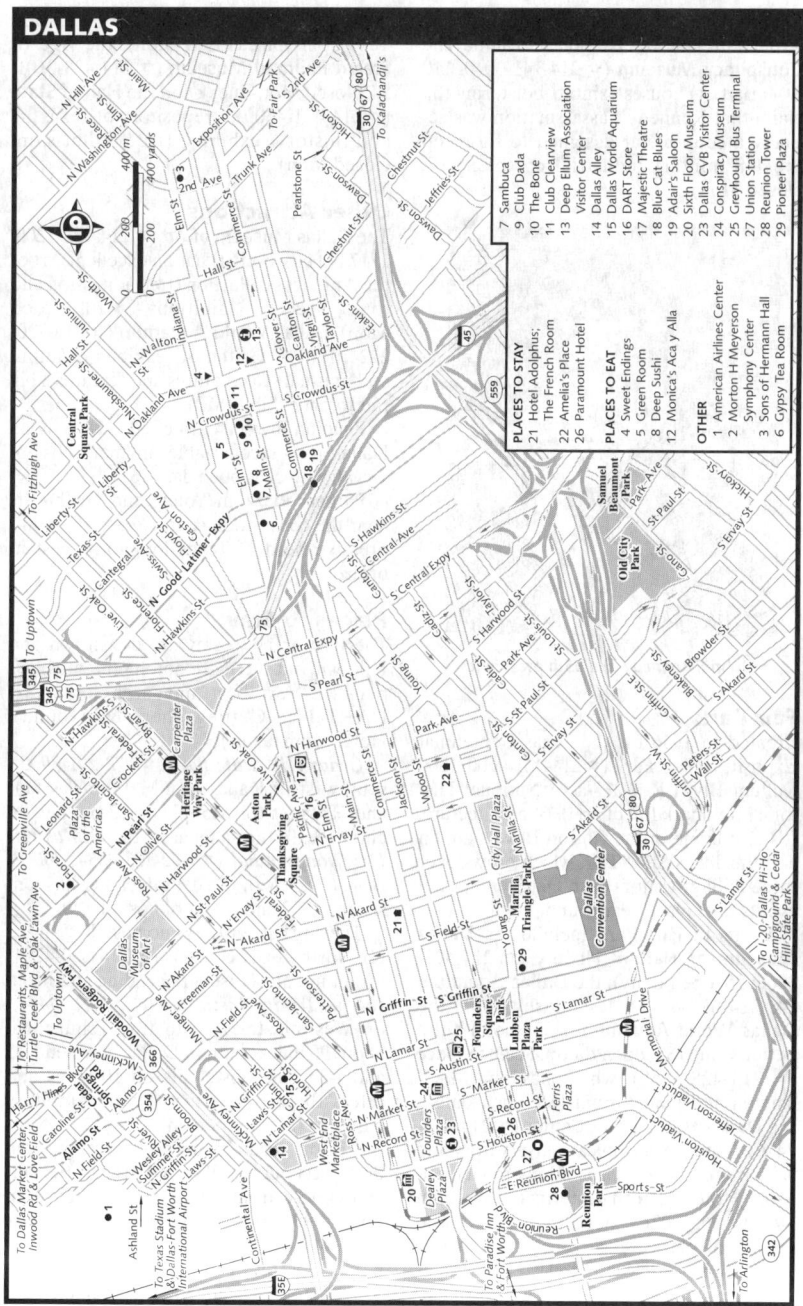

DALLAS

PLACES TO STAY
21 Hotel Adolphus;
   The French Room
22 Amelia's Place
26 Paramount Hotel

PLACES TO EAT
4 Sweet Endings
5 Green Room
8 Deep Sushi
12 Monica's Aca y Alla

OTHER
1 American Airlines Center
2 Morton H Meyerson
   Symphony Center
3 Sons of Hermann Hall
6 Gypsy Tea Room
7 Sambuca
9 Club Dada
10 The Bone
11 Club Clearview
13 Deep Ellum Association
   Visitor Center
14 Dallas Alley
15 Dallas World Aquarium
16 DART Store
17 Majestic Theatre
18 Blue Cat Blues
19 Adair's Saloon
20 Sixth Floor Museum
23 Dallas CVB Visitor Center
24 Conspiracy Museum
25 Greyhound Bus Terminal
27 Union Station
28 Reunion Tower
29 Pioneer Plaza

TEXAS

Polls have shown that fewer than 15% of Americans believe Oswald acted alone. The **Conspiracy Museum** (☎ 214-741-3040, 110 S Market St) houses exhibits bolstering the claim that Kennedy's assassination was actually a coup d'état designed to shore up the US military-industrial complex ($7; closed Mon).

John F Kennedy, the 35th president

Fair Park

Created in 1936 for the Texas Centennial Exposition, Fair Park (☎ 214-421-9600, 1300 Cullum Blvd) is a 277-acre National Historic Landmark full of art deco architecture. It's also home of the Cotton Bowl stadium and the Texas State Fair, which draws over three million visitors each October. Special events take place year round.

Sights in Fair Park include the **Dallas Museum of Natural History** (☎ 214-421-3466; $5; open daily); the **Dallas Aquarium** (☎ 214-670-8443), less flashy than the **Dallas World Aquarium** (see below) but a better value ($3; open daily); **Science Place** (☎ 214-428-5555), which has an IMAX cinema and planetarium ($6; open daily); the **Dallas Horticulture Center** (☎ 214-428-7476), featuring a tropical conservatory and a fragrance garden (free admission; closed Mon); the **African-American Museum** (☎ 214-565-9026), detailing the art and history of blacks since precolonial Africa (free admission; closed Mon); the **Women's Museum** (☎ 214-915-0860), a Smithsonian-affiliated museum focusing on women's his-

torical achievements ($5; free admission Tues 5pm-9pm; closed Mon); the **Age of Steam Railroad Museum** (☎ 214-428-0101; $4; closed Mon-Tues); and the **Hall of State** (☎ 214-421-4500), a repository of Texas art and history exhibits (free admission; closed Mon).

Other Attractions

The **Dallas Museum of Art** (☎ 214-922-1200, 1717 N Harwood St) has an excellent Art of the Americas collection (free admission and tours, special exhibitions $8-10; closed Mon). **Dallas World Aquarium** (☎ 214-720-2224, 1801 N Griffin St) exhibits beautiful and unusual sea creatures and features a big rainforest exhibit ($12).

Reunion Tower (☎ 214-651-1234) is among Dallas' most recognizable landmarks. Its observation deck is open daily ($2).

Pioneer Plaza, at Young and Griffin Sts near the convention center, features an impressive herd of Texas longhorns cast in bronze.

Places to Stay

The best areas to stay are downtown and Uptown, but these are among the most expensive. Next best: any area served by DART (see Getting There & Around). Hotel room tax is 15%.

Cedar Hill State Park (☎ 972-291-3900), southwest of Dallas on FM 1382, has tent and RV sites for $15, plus a $5-per-person entry fee. In the same area, the *Dallas Hi-Ho Campground* (☎ 972-223-4834, 200 W Bear Creek Rd), in Glenn Heights, has tent sites for $12 and full hookups for $20.

The city currently has no hostels. Call the HI North Texas Council (☎ 214-350-4294) for an update. Hostelers heading south can stay at *Trinity Institute* (☎ 254-395-4444), on Westminster Ave in tiny Tehuacana, about 90 miles south of Dallas between I-45 and I-35. The hostel sits on 10 acres and offers three rooms in converted military barracks ($15 per person).

Visitors requiring lowest-budget digs can drive west out Fort Worth Ave (past the jail) and choose from a number of seedy flophouses. The ridiculously named *Paradise Inn* (☎ 214-748-3939, 1736 Fort Worth Ave) is perhaps the least objectionable (from $30/40 singles/doubles). The management would appreciate you not conducting drug deals on the premises. On the east side, **Welcome Inn** (☎ *214-826-3510, 3243 Merrifield Ave)*, at I-30's Dolphin Rd exit, has friendly management and no-frills rooms ($35/40). Nearby on Samuell Blvd are a couple of questionable dirt-cheapies.

Sixteen Motel 6 locations, including three Studio 6 versions, are in the greater Dallas area. A **Motel 6** (☎ *972-915-3993, 7800 Heathrow Dr)*, in Irving, is by DFW airport ($40/44 singles/doubles), while **Studio 6 Northwest** (☎ *214-904-1400, 2395 Stemmons Trail)* is about 10 miles from downtown off I-35 E (from $229/249 per week).

The old **Paramount Hotel** (☎ *214-761-9090, 302 S Houston St)* is undergoing a $14 million metamorphosis into the new Hotel Lawrence. It has a superb location near Dealey Plaza, and rates are low. If you arrive on Greyhound or Amtrak, you can get a $49 room by showing your ticket. Rack rates are $77 weekends, $109 weekdays, but deep discounts are often available. When the Lawrence emerges from the chrysalis, rates will probably be higher.

Super 8 Dallas Market Center (☎ *214-631-6633, 9229 Carpenter Fwy)*, at Regal Row, has rack rates of $50/55. **Sheraton Dallas Brookhollow** (☎ *214-630-7000, 1241 W Mockingbird Lane)* has weekend rates from $70. The weekday rack rate is $109. Sheraton's shuttle takes guests to Love Field and anywhere else within a 5-mile radius.

Ramada Limited Park Cities Inn (☎ *214-521-0330, 6101 Hillcrest Ave)*, four blocks north of Mockingbird on the west side of US 75, is in a nice neighborhood with bookstores and coffeehouses edging the Southern Methodist University campus. Rooms start at $69.

Amelia's Place (☎ *214-651-1775, 888-651-1775,* Ⓦ *www.flash.net/~ameliaj, 1775 Young St)* is a quirky B&B in a warehouse-style downtown loft. It's the domain of 60-something proprietor Amelia Core Jenkins. As her Web site proclaims, Amelia 'welcomes: people of any color, unmarried couples, same-sex couples, smokers…not suitable for pets, children, snobs, bigots, nor fanatics.' (Smoking areas are provided, but guestrooms are smoke-free.) Rooms run $95-115, including breakfast, wine and cheese.

Downtown's **Hotel Adolphus** (☎ *214-742-8200, 800-221-9083, 1321 Commerce St)* epitomizes old Dallas: rich and refined. Rooms cost $225-455. You can't afford it, but the **Mansion on Turtle Creek** (☎ *214-559-2100, 800-527-5432, 2821 Turtle Creek Blvd)* is worth a look. It sits on a beautiful 4½-acre estate and represents the ultimate in opulence.

Places to Eat

With about 5000 restaurants, Dallas has something for every taste and budget. The highest concentration of restaurants is in Uptown and Deep Ellum.

Start the day at **Bread Winners** *(3301 McKinney Ave)*. Great food and comfortable ambience make this bakery/cafe the city's favorite breakfast place ($8-10). For late-night munchies in Deep Ellum, look to **Sweet Endings** *(2901 Elm St)*, where excellent carrot cake is $4.

John's Cafe *(2724 Greenville Ave)* has basic food at hard-to-beat prices: $4 for a huge breakfast, $7 for a lunch of rib eye steak with potatoes and salad. (The *Dallas Observer* named John's the 'Best Hangover Recuperation Spot.') **Sonny Bryan's Smokehouse** *(2202 Inwood Rd)*, near Harry Hines Blvd, serves the city's best barbecue for lunch only. Beef on a bun costs $4.

Monica's Aca y Alla *(2914 Main St)* serves gourmet Mexican fare for the Deep Ellum crowd (lunch $5-6, dinner $10-12). Also drawing raves is Monica's haute-Mex **Ciudad DF** *(3888 Oak Lawn Ave)*, in Turtle Creek Village (dinner $16-25). More Mexican food is available at low-key **Blue Goose Cantina** *(2905 Greenville Ave)*, a prime people-watching hangout and regular Sunday-brunch stop for the Harley-Davidson crowd (lunch $6-10, dinner $10-20).

Kalachandji's *(5430 Gurley Ave)*, east of downtown (take exit 49A off I-30), serves vegetarian buffets (lunch $7, dinner $10) in a Hare Krishna temple 2 miles east of downtown. **Cosmic Cafe** *(2912 Oak Lawn Ave)* also offers delicious Indian-influenced vegetarian fare ($6-9). In Deep Ellum, **Deep Sushi** *(2624 Elm St)* specializes in just that for $5-15.

Steak-lovers stampede to **Star Canyon** (☎ *214-520-7827, 3102 Oak Lawn Ave)* for the mouthwatering 'cowboy' bone-in rib eye ($28). For fresh and simple seafood, try **S&D Oyster Company** *(2701 McKinney Ave)*, which offers a dozen oysters for $7.

Salve! (☎ *214-220-0070, 2120 McKinney Ave)* offers Tuscan-style Italian fare (dinner entrées $26-36). At the **Green Room** (☎ *214-748-7666, 2715 Elm St)*, chef Marc Cassel prepares a four-course mystery meal ($36; $58 with wine) drawing from the menu and the day's market specials. The beef tenderloin ringed with sun-dried tomato grits encircled by a blackeye pea molé was nirvana. Save room for the crème brûlée.

Trendsetters with decor as interesting as the food include *Abacus* (☎ *214-559-3111, 4511 McKinney Ave)*, with an international-eclectic menu (entrées $26-36), and almost-over-the-top *Voltaire* (☎ *972-239-8988, 5150 Keller Springs Rd)*, at the North Dallas Tollway, featuring superb French-Asian cuisine (entrées $16-32).

The French Room, in the Hotel Adolphus (see Places to Stay), offers drop-dead opulence and prices to match ($59-77 for two to four courses). The *Mansion on Turtle Creek* (see Places to Stay) also offers the hoitiest of toit ($65 for three courses).

Entertainment

Check the *Dallas Observer* for complete entertainment listings.

The *Dallas Symphony Orchestra* (☎ *214-692-0203, 2301 Flora St)* performs at the IM Pei–designed Morton H Meyerson Symphony Center. Fair Park Music Hall is home to the *Dallas Opera* (☎ *214-443-1000)*. Music, dance and drama are all presented at the exquisitely restored 1921 *Majestic Theatre* (☎ *214-880-0137, 1925 Elm St)*.

Deep Ellum is live-music central. Both local and big-name touring bands in all styles play the beloved *Gypsy Tea Room* (☎ *214-744-9979, 2548 Elm St)*. Local bands play at *Club Clearview* (☎ *214-939-0077, 2806 Elm St)* and *Club Dada* (☎ *214-744-3232, 2720 Elm St)*.

Stay in Deep Ellum for blues at *The Bone* (☎ *214-744-2663, 2724 Elm St)* or *Blue Cat Blues* (☎ *214-744-2287, 2612 Commerce St)*, for nightly jazz at *Sambuca* (☎ *214-744-0820, 2618 Elm St)*, and for boot-scootin' honky-tonkin' at *Adair's Saloon* (☎ *214-939-9900, 2624 Commerce St)*. In Deepest Ellum, *Sons of Hermann Hall* (☎ *214-747-4422, 3414 Elm St)* is the place to hear authentic country music and other acoustic delights. If yodeler Don Walser is on the bill, be there.

Elsewhere in town, *Muddy Waters* (☎ *214-823-1518, 1518 Greenville Ave)* books blues, rockabilly and more, while Tejano is on tap at *Tejano West* (☎ *214-361-6083, 6532 E Northwest Hwy)*. *Dallas Alley* (☎ *214-720-0170, 2019 N Lamar St)*, at West End Marketplace, is a multiclub venue offering varied musical styles.

Cedar Springs Rd is the main drag for gay nightlife. Look for perennial favorite *JR's* (☎ *214-528-1004, 3923 Cedar Springs Rd)*, or catch the Tuesday-night mixer at the *Crew's Inn* (☎ *214-526-9510, 3215 N Fitzhugh Ave)*. *Sue Ellen's* (☎ *214-559-0650, 3903 Cedar Springs Rd)* is Dallas' biggest lesbian bar; rope yourself a cowgirl on two-step Tuesdays. Popular *Buddies II* (☎ *214-526-0887, 4025 Maple Ave)* attracts a diverse crowd of women-lovin' women.

Spectator Sports

The Dallas Cowboys (☎ 972-579-5000) play NFL football at Texas Stadium in Irving, about 20 minutes from downtown Dallas. The Texas Rangers (☎ 817-273-5100) play pro baseball at the Ballpark in Arlington, between Dallas and Fort Worth. The Dallas Mavericks NBA basketball team (☎ 972-988-3865) and the Dallas Stars NHL hockey team (☎ 214-467-8277) play at the new American Airlines Center, between the Woodall Rodgers Fwy and I-35 E, just north of the West End district. The Dallas Burn (☎ 214-979-0303) play pro soccer at the Cotton Bowl.

Getting There & Away

Air Dallas is the main domestic and international gateway to Texas. Dallas–Fort Worth International Airport (DFW; ☎ 972-574-4420) is 16 miles northwest of the city via I-35 E, Hwy 183 and Hwy 121. Southwest Airlines uses smaller, more convenient Love Field, just northwest of downtown (take Inwood Rd northeast from Harry Hines Blvd and turn left on Cedar Springs).

Bus & Light Rail Greyhound buses run from the Dallas station (☎ 214-655-7085, 205 S Lamar St) to Fort Worth ($7; 1 hour), San Antonio ($34; 5 hours), Austin ($27; 3 hours), Houston ($33; 5 hours) and El Paso ($60; 14 hours).

Train Amtrak's *Texas Eagle* stops at downtown's Union Station (☎ 214-653-1101, 401 S Houston St).

Getting Around

To/From the Airport Bus No 202 ($2) runs downtown from DFW; bus No 39 ($1) heads downtown from Love Field. From DFW you can also catch the Trinity Railway Express train to downtown's Union Station ($2). Discount Shuttle (☎ 817-267-5150) and SuperShuttle (☎ 817-329-2000) run shuttles from DFW to downtown Dallas for around $15, and from Love Field for $15-19. A taxi between DFW and central Dallas will cost $40-45.

Bus, Light Rail & Trolley Dallas Area Rapid Transit (DART; ☎ 214-979-1111), the city's public transportation system, operates buses, trolley buses and light-rail trains throughout downtown and the outlying areas. Its Trinity Railway Express connects downtown Dallas with DFW and will eventually be extended to Fort Worth; call for an update. Pick up a DART route map downtown at the DART store, Elm St at Ervay St, or call for route and schedule information. Fares are 50¢ around downtown, $1-2 elsewhere.

Uptown and downtown Dallas are connected by the McKinney Ave Trolleys (☎ 214-855-0006), which run daily between the Dallas Museum of Art and Hall St ($1.50).

Car Masochists count driving in Dallas among life's peak experiences. Stay off the road during rush hours. There's little free parking in downtown Dallas. Meters must be plugged (and are read) well into the evening in many areas. Many lots are self-pay, so carry plenty of $1 bills. Park in a secure, well-lit area at night. Parking is particularly difficult in Deep Ellum at night; take a cab (about $5 from downtown).

AROUND DALLAS

Arlington, between Dallas and Fort Worth, is a good place for family fun. Some highlights are the mega-amusement park **Six Flags Over Texas** (☎ 817-530-6000), famous for scary coasters ($40, kids under 48 inches $20, parking $8); **Hurricane Harbor Six Flags** (☎ 817-265-3356), a humongous waterpark

($27/14, parking $5); **Air Combat School** (☎ 817-640-1886), a high-tech flight-simulator attraction ($40; reservations required); and the **Ballpark in Arlington**, home of the Texas Rangers pro baseball team (☎ 817-273-5100). All are off I-30 just west of Hwy 360.

FORT WORTH

This city is proud of its nickname, 'Cowtown,' but the livestock industry is just a small part of what's happening here. Fort Worth has done such a good job preserving yet transforming itself for the 21st century that even Dallas visionaries cite it as an example of how a city should work. It's far more user-friendly than Dallas and offers lots of attractions, all easily accessible by public transportation. Despite the skyscrapers, the city feels like an overgrown small town.

The town's biggest event is the Southwestern Stock Show and Rodeo, held late January or early February each year at Will Rogers Coliseum. Fort Worth is also home to the prestigious two-week Van Cliburn International Piano Competition, held every four years in spring (the next is in 2005).

History

In 1849 Camp Worth was one of a string of US forts on the Texas frontier. By 1853 the army had withdrawn, and settlers took over the old post buildings.

Fort Worth became famous during the great open-range cattle drives of the late 19th century. More than 10 million head of cattle were trooped through the city on the Chisholm Trail, from Texas north to Kansas.

The late 19th and early 20th centuries saw rampant lawlessness. Robert Leroy Parker and Harry Longbaugh – better known as Butch Cassidy and the Sundance Kid – hid out in town, as did Great Depression–era hold-up artists Bonnie Parker and Clyde Barrow.

The cattle business remained king here throughout the 1920s, even as major finds in nearby oil fields turned the city into an important petroleum-industry operations center. Philanthropists wrote much of the city's mid- to late-20th century history. Amon Carter, oilman and early publisher of the *Star-Telegram*, put the city on the arts map. The Bass family, among the world's richest, lives here; collectively, they've transformed Sundance Square into an urban showplace.

Visitors will notice a couple of downtown skyscrapers with sheets of plywood where glass windows should be. A tornado hit the city hard in March 2000, killing two people and trashing many buildings, including the local FBI office. (Sensitive files were blown as far away as Dallas.)

Orientation

The three areas most interesting to visitors – downtown, the Cultural District and the Stockyards – form a lopsided triangle. North Main St runs between downtown and the Stockyards, Lancaster Ave connects downtown to the Cultural District, and University Ave and Northside Dr connect the Cultural District to North Main St near the Stockyards. All these areas are north of and easily accessed from I-30.

Information

The Fort Worth Convention and Visitors Bureau has visitor centers downtown (☎ 817-336-8791, 415 Throckmorton St), in the Stockyards (☎ 817-624-4741, 130 E Exchange Ave) and in the Cultural District (☎ 817-882-8588, 3401 W Lancaster Ave). Internet access is available at the palatial (if sterile) downtown library (☎ 817-871-7323, 500 W 3rd St).

Downtown

The highlight here is vibrant 14-block **Sundance Square**, full of colorful architecture and public art. The area is safe to explore on foot day or night – it's crawling with cops on mountain bikes. (They're friendly and low-key.)

Museums here include the **Sid Richardson Collection of Western Art** (☎ 817-332-6554, 309 Main St), featuring paintings and bronzes by Frederic Remington and Charles Russell (free admission; closed Mon), and the **Modern at Sundance Square** (☎ 817-335-9215, 410 Houston St), the Modern Art Museum's downtown gallery (free admission; open daily).

South of Sundance Square, between Houston and Commerce Sts at 15th St, is the 5½-acre **Water Gardens**, an elaborate series of fountains created by architect Philip Johnson.

Cultural District

The city's impressive Cultural District is a museum-lover's nirvana. And within easy walking distance from one another are several first-rate museums (free admission; closed Mon), each trying to outdo the next in architectural merit. The district is under extensive expansion and renovation.

A visit to the recently rebuilt **Amon Carter Museum** (☎ 817-738-1933, 3501 Camp Bowie Blvd) is a visual tour of the USA – from Yosemite with Albert Bierstadt to Taos with Georgia O'Keeffe, to Pike's Peak with George Caleb Bingham and Narragansett Bay with Martin Johnson Heade. The museum also boasts a collection of 350,000 photos, including early masterworks by Mathew Brady, William Henry Jackson, Henri Cartier-Bresson and Laura Gilpin.

Kimbell Art Museum (☎ 817-332-8451, 3333 Camp Bowie Blvd) is relatively small but hosts excellent touring exhibitions and houses a fine collection spanning ancient times to modern.

The **Modern Art Museum of Fort Worth** (☎ 817-738-9215, 1309 Montgomery St) holds works by Picasso, Warhol, Motherwell, Rauschenberg and Pollock. It's moving into stunning new digs opposite the Kimbell in 2002.

The **Museum of Science & History** (☎ 817-255-9300, 1501 Montgomery St) is full of fossils, dinosaurs and kid-friendly interactive stuff ($6.50/4.50 adults/kids). It also has a planetarium ($3.50) and IMAX theater ($6.50/4.50 adults/kids).

Stockyards National Historic District

Once the livestock industry's trading center, the Stockyards are now a tourist-oriented entertainment and shopping district. But the original buildings remain, giving the district a respectably authentic ambience.

The former sheep and hog pens of **Stockyards Station** (140 E Exchange Ave) now house shops selling Western wear, Western art and Western furnishings. Lone Star Wines (☎ 817-626-1601) offers tastings of the best wines made in Texas. Also in the station is the depot of Tarantula Railroad (☎ 817-625-7245), a tourist excursion train.

Next to Stockyards Station, the visitor information center (see Information) is the departure point for walking tours ($6) of the district. Across the street, inside the Live Stock Exchange, the small **Stockyards Museum** (☎ 817-625-5087, 131 E Exchange Ave) displays photos and memorabilia from the heyday of Fort Worth's cattle industry (free admission; closed Sun).

City-paid cowboys on horseback roam the district, answering tourist questions and posing for photos. Twice a day, at 10am and 4pm, they drive a small herd of Texas longhorns around the block for the benefit of visitors. It's a goll-dang Kodak moment, pardner. After sundown, the area's many restaurants, bars and music halls become the main attractions.

Pay parking lots are numerous; two lots straddling the easternmost end of Exchange Ave are free.

Places to Stay

Several Army Corps of Engineers *campgrounds* (☎ 817-292-2400), on Benbrook Lake southwest of Fort Worth, have sites for tent campers ($10) and RVs ($18.50). *Midtown RV Park* (☎ 817-335-9330, 2906 W 6th St), a few blocks from the Cultural District and only about a mile from downtown, has showers and laundry facilities ($25; full hookups).

Small *Sims Motel* (☎ 817-332-2078, 901 N Henderson Rd) has acceptable rooms (with Magic Fingers!) for $37. It's near two popular blues venues (see Entertainment). *Great Western Inn* (☎ 817-877-3500, 1815 E Lancaster Ave) offers standard rooms for $35/40 singles/doubles. The well-kept *Green View Inn* (☎ 817-624-1698, 1816 Jacksboro Hwy) charges $40/45; rooms with kitchens are available as weekly rentals.

Park Central Hotel (☎ 817-336-2011, 1010 Houston St) has some of the cheapest rooms downtown ($65). *Clarion Hotel* (☎ 817-332-6900, 600 Commerce St) is across from Bass Hall and has rack rates from $89/99; check the Internet for discounts. The big *Ramada Plaza Hotel* (☎ 817-335-7000, 1701 Commerce St) has an indoor pool and gym. Rates are $89-149, depending on occupancy level.

Noteworthy splurges in Sundance Square include *Etta's Place* (☎ 817-654-0267, 200 W 3rd St), a 10-room B&B/boutique hotel named for Etta Place, the Sundance Kid's gorgeous girlfriend ($125-165), and the big *Renaissance Worthington Hotel* (☎ 817-870-1000, 200 Main St), modern and thoroughly luxurious ($134-189).

In the Stockyards, the small and charismatic old *Texas Hotel* (☎ 817-624-2224, 2415 Ellis Ave) has an excellent location near the action. Rooms cost $40/50. The Stockyards splurge is the posh *Stockyards Hotel* (☎ 817-625-6427, 109 E Exchange Ave), with rooms from $129.

Places to Eat

For breakfast, head to *Cactus Flower*, downtown at 150 Throckmorton St or near the Cultural District at 509 University, where you can fill up for under $6. The best Sunday brunch ($30) is at *Renaissance Worthington Hotel* (see Places to Stay). *La Madeleine* (☎ 817-332-3639, 305 Main St) is a casual French-inspired bistro with good coffee and pastries, along with salads and sandwiches ($3-9).

Trendy *Angeluna* (☎ 817-334-0080, 215 E 4th St), in Sundance Square, offers a wide-ranging international menu (dinner entrées $14-29) and Fort Worth's most beautiful clientele; make reservations and dress appropriately. For French with a Mediterranean accent, try acclaimed *Bistro Louise* (☎ 817-922-9244, 2900 S Hulen St), which serves up such delicacies as macadamia-crusted shrimp ($9) and tea-smoked duck ($20). The desserts are probably illegal.

Steak is big in Cowtown. At clubby *Del Frisco's Double Eagle Steak House* (812 Main St), a slab of steer costs $25-47. For barbecue, try *Railhead Smokehouse* (2900 Montgomery St), just south of I-30, or venerable *Angelo's Barbecue* (2533 White Settlement Rd); both are inexpensive.

Joe T Garcia's (2201 N Commerce St), between downtown and the Stockyards, started as a shack. Four generations later, it takes up a city block, with extensive outdoor dining amid fountains and pools. This Tex-Mex place has a limited lunch menu ($6-10) and only enchiladas ($9) or fajitas ($11) for dinner. It's usually packed and only accepts cash.

Italian-food fans are drawn to *Sardine's* (☎ 817-332-9937, 3410 Camp Bowie Blvd), across from Amon Carter Museum. Among the city's most romantic restaurants, it's faced with closure thanks to the Cultural District's expansion plans. Vegetarians will appreciate *Maharaja*

(6308 Hulen Bend Blvd), an excellent Indian restaurant.

Entertainment

Downtown's Sundance Square becomes a hot spot after dark. The exquisite *Bass Performance Hall* (☎ 817-212-4325, 888-597-7827, 555 Commerce St) is home to the Fort Worth Symphony (☎ 817-665-6000), the Fort Worth Opera (☎ 817-731-0833) and the Fort Worth-Dallas Ballet (☎ 817-377-9988). *Caravan of Dreams* (☎ 817-429-4000, 312 Houston St) is an equally beautiful gem. Its theater hosts big-name musicians from all over the musical map, and its Rooftop Grotto Bar is an open-air spot perfect for sipping a midsummer-night's margarita.

Bars are three to a block around Sundance Square. The *Flying Saucer (111 E 4th St)* offers about 80 beers on tap. Nondrinkers can check out *Coffee Haus (404 Houston St)*, a hip caffeinery with a jazz soundtrack.

In the Stockyards, *Billy Bob's Texas* (☎ 817-624-7117, 2520 Rodeo Plaza) draws top country & western stars to its main stage. The cavernous club also offers live bull-riding, country dance lessons, pool tables, games and memorabilia of the famous performers who've played at the place. Though it touts itself as the world's largest honky-tonk, Billy Bob's feels more like Las Vegas. A low-key alternative is *White Elephant Saloon (106 E Exchange Ave)*, a quintessential cowboy bar with live country music nightly. Bar scenes in the TV program *Walker, Texas Ranger* were filmed here.

Blues venues in town include *J&J Blues Bar (937 Woodward Ave)*, a down-and-dirty roadhouse where the blues are a way of life; *Bad to the Bone (702 N Henderson St)*, a hole-in-the-wall around the block from J&J; and the *Thirsty Armadillo (2467 N Main St)*, in the Stockyards. For jazz, try the *Jazz Cafe (2504 Montgomery St)* or *Sardine's* (see Places to Eat). For alternative rock, go to the *Wreck Room (3208 W 7th St)*, near the Cultural District, or check the schedule at the popular *Ridglea Theater* (☎ 817-738-9500, 6025 Camp Bowie Blvd).

Ye Olde Bull & Bush (2300 Montgomery St) is a classic pub between I-30 and the Cultural District. It offers pints of Bass, Watneys and Guinness, along with dartboards, old copies of the *Sunday Times* and maybe even bagpipe music.

Magnolia St Station (600 W Magnolia St) is the city's most popular gay bar.

Getting There & Around

From the Greyhound station (☎ 817-429-3089, 901 Commerce St), buses travel to/from Dallas ($6; 1 hour), San Antonio ($32; from 6 hours) and Houston ($31; from 6 hours).

Amtrak's *Texas Eagle* stops at the depot (☎ 817-332-2931, 1501 Jones St). Longhorn Trolley (☎ 817-215-8600) connects the three major tourist areas. Trolleys run every 20 minutes from 11am to 6pm (Cultural District) or 11pm (Stockyards and downtown). The fare is $2 one way, $5 all day.

Watch for the Fort Worth extension of Dallas' Trinity Railway Express, a light-rail connection now linking DFW and downtown Dallas; for information call Dallas Area Rapid Transit (☎ 214-979-1111).

South-Central Texas

If you've only got a short time in Texas, this would be a good place to head. Here you'll find San Antonio, home of the Alamo; Austin, the state's capital and music-scene epicenter; and the Hill Country, an undulating, unhurried place a world away from the rat race. Perhaps you've heard of the Heart of Texas? Well, here it is.

AUSTIN

Though it *is* the state capital, supercool Austin is better known for musicians than politicians. Americans who watch public TV's *Austin City Limits* have seen many of the stars who cut their teeth in this self-proclaimed 'live music capital' of the USA.

In the early 1960s, Wednesday-night jam sessions at Threadgill's gas station and beer joint attracted musicians from around Texas, including Port Arthur's soon-to-be-famous rock diva, Janis Joplin. In 1970 Eddie Wilson opened his legendary Armadillo World Headquarters here, and for the next decade the Armadillo was ground zero for the Cosmic Cowboy movement – *the* musical hangout for guys like Waylon Jennings, Kinky Friedman, Asleep at the Wheel, Steven Fromholz, the Lost Gonzo

Band and for seminal acts like the Clash, Bruce Springsteen, Frank Zappa, Van Morrison and BW Stevenson. Later Austin performers and bands that would make their mark include the Butthole Surfers, Jimmie Vaughan, Stevie Ray Vaughan and Double Trouble, Joe Ely and Jerry Jeff Walker.... Austin rocks.

Orientation & Information

Guadalupe (**gwad**-ah-loop) St runs west of Congress Ave and becomes, near the University of Texas (UT) campus, the Drag. East 6th St, between Congress Ave and Sabine St, harbors a dizzying collection of nightclubs packed with 20-somethings. A few blocks away, the Warehouse District draws a slightly older, mellower crowd to generally more upscale restaurants and clubs. As one local put it, 'You graduate from 6th St to the Warehouse District, where you find a wife then move to a house in the hills – hopefully.'

The local Austin Visitor Information Center (☎ 512-583-7235, 800-926-2282, Ⓦ www.austintexas.org, 201 E 2nd St) is open daily. It sponsors free walking tours (☎ 512-454-1545) and offers Internet access for a small fee. Free Internet access is available at Austin's large public library (☎ 512-499-7300, 800 Guadalupe St). The Austin Gay & Lesbian Chamber of Commerce (☎ 512-472-8299) is at 3004 Medical Arts St. Book People Inc (☎ 512-472-4288, 603 N Lamar Blvd) sells, of all things, books!

Capitol Complex

The 1888 Texas State Capitol (☎ 512-463-0063) appears like a pink mirage downtown. Nearby is the Greek Revival–style 1856 Governor's Mansion (☎ 512-463-5516, 1010 Colorado St); free tours are available. The Capitol Complex Visitors Center (☎ 512-305-8400, 112 E 11th St), in the German-Romanesque former General Land Office (1857), has information on capitol tours.

University of Texas at Austin

The Lyndon B Johnson Library & Museum (☎ 512-916-5136, 2313 Red River St) contains the expected propaganda but also offers solid exhibitions on JFK, the Bay of Pigs, the civil-rights movement and the Vietnam War (free admission; open daily).

The Jack S Blanton Museum of Art (☎ 512-471-7324) is in two buildings: Harry Ransom Center (21st St at Guadalupe St) and the Art Building (23rd St at San Jacinto Blvd). The collection focuses on 20th-century American and Latin American art (free admission; open daily).

The striking new Bob Bullock Texas State History Museum (☎ 512-936-8746), MLK Blvd at N Congress Ave, opened in spring 2001 ($5; open daily). Inside are exhibits focusing on 'The Story of Texas,' as well as an extra-charge 200-seat multimedia theater and 400-seat IMAX theater.

Austin's most infamous structure is the **University of Texas Tower**, where in August 1966 Charles Whitman opened fire on passersby for 99 minutes before being killed by police. Visitors must now pass through a metal detector before climbing to the top for killer views (☎ 512-475-6633; $3; reservations required).

Downtown Museums

Austin's excellent Mexic-Arte Museum (☎ 512-480-9373, 419 Congress Ave) has rotating exhibitions by Mexican artists ($2). The Austin Museum of Art (☎ 512-495-9224, 823 Congress Ave) also features rotating exhibitions and has a small permanent collection of 20th-century art ($3; $1 Thurs; closed Mon).

Parks

Just south of the Colorado River, 351-acre **Zilker Park** (☎ 512-472-4914) has hiking and biking trails, a nature center, botanical gardens, a sculpture garden and **Barton**

Austin's Bats

Up to 1½ million Mexican free-tailed bats make their home upon a platform beneath the Congress Ave Bridge (Mar-Nov). It's become an Austin tradition to watch around sunset as the bats swarm out to feed on an estimated 10,000 to 30,000 pounds of insects. Capitol Cruises (☎ 512-480-9264), behind the Hyatt Hotel, offers bat-watching cruises on Town Lake below the bridge ($8). Bat Conservation International runs a Bat Hotline (☎ 512-416-5700 category 3636).

TEXAS

AUSTIN

PLACES TO STAY & EAT
5 La Quinta Capitol
6 Super 8-Central
7 Aquarelle
8 Extended Stay America
10 Jean-Luc's French Bistro
15 Waterloo Brewing Company
19 Driskill Hotel
25 6th St Hostel
26 Kaya Blue
29 Bitter End Bistro & Brewpub
30 Alamo Drafthouse Cinema
34 Las Manitas Avenue Café
37 Austin Motel
38 El Sol y La Luna
40 Hotel San José

OTHER
1 Bob Bullock Texas State History Museum
2 Brackenridge Hospital
3 Governor's Mansion
4 General Land Office
9 Austin Public Library
11 Paramount Theatre
12 Austin Museum of Art
13 Stubb's BBQ
14 La Zona Rosa
16 Azucar
17 Rainbow Cattle Co
18 Antone's
20 Jazz
21 Joe's Generic Bar
22 Ritz Lounge
23 The Metro
24 Emo's
27 Austin Music Hall
28 Oilcan Harry's
31 Speakeasy
32 Mexic-Arte Museum
33 Elephant Room
35 Austin Visitor Information Center
36 Bat Colony
39 Continental Club

TEXAS

Springs Pool (☎ 512-476-9044), a locally beloved spring-fed swimming hole with chilly, sparkling clear waters ($3; closed Thurs).

Mt Bonnell (elevation 785 feet), northwest of downtown, offers panoramic city views. Take 35th St west, turn left on Old Bull Creek Rd, and turn right on Mt Bonnell Rd. Once there, it's a steep climb up 99 stone steps to the summit.

Special Events

In mid-March, one of the American music industry's biggest events, **South by Southwest** (SXSW; ☎ 512-467-7979), draws an overwhelming 1000-some bands and solo artists from around the world to 50 different Austin venues. Almost every popular musical style is represented. The *San Antonio Express-News* called it 'an alt-rock, hip-hop, Tejano thing,' and as one music-loving wag put it, 'It's like a mile-long buffet where your stomach is ready to burst after 20 feet!'

Another big event is February's **Mardi Gras** celebration, which brings breast-baring and bead-groveling inebriates to 6th St.

Places to Stay

Avoid the seedy motels on S Congress Ave (approximately south of the Continental Club). Book early for SXSW and expect peak prices.

Camping Just over 6 miles north of downtown, *Emma Long Metropolitan Park* (☎ 512-346-1831) has tent ($6) and RV ($15) sites (entry fee $5-8 per car). Take MoPac Expressway (Hwy 1) north to RR 2222, turn west past the intersection of Hwy 360 and turn left at City Park Rd.

McKinney Falls State Park (☎ 512-243-1643, 5808 McKinney Falls Pkwy), southeast of the city, has primitive sites ($12 per site, plus $2 per person daily entry fee). *Austin Lone Star RV Resort* (☎ 512-444-6322, 7009 I-35 S), south of downtown, has tent and RV sites for $36-38.

Hostels For a prime location, you can't beat *6th St Hostel* (☎ 512-495-9772, 604 E 6th St), right by the entertainment district. The front desk is open 24 hours, and no chores are required. Amenities include a TV room, library, game room, lockers and Internet access (no kitchen, laundry or private rooms). Bike rentals and local tours are available. Dorm bunks run $18-20.

HI Austin (☎ 512-444-2294, 2200 S Lakeshore Blvd) is a cheerful place on Town Lake. Amenities include a kitchen, common area, laundry, Internet access and canoe and kayak rentals. Beds cost $16/19 for members/nonmembers (no private rooms).

Motels & Hotels Two independent motels near each other on S Congress Ave are *the* hip Austin stays. 'So close, yet so far out,' the inimitable *Austin Motel* (☎ 512-441-1157, 1220 S Congress Ave) offers classic digs and friendly service (from $53/61 singles/doubles). Just up the street, *Hotel San José* (☎ 512-444-7322, 800-574-8897, 1316 S Congress Ave) is a chic, contemporary redesign of an old road motel. Very trendy. Rates are $69-175.

Chain places line the interstate. Driving downtown is the pits, so lodgings within walking distance are highly recommended. *Super 8 Central* (☎ 512-472-8331, 1201 N I-35), just across I-35 at 12th St, is an easy walk to downtown and a good deal for the location (from $55/62). *La Quinta Capitol* (☎ 512-476-1166, 300 E 11th St) is by the capitol and has clean and comfortable rooms for around $95-110. A short walk from both the E 6th St and Warehouse Districts, *Extended Stay America* (☎ 512-457-9994, 600 Guadalupe St) is a reasonably good deal for stays of a week or more (from $439/week).

Downtown's famous *Driskill Hotel* (☎ 512-474-5911, 800-252-9367, 604 Brazos St) is a wonderful place with a colorful history ($205-255; suites higher). It's nice to walk through, even if you're not staying there.

Places to Eat

For healthy food any time of day or night, head to *Kerbey Lane Cafe* (2606 Guadalupe St), on the Drag and at three other locations. Kerbey Lane makes great breakfasts using homegrown, pesticide-free veggies and free-range beef and pork (open 24 hours). Inexpensive and *sabroso* Mexican breakfasts are available at *El Sol y La Luna* (1224 S Congress Ave) and *Las Manitas Avenue Café* (211 Congress Ave).

Coffeehouse denizens will love *Spider House (2908 Fruth St)*, a block east of Guadalupe between 29th and 30th, just north of the Drag. The old house has a dark, meditative interior and a pleasantly entropic patio. It's frequented by interesting artsy types and offers bottled beers in addition to coffee.

For a cheap Vietnamese lunch (under $5), check out *Kim Phung (7601 N Lamar Blvd)*, near Anderson Lane (Hwy 183). For healthy veg-Mex lunches (around $6), the award goes to *Mr Natural (1901 César Chávez St)*.

Waterloo Brewing Company (401 Guadalupe St) has great beer and tasty pub grub (most $5-8) along with a casual, convivial atmosphere. *Bitter End Bistro & Brewpub (☎ 512-478-2337, 311 Colorado St)* also produces excellent beer and offers an upscale menu. Both are in the Warehouse District.

Mother's Cafe (4215 Duval St), at 43rd St, is a vegetarian mecca with an extensive menu that runs the gamut from fresh salads to curried lentil soup (lunch $6-9). It has a nice patio. *Veggie Heaven (1914A Guadalupe St)* has a Chinese vegetarian menu with more than 40 entrées. Everything's under $8.

At *Alamo Drafthouse Cinema (☎ 512-867-1839, 409 Colorado St)* you can eat dinner and watch a movie at the same time. One recent offering was a Spaghetti-Western Spaghetti Feast. You must be 18 or older to enter.

If you like fat, head to ramshackle *Sam's Bar-B-Cue (2000 E 12th St)* for delicious artery-clogging 'cue. Another Austin tradition, *Ruby's BBQ (512 W 29th St)* serves hormone-free, USDA choice meats. *Stubb's BBQ* (see Entertainment) is no slouch either; try the turkey breast. But for the ultimate in barbecue, locals head out to *The Salt Lick (☎ 512-858-4959, 18300 FM 1826)*, about 22 miles southwest of town in Driftwood (take the MoPac Expressway south to Hwy 290, then west to FM 1826). It's open daily; no credit cards are accepted. Bring your own alcohol.

Austin has many excellent fine-dining restaurants. *Kaya Blue (☎ 512-478-8788, 621A E 6th St)* serves exciting fusion cuisine (entrées $10-25). More traditional is upscale *Jeffrey's (☎ 512-477-5584, 1204 W Lynn)*, at 12th St, between the capitol and MoPac. It offers a daily-changing menu of Southwest regional cuisine (entrées $24-26). *Green Pastures (☎ 512-444-4747, 811 W Live Oak St)* occupies a grand Victorian mansion on 7 oak-studded acres off Congress Ave in south Austin. The menu offers 'Southwest-continental' fare (entrées $20-40). When only escargots and a bottle of Chateau Neuf du Pape will do, head to *Jean-Luc's French Bistro (☎ 512-494-0033, 705 Colorado St)*, with entrées for $20-29, or *Aquarelle (☎ 512-479-8117, 606 Rio Grande St)*, with entrées for $24-35.

Entertainment

The *Austin Symphony Orchestra (☎ 512-476-6064)* is the state's oldest symphony (but the geezers can still play). Their venue is Bass Concert Hall, on the UT campus near the intersection of 23rd and Trinity Sts. *Austin Lyric Opera (☎ 512-472-5927)* sings artful arias at Bass Hall. The well-respected *Austin Musical Theatre (☎ 512-428-9696)* presents classic musicals at the Paramount Theatre, 713 Congress Ave.

For club listings, check the free weekly *Austin Chronicle*, available citywide. On any Friday night, hundreds of bands will be playing at more than 100 venues.

Antone's (☎ 512-474-5314, 213 W 5th St) calls itself the 'Home of the Blues' but books big-name acts in all genres. A sure bet for blues is *Joe's Generic Bar (☎ 512-480-8171, 315 E 6th St)*. The venerable *Continental Club (☎ 512-441-2444, 1315 S Congress Ave)*, south of the river, is a well-respected venue offering consistently good blues, rockabilly and country.

Stubb's BBQ (☎ 512-480-8341, 801 Red River St) has a backyard amphitheater and live music nightly – lots of insurgent country acts plus blues and more. For jazz, try the *Elephant Room (☎ 512-473-2279, 315 Congress Ave)* or *Jazz (☎ 512-479-0474, 214 E 6th St)*.

La Zona Rosa (☎ 512-472-2293, 612 W 4th St) offers a variety of music, including a healthy share of Cuban and other Latino fare. *Azucar (☎ 512-478-5650, 400 Lavaca St)* is a great place to salsa the night away. *The Metro (☎ 512-478-9500, 505 E 6th St)* offers live bands tending toward rock and metal.

Look for local bands at *Hole in the Wall (☎ 512-472-5599, 2538 Guadalupe St)* and the *Ritz Lounge* (☎ *512-474-9574, 320 E 6th St)*. Degenerate punks play nightly at *Emo's* (☎ *512-477-3667, 603 Red River St)*. (Red River between 6th and 10th Sts hums with high-voltage club energy.) Dressy, martini-esque *Speakeasy* (☎ *512-476-8017, 412 Congress Ave)* gets the atmosphere award for its sneaky alley entrance and cool rooftop deck.

For country & western, head for the *Broken Spoke* (☎ *512-442-6189, 3201 S Lamar Blvd)*. On Riverside Dr east of I-35, almost every strip mall has a packed Tejano bar; try *Club Latino* (☎ *512-441-2999, 1907 E Riverside Dr)*.

Big-time bands play *Austin Music Hall* (☎ *512-495-9962, 208 Nueces St)*; the *Backyard/Live Oak Amphitheatre* (☎ *512-263-4146)*, Hwy 71 at Hwy 620, about 30 or 40 minutes west of town; and the intimate, not-to-be-missed *One World Theatre* (☎ *512-329-6753, 7701 Bee Cave Rd)*, also west of town.

Gay and lesbian clubs include *Rainbow Cattle Co* (☎ *512-472-5288, 305 W 5th St)*, featuring country & western music and an enormous dance floor, and *Oilcan Harry's* (☎ *512-320-8823, 211 W 4th St)*, also popular and usually packed.

Getting There & Around

Austin Bergstrom International Airport (☎ 512-530-2242) is off Hwy 71 southeast of downtown. Bus No 100 (50¢) runs hourly between the airport and downtown. Super-Shuttle (☎ 512-258-3826) runs as needed and charges $10 to downtown. A taxi between the airport and downtown costs $17-21.

The station for Greyhound and the Kerrville Bus Co (☎ 512-458-4463 for both) is at 916 E Koenig Lane, on the north side of town off I-35; take bus No 7/Duval to downtown. One bus a day heads to the Hill Country at 6:30pm – to Fredericksburg ($18; 1½ hours) and Kerrville ($24; 2½ hours). Other destinations include Dallas ($27; from 3½ hours), Houston ($21; from 3 hours), El Paso ($111; from 12 hours), San Antonio ($15; from 1½ hours) and Laredo ($28; from 4½ hours).

Bus company Capital Metro (☎ 512-474-1200, Ⓦ www.capmetro.org) runs Austin's public transit and has an information center at 106 E 8th St. In addition to regular city buses (standard fare 50¢), the company operates the 'Dillo Lines, a free shuttle service with five routes blanketing downtown. One route connects with two park-and-ride lots – a good strategy if you must drive into the city.

Austin's Amtrak station (☎ 512-476-5684, 250 N Lamar Blvd) is served by the *Texas Eagle* and *Sunset Limited* trains.

Rent bikes from Waterloo Cycles (☎ 512-472-9253, 2815 Fruth St), just off Guadalupe St south of 29th, from $10 a day. Almost all city buses are equipped with bicycle racks (free).

AROUND AUSTIN

Northwest of Austin along the Colorado River, **Lake Travis** and **Lake Austin** are popular recreation areas, while **Lake Buchanan** is more serene.

You must be over 18 to enter **Hippie Hollow**, Texas' only official clothing-optional beach. It has excellent lake views, swimming and hiking trails. From RR 620 at FM 2222, take RR 620 south 1.3 miles to Comanche Trail and turn right. The entrance is 2 miles ahead on the left.

Camping is available at a series of parks along the Colorado. The Lower Colorado River Authority (☎ 800-776-5272) can send you a copy of its free *Park Pack*, which details hiking and camping in the parks.

The reason to come to the little town of **Lockhart**, about 20 minutes south of Austin on US 183, is to stuff yourself silly on barbecue – by far the best in Texas. In 1895 Charles Kreuz established a meat market and grocery store here. In 1900 it was bought by the Schmidt family, who've run it ever since as Kreuz Market (☎ 512-398-2361, 619 N Colorado St). In eight indoor open pits, immense oak branches heat succulent pork chops tender enough to cut with a spoon, brisket and prime rib ($8-14 per pound; closed Sun). Greyhound has service from Austin daily at 11:45am ($11).

HILL COUNTRY

West of I-35 between Austin and San Antonio lies the Hill Country, one of the state's biggest draws. Here, peaceful little towns lie among gently rolling hills and valleys, and clear-running rivers and streams cut through cactus-speckled cattle ranches. German and Czech settlers established roots here, and the area still has a European flavor, most obvious in Fredericksburg. Elsewhere in the region, dude ranches attract cityfolk intent on experiencing a bit of the cowboy life, and numerous vineyards produce some of the state's best wine (pick up a free copy of *Texas Hill Country Wine Trail* at local tourist offices or any Texas Travel Information Center).

Johnson City

Named for hometown-boy Lyndon Baines Johnson (1908–73), the country's 36th president, Johnson City is home to **Lyndon B Johnson National and State Historical Park**. The park encompasses two historical sites, both of which are open daily (day-use only). In town are the Johnson settlement, which includes a visitor center and LBJ's boyhood home. Admission, including a guided tour, is free.

About 14 miles west along US 290 is Johnson Ranch, LBJ's 'Texas White House.' The visitor center here is free, but to see the actual ranch sites and buildings you have to take the NPS bus tour ($3). For more information, call the NPS office (☎ 830-868-7128) or the state park office (☎ 830-644-2252, 800-792-1112). The bus between Austin and Fredericksburg stops in Johnson City ($9 from Austin).

Fredericksburg

Center of the Hill Country, Fredericksburg was founded by German immigrants in 1846. After successfully negotiating a goodwill treaty with local Comanches, the enterprising pioneers were allowed to settle here in peace – maybe good German beer helped grease the wheels. Today the picturesque town celebrates its heritage with plenty more of that beer, along with heavenly breads, pastries and other German food. The Fredericksburg Convention and Visitors Bureau (☎ 830-997-6523, 888-997-3600, ⓦ www.fredericksburg-texas.com, 106 N Adams St) is open daily. Kerrville Bus Co runs a bus from Austin daily at 6:30pm ($17-18; 1½ hours), returning from Fredericksburg at 9am.

The 7-acre **National Museum of the Pacific War** (☎ 830-997-4379, 340 E Main St) features the life and times of homeboy Admiral Chester Nimitz ($5; open daily). At the town plaza, between Crockett and Adams on Main St, is a 1935 replica of the original 1847 **Vereins Kirche** ('Society Church'). It's now a county-history museum (☎ 830-997-2835); free admission. The **Pioneer Museum** complex (☎ 830-997-2835, 309 W Main St) preserves nine historical buildings ($3; open daily). Guided walking tours of town ($10) are led by K&K Historic Tours of Fredericksburg (☎ 830-990-0155).

Places to Stay & Eat Just over 3 miles south of town on Hwy 16, *Lady Bird Johnson Municipal Park* (☎ 830-997-4202) has primitive/developed campsites by the Pedernales River for $8/18. *Fredericksburg Heritage KOA* (☎ 830-997-4796), 5 miles east of town at the junction of Hwy 290 and FM 1376, is a tidy park with a pool, hot tub and laundry. Tent and RV sites cost $19-29 for one or two people; cabins cost $39.

Antiseptically clean *Dietzel Motel* (☎ 830-997-3330), Hwy 290 W at Hwy 87 N (at the town's west end), is a good deal (from $42/45 for singles/doubles). The *Deluxe Inn Budget Host Hotel* (☎ 830-997-3344, 901 E Main St) has a friendly staff and continental breakfast (from $34/40).

Nearly 300 B&Bs do business in the county. To narrow your search and find a room ($65-180), use one of the city's reliable and efficient booking services, among them Bed & Breakfast of Fredericksburg (☎ 830-997-4712) and Gästehaus Schmidt Reservation Service (☎ 830-997-5612).

Popular for breakfast, the *Old German Bakery & Restaurant* (225 W Main St) makes some mean French toast but can be erratic and noisy when crammed with tourists (open Thurs-Mon). For exquisite German pastries and breads, try family-run *Dietz Bakery* (218 E Main St).

Altdorf Biergarten Restaurant (301 W Main St) is the town's best German place, with a sunny patio, big mugs of beer, German music and typical Bavarian specialties ($10-12; closed Tues). *Fredericksburg Brewing Company* (245 E Main St) makes superb beers and serves good food ($8-22).

Th chic-est dining in town is at *Navajo Grill* (209 E Main St), featuring gourmet recipes drawn from across the southern US; try the chile-rubbed Gulf shrimp ($19) or the grilled pork chop with Creole mashed potatoes ($18). The Tex-Mex-inspired

Sunday brunch ($8) is also popular. The restaurant's adjacent wine bar offers about 15 wines by the glass ($5-8; closed Mon).

Enchanted Rock State Natural Area

The exposed pink granite batholith here rises 425 feet and covers 640 acres. The park (☎ 915-247-3903, 16710 Ranch Rd 965), 18 miles north of Fredericksburg, offers hiking, rock climbing and primitive walk-in tent camping ($7-9; no RVs). Park admission is $5 per person. A daily visitor quota is enforced; call ahead to make sure there's room for you.

Luckenbach

With a population under 10, Luckenbach is less a town than a state of mind. Its 'downtown' consists solely of a creaky old general store/beer joint and an adjacent dance hall, sitting on 10 creekside acres in the bucolic countryside. But Luckenbach has been a mecca for country music fans ever since Waylon Jennings sang about it in 1977. Pilgrims and devotees have left their handscrawled howdies on the walls. One, in the men's bathroom, informs us that 'Willie Nelson peed here.' He undoubtedly did, more than once.

The store (☎ 830-997-3224, 888-311-8990) hosts Sunday afternoon acoustic jam sessions and regular weekend concerts. You can count on a crowd on the Labor Day and Fourth of July weekends, when Jennings and Nelson often perform, along with dozens of country music's finest. Lodging is available just down the road at *Luckenbach Inn (☎ 830-997-2205, 800-997-1124, 3234 Luckenbach Rd)*, a country B&B ($125-150).

From Fredericksburg, take Hwy 290 east to FM 1376 and go south about 3 miles.

Kerrville

Central, friendly Kerrville, a large workaday town on the Guadalupe River, has accommodations and restaurants in all price ranges. The Kerrville Convention and Visitors Bureau (☎ 830-792-3535, 800-221-7958, Ⓦ www.kerrvilletexas.cc, 2108 Sidney Baker) is open daily and has information about local horseback riding, dude ranches and the big **Kerrville Folk Festival**, an 18-day musical extravaganza around Memorial Day weekend.

The biggest draw here is the **Cowboy Artists of America Museum** (☎ 830-896-2553, 1550 Bandera Hwy), a first-rate showcase of artwork about cowboys, Indians and that proverbial home on the range. From downtown, take Hwy 16 south to Hwy 173 (Bandera Hwy) and turn left; it's half a mile ahead on the right ($5; open daily).

Kerrville-Schreiner State Park (☎ 830-257-5392, 2385 Bandera Hwy), past the museum about 1½ miles down Hwy 173, is fun for hiking, biking, swimming, tubing and camping (day-use $3; campsites $9-15).

Kerrville Bus Co (☎ 830-257-7454, 701 Sidney Baker St) runs service to Austin ($22-24; 2¼ hours) and Fredericksburg ($7; 30 minutes) at 8:30am daily and to San Antonio ($13-14; 1¾ hours) several times daily.

Bandera

South of Kerrville on Hwy 173, Bandera has the look and feel of an old Western movie set. The little town is the self-proclaimed Cowboy Capital of the World, and wanna-be cowpokes can bond with Ol' Paint at one of the many dude ranches dotting the surrounding hills. Visitors with less horse sense will find Bandera a good base for kayaking or tubing the Medina River. Nearby, Lake Medina and the Hill Country State Natural Area are pleasant diversions. The friendly Bandera County Visitors Bureau (☎ 830-796-3045, 800-364-3833, Ⓦ www.tourtexas.com/bandera, 1808 S Hwy 16) can provide information on these attractions (open daily).

The best food in town is at *Fool Moon (204 Main St)*, a casual and cozy eatery/coffeehouse with fresh gourmet fare for breakfast, lunch (both $5-8) and dinner ($16-21). *Bandera Saloon (402 Main St)* is a real locals' bar, with friendly folks and regular live music.

Lost Maples State Natural Area

This 2174-acre spread along the Sabinal River southwest of Kerrville (5 miles north of Vanderpool on RR 1871) preserves the state's only maple forest. Though most popular in late October and early November, when the leaves turn colors, the park (☎ 830-966-3413) offers good hiking, picnicking and camping year round.

TEXAS

The Cowboys

Perhaps no other figure in literary or cinematic history has been so romanticized as the cowboy, who has come to symbolize the freedom of the plains and the industrious and untamable nature of the American people themselves.

Normally reticent Europeans will drop all pretense of superiority and giggle delightedly given the chance to throw on spurs, chaps and gloves and take to the trail at a dude ranch. And the image of the American West – the one Hollywood exported through its Westerns – is engraved in the minds of people from Delhi to Dublin.

The origins of the American cowboy go back to 16th-century Spain, where cattle were allowed to graze freely and were herded by ranch hands on horseback. The Spaniards brought this practice to Mexico, and Mexican *vaqueros* (wranglers) later passed on their methods to settlers in Texas. The Americans mispronounced *vaquero*, corrupting it to 'buckaroo.'

With westward expansion and the capture of new lands from the Indians, cattle drives became common. Cowboys, under the direction of a foreman, would herd together thousands of cattle to be driven north. The cowboys caught calves using a *lariat* (from the Spanish *la reata*) and marked them for identification using the heated-iron design that comprised the owner's brand.

The cattle drive was led by a scout and chuck wagon, which would prepare food in advance of the herd's arrival. Cowboys would ride in packs at the front, sides and, if they were unlucky, the rear of the herd, eating dust the whole way. To filter the dust, cowboys used bandana handkerchiefs tied over their noses and mouths.

Though horses would be changed in relays along the trail, the cowboy always kept his own saddle. Masterfully crafted and as comfortable as possible for rides that were often 24 hours or more, a cowboy's saddle was his most important tool and the last thing he sold in hard times.

The lives of cowboys changed drastically after the fencing of the range. With smaller areas for grazing cows, the duties of a cowboy are far different today, though there are still cowboys throughout the western USA.

But the cowboy culture lives on. One spectacular place to gain insights into the life of a cowboy is at the remarkable Cowboy Artists of America Museum at Kerrville.

SAN ANTONIO

San Antonio is the nation's ninth-largest city, but its Tex-Mex culture gives it a laid-back feel. Locals joke that everyone's on 'San Antonio Standard Time.' The city's eminently walkable downtown holds that supreme butch monument to American courage, the Alamo, as well as Riverwalk, the gentrified renovation of a once-seedy flood-control canal. Other attractions in greater San Antonio include two big theme parks: SeaWorld and Six Flags Fiesta Texas.

Big San Antonio events include the San Antonio Stock Show & Rodeo in early Feb-

ruary; Fiesta San Antonio, a citywide celebration held in mid-April; and Las Posadas, a candlelight procession along Riverwalk at Christmastime.

History

The Spanish established San Antonio as a military garrison in 1718 and built missions in the area. In 1731 Spanish settlers from the Canary Islands founded a town here; by 1791 the area was attracting Mexican and American settlers.

During the Texas War for Independence (1835–6), the legendary Battle of the Alamo was fought here. After the state's independence from Mexico, San Antonio, at the southern end of the Chisholm Trail, boomed as a cattle town.

The city's 20th-century growth was largely military. Fort Sam Houston (1879) was later joined by Kelly, Lackland, Randolph and Brooks Air Force Bases. Today's economy revolves around the tourism, oil, livestock and technology industries.

Information

The San Antonio Convention and Visitors Bureau (☎ 210-207-6700, 800-447-3372, W www.sanantoniocvb.com) runs a visitor center opposite the Alamo (☎ 210-207-6748, 317 Alamo Plaza), which has information on city tours. The San Antonio Gay & Lesbian Community Center (☎ 210-732-4300, 3126 N St Mary's) is open daily. The San Antonio Central Library (☎ 210-207-2500, 600 Soledad St) offers Internet access.

The Alamo

In the early 18th century, the Spanish constructed five San Antonio–area missions as way stations for colonial expansion. Mission San Antonio de Valero, better known as the Alamo (☎ 210-281-0710, 300 Alamo Plaza), is the most famous (free admission; open daily).

In December 1835, Texan troops captured San Antonio and occupied and fortified the Alamo throughout the winter. On February 23, 1836, Mexican general Antonio López de Santa Anna led 2500 Mexican troops in an attack against it. Santa Anna's troops pounded the Alamo for 13 days before retaking it and executing almost all of the surviving defenders, including James Bowie, William Travis and Davy Crockett. Bowie's and Travis' black slaves (Sam and Joe, respectively) fought alongside their masters during the battle and survived the attack.

Mission Trail

South of the Alamo lie the other four missions, including (from north to south) Concepción (1731), San José (1720), San Juan (1731) and Espada (1745–56). Together, these four missions make up San Antonio Missions National Historical Park (☎ 210-932-1001). Mission San José, the most beautiful, is the site of the national-park visitor center. From the Alamo, take S St Mary's south until it becomes Mission Rd, which leads to all the missions. Parts of the Mission Trail are served by VIA (the city's bus system) and local tour companies.

Riverwalk

Though touristy, Riverwalk is still a pleasant strolling ground, and even hard-boiled visitors will probably enjoy a cruise along it with Yanaguana River Cruises (☎ 210-244-5700). Get tickets ($5.25) at Rivercenter Mall, Holiday Inn Riverwalk or on the Riverwalk opposite Hilton Palacio del Rio. Signs throughout downtown point out stairways down to Riverwalk, which is well below street level.

Museums

The McNay Art Museum (☎ 210-824-5368, 6000 N New Braunfels Ave) exhibits an outstanding collection of European and American modern art, including works by Van Gogh, Toulouse-Lautrec, Chagall, Cézanne, Hopper, Dali and Matisse (free admission; closed Mon).

San Antonio Museum of Art (SAMA; ☎ 210-978-8100, 200 W Jones Ave) houses rotating exhibitions and a core collection of Asian, Egyptian and ancient art ($5). Next door, the Nelson A Rockefeller Center for Latin American Art exhibits SAMA's impressive collection of Spanish Colonial, Mexican and pre-Columbian works (included in the SAMA admission price).

Buckhorn Saloon & Museum (☎ 210-247-4000, 318 E Houston St) has been around since 1881, when founder Albert Friedrich offered a free beer or shot of whiskey to any patron bringing in a rack of antlers. Today it's a two-story museum ($8) housing big-game taxidermy, cheezoid Americana and a camp wax museum.

Other Attractions

At the southern city center is HemisFair Park, site of the 1968 World's Fair and the Tower of the Americas (☎ 210-207-8615), which has an observation platform ($3) and a revolving restaurant/lounge. The park also holds the superb Institute of Texan Cultures (☎ 210-458-2300, 801 S Bowie St), which explores the diverse nature of the state's settlers with sections devoted to 27 ethnic and national groups ($4; closed Mon).

TEXAS

SAN ANTONIO

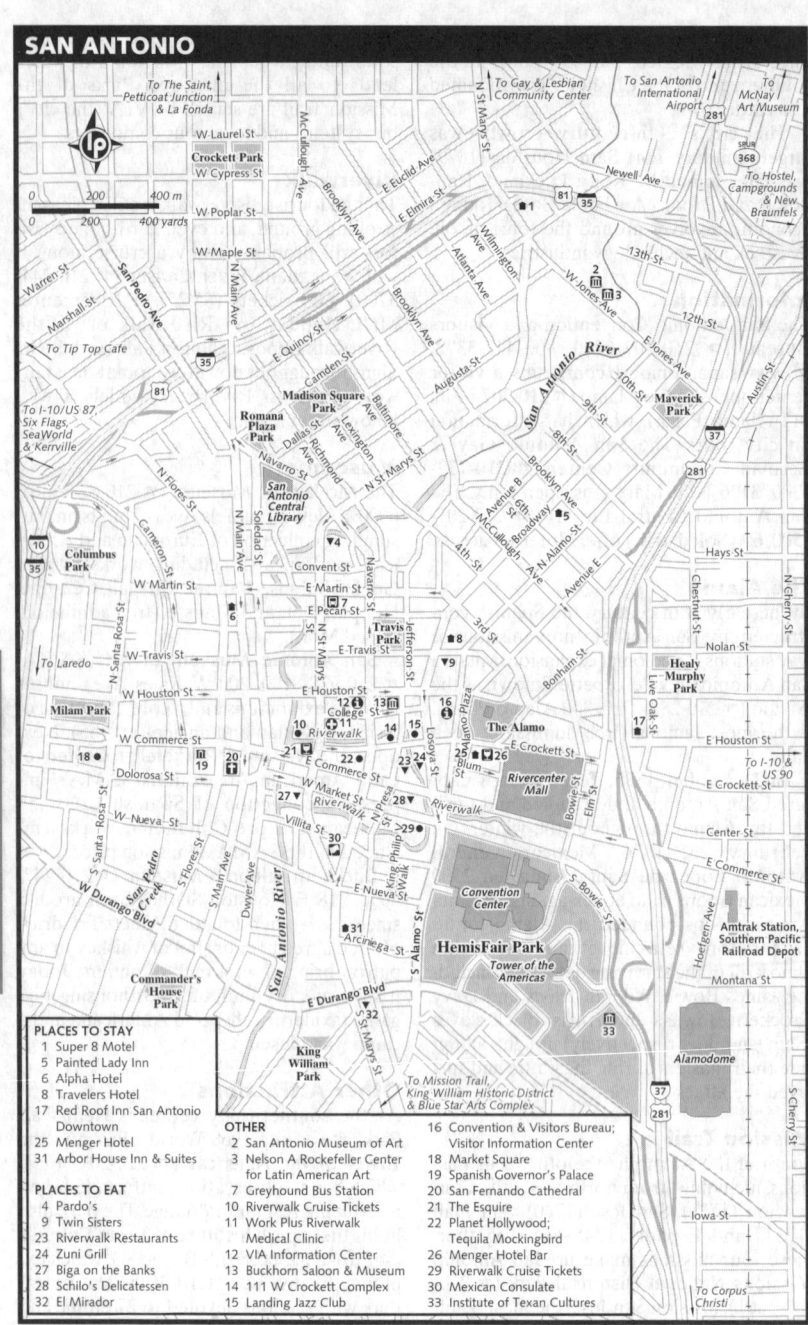

To The Saint,
Petticoat Junction
& La Fonda

To Gay & Lesbian
Community Center

To San Antonio
International
Airport

To
McNay
Art Museum

W Laurel St

Crockett Park

W Cypress St

W Poplar St

0   200   400 m
0   200   400 yards

W Maple St

281

Newell Ave

368

To Hostel,
Campgrounds
& New
Braunfels

13th St

1

2

3

12th St

To Tip Top Cafe

San Antonio River

E Jones Ave

Maverick
Park

Madison Square
Park

Romana
Plaza
Park

37

281

To I-10/US 87,
Six Flags,
SeaWorld
& Kerrville

San
Antonio
Central
Library

5

Hays St

10
35

Columbus
Park

Convent St

Healy
Murphy
Park

7

Travis
Park

8

9

Milam Park

The Alamo

17

18

10 11

14 15 16

12

13

19

20

21

22

23 24

25 26

Rivercenter
Mall

27

28

29

30

Convention
Center

31

HemisFair Park
Tower of the
Americas

33

Alamodome

Commander's
House
Park

32

King
William
Park

To Mission Trail,
King William Historic District
& Blue Star Arts Complex

Amtrak Station,
Southern Pacific
Railroad Depot

To I-10 &
US 90

To Corpus
Christi

PLACES TO STAY
1 Super 8 Motel
5 Painted Lady Inn
6 Alpha Hotel
8 Travelers Hotel
17 Red Roof Inn San Antonio
    Downtown
25 Menger Hotel
31 Arbor House Inn & Suites

PLACES TO EAT
4 Pardo's
9 Twin Sisters
23 Riverwalk Restaurants
24 Zuni Grill
27 Biga on the Banks
28 Schilo's Delicatessen
32 El Mirador

OTHER
2 San Antonio Museum of Art
3 Nelson A Rockefeller Center
   for Latin American Art
7 Greyhound Bus Station
10 Riverwalk Cruise Tickets
11 Work Plus Riverwalk
    Medical Clinic
12 VIA Information Center
13 Buckhorn Saloon & Museum
14 111 W Crockett Complex
15 Landing Jazz Club

16 Convention & Visitors Bureau;
    Visitor Information Center
18 Market Square
19 Spanish Governor's Palace
20 San Fernando Cathedral
21 The Esquire
22 Planet Hollywood;
    Tequila Mockingbird
26 Menger Hotel Bar
29 Riverwalk Cruise Tickets
30 Mexican Consulate
33 Institute of Texan Cultures

Just east of I-35, touristy **Market Square** (514 W Commerce St) re-creates a Mexican marketplace, with shops selling fabrics, craftwork and clothing, plus restaurants and food kiosks serving decent Mexican food. A Smithsonian-affiliated Latino Museum is scheduled to open here by spring 2002.

Other downtown attractions include the 1749 **Spanish Governor's Palace** (☎ 210-224-0601, 105 Plaza de Armas), behind city hall ($1.50), and **San Fernando Cathedral** (115 Main Plaza), on N Main St just south of E Commerce St, which was established by the Canary Islanders (see History) and is the nation's oldest surviving cathedral.

King William Historic District, south of downtown, is a charming residential neighborhood featuring many late-19th-century homes built by wealthy German settlers. The architecture is predominantly Victorian, though you'll also see Italianate, Colonial Revival, beaux arts and even modern styles. Nearby is **Blue Star Arts Complex** (1400 S Alamo St), which houses art galleries, art-related businesses and the Blue Star Brewing Co (see Places to Eat).

Off the outer loop (Loop 1604), **Sea-World San Antonio** (☎ 210-523-3611), Ellison Dr at Westover Hills Blvd, features marine-life displays and shows along with water slides and a kick-ass roller coaster ($34/24; open Mar-Nov). **Six Flags Fiesta Texas** (☎ 210-697-5050), Loop 1604 at I-10, offers more gravity-defying coasters, a water park and other entertainment ($39/$20 kids under 48 inches tall, $7 parking).

Places to Stay
Everything's booked solid during major college sporting events, festivals and large conventions.

Dixie Kampground (☎ 210-337-6501, 1011 Gembler Rd), 3½ miles northeast of downtown, has tent sites for $18. Closer is the cheery *San Antonio KOA* (☎ 210-224-9296, 602 Gembler Rd), with tent sites for $20. To reach the campgrounds, take I-35 north to exit 159B, turn right onto Coliseum Ave and left on Gembler.

HI San Antonio Hostel (☎ 210-223-9426, 621 Pierce St) is 2 miles north of city center. It has a pool, kitchen and common area. Dorm beds are $16/19 for members/nonmembers. Private rooms run from $39/44

singles/doubles. From downtown, head north to I-35 exit 159A, turn left, go to Grayson, turn left again and go two blocks to Pierce St.

Spartan (with a capital S) lodgings downtown include *Travelers Hotel* (☎ 210-226-4381, 220 N Broadway), with cleanish rooms from $26/37 without bath, $36/43 with bath; and *Alpha Hotel* (☎ 210-223-7644, 315 N Main St), with worn rooms for $31/37.

Good chain-motel deals near downtown include *Super 8 Motel* (☎ 210-222-8833, 1614 N St Mary's), with rooms for $50-80, and *Red Roof Inn San Antonio Downtown* (☎ 210-229-9973, 1011 E Houston St), just across I-37, which is relatively new, totally spotless and has big rooms from as low as $49/54.

Quirky-artsy *Arbor House Inn & Suites* (☎ 210-472-2005, 888-272-6700, 540 S St Marys) has a great location near Riverwalk and the Alamo. Rooms are spread across four historic houses on the property, which has a comfortable, intimate feel. Rates are $110-175 peak season ($95-140 off season).

Downtown has several top-end hotels with historic style. Most famous is the *Menger Hotel* (☎ 210-223-4361, 800-345-9285, 204 Alamo Plaza), which dates from 1859 and has hosted presidents and celebrities throughout its history. Legend has it that General Robert E Lee once rode his horse into the lobby. Today the Menger has been modernized, but it's full of historic art and furnishings, and it's as close as you can sleep to the Alamo. Rooms cost $155/165; occasional specials start at $100.

A good B&B choice is the gay/lesbian-friendly *Painted Lady Inn* (☎ 210-220-1092, 620 Broadway), in a convenient (if not aesthetic) part of town. The interior is a gorgeous work of art, and amenities include a private rooftop hot tub. Rooms, all with private bath, go for $89-219.

Places to Eat
Low-budget gourmands will love *Tip Top Cafe* (2814 Fredericksburg Rd), between West Ave and Babcock Rd. The colossal chicken-fried steak ($6.25) is enough to make you weep, and the heaving plates of crunchy and enormous onion rings ($3) are just spectacular. *Schilo's Delicatessen* (424 E Commerce St), by Riverwalk, has wonderful split-pea soup ($2.25) and beef stew ($4.75,

TEXAS

served Mon 11am-3pm). It's pronounced **shee**-lows.

***Twin Sisters** (124 Broadway)* offers healthy, natural food – including many vegetarian dishes – for breakfast and lunch (closed Sat-Sun). On Saturday head for ***El Mirador** (722 S St Mary's)* for its famous *sopa Azteca,* a heavenly chicken-and-vegetable soup ($5). ***La Fonda** (☎ 210-733-0621, 2415 N Main St),* in the beautiful Monte Vista Historic District, is a good choice for authentic Mexican fare ($7-12).

Casual ***Blue Star Brewing Co** (1414 S Alamo St),* in the Blue Star Arts Complex just south of downtown, makes excellent beers and serves better-than-average pub fare (most items $6-8).

Riverwalk's fine-dining choice is ***Biga on the Banks** (☎ 210-225-0722, 203 S St Marys St),* which features an acclaimed chef and creative international-eclectic cuisine for dinner ($17-35) and Sunday brunch. At the edge of Riverwalk, out of the tourist fray, is upscale yet comfortable ***Pardo's** (☎ 210-228-9999, 700 N St Marys St),* which has perhaps the best atmosphere around and serves steak, seafood and chicken (entrées $13-22; closed Sun). ***Zuni Grill** (☎ 210-227-0864, 223 Losoya St)* offers tasty Southwest cuisine and outdoor seating along Riverwalk. Open for lunch ($7-9) and dinner ($14-25).

Just northeast of downtown, ***Josephine Street** (400 E Josephine St)* and ***Liberty Bar** (328 E Josephine St),* in adjacent creaking Victorian houses, offer tremendous bang for the buck. Josephine Street has an incredible blackened sirloin steak for $10.50, and discounts dishes on Tuesday. Liberty Bar consistently has super everything, including some vegetarian options. Many main courses are under $10, though the glorious crab cakes cost $16.

Entertainment

Check *The Current* or the *Express-News* for listings of clubs, local music and cultural events.

***The Esquire** (155 E Commerce St)* has cheap drinks, colorful regulars and the longest bar in Texas (or so they claim). The little ***Menger Hotel Bar** (204 Alamo Plaza),* is a great rainy-day hideaway with dark wood and subdued lighting.

Two of the best live-music clubs are some distance from downtown. Rock-oriented

***Jewel's** (☎ 210-691-3000, 5500 Babcock Rd),* at Eckhert, is northwest of downtown near South Texas Medical Center. ***Far West Rodeo** (☎ 210-646-9378, 3030 NE Loop 410),* at the I-35/Loop 410 intersection northeast of downtown, is a huge country-music dance hall attracting big-name performers. It also features a mechanical bull and indoor pro rodeo.

Several downtown venues offer regular live music. Try ***Tequila Mockingbird** (☎ 210-226-2473, 245 E Commerce St),* behind and underneath Planet Hollywood, or the *111 W Crockett complex* on Riverwalk, where at least one of the several establishments usually has someone playing.

A San Antonio tradition is jazz at the ***Landing Jazz Club** (☎ 210-223-7266, 123 Losoya St),* on Riverwalk at the Hyatt Regency. The Jim Cullum Jazz Band plays Mon-Sat nights.

The city's most popular gay bar is ***The Saint** (☎ 210-225-7330, 1430 N Main St).* Lesbians like ***Petticoat Junction** (☎ 210-737-2344, 1812 N Main St).*

Spectator Sports

The San Antonio Spurs (☎ 210-554-7787) play NBA basketball at the Alamodome, 100 Montana St, across I-37 from downtown.

Getting There & Around

Air San Antonio International Airport (☎ 210-207-3411) is about 10 miles north of downtown, just north of the Loop 410/US 281 intersection. City buses (75¢) run to downtown San Antonio about every 45 minutes at peak times and far less frequently at other times. SATrans (☎ 210-281-9900) runs shuttle buses to downtown ($8). A cab to downtown will cost $15-17.

Bus Greyhound (☎ 210-270-5824) and Kerrville Bus Lines (☎ 210-227-5669) share a terminal at 500 N St Mary's downtown. Greyhound goes to Austin ($14-15; from 1½ hours), Houston ($23; from 3¼ hours), Galveston ($45-48; from 5 hours) and Dallas ($32-34; from 5 hours).

VIA (☎ 210-362-2020), San Antonio's city bus system, has a downtown information center at 260 E Houston St, where you can pick up a systemwide route map ($2). The company runs four handy streetcar routes across downtown (50¢ one way, $2 all day); streetcars pass each stop about every 10 minutes. Outside downtown, regular buses can get you most anywhere; call for route and schedule information.

Train Amtrak's *Sunset Limited* and *Texas Eagle* trains stop at the beautiful depot (☎ 210-223-3226, 350 Hoefgen Ave), just east of I-37 north of the Alamodome.

Car San Antonio is a driving nightmare, and then you have to park, which is nearly impossible. Many downtown-area lodgings offer free guest parking. Otherwise, the metered spaces around Travis Park would be a good place to start looking.

Taxi Taxi rates are $1.60 flagfall ($2.60 after 9pm) plus $1.50 per mile. The biggest company in town is Yellow–Checker Taxi (☎ 210-222-2222).

AROUND SAN ANTONIO

The area directly north of San Antonio is a haven for shoppers, who stream into the cheap factory outlet malls lining I-35. Prices are extraordinarily low.

New Braunfels

Water is the summer focus here. Rafting and tubing down the Guadalupe River is popular, and a great place to access the river is at Gruene (say 'green') Historic District, just north of town. Take FM 306 west from I-35 exit 191 and follow the signs. Raft and tube rentals are available.

Gruene was settled by German farmers in the 1840s. The hamlet's highlight is **Gruene Hall** (☎ 830-606-1281), an 1880s dance hall that draws folks from across Texas for live music and lively down-home atmosphere.

Elsewhere in New Braunfels, **Schlitterbahn Waterpark Resort** (☎ 830-625-2351) is one of the country's best ($27; open April-Sept).

Be sure to stop by New Braunfels Visitor Center (☎ 830-625-2385, 800-572-2626, Ⓦ www.nbcham.org, 390 S Seguin) for more information (closed Sat-Sun). A second visitor center off I-35 at Post Rd is open daily.

San Marcos

Big-game bargain hunting is the draw here. **Prime Outlets–San Marcos** and the similarly gargantuan **Tanger Outlet Center** (both off

I-35, exit 200) provide hundreds of name-brand factory outlet shops offering 30% to 70% off retail prices.

The town also offers charming historic districts, tranquil tubing on the San Marcos River, glass-bottom boating ($6) at **Aquarena Center** (☎ 800-999-9767), and family fun at **Wonder World** (☎ 512-392-3760), a small theme park ($11-16) around natural caverns.

Music lovers should check out *Cheatham Street Warehouse (☎ 512-353-3777, 119 Cheatham)*, a historic breeding ground for Texas singer-songwriters.

Open daily, the San Marcos Visitor Information Center (☎ 512-393-5930, 888-200-5620, Ⓦ www.sanmarcostexas.com/tourism, 617 I-35 N) has information on the city's many B&Bs.

Houston

The state's largest city, and the nation's fourth-largest, sprawling Houston offers a unique urban experience. Thanks to a historic lack of zoning laws, the city has skyscrapers not just downtown but in several areas. And in summer, the downtown streets are eerily deserted; to combat the sweltering heat and humidity, many buildings are linked by a network of air-conditioned underground pedestrian tunnels.

Houston got its big break in the 1970s, when oil *was* the economy and Houston was the industry's capital. When oil reached $40 a barrel in 1981, Houston was awash in money. It's been up and down ever since, but Houston's economy has long-since diversified into medical services and high-tech (including aerospace and computer-related industries), and the city still oozes big bucks from every pore.

Seeing Houston's sights won't take more than a day or two, but if you stay longer you can sample from the scores of restaurants, bars and clubs enjoyed by Houston's generally young and ebullient population, or head down to the Clear Lake area to see NASA's Johnson Space Center (see Around Houston, later).

Orientation

Houston's street names can be very confusing. Most have no official suffix such as St,

TEXAS

Rd, Ave etc. A city official remarked, 'You can call them what you want – we do.' Furthermore, there is no official boundary between north and south or east and west designations on streets. Good luck.

Most areas of visitor interest lie between downtown and the Galleria mall, 6 miles to the west. If you're just passing through, bypass the Bangkokian traffic congestion by taking the Sam Houston Tollway around the city.

A tour of the most interesting districts would look something like this: Starting from downtown, take Bagby/Dallas west to Montrose St and turn south. The Montrose District has a good mix of shops and clubs and is the center of Houston's gay scene. Continue south on Montrose St to the Museum District, just north of Hermann Park. West of Montrose, around the Southwest Freeway on Kirby is the hopping-for-shopping Upper Kirby District, marked by an abundance of red British phone booths (Upper Kirby – UK – get it?). Continuing north, Kirby heads through chichi River Oaks and bends east, becoming the Allen Parkway and continuing posthaste into downtown. This is a quick and scenic route between Kirby and city center.

Heading south of the freeway on Kirby will take you toward University Village, just west of Rice University. This compact area – a good place to explore on foot – is full of restaurants and nightlife.

Farther west, just off the loop (I-610), is Uptown, home to the glitzy Post Oak District, the immense Galleria shopping mall and loads of high-priced chain shops. Just south of there is the Richmond Strip, another prime nightlife area.

Information

The Greater Houston Convention and Visitors Bureau (☎ 713-437-5200, 800-446-8786, Ⓦ www.houston-guide.com, 901 Bagby), downtown in City Hall, has a huge visitor center with thousands of brochures; open daily. Staff can provide information on city tours.

Much of central Houston uses the original 713 area (telephone) code. Other local area codes currently include 281 and 832. New phone numbers may be assigned any one of these area codes without regard to geography, so you need to know all ten digits.

Public libraries with Internet access include the downtown branch (☎ 713-236-1313, 500 McKinney) and the Montrose branch (☎ 713-284-1958, 4100 Montrose St).

Currency exchange is available at both airports, as well as at Bank of America (☎ 713-247-6000, 700 Louisiana) and Chase Bank (☎ 713-216-4865, 712 Main St).

Downtown

The skyline is best seen at night, when many buildings have special lighting. Tallest of the skyscrapers is **Chase Tower** (600 Travis), which has a free 60th-floor observation deck (open Mon-Fri). Downtown's oldest buildings – a few survivors from the mid-19th century – can be found around Market Square Park and Allen's Landing Park. The Heritage Society (☎ 713-655-1912) manages eight 19th-century buildings and a small museum in **Sam Houston Park**, 1100 Bagby (tours $6; open daily).

Downtown is home to the **Theater District**, centered around the Bayou Place entertainment complex (Texas Ave at Smith). The complex holds clubs, restaurants, the Angelika Film Center (screening a mix of first-run, foreign, art and indie films) and the Aerial Theater, a prime concert venue. Several other theaters and the impressive new Hobby Center for the Performing Arts are nearby. East out Prairie a short way is Enron Field, the downtown ballpark of the Houston Astros baseball team.

Air-Con

The two most important words in Houston's history are not oil and cattle – although they've been extremely important – but rather 'air' and 'conditioning.' From its founding in 1836 up until the 1930s, Houston was a sleepy, mosquito-ridden regional center. In July, when the average daytime temperature is a sweltering 94°F, work melted away as Houstonians fled to the Gulf Coast in search of breezes. The advent of climate control made the city bearable year round, and the city's population boomed. (In summer, always carry a sweater – Houstonians crank their air-conditioning levels to the 'arctic' setting.)

River Oaks & Montrose District

Along Buffalo Bayou in River Oaks, **Bayou Bend** (☎ 713-639-7750, 1 Westcott) is the former home of the unfortunately named Ima Hogg, philanthropist and daughter of Texas Governor James S Hogg. It's now a museum with an impressive American decorative-arts collection and 14 acres of gardens ($10-14; free on the third Sunday each month; closed Mon).

Nearby **Rienzi** (☎ 713-639-7800, 1406 Kirby), the former home of Houston art patrons Harris and Carroll Masterson, holds an equally fine collection of European decorative arts (from $4; open Thurs-Mon; reservations required).

A few more sights are west of Montrose between Alabama St and Richmond Ave. Housed in a magnificent building, the outstanding **Menil Collection** (☎ 713-525-9400, 1515 Sul Ross Dr) contains several rooms devoted to surrealists, including René Magritte. Two annexes house works by Cy Twombly and Dan Flavin (free admission; open Wed-Sun).

A block east, **Rothko Chapel** (☎ 713-524-9839, 3900 Yupon St) holds 14 large paintings by Mark Rothko (free admission; open daily). The nearby **Byzantine Fresco Chapel Museum** (☎ 713-521-3990, 4011 Yupon) contains stunning 13th-century frescoes that arrived from Cyprus under Maltese Falcon-esque circumstances (free admission; open Wed-Sun).

Museum District & Hermann Park

Unless noted otherwise, all the following museums are closed Monday (except federal holidays, when they are open).

The **Museum of Fine Arts, Houston** (☎ 713-639-7300, 1001 Bissonnet) has a large collection (in two separate buildings), heavy on works by American (especially Texan) artists as well as 19th-century impressionists and postimpressionists, plus a sculpture garden holding works by Rodin, Matisse and others ($5; free Thurs). The museum's cafe offers excellent gourmet fare.

The **Children's Museum of Houston** (☎ 713-522-1138, 1500 Binz) has fun interactive exhibits, including a mechanical cow for tots to milk (admission $5; $3 after 3pm; free 5pm-8pm Thurs). Kids will also love the Museum of Health and Medical Science (☎ 713-521-1515, 1515 Hermann) for its huge models of human innards…'eww, gross!' ($4; free Thurs 4pm-7pm).

The excellent **Houston Museum of Natural Science** (☎ 713-639-4629, 1 Hermann Circle) in Hermann Park comprises exhibit halls ($5; free Tues 2pm-6pm); a planetarium ($4); IMAX theater ($6.50); and the Cockrell Butterfly Center ($4), a three-story dome where you can walk among thousands of butterflies (open daily; parking $3).

Hermann Park itself is a 407-acre refuge holding the **Houston Zoo** (☎ 713-523-5888), which charges $2.50; a golf course; garden center; and Miller Outdoor Theatre, a popular summer performance venue.

Other Attractions

The **Galleria** (5075 Westheimer Rd), at Post Oak Blvd, holds more than 300 shops, two hotels, a bevy of restaurants and an ice-skating rink. Nearby at the base of Williams Tower (near the corner of Post Oak Blvd and Hidalgo St) is the **Water Wall**, a 64-foot-tall U-shaped waterfall.

The aging **Astrodome** (8400 Kirby) is home to the big Houston Livestock Show and Rodeo, held each February and March. Next door is Reliant Park, home field for the new Houston Texans NFL-football franchise. Opposite, **Six Flags AstroWorld** theme park (☎ 713-799-1234, 9001 Kirby) features killer coasters and thrill rides ($36), while affiliated **WaterWorld** provides slides, pools, beaches and other watery pleasures ($20). A combined ticket good for one day at both parks costs $40.

Places to Stay

Half a mile south of Sam Houston Pkwy off Aldine-Westfield Dr, *KOA Houston Central* (☎ 281-442-3700, 1620 Peachleaf) has tent sites from $18.

As comfortable as a favorite old slipper gently chewed by the dog, the Hostels of America–affiliated *Houston International Hostel* (☎ 713-523-1009, 5302 Crawford) enjoys a great location in a quiet residential neighborhood near the Museum District. It's a fine place to call home during your stay ($15). Low-budget digs ($25-36) are also available at the *YMCA* (☎ 713-659-8501, 1600 Louisiana).

TEXAS

Motel 6 offers 17 locations in greater Houston (most from $38/44 singles/doubles), including six 'Studio 6' extended-stay versions (from $200/220 weekly). Its ***Motel 6 Hobby Airport*** *(☎ 713-941-0990, 8800 Airport Blvd)* is half a mile from the runway.

Among the faded motels near the Astrodome is ***Grant Palm Court Inn*** *(☎ 713-668-8000, 8200 S Main St),* with big rooms (from $41) and free donuts. ***Days Inn*** *(☎ 713-523-3777, 4640 S Main St)* is near Montrose and the Museum District ($54/59).

In the convenient Greenway Plaza area are ***La Quinta Inn Astrodome*** *(☎ 713-668-8082, 9911 Buffalo Speedway),* with big rooms for $69-76, and ***Extended Stay America*** *(☎ 713-521-0060, 2330 Southwest Fwy),* with rooms from $59/64, $289/310 per week.

Gay-friendly B&Bs include ***Lovett Inn*** *(☎ 713-522-5224, W www.lovettinn.com, 501 Lovett Blvd),* which has a pool and rooms from $75, and the exclusively gay-and-lesbian ***Montrose Inn*** *(☎ 713-520-0206, 408 Avondale),* with rooms from $59.

TEXAS

Places to Eat

You could gain some serious weight on a gastronome's tour of Houston. Cooks from every corner of the world prepare their home-country recipes here. The local favorites listed below are just the tip of the iceberg.

Haggard vegetarians finally find peas at ***Whole Foods Market*** *(☎ 713-520-1937, 2955 Kirby),* in Upper Kirby (and other Houston locations). Healthy fruits and veggies are the raisins d'être at ***Hobbit Cafe*** *(2243 Richmond Ave),* though meat dishes are available too ($8-10).

Goode Co Barbeque *(5109 Kirby)* draws crowds ostensibly for the right-on barbecue but really for the sinful pecan pie. Relaxed ***Luling City Market*** *(4726 Richmond Ave),* in upper crust Uptown, also comes in right on 'cue. For steaks, try ***Capital Grille*** *(5365 Westheimer Rd),* with entrées for $27-33.

Two Rows Restaurant & Brewery *(2400 University),* in University Village, hops after 5pm, as the wage slaves pour in for heady brew and fine food. ***Backstreet Cafe*** *(1103 S Shepherd),* in River Oaks, was voted 'Best Alfresco Dining' in a *Houston Press* readers' poll. It serves excellent soups, salads and sandwiches on a flower-filled patio.

At ***Bayou City Seafood N' Pasta*** *(4730 Richmond Ave and 2414 University),* fresh gulf shrimp and oysters are priced righter than Bob Barker. Buy a platter for your sweetheart, and bayou one too ($13). For more great seafood with a Cajun beat, try down-home ***Floyd's Cajun Kitchen*** *(1200 Durham),* where you can *étouff* yourself on Houston's best crawfish étoufée for $11.

Nationally renowned ***Kim Son*** *(2001 Jefferson St, 7531 Westheimer Rd and 12750 SW Fwy)* is a local legend run by the La family, who escaped in a boat from Vietnam in 1979. The 280-item menu ranges from rice-noodle soup to jellyfish and lotus root (lunch specials average $5). Former president George Bush (Dubya's dad) and wife Barbara are regulars at ***Hunan*** *(1800 Post Oak Blvd),* near the Galleria, where they rave about their dim son (entrées $13-19).

Trés chic and trés cher, ***Tony's*** *(☎ 713-622-6778, 1801 Post Oak Blvd)* is Houston's celebrity hangout. The 'New European' cuisine draws from a mix of Italian and French influences (entrées $25-45; closed Sun). For new American fare, head to ***Mark's American Cuisine*** *(☎ 713-523-3800, 1658 Westheimer Rd),* where owner-chef Mark Cox is a culinary conjurer extraordinaire (entrées $15-25).

Many say upscale ***McCormick & Schmick's*** *(☎ 713-840-7900, 1151 Uptown Park)* is the town's best seafood place; some call it Houston's best restaurant, period (entrées $8-25). Less formal is ***Goode Co Seafood*** *(2621 Westpark),* off Kirby, where Jim Goode and crew do fish with multicultural Gulf Coast flair ($6-25).

Américas *(☎ 713-961-1492, 1800 Post Oak Blvd),* offers outrageous Amazon-rainforest decor and fine-dining South American cuisine. The beef tenderloin in chimichurri sauce ($23) will leave you speechless.

Entertainment

Houston's nightlife is happening. Whatever your style, the city has someplace for you to step out at night.

Performing Arts The highbrow heart of Houston's entertainment scene is downtown's Theater District. The ***Aerial Theater*** *(☎ 713-230-1600, 520 Texas Ave),* in Bayou

Place, is a major venue for popular music and entertainment, while *Alley Theatre* (☎ 713-228-8421, 615 Texas Ave) presents first-rate drama.

The *Houston Symphony* (☎ 713-224-7575) performs at Jones Hall (615 Louisiana). The *Houston Grand Opera* and *Houston Ballet* (☎ 713-227-2787, 800-828-2787 for both) are based at Wortham Center (500 Texas Ave).

The *Society for the Performing Arts* (☎ 713-227-4772) brings Broadway musicals to the spiffy new Hobby Center for the Performing Arts, on Bagby (opening fall 2002). The Hobby Center will also be the home venue for Houston's acclaimed *Theatre Under the Stars* (☎ 800-678-5440).

Nightclubs Check out the weekly *Houston Press* or the alternative *Houston's Other* for comprehensive club listings.

Downtown's upscale art deco *Mercury Room* (☎ 713-225-6372, 1008 Prairie) has great decor, a trendy crowd and DJ or live entertainment Wed-Sat. To rock out, try the *Engine Room* (☎ 713-654-7846, 1515 Pease) or *Fitzgerald's* (☎ 713-862-3838, 2706 White Oak).

Local bands are featured at the following clubs: *Fabulous Satellite Lounge* (☎ 713-869-2665, 3616 Washington Ave), which also draws some big names; the *Sidecar Pub* (☎ 281-807-4040, 11202 Huffmeister), at Hwy 290, which has a great sound system and beer selection; and *Rudyard's Pub* (☎ 713-521-0521, 2010 Waugh St), a local institution offering live music Tues-Sun.

The *Continental Club* (☎ 713-529-9899, 3700 Main St) presents a variety of top-notch music at least five nights a week. Equally eclectic, if smaller-time, is *Mausoleum* (☎ 713-526-4648, 411 Westheimer Rd), which has regular jazz jams and open-mike poetry readings.

For down-and-out 12-bar blues, try the appropriately divey *Big Easy* (☎ 713-523-9999, 5731 Kirby), the *Shakespeare Pub* (☎ 281-497-4625, 14129 Memorial) or *Dan Electro's Guitar Bar* (☎ 713-862-8707, 1031 E 24th St), which hosts a Thursday night blues jam.

Cozy little *Cézanne* (☎ 713-522-9621, 4100 Montrose St), near Richmond Ave (above the Black Labrador), offers superb live jazz in a setting that calls for Cognac. Not far away, *Scott Gertner's Skybar*

(☎ 713-520-9688, 3400 Montrose St), at Hawthorne, offers jazz along with nice penthouse views. Downtown's *Sambuca Jazz Cafe* (☎ 713-224-5299, 900 Texas Ave), in the Rice Hotel, is a supper club serving Mediterranean cuisine and live jazz nightly. For wild Latin rhythms, head on down to *Elvia's International* (☎ 713-266-9631, 2727 Fondren), at Westheimer Rd, which offers live music and dancing Tues-Sat nights. Serious two-steppers step out to *Blanco's* (☎ 713-439-0072, 3406 W Alabama), Houston's best honky-tonk.

Montrose is the heart of Houston's gay-and-lesbian club scene. Here you'll find popular *Pacific Street* (☎ 713-523-0213, 710 Pacific St) and *JR's Bar & Grill* (☎ 713-521-2519, 808 Pacific St), where 'happy hour' lasts almost all day. *Rich's* (☎ 713-959-9606, 2401 San Jacinto) is another local favorite. *Chances* ☎ 713-523-7217, 1100 Westheimer Rd) is a popular lesbian bar with dancing until 2am.

Pubs & Bars European-style pubs include the *Black Labrador* (4100 Montrose St), offering upscale atmosphere, British pub fare and the requisite pints of Guinness and Bass; *The Harp* (1625 Richmond Ave), between Montrose and Upper Kirby, a lovely low-key neighborhood Irish pub; and *Slainte* (509 Main St), downtown, which takes its name from a Gaelic drinking toast and offers good food.

Less European in flavor but popular with beer connoisseurs are *Ginger Man* (5607 Morningside), a University Village pub with 69 beers on tap, the *Mercantile* (1010 Prairie), a downtown brew house in a restored 1912 theater, and the huge *Flying Saucer Draught Emporium* (705 Main St), with 85 taps.

Spectator Sports

The Houston Astros (☎ 713-259-8000) play pro baseball downtown at Enron Field, 501 Crawford. The Houston Rockets (☎ 713-627-3865) and Houston Comets (☎ 713-627-9622) play men's and women's basketball, respectively, at Compaq Center, Greenway Plaza, just off the Southwest Fwy. Compaq Center is also home ice of the Houston Aeros IHL hockey team (☎ 713-627-2376). The new Houston Texans NFL franchise will kick off its inaugural season in August 2002 at Reliant Park. Billed as 'The World's

TEXAS

Largest Rodeo,' Houston's Livestock Show & Rodeo draws more than a million visitors to the Astrodome each Feb.

Getting There & Around

Air George Bush Intercontinental Airport (IAH; ☎ 281-230-3100), 22 miles north of city center, is served by major domestic and international airlines. William P Hobby Airport (HOU; ☎ 713-640-3000) is a major domestic hub.

Bus No 102 ($1.50) runs between IAH and downtown daily. Bus No 88 ($1) serves HOU twice in the morning and twice in late afternoon (weekdays only). Express Shuttle USA (☎ 713-523-8888) offers van service from both Bush ($19) and Hobby ($14) airports. A taxi to downtown runs about $35/20 from IAH/HOU.

Bus The Houston bus terminal (☎ 713-759-6565, 2121 Main St) is between downtown and the Museum District. Greyhound has service to Brownsville ($25; from 6 hours), Corpus Christi ($22; from 4 hours), Dallas ($33; from 4 hours) and San Antonio ($23; from 3 hours).

Metro (☎ 713-635-4000) runs a network of bus lines throughout Houston. Weekend service is sketchy. Standard fare is $1, $2 for a day pass. A free trolley system serves downtown.

Train Amtrak's *Sunset Limited* stops at the downtown depot (☎ 713-224-1577, 902 Washington Ave).

Taxi Cab rates are $3 flagfall and $1.50 for each additional mile. Note that given Houston's sprawl, your cab tab can quickly surpass car rental rates. You must call for a cab; companies include United (☎ 713-699-0000) and Yellow (☎ 713-236-1111).

AROUND HOUSTON

Houston, we have a problem. It seems that one of the city's biggest attractions, NASA's world-famous Johnson Space Center, is actually down I-45 halfway to Galveston. But combined with a few other attractions in the area, it makes for a good day trip.

San Jacinto

The Texas War for Independence was won at the Battle of San Jacinto, where Mexican general Antonio López de Santa Anna was finally defeated. As San Jacinto Battleground State Historical Complex (☎ 281-479-2421) more than 1000 acres of the battleground are preserved (free admission; open daily). The complex includes the 570-foot-tall San Jacinto Monument, which has an observation deck ($3); the San Jacinto Museum of History; and the vintage 1914 battleship *Texas,* a veteran of both World Wars.

Johnson Space Center

This center, 25 miles southeast of downtown Houston, is among the state's most popular tourist destinations. The NASA/Clear Lake Convention & Visitors Bureau (☎ 281-488-7676, 1201 NASA Rd 1) is open 9am-5pm Mon-Fri.

While all manned US space missions are launched at Kennedy Space Center in Florida, this is where they are planned and controlled. Unfortunately, tours are available only as part of admission to the **Space Center Houston** (☎ 281-244-2100, 1601 NASA Rd 1), the official NASA visitor center and a commercial nightmare. The fun begins with a $3 parking fee and continues with corporate sponsors for almost every section except the toilets (they're probably working on it). If you look past the hype, you'll find a serious description of the space program. But you leave confident that, if it were to happen today, Neil Armstrong's first steps on the moon would leave the impression of the Nike swoosh. Admission ($15) includes the visitor center exhibits plus a tram tour of Johnson Space Center covering Mission Control, the shuttle training facilities, zero-gravity labs and more. It's mercifully free to view the fascinating display of NASA hardware at neighboring **Rocket Park**. Take I-45 to the NASA Rd 1 exit and drive east.

For a more down-to-earth astronaut experience, find your way to *Outpost Tavern*, NASA Rd 1 at Egret Bay Rd, in nearby Webster. NASA engineers and even astronauts frequent this rickety old beer bar, which has a friendly crowd of regulars and astronaut portraits lining the walls.

Clear Lake

Houston's boating center and a great place to beat the summer heat, Clear Lake has a definite happy-go-lucky resort feel. Restaurants galore overlook the water and the parades of billowing sails, while margarita bars play Jimmy Buffet into the wee hours for the perennially shorts-clad crowd.

Though getting out on the water is the main event here, the area has a couple of other attractions. **Armand Bayou Nature Center** (☎ 281-474-2551, 8500 Bay Area Blvd) is a pristine 2500-acre nature preserve with trails and exhibits ($3; closed Mon). It's also the Houston area's best place for canoeing; guided trips ($20) run every Sat morning. Out on Galveston Bay, touristy **Kemah Boardwalk** (☎ 877-285-3624) beckons with shops, restaurants and amusement-park rides.

Gulf Coast

America's 'Third Coast,' as folks there like to call it, is a relaxed and lovely place. Quiet small towns line the coast, which wends its way around coves, bayous, rivers, bays and hundreds of miles of almost untouched beaches. If your idea of heaven is a tent on the beach far from another person, you could spend an eternity wandering these sands.

GALVESTON

Sultry Galveston is as close as you'll get in Texas to the Deep South. Gorgeous Victorian homes and mansions in several different historic neighborhoods give the city a genteel sensuality found nowhere else in the state.

Memories of the 1900 hurricane that took 6000 lives, the country's worst natural disaster ever, run deep. But Galveston knows how to party, and its Mardi Gras festivities are the state's biggest.

Orientation & Information

Galveston Island is 30 miles long and no more than 3 miles wide. Seawall Blvd follows the gulf shore for more than 10 miles; the Strand centers the city's historic downtown along the ship channel. Both areas are usually safe, but be wary west of 25th St and a block or two north of Seawall.

The local Galveston Island Visitors Center (☎ 409-763-4311, 888-425-4753, ⓦ www.galvestoncvb.com, 2428 Seawall) provides visitor information. Rosenberg Library (☎ 409-763-8854, 2310 Sealy) offers public Internet access.

Things to See & Do

Incorporating multimedia attractions, an IMAX theater, artificial beach, paddlewheeler and high-tech aquarium, glitzy **Moody Gardens** (☎ 409-744-4673, 800-582-4673, 1 Hope Blvd) is Galveston's top tourist draw. But it seems both overhyped and overpriced ($25 for everything, $7.50-11 for a single attraction). The best component is the aquarium ($11), which holds more than 8,000 sea creatures, including kid-aweing sharks, in some two million gallons of tank space.

The historic Strand district is bounded by 20th and 25th Sts, Mechanic St and Harborside Dr. Museums here include the free **Galveston County Historical Museum** (☎ 409-766-2340, 2219 Market) and the **Galveston Railroad Museum** (☎ 409-765-5700, 123 25th; $5). Both are open daily.

North of Harborside Dr at 21st St, **Pier 21** holds shops, restaurants and museums around a converted old dock. Here the **Texas Seaport Museum** (☎ 409-763-1877) details Galveston's seaport life during its 19th-century heyday ($6). It's home to the tall-ship *Elissa,* a beautiful 1877 Scottish barque. At nearby Pier 20, the **Ocean Star** (☎ 409-766-7827) is a retired offshore rig with excellent exploration exhibits ($5).

The **Sea Turtle Center** (☎ 409-766-3670), on Science Dr S (off the 5000 block of Ave U), is devoted to saving the endangered Kemp's ridley sea turtle. Free tours run Tues, Thurs and Sat.

The 1886 **Bishop's Palace** (☎ 409-762-2475, 1402 Broadway), the 1895 **Moody Mansion** (☎ 409-762-7668, 2618 Broadway) and the 1859 **Ashton Villa** (☎ 409-762-3933, 2328 Broadway) have all been restored to their original splendor and are open daily for tours ($6, $6 and $5, respectively).

Take the 51st St Causeway to Pelican Island and **Seawolf Park** (☎ 409-744-5738), where the kids can clamor in and all over two real WWII-era ships: the submarine USS *Cavalla* and the destroyer escort USS *Stewart* ($4 adults, $2 kids; $5 parking). The rest of the park is a nice place for a picnic overlooking Galveston Bay. Kids will also enjoy the **Bolivar Ferry**, which makes a short run over to Port Bolivar and back. You'll get views of the Galveston skyline and big ships in the bay, and best of all, it's absolutely free. The landing is northeast of the Strand, at the end of Ferry Rd (off 2nd St).

Places to Stay & Eat

Six miles southwest of Galveston on Seawall, *Galveston Island State Park* (☎ 409-737-1222, 14901 FM 3005) has tent sites for $12-20, plus a $3 per person daily fee; book ahead in summer.

Seawall Blvd is lined with motels in all price ranges, from cheap dumps to luxury stays. The rattiest among them start at $25-30 for a single, but that's midweek, off-season. In summer, their rates can run to well over $50. The *HI Galveston Hostel* (☎ 409-765-9431, 201 E Seawall), in the Sandpiper Motel, is right on the beach and the best bet for the budget traveler. It's old but hasn't thoroughly gone to seed, and the hostel section has a nice common room with a TV, small library and Internet access. Hostel bunks are $17.50; motel rooms are $50-120, depending on season.

Of the several moderately priced chain motels along Seawall, newest is *Holiday Inn Express* (☎ 409-766-7070, 102 E Seawall). It's on the quiet east end of Seawall and has an outdoor pool ($69-209, depending on season).

Luxury digs include the *Wyndham Tremont House* (☎ 409-763-0300, 2300 Ship's Mechanic Row), in the Strand district ($119-195), and *Hotel Galvez* (☎ 409-765-7721, 2024 Seawall), a grande dame down by the beach ($225-245). Also luxurious is the *Harbor House* (☎ 409-763-3321, 800-874-3721, www.harborsidepier21.com, Pier 21 No 28), an intimate inn in a converted dockside warehouse ($158-165). A unique, romantic lodging is the *Stacia Leigh* (☎ 409-750-8858), Harborside Dr at Pier 22, a B&B on Mussolini's old yacht. It has 11 rooms ($125-150), eight with Jacuzzis, and there's a hot tub on the dock.

For a haute breakfast go to *Mosquito Cafe (628 14th)*, where the sophisticated menu includes frittatas, quiches, fresh-baked muffins and even granola with yogurt and fresh fruit. For fancy fish, flounder your way over to *Gaido's (3800 Seawall)*.

The *Original Mexican Cafe (1401 Market)* has served Mexican food since 1916; various taco, tamale and enchilada combos cost under $5. For the best purely Mexican food, head to *Claudia's (1220 Tremont)*. Five bucks will get you a good barbecued-beef sandwich at either *Leon's World's Finest In & Out B-B-Q House (5427 Broadway)* or *Queen's Barbecue (3428 Ave S)*, near Seawall.

Food and an oceanfront beach scene are available at *Fish Tales (2502 Seawall)*, which has a nice upstairs deck. But the quintessential beach bar, and there's really only one, is *Woody's (1726 Seawall)*. Look for the Harleys out front.

Near the Strand, *Molly's Pub (2013 Postoffice St)* has a good draft beer selection and jovial atmosphere.

Getting There & Around

Kerrville Bus Lines (☎ 409-765-7731, 714 25th) runs four buses a day to Houston ($13-14; 1 hour). The Galveston Island Rail Trolley (☎ 409-763-4311) links the Strand with Seawall via 25th St (60¢). A small Strand loop is free. The city also operates a fleet of electric shuttle buses serving many hotels and visitor attractions. The shuttles operate Thurs-Sun ($1).

ARANSAS NATIONAL WILDLIFE REFUGE

This 70,504-acre refuge (☎ 361-286-3559) is the Texas coast's premier bird-watching site (admission $5 per car). The birding frenzy peaks in March and November. Most watched are the whooping cranes (one of the continent's rarest creatures) who winter here. You also might see wild boars, alligators, armadillos, white-tailed deer and many other species. The refuge is 35 miles northeast of Rockport; take Hwy 35 to FM 774 and follow the signs.

Cuddle up to an armadillo.

CORPUS CHRISTI

Corpus is a pleasant enough port town, but you wouldn't book your honeymoon here. The visitor center (☎ 361-881-1888, 1823 N Chaparral) opens daily. Nearby are **Heritage Park**, with restored old buildings, and the **Museum of Science & History** (☎ 361-883-2862). Admission is $5; closed Mon.

Something's fishy at **Texas State Aquarium** (☎ 361-881-1200, 2710 N Shoreline), across the bridge from downtown ($9, plus $3 parking; open daily). Guarding the aquarium is the 900-foot aircraft carrier **USS Lexington** (☎ 361-888-4873), permanently docked here and open daily as a museum ($9). Not quite as big is a Spanish replica of Columbus' *Niña*, usually moored in front of downtown.

Several budget motels on the beach provide basic accommodations in the $35-50 range. At night, grab dinner at *Padre Island Brewing Company (405 Chaparral)*, then walk down to *Dr Rockit's Blues Bar (709 Chaparral)*, featuring live music nightly.

PADRE ISLAND NATIONAL SEASHORE

One of the longest stretches of undeveloped seashore in the US, Padre Island has 70 miles of white-sand beaches backed by grassy dunes (admission $10 per vehicle). It's home to all the wildlife found elsewhere along the coast and then some.

The visitor center (☎ 361-949-8068) is on the beach just before the end of the paved road (open daily). A small grocery store has mainly convenience foods and drinking water, which is unavailable farther south. Hikers and campers who trek south on the island need 1 gallon of water per person per day, sunscreen, insect repellent and good shady hats.

The developed campground near the entrance costs $8 (no hookups). Camping on the beaches is free.

SOUTH PADRE ISLAND

Don't confuse the national seashore with South Padre Island, a condo-crammed resort comprising the island's southern 5 miles. SPI is separated from the north by Mansfield Channel and only accessible via the 2½-mile-long Queen Isabella Causeway from the mainland. South Padre Island is developed, but its beaches are clean, its water warm for much of the year and the locals ready to make your acquaintance. SPI is also the state's prime spring-break destination; it's infested with partying college students most of March (when all motels are booked solid at inflated prices).

For more information, contact the South Padre Island Visitor Center (☎ 956-761-6433, 800-767-2373, 600 Padre Blvd).

The Border

The Rio Grande (which Mexicans call the Río Bravo) forms Texas' international boundary with Mexico. The dramatic clash of Third World meeting First World is unique to the US/Mexico border. The border towns offer the visitor an easily accessible and fascinating bicultural experience.

In the east, near the Gulf of Mexico, the lush Rio Grande Valley is an agriculture center, where sweet citrus grows to Texas-size proportions. Farther west, the land becomes drier, eventually becoming desert. The twin towns of Laredo (US) and Nuevo Laredo (Mexico) comprise the Texas border's most popular tourist crossing.

LOS DOS LAREDOS

The Two Laredos are divided by the Rio Grande, but their economies are inseparable. Thousands of locals commute to work across the border, and long lines of trucks wait to cross in either direction.

More than 90% of the Laredo population is Latino, and most are bilingual. 'Spanglish,' the commonly used name for the local linguistic mixture, is the common tongue.

Orientation

Historic Laredo is a compact area on the Rio Grande's north bank. Across the river, Nuevo Laredo spreads out around Avenida Guerrero, the city's main street. For a small fee, walk across the border into Mexico on International Bridge No 1 (IB1), which leads you right onto the north end of Guerrero; Nuevo Laredo's main plaza is seven blocks down the street.

Information

The friendly Laredo Convention and Visitors Bureau (☎ 956-795-2200, 501 San

TEXAS

Augustín) is closed Sunday. The Nuevo Laredo tourist office (☎ 8-712-73-97), Calle Herrera at Avenida Juárez, is open daily.

Most *casas de cambio* (exchange offices) won't change traveler's checks, but most businesses will accept them if you want to buy something. Border formalities are as with any US entry point on your return.

A warning about water: In Mexico, don't drink it, and on the border, don't swim in it. The Rio Grande is horribly polluted. Keep purses and wallets guarded on both sides of the border. In Nuevo Laredo, be wary of walking down dark streets away from the tourist area at night.

Things to See & Do

Laredo's cobblestoned and oak-lined San Augustín Plaza dates to 1767; at its east is the Gothic Revival San Augustín Church. Nearby, the Republic of the Rio Grande Museum (☎ 956-727-3480, 1003 Zaragoza St) has excellent historical exhibits ($1; closed Mon and Tues).

Nuevo Laredo has an interesting market and many restaurants, bars and souvenir shops catering to day-trippers from the US – most of them accept US currency and quote prices in dollars.

Places to Stay & Eat

Lake Casa Blanca State Park (☎ 956-725-3826, 5102 Bob Bullock Loop) has tent sites ($6, plus $3 per person park-entrance fee). Most of Laredo's lodgings are along I-35, an inconvenient distance from downtown. The *Motel 6 (☎ 956-722-8133, 5920 San Bernardo Ave),* off I-35 exit 4, has rooms that are better than the chain's usual standard ($44/50 singles/doubles).

In Nuevo Laredo, *Hotel Romanos (☎ 8-172-23-91, Calle Dr Mier 2420),* just east of the plaza, has clean, air-conditioned doubles for $34. *Hotel Mesón Del Rey (☎ 8-712-63-60, Avenida Guerrero 718),* on the plaza, is comfortable and a good value ($43/48).

In Laredo, *907 Zaragoza (☎ 956-712-9825, 907 Zaragoza)* is the swank-du-jour of Laredo's fine-dining scene. In Nuevo Laredo, *Victoria 3020 (☎ 8-713-30-20, Victoria 3020),* two blocks south and one block west of IB1, is the town's nicest restaurant, specializing in elegantly prepared regional dishes ($13-27). The bars in town get rowdy at night – tequila's cheap and so are the crowds.

Getting There & Around

Greyhound (☎ 956-723-4324, 610 Salinas) offers service to San Antonio ($15-16; from 2¾ hours), Houston ($30; 6¾ hours) and Brownsville ($26; 5 hours).

Panhandle Plains

The Northwest Texas Panhandle is a land of sprawling cattle ranches, where people can still make a living on the back of a horse. Its landscape seems endlessly flat, punctuated only by utility poles and windmills, until a vast canyon materializes almost miragelike to play tricks on the horizon. The canyonlands, formed by eroding caprock (the layer of caliche, marl, chalk and gravel that lies beneath the plains), make for classic Western scenery.

LUBBOCK

Home of Texas Tech University and a star on the Texas wine scene, Lubbock is unquestionably the Panhandle's culture capital. 'The Hub City,' as it's known, enjoys a fun college-town atmosphere, good restaurants, an abundance of bars and nightclubs, several performing-arts venues and two excellent museums. Lubbock Convention & Visitors Bureau (☎ 806-747-5232, 800-692-4035,

W www.lubbocklegends.org, 1301 Broadway, Suite 200) has visitor information.

Things to See & Do

Lubbock was hometown to the late rocker Buddy Holly, killed in a 1959 plane crash. The **Buddy Holly Statue & Walk of Fame** at the Civic Center, 8th St at Ave Q, is surrounded by plaques honoring the rock pioneer and other famous West Texans, including Joe Ely, Roy Orbison, Bob Wills and Tanya Tucker. The **Buddy Holly Center** (☎ 806-767-2686, 1801 Ave G) houses a small gallery dedicated to Holly ($3). Among the exhibits: a couple of Holly's guitars, his trademark glasses – recovered from the crash site – and photos of Holly and his band. Visitors still leave guitar picks at **Buddy Holly's grave** in Lubbock City Cemetery, 31st and Teak Ave.

On Texas Tech's north side, two outstanding university-affiliated museums sit side by side. The **National Ranching Heritage Center** (☎ 806-742-0498, 3121 4th St) details ranch life on the High Plains since the late 18th century (free admission). Inside are historical photos and exhibits culled from the museum's huge collection of Western paraphernalia. Out back are 36 historic structures – everything from an opulent 1909 Queen Anne ranch house to a rickety sticks-and-sod pioneer cabin that would make the Big Bad Wolf think pork chops.

Next door is the superb **Museum of Texas Tech University** (☎ 806-742-2490), primarily an art museum but also a gallery dedicated to life-size castings of dinosaur skeletons (free admission; closed Mon). The permanent collection is heavy on art from the American West; the diverse rotating exhibitions have recently included West African sculpture and Andy Warhol prints. Presentation is superb. Budget plenty of time to view the extensive galleries.

Two of the state's top wineries are just south of town, and both offer free tours and tasting. The excellent **Llano Estacado Winery** (☎ 806-745-2258) is on the south side of FM 1585, east of US 87; try the Cellar Select cabernet. A little farther south, east from the US 87 Woodrow Rd exit, is Cap Rock Winery (☎ 806-863-2704), which has an impressive Mission-style headquarters; try the luscious Toscano Rosso.

Places to Stay & Eat

In Yellowhouse Canyon, *Buffalo Springs Lake* (☎ 806-747-3353) has tent sites for $10; take 50th St east off the loop 5 miles. *Lubbock RV Park* (☎ 806-747-2366), I-27 exit 9, has tent/RV sites for $12/18.

Texas Motor Inn (☎ 806-744-0444, 2121 Amarillo Hwy), $26/36, and *El Tejas Motel* (☎ 806-763-9343, 1000 N Ave Q), $25/40, are among Lubbock's cheapest sleeps. Both are north of town off I-27. *Motel 6* (☎ 806-745-5541, 909 66th St), three exits south of downtown on the interstate, is above average for the chain ($37/43). Three ritzier places – La Quinta, Holiday Inn and Sheraton Four Points – lie along Ave Q between 4th St and Broadway.

In the Depot District, *Hub City Brewery* (☎ 806-747-1535, 1807 Buddy Holly Ave) offers good food and great beer. For barbecue, head north to the *County Line Smokehouse & Grill* (☎ 806-763-6001), which sits on expansive, parklike grounds out near the airport – easily the best atmosphere of any place in town. Take the first airport exit and turn left, or take University all the way north to the restaurant's big billboard and turn right. For a splurge, visitors can can-can over to *Chez Suzette* (☎ 806-795-6796, 4423 50th St) for upscale French fare.

Entertainment

For complete entertainment information, pick up the free monthly *Caprock Chronicle*, available all over town.

The delightful Depot District, centered around Buddy Holly Ave at 19th St, is the town's premier nightlife center. Here you'll find a sports bar, a daiquiri bar, a martini bar, a brewpub, a mellow cocktail lounge and several big dance clubs.

In other areas, places to check out include *Jazz* (☎ 806-799-2124, 3703 C 19th St), which regularly serves its namesake music along with Louisiana Cajun cuisine; *Cap Rock Cafe* (☎ 806-784-0300, 3405 34th St), an indoor/outdoor beer bar full of sweet young thangs and older oglers; and *Midnight Rodeo* (☎ 806-745-2813, 7301 S University), a large nightspot featuring both country and rock music and dancing.

For more highbrow entertainment, attend a performance of *Lubbock Symphony Orchestra* (☎ 806-762-1688), *Ballet Lubbock* (☎ 806-785-3090) or *Lubbock*

TEXAS

Community Theater (☎ 806-741-1640).
Many events are presented on campus; for
information call the campus box office
(☎ 806-742-3610).

Getting There & Away

From the unlucky depot at 1313 13th St
(☎ 806-765-6641), buses go to Amarillo
($22; from 2½ hours), Dallas ($52; from 8
hours) and San Antonio ($58; from 9
hours). The optimistically named Lubbock
International Airport (☎ 806-775-3126,
Ⓦ www.flylia.com) is north of town at 5401
N Martin Luther King and served by Southwest, Continental, American Eagle and
Delta Air Lines.

NORTH OF LUBBOCK

Near Amarillo, the former heart of fabled
Route 66, you can still get your kicks at
Cadillac Ranch. This salute to the Route features 10 Cadillacs buried hood first in a
wheat field off I-40 exit 60 (Arnot Rd, 16
miles west of Amarillo).

South of Amarillo in Canyon, the huge
and superb **Panhandle Plains Historical
Museum** (☎ 806-651-2244, 2401 4th Ave)
features exhibits on the petroleum industry,
pioneer life and the cultural history of the
southern Great Plains ($4, free Sun).

East of Canyon 12 miles on Hwy 217, at
Palo Duro Canyon State Park (☎ 806-488-
2227), the Prairie Dog Town Fork of the
Red River carves its way spectacularly
through the caprock. A paved road leads
down into the canyon to great camping,
horseback riding (rentals available), hiking
and mountain biking – though it's dang hot
in summer (day-use $3 per person).

If you're heading toward Dallas, check
out **Caprock Canyons State Park** (☎ 806-
455-1492) near Quitaque. It's more of the
same beautiful canyon scenery as at Palo
Duro, with a lake, bison herd and a 64-mile
hike/bike trail along an abandoned railroad
right-of-way. In nearby Turkey, the free **Bob
Wills Museum** (☎ 806-423-1253) is a shrine
to the King of Western Swing.

West Texas

In many ways, the western reaches of Texas
have more in common with both New
Mexico and old Mexico than with the rest of

Texas. El Paso is closer to Santa Fe than to
Austin, and Spanish is spoken here as often
as English. The frontier spirit seems very
much alive in these wide-open desertlands,
which hold two of the state's biggest, wildest
parks: Guadalupe Mountains National Park
and Big Bend National Park.

Note that El Paso and the rest of far-west
Texas are in the Mountain Time Zone, one
hour behind the rest of the state.

GUADALUPE MOUNTAINS
NATIONAL PARK

Guadalupe Peak (8749 feet) is the highest
point in Texas, and McKittrick Canyon has
the state's best fall foliage. If you seek high-
desert splendor, this park is a must. The
park headquarters and visitor center
(☎ 915-828-3251) are at Pine Springs, off US
62/180. Admission is free; open daily. No
gasoline, food or beverages are available.

The park has more than 80 miles of trails,
from short nature walks to strenuous treks.
The most popular day hike is McKittrick
Canyon Trail, especially scenic in fall, when
the hardwoods turn color. The strenuous
trail to Guadalupe Peak is 8½ miles
roundtrip and gains 3000 feet in elevation.

Ten backcountry campsites dot the park.
Overnight hikers must get a permit (free) at
either Pine Springs visitor center or Dog
Canyon ranger station on the park's north
side, reached via New Mexico Hwy 137;
both places have primitive campgrounds
($8). No water is available in the backcoun-
try. Silver Stage Lines (☎ 915-778-0162) runs
a shuttle past the park.

HUECO TANKS STATE
HISTORICAL PARK

About 32 miles east of El Paso off US
62/180, the Hueco Tanks have attracted
humans and animals for thousands of years.
Three small granite mountains here are
pocked with depressions *(hueco* is Spanish
for 'hollow') that hold rainwater, creating
an oasis in the barren desert. Wildlife is
abundant, and so is evidence of human
habitation in the form of pictographs, pot-
sherds and bits of worked flint. The 860-acre
park is also a magnet for rock climbers. Free
guided pictograph tours are offered, as are
bouldering tours and bird-watching tours.

To minimize human impact on the fragile
park (☎ 915-857-1135), a daily visitor quota

is enforced; call ahead to check status. Day-use fee is $4. Twenty campsites are available ($9-11), and reservations are suggested. You can also camp down the road at Pete's Country Store, a longstanding climbers' haven. Silver Stage Lines (☎ 915-778-0162) runs a shuttle from El Paso to the park for $20 each way per person.

EL PASO

Isolated at the state's far-western tip – farther west than most of New Mexico – El Paso has little in common with the rest of Texas. Without the bounties of big oil or high tech, El Paso seems disproportionately poor for a city its size. Commercial buildings – from storefronts to skyscrapers – sit vacant, and attempts to attract new business are hampered by the city's lack of a marketable identity. Nevertheless, most El Pasoans seem content and proud of what the city's got: an unpretentious, bicultural society with a strong independent streak.

Across the Rio Grande lies Ciudad Juárez (population approaching two million), Mexico's fourth-largest city. Though the US Border Patrol tries to keep the two countries neatly separated, Mexican culture has always been dominant in El Paso. As about 80% of the residents are Latino, Spanish is the default language. You don't find Tex-Mex food here – it's Mexican food.

History

For centuries, the broad pass for which the city is named has been traversed by an anthropologist's laundry list of peoples.

The years between 1881 (when the railroad arrived) and 1920 might well be called the city's glory days. El Paso became a major rail hub, bringing wealth and urban sophistication. One noted architect of the era, Henry C Trost, designed and built many exceptional structures downtown, most of which still stand. The railroads also brought some of the Wild West's most colorful characters to town: Gunfighter John Wesley Hardin lived and died here, and Mexican revolutionary Pancho Villa holed up in El Paso for a time.

Orientation

The Franklin Mountains pin the downtown area against the border and cleave the rest of the city into eastern and western sides.

The airport is on the east side, while the University of Texas at El Paso (UTEP) and the New Mexico border lie on the west. The two sides are connected by I-10, which squeezes between the mountains and downtown, and by scenic Transmountain Rd, which traverses the Franklins farther north. The soul of El Paso lies right downtown by the border.

Information

The El Paso Visitors Center (☎ 915-534-0600, 800-351-6024, Ⓦ www.visitelpaso.com) is on Santa Fe St at the Civic Center (open daily). El Paso Public Library (☎ 915-544-6772, 501 N Oregon) offers free Internet access. Adelante (☎ 915-533-9875) is a bilingual gay-and-lesbian information and help line. *StantonStreet.com* is an excellent online magazine about El Paso. *Bridge,* the quarterly published by the Bridge Center for Contemporary Art, is a fascinating read for its articles on border art and culture.

Things to See & Do

The historic heart of El Paso is **San Jacinto Plaza**, which once held a pond containing live alligators. Today a sculpture by El Paso native Luis Jimenez memorializes the former reptilian residents.

Another Jimenez sculpture, *Vaquero,* stands nearby in front of the **El Paso Museum of Art** (☎ 915-532-1707, 1 Arts Festival Plaza). The museum holds a permanent collection of European, Mexican and American art and presents about 15 rotating exhibits annually ($1; closed Monday). Between the plaza and the museum, the windows of **Ruly's Barber Shop**, on the north side of Mills Ave, tell a capsule history of El Paso, with photos of Pancho Villa, John Wesley Hardin, the alligators and other characters from the city's past. Hardin and other early notables are buried in historic **Concordia Cemetery**, near the I-10/US 54 interchange.

The **Wilderness Park Museum** (☎ 915-755-4332, 4301 Transmountain Rd), on the east side of the Franklins, holds early Native American pottery and artifacts, as well as great dioramas depicting the lifestyles of the region's early peoples ($1; closed Mon).

Franklin Mountains State Park (☎ 915-566-6441) is a 24,000-acre preserve offering day-use ($3) picnicking, hiking, mountain biking and rock climbing, as well as camping in a limited number of primitive, tents-only sites ($8). The park's main entrance is near the bottom of Transmountain Rd on El Paso's west side.

For a sweeping panorama across El Paso and sprawling Juárez, take the **Wyler Aerial Tramway** (☎ 915-566-6622, 1700 McKinley) to the top of 5632-foot Ranger Peak ($7; closed Tues-Wed). Acrophobes get a comparable view from the turnout along **Scenic Dr**, right above downtown. Go at night when the sea of lights is breathtaking.

Die-hard history buffs might enjoy the lower valley's Mission Trail, a driving route southeast of town that connects several early Spanish missions. **Mission Ysleta** (originally built in 1691) is on the Tigua reservation (take I-10 east to the Zaragoza exit, turn right and continue 3 miles), where it stands in bizarre juxtaposition to the tribe's modern **Speaking Rock Casino** (☎ 915-860-7777). Also here, the **Tigua Cultural Center** (☎ 915-859-5287, 305 Yaya Lane) explains tribal history and hosts traditional dance performances on weekends (closed Mon). Follow signs east to **Socorro Mission** (1691) and **San Elizario Chapel** (1877). For information on the missions, call the Mission Trail Association (☎ 915-534-0677).

When you've finished exploring El Paso, cross the border to **Ciudad Juárez, Mexico**. The El Paso-Juarez Trolley Co (☎ 915-544-0061, 1 Civic Center Plaza) operates the Border Jumper, a trolley looping hourly from El Paso Civic Center through Juárez and back, making 11 stops en route. The $12 ticket allows you to get off and on at will. Or you can just walk across the Santa Fe St bridge (25¢ for pedestrians) into Mexico. The bridge leads right onto Av Juárez, the city's main tourist strip. Stroll down Juárez to the vibrant cathedral area and back, passing restaurants and shops galore. Don't forget your passport.

Places to Stay

Tent camping is available at Franklin Mountains State Park (see Things to See & Do, above). **Roadrunner RV Park** (☎ 915-598-4469, 1212 Lafayette Dr), east of downtown at the I-10 Yarbrough Dr exit (exit 28B), has RV sites ($22), tent sites ($18), a pool and a playground.

The vintage 1922 **Gardner Hotel/El Paso International Hostel** (☎ 915-532-3661, Ⓦ www.gardnerhotel.com, 311 E Franklin Ave) has a great downtown location, comfortable facilities and a super-friendly staff. Ask Manager Joe Nebhan to point you to some of his favorite area haunts. The hostel is affiliated with Hostels of America. Bunks cost $15; hotel rooms cost $22/33 singles/doubles for shared bath, $43 for private bath. Legend has it that Depression-era gangster John Dillinger stayed here shortly before his capture in Tucson, Arizona.

A reasonable runner-up choice would be **Budget Lodge Motel** (☎ 915-533-6821, 1301 N Mesa St), which offers rooms for $25/29 and has a coffee shop. Farther out Mesa, the **Mesa Inn** (☎ 915-532-7911, 4151 N Mesa) charges $25.

For a splurge, head to **Hilton Camino Real** (☎ 915-534-3000, 101 S El Paso St), a beautifully modernized historic hotel downtown (rooms from $99). Even if you don't stay there, it's worth having a drink at the hotel's stunning (and stunningly overpriced) Dome Bar.

Places to Eat

Fine-dining honors go to trendy **Cafe Central** (☎ 915-545-2233, 1 Texas Court), across from the Hilton Camino Real (behind the Fray Garcia statue). Its European-bistro styling complements a creative nouvelle menu with regional accents (reservations suggested; closed Sun).

Get a Mexican breakfast and a car wash at **H&H Coffee Shop** (701 E Yandell Ave), a tiny hole-in-the-wall with character. **The Tap** (408 E San Antonio Ave) is a classic downtown dive serving delicious Mexican cuisine. More traditional are **La Hacienda Restaurant** (1720 W Paisano), in a historic ranch house on the river, and **Kiki's** (2719 N Piedras Ave), which perennially wins Best of El Paso awards.

Somewhat out of town but locally recommended for steaks and atmosphere is the **Cattleman's Steakhouse** (☎ 915-544-3200), at Indian Cliffs Ranch. It is a great place to watch the sunset from the veranda. Drive 20 miles east of town on I-10 to the Fabens exit (exit 49), then drive north 5 more miles.

Entertainment

For extensive entertainment listings, pick up the free weekly *What's Up*, the free monthly *El Paso Scene* or the Friday *Tiempo* supplement to the *El Paso Times*.

You can also drop by the **Bridge Center for Contemporary Art** (☎ 915-532-6707, 1 Union Fashion Center, Suite B), at Stanton St and San Antonio Ave. It's a gallery/bookstore/coffeehouse/performance venue, and director David Romo can tell you everything about the El Paso art and music scene. Live entertainment – from open mikes to jam sessions to drum circles – takes place here most nights.

The **El Paso Symphony** (☎ 915-532-3776) performs at Abraham Chavez Theatre in the Civic Center September through April ($7.50-25).

Cincinnati St between Mesa and Stanton, near UTEP, draws students and others to **Dolce Vita's** (205 Cincinnati Ave), El Paso's coolest coffeehouse; the **Cincinnati Club** (207 Cincinnati), a character-filled bar that touts its house-special chili; and **Fellini's Film Cafe** (☎ 915-544-5420, 220 Cincinnati), which rents and screens art films and serves sandwiches and coffee drinks.

Getting There & Around

El Paso International Airport (☎ 915-772-4271) is 8 miles northeast of downtown. Bus No 33 ($1) runs between the airport and downtown. A cab or shuttle to downtown costs $15-17. Try Southwest Shuttle (☎ 915-771-6661), which requires reservations, or United Independent Cab (☎ 915-590-8294). Car rental companies at the airport include Budget (☎ 915-778-5287) and Dollar (☎ 915-778-5445).

Greyhound (☎ 915-532-2365, 200 W San Antonio Ave) has service to Las Cruces ($10; 1 hour), Albuquerque ($38; 7 hours), Dallas ($57-63; from 11 hours) and San Antonio ($82; 10 hours).

Sun Metro (☎ 915-533-3333) is the city-wide bus service. Incredibly, the company offers no systemwide route map. Get individual route schedules at the bus information booth, across from San Jacinto Plaza on the corner of Oregon and Main Ave, or inside the Jack in the Box across the street. Standard fare is $1. Two trolley routes transport folks around downtown's historic areas (25¢).

Amtrak's *Sunset Limited* stops at Union Depot (☎ 915-545-2247, 700 San Francisco Ave).

BIG BEND NATIONAL PARK

This park is vast enough for a lifetime of discovery but has enough roads and trails to permit short-term visitors to see a lot in two to three days. Its diverse geography makes for an amazing variety of critters: mountain lions, black bears, collared peccaries and white-tailed deer, as well as 56 species of reptiles and amphibians and more than 100 bird species. Big Bend Birding Expeditions (☎ 915-371-2356) offers area bird-watching trips. Spring and fall are the best times to visit. Summer is scorching. Spring means moderate temperatures and lots of wildflowers (and crowds), while fall is a great time for river-running. Winter storms bring snow and freezing temperatures.

The main visitor center (☎ 915-477-2251) is along the main park road, 29 miles from the Persimmon Gap entrance and 26 miles from the Maverick entrance at Study Butte (open daily). Admission is $10 per car, $5 for bicyclists and pedestrians. Near the park, the towns of Study Butte, Terlingua and Lajitas – with a total population of a few hundred at most – are outfitting centers. Together, they offer a good selection of visitor services.

The park's 110 miles of paved road and 150 miles of dirt road make scenic driving the most popular activity. But 150 miles of **hiking trails** also web the park; the Chisos Mountains have the most. Several short hikes offer quick introductions to the Chihuahua Desert and Rio Grande. Free backcountry permits, available at all visitor centers, are required for **backpacking** and camping.

Several companies offer guided **river trips** in and around Big Bend. Try Terlingua's Far Flung Adventures (☎ 915-371-2489, 800-359-4138).

Undeveloped campgrounds at **Rio Grande Village**, **Chisos Basin** and **Cottonwood**, near Castolon, have tent sites for $7. Rio Grande Village has RV sites for $14.50. **Chisos Mountain Lodge** (☎ 915-477-2291) is good for accommodations and so-so for food. Its cottages ($84) sleep three; No 103 has the best view in Texas. Outside the park, Terlingua, Lajitas and Alpine all have lodgings. It's best to bring in your own food from outside the park.

No public transportation serves the park. Amtrak's *Sunset Limited* stops in Alpine, and Trans-Pecos Transport (☎ 915-837-0100, 877-388-1776) offers shuttles from there to the park.

NORTH OF BIG BEND

Several interesting towns lie between Big Bend and I-10. **Marfa** is home to the Chinati Foundation, an art center for large-scale sculpture. The town is also known for the unexplained 'Marfa lights,' which flash across the desert sky; even Scully and Mulder don't know what causes them.

Fort Davis (elevation 5,000 feet) is the highest town in Texas. It's home to McDon- ald Observatory, which hosts occasional public star parties, and to Blue Mountain Vineyards, which makes a stellar cabernet. **Balmorhea**, up on I-10, has a small state park around a huge spring-fed swimming pool.

Alpine, a pretty college town with a good art scene, coffeehouse and museum, could make a nice base for Big Bend explorations. Farther east is **Marathon**, an artsy hamlet home to the incongruously upscale *Gage Hotel* (☎ 915-386-4205, 800-884-4243). North of Marathon on I-10 is **Fort Stockton**, where backpack-toting budgeteers can hole up at *Comanche Motel and Hostel* (☎ 915-336-8447, 1301 E Dickenson Blvd); hostel bunks cost $14.

Great Plains

Great Plains

Ridiculed as a flat 'fly-over zone' and raced through by travelers heading somewhere else, the Great Plains is likely the USA's least understood (or thought about) region. Those who do venture off the interstates – and onto pink roads of quartzite or old Route 66 – find there's more than meets the eye at 75mph. Each of the Great Plains' seven states – Missouri, Oklahoma, Kansas, Iowa, Nebraska, South Dakota and North Dakota – are home to diverse bumps in the landscape: forested Ozarks, rugged Wichitas, grass-bearded Sand Hills, rock-solid canyons, soft loess hills, badlands and sacred Black Hills.

Even the noted farmlands can be varied. Along Kansas' wheat-lined I-70, the Plains quickly roll into something new. If a horizon seems short, detour toward it and discover a canyon dropping out of nowhere.

No guest of the Great Plains can escape its history – this is where cowboys became cowboys, 60 million buffalo ran wild, pioneers blazed trails west and the heroic Plains Indians fought overpowering forces.

Stories are also told by plugged oil wells and abandoned farmhouses. In recent years, falling populations have brought back the 'frontier' to some areas of the western Plains, where you'll find just one smiling face per square mile, if that. Those proud folk who stuck it out here have faced droughts, dust bowls, tornadoes, insects, battles, reservations and – for family farmers – corporations. A South Dakotan might feel no real bond with an Oklahoman, but both will tribute the 'Great Plains' by branding their airlines, tractor dealership or large-animal veterinarian clinic with the name.

Most visitors to the region will stop for St Louis' Arch, Kansas City's barbecue or South Dakota's Mt Rushmore. Others are curious to see the great Mississippi and Missouri Rivers, or where movies like *Field of Dreams* were filmed and TV shows like *Gunsmoke* were set. Some travelers stop in 'corntowns' to chat with ballcap-wearing diners or watch a rodeo in the land it was made.

But if even the region's most celebrated tourists, Lewis and Clark, were just passing through, why should you stop? Because the Great Plains' greatest gift to travelers isn't in the destination, it's in the discoveries made when traveling without one.

Highlights

- South Dakota's Black Hills – gigantic sculptures of four US presidents and Crazy Horse
- Badlands – ruggedly beautiful landscapes in the Dakotas and Nebraska
- St Louis & Kansas City – cool blues and jazz, hickory-smoked barbecue

History

The first Plains Indians were paleo-Indian nomadic groups, known to have hunted mammoths in the region 10,000 years ago. About 1500 years ago, Mississippi cultures began practicing horticulture, fashioning pottery and establishing sophisticated cities, such as Cahokia (in present-day Illinois). Around 500 BC, Woodland cultures set up smaller cities, such as Effigy (in present-day Iowa).

The Spaniards introduced the horse around AD 1630, and its use reached the far ends of the Plains by the mid-18th century. Increased mobility led to complete cultural changes – buffalo meat became the staple, the tipi and travois (A-shaped sledge) characterized a new hunting lifestyle, and tribes practiced the 'sun dance.'

In the early 1540s, Francisco Vásquez de Coronado wandered into present-day Kansas unsuccessfully looking for Quivira, a legendary city of gold. French explorers, following the Mississippi and Missouri Rivers, later claimed a huge region west of the Mississippi for France. It passed to Spain in 1763, was returned to France in 1800, and was sold to the USA in the 1803 Louisiana Purchase, which included the seven states in this chapter. President Thomas Jefferson then sent Meriwether Lewis and William Clark to explore the new lands from 1804 to 1806.

The prairie west of the Mississippi River was later settled in waves. The acquisition of land west of the Continental Divide made territorial expansion to the Pacific Ocean the USA's new goal, and economic depression in the late 1830s spurred the first immigrants toward it. The Santa Fe Trail became the first corridor of commerce between Missouri and Santa Fe (then part of Mexico). Meanwhile, the settlers' hunger for land forced the Indian tribes westward, often forcibly, as in the infamous resettlement of the Five Civilized Tribes via the 1838–9 'Trail of Tears' (see the Oklahoma section).

Between 1840 and 1870, more than 400,000 people pushed their way along the Oregon Trail, which went up Nebraska's Platte River and over the divide. In 1846–7 about 70,000 Mormons took their own trail, from Nauvoo, Illinois, to present-day Salt Lake City. The Pony Express mail route (1860–61) rushed between St Joseph, Missouri, and Sacramento, California.

This mass migration forced Native Americans off their lands, while the buffalo hunters destroyed their livelihood. Land rushes following the 1862 Homestead Act and the discovery of gold in the sacred Black Hills in 1874 spelled the end of tradi-

tional ways for the Plains Indians – despite a heroic resistance (see the South Dakota section).

Meanwhile a new mythology was in the making – that of the cowboy. Cattle drives along the Chisholm Trail (1867–80); wild towns such as Dodge City, Deadwood and Abilene; the Range Wars of the 1880s; gamblers and gunfighters; train robberies; and a practical means of dress for long-distance horseback riding were all contributing factors.

At the same time, the railroad expanded the possibilities for agriculture and the movement of produce, and open prairie was transformed into farms and towns, surrounded by barbed-wire fences, windmills and barns. Slowly the Plains were incorporated into the USA, first as territories, then as states.

The early 20th century was witness to an oil boom, but by the mid-1930s the neglect and mismanagement of the prairies resulted in a lot of topsoil being blown away during the dust bowl, especially in Oklahoma. Improved land management and environmental controls have enabled the evolution of thriving agribusiness throughout the Plains and industrial growth in the larger cities.

Today the Plains are the breadbasket of the country, but vast, remote areas in its west are dying off, evident in Kansas' 6000 ghost towns and falling populations in 70% of the Plains. Academics Frank and Deborah Popper have argued than an ailing chunk of the Plains (about the size of Montana) should not be farmed but returned to nature – for prairie and buffalo restoration and ecotourism. Some Plains farmers have started to warm up to the alternative, as buffalo numbers (and buffalo meat sales) have risen beyond expectation.

Geography

The Plains are not completely flat but rise gradually from the Mississippi River to the Rocky Mountains. Much of the terrain is low, rolling hills, with the Ozark Plateau and Oklahoma's Ouachitas rising in the southeast, and the Black Hills rising in western South Dakota. One aberration is the convoluted, below-the-plains badlands of the Dakotas. The seven states covered in this chapter span roughly 650 miles east to west, 1000 miles north to south.

GREAT PLAINS

GREAT PLAINS

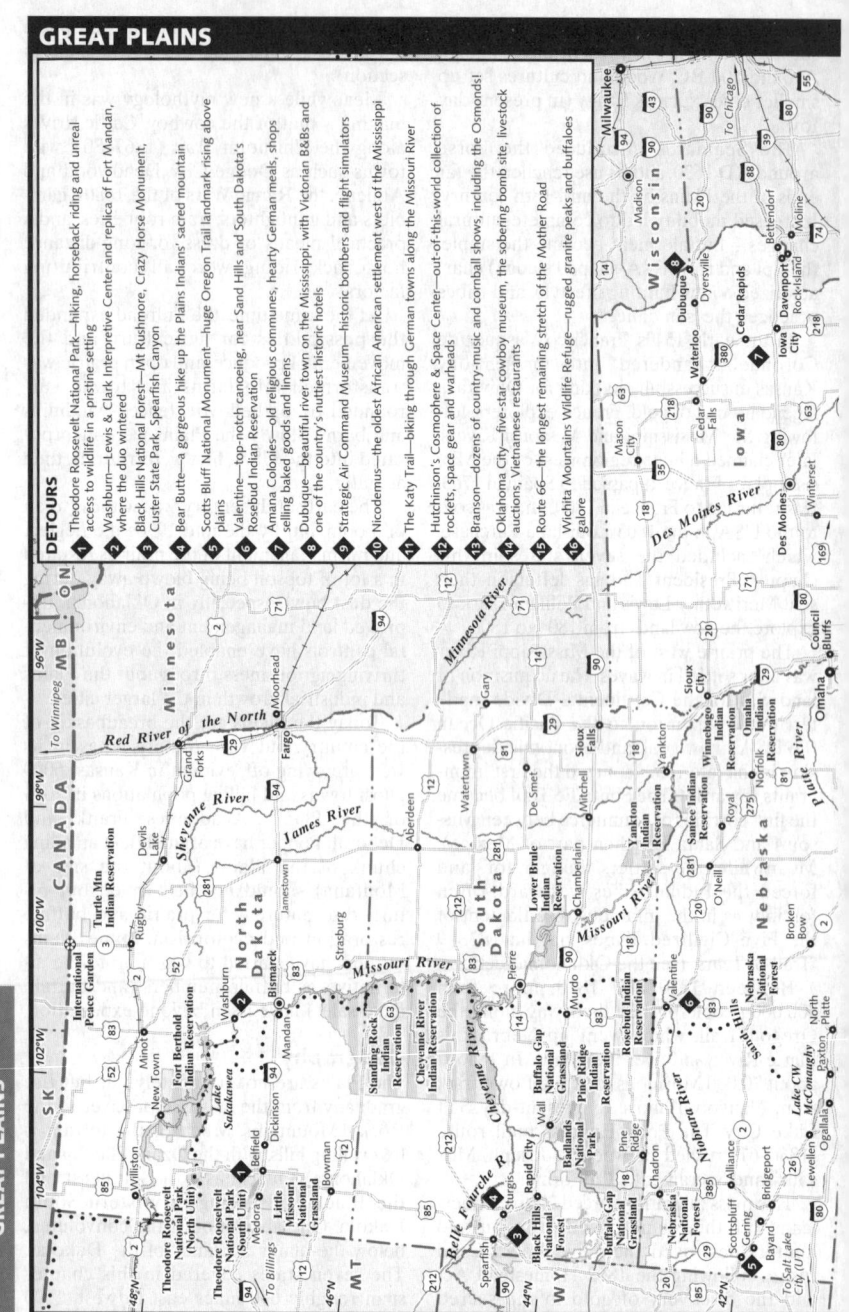

DETOURS

1. Theodore Roosevelt National Park—hiking, horseback riding and unreal access to wildlife in a pristine setting

2. Washburn—Lewis & Clark Interpretive Center and replica of Fort Mandan, where the duo wintered

3. Black Hills National Forest—Mt Rushmore, Crazy Horse Monument, Custer State Park, Spearfish Canyon

4. Bear Butte—a gorgeous hike up the Plains Indians' sacred mountain

5. Scotts Bluff National Monument—huge Oregon Trail landmark rising above plains

6. Valentine—top-notch canoeing, near Sand Hills and South Dakota's Rosebud Indian Reservation

7. Amana Colonies—old religious communes, hearty German meals, shops selling baked goods and linens

8. Dubuque—beautiful river town on the Mississippi, with Victorian B&Bs and one of the country's nuttiest historic hotels

9. Strategic Air Command Museum—historic bombers and flight simulators

10. Nicodemus—the oldest African American settlement west of the Mississippi

11. The Katy Trail—biking through German towns along the Missouri River

12. Hutchinson's Cosmosphere & Space Center—out-of-this-world collection of rockets, space gear and warheads

13. Branson—dozens of country-music and cornball shows, including the Osmonds!

14. Oklahoma City—five-star cowboy museum, the sobering bomb site, livestock auctions, Vietnamese restaurants

15. Route 66—the longest remaining stretch of the Mother Road

16. Wichita Mountains Wildlife Refuge—rugged granite peaks and buffaloes galore

GREAT PLAINS

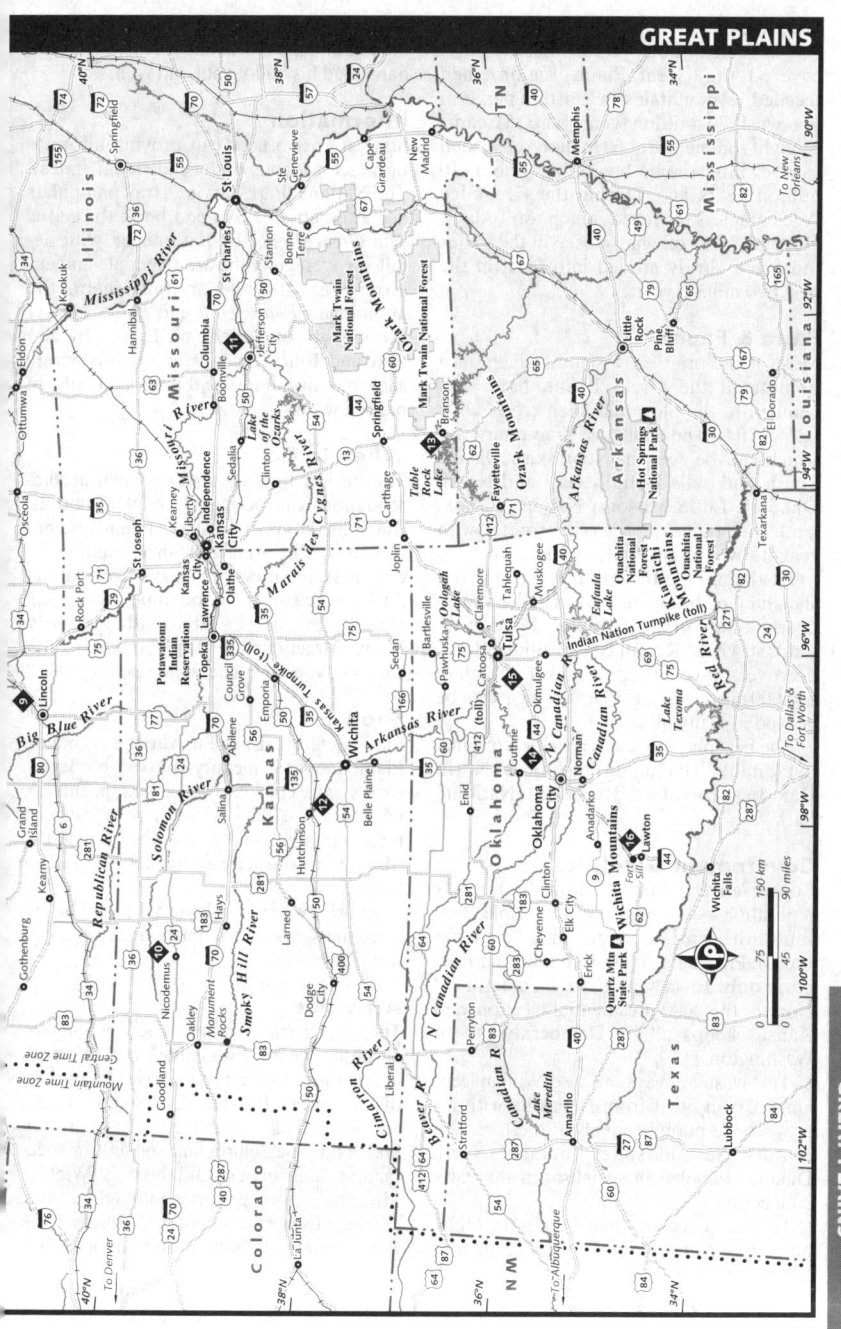

Geology

For a half-billion years, shallow seas covered the Great Plains region, then receded as mountains began to emerge in the west 70 million years ago. Streams brought sediments for 60 million years, then carved into them, beginning about 10 million years ago. During the Great Ice Age, glaciers covered much of today's Dakotas. Most of what we see in the Plains today has slowly eroded into form in the past two million years.

Flora & Fauna

Most of the prairie grasslands, which once dominated the Great Plains, have succumbed to the plow and alien crops. Only 0.1% of its original tallgrass prairie survives, which can be seen in Nebraska's Oglala, South Dakota's Buffalo Gap and North Dakota's Little Missouri National Grassland. The original prairie is interpreted with zeal at Iowa's Neal Smith NWR.

In the mid-19th century, the wanton slaughter of bison (usually called buffalo) nearly killed off all 60 million. Mere thousands survived. Recent conservation efforts, however, have brought back more than 150,000 bison to the Plains, which can be viewed in many places.

The best place to see the prairie's original inhabitants (including bison) is North Dakota's Theodore Roosevelt National Park.

Government & Politics

Conservative politics reaffirm the region's reputation as the buckle of the 'Bible Belt' (note the anti-abortion signs in some states). Five states have Republican governors; only Iowa voted for Democrat Al Gore in the 2000 presidential election; and Kansas keeps all its Democrats out of Washington, DC.

This wasn't always the case. William Jennings Bryan burst from Nebraska with his progressive populist ideals in the late 19th century. Several states (notably North Dakota) dabbled in socialism in the early 20th century.

Half a dozen football heroes in Oklahoma and Nebraska now play ball in suits and ties in the US Congress.

Missouri's 2000 US Senatorial election was a bizarre one: Just weeks before the election, Democrat governor Mel Carnahan died in a plane crash. His wife, Jean Carnahan, filled his ballot spot and won.

Information

State tourist offices can provide information (see sections under individual states). The National Park Service's trail pamphlets are indispensable. A good book to read is *The Great Plains,* by Ian Frazier, with detailed coverage of the area's people and environment. If you can find them, the anthologies *Plains Folk* and *Plains Folk II* (University of Oklahoma Press), by Jim Hoy and Tom Isern, give glory to concrete silos, rodent hunters and discarded balls of barbed wire.

When to Go

The busiest time is summer, when accommodations can be heavily booked and attractions choked; it's usually humid and hot (about 90°F). Spring and fall are mild in the central Plains area, with an average of about 50°F, so these are good times to travel. Winters are harsh, often with blizzards. Many attractions are closed, travel is difficult, and you need adequate clothing.

Food

Like beef? Meat in all its varieties is big on Plains menus – hickory-smoked barbecue, strip steaks, chicken-fried steaks, prime rib, meatloaf. You'll find a fair share of Mexican restaurants in some of the southern states. Many Native American sites cook up Indian tacos.

Prairie oysters (or lamb fries) are an interesting snack, if you fancy deep-fried calf testicles.

Activities

These seven states offer a variety of things to do outdoors, from watching sandhill cranes in Nebraska to bicycling across Missouri on the Katy Trail. In South Dakota's Badlands and Black Hills, adventurous travelers can hike, bike, rock climb and spelunk in spectacular landscapes. Oklahoma's Wichita Mountains make for challenging rock climbs. Missouri's water-filled Bonne Terre mine is open for scuba diving! Canoeists will be giddy on Nebraska's Niobrara River. Wanna-be cowboys and cowgirls can learn to rope and ride on North Dakota's (and other states') ranches, or take square dance or two-step lessons in many spots. In winter, hiking trails become tracks for cross-country skiing or snowmobiling.

Getting There & Around
Air The region's main airport is Lambert-St Louis International (see the St Louis section), but it has few direct international flights. Foreign visitors may be better off getting a connection from O'Hare Airport in Chicago.

Bus The carless brave won't be able to see much of the Plains beyond the major highways. Greyhound buses work the interstates except for South Dakota's I-90, which is served by Jack Rabbit (see the Rapid City section), and I-29 between Sioux Falls, South Dakota, and Fargo, North Dakota.

Train A few Amtrak routes cross the Plains states (mostly at night):

Empire Builder – between Chicago and Seattle, Washington, via North Dakota (including Fargo)

California Zephyr – between Chicago and San Francisco via Iowa (including Osceola, south of Des Moines) and Nebraska (including Omaha and Lincoln)

Southwest Chief – between Chicago and Los Angeles via Missouri (including St Louis and Kansas City) and Kansas (including Newton, north of Wichita)

Ann Rutledge – daily between Chicago and Kansas City (including St Louis)

Texas Eagle and *State House* – daily between Chicago and St Louis

Kansas City Mule – daily between St Louis and Kansas City

Heartland Flyer – daily between Fort Worth, Texas, and Oklahoma City

Car & Motorcycle For traveling in the Plains states, driving sure beats public transport. Six interstate highways cross the Plains states going east-west; north-south routes are less developed and less direct. I-44 has been built over and around the original Route 66 across Missouri and Oklahoma, but substantial stretches survive (see the Oklahoma section). US 50, the last surviving transcontinental route that is not a modern interstate, crosses Kansas and Missouri. The Great River Rd is a well-signed

network of roads and highways that runs along the Mississippi River.

Missouri

Missouri is the Great Plains' most consistently scenic state, as it has a good mix of urban attractions, wilderness areas, the Mississippi and Missouri Rivers, and Branson – the Ozarks' answer to Nashville.

Historically the Gateway to the West, St Louis is known for its Arch and its blues. A number of musical legends – Chuck Berry, Tina Turner and Miles Davis – got their start here in the 'Home of the Blues.' Kansas City is known for its barbecue, fountains and jazz. It was another important launching pad for many great jazz performers, including Count Basie and Charlie Parker.

The plateaus, hills and valleys of the Ozarks are great recreational areas. Historic river towns possess their own charm. There have been many jokes about Missouri's nickname, the 'Show Me State.' It's based on the legendary skepticism.

History
The junction of the Mississippi and Missouri Rivers was once an extremely fertile region, so it isn't surprising that Cahokia, the most sophisticated pre-Columbian Native American civilization north of Mexico, was founded in the area. It is estimated that the Mississippi people lived in this city of mounds (just over the river in present-day Illinois) from AD 700 to 1500.

The French missionaries Louis Jolliet and Père Jacques Marquette descended the Mississippi from the north in 1643. In 1720 the first lead ore (galena) mine was built. Fur trappers followed, establishing outposts – Ste Genevieve in 1725, St Louis in 1764.

Missouri was organized as a territory in 1812, and immigration increased markedly. The first steamboat reached St Louis in 1816. Missouri was admitted to the Union as a slave state in 1821, per the Missouri Compromise (which permitted slavery in Missouri but prohibited it in any other part of Louisiana Territory above the 36°30' parallel). In 1846, Dred Scott, a slave from Missouri, brought suit on grounds that temporary residence in free territory released

Missouri

Nickname: Show Me State

Population: 5,595,200 (16th)

Area: 69,710 sq miles (21st)

Admitted to Union: August 10, 1821 (24th)

Capital city: Jefferson City (population 34,900)

Other cities: Kansas City (441,600), St Louis (348,200), Springfield (142,900)

Birthplace of: Samuel Clemens (Mark Twain), Jesse James, George Washington Carver, Harry S Truman, TS Eliot, singer Sheryl Crow, author Maya Angelou

Famous for: Gateway Arch; Budweiser; first ice-cream cone, hot dog and iced tea (1904)

him from slavery. A series of courts ruled against him, ending in the Supreme Court – the decision further divided Missouri's pro- and antislavery factions. By the time the Civil War began, feelings were particularly bitter, especially along the Missouri-Kansas border. One of the Civil War's fiercest battles was fought on Missouri soil on August 10, 1861, at Wilson's Creek.

Following the war, the state prospered with increased westward expansion and railroad development. Local ore deposits fueled manufacturing companies, and Kansas City and St Louis emerged as important industrial centers.

Missouri last hit the world stage in 1993, when massive efforts prevented flooding of low-lying towns such as Hannibal and Ste Genevieve.

Information

The informative Missouri Division of Tourism (☎ 573-751-4133, 800-877-1234, W www.missouritourism.org, PO Box 1055, Jefferson City, MO 65102) has seven Welcome Centers. The most convenient centers are in St Louis (I-270), Joplin (I-44), Kansas City (I-70) and Rock Port (I-29).

For road conditions, call ☎ 573-751-2551 or 888-275-6636. Statewide sales tax is 4.225%. (Lodgings may add 5.5%, food and beverage up to 4% more.)

For information about camping in state parks, call ☎ 800-334-6946. Bed & Breakfast Inns of Missouri (☎ 800-213-5642) has information on statewide B&Bs.

ST LOUIS

It was inevitable that one of the frontier's earliest outposts would be established at the junction of the country's two mightiest rivers. Fur trapper Pierre Laclede chose the site in 1764, and settlers and trappers followed. The trickle of new residents following the Louisiana Purchase became a flood after the 1857 railroad link. By the 1870s the population was 300,000. In 1904 St Louis hosted two international events – the World's Fair and Olympics – and established itself as an innovator and growth center.

Things went downhill, however. People didn't 'meet' in St Louis; they left it. The central corridor cleared out, leaving incredible red-brick townhouses abandoned, boarded up and awaiting a date with the bulldozer. (The trend persists – the export of red bricks remains a big source of income – along with the automobile, aerospace and aircraft industries based here.) In the 1990s, St Louis' population declined by a further 50,000.

Despite the stats – and Chevy Chase's experiences here in the film *Vacation* – St Louis is fun to visit. Several flourishing neighborhoods in town – including Soulard and Benton Park – preserve their past. Popular events include the Blues Heritage Festival on Labor Day weekend. And there's the giant Gateway Arch, which symbolizes St Louis' historical role as Gateway to the West.

Orientation

The landmark Gateway Arch is in the riverside Jefferson National Expansion Memorial. Just north is Laclede's Landing historic district. To the west is downtown and its central artery, Market St, along which is the shopping and restaurant enclave Union Station.

Neighborhoods of particular interest are Forest Park; the Loop (also called University City Loop); posh Central West End; the Hill, an Italian American neighborhood; bohemian Grand South Grand; the Ville, the most significant of the African American neighborhoods; and Soulard, the city's Latin quarter.

East St Louis, in Illinois, is not a pleasant place after dark.

Information

The St Louis Convention & Visitors Commission (☎ 314-421-1023, 800-888-3861) is at 1 Metropolitan Square, Suite 1100. More convenient is the visitor center (☎ 314-342-5160), at 7th St and Washington Ave.

Tune into community-run KDHX FM 88.1, which plays folk, blues and odd rock. Check email at the amazing St Louis Public Library (☎ 314-241-2288, 1301 Olive St).

There are plenty of parking lots downtown, including at Laclede's Landing, a short walk from the Arch ($5 for eight hours).

Riverfront & Downtown

Many St Louisans roll their eyes about it, but the **Gateway Arch** (1965; ☎ 314-982-1410, 707 N 1st St) is a five-star structure – the Great Plains' own Eiffel Tower. Designed by Finnish American architect Eero Saarinen, the Arch stands 630 feet tall and just as wide at its base. Unless you're particularly claustrophobic or faint from heights, take the four-minute tram ride to the observatory ($7; open daily) – it's wise to buy tickets in advance at Ⓦ www.stlouisarch.com. Anyone can enjoy views of the Arch from the park below. The subterranean **Museum of Westward Expansion**, under the Arch, has coverage of the Plains Indians, Lewis and Clark, and buffalo soldiers (free admission). There are three huge-screen movies to see ($6).

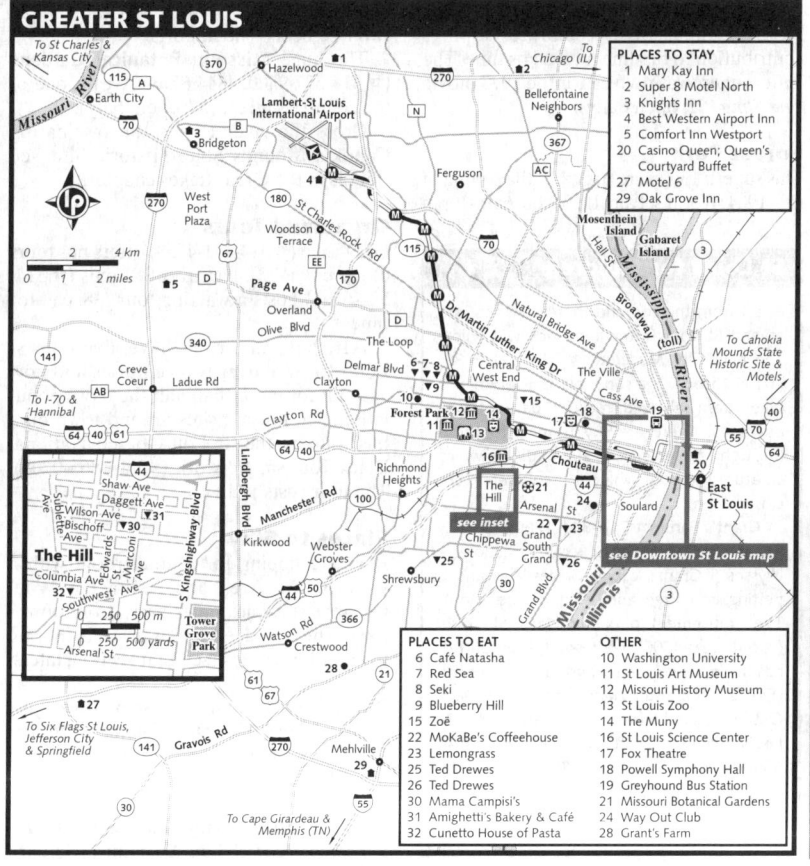

GREATER ST LOUIS

PLACES TO STAY
1 Mary Kay Inn
2 Super 8 Motel North
3 Knights Inn
4 Best Western Airport Inn
5 Comfort Inn Westport
20 Casino Queen; Queen's Courtyard Buffet
27 Motel 6
29 Oak Grove Inn

PLACES TO EAT
6 Café Natasha
7 Red Sea
8 Seki
9 Blueberry Hill
15 Zoë
22 MoKaBe's Coffeehouse
23 Lemongrass
25 Ted Drewes
26 Ted Drewes
30 Mama Campisi's
31 Amighetti's Bakery & Café
32 Cunetto House of Pasta

OTHER
10 Washington University
11 St Louis Art Museum
12 Missouri History Museum
13 St Louis Zoo
14 The Muny
16 St Louis Science Center
17 Fox Theatre
18 Powell Symphony Hall
19 Greyhound Bus Station
21 Missouri Botanical Gardens
24 Way Out Club
28 Grant's Farm

GREAT PLAINS

Facing the Arch, the 1845 **Old Court-house & Museum** (☎ 314-655-1600, 11 N 4th St) is where the famed Dred Scott case was first tried (free admission; open daily).

There are a number of steamboats moored nearby – Gateway Riverboat Cruises (☎ 314-621-4040), just south of the Arch, has one-hour trips four times a day ($9).

You can walk north along the waterfront under the historic Eads railway bridge to the historic **Laclede's Landing**, a lackluster (but convenient) precinct of shops, restaurants and bars.

You can bowl on a 1922 attendant-sets-up-the-pins lane *and* pay tribute to the city's beloved baseball team at the **International Bowling & Cardinals Hall of Fame** (☎ 314-231-6340, 111 Stadium Plaza). Admission is $6; open daily.

The **Scott Joplin House** (☎ 314-340-5790, 2658A Delmar Blvd) celebrates Joplin's contribution to ragtime music. His tune 'The Entertainer' was revived for the 1973 movie *The Sting* ($2; open daily).

Forest Park

This superb 1300-acre park was the setting of the 1904 World's Fair. It's open 6am-10pm

St Louis for Children

Apart from the zoo and the Arch, there are several St Louis attractions kids will enjoy. The new **City Museum** (☎ 314-231-2489, 701 N 15th St) is a super place. Everything's made from salvaged, recycled parts of area buildings. There are sky tunnels to climb through, secret caves 'guarded' by weird creatures and a whale of concrete ($6; closed Mon).

Grant's Farm (☎ 314-843-1700), Gravois Rd at Grant Rd, has several attractions – Ulysses S Grant's cabin, Clydesdales and a petting zoo (free admission; closed Mon). The amusement park **Six Flags St Louis** (☎ 636-938-4800), off I-44 at Allenton Rd, has five roller coasters – and calmer rides too ($40/20 for adults/kids; open daily Apr-Oct). Kids can build their own Arch at the **St Louis Science Center** (☎ 314-289-4444, 5050 Oakland Ave), with 700 other hands-on exhibits (free admission; open daily).

daily. On the grounds is the **St Louis Art Museum** (☎ 314-721-0072), on Art Hill. Built for the fair, it has a collection of 30,000 international works (free admission; closed Mon).

Also on the grounds is the **St Louis Zoo** (☎ 314-781-0900, 1 Government Dr). The apes, lions and seals are free to see, but it's $4 extra to see the insectarium or children's zoo (open daily). The **Missouri History Museum** (☎ 314-454-3124) focuses on the city and has an interesting World's Fair exhibit (free admission; open daily).

Other Attractions

The world's largest beer plant, the **Anheuser-Busch Brewery** (☎ 314-577-2626), at 12th and Lynch Sts, gives free tours (open daily). You get to see the bottling plant and famous Clydesdale horses – names include 'Bruce' and 'Scott.' Visitors (with ID) can sample two free beers – no imports.

The huge **Missouri Botanical Gardens** (☎ 314-577-9400, 4344 Shaw Ave) is one of the country's nicest ($7; open daily).

Cross the river to see the fascinating Cahokia Mounds State Historic Site; see Illinois in the Great Lakes chapter.

Organized Tours

Gray Line (☎ 314-421-4753) offers bus tours of the city ($22). Discover St Louis (☎ 314-522-6367) hosts a walking tour ($8; call for times).

African Americans have lived in St Louis for well over two centuries and now account for more than half the city's population. See historic sites around town on a bus tour by the St Louis–based National Black Tourism Network (☎ 314-865-0708). The tour costs $29.

Places to Stay

If you're hoping for a hotel room with a view of the Arch, it's gonna cost you. Cheaper stays are miles away from downtown. The best deals are in the neighboring town of St Charles (see that section, later).

Budget Twenty miles west of town, just north of Hwy 100, *Dr Edmund A Babler State Park* (☎ 636-458-3813) has developed tent/RV sites for $7/15. Illinois' Casino Queen (see below) has $23 RV sites (no tents).

The *HI Huckleberry Finn Hostel* (☎ 314-241-0076, 1904 S 12th St) is in a Soulard

DOWNTOWN ST LOUIS

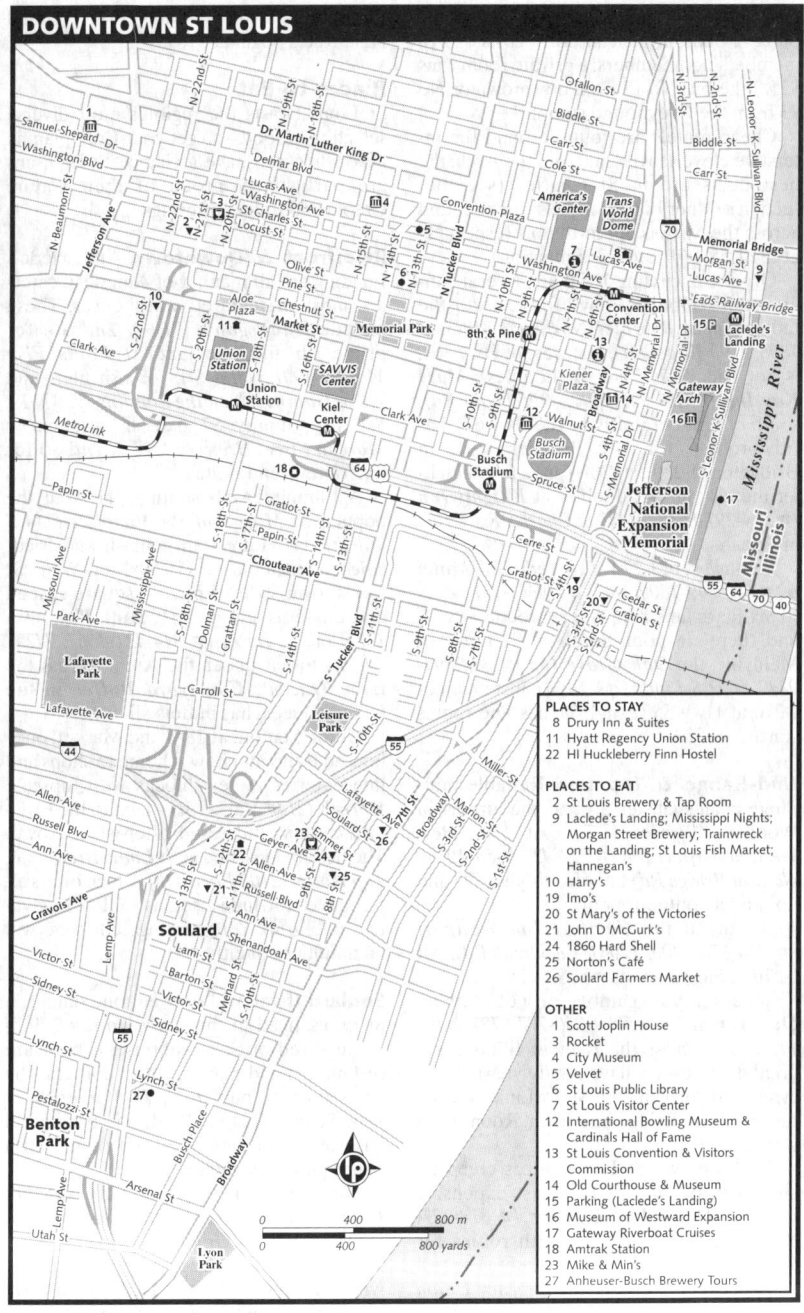

PLACES TO STAY
8 Drury Inn & Suites
11 Hyatt Regency Union Station
22 HI Huckleberry Finn Hostel

PLACES TO EAT
2 St Louis Brewery & Tap Room
9 Laclede's Landing; Mississippi Nights;
   Morgan Street Brewery; Trainwreck
   on the Landing; St Louis Fish Market;
   Hannegan's
10 Harry's
19 Imo's
20 St Mary's of the Victories
21 John D McGurk's
24 1860 Hard Shell
25 Norton's Café
26 Soulard Farmers Market

OTHER
1 Scott Joplin House
3 Rocket
4 City Museum
5 Velvet
6 St Louis Public Library
7 St Louis Visitor Center
12 International Bowling Museum &
   Cardinals Hall of Fame
13 St Louis Convention & Visitors
   Commission
14 Old Courthouse & Museum
15 Parking (Laclede's Landing)
16 Museum of Westward Expansion
17 Gateway Riverboat Cruises
18 Amtrak Station
23 Mike & Min's
27 Anheuser-Busch Brewery Tours

GREAT PLAINS

townhouse – a handy location for nearby pubs. A bunk in a clean dorm costs $15/18 members/nonmembers; a private room runs $35. Take bus No 17 from downtown or No 73 from the Greyhound station.

Cheap motels are found around the interstate cloverleaves, far from the Arch; the best deals are in St Charles (see that section). Other budget motels can be found across the Mississippi in Illinois (especially at the I-55, I-70 and I-255 junction).

Off city-encircling I-270 are several congregations of budget stays. To the north, the fading *Super 8 Motel North* (☎ 314-355-7808, 2790 Target Dr), just west of Hwy 367, is not bad ($47/52 singles/doubles). *Mary Kay Inn* (☎ 314-921-4400, 8911 Dunn Rd), south of Lindbergh Blvd exit (Hwy 67), has tidy rooms for $40. Farther west in Bridgeton (I-270 exit 20B) are a few sketchier motels; the $41 doubles at *Knights Inn* (☎ 314-291-8545, 12433 St Charles Rock Rd) are clean.

Southwest of I-270 at I-44 exit 274, *Motel 6* (☎ 636-349-1800, 1860 Bowles Ave) caters to Six Flags fans; rooms cost around $48/54, and there's a pool. South of St Louis in Mehlville, the *Oak Grove Inn* (☎ 314-894-9449, 6602 S Lindbergh Blvd), just north of I-270 at Hwy 55 (exit 197), has fine rooms starting at $50.

Mid-Range & Top End Reliable mid-range chains cluster around the airport in Woodson Terrace (I-70 exit 236). *Best Western Airport Inn* (☎ 314-427-5955, 10232 Natural Bridge Rd) has nice rooms ($75 and up) and an outdoor pool.

Rooms at the *Comfort Inn Westport* (☎ 314-878-1400, 12031 Lackland Rd), off I-270 at Page Ave, start at $89.

Whether you gamble or not, *Casino Queen* (☎ 618-874-5000, 800-777-0777, 200 S Front St), across the river in Illinois, is a good deal. Rooms have dandy views of the Arch, and you can take MetroLink over the historic Eads Bridge into town. Room rates start at $99.

In downtown St Louis, prices creep up significantly. One of the least expensive hotels is *Drury Inn & Suites* (☎ 314-231-8100, 711 N Broadway), with rooms for $99/109 and an indoor pool. A notch or two up is the ultra-classy *Hyatt Regency Union Station* (☎ 314-231-1234, 1820 Market St).

Its lobby is in the station's former Grand Hall. Rates begin at $109.

Places to Eat
St Louis boasts the region's most diverse selection of food – so get your Ethiopian fix here while you have a chance. St Louisans are particularly proud of their Cajun, Creole and Italian offerings.

Riverfront & Downtown At Laclede's Landing are all manner of American eateries, most in restored warehouses. These include *Hannegan's* (719 N 2nd St), for prime rib and live jazz; *St Louis Fish Market* (901 N 1st St), for fish filets and sushi; *Trainwreck on the Landing* (720 N 1st St), for yummy $7 ostrich burgers; or *Morgan Street Brewery* (721 N 2nd St) for microbrews and pasta.

A 10-minute walk south of the Arch, the popular *St Mary's of the Victories* (744 S 3rd St) has Hungarian goulash and fried-chicken lunch buffets ($6.50; Mon-Wed). St Louis' own style of pizza – square-shaped and thin-crusted – is tasty stuff: Pick up a $7.50 pie at *Imo's* (☎ 314-421-4667, 742 S 4th St) to eat under the Arch. Across the river, *Queen's Courtyard Buffet*, in the Casino Queen, has buffets all day.

Union Station, at 18th and Market, once housed trains and now is home to shops and fine eateries. A few blocks west, upscale *Harry's* (2144 Market St) – next to the FBI – attracts a well-dressed after-work crowd. The ties are loosened at *St Louis Brewery & Tap Room* (2100 Locust St), which offers alternatives to Budweiser, as well as innovative pub grub. Your ringing cellphone will go unnoticed at either.

Soulard If you will only eat one dinner in St Louis, head to this leafy 'hood of 19th-century red-brick townhouses. There are restaurants and pubs on most corners. The city's favorite pub, *John D McGurk's*, at 12th St and Russell Blvd, has traditional Irish dishes (a good stew is $9), and Irish bands play most nights.

For Cajun and Creole food, try *Norton's Café* (808 Geyer Ave) for jambalaya ($9) or crawdad specials. Or go to *1860 Hard Shell* (1860 S 9th St), a three-part restaurant-bar with delicious broiled cod fish ($13) and live blues every night. You can pick up vittles at the **Soulard Farmers Market**, at Lafayette Ave and 7th St (Tue-Sat).

The Hill This neighborhood – marked with 'Italian-flag' fire hydrants – features some of the best Italian food this side of the Mississippi. Try **Cunetto House of Pasta** (5453 Magnolia Ave), for veal dishes and low-salt pastas; **Amighetti's Bakery & Café** (5141 Wilson Ave), a traditional place; and **Mama Campisi's** (2132 Edwards St), for delicious toasted ravioli.

Grand South Grand Running along S Grand Blvd, this area thrives with a youthful lot and is a good area to find vegetarian fare. **MoKaBe's Coffeehouse** (3606 Arsenal St), at Grand, is famous for its grilled veggie sandwich ($5) and the sprawling all-vegetarian Sunday brunch ($10). **Lemongrass** (3216 S Grand Blvd) is a cheap authentic Vietnamese restaurant, with many meatless dishes.

Do not leave St Louis without gorging on frozen custard at **Ted Drewes** (4224 S Grand Blvd), in summer only. (The original location, at 6726 Chippewa St, is open all year.) On a warm evening, bring a book; lines get long.

Central West End & the Loop Just northeast of Forest Park, along Euclid St in Central West End, is a posh enclave of shops and restaurants, many with sidewalk tables. **Zoï** (4753 McPherson) serves carefully prepared pan-Asian dishes; seared salmon with spinach and vermicelli costs $13.

Near Washington University, 'the Loop' runs along Delmar Blvd and has many international eateries catering to a younger crowd. For hands-on food, **Red Sea** (No 6511) prepares Ethiopian specialties. Japanese box lunches are tasty at **Seki** (No 6335). More upscale is **Café Natasha** (No 6623), with good Persian dinners. **Blueberry Hill** (No 6504) offers heaps of rock memorabilia and good burgers.

Entertainment

Travelers have stopped in St Louis to let loose since before Lewis and Clark endured pre- and post-journey hangovers in the early 19th century. Grab a free weekly **Riverfront Times** for listings.

Pubs & Clubs Most bars around town close at 1am, when the action moves to '3am licensed' downtown clubs (centered on Washington Ave, west of Tucker Blvd). **Rocket** (☎ 314-588-0055, 2001 Locust St) is a good bar on the indie-rock circuit. Lone Star beer costs $2. For DJ-blasting trance, house and techno, hit the laser-lit dance floor at **Velvet** (☎ 314-241-8178, 1301 Washington Ave), open until 3am ($5 cover).

Most of the Laclede's Landing and Soulard restaurants and pubs are archetypal drinking holes with live music on weekends. In the Landing, **Mississippi Nights** (☎ 314-421-3853, 914 N 1st St) is a club hosting big-name acts. In Soulard, go to **Mike & Min's** (☎ 314-421-1655, 925 Geyer Ave) to sit side-by-side with Soulardians chugging Bud Light and listening to blues bands (Wed-Sat). Farther west, **Way Out Club** (☎ 314-664-7638, 2525 S Jefferson Ave) is another worthy venue.

St Louis' best show is held once a month (on the third Thursday) when St Louis native Chuck Berry rocks the small basement bar at **Blueberry Hill** (☎ 314-727-0880, 6504 Delmar Blvd) – the $22 tickets sell out quickly.

Performing Arts Try to catch a concert, dance or Broadway show at the 1929 **Fox Theatre** (☎ 314-534-1111, 527 N Grand Blvd). Seeing its ornate interior is worth it. For a tour, call ☎ 314-534-1678. The St Louis Symphony Orchestra raises their bows and tubas at the nearby **Powell Symphony Hall** (☎ 314-534-1700, 718 N Grand Blvd). The Municipal Opera Association, **The Muny** (☎ 314-361-1900), hosts nightly summer shows in Forest Park; some of the 12,000 seats are free.

Spectator Sports

They're sports mad in St Louis. Busch Stadium (250 Stadium Plaza) is a baseball shrine to the Cardinals (☎ 314-421-2400), whose fortunes have risen with the exploits of slugger Mark McGwire, heir to Roger Maris' home-run record.

The Rams (☎ 314-425-8830), the NFL football team, play downtown at Trans World Dome at America's Center. The St Louis Blues (☎ 314-622-2500) play NHL hockey at the SAVVIS Center.

GREAT PLAINS

Getting There & Away

Lambert–St Louis International Airport (☎ 314-426-8000) is the home base of TWA, which has services to all major US cities as well as Omaha, Nebraska; Des Moines, Iowa; and Oklahoma City, Oklahoma. The airport is 12 miles northwest of downtown, connected by bus, light-rail system, taxi (about $25), or Exit Express (☎ 314-646-1166) for $11 per person.

The Greyhound bus station (☎ 314-231-4485) is at 1450 N 13th St, though some buses stop at the airport. Every day, 12 buses leave for Chicago ($31; from 6½ hours); six head to Indianapolis, Indiana ($23; 4½ hours); seven go to Memphis, Tennessee ($41; from 7 hours); and eight go to Oklahoma City ($79; 12½ hours).

The Amtrak station (☎ 314-331-3300, 550 S 16th St) is a couple blocks east of Union Station. Three trains travel to Chicago daily ($27-58; 5½ hours); there are also trains bound for Kansas City ($26-52; 5½ hours) and Memphis (with bus connection; $69-100; 7½ hours).

Getting Around

The Bi-State Transit System (BSTS; ☎ 314-231-2345) runs local buses as well as the excellent MetroLink light rail (fares are $1.25 on both; a day pass is $4). The Levee Line is a free rail service between Union Station and Laclede's Landing (weekdays only). Yellow Cabs (☎ 314-361-2345) charge $1.50 per mile.

RIVER TOWNS

Interesting towns that make popular weekend excursions for St Louisans lie north and south of St Louis on the Mississippi River and just west on the Missouri.

St Charles

This 19th-century river town, on the Missouri River 20 miles northwest of St Louis, is now almost a suburb. The St Charles Convention & Visitors Bureau (CVB; ☎ 636-946-7776, 230 S Main St) has information.

St Charles was founded in 1769 as Les Petites Côtes (The Little Hills) by the French fur baron Louis Blanchette. A few miles off the interstate is the picturesque, historic nine-block downtown with the first state capitol, on S Main St. The historic 26-block Frenchtown neighborhood, on N Main St, is just north.

Lewis and Clark heritage days are reenacted in the third week of May, and the Lewis & Clark Center (701 Riverside Dr) has a few exhibits ($1).

For bikers, St Charles is the eastern gateway to the Katy Trail (see Along US 50, Highway 94 & Highway 100, later). There's also good canoeing in the area (not on the swift Missouri, though).

Near the small town of Defiance, on Hwy 94, 20 miles southwest of St Charles, the **Daniel Boone Home** (☎ 636-798-2005) is where the frontier legend lived off and on from 1803 until his death in 1820 ($7; closed Mon and winter).

Along St Charles' three I-70 exits are newer, better-value motels than those in St Louis. The reliable ***Red Roof Inn*** (☎ 636-947-7770, 2010 Zumbehl Rd) has clean $46/51 singles/doubles. St Charles has several good B&Bs, including ***Boone's Lick Trail B&B*** (☎ 636-947-7000, 1000 S Main St), with rooms starting at $105.

Finding good food is easy. ***Eckert's*** (515 S Main St) has light sandwiches on a pleasant outdoor patio; plus there's a bocce court. To keep it real in St Charles, eat French: ***Bonaparte's*** (140 N Main St) is a fancy brasserie with a prix-fixe menu ($28; dinner only).

Hannibal

From the look of things in this weary birthplace of Mark Twain, 105 miles north of St Louis, the author's appeal to travelers began to wane around the time MTV got

Mark Twain, Hannibal's famous son

rolling. No new motels have been built since around then, and most attractions are dated.

Still, for big-time fans, the scenes of Tom Sawyer and Huck Finn's great adventures are irresistible: You can see the white fence Tom *didn't* paint and the cave where he and Becky Thatcher got lost. Follow school kids to the big **Mark Twain Boyhood Home & Museum** (☎ 573-221-9010, 208 Hill St), featuring four replica buildings, two films and *three* gift shops ($6). Get a new copy of *Life of Mississippi* stamped with the museum logo. Afterward, climb Cardiff Hill, just past the Tom and Huck statue. Trips on the *Mark Twain* riverboat (☎ 573-221-3222) cost $9.

The *Mark Twain Cave Campground (☎ 573-221-1656 ext 23),* 2 miles south on Hwy 79, has tent/RV sites for $16/20. *Hannibal Inn (☎ 573-221-6610, 4141 Market St),* off Hwy 61, has an indoor pool and $59/67 singles/doubles in summer.

Just below the giant rotating mug, the *Mark Twain Dinette (400 N 3rd St)* won't let you leave without sampling the homemade root beer; there's a cheap breakfast and lunch buffet.

Ste Genevieve

This little town, 60 miles south of St Louis, was the first permanent settlement in Missouri (1725). French influences are evident in many buildings; several can be toured, including the Bolduc-Le Meilleur House and Bolduc House ($4 to tour both). The Ste Genevieve Museum (☎ 573-883-3461), at Merchant and 3rd Sts, has many relics relating to the town's heyday ($1.50). The Great River Road Interpretive Center (☎ 573-883-7097, 66 S Main St) has exhibits on the Mississippi River and information on B&Bs. *Family Budget Inn (☎ 573-543-2272, 17030 New Bremen Rd)* has $40 singles and a pool.

Cape Girardeau

Another pleasant river town, 115 miles downstream from St Louis, Cape Girardeau was a steamboat stop as early as 1835. Drop by the CVB (☎ 573-335-1631, 100 Broadway) for brochures and perhaps the free *Rush Limbaugh Hometown Tour* – a map showing childhood sites of the megaconservative radiohead, who was born here. The Cape Heritage Museum (☎ 573-334-0405, 538 Independence St) tells the story of

the town ($2). Downtown's Water St and the nearby riverfront are fine places for a stroll.

Some 10 miles north on Hwy 177 is **Trail of Tears State Park** (☎ 573-334-1711), a beautiful region that belies its sad past as part of the Cherokees' forced march to Oklahoma. There are trails, Mississippi overlooks and *camping*; developed tent/RV sites cost $7/15.

ALONG INTERSTATE 70

The fastest route between St Louis and Kansas City is I-70, but it's not particularly interesting. Halfway across the state, **Columbia** is a nice college town, home to the University of Missouri – the oldest university west of the Mississippi. Contact the Columbia CVB (☎ 573-875-1231, 300 S Providence).

Boone's Lick State Historic Park, northwest of Boonville on Hwy 87, is where Daniel Boone's sons manufactured salt from the 'licks,' natural saltwater springs (free admission). Just across the Missouri (but reached by Hwy 41), tiny **Arrow Rock** was first settled in 1810 and was later an important stopover on the Santa Fe Trail. It's now a state historic site (☎ 660-837-3330), with more than a dozen historic buildings and a superb visitor center that interprets the Boone's Lick region (free admission; open daily). The site has developed (and good) *campsites* ($7/12 for tents/RVs).

ALONG US 50, HIGHWAY 94 & HIGHWAY 100

A slower alternative from St Louis to Kansas City is US 50, and frankly it's not much more attractive. Better drives between St Louis and Jefferson City hug the banks of the Missouri: To the north, Hwy 94 runs alongside the Katy Trail; to the south, Hwy 100 passes through the pretty German town of Hermann, home to wineries and the *Acorn Bunk & Bagel (☎ 573-486-4003, 236 W 4th St),* with cozy rooms for $36 and $41.

So little is going on in the small state capital, **Jefferson City** ('Jeff City'), on US 50, that a law had to be passed requiring state officials to live here. But the handsome State Capitol (☎ 573-751-4127) is worth a look for its good Thomas Hart Benton murals (free admission; open daily). The Jeff

City CVB (☎ 573-634-3616, 213 Adams St) has information on the nearby Katy Trail (see below).

The nicest way to cross most of Missouri's belly is on a bike. The **Katy Trail State Park** boasts a superb 225-mile biking and hiking trail that connects St Charles and Clinton, 65 miles southeast of Kansas City. Open since 1986, the trail runs along the former Missouri-Kansas-Texas (MKT) railroad (the 'Katy'). On its course are a variety of habitats – ideal for the bird-watching crowd. Along its eastern two-thirds, the trail snakes between high bluffs and the Missouri River. Some of its most scenic bits are west of Defiance, where wee German towns make up 'Missouri's Rhineland,' including hilltop Hermann. Another highlight is the stretch between Jefferson City and New Franklin, including areas inaccessible to cars. Amtrak stops in Hermann, Jeff City and Sedalia (see below), and bike rentals and accommodations are available in each (and also in Defiance). For more information, call ☎ 800-334-6946 or check the Web site Ⓦ www.katytrailstatepark.com.

Ragtime immortal Scott Joplin once lived in **Sedalia**, 75 miles east of Kansas City. The town hosts a Ragtime Festival in June and the Missouri State Fair in August. The chamber of commerce (☎ 816-826-2222, 113 E 4th St) provides information.

ALONG INTERSTATE 44

Between St Louis and the state's southwest border with Oklahoma, I-44 is built over Route 66, and derelict gas stations, diners and motels dot the roadsides. Just south of Stanton, the **Meramac Caverns** (☎ 314-468-2283) are as interesting for their Civil War history and hokey charm as for their stalactites ($12.50; open daily). Watch for more Route 66 relics toward Springfield, which is the turnoff to the Ozarks (see below).

West of Springfield, a 40-mile stretch of Route 66 survives as Hwy 96, and 19th-century **Carthage** provides serious nostalgia appeal. South of Joplin on Hwy 71, the **George Washington Carver National Monument** (☎ 417-325-4151) has displays on the African American scientist, known for developing 105 ways to prepare the peanut (free admission; open daily).

OZARKS

Most of the Ozarks are in Arkansas, but the charming hill country extends into the southern fourth of Missouri and into eastern Oklahoma. Much of the Missouri Ozarks were stripped of timber in the late 19th century, and many rivers have been dammed to create a network of lakes.

The **Ozark Trail** (☎ 573-751-2479) is a 300-mile hiking trail through parts of the Mark Twain National Forest. One day it will run 500 miles from St Louis to Arkansas' Ozark Highland Trail.

North of US 60, midway between Cape Giradeau and Springfield, the **Ozark Scenic Riverways** (☎ 573-323-4236) – Current River and Jack's Fork – boasts 134 miles of splendid canoeing and tubing. There are six campgrounds. Van Buren, on Hwy 60, has motels and canoe rentals. Take the fun car ferry across the river, off Hwy KK near Rector.

About 70 miles southwest of St Louis, **Bonne Terre Mine** is near the intersection of Hwys 47 and 67 (open daily Apr-Oct, Fri-Sun the rest of the year). The water-filled, 80-sq-mile mine, built in 1864 to mine lead, is open for **scuba diving** on weekends (dives start at $60); call ☎ 314-731-5003. Boat tours (☎ 573-358-2148) are $17.50.

Branson

This love-it-or-hate-it tourist town (population 6050) is to country music what Disney is to history. The main attractions are the 47 theaters hosting 70 country music and corny comedy shows. During peak season – June and July, and between Labor Day and Christmas – the population swells to 150,000.

The neon-lit '76 Strip' (Hwy 76) looks like an Ozark Vegas, with several miles of theaters, hotels, restaurants and wax museums. When shows let out, traffic crawls. Watch for the color-coded routes that bypass it.

The Branson Visitors Center (☎ 417-334-4136), on Hwy 248 just west of the US 65 junction, has town and lodging information. The scores of 'Visitor Information' centers around town give free tickets to shows *if* you'll sit through a 90-minute timeshare plug.

Many **theater shows** are associated with particular performers (often performing in

GREAT PLAINS

peak season only) – for example, and in no particular order of merit, Wayne Newton, Andy Williams, Glen Campbell, the Osmond Brothers (but not Tito, he's a Jackson), Bobby Vinton, Yakov Smirnoff and Mel Tillis. Other shows include the long-running, hokey 'Baldknobbers Jamboree.' Branson's show prices are $17-42 a head; theaters run three shows a day. For tickets, call Ozark Ticket & Travel (☎ 417-335-3132, 888-998-4253). Reserve a week in advance during peak season.

Two outdoor attractions, open since 1959, spurred the Branson boom. Huge **Silver Dollar City** (☎ 417-336-7180, 800-952-6626), west of town, is a popular amusement park that relives the Mark Twain era, with its music shows, replica buildings and Ozark crafts shops ($36/24 for adults/children). The **Shepherd of the Hills** (☎ 417-334-4149, 5586 W Hwy 76) is a show based upon a homespun novel of Ozark life ($30 with dinner).

Around popular Table Rock Lake, southwest of town, are tons of *campsites* (most geared to RVs). Branson fills up with package-tour visitors during peak times. To snare any of the overpriced accommodations, you might have to use a reservation service: Branson Hotline (☎ 800-523-7589) books rooms for $55 and up, and Branson Vacation Reservations (☎ 800-221-5692) has package deals (three shows and two nights is $209).

There are cute cabins along narrow Lake Taneycomo (just east of downtown) that predate Silver Dollar City. *Shady Lane Resort* (☎ 417-334-3823, 404 N Sycamore St) has clean cabins with kitchenettes for $45 and $55.

KANSAS CITY

It's said that St Louis looks east and Kansas City looks west. This bustling farm-distribution and industrial center was, for generations, a serious 'cowtown.' Its giant stockyards closed in 1991.

KC started life as a trading post in 1821 and expanded rapidly after the arrival of the steamboats and, later, westward expansion (it was then called Westport). Prior to the Civil War, KC was caught up in the maelstrom of 'Bleeding Kansas,' a conflict between pro- and antislavery groups. During KC's roaring gangster days of the 1930s, rabble-rousing mayor Tom Pendergast built lovely buildings and winding Brush Creek – profiting his own cement company.

Today, Kansas City – including its smaller neighbor KC Kansas – is a very livable (and large) metropolis. Within its sprawl is more 'elbow room' than any other US metropolis: Each person gets 85,842 sq feet.

Orientation

I-70 is the main east-west route into the city, and it connects the two halves of KC across the Kansas River. In downtown, I-70 meets I-35, which runs northeast-southwest (crossing the Missouri River), as well as I-29, which heads north to the airport. The encircling I-435 takes in all of KC's sprawl, from the airport in the north, to near Independence in the east, and the Kansas suburb of Overland Park in the southwest.

North-south running State Line Rd divides KC Missouri and KC Kansas (which has little to offer travelers). KC Missouri has some distinct areas, including the historic River Market (also called City Market), centering at 5th St and Walnut St north of downtown; the historic African American 18th & Vine District; the historic Westport District, based on Westport Rd near Broadway; and the huge Country Club Plaza shopping and dining precinct, based on Broadway between 46th and 48th Sts.

Information

The Greater Kansas City CVB (☎ 816-221-5242, 800-767-7000, @ gointokansascity.com) is on the 25th floor of City Center Square, 1100 Main St (open Mon-Fri). A good resource is the Missouri Welcome Center (☎ 816-889-3330, 4010 Blue Ridge Cutoff), off I-70 east of I-435 (open daily).

Kansas City's Main Library (☎ 816-701-3400, 311 E 12 St) and Westport Branch (☎ 816-701-3635, 118 Westport Rd) have free Internet access.

Museums

The **Museums at 18th & Vine** (☎ 816-474-8463, 1616 E 18th St) are well worth visiting. You can 'play drums' to Sonny Rollins at the interactive Kansas City Jazz Museum, which also has displays on key players, including KC Kansas native Charlie Parker. Visit the Negro Leagues Baseball Museum

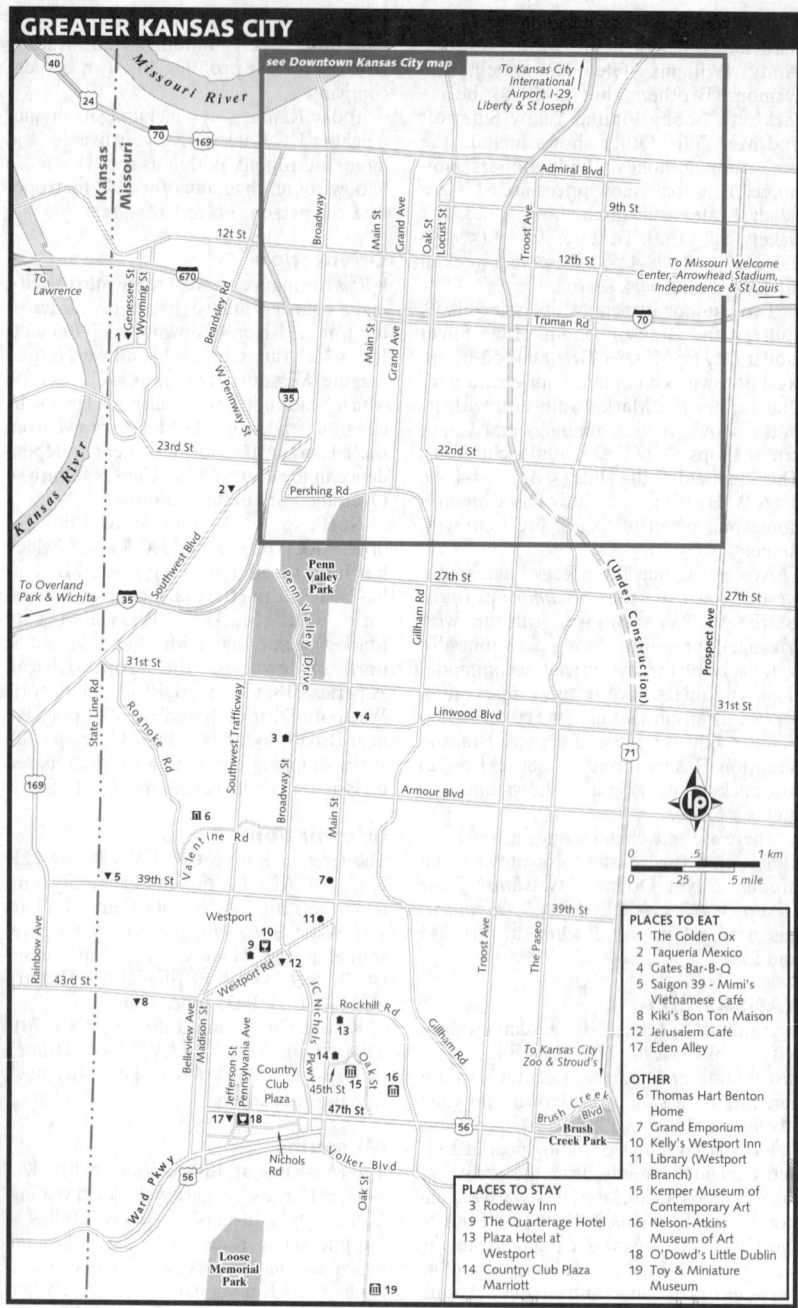

GREATER KANSAS CITY

see Downtown Kansas City map

To Kansas City International Airport, I-29, Liberty & St Joseph

To Missouri Welcome Center, Arrowhead Stadium, Independence & St Louis

To Lawrence

To Overland Park & Wichita

To Kansas City Zoo & Stroud's

PLACES TO EAT
1 The Golden Ox
2 Taquería Mexico
4 Gates Bar-B-Q
5 Saigon 39 – Mimi's Vietnamese Café
8 Kiki's Bon Ton Maison
12 Jerusalem Café
17 Eden Alley

OTHER
6 Thomas Hart Benton Home
7 Grand Emporium
10 Kelly's Westport Inn
11 Library (Westport Branch)
15 Kemper Museum of Contemporary Art
16 Nelson-Atkins Museum of Art
18 O'Dowd's Little Dublin
19 Toy & Miniature Museum

PLACES TO STAY
3 Rodeway Inn
9 The Quarterage Hotel
13 Plaza Hotel at Westport
14 Country Club Plaza Marriott

GREAT PLAINS

to learn about African American teams (eg, the KC Monarchs and New York Black Yankees) that flourished until baseball became fully integrated in 1959. Displays cover stars such as Satchel Paige and Jackie Robinson. Entry costs $6/8 for one/two museums (closed Mon).

Home to 200 tons of salvaged 'treasure' from a riverboat that was snag-struck and then sunk in 1856, the *Arabia* **Steamboat Museum** (☎ 816-471-4030), located in River Market, offers good insight to the crafty Missouri River, which claimed 289 steamboats ($7.50; open daily).

The recently reopened **Union Station** (1914), at Main St and Pershing Rd, has a restaurant, small historical museum, several giant-screen movies ($7) and the new **Science City** (☎ 816-460-2000), which is a metropolis with kid-friendly exhibits, including an astronaut-training program and foamy floored 'sewer' ($12.50; open daily). Free parking is available. Across Pershing Rd is the towering Liberty Memorial, built for WWI veterans.

The grand **Nelson-Atkins Museum of Art** (☎ 816-561-4000, 4525 Oak St) has giant shuttlecocks on its lawn and an excellent collection of American, Asian and European art. Be sure to see the 14th-century Chinese temple and Duane Hanson's *Museum Guard*, which amazes school kids ($5; closed Mon). Nearby is the free **Kemper Museum of Contemporary Art** (☎ 816-753-5784, 4420 Warwick Blvd).

The **Toy & Miniature Museum** (☎ 816-333-2055, 5235 Oak St) draws an older crowd for its detailed dollhouses and antique toys ($4; closed Mon-Tue). You can tour the Victorian-style **Thomas Hart Benton Home** (☎ 816-931-5722, 3616 Belleview Ave), where the artist lived from 1939 to 1975 ($2; open daily).

Other Attractions

The outdoor deck observatory of **City Hall** (414 12th St) has great views and is free. The **Hallmark Visitors Center** (☎ 816-274-5672, 2450 Grand Blvd), in Crown Center, is a celebration of the syrupy sentimentality of greeting cards. Kids can design their own cards (free admission; closed Mon).

The **Country Club Plaza**, the USA's oldest outdoor shopping center (1922), is a delightful place with fountains, statues and

Kansas City Barbecue

Savoring hickory-and-oak-smoked brisket, pork or ribs at one of the classic barbecue joints around town is a must-meal for any meat-eater. KC's own style of barbecue – pit-smoked and spicily sauced – is rooted in the 1920s, when an African American entrepreneur set up a newspaper-wrapped-brisket stand. By the 1940s, the city was hooked.

Squeaky-doored *Arthur Bryant's (1727 Brooklyn Ave)*, east of the Museums at 18th & Vine, flops two handfuls of barbecue between outmatched bread slices ($5). The city's most famous barbecue is at *Gates Bar-B-Q (1221 12th St)*, at Brooklyn Ave, where it's assumed you'll want a frosted mug of beer with your brisket or turkey. (There are four other locations, including one at 3205 Main St.) At the roadhouse *BB's Lawnside Bar-B-Q (☎ 816-822-7427, 1205 E 85th St)*, east of Hwy 71 in southeast KC, diners chomp on famed ribs while blues bands blare in front of a wall-to-wall mural.

Moorish-style architecture patterned after Seville, Spain. The Plaza also has a canal, upscale shops and restaurants, and a visitor center (222 W 47th St) in the clock tower.

Swope Park (☎ 816-444-4656), at 63rd St and Swope Parkway (southeast of the Plaza), is home to the **Kansas City Zoo** (☎ 816-513-5701), popular for its gibbons and rhinos ($6/3 for adults/kids). Another kid favorite, the amusement park **Worlds of Fun** ($33.50/12) and adjoining waterpark **Oceans of Fun** ($23/12) is a few miles northeast of downtown (I-435 exit 54). Call ☎ 816-454-4545 for information.

Take an eerie drive in the 800-acre **Sub-Tropolis**, just east of I-435 on Hwy 210 (northeast of downtown), a subterranean free-trade zone built in limestone.

Places to Stay

About 8 miles northwest of the airport, riverside *Weston Bend State Park* (☎ 816-640-5443), on Hwy 45 north of Hwy 92, has hiking trails and tent/RV sites for $7/12.

Cheap motels are way outside city center. You'll find some near the KC airport to the north (I-29 exits 12 and 13), around the city at

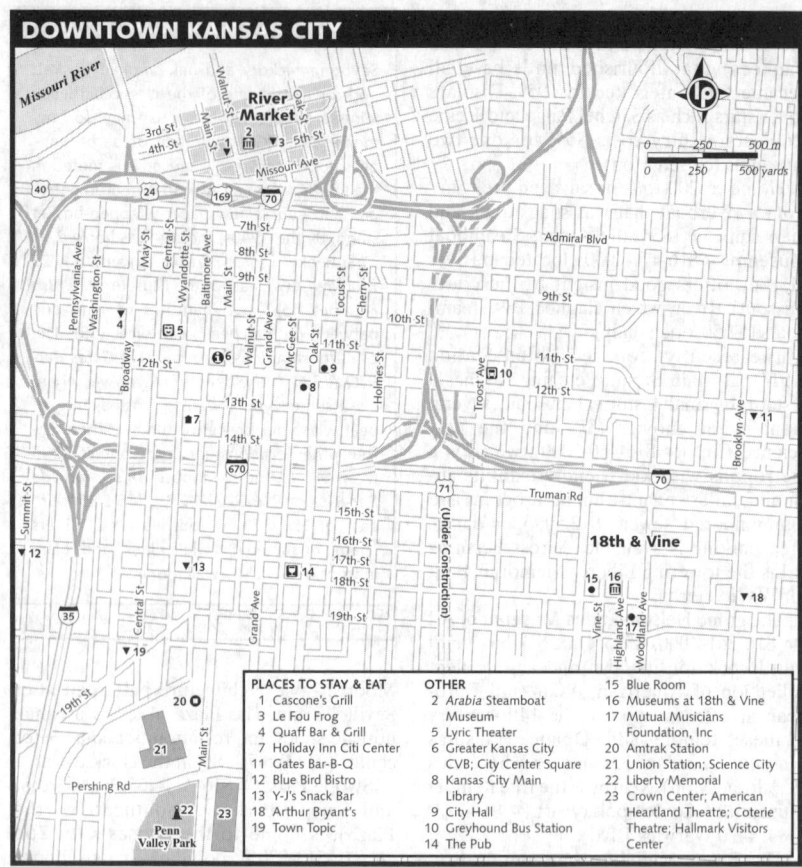

DOWNTOWN KANSAS CITY

PLACES TO STAY & EAT
1 Cascone's Grill
3 Le Fou Frog
4 Quaff Bar & Grill
7 Holiday Inn Citi Center
11 Gates Bar-B-Q
12 Blue Bird Bistro
13 Y-J's Snack Bar
18 Arthur Bryant's
19 Town Topic

OTHER
2 *Arabia* Steamboat Museum
5 Lyric Theater
6 Greater Kansas City CVB; City Center Square
8 Kansas City Main Library
9 City Hall
10 Greyhound Bus Station
14 The Pub

15 Blue Room
16 Museums at 18th & Vine
17 Mutual Musicians Foundation, Inc
20 Amtrak Station
21 Union Station; Science City
22 Liberty Memorial
23 Crown Center; American Heartland Theatre; Coterie Theatre; Hallmark Visitors Center

I-435 exits and in Independence (see that section). Comfortable *Econo Lodge KCI Airport* (☎ 816-464-5082, 11300 NW Prairie View Rd), off I-29 exit 12, has $55/59 singles/doubles in summer. Near Worlds of Fun, *Crossland* (☎ 816-413-0068, 4301 N Garrington Ave) has clean rooms for $54/59. Farther south on I-435, *Motel 6* (☎ 816-333-4468, 6400 E 87th St) has good rooms for $39/49, but the area is a bit sketchy. Off I-435 in Overland Park (about 12 miles southwest of downtown), *Red Roof Inn* (☎ 913-341-0100, 6800 W 108th St) has standard rooms for $39/46.

Many mid-range chains are found near the airport and at the junction of I-435 and US 169/50 in Overland Park. In town, you'll find several good accommodations near the Westport District. *Plaza Hotel at Westport* (☎ 816-561-9600, 4309 Main St) has $89 rooms. Up a notch is the *Quarterage Hotel* (☎ 816-931-0001, 800-942-4233, 560 Westport Rd), with excellent $99 rooms, free cocktails from 5 to 7pm, and health club access. The *Rodeway Inn* (☎ 816-531-9250, 3240 Broadway) has slightly worn doubles for $69.

Country Club Plaza Marriott (☎ 816-531-3000, 4445 Main St) is the height of luxury but affordable, with B&B specials for $99 on weekends. Downtown accommodations are all costly; try the historic *Holiday Inn Citi Centre* (☎ 816-471-1333, 1215 Wyandotte St). Rates begin at $119.

Places to Eat

In River Market, *Cascone's Grill (20E 5th St)* is an old favorite for cheap breakfasts, sandwiches and minestrone soup. The exquisite *Le Fou Frog (400 E 5th St)* is a French bistro with daily menus. On Sunday nights there's live music.

Downtown workers laze in vinyl booths at *Quaff Bar & Grill (1010 Broadway);* $5 tuna melts are served on plastic plates. At *Town Topic (2021 Broadway)*, burgers sizzle on the grill all night long. Near many art galleries, tiny *Y-J's Snack Bar (128 W 18th St)* is crammed with 1950s whatnots. It's good for coffee and sandwiches. To the west are several authentic Mexican restaurants along Southwest Blvd, including *Taquería Mexico (No 910)*, at 24th St, with combo deals for $6.

Vegetarians flock to *Blue Bird Bistro (1700 Summit)*, at 17th St. Try the green curry with rice ($8.50). The city's best steaks are at *The Golden Ox (☎ 816-842-2866, 1600 Genessee)*, near the old stockyards. A KC strip costs $20.

Westport is KC's nightlife center and has many restaurants. For Middle-Eastern fare, try *Jerusalem Café (431 Westport Rd)*. The $11 kebabs are popular. Farther west, *Kiki's Bon Ton Maison (☎ 816-931-9417, 1515 Westport Rd)* offers Cajun delights, including alligator sausage.

The Plaza has many choices, some quite upscale. One unlike the rest is *Eden Alley (707 W 47th St)*, at the Unity Temple on the Plaza, which is popular for its vegetarian options (pizzas, pastas, sandwiches).

Along W 39th St, close to the Kansas border, is a strip of coffeehouses and restaurants; try *Saigon 39 – Mimi's Vietnamese Café (1806½ W 39th St)* for good noodles.

At *Stroud's (1015 E 85th St)*, near Hwy 71, scurrying waitstaff hoist giant dinners for a devoted crowd. Three pieces of chicken, green beans, mashed potatoes, salad and *two* cinnamon rolls is $10. You can't beat it.

Entertainment
Pick up the free *Pitch Weekly* for entertainment listings.

Pubs & Clubs There are live-music venues in Westport and the River Market. Next to the Museums at 18th & Vine, the slick *Blue Room (☎ 816-474-2929)* hosts jazz shows on Monday, Thursday, Friday and Saturday nights ($5). Nearby, the one-of-a-kind

Mutual Musicians Foundation, Inc (☎ 816-471-5212, 1823 Highland), next to a transient hotel, is 'home' to all musicians. Weekend impromptu jazz sessions roll from midnight on.

A diverse crowd meets at the friendly downtown bar *The Pub (1721 McGee St)*. The bubbling grease fry drowns out the jukebox. Check to see what blues, rock or jazz show is on at the barroom *Grand Emporium (☎ 816-531-1504, 3832 Main St)*.

In KC's oldest building, the Irish pub *Kelly's Westport Inn (500 Westport Rd)* sells short beers to crusty regulars and has $2 pizza slices in the back. The bartender says 'God bless' if you tip. In the Plaza, *O'Dowd's Little Dublin (4742 Pennsylvania Ave)* is an upscale Irish pub with food and live music.

Performing Arts KC kids dig the plays staged at *Coterie Theatre (☎ 816-474-6552)*, in Crown Center (tickets are $8/6 for adults/kids). Broadway-style productions are performed in the *American Heartland Theatre (☎ 816-842-9999)*, in Crown Center, and the outdoor *Starlight Theatre (☎ 816-363-6601)*, in Swope Park. The *Lyric Opera of Kansas City (☎ 816-471-7344)* and the *Kansas City Symphony (☎ 816-471-0400)* perform downtown at the Lyric Theater (1029 Central St at 11th St).

Spectator Sports
The Chiefs NFL football and Wizards pro soccer teams play at Arrowhead Stadium (☎ 816-920-9300), east of downtown at I-70 and the Blue Ridge Cutoff. The neighboring Truman Sports Complex (☎ 800-676-9257) hosts the Royals baseball squad.

Getting There & Around
KC International Airport (☎ 816-243-5237) is 17 miles northwest of downtown. A taxi into town costs about $35; call Yellow Cab (☎ 816-471-5000). The KCI Shuttle (☎ 816-471-2015) is cheaper ($13-17).

Greyhound (☎ 816-221-2885), at 12th and Troost Sts, sends buses daily to Omaha ($29; 4 hours), Chicago ($47; 12½ hours), Denver ($65; from 11 hours), St Louis ($32; 4½ hours) and Tulsa, Oklahoma ($57; 5 hours).

Amtrak (☎ 816-421-3622), just behind Union Station, has trains departing for St Louis ($26-52; 5½ hours), Denver ($104-160,

GREAT PLAINS

including van to Omaha; from 14 hours) and Santa Fe, New Mexico ($124-208, including van connection; 19 hours).

Local transport is with Metro buses (☎ 816-221-0660); the minimum fare is 60¢. The KC Trolley (☎ 816-221-3399) runs every 30 minutes daily, stopping at sites between River Market and the Plaza ($7).

AROUND KANSAS CITY
Independence

Several miles east of Kansas City, Independence was the home of Harry S Truman, US president from 1945 to 1953. The **Truman Presidential Library & Museum** (☎ 816-833-1400, 500 W US 24) has exhibits. Harry 'speaks' to you in the White House Oval Office replica ($5). See how Harry and Bess lived at the **Truman Home** (219 N Delaware St), packed with unmoved original belongings. Tour tickets are sold at the Information Center (☎ 816-254-2720, 223 N Main St) from 8:30am ($3). All the Truman sites are open daily. The courthouse where Harry began his political career is in nearby Independence Square.

Independence was the starting point of the Santa Fe Trail in the 1820s, and the California and Oregon Trails in the 1840s. The **National Frontier Trails Center** (☎ 816-325-7575, 318 W Pacific Ave) has good exhibits on westward migration and on Lewis and Clark ($3.50; open daily).

Towering west of downtown, the Community of Christ temple looks like a soft-serve sundae made of silver.

There are a number of motels around the junction of I-70 and Noland Rd (exit 12). The garish red-white-and-blue *American Inn* (☎ 816-373-8300, 4141 S Noland Rd) has some $27 rooms, plenty of room to park the 18-wheeler, and a karaoke bar that (according to one local) 'gets pretty wild' on weekends – ain't that America? The great-value *Serendipity B&B* (☎ 816-833-4719, 116 S Pleasant Ave), near Truman's home, has seriously Victorian rooms for $30 and up.

St Joseph

As the western terminus of the railways before the Missouri River was bridged, St Joseph was the departure point for many pioneers traveling west. In 1860, the first Pony Express carried messages from 'St Jo' 1900 miles west to California, a service that lasted just 18 months before going bust. The **Pony Express Memorial** (☎ 816-279-5059, 914 Penn St) tells the story of the Express and its riders: 'skinny, wiry fellows' recruited to face death daily – 'orphans preferred' ($4; open daily).

St Jo was also home to Jesse James and jazz great Coleman Hawkins, the namesake of a mid-June festival. Pick up a downtown walking tour map at the St Joseph CVB (☎ 816-233-6688, 109 S 4th St).

Housed in a former mental hospital, the large **Glore Psychiatric Museum** (☎ 816-387-2310, 3406 Frederick Ave) is fascinating. Simple displays show how lobotomies accidentally began and how 'treatment' has advanced from the 'bath of surprise' to occupational therapy, such as painting (free admission; open daily).

The **Albrecht-Kemper Museum of Art** (☎ 816-233-7003, 2818 Frederick Ave) houses a fine 1300-piece collection, specializing in American art ($3; closed Mon).

The James Gang

Outlaw Jesse James got his gun, shot his gun and got killed by one in the region around Kansas City. Born in 1847 in **Kearney**, about 25 miles northeast, Jesse lived with his brother on a farm in their early years; the farm is now open to visitors ($5.50). In nearby **Liberty** is the bank (103 N Washington St) where the James Gang carried out the first successful daylight bank robbery in the USA ($4).

In St Joseph, visit the **Jesse James Home**, at 12th and Penn Sts, where Jesse got himself shot dead in 1882 ($2). Gang member Bob Ford did the deed as Jesse straightened a crooked painting.

Jesse rode again (briefly) in 1995, when his body was exhumed and DNA-tested to prove that he – and not some other bloke – was the actual Jesse James: They're 99% sure. Explore the 1% chance that James *didn't* die in 1882 at the Jesse James Wax Museum, in Stanton on I-44 ($5).

Note: Lest you be seduced by Jesse's legend, remember what Bobby learned on a *Brady Bunch* episode – Jesse was 'a mean dirty killer.'

Several motels are near the junction of I-29 exit 47 (at Hwy 6/Frederick Blvd), including *Motel 6* (☎ *816-232-2311, 4021 Frederick Blvd*), with $44 rooms. Downtown, *Holiday Inn* (☎ *816-279-8000, 102 S 3rd St*) is a great value ($76 single or double).

Go for barbecue at the *Old Town Smokehouse (1120 Penn St)*, near Jesse's old home. *Barbosa's Castillo (4804 Frederick Ave)*, in a 19th-century 'castle,' is loved for its Mexican food.

Oklahoma

Oklahoma rightly touts itself as 'Native America' – referring to both its natural beauty and its Native American roots (it still has the country's biggest Native American population). Oklahoma also has surprisingly diverse scenery – lush Green Country in the northeast, the pine-covered Ouachita and Kiamichi Mountains in the southeast and rugged Wichita Mountains in the southwest.

Oklahoma has more miles of Route 66 than any other state (400 miles). While on the roads, look out for old 'Oklahoma is OK' license plates – a much maligned slogan that adorned the state's vehicles for many years.

History

Evidence has been found of Native American settlement beginning 10,000 years ago in the Oklahoma area. Much later, Wichita, Comanche and Osage occupied the area. In 1834 Oklahoma was declared an Indian Territory, and thousands of Choctaw, Creek, Cherokee, Chickasaw and eventually Seminole (collectively, the Five Civilized Tribes) were forced here from their homelands in the southeastern states. During the winter of 1838–39, more than 15,000 Cherokee were marched along the infamous 'Trail of Tears'; 4000 perished of cold and hunger before they reached Oklahoma.

In the 1880s, eager homesteaders ('Sooners') crossed territory lines to stake claims *before* the US gave the go-ahead to parcel out former Native American lands. There were many legal 'land runs' following, but the most famous one occurred on April 22, 1889, when land-seekers streamed in and tent cities grew up overnight.

Oklahoma
Nickname: Sooner State
Population: 3,450,700 (27th)
Area: 69,900 sq miles (20th)
Admitted to Union: November 16, 1907 (46th)
Capital city: Oklahoma City (population 475,300)
Other cities: Tulsa (385,000), Norman (94,200)
State song: 'Oklahoma!' (Rodgers & Hammerstein)
Birthplace of: Woody Guthrie, athlete Jim Thorpe, parking meters (1935), Will Rogers, Boy Scouts of America, Garth Brooks, Brad Pitt, bands Flaming Lips and Hanson
Famous for: 1930s Dust Bowl, tornadoes, football, 1995 Oklahoma City bombing

The Indian nations formed their own confederation but were refused statehood, so they joined with Oklahoma Territory and the two sections were admitted to the Union as a state in 1907.

The discovery of oil brought wealth to Oklahoma in the 1920s, but the Depression, dust bowl and the plunge of oil prices affected the state badly. Settlers had plowed the sensitive grasslands with a vengeance, taking no notice of conservation measures. The western half of Oklahoma's topsoil literally blew away after severe drought, and thousands of disillusioned 'Okies' migrated westward to states offering a better future. Today, improved conservation techniques and greater care for the fragile Plains environment have revitalized Oklahoma's agricultural industry.

Information

The state has 12 conveniently positioned, state-operated Welcome Centers (open daily), including one at either end of I-40. The Oklahoma Tourism & Recreation Dept (☎ 405-521-2409, 800-652-6552, Ⓦ www .travelok.com) provides an information pack.

For highway conditions, call ☎ 405-425-2385. For information on Route 66, call ☎ 405-348-3589. The statewide sales tax is

4.5%; another 4% is assessed on lodging and restaurants.

OKLAHOMA CITY

Oklahoma's capital is like a four-door 1976 Coup de Ville with a broken bumper and bullhorns on the front: It's big and ugly but oozes with a style all its own. Its fistful-plus of attractions transform the flat, fairly tree-less city into a pretty good place to spend a few days.

Oklahoma City ('OKC') sprang up on April 22, 1889, as 10,000 legitimate land claimants staked out land around the Santa Fe railroad station. The city yanked capital honors from Guthrie in 1910 and was cata-pulted into wealth in 1928, when OKC's first gusher erupted above a vast oil field.

Amid all the fun, OKC forgot to think much about city planning, and in 1965 asked urban architect IM Pei for a makeover – long-awaited gardens and green belts and a concourse of skywalks and tunnels helped improve the city's appearance. In 1993 city voters passed a landmark $310 million tax for another downtown building spree. The results include a new canal and baseball park in the historic Bricktown district – both big hits. By 2003 OKC will have a new convention center, library, capitol dome and 7 miles of trails and parks along North Canadian River.

Orientation & Information

Oklahoma's main interstates (I-44, I-35, I-40 and Route 66) pass through OKC. Down-town is bordered by I-40 on the south, 5th St to the north, Shartel Ave to the west and the Santa Fe train track to the east. The Brick-town District is just east.

The Oklahoma City CVB (☎ 405-297-8912, 800-225-5652, W www.visitokc.com, 189 W Sheridan Ave) is open weekdays. The downtown library (☎ 405-231-8650, 131 McGee Ave) has Internet access (closed Sun). 'King Country' 93.3 FM gives OKC a steel-guitar soundtrack.

Things to See & Do

The city's most worthwhile attraction is the huge **National Cowboy & Western Heritage Museum** (☎ 405-478-2250, 1700 NE 63rd St), formerly the Cowboy Hall of Fame. Highlights include cowboy art by Charles M Russell and Frederic Remington, James Earle Fraser's 18-foot statue *The End of the Trail*, Native American artifacts and a rodeo room with an exhibit on African American bulldogger Bill Pickett. The Children's Cowboy Corral is a hit with the young'uns. Sadly the museum's focus leaves most cow-*girls* in the dust ($8.50/4.25 for adults/chil-dren; open daily).

In the seven-story Crystal Bridge at the **Myriad Botanical Gardens** (☎ 405-297-3995), at Reno and Robinson Aves, you can witness three ecosystems in action ($4; open daily). The **Calvary Baptist Church** (300 N Walnut Ave) played a big role in Okla-homa's Civil Rights movement.

The **State Capitol** (☎ 405-521-3356, 2300 Lincoln Blvd) has stood patiently domeless since funds dried up in 1917 but will get its dome in 2003. Outside, oil derricks stand sentry over huge (plugged) oil wells under the grounds. The **Oklahoma State Museum**

The Oklahoma City Bombing

On April 19, 1995, OKC's security and self-confidence were destroyed in mere moments with the tragic bombing of the Alfred P Murrah Federal Building by right-wing extremists. Some 168 lives were lost, including those of 16 preschoolers. The devastated city block, at 5th St and Harvey Ave – now called the Oklahoma City National Memorial – immediately became a macabre attrac-tion, with many visitors pinning mementos to a chain-link fence.

Today there are two new memorials to see: The chilling Outdoor Symbolic Memorial has walls marked '9:01' and '9:03' to frame the time of the blast; 168 empty chairs represent each of the victims and are illuminated at night (free admission; open daily). The Memorial Center Museum (☎ 405-235-3313, 620 N Harvey Ave) has comprehensive and sometimes graphic exhibits ($7; open daily). It starts in a 'conference room' where an actual recording of the blast is played. Parking garages and meters are near the site.

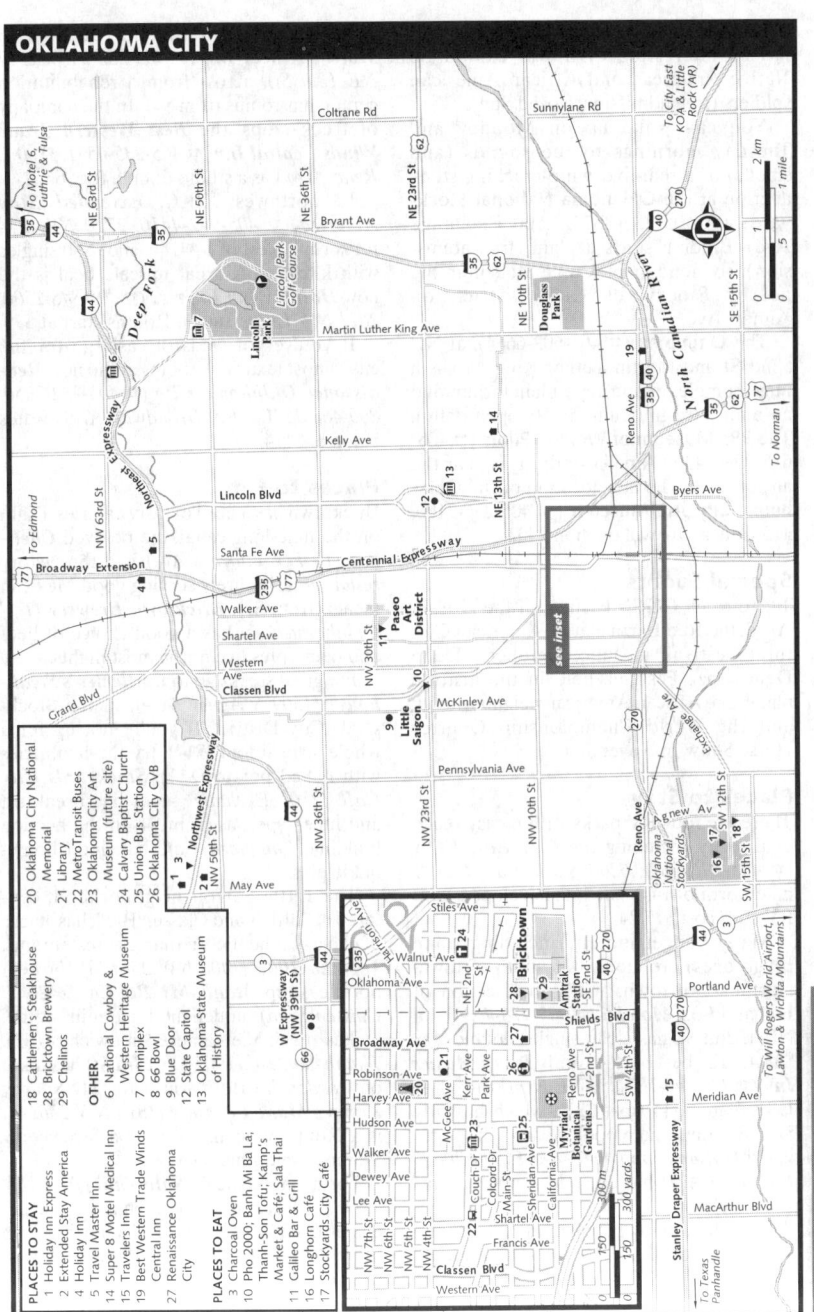

OKLAHOMA CITY

PLACES TO STAY
1 Holiday Inn Express
3 Extended Stay America
4 Holiday Inn
5 Travel Master Inn
14 Super 8 Motel Medical Inn
15 Travelers Inn
19 Best Western Trade Winds
   Central Inn
27 Renaissance Oklahoma
   City

PLACES TO EAT
8 Charcoal Oven
10 Pho 2000; Banh Mi Ba La;
   Thanh-Son Tofu; Kamp's
   Market & Café; Sala Thai
11 Galileo Bar & Grill
16 Longhorn Café
17 Stockyards City Café

18 Cattlemen's Steakhouse
28 Bricktown Brewery
29 Chelinos

OTHER
6 National Cowboy &
   Western Heritage Museum
7 Omniplex
9 Blue Door
12 State Capitol
13 Oklahoma State Museum
   of History

20 Oklahoma City National
   Memorial
21 Library
22 MetroTransit Buses
23 Oklahoma City Art
   Museum (future site)
24 Calvary Baptist Church
25 Union Bus Station
26 Oklahoma City CVB

of History (☎ 405-521-2491, 2100 N Lincoln) has an interesting Civil War exhibit on Native American and African American soldiers (free admission; closed Sun).

You can wake up on Monday and Tuesday mornings to the sounds (and smells) of a real-live, whip-cracking stock auction at the **Oklahoma National Stockyards** (☎ 405-235-8675, 2500 Exchange Ave). Bidding starts at 8am (free admission). To blend in, pick up a Stetson in the nearby Stockyards City District, on Agnew Ave.

The **Omniplex** (☎ 405-602-6664), at NE 52nd St and Martin Luther King Ave, is a huge complex featuring a planetarium and air-and-space museum ($6.50; open daily). The **99s Museum of Women Pilots** (☎ 405-685-9990, 4300 Amelia Earhart) is near the airport ($5). The new location of the **Oklahoma City Art Museum** (☎ 405-236-3100, 415 Couch Dr) will open in 2003.

Special Events

Try to catch OKC's Festival of the Arts, in April; the Red Earth Native American Cultural Festival, in June; October's Deep Deuce Jazz Festival, held in the historic namesake African American neighborhood; and the World Championship Quarter Horse Show, in November.

Places to Stay

There are four RV parks within easy reach of the city, including the **City East KOA** (☎ 405-391-5000, 6200 S Choctaw Rd), 1 mile north of I-40 exit 166; developed tent/RV sites cost $17/24.

Many budget motels (including some rough ones) are along I-35 south of town. Northeast of town, at the intersection of I-44 and I-35, **Motel 6** (☎ 405-478-4030), on NE 122nd St, has clean singles/doubles for $33/42. The best buck-saver is **Travel Master Inn** (☎ 405-840-1824, 33 NE Expressway), at US 77 and I-44 (exit 127), which has tidy $28/38 rooms and a pool. Nearby, the renovated **Holiday Inn** (☎ 405-843-5558, 6200 N Robinson Ave) has an indoor pool; rooms start at $80.

There are many hotels (and restaurants) north and south of I-40 on busy Meridian Ave, including **Travelers Inn** (☎ 405-942-8294, 504 S Meridian Ave). Clean rooms cost $45/50.

Just east of downtown, the cute **Super 8 Motel Medical Inn** (☎ 405-232-0404, 1117 NE 13th St), across from a rehabilitation center, has rooms from $41. In the company of truck stops, the **Best Western Trade Winds Central Inn** (☎ 405-235-4531, 1800 E Reno Ave) has a studio double for $66.

In northwest OKC, **Extended Stay America** (☎ 405-942-4410, 2720 NW Expressway), west of I-44, has nice $50 singles with kitchens. A great upscale deal is the new **Holiday Inn Express** (☎ 405-848-1500, 2811 NW Expressway). Rooms start at $79.

If you've got wads of cash, go for the city's most luxurious rooms at the new **Renaissance Oklahoma City** (☎ 405-232-2050, 800-468-3571, 10 N Broadway Ave). Rates begin at $124.

Places to Eat

Bricktown has a herd of tasty eateries. Right on the mile-long canal, the beloved **Chelinos** (15 E California Ave) is a three-story *restaurante*, leisurely serving good Mexican meals (from $7). **Bricktown Brewery** (1 N Oklahoma Ave) has a good choice of beef and beers, plus live music most nights.

For great steaks go to **Cattlemen's Steakhouse** (1309 S Agnew Ave), in the Stockyards City District. If you're not up for a whole strip sirloin ($17), try the lamb fries with baked potato ($11). **Stockyards City Café** (2501 Exchange Ave) has breakfast and lunch specials from $4. In the auction building, **Longhorn Café** has good homemade pies.

The Little Saigon neighborhood, centered at 23rd St and Classen Blvd, has stacks of cheap, authentic Vietnamese restaurants. Try **Pho 2000** (1400 NW 23rd St) for beef noodle soup. **Banh Mi Ba La** (2426 N Classen Blvd), under the huge milk bottle, makes quick Vietnamese sandwiches ($2). **Thanh-Son Tofu** (905 SW 23rd St) has takeout *lo dau hu* (tofu soup) for $1. Nearby **Kamp's Market & Café** (1310 NW 25th St) is a Route 66 icon. Stop for a Strawberry Wampus smoothie ($4).

For meatless meals, **Sala Thai** (1614 NW 23rd St) has many good Thai vegetarian dishes from $8. Several blocks northeast, in the colorful Spanish-style Paseo Art District, **Galileo Bar & Grill** (3009 Paseo Dr) makes sandwiches and iced coffee. The timeless drive-in **Charcoal Oven** (2701 NW

Expressway) has served hickory burgers since 1958 ($5 with fries and drink) – ask for the sauce.

Entertainment

For listings, pick up the free *Oklahoma Gazette*. Bricktown usually has some action in the evenings. The *66 Bowl* (☎ *405-946-3966, 3810 NW 39th St)*, on Route 66, is a bowling alley that often hosts rockabilly and punk shows. You can bring your own beer or wine to low-key concerts at *Blue Door* (☎ *405-524-0738, 2805 N McKinley Ave)*.

Getting There & Around

Will Rogers World Airport is several miles southwest of downtown. Take I-44 south from I-40, or I-240 west from I-35. Getting downtown in a Yellow Cab (☎ 405-232-6161) costs $17; the Blue Vans Shuttle (☎ 405-681-3311) charges $13.

Greyhound buses depart from the Union Bus Station (☎ 405-235-6425, 427 W Sheridan Ave). Daily buses leave for Dallas ($41; from 4 hours); Tulsa ($16; 2 hours); Kansas City ($70; 7 hours); Little Rock, Arkansas ($70; from 7 hours); and Albuquerque, New Mexico ($61; 12 hours). Jefferson Lines (☎ 405-239-6831) also runs buses out of the station.

Daily Amtrak trains connect Fort Worth, Texas, and OKC's Santa Fe Depot at 100 S EK Gaylord Blvd ($26-50; 4½ hours).

Fares on MetroTransit city buses (☎ 405-235-7433, 200 N Shartel) are $1.

AROUND OKLAHOMA CITY
Guthrie

Oklahoma's first capital, 20 miles north of Oklahoma City, is one of the Great Plains' best-preserved towns. Its 12-sq-block downtown, lined with hundred-year-old buildings, teems with life on many summer weekends and during April's '89er Celebration. Tom Cruise and Dustin Hoffman came here to film the crosswalk scene for *Rain Man*. The CVB (☎ 405-282-1947, 212 W Oklahoma Ave) has brochures.

At the excellent **Oklahoma Territorial Museum** (☎ 405-282-1889, 406 E Oklahoma Ave), see a copy of the state's first flag, changed in 1922 for looking 'too communist' ($2). The Texas-sized **Scottish Rite Temple** (☎ 405-282-1281, 900 E Oklahoma Ave) has two tours daily ($5).

Osage Indian Nation

This large area, northwest of Tulsa on pleasant SR 11, is technically Osage County but is marked with 'Osage Indian Nation' signs. Since 1872 it's been home for the twice-removed tribe (originally from present-day Missouri and Arkansas). When oil was discovered on their lands in 1920, the Osage became the world's richest nation, sadly prompting the 'Reign of Terror,' when hundreds of Osage were shot and bombed by lowlifes seeking wealth. (The Osage ended up *paying* the FBI to investigate.)

In 1927, the local Hominy Indians football team played the champion New York Giants and, surprisingly, they whipped them in **Pawhuska**, 28 miles west of Bartlesville on US 60, where today you can visit a few interesting museums. The surrounding Osage Hills (including the Tallgrass Prairie Reserve) make for nice drives. Take the gravel roads, and check local cemeteries for those who died in the '20s.

Guthrie has a dozen historic B&Bs, including *Harrison House* (☎ *405-282-1000, 124 Harrison)*, with rooms for $72.

Norman

Oklahoma's third-largest city is the home of the University of Oklahoma (OU) and its worshipped Sooners football team. The OU Visitor Center (☎ 405-325-2151), in Jacobson Hall at Boyd and Parrington Oval, can arrange tours. Across the oval, the free Fred Jones Jr Museum of Art is worth a peek. OU's best attraction is the new, dinosaur-packed **Sam Noble Oklahoma Museum of Natural History** (☎ 405-325-4712, 2401 S Chautauqua Ave), a mile south of Lindsey St ($4; open daily). In the wee campus corner, a three-block area centered at Boyd and Asp Sts, *Midway* on Buchanan St, is a convenience store/hangout where a reluctant owner makes sandwiches 'with love.'

OKLAHOMA CITY TO TULSA (ROUTE 66)

Route 66 between Oklahoma's two biggest cities is the country's longest remaining continuous stretch of the Mother Road. Take it

GREAT PLAINS

and save the $3.50 toll required for the I-44 route, which Route 66 snakes around.

In **Arcadia**, stop at the famed Round Barn (free admission), then grab a burger at *Hillbillee's Café & B&B* (☎ 405-396-2982). The rooms cost $75 on weekends, when bands play foot-stompin' tunes at the cafe.

About halfway to Tulsa, **Chandler** is the route's nicest town and has old Route 66 filling stations and the *Lincoln Motel* (☎ 405-258-0200), with a US flag hanging outside each of its $35 rooms. About 3 miles west, *Read Ranch* (☎ 405-258-2999) has rustic cabins ($35) and horseback-riding packages ($125 per person). In **Stroud**, 14 miles east, *Rock Café* serves some intense peach cobbler.

TULSA

Oklahoma's second-largest city is its nicest. From the highways, Tulsa's downtown pops out of a sea of oaks that give the area its 'Green Country' nickname. Tulsa's name comes from the Creek Indians who camped on the Arkansas River here in 1828: Their word 'Tallahassee' (Old Town) evolved to 'Tulsey Town' and finally 'Tulsa.'

Known as the 'Oil Capital of the World' in the early to mid-20th century, Tulsa actually didn't have much oil – just heaps of oil companies that reaped the rewards of statewide wells. Some of the riches have been transformed into a wide range of landmarks, including the 76-foot *Golden Driller* on 21st St between Harvard and Yale.

The SE Hinton book *The Outsiders* – and subsequent film – took place in Tulsa. And you can credit Tulsa for raising the teen pop stars Hanson.

Orientation & Information

I-44 rolls through town from the southwest to the northeast, and I-244, US 75 and US 64 conveniently lead into downtown from it. The CVB (☎ 918-477-1000, 616 S Boston St) has brochures (open Mon-Fri). The nearest state Welcome Center (☎ 918-439-3212) is east of town on I-44 in Catoosa. Radio station KVOO 1170 AM has given Tulsa its country twang since 1926.

Things to See & Do

The **Thomas Gilcrease Museum** (☎ 918-596-2700, 1400 Gilcrease Museum Rd), off US 64 northwest of downtown, has a tremendous collection of art depicting the American West, Native American art and a detailed Las Artes de Mexico exhibit ($3; closed Mon).

The **Philbrook Museum of Art** (☎ 918-749-7941, 2727 S Rockford Rd), east of Peoria Ave, is housed in a villa of Italian Renaissance style with surrounding gardens. The collection is superb – Asian, Native American and European ($5.50; closed Mon).

The Historic Greenwood District, a few blocks northeast of downtown, is where 'Black Wall Street' thrived in the early 20th century. Its **Greenwood Cultural Center** (☎ 918-596-1030, 322 N Greenwood Ave) displays photos of the area before and after the 1921 Tulsa Race Riot (see the boxed text 'African Americans in Oklahoma'), and houses the Oklahoma Jazz Hall of Fame (free admission; closed Sun).

Named for the TV evangelist, **Oral Roberts University** (ORU; 7777 S Lewis Ave) flaunts a retro-futuristic campus that looks like the Jetsons meet Jesus. To prompt funds, Oral once camped out in the 200-foot glass Prayer Tower (☎ 918-495-7910), east of the huge praying hands. Go up it for a view; there's no pressure to 'talk to God.'

Tulsa is famed for its **art deco buildings**, though most are spaced apart. The 1931 Tulsa Union Depot, on 1st St downtown, is closed to the public, but you can view the outside. A collection of 40-plus art deco buildings is found between 2nd, 6th, Cheyenne and Cincinnati Sts. Downtown's most distinctive building is the skyscraper United Methodist Church (1301 S Boston Ave).

Western swing hero Bob Wills was taken back to Tulsa after his death in 1975. Visit **Bob Wills' grave** at Memorial Park (5115 S Memorial Dr).

Places to Stay

The *Tulsa KOA* (☎ 918-266-4227, 19605 E Skelly Dr), east of Tulsa in Catoosa (I-44 exit 240A), has tent/RV sites for $18/24.

West of the Arkansas River on I-44 are some old-timer motels, some a bit haggard. A good one is *Gateway Motor Hotel* (☎ 918-446-6611, 5600 W Skelly Dr), with $35 doubles. In town, *Village Inn* (☎ 918-743-2009, 114 E Skelly Dr), off I-44 exit 226, has clean singles for $43. Close to the airport, **Super 8** (☎ 918-836-1981, 6616 E Archer) has a pool and $51 singles.

The centrally located **Fairfield by Marriott** (☎ 918-663-0000, 3214 S 79th E Ave), at the junction of I-44 and SR 51, is a good mid-range choice with $59/69 singles/doubles and an indoor pool.

Places to Eat

There's good dining in the Brookside neighborhood, on Peoria Ave between 31st and 51st Sts. Try the busy-at-breakfast **Brookside By Day** (3313 Peoria Ave). Just north, Cherry Street, along 15th St just east of Peoria, has several tasty options. Many locals swear that **Ron's Hamburgers & Chili** (3239 E 15th St) grills Tulsa's best burger. The classic downtown diner **Nelson's Buffeteria** (514 S Boston Ave) is popular for its $5 chicken-fried steaks.

Open to midnight daily, **Jamil's** (☎ 918-742-9097, 2833 E 51st St), near Harvard Ave, is a great little steakhouse serving hickory-grilled steaks (from $16); each come with Lebanese hors d'oeuvres.

Between ORU and I-44, **India Palace** (6963 S Lewis Ave) has some of the best Indian food this side of Punjab. A huge lunch buffet costs $7, and the cups of chai are bottomless. You might want to follow (some) regulars' tradition by thanking the chefs in person.

Ri Le (4932 E 91st St), at Yale Ave, serves good Vietnamese meals, including the all-vegetarian pineapple soy with fake beef ($7).

Entertainment

Although on the quiet side, Tulsa has something happening on many nights; check the *Urban Tulsa Weekly* for what's going on. Aside from Brookside bars, catch a show at historic **Cain's Ballroom** (☎ 918-584-2309, 423 N Main St), which has seen the likes of Bob Wills and the Sex Pistols. **Caravan Cattle Company** (☎ 918-663-5468, 7901 E 41st St) gives free two-step lessons on Tuesday nights. In summer, there's a dandy production of *Oklahoma!* at **Discoveryland!** (☎ 918-742-5255), in Sand Springs, 5 miles northwest of Tulsa ($16).

Getting There & Around

Tulsa International Airport (☎ 918-838-5046), off Hwy 11, is northeast of downtown. Greyhound (☎ 918-584-4428, 317 S Detroit Ave) has daily buses bound for Oklahoma City ($17; 2 hours) and Kansas City ($57; from 5 hours). Tulsa Transit metro buses (☎ 918-582-2100) run limited routes.

GREEN COUNTRY

Full of lakes and subtle, forested hills, Oklahoma's northeast corner (including Tulsa) is called 'Green Country.' Drivers heading to Missouri can go along segments of Route 66. Catoosa's Blue Whale (a smiling pond-moored, wooden thing) is a favorite stop.

Bartlesville & Woolaroc

North of Tulsa, the oil town Bartlesville is noted for Frank Lloyd Wright's tallest skyscraper **Price Tower**, which is filled with original Wright-designed furnishings from the 1950s. (It was originally intended to be a New York City apartment building.) Tours are at 11am and 2pm ($5; closed Mon).

Kids love Woolaroc (☎ 918-336-0307), 12 miles southwest on SR 123, one of the state's best attractions. Frank Phillips, the founder of Phillips Oil, poured a good deal of his fortune into this eclectic collection of Native American and Wild West artifacts. You can tour Phillips' lodge, a Native American center and an oil site, and see scores of buffalo. If you touch the stuffed buffalo, next to the buffalo burger stand, it'll scold you ($5/free for adults/kids; closed Mon in winter).

Claremore

Many folks don't know who Will Rogers was these days, but don't say this in his home town of Claremore, on Route 66 northeast of Tulsa. Will, born in 1879, was a Cherokee cowboy, movie star, comedian and homespun philosopher. Two hours at the smashing **Will Rogers Memorial Museum** (☎ 918-341-0719), a mile west of Route 66, will give you a sense of his importance when he was alive ($4).

Trail of Tears Country

The Five Civilized Tribes (Cherokee, Choctaw, Chickasaw, Creek and Seminole) were moved into this region, southeast of present-day Tulsa, in the late 1830s. Anyone interested in learning about Native American culture should stop here for a few days.

Known from the Merle Haggard song 'Okie from Muskogee,' **Muskogee** (49 miles

African Americans in Oklahoma

The history of Oklahoman African Americans is important in the story of the USA's settlement. Many came as slaves of the Five Civilized Tribes during the infamous Trail of Tears. The first African American troop to defeat the Confederacy during the Civil War did so at the Battle of Honey Springs (July 1863), near today's Muskogee. Many of the soldiers went on to become members of the 9th and 10th Cavalries of Fort Sill, fought in Indian Wars and earned the title 'buffalo soldiers' (as Native Americans likened their hair to a buffalo's).

After the war, the 'freedmen' established businesses and created towns. At the time of Oklahoma statehood, African Americans made up the majority of the population, outnumbering both Native Americans and whites. Even during the periods of segregation and the Jim Crow laws, the African Americans in Oklahoma thrived in boom towns such as Boley and Rentiesville. But most prosperous was Tulsa's Greenwood Ave, dubbed 'Black Wall Street.'

In 1921 Greenwood Ave became the scene of the nation's worst racial violence. An 'army' of white looters stormed the area while planes flew overhead. The police stood back as 36 people died (officially – the real number could be in the hundreds). Scores of families lost all property and savings, but no compensation has ever been granted. The fight for justice by survivors and descendants continues in the 21st century.

Many famous names emerged from Oklahoma: Deputy US Marshal Bass Reeves arrested some 3000 outlaws. Bill Pickett invented the sport of bulldogging (steer wrestling) and could pull a bull down by biting its lip. Henry Clay of the 101 Ranch Wild West Show taught Will Rogers roping tricks. Edwin P McCabe, who founded Langston City as part of the 'all-black town movement,' pushed for a black state for 19 years. And a host of jazz and bebop musicians started off with the Oklahoma City Blue Devils, including saxophonist Lester Young, jazz violin innovator Claude Williams and pianist William 'Count' Basie.

southwest of Tulsa) is home to the Five Civilized Tribes Museum (☎ 918-683-1701), on Honor Heights Dr (east of the US 62 and 69 junction), which is housed in the 1875 Union Indian Agency building ($2).

West on US 62, **Tahlequah** has been the Cherokee capital since 1839. The Cherokee Heritage Center (☎ 918-456-6007), south of town, has good displays of the Trail of Tears forced march ($8.50). In July and August, see *Tsa-La-Gi* ('Cherokee'), a great outdoor production ($15). The nearby Illinois River is popular for canoe trips in spring and summer. *Oak Hill Motel Suites* (☎ 918-458-1200, 2600 S Muskogee Ave) has single rooms for $59.

Downtown **Okmulgee** looks like the set of a 1950s film, with shops such as Boy Howdy Variety Store going strong. The Creek Council House Museum (☎ 918-756-2324, 106 W 6th St) is in the former capital of the Muscogee (Creek) Nation. Don't miss the stick-ball display, a ritual so fierce that 'limbs were frequently broken' (free admission; closed Sun and Mon).

The region also hosts a few **African American rodeos**, in Okmulgee in August and in the African American historic town of Boley on Memorial Day weekend.

WESTERN OKLAHOMA

West of Oklahoma City on I-40, Oklahoma opens into the 'real West.' Amid expansive fields of prairie and jarring Wichita Mountains, you'll find much evidence of Native American and pioneer heritages, plus heaps of worthy Route 66 sites.

Oklahoma City to Texas Panhandle

West of Oklahoma City, I-40 runs to Texola, on the state's western border. Route 66 frequently twists on and off the interstate; get the free *Official Oklahoma Route 66 Association Trip Guide* to help locate its many landmarks.

Red Rock Canyon State Park (☎ 405-542-6344), south of I-40 on US 281, has rock-climbing walls and $7 tent sites.

GREAT PLAINS

In Clinton, at the junction of US 183, the neon-lit **Route 66 Museum** (☎ 580-323-7866, 2229 W Gary Blvd) has six decades of memorabilia ($3).

Other points of interest along the western section of the state's I-40/Route 66 include Elk City, with chain motels and the **National Route 66 Museum** (☎ 580-225-6266), which charges a $5 admission.

Cheyenne, 24 miles north of I-40, is worth a detour. Its **Washita Battlefield Site** is where George Custer's troops launched the 1868 attack of the slumbering (and peaceful) village of Chief Black Kettle. Learn more at the Black Kettle Museum (☎ 580-497-3929). *Coyote Hills Guest Ranch* (☎ 580-497-3931), west of the battlefield, has rooms for $135 per person, including meals, horseback riding and mountain biking.

Anadarko

Founded in the 1901 land rush, when settlers claimed former Native American lands, Anadarko and the surrounding area, west of I-44 via US 62, is still home to 64 tribes and calls itself the 'Indian Capital of the Nation.' Anadarko hosts powwows and rodeos most months; get information from the chamber of commerce (☎ 405-247-6651), at Mission and Kentucky Sts.

The **Southern Plains Indian Museum** (☎ 405-247-6221), on US 62, has exhibits on Native American art as well as a store ($3; closed Mon). The nearby **National Hall of Fame for Famous American Indians** (☎ 405-247-5555) is a 40-acre park with 43 bronze busts. The post office, at SR 8 and Oklahoma St, has 16 impressive murals.

Indian City USA (☎ 405-247-5661), 2 miles south on SR 8, is worth visiting for the guided tour of seven authentic Native American villages scattered along a hilltop trail. Ask about Tonkawa ghosts seen in the area ($7.50; open daily).

Payless Inn (☎ 405-247-2538, 1603 E Central), on US 62, has $50 doubles. Oklahoma's best barbecue is at *Jake's Rib*, 19 miles east in Chickasha.

Lawton & Fort Sill

The last of the land-rush cities, Lawton ain't one of Oklahoma's lovelier places, but the **Museum of the Great Plains** (☎ 580-581-3460, 601 NW Ferris St) has magnificent collections of Plains Indian artifacts and prairie dogs outside ($3; closed Mon).

North of town, Fort Sill, established in 1869 as an Indian-fighting outpost, is an active base with a frontier flavor. Follow signs from the fort to **Geronimo's grave**. The Fort Sill Museum (☎ 580-442-5123) has photos and a film of the African American troop that built the fort. Missile Park is an outdoor display of artillery used from WWII to Desert Storm, a far cry from that used to subdue the Plains Indians (free admission).

Wichita Mountains

One of the Great Plains' most beautiful settings, the **Wichita Mountains Wildlife Refuge**, on SR 49 west of I-44 (northwest of Fort Sill), is a superb destination for hiking and wildlife viewing (more than 600 buffalo roam the refuge). The Wichitas' granite peaks are ideal for rock climbing; check the Wichita Mountains Climbers Coalition (Ⓦ www.wichitamountains.org) for tips.

The visitor center (☎ 580-429-3222) shows a good film on buffalo. Drive up Mt Scott or, if you're feeling energetic, hike up Elk Mountain for incredible views. *Doris Campground* has developed tent/RV sites on the refuge for $6/10.

Nearby **Medicine Park** is a cobblestone village unknown to most Oklahomans. For generations, Native Americans used the water from the area's creek for healing purposes. Hollywood stars and gangsters splashed in it in the early 20th century. *Haile Hideaway* (☎ 580-529-2341) has two randomly decorated rooms (from $65) across from a music hall. Have a steak and hot roll at the timeless *Old Plantation Restaurant* (☎ 580-529-9641); be sure to ask 'GrandMa' about how she liked meeting Twisted Sister's Dee Snider.

Another extension of the Wichitas is 51 miles west at the gorgeous 4500-acre **Quartz Mountain State Park**, on Lake Altus-Lugert. There are mountain trails and developed *campsites* (☎ 580-563-2238) for $7. The new *Quartz Mountain Resort* (☎ 580-563-2424, 877-999-5567) is a great place to get some rest and relaxation; rooms start at $109.

Kansas

The vast, rolling prairies of Kansas are blanketed with wheat and occasionally battered by tornadoes – such as the mythical one that whisked Dorothy and Toto away in the *Wizard of Oz*. Though the state's tourist attractions are few, the Kansas Plains dwellers are some of the friendliest folks you could hope to meet.

History

Kansas has historically been a place people passed through – Coronado seeking Quivira, cowboys driving cattle, pioneers following the Santa Fe Trail, the Pony Express delivering mail, railroads transporting people and goods, and carloads of college kids heading to Colorado ski slopes.

The Kansas-Nebraska Act of 1854, which allowed settlers in Kansas and Nebraska to vote for or against slavery, triggered 'Bleeding Kansas,' a conflict between the pro- and antislavery settlers that hastened the Civil War. In 1856, Lawrence was ransacked by proslavery border 'Ruffians'; retaliatory raids by antislavery forces followed, including one led by the abolitionist John Brown. Kansas was admitted as a free state shortly after the Southern states seceded from the Union in 1860.

The buffalo were wiped out, the Native Americans (even the state's namesake Kansa, who were relocated to present-day Oklahoma in 1873) pushed off and the settlers moved in, after which Kansas changed quickly from rip-roaring open range to some of the most productive wheat lands in the world. Aviation industries, based in Wichita, have been big moneymakers too.

Information

Kansas runs four information centers – in Kansas City on I-70, in Olathe at I-35 exit 220, in Belle Plaine on the I-35 (south of Wichita) and way out west in Goodland on I-70. Ask for information from Kansas Travel & Tourism (☎ 785-296-2009, 800-252-6727, Ⓦ www.kansascommerce.com).

All state parks require a daily vehicle permit ($5). For more information, call ☎ 620-672-5911. For road conditions, call ☎ 800-585-7623.

Kansas

Nickname: Sunflower State

Population: 2,478,100 (32nd)

Area: 82,280 sq miles (15th)

Admitted to Union: January 29, 1861 (34th)

Capital city: Topeka (population 120,300)

Other cities: Wichita (311,800), Lawrence (67,800)

State song: 'Home on the Range'

Birthplace of: Amelia Earhart, Charlie Parker, Annette Bening, Melissa Etheridge, silent-film star Buster Keaton

Famous for: Turkey Red wheat, starting prohibition, fictional residents Dorothy and Toto (of Oz fame)

The statewide tax is 4.9%, with increments up to 2%; extra lodging taxes range from 1% to 5%.

WICHITA

This now-prosperous city on the confluence of the Big and Little Arkansas Rivers had a humble beginning as a cowtown on the Chisholm Trail in the 1860s. The railroad's arrival in 1872 triggered a boom, and burgeoning wheat and oil industries fanned its growth. Following WWI Wichita began producing heaps of airplanes. Boeing, Beech and Cessna have manufacturing plants near the city.

Ongoing riverfront development, including river walks, is helping transform a ho-hum downtown into something special (as a guide said, 'even folks from *Kansas City* are starting to visit'). Wichita's McConnell Air Force Base treats the town with an air show in June, and the city hosts the Mid-America All Indian Center Inter-Tribal Powwow in July.

Incidentally, Wichitans have bickered over the pronunciation of the Arkansas River for well over 100 years. Most locals continue to refer to it as 'areKANsas.' Conform or be cast out.

The Wichita CVB (☎ 316-265-2800, 800-288-9424, Ⓦ www.wichita-cvb.org, 100 S Main St) is open weekdays. A boathouse visitor center (335 W Lewis) is open daily. Tune in to KFDI 1070 AM for old-time country tunes and a lost-dog report.

Things to See & Do

Across the Arkansas from downtown are several quite interesting museums. The new **Exploration Place** (☎ 316-263-3373, 300 N McLean Blvd) has lots of kid-friendly science exhibits, including a touchable tornado ($7/5 adults/kids; open daily). Outside there's a bizarre minigolf course – you aim for one hole with lasers ($5).

The **Indian Center Museum** (☎ 316-262-5221, 650 N Seneca St) has a Native American flag collection, plus a new grass house (the traditional Wichita dwelling). Events are scheduled here year round ($6; closed Mon). For another version of the Wild West, visit **Old Cowtown** (☎ 316-264-6398, 1871 Sim Park Dr), featuring pioneer-era buildings and gunfights ($7/3.50; open Apr-Oct). The **Wichita Art Museum** (☎ 316-268-4921, 619 Stackman Dr) will be closed until the end of 2002 to add a new wing for its American collection.

The prairie-style **Allen-Lambe House** (☎ 316-687-1027, 255 N Roosevelt St) was designed by Frank Lloyd Wright in 1915; Frank ranked it among his best ($8). Call to schedule a tour of the **Kansas African American Museum** (☎ 316-262-7651, 601 N Water St) in a historical church (free admission).

In the fascinatingly unrestored old airport, the **Kansas Aviation Museum** (☎ 316-683-9242, 3350 George Washington Blvd) has a bunch of planes inside and a view of the air force base from the tower ($2; closed Sun and Mon).

Places to Stay

The **USI RV Park** (☎ 316-838-8699, 2920 E 33rd N St) has RV and tent sites with full hookups for $20.

On the East Corridor just west of US 54 and I-35, there are piles of motels, including the well-kept **Mark 8 Lodge** (☎ 316-685-9415, 888-860-7268, 8136 E Kellogg), near Rock Rd, which has $33 doubles with kitchenettes. Another concentration of motels is near the airport, around US 54 and I-235. Try **Scotsman Inn West** (☎ 316-943-3800, 5922 W Kellogg), with $38 doubles.

For location, you can't beat the **Hotel at Oldtown** (☎ 316-267-4800, 877-265-3269, 830 1st St), steps away from restaurants and bars. Rooms start at $92 on weekends.

Places to Eat

Though Wichita is home of Pizza Hut (there are 21 outlets here), Wichitans' favorite eateries are in Old Town, the eight-block historic district just east of downtown. You're likely to wait for a seat at dinner.

On sunny days, locals crowd the outside patio at **Larkspur Restaurant** (904 E Douglas), popular for pastas and steaks ($15 and up, cheaper at lunch). **Rowdy Joe's** (231 N Mosley St) has buffalo heads on the wall and $6 buffalo burgers on the menu. **Herb Garden Restaurant** (626 E Douglas), a block west, has a few veggie sandwiches at lunch.

Open since 1930, **Nu Way Café** (1416 W Douglas), west of the museums, serves unique shredded-beef burgers ($3) and homemade root beer ('made from a ton of sugar').

Getting There & Around

The Mid-Continent Airport is 5 miles southwest of downtown on US 54 (Kellogg Dr).

The Greyhound station (☎ 316-265-7711, 312 S Broadway) sends buses to Kansas City ($32; from 3 hours), Oklahoma City ($31; from 2 hours) and Denver, Colorado ($72; from 12 hours).

The nearest Amtrak station (☎ 316-283-7533), 27 miles north in Newton on I-135, has trains leaving around 3am, on their way to Kansas City and Albuquerque, New Mexico; a local bus connects to Wichita.

Wichita Metro Transit Authority buses (WMTA; ☎ 316-265-7221, 214 S Topeka St) run a few routes around town ($1). For a taxi, call Best Cabs (☎ 316-838-2233).

ALONG INTERSTATE 70

This is Kansas' 'main street' running east-west across the state, from Kansas City west to the Colorado border. Kansas' part of I-70 westward commences in Kansas City, but most of the city and points of interest are in Missouri; see the Missouri section, earlier.

Lawrence

The nicest city in Kansas, Lawrence was founded in 1854 by abolitionists and was often a hotbed for clashing forces. The city was an important stop on the Underground

Dorothy & the Land of Oz

No trip to Kansas is complete without a visit to Oz. L Frank Baum's classic fantasy books are firmly etched in everyone's memory via the great Hollywood film the *Wizard of Oz* (1939). In **Liberal**, the Land of Oz (☎ 620-624-7624) is at, of course, 567 Yellow Brick Rd; a fake 'twister' will transport you to a replica of Dorothy's pad ($5/3.50 adults/kids; open daily).

Another place for Oz-heads to visit is **Sedan**, which has a mile-long yellow brick road around its historic downtown. The Yellow Brick Road Visitor Center (☎ 316-725-5797) has a gift shop (closed Sun). Watch out for munchkin droppings.

Railroad, but it suffered for its antislavery zeal in 1863 when the Confederate Quantrill's Raiders swooped down, killing around 150 civilians.

Today Lawrence is home to Kansas University (KU), which has a few free museums worth seeing, and Haskell Indian Nations University, the country's only intertribal university (where Olympian Jim Thorpe studied). Best of all is Lawrence's active downtown, perhaps one of the country's nicest. Pick up brochures at the visitor center (☎ 785-865-4499), at N 2nd and Locust Sts (open daily). Call ☎ 877-942-0544 for a shuttle to or from the KCI airport ($29).

Camp at *Lawrence/Kansas City KOA* (☎ 785-842-3877), north of the I-70 and US 59 intersection (tent sites cost $20), or at lovely *Clinton State Park* (☎ 785-842-8562), southwest of town.

The presence of KU jacks up the motel rates. Try *Super 8 Motel* (☎ 785-842-5721, 515 McDonald Dr), south of I-70, one of the better deals with $53/63 singles/doubles. Downtown, the historic rooms at *Eldridge Hotel* (☎ 785-749-5011), at 7th and Massachusetts Sts, are $78 during the week; a few blocks west, *Halcyon House B&B* (☎ 785-841-0314, 1000 Ohio) has cozy rooms starting at $49.

Dining is a good reason to stop in Lawrence; head to 'Mass St' – downtown's chainless strip. Transformed from a bank, *Teller's Restaurant* (746 Massachusetts) has good pastas ($12 and up) and a 'vault' bathroom. *Rudy's Pizzeria* (704 Massachusetts) is famous for spicy $2 slices. Nearby, the appropriately named *Wheatfields* (904 Vermont St), serves local breads and pastries.

See a live show or movie at historic *Liberty Hall* (☎ 785-749-1972, 644 Massachusetts St).

Topeka

Kansas' rather grim capital has a few attractions worth seeing. The CVB (☎ 785-234-1030, 1275 SW Topeka Blvd) has brochures.

The quiet **Brown vs Board of Education Historic Site** (☎ 785-354-4273, 424 S Kansas Ave, Suite 215) shows an interesting video on the landmark 1954 Supreme Court case, which banned segregation in US schools (free admission; open Mon-Fri). There are plans to open a new museum at the historic Monroe Elementary School, at 15th and Monroe Sts.

The impressively domed **State Capitol** (☎ 785-272-8681, 6425 SW 6th Ave) houses a famous mural of John Brown (free tours Mon-Fri).

The **Menninger Foundation** (☎ 785-350-5860, 5800 SW 6th St) is a leader in mental health treatment. There's a collection of old mechanical restraints to see (free admission; open Mon-Fri).

There are several chain motel options off I-70 on Wanamaker Rd, west of town, and at the reliable *Motel 6* (☎ 785-272-8283, 709 Fairlawn Rd), off I-70 exit 357A, which has $45 rooms.

You can find chain restaurants along Wanamaker Rd. For more local flavor, the *Dutch Goose Bar and Grill* (3203 SW 10th St) emphasizes 'bar' rather than 'grill'; there's another location at 5630 SW 29th St. *Hanover Pancake House* (1034 S Kansas Ave) has $2 fried pickles.

Abilene

Driving into Abilene from I-70 is like a summer rain rinsing a muddy face. This friendly town, tucked away south of the interstate, is one of Kansas' highlights, with a priceless tourist center; the Abilene CVB (☎ 785-263-2231, 800-569-5915, 201 NW 2nd St) provides coffee and cookies, smiles and information.

In the late 19th century, however, Abilene was one of the rowdiest spots you could find – where cussin' cowboys and huge herds of Texas longhorns ended their trip up the Chisholm Trail. Today Abilene prefers to celebrate onetime resident and former president Dwight D Eisenhower. The **Eisenhower Center** (☎ 785-263-4751, 200 SE 4th St) includes his boyhood home (free admission), museum ($3.50), library (free) and grave. Dog lovers should go across the street to the **Greyhound Hall of Fame** (☎ 785-263-3000, 409 S Buckeye), where retired racers 'Sharon' and 'Chig' greet visitors (free admission; open daily).

Lovingly run, the *Diamond Motel* (☎ 913-263-2360, 1407 NW 3rd St) has great singles/doubles for $30/34. The best place in town to eat is the historic *Kirby House* (☎ 913-263-7336, 205 NE 3rd St), with steaks and changing dinner specials.

Western Kansas

West of Abilene, I-70 opens up into rolling, wide-open plains, where winds can knock over 18-wheelers and monotonous scenery can send the perpetually curious into a freefall of boredom. But there are a few interesting detours.

Hays sprang to life in the 1860s when Fort Hays was built to protect railroad workers. Today, some original buildings stand at the Fort Hays Historical Site (☎ 785-625-6812), 4 miles south of I-70 on US 83 (free admission). The domed Sternberg Museum of Natural History (☎ 785-628-4286, 3000 Sternberg Dr) has an unusual fish-within-a-fish fossil and animated dinosaurs ($5).

Founded in 1877 by African American settlers seeking the 'promised land,' lonely but friendly **Nicodemus** (population 25), 59 miles northwest of Hays, is one of the oldest surviving towns of its kind in the US. There are five historic buildings (and a lone parking meter). The visitor center (☎ 785-839-4233), in the former Township Hall, has a film and gives guided tours (free; call for hours). Nicodemus' Homecoming, in late July, is a big event. In little Bogue, just west, *Blue Bottle Café* serves, of all things, a veggie pita for $4.

Back on I-70, **Oakley** has a free fossil museum with heaps of prehistoric shark teeth. South on US 83 are the surprising **Monument Rocks**, 80-foot chalk formations that look like a Jawa hangout (think *Star Wars*). At *Lake Scott State Park* (☎ 620-872-2061), 10 miles farther south, the Plains suddenly break into a lovely canyon. Tent/RV sites cost $7/13.

ALONG US 50 & US 56

Alternatives to taking I-70 across Kansas are US 50 and US 56. Both pass through the Flint Hills in the east, then meet out west and enter Dodge City together.

Fabled US 50 pairs up with I-35 southwest from Kansas City; after crossing I-135, it heads out on its own again as it passes through **Chase County**, which William Least Heat-Moon examined in his book *Prairyerth*. Just west, *Jones Sheep Farm B&B* (☎ 620-983-2815), in Peabody, is a private farmhouse ($55). If you can't fall asleep, try counting the sheep.

Hutchinson, on US 50 west of I-135, is the unlikely home of the amazing **Cosmosphere & Space Center** (☎ 620-662-2305, 1100 N Plum Ave), where you can see the original *Apollo 13*, a nuclear warhead found rotting in an Alabama warehouse and cool Soviet cosmonaut outfits. There's a fun astronaut training program for the kids ($5; open daily).

Another route is US 56 southwest, which follows the old Santa Fe Trail (a little north of US 50). **Council Grove** used to be a good place to fix the Conestoga wagon. The *Cottage House Hotel* (☎ 620-767-6828, 25 N Neosho) has inviting, squeaky-floored rooms for $72.

The large **Mennonite communities** around Hillsboro, on US 56 west of Marion, are descendants of Russian immigrants who brought the Turkey Red strain of wheat to the Plains, where it thrived despite harsh conditions. Cute **Lindsborg**, about 15 miles north of US 56, on SR 4 west of I-135, flaunts its Swedish roots.

GREAT PLAINS

There are B&Bs, restaurants and events; for information call ☎ 888-227-2227. Don't miss the views from **Coronado Heights**, just north, where the Spanish explorer once cursed his feckless pursuit of gold.

Back on US 56, continue west to Great Bend, then southwest to **Larned**, where you can see the Santa Fe Trail Center Museum (☎ 620-285-2054) for $3 and, just west, the restored Fort Larned National Historic Site (☎ 620-285-6911), the only fort set up along the Santa Fe Trail ($2; open daily).

Dodge City
Modern Dodge, on US 50/56 southwest of Larned, revels in its infamous Wild West past, but today's humming grain elevators all but drown out the distant echo of the hell-raisin' days. You can find a few historic reminders, but real gunslingers, one-eyed buffalo hunters, card sharks and brothel keepers are a thing of yesteryear. For brochures, saunter into the CVB (☎ 620-225-8186, 400 W Wyatt Earp Blvd).

The touristy **Boot Hill Museum & Front Street** (☎ 620-227-8188) includes a cemetery, jail and saloon, where reenactments invoke the memory of Wyatt Earp and Bat Masterson ($7).

More fetching is **Fort Dodge** (☎ 620-227-2121), southeast on US 154. This mix of old and new buildings is home to retired soldiers, who tend to wave at visitors. There's a museum and a house that General Custer once spent the night in (free admission). About 9 miles west of town on US 50 are Santa Fe Trail **wagon wheel ruts**, most visible at dusk. None of Dodge's towering grain elevators are open for tours, but if you're in town between harvests, drop by and ask for one – you might just get lucky.

Thunderbird Motel (☎ 620-225-4143, 2300 W Wyatt Earp Blvd) has good-value singles/doubles for $37/44 (plus a ferret in the office).

Escape the Plains at **Pho 2000** (415 S 2nd Ave), south of Boot Hill, which serves Vietnamese beef noodle soup ($4.50). If you're craving a super burrito, Dodge also has many authentic Mexican restaurants (and taco trucks).

Iowa

This predominately agricultural state is a pleasant destination. Most visitors are keen to see the Madison County bridges or pose in front of Grant Wood's *American Gothic* house. More rewarding detours can be found too, particularly the drives along the Mississippi valley in the east, or through the Loess Hills in the west. Iowa's 13 well-signed scenic drives negate any notion that growing crops makes for ugly scenery.

Author Bill Bryson jokes that he's from Iowa because 'someone has to be,' but actually Iowans burst with as much state pride as Texans do.

History
Iowa was long traversed by Native Americans crossing to the main arteries of the Missouri, Big Sioux and Mississippi Rivers. Their burial and ceremonial mounds, dating from 500 BC to AD 1300, can still be seen near the western banks of the Mississippi (such as the Effigy Mounds, north of Dubuque).

Iowa was part of the Louisiana Purchase of 1803 but was not settled by whites until the 1830s. When the Black Hawk War against local Native Americans ended in 1832, the US government traded salt and tobacco for Iowa's fertile Mississippi valley region. Soon afterward, dragoons (lightly armed cavalry) 'pacified' the region and established a string of forts north of Des Moines. Immigrants then flooded in from all parts of the world, some of whom established experimental farming communities. (Of these, only the Amana Colonies remain, listed later in the chapter.)

Today Iowa is a patchwork quilt of carefully tended farms (95% of the land is fertile). Iowa – the 'food capital of the world' – leads the US in corn, soybean and hog production. A quarter of its crops gets exported overseas.

Information
You can't throw a hog in Iowa without it landing on a Welcome Center – there are 23 in all. The handiest ones are near the borders, just off the interstates, in Council Bluffs (I-80 exit 1B); Lamoni (I-35 exit 4);

Iowa

Nickname: Hawkeye State

Population: 2,869,400 (30th)

Area: 56,275 sq miles (26th)

Admitted to Union: December 28, 1846 (29th)

Capital city: Des Moines (population 193,200)

Other cities: Cedar Rapids (108,800), Davenport (95,300)

Birthplace of: John Wayne, author Bill Bryson, bandleader Glen Miller, Herbert Hoover, 'Buffalo Bill' Cody, Capt James T Kirk of *Star Trek*

Famous for: *American Gothic*, Madison County's bridges, John Deere tractors, hogs (number one in US pork production)

☺☺☺☺☺☺☺☺☺☺☺☹☺

Le Claire, off I-80 in the Mississippi valley; and Northwood (I-35 exit 214) at the 'top of Iowa.'

For information, contact the Iowa Division of Tourism (☎ 515-242-4705, 800-345-4692, w/eb www.traveliowa.com).

For highway conditions, call ☎ 515-288-1047 or 800-288-1047. The state sales tax is 5%, with city increments up to 2%; extra lodging taxes go up to 7%.

DES MOINES

Iowa's capital city, home to many insurance companies, is sometimes chided as 'Dead Moans' by locals mocking the city's lackluster nightlife. But Des Moines' few attractions are really good ones, and the downtown – positioned between a working-class east side and an upscale west side – is struggling for a little life. Perhaps the city would have had more character if it stuck with its original name, Fort Raccoon (the garrison built in 1843). The city's current name comes from 'La Rivière des Moines' (River of the Monks), bestowed by early French *voyageurs*.

I-80 and I-35 skirt Des Moines to the north; I-235 cuts through its center. The Des Moines CVB (☎ 515-286-4960, 800-451-2625, 405 6th Ave at Locust) provides city information.

Things to See & Do

The **State Capitol** (1883; ☎ 515-281-5591), at E 9th St and Grand Ave, must have been Liberace's favorite government building. Its every detail – from the sparkling gold dome to the smell of fried chicken wafting up from the basement cafeteria – seems to strive to outdo the other. On no account miss the collection of first-ladies-of Iowa dolls (open daily). The ambitious **Iowa Historical Museum** (☎ 515-281-5111, 600 E Locust St) has a 'favorite things of the 20th century' exhibit, which includes pacemakers and miniskirts (free admission; closed Mon).

The **Des Moines Art Center** (☎ 515-277-4405, 4700 Grand Ave), south of I-235 42nd St exit, is worth a look for both its interesting architecture and collection of modern art. Best is IM Pei's sculpture garden, featuring Red Grooms' Germanic 'butter cow' (free admission; closed Mon).

The amazing, 600-acre **Living History Farms** (☎ 515-278-5286), off I-80/I-35 at Hickman Rd  (in Urbandale, west of town), has four re-created villages ranging from a 1700 Ioway village to a 1900 big-red-barn farm. Visitors see how the introduction of livestock and new tools revolutionized farming. Dedicated historians farm with period tools all year. Kids love seeing the piglets ($10/5 adults/children; open daily May-Oct).

Places to Stay

Five public campgrounds are in the area. To reach *Bob Shetler* (☎ 515-276-0873), on Saylorville Lake, go 2 miles north on Hwy 401 (Merle Hay Rd), then a mile north on NW Beaver Dr. Tent/RV sites cost $8/12.

There are several chain motels at I-80/I-35 exit 131 in Urbandale, such as *Best Inn* (☎ 515-270-1111, 5050 Merle Hay Rd), with $54/61 singles/doubles and a Special K breakfast.

Across from the airport, the recently renovated *Motel 6* (☎ 515-287-6364, 4817 Fleur Dr) has good rooms for $40/45. At the I-80/I-35 exit 124 in Clive, *Fairfield Inn by Marriott* (☎ 515-226-1600, 1600 114th St) has a heated pool and $85 rooms. A great downtown place, the 1930s art deco *Kirkwood Civic Center Hotel* (☎ 515-244-9191, 400 Walnut St) has good rooms for $54.

Places to Eat

The food is good in Des Moines, but don't ask Ozzy Osbourne about it. He bit a head off a bat here in 1982.

For tasty tacos go to *Tasty Tacos (5847 SE 14th St)*, near the capitol. The beloved local chain has served fried-flour steak, chicken and bean tacos since 1961 ($2).

Downtown's Court Ave has several lively restaurants. Out next to Living History Farms, *Machine Shed Restaurant (11151 Hickman Rd)* does some fine country cooking. The 1950s-style *Drake Diner (1111 25th St)* is popular with students of nearby Drake University.

At the excellent Vietnamese restaurant *A-Dong (1905–7 Cottage Grove)*, just south of the Martin Luther King Jr exit off I-235, *mi xao don chay* (crispy egg noodles with tofu) costs $5.

Entertainment

If you need to rock, pick up the free weekly *Cityview* and see who's playing at *Hairy Marys* (☎ 515-255-2456, 2307 University), near Drake University. *JavaJoes Coffeehouse (214 4th St)*, around the corner from Court Ave, has live music nightly (and serves $5 veggie sandwiches).

Getting There & Around

There are limited air services to Des Moines International Airport, southwest of downtown. Greyhound buses (☎ 515-243-1773, 1107 Keosauqua Way) leave daily for Chicago ($41; from 7 hours) and Omaha ($24; 2½ hours). Amtrak's nearest stop is in Osceola, Iowa (39 miles south).

At 6th and Walnut Sts, you can hop on MTA metro buses (☎ 515-283-8100), with several routes.

AROUND DES MOINES
Madison County

This sleepy county, about 30 miles southwest of the capital, slumbered for half a century until Robert James Waller's blockbusting, tear-jerking novel *The Bridges of Madison County* and its movie version brought in scores of fans to check out the sites. The seven **covered bridges** where Robert and Francesca fueled their affair are here. Pick up a map at the Madison County Visitor Center (☎ 641-462-1185) in Winterset. The best is the Cedar Bridge, northeast

of the town. The Covered Bridges Festival is held in mid-October.

Another popular site is the well-signed movie set location of **Francesca's House**, 16 miles northeast of Winterset ($5; daily May-Oct). The **birthplace of John Wayne** (also known as Marion Robert Morrison) is a humble dwelling at 216 S 2nd St in Winterset ($2.50).

Featured in the film, Winterset's *Northside Café (61 Jefferson St)* is known for its chicken-fried steaks. If you are with Madonna, go to *Espresso Yourself*, on the square; sandwiches are $4.

Neal Smith NWR

About 20 miles east of Des Moines on Hwy 163, near Prairie City, this wonderful, 5000-acre (and hopefully growing) wildlife refuge is the site of an unprecedented tallgrass reconstruction project. See the film and displays at the Prairie Learning Center (☎ 515-994-3400) to learn about the Great Plains' ecosystems that began to vanish with the arrival of pioneers, farming, livestock, cities and interstates. Outside are herds of buffalo and elk, plus a 5-mile auto tour and 2-mile hiking trail (free admission; open daily).

Eldon

About 90 miles southeast of Des Moines, on Hwy 16 near Ottumwa, tiny Eldon lives in infamy as the source of Grant Wood's iconic (and often parodied) *American Gothic* (1930). You can see the house, on the subsequently named American Gothic St, and strike your own grimacing pose with whatever 'tool' you have on you – be it pitchfork or cricket bat. (The actual painting is in the Art Institute of Chicago.)

ALONG INTERSTATE 80

Most of Iowa's attractions are within an easy drive of I-80, which runs east-west across the center of the state. I-80 connects the **Quad Cities** (Bettendorf and Davenport, Iowa; and Moline and Rock Island, Illinois – see the Great Lakes chapter for details) with Council Bluffs (and Omaha, Nebraska). Des Moines (see above) is about midway.

Iowa City

The former territorial and state capital is a busy student town that has outgrown its infrastructure. The University of Iowa campus spills over both sides of the Iowa River; on the east side (at Iowa Ave and Clinton St) it mingles with riverfront parks and downtown's restaurants and bars. A lot goes on. In summer (when the student-to-townie ratio evens out) bands often play at the pedestrian mall. The Iowa City/Coralville CVB (☎ 319-337-6592, 800-283-6592, 408 1st Ave), in neighboring Coralville, has information. The Greyhound bus station (☎ 319-337-2127) is at 404 E College St.

The university has a few good (free) museums, including the old capitol, a natural history museum (with a huge sloth) and the **University of Iowa Museum of Art** (☎ 319-335-1727, 150 N Riverside Dr) with a particularly good African collection. The new **Iowa Children's Museum** (☎ 319-625-6255) is in Coralville's Coral Ridge Mall, near I-80 exit 240 ($4.50; closed Mon).

Near Coralville Lake, the **Devonian Fossil Gorge**, 4 miles north of I-80 on Dubuque St, is a Devonian-era seafloor with countless fossils. It was exposed by the 1993 floods (free admission).

In West Branch, 11 miles east on I-80, is the worthwhile **Herbert Hoover Birthplace & Library** (☎ 319-643-2541). Hoover was the 31st US president (1928–32) and a famous relief administrator, but he's more remembered (deservedly or not) as the namesake of Depression-era 'Hoovervilles.' The site includes the tiny cottage where lil' Herb was born ($2; open daily).

Coralville Lake (☎ 319-338-3543) has developed campsites. For a motel, take I-80 exit 242: Comfortable *Big Ten Inn* (☎ 319-351-0400, 707 1st Ave) has $36/42 singles/doubles. The riverside *Iowa House Hotel* (☎ 319-335-3513), at Madison and Jefferson Sts, adjoins the student union; rooms cost $74/84. The best value in Iowa City is *Haverkamp's Linn Street B&B Homestay* (☎ 319-337-4363, 619 N Linn St), with neat rooms for $35-50.

It's food and beer galore around downtown. Slick *Atlas World Grill* (1½ Dubuque St) has a Thai salad for $9 and jerk chicken for $11. For meatless meals, *Masala* (9 Dubuque St) serves several veggie curries; the busy lunch buffet costs $6.

Cedar Rapids

Iowa's second-largest city, 24 miles north of Iowa City, is a major manufacturing center along the Cedar River. Stop at the CVB (☎ 319-398-5009, 119 1st Ave) for brochures.

Cedar Rapids has several museums, including the terrific **Museum of Art** (☎ 319-366-7503, 410 3rd Ave). The museum has comprehensive coverage of Grant Wood's work ($4; closed Mon). The National Czech & Slovak Museum (☎ 319-362-8500, 30 16th Ave SW) is around the corner from the Czech Village eateries.

South of downtown at the junction of I-380 and US 30, *Red Roof Inn* (☎ 319-366-7523, 3325 Southgate) will set you up with $55/61 rooms.

Amana Colonies

These seven villages, 18 miles northwest of Iowa City, are stretched along a 15-mile loop. All were established as German religious communes in the 1850s by 'Inspirationists,' who follow a belief in *werkzeuge,* the divine revelation of inspired prophets. Unlike the Amish and Mennonite religions, Inspirationists embrace modern technology, evident in their booming refrigerator business (note the imposing plant in Middle Amana).

Today the well-preserved villages offer a glimpse at the unique culture, and there are lots of arts, crafts, cheeses, baked goods and wines to buy. Stop at the Amana Colonies CVB (☎ 319-622-7622), at I-80 exit 225, for the indispensable guide map.

There's a handful of museums around the villages (open daily May-Oct). Popular stops include the Amana Woolen Mill (linens cost $13 and up), the Barn Museum in South Amana and the communal kitchen in Middle Amana. Best for insight to the villages' origins is the **Museum of Amana History**, in Amana ($3).

The villages are home to a campsite and many good-value B&Bs, including Homestead's timeless *Die Heimat* (☎ 319-622-3937), with $69 rooms. A few good motels can be found at interstate exits.

One of the Amanas' top draws is the hefty-portioned, home-cooked German cuisine. Closest to I-80 is Homestead's *Zubers Restaurant*, which serves great pork chop and spatzle meals for $6.50. In Amana, *Ox Yoke Inn* and *Colony Inn Restaurant* have good German food too. South Amana's *Marketplace* has fish and vegetarian dishes. Middle Amana's *Hahn's Hearth Oven Bakery* usually sells out its cakes after lunch.

Council Bluffs

At Iowa's west end of I-80 is Council Bluffs, a traffic-choked town known for its casinos and budget motels, which make it a good base for exploring its big brother across the Missouri River – Omaha, Nebraska.

The Iowa Welcome Center here doubles as the interesting Western Trails Historic Center (☎ 712-366-4900, 3434 Downing Ave), I-80 exit 1B, with displays on Lewis and Clark.

Off I-80/I-29 exit 3 are many budget motels, including the reliable *Motel 6* (☎ 712-366-2405, 3032 S Expressway), with $50 rooms.

Loess Hills Byway

Many travelers seeing signs for the Loess Hills Byway – a 200-mile network of roads that run along Iowa's western edge parallel to I-29 – wonder, 'What is this loess anyway?' Loess (rhymes with Gus) is a windblown glacier-ground soil that began piling up into these unique formations about 18,000 years ago. Dramatic (and soft) 'catwalk' slopes step down steep hills. Nowhere else but China do loess hills reach these heights.

The hills' most dramatic scenery is off I-29 (north of Council Bluffs), in Harrison and Monona Counties; exit I-29 at Hwy 183 at Missouri Valley, and head north. In Moorhead, stop at the Loess Hills Hospitality Association (☎ 712-886-5441) for route maps and tips on hikes (open daily). Pick up the helpful *Iowa's Loess Hills Scenic Byway* booklet at any Iowa Welcome Center.

ALONG US 20

Most scenery along US 20, Iowa's northern passage from Dubuque on the Mississippi River to Sioux City on the Missouri River, is brick-smacked flat. But detours along the Mississippi valley pass breathtaking scenes of implausibly farmed lands that ripple like lime-green waves. Much of the movie *Straight Story* was filmed in Iowa north of US 20.

Dubuque

One of the Mississippi's nicest river towns, Dubuque makes for a great stop: 19th-century Victorian homes line its narrow, and surprisingly urban, streets between the river and seven steep hills. Those seeking action can canoe on area rivers, bike the 26-mile Heritage Trail or square dance (for information, call ☎ 563-556-1253). The film *Take This Job and Shove It* was filmed here.

Get information at the Welcome Center (☎ 563-556-4372, 400 E 3rd St) near the river. Greyhound buses (☎ 563-583-3397) leave from the Julien Inn (see below).

The short **4th Street Elevator** at the Fenelon Place Elevator Company, at 4th St and Fenelon, climbs a steep hill for huge views. Ring the bell to begin the ride ($1.50; open daily to 10pm Apr-Nov). Learn about 300 years of life on the Mississippi at the **Mississippi River Museum** (☎ 563-557-9545), at 3rd St near Ice Harbor. The film is the highlight ($6; open daily). Nearby, the *Spirit of Dubuque* (☎ 563-583-8093) offers Mississippi cruises ($9.50). Bird-watchers may see the national bird at Eagle Point Park, north of downtown (take Rhomberg to Shiras).

Places to Stay & Eat Camp on Schmidt Island at *Miller Riverview Park* (☎ 563-589-4238); developed sites cost $6. The historic *Julien Inn* (☎ 563-556-4200, 800-798-7098, 200 Main St) is pure fun. The lobby flaunts its 1960s makeover; fleur-de-lis signs hang over carpeted doors; a little bedside bulb lights up when guests have a message. Singles/doubles cost $49/59; the compact single is just $24. Dubuque has great Victorian B&Bs too. The most economical is the *Richards House* (☎ 563-557-1492, 1492 Locust). Spacious rooms go for $40 and $50 weekdays ($85 on weekends).

At the Julien Inn, *Alte Gocke* has a loyal, cackling crew of breakfast diners. The jolly, saucy *Europa Haus* (1301 Rhomberg) has German beers on tap; sauerbraten is $9. Try to make it to *Breitbach's Country Dining* (☎ 563-552-2220), in Balltown, a rewarding 17-mile drive north. Breitbach's has been serving gut-busting cod and chicken dinners since 1852. Don't miss the Depression-era gypsy-drawn mural and the nearby overlook of the Mississippi.

Dyersville & Around

An otherwise quiet farm town, Dyersville attracts thousands of visitors each year for two reasons: baseball and toys. The *Field of Dreams* baseball diamond, as seen in the 1989 film, is 3 miles northeast of town. You can run around the bases for free (open Apr-Nov).

Dyersville's farm-toy show in November attracts more than 20,000 fans, and four 'farm-toy manufacturers' are here. Plus there's the surprising **National Farm Toy Museum** (☎ 563-875-2727, 1110 16th Ave) with a fun film and 30,000 historic toy tractors and barns ($4/1 adults/kids; open daily). You can take home a tiny John Deere for $7; bigger, more detailed ones (made locally) start at $40.

About 65 miles west, stop to see the lovely Frank Lloyd Wright–designed **Cedar Rock** (☎ 563-934-3572), near the cute town of Quasqueton. The 1950 house, overlooking the Wapsipinicon River, is an example of Frank's 'simplified residential architecture' (free admission; open daily May-Oct).

Waterloo
Home of four John Deere tractor plants, Waterloo is the place to get one of those prized green-and-yellow caps that you've seen all over middle America. Fun tractor-driven tours of the **John Deere Tractor Assembly** (☎ 319-292-7697, 3500 E Donald St), near US 63, show how these monstrously sized vehicles get made ('with pride'). Free tours are at 8am, 10am and 1pm weekdays (minimum age 12; reserve ahead).

You can sleep at the *Twister Film Site* (☎ 641-858-5133), off Hwy 75 southwest of Waterloo, where the film *Twister*'s final tornado showdown was shot. Rooms cost $25.

Sioux City
The Missouri and Big Sioux Rivers meet at this city of 80,500 – also called Siouxland – known for its tasty Sue Bee Honey (and its cute logo) and perhaps for being the site of an 1989 United plane crash. The CVB (☎ 712-279-4800, 801 4th St) has some brochures.

The **Sgt Floyd Monument**, off I-29 south of town, marks the burial site of the only explorer to die during the Lewis and Clark expedition. North and south of town are drives, hikes and lookouts along the Loess Hills Byway (see earlier).

Stone State Park (☎ 712-255-4698), north of town on Hwy 12, has $8 developed campsites. Across the river in Nebraska, *New Marina Inn* (☎ 402-494-4000) has riverfront rooms starting at $84.

By all means, stop at the huge *Uncle John Music Café* (☎ 712-277-3922, 1101 4th St), a coffeehouse with a bar serving burgers, a stage for live shows and a 1980 Rolling Stones pinball machine.

Nebraska

Apart from the cities of Omaha and Lincoln, which sit at the state's eastern edge near the Missouri River, Nebraska is a vast, scantily inhabited prairie grassland that imperceptibly rises to the foothills of the Rockies. Crossing this expanse makes for an interesting journey – following in the footsteps of the Pony Express and the pioneers in Conestoga wagons ('prairie schooners') who blazed the Oregon, Mormon and California Trails.

The modern traveler in a motorized wagon now welcomes the same landmarks that the pioneers craved after long days in a monotonous landscape (but with the benefit of some interesting cowtowns and corntowns). There are also rewarding wildlife refuges, forests, sand hills, canoeable rivers (such as the Niobrara) and recreational lakes.

I-80 is the state's major east-west artery, although much of its length is boring. Those traveling to South Dakota's Black Hills may prefer the more scenic US 275 and US 20 northwest of Omaha, or Hwy 2 through the Sand Hills.

History
Lewis and Clark followed the Missouri along Nebraska's eastern fringe and met with Native Americans here in 1804. It took another 20 years before the Platte River was used by trappers.

The trickle of white visitors turned to a flood after 1841, when the first covered wagon passed through on its way to Oregon. The Platte Valley was soon swarming with settlers – some 400,000 hopefuls – looking for a new start in the mythical West.

The arrival of transcontinental railroads, such as the Union Pacific, made covered wagons unnecessary, and the trail ruts succumbed to pasture as settlers rushed in after the 1862 Homestead Act. Settlers took advantage of the rich soils and abundant grasslands, and Nebraska developed into a productive agricultural state.

Nebraska

Nickname: Cornhusker State

Population: 1,711,300 (37th)

Area: 77,360 sq miles (16th)

Admitted to Union: March 1, 1867 (37th)

State tree: cottonwood

Capital city: Lincoln (population 225,600)

Other cities: Omaha (390,000), Grand Island (42,900)

Birthplace of: Lakota leader Red Cloud, Malcolm X, Gerald Ford, author Willa Cather, Johnny Carson, Marlon Brando, Nick Nolte, Kool-Aid

Famous for: first rodeo (1882), only unicameral state legislature (1934), Chimney Rock (Oregon Trail landmark), football

Information

Nebraska has about 30 state information centers (half of which are staffed), especially along I-80 between Omaha and Kimball. You can get information in advance from the Nebraska Travel and Tourism Division (☎ 402-471-3796, W www.visitnebraska.org). The Nebraska Game and Parks Commission runs a good Web site (W www.ngpc.state.ne.us).

Visitors to Nebraska state parks must purchase a vehicle sticker, which is good at any park ($2.50 daily, $14 annual). For more information, call ☎ 800-826-7275.

For highway information, call ☎ 800-906-9069; if you're out of state, call ☎ 402-471-4533. The statewide sales tax is 1.5%, with local increases of up to 5%; lodging is 3% more.

OMAHA

Nebraska's largest city is not its prettiest, but Omaha has a rich history as a prairie outpost. Its location on the Missouri River and its proximity to the Platte made it a favored jumping-off point for the Oregon and Mormon Trails. Fort Omaha was built in 1868 as a staging post for troops fighting in the Indian Wars.

These days Omaha is home to more millionaires per capita than any other US city (leading Omaha's list is Warren Buffet).

Some of the extra greenbacks have been pumped into museums, galleries and downtown's now-trendy Old Market area.

Omaha has a strained relationship with its Iowan neighbor, Council Bluffs. (An Omaha mayor once called Council Bluffs 'the XXX city' because of its casinos and adult novelty shops.)

Information

The Omaha CVB (☎ 402-444-4660, 6800 Mercy Rd, Suite 202) in the AK-SAR-BEN complex, is tough to find (take I-80 exit 449). More convenient is the Nebraska I-80 Information Center (☎ 402-595-3990, 212 Bob Gibson Blvd) near the Missouri River (open daily). The W Dale Clark Library (☎ 402-444-4800, 215 S 15th St) has free Internet access.

Things to See & Do

The grand **Old Market**, between 10th and 13th Sts and Farnam and Jackson Sts, has century-old warehouses, cobblestone streets and nightlife to enjoy. A few blocks west, the art deco **Joslyn Art Museum** (☎ 402-342-3300, 2200 Dodge St) houses a great collection of Renaissance and 19th- and 20th-century American and European art ($6; closed Mon).

The ever-expanding **Henry Doorly Zoo** (☎ 402-733-8401, 3701 S 10th St), I-80 exit 454, has a giant cat complex, plus up-close looks at Plains animals. New desert and cave exhibits are due to open in 2002 ($7.50/3.75 for adults/kids; open daily).

Omaha was the birthplace of an unlikely pair, 38th president Gerald Ford and civil-rights leader Malcolm X. One proved that it was difficult to 'walk and chew gum at the same time'; the other swayed crowds of African Americans with his eloquence. The swank **Gerald R Ford birth site** (☎ 402-444-5955), at 32nd St and Woolworth Ave, can be visited for free. The **Malcolm X birth site** (3448 Pinkney St) is closed for restoration. One day it might also include the historical exhibits of the **Great Plains Black Museum** (☎ 402-345-2212), presently located at 2213 Lake St ($2).

One of Nebraska's top attractions owes its fortune to the state's central location in the USA, which surely helped it become the headquarters of the Strategic Air Command (SAC). Midway between

Omaha and Lincoln, the fascinating **Strategic Air Command Museum** (☎ 402-827-3100, 800-358-5029), at I-80 exit 426, boasts the 'best' of SAC offerings. Two massive hangars house more than 30 aircraft (including the bomb-dropping B-36 *Peacemaker)* and 20 missiles. Take a jolting ride on the real 'Desert Storm' flight simulator – if you can handle waiting for Boy Scouts to finish their flight ($6/3 adults/kids; open daily).

Places to Stay

West of town, ***Louisville State Lakes*** *(☎ 402-234-6855),* south of I-80 exit 440, has developed tent/RV sites for $8/11; ***Platte River State Park*** *(☎ 402-234-2217),* 25 miles south of I-80, has good cabins ($30-85) and plenty of wild turkeys.

Omaha motels abound along I-80 and I-680 N exits. (The best deals, however, are over in Council Bluffs.)

The ***Motel 6*** *(☎ 402-331-3161, 10708 M St),* at I-80 exit 445, has singles/doubles for $52/58. The ***Cornhusker Inn & Suites*** *(☎ 402-391-5757, 7101 Grover St),* at I-80 exit 449, has clean (but overpriced) rooms for $60/80.

A reasonably priced downtown hotel is ***Best Western Redick Tower Hotel*** *(☎ 402-342-1500, 1504 Harney St),* near Old Market; standard singles cost $70-109.

Places to Eat

Omaha's huge stockyards closed in 1998, but you still can't swing a stick in town without hitting a great steakhouse. The best is ***Johnny's Café*** *(☎ 402-731-4774, 4702 S 27th St),* next to the former stockyards. Iron cow-sculpture doors lead to meat-eating bliss; the Omaha strip steak costs $18.50 (closed Sun).

The Old Market has many restaurants and bars. ***Ahmad's*** *(1006 Howard St)* serves Persian dishes in a dressed-up setting. Choose one of several vegetarian meals, or get what Harrison Ford did – the beef keimah in cinnamon potato sauce ($15).

Sprightly ***Bohemian Café*** *(1406 S 13th St),* a few blocks south, serves Czech meals. The half-a-roasted-duck dinner costs $11.50; a white mug of pilsner beer is $4.50. In north Omaha, near the Great Plains Black Museum, try the ***Fair Deal Café*** *(2118 N 24th St)* for soul food.

Getting There & Around

Omaha's Eppley Airfield (☎ 402-422-6817), northeast of downtown, has links to a number of other nearby cities. One major carrier is Midwest Express (☎ 800-452-2022). A ride downtown with Happy Cab (☎ 402-339-8294) costs about $10.

Greyhound (☎ 402-341-1906, 1601 Jackson St) has daily buses bound for Lincoln ($12; 1 hour); Kansas City ($32; from 3 hours); Rapid City, South Dakota ($90; 13 hours) and Denver, Colorado ($72; from 11 hours).

Amtrak (☎ 402-342-6699, 1003 9th St) has daily train service to Lincoln ($9-16; 1 hour), Chicago ($68-122; 9½ hours) and Denver ($72-128; 9 hours).

Metro Area Transit city buses (☎ 402-341-0800) run limited routes.

LINCOLN

Nebraska's capital ('Star City') is a good place for an overnight stop. The downtown and historic Haymarket District are within easy walking distance of several museums, the University of Nebraska campus and the state capitol. Named for honest Abe (former US president), Lincoln has a low crime rate, as well as low cost of living and more city parks per capita than any other US city. Younger folks dig Lincoln; its median age is 31.3. Get information from the helpful visitor center (☎ 402-434-5348, 201 N 7th St) in Lincoln Station in the Haymarket (open daily).

Things to See & Do

The remarkable 400-foot **State Capitol** (☎ 402-471-0448), at 14th and H Sts, represents the best in phallic capitol buildings. The outside view will be marred until 2007, when a restoration will be complete, but indoor tours of the lovely 1932 art deco interior are given daily and are free.

The **Museum of Nebraska History** (☎ 402-471-4754), at P and 15th Sts, has a worthwhile First Nebraskans exhibit (free admission; open daily). Nearby, the new **Lincoln Children's Museum** (☎ 402-477-4000, 1420 P St) has a whole indoor, whippersnapper-sized town ($4; closed Mon). Another good diversion is the **University of Nebraska State Museum** (☎ 402-472-2642), in Morrill Hall, which has

Abe Town just didn't sound right.

mammoth bones supposedly found by a Nebraska chicken ($2 donation; open daily).

The prized Nebraska Cornhuskers football team plays home games here in fall. On most weekdays, you can tour the team's field and hall of fame at Memorial Stadium (☎ 402-472-1905).

Places to Stay

The budget *HI Cornerstone Hostel* (☎ 402-476-0926, 640 N 16th St), in a church between two fraternity houses, has a few basic dorm rooms with beds for $10/13 (members/nonmembers).

There are budget motels aplenty on W 'O' St/Hwy 6, near I-80 (exits 395, 396 and 397), including *Welcome Home Inn & Suites* (☎ 402-474-7666, 2231 W 'O' St) with $47 doubles and indoor pool. Pickings are slightly better off I-80 at the Cornhusker Hwy (NW 12th St) exit; *Horizon Inn* (☎ 402-474-5252, 2901 NW 12th St) has clean doubles for $40 with a VCR in each.

The new *Embassy Suites Hotel* (☎ 402-474-1111, 1040 P St), across from the Haymarket, has a number of luxurious rooms starting at $119.

Places to Eat

Lincoln's Haymarket District, a rejuvenated six-block warehouse area dating from the early 20th century, has a good variety of grub. *The Oven* (201 N 8th St) is an upscale Indian restaurant with 14 vegetarian entrées on the menu. *Maggie's Vegetarian Vittles* (311 N 8th St) serves vegan meals. University students and downtown workers soak in the afternoon sun on the dock at *The Mill* (800 P St), which serves coffees and snacks and offers Internet access.

Star City's serious meat-eaters head to *Misty's* (☎ 402-466-8424, 6235 Havelock) for a New York strip steak ($20).

Entertainment

Lincoln usually has something going on to help you unwind from a day's drive. The university *Nebraska Union* (☎ 402-472-8146), at 14th and R Sts, hosts many films and concerts. *The Zoo* (☎ 402-435-8754, 136 N 14th St) has a blues or rock show every night. *Q* (☎ 402-475-2269, 226 S 9th St) is a popular gay bar.

Getting There & Around

Greyhound (☎ 402-474-1071, 940 P St) has four daily buses to Omaha ($12; 1 hour). Amtrak trains (☎ 402-476-1295, 201 N 7th St) arrive in the wee hours; trains head west to Denver, Colorado ($70-125; 8 hours), and east to Omaha ($9-16; 1 hour). A ride with Husker Cabs (☎ 402-477-4111) from either station to the budget hotels is about $14.

ALONG INTERSTATE 80

Unfortunately, I-80 (also called the Great Platte River Rd) – the shortest route across the Plains – is also the least interesting, but there are a few diversions.

West of Lincoln in **Grand Island**, near the junction of US 281, is the modern Stuhr Museum of the Prairie Pioneer (☎ 308-385-5316), which has the building where Henry Fonda was born, plus a well-interpreted collection of artifacts ($7.50). *Oak Grove Inn* (☎ 308-384-1333, 3205 S Locust) has comfy doubles for $36.

At Grand Island, Hwy 2 branches northwest through Broken Bow to Alliance in the panhandle. Hwy 2 is slow but scenic. Its 20,000 sq miles of **Sand Hills** – sand dunes covered in grass – is one of the country's most isolated areas. Keep your gas tank full.

Fort Kearny State Historical Park (☎ 308-865-5306), west of Grand Island near the junction of I-80 and Hwy 44, is a partial reconstruction of the Oregon Trail outpost built here in 1848. The small museum has an exhibit on Moses Sydenham, a nutty pioneer who fought to move the nation's capital to Kearney ($2.50 per car).

There's no missing the new **Great Platte River Road Archway Monument** (☎ 877-511-2724), which hangs perilously over I-80 a few miles east of Kearney. The gadget-heavy museum traces Nebraska's history ($7.50; open daily).

Farther west at Gothenburg is an original **Pony Express station**, in Ehmen Park at 15th and Lake Sts, which was used from 1860 to 1861 (free admission). Equally as impressive is *Lasso Espresso*, right off I-80. Lasso is a walk-up stand with chai tea and cappuccinos.

North Platte is home to the mammoth Union Pacific Bailey reclassification yards – an area of train tracks the size of 3097 football fields. Construction for a new observatory and museum, 3 miles west of town, should be completed by mid 2002. The **Buffalo Bill Ranch State Historic Park** (☎ 308-535-8035), on Scouts Rest Ranch Rd 6 miles north, celebrates Bill Cody, the father of rodeo and the famed Wild West Show. His house and big red barn are packed with memorabilia (free admission; $2.50 parking). Hour-long trail rides cost $12. For a taste of country livin', hang your hat at *Knoll's Country Inn* (☎ 308-368-5634), a farmhouse B&B southwest of town ($60-75).

To the west near **Paxton**, Central Time changes to Mountain Time. You can spend the extra hour at *Ole's Big Game Lounge* looking at stuffed versions of what you are probably eating. Buffalo burgers cost $5; prime rib dinner is $14 (open to 10pm).

ALONG US 26 (OREGON TRAIL)

Branch off I-80 at Ogallala, and follow the Oregon Trail (basically the North Platte River) along US 26 to the huge landmarks of Nebraska's panhandle. At Windlass Hill in **Ash Hollow State Historical Park** (☎ 308-778-5651), near Lewellen, you can see wagon ruts made in the 19th century. Near Bridgeport, 56 miles northwest, stand the **Courthouse & Jail Rocks**, the first of the major landmarks. From Bridgeport, take a detour 40 miles north on US 385 to rural Alliance, the quiet (somewhat reluctant) home to **Carhenge**, in a field 2 miles north. This Stonehenge replica is made from 34 discarded car bodies to 'surprise people.' You might bump into a few happy teens drinking beer here.

Continuing west on US 26, you'll find the impressive **Chimney Rock**, the most frequently mentioned trail landmark in pioneer diaries – and the model for the artwork on new Nebraska license plates. The excellent visitor center (☎ 308-586-2581) interprets the pioneer trails ($2; open daily). South, past the center, is a short trail.

Relive pioneer days on an overnight prairie schooner trip by **Oregon Trail Wagon Train** (☎ 308-586-1850), just northwest of Chimney Rock; trips run $175 and up, including meals and bedding. There are also chuckwagon cookouts, canoes and cabins.

Visible for miles, the most impressive Trail landmark, **Scotts Bluff National**

500,000 Sandhill Cranes Can't Be Wrong

The area along I-80 may be dullsville to many travelers, but it's had, for 9 million years and counting, very devoted fans in sandhill cranes. In February and March, more than half a million of these 4-foot-tall, reddish-brown birds stop in the North Platte River valley between Grand Island and Kearney to roost and dine before heading north for a Canadian summer. Endangered whooping cranes also roost here.

Sandhill cranes are romantic: Pairs mate for life, which lasts about 25 years, or until a hunter in Kansas, Oklahoma or Texas takes one down (hunting cranes is prohibited in Nebraska). And, while in Nebraska, couples renew 'vows' through an odd jumping dance.

Any time of year, stop by Crane Meadows Nature Center (☎ 308-382-1820), just south of I-80 exit 305, to see exhibits on cranes and area wildlife ($3), hike 7 miles of trails along the Platte and go up a tower for views of the river habitat ($3).

GREAT PLAINS

Monument (☎ 308-436-4340) is 3 miles west of Gering on Hwy 92. The Sioux called it *me-a-pa-te* (hill that is hard to go around) millennia ago. Today you can drive up it in a flash, or take the 1½-mile hike. The views of Wyoming's Laramie Peak 90 miles west and North Platte River 800 feet below are outstanding. (Five million years ago this was level ground.) The visitor center's museum has a funny display of the bluff's namesake, Hiriam Scott, a fur trader who died here in 1828 ($5 per vehicle). The windswept town of Scottsbluff, 5 miles north, has little life off US 26. Better stayovers are in Chadron and Fort Robinson (see below).

ALONG US 20

This route is a nice (if lonesome) route across Nebraska. The farther west you go, the more space you'll see between towns, trees and pickup trucks. Be sure to snare the free *Highway to Adventure: US 20* brochure, available at visitor centers.

Running on converted railroad lines, the in-progress **Cowboy Trail** (☎ 402-370-3374) is a network of good biking, hiking and horseback-riding trails. When completed, the route will run nearly 200 miles. It will begin in the east at Norfolk (US 275 about 24 miles south of US 20), catch up with US 20 a bit east of O'Neill and continue west to Valentine. Finished stretches include Norfolk to Neligh and Ewing to O'Neill (mostly along US 275), and 5 miles around Valentine (on US 20). While in Neligh, drop by the Neligh Mill Historic Site (☎ 402-887-4303), on US 275, for a neat vintage flour sack ($1).

At **Ashfall Fossil Beds State Historical Park** (☎ 402-893-2000), off US 20 north of Royal, you can see unearthed prehistoric skeletons of more than 200 critters, buried 10 million years ago by ash from a 'Pompeii-like' explosion in what is now Idaho. Some still have grass in their mouths. On-site paleontologists can answer questions ($3, plus $2.50 vehicle pass).

A good place to stay is 40 miles west at the *Historic Golden Hotel* (☎ 402-336-4436, 800-658-348, 406 E Douglas St), in O'Neill (Nebraska's 'Irish capital'). Singles/doubles cost $29/45. US 20 enters flatter territory west of O'Neill, with increasingly greater space between trees, towns and pickup trucks.

Valentine

On the northern edge of the Sand Hills, the 'Cupid Capital of Nebraska' is the hub for remarkable canoeing, kayaking and inner-tubing in the nearby Niobrara River. The CVB (☎ 402-376-2969), at US 20 and US 83, has information on the dozen outfitters in town. River routes east of town are the most rewarding, but you'll see fewer folks floating to the west.

About 12 miles east on Hwy 12, an impressive waterfall can be seen at **Smith Falls State Park** (☎ 402-376-1306), which is also a great place for *camping*. Tent and RV sites cost $3 per person (plus $2.50 vehicle pass).

In town, stay at the red-brick *Valentine Motel* (☎ 402-376-2450), on Main St, which has cute $30 rooms and a 1953 Ford parked out front. *Lovejoy Ranch* (☎ 402-376-2668, 800-672-5098), 17 miles south, is a B&B ranch with rooms starting at $75.

Northern Panhandle

Friendly **Chadron** was the setting for part of Jim Harrison's novel *Dalva*. The **Museum of the Fur Trade** (☎ 308-432-3843), 3 miles east of town, covers 400 years of trading in North America. It also has the restored Bordeaux Trading Post, which was shut down for trading guns with the Native Americans who wiped out Custer ($2.50; call for times).

Surrounded by the Nebraska National Forest, *Chadron State Park* (☎ 308-432-6167), 10 miles south on US 385, has pine-scented tent/RV sites for $7/11. In Chadron, stay at the clean *Grand Westerner Motel* (☎ 308-432-5595, 1050 W US 20), with $32 rooms and a Cornhusker shrine in the office. For breakfast, go to *Helen's Pancake & Steak House*, on US 20, where a ballcap-wearing coffee club rolls dice on weekday mornings.

Northwest of Crawford (which is 18 miles west of Chadron) are a few paleontological wonders. **Toadstool Geological Park** is a mini-badlands with a wide variety of fossils (free admission; open daily) and a hiking trail through the surrounding Oglala National Grassland (☎ 308-432-0300). The nearby Hudson-Meng Bison Bonebed (☎ 308-665-3900) displays the site where 1000 bison enigmatically perished more than 10,000 years ago ($3; open May-Sept).

Beautiful **Fort Robinson State Park** (☎ 308-665-2900), 3½ miles west of Crawford ($2.50 per vehicle), was where Crazy Horse was killed in 1877 while in captivity – a plaque marks the spot. The Fort Robinson Museum gives a disappointingly one-sided version of the Sioux Wars but has good displays on the fort's reputation as the 'country club of the army' ($2). West of the fort is the 3-mile Smiley Canyon Scenic Drive. From April to November, there's cozy *lodging* in the 1909 barracks ($35) and 1874 quarters ($85). In summer the Post Playhouse (☎ 308-665-1976) puts on a play six nights a week ($10).

Farther west on US 20, at Harrison, drive 23 miles south on Hwy 29 to reach **Agate Fossil Beds National Monument** (☎ 308-668-221), a rich source of unusual fossils dating 10 to 20 million years. The most interesting is the *Daemonelix*, a fossilized corkscrew tunnel dug by prehistoric beavers. There are two trails and a collection of Native American artifacts ($2; open daily).

South Dakota

South Dakota is the highlight of a visit to the Plains states, offering excellent introductions to Native American culture and the Old West, and it has the region's most beautiful natural attractions, including the rugged Badlands and the beautiful Black Hills. No visitor should miss the giant sculptures of Mt Rushmore and Crazy Horse.

I-90 gives good access to the state's premier attractions, crossing the state from Sioux Falls in the east, to Spearfish in the west. Get off the interstate to enjoy South Dakota's unique 'pink' two-lane highways, made from the state's abundant reddish quartzite.

History

South Dakota, best remembered for the Great Sioux Nation's struggle to retain its traditional lands in the late 19th century, has a long history of settlement, reaching as far back as warrior-hunters around 8000 BC; by AD 900 large settlements had been established by the Arikara. The Sioux arrived in the mid-18th century.

The first Europeans to leave their mark were the Vérendrye brothers, whose etched lead plate, deposited in 1743, claimed the

South Dakota

Nicknames: Sunshine State, Mt Rushmore State

Population: 754,900 (45th)

Area: 77,125 sq miles (17th)

Admitted to Union: November 2, 1889 (40th)

Capital city: Pierre (population 13,900)

Other cities: Sioux Falls (124,000), Rapid City (59,600)

State tree: Black Hills spruce

State fossil: triceratops

Birthplace of: Sitting Bull, Crazy Horse, Black Elk, Calamity Jane, news anchor and author Tom Brokaw, Catherine 'Daisy Duke' Bach, quarterback Josh Heupel

Famous for: Mt Rushmore, Black Hills, the Sioux, *Little House on the Prairie*

region for France. When the USA acquired it with the 1803 Louisiana Purchase, the region was very much the domain of the Sioux and a few brave fur trappers.

It wasn't until the 1850s that the rich Dakota soil attracted the interest of settlers. The 1868 Fort Laramie Treaty between the USA and the Sioux promised the Sioux large tracts of land to roam freely upon.

The treaty was irrevocably broken in 1874 when Lieutenant Colonel George Custer led an expedition into the Black Hills in search of gold – unfortunately, he was successful. Miners and settlers soon streamed in illegally, and the Sioux retaliated in the biggest of the Indian Wars.

By the late 1870s, it became obvious to the emergent USA that there was one remaining obstacle to the unfettered development of the Plains: the independent Plains Indians. In 1876 the army supremo General Sherman, responding to the Indians' decision not to return to their reservations, planned to eliminate all opposition in a three-pronged attack. The Sioux and other tribes gathered at Rosebud, South Dakota, for their last great year on the Plains, a last taste of the old way of life. Thousands of warriors came – including chiefs Crazy Horse, Sitting Bull, Red Cloud, Little Big Man and Two Moons.

GREAT PLAINS

Sioux chief Sitting Bull

Sitting Bull entered a trance and foresaw the death of white soldiers.

Three forces then converged on the Sioux and their allies. The charismatic chief Crazy Horse and 1500 bedecked braves held off the southern force at Rosebud, killing 90. Shortly afterward, Crazy Horse led the charge that annihilated Custer and the 7th Cavalry at the Battle of Little Big Horn.

It was to be the Plains Indians' last real victory over the invaders. Faced with overwhelming force, they split up. Sitting Bull fled to Canada, Crazy Horse turned in his gun in 1877, and the railroads and settlers inched forward. The final decimation of Sioux resistance came at Wounded Knee in 1890, when the army reacted strongly to a revival of the Ghost Dance religion and ruthlessly massacred some 300 men, women and children. (Much later, in 1973, Oglala Sioux loyal to the American Indian Movement occupied Wounded Knee and kept federal officers at bay for 70 days.)

After the captured Plains Indian lands were 'freed,' settlers flooded in to face drought, dust storms and depression (another story) in their efforts to establish a viable agricultural base. Today South Dakota is one of the poorest states in the USA, but it has a vibrant tourism industry.

Information

The South Dakota Dept of Tourism (☎ 800-732-5682, Ⓦ www.state.sd.us/tourism, 711 E Wells Ave, Pierre, SD 57501) provides an information pack. Most state information centers, along I-90 and I-29, are staffed only in summer. Good brochures include the *South Dakota Guide to Indian Reservation & Art* and *Lewis and Clark: The South Dakota Adventure*.

In the center of the state, roughly along the Missouri River, Central Time changes to Mountain Time.

Call ☎ 800-710-2267 for state park campground information or reservations. For winter road conditions, call ☎ 605-394-2255; for details on road construction (and there is plenty), call ☎ 605-773-3571. The statewide sales tax is 4%, with city increments up to 2%. In some places another 1% may be added.

SIOUX FALLS

South Dakota's biggest city, at the intersection of I-90 and I-29, is a regional center for marketing, banking and agriculture – not to mention lottery 'casinos' (Sioux Falls has 64). The world's largest hog kill-and-pack plant is here too. The Sioux Falls CVB (☎ 605-336-1620, 200 N Phillips Ave) provides information.

See the Big Sioux River splash over quartzite rocks at **Falls Park** (☎ 605-367-7430), off Weber Ave north of downtown; the park has a good visitor center, with an observatory. The restored **Old Courthouse Museum** (☎ 605-367-4210), at 6th St and Main Ave, has a good display on Plains Indians (free admission); it also hosts free concerts on Friday in summer.

At I-29 exit 77, in the city's southwest, the slightly aged *Empire Inn* (☎ 605-361-2345, 4208 W 41st St) has an indoor pool and clean singles/doubles for $47/57. The best mid-range deal is at *Country Inn & Suites* (☎ 605-373-0153, 200 E 8th St) with $78 rooms near the falls; its *Falls Landing Restaurant* is open at dinner. *Bagel Boy (1911 S Minnesota St)* makes good sandwiches. Along downtown's Phillips Ave, try *Touch of Europe (No 337)* for Eastern European food (and live jazz on weekends), or *Kristina's Café & Bakery (No 334)* for weekend brunch.

AROUND SIOUX FALLS

About 80 miles southwest of Sioux Falls, **Yankton** is the former territorial capital. It's a well-preserved town at the east end of Lewis and Clark Lake, a boaters' paradise. The CVB (☎ 605-665-3636, 218 W 4th St) has brochures. Camp in one of 400 tent/RV sites ($10/15) at the **Lewis & Clark Recreation Area** (*☎ 605-668-2985*). The homey **Gavins Point B&B** (*☎ 605-668-0691, 252 Gavins Point Rd*) has $70 rooms overlooking the lake. North of town on US 81, **JoDean's** packs 'em in for its hearty 50-foot buffet ($7).

The only interstate linking the two Dakotas is Interstate 29, on the eastern edge of the states. *Little House on the Prairie* fans (only) should head 40 miles west on US 14, from Brookings, to Laura Ingalls Wilder's former home in **De Smet**. There are two original Wilder homes (☎ 605-854-3383), which charge $5 admission, a drive-by tour of sites featured in her books and an outdoor play (☎ 605-692-2108) in June and July.

The remote **HI Pleasant Valley Hostel** (*☎ 605-272-5614*) is on the Minnesota border near Gary (west of I-29 on SR 22). Run by a worldly local who can suggest day trips, the hostel is near hikes and a swimming hole. Bunks cost $15.

ALONG INTERSTATE 90
I-90 from Sioux Falls to Rapid City (the gateway to the Black Hills) is a straight, boring stretch, but north and south of it lie some of the state's most scenic parts.

Mitchell
This city, 66 miles west of Sioux Falls, is overwhelmingly the home of the kitschy, Moorish-style **Corn Palace**, at 6th and Main Sts, which is redecorated with 275,000 ears of corn annually (tours are free). It serves as Mitchell's civic center, active all year; stop by for a basketball game in winter.

The domed **Mitchell Prehistoric Indian Village Museum** (☎ 605-996-5473), north of the palace, contains two unearthed 11th-century Mandan lodges. Archaeologists dig up relics on most days ($5; open daily, by appointment in winter).

Motel rates go way up in summer. The **Corn Palace Motel** (*☎ 605-996-5559, 902 S Burr*) has good-value doubles for $40. **Super 8 Motel** (*☎ 605-996-9678*), at I-90 and SR 37, has $65 rooms and a few pools. For food, **Cottonwood Canyon** (*512 N Main*) has

tasty jerk chicken ($5.50), plus Internet access. A toy train runs through *The Depot*, at the south end of Main, which has pub fare and a happy hour at 5:30pm.

Chamberlain
I-90 crosses the Missouri at Chamberlain, where you can see the excellent **Akta Lakota Museum & Cultural Center** (☎ 605-734-3452, 800-798-3452), at St Joseph's Indian School, with Sioux and other Native American artifacts plus movie props from *Dances with Wolves* (free admission). History buffs should pop into the hilltop welcome center, east of town, where the new **Lewis & Clark Information Center** (☎ 605-734-4562) has exhibits on the duo (summer only).

Pierre
South Dakota's pleasant capital is 30 miles north of I-90 on US 83 but is more rewardingly approached from Chamberlain via Hwys 50 and 34, an 87-mile drive through the Crow Creek Indian Reservation with views of the Missouri that seem to pop out of a George Catlin painting. The area north of Pierre (pronounced peer – no one is sure why) was the setting for many scenes in *Dances with Wolves*. The Pierre CVB (☎ 605-224-7361, 800 W Dakota Ave) has brochures.

The photogenic **State Capitol** (☎ 605-773-3765, 500 E Capitol Ave) has a self-guided tour available; search the capitol's tile floors for 11 never-found 'signature stones' set in 1910 (no reward). Don't blame legislators for the faint stench outside; it's natural gas flowing into nearby Capitol Lake, home to many Canadian geese in winter. Exhibits at the fascinating **South Dakota Cultural Heritage Center** (☎ 605-773-3458, 900 Governor's Dr) include a bloody ghost dance shirt from Wounded Knee ($3; open daily). On the Missouri River, Framboise Island (where Lewis and Clark had a rough encounter with the Sioux) has trails.

Farm Island State Park (*☎ 605-224-5606*), 5 miles east on Hwy 34, has developed campsites for $10. The **Budget Host Inn/State Motel** (*☎ 605-224-5896, 640 N Euclid St*) has a recliner in each room ($37 singles). **Mad Mary's Steakhouse** (*110 E Dakota Ave*) serves cod fish ($8) in addition to beef. Don't mention Mary at the lively, sawdust-floored **Cattleman's Club** (*29608*

GREAT PLAINS

Hwy 34), a steak-eater's paradise. (Mary is the owner's ex.)

Rosebud Indian Reservation

At Murdo on I-90, detour 40 miles south on US 83 to Rosebud Indian Reservation, the home of the Sicangu Lakota Oyate; for information call ☎ 605-856-2538. The friendly **Buechel Memorial Lakota Museum** (☎ 605-747-2745), in St Francis (7 miles southwest of Rosebud town), has artifacts, including some Crazy Horse belongings (free admission). In Rosebud, *Salt Camp Cabins* *(☎ 605-747-2206)* overlook the lovely Crazy Horse Canyon, which has a nice lake for a dip; cabins cost $100.

Back in Murdo, **Elvis' Harley-Davidson** can be seen at the Pioneer Auto Museum ($7).

Pine Ridge Indian Reservation

The home of the Lakota Oglala Sioux, south of the Badlands, is the nation's poorest 'county' and makes for a sobering experience for visitors, as wrecked cars dot the yards of run-down homes and carless residents walk along dusty roads. The Sioux have rejected government compensation offers for the Black Hills because taking money for their traditional home would bring them 'spiritual poverty.' Plus, as an Oglala priest said, 'There's no controversy over the Black Hills – they're ours.'

Wounded Knee Massacre Site, 20 miles northeast of Pine Ridge town, is the reservation's top attraction, but it is *not* a feted part of South Dakota. Tourist literature neglects it, and the site has little more than a ramshackle cemetery, a roadside sign and a few souvenir sellers in summer.

In Pine Ridge town, stop at the **Red Cloud Indian School** (☎ 605-867-5491), 4 miles north on US 18, to visit Chief Red Cloud's grave and the Heritage Center, which has a shop selling art and Lakota flash cards. In town, the heroic youth center Visions of SuAnne Big Crow includes the *Happytown USA* diner, open to all. At the farmhouse *Wakpamni B&B (☎ 605-288-1800)*, 20 miles east of Pine Ridge, guests can enjoy a sweat-lodge ceremony and talk with an Oglala guide ($60 and up).

Look for the locally produced *Welcome to the Oglala Lakota Nation* brochure, which includes listings of the area's frequent powwows.

Wall

If you don't know about Wall (on I-90) before you arrive in South Dakota, you soon will. Billboards for its famous 'drugstore' infest the state. The block-long **Wall Drug** (☎ 605-279-2271, 510 Main St) is pretty much what it advertises: 5¢ coffee, 1970s-era Wild West toys, Black Hills gold, moccasins, fudge, leather, books on Wall Drug, shirts that say 'Wall Drug,' singing cowboy machines and big gorillas. Go crazy.

Just south of Wall is the **Buffalo Gap National Grassland**, an area of prairie and badlands. The National Grassland Visitor Center (☎ 605-279-2125, 708 Main St) interprets the history, flora and fauna of the region.

Dandy *Welsh's Motel (☎ 605-279-2271, 312 South Blvd)* has clean singles for $60. For food, there's always *Wall Drug Café*. Morning eggs cost $2.50; sandwiches start at $2.

Badlands National Park

The desolate lunar landscape of this region was referred to as *mako sica* (badland) by Native Americans. The views from the corrugated 'walls' surrounding the Badlands are spectacular – colorful eroded spires, pinnacles and canyons stretch into the distance. The setting was perfect for a frightening battle scene in the sci-fi film *Starship Troopers*. Today the Badlands Park protects a remnant of one of the world's greatest prairie grasslands, several species of Plains mammals and golden eagles.

The park's north unit is the most developed; the Hwy 240 loop road is easily reached from I-90. The gravel Sage Creek Rim Rd goes west of the loop, above the Badlands Wilderness Area, which is open for backcountry hiking and camping. The less-accessible south units are in Pine Ridge Indian Reservation.

The Ben Reifel Visitor Center (☎ 605-433-5361), at Cedar Pass, is open all year; White River Visitor Center, in the southern section, is open in summer. If you visit in winter, watch for snowdrifts. A seven-day pass costs $10 for cars, $5 for hikers and cyclists.

The *Badlands Circle 10 Campground (☎ 605-433-5451)*, half a mile south of I-90 exit 131, has developed sites for $15. Motels can be found on I-90 in Kadoka and Wall (see earlier), or in the park at the Oglala Sioux–operated ***Cedar Pass Lodge*** (☎ 605-433-5460). A cabin for two people costs $52 (open Apr-Oct). Drop by its ***Buffalo Dining Room*** for breakfast or Indian tacos.

BLACK HILLS

This 8000-sq-mile mountainous region on the Wyoming–South Dakota border boasts 7000-foot 'hills' (the ironic highlight of the Plains states). The region's name – the 'black' comes from the dark Ponderosa pine-covered slopes – was conferred by the Lakota Sioux, to whom the hills were a sacred, spiritual and ancestral home. In 1868 Fort Laramie Treaty, they were assured that the hills would be theirs for eternity, but the discovery of gold changed that, and the Sioux were pushed north, and later to reservations. Today the Sioux continue their struggle to reclaim the lands.

You'll need several days (at least) to explore the area, which covers more ground than Rocky Mountain, Grand Canyon or Yosemite National Parks. Throughout are incredible backroad drives, rock climbing, mines, caves, Custer State Park, Mt Rushmore and Crazy Horse monuments, the Black Hills National Forest, myriad activities (eg, ballooning, biking, boating, hiking, skiing and panning for gold) and heaps of kitsch sandwiched in between.

About half the 4½ million annual visitors choose one place as a base; others split their stay between the North Hills (Spearfish, Deadwood, Sturgis) and the more visited

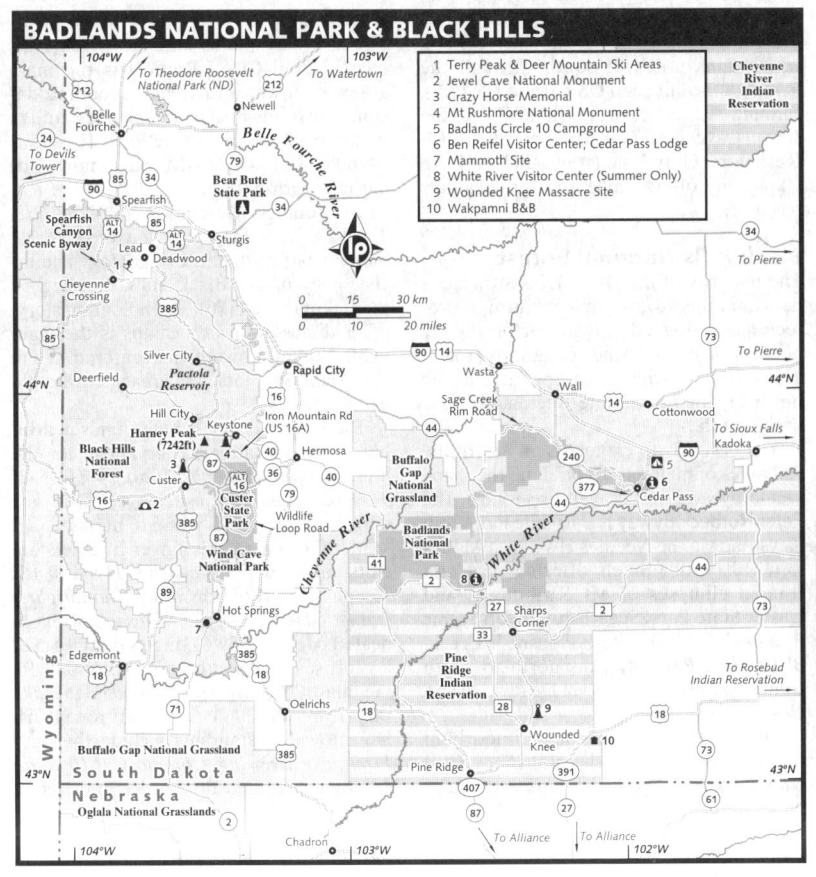

BADLANDS NATIONAL PARK & BLACK HILLS

1 Terry Peak & Deer Mountain Ski Areas
2 Jewel Cave National Monument
3 Crazy Horse Memorial
4 Mt Rushmore National Monument
5 Badlands Circle 10 Campground
6 Ben Reifel Visitor Center; Cedar Pass Lodge
7 Mammoth Site
8 White River Visitor Center (Summer Only)
9 Wounded Knee Massacre Site
10 Wakpamni B&B

South Hills (Custer, Keystone, Hot Springs). At the cusp of the hills stand the 'gateway' towns on I-90 (Rapid City, Sturgis, Spearfish). Between Memorial Day and Labor Day, room rates skyrocket – sometimes even 300% above off-season rates – and reservations are essential.

Each of the main attractions and towns has an information office or CVB. The best is Rapid City's Black Hills Visitor Center (☎ 605-355-3700, 1851 Discovery Circle), I-90 exit 61, north on Elk Vale Rd. Black Hills Central Reservations (☎ 800-529-0105, 68 Sherman St), in Deadwood, will find last-minute motel and cabin vacancies around the Black Hills.

I-90 skirts the north of the Black Hills, and three major access roads head into the hills from it: US 14A, which loops from Spearfish to Sturgis via Deadwood; the US 385 Black Hills Parkway (initially US 85), which runs north to south through the length of the hills; and US 16 (and US 16A), running east to west from Rapid City to the Jewel Cave National Monument via Mt Rushmore. Gray Line (☎ 605-342-4461), in Rapid City, offers a nine-hour, greatest-hits bus tour.

Black Hills National Forest

The majority of the Black Hills attractions lie within this 1875-sq-mile mixture of protected and logged forest, perforated by pockets of private land along most roads. The forest stretches from Spearfish in the north to Angostura State Recreation Area in the south.

The best way to explore is on any of the 353 miles of hiking trails or along the many scenic byways and gravel 'fire roads.' The Peter Norbeck Byway is a 70-mile loop from Keystone via the Needles Hwy, Iron Mountain Rd (with tunnels offering perfectly framed glimpses of Mt Rushmore) and Custer State Park. Spearfish Canyon Scenic Byway (US 14A) follows Spearfish Creek. Black Hills Parkway runs north to south from I-90 to Hot Springs via Deadwood and Custer.

Many side roads are mapped poorly in the free and otherwise helpful *Black Hills National Forest Recreation Guide;* if you're planning to explore the area, pick up the widely available Black Hills National Forest map ($6).

For biking, the 114-mile George S Mickelson Trail cuts through much of the forest, running from Lead through Hill City and Custer to Edgemont. (Deadwood's Penny Motel runs a shuttle to pick up or drop off bikers at various points on the trail.)

There are six ranger stations around the forest and a visitor center at Pactola Reservoir, near the junction of US 385 and Hwy 44 (open daily May 15-Oct 1). The Black Hills National Forest office (☎ 605-673-9200) is in Custer.

Good *camping* abounds in the forest. There are 30 basic campgrounds ($9-18), and backcountry camping is allowed anywhere (free; no open fires). You can call ☎ 877-444-6777 to make reservations (recommended for summer weekends).

Rapid City

This is where plains and the Black Hills meet. Rapid City ('Rapid') is the main gateway town, and it has accommodations, restaurants, tour services and a junkpile of kitschy attractions. The CVB (☎ 605-343-1744, 444 Mt Rushmore Rd) has city information.

The Journey Museum (☎ 605-394-6923, 222 New York St) takes you through 2½ billion years of the history, geology and archaeology of the Black Hills, focusing on the Lakota Sioux ($6). The hologram storyteller discussing *wicoti* camps is the highlight. Around downtown (centered at 6th and Main Sts), look for great decades-old neon signs.

There are a dozen campgrounds nearby, but if you are after scenery, head for the hills. Friendly *Robert's Roost (☎ 605-341-3434, 627 South St),* just east of US 16, is a duplex-turned-hostel with $16 bunks.

Many chain motels linger at interstate exits, and older motels line Hwy 79 (St Joseph St), east of downtown. *Lamplighter Inn (☎ 605-342-3385, 27 St Joseph St)* has a heated pool and $59/69 singles/doubles ($20 less off season). South of Rapid on US 16, the hilltop *Big Sky Motel (☎ 605-348-3200, 4080 Tower Rd)* has clean rooms for $48/64. Downtown's restaurants include the busy *Firehouse Brewing Company (610 Main St),* which brews a dozen ales and has $7 buffalo burgers.

The Rapid City Regional Airport (☎ 800-357-9998, 605-393-9924) is on Hwy 44 southeast of town. The Airport Express Shuttle (☎ 605-399-9999) charges $12 to get downtown, $60 to Deadwood or Custer. Greyhound buses don't serve the Black Hills; Jack Rabbit buses (☎ 605-348-3300, 800-556-0519, 333 6th St) connect Rapid with Denver, Colorado ($80), and Sioux Falls ($68). The orange Rapid Taxi cabs (☎ 605-348-8080) charge $1.40 per mile.

Sturgis

Pokey little Sturgis is known the world over as the annual gathering ground of up to half a million 'hog' (Harley-Davidson motorcycle) lovers, at the Sturgis Rally & Races (☎ 605-347-9190) in early August. Balloonists congregate here over Mother's Day weekend. The chamber of commerce (☎ 605-347-2556, 2040 Junction Ave) has town information.

At the new **Sturgis Motorcycle Museum & Hall of Fame** (☎ 605-347-0849, 1344 Main St), fans who missed the rally can ogle over 38 Harleys ($3; open daily). Don't forget to pick up a rally T-shirt for your hog-lovin' chums back home.

Standing stoically apart from the Black Hills, the namesake mountain of **Bear Butte State Park** (☎ 605-347-5240), 12 miles north of Sturgis on Hwy 79, juts 1400 feet above the plains. Once the stronghold of Crazy Horse, it remains of great spiritual significance to the Plains Indians, evident in hundreds of prayer cloths strung along the 1.7-mile climb up to the summit ($3). Bear Butte is the north end of the **Centennial Trail**, a 111-mile riding/hiking trail to Wind Cave National Park.

Unless you're a 'rider,' you'll likely not linger long in Sturgis. During the rally, temporary campsites are set up around town, and motels boost rates to hundreds of dollars a night. Check the rally Web site for vacancies (Ⓦ www.sturgismotorcyclerally.com).

Basic campsites at **Bear Butte State Park** cost $6. Sturgis has a few chain motels around I-90 exit 32 and cheaper places along Junction Ave. **Super 8 Motel** (☎ 605-347-4447), off I-90 exit 30, has $64/73 singles/doubles. **Hog Heaven Resort** (☎ 605-347-0023), a mile south, has $15 campsites and $50 cabins.

One-Eyed Jack's Saloon (1304 Main St) is a biker bar with burgers and a happy hour (4-7pm) most nights.

Spearfish

Another base on I-90 is Spearfish, near Wyoming and at the mouth of the scenic **Spearfish Canyon Scenic Byway** (US 14A). The chamber of commerce (☎ 605-642-2626, 106 W Kansas) has regional information. The outdoor 'Black Hills Passion Play' (☎ 605-642-2646) is staged in summer ($12-18). In winter, many skiers come to hit nearby downhill slopes and cross-country trails. Ski Cross Country (☎ 605-722-3851, 705 3rd St) has rentals.

There are four nearby campgrounds. **Spearfish KOA** (☎ 605-642-4633), southwest of I-90 exit 10, has tent/RV sites for $18/25; 'kabins' cost $38. There are motels around I-90 exit 14, including the renovated **Black Hills Inn** (☎ 605-642-8105, 323 S 27th St), with indoor pool and $75/85 singles/doubles ($35 less off season). Just south of I-90 exit 12, **Kelly Inn** (☎ 605-642-7795, 540 E Jackson St) has comfy rooms for $79/89.

The **Spearfish Canyon Resort** (☎ 605-584-3435), 13 miles south, sits triumphantly in its namesake, near trails, streams and a **Dances with Wolves** film site. Rooms start at $109. The resort's **Latchstring Restaurant** serves tasty grilled rainbow trout with almonds ($14).

Back in town, **Common Ground** (111 E Hudson), off Main St, has a $4 veggie burger. **Roma's** (701 5th St), in a nice sandstone building, serves gourmet Italian meals.

Deadwood & Lead

Settled illegally by anxious gold rushers in the 1870s, Deadwood today is a proud (and respectable) National Historic Landmark. Its Main St is lined with many fine (and recently restored) Gold Rush–era buildings. The town's hell-raisin' days are long gone, replaced by a gentler crowd of poker players who are taking advantage of the town's legalized limited-stakes gambling, which jumpstarted the town's tourism appeal in the 1990s.

Deadwood plays up its pioneer days, and some famous names crop up repeatedly: Wild Bill Hickok, shot in the back here in 1876; Jack McCall, the drifter who shot Hickok; Calamity Jane (also known as Martha Canary); gunslingers Doc Holliday and Wyatt Earp; the prospector Potato Creek Johnny; and brothel owner Poker

Alice Tubbs. Hickok and Jane now rest side by side, up in Boot Hill at **Mt Moriah Cemetery** ($1; open daily). Less is said about Harvey Fellows, a pioneer stagecoach driver. After decades of life-risking adventures, Harvey fell to his death from his coach seat during a Main St parade in 1929.

The Deadwood CVB (☎ 605-578-1876, 800-999-1876, 735 Main St) has brochures, as does the more helpful History & Information Center (☎ 605-578-2507), a block west of Main St, at Pine St and US 85/14A (open daily).

In nearby Lead (pronounced leed), peek at the 944-foot-deep open cut of the **Homestake gold mine** (160 E Main St) to see what mining will do to a mountain (free admission; van tours $5). It's the USA's largest operating gold mine but will shut down in late 2002.

Places to Stay There are six campgrounds near Deadwood. *Deadwood KOA* (☎ 605-578-3830), just a mile west on US 14A, has $18 campsites and $39 'kabins.' The bald 'mountain' across US 14A was made from dug-up rock from the Homestake mine. *Wild Bill's Campground* (☎ 605-578-2800), 5½ miles south on US 385, has tent/RV sites for $13/19; cabins cost $58.

Budget motels in Deadwood, all on Main St, include the spotlessly clean *HI Penny Motel* (☎ 605-578-1842, 877-565-8140, 818 Upper Main St), with $15 bunks in a dorm and good $49 singles ($20 less off season). Penny also rents bikes ($25 per day) and offers drop-off service for the Mickelson Trail. In downtown, you can't beat the *Historic Franklin Hotel* (☎ 605-578-2241, 700 Main St); many rooms are named for celebrities who've stayed in them (rates start at $95 in summer).

Near Lead, *Ponderosa Motor Lodge* (☎ 605-584-3321), on US 14A, has cute cabins for $60. The brookside *Whitetail Court Motel* (☎ 605-584-3315), 2½ miles southwest of town on US 85/14A, has cabins with VCRs (from $49), plus two hot tubs.

Places to Eat Nearly all gambling houses have a menu of sorts. The *First Gold Hotel* (270 Main St) has a 79¢ (!) breakfast, and the *Silverado Gaming Establishment* (709 Main St) has a big juicy buffet ($6 at lunch, $11 at dinner). If you prefer eating without

slot machines at your elbow, your best bet is the *Deadwood Social Club* (657 Main St), above Saloon No 10, where Hickok got rubbed out. A 'veggie junction pasta' is $10 at dinner.

Mt Rushmore National Monument

The 60-foot faces of George Washington, Thomas Jefferson, Abraham Lincoln and Theodore Roosevelt – carved in the granite of a Black Hills outcrop – are some of the most famous images in the USA (the monument gets 3 million visitors each year). You can't help but be overwhelmed by its sheer scale and the massive physical effort of the team (led by sculptor Gutzon Borglum) that created it. If Washington were depicted from head to toe, he would be 465 feet high. The site was dedicated in 1927, and 14 years of work commenced – Washington emerged in 1930, Jefferson in 1936, Lincoln in 1937 and Roosevelt in 1939. Borglum died in March 1941, and his son Lincoln supervised the completion in October 1941.

The visitor center (☎ 605-574-2523) has information, exhibits, a new film, bookstore and a *snack shop* selling sandwiches and fudge. You pass through an avenue of all 50 state flags before reaching the Grand View Terrace, which is above the spacious amphitheater. The closest you can get to the monument is around the Presidential Trail loop, which has good nostril views (free admission). There's a 9pm light show in summer. You can park near the center ($8 annual permit) or at a free lot a quarter-mile away. The monument is 3 miles south of Keystone (see below) via US 16A and 25 miles southwest of Rapid City via US 16.

Keystone

The nearest lodging and restaurants to Mt Rushmore are in Keystone, a one-time mining town now solely devoted to the monument. You can learn more about Mt Rushmore's enigmatic creator by visiting the **Rushmore-Borglum Story** (☎ 605-666-4448), on US 16A ($7).

A tramway runs in summer, but frankly you get better views of the monument from 17-mile Iron Mountain Rd to the south. Also in summer, Rushmore Helicopters (☎ 605-666-4461) offer good-value short flights for $20 and $40.

There are several chain motels in town, but better stays are just north on US 16A: the bush-clad *Powder House* (☎ 605-666-4646), with cabins starting at $55, and *Holy Smoke Resort* (☎ 605-666-4616), with rustic log cabins for $80 and $95. If you *must* sleep under the gaze of stone men, *Mt Rushmore's Presidents View Resort* (☎ 605-666-4212), in town, has exactly one room with a view, the $130 suite.

Along Keystone's tacky strip of 'old-time' shops and restaurants is the cozy *1880 Railhead Family Restaurant*, which has a lunch/dinner buffet for $9/15.

Hill City

In between Rapid, Custer and Mt Rushmore, little Hill City is a good place to base yourself. Keen rock climbers can contact the Sylvan Rocks Climbing School (☎ 605-574-2425, 301 Main St). Group courses (including equipment) start at $150. The shop up front sells climbing gear. High Country Guest Ranch (☎ 888-222-4628) arranges three-hour horse rides ($41).

There are lots of sleeping places around town, including *Pine Rest Cabins* (☎ 605-574-2416, 800-333-5306), a mile south, with rustic cabins from $85 (and a spotless dog named Spot).

Crazy Horse Memorial

The world's largest monument, 4 miles north of Custer, is, as author Ian Frazier describes, 'a ruin, only in reverse.' Lookers-on of the 563-foot work-in-progress can gawk at what will be – the Sioux leader astride his horse, pointing to the horizon saying, 'My lands are where my dead lie buried' – rather than what was.

Never photographed, defeated in battle or found on the dotted line of a meaningless treaty, the great Crazy Horse was the obvious choice for a 'monument for all Native Americans.' Lakota Sioux elders hoped one would balance the presidential focus of Mt Rushmore, and in 1948 they asked Boston-born sculptor Korczak Ziolkowski to build it. He fervently blasted at the mountain until his death in 1982. Often mountain goats were his only companions.

Korczak's (large) family completed Crazy Horse's 88-foot face in 1998. Next up is the horse's head, then Crazy Horse's (which will be larger than Mt Rushmore's four presidents combined). No one can guess when it will be complete. Depending on weather, you can see (and hear) blasts on most days year round.

The huge visitor center (☎ 605-673-4681) charts the progress, exhibits scale models and has a viewing deck. During the Volksmarch, held the first weekend of June, there are trips up to the mountain, which is lit nightly. Adjacent to the center is the impressive Indian Museum of North America and Korczak's studio. Blasted-off pieces of the monument are available for free (but heavy) souvenirs. There's also a restaurant and a gift shop with books on Crazy Horse.

Offers of federal funding have been turned down flat. Korczak felt the 'American people' – not the government – should finance such a work. Entry to the visitor center, museum and studio costs $8/19 per person/car and is free for Native Americans (open daily).

Heritage Village (☎ 605-673-4761), a mile south of Crazy Horse, has tent sites for $14 and tipis for $22.

Custer

This town gets its name from the enigmatic general who found gold in the hills in 1874. Today Custer isn't too much to look at, but it has a great location near Custer State Park. The chamber of commerce (☎ 605-673-2244) is at 615 Washington St.

An hour-long sunrise **balloon flight** with Black Hills Balloons (☎ 605-673-2520) over the monuments is fantastic but expensive at $210/165 adults/children (no kids under six).

There are 17 campgrounds in the region. The popular *Flintstones Bedrock City* (☎ 605-673-4664), a mile south on US 385, has rather treeless tent/RV sites for $16/20, but there's a wealth of activities for the kids.

Chief Motel (☎ 605-673-2318, 120 Mt Rushmore Rd) has a pool, hot tub and $65/87 singles/doubles in summer. Comfier are the yellow-and-red 1930s cottages at *Shady Rest Motel* (☎ 605-673-4478, 238 Gordon), two blocks south of Mt Rushmore Rd ($55 and $65).

Skyway Restaurant (511 Mt Rushmore Rd) has a $5 veggie pita at lunch. The lively *Bavarian Restaurant*, north on US 16/385, has live music and good German food; try the *rouladen* for $10.

Custer State Park

This superb 114-sq-mile park is one of the state's highlights. The only reason it isn't a national park is the state grabbed it first. It boasts one of the largest free-roaming buffalo herds in the world (about 1500), the famous 'begging burros' (donkeys seeking handouts) and more than 200 species of birds. Elk, whitetail and mule deer, pronghorns, mountain goats, bighorn sheep, coyotes, prairie dogs, mountain lions and bobcats may also be seen along the 18-mile Wildlife Loop Rd, Iron Mountain Rd and the incredible 14-mile Needles Hwy.

Every year in October there is a roundup of the park's buffalo, and 500 are sold at the November auction (get one for $500-1000).

The Peter Norbeck Visitor Center (☎ 605-255-4464), 15 miles east of Custer (on US 16A), in the center of the park, has exhibits and offers activities ($5/10 per person/car in summer, $2/5 otherwise). In summer, the center offers daily gold-panning demonstrations at 1pm (free admission).

Hiking through the prairie grassland and pine-covered hills gives you a great opportunity to observe wildlife. Trails such as Sylvan Lake Shore, Cathedral Spires, French Creek Natural Area and Centennial allow visitors to explore a variety of habitats. A popular hike is up the state's tallest mountain, Harney Peak; the trailhead is at Sylvan Lake. Swimming, fishing and boating on the park's lakes – as well as climbing on its jagged rock spires – are also very popular.

You can camp in eight developed *campsites* around the park ($12-16). Reservations are recommended in summer; call ☎ 800-710-2267. French Creek Natural Area has primitive camping for $2.

The park has four impressive *resorts* (☎ 800-658-3530), each with cabins and campsites: the State Game Lodge, Sylvan Lake, the Blue Bell and the Legion Lodge. Summer rates for a lodge room or cabin start at $75.

Wind Cave National Park

The park, just south of Custer State Park, covers nearly 47 sq miles. The park is three-quarters prairie grassland and one-quarter forest and home to stacks of wildlife. The visitor center (☎ 605-745-4600) has displays and conducts interpretive walks.

The central (but hidden) feature is, of course, the cave, which is 98 miles long and growing (new tunnels are frequently discovered). It has scores of unique 'boxer' formations, dating 60 to 100 million years. Plus there are the strong gusts – felt at the entrance, not inside – that give its name (these inhalations and exhalations are caused by changes in atmospheric pressure, not a snoring Cave Demon). There are five tours, ranging from one to four hours (from $6 to the $20 down-and-dirty spelunking tour).

Hiking is a popular activity in the park, where you will find the south end of the 111-mile Centennial Trail. Be sure to hit the short trail up to the summit of Rankin Ridge (5013 feet).

Camping in summer costs $10 per site ($5 in winter).

Jewel Cave National Monument

The best of the Black Hills' many caves is 125-mile-long Jewel Cave, 13 miles west of Custer on US 16. It's known for the nailhead calcite crystals that line its walls. There are three popular tours – the Scenic ($8), two-hour candlelit Historic ($8) and four-hour hard-hat-with-headlight Spelunking ($20; adults only). The visitor center (☎ 605-673-2288) is open daily.

Hot Springs

This attractive town, a bit south of the main Black Hills circuit, boasts beautiful 1890s sandstone buildings and warm mineral springs (*minnekahta* – 'hot water' to the Lakota Sioux). The chamber of commerce (☎ 605-745-4140, 801 S 6th St) has lots of information.

The water at Evans Plunge (☎ 605-745-5165, 1145 N River St), a giant indoor geothermal springs pool, is 87° all year ($8; open late in summer). Locals like to wade in Fall River Park, off S River St, or swim at Cascade Falls, 10 miles south on US 71 (free, and warm all year).

The remarkable Mammoth Site (☎ 605-745-6017), on the US 18 bypass, is the country's only left-as-found mammoth fossil display. Hundreds of animals perished in a sinkhole here over a 300- to 700-year period about 27,000 years ago. A lot of mommy-mammoth tears must have been shed here too – most of the 52 mammoths found so far are adolescents (and all are male!); in July you can cheer on paleontologists digging for more bones ($6).

Angostura State Recreation Area (☎ 605-745-6996), 10 miles south on US 18, has campsites for $10. You'll find several good motels in town. The fun, hilltop *Historic Log Cabin Motel* (☎ 605-745-5166), on US 385 north of town, has a petting zoo, basketball court and bikes; kitchenette cabins start at $44. The *Bison Motel* (☎ 605-745-5191, 646 S 5th St) has basic rooms for $64 and up.

Elk Horn Café (310 S Chicago St) serves good breakfasts all day.

North Dakota

Travelers crossing the USA's least-visited state on I-94, the alternate US 2, or Amtrak's *Empire Builder* should be ready for 300 miles of uninterrupted rolling plains that often look like a big guy sat on them. Theodore Roosevelt National Park is North Dakota's highlight, with an amazing amount of wildlife. Other attractions are the 200-mile-long Lake Sakakawea, Lewis & Clark State Park and seeing 'thunder boomers' form in the big skies long before the rain hits you.

Though linked by name with South Dakota, North Dakota tends to be more chummy with its eastern neighbor, Minnesota, which locals like to point out is colder. So concerned are some North Dakotans over perception of their state as a frozen, lifeless flatland, that in 1947 and 1989 legislation nearly passed to drop the 'North' in the state name. The drama resurfaced in 2001, as the name-change proposal was once again put forth. (Governor Ed Schafer said it would be 'fun' to change the name.)

History
During their epic trip, Lewis and Clark spent more time in present-day North Dakota than any other state, meeting up with Shoshone guide Sacagawea on their way west. In the mid-19th century, small pox epidemics came up the Missouri River, decimating the populations of the Arikara, Mandan and Hidatsa tribes, who affiliated and established the Like-a-Fishhook Village in the mid-19th century.

When the railroad arrived in the 1870s, thousands of settlers flocked in to take up allotments under the Homestead Acts. As farmers adopted new machines and techniques, the state's grain farms became so productive they were called 'Bonanza Farms.' By 1889 the state population was more than 250,000, half foreign-born (one in eight were from Norway).

North Dakota has been good to its people. The young Theodore Roosevelt came here to hoop, holler and work the 'dogies,' and later became the president who created the first national parks. In the early 20th century, farmers were being exploited by monopolized grain-elevator companies, so North Dakota set up state-owned banks and a state-run grain elevator that paid fair prices.

Mining of coal, oil, natural gas and uranium has increased in recent years. Many family farms have been taken over by big agricultural companies, but the state population continues to grow slightly.

Information
The helpful state Tourism Dept (☎ 701-328-2525, 800-435-5663, ⓦ www.ndtourism.com) has information. North Dakota Parks and

Recreation (☎ 701-328-5357, 1835 Bismarck Expressway) is in Bismarck. Visitors to state parks will need to purchase a $4 daily vehicle permit. For information on the parks' campsites (or to make reservations), call ☎ 800-807-4723.

For highway conditions, especially in the harsh winters, call ☎ 701-328-7623. State and local taxes add roughly 6% to prices.

ALONG INTERSTATE 94

The quickest route across North Dakota, I-94 also provides easy access to most of the state's top attractions.

Fargo

North Dakota's biggest city sits along the north-running Red River, across from Moorhead, Minnesota. Fargo has been a fur-trading post, a frontier town, a quick-divorce capital and a frequent destination for folks in the Federal Witness Protection Program. But Fargo is best known from the wacky characters in the film *Fargo,* still a source of debate in town (though it was filmed in Minnesota). Fewer people seem upset that Fuji Film called Fargo the 'most unphotogenic city in the US.' Fargo is flat and teems with construction crews (who will be expanding roads into the next decade), but its friendly vibe can't be put on film. Fargo is, as some say here, 'for neat.'

Housed in a humongous 'grain elevator,' the Fargo-Moorhead CVB (☎ 701-282-3653, 800-235-7654, 2001 44th St), I-94 exit 348, showers visitors with free popcorn, coffee and brochures.

Things to See & Do The Walk of Fame outside the CVB includes George W Bush and Def Leppard. In the historic downtown, the 1926 art deco **Fargo Theatre** (☎ 701-235-4152, 314 Broadway) has an old Wurlitzer organ and screens independent films. Across the river in Moorhead, the **Hermkomst Center** (☎ 218-299-5511, 202 1st Ave N) has a cool 76-foot replica of a 9th-century Viking ship – it was sailed to Norway in 1982. A film tells the story ($3.50; open daily).

Places to Stay & Eat You can camp right in town on the riverfront **Linwood Campground** (☎ 701-232-3987), at 17th Ave and 5th St (near I-94 exit 351); developed tent/RV sites cost $8/15. **Motel 6** (☎ 701-232-9251, 1202 36th St), just north of I-29 13th St exit, has $40/46 singles/doubles. A bit more upscale, **C'mon Inn** (☎ 701-277-9944, 4338 20th Ave), near the CVB, beckons guests with nice $59 rooms, an indoor pool and a Jacuzzi.

Wacky **Space Aliens** (1840 45th St), off I-94, is a cross of 1950s diner and *Mars Attacks!*; it's known for its barbecue (ribs start at $8). Downtown, the **Dakota Soda** (420 Broadway), in the Zandbroz Variety shop, has $4 pasta lunches. Students and musicians hang out at **Trentino** (311 Broadway), a cafe with snacks.

Entertainment Some rocking gets done in town. Check out the **Moose Lodge** (309 Broadway), the unlikely spot for open-mic rap gigs. In Moorhead, live shows at both **Kirby's** and **Ralph's Corner**, at 4th and Main Sts, attract a mix of old-timers and punk rockers.

Getting There & Around There are stations for Greyhound (☎ 701-293-1222, 402 Northern Pacific Ave) and Amtrak (☎ 701-232-2197, 420 4th St N). If you get drunk, call Doyle's cabs (☎ 701-235-5535).

Around Fargo

Built in the 1880s, the restored **Bagg Bonanza Farm** (☎ 701-274-8989), 45 miles south on I-29, offers a unique glimpse at the area's wheat-boom days. Guided tours are given Friday to Sunday in summer, or by appointment ($3.50).

In **Jamestown**, 93 miles west on I-92, the world's largest buffalo – a statue – stands at the end of Frontier Village (☎ 701-252-6307), a collection of old buildings (free admission; open May-Aug). Nearby, the **National Buffalo Museum** (☎ 701-252-8648) has exhibits on our hairy friends. A rare albino buffalo roams the grounds ($3).

Bismarck & Mandan

Bismarck, North Dakota's state capital, was named after the German chancellor to make it attractive to European investors and settlers. Most of the town has since surrendered to commercial sprawl, but a handful of sights (plus great sidetrips) make it a nice stopover. There are pleasant beaches and trails along the Missouri River. Mandan, named after the area's original riverside dwellers, is a somewhat run-down railway town across the river.

The Bismarck-Mandan CVB (☎ 701-222-4308, 800-767-3555, 1600 Burnt Boat Dr), in Bismarck, has brochures.

Things to See & Do In Bismarck, the impressive 1930s art deco **State Capitol** (☎ 701-328-2480), at the end of N 7th St, is often referred to as the 'skyscraper of the prairie' and looks something like a Stalinist school of dentistry. There's an observatory deck on the 18th floor. Behind the Sacagawea statue, the huge **North Dakota Heritage Center** (☎ 701-328-2666), on Capitol Mall, offers comprehensive displays of the state's history. By all means listen to the recording of the State March (free admission; open daily). The **Bank of North Dakota** (BND; ☎ 701-328-5700), at 9th and Main Sts, is the USA's only state-owned bank; ask for a tour.

Some 7 miles south of Mandan on SR 1806 is **Fort Abraham Lincoln State Park** (☎ 701-663-9571), well worth the detour. Its On-A-Slant Indian Village has three re-created Mandan earthlodges. Nearby you can tour full-scale replicas of the fort's cavalry post, including Custer's house (from where he set out for his 'last stand'). Up the hill, the infantry blockhouses have top-notch views ($4, plus $4 vehicle permit).

Places to Stay & Eat Fort Abraham Lincoln State Park has *campsites* on the river ($7/12 for tents/RVs); *cabins* with bunks cost $30. In Bismarck, there is a congregation of motels around I-94 exit 159 and State St. *Select Inn* (☎ 701-223-8060, 505 Interchange Ave) has good-value $43/50 singles/doubles with free breakfast. Bismarck's action – amid malls and megastores – is centered at Bismarck Expressway Ave and S Washington St. Here you'll find rooms for $44 and up at *Expressway Inn* (☎ 701-222-2900, 200 Bismarck Expressway Ave) as well as chain restaurants. For food downtown, try *Fiesta Villa*, on Main St, for Mexican food in an old Spanish-style depot. For location, you can't beat a meal at *Meriwether's (1700 River Rd)*, on the banks of the Missouri. A veggie sandwich costs $7.

Around Bismarck

North of Bismarck are several worthwhile attractions near the spot that Lewis and

Clark wintered with the Mandan in 1804–5. The best is the **Lewis & Clark Interpretive Center** (☎ 701-462-8535), in Washburn (take US 83 north to Hwy 200A), where you can learn about the duo's epic expedition and the Native Americans who helped out. There's an interesting new exhibit on Fort Clark, a trading post established nearby in 1830 ($5). **Fort Mandan**, a replica of the 30-acre fort built by Lewis and Clark, is 2½ miles west on CR 17 (10 miles downstream from the flooded original site). Just north of Stanton on CR 37, the **Knife River Indian Villages** (☎ 701-745-3309) feature the sites of three Hidatsa and Mandan villages that were occupied for 900 years. Sacagawea joined Lewis and Clark from here. Trails lead past depressions where earthlodges once stood. The visitor center runs a great video (free admission; open daily).

West of Bismarck on I-94, stop and see Sue, the **World's Largest Holstein Cow**, in New Salem. No offense to the udders, but the view from the hill just above is the highlight. In Dickinson, 65 miles west, the **Dakota Dinosaur Museum** (☎ 701-225-3466) has 10 dinosaur reconstructions, a risky revolutionary skulls display and a full triceratops skull. You'll learn the most by speaking with the friendly fossil finder, who is usually around ($6). Dickinson has several budget motels; the *Hartfiel Inn (☎ 701-225-6710, 509 3rd Ave W)* has B&B rooms for $59.

South of Bismarck, scenic SR 24/1806 goes through Standing Rock Indian Reservation and into South Dakota. The **burial site of Sitting Bull** is at Fort Yates, not far from Lake Oahe. On the other side of the Missouri, US 83 leads south of Bismarck to **Lawrence Welk Farmstead** (☎ 701-336-7470), 2 miles west of Strasburg. You can tour this childhood home of the legendary bandleader responsible for 'champagne-bubble music' ($3; open May-Sept).

Theodore Roosevelt National Park

Undoubtedly North Dakota's highlight, this superb park near the state's western border has two very different units. The South Unit, near I-94 at Medora, has rolling badlands and a 36-mile scenic loop. The remote North Unit, 68 miles north on US 85, offers more rugged scenery, deeper crags and a 14-mile drive – as well as fewer visitors. An extensive area around the units is protected as the Little Missouri National Grassland.

Wildlife is everywhere – some 200 species of birds, mule and whitetail deer, wild horses, bighorn sheep, elk and car-surrounding herds of bison. And there's no missing the squeaking prairie dogs, whose sprawling 'towns' show that they knew about urbanization long before we humans did.

There are opportunities for **hiking** on 85 miles of backcountry trails (a permit is required) as well as many **horseback-riding** trails. You can hike, ride or bike the 110-mile Maah Daah Hey Trail between the park units too; for information call ☎ 701-225-5151.

The park has three visitor centers, including the Medora Visitors Center (☎ 701-623-4466), with Theodore Roosevelt's old cabin out back. Theodore credited his rise to presidency to his experiences in North Dakota. He described this area as 'a land of vast, silent spaces, of lonely rivers, and of plains, where the wild game stared at the passing horsemen' – which still rings pretty true today. Park entry costs $5/10 per person/vehicle.

The park has two developed ***campgrounds*** with sites for $10. Free backcountry camping is allowed throughout the park. There are accommodations

and restaurants in Medora (see below), Belfield and Dickinson.

Medora

This partially restored frontier town cashes in on its proximity to one of the country's best parks. The Medora Musical (☎ 800-633-6721), a downright unabashed 'Teddy dedication,' is staged in the Burning Hills Badlands Amphitheater from mid-June to Labor Day ($19).

Open all year, the quaint ***Sully Inn*** (☎ 701-623-4455), at 4th St and Broadway, has clean rooms for $50 ($10 less in the basement). For food, don't expect McDonald's; all eating places are privately run. ***Cowboy Café***, at 4th St and 3rd Ave, has great breakfasts and a talkative cook. ***Iron Horse Saloon***, at Pacific Ave and 3rd St, serves good pan-fried pike with potatoes for $9.50. Greyhound buses stop in town.

ALONG US 2

Once the Great Northern Rd, US 2 offers more prairie feel than I-94. There are some vintage small towns like Rugby, the proud geographical center of North America. The route goes by many **missile silos** buried in the prairie too, particularly between Grand Forks and Devils Lake and around Minot. Watch for a parking garage or small field surrounded by a chain-link fence. These are *not* open to the public.

Grand Forks

An island of suburbia in a sea of prairie, Grand Forks is home to the University of North Dakota (UND) and an air force base, which is a big employer. The town was hit hard by the Red River flood in 1997 but has recovered well. Get brochures at Greater Grand Forks CVB (☎ 701-746-0444, 4251 Gateway Dr), open daily.

UND, near DeMers Ave east of I-29, is a civilizing influence on the town, and its Museum of Art (☎ 701-777-4195), on Centennial Dr, is worth seeing (free admission). The university's school of Aerospace Sciences has tours; call ☎ 701-777-2791. Pick up a cool $1 flour bag from the state-owned North Dakota State Mill, on Mill Rd north of Gateway Dr.

For sleeping, it's futile to resist the charms of the ***Fabulous Westward Ho***

'Who are you calling cute?' – prairie dog

Motel (☎ 701-775-5341, *3400 Gateway Dr*), east of I-29 (exit 141). Rooms have comfy beds and old-style phones ($41).

Grand Forks is the birthplace of cream of wheat; get a $1.75 bowl of it at *2-29 Café (4720 Gateway Dr)*, a friendly truck stop open all day. Over in East Grand Forks, Minnesota, *Whitey's Wonderbar Café (121 DeMers Ave)* serves tasty walleye pike sandwiches for $6.50.

For fun, the huge, lit-up *Westward Ho Entertainment Complex* (☎ 701-772-2222), next to the hotel, has a 1920s-style ballroom that hosts a UND comedy group and concerts; Amber Bock beer costs $1.50.

Devils Lake
This nice town shares its name with the popular lake here. There's a restored 19th-century downtown and inexpensive lodgings along the highway. The CVB (☎ 701-662-4903) has information.

The lake was called Miniwakan (Spirit Water) by the Sioux and later misinterpreted as 'Evil Spirits' by settlers. Today it is surrounded by campgrounds and a few state parks. *Grahams Island State Park* (☎ 701-766-4015) has developed tent/RV sites for $7/12, and new cabins for $30.

The Spirit Lake Sioux Indian Reservation includes the well-preserved **Fort Totten** (☎ 701-766-4441), south of town ($4; May-Sept).

International Peace Garden
If you've wondered why North Dakota is the 'Peace Garden State,' venture 46 miles north of Rugby to this 2339-acre garden (☎ 701-263-4390), set in the wee Turtle Mountains and packed with 150,000 flowers (in summer). North Dakota and the Canadian province of Manitoba created it following WWI as a symbol of everlasting international harmony: It didn't work, but it's pretty. There are symbolic sculptures, a hike on the Canada side and good *camping* in the US ($11). You'll go through US customs to 'reenter' North Dakota. Resist the temptation to tell the agent to 'give peace a chance' ($10 per vehicle; May-Sept).

Minot
The main interests in Minot (rhymes with 'shine it') are the big state fair in July and

---

Range Life

Many city slickers long for the opportunity to live out fantasies as cowboys or cowgirls. Western North Dakota is a good place to do it, à la Teddy Roosevelt.

Near Medora, the *Dahkotah Lodge Guest Ranch* (☎ 701-623-4897) has three-night packages from $290 per person for full board and riding. Real roughriders go with *Little Knife Outfitters* (☎ 701-628-2747, 800-438-6905), in Watford City. A five-day ride on the Maah Daah Hey Trail runs $420 if you book ahead (including horse and meals).

The relaxing 7500-acre *Knife River Ranch* (☎ 701-983-4290), in Golden Valley northwest of Dickinson, has $55 cabins. For $162 per day you can ride, canoe and eat all you can handle.

Other Plains states have these ranches too. Poke around and you'll find plenty of places – particularly in South Dakota and Nebraska – that provide bunkhouses, stage a steakfry, demonstrate how to 'punch dogies' and offer horse-drawn feed-wagon rides.

---

the October Norsk Hostfest, a Scandinavian shindig in which *lefse* (potato flatbread) predominates. The CVB (☎ 701-857-8206, 1020 S Broadway) has information. The infrequent tours of the **Minot Air Force Base** (☎ 701-723-6212), 15 miles north on US 83, include a visit to a missile silo used to train military folk (call ahead).

Several motels and restaurants are near the intersection of US 83 and US 2; the *Ho-Hum Motel* (☎ 701-852-2191), just west on US 2, has a hey-ho view of the plains ($31 singles).

New Town
About 15 miles south of Stanley (on US 2) in the Fort Berthold Indian Reservation, New Town is worth a detour. Drive up Crow Flies High Butte, 4 miles west of town, for views of Lake Sakakawea. Across the bridge, the splendid **Three Tribes Museum** (☎ 701-627-4477), next to a casino, explains why the Mandan, Hidatsa and Arikara peoples affiliated in the 19th century ($3; open daily Apr-Oct). The reservation is host to several

summer powwows. The *West Dakota Inn* (☎ 701-627-3721) has $35 rooms.

West to Montana

Small prairie towns are spaced along US 2 west of Minot, some picturesquely decrepit – all dotted with empty buildings. Williston has a 35-foot monument to agriculture and several motels. Try *Travel Host* (☎ 701-774-0041), at US 2 and US 85 N, with $38 rooms.

West on SR 1804, **Fort Buford** (☎ 701-572-9034) was the army outpost where Sitting Bull surrendered ($4); note the causes of death marked on tombstones at the cemetery. A bit farther is the **Fort Union Trading Post** (☎ 701-572-9083), a reconstruction of the American Fur Company post built in 1828 (open daily). Its colorful walls look like a clown palace from a distance.

Rocky Mountains

Rocky Mountains

Home to some of the USA's most gorgeous wilderness, this region of soaring peaks, alpine valleys and windswept prairies is also the birthplace of the fabled Wild West. This is where explorers Lewis and Clark made their names, Custer met his fate at Little Bighorn and Butch Cassidy's Wild Bunch robbed the railroad. Besides countless scenic wonders, a tour through modern Colorado, Wyoming, Montana or Idaho offers a fascinating look at this land of legend – though careful observers will find the real Wild West quite different from that portrayed by Hollywood and mainstream US history.

National parks are arguably the Rockies' biggest draw. Yellowstone Park in Wyoming and Rocky Mountain Park in Colorado both reward visitors with amazing scenery, but equally impressive vistas (minus the crowds) can be enjoyed at wilderness areas such as Colorado's San Juan National Forest and Montana's Bob Marshall Wilderness Area. If you love the great outdoors, the Rockies should be a priority destination, whether for hiking, biking, climbing, camping, fishing, rafting, kayaking or even hot-air ballooning.

Historical sites also abound, from the ancient cliff dwellings of Mesa Verde's Ancestral Puebloans to old mining and frontier towns like Telluride, Leadville and Laramie. Amid their pleasant restaurants, bars and shops, towns like these shelter museums and historical sites which show that, especially for Native Americans, a lot was lost when the West 'was won.'

History

The Rockies' first inhabitants were nomadic hunter-gatherers who lived in small bands; artifacts from eastern Colorado provide evidence of bison-hunting 11,000 years ago. The most complex societies in North American antiquity flourished on the Colorado Plateau, including those at Mesa Verde, near present-day Cortez, Colorado.

Many different groups occupied the region at the time of European contact, including the Nez Percé and Shoshone in Idaho and western Wyoming, the Crow and

Highlights

- Denver – world-class museums, theater and music, and a growing culinary scene
- Rocky Mountain National Park – touristed, but hard to beat for scenery and wildlife
- Boulder – liberal and collegial, where old-time hippies meet new-money yuppies
- Telluride & Crested Butte – great skiing, Old West mining history
- Mesa Verde National Park – awe-inspiring cliff dwellings and pueblos
- Yellowstone National Park – spectacular geysers, forests, alpine lakes and wildlife
- Grand Teton National Park – jagged granite spires and great hiking and climbing
- Glacier National Park – gorgeous alpine scenery and wilderness
- Sun Valley – synonymous with celebrity, and one of the country's top ski resorts

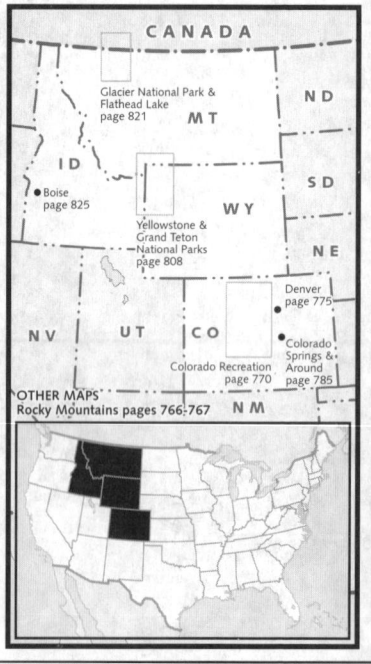

Lakota in Montana, and the Utes in Colorado. Among the first Europeans to see the Rocky Mountain area were Spaniards moving north from Mexico in the late 18th century and French trappers and fur traders.

In 1803 the upstart USA, under Thomas Jefferson, bought from France nearly all of present-day Montana and Wyoming and the eastern half of Colorado as part of the Louisiana Purchase. To assess this enormous acquisition, Jefferson ordered an expedition led by explorers Meriwether Lewis and William Clark, who proceeded to cover 8000 miles in three years.

Subsequent explorers like John Colter, Jim Bridger and Jim Beckwourth came to know the backcountry of the Rockies better than anyone except the Native Americans, with whom most of the explorers had good relationships. The local knowledge of the mountain explorers paved the way for those heading to the West Coast.

Even into the 20th century, hundreds of thousands of emigrants followed the Oregon Trail up the Missouri River and across the Continental Divide to South Pass and farther west. In the late 1860s, completion of the Transcontinental Railroad across southern Wyoming slowed, but did not halt, the inexorable march of wagon trains, pioneers and their possessions across the continent.

To make room for more settlers, the USA purged the western frontier of the Spanish, the British and, in one of the country's most shameful eras, most of the Native American population. The US government signed endless treaties to defuse Native American objections to increasing settlement. But, pressured by miners and other immigrants, the government always reneged and shunted tribes onto increasingly smaller reservations. Gold miners' incursions into Native American territory in Montana and the building of US Army forts along the Bozeman Trail ignited a series of wars with the Lakota (Sioux), Cheyenne, Arapaho and others. In 1876 the Lakota and their allies stunned the entire country by obliterating Lieutenant Colonel George Armstrong Custer's 7th Cavalry at Little Bighorn Valley in Montana. But the army eventually prevailed – its virtually unlimited supplies

Cheyenne Indian and son on the Tongue River Reservation, Montana (1939)

ROCKY MOUNTAINS

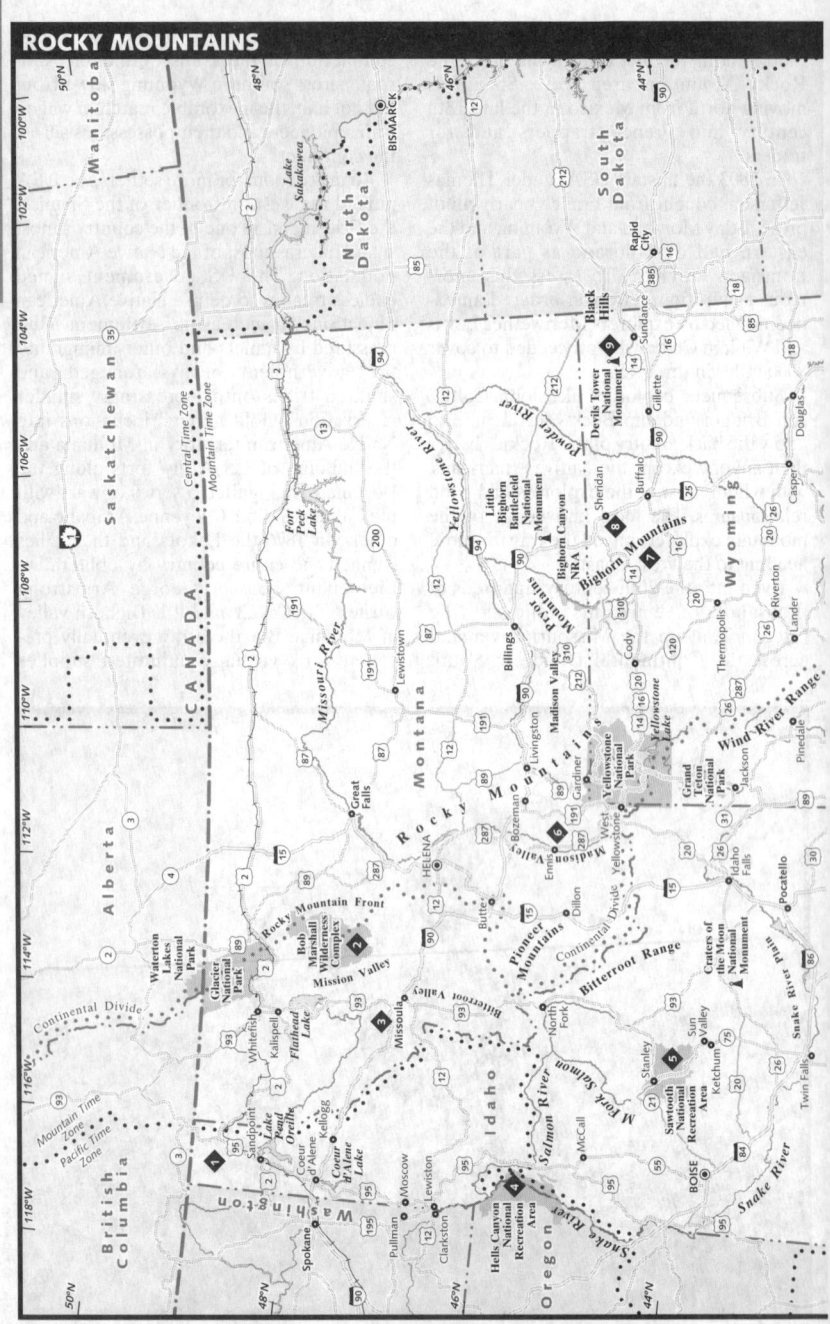

ROCKY MOUNTAINS

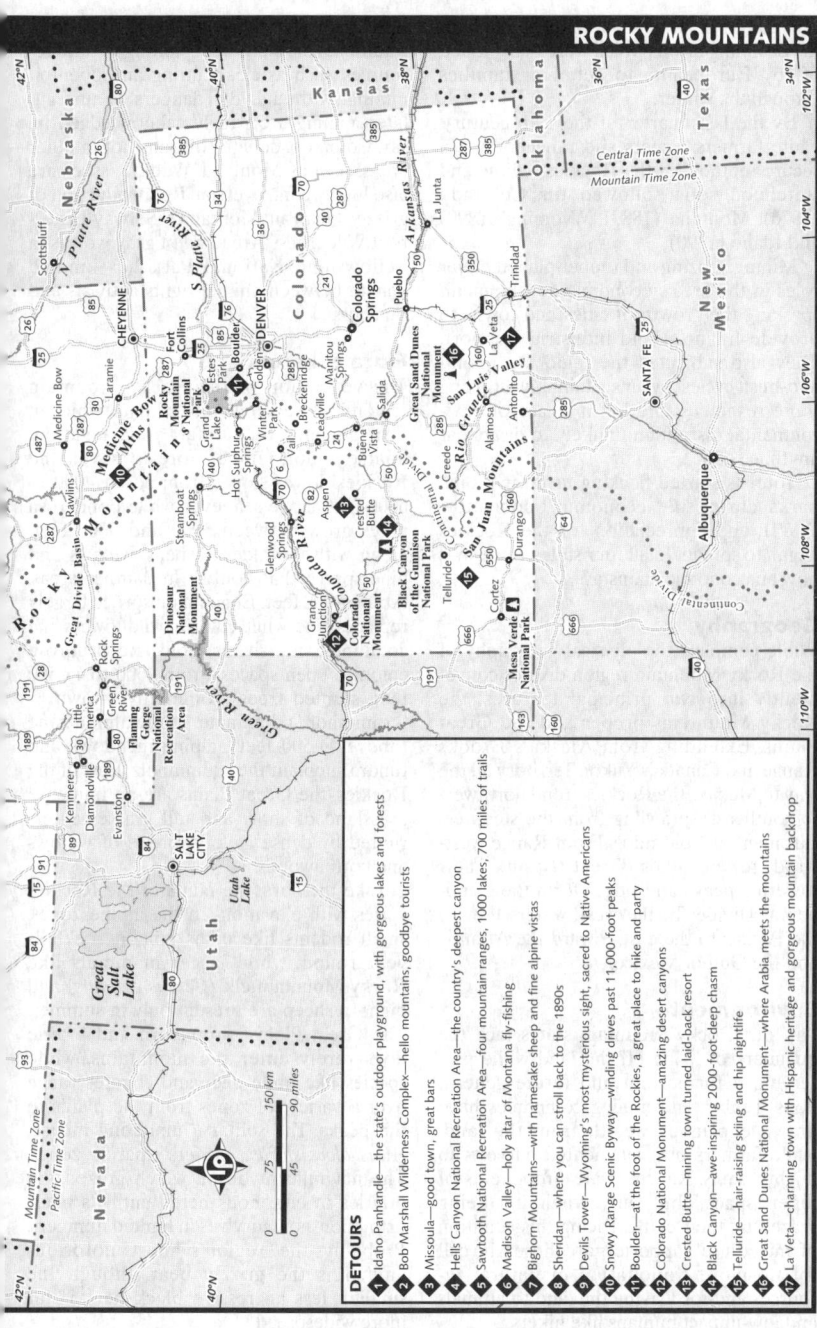

DETOURS

1. Idaho Panhandle—the state's outdoor playground, with gorgeous lakes and forests
2. Bob Marshall Wilderness Complex—hello mountains, goodbye tourists
3. Missoula—good town, great bars
4. Hells Canyon National Recreation Area—the country's deepest canyon
5. Sawtooth National Recreation Area—four mountain ranges, 1000 lakes, 700 miles of trails
6. Madison Valley—holy altar of Montana fly-fishing
7. Bighorn Mountains—with namesake sheep and fine alpine vistas
8. Sheridan—where you can stroll back to the 1890s
9. Devils Tower—Wyoming's most mysterious sight, sacred to Native Americans
10. Snowy Range Scenic Byway—winding drives past 11,000-foot peaks
11. Boulder—at the foot of the Rockies, a great place to hike and party
12. Colorado National Monument—amazing desert canyons
13. Crested Butte—mining town turned laid-back resort
14. Black Canyon—awe-inspiring 2000-foot-deep chasm
15. Telluride—hair-raising skiing and hip nightlife
16. Great Sand Dunes National Monument—where Arabia meets the mountains
17. La Veta—charming town with Hispanic heritage and gorgeous mountain backdrop

arrived by rail, while the Lakota had to hunt the declining bison (which were being killed off by Europeans) to get their families through the winter.

By the last quarter of the 19th century, white farmers, miners and ranchers had a secure foothold in the Rockies region, and statehood soon followed for Colorado (1876), Montana (1889), Wyoming (1890) and Idaho (1890).

Mining, grazing and timber played major roles in the area's economic development, sparking the growth of cities and towns to provide financial and industrial support. They also subjected the region to boom-and-bust cycles by unsustainably utilizing those resources, and left a legacy of environmental disruption unlikely to disappear anytime soon.

Tourists started flocking to the national parks during the economic boom after WWII, and appreciation for the Rockies began to spread. In all four states, tourism is now an economic mainstay.

Geography

While complex, the physical geography of the Rocky Mountain region divides conveniently into two principal features: the Rocky Mountains proper and the Great Plains. Extending from Alaska's Brooks Range and Canada's Yukon Territory all the way to Mexico, the Rockies trend northwest to southeast, sprawling from the steep escarpment of Colorado's Front Range westward to Nevada's Great Basin. Their towering peaks and ridges form the Continental Divide: To the west, waters flow to the Pacific; to the east, toward the Atlantic and the Gulf of Mexico.

Environment

All four Rocky Mountain states face the quandary of living off the land while preserving it for current and future generations. Timber and mining companies have drawn enormous wealth from the land, while farmers owe augmented harvests to mighty dams. Ranchers are proponents of 'open space,' but only when it's being grazed by their cattle. Facing this coalition of 'mixed-use' supporters are those who call for no more exploitation of natural resources and for leaving the land to animals and low-impact humans like hikers.

Already there's been a marked drop in traditional methods of exploiting natural resources, such as clear-cutting and open-pit mining. Although the dangers of unregulated mining are widely acknowledged in, say, Colorado, debate still runs hot in other areas, such as Montana. Wildlife issues are also highly controversial. Reintroduction of grizzly bears in Montana's Selway-Bitterroot Wilderness Area and of gray wolves in Yellowstone National Park has kindled debate between animal-rights activists and ranchers.

Flora & Fauna

The vegetation of the Rocky Mountain region is closely linked to climate, which in turn depends on rainfall and elevation. Sparse piñon-juniper forests cover the Rockies' lower slopes from about 4000 to 6000 feet above sea level, while ponderosa pines grow between 6000 and 9000 feet, along with the alders, aspens, willows and blue spruce that flourish in damper areas. Above 9000 feet, Engelmann spruce largely replaces pine, while colorful wildflowers like columbine, marsh marigold and primrose colonize open spaces. From 9000 to 11,500 feet, stunted trees (commonly known as 'krummholz') dominate. In the alpine zone (above 11,500 feet), alpine meadows and tundra supplant the krummholz. East of the Rockies, the Great Plains are an immense grassland of short and tall grasses, interrupted by dense gallery forests of willows and cottonwoods.

Like the flora, the fauna of the Rockies varies with elevation. In the alpine zones, small rodents like pikas inhabit rockfalls year round, while larger mammals like Rocky Mountain elk (Cervus elaphus) and bighorn sheep are present only in summer. The Great Plains' pronghorn and prairie dogs rarely enter the mountains, while species like mule deer and coyotes range over a variety of zones from the plains to the peaks. The solitary, lumbering moose, Alces alces shirasi, prefers riparian zones. The magnificent bison, which grazed the prairies in enormous herds until its near-extinction, now survives in limited numbers. Probably the region's most notorious animal is the grizzly bear, though the smaller, less aggressive black bear is far more widespread.

Government & Politics

The Rocky Mountain West is generally conservative in its politics, usually supporting the Republican party in presidential elections, but there are enclaves of liberal and even radical politics. Colorado is the most diverse and liberal state.

Political battles are often influenced by powerful business interests supporting natural-resource development, such as large-scale agriculture, mining, energy or ranching.

When to Go

For many travelers, the Rockies are a summer destination, but the winter ski season also draws a large number of visitors. Some prefer the fall, when the aspens flaunt their autumn gold, or the spring wildflower season.

It starts to feel like summer in Rockies around June, and the warm weather lasts until about mid-September. While winter doesn't usually hit until late November, snowstorms can start in the mountains as early as September! Winter usually lasts until March or early April. In the mountains, the weather is constantly changing (snow in summer is not uncommon), so always be prepared.

Summer is the high season, which means more crowds and increased lodging rates. At ski resorts, peak-season rates and conditions also apply in winter. Accommodation prices can increase by up to 30% during peak seasons, depending on where you are. The best off-season time is mid-September through October, as the weather usually stays warm and services aren't totally shut down yet.

Gay & Lesbian Travelers

With the conservatism that prevails in the Rockies, attitudes towards gay people can sometimes be rather primitive. Gay travelers should be careful, especially in rural areas, where just the sight of two men or two women holding hands can be received with abuse.

Gay and lesbian groups are still targeted by conservative groups in Colorado, especially right-wing religious organizations. Violent incidents, such as the 1998 murder of University of Wyoming student Matthew Shepard in Laramie, Wyoming, are reminders that even the more open college towns are not predictable. But at the same time awareness and attitudes have improved, especially in the Denver area, which is home to a vibrant gay community.

You may search in vain for gay bars in Wyoming, Montana or Idaho, but you will find meetings and events hosted by gay, lesbian, bisexual and transgender groups. These are often associated with universities, so you're most likely to find such groups in college towns like Laramie, Bozeman, and Missoula, as well as Moscow and Boise.

Activities

The national parklands, wilderness areas and forests of the Rocky Mountains offer some of the world's best opportunities to enjoy all kinds of recreational activities, from backpacking and mountain biking to caving and windsurfing.

There is perhaps no better way to appreciate the region's lofty glacial peaks, peaceful dense forests, remote mountain meadows and high alpine lakes than by hiking. Remember that once you get into the backcountry, much of the scenery looks the same throughout the Rocky Mountain region. So unless you're longing specifically to see the Tetons, time may be better spent on a nearby trail than in the car trying to get to a more famous spot farther away. Hiking in one of Wyoming's wilderness areas may be much more rewarding, just as beautiful and half as crowded as hiking in Yellowstone National Park.

The Rockies are also a hot spot for mountain biking. Bike-friendly cities where you can ditch the car and ride to museums and other attractions on a network of routes include Missoula, Denver, Boulder, Fort Collins, Durango and Pueblo. Multiple-day mountain-bike tours are possible using the San Juan Hut System, which extends from Telluride across the Colorado Plateau to Moab, Utah. Idaho's Taft Tunnel Bike Trail follows a converted rail line through mountain tunnels (including the 8771-foot-long Taft Tunnel, constructed in 1909) and over high railway trestles across to Montana.

The high mountains and reliable snow conditions have made the Rocky Mountain states, Colorado in particular, one of the country's most popular skiing destinations, attracting investors and multimillion-dollar ski resorts equipped with the latest in chairlift technology, snow-grooming systems and

COLORADO RECREATION

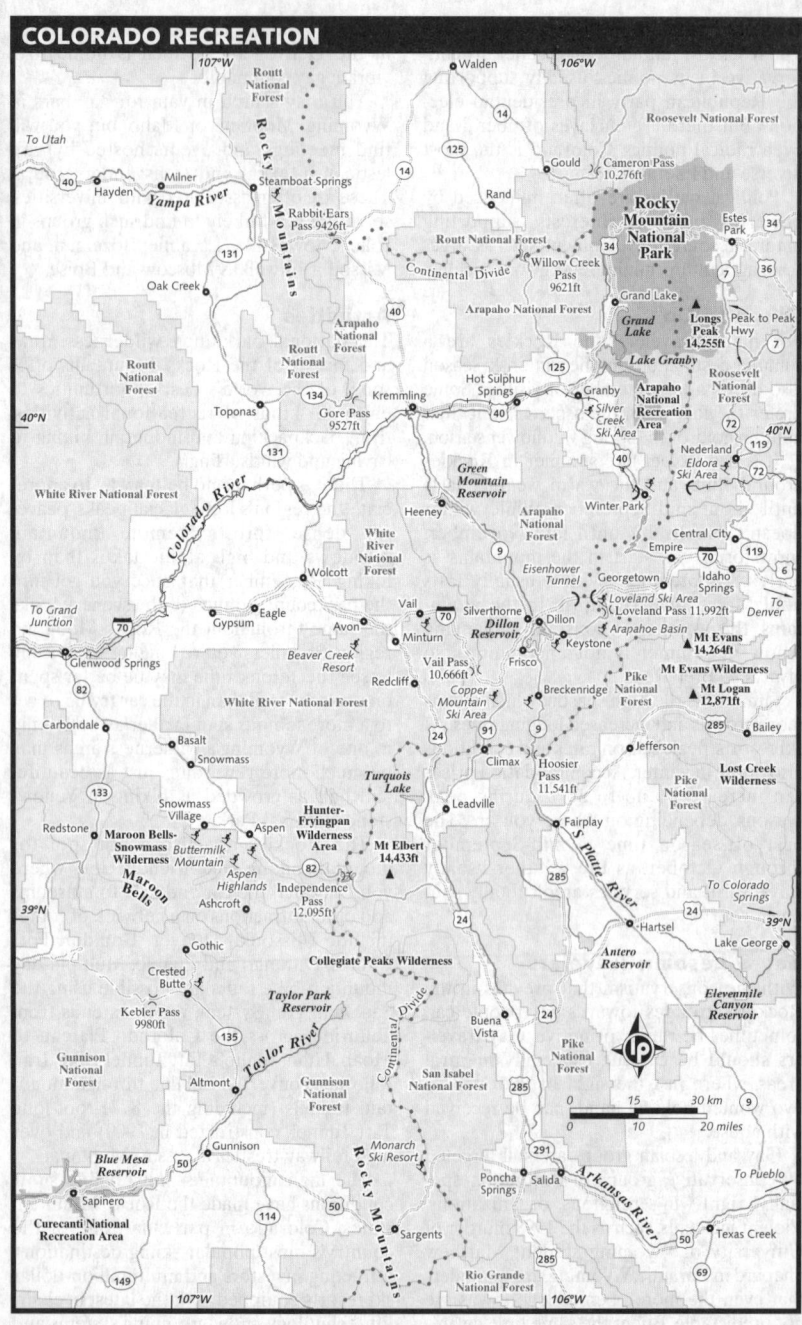

facilities. Along with the big names – like Aspen, Vail, Jackson Hole, Big Sky and Sun Valley – are small operations with a handful of lifts, cheaper ticket prices and terrain that is often as challenging as that of their glitzier neighbors. In addition to downhill skiing and snowboarding, many national parks, notably Yellowstone, close their roads during the winter and maintain cross-country trails into the parks' interiors.

Opportunities for rock climbing and mountaineering are almost unlimited in the Rockies – Colorado alone has 54 peaks over 14,000 feet above sea level, more than the rest of the US combined. Popular spots include Jackson Hole and Estes Park (the access points to Grand Teton and Rocky Mountain National Parks), Wyoming's Wind River Range, Penitente Canyon in Colorado's San Luis Valley and Hyalite Canyon, near Bozeman, Montana. For nontechnical peaks, head to the Bitterroot Range or the Gallatin Valley, where trails are well marked.

People may have trouble choosing from the myriad white-water rafting alternatives in the Rockies. Commercial outfitters in all four states provide white-water experiences ranging from inexpensive half-day trips to multiple-day expeditions. In Colorado, good choices are the Arkansas River between Buena Vista and Cañon City and the un-dammed Yampa River west of Steamboat Springs. Popular Wyoming spots include the Snake River between Hoback Junction and Alpine, the Shoshone River west of Cody and the Wind River south of Thermopolis. Just outside Yellowstone National Park near Gardiner, Montana, the Yellowstone River is the longest free-flowing river in the entire country. The stretch of the Clark Fork River through Alberton Gorge, west of Missoula, is considered western Montana's best white water, with Class III and IV rapids. In Idaho, rivers include the Upper Salmon River, St Joe National Wild & Scenic River in the Panhandle, the Snake River and the Payette River. While river rafting is the most popular water sport in the Rocky Mountain states, many raft-laden rivers are just as good for canoeing or more sedate float or tube trips.

A noteworthy online source for outdoor activities is the extensive Great Outdoor Recreational Pages (W www.gorp.com).

Getting There & Around

Air Denver International Airport is the region's main hub. From here you can fly to the small airports dotting the area (see Denver under Colorado, later in this chapter). Salt Lake City (see Utah in the Southwest chapter) also has connections with destinations in all four states.

Most short flights within the region carry high price tags. The best way to cut costs for regional flights is to book them at the same time you book a ticket to Denver or Salt Lake City.

Bus Greyhound (☎ 303-293-6555, 800-231-2222, W www.greyhound.com) has fixed routes throughout the Rockies, but it has reduced or eliminated services to smaller rural communities. TNM&O (☎ 719-635-1505) is affiliated with Greyhound and serves the same lines through Colorado and parts of Wyoming. Powder River Coach USA (☎ 800-442-3682) primarily serves eastern Wyoming, but it also goes to Denver, Colorado; Billings, Montana; and Rapid City, South Dakota. Rim Rock Stages (☎ 800-255-7655) also serves Montana destinations. Denver is the main hub.

Train Amtrak services that run to and around the region include the following:

Empire Builder – running daily from Seattle to Chicago, with 12 stops in Montana (including East Glacier and Whitefish) and one stop in Idaho at Sandpoint

California Zephyr – running daily between Emeryville, California (in the San Francisco Bay Area) and Chicago, stopping in Colorado at Denver, Fraser-Winter Park, Glenwood Springs and Grand Junction

Southwest Chief – linking Los Angeles with Chicago via Albuquerque, New Mexico, with stops in the southern Colorado towns of Trinidad, La Junta and Lamar

Car & Motorcycle The Rockies are vast and public transport limited, so it's best to have your own vehicle. The most convenient and cheapest place to rent or buy a car is Denver, which is also where you'll find the most drive-away opportunities.

The scenic drives in this region could justify a separate book. Along with famous ones like Rocky Mountain Park's Trail Ridge Rd and Glacier National Park's

Going-to-the-Sun Rd, great drives can be found throughout most of central and western Colorado, western Wyoming and Montana, and the central Idaho Rockies. Others include Colorado's Peak to Peak Hwy and the San Juan Skyway.

Colorado

The best known of the Rocky Mountain states, Colorado owes its fame to its mountains, which soar to majestic heights and create unrivaled vistas and recreational opportunities. This wealth of alpine scenery means that during the peak summer season, when millions of tourists flood the state, visitors can still find solitude at a remote mountain lake or meadow or atop a craggy summit.

The eastern edge of the Rocky Mountains, Colorado's Front Range, stretches from Wyoming to New Mexico and is the most heavily populated part of the state. The star of the northern Front Range is Rocky Mountain National Park, worth visiting year round, though summer crowds can be oppressive. Along the southern Front Range, top draw Colorado Springs gets mixed reviews: Some love all the action and attractions, like Pikes Peak and Garden of the Gods, while others find it tawdry and

overblown. Farther south, to the west of Trinidad, the meadows and alpine forests around La Veta and Cuchara offer a chance to take a scenic tour off the beaten path.

The Mountain Region boasts some of Colorado's most impressive alpine scenery and outstanding ski resorts. In the spring, summer and autumn, there's great hiking and biking in state and national parks, national forests and even the ski resorts. Gold-medal trout fishing, rafting and kayaking as well as opportunities to explore weathered ghost towns also lure visitors in warm weather.

Western Colorado stands out from the rest of the state. The beautiful desert canyons and mesas like Colorado National Monument, the archaeological wonders of Mesa Verde National Park and the near-deserted Dolores River Canyon are all starkly different from the alpine wilderness that most associate with Colorado.

History

US expansion spread to Colorado with the discovery of gold west of Denver in 1859, and by 1870 railroads linked the state with Wyoming and Kansas. The mining emphasis shifted from gold to silver during the 1870s, as the mountain smelter sites like Leadville and Aspen developed into thriving population centers almost overnight. Political expedience led the fledgling territory to statehood in 1876, the centennial of US independence. The following century saw the state's natural-resource-dependent economy swing through repeated boom-and-bust cycles, traces of which can be seen in larger cities and old mining towns. Tourism, and more recently the high-tech industry, have come to the rescue, making Colorado the most prosperous of the Rocky Mountain states.

Information

The Colorado Travel & Tourism Authority (☎ 800-265-6723, Ⓦ www.colorado.com, PO Box 3524, Englewood, CO 80155) publishes a useful state vacation guide and regional information packages. It also operates Colorado Welcome Centers at the entry points of Burlington, Cortez, Dinosaur, Fort Collins, Fruita, Julesburg, Lamar and Trinidad, where you'll find free state-highway maps and travel information covering the entire state.

To check on road conditions in Colorado, call ☎ 303-639-1234.

Colorado

Nickname: Centennial State

Population: 4,301,000 (24th)

Area: 104,100 sq miles (8th)

Admitted to Union: August 1, 1876 (38th)

Capital city: Denver (population 2,300,000)

Other cities: Colorado Springs (358,500), Boulder (101,000), Grand Junction (42,000)

State animal: Rocky Mountain bighorn sheep

State dinosaur: stegosaurus

Birthplace of: Jack Dempsey, Florence Sabin, Douglas Fairbanks

Famous for: skiing, rodeo, John Denver's 'Rocky Mountain High,' Coors

☺ ☺ ☺ ☺ ☺ ☺ ☺ ☺ ☺ ☺ ☹ ☺

The Real Wild West

The romantic notion of the Wild West, one of the most misleading images in US history, is based on tales of men like Wyatt Earp, Doc Holliday and Wild Bill Hickok who faced enemies in the street to defend their honor, even against overwhelming odds.

While these battles often took place between individuals or small groups, they represented something much greater: a struggle among merchants, mining czars and cattle barons, and the little guys, like homesteaders, miners and mavericks, for control of Western resources.

Figures like the legendary Butch Cassidy – whose Wild Bunch audaciously robbed the Union Pacific Railroad, which dominated Wyoming political and economic life – proved difficult to apprehend because many ordinary citizens admired or sympathized with their exploits.

The Hollywood legacy of cowboys and Indians shows how one-sided US interpretation of history has been. Cowboys were actually invaders on Native American lands, as cattle herds replaced bison on plains and prairies. The same is true of the US Army. Romantically viewed as heroic defenders of pioneer emigrants and settlers, the ill-trained or vengeful enlistees were often responsible for savage attacks against defenseless tribes.

Of course, Native Americans also committed atrocities, often in response to military or settler provocation. And though often viewed as a single entity pitted against the invaders, they were, in fact, a variety of peoples, often no more similar than Spaniards and Swedes, and were often bitter rivals. The Pawnee, for instance, often served as US Army scouts against their Lakota enemies.

The state sales tax is 3%. Many towns also have a lodging tax of 2% or less, except Denver, where lodging tax is 12%. Denver also levies a dining tax of 4%.

Colorado's abundant natural beauty (and relatively high motel prices) make camping one of the best accommodation options. Public campgrounds blanket the state, though more popular areas may require reservations. USFS sites can be reserved by calling ☎ 877-444-6777, or online at ⓦ www.reserveusa.com. In addition to national-park and forest campgrounds, you can reserve sites at some state parks by calling ☎ 800-678-2267, in Denver ☎ 303-470-1144. Most state parks charge a $4 daily parking fee per vehicle.

DENVER

Known as the 'Mile High City' due to its 5280-foot elevation, Denver is a former cow town that in recent years has developed into a lively, friendly city. The economic hub of the Rockies, it's also home to an array of museums and galleries and some fine restaurants, bars and clubs. Though not large by US standards, Denver is the only urban metropolis in the region.

History

When the gold seekers began flocking to the South Platte River Valley in 1859, Arapaho and Cheyenne buffalo hunters already occupied hundreds of camps in the area. General William H Larimer made a shameless attempt to sway the Kansas territorial governor, James W Denver, into granting Larimer and his partners a township at the confluence of Cherry Creek and the South Platte River by proposing to name the new town 'Denver.' It worked, and the Denver City Township Company was set up in late 1859. Gold discoveries west of Denver that same year sparked a rush, and the city boomed as a center for transport and finance. It got a further boost when the Denver Pacific and Kansas Pacific railroads arrived in 1870, linking the city with Wyoming and Kansas, respectively. Finally, in 1928, the Moffat Tunnel was opened to bring transcontinental rail traffic through Denver.

WWII brought jobs at hastily built munitions and chemical-warfare plants in and around the city. But growth suffered in the 1970s and '80s, when oil prices plummeted. The cycle reversed in the 1990s, as Denver became home to computer, telecommunications and other high-technology firms and service providers, which now underpin the local economy.

Orientation & Information

Most of Denver's sights are in the downtown district, which roughly comprises a square defined to the south and east by Colfax Ave and Broadway. The 16th St Mall is the focus of most retail activity, while Lower Downtown (or 'LoDo'), which includes historic Larimer Square near Union Station, is the heart of Denver's restaurant and nightlife scene.

Denver's Visitors Bureau (☎ 303-892-1112, 800-645-3446 for lodging reservations, W www.denver.org, 1668 Larimer St), in the Tabor Center, is open daily.

The best source for local events is the free weekly *Westword,* an irreverent newspaper with informative music, art and restaurant listings.

Just north of the Cherry Creek Shopping Center, the Tattered Cover Bookstore (☎ 303-322-7727, 2955 E 1st Ave) boasts a great selection. There is a convenient branch in LoDo (☎ 303-436-1070, 1628 16th St).

The main downtown post office (951 20th St) is open weekdays.

Things to See & Do

Resembling a modern high-rise jail downtown, the **Denver Art Museum** (☎ 303-640-4433, 100 W 14th Ave) houses one of the largest Native American art collections in the USA ($4.50; open Tue-Sat).

Lively exhibits at the **Colorado History Museum** (☎ 303-866-3682, 1300 Broadway), across from the Civic Center, include beautiful Native American rugs and life-size mining and transportation displays ($4.50; open daily).

The **Denver US Mint** (☎ 303-405-4761, 320 W Colfax Ave) is one of three gold depositories in the US, producing more than 5 billion coins annually. Free 20-minute tours are offered weekdays.

Other worthwhile downtown museums include the **Byer-Evans House & Denver History Museum** and **Molly Brown House**.

In spacious City Park, east of downtown, the **Denver Museum of Nature & Science** (☎ 303-322-7009, 2001 Colorado Blvd) is one of the premier natural-history museums in the country, featuring excellent wildlife and geological and dinosaur exhibits ($7; open daily). Also housed in the complex is a giant-screen (4½ stories high) IMAX theater and **Gates Planetarium**. To get here from downtown, take eastbound bus No 20 from 17th and Blake Sts.

North of downtown in the Five Points neighborhood, the **Black American West Museum & Heritage Center** (☎ 303-292-2566, 3091 California St) helps amend mainstream history by explaining the role of African Americans in developing the west ($4; open daily, closed Mon-Tue in winter). Southeast of downtown, **Museo de las Américas** (☎ 303-571-4401, 861 Santa Fe Dr) focuses on Latino art, history and contributions to the Southwest ($3; closed Sun).

Hands-on exhibits at the **Children's Museum of Denver** (☎ 303-433-7444, 2121 Crescent Dr), across from Mile High Stadium, include a mini TV studio and supermarket ($6.50; closed Mon). From 15th and Blake Sts downtown, bus No 10 leaves for the museum.

Places to Stay

Budget Denver's three hostels are all fairly close to downtown. Reservations are strongly advised, especially April to November. *Melbourne International Hotel & Hostel (☎ 303-292-6386, 607 22nd St)* has basic but clean dorms ($12/15 for HI-AYH members/nonmembers) and private rooms (from $27). The cheapest beds in town ($8.60 plus $1 per week linen rental) are at *Denver International Hostel (☎ 303-832-9996, 630 E 16th Ave).* Separate dorm rooms for females and families are available. The newer *Hostel of the Rocky Mountains (☎ 303-861-7777, 1530 Downing St)* has 80 beds ($15) plus private rooms with shared bath ($36). The hostel offers free pickup from the bus and train stations.

Tattered *Standish Hotel (☎ 303-534-3231, 1530 California St)* is close to the 16th

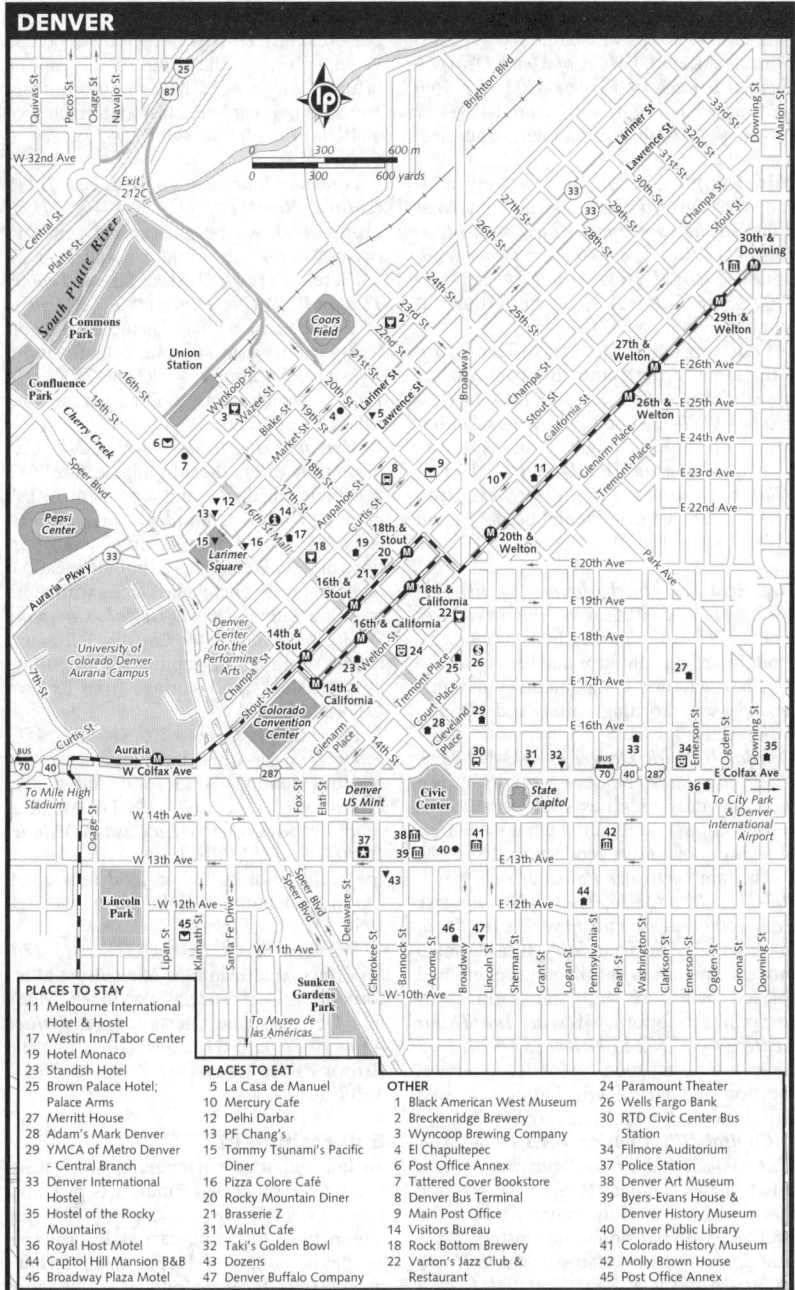

DENVER

PLACES TO STAY
11 Melbourne International
   Hotel & Hostel
17 Westin Inn/Tabor Center
19 Hotel Monaco
23 Standish Hotel
25 Brown Palace Hotel;
   Palace Arms
27 Merritt House
28 Adam's Mark Denver
29 YMCA of Metro Denver
   - Central Branch
33 Denver International
   Hostel
35 Hostel of the Rocky
   Mountains
36 Royal Host Motel
44 Capitol Hill Mansion B&B
46 Broadway Plaza Motel

PLACES TO EAT
5 La Casa de Manuel
10 Mercury Cafe
12 Delhi Darbar
13 PF Chang's
15 Tommy Tsunami's Pacific
   Diner
16 Pizza Colore Café
20 Rocky Mountain Diner
21 Brasserie Z
31 Walnut Cafe
32 Taki's Golden Bowl
43 Dozens
47 Denver Buffalo Company

OTHER
1 Black American West Museum
2 Breckenridge Brewery
3 Wyncoop Brewing Company
4 El Chapultepec
6 Post Office Annex
7 Tattered Cover Bookstore
8 Denver Bus Terminal
9 Main Post Office
14 Visitors Bureau
18 Rock Bottom Brewery
22 Varton's Jazz Club &
   Restaurant

24 Paramount Theater
30 RTD Civic Center Bus
   Station
34 Filmore Auditorium
37 Police Station
38 Denver Art Museum
39 Byers-Evans House &
   Denver History Museum
40 Denver Public Library
41 Colorado History Museum
42 Molly Brown House
45 Post Office Annex

St Mall and has singles/doubles with shared bath ($38/43) or private bath ($40/47). Also centrally located, **YMCA of Metro Denver – Central Branch** (☎ 303-861-8300, 25 E 16th Ave) also has rooms with shared ($37) or private ($44) bath; reservations are advised.

Mid-Range One of the few truly mid-range downtown places is the somewhat dingy **Broadway Plaza Motel** (☎ 303-893-3501, 1111 Broadway), at $55/59 for singles/doubles. **Royal Host Motel** (☎ 303-831-7200, 930 E Colfax Ave) is a bit farther out and has similar rooms ($40/45).

Only two hotels are next to Denver International Airport; both offer comfortable, upscale rooms. **Fairfield Inn DIA** (☎ 303-576-9640, 800-228-2800, 6851 Tower Rd) has rooms from $59. Singles/doubles at the nearby **Hampton Inn DIA** (☎ 303-371-0200, 6290 Tower Rd) are $69/79. Both places offer free Continental breakfast and 24-hour airport shuttle.

Top End The **Hotel Monaco** (☎ 303-296-1717, 800-397-5380, 🆆 www.monaco-denver.com, 1717 Champa St) boasts a bright, modern art deco interior and sees to all the details (including complimentary national newspapers, morning coffee and evening wine). Rates are $125-175.

Adam's Mark Denver (☎ 303-893-3333, 1550 Court Place) boasts a great downtown location and amenities such as a fitness room, sauna, pool and business center. Singles/doubles are a good value at $89/199.

The famous **Brown Palace Hotel** (☎ 303-297-3111, 800-321-2599, www.brownpalace.com, 1600 17th St) is a Denver historic landmark with rooms from $195. It lacks some modern amenities, but the atmosphere and service justify its four-star rating. For something modern, **Westin Inn/Tabor Center** (☎ 303-572-9100, 800-937-8461, 1672 Lawrence St) is a good bet for decor, service, location and facilities including a heated indoor/outdoor pool. Rates are $89-250.

Capitol Hill Mansion B&B (☎ 303-839-5221, 800-839-9329, 1207 Pennsylvania St) is listed in the National Register of Historic Places and is one of the country's top-rated B&Bs ($90-165). Another fine historic B&B near downtown is the 10-room **Merritt House** (☎ 303-861-9009, 877-861-5230, 941 E. 17th Ave), an 1889 Victorian mansion ($90-150).

Places to Eat

For breakfast, **Dozens** (☎ 303-572-0066, 236 W 13th Ave), to the south of the capitol, offers hearty egg dishes and muffins. Another popular breakfast and lunch spot is **Walnut Cafe** (☎ 303-832-5108, 338 E Colfax Ave).

For cheap lunches, it's hard to beat **Taki's Golden Bowl** (☎ 303-832-8440, 341 E Colfax Ave), where you can get generous rice bowls, yakisoba or udon noodles for $3-5. There's more good Asian fare at **Tommy Tsunami's Pacific Diner** (☎ 303-534-5050, 1432 Market St), a funky Japanese eatery offering good sushi specials. Slightly more stylish is **PF Chang's** (☎ 303-260-7222, 1415 15th St), which earns good marks for nouvelle Chinese fare.

Mercury Cafe (☎ 303-294-9281, 2199 California St) offers 'healthy hippie fare' like vegetable enchiladas and tofu, meat, or fish dinners. **Rocky Mountain Diner** (☎ 303-293-8383, 1800 Stout St) serves large portions of tasty Western fare (buffalo meatloaf and roast-duck enchiladas) along with more traditional items. **Denver Buffalo Company** (☎ 303-832-0880, 1109 Lincoln St), a few blocks south of the capitol, serves buffalo burgers, steaks and sausage from its own Colorado ranch.

Pizza Colore Cafe (☎ 303-534-6844, 1512 Larimer St) is open late and has ample outdoor seating, good food and hearty dinner entrées for around $8. For Mexican food, locals reckon that **La Casa de Manuel** (☎ 303-295-1752, 2010 Larimer St) is one of the better choices. Indian-food fans enjoy the $6 lunch buffet at **Delhi Darbar** (☎ 303-595-0680, 1514 Blake St).

Brasserie Z (☎ 303-293-2322, 815 17th St) offers American nouvelle cuisine at affordable prices, especially at lunch. Many feel Denver's finest restaurant is **Palace Arms** (☎ 303-297-3111, 321 17th St), in the Brown Palace Hotel (see Places to Stay – Top End).

Entertainment

To find out what's happening with music, theater and other performing arts, pick up a free copy of *Westword*. The biweekly gay newspaper *Out Front* carries informative articles about the local scene and entertainment listings. It can be found in coffee shops around Capitol Hill.

Occupying almost four city blocks south of 14th St, between Arapahoe and Champa Sts, the vast *Denver Center for the Performing Arts* (☎ 303-893-4300), the world's largest performing-arts center under one roof, hosts the resident Colorado Symphony Orchestra, Opera Colorado, Denver Center Theater Company, Colorado Ballet and touring Broadway shows.

Denver's numerous brew pubs offer fine beer and good food. The pioneer *Wyncoop Brewing Company* (☎ 303-623-9518), at 18th and Wyncoop Sts, is probably the most rocking spot. Another place that sees a lot of action is *Rock Bottom Brewery* (☎ 303-534-7616, 1001 16th St), offering patio seating on the pedestrian mall. Near Coors Field, *Breckenridge Brewery* (☎ 303-297-3644, 2200 Blake St) has some outstanding beers and is the place to be before a Colorado Rockies game.

An eclectic mix of performers, ranging from Cajun and blues to big-band swing, plays weekends at *Mercury Cafe* (☎ 303-294-9281, 2199 California St). *El Chapultepec* (☎ 303-295-9126, 1962 Market St), near the ballpark, is a cozy venue for top jazz. More sedate is *Varton's Jazz Club and Restaurant* (☎ 303-399-1111, 1800 Glenarm Place). In town, the main venues for national acts are *Paramount Theater* (☎ 303-534-8336, 1631 Glenarm Place) and *Filmore Auditorium* (☎ 303-837-0360, 1510 Clarkson St).

Spectator Sports

Denver, a city known for manic sports fans, boasts five professional teams. The Colorado Rockies (☎ 303-262-0200, 800-388-7625) play baseball at the highly rated Coors Field. The Pepsi Center (☎ 303-405-1111) hosts the Denver Nuggets basketball team (☎ 303-830-8497) and the 2001 Stanley Cup champion Colorado Avalanche hockey team (☎ 303-893-6700). The popular Denver Broncos football team (☎ 303-299-6000) and the Colorado Rapids soccer team (☎ 303-649-9000, 800-844-7777) play at Mile High Stadium.

Getting There & Away

Air Denver International Airport (DIA) is served by around 20 airlines and offers flights to nearly every major US city. Located 24 miles from downtown, DIA is connected with I-70 exit 238 by the 12-mile-long Peña Blvd. Plan on getting to DIA an hour before flight time, as it takes around 20 minutes just to reach the gates.

Tourist and airport information (☎ 303-342-2000, 800-247-2336) is available from a booth in the terminal's central hall.

Bus Greyhound and the affiliate TNM&O buses stop at the Denver Bus Terminal (☎ 303-293-6555), at 19th and Arapahoe Sts in downtown Denver (open 6am-midnight). Powder River Coach USA (☎ 800-442-3682) also stops here and offers service north to Cheyenne, Wyoming, and on to Montana and South Dakota.

Train Amtrak's *California Zephyr* runs daily between Chicago and San Francisco via Denver. Trains arrive and depart from Union Station (☎ 303-825-2583). For recorded information on arrival and departure times, call ☎ 303-534-2812. Amtrak (☎ 800-872-7245, Ⓦ www.amtrak.com) can also provide schedule information and train reservations.

Denver's *Ski Train* (☎ 303-296-4754, Ⓦ www.skitrain.com) to Winter Park operates on weekends throughout the ski season.

Getting Around

To/From the Airport All transportation companies have booths near the baggage claim. Public RTD (☎ 303-299-6000, 800-366-7433, Ⓦ www.rtd-denver.com) buses link the airport with downtown Denver hourly ($6; 1 hour). RTD also runs buses to Boulder ($8; 1½ hours). Super Shuttle (☎ 303-370-1300, 800-258-3826) and Denver Express Shuttle (☎ 303-342-3424, 800-448-2782) offer frequent van service to downtown hotels ($15). For door-to-door service, Shuttle King (☎ 303-363-8000) charges $20-35 to destinations in and around Denver. Taxis to downtown Denver charge a flat fare of $43, excluding tip.

Airport shuttles to the Front Range and Mountain areas are also available; see those sections later in this chapter for details.

Car & Motorcycle Nearly all the major car rental firms have counters at DIA, though a few have offices in downtown Denver; check the yellow pages.

For those lacking credit cards, A-Courtesy Rent A Car (☎ 303-733-2218, 800-441-1816,

270 S Broadway) accepts cash deposits, but its vehicles cannot be driven outside of Colorado.

For drive-aways, try Auto Driveaway Co (☎ 303-757-1211, ☻ autodriveaway@ quest.net), 5777 E Evans Ave. Also check the ride boards at the hostels.

Taxi Three taxi companies serve Denver: Metro Taxi (☎ 303-333-3333), Yellow Cab (☎ 303-777-7777) and Zone Cab (☎ 303-444-8888).

Local Transportation The Regional Transit District (RTD; ☎ 303-299-6000, 800-366-7433) provides public transportation throughout the Denver and Boulder area. Local buses cost $1.25 during peak weekday hours (6am-9am and 4pm-6pm), 75¢ during off-peak hours. Free shuttle buses operate along the 16th St Mall.

From April to early September, RTD's Cultural Connection Trolley makes the rounds of numerous Denver sights (all-day fare $3). The trolley leaves the Denver Center for the Performing Arts every half hour 9:30am-5:30 pm.

RTD also operates a light-rail line serving 16 stations on a 12-mile north-south route that passes through downtown. Fares are the same as for local buses.

AROUND DENVER
Golden

This city (population 17,150) has earned a place on the map thanks to the Coors Brewery. Aside from this dubious distinction, the town has a small historic district and a few interesting museums.

The helpful visitor center (☎ 303-279-3113, 800-590-3113, ⓦ www.goldencochamber.org), at the corner of 10th and Washington Sts, is open daily.

Most visitors to Golden head to the **Coors Brewing Company** (☎ 303-277-2337) for free 1½-hour tours of the huge copper vats, bottling plant and other beer-production facilities, as well as free samples at the end.

The 1867 **Astor House Hotel Museum** (822 12th St) is a fine example of a late-Victorian western hotel ($3; open 10am-4:30pm Tue-Sat). Nearby, the intriguing **Clear Creek History Park** features several reconstructed 19th-century buildings. From May through October 45-minute tours start on the hour 11am-4pm ($3). A combined ticket for the two sites (☎ 303-278-3557) costs $4.50.

Golden Pioneer Museum (☎ 303-278-7151, 923 10th St) exhibits memorabilia from Golden's Territorial Capital years, 1859 to 1930 (free admission; open 10am-4:30pm Mon-Sat).

Kids and railroad buffs will love the **Colorado Railroad Museum** (☎ 303-279-4591, 17155 W 44th Ave), 2 miles east of Golden – take 10th St from downtown. It has 50 locomotives and train cars on display ($6; open daily).

About 5 miles west of Golden, **Lookout Mountain Park** is the gateway to the Denver Mountain Parks system. The summit offers great views and the **Buffalo Bill Museum & Grave** (☎ 303-526-0747). Admission to the museum is $3 (closed Mondays).

Good **mountain-bike trails** are in Matthews/Winters Park, just south of I-70 along Hwy 26, and the White Ranch Open Space Park, a few miles north of town.

Nice primitive and developed campsites ($6-10) are available at beautiful *Golden Gate State Park (☎ 303-582-3707, 800-678-2267)*, about 16 miles northwest of Golden up Golden Gate Canyon Rd. Reservations are advised.

Other options include the neat *Golden Motel (☎ 303-279-5581, 510 24th St)*, which charges $44/48 for singles/doubles, and the rustic 1860s *Stage Shop Guest Cottages (☎ 303-279-2667, 807 9th St)*, where rooms run $80.

Hilltop Cafe (☎ 303-279-8151, 1518 Washington Ave) offers light bistro fare. *Mesa Bar & Grill (☎ 303-277-9898, 1310 Washington Ave)*, in the Table Mountain Inn, offers fine Southwestern cooking.

RTD (☎ 303-299-6000) buses Nos 16 and 16L run between Golden and downtown Denver (California and 15th Sts).

Mountain Parks

Denver's outdoor playground, this system of 27 parks stretches from 15 to 60 miles west of the city. One of the most interesting spots is **Red Rocks Park**, home of a wonderful natural amphitheater used for summer concerts. It's just north of the tiny town of **Morrison**, a National Historic District 32 miles southwest of Denver. Park maps and information are available from the Denver visitor center.

South Platte River

This portion of the Pike National Forest southwest of the Chatfield Reservoir has several hiking and biking opportunities, including the start of the 500-mile **Colorado Trail** and the **Buffalo Creek Mountain Bike Area**. Maps and information are available at the USFS South Platte Ranger Station (☎ 303-275-5610), on US 285, 6½ miles west of the Hwy 470 exit and about 5 miles from Morrison.

Idaho Springs & Georgetown

These two 19th-century mining towns, respectively 20 and 35 miles west of Denver along I-70, still have a historical feel, with antique shops, galleries and restaurants, as well as the dramatic backdrop of the rising Rocky Mountains. For tourist information, visit the Idaho Springs visitor center & museum (☎ 800-685-7785, ☒ www .idahospringschamber.com, 2060 Miner St) and the Historic Georgetown visitor center (☎ 888-569-0750, ☒ www.georgetowncolorado .com), at exit 228 off I-70.

From late May to early October you can ride the steam train around the **Georgetown Loop Railroad** (☎ 303-569-2403, 800-691-4386, ☒ www.georgetownloop.com) through the mountains between Devil's Gate (Georgetown) and Silver Plume ($13).

Hot-springs buffs will appreciate *Indian Springs Resort* (☎ *303-989-6666, 302 Soda Creek Rd*, ☒ *www.indianspringsresort.com*) in Idaho Springs. Pleasant doubles cost $55-79, and campsites are $18. The geothermal caves, pool and 'Club Mud' are open to day-trippers.

Drive to the 14,264-foot summit of **Mt Evans** via the Mt Evans Hwy, off I-70 exit 240 at Idaho Springs. Near the exit, the USFS Clear Creek Ranger Station (☎ 303-567-2901) is open daily and has information, books and topo maps. Reservable USFS campsites are found at *Echo Lake Campground* (☎ *800-280-2267*) at $10, plus an $8.65 reservation fee.

Loveland Ski Area

About 55 miles west of Denver, Loveland Basin Ski Area (☎ 800-736-3754, ☒ www .skiloveland.com), on the Continental Divide off I-70, is popular for its proximity to the city, good snow conditions, unassuming atmosphere and $41 lift tickets.

BOULDER

In conservative Colorado, scenic Boulder (population 101,000) has long been a bastion of liberal politics and alternative lifestyles and social attitudes. This lively city is also an intellectual and cultural center, mainly due to the University of Colorado – Boulder, with its 20,000 students. Though not filled with sights, Boulder is fun and boasts an extensive mountain-parks system.

Orientation & Information

Boulder's two major areas of interest are the downtown Pearl St Mall and the University Hill district (next to the university campus). Overlooking the city from the west are the Flatirons, an eye-catching rock formation that looks like a row of giant arrowheads.

At Folsom St, the Boulder Convention & Visitors Bureau (☎ 303-442-2911, ☒ www .bouldercoloradousa.com, 2440 Pearl St) is open weekdays. For information about the Arapaho and Roosevelt National Forests, contact the US Forest Service Boulder Ranger District Office (☎ 303-444-6600, 2995 Baseline Rd). For books on the area, try Boulder Bookstore (☎ 303-447-2074, 1107 Pearl Street).

Downtown

The main feature of downtown Boulder is the **Pearl St Mall**, a lively and sometimes offbeat pedestrian zone filled with shops, bars, galleries and restaurants. Guided and self-guided tours of Boulder's historic homes and downtown buildings are available weekdays from Historic Boulder (☎ 303-444-5192, 646 Pearl St). Nearby is Mapleton Hill, home to Boulder's oldest and most magnificent homes.

Activities

From Chautauqua Park, at the west end of Baseline Rd, **hiking** trails head in many directions, including up to the Flatirons. Other nice hikes head up Gregory Canyon and Flagstaff Mountain, which can also be accessed by car via Baseline Rd. The easy Mesa Trail runs north 7 miles from Chautauqua to Eldorado Canyon and offers access to more difficult routes, such as Shadow Canyon, Fern Canyon and Bear Canyon, which leads up to Bear Peak (elevation 8461ft). The Boulder Mountain Parks Ranger Cottage (☎ 303-441-3408) at

Chautauqua offers maps and information weekdays.

The 9-mile Boulder Creek Trail is the main **bicycling** route in town and leads west to an unpaved streamside path to Four Mile Canyon. Those seeking a challenge can ride 4 miles up Flagstaff Rd to the top of Flagstaff Mountain.

Most Boulder Mountain Parks trails are off-limits to mountain bikes. Exceptions include Doudy Draw, near Eldorado Springs, and Marshall Mesa, off Marshall Rd south of town. Far more challenging is the 10-mile loop at Walker Ranch, 10 miles west of Boulder via Flagstaff Rd.

Bike rentals, maps and information are available from University Bicycles (☎ 303-444-4196), at 9th and Pearl Sts, and Full Cycle (☎ 303-440-7771, 1211 13th St).

Eldorado Canyon State Park (☎ 303-494-3943) is one of the country's most popular **rock-climbing** areas, offering Class 5.6 to 5.9 climbs. The park entrance is on Eldorado Springs Dr, 3 miles west of Hwy 93.

Places to Stay

The *Boulder Mountain Lodge* (☎ 303-444-0882, 91 Four Mile Canyon Rd), just west of town on Hwy 119, has 15 tree-shaded sites ($14), as well as motel-style rooms ($52-58).

In the University Hill district, *Boulder International Youth Hostel* (☎ 303-442-0522, W www.boulderhostel.com, 1107 12th St) offers dorm beds ($15, three-day limit) and private rooms with shared bath ($36 per day, $170 per week, $290 for two weeks, $540 per month).

Near the entrance to Boulder Canyon, *Foot of the Mountain Motel* (☎ 303-442-5688, 200 Arapahoe Ave) has cozy though small wood-paneled rooms (from $50/65 in winter/summer).

North of the CU campus, singles/doubles cost $115/130 (peak season) and $75/85 (off-peak) at *Quality Inn & Suites* (☎ 303-449-7550, 888-449-7550, 2020 Arapahoe Ave). Rates include full breakfast, use of an indoor pool and hot tub, and 24-hour Internet access. There is a string of other chain motels east of the university campus on 28th St, with rates around $60-90 for a double in summer.

Hotel Boulderado (☎ 303-442-4344, 800-433-4344, W www.boulderado.com, 2115 13th St), a block from the Pearl St Mall, is a beautifully restored 1909 brick building with antique-furnished rooms (from $130/159 winter/summer).

The *Boulder Victoria Historic Bed & Breakfast* (☎ 303-938-1300, W www.bouldervictoria.com, 1305 Pine St) is a beautifully restored mansion close to downtown. Its seven rooms cost $119-215 in summer, $99-169 in winter.

Places to Eat

A cheap way to get started is to take advantage of the 7am-9am early-bird special at *Dot's Diner* (☎ 303-447-9184, 1333 Broadway). Eggs, hash browns and toast costs $2.50. Another good spot is the long-standing *Rocky Mountain Joe's* (☎ 303-442-3969, 1410 Pearl St Mall).

Pan Asia Fusion (☎ 303-447-0101, 1175 Walnut St) serves up great Pacific Rim specialties and good-value $6 lunch specials. The unique *Boulder Dushanbe Teahouse* (☎ 303-442-4993, 1770 13th St) is a traditional Tajik teahouse presented by Boulder's Russian sister city, Dushanbe.

Up on University Hill, *Illegal Pete's* (☎ 303-444-3055, 1320 College Ave) has won rave reviews from locals for its tasty over-sized burritos.

Among the many top-end restaurants in town, the most spectacular is the *Flagstaff House* (☎ 303-442-4640, 1138 Flagstaff Rd), perched on the north side of Flagstaff Mountain and offering excellent continental dishes and local game.

Entertainment

Boulder is known for its scores of bars and brew pubs. Popular spots include *West End Tavern* (☎ 303-444-3535, 926 Pearl St), with a great rooftop deck; *Walnut Brewery* (☎ 303-447-1345, 1123 Walnut St), a more sedate spot with locally brewed beer; and *Mountain Sun Pub & Brewery* (☎ 303-546-0886, 1535 Pearl St), where long hair, tie-dyes and dreadlocks are the norm.

Getting There & Around

RTD (☎ 303-299-6000) buses provide fairly frequent service in and around Boulder; maps are available at Boulder Station, 14th and Walnut Sts. RTD buses (route B) operate between Boulder Station and Denver's Market St Station ($3; 1 hour). RTD's Skyride bus (route AB) offers hourly service to Denver International Airport ($8; 1½ hours). Hotel and door-to-door shuttle service ($18 and $22, respectively) is available from Super Shuttle (☎ 303-444-0808).

AROUND BOULDER

Heading west 17 miles up scenic Boulder Canyon is **Nederland**, a lively, gritty town near the base of the beautiful **Indian Peaks Wilderness Area**. Four miles west of Nederland, **Eldora Ski Area** (☎ 303-440-8700, W www.eldora.com) is small but offers some interesting downhill ski runs and good terrain for Nordic skiing.

The Indian Peaks area has many fine hiking and camping opportunities, including the trail to the 12,000-foot **Arapaho Pass**, accessed from the Fourth of July campground.

Stretching some 40 miles between Nederland and Estes Park (see that section, later), the **Peak to Peak Highway** takes you past breathtaking mountains (including 14,255-foot Longs Peak), lush valleys, grassy meadows and small mountain towns.

ROCKY MOUNTAIN NATIONAL PARK

Some 3 million visitors swarm Rocky Mountain National Park every year to take in the stunning natural beauty and view wildlife such as elk, bighorn sheep, moose and beaver. Most are attracted to **Trail Ridge Rd**, which winds through spectacular alpine tundra environments, or the shorter trails. However, you don't have to hike or camp with everyone else; those who venture on foot to areas away from the road corridor will be rewarded with superlative scenery and even solitude.

Hotel construction and road building in the settlement of Estes Park during the late 19th century prompted naturalist Enos Mills to campaign in 1909 to protect the area. He faced opposition from private grazing and timber interests, including the US Forest Service (USFS). But in early 1915, Congress approved the bill creating Rocky Mountain National Park. Workers completed Fall River Rd over the Continental Divide in 1920, and the Trail Ridge Rd opened in 1932 to provide an alternative that traversed 10 miles of treeless alpine tundra.

Orientation

Trail Ridge Rd (US 34) is the only east-west route through the park; the US 34 eastern approach from I-25 and Loveland follows the Big Thompson River Canyon. The most direct route from Boulder follows US 36 through Lyons to the east entrances. Another approach from the south, mountainous Hwy 7, provides access to campsites and trailheads (including Longs Peak) on the east side of the Continental Divide. Winter closure of US 34 through the park makes access to the west side dependent on US 40 at Granby.

There are two entrance stations on the east side: at Fall River (US 34) and Beaver Meadows (US 36). The Grand Lake Station (US 34) is the only entry on the west side.

Information

Three of the park's six visitor centers are outside the park's entrances. The Beaver Meadows Visitors Center/Park Headquarters (☎ 970-586-1206), on US 36, and Kawuneeche Visitors Center (☎ 970-627-3471), north of Grand Lake on US 34, are open year round. Lily Lake, on Hwy 7 south of Estes Park, is open May to November. Within the park, the Alpine Visitors Center and Moraine Park Visitors Center are open in summer and fall. Fall River Visitor Center is located in the park's northeast. General park information is broadcast on 1610 AM; for road and weather information, call ☎ 970-586-1333.

Entry to the park ($10 for vehicles, $5 for hikers/cyclists) is valid for seven days. Backcountry permits ($15) are required for overnight stays outside developed campgrounds. Reservations by mail or in person are accepted after March. Phone reservations can be made November to April. The Backcountry Office (☎ 970-586-1242), east of the Headquarters Visitors Center, is open daily. For a reservation form and a map of backcountry campsites, write to Backcountry Office, Rocky Mountain National Park, Estes Park, CO 80517.

Hiking

Families might consider the easy hikes in the Wild Basin to Calypso Falls or to Gem Lakes in the Lumpy Ridge area.

The very popular **Bear Lake Trailhead** offers easy hikes to several lakes and beyond. Another busy area is **Glacier Gorge Junction Trailhead**. Both are serviced by the Glacier Basin–Bear Lake shuttle.

Forested Fern Lake, 4 miles from the Moraine Park Trailhead, is dominated by craggy Notchtop Peak. You can complete a loop to the Bear Lake shuttle stop in 8½ miles for a rewarding day hike, or head into the upper fern creek drainage to explore the backcountry. The strenuous **Flattop Mountain Trail** is the only cross-park trail, linking Bear Creek on the east side with either Tonahutu Creek Trail or the North Inlet Trail on the west side.

One of the easiest peak climbs in the area is the 1½-mile trail up **Lily Mountain** (great views), 6 miles south of Estes Park on Hwy 7. At the other extreme is the strenuous hike to the 14,255-foot summit of Longs Peak. An easier option near here is the hike to Chasm Lake (11,800 feet).

Trail Ridge Rd crosses the Continental Divide at **Milner Pass** (10,759 feet), where trails head 4 miles (and up 2000 feet!) southeast to Mt Ida, which offers fantastic views.

Before July, many of the trails are snowbound, and high water runoff makes passage difficult.

Other Activities

All **bicycling** is restricted to paved surfaces like Trail Ridge Rd and the Horseshoe Park/Estes Park Loop. The only exception is the 9-mile, 3000-foot climb up Fall River Rd (head back down on Trail Ridge Rd).

On the east side, the Bear Lake and the Glacier Gorge Junction trailheads offer good routes for **cross-country skiing** and **snowshoeing**. Backcountry skiing is also possible; check with the visitor centers.

Places to Stay

The only overnight accommodations in the park are at campgrounds; the majority of motel or hotel accommodations are around Estes Park or Grand Lake.

The park's five formal campgrounds *Moraine Park*, *Longs Peak*, *Aspenglen* and *Glacier Basin* on the east side, and *Timber Creek* on the west side. All provide campfire programs and have public telephones and a seven-day limit during summer months; all except Longs Peak take RVs (no hookups). Camping fees are $16 ($10 in winter, when the water supply is off). All except Longs

Peak take RVs (no hookups) and have a seven-day limit in summer. Reservations are essential in summer. You will need a permit to stay in backcountry campgrounds (see Information, earlier).

The Moraine Park and Longs Peak campgrounds are open year round. The location of Longs Peak Campground, 12 miles south of Estes Park on Hwy 7, is intended to provide Longs Peak hikers with an early trail start. It has 26 tent sites available on a first-come, first-served basis for seven-day stays. Aspenglen, 5 miles west of Estes Park on US 34, also has 54 first-come, first-served sites early May to early September. Moraine Park (247 sites) and Glacier Basin (150 sites) accept reservations (with Visa or Master Card) up to five months in advance through the National Park Reservation Center (☎ 800-365-2267, PO Box 85705, San Diego, CA 92186-5705, or online (Ⓦ reservations.nps.gov). Both campgrounds are served by the shuttle buses on Bear Lake Rd. Glacier Basin is open June to September.

At the southeast boundary of the park near Wild Basin, the USFS *Olive Ridge Campground* (☎ 877-444-6777 for reservations) has 56 heavily used sites for $12; it's open mid-May to November.

Timber Creek, 7 miles north of Grand Lake, remains open in winter and has 100 sites (no reservations).

Getting Around

A free shuttle bus provides frequent summer service from the Glacier Basin parking area to Bear Lake. During the summer peak, a second shuttle operates between Moraine Park campground and the Glacier Basin parking area. Shuttles run on weekends only mid-August to September.

FRONT RANGE
Fort Collins & Around

Home to Colorado State University, Fort Collins boasts a lively **Old Town** district where restored late-19th-century buildings house fun restaurants, bars and brew pubs. Proximity to the beautiful **Cache la Poudre River Valley** and **Red Feather Lakes** also make Fort Collins an excellent jumping-off point for wilderness excursions.

There's a small downtown tourist information counter in the Walnut St police station, but for more extensive information head for the Colorado Welcome Center (☎ 970-491-3388, 800-274-3678, 3545 E Prospect Rd), just off the Prospect Rd exit of I-25. At the same address, Colorado State Parks (☎ 970-491-1168) has information about access to local recreational areas and campsites. The USFS headquarters for the Arapaho and Roosevelt forests and the Pawnee National Grasslands is at 240 W Prospect Rd and Colorado Blvd. Their information center (☎ 970-498-2770, 1131 S College Ave) offers extensive maps and trail information.

Airport Express (☎ 970-482-0505) provides hourly shuttle service between Denver's airport and Fort Collins ($18; 1½ hours). Greyhound/TNM&O and Powder River buses connect Fort Collins to Denver. The bus terminal (☎ 970-221-1327, 501 Riverside Ave) is closed Sunday.

Estes Park

This is the eastern gateway to Rocky Mountain National Park, where the year-round population of 10,000 can explode to 30,000 on summer weekends. With countless motels and tacky craft and souvenir shops, the town may disappoint some, but it has a certain charm, especially in the off-season, and nearly any convenience a traveler might need.

Try the Estes Park Visitors Center (☎ 970-586-4431, 800-443-7837, W www.estesparkresort.com, 500 Big Thompson Ave), at US 34 just east of the US 36 junction, for help finding lodgings (open daily).

Everything's booked during the peak July and August period, so advance reservations are essential. Off-season rates may be half the summer prices, though many places close for the winter. Most of the cheaper motels (which aren't that cheap) are east of town along US 34 or Hwy 7.

Mary's Lake Campground (☎ 970-586-4411, 2120 Mary's Lake Rd) offers 40 tent/RV sites ($22/27). Five miles southeast of Estes Park at the end of Hwy 66, *Estes Park Campground* (☎ 970-586-4188) caters to tent campers ($23).

In town, *Colorado Mountain School* (☎ 970-586-5758, 351 Moraine Ave) has comfortable, clean dorm rooms ($20) – a great choice if there's space. The 860-acre *YMCA of the Rockies* (☎ 970-586-3341, W www.ymcarockies.org, 800-777-9622) is on the town outskirts and offers campsites

($17-21), over 530 lodge rooms ($64-92) and around 200 cabins and vacation homes ($116-279).

Estes Park has more than 40 motels to choose from. One of the cheaper places is *Lazy T Motel* (☎ 970-586-4376, 1340 Big Thompson Ave), with a pool, sauna and rooms from $40. *Four Winds Motor Lodge* (☎ 970-586-3313, 1120 Big Thompson Ave) has a pool and hot tub and kitchens (from $61).

Cottages, though sometimes quite basic, often offer more scenic locations and privacy than motels. One-room cottages ($80) are not a bad deal at *Triple R Cottages* (☎ 970-586-5552, 1000 Riverside Dr). *Telemark Resort* (☎ 970-586-4343, 650 Moraine Ave) has two-person cottages ($90) near the Big Thompson River.

Black Canyon Inn (☎ 970-586-8113, 800-897-5123, W www.blackcanyoninn.com, 800 MacGregor Ave) is a secluded 14-acre property offering luxury suites (one/two/three bedrooms from $160/225/385) and rustic log cabins from $160.

The landmark *Stanley Hotel* (☎ 970-577-4018, 800-976-1377, 333 Wonderview Ave), the grand dame of northern Colorado's historic resort hotels, offers great mountain views ($165-250).

One of the best spots in town for tasty and healthy meals is *Notchtop Bakery & Cafe*, in the Stanley Village shopping complex. *Molly B Restaurant* (☎ 970-586-2766, 200 Moraine Ave) has hearty, reasonably priced dishes for vegetarians and carnivores. *Mama Rosa's* (☎ 970-586-3330, 338 E Elkhorn Ave) offers outdoor seating and family-style Italian lunches and dinners. For amazing steak dinners, make a reservation at the upmarket *Twin Owls Steakhouse* (☎ 970-586-9344, 800 MacGregor Ave), north of town at the historic Black Canyon Inn.

From Denver International Airport, Estes Park Shuttle (☎ 970-586-5151, 800-950-3274) provides four daily trips to Estes Park for $39/75 one way/roundtrip.

Grand Lake

The western gateway to Rocky Mountain National Park, Grand Lake (population 450) is a tourist haven like Estes Park, though its namesake lake is indeed beautiful. The Grand Lake Area Chamber of Commerce (☎ 970-627-3402, 800-531-1019,

W www.grandlakechamber.com), at the junction of US 34 and W Portal Rd, is open daily. There's also an office (928 Grand Ave) in town.

The Arapaho National Forest, to the west of town, has some good **mountain-biking** trails; get a map from the Grand Lake Metro Recreation District (☎ 970-627-8328). Rocky Mountain Sports (☎ 970-627-8124, 711 Grand Ave) rents and sells bikes. Several Rocky Mountain National Park **hiking** trailheads are just outside the town limits, including those to the Tonahutu Creek Trail and the Cascade Falls/North Inlet Trail, both near Shadowcliff Lodge. Monarch Guides (☎ 970-627-2409, 888-463-5628) runs half-day, day and overnight **rafting** trips on the upper Colorado and Eagle Rivers.

The *Elk Creek Campground* (☎ *970-627-8502, 800-355-2733*), on Golf Course Rd just west of US 34 and south of the park entrance, is open year round and has sites for around $20. *Winding River Resort* (☎ *970-627-3215*), off Grand County Rd 491 opposite the Kawuneeche Visitors Center, has tent/RV sites for $18/20.

Overlooking Grand Lake from Summerland Park Rd, just north of W Portal Rd, the nonprofit *HI Shadowcliff Lodge* (☎ *970-627-9220*) is a great value, with a beautiful setting and comfortable dorm beds ($11/13 members/nonmembers); guests should bring sheets or a sleeping bag. It also has private singles/doubles ($25/30) and five-person cabins with kitchens ($65-80). Reservations are essential.

Next to the Tonahutu River, *Rapids Lodge* (☎ *970-627-3707, 209 Rapids Lane*) offers cozy, uniquely decorated rooms ($65-105) in a historic building. *Waconda Motel* (☎ *970-627-8312, 725 Grand Ave*) is also a good bet (from $65).

EG's Garden Grill (☎ *970-627-8404, 1000 Grand Ave*) has a festive beer garden, serves varied cuisine (from interesting salads to seafood) and occasionally features live music. Nearby, *Pancho & Lefty's* (☎ *970-627-8773, 1120 Grand Ave*) dishes up a commendable mix of American and Mexican classics.

Home James Transportation Services (☎ 970-726-5060, 800-359-7536, W www.homejames-shuttle.com) runs door-to-door shuttles to Denver International Airport ($58; 2½ hours); reservations are necessary.

Colorado Springs & Around

Colorado Springs (population 358,500) is arguably the state's most overrated tourist destination. Worthwhile sights like the Pioneer Museum, Pikes Peak Toll Rd and Garden of the Gods are often crowded and compete with tawdry attractions such as the Ghost Town Wild West Museum and the Cave of the Winds. Despite the hype, the Springs is not a 'must see' destination; Colorado has plenty of other 14,000-foot peaks, hot-springs resorts and fine museums in nicer, less crowded settings. Visiting sports buffs, however, won't want to miss the Museum of the American Cowboy and Olympic Training Complex.

Orientation & Information I-25 bisects the metropolitan area; to the east is the central business district and to the west are Old Colorado City, Garden of the Gods and Manitou Springs.

The Colorado Springs Visitor Information Center (☎ 719-635-7506, 800-368-4748, W www.coloradosprings-travel.com), downtown at the corner of Cascade and Colorado Aves, is open daily in summer, weekdays in winter.

Wells Fargo Bank (90 S Cascade Ave) is opposite the visitor center.

The impressive Chinook Bookstore (☎ 719-635-1195, 210 N Tejon St) and Gateway Books (☎ 719-635-4514, 119 E Bijou St) are both across from Acacia Park.

Things to See & Do Housed in the 1903 El Paso County Courthouse, the **Colorado Springs Pioneer Museum** (☎ 719-578-6650, 215 S Tejon St) is well worth a visit for its exhibits of frontier life in the area (free admission; open Tue-Sat year round, plus Sun afternoon May-Oct).

The **US Air Force Academy** is one of Colorado Springs' most popular attractions. No guided tours are offered, but a self-guided tour map is available from the visitor center (☎ 719-333-2025), open daily. Notable stops along the route include a B-52 bomber near the north entrance and the spires of the stunning Cadet Chapel. The Academy is off I-25 exit 156B.

The bizarre and beautiful red sandstone formations at the **Garden of the Gods** draw more than two million visitors each year to see highlights like Balanced Rock, High Point

COLORADO SPRINGS & AROUND

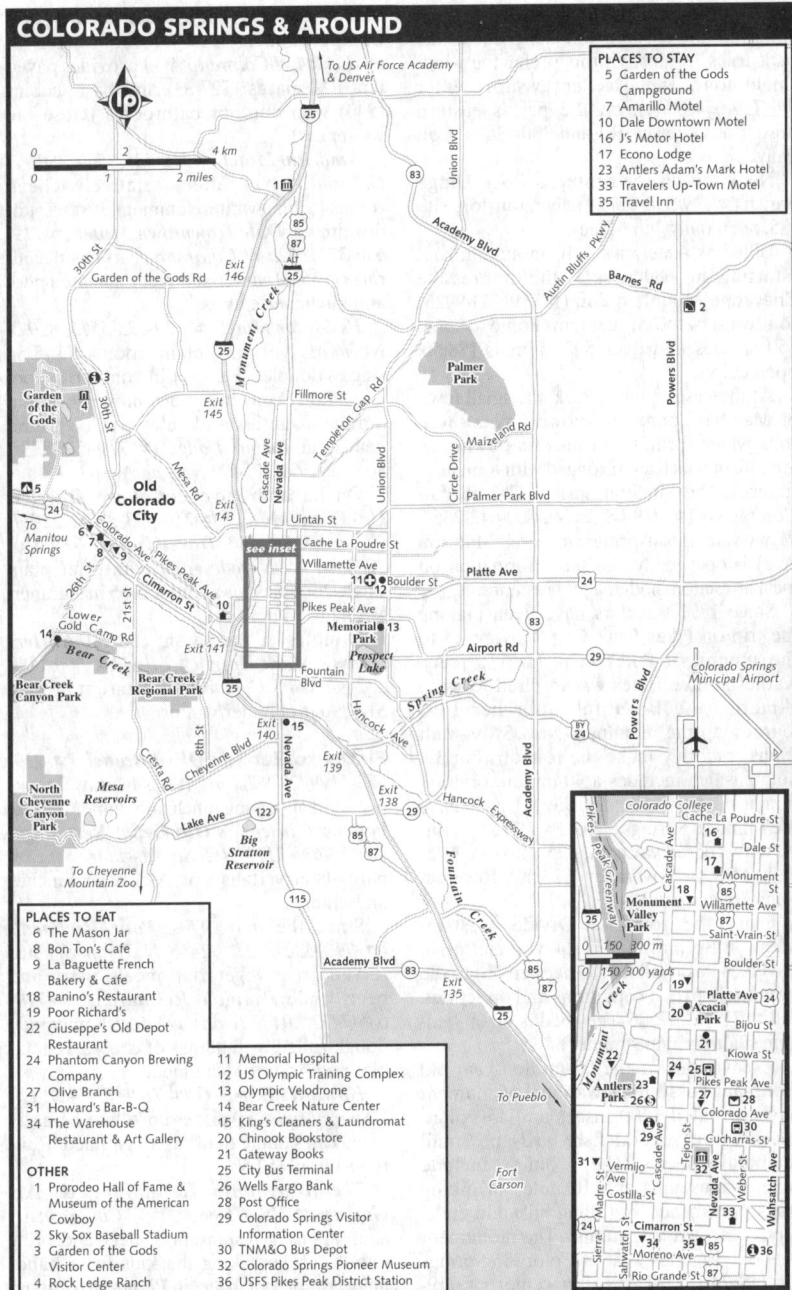

and Central Garden. The best way to see it and avoid the crowd is to take to one of the park trails, as most visitors prefer the windshield tour. The excellent visitor center (☎ 719-634-6666), on the park's eastern border at Gateway Rd and 30th St, is open daily.

Near the visitor center is **Rock Ledge Ranch** (☎ 719-578-6777), a living-history site ($5, open daily June-Dec).

Billed as America's only 'mountain zoo' (starting at 6800 feet), the impressive **Cheyenne Mountain Zoo** (☎ 719-633-9925) southwest of the city center is home to some 150 species and over 500 animals ($8.50; open daily).

At the base of Pikes Peak, the small town of **Manitou Springs** is known for its seven soda-water springs and historic downtown area, all of which are thronged with tourists in summer. The Manitou Springs Chamber of Commerce (☎ 719-685-5089, 800-642-2567, W www.manitousprings.org, 354 Manitou Ave) is open daily and has information on local attractions, lodging and restaurants.

Since 1891 travelers have been making the trip on **Pikes Peak Cog Railway** up to the summit of Pikes Peak (14,110 feet). Katherine Lee Bates was inspired to write 'America the Beautiful' after her 1893 journey up the mountain. Now Swiss-built trains smoothly make the roundtrip in 3¼ hours, which includes a 40-minute orientation at the top (bring a jacket). Trains leave the Manitou Springs depot (☎ 719-685-5401, W www.cograilway.com, 515 Ruxton Ave) daily May to November ($23.50). Reservations are essential.

From the town of Divide, west of Manitou Springs on US 24, you can drive the **Pikes Peak Toll Rd** ($6 per person) to the summit. For road conditions and directions, call ☎ 719-635-7506. The road is open 9am-3pm (7am-7pm in summer).

Excavations at the 35-million-year-old **Florissant Fossil Beds National Monument** have revealed 1200 insect and 150 plant species plus several fish, bird and small mammal species. The grounds include several museums and 10 miles of hiking trails past meadows, rolling hills and enormous petrified tree stumps. The monument is about 30 miles west of Colorado Springs via US 24 ($2). The visitor center (☎ 719-748-3253) is open daily.

Places to Stay The *Garden of the Gods Campground* (☎ 719-475-9450, 800-248-9451, 3704 W Colorado Ave) provides paved tent/RV spaces ($27/33) and basic cabins ($40) with outdoor bathrooms (closed in winter).

Amarillo Motel (☎ 719-635-8539, 2801 W Colorado Ave) offers relatively cheap rooms ($35/50 winter/summer). Just west of downtown, *Dale Downtown Motel* (☎ 719-636-3721, 620 W Colorado Ave) has decent rates ($35/40 winter/summer), a heated pool and kitchenette units.

J's Motor Hotel (☎ 719-633-5513, 820 N Nevada Ave) has plain rooms ($45/55 singles/doubles, $15 less in winter), a pool and a fairly convenient downtown location. Similar facilities and rates can be found nearby at *Econo Lodge* (☎ 719-636-3385, 800-553-2666, 714 N Nevada Ave).

On the south end of downtown, *Travelers Up-Town Motel* (☎ 719-473-2774, 220 E Cimarron St) and *Travel Inn* (☎ 719-636-3986, 512 S Nevada Ave) both offer plain singles/doubles for about $55/65 in summer, $32/42 in winter.

Doubles at the swish, central *Antlers Adam's Mark Hotel* (☎ 719-473-5600, 800-222-8733, 4 S Cascade Ave) start at around $120/90 in summer/winter.

Places to Eat The *Olive Branch* (☎ 719-475-1199, 23 S Tejon St) has healthy breakfasts and appealing lunch and dinner menus. Popular *Giuseppe's Old Depot Restaurant* (☎ 719-635-3111, 10 S Sierra Madre St) prepares hearty Italian or American lunches and dinners.

Since the mid-1970s, *Poor Richard's* (☎ 719-632-7721, 324½ N Tejon St) has served great vegetarian meals, pizza and beer, while *Panino's Restaurant* (☎ 719-635-7452, 604 N Tejon Ave) does homemade dough rolled with fillings of cheese, vegetables and beans or lean meats.

Howard's Bar-B-Q (☎ 719-473-7427, 114 S Sierra Madre St) dishes up killer ribs; early risers can sample their tasty egg-filled 'Railroad Wrap' ($2.50).

The Warehouse Restaurant & Art Gallery (☎ 719-475-8880, 25 W Cimarron St) is an amusing restaurant, gallery and brew pub. Consider taking the kids for a handmade draft root beer at *Phantom Canyon Brewing Company* (☎ 719-635-2800, 2 E

Pikes Peak Ave), which also serves fine beers and tasty entrées.

In Old Colorado City, *The Mason Jar* (☎ *719-632-4820, 2925 W Colorado Ave)* serves inexpensive American fare for breakfast, lunch or dinner. *La Baguette French Bakery & Cafe* (☎ *719-577-4818, 2417 W Colorado Ave)* is a bright, spacious eatery that serves espresso. *Bon Ton's Cafe* (☎ *719-634-1007, 2601 W Colorado Ave)* serves breakfast and lunch to a casual crowd on its large patio.

Getting There & Around The Colorado Springs Municipal Airport (☎ 719-550-1900) offers a viable alternative to Denver International Airport. The Yellow Cab (☎ 719-634-5000) fare from the airport to the city center is around $20-25.

TNM&O buses between Cheyenne, Wyoming, and Pueblo stop daily at the depot (☎ 719-635-1505, 120 Weber St).

The City Bus Terminal (☎ 719-475-9733, 127 E Kiowa) offers schedule information and route maps for all 13 city bus lines.

Trinidad & Around
Trinidad sits on the Purgatoire River where it flows down from the heights of the Sangre de Cristo Mountains out to the Eastern Plains. The town's past is documented in several good museums and on the brick-paved streets in **Corazon de Trinidad**, the 'heart' of downtown that has been designated a National Historic District. The Trinidad–Las Animas County Chamber of Commerce (☎ 719-846-9285, W www.trinidadco.com, 309 Nevada Ave) is in the Colorado Welcome Center, near I-25 exit 14A (open daily).

Trails End Motel (☎ *719-846-4425, 616 E Main St)* offers convenient access to downtown ($33/40 singles/doubles). The excellent *Main Street Bakery & Cafe* (☎ *719-846-8779, 121 W Main St)* serves fresh breads and pastries, deli sandwiches, pizzas, pastas and salads.

Two hundred miles south of Denver on I-25, Trinidad lies at the junction of Hwy 12 (designated the Scenic Hwy of Legends), leading into the Sangre de Cristo Mountains, and US 350, the historic Mountain Branch of the Santa Fe Trail. Greyhound/TNM&O buses stop at JR's Travel Shoppe (☎ 719-846-6390, 639 W Main St), a Conoco gas station near I-25 exit 13B. Amtrak's

Southwest Chief passes through Trinidad on its daily Chicago–Los Angeles route.

Consider a pleasant little excursion to **Bent's Old Fort** (☎ 719-383-5010), on Hwy 194, 8 miles east of La Junta ($2; open daily). This impressive reconstructed site was a hub on the Santa Fe Trail from 1833 to 1849. At the fort you can view a 20-minute film, take a 45-minute tour with a ranger dressed in period costume, or simply walk through the various rooms.

While in La Junta, be sure to stop in at the fascinating **Koshare Indian Museum** (☎ 719-384-4411, 115 W 18th St), which is open daily ($2).

La Veta & Around
Tiny La Veta is the gateway to the Cuchara Valley and the Great Dikes of the Spanish Peaks. Artists and writers have been drawn to La Veta's splendor, and the town makes a pleasant base from which to explore the beautiful surrounding countryside.

Go to the La Veta/Cuchara Chamber of Commerce (☎ 719-742-3676, W www.ruralwideweb.com, 131 E Ryus Ave) for information on the few motels and restaurants in town (open weekdays). The USFS San Isabel National Forest ranger station (☎ 719-742-3681, 103 E Field St) has maps and information on hiking and mountain biking in the area.

In town, explore La Veta's history and Hispanic culture at **Fort Francisco Museum** ($2) or check out the works of local artists at **The Gallery**, both open Memorial Day to Oktoberfest weekend.

Eleven miles south of La Veta on Hwy 12, **Cuchara** is an attractive one-street town that comes to life in winter, when it serves patrons of the nearby **Cuchara Mountain Resort** (☎ 877-282-4272, W www.cuchara.com), a small ski mountain that boasts good snow and a casual atmosphere. *River's Edge B&B* (☎ *719-742-5169, W www.ruralwideweb.com/rebb.htm)* is a cozy wooden building with a delightful riverside setting and friendly owners ($85-138).

Pizza, steaks, booze and occasional live entertainment attract revelers and their dogs to *Boardwalk Saloon* (☎ *719-742-3450)*. At the other end of the spectrum, *The Timbers* (☎ *719-742-3838)* is an upscale restaurant somewhat modeled on La Veta's food-art-music theme.

Another 18 miles south of La Veta lies **Monument Park**, a beautiful evergreen-filled basin surrounding a mountain reservoir (admission $4). The campsites ($10) and adobe-style lodge and cabins ($63-83) of *Monument Lake Resort* (☎ 719-868-2226, 800-845-8006) make a good base for exploring nearby trails. The park and resort are closed in winter.

MOUNTAIN REGION
Steamboat Springs
Steamboat Springs is one of Colorado's more appealing high-class ski resorts. Far from the glitter of Vail, it retains some of its original character and charm. Summer is almost as popular, owing to all the outdoor activities offered.

Steamboat Springs' two major areas are Old Town and, 5 miles south, the newer warren of curving streets at Steamboat Village, centered on the ski resort. US 40 is known as Lincoln Ave through Old Town.

The Steamboat Springs visitor center (☎ 970-879-0880, 800-922-2722, Ⓦ www.steamboat-chamber.com, 1255 S Lincoln Ave) is opposite Sundance Plaza. The USFS Hahn's Peak Ranger Office (☎ 970-879-1870, 925 Weiss Dr) is at the southeast end of town.

With a well-earned reputation for consistently good powder **skiing**, Steamboat Ski Area (☎ 970-879-6111, 800-922-2722) features a 3600-foot vertical drop. Lift tickets are $50.

Ike's

Barring the blizzard of the century, no one approaching Craig on US 40 from Steamboat Springs can miss the rolling hillsides covered by something that, according to local yellow pages, is Ike's Automatic Transmission Shop. In fact, Ike's is a sprawling junkyard that may hold more wrecks than there are licensed vehicles in Moffat County. According to local legend, the sight so aggravated Lady Bird Johnson that it prompted her to launch her famous nationwide beautification program during her husband Lyndon's presidency. Ike's is not really photogenic, but it is unforgettable.

☺ ☺ ☺ ☺ ☺ ☺ ☺ ☺ ☺ ☹ ☺

For **mountain biking**, pick up the 'Steamboat Trails Map' at the visitor center; there are also bike trails accessible by the gondola at the ski resort. Buggywhips (☎ 970-879-8033, 800-759-0343, 720 Lincoln Ave) offers white-water rafting and fishing trips on the Yampa, Colorado, Eagle and Arkansas Rivers.

Steamboat Central Reservations (☎ 970-879-4074, 800-922-2722) helps book accommodations. Rates quoted are for winter; summer prices are usually lower.

Steamboat Springs KOA Kampground (☎ 970-879-0273), on US 40 about 2 miles west of downtown, is a nice spot with tent sites ($19) on a small island in the Yampa River.

Steamboat's best motel value is *Nordic Lodge Motel* (☎ 970-879-0531, 800-364-0331, 1036 Lincoln Ave), with sparkling singles/doubles ($80/95), a hot tub and a sauna. Other 'cheap' spots include bland *Western Lodge* (☎ 970-879-1050, 800-622-9200, 1122 Lincoln Ave), at $70/80, and *Nite's Rest Motel* (☎ 970-879-1212, 800-828-1780, 601 Lincoln Ave), at $80/90. In Old Town, *Steamboat Valley Guest House* (☎ 970-870-9017, 800-530-3866, Ⓦ www.steamboatvalley.com, 1245 Crawford Ave), is a wooden ski-lodge affair with rooms from $80-125. In Steamboat Village, Best Western's *Ptarmigan Inn* (☎ 970-879-1730, 2304 Apres Ski Way) is right next to the Steamboat gondola (singles/doubles $99/110).

Among the best meal deals in town are the $7 homemade dinners at *Johnny B Goode's Diner* (☎ 970-870-8400, 738 Lincoln Ave). Caffeine boosts (as well as healthy meals) are offered at *Mocha Molly's Coffee Saloon* (☎ 970-879-0587, 635 Lincoln Ave). *Cugino's Pizzeria* (☎ 970-879-5805, 825 Oak St) has an appealing Italian menu and atmosphere. A bit more upscale, well-made entrées and beer can be had at *Steamboat Brewery & Tavern* (☎ 970-879-2233), at 5th St and Lincoln Ave.

Steamboat Springs is served by the Yampa Valley Regional Airport, near Hayden, 22 miles west.

Alpine Taxi/Limo (☎ 970-879-2800, 800-232-7433) serves both the Yampa Valley Regional Airport ($22) and Denver International Airport ($60; 4 hours).

Greyhound's US 40 service between Denver and Salt Lake City inconveniently stops at the Phillips 66 gas station (30475 Hwy 40), about 1 mile west of town. There is a Steamboat Springs Transit bus stop about 30 feet west of the gas station where you can catch a bus into town.

Steamboat Springs Transit (☎ 970-879-5585) runs a free bus service between Old Town and the ski resort.

Steamboat Springs to Winter Park

Along with some fine scenery, there are a few points of interest along US 40 between these two ski resort towns. **Kremmling** isn't much of a town, but there is some good hiking and mountain biking in the area; check with the USFS Middle Park Ranger District Office (☎ 970-724-9004, 210 S 6th St/Hwy 9). **Hot Sulphur Springs** (🆆 www .hotsulphursprings.com) shelters an interesting museum and the pleasant *Hot Sulphur Springs Resort & Spa* (☎ 970-725-3306, 5617 County Rd 20), where you can either stop for a soak ($13.50) or spend the night ($74-108).

Winter Park

Less than a two-hour drive from Denver, Winter Park is one of Colorado's most convenient and least pretentious ski resorts, as well as a great place for summer recreation. Most services are along US 40 (which runs the length of Winter Park), including the visitor center (☎ 970-726-4118, 800-903-7275, 🆆 www.winterpark-info.com), open daily.

South of town, **Winter Park Resort** (☎ 970-726-5514, 800-525-2466, 🆆 www .skiwinterpark.com) covers four mountains and has a vertical drop of more than 3000 feet (lift tickets $54). Winter Park also has 45 miles of lift-accessible **mountain-biking** trails connecting to a 600-mile trail system running through the valley. Other good rides in the area include the road up to **Rollins Pass**.

Winter Park Central Reservations (☎ 970-726-5587, 800-453-2525) is the area's central booking agent.

The USFS *Idlewild Campground*, at the south end of Winter Park, is the closest camping area to town. The 26 sites ($10) can fill up early. Five miles south on US 40, *Robbers Roost Campground* has 11 sites.

Viking Lodge (☎ 970-726-8885, 800-421-4013), on US 40 between Vasquez Rd and

Cooper Creek Way, offers nice rooms ($65-105), a ski/bike shop, hot tub, sauna and discounts for HI-AYH members. Doubles at *Arapahoe Ski Lodge* (☎ 970-726-8222), on US 40 just north of Lions Gate Rd, are $65 in summer (including breakfast). During ski season rates are $178 (including dinner and breakfast). *Pines Inn* (☎ 970-726-5416, 800-824-9127), a pleasant B&B within walking distance from Winter Park Ski Resort, offers singles/doubles from $100/110 in summer, $70/120 in ski season.

Carver's Bakery Cafe (☎ 970-726-8202, 93 Cooper Creek Way) has superb, reasonably priced breakfasts and lunches, while *Deno's Mountain Bistro* (☎ 970-726-5332), across from Cooper Street Square, is popular with skiers and bikers. For spicy Mexican delights, look for *La Taqueria* (☎ 970-726-0280), in Park Place Center.

Home James Transportation Services (☎ 970-726-5060, 800-359-7536, 🆆 www .homejames-shuttle.com) runs shuttles to Denver International Airport ($39; 2 hours). Amtrak's *California Zephyr* stops daily in Fraser (near Winter Park), while the scenic *Ski Train* (☎ 303-296-4754) links Denver with Winter Park Resort weekends between mid-December and early April ($38 roundtrip).

Greyhound buses stop at the Winter Park visitor center.

Summit County

This mountain playground, just over an hour's drive from Denver, is a center for winter and summer recreation. The Summit County Chamber of Commerce (☎ 970-668-5800, 🆆 www.summitnet.com, 11 S Summit Blvd) is in Frisco. Summit County Central Reservations (☎ 970-468-6222, 800-365-6365) arranges lodging, transportation, lift tickets and activities.

The town of **Dillon**, east of the large Dillon Reservoir, serves mainly as a service center for day skiers up from Denver, though it does offer some (relatively) cheap accommodations. North of Dillon, on the other side of I-70, **Silverthorne** has the Arapaho National Forest (Dillon) ranger station (☎ 970-468-5400), a small visitor center and some ugly factory outlet stores. On the reservoir's west end, the town of **Frisco** is another convenient service hub, with moderately priced lodging and visitor information.

Skiing & Snowboarding The aptly named Summit County is home to four ski mountains. **Arapahoe Basin Ski Area** (☎ 970-468-0718, 888-272-7246, ⓦ www.arapahoebasin.com) is a spartan, high-altitude spot favored by expert skiers and is often open until June (lift tickets $40). **Keystone Ski Resort** (☎ 970-496-2316, 800-258-9553, ⓦ www.keystoneresort.com) is more family oriented, and the mountain has terrain for all ability levels, as well as night skiing (lift tickets $52).

Breckenridge (☎ 800-789-7669) covers four mountains, making it Summit County's largest ski area (lift tickets $53). The mountain has the added advantage of proximity to the interesting and lively former mining town of Breckenridge (see that section, later). **Copper Mountain Resort** (☎ 970-968-2882), like Keystone, is a modern, self-contained resort (lift tickets $55); the terrain is mainly suited for intermediate skiers.

Other Activities The Summit County network of paved paths connects Frisco with Dillon (5 miles), Breckenridge (10 miles), Copper Mountain (8 miles), Keystone (12 miles) and Ten Mile Canyon over Vail Pass (14 miles; see Vail, later). Cyclists and in-line skaters are not the only ones to benefit from the trails – Nordic skiers also enjoy them in winter. Gear stores in Frisco rent bikes and other equipment.

Places to Stay & Eat Four large USFS Arapaho National Forest campgrounds (☎ 970-468-5400, 877-444-6777 for reservations) line the shores of Dillon Reservoir: *Heaton Bay* (72 sites, $12), *Peak One* (79 sites, $12), *Pine Cove* (50 sites, $9) and *Prospector* (109 sites, $11).

Silverthorne's *HI-AYH Alpen Hütte Lodge* (☎ 970-468-6336, 471 Rainbow Dr) is a fine facility where comfortable beds ($28/18 peak season/off-season) and the babbling Blue River lull you to sleep. Standard chain motels can also be found along Silverthorne Lane. In Dillon, the clean *Best Western Ptarmigan Lodge* (☎ 970-468-2341, 800-842-5939, 652 Main St) has a pool, sauna and whirlpool (from $75).

In Frisco, the cozy *Woods Inn* (☎ 970-668-2255, 877-664-3777, ⓦ www.woodsinnbandb.com, 205 S Second Ave) is a good-value B&B that offers rooms with shared bath

from $25 and rooms/suites with private bath from $75/125. Amenities include a cozy living area with a fireplace and a hot tub. Frisco also has a number of motels, including the centrally located *Snowshoe Motel* (☎ 970-668-3444, 800-445-8658, 521 Main St), at $45/59 in summer/winter.

The *Arapahoe Cafe & Pub* (☎ 970-468-0873, 626 Lake Dillon Dr) has healthy fare such as trout and vegetarian pasta. *Sunshine Cafe* (☎ 970-468-6663), across from City Market in Silverthorne, is open daily and is a locals' favorite for good food and low prices. Both spots serve breakfast.

Frisco's *Butterhorn Bakery & Deli* (☎ 970-668-3997, 408 W Main St) is the place to 'carb up' for a day on the slopes or trails. For mountain haute cuisine, head for the award-winning *Uptown Bistro* (☎ 970-668-4728, 304 Main St).

Getting There & Around Greyhound buses (☎ 970-668-8917) stop at the Frisco Transfer Center (1010 Meadow Dr) behind Safeway and Wal-Mart en route to Denver and Grand Junction. Use the free Summit Stages buses (☎ 970-668-0999), which carry skis and bikes, to get to Copper Mountain, Keystone, Breckenridge, Frisco and Silverthorne.

Resort Express (☎ 970-468-7600, 800-334-7433, ⓦ www.resort-express.com) offers service between Denver International Airport and Summit County for $49 each way.

Breckenridge

With its 19th-century mining feel, Breckenridge has more character than other Summit County spots. Stop by the Breckenridge information center (☎ 970-453-6018, 309 N Main St) and activity center (☎ 970-453-5579, 137 S Main St) for information on accommodations, restaurants and the great hiking and mountain biking to be had in the area. The free *Breckenridge Magazine* outlines a walking tour of the historic town. The Summit Historical Society sells tickets for guided tours of the Edwin Carter Museum, Lomax Placer Mine, Washington Mine and the Breckenridge Historic District.

Breckenridge Resort Central Reservations (☎ 970-453-2918, 311 S Ridge St) can help book condominiums, the main form of accommodations in town.

The tattered *Fireside Inn B&B and Hostel* (☎ 970-453-6456, 114 N French St) has dorm beds (from $23), private rooms (from $65), ski and bike storage and a hot tub. The clean, well-run *Swiss Inn* (☎ 970-453-6489, 888-794-7750, 205 S French St) is the budget traveler's best bet, with dorm beds ($39) and private rooms (from $69).

Whole-wheat pancakes are a bargain at *Blue Moose* (☎ 970-453-4859, 540 S Main St), open only to 2pm. Get your bagel fix at *Pika Bagel Bakery & Cafe* (☎ 970-453-6246, 500 S Main St) or *Love Bagels!* (☎ 970-547-1115, 325 S Main St). The colorful *Rasta Pasta* (☎ 970-453-7467, 411 S Main St) serves up big plates of pasta for lunch and dinner. *Bubba's Bones* (☎ 970-547-9942, 110 S Ridge St) is the locals' favorite place for Southern-style barbecue.

Leadville

Nicknamed 'Cloud City' for its 10,200-foot altitude, Leadville has a fascinating mining legacy that once made it Colorado's second-largest city.

The visitor center (☎ 719-486-3900, 800-939-3901, W www.leadvilleusa.com) is at 809 Harrison Ave, and the USFS Leadville Ranger Station (☎ 719-486-0749, 2015 Poplar St) is on the north end of town.

The town's **historic buildings** include the Tabor Opera House, the National Mining Hall of Fame & Museum and the Heritage Museum & Gallery. Historic **mining areas** are a short drive away and can also be viewed via the Leadville, Colorado & Southern Railroad (☎ 719-486-3936), which runs daily late May to early October ($22.50).

For **hiking**, the stunning mountains surrounding Leadville include two 14,000-foot peaks, Mt Massive and Mt Elbert, the latter being Colorado's highest (14,433 feet). There's also good **mountain biking**. Rent bikes and get information at Bill's Sport Shop (☎ 719-486-0739, 225 Harrison Ave). **Ski Cooper** (☎ 719-486-2277), 9 miles north of Leadville, is a small mountain with $29 lift tickets.

In town, pitch your tent at *Leadville RV Corral* (☎ 719-486-3111, 135 W 2nd St) for $15. The USFS's *Halfmoon* and *Elbert Creek* campgrounds are 10 miles southwest of Leadville ($8). There are also six USFS campgrounds on Turquoise Reservoir ($11-12).

If you're feeling adventurous, try *Leadville Hostel* (☎ 719-486-2202, 500 E 7th

St). It's a bit worn down but costs only $20 a night. *Alps Motel* (☎ 800-818-2577, 207 Elm St) is the town's best motel, with clean, modern singles/doubles ($39/45). *Mountain Peaks Motel* (☎ 719-486-3178, 1 Harrison Ave) offers budget rooms ($30/35).

Cloud City Coffee House & Deli (☎ 719-486-1317, 711 Harrison Ave) has art exhibits, music, good coffee and fine food. *Callaway's* (☎ 719-846-1418), in the Delaware Hotel, offers exceptional value, with breakfasts under $5 and hearty lunches/dinners ($6/10). *Wild Bill's Restaurant* (☎ 719-486-0533, 200 Harrison Ave) is the place to go for $1 flame-broiled hamburgers.

Dee Hive Tours & Transportation (☎ 719-486-2339, 506 Harrison Ave) charges $61 one way to Denver and has a four-passenger minimum.

Vail

Vail is the nation's largest ski resort, and while the skiing can be amazing, the town gets mixed reviews for its 'instant Tyrolia' design. But skiing – not architecture – is what attracts visitors, and the resort consistently ranks among the top five in surveys of North American ski areas. The surrounding alpine country offers plenty to do in summer as well.

Orientation & Information Vail Village is the principal center of activity. Motorists must park at the Vail Transportation Center & Public Parking garage before entering the pedestrian mall near the chairlifts. Lionshead is a secondary center and lift about a half-mile to the west.

The Vail Visitor Center (☎ 970-479-1385, 800-525-3875, W www.vail.net) is at the Transportation Center (open daily). The Web sites W www.visitvailvalley.com and www.vailsource.com are excellent trip-planning tools. The White River National Forest Holy Cross Ranger Station (☎ 970-827-5715) is at the corner of I-70 exit 176 and US 24.

Skiing & Snowboarding Vail Mountain, with 6¼ miles of ski terrain, has trails for all ability levels. Lift tickets cost $62. For more information, call Vail Associates (☎ 970-476-5601).

Cross-country skiers can head to the Nordic Center at the Vail golf course

(☎ 970-479-4391) or the larger Cordillera Nordic Center (☎ 303-926-5100), 15 miles west of Vail. Check with the USFS Holy Cross Ranger Station (see Orientation & Information) for information on nearby backcountry ski routes like Shrine Pass.

Bicycling On the south side of I-70, a paved bike route extends through Vail and continues east to the Ten Mile Canyon Trail over Vail Pass to Frisco, the hub of Summit County bike trails. Another popular but physically demanding ride climbs over Tennessee Pass to Leadville on the narrow shoulders of US 24. Vail Mountain has about 20 well-marked mountain-bike trails crisscrossing the ski runs. Pick up a free copy of the 'Biking & Hiking Map,' as well as a list of where to rent bikes, at the visitor center.

Hiking The Holy Cross Wilderness Area has a wealth of great hikes such as the strenuous Notch Mountain Trail, which affords great views of Mt of the Holy Cross. The Half Moon Pass Trail leads up Mt of the Holy Cross. The Eagles Nest Wilderness Area also has some fine hiking destinations, including Booth Falls, Gore Lake and Two Elk Pass.

Places to Stay & Eat Don't expect any budget lodgings near Vail. Vail Central Reservations (☎ 970-476-1000, 800-525-3875, 100 E Meadow Rd) handles most properties.

The forested USFS *Gore Creek Campground*, at the east end of Bighorn Rd, offers 25 campsites ($8) June to Labor Day Weekend. It's 6 miles from Vail Village by bike or bus.

Among the least expensive places is *Roost Lodge (☎ 970-476-5451, 800-873-3065, 1783 N Frontage Rd)*, in West Vail. Its plain contemporary rooms sleep four comfortably. Summer/winter rates start at $40/62. Vail's other 'budget' place, *Park Meadows Lodge (☎ 970-476-5598, 1472 Matterhorn Circle)*, on the other side of the freeway, offers 28 one- and two-bedroom condos starting at $64/119 summer/winter.

One block from four lifts in Vail Village, the small European-style *Tivoli Lodge (☎ 970-476-5615, 800-451-4756, 386 Hanson Rd)* has cozy rooms ($139/69 winter/summer), a pool, hot tub and sauna.

At the top of Bridge St, *The Daily Grind (☎ 970-476-5856)* begins serving muffins and coffee at 6:30am. Even if you sleep until noon, you can start your day at *Blu's (☎ 970-476-3113, 193 E Gore Creek Dr)*, which serves breakfast until 5pm. *KB Ranch Co (☎ 970-476-1937)*, in Lionsquare Lodge, next to the Lionshead gondola, offers unpretentious dinners with a great salad bar ($10-15).

Getting There & Around From December to early April, the Eagle County Airport, 35 miles west of Vail, has direct jet service to destinations across the country, but it shuts down the rest of the year.

Colorado Mountain Express (☎ 970-949-4227, 800-525-6363, Ⓦ www.cmex.com) offers shuttle service to and from Denver International Airport. Greyhound buses stop at the Vail Transportation Center (☎ 970-476-5137) en route to Denver or Grand Junction.

Check the *Vail Valley* magazine for information on Vail's useful free bus system.

Around Vail

Three miles west of Vail on US 24, **Minturn** is a quaint railroad town that still retains its charm amid all the luxury development in surrounding areas. It's worth a stop to check out the art galleries and a couple of good restaurants, and possibly stay at *Minturn Inn (☎ 800-646-8876, Ⓦ www.minturninn.com, 442 Main St)*, a delightful B&B ($79-269). Another 10 miles south on US 24 is **Redcliff**, a tiny old lumber town with an unadulterated Old West feel to it. For a complete contrast, staying at the high-rent, neo-Tyrolean village at the base of the excellent **Beaver Creek Ski Area** will cost at least $200 per night.

Glenwood Springs

Glenwood Springs offers natural hot springs, a mild climate and a range of summer activities next to the Colorado River. The **Hot Springs Lodge and Pool** (☎ 970-945-7131, 401 N River St) is one of Colorado's most popular vacation destinations ($8.75). Only 45 minutes from both Vail and Aspen, the town's inexpensive winter accommodations also make a good alternative skiing base.

The Chamber Resort Association visitor center (☎ 970-945-6589, 888-445-3696), at 11th

St and Grand Ave, is open daily. The USFS White River National Forest headquarters (☎ 970-945-2521) is at 900 Grand Ave.

There's good road and mountain **biking** as well as plenty of **hiking** around Glenwood Springs; pick up the free topographic *Glenwood Springs Trails Guide* from the visitor center and the USFS. You can rent bikes at BSR Sports (☎ 970-945-7317, 210 7th St).

Glenwood Canyon offers Class III and IV white water below the Shoshone Dam, 7½ miles east of town. For guided tours, try Rock Gardens Rafting (☎ 970-945-6737, 800-958-6737, W www.rockgardens.com).

The *Glenwood Springs Hostel* (☎ 970-945-8545, 800-946-1295, 1021 Grand Ave) has over 40 dorm beds (from $12) and private rooms ($20-26). Discount mountain-bike rentals and kayaking trips are offered to guests. *Back in Time B&B* (☎ 970-945-6183, 888-854-7733, 927 Cooper Ave) is housed in a pleasant 1903 Victorian home. Singles/doubles start at $55/75.

About 20 motels and hotels are in the Glenwood area, and those closest to the city center fill up quickly during summer. South of town, *Frontier Lodge* (☎ 970-945-5496, 888-606-0602, 2834 Glen Ave) is a great value (from $50). *Glenwood Motor Inn* (☎ 970-945-5438, 800-543-5906, 141 W 6th St) is clean, comfortable and close to the town center ($45-96). There is also a string of slightly cheaper motels in West Glenwood, 1 to 2 miles from town on Hwy 6.

The historic Victorian *Hotel Colorado* (☎ 970-945-6511, 800-544-3998, 526 Pine St) is a great choice if you're not on a budget, with antique-furnished rooms from $98.

Wild Rose Bakery (☎ 970-928-8973, 310 7th St) serves delicious muffins, Danishes, scones and fresh bread. Lunch in Hotel Colorado's formal *Devereux Room* is a good value, with sandwiches, burgers and pasta for under $8. Dinner entrées (around $20) are more elaborate. *Brew Pub* (☎ 970-945-1276, 402 7th St) has delicious sandwiches and handcrafted beers on tap. Carnivores will enjoy the mountain-smoked-meat selections at *Smokin' Willies Bar-B-Que* (☎ 970-945-2479, 101 W 6th St).

Colorado Mountain Express (☎ 970-949-4227, 800-525-6363, W www.cmex.com) offers shuttle service to and from Denver International Airport. Amtrak's *California Zephyr* stops daily at the Glenwood train depot (☎ 970-945-9563) on South River St. Greyhound buses between Grand Junction and Denver stop at the Ramada Inn (124 W 6th St).

Roaring Forks Transit Authority (☎ 970-925-8454) offers bus connections with Aspen from the Glenwood Mall.

Aspen

Home to great skiing and beautiful alpine scenery, Aspen is nonetheless best known for its visitors – some of the wealthiest skiers in the world. Viewing the parade of personalities strutting about in garish attire is like peeking into the royal court. Even the police drive Saabs. Don't worry, though; the natural scenery is even more captivating.

The Aspen Chamber Resort Association (☎ 970-925-9000, 800-262-7736, W www.aspenchamber.org), in the City Parking Garage near N Mill St, is open weekdays. On weekends information is available at the historic Wheeler Opera House (☎ 970-920-7148, 320 E Hyman Ave).

The White River National Forest Aspen Ranger Station (☎ 970-925-3445, 806 W Hallam) has maps and information on the forest and three wilderness areas surrounding Aspen: Hunter Fryingpan, Maroon Bells–Snowmass and Collegiate Peaks.

Skiing & Snowboarding Four ski areas are operated by Aspen Skiing Company. Aspen (or Ajax), overlooking the town, is an athlete's mountain, offering more than 3000 feet of steep vertical drop. Aspen Highlands, about 1 mile west of town, has outstanding extreme skiing, breathtaking views and the longest vertical drop in Colorado (3800 feet). Buttermilk Mountain, 2 miles west of Aspen, provides gentle slopes for beginners and intermediate skiers. Snowmass, 12 miles northwest of Aspen on Hwy 82, offers a nice mix of intermediate and extreme expert terrain. Call ☎ 970-925-1220 or 800-525-6200 for information on lift tickets, hotels or rentals.

The best cross-country skiing in the area is at Ashcroft (☎ 970-925-1971), in the beautiful Castle Creek Valley, with 20 miles of groomed trails passing through a ghost town. For backcountry skiing, the 10th Mountain Division Hut Association (☎ 970-925-5775, 1280 Ute Ave) offers nearly 300 miles of trails connecting 14 overnight cabins. Getting to them requires both skill and advance reservations. The office also handles reservations for the Braun Hut System, which covers Aspen, Vail, Leadville and Hunter Creek.

Hiking & Backpacking The three wilderness areas surrounding Aspen offer plenty of trails in summer and early fall. The Hunter Valley Trail leads through wildflower meadows and on into the Hunter-Fryingpan Wilderness Area. Conundrum Hot Springs is the reward after 8½ miles of moderate climbing on the Conundrum Creek Trail. You can continue over Triangle Pass and return on East Maroon Creek Trail to get a bus from Maroon Lake back to Aspen. Other trails in the Hunter-Fryingpan or Collegiate Peaks Wilderness Areas, east of Aspen, tend to be less used than the popular Maroon Bells–Snowmass area.

Mountain Biking There are plenty of heavily used routes on Aspen Mountain and Smuggler Mountain. Hunter Valley and the Sunnyside trails provide a challenging single-track loop north of town. The Montezuma Basin and Pearl Pass rides offer extreme cycling experiences, well above timberline, south of town from Castle Creek Rd. The Hub (☎ 970-925-7970, 315 E Hyman Ave) rents mountain bikes.

Places to Stay & Eat The USFS White River National Forest's Aspen Ranger District (☎ 970-925-3445) operates nine *campgrounds* ($11-12).

Aspen Central Reservations (☎ 970-925-9000, 800-262-7736, ⓦ www.aspen4U.com, 425 Rio Grande Place) can help book B&Bs, hotels and condos. The European-style *St Moritz Lodge* (☎ 970-925-3220, 334 W Hyman Ave) has dorms with shared bath ($44/29 winter/summer). *The Mountain Chalet* (☎ 970-925-7797, 800-321-7813, 333 E Durant Ave) is the closest to the lifts and town center. Standard rooms cost $78-105 during ski season, less during summer – and there's a pool, sauna and whirlpool. Similar rates and facilities are at *Innsbruck Inn* (☎ 970-925-2980, 233 W Main St). *L'Auberge d'Aspen* (☎ 970-925-8297, 877-282-3743, 435 W Main St) offers cozy cottages with fireplaces in the $80-250 range.

Budget diners rely on *The Popcorn Wagon* (☎ 970-925-2718, 305 S Mill St), which has outdoor seating and serves tasty crêpes and sandwiches. *Main St Bakery* (☎ 970-925-6446, 201 E Main St) is a good place for dinners such as vegetarian lasagna or chicken potpie. Crowds flock to *The Mother Lode* (☎ 970-925-7700, 314 E Hyman Ave), where they've been serving delectable pasta dishes since 1959.

Entertainment A popular watering hole for the local ski patrol, *The Red Onion* (☎ 970-925-9043, 420 E Cooper Ave) first opened in 1892. *Cooper St Pier* (☎ 970-925-7758, 508 E Cooper Ave) is a good place to shoot pool or have some pub food.

Near the gondola base, *The Tippler* (☎ 970-925-4977, 535 E Dean St) features late-night dancing, while top rock and blues acts occasionally gig at *Double Diamond* (☎ 970-920-6905, 450 S Galena St).

Getting There & Around Sardy Field, 4 miles north of Aspen on Hwy 82, has commuter flights from Denver and nonstops to Minneapolis and Los Angeles. Colorado Mountain Express (☎ 970-949-4227, 800-525-6363, ⓦ www.cmex.com) offers frequent service to Denver International Airport ($100; 4 hours).

Roaring Fork Transit Agency (☎ 970-925-8484) buses connect Aspen with the ski mountains and Glenwood Springs.

Buena Vista & Salida

South of Leadville on US 24, Buena Vista and Salida have beautiful settings near the Collegiate Range. These towns are at the heart of the outstanding **white-water rafting** on the Arkansas River Headwaters Recreation Area, a 148-mile stretch of state-run recreation facilities and wildlife areas. Narrow Brown's Canyon, south of Buena Vista, is the most popular stretch of the river in Colorado. For maps and complete information, check out the Arkansas Headwaters Recreation Office (☎ 719-539-7289, 307 W Sackett St) in Salida. Buffalo Joe River Trips (☎ 719-395-8757, 800-356-7984, 113 N Railroad St) has a good reputation for safe and enjoyable trips.

The alpine country around both towns offers fine hiking, mountain biking and fishing. In Buena Vista, check with the

visitor center (☎ 719-395-6612, W www
.buenavistacolorado.org, 343 S US 24), open
weekdays, and the Trailhead (☎ 719-395-
8001, 707 N US 24), a sporting-goods store.
In Salida, the Heart of the Rockies
Chamber of Commerce (☎ 719-539-2068,
W www.salidachamber.org, 406 W US 50) is
open daily in summer. The Salida USFS
Ranger Station (☎ 719-539-3591) is at 325
W Rainbow Blvd.

The USFS has two campgrounds west of
Buena Vista and several in the Salida area.
There are plenty of motels in both towns,
though they fill up in summer. A good bet in
Buena Vista is *Vista Court Cabins & Lodge*
(☎ 719-395-6557, 1004 W Main St), from
$45, while *Liar's Lodge (☎ 719-395-3444,*
888-542-7756, W *www.liarslodge.com, 30000*
County Rd 371) is a handsome log cabin inn
on the banks of the Arkansas River ($65/95
off-peak/peak season). In Salida the attractive *Mountain Motel (☎ 719-539-4420, 1425*
E Rainbow Blvd) has cabin-style rooms
with kitchens (from $50).

Those looking for a soak can try *Mt*
Princeton Hot Springs Resort (☎ 719-395-
2361, 888-395-7799, W *www.mtprinceton*
.com), south of Buena Vista, where you can
just bathe ($6) or stay the night (from $62/70
winter/summer).

San Luis Valley

The vast San Luis Valley lies between the
jagged 14,000-foot peaks of the Sangre de
Cristo Range to the east and the San Juan
Mountains to the west.

The main attraction of this area is the
Great Sand Dunes National Monument, a
55-sq-mile sea of sand dunes, the tallest of
which rise 700 feet from the valley floor.
Whether viewed from afar or from atop one
of the dunes, it's a surreal place and well
worth a visit. For information on camping
and hiking in the dunes or the surrounding
alpine forests, check with the visitor center
(☎ 719-378-2312), 3 miles north of the entry
gate (entry $3). There's also some good
mountain biking in this area. The main
campground in the monument is the 88-site
Pinyon Flats, open year round ($10).

The monument is 34 miles northeast of
Alamosa, the largest town in the area, with
numerous motels. For more information,
contact the Alamosa County Chamber of
Commerce information depot (☎ 719-589-

4840, 800-258-7597, W www.alamosa.org), in
Cole Park at 3rd St and the west bank of the
Rio Grande.

About 40 miles southeast of Alamosa is
the Hispanic town of **San Luis**, an appealing,
friendly spot where you can kick back and
appreciate the rare character and sense of
community this place has enjoyed since its
1851 founding. The San Luis Visitors Center
(☎ 719-672-3321), on Main St opposite the
Hwy 142 intersection, is open 9am-1pm
Thursday to Sunday.

Farther south, about 5 miles north of the
New Mexico border, the dusty town of Antonito is the northern terminus of the
Cumbres & Toltec Scenic Railroad (☎ 719-
376-5483, W www.cumbrestoltec.com), a
narrow-gauge railway that winds its way
through the mountains to Chama, New
Mexico, from Memorial Day to mid-October
(13 trip options for $29-60). Nearby is a
highway that follows the **Conejos River** into
the Rio Grande National Forest, where you
can camp, fish, observe wildlife or watch the
steam train wind through Cumbres Pass.

Crested Butte

Remote, beautiful and laid-back, Crested
Butte is arguably Colorado's best ski resort.
Though the terrain on Crested Butte Mountain is aimed mainly at expert skiers, the
friendly, unpretentious atmosphere and
wealth of summer outdoor activities
welcome everyone. Most everything in town
is on Elk Ave, including the visitor center
(☎ 970-349-6438, 800-545-4505, W www
.crestedbuttechamber.com), at Hwy 135 and
Elk Ave (open daily).

Crested Butte Mountain Resort (☎ 970-
349-2333, 800-544-8448, W www.skicb.com)
sits 2 miles north of the town at the base of
the impressive mountain of the same name.
The area is surrounded by forests, rugged
mountain peaks and the West Elk, Raggeds
and Maroon Bells–Snowmass Wilderness
Areas. Lift tickets cost $53, but they're $27
at the start and finish of the season, usually
late November to mid-December and early
to mid-April.

Crested Butte has also become a
mountain-biking mecca, and the Crested
Butte Mountain Heritage Museum even
sports a Mountain Bike Hall of Fame. The
area is littered with excellent high-altitude
single-track trails. The best place for maps

and information is The Alpineer (☎ 970-349-5210, 800-223-4655), near the intersection of Elk St and Hwy 135, which also rents mountain bikes.

Places to Stay The chamber of commerce reservation center (☎ 970-349-7048, 800-215-2226, ⓔ cbreserve@rmi.net) can help book lodgings.

The Gunnison National Forest's Taylor River Ranger District (☎ 970-641-0471, 216 N Colorado St), in Gunnison, operates 18 campgrounds between Crested Butte and Gunnison. The closest large campground is the USFS *Lake Irwin* (☎ 877-444-6777 for reservations), west of town before Kebler Pass ($10).

Crested Butte International Hostel (☎ 970-349-0588, 888-389-0588, ⓔ hostel@crestedbutte.net, 615 Teocalli Ave) has 52 beds ($17-28), a kitchen, laundry and fireplace. Reservations are advised.

The atmospheric 1881 *Forest Queen* (☎ 970-349-5336, 800-937-1788, 129 Elk Ave) has off-season/peak-season rooms with shared bath ($49/59) and private bath ($59/69). The *Inn at Crested Butte* (☎ 970-349-1225, 800-949-4828, ⓔ innatcb@rmii.com, 510 Whiterock Ave) offers fairly comfortable doubles (from around $85 in winter).

For something truly out of the ordinary, book one of the six funky guest rooms ($99-139) at *The Claim Jumper* (☎ 970-349-6471, fax 970-349-7757, 704 Whiterock Ave), a museumlike inn feverishly decorated with colorful paraphernalia.

The cheapest, and smallest, rooms on Mt Crested Butte are at *Manor Lodge* (☎ 970-349-5365, 650 Gothic Rd), at $99/59 winter/summer.

Places to Eat & Drink In the morning, locals congregate at *Butte Bagels* (☎ 970-349-2707), on Elk Ave, and at *Camp 4 Coffee* (☎ 970-209-0346, 402½ Elk Ave), a building *covered* in old car license plates where they serve great coffee and baked goods. For heartier American-style breakfasts and lunches, try the nearby *Paradise Cafe* (☎ 970-349-6233), at 4th St and Elk Ave, which has a nice terrace for warm-weather eating.

Butte Bayou (☎ 970-349-9761), near 1st St and Elk Ave, whips up great po'boy sandwiches and spicy Cajun food. *Pitas in Paradise* (☎ 970-349-0897, 313 3rd St) does great gyros and Mediterranean food. *Teocalli Tamale* (☎ 970-349-2005, 311½ Elk Ave) is good lunch choice for burritos, tacos and tamales in the $5 range.

For top-end dining, *Timberline* (☎ 970-349-9831, 21 Elk Ave) and *Le Bousquet* (☎ 970-349-5808), at 6th and Belleview, have earned kudos from locals.

Bars worth checking out include the 1890s *Kochevar's* (☎ 970-349-6745, 127 Elk Ave) and *The Eldo* (☎ 970-349-6125, 215 Elk Ave), which has a great outdoor deck and occasional live music.

Getting There & Around Crested Butte's air link to the outside world is Gunnison County Airport, 28 miles south. Alpine Express (☎ 970-641-5074, 800-822-4844) meets all commercial flights in the winter but requires reservations in summer months. The roundtrip fare to Crested Butte is $38.

The free Mountain Express (☎ 970-349-5616) connects Crested Butte with Mt Crested Butte hourly 7am-11:40pm.

San Juan Mountain Towns

The lush, volcanic San Juan Mountains spread over most of southwest Colorado, offering some of the finest alpine scenery in the state. Several small towns make pleasant way stations for enjoying the natural beauty and offer a good look at frontier history.

Near the Rio Grande headwaters on Hwy 149, the tiny mining town of **Creede** (population 500) has little to show for its boomtown days, when it was filled with 10,000 rowdy citizens. Since the last silver mine closed in 1988, the town has relied on its historic main street (filled with galleries and shops), the Creede Repertory Theatre and neighboring wilderness areas to attract visitors. In summer there's plenty of good hiking, mountain biking, rafting and fishing. Contact the Creede Chamber of Commerce (☎ 719-658-2374, 800-327-2102, ⓦ www.creede.com) for information on lodging, restaurants and activities (open weekdays). In winter Creede is almost a ghost town, and only one of its several lodgings remains open year round.

Equally tiny **Lake City**, farther north on Hwy 149, was grandly called the 'Metropolis of the Mines' in the 1870s. But unlike many mining towns, it attracted optimistic settlers rather than itinerants, which perhaps accounts for the Greek and Gothic Revival architecture and pleasant tree-lined streets. In addition to fine hiking, the area is known for the Alpine Loop Byway, a rugged unpaved route over Engineer Pass to Ouray for 4WD vehicles and mountain bikes. The Lake City Chamber of Commerce (☎ 970-944-2527, 800-569-1874, W www.hinsdale-county.com) is on Silver St.

Spectacular alpine peaks leave barely a quarter mile of valley floor for the 800 residents of **Ouray**, a town known for the Ouray Hot Springs and more recently for Ouray Ice Park, the world's first dedicated ice-climbing area. The visitor center (☎ 970-325-4746, 800-228-1876, W www.ouraycolorado.com) at the hot springs has information on lodging, dining, and jeep tours and hiking in the nearby Mt Sneffels and Uncompahgre Wilderness Areas (open daily).

South of Ouray via Hwy 50, across the sometimes harrowing Red Mountain Pass, lies **Silverton**, a National Historic Landmark that also serves as the northern terminus for the Durango & Silverton Narrow Gauge Railroad (☎ 970-387-5416), which runs early May to mid-October (see Durango, later). The visitor center (☎ 970-387-5654, 800-752-4494, W www.silverton.org), south of town at the junction of Greene St and US 550, is open daily.

Between Silverton and Ouray, US 550 is known as the **Million Dollar Highway**. The route passes many old mine headframes (the supports that lowered people and supplies into the mines) and some extraordinary Alpine scenery.

Telluride

This town has it all: 300 inches of snow annually, a 3000-foot vertical drop to ski lifts in town, a dramatic box-canyon setting, a rich mining history and a well-preserved Victorian downtown. The town's small size means you can get everywhere on foot, so leave your car at the 'intercept parking lot' by the visitor center (☎ 970-728-3041, 888-288-7360), at the town entrance. In the same building is Telluride Central Reservations (☎ 888-355-8743, W www.telluride.com), which handles accommodations and festival tickets. Online information on lodgings, restaurants, skiing and other activities is at W www.telluride.com and W www.telluridemm.com.

Covering three distinct areas, **Telluride Ski Area** (☎ 970-728-7533, 888-288-7360, W www.telluride-ski.com) is served by 12 lifts. Much of the terrain is for advanced skiers, but there's still plenty for beginners and intermediates (lift tickets $61, $40 before mid-December). There is plenty of great **mountain biking** and **hiking** in the surrounding mountains. Easy Rider (☎ 970-728-4734, 101 W Colorado Ave) has information and bikes for rent. Telluride Sports (☎ 970-828-7547, 150 W Colorado Ave) has topo maps and USFS Uncompahgre Forest maps. Telluride Central Reservations (☎ 888-288-7360) can provide information on lower-rate periods and ski-free packages.

Right in town, *Telluride Town Park Campground* (☎ 970-728-3071) offers 42 campsites ($10, with parking $12) with shower access. Spartan rooms with shared bath at *Oak Street Inn* (☎ 970-728-3383, 134 N Oak St) are the least expensive in town ($42).

The popular *Baked & Brewed in Telluride* (☎ 970-728-4775, 127 S Fir St) offers baked goods, pizza, daily specials and home-brewed beer at reasonable prices. *Wildflower Cooking Co* (☎ 970-728-8887), right at the base of the gondola, does great fresh baked treats for breakfast and lunch. *Fat Alley* (☎ 970-728-3985, 122 South Oak St) does Southern-style barbecue as well as good veggie choices.

Commuter aircraft serve the mesa-top Telluride Airport, 5 miles east of town, when the weather is good. At other times, planes fly into Montrose, 65 miles north. Shuttles between the Montrose airport and Telluride ($32) are run by Telluride Express (☎ 970-728-6000, 888-212-8294) and Mountain Limo (☎ 970-728-9606, 888-546-6894).

Durango

Tourists flood Durango in summer to ride the steam-driven **Durango & Silverton Narrow Gauge Railroad** (☎ 970-247-2733, 888-872-4607), which makes a scenic 45-mile trip north to Silverton ($53 roundtrip). Those who haven't booked a train ticket a month in advance can enjoy mountain biking and rafting during the summer and skiing during winter at **Durango Mountain Resort** (☎ 970-247-9000, 800-982-6103, W www.durangomountainresort.com), 25 miles north of Durango on US 550.

The visitor center (☎ 970-247-0312, 800-525-8855, W www.durango.org, 111 S Camino del Rio), south of town at the Santa Rita exit from US 550, is open daily. The San Juan–Rio Grande National Forest Headquarters and BLM office (☎ 970-247-4874, 15 Burnett Court) offers camping and hiking information and forest maps (open weekdays).

Rivers West (☎ 970-259-5077, 520 Main Ave) and Mountain Waters Rafting (☎ 970-259-4191, 800-748-2507, 108 W College Ave) offer raft trips on the Animas River.

USFS campsites ($10) can be reserved (☎ 877-444-6777) at *Haviland Lake*, 18 miles north of Durango, while the large *Junction Creek* ($10), 3 miles west of Main Ave and 25th St, is first-come, first-served. Eight miles north of Durango, *Hermosa Meadows Camper Park (☎ 970-247-3055, 800-748-2853)* offers 90 shaded tent sites ($20) with laundry and showers next to the Animas River.

Nearly all of Durango's 40-plus motels are expensive and full in summer; call Durango Central Reservations (☎ 970-247-8900, 800-979-9742) to help book a room. *Durango Hostel (☎ 970-247-9905, 543 E 2nd Ave)* offers the bare necessities; dorm beds are $13/15 for HI members/nonmembers. One of the best motel values in town is the low-key *End O' Day Motel (☎ 970-247-1722, 350 E 8th Ave)*, at $34/42 for singles/doubles. At the northern tip of town, *Silver Spur Motel (☎ 970-247-5552, 800-748-1715, 3416 Main Ave)* is also reasonable (singles/doubles $65/85 in summer, $40/44 in winter) and has a pool. *Gable House (☎ 970-247-4982, @ ghbb@frontier.net, 805 E 5th Ave)* is a splendid 1892 Queen Ann Victorian home. Shared-bath rooms run $75-135.

You can caffeine up and surf the Net at *Steaming Bean Coffee Co (☎ 970-385-7901, 915 Main Ave)*. *Carver Brewing Co (☎ 970-259-2545, 1022 Main Ave)* has built up a strong following for its cool outdoor beer garden. The historic-looking *Olde Tymer's Cafe (☎ 970-259-2990, 1000 Main Ave)* offers good lunches and outdoor patio seating.

Durango–La Plata County Airport, 18 miles southeast of Durango via US 160 and Hwy 172, has regular commuter flights to and from Denver, Phoenix and Albuquerque. Durango Transportation (☎ 970-259-4818)

has frequent airport shuttles ($15). Greyhound/TNM&O buses run daily from the Bus Center (☎ 970-259-2755, 275 E 8th Ave) north to Grand Junction and south to Albuquerque.

The Durango Lift (☎ 970-259-5438) operates a frequent trolley bus service along Main Ave.

WESTERN COLORADO
Grand Junction
Western Colorado's main urban center, Grand Junction boasts a pleasant downtown historic district, but its main use for travelers is as a base for exploring the nearby scenic wonders of the Colorado National Monument and the Grand Mesa.

The Visitor & Convention Bureau Information Center (☎ 970-244-1480, 800-962-2547), at the junction of I-70 and Horizon Dr, is open daily. Tourist information is also available from the downtown chamber of commerce (☎ 970-242-3214, W www.grand-junction.net, 360 Grand Ave). The USFS Grand Junction office (☎ 970-242-8211, 764 Horizon Dr) and the BLM Grand Junction Area Office (☎ 970-244-3000) are opposite Walker Field Airport at 2815 H Rd.

Some of Colorado's finest **mountain biking** can be found around Grand Junction, particularly near the town of Fruita, 13 miles west. Tompkin's Cycle Center (☎ 970-241-0141, 301 Main St) and Bicycle Outfitters (☎ 970-245-2699, 227 Ute Ave) are two good places to rent bikes. In Fruita, the best bike shop is Over the Edge Sports (☎ 970-858-7220, 202 E Aspen Ave).

The *RV Ranch (☎ 970-434-6644, 3238 E I-70 Business Loop)*, reached by I-70 exit 37, has tent/RV sites ($30/32).

Hotel Melrose (☎ 970-242-9636, 800-430-4555, W www.hotelmelrose.com, 337 Colorado Ave) is close to downtown, Greyhound and Amtrak, and offers dorm beds ($15) and rooms with shared/private bath (from $30/45) in a restored 1908 building – the best deal in town.

One of the cheapest motels near downtown is basic *Daniel's Motel (☎ 970-243-1084, 333 North Ave)*, at $30/40 for singles/doubles. Closer to downtown is *Value Lodge (☎ 970-242-0651, 104 White Ave)*, which has a pool ($35/38).

Try the attractive *Crystal Cafe & Bake Shop (☎ 970-242-8843, 314 Main St)* for excellent breakfasts, lunches and baked goods. **Main Street Bagels** (☎ 970-241-2740, 559 Main St) bakes scrumptious New York–style bagels. **Rockslide Brewery** (☎ 970-245-2111, 401 Main St) has decent food, though locals like it more for the beer.

Walker Field, Grand Junction's commercial airport, is 8 miles northeast of downtown (I-70 exit 31) and offers daily flights to Denver, Phoenix and Salt Lake City. Buses leave the Greyhound depot (☎ 970-242-6012, 830 S 5th St) for Denver, Durango, Las Vegas, Salida and Salt Lake City. Amtrak's daily *California Zephyr* stops at the train depot (☎ 970-241-2733, 339 S 1st St).

Grand Mesa

Towering above the Grand Valley, this 'island in the sky' is a lava-capped plateau rising more than 11,000 feet above sea level at its highest point. Its broad summit offers a delightful respite from the Grand Valley's summer heat, as well as beautiful Alpine scenery and an interesting four-hour loop drive from Grand Junction (via I-70, Hwy 65 and US 50) with plenty of opportunities for side trips and stopovers. You can get maps and information at the Grand Junction visitor center; the Grand Mesa Byway Welcome Center (☎ 970-856-3100), at the southern side of the mesa on Hwy 65 in Cedaredge (open May to mid-Oct); or several smaller information stations atop the mesa. In winter try the fine powder and intermediate runs of **Powderhorn Ski Area** (☎ 970-268-5700, 800-241-6997), on the mesa's northern slope.

There are 12 USFS *campgrounds* in Grand Mesa National Forest, most of which charge $7-10. Lodges at Alexander Lake (☎ 970-856-6700), Grand Mesa (☎ 970-856-3250) and Powderhorn (☎ 970-268-5700) have rooms ($35-55) and cabins ($65-75), though some close in winter.

Colorado National Monument

From the Uncompahgre Uplift of the Colorado Plateau, 2000 feet above the Grand Valley of the Colorado River, about half a dozen accessible colorful sandstone canyons precipitously descend to the flatlands. Once dinosaur country, this 32-sq-mile scenic wonder is one of the most rewarding side trips possible off an interstate highway – well worth an automobile detour but even better for backcountry exploration. Open year-round, it's an exceptional area for hiking and camping, as well as biking on Rim Rock Rd, which links the eastern and western entrances.

The monument is 4 miles west of Grand Junction, though its western entrance is closer to Fruita. The visitor center (☎ 970-858-3617), on the plateau at the north end of the park, is open daily. Park entry is $5 per automobile, $3 for pedestrians or cyclists.

Saddlehorn Campground, close to the visitor center, has the only formal sites ($10) within the park proper. Backcountry camping is free (permits required).

Black Canyon of the Gunnison National Park

Visitors often feel awe (and vertigo) peering down this dark, 2000-foot-deep chasm over the Gunnison River. The south rim has more facilities than the remote north rim. The 6-mile South Rim Rd winds along the canyon edge and past 11 overlooks (some reached by short trails) and makes for a great bike ride. The visitor center (☎ 970-249-1915, 800-873-0244) is at Gunnison Point, the second viewpoint. Entry is $7 per vehicle or $4 for bikes and is good for seven days.

South Rim Campground has over 100 campsites. Sites near the river are also available at **East Portal Campground**, part of the nearby Curecanti National Recreation Area. **North Rim Campground** is closed in winter. The camping fee is $8.

Dolores River Canyon

Stark sandstone formations, juniper-covered mesas and sagebrush valleys flank the curves of Hwy 141 as it winds through the isolated Dolores River Canyon. The canyon, which stretches 159 miles between Dove Creek and the US 50 turnoff to Unaweep Canyon, 9 miles south of Grand Junction, is one of the least-visited scenic spots in Colorado. The few towns along the way include tiny **Dove Creek** and **Naturita** and the one-store town of **Bedrock**. Parts of the Dolores River offer excellent white-water rafting. Wilderness Aware (☎ 800-462-7238, W www.inaraft.com) offers trips that explore the cultural and natural history along the river.

A brochure describing sights along the route is available at the Colorado Welcome

ROCKY MOUNTAINS

Centers in Cortez and Fruita. The Nucla-Naturita Chamber of Commerce (☎ 970-865-2350, 217 W Main St/Hwy 141), in Naturita, and the Dove Creek Chamber of Commerce (☎ 970-677-2245, 128 Hwy 666) also offer such information.

Mesa Verde National Park

Among national parks, Mesa Verde National Park is unique for its focus on preserving cultural relics of the fascinating Ancestral Puebloan culture. Opportunities for hiking and road biking are limited; the main reason to come here is to view history. Magnificent sites dot the canyons and mesa tops. The park is a high plateau lying south of US 160, midway between Cortez and Mancos.

Ancestral Puebloan dwellings in Mesa Verde evolved from simple structures in AD 450 to the great cliff cities that were mysteriously abandoned in 1300. The Puebloans moved to the cliff faces around 1200. Communities ranged from a few rooms to over 200 compartments, many connected with internal passageways. Their disappearance after only a century still defies explanation.

The cliff dwellings remained undisturbed until 1849, when a US Army lieutenant stumbled upon them. Discovery of the magnificent Cliff Palace occurred only when two local cowboys were searching for stray cattle after an 1888 snowfall. Subsequent looting prompted calls to protect the ruins, and Congress established Mesa Verde National Park in 1906.

From the entrance, it's 21 miles to Park Headquarters (☎ 970-529-4461), open weekdays, and the nearby Chapin Mesa Museum (☎ 970-529-4475), open daily. Along the way are Morefield Campground (4 miles), the panoramic viewpoint at Park Point (10 miles) and the Far View Visitor Center (☎ 970-529-4543), open daily from late spring to early autumn (15 miles). Visitors must stop at Far View to obtain the required tickets ($1.75) for tours of Cliff Palace or Balcony House. Entry costs $10 per vehicle, $5 per hiker or cyclist. Many portions of the park are closed in winter. Entry is $10 per vehicle passenger, $5 for bicyclists, hikers and motorcyclists, and is valid for seven days.

ARAMARK Mesa Verde (☎ 970-529-4421) offers guided tours from May to mid-

Anasazi: A Misnomer

The people of Mesa Verde have been commonly referred to as 'Anasazi,' a term archaeologists in the 1930s borrowed from a Navajo word thought to mean 'the ancient ones.' They almost got it right: It actually means 'enemy ancestors,' and modern-day descendants in Arizona and New Mexico have understandably pressed for a more accurate name, especially since their ancestors weren't even related to the Navajo. The National Park Service has changed its literature to reflect this situation, now using the term 'Ancestral Puebloans.' Likewise, it has become politically correct to use the term 'sites,' as opposed to the commonly used 'ruins,' when referring to the archeological relics of the region.

October. The largest concentration of Ancestral Puebloan sites in the area is at **Chapin Mesa**, including the densely clustered Far View Site and the large Spruce Tree House.

South from Park Headquarters, the 6-mile **Mesa Top Rd** connects excavated mesa-top sites, accessible cliff dwellings and vantages of inaccessible cliff dwellings from the mesa rim. Sites include the oft-photographed Square Tower House, Cliff Palace and Balcony House.

At **Wetherill Mesa**, the second-largest concentration of sites, visitors may enter stabilized surface sites and two cliff dwellings, including the Long House.

The *Morefield Campground (☎ 970-529-4421)*, open May to mid-October, has 445 tent/RV sites ($18/25). *Far View Lodge (☎ 970-529-4421)*, 15 miles from the park entrance, has nice Southwestern-style rooms ($90/107 off-peak/peak season) with good views. There are also plenty of motels in Cortez and a few places in the towns of Dolores and Mancos. Restaurants are in Morefield Village, Far View Terrace, near Chapin Mesa Museum and at Far View Lodge.

Cortez & Around

Cortez is the main lodging spot for visitors to Mesa Verde National Park. The Colorado

Welcome Center (☎ 970-565-4048, 928 E Main St) has local and statewide information and is open daily.

The only decent campground with tent/RV sites ($20/25) is the **Cortez–Mesa Verde KOA** (☎ 970-565-9301, 27432 E Hwy 160), at the east end of town (open mid-May to mid-Sept).

There is a good selection of motels in Cortez, though reservations are advised in summer. The basic but clean **Ute Mountain Motel** (☎ 970-565-8507, 531 S Broadway) is a pretty good value ($28/45 singles/doubles), as is **Budget Host Inn** (☎ 970-565-3738, 2040 E Main St), which boasts a pool, a hot tub and spacious, spotless rooms ($78 in summer, around half that in winter).

In Mancos, the charming **Old Mancos Inn** (☎ 970-533-9019, fax 970-533-7138, 200 W Grand Ave) is one of the few truly gay-friendly hotels in Colorado. Shared-bath singles/doubles cost $30/35; rooms are $45/50 with attached bath.

Cortez Municipal Airport, 2 miles southwest of town, has daily flights to Denver and Farmington, New Mexico.

In the shadow of Sleeping Ute Mountain, 12 miles south of Cortez, the Ute Mountain Reservation is home to both a casino and the **Ute Mountain Tribal Park** (☎ 970-565-9653, 800-847-5485), 3 miles west of US 160/US 666, where you can take tribe-arranged tours of Ancestral Puebloan cliff dwellings. Six sets of unique tower ruins lie at the desolate **Hovenweep National Monument** (☎ 970-749-0510), 42 miles west of Cortez. If you like barren scenery, make the 38-mile trip southwest to **Four Corners**, the only place in the country where four state borders (Colorado, New Mexico, Arizona and Utah) intersect.

Wyoming

Wyoming's colorful history of pioneer migration and settlement overlays the enduring presence of the Shoshone and Arapaho people, who today live on the Wind River Indian Reservation. While its romantic Wild West image is at odds with actual history, the 'Cowboy State' still promotes the myth: Almost every town has a rodeo, and the era of mountain men and Indians is reenacted in pageants statewide.

Wyoming is a state of physical contrasts, where broad, arid basins and sagebrush plains yield to forested mountains. Pronghorn herds cross the high desert, and moose, elk and bear roam the mountain country. Such remarkable diversity provides an excellent arena for outdoor activities, from fishing and boating to hiking, backcountry camping, climbing and skiing.

Most visitors head straight to northwest Wyoming, home to the geysers of Yellowstone National Park, the granite summits of the Teton and Wind River mountains, and the world-famous Jackson Hole ski resort. Northern Wyoming's other draws include the Bighorn Mountains and the enigmatic Devils Tower National Monument. The state's southern part sees far fewer visitors, but does boast the beautiful Medicine Bow Mountains and historic Laramie.

History

Construction of the Transcontinental Railroad in the 1860s opened up the Wyoming territory, which had its boundaries officially designated in 1868. This was largely the work of the Union Pacific (UP) Railroad, which dominated local economic and political life. Wyoming's first legislators enacted an extraordinary statute in 1869 granting women 21 years of age and older the right to vote and hold office. When it obtained statehood in 1890, Wyoming became known

---

Wyoming

Nicknames: Equality State, Cowboy State

Population: 493,782 (50th)

Area: 97,820 sq miles (10th)

Admitted to Union: July 10, 1890 (44th)

Capital city: Cheyenne (population 55,000)

Other cities: Casper (49,000), Laramie (25,000)

State mammal: bison

Famous for: extreme weather, cowboys and cattle barons, population scarcity, endless dirt roads, giving women the vote first (1869)

Home of: the USA's first national park (Yellowstone, 1872), yellow pages (1883)

as the 'Equality State.' While some legislators saw it as an issue of principle, others voted for it to attract more female settlers; in the 1870 census, men over 21 outnumbered women six to one.

Information

The main Wyoming Information Center (☎ 307-777-7777, 800-225-5996, W www.wyomingtourism.org), I-25 exit 7 at College Drive in Cheyenne, is open daily. Other Wyoming Information Centers are off the interstate in Pine Bluffs, Evanston, Jackson, Laramie, Sundance and Sheridan. Request the very helpful seasonal 'Wyoming Vacation Guide,' which includes a state highway map. For online information, check out W www.state.wy.us. For road conditions across the state, dial ☎ 307-772-0824 or 888-996-7623 in Wyoming.

State sales tax is 4%; county sales tax ranges from zero to 2%. State bed tax is no more than 8%, including the 1% to 2% bed tax most counties add.

Getting There & Around

Towns with airports include Casper, Cheyenne, Cody, Gillette, Jackson Hole, Laramie, Pinedale and Sheridan. Most are not linked by air to one another, but instead have service to Denver or Salt Lake City. There is no passenger train service in Wyoming, and bus routes are limited. As in other Rockies states, a car is the best way to go.

CHEYENNE

At the Great Plains' western edge, Cheyenne is Wyoming's capital and largest city. For visitors, it serves mainly as a gateway. The Cheyenne Area Convention & Visitors Bureau (☎ 307-778-3133, 800-426-5009, W www.cheyenne.org, 309 W Lincolnway) is open weekdays, daily in summer.

Historically a cattle town, Cheyenne also owes its development to the UP Railroad and, later, the US military. Once known as a lawless 'Hell on Wheels,' the city shelters a historic downtown, the somewhat somber **Wyoming State Museum** (☎ 307-777-7022 weekdays, ☎ 307-777-7024 weekends, 2301 Central Ave) and the **Frontier Days Old West Museum** (☎ 307-778-7290, 4501 N Carey Ave), at I-25 exit 12, which takes a livelier look at early Cheyenne ($4).

Beginning the last full week in June, the city stages Wyoming's largest and longest-running (since 1897) celebration, Cheyenne Frontier Days, featuring 10 days of rodeos, concerts, dances, air shows, free pancake breakfasts, chili cook-offs, a carnival and most every other sort of shindig. Enter the ticket office (☎ 307-778-7222, 800-227-6336, W www.cfdrodeo.com, 4501 N Carey Ave) from 8th Ave at Frontier Park.

Places to Stay & Eat

Reservations are essential during Frontier Days, when everything within 50-miles is booked and rates double as far away as Laramie and Greeley, Colorado. Rates (and temperatures!) drop during the dead of winter.

Cheyenne's nicest RV park is the well-landscaped **AB Camping** (☎ 307-634-7035, 1503 W College Dr), I-25 exit 7, with tent/RV sites for $13/20 (open Mar-Oct). The closest public camping is 25 miles west, in Curt Gowdy St Park.

A string of motels lines noisy Lincolnway (I-25 exit 9), including **Wyoming Motel** (☎ 307-632-8104, 1401 W Lincolnway), with rooms under $25; the friendly **Guest Ranch Motel** (☎ 307-634-2137, 1100 W Lincolnway), from $30; and **Home Ranch Motel** (☎ 307-634-3575, 2414 E Lincolnway), at $28/30 for singles/doubles.

Friendly **Chloe's Java Joint** (1711 Carey Ave) offers light, veggie-friendly breakfasts and lunches in funky downtown digs. Non-smoking **Lexie's** (216 E 17th St) has an appealing menu of reasonably priced breakfasts, sandwiches and Italian and Mexican dishes. **Sanford's Grub & Pub** (115 E 17th St) features hearty eats and a good selection of non-macrobrews.

Getting There & Around

Cheyenne Municipal Airport (☎ 307-634-7071, 200 E 8th Ave) has daily United Express flights to Denver. The Armadillo Express DIA Shuttle (☎ 307-632-2223, 888-256-2967) picks up several times daily at Best Western Hitching Post Inn and Holiday Inn ($28 one way). All bus lines use the depot at 222 E Deming Drive (US 85 at I-80 exit 362), which has daily departures to Billings, Montana (some via Bighorn Basin); Denver; Chicago; and San Francisco.

On weekdays, the Cheyenne Transit Program (CTP; ☎ 307-637-6253) operates seven local weekday bus routes.

WEST OF CHEYENNE

Happy Jack Rd (Hwy 210) leads west from Cheyenne, past scenic camping at Curt Gowdy State Park ($9), toward Vedawoo Glen. It continues into the Medicine Bow National Forest and on to Laramie. This lovely rural area has guest ranches, including the luxurious 120-acre *A Drummond's Ranch* (☎ 307-634-6042, W *www.cruising-america .com/drummond, 399 Happy Jack Rd*) and *Bit-O-WYO Ranch B&B* (☎ 307-638-8340, W *www.bitowyo.com, 470 Happy Jack Rd*).

LARAMIE

Home to Wyoming's only four-year university, Laramie is the state's cultural capital, with an abundance of museums, a thriving historic downtown and a vibrant student atmosphere. Unfortunately, in 1998 the town was often in the press after Matthew Shepard, a gay student, was beaten to death here.

The Laramie Area Chamber of Commerce (☎ 307-745-7339, 800-445-5303, 800 S 3rd St) is open weekdays. The USFS Medicine Bow–Routt National Forest & Thunder Basin National Grassland Headquarters (☎ 307-745-2300, 2468 Jackson St) are at the Hwy 230/130 junction. Dial ☎ 307-721-7345 for the Laramie Area Events Hot Line.

Spend an afternoon wandering Laramie's 1860s-era **historic district**, one of Wyoming's most interesting. Other attractions include the stately campus and myriad museums of the **University of Wyoming** (UW; ☎ 307-766-4075, W *www.uwyo.edu*) and the **Wyoming Territorial Prison & Old West Park** (☎ 307-745-6161, 800-845-2287, 975 Snowy Range Rd), at I-80 exit 311, a curious restoration of an early prison and frontier town with a theme-park feel ($5; open mid-May to Sept).

Reservations are recommended (and rates are much higher) for UW graduation (mid-May), Fourth of July, Cheyenne Frontier Days (last full week in July) and fall UW football weekends.

The best camping options are *USFS sites* ($10) in the Pole Mountain area, 10 miles east of town. *Laramie KOA* (☎ 307-742-6553, 800-562-4153, 1271 W Baker St), I-80 exit 310, charges $15 for tent sites, $22 for full hookups and $30 for klapboard kabins.

Last-ditch *Riverside Campground* (☎ 307-721-7405), on Curtis St east of I-80 exit 310, begs $9 for bleak tent sites.

Numerous places are off I-80 exit 313. The best deal is *Motel 6* (☎ 307-742-2307, 621 Plaza Lane), at $38/45 for singles/doubles. *Motel 8* (☎ 307-745-4856, 888-745-4800, 501 Boswell Dr*) has comfortable singles/doubles ($42/50), while the attractive *Sunset Inn* (☎ 307-742-3741, 800-308-3744, 1104 S 3rd St*) has a pool and hot tub ($50/56).

Laramie has some of Wyoming's better restaurants, including the tasty (entrées under $10) *Jeffrey's Bistro* (123 Ivinson Ave) and *Café Jacques* (216 E Grand Ave). *Old Buckhorn Bar* (114 Ivinson St) is a favorite with rowdy university students, while *Cowboy Saloon* (108 S 2nd St) attracts country & western diehards and agile line dancers.

Laramie Regional Airport, 4 miles west of town via I-80 exit 311, has daily flights to Denver. The Armadillo Express DIA Shuttle (☎ 307-632-2223, 888-256-2967) stops on the UW campus and at Holiday Inn (2313 Soldier Springs Rd), I-80 exit 311 ($52 one way). Greyhound (☎ 307-742-5188) and Powder River (☎ 800-442-3682) buses stop at the Tumbleweed Express gas station (4700 Bluebird Lane) at the east end of town (I-80 exit 316).

MEDICINE BOW MOUNTAINS & SNOWY RANGE

The Snowy Range's 11,000-foot summits cap the rugged Medicine Bow Mountains west of Laramie. Southwest are the Sierra Madre and the Continental Divide. The Medicine Bow National Forest extends across both mountain ranges. Between them is the North Platte River Valley, where the upscale hot-springs resort of **Saratoga** (population 1800) is the main settlement. The low-key twin towns of **Riverside** and **Encampment** are the gateways to the Sierra Madre along the Continental Divide.

The 79-mile **Snowy Range Scenic Byway** (Hwy 130) traverses Snowy Range Pass (10,847 feet; typically plowed Memorial Day to mid-Oct) between Centennial and Saratoga, providing easy access to lovely scenic overlooks, trails, winter sports, fishing areas and campgrounds. Maps and information are available at the year-round

Centennial Visitor Center (☎ 307-745-7339), a mile west of Centennial on Hwy 130, and the summer-only Brush Creek Information Center (☎ 307-326-5562), 20 miles east of Saratoga on Hwy 130.

SUNDANCE

Rumped up against the Black Hills of remote northeastern Wyoming, Sundance (population 1275) is known for its rich history, ranching tradition and natural beauty. Founded in 1879, the town is most famous for giving Butch Cassidy's companion Harry Longabaugh his nickname, the Sundance Kid. Sundance's pleasant atmosphere and convenient location along I-90 make it the perfect base for exploring Devils Tower National Monument, the Bearlodge Mountains and the Black Hills of South Dakota.

The Sundance Area Chamber of Commerce (☎ 307-283-1000) runs a summer-only tourist information kiosk at the I-90 exit 189 rest area.

The year-round *Mountain View Campground* (☎ 307-283-2270, 800-792-8439), Government Valley Rd a mile east of town, has little shade but is well maintained, with a pool and laundry (tents/RVs $13/18). *Deane's Pine View Motel* (☎ 307-283-2262, 117 N 8th St) has basic rooms ($45) and rooms with kitchenettes ($55).

Powder River Coach USA buses run daily between Gillette and Rapid City, South Dakota, and stop at Sundance's Bear Lodge Motel (218 Cleveland Ave).

BEARLODGE MOUNTAINS & BLACK HILLS

The Bearlodge Mountains north of Sundance are bounded by US 14, I-09, and Hwys 24 and 11. Blanketed by ponderosa pine, aspen and oak forests, the Black Hills extend from South Dakota into northeastern Wyoming. The USFS Black Hills National Forest Bear Lodge Ranger District (☎ 307-283-1361), 1 mile east of town on US 14 E, has information on outdoor activities.

Notable spots include **Warren Peak Lookout**, with views of four states, Devils Tower (see below) and the Bighorn Mountains; and the picturesque **Cook Lake Recreation Area**, with its abundant wildlife and limestone bluffs. Ask the USFS about the northern Black Hills' **ghost towns**.

USFS campgrounds are located near Sundance, en route to Warren Peak Lookout, Cook Lake and along Hwy 24 between the towns of Alva and Aladdin.

DEVILS TOWER NATIONAL MONUMENT

'The heart of everything that is,' is how Lakota leader Arvol Looking Horse once described Devils Tower National Monument, a 60-million-year-old volcanic mass that retains strong cultural and religious significance today for 23 Native American tribes. Rising dramatically above the Belle Fourche Valley, it gained national fame in 1977 when it starred as the point of alien contact in Steven Spielberg's *Close Encounters of the Third Kind*. The national monument, which covers only about 2 sq miles, offers hiking, wildlife viewing, bird-watching, picnicking and camping. It's a mandatory stop for those traveling between the Black Hills and western Wyoming's national parks.

The visitor center (☎ 307-467-5283, W www.nps.gov/deto), 3 miles beyond the entrance station ($8), is open mid-spring to fall. The National Park Service's *Belle Fourche Campground* is open April to October; sites ($12) fill up early. Camping is also available in the Bearlodge Mountains, Black Hills and in Sundance (see above). The nearest motels are in Hulett, Sundance and Moorcroft.

BUFFALO

At the eastern foot of the Bighorn Mountains, the town of Buffalo (population 3750) literally bears the brand of Wyoming's ranching heartland – ranchers' marks cover the benches in the pleasant riverside park over Clear Creek, in downtown's **historic district**. Check out the haphazard collection of Indian artifacts and Bozeman Trail memorabilia at the **Jim Gatchell Memorial Museum** (100 Fort St), where admission is $2. A scenic loop drive northwest of Buffalo through the **Bud Love Winter Range** is recommended for late-afternoon roadside wildlife viewing.

The Buffalo Chamber of Commerce visitor center (☎ 307-684-5544, 800-227-5122, 55 N Main St) is open daily. The USFS Bighorn National Forest Buffalo Ranger District and the Buffalo Area BLM are at 1425 Fort St (US 16 W).

Shady tent/RV sites ($16/21) at *Indian Campground* (☎ 307-684-9601, 660 E Hart St) are well maintained. Most motels are on E Hart St (US 16) and Fort St (US 16 W). *Mountain View Motel* (☎ 307-684-2881, 585 Fort St) has rustic cabins ($40-75). Rates may be a bit cheaper at the friendly *Z-Bar Motel* (☎ 307-684-5535, 888-313-1227, 626 Fort St).

Powder River Coach USA buses stop at Just Gone Fishing (777 Fort St), at Spruce.

SHERIDAN

At the eastern foot of the Bighorn Mountains in the Big Goose Valley, Sheridan (population 15,000) has one of Wyoming's more interesting **historic districts**, which includes the 1893 Sheridan Inn, occasional home to Buffalo Bill Cody.

The Wyoming Information Center (☎ 307-672-2485, 800-453-3650) on Valley View Drive (Hwy 336 at I-90 exit 23) is open daily. The USFS Bighorn National Forest Headquarters office (☎ 307-672-0751) is at 1969 S Sheridan Ave.

Sheridan/Big Horn Mountains KOA (☎ 307-674-8766, 800-562-7621, 63 Decker Rd), I-90 exit 20, is north of town (tents/RVs $16/20; open May-Oct). The closest public camping is in the Bighorn National Forest. Most motels are along Main St north of 5th St, and along Coffeen Ave. *Guest House Motel* (☎ 307-674-7496, 800-226-9405, 2007 N Main St) is the best budget choice.

Buffalo Jumps

Buffalo jumps, or *pishkun*, were used by many Indian tribes as mass hunting tools. In the fall, when bison cows were fat, tribes journeyed to their pishkun site, where they camped and performed sacred dances and rituals to ensure a successful task. The site had to be a flat, wide expanse with a long, sheer cliff of at least 30 feet on one side.

Runners, chosen for their speed and agility, purified themselves in the sweat lodge to rid themselves of human odor, then put on buffalo, antelope or wolf skins. In disguise they coaxed a bison herd into a roundup area that led to a drive lane marked by large decorated cairns called 'dead men.' The head runner, dressed in a full buffalo robe with head and horns still attached (imagine the weight of this!), would then catch the attention of the lead bison and begin to run towards the cliff. The trick was to run at a pace fast enough that the bison had too much momentum when they reached the cliff's edge, but slow enough that they wouldn't get spooked and escape the herd.

Other people hiding behind the dead men kept the bison within the drive lanes – by spooking or swatting them – and when the herd reached the cliff the head runner jumped out of the way, usually into a hole that had been dug by the cliff's edge. The bison that survived the fall were killed by hunters waiting near the bottom of the fall.

Casual yet sophisticated **Ciao Bistro** (☎ 307-672-2838, 120 N Main St) is one of Wyoming's best restaurants outside Jackson Hole. Lunch is first-come, first-served, although waiting is not unusual; dinner reservations are recommended.

For rental cars, try Enterprise (☎ 307-672-6910), near the Sheridan County Airport. The airport, at the south end of town via Big Horn Ave (Hwy 332), has daily flights to Denver. Northbound and southbound Powder River Coach USA buses stop twice daily at the Evergreen Inn (580 E 5th St).

BIGHORN MOUNTAINS

The Bighorn Mountains are a jewel that should not be missed by those traveling to or from Yellowstone and Grand Teton National Parks. This dramatic range is home to large meadows of grass and wildflowers, conifer forests and wildlife such as bighorn sheep, elk and black bears.

Three scenic east-west roads cross the Bighorns. US 16 (Cloud Peak Skyway), between Buffalo and Worland via Powder River Pass (9666 feet), skirts the pristine **Cloud Peak Wilderness Area**. US 14 (Bighorn Scenic Byway) runs between Ranchester and Greybull via Granite Pass (8950 feet), and US 14 Alternate (Medicine Wheel Passage) connects Burgess Junction and Lovell via Baldy Pass (9430 feet). The latter passes **Medicine Wheel National Historic Landmark**, on the western slope of Medicine Mountain (10,000 feet). Dating from AD 1200 to 1700, this sacred site is a mystery; it may represent a likeness of the Sun Dance Lodge of Crow legend or might have been used for astronomy.

Along these roads are numerous trailheads, picnic areas and scenic overlooks, and dozens of inviting USFS and BLM campgrounds. Detailed information is available from the USFS offices in Buffalo, Sheridan, Greybull and Worland. A few private lodges offer basic accommodations, campsites and services.

CODY

Cody's brash Wild West bluster contrasts with the Bighorn Basin's sleepy agricultural towns. A popular Yellowstone stopover, it rivals Jackson as Wyoming's premier tourist town, at least during summer. Original storefronts give Cody (population 7900) a veneer of authenticity, but its tourist pitch is still palpable. The visitor center (☎ 307-587-2777, 836 Sheridan Ave) is open daily. The USFS Shoshone National Forest Wapiti Ranger District (☎ 307-527-6921) is at 203A Yellowstone Ave.

Cody's major tourist attraction is the **Buffalo Bill Historical Center** (☎ 307-587-4771, Ⓦ www.bbhc.org, 720 Sheridan Ave). Its four museums are homage to the male Anglo-Saxon Western myths that have been molded into the enduring image of the region ($10). Also popular is the **Cody Nite Rodeo** (☎ 307-587-5155), which takes place nightly June to August ($12) at Stampede Park (421 W Yellowstone Ave).

Try Cody Area Central Reservations (☎ 888-468-6996) for accommodation bookings. Prices in Powell (24 miles northeast) are slightly lower for similar accommodations. The closest public campgrounds are 6 miles west of town off US 14/16/20 at Buffalo Bill Park and farther along toward Yellowstone in the Wapiti Valley.

Gateway Campground (☎ 307-587-2561, 203 Yellowstone Ave) has shady tent sites ($12). Friendly **Uptown Motel** (☎ 307-587-4245, 1562 Sheridan Ave) starts under $50. Downtown, historic **Pawnee Hotel** (☎ 307-587-2239, 1032 12th St) has a nice garden ($32/36 singles/doubles).

Maxwell's Fine Food & Spirits (☎ 307-527-7749, 937 Sheridan Ave) has a nice selection of salads, sandwiches and bistro dinners. Their adjacent bakery serves good espresso.

SkyWest/Delta flies daily to Salt Lake City from Yellowstone Regional Airport (☎ 307-587-5096), 1 mile east of Cody at the US 14/16/20 and Hwy 120 junction. Powder River Coach USA buses stop at Daylight Donuts (1452 Sheridan Ave) en route to Casper and Billings, Montana.

LANDER & AROUND

At the foot of the Wind River Range, genial Lander (population 7500) is a base for many outdoor activities. According to an enthusiastic native, the best thing about Lander is 'you can grab a bucket o' chicken downtown, head for the hills and have a picnic in the wilderness while it's still warm.' The presence of the National Outdoor Leadership School

(NOLS; W www.nols.edu) lends a college-town atmosphere.

The rugged areas around Lander are popular for **rock climbing** and **mountain biking**. Wild Iris Mountain Sports (☎ 307-332-4541, 888-284-5968, 333 Main St) is the climbers' mecca, while cyclists and powder hounds hang out at Freewheel Ski & Cycle (☎ 307-332-6616, 800-490-6616 in Wyoming, 378 W Main St).

The Lander Area Chamber of Commerce (☎ 307-332-3892, 800-433-0662, 160 N First St) is open weekdays. The USFS Shoshone National Forest Washakie District Ranger Station (☎ 307-332-5460, 333 Hwy 789 S) has useful information on the **Popo Agie** (pronounced pah-poh-sha) **Wilderness Area** and the other nearby backcountry destinations. Wind River Transportation Authority (WRTA; ☎ 307-856-7118) provides scheduled weekday service between Lander, Riverton, Dubois, Rock Springs and Riverton Regional Airport ($13).

National Geographic Traveler once named **Sinks Canyon State Park** one of the USA's top 50 state parks. The Middle Fork of the Popo Agie River flows through the narrow canyon, disappearing into the soluble Madison limestone called 'the Sinks,' and pops up faster and warmer a quarter-mile downstream in a trout-filled pool called the 'Rise.'

The park's summer-only visitor center (☎ 307-332-3077) is near two campgrounds ($9). The park entrance is 6 miles south of Lander on Sinks Canyon Rd (Hwy 131), also known as 'the Loop.' Follow this road into the national forest for epic rock climbing, mountain biking, hiking and fishing spots.

Camping is free (three-night maximum) at *Lander City Park* (☎ 307-332-4647, 405 Fremont St), off 3rd St, but count on meeting rowdy teenagers. *Holiday Lodge* (☎ 307-332-2511, 800-624-1974, 210 McFarlane Dr), with riverfront tent sites ($5 per person), hot-tub use and showers ($3 for nonguests), is the best in-town tenting option. The closest public campsites are at Sinks Canyon State Park.

Most Main St motels offer kitchenettes and family rooms for a few bucks extra. *Western Motel* (☎ 307-332-4270, 151 N 9th St), at $28/30 for singles/doubles, and *Maverick Motel* (☎ 307-332-2300, 877-622-2300, 808 Main St), at $35/50, are the best bets.

Grains of Lander grocery (☎ 307-332-5966, 388 Main St) has a good health food selection. *The Magpie* (☎ 307-332-5565, 159 N Second St) is the best spot for pastries, espresso or a light lunch. *Gannett Grill* (☎ 307-332-8228, 126 Main St), next to the Lander Bar, sustains the outdoor crowd with good pub grub.

YELLOWSTONE NATIONAL PARK

The country's first national park, Yellowstone was established to preserve its spectacular and unique geography: the geothermal phenomena, the vivid Grand Canyon of the Yellowstone, the fossil forests and Yellowstone Lake. In addition to housing half the world's geysers, Yellowstone is also home to the largest concentration of wildlife in the lower mainland USA. Its abundant alpine lakes, rivers and waterfalls are world-renowned. In 1912 *National Geographic* published its first article about Yellowstone, recommending visitors allow 5½ days to visit the park. The same holds true today, although it is easy to spend more time. This cornucopia of natural features attracts up to 30,000 visitors daily and more than 3 million each year, though the park's extreme popularity is the single greatest threat to its environment. It's still possible to escape the hordes, but only if you're willing to hike.

History

In 1807, when John Colter was the first white man to visit the area, the only inhabitants were Tukudikas, a Shoshone-Bannock people who hunted bighorn sheep. Other tribes occasionally passed through Yellowstone country even after its declaration as a national park, including the Nez Percé, who in 1877 kidnapped several tourists on their way north to evade the US Army; they were eventually captured in Montana.

Fur trappers and miners came after Colter but never gained a firm foothold. Colter's reports of Yellowstone's soaring geysers and boiling mud holes, at first dismissed as tall tales, brought increased scientific interest and led to several expeditions. Spurred by lobbying, the US Congress designated Yellowstone a national park in 1872.

The US Cavalry managed the area from 1886 until the creation of the National Park Service (NPS) in 1918. With the transfer of

YELLOWSTONE & GRAND TETON NATIONAL PARKS

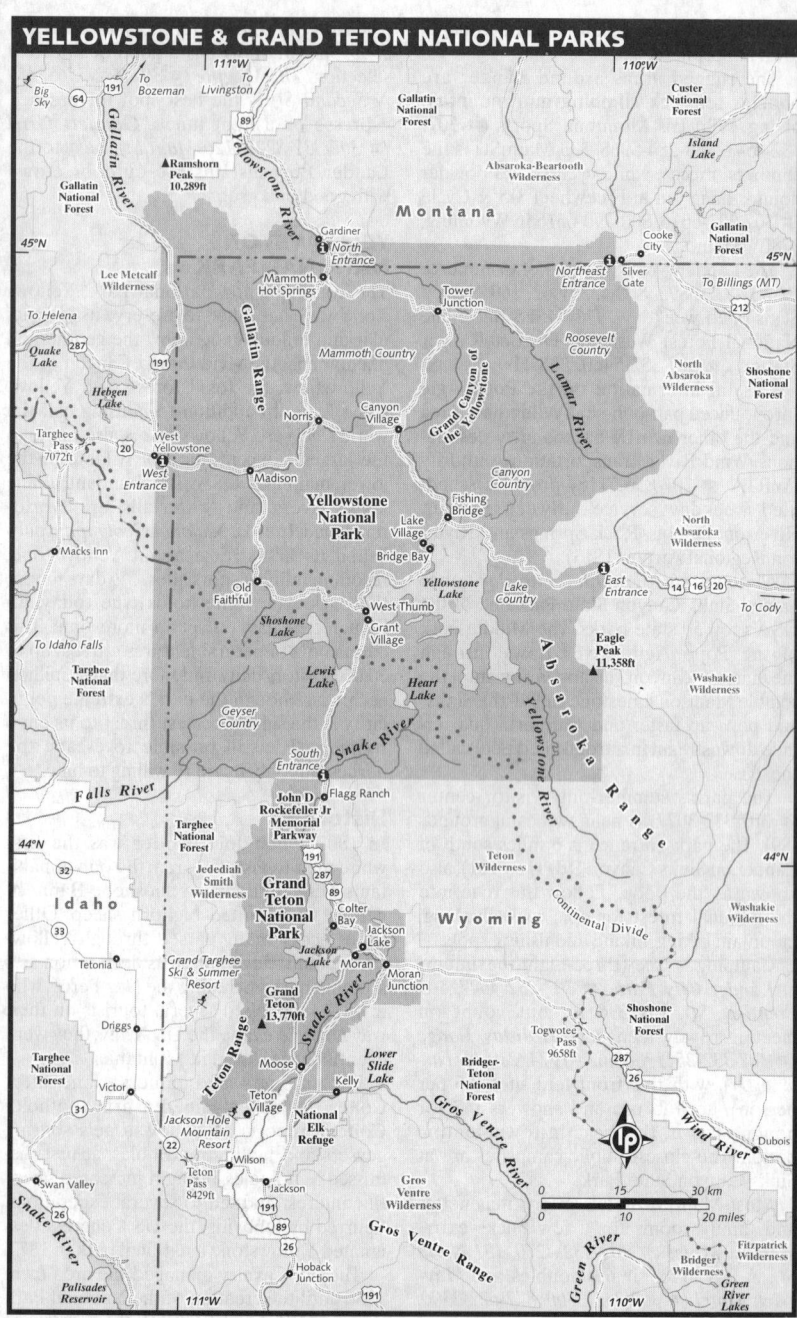

power came policies such as predator eradication, forest-fire suppression and tourist development – all still subjects of debate.

Orientation

Five distinct regions comprise the 3472-sq-mile park. Starting clockwise from the north, they include Mammoth Country, Roosevelt Country, Canyon Country, Lake Country and Geyser Country.

Of the park's five entrance stations, only the historic arched North Entrance, near Gardiner, Montana, is open year round. The others, typically open May to October, are the Northeast Entrance (Cooke City, Montana), the East Entrance (Cody), the South Entrance (north of Grand Teton National Park) and the West Entrance (West Yellowstone, Montana). The 142-mile Grand Loop Rd scenic drive is the park's main road.

Information

Contact the National Park Service, Visitor Services Office, Box 168, Yellowstone National Park, WY 82190 (W www.nps.gov/yell) for a park information packet. The park headquarters (☎ 307-344-7381), at Fort Yellowstone, Mammoth Hot Springs, is open 9am-6pm daily. AmFac Parks & Resorts (☎ 307-344-7311, W www.travelyellowstone .com, Box 165, Yellowstone National Park, WY 82190-0165), is the park's activities, camping and accommodations concessionaire.

The park is open year round, although some roads and entrances close during winter. Park entrance permits ($20 per vehicle or $10 per hiker/cyclist) are valid for seven days for entry into both Yellowstone and Grand Teton National Parks.

A series of summer-only visitor centers are evenly spaced every 20 to 30 miles along Grand Loop Rd. Albright Visitor Center is open year round. Old Faithful Visitor Center is open April to October and December to March. Dial ☎ 307-344-2114 for current road and weather conditions.

Things to See & Do

Known for its fossil forests and geothermal areas at Mammoth Hot Springs and Norris Geyser Basin, **Mammoth Country** is North America's most volatile and oldest known continuously active (115,000 years) geothermal area. The peaks of the Gallatin Range rise to the northwest, towering above the lakes, creeks and the area's numerous hiking trails.

Fossil forests, the commanding Lamar River Valley and its tributary trout streams, Tower Falls and the Absaroka Mountains' craggy peaks are the highlights of **Roosevelt Country**, the park's most remote, scenic and undeveloped region. Several good hikes begin near the Tower-Roosevelt Junction.

A series of scenic overlooks and a network of Grand Canyon of the Yellowstone rim trails highlight the beauty of **Canyon Country**. South Rim Dr leads to the canyon's most spectacular overlook, at Artist Point. Mud Volcano is Canyon Country's primary geothermal area. Notable trails include the Seven Mile Hole Trail, which descends from the north rim into the canyon and tracks up Mt Washburn, the park's highest peak (10,243 feet).

Yellowstone Lake, the centerpiece of **Lake Country** and one of the world's largest alpine lakes, is also' home to the country's largest inland population of cutthroat trout. The often snowcapped Absaroka Mountains rise dramatically east and southeast of the lake. Lake Village's 1890 **Lake Yellowstone Hotel** is on the National Register of Historic Places.

Geyser Country has the most geothermal features in the park. Upper Geyser Basin contains 180 of the park's 200 to 250 geysers. The most famous is Old Faithful, which spews over 8000 gallons of water 100 to 180 feet into the air every 79 minutes or so. The Firehole and Madison Rivers offer superb fishing and wildlife viewing.

Hikers can explore Yellowstone's backcountry from over 85 trailheads that give access to 1200 miles of **hiking** trails. A free backcountry use permit, available at visitor centers and ranger stations, is required for overnight trips. Backcountry camping is allowed in 300 designated sites, 60% of which can be reserved in advance by mail; a $15 fee applies regardless of the number of nights.

Bicycling is best April to October, when the park's roads are usually snow-free. Cyclists are permitted to ride on public roads and a few designated service roads, but are banned from backcounty trails.

Most park trails are not groomed, but unplowed roads and trails are open for

cross-country skiing. A backcountry use permit is required for overnight trips.

Places to Stay & Eat

National Park Service and private campgrounds, cabins, lodges and hotels are in the park. During summer, high demand for all types of accommodations makes it difficult to bed down without a reservation. Contact park concessionaire AmFac (☎ 307-344-7311) to reserve a spot at its campsites, cabins or lodges.

AmFac operates the five campgrounds that accept reservations: **Bridge Bay Campground** in Lake Country, with 429 sites ($15/23 tents/RVs); **Canyon Campground** in Canyon Country, with 271 sites ($15/23); **Fishing Bridge RV Park** in Lake Country with 341 sites for hard-shell RVs only ($25); **Grant Village Campground** in Lake Country, with 425 sites ($15/23); and **Madison Campground** in Geyser Country, with 280 sites ($15/23).

Seven other campgrounds, in Mammoth, Roosevelt and Geyser Countries, are operated by the National Park Service on a first-come, first-served basis (tent sites $10-12, RVs $23).

Most hotels and cabins operated by AmFac are open May to October:

Canyon Lodge & Cabins – in Canyon Country ($54-106)

Old Faithful Inn – in Geyser Country ($85-329)

Old Faithful Lodge Cabins – in Geyser Country ($35)

Old Faithful Snow Lodge & Cabins – in Geyser Country ($75-125)

Grant Village – in Lake Country ($90-120)

Lake Lodge Cabins – in Lake Country ($50-106)

Lake Yellowstone Hotel & Cabins – in Lake Country ($83-155)

Mammoth Hot Springs Hotel & Cabins – in Mammoth Country ($50-83)

Roosevelt Lodge Cabins – in Roosevelt Country ($43-83)

The rustic Lake Lodge is the most peaceful, while Roosevelt Lodge offers the most authentic Western experience. Lake Yellowstone Hotel is a grand reminder of a bygone era, but its cabins are, like most others in the park, tiny boxes scattered in a shadeless area near ye olde parking lot. Other top-end park properties include Mammoth Hot Springs Hotel and Old Faithful Inn. Other accommodations, notably Grant Village, are more generic and modern.

There are plenty of accommodations in the gateway towns of Gardiner and West Yellowstone that offer visitors little more than a place to grab a meal and catch some shut-eye. Motels are nearly identical, the only variations being location and amenities. For more information, contact the chamber of commerce in West Yellowstone (☎ 406-646-7701) or Gardiner (☎ 406-848-7971).

In West Yellowstone, historic **Madison Motel** (☎ 406-646-7745, 800-838-7745, 139 Yellowstone Ave), open May to October, has dorm beds ($15) and rooms without/with private bath (from $30/35). A real gem, **Sleepy Hollow Lodge** (☎ 406-646-7707, 124 Electric St) has small log cabins with kitchens ($65).

In Gardiner, try the remodeled **Town Motel** (☎ 406-848-7322), on Park St between 1st and 2nd Sts ($52/60 singles/doubles), or **Hillcrest Cottages** (☎ 406-848-7353), at 4th and Scotts Sts, which has cottages with kitchenettes from $60.

There are snack bars, delis and grocery stores scattered around the park. At Canyon Lodge, Lake Lodge, Old Faithful Lodge, Grant Village Lake House Restaurant, Mammoth Hot Springs Hotel and Roosevelt Lodge Dining Room, which requires reservations, lunch is reasonably priced but can be crowded. Dinners are more expensive and require reservations (☎ 307-344-7901 for any of the restaurants).

Getting There & Away

Year-round airports near the park are in Cody (52 miles); Jackson (56 miles); Bozeman, Montana (65 miles); and Idaho Falls, Idaho (107 miles). The airport in West Yellowstone, Montana, is usually open June to September. It's usually more affordable to fly into Salt Lake City, Utah (390 miles), or Denver, Colorado (563 miles) and rent a car.

No public transport exists to or within Yellowstone National Park. During the summer, commercial buses operate from Jackson and Cody. Buses operate to West Yellowstone and Gardiner from Bozeman year round.

GRAND TETON NATIONAL PARK

South of Yellowstone, the Teton Range's jagged granite spires are the centerpiece of spectacular Grand Teton National Park. Twelve glacier-carved summits rise above 12,000 feet, crowned by the singular Grand Teton (13,770 feet). This 40-mile-long range towers above Jackson Hole, where lakes and streams, including the nascent Snake River, mirror the soaring peaks.

Orientation & Information

The park has two entrance stations: Moose (south), on Teton Park Rd west of Moose Junction; and Moran (east), on US 89/191/287 north of Moran Junction.

Grand Teton National Park headquarters (☎ 307-739-3600, W www.nps.gov/grte, Box 170, Moose, WY 83012) shares the building with the year-round Moose Visitor Center (☎ 307-739-3399, 307-739-3309 for back-country permits), on Teton Park Rd, half a mile west of Moose Junction. There are also summer-only visitor centers at Jenny Lake and Colter Bay.

Three concessionaires operate accommodations, restaurants and activities: *Dornan's* (☎ 307-733-2522, W www.dornans.com), *Grand Teton Lodge Company* (☎ 307-543-3100, 800-628-9988, W www.gtlc.com) and *Signal Mountain Lodge* (☎ 307-543-2831, W www.signalmtnlodge.com).

The park is open year round, although some roads and entrances close during winter. Fees are the same as for Yellowstone Park (see above), and the seven-day pass is valid for both parks.

Things to See & Do

Some interesting **historic buildings** can be found at Menor's Ferry, half a mile north of Moose Village, and along Mormon Row, east of Blacktail Butte.

The 5-mile **Signal Mountain Summit Rd**, east of Teton Park Rd, goes to Signal Mountain's summit. Another nice route is the **Jenny Lake Scenic Loop Rd**, which abuts Grand Teton.

The park has 200 miles of **hiking trails**. Pick up the 'Day Hikes' or 'Backcountry Camping' brochures. A free backcountry use permit, available at visitor centers, is required for overnight trips. Backcountry reservations can be made by mail January to May; write the park headquarters (see

Orientation & Information, earlier). The north-south **Teton Crest Trail**, which runs just west of the main summits, can be accessed from trailheads that wind up steep canyons.

The Tetons offer great **rock climbing**. Excellent short routes abound, as well as classic longer summits like Grand Teton, Mt Moran and Mt Owen. The Jenny Lake Ranger Station (☎ 307-739-3343), open daily in summer, is ground zero for climbing information. The American Alpine Club's *Climbers Ranch* (☎ 307-733-7271), on Teton Park Rd, operates a summer dormitory for climbers. For instruction and guided climbs, contact Exum Mountain Guides (☎ 307-733-2297, W www.exumguides.com) or Jackson Hole Mountain Guides (☎ 307-733-4979, 800-239-7642, W www.jhmg.com).

Adventure Sports (☎ 307-733-3307), at Dornan's Market in Moose Village, has maps, rents bikes and can suggest **road-** and **mountain-biking** routes.

Fishing is also good, with abundant whitefish and cutthroat, lake and brown trout in park rivers and lakes. Get a license at the Moose Village store, Signal Mountain Lodge or Colter Bay Marina.

Places to Stay & Eat

The park features NPS campgrounds and private cabins, lodges and motels. Most campgrounds and accommodations are open May to October, weather depending.

The NPS (☎ 307-739-3603 for recorded info) operates the park's only five campgrounds on a first-come, first-served basis: *Colter Bay Campground* near Jackson Lake Junction, with 310 sites ($12/27 tents/RVs); *Gros Ventre Campground* near Gros Ventre Junction, with 360 sites, 100 tent-only ($12); *Jenny Lake Campground* near Moose Junction, with 49 tent-only sites ($12); *Lizard Creek Campground* near Colter Bay Junction, with 60 sites ($12); and *Signal Mountain Campground* near Jackson Lake Junction, with 86 sites ($12).

Demand for campsites is high early July to Labor Day. Most campgrounds fill by 11am (Jenny Lake fills much earlier; Gros Ventre fills last). Colter Bay and Jenny Lake have tent-only sites reserved for backpackers and cyclists.

Grand Teton Lodge Company runs *Colter Bay Village* (canvas tents $35, cabins

$32-125), *Jackson Lake Lodge* (motel rooms $115-200, cottages $135-200) and exclusive *Jenny Lake Lodge* (all-inclusive packages $325-400). *Signal Mountain Lodge* offers cabins ($80-100), motel rooms ($100-155) and bungalows (from $175). In Moose, there's Dornan's *Spur Ranch Log Cabins* ($140-170, $35-60 less in winter). Contact the appropriate concessionaire (see Orientation & Information, earlier) for reservations.

There are several reasonably priced restaurants in and around Colter Bay Village, Jackson Lake Lodge and Moose Village. Jackson Lake Lodge's *Mural Room* features 'Rocky Mountain cuisine' and is considerably more upscale, as is *Jenny Lake Lodge Dining Room*; both require dinner reservations and expect men to wear jackets.

JACKSON HOLE

Recreation drives Jackson Hole's popularity, and it's Wyoming's most expensive destination. Though downhill skiing dominates, summer visitors can hike, bike, raft and faux-cowboy. Moose, elk and bison roam the valley floor, set against the backdrop of the snowcapped Tetons.

Jackson (population 6000) is disparaged by die-hard Wyomingites as a tourist enclave where jet-set celebrities frequent fancy restaurants, rapacious realtors push overpriced timeshares and fatuous shoppers swarm kitschy boutiques. However, the town also supports a vigorous cultural life and is the hub of a truly world-class ski resort.

The helpful visitor center (☎ 307-733-3316, W www.jacksonholechamber.com, 532 N Cache Dr) is open daily. The USFS Bridger-Teton National Forest Headquarters (☎ 307-739-5500) is at 340 N Cache Dr. Valley Bookstore (☎ 307-733-4533, 800-647-4111), in Gaslight Alley at the corner of N Cache Drive and Deloney Ave, has a superb selection of Western and general-interest books.

Things to See & Do

Jackson's downtown has a handful of **historic buildings** worth a look, and a silly reenactment of a **Town Square shoot-out** occurs nightly in summer. More worthwhile is a visit to the **National Elk Refuge** (☎ 307-733-9212), northeast of Jackson via Elk Refuge Rd, which offers winter sleigh rides, or the **National Museum of Wildlife Art** (☎ 307-733-5771, 2820 Rungius Rd), 3 miles north of town ($6).

From the 6311-foot base at Teton Village to the summit of Rendezvous Mountain (10,450 feet), **Jackson Hole Mountain Resort** (☎ 307-733-2292, 888-333-7766, www.jacksonhole.com) boasts the USA's greatest continuous vertical rise and is one of the country's top ski destinations, with mostly advanced terrain (full-day lift tickets $54). The year-round resort is 12 miles northwest of Jackson, offering hiking, aerial tram rides ($16), mountain biking and horseback riding.

Right in town, the year-round 400-acre **Snow King Resort** (☎ 307-733-5200, 800-522-5464, W www.snowking.com) offers skiing, ice-skating, horseback riding and mountain biking (lift tickets $30/20 adults/kids, summer scenic rides $7/5).

Places to Stay

Reservations are essential in summer and winter. Cheap weekly rates are available October 1 until the first big snowfall, and after the snow melts to Memorial Day. Jackson Hole Central Reservations (☎ 800-443-6931) is the one-stop shop for top-end lodgings.

Cramped *Wagon Wheel Campground* (☎ 307-733-4588, 435 N Cache Drive) attracts climbers and backpackers (tents/RVs $11/27). The closest USFS campground is *Curtis Canyon*, just east of the Elk Refuge off USFS Rd 30440. *The Bunkhouse* (☎ 307-733-3668, 215 N Cache Dr) has basement hostel beds ($18), nonguest showers ($5) and a kitchen.

The best budget bet is friendly *Teton Inn* (☎ 307-733-3883, 800-851-0070, 165 W Gill Ave), from $40. Other affordable options include sprawling *Virginian Lodge* (☎ 307-733-2792, 800-262-4999, 750 W Broadway), from $45, and hospitable *Sundance Inn* (☎ 307-733-3444, 888-478-6326, W www.sundanceinnjackson.com, 135 W Broadway), with a hot tub, thoughtful free breakfast and afternoon snacks (from $50).

Teton Village's only budget option is *Hostel X* (☎ 307-733-3415, W www.hostelx.com), with basic double-occupancy rooms with private bath from $45 in summer and $50 in winter (five-night minimum, book ahead).

Places to Eat & Drink

Jackson is home to Wyoming's most sophisticated grub. Budget-conscious self-caterers should shop **Food Town** (cheapest) or **Albertsons**, both at the west end of town off Broadway; or health-conscious **Harvest Natural Foods** (130 W Broadway).

Jedediah's (135 E Broadway) is popular for cheap breakfasts and also serves lunch and dinner (summer only). BYOB **Bubba's Bar-B-Que** (515 W Broadway) has meaty ribs and a decent salad bar. Upscale **Snake River Grill** (84 E Broadway) comes highly recommended for gourmet dining. Where's the beef? **Gun Barrel Steakhouse** (862 W Broadway), pardner.

Jackson's nightlife landmark is the touristy **Million Dollar Cowboy Bar** (25 N Cache Dr). **The Rancher** (20 E Broadway) is a local happy-hour favorite pool hall. The beer's better than the grub at **Snake River Brewing Co** (265 S Millward St). Wilson's **Stagecoach Bar** (5755 W Hwy 22) is worth the 5-mile drive: Every Sunday the famous (and aging) Stagecoach Band recites country & western favorites until 10pm. Herb tokers and cowpokers mingle here more than any other place in the wild West.

Getting There & Around

Jackson Hole Airport is 7 miles north of Jackson off US 26/89/191 within Grand Teton National Park. Daily flights serve Denver and Salt Lake City, while weekend flights connect Jackson with Chicago. Jackson Hole Express (☎ 307-733-1719, 800-652-9510) buses shuttle daily between Salt Lake City and Jackson, via Idaho Falls ($47 one way; 5½ hours). The Jackson depot is the Mini-Mart (395 W Broadway) near Burger King. Southern Teton Area Rapid Transit (Start) runs between Jackson and Teton Village.

Montana

Though its name translates to 'mountain,' Montana is known for its ever-changing 'Big Sky', which dominates any view. Artists, authors, real-estate developers, students and movie stars have found Montana increasingly attractive for its space, recreational opportunities and 'live and let live' ethic. Some Montanans welcome this influx, while others feel that their lifestyle will be threatened by outside influence.

Sparsely populated, the state offers plenty of wild territory. Even the biggest draws, Glacier National Park and Flathead Lake, offer alpine beauty and solitude for those willing to hike.

Famous trout-filled rivers flow from Yellowstone Park toward Bozeman (Montana's fastest-growing town) through several mountain ranges – Gallatin, Madison, Absaroka – that are wonderful for backcountry camping and exploration. Slightly east, the high Alpine tundra atop the Beartooth Plateau is unique in its geology and accessibility to motorists – via the highest road in the USA. There's also history to explore, from old mining towns such as Butte to the site of the Battle of the Little Bighorn, where Custer made his infamous last stand.

History

Gold was discovered near Bannack in 1863, and gold strikes continued – notably Last Chance Gulch (Helena) and Alder Gulch (Virginia City). Just as electricity began to create enormous demand for copper wire, Marcus Daly struck the world's largest and purest copper vein in Butte, which continued to be mined for the next 100 years. Montana was here to stay, and in 1889 it became the 41st state of the Union.

Montana

Nicknames: Big Sky Country, Treasure State

Population: 902,200 (46th)

Area: 147,045 sq miles (4th)

Admitted to Union: November 8, 1889 (41st)

Capital city: Helena (population 29,100)

Other cities: Billings (92,300), Missoula (58,500)

State motto: Oro y plata (Gold and silver)

Birthplace of: Gary Cooper, artist Charles Russel, the Missouri River

Famous for: big sky, fly-fishing, Custer's last stand

Information

Montana's statewide tourist board, Travel Montana (☎ 406-444-2654, 800-847-4868, W www.visitmt.com, 1424 9th Ave, PO Box 200533, Helena, MT 59620) offers free publications available throughout the state, including a state road map and the *Montana Vacation Guide*. Also free, but usually available only by contacting Travel Montana, are the *Montana Travel Planner*, which has details on accommodations and outfitters, and *Montana Winter Guide*.

For information on road conditions, call ☎ 800-226-7623 or check W www.mdt .state.mt.us.

There is no sales tax in Montana, but there is a 4% bed tax and, in some towns, a resort tax of 4% applied as a sales tax.

BOZEMAN

Bozeman's appeal is tied to the student population of Montana State University (MSU), its 'small-town' agricultural roots and its natural setting at the foot of the Bridger Mountains. Farmers and ranchers walk past boutiques and gift shops that fill the picturesque buildings along Main St. MSU's **Museum of the Rockies** (☎ 406-994-3466, S 7th Ave), at Kagy Blvd, is the largest and most entertaining natural-history museum in Montana, with dinosaur exhibits, early Native American art, a planetarium and laser shows ($9). South of town, Hyalite Canyon is great for climbing, trail running and mountain biking. North of town, the Bridger Mountains offer excellent hiking and skiing at **Bridger Bowl Ski Area** (☎ 406-587-2111) and **Bohart Ranch Cross-Country Ski Center** (☎ 406-586-9070).

Bozeman's chamber of commerce (☎ 406-586-5421, 800-228-4224) maintains a useful Web site (W www.bozemanchamber .com) and staffs a small Visitors Information Center (1001 N 7th Ave) near I-90. Barrel Mountaineering (☎ 406-582-1335, 240 E Main St) has maps, trail guides and gear rentals. Call ☎ 406-587-9784 for current trail, road and weather conditions.

Places to Stay & Eat

There are three USFS campgrounds ($11) at *Hyalite Canyon Recreation Area*, 11 to 18 miles from Bozeman on Hyalite Canyon Rd. *Bear Canyon Campground* (☎ 406-587-1575), 3 miles east of Bozeman off I-90 exit

313, has tent/RV sites ($12/17), a heated pool, laundry facilities and a store (open May 1 to Oct 31). *Bozeman Backpacker's Hostel* (☎ 406-586-4659, 405 W Olive St) is an independent hostel that serves a young, international, active clientele ($14).

The full gamut of chain motels lies north of downtown on 7th Ave, near I-90. A half-mile east of downtown, near the bus depot, *Blue Sky Motel* (☎ 406-587-2311, 800-845-9032, 1010 E Main St) has clean rooms ($58), and *Alpine Lodge* (☎ 888-922-5746, 1017 E Main St) has rooms and suites with a kitchen that sleep six for $35-68.

Community Food Co-Op (908 W Main St) has a fantastic deli, salad bar, juice bar and bakery. *Leaf & Bean* (35 W Main St) is Bozeman's primary caffeine merchant, while *La Parilla – The Grill* (1533 W Babcock) serves a variety of wraps (under $6). For dinner try chicken potpie ($7) or a grilled tuna sandwich ($6) at cozy *Cateye Café* (23 N Tracy Ave) or head to *Montana Ale Works* (611 E Main St) for food ($5-13), beer, pool and people-watching.

Getting There & Away

The ever-expanding Gallatin Airport (☎ 406-388-6632), 8 miles northwest of downtown, has flights to Salt Lake City, Portland and Seattle. The bus depot (☎ 406-587-3110, 1205 E Main St) is half a mile from downtown. Greyhound and Rimrock Trailways service all Montana towns along I-90. Karst Stages (☎ 406-388-9923, 800-287-4759) runs five buses daily from the airport to Big Sky ($18) and two to West Yellowstone ($25). Service is limited November to June.

EAST OF BOZEMAN
Missouri Headwaters

The Madison, Jefferson and Gallatin Rivers converge here to form the headwaters of the Missouri-Mississippi River drainage (the largest in North America), 2464 miles above its mouth. Before Lewis and Clark arrived in 1805, explorers looking for the headwaters could almost smell the salt water from here, believing the mighty river was part of a northwest passage to the Pacific Ocean and the exotic 'Orient' beyond it. **Missouri Headwaters State Park** offers an up-close view of the headwaters, as well as a nice place to picnic and shadeless places to camp ($12). Another worthwhile stop is **Lewis & Clark Caverns State Park** (☎ 406-287-3541), where you can take two-hour tours ($6) of the spectacular gravity-defying cave formations. The park has a nice campground ($11) open May to September.

Madison Valley

Hardly visible to passers-through, the Madison Valley began development with gold finds around **Pony** in the 1860s and continues today with the world's largest talc-producing district, in the Gravelly Range. At the foot of the Tobacco Root Mountains, Pony remains a picturesque outpost with glorious old brick buildings, unpaved streets and the still lively *Pony Bar*.

More important to most people is that the Madison River from Ennis south to West Yellowstone has some of the finest 'blue ribbon' fishing in the USA. The best fishing is said to be between Ennis and Quake Lake, accessible from six fishing access sites along US 287. **Ennis**, a fishing mecca if there ever was one, is a good stop for lodging, supplies, guides and information.

Gallatin Valley

The Gallatin River cuts through a narrow, rugged gorge between the Madison and Gallatin Ranges, paralleled by US 191. This route is peppered with enough trailheads to keep hikers and skiers busy for years. Development in the valley is limited to occasional tourist services – guest ranches, lodges, outfitters – spread out every 10 miles or so. The exception is around the turnoff to **Big Sky** (☎ 800-548-4486), the valley's foremost destination for skiing and, in summer, gondola-served hiking and mountain biking. But for backpacking and backcountry skiing, head to the **Lee Metcalf Wilderness Complex**, which covers 389 sq miles of Gallatin and Beaverhead National Forest land west of US 191. Numerous USFS campgrounds snuggle up to the Gallatin Range on the east side of US 191, making it easy to find a spot to pitch your tent and enjoy the scenery.

Paradise Valley

Aptly named Paradise Valley has many fishing access sites that put you right down at river's edge and USFS roads leading to hiking, mountain-biking and ski trails in the Absaroka-Beartooth Wilderness. Rafts,

kayaks and canoes take to the river June to August.

Livingston is a small town at the north end of the valley that still has a rough-and-tumble feel, despite the recent influx of art galleries and snazzy antique stores. The saloons that Calamity Jane and Kitty O'Leary frequented during Livingston's railroad days have gone relatively unchanged, however. Anyone even slightly interested in fly-fishing should make a detour to the **Federation of Fly Fishers Fly Fishing Museum** (☎ 406-222-9369) and **Dan Bailey's Fly Shop** (☎ 406-222-1673, 800-356-4052), known as one of the world's best for Goofus Bugs, Humpy Flies, Trudes, Green Drakes and Hair Wing Rubber Legs.

Twenty miles south of Livingston, **Chico Hot Springs** (☎ 406-333-4933) was established in 1900. The place is unpretentiously elegant and restored with great attention to rustic detail. A plunge costs $5 for nonguests, rooms start at $45 and dinner at the well-known restaurant will cost around $35.

Absaroka Beartooth Wilderness

Bordered by Paradise Valley in the west and Yellowstone National Park in the south, this is the third-most-visited wilderness area in the US. The thickly forested Absaroka Range dominates the area's west half and is most easily reached from Paradise Valley or the Boulder River Corridor. The Beartooth Range's jagged peaks and Alpine tundra are best reached from Hwy 78 and US 212 near Red Lodge. Because of its proximity to Yellowstone National Park, the Beartooth portion gets two-thirds of the area's traffic – most of it concentrated near the wilderness boundaries. But there is plenty of uncrowded alpine scenery to be enjoyed in the rugged interior.

A quaint old mining town with fun bars and restaurants, **Red Lodge** is a destination in its own right, with a wealth of day hiking, backpacking and, in winter, skiing opportunities right near town. The Red Lodge Chamber of Commerce (☎ 406-446-1718, 601 N Broadway Ave) has accommodation information, while the Beartooth Ranger Station (☎ 406-446-2103), 3 miles south of Red Lodge on US 212, is the best resource for recreation maps and information.

The **Beartooth Hwy** (US 212) connects Red Lodge to Cooke City and Yellowstone's

Bad girl Calamity Jane (1895)

north entrance by an incredible 68-mile journey that passes soaring peaks and alpine tundra – a destination as well as a travel corridor (open June to Oct 15).

Little Bighorn Battlefield

This is one of the few reasons visitors ever see the endless prairies and pine-covered hills of Montana's southwest Plains. Sited on the Crow Indian Reservation (Montana's largest), the Little Bighorn Battlefield National Monument is where General George Custer made his infamous 'last stand' and where numerous other battles between Native Americans and the US Cavalry were fought.

The monument's visitor center (☎ 406-638-2621) has good displays, videos and maps. It's difficult to grasp the full story of Little Bighorn in an afternoon's visit, but listening to the lectures and attending one of the free guided tours gives a good overall view of what happened. Beyond the visitor center, the battlefield is best visited by car. Entrance to the monument ($5 per car; open daily) is 1 mile east of I-90 on US 212. **Hardin**, the area's hub and the only major service center around, has a few small motels and restaurants.

BUTTE

A mining metropolis during the late 19th century, Butte today looks like 'Chicago meets the Wild West,' with ornate buildings lying vacant and accented by a skyline of massive headframes (mining supports). Butte is not a feel-good place, but its history is fascinating – significant beyond Montana's development and loaded with political intrigue. Its bars, restaurants and B&Bs make it a good place to spend a night or two. Get a walking tour map of Uptown Butte, one of the USA's largest **historic districts**, from the visitor center (☎ 406-723-3177, 800-735-6814, 1000 George St), north of I-15/I-90, or just walk along Granite, Broadway and Park Sts, read the National Register of Historic Places plaques and poke your nose in any building open to the public.

Other sites worth seeing are the **Mineral Museum** and **World Museum of Mining**, both near the Montana Tech campus, and the **Dumas House Brothel Museum** (☎ 406-723-6128), the only building in the USA originally constructed as a brothel and never used as anything else.

Butte KOA (☎ *406-782-0663*), near I-90 exit 126, charges $18/23 for tent/RV sites. Good motel options include *Capri Motel* (☎ *406-723-4391, 220 N Wyoming St*), at $36, and *Historic Finlen Hotel* (☎ *406-723-5461, 100 E Broadway at Arizona Ave*), at $50-55.

A few dining 'institutions' left from better days are *Gamer's* (*15 W Park St*), with American breakfasts and lunches (under $5) and *Pekin Noodle Parlor*, upstairs on Main St between Park and Galena Sts, whose individual 'dining cabins' and Pepto-Bismol pink walls show grease from years of lively activity (open late).

Greyhound and Rimrock Bus lines use Butte's Greyhound depot (☎ 406-723-3287, 101 E Front St); destinations include Dillon ($12.50), Missoula ($13.50), Helena ($12.50) and Bozeman ($15.50).

HELENA & AROUND

As the state capital, Helena enjoys a stable economy and hustle-bustle pace set by well-dressed businessfolk and politicians, sort of a novelty for Montana. Sights include the neoclassical State Capitol Building, the elegant old buildings along Last Chance Gulch (Helena's pedestrian shopping district), the Holter Museum of Art and Archie

Bray Foundation, one of the nation's most important training grounds for ceramics and pottery artists. Pick up a walking-tour map at the visitor center (☎ 406-447-1540, 2003 Cedar St), just east of I-15. In summer a tour train ($5) leaves from in front of the capitol and circles the Last Chance Gulch area.

Mount Helena City Park has **hiking** and **mountain biking** trails that wind around the base and to a 5460-foot-high summit with great views.

Less than 20 miles from Helena, the **Gates of the Mountains Wilderness Area** sees few visitors and offers excellent hiking and backpacking. Its name comes from Gates of the Mountains Canyon, which can be viewed by tour boat (☎ 406-458-5241). About 15 miles west of Helena, **MacDonald Pass** provides access to the Continental Divide Trail, a forest service campground ($6) and, in winter, a great network of cross-country ski trails. Also outside Helena are the **ghost towns** of Marysville and Elkhorn, and the developed **hot springs** of Boulder.

The Helena National Forest Office (☎ 406-449-5201, 2880 Skyway Dr), across from the Helena Regional Airport, has topographical maps and recreation information. The Base Camp (☎ 406-443-5360, 333 N Last Chance Gulch) rents outdoor gear (closed Sun).

The *Iron Front Hotel* (☎ 406-443-2400, 415 N Last Chance Gulch) has two rooms ($29 without bath). Conveniently located, *Helena Inn* (☎ 406-442-6080, 877-387-0102, 910 Last Chance Gulch) and *Budget Inn* (☎ 406-442-0600, 800-862-1334, 524 N Last Chance Gulch) both have rooms starting at $45. East of downtown near I-15 is a string of chain motels, each with free breakfast, pool, Jacuzzi, fitness center and rooms for $58-85. If you stay in one B&B in Montana, make it *The Sanders* (☎ 406-442-3309, 328 N Ewing St), where elegant rooms are $90-105.

At the corner of Fuller and Placer Aves, *The Real Foods Store* has an outstanding deli and natural foods, while adjacent *Morning Lights* is the place for coffee and pastries. *No Sweat Café* (427 N Last Chance Gulch) uses mostly organic ingredients in its hearty egg dishes, sandwiches and Mexican fare ($4-7).

Miller's Crossing (52 S Park Ave) offers pastas and burgers (under $10). *Bert & Ernie's*, on the corner of Last Chance Gulch and Lawrence St, is similar but nonsmoking.

Helena Regional Airport (☎ 406-442-2821) is 2 miles north of downtown and operates flights to most other airports in Montana, Salt Lake City and Spokane, Washington. Rimrock Stages services Helena's bus depot (☎ 406-442-5860), 7 miles east of town on US 12, where buses go to Great Falls ($13), Butte ($13), Missoula ($19), Billings ($31) and Bozeman ($15). Taxis (☎ 406-449-5525) run from the depot to downtown ($7).

MISSOULA

Home to the University of Montana cultural events and cafes, Missoula is arguably Montana's most enjoyable town and a good starting point. Its museums are OK, but most people head for the outdoors: The **Rattlesnake Recreation Area** is spittin' distance from town, the Bitterroot Range spans its western edge and the Clark Fork River courses right through it.

Stop by the chamber of commerce (☎ 406-543-6623, 800-526-3465, 825 E Front St), one block south of the I-90 Van Buren St exit, or the Trail Head (☎ 406-543-8440), on the corner of Higgins and Pine Sts, for maps and information.

Things to See & Do

In town you can look at the contemporary exhibits and installations of the **Missoula Museum of the Arts** (335 N Pattee St), which charges a $2 admission (closed Sun), and ride **Missoula's Carousel**, in Caras Park near the river, the first hand-carved carousel made in the USA in over 60 years (50¢).

One of the most accessible **hikes** around is along the south side of Clark Fork from McCormick Park (west of the Orange St bridge) back into Hellgate Canyon. Ascend the steep Mt Sentinel Trail (about a mile past the university) to reach Mt Sentinel's 5158-foot summit.

Advanced skiers like **Snowbowl Ski Area** (☎ 406-549-9777), 17 miles north of Missoula, for its 2600-foot vertical drop (the biggest in Montana). 10,000 Waves (☎ 406-549-6670, 800-537-8315) offers two-hour ($30), half-day ($47) and full-day ($72) **rafting** and **kayaking** trips on the Class III and IV rapids of Alberton Gorge or on gentler Blackfoot River.

Places to Stay & Eat

Most lodging is on Broadway between Van Buren and Orange Sts, within walking distance to the campus and downtown.

The best budget motels are *Downtown Motel* (☎ 406-549-5191, 502 E Broadway), *City Center Motel* (☎ 406-543-3193, 338 E Broadway), and *Ponderosa Motel* (☎ 406-543-3102, 800 E Broadway), which offer dated, no-frills rooms ($45). *Royal Motel* (☎ 406-542-2184, 388 Washington St), one block north of Broadway, and *Uptown Motel* (☎ 406-549-5141, 800-315-5141, 329 Woody St), near the courthouse, have quieter locations and more modern rooms ($48); the Uptown Motel also has one three-bed room that sleeps six ($70).

Bernice's Bakery (190 S 3rd St), south of the river, is a mainstay for pastries, bread and strong coffee. *Food For Thought*, across from the university at the corner of Arthur and Daly Sts, has creative breakfasts, sandwiches and salads for around $5. The only (South Asian) Indian restaurant in Montana, *Tipu's* (115½ S 4th St) and the slightly fancier *Tipu's Tiger* (531 S Higgins) both create tasty vegetarian dishes ($6-8) using lentils, garbanzos, seasonal vegetables and lots of spices; their *chai* is as good as it gets this side of Delhi.

Cozy *Hob Nob* (208 E Main St), in the back of the Union Club, has excellent burgers (salmon, beef, or veggie) served with sweet-potato fries ($5), nightly specials ($10-13) and occasional live jazz.

Entertainment

Pick up a copy of the *Independent* or look in the Entertainment section of Friday's *Missoulian* for what's on around town. Missoula's bars are squarely on the Montana booze map. Near the north end of Higgins Ave, *Iron Horse Brewpub* has a good student scene. Nearby, *Charlie B's* is a Missoula institution for billiards, Cajun grub and a good selection on tap. For live music try *Top Hat* (134 W Front St), *Jay's Upstairs* (119 W Main St) or Missoula's best jazz spot, *The Old Post* (103 W Spruce St). *The Raven Café* (130 E Broadway) has several pool tables, comfy chairs and shelves of books, but no smoking or alcohol.

Getting There & Around

Delta, Horizon Air, Northwest Airlines and United fly to Kalispell; Seattle, Washington; Salt Lake City, Utah; and Minneapolis, Minnesota, from the Missoula County International Airport (☎ 406-728-4381), 5 miles west of Missoula on US 12 W.

All bus lines arrive and depart from the slightly run-down Greyhound bus depot (☎ 406-549-2339, 1660 W Broadway), 1 mile west of town. Daily departures include Kalispell, Whitefish, Helena and Bozeman.

The free Emerald Line Trolley makes a full loop downtown every 20 minutes, weekdays until 4pm. Mountain Line Buses (☎ 406-721-3333) radiate from the transfer center on Pine St between Woody and Ryman Sts; bus No 10 goes to the Greyhound station and, upon request, the airport.

BITTERROOT VALLEY

Past the service centers and log-home manufacturers along Hwy 93, the Bitterroot Range offers tons of opportunities for hiking, fishing and skiing. Parallel to Hwy 93, East Side Rd offers a glimpse of the Bitterroot's agricultural soul and a few historical sites, including St Mary's Mission and the 24-bedroom Marcus Daly Mansion.

About halfway down the valley, Hamilton is home to the Bitterroot Chamber of Commerce (☎ 406-363-2400) and Forest Supervisor's Office (☎ 406-363-7117), which has the widest selection of maps and literature for surrounding wilderness areas. Good lodging options include *Deffy's Motel* (☎ 406-363-1244, 321 S 1st St) and *City Center Motel* (☎ 406-363-1651, 415 W Main St), both with singles doubles for $35/40.

At the valley's south end, Darby has one main street with the Darby Historical Ranger Station on the north end and some classic Western bars on the south. *Darmont* has a great collection of old saws hanging (yikes!) from the ceiling. Down in Sula, Lost Trails Hot Springs Resort (☎ 046-821-3574) charges $4.50 for a soak in its hot outdoor pool.

The 29 drainages that cut through the Bitterroot Range create dramatic canyons and hiking possibilities. Trailheads are well signed off US 93, usually 2 to 8 miles west via maintained roads. The 7-mile Lake

Como National Recreation Loop Trail begins 4 miles west of US 93, where there is a swimming beach, boat launch and picnic area. The trail encircles the lake, crossing the **Rock Creek Trail**, which leads to the Selway-Bitterroot Wilderness Area.

FLATHEAD LAKE

With 128 miles of wooded shoreline, picturesque bays and a large population of fish, Flathead Lake is one of Montana's most popular destinations. It's a good day trip from Missoula, Kalispell/Whitefish or Glacier National Park, and an excellent place to spend a few days camping, swimming or, in winter, skiing. The **Flathead Lake Marine Trail** makes paddling from one access point to another a fun way to explore. You can easily drive around the lake in four hours, but plan for stops along the way.

At the south end, **Polson** is the area's service center, with the biggest concentration of motels, restaurants and gas stations. Its funky Miracle of America Museum, 2 miles south of town on US 93, is definitely worth a stop. At the lake's opposite end, **Bigfork** is a quaint tourist village with artsy shops, good restaurants and an excellent live performance theater on Electric Ave, its main drag. Between the two you've got campgrounds, summer-camp-style resorts, and, on the lake's east side, orchards that produce fat, mahogany-red cherries.

In either town you can catch a boat tour to visit **Wild Horse Island**, where wild horses thought to be descendants of Pend d'Oreille and Flathead horses roam, and **Painted Rock**, a large outcropping with ancient pictographs. Keep a lookout for Flathead Nessie, a distant cousin to the Loch Ness Monster who has been lurking in the lake since the 1930s.

A good Web site is W www.gonorthwest .com/Montana/northwest/Flathead-Lake.htm. The Polson Chamber of Commerce (☎ 406-883-5969, 302 Main St) has information about accommodations, while Bear Dance (☎ 406-883-1700), on US 93 at 1st St, has outdoor activity information, sells maps and rents kayaks. On the north end, stop by the Swan Lake Ranger District Station (☎ 406-837-5081), west of Bigfork on Ranger Station Drive, for maps and campground information.

WHITEFISH & KALISPELL

Once a major hub for the Great Northern Railroad and now a gateway to Glacier National Park, Whitefish sports an Old West ambience with new West restaurants, shops and bars. It sits in the shadow of **Big Mountain**(☎ 406-862-2900, W www.bigmtn.com), one of Montana's premier year-round resorts, with downhill skiing (lift tickets $44) plus gondola-served hiking and mountain biking in summer. Glacier Cyclery (☎ 406-862-6446, 336 2nd St) has maps and guided rides and rents bikes at $15/20 for a half-/full-day.

Kalispell, 13 miles south of Whitefish, is Flathead Valley's commercial center – not a particularly charming city, but home to the restored 1895 Norman-style **Conrad Mansion** (☎ 406-755-2166). Glacier National Park is about an hour's drive from either city.

Check out W www.whitefishmt.com for local weather and a variety of useful links. The Whitefish Chamber of Commerce (☎ 406-862-3501, 877-862-3548) is in the Whitefish Mountain Mall at 6475 US 93 S. The Kalispell Area Chamber of Commerce (☎ 406-752-6166) is on the corner of Center and Main Sts. The Tally Lake Ranger Station (☎ 406-862-2508), 1 mile west of Whitefish on US 93 W, has information about the surrounding Flathead National Forest. Free Internet access is available at the public library in both towns.

The *Whitefish KOA & Buffalo Bobs Pizza (☎ 406-862-4242)*, four miles south of Whitefish on US 93, caters to RVs ($22, $32 with water) but has 15 tent sites ($18). *Whitefish Lake State Park* campground, on the southwest edge of the lake, has $6 first-come, first-served sites.

Whitefish has two terrific year-round hostels. *HI-AYH Bunkhouse Travelers Inn & Hostel (☎ 406-862-3377, 217 Railway St)* charges $13 for a bunk and $30 for a private room. Up the street, *Non-Hostile Hostel (☎ 406-862-7447, 300 E 2nd St)* sleeps six people ($15 each) and accepts reservations.

Motel reservations are necessary during summer and winter. South of Whitefish on US 93 you'll find chain motels as well as *Chalet Motel (☎ 406-862-2548, 800-462-3266)*, with a pool and hot tub ($60-80); *Allen's Motel (☎ 406-862-3995, 6540 US 93 S)*, at $45-80; and *Duck Inn (☎ 406-862-3825,*

800-344-2377), where rooms ($60-85) have decks, fireplaces and views. The best deal in Kalispell is ***Kalispell Grand Hotel*** (☎ *406-755-8100, 800-858-7422, 100 Main St),* at $68-81, including breakfast.

Air Glacier Park International Airport (☎ 406-257-5994), halfway between Whitefish and Kalispell on US 2, has flights to Missoula, Salt Lake City and Seattle. The Airport Shuttle Service (☎ 406-752-2842) charges $15 per person for trips between the airport and Whitefish or Kalispell.

Amtrak's *Empire Builder* stops at Whitefish's railroad depot (☎ 406-862-2268), at the north end of Central Ave; a roundtrip ticket to West Glacier is $15. Intermountain Transport (☎ 406-755-4011) connects Whitefish to Kalispell ($7.50), Missoula ($24), Helena ($33), Bozeman ($45) and Seattle ($81). Buses stop at the Your C-Stop gas station (403 2nd St), in Whitefish, and the bus depot (15 13th St E) in Kalispell. The free Shuttle Network of Whitefish (SNOW) bus runs between Whitefish and Big Mountain during ski season.

BOB MARSHALL WILDERNESS COMPLEX

The Bob Marshall Wilderness Complex, affectionately called 'the Bob,' runs roughly from the southern boundary of Glacier National Park in the north to Rogers Pass (on Hwy 200) in the south. Within the complex are three designated wilderness areas: Great Bear, Bob Marshall and Scapegoat. National Forest lands surround most of the complex, offering developed campgrounds, road access to trailheads and quieter country when the Bob gets loaded with hunters in autumn. The core lands (not including the surrounding 1563 sq miles of National Forest) encompass 2344 sq miles, 3200 miles of trails and sections that are more than 40 miles from the nearest road. The chances of finding total solitude here are very good, and the diversity of geology, plants and wildlife is immense.

You can access the Bob from the Seeley-Swan Valley in the west, Hungry Horse Reservoir in the north, the Rocky Mountain Front in the east and off Hwy 200 in the south. The easiest (and most popular) access routes are from the Benchmark and Gibson Reservoir trailheads in the Rocky Mountain Front.

Other good access points are the Holland Lake and Pyramid Pass trailheads on the Seeley-Swan side. Trails in this range generally start very steeply, reaching the wilderness boundary after about 7 miles. It takes another 10 miles or so to really get into the heart of the Bob. There are good day hikes from all sides.

Ranger stations that tend to the Bob include the following:

Augusta Information Station (☎ 406-562-3247, 405 Manix St, Augusta)

Flathead National Forest Headquarters (☎ 406-758-5204, 1935 3rd Ave E, Kalispell)

Hungry Horse Ranger Station (☎ 406-387-3000), on Hwy 2 in Hungry Horse

Lewis & Clark National Forest Supervisors Office (☎ 406-791-7700, 1101 15th St N, No 401, Great Falls)

Seeley Lake Ranger Station (☎ 406-677-2233), 3 miles north of Seeley Lake on Hwy 83

Spotted Bear Ranger District (☎ 406-758-5376), 55 miles south of Hungry Horse (open summer only)

Swan Lake Ranger District (☎ 406-837-7500), in Bigfork

Rocky Mountain Ranger District (☎ 406-466-5341, 1102 Main Ave NW, Choteau)

GLACIER NATIONAL PARK

Small but rich in scenery and biological diversity, Glacier National Park is Montana's most revered attraction. It draws large crowds in July and August, but most visitors stick close to roads, developed areas and short hiking trails. Head into the backcountry to be alone.

Those who don't have the time or desire to explore the remote reaches may be satisfied with a drive over Going-to-the-Sun Rd, from which you can see tremendous examples of glacial activity and often mountain goats and bighorn sheep. In winter, when Going-to-the-Sun Rd is closed but surrounding access roads lead to snowshoe and cross-country ski trails, the park is left to wildlife and hearty souls.

The less crowded Waterton Lakes National Park extends north into Canada. Together the two parks are a designated International Peace Park, signifying harmonious relations between the countries, and as a World Heritage Site to protect the parks' vast cross section of plant and animal species.

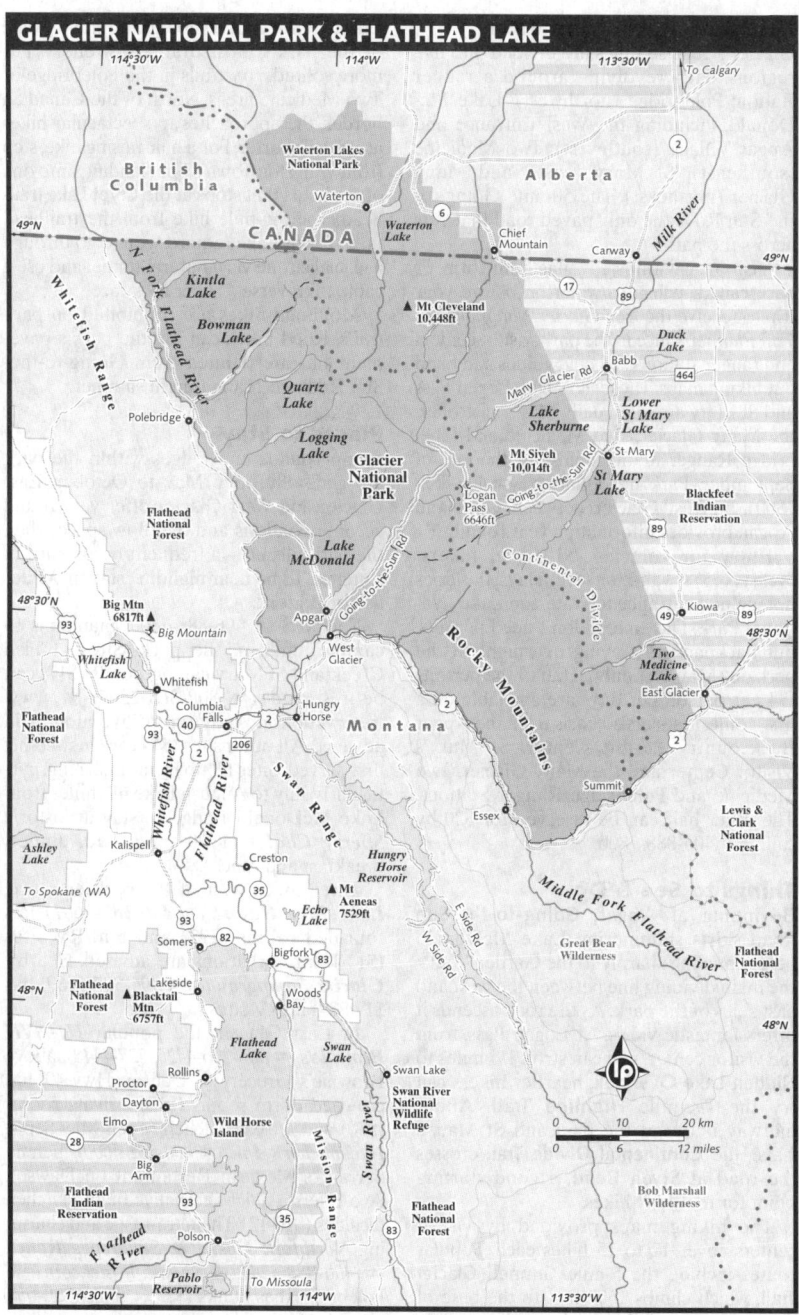

GLACIER NATIONAL PARK & FLATHEAD LAKE

Orientation & Information

Glacier's 1562 sq miles are divided into five regions, each revolving around a ranger station: Polebridge (northwest); Lake Mc-Donald, including the West Entrance and Apgar Village (southwest); Two Medicine (southeast); St Mary (east); and Many Glacier (northeast). The 50-mile Going-to-the-Sun Rd is the only paved road that cuts across the park.

Visit W www.nps.gov/glac/home.htm or parkscanada.pch.gc.ca/waterton before your trip to receive the free *Glacier National Park Trip Planner*. Once in the park, visitor centers and ranger stations sell field guides and hand out hiking maps. Those at Apgar, Logan Pass and St Mary are open daily May to October; the Many Glacier, Two Medicine and Pole-bridge Ranger Stations close at the end of September. Park headquarters (☎ 406-888-7800), in West Glacier between US 2 and Apgar, provides information year round.

Entry for vehicles ($10) and hikers/cyclists ($5) is valid for seven days; this does not include entrance to Waterton Lakes National Park. Day hikers don't need permits, but backpackers staying overnight in the park do (May-Oct only). Half of the permits ($4 per person per day) are available on a first-come, first-served basis from the Apgar Backcountry Permit Center, St Mary's Visitor Center and the Many Glacier, Two Medicine and Polebridge Ranger Stations. The other half can be reserved for $20 by calling ☎ 406-888-7800.

Things to See & Do

Beginning at Apgar, **Going-to-the-Sun Road** skirts shimmering Lake McDonald before angling sharply to the Garden Wall – the main dividing line between the west and east sides of the park. As the road ascends it offers fantastic views. At Logan Pass, from the visitor center, you can stroll 1½ miles to **Hidden Lake Overlook**; heartier hikers can try the 7½-mile **Highline Trail**. About halfway between the pass and St Mary's Lake, the **Continental Divide Trail** crosses the road at Siyeh Bend, a good starting point for multiday hikes.

The hiking maps provided by visitor centers cover 12 to 15 hikes each. Popular routes include the 5-mile **Grinnell Glacier Trail**, which climbs 1600 feet to the base of the park's most visible glacier, and the 6-mile **Cracker Lake Trail**, a 1400-foot climb to some of the park's most dramatic scenery. For more solitude, try trails in the Polebridge or Two Medicine areas. North of the Canadian border, the approaches to spectacular hikes are much shorter. For a hair-raising hike, step from Waterton Town's boat landing onto one of the boats that stops at the **Crypt Lake** trailhead. The 5½-mile hike from the trailhead up to Crypt Lake requires you to go through a glacial cirque via a natural tunnel and use a cable to traverse a sheer rock face.

Mountain bikes are prohibited on park trails. Road bikes can ply the park's pavement but are banned from Going-to-the-Sun Rd from 11am-4pm in summer.

Places to Stay

Campgrounds and lodges within the park are generally open May to October. East Glacier and West Glacier offer year-round accommodations and overflow space when the park fills up – a frequent occurrence in summer. To be near nightlife, stay in White-fish or Bigfork.

The NPS (☎ 406-888-7800) maintains 13 campgrounds in the park. Sites at Fish Creek and St Mary campgrounds ($17) can be reserved (☎ 800-365-2267, W www .reservations.nps.gov) up to five months in advance. All other sites ($14) are first-come, first-served. Sites fill up by midmorning, particularly July to August. Hike 6½ miles from Lake McDonald Lodge to stay at historic *Sperry Chalet* ($100 for a bed, dinner, breakfast and lunch).

Three miles west of the park entrance, *Lake Five Resort* (☎ 406-387-5601) has four-bed cabins ($92) and tent/RV sites ($14/18); reservations are advised. Nearby, *Glacier Campground* (☎ 406-387-5689) has $17/22 tent/RV sites.

In East Glacier, the popular *HI-AYH Brownie's* (☎ 406-226-4426, 727-4448), above Brownie's Grocery & Deli on Hwy 49, has crowded dorm rooms ($12), private rooms ($30) and a clean kitchen (open May-Sept). *Backpacker's Inn* (☎ 406-862-5600), behind Serrano's Mexican Restaurant on Dawson Ave, offers a quiet alternative but no kitchen facilities ($10-12). The ultra-rustic and charming *Northfork Hostel & Squarepeg Ranch* (☎ 406-888-5241, W www.nfhostel.com), in Polebridge, has bunks ($13), cabins ($30-65), plus a kitchen and free use of mountain bikes, cross-country skis and snowshoes. A ride from the Amtrak station in West Glacier is $25.

In West Glacier, *Vista Motel* (☎ *406-888-5311, 800-831-7101*), 2 miles west of the park entrance, has 26 rooms ($55-60) and an outdoor pool. *Glacier Highland Resort Motel* (☎ *406-888-5427, 800-766-0811*), across from the train station, has 33 motel units ($65). In East Glacier, *Sears Motel & Campground* (☎ *406-226-4432*) and the *Whistling Swan Motel* (☎ 406-226-4412) have similar rooms for around $55.

Dating from the early 1900s, Glacier's historic lodges are now operated by Glacier Park Inc (☎ 406-756-2444, 602-207-6000 for advance reservations) and cost $88-135 per room; cheapest are the $41 cottages (no bath) at the *Swiftcurrent Motor Inn*.

The flagship *Glacier Park Lodge* (☎ *406-226-9311*) has interior balconies supported by sixty Douglas fir timbers (estimated to be 500 to 800 years old). *Lake McDonald Lodge* (☎ *406-888-5431*) has a cozy hunting-lodge atmosphere and many rooms facing the lake. The majestic and much-photographed *Prince of Wales Hotel* (☎ *406-859-2231*) sits on a pile of glacial till overlooking icy-blue Waterton Lake.

Places to Eat

Most restaurants are open year round. In summer there are grocery stores with an array of camping supplies in Apgar, Lake McDonald Lodge, Rising Sun and at the Swiftcurrent Motor Inn.

In East Glacier, *Serrano's Mexican Restaurant* serves up good Mexican food (under $10) and has a rousing bar scene in summer. *Brownie's Grocery & Deli* has a well-rounded grocery supply and makes all its own breads. Dining options in West Glacier are unexciting at best; if you can, head to Whitefish.

Getting There & Around

Glacier International Airport is 20 miles southeast of the park's west entrance (see Whitefish & Kalispell, earlier). Amtrak's *Empire Builder* stops at East Glacier (Glacier Park Station) and West Glacier (Belton Station). Glacier Park (☎ 406-888-9187) runs shuttles over Going-to-the-Sun Rd, including the Hikers Express, which drops passengers off at Siyeh Bend ($13), Logan Pass ($17) and The Loop ($20).

Idaho

Idaho is synonymous with wilderness. The sparsely populated state has more than 28,000 sq miles of federally protected national forests and wilderness areas – only Alaska has more. Idaho's 3100 white-water miles give it more runnable river than any other state; names like the 'River of No Return' and 'Hells Canyon' elicit yips of joy from river rats worldwide. Much rare wildlife – grizzly bears, woodland caribou, wolves and wolverines – is found here.

Idaho's backcountry may be protected from further exploitation, but the adventure-tourism boom – and the state's aggressive marketing of its natural beauty – threaten the wilderness ethos just as surely. The woods of central and northern Idaho attract legions of hikers, mountain bikers, hunters, snowmobilers and skiers, while the state's arid southern plain is a major agricultural area, producing Idaho's famous potatoes. Like the landscape, the state's population has its contrasts: insular Mormon farm towns below the 45th parallel, trendy Boise city slickers, the Panhandle's ostracized white supremacists.

Idaho is not particularly destination-driven. Most visitors travel I-84 and US 95, but those who escape the interstate are quickly rewarded with unlimited recreational opportunities. Whether you're headed 'up a crick,' through the rapids or

***

Idaho

Nicknames: Gem State, Spud State

Population: 1,294,000 (40th)

Area: 83,575 sq miles (13th)

Admitted to Union: July 3, 1890 (43rd)

Capital city: Boise (population 170,000)

Other cities: Pocatello (53,000), Idaho Falls (50,000)

State folk dance: square dance

Birthplace of: Lana Turner, Ernest Hemingway

Famous for: potatoes, hot springs, wilderness, wildlife

down the slopes, the kaleidoscopic scenery is spectacular, and the cost of travel relatively inexpensive.

History

Real settlement of Idaho did not come until gold was discovered at Pierce on Orofino Creek in 1860. Miners rushed to Idaho's mountains, establishing gold camps and trade centers like Lewiston and Boise. Rich silver and lead veins spurred further growth, and by 1890 Idaho was granted statehood, laying ground for a homesteading boom.

Information

The Idaho Travel Council (☎ 208-334-2470, 800-635-7820, ⓦ visitid.org, 700 W State St, Boise) furnishes several useful state guides and maps. Idaho's Welcome Centers are on I-15 near Malad City, I-84 near Payette and I-90 near Post Falls. There are also regional travel bureaus in Boise, Coeur d'Alene, Idaho Springs, Lava Hot Springs, Lewiston and Twin Falls. The Idaho Outfitters & Guides Association (☎ 208-342-1919, 800-494-3246, ⓦ www.ioga.org, 711 N 5th St, Boise) provides a list of certified outdoors outfitters.

For information on road conditions, dial ☎ 208-336-6600 or 888-432-7623 (in Idaho only).

State sales tax is 5%. State bed tax is a minimum of 6%; a few cities add 1% to 3% more.

Getting There & Around

Idaho's main airport is in Boise, which has commuter links to Hailey, Lewiston, McCall, Salmon and Stanley. The Idaho Falls, Pocatello and Twin Falls airports have flights to Denver and Salt Lake City. Amtrak's daily *Empire Builder* stops in Sandpoint.

BOISE

Idaho's capital, largest city and home to its state university, Boise (population 170,000) is an enjoyable city that manages to meld urbane sophistication with vestiges of the cowboy Wild West. It's a worthy destination for travelers who enjoy a hip, easygoing 'small big town' focused on the outdoors. Much of the city's late-19th-century architectural core remains. Street life abounds:

Cafes and restaurants stay open late, and on hot summer evenings crowds from nightspots spill out into the streets.

Facing the Grove in Boise Centre, Boise's Information Center (☎ 208-344-5338, ⓦ www.boise.org, 850 Front St) is open weekdays. Boise Parks & Recreation (☎ 208-384-4240, 1104 Royal Blvd) produces a free map of the 20-mile Boise River Greenbelt that details its parks and museums. The USFS Boise National Forest office and the Idaho State BLM share a common visitor center (☎ 208-384-3200, 1387 S Vinnell Way).

Things to See & Do

The main business district is bounded by State, Grove, 4th and 9th Sts. Restaurants and nightspots are concentrated downtown in the brick-lined pedestrian plaza of **The Grove**, the gentrified former warehouse district at **8th St Marketplace** and **Old Boise**, just east of downtown.

Worthwhile sights include the impressive state capitol; riverfront Julia Davis Park, home to the free Idaho Historical Museum; Boise Art Museum ($4); and the creepy but fascinating Old Idaho Penitentiary ($4), 1½ miles east of Broadway Ave off Warm Springs Rd.

Northeast of Boise, **hiking** trails span the mountains of the Boise Front. **Bogus Basin Resort** (☎ 800-367-4397, ⓦ www.bogusbasin .com), 16 miles north of Boise, offers downhill and cross-country skiing during winter (full-day lift tickets $35) and hiking and mountain biking in summer.

Places to Stay & Eat

Stay close to downtown to enjoy the evening street life; reservations are a good idea. Boise's bed tax is 11%.

On the River RV Park (☎ 208-375-7432, 800-375-7432, 6000 N Glenwood St) offers swimming and fishing in the Boise River ($15/20 tents/RVs). It's 4 miles north of I-84 exit 46, then 4 miles east on US 20/26.

Budget places west of downtown include *Sands Motel* (☎ 208-343-2533, 1111 W State St), at $35/40 for singles/doubles; *Cabana Inn* (☎ 208-343-6000, 1600 Main St), at $35/40; and *Budget Inn* (☎ 208-344-8617, 2600 Fairview Ave), with a sauna and restaurant ($40/45). There's another budget area along Capitol Blvd near the university.

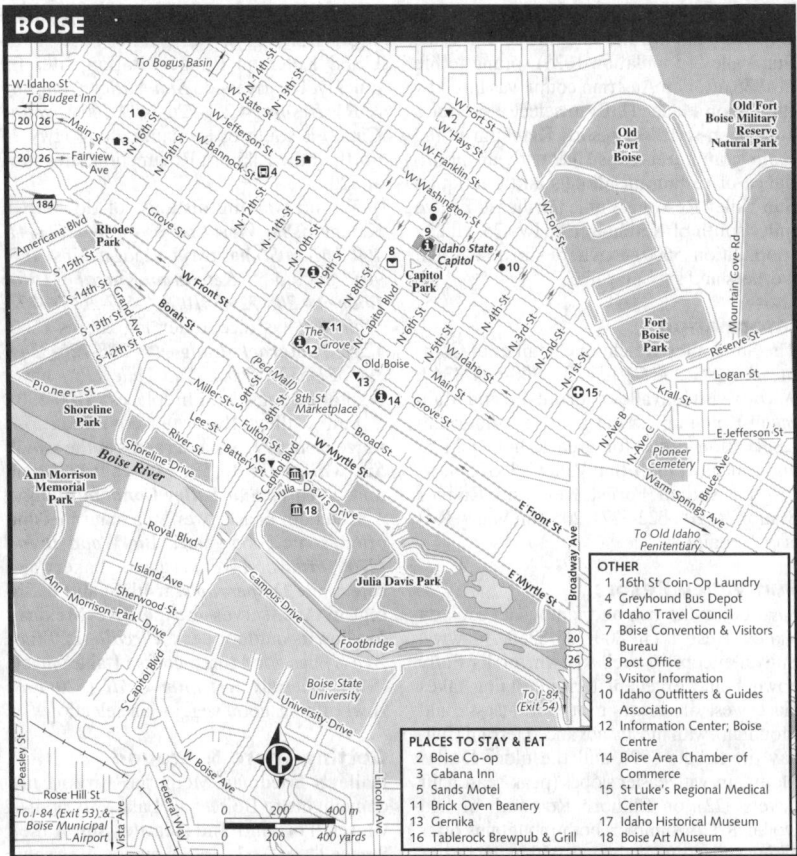

BOISE

PLACES TO STAY & EAT
2 Boise Co-op
3 Cabana Inn
5 Sands Motel
11 Brick Oven Beanery
13 Gernika
16 Tablerock Brewpub & Grill

OTHER
1 16th St Coin-Op Laundry
4 Greyhound Bus Depot
6 Idaho Travel Council
7 Boise Convention & Visitors Bureau
8 Post Office
9 Visitor Information
10 Idaho Outfitters & Guides Association
12 Information Center; Boise Centre
14 Boise Area Chamber of Commerce
15 St Luke's Regional Medical Center
17 Idaho Historical Museum
18 Boise Art Museum

On the Grove, **Brick Oven Beanery**, at 8th and Main Sts, offers outdoor seating and hearty salads and burgers (most dishes under $7). On the Basque Block, friendly **Gernika** (202 S Capitol Blvd) has the state's best pork tenderloin sandwiches (everything under $8), as well as draft beers, Basque wine and sidewalk seating. Boise's best microbrewery, **Tablerock Brewpub & Grill** (705 Fulton St) also has good grub. **Boise Co-op** (888 W Fort St) is Idaho's largest natural-foods store.

Getting There & Around

Boise Municipal Airport (BOI; I-84 exit 53) has daily flights to Denver, Las Vegas, Phoenix, Portland, Salt Lake City, Seattle and Spokane. Greyhound (☎ 208-343-3681) and Northwestern Trailways (☎ 208-336-3300, 800-366-3830) depart from the bus station at 1212 W Bannock St. Buses serve cities along three principal routes: I-84, US 95 and I-15/20/287/91.

Boise Urban Stages (BUS; ☎ 208-336-1010) operates local buses, including an airport route.

KETCHUM & SUN VALLEY

Ketchum and Sun Valley are Idaho's premier destinations. Sun Valley, according to *Condé Naste* and *Ski* magazines, is the USA's top-ranked ski resort. Synonymous with celebrity, the Ketchum and Sun Valley area is a year-round destination, where the truly wealthy live in their 'trophy homes.'

Ketchum (population 3875) began in the 1880s as a mining and smelting center, while Sun Valley (population 1025) sprang to life in 1936 after an Austrian count was hired by the Union Pacific (UP) to select a site for a European-style ski resort. Ketchum is the main commercial district, with an abundance of restaurants, hotels and boutiques. Sun Valley Resort is 1 mile northeast. Twelve miles south of Ketchum on Hwy 75, Hailey (population 5600) is where most seasonal workers and ski bums live.

Information

The Sun Valley/Ketchum Chamber of Commerce (☎ 208-726-3423, 800-634-3347, W www.visitsunvalley.com), at 4th and Main Sts in Ketchum, acts as a visitor center and reservation office for area lodging, skiing and transportation. Sun Valley's USFS Sawtooth National Forest Ketchum Ranger Station (☎ 208-622-5371, 206 Sun Valley Rd) is open daily.

Sun Valley Resort

Favored by the rich and famous jet set, Sun Valley Resort (☎ 800-786-8259, W www .sunvalley.com) is well known for its fluffy powder and excellent terrain. Skiing takes place west of Ketchum at world-class Bald Mountain, with mostly advanced terrain (full-day lift tickets $59), and the older Dollar Mountain, with easier slopes (peak-season lift tickets $22), on Elkhorn Rd south of Old Dollar Rd. In summer, both mountains offer hiking and mountain biking. Within the resort, the Sun Valley Mall has restaurants and shops along an outdoor pedestrian boardwalk.

Hiking & Mountain Biking

The well-maintained Wood River Trail System (WRTS) winds 20 miles through Ketchum and Sun Valley. The 10-mile Sun Valley Trail connects to the WRTS. Several other excellent hiking trails near Ketchum also permit mountain biking, including the 5½-mile Adams Gulch loop and Fox Creek, a 5-mile loop with mountain views that connects with three other trails.

Places to Stay & Eat

The chamber of commerce provides a helpful free reservation service. Most campgrounds and accommodations have a pool and hot tub. The bed tax is 9%.

The free **USFS Boundary Campground** is off Trail Creek Rd, 3 miles east of the USFS Ketchum Ranger Station; sites fill quickly. The riverside **Sun Valley Camping & RV Resort** (☎ 208-726-3429, 106 Meadow Circle) is south of Ketchum along Hwy 75 north of the Elkhorn Rd junction; sites start at $20.

Within walking distance of downtown Ketchum, **Ski View Lodge** (☎ 208-726-3441, 409 S Main St) has two-bed log cabins ($65-90). Secluded **Ketchum Korral Motor Lodge** (☎ 208-726-3510, 800-657-2657, 310 S Main St) has nice, older log cabins ($60-125). **Tamarack Lodge** (☎ 208-726-3344, 800-521-5379, 500 E Sun Valley Rd) has a pool and rooms with fireplaces ($100-130).

Sun Valley Resort accommodations range from $99 for basic rooms at the swank **Sun Valley Inn** to $319 for four-bedroom units at cushy **Sun Valley Condominiums**.

Ketchum boasts over 80 restaurants and offers some good values. **Big Wood Bread** (270 Northwood Way) is a good bakery and cafe, while **Desperado's**, at 4th St and Washington Ave, serves inexpensive Mexican food on its outdoor deck. **Piccolo** (220 East Ave N) has good three-course Italian meals ($15). Friendly **Ketchum Grill** (520 East Ave) offers a good vegetarian selection.

Getting There & Around

Hailey's Friedman Memorial Airport has daily flights to Boise, Salt Lake City and, in winter, Portland and Seattle. Sun Valley Stages (☎ 800-574-8661) runs winter shuttles between Sun Valley and the Boise Municipal Airport ($45 one way; 3 hours).

Ketchum Area Rapid Transit (KART; ☎ 208-726-7140) operates free daily bus service between Ketchum and Sun Valley.

CRATERS OF THE MOON NM

Craters of the Moon National Monument (☎ 208-527-3257) is an 83-sq-mile volcanic showcase. Lava flows, cinder cones and lava tubes lie along the 7-mile **Crater Loop Rd**, accessible by car or bicycle (open 24 hours daily Apr-Nov). Short trails lead from Crater Loop Rd to crater edges, onto cinder cones and into tunnels and lava caves. Entry costs $5, and there's a surreal **campground** ($10) near the entrance station. The monument is on US 20/26, 18 miles west of Arco, or a one-hour drive southeast of Ketchum.

SAWTOOTH NATIONAL RECREATION AREA

Heading north from Ketchum, Hwy 75 winds its way past timbered slopes and along the Salmon River before ascending Galena Summit (8701 feet), which has truly breathtaking views. The 1180-sq-mile Sawtooth National Recreation Area spans the Sawtooth, Smoky, Boulder and Salmon River mountains and has 42 peaks over 10,000 feet, 1000 lakes, 100 miles of streams and 700 miles of trails. The adjacent 340-sq-mile Sawtooth Wilderness Area centers on the rugged Sawtooth Range.

Recreation around here is limited to July, August and winter. It can snow anytime. Summer activities include hiking, fishing, rafting, horseback riding, boating and camping. Snowmobiling, hunting and cross-country skiing are the most popular winter activities. The area headquarters (☎ 208-727-5013, 800-260-5970), Hwy 75 (Star Route), 8½ miles north of Ketchum, has guides for camping, hiking, mountain biking and rafting. This is also where you must buy your Trailhead Parking Pass ($5 per day or $15 per year).

Hwy 75 offers access to most of the lakes, trailheads and campgrounds, including the popular Alturas, Pettit and Redfish Lakes.

Pockets of privately owned land dot the area, primarily along Hwy 75, including the old ranching and mining community of **Stanley**, which still retains a low-key demeanor and makes an excellent base for exploring. The Stanley-Sawtooth Chamber of Commerce (☎ 208-774-3411, 800-878-7950, W www.stanleycc.org), in the community building on Hwy 21, is open daily. Good lodging options include *Cole's Sawtooth Hotel & Cafe (☎ 208-774-9947),* where rooms with shared/private bath start at $27/45, and welcoming *Valley Creek Motel (☎ 208-774-3606),* with its Sawtooth-view rooms ($50-90).

MCCALL

At the northern end of Long Valley, McCall (population 3200) sits along Payette Lake's southern shore. This pleasant year-round resort community – unlike others in Idaho – tries to minimize the hype and glitz and maintain a relaxing pace of life, offering water sports, great skiing at nearby Brundage Mountain (☎ 800-888-7544, W www.brundage.com), good restaurants and lodgings. The McCall Chamber of Commerce (☎ 208-634-7631, 1001 State St) is one block south of W Lake St. Detailed recreation information is available from the USFS Payette National Forest offices: McCall Ranger District (☎ 208-634-0400, 102 W Lake St) and Forest Krassel Ranger District (☎ 208-634-0600, 500 N Mission St).

HELLS CANYON NATIONAL RECREATION AREA

North America's deepest gorge, Hells Canyon is thousands of feet deeper than the Grand Canyon, plunging 8913 feet from Mt Oore's He Devil Peak on the east rim to the Snake River at Granite Creek. The remote 1000-sq-mile Hells Canyon National Recreation Area offers hiking, fishing, swimming, camping and some dramatic scenery. The **Snake National Wild & Scenic River** through Hells Canyon is a favorite spot for rafting and jet-boat trips.

The Hells Canyon NRA spans the Idaho-Oregon state line, but the Oregon section is not readily accessible from Idaho. US 95 parallels its eastern boundary; a few unpaved roads lead from US 95 between the tiny towns of Riggins and White Bird into the NRA. Only one road leads from US 95 to the Snake River itself, at Pittsburg Landing.

The Hells Canyon NRA Riggins office (☎ 208-628-3916) has maps and information on campgrounds, roads, trails and fishing. The Riggins Chamber of Commerce (☎ 208-628-3778, W www.rigginsidaho.com) has information on the area's numerous outfitters.

Travelers with time (and high-clearance vehicles) can drive to the canyon rim on unpaved roads for dramatic views: USFS Rd 517 (open July-Oct), a quarter-mile south of the Hells Canyon Riggins office on US 95, climbs 17 miles to the rim and ends 2 miles later at the breathtaking **Heaven's Gate Lookout**.

IDAHO PANHANDLE

Though Idaho's largely unpopulated sliver is notorious for solitude-seeking survivalists and white supremacists, visitors are far more likely to encounter a moose than a militia. This beautiful lake-studded area is speckled with resorts and old mining towns.

Coeur d'Alene, **Kellogg** and **Sandpoint** are prime destinations for skiers, anglers and water-sports enthusiasts, while the old silver-mining town of **Wallace** preserves the Western flavor of its historic town center. Sixty lakes lie within 60 miles of Coeur d'Alene, including Hayden, Priest and Pend Oreille, all surrounded by campgrounds. Outdoor activities are everywhere, from white-water rafting near Bonners Ferry to Jet-skiing on Lake Coeur d'Alene to back-packing through the primeval forest around Priest Lake.

The Coeur d'Alene visitor center (☎ 208-773-4080, 800-292-2553) is downtown on Northwest Blvd. The USFS Idaho Panhandle National Forest office (☎ 208-765-7223) is at 3815 Schreiber Way. The Greater Sandpoint Chamber of Commerce (☎ 208-263-2161, 800-800-2106) is at 100 US 95 N. And the USFS Idaho Panhandle National Forest Sandpoint office (☎ 208-263-5111) is located at 1500 US 2.

Good, centrally located Coeur d'Alene lodging options include the *Flamingo Motel (☎ 208-664-2159, 800-955-2159, 718 Sherman Ave)*, from $65, and the *Inn at the Lake (☎ 208-676-1225, 621 Sherman Ave)*, from $50. In Sandpoint, for comparatively inexpensive lake access, *Lakeside Inn (☎ 208-263-3717, 800-543-8126, 106 Bridge St)* is unsurpassed (singles/doubles $70/85). Closer to downtown is the basic *K2 Inn (☎ 208-263-3441, 501 N 4th Ave)*, at $50/60.

Southwest

America's Southwest is a mythic land, much of it an immense desert that is at once beautiful, awe-inspiring and hopelessly desolate. It includes the dramatic canyons carved by the mighty Colorado River, the cactus-filled Sonoran Desert, the colorful cliffs of the Grand Staircase and the most inhospitable mountain ranges in the country. The most rugged portions of the Southwest remain virtually untouched, with seemingly endless miles of eroded rock, blue sky and blazing sunshine.

The people who have chosen to live in this harsh environment have also acquired the patina of myth: the ancestral Indians and their modern descendants; the Spanish explorers and missionaries; the persecuted Mormons who settled Utah; the rough-and-ready miners who dug for silver and gold, and then uranium; the cowboys, outlaws, trappers and ranchers; and even the US military, which closed off vast, uninhabited stretches for nuclear and other weapons testing.

In addition to experiencing this fabled terrain, visitors to the Southwest today can enjoy the chic restaurants and galleries of Santa Fe and Sedona, the buzz of Las Vegas' neon-lit casinos and the world-class skiing in Utah and northern New Mexico. Crowds and prices vary dramatically according to season (see When to Go, later).

History

Native Americans The oldest evidence of human habitation in the Southwest was discovered in Clovis, New Mexico, where woolly-mammoth bones and spearheads suggest that hunter-and-gatherer Indians roamed the area 12,500 years ago. By about AD 100, three dominant cultures were emerging in the Southwest: the Hohokam of the desert, the Mogollon of the central mountains and valleys, and the Ancestral Puebloans (formerly known as the Anasazi) of the northern plateaus.

In one of the Southwest's most puzzling mysteries, the Hohokam inexplicably disappeared by about 1450. The Mogollon people became more or less incorporated into the Ancestral Puebloans, who themselves

Highlights

- Grand Canyon – mile-deep, stunning, surreal and superb
- Zion National Park – great hikes through verdant valleys and brilliant red rock
- Chaco Culture National Historic Park – massive, ancient, remote Ancestral Puebloan site
- Bryce Canyon – spectacular pinnacles of otherworldly rock formations
- Santa Fe – the USA's highest capital city, an adobe wonderland of Southwest style ringed by mountains and desert
- Las Vegas – quintessential Americana, glitz and gambling in Glitter Gulch

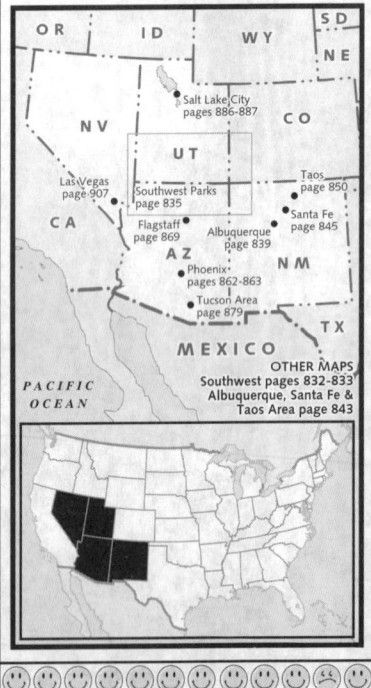

began to abandon their homes in the 15th century. By the 16th century the Ancestral Puebloans had moved mainly to the pueblos now found along the Rio Grande and also settled the Acoma Pueblo of New Mexico's northwest corner and the Hopi villages in Arizona. Nomadic bands of Indians from two distinct language groups moved into the Southwest between AD 1300 and 1600.

One of the highlights of a trip to the Southwest is exploring ancestral sites, including the Canyon de Chelly National Monument in Arizona; Mesa Verde, Colorado; and the Bandelier National Monument, New Mexico. The most ancient links with the Ancestral Puebloans are found among the Hopi tribe of northern Arizona. Here, perched on top of a mesa, the village of Old Oraibi has been inhabited continuously since about 1150.

Spanish Settlement European presence in the Southwest began with Spanish fortune seekers of the 16th century. In 1540 Francisco Vásquez de Coronado set off from Mexico City with 336 Europeans, 1000 Indians and 1100 pack and riding animals in search of the fabled and immensely rich 'Seven Cities of Cibola.' For two years they traveled through what is now Arizona and New Mexico, but instead of gold they found Indian pueblos of mud bricks and wooden sticks.

In 1598 Juan de Oñate headed north from Mexico to the pueblos near the confluence of the Rio Chama and Rio Grande. He set up headquarters at the Tewa-speaking pueblo of Ohke (he renamed it San Juan) but soon moved across the river to San Gabriel, which became the first capital of New Mexico. In 1608, after political problems, de Oñate returned to Mexico, San Gabriel was abandoned, and the present capital of Santa Fe was laid out by Pedro de Paeralta from 1609 to 1610. For the next 200 years, Spanish settlers, missionaries and Indians shared the region, often with conflict, violence and bloodshed, and sometimes with uneasy calm.

Concurrent with the Louisiana Purchase of 1803, the Spanish colonies of the Southwest abutted US territory for the first time. Zebulon Pike illegally entered the Spanish territory during his expedition from 1806 to 1807, and in his report of 1810 he declared the region part of the 'Great American Desert,' unfit for settlement but rich with trade potential. Upon Mexican independence in 1821 and the lifting of Spain's trade restrictions, William Becknell, a trader from Missouri, began traveling the 800-mile Santa Fe Trail from St Louis to Santa Fe. Taos, New Mexico, became a primary trading center for British, American, Indian and Spanish traders.

US Settlement Trade was one of the primary American objectives in the Mexican-American War of 1846–7, which gave the USA control of most of Arizona and New Mexico. In 1853 the Gadsden Purchase brought southern Arizona into US hands. Meanwhile, to the north, in present-day Utah, a Christian sect called the Church of Jesus Christ of Latter Day Saints sought refuge from persecution.

Explorations during the 19th century paved the way for US settlement and economic development. Development was primarily due to the railroad surveys of the mid-1850s and the geological surveys of the 1860s and 1870s, combined with the Indian Wars and the forcible removal of whole tribes of Native Americans by the US Army. Gold and silver drew miners to the region, and mining towns, often with more saloons and bordellos than any other kind of establishment, mushroomed overnight near the richest mines. Not surprisingly, law and order was practically nonexistent in many parts of the Southwest during the latter part of the 19th century. At the turn of the century, the joint efforts of the Fred Harvey Company and the Atchison, Topeka and Santa Fe Railroad created a tourist empire predicated upon the natural wonders and Indian cultures of the region.

20th Century The history of modern settlement in the arid Southwest is closely linked to the development of water use. Following the Reclamation Act of 1902, huge federally funded dams were built throughout the West to control the rivers, irrigate the desert and encourage development. The constant disagreements and rancorous debates within each state as to who should be allowed to use these rivers' water continue today.

Recent additions to the Southwest's water supply are underground water reserves, or aquifers. The most famous of these is the Ogallala Aquifer of the Great

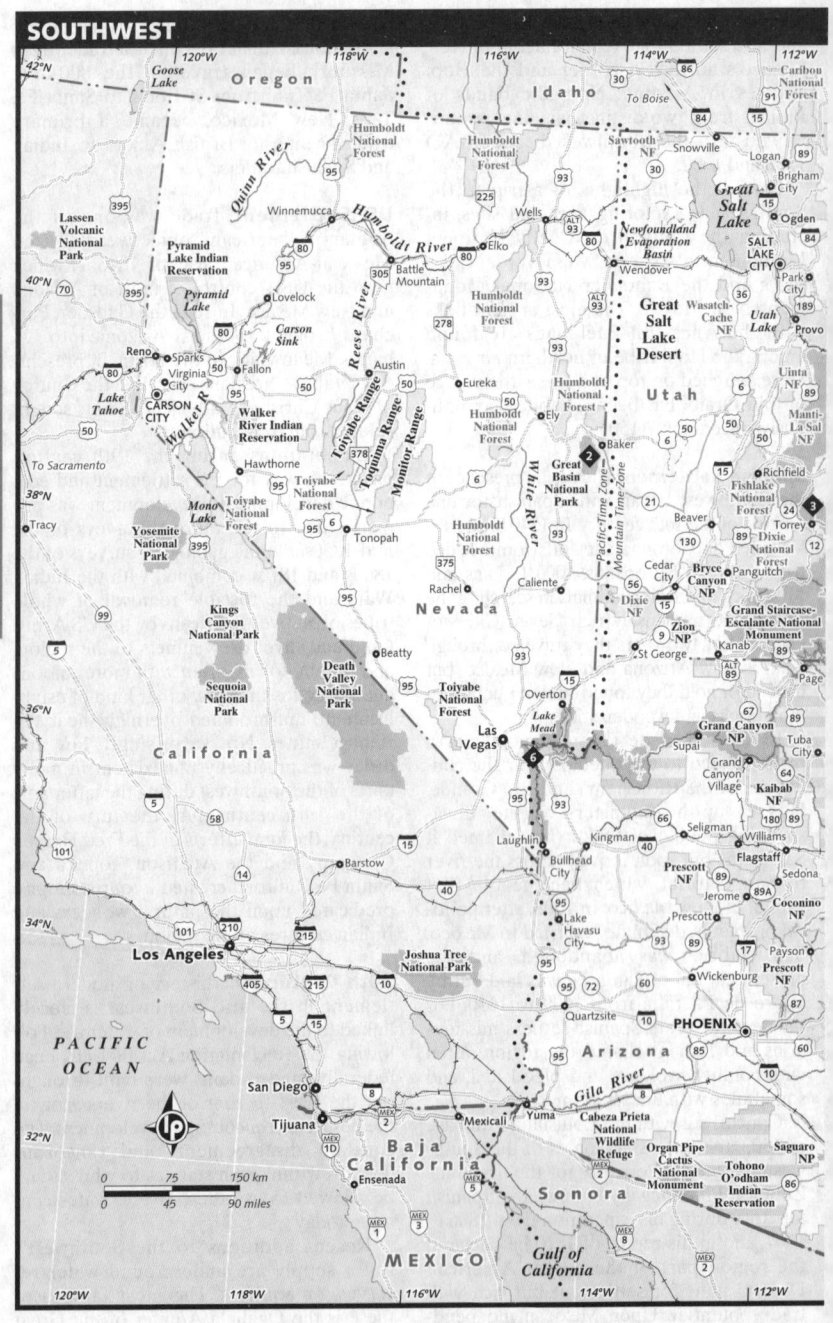

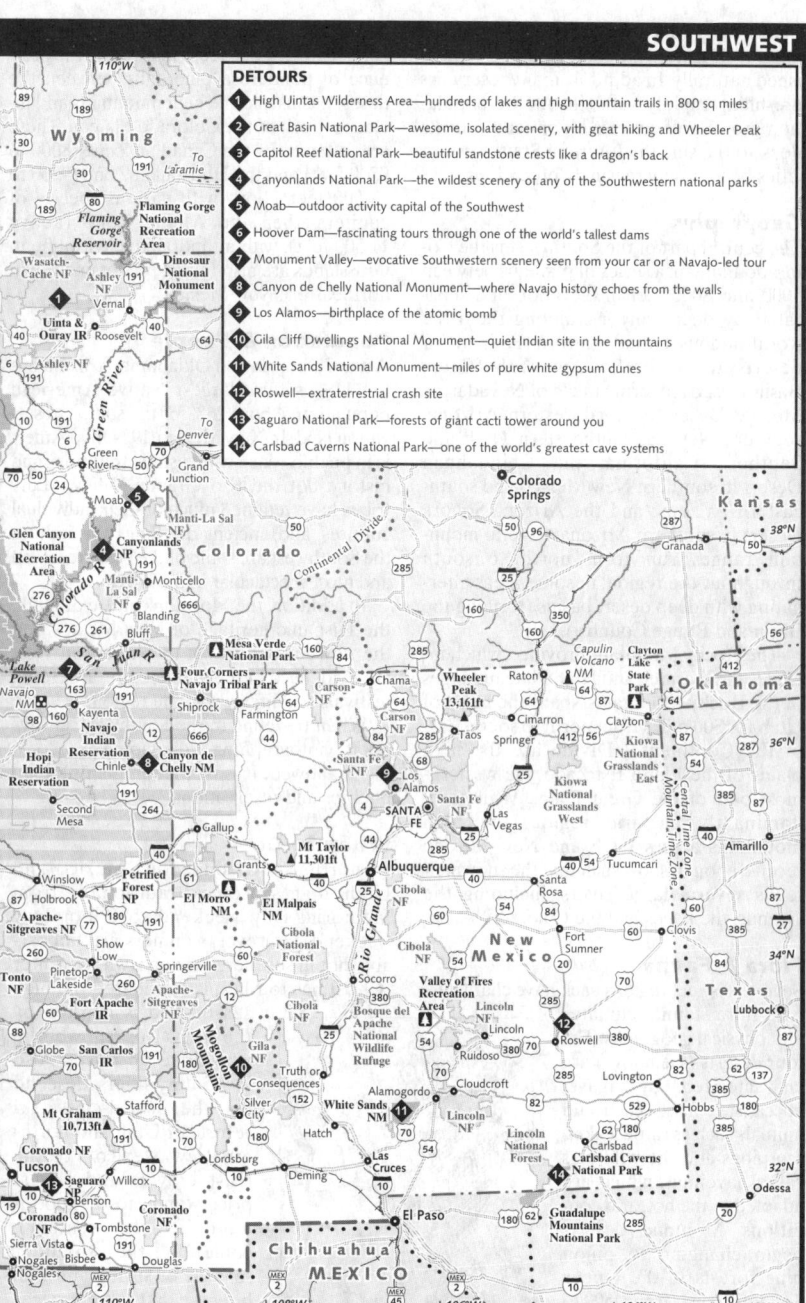

DETOURS

1. High Uintas Wilderness Area—hundreds of lakes and high mountain trails in 800 sq miles
2. Great Basin National Park—awesome, isolated scenery, with great hiking and Wheeler Peak
3. Capitol Reef National Park—beautiful sandstone crests like a dragon's back
4. Canyonlands National Park—the wildest scenery of any of the Southwestern national parks
5. Moab—outdoor activity capital of the Southwest
6. Hoover Dam—fascinating tours through one of the world's tallest dams
7. Monument Valley—evocative Southwestern scenery seen from your car or a Navajo-led tour
8. Canyon de Chelly National Monument—where Navajo history echoes from the walls
9. Los Alamos—birthplace of the atomic bomb
10. Gila Cliff Dwellings National Monument—quiet Indian site in the mountains
11. White Sands National Monument—miles of pure white gypsum dunes
12. Roswell—extraterrestrial crash site
13. Saguaro National Park—forests of giant cacti tower around you
14. Carlsbad Caverns National Park—one of the world's greatest cave systems

Plains, from which water is being extracted at a much faster rate than it can be replenished naturally. In addition, many reservoirs are filling rapidly with silt. As the population grows, golf courses bloom and tourists flock to the sun, the future of Southwestern cities becomes increasingly precarious.

Geography

The central part of the Southwest is the Colorado Plateau, a series of plateaus between 5000 and 8000 feet in elevation and separated by deep canyons, among them the world-famous Grand Canyon. Four major deserts are in the Southwest: the Great Basin Desert, covering much of Nevada; the Mojave Desert of northwestern Arizona, southern Nevada, southeastern Utah and Southern California; the Chihuahuan Desert in southern New Mexico and southeastern Arizona; and the Arizona-Sonora Desert in southern Arizona. Several mountain ranges run from north to south throughout the region, in some areas alternating with deep desert basins (forming the Basin and Range Country).

The Rocky Mountain Province, which includes the Wasatch and High Plateau ranges of the Rocky Mountains, spans the heart of Utah for 300 miles from north to south. East of the Continental Divide are the high plains of the Llano Estacado, the westernmost part of the Great Plains. While predominantly an arid region, the high mountains across Utah and New Mexico receive enough snow such that the snowmelt feeds several large rivers, including the Grande, the Pecos and the Colorado.

Flora & Fauna

Several distinct regions each have characteristic flora, fauna, climates and physical geography. The four deserts (see above) are characterized by agave, yucca, sagebrush, cacti and animals such as rattlesnakes, scorpions and the wild pigs called javelinas, which are adapted to the hot, arid conditions. Montane deserts begin changing to piñon pine forests in the Upper Sonoran Zone (from 4500 to 6500 feet), with its black

bears and mountain lions. The transition zone (6500 to 8000 feet), marked by the presence of ponderosa pine, falls between the desert basins and the high mountains and includes much of the Colorado Plateau. These are followed by the Canadian Zone (8000 to 9500 feet) and the Hudsonian Zone (9500 to 11,500 feet), both with various species of conifers, then the Alpine Zone (above 11,500 feet), with a tundralike environment. Grasslands are also found, predominantly in northeastern New Mexico.

Population & People

After California and Oklahoma, Arizona has the USA's third-largest Native American population. About 26% of the state is reservation land. In New Mexico, 19 Native American pueblos, each with distinct traditions and history, dot the Rio Grande Valley. Many tribes have retained much of their individual cultures, and ancient dwellings throughout the Southwest are some of the best preserved and most spectacular in the USA.

In addition, the Mormon culture of Utah, the Hispanic heritage of New Mexico and the 'cowboy culture' of the American West are evidenced in the architecture, arts, food, festivals and lifestyle of the region.

When traveling in the Southwest, always ask if photographing, videotaping or recording is allowed. It is banned in many Indian pueblos and reservations.

When to Go

In northern Arizona, New Mexico and Utah, high season is traditionally from Memorial Day weekend to Labor Day weekend. However, summers are unbearably hot in southern Arizona, where winter (Christmas to May) is considered the high season and is marked by the arrival of 'snowbirds,' who drive up prices. Also in winter, skiers descend on the world-class ski resorts of Utah and northern New Mexico. For the least crowds and lowest prices (and mostly good if unpredictable weather), come in the shoulder seasons of spring and fall, but note that some services may be closed.

SOUTHWEST PARKS

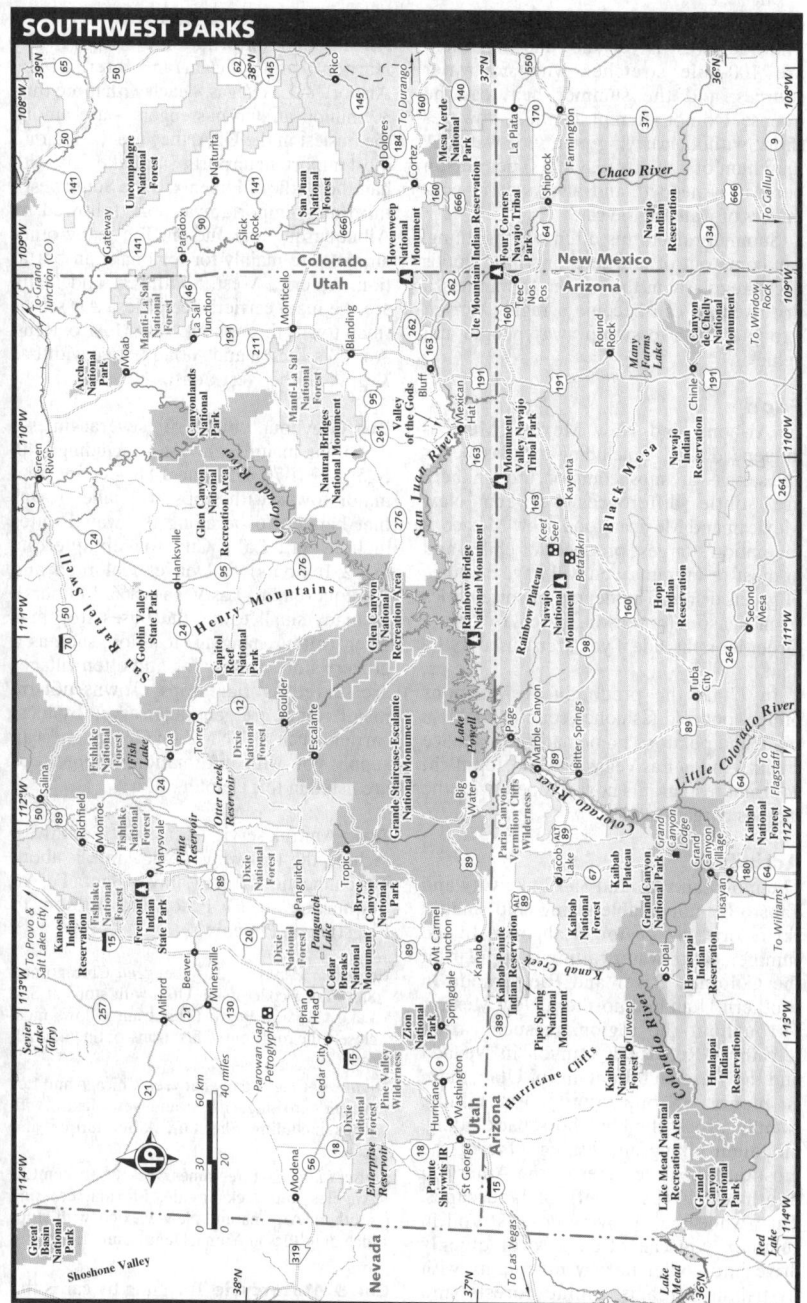

Dangers & Annoyances

The Southwest is very hot and dry. There are 100-mile stretches with no water sources, and the summer heat can be intense. Do not attempt any hike, however short, without carrying plenty of water. A minimum of 4 quarts (3.8 liters) per person per day is needed, and always carry containers of water in the car.

Summer rainstorms, often with lightning, can come out of nowhere, and flash floods occur regularly in the region. In minutes, a dry riverbed can become a raging torrent strong enough to sweep away people and vehicles.

Food

In Arizona and New Mexico, Mexico-influenced food – including tortillas, beans and salsas – are most common, though there are subtle differences between New Mexican and Mexican food. New Mexico is the nation's largest producer of chiles, and in most restaurants, you will have a choice of green or red. The degree of spice varies from season to season, batch to batch. Order it on the side if you aren't used to the heat.

In Utah, the predominant Mormons prefer good, old-fashioned country cooking: steak and potatoes, homemade pies and ice cream. And in Las Vegas, Nevada, top-flight gourmet restaurants now compete with the famous bargain buffets.

Activities

The mountains around Salt Lake City and Taos offer unbeatable skiing, and smaller ski resorts can be found all over. In the summer, white-water rafting is popular on the Colorado River and Rio Grande in southern Utah and northern New Mexico. Throughout the region, in such varied terrain as Red Rock Canyon in Nevada and the Wasatch Mountains of Utah, there is plenty of opportunity for hiking, camping, rock climbing, horseback riding, mountain biking and fishing. One of the most distinctive features of the American Southwest is the variety of landscapes. Thus, while the low-lying deserts broil in summer, you can often hike or quickly drive into cooler nearby mountains, with fly-fishing streams, alpine forests and meadows of wildflowers.

Getting There & Around

Air Phoenix International Airport (Sky Harbor) and McCarran International Airport, in Las Vegas, – each with more than 30 million annual passengers – are among the busiest in the USA; they are the region's most important airports. Salt Lake City, with half the traffic of Phoenix, is the Southwest's third-most-important airport, followed by Albuquerque and Tucson. The many other airports are mainly for regional transportation. America West, Southwest and Delta are the main carriers here. Mesa Air serves small towns throughout New Mexico. Reno Air links Tucson and Albuquerque with Las Vegas and the West Coast.

Bus Greyhound buses run several times a day along major highways – including I-40, I-25, I-17, I-70, I-10 and I-80 – connecting major towns with stops at smaller towns that happen to be along the way. Routes include Salt Lake City to Albuquerque ($102; 16 hours) via Denver, Colorado; and Albuquerque to Las Vegas ($66; 14 hours). In many small towns the buses stop at a given (often changing) location, such as a grocery store parking lot, and often villages are served as 'flag stops.' Towns not on major routes are generally served by local carriers such as TNM&O; Greyhound can supply you with information. Major stops are listed in this chapter.

Train Amtrak services across the Southwest include the following. (Ask Amtrak about bus connections from Lamy to Santa Fe, Albuquerque to El Paso, and Tucson to Flagstaff via Phoenix.)

California Zephyr – daily between Chicago and San Francisco, crossing Utah with stops at Salt Lake City and Provo (This train follows most closely the route of the first transcontinental railroad.)

Southwest Chief – daily between Chicago and Los Angeles, crossing Arizona and New Mexico, with stops including Flagstaff, Albuquerque and Raton

Sunset Limited – three times weekly between Los Angeles and Jacksonville, Florida, crossing southern Arizona and New Mexico, with stops including Tucson, Yuma, Deming and El Paso

Car & Motorcycle Traveling by car is the best way to explore the Southwest, much of which is small villages, dispersed national parks and dirt roads through high mountains and rough desert; a 4WD is ideal. Always carry detailed maps and water, and ask about road conditions before venturing off paved roads. The fabled Route 66 traversed the Southwest across New Mexico and Arizona, though most of the original road is now buried under I-40. The longest section is in scenic western Arizona. Shorter sections also survive where I-40 bypassed small towns like Tucumcari, Santa Rosa, Grants, Gallup, Holbrook and Kingman – where old diners, motels and gas stations are classics of roadside Americana.

New Mexico

The New Mexico license plate is the only one in the country with 'USA' on it, a reminder that New Mexico is indeed a part of the contiguous 48 states. New Mexico – with its strong Native American, Hispanic and Anglo heritages and influences; its luminescent desert landscape and its desolate mountains – is as much a unique culture as a place to visit. Wandering through the dusty villages of the northern mountains, studying ancient Indian sites, exploring the 'atomic city' of Los Alamos and the alien magnet of Roswell, eating green-chile burritos from roadside stands, hiking among ponderosa pines and lava flows, skiing in Taos and soaking in natural hot springs along the Rio Grande – this is New Mexico. It's no wonder the license plate also reads 'land of enchantment.'

History
As far back as 10,500 BC, Indians roamed the land. Through raiding, war, immigration and trade, individual tribes were blended and transformed, and by Coronado's arrival in the 16th century, the dominant culture was that of the Pueblo tribes.

Upon the establishment of Santa Fe as the colonial capital in 1610, Spanish settlers fanned out across northern New Mexico, digging irrigation ditches (still used today) and farming mainly beans, wheat and corn. More than 50 churches were built in the span of 10 years, many of which are still in use, and missionaries began their often violent efforts to convert the area's Pueblo

New Mexico	
Nickname: Land of Enchantment	
Population: 1,713,800 (36th)	
Area: 121,598 sq miles (5th)	
Admitted to Union: January 6, 1912 (47th)	
Capital city: Santa Fe (population 66,500)	
Other cities: Albuquerque (678,800), Farmington (40,000)	
State bird: roadrunner	
Birthplace of: hotelier Conrad Hilton (1887–1979); USFS antifire spokesbear, Smokey	
Famous for: green chiles, ancient pueblos, Santa Fe style, the first atomic bomb (1945)	
Home of the USA's oldest: road (the Camino Real), public building (Santa Fe governors' palace, 1610)	
Percentage of the population below poverty line: 20.8% (1st)	

Indians to Catholicism. When the San Juan Pueblo leader Popé was persecuted for his religious practices, he hid in the Taos Pueblo and planned what would be the successful Pueblo Revolt of 1680. Indians occupied Santa Fe until 1692, when Diego de Vargas recaptured the city.

In 1851 New Mexico became US territory. Indian wars, particularly against the Navajo and Apache in western New Mexico and eastern Arizona, settlement by cowboys and miners, and trade among hunters, trappers, Indians and Santa Fe Trail merchants further transformed the region. The arrival of the railroad in the 1870s opened the state to an economic boom, and fortunes were made and lives lost in the lawless days of the Wild West.

Painters and writers, the most famous being Georgia O'Keeffe, set up art colonies in Santa Fe and Taos in the early 20th century. In 1943 a scientific community descended on Los Alamos (see 'Atomic City,' later). The interstate arrived in Albuquerque as late as the 1960s, and until the 1970s most of the roads in Santa Fe were unpaved. Land development and the influx of tourists have altered the landscape, and today million-dollar homes abut some of the poorest counties in the country. The primary issues of the 21st century will be overdevelopment, the ramifications of the nuclear age, the allocation and preservation of water, and problems arising from the state's economic and cultural diversity.

Information

You can contact the New Mexico Department of Tourism (☎ 505-545-2070, 800-733-6396, ⓦ www.newmexico.org, 491 Old Santa Fe Trail, Santa Fe, NM 87503) for various sorts of information. The convenient Public Lands Information Center (☎ 505-438-7542, ⓦ www.publiclands.org, PO Box 27115, Santa Fe, NM 87502) provides camping and recreation information for all public lands in New Mexico.

Sales tax is around 6%, with an additional tax on accommodations in some counties.

The area code in Albuquerque, Santa Fe and Los Alamos is scheduled to change to 575 in June 2002. Local objections, however, may delay the changeover.

Arts

Indian arts – predominantly silver and turquoise jewelry, pottery and basketwork – are for sale from artists' private homes in the pueblos, trading posts and upscale galleries throughout the state. Visitors will also find Hispanic arts, including Santos and woodcarvings. Santa Fe style, with its fusion of Spanish, Mexican and Native American crafts, has developed into a distinct and widely recognized architectural, graphic and decorative aesthetic. Santa Fe and Taos, both artists' colonies since the early 20th century, offer nationally acclaimed visual and performing art.

ALBUQUERQUE

The largest and most populous city in New Mexico has long been a dot on the map of Route 66. You won't find the tourist schlock or the tourist prices of nearby Santa Fe (one hour north); Albuquerque offers inexpensive accommodations and a convenient base for exploring nearby mountains, deserts and Indian sites.

Orientation & Information

Albuquerque's major boundaries are Paseo del Norte Dr to the north, Central Ave to the south, Rio Grande Blvd to the west and Tramway Blvd to the east. Central Ave (I-25 exit 224B or I-40 exit 167) is the city's main artery, passing through Old Town, downtown, the university and Nob Hill. The city is divided into four quadrants (NW, NE, SW and SE). The intersection of Central Ave and the railroad tracks just east of downtown serves as the center point.

The Albuquerque Convention & Visitors Bureau (CVB; ☎ 505-842-9918, 800-733-9918, ⓦ www.abqcvb.org, 20 First Plaza Bldg, Suite 601), in the Galleria, is open weekdays. The Cibola National Forest

---

New Mexico Pueblo Indians

New Mexico's Pueblo Indians are descendants of Ancestral Puebloans (formerly referred to as the Anasazi), who populated much of the Southwest by AD 700. A complex and sophisticated civilization, Ancestral Puebloan culture peaked during the 11th century, with populations centered at Chaco Canyon in northwest New Mexico and Mesa Verde in southwest Colorado (both easily accessible from Farmington, New Mexico). Despite complex irrigation systems and an elaborate network of roads, Chaco Canyon was abandoned at the end of the 12th century for reasons still not clear (perhaps because of drought and a depleted environment).

The Ancestral Puebloans migrated into smaller communities, settling in pueblo villages along the Rio Grande and throughout New Mexico and the Four Corners region, and by the time of Coronado's expedition in 1540, perhaps hundreds of pueblo communities dotted the region. Today, descendants of the Ancestral Puebloans are found in the Pueblo Indian groups throughout New Mexico, particularly along the Rio Grande Valley. The living pueblos at Acoma (circa 12th century) and Taos (circa 1450) are among the oldest continuously inhabited settlements in North America (along with the Hopi village of Old Oraibi in northern New Mexico).

ALBUQUERQUE

PLACES TO EAT
3 Sadies
3 Taco Cabana
5 Flying Star Café
7 Flying Star Café
18 El Patio
19 The Frontier
20 Il Vicino
21 Flying Star Café
22 Scalo's
26 Los Cuates
32 Seasons
35 High Noon Restaurant & Saloon
36 Church St Café
39 Old Route 66 Diner

OTHER
1 Visitor Center
4 Midnight Rodeo
6 Page One
8 Rio Mountainsport
9 Indian Pueblo Cultural Center
13 Visitors Bureau
14 Main Post Office
15 Galleria; Albuquerque Convention & Visitors Bureau
16 Amtrak Station; Albuquerque Bus Transportation Center
17 Presbyterian Hospital
25 Pulse
27 Tingley Coliseum
28 National Hispanic Cultural Center of New Mexico
29 UNM Arena; The Pit
30 UNM Stadium
31 National Atomic Museum
33 REI
34 New Mexico Museum of Natural History & Science
37 Albuquerque Museum
38 Old Town Information Center

PLACES TO STAY
10 El Vado
11 HI/AYH Route 66
12 La Posada de Albuquerque
23 University Lodge
24 Nob Hill Motel

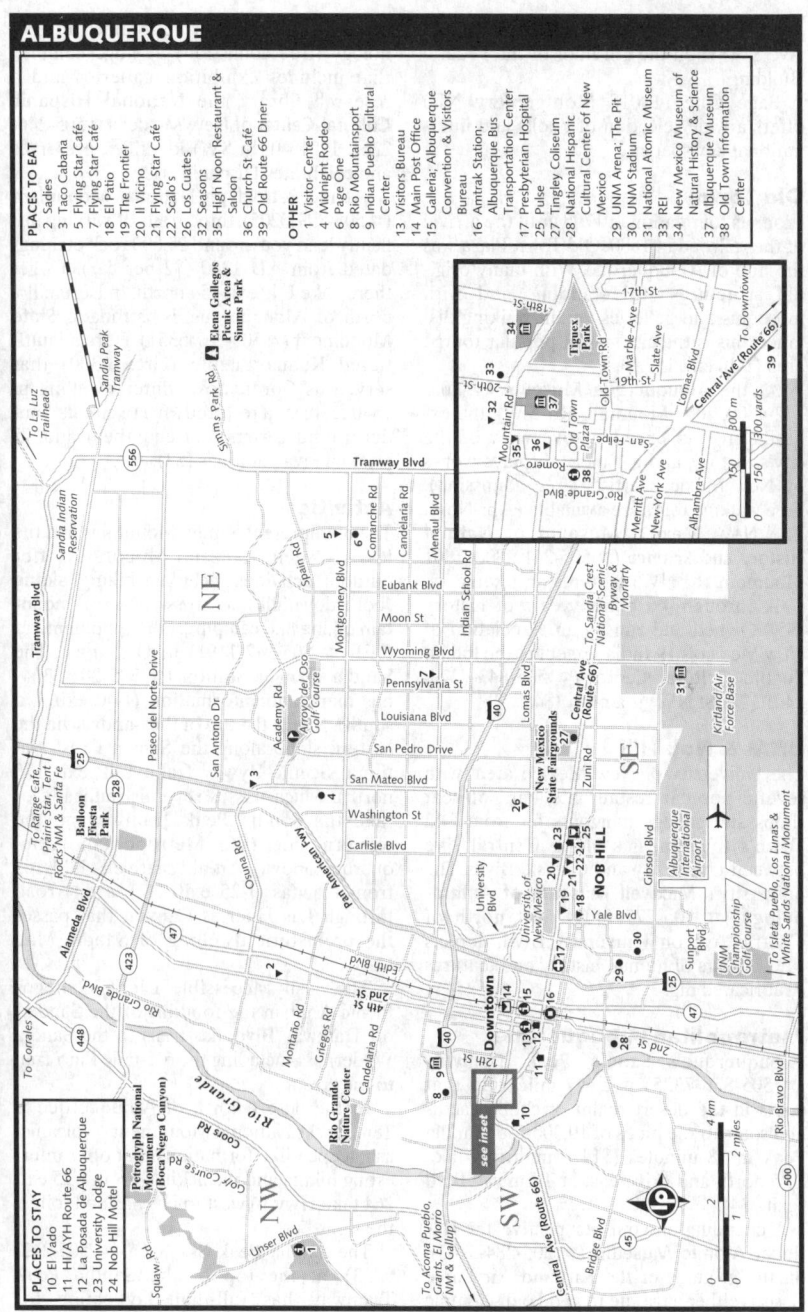

SOUTHWEST

Service office (☎ 505-842-3292, 517 Gold Ave SW) is on the 5th floor of the Federal Building.

Page One (11018 Montgomery NE) offers a wide selection of books and international newspapers.

Old Town

From its foundation in 1706 until the arrival of the railroad in 1880, Old Town Plaza was the hub of Albuquerque. With many original structures still standing, and with museums and galleries within walking distance, this is the city's most popular tourist area (I-40 exit 157A).

At the **Albuquerque Museum** (☎ 505-242-4600, 2000 Mountain Rd NW), the exhibits give an excellent overview of the city's history, and a gallery displays works by New Mexican artists (free admission). Free walking tours are available (Apr-Nov). The **New Mexico Museum of Natural History and Science** (☎ 505-241-2800, 1801 Mountain Rd NW) features an interactive walk through 4.6 billion years of history ($5). Owned and run by an association of New Mexico's 19 Indian pueblos, the **Indian Pueblo Cultural Center** (☎ 505-843-7270, 2401 12th St NW) is a must ($4).

UNM & Nob Hill

The University of New Mexico area, with several popular restaurants, bars, offbeat shops and college hangouts far from Old Town's tourism, lies along Central Ave between University and Carlisle Blvds. The university's **Maxwell Museum of Anthropology** (☎ 505-277-4404), just north of Central Ave on University Blvd, depicts 11,000 years of human history and features a fabricated dig.

Metropolitan Albuquerque

Albuquerque's **Sandia Peak Tramway** (☎ 505-856-7325) is a 2.7-mile ride that starts in the desert realm of cholla cactus and soars to the pines of 10,300-foot Sandia Peak in 18 minutes ($14 roundtrip). Take I-25 north and drive east at Tramway Blvd (exit 234).

Depending on your perspective, the **National Atomic Museum** (☎ 505-284-3243), on the grounds of the Kirtland Air Force Base, is either a tribute to good old scientific know-how or a bizarre public-relations center extolling the virtues of nuclear technology (free admission). A huge complex that includes exhibition galleries and a research library, the **National Hispanic Cultural Center of New Mexico** (☎ 505-246-2261, 1701 4th St SW) identifies, preserves and celebrates Hispanic arts.

At the **Petroglyph National Monument** (☎ 505-899-0205), three trails of varying difficulty lead you around 25,000 rock etchings dated from AD 1300 ($2 per car). To get there, take I-40 exit 154 north. In Bernalillo, north of Albuquerque, is **Coronado State Monument** (☎ 505-867-5351). Here a multitiered Kuaua Pueblo (circa 1300) that served as Coronado's winter dwelling in 1540 features a restored *kiva* (a circular, underground ceremonial chamber) and 15 original kiva paintings ($3).

Activities

The omnipresent Sandia Mountains and the less crowded Manzano Mountains offer outdoor activities including **hiking, skiing** (both downhill and cross-country), **mountain biking** and **camping**. For equipment, try REI (☎ 505-247-1191) in Old Town. The Sandia Ranger Station (☎ 505-281-3304) has maps and information (I-40 exit 175 south). Reach the top of the Sandias via the eastern slope along the Sandia Crest National Scenic Byway (take I-40 exit 175 north), which passes several trailheads, or take the Sandia Peak Tramway up the western side (see Metropolitan Albuquerque above). An alternative is NM 165 from Placitas (I-25 exit 242), a dirt road through Las Huertas Canyon that passes the prehistoric dwelling of Sandia Man Cave.

The easily accessible Elena Gallegos Picnic Area, in the foothills of the Sandias off Tramway Blvd, has trails to the Sandia Wilderness, including the 6½-mile Pino Trail to the crest.

In the desert north of Albuquerque is Tent Rocks National Monument – volcanic-ash, teepee-like formations that offer interesting hiking and picnicking. From I-25 exit 264 take Hwy 16 west to Hwy 22 and follow the signs.

The Sandia Peak Ski Area (☎ 505-242-9133), at the top of the Sandia Peak Tramway, has full-/half-day skiing for $34/25. On weekends (May-Oct), one lift remains open, and mountain-bike rental is available. If you only have time for one hike, take the 8-mile La Luz Trail to the top of the Sandias. To get to the trailhead, take I-25 north to Tramway Blvd, head east, and take the first road on the left (USFS Rd 444) to the end.

Organized Tours

Gray Line (☎ 505-242-3880) offers, among other things, bus tours of Albuquerque ($23) and Acoma Pueblo ($39). For a complete listing of the more than 30 organized tour companies, including those offering specialty tours such as pueblo-art and adventure trips, contact the visitors bureau.

Special Events

Hundreds of hot-air-balloon pilots, with all shapes of balloons (including Noah's Ark and a cow) attract almost one million spectators to the International Balloon Festival in early October. If at all possible, take a balloon ride during one of the 6am ascents.

Places to Stay

Hotel chains hug the interstates and cluster around the airport; try I-40 exit 155.

Contact the Sandia Ranger Station (☎ 505-281-3304) for information on good camping in the Sandia Mountains and Manzano Mountains. Adjacent to Coronado State Monument is a small *campground* (☎ 505-980-8256) with nice views of the Sandia Mountains and the Rio Grande.

Downtown, the friendly **Route 66** (☎ 505-247-1813, 1012 Central SW) offers shared/private rooms for $14/24. Twenty miles east of the city (I-40 exit 175 north), the rural **Sandia Mountain Hostel** (☎ 505-281-4117) affords easy access to mountains ($12/30 shared/private).

Central Ave (I-25 exit 224B) offers plenty of cheap and quirky options. The following have rooms in the $25-35 range. In Old Town, **El Vado** (☎ 505-243-4594, 2500 Central SW), built in 1936, claims to be the purest surviving Route 66 motel in Albuquerque. Just east of the university in trendy Nob Hill are the **Nob Hill Motel** (☎ 505-255-3172, 3712 Central Ave SE) and **University Lodge** (☎ 505-266-7663, 3711 Central Ave NE). There are many other cheapies east of Carlisle, but the neighborhood becomes increasingly seedy the more you head east.

Built in 1939 and registered with Historic Hotels of America, the fine tile, wood and leather lobby of **La Posada de Albuquerque** (☎ 505-242-9090, 800-777-5732, 125 2nd St NW) has a great bar with weekend jazz. Rooms cost $80-180.

In Corrales, a farming village 20 minutes north of town, the friendly **Nora Dixon Place** (☎ 505-898-3662, 888-667-2349, W *www.noradixon.com, 312 Dixon Rd*) has rooms from $75 nestled in the Rio Grande bosque.

Places to Eat

If the chile ain't hot enough, the cook's not mad enough.

– New Mexican adage

Albuquerque offers the traveler plenty of good, cheap food, particularly if you like New Mexican fare. You won't find the trendy, upscale venues like in Santa Fe, but you won't find Santa Fe prices either.

Stay away from the tourist traps around Old Town Plaza. Housed in a tiny home, **Church St Café** (2111 Church St NW) has Mexican food with patio dining. **High Noon Restaurant & Saloon** (425 San Felipe St NW) serves up grilled fare in a rough-hewn, 18th-century adobe. **Seasons** (☎ 505-766-5100, 2031 Mountain Rd NW), with bright yellow walls and high ceilings, has a rooftop cantina (meals cost $7-20). Stop in the tiny **Old Route 66 Diner** (1720 Central Ave SW) for a great green-chile cheeseburger or hot pastrami sandwich ($5).

Near the university, restaurants and bars line Central Ave. Don't miss the **Flying Star Café** (3416 Central SE), with lines going out the door for its creative meals and desserts; there are other locations in the city. Place an order and take a number at **The Frontier**, on Central Ave across from the university, an Albuquerque tradition for delicious but inexpensive meals; it's open 24 hours a day. Students enjoy **El Patio** (142 Harvard Dr SE) for New Mexican food. **Il Vicino** (3403 Central Ave SE) serves wood-oven pizza and microbrewed beer. **Scalo's** (☎ 505-255-8781, 3500 Central Ave SE) is a great spot for upscale Italian.

Los Cuates, on Lomas Blvd at Monroe St, and **Sadies** (6230 4th St NW) are Albuquerque favorites for reasonably priced

Southwestern specialties. North of the city, the expensive *Prairie Star* (☎ 505-867-3327), I-25 exit 242 west, offers Albuquerque's best views of the mountains; come for a sunset drink on the patio. *Range Café*, I-25 exit 240 west then north on Camino del Pueblo, is a hidden jewel for stylized diner fare. Next door, knock to get into *Silva's Saloon*, the quintessential Old West bar that's been setting 'em up since 1933. *Taco Cabana (6500 San Mateo Blvd NE)*, open 24 hours, serves New Mexican food, beer and margaritas.

Entertainment

The free *Weekly Alibi* has information on art and entertainment. The University of New Mexico Box Office (☎ 505-277-4569) sells tickets for performing arts at *Popejoy Hall*. *The Guild* (☎ 505-255-1848), on Central Ave just west of Carlisle Blvd, screens foreign and alternative films.

There are several live music clubs and bars along Central Ave downtown and in the UNM/Nob Hill area. *Anodyne (409 Central Ave NW)*, with book-lined walls, pool tables, more than 100 bottled beers and a long window, is an excellent spot to relax. For country line dancing, try *Midnight Rodeo (☎ 505-888-0100, 4901 McLeod Rd NE)*. Just east of Nob Hill, *Pulse (☎ 505-255-3334, 4100 Central Ave SE)* is a popular gay venue.

Spectator Sports

The University of New Mexico Lobos draw huge crowds to the Pit (☎ 505-925-5626) for basketball. The new New Mexico Slam plays International Basketball League (IBO) basketball at the Convention Center (☎ 505-924-2255). Call the New Mexico Rodeo Association (☎ 505-873-7770) for information on local rodeos.

Getting There & Around

Air Most major US airlines service Albuquerque International Airport (☎ 505-842-4366). Mesa Airlines (☎ 505-842-4218, 800-637-2247) provides local service to cities within New Mexico; to Durango and Colorado Springs, Colorado; and to Dallas, Texas. Rio Grande Air (☎ 505-764-3041, 877-435-9742) services Albuquerque, Farmington, Taos and Durango. Most hotels have free shuttles to the airport.

Bus The Albuquerque Bus Transportation Center (☎ 505-243-4435, 300 2nd St SW) has daily Greyhound buses to Santa Fe ($12; 1 hour), Farmington ($33; 3½ hours), Taos ($22; 3 hours), Alamogordo ($36; 4 hours) and beyond. Sandia Shuttle (☎ 505-243-3244) goes to Santa Fe 10 times daily ($20; 1 hour). For shuttle service to Taos ($20; 3 hours), call Twin Hearts (☎ 505-751-1201, 800-654-9456); it operates four times daily.

Train Amtrak's *Southwest Chief* stops daily at Albuquerque's train station (☎ 505-842-9650, 214 1st St SW), heading east to Kansas City, Missouri (from $116; 17 hours) and Chicago (from $131; 25 hours) at 12:55pm, and west to Flagstaff, Arizona (from $59; 5 hours), and Los Angeles (from $67; 16 hours) at 5:32pm. Service to Santa Fe (from $32) is via the 12:55pm train to Lamy, connecting with a bus to arrive in Santa Fe at 3:40pm.

Local Transportation SunTran (☎ 505-843-9200) buses stop running around 9pm. Three Sun Trolleys serve Central Ave and downtown 10am-6pm daily. Yellow Cab (☎ 505-247-8888) is open 24 hours. Rio Mountainsport (☎ 505-766-9970, 1210 Rio Grande Blvd NW), just north of I-40, rents mountain bikes (from $14 for a half day).

EAST ALONG I-40

Moriarty (35 miles east), Santa Rosa (114 miles east) and especially Tucumcari (173 miles east) make convenient stops for cheap motels.

In Santa Rosa, the **Route 66 Auto Museum** (☎ 505-472-1966, 2766 Old Route 66) pays homage to the mother of all roads. Eight miles north of town, **Santa Rosa State Park** (☎ 505-472-3110) has swimming ($3 per vehicle) and tent/RV sites for $10/14. For a Route 66 original, try the *Blue Swallow Motel (☎ 505-461-9849, 815 E Tucumcari Blvd)* in Tucumcari (from $30). The simple *HI-AYH Redwood Lodge (☎ 505-461-3635, 1502 W Tucumcari Blvd)* has private rooms for $15.

WEST ALONG I-40

Although you can drive to Arizona in about two hours, national monuments and pueblos along the way are worth stopping at for a visit.

ALBUQUERQUE, SANTA FE & TAOS AREA

SOUTHWEST

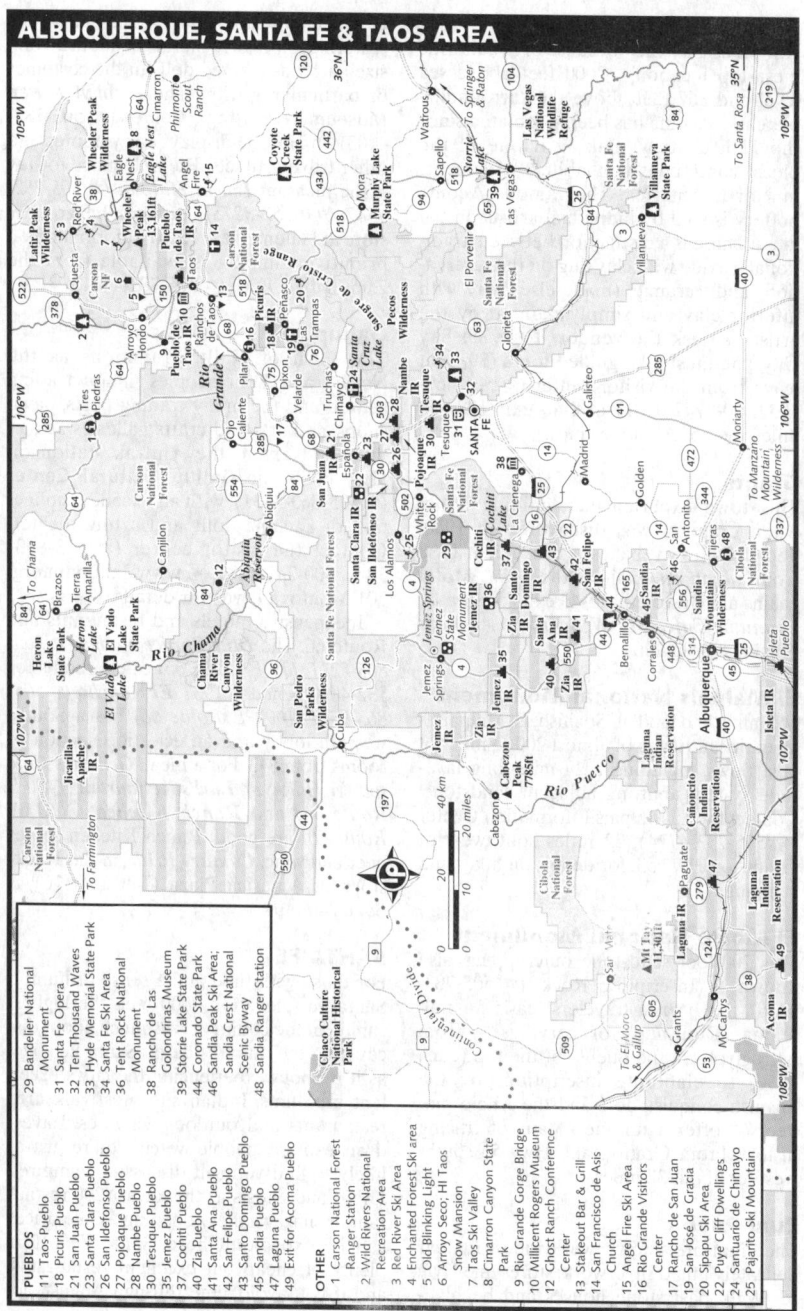

PUEBLOS

11 Taos Pueblo
18 Picuris Pueblo
21 San Juan Pueblo
23 Santa Clara Pueblo
26 San Ildefonso Pueblo
27 Pojoaque Pueblo
28 Nambe Pueblo
30 Tesuque Pueblo
35 Jemez Pueblo
37 Cochiti Pueblo
40 Zia Pueblo
41 Santa Ana Pueblo
42 San Felipe Pueblo
43 Santo Domingo Pueblo
45 Sandia Pueblo
47 Laguna Pueblo
49 Exit for Acoma Pueblo

29 Bandelier National Monument
31 Santa Fe Opera
32 Ten Thousand Waves
33 Hyde Memorial State Park
34 Santa Fe Ski Area
36 Tent Rocks National Monument
38 Rancho de Las Golondrinas Museum
39 Storrie Lake State Park
46 Sandia Peak Ski Area; Sandia Crest National Scenic Byway
48 Sandia Ranger Station

OTHER

1 Carson National Forest Ranger Station
2 Wild Rivers National Recreation Area
3 Red River Ski Area
4 Enchanted Forest Ski area
5 Old Blinking Light
6 Arroyo Seco; Hi Taos
7 Snow Mansion
8 Cimarron Canyon State Park
9 Rio Grande Gorge Bridge
10 Millicent Rogers Museum
12 Ghost Ranch Conference Center
13 Stakeout Bar & Grill
14 San Francisco de Asis Church
15 Angel Fire Ski Area
16 Rio Grande Visitors Center
17 Rancho de San Juan
19 San José de Gracia
20 Sipapu Ski Area
22 Puye Cliff Dwellings
24 Santuario de Chimayo
25 Pajarito Ski Mountain

SOUTHWEST

Acoma Pueblo

Known as 'Sky City' because of its fantastic mesa-top location – 7000 feet above sea level and 367 feet above the surrounding plateau – Acoma has been populated since the 12th century, making it one of the oldest continuously inhabited settlements in North America. The famous Acoma pottery is sold by individual artists on the mesa. There is a distinction between 'traditional' (made with clay dug on the reservation) and 'ceramic' (made elsewhere with inferior clay and simply painted by the artist), so ask the vendor. To reach Sky City, you must take guided tours ($9) that leave from the visitor center (☎ 505-469-1052, 800-747-0181) at I-40 exit 108 (50 miles west of Albuquerque).

Grants

This town experienced a mining boom when uranium was discovered in 1950. Today the town makes a convenient base from which to explore the area. Motel chains are clustered at I-40 exit 85. Stop by ***Uranium Café*** *(519 W Santa Fe Ave)* for breakfast or lunch.

El Malpais National Monument

Meaning 'bad land' in Spanish, El Malpais is an eerie landscape of almost 200 sq miles of lava flows, including a 17-mile-long lava-tube system abutting adjacent sandstone. Contact the El Malpais Information Center (☎ 505-783-4774), 22 miles southwest of Grants on Hwy 53, for details on hikes and camping.

El Morro National Monument

This 200-foot sandstone outcropping, also known as 'Inscription Rock' (☎ 505-783-4226), has been a travelers' oasis for millennia. Thousands of carvings – from petroglyphs in the pueblo at the top (circa 1250) to elaborate inscriptions by the Spanish conquistadors and the Anglo pioneers – offer a unique means of tracing history. From Grants, take Hwy 53 southwest for about 38 miles.

Zuni Pueblo

The Zuni are known worldwide for their delicately inlaid silverwork; stores line Hwy 53. Walk past stone houses and beehive-shaped mud ovens to the massive **Our Lady of Guadalupe Mission** (☎ 505-782-4477), featuring impressive murals of about 30 life-size kachinas (carved dolls in the costumes of particular spirits). The **A:shiwi A:wan Museum & Heritage Center** (☎ 505-782-4403) on Hwy 53 displays early photos and other tribal artifacts. The only place to stay is the pleasant ***Inn at Halona*** *(☎ 505-782-4547, 800-752-3278),* behind the grocery store at Halona Plaza ($85). Information on primitive camping is available from the Zuni Tribal Office (☎ 505-782-4481).

Gallup

The town of Gallup functions as the Navajo and Zuni peoples' major trading center, and the many trading posts, pawn shops, and arts-and-crafts galleries attract visitors. Next to the Amtrak station on Hwy 66 is the **Gallup Cultural Center** (☎ 505-863-4131), with an excellent collection of kachina dolls and a tiny theater. Contact the visitor center (☎ 505-863-3841, 800-242-4282, W www.gallupnm.org, 701 Montoya Blvd) for details.

Inexpensive motels and restaurants line Route 66. The ***Blue Spruce Lodge*** *(☎ 505-863-5211, 119 E Route 66)* offers rooms for $32-40. Opened in 1937, ***El Rancho*** *(☎ 505-863-9311, 1000 E Route 66)* has a Southwestern lobby and an eclectic selection of rooms from $43. For a meal, ***Genaro's Café*** *(600 W Hill Ave),* ***Earl's Restaurant*** *(1400 E Route 66)* and ***Ranch Kitchen*** *(3001 W Route 66)* are good; Ranch Kitchen serves beer and wine. ***Country Pride***, in the Truckstops of America Plaza (I-40 exit 16), is open 24 hours.

SANTA FE

For those with time and a sense of humor, Santa Fe (elevation 7000 feet, the highest capital in the country) is as much about discovering the quirky side of 'Santa Fe style' as it is about experiencing the city's excellent museums, Indian sites, festivals, arts, restaurants and outdoor activities. Eavesdrop, explore, people-watch; you're just as likely to find yourself discussing vampires, UFOs and ghosts as the latest $200 restaurant or snazzy gallery opening. While prices can be exorbitant here, Santa Fe offers plenty of cheap but excellent restaurants, and if you avoid June through August, accommodations can be reasonable.

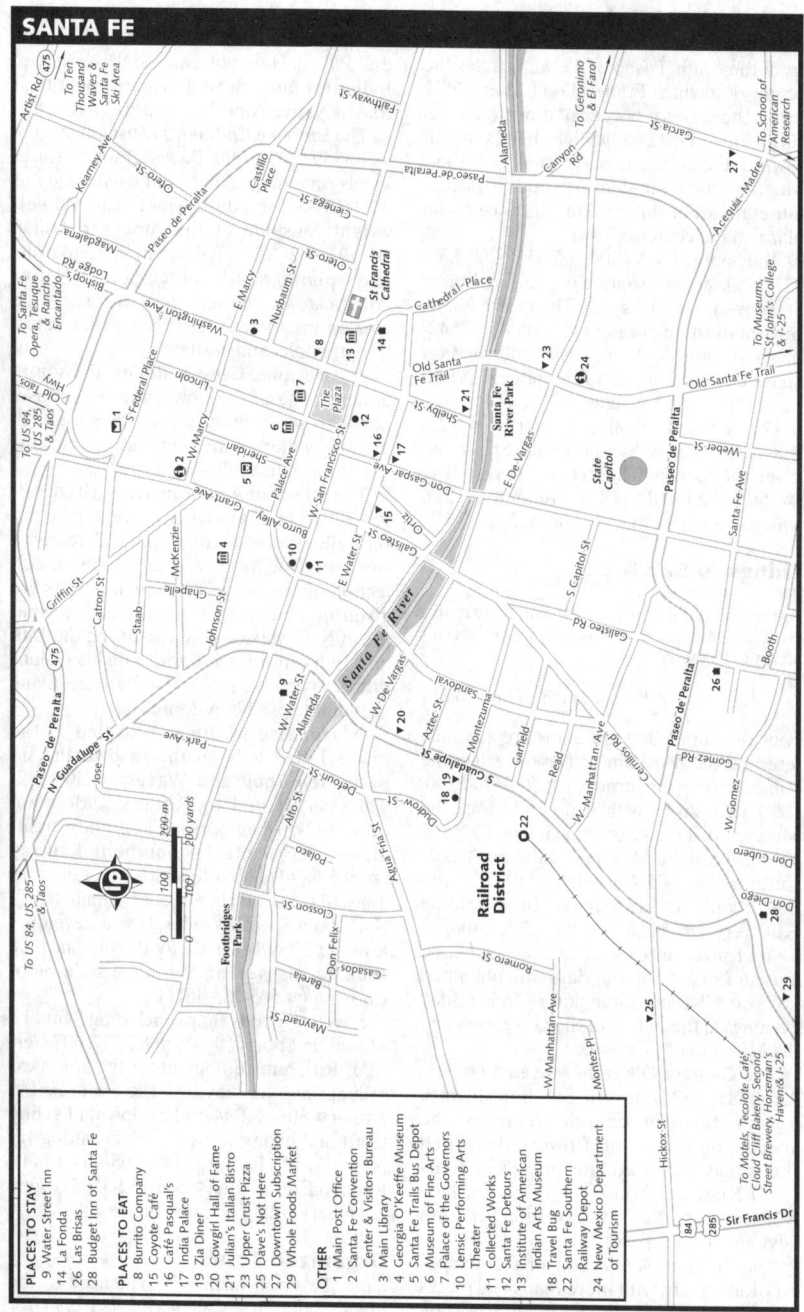

SANTA FE

PLACES TO STAY
9 Water Street Inn
14 La Fonda
26 Las Brisas
28 Budget Inn of Santa Fe

PLACES TO EAT
8 Burrito Company
15 Coyote Café
16 Café Pasqual's
17 India Palace
19 Zia Diner
20 Cowgirl Hall of Fame
21 Julian's Italian Bistro
23 Upper Crust Pizza
25 Dave's Not Here
27 Downtown Subscription
29 Whole Foods Market

OTHER
1 Main Post Office
2 Santa Fe Convention
   Center & Visitors Bureau
3 Main Library
4 Georgia O'Keeffe Museum
5 Santa Fe Trails Bus Depot
6 Museum of Fine Arts
7 Palace of the Governors
10 Lensic Performing Arts
   Theater
11 Collected Works
12 Santa Fe Detours
13 Institute of American
   Indian Arts Museum
18 Travel Bug
22 Santa Fe Southern
   Railway Depot
24 New Mexico Department
   of Tourism

Orientation & Information

Cerrillos Rd (I-25 exit 278) enters town from the south; Paseo de Peralta circles the center of town; St Francis Dr (I-25 exit 282) forms the western border of downtown and turns into US 285, which heads north toward Española, Los Alamos and Taos. Most of the 19th-century buildings and museums are within walking distance of the plaza, in the center of town.

The Santa Fe CVB (☎ 505-955-6200, 800-777-2489, W www.santafe.org, 201 W Marcy St) is open weekdays only. The Public Lands Information Bureau (☎ 505-438-7542, W www.publiclands.org), with information on outdoor activities and camping, is at I-25 exit 282B. Look for signs.

For books, try Collected Works (☎ 505-988-4226, 208B W San Francisco St), across from the Lensic Theater, or Travel Bug (☎ 505-992-0418, 328 S Guadalupe St), which specializes in travel books.

Things to See & Do

If you don't feel the energy when you get to northern New Mexico, then you know you weren't meant to be there.

– A Santa Fean to an Iowa tourist

Four recommended museums are administered by the **Museum of New Mexico**: the Palace of the Governors (☎ 505-476-5100, 100 Palace Ave); with regional history, the Museum of Fine Arts (☎ 505-476-5072, 107 Palace Ave); the Museum of Indian Arts & Culture (☎ 505-476-5072, 710 Camino Lejo); and the Museum of International Folk Art (☎ 505-476-1200, 706 Camino Lejo). Entrance costs $5 for one visit to one museum, or $10 for four days with unlimited visits to all four; admission is free Friday evenings at the Palace of the Governors and the Museum of Fine Arts.

The **Georgia O'Keeffe Museum** (☎ 505-995-0785, 217 Johnson St), housed in a former Spanish church, features the artist's paintings of flowers, bleached skulls and adobe architecture ($5). Tours of O'Keeffe's house in Abiquiu (see Northwestern New Mexico, later) require advance reservations.

The National Collection of Contemporary Indian Art, with more than 8000 pieces of basketry, beadwork and other arts, is on display at the **Institute of American Indian Arts Museum** (☎ 505-983-8900, 108 Cathedral Place). Here you can see the variety of Indian art forms as well as learn about their role in Native American culture ($4).

The **Santa Fe Children's Museum** (☎ 505-989-8359, 1050 Old Pecos Trail) features hands-on exhibits that adults will enjoy as well ($4/3 for adults/kids). The **Wheelwright Museum of the American Indian** (☎ 505-982-4636, 704 Camino Lejo) displays photographs, contemporary Native American art and historical artifacts (free admission); the gift store has a wide selection of books and crafts.

At one time, **Canyon Rd**, on the southeastern edge of the downtown area, was a dusty artists' community. Today about 100 upscale galleries and several restaurants hug this small, adobe-lined street.

The **School of American Research** (☎ 505-954-7205, 660 E Garcia St), a center for anthropological and archaeological research since 1907, features a comprehensive collection of textiles and Indian art. Tours are given on Friday by reservation. See what life in New Mexico was like during the 18th and 19th centuries at **Rancho de las Golondrinas** (☎ 505-471-2261), a 200-acre living museum (closed Nov-March).

A Japanese health spa nestled in the piñon-dotted hills on the road to the ski basin, **Ten Thousand Waves** (☎ 505-982-9304, 3451 Hyde Park Rd) has outdoor hot tubs ($13-26 per person) and body treatments. The **Santa Fe Southern Railway** (☎ 505-989-8600) offers rides to Lamy, 18 miles to the south, in a 1920s Pullman ($30). Ask about specialty rides. If you develop a love for New Mexican food, you can take **cooking classes** at Santa Fe School of Cooking (☎ 505-983-4511).

Sporting-goods shops, including Santa Fe Mountain Sports (☎ 505-988-3337, 607 Cerrillos Rd), rent equipment for the area's excellent outdoor activities. The Santa Fe Ski Area (☎ 505-982-4429) has downhill **skiing** ($40) and **hiking** trails. For **river rafting** try New Wave Rafting (☎ 505-984-1444). Rancho Encantado (☎ 505-982-3537) offers **horseback riding** through the desert.

Organized Tours

Santa Fe's rich history is evidenced in the town's buildings. Call ☎ 505-988-2774 for walking tours ($10). Many companies offer guided tours, including outdoor trips, around Santa Fe and northern New Mexico. Try Santa Fe Detours (☎ 505-983-6565, 800-338-6877, W www.sfdetours.com) and Outback Tours (☎ 505-820-6101, 800-800-5337, W www.outbacktours.com).

Special Events
On the third weekend in August, collectors and nonaficionados alike deluge Santa Fe for the Indian Market (☎ 505-983-5220), a judged show featuring work by more than a thousand Indian artists.

Places to Stay
Rates, often excruciatingly high, vary for no apparent reason – you can haggle. Rates below are for high season (June-Aug). Santa Fe Stay (☎ 505-820-2468, 800-995-2272) specializes in home stays, ranch resorts and *casitas* (adobe cottages). Access the visitor center Web site at W www.santafe.org for other reservation services.

The nearest USFS campgrounds are along the road to the ski basin ($5). Eleven miles east of downtown at I-25 exit 290 is *Rancheros de Santa Fe Camping Park* (☎ 505-466-3482), with tent/RV sites for $17/23 (Mar-Nov). *Santa Fe International Hostel* (☎ 505-988-1153, ☻ santafehostel@quest.net, 1412 Cerrillos Rd) has shared rooms for $15 and private rooms for $25-34.

The usual chains and the cheapest motels line Cerrillos Rd; for rooms in the $55-70 range, try *King's Rest Court* (☎ 505-983-8879, 1452 Cerrillos Rd), *Cottonwood Court* (☎ 505-982-5571, 1742 Cerrillos Rd) and the Route 66–style *Thunderbird Inn* (☎ 505-983-4397, 1821 Cerrillos Rd). *El Rey Inn* (☎ 505-982-1931, 800-521-1349, 1862 Cerrillos Rd), on three grassy acres, has rooms for $60-155. Within walking distance of downtown is *Budget Inn of Santa Fe* (☎ 505-982-5952, 800-288-7600, 725 Cerrillos Rd), with rooms from $82.

Water Street Inn (☎ 505-984-1193, 800-646-6752, 427 W Water St) offers lovely rooms from $125, including breakfast, evening wine and snacks. Two-bedroom Southwest-style condos cost $207 at *Las Brisas* (☎ 505-982-5795, 624 Galisteo Rd); one-bedrooms are available.

Places to Eat
With an overwhelming selection of excellent restaurants, many of them incredibly expensive, choosing a place to eat can be a daunting task.

Around the plaza, the *Burrito Company (111 Washington Ave)* is quick and cheap (burritos under $5). Try *Upper Crust Pizza (329 Old Santa Fe Trail)* too. Despite the wait, don't miss *Café Pasqual's (121 Don Gaspar Ave)*, deservedly famous for its creative and hearty food. *India Palace*, across the street, has a tasty $7 lunch buffet. *Julian's Italian Bistro* (☎ 505-988-2355, 221 Shelby St) is housed in a tiny adobe with a back patio. The rooftop cantina at *Coyote Café (132 Water St)* offers delicious food at half the price of the overhyped main restaurant (from $7; Apr-Oct).

For reasonably priced upscale diner fare in the Guadalupe St area, try *Zia Diner (326 S Guadalupe St)*. Across the street, *Cowgirl Hall of Fame*, with iron-saddle bar chairs, offers live music and barbecue. On Hickox St several blocks west of the south side of Guadalupe St is *Dave's Not Here*, legendary for cheap, delicious New Mexican fare.

Far from the tourist crowds and Santa Fe frills, *Tecolote Café (1203 Cerrillos Rd)* and *Horseman's Haven (6500 Cerrillos Rd)*, on the strip's far south end, serve up huge plates of outstanding New Mexican food ($3-9). Just east of Cerrillos Rd on 2nd St, try Santa Fe hangouts *Cloud Cliff Bakery* (for great breakfasts) and *Second Street Brewery* (with live music).

Check out *Downtown Subscription* for light meals, desserts and a wide range of newspapers and magazines. Head to *Geronimo* (☎ 505-982-1500, 724 Canyon Rd), housed in a 1756 adobe, for a splurge that won't disappoint.

Secluded in the desert silence about 45 minutes northwest of town is the intimate *Rancho de San Juan* (☎ 505-753-6818, W www.ranchodesanjuan.com). The set menu is $45 (rooms are available for rent too). Ask to tour the chapel carved into the sandstone hillside.

Entertainment
Check the free *Santa Fe Reporter* for a thorough listing. The old bar at *El Farol* (☎ 505-983-9912, 808 Canyon Rd) offers live

flamenco, jazz and blues (Thurs-Sat). For a sunset drink, try the rooftop bar at *La Fonda*, a hotel across from St Francis Cathedral, or *Rancho Encantado* (☎ 505-982-3537), 8 miles north of town in Tesuque.

On summer weekends, picnic on the grass for free at the *Shakespeare in the Park* program (☎ 505-982-2910) at St John's College. Even if you're not an opera fan, try to see a summer performance at the open-air *Santa Fe Opera* (☎ 505-986-5900). The tailgate dinners (with crystal and linen) in the parking lot are a Santa Fe tradition ($8-128). Catch a performance at the renovated *Lensic Performing Arts Center* (☎ 505-982-0301, 211 W San Francisco Ave).

Shopping

With everything from carved howling coyotes to turquoise jewelry to fine art, Santa Fe attracts shoppers of all budgets. Pick up a free *Wingspread Collectors Guide* at hotels. On weekends, individual vendors at the Tesuque Pueblo Flea Market, on US 285 north of town, offer everything from 19th-century doors to handcrafted chile-pepper picture frames (May-Oct).

Getting There & Around

TNM&O/Greyhound (☎ 505-471-0008), at St Michael's Dr and Calle Lorca, runs daily buses to Albuquerque ($12; 80 minutes), Taos ($17; 1½ hours) and beyond. Sandia Shuttle (☎ 505-474-5696, 888-775-5696) services Albuquerque Airport ($20; 10 daily), and Twin Hearts (☎ 505-751-1201, 800-654-9456) services Taos ($30; 4 daily). Amtrak's *Southwest Chief* stops at Lamy, where buses take passengers 17 miles to Santa Fe. Santa Fe Trails (☎ 505-438-1464), on Sheridan Ave, provides local service. Call Capital City Cab (☎ 505-438-0000) for a taxi.

AROUND SANTA FE

At the Puye Cliff Dwellings (☎ 505-753-7326), home to the ancestors of today's Santa Clara Indians, you used to be able to climb around in the 740 apartment-like rooms. Fire damage has closed it since 1998, but call for current information. The cliff dwellings are in the Santa Clara Pueblo. Take Hwy 285 north to Española and drive southwest on Hwy 30 for 1.3 miles. Rooms and food in **Española** are cheaper than

Santa Fe, with motels in the $35-60 range. Billed as the 'USA's oldest health resort,' *Ojo Caliente Mineral Springs and Resort* (☎ 505-583-2233, 800-222-9162, ⓦ www .ojocalientespa.com) is a quiet bathhouse spa, with horseback riding, a pool and body treatments (doubles from $100).

PAJARITO PLATEAU & JEMEZ MOUNTAINS

Red rocks, pine forest and streams in this region offer hiking, natural hot springs and fishing. Within miles of each other, the Valles Grande Caldera, Bandelier National Monument and Los Alamos evidence the iconographic geological, human and atomic history of the American West.

Los Alamos

Home to the atomic bomb and perched atop fingerlike mesas, Los Alamos is an interesting spot. The Los Alamos Chamber of Commerce & Visitors Center (☎ 505-662-8105, 800-444-0707, ⓦ www.visit.losalamos.com), in Central Park Square, is open weekdays.

On Central Ave, the well-designed **Bradbury Science Museum** (☎ 505-667-4444) covers atomic history (free admission). Next door, the Otowi Station Museum Shop and Bookstore has a thorough selection of regional and atomic books. With atomic popular-culture artifacts and exhibits on the social history of life 'on the hill' during the secret project, the tiny **Los Alamos Historical Museum** (☎ 505-662-4493), in Fuller Lodge (circa 1928), is worth a visit (free admission). Ask for a self-guided downtown walking-tour pamphlet. The small Pajarito Ski Mountain (☎ 505-662-5725) offers challenging **skiing** on weekends ($33).

The few chain motels in town start at $60. May to October, free basic *camping* is available at the top of the ski mountain. Locals flock to the excellent and cheap *LA Chili Works (1743 Trinity Dr)* for walk-up New Mexican fare (6am-1pm Tue-Fri, 7am-11am Sat). For a beer, live music and bar fare, head to the *Canyon Bar & Grill* (☎ 505-662-3333) on the far north side of Central Park Square.

Bandelier National Monument

Rio Grande Puebloans lived here until the mid-16th century. Today several sites (none restored), a convenient location and a spec-

Atomic Southwest

In 1943, Los Alamos, then a boys' school perched on a 7400-foot mesa, was chosen as the top-secret headquarters of the Manhattan Project (the code name for research and development of the atomic bomb). The 772-acre site, accessed by two dirt roads, had no gas or oil lines, only one wire service and was surrounded by forest. Guarded by barbed wire, Los Alamos was unknown even to nearby Santa Fe; its residents' postal address was simply 'Box 1663, Santa Fe.'

Here, a makeshift community lived under the oddest of circumstances. Unless directly related to the essential details of the project, those who lived on 'the hill' – including scientists' spouses, army personnel and local Latinos and Native Americans recruited to work in the labs and homes – had no idea why they were there or what kind of work was being done.

On July 16, 1945, its scientists first detonated an atomic bomb at the Trinity Site in southern New Mexico, which is now part of White Sands Missile Range. (The precise site is open to visitors twice a year, the first Saturday in April and October.) Upon the USA's detonation of atomic bombs in Japan, the secret city of Los Alamos was exposed to the public. The city continued to be clothed in secrecy, however, until 1957, when restrictions on visiting were lifted.

Today, the lab is still the backbone of the town, and a budding tourist industry proudly embraces the town's atomic history with souvenirs like Atomic City T-shirts (emblazoned with a red and yellow exploding bomb) and La Bomba wine.

tacular landscape make Bandelier (☎ 505-672-3861) a good choice for those interested in ancient pueblos ($10). Almost 50 sq miles of canyons, with backpacking trails and camping, are protected within the monument.

Jemez Springs
This tiny town squeezed into a narrow valley offers several small B&Bs and restaurants, a bathhouse with body treatments, a few monasteries and a Zen Buddhist center. Ask about natural hot springs and camping at the Santa Fe National Forest Ranger Station (☎ 505-829-3535).

Cuba
An old adobe lodge set in 330 acres of the Nacimiento Mountains, the friendly and beautiful *Circle A Ranch Hostel* (☎ 505-289-3350, PO Box 2142, Cuba, NM 87013) is a sworn favorite among those looking for a quiet retreat. Dorms cost $13; private rooms are $38-48. You can take Greyhound to Cuba and call for a pickup (open May-Oct).

TAOS
The first permanent residents of this area were Ancestral Puebloans, who arrived around AD 900. Spanish missionaries in the 16th century, French trappers in the 18th century, American traders in the 19th century, and artists, hippies and outdoor enthusiasts in the 20th century have all left their mark in this relaxed town. At 6967 feet, bordered by the Rio Grande and the Taos Plateau to the west and the Sangre de Cristo Mountains to the north, Taos offers a spectacular landscape and year-round outdoor activities.

Orientation & Information
Entering from the south, Hwy 68 turns into Paseo del Pueblo Sur, with motels and the Taos Visitors Center (☎ 505-758-3873, 800-732-8267, W www.taosguide.com). It goes through town, turning into Paseo del Pueblo Norte, and forks northeast toward Taos Pueblo and northwest toward the ski valley. The Carson National Forest Supervisor's Office (☎ 505-758-6200, 208 Cruz Alta) is east of the strip, and the Bureau of Land Management (BLM; ☎ 505-758-8851) is next door.

Things to See & Do
Built around AD 1450 and continuously inhabited ever since, **Taos Pueblo** (☎ 505-758-1028) is the largest existing multistory pueblo structure in the USA and one of the best surviving examples of traditional adobe construction – well worth a visit. An informal tour is offered daily (no fee, but you should tip the guide). The pueblo may

be closed for sacred ceremonial dances in February, March and August; call for current information on hours and festivals. Taos Indian Horse Ranch (☎ 505-758-3212) offers **horseback riding** through Indian land (from $40).

The historic homes of three influential local figures reflect three distinct elements of Taos history – the mountain man, the artist and the trader. Tickets to the **Kit Carson Home** (☎ 505-758-4741), one block from the plaza on Kit Carson Rd; the **Blumenschein Home** (☎ 505-758-0505, 222 Ledoux St); and the **Martínez Hacienda** (☎ 505-758-1000), a colonial trader's former home on Ranchitos Rd, cost $5/7.50/10 for one/two/three homes. Housed in a 19th-century adobe compound, the **Harwood**

Foundation Museum (☎ 505-758-9826, 238 Ledoux St) features paintings, sculpture and photography by northern New Mexico artists ($5).

Works from the Taos Society of Artists (1912–26) are on display at the **Van Vechten–Lineberry Taos Art Museum** (☎ 505-758-2690), on Camino del Pueblo ($6). Originally home to Russian artist Nicolai Fechin, who meticulously carved its interior in the 1920s, the **Fechin Institute** (☎ 505-758-1710, 227 Paseo del Pueblo Norte) showcases his paintings ($4). The **Millicent Rogers Museum** (☎ 505-758-2462), filled with pottery, jewelry, baskets and textiles, is considered one of the best collections of Indian and Spanish colonial art in the USA ($6). It's on Millicent Rogers

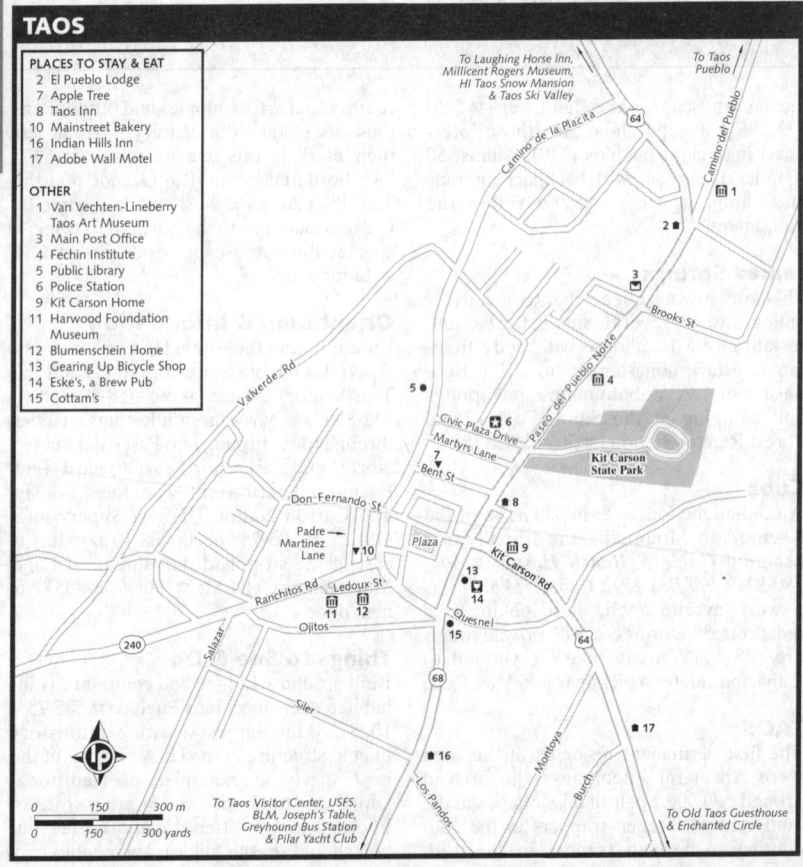

TAOS

PLACES TO STAY & EAT
2   El Pueblo Lodge
7   Apple Tree
8   Taos Inn
10 Mainstreet Bakery
16 Indian Hills Inn
17 Adobe Wall Motel

OTHER
1   Van Vechten-Lineberry
    Taos Art Museum
3   Main Post Office
4   Fechin Institute
5   Public Library
6   Police Station
9   Kit Carson Home
11 Harwood Foundation
    Museum
12 Blumenschein Home
13 Gearing Up Bicycle Shop
14 Eske's, a Brew Pub
15 Cottam's

To Laughing Horse Inn,
Millicent Rogers Museum,
HI Taos Snow Mansion
& Taos Ski Valley

To Taos Pueblo

Camino de la Placita
Camino del Pueblo
Brooks St
Valverde Rd
Paseo del Pueblo Norte
Civic Plaza Drive
Martyrs Lane
Bent St
Don Fernando St
Padre Martinez Lane
Plaza
Kit Carson Rd
Kit Carson State Park
Ranchitos Rd
Ledoux St
Ojitos
Quesnel
Salazar
Siler
Los Pandos
Montoya
Burch

To Taos Visitor Center, USFS,
BLM, Joseph's Table,
Greyhound Bus Station
& Pilar Yacht Club

To Old Taos Guesthouse
& Enchanted Circle

0   150   300 m
0   150   300 yards

Museum Rd about 4 miles north of the plaza.

At 650 feet above the Rio Grande, the steel **Rio Grande Gorge Bridge** is the second-highest suspension bridge in the USA. Call for information on Spanish and English services at the 16th-century **San Francisco de Asis Church** (☎ 505-758-2754), at the southern end of the strip in Rancho de Taos, south of Taos itself. Designed by Michael Reynolds to 'eliminate stress from both the planet and its inhabitants,' **Earthships** (☎ 505-751-0462, Ⓦ www.earthship.org) are environmentally friendly houses built with used automobile tires and cans and set in the Taos Plateau ($5). Ask about overnight accommodations.

The major attraction in the summer is **white-water rafting** in the Taos Box, the steep-sided cliffs that frame the Rio Grande; trips average $45/80 for a half/full day. There are **hiking** trails for all levels; several trailheads line the road to the ski valley. Cottam's (☎ 505-758-2822) and Gearing Up Bicycle (☎ 505-753-7559), both on Paseo del Pueblo Sur just south of the plaza, rent bikes and have information on trails.

With a peak elevation of 11,819 feet and a 2612-foot vertical drop, Taos Ski Valley offers some of the most challenging **skiing** in the US and yet remains low-key and relaxed ($45). Contact Taos Ski Valley, Inc (☎ 505-776-2291, Ⓦ www.skitaos.org) for details on accommodations, summer activities and week-long ski packages (from $1250).

Places to Stay

The Taos Ski Valley Visitors Bureau and New Mexico Reservations (☎ 505-776-2233, 800-776-1111, Ⓦ www.taosskivalley.com, PO Box 90, Taos Ski Valley, NM 87525) books condos, cabins and hotels.

Campers will find plenty of seasonal basic camping in the *Carson National Forest*; the closest campgrounds are east of Taos nestled between Hwy 64 and a creek. The *Questa Ranger Station* (☎ 505-586-0520) maintains five free campgrounds along the stream on the road to Taos Ski Valley. In Pilar, the *Orilla Verde National Recreation Site* (☎ 505-758-4060) has pleasant desert sites along the Rio Grande ($8). At the desolate BLM *Wild Rivers National*

Recreation Area, 26 miles north of town, you can camp and grill at the piñon-studded sites overlooking the Rio Grande Gorge or hike down the gorge to backcountry sites by the river ($7; no hookups).

Ten minutes north of Taos in the tiny town of Arroyo Seco is the *HI Taos Snow Mansion* (☎ 505-776-8298), with bunk-style lodging ($20), private rooms and teepees (from $28), and camping ($10 for one, $5 for each additional person).

Greyhound will drop you at the *Pilar Yacht Club* (☎ 505-758-9072), set next to the Rio Grande in Pilar; doubles cost $40/125 for a night/week. Rooms at *Indian Hills Inn* (☎ 505-758-4715, 233 Paseo del Pueblo Sur), *El Pueblo Lodge* (☎ 505-758-8700, 800-433-9612, 412 Paseo del Pueblo Norte) and *Adobe Wall Motel* (☎ 505-758-3972, 227 E Kit Carson Rd) cost $50-100. Listed on the National Register of Historic Places, the *Taos Inn* (☎ 505-758-2233, 800-826-7466, 125 Paseo del Pueblo Norte) has a great bar with live music and rooms from $90.

A travelers' hangout with bikes for loan, an honor-system kitchen and a hot tub, the quirky *Laughing Horse Inn* (☎ 505-758-8350, 800-776-0161, 729 Paseo del Pueblo Norte) is a treat. Rates vary from $47 for a single to $150 for a guesthouse sleeping four. The friendly and peaceful *Old Taos Guesthouse* (☎ 505-758-5448, 505-758-5548), east of town off Kit Carson Rd, has Southwestern rooms from $75.

Places to Eat

Try *Mainstreet Bakery* on Guadalupe Plaza for plates of 'all organic – all natural …almost' (under $7). On Paseo del Pueblo Norte, *Orlando's* is good for New Mexican fare. The *Apple Tree* (☎ 505-758-1900, 123 Bent St), housed in an adobe home, has a patio and good upscale food. *El Pueblo Café* (625 Paseo del Pueblo Norte) is a no-frills cafe open until 2:30am on weekends. A quiet spot with a low-beamed ceiling, *Joseph's Table* (☎ 505-751-4512, 4167 Paseo del Pueblo Sur) serves excellent food ($20). For a slice, stop by *Outback Pizza* (712 Paseo del Pueblo Norte). Try a green-chile beer or Dead Presidents Ale and cheap, tasty pub fare, and listen to live music at *Eske's, a Brew Pub*, just south of the plaza off Paseo del Pueblo Sur.

Just east of the blinking light on the way to the ski valley, **Old Blinking Light** is good. Isolated in the hills 9 miles south of town with views of Taos Valley, **Stakeout Grill & Bar** (☎ *505-758-2042*) specializes in steaks. It's pricey, but you can always come for a drink.

Getting There & Around

From Santa Fe, take either 'the high road' along Hwy 76 and Hwy 518, with galleries, Hispanic villages and sites worth exploring (in particular, San Jose de Gracia and Sanctuario de Chimayo), or follow the Rio Grande on Hwy 68.

TNM&O/Greyhound (☎ 505-758-1144, 1238 Gustorf Rd) has daily service to Santa Fe ($16; 1½ hours) and Albuquerque ($24; 2¼ hours).

Twin Hearts Express (☎ 505-751-1201, 800-654-9456) shuttles to Albuquerque Airport ($40; 3 hours), Santa Fe ($25; 1½ hours) and Taos Ski Valley ($10, 40 minutes); call for other shuttle destinations.

ENCHANTED CIRCLE

This 84-mile loop takes you north and east of Taos through barren windswept high desert, alpine forests and mountain streams. North of Questa is the spectacular **Wild Rivers National Recreation Area** (see Camping under Taos) and the 20,000-acre Latir Peak Wilderness. **Red River** (☎ 505-754-2366, 800-348-6444), originally a gold-mining town, is an 'Old West' family spot with a small ski slope.

NORTHEASTERN NEW MEXICO

Dinosaur tracks and the tracks of the Santa Fe Trail contribute to the ancient allure of these high plains.

Las Vegas

Don't be fooled. This Las Vegas is a far cry from its neon namesake in Nevada.

The area was inhabited mainly by Comanches until 15 Latino families received a grant to found Las Vegas in 1835. In 1846 the USA assumed possession. Historians claim that more than 900 19th-century buildings in Las Vegas are listed on the National Register of Historic Places. Ask for a walking-tour brochure from the chamber of commerce (☎ 505-425-8631, 800-832-5947, Ⓦ www.lasvegasnewmexico.com, 513 6th

St). The Santa Fe National Forest Ranger Station (☎ 505-425-3534, 1926 7th St) has information on the area's outdoor activities and camping.

The **Inn on the Santa Fe Trail** (☎ *505-425-6791, 1133 Grand Ave*) offers Southwestern decor (rooms cost $60-70). Built in 1882, the **Plaza Hotel** (☎ *505-425-3591, 800-328-1882, 230 Old Town Plaza*) has doubles for $92. **El Rito de San José** (☎ *505-425-7027*), north of Las Vegas in Porvenir, offers 10 rustic and isolated cabins for $55-75 (May-Oct). In the tiny village of Sapello, the **Star Hill Inn** (☎ *505-425-5605*) is 'an astronomer's retreat in the Rockies,' with telescopes and 195 acres for hiking. Cottages with fireplaces cost $70-120.

The best spot for New Mexican food is the casual **Estellas** on Bridge St.

Cimarron

Home of Ute and Apache Indians, Cimarron was a Wild West town following Anglo settlement. The old St James Hotel alone saw the deaths of 26 men. Today Cimarron is a quiet village of less than 1000 inhabitants. At **Cimarron Canyon State Park**, a steep-walled canyon with several hiking trails and excellent trout fishing, there are three basic **campgrounds** (☎ *505-377-6271*) nestled along the Cimarron River ($10). The **St James Hotel** (☎ *505-376-2664, 800-748-2694*), originally a saloon in 1873 (as evidenced by the bullet holes in the ceiling), has a cozy bar with a pool table and simple late-19th-century-style rooms for $90-120.

Raton

This town's visitor center (☎ 505-445-3689, 800-638-6161, Ⓦ www.raton.com, 100 Clayton Rd) has statewide information and a walking tour that takes in New Deal murals and buildings from the town's mining and railroad days.

In the foothills of the Rockies (7800-foot elevation), 10 miles northeast of Raton, **Sugarite Canyon State Park** (☎ 505-445-5607) has hiking, cross-country skiing and ice-skating. Tent/RV sites cost $7/13. For early Western ambience, try the recommended **El Portal Hotel** (☎ *505-445-3631, 101 N 3rd St*), with rooms for $45/140 per day/week. For New Mexican food, try **La Cosina Café** (*745 S 3rd St*).

Capulin Volcano National Monument

Rising 1300 feet above the surrounding plains, Capulin Volcano ($5) is the easiest to visit of several volcanoes in the area. From the visitor center (☎ 505-278-2201), a 2-mile road spirals up the mountain to a parking lot at the crater rim (8182 feet), where trails lead around and into the crater. The entrance is 3 miles north of the village of Capulin, which is 30 miles east of Raton on Hwy 87.

Clayton Lake State Park

This park (☎ 505-374-8808), 12 miles northwest of Clayton on Hwy 370, contains more than 500 footprints of eight dinosaur species ($4). Tent/RV sites cost $7/11. Nearby Clayton has chain motels and the historic *Eklund Dining Room & Saloon* (☎ 505-374-2551, 15 Main St).

SOUTHEASTERN NEW MEXICO

Often overlooked for the tourist mecca of the north, some of the state's most awesome and recommended sites dot the southeast's vast expanses of desert, ranchland, nondescript towns and oil rigs.

Alamogordo & Around

Alamogordo (Spanish for 'fat cottonwood') lies at 4350 feet in the Tularosa Basin, with the Sacramento Mountains to the east. The Alamogordo Visitor Center (☎ 505-437-6120, 800-826-0294, W www.alamogordo.com) is at 1301 N White Sands Blvd (WSB).

The **International Space Hall of Fame** (☎ 505-437-2840, 877-333-6589), a five-story glass cube at the east end of Indian Wells Rd, looms over town. Inside are exhibits about space research and flight ($5.50) and a huge wraparound screen theater featuring multimedia presentations ($5.50).

To reach the **Three Rivers Petroglyph National Recreation Area** (☎ 505-525-4300), drive 17 miles north on Hwy 43. It showcases 20,000 petroglyphs inscribed 1000 years ago by the Jornada Mogollon people ($2). There are free campsites with water and toilets.

At **White Sands National Monument** (☎ 505-679-2599), gypsum, a chalky mineral used in making plaster of paris, covers 275 sq miles to create a dazzling white sea of sand. From beyond the visitor center, 16

miles southwest of Alamogordo, a 16-mile loop leads into the heart of the park. You are encouraged to climb and play in the dunes, and several hiking trails leave the parking areas ($3). Apply for backcountry camping permits ($3) at the visitor center.

Abundant developed and free camping is available in *Lincoln National Forest*, paticularly along forest roads branching off from Hwy 82 east of Alamogordo. The *Oscuro High Desert Hostel* (☎ 505-648-4007), a working ranch on 240 acres 15 miles south of Carrizozo (between mile markers 108 and 107 on Hwy 54), has dormitory/private rooms for $14/27. The hostel is a 1½-mile walk from the Greyhound stop in Oscuro; call for a pickup. Hotels and cheap motels stretch out along WSB.

Stop by *Plaza Pub* on the corner of WSB and 10th St for great green-chile stew, a wide selection of beer and a game of pool. *Keg's Brewery* (817 Scenic Dr) has '60s decor and bands (everything from heavy metal to country) on some weekends.

TNM&O/Greyhound (☎ 505-437-3050, 601 N WSB) has several daily buses heading north to Albuquerque ($36; 4½ hours) and south to Carlsbad ($35; 4½ hours).

The El Paso Shuttle (☎ 505-437-1472, 800-872-2701) services El Paso International Airport ($21; 1½ hours), and Shuttle Ruidoso (☎ 800-872-2701) services Ruidoso ($25; 1 hour) by reservation only. Shuttles depart from the Best Western at 1020 S WSB.

Cloudcroft

Hwy 82 climbs from 4315 to 9000 feet within 16 miles to pleasant Cloudcroft, a welcome relief from the desert. The chamber of commerce (☎ 505-682-2733, W www.cloudcroft.net) is on Hwy 82.

Beyond the many camping options, most accommodations in Cloudcroft are cabins. *The Lodge* (☎ 505-682-2566, 800-395-6343), built in 1911, stands out as one of the best historic hotels in the state (from $80). Inside, *Rebecca's* offers good food with views. The popular *Western Bar & Café*, on Burro Ave, is straight out of a Wild West movie.

Ruidoso

Located in the Sacramento Mountains, this resort town (elevation 7000 feet) is famous

SOUTHWEST

for top-notch horseracing at **Ruidoso Downs Racetrack** (☎ 505-378-4431) and outdoor activities. American West enthusiasts will enjoy the more than 10,000 western-related items in the **Hubbard Museum of the American West** (☎ 505-378-4142), about 4½ miles east of downtown on Hwy 70 ($6). Ski Apache (☎ 505-336-4356) offers good **skiing** ($42). Tourist information is available at the chamber of commerce (☎ 505-257-7395, 800-253-2255, W www.ruidoso.net, 720 Sudderth Dr).

Beyond camping and chain hotels, accommodations are mainly condos and mountain cabins. Call Central Reservations of Ruidoso (☎ 505-257-7477, 888-257-7577).

The once-grand *Inn of the Mountain Gods* (☎ 505-257-5141, 800-545-9011), beautifully set on the Mescalero Apache Reservation, offers a casino and activities, including horseback riding, hunting, swimming and archery (double rooms start at $100). *Ruidoso Lodge Cabins* (☎ 505-257-2510, 800-950-2510, 300 Main St) has cabins along the river for $80-150. Seventeen simple but nice rooms with refrigerators and microwaves start at $50 at the *Sitzmark Chalet* (☎ 505-257-4140, 800-658-9694, 627 Sudderth Dr).

Lively *Casa Blanca* (501 Mechem Dr) serves Mexican food in a renovated Spanish-style house. Great for kids, the *Flying J Ranch* (☎ 505-336-4330), on Hwy 48 about 1½ miles north of Alto, is a 'Western village' offering a Wild West gunfight, a chuckwagon, dinner, and a stage show with Cowboy music (June-Sept; $16). For more elegance, try *La Lorraine* (☎ 505-257-2954, 2523 Sudderth Dr), with food for $12-22.

TNM&O/Greyhound (☎ 505-257-2660, 138 Service Rd) has daily buses to Alamogordo ($11; 1 hour), Roswell ($16; 1½ hours) and beyond. Shuttle Ruidoso (☎ 505-336-1683) goes to Alamogordo four times daily ($25), by reservation only. Enterprise (☎ 505-257-1154, 643 Sudderth Dr) rents cars.

Valley of Fires Recreation Area

Just west of the intersection of Hwy 380 and Hwy 54, 58 miles from Alamogordo, this recreation area (☎ 505-648-2241) features the most recent lava flows in the continental USA ($5). Primitive camping and RV

hookups cost $5-11. In nearby Carrizozo, Outpost Bar & Grill serves excellent green chile.

Lincoln

For fans of Western history, a visit to tiny Lincoln – where a gun battle turned Billy the Kid into a legend – is a must. Modern influences (neon-lit motels, souvenir stands, fast-food joints) are not allowed. Main St is designated as **Lincoln State Monument** (☎ 505-653-4372), and a joint ticket to the local museum and 19th-century buildings costs $6. The recommended *Casa de Patrón B&B* (☎ 505-653-4676, 800-524-5202) has rooms from $87.

Roswell

Oddly famous as both the country's largest producer of wool and its UFO capital, Roswell has built a tourist industry around the alleged 1947 UFO crash here. The visitors bureau (☎ 505-624-0889, 888-767-9355, W www.roswell-usa.com) is at 426 N Main St.

Believers and skeptics alike will want to check out the **UFO Museum & Research Center** (☎ 505-625-9495, 114 N Main St). With 17 galleries filled with Southwestern art and an eclectic mix of historical artifacts, the **Roswell Museum & Goddard Planetarium** (☎ 505-624-6744, 100 W 11th St) is worth a visit.

At *Bottomless Lakes State Park* (☎ 505-624-6058), east of Roswell off Hwy 380, tent/RV sites cost $10/14. Hotels and cheap motels, including *Budget Inn West* (☎ 505-623-3811, 2200 W 2nd St), with rooms from $32, line Main and 2nd Sts. The *Nuthin' Fancy Café* (2103 N Main St) features blue-plate specials (meatloaf, chicken-fried steak and other American diner fare) and 14 beers on tap.

Buses leave daily for Albuquerque ($35; 4 hours) and Carlsbad ($20; 1½ hours) from the TNM&O/Greyhound bus station (☎ 505-622-2510, 1100 N Virginia Ave), behind Wendy's.

Carlsbad

Travelers use Carlsbad as a base for visits to nearby Carlsbad Caverns National Park (see below) and the Guadalupe Mountains (see the Texas chapter). The National Parks Information Center (☎ 505-885-8884, 3225

National Parks Hwy) and the chamber of commerce (☎ 505-887-6516, 800-221-1224, W www.chamber.caverns.com, 302 S Canal St) have information on both.

The **Living Desert State Park** (☎ 505-887-5516) spread out over the Ocotillo Hills on the northwestern outskirts of town (on Miehls Dr off US 285) exhibits the wildlife of the Chihuahuan Desert ($4).

Many motels line Canal St. Try the *Economy Inn* (☎ 505-885-4914, 1621 S Canal St), with rooms starting at $30. Locals and visitors crowd *Lucy's* (701 S Canal St) for cheap, tasty New Mexican. *Jerry's* (3720 National Parks Hwy) serves American fare 24 hours.

TNM&O/Greyhound buses leave daily from the bus depot (☎ 505-887-1108, 1000 S Canyon St) for Albuquerque ($47; 5 hours) and El Paso ($32; 3 hours).

Carlsbad Caverns National Park

Who in their right mind would drive for hours across the desert just to see a cave? You'll see. The park covers 73 sq miles and includes more than 85 caves, including the 60-mile **Lechugilla Cave**. A 2-mile subterranean walk from the cave mouth reaches an underground chamber 1800 feet long, 255 feet high and more than 800 feet below the surface.

The park's second attraction is the Mexican free-tail **bat colony** that roosts here (Apr-Oct). For more than self-guided tours, call the park (☎ 505-785-2232, 800-967-2283). Backpacking trips into the desert backcountry are allowed by permit (free).

Fort Sumner

Famous for the atrocious Bosque Redondo Indian Reservation disaster (see the boxed text) and Billy the Kid's last showdown with Sheriff Pat Garrett, this area is full of Indian and outlaw history. Camping and inexpensive accommodations are nearby.

SOUTHWESTERN NEW MEXICO

Dominated by the Chihuahuan Desert, this is sparsely populated ranching country with a mining and railroad history. In the north, the countryside rises to the mountains of the Gila National Forest.

Tragedy at Bosque Redondo

With the Union victory at Glorietta Pass in March 1862, the threat of Confederate control of the Southwest ended and the troops turned all their force on the Native Americans. The battles that followed were cruel and bloody, involving broken treaties and several massacres.

Brigadier General James H Carleton directed Kit Carson of the New Mexico volunteers to invade the Mescalero Apache and Navajo. Despite his initial reluctance to fight Indians, arguing that he had volunteered to fight Confederates, and threatening to resign, Carson eventually followed orders. During a cold and snowy March in 1863, Carson marched into Canyon de Chelly, the Navajo stronghold, and destroyed crops, orchards and livestock. Six thousand Navajo surrendered out of starvation, and so began the nearly 400-mile 'Long Walk' from Canyon de Chelly to Bosque Redondo. Hundreds of Navajo died from hunger or the elements before reaching the reservation.

Chiefs Manuelito, Barboncito and Armicjo, refusing to surrender, hid in the mountains with their people. Others escaped the reservation, and Carleton posted guards for 40 miles around Fort Sumner. For years, Carleton hunted Navajos, and for years Manuelito and other warriors resisted capture. On September 1, 1866, a worn-down Manuelito finally surrendered, and soon after, Barboncito, the last of the Navajo chiefs, surrendered.

Carleton had hoped to convert the defeated Indians to Christian farmers, but the land was harsh and unsuitable for agriculture, and brackish water spurred disease. Eighteen days after Manuelito's surrender, General Carleton was removed from command in New Mexico, and for two years, officials from Washington, DC, came to assess the situation. In 1868, under the direction of General William Sherman and after four years of starvation and deprivation, the surviving Indians were allowed to return to their homelands. About 3000 had died since their imprisonment at Bosque Redondo. (See Navajo Indian Reservation, under Northeastern Arizona, for more information.)

Socorro & Around

Stop by the chamber of commerce (☎ 505-835-0424), on the plaza, for information on the area. Thousands of minerals, fossils and other geological exhibits are displayed at the **Mineral Museum** (☎ 505-835-5420), on the campus of the New Mexico Institute of Mining & Technology (free admission). The **Very Large Array** radio telescope facility, 27 huge antenna dishes sprouting like giant mushrooms in the high plains, is 20 miles to the west of Magdalena, on Hwy 60. Endangered whooping cranes winter in the 90 sq miles of fields and marshes at **Bosque del Apache National Wildlife Refuge** (☎ 505-835-1828); entrance costs $3 per car. On the way from I-25 (exit 139), stop at the *Owl Bar Cafe* for amazing green-chile cheeseburgers (closed Sun).

Socorro RV Park (☎ *505-835-2234*), at I-25 exit 147, has RV sites for about $20. *Sands Motel* (☎ *505-835-1130, 400 California NE*) and the *Economy Inn* (☎ *505-835-0276, 205 California NW*) offer clean rooms in the high $20s. Motel 6 and other chains are represented. On the east side of the plaza, *Martha's Black Dog Coffeehouse* serves tasty coffees, breakfasts, sandwiches and salads, while *Socorro Springs Brewing Co*, just north, has good pizzas, pastas and microbrews.

Call Greyhound (☎ 505-835-1767) for bus information.

Truth or Consequences

Built on the site of natural hot springs in the 1880s, today 'T or C' is a funky little town named for a 1940s radio program. Wander around the little hole-in-the-wall cafes and check out the junk shops. Elephant Butte Lake State Park (☎ 520-744-5421) and other local lakes offer excellent fishing. For a soak ($6), try Charles Motel & Bath House with massage, sauna, reflexology, holistic healing available, or the Riverbend Hot Springs, with six outdoor tubs by the river.

Riverbend Resort (☎ *505-894-6183, 100 Austin Ave)* includes a friendly riverside HI-AYH hostel with cabins, trailers and teepees. Dorms cost $15 and doubles start at $30, including free hot mineral baths. Basic, ragged, cheap motels are along Date St between 6th and 9th Sts (all around $20). Better bets are the *Ace Lodge* (☎ *505-894-2151), Desert View Motel* (☎ *505-894-3318)* and the *Charles Motel* (☎ *505-894-7154, 601*

Broadway), with rooms in the $30s, For a meal, head to *Hilltop Cafe (1301 N Date St)* or *La Cocina*, I-25 exit 79.

Greyhound/TNM&O (☎ 505-894-3649) runs two daily buses north and south.

Las Cruces & Around

This town is a farming center for chiles, pecans and apples; most farms are small and family owned. The village of Hatch, 40 miles north, is considered New Mexico's chile capital. New Mexico State University (NMSU), with some 15,000 students, gives the town a friendly college feel and offers interesting museums. The city is at 4200 feet, between the Rio Grande Valley and the strangely fluted Organ Mountains, rising to the east. The visitors bureau (☎ 505-541-2444, 211 N Water St) is open weekdays.

Three miles southwest of downtown Las Cruces is **Mesilla**, established in 1850 for Mexican settlers who wished to avoid becoming part of the USA after the Mexican-American War. Despite the souvenir shops and tourist-oriented restaurants, the Mesilla Plaza and surrounding blocks are a step back in time. Wander around to get the feeling of an important mid-19th-century Southwestern town.

For bird-watching, head to **Dripping Springs National Recreation Area** (☎ 505-522-1219), located in the Organ Mountains (head east on University Ave). En route to the area you'll find the **New Mexico Farm & Ranch Heritage Museum** (☎ 505-522-4100), 'the largest farm and ranch museum in the country.'

For camping, *Siesta RV Park* (☎ *505-523-6816, 1551 Avenida de Mesilla)* charges $19 with hookups and has a few tent sites. A number of cheap places with doubles in the $20s are clustered along Picacho Ave east of Hwy 292. Try *Royal Host Motel* (☎ *505-524-8536)* or *Economy Inn* (☎ *505-524-8627)*. Nearby, the pleasant *Day's End Lodge* (☎ *505-524-7753, 755 N Valley Dr)* has a pool and charges $30/35 for singles/doubles, including breakfast.

Of the several B&Bs, *Lundeen Inn of the Arts* (☎ *505-526-3326, 888-526-3326,* ⓦ *www.innofthearts.com, 618 S Alameda Blvd)* stands out. It's a large, turn-of-the-19th-century adobe house with 20 guest rooms and an art gallery. Doubles cost $75-105, including full breakfast.

The university crowd hangs out at *Spirit Winds Coffee Bar (2260 S Locust St)*, with occasional live entertainment. For Mexican lunches, head to *Nellie's Cafe (1226 W Hadley Ave)*; no alcohol is served. *High Desert Brewing Company (1201 W Hadley Ave)* is a microbrewery with pub food and live music. *My Brother's Place (334 Main St)* has Mexican and American food and pool tables. In Mesilla, several good but pricey eateries sit around the plaza. A few blocks away, the recommended *El Comedor (2190 Avenida de Mesilla)* serves good, cheap Mexican meals indoors or on a small patio.

Greyhound/TNM&O (☎ 505-524-8518) is at 490 N Valley Dr. Las Cruces Shuttle (☎ 505-525-1784, 800-288-1784) has vans from Las Cruces to El Paso Airport ($28) and to Deming and Silver City.

Rock Hound State Park

Dig and chip for rocks bearing (perhaps) agate, opal, jasper or quartz crystals – there's a 15lb limit! Tent/RV sites cost $10/14. The park (☎ 505-546-6182) is 14 miles southeast of Deming.

Silver City & Around

On the southern edge of the mountainous **Gila National Forest** – rugged country suitable for remote backpacking, camping, fishing, cross-country skiing, river floating and horseback riding – the mining town of Silver City offers a few outfitters and rental options. Call the chamber of commerce (☎ 505-538-3785, 800-548-9378) or forest ranger (☎ 505-538-2771) for information.

Up a winding 42-mile road north of Silver City, the recommended **Gila Cliff Dwellings National Monument** (☎ 505-536-9461) was occupied in the 13th century by Mogollon Indians. The site's relative isolation dissuades visitors who crowd many other Southwestern archaeological sites. There's free basic *camping* here. On the way up, stop in tiny Pinos Altos for a beer and a bite at the *Buckhorn Saloon* and investigate the hot springs along the way.

Strangely rounded volcanic towers make up **City of Rocks State Park** (☎ 505-536-2800), southeast of Silver City on Hwy 61, where secluded camping among the towers costs $10/14 for tents/RVs. Nearby, **Faywood**

Hotsprings (☎ 505-536-9663) has both clothing-required and clothing-optional pools, as well as tent and RV sites and trailers for rent.

The ranger station has more information on camping. The restored *Palace Hotel (☎ 505-388-1811, 106 W Broadway)* dates from 1882 ($33-53). East Hwy 80 has several motels. In Pinos Altos, *Bear Creek Motel & Cabins (☎ 505-388-4501, 888-388-4515)* has 15 cabins with fireplaces ($100-150). Built in 1928 and surrounded by 160 acres of trails, *Bear Mountain Lodge (☎ 505-538-2538, 877-620-2327)* is operated by the Nature Conservancy and has a resident naturalist. Double rooms cost $80-175 with breakfast.

Vicki's Deli & Eatery (107 W Yankie St) serves good sandwiches and light meals. The unpretentious and good *Jalisco Cafe (100 S Bullard St)* is a local Mexican food favorite (closed Sun); no alcohol is served.

Silver Stage Lines (☎ 800-522-0162) and Las Cruces Shuttle (☎ 800-288-1784) have daily vans to El Paso Airport.

NORTHWESTERN NEW MEXICO

Here, some of the Southwest's most fabulous ancient Indian sites coexist with reflections of the USA's mining and atomic history, offering an ironic perspective on the American West.

Abiquiu & Around

A tiny farming valley on Hwy 84 about 45 minutes northwest of Santa Fe, Abiquiu is famous as the home of artist Georgia O'Keeffe. The Georgia O'Keeffe

Georgia O'Keeffe, Abiquiu artist

SOUTHWEST

Foundation (☎ 505-685-4539) offers one-hour tours of **O'Keeffe's home** with reservation (Tue, Thurs, Fri Apr-Nov; $22). Basic *camping* is available at Abiquiu Reservoir.

The beautiful **Ghost Ranch Conference Center** (☎ 505-685-4333, 877-804-4678, Ⓦ www.ghostranch.org) has a small dinosaur museum (free admission) and hiking trails. Double rooms with dorm-style/shared/private bath cost $47/55/65 per person, including meals at the cafeteria. For a local bar and diner, head north on Hwy 554 to El Rito.

Chama

The town of Chama is famous for the open-carriage **Cumbres & Toltec Scenic Railroad** (☎ 505-756-2151, 800-323-9469, Ⓦ www.cumbresandtoltec.com), both the longest (64 miles) and highest (over the 10,015-foot-high Cumbres Pass) narrow-gauge steam railroad in the USA (open May-Oct). The train runs between Chama and Antonito, Colorado. You can take the full trip ($30/60 for children under 12/adults; eight hours including return trip by van or train) or go to the midpoint of Osier, Colorado, and be picked up at a later date ($40/20). This allows the option of backpacking and fishing in the San Juan Mountains.

Reservations are required at the *Conejos River Hostel* (☎ 719-376-2518), a 6-mile hike from the sublet water station between Antonito and Osier ($12/15 for members/nonmembers). Call for directions from Antonito (10 miles). The hostel is likely closed November to April, but call to confirm.

Aztec Ruins National Monument

An alternative to the bigger and more visited sites of Chaco Culture National Historic Park (see below) and Mesa Verde National Park (see the Rocky Mountains chapter), this site (☎ 505-334-3160) features the largest reconstructed kiva in the country, with an internal diameter of almost 50 feet ($4 per car).

In adjoining Aztec, *Miss Gail's Inn* (☎ 505-334-3452, 888-534-3452, 300 S Main St) offers historic (circa 1907) singles/doubles for $65/75. Inside, *Giovanni's* serves a tasty lunch.

Navajo Dam & Navajo Lake State Park

Stretching over 30 miles northeast and across into Colorado, this lake (☎ 505-632-2278) has camping and boating ($4). Locals call the trout fishing in the San Juan River 'world class.' Outfitters include Born-n-Raised on the San Juan River, Inc (☎ 505-632-2194). Secluded under the cliffs against the river, *Soaring Eagle Lodge* (☎ 505-632-3721, 800-866-2719), south of Navajo Dam on Hwy 539, offers simple suites for $125.

Chaco Culture NHP

Featuring massive Ancestral Puebloan buildings set in an isolated high-desert environment, this intriguing National Historic Park ($8 per vehicle) contains evidence of 5000 years of human occupation. Pueblo Bonito is four stories tall and may have had 600 to 800 rooms and kivas. Sites have been stabilized but not reconstructed. Apart from taking the self-guided loop tour, you can hike **backcountry trails** to see remote sites.

The nearest provisions are along Hwy 44, 21 miles from the visitor center (☎ 505-786-7014). *Gallo Campground*, 1½ miles from the visitor center, is open year round on a first-come, first-served basis ($10; no hookups). Also see the Cuba (earlier) and Farmington (next) sections. All routes to the park involve rough dirt roads, which tend to become impassable after heavy rains or snow.

Farmington & Around

Farmington has plenty of facilities and serves as a pleasant base from which to explore the Four Corners area. Contact the visitor center (☎ 505-326-7602, 800-448-1240, Ⓦ www.farmingtonnm.org, 203 W Main St) and the BLM (☎ 505-599-8970, 1235 La Plata Hwy) for information. Moore Anthropological Research (☎ 505-334-6675) offers tours to nearby Indian sites ($85 per half-day for two people).

Shiprock, a 1700-foot-high volcanic plug that rises eerily over the landscape to the west, was a landmark for the Anglo pioneers and is a sacred site to the Navajo. The Navajo community of Shiprock hosts an annual Navajo Fair with a rodeo, powwow and traditional dancing (late Sept or early Oct). About 35 miles south of Farmington along Hwy 371, the **Bisti Badlands and De-Na-Zin Wilderness**, an undeveloped BLM area, offers a barren but geologically interesting landscape, with many eroded and colorfully pigmented formations.

Reliable trading posts, with a variety of Indian crafts, are found along Hwy 64 west of town. Founded in 1875, the Fifth Generation Trading Company (232 W Broadway) has a big selection.

Several motels along Airport Dr offer rooms in the $30s; try *Budget Inn* (☎ 505-326-5521, 652 E Main St). The usual hotel chains are clustered around Scott Ave and Broadway. Three miles from downtown, *Silver River Adobe B&B* (☎ 325-8219, 800-382-9251) offers a peaceful respite among the trees on the San Juan River (from $80). Friendly and low-key, *Three Rivers Eatery & Brewhouse* (101 E Main St) bustles with locals for lunch and dinner. *Something Special Bakery and Tearoom* (116 N Auburn Ave) serves coffee and pastries (7am-2pm Mon-Fri).

TNM&O/Greyhound (☎ 505-325-1009) stops at 101 E Animas St with daily buses to Albuquerque ($33; 4 hours). Navajo Transit System (☎ 520-729-4111) offers a weekday bus to Window Rock (see Navajo Indian Reservation in the Northeastern Arizona section). KB Cab (☎ 505-325-2999) has 24-hour taxi service.

Arizona

Many visitors come here with images of 'Roadrunner' cartoons, saguaro cacti and rattlesnakes, but Arizona offers more than the Grand Canyon and Arizona-Sonora Desert. Forested mountains, with skiing in the winter and fishing streams in the summer, ring important cities, and artificial lakes dot the state. Arizona is popular with American tourists, some of whom come during the winter to enjoy the sunny skies or posh resorts. Unlike neighboring New Mexico, Arizona has many full-service hotels and retirement communities. Travelers will find that the landscape and culture offer a rich variety of unexpected attractions. You can chow down on steak 'n' beans at a 'cowboy ranch'; ride stagecoaches and watch modern-day 'shootouts' in self-styled Wild West towns; learn about Indian history, religion and culture at the Navajo and Hopi Reservations; poke around the remnants of Arizona's mining history in ghost towns; explore wildlife refuges; and enjoy outdoor activities all year round.

History

By the time of European contact, Arizona was home to the Hopi, Navajo, Tohono O'odham, Yuman, Apache and several other tribes. The Spanish explorer Francisco Vásquez de Coronado passed through here on his failed quest for the mythical Seven Cities of Cibola, and settlers and missionaries followed in his path. By the mid-19th century, the US controlled Arizona, and in 1863, President Abraham Lincoln created the Arizona Territory.

The Indian Wars, in which the US Army battled Indians to 'protect' settlers and to wrest land from those who had little use for European concepts of land ownership, officially ended in 1886 with the surrender of Apache warrior Geronimo. The railroad had arrived a few years earlier, and wild frontier mining towns grew up almost overnight. In 1912, President Theodore Roosevelt's support for damming the territory's rivers paved the way to statehood, and Arizona became the 48th state. Over the next decades, more dams were built, copper mining flourished, and tourists flocked to the state. After WWII, air conditioning became widely available, and growth was phenomenal.

SOUTHWEST

Arizona

Nickname: Grand Canyon State

Population: 5,130,700 (20th)

Area: 114,006 sq miles (6th)

Admitted to Union: February 14, 1912 (48th)

Capital city: Phoenix (population 1,322,000; metro area 3.25 million)

Other cities: Tucson (487,000), Mesa (396,400), Yuma (77,500)

State reptile: Arizona ridge-nosed rattlesnake

State neckwear: bolo tie

Famous for: the Grand Canyon, the cactus

Home of: Apache chief Geronimo (1829–1909), Supreme Court justice Sandra Day O'Connor (b 1930), first US rodeo (1888)

Daylight saving time: Arizona doesn't use it (except on the Navajo Reservation)

Scarcity of water resources remains among the foremost issues in Arizona. The simple solution, of course, is to stop further building and development, but things don't work that way. Growth continues, and the state desperately searches for water for its burgeoning desert cities.

Flora & Fauna
The tall, majestic saguaro and organ-pipe cacti, home to dozens of desert species of insects, birds and mammals, are found only in parts of southern Arizona and Mexico. Southeastern Arizona is the undisputed hummingbird capital of the country, and many other rare birds fly in from Mexico, including two species of tropical trogons.

Information
The Arizona Office of Tourism (☎ 602-230-7733, 800-842-8257, W www.arizonaguide.com, 2702 N 3rd St, Suite 4015, Phoenix, AZ 85004) will send free information. The Arizona Public Lands Information Center (☎ 602-417-9300, W www.publiclands.org, 222 N Central Ave, Phoenix, AZ 85004) provides information about USFS, NPS, BLM and state lands and parks. The Arizona Association of B&B Inns (☎ 602-488-9636, 888-820-8299, PO Box 4948, Cave Creek, AZ 85327) can provide a statewide list of its members. Basic sales tax is 5.6%.

Arizona is on Mountain Standard Time but is the only western state that does not observe daylight saving time from spring to early fall. The exception is the Navajo Reservation, which does observe daylight saving time.

PHOENIX
Phoenix and surrounding cities create a 1000-sq-mile metropolitan sprawl of strip malls, chic resorts, retirement RV parks and golf courses, collectively known as the 'Valley of the Sun.' With more than 300 days of sunshine a year, outdoor activities in the surrounding mountains and a cultivated 'cowboy' tourist appeal, Phoenix is a primary resort destination and a magnet for 'snow birds' seeking refuge from northern winters.

History
As early as 300 BC, the area's dry desert soil began yielding crops for the Hohokam people, who spent centuries developing a complex system of irrigation canals, only to mysteriously abandon them around AD 1450. In the mid-1860s, the US Army built Fort McDowell northeast of Phoenix. After the railway arrived in 1887, the lack of water impeded further growth until the completion of the Roosevelt Dam on the Salt River in 1911. Since then, recreation and ancient culture have become this area's main attractions. From WWII to the present day, the valley's population has grown more than sevenfold.

Orientation
At about 1100 feet above sea level, the valley is ringed by mountains that range from 2500 to more than 7000 feet in elevation. Central Ave, running north-south in Phoenix, divides west addresses from east addresses; Washington St, running west-east in Phoenix, divides north addresses from south addresses. To the east, Mesa's Main St becomes the Apache Trail in Apache Junction, heading northeast along to Hwy 88 into the Tonto National Forest. Of the major freeways leaving Phoenix, I-17 N (Black Canyon Hwy) has the most motels.

Information
The Greater Phoenix Convention & Visitors Bureau (☎ 602-254-6500, 877-225-5749, 50 N 2nd St) is open weekdays. The main library (☎ 602-262-4636) is at 1221 N Central Ave. Wide World of Maps (☎ 602-279-2323, 2626 W Indian School Rd) has maps and guidebooks. The Book Store (☎ 602-279-3910, 4230 N 7th Ave) has many periodicals and magazines.

Central Phoenix
For Southwestern Indian history and culture, the **Heard Museum** (☎ 602-252-8840, 2301 N Central Ave), with a kachina-doll room, is outstanding and should be at the top of your list ($7). The **Phoenix Art Museum** (☎ 602-257-1880, 1625 N Central Ave) shows worldwide works from between the 14th and 20th centuries; don't miss the collection of clothing from the last two centuries ($7, free on Thurs).

At **Heritage Square** (☎ 602-262-5029), 19th-century buildings house several interesting museums and shops. Adjoining the square is the **Arizona Science Center** (☎ 602-716-2000), with 350 exhibits that encourage hands-on experimentation, a five-story theater with hourly shows and a planetarium ($8, plus $3 for shows). Displays at the nearby **Phoenix Museum of History** (☎ 602-253-2734) range from 2000-year-old archaeological artifacts to an exhibit about the sinking of the USS *Arizona* at Pearl Harbor in 1941 ($5).

Outer Phoenix

The 145-acre **Desert Botanical Garden** (☎ 480-941-1225, 1201 N Galvin Parkway), with thousands of arid-land plant species from Arizona and around the world, provides insight into how plants survive in the desert. The surrounding Papago Park has biking and equestrian trails, as well as the **Phoenix Zoo** (☎ 602-273-1341), with a $10 admission. Opposite Papago Park, the **Hall of Flame** (☎ 602-275-3473) exhibits more than 90 firefighting machines dating from 1725 ($5). At the **Pueblo Grande Museum** (☎ 602-495-0900, 4619 E Washington St), parts of an excavated Hohokam village remain exposed for the visitor ($2).

Tempe

With almost 45,000 students, **Arizona State University** (ASU; ☎ 480-965-9011) is the largest college in the Southwest. It has several museums, trendy hangouts, and sporting and cultural events year round. Its unique architecture, including the Frank Lloyd Wright–designed Gammage Auditorium, is worth exploring. Call ☎ 480-965-2278 for campus events.

Scottsdale

Scottsdale is popular with visitors for its 19th-century downtown area (with upscale galleries and crafts stores), posh resorts and variety of restaurants. Up north, the **Fleischer Museum** (☎ 480-585-3108, 17207 Perimeter Dr) is dedicated to American impressionism of the California School (free admission). **Rawhide** (☎ 480-502-5600, 23023 N Scottsdale Rd) is an 'Old West' town with saloons, showdowns, stagecoaches and all that stuff.

Mesa

The interactive **Mesa Southwest Museum** (☎ 480-644-2230, 53 N MacDonald St) features animated dinosaurs, an eight-cell territorial jail and gold panning ($6). With 33 flyable airplanes from WWI to the Vietnam War on display, the **Champlin Fighter Museum** (☎ 480-830-4540, 4800 E McKellips Rd), in Falcon Field Airport, has one of the largest collections of fighter aircraft in the world ($6.50).

Activities

Several large parks in the mountains ringing the valley offer **hiking**, **cycling**, **horseback riding** and camping. On the southwestern outskirts of the valley (take I-10 west from downtown), the 31-sq-mile Estrella Mountain Regional Park (☎ 623-932-3811) provides 34 miles of multiuse trails and camping. One of Phoenix's most popular hikes climbs to the 2608-foot summit of Squaw Peak. (The parking lots are along Squaw Peak Dr, northeast of Lincoln Dr between 22nd and 24th Sts.) These and other parks charge $3 per vehicle for day use.

Along the Bush Hwy (take Power Rd north from 6800 E Main St in Mesa, which turns into Bush Hwy), Salt River Recreation (☎ 480-984-3305) rents tubes and provides van shuttles for **inner-tubing** down the Salt River ($10, includes tube and shuttle) from mid-April to September. Nearby, from fall to spring, Saguaro Lake Ranch Resort (☎ 480-380-1239) has horseback riding.

Places to Stay

From very basic motels to ritzy resorts, the valley's hundreds of accommodations share one common feature...prices *plummet* in summer, often to half of the winter rates.

Camping & Hostels The *Estrella Mountain Regional Park* (see Activities) charges $8-15 for campsites. Head northeast of Apache Junction along Hwy 88 for camping in the *Tonto National Forest* (☎ 602-417-9300). Nestled at the foot of the Superstition Mountains, *Lost Dutchman State Park* (☎ 480-982-4485) has 35 tent sites ($10). About 120 RV parks are listed in the yellow pages!

The friendly *HI Phoenix, Metcalf House* (☎ 602-254-9803, 1026 N 9th St) offers dorms for $15 apiece. The *YMCA* (☎ 602-253-6181, 350 N 1st Ave) rents single rooms with shared bath for $28/125 per night/week.

Motels & Hotels Chains dominate the Phoenix hotel scene. There are 17 (!) *Motel 6*s in the greater Phoenix area charging

SOUTHWEST

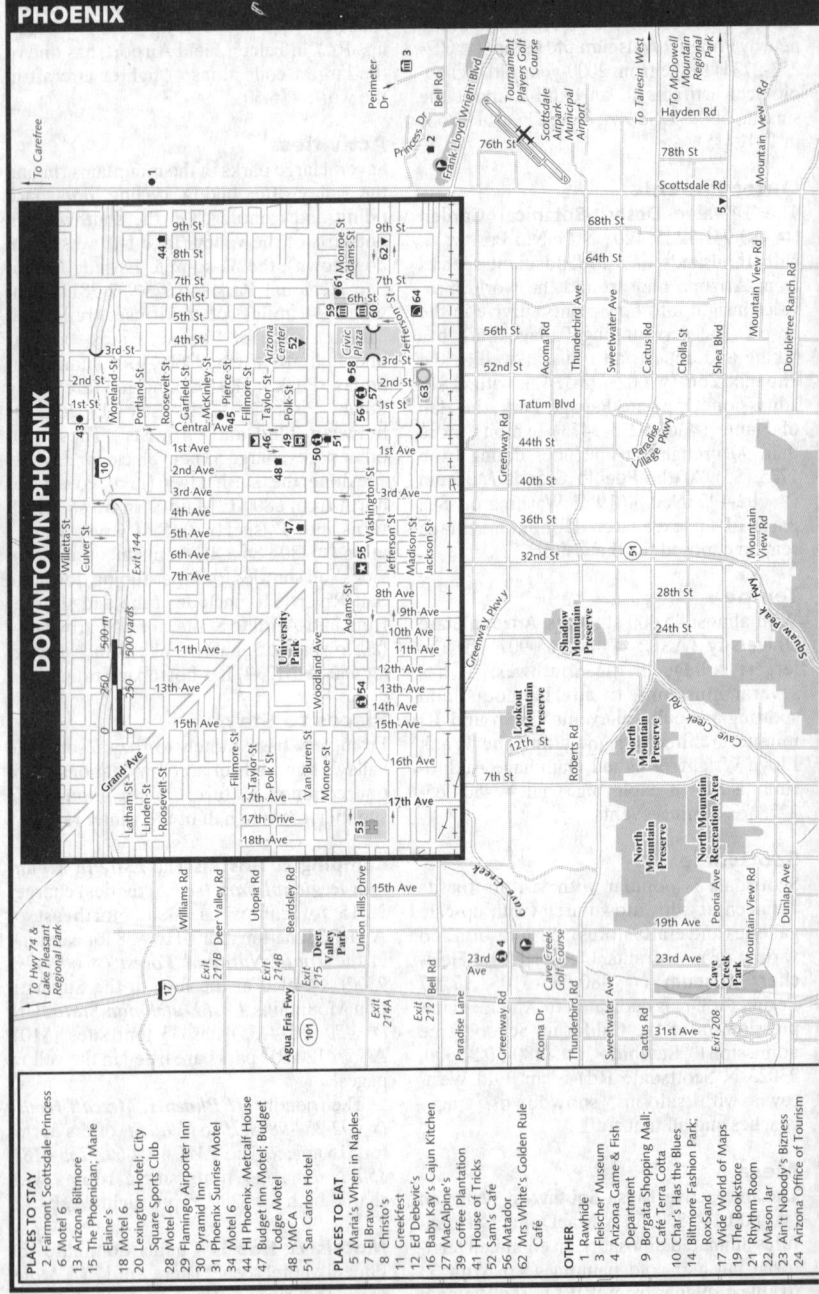

PLACES TO STAY
2 Fairmont Scottsdale Princess
6 Motel 6
13 Arizona Biltmore
15 The Phoenician; Marie Elaine's
18 Motel 6
20 Lexington Hotel; City Square Sports Club
28 Motel 6
29 Flamingo Airporter Inn
30 Pyramid Inn
31 Phoenix Sunrise Motel
34 Motel 6
44 HI Phoenix, Metcalf House
47 Budget Inn Motel; Budget Lodge Motel
48 YMCA
51 San Carlos Hotel

PLACES TO EAT
5 Maria's When in Naples
7 El Bravo
8 Christo's
11 Greekfest
12 Ed Debevic's
16 Baby Kay's Cajun Kitchen
27 MacAlpine's
39 Coffee Plantation
41 House of Tricks
52 Sam's Cafe
56 Matador
62 Mrs White's Golden Rule Café

OTHER
1 Rawhide
3 Fleischer Museum
4 Arizona Game & Fish Department
9 Borgata Shopping Mall; Café Terra Cotta
10 Char's Has the Blues
14 Biltmore Fashion Park; RoxSand
17 Wide World of Maps
19 The Bookstore
21 Rhythm Room
22 Mason Jar
23 Ain't Nobody's Bizness
24 Arizona Office of Tourism

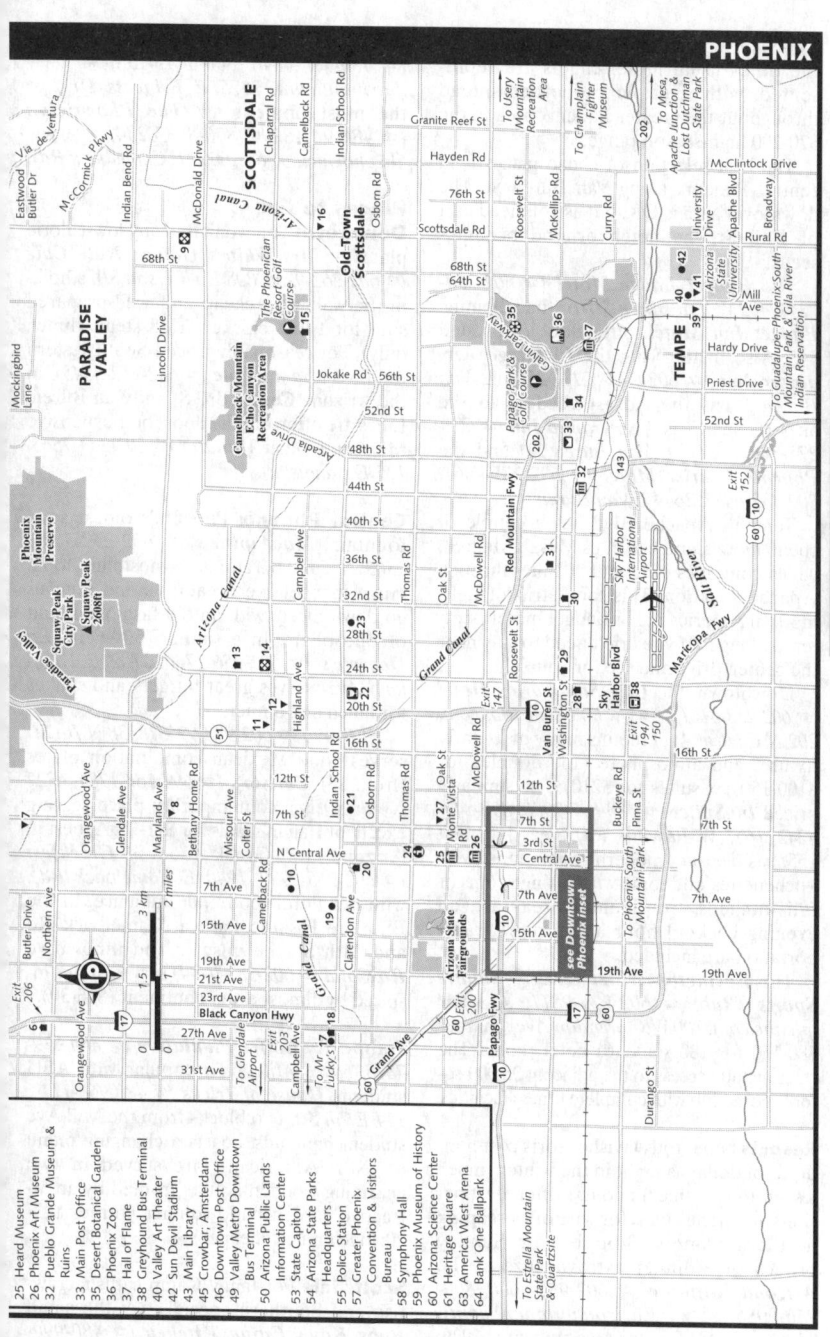

PHOENIX

SOUTHWEST

25 Heard Museum
26 Phoenix Art Museum
32 Pueblo Grande Museum &
   Ruins
33 Main Post Office
35 Desert Botanical Garden
36 Phoenix Zoo
37 Hall of Flame
38 Greyhound Bus Terminal
40 Valley Art Theater
42 Sun Devil Stadium
43 Main Library
45 Crowbar; Amsterdam
46 Downtown Post Office
49 Valley Metro Downtown
   Bus Terminal
50 Arizona Public Lands
   Information Center
53 State Capitol
54 Arizona State Parks
   Headquarters
55 Police Station
57 Greater Phoenix
   Convention & Visitors
   Bureau
58 Symphony Hall
59 Phoenix Museum of History
60 Arizona Science Center
63 Heritage Square
63 America West Arena
64 Bank One Ballpark

$40-50 in summer and $70-80 in winter. All the other usual motel chains are represented, with multiple properties spread throughout the greater Phoenix area in the $70-200 high-season range.

The best selection of cheap places is in central Phoenix along Van Buren St. The downtown area is OK, but as you head east of 10th St, the neighborhood becomes seedy.

The **Budget Lodge Motel** (☎ 602-254-7247, 402 W Van Buren St), or the adjoining **Budget Inn Motel**, offer doubles around $45. Also in the $40s, the **Flamingo Airporter Inn** (☎ 602-275-6211, 2501 E Van Buren St) is the closest cheapie to the airport. Nearby is the **Pyramid Inn** (☎ 602-275-3691, 3307 E Van Buren St) and the **Phoenix Sunrise Motel** (☎ 602-275-7661, 800-432-6483, 3644 E Van Buren St).

Tempe's Apache Blvd has a couple of cheap motels, and becomes Mesa's Main St, which continues for about 20 miles through Apache Junction. This long strip of ugly, modern Americana has budget motels scattered along it. If you don't need to stay near the center, drive and see for yourself.

Downtown, the 1927 **San Carlos Hotel** (☎ 602-253-4121, W www.hotelsancarlos.com, 202 N Central Ave) retains many of its early fixtures and atmosphere (130 doubles for $100-150; six suites for $210). The similarly priced **InnSuites** (☎ 480-897-7900, 800-842-4242, 1651 W Baseline Rd), near I-10 exit 155, has pleasant modern rooms, most with kitchenettes, and some with sitting rooms or full kitchens. Continental breakfast, an evening cocktail hour and airport transportation are included.

The **Lexington Hotel & City Square Sports Club** (☎ 602-279-9811, W www.phxihc.com, 100 W Clarendon Ave) charges $80-130 for 180 standard hotel rooms. The rates include access to the adjacent 35,000-sq-foot sports club with complete fitness facilities.

Resorts Numerous lavish resorts cost hundreds of dollars a night in the winter (much less in the summer) and are often destinations in themselves for visitors escaping northern winters. Stop by for Sunday brunch or a dinner extravaganza at the **Arizona Biltmore** (☎ 602-955-6600, 800-950-0086, W www.arizonabiltmore.com), 24th St and E Missouri Ave, built circa 1929;

the 450-acre **Fairmont Scottsdale Princess** (☎ 480-585-4848, 800-344-4758, W www.fairmont.com, 7575 E Princess Dr); or the most opulent all, **The Phoenician** (☎ 480-941-8200, 800-888-8234, W www.thephoenician.com, 6000 E Camelback Rd).

Places to Eat

Downtown You won't find any low-calorie plates at **Mrs White's Golden Rule Café** (☎ 602-262-9256, 808 E Jefferson St), a hole-in-the-wall with cheap and well-prepared soul food like chicken-fried steak (lunch only). For reasonably priced Southwestern food, visit **Sam's Cafe** (☎ 602-252-3545), in the Arizona Center, 3rd St and Van Buren. Lines are often out the door for inexpensive Mexican food at **Matador** (☎ 602-254-7563, 125 E Adams St).

Central Phoenix Phoenix's oldest soda fountain, **MacAlpine's** (☎ 602-252-3039, 2303 N 7th St) retains its nostalgic look. Huge inexpensive breakfasts and lunches go down nicely with an old-fashioned malt or phosphate. In a similar '50s vein, **Ed Debevic's** (☎ 602-956-2760, 2102 E Highland Ave) serves great burgers and shakes for lunch and dinner.

El Bravo (☎ 602-943-9753, 8338 N 7th St) serves good Mexican combination plates (from $5). **Christo's** (☎ 602-264-1784, 6327 N 7th St) is a contemporary place serving excellent Italian meals for $11-25. A 'best in Arizona' for Greek food is **Greekfest** (☎ 602-265-2990, 1940 E Camelback Rd), with delightful food and ambience. In the Biltmore Fashion Park at Camelback Rd and 24th St, the upscale and innovative **RoxSand** (☎ 602-381-0444) serves dishes inspired by almost every continent ($16-30).

Tempe Try **Coffee Plantation** (☎ 480-829-7878, 680 S Mill Ave), popular with ASU students. **House of Tricks** (☎ 480-968-1114, 114 E 7th St), two blocks from the Mill Ave student hangouts, boasts a changing menu of 'New American' fare served in two charming wooden houses fronted by an attractive garden patio (dinner entrées $13-20; lunch much cheaper).

Scottsdale For tangy Cajun catfish, crawfish and Southern specials, try the small **Baby Kay's Cajun Kitchen** (☎ 480-990-

9080, 7216 E Shoeman Lane); meals cost
$8-15. *Maria's When in Naples* (☎ 480-991-
6997, 7000 E Shea Blvd) serves lunches and
homemade pasta dinners (from $13). *Café
Terra Cotta (☎ 480-948-8100, 6166 N Scottsdale Rd)* serves good New Southwestern
lunch and dinner ($8-24) and heavenly
desserts. *Marie Elaine's,* in the swanky
Phoenician resort, requires jackets and ties
for men, has the valley's most expensive
menu and is the only Mobil five-star restaurant in Arizona.

Entertainment
Ask at the visitors bureau for information
on the city's rich performing arts. The free
alternative weekly *New Times* has a thorough listing of events. Alternative film is
featured at the *Valley Art Theater* (☎ 602-
222-4275 ext 027, 509 S Mill), in Tempe.

Mill Ave between 3rd and 7th Sts in
Tempe is the heart of ASU bars and nightclubs. *Mr Lucky's* (☎ 602-246-0686, 3660
NW Grand Ave) has live country & western
and a corral outside with bull-riding competitions on weekends. Several fun bars are in
the Arizona Center. The loud *Mason Jar*
(☎ 602-956-6271, 2303 E Indian School Rd)
attracts a young crowd; they have a no-
alcohol area. *Char's Has the Blues* (☎ 602-
230-0205, 4631 N 7th Ave) and the *Rhythm
Room* (☎ 602-265-4842, 1019 E Indian
School Rd) are the best live blues bars.
Ain't Nobody's Business (☎ 602-224-9977,
3031 E Indian School Rd) is a friendly
lesbian bar. Gay men dance at *Crowbar*
(702 N Central Ave) and *Amsterdam (718 N
Central Ave).*

Spectator Sports
The Phoenix Suns men's team (☎ 602-379-
7867) and the Phoenix Mercury women's
team (☎ 602-252-9622) play basketball at
America West Arena. The Arizona Cardinals (☎ 602-379-0102) play football at ASU
Sun Devil Stadium in Tempe. The Arizona
Diamondbacks (☎ 602-514-8400) play baseball at the Bank One Ballpark.

Getting There & Around
Phoenix's Sky Harbor International Airport
(☎ 602-273-3300) is 3 miles southeast of
downtown. Valley Metro's Red Line operates buses from the airport to Tempe and
Mesa along Apache Blvd and Main St and

to downtown Phoenix ($1.25; no service
on Sun).

The Greyhound bus terminal (☎ 602-389-
4200, 2115 E Buckeye Rd) has buses all
over the country: Tucson ($14; from 2
hours), Flagstaff ($21; from 2½ hours), Los
Angeles ($33; from 6½ hours), El Paso ($35;
from 7½ hours).

The Arizona Shuttle Service (☎ 800-888-
2749) has many vans linking Phoenix
Airport with Tucson ($28; 2 hours).

Valley Metro (☎ 602-253-5000) operates
buses all over the valley on weekdays and
on a limited basis on Saturday ($1.25), with
free FLASH service around the ASU area
and free DASH service around downtown
Phoenix. For 24-hour taxis, call Yellow Cab
(☎ 602-252-5252).

EAST-CENTRAL ARIZONA
East of Phoenix, between the high desert of
northeastern Arizona and the low Sonoran
Desert of southeastern Arizona, lies mainly
mountainous and forested land dotted with
small villages and lodges. The area, particularly popular with the citizens of Phoenix
and Tucson, offers a cool respite from the
summer heat, as well as year-round outdoor
recreation (including cross-country skiing
and natural hot springs).

Sunrise Park Resort (☎ 928-735-7669), on
the White Mountain Apache Indian Reservation, offers downhill skiing and a hotel.
Within 30 miles or less, you can stay at
Pinetop-Lakeside (☎ 928-367-4290, 800-573-
4031, W www.whitemtns.com), with many
mid-priced motels, cabin complexes and
restaurants; Show Low, with the cheapest
motels; tiny Greer, with cabins and mountain lodges; and Springerville-Eagar (☎ 928-
333-2123, W www.az-tourist.com), with
motels and nearby archaeology sites. Call
about inexpensive guided tours.

Coronado Trail
Hwys 180 and 191, ascending to 9000 feet
from Springerville before dropping to
Clifton at 3500 feet, run roughly parallel to
Francisco Vásquez de Coronado's 1540
route and offer campgrounds, a few motels
and access to pristine wilderness. In
Alpine (population 650) the Apache-Sitg-
reaves Alpine Ranger Station (☎ 928-339-
4384) is open weekdays. The south end of
the trail is very slow, with many hairpin

bends. A few miles above Clifton is the country's biggest copper-producing mine; views of the 2-mile-long open-pit mine with 200-ton trucks crawling like insects down below might give you disturbing dreams. The nearest town at the south end of the route is **Safford**, with about a dozen motels.

Globe

This town (☎ 928-425-4495, 800-804-5623) offers the cheapest accommodations in the area and is a rural alternative to Phoenix, 80 miles west. *El Rey Motel (☎ 928-425-4427, 1201 E Ash St)* is an old-fashioned American motor-court with basic, clean rooms at $22/32 singles/doubles. Several other chain and nonchain motels are spread out along Hwy 60.

Apache Trail

The steep and winding Apache Trail (Hwy 88) loops northwest from Globe, past a few campgrounds and motels, then 45 miles to the greater Phoenix area. The 22 miles west of Roosevelt Dam are unpaved. **Tonto National Monument** (☎ 928-467-2241) protects a two-story Salado pueblo built in a cave ($3).

Constructed of bricks in 1911, **Theodore Roosevelt Dam** was the earliest of the large dams in the Southwest and, at 280 feet, is the world's highest masonry dam. The Wild West look of **Tortilla Flat** makes the little village a popular stop.

CENTRAL ARIZONA

Here visitors will find Indian sites, cowboy dude ranches, nostalgic old mining towns and New Age culture, all blended together in that odd mishmash that is the American West. From Phoenix, you can take 1-17 north to Flagstaff, the 'gateway to the Grand Canyon,' in three hours, or you could spend a few days wandering through the mountains and intriguing small towns along and near Hwy 89A.

Wickenburg

An hour northwest of Phoenix, Wickenburg has a 19th-century center and several dude ranches offering cowboy-style vacations in fall, winter and spring. Contact the chamber of commerce (☎ 928-684-5479, 800-9242-5242, W www.wickenburgchamber.com) for a listing. Desert Caballeros Western Museum (☎ 928-684-2272, 21 N Frontier) features canvases and bronzes by famous Western artists such as Frederic Remington, George Catlin and Charles M Russell ($5).

Prescott

Outdoor activities, two colleges, a small artists' community and galleries add to Prescott's bohemian air. The chamber of commerce (☎ 928-445-2000, 800-266-7534, W www.prescott.org, 117 W Goodwin St) is open daily, and the Prescott National Forest (☎ 928-771-4700, 344 S Cortez) has information on hiking, camping and fishing.

Prescott Transit Authority/Greyhound (☎ 928-445-5470, 820 E Sheldon St) and Shuttle U (☎ 800-304-6114) go to Phoenix (around $24; 2 hours).

The first territorial capital, Prescott retains its Wild West heritage in the once-infamous **Whiskey Row**, where cowboys and miners would wander from saloon to saloon until they had consumed a drink at each of its 40 drinking establishments. Many early buildings remain, and you can still have a shot in an early saloon on Montezuma St by the Courthouse Plaza.

Six miles north of town on Hwy 89, the **Phippen Museum of Western Art** (☎ 928-778-1385) features the work of cowboy artist George Phippen and a good collection of other Western art ($3). With 19th-century structures from all over Arizona (including two former governors' mansions), stagecoaches and ranch furnishings from Arizona's territorial past, the **Sharlot Hall Museum** (☎ 928-445-3122, 415 Gurley St) is worth a stop ($5).

An old Whiskey Row hotel, *Hotel St Michael (☎ 928-776-1999, 800-678-3757, 205 W Gurley St)* has 72 older but clean rooms for $49-59 ($20 surcharge on weekends). The wooden bar at *Hotel Vendome (☎ 928-776-0900, 888-463-3583, 230 S Cortez St)* is a good spot for a drink (rooms start at $80). When it opened in 1927, *Hassayampa Inn (☎ 928-778-9434, 800-322-1927, 122 E Gurley St)* was one of Arizona's most elegant hotels; today it is one of Prescott's classiest ($100-200 with full breakfast). For a listing of 14 Prescottian B&Bs, visit W www.prescott-bed-breakfast.org.

Near the courtyard plaza on Gurley St, try *Gurley St Grill* or the *Prescott Brewing Company* for a burger and a brew. On Montezuma St, *Zuma's* has wood-oven pizzas, an above-average selection of libations and a slightly alternative atmosphere, while *Palace Restaurant & Bar* has good food and waitstaff in late-19th-century clothing.

Jerome

A thriving copper-mining town in the 19th century, Jerome is now a national historic district. The setting is quite extraordinary – the entire town looks like it's about to slide off the mountainside. Indeed, many buildings have done just that. The famous 'sliding jail' can be seen 225 feet below its original location. Artists have replaced miners, and today antique shops and galleries line the winding streets. The chamber of commerce (☎ 928-634-2900, ⓦ www.jeromechamber.com) lists local hostelries and B&Bs. The **Mine Museum** (☎ 928-634-5477) and **Jerome State Historic Park** (☎ 928-634-5381), housed in a 1916 mansion 2 miles beyond Jerome off Hwy 89A, present the town's mining history.

Cottonwood

This small town has several motels and is near the **Verde Canyon Railroad** (☎ 928-639-0010, 800-293-7245), which has vintage engines pulling indoor and open-air coaches on a four-hour round-trip ride through splendid country to the north – Arizona's most scenic private train ride. Trains leave several times a week, reservations are required, and tickets cost $55 for 1st class and $36 for 2nd class.

Sedona

Four million visitors a year come to Sedona for its fine resorts, excellent restaurants, art galleries and the psychic 'cosmic energy' of the landscape. The town offers good arts-and-crafts shopping and many outfitters to arrange theme-oriented tours of the surrounding red-rock country by 4WD, van, bicycle or hot-air balloon, and there are plenty of day hikes and scenic drives. Day trips to Jerome, Cottonwood, the Grand Canyon and other surrounding sites are popular. Sedona is a relatively expensive and upscale base; budget travelers usually head to Flagstaff.

In the middle of town is the 'Y,' the junction of Hwys 179 and 89A. The bustling and helpful chamber of commerce (☎ 928-282-7722, 800-288-7336), at Hwy 89A and 4th St,

is open daily and has masses of information. Much of the surrounding National Forest land requires a Red Rock Parking Pass ($5/15 daily/weekly). The Sedona-Phoenix Shuttle (☎ 928-282-2066, 800-448-7988) offers several airport shuttles a day ($35).

The 27-mile **Oak Creek Canyon** drive (Hwy 89A) from Sedona to Flagstaff follows Oak Creek as it squeezes among red, orange and white cliffs into ponderosa forest. At **Slide Rock State Park** (☎ 928-282-3034), Oak Creek sweeps swimmers past placid pools and through a natural rock chute ($5 per car).

The USFS (☎ 928-282-4119) runs campgrounds in *Oak Creek Canyon* ($12, no hookups; May-Sept). Ask about other camping options. *Hostel Sedona* (☎ 928-282-2772, 5 Soldiers Wash Dr) has dorms for $18 and two doubles.

Chain *motels* include Super 8, two Best Westerns, Days Inn, Comfort Inn and

SOUTHWEST

In Search of the New Age

Sedona is the Southwest's foremost New Age center and one of the most important anywhere. The term 'New Age' refers to a trend toward seeking alternative explanations or interpretations of health, religion, the psyche and enlightenment. Drawing upon new and old factual and mystical traditions from around the world, New Agers often seek to transform themselves psychologically and spiritually in the hopes that such personal efforts will eventually transform the world at large.

Sedona offers mainstream services such as massages, nutrition counseling and yoga classes, through increasingly esoteric practices such as herbology, psychic channeling, aura photography, tarot, past-life regressions, crystal healing and drumming workshops. You can't miss the New Age stores in town; many have the word 'crystal' in their names.

The four best-known vortexes in the Sedona area are on the local red-rock mountains; for information and guided tours of other important New Age sites, stop by the Center for the New Age (☎ 928-282-2085, 341 Hwy 179).

Quality Inn. Of about 25 B&Bs in town, many are featured online at W http://bb.sedona.net. For 'budget' rooms in the $50-80 range, try the *White House Inn* (☎ 520-282-6680, 2986 W Hwy 89A); the *Sedona Motel* (☎ 928-282-7187), on Hwy 179 near 89A; or the *Village Lodge* (☎ 928-284-3626, 800-890-0521), in Oak Creek Village, 7 miles south.

In the $80-130 range, the *Sky Ranch Lodge* (☎ 929-282-6400, 888-708-6400), on Airport Rd, is a good value by Sedona standards. Its 94 rooms, pool and hot tub are in a nicely landscaped setting above town.

For breakfast, the *Coffeepot Restaurant* (2050 W Hwy 89A) has been the place to go for decades. Grab a sandwich or fix your own meal from *New Frontiers Natural Foods & Deli* (1420 W Hwy 89A), open 8am-8pm daily. Hankering for rattlesnake ribs with cactus condiments? Head over to *Cowboy Club* (241 Hwy 89A).

Thai Spices (2986 W Hwy 89A) serves spicy and inexpensive Thai food. The *Hideaway* (251 Hwy 179) serves good Italian lunches and dinners on a patio overlooking wooded Oak Creek. The bustling and popular *Javelina Cantina* (671 Hwy 179) does a slightly Americanized Mexican lunch and dinner.

René at Tlaquepaque, on Hwy 179 south of Hwy 89A, long considered one of Sedona's best, offers upscale cuisine including pronghorn antelope and ostrich. The best place for a view and outstanding Southwestern fare is *Yavapai Dining Room* (525 Boynton Canyon Rd), at the Enchantment Resort ($15-25; $29 champagne brunch Sun).

Flagstaff

Set among cool ponderosas, 1½ hours from the Grand Canyon and home to Northern Arizona University (NAU), 'Flag' is a friendly and affordable hub from which to explore the surroundings. The mountains and forests around Flagstaff offer scores of hiking, mountain-biking and skiing (☎ 928-779-1951, 928-779-4577) possibilities. For rentals and maps, stop by Peace Surplus (☎ 928-779-4521), Babbitt's (☎ 928-774-4775) or Sinagua Cycles (☎ 928-779-1092).

Orientation & Information The main drag and motel strip, Route 66 (Santa Fe Ave) roughly parallels I-40. The visitor center (☎ 928-774-9541, 800-842-7293, 1 E Route 66), in the historic railway depot downtown, is open daily. The Coconino National Forest Supervisor's Office (☎ 928-526-0866) is at 2323 Greenlaw Lane.

Things to See & Do A Hopi kiva is one of several excellent exhibits at the Museum of Northern Arizona (☎ 928-774-5211, 3001 N Fort Valley Rd). Ask about museum-led tours of the region. Of many important observations made at Lowell Observatory (☎ 928-774-2096, 1400 W Mars Hill Rd), the most famous was the discovery of the planet Pluto in 1930 ($4, including tours and special events; open 9am-5pm in summer and sporadic hours other times; call for nighttime viewing hours).

Accessed from Hwy 89N, the 1000-foot-tall volcano cone at Sunset Crater National Monument (☎ 928-526-0502) was formed by volcanic eruptions in AD 1064–5. Trails give great views; climbing is prohibited. Continue past the crater to Wupatki National Monument (☎ 928-679-2365), with hundreds of Ancestral Puebloan sites, five of which are easily accessible. Crack-In-Rock Pueblo can be visited only on a ranger-led, 16-mile roundtrip backpacking tour (weekends in Apr and Oct; reservations essential). The Sinagua buildings at Walnut Canyon National Monument (☎ 928-526-3367), near I-40 exit 204, are eerily set in caves within near-vertical walls of a butte jutting splendidly from a wooded canyon. These monuments charge $3 for adults. Camping is not allowed.

Places to Stay & Eat The *Grand Canyon International Hostel* (☎ 928-774-9421, 19 S San Francisco St) and the nearby *Dubeau International Hostel* (☎ 928-774-6731) are jointly owned (☎ 888-442-2696 for reservations). Dorms cost $14-16, and doubles (shared bath) cost $28-35, including breakfast, kitchen, laundry, TV/video room and Greyhound station pickup.

Many cheap and basic motels (about $30 in summer) line Route 66, and dozens of chains (including four Motel 6s) are in the area. There are also numerous B&Bs here. The *Weatherford Hotel* (☎ 928-779-1919, 23 N Leroux St) dates back to 1898, when it was northern Arizona's finest hotel. Eight

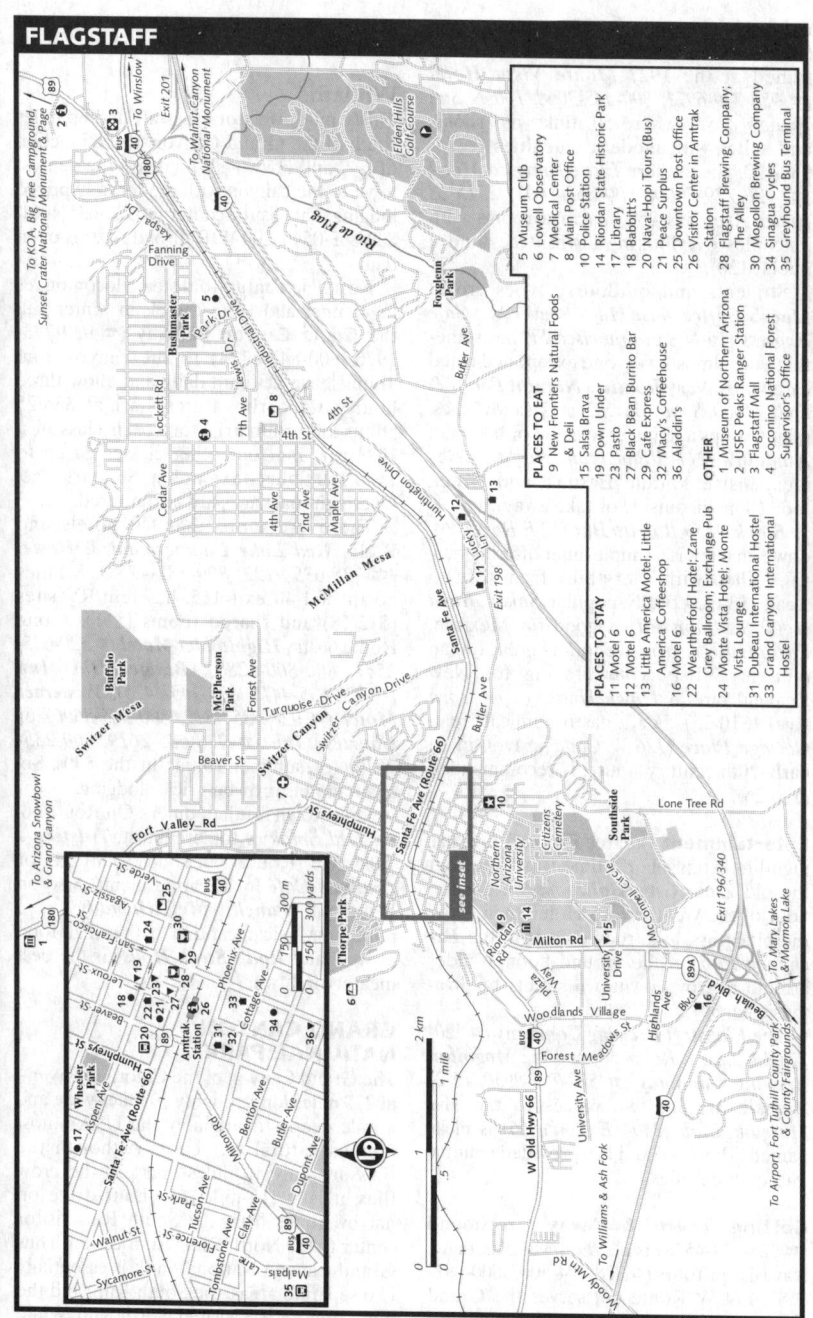

FLAGSTAFF

PLACES TO EAT
9 New Frontiers Natural Foods & Deli
15 Salsa Brava
19 Down Under
23 Pasto
27 Black Bean Burrito Bar
29 Cafe Express
32 Macy's Coffeehouse
36 Aladdin's

OTHER
1 Museum of Northern Arizona
2 USFS Peaks Ranger Station
3 Flagstaff Mall
4 Coconino National Forest Supervisor's Office
5 Museum Club
6 Lowell Observatory
7 Medical Center
8 Main Post Office
10 Police Station
14 Riordan State Historic Park
17 Library
18 Babbitt's
20 Nava-Hopi Tours (Bus)
21 Peace Surplus
25 Downtown Post Office
26 Visitor Center in Amtrak Station
28 Flagstaff Brewing Company; The Alley
30 Mogollon Brewing Company
34 Sinagua Cycles
35 Greyhound Bus Terminal

PLACES TO STAY
11 Motel 6
12 Motel 6
13 Little America Motel; Little America Coffeeshop
16 Motel 6
22 Weatherford Hotel; Zane Grey Ballroom; Exchange Pub
24 Monte Vista Hotel; Monte Vista Lounge
31 Dubeau International Hostel
33 Grand Canyon International Hostel

old-fashioned rooms (no TV or phone) cost $50-60. Scenes from *Casablanca* were filmed at the 1927 *Monte Vista Hotel* (☎ *928-779-6971, 800-545-3068, 100 N San Francisco St*), where 50 funky old rooms and suites with modern amenities go for $60-120. The modern *Little America Motel* (☎ *928-779-7900, 800-865-1401, 2515 E Butler Ave*) has 250 spacious rooms with balconies overlooking lawns, trees and a pool ($120).

Students and outdoorsy types crowd *Macy's Coffeehouse (14 S Beaver St)*. *Cafe Express (16 N San Francisco St)* has something for almost everyone except dedicated carnivores. *New Frontiers Natural Foods & Deli (1000 S Milton Rd)* has sandwiches, salads, soups and juices to eat in or take out. *Aladdin's (211 S San Francisco St)* serves inexpensive Middle Eastern and Greek food (dine in, outside or take away).

Black Bean Burrito Bar (12 E Route 66), down an alley, is a simple diner offering burritos filled with everything from tofu to steak ($3-6). Locally popular *Salsa Brava (1800 S Milton Rd)* is good for Mexican. *Pasto (19 E Aspen Ave)* offers great Italian dinners. Satisfy your craving for New Zealand fare at *Down Under (6 E Aspen Ave)* ($10-25). For a gastronomical treat, *Cottage Place (126 W Cottage Ave)*, in an early-20th-century house, is recommended ($16-26).

Entertainment The free *Flagstaff Live* has nightlife listings. For a time-trip, check out the old *Zane Grey Ballroom*, on the top floor of the Weatherford Hotel, then enjoy the bluegrass, folk, rock or jazz in the *Exchange Pub* on the ground floor. Wander around nearby downtown streets for live-music bars.

The *Flagstaff Brewing Company (☎ 520-773-1442, 16 E Route 66)* and the *Mogollon Brewing Company (☎ 520-773-8950, 15 N Agassiz St)* are two places to try. The *Museum Club (3404 E Route 66)* is nicknamed 'The Zoo' and has provided country music for decades.

Getting There & Away Greyhound (☎ 928-774-4573) is at 399 S Malpais Lane. Nava-Hopi Tours (☎ 928-774-5003, 800-892-8687, 114 W Route 66) serves the Grand Canyon ($14) and Phoenix Airport. There

are no buses to Page. Ask around about summer shuttles.

Williams

Thirty miles west of Flagstaff and 60 miles south of the Grand Canyon at the junction of I-40 and Hwy 64, Williams is the nearest town to the canyon with moderately priced lodging. The visitor center (☎ 928-635-4061, 800-863-0546, 200 W Railroad Ave) is open daily.

Nostalgic, century-old steam locomotives in summer and 1950s diesels in winter pull the **Grand Canyon Railway** (☎ 928-773-1976, 800-843-8724) to the canyon rim. Trains leave at 10am daily and allow three hours at the rim. Rates start at $55/25 adults/kids roundtrip for coach class in a 1923 car, and four other classes go up to $140/110, plus tax and a $6 park fee. Overnight packages are also offered.

There are more than 40 hotels and B&Bs. *Red Lake Campground & Hostel* (☎ *928-635-9122, 800-581-4753)*, 8 miles north of I-40 exit 165, has tent/RV sites ($12/18) and shared rooms ($11). Along Route 66, try *Highlander Motel (☎ 520-635-2541, 800-800-8288)*, *Budget Host Inn* (☎ *928-635-4415, 800-745-4415)*, *Westerner Motel (☎ 928-635-4312, 800-385-8606)* or *Courtesy Inn (☎ 928-635-2619, 800-235-7029)* for summer rooms in the $40s. Six chain motels provide pricier lodging.

Downtown is full of diners. On Route 66, try *Old Smoky's* for breakfast; *Twisters*, a '50s-style Route 66 soda fountain; or *Cruiser's Café* for a varied menu. Also on Route 66, *Pancho McGillicuddy's* is a popular 'Mexican cantina' with gringo food as well, and *Rod's Steak House* is the best meatery in town.

GRAND CANYON NATIONAL PARK

The Grand Canyon of the Colorado River – at 277 miles long, roughly 10 miles wide and a mile deep – is arguably the USA's most famous natural attraction. Although the rims are only 10 miles apart as the crow flies, it is a 215-mile, five-hour drive on narrow roads from the South Rim visitor center to the North Rim visitor center. Thus Grand Canyon National Park is essentially two separate areas: the South Rim, and the more remote, less-visited North Rim. While camera-draped tourists throng the South Rim in summer, many only stay long enough to look out at the designated 'scenic views.' You can generally escape the crowds if you visit the South Rim during cooler autumn and winter months, the North Rim in the summer or hike down into the canyon.

Information

Grand Canyon Village, about 6 miles north of the South Entrance Station, has hotels, camping, restaurants, stores, showers, rim trails, a train depot, a clinic, a bank, a post office, a free shuttle bus system and other services. Canyon View Information Plaza, at the northeast end of the village, has extensive visitor information and a large book/map store (open daily 8am-6pm). The center can be reached only by foot (about a quarter-mile) or by frequent free bus shuttles. Ask about free ranger-led walks and talks. An automated system (☎ 928-638-7888) has recorded information on everything from weather conditions to applying for a river-running permit. Contact Grand Canyon National Park (PO Box 129, AZ 86023) for the free *Grand Canyon Trip Planner*, or check ⓦ www.nps.gov/grca for comprehensive information.

Entrance to the park is $20 per private vehicle; $10 for bicyclists and pedestrians (valid for seven days). One rim-to-rim shuttle (☎ 928-638-2820 for required reservations) runs daily ($60/100 one way/roundtrip; May-Oct). Permits are required for all activities (camping, backpacking, boating, horseback riding, fishing) except day hikes.

The Grand Canyon Association (☎ 928-638-2481, ⓦ www.grandcanyon.org, PO Box 399, AZ 86023) sells more than 350 different books, maps, trail guides and informational videos, and will send out a mail-order catalog.

When to Go June is the driest month; July and August are the wettest. January has average overnight lows of 13° to 20°F and daytime highs of around 40°F. Summer temperatures inside the canyon rise above 100°F almost every day. Although the South Rim is open all year, the majority of visitors come between Memorial Day (late May) and Labor Day (early

September), when it is very crowded. The North Rim is open only mid-May to mid-October.

Backpacking Permits Permits cost $10 plus $5 per person per night. Applications can be sent or faxed to the Backcountry Office (☎ 928-638-7875, fax 928-638-2125, PO Box 129, Grand Canyon, AZ 86023). Alternatively, go to ⓦ www.nps.gov/grca on the NPS Web site or deliver applications in person.

Applications are accepted for the current month and the next four months *only*. Your chances are pretty good if you apply early and provide alternative hiking itineraries. If you arrive without a backcountry permit, don't despair. Head to the Backcountry Office (open 1pm-5pm Mon-Fri), by the Maswik Lodge, and get on the waiting list for cancellations. You'll likely get a permit within one to six days, depending on season and itinerary.

River Running

Every year more than 20,000 people run the canyon's white-water rapids in a variety of motorized and nonmotorized boats. Clients paddle on some trips – your choice. Most are commercial trips that get fully booked many months in advance, although occasional cancellations allow clients to pick up a trip with just a few weeks' notice. Expect to get soaked, to spend nights camping on beaches and to pay about $200 per person per day (including meals). Trips last from three to 15 days (Apr-Oct). Sixteen companies have permits to run the river; contact the park for a complete list.

One-day trips can be made outside the park from Page or with Hualapai Tours (☎ 888-255-9550, ⓦ www.hualapaitours.com), on the Hualapai Indian Reservation, west of the park.

South Rim

The South Rim, at an elevation of 7000 feet and much more accessible than the North Rim, gets 90% of park visitors. Hwy 64 north from Williams (60 miles) or west from the junction of Hwy 89 (53 miles) reaches the Grand Canyon at Grand Canyon Village. Here, the **Yavapai Museum** has geology exhibits, and the **Tusayan Museum** showcases Ancestral Puebloan history.

While the foremost attraction is the 33-mile rim itself, exploring the canyon is also highly recommended.

Scenic Drives East of Grand Canyon Village, Hwy 64 follows Desert View Dr, with numerous scenic overlooks en route to the East Entrance Station. West of the village, the Hermit's Rest Route also passes many overlooks but is closed to private vehicles. Take one of the frequent free shuttles, which stop at every overlook.

Hiking & Backpacking There are lots of trails in and around the canyon. The popular and recommended 12.2-mile roundtrip hike along **Bright Angel Trail** from the South Rim (6900 feet) to Plateau Point (3800 feet) is a strenuous all-day trek. There are rest houses after 1½ miles (1130-foot elevation drop) and 3 miles (2110-foot elevation drop). From Indian Gardens, a campground 4½ miles from the rim, you can continue to the Colorado River and the Bright Angel Campground (9½ miles from the rim). A few hundred yards beyond is Phantom Ranch (see Places to Stay & Eat, below), with water, food and a ranger station.

Hike safely – carry plenty of water and watch your footing. Lock your car and leave valuables out of sight. The National Park Service recommends that rim-to-river hikes be done as an overnight trip, because climbing out after a long descent is very strenuous.

Organized Tours Within the park, most tours are operated by Amfac (☎ 303-297-2757, fax 303-297-3175, W www.amfac.com). Various bus tours are offered several times a day.

Mule trips usually require advance reservation. A one-day mule trip to Plateau Point takes about seven hours roundtrip ($120). Overnight mule trips to Phantom Ranch are offered daily ($335/600 one/two persons, including meals and dormitory accommodations). During the winter only, when reservations are often unnecessary, three-day/two-night trips to Phantom Ranch cost $770 for two people. Riders must weigh less than 200lb clothed (75kg) and be at least 4 feet, 7 inches (142cm) tall.

Air tours, much criticized for ruining the natural quiet of the canyon, are available from the airport in Tusayan (listed later).

Places to Stay & Eat If you can't find accommodations in the national park, try Tusayan (see below), Valle (31 miles south), Cameron (53 miles east), Williams (about 60 miles south) or Flagstaff (about 80 miles south).

To tent camp at *Mather Campground*, at Grand Canyon Village ($15), you should make reservations (☎ 301-722-1257, 800-365-2267, W www.nps.gov/grca) up to five months in advance, though same-day availability is possible in the low season. Next door, *Trailer Village* (☎ 303-297-2757, W www.nps.gov/grca) charges $24 for RV sites. *Desert View Campground*, near the east entrance, is $10 per site on a first-come, first-served basis (May-Oct).

Six lodges are all operated by Amfac (see Organized Tours, earlier). On the rim, the most famous lodge is the 1905 *El Tovar Hotel*. Rooms start at $120, and suites go to $300; some have canyon views. The El Tovar Dining Room is the canyon's best and requires dinner reservations. Budget travelers go to the rustic 1935 *Bright Angel Lodge & Cabins*, with simple lodge rooms ($48-68), many with shared bath, and cabins ($76-236). There is a restaurant and ice-cream shop. The four other lodges have standard motel rooms ($76-126); two have cafeterias. In the *Village Marketplace*, there's a deli and grocery store. Some restaurants may close in winter.

Phantom Ranch, by the Colorado River in the canyon, has 11 rustic cabins with double bunk beds ($65) and two segregated 10-bunk dorms ($22), which are often full with mule riders. Meals (by reservation), snacks, limited supplies, beer and wine are sold.

Getting There & Away Most people drive or arrive on a bus tour. See the Flagstaff section for information on Nava-Hopi Tours, which is the only regularly scheduled bus service into the park. See the Williams section for the Grand Canyon Railway.

North Rim

The differences between the North and South Rims of the Grand Canyon are elevation, accessibility and number of visitors. The North Rim is more than 8000 feet above sea level. Summers are cooler, winters are colder, the climate is wetter and the spruce-fir forest above the rim is much thicker than the forests of the South Rim. Winter storms close the canyon by December 1, or earlier if there's heavy snow.

Orientation & Information The North Rim Visitor Center (☎ 928-638-7864), by the Grand Canyon Lodge, is 44 miles on Hwy 67 from Alt Hwy 89. The Backcountry Office is in the ranger station near the campground. Other services at the North Rim are a restaurant, gas station, bookshop, general store, coin laundry and showers, medical clinic and tours. From mid-October to mid-May, all services are closed except the campground, which stays open as weather permits (no later than Dec 1). In winter, you can ski in and camp (with a backcountry camping permit). It takes about three days to ski in from where the road is closed, so this trip is only for adventurous and highly experienced winter campers/skiers.

Scenic Drives From the visitor center, about 20 miles of roads lead to several scenic overlooks with picnic areas, including Point Imperial (elevation 8803 feet), the highest overlook in the entire park.

The Toroweap Overlook, with primitive camping, offers a remote overlook. To get there, drive 9 miles west of Fredonia on Hwy 389 and take a rough unpaved road 55 miles southwest to the Tuweep Ranger Station, which is staffed year round. (An alternative route is a 90-mile dirt road from St George, Utah.) It is five more miles from Tuweep to the overlook. (Note that you must leave and reenter the national park to reach Toroweap.)

Hiking & Backpacking The North Kaibab Trail plunges down to the Colorado River, 5750 feet below and 14 miles away, connecting with trails to the South Rim. The first 4.7 miles drop well over 3000 feet to **Roaring Springs**, a popular all-day hike and mule-ride destination. If you prefer a shorter day hike below the rim, you can walk just three-quarters of a mile down to the **Coconino Overlook** or 1 mile to the **Supai Tunnel**, 1400 feet below the rim.

Cottonwood campground is 7 miles and 4200 feet below the rim and is the only campground between the North Rim and the river. Phantom Ranch and Bright Angel

(see South Rim, above) are 7 and 7½ miles below Cottonwood. Because it's twice as far from the North Rim to the river as from the South Rim, rangers suggest three nights as a minimum to enjoy a rim-to-river and return hike.

Organized Tours Canyon Trail Rides (☎ 435-679-8665, 435-834-5500) offers mule rides into the Grand Canyon (from $20/100 for an hour/all-day tour). Advance reservations are recommended, or stop by their desk in the Grand Canyon Lodge. Note that mule rides are not available to the Colorado River except from the South Rim.

Places to Stay & Eat A mile and a half north of the Grand Canyon Lodge, *North Rim Campground* (☎ 301-722-1257, 800-365-2267) has 82 sites ($15; no hookups) and a grocery store. Make reservations up to five months in advance. You can also camp in *Kaibab National Forest*, farther north along Hwy 67.

The North Rim's only hotel is the *Grand Canyon Lodge* (☎ 928-638-2611, 303-297-2757 for reservations), with 200 cabins and double rooms ($80-120). A restaurant (dinner reservations required), cafeteria, coffee shop and saloon bar serve food.

Tusayan

This town, 8 miles south of Grand Canyon Village, offers several pricey chain motels and restaurants strung along Hwy 64. Free dispersed camping is allowed in the Kaibab National Forest. *Grand Canyon Camper Village* (☎ 928-638-2887) often has tent/RV sites ($17/24) when everywhere else is full.

Havasupai Indian Reservation

Tribal headquarters of the Havasupai Indians are in **Supai**, the only village within the Grand Canyon, which has been here for centuries. The Supai post office uses pack animals – mail from here is postmarked to prove it! The 8-mile hike down to Supai follows Havasu Creek, but the most memorable, waterfall-lined sections are along the 4 or 5 miles of trail below the village. Allow three days and two nights here. Get information and camping reservations from Havasupai Tourist Enterprise (☎ 928-448-2141, 928-448-2121, Supai, AZ 86435). All visitors pay a $15 fee.

SOUTHWEST

To reach Supai, look for a signed turnoff to Hualapai Hilltop 7 miles east of Peach Springs on Route 66. Drive 62 miles (no services), park your car, lock up, lace your boots and head about 8 miles out and 2000 feet down! Havasupai Tourist Enterprise can arrange horses or mules by advance reservation: $80 from hilltop to Supai, $110 from hilltop to the campground, $40 from Supai to the campground. Helicopter day trips ($450) can be arranged.

In Supai, the **Havasupai Lodge** (☎ 928-448-2111, 928-448-2201) has 24 modern rooms ($75-96 in summer) with canyon views. Two miles below Supai is **Havasupai Campground**, with 400 tent sites stretching along the river ($10 per person). Reservations are essential and should be made well in advance in the summer.

LAKE POWELL
In the 1950s Glen Canyon was the heart of the largest 'roadless' area in the continental USA. And in 1956 conservationists fought hard against the construction of the Glen Canyon Dam but lost. When the dam was finished in 1963, the Colorado River and its tributaries began backing up for 186 miles. By 1980 Lake Powell had flooded the canyon to a depth of 560 feet and had created almost 2000 miles of shoreline, becoming the second-largest artificial reservoir in the country.

Lake Powell is part of the 1933-sq-mile **Glen Canyon National Recreation Area** (GCNRA). Houseboating is particularly popular, and despite hundreds of vessels, the lake is large enough that you can get away from the crowds. The Carl Hayden Visitor Center (☎ 928-608-6404) is at the dam, 2 miles north of Page. Five miles north of the visitor center is **Wahweap Marina Lodge** (☎ 928-645-2433), the largest of the four marinas on Lake Powell, with complete visitor services.

Aramark (☎ 602-278-8888, 800-528-6154, Ⓦ www.visitlakepowell.com, PO Box 56909, Phoenix, AZ 85079) is the concessionaire for houseboats and lodges at the lake; advance reservations are recommended. Summer rates for boats sleeping six to 12 range from about $1800 to $5500 weekly (up to 40% less Nov-Apr). Boat tours from 90 minutes to all day cost $25-100. On the south shore of Lake Powell, **Rainbow Bridge National Monument**, usually reached by tour boat, is the largest natural bridge in the world and a site of religious importance to the Navajo.

Five miles from Lake Powell, **Page** is a regional center and offers plenty of accommodations and services. The cheapest motels, which have simple, clean rooms from about $50 in summer, include **Uncle Bill's** (☎ 928-645-1224, 115 8th Ave) and **LuLu's Sleep Ezze** (☎ 928-608-0273, 105 8th Ave), both with shared bathrooms, or **Bashful Bob's Motel** (☎ 928-645-3919, 750 S Navajo Dr) and **Page Boy Motel** (☎ 928-645-2416, 150 N Lake Powell Blvd). Chain motel rooms cost $80-200 in summer, when reservations are recommended.

NORTHEASTERN ARIZONA
Here Navajo hogans (octagonal homes made of wood and earth, with the door facing east) and Hopi kivas nestle against some of the most spectacular landscape in North America. Equally impressive are the ancient pueblos in the Canyon de Chelly and Navajo National Monuments.

Navajo Indian Reservation
After the infamous 'Long Walk' (see the boxed text 'Tragedy at Bosque Redondo,' earlier), the surviving Navajo returned to their homeland in 1868 under a treaty that created a reservation of about 5500 sq miles. Today, the Navajo Nation, as the Navajo prefer to call it, covers about 27,000 sq miles of high desert and forest and is the largest reservation in the USA. Half of the approximately 175,000 members of the Navajo Nation live here.

The US military used Navajo servicemen speaking their native tongue to create a secret code during WWII – it was never broken. Tune in to KTNN AM 660/KWRK 96.1 out of Window Rock for Navajo programming every day.

The biggest Native American event in the country is the Annual Navajo Nation Fair, held over Labor Day weekend in Window Rock. Most visitors stay in Gallup, New Mexico.

Information The Navajo Tourism Office (☎ 928-871-6436, 928-871-7371, Ⓦ www.navajo.org) provides a free tourist information magazine, available on the reservation and nearby towns. All backcountry activities require a permit from the Navajo Parks & Recreation Department (☎ 928-871-6647, fax 928-871-6637), next to the zoo and botanical park at the east end of Window Rock.

Window Rock In the tribal capital, the Navajo Council Chambers (☎ 928-871-6417) can be visited; it's just off Hwy 12, almost 2 miles north of Hwy 264. On Hwy 264 just east of Hwy 12 are the tourist facilities, including the FedMart shopping plaza (where the Navajo Transit System bus leaves from; see below), the museum and a bank. For Navajo crafts, stop by the Navajo Arts and Crafts Enterprise (☎ 928-871-4090).

Hubbell Trading Post NHS This trading post (a National Historic Site) looks much as it would have soon after it was established by John Lorenzo Hubbell at Ganado (just off Hwy 264, 30 miles west of Window Rock) in 1878. Indian artists still trade here and often give weaving and silversmithing demonstrations (8am-6pm).

Canyon de Chelly National Monument This many-fingered canyon and National Monument (pronounced **duh**-shay) contains several Ancestral Puebloan pit dwellings (circa AD 350) and some large cliff dwellings in the canyon walls (circa 1200). Two scenic rim drives, each taking about three hours to appreciate, are free, but you must have a Navajo guide to visit the canyon. At the visitor center (☎ 928-674-5500), just east of Chinle, ask about guided hikes ($15; 4 hours), 4WD trips ($40 for a half day) and horseback rides ($10/hour plus $10 for a guide).

By the visitor center is the free *Cottonwood Campground* and attractive *Thunderbird Lodge* (☎ 928-674-5841, 800-679-2473), with rooms for $100-150. A Holiday Inn and Best Western are within 3 miles. *Spider Rock Campground* (☎ 928-674-8261), 10 miles east along South Rim Dr, is pleasantly quiet ($10). Neither campground has hookups.

Four Corners Navajo Tribal Park You can put a foot into Arizona, another into New Mexico, a hand into Utah and another into Colorado here – the only place in the USA where four states come together

($2.50). Navajo food stands and dozens of the inevitable crafts stalls surround the site, which is off Hwy 160.

Monument Valley Navajo Tribal Park The magnificent mesas and buttes of Monument Valley, immortalized through westerns like John Ford's 1939 *Stagecoach* and the 1962 *How the West Was Won,* is 24 miles north of Kayenta on Hwy 163. From the visitor center, you can drive the 17-mile unpaved road yourself ($3) or arrange Jeep and horseback tours ($30, though not always in winter). *Mitten View Campground* has tent sites ($10). The closest hotel is in Utah (see Monument Valley in Utah, later in the chapter).

Navajo National Monument The Ancestral Puebloan sites of Betatakin and Keet Seel are open for public visitation (summer only) and are both exceptionally well preserved, extensive and impressive. Because you need to hike 5 miles roundtrip to Betatakin and 17 miles roundtrip to Keet Seel (camping permitted), this is a good place to check out pueblo sites away from crowds. There are only 20 daily hiking permits (free), so call for reservations up to two months in advance. The visitor center (☎ 928-672-2700) is 9 miles north of Hwy 160 along paved Hwy 564 (8am-5pm). Free camping here is on a first-come, first-served basis.

Places to Stay Navajo guides arrange stays with local families or in a traditional hogan (bring a sleeping bag; bathroom facilities are minimal) starting at $90. The Navajo Tourism Office has a list of approved guides.

Navajo Nation Inn (☎ 928-871-4108, 800-662-6189), in Window Rock, has rooms starting at $65. West of town is a *Days Inn* (☎ 928-871-5690).

Kayenta provides convenient (although pricey) tourist services for visitors to nearby Monument Valley and Navajo National Monument. Chain motels include a Best Western, Hampton Inn and Holiday Inn.

In Tuba City, students operate the *Grey Hills Inn* (☎ 928-283-6271) in the Grey Hills High School, on Hwy 160 just past Hwy 264 ($42-58 for one to four people, with shared bath). There's a Quality Inn here as well.

Getting There & Away The Navajo Transit System (☎ 928-729-4002, 928-729-4110), in Window Rock, runs three or four buses to Gallup, New Mexico (Mon-Sat), and one bus on weekdays to Tuba City ($14; 4 hours), with stops along Hwy 264 via the Hopi Reservation. There are also weekday buses to Kayenta and Farmington, New Mexico.

Hopi Indian Reservation

The oldest, most traditional and religious tribe in Arizona (if not the entire continent), the Hopi are a private people who have received less outside influence from most other tribes. Villages, many built between AD 1400 and 1700, dot the isolated mesas. **Old Oraibi**, inhabited since the early 12th century, vies with Acoma Pueblo in New Mexico for the title of the oldest continuously inhabited town in North America.

Hwy 264 runs past the three mesas (First, Second and Third Mesa) that form the heart of the reservation. There are no banks, and cash is preferred for most transactions. Call ☎ 928-734-3283 for information. Photography is rarely allowed.

At the end of First Mesa, the tiny village of **Walpi** (circa 1200) has a spectacular setting on a finger mesa (too narrow to drive) jutting out into space; it's the most dramatic of the Hopi villages. From the parking area near the village entrance, a tourist office (☎ 928-737-2262) can arrange a Hopi guide for a 45-minute walking tour ($8); it's well recommended. The Hopi are known for their kachina dolls, and these and other crafts can be purchased from individual artists in the villages and at the Hopi Cultural Center.

The *Hopi Cultural Center Restaurant & Inn* (☎ 928-734-2401), in Second Mesa, is the only motel (rooms cost $90-100).

Winslow

The Eagles' hit 'Take It Easy,' in which a hitchhiker, standing on a corner in Winslow, Arizona, gets checked out by a girl ('my Lord!') in a flatbed Ford, has generated civic pride. The corner of Route 66 at Kingsley Ave and 2nd St has a small plaza with a statue and wall mural telling the story – a popular photo opportunity.

Winslow also provides the closest off-reservation accommodations to the Hopi mesas. Several old Route 66 motels line 2nd and 3rd Sts ($20-30), and motel chains are represented. The most memorable place is the recently restored *La Posada* (☎ 928-289-4366, 🌐 www.laposada.org, 303 E 2nd St), complete with period furnishings. The finest hotel in northeastern Arizona during the 1930s, it is once again the finest hotel in the region ($79-99).

Petrified Forest National Park

Conifers from the Triassic (225 million years ago, meaning they were contemporary with ancient reptiles and predated the dinosaurs) make up this 'forest' ($10 per vehicle; 8am-5pm). Apart from the petrified logs, visitors see a few small ancient Indian sites, some petroglyphs and the otherworldly scenery of the **Painted Desert** – some 67 sq miles of picturesque lands that change colors as the sunlight plays tricks with the minerals in the earth.

From the **Rainbow Forest Museum**, on Hwy 180 19 miles southeast of Holbrook, a park road heads 28 miles north, passing short trails, many signed pullouts and the Painted Desert Visitor Center (☎ 928-524-6228), emerging at I-40 exit 311.

Holbrook

This town is the closest to Petrified Forest National Park. It's west of the park, on I-40 near Hwy 77. Plenty of cheap and chain motels line the main drags, Navajo Blvd and Hopi Dr. Native American dancers perform for free (tips appreciated) outside the 1898 county courthouse at 7pm in summer. Photography is permitted.

WESTERN ARIZONA

Artificial lakes, with year-round recreational activities, dot the Colorado River along the state's western border. The area around the lower Colorado south of I-10 contains some of the West's wildest and most rugged areas.

Kingman & Around

Kingman is the major town along I-40 between California and Flagstaff. It offers plenty of inexpensive and mid-range accommodations and provides an excellent base for exploring the northwest corner of the state. Founded by Lewis Kingman in 1880 as a railway stop, the town retains many of its late-19th-century buildings. The visitor center (☎ 928-753-6106, 120 W Andy Devine Ave) is open daily and features a **Route 66 Museum** ($3). Greyhound (☎ 928-757-8400, 3264 E Andy Devine Ave) has a bus stop behind the McDonald's restaurant.

The longest extant stretch of Route 66, once called the 'Main Street of America,' winds 160 miles through empty northwestern Arizona countryside, running from Seligman to Topock on the Arizona-California border. Two million ounces of gold were extracted at **Oatman** before the last mine closed in 1942. Today 500,000 visitors annually come through this self-styled 'ghost town' in the rugged Black Mountains, with gunfights at high noon and Western dancing at night. Old Route 66 winds through town.

Founded in 1862 by silver miners, the quiet town of **Chloride** is Arizona's oldest mining town. From Kingman, head northwest on Hwy 93 for 19 miles; turn right and drive 3½ miles into town.

Hualapai Mountain Park (☎ 928-757-3859), 14 miles southeast of Kingman, surrounds 8417-foot Hualapai Peak and offers camping ($6/12 tents/RVs). Motels line Andy Devine Ave (between I-40 exits 48 and 53). For rooms starting in the $20s, try *Arcadia Lodge (☎ 928-753-1925)*, *Lido Motel (☎ 928-753-4515)* or *High Desert Inn (☎ 928-753-2935)*. Many chain motels cluster around exit 53. *Silver Spoon Family Restaurant (2011 E Andy Devine Ave)* is a popular local place (open 5am-10pm). *Dambar & Steak House (1960 E Andy Devine Ave)* specializes in big steaks ($10-20) for dinner.

In Oatman, the two-story adobe *Oatman Hotel (☎ 928-768-4408)* is on the National Register of Historic Places, and the simple rooms are almost unchanged since Hollywood legends Clarke Gable and Carole Lombard honeymooned here in the 1930s ($35 with shared bathroom).

In Chloride, *Sheps Miners Inn B&B (☎ 928-565-4251, 877-565-4251)* rents 12 rooms ($35-65).

Lake Havasu City

When the city of London auctioned off its 1831 bridge in the late 1960s, developer Robert McCulloch bought it for $2.5 million, disassembled it into 10,276 granite slabs, transported the 10,000 tons of stone and reassembled it at Lake Havasu City. Perhaps one of the oddest experiences in Arizona is sitting at a pseudo-English pub in the 'English Village' and looking out at London Bridge. Locals claim that the bridge and water activities attract more tourists than anywhere in Arizona except the Grand Canyon, and it certainly can be a madhouse of jet boats and tourists. Students cram the town during spring break. Summer temperatures reach more than 100°F for weeks on end.

Windsor Beach Campground (☎ 928-855-2784), 2 miles north on London Bridge Rd, has showers, a boat launch and camping (no hookups) for $12 per day. The cheapest motels ($50 in summer) include *Havasu Motel (☎ 928-855-2311, 2035 Acoma Blvd)* and *Lakeview Motel (☎ 520-855-3605, 440 London Bridge Rd)*. There are several chain motels in the area.

Several restaurants are on or near the half-mile of McCulloch Blvd between Smoketree Ave and Acoma Blvd. The locally popular *Taco Hacienda (2200 Mesquite Ave)* has been feeding folks here for two decades (eons by Lake Havasu City standards).

Greyhound buses (☎ 928-764-4010) leave from the Busy 'B' Shell Service Station (3201 N Hwy 95), 4 miles north of town.

Quartzsite

This town has about 3400 permanent residents, but in January and February, gem-and-mineral shows attract more than one million visitors, who come to buy, sell, trade and admire. These folks can't quite squeeze into the town's four tiny motels, so thousands upon thousands of RVs stretch out as far as the eye can see – a strange sight indeed. The chamber of commerce (☎ 928-927-5600) is north of I-10 exit 17.

Yuma

This town of 77,515 people is Arizona's third-largest metropolitan area and is one of the sunniest and driest. Weather records indicate that 93% of daylight hours are sunny, and rainfall averages about 3 inches annually. At the gruesome and offbeat **Yuma Territorial Prison State Historic Park,** you can visit buildings that housed more than 3000 of Arizona's most feared criminals between 1876 and 1909. The prison (☎ 928-783-4771) is open daily ($3). I-8 exit 2 takes you to 16th St (Hwy 95), which crosses 4th Ave (Hwy 80). These streets are the main hotel/restaurant drags. The Convention & Visitors Bureau (☎ 928-783-0071) is at 377 S Main St.

The Yuma Railway (☎ 928-783-4400) makes two-hour runs in historic carriages from 8th St, 6 miles west of downtown ($13; Sat-Sun Oct-May). *Colorado King* (☎ 928-782-2412), a two-deck paddleboat, gives three-hour narrated boat tours ($30).

Yuma offers several chain motels by I-8 exit 2. Many cheaper ones ($30-40 in summer, $50-60 in winter) are along 4th Ave. Try *El Rancho Motel* (☎ 928-783-4481), the *Regalodge* (☎ 928-782-4571) or the better *Yuma Cabaña* (☎ 928-783-8311). *La Fuente Inn & Suites* (☎ 928-329-1814, 800-841-1814, 1513 E 16th St) is a modern Spanish-colonial-style building around a landscaped garden and pool. Winter rates start at $100.

Eclectic *Lutes Casino* (221 Main St) serves burgers and claims to be Arizona's oldest pool hall. The *Garden Café* (250 Madison Ave) serves breakfast and lunch in an elegant patio. Among Yuma's many Mexican restaurants, try *Chretin's* (485 15th Ave), tucked away on a residential street. *Hunter Steakhouse* (2335 4th Ave) does good steaks and prime rib. *Red's Bird Cage Saloon* (231 Main St) has pool, darts and drinking after Lutes closes.

The Greyhound station (☎ 928-783-4403) is at 170 E 17th Place. American Shuttle Express (☎ 928-726-0906, 888-749-9862) provides vans to Phoenix Airport ($48; 3½ hours).

TUCSON

Rich in Latino roots and home to the University of Arizona (U of A), Tucson is set in a Sonoran Desert valley at 2500 feet, surrounded by mountains, some reaching more than 9000 feet. With 843,746 metro-area inhabitants, it is Arizona's second-largest city.

Contact Off the Beaten Path Tours (☎ 520-529-6090) and Trail Dust Jeep Tours (☎ 520-747-0323) for tours of the city and surrounding area.

The Tucson Gem and Mineral Show, in early February, is the largest of its kind in the world. The Fiesta de los Vaqueros (locally called 'Rodeo Week'), held from Thursday to Sunday in the last week of February, features a huge nonmotorized parade.

Orientation & Information

Downtown Tucson and the historic district are east of I-10 exit 258. Stone Ave, at its intersection with Congress St, forms the zero point for Tucson addresses. About a mile northeast of downtown is the U of A campus, and a mile south of downtown is the square mile of South Tucson, with funky Mexican restaurants.

The Convention & Visitors Bureau (☎ 520-624-1817, 800-638-8350, W www .visittucson.org, 110 S Church Ave) is open daily. The Coronado National Forest Supervisor's Office (☎ 520-670-4552, 300 W Congress St) is open weekdays, and the Sabino Canyon Ranger Station (☎ 520-749-8700) is open daily (see Things to See & Do). The main library (☎ 520-791-4393, 101 N Stone Ave) is open daily and offers Internet access, as does Hotel Congress (see Places to Stay).

Things to See & Do

In downtown Tucson, you can stroll through the 19th-century buildings and craft stores in the Presidio Historic District. The **Tucson Museum of Art** (☎ 520-624-2333, 140 N Main Ave) houses a small collection of pre-Columbian artifacts from South America as well as various works of 20th-century Western art ($5, free on Sun; closed Mon in summer).

The **University of Arizona** campus, a worthwhile stop, houses some excellent museums and several notable outdoor sculptures. A visitor center (☎ 520-621-5130) at the southeast corner of University Blvd and Cherry Ave is open weekdays.

With a nice collection of works by American photographers and a remarkable archive (including most of Ansel Adams' and Edward Weston's work), the internationally renowned **Center for Creative Photography** (☎ 520-621-7968, 1030 N Olive Ave) is a must for anyone interested in photography (free admission). Opposite is the UA Museum of Art (☎ 520-621-7567).

TUCSON AREA

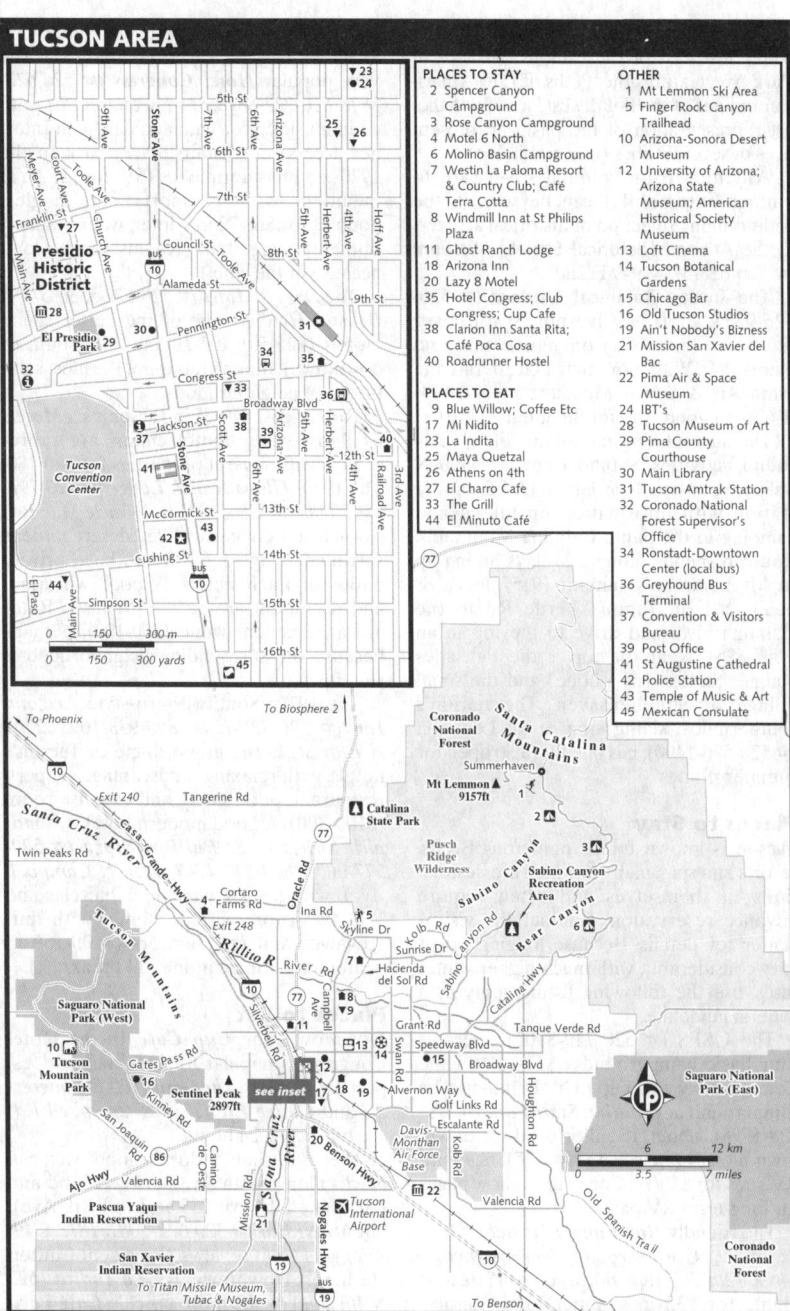

PLACES TO STAY
2 Spencer Canyon Campground
3 Rose Canyon Campground
4 Motel 6 North
6 Molino Basin Campground
7 Westin La Paloma Resort & Country Club; Café Terra Cotta
8 Windmill Inn at St Philips Plaza
11 Ghost Ranch Lodge
18 Arizona Inn
20 Lazy 8 Motel
35 Hotel Congress; Club Congress; Cup Cafe
38 Clarion Inn Santa Rita; Café Poca Cosa
40 Roadrunner Hostel

PLACES TO EAT
9 Blue Willow; Coffee Etc
17 Mi Nidito
23 La Indita
25 Maya Quetzal
26 Athens on 4th
27 El Charro Cafe
33 The Grill
44 El Minuto Café

OTHER
1 Mt Lemmon Ski Area
5 Finger Rock Canyon Trailhead
10 Arizona-Sonora Desert Museum
12 University of Arizona; Arizona State Museum; American Historical Society Museum
13 Loft Cinema
14 Tucson Botanical Gardens
15 Chicago Bar
19 Old Tucson Studios
19 Ain't Nobody's Bizness
21 Mission San Xavier del Bac
22 Pima Air & Space Museum
24 IBT's
28 Tucson Museum of Art
29 Pima County Courthouse
30 Main Library
31 Tucson Amtrak Station
32 Coronado National Forest Supervisor's Office
34 Ronstadt-Downtown Center (local bus)
36 Greyhound Bus Terminal
37 Convention & Visitors Bureau
39 Post Office
41 St Augustine Cathedral
42 Police Station
43 Temple of Music & Art
45 Mexican Consulate

SOUTHWEST

The **Arizona State Museum** (☎ 520-621-6302), just east of the campus entrance at Park Ave, features the 'Paths of Life: American Indians of the Southwest,' a state-of-the-art representation of the past and present lives of several tribes (free admission).

Anything from colonial silverware to vintage automobiles can be seen in the wide-ranging selection of historical artifacts at the **Arizona Historical Society Museum** (☎ 520-628-5774, 949 E 2nd).

The **Tucson Botanical Gardens** (☎ 520-326-9255, 2150 N Alvernon Way) cover 5½ acres and focus on native dry-land plants ($4). With more than 200 aircraft, the **Pima Air & Space Museum** (☎ 520-574-0462) is a good stop for flight buffs ($10).

The surrounding mountains offer year-round activities. Sabino Canyon (5900 N Sabino Canyon Rd) has a USFS ranger station with information on **hiking** and camping in the Santa Catalina Mountains. You can spend a couple of days hiking up to Mt Lemmon's summit (9157 feet), or head east on Tanque Verde Rd to the Catalina Hwy and drive to the top in an hour ($5). Near the top is the Palisades Ranger Station (no phone) and the small village of Summerhaven. The nation's southernmost **skiing** area, at Mt Lemmon (☎ 520-576-1400), has one lift (also open for summer riding).

Places to Stay

Tucson is known for its numerous B&Bs, resorts and spas, many of which are destinations in themselves and often require advance reservation. Contact the visitor center for details. Because lodging prices vary considerably, with much higher winter rates, use the following listings only as a general guideline.

The USFS (☎ 520-749-8700) operates four basic campgrounds ($12-14) on the Catalina Hwy going up to Mt Lemmon. The campground at **Catalina State Park** (☎ 520-628-5798), about 15 miles north of downtown along Oracle Rd (Hwy 77), has tent/RV sites for $10/15. Check the yellow pages for long-term RV parks.

The friendly **Roadrunner Hostel** (☎ 520-628-4709, Ⓦ www.roadrunnerhostel.com, 346 E 12th St) offers dorm rooms ($16; four nights for $32 in summer) and doubles ($35). Free Internet access, kitchen privileges, TV/video room and coin laundry are included; bicycles can be rented ($7). The very popular **Hotel Congress** (☎ 520-622-8848, 800-722-8848, 311 E Congress St), with a hip music club, a cafe and bar (with Internet access) downstairs, dates back to the 1920s and has dorm beds ($17 for HI-AYH members with passport) and singles/doubles for $68/72 in winter, when reservations are suggested. (Rooms can be loud because of the club.)

The **Lazy 8 Motel** (☎ 520-622-3336, 314 E Benson Hwy) is one of the better cheap motels ($25-50) at I-10 exit 261 (south of downtown), though this is not the most salubrious of neighborhoods.

Rooms cost $40-65 in Tucson's six **Motels 6**s. Most other motel chains are represented, with several properties for $60-180. The 1940s **Ghost Ranch Lodge** (☎ 520-791-7565, 800-456-7565, 801 W Miracle Mile Rd) sits in 8 acres of cactus-filled desert gardens surrounded by rooms. Some have private patios or kitchenettes. A pool, whirlpool and restaurant are on the premises. Rates are an excellent value ($50-100), perhaps because the surrounding neighborhood is run-down.

The 1930s Southwestern-style **Arizona Inn** (☎ 520-325-1541, 800-933-1093, 2200 E Elm St) is the grand dame of Tucson's hotels, with relaxing landscaping, a superb restaurant, pool, sauna and exercise room ($100-300). A good modern hotel is **Windmill Suites at St Phillips Plaza** (☎ 520-577-0007, 800-547-4747, 4250 N Campbell Ave), with a pool, whirlpool, bicycles and 120 two-room suites, some with microwaves and refrigerators ($100-150 in winter, including continental breakfast).

Places to Eat

Downtown, the **Cup Cafe**, in the Hotel Congress, is popular for breakfast and, especially, desserts. **The Grill** (100 E Congress St) and **Coffee Etc** (2830 N Campbell Rd) are both open 24 hours.

There are half a dozen good Mexican places along S 4th Ave between 22nd and I-10 (take I-10 exit 259 east to S 4th Ave), but **Mi Nidito** (☎ 520-622-5081, 1813 S 4th Ave) gets great reviews. (President Clinton ate here.) Downtown, try **La Indita** (622 N 4th Ave) or the more upscale **Café Poca Cosa** (☎ 520-622-6400, 88 E Broadway

Blvd), at the Clarion Inn Santa Rita. The oldest place in town is *El Charro Cafe* (☎ *520-622-1922, 311 N Court Ave)*, which they say has been in the same family since 1922 and is very popular with tourists and locals alike. *El Minuto Café (345 S Main Ave)* is famous for its chiles rellenos.

Maya Quetzal (429 N 4th Ave) is a small and friendly place serving inexpensive Guatemalan food. *Athens on 4th (500 N 4th Ave)* has tasty Greek food at moderate prices. For excellent upscale Southwestern fare, try *Café Terra Cotta* (☎ *520-577-8100, 3500 E Sunrise Dr)*, near the Westin La Paloma Resort. *Blue Willow (2616 E Campbell Rd)* emphasizes vegetarian choices and attracts a slightly alternative clientele of all ages.

Entertainment
Read the free alternative *Tucson Weekly* for updates on local happenings. The *Loft Cinema* (☎ *520-795-7777, 3233 E Speedway Blvd)* often screens foreign flicks.

Downtown, 4th Ave near 6th St is a good spot to bar hop. Students head to *Chicago Bar (5954 E Speedway Blvd)* for blues and rock. *Club Congress*, in the Hotel Congress, has alternative dance music (recorded and occasionally live). For Latin music, try *Irene's (254 E Congress St)*. *IBT's (616 N 4th Ave)* is Tucson's best gay dance club, while *Ain't Nobody's Bizness (2900 E Broadway Blvd)*, in a shopping plaza, attracts lesbians.

The *Temple of Music & Art* (☎ *520-884-4875, 330 S Scott Ave)*, the *Tucson Convention Center* (☎ *520-791-4266, 260 S Church St)* and the U of A *Centennial Hall* (☎ *520-621-3341, 1020 E University Blvd)* host various cultural events.

Getting There & Around
Tucson International Airport (☎ 520-573-8000) is 9 miles south of downtown.

The Amtrak station is at 400 E Toole Ave. Greyhound (☎ 520-792-3475, 2 S 4th Ave) runs buses to Phoenix ($30; 2 hours). The Arizona Shuttle Service (☎ 520-795-6771, 5350 E Speedway Blvd) has hourly vans to Phoenix Airport. Arizona Stagecoach (☎ 520-889-1000) has door-to-door, 24-hour airport service.

The Ronstadt-Downtown Center is one of three major transit centers in Tucson. Sun Tran (☎ 520-792-9222) buses serve metropolitan Tucson. Yellow Cab (☎ 520-624-6611) has 24-hour service. For bike rental, try Bargain Basement Bikes (☎ 520-624-9673, 428 N Fremont Ave).

AROUND TUCSON
Mission San Xavier del Bac
Founded by the Jesuit Padre Kino in 1700, the San Xavier mission (☎ 520-294-2624) is Arizona's oldest European building still in use. Catholic masses are held daily. To get there, drive south on I-19 to exit 92.

Arizona-Sonora Desert Museum
Coyotes, javelinas, bobcats, snakes, hummingbirds, scorpions and just about any other local desert animals you can think of are displayed in natural-looking outdoor settings at this excellent living museum (☎ 520-883-2702, 2021 N Kinney Rd) off Hwy 86; it's one of the best zoos of its kind ($10).

Old Tucson Studios
A film set from 1939 onward, Old Tucson (☎ 520-883-0100), a few miles southeast of the Arizona-Sonora Desert Museum, is now a Western theme park with Wild West events galore ($16).

Biosphere 2
Built to be completely sealed off from Biosphere 1 (the biosphere on which we live), Biosphere 2 (☎ 520-896-6200, Ⓦ www .bio2.edu) is a 3-acre glassed dome housing seven separate microhabitats and designed to be self-sustaining. In 1991 eight 'bionauts' entered Biosphere 2 for a two-year tour of duty, during which they were physically cut off from the outside world. They emerged two years later, thinner but in pretty fair shape. Although this experiment could be used as a prototype for future space stations, it was a privately funded endeavor and was engulfed in controversy. Now, various research projects are ongoing. Biosphere 2 is about 30 miles north of Tucson on Hwy 77 ($13 with an outside guided tour, another $10 to go inside).

Saguaro National Park
With two separate units, east and west of Tucson, this park's main purpose is to preserve large stands of the giant saguaro cactus and its associated habitat and

wildlife. The Saguaro East Visitors Center (☎ 520-733-5153), 15 miles east of downtown along Old Spanish Trail (take E Broadway), has information regarding day hikes, horseback riding and park camping (free permits must be obtained by noon on the day of your hike). The park boasts 130 miles of trails, including the Tanque Verde Ridge Trail, which climbs to Mica Mountain (8666 feet). Admission is $6 per car.

Two miles northwest of the Arizona-Sonora Desert Museum (see above) is the Saguaro West Visitors Center (☎ 520-733-5158). Admission to the park is free (for now, anyway). Although night hiking is permitted, camping is not.

WEST OF TUCSON

Hwy 86 heads west of Tucson toward some of the driest parts of the Sonoran Desert.

West of Sells on Hwy 86, **Kitt Peak National Optical Observatory** is the largest optical observatory in the world. Contact the visitor center (☎ 520-318-8726) for information on guided tours. You don't get to look through the telescopes except for during the nightly three-hour sessions ($35), which are booked up weeks in advance. Self-guided tours are available (9am-3:45pm daily except major holidays).

Two unpaved loop drives (21 and 53 miles) and six hiking trails take you into the undisturbed Sonoran Desert habitat at **Organ Pipe Cactus National Monument**, with three types of large columnar cacti and an excellent variety of other desert flora and fauna. The visitor center (☎ 520-387-6849) is 22 miles south of the Hwy 86 junction at Why. Admission is $5 per car. Campsites cost $10 (no RV hookups); backcountry camping is allowed by $5 permit only.

SOUTH OF TUCSON

Several sites of interest are near I-19 en route to Mexico.

The **Titan Missile Museum** is a National Historic Landmark (☎ 520-625-7736 for tour reservations), at I-19 exit 69, featuring an underground launch site for Cold War–era intercontinental ballistic missiles ($7.50).

If history and/or shopping for crafts interest you, the small village of **Tubac** (I-19 exit 34), with more than 80 galleries and the like, is a worthwhile stop. The 1752 Tubac Presidio (☎ 520-398-2252) now lies in ruins, but an 1885 schoolhouse and a museum tell the history. At I-19 exit 29, **Tumacacori National Historic Site** (☎ 520-398-2341) is the well-preserved ruin of a never-completed Franciscan church started in 1800. A visitor center, museum and gift shop are on site ($3).

Arizona's most important gateway to Mexico, **Nogales** is bustling with activity and tourists buying Mexican goods. (There's a Nogales on each side of the border.) The chamber of commerce (☎ 520-287-3685), in Kino Park off Grand Ave, is open weekdays. The Mexican Consulate (☎ 520-287-2521) is at 571 Grand Ave. Chain *motels*, with rooms at $40-100, are clustered at I-19 exit 4 and along Business Hwy 19.

Greyhound (☎ 520-287-5628) and other companies leave from 35 N Terrace with hourly buses to Tucson ($7). From the bus terminal about 3 miles south of the border, there are frequent departures farther into Mexico and a daily train south to Guadalajara and Mexico City. Drivers into Mexico can obtain car insurance from Sanborn's (☎ 520-281-1873, 2921 Grand Ave) or in the Holiday Inn Express (I-19 exit 4).

SOUTHEASTERN CORNER

This is Cochise County – land of Indians, cowboys, miners, outlaws, ranchers, gunslingers and Western lore. The Huachuca and Chiricahua Mountains provide scenic beauty.

Benson & Around

This rural town is a quiet travelers' stop with a few chain motels clustered at I-10 exits 304 and 302, and basic old motels along 4th St (Hwy 80). **Kartchner Caverns State Park** (9 miles south on Hwy 90), a 2½-mile-long wet limestone cave, is touted as one of the world's 10 best living (ie, stalactites, stalagmites and other features are still forming) caves. Entrance is by guided tours ($14), limited to 20 people leaving 25 times a day; advance reservations are required (☎ 520-586-2283). Each morning 100 same-day tour tickets are sold; travelers wait from before dawn to snag one in the busy winter high season.

The excellent **Amerind Foundation** (☎ 520-586-3666), in Dragoon, 15 miles east of Benson (I-10 exit 318 east), features exhibits of American Indian archaeology, history and culture ($3).

Willcox

This fruit-growing center is busy with visitors during the apple harvest and with bird-watchers, who flock to the nearby wintering grounds of thousands of sandhill cranes. The chamber of commerce (☎ 520-384-2272, 800-200-2272), by I-40 exit 320, has information. Chain motels are clustered at this exit. Greyhound (☎ 520-384-2183) stops at 622 N Haskell Ave (at the Lifestyle RV Resort).

Chiricahua National Monument

This small and remote National Park Service area in the Chiricahua Mountains offers strangely eroded volcanic geology and abundant wildlife. The **Bonita Canyon Scenic Drive** will take you 8 miles to Massai Point at 6870 feet, and there are numerous hiking trails. The monument (☎ 520-824-3560) is 40 miles southeast of Willcox off Hwy 186 ($6 per car). You can camp in basic tent sites ($8), but wilderness camping is not permitted.

Sierra Vista & Around

A modern town, Sierra Vista (elevation 4623 feet) is a good center from which to visit local attractions. The chamber of commerce (☎ 520-458-6940, 800-288-3861) is at 21 E Wilcox Dr.

At 5500 feet, in the Huachuca Mountains south of Sierra Vista, the **Ramsey Canyon Preserve** (☎ 520-378-2785, 520-378-2640) is famous as one of the best places in the USA to see about 14 species of hummingbirds. Large RVs can't make it up the road here. *Ramsey Canyon Inn B&B (☎ 520-378-3010)* has eight rooms for ($121-158); reservations are essential.

Sitting along the San Pedro, the longest remaining undammed river in Arizona, the **San Pedro Riparian National Conservation Area** is a part of the Nature Conservancy's 'Last Great Places' program. Backcountry camping (☎ 520-458-3559) is allowed here by permit ($2); self-pay stations are in the parking lots. The area is reached by several roads east of Sierra Vista.

In Sierra Vista, chain motels with rooms for $40-90 line Fry Blvd. Also try *Western Motel (☎ 520-458-4303, 43 W Fry Blvd)*, with microwaves and refrigerators.

Golden State (☎ 520-458-3471, 28 Fab Ave) has daily buses to Bisbee, Douglas, Tucson and Phoenix.

Tombstone

> Here lies
> Lester Moore
> Four slugs from a .44
> No Les
> No more
>
> – Tombstone grave headstone

A rip-roaring, brawling, 19th-century silver-mining town, and the site of the famous 1881 shootout at the OK Corral, Tombstone is a National Historic Landmark that attracts crowds of tourists with its old Western buildings, stagecoach rides, Wild West festivals, saloons and reenactments of gunfights.

The Visitor & Information Center (☎ 520-457-3929, 800-457-3423, W www.tombstone.org) is at the corner of 4th and Allen Sts. Budget motels ($40-60) include the *Larian Motel (☎ 520-457-2272, 410 E Fremont St)* and *Trail Riders Inn (☎ 520-457-3573, 800-574-0417, 13 N 7th St)*. There are also several B&Bs and a Best Western.

Bisbee

Many buildings in Bisbee date from the heyday of the early-20th-century copper-mining boom. The town has more of a Victorian feel to it than any other in Arizona, as well as an intriguing mix of aging miners and gallery owners, hippies and artists. The chamber of commerce (☎ 520-432-5421, 866-224-7233, 31 Subway St) is open daily. The **Queen Mine** (☎ 520-432-2071) can be visited in underground mine cars ($10).

Shady Dell RV Park (☎ 520-432-3567, 1 Douglas Rd), at the Lowell traffic circle, rents seven antique aluminum camping trailers ($35-75). The funky, arty *Red Metal Miners' Hostel (☎ 520-432-6671, 59-B Subway St)* sleeps up to 12 folks in dorms ($18) or in private rooms ($40); it has Internet access, kitchen, laundry and bike rental. The 1902 *Copper Queen Hotel (☎ 520-432-2216, 800-247-5829, 11 Howell St)* retains its turn-of-the-century feel ($70-136).

One World Travel (☎ 520-432-5359, 7 OK St) sells bus tickets.

Utah

Four-wheel-drive vehicles, loaded down with mountain bikes, river rafts or skis, are as ubiquitous in Utah as green chilies in New Mexico and poker chips in Nevada. The rugged state, with its vast expanses of undeveloped mountains, red-rock canyons, lonely deserts and wild rivers, is one of the nation's most popular recreation spots.

In addition, Utah's two defining cultures – the ancestral Indians who left their traces on the rocks and the modern Mormons who chose this land as their home – can be encountered everywhere. The southern half of the state contains the majority of the national parks and desert wilderness (where John Ford Westerns and *Thelma & Louise* were filmed), while the northern half of Utah contains forested mountains with world-class skiing and attractive Mormon towns, including the capital, Salt Lake City.

In early 2002, Utah hosted the Winter Olympics, which brought the state a level of international attention heretofore unknown and left in its wake a number of first-class skate and ski facilities, most of which can be used by the public.

History

In prehistoric times, beginning more than 8000 years ago, the nomadic Ute (from whom Utah gets its name), Paiute and Shoshone peoples lived in the Great Basin desert of Utah. While the Europeans arrived as early as 1776, the Indians inhabited the region freely until the mid-19th century.

The Mormon pioneers, fleeing religious persecution and led by Brigham Young, traveled the Mormon Trail; though it paralleled the Oregon Trail, Mormons and other pioneers avoided one another. The Mormons founded Salt Lake City on July 24, 1847. Calling their state Deseret (which means 'honeybee' according to the Book of Mormon), this communitarian society transformed the 'Great American Desert' into flourishing farms. In 1848, when a late frost followed by a plague of crickets threatened to wipe out the crops, a flock of gulls flew in, ate the crickets and miraculously saved the remaining crop; hence the state bird is a gull. In 1849 Mormons thrived by catering to the flood of Gold Rush travelers who passed through their settlements.

But their self-imposed isolation did not last long, and the second half of the 19th century was marked by conflict between the federal government and the Mormon church. In 1848 the USA acquired the region from Mexico, and in 1850 the Territory of Utah was created. The Mormons petitioned Congress for statehood six times, the first as far back as 1856, but these petitions were consistently rejected because of Mormon polygamy (the practice of having more than one spouse at the same time), which was outlawed by the US government in 1862. Church leaders, who considered the practice protected by the First Amendment (which guarantees the freedom of religion), continued the practice, but the US Supreme Court ruled against them in 1879. With the coming of non-Mormons to Utah, the polygamy issue became more difficult to ignore, and more than 1000 Mormon men were jailed in the 1880s for the practice. The relationship between the largely Mormon territory and the federal government steadily deteriorated, and some Congressmen proposed a bill to withdraw voting rights from all Mormon men.

Utah

Nicknames: Beehive State, Mormon State

Population: 2,233,200 (34th)

Population under 18 years old: 32.2% (1st)

Area: 84,904 sq miles (13th)

Admitted to Union: January 4, 1896 (45th)

Capital city: Salt Lake City (population 181,800; metro area 1.7 million)

State bird: California gull

Official state snack food: Jell-O (traditionally lime green with carrots)

Birthplace of: machine-gun inventor John M Browning (1855–1926), beloved bad guy Butch Cassidy (1866–1908)

Famous for: Mormons, dramatic red-rock desert, 2002 Winter Olympics

The tense situation was settled in 1890, when Mormon Church President Wilford Woodruff announced that God had told him that Mormons should abide by US law, and polygamy was discontinued. Soon afterward, Utah's sixth attempt at statehood was successful; it was admitted to the Union in 1896 as the 45th state.

In 1905 Brigham Canyon Copper Mine began producing copper; in 1907 oil production began in the Virgin River area; and in 1952 uranium was discovered near Moab. Utah has struggled ever since with the environmental repercussions of its mining history, as well as with its history of military-weapons testing in the Great Salt Lake Desert.

Religion

Mormons – members of the Church of Jesus Christ of Latter Day Saints (LDS) – remain in the majority in Utah, although the margin is slimmer now than it ever has been. About 70% of the state's population is Mormon, and Mormons continue to exert a powerful conservative influence on life in the state.

The church prizes the family above all else; Mormon families tend to be large, and Mormon communities are supportive of one another. Hard work, tithing (donating 10% of one's annual income) and a strict obedience to church leaders are very important. Smoking and drinking alcohol, tea or coffee are forbidden. The LDS church is very conservative. Women are not allowed to take leadership roles, nor were African Americans until 1978. In Mormon schools and colleges, dress codes are strict; for example, wearing shorts or skirts above the knee is not allowed, nor are body piercings (except for a single pair of earrings on women).

Public services with hymns and sermons are held in tabernacles. Private ceremonies, including weddings and baptisms, are open only to practicing Mormons and are kept secret from outsiders.

Many young adults perform a voluntary missionary service to spread the faith around the world, but members of any age may also go on missions. Women are called Sisters during their service, which lasts for 18 months; the men, called Elders, spend two years. There are now around 11 million Mormons worldwide.

Information

The Utah Tourism & Recreation Information Center (☎ 801-538-1030, 800-200-1160, Ⓦ www.utah.com, Council Hall, Capitol Hill, Salt Lake City, UT 84114) is run by the Utah Travel Council. For information on skiing, ask for the *Utah Winter Vacation Planner* (and visit Ⓦ www.skiutah.com). Utah State Parks (☎ 800-322-3770, Ⓦ parks.state.ut.us, 1594 W North Temple, Salt Lake City, UT 84114) sells an annual day-use permit ($65 per car) and arranges camping reservations. For road conditions, call ☎ 800-492-2400. The sales tax rate is 6.6%; hotel-room taxes vary from 10% to 15%.

SALT LAKE CITY

Next day we strolled about everywhere through the broad, straight, level streets, and enjoyed the pleasant strangeness of a city of fifteen thousand inhabitants with no loafers perceptible in it; and no visible drunkards or noisy people.

– Mark Twain describing Salt Lake City in 1872

Spectacularly set at the foot of the Wasatch Mountains, Salt Lake City is the headquarters of the Mormon Church and was the host of the 2002 Winter Olympics. While the Great Salt Lake and the impressive architecture and culture of the Mormon Church are the two most famous attractions, nearby mountains offer excellent skiing, hiking, camping and boating.

Gray Line (☎ 801-521-7060) offers city tours ($18; 3½ hours). Salt Island Adventures (☎ 801-252-9336) runs one-hour scenic cruises on the lake ($12).

Orientation

Salt Lake City (as is true of most Mormon towns) is laid out in a spacious grid with streets aligned north-south and east-west. The city's most important block is Temple Square (I-15 exit 312), and addresses are numbered from this zero point, with 100 being equivalent to one city block.

Information

The Visitor Information Center (☎ 801-944-4240) and the Convention & Visitors Bureau (CVB; ☎ 801-521-2822, 800-541-4955, Ⓦ www.visitsaltlake.com, 90 S West Temple St, Salt Lake City, UT 84101) are both in the modern Salt Palace Convention

SOUTHWEST

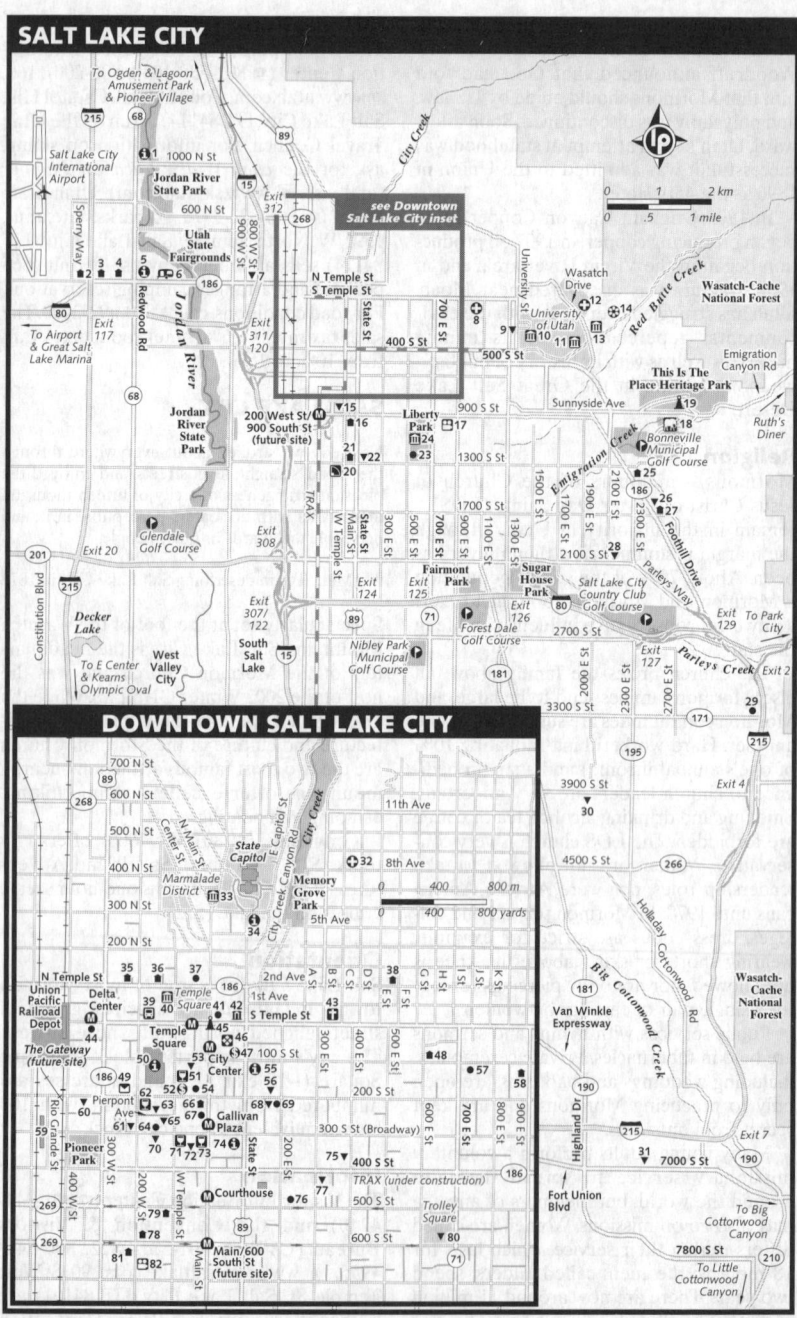

SALT LAKE CITY

PLACES TO STAY
2   Holiday Inn Express
3   Motel 6 Airport
4   Days Inn
6   Salt Lake City KOA
16   Holiday Inn
21   Ute Hostel
25   Scenic Motel
27   Skyline Inn
35   City Creek Inn
36   Travelodge Temple Square
38   HI The Avenues
48   Anton Boxrud B&B
58   Saltair
66   Hotel Monaco
78   Motel 6
79   Travelodge City Center
81   Super 8 Motel

PLACES TO EAT
7   Red Iguana
9   Pie Pizzeria
15   Cafe Trang
22   House of Tibet
26   Bombay House
28   Blue Plate Diner
30   Café Madrid
31   Lone Star Taqueria
53   Mikado
56   Star of India
60   A Cup of Joe
61   Red Rock Brewing Company
63   Pierpont Cantina
65   Marmot Mesa
68   Cedars of Lebanon

70   Squatter's Pub Brewery
72   Market Street Grill
75   Ichiban Sushi
77   Salt Lake Roasting Company
80   Desert Edge Brewery

OTHER
1   Jordan River State Park
     Ranger Station
5   Utah State Parks
     & Recreation Office
8   Salt Lake Regional Hospital
     and Medical Center
10   Utah Museum of Natural
     History
11   Utah Museum of Fine Arts
12   University Hospital
13   Fort Douglas; Military
     Museum
14   Red Butte Gardens
     and Arboretum
17   Tower Theater
18   Hogle Zoo
19   This Is The Place Monument
20   Franklin Covey Field
23   Tracy Aviary
24   Chase Home Museum
     of Utah Folk Art
29   REI
32   LDS Hospital
33   Pioneer Memorial Museum
34   Council Hall; Utah Tourism
     & Recreation Information
     Center
37   LDS Conference Center

39   Greyhound Bus Depot
40   Museum of Church History
     & Art
41   Joseph Smith Memorial
     Building
42   Beehive House
43   Cathedral of the Madeleine
44   Delta Center
45   Brigham Young
     Monument/Meridian
     Marker
46   ZCMI Shopping Center
47   First Security Bank
49   Post Office
50   Salt Palace Convention
     Center; Visitor Information
     Center; Salt Lake Convention
     & Visitors Bureau
51   Dead Goat Saloon
52   American Express
54   Capitol Theater
55   USFS Office
57   Wasatch Touring
59   Rio Grande Depot
     & Utah Historical Society
62   Zipperz
64   Rose Wagner Performing
     Arts Center
67   Sam Weller's Books
69   Guthrie Bicycle
71   Zephyr
73   Ya'Buts
74   BLM Office
76   Library
82   Brewvies

Center. General delivery mail goes to the downtown post office (☎ 801-978-3001, 230 W 200 South). The free *City Weekly,* with arts and entertainment coverage, is Salt Lake's alternative press. The main library (☎ 801-524-8200, 209 E 500 South) has free Internet access and a great periodicals room. Sam Weller's Books (☎ 801-328-2586, 254 S Main St) has a comprehensive selection of outdoor guides and maps.

Downtown
Enclosed by 15-foot-high walls, **Temple Square** (☎ 801-240-2534) features 19th-century Mormon buildings and Mormon history exhibits. You should make every effort to visit **The Tabernacle** when the famous Mormon Tabernacle Choir is singing or when the daily organ recital is in progress.

Adjoining Temple Square, the **Museum of Church History and Art** (☎ 801-240-3310)

has impressive exhibits of pioneer history. You can research your family's genealogy at the **Joseph Smith Memorial Building** (☎ 801-240-1266), an elegant hotel from 1911 to 1987; also here are daily screenings of *Testament,* an hour-long film about Mormon beliefs. Brigham Young's home, the **Beehive House** (☎ 801-240-2671), circa 1854, has been meticulously maintained and contains period furnishings. The Mormon Church's new **LDS Conference Center** (☎ 801-240-0075) has great views from its rooftop gardens. Admission is free to all these sites.

You'll find many Daughters of Utah Pioneers (DUP) museums throughout the state, but the **Pioneer Memorial Museum** (☎ 801-538-1050, 300 N Main) is by far the best, a vast treasure trove of pioneer artifacts (free admission). The walls of the impressive **Utah State Capitol** (☎ 801-538-1563) are covered with historical murals. Next to the capitol, City Creek Canyon is a favorite spot for runners and bicyclists.

Around Downtown

Site of the Olympic Village in 2002, the University of Utah (☎ 801-581-7200) east of downtown has several museums, including the **Utah Museum of Fine Arts** (☎ 801-581-7332), which expanded into a beautiful new building in 2001 (free admission). In the Wasatch foothills, the lovely **Red Butte Gardens and Arboretum** (☎ 801-581-4747) spreads over a relaxing 25 acres with terrific city views ($5).

At **This Is The Place Heritage Park** (☎ 801-584-8391), at the mouth of Emigration Canyon, actors in period dress work among buildings typical of the early Mormon settlements ($6). The small **Hogle Zoo** (☎ 801-582-1631) is nearby ($5).

South of downtown, the popular **Liberty Park** (☎ 801-972-7800) offers a swimming pool, a children's amusement park, formal flower gardens, the Chase Home Museum of Utah Folk Art and the cheerful Tracy Aviary ($3).

At **Kearns Olympic Oval** (☎ 968-6825, 5624 S 4800 West), you can cruise the same oval the Olympic speed skaters raced around ($4). The adjoining recreational facility has large pools for playing, diving and swimming ($5.50).

Activities

The Wasatch Mountains offer abundant opportunities for hiking, mountain biking, camping and cross-country skiing. For maps, guides and rental equipment, try Wasatch Touring (☎ 801-359-9361, 702 E 100 South); Guthrie Bicycle (☎ 801-363-3727, 156 E 200 South); or REI (☎ 801-486-2100, 3285 E 3300 South).

Places to Stay

The huge *Salt Lake City KOA* (☎ 801-328-0224, 800-226-7752, 1400 W North Temple) charges $19/27 for tents/RVs. The USFS (☎ 801-524-5042) maintains four basic seasonal campgrounds in the Wasatch Mountains ($12) in Big Cottonwood and Little Cottonwood Canyons.

The no-frills *HI The Avenues* (☎ 801-359-3855, 888-884-4752, 107 F St) has dormitories ($17) and doubles ($25-$40). The

smaller and homier *Ute Hostel* (☎ 801-595-1645, 21 E Kelsey Ave) has dorms/private rooms for $15/35.

Summer and winter are the high seasons; prices may be lower in late spring and fall. Ideally located, *City Creek Inn* (☎ 533-9100, 230 W North Temple) is one of the few attractive budget choices in town (doubles are $58). *Scenic Motel* (☎ 801-582-1527, 1345 S Foothill Dr) has clean, decent doubles for $48. For about the same price, Motel 6 has several locations, and a few frayed bottom-end places line North Temple St west of I-15.

Most mid-range hotels are dependable chains such as Travelodge, Days Inn, Holiday Inn and Super 8. *Skyline Inn* (☎ 801-582-5350, 2475 E 1700 South) is a good choice, with doubles for $70. Two pleasant B&Bs are *Anton Boxrud* (☎ 801-363-8035, 800-524-5511, 57 S 600 East) and *Saltair* (☎ 801-533-8184, 800-733-8184, 164 S 900 East); both have pretty rooms for $70-150 with homecooked breakfasts. A worthwhile splurge is the arty, over-the-top *Hotel Monaco* (☎ 595-0000, 877-294-9710, 15 W 200 South). Unusually designed rooms are $170/120 midweek/weekends; ask for your companion goldfish.

Places to Eat

The *Salt Lake Roasting Company* (320 E 400 South) may be the best coffeehouse in town, while *A Cup of Joe* (353 W 200 South) is a relaxing, artsy hangout.

Blue Plate Diner (2041 S 2100 East) is a '50s diner with modern sensibilities: tasty all-you-can-eat specials are $5-10. About five minutes east of town in Emigration Canyon, *Ruth's Diner* serves the meanest breakfast on the sunniest patio.

Savvy locals head to *Red Iguana* (736 W North Temple) for great, unpretentious Mexican food ($7-13), and it's worth the trek south for the fish tacos at *Lone Star Taqueria* (2265 E Fort Union Blvd). For a more lively atmosphere, try *Pierpont Cantina* (122 W Pierpont Ave).

What do locals know? They voted *Pie Pizzeria* (1320 E 200 South), a university hangout, the state's 'best pizza' – and they're right.

Enjoy Salt Lake's good ethnic restaurants, as they are few and far between elsewhere in Utah. *Cedars of Lebanon* (152 E

200 South) has all-you-can-eat Middle Eastern weekday lunch buffets ($7). For Indian, *Star of India (177 E 200 South)* and *Bombay House (1615 S Foothill Dr)* are good. *House of Tibet (145 E 1300 South)* serves authentic Tibetan cuisine, and *Cafe Trang (818 S Main)* is a well-regarded Vietnamese place. For Japanese dinners, *Mikado (67 W 100 South)* has nice ambience, while *Ichiban Sushi (336 S 400 East)* concocts inventive sushi in a renovated church.

The beer is great and the food reasonable at any of these popular brewpubs: *Squatter's Pub Brewery (147 W Broadway); Red Rock Brewing Company (254 S 200 West); Desert Edge Brewery*, in Trolley Square, and the low-key *Marmot Mesa (163 W Pierpont Ave)*.

Grab the early-bird special ($15) at *Market Street Grill (☎ 801-322-4668, 48 W Market)* for well-priced, perfectly grilled fish. The cozy *Café Madrid (☎ 801-273-0837, 2080 E 3900 South)* prepares authentic Spanish cuisine ($14-25) that's the envy of Spain's capital (dinner only Mon-Sat). For a romantic evening, drive up Mill Creek Canyon to *Log Haven (☎ 801-272-8255)*; open nightly.

Entertainment

Watch a first-run movie while enjoying a beer and burger at *Brewvies (☎ 801-355-5500, 677 S 200 West)*. *Tower Theater (☎ 801-412-1824, 876 E 900 South)* has alternative films.

Because of the Mormon influence, most nightclubs are private. You must buy a two-week membership ($5 for five guests), or ask at the entrance and a member inside might sponsor you for the night.

You'll find several nightspots along S West Temple St, including *Dead Goat Saloon* and *Zephyr*, both are very popular and have live music almost nightly. *Ya'Buts (45 W 300 South)* is a hipster's pool hall. Salt Lake has the only gay club scene in Utah; go to the friendly *Zipperz (155 W 200 South)* to find out more.

The Salt Lake City Arts Council (☎ 801-596-5000) has information about various local cultural events, including theater, dance, opera and symphony. The *Capitol Theater (☎ 801-355-2787, 50 W 200 South)* and the *Rose Wagner Performing Arts Center (☎ 801-323-6800, 138 W 300 South)* are two main venues.

Spectator Sports

The men's professional basketball team, the Utah Jazz, and the women's professional basketball team, the Utah Starzz, play at the Delta Center (☎ 801-325-2500). The International Hockey League's Utah Grizzlies (☎ 801-988-7825) play at the city's E Center (☎ 801-988-8888), which hosted most of the men's ice hockey competitions during the Olympics.

Getting There & Around

Air Salt Lake City International Airport (☎ 801-575-2400) is about 6 miles west of downtown. The local Alpine Air (☎ 801-575-2839, 801-521-9215) flies between Salt Lake City and Moab daily (call for prices).

The transportation desk (☎ 801-575-2477) at the airport has information on shuttle services throughout the Salt Lake City/Wasatch Front area.

Bus Greyhound (☎ 801-355-9579) has several buses a day heading south through Provo, Cedar City and St George to Las Vegas, Nevada ($46; 8½ hours) and Los Angeles ($86; 15 hours); west to San Francisco ($66; 16 hours); east through Heber City to Denver ($46; 13 hours); and north through Ogden to Seattle ($76; 24 hours).

Train Amtrak's *California Zephyr* stops daily at the Rio Grande Depot (☎ 801-531-0188) going east to Chicago ($215; 36 hours) and west to Oakland, California ($110; 17 hours).

Local Transportation UTA (☎ 801-287-4636) serves Salt Lake City with buses (6am-7pm, no Sunday service) and light rail (called TRAX, with similar hours, plus Sunday service). Several buses a day go to the cities of Provo, Tooele, Ogden and the towns and suburbs in between ($1). The center of downtown Salt Lake is a free-fare zone.

UTA Ski Buses serve the four local ski areas well ($1.75). Yellow Cab (☎ 801-521-2100) offers 24-hour taxi service.

AROUND SALT LAKE CITY

Float in the Great Salt Lake's saline waters and see what it feels like to be unsinkable at beaches near the **Great Salt Lake Marina** (☎ 801-250-1822, I-80 west exit 104). **Lagoon**

Amusement Park & Pioneer Village (☎ 385-451-8000, 800-748-5246) has water slides, roller coasters, steam trains and gunslingers shooting it out daily (all-day rides $30/24 for adults/kids; parking $6; open Sat-Sun mid-Apr-late Sept, daily from Memorial Day to Labor Day). To get there, take I-15 north to the Lagoon Dr exit.

Billed as the 'Richest Hole on Earth,' Bingham Canyon Copper Mine (☎ 801-252-3234, I-15 exit 301) is reportedly the largest excavation that humans have ever dug. The 2½-mile-wide and three-quarter-mile-deep gash can be seen from space and also from a stunning overlook ($4).

Within 40 minutes of Salt Lake City are four world-class ski resorts in Little Cottonwood and Big Cottonwood Canyons: Snowbird Ski Area (☎ 801-742-2222, W www.snowbird.com) has excellent snowboarding; laid-back, less-expensive Alta Ski Area (☎ 801-742-3333, W www.alta.com) is the skier's choice; Brighton Ski Area (☎ 801-532-4731, W www.skibrighton.com) has a popular half-pipe; and Solitude Ski Area (☎ 801-534-1400, W www.skisolitude.com) also has cross-country ski trails. There are plenty of accommodations at the ski resorts, but they're outrageously expensive.

WASATCH MOUNTAINS REGION
The Wasatch Mountains are home to 11 ski resorts (including the Cottonwood Canyon resorts, above) within 55 miles of Salt Lake City, and also offer abundant hiking, camping, fly-fishing and mountain biking.

Antelope Island State Park
This pretty, 15-mile-long island (☎ 801-725-9263, I-15 exit 335) has nice hiking as well as the best beaches for experiencing the Great Salt Lake. It is also famous as the home to one of the largest bison herds in the country, and the fall corralling of these animals is one of the area's most famous wildlife spectacles. A basic campground (☎ 800-322-3770) has sites for $10.

Ogden
Home to Weber State University, Ogden offers the pleasures of a university town and a mid-19th-century center about 35 miles north of Salt Lake City. After the completion of the first transcontinental railway in 1869, Ogden became an important railway town.

The restored Union Station, at 25th St and Wall Ave, contains the visitors bureau (☎ 385-627-8288, W www.ogdencvb.org) and several worthy museums covering vintage trains, firearms, cars and more ($3). Also in Union Station is the National Forest Information Center (☎ 385-625-5306), with maps and information on area hiking, biking and kayaking (on the Ogden and Weber Rivers).

The Ice Sheet (☎ 385-399-8750), at Weber State University, hosted curling in the 2002 Winter Olympics; learn to curl yourself or just come to skate ($3.25).

The steep-walled Ogden Canyon heads 40 miles northeast through the Wasatch Mountains to Monte Cristo Summit (9148 feet), passing the following: Nordic Valley Ski Area (☎ 385-745-3511), a tiny 85-acre resort with the cheapest skiing in the state; Snowbasin Ski Area (☎ 385-399-1135, W www.snowbasin.com), a 3200-acre resort that hosted downhill and super G skiing events in the 2002 Olympics; and Powder Mountain Ski Area (☎ 385-745-3771, W www.powdermountain.net), with lots of, well, powder.

Millstream Motel (☎ 385-394-9425, 1450 Washington Blvd) retains the flavor of its 1940s heyday; decent doubles are $44. Other, more down-at-the-heels budget places line Washington Blvd. The best mid-range options are chain motels; several are in town and at the Ogden freeway exits.

In the 19th century, historic 25th St between Union Station and Grant Ave was lined with brothels and raucous saloons; now it has Ogden's nicest selection of restaurants and bars.

Park City
Forty minutes east of Salt Lake City on I-80, the well-preserved, 19th-century silver-mining town of Park City (elevation 6900 feet) is the Southwest's largest ski town and a hub of outdoor activity in the summer. It is also the most liberal town in this most conservative state. The main Visitor Information Center (☎ 435-649-6104, 800-453-1360, W www.parkcityinfo.com) is at 528 Main St; a second location (☎ 435-658-4541) is at 750 Kearns Blvd.

Activities Popular for skiing, Park City is home to three of Utah's preeminent ski

resrts. A chairlift right in town can take you to Park City Mountain Resort (☎ 435-649-8111, Ⓦ www.parkcitymountain.com), which hosted the giant slalom and snowboarding events in the 2002 Winter Olympic Games. The posh, skiers-only Deer Valley Resort (☎ 435-649-1000, 800-424-3337, Ⓦ www.deervalley.com) is also the most expensive, and The Canyons (☎ 435-649-5400, Ⓦ www.thecanyons.com) has expanded and upgraded to become Utah's largest ski area, with 14 lifts, 134 runs and a popular half-pipe for snowboarding.

At the Utah Winter Sports Park (☎ 435-658-4200), on Hwy 224 outside Park City, the Olympians are gone, but you can test your nerve by **bobsledding** and **ski jumping** on the same tracks and slopes, or just come to watch the pros practice (call for rates, schedules and reservations).

In summer, Park City and Deer Valley have **biking** and **hiking** accessible by chairlifts; The Canyons has scenic gondola rides and hiking. For a thrill, ride Park City's 'alpine slide,' a wheeled sled that races down a cement track ($8).

Special Events Arts and music events occur throughout the summer, and ski season sees many competitions. However, everything stops during the last two weeks in January for the Sundance Film Festival (☎ 801-328-3456, Ⓦ www.sundance.org), which showcases independent filmmakers. Tickets often sell out well in advance.

Places to Stay The 2002 Olympics caused a miniboom in hotels in this already booming town, which offers more than 100 condo complexes, upscale hotels and B&Bs. Winter rates are high (and are quoted below), but prices drop considerably in summer, and often vary from weekend to weekday. Dozens of companies can organize ski packages and offer reservation services. Try Park City Reservations (☎ 435-649-9598, 800-453-5789, Ⓦ www.parkcityres.com) for ski packages or Central Reservations of Park City (☎ 435-649-6606, 800-519-4764, Ⓦ www.parkcityski.com) for rooms.

The nearest campsite is the streamside *Hidden Haven Campground* (☎ 435-649-8935), 1 mile northwest of I-80 exit 145 ($20/25 tents/RVs). New in 2001, *Park City International Hostel* (☎ 435-655-7244, 268 Main) has a perfect location, pristine four-bed dorms ($30), a laundry, a kitchen and a multimedia room. Also well located, *Chateau Après Lodge* (☎ 435-649-9372, 1299 Norfolk Ave) has dormitories ($28) and worn doubles ($82).

Star Hotel (☎ 435-649-5746, 227 Main), in an older family house, offers singles/doubles for $85/150, including breakfast and dinner. *Edelweiss Haus* (☎ 435-649-5100, 800-245-6417, 1482 Empire Ave) has both hotel rooms ($100) and condos ($200-400). If you want the best (and who doesn't?), *Stein Eriksen Lodge* (☎ 435-649-3700, 800-435-1302), at Deer Valley Ski Resort, is without peer. Rooms in winter start at $575.

Places to Eat Gourmets and gourmands will find everything they desire along Park City's historic Main St and at the resorts. Open early and closing late, *Morning Ray Café & Bakery* flies in New York bagel dough to bake fresh, and that's all some people need to know. *Wasatch Brew Pub* is a fine microbrewery with excellent pub grub ($8-16). *The Eating Establishment* is one of the area's most enduring and reasonably priced spots. More upscale, *Wahso* serves a heady fusion of Asian cuisines, and *Chimayo* captures the Southwest.

At Deer Valley, Snow Park Lodge's *Seafood Buffet* (☎ 435-645-6632, reservations required) puts Vegas spreads to shame ($45), and Stein Eriksen Lodge's *Glitretind* (☎ 435-649-6455) is fairly regarded as the most romantic gourmet restaurant in Utah.

Entertainment A half dozen crowded private clubs, most with live music, line Main St; to gain admission, you must either obtain a guest membership ($5) or be sponsored by a member, but both are easy to do. *Harry O's* is the hot place for dancing. The nicely restored *Egyptian Theater* (☎ 435-649-9371) has plays in summer.

Getting There & Around Neither Greyhound nor Amtrak serve Park City. Lewis Bros Stages (☎ 435-649-2256 in Park City, 801-359-8677 in Salt Lake City) offers year-round shuttles to/from Salt Lake City several times a day ($26).

Park City Transit runs frequent, free buses around town and to the ski resorts, making it easy not to rent a car.

Heber City & Around

This town, about 40 miles east of Salt Lake City at the junction of Hwys 40 and 189, makes a good base for exploring the scenic Wasatch Mountains.

Call the **Heber Valley Historic Railroad** (☎ 435-654-5601) for sightseeing trips ($19; 3½ hours).

In winter, **Wasatch Mountain State Park** (☎ 435-654-1791) has cross-country skiing and snowshoeing at Soldier Hollow, site of the Nordic events in the 2002 Winter Olympics. **Jordanelle State Park** (☎ 435-649-9540) offers summer water activities on its large reservoir and birding along the Provo River in spring and fall.

Approximately 15 miles southwest of Heber City, Hwy 189 squeezes through the steep-walled **Provo Canyon** on its way to Provo. For information on camping and hiking, contact the Uinta National Forest Heber City Ranger Station (☎ 435-654-0470, 2460 S Hwy 40).

Another attractive drive is **Alpine Loop Rd**; exit north off Hwy 189 onto the narrow and twisting Hwy 92. Tucked under Mt Timpanogos, Robert Redford's **Sundance Resort** (☎ 385-225-4107, 800-892-1600, W www.sundanceresort.com) offers an elegant, rustic getaway in a wilderness setting, with excellent skiing, a year-round arts program and hiking and mountain biking during the summer. The three beautiful caves in **Timpanogos Cave National Monument** (☎ 385-756-5238) can be seen only as part of a ranger-led trip. Buy tickets in advance ($6; open May-Oct).

You can camp in the surrounding national forest and nearby state parks (see above). Affordable Heber City is increasingly popular with Park City skiers. The following are all on Main St. *Mac's Motel* (☎ 435-654-0612) has simple rooms from $40. *Beaver Mountain Motel* (☎ 435-654-2150) is a good value ($40-60), and the quaint *Swiss Alps Inn* (☎ 435-654-0722) is also recommended ($50-80). A new *Holiday Inn Express* (☎ 435-654-9990) is the largest hotel in town by far and appeals to skiers; rooms start at $80.

Seven miles west of Heber City, in Midway, the fun-packed *Homestead Resort* (☎ 435-654-1102, 800-327-7220, 700 N Homestead Dr) offers natural hot springs (with scuba diving!), golf, cross-country skiing, sleigh rides and more. Rooms are $119, suites $189.

In addition to a few greasy spoons and average restaurants, Heber has the *Sidetrack Café* (94 S Main), serving espresso and light lunches, and *Snake Creek Grill* (☎ 435-654-2133, 650 W 100 South), which prepares interesting gourmet fare at reasonable prices ($12-16; dinner only Wed-Sun).

Provo & Around

This Mormon city features late-19th-century buildings and Brigham Young University. Sundance Resort (see above) is nearby, as is Utah Lake, the state's largest freshwater lake.

For area information, head to the Utah Valley Visitors Bureau (☎ 385-370-8393, W www.utahvalley.org/cvb, 51 S University Ave) and the Uinta National Forest Ranger Station (☎ 385-377-5780, 88 W 100 North). The historic main library (☎ 385-852-6650, 550 N University) has free Internet access.

Clean-cut Brigham Young University (BYU; ☎ 385-378-4636) has several interesting museums, including the surprisingly sophisticated **Museum of Art** (☎ 385-378-2787), one of the biggest in the Southwest. The 150-sq-mile **Utah Lake State Park** (☎ 385-375-0733), west on Center St, offers year-round water activities ($6). Built for the 2002 Olympics, **The Peaks Ice Arena** (☎ 385-377-8777, 100 N Seven Peaks Blvd) hosted hockey competitions and now offers public skating year-round ($4).

Ten minutes north near Lehi, at Thanksgiving Point on I-15 (exit 287), the **North American Museum of Ancient Life** (☎ 385-766-5000) has interactive, walk-through exhibits containing approximately 60 dinosaur skeletons, one of the world's largest collections ($9).

Six miles south of Provo in Springville is the **Springville Museum of Art** (☎ 385-489-2727, 126 E 400 South). The historic building makes a lovely setting for the eclectic collection, which emphasizes Utah and Soviet artists (free admission).

Lakeside Campground (☎ 385-373-5267), near Utah Lake State Park, charges $16/23 for tent/RV sites. Provo has a number of basic budget motels. *Safari Motel* (☎ 385-373-9672, 250 S University Ave) is a better one ($38-48). Mid-range chains here include Travelodge, Super 8 and Days Inn. Near BYU, *Best Inn & Suites* (☎ 385-374-6020, 1555 Canyon Rd) has very nice rooms for $55-70.

The historic buildings in Provo Town Square (Center at University Ave) now contain a variety of restaurants. Try *Los Hermanos* (16 W Center) for Mexican, *La Dolce Vita* (61 N 100 East) for good-value Italian and *Bombay House* (463 N University) for Indian.

Greyhound (☎ 385-373-4211, 124 N 300 West) has several buses daily north and south on I-15. Amtrak (☎ 800-872-7245, 600 S 300 West) has one daily train, the *California Zephyr*, to Denver ($85; 14½ hours) and points east and to Oakland, California ($124; 19 hours), via Salt Lake City ($9; 1 hour).

NORTHERN UTAH

North of Ogden, the mountains get smaller but no less beautiful. In sharp contrast, north and northwest of the Great Salt Lake, the land is very arid, saline and extremely barren; few people inhabit, or visit, the desolate northwest corner of Utah.

Golden Spike NHS

On May 10, 1869, the westward Union Pacific Railroad and eastward Central Pacific Railroad met at Promontory Summit. With the completion of the transcontinental railroad, the face of the American West changed forever. This National Historic Site (☎ 435-471-2209), 32 miles west of Brigham City on Hwy 83, has daily demonstrations using replicas of the original steam engines and other informative talks on life in the 1860s ($7).

Logan

Founded in 1859 and home to Utah State University, Logan is a quintessential old-fashioned American community with strong Mormon ties. Situated in bucolic Cache Valley, it offers year-round outdoor activities, particularly hiking, camping, snowmobiling and cross-country skiing.

You can visit the Bridgerland Travel Region office (☎ 800-882-4433, W www.bridgerland.com, 160 N Main) and the Logan Ranger Station (☎ 435-755-3620, 1500 E Hwy 89) for information.

Perhaps the best of its kind, the **American West Heritage Center** (☎ 435-245-6050), on Hwy 89 south of town, offers authentic re-creations of frontier communities with plenty of hands-on activities ($5). It also hosts the popular weeklong Festival of the American West in July, a must for frontier buffs.

The **Wellsville Mountain range** is reputedly one of the highest in the world rising from such a narrow base. The only access to the mountains is via steep trails up their almost-vertical sides; the area is about 10 miles from Logan. Get information and maps from the Logan ranger.

The 40-mile drive through **Logan Canyon** (Hwy 89 to Garden City) is beautiful any time of year, but in fall it is jaw-dropping. Enjoy hiking and biking trails, rock climbing, fishing spots and seasonal campgrounds. The Beaver Creek Lodge (☎ 435-753-1076) rents horses and snowmobiles.

Riverside RV Park (☎ 435-245-4469, 445 W 1700 South) charges $10/17 for tent/RV sites. Mid-range chain hotels are your best choice, such as Days Inn, Super 8, Comfort Inn and Best Western ($45-70).

For a meal, try the 1920s-style *Bluebird Restaurant* (19 N Main). Popular with the university crowd, *Caffé Ibis* (52 Federal Ave) serves gourmet coffees and healthy sandwiches. Get a burger and a microbrew at *The White Owl* (36 W Center), Logan's watering hole for non-Mormons.

Garden City & Bear Lake

Tiny Garden City provides lake visitors with modest places to stay and eat; it is very busy in summer. Pleasant Bear Lake State Park (☎ 435-946-3343) offers lots of camping and lake activities.

NORTHEASTERN UTAH

Despite being hyped as 'Utah's Dinosaurland,' this region offers only one standout dinosaur site, but the high wilderness terrain – all towns are a mile above sea level – and the Uinta Mountains make for gorgeous outdoor excursions.

Mirror Lake Highway

This alpine route, beginning in **Kamas**, 16 miles southeast of I-80 exit 156, covers 65 miles as it climbs to elevations of more than 8000 feet into Wyoming. The road provides some beautiful vistas of the western Uintas and passes by scores of lakes, campgrounds (no RV sites) and trailheads. Contact the Wasatch-Cache National Forest Kamas Ranger Station (☎ 435-783-4338, 50 E Center) for information.

Uinta Mountains

You have to hike or ride a horse in the rugged 800-sq-mile High Uintas Wilderness Area, as there are no roads, and even mountain bikes are prohibited. The high country has hundreds of lakes, most of which are stocked annually with trout and whitefish. Come for the excellent fishing and the rare experience of remote wilderness. The Ashley National Forest Roosevelt Ranger Station (☎ 435-722-5018), at 244 W Hwy 40 in Roosevelt, has information.

Basic campgrounds ($8-10) are in the national forest surrounding the wilderness area. Nearby lodges include *Defa's Dude Ranch* (☎ 435-848-5590), with inexpensive cabins, and *Rock Creek B&B* (☎ 435-454-3853), in Mountain Home, with rooms for $40-95.

Flaming Gorge
National Recreation Area

Named for its fiery red sandstone, Flaming Gorge offers 375 miles of shoreline around Flaming Gorge Reservoir. There's fly-fishing and rafting upon the Green River, boating and world-record fishing in the reservoir (eg, a Mackinaw trout weighing 51lb 8 oz), hiking, cross-country skiing and great scenery. Information is available from the USFS Flaming Gorge Headquarters (☎ 435-784-3445, PO Box 278, Manila, UT 84046). The Flaming Gorge Visitor Center (☎ 435-885-3135), on US 191 at the dam, is open daily year-round; the Red Canyon Visitor Center (☎ 435-889-3713),

4 miles west of Greendale Junction, is open May-Oct.

Sheep Creek Canyon, a dramatic 13-mile paved loop through the Sheep Creek Canyon Geological Area, leaves Hwy 44 about 15 miles west of Greendale Junction.

More than 20 campgrounds ($13-30) in and around Flaming Gorge are mostly open May-Oct. *Red Canyon Lodge* (☎ 435-889-3759) provides simple cabins with shared baths from $40 Apr-Oct. *Flaming Gorge Lodge* (☎ 435-889-3773) offers motel rooms (from $63) and condominiums (from $111) all year.

Vernal

This town is the region's largest and has plenty of motels and area information. The local visitor center (☎ 435-789-7894, Ⓦ www.dinoland.com, 235 E Main St) is attached to a good natural-history museum (with dinosaurs) and has brochures on driving tours; the Red Cloud Loop & Petroglyphs tour is a highlight. The Ashley National Forest Vernal Ranger Station (☎ 435-789-1181, 355 N Vernal Ave) has information on area camping and hiking.

Red Fleet State Park (☎ 435-789-4432), 12 miles northeast of Vernal on Hwy 191, has boating, basic camping ($10) and a 1½-mile hike (roundtrip) to fossilized dinosaur tracks (day use $4).

The Green and Yampa Rivers are the main waterways in the area, and both have rapids to satisfy the white-water enthusiast as well as calmer areas for gentler float trips. For one- to five-day trips for $65-700, try Hatch River Expeditions (☎ 435-789-4316) or Dinosaur River Expeditions (☎ 435-781-0717). River Runners Transport (☎ 435-781-1180) rents rafts and kayaks.

Dinosaurland KOA (☎ 435-789-2148, 930 N Vernal Ave) has nice facilities and sites ($17-22). *Sage Motel* (☎ 435-789-1442, 54 W Main St) is popular with Europeans; roomy singles/doubles are $45/55. For the same price, also try *Split Mountain Lodge* (☎ 435-789-9020, 1015 E Hwy 40) or *Weston Lamplighter Inn* (☎ 435-789-0312, 120 E Main). Chains in Vernal include Motel 6, Days Inn and Rodeway

Inn. Restaurants are simple, inexpensive affairs.

Greyhound (☎ 435-789-0404, 72 S 100 West) runs buses twice daily to Salt Lake City ($32; 5 hours).

Dinosaur National Monument
One of the largest dinosaur fossil beds in North America was discovered here in 1909. The quarry was enclosed, hundreds of bones were exposed but left in the rock, and visitors can now come to marvel at the find (and at the daunting challenge of paleontology). Apart from visiting the quarry, you can drive, hike, backpack and raft through the starkly eroded, dramatic canyons of the national monument.

Dinosaur National Monument straddles the Utah-Colorado state line. Visit the headquarters (☎ 970-374-3000, 4545 Hwy 40) in tiny Dinosaur, Colorado; the quarry is in Utah ($10 per vehicle; open Mon-Fri, daily in summer). The monument has several basic, summer-only campgrounds ($6-12), but no lodge.

WESTERN UTAH
Grim names on local maps describe western Utah: Snake Valley, Skull Valley, Blood Mountain, Disappointment Hills, Confusion Range. This is harsh desert country, much of it BLM land or used for military testing (as well as, today, destroying banned chemical weapons). Thousands of acres in the **Bonneville Salt Flats** (the remnants of ancient Lake Bonneville, which once covered all of northern Utah) provide a super-smooth surface for car racing and setting speed records. After marveling at the endless salt, you can gamble in the casinos at nearby **Wendover**, along I-80 on the Utah/Nevada state line.

The best way to experience Utah's remote Great Basin is to drive the original **Pony Express Trail**, a good dirt road (passable only in dry weather) running more than 130 miles from Fairfield (on Hwy 73) to the village of Ibapah near Nevada (allow 5-7 hours). The Salt Lake City BLM (☎ 801-977-4300) has information; primitive camping is allowed. Along the trail, Fish Springs is a literal oasis in the desert and an important migratory bird refuge.

19th-Century Federal Express

Those who complain that mail delivery is too slow would not have been happy in the mid-19th century, when a letter took two months to reach California from the East Coast. Delivery was by boat to Caribbean Panama, by mule to the Pacific Coast, and by boat again up to San Francisco.

The Pony Express was founded in 1860 to speed mail across the country. Expert horsemen who weighed under 120lb were hired to ride the almost 1900 miles from St Joseph, Missouri, to Sacramento, California. They rode in relay, passing through home stations – roughly 60 miles apart – where riders changed, and through swing stations about 12 miles apart, where horses were changed. Distances averaged 190 miles per day, though 'Buffalo Bill' (William C Cody) rode a record 322 miles in under 22 hours, using 21 different horses. The fastest run was the delivery of President Lincoln's inaugural address, which took just 7½ days. The service lasted only 19 months; its end came with the completion of a transcontinental telegraph system in 1861.

CENTRAL UTAH
Most folks speed through central Utah on one of the north-south highways (I-15, Hwy 89 and Hwy 6), but the mountains and valleys contain some pretty driving detours, hiking, camping and interesting Mormon towns.

Along Interstate 15
The small towns along Utah's main north-south artery see few tourists; most motels and services are near the highway exits.

A lovely detour is the **Nebo Loop Scenic Byway**. From Payson (just south of Provo on I-15), take 600 E southbound to this paved road, which climbs through the Wasatch Mountains in the Uinta National Forest before dropping to Nephi, about 40 miles away. The route is open June-Oct and offers plenty of excellent fishing and hiking. Several basic forest-service campgrounds ($12) are open in summer.

The territorial capital in 1851, **Fillmore** today is a quaint rural town. Territorial Statehouse State Park (50 W Capitol Ave) contains Utah's oldest government building, which is filled with pioneer memorabilia ($5). The BLM (☎ 435-743-3100, 35 E 500 North) provides information about BLM areas west of Fillmore, and the Fishlake National Forest Fillmore Ranger Station (☎ 435-743-5721, 390 S Main St) has maps for nearby camping and hiking.

Thirty miles south of Fillmore (I-15 exit 135) is the fully restored **Cove Fort**, circa 1867; Mormon guides explain the fort's history.

The unpaved **Paiute ATV Trail**, for all-terrain vehicles, is a 200-mile loop in the Fishlake National Forest east of I-15; it crosses three mountain ranges, mostly in USFS and BLM lands. The trail can be accessed at Fillmore, Richfield, Marysvale and other places.

Along Highway 89

The towns along Hwy 89, with their late-19th-century Main St architecture, magnificent temples and traditional, clean-living inhabitants, have a definite early-Mormon feel. The route is a much more pleasant, slightly slower alternative to the parallel I-15.

Tiny **Fairview** attracts visitors with its fine Fairview Museum of History & Arts (☎ 435-427-9216, 85 N 100 East), featuring a life-size replica of a 15,000-year-old Columbian mammoth, Indian exhibits and interesting Utah art (free admission). East of Fairview, Hwy 31 is a gorgeous mountain drive to Huntington.

The entirety of sleepy **Spring City** is on the National Historic Register; it's a model of Mormon town planning. **Manti**, one of Utah's earliest towns (1849), is famous for its summer Mormon Miracle Pageant (☎ 435-835-3000). In town, *Temple Hill Resort* (☎ 435-835-2267, 296 E 900 North) has tent/RV sites for $15/22. Two attractive

budget motels (around $40) are **Manti Motel** (☎ 435-835-8533, 445 W Main) and **Temple View Lodge** (☎ 435-835-6663, 260 E 400 North).

Richfield is the largest town for 100 road miles in any direction, and it has the best selection of motels and restaurants (all along Main St). Best choices are *Topsfield Lodge & Steak House* (☎ 435-896-5437, 1200 S Main), with rooms in the $30s, and *Romanico Inn* (☎ 435-896-8471, 1170 S Main), with pleasant rooms for $44.

In the conservative Mormon farming community of **Monroe** is the very unconservative *Mystic Hot Springs* (☎ 435-527-3286, 475 E 100 North), an almost nostalgic hippy oasis. Soak ($5), camp ($10) or stay in a cabin ($25); outdoor concerts are held year round.

Containing more than 500 panels of rock art on nearby cliffs and an excavated village, **Fremont Indian State Park** (☎ 435-527-4631), I-70 exit 17, is an excellent place to learn more about the Fremont, who inhabited Utah from AD 500 to 1300 and were contemporaries of the Ancestral Puebloans ($5).

Local businesses in **Marysvale** rent out ATVs and horses for the Paiute ATV Trail (see above). Five miles north on Hwy 89 is *Big Rock Candy Mountain Resort* (☎ 435-326-2000), with nine modern motel rooms ($59) and seven cabins ($39-89).

Skyline Drive

One of Utah's most spectacular wilderness roads, this dirt road parallels Hwy 89, traversing 90 miles along the crest of the Wasatch Plateau at elevations in excess of 10,000 feet. 4WD vehicles are needed to complete the drive (open summer and fall only), although easier sections can be accessed from towns along Hwy 89 (such as Fairview and Ephraim) or Hwy 10 (such as Huntington and Castle Dale).

Most of the drive is within the Manti-La Sal National Forest; ranger stations in Price (see below) and Ephraim (☎ 435-283-4151) have information. The drive begins near the Tucker Rest Area, 30 miles east of Spanish Fork along Hwy 6, and follows USFS Rd 150 for most of its length.

Carbon County & Castle Valley

The imposing buttes and austere eroded formations of 'Castle Country' dominate this colorful but dry region, traversed by Hwys 6 and 10. The discovery of coal and the arrival of the railway in 1883 attracted immigrants from diverse backgrounds to Carbon County, diluting the Mormon heritage that predominates in the valleys west of here.

The mining town of **Price** has the best range of motels and restaurants. The Manti-La Sal National Forest Price Ranger Station (☎ 435-637-2817, 599 W Price River Dr) and the Castle Country Travel Office (☎ 435-637-3009, W www.castlecountry.com, 90 N 100 East) have thorough information on regional sites and outdoor activities. The excellent **College of Eastern Utah Prehistoric Museum** (☎ 435-637-5060, 155 E Main St) displays dinosaur skeletons and Indian artifacts (free admission).

South of Wellington on Hwy 6 is the turnoff for **Nine-Mile Canyon**, which is famous for its numerous Fremont Indian pictographs and petroglyphs. The dusty dirt road is actually almost 50 miles long (allow 3-4 hours), and the rock art can be hard to spot; get information first at the Price BLM (☎ 435-636-3600, 125 S 600 West).

In the 19th century, outlaws used the remote **San Rafael River and Swell** region as a hideout. Dirt roads, most accessible by 4WD only, crisscross the area, and backcountry camping is allowed. The best road, which passes both a spur to the awesome Wedge Overlook and the Buckhorn Wash Pictographs, is a gravel one that leaves Hwy 10, 2 miles north of Castle Dale; the entire route is more than 60 miles (allow 3 hours). Always carry extra water when exploring.

SOUTHEASTERN UTAH

This portion of Utah contains some of the most inhospitable and beautiful terrain in the world. Over millennia, the Colorado, Green and San Juan Rivers have carved a landscape of such sheer-walled majesty and otherworldly desolation that it can challenge one's capacity for wonder. Every year, millions come to experience this country in every conceivable way: by foot, horseback, bicycle, car, 4WD, all-terrain vehicle, plane, helicopter and raft. You can camp alone in the silent desert or be catered to in exclusive lodges. But however you visit, remember to tread lightly; millions of footsteps are taking their toll on this deceptively fragile environment.

This section is organized roughly north to south, beginning with Green River, on I-70, and following US 191 into the southeast corner of the state. See the Southwest Parks map.

Green River

The 'world's watermelon capital,' Green River is the only town of any size along I-70 between Salina and Grand Junction, Colorado. It offers a good base for river running, and accommodations are cheaper here than in Moab, about 40 miles southeast. Moki Mac River Expeditions (☎ 435-564-3361) and Holiday River Expeditions (☎ 435-624-6323) offer river trips.

Motels and most businesses line Main St. For basic budget rooms ($35-45), try *Mancos Rose Motel* (☎ 435-564-9660), *Oasis Motel* (☎ 435-564-8272) or *Bookcliff Lodge* (☎ 435-564-3406). River rafters go to *Ray's Tavern*, which serves microbrews and great hamburgers and steaks.

Greyhound (☎ 435-564-3421, 525 E Main St), in the Rodeway Inn, has daily service to Salt Lake City ($32; 4 hours), Las Vegas ($58; 7½ hours) and beyond. Amtrak's *California Zephyr* stops here daily on its run between Salt Lake City ($48; 5 hours) and Denver ($59; 11 hours). The station (☎ 435-872-7245) is at 250 S Broadway. It's the only Amtrak stop in southeastern Utah. See Moab, below, for shuttle services.

Moab

The 1950s uranium boom put Moab on the map. The boom slowed in the 1960s, but then tourists began to arrive steadily, word having spread about the area's striking landscape. However, it wasn't until mountain biking took off in the mid-1980s that tourism reached its current craze – everyone wanting to experience writer Edward Abbey's slickrock desert. Hollywood has a long history of filming in the spectacular terrain here, including some John Wayne Westerns and Indiana Jones footage. Today Moab is a semirural yet trendy town with chic restaurants and art galleries and more than 50 companies offering biking, river running, backpacking, horseback riding and 4WD tours and rentals. Despite a ton of hotels, B&Bs and campgrounds, the town is packed with visitors from spring to fall, and reservations are advised.

SOUTHWEST

Information The multiagency Moab Information Center, at the corner of Main and Center, can answer questions about Moab and all the area's public lands, parks and forests. Contact the Grand County Travel Council (☎ 435-259-8825, 800-635-6622, ⓦ www.discovermoab.com, PO Box 550, Moab, UT 84532) for advance information. Get in touch with Central Reservations (☎ 435-259-5125, 800-748-4386, 50 E Center St) for accommodations and tour reservations. The Canyonlands Natural History Association (☎ 435-259-6003, 800-840-8978, ⓦ www.cnha.org) will send a free mail-order catalog of books on the region.

Activities Rafting, biking and 4WD exploration are *the* things to do. Good outfitters include the following:

Adrift Adventures (☎ 435-259-8594, 800-874-4483, ⓦ www.adrift.net) 378 N Main St; PO Box 577, Moab, UT 84532

Canyon Voyages (☎ 435-259-4121, 800-733-6007, ⓦ www.canyonvoyages.com) 211 N Main St; PO Box 416, Moab, UT 84532

Canyonlands Field Institute educational expeditions (☎ 435-259-7750, 800-860-5262, ⓦ www.canyonlandsfieldinst.org) 1320 S Hwy 191; PO Box 68, Moab, UT 84532

Rim Tours (☎ 435-259-5223, 800-626-7335, ⓦ www.rimtours.com) 1233 S Hwy 191, Moab, UT 84532

Tex's Riverways (☎ 435-259-5101, ⓦ www.texsriverways.com) 691 N 500 West; PO Box 67, Moab, UT 84532

Places to Stay The backpacker's choice is *Up the Creek Campground* (☎ 435-259-2213, 210 E 300 South) for tents only ($10). *Moab Valley RV & Campark* (☎ 435-259-4469) and *Riverside Oasis* (☎ 435-259-3424) are on Hwy 191 close to Arches National Park; sites are $16-24.

The friendly *Lazy Lizard International Hostel* (☎ 435-259-6057, 1213 S Hwy 191) attracts relaxed outdoor enthusiasts (dormitories/doubles cost $8/22).

For doubles around $50, try the delightfully decorated *Hotel Off Center* (☎ 435-259-4244, 96 E Center St), *Silver Sage Inn* (☎ 435-259-4420, 840 S Main St) or *Inca Inn Motel* (☎ 435-259-7261, 570 N Main). For $67 a double, good values are the charming *Kokopelli Lodge* (☎ 435-259-7615, 888-530-

3134, 72 S 100 East) and the rustic-looking *Redstone Inn* (☎ 435-259-3500, 535 S Main).

Places to Eat & Drink The *Jailhouse Café* (101 N Main) dishes up delicious breakfasts daily until noon. Popular with the biking and outdoor crowd, *Slickrock Cafe* (5 N Main) serves Southwestern food. *Eddie McStiff's* (57 S Main) is a lively microbrewery and restaurant with the best pizza in town. Venerable *Poplar Place Pub & Eatery* (11 E 100 North) remains quite 'poplar' for libations. *La Hacienda* (754 N Main) serves excellent Mexican meals ($7-14). For a truly gourmet dinner, make a reservation at *Center Cafe* (☎ 435-259-4295, 60 N 100 West); it's regarded as the best in southern Utah ($20-27).

Getting There & Around Bighorn Express (☎ 888-655-7433) has a daily shuttle van between Moab and the Salt Lake City airport ($49; 4½ hours). Taxis and bike shuttles are available from Coyote Shuttle (☎ 435-259-8656) and Roadrunner Shuttle (☎ 435-259-9402).

Arches National Park

No one comes to southeast Utah without visiting this national park (☎ 435-719-2299), which boasts the greatest concentration of sandstone arches in the world. Of course, that means that Arches, five quick miles north of Moab on Hwy 191, is often very crowded (and the park is contemplating instituting a shuttle system). Many of the most spectacular arches are easily reached by paved road and relatively short hiking trails. Highlights are Balanced Rock, the oft-photographed Delicate Arch, the spectacularly elongated Landscape Arch and ranger-led trips into the Fiery Furnace. Because of the heat and scarcity of water, few visitors backpack, though this is allowed with free permits (available from the visitor center). Entry costs $10 per vehicle. The scenic *Devils Garden* campground ($10) is open year round.

Dead Horse Point State Park

This tiny state park (☎ 435-259-2614) packs a wallop: drop-dead gorgeous views of the Colorado River, Canyonlands National Park and the distant La Sal Mountains ($6). It's a worthwhile side trip off of Hwy 313 (north of Moab), especially if you're heading to/from Canyonlands. *Kayenta Campground* has sites for $13.

Canyonlands National Park

Wherever we look there is but a wilderness of rocks – deep gorges where the rivers are lost below cliffs and towers and pinnacles, and ten thousand strangely carved forms in every direction, and beyond them mountains blending with the clouds.

– John Wesley Powell describing
Canyonlands in 1869

Covering 527 sq miles, this is the largest and wildest national park in Utah. Indeed, parts of it are as rugged as almost anywhere on the planet. Canyons tipped with white cliffs tumble down to the river, 2000 feet below. Arches, bridges, needles, spires, craters, mesas, buttes – Canyonlands is a crumbling beauty, a vision of ancient earth.

You can hike, raft and 4WD (Cataract Canyon offers some of the wildest white water in the West), but be sure that you have plenty of gas, food and water before leaving Moab. The difficult terrain and lack of water make this the least developed and least visited of the major Southwestern national parks.

The canyons of the Colorado and Green Rivers divide the park into three districts: 'Island in the Sky' (most easily reached – Hwy 313 from Hwy 191 north of Moab); 'The Needles' (Route 211 west from US 191, 40 miles south of Moab); and the 'Maze' (one of the wildest and most remote areas in the Southwest, accessible by 4WD only). In Horseshoe Canyon, along the 32-mile-long road from Hwy 24 to the Maze, is the Great Gallery, with superb life-size rock art left by prehistoric Indians.

Permits, ranging from $15 to $30, are required for all activities except day trips. You can make reservations in writing or by fax (at least two weeks in advance) through the Canyonlands National Park Reservation Office (☎ 435-259-4351, fax 435-259-4285, 2282 S West Resource Blvd, Moab, UT 84532). Or you can just show up, though reservations are recommended in the busy spring and fall. The main visitor center (☎ 435-259-4712) is in Island in the Sky;

another is at The Needles (☎ 435-259-4711). The entrance fee is $10 per vehicle. For recorded information and to request mailed material, call ☎ 435-259-7164.

Monticello

At a cooler elevation in the Abajo Mountain foothills, this small town contains the multi-agency San Juan Visitors Center (☎ 435-587-3235, 800-574-4386, W www.southeastutah.com, 117 S Main St) which has complete information on outdoor activities, national parks and forests, camping and hotels in this corner of Utah.

Blanding

This town is a worthwhile stop for the **Edge of the Cedars State Park** (☎ 435-678-2238, 660 W 400 North), which contains partially excavated Ancestral Puebloan buildings and a great collection of pottery and other artifacts ($5).

Hovenweep National Monument

The beautiful, little-visited Hovenweep, meaning 'deserted valley' in the Ute language, contains six sets of prehistoric Ancestral Puebloan Indian sites, five of which require long hikes to reach ($6). There is a ranger station (☎ 970-560-4282), a new visitor center and a basic campground ($10), but no facilities. The main access is east of Hwy 191 on Hwy 262 via Hatch Trading Post, more than 40 miles from Bluff or Blanding.

Bluff

Surrounded by red rock, tiny Bluff makes a comfortable, laid-back home base for exploring the region. It's an ideal starting point for San Juan River trips. Wild Rivers Expeditions (☎ 435-672-2244) has been guiding educational river trips for four decades (day trips are $120). Far Out Expeditions (☎ 435-672-2294) arranges off-the-beaten-track trips to Monument Valley; a day trip includes lunch with a Navajo family and a weaving demonstration ($100). Groups should ask about their fabulous bunkhouse.

The BLM's *Sand Island Recreation Area*, west of town off Hwy 163, has a basic campground ($6). Bluff has a great selection of lodgings and several good restaurants; most are along Main St. For $45-55, try

Mokee Motel (☎ *435-672-2242*), *Kokopelli Inn* (☎ *435-672-2322*) or the always hospitable *Recapture Lodge* (☎ *435-672-2281*). *Pioneer House Inn* (☎ *435-672-2446, 3rd East and Mulberry Ave)* has enormous suites ($70) with breakfast; they also arrange private tours.

Natural Bridges National Monument

Forty miles west of Blanding, this became Utah's first National Park Service land in 1908. The highlight is a dark-stained, white sandstone canyon containing three easily accessible natural bridges. The oldest, the Owachomo Bridge, spans 180 feet but is only 9 feet thick ($6). Basic camping is available ($10).

Hwy 261 & Moki Dugway Backway

Magnificently scenic Hwy 261 leaves Hwy 95 and heads south to Hwy 163, about 33 miles away, passing a number of interesting spots.

The **Grand Gulch Primitive Area**, south of Hwy 95 in Cedar Mesa, features hundreds of Ancestral Puebloan sites. Thirty miles south of Hwy 95 Cedar Mesa ends dramatically but the road doesn't: the unpaved, hairpin-turned **Moki Dugway** descends 1100 feet in three fist-clenching miles. The panoramic views from the top are among the best in the country. At the bottom, a dirt road heads east into the **Valley of the Gods**, a 17-mile drive through monoliths of sandstone that locals call a 'mini-Monument Valley.' Near the southern end of Hwy 261, a 4-mile paved road heads west to **Goosenecks State Park**, a small lookout with memorable views of the San Juan River, 1100 feet below.

Monument Valley

Hwy 163 winds southwest past the village of Mexican Hat (which has a few simple motels) and enters the Navajo Indian Reservation and, after about 30 miles, Monument Valley Navajo Tribal Park (see the Northeastern Arizona section). Just inside the Utah border, *Goulding's Lodge* (☎ 435-727-3231, Ⓦ www.gouldings.com) is the only hotel near Monument Valley. Rooms are $155/62 in high/low season; each has a balcony with a million-dollar view of the colossal red buttes. Goulding's also has a museum, tours, store, gas and campground ($15/25 for tents/RVs).

SOUTH-CENTRAL & SOUTHWESTERN UTAH

This section is organized roughly northeast to southwest: from Hanksville, along Hwy 24 through Capitol Reef National Park and southwest along Hwy 12, which passes the Grand Staircase-Escalante National Monument and Bryce Canyon and is one of the most scenic roads in the country. From Hwy 12, US 89 goes south to Kanab (and continues to the North Rim of the Grand Canyon). I-15, the major north-south route, leads to Cedar City, St George and Zion National Park (along Hwy 9). See the Southwest Parks map.

Hanksville

This village is a convenient stopping place at the junction of Hwys 95 and 24. The BLM (☎ 435-542-3461, 406 S 100 West) has information on the nearby **Henry Mountains**, a remote, 11,000-foot-high range. About 40 miles north off of Hwy 24 is **Goblin Valley State Park**, full of delightful, alien rock formations ($5).

Whispering Sands Motel (☎ *435-542-3238, 132 S Hwy 95)* is the best of Hanksville's few simple motels ($60).

Capitol Reef National Park

Not as crowded as Utah's other national parks, but equally scenic, Capitol Reef contains much of the 100-mile **Waterpocket Fold**, created 65 million years ago when the earth's surface buckled up and folded, exposing a cross-section of geologic history that is almost painterly in its intensity of color. On Hwy 24, the visitor center (☎ 435-425-3791) is at the start of the park's 12½-mile scenic drive, which leads to numerous hiking trails. Also in the park is the Mormon pioneer town of Fruita, containing historic buildings, working fruit orchards and a grassy, basic *campground* ($10). Other long dirt roads lead through the park. Backcountry camping is free with a permit, but this is a desert wilderness, so be prepared. For more information, contact the Superintendent, Capitol Reef National Park, HCR 70, Box 15, Torrey, UT 84775. Day use is $4.

Torrey

A rural village on Hwy 12, 11 miles west of Capitol Reef National Park's visitor center, Torrey is an unexpectedly hip enclave. Wayne County Travel Council (☎ 435-425-3365, 800-858-7951, Ⓦ www.capitolreef.org) runs a summer-only information booth at the junction of Hwys 24 and 12. Several outfitters can arrange area hiking, biking, horse and jeep expeditions; try Hondoo Rivers & Trails (☎ 435-425-3519, 800-332-2696).

In addition to good campgrounds, Torrey has nice motels and B&Bs and some standout restaurants. The appealing *Capitol Reef Inn & Café* (☎ *435-425-3271, 360 W Main*) has 10 rooms ($44). *Rim Rock Inn* (☎ *435-425-3398),* on Hwy 24 just outside the national park, has great views and doubles for $60, a good deal. In town, *Café Diablo* (*599 W Main*) prepares first-rate Southwest cuisine ($18-25) in summer only.

Boulder

This tiny village is 32 miles south of Torrey on Hwy 12. From here, the attractive **Burr Trail** heads east as a paved road across the northeastern corner of the Grand Staircase-Escalante National Monument, crosses Capitol Reef National Park as an unpaved road and continues to Bullfrog Marina on Lake Powell (see the Arizona section), about 70 miles from Boulder. *Pole's Place* (☎ *435-335-7422),* on Hwy 12 in town, has 12 nice motel rooms ($50-60).

Escalante

The Escalante Interagency Office (☎ 435-826-5499, PO Box 246, Escalante, UT 84726) has complete information on all area public lands. Fifteen miles east on Hwy 12, *Calf Creek Recreation Area* (☎ *435-826-5499)* has a nice basic campground ($7) and a recommended 3-mile hike to Lower Calf Creek Falls.

Escalante has a few budget motels; the best deal is *Circle D Motel* (☎ *435-826-4297, 475 W Main),* with recently refurbished rooms ($35-45).

Grand Staircase-Escalante NM

This 2656-sq-mile monument, established in 1996, links the area between Bryce Canyon National Park in the west with Capitol Reef National Park in the east and Glen Canyon National Recreation Area (see the Arizona section) in the southeast. Tourist infrastructure is minimal, leaving a vast, remote desert for adventurous travelers who have the time and necessary outdoor equipment to explore.

Three unpaved roads – Skutumpah/Johnson Canyon Rd (the least used and most westerly route), Cottonwood Canyon Rd and Smoky Mountain Rd – cross the monument roughly north to south between Hwys 12 and 89. A fourth unpaved road – the Hole-in-the-Rock Rd – begins from Hwy 12 and dead-ends at the Glen Canyon National Recreation Area. The park has only two basic *campgrounds* on Hwy 12. Wilderness camping is allowed in established areas, and a permit is required. As of 2001, permits were free, but that may change. Current information is available from the Escalante Interagency Office (see Escalante above).

A popular hike is along the Escalante River in **Escalante Canyon**. Adventurers can hike the entire length to Lake Powell but will get wet. The 'trail' frequently crosses the river. The canyon scenery is marvelous, with sheer cliffs and soaring arches, waterfalls and pools, as well as many side canyons where the chances of seeing anyone are slim indeed.

Kodachrome Basin State Park

Dozens of red, pink and white sandstone chimneys make this a colorful state park ($4). Call ☎ 435-679-8562 for park information. The campground is open all year ($13).

Bryce Canyon National Park

The Grand Staircase, a series of steplike uplifted rock layers stretching north from the Grand Canyon, culminates at this very popular park in the Pink Cliffs formation, full of wondrous pinnacles and points, steeples and spires, and odd formations called 'hoodoos.' The 'canyon' is actually an amphitheater eroded from the cliffs.

From Hwy 12, Hwy 63 heads 4 miles south to Rim Rd Dr (8000 feet), an 18-mile dead-end road that follows the rim of the canyon, passing the visitor center (☎ 435-834-5322), the lodge, two campgrounds, viewpoints and trailheads, ending at Rainbow Point, 9115 feet above sea level.

Entrance costs $10 per person, $20 per vehicle. There is a free shuttle system. For further information, contact the Superintendent, Bryce Canyon National Park, Bryce Canyon, UT 84717.

Hikes from the rim down into the canyon and among the spires can range from 1 to 30 miles. Canyon Trail Rides (☎ 435-679-8665) operates backcountry horse or mule tours. Rangers lead new- and full-moon stargazing evenings in summer. In winter, certain trails are open to cross-country skiing and snowshoeing.

With a permit ($5), you can camp at 10 designated backcountry sites below the rim. The park's two campgrounds ($10) fill by noon in summer.

The attractive, historic *Bryce Canyon Lodge* (☎ 303-297-2757) is open April to October (from $92). A general store offers camping supplies and coin-operated showers seasonally. On Hwy 63 just north of the park, *Best Western Ruby's Inn & Campground* (☎ 435-834-5341) is a huge, unrelentingly 'Western' complex with two hotels (from $60 in summer), a campground ($16/25 for tents/RVs), restaurants, a nightly rodeo, tours, groceries, gift shops and more.

Panguitch & Around

A popular stop on Hwy 89 and surrounded by 'Scenic Byways' (Hwy 89 itself, Hwy 143 to the west and Hwy 12 to the east), Panguitch is 24 miles from Bryce Canyon National Park and 70 miles from Zion. Garfield County Travel Council (☎ 800-444-6689) has regional information. For camping and outdoor activities, head southwest on Hwy 143 to Panguitch Lake. Farther west on Hwy 143, Brian Head Ski Resort (☎ 435-677-2035, Ⓦ www.brianhead.com) offers downhill and cross-country skiing in winter. In summer, you can reach the 11,307-foot Brian Head Summit – great views.

In town, motels with rooms for about $50 line Main St. Try *Horizon Motel* (☎ 435-676-2651), *Blue Pine Motel* (☎ 435-676-8197) or *Canyon Lodge* (☎ 435-676-8292).

Along Highway 14

This paved, scenic road crosses the beautiful Markagunt Plateau between I-15 and Hwy 89 and gives access to hiking trails, fishing lakes and lodges. In winter, it's kept open by snowplows.

A few miles north on Hwy 148, Cedar Breaks National Monument (☎ 435-586-9451), at 10,400 feet, is only open in summer. Its stunning amphitheater features wonderfully eroded, almost neon-colored spires ($3 per person).

Kanab

Surrounded by desert wilderness on all sides, Kanab was an isolated Mormon community until the advent of roads. In the 1930s, the film industry 'discovered' the area, and almost 100 movies have been filmed here. Paved roads lead to the area's famous national parks: Zion (40 miles), Bryce Canyon (80 miles), the north rim of the Grand Canyon (80 miles) and Glen Canyon National Recreation Area (74 miles; see Lake Powell in the Arizona section).

Hwy 89 snakes through town, and a good selection of motels and restaurants lie along it. The county Travel Information Center (☎ 435-644-5033, Ⓦ www.kaneutah.com, 78 S 100 East) and the BLM office (☎ 435-644-2672, 180 W 300 North) have area information.

The private, no-frills *Canyonlands International Hostel* (☎ 435-644-5554, 143 E 100 South) attracts international travelers (dorms cost $10). A good bargain is *Bob-Bon Inn Motel* (☎ 435-644-5094, 236 N 300 West), with rooms under $40. *Parry Lodge* (☎ 435-644-2601, 89 E Center St) has long been *the* place to stay in Kanab (around $60).

Cedar City

Less than an hour's drive northeast of Zion on I-15, with plenty of hotels and places to eat, Cedar City is a natural stopping place. For area information, head to the Iron County Tourism Bureau (☎ 435-586-5124, Ⓦ www.scenicsouthernutah.com, 581 N Main), Dixie National Forest Cedar City Ranger Station (☎ 435-865-3200, 82 N 100 East) and the BLM (☎ 435-586-2401, 176 E DL Sargent Dr). From June to September, the nationally renowned Shakespearean Festival (☎ 435-586-7878) keeps the town buzzing.

Chain motels line Main St. For basic rooms ($40-60 in summer), try *Zion Inn* (☎ 435-586-9487), *Best Travel Inn* (☎ 435-586-6557) or *Super 7 Motel* (☎ 435-586-6566). B&Bs are popular here; one of the best is *Big Yellow Inn* (☎ 435-586-0960, Ⓦ www.bigyellowinn.com, 234 S 300 West), with sumptuous rooms ($85-$180).

Cedar City has a lot of restaurants, but few stand out. The old-world *Adriana's (164 S 100 West)* is popular with festivalgoers.

The Greyhound bus stop (☎ 435-586-9465, 1744 Royal Hunte Dr) is in a Chevron gas station at I-15 exit 57. Several daily buses run to Las Vegas ($31; 3½ hours), Salt Lake City ($40; 5 hours) and elsewhere.

St George

A spacious Mormon town with wide streets and pioneer buildings, St George is popular with retirees and visitors to Zion and other nearby parks. With eight golf courses, it claims to have the best year-round golf in the state. Get local information at the chamber of commerce (☎ 435-628-1658, W www.stgeorgechamber.com, 97E St George Blvd). Nine miles north on Hwy 18, **Snow Canyon State Park** (☎ 435-628-2255) has volcanic landscapes, petroglyphs and hiking trails to lava caves. The Greyhound stop (☎ 435-673-2933, 1235 S Bluff), inside McDonald's, is the closest stop to Zion.

Campgrounds in town cater mainly to RVs. St George has the biggest selection of accommodations in southern Utah; most are chains, and many line St George Blvd. *Chalet Motel (☎ 435-628-6272, 664 E St George Blvd)* is a good deal ($30s). For recommended doubles in the $40s, try *Sun Time Inn (☎ 435-673-6181, 420 E St George Blvd)* or *Sullivan's Rococo Inn & Steak House (☎ 435-628-3671, 511 S Airport Rd)*, which has great views and better steaks.

Budget travelers may wish to drive 17 miles east to the tiny town of Hurricane (on Hwy 9 to Zion National Park), where the clean, well-run *HI Hurricane Dixie Hostel (☎ 435-635-8202, 73 S Main)* has dorms for $15.

Springdale

A pleasant, relaxed community at the southeast entrance to Zion National Park, Springdale caters to park visitors with a relative abundance of nice lodgings and good restaurants. The chamber of commerce (☎ 435-722-3757) has information. Bicycles, kayaks and inner tubes (for tubing down the Virgin River) are available for rent – just look for signs.

All businesses are along the main highway; summer rates are high. The large, riverside *Zion Canyon Campground* (☎ 435-772-3237) has tent/RV sites for $16/20. Friendly *El Rio Lodge (☎ 435-772-3205)* has rooms for $52, and *Terrace Brook Lodge (☎ 435-772-3932)* is $65. The *Bit & Spur Restaurant & Saloon* serves tasty Mexican and Southwestern cuisine and has a lively bar.

Zion National Park

The white, pink and red rocks of Zion are so huge, overpowering and magnificent that few photos can do them justice – though people try, *lots* of people. In summer, so many cars crowd the 6-mile drive into Zion Canyon – a half-mile-deep slash formed by the Virgin River – that the park now shuts the road April through October and runs a free shuttle bus. This has resulted in a much quieter park, but it hasn't lessened the number of people. Escaping the tourist hordes is relatively easy, however: Simply hike, or take a guided horseback-riding trip, into the spectacularly wild country beyond the scenic pullouts.

Three roads enter the park. The most popular, Zion-Mt Carmel Hwy (Hwy 9 between Mt Carmel Junction and Springdale) enters the south side, leads past the entrance to Zion Canyon and has a tunnel so narrow that escorts must accompany vehicles more than 7 feet 10 inches wide or 11 feet 4 inches high. The road leads to the newly expanded Zion Canyon Visitor Center (☎ 435-772-3256) and the new Zion Museum (scheduled to open in 2002); entrance to the park via this route is $20 per vehicle.

It costs nothing to enter the park along Kolob Terrace Rd (closed Nov-May), which leaves Hwy 9 at the village of Virgin and climbs more than 4000 feet to Lava Point. However, there are no facilities, only a ranger station and primitive campground.

At the park's north end, it costs $10 to enter via Kolob Canyons Rd (I-15 exit 40), which leads to the much smaller Kolob Canyons Visitor Center (☎ 435-586-9548) and wonderful views and hikes.

Maps and books can be ordered in advance from the Zion Natural History Association (☎ 435-772-3264, 800-635-3959 for credit-card orders), Springdale, UT 84767).

More than 100 miles of trails offer everything from leisurely strolls to wilderness **backpacking** and camping. The most famous backpacking trip is through **The Narrows**, a

16-mile journey through canyons along the Virgin River (June-Sept). In places, the canyon walls are only 20 feet apart and tower hundreds of feet above; wading and sometimes swimming the river is required. Overnight permits ($5) from the visitor centers are issued only the day of or the day before your hike.

At the south gate, two basic campgrounds have more than 300 first-come, first-served sites ($14), but come early. A few sites can be reserved (☎ 800-365-2267). *Zion Lodge* (☎ 303-297-2757), beautifully set in the middle of Zion Canyon, offers motel rooms from $97 and cabins from $107, most with excellent views and private porches. A restaurant and cafe are also here.

Nevada

You know you're in Nevada when even the roadside gas station has a slot machine. Or when the waitress at a 24-hour coffee shop asks if you want a keno ticket with your eggs. Brochures enjoin visitors to 'discover both sides of Nevada,' and for many travelers this means driving all night to reach Las Vegas, a few minutes of pure adrenaline at the gaming tables, and the hangover that ensues after blowing $100 in less than 10 minutes. As the signs say, 'Welcome to Fabulous Nevada.'

It's not always obvious, but Nevada – from a Spanish word meaning 'snow-clad' – is more than just slot machines and cheap casino buffets. For starters, there's lots of rugged, beautiful terrain to explore, from the mountains of Great Basin National Park to the empty highways and sweeping desert valleys. Immerse yourself in Western history in towns like Virginia City and Elko, or just pitch a tent and spend the evening under the huge, star-dotted sky. If you're lucky, you might even see a UFO.

History
Ancient Lake Lahonton covered much of western Nevada until about 7000 years ago, and prehistoric communities fished and hunted on its shores. After the lake dried up, the region was inhabited by the northern Paiute people, who adapted to life in the desert. There was also an Ancestral Puebloan presence in the southeast around 2500 years ago.

Though claimed by Spain, Nevada was scarcely touched by Europeans until the 1820s, when trappers ventured into the Humboldt River Valley. Jedediah Smith explored southern and central Nevada in 1826, and the springs and grasslands of Las Vegas ('the meadows') later became a stop on the Spanish Trail from Santa Fe to California. US Army Lieutenant John Frémont came south from Oregon in 1843, naming the Carson Valley after his guide, Kit Carson. Two years later, Frémont returned to chart what became the Humboldt Emigrant Trail across northern Nevada.

After the Mexican War, Nevada became part of the new Utah Territory, but most emigrants headed straight through to the California gold fields. That all changed in 1859, when the Comstock Lode – the largest silver deposit ever mined – was discovered south of Reno. The US government needed money to wage the Civil War, and so Nevada was soon incorporated and admitted to the Union in 1864; it provided the extra vote needed to ratify the 13th Amendment, which abolished slavery.

As the Comstock Lode was mined out, Nevada's population declined. In the early 20th century, new mineral discoveries tem-

---

Nevada

Nicknames: Silver State, Sagebrush State

Population: 1,998,300 (35th)

Area: 110,567 sq miles (7th)

Admitted to Union: October 31, 1864 (36th)

Capital city: Carson City (population 52,500)

Other cities: Las Vegas (483,500; metro area 1,425,700), Reno (180,500)

State fossil: ichthyosaur

Birthplace of: First lady Thelma 'Pat' Nixon (1912–93), Andre Agassi (b 1970)

Famous for: Las Vegas, UFOs and Area 51, lonesome desert highways, legal prostitution

porarily revived the state's fortunes, and there was some diversification into grazing and agriculture. The Great Depression brought a collapse in mineral and crop prices, so in 1931 the state government legalized gambling and created agencies to tax it, turning an illegal activity into a revenue source and tourist attraction. Las Vegas grew into a major city, thanks to gangsters in the 1940s and 1950s who bankrolled its growth, and thanks to Hoover Dam, a New Deal project that provided water and electricity.

Since WWII, Nevada's wide-open spaces have been used to test nuclear weapons and military aircraft; its next controversial industry may be nuclear-waste storage. Tourism and gambling are the state's biggest industries, followed by mining and agriculture.

Geography
Roughly three-quarters of Nevada are in the Great Basin, so called because its rivers drain to inland lakes and sinks, not to the sea. The basin is crossed by parallel north-south ranges and broad valleys and is more descriptively known as the Basin and Range Country.

Flora & Fauna
The Great Basin is a high desert. Sagebrush makes up about 70% of the ground cover and provides a habitat for small animals like rabbits, squirrels, snakes, lizards and sage grouse (one of the few species that can survive by eating sage). Larger animals include coyotes, pronghorn antelope and mountain lions, as well as thousands of feral horses and burros.

Life zones that vary with altitude are a feature of Nevada's ecology. Desert vegetation dominates up to about 6500 feet, followed by various types of forest up to 11,500 feet. Bristlecone pines survive in the highest, coldest, harshest environments and are the longest-lived things on earth (some are nearly 5000 years old). One of the best places to see life-zone transitions, and bristlecones, is Great Basin National Park in eastern Nevada.

Gambling
Except for poker, all gambling pits the player against the house, and the house always has a statistical edge. Some casinos offer introductory lessons in blackjack, roulette and craps. To enter a gambling area, you must be at least 18 years old. To gamble and/or drink alcohol in the casino, you must be 21 years old.

Information
The Nevada Commission on Tourism (☎ 800-638-2328, Ⓦ www.travelnevada.com) sends free books, maps and information on accommodations, campgrounds and events. The Las Vegas Convention and Visitors Authority (☎ 702-892-0711, Ⓦ www.lasvegas 24hours.com, 3150 Paradise Ave, Las Vegas, NV 89109) is another helpful organization.

For highway conditions, call ☎ 877-687-6237, or check the Web (Ⓦ www.nvroads .com). Sales tax is around 7%, with an additional tax on accommodations in some counties.

Note that prostitution is definitely illegal in Clark County (which includes Las Vegas) and Washoe County (which includes Reno), though there are legal brothels in many smaller counties.

In May 1999 Nevada's phone area code split, with Las Vegas and vicinity keeping 702 and the rest of the state adopting 775.

LAS VEGAS
'Fabulous' Las Vegas has grown in 90 years from nothing to a city of nearly a half-million people. If you've come for the gambling and glitter, you'll love it. At least for a few days, until your money disappears and sunshine seems unnatural.

A few years back, Vegas was known as a place filled with tour buses, elderly vacationers and high-rolling mafioso types. Recently, with help from such movies as *Swingers* and *Fear & Loathing in Las Vegas,* it has become a hip playland for twenty- and thirty-somethings looking for a weekend of excess and faux glamour. Also, unlike the rest of the USA, there is no 'last call,' and you can drink and smoke pretty much everywhere 24 hours a day. Las Vegas is not only a refuge for those who are over the legal gambling age of 21; it has become a popular family destination with many of the hotels boasting amusement parks, waterslides and movie theaters for the kids.

Even if you can't stand lounge singers, the incessant 'ding-ding-ding' of the slot

Tying & Untying the Knot

Looking to get hitched? You can do so quickly in Nevada if you're over 18 years old and have proof of identity. If your or your beloved has been married before, though, make sure the divorce is final; you must know the date of the divorce and the city and state where it was granted. When you're ready, head to the nearest county courthouse, where marriage licenses cost $50 (cash only). To seal the deal, a ceremony must also be performed (one witness is required). For an experience that's as much kitsch as romance, try tying the knot at one of Nevada's famous wedding chapels. A mind-boggling variety of wedding packages is available; many involving white limos and Elvis impersonators. The simplest start at around $100. The Web site W www.travelnevada.com/marriage_info.asp has basic marriage information with links to several county courthouses and, in turn, some wedding chapels. To find a chapel you can also just check the local yellow pages.

Divorces are another story. First of all, one member must reside in Nevada for at least six weeks; then the divorce-seeker can head over to a lawyer or paralegal service and complete the required papers. The Web site W www .divorcesource.com/NV/index.shtml is one place to start looking for legal assistance. An uncontested divorce may take as little as a month; contested cases, much longer. Prices will, of course, vary accordingly.

machines and the haggard countenances of down-and-out gamblers, Vegas is a place like no other and a great stop between California and points east.

History

A small spring north of downtown was used by Paiute Indians and later by emigrants en route to California. Mormons established a small mission, but in 1902 most of the land was sold to a railroad company, and Las Vegas became a railroad town with ice works, hotels and saloons. There were gambling houses, too, but local Mormon conservatism did not encourage gaming even after it was legalized. The first casinos were built by Los Angeles developers and

Mafia associates. In 1946, Bugsy Siegel's Fabulous Flamingo pioneered the new style of casinos – big and flashy with lavish entertainment to draw in the gamblers.

Orientation & Information

Downtown Las Vegas is the original town center; its main artery, Fremont St, is now a covered pedestrian mall lined with low-key casinos and hotels. Las Vegas Blvd goes through downtown and continues south for about 10 miles. A 3-mile stretch of this boulevard, known as 'the Strip,' has most of the newer, bigger hotel/casinos.

The Las Vegas Visitor Center (☎ 702-892-7575, W www.lasvegas24hours.com) is in the Convention Center at 3150 Paradise Rd.

The Gay & Lesbian Community Center (☎ 702-733-9800, 912 E Sahara Ave) gives referrals for gay-friendly hotels, clubs and such. Like most of Nevada, Las Vegas is not particularly gay friendly.

Most of the tourist areas are safe, but Las Vegas Blvd between downtown and the Strip can feel a bit threatening.

Casinos

Most casinos entice gamblers with free booze (don't forget to tip the waitstaff!), cheap food and glitzy entertainment. Inside, casinos are hideously gaudy, noisy and deliberately disorienting, with no clocks or windows. The Strip's new megacasinos also feature gimmicky themes, attention-grabbing architecture and some nongambling amusements.

The casinos listed below (from north to south) are worth visiting as attractions in themselves.

Stratosphere – This casino's landmark is its 1149-foot tower with two rides up top – the world's highest roller coaster ($5) and the free-fall Big Shot ($8)   and a restaurant (☎ 800-998-6937).

Las Vegas Hilton – Just east of the Strip, this casino has a flashy sci-fi theme, plus the Star Trek: The Experience ride ($15), which is popular with trekkies (☎ 800-732-7117).

Circus Circus – One of the original casino-cum-theme-parks, this place has the small amusement park, Adventuredome (day pass $19), and free circus acts (☎ 702-794-3939).

Treasure Island – The pirate ship and man-of-war in the lagoon out front stage a sea battle every 1½ hours 4:30pm-midnight (☎ 800-944-7444).

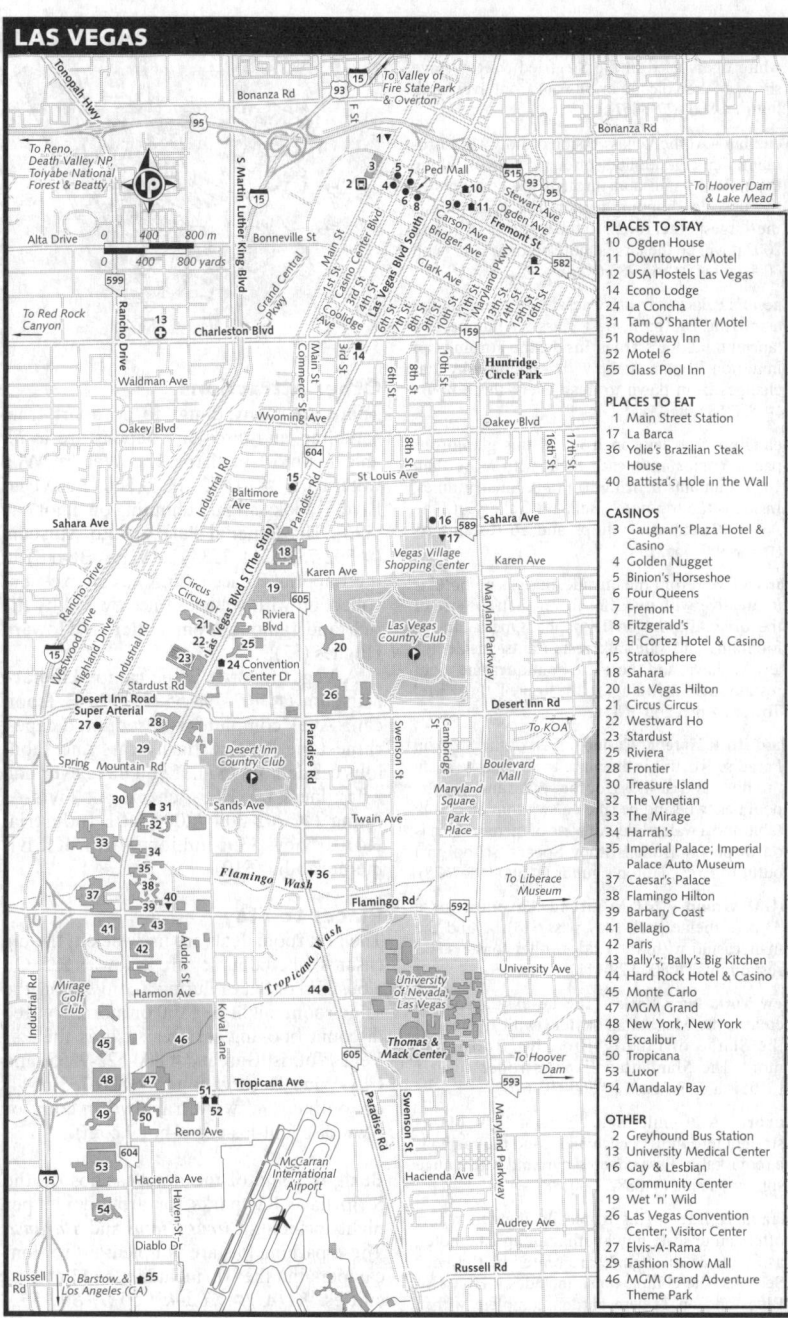

LAS VEGAS

SOUTHWEST

PLACES TO STAY
10 Ogden House
11 Downtowner Motel
12 USA Hostels Las Vegas
14 Econo Lodge
51 La Concha
31 Tam O'Shanter Motel
51 Rodeway Inn
52 Motel 6
55 Glass Pool Inn

PLACES TO EAT
1 Main Street Station
17 La Barca
36 Yolie's Brazilian Steak House
40 Battista's Hole in the Wall

CASINOS
3 Gaughan's Plaza Hotel & Casino
4 Golden Nugget
5 Binion's Horseshoe
6 Four Queens
7 Fremont
8 Fitzgerald's
9 El Cortez Hotel & Casino
15 Stratosphere
18 Sahara
20 Las Vegas Hilton
21 Circus Circus
22 Westward Ho
23 Stardust
25 Riviera
28 Frontier
30 Treasure Island
32 The Venetian
33 The Mirage
34 Harrah's
35 Imperial Palace; Imperial Palace Auto Museum
37 Caesar's Palace
38 Flamingo Hilton
39 Barbary Coast
41 Bellagio
42 Paris
43 Bally's; Bally's Big Kitchen
44 Hard Rock Hotel & Casino
45 Monte Carlo
47 MGM Grand
48 New York, New York
49 Excalibur
50 Tropicana
53 Luxor
54 Mandalay Bay

OTHER
2 Greyhound Bus Station
13 University Medical Center
16 Gay & Lesbian Community Center
19 Wet 'n' Wild
26 Las Vegas Convention Center; Visitor Center
27 Elvis-A-Rama
29 Fashion Show Mall
46 MGM Grand Adventure Theme Park

The Mirage – This casino is a re-created tropical rain forest, complete with a dolphin tank and the white tigers used in the Siegfried & Roy stage show; a fake volcano erupts out front every half hour (☎ 800-627-6667).

Venetian – At the Vegas version of Italy's most romantic city, gondoliers offer rides ($10) along the indoor canal and through the corridors of the upscale shopping center. The hotel boasts the 'largest hotel rooms in the world,' and by late 2002 it will be the largest hotel in the world, with 6000 suites (☎ 888-283-6423).

Caesar's Palace – Stylish Caesar's is entered along a moving footpath, past classic columns and 'ancient' talking statues. Inside, the Forum is an imitation Roman street, with a painted sky that changes from dawn to dusk every three hours (☎ 800-634-6001).

Bellagio – The lake in front of this glamorous palace comes alive each night with more than 1000 fountains dancing to Frank Sinatra tunes. Inside is the top-notch Bellagio Gallery of Fine Art ($12), amazing shops and 16 restaurants (☎ 888-987-6667).

Paris – Even from the outside, this casino/hotel is impressive, with its Eiffel Tower (half the size of the original), Arc de Triomphe, Opera House, fountains and sidewalk restaurants. Inside, it's always dawn, and there are boutiques and eight restaurants, including at the top of the Eiffel Tower (☎ 888-266-5687).

Hard Rock Hotel & Casino – East of the Strip on Paradise Rd, this is the place to see and be seen; this hotel and casino is for the young and hip. The pool has two sand beaches, a swim-up blackjack table and a waterslide. All sorts of memorabilia is on display – from Britney Spears' school girl outfit to Eric Clapton's guitar (☎ 800-693-7625).

MGM Grand – MGM Grand Adventure is a 33-acre theme park (day pass $13) behind the main casino, with water rides, roller coasters and restaurants (☎ 800-929-1111).

New York, New York – The hotel's facade re-creates the Manhattan skyline, with replicas of the Statue of Liberty, Brooklyn Bridge and more. The Manhattan Express roller coaster ($10) is a major rush (☎ 800-693-6763).

Luxor – A 10-mile-high beam of light blazes straight into the sky each night, and the casino is a remarkable glass-covered pyramid with a huge sphinx outside (☎ 888-777-0188).

Mandalay Bay – This tropically themed resort offers an upscale hotel within an upscale hotel, as Floors 35 through 39 are rented by the Four Seasons. The complex also includes a House of Blues and an 11-acre garden complete with a manmade beach (☎ 877-632-7000).

Other Attractions

There are many things to do apart from gambling, and discount coupons are available for most of them. The **Wet 'n' Wild** water park (☎ 702-734-0088, 2601 Las Vegas Blvd S) looks mighty tempting on a hot day ($26). The **Imperial Palace Auto Museum** (☎ 702-731-3311, 3535 Las Vegas Blvd S), at the Imperial Palace casino, has an excellent collection with vehicles once owned by the rich and famous, from Hitler to Howard Hughes ($7).

A Vegas favorite is the campy **Liberace Museum** (☎ 702-798-5595, 1775 E Tropicana Ave), complete with sequined capes, rhinestone jewelry, flashy cars and fabulous candelabra ($7). If you have ever had a fondness for Elvis, check out **Elvis-A-Rama** (☎ 702-309-7200, 3401 Industrial Rd) to view $3½-million worth of Elvis memorabilia ($10).

Places to Stay

The best room deals are midweek at the big casinos, when doubles are as low as $35. On a busy Fri or Sat or during a convention, the same room might be $100 or more. Try free discount booking services such as the Las Vegas Tourist Bureau (☎ 800-522-9555) and City Wide Reservations (☎ 800-733-6644) or online (Ⓦ www.travelworm.com or www.discount-las-vegas-hotel.com).

Budget Some of the hotel/casinos on the Strip have RV parks for around $15 per night, including *Circus Circus* and *Stardust*. These parking lots are not pleasant for tent campers, but they do include use of hotel facilities. *KOA* (☎ 702-451-5527, 800-562-7782, 4315 Boulder Hwy), a few miles south of town, has tent and RV sites ($24 for two people) and a swimming pool.

USA Hostels Las Vegas (☎ *702-385-1150, 1322 Fremont St*) is on the not-so-nice outskirts of downtown, but the facilities, including a pool, jacuzzi and bar, are top-notch and the staff are incredibly accommodating. Dorm beds are $15, singles $35, doubles $45. Call for free pickup from the Greyhound station. *Downtowner Motel* (☎ *702-384-1441, 129 N 8th St*) is not very appealing but has cheap singles/doubles for $39/49. The pleasant but older *El Cortez Hotel & Casino* (☎ *702-385-5200, 800-634-6703, 600 E Fremont St*) charges $20/35 midweek. Budget-friendly casinos include *Circus Circus* (☎ *800-634-3450*), *Stardust* (☎ *800-824-6033*) and *Riviera* (☎ *800-634-6753*).

Mid-Range Steps away from the south end of the Strip, *Rodeway Inn* (☎ *702-795-3311*) and *Motel 6* (☎ *702-798-0728*), both on E Tropicana Ave, are good options with clean rooms for $33/48 singles/doubles. Also on the south end is the *Glass Pool Inn* (☎ *702-739-6636, 4613 Las Vegas Blvd S*), with consistently low-priced rooms ($48/59) and, of course, the infamous 'glass' pool.

Mid-strip, *La Concha* (☎ *800-331-2431, 2955 Las Vegas Blvd S*) is convenient, with rooms at $38 midweek and $68 weekends. *Tam O'Shanter Motel* (☎ *702-735-7331, 3317 Las Vegas Blvd S*) is popular with budget travelers and charges around $45 for doubles.

Downtown, *Gaughan's Plaza Hotel & Casino* (☎ *702-386-2110, 1 Main St*) is right on top of the bus station and has above-average rooms from $40 midweek and $65 weekends.

Top End Even the 'nice' casinos in town have packages – rooms plus dinner shows and discounted meals – so call around. Standard rates are $70 to $95 midweek, $125 and up on the weekends. For the money, the nicest spot on the Strip is *Caesar's Palace* (☎ *800-634-6001*), followed by the *Luxor* (☎ *800-288-1000*) and *MGM Grand* (☎ *800-929-1111*). See Casinos (earlier) for more options.

Places to Eat

The larger casinos have multiple restaurants ranging from moderately priced cafes to top-end gourmet restaurants. The all-you-can-eat buffet, a Las Vegas institution, is where gluttonous gamblers pile plates with wide and heavy loads, only to return later for dessert. The best buffet in town is a subject of debate, but those commonly mentioned include the *Main Street Station* ($14 dinner), *Bally's Big Kitchen* ($16) and the *Palatium Buffet* at Caesar's Palace ($20). The cheapest buffet is at *Circus Circus* ($6/7/8 breakfast/lunch/dinner), and you get what you pay for.

When you need a break from casino life, try *La Barca*(☎ *702-657-9700, 953 E Sahara Ave*), where you'll be served authentic Mexican seafood dishes (from $10) in a festive atmosphere. You'll have a ball at *Battista's Hole in the Wall* (☎ *702-732-1424, 4041 Audrie St*), where for a set price of $17-30, depending on the entrée, you get minestrone or salad, a pasta side, an entrée, a cappuccino and all the house wine you can drink. *Yolie's Brazilian Steak House* (*3900 Paradise Rd*) cooks outstanding grilled meats ($9-15).

Entertainment

An incredible amount of entertainment is offered every night; for listings, get a copy of *What's On* (🖳 www.ilovevegas.com) or *Showbiz.* 'Big-room' casino shows can be either concerts by famous musicians, Broadway musicals or flashy song-and-dance spectacles.

The hottest show in town is Cirque du Soleil's aquatic show, *O* (☎ *888-488-7111*), performed at the Bellagio in and around a 1¹⁄₂-million-gallon pool. Tickets are pricey at $93/121, depending on seats, but since the show is sold out weeks in advance, it gives you time to save up. Also recommended is Cirque du Soleil's *Mystère* (☎ *800-392-1999*), at Treasure Island (from $70), and *Siegfried & Roy* (☎ *800-963-9634*), at the Mirage ($100). For the more budget-conscious, try the Riviera's *Evening at La Cage* (☎ *877-892-7469*), with a cast of over-the-top female impersonators ($30), and the Stratosphere's daytime classic *Viva Las Vegas* ($12, or $14 including buffet).

Getting There & Around

McCarran International Airport (☎ *702-261-5743*) has direct flights from most US cities and a few from Canada and Europe.

Bell Trans (☎ 702-739-7990) and Gray Line (☎ 702-384-1234) both provide airport shuttle service ($3.50-5 per person).

The Greyhound bus station (☎ 702-384-9561), downtown on Main St, has regular buses to/from Los Angeles ($35; 5½ hours) and San Diego ($42; 8½ hours), plus connections to San Francisco via Reno ($70; 14 hours).

Amtrak does not run trains to Las Vegas, although they do offer bus service from Los Angeles ($35).

Local bus service is provided by Citizens Area Transport (CAT; ☎ 702-228-7433); bus No 301 runs up and down the Strip 24 hours a day, all the way to downtown ($1.50).

The Strip Trolley (☎ 702-382-1404) does a loop from Mandalay Bay to the Stratosphere and out to the Las Vegas Hilton every 25 minutes until 2am ($1.50).

Dozens of agencies along the Strip rent cars for $25-45 per day. Try either Budget (☎ 702-736-1212) or Thrifty (☎ 702-896-7600).

AROUND LAS VEGAS
Red Rock Canyon
Only 20 miles west of Vegas, this dramatic valley is noted for the steep Red Rock escarpment, rising 3000 feet on its western edge. A 13-mile, one-way scenic loop starts at the BLM visitor center (☎ 702-363-1921), near Hwy 159. The canyon is especially impressive at sunset and sunrise. Day use is $5. Camping at the Oak Creek site is available year round on a first-come, first-served basis.

Toiyabe National Forest
The Spring Mountains form the western boundary of the Las Vegas Valley, with higher rainfall, lower temperatures and fragrant pine forests. The village of Mt Charleston has a USFS ranger station (☎ 702-872-5486) on Hwy 157, and several hikes, including the demanding 9-mile trail up to Charleston Peak (elevation 11,008 feet), can be accessed from the village. Campgrounds are open mid-May to Oct ($6).

Hoover Dam
The strong and graceful curve of 726-foot Hoover Dam spans a massive ravine and riverbed, its art deco style contrasting superbly with the stark landscape. To some people, Hoover is only a dam, but to many it's the best nongambling attraction in Nevada.

Hoover Dam, a New Deal project completed in 1935 at a cost of $175 million, was built to control floods on the lower Colorado River. The hydroelectricity and water supply were bonuses that enabled Las Vegas to grow. The visitor center (☎ 702-294-3517), 35 miles southeast of Las Vegas on Hwy 93, has interesting exhibits, as well as a great rooftop view of the dam. Tickets cost $4, or you can take one of two highly recommended tours – a 35-minute introductory tour ($10) and an hour-long hardhat tour ($25). Both are offered daily year round. A walk across the dam not only gives great perspectives but also allows you to cross the Nevada-Arizona border, as well as the Pacific/Mountain time zones.

Lake Mead
National Recreation Area
With 500 miles of shoreline, Lake Mead is popular for fishing, boating, swimming, water skiing and even scuba diving. The visitor center (☎ 702-293-8906) is on Hwy 93 about 26 miles from Las Vegas. From there, the scenic **North Shore Rd** winds around the lake, passing several campgrounds.

Just to the south of Hoover Dam on Hwy 163, close to the California-Arizona-Nevada border, **Laughlin** is a booming but tacky resort town with a dozen large casinos/hotels along the west bank of the Colorado River.

Valley of Fire State Park
Near the north end of Lake Mead NRA, easily accessible from Las Vegas, Valley of Fire is a masterpiece of desert scenery, with psychedelically shaped sandstone. Hwy 169 runs through the park ($5), right past the visitor center (☎ 702-397-2088), which has hiking information and excellent exhibits. The winding side road to **White Domes** is especially scenic. The valley is at its most fiery at dawn and dusk, so consider staying overnight in one of the park's two year-round campgrounds ($7).

Overton
More than a thousand years ago, a community of Ancestral Puebloan Indians farmed here, but they mysteriously abandoned their pueblolike structures. Overton's **Lost City**

Museum (☎ 702-397-2193), on Hwy 169, has a collection of artifacts going back 10,000 years and some adobe dwellings reconstructed on original foundations ($2).

WESTERN NEVADA

The western corner of Nevada was the site of the state's first trading post, first farms and the famous Comstock silver lode, which spawned towns, financed the Union side in the Civil War and earned Nevada its statehood. For information about the Nevada side of Lake Tahoe, see the Sierra Nevada section of the California chapter.

Reno

The 'Biggest Little City in the World' is smaller and less glitzy than Las Vegas. Blue-collar Reno and its gritty downtown don't make a sterling first impression, but there are cheap accommodations and gaming tables aplenty, plus easy access to Lake Tahoe and Virginia City.

In the 1850s, travelers on the Humboldt Trail to California needed to cross the Truckee River. Toll bridges, hotels and saloons soon sprang up, followed by a railroad depot that helped Reno cash in on the mining boom. When the mines played out, Reno made an economic virtue of gambling and prostitution, which were suppressed enterprises in increasingly respectable California. Agriculture, light industry and tourism have since helped diversify the economy.

Reno does have historic buildings, such as the 1911 Washoe County Courthouse, 117 S Virginia St, where Clark Gable and Marilyn Monroe met in *The Misfits*. Sadly, however, the city seems increasingly bent on erasing its past. For instance, the beloved Mapes Hotel, Nevada's prototype hotel/casino and once on the National Register of Historic Places, is now a pile of rubble.

Orientation & Information Reno's downtown is north of the Truckee River and south of I-80. Most of the action is along Virginia St, between 1st and 6th Sts.

The visitor center (☎ 800-367-7366) is in the lobby of the National Bowling Stadium (300 N Center St), between 3rd and 4th Sts. With 80 lanes upstairs, it's worth a quick look.

Casinos Many Reno casinos lack flash, though Vegas-style theme palaces are

catching on. Older establishments include **Fitzgeralds**, on N Virginia St, and the **Eldorado**, on 2nd St. **Harrah's** (219 N Center St) aims for a classier crowd, while the **Silver Legacy**, on N Virginia St at W 5th St, shows off with a 19th-century streetscape plus sound-and-light shows inside a 120-foot dome. **Circus Circus** (500 N Virginia St) has free circus acts and a game-filled midway.

Away from downtown are the swank **Peppermill** (2707 S Virginia St); the grass-hut-themed **Atlantis** (3800 S Virginia St); the huge **Reno Hilton**, on E 2nd St near Hwy 395; and **John Ascuaga's Nugget**, off I-80 in nearby Sparks.

Museums Downtown, at the corner of Lake and Mill Sts, the **National Automobile Museum** (☎ 775-333-9300) has one-of-a-kind vehicles, including James Dean's 1949 Mercury and a 1938 Phantom Corsair ($7.50). The **Nevada Historical Society Museum** (☎ 775-688-1190), off N Virginia St on the University of Nevada campus, has a good account of the region's indigenous cultures ($2). **Fleischmann Planetarium** (☎ 775-784-4811), on N Virginia St directly across from the historical museum, has fun science exhibits (free admission) and plays nature films on a massive 70mm screen ($7).

Places to Stay The casinos are cheapest midweek, with doubles beginning around $35. Phone ahead: Rooms can fill up fast, and you sometimes get a better rate if you do. The hotel referral hotline at the visitor center (☎ 800-367-7366) is useful on weekends and during special events, when prices rise considerably and rooms are hard to find.

The following are listed roughly in order from cheapest ($35 midweek at the Sundowner) to most expensive ($69 midweek, from $200 weekends at the Hilton): *Sundowner* (☎ 775-786-7050, 450 N Arlington St), *Fitzgeralds* (☎ 775-785-3300, 800-648-5022, 255 N Virginia St), *Circus Circus* (☎ 775-329-0711, 500 N Sierra St), *Peppermill* (☎ 775-826-2121, 2707 S Virginia St) and *Reno Hilton* (☎ 775-789-2000, 800-648-5080, 2500 E 2nd St).

Cheap motels can be found along W 4th and E 5th Sts. The 1931 art deco *El Cortez* (☎ 775-322-9161, 239 W 2nd St) was once the tallest building in town. Rooms are adequate, and rates run $26-34. *Seasons Inn (☎ 800-322-8588, 495 West St)* has clean rooms that are fairly quiet for Reno (singles $38 midweek, $99 Sat).

Places to Eat The casinos' all-you-can-eat buffets are worth it if you're seriously hungry. The weekday brunch at *Harrah's* is $8 and includes fresh fruit and salads; dinner is $10. *Brew Brothers*, in the Eldorado, has tasty late-night pizzas ($7) and excellent microbrews ($3). Reno's cheapest meal is at the *Cal Neva*, where eggs and bacon are only 99¢ from 10pm-8am ($1.74 otherwise).

For healthier fare, abandon the casinos for the quirky *Deux Gros Nez (349 California Ave)*, behind the Cheese Board, serving excellent smoothies, sandwiches and pasta dinners ($3-7). Or try a taste of Nevada's Basque culture at *Louis' Basque Corner (301 E 4th St)*, where $17 gets you a complete meal.

Getting There & Around Reno-Tahoe International Airport (☎ 775-328-6499) is a few miles southeast of downtown. The Greyhound station (☎ 775-322-2970), near W 1st St and Arlington Ave, has frequent buses to San Francisco ($37), Los Angeles ($61), and Las Vegas ($72). The Amtrak station (☎ 775-329-8638, 800-872-7245), on Commercial Row, has daily service to Sacramento ($53) and San Francisco ($60).

The RTC Citifare bus system (☎ 775-348-7433) covers most of the metropolitan area ($1.25). The main transfer station is at E 4th and Center Sts. Gray Line (☎ 775-331-1147) runs shuttles to Lake Tahoe ski areas; package prices (call for the latest) include lift tickets.

Pyramid Lake
Beautiful blue Pyramid Lake is 25 miles north of Reno on the Paiute Indian Reservation. Permits ($5/6 night camping/day fishing) and supplies are available at the ranger station (☎ 775-476-1155), on Hwy 445 in Sutcliffe. The shores are lined with beaches, and there are also interesting tufa formations (a porous rock formed by water deposits). Anaho Island, near the eastern shore, is a bird sanctuary for the American white pelican.

Carson City
Nevada's sleepy state capital has tree-lined streets, some handsome old buildings and a couple worthwhile museums.

Carson City was named after the Carson River, which itself was named after frontiersman Kit Carson. It gained official recognition in 1861 as the capital of the Nevada Territory, and again in 1864 as capital of the newly created state of Nevada. With the discovery of gold and silver in nearby hills, Carson City prospered as a railway depot and service center for the mines.

Along Hwy 395 (Carson St), you'll find motels, restaurants and tired-looking casinos. The visitors bureau (☎ 775-882-1565), a mile south of downtown at 1900 S Carson St, gives out a map with historical walking and driving tours. For hiking and camping information, stop by the USFS station at 1536 S Carson St.

The **Nevada State Capitol**, downtown at 101 N Carson St, was completed in 1871 with local sandstone from a prison-run quarry. There's an interesting free museum on the 2nd floor. Housed inside the 1869 US Mint building, the excellent **Nevada State Museum** (☎ 775-687-4810, 600 N Carson St) has dioramas showing Indian life and, in the basement, a re-created gold mine ($3).

Camping is available at *Washoe Lake State Park (☎ 775-687-4319)*, off Hwy 395, a few miles north of Carson City ($13).

On downtown's northern fringe, you can't miss the neon cowboy outside the *Frontier Motel (☎ 775-882-1377, 1718 N Carson St)*. Doubles run $35-69. The respectable *Desert Hills Motel (☎ 775-882-1932, 800-652-7785, 1010 S Carson St)* charges from $39.

Downstairs from the 1862 St Charles Hotel, the handsome *Cafe Del Rio (302 S Carson St)* serves Mexican meals for under $10. Bargain hunters will enjoy the $5 prime rib dinner at the *Carson Nugget (507 N Carson St)*.

Greyhound buses (☎ 775-882-3375) stop at the Frontier Motel on the way to/from Reno ($12), Los Angeles ($77) and Las Vegas ($72).

Virginia City
As early as the 1860s, this mining boomtown had gas lines, a sewer system, the West Coast's first elevator and a popula-

tion of 15,000 (including newspaperman Samuel Clemens, alias Mark Twain). A mining technique developed here, square-set timbering, kept the 750 miles of tunnels from collapsing. Population peaked at 30,000 in 1875, when a fire swept through and destroyed more than 2000 buildings. Virginia City (named after miner James 'Old Virginny' Finney) was miraculously rebuilt within a year at an estimated cost of $125 million, but the city never again achieved its former rough-and-tumble glory.

Today the town is a National Historic Landmark, with a main street of Victorian buildings, wooden sidewalks and some pretty hokey 'museums.' The main drag is C St, with the chamber of commerce (☎ 775-847-0311) housed in a yellow railroad car. The staff distributes lodging lists and the informative *Guide to Virginia City* and sells tickets for a 35-minute ride on the **Virginia & Truckee Railroad** ($5.50; closed in winter). The smart and sassy *Comstock Chronicle*, a local weekly, also publishes a visitors guide during the summer.

Many of the town's attractions are seriously silly, though some are true gems, such as the **Fourth Ward School** (☎ 775-847-0975, 537 C St), a monumental four-story building that once housed 1025 students. The quirky **Way It Was Museum**, at the north end of C St, gives some good background on mining the lode ($2.50), as does the half-hour tour of the **Chollar Mine** (☎ 775-847-0155), at the south end of F St ($5; closed in winter). To see how the mining elite lived, stop by the Mackay Mansion, on D St, and The Castle, on B St. Dozens of played-out miners are buried at the picturesque **Silver Terrace Cemetery**, off Carson St.

While not as cheap, Virginia City is a more peaceful and pleasant place to spend the night than Carson City or Reno. *Gold Hill Hotel* (☎ 775-847-0111), south of town on Hwy 342, has beautiful old rooms beginning at $45 a double. The lavender-colored *Crooked House* (☎ 775-847-4447, 800-340-6353, 8 F St) is another attractive choice (rooms $75-125, including breakfast).

For breakfast, the *Miner Diner* (465 C St) has tasty baked goods. Noodle and rice plates at the *Mandarin Garden* (30 B St) are affordable and delicious, and the restaurant is vegetarian friendly.

The Comstock Lode

In 1859 two Irish prospectors discovered gold in Six-Mile Canyon and followed the lode up to what is now the north end of C St in Virginia City. Another prospector, Henry Comstock, fraudulently claimed that the dig was on his land and tricked the Irishmen into giving him a piece of their pay dirt.

It is appropriate that the Comstock Lode was named after a con man, for though it yielded perhaps $400 million in precious metals, several times this amount was traded in mining stocks by speculators in San Francisco. The Comstock's patchwork of overlapping lots, providing access to a labyrinth of shafts that connected more than 750 miles of tunnels, was further contested by crooked lawyers in corrupt courts. Only when Nevada was admitted to the Union in 1864 – thanks partly to President Abraham Lincoln's hope that Comstock ore would help keep the Union solvent – were federal judges able to come in and sort out the mess.

If you're thirsty, C St offers plenty of choices. The crusty **Red Dog Saloon** once hosted psychedelic-rock pioneers like the Charlatans, Jefferson Airplane and the Grateful Dead in 1965, and the **Delta Saloon** is where you can literally 'read the walls,' which are covered with articles and photographs.

NEVADA GREAT BASIN

Most travelers pass through Nevada on one of several desert highways, all of which have interesting stops and detours to remote areas.

Along Interstate 80

The old fur trappers' route followed the Humboldt River from northeast Nevada to Lovelock, near Reno. The same route was used by the early Emigrant Trail, the Central Pacific Railroad, Hwy 40 ('the Victory Hwy') and I-80.

Lovelock has motels, but most people press on to Reno or **Winnemucca**. Here, there's a great detour 50 miles north to the Santa Rosa Mountains; for information, stop by the USFS Santa Rosa ranger station (☎ 775-623-5025 ext 5, 1200 E Winnemucca Blvd). Southwest of Winnemucca is the folk-art sculpture garden **Thunder Mountain**, directly off I-80 in Imlay. Built by WWII veteran Chief Rolling Mountain Thunder as a monument to the injustices against Native Americans, it has free self-guided tours and is full of spooky figures and curious structures.

In 1861 pioneers battled Shoshone Indians in the area around **Battle Mountain**. The culture of the cowboy and the American West is most diligently cultivated in **Elko**, a better stop. Northeastern Nevada Museum (☎ 775-738-3418, 1515 Idaho St) has excellent displays on pioneer life, Basque settlers and modern mining technology ($5). The Western Folklife Center (☎ 775-738-7508, 501 Railroad St) organizes art and history exhibits and the annual Cowboy Poetry Gathering each January. Motels on Idaho St, east of the town center, include *Motel 6 (☎ 775-738-4337)*, charging $42-46, and the cheaper *Elko Motel (☎ 775-738-4433)*, charging $30.

For information about the Elko backcountry, visit the USFS office (☎ 775-738-5171, 976 Mountain City Hwy). North of Elko are old mining towns like Jarbridge and Tuscarora. To the south, the **Ruby Mountains** are a superbly rugged range. The picture-perfect village of **Lamoille** has food and lodging and one of the most-photographed rural churches in the USA.

Along Highway 50

'The loneliest road in America' crosses picturesque Great Basin terrain – desert mountains and wide, see-for-miles valleys – and towns are few. Once part of Lincoln Hwy, lonesome Hwy 50 follows the route of the Overland Stagecoach, the Pony Express and the first transcontinental telegraph line.

Fallon is an agricultural and military town, home to a naval air base where top gunners streak through the skies. Fallon's other charms include a good county museum (☎ 775-423-3677, 1050 S Maine St) and a few motels, such as the *Lariat (☎ 775-423-3181, 850 W Williams St)*, where doubles are $38. Three miles west on Hwy 50 is *Bob's Root Beer*, a vintage drive-in with tasty root-beer floats.

Farther east at **Grimes Point Archaeological Area** are dozens of boulders covered in petroglyphs. The next substantial town is **Austin**, rundown since its 1880s heyday. The mountainous area, though, is beautiful, and Austin's USFS office (☎ 775-964-2671) can recommend good hiking and driving loops. Mountain biking is also popular, and the friendly shop Tyrannosaurus-Rex (☎ 775-964-1212, 270 Maine St), just east of town, has maps, frozen yogurt and bikes for rent ($25 a day).

To the southwest of Austin, **Berlin-Ichthyosaur State Park** (☎ 775-964-2440) features the ghost town of Berlin and the fossil remains of half a dozen ichthyosaurs (carnivorous marine reptiles that lived here 225 million years ago). Daily fossil tours are offered in summer ($2), and there's a good year-round campground ($10).

During the late 19th century, $40-million worth of silver was extracted from the hills near **Eureka**. The town is now fairly well preserved, possessing a handsome courthouse, a newspaper museum (☎ 775-237-5484), a beautifully restored 1880 opera house and a few well-kept motels.

Larger **Ely**, another silver- and copper-mining town, had its own railroad; today the Nevada Northern Railway Museum (☎ 775-289-2085, 1100 Ave A) includes the old station, depot and workshops ($3; closed in winter). Downtown also has beautiful historic murals and great old neon signs, along with some decent motels.

Near the Nevada-Utah border is the awesome, uncrowded **Great Basin National Park**. It encompasses 13,063-foot Wheeler Peak, rising abruptly from the desert. Hiking trails near the summit take in superb country with glacial lakes, ancient bristlecone pines and even a permanent ice field. The park visitor center (☎ 775-234-7331) arranges guided tours of **Lehman Caves** ($2-8), which are richly decorated with rare limestone formations. There are four developed campgrounds within the park ($10), and one is open year round.

Nearby **Baker** has a couple motels and restaurants.

Along Highway 95

Hwy 95 goes roughly north-south through the western part of the state via Winnemucca, Hawthorne, Tonopah and Goldfield.

The southern section of Hwy 95 is starkly scenic as it passes the Nevada Test Site (where more than 720 nuclear weapons were exploded in the 1950s). Side roads head west to California and Death Valley. In Beatty, the *HI Happy Burro Hostel (☎ 775-553-9130)* has beds for $18.

Along Highways 375 & 93

Hwy 375, dubbed the 'Extraterrestrial Hwy,' intersects Hwy 93 near top-secret **Area 51**, part of Nellis Air Force Base and a supposed holding area for captured UFOs. In the tiny town of **Rachel**, on Hwy 375, *Little A-le Inn (☎ 775-729-2515)* accommodates earthlings and aliens alike (doubles $40) and sells extraterrestrial souvenirs. In a nearby trailer, the nongovernment **Area 51 Research Center** (☎ 775-729-2648) has books, maps, and photographic displays.

Continuing east, Hwy 93 passes through a gorgeous Joshua tree grove before arriving in **Caliente,** a former railroad town with a mission-style 1923 depot. The Intellectual Cowboy Bookstore (☎ 775-726-3813) offers tourist information, and the shady *Caliente Hot Springs Motel (☎ 888-726-3777)* has rooms for $45. Area attractions include the Rainbow Canyon scenic drive and nearby **Cathedral Gorge State Park**, with campsites amidst badlands-style cliffs.

Two dozen miles north is **Pioche**, an attractive hillside mining town overlooking beautiful Lake Valley. The Million Dollar Courthouse and Lincoln County Historical Museum are both worth exploring, and if you need somewhere to lay your hat, the *Overland Hotel & Saloon (☎ 775-962-5895)* has rooms for $39.

SOUTHWEST

California

California

California is like a country in itself. It is home to top-notch cities and offers amazing and diverse landscape in every direction. In one day you can travel from the beautiful pine forests of the Sierra Nevada to palm-lined beaches or desert dunes. Of course, you need more than a day to discover this awe-inspiring state. Even longtime Californians find they don't have enough time to explore everything their state has to offer. After all, California is larger than Britain and has enough road mileage to circle the globe – three times.

Most people have Hollywood-inspired visions of California – the surfers, Beverly Hills mansions, Deadhead hippies, freeways and fancy cars can look very familiar. Many travelers limit themselves to San Francisco, LA and the most famous national parks, but that barely scratches the surface. There's another California happening at 24-hour truck stops on I-5, on parched salt flats and anywhere you see a sign warning 'Next Gas 112 Miles.' Go ahead: Do Disneyland and Alcatraz, ride a cable car, and lounge on a beach, but don't forget about the block-long towns, rolling green hills and wide open spaces beyond the tourist landmarks.

History

Prehistory Stone tools found at sites in the Bakersfield area have been dated to around 10,000 BC, which is about the same period that the early stone spear points discovered in Clovis, New Mexico, were produced. Archaeological evidence, combined with accounts from early European visitors, suggests that California was home to 300,000 indigenous people, with more than 20 language groups and 100 dialects. Conflict between the groups was almost nonexistent, and they had no class of warriors and no tradition of warfare – at least until the Europeans arrived.

European Discovery Following their conquest of Mexico in the early 1500s, the Spanish began exploring the limits of their new empire. The southern tip of California was settled in 1535, but it was not until 1539 that an exploration by Francisco de Ulloa

Highlights

- Venice Beach, LA – kick back, roll on, chill out at SoCal central
- Disneyland – the original theme park, where the mouse still delivers
- Golden Gate Bridge – spectacular sculptural symbol of stylish San Francisco
- San Francisco's Halloween and Gay Pride parades – dress for excess
- Tall timber – superb sequoias and rad redwoods
- Big Sur – gorgeous cliffside area along Hwy 1
- Joshua Tree – skull-shaped rocks and millions of unique yuccas
- Yosemite – walk away from four million tourists to see the sublime Sierra
- Death Valley – a desert to die for

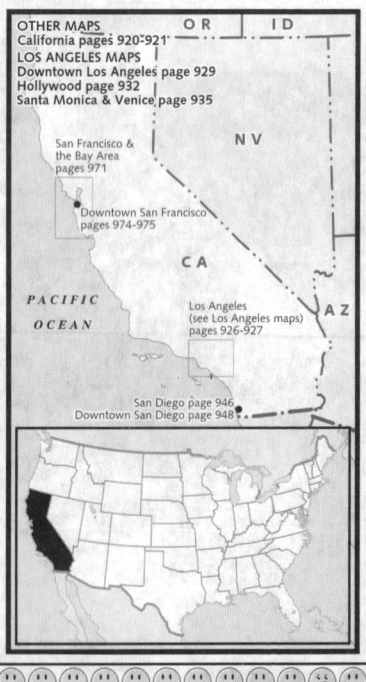

OTHER MAPS
California pages 920-921
LOS ANGELES MAPS
Downtown Los Angeles page 929
Hollywood page 932
Santa Monica & Venice page 935

San Francisco & the Bay Area pages 971

Downtown San Francisco pages 974-975

Los Angeles (see Los Angeles maps) pages 926-927

San Diego page 946
Downtown San Diego page 948

established that it was a peninsula rather than an island. The peninsula became known as Baja (Lower) California, and the coast to the north was called Alta (Upper) California.

In the 1700s, as Russian ships were sailing south to California's coast in search of sea otter pelts and British trappers and explorers were spreading throughout the West, the Spanish government decided it was time for a permanent settlement. Padre Junípero Serra established a mission in San Diego, while Gaspar de Portolá continued north with instructions to form a second outpost at Monterey. Another group came overland from Sonora, led by Juan Bautista de Anza. This group settled on the San Francisco peninsula in 1776 and named the place Yerba Buena. Other civilian settlements were later established at San Jose (1777) and Los Angeles (1781).

Bear Flag Republic When Mexico won independence from Spain in 1821, the new government regarded the church with mistrust and sought ways to make California a profitable possession. When frontiersman Jedediah Smith turned up in San Diego in 1827, the Mexican authorities were alarmed to discover the route from the east was not impassable. Another frontiersman, Kit Carson, pioneered an immigrant route across the Sierra Nevada to Los Angeles. While the USA made proposals to buy the territory from Mexico, settlers in northern California plotted a more direct approach: Rebels seized the town of Sonoma, hoisted an improvised flag depicting a crudely drawn bear and proclaimed California the 'Bear Flag Republic.' It was one of the shortest-lived republics in history, but the bear and the words 'California Republic' still survive on the state flag.

Mexican-American War & Statehood In May of 1846 the USA declared war on Mexico, resulting in the 1848 Treaty of Guadalupe Hidalgo, which turned over California to the USA, along with most of New Mexico and Arizona. By coincidence, gold was discovered in northern California almost simultaneously. In 1848 and '49, more than 90,000 people from other parts of the country and the world rushed to California. The state population boomed by

California

Nickname: Golden State, Bear Flag Republic

Population: 33,871,000 (1st)

Area: 163,710 sq miles (3rd)

Admitted to Union: September 9, 1850 (31st)

Capital city: Sacramento (population 406,900)

Other cities: Los Angeles (3,820,000), San Diego (1,255,400), San Francisco (777,000)

Birthplace of: writer John Steinbeck (1902–68), photographer Ansel Adams (1902–84), chef Julia Child (b 1912), pianist-composer Dave Brubeck (b 1920), filmmaker George Lucas (b 1944)

Famous for: Disneyland, earthquakes, *Baywatch*, hippies, skateboards, Silicon Valley, self-actualization therapy

565%. San Francisco became a hotbed of gambling, prostitution and chicanery. In 1850, California gained admittance to the USA as a non-slave state.

Railroad building was a mania in the USA during the mid-19th century. The track going east from Sacramento was the work of the Central Pacific Railroad and thousands of Chinese laborers. The new railroad meant that the trip from New York to San Francisco could be done in four or five comfortable days, rather than two arduous months.

20th Century The big San Francisco earthquake and fire of 1906 destroyed most of California's largest and wealthiest city, but it was barely a hiccup in the state's ongoing development – population increased by 60% in the decade to 1910.

WWII had a major impact on California, mainly from the influx of military workers and the development of new industries. Anti-Asian sentiments resurfaced, and numerous Japanese Americans were interned. Mexicans came to the state to fill labor shortages. Many of the service people who passed through California liked the place so much that they returned to settle after the war. In the 1940s the population grew by 53%; in the '50s, by another 49%.

CALIFORNIA

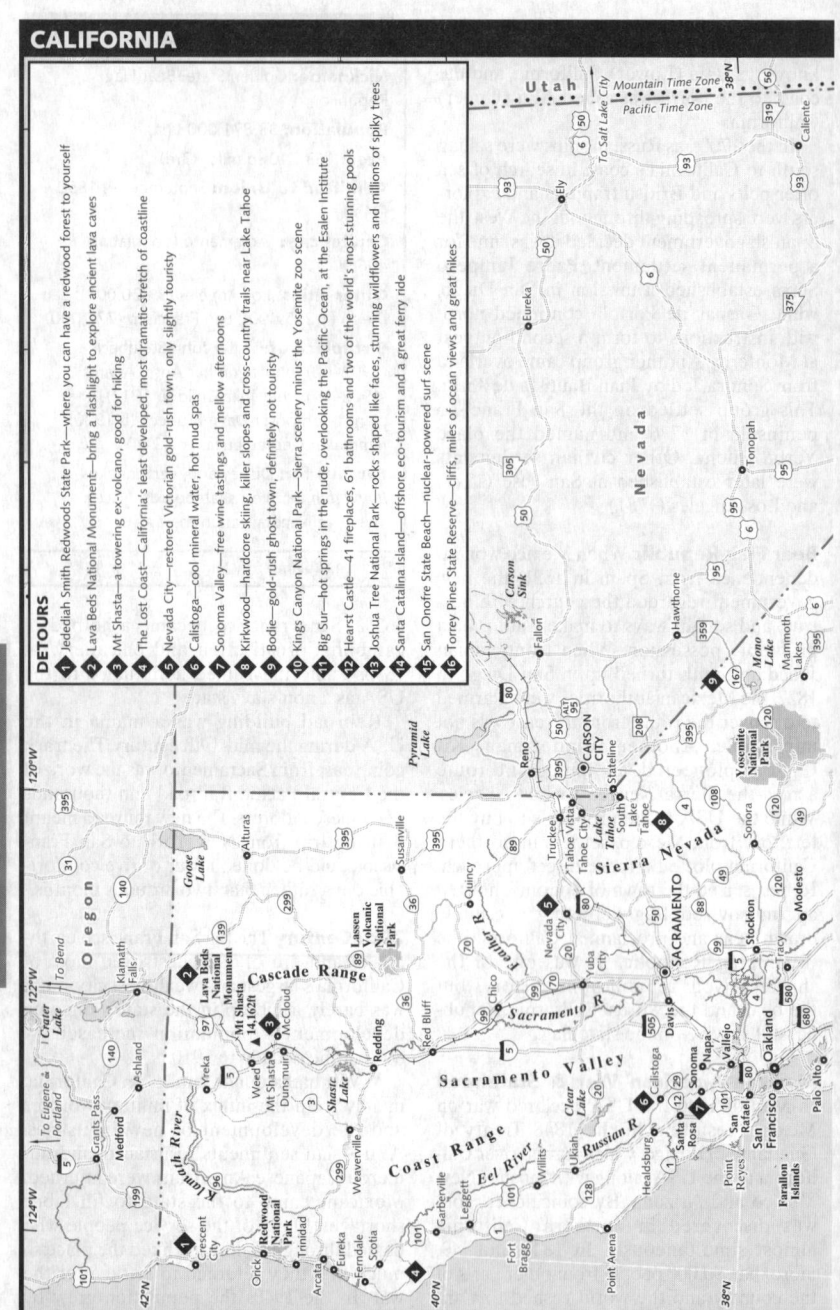

DETOURS

1. Jedediah Smith Redwoods State Park—where you can have a redwood forest to yourself
2. Lava Beds National Monument—bring a flashlight to explore ancient lava caves
3. Mt Shasta—a towering ex-volcano, good for hiking
4. The Lost Coast—California's least developed, most dramatic stretch of coastline
5. Nevada City—restored Victorian gold-rush town, only slightly touristy
6. Calistoga—cool mineral water, hot mud spas
7. Sonoma Valley—free wine tastings and mellow afternoons
8. Kirkwood—hardcore skiing, killer slopes and cross-country trails near Lake Tahoe
9. Bodie—gold-rush ghost town, definitely not touristy
10. Kings Canyon National Park—Sierra scenery minus the Yosemite zoo scene
11. Big Sur—hot springs in the nude, overlooking the Pacific Ocean, at the Esalen Institute
12. Hearst Castle—41 fireplaces, 61 bathrooms and two of the world's most stunning pools
13. Joshua Tree National Park—rocks shaped like faces, stunning wildflowers and millions of spiky trees
14. Santa Catalina Island—offshore eco-tourism and a great ferry ride
15. San Onofre State Beach—nuclear-powered surf scene
16. Torrey Pines State Reserve—cliffs, miles of ocean views and great hikes

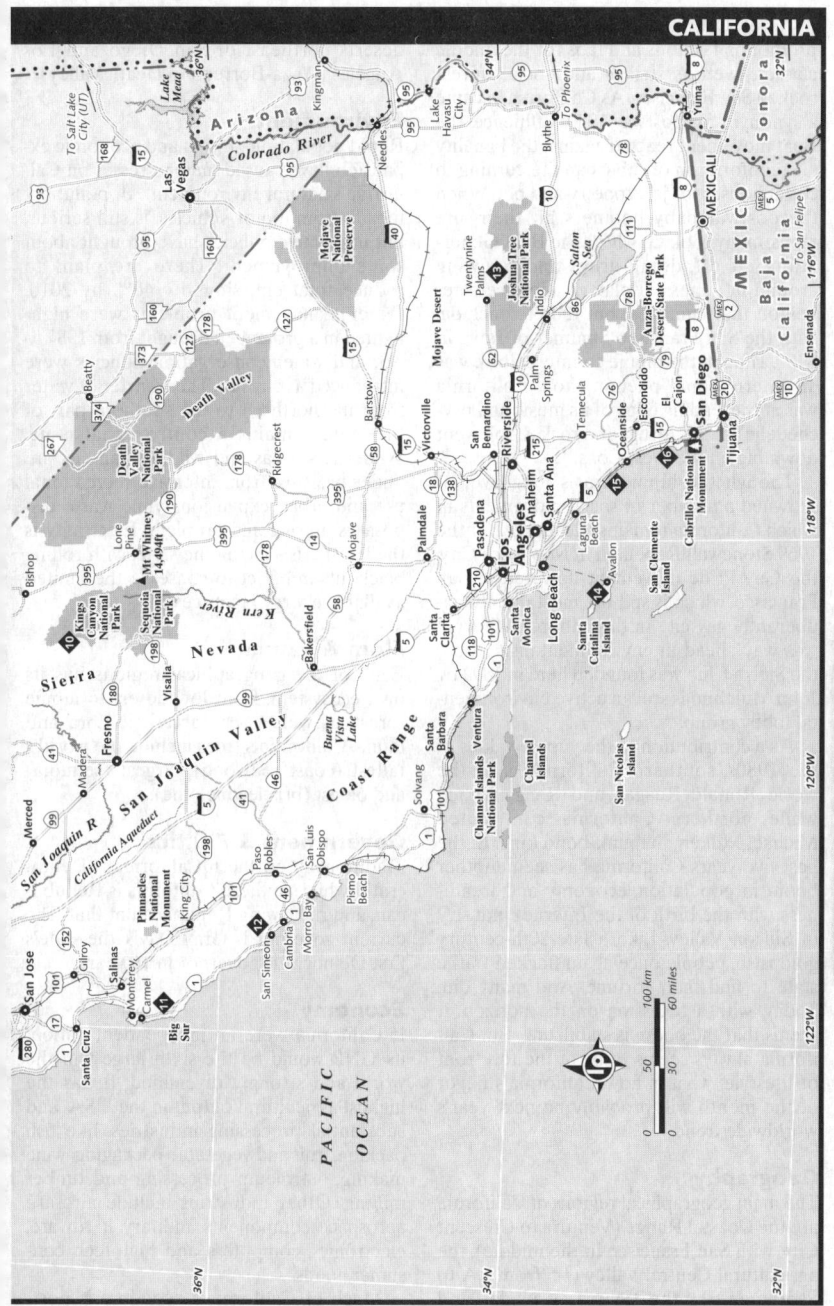

CALIFORNIA

As early as the 1930s, Hollywood was promoting fashions and fads for the middle classes, even as strikes and social unrest rocked San Francisco. As California became a synonym for postwar 1950s affluence, the Beat movement reacted against the banality and conformism of suburban life, turning to coffeehouses for jazz, poetry and pot. When the postwar baby boomers hit their late teens, many took up where the Beat Generation left off, doing drugs and screwing around in a mass display of adolescent rebellion that climaxed, but didn't conclude, with the San Francisco Summer of Love in 1967. Though the hippie counterculture was an international phenomenon, California was at the leading edge of its music and psychedelic art. Sex, drugs and rock & roll went down big on the West Coast.

Though the hippie era is long over, it spawned a number of social movements in which California remains a leader. After the 1969 Stonewall Rebellion in New York City, the Gay Pride movement flowered in San Francisco, which is still the most openly, exuberantly gay city in the nation. California was way ahead in environmentalism, too – the Sierra Club was founded here in 1892 by John Muir and is still an active environmental lobby group.

As a contribution to the yuppie values of the 1980s, southern California gave the world Ronald Reagan and Reaganomics, while northern California contributed Michael Milken, the junk-bond king. In the past five years California has seen another boom in population, economy and trendiness with the birth of the Internet industry in Silicon Valley. Like a late-20th-century gold rush, people once again flocked to the state to find their fortune. And many did. Today, with a recession on the horizon, it seems that the boom is stabilizing. But California always seems to be at the forefront of lifestyle; what is now California's flavor of the month will probably be next year's worldwide trend.

Geography

The main geographical regions of California are the Coastal Range (Ventura to Crescent City, with San Francisco in the middle), the agricultural Central Valley (I-5 from LA to Sacramento), the Sierra Nevada and Cascade mountain ranges (Bakersfield to the California-Oregon border) and the vast deserts northeast of San Diego and Los Angeles (Anza-Borrego to Death Valley).

Environment

Rapid population growth and economic expansion have caused major stresses on California's natural environment. Air pollution, mostly from motor vehicles, is still serious, but innovative policies have brought about some improvement. There are plans to reduce total emissions by 40% by 2010. Water management problems were highlighted in a prolonged drought from 1987 to '93, and water conservation policies were introduced as a result. The transfer of water from the northern to the southern part of the state remains a controversial issue. Wilderness areas and wildlife habitats are under pressure from intensive recreational use and urban expansion, while waste disposal is an ongoing problem. Electricity is the latest crisis facing the state, with rolling blackouts in effect to conserve the limited available energy resources.

Flora & Fauna

Each of the geographical regions has its own ecosystem, from low desert to alpine forest, as well as characteristic flora and fauna. California's trees include the world's tallest (coast redwood), largest (sequoia) and oldest (bristlecone pine).

Government & Politics

Traditionally, northern California is Democratic, while southern California is Republican, and right-wing Republican at that. The current governor is Gray Davis, the state's first Democratic governor in 16 years.

Economy

If California were an independent nation, its GNP would be the sixth largest in the world and strongly diversified. It has the highest agricultural output in the USA, and substantial processing industries, like fish packing, fruit and vegetable packaging, wine making, petroleum processing and timber milling. Other industries include aircraft, aerospace components, military hardware, electronics, computers and high-tech consumer goods.

Much of California's economy is postindustrial, with banking, finance, education,

CALIFORNIA

research and development, computer software, TV, movies, tourism and corporate services all being major money spinners. Though the state was founded on mining, this is now of minor importance.

Population & People

California is the most populous state in the USA, with a population of 33,871,000 in 2000 comprising about 10% of the nation's total population. The people are about 47% white, 32% Hispanic, 11% Asian and Pacific Islander, 7% black and 1% Native American. More than 20% of those living in California are foreign-born.

Arts

There are identifiably Californian trends in music, literature and visual arts, though they are often difficult to distinguish from national and international developments. Movies and TV shows are the state's most characteristic art forms and also its most conspicuous exports. Much of California's self-image and international identity has been defined on the screen, so pretrip research viewing could include *San Francisco* (1936), *Citizen Kane* (1941), *Vertigo* (1958), *The Graduate* (1967), *Harold & Maude* (1971), *American Graffiti* (1973), *Chinatown* (1974), *Valley Girl* (1983), *LA Story* (1991), *Tales of the City* (1993), *Swingers* (1996) and *LA Confidential* (1997).

Also distinctively Californian are the Spanish Revival and Mission styles of architecture. Though very few buildings from the state's Spanish-Mexican era remain, these styles were romantically revived during the early 1900s. Following the 1849 gold rush, grand Victorian mansions were constructed throughout California, especially in San Francisco and along the north coast.

Religion

Californians are 70% Christian, 5% Jewish, and 7% 'other faiths,' including Muslim, Hindu, Buddhist, Sikh and Baha'i. California is also home to a number of unique religious practices, from gay churches and faith healers to utopian communities and self-realization gurus.

Information

The California Office of Tourism (☎ 916-322-2881, 800-862-2543, ⓦ www.gocalif.ca.gov, 1011 10th St, Sacramento, CA 95814) will send out a wad of tourist brochures and maps. The state sales tax is around 7% or 8%, depending on the county. For statewide highway conditions, call ☎ 916-445-7623 or 800-427-7623.

Because of the rapidly increasing use of available telephone lines, California is adding new area codes (the first three digits of each phone number) on an almost monthly basis. If you have problems calling a telephone number, call Pacific Bell information (☎ 800-310-2355, ⓦ www.pacbell.com/about-pb/areacode) to find out if the area code has been changed.

When to Go

California is a large state, so it's best to consider the weather conditions of the particular region you are planning to visit. The best time to visit northern California, especially San Francisco, is in September or October when the days are warm and most of the summer fog has dissipated. The mountain regions are wonderful both in the summer and in the winter, although many parts become inaccessible in the winter months due to large amounts of snow. The deserts are best visited in early spring, when the wildflowers are blooming and before the stifling heat becomes unbearable. Southern California is pleasant year round, but the best months for outdoor and beach activities are May to October.

Accommodations

California has a full range of accommodations, with plenty of cheap motels along the highways. For low-budget backpackers, it has a number of HI and independent hostels and a plethora of camping options. Call ParkNet (☎ 800-444-7275, ⓦ www.reserveamerica.com) to reserve space at any California state park or the National Park Service (☎ 800-365-2267, ⓦ reservations.nps.gov) for national parks.

Activities

There are dozens of state and national parks in California offering excellent hiking. Joshua Tree, Anza Borrego and Death Valley encompass dramatic deserts; Kings Canyon, Sequoia and foggy Redwood are tree-clad mountain retreats; and Yosemite is an all-around wonderland, with lakes, granite peaks and alpine meadows. The spectacular 2638-mile Pacific Crest Trail passes through the length of the state and on to Oregon and Washington.

The state's current mountain-biking mecca is Mammoth Mountain, though Marin County, just north of San Francisco, is right up there too. In winter Mammoth and the resorts around Lake Tahoe offer good skiing and snowboarding. There are great surf beaches all along the coast, but the water is usually cold (wear a wet suit). The best sites for scuba diving are Monterey, Catalina Island and La Jolla.

Getting There & Around

Air Los Angeles and San Francisco are major international airports and important regional air hubs. Within the state, there are a number of smaller airports, including Sacramento, Oakland, San Jose, Burbank, Ontario, Orange County and San Diego.

Bus The state's cities and major towns are served by Greyhound (☎ 800-231-2222). A more interesting – and cheaper – option for the open-minded is Green Tortoise (☎ 415-956-7500, 800-867-8647, Ⓦ www .greentortoise.com). It operates buses with sleeping bunks to cities in and around California as well as to national parks.

Train There are four main Amtrak (☎ 800-872-7245, Ⓦ www.amtrak.com) routes connecting California with the rest of the USA:

California Zephyr – daily service between Chicago and San Francisco (Emeryville), with stops in Denver, Colorado; Salt Lake City, Utah; and Reno, Nevada

Coast Starlight – daily service along the West Coast, from Seattle, Washington, to San Diego, via Portland, Oregon; Sacramento; Oakland; Santa Barbara; and Los Angeles

Southwest Chief – daily service between Chicago and Los Angeles via Kansas City, Missouri; Albuquerque, New Mexico; and Flagstaff, Arizona

Sunset Limited – service three times a week between Jacksonville, Florida, and Los Angeles, via New Orleans, Louisiana; San Antonio, Texas; and Tucson, Arizona

Within the state, useful rail routes include the *San Diegan,* which links San Diego and Los Angeles, continuing on to San Luis Obispo; the *Capitol Corridor,* between San Jose and Reno; and the *San Joaquin,* connecting the Bay Area to Bakersfield and southern California.

Car & Motorcycle Los Angeles, San Diego and San Francisco are probably the best places to rent a car, with many national and local operators. See those cities' sections, later, for details.

Los Angeles

So maybe you *think* you hate LA. Maybe you crack jokes about '40 suburbs in search of a city' and about plastic people living shallow *Baywatch* lives. Perhaps there's even an element of truth to that. But what makes LA so fascinating is its wealth of human experience, its near-utopian mosaic of cultures living side by side in relative peace, its beautiful setting by the sea and framed by mountains. Say what you like, but LA is a true survivor. Despite devastating earthquakes and brush fires, despite smog and jam-packed freeways, despite race riots and crimes of passion that make soap operas look maudlin, LA continues to grow, and even flourish.

It doesn't matter whether you dread spending a single day in LA, or can't wait to meet a real Hollywood star or muscle-bound surfer. LA is the West Coast's busiest travel hub, and it's worth spending a few nights in the City of Angels.

There are hundreds of things to see and do here – that's the good news. The bad news is that LA can, at first glance, be confusing, even intimidating, because of its size and sprawl. LA is not a single city with a well-defined center, but an urban patchwork of 88 cities, of which the City of Los Angeles itself is just one. Others include Santa Monica, Pasadena, Beverly Hills and Long Beach – all independent cities with their own identities. Each one of these makes for a good base from which to explore LA, the most exciting of urban areas.

You'll need a car – or plenty of patience traveling on local buses – to get from point to point, though a car is not strictly necessary within each minicity. If you're in a rush, concentrate on downtown, Hollywood, the Mid-Wilshire museums and Santa Monica and Venice. Each area *could* be covered in a few hours, but try to budget a full day to avoid sensory overload.

History

As early as 6000 BC, the LA area was settled by the Gabrieleño and Chumash Indians. The first non-Indians to live in the region were Spanish missionaries, who founded Mission San Gabriel Archangel in 1771 and the Mission San Fernando Rey de España in 1797. Forty-four *pobladores,* or settlers, were assigned to establish a new town near the Indian village of Yangna in 1781. The town they established, El Pueblo de Nuestra Señora la Reina de los Angeles del Río Porciúncula (The Town of Our Lady the Queen of the Angels of the Porciúncula River), was named after a saint whose feast day had just been celebrated.

Joseph Chapman, a Boston millwright-cum-pirate, became the first Yankee, or *yanqui*, Angeleno in 1818. Most Easterners didn't know much about LA until 1840, when Richard Henry Dana's *Two Years Before the Mast* gave an account of his mid-1830s experience in the local hide-and-tallow trade. 'In the hands of an enterprising people, what a country this might be,' Dana wrote of LA, which then had a population of just over 1200.

With California statehood, Los Angeles was incorporated (on April 4, 1850) and was made the seat of broad Los Angeles County. In 1885 the Atchison, Topeka & Santa Fe Railroad directly linked LA with the East Coast. As a result, LA's population skyrocketed from 2300 in 1860 to more than 50,000 in 1890. By 1920 there were a million people, and after the local discovery of oil in 1930 LA claimed two million citizens.

During WWI the Lockheed brothers and Donald Douglas established aircraft manufacturing plants in LA. Two decades later a real-estate boom generated new suburbs south of LA. Today nearly 16 million people live within a 60-mile radius of the city center. LA County boasts 9.9 million people, while the City of LA proper has 3.82 million. The county population breakdown is 45.6% Latino, 32.2% white, 12.6% Asian or Pacific Islander and 9.43% African American. If LA County were a nation, its gross product would rank 19th in the world, before Switzerland and Sweden. Tourism ($11.9 billion a year) and entertainment ($4.2 billion) rank high on the list of most productive industries.

Orientation

Most areas of interest to visitors are in and west of downtown LA. Hollywood is a vast area that encompasses such neighborhoods as bohemian-turned-trendy Silver Lake and fashionable Melrose Ave. On its western edge ensues West Hollywood, LA's gay and lesbian center. Farther west, Bel Air, Brentwood and Beverly Hills all epitomize the 'lifestyles of the rich and famous.' North of the Hollywood Hills is the San Fernando Valley, both quintessential suburbia and home of the major TV and movie studios. Hugging the northern county coast are three more posh areas: Malibu, Pacific Palisades and Santa Monica. Coastal towns farther south, such as Venice, Marina del Rey and Hermosa Beach, are more relaxed middle-class enclaves. San Pedro and Long Beach, farther south, are both port towns and jumping-off points for Mediterranean-flavored Santa Catalina Island.

Information

Tourist Offices Maps, lodging information and discounted tickets to theme parks and other attractions are available from the LA Convention & Visitors Bureau (☎ 213-689-8822, W www.lacvb.com, 685 S Figueroa St), downtown, and the Hollywood Visitor Information Center (no ☎, 6541 Hollywood Blvd) in Hollywood. Both are closed Sunday.

Bookstores Book Soup (☎ 310-659-3110, 8818 Sunset Blvd), in West Hollywood, is a good place for international magazines and newspapers. Other good stores include Dutton's Brentwood (☎ 310-476-6263, 11975 San Vicente Blvd); the Midnight Special Bookstore (☎ 310-393-2923, 1318 Third Street Promenade), in Santa Monica; Nations Hermosa Beach (☎ 310-318-9915, 502 Pier Ave), in Hermosa Beach; and Vromans (☎ 626-449-3220, 695 E Colorado Blvd) and Distant Lands (☎ 626-449-3220, 56 S Raymond Ave), in Pasadena.

Gay & Lesbian Travelers The LA Gay & Lesbian Center (☎ 323-993-7400, 1625 N Schrader Blvd), in Hollywood, is one of the largest such organizations in the world. The center offers lots of services, recommends

CALIFORNIA

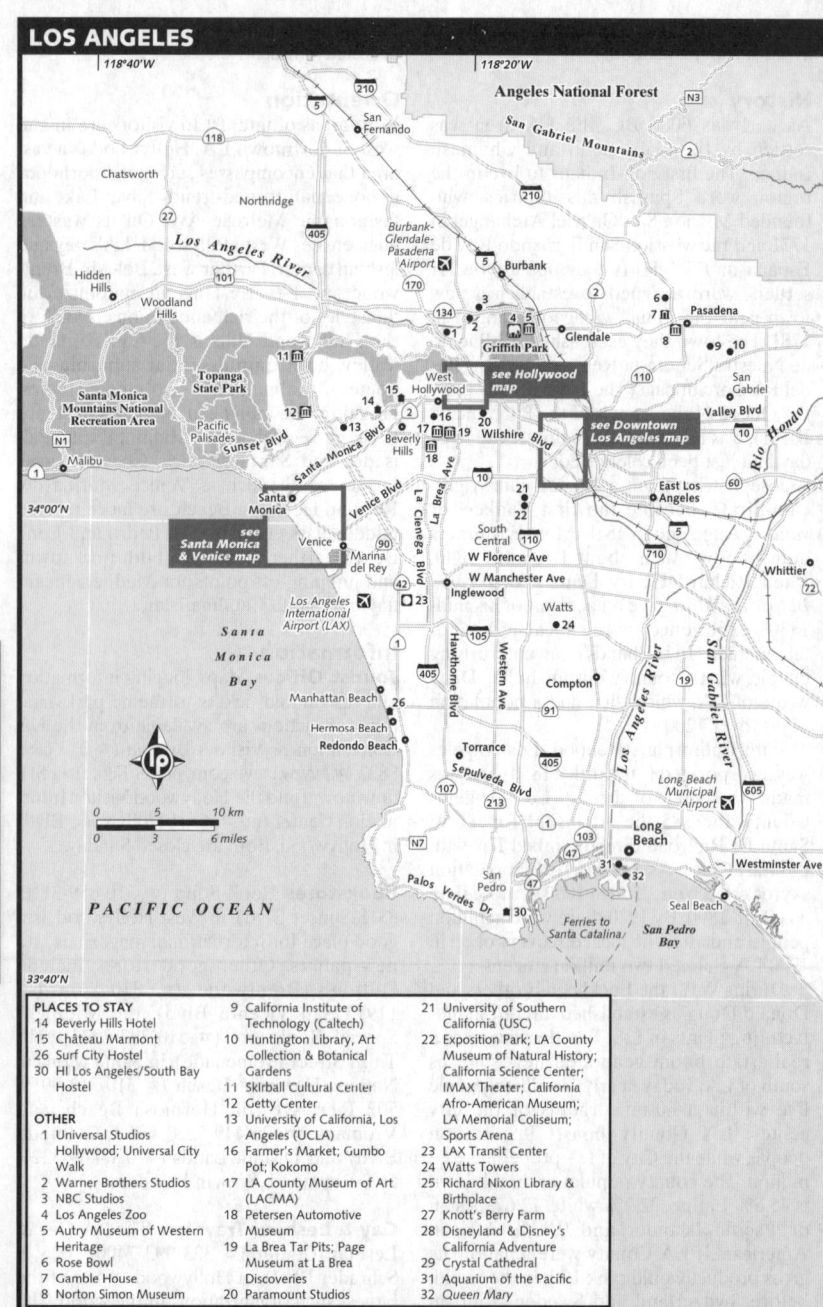

LOS ANGELES

PLACES TO STAY
14 Beverly Hills Hotel
15 Château Marmont
26 Surf City Hostel
30 HI Los Angeles/South Bay Hostel

OTHER
1 Universal Studios Hollywood; Universal City Walk
2 Warner Brothers Studios
3 NBC Studios
4 Los Angeles Zoo
5 Autry Museum of Western Heritage
6 Rose Bowl
7 Gamble House
8 Norton Simon Museum

9 California Institute of Technology (Caltech)
10 Huntington Library, Art Collection & Botanical Gardens
11 Skirball Cultural Center
12 Getty Center
13 University of California, Los Angeles (UCLA)
16 Farmer's Market; Gumbo Pot; Kokomo
17 LA County Museum of Art (LACMA)
18 Petersen Automotive Museum
19 La Brea Tar Pits; Page Museum at La Brea Discoveries
20 Paramount Studios

21 University of Southern California (USC)
22 Exposition Park; LA County Museum of Natural History; California Science Center; IMAX Theater; California Afro-American Museum; LA Memorial Coliseum; Sports Arena
23 LAX Transit Center
24 Watts Towers
25 Richard Nixon Library & Birthplace
27 Knott's Berry Farm
28 Disneyland & Disney's California Adventure
29 Crystal Cathedral
31 Aquarium of the Pacific
32 Queen Mary

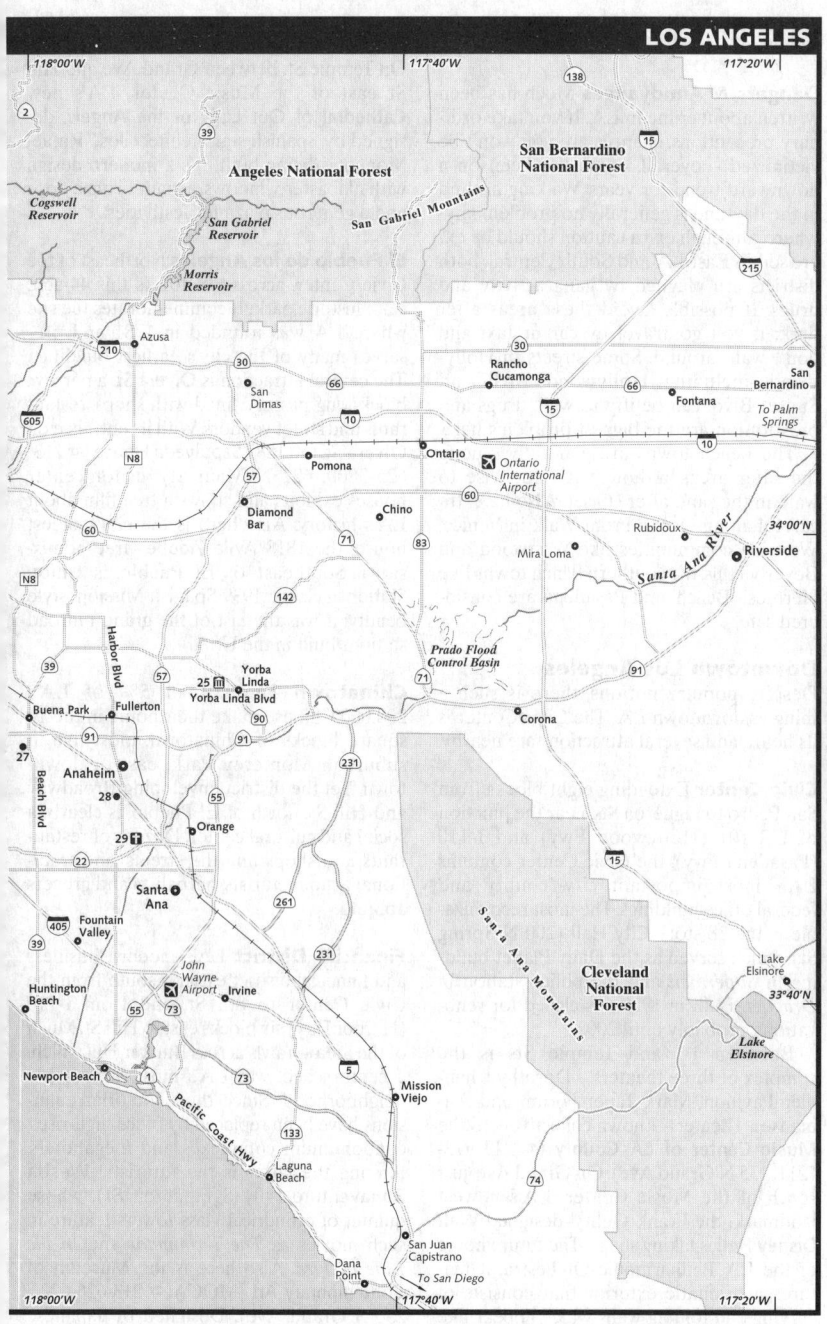

CALIFORNIA

gay-friendly hotels and hosts workshops and activities.

Dangers & Annoyances Much has been written about crime in LA. If you take ordinary precautions, chances are you won't be victimized – overall, crime has been on a downward trend for years. Walking around in the daytime is generally no problem anywhere, although extra caution should be exercised in East LA and South Central; both districts are plagued by gang activity and drugs. If possible, avoid these areas after dark; if you go, travel by car or taxi and don't walk around. Some streets in Hollywood, including Hollywood Blvd and Sunset Blvd, can be iffy as well; drugs and prostitution are the biggest problems here.

The beach towns are generally among the safer areas, although it's not wise to walk in the sand after sunset. Also be extra careful along Ocean Front Walk in Venice. Westside communities like Westwood and Beverly Hills, the southern beach towns like Hermosa Beach, and Pasadena are considered safe.

Downtown Los Angeles

Despite popular notions, there is such a thing as downtown LA. The Civic Center is its heart, and several attractions are nearby.

Civic Center Extending eight blocks from San Pedro to Figueroa Sts, near the junction of US 101 (Hollywood Fwy) and I-110 (Pasadena Fwy), the Civic Center contains LA's most important city, county and federal office buildings. The most recognizable is the 28-story **City Hall** (200 N Spring St), which served as the Daily Planet building in *Superman* and the police station in *Dragnet*. Built in 1928, it's closed for renovations, probably until 2002.

Between 1st and Temple Sts is the complex of three theaters – Dorothy Chandler Pavilion, Mark Taper Forum and Ahmanson Theater – known collectively as the **Music Center of LA County** (☎ 213-972-7211, 135 N Grand Ave). On Grand Ave, just south of the Music Center, LA's newest landmark, the Frank Gehry–designed **Walt Disney Hall** is taking shape. The future home of the LA Philharmonic Orchestra, it features a dramatic exterior that consists of curving and folding walls which appear like an architectural interpretation of a ship caught in a rough sea. It will 'set sail' in 2003. On Temple St, between Grand Ave and Hill St east of the Music Center, LA's new **Cathedral of Our Lady of the Angels**, designed by Spanish star architect José Rafael Moneo, is being built. It's a modern design with alabaster windows, a giant bronze door and a generous plaza for festivities.

El Pueblo de los Angeles Northeast of the Civic Center, across US 101, is this 44-acre state historic park. It commemorates the site where LA was founded in 1781 and preserves many of the city's earliest buildings. The central attraction is **Olvera St**, a narrow, block-long passage lined with shops, restaurants and street vendors. With its entrance on Olvera St, the 1887 **Sepulveda House** (☎ 213-625-3800, 622 N Main St) visitor center houses exhibits and shows a free film about LA's history. Also here is the city's oldest house, the 1818 **Avila Adobe** (free admission). Southeast of El Pueblo is **Union Station**, a classic 1939 Spanish Mission–style beauty; it was the last of the grand railroad stations built in the USA.

Chinatown Fewer than 5% of LA's 200,000 Chinese make their home in the 16 square blocks of Chinatown; most live in suburban Monterey Park, east of downtown. Yet the district enveloping Broadway and Hill St, north of El Pueblo, is clearly a social and cultural center. Dozens of restaurants and shops line the streets, and traditional acupuncturists, herbalists and grocers abound.

Financial District LA's modern business and financial district extends south from the Civic Center to 8th St, and from I-110 (Harbor Fwy) six blocks east to Hill St. Much of the area sprawls across Bunker Hill which, a century ago, was LA's most fashionable neighborhood. Since then, Victorian mansions have been replaced by office high-rises, condominium complexes and megahotels. Among the latter is the futuristic **Westin Bonaventure** (404 S Figueroa St), whose quintet of cylindrical glass towers feature in such movies as *The Terminator* and *In the Line of Fire*. Also here is the **Museum of Contemporary Art** (MOCA; ☎ 213-626-6222, 250 S Grand Ave). Designed by Japanese

CALIFORNIA

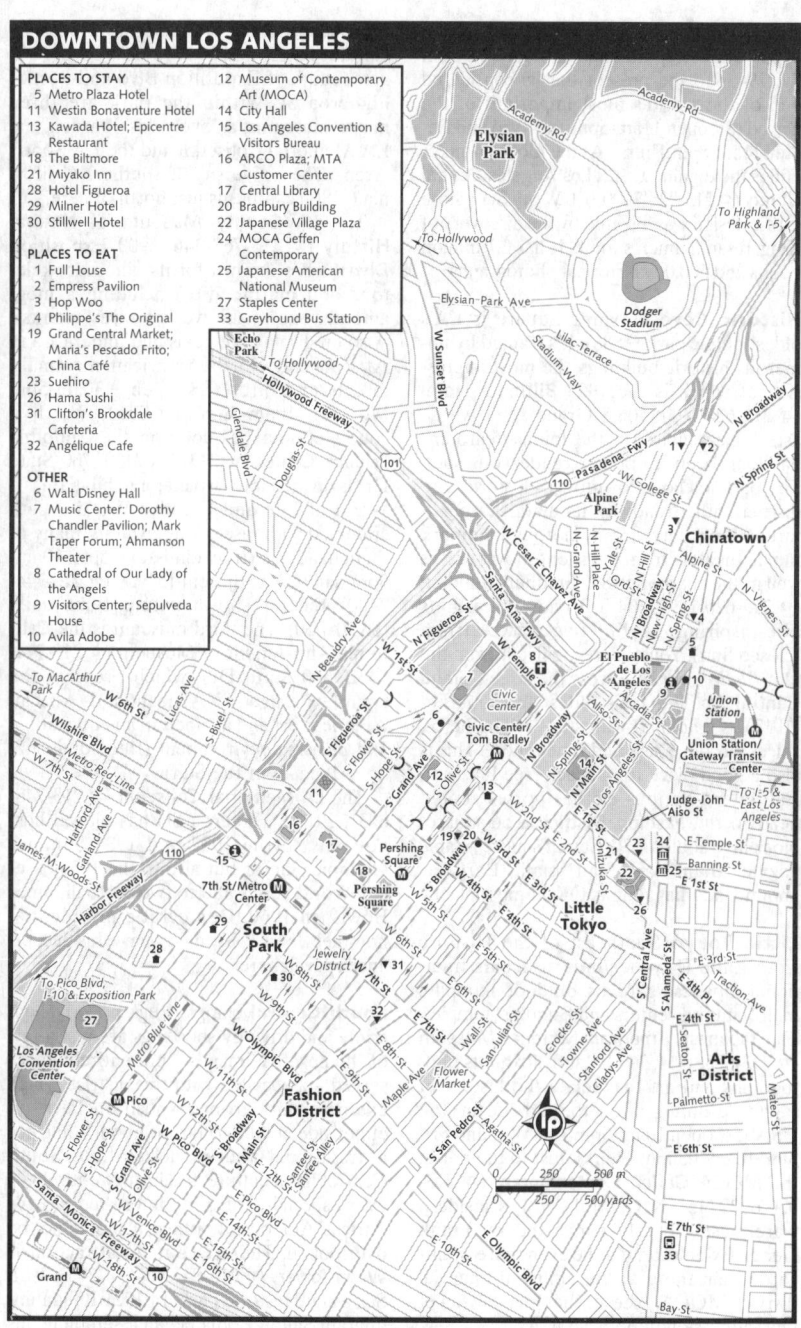

DOWNTOWN LOS ANGELES

PLACES TO STAY
5   Metro Plaza Hotel
11 Westin Bonaventure Hotel
13 Kawada Hotel; Epicentre Restaurant
18 The Biltmore
21 Miyako Inn
28 Hotel Figueroa
29 Milner Hotel
30 Stillwell Hotel

PLACES TO EAT
1   Full House
2   Empress Pavilion
3   Hop Woo
4   Philippe's The Original
19 Grand Central Market; Maria's Pescado Frito; China Café
23 Suehiro
26 Hama Sushi
31 Clifton's Brookdale Cafeteria
32 Angélique Cafe

OTHER
6   Walt Disney Hall
7   Music Center: Dorothy Chandler Pavilion; Mark Taper Forum; Ahmanson Theater
8   Cathedral of Our Lady of the Angels
9   Visitors Center; Sepulveda House
10 Avila Adobe

12 Museum of Contemporary Art (MOCA)
14 City Hall
15 Los Angeles Convention & Visitors Bureau
16 ARCO Plaza; MTA Customer Center
17 Central Library
20 Bradbury Building
22 Japanese Village Plaza
24 MOCA Geffen Contemporary
25 Japanese American National Museum
27 Staples Center
33 Greyhound Bus Station

CALIFORNIA

architect Arata Isozaki, it houses a collection of paintings, sculptures and photographs from the 1940s to the present that is considered one of the world's most important of the period ($6; open 11am-5pm Tue-Wed and Fri-Sun, 11am-8pm Thurs). At the foot of Bunker Hill is the dignified 1922 **Los Angeles Central Library** (☎ 213-228-7000, 630 W 5th St), whose exotic design was inspired by the discovery of King Tutankhamen's tomb. It has 2.1 million books and 500,000 historical photographs.

Historic Core Pershing Square is LA's oldest public park (1886). It's framed by numerous historic buildings, the most impressive of which is the 1923 **Biltmore Hotel** (☎ 213-624-1011, 506 S Grand Ave), whose astrological clock (in the lounge/tearoom) has long been a popular rendezvous spot. The park anchors downtown's historic core district with Broadway, its main thoroughfare. Along here are numerous landmark movie theaters from the silent-movie era, as well as the charming 1893 **Bradbury Building** (☎ 213-626-1893, 304 S Broadway), with its awe-inspiring skylit, five-story atrium (closed Sun). You may recognize it from the film *Blade Runner*. Across the street, **Grand Central Market**, LA's oldest food market (1917), is crammed with stalls selling herbs, spices, produce, fish and much more. This is also a good place for a snack (see Places to Eat, later). Serious clothes horses should head to the **Fashion District**, a 56-square-block area south of 7th St that's more Arabic bazaar than American mall. Bargains abound, and haggling is OK in most places.

Little Tokyo Southeast of the Historic Core, Little Tokyo features sushi bars, traditional Japanese gardens, outdoor shopping malls, cultural centers and Buddhist temples. The **Japanese American National Museum** (☎ 213-625-0414, 369 E 1st St) exhibits photographs and art that relate the history of Japanese immigration to, and life in, the USA ($6; open 10am-5pm Tue-Wed and Fri-Sun, 10am-7:30pm Thurs). Just to the north, the **MOCA Geffen Contemporary** (☎ 213-626-6222, 152 N Central Ave) is inside a warehouse cleverly converted by Frank Gehry. Exhibits tend to be even more avant-garde than those at the affiliated financial district MOCA (see earlier). A $6 ticket buys admission to both MOCAs.

Exposition Park What began as an agricultural fairground in 1872 now covers 160 acres south of Exposition Blvd and west of Figueroa St. Within the park are three major museums, a lovely rose garden, the LA Memorial Coliseum and the LA Sports Arena. The University of Southern California (USC) campus is just north of here.

The **LA County Museum of Natural History** (☎ 213-763-3466, 900 Exposition Blvd) is best known for its dinosaur skeletons and marine life (including a megamouth, one of the world's rarest sharks). Also on display are gems and minerals, and African and North American mammals, insects and birds ($8; open 9:30am-5pm Mon-Fri, 10am-5pm Sat-Sun). Worth a couple of hours' exploration, the **California Science Center** (☎ 213-744-7400, 700 State Dr) is divided into two major exhibit areas – World of Life and Creative World – both crammed with fascinating exhibits, many of them hands-on (free admission; open 10am-5pm daily). An adjacent IMAX (☎ 213-744-7400) theater shows nature films daily ($6.50-7.50). The third museum is the **California Afro-American Museum** (☎ 213-744-7432, 600 State Dr), which presents the complex range of African and African American art and artifacts in an educational and pleasing environment (free admission; open 10am-5pm Tue-Sun).

The **LA Memorial Coliseum** (☎ 213-748-6131, 3911 S Figueroa St) has played host not only to the 1932 and 1984 Summer Olympic Games, but also to the 1959 baseball World Series and to two football Super Bowls. In 1960, Democratic presidential nominee John F Kennedy gave his acceptance speech here.

South Central Gangs, drugs, poverty, high crime and drive-by shootings are just a few of the negative images – not entirely undeserved – associated with this district, which extends south from Exposition Park on either side of I-110 (Harbor Fwy). While not a traditional tourist destination, South Central has a culture and history entirely its own; especially for those interested in LA's African American heritage, it should not be overlooked. The area's main attraction is **Watts Towers** (☎ 213-847-4646, 1727 E 107th St), a state historic park. In 1921 Italian immigrant Simon Rodia began assembling this free-form sculpture, now considered among the world's finest examples of folk art. Supporting his towers are slender columns containing steel reinforcement, which he tied with wire, wrapped with wire mesh and covered by hand with cement. Incorporated into the facade are glass, mirrors, seashells, rocks, ceramic tile and pottery.

Mid-Wilshire

Wilshire Blvd passes through an eclectic mix of neighborhoods. West of downtown is the sprawling **Koreatown**, home not just to Koreans but increasingly also to Latin American immigrants. The Korean presence is most prevalent along Vermont, Normandie and Western Aves and Wilshire Blvd, which are lined with shops and restaurants.

Farther west, in the Hancock Park neighborhood, is LA's 'Museum Row.' The **Page Museum at La Brea Discoveries** (☎ 323-936-2230, 5801 Wilshire Blvd) displays the fossilized skeletons of long-extinct mammals that died in the adjacent La Brea Tar Pits. Excavations have yielded more than a million bones, including those from saber-toothed tigers, ground sloths, mammoths and mastodons, along with 200 different bird, reptile, insect and plant species ($6; open 9:30am-5pm Mon-Fri, 10am-5pm Sat-Sun). Just west is the **LA County Museum of Art** (Lacma; ☎ 323-857-6000, 5901 Wilshire Blvd), considered one of the country's leading art museums. Its vast collection encompasses fine art, sculpture and decorative arts from Europe, Asia and America as well as ancient and Islamic art and a Far Eastern section ($7; open noon-8pm Mon-Tue and Thurs, noon-9pm Fri, 11am-8pm Sat-Sun).

LA's love affair with the automobile is celebrated at the **Petersen Automotive Museum** (☎ 323-930-2277, 6060 Wilshire Blvd). Even non–car buffs will enjoy the mock streetscape of LA in the 1920s and '30s, which shows how its growth into a megacity is intricately tied to the evolution of the automobile. The upper galleries have changing car exhibits ($7).

Orthodox and Hassidic Jews are a major presence in the **Fairfax District**, which centers on Fairfax Ave between Santa Monica and Wilshire Blvds. For visitors the main point of interest is the daily Farmers' Market (6333 W 3rd St), which offers dozens of fun eateries and food stands.

Hollywood

Hollywood is back – at least if the dreams of developers come true. For decades, glamour was banished from this fabled part of Los Angeles forever synonymous with the movie industry. But now revamped historic movie theaters, the completion of the Metro Red Line subway and especially the construction of the Hollywood & Highland Entertainment Complex (the planned home of the Academy Awards from 2002) have breathed new life into the grimy streets of the former dream factory. Looking down on all this activity is the HOLLYWOOD sign up in the Hollywood Hills. Hiking to the sign is no longer legal, but good views can be had from the end of Beachwood Dr and from the Griffith Park Observatory.

Pick up tourist information in the historic **Janes House** (☎ 213-689-8822, 6541 Hollywood Blvd).

Central Hollywood The heart of Hollywood is along Hollywood Blvd between La Brea Ave and Vine St. Here the sidewalks are paved in stars: The **Hollywood Walk of Fame** honors more than 2000 celebrities from film, television, radio, theater and the recording industry.

Mann's Chinese Theater (☎ 323-464-8111, 6925 Hollywood Blvd) is famous for its forecourt, where more than 150 screen legends have left their marks in the cement – from Betty Grable's legs to Jimmy Durante's nose. Other historic theaters on this stretch include the 1926 **El Capitan** (☎ 323-467-7674, 6838 Hollywood Blvd), where *Citizen Kane* premiered, and the **Egyptian Theatre** (☎ 323-466-3456, 6712 Hollywood Blvd), now the home of American Cinemathèque, a nonprofit film organization. The **Hollywood Entertainment Museum** (☎ 323-465-7900, 7021 Hollywood Blvd) employs state-of-the-art technology to give visitors a simplified yet fun look at the history and mystery of moviemaking. Highlights include original sets from *Cheers* and *Star Trek*. For a free history of Hollywood, visit the mezzanine of the **Hollywood Roosevelt Hotel** (☎ 323-466-7000, 7000 Hollywood Blvd), the location of the first Academy Awards ceremony.

Farther east, near Highland Ave, is a trio of kitschy museums: Ripley's Believe It or Not!, the Hollywood Wax Museum and the Guinness World of Records Museum.

CALIFORNIA

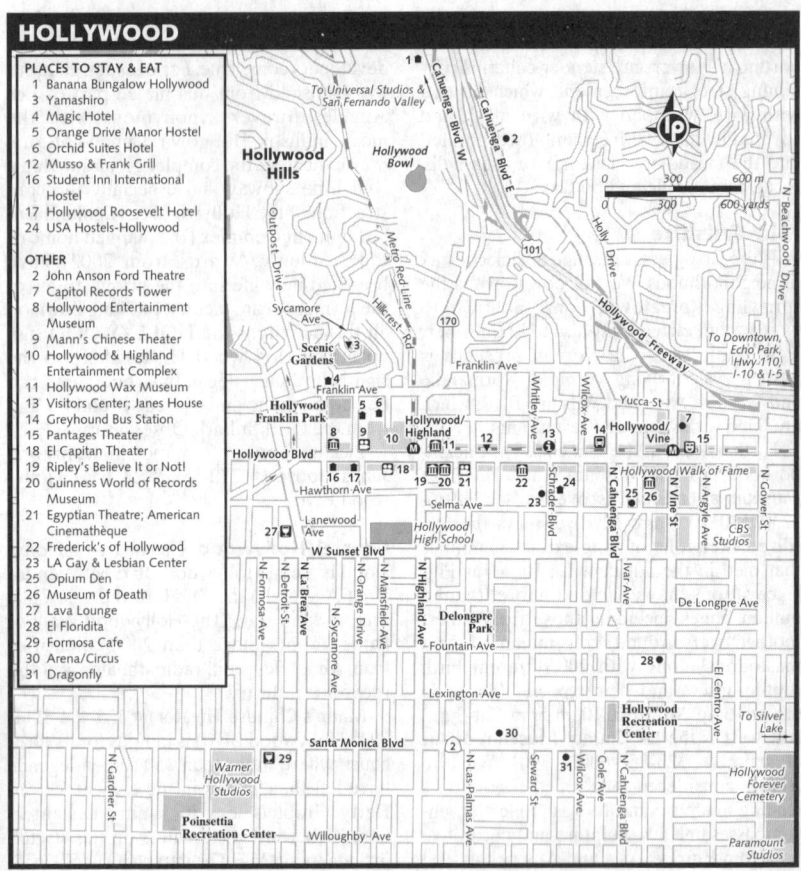

HOLLYWOOD

PLACES TO STAY & EAT
1 Banana Bungalow Hollywood
3 Yamashiro
4 Magic Hotel
5 Orange Drive Manor Hostel
6 Orchid Suites Hotel
6 Musso & Frank Grill
16 Student Inn International Hostel
17 Hollywood Roosevelt Hotel
24 USA Hostels-Hollywood

OTHER
2 John Anson Ford Theatre
7 Capitol Records Tower
8 Hollywood Entertainment Museum
9 Mann's Chinese Theater
10 Hollywood & Highland Entertainment Complex
11 Hollywood Wax Museum
13 Visitors Center; Janes House
14 Greyhound Bus Station
15 Pantages Theater
18 El Capitan Theater
19 Ripley's Believe It or Not!
20 Guinness World of Records Museum
21 Egyptian Theatre; American Cinematheque
22 Frederick's of Hollywood
23 LA Gay & Lesbian Center
25 Opium Den
26 Museum of Death
27 Lava Lounge
28 El Floridita
29 Formosa Cafe
30 Arena/Circus
31 Dragonfly

Admission to each costs about $11. Down the street, **Frederick's of Hollywood** (☎ 323-466-8506, 6608 Hollywood Blvd) has a free exhibit of celebrity lingerie (open 10am-6pm Mon-Sat, noon-5pm Sun). Nearby, the new **Museum of Death** (☎ 323-466-8011, 6340 Hollywood Blvd) is a macabre compilation of death-related artifacts, memorabilia, photographs and even art by serial killers like John Wayne Gacy ($7; open noon-10pm Sun-Thurs, noon-midnight Fri-Sat).

Also of note is the landmark **Capitol Records Tower** (1750 N Vine St), designed to represent a stack of vinyl records topped by a stylus.

West Hollywood The city of West Hollywood is the heart of LA's gay and lesbian community, which makes up one third of its 36,000 residents. Recent Russian Jewish immigrants account for 12% of the local population. West Hollywood is one of LA's hippest areas, teeming with legendary nightclubs, restaurants and hotels, especially along the famous Sunset Strip. (In)famous spots include the 1927 **Château Marmont Hotel** (☎ 323-656-1010, 8221 Sunset Blvd), where comedian John Belushi died of a drug overdose, and the Johnny Depp–owned **Viper Room** (☎ 310-358-1880, 8852 Sunset Blvd), where actor River Phoenix died of drug-related complications in 1993. Nearby are LA's trendiest hotel, the **Mondrian** (☎ 323-650-8999, 8840 Sunset Blvd), with its exclusive Sky Bar, and the original **House of Blues** (☎ 323-848-5100, 8430 Sunset Blvd).

Melrose Ave This street is LA's former and once-again epicenter of cool and a good place to pick up eccentric fashions and vintage clothing. Flashy boutiques, many of the wacky and unique variety, flank both sides of this thoroughfare. Restaurants, bars and theaters are also part of the eclectic mix. Melrose is one of the funnest places in town to stroll around. The action is concentrated in the section between Fairfax and La Brea Aves. To the west, around the Pacific Design Center, Melrose goes chic with cutting-edge art galleries, upscale shops and designer boutiques. To the east is **Paramount Studios** (☎ 323-956-1777, 5555 Melrose Ave), the only major movie studio still in Hollywood proper. Two-hour studio tours run hourly ($15; 9am-2pm Mon-Fri). Audience tickets to TV shows, mostly sitcoms, are available by phone or in person five days before the live tapings.

Griffith Park The nation's largest city park, Griffith Park covers 4107 acres and includes two 18-hole golf courses, sports facilities, the historic outdoor **Greek Theater** (☎ 323-665-1927) and plenty of hiking trails. Access to Griffith Park Dr is easiest via the Griffith Park Dr or Zoo Dr exits off I-5 (Golden State Fwy). The **Los Angeles Zoo** (☎ 323-644-4200), on the park's northern edge, is home to some 1200 animals representing 350 species ($8.25; open 10am-5pm, longer in summer). The undisputed highlight is the Chimpanzees of Mahale Mountains exhibit, where 13 Tanzanian chimps dwell in a re-created habitat. Anyone interested in the history of the American West will hit the mother lode at the **Autry Museum of Western Heritage** (☎ 323-667-2000, 4700 Western Heritage Way), which has perhaps the definitive collection ($7.50; open 10am-5pm Tue-Wed and Fri-Sun, 10am-8pm Thurs).

On the upper slopes of Mt Hollywood, the landmark 1935 **Griffith Observatory & Planetarium** (2800 E Observatory Rd) is closed for renovation until 2004. You may recognize it from *Rebel Without a Cause*.

Beverly Hills

The reality of this sophisticated city-within-a-city is not so different from the myth. This is a place where the rich and famous frolic and where opulent mansions line winding,

---

Star Gazing

To see a particular TV star while in LA, your best bet is to watch a taping of his or her show. The easiest way to get tickets is through Audiences Unlimited (☎ 818-753-3483, Ⓦ www.tvtickets.com), which handles the distribution for 30 shows, including *Friends* and *Spin City*.

NBC Studios (☎ 818-840-3537, 3000 W Alameda Ave), in Burbank, runs an informative studio tour ($7; 9am-3pm daily, extended summer hours; reservations are recommended). Free tickets are available for live tapings of *The Tonight Show* with Jay Leno. Close by, the **Warner Bros Studio** (☎ 818-972-8687, 4000 Warner Blvd) has excellent, if pricey, two-hour tours of its museum, sets and studios ($32; 9am-4pm Mon-Fri in summer, 9am-3pm in winter).

Universal Studios Hollywood (☎ 818-622-3801), off US 101 (Hollywood Fwy) in Universal City, is one of LA's top attractions. There are gut-wrenching rides, mind-blowing special-effects shows and the Studio Tour, a part-educational, part-thrill ride behind the scenes of moviemaking ($41; open 8am-10pm in summer, 9am-7pm rest of year). Also here is **Universal City Walk**, a cleverly designed but overcommercialized shopping, dining and entertainment promenade (free admission; parking $7).

---

tree-lined streets. The landmark **Beverly Hills Hotel** (☎ 310-276-2251, 9641 Sunset Blvd), also known as the Pink Palace, has served as unofficial hobnobbing headquarters of the Hollywood power elite since 1912 (think Chaplin to Harrison Ford). Its Polo Lounge is a prime spot for celebrity gazing (dress nicely and come with a fat wallet). World-famous **Rodeo Drive** is lined with haute-couture designer stores. At the **Museum of Television & Radio** (☎ 310-786-1000, 465 N Beverly Dr) you can easily spend a few hours watching old movies, TV shows and documentaries ($6; open noon-5pm Wed-Sun, except noon-9pm Thurs). The **Museum of Tolerance** (☎ 310-553-8403, 9786 W Pico Blvd) offers a multimedia Holocaust experience while making visitors confront their closely held beliefs about racism ($8; open 10am-4pm Mon-Thurs, 10am-1pm Fri, 11am-5pm Sun).

Brentwood & Westwood

LA's Westside is dominated by the quiet, affluent neighborhoods of Bel Air and Brentwood and the 419-acre, 35,000-student campus of the **University of California at Los Angeles** (UCLA). The **UCLA Hammer Museum** (☎ 310-443-7000, 10899 Wilshire Blvd) presents exhibits drawn from the late industrialist's collections. Armand Hammer was an entrepreneur and art collector who had extensive import-export dealings with the Soviet Union and personal contact with Lenin during the 1920s. He later went into the oil business and became head of the Occidental Petroleum Corporation. His collections of impressionist and postimpressionist paintings and lithographs by Honoré Daumier and contemporaries are on show. Other exhibits showcase emerging and established artists, many from California ($4.50; open 11am-7pm Tue-Wed and Fri-Sat, 11am-9pm Thurs, 11am-5pm Sun).

The $1 billion **Getty Center** (☎ 310-440-7300, 1200 Getty Center Dr) is a magnificent Richard Meier–designed campus on a hilltop above I-405 (San Diego Fwy). The vast collection ranges from Italian Renaissance to David Hockney (free admission, $5 parking; open 10am-7pm Tue-Wed, 10am-9pm Thurs-Fri, 10am-6pm Sat-Sun).

Close by, the fascinating **Skirball Cultural Center** (☎ 310-440-4500, 2701 N Sepulveda Blvd) chronicles the art and history of Judaism with a strong focus on Jewish life in America ($8; open noon-5pm Tue-Sat, 11am-5pm Sun).

Santa Monica & Venice

The seaside city of Santa Monica is one of the most agreeable in LA, with its early-20th-century pier, pedestrian-friendly downtown and colorful Main St shopping area. The **Santa Monica Visitors Bureau** (☎ 310-393-7593, 1400 Ocean Blvd), in a little kiosk, has brochures, maps and public transportation information (open 10am-5pm). The **Santa Monica Museum of Art** (☎ 310-586-6488, 2525 Michigan Ave) is a saucy and irreverent home of cutting-edge art ($3; open 11am-6pm Tue-Sat, noon-5pm Sun). It's integrated into **Bergamot Station**, a former

trolley stop that's been converted into a nexus of the LA art scene with some 40 galleries. **Third Street Promenade**, a tremendously popular pedestrian mall, extends for three long blocks from Wilshire Blvd south to Broadway. Ocean Ave parallels **Palisades Park**, perched on a bluff overlooking the Pacific Ocean (great sunsets). The famous **Santa Monica Pier** has a Ferris wheel and other rides in its Pacific Park, as well as the quaint 1920s carousel featured in *The Sting*.

Inland, another highlight is the **Museum of Flying** (☎ 310-392-8822), at the Santa Monica Municipal Airport. You can take a self-guided tour of exhibits examining the beginnings of flight and highlighting aerial milestones and pioneers ($7; open 10am-5pm Wed-Sun).

The quintessential bohemian playground, Venice is famous for its **Ocean Front Boardwalk**, Muscle Beach, canals and unique blend of hippies, New Agers, artists, industry types and students. In recent years, though, gentrification and rising real-estate prices have begun whittling away at the community's character, and it is slowly becoming yuppified.

DAVID PEEVERS

The Getty Center – fabulous and free

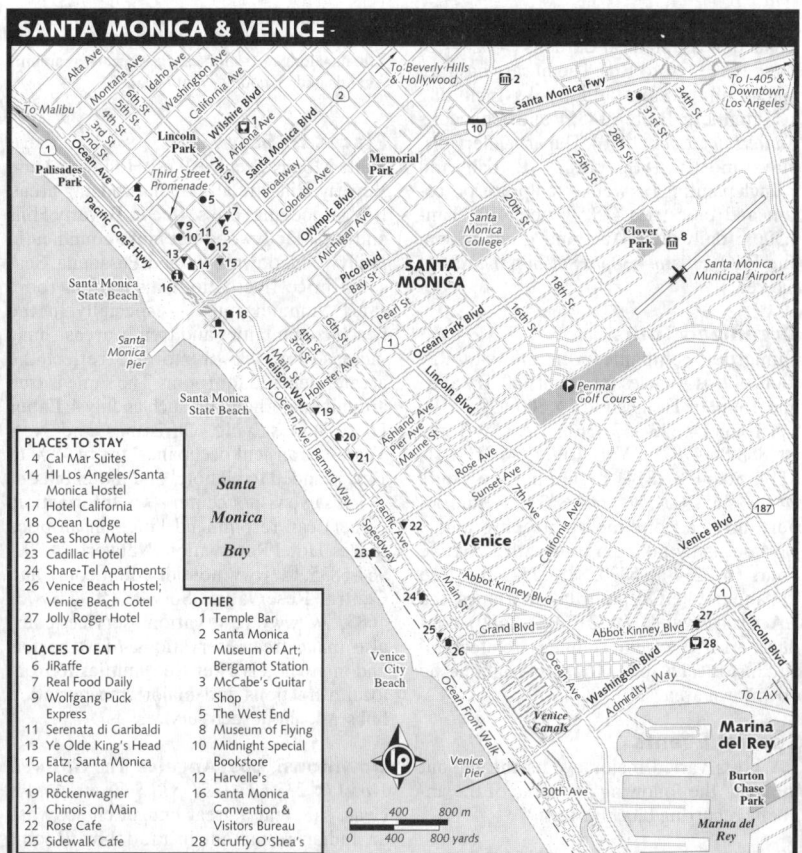

SANTA MONICA & VENICE

PLACES TO STAY
4 Cal Mar Suites
14 HI Los Angeles/Santa Monica Hostel
17 Hotel California
18 Ocean Lodge
20 Sea Shore Motel
23 Cadillac Hotel
24 Share-Tel Apartments
26 Venice Beach Hostel; Venice Beach Cotel
27 Jolly Roger Hotel

PLACES TO EAT
6 JiRaffe
7 Real Food Daily
9 Wolfgang Puck Express
11 Serenata di Garibaldi
13 Ye Olde King's Head
15 Eatz; Santa Monica Place
19 Röckenwagner
22 Rose Cafe
25 Sidewalk Cafe

OTHER
1 Temple Bar
2 Santa Monica Museum of Art; Bergamot Station
3 McCabe's Guitar Shop
5 The West End
8 Museum of Flying
10 Midnight Special Bookstore
12 Harvelle's
16 Santa Monica Convention & Visitors Bureau
28 Scruffy O'Shea's

CALIFORNIA

Malibu

Fabled Malibu parallels the coastline for 27 miles north of Santa Monica. It is home to numerous celebrities who are holed up in exclusive residential enclaves that are off-limits to the public. Walking along the beach, though, is legal below the high-tide mark. A handful of state parks and beaches offer the best access. Traveling from east to west, they include Las Tunas, Malibu Surfrider, Pt Dume, Zuma and Leo Carrillo.

Pasadena

Resting in the shadow of the lofty San Gabriel Mountains, northeast of downtown LA, Pasadena is the site of the famed Tournament of Roses (see Special Events, later) and the acclaimed California Institute of Technology (CalTech). **Old Town** is the heart of Pasadena, a 20-block historic district stretching out along Colorado Blvd between Arroyo Pkwy and Pasadena Ave. A short walk west is the **Norton Simon Museum** (☎ 626-449-6840, 411 W Colorado Blvd), with an outstanding collection of European art from the Renaissance to the 20th century as well as Asian sculpture ($6; closed Tue).

Northwest of here is the 1908 **Gamble House** (☎ 626-793-3334, 4 Westmoreland Place). Designed by architects Charles & Henry Greene, it is considered the world's best example of Craftsman-style bungalow architecture ($5; open noon-3pm Thurs-Sun).

Southeast of Pasadena, in San Marino, Henry Huntington's 1910 mansion and its grounds house the **Huntington Library, Art Collection & Botanical Gardens** (☎ 626-405-2100, 1151 Oxford Rd). The library has rare maps, manuscripts and books including a Gutenberg Bible (1455) and Chaucer's *Canterbury Tales* (1410). The art gallery displays mostly 18th-century British and French paintings as well as sculpture, porcelain and tapestries ($8.50; open 10:30am-4:30pm daily June-Aug, and noon-4:30pm Tue-Fri, 10:30am-4:30pm Sat-Sun the rest of the year).

Organized Tours

Numerous companies run minivan day tours of Los Angeles for about $40. Try Starline Tours of Hollywood (☎ 800-959-3131), LA Tours (☎ 323-937-3361), LA City Tours (☎ 888-800-7878), VIP Tours (☎ 310-641-8114, 800-438-1814) or GuideLine Tours (☎ 323-465-3004, 800-604-8433). A fun opportunity to combine sightseeing and a workout is by taking a tour with LA Bike Tours (☎ 323-466-5890, 888-775-2453), also for about $40. On Saturday mornings, the LA Conservancy (☎ 213-623-2489) conducts a series of entertaining architectural and historical walking tours throughout the downtown area ($8).

Special Events

LA hosts varied major events throughout the year; the following are some of the annually recurring blockbusters:

Tournament of Roses Parade (☎ 626-449-7673) is an enormous cavalcade of flower-coated floats along Pasadena's Colorado Blvd on New Year's Day. The Rose Bowl football game (☎ 626-449-4100) takes place later the same day.

Cinco de Mayo (☎ 213-625-5045) is celebrated with bands and parades in the Pueblo area of downtown on May 5.

Gay Pride Week (☎ 323-860-0701) brings some 250 vendors and food stalls to West Hollywood in June.

Los Angeles County Fair (☎ 909-623-3111), the world's largest, takes place in Pomona, in eastern LA County, every September.

West Hollywood's Halloween Party is a rambunctious street fair with eccentric, and occasionally X-rated, costumes all along Santa Monica Blvd on Oct 31.

Doo Dah Parade (☎ 626-440-7379), in Pasadena, is a wacky parody of the traditional Rose Parade on the Saturday after Thanksgiving.

Hollywood Christmas Parade (☎ 323-469-2337) features celebrities from film and TV on flashy floats, along with horses, classic cars, marching bands and, of course, Santa Claus.

Places to Stay

Santa Monica, Venice, West Hollywood and Beverly Hills are all popular lodging areas. Budget lodgings are scarce in Beverly Hills and West Hollywood but more abundant in Hollywood, downtown and Pasadena. Seasonal price fluctuations also affect room rates. Summer rates – especially in the beach communities and trendy areas – may increase by 50% or more to reflect the greater demand for rooms. The same is true around major holidays such as July 4, Labor Day, Thanksgiving, Christmas and New Year. A 'transient occupancy' tax of 12% to 14% is added to all hotel and motel bills.

LA's two visitor centers (see Information, earlier) can recommend hotels in all price ranges. Hotel Reservations Network (☎ 800-964-6835, Ⓦ www.hoteldiscount.com) and Central Reservation Service (☎ 800-873-4683, Ⓦ www.reservations-services.com) also make free reservations. Most hostels and many hotels offer free shuttles to/from local attractions and major transportation hubs; ask about such services.

Downtown Los Angeles The *Stillwell Hotel* (☎ 213-627-1151, 838 S Grand Ave) is clean, safe and a great budget choice, with an Indian restaurant in the lobby. Rooms cost $49-80; some have shared bathroom.

Milner Hotel (☎ 213-627-6981, 813 S Flower St) doesn't look like much from the outside, but the rooms ($60-70) are spacious and clean. On the edge of Chinatown near Union Station, *Metro Plaza Hotel* (☎ 213-680-0200, 711 N Main St) has rooms with refrigerators and microwave ovens ($69-84). Easily the mid-range favorite, *Hotel Figueroa* (☎ 213-627-8971, 939 S Figueroa St) has a striking tiled lobby, outdoor pool and large rooms ($88-124).

Little Tokyo's *Miyako Inn* (☎ 213-617-2000, 328 E 1st St) has full spa facilities and Japanese-style rooms with tatami floors and shoji screens ($114-168). *Kawada Hotel* (☎ 213-621-4455, 200 S Hill St) is another good choice, with a TV and VCR in each room ($139) and the dependable Epicentre restaurant on the premises. Featured in numerous movies, the **Westin Bonaventure Hotel** (☎ 213-624-1000, 404 S Figueroa St) has 1199 guest rooms ($247), 20 restaurants and a fitness deck the size of a football field.

Mid-Wilshire Rooms are OK if nothing special at the convenient **Dunes Wilshire Motor Hotel** (☎ 323-938-3616, 4300 Wilshire Blvd), where rates are $64-74; the swimming pool is a bonus. The gracious **Wilshire Royale Howard Johnson** (☎ 213-387-5311, 2619 Wilshire Blvd) is a restored art deco palace with rooms in the $109-149 range.

Hollywood There are a few hostels to choose from in Hollywood. **Banana Bungalow Hollywood** (☎ 323-851-1129, 2775 N Cahuenga Blvd) is the quintessential party place, with a pool, cafe and small store. Beds cost $15-20, private rooms cost $59/68/76 double/triple/quad, including breakfast; a passport is required. At **USA Hostels Hollywood** (☎ 323-462-3777, 1624 Schrader Blvd), free comedy nights, breakfast and a great kitchen are distinctive assets. Beds cost $16, private rooms $36-44. The **Student Inn International Hostel** (☎ 323-469-9269, 7038½ Hollywood Blvd) has dorms, including large beds for couples, for $11-13 (non-US passport required). **Orange Drive Manor** (☎ 323-850-0350, 1764 N Orange Dr) is very low-key. This friendly hostel offers plenty of privacy and a peaceful atmosphere. Beds cost $18-22, singles/doubles cost $33/39. In the Fairfax District an excellent choice is the newish **Orbit Hostel** (☎ 323-655-1510, 7950 Melrose Ave), which offers bold-colored retro decor, a convenient location and clean and carpeted dorms. Beds cost $15-17, private rooms cost $45-59. Passports are required for dorms.

There are some noteworthy hotels and motels in the area. In the heart of Hollywood the popular **Orchid Suites Hotel** (☎ 323-874-9678, 1753 N Orchid Ave) occupies a converted apartment block, so all rooms ($59-109) have kitchens and private bathrooms. Spacious rooms ($69-125) in the nearby **Magic Hotel** (☎ 323-851-0800, 7025 Franklin Ave) also have kitchens, and there's a swimming pool. The stylish 1927 **Hollywood Roosevelt Hotel** (☎ 323-466-7000, 7000 Hollywood Blvd) has a great lobby, the Cinegrill lounge and comfortable rooms ($99-299).

In the Fairfax District you'll find pleasant rooms at **Bevonshire Lodge Motel** (☎ 323-936-6154, 7575 Beverly Blvd) for $49-58. The **Farmer's Daughter Motel** (☎ 323-937-3930, 115 S Fairfax Ave), directly opposite the Farmers' Market, has plain, clean doubles for $58-95. Your best bet is the **Beverly Laurel Hotel** (☎ 323-651-2441, 8018 Beverly Blvd). Largish rooms ($75-79) are furnished with style and wrap around a nice pool. There's a cool coffee shop attached.

In trendy West Hollywood prices are lowest at **Holloway Motel** (☎/fax 323-654-2454, 8465 Santa Monica Blvd). Rooms have voice mail, data ports and safes and cost $70-100. Those with more money should check into **The Standard** (☎ 323-650-9090, 8300 Sunset Blvd), where the pool is pink and hip rooms ($99-225) have platform beds.

One of the cheapest choices near UCLA is **Royal Palace Westwood Hotel** (☎ 310-208-6677, 1052 Tiverton Ave), where comfortable rooms cost $70-119.

Santa Monica & Venice The 200-bed **HI Los Angeles/Santa Monica** (☎ 310-393-9913, 1436 2nd St) is one block from Third Street Promenade and one from the beach. Bunks cost $23-28; private rooms cost $62. Venice has plenty of backpacker hostels, most no more than a block from the beach. **Share-Tel Apartments** (☎ 310-392-0325, 20 Brooks Ave) is excellent but only takes non-US travelers. Each dorm has a kitchen and full bathroom. Rates ($20 dorms, $46-50 private rooms) include daily breakfast and weekday dinner. **Venice Beach Cotel** (☎ 310-399-7649, 25 Windward Ave) has plenty of facilities. Its party atmosphere can make it noisy. Americans with passports are welcome. Some dorms have ocean views. Bunks cost $15-17.50, private cost $35-49. A block away is **Venice Beach Hostel** (☎ 310-452-3052, 1515 Pacific Ave), another convivial place. US citizens need a passport or driver's license. Dorm beds cost $19-21, private rooms $55. See also Cadillac Hotel later.

Hotels and motels worth checking out include **Ocean Lodge** (☎ 310-451-4146, 1667 Ocean Ave), in Santa Monica. Central and unpretentious, this motel counts updated and nicely furnished rooms and free Internet access among its assets. Rates fluctuate wildly, starting at $69. **Sea Shore Motel** (☎ 310-392-2787, 2637 Main St), in southern

Santa Monica, is a good value, clean, well run and only two blocks from the beach. Rooms cost $70-119. The older *Cal Mar Hotel Suites* (☎ 310-395-5555, 220 California Ave) is an all-suite property well suited to families. Large rooms with full kitchens cost $99-159. For quirky surf ambience with upscale amenities, try *Hotel California* (☎ 310-393-2363, 1670 Ocean Ave), where rooms cost $160-350.

In Venice, the best bargain is the *Cadillac Hotel* (☎ 310-399-8876, 401 Ocean Front Walk), an art deco beachside classic. It has 30 rooms ($69-79) and four-person dorms ($20 per person) plus a sauna and rooftop sundeck. The *Jolly Roger Hotel* (☎ 310-822-2904, 2904 Washington Blvd) is a hip place friendly to international travelers. Rooms cost $75-85, $20 less in the older annex.

LAX Area In the ultimate beach town of Hermosa Beach, south of LAX, is the grungy but popular *Surf City Hostel* (☎ 310-798-2323, 26 Pier Ave), right on 'bar row.' Dorms cost $15-18, private rooms $35-40. All travelers are welcome. Even farther south, in the suburb of San Pedro, is *HI Los Angeles/South Bay* (☎ 310-831-8109, 3601 S Gaffey St No 613). It is on a hilltop overlooking the ocean and is convenient to Santa Catalina Island ferries but little else. Dorms cost $14-17, rooms $39. Take MTA bus No 466 South to the Korean Bell stop ($1.85).

The cheapest hotels and motels near LAX are the chains, including *Super 8* (☎ 310-670-2900, 9250 Airport Blvd), where rooms cost $65-85. There's an on-site restaurant. The large *Furama Hotel* (☎ 310-670-8111, 8601 Lincoln Blvd) is a pleasant, resort-style property with rates of $99-119. Both places have free shuttle service to/from LAX.

Places to Eat

Eating out is one of the great delights in cosmopolitan LA, one of the places that invented California cuisine back in the mid-1980s. Dishes are prepared in a low-fat and healthful way, characterized by fresh seasonal ingredients, unusual flavor fusions and artistic presentation. Budget restaurants charge less than $10 for a main dish, mid-range restaurants $10-20 and top-end restaurants over $20.

Downtown Los Angeles In LA's historic core, the Grand Central Market (317 S Broadway) is a dream come true for the cash-strapped. Fill up for under $5 at such places as *Maria's Pescado Frito* (central aisle), with great fish tacos and ceviche tostadas, or *China Café* (upper level), with steamy bowls of soup or giant platters of chow mein. The buffet-style *Clifton's Brookdale Cafeteria* (☎ 213-627-1673, 648 S Broadway) has been an integral part of downtown since the 1930s. It's no booze, cash only and very groovy. A lunchtime favorite is *Angélique Cafe* (☎ 213-623-8698, 840 S Spring St), near the Fashion District, which serves delicious homemade French cuisine for under $10.

Chinatown has plenty of cheap chow houses where $5-8 buys huge plates of lemon chicken or Mongolian beef. *Full House* (☎ 213-617-8382, 963 N Hill St) and *Hop Woo* (☎ 213-617-3038, 855 N Broadway) are recommended. *Empress Pavilion* (☎ 213-617-9898, 988 N Hill St), on the 3rd floor of Bamboo Plaza, is a great place for dim sum; full midday meals cost $12-15. Near Union Station *Philippe's The Original* (☎ 213-628-3781, 1001 N Alameda St) has been a beloved landmark since 1908 and is the self-proclaimed home of the French-dip sandwich ($4).

In Little Tokyo *Suehiro* (☎ 213-626-9132, 337 E 1st St) has soups, rice dishes, sukiyaki (stew) and other Japanese dishes for $4-15

(open until 1am Mon-Fri, 3pm Sat-Sun). Serious sushi lovers should try **Hama Sushi** (☎ 213-680-3453, 355 E 2nd St), where combinations cost $12-15.

Mid-Wilshire Eateries abound at the Farmers' Market (6333 W 3rd St). Good choices are **Gumbo Pot**, where you can sink teeth into Southern-style stew or a po'boy sandwich ($4-8), and **KoKoMo**, a hip art deco eatery with big breakfasts for under $8. **Damiano Mr Pizza** (412 N Fairfax Ave) is a night-owl favorite that sells energy-restoring slices from $1.71, full pies from $9.25 and pasta from $4.50. For an exotic experience, try **Nyala** (☎ 323-936-5918, 1076 S Fairfax Ave), where the best deal is the all-you-can-eat, all-vegetarian lunch buffet for $5.

Hollywood In central Hollywood the hilarious **Old Spaghetti Factory** (☎ 323-469-7149, 5939 Sunset Blvd) has over-the-top decor and full meals for $6-9, including pasta, salad, bread, dessert and coffee. For superb Thai, try **Sanamluang** (☎ 323-660-8006, 5176 Hollywood Blvd), tucked away in a mini-mall. Meals cost $4-6. Armenian-style rotisserie chicken is the lip-smacking favorite at **Zankou Chicken** (5065 Sunset Blvd); half a bird plus side dishes costs $6. In the Los Feliz District, in eastern Hollywood, **Palermo** (☎ 323-663-1178, 1858 Vermont Ave) is a boisterous budget Italian eatery with huge, satisfying portions.

Some restaurants are worth a splurge. Hemingway and Raymond Chandler are among those who've hoisted martinis and tucked into steaks at the **Musso & Frank Grill** (☎ 323-467-7788, 6667 Hollywood Blvd), a timeless classic since 1919 (entrées $20-35). **Yamashiro** (☎ 323-466-5125, 1999 N Sycamore Ave) is a beautiful Japanese restaurant with stunning views of LA.

On Melrose Ave **Pink's Hot Dogs**, at La Brea Ave, is a landmark 'doggeria' famous for its chili dogs. Along the most frenetic section of Melrose – between La Brea and Fairfax – look for **Caffe Luna** (☎ 323-655-8647, 7463 Melrose Ave), a hip Italian spot with a romantic courtyard. Main dishes cost $9-13. **Bouchon** (☎ 323-852-9400, 7661 Melrose Ave) is a popular French bistro with similar prices. Many Angelenos consider the French restaurant **Patina** (☎ 323-467-1108, 5955 Melrose Ave) to be the city's single

best dining experience. Main dishes start at $20, set dinners at $70.

In West Hollywood **Hugo's** (☎ 323-654-3993, 8401 Santa Monica Blvd) draws stars and producers for power breakfasts ($8-10). The **French Quarter Market** (☎ 323-654-0898, 7985 Santa Monica Blvd) is popular with gay people, but everyone will feel welcome. The vast menu offers great salads, burgers and other classic fare, mostly for under $10. **Cobalt Cantina** (☎ 310-659-8691, 616 N Robertson Blvd) does tapas ($3-9), interesting Cal-Mex sandwiches and main dishes ($11-18) and has promotions (usually Sun-Tue) like two-for-one specials.

Santa Monica & Venice There are plenty of restaurants and cafes on Third Street Promenade, including **Wolfgang Puck Express** (1315 3rd St), upstairs, where gourmets on a budget can sample such Puck best-sellers as the Chinese chicken salad. **Eatz**, the food court on the ground floor of the Santa Monica Place mall, also has plenty of budget choices. **Ye Olde King's Head** (116 Santa Monica Blvd) is famous for its authentic fish and chips (from $8.50).

Real Food Daily (☎ 310-451-7544, 514 Santa Monica Blvd) is one of LA's best vegan restaurants ($6-12). **La Serenata di Garibaldi** (☎ 310-656-7017, 1416 4th St) is an upscale Mexican place with cheerful decor where main dishes average $15. Recommended top-end restaurants include **Röckenwagner** (☎ 310-399-6504, 2435 Main St), for Franco-German cuisine with a California flair; Wolfgang Puck's **Chinois on Main** (☎ 310-392-3037, 2709 Main St), for innovative Cal-Asian fare; and the elegant **JiRaffe** (☎ 310-917-6671, 502 Santa Monica Blvd), for Cal-French food.

On Venice's Ocean Front Walk, you can't beat the views or the people-watching at the **Sidewalk Cafe** (☎ 310-399-4457, 1401 Ocean Front Walk), which serves breakfasts, burgers, salads, nachos and more for under $10. The **Rose Cafe** (☎ 310-399-0711, 220 Rose Ave), two blocks off the beach, has budget-friendly salads and sandwiches. Prices are higher in the restaurant section.

Entertainment

The best sources of information for LA's many entertainment options are the free *LA Weekly* and the 'Calendar' section of the daily *Los Angeles Times*. For most events tickets are available from the venue box offices and from TicketMaster (☎ 213-480-3232).

Bars & Clubs Unless otherwise specified, you must be at least 21 years old to enter bars and nightclubs. At the latter, expect to pay a cover charge of $5-20. Club dress codes, often enforced but usually unofficial, generally prohibit torn jeans, shorts and bare feet.

In Hollywood, *Dragonfly* (☎ 323-466-6111, 6510 Santa Monica Blvd) books mostly rock bands, plus the occasional reggae or Latin group (open Thurs-Sat). *Arena* (☎ 323-462-0714, 6655 Santa Monica Blvd) has theme nights from retro to house to hip-hop to salsa (Thurs-Sun) and usually goes gay on Saturday. The *Formosa Cafe* (☎ 323-850-9050, 7156 Santa Monica Blvd) is a groovy hipster bar that was once a favorite watering hole of Bogart, Monroe and Gable. For local talent, head to the tiki-themed *Lava Lounge* (☎ 323-876-6612, 1533 N La Brea Ave), where the Blue Hawaiian will give you that special Maui buzz. *Opium Den* (☎ 323-466-7800, 1608 Cosmo St) is an exotic island with an ambience that's low in attitude but high in energy. Bands are mostly of the home-grown variety. Popular *El Floridita* (☎ 323-871-8612, 1253 N Vine St) is a Cuban restaurant and dance club where Monday is the most happening night.

In eastern Hollywood, in hip Silver Lake, the *Good Luck Bar* (☎ 323-666-3524, 1514 Hillhurst Ave) is a Chinese fantasy world in carmine red with seductively strong drinks (try Yee Mee Loo Blue). Nearby *Tiki Ti* (☎ 323-669-9381, 4427 Sunset Blvd) is a garage-size tropical tavern stuffed with wickedly wonderful nautical kitsch. In the adjacent Los Feliz neighborhood is *The Derby* (☎ 323-663-8979, 4500 Los Feliz Blvd), a classy club with live bands that is LA's swing central.

In Koreatown the barely lit and old-timey *HMS Bounty* (☎ 323-385-7275, 3357 Wilshire Blvd) now woos a new generation of scenesters with its worn plastic booths and stiff, wallet-friendly drinks. The Mid-Wilshire *Conga Room* (☎ 323-549-9765, 5634 Wilshire Blvd) sizzles with big-name salsa acts like Tito Puente; dress nicely.

In West Hollywood along Sunset Strip there are several legendary LA rock clubs,

including *Coconut Teaszer* (☎ 323-654-4773, 8117 Sunset Blvd), Johnny Depp's celebrity-heavy *Viper Room* (☎ 310-358-1880, 8852 Sunset Blvd), *Whisky a Go Go* (☎ 310-652-4202, 8901 Sunset Blvd) and *The Roxy* (☎ 310-276-2222, 9009 Sunset Blvd). Except for the Viper Room, ages 18 and up are OK. Next to the Whisky, *Cat Club* (☎ 310-657-0888, 8911 Sunset Blvd) is an small, unpretentious club owned by former Stray Cat member Slim Jim Phantom. Theme parties with a naughty bent (drag, gothic, male and female strip shows etc) are the specialty of *Club 7969* (☎ 323-654-0280, 7969 Santa Monica Blvd). Whips and worse come out during Saturday's 'Sin-a-Matic' club.

Most of LA's gay bars are on Santa Monica Blvd in West Hollywood. *The Palms* (☎ 310-652-6188, 8572 Santa Monica Blvd) is the oldest lesbian bar and party venue, with karaoke, live bands and salsa nights. *Rage* (☎ 310-652-7055, 8911 Santa Monica Blvd) is a high-energy men's bar and dance club. *The Abbey* (☎ 310-289-8410, 692 N Robertson Blvd) is a fashionable cafe-bar, where you can sip flavored martinis on a divan in a private booth. The audience is mixed.

In Santa Monica, a block north of Third Street Promenade, *Harvelle's* (☎ 310-395-1676, 1432 4th St) has long been a leading live blues club. *The West End* (☎ 310-313-3293, 1301 5th St) attracts lots of expat Brits and other Euro types to its lively, partylike dance nights, while *Temple Bar* (☎ 310-393-6611, 1026 Wilshire Blvd) books bands nightly, most of them of the funk, hip-hop and rock persuasion. *McCabe's Guitar Shop* (☎ 310-828-4403, 3101 Pico Blvd) is LA's longtime main folk venue where nearly everyone worth his or her salt – Joni Mitchell and John Lee Hooker among them – has played (all ages OK).

In Venice, *Scruffy O'Shea's* (☎ 310-821-0833, 822 Washington Blvd) is party central most nights. It has a happening happy hour, English pub grub and live bands nightly.

Classical Music Downtown, the *Dorothy Chandler Pavilion* (☎ 213-972-7211, 135 N Grand Ave), in the Music Center of LA County, is the city's main venue for highbrow music. It is home to the LA Philharmonic Orchestra, the LA Opera and the LA Master Chorale (tickets $10-150). A summer concert at the *Hollywood Bowl* (☎ 323-850-2000,

2301 N Highland Ave) is a great experience. Start off the evening with a picnic on the parklike grounds or in the bleachers before show time, then relax with a glass of wine (bring your own) beneath the starry skies to the sounds of Beethoven, Wynton Marsalis or mariachi music. Nearby, the ***John Anson Ford Theatre*** *(☎ 323-461-3673, 2580 Cahuenga Blvd E)* has a summer series that includes music, dance and theater.

Theater & Dance There are more than 200 stage groups and venues in the metropolis. Half-price theater tickets for same-day evening or next-day matinee shows are sold by Theatre LA (Ⓦ www.theatrela.org).

The ***Mark Taper Forum*** *(☎ 213-628-2772, 135 N Grand Ave),* at the Music Center of LA County, is one of the West Coast's leading theaters. It emphasizes the development of new plays and presents US and world premieres. The ***Ahmanson Theater*** *(☎ 213-628-2772),* in the same complex, stages major Broadway productions. You will also see top dance shows and musicals at the ***Shubert Theater*** *(☎ 800-447-7400, 2020 Ave of the Stars),* in Century City, and the historic ***Pantages Theater*** *(☎ 323-468-1770, 6233 Hollywood Blvd),* in Hollywood.

Comedy Comedy clubs abound in Hollywood. The excellent ***Groundlings Theater*** *(☎ 323-934-9700, 7307 Melrose Ave)* is a first-rate improv school and company whose alumni include Paul Reubans (Pee-wee Herman), the late Phil Hartman and Julia Sweeney. Top-rated stand-ups appear regularly at ***The Improv*** *(☎ 323-651-2583, 8162 Melrose Ave).* Nearby is *Acme Comedy Theater (☎ 323-525-0202, 135 N La Brea Ave).*

Spectator Sports
The Los Angeles Dodgers play 81 baseball games from April to October at Dodger Stadium (☎ 323-224-1500, 1000 Elysian Park Ave), just north of downtown LA (tickets $6-17). The city has three professional basketball teams, all of which play at the splendid new Staples Center (☎ 213-742-7340, 1111 S Figueroa St), in downtown LA. The top team is the LA Lakers, home of Shaquille O'Neal and Kobe Bryant. More than often, tickets ($21-160) are sold out. The LA Sparks are the city's successful

women's team, while the LA Clippers are its secondary men's team. The Los Angeles Kings professional ice hockey team also plays at the Staples Center. The Los Angeles Galaxy pro soccer team plays at the Rose Bowl (☎ 877-342-5299, 1001 Rose Bowl Dr), in Pasadena.

Getting There & Away
Air Los Angeles International Airport (LAX; ☎ 310-646-5252) is the fourth-busiest airport in the world. Some 17 miles southwest of downtown, LAX has nine terminals, with all but one around a two-level, central traffic loop. Ticketing and check-in are on the upper (departure) level, while baggage-claim areas are on the lower (arrival) level. The hub for international flights is the Tom Bradley International Terminal. To travel between terminals, board the free Shuttle A beneath the LAX Shuttle sign on islands outside each terminal on the lower level. Hotel courtesy shuttles stop here as well.

Some 14 miles northwest of downtown is the Burbank-Glendale-Pasadena Airport (☎ 818-840-8847), which handles mostly regional domestic air travel. It is worth considering if you are staying in Hollywood.

Bus Greyhound Bus Lines (☎ 800-231-2222) serves LA from cities all over North America. The 24-hour main terminal (☎ 213-629-8421, 1716 E 7th St), at Alameda St, is downtown. The area's a bit rough, but the station is safe enough inside. Other LA-area Greyhound stations are in Hollywood (☎ 323-466-6381, 1715 N Cahuenga Blvd), Pasadena (☎ 626-792-5116, 645 E Walnut Ave) and Anaheim (☎ 714-999-1246, 100 W Winston Rd). There are several buses a day to San Francisco ($42; from 7½ hours); Seattle, Washington ($85; from 25½ hours); San Diego ($13; from 2¼ hours); Phoenix, Arizona ($33; from 6½ hours); and Las Vegas, Nevada ($33; from 5 hours).

Green Tortoise (☎ 415-956-7500, 800-867-8647) buses travel weekly up and down the West Coast and into Mexico. Fares cost $35 to San Francisco, $89 to Seattle.

Train Amtrak trains (☎ 800-872-7245) arrive and depart from downtown's Union Station (800 N Alameda St). Trains serve San Francisco ($56 one way; 9½-12½ hours), Seattle ($173; 34½ hours), San

Diego ($26; 2¾ hours) and Phoenix via Tuscon ($106; 12 hours).

Getting Around

The Metropolitan Transportation Authority (MTA; ☎ 800-266-6883, ⓦ www.mta.net) oversees an extensive system that includes buses, light and heavy rail and a new subway. Its customer center (515 S Flower St) is on Level C of ARCO Plaza, downtown.

To/From the Airport

Shuttle Bus C, which stops outside each LAX terminal every 10 to 20 minutes, goes to the LAX Transit Center at 96th St and Vicksburg Ave in El Segundo, about a five-minute ride from the airport. Here you can connect to public buses that will take you anywhere in Greater LA. MTA bus No 42 goes straight to downtown LA ($1.35). For Hollywood take MTA bus No 42 then switch to No 212 at Overhill & La Brea ($1.60). Bus No 3 of the Big Blue Bus company heads for Venice and Santa Monica (50¢).

For door-to-door van service, inquire at the ground-transportation desk at each terminal's lower level. Most shuttles operate 24 hours a day and drop you off right at your destination. Expect to pay $12 to downtown, $19 to Hollywood and $14 to Santa Monica. Try Prime Time (☎ 800-473-3743) and Xpress Shuttle (☎ 800-427-7483). Taxis are plentiful and cost about $25 to Santa Monica, $30 to downtown or Hollywood and up to $80 to Disneyland.

Bus & Metro Rail

A network of 200-plus MTA bus routes spans the metropolis. The fare is $1.35, plus another 25¢ for each transfer you require. The new Metro Rapid is a fast and frequent priority bus: Bus No 720 travels along Wilshire Blvd between Santa Monica and East LA, while bus No 750 connects Universal City with other Valley communities. Downtown LA and some neighborhoods like Hollywood and the Fairfax District are also served by DASH (☎ 213-808-2273) minibuses (25¢; Mon-Sat). The Santa Monica–based Big Blue Bus company (☎ 310-451-5444) serves much of western Los Angeles, including Santa Monica, Venice, Westwood and LAX (50¢). Express bus No 10 runs from Santa Monica to downtown ($1.25).

MTA-operated Metro Rail (☎ 800-266-6883) consists of three lines: the Blue Line between downtown LA and Long Beach, the Red Line subway from downtown's Union Station to North Hollywood (via Central Hollywood and Universal Studios), and the Green Line from Norwalk to Redondo Beach. Tickets are dispensed by coin-operated machines ($1.35).

Car & Motorcycle

If you're going to rent a car, do it at the airport upon arrival. Agencies are throughout the LA area, but bargaining power goes farthest at LAX. Expect to pay $25-45 per day, or $120-200 per week, for the smallest model. Most rental agencies require that drivers be at least 21 years old; drivers under 25 must normally pay a surcharge of $5-15 per day. Rates do not include the 8% sales tax...or insurance ($9-14 a day). Independent agencies that may have lower rates include Midway (☎ 800-366-0643, 1901 Ocean Ave), in Santa Monica, and Rent-A-Wreck (☎ 310-478-0676, 12333 W Pico Blvd), in West LA.

Taxi

Except for those lined up outside airports, train stations, bus stations and major hotels, cabbies will only respond to phone calls. Fares are metered: $2 flagfall plus $1.80 per mile. Try Checker (☎ 800-300-5007) or Independent (☎ 800-521-8294).

AROUND LOS ANGELES
Long Beach

The port town of Long Beach is LA County's southernmost city and its second largest. For an easy day trip take the Metro Rail Blue Line from downtown LA. Long Beach has a small, vibrant downtown, with most of the action centered on Pine Ave. It also has a pleasant shoreline where the elegant British ocean liner **Queen Mary** (☎ 562-435-3511, 1126 Queens Hwy) has been moored since 1967. Larger and more luxurious than even the *Titanic,* it transported royals, dignitaries and immigrants during its 1001 Atlantic crossings between 1934 and 1964 ($17).

Long Beach's other flagship attraction is the fabulous **Aquarium of the Pacific** (☎ 562-590-3100, 100 Aquarium Way). Seventeen large habitats and 30 smaller focus tanks house more than 10,000 fish, mammals and birds from three Pacific Rim regions: Southern California & Baja, Northern Pacific and Tropical Pacific ($15).

Santa Catalina Island

Santa Catalina is one of the largest of the Channel Islands, a chain of semisubmerged mountains between Santa Barbara and San Diego. It was bought in 1919 by William Wrigley Jr (the heir to the chewing-gum fortune), who built a mansion and an art deco casino in Avalon. He also briefly made Catalina the spring training headquarters for his baseball team, the Chicago Cubs.

The Mediterranean-flavored port town of **Avalon** has attracted tourists since the 1930s. Catalina's interior and most of its coastline are largely undeveloped. It's possible to visit Avalon on a day trip, but it's better to spend at least one night and take an island tour. Jeep Eco-Tours (☎ 310-510-2595 ext 0), run by the Santa Catalina Island Conservancy, offers three-hour journeys on the island's backroads ($98). To see Santa Catalina's rich underwater gardens, take a trip on a glass-bottom boat; Santa Catalina Discovery Tours (☎ 310-510-8687) and Catalina Adventure Tours (☎ 310-510-2888) both operate tours from the Avalon pier ($8).

Catalina Express (☎ 310-519-1212) offers year-round service to Santa Catalina from Long Beach and San Pedro with up to 30 departures in summer ($42 roundtrip). The first boat leaves around 6:30am, the last boat around 8pm.

Campers should reserve a site at *Hermit Gulch Campground* (☎ *310-510-8368),* in Avalon Canyon. It's a 1½-mile hike or bus ride ($6-12). For information on camp-grounds in the interior call ☎ 888-510-7979.

In Avalon the cheapest accommodations option is *Hostel La Vista* (☎ *310-510-0603, 145 Marilla Ave),* with basic facilities ($15; open June-Oct). Half a block from the shore, the friendly *Hermosa Hotel* (☎ *310-510-1010, 131 Metropole St)* is a great value ($35-55 weekdays, $50-100 weekends). The newly remodeled *Catalina Beach House* (☎ *310-510-1078, 200 Marilla Ave)* charges $35-145.

San Bernardino Mountains

Surrounded by the San Bernardino National Forest, 110 miles east of LA, **Big Bear** is a family-oriented mountain town built around a big lake. In summer there's water sports, mountain biking and hiking; in winter there's skiing at Bear Mountain (☎ 909-585-2519) and Snow Summit (☎ 909-866-5766);

ski passes cost $35-40. The local chamber of commerce (☎ 909-866-4607, 630 Bartlett Rd) has area maps and other information. The excellent Discovery Center (☎ 909-866-3437), on the north shore of Big Bear Lake, has camping information and wilderness permits. Lodges, hotels, motels and cabins line Hwy 18. Hotel rooms cost around $50 weeknights, double on weekends; for free reservations, call ☎ 800-424-4232.

Mountain Area Regional Transit Authority (MARTA; ☎ 909-584-1111) buses connect Big Bear with the Greyhound bus station and the Metrolink train station in San Bernardino ($5). Groups up to 10 people can reserve the door-to-door Big Bear Shuttle (☎ 909-585-5514), which costs $150 plus $10 per person.

Big Bear Lake is about a 2½-hour drive from LA. Take I-10 (San Bernardino Fwy) east to Hwy 30 in Redlands. Follow Hwy 30 to Hwy 330 and then Hwy 18. For a more scenic route, exit Orange St N in Redlands and follow the signs to Hwy 38.

Disneyland

Opened in 1955 by Walt Disney himself, Disneyland (☎ 714-781-4000, 1313 Harbor Blvd) is billed as the 'Happiest Place on Earth' and is certainly an integral part of an American childhood. The park is divided into seven thematic 'lands,' including the Western-style Frontierland, the jungle-themed Adventureland, the space-age Tomorrowland, and Fantasyland, peopled by Disney characters. Each features several rides – favorites include Space Mountain, the Indiana Jones Adventure and Pirates of the Caribbean.

In February 2001, a second park called **Disney's California Adventure** opened right next to the original. It too is subdivided into several sections, each of which celebrates a California region, from Hollywood to San Francisco. Rides are exciting and imaginative but don't have the heart-stopping velocity of Disneyland's. Connecting the two parks is the new **Downtown Disney**, a pedestrian mall (free admission) with a fun, though sanitized, mix of dining, shopping and entertainment venues, including a House of Blues branch and the ESPN Zone, a vast sports bar with 175 TV monitors.

You can see either park in a day, but it requires at least two days to go on all the

CALIFORNIA

Disney Facts

- Disneyland welcomed its millionth visitor in 1955 after seven weeks in operation.
- In 1959 Nikita Khrushchev was denied park entry.
- Each year park visitors consume four million hamburgers and 3.4 million orders of fries. On a busy day, 30 tons of trash are collected.
- Comedian Steve Martin once worked at a Disneyland magic shop.
- The Jungle Cruise was planned to showcase live tigers, lions and snakes, until park officials realized the animals would sleep all day and possibly eat visitors.

rides (three if visiting both parks), especially in summer when lines are long – visit midweek or arrive when the gates open. A one-day pass, including all rides, costs $43/$33 adults/kids ages three to nine; kids under age three go free. Three-day passes good for admission to both parks cost $111/87 adults/kids, four-day passes $137/107. Parking costs $8. Hours change constantly, though 10am-8pm off-season and 8am-10pm in summer are rough guidelines. Call ahead to be sure.

The friendly *HI Fullerton Hostel* (☎ 714-738-3721, 1700 N Harbor Blvd), 5 miles from the park, has the cheapest accommodations around (beds $13-15; nonmembers $3 more). There are dozens of chain motels surrounding the park offering rooms with basic amenities from around $70. The pleasant *Castle Inn & Suites* (☎ 714-774-8111, 1734 S Harbor Blvd) is often booked but has nice rooms ($80-110), a pool and free parking. If it's full, try the *Candy Cane Inn* (☎ 714-774-5284, 1747 S Harbor Blvd), across the street, which has similar prices.

Around Disneyland

Travelers usually stay away from the smog- and strip-mall-filled interior Orange County, but there are a few diamonds in this urban rough. **Knott's Berry Farm** (☎ 714-220-5200), 4 miles northwest of Disneyland, is a high-tech amusement park with an Old West theme, roller coasters,

gold-panning demonstrations and staged gun fights. It's less crowded than Disneyland and plenty of fun ($40). Second-tier sights include Robert Schuller's psychedelic **Crystal Cathedral** (☎ 714-971-4000), off I-5 at Chapman Ave in Garden Grove, and the **Richard Nixon Library & Birthplace** (☎ 714-993-3393, 18001 Yorba Linda Blvd), in Yorba Linda, 15 minutes northeast of Disneyland.

Orange County Beaches

Surfers, artists and retirees give Orange County's beach towns their distinct vibe. South of Long Beach, the first official 'beach town' is **Seal Beach**, with a pleasantly walkable downtown that lies along a few blocks of Main St. Farther south, sophisticated **Newport Beach** has good shopping and a huge pleasure-craft harbor. The main tourist area, south of Hwy 1 via Balboa Blvd, has beaches, the 1905 Balboa Pier and a family-oriented amusement center. At the very tip of the peninsula is The Wedge, a bodysurfing spot with waves up to 30 feet high.

Secluded beaches, glassy waves and a host of art galleries make **Laguna Beach** incredibly popular. Crowds are thick on summer weekends. Each July Laguna hosts the well-respected Festival of the Arts, the less high-brow Sawdust Festival (also an arts festival) and the Pageant of the Masters, where human models stand perfectly still to recreate famous paintings. Tickets to the Pageant ($10-60) must be ordered weeks in advance (☎ 800-487-3378).

Mission San Juan Capistrano, off I-5 a few miles north of Hwy 1, is one of California's most visited missions, with a lush garden and graceful arches ($6). The *HI San Clemente* (☎ 949-492-2848, 233 Ave Granada), in San Clemente, is situated five blocks from the beach (beds $13-16; open May-Oct).

San Diego

Conservative, comfortable and affluent San Diego is a great place to enjoy the laid-back California lifestyle. The city is more accessible and far friendlier than Los Angeles, and there are plenty of sights and activities – museums, zoos, animal parks, beaches and more – to keep you busy for a few days.

History

The indigenous Kumayaay people lived in small villages around the bay, catching fish and birds, collecting shellfish, and using local plants for food. They made seasonal trips to hunt and gather acorns in the Cuyamaca mountains, where grinding holes are about the only tangible remains of their long habitation. The first contacts with Europeans were fleeting, but in 1769, Father Junípero Serra founded the first of the California missions here. Initially ravaged by disease and Indian attack, the mission eventually achieved some stability and had as many as 1500 converted Kumayaay in the congregation. The other missions in the area included San Luis Rey Francia (1798), San Antonio de Pala (1815) and Santa Ysabel (1818).

After Mexico won independence, the missions were dissolved and their lands were granted to large cattle runs called 'ranchos.' The small community of San Diego became a civilian pueblo in 1835. Despite the prosperity of the rancheros, San Diego remained a ramshackle village at the base of the Presidio Hill, while the displaced Kumayaay fell into poverty.

San Diego was a backwater until the early 20th century, when it acquired some importance in aviation and as a minor naval base. When Pearl Harbor, Hawaii, was bombed, the headquarters of the US Pacific Fleet moved to San Diego, and the boom in wartime activity transformed the city. Since WWII, growth has been phenomenal, with the climate and the seafront location attracting businesses, tourists, and educational and research institutions.

Orientation & Information

The downtown area is a compact grid east of San Diego Bay, with the train station, Greyhound terminal and airport close by. Most attractions are also within easy reach of downtown. The International Visitors Information Center (☎ 619-236-1212) is on 1st Ave at the west side of Horton Plaza (closed Sun in winter). The smaller International Information Center (☎ 619-232-8583, 170 6th Ave) is opposite the Gaslamp Quarter gateway (Tue-Sat). A third visitor center (☎ 619-276-8200), beside E Mission Bay Dr, is convenient if you are coming into San Diego on I-5. All three stock discount coupons for major sights, such as SeaWorld and the San Diego Zoo.

For all your reading needs, try the Upstart Crow (835 W Harbor Dr) or Le Travel Store (739 4th Ave) bookstores. In Coronado visit Bay Books (1029 Orange Ave).

Hillcrest is the center of San Diego's gay community. Here the Lesbian & Gay Men's Center (☎ 619-692-2077, 3909 Centre St) provides information and counseling. The *Gay & Lesbian Times* (☎ 619-299-6397) is a free weekly published in San Diego. Also check out the Gay San Diego Web site (Ⓦ www.gaysandiego.com).

Downtown

After San Diego's downtown was subdivided by the speculator Alonzo Horton in 1867, its main street, 5th Ave, became known as the Stingaree, a notorious strip of saloons, gambling joints and bordellos. It was so seedy that its buildings survived the later office-development boom, and the restored buildings now house restaurants, bars, theaters and galleries.

With new brick sidewalks and old-style wrought-iron streetlamps, the **Gaslamp Quarter** is at its most enjoyable on warm evenings, when people throng the streets and crowd the restaurants' outdoor tables. The Gaslamp Quarter Historical Foundation, headquartered at the **William Heath Davis House** (☎ 619-233-4692, 410 Island Ave), conducts historical walking tours ($5; 11am Sat). The house itself, now an interesting museum, was built on the East Coast in 1850 and later shipped to San Diego via Cape Horn.

Downtown's main drag is Broadway, a functional street that goes from the waterfront, past the impressive Santa Fe Depot, the trolley depot and some new high-rise buildings. The postmodern **Horton Plaza** shopping mall occupies a seven-block area south of Broadway, with cinemas, theaters, restaurants and 140 shops in a wildly colorful, crescent-shaped open courtyard – it's like an Escher drawing.

Opposite the Santa Fe Depot, the **Museum of Contemporary Art** (☎ 619-234-1001) has changing exhibitions of painting and sculpture (free admission; closed Wed).

San Diego Children's Museum (☎ 619-233-8792, 200 W Island Ave) has giant construction toys, craft activities, storytelling and music for the kiddies ($6).

SAN DIEGO

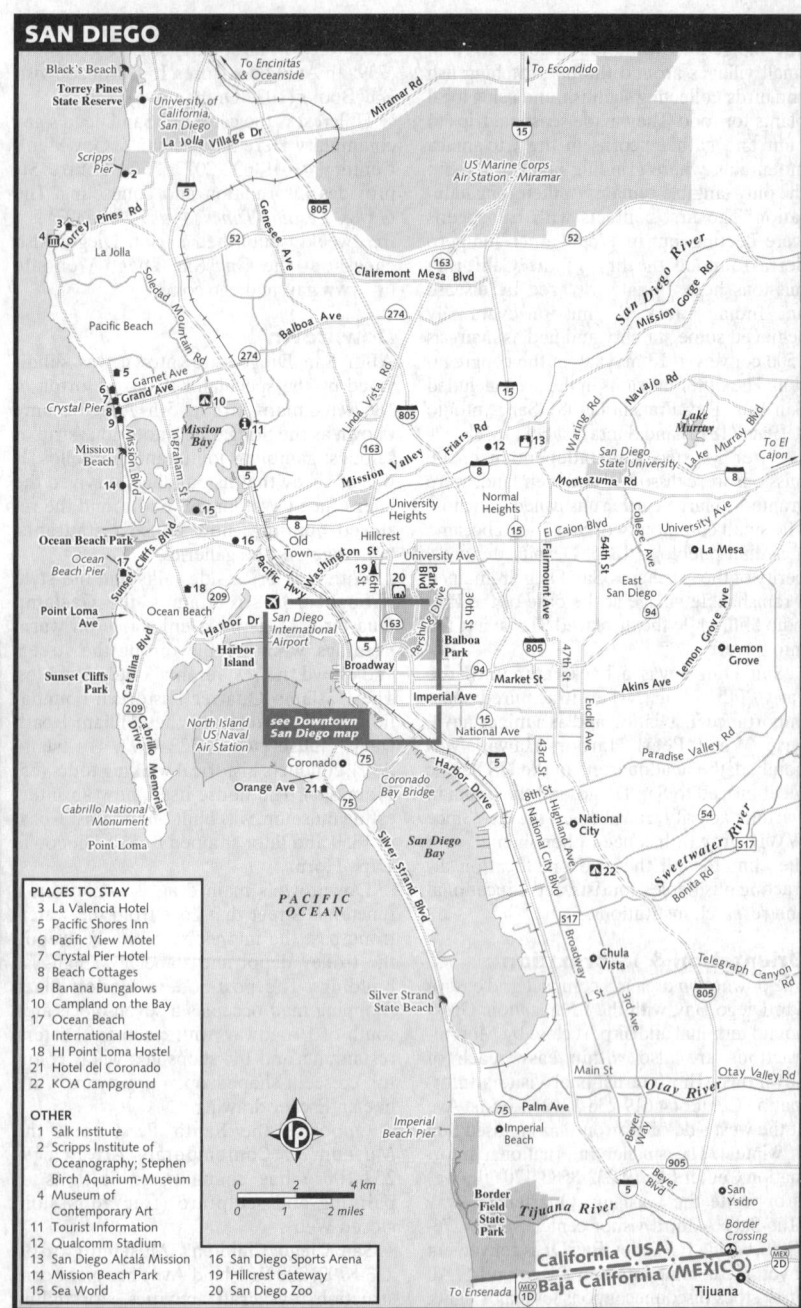

Black's Beach
Torrey Pines
State Reserve
1
University of
California,
San Diego
La Jolla Village Dr
To Encinitas
& Oceanside
To Escondido
Miramar Rd
15
US Marine Corps
Air Station - Miramar
Scripps
Pier
2
5
805
Torrey Pines Rd
3
4
La Jolla
52
52
San Diego River
Clairemont Mesa Blvd
163
Mission Gorge Rd
Pacific Beach
Balboa Ave
274
274
Watson Rd
Navajo Rd
Lake
Murray
5
Garnet Ave
6
Grand Ave
8
9
10
Mission
Bay
11
805
15
163
12
13
San Diego
State University
Lake Murray Blvd
To El
Cajon
Mission
Beach
Ingraham St
Linda Vista Rd
Friars Rd
Mission Valley
Montezuma Rd
College Ave
8
14
15
8
University
Heights
Normal
Heights
El Cajon Blvd
University Ave
Ocean Beach Park
16
Old
Town
Hillcrest
15
54th St
East
San Diego
La Mesa
Ocean
Beach Pier
17
Sunset Cliffs Blvd
Pacific Hwy
Washington St
University Ave
Fairmount Ave
Point Loma
Ave
18
209
Ocean Beach
Harbor Dr
19
20
Park
Blvd
30th St
805
47th St
Lemon Grove Ave
Lemon
Grove
Sunset Cliffs
Park
Catalina Blvd
Cabrillo Memorial Drive
209
Harbor
Island
San Diego
International
Airport
163
Balboa
Park
94
Akins Ave
Euclid Ave
North Island
US Naval
Air Station
Broadway
Imperial Ave
94
Market St
Paradise Valley Rd
see Downtown
San Diego map
National Ave
43rd St
8th St
Cabrillo National
Monument
Point Loma
Coronado
75
Orange Ave
21
75
Coronado
Bay Bridge
San Diego
Bay
Harbor Drive
Silver Strand Blvd
National City Blvd
National
City
54
517
Sweetwater River
Bonita Rd
22
PACIFIC
OCEAN
517
Broadway
Chula
Vista
3rd Ave
Telegraph Canyon Rd
805
Silver Strand
State Beach
L St
Main St
Otay River
Otay Valley Rd
75
Palm Ave
905
Imperial
Beach Pier
Imperial
Beach
Beyer Way
Beyer Blvd
San
Ysidro
Border
Field
State
Park
Tijuana River
Border
Crossing
California (USA)
MEX
2D
To Ensenada
MEX
1D
Baja California (MEXICO)
Tijuana

PLACES TO STAY
3 La Valencia Hotel
5 Pacific Shores Inn
6 Pacific View Motel
7 Crystal Pier Hotel
8 Beach Cottages
9 Banana Bungalows
10 Campland on the Bay
17 Ocean Beach
   International Hostel
18 HI Point Loma Hostel
21 Hotel del Coronado
22 KOA Campground

OTHER
1 Salk Institute
2 Scripps Institute of
   Oceanography; Stephen
   Birch Aquarium-Museum
4 Museum of
   Contemporary Art
11 Tourist Information
12 Qualcomm Stadium
13 San Diego Alcalá Mission
14 Mission Beach Park
15 Sea World

16 San Diego Sports Arena
19 Hillcrest Gateway
20 San Diego Zoo

0   2   4 km
0   1   2 miles

CALIFORNIA

Embarcadero

The San Diego waterfront is remarkably clean and attractive. One conspicuous attraction is the *Star of India,* with its tall masts and rigging. The ship is the highlight of the **Maritime Museum** (☎ 619-234-9153), which has two other restored sailing vessels ($6; open 9am-9pm). Aircraft carriers park across the harbor. Farther south are piers for cruise ships and harbor ferries, the fishing boat harbor and **Seaport Village** (☎ 619-235-4014), a touristy collection of novelty shops, restaurants and snack outlets.

Balboa Park

Northeast of downtown, the beautiful landscaping of Balboa Park is attributable to horticulturalist Kate Sessions, who planted some 10,000 trees and shrubs here. Spanish colonial-style buildings, constructed as temporary structures for the 1915–16 Panama-California Exposition, were so popular that many were retained and rebuilt and now house museums along El Prado promenade. You can stroll around the park anytime, but be cautious after dark. Balboa Park is easily reached from downtown San Diego on bus Nos 7, 7A and 7B along Park Blvd.

The Balboa Park Information Center (☎ 619-239-0512), in the House of Hospitality on El Prado, sells park maps ($1) and the Balboa Passport ($21), which allows a single admission to nine of the park's museums (excluding the zoo) for one week. Individual museum admissions are $5-10; museums offer free entry Tuesday on a rotating schedule. Unless noted otherwise, the museums are closed Monday.

Coming from the west, El Prado passes under a decorated archway and into a quadrangle, with the **Museum of Man** (☎ 619-239-2001) on its north side. The museum has artifacts from all over the world as well as excellent temporary exhibits such as Inquisition: Torture & Intolerance, a medieval torture-device exhibit (open daily). The **Simon Edison Centre for the Performing Arts** (☎ 619-239-2255) has three venues, including The Old Globe Theatre, which has a top-notch summer Shakespeare series. At the southwest corner of the Plaza de Panama is the **Mingei International Museum** (☎ 619-239-0003), with a fascinating collection of folk art from around the globe.

One of the country's largest art museums, the **San Diego Museum of Art** (☎ 619-232-7931) includes European masterpieces, fine American landscapes and interesting Asian galleries. The nearby **Timken Museum of Art** (☎ 619-239-5548), in a boxy 1965 building, houses a small but impressive collection, with paintings by Rembrandt, Rubens, El Greco, Cézanne and Pissarro, plus some very appealing Russian icons. The **Museum of Photographic Arts** (☎ 619-238-7559) exhibits fine art photography from the late 19th century to the present, as well as an ongoing film series.

The **Reuben H Fleet Science Center** (☎ 619-238-1233) has hands-on exhibits to teach children about the scientific world. It also has San Diego's only IMAX theater, featuring everything from planetarium shows to *Michael Jordan to the Max.* Recently renovated, the **Natural History Museum** (☎ 619-232-3821) is far more interesting, with good exhibits on gems, bugs, ocean ecology, reptiles and dinosaurs (open daily).

Buildings south of Plaza de Panama date from the 1935 Pacific-California Exposition. Most interesting are the **San Diego Automotive Museum** (☎ 619-231-2886), with a

---

The Legacy of Kate Sessions

Kate O Sessions graduated with a degree in botany from the University of California at Berkeley in 1881, a time when few women attended college and even fewer studied the natural sciences. She came to San Diego as a schoolteacher but soon began working as a horticulturist, establishing gardens for the fashionable homes of the city's emerging elite. In 1892, in need of space for a nursery, she proposed an unusual deal to city officials: She would have the use of 30 acres of city-owned Balboa Park for her nursery in return for planting 100 trees a year and donating 300 others for placement throughout San Diego. The city agreed to the arrangement, and Kate Sessions more than fulfilled her side of the bargain. Within 10 years, Balboa Park had shade trees, lawns, paths and flower beds. Grateful San Diegans soon began referring to her as 'The Mother of Balboa Park.'

DOWNTOWN SAN DIEGO

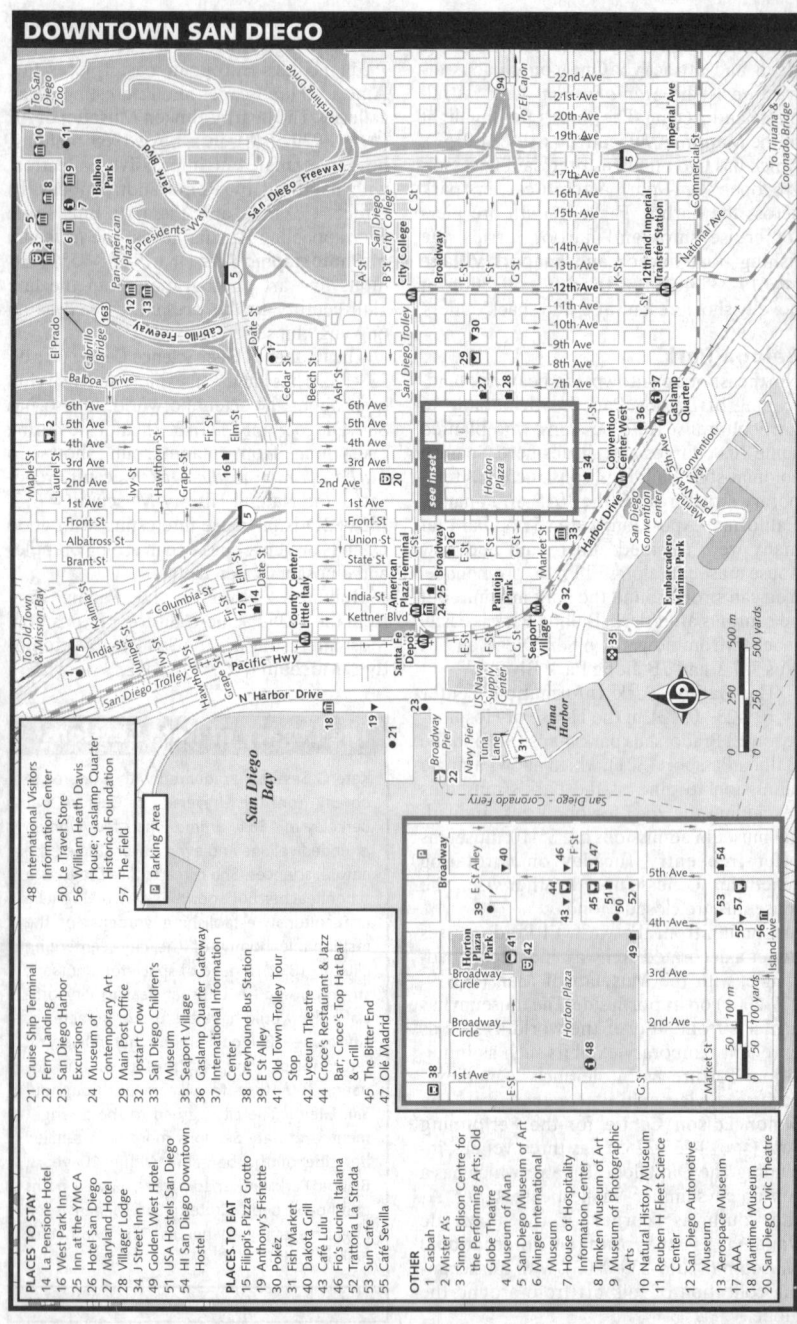

PLACES TO STAY
14 La Pensione Hotel
16 West Park Inn
25 Inn at the YMCA
26 Hotel San Diego
27 Maryland Hotel
28 Villager Lodge
34 J Street Inn
49 Golden West Hotel
51 USA Hostels San Diego
54 HI San Diego Downtown Hostel

PLACES TO EAT
15 Filippi's Pizza Grotto
19 Anthony's Fishette
30 Pokéz
31 Fish Market
40 Dakota Grill
43 Café Lulu
46 Fio's Cucina Italiana
52 Trattoria La Strada
53 Sun Cafe
55 Café Sevilla

21 Cruise Ship Terminal
22 Ferry Landing
23 San Diego Harbor Excursions
24 Museum of Contemporary Art
29 Main Post Office
32 Upstart Crow
33 San Diego Children's Museum
35 Seaport Village
36 Gaslamp Quarter Gateway
37 International Information Center
38 Greyhound Bus Station
39 E St Alley
41 Old Town Trolley Tour Stop
42 Lyceum Theatre
44 Croce's Restaurant & Jazz Bar; Croce's Top Hat Bar & Grill
45 The Bitter End
47 Ole Madrid

48 International Visitors Information Center
50 Le Travel Store
56 William Heath Davis House; Gaslamp Quarter Historical Foundation
57 The Field

OTHER
1 Casbah
2 Mister A's
3 Simon Edison Centre for the Performing Arts; Old Globe Theatre
4 Museum of Man
5 San Diego Museum of Art
6 Mingei International Museum
7 House of Hospitality Information Center
8 Timken Museum of Art
9 Museum of Photographic Arts
10 Natural History Museum
11 Reuben H Fleet Science Center
12 San Diego Automotive Museum
13 Aerospace Museum
17 AAA
18 Maritime Museum
20 San Diego Civic Theatre

☑ Parking Area

well-presented collection of more than 80 cars and motorbikes, and the **Aerospace Museum** (☎ 619-234-8291), which has models as well as replica and original aircraft.

The most famous site in Balboa Park is the world-class **San Diego Zoo** (☎ 619-234-3153, W www.sandiegozoo.org), with more than 4000 animals in a beautifully landscaped setting. Highlights include the bioclimatic exhibits, such as Tiger River (a re-created Asian rainforest environment) and Gorilla Tropics (an African rainforest). Arrive early, when animals are most active. Admission costs $18/8 adults/kids or $27/15 with a 40-minute guided bus tour and aerial tram ride. Discount coupons are available. The zoo is open daily year round. Joint tickets to the zoo and San Diego Wild Animal Park (see Around San Diego, later) cost $41/26.

Presidio Hill, Mission Valley & Old Town

In 1769 the first Spanish mission in California was established on the Presidio Hill, overlooking the valley of the San Diego River. Though none of the original structures remains, the attractive site is now occupied by the **Junípero Serra Museum** (☎ 619-297-3258), an imitation Spanish colonial building with artifacts and pictures from the Mission and Rancho periods ($5; open 10am-4:30pm Fri-Sun).

In 1773 the settlement, **Mission San Diego de Alcalá**, was moved a few miles upriver. Rebuilt several times after Indian attack, earthquake and deterioration, it now has a small congregation, a visitor center (☎ 619-281-8449) and a sleepy old Spanish ambience ($2). I-8 runs the length of the valley, past hotels, golf courses, shopping centers and the spectacular multilevel interchange at I-805.

The land beneath the hill was laid out with a plaza, and by the 1830s Pueblo de San Diego had 40 huts and a few large adobe houses. After it was established as a state historic park in 1968, archaeological work was done and old buildings were reconstructed. Now **Old Town** is a pleasant but touristy pedestrian precinct with shops and restaurants. The visitor center (☎ 619-220-5422), near the Old Town Theatre, has free guided tours at 10:30am and 2pm daily.

Hillcrest

Some ornate Victorian mansions survive in the once-fashionable hills north of downtown. The corner of University and 5th Aves is the heart of Hillcrest. This is the colorful center of San Diego's gay community, marked by a big suspended neon sign. Nearby are bars, restaurants, bookstores and record shops. Stop at Gaymart (☎ 619-543-1221, 550 University Ave) for sex toys, tight polyester shorts and gay newspapers and bulletins.

Point Loma

This peninsula extends across the entrance to San Diego Bay. At its southern tip, **Cabrillo National Monument** (☎ 619-557-5450) – where Juan Rodríguez Cabrillo landed briefly in 1542 – offers stunning panoramas over the bay. The visitor center has good exhibits on the native inhabitants and natural history. Also interesting are the 1854 lighthouse, the tide pools on the ocean side and whale-watching in winter. Access is via Catalina Blvd or bus No 6A from downtown ($5 per car, $2 walk-in).

Beaches

There are three main beaches in San Diego. The farthest south is Ocean Beach, which has a long fishing pier, beach volleyball, sunset barbecues and good surf. Newport Ave is well stocked with bars, eateries and shops selling beachwear and surf gear. Farther north are Mission Beach and Pacific Beach. Ocean Front Walk lines both beaches and attracts skaters and cyclists year round. In summer it's 3 miles of *Baywatch* California beach scene, with end-to-end bodies, cafes, beach bars, surf rental shops and impossible parking. Mission Beach Park has a classic wooden roller coaster and a large indoor pool. Pacific Beach (or PB) activity spreads inland along Garnet Ave, with many lively bars and restaurants. There are more beaches in La Jolla and Coronado.

Coronado

Not quite an island, the oh-so-respectable community of Coronado is joined to the mainland by a spectacular 2-mile bridge and a long, narrow sand spit that runs south to Imperial Beach. North Island Naval Air Station occupies a big chunk of northern

CALIFORNIA

Coronado. Hourly ferries to Coronado leave from Broadway Pier, a few blocks south of the Maritime Museum ($4 roundtrip). You can also come across by ferry and rent a bike at Holland's Bicycle Shop (☎ 619-435-3153, 977 Orange Ave) to cruise around.

The Hotel del Coronado (see Places to Stay, later), on the island's southeast corner, is a much-loved local institution. It has conical towers, cupolas and dormer windows. A gallery features famous guests of the 'Hotel Del,' including Marilyn Monroe, Frank Sinatra and Hillary Clinton.

Mission Bay

Coastal engineering turned the swampy mouth of the San Diego River into a 7-sq-mile playground of beaches, bays and parks. Facilities run from luxurious resort hotels to free outdoor activities. Kite flying is popular, along with water sports and cycling on the miles of bike paths.

San Diego's star attraction, **Sea World** (☎ 619-226-3901, W www.seaworld.com) started here in 1964. It's very commercial, but the Shamu show and dolphin acts are entertaining, while the Shark Encounter and Hidden Reef are almost educational. Expect long waits for shows in peak season ($42/32 adults/kids, $6 parking; open 9am-11pm daily in summer, otherwise until sunset). Take bus No 9 from downtown.

La Jolla

This swanky and status-conscious suburb (pronounced la-**hoy**-a) has upscale shopping and a scenic seafront. Noteworthy sights include the Children's Pool, La Jolla Cove and, marked by buoys, the offshore San Diego–La Jolla Underwater Park, a great spot for scuba diving (see Activities, later). The **Museum of Contemporary Art** (MCA; ☎ 858-454-3541, 700 Prospect St) has been the cultural focus of La Jolla since 1941 ($4; closed Wed).

The area is home to the University of California at San Diego (UCSD) and renowned research institutes. The **Salk Institute** (☎ 858-453-4100), a biomedical research center on the UCSD campus, is a masterpiece of modern architecture, designed in 1965 by Louis Kahn; you can call to arrange a free weekday tour. At UCSD's Scripps Institute of Oceanography, the **Stephen Birch**

Aquarium-Museum (☎ 858-534-3474) presents brilliant displays of marine life and sciences and is definitely worth a visit ($8.50). There's superb coastline at **Torrey Pines State Reserve** ($2 per car) with gorgeous ocean-view trails. The cliffs attract hang gliders. Separate **Blacks Beach** is popular with nudists and gays.

Activities

San Diego has good **surfing**, but it can get crowded. For surf reports call ☎ 619-221-8824. First-timers should try Pacific Beach Surf School (☎ 858-488-9575), and soon you'll be surfin' like the pros ($45 for 1½ hours; reservations required). The best **scuba diving** is in the San Diego–La Jolla Underwater Park, with giant kelp forests and the 100-foot-deep La Jolla Canyon; the Diving Locker (☎ 858-272-1120, 1020 Grand Ave) and Blue Escape (☎ 619-223-3483, 888-500-3483, 1617 Quivira Rd, Suite B) charge $40 to $65 per dive. Harbor Excursions (☎ 619-234-4111, 800-442-7847) conducts three-hour **whale-watching** trips ($23; mid-Dec to Mar) that depart from Broadway Pier.

Organized Tours

Old Town Trolley Tours (☎ 619-298-8687, 800-868-7482), in Horton Plaza, does a loop around the main attractions near downtown; you get on and off as you please ($21). Other tours are offered by Grayline (☎ 619-491-0011, 1775 Hancock St, Suite 130). Hourlong harbor cruises with Hornblower Cruises (☎ 619-686-8700) or San Diego Harbor Excursions (☎ 619-234-4111) depart daily from Broadway Pier ($13).

Places to Stay

Accommodations in summer, particularly beachside, are heavily booked and highly priced. A good way to save a few dollars is by booking your room with a discount reservation service such as Save Cash (☎ 800-728-3227, W www.savecash.com) or San Diego Hotel Discounts (☎ 619-238-0900, W www.sandiegodiscounts.com). No matter where you stay, county taxes add 10.5% to the bill.

Camping The *Campland on the Bay* *(☎ 800-422-9386),* on Mission Bay, has a restaurant, pool, sauna and bike and boat rentals, but the tent area is unattractive. The most expensive sites face the water ($50/100 tent/RV, cheaper Mon-Fri). **KOA** *(☎ 619-427-3601, 800-562-9877, 111 N 2nd Ave)*, in Chula Vista, is about 5 miles southeast of downtown ($30/35 tent/RV). Take the trolley at 12th and Market Sts to Chula Vista, then bus No 706.

Hostels San Diego's hostels are open year round, and none has a curfew. In the Gaslamp Quarter, the **HI San Diego Downtown Hostel** *(☎ 619-525-1531, 521 Market St)* is clean and convenient, offering four- and six-bed dorms both for $18, $20 nonmembers, and a handful of doubles for $50. A much better option is **USA Hostels San Diego** *(☎ 619-232-3100, 726 5th Ave)*, housed in a renovated Victorian, with extremely friendly staff, cozy rooms and free waffles and pancakes for breakfast. Dorm beds cost $19 and private rooms $40. Prices go up slightly in summer. Close to the beach, the laid-back **Ocean Beach International Hostel** *(☎ 619-223-7873, 800-339-7263, 4961 Newport Ave)* has a great location ($15-17). Proof of international travel is required. Up in Pacific Beach, **Banana Bungalows** *(☎ 858-273-3060, 707 Reed Ave)* is a great place for a beachside party but a tough place to get a good night's sleep ($16-20). The 61-bed **HI Point Loma Hostel** *(☎ 619-223-4778, 3790 Udall St)* is about a mile from Ocean Beach in what looks like suburbia and is inconvenient without a car (take the SeaWorld Dr exit off I-8). Otherwise it's clean and comfortable ($15-18).

Motels & Hotels Budget hotels can be hard to come by, especially in the summertime, but there are still a few available. On the very budget, almost sketchy end are **Golden West Hotel** *(☎ 619-233-7594, 720 4th Ave)*, a once-stylish hotel from the 1940s, with singles/doubles for $29/32; the art deco **Hotel San Diego** *(☎ 619-234-0221, 339 W Broadway)*, with doubles from $39; and the simpler **Maryland Hotel** *(☎ 619-239-9243, 630 F St)*, with rooms for $35/40. The **Inn at the YMCA** *(☎ 619-234-5252, 500 W Broadway)* is a surprisingly stylish 1920s building offering clean doubles (from $30) with access to the Y's gym, pool and sauna. **J Street Inn** *(☎ 619-696-6922, 222 J St)* is a converted apartment complex with spacious rooms ($35/40) and

friendly staff. **Villager Lodge** *(☎ 619-238-4100, 660 G St)* has a bit more character than the chain hotels and offers free off-street parking ($69 Mon-Fri, $99 Sat-Sun).

Close to downtown in Little Italy, **La Pensione Hotel** *(☎ 619-236-8000, 606 W Date St)* is a contemporary European-style guesthouse with clean, simple rooms overlooking the bay or the city ($50/60). Halfway between downtown and Hillcrest, **West Park Inn** *(☎ 619-236-1600, 1840 4th Ave)* is yet another converted apartment block, with fully equipped doubles ($55) facing a shady courtyard.

In Hillcrest, **Studio 819** *(☎ 619-542-0819, 819 University Ave)* is a residential hotel with a welcoming staff and clean doubles ($55). **Hillcrest Inn** *(☎ 619-293-7078, 3754 5th Ave)*, is a gay-friendly hotel in a spectacular location with rooms surrounding a pool, Jacuzzi and garden (doubles $55-79).

Motels near the beach can be a good value off-season, but summer prices increase by 30% or more. Pacific Beach has the best selection. Try the **Pacific View Motel** *(☎ 858-483-6117, 610 Emerald St)*, which is not the cleanest motel but is right on the beach ($45-65). **Pacific Shores Inn** *(☎ 619-483-6300, 4802 Mission Blvd)* is a good deal with spacious doubles and a pool ($69). The **Beach Cottages** *(☎ 858-483-7440, 4255 Ocean Blvd)*, next to the Banana Bungalow hostel, offers one- and two-bedroom cottages ($130/200). At **Crystal Pier Hotel** *(☎ 858-483-6983, 4500 Ocean Blvd)* the rooms ($165-195) are built on the pier above the beach and ocean.

There's a bunch of chain motels along Pacific Hwy as you approach downtown from the north, and Mission Bay Dr has more possibilities. There are more on El Cajon Blvd if you come from the east.

The famous **Hotel del Coronado** *(☎ 619-435-6611, 1500 Orange Ave)* has tennis courts, a pool, restaurants and the Pacific Ocean out back. Only half the rooms are in the old timber building, and they're not that special (doubles $150-400). La Jolla has lots of top-end choices, notably the Mediterranean-style **La Valencia** *(☎ 800-451-0772, 1132 Prospect St)*, with posh doubles from $230.

Places to Eat

Downtown Asian places along Broadway are good and cheap. In Horton Plaza, the

CALIFORNIA

top-floor food court has at least a dozen restaurants from budget to top end serving everything from sushi to Mongolian barbecue. In Little Italy, *Filippi's Pizza Grotto (1747 India St)* makes excellent, inexpensive pizzas. On the waterfront, *Anthony's Fishette* is the simplest of the three Anthony seafood eateries – enjoy fish and chips ($5) on the harborside veranda. Farther south at Tuna Harbor, *Fish Market* has inexpensive sushi, oysters and fresh fish.

Gaslamp Quarter Over 60 places here offer everything from a quick breakfast to a gourmet dinner. *Café Sevilla (555 4th Ave)* creates authentic tapas ($5) and has music and dancing nightly until 2am. *Pokéz (947 E St)* serves up delicious Mexican and vegetarian cuisine for less than $5. For cheap breakfast specials ($3), try the 1950s-era *Sun Cafe (421 Market St)*. *Café Lulu (419 F St)* has snacks and drinks with a nice front patio for people-watching. Nearby, on 5th Ave just north of G St, is a group of upscale Italian restaurants, including *Trattoria La Strada (702 5th Ave)*. Fashionable *Fio's Cucina Italiana (801 5th Ave)* is pricey but not outrageous, with excellent pastas and a long wine list. *Dakota Grill (☎ 619-234-5554, 901 5th Ave)*, at E St, serves good California cuisine (entrées $13-18).

Hillcrest You can watch the busy workers at *Bread & Cie (350 University Ave)* bake unique flavored homemade breads in an oven imported from France. Enjoy one of their many delicious sandwiches out on the sunny patio. Numerous ethnic restaurants along both University and 5th Ave serve up everything from Sicilian to Thai. For something a little different, try *Kyber Pass (523 University Ave)*, serving traditional Afghani cuisine including curries, kabobs and rice dishes ($7-12). Next door is the popular *Taste of Thai (527 University Ave)*, which has an extensive menu offering exotic Thai dishes for under $10. *California Cuisine (1027 University Ave)* serves seafood, pasta and game and has a good wine list; dinner entrées start at $14.

Beaches The *South Beach Bar & Grille*, on Newport Ave in Ocean Beach, is justly famous for its grilled fish tacos ($4). In Pacific Beach, *Joe's Crabshack (4325 Ocean Blvd)* is a lively place to watch the sunset while eating delicious fried clams and other seafood items ($7-12). A great breakfast spot on the beach is *Green Flash (701 Thomas Ave)*. For a budget option in La Jolla try *Don Carlos Taco Shop (737 Pearl St)*, which serves outstanding Mexican food. The fish potato burrito is highly recommended.

Entertainment

Live theater thrives in San Diego. Ticket-Master (☎ 619-220-8497) has information and books tickets. The free weekly *San Diego Reader*, available in shops around the city, has detailed nightlife listings. Arts Tix (☎ 619-497-5000), on Broadway in front of Horton Plaza, sells performing-arts tickets for half price on the day of a performance (closed Sun).

The *San Diego Opera (☎ 619-570-1100)* and *California Ballet (☎ 858-560-6741)* perform downtown at the San Diego Civic Theatre, on 3rd Ave at B St. The *San Diego Repertory Theatre (☎ 619-544-1000)* performs at Horton Plaza's Lyceum Theatre.

Downtown, the *Casbah (☎ 619-232-4355, 2501 Kettner Blvd)*, near the airport, is San Diego's best alternative club, with live bands most nights, a garden area for smokers and a few pool tables out back. Stylish *Mister A's (☎ 619-239-1377, 2550 5th Ave)* is a rooftop cocktail bar with incredible views of downtown; dress nicely.

The family of late bluesman Jim Croce runs *Croce's Restaurant & Jazz Bar (☎ 619-233-4355, 802 5th Ave)* and the adjacent *Croce's Top Hat Bar & Grill (☎ 619-232-4338)*, a blues/R&B venue. Also in the Gaslamp Quarter, *E-Street Alley (☎ 619-979-9999)*, between 4th and 5th Aves, is a high-energy dance club with DJs spinning house, trance and hip-hop. *Olé Madrid (☎ 619-557-0146, 751 5th Ave)* is also good for dancing. *The Bitter End (☎ 619-338-9300, 770 5th Ave)* mixes martinis with DJ dance tunes. For an authentic Guinness try *The Field (☎ 619-232-9840, 544 5th Ave)*. The entire bar was shipped piece by piece from Ireland.

Nearly all the bars in Hillcrest cater to a mainly gay clientele. Some of the most popular are *Rich's (☎ 619-295-2195, 1051 University Ave)*, *Hamburger Mary's/Kickers (☎ 619-491-0400, 308 University Ave)* and *Flick's (☎ 619-297-2056, 1017 University*

Ave). The Flame (3780 Park Blvd) is a lesbian dance club with different theme nights. If you're not into the gay scene and want a drink in Hillcrest, try the oldest bar in the 'hood, *The Alibi (☎ 619-295-0881, 1403 University Ave)*, where hipsters, local working-class folks and yuppies all come to share in the $2, 23oz beer deal.

In Pacific Beach, *Blind Melons (☎ 858-483-7844, 710 Garnet Ave)* presents mainly blues and some rock. Both *Plan B Club (☎ 858-483-9920, 945 Garnet Ave)* and *Tremors (☎ 858-272-7278, 860 Garnet Ave)* play industrial dance music to young crowds. In Mission Beach, *'Canes (☎ 858-488-9690, 3105 Ocean Front Walk)* is a bar and grill with dancing and some big-name alternative bands. Over in Ocean Beach, *Winston's (☎ 858-222-6822, 1921 Bacon St)* features live reggae and blues.

Spectator Sports
Qualcomm Stadium (☎ 619-283-4494, 9449 Friars Rd) is in Mission Valley, near the intersection of I-8 and I-15. The stadium is home to the San Diego Chargers football team (☎ 619-280-2121) and San Diego Padres baseball team (☎ 619-283-4494). San Diego Sports Arena (☎ 619-224-4171, 3500 Sports Arena Blvd) hosts concerts and family shows and is home to San Diego's minor-league ice hockey team, the Gulls, and the indoor soccer team, the Sockers.

Getting There & Around
Air San Diego International Airport (☎ 619-231-2100) is 2 miles west of downtown. It is easily reached by bus Nos 2 and 2A ($2.25; 5am-12:40am) or by The Flyer express bus No 992, which stops at the Santa Fe train station and along Broadway ($2.25; 5am-1:15am). Airport shuttle services ($6.50) include Cloud Nine (☎ 858-278-8877) and Coastline Shuttles (☎ 800-816-3520). A taxi downtown costs $8-13.

Bus The Greyhound station (☎ 619-239-8082, 120 W Broadway) has frequent buses to Los Angeles ($13; 2½ hours); El Centro ($19; 2½ hours); Phoenix, Arizona ($44; 8 hours); and San Ysidro/Mexican border ($7; 30 minutes).

Train The elegant Santa Fe Depot, at the west end of C St, is used by both Coaster (☎ 619-233-3004, 800-266-6883) commuter trains serving north San Diego county and by Amtrak (☎ 619-239-9021), which has regular connections to Los Angeles ($23; 2½ hours), Santa Barbara ($26; 5 hours), San Francisco ($62; 11 hours) and Phoenix, Arizona ($116; 14 hours).

Car & Motorcycle The west terminal at the airport has free direct phones to a bunch of car rental companies ($40 a day). You will get a better rate out of Thrifty (☎ 619-233-9333, 800-367-2277), West Coast (☎ 619-544-0606) and Getaway (☎ 619-233-3777).

Local Transportation Buses and trolleys are run by Metropolitan Transit Service (MTS; ☎ 619-233-3004). The MTS Transit Store, downtown at Broadway and 1st Ave, has route information and sells day passes ($5), valid for unlimited travel on local buses, ferries and trolleys. A bus ticket ($1.75) is good for an hour – have correct change and ask for a transfer ticket in case you need to change. Trolleys run from the American Plaza terminal near Santa Fe Depot. Ferries to Coronado cost $2.

AROUND SAN DIEGO
San Diego County (4200 sq miles) has a great variety of landscapes, 60 miles of superb coastline, a near-perfect climate and a growing population of over 2.5 million.

North County
North of La Jolla there's an almost continuous string of seaside suburbs up to the Camp Pendleton Marine Base. The best surf is at Swami's, near Encinitas, and at Oceanside. North of Oceanside there's camping and some decent surfing at **San Onofre State Beach**, which is overshadowed by a set of nuclear reactors. If you're interested in surfing, check out Oceanside's free **California Surf Museum** (☎ 760-721-6876, 223 N Coast Hwy), open 10am-4pm Thursday to Monday.

The **Lawrence Welk Resort** (☎ 760-749-3000, 8860 Lawrence Welk Dr), in Escondido, incorporates a groovy museum and summertime dinner theater (light musicals and that sort of thing). The famed 1800-acre **San Diego Wild Animal Park** (☎ 619-234-6541), 32 miles north of downtown San Diego, has herds of giraffe, zebra, rhino and other animals roaming the valley floor ($25, $42 combined ticket with San Diego Zoo; open 9am-8pm). From I-15 take the Via Rancho Parkway exit and follow the signs.

Tijuana (Mexico)

With over 1½ million people, Tijuana (tee-**hwah**-na) is just across the border from San Diego. The archetypal border town, Tijuana is not at all like most Mexican cities, but it's worth visiting to experience the contrast between Mexico and the USA. Young US citizens come here to get legally drunk from age 18, and others come for cheap car repairs, discount dental work, leather goods and sleaze. The streets can get pretty sketchy after nightfall.

Before you arrive you can call the Baja California tourist office (☎ 800-225-2786 in San Diego) for information. English-speaking staff offers information at the Tijuana-based Cotuco (☎ 684-16-85), on Avenida Revolución between Calles 3a and 4a, or the state-run Secure on Avenida Revolución at Calle 1a. US citizens don't need a visa or a passport for a short visit to Tijuana but should bring a photo ID; visas are not required for travelers from Australia, New Zealand and the EU, but you do need a Mexican government tourist card, available at your embassy or at the border crossing. Returning to the USA, non-Americans must have a passport with a US visa. If your US immigration card has nearly expired, you will have to apply for a new one, and the INS

may want to see your onward airline ticket, sufficient funds and so on.

Prices are mostly in dollars. Bring small notes and coins or you may get change in pesos at a low rate. Haggling is the norm at many tourist shops – you might get a better price in pesos. Numerous *casas de cambio* will change money and traveler's checks. When calling Mexico from the USA, you must dial ☎ 011-52; once there, dial ☎ 95 before calling a US number or ☎ 98 before any other foreign numbers. For more information about Tijuana, see Lonely Planet's *San Diego & Tijuana* and *Mexico* guides.

The main attraction is **Avenida Revolución**, with restaurants, seedy bars, tacky souvenir shops, zappy dance clubs and street photographers with zebra-striped burros. A highlight is **Frontón Palacio Jai Alai** (Avenida Revolución 1100), which hosts evening matches of jai alai, a fast-moving hybrid of lacrosse and handball ($2).

Centro Cultural Tijuana (☎ 684-11-11), 1 mile west of Avenida Revolución on Paseo de los Héroes, has exhibitions on Mexican culture, a free art gallery and an IMAX theater. Sunday **bullfights** take place July to October at the Plaza Monumental stadium and at the more convenient Toreo de Tijuana stadium on Agua Caliente (the southern extension of Avenida Revolución). Tickets cost $4-12 locally or $14-45 in advance from San Diego's Five Star Tours (☎ 619-232-5049).

Tijuana's hotels range from terrible to awful, especially the by-the-hour places along Avenida Revolución. One exception (sort of) is *Hotel Nelson* (☎ 685-43-03, *Avenida Revolución 721),* with basic windowless doubles for $40 and some nicer ones starting at $50. *Hotel Villa de Zaragoza* (☎ 685-18-32), two blocks east of Frontón Palacio Jai Alai, has clean, air-con rooms ($40).

Don't drive to Tijuana – parking is difficult, and there may be a long wait at the border coming back. Leave your car at a parking lot in San Ysidro (about $5), cross the border on foot and walk to Avenida Revolución. Alternatively, you can take a trolley from downtown San Diego ($2) or a bus from the San Diego Greyhound station ($5).

California Deserts

Forget about green. After a while the starkness of the desert landscapes and the clarity of the light become beautiful in their own way. Be warned that these deserts present real dangers – extreme temperatures (120°F and up), freezing windy nights and the potential for flash floods. Don't enter or explore abandoned mine shafts. And bring lots of water; being stranded without water is the biggest danger in the desert.

ANZA-BORREGO DESERT STATE PARK

This park is for people who want to be *in* the desert. The park is large, some 937 sq miles, and you must have a car, preferably a 4WD, to get around. You can drive most anywhere, so pack in some water and groceries and pitch a tent in the absolute middle of nowhere. Several paved roads run through Anza-Borrego, and numerous dirt side roads offer hard-core 4WD possibilities. At sunrise try the 4-mile dirt road that goes south from Hwy S22 to **Font's Point**, overlooking the Borrego Badlands. A good full-day odyssey is Hwy S2, which traverses the park's southwestern corner and parallels an 1850s stagecoach route known as the Southern Emigrant Trail; watch for signs and a bumpy dirt road to the oasis at Palm Spring. The desert is riddled with short walks. The self-guided **Borrego Palm Canyon Nature Trail** goes northeast from the Borrego Palm Canyon campground, climbing 350 feet in 1½ miles to a palm grove and waterfall. Park admission is free.

The best time to visit Anza-Borrego is in wildflower season, usually February to mid-April; for recorded wildflower updates, call ☎ 760-767-4684.

The wearisome town of Borrego Springs is a small span of road offering shops, restaurants and gas to desert folk. The staff at the visitor center (☎ 760-767-4205), 2 miles west of Borrego Springs, is well informed (open 9am-5pm daily, Sat-Sun in summer) and has a small indoor/outdoor nature exhibit. If you venture off the main highways, there's a $5 day-use fee, which is payable at the visitor center or at major trailheads.

The **Borrego Palm Canyon** campground, 2½ miles west of the visitor center, has tent sites with full amenities, but don't expect a shady haven. **Tamarisk Grove Campground**, on Hwy S3 near Hwy 78, is smaller but with a pleasant grove of trees. Both cost $10-15 and can be reserved through ParkNet (☎ 800-444-7275, W www.reserveamerica.com). Backcountry camping is allowed just about everywhere, though not within 200 yards of water. Register at the visitor center.

In Borrego Springs, the **Oasis Motel** (☎ 760-767-5409, 366 Palm Canyon Dr) has kitchenettes and is about the cheapest place in town ($55). Nearby **Hacienda del Sol** (☎ 760-767-5442) has similar prices. All rooms at the new **Borrego Valley Inn** (☎ 760-767-0311), on the road to the visitor center, have private patios; many have small kitchenettes ($100-150).

SALTON SEA & IMPERIAL VALLEY

From miles away, the Salton Sea, California's largest lake, looks refreshing and almost like a tropical resort in the middle of the desert. In reality it is murky brown and eerily desolate, bordered by a few small trailer-park towns and date farms. However, the **Sonny Bono Salton Sea National Wildlife Refuge**, off Hwy 111, is a great place for bird-watching. The area also encourages camping, fishing (although eating the fish is

---

The Salton Sea

In 1905 the Colorado River flooded and overflowed into irrigation channels, nearly inundating the entirety of the Imperial Valley. It took 18 months, 1500 workers, $12 million and half a million tons of rock to put the Colorado River back on its course to the Gulf of Mexico. As a result the previously dry Salton Sink became a lake, 45 miles long and 17 miles wide. It had no natural outlet and, as evaporation reduced its size, the natural salt levels became more concentrated. The Salton became an inland sea, with its surface actually 228 feet below the level of the sea in the Gulf of California and its water over 1½ times as salty.

☺☺☺☺☺☺☺☺☺☺☹☺

not encouraged) and boating. Unfortunately swimming is not the best idea, as the salt content is so high it stings the eyes. Southeast of the lake, the **Algodones and Imperial Dunes**, off Hwy 78, are definitely worth a visit. Up to 300 feet high, these sand dunes are similar to those found in Death Valley and are popular with off-road vehicles.

PALM SPRINGS

The four so-called Resort Cities – Palm Springs, Cathedral City, Rancho Mirage and Palm Desert – extend the length of the Coachella Valley, forming an almost continuous sprawl of immaculately clean suburbs, gated retirement communities and private golf courses. Palm Springs is the original and most visited resort, famous as a winter retreat for Hollywood stars and a home for the moderately rich. Its former mayor was the late Sonny Bono (of Sonny and Cher fame). There's a growing gay scene here. Every March Palm Springs hosts the biggest lesbian happening in the country, the Dinah Shore Weekend, which is attended by up to 25,000 people. College students by the thousands crowd the town during spring break. However, there's not much to do except hang around a pool or play golf; the real interest is in visiting the nearby canyons, mountains and deserts.

Orientation & Information

Palm Springs has a reasonably compact downtown area, with shops, galleries, banks and restaurants centered on roughly four blocks of Palm Canyon Dr, which runs one way north to south. The parallel Indian Canyon Dr runs one way south to north. The Palm Springs Visitor Center (☎ 760-778-8418, 2781 N Palm Canyon Dr), 2 miles north of downtown, is open daily year round. Staff can book discounted hotel rooms, desert tours and golf packages.

Things to See & Do

North of the visitor center is a turnoff to the world's largest rotating **Aerial Tramway** (☎ 760-325-1391), boasting '360° of WOW'; the individual cars rotate. The 6000-foot climb (15 minutes) is said to be like traveling through vegetation zones from Mexico to Canada. The tramway operates daily (closed two weeks in August) and costs $20 roundtrip or $25 including dinner at the mountaintop restaurant. The **San Jacinto Wilderness State Park** at the top is a great place for hiking, snowshoeing or cross-country skiing. Sights downtown include **Palm Springs Desert Museum** (☎ 760-325-7186, 101 Museum Dr), which is worth a visit ($7.50; open 10am-5pm Tue-Sat, noon-5pm Sun); the **Village Green Heritage Center** (☎ 760-323-8297, 221 S Palm Canyon Dr), with a reproduction of a 1930s general store ($2); and **Oasis Water Park** (☎ 760-327-0499, 1500 Gene Autry Trail), with 12 water slides and a wave pool that feels oh-so-soothing on a blistering summer day ($22/15 adults/kids, $4 parking; open Mar-Oct).

If **golf** is a favorite pastime then Palm Springs is a dream come true. With over 100 lusciously green golf courses the choices are endless, although many of the courses are private and very expensive. A few of the best public courses include Tahquitz Creek Golf Resort (☎ 760-328-1005, 1885 Golf

---

Palm Springs Celebrities

A long list of Hollywood stars have lived or stayed in Palm Springs, including Jean Harlow, Al Jolson, Nat King Cole, Liberace, Dean Martin, Jack Warner, Liz Taylor, Spencer Tracy, Bing Crosby, Lawrence Olivier, Goldie Hawn and Kirk Douglas. Name-dropping comes easy in a place with streets like Dinah Shore Drive and Gene Autry Trail. Former president Gerald Ford makes frequent golfing forays to the valley and also has a drive named after him.

The town is associated with some well-known scandals, romances and marriages – Clark Gable and Carole Lombard, Frank Sinatra and Ava Gardner, Elvis and Priscilla Presley (who honeymooned here), Bob and Dolores Hope (Dolores is much more popular in Palm Springs than Bob), the former evangelical team of Jim and Tammy Faye Bakker, and Zsa Zsa Gabor plus six or eight of her husbands.

The late Sonny Bono, of Sonny and Cher, owned a fashionable restaurant here and was once mayor of Palm Springs. His accidental, premature death was cause for mourning and flags flying at half-mast throughout the city.

☺☺☺☺☺☺☺☺☺☺☹☺

Club Dr) and Mesquite Country Club (☎ 760-323-9377, 2700 E Mesquite Ave).

Palm Springs is surrounded by Indian Canyons, once home to the Cahuilla Indians and now part of the **Agua Caliente Reservation** (☎ 760-325-3400). A walk up these canyon oases, surrounded by towering cliffs, is a pleasure. From downtown go south on Palm Canyon Dr for about 2 miles to the reservation entrance ($6). The 1200-acre **Living Desert** (☎ 760-346-5694, 47-900 Portola Ave), in Palm Desert, is a wildlife preserve with lots of pleasant walking trails and animal exhibits with everything from antelope to zebra ($8.50; closed August).

Places to Stay & Eat
Budget options are hard to come by in Palm Springs; the best bet is the chain motels on S Palm Canyon Dr. Other options include the well-maintained *Palm Court Inn (☎ 760-416-2333, 1983 North Palm Canyon Dr)*, with singles/doubles for $69/89, and *Budget Host Inn (☎ 760-325-5574, 1277 S Palm Canyon Dr)*, where rooms cost from $79. *Chestnutz (☎ 800-621-6973, 641 San Lorenzo Rd)* is a clothing-optional resort catering to gay males, with a pool and spa (doubles $89-119). *Bee Charmer Inn (☎ 760-778-5883, 1600 E Palm Canyon Dr)* is a well-known resort for women (doubles $115-145).

A good breakfast option is *Rock Garden Café (777 S Palm Canyon Dr)*, serving all your breakfast favorites. An extensive lunch and dinner menu offers everything from roast beef sandwiches to vegetarian quiche for under $10. An old favorite eatery is the original *Las Casuelas (368 N Palm Canyon Dr)*, serving authentic Mexican fare ($7-12). *Blue Coyote Grill (☎ 760-327-1196, 445 N Palm Canyon Dr)* is a great place to sit outside and enjoy the desert air while sipping on delicious fruit-flavored margaritas. The Southwestern-style entrées are tasty (around $15). *Riccio's (2155 N Palm Canyon Dr)* does semipricey Italian food in an authentic 1960s dining room.

Entertainment
The Palm Springs Follies revue includes music, showgirls and comedy at the 1936 *Plaza Theater (☎ 760-327-0225, 128 S Palm Canyon Dr)*. The twist is that all the performers are women over age 50 ($35-65).

Zeldaz Nightclub & Beachclub (☎ 760-325-2375, 169 N Indian Canyon Dr) attracts a mixed crowd for drinking and dancing. The local gay scene centers on the *Toolshed (☎ 760-320-3299, 600 E Sunny Dunes Rd)*.

Getting There & Around
The local SunBus (☎ 760-343-3451) connects Palm Springs with the surrounding resorts and with the Indio Amtrak station (75¢). The downtown Greyhound station (☎ 760-325-2053, 311 N Indian Canyon Dr) has daily service to Los Angeles ($18) and San Diego ($26). Amtrak's (☎ 800-872-7245) *Sunset Limited* route between Los Angeles and Miami stops in Palm Springs at Indian Canyon Dr and I-10. The fare to Los Angeles is $29, to Orlando $250. By car I-10 is the main route to/from Los Angeles (2 hours). For those who have an extra hour or two, Hwy 74 winds through the scenic San Bernadino National Forest and the Santa Rosa mountains and is well worth the detour.

JOSHUA TREE NATIONAL PARK
This small desert park, visited each year by 1.25 million people, is known for its spiky Joshua trees (remember the U2 album?) and plump, climber-friendly rock formations. It's possible to drive across Joshua Tree in about two hours, but you must get away from your car to appreciate the wide open spaces. Two visitor centers have maps and can suggest short hiking trails, as well as 4WD and mountain-biking routes. A panoramic spot for sunsets is Keys View, at 5185 feet; for sunrises try the Cholla Cactus Garden. Good hiking spots include Hidden Valley and Lost Horse mine. Bring plenty of water. Park admission for vehicles ($10) and walk-ins ($5) is good for seven days.

Right by the north entrance to the park, Twentynine Palms is a service town for the park and nearby Marine Corps base. The west entrance is off Hwy 62, near the forgettable town of Joshua Tree; you'll find more and better services in nearby Yucca Valley. The park headquarters, open daily year round, is at the Oasis Visitor Center (☎ 760-367-7511), on National Monument Dr in Twentynine Palms, just outside the park's northern boundary. The smaller Cottonwood Visitor Center (no ☎), off Hwy 195, is a few miles inside the park's south entrance. For emergency assistance, call ☎ 909-383-5651.

There are nine campgrounds in the park, mostly available on a first-come, first-served basis (☎ 800-365-2267, W www.nps.gov/jotr). *Black Rock Canyon* ($10) and *Cottonwood* ($8) have water available; the other campgrounds are free, but you must bring your own water. Backcountry camping is permitted, but not less than a mile from the nearest road or 500 feet from the nearest trail – register at one of the 12 backcountry boards listed in the free *Joshua Tree Guide* newspaper (available from the visitor center). No fires are permitted.

Twentynine Palms is the best town to stay in. *Motel 6 (☎ 760-367-2833, 72562 Hwy 62)* is nice and clean ($39). The most attractive and laid-back spot is the family-run *29 Palms Inn (☎ 760-367-3505, 73950 Inn Ave)*, built around the Oasis of Mara. The staff is extremely friendly and the accommodations are in comfortable cabins or adobe bungalows ($75-100). Even if you don't stay here, have a meal at the poolside restaurant, where all vegetables and fruits are grown in the on-site garden, and the bread and pastries are baked daily in a stone oven behind the restaurant.

In Joshua Tree the *High Desert Motel (☎ 760-366-1978, 61310 Hwy 62)* has basic doubles starting at $45. North of Yucca Valley, off Hwy 62, *Rimrock Ranch Cabins (☎ 760-228-1297)* rents out homey pine cabins with private patios for $75-125. A two-night minimum stay is required.

MOJAVE DESERT

The Mojave (mo-**ha**-vee) Desert covers a vast area, from the northern edge of LA County to the remote, almost unpopulated Mojave National Preserve. Most people quickly pass through this parched desert basin on their way to/from Death Valley or Las Vegas, and there's little reason to linger.

Lower Mojave

Coming from Los Angeles, the first 'major' stop on I-15 is Victorville, home to the offbeat **Roy Rogers–Dale Evans Museum** (☎ 760-243-4547), with a mind-boggling collection of photographs and mementos of the late Hollywood film star Roy Rogers, his wife Dale Evans and their horse, Trigger ($7). Exit I-15 at Roy Rogers Dr, go west and take the first left. At the junction of I-15 and I-40, Barstow is about halfway between Los Angeles and Las Vegas, and lots of travelers break their journeys at one of the *budget motels* lining E Main St. They're not looking for charm, and they don't find any. Eight miles from Barstow, the **Rainbow Basin National Natural Landmark** has effulgent layers of sedimentary rock, folded and distorted into psychedelic formations. There's a scenic drive and several short hiking trails. Take Fort Irwin Rd north of Barstow for 6 miles, then Fossil Bed Rd west for 2 miles. The infamous **Calico Ghost Town** (☎ 760-254-2122) is an old mining camp off I-15, 10 miles north of Barstow. Abandoned until 1951, when Walter Knott (of Knott's Berry Farm fame) began to rebuild it, Calico is now only marginally more authentic than Disney's Frontierland but a fun place to stop and take a break.

Upper Mojave

About 55 miles north of LA you come to the town of **Mojave**. Sierra Hwy (Hwy 14) is the main drag, with the railroad on the west side and motels and fast-food restaurants on the east side. Driving through, you might think Mojave had a huge international airport, but all those airliners here are actually in storage, because deterioration is minimal in the dry desert air. Southeast of Mojave the 470-sq-mile **Edwards Air Force Base** (☎ 661-277-3517) is a flight-test facility for NASA and the US Air Force. It was here that Chuck Yeager flew the Bell X-1 on the world's first supersonic flight in 1947. Free tours of the base are given on Friday by appointment. The **NASA-Dryden Flight Research Facility** (☎ 661-276-3446) offers guided tours on weekdays; reservations are required.

Red Rock Canyon State Park (☎ 661-942-0662) straddles Hwy 14, about 25 miles north of Mojave. Its sandstone cliffs – used in the opening scenes of the movie *Jurassic Park* – present a spectacular range of colors at sunrise and sunset ($2; $8 camping). **Ridgecrest** is the last sizable town before Death Valley and not a bad place to stock up on water, gas and supplies, or to spend a night in a reasonably priced motel.

DEATH VALLEY

The name itself evokes all that is harsh, hot and hellish – a lifeless place of Old Testament severity. Naturalists are keen to point out that many plants and animals thrive here, but it's hard to believe that anything can survive in a place that holds the world's second-hottest temperature record, at 134°F (56°C), measured in 1913 at Furnace Creek; the world record, 136°F (58°C), belongs to the Libyan desert. Winter is the peak season, when accommodations can be booked solid and campgrounds fill before 11am. Wildflower season (Feb to mid-Apr) is also popular. **Death Valley National Park** covers 4687 sq miles and is the largest national park in the continental USA. The actual valley is about 100 miles long and 5 to 15 miles wide. There is no scheduled bus or train service to Death Valley, though some charter buses operate from Las Vegas.

Orientation & Information

Furnace Creek, toward the valley's southern end, has the most facilities, including a visitor center (☎ 760-786-2331), a well-stocked general store (open 7am-10pm), a gas station, a campground, a restaurant and a hotel. In Stovepipe Wells there's a ranger station (☎ 760-786-2342), a store with an ATM, a hotel, a campground and a restaurant. Food, water and gas are also available at Scotty's Castle and Panamint Springs. The park's entry fee, $10 per vehicle, is valid for multiple entries over 10 days and includes a Death Valley map.

Driving Tour

This tour, traveling south to north and back, can be done in a single day (even starting outside the valley) if you begin early. Start by driving up to **Dante's View** for the best overall view of the valley; it's absolutely brilliant at sunrise. Heading down toward the central valley, take a short walk out to **Zabriskie Point**, another good sunrise/sunset spot. Follow the signs to **Furnace Creek**, where you can get some breakfast and sit in the shade. From Furnace Creek, drive 50 miles straight through to the north end of the valley. Go a few hundred yards past the Grapevine ranger station and turn right to **Scotty's Castle** (☎ 760-786-2392), which is nearly 3000 feet above sea level and noticeably cooler. The Spanish-Moorish mansion was built in the 1920s by Walter E Scott, alias 'Death Valley Scotty,' for Chicago insurance magnate Albert Johnson. Head back down the valley, and by the time you reach the scenic loop at the **Mesquite Flat**

Sand Dunes, the temperature should be more bearable. Nearby is Stovepipe Wells Village, with a pool you can use for $2. A few miles southwest, the valley floor is filled with lumps of crystallized salt in what is called the **Devil's Golf Course**. In the middle of this salt pan is the deepest part of the valley, 282 feet below sea level, the lowest point in the USA and the fifth-lowest in the world (the Dead Sea between Jordan and Israel owns the record).

Eureka Sand Dunes, an arduous but recommended side trip, rise up to 680 feet from a dry lake bed. From the north end of the valley, near Ubehebe Crater, 44 miles of dirt road lead to the dunes. Unless there has been wet weather the road can be traveled by a regular car, but budget at least five hours roundtrip.

Places to Stay & Eat

You can camp free in most parts of Death Valley, as long as you are 1 mile from the nearest road and a quarter mile from any water source. Check with the visitor center first and fill out the required backcountry registration form. Just north of the visitor center, **Furnace Creek Campground** has 136 sites ($16). It's open all year but fills up early in winter and is very hot in summer. Nearby **Texas Springs** has a little more shade ($10; open Oct-Apr). **Stovepipe Wells Campground** has very little shade and lots of RVs ($10; open Oct-Apr). Year-round **Mesquite Springs**, near Scotty's Castle, is somewhat cooler thanks to its 1800-foot elevation ($10). For reservations at all campsites call ☎ 800-365-2267.

The **HI Johannesburg Hostel** (☎ 760-374-2323) is off I-395 in sleepy Johannesburg, about 80 miles southwest of Death Valley. It sponsors trips to the Valley as well as many of the area's other parks. Call ahead and check in to the hostel at the local visitor center ($12; closed Aug). **HI Desertaire Hostel** (☎ 760-852-4580) is in Tecopa, 5 miles east of Hwy 127 and about an hour by car from Death Valley. Beds are in small, simple single-sex trailer-dorms ($13-16); call for directions and ask the friendly owner about the nearby hot springs.

Furnace Creek Ranch & Inn (☎ 760-786-2345) has cabins ($97) and lodge rooms ($150-250) as well as a hillside five-star inn with luxury rooms ($175-325). All accommodations allow use of the spring-fed swimming pool, tennis courts and the world's lowest golf course. Accommodations at **Stovepipe Wells Village** (☎ 760-786-2387) include standard rooms ($67) and 'deluxe' rooms ($88). There are also more basic 'patio rooms' ($47), but you must ask for these specifically. This place fills up quickly, so make reservations. **Panamint Springs Resort** (☎ 702-482-7680), on Hwy 190 near the park's western boundary, has basic doubles ($65-79) and cabins ($139).

Restaurants are few and far between in Death Valley; you may want to consider self-catering, and bring snacks. **Forty-Niner Café**, in Furnace Creek, has sandwiches and pizzas for under $10. The dining room at Stovepipe Wells Village serves up decent meals for around the same price.

Central Coast

California's Central Coast, stretching from Ventura north to Monterey Bay, covers nearly 300 miles of prime shoreline. Hwy 101 is the region's main artery, though for outstanding coastal views travel along the Pacific Coast Hwy (Hwy 1) between San Luis Obispo and Monterey.

VENTURA & THE CHANNEL ISLANDS

Heading north from Los Angeles, Hwys 1 and 101 merge just south of Ventura, a large beach town with a few museums clustered around the 1782 **Mission San Buenaventura** (☎ 805-643-4318, 211 E Main St). The main drag has many antique shops, cafes and restaurants. Ventura Harbor, southwest of Hwy 101 via Harbor Blvd, is where boats depart for the five Channel Islands.

Also dubbed 'America's Galápagos,' the Channel Islands, from Newport Beach to Santa Barbara, comprise **Channel Islands National Park**. Anacapa is closest to the mainland and thus gets the most visitors. San Miguel is known for its abundance of seals, sea lions and sea otters. Santa Cruz is the largest island, most of which is privately owned by the Nature Conservancy. All the islands have primitive **campgrounds** ($2.50); bring food and water. Permits are required and free of charge at the park headquarters. For campsite reservations call ☎ 800-365-2267 or book online at Ⓦ reservations.nps.gov.

You can catch ferries to all five islands next to the park headquarters at Islands Packers (☎ 805-642-7688). Ferries cost $37-65, depending on which island you're going to. Also available are half-day tours around Santa Cruz ($22) and full-day trips, including ranger-led hikes, to Anacapa ($37) and Santa Cruz ($42). Ferries also run from Santa Barbara with Truth Aquatics (☎ 805-962-1127, 301 W Cabrillo Blvd) for $60. Channel Islands Aviation (☎ 805-987-1301) runs year-round flights from Santa Barbara's airport. Day trips to Santa Rosa and Santa Cruz cost $139; other packages are available.

SANTA BARBARA

This city markets itself as the 'California Riviera,' thanks to its mild climate, seaside location, affluent population and

LINDA BROWN

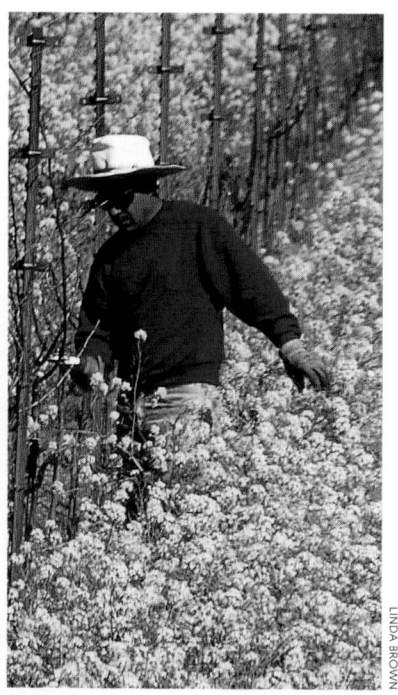

Worker trimming vines; Napa Valley, California

RICK GERHARTER

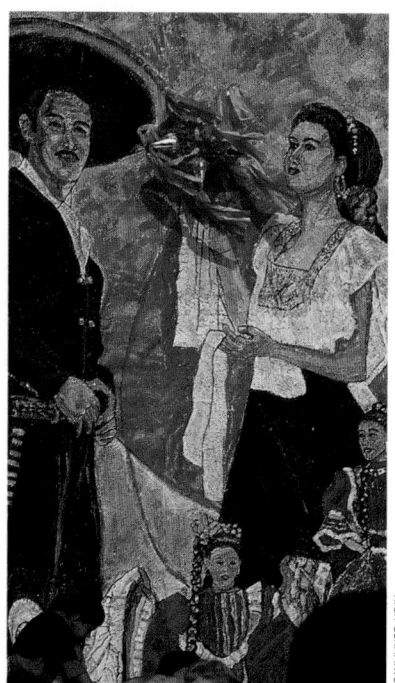

Mural in East Los Angeles, California

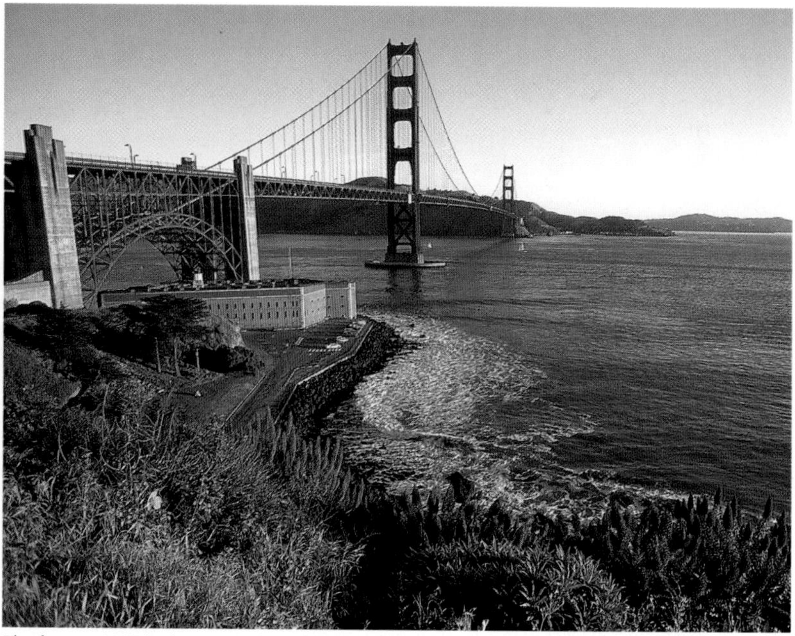
JOHN ELK III

The famous 1937 bridge spans the Golden Gate entrance to San Francisco Bay, California.

JOHN ELK III

A good place to reflect – Mt Hood towers over Trilium Lake, Oregon.

RICHARD CUMMINS

Buoys will be buoys. Westport, Washington

Mediterranean architecture. Beyond its snobbish boutiques and white-tablecloth eateries, Santa Barbara is an affable beach town with water sports, several notable museums and miles of bike trails. Five colleges in the area, including the University of California at Santa Barbara (UCSB), keep the cafes and bars boisterous – though the real college scene is centered off Hwy 101 in Isla Vista, 10 miles north of downtown.

Orientation & Information

Exit Hwy 101 at State St, downtown Santa Barbara's main drag. Close to the beach, the visitor center (☎ 805-965-3021, 1 Santa Barbara St) has maps and brochures. Hot Spots (☎ 805-564-1637, 36 State St) is a 24-hour coffeehouse with a helpful visitor center in the back.

Things to See &Do

The **Santa Barbara County Courthouse** (☎ 805-962-6464, 1100 Anacapa St) is probably the city's most impressive architectural site. Completed in 1929, the courthouse is in Moorish Revival style, with tiles from Tunisia and Spain. The 85-foot clock tower offers flawless views of the city. Free docent-led tours are given daily except Sunday. The **Santa Barbara Museum of Art** (☎ 805-963-4364, 1130 State St) has a varied collection with works by Monet, Matisse, Chagall, Hopper and O'Keeffe. Asian art and classical sculpture are on the ground floor ($5; closed Mon). The **Santa Barbara Historical Museum** (☎ 805-966-1601, 136 E De La Guerra St) occupies an 1817 adobe that housed the last Mexican capital of California. The historical collections are top-notch. **Stearns Wharf**, a rough wooden pier that extends into the harbor from the south end of State St, is a favorite place to eat seafood, watch sea lions and get a good view of Santa Barbara from a distance. The wharf's Sea Center (☎ 805-963-1067) has touch tanks filled with starfish and sea anemones ($3).

Called the Queen of the Missions, **Mission Santa Barbara** (☎ 805-682-4713, 2201 Laguna St) sits at the foot of the Santa Ynez Mountains a half-mile north of downtown. The tenth to be built in California, the mission was established in 1786 on the feast day of St Barbara, December 4. Behind the church is an extensive cemetery with 4000 Chumash Indian graves. Visit the **Museum of Natural History** (☎ 805-682-4711, 2559 Puesta del Sol Rd), a half-mile north of the mission, just to see its beautiful architecture and lovely landscaping ($6). Another mile farther into the hills is Santa Barbara's **Botanic Garden** (☎ 805-563-2521, 1212 Mission Canyon Rd). This extensive garden is devoted entirely to California's native flora, with 5 miles of trails meandering through cacti, redwoods and wildflowers ($5).

For sunset cruises ($25), contact Sunset Kidd (☎ 805-962-8222, 125 Harbor Way). To venture out on a whale-watching trip ($27 per half day) contact Captain Don's (☎ 805-969-5217), on Stern's wharf. Cycles-4-Rent (☎ 805-652-0462, 101 State St) rents all sorts of bikes, including mountain bikes, tandems and quadricycles, by the hour ($6-10) and day ($20-45). Pedal & Paddle (☎ 805-687-2912) has guided kayak trips around the bay (from $45).

Places to Stay

Santa Barbara's budget accommodations are concentrated on upper State St, where many small motels have decent rooms for under $50. Note that rooms are booked far in advance in summer and on most weekends. State beach camping is available year round at many of Santa Barbara's nearby beaches, including *Refugio* and *El Capitan* ($12). The closest is *Carpentieria State Beach* (☎ 805-968-1033), 12 miles south of downtown ($12/18 tent/RV). Reservations can be made at Ⓦ www.reserveamerica.com or by calling ☎ 800-444-7275.

In downtown Santa Barbara, *Banana Bungalow* (☎ 800-346-7835, 210 E Ortega St) is a great place to stay if you're looking to meet fellow travelers or just want a cheap place to crash. The hostel organizes beach barbecues, pub crawls and volleyball competitions. Beds cost $16 in the 'big' dorm, $22 in six- or eight-bed rooms. *Hotel State Street* (☎ 805-966-6586, 121 State St) is a clean, European-style B&B that attracts sophisticated budget travelers. Rooms have shared bathroom and breakfast is included ($39 Mon-Thurs, $79 Fri-Sun). Closer to downtown and on a nicer stretch of State St, *Hotel Santa Barbara* (☎ 805-965-4572, 533 State St) has a spiffy lobby and equally spiffy singles/doubles ($99/139).

Built by Charlie Chaplin in 1928, the *Montecito Inn* (☎ 800-969-7854, 1295 Coast

CALIFORNIA

Village Rd) is a quaint hotel in the upscale neighborhood of Montecito. The rooms are pleasantly decorated (from $185). Nestled among 10 acres of lush gardens, *El Encanto Hotel & Garden Villas (☎ 805-687-5000, 1900 Lasuen Rd)* sits on a hill above the mission. Secluded cottages start at $179.

Places to Eat
Santa Barbara's 'restaurant row' is along the 500 and 600 blocks of State St. If you want a really good meal for around $5, head to Isla Vista and eat with UCSB students.

Jump-start your morning with the locals at *Santa Barbara Roasting Company (321 State St),* which serves freshly roasted coffee to flip-flop-clad clientele. *Natural Café (508 State St)* is a totally California experience, with delicious good-for-you meals. For a little peace of mind, try the Good Karma Burger, Buddha Burrito or Yogi Special, all under $8. *La Playa Azul (914 Santa Barbara St)* serves moderately priced Mexican food on a sunny deck. No-frills *La Tolteca (614 E Haley St)* is a 'mexicatessen' famous for its enchiladas and tamales ($3-8). The *Santa Barbara Shellfish Co*, on Stearns Wharf, is a fish counter where you get fresh crab, chowder and grilled fish for less than $12.

Entertainment
The downtown scene revolves around lower State and Ortega Sts. *The Tank (416 State St)* is a bar and dance club where you can sip cocktails and stare at hypnotic wall-length aquariums. *Q's Sushi-a-GoGo (409 State St)* is a sushi bar as well as a three-story club. The club heats up after midnight with UCSB students dancing to popular hip-hop and dance tunes. *SOhO (☎ 805-962-7776, 1221 State St)* has live jazz, rock and blues nightly.

Ballet, light opera and orchestral music are staged at the *Granada Theatre (☎ 805-966-2324, 1216 State St)* and *Arlington Theatre (☎ 805-963-4408, 1317 State St).*

Getting There & Around
Greyhound (☎ 805-965-7551) sends daily buses to Los Angeles ($13) and San Francisco ($32) from the downtown depot at 34 W Carrillo St. Amtrak (☎ 805-963-1015) trains leave daily from the station at 209 State St for Los Angeles ($22) and San Francisco via Oakland ($67).

The convenient Downtown-Waterfront Shuttle (☎ 805-638-3702) runs from Stearns Wharf to the north end of State St, and along Cabrillo Blvd from the Yacht Harbor to the zoo (25¢; 10am-6pm).

SANTA BARBARA TO SAN LUIS OBISPO
North of Santa Barbara, Hwy 101 snakes along the coast and turns inland at Gaviota, continuing past the turnoff for Solvang, a quasi-Danish village with bakeries and kitschy gift shops. Hwy 101s and 1 rejoin 75 miles later at Pismo Beach, a dog-eared tourist town known for clams and sand dunes. Back at Gaviota, Hwy 1 swings northwest past Vandenberg Air Force Base and endless patches of sugar beets and lettuce. The largest town along this not-so-scenic stretch of Hwy 1 is Lompoc, a quiet military community.

SAN LUIS OBISPO
Known as SLO, this town is large enough to support a major university (California Polytechnic State University), some diverse nightlife and a variety of good restaurants, yet small enough to inspire sobriquets like 'charming' and 'off the beaten path.' The chamber of commerce (☎ 805-781-2777, Ⓦ www.slochamber.org, 1039 Chorro St), off Higuera St, gives hotel referrals and sells tickets to Hearst Castle and other events in the area.

Things to See & Do
Founded in 1772, **Mission San Luis Obispo De Toloso** (☎ 805-543-6850) occupies a block of Monterey St between Chorro and Broad Sts. It has an excellent museum with extensive Chumash Indian exhibitions. The mission church is still active, and mass is celebrated on weekends and religious holidays. In front of the mission, **Mission Plaza** is a pleasant spot with several restored adobes and an amphitheater overlooking San Luis Creek. On the plaza's south end is the **San Luis Obispo Art Center** (☎ 805-543-8562), showcasing local artists, sculptors and photographers (free admission). Across from the mission, the **San Luis Obispo County Historical Museum** (☎ 805-543-0430), housed in the 1904 Carnegie Library Building, is definitely worth a visit (free admission). The **Children's Museum** (☎ 805-544-5437, 1010 Nipomo St)

has amusing hands-on displays ($4). The **farmers' market** along Higuera St is a great way to get a feel for the SLO scene. The street is closed off to traffic and local vendors line the streets selling fresh fruits and vegetables as well as everything from barbecued corn to freshly grilled salmon (open 6-9pm Thurs).

Places to Stay

The ***HI Hostel Obispo*** *(☎ 805-544-4678, 1617 Santa Rosa)* is a quaint, clean hostel in a homey Victorian close to downtown. Check-in is 5pm-10pm; it's closed 9:30am-4:30pm (beds $16-18, private rooms $40). SLO's budget motels are concentrated at the north end of Monterey St. Owned by a friendly family, ***Villa Motel*** *(☎ 805-543-8071, 1670 Monterey St)* has newly renovated rooms ($65). ***Adobe Inn*** *(☎ 805-549-0321, 1473 Monterey St)* offers comfortable rooms and a morning breakfast buffet ($55-100). For something a bit funky, ***Madonna Inn*** *(☎ 805-543-3000, W www.madonnainn.com)*, off Hwy 101 on Madonna Rd, is a crazy and kitschy hotel with 109 theme rooms ($137-250). The Caveman Room is carved out of solid rock with a waterfall shower, the Safari Room is...well, you get the idea. Even if you're not staying here, it's worth a stop to peruse the grounds.

Places to Eat & Drink

The ***SLO Brewing Co*** *(1119 Garden St)*, known for its delicious home-brewed beer, has good veggie burgers, grilled meats and fish and large salads for under $10. ***Big Sky Café*** *(1121 Broad St)* has a fantastic breakfast menu and an extensive lunch and dinner selection offering everything from zydeco fried chicken salad to local fresh fish dishes. Entrées are a bargain ($5-12). For top-notch Mexican food, line up with the locals at ***Tio Alberto's*** *(1131 Broad St)*. ***Mo's BBQ*** *(970 Higuera St)* is a good bet for juicy pork and beef ribs.

The SLO Brewing Co, ***McCarthy's*** *(☎ 805-544-0268, 1019 Court St)* and ***Mother's Tavern*** *(729 Higuera St)* are the college crowd's favorites for boozing.

Getting There & Away

Greyhound departs daily from the SLO station (☎ 805-543-2121, 150 South St) to Los Angeles ($26), Santa Barbara ($19) and San Francisco ($38). There are once-daily trains from SLO to Los Angeles ($26), Santa Barbara ($19) and San Francisco ($38) from the Amtrak station (☎ 805-541-0505), at the southern end of Santa Rosa St.

Driving Highway 1

Completed in 1937 after 18 years of construction (mostly with convict labor), Hwy 1 is California's premier scenic highway, and it certainly deserves the title. The curvy two-lane road isn't meant for quick travel; driving straight from Carmel to San Luis Obispo takes about five hours. But motoring it is well worth the detour. Taking in the brilliant coastal scenery here is mandatory; towering, golden cliffs plummet down to the rock-strewn sea, which can change from peacock blue to the deep purple of a marlin's back in a heartbeat.

Photographers are advised to load up on film and to spend all the daylight hours making the trip. You will find yourself pulling off the road every hundred yards or so for that perfect shot. From December to March, whales migrating north from Baja make a fantastic roadside attraction, and breeding elephant seals lying along the highway's beaches make for another good reason to pull over.

If you enjoy driving, you will love the banks and swerves of this road. But your patience can be tested: Summer brings fog and heavy traffic, and the highway is often closed during winter storms. Just relax and let the road reveal one incredibly beautiful vista after another. Buy gas in Carmel or San Luis Obispo to avoid exorbitant gas prices (sometimes more than double the regular price), and bring your own food for picnicking. Beach access is limited since much of the land along Hwy 1 is private (trespass laws are strictly enforced), and swimming is discouraged because of undertows and rip currents. Trails that do lead to the beach require tennis shoes or sturdy sandals.

MORRO BAY TO HEARST CASTLE

Apart from its gift-shop-infested Embarcadero, Morro Bay is an honest-to-goodness fishing town whose livelihood depends

more on the day's catch than on tourism. The town's landmark is 576-foot Morro Rock, dubbed 'El Morro' by explorer Juan Cabrillo for the domed turban hats worn by the Moors of Spain. The chamber of commerce (☎ 805-772-4467, 800-231-0592, 880 Main St) is open 8am-5pm weekdays and 10am-3pm Saturday.

Tiger's Folly II, an old paddle wheeler, makes $10 harbor tours with a Dixieland jazz serenade; buy tickets at Harbor Hut Restaurant (☎ 805-772-2255, 1205 Embarcadero). Virg's Landing (☎ 805-772-1222), at the north end of the Embarcadero, runs fishing trips ($25-35) and whale-watching trips ($20). Fifteen miles north of Morro Bay, just off Hwy 1, **Harmony** (population 16) has an old creamery housing artists' workshops and art galleries. Four miles farther north, **Cambria** is a self-proclaimed artists' village surrounded by hills.

Nearby, 'new' San Simeon is a bland mile-long strip of motels and restaurants along Hwy 1; 'old' **San Simeon** is a small beachside settlement on the west side of Hwy 1, across from the entrance to Hearst Castle. The Hearst Corporation still owns most of the land here, including a 125-sq-mile cattle ranch. Overlooking the Pacific Ocean, **Hearst Castle** is California's most famous monument to wealth and ambition. William Randolph Hearst, the newspaper magnate, based his 'enchanted hill' on a Mediterranean village, with 165 rooms, four guest houses, unbelievable swimming pools and gardens all surrounding a central plaza. The visit is worthwhile, if only to see something so ostentatious. Four estate tours are offered ($14 each); tour 1 is best for first-time visitors. All tours last about two hours and leave by bus from the visitor center (☎ 800-444-4445). Reservations are recommended on summer weekends.

Five miles north of Hearst Castle is a stretch of beach that offers fantastic viewing of the new mainland breeding colony for the noisy and immense elephant seals. The seals come here for breeding, molting and sleeping, and are easily viewed year round. The spot is unmarked; keep your eyes peeled for a crowded parking lot.

As you continue north, Hwy 1 leaves civilization far behind, hugging the rugged Pacific shore and traversing vast stretches of coast where services – let alone towns – are few and far between. After about 60 miles you hit tiny Gorda, with an expensive gas station, deli and cafe. Next stop is the Central Coast's blockbuster attraction – Big Sur.

A bus service between San Luis Obispo, Morro Bay and San Simeon is run by Central Coast Area Transit (☎ 805-541-2228) on weekdays only ($1.75).

The *Morro Bay State Park Campground* (☎ 800-444-7275 ParkNet), 2 miles south of town, has beautiful sites surrounded by eucalyptus and cypress trees ($12). In Morro Bay itself *Pleasant Inn Motel* (☎ 805-772-8521, 235 Harbor St) is a small, B&B-type motel ($55-65). *Ascot Inn* (☎ 805-772-4437, 845 Morro Ave) has spiffy singles/doubles for $35/75. Adjacent to the inn is the newly built *Ascot Suites* (same ☎), with ocean-view rooms, some with hot tubs (from $175).

Cambria's oceanside Moonstone Beach Dr is lined with lodging choices, though there are cheaper options on and around the village's Main St. Six miles south of 'old' San Simeon are the adjacent *San Simeon Creek Campground* ($22) and the far more basic *Washburn Campground* ($8). In San Simeon, along Hearst and Castillo Drs, the *Sands Motel* (☎ 805-927-3243) has oceanside rooms ($55-65) and an indoor pool.

Morro Bay has many seafood eateries along Embarcadero, including the *Harbor Hut Restaurant*, *Galley Restaurant* and *Great American Fish Company*. For a good meal (under $10) in Cambria, try the California-Mexican-style *Creekside Gardens Café (2114 Main St)*. For a slightly more upscale dining experience, *Sow's Ear Café* offers delicious steaks, seafood and pastas for less than $20.

BIG SUR

This area is simply awe-inspiring. There are no traffic lights or shopping centers, and when the sun goes down, the moon and stars are the only streetlights. 'Big Sur' refers to a vast stretch of sparsely populated, spectacular coast along Hwy 1. If there is a hub, it is **Big Sur Center** (called 'the village'). Here lie the post office and Big Sur Bazaar (☎ 831-667-2197), a combination market, deli and all-purpose shop. Three miles south, the USFS Big Sur Ranger Station (☎ 831-667-2315) issues backcountry permits and has trail information.

Elephant Seals

Elephant seals follow a precise calendar: Between September and November young seals and the yearlings, who left the beach earlier in the year, return and take up residence. In November and December, the adult males return and start the ritual struggles to assert superiority; only the largest, strongest and most aggressive 'alpha' males gather a harem. From December through February, the adult females arrive, pregnant from last year's beach activities, give birth to their pups and, about a month later, mate with the dominant males.

At birth an elephant seal pup weighs about 80 pounds and, while being fed by its mother, puts on about 7lb a day. A month's solid feeding will bring the pup's weight up to about 300lb, but around March the females depart, abandoning their offspring on the beach. For the next two to three months the young seals, now known as 'weaners,' lounge around in groups known as 'pods,' gradually learning to swim, first in the rivers and tidal pools, then in the sea. In April, the young seals depart, having lost 20% to 30% of their weight during this prolonged fast.

Because street signs are rare in Big Sur, locals use the following sights (listed in south-north order) as highway reference markers. **Esalen Institute** (☎ 831-667-3000, Ⓦ www.esalen.org), marked only by a sign reading 'Esalen Institute, By Reservation Only,' is a renowned New Age resort with expensive workshops that 'promote human values and potentials.' If touchy-feely gobbledygook isn't of interest, the Institute also offers such pampering activities as massages and hot springs as well as classes in meditation, yoga and Chi Gung.

The highlight at **Julia Pfeiffer Burns State Park**, a few miles north of Esalen, is 50-foot McWay Falls, which drops straight into the sea. To reach the waterfall viewpoint, take the trail that heads west from the park entrance and cross beneath Hwy 1. Note that the park's $3 entrance fee is also valid for Pfeiffer Big Sur and Andrew Molera State Parks (see below).

Housed amid gardens and sculptures, the **Henry Miller Memorial Library** (☎ 831-667-2574) has reams of Miller's written works and a great collection of Big Sur and Beat Generation material (call for hours and admission). Immediately south of the USFS Big Sur Ranger Station, **Pfeiffer Big Sur State Park** occupies 680 acres, has plenty of coastal hiking trails and is named after Big Sur's first European settlers – Michael and Barbara Pfeiffer, who arrived in 1869.

Ventana Wilderness is popular with backpackers; a favorite destination is the mineral pools at Sykes Hot Springs, about 11 miles from the wilderness boundary via the Pine Ridge Trailhead (accessible from the ranger station parking lot). **Andrew Molera State Park**, a few miles past Big Sur Center, features a gentle half-mile trail that leads to a beautiful beach. From here several trails head south along the bluffs above the ocean. Molera Trail Rides (☎ 831-625-5486) runs guided horseback rides ($40; 2 hours).

Point Sur is that imposing volcanic rock that looks like an island, but is actually connected to land by a sandbar. On weekends (also Wed, Apr-Oct) you can take a tour of the 1899 Point Sur Light Station atop the rock; for tour information call ☎ 831-625-4419 ($5; 3 hours).

Big Sur is an extremely popular weekend getaway, and accommodations fill up on weekends. Most places take reservations, so plan ahead or arrive early.

All three of the state parks in Big Sur contain campsites ($14-22). Reserve through ParkNet (☎ 800-444-7275, Ⓦ www.reserveamerica.com). A good – but often crowded – private campground is *Big Sur Campground & Cabins* (☎ 831-667-2322), 2 miles north of Pfeiffer Big Sur State Park. It has trailer and tent sites ($24), tent cabins ($44) and deluxe cabins (from $80), as well as a store and hot showers. The area's most scenic (and peaceful) campground is the USFS *Bottcher's Gap* (☎ 805-434-1996), with 14 first-come, first-served sites overlooking the Ventana Wilderness ($12). Bottcher's Gap is nearly 8 miles up the steep Palo Colorado Rd, which intersects Hwy 1 about 6 miles north of Andrew Molera State Park (12 miles south of Carmel; see later).

Popular *Deetjen's Big Sur Inn* (☎ 831-667-2377), about 2 miles south of the USFS

CALIFORNIA

ranger station, is a pleasant and cozy lodging and dining choice; reservations are advised ($99-165). Just north of Big Sur Center, **Ripplewood Resort** (☎ *831-667-2242)* has cabins with kitchens and private bathrooms ($65-105). The coffee shop serves breakfast and lunch, and a market stocks fresh produce and picnic supplies. Next door, the quaint **Glen Oaks Motel** (☎ *831-667-2105)* has clean, simple rooms ($65-100). Singles/doubles at the nearby **Big Sur River Inn** (☎ *831-667-2700)* have views of the Big Sur River and include access to a heated pool ($80/150).

The **Six Bells Pub**, next to Big Sur River Inn, is a bar-restaurant that serves reasonably priced seafood, steaks and veggie burgers in the cozy dining room or outside on the deck overlooking the river and redwood forest. Known for its elaborate gardens and ocean views, **Nepenthe** (☎ *831-667-2345)*, near Deetjen's, is good for an elegant meal. Below the main restaurant, **Cafe Kevah** has salads and sandwiches (under $10).

CARMEL & AROUND

Begun as a planned seaside resort in the 1880s, by the early 1900s **Carmel-by-the-Sea** had established a reputation as a slightly bohemian retreat. Though the artistic flavor survives, Carmel is thoroughly affluent and a bit stodgy. The town's picturesque appearance is ensured by local bylaws that forbid streetlights, sidewalks and, in the central area, mailboxes. Since there's no mail delivery, there are also no street numbers in the compact downtown area.

The **San Carlos Borromeo del Rio Carmelo Mission** (☎ 831-624-3600, 3080 Rio Rd) was founded by Padre Junípero Serra in 1769. He died here in 1784 and is buried on the grounds beside his compatriot, Padre Juan Crespi. The mission itself is one of the most complete in California and has an interesting museum ($2). Poet Robinson Jeffers – one of the creators of the Carmel ethos – built his rugged home, **Tor House** (☎ 831-624-1813, 26304 Ocean View Ave), a few blocks from Carmel Bay. Tours are offered, but numbers are limited so it's wise to book in advance ($7; Fri-Sat).

Dubbed 'the greatest meeting of land and sea on earth,' **Point Lobos State Reserve** (☎ 831-624-4909), 4 miles south of Carmel, is a rocky coastline encompassing 554 aboveground acres and 750 submerged acres that are ideal for scuba diving ($3 per vehicle). There's a good selection of short walks, most of them less than a mile long. One favorite destination is Devil's Cauldron, a blowhole and whirlpool that gets splashy at high tide.

Carmel and Monterey are linked by Hwy 1 and by the spectacularly scenic **17-Mile Drive**, which winds through easygoing Pacific Grove, by the famed Lone Cypress (the well-photographed unofficial symbol of Carmel) and the million-dollar homes and golf courses of Pebble Beach, an unapologetic symbol of the Monterey Peninsula's wealth. There are five entry gates to Pebble Beach ($7.50 per car for nonresidents; free admission for bicycles). On weekends bicycles can use only the Pacific Grove gate. Continue through Pacific Grove to the northern tip of the peninsula to reach the 1855 **Point Piños Lighthouse** (☎ 831-648-3116), the oldest continuously operating lighthouse on the West Coast (free admission; open 1pm-4pm Thurs-Sun).

Many places in Carmel are quite expensive and impose a two-night minimum stay on summer weekends. Campers can go 4 miles up Carmel Valley Rd to the campgrounds at **Saddlemountain** (☎ *831-624-1617)* or **Riverside** (☎ *831-624-9329)*. In the town center **The Homestead** (☎ *831-624-4119)*, on the corner of Lincoln and 8th Aves, has rooms and cottages from $75. The friendly and convenient **Carmel Oaks Inn** (☎ *831-624-5547)*, on the corner of 5th Ave and Mission St, has comfortable singles/doubles for $99/119.

Carmel's ex-mayor and most famous resident, Clint Eastwood, once owned the **Hog's Breath Inn**, on San Carlos between 5th and 6th Aves. It still serves moderately priced Eastwood-movie-themed food and drinks, such as the Dirty Harry Burger and Pale Rider Ale.

MONTEREY

Nowhere is California's Latino heritage richer than in Monterey, the capital of Alta and Baja California in the 18th century and a provincial capital after Mexico broke from Spain in 1821. Downtown 'Old Monterey' has numerous adobe buildings from the Spanish and Mexican periods, and it's a pleasant place for a stroll. Through the Lighthouse Ave tunnel is 'New Monterey,' where you'll find the world-famous aquarium, the hostel and the tourist traps of Cannery Row.

The helpful Monterey Chamber of Commerce (☎ 831-649-1770), at Camino El Estero and Franklin St, provides driving advice and direct-dial phones to more than 40 hotels.

Monterey State Historic Park

Near the water just north of downtown, this park (☎ 831-649-7118) includes six of Monterey's finest historical buildings ($5). Tickets are available from the visitor center desk just inside the lobby of the Maritime Museum.

In 1822 newly independent Mexico stipulated that any cargo brought to Alta California would have to be unloaded at **Monterey Custom House**. The restored building displays a collection of antique goods. Thomas Larkin arrived from New England in 1832 and made a fortune in trade; later he was the US consul in Monterey when the US Army annexed California in 1846. He commenced building **Larkin House** in 1834; its combination of New England design and adobe construction is known today as 'Monterey colonial.' Robert Louis Stevenson came to Monterey in 1879 to meet with his wife-to-be, Fanny Osbourne. The **Stevenson House**, then the French Hotel, was where he stayed and reputedly wrote *Treasure Island*. The building now houses a superb collection of Stevenson memorabilia.

Nearby, the **Maritime Museum of Monterey** (☎ 831-373-2469), on Custom House Plaza, has a great ship-in-a-bottle collection plus displays on the rise and rapid fall of the local sardine business ($5). A short walk from the state historic park, **Fisherman's Wharf** is just a tourist trap at heart, but it's good fun nevertheless. It features plenty of restaurants, gift shops and fresh-seafood stands.

Monterey Museum of Art

This museum (☎ 831-372-5477) has two downtown branches. Both have rotating and permanent exhibits; the Civic Center collection (559 Pacific St) emphasizes Californian artists and photographers, while La Mirada branch (720 Via Mirada) explores Monterey life in the early 20th century ($5).

Cannery Row

In its heyday Cannery Row was a hectic and very smelly place. The American Can Company began operations here in 1926 and within a year churned out 26 million cans of sardines. In 1945 Monterey's sardine catch reached a peak of 250,000 tons, though by 1950 the catch crashed to 33,000 tons, forcing most of the sardine canneries to close down. Nowadays Cannery Row is a tacky seven-block enclave of restaurants and souvenir shops. The innovative 'New Cannery Row Mural,' completed in 1998, is worth a look; it features unique historical panels by different artists. A statue of John Steinbeck (1902–68) presides over the scene – his novel *Cannery Row* paid dark homage to the local sardine industry.

Monterey Bay Aquarium

New Monterey's one truly amazing attraction is the mighty Monterey Bay Aquarium (☎ 831-648-4888), devoted to the marine life of the area. Highlights include the two-story Kelp Forest tank, where you can view sharks and other sea creatures swimming between towering fronds of kelp, and the Outer Bay exhibit, with its soothing tanks of colorful, mesmerizing jellyfish. The tickets ($16/8 adults/kids) are worth it – nearly two million visitors a year think so, making entry lines long. Beat the crowds by reserving tickets (☎ 800-756-3737) for a small fee.

Activities

For surfing gear and rentals, head to On the Beach (☎ 831-646-9283, 693 Lighthouse Ave). Guided scuba dives cost $50/80 for one dive/two dives, equipment extra, at the Aquarius Dive Shop (☎ 831-375-1933). Aquarius has two waterfront locations, at 32 Cannery Row and 2040 Del Monte Ave. Rent a kayak for $30 a day from Monterey Bay Kayaks (☎ 831-373-5357, 693 Del Monte Ave). Randy's (☎ 831-372-7440) runs three-hour whale-watching trips ($27) and deep-sea fishing tours ($40) from Fisherman's Wharf.

Places to Stay & Eat

Tent camping costs $18 at the 185-site *Laguna Seca Recreation Area* (☎ *831-758-3604*),

CALIFORNIA

which is 9 miles east of Monterey on Hwy 68 toward Salinas.

The new, squeaky-clean *HI Monterey Hostel* (☎ 831-649-0375), in the Carpenter's Union Hall at the corner of Irving and Hawthorne Sts, has 45 beds and a guest parking lot ($17-19). As far as motels go, the Monterey Peninsula ain't cheap, especially in summer. There's a cluster of economical motels on N Fremont St, 2½ miles from downtown and east of Hwy 1 (Casa Verde exit). Both *Motel 6* (☎ 831-646-8585) and *Vagabond Motel* (☎ 831-372-6066) charge $60-80.

Close to Old Monterey, *El Dorado Inn* (☎ 831-373-2921, 900 Munras Ave), at El Dorado St, has doubles for $100. Nearby Pacific Grove offers some nicer, quieter options, such as *Butterfly Inn* (☎ 831-373-4921, 1073 Lighthouse Ave), where rates run $89-159.

Restaurants on Cannery Row and Fisherman's Wharf are generally touristy and overpriced, though the seafood is certainly fresh. *Indian Summer* (☎ 831-372-4744, 220 Oliver St), behind the Doubletree Hotel, serves lunch and dinner in a beautiful garden setting ($9-15). For those low on cash, *Papá Chano's* (462 Alvarado St) makes great $5 burritos.

Getting There & Around
Greyhound buses traveling between Los Angeles ($40) and San Francisco ($19) stop at the Exxon gas station (1024 Del Monte Ave), just east of El Estero Lake. Monterey-Salinas Transit (MST; ☎ 831-899-2555) operates buses around the peninsula to Carmel and Pacific Grove, and south to Big Sur. The Monterey Transit Plaza, at the south end of Alvarado St, is the main MST terminal.

SANTA CRUZ
Santa Cruz is just as beautiful as Monterey, and its 'beach town' vibe is more authentic. Restaurants and businesses here cater more to health-conscious hippies than wealthy yuppies. It's also home to the University of California at Santa Cruz (UCSC) and its 10,000 left-of-center students.

Santa Cruz grabbed national headlines after the 1989 Loma Prieta earthquake, when downtown's Pacific Garden Mall was decimated and a number of people were killed. Things are mostly back to normal –

but 'normal' in an offbeat Santa Cruz way. The city is serene and quiet most of the year, except on summer weekends, when crowds swarm the beaches and the Santa Cruz Beach Boardwalk.

Orientation & Information
Restaurants and shops line parallel Pacific Ave and Front St, the unofficial main drags. For the beach and Boardwalk, head south on Front St and turn left on Beach St. The visitor center (☎ 831-425-1234, 701 Front St) can help with maps and accommodations.

Things to See & Do
The 1906 **Boardwalk** (☎ 831-426-7433) is the oldest beachfront amusement park on the West Coast, with a 1923 Giant Dipper coaster and a 1911 Looff carousel – both National Historic Landmarks. It is open daily in summer, weekends all year and some winter holidays. Individual rides cost $2-3; an unlimited all-day ticket costs $23.

The **Museum of Art & History** (☎ 831-429-1964, 705 Front St) and the adjacent Octagon Gallery (same ☎) are worth a quick look ($4). The **Santa Cruz City Museum of Natural History** (☎ 831-420-6115, 1305 E Cliff Dr), east of the San Lorenzo River, displays the fossilized skeleton of a 10-million-year-old sea cow, an extinct relative of the Australasian dugong. The tiny **Surfing Museum** (☎ 831-420-6289), at Lighthouse Point on W Cliff Dr, overlooks Steamer's Lane, Santa Cruz's most popular surfing break (free admission; open noon-4pm Thurs-Mon).

Natural Bridges State Beach, just north of Santa Cruz at the end of W Cliff Dr, has a good beach, tidal pools and trees where monarch butterflies hibernate in bunches from November to March. The natural bridge, unfortunately, has washed away.

Although there are no railway connections to modern Santa Cruz, there are two scenic, historical **train rides** (☎ 831-335-4484). From the Boardwalk, the Santa Cruz, Big Trees & Pacific Railway takes an hour to reach Roaring Camp, a re-created 1880s logging town ($17). From Roaring Camp, narrow-gauge steam locomotives of the Roaring Camp & Big Trees Railroad make the 75-minute roundtrip journey to Big Trees Redwood Forest ($15).

There's good, clean fun at the **Mystery Spot** (☎ 831-423-8897), a fine old-fashioned tourist trap. Mysterious forces push you around and make balls roll uphill, while buildings lean at silly angles ($5/3 adults/ kids). It is 3 miles north of town on Branciforte Dr; take Water St to Market St, turn left and continue up into the hills.

Santa Cruz's New Agey **spas** are ideal places to unwind. The Well Within (☎ 831-458-9355, 112 Elm St) has private tub and sauna rentals for $27 an hour. Kiva House (☎ 831-429-1142, 702 Water St) has a communal tub that's $16 all day.

Activities
Either **hiking** or **biking** along the beautiful W Cliff Dr is a satisfying way to enjoy the sunset. From the Boardwalk it's 1 mile to Lighthouse Point, 3 miles to Natural Bridges. Check Beach St for bike-rental shops.

Rent **surfing** gear from Go Skate (☎ 831-425-8578, 601 Beach St) or Freeline Design (☎ 831-476-2950, 821 41st Ave). For **kayaking**, Kayak Connection (☎ 831-479-1121, 413 Lake Ave) has four-hour rentals from $27. **Whale-watching** trips depart from the pier. Ocean Odyssey (☎ 831-475-3483, 2345 S Rodeo Gulch Rd) has the skinny on **scuba diving**.

Places to Stay & Eat
You can **camp** (☎ 800-444-7275) among the redwoods in nearby Henry Cowell and Big Basin State Parks, north of town off Hwy 9, and at New Brighton State Beach, about 4 miles south of Santa Cruz near Capitola. Tent sites cost $12, and reservations are advised.

HI Carmelita Cottages Hostel (☎ 831-423-8304, 321 Main St) is just two blocks from the beach and one of the finest along the Central Coast ($15-17; reservations advised). For motels, try Riverside Ave, Ocean St, Mission St or the streets running back from the Boardwalk. Beware, though, that lodging isn't cheap here, especially during summer. Among the lowest is the no-frills *Islander Motel* (☎ 831-426-7766, 522 Ocean St), charging $69-95. If you're going to stay overnight, you might as well do it right; pleasant *Sea & Sand Inn* (☎ 831-427-3400, 201 W Cliff Dr) has rooms overlooking the ocean (from $139).

Downtown Santa Cruz, especially Pacific Ave and Front St, is a good place to browse for cheap pizza slices, Mexican eateries, brunch spots, and java joints. For breakfast, it's hard to beat the super-friendly *Silver Spur* (2650 Soquel Dr), a mile north of Hwy 1 on Santa Cruz' east end. On the pier, the *Dolphin* serves straightforward, sit-down or takeout seafood ($5 and up) and offers good views. The *Seabright Brewery* (519 Seabright Ave) serves good pub food and great beer to a loud, lively crowd. *Azur* (☎ 831-427-3554, 1001 Center St) is a new Mediterranean restaurant ($10-20).

Entertainment
There's regular live music at the all-ages *Kuumbwa Jazz Center* (☎ 831-427-2227, 320 Cedar St), *Palookaville* (☎ 831-454-0600, 1133 Pacific Ave) and *The Catalyst* (☎ 831-423-1336, 1011 Pacific Ave); check the weekly *Metro Santa Cruz* for schedules. *Blue Lagoon* (☎ 831-423-7117, 923 Pacific Ave) is a loud dance club popular with the local gay crowd and students.

Getting There & Away
Santa Cruz Metropolitan Transit (831-425-8600) operates from the Santa Cruz Metro Transit Center (920 Pacific Ave) and serves the greater Santa Cruz region ($1, day pass $3). Greyhound (☎ 831-423-1800, 425 Front St) runs daily buses to/from San Francisco ($12) and Los Angeles ($42). Bus connections from the CalTrain/Amtrak station in San Jose cost $6 and leave regularly from the Metro Transit Center.

San Francisco & the Bay Area

SAN FRANCISCO
Visually spectacular, historically colorful and a regular trendsetter in everything from flower power to gay liberation, San Francisco consistently tops the polls as America's favorite city. Streets soar up and plunge down steep hills, framing dramatic views and concealing quiet neighborhoods within the urban chaos. In the background, there's always the bay, crossed by two of the world's most famous bridges.

History
Although the Miwok and Ohlone Indians inhabited the area for centuries, it was less

than 250 years ago that the first Europeans, the overland party of Gaspar de Portolá, encountered the bay. In 1775, Juan Manuel de Ayala sailed into San Francisco Bay, becoming the first European to enter the narrow passage that would later become known as the Golden Gate.

After the Mexican-American War, California was ceded to the USA in 1846, just two years before gold was discovered in the Sierra Nevada. During the first year of the gold rush that followed, the young city's population exploded from 500 to 25,000.

In the latter half of the 1800s, the area around Portsmouth Square was a labyrinth of casinos, saloons and opium dens. The 'Barbary Coast' (now Chinatown and Jackson Square) was known the world over as a dangerous place, where sailors were routinely knocked out, robbed and 'Shanghai'd' – awaking to find themselves indentured to a ship that was already out to sea.

The 1906 earthquake and fire leveled most of the city, and frantic years of construction followed. This continued through the 1930s, when large-scale public works projects gave the region a lift during the Great Depression – the most outstanding examples being the San Francisco–Oakland Bay Bridge (1936) and the Golden Gate Bridge (1937).

During WWII the Bay Area became a major launching pad for military operations in the Pacific; gigantic shipyards soon sprang up around the bay. Although military spending continued to be a boon to the local economy for several decades, the postwar years were distinguished by the city's colorful countercultures: The Beats spearheaded the '50s poetry movement, and the hippies brought flower power and free love to the city in the '60s. The 'Summer of Love' kicked off in 1967, when 20,000 people congregated in Golden Gate Park for a free concert.

In the '60s, San Francisco also became known for its relatively accepting attitude toward gays. The AIDS epidemic, which struck in the early '80s, has had a tremendous impact, but the city's gay community continues to thrive. The economic booms of the '80s and '90s attracted large numbers of young urban professionals, known as

'yuppies' and 'dot-commers,' to San Francisco. With so much disposable income in people's pockets, the city's restaurant industry blossomed, and San Francisco gained a reputation for being at the vanguard of the country's culinary renaissance.

Orientation

San Francisco is compact, covering the tip of a 30-mile-long peninsula, with the Pacific Ocean to the west and the San Francisco Bay to the east. The city can be divided into three sections. The downtown district is in the northeast between Van Ness Ave, Market St and the bay, and includes the Embarcadero, Union Square, the financial district, Civic Center, Chinatown, North Beach, Nob Hill, Russian Hill and Fisherman's Wharf.

The South of Market District, or SoMa, is a trendy warehouse zone that fades into the Mission, the city's Latino quarter, and then the Castro, the city's gay quarter.

The western part of the city is mostly residential and stretches from Van Ness Ave all the way to the Pacific Ocean, encompassing upscale neighborhoods like the Marina and Pacific Heights, less pricey zones like the Richmond and Sunset Districts, and Golden Gate Park, Japantown and the Haight.

Information

San Francisco's Visitor Information Center (☎ 415-391-2000) is at Market and Powell Sts, on the lower level of Hallidie Plaza (open daily).

For a good read, City Lights (☎ 415-362-8193, 261 Columbus Ave), in North Beach, has a great selection of Beat poetry and

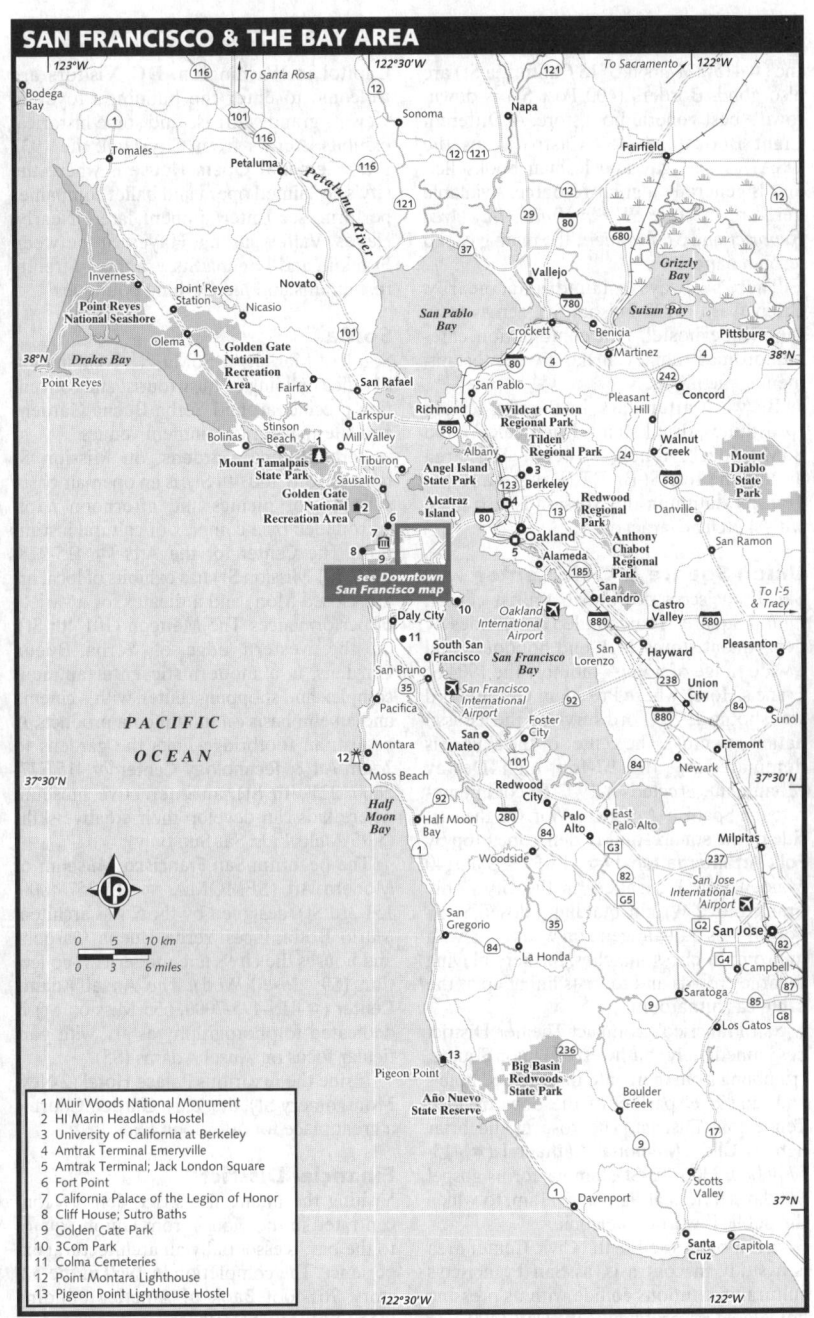

SAN FRANCISCO & THE BAY AREA

1 Muir Woods National Monument
2 HI Marin Headlands Hostel
3 University of California at Berkeley
4 Amtrak Terminal Emeryville
5 Amtrak Terminal; Jack London Square
6 Fort Point
7 California Palace of the Legion of Honor
8 Cliff House; Sutro Baths
9 Golden Gate Park
10 3Com Park
11 Colma Cemeteries
12 Point Montara Lighthouse
13 Pigeon Point Lighthouse Hostel

see Downtown San Francisco map

CALIFORNIA

progressive literature. Staceys Bookstore (☎ 415-421-4687, 581 Market St) and Books Inc (☎ 415-221-3666, 3515 California St) are also good. Borders (400 Post St) is downtown's best general bookstore. A Different Light Bookstore (489 Castro St) is the USA's largest gay and lesbian bookseller, and is generally a great resource. Available here are the free *SF Bay Times, Bay Area Reporter* and *SF Frontiers,* the main gay and lesbian papers.

There's always a laundromat nearby. Brain Wash (1122 Folsom St), across from the Globe hostel, is a combination cafe-laundromat that even has live entertainment some nights.

Be wary after dark in the Tenderloin (prostitutes, drunks and drug dealers) and SoMa (dark, lonely streets). The area around the 16th St BART (Bay Area Rapid Transit) station in the Mission is also filled with sketchy characters.

Union Square & Civic Center

San Francisco's downtown tourist center, Union Square, is surrounded on all sides by department stores, high-end boutiques and a wide range of hotels – notably the 1904 St Francis Hotel, where President Gerald Ford was shot in 1975 (Ford survived the assassination attempt). The center of the square is dominated by the 97-foot-high Dewey Monument, erected in 1903 to commemorate the Spanish-American War. On the east side of the square, on Maiden Lane, stop by Folk Art International (☎ 415-392-9999, 140 Maiden Lane), a gallery in the city's only Frank Lloyd Wright building (closed Sun). Powell St is quite a scene on weekends, with impromptu chess matches, buskers playing to large crowds and tourists lining up at the cable car turnaround.

San Francisco's compact Theater District lies immediately southwest of Union Square, crumbling from there into the blighted hotels and 'massage' parlors of the downtrodden Tenderloin District. The rose in the briar here is Glide Memorial Cathedral (☎ 415-674-6000, 330 Ellis St), famous for its gospel Sunday services at 9am and 11am, to which the public is warmly welcome.

A few blocks south, the Civic Center area is a study in contrasts, as San Francisco's cultural institutions collide with its pressing homelessness problem. City Hall (400 Van Ness Ave), built in 1915 in the beaux arts style, has a taller dome than that of the US Capitol in Washington, DC. Visitors are welcome to enter the building's foyer to view its grand staircase and some historical exhibits. Across from City Hall, the 1932 War Memorial Opera House is where the city's acclaimed opera and ballet companies perform (see Entertainment, later). Nearby Hayes Valley, along Hayes St between Franklin and Laguna Sts, is a mix of trendy restaurants and hip clothing boutiques.

SoMa

South of Market, or SoMa, is a combination of office buildings, a busy tourist and convention precinct around Yerba Buena Gardens and late-night entertainment venues.

Yerba Buena Gardens, on Mission St between 3rd and 4th Sts, is an open-air oasis, suitable for picnics and afternoon naps, surrounded by a complex of cultural institutions. The Center for the Arts (☎ 415-978-2710, 701 Mission St) has exhibits of local art ($6; closed Mon) and a theater for a variety of performances. The Metreon (101 4th St), on the western edge of Yerba Buena Gardens, is a modernistic entertainment complex and shopping center, with a cinema and an emphasis on multimedia products. A pedestrian footbridge links the gardens to Zeum Art & Technology Center (☎ 415-777-2800, 221 4th St), an interactive museum where kids can develop their creative skills ($7/5 adults/kids; Sat-Sun only).

The beautiful San Francisco Museum of Modern Art (SFMOMA; ☎ 415-357-4000, 151 3rd St), designed by the Swiss architect Mario Botta, faces Yerba Buena Gardens and houses the city's fine modern art collection ($9; closed Wed). The Ansel Adams Center (☎ 415-495-7000, 655 Mission St) is dedicated to photography as art, with particular focus on Ansel Adams ($5).

Inside the luxurious Palace Hotel (2 New Montgomery St), the leafy Garden Court is a great place for afternoon tea.

Financial District

Visiting the financial district, densely concentrated in the blocks from Union Square to the bay, is essentially an architectural experience. The completion in 1969 of the 52-story, 761-foot Bank of America building (555 California St) ushered in a new era for

San Francisco's previously low-rise skyline. Tipple expensive cocktails and admire an amazing view at the building's top-floor Carnelian Room (☎ 415-433-7500). San Francisco's tallest building, the 853-foot **Transamerica Pyramid** (600 Montgomery St) was completed in 1972. Summer lunchtime concerts take place Friday on the Pyramid's Redwood Plaza (free admission).

The **Wells Fargo** bank building (420 Montgomery St) has a free museum chronicling the Pony Express and Wells Fargo's own colorful history. The **Ferry Building**, where the Embarcadero meets Market St, is an enduring San Francisco landmark, and ferries continue to run from here to points around the bay.

Other highlights in the district include the 1930 **Pacific Coast Stock Exchange** (301 Pine St), with some impressive statues gracing its front steps, and the 1908 **Bank of California** building (400 California St), fronted by Corinthian columns.

Chinatown

This is the city's most colorful and crowded neighborhood. The sightseers' nexus is **Grant Ave**, which in the late 1800s was, like many of the nearby streets, a notorious strip of brothels, opium dens and gambling parlors. Originally called Dupont St ('Du Pon Gai' to the Chinese), it was renamed in 1885 in honor of president and Civil War hero Ulysses S Grant. The dragon-studded **Chinatown Gate**, on Grant Ave at Bush St, is a good place to start a tour of the neighborhood. At Grant Ave and California St, **Old St Mary's Church**, with a 90-foot clock tower, was the tallest building in the city when it was completed in 1854.

Portsmouth Square, at Kearny and Washington Sts, was the heart of San Francisco during the gold rush, and to residents of the surrounding apartments it is still Chinatown's 'living room.' Children romp in the park's playground and older folks gamble on the benches.

For a glimpse of the 'real' Chinatown, venture down some of the dark alleys. **Waverly Place**, a narrow street between Grant and Stockton Sts, is lined with open balconies and upstairs temples. Ross Alley is another picturesque lane. At the **Golden Gate Cookie Company** (56 Ross Alley) you can see how fortune cookies are made and

then buy a fresh bag (risqué 'French adult' fortunes available). The most festive time to visit Chinatown is during Chinese New Year (see Special Events, later).

North Beach

This area is the city's Italian quarter, which explains all the pasta restaurants and cappuccino cafes. During the '50s, North Beach was the Beatniks' neighborhood of choice, and some of their old hangouts are still hanging on. Along Broadway a few lurid neon signs remain from the early 1960s, the golden age of topless and bottomless dancing.

The green 1905 **Sentinel Building** (916 Kearny St) is owned by filmmaker Francis Ford Coppola, who runs a small restaurant on the ground floor. **Vesuvio** (255 Columbus Ave) is an old Beat bar. Next door, **City Lights Bookstore** is still owned by poet Lawrence Ferlinghetti, who opened the store in 1953.

Atop Telegraph Hill, the 210-foot **Coit Tower** (☎ 415-362-0808) is one of San Francisco's most prominent landmarks. It was built in 1934, financed by San Francisco eccentric Lillie Hitchcock Coit, who harbored a peculiar passion for fire and firefighters. The tower's lobby is adorned with superb murals painted in the 1930s. Elevator rides to the top cost $3.

Russian Hill & Nob Hill

West of North Beach are the steep streets of Russian Hill, with some scenic stairway gardens as well as the famous 1000 block of **Lombard Street**, which wiggles downhill from Hyde St to Leavenworth St and is billed as 'the world's crookedest street.'

At the **San Francisco Art Institute** (800 Chestnut St), the Diego Rivera Gallery features a fine fresco by the Mexican muralist. The campus has a cafe, and its terraces afford views of the bay.

In the 1870s wealthy nabobs desired hilltop estates, but dreaded the horse-and-buggy accidents one risked in scaling the steep streets to the summit of Nob Hill. To solve the problem, the cable car was invented. The city's ruthless 'Silver Kings' – Mark Hopkins, Collis P Huntington, James Grantham Fair and Leland Stanford, who made their fortunes from the Comstock Lode strike – took up residence here. The **Cable Car Barn & Museum** (☎ 415-474-1887,

DOWNTOWN SAN FRANCISCO

PLACES TO STAY
2 HI San Francisco
   Fisherman's Wharf
13 San Remo Hotel
21 Hotel Bohème
27 Green Tortoise Hostel
32 Fairmont Hotel; Tonga
   Room
38 Pacific Tradewinds Guest
   House
44 Petite Auberge
45 Mark Hopkins
   Inter-Continental Hotel
46 Cartwright Hotel
47 Sheehan Hotel
47 Grant Plaza
48 Astoria Hotel
50 Triton Hotel
56 Dakota Hotel
58 Adelaide Inn
61 Maxwell Hotel
64 Palace Hotel
69 Central YMCA Hotel
71 HI San Francisco
   Downtown
72 Foley's Inn
74 Mosser's Victorian Hotel
81 Aida Hotel
88 Grand Central Hostel
90 San Francisco
   International Student
   Center
94 Globe Hostel
105 Edwardian San Francisco
   Hotel
111 24 Henry
113 Twin Peaks Hotel
114 The Willows Inn

PLACES TO EAT
1 Greens
5 McCormick & Kuleto's
6 Buena Vista Café
16 PlumpJack Cafe
17 L'Osteria del Forno
19 Mario's Bohemian Cigar
   Store
20 Golden Boy Pizza
22 Gold Mountain
25 House of Nanking
28 Caffè Macaroni
33 Lucky Creation
36 R&G Lounge
51 Tadich Grill
51 Café Claude
59 Yank Sing
59 Postrio
60 Farallon
66 Viet Nam II
82 LuLu
83 South Park Cafe
84 Powell's Place
93 Julie's Supper Club
96 Fringale
101 Squat & Gobble Cafe
102 Thep Phanom
104 Kate's Kitchen
106 Zuni Café
115 Chow
116 Cafe Flore
117 Bagdad Cafe
119 Ti Couz
121 Slanted Door
122 Taquería Pancho Villa

ENTERTAINMENT
9 Lou's Pier 47
18 Club Fugazi
23 The Saloon
24 Vesuvio Cafe
26 Tosca Cafe
55 Edinburgh Castle
57 C Bobby's Owl Tree
62 Harry Denton's
   Starlight Room
67 Backflip
80 Sound Factory
92 Up & Down Club
95 Endup
99 Toronado
100 Mad Dog in the Fog
103 Nickie's
107 Zeitgeist
108 Paradise Lounge
109 Slim's
110 The Stud
112 Cafe du Nord
120 Roxie Cinema
123 Detour
124 The Café
125 Castro Theatre
126 Elbo Room

OTHER
3 San Francisco National
   Maritime Museum
4 Ghirardelli Square
7 Hyde St Historic Ships
   Pier
8 The Cannery; Jack's
   Cannery Bar
10 Exploratorium
11 Palace of Fine Arts
12 San Francisco Art
   Institute
14 Saints Peter & Paul
   Church
15 Coit Tower
29 Haas-Lilienthal House
30 Grace Cathedral
31 Cable Car Barn &
   Museum
34 Old St Mary's Church
35 Portsmouth Square
37 Chinese Culture Center
39 Transamerica Pyramid
40 Wells Fargo Bank
   Building

41 Bank of California
   Building
43 Ferry Building
49 Chinatown Gate
52 Bank of America
   Building
53 Pacific Coast Stock
   Exchange
63 Dewey Monument
65 Transbay Terminal
68 Civic Center Post Office
70 Glide Memorial United
   Methodist Church
73 Visitors Information
   Center
75 Metreon
76 Yerba Buena Center for
   the Arts; Yerba Buena
   Gardens
77 Ansel Adams Center for
   Photography
78 San Francisco Museum
   of Modern Art
   (SFMOMA)
79 George R Moscone
   Convention Center
85 War Memorial Opera
   House
86 Davies Symphony Hall
87 City Hall
91 Main Library
91 Brain Wash
97 CalTrain Depot
98 Pacific Bell Park
118 Mission Dolores

Aquatic
Park

Marina Green Drive
Marina Green

Fort
Mason

Marina Blvd

Jefferson St

Beach St

North Point St

Bay St

Francisco St

The Marina

George R Moscone
Recreation Center

Bay St

To Golden
Gate Bridge

Richardson Ave

Francisco St

Chestnut St

The
Presidio

Lombard St

Greenwich St

Filbert St

Union St

Green St

Vallejo St

Broadway

Pacific Ave

Jackson St

Alta
Plaza
Park

Washington St

Clay St

Sacramento St

California St

Pine St

Bush St

Sutter St

Post St

Pacific
Heights

Japantown

Japan Center

Lafayette
Park

Geary Blvd

Raymond
Kimbell
Playground

Eddy St

Turk St

Golden Gate Ave

McAllister St

Fulton St

Alamo
Square

Hayes
Valley

Hayes St

To Golden Gate Park

Fell St

Oak St

Page St

Haight St

Waller St

Lower Haight

Duboce
Park

Hermann St

Duboce Ave

Corona
Heights
Park

Castro St
Muni
Station

17th St

The Castro

Church St
Muni Station

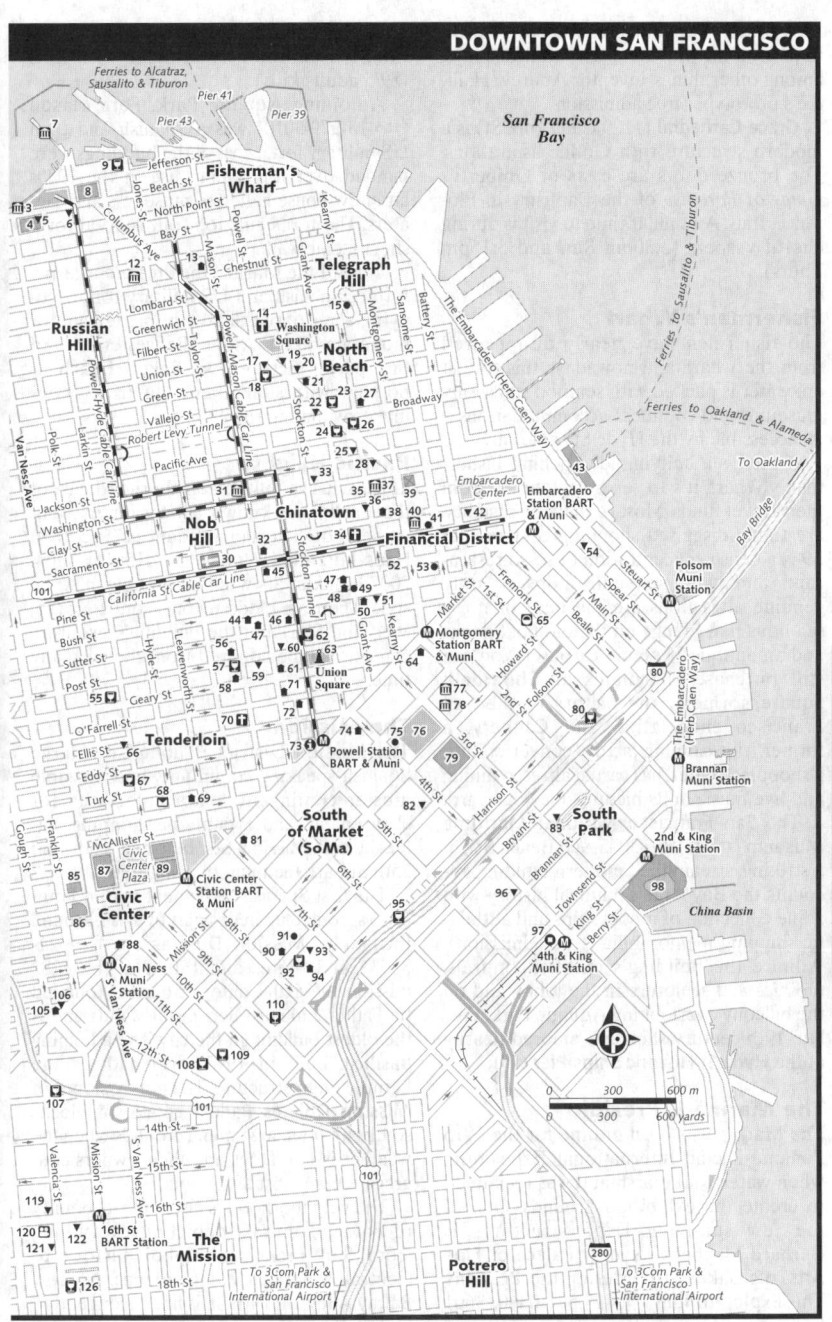

DOWNTOWN SAN FRANCISCO

Ferries to Alcatraz,
Sausalito & Tiburon
Pier 41

Pier 43

Pier 39

San Francisco
Bay

Ferries to Sausalito & Tiburon

Ferries to Oakland & Alameda

To Oakland

Bay Bridge

Jefferson St
Fisherman's
Wharf
Beach St
North Point St
Bay St
Columbus Ave
Jones St
Powell St
Mason St
Chestnut St
Telegraph
Hill
Grant Ave
Kearny St
Battery St
Sansome St

Lombard St
Greenwich St
Taylor St
Washington
Square
North
Beach
Montgomery St
Filbert St
Union St
Green St
Broadway
Vallejo St
Robert Levy Tunnel
Stockton St
Pacific Ave
Powell-Mason Cable Car Line

Russian
Hill

Van Ness Ave
Polk St
Larkin St
Powell-Hyde Cable Car Line

Jackson St
Washington St
Clay St
Sacramento St
101
California St Cable Car Line

Nob
Hill
Chinatown
Financial District
Stockton Tunnel

Embarcadero
Center
Embarcadero
Station BART
& Muni

Folsom Muni
Station

Pine St
Bush St
Sutter St
Post St
Geary St
Hyde St
Leavenworth St

O'Farrell St
Ellis St
Eddy St
Turk St
Tenderloin
Union
Square
Powell Station
BART & Muni
Montgomery
Station BART
& Muni
Market St
1st St
Fremont St
Beale St
Main St
Spear St
Steuart St

The Embarcadero (Herb Caen Way)

Howard St
2nd St
Folsom St
80
Brannan
Muni Station
2nd & King
Muni Station

McAllister St
Civic
Center
Plaza
Civic Center
Station BART
& Muni
Civic
Center
South
of Market
(SoMa)
5th St
Harrison St
South
Park
Bryant St
Brannan St
Townsend St
King St
Berry St
China Basin

Franklin St
Gough St
Van Ness Ave
S Van Ness Ave
7th St
6th St
8th St
9th St
10th St
11th St
12th St
Mission St
4th & King
Muni Station

101
14th St
15th St
16th St
Valencia St
Mission St
S Van Ness Ave
16th St
BART Station
The
Mission
18th St
101
Potrero
Hill
280
To 3Com Park &
San Francisco
International Airport
To 3Com Park &
San Francisco
International Airport

0   300   600 m
0   300   600 yards

CALIFORNIA

1201 Mason St) showcases the power plant that tows all the cable cars and displays, among other things, inventor Andrew Hallidie's prototype (free admission).

Grace Cathedral (1100 California St) is a modern structure with Gothic aspirations. The bronze doors are casts of Ghiberti's *Gates of Paradise* of the Baptistry in Florence, Italy. A popular time to visit is during choral vespers (3:30pm Sun and 5:15pm Thurs).

Fisherman's Wharf

The fishermen have nearly disappeared from the wharf, and nowadays this tourist epicenter is packed with seafood stalls, silly museums and countless accommodations – all accessible by the Hyde St cable car.

If there's a unifying idea behind Fisherman's Wharf, it's to separate tourists from their travel funds. Most of the area's 'sights' are thinly disguised shopping centers. **Pier 39** is a dense concentration of so-so restaurants and tacky souvenir shops; its only genuine attractions are the herd of noisy sea lions that lounge on the old boat docks and an antique Venetian carousel. You can still purchase chocolates at **Ghirardelli Square**, formerly the factory of the San Francisco chocolatier. **The Cannery**, a former fruit-canning factory converted into a shopping center, has casual alfresco dining and live music in its picturesque courtyard.

The **San Francisco National Maritime Museum** (☎ 415-556-3002, 900 Beach St), in a striking, streamlined modern building, recounts the Bay Area's nautical history with a fine collection of model ships and authentic shipping memorabilia (free admission). Admire the building's excellent murals, mosaics and sculpture in the lobby and on the balcony overlooking Aquatic Park. Five late-19th-century ships are moored nearby at the **Hyde St Historic Ships Pier** ($5).

The Marina & Presidio

The Marina was born in time for the 1915 Panama-Pacific International Exposition, when waterfront marshland was reclaimed to create the exhibition grounds. One of the few surviving Expo structures is Bernard Maybeck's stately **Palace of Fine Arts**, off Baker St bordering the Presidio. The **Exploratorium** (☎ 415-561-0360, 3601 Lyon St) was established in 1969 as a museum of art, science and human perception; it's enormously popular with kids ($9/5 adults/kids).

Adjoining Aquatic Park, **Fort Mason** (☎ 415-979-3010) was a Spanish and then US military fort. Most of the buildings were handed over for civilian use in the 1970s and now house galleries, museums and theaters. The fort's cliff-top trail is good for a short scenic walk.

West of the Marina, the **Presidio** is also a former Spanish and US military fort, occupying acres of parkland – prime terrain for mountain bikers. Along the western rim of the park, picturesque **Baker Beach** is popular with sunbathers, but tricky tides make swimming risky.

Pacific Heights

This exclusive hilltop neighborhood east of the Presidio is known chiefly for its well-preserved Victorian residences. The 1886 **Haas-Lilienthal House** (☎ 415-441-3004, 2007 Franklin St) was built in Queen Anne style. There's a plodding one-hour tour ($5; Wed and Sun), but the building's exquisite exterior can be admired from the curb any time.

The Mission

The Mission District is home to a large Spanish-speaking community and a sizable hipster contingent. It's a great area for cheap meals and evening bar-hopping. Valencia and Mission Sts, between 16th and 25th Sts, are the main thoroughfares.

The first Spanish settlement in San Francisco sprouted up in this part of town, around the adobe **Mission Dolores** (☎ 415-621-8203), at Dolores and 16th Sts. The 1782 mission, the sixth California mission founded by Father Junípero Serra, still stands and is the oldest building in the city. The adjoining basilica, built in 1913, overshadows the humble older structure. The grassy slopes of **Mission Dolores Park**, a couple of blocks south, are popular sunning grounds when the weather is fair. Dogs and their owners congregate here most afternoons.

The neighborhood is noted for its bounty of colorful murals depicting everything from San Francisco's labor history to Central American independence. Narrow **Balmy Alley**, off 24th St, is lined from end to end with murals.

The Castro

The compact Castro, the gay center of San Francisco, is great for strolling, people-watching and getting your body pierced. The magnificent **Castro Theatre**, where the city's most important film festivals are held, is the primary landmark on busy Castro St. Most of the neighborhood's attractions qualify as entertainment and are listed in that section.

The Haight

The epicenter of San Francisco's hippie movement only hints at the idealism of the '60s. In January 1966, author Ken Kesey's psychedelic Trips Festival – anticipating the Golden Gate Park's Human Be-In, one year later – laid the path for the Summer of Love. Around the same time, bands like the Grateful Dead, Big Brother and the Holding Company, and Jefferson Airplane were establishing the city's rock & roll sound. Today, despite the throngs of tie-dyed stragglers still cluttering Haight St, the Summer of Love is only a purple-haze-like memory.

The **Upper Haight**, also called Haight-Ashbury, stretches from Golden Gate Park to Buena Vista Park and is lined with funky clothing shops, cafes and cheap restaurants. Deadheads will want to snap a photo at 710 Ashbury St, the onetime communal home of the Grateful Dead (now a private residence). On Haight St east of Divisadero St, the **Lower Haight** is a scruffy few blocks of music clubs, cafes and top-notch dive bars.

Golden Gate Park & Around

San Francisco's biggest park was designed in 1871 by 24-year-old William Hammond Hall, who transformed 1017 acres of windswept sand dunes into the largest developed city park in the world. Information is available at McLaren Lodge (☎ 415-831-2700), near the park's Fell St entrance.

The oldest building in Golden Gate Park is a Victorian glasshouse called the **Conservatory of Flowers**; it was seriously damaged by winter storms a few years ago, and while it's closed indefinitely you can admire it from the outside. The **California Academy of Sciences** (☎ 415-750-7145) is a large natural-history museum with a wide variety of child-pleasing exhibits, including the Steinhart Aquarium and Morrison Planetarium ($8.50/2 adults/

Gay San Francisco

In the early 1950s, a chapter of the Mattachine Society, the first serious homosexual-rights organization in the USA, sprang up in San Francisco, and in 1955 the Daughters of Bilitis (DOB), the nation's first lesbian organization, was founded here. During the 1959 mayoral campaign, challenger Russell Wolden accused incumbent mayor George Christopher of turning San Francisco into 'the national headquarters of the organized homosexuals in the United States.' Christopher was reelected, but was not about to be accused of being soft on queers. He responded with a massive police crackdown on gay male cruising areas, raids that resulted in a public blacklist of gay citizens.

Resistance to this persecution did not come out of the homophile movement but out of bars, and one in particular: the Black Cat, dubbed by Allen Ginsberg as 'the greatest gay bar in America.' (José Sarria, a drag performer at the Black Cat, ran for city supervisor in 1961, becoming the first openly gay person to run for public office in the USA.)

The age of tolerance had not yet arrived, however. In 1965 a dance sponsored by the Council on Religion and the Homosexual was raided by the police, and everyone in attendance was arrested and photographed. The city was outraged, and even the media denounced the police behavior. This event helped to turn the tide in the city's perception of the gay community. The crackdown on gay bars stopped, and a gay person was appointed to sit on the police community-relations board.

With the 1977 election of gay activist Harvey Milk to the Board of Supervisors, recognition of the gay-rights movement reached a new peak, but the euphoria was to be short-lived. The following year, Milk and Mayor George Moscone were assassinated by Dan White, an avowedly antigay former police officer.

kids). The **Japanese Tea Garden** (☎ 415-831-2700) is an immaculate garden with a stylized pagoda and a horseshoe-shaped footbridge that clears an elegant little stream ($2).

The park is packed with sporting facilities, including 7½ miles of bicycle trails, 12 miles of bridle trails, a challenging nine-hole golf course and 21 tennis courts. Rowboats, pedal boats and electric boats can be rented on **Stow Lake** (☎ 415-752-0347) for around $12 an hour. You'll find places renting bikes and skates along the park's periphery.

Standing just north of Golden Gate Park, along the Great Hwy, is the landmark **Cliff House** (☎ 415-386-3330), originally built in 1863. In 1896 Adolph Sutro transformed the building with art galleries, dining rooms and an observation deck. A fire in 1909 destroyed the stunning second Cliff House, which was replaced by the rather dull current building, which houses a popular restaurant with great views and so-so food. The very cool **Musée Mécanique** (☎ 415-386-1170), downstairs from Cliff House, has cacophonous arcade games and other antique amusements; bring lots of quarters (free admission). The ruins in the cove just to the north are all that remain of **Sutro Baths**, an immense swimming palace that went up in 1886 and burned down in 1966.

The **California Palace of the Legion of Honor** (☎ 415-750-3600), in Lincoln Park north of Golden Gate Park, is one of San Francisco's premier art museums, with a world-class collection of European art from medieval times to the 20th century ($8; closed Mon).

San Francisco Bay

Designed by Joseph Strauss and constructed between 1933 and 1937, the beautiful **Golden Gate Bridge** (☎ 415-921-5858), 2 miles in length with a main span of 4200 feet, links San Francisco with Marin County. At the time of completion it was the longest suspension bridge in the world. Painting the bridge is a never-ending job – a team of 25 painters adds another 1000 orange gallons every week. A prime starting point for bridge gazing is **Fort Point Lookout**, on Marine Dr at the bridge's southern end. Cars pay a $3 toll for southbound (Marin to San Francisco) travel; pedestrians can cross free via the sidewalk along the bridge's east side.

From 1933 to 1963, the rocky island in the middle of San Francisco Bay was home to some of the most notorious convicts in the USA, including Al Capone, 'Machine Gun' Kelly and Robert Stroud, otherwise known as the 'birdman of Alcatraz.' Twelve-acre **Alcatraz** was not altogether escape-proof, but while several inmates got themselves off the island, none is known to have reached land alive (still, the unexplained disappearance of some escapees leaves room for wonder). Blue & Gold Ferries (☎ 415-773-1188, 705-5555 reservations) runs to the island from Pier 41; tickets ($14.50) include the ferry trip and an audio tour, and must be booked in advance.

Activities

For **mountain-biking**, rent from Start to Finish Bike Shop (☎ 415-750-4760, 672 Stanyan St), on the eastern edge of Golden Gate Park. **In-line skates** can be rented at Skates on Haight (☎ 415-752-8376, 1818 Haight St), also near the park. For **sailing** lessons, try Spinnaker Sailing (☎ 415-543-7333), at Pier 40, which also has tours aboard a sleek old brigantine.

Ocean Beach is one of the most challenging places for **surfing** in California, with cold swells rising 12 feet or higher. There are no lifeguards and the riptide is extremely dangerous. You should never surf alone or without at least a 3mm full-length wetsuit. For a recorded message of the latest surfing conditions at Ocean Beach, call Wise Surfing (☎ 415-665-9473).

Organized Tours

The visitor center (see Information, earlier) offers an excellent line of walking-tour leaflets. The Chinese Culture Center (☎ 415-986-1822) conducts a Chinese Heritage Walk ($15; Sat) and a Chinese Culinary Walk and Luncheon ($30; Fri). The Mission District Mural Walk (☎ 415-285-2287) points out the neighborhood's resplendent murals ($10). Cruisin' the Castro (☎ 415-550-8110), with an emphasis on gay history and culture, costs $40 and includes brunch. Haight-Ashbury Tours (☎ 415-863-1621) offers walks around the Haight ($15; Tue and Sat). The Public Library's City Guides (☎ 415-557-4266) organizes free walking tours led by local historians.

Special Events

Chinatown's Golden Dragon Parade, led by a 75-foot-long dragon, kicks off Chinese New Year in January or early February, depending on the year. The Bay to Breakers

12km race (☎ 415-777-7770), on the third Sunday in May, features over 100,000 Bay Area joggers (many in crazy costumes) puffing their way from the Embarcadero to the Pacific Ocean.

Gay Pride Week makes June a celebratory month for San Francisco's queer community, kicking off with the Gay & Lesbian Film Festival at the Castro Theater. On the last Sunday in June the often outrageous Gay Freedom Day Parade is held; up to 500,000 people congregate along Market St during the city's biggest annual parade.

The Santa Maria del Lume (patron saint of fishermen) procession in October makes its way from Sts Peter & Paul Church in Washington Square, North Beach, down Columbus Ave to Fisherman's Wharf. Halloween sees thousands of costumed revelers take to the streets, particularly Castro St around 18th St, on October 31.

Places to Stay

Advance bookings are sometimes imperative on summer weekends and holidays. In a pinch, Fisherman's Wharf and Lombard St (Hwy 101) are packed with motels.

Budget San Francisco has no shortage of hostels. Hostelling International has two locations. The large, well-equipped *HI San Francisco Downtown* (☎ 415-788-5604, 312 Mason St), also known as the Hostel at Union Square, is a stone's throw from said square (dorm beds $22-25). *HI San Francisco Fisherman's Wharf* (☎ 415-771-7277), at Fort Mason, Bldg 240, overlooks the bay near Fisherman's Wharf and has top-notch facilities ($21-23).

In the Union Square and Civic Center area, the cheapest of the decent hotels charge $35-60 a night for a room. The *Adelaide Inn* (☎ 415-441-2261, 5 Isadora Duncan Court) is a comfy, small place where rooms have shared bathrooms. The *Aida Hotel* (☎ 415-863-4141, 1087 Market St) is worn but tidy. *Grand Central Hostel* (☎ 415-703-9988, 1412 Market St) has private rooms and dorm the rooms (beds $17, doubles $45-55). *Foley's Inn* (☎ 415-397-7800, 235 O'Farrell St) is in a very central block and is above an Irish pub ($55-75 shared bathroom, $85-135 private bathroom).

SoMa is a good choice if you want to be near bars and live music. The large *Globe Hostel* (☎ 415-431-0540, 10 Hallam Place), off Folsom St between 7th and 8th Sts, is in the thick of the action and attracts an international crowd (beds $19, private rooms $47); US citizens need to show a passport to stay. Nearby, the *San Francisco International Student Center* (☎ 415-255-8800, 1188 Folsom St) is upstairs from a noisy dance club, but it's still booked solid on weekends (beds $15-17); US citizens must show a passport.

In Chinatown *Grant Plaza* (☎ 415-434-3883, 465 Grant Ave) and the *Astoria Hotel* (☎ 415-434-8889, 510 Bush St) have very basic rooms starting around $60. A standout convenient to North Beach and Fisherman's Wharf is the pleasantly old-fashioned *San Remo Hotel* (☎ 415-776-8688, 2237 Mason St), with doubles for $50-85. In North Beach, on a sleazy but safe strip, *Green Tortoise Hostel* (☎ 415-834-1000, 494 Broadway) has clean rooms and good facilities (beds $19-22, rooms $48). The friendly *Pacific Tradewinds Guest House* (☎ 415-433-7970, 680 Sacramento St) has orderly rooms, a kitchen and a travel-savvy staff ($18-20).

The *Central YMCA Hotel* (☎ 415-885-0460, 220 Golden Gate Ave) is on a somewhat sketchy block, but it offers simple, clean singles/doubles with shared bathroom ($43/61).

In the Castro, *Twin Peaks Hotel* (☎ 415-863-2909, 2160 Market St) has basic and cheap rooms with shared/private bathroom for $50/65.

Mid-Range Near Union Square the old-fashioned *Dakota Hotel* (☎ 415-931-7475, 606 Post St) has TVs, microwaves and small refrigerators in most rooms ($79-119). The *Sheehan Hotel* (☎ 415-775-6500, 620 Sutter St) has fitness facilities and an indoor swimming pool ($65-99 shared bathroom, $89-169 private bathroom). *Edwardian San Francisco Hotel* (☎ 415-864-1271, 1668 Market St) is a charming pensione-style place where rooms with shared bathroom cost $70-110.

In SoMa, *Mosser's Victorian Hotel* (☎ 415-986-4400, 54 4th St) has rooms with shared bathroom for $69-89 (private bathrooms cost a lot more). An excellent spot in the heart of North Beach, the small *Hotel Bohème* (☎ 415-433-9111, 444 Columbus Ave) is heavily into stylized Beat decor (doubles $149-169).

In the Mission, the *Inn San Francisco* (☎ 415-641-0188, 943 S Van Ness Ave), near 20th St, is a classy Victorian B&B. Rooms with shared bathroom cost $105-145; deluxe rooms, with private bathroom and extras like hot tubs, spas or fireplaces, cost a lot more.

A few places in the Castro cater to same-sex couples. *24 Henry* (☎ 415-864-5686, 800-900-5686, 24 Henry St) is a quiet and friendly hotel in an old Victorian house, just a few blocks from the heart of the Castro ($65-120). *The Willows Inn* (☎ 415-431-4770, 710 14th St) is a stylish B&B that draws an international crowd ($100-140).

Haight-Ashbury's *Red Victorian* (☎ 415-864-1978, 1665 Haight St) is a New Agey B&B with comfy, quiet rooms and plenty of 1960s character. Rooms cost $86-126 (most have shared bathroom).

Top End Not-too-snooty hotels in the Union Square area, with doubles from $140-200, include the attractive *Cartwright Hotel* (☎ 415-421-2865, 524 Sutter St); the theatrical *Maxwell Hotel* (☎ 415-986-2000, 386 Geary St), with its stylish rooms; and the romantic *Petite Auberge* (☎ 415-928-6000, 863 Bush St). The oh-so-stylish *Triton Hotel* (☎ 415-394-0500, 342 Grant Ave) is an over-the-top designer hotel that's a lot of fun for the cheeky glam set.

The city's poshest spots, where the sky's the limit in terms of price, are the *Palace Hotel* (☎ 415-512-1111, 2 New Montgomery St) and two Nob Hill landmarks – the *Fairmont Hotel* (☎ 415-772-5000, 950 Mason St) and the *Mark Hopkins Inter-Continental* (☎ 415-392-3434, 999 California St).

Places to Eat

While in San Francisco, you're going to want to see if the city is really the culinary hot spot it's cracked up to be. In recent decades it has fostered a reputation for cutting-edge restaurants, but the array of international cuisines in the city is San Francisco's true strength. Try Chinatown for Chinese, North Beach for Italian and the Mission for Mexican and Latin American. Japantown has a preponderance of noodle shops and sushi restaurants, and Thai and Vietnamese eateries can be found all over town.

Downtown The downtown area has all sorts of quick-grab lunch spots that don't really distinguish themselves in any way, but they're convenient for the traveler interested in sightseeing. For more character, try one of the many French bistros between Union Square and the financial district. *Cafe Claude* (☎ 415-392-3515, 7 Claude Lane) is a small and very pleasant bistro with outdoor tables and evening music. Italian and French restaurants with outdoor tables also line nearby Belden St. The mid-range *Tadich Grill* (240 California St), the city's oldest restaurant, serves up solid traditional seafood and grill fare.

Some of the city's most renowned (and expensive) restaurants are around Union Square. *Postrio* (☎ 415-776-7825, 545 Post St) is a prime exponent of California cuisine, as dreamed up by Wolfgang Puck. *Farallon* (☎ 415-956-6969, 450 Post St) is a stylish and innovative seafood restaurant.

The area around the Civic Center has some great restaurants. *Zuni Café* (☎ 415-552-2522, 1658 Market St) is a casually chic city institution with delicious and pricey meals. In Hayes Valley a much cheaper choice is *Powell's Place* (511 Hayes St), for soul food and tasty fried chicken. For rice, noodles and Vietnamese seafood dishes, try *Viet Nam II* (701 Larkin St), in the Tenderloin.

SoMa Hip and noisy *LuLu* (☎ 415-495-5775, 816 Folsom St) specializes in French-California dishes and rotisserie meats. *Julie's Supper Club* (☎ 415-861-0707, 1123 Folsom St), near the Globe Hostel, has an uneven menu (appetizers stand out), swinging decor, a great bar and late-night dancing. *Fringale* (☎ 415-543-0573, 570 4th St) is an exceptional French-Basque bistro, crowded and noisy and a surprisingly good value. For some of the city's best dim sum, try *Yank Sing* (101 Spear St), in the Rincon Center. In a curious patch of green in the heart of Multimedia Gulch, *South Park Cafe* (108 South Park) has a very French flavor and reasonable prices.

Chinatown & North Beach Inexpensive Chinese restaurants include the always-packed *House of Nanking* (919 Kearny St) and the less hectic *R&G Lounge* (631 Kearny St). *Lucky Creation* (854 Washington St) offers simple Chinese vegetarian dishes. *Gold Mountain* (644 Broadway) is

Chinatown's biggest and liveliest dim sum palace and is also open for less exciting dinners.

North Beach has a bevy of Italian eateries. Despite its edgy attitude, **Golden Boy Pizza** *(542 Green St)* serves terrific pan pizza by the slice. **L'Osteria del Forno** *(☎ 415-982-1124, 519 Columbus Ave)* is an intimate place that dishes out wonderful handmade raviolis and pizzas for dinner and inexpensive sandwiches for lunch (closed Tue). **Mario's Bohemian Cigar Store** *(566 Columbus Ave)* is a casual cafe-bar-restaurant that looks out onto Washington Square and has tasty focaccia sandwiches. A worthwhile semisplurge is the cramped, very Italian **Caffè Macaroni** *(☎ 415-956-9737, 59 Columbus Ave)*. It's open for dinner (closed Sun), but its other shop, across the street, is open for lunch.

Fisherman's Wharf Chowder served in hollow sourdough rounds are available from takeout food stalls. Most of the older Italian American establishments on the wharf are expensive and not particularly good, but they do offer traditional Fisherman's Wharf atmosphere, if that's what you came for. A cut above is the newer **McCormick & Kuleto's** *(☎ 415-929-1730)*, in Ghirardelli Square, with an extensive seafood menu (for economical choices, sit in the Crab Cake Lounge). **Buena Vista Café** *(☎ 415-474-5044, 2765 Hyde St)* is a historic bar and grill that serves booze and three square meals daily.

The Marina & Fort Mason In this affluent residential neighborhood, most restaurants open only for dinner, but grocery stores and delis can help you assort your own lunch before heading off to explore the nearby Presidio. **PlumpJack Cafe** *(☎ 415-563-4755, 3127 Fillmore St)* serves Mediterranean-Californian cuisine for lunch and dinner (closed Sun). At Fort Mason, the city's best-known vegetarian restaurant, **Greens** *(☎ 415-771-6222)*, in Bldg A, has an elegant dining room and a basic takeout lunch cafe.

The Mission The junction of 16th and Valencia Sts is a major restaurant corner, with a dozen good choices within one block. For casual Mexican fare (especially burritos), head to **Taquería Pancho Villa** *(3071 16th St)*. Deeper into the Mission, **La Taquería** *(2889 Mission St)* is often singled out as the best place for inexpensive tacos and burritos.

The Mission also has plenty of international restaurants. **Ti Couz** *(☎ 415-252-7373, 3108 16th St)* turns out a huge variety of sweet and savory crepes at reasonable prices. A good splurge is the chic **Slanted Door** *(☎ 415-861-8032, 584 Valencia St)*, with its innovative approach to Vietnamese food (closed Mon; reservations essential).

The Castro The Castro has several round-the-clock diners. The best of them is **Bagdad Cafe** *(2295 Market St)*, where huge breakfasts, sandwiches and burgers satisfy many a hungry late-night scenester. **Chow** *(☎ 415-552-2469, 215 Church St)* is a lively and friendly spot for tasty, reasonably priced pizzas, pastas and meat dishes (lunch Sun-Thurs, dinner nightly). **Cafe Flore**, at Market and Noe Sts, is a relaxed cafe with a great patio and a stylish, cruisy crowd.

The Haight Lower Haight's **Squat & Gobble Cafe** *(237 Fillmore St)* and **Kate's Kitchen** *(471 Haight St)* serve all meals but are known for their hearty breakfasts. **Thep Phanom** *(☎ 415-431-2526, 400 Waller St)* is considered one of San Francisco's better budget Thai restaurants – try the nightly specials.

In the Upper Haight, **Magnolia Pub & Brewery** *(☎ 415-864-7468, 1398 Haight St)* gratifies those hungering for contemporary American food and thirsting for lovingly crafted ales. **Cha Cha Cha** *(1801 Haight St)* is a crowded, lively place with excellent Caribbean-influenced tapas; reservations aren't accepted, and there's often a long wait for a table.

Entertainment
The city's most extensive entertainment listings are found in the free weeklies, the *San Francisco Bay Guardian* and *SF Weekly*. For tickets to the theater, big music acts and other shows, call BASS (☎ 415-776-1999, W www.tickets.com). TIX Bay Area (☎ 415-433-7827, 251 Stockton St), on Union Square, sells half-price tickets to opera, dance and theater events (closed Sun-Mon).

Bars & Clubs There are a few exceptions, but most of the city's nightlife is reserved

CALIFORNIA

for the 21-and-up set. The ritzy hotel lounges around Union Square are ideal for cocktails and swell views. *Harry Denton's Starlight Room (450 Powell St)*, on the top floor of the Sir Francis Drake Hotel, has stellar views and nightly dancing. The Fairmont Hotel's *Tonga Room*, at California and Mason Sts, wins the award for Polynesian kitsch, and every half hour the city's only artificial 'monsoon' blows through.

The walls of *C Bobby's Owl Tree (601 Post St)* are a who's-who of ancient owldom, and *Edinburgh Castle (950 Geary St)* has a big selection of British beers, Scotch whiskies and occasional live performances. *Backflip (601 Eddy St)*, in the Tenderloin, is an ultrachic lounge – an Austin Powers set that takes itself a mite too seriously (closed Sun-Mon).

SoMa is where the greatest concentration of dance and music clubs is. The *Up & Down Club (☎ 415-626-2388, 1151 Folsom St)* is a hip spot to dance (upstairs) or hear local jazz (downstairs). *Slim's (☎ 415-621-3330, 333 11th St)* books live R&B artists. On the corner of 11th and Folsom Sts, *Paradise Lounge (☎ 415-861-6906)* is a noisy, crowded hipster hangout with three stages and a dance floor. The *Stud (☎ 415-252-7883, 399 9th St)* is a legendary gay dance club that hosts 'Trannyshack' for cross-dressers. On Saturday night the *Sound Factory (☎ 415-979-8686, 525 Harrison St)* draws a large college crowd with its 18-and-up admission policy. *EndUp (☎ 415-357-0827, 401 6th St)* is one of the most popular dance clubs in the city, particularly on 'Fag Fridays' and during its all-day Sunday tea dance.

In North Beach the former Beat hangout *Vesuvio (255 Columbus Ave)* continues to be a popular neighborhood bar. Elegantly aged *Tosca Cafe (242 Columbus Ave)* is famous for its all-opera jukebox. *The*

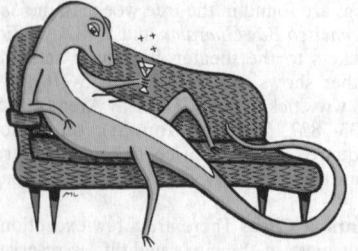

Saloon (1232 Grant Ave) is a worn-out local watering hole that features blues and '60s rock bands.

Of the many places around Fisherman's Wharf, the pleasant patio tables at *Jack's Cannery Bar*, in the Cannery, are always in demand on warm evenings. *Lou's Pier 47 (☎ 415-771-0377, 300 Jefferson St)* features your basic blues musicians nightly.

The Mission is the epicenter of San Francisco's hip nightlife. Valencia St between 16th and 22nd Sts, with several bars on nearly every block, is particularly conducive to pedestrian bar-hopping. The always-packed *Elbo Room (☎ 415-552-7788, 647 Valencia St)*, near 17th St, prominently features a long, curvaceous bar downstairs and a dance floor and stage upstairs. The *Latin American Club (3286 22nd St)* is a hip but casual hangout. Just down the street, the *Make Out Room (3225 22nd St)* has similar attributes but also features live alternative rock and country punk bands some nights. Young, hip lesbians hang out at the *Lexington Club (3464 19th St)*. The back beer garden at *Zeitgeist (199 Valencia St)* is the in spot for city bikers and a rugged band of independent-minded hipsters.

In the lively Castro neighborhood, *Twin Peaks (401 Castro St)*, at Market St, draws an older gay-male crowd. *The Café (2367 Market St)* is a multifaceted club with a dance floor, a large deck overlooking Market St and a pool table. The more hardcore *Detour (2348 Market St)* has DJs, beefy go-go dancers and a cruisy crowd.

Basement-level *Cafe du Nord (☎ 415-861-5016, 2170 Market St)*, at Sanchez St, is a former speakeasy that books live jazz and alternative rock bands.

In the Haight, at the distinctly retro *Club Deluxe (☎ 415-552-6949, 1511 Haight St)* the crowd dresses the part, enjoying the swing and big-band tunes. In the Lower Haight, the *Toronado (547 Haight St)* has one of the city's broadest beer selections. *Nickie's (☎ 415-621-6508, 460 Haight St)* is a noisy bar and dance club. *Mad Dog in the Fog (530 Haight St)* pours Guinness and British ales, serves hearty pub grub and is packed most nights with a friendly mix of locals and foreigners.

Classical Music & Dance The San Francisco Symphony performs September to

May in **Davies Symphony Hall** (☎ 415-864-6000, 201 Van Ness Ave). The acclaimed San Francisco Opera performs from early September to mid-December at the **War Memorial Opera House** (☎ 415-864-3330, 301 Van Ness Ave). The **San Francisco Ballet** (☎ 415-865-2000), the oldest ballet company in the USA, performs at the opera house or at the Yerba Buena Center for the Arts.

Theater San Francisco has numerous small theater companies – check the free weekly papers for listings – and one major company, the American Conservatory Theater (ACT; ☎ 415-749-2228), which performs primarily at the **Geary Theater** (415 Geary St). The touring Broadway productions play at the **Curran Theatre** (☎ 415-551-2000, 445 Geary St), the **Golden Gate Theatre** (☎ 415-551-2000, 1 Taylor St) and the **Orpheum Theatre** (☎ 415-551-2000, 1192 Market St).

San Francisco's longest-running theater-comedy extravaganza is 'Beach Blanket Babylon' at **Club Fugazi** (☎ 415-421-4222, 678 Green St). You must be over 21 years of age, except at matinees.

Cinema The city's grandest surviving old-style cinema is the **Castro Theatre** (☎ 415-621-6120, 429 Castro St), which always has a great calendar of art films, foreign films and gay and lesbian screenings. For a more eclectic repertory, check out the **Roxie Cinema** (☎ 415-863-1087, 3117 16th St), in the Mission, and Upper Haight's **Red Victorian** (☎ 415-668-3994, 1727 Haight St).

Spectator Sports

The local NFL football team, the San Francisco 49ers (☎ 415-468-2249), plays at windy 3Com (formerly Candlestick) Park, off Hwy 101 in the southern part of the city. The city's major-league baseball club, the San Francisco Giants (☎ 415-467-8000), plays at the more congenial Pacific Bell Park, along the Embarcadero near downtown. Sporting-event tickets are not always easy to come by. Try BASS and Ⓦ www.tickets.com. Before games, scalpers are usually selling tickets (illegally) near the stadiums.

Getting There & Away

Air San Francisco International Airport (SFO; ☎ 650-876-7809) is 14 miles south of downtown off Hwy 101. Southwest and United are two widely used airlines that fly in and out of SFO. A jaunt down to Los Angeles or up to Seattle or Portland will cost around $100. Information booths on the lower levels of all the terminals are open 8am-1:30am daily. Travelers' Aid information booths on the upper levels are open 9am-9pm daily.

Bus The Transbay Terminal (425 Mission St), at 1st St in SoMa, is the city's major bus station. If you're heading out to neighboring communities, you can take AC Transit (☎ 415-839-2882) buses to the East Bay, Golden Gate Transit (☎ 415-923-2000) buses north into Marin and Sonoma Counties, and SamTrans (☎ 800-660-4287) buses south to Palo Alto and along the Pacific Coast.

Greyhound (☎ 415-495-1575, 800-229-9424) has several buses daily to Los Angeles ($35-41; from 8 hours), Lake Tahoe ($45-70 roundtrip; from 5 hours) and other destinations. Buses leave from the Transbay Terminal. Green Tortoise buses (☎ 415-956-7500, 494 Broadway) are always a fun alternative for getting to LA ($35), Seattle ($69) and the East Coast (call for prices).

Train Caltrain (☎ 800-660-4287) operates down the Peninsula, linking Palo Alto (45 minutes), home of Stanford University, and San Jose (1¼ hours) to its San Francisco depot at 4th and Townsend Sts in SoMa. A free shuttle bus takes passengers to San Francisco's Ferry Building and Caltrain station from the Amtrak (☎ 800-872-7245) terminals in Emeryville and Oakland's Jack London Square. Getting to San Francisco from the Amtrak stations is extremely inconvenient if you don't get the shuttle bus. Trains arriving from the north connect with the bus at Emeryville, so get off the train there, not at Oakland; those from the south connect with the bus at Oakland.

Getting Around

To/From the Airport SamTrans (☎ 800-660-4287) buses depart several times an hour from the lower level on the center island at Central Terminal and curbside at North and International terminals. Bus No KX ($3) takes about half an hour to reach downtown; bus No 292 ($2.20) is not an express and takes twice as long. Bus BX

($1.10) takes 20 minutes to reach the Colma BART station, where you can catch the BART subway train to downtown San Francisco ($2.25).

The SFO Airporter (☎ 415-641-3100) bus departs from the baggage claim areas and stops at major hotels ($12). Door-to-door shuttles typically cost $12-15; try Super-Shuttle (☎ 415-558-8500) or Lorrie's (☎ 415-334-9000).

Taxis to downtown San Francisco cost about $35 – a good deal if three people can share.

Local Transportation San Francisco's Municipal Transit Agency (Muni; ☎ 415-673-6864) operates bus lines, streetcars and cable cars. A detailed Muni *Street & Transit Map* ($2) is available at the visitor center. General fare for buses or streetcars is $1; cable car fare is $2. A Muni Passport, available in one-day ($6), three-day ($10) or seven-day ($15) versions, allows unlimited travel on all Muni transport, including cable cars; it's sold at the visitor center and at the TIX Bay Area kiosk on Union Square.

The Bay Area Rapid Transit system (BART; ☎ 650-992-2278) is the commuter train system linking San Francisco with the East Bay. In the city, BART runs beneath Market St, down Mission St and south to Colma (eventually it will serve the airport). Fares are $1.10-4.70. Most ticket machines won't make change, so it's best to have change in hand.

Car & Motorcycle All the big rent-a-car operators can be found in San Francisco, most at the airport. Downtown offices include the following: Alamo (☎ 415-693-0191, 750 Bush St), Avis (☎ 415-885-5011, 675 Post St), Budget (☎ 415-775-5800, 321 Mason St), Dollar (☎ 415-771-5301, 364 O'Farrell St), Hertz (tel 415-771-2200, 433 Main St) and Thrifty (☎ 415-788-8111, 520 Mason St).

Some of the major cab companies are DeSoto Cab (☎ 415-970-1300), Veteran's Taxicab (☎ 415-552-1300) and Yellow Cab (☎ 415-626-2345). Fares are around $1.70 per mile.

Ferry Blue & Gold Ferries (☎ 415-705-5555) runs the Alameda-Oakland ferry from Pier 41 and the Ferry Building. It also serves Alcatraz Island. Golden Gate Ferry (☎ 415-923-2000) has regular service from the Ferry Building to Larkspur and Sausalito in Marin County.

MARIN COUNTY

Just a short drive across the Golden Gate Bridge from San Francisco, Marin County is a wealthy, laid-back region with stunning views and great hiking and biking trails. **Sausalito** is the first town you encounter after crossing the Golden Gate from San Francisco. Once a small seafaring center, this tiny bayside community is now an expensive tourist haven with a scenic waterfront promenade.

Occupying a 750-acre island in San Francisco Bay, **Angel Island State Park** (☎ 415-435-1915) is a popular place for walking and biking. The ferry ride from Tiburon (☎ 415-435-2131) costs $6, plus $1 to bring a bicycle. Blue & Gold Ferries (☎ 415-705-5555) charges $12 roundtrip and departs from Pier 41 at Fisherman's Wharf (weekends only off-season).

Marin Headlands

These hilly, windswept headlands are interlaced with prime hiking trails and offer spectacular views of San Francisco. To reach the hiking trailheads, take the Alexander Ave exit from the Golden Gate Bridge, go past Fort Baker and head west on Conzelman Rd. Fort Baker is generally a mob scene to avoid, though its **Bay Area Discovery Museum** (☎ 415-487-4398) is a first-rate children's museum housed in converted military barracks ($7).

At the *HI Marin Headlands Hostel* (☎ *415-331-2777*), near the visitor center at Fort Barry, beds cost $13-15, $39 for a private double room.

Mt Tamalpais State Park

Majestic 2571-foot Mt Tamalpais, or Mt Tam, has breathtaking views of the ocean, bay and hills rolling into the distance. Mt Tamalpais State Park was formed in 1928 and encompasses 6300 acres of wilderness plus over 200 miles of hiking and biking trails. Panoramic Hwy climbs from the sleepy town of Mill Valley through the park to Stinson Beach. Pantoll Station (☎ 415-388-2070, 801 Panoramic Hwy) is the park headquarters; pick up a map for $1. The adjacent campground is first-come, first-served ($12). Pantoll is an excellent place to start a hike. Steep Ravine Trail follows a wooded creek to the coast (about 2 miles each way), where there are six magnificent tent sites (reserve at ☎ 415-388-2070).

Muir Woods National Monument
The slopes of Mt Tam were once carpeted with mighty redwoods. The only surviving remnant is 550-acre Muir Woods, a national monument since 1908, which was named after Sierra Club founder John Muir. For an easy walk try the 1-mile Main Trail Loop, which runs along Redwood Creek to the 1000-year-old trees at Cathedral Grove and returns via Bohemian Grove. Muir Woods is just 12 miles north of the Golden Gate Bridge via Hwy 101 (take the Hwy 1 exit and follow the signs). There's a ranger station (☎ 415-388-2595) and a crowded parking area. Arrive early or stay late to avoid the crowds. Camping is prohibited ($2; open 8am to sunset daily).

In the hills above Muir Beach, along Hwy 1, the Green Gulch Farm & Zen Center operates the 12-room *Lindisfarne Guest House* (☎ 415-383-3134, 1601 Shoreline Hwy). Doubles cost $125-155, including breakfast.

John Muir, tree hugger

Point Reyes National Seashore
Divided off from the mainland by Tomales Bay, the triangle-shaped peninsula of Point Reyes National Seashore comprises 110 sq miles of windswept beaches, lagoons and forested cliffs. The westernmost point of the peninsula, Point Reyes Headlands, is crowned by the **Point Reyes Lighthouse**, the best spot in the Bay Area for onshore whale-watching.

The small towns of Olema, Point Reyes Station and Inverness are convenient park entry points. The Bear Valley Visitor Center (☎ 415-663-1092) is the park headquarters and has trail maps and park displays. Point Reyes has four hike-in campgrounds (sites $10); closest to the beach are *Coast* and *Wildcat*, respectively 1.8 miles and 6.3 miles from the Bear Valley Visitor Center. For camping reservations, call ☎ 415-663-8054.

The *HI Point Reyes Hostel* (☎ 415-663-8811) is off Limantour Rd, 8 miles from the Bear Valley Visitor Center (beds $13). Bring food, as the nearest supplies are in Point Reyes Station.

BERKELEY
Erstwhile seat of radical student politics, Berkeley (population 106,000) has mellowed since its 1960s heyday but is still a mecca of liberalism and the bizarre – the sort of place where bumper stickers read 'Subvert the Dominant Paradigm.'

The 'People's Republic of Berkeley' itself is subverted by the 30,000-student campus of the **University of California at Berkeley** ('Cal' to most students and locals), founded in 1873. Campus maps and information are available at the university's Visitor Services center (☎ 510-642-5215, 101 University Hall, 2200 University Ave), at Oxford St. It also offers free campus tours (10am Mon-Sat, 1pm Sun). The campus landmark is the 307-foot Sather Tower, which was modeled on St Mark's Basilica in Venice (students call it the 'Campanile'). Rides to the top cost $2. The Bancroft Library displays the surprisingly small gold nugget – 'roughly half the size of a pea' – that started the California gold rush when it was discovered by James Marshall in 1848.

Other campus sights include the Berkeley Art Museum (☎ 510-642-0808, 2626 Bancroft Way), east of Telegraph Ave, with six galleries of Asian and modern art ($6). The museum also houses the highly respected Pacific Film Archive (enter at 2621 Durant Ave), which screens little-known independent and international films throughout the year.

Leading directly up to the main south gate of the Cal campus, **Telegraph Avenue** is a prime student hangout packed with bookstores, including the acclaimed Cody's Books (☎ 510-845-9033, 2454 Telegraph Ave), record stores, cafes and cheap eateries.

Basic and mid-range motels are clustered west of campus along University Ave. In the heart of downtown Berkeley, the **YMCA** (☎ *510-848-6800, 2001 Allston Way*) has cubicle-like singles with shared bathroom ($33). Students' parents stay at the 22-room, nonsmoking **Bancroft Club Hotel** (☎ *510-549-1000, 2680 Bancroft Way*) and the 140-room **Hotel Durant** (☎ *510-845-8981, 2600 Durant Ave*). Doubles at both cost $140-195.

Top student restaurant picks include **Café Intermezzo** (☎ *510-849-4592, 2475 Telegraph Ave*) for huge salads and **Blue Nile** (☎ *510-540-6777, 2525 Telegraph Ave*) for Ethiopian food. The **Gourmet Ghetto**, on Shattuck Ave north of University Ave, is home to many highly regarded restaurants. The most conspicuous, and widely considered the birthplace of California cuisine, is Alice Waters' **Chez Panisse** (☎ *510-548-5525, 1517 Shattuck Ave*). Downstairs is very formal, with fixed-course menus for $45-75 per person (the price of a meal rises as the week progresses); upstairs, a more relaxed cafe has entrées from $15.

AC Transit (☎ *510-839-2882*) runs local buses in Berkeley as well as between Berkeley/Oakland ($1.35) and San Francisco ($2.50).

From San Francisco, it's a short trip on BART to the Downtown Berkeley station ($2.65). From that station, walk south on Shattuck Ave and turn left at Bancroft Way. Telegraph Ave and the main UCB campus gate are four blocks ahead.

OAKLAND

Despite its rough reputation, Oakland (population 388,000) is a city of remarkable racial and economic diversity. Parts of the nation's fifth-busiest port may suffer from urban decay and street crime, but don't worry too much during daylight hours in the busy downtown area. The Oakland Convention and Visitors Bureau (☎ 510-839-9000) is at suite 120, 475 14th St.

A block west of the 12th St BART station is the 1914 **City Hall**, at 14th and Washington Sts. A few blocks south, along 9th St, is Old Oakland's **Victorian Row**, with prime examples of architecture from the 1860s. Oakland's **Chinatown**, a less touristy version of the one in San Francisco, is east of Broadway between Franklin and Webster Sts. The 1931 **Paramount Theater** (☎ 510-465-6400, 2025 Broadway), at 21st St, is an art deco movie theater that screens a variety of films and hosts performances by the Oakland Ballet and Oakland East Bay Symphony.

The waterfront **Jack London Square**, at the south end of Broadway, is a low-key tourist zone filled with restaurants and shops. The square itself is named for Jack London (1876–1916), author of *Call of the Wild* and a native of San Francisco. Two sites in the square relate to London: Heinhold's First & Last Chance Saloon (☎ 510-839-6761, 56 Jack London Square), an 1880 watering hole where the author reputedly pissed away a few evenings; and a replica of London's Yukon cabin, just across the way. The nearby **Ebony Museum** (☎ 510-763-0745) has displays of African American art.

Oakland's visual centerpiece is **Lake Merritt**, created in 1869 by damming an arm of the Oakland estuary. In the late 19th century, Lake Merritt was lined with fine homes; today, however, there is just one survivor, the **Camron-Stanford House** (☎ 510-444-1876, 1418 Lakeside Dr), open 11am-4pm Wednesday, 1pm-5pm Sunday ($4).

The **Oakland Museum of California** (☎ 510-238-2200, 1000 Oak St), at 10th St, is home to the superb Cowell Hall of California History and the less compelling Hall of California Ecology ($6; open Wed-Sun).

Near Jack London Square, **Jack London Inn** (☎ 510-444-2032, 444 Embarcadero West) has $135 doubles. San Francisco has far better lodging options.

There are many inexpensive Asian restaurants in Chinatown, within easy access of BART. Try **Pho Hoa Lao II** (☎ *510-763-8296, 333 10th St*) for Vietnamese and **Battam Bang** (☎ *510-839-8815, 850 Broadway*) for Cambodian. Also downtown, **Pacific Coast Brewing Co** (☎ *510-836-2739, 906 Washington*) is a fun place to grab a beer and tasty American food.

All that's left of Oakland's once-thriving blues scene is gritty **Eli's Mile High Club** (☎ *510-655-6661, 3629 Martin Luther King Jr Way*) and the intimate **5th Amendment** (☎ *510-832-3242, 3255 Lakeshore Dr*). Taxis are safest late at night to/from either club. **Yoshi's** (☎ *510-238-9200*) is a top-flight jazz club and sushi restaurant at Jack London Square.

From Oakland International Airport (☎ 510-577-4000), shuttle buses to the Coliseum BART station run about every

10 minutes until midnight daily. SuperShuttle (☎ 510-595-3000) offers door-to-door service to Oakland ($15) and San Francisco ($24). A taxi to downtown Oakland costs about $15; the fare across the bay to San Francisco costs about $50.

Oakland's Greyhound station (☎ 510-834-3213, 2103 San Pablo Ave) is rather seedy. AC Transit (☎ 510-839-2882) runs local buses between San Francisco and Oakland ($2.50); bus No O is the most convenient. There is an Amtrak station (☎ 510-238-4306) at Jack London Square. From San Francisco, take BART to the 12th St station in downtown Oakland ($2.10). Far more pleasant is the Alameda-Oakland ferry (☎ 510-522-3300), which operates from two locations in San Francisco (Pier 41 and the Ferry Building) to Jack London Square up to 12 times daily ($9 roundtrip).

PENINSULA & SOUTH BAY

San Francisco is the tip of a 30-mile-long peninsula sandwiched between the Pacific Ocean and San Francisco Bay. Heading south along Hwy 101 or the more scenic I-280 leads to suburban **Colma**, San Francisco's graveyard ever since cemeteries were banned within the city limits. The notables interred here include gunslinger Wyatt Earp, jeans inventor Levi Strauss and Tina Turner's poodle. Many of the cemeteries are along El Camino Real, just east of I-280 from the Serramonte exit. Get a cemetery tour leaflet from the Colma Town Hall (☎ 650-997-8300, 1198 El Camino Real), at Serramonte Blvd.

Filoli (☎ 650-364-2880) is a superb 1915 mansion and country estate, near the small town of Woodside, that was used as a backdrop in *Dynasty*. Tours, both guided (Tue-Sat) and self-guided (Fri-Sat), include the gardens and surrounding countryside ($10). Guided tours require reservations. Exit I-280 at Edgewood, head west to Cañada Rd, then turn right.

Along Hwy 1

Far more scenic than either freeway is narrow, coastal Hwy 1. Just north of Montara, **Gray Whale Cove State Beach** is a popular clothing-optional strand. Close by, the *HI Point Montara Lighthouse Hostel* (☎ 650-728-7177), on Hwy 1 at 16th St, is a busy hostel with a hot tub (beds $17; reserve

ahead). Farther south on Hwy 1, **Half Moon Bay** is a growing tourist town with a good beach. Ten miles south, at the Hwy 84 junction, is tiny **San Gregorio**, where the general store–cafe is a good stop for a beer and, on weekends, live music. Another 5 miles leads to **Pescadero**, home to comfy *Duarte's Tavern* (☎ 650-879-0464), serving up daily the best artichoke soup and ollalaberry pie you've likely tasted; dinner are reservations recommended. Nearby Butano State Park is good for day hikes. Just off Hwy 1, south of Pescadero by another 5 miles, *HI Pigeon Point Lighthouse Hostel* (☎ 650-879-0633) is, like the Point Montara hostel, frequently busy (beds for $18).

A visit to the elephant seal colony at **Año Nuevo State Reserve** (☎ 650-879-0227), 5 miles south of Pigeon Point off Hwy 1, is a wonderful experience. However, during the mating and birthing season (Dec-Mar), visitors are allowed only on heavily booked guided tours ($2 parking, $4 each additional person); for reservations call ☎ 800-444-4445. Reservations are not required the rest of the year.

Palo Alto

At the south end of the Peninsula, Palo Alto is home to internationally renowned Stanford University. Unlike Berkeley, Palo Alto is noticeably more affluent and conservative. It's also a major high-tech center on the northern fringe of Silicon Valley, home to companies like Hewlett-Packard and the **NASA-Ames Research Center** (☎ 650-604-6497), a must for tech-heads and space fanatics (free admission).

Stanford University opened in 1891, just two years before founder Leland Stanford's death. The lovely campus was built on the Stanford family homestead and, as a result, is still called 'the farm.' From downtown Palo Alto, University Ave spears straight into the heart of the spacious campus. The Stanford University Information Booth (☎ 650-723-2560) is in Memorial Hall, in front of Hoover Tower, which you can climb for $2.

The *HI Hidden Villa Hostel* (☎ 650-949-8648, 26870 Moody Rd), in the Los Altos Hills south of Palo Alto, is the country's oldest hostel. It's part of the calm, secluded Hidden Villa farm and preserve, 2 miles west of I-280 and worlds away from Silicon

CALIFORNIA

Just Where *Is* Silicon Valley?

Don't look for Silicon Valley on the map – it doesn't exist. Since the Santa Clara Valley – stretching from Palo Alto down through Mountain View, Sunnyvale, Cupertino and Santa Clara to San Jose – is thought of as the birthplace of the microcomputer, it's been dubbed 'Silicon Valley.' Silicon is the basic element used to make the silicon chips that form the basis of microcomputers.

Not only does the valley not exist on the map, it's pretty hard to define on the ground. The Santa Clara Valley is wide and flat, and its towns are essentially a string of shopping centers, suburbs and industrial parks linked by a maze of freeways. It's hard to imagine that this was an expanse of orchards and farms as late as WWII. There's little to see in Silicon Valley; the cutting-edge computer companies are secretive and not keen on factory tours. Their anonymous-looking buildings – expanses of black glass are an architectural favorite – hint at their attitude. However, since the computer business is famed for its garage start-ups, enthusiasts may want to drive by 367 Addison Ave, just five blocks south of University Ave in downtown Palo Alto, to see the garage where William Hewlett and David Packard started their eponymous computer giant.

Valley (beds $14; closed June-Aug for summer camp). Cheap motels line El Camino Réal. In downtown Palo Alto the resolutely old-fashioned *Cardinal Hotel* (☎ 650-323-5101, 235 Hamilton Ave) has a terrific location (from $125 for standard doubles).

Don't worry about finding a place to eat here. In the compact blocks of downtown Palo Alto, every food requirement a university population could conjure up can be satisfied.

SAN JOSE

Founded in 1777 and briefly established as California's state capital (1849–51), San Jose is a flat, sprawling city with more than a hint of Los Angeles in its makeup. Boosters note that it's grown astonishingly fast in the last 30 years and is now among the largest cities in the USA. It's also the undisputed 'capital' of Silicon Valley. A handful of downtown sights will keep you busy for an afternoon on the way to/from San Francisco.

Downtown San Jose is at the junction of Hwy 87 and I-280. The helpful visitor center (☎ 408-283-8833, 150 W San Carlos St) is inside the convention center. Across the street is the fine **Technology Museum of Innovation** (☎ 408-294-8324, 201 S Market St), with various high-tech displays ($9) as well as an IMAX theater. The underappreciated **San Jose Museum of Art** (☎ 408-271-6855, 110 S Market St) has permanent and major touring exhibitions ($7). Continue north on Market St and turn left at San Pedro St for the **Peralta Adobe** and adjacent **Fallon House** (☎ 408-993-8182). The former dates from 1797 and was part of San Jose's original Spanish pueblo. The latter was built in 1854–55 by Thomas Fallon, who married the daughter of an important Mexican landowner and went on to become the mayor of San Jose. Tours include both structures ($6; Tue-Sun).

Other sights include the **Rosicrucian Egyptian Museum** (☎ 408-947-3636), at Naglee and Park Aves, about 5 miles from downtown. The Rosicrucians are devoted to the study of mysticism and metaphysics; displays include pharaonic artifacts, mummies and models of pyramids, temples and tombs ($9; closed Mon). **History Park** (☎ 408-287-2290, 1650 Center Rd), in Kelley Park, is a notable collection of historic buildings brought from all over San Jose (free admission Tue-Fri; $6 Sat-Sun). The overhyped **Winchester Mystery House** (☎ 408-247-2101) is not worth the $16 admission, but if you're still curious, it's on Winchester Blvd 10 miles west of downtown.

Craving high-speed adventure? Paramount's **Great America** theme park (☎ 408-988-1776), off Hwy 101 in nearby Santa Clara, has high-adrenaline rides that recreate various Paramount movies, including *Top Gun* and *Star Trek* ($43; closed winter).

The *HI Sanborn Park Hostel* (☎ 408-741-0166) is a beautiful log building in dense, woodsy Sanborn County Park (beds $12). The park is off Hwy 9 (Congress Springs Rd), 4 miles west of Saratoga and 12 miles west of San Jose. Just west of downtown San Jose, *The Alameda Motel* (☎ 408-295-7201, 1050 The Alameda) has rooms for $75.

Cafe Matisse (*371 S 1st St*) has bagels, coffee and a relaxed atmosphere. For dinner there are several good choices downtown on San Pedro St, including the *Tied House* brewpub (☎ *408-295-2739*).

Northern California

Whether you're winding along the coastal highway, surveying the rolling vineyards of the Napa Valley, craning your neck at massive redwoods or exploring the hills where gold was mined, you'll find the northern half of California strikingly different from its southern reaches.

NORTH COAST

From Bodega Bay up to the Oregon border, California's north coast is famous for its lush redwood forests and rocky, brooding coastline. North of the Golden Gate Bridge, the Pacific Coast Hwy (Hwy 1) and the Redwood Hwy (Hwy 101) separate. Hwy 1 snakes along the coast, while Hwy 101 heads through fertile inland valleys before entering the great redwood forests. The two highways finally rejoin at Leggett.

Bodega Bay to Fort Bragg

This stretch of grand coastline is mostly cool and foggy in summer, cold and rainy in winter. The best times to visit are spring and fall. Whale-watching is popular November to April, when California gray whales migrate down the coast; boats leave from Bodega Bay and Fort Bragg.

Bodega Bay is a small fishing town with nice beach hikes. Along with its inland sister city, endearing little Bodega, it was a location for Hitchcock's 1963 thriller *The Birds*. Whale-watching trips with Bodega Bay Sport Fishing Center (☎ 707-875-3495) cost $25. Bodega Bay Pro Dive (☎ 707-875-3054, 1275 Hwy 1) offers diving trips and gear rental. The Surf Shack (☎ 707-875-3944) rents surfboards ($13 a day).

Jenner is perched on the picturesque coastal hills at the mouth of the Russian River; north of town, stop at the Hwy 1 turnouts for a view of the harbor seal colony. Look for whale spouts, too. An 1812 Russian trading post is now **Fort Ross State Park** (☎ 707-847-3286), a pleasant coastal park with historic displays and reconstructed buildings ($2).

Salt Point State Park (☎ 707-847-3221) has hiking trails, tide pools, two campgrounds ($12) and an underwater diving reserve at Gerstle Cove (park admission $2). Adjacent is **Kruse Rhododendron State Reserve**, where pink blooms spot the green, wet woods in springtime.

Gualala (wah-la-la), founded in 1858 as a lumber mill, has a breathtaking coastal location. A mile south of town, Gualala Point Regional Park (☎ 707-785-2377) has an attractive campground ($16), hiking trails and a windswept beach (park admission $3).

Charming **Point Arena** has interesting old buildings and a fishing pier. A few miles north, the 1908 Point Arena Lighthouse & Museum (☎ 707-882-2777) offers knockout coastal views. Tours are worth the detour ($3).

Eight miles north of Elk, **Van Damme State Park** (☎ 707-937-5804) has the popular

---

High Grass & Tall Trees

The upper North Coast is famous for marijuana, especially the sinsemilla ('without seeds' in Spanish) grown in Humboldt and Mendocino Counties. In the 1970s the hills were full of hippies and 'back-to-the-land' types growing marijuana. All that changed in the 1980s with the government's Campaign Against Marijuana Planting (CAMP). CAMP sent helicopters buzzing over the hills with infrared scopes that could detect marijuana plants. CAMP is controversial but still in operation, and is largely responsible for the atmosphere of paranoia and suspicion – people arming themselves to defend their crops and worrying about police informers.

The region's other famed verdure is the coast redwood *(Sequoia sempervirens)* found in a narrow 450-mile coastal strip from central California to southern Oregon. Redwoods can live up to 2200 years, grow to 367 feet tall and reach a base diameter of 22 feet. Unlike most trees, coast redwoods have no taproot, and their root system is shallow in relation to their height, similar to a nail standing on its head. Thick bark insulates the trees from disease and insects, and protects them from forest fires.

Fern Canyon Trail, an unusual pygmy forest and a visitor center with a good museum ($2 per car).

Photogenic **Mendocino**, perched upon a bluff overlooking the Pacific Ocean, is noted for its Cape Cod–style architecture and numerous shops. The Sweetwater Gardens Lodge (☎ 707-937-4140, 955 Ukiah St) offers hot tubs and massages. At Big River, just south of Mendocino, Catch a Canoe & Bicycles, Too! (☎ 707-937-0273) rents mountain bikes, canoes and kayaks.

Fort Bragg is more of a blue-collar town than touristy Mendocino, and food and lodgings are cheaper. Fort Bragg's pride and joy is the 1885 Skunk Train (☎ 704-964-6371, 800-777-5865), with historic engines running east to Willits ($39). For fishing and whale-watching trips, try Anchor Charters (☎ 707-964-4550), in Noyo Harbor at the south end of town. North of downtown is Glass Beach; site of an old bottle factory, it's covered with bits of colored glass worn smooth by the sea.

The *Bodega Harbor Inn* (☎ 707-875-3594, 1345 Bodega Ave) has cottage-style rooms ($60-82). The historic *Gualala Hotel* (☎ 707-884-3441), on Hwy 1, has a passable restaurant and old but decent rooms (from $48). Beware the loud bar noise at night. In the morning, friendly *PB Espresso* is just a short walk north. There are a surprising number of gourmet (and pricey) restaurants along Hwy 1; a favorite local place is *Pangaea* (☎ 707-882-3001), in downtown Point Arena.

Manchester Beach KOA (☎ 707-882-2375), half a mile from tiny Manchester, is a good family campground, attractively manicured and sporting a pool and hot tub ($26-29 tent sites, $41-120 'kabins'). Low-key *Queenie's Roadhouse Cafe*, in Elk, has quality breakfasts and lunches at reasonable prices ($5-8).

Mendocino hotels and B&Bs, most of them in restored Victorians, are expensive. If you're determined to stay here, try calling Mendocino Coast Reservations (☎ 707-937-1913).

Fort Bragg has more down-to-earth options. The *Coast Motel* (☎ 707-964-2852, 18661 Hwy 1) has basic rooms from $45. On the nicer end is the 1912 *Colonial Inn* (☎ 707-964-1384, 533 Fir St), several blocks from busy Hwy 1, with 10 rooms ($90-140).

The nearby *North Coast Brewing Co* (444 N Main St) makes a great rockfish sandwich ($9) as well as the excellent Red Seal Ale. The *Headlands Coffeehouse* (120 Lamel St) has good brews, too.

In Caspar, 5 miles north of Mendocino, laid-back *Jug Handle Farm & Nature Center* (☎ 707-964-4630) offers private accommodations ($20 per person; bring a sleeping bag) in a beautiful old farmhouse with a fully equipped kitchen, plus 39 acres of forest and trails.

The Mendocino Transit Authority (MTA; ☎ 800-696-4682) sends bus No 65 every morning from Fort Bragg south to Santa Rosa via Willits and Ukiah ($16; 3 hours); at Santa Rosa you can catch a San Francisco–bound bus No 80 ($6) operated by Golden Gate Transit (☎ 415-923-2000). Greyhound and Amtrak do not serve towns along Hwy 1.

Russian River

North of San Francisco, about two hours by car via Hwys 101 and 116, the lower Russian River courses through redwoods, vineyards and a few tiny towns. **Guerneville** is the region's biggest town, with plenty of hotels and restaurants. It's also a popular gay and lesbian vacation destination. The local chamber of commerce (☎ 707-869-9000, 16209 1st St) has maps and lodging guides. Korbel Cellars (☎ 707-824-7004, 13250 River Rd) a picturesque 1886 winery noted for its sparkling wines, gives free tours daily. **Armstrong Redwoods State Reserve** (☎ 707-869-2015), about 2 miles north of Guerneville, has a magnificent stand of old-growth redwood trees ($2). *Camping* at nearby Austin Creek costs $12.

Nine miles west from Guerneville **Duncans Mills** is a tiny historic town with the friendly *Blue Heron* restaurant. Kayaks can be rented at Gold Coast Coffee & Kayaks (☎ 707-865-1441). Quaint **Occidental**, 11 miles south of Guerneville via the Bohemian Hwy, is a good destination for scenic drives. Continue south to Freestone, where the *Wild Flour Bakery* sells amazing breads. Burke's Canoe Trips (☎ 707-887-1222), 1 mile north of Forestville, rents canoes ($40), and its do-it-yourself paddle to Guerneville is highly recommended.

Healdsburg to Scotia

Small, quiet **Healdsburg** is centered around a green, shady Spanish-style plaza. The Russian River – and over 60 wineries within a 30-mile radius – attract more than a million visitors each year to this area. Grab a Wine Country map from the Healdsburg Visitor Center (☎ 707-433-6935, 217 Healdsburg Ave). Taste local vintages at the Hop Kiln Winery (☎ 707-433-6491, 6050 Westside Rd).

A detour to **Anderson Valley**, which is studded with vineyards and apple orchards, is far prettier than the equivalent stretch of Hwy 101; take Hwy 128 west to tiny Boonville, then Hwy 253 northeast to Ukiah. **Hopland**, 15 miles south of Ukiah on Hwy 101, is so named for the hop vines that used to be grown around here. You can still taste that heady past at the Mendocino Brewing Company (☎ 707-744-1015). One of California's best brew pubs, it's a popular stop for its fresh Red Tail Ale and laid-back beer garden. Another worthwhile attraction is the Real Goods Solar Living Center (☎ 707-744-2100, 13771 Hwy 101 S). The beautifully landscaped garden shows off environmentally friendly building methods and a range of water, solar and wind power options. The Fetzer winery (☎ 707-744-1250, 13601 Eastside Rd) is also here.

Ukiah, the largest town for miles, is surrounded by vineyards and pear orchards. Despite few tourist attractions, it offers plenty of places to stay and eat. Orr Hot Springs (☎ 707-462-6277), 15 miles west of Ukiah (Hwy 101 to N State St exit), is a small, clothing-optional hot springs ($22 day use). Facilities include hot tubs, dorm rooms ($40-45), private rooms and cottages ($115-185) and a communal kitchen.

Traveling north, **Leggett**, beside the South Fork of the Eel River, is where you'll catch your first glimpse of a giant redwood forest. The town itself is small and easy to miss. Standish-Hickey State Recreation Area (☎ 707-925-6482), 5 miles north of Leggett on Hwy 101, has old-growth redwoods, swimming holes and hiking trails.

Garberville, along with its more ragged sister town of Redway 2 miles away, became famous in the 1970s for the sinsemilla marijuana grown in the surrounding hills. Today Garberville is a quiet town with basic services and a few good places to eat.

The **Lost Coast** became 'lost' when the state's highway system bypassed the rugged mountains of the King Range, which rises to around 4000 feet only a few miles from the ocean. Today the region is mostly untouched and undeveloped. From Garberville it's 23 miles on a rough road to Shelter Cove, a seaside resort with a deli and hotels. The views are stunning from here to Honeydew, a dot on the road with a gas station that's open sporadically. From Honeydew, you can return to Hwy 101 via Bull Creek (one hour) or via Petrolia and lovely Ferndale (up to three hours). The latter has attractive Victorian buildings, plus several places to stay and eat.

On Hwy 101, 80-sq-mile **Humboldt Redwoods State Park** (☎ 707-946-2263) has some of the world's oldest redwood trees. The park's awe-inspiring Avenue of the Giants, a 32-mile stretch of two-lane road winding through wonderful old-growth forests, runs parallel to Hwy 101 and the Eel River.

Scotia is a rarity in the modern world: a 'company town' entirely owned and operated by the Pacific Lumber Company. It's a wholesome little place with housing and services for a few hundred families. Free self-guided mill tours are offered weekdays; contact the Scotia Museum & Visitors Center (☎ 707-764-4247), on Main St. In winter, when the visitor center is closed, follow signs straight to the mill.

Places to Stay & Eat Near Leggett, *Standish-Hickey State Recreation Area (reservations ☎ 800-444-7275)* has $12 campsites. The $12 campsites at *Humboldt Redwoods State Park* are magnificent but hard to come by; book ahead *(☎ 800-444-7275)*.

On the northern edge of Healdsburg, *Healdsburg Travel Lodge (☎ 707-433-0101, 178 Dry Creek Rd)* has rooms from $89 midweek. A string of older budget motels lines Healdsburg Ave, a few blocks south of the plaza.

Many motels line S State St in Ukiah; try the *Rodeway Inn (☎ 707-462-2906),* which has a swimming pool (doubles $49-65). *Sanford House B&B (☎ 707-462-1653, 306 S Pine St)* has five rooms in a 1904 Queen Anne–style Victorian close to downtown ($100).

The fancy, Tudor-style *Benbow Inn (☎ 707-923-2124),* just south of Garberville off Hwy 101, has rooms from $120; it's also a nice place for a cocktail or, if you're splurging, dinner. Garberville proper has several budget motels on Redwood Dr, including the *Motel Garberville* (☎ 707-923-2422), with doubles from $48.

At the two-room *Lost Inn* (☎ 707-629-3394), on the Lost Coast in the hamlet of Petrolia, $95 gets you deluxe accommodations and breakfast. Several of the tiny towns along the Avenue of the Giants in Humboldt Redwoods State Park have attractive accommodations. *Miranda Gardens Resort* (☎ 707-943-3011), in Miranda beside the Eel River, is a lovely place with a heated swimming pool and cottages from $75.

Garberville's *Woodrose Cafe (911 Redwood Dr)* has numerous organic and vegetarian options for breakfast and lunch. In addition to wineries, Northern California is home to several excellent brew pubs. *Bear Republic (345 Healdsburg Ave)* is a relaxing spot in downtown Healdsburg. In Boonville, the Anderson Valley Brewing Company sells its classic Boont Amber in its downtown *Buckhorn Saloon*.

Getting There & Around

Greyhound (☎ 707-442-7654) has frequent service from San Francisco to many towns along Hwy 101, including Ukiah ($23). The Redwood Transit System (☎ 707-443-0826) operates buses on weekdays between Scotia in the south and Trinidad in the north.

Eureka to Crescent City

At first glance, the largest town on California's far north coast, **Eureka**, is a thunder of traffic, motels and fast-food joints. Away from Hwy 101, however, Eureka's relaxing Old Town has historic Victorian buildings, interesting shops and good restaurants; it makes for a worthwhile stroll. Stop by the Eureka Chamber of Commerce (☎ 707-442-3738, 2112 Broadway) for maps and information.

The Clarke Memorial Museum (☎ 707-443-1947), at 3rd and E Sts, has an impressive American Indian collection. Blue Ox Millworks (☎ 707-444-3437), at the ocean end of X St, displays antique tools used in the production of gingerbread trim on Victorian houses and is well worth the $5 admission. Also consider a harbor cruise on the 1910 *Madaket* (☎ 707-445-1910), which departs from the foot of L St ($11; May-Oct).

Nine miles north of Eureka, **Arcata** is a laid-back university town where old-school hippie values and other alternative lifestyles are alive and well. Around downtown's Arcata Plaza are decent restaurants, shops and historic buildings. Taking up most of the northeast side of town, Humboldt State University (☎ 707-826-3011) has an attractive campus and a good art gallery. Unwind in a sauna or private hot tub at the blissful Finnish Country Sauna & Tubs (☎ 707-822-2228), at the corner of 5th and J Sts ($15 an hour).

Trinidad, about 12 miles north of Arcata, is an affluent historic town. The Trinidad Memorial Lighthouse and Trinidad Museum (☎ 707-677-3883), both on Edward St, are worth a look (museum open Sat-Sun May-Oct). You can also hike at Trinidad Head and beautiful Trinidad State Beach. Scenic Dr, which is indeed a scenic drive along coastal bluffs, eventually leads to Luffenholtz Beach, a raging surf spot.

The tiny town of **Orick** is unremarkable in itself, but the Redwood National & State Parks Information Center, on Hwy 101 a mile south of town, is a great resource for hikers and campers; rangers here also issue free permits to visit Tall Trees Grove. For information on the state and national parks described below, call the information center (☎ 707-822-7611).

The highlights at **Redwood National Park** are the Lady Bird Johnson Grove and Tall Trees Grove, home to several of the world's tallest trees. Both are a few miles off Hwy 101 on Bald Hills Rd (free admission).

Prairie Creek Redwoods State Park is famous for Fern Canyon, a sheer 60-foot fissure overgrown with ferns. The park, home to amiable herds of Roosevelt elk, has over 70 miles of trails and some spectacular scenic drives; the 8-mile Newton B Drury Scenic Parkway, passing through virgin redwood forests, runs parallel to Hwy 101. The Prairie Creek Visitor Center is on the parkway, 6 miles north of Orick ($2).

There's not much in **Klamath** except a giant redwood carving of Paul Bunyan and Babe the Blue Ox at the entrance to the silly Trees of Mystery (☎ 707-482-2251). A 30-minute walk leads past some oddly shaped redwood trees ($7). More interesting is the nearby End of the Trail Museum, with an outstanding collection of American Indian artifacts (free admission). A few miles north,

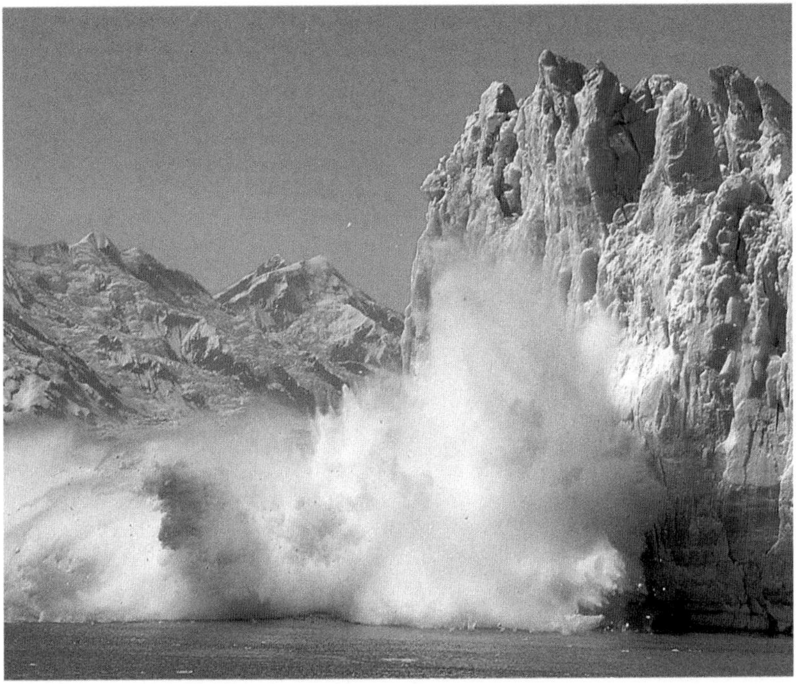

JIM DUFRESNE

A glacier calves into the ocean in Alaska.

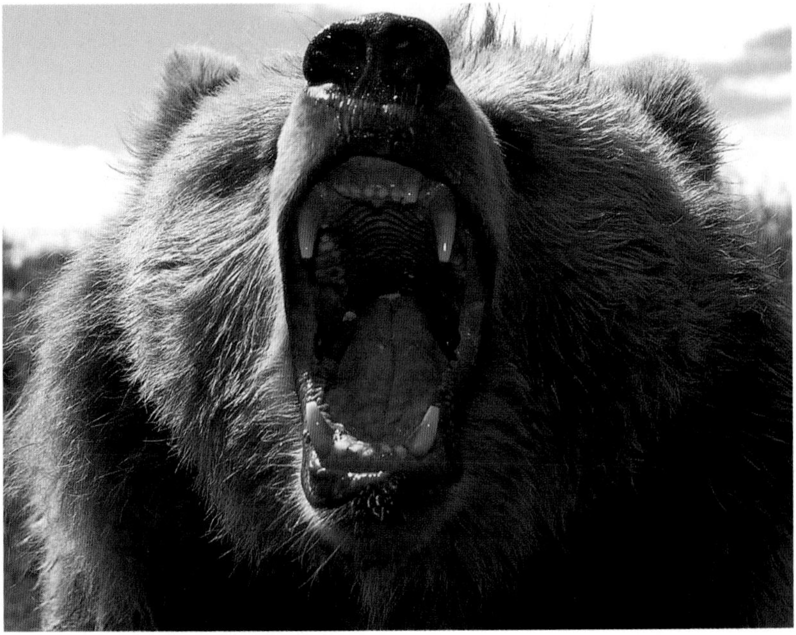

MARK NEWMAN

Someone's got a headache. Grizzly bear, Alaska

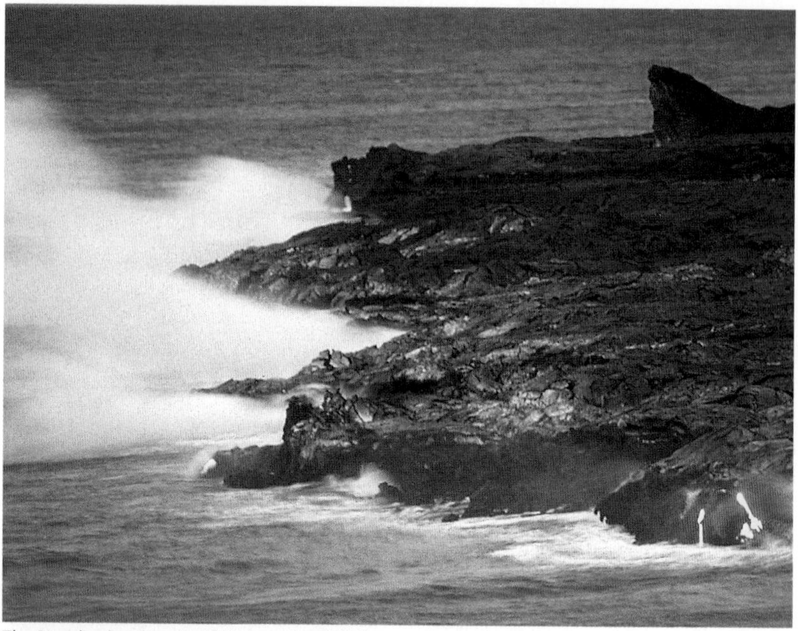
CASEY & ASTRID WITTE MAHANEY

The Big Island making itself bigger, Hawaii Volcanoes National Park

LEE FOSTER

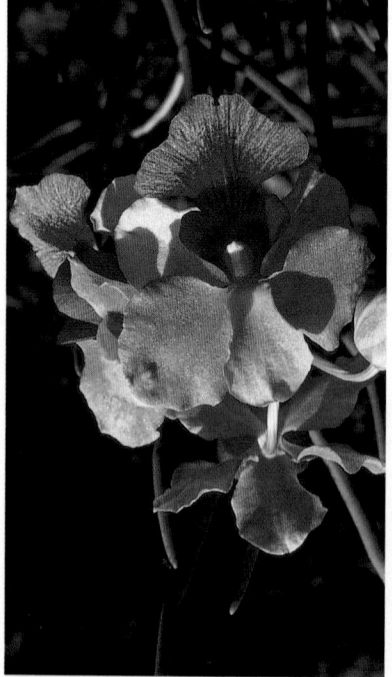

Traditional lei orchid, Hawaii

CASEY & ASTRID WITTE MAHANEY

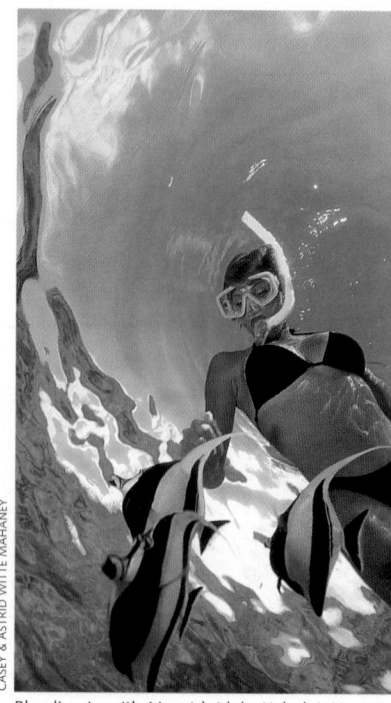

Blending in with Moorish idols; Kahului, Hawaii

Del Norte Coast Redwoods State Park contains beautiful redwood groves and 8 miles of unspoiled coastline ($2).

On a crescent-shaped bay, **Crescent City** is the only sizable coastal town north of Arcata. It has few old buildings, as over half the town was destroyed by a tidal wave in 1964. The 1865 Battery Point Lighthouse (☎ 707-464-3089), at the south end of A St, is accessible whenever the tide is out. Tours are offered ($2; Apr-Sept).

Jedediah Smith Redwoods State Park, 5 miles northeast of Crescent City, is less crowded than other North Coast nature areas, and dozens of hiking trails loop through thick, lush stands of old-growth redwoods ($2). In summer, park rangers lead popular, economically priced kayak trips down the Smith River. Maps and park information are available at the Hiouchi Information Center, on Hwy 199 in Hiouchi, 5 miles east of Hwy 101.

Places to Stay & Eat Each of the state and national parks has campgrounds ($12); for reservations call ☎ 800-444-7275.

Dozens of motels are along Hwy 101 in Eureka, but you'll get more peaceful sleep away from the highway. *Bayview Motel* (☎ 707-442-1673, 2844 Fairfield St) has quiet, clean rooms for $75. The popular *Samoa Cookhouse* (☎ 707-442-1659), on the Samoa Peninsula four minutes from town, is an 1893 lumber camp with a massive, family-friendly dining hall full of historic photographs. All-you-can-eat meals cost $7-12.

The 1915 *Hotel Arcata* (☎ 707-826-0217, 708 9th St) is a beautifully restored inn on the town square; comfortable queen-bed rooms cost $72-82. Two miles north of Trinidad on Patrick's Point Dr, the *Trinidad Inn* (☎ 707-677-3349) has 10 uniquely decorated rooms from $80.

The *HI Redwood Hostel* (☎ 707-482-8265, 14480 Hwy 101), 8 miles north of Klamath, is right on the coast near hiking trails ($15; reservations advised).

Half a mile south of Crescent City, modest but charming *Curly Redwood Lodge* (☎ 707-464-2137, 701 Hwy 101 S), built from a single redwood tree, offers large, attractive rooms ($39-60). In town on 3rd and G Sts, *Glen's Bakery* has pink booths, tasty glazed donuts and diner-style meals.

Getting There & Around Greyhound (☎ 707-442-7654) hits most major towns along Hwy 101 from San Francisco ($36; 8 hours). Redwood Transit System buses (☎ 707-443-0826) stop in Arcata on their weekday Trinidad-Scotia and Eureka–Blue Lake routes.

WINE COUNTRY

According to local lore, California's Wine Country got its start in 1857, when Hungarian Count Agoston Haraszthy purchased a defunct vineyard in Sonoma. These days the parallel Sonoma and Napa Valleys are home to more than 240 wineries, with 75 or so in less famous but equally fertile neighboring valleys. Only about 5% of California wine comes from the Wine Country, but it's generally the top 5%.

The Wine Country is an easy day trip from San Francisco, but an overnight stay gives a much better taste of the vineyards. Few Napa wineries offer free tastings anymore; fees run $2-7 for several varieties. In Sonoma Valley, free tastings are the rule rather than the exception. Many wineries scale down their tours and tastings in winter; call ahead. A deluxe way to explore the Wine Country is by rail on the Napa Valley Wine Train (☎ 707-253-2111), which offers three-hour lunch ($70) and dinner ($78) trips daily.

Napa Valley

There are over 200 wineries in the 30-mile-long Napa Valley, and most are open for tastings 11am-4pm daily. **Napa**, at the valley's southern end, is of little interest except for the Napa Valley Visitors Bureau (☎ 707-226-4759, 1310 Napa Town Center); follow signs. It's good place to get your bearings, the clerks are friendly and there

are brochures galore. Look for the helpful free tabloid *Inside Napa Valley*, which includes a map and tasting schedule.

Far more charming are **St Helena** – don't miss the town's fascinating Silverado Museum, which is on Library Lane – and **Calistoga**, at the top of the valley. Two roads run south-north along the valley: the busy St Helena Hwy (Hwy 29) and the more scenic Silverado Trail, just a mile or two east.

The following wineries are listed in south-north order. Wine and art merge at the classy **Hess Collection** (☎ 707-255-1144, 4411 Redwood Rd), several miles west of Napa. Good modern works by Francis Bacon, Louis Soutter and others are spread over three floors, with the tasting room downstairs. Napa's **Stag's Leap** (☎ 707-944-2020, 5766 Silverado Trail) produces an award-winning cabernet sauvignon.

In Yountville, **Domaine Chandon** (☎ 707-944-2280), west of Hwy 29, makes excellent 'sparkling wines' (it ain't champagne unless it's grown in Champagne, France) and has an exquisite restaurant. On the St Helena Hwy in Oakville, **Robert Mondavi** (☎ 707-226-1395) is a big commercial winery with an interesting tour ($10) on the wine-making process.

In Rutherford the historic 1882 Atkinson House fronts modern **St Supéry** (☎ 707-963-4507, 8440 St Helena Hwy), highlighted by its innovative wine displays. **Beaulieu** (☎ 707-967-5230, 1960 St Helena Hwy) was founded in 1900 by a French immigrant and is now one of the larger Napa Valley wineries. The nearby **Niebaum-Coppola Winery** (☎ 707-963-9099) is owned by filmmaker Francis Ford Coppola; the wines are good, and there's a small 'museum' with props from the *Godfather* and *Dracula* movies. The small **Heitz Cellars** (☎ 707-963-3542), off Hwy 29 in St Helena, is a friendly winery with excellent cabernets.

In Calistoga, architecture, art and wine attempt harmony at **Clos Pegase** (☎ 707-942-4981, 1060 Dunaweal Lane). Aside from the spas (see later), Calistoga has one nonintoxicating sight, the hokey **Old Faithful Geyser** (☎ 707-942-6463, 1299 Tubbs Lane), 2 miles north of town, which spouts off every 50 minutes or so ($6).

Sonoma Valley

About 15 miles in length, Sonoma Valley is less commercial than Napa and has far fewer wineries (40 or so). Quaint, popular **Sonoma**, at the valley's southern end, is a good base for bicycling tours. Downtown's historic Sonoma Plaza was laid out by Mexican general Mariano Guadalupe Vallejo in 1834 and is these days surrounded by restaurants and shops. Adjacent is Sonoma Mission, built in 1823 and now part of Sonoma State Historical Park (☎ 707-928-1519); it's worth a look. The $1 admission also covers the Sonoma Barracks, the Vallejo home a half-mile away and the Petaluma Adobe, 15 miles west near suburban Petaluma, itself a pleasant, picture-perfect slice of small-town California. **Santa Rosa**, at the valley's northern end, is bigger but lacks charm.

The following wineries are listed south-north and are accessible from Hwy 12. Sonoma's **Gundlach-Bundschu** (☎ 707-938-5277, 2000 Denmark St) was founded by a Bavarian immigrant in 1858. Follow the very winding road to the winery, which also has a lake, hiking trail and picnic area. Historic **Buena Vista** (☎ 707-938-1266, 800-926-1266, 18000 Old Winery Rd) dates back to 1857, when it was purchased by the pioneering Hungarian vintner Count Agoston Haraszthy.

The small, relaxed **Valley of the Moon** (☎ 707-996-6941, 777 Madrone Rd), in Glen Ellen, is far enough off busy Hwy 12 to escape the crowds. **Benziger** (☎ 707-935-3000), also in Glen Ellen but on the road up to lovely Jack London State Historic Park, is a highly educational winery with do-it-yourself vineyard walks and tractor-driven tours of the whole winery.

At the northern end of the valley in Kenwood, **Chateau St Jean** (☎ 707-833-4134, 8555 Sonoma Hwy) has pleasant grounds and a picnic area.

Sprawled-out Santa Rosa has no wineries but does have cheap hotels and **Snoopy's Gallery** (☎ 707-546-3385, 1667 W Steele Lane), with an awesome collection of *Peanuts* paraphernalia created by the late cartoonist Charles Schulz, who lived in Santa Rosa.

Spas & Mud Baths

Spa packages last about an hour and start at around $50, with added massages and facials pushing the cost much higher. Well-regarded Calistoga spas include Dr Wilkinson's Hot

Springs (☎ 707-942-4102, 1507 Lincoln Ave) and Indian Springs (☎ 707-942-4913, 1712 Lincoln Ave).

Popular Harbin Hot Springs (☎ 707-987-2477) is 4 miles north of Middletown, which in turn is 12 miles north of Calistoga. The day-use fee is $20-30; dorms cost $35-50 (bring your own linen). The vibe here is *very* New Age, with clothing-optional pools and a vegetarian restaurant.

Places to Stay & Eat
The *Sugarloaf Ridge State Park (☎ 707-833-5712)*, north of Kenwood on Adobe Canyon Rd, has campsites for $12.

Calistoga has the best selection of lodging in the Wine Country. *Golden Haven Hot Springs (☎ 707-942-6793, 1713 Lake St)* has doubles from $59 midweek, including pool and hot-tub use. The *Calistoga Inn (☎ 707-942-4101, 1250 Lincoln Ave)* serves nice meals and its own Napa Valley Brewing Co ales on a beautiful outdoor patio. Rooms run $65-90. One mile west of downtown Sonoma, *El Pueblo Inn (☎ 707-996-3651, 896 W Napa St)* has doubles from $95. Several stylish older hotels are right on Sonoma Plaza, including the *Sonoma Hotel (☎ 707-996-2996)*, which has rooms from $160.

Sonoma's *Artisan Bakers (☎ 707-939-1765, 750 W Napa St)* sells pastries, sandwiches, pizza and its award-winning breads. In Napa Valley you better have a reservation (and a sizable bankroll) to dine at renowned *French Laundry (☎ 707-944-2380, 6640 Washington St),* in Yountville. For the rest of us, the casual *Gordon's Cafe and Wine Bar (6770 Washington St)* is open Tuesday to Sunday for breakfast and lunch. Right on Hwy 29 in minuscule Oakville, the lovely *Oakville Grocery (☎ 707-944-8802)* sells gourmet picnic fixings and deli sandwiches.

Getting There & Around
Public transportation can get you to the valleys but is not ideal for vineyard hopping. Greyhound buses (☎ 800-231-2222) run twice daily from San Francisco up Napa Valley to Calistoga ($15). Golden Gate Transit (☎ 415-923-2000, 707-541-2000) has buses from San Francisco to Sonoma ($6), Petaluma and Santa Rosa. Sonoma County Transit (☎ 707-576-7433) serves Sonoma Valley.

The Wine Country is an hour's drive north from San Francisco via Hwy 101 or I-80.

Rent bicycles ($25-30 a day) in Napa at Napa Bike Tours (☎ 707-255-3377), in Calistoga at Getaway Adventures (☎ 707-942-0332) and in Sonoma at Sonoma Valley Cyclery (☎ 707-935-3377).

SACRAMENTO
Sitting flat and low amid a largely agricultural landscape, sprawling, suburban Sacramento lacks the picturesque coastal or mountain beauty to make it a vital tourist destination. As the state capital, however, it has a good deal of history, tracing back to gold rush days; and as a modern urban center, it sports a youthful buzz unique in the primarily rural Central Valley. Sacramento also has one of the country's busiest harbors, two top-drawer universities and plenty of good restaurants and museums.

In 1839 Swiss immigrant John Sutter proposed building an outpost north of San Francisco at the confluence of the Sacramento and American Rivers. When James Marshall discovered gold at Sutter's lumber mill near Coloma in 1848, thousands of people flocked to California, most of whom traveled through Sutter's Fort. John Sutter eventually deeded the land to his son, who christened the newly sprung town 'Sacramento.' In 1854, after several years of legislative indecision, the riverfront settlement became California's permanent capital.

The Visitor Information Center (☎ 916-442-7644, 1101 2nd St), in Old Sacramento, has free city maps and can recommend hotels in all price categories.

Things to See & Do
The 19th-century **California state capitol** is at 10th St and Capitol Mall. Rooms on the ground floor, called the Capitol Museum (☎ 916-324-0333), contain furniture, photographs and documents from various periods. The Assembly and Senate rooms are open to the public whenever they're in session.

A few blocks west toward the river, **Old Sacramento** (Old Sac) contains California's largest concentration of buildings on the National Register of Historic Places, now housing candy stores, T-shirt shops and restaurants. The *Spirit of Sacramento* (☎ 916-552-2933), an 1842 paddle wheeler docked next to the visitor center, makes one-hour narrated tours of the Sacramento River and is worth the $10 ticket.

At Old Sac's northern end is the excellent **California State Railroad Museum** (☎ 916-324-0539), with self-guided tours ($3-6). Next door, the **Discovery Museum** (☎ 916-264-7057) has hands-on science exhibits and a good display of gold-rush-era artifacts ($5).

Sutter's Fort (☎ 916-324-0539), at the corner of 27th and L Sts, was once the only trace of civilization for hundreds of miles. It's been restored to its 1850s appearance and offers self-guided tours ($1-3). On the north side of the fort, the popular **California State Indian Museum** has a thorough display of Native American costumes and basketry ($1).

Housed in Judge Edwin B Crocker's Victorian home – a piece of art in itself – the **Crocker Art Museum** (☎ 916-264-5423), at 3rd and O Sts, holds the West Coast's first publicly displayed art collection ($6).

The 700-acre **Cal Expo** (☎ 916-263-3000), east of I-80, is the site of the annual California State Fair in mid-August and a variety of other events year round. Also here is **Waterworld USA** (☎ 916-924-0556), a tangle of water slides and carnival games ($22).

Places to Stay & Eat

Campgrounds are scarce around Sacramento, so the Sacramento **KOA** (☎ 916-371-6771, 3951 Lake Rd W) is your only real option, with both tent ($25) and RV ($33) sites. The **HI Sacramento Hostel** (☎ 916-443-1691, 900 H St), in a restored 1885 Victorian, is walking distance to the capitol, Old Sac and the train station (beds $12-17). The **Quality Inn** (☎ 916-444-3980, 818 15th St) is a nice budget hotel, centrally located with clean doubles for $74. **Hartley House** (☎ 800-858-1568, 700 22nd St) is a five-room B&B with weekend rates from $159.

Cafe Bernardo (2726 Capitol Ave) has a casual atmosphere and inexpensive, excellent food. **Fanny Ann's** (1023 2nd St) serves burgers and beer in a popular Old Sac bar. In an old barge on the north bank of the American River, **Virgin Sturgeon** (1577 Garden Hwy) is a local favorite for seafood and barbecued ribs.

Getting There & Around

Sacramento is 91 miles east of San Francisco via I-80, and 386 miles north of LA via I-5. It's also served by Hwy 99. Sacramento International Airport (☎ 916-929-5411), 15 miles north of downtown off I-5, is serviced by several major airlines. Greyhound (☎ 916-922-2795, 1924 El Camino Ave), off I-80, serves San Francisco ($15), Los Angeles ($45), Seattle ($65) and other major towns. Sacramento's Amtrak (☎ 800-872-7245) depot is between downtown and Old Sac at 4th and I Sts. Trains leave daily for San Francisco ($18), Los Angeles ($63), Reno ($53), Seattle ($147) and beyond.

Sacramento Regional Transit (☎ 916-321-2877) runs a bus system and a light rail line, the latter mostly serving commuters. Fares cost $1.50.

GOLD COUNTRY

Hugging the foothills of the western Sierra Nevada, California's Gold Country winds 300 miles north to south along Hwy 49; the most interesting stretch is from Nevada City to Sonora. Besides beautiful scenery and an abundance of hiking and camping, the Gold Country area has a wealth of restored mining towns, fascinating old buildings and historic hotels soaked in Old West atmosphere.

The gold rush started on January 24, 1848, when James Marshall was inspecting the lumber mill he was building for John Sutter, near present-day Coloma. From the mill's tailrace water Marshall pulled out a gold nugget 'roughly half the size of a pea' – an inauspicious beginning to a legendary era.

The first true rush came from San Francisco in the spring of 1848. During this wave, men found gold so easily that they thought nothing of spending (or gambling) all they had in one night. News spread to Oregon, the East Coast and South America, and by the end of 1848 over 30,000 people had come. By 1849 the real gold rush was on, with an additional 60,000 people (known as the 49ers) migrating to California in search of the 'Mother Lode.'

You can experience a different sort of rush rafting the American, Tuolumne, Kings and Stanislaus Rivers in Class III and IV rapids. Whitewater Connection (☎ 800-336-7238) and Zephyr Whitewater Expeditions (☎ 800-431-3636) offer half-day trips for $79 and up as well as longer excursions.

Northern Mines

Stretching from Nevada City to Placerville, the Northern Mines are some of the most picturesque area mines. Perched on mountainsides and entrenched in canyons, they are bordered by the Tahoe National Forest.

With well-preserved Victorians and an attractive woodsy location, **Nevada City** is a charming tourist town peopled with friendly New Agers and outdoors types, as well as those with gun racks on their pickup trucks. The chamber of commerce (☎ 530-265-2692, 132 Main St) has a large selection of brochures on recreation and lodging, and the Tahoe National Forest Headquarters (☎ 530-265-4531), on Hwy 49 at the north end of Coyote St, has information about backcountry trips. Housed in Nevada City's original firehouse, the Firehouse Museum (☎ 530-265-5468, 214 Main St) has an extensive Chinese collection and a 'haunted' photograph that attracts parapsychologists by the busload (admission by donation). Built in 1856, the foundry that produced the first Pelton waterwheel – which revolutionized hydraulic mining – is now the Miners Foundry Cultural Center (☎ 530-265-5040, 325 Spring St).

About 5 miles southwest is **Grass Valley**, where locals buy groceries and service their cars. Though not as cute as Nevada City, Grass Valley does have a historic downtown district, cheap accommodations and two blockbuster museums. The Empire Mine State Historic Park (☎ 530-273-8522), 2 miles east of town off Hwy 49, sits atop 367 miles of mine shafts that, from 1850 to 1956, produced six million ounces of gold (about $2 billion worth). It's definitely worth a half day's exploration ($1). Grass Valley's North Star Mining Museum (☎ 530-273-4255), at Mill St's south end, has a good collection of Pelton waterwheels and mining equipment (admission by donation; open May-Sept).

Auburn, because of its proximity to I-80, is one of the Gold Country's most visited – though not picturesque – towns. Part of the attraction are the history displays at the Placer County Museum (☎ 530-889-6500), on Maple St in the Placer County Courthouse ($1). The nearby Bernhard Museum Complex (291 Auburn-Folsom Rd) displays typical 19th-century farm life ($1).

Originally known for its proximity to Sutter's Mill (the first gold-discovery site), **Coloma** is now equally famous for its whitewater rafting. All that make up the 'town' are a few campgrounds along Hwy 49 and the Marshall Gold Discovery State Historic Park (☎ 530-622-3470), which has hiking trails, restored buildings and a replica of Sutter's Mill ($2 per car).

Once an important point on the California-Nevada stagecoach route, **Placerville** – or 'Old Hangtown' – is now chiefly a gas and food stop for travelers on Hwy 50. On the upside, most buildings along Main St date back to the 1850s, including the El Dorado County Courthouse and Placerville Hardware, the oldest hardware store west of the Mississippi River.

Southern Mines

The Southern Mines extend from Placerville south to Sonora and are bordered by the Stanislaus National Forest and Yosemite National Park. Tiny **Amador City** was once home to the Keystone Mine, one of the most prolific gold producers in California. The town was abandoned until the 1950s, when a family from Sacramento converted the dilapidated buildings into antiques shops.

In the 1860s and '70s **Sutter Creek** was California's main foundry center. Now it's one of the Gold Country's most endearing (and busiest) towns, with raised sidewalks and high-balconied buildings that are free of modern additions. From Sutter Creek, take Ridge Rd east for about 12 miles to the **Chaw'Se Indian Grinding Rock State Historic Park**, sacred ground for the local Miwok Indians ($2 per car). The park has ancient petroglyphs along with mortar holes called *chaw'Ses*, used for grinding acorns into meal. Camping is available ($12), and adjacent is the good Regional Indian Museum (☎ 209-296-7488).

Tiny, quiet **Volcano**, 14 miles east of Sutter Creek via Sutter Creek Rd, is refreshingly off the main tourist track. The 1862 *St George Hotel* (☎ 209-296-4458) is the town's chief business, with historic rooms (doubles $75-98, including breakfast), weekend meals and a great old bar. Nearby Daffodil Hill is an impressive sight each spring.

In **Jackson** the Amador County Museum (☎ 209-223-6386, 225 Church St) has Gold Country history displays, a curious collection of old Victrolas and the infamous 'heart-shaped plaque.' Excellent, unique 'model mine' tours take place on weekends ($2), worth seeing before visiting the actual Kennedy Gold Mine (☎ 209-223-9542) itself ($5). Five miles southeast of Jackson **Mokelumne Hill** was the principal mining town of Calaveras County and the county seat from 1853 to 1856. Now 'Moke Hill' is a good place to see historic buildings without the common barrage of antiques stores and gift shops.

In Cave City, 9 miles east of San Andreas, the spectacular **California Caverns** (☎ 209-736-2708) were described by John Muir as 'graceful flowing folds deeply pleated like stiff silken drapery' (80-minute tours $10; open mid-May to Dec).

With a main street that looks like a cross between a Norman Rockwell painting and a Randolph Scott Western, **Murphys** is thoroughly charming and, consequently, very popular. Mercer Caverns (☎ 209-728-2101), open year round, are 1 mile north of town via a well-marked road from the east end of Main St (50-minute tours $9).

Known as the 'Gem of the Southern Mines,' **Columbia** is now a state historic park (☎ 209-536-1672), with four blocks of 1850s buildings and concessionaires in period costumes.

In its heyday **Sonora** was a cosmopolitan center with Spanish plazas, elaborate saloons and the Southern Mines' largest concentration of gamblers and gold. Still bustling as the Tuolumne County seat, Sonora is a good place to gas up and eat, though expect traffic jams. There is a visitor center (☎ 209-533-4420, 800-446-1333, 542 S Stockton Rd). Nearby **Jamestown** has a restored Main St, nice old hotels and Railtown 1897 (☎ 209-984-3953), with steam-train displays and rides on summer weekends ($6).

Places to Stay & Eat

In Nevada City a double at the *Northern Queen Inn* (☎ 530-265-5824, 400 Railroad Ave) costs $77. Auburn's *Foothills Motel* (☎ 530-885-8444), on Bowman Rd west of I-80, charges $60-65, including pool and spa use. The classy *Imperial Hotel* (☎ 800-242-5594), in Amador City, has $80-110 rooms and pricey but popular dinners (entrées from $20).

An exception to Sutter Creek's expensive lodging scene, *Bellotti Inn* (☎ 209-267-5211, 53 Main St) has musty, TV-free rooms for about $45 atop the town's oldest bar. In low-key Mokelumne Hill, the friendly 1851 *Hotel Leger* (☎ 209-286-1401) has mediocre food but nice rooms from $55.

Jackson has several inexpensive motels along Hwy 49, but the *Country Squire Motel* (☎ 209-223-1657), a half-mile north of downtown across from pleasant Kennedy Tailing Wheels Park, is removed from traffic ($62-68). *Calaveras Big Trees State Park* (☎ 209-795-2334), 15 miles north of Murphy's on Hwy 4, has giant sequoia groves (entrance $2) and nice campsites ($12).

Sonora's lovely *Gunn House Hotel* (☎ 209-532-3421, 286 S Washington St) has rooms from $50 and a restaurant upstairs. The tidy *Sonora Gold Lodge* (☎ 209-532-3952, 480 W Stockton St) charges $59-79.

In Sutter Creek the *Sutter Creek Coffee Roasting Co (20 Eureka St)* pours a fine cup. In Columbia the *Old Stamp Mill Brewery* (☎ 209-532-3089) is an excellent stop for a glass of beer or wine (from the Gold Mine Winery), with crab dinners ($15) on summer weekends. In Sonora, *Josephine's* (☎ 209-533-4111) trattoria is above the Gunn House Hotel (entrées $15). There's also *Garcia's Taqueria (145 S Washington St)*, with $4 burritos and outdoor seating.

Getting There & Around

About 26 miles east of Sacramento, Hwy 49 intersects I-80 in the town of Auburn. Greyhound (☎ 916-922-2795) runs buses from Sacramento to Auburn ($9), Placerville ($11) and Stockton ($11).

Local bus systems include Gold Country Stage (☎ 530-477-0103), which charges $1 between Grass Valley and Auburn, and Placer County Transit (☎ 530-889-7570).

NORTHERN MOUNTAINS

North of Redding are some of California's most beautiful – and least visited – features, including majestic Mt Shasta, Lassen Volcanic National Park and Lava Beds National Monument.

Redding to Yreka

At the north end of the Sacramento Valley, **Redding** is an unremarkable town, but highly convenient as a stopover when exploring nearby areas. Maps and camping permits for northern California's national forests are available at the Shasta-Trinity National

Forest Headquarters (☎ 530-244-2978, 2400 Washington Ave), open weekdays.

If you have time for a detour, or if you're heading to/from the coast, consider taking Hwy 299 – especially in autumn, when the leaves change colors. Known as the Trinity Scenic Byway, it winds through the foggy, tree-clad **Trinity Alps**. Stop in Weaverville, a beautiful mountain town at the heart of the region.

North of Redding along I-5, **Shasta Lake** has hiking trails, campgrounds, and boat rentals along its shores. The lake exists because of massive Shasta Dam, which dominates its southern end. Free dam tours are given daily (☎ 530-275-4463). Tours of Lake Shasta Caverns (☎ 530-238-2341) include a catamaran ride across Shasta Lake ($17).

The railroad town Dunsmuir is surrounded by pristine scenery and good fishing. The larger town of **Mt Shasta** is dwarfed by its namesake mountain, which towers above it. Originally called Strawberry Valley, the town was renamed Sisson, then given the name Mt Shasta in the 1920s, after the local Shasta Indian tribe. Today it makes an excellent base, with several decent places to stay and eat. The Mt Shasta Visitor Center (☎ 530-926-4865, 300 Pine St) provides regional information. The Sisson Museum (☎ 530-926-5508), open in summer only (free admission), and the Mt Shasta Fish Hatchery (☎ 530-926-2215), are side by side at 1 Old Stage Rd, half a mile west of I-5.

Mt Shasta itself, California's sixth-highest mountain (14,162 feet), seems especially magnificent because it rises alone on the landscape. The area's prime activities are hiking, mountain biking, climbing and skiing. Everitt Memorial Hwy goes up the mountain to 7900 feet; to access it, simply head east from town on Lake St and keep going. Rangers can suggest a number of good hiking trails, depending on the weather conditions. To climb higher than 10,000 feet, obtain a $15 permit from the Mt Shasta Ranger Station (☎ 530-926-4511, 204 W Alma St). On the south slope, off Hwy 89, Mt Shasta Ski Park (☎ 530-926-8610) offers skiing in winter and mountain biking and chairlift rides in summer.

McCloud, a quaint, historic mill town 10 miles east of I-5, is on Hwy 89 at the foot of Shasta's southern slope. Hiking is good in the area, especially the Squaw Valley Creek Trail, an easy 5-mile loop south of town.

Yreka (why-**ree**-ka), inland California's northernmost city, is a pleasant spot to stay and eat. Locals are proud of the Yreka Western Railroad (☎ 530-842-4146), a 1915 Baldwin steam engine that chugs to the tiny town of Montague in summer ($12; 3 hours).

Redding has several older budget motels right downtown, including the *Thunderbird Lodge* (☎ 530-243-5422, 1350 Pine St), which charges $37-40. In Dunsmuir, the pleasant, shady *Cedar Lodge* (☎ 530-235-4331, 4201 Dunsmuir Ave) has $44-52 rooms. The town's most unusual place to stay, however, is in a vintage railroad caboose at *Railroad Park Resort* (☎ 530-235-4440), off I-5 just south of town (doubles from $85). Mt Shasta's nice *Strawberry Valley Inn* (☎ 530-926-2052, 1142 S Mt Shasta Blvd) has doubles from $53. McCloud has several B&Bs, including the friendly *Stoney Brook Inn* (☎ 530-964-2300, 309 W Colombero), with a hot tub, sauna and doubles from $54. Several comfortable motels line Yreka's Main St, including the *Klamath Motor Lodge* (☎ 530-842-2751, 1111 S Main St), with a swimming pool and a shady lawn ($48).

Popular *Buz's Crab* (2159 East St), in Redding, serves fresh, affordable ($6-8) seafood baskets daily. In Mt Shasta the taco stand *Pancho & Lefkowitz*, on Chestnut St at Mt Shasta Blvd, is a low-key local favorite. In McCloud *Raymond's Ristorante* (☎ 530-964-2099, 424 Main St) serves fine, filling Italian meals (closed Tue).

Greyhound and Amtrak service Redding, Dunsmuir and Yreka. By car, San Francisco to Redding is 215 miles (4 hours); Redding to Portland, Oregon, is 420 miles (7 hours). STAGE buses (☎ 530-842-8295) run from Dunsmuir to Yreka ($3.50; 1¼ hours).

Northeast Corner

Many native Californians never see the places mentioned in this section, even though **Lava Beds National Monument** is surely one of the state's more remarkable attractions ($5). This 9-by-8-mile volcanic park features lava flows, craters and hundreds of lava tubes. 'Captain Jack's Stronghold' is named after a bloody battle in 1872, when fed-up Modoc Indians led by 'Captain Jack' confounded US forces by hiding in the lava beds. Near the visitor center (☎ 530-667-2282), on

Hill Rd off Hwy 161 on the park's south side, a short loop drive gives access to the lava tubes. Rangers at the center provide free flashlights for self-guided exploring. Take their safety tips seriously.

The **Klamath Basin National Wildlife Refuges** lie along the Pacific Flyway, providing safe havens for migrating birds. The visitor center (☎ 530-667-2231) is on Hill Rd, about 5 miles west of Tulelake. Ten-mile auto tours cost $3.

Modoc National Forest covers almost 3125 sq miles of California's northeast corner. At **Medicine Lake Highlands**, 14 miles south of Lava Beds Monument, Medicine Lake is a beautiful crater lake surrounded by pine forest, volcanic formations and campgrounds.

Alturas, at the junction of Hwys 299 and 395, is the Modoc County seat and principal service town for local ranchers. 'Where the West still lives' – the Modoc County slogan – is a fitting description. The Modoc National Forest Supervisor's Headquarters (☎ 530-233-5811), on W 12th St, has hiking information and maps (open Mon-Fri). The **Modoc National Wildlife Refuge**, 3 miles southeast of Alturas, is definitely worth a visit. A signboard posts a map of the refuge and suggests an auto tour, with tips for birdwatchers. Just 24 miles east of Alturas, on the California-Nevada border, is beautiful **Surprise Valley**, home to ranches, the tiny town of Cedarville, and plenty of hiking, camping and solitude in the wild Warner Mountains.

Susanville is primarily a service town for the surrounding cattle and timber district. The few travelers passing through Susanville are invariably on the way to/from **Lassen Volcanic National Park**. In addition to spectacular Lassen Peak (10,457 feet), the world's largest plug-dome volcano, the park contains boiling hot springs, steaming sulfur vents and tube caves. Hwy 89 wraps around Lassen Peak and provides access to geothermal areas, hiking trails and campgrounds. The park ($10 per car) has two entrances, both with visitor centers: one on Hwy 44 at Manzanita Lake, and one in the south off Hwy 89, via a turnoff 5 miles east of Mineral, where the park headquarters (☎ 530-595-4444) is located.

At the Lava Beds monument, there's a tree-shaded campground beside the visitor center ($10). There are **campgrounds** in Lassen Volcanic National Park ($8-14; first-come, first served) and various lodges, cabins and such near the main entrance.

Overall, the region has few commercial services, though there is the cute little **Ellis Motel** (☎ 530-667-5242), 2 miles north of Tulelake on Hwy 139 (doubles $39). Alturas has several affordable motels, including the **Essex Motel** (☎ 530-233-2821, 1216 N Main St), with comfortable rooms for $38. The impressive **Niles Hotel** (☎ 530-233-3261, 304 S Main St) is a restored historic landmark with attractive $65 rooms.

The cozy restaurant named **Captain Jack's Stronghold** (☎ 530-664-5566) sits alone 5 miles south of Tulelake on Hwy 139 (dinners $6-10).

In Alturas, dinners are served downstairs on weekends at the Niles Hotel; for lunch try **Sweet Things** (123 S Main St). In Cedarville, the **Cedarville Cafe and Saloon** serves satisfying food (dinners $8-12), including a mean ham and barley soup.

Sierra Nevada

The mighty Sierra Nevada mountain range stretches 400 miles along the California-Nevada border. The highest peaks, including Mt Whitney at 14,494 feet, are along the Sierra Nevada Crest in the east, while Yosemite, Kings Canyon and Sequoia National Parks are mostly accessible from the west. Between the mountains and foothills lies a granite world woven with canyons, rivers, lakes and alpine meadows.

LAKE TAHOE

The California-Nevada state border cuts lengthwise through brilliantly blue Lake Tahoe, a stunning natural wonder nestled among rugged peaks. Parks abound everywhere, though along the highway much of the land is developed, with towering casinos flashing from the Nevada side. Lake Tahoe's north shore (accessible via I-80) has numerous ski resorts, while the south shore (via Hwy 50) has flashy casinos and loads of cheap motels. Driving around Lake Tahoe isn't necessarily the best strategy for exploring – better to pick a spot and settle in for hiking, picnicking or simply taking in the view.

In winter, Hwy 89 (Emerald Bay Rd) is usually closed, and tire chains are often required on I-80 and Hwy 50; for winter road information, call ☎ 800-427-7623.

North & East Shores
On I-80 northwest of Tahoe, Truckee is a onetime mining and railroad town with restaurants, shops and hotels. Adjacent **Donner Lake** is surrounded by small, woodsy resorts and is a low-key alternative to the Tahoe action. At the east end of Donner Lake, the Emigrant Trail Museum (☎ 530-582-7894) does a great job chronicling the Donner Party's fateful journey in the winter of 1846, when a combination of winter storms and poor planning wiped out half of the 87-person Donner Party; survivors were forced to eat human flesh to avoid starvation.

Tahoe City is the north shore's largest town. Visit the North Lake Tahoe Chamber of Commerce (☎ 530-581-6900), near the junction of Hwys 89 and 28, for lodging, dining, hiking and skiing information. A popular activity, especially with kids, is crowding onto Fanny Bridge and watching the fish swim by underneath.

Heading northeast on Hwy 28, Tahoe Vista and Kings Beach have attractive motels and some well-preserved 1950s charm. Hiking, biking and cross-country skiing can be enjoyed at North Tahoe Regional Park, north of Hwy 28 at the end of National St.

Tahoe's northeastern shore is dominated by **Lake Tahoe–Nevada State Park** (☎ 775-831-0494), which has cross-country skiing in winter and a nice (albeit often crowded) beach at Sand Harbor (parking $6). Crystal Bay is an aging casino town, while affluent Incline Village – the source of the wood that shored up Virginia City's mines (see Nevada in the Southwest chapter) – is home to the tacky Ponderosa Ranch (☎ 775-831-0691), where the TV Western *Bonanza* was filmed ($10.50).

West & South Shores
If you only have one day here, **DL Bliss State Park** (☎ 530-525-7232) is a good place to spend it; there's clear turquoise water, white sand and access to unspoiled hiking trails (parking $5).

It's hard to miss **Vikingsholm Castle** (☎ 530-525-7277), off Hwy 89 at the lake's edge and reached by boat or a steep 1-mile descent. Tours of this dowdy Scandinavian mansion, built in 1928, are given daily ($1; open daily June-Sept, Sat-Sun off-season). Narrow **Emerald Bay** is one of Tahoe's major attractions, containing the lake's only island and waters that truly justify its name. About 3 miles southeast on Emerald Bay Rd, the **Tallac Historic Site** (☎ 530-541-5227) encompasses three historic estates and a museum, all worth an hour or so.

Few people, even locals, have good things to say about South Lake Tahoe and its faceless motels and shopping malls. It does, though, have relatively cheap accommodations and a helpful visitor center (☎ 530-541-5255). Immediately across the Nevada border is **Stateline**, where you can gamble away your future at Caesar's Tahoe, Harrah's and Harvey's.

Activities
The lake is surrounded by skiing areas, including the following:

Alpine Meadows (☎ 530-581-8375) – large, family-friendly resort; 12 lifts ($52); off Hwy 89 near Tahoe City

Heavenly (☎ 775-586-7000) – best all-around resort; 28 lifts ($57); near Stateline in South Lake Tahoe

Kirkwood (☎ 209-258-6000) – locals' choice and popular with snowboarders; 13 lifts ($52); 35 miles south of Lake Tahoe on Hwy 88

Squaw Valley USA (☎ 530-583-6985) – world-class resort, host of 1960 Winter Olympics; 33 lifts ($54); off Hwy 89, 10 miles north of Tahoe City

There are marked cross-country and snowshoe trails at Camp Richardson (☎ 530-542-6584), on Hwy 89 a few miles north of South Lake Tahoe. Other good spots are Lake Tahoe–Nevada State Park and Tahoe Cross Country Ski Area (☎ 530-583-5475), in Tahoe City. Further winter activities include two-hour snowmobile tours, which don't come cheap ($89 one rider, $124 two). Reserve through Zephyr Cove Snowmobile Center (☎ 775-588-3833).

During the summer, enjoy the nice beaches along Emerald Bay Rd, rent a canoe or kayak from Ski Run Boat Company (☎ 530-544-0200) or follow one of many good hiking and biking trails. A favorite trek is the 5-mile climb up Mt Tallac in the Desolation Wilderness. Pick up maps and permits

CALIFORNIA

at the USFS Visitor Center (☎ 530-573-2674) near the Tallac Historic Site.

Places to Stay & Eat

On Hwy 89 south of Truckee, the USFS campground *Goose Meadow* *(reservations ☎ 800-280-2267)* has $10 tent sites protected from highway noise. *Sugar Pine Point State Park (reservations ☎ 530-525-7982, 800-444-7275)*, on the western shore, has $12 sites among the trees.

In South Lake Tahoe, *Doug's Mellow Mountain Retreat (☎ 530-544-8065, 3787 Forest Ave)* is an independent hostel in a suburban house run by a ski bum (beds $15). Motel prices can vary hugely depending on the season and day of the week. Summer weekends are highest, with rates at even modest motels sometimes climbing over $100 a double.

The South Lake Tahoe Visitor's Authority (☎ 800-288-2463) makes free room reservations, sometimes with discounted casino shows and lift tickets. Some South Tahoe motels and casinos also have ski packages: *Caesar's Tahoe (☎ 800-648-3353)* offers a two-night stay and lift tickets for about $300 per couple, and at the *Tahoe Sunset Lodge (☎ 530-541-2940)*, a room and lift tickets can be as low as $120 per couple midweek.

Dozens of budget motels line Hwy 50, from Stateline west to the junction with Hwy 89, an area still commercial but removed from the casino madness. Typical is the *Tahoe Sundowner (☎ 530-541-2282)*, just south of the Hwy 50/89 split, with $35 midweek specials.

In Tahoe City, above-average rooms at *Tahoe City Inn (☎ 800-800-8246, 790 N Lake Blvd)* begin at $75 weekends. Worth a splurge is dinner (entrées from $20) at *Wolfdale's (☎ 530-583-5700, 640 N Lake Blvd)*.

In Kings Beach, the *North Lake Lodge (☎ 530-546-2731, 8716 N Lake Blvd)* has rooms from $45, and the nearby *Char Pit* serves burgers and excellent milkshakes.

Getting There & Around

The tiny South Lake Tahoe Airport (☎ 530-542-6180) is south of Tahoe on Hwy 50/89. Major commercial flights, however, fly out of the Reno-Tahoe International Airport (☎ 775-328-6499). The Tahoe Casino Express (☎ 800-446-6128) runs shuttles between Reno-Tahoe International Airport and South Lake Tahoe casinos ($17).

Greyhound buses (☎ 530-543-1050) leave from the Tahoe Colony Inn (3794 Montreal Rd) daily for Sacramento ($23) and San Francisco ($30).

Tahoe Area Rapid Transit (TART; ☎ 800-736-6365) buses connect Tahoe City, Truckee, Tahoe Vista and other towns. In summer service is extended down the west shore to Meeks Bay Resort, where you can transfer to the South Lake Tahoe Stage (☎ 530-542-6077) network ($1.25). Larger casinos run free shuttles until 2am, stopping at any Stateline/South Tahoe motel.

YOSEMITE NATIONAL PARK

The fact that 4.1 million people a year visit Yosemite suggests that the USA's premier national park is a place of ravishing natural beauty – and that sometimes, to the dismay of first-time visitors, it is brutally crowded. Yet with tourist activity concentrated in only 6% of the park (mostly Yosemite Valley), outdoors enthusiasts need only hit the trails to find honest-to-goodness wilderness and that precious commodity – solitude.

In 1864 President Abraham Lincoln signed a bill preserving the park under the Yosemite Grant to California. Thanks to the passionate campaigning of naturalist John Muir, the area was established as Yosemite National Park in 1890. Balancing tourists' needs with those of the environment is an ongoing battle in Yosemite, which is plagued by heavy crowds, traffic, and smog. One idea under study would ban most vehicles in the park, thus eliminating one of Yosemite's major summertime blemishes.

Orientation & Information

Yosemite's entrance fee ($20 per vehicle, $10 for those on bicycle or foot) is valid for seven days. There are four primary entrances to Yosemite: South Entrance (Hwy 41), Arch Rock (Hwy 140), Big Oak Flat (Hwy 120 west) and Tioga Pass (Hwy 120 east). Hwy 120 traverses the park as Tioga Rd (closed in winter), connecting the valley with Mono Lake via 9945-foot Tioga Pass. Yosemite Valley, on the southwest side of the park, is the foremost destination and home to most visitor facilities and campgrounds. Tuolumne Meadows, off Tioga Rd (closed in winter), is a hub for backpackers and serious backcountry hikers. Wawona, at the southern entrance, has a hotel, store, pioneer museum and Mariposa Grove of giant sequoias.

The visitor center in Yosemite Valley (☎ 209-372-0299) is the park's main information source, though there are ranger stations with maps and posted campground availability at all park entrances. For recorded Yosemite information and road/weather conditions, call ☎ 209-372-0200.

Wilderness permits are required year round for overnight trips. A quota system limits the number of people leaving from each trailhead. Half of the permits are available free of charge on a first-come, first-served basis no more than 24 hours in advance; the other half can be reserved through the Yosemite Wilderness Center (☎ 209-372-0740) no earlier than 24 weeks and no later than two days before your trip ($5). Know how many people are in your party, entry and exit dates, starting and ending trailheads and your principal destination.

There are gas stations at Wawona, El Portal, Tuolumne Meadows and the Tioga Rd/Big Oak Flat Rd junction (closed in winter). Bank of America has an branch and 24-hour ATM in Yosemite Village, next to the Village Store. There is a 24-hour medical clinic (☎ 209-372-4637) close to Yosemite Village.

Yosemite Valley

On the park's southwest side, Yosemite Valley is 35 miles from the South Entrance, 13 miles from Arch Rock, 29 miles from Big Oak Flat and 58 miles from Tioga Pass. A one-way road makes an 8½-mile loop around the valley floor, with access to campgrounds and visitor facilities. The hub is **Yosemite Village**, with a visitor center, museums, stores, restaurants and a post office.

West of the village, there's an easy path to the base of **Yosemite Falls**, visible from all over the valley. Together the upper and lower falls cascade 2425 feet – the tallest waterfall in North America. At the valley's southeast end, where the Merced River rushes around two small islands, **Happy Isles** is the starting point for several popular hikes and home to the Happy Isles Family Nature Center (open May-Oct).

One of the park's best views is from **Glacier Point**, 3214 feet above the valley floor. It is accessible via Glacier Point Rd (off Hwy 41) by car and tour bus, and by cross-country skis or on foot via the steep Panorama or Four Mile Trails.

On the north side of the valley, the Valley View Turnout is a good place to ogle **El Capitan**, the largest granite monolith in the world (3593 feet from base to summit). For a wider, 'classic' Yosemite Valley view – one encompassing El Capitan, Half Dome and Bridleveil Falls – stop at the pullout on the road toward Badger Pass, just before the tunnel.

Tuolumne Meadows

At 8500 feet, Tuolumne (too-**ahl**-uh-mee) Meadows is the largest subalpine meadow in the Sierra. Its wide open fields and clear blue lakes are a dazzling contrast to Yosemite's densely forested valley. Tioga Rd (Hwy 120) provides access to Tuolumne and is the only road to traverse the park from east to west. At the meadow's west end, Tuolumne Meadows Visitor Center (☎ 209-372-0263) has a large selection of maps and general guidebooks. About a mile east, the Tuolumne Meadows Store (☎ 209-372-8428) offers some maps, as well as camping supplies. A ranger kiosk, off the road near Tuolumne Meadows Lodge, issues wilderness permits.

Impassable Tioga Pass

Hwy 120, the main route into Yosemite National Park from the Eastern Sierra, climbs through Tioga Pass, the highest pass in the Sierra, at 9945 feet. On most maps of California, you'll find a parenthetical remark – 'closed in winter' – printed on the map near the pass. While true, this statement is also misleading. The Tioga Rd is usually closed from the first heavy snowfall in October to May or June. If you are planning a trip through Tioga Pass in the spring, you're likely to be out of luck. According to the park's official policy, the earliest date that the road through the pass will be plowed is April 15, yet the pass has only been open in April once since 1980. So call ahead (☎ 209-372-0200) for road and weather conditions before heading for Tioga Pass.

Besides great scenery, Tioga Rd offers relatively uncrowded campgrounds, excellent day hikes and the chance to watch climbers at close range. At the road's west end, just after the Big Oak Flat Rd junction, are two giant sequoia groves: **Merced Grove**, reached by a 2-mile hike (the trailhead is on the south side of the road, near a post marked B-10), and **Tuolumne Grove**, cut through by a 6-mile loop road.

Activities

Yosemite has over 800 miles of trails that go far beyond the beaten tourist path. Several heavily trodden hiking trails start in the valley. Most popular is the paved **Mist Trail**, from Happy Isles Family Nature Center to Vernal Falls. **Panorama Trail** – good for viewing waterfalls, Half Dome and the valley – goes from Happy Isles Family Nature Center to Glacier Point; it's a tough, steep climb, however, even for hearty trekkers.

Keen eyes might pick out climbers working their way up Half Dome and El Capitan. It's not something to try on a whim, but if you're curious, the Yosemite Mountaineering School (☎ 209-372-8435) does offer beginner and intermediate rock-climbing classes ($70 all-day classes). For climbing and camping supplies, try Curry Village Mountain Sport Shop (☎ 209-372-8396), in Yosemite Valley, or the Tuolumne Meadows Store (☎ 209-372-1328), open May-Oct.

Yosemite is a magical place when snow falls – not only is it eerily beautiful, but accommodations are cheaper and the park far less crowded. Roads in the valley are plowed, and Hwys 41, 120 and 140 are kept open (Tioga Rd closes with the first snowfall). Buy snow chains before approaching the park. Downhill **skiing** is available at Badger Pass (☎ 209-372-1000), cross-country skiing at Badger Pass, Crane Flat and Mariposa Grove. Two backcountry ski huts – with beds, cooking facilities, woodstoves and water – are available for overnight stays. The Yosemite Association (☎ 209-372-0740) operates the Ostrander Ski Hut, and Yosemite Concession Services (☎ 209-252-4848) operates the Glacier Point Hut; reservations are required for both.

Curry Village has **bike** rentals and an **ice-skating** rink (open Nov-Mar).

Places to Stay

Yosemite campgrounds can fill up fast any time of year – 'If you find a spot, don't give it up,' advise rangers – so for peace of mind it's best to reserve (☎ 800-436-7275) up to five months in advance. Last-minute campers might have better luck outside park borders at USFS and private facilities. Don't expect a wilderness experience: In summers especially, valley camping is like living in an apartment building with very thin walls.

Campsites on the reservation system, including those in most valley campgrounds, include flush toilets, picnic tables, fire rings and food-storage boxes ($18). Additional campgrounds, such as *Bridleveil Creek* and peaceful *White Wolf*, provide water and are first-come, first-served ($12). This goes for primitive sites as well ($8), including *Tamarack Flat* and *Yosemite Creek*, which are both down rugged roads that discourage RVs.

The 55-site *Tuolumne Meadows Campground* is half first-come, first-served, with nice spots along a creek (open July-Sept). Near Yosemite Lodge, popular 35-site *Sunnyside Walk-In* (also called Camp 4) is first-come, first-served ($5 per person; open year round).

In Midpines, friendly *HI Yosemite Bug Hostel* (☎ 209-966-6666), 20 miles from the park on Hwy 140, has dorm beds ($16), private rooms ($40-105), tent cabins ($30-50) and tent sites ($17).

All cabin and hotel room reservations/cancellations are made through *Yosemite Concession Services* (*YCS*; ☎ 209-252-4848, 5410 E Home Ave, Fresno, CA 93727). From November to March it's possible to reserve a spot through the YCS Web site (Ⓦ www.yosemitepark.com). Wherever you stay, make reservations as early as possible, as some cabins are booked a year in advance. Most rates go down off season.

In Yosemite Valley, *Housekeeping Camp* has tent cabins, a grocery store, laundry and pay showers. Cabins – concrete slabs with plastic sides and roofs – cost $57.

Curry Village is a privately run enterprise founded in 1899. It started with seven tents, but today it looks like a labor camp, with tent cabins ($48) crowded close together. Each has four beds on a wooden platform. Wooden cabins without bathrooms ($58) are a bit nicer, while those with bathrooms ($75) are spacious. Modern rooms, right in the thick of Curry Village, cost $103.

Tuolumne Meadows Lodge has canvas tent cabins with four beds, a woodstove and candles (no electricity) for $56. Expensive breakfasts and dinners are served in the dining room. A mile north of the highway, the ***White Wolf*** lodge has a rustic dining room and cabins ($52-71).

Character-lacking ***Yosemite Lodge*** gets large tour groups and has the park's most popular restaurant and bar. Standard rooms cost $103; modern 'lodge' rooms with TV and phone cost $142 (cheaper in winter).

The valley's deluxe accommodations are at the elegant ***Ahwahnee Hotel***, with rooms and cottages for $320. Near the park's south entrance is another upscale option, the 1879 ***Wawona Hotel***, with rooms for $96-160. Both hotels also serve cocktails and elegant, but expensive, dinners.

Places to Eat
In Yosemite Village, ***Dengan's Deli*** makes hearty sandwiches, and the ***Village Store*** sells the fixings to build your own. Close by, ***The Loft Pizzeria*** serves pastas and salads. At the Curry Village, ***Dining Pavilion*** is an outdoor pizza window and, inside, a self-service cafeteria with breakfast, lunch and dinner for less than $10.

Getting There & Around
Amtrak (☎ 209-722-6862, 800-872-7245) runs a train/bus system from cities like San Francisco ($37) and Los Angeles ($39) into Yosemite Valley via its Merced depot. Yosemite Area Region Transportation (Yarts; ☎ 877-989-2787) runs daily buses to the valley from Merced ($10), Midpines ($7) and other towns. Another Yarts bus (☎ 800-626-6684) runs in summer only from Mammoth ($15), stopping in Tuolumne Meadows.

A free shuttle bus (☎ 209-372-1240) is available year round for getting to points within Yosemite Valley itself.

SEQUOIA & KINGS CANYON NATIONAL PARKS
South of Yosemite, the adjacent Sequoia and Kings Canyon National Parks encompass some of California's finest alpine scenery, as well as groves of giant sequoia trees. Despite this superlative terrain,

crowds are sparse thanks to the parks' location – and the fact that no highways cross the Sierras here. Compared to Yosemite in summer, they're practically empty.

Orientation & Information
Sequoia was designated a national park in 1890 (the second in the USA), Kings Canyon in 1940. The two parks, though distinct, are operated as one unit with a single admission of $10 per car, $5 for people on bicycle or foot. Admission is valid for seven days.

Enter the parks via Grant Grove (Hwy 180) or Ash Mountain (Hwy 198), the latter a series of narrow switchbacks.

The main north-south road is the 48-mile Generals Highway, and **Grant Grove** (☎ 559-335-2856) and **Lodgepole** (☎ 559-565-3782) are the two hubs. Each has a visitor center, a market, showers, a post office and ATMs. Grant Grove and Lodgepole facilities are open year round. The **Foothills** visitor center (☎ 559-565-3135), at the Ash Mountain entrance, is also open year round. The **Cedar Grove** visitor center (☎ 559-565-3793) and ranger station at remote **Mineral King** (☎ 559-565-3768), however, are open in summer only. For current trail conditions and backcountry information, call ☎ 559-565-3708.

Gas is not currently available in the park, but it is sold at Kings Canyon Lodge and Hume Lake, both private facilities north of Grant Grove.

Sequoia National Park
A good destination for first-time visitors is **Giant Forest**, home to the massive General Sherman Tree, the world's largest. From the parking lot you can also access the Congress Trail, a worthwhile 2-mile paved pathway passing impressive trees. For more solitude, continue to the 5-mile Trail of the Sequoias, which puts you deeper into the forest.

The nearby **Giant Forest Museum**, opened in 2001, has exhibits about sequoia ecology and history. For mind-boggling views of the Great Western Divide, climb the steep quarter-mile staircase up **Moro Rock**.

Discovered in 1918 by two fishermen, **Crystal Cave** extends around 3 miles into the earth and has formations estimated to be 10,000 years old. The 45-minute cave tour covers a half mile of chambers; tickets are available at the Lodgepole and Foothills visitor centers, not at the cave ($8).

Giant Sequoias

In the same family as the California coast redwood and Dawn sequoia (recently discovered in China), the giant sequoia (*Sequoiadendron giganteum*) grows only on the Sierra's western slope, between 5000 and 7000 feet. Giant sequoias are the largest living things on earth in terms of volume. They can grow to 300 feet tall and 40 feet in diameter, and live up to 3000 years – the eldest is estimated to be 3500 years old. Aside from Yosemite, look for sequoia groves around Kings Canyon and Sequoia National Parks and the similarly gigantic California coast redwood tree along the Pacific Coast.

Kings Canyon National Park

Grant Grove was originally General Grant National Park, but in 1940 it was absorbed into Kings Canyon National Park. One mile north of the village, **General Grant Grove** includes the General Grant Tree and several other impressive giants. North of Grant Grove, Kings Canyon Hwy drops 2000 feet to Cedar Grove, along the South Fork of the Kings River. The 36-mile drive takes about an hour and is among the most magnificent in any national park. Views from the road into the valley are spectacular, with roaring

rivers, rugged peaks and steep granite cliffs. The canyon itself, plunging 8200 feet, is the deepest in the contiguous 48 states. Six miles beyond Cedar Grove, **Roads End** is just that, with trailheads, overnight parking and a ranger kiosk that issues wilderness permits. Beautiful Zumwalt Meadow is an easy half-hour hike from the parking lot.

Activities

With trail mileage 10 times greater than road mileage, the parks are a **backpacking** heaven. Kings Canyon and the Mineral King region of Sequoia offer the best back-country access, while the Jenny Lakes Wilderness Area (accessible from Big Meadows Trailhead near Big Meadows Campground) has pristine meadows and lakes at lower elevations. Wilderness permits are required for all overnight trips and are available free of charge at visitor centers and ranger stations. There is a $10 reservation fee by fax or post; write to Wilderness Permit Reservations, Sequoia and Kings Canyon NP, HCR 89, Box 60, Three Rivers, CA 93271. Trails are usually open by mid-May, and quotas go into effect when necessary (usually July-Aug).

In winter, Grant Grove Village (including the market and restaurant) is in full swing, with plenty of accommodations (☎ 559-335-5500). Further **skiing** activity is centered on the Sequoia Ski Touring Center (☎ 559-565-3435) in Wolverton, 2½ miles south of Lodgepole. Both regions provide rental equipment and marked trails.

Places to Stay & Eat

Sites at *Lodgepole* and Dorst can be reserved by calling ☎ 800-365-2267. Others are available on a first-come, first-served basis only, including *Sunset*, which is forested and hilly, and *Azalea*, where sites are well dispersed ($8-16). *Lodgepole*, *Azalea*, *Potwisha* and *South Fork* campgrounds are open year round; the rest, including the four down inside Kings Canyon, are usually open May to October. Call ☎ 559-565-3341 for updates.

If you want a pampered camping experience, consider staying at *Bearpaw Meadow Camp* (☎ 888-252-5757), in Sequoia. From Crescent Meadow trailhead, Bearpaw is an 11½-mile hike along the stunning High Sierra Trail. The camp, overlooking an awesome granite valley, has tent cabins, hot showers, linens and full meals. A one- to three-person cabin costs $300; reservations are required.

For advance reservations at Kings Canyon lodges, call ☎ 866-522-6966. The year-round **Grant Grove Lodge** has tent cabins ranging from rustic ($38) to deluxe ($93), with private bathrooms and electricity. **Grant Grove Restaurant**, open year round, is an above-average coffee shop with meals under $10. **Cedar Grove Lodge** has motel-style rooms for $90. Halfway between Grant Grove and Cedar Grove, the privately run **Kings Canyon Lodge** (☎ 559-335-2405) is a better value, with rooms and cabins from $69. Its cozy, rustic cafe-bar, built in the 1930s, serves meals and cocktails daily. Even the gas pumps are antiques.

Budget motels line the highways outside the park borders. The cheapest is likely the **Mineral King Motel** (☎ 559-592-4917), 25 miles east of Ash Mountain in Exeter, with adequate rooms from $30.

EASTERN SIERRA

The eastern side of the Sierra Nevada mountains is a captivating region where granite peaks abruptly plunge into the Great Basin desert. At the center of the region is sun-blasted Owens Valley, but gain a few thousand feet and you're suddenly surrounded by high-altitude lakes and breezy alpine meadows.

Busy Hwy 395 runs the length of the range, with turnoffs offering side trips to the region's lakes and mountains. Towns like Bishop, Mammoth Lakes, Lee Vining and Bridgeport make good jumping-off points for hikers, bikers, fishers and skiers.

A worthwhile detour is **Bodie State Historic Park**, on Hwy 270, which intersects Hwy 395 about 7 miles south of Bridgeport. The drive is 13 miles, the last three unpaved and often closed in winter. The combination of a remote location and the large number of original, well-maintained gold-rush-era buildings makes Bodie, founded in 1859, one of the West's most picturesque ghost towns. The visitor center (☎ 760-647-6445) is excellent (open winter). Park admission costs $1.

Mono Lake is an Ice Age remnant formed more than 700,000 years ago. Appearing like drip sand castles on and near the lakeshore, Mono's ancient tufa towers form when calcium-bearing freshwater bubbles up through the alkaline lake. The most photogenic concentration is at the South Tufa Reserve, on the lake's southern rim. Perched alongside the lake, Lee Vining acts as a gateway to the area and has two helpful information centers. Immediately north of town, the USFS runs the Mono Basin Scenic Area Visitor Center (☎ 760-647-3044), which has informative displays, camping information and a gorgeous view. In town, the Mono Lake Committee bookstore (☎ 760-647-6595) is another good source for maps and regional information.

Unless you're truly in a rush, take the time to drive and dawdle along the 14-mile **June Lake Loop**. The scenic road, signposted midway between Mono Lake and Mammoth, follows Hwy 158 west into the mountains, passing Grant, Silver, Gull and June Lakes. The town of June Lake is a small resort community with grocery stores and motels.

Mammoth Lakes (population 4500) is an unattractive conglomeration of shopping centers and condominiums. Despite its lack of charm, it sports a laid-back atmosphere, decent restaurants and stellar mountain surroundings. In summer the lakes are a popular destination for hikers. The area's main attraction, though, is **Mammoth Mountain** (☎ 888-462-6668), with world-class skiing (lift tickets $56) and a summertime mountain-bike park (lift tickets $28; $61 including bike rental). The Mammoth Lakes Ranger Station (☎ 760-924-5500) and Mammoth Lakes Visitor Bureau (☎ 800-367-6572) share a building on the north side of Route 203, just before Old Mammoth Rd. This one-stop information center issues wilderness permits, has campground listings, and offers a 24-hour courtesy phone to local hotels.

Before dropping down into Owens Valley, look for a road marked 'Tom's Place,' which branches west of Hwy 395 and climbs up Rock Creek Canyon, past big boulders and wide meadows. It ends at the Mosquito Flat parking lot (10,300 feet), the highest point accessible by car in the Eastern Sierra. Easy trails lead to Little Lakes Valley, the scenery about as good as it gets on a day hike.

Bishop, the largest town south of Mammoth Lakes, is a major stop for skiers and hikers. The central district has some

CALIFORNIA

character, with covered sidewalks, 1950s neon signs and hunting and fishing stores. Restaurants, motels and gas stations line the highway on either end of town. Worth at least an hour's stop, **Laws Railroad Museum** (☎ 760-873-5950), 4 miles northeast of Bishop on Hwy 6, is an extensive collection of Old West buildings, including the 1883 Laws railroad depot ($2 donation).

For stunning views, take the hourlong drive up to the **Ancient Bristlecone Pine Forest** (☎ 760-873-2500). From Bishop drive 15 miles south to Big Pine, then head east on Hwy 168 another 13 miles to the marked turnoff ($2 per person). Above 10,000 feet in the White Mountains, these gnarled, picturesque trees are Earth's oldest living things, some dating back 4000 years. The road (closed in winter) is paved to the top, where there are hikes of varying length, primitive camping and a visitor center. Wear sunscreen and a hat.

Places to Stay & Eat

Campgrounds abound in the Eastern Sierras. On public land outside developed campsites, however, you'll need a fire permit, even for a camp stove. They're free, valid for the calendar year, and obtainable at ranger stations including those in Bridgeport (☎ 760-932-7070), Mammoth (☎ 760-924-5500) and Bishop (☎ 760-873-2500).

On Bridgeport's Main St, next to the historic Mono County Courthouse, the *Silver Maple* (☎ 760-932-7383) is a lovely motel with a big yard (doubles $65). In Lee Vining, *El Mono* (☎ 760-647-6310) has basic rooms ($49-80).

Mammoth Lakes' excellent *Davison St Guesthouse* (*reservations* ☎ 760-924-2188, 619-544-9093, 19 Davison St) has dorm beds ($22) and a few private doubles ($30) – book ahead. Rooms at the *Holiday Haus Motel* (☎ 760-934-2414, 3905 Main St) run $55-95. The *Sierra Nevada Rodeway Inn* (☎ 800-824-5132, 164 Old Mammoth Rd) has a hot tub and standard rooms for $69-99. For breakfast and lunch try the *Good Life Cafe*, in the Mammoth Mall.

Nearby June Lake is loads more charming than Mammoth. At *Lake Front Cabins* (☎ 760-648-7527), double rooms cost $80-85. Farther up Hwy 158, cabins at *Fern Creek Lodge* (☎ 800-621-9146) begin at $50. *Rock Creek Lodge* (☎ 760-935-4170), on Rock Creek Rd near Mosquito Flat, has cabins (from $80), a dining room and a general store.

In Bishop, the cozy *Elm's Motel* (☎ 760-873-8118, 233 E Elm St) has doubles for $40. The tidy *Inyo Country Store* (☎ 760-872-2552, 177 Academy St) serves breakfast and lunch daily, dinner by reservation only. Another place in Bishop is the *Bishop Grill*, on Main St at Willow St, an older diner with nice booths and basic chow.

The *HI Winnedumah Hotel & Hostel* (☎ 760-878-2040) is 40 miles south of Bishop in the small town of Independence (beds $18, including breakfast, private rooms from $55).

Getting There & Around

Greyhound (☎ 775-882-3375 in Carson City) buses travel Hwy 395 between Los Angeles and Carson City, Nevada, stopping in most towns. Free Mammoth Mountain shuttle buses (☎ 760-934-0687) make loops through Mammoth during ski season.

Pacific Northwest

The states of Washington and Oregon have some of the most diverse and dramatic landscape in the country, from the cliff-hung Oregon coast to the sleepily rural islands of Puget Sound, the volcanic peaks of the Cascade Range and precipitous gorge of the Columbia River. These evocative landscapes aren't just for looking at. In the Northwest, you're expected to get outdoors and enjoy yourself. The forests and coastlines are webbed with hiking trails, the rivers churn with white water for rafting and kayaking, and every mountain peak is fair game for rock climbers and mountaineers.

The cities of the Northwest are noted for their high standard of living and vibrant cultural life; Seattle especially is a hot spot of youth culture and high-tech industry. And although the Northwest is in the far corner of mainland USA, it offers plenty of options for onward travel into Canada, north to Alaska and east to the Rocky Mountains.

History

If the ancestors of the Native Americans did arrive via a land bridge from Russia to Alaska, then it's probable that the coasts, islands and river valleys of the Pacific Northwest were some of the continent's first populated areas. When Europeans arrived in the 18th century, societies like the Chinook and the Salish already had well-established, prosperous communities based on the rich supply of seafood. Their trading routes extended hundreds of miles, and superbly made longhouses, canoes and other artifacts show elaborate and distinctive decorations. The aristocracy of these cultures regularly shared much of their material wealth with their community in ceremonial feasts called potlatches. Inland, on the arid plateaus between the Cascades and the Rocky Mountains, cultures like the Nez Percé and the Spokane were founded on seasonal migration between river valleys and temperate uplands.

Three hundred years after Columbus landed in the New World, Spanish and British explorers were probing the northern Pacific Coast, still seeking the fabled Northwest Passage. Captain George Vancouver

Highlights

- Seattle – postgrunge music scene, coffee culture and a superb setting
- Olympic National Park – snowcapped peaks rising from the rainforest; excellent wilderness hiking
- North Cascades National Park – dramatic alpine scenery and rafting on the Skagit River
- Mt St Helens – eerie, postapocalyptic landscape
- Crater Lake – the deepest, bluest and perhaps the prettiest lake in the USA
- Portland – perhaps USA's most livable city, with rivers, trees and a relaxed atmosphere
- Oregon Coast – magnificent cliffs and dunes; whale- and bird-watching
- Columbia River Gorge – scenic drives along a majestic river

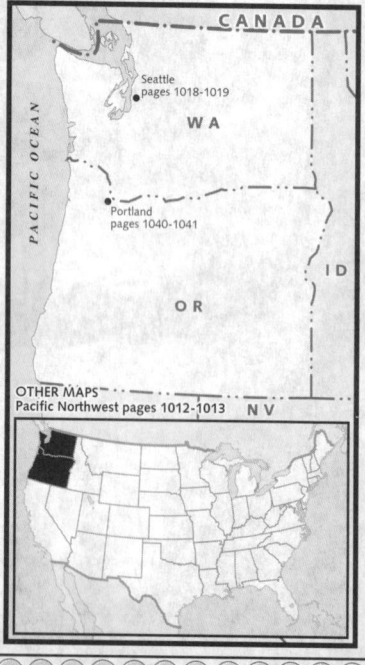

was, in 1792, the first explorer to sail the waters of Puget Sound, claiming British sovereignty over the entire region. At the same time, an American, Captain Robert Gray, found the mouth of the Columbia River. In 1805 the explorers Lewis and Clark crossed over the Rockies and made their way down the Columbia River to the Pacific Ocean, extending the US claim on the territory.

By 1809 trappers from two competing British fur-trading companies, the Hudson's Bay Company and the North West Company, had ventured into present-day British Columbia, Montana, Idaho and eastern Washington to establish fur-trading forts. Fort Vancouver was established by the Hudson's Bay Company in 1824 to serve as the headquarters for the entire Columbia region. The nearly self-sufficient agricultural community thrived and encouraged settlement in its environs. The trade had a devastating impact on the indigenous cultures, however, assailed as they were by the double threat of European diseases and alcohol.

During the 1830s American missionaries, intent on converting the indigenous inhabitants to Christianity, established farmsteads throughout the Willamette Valley. In 1843 settlers at Champoeg, on the Willamette River south of Portland, voted to organize a provisional government independent of the Hudson's Bay Company, thereby casting their lot with the USA, which formally acquired the territory from the British by treaty in 1846. Over the next decade, some 53,000 settlers came to the Northwest via the 2000-mile-long Oregon Trail.

Relations between settlers and the area's native inhabitants reached a tragic low in 1847 when Cayuse Indians, believing the Whitman mission in Walla Walla had introduced an epidemic of measles, killed a dozen missionaries. Settlers now felt justified in rounding up the indigenous people and moving them to reservations, where increased illness, starvation and dislocation led almost to their extinction. By 1860 much of the Pacific Northwest was settled, and most major cities had been established.

Speculation and competition to become the terminus of the transcontinental railroads led to the development of several western Washington towns. But with the naming of Tacoma as the terminus of the Northern Pacific Railroad (1873) and the arrival of the Great Northern Railroad in Seattle (1893), the future of the region was set. Agriculture and lumber became the pillars of the regional economy until 1914, when the opening of the Panama Canal and WWI brought increased trade to Pacific ports. Shipyards opened along Puget Sound, and the Boeing aircraft company set up shop near Seattle.

Big dam projects in the 1930s and '40s provided cheap hydroelectricity and irrigation to the Pacific Northwest. WWII offered another boost for the aircraft manufacturing and shipbuilding industries, and agriculture continued to be a big earner throughout the region. The postwar period saw major growth, above all in the urban areas around Puget Sound. Washington's population grew to be twice that of Oregon's.

All this rapid growth was not without environmental cost. The continued production of cheap hydroelectricity and the massive irrigation projects along the Columbia have led to the nearly irreversible destruction of the Columbia River ecosystem. Logging also has left its scars, especially in Oregon.

Despite the damage, the Pacific Northwest has gained a reputation as a sort of ecological utopia, attracting newcomers in search of cleaner, greener lands. Oregon in particular became a magnet for politically progressive and environmentally minded individuals. In the 1980s and '90s, high-tech industry, embodied by Microsoft in Seattle and Intel in Portland, encouraged a different kind of migration, this time of wired entrepreneurs.

Geography & Environment

The major geographical regions are the coastal mountains and islands, the Cascade Range, and the plateaus stretching from east of the Cascades to the Rocky Mountain foothills. The mighty Columbia River drains nearly all of Oregon, Washington and Idaho, as well as parts of the neighboring states and provinces.

The environment is a contentious issue in the Northwest; flash points are the logging of old-growth forests and the destruction of salmon runs in streams and rivers.

Flora & Fauna

In the high-rainfall area west of the Cascades, forests are fast growing and dense

PACIFIC NORTHWEST

PACIFIC NORTHWEST

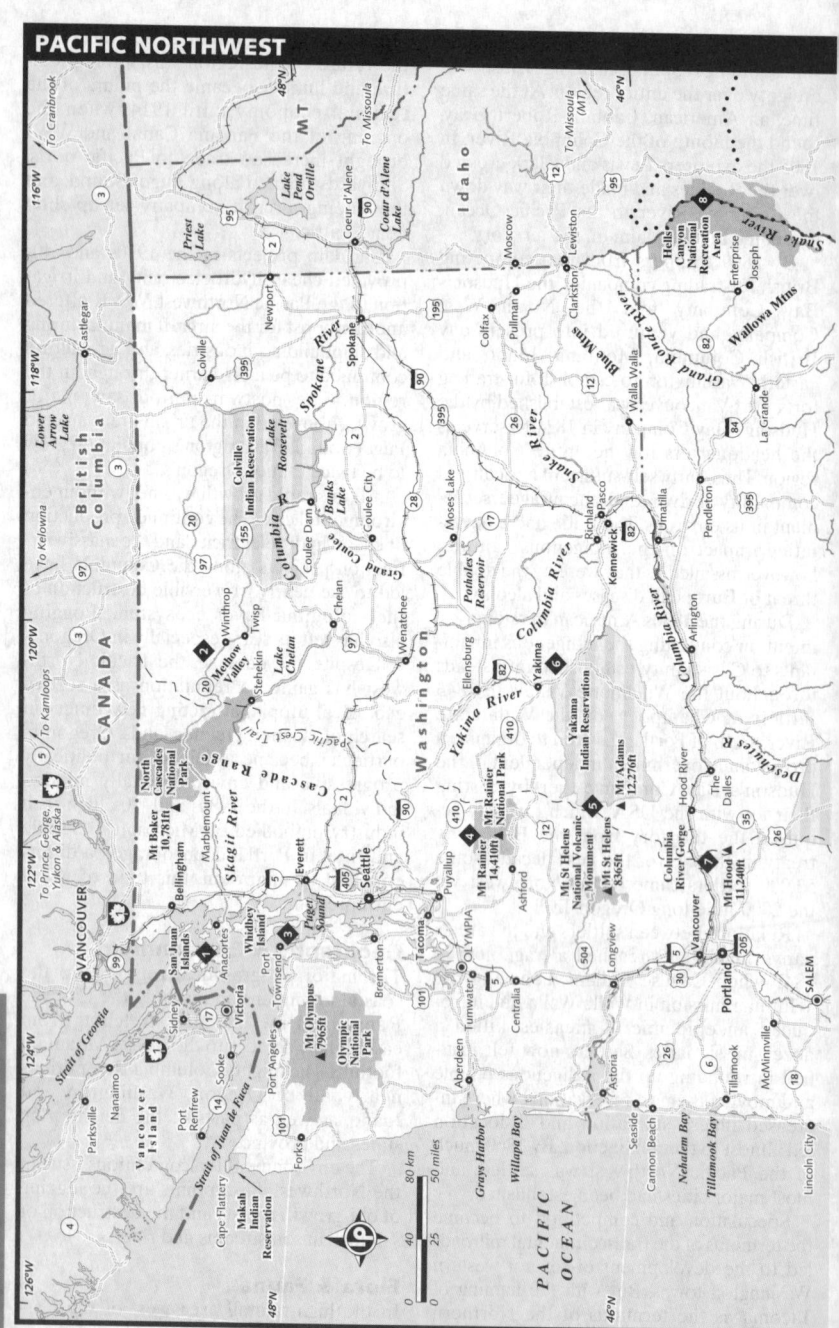

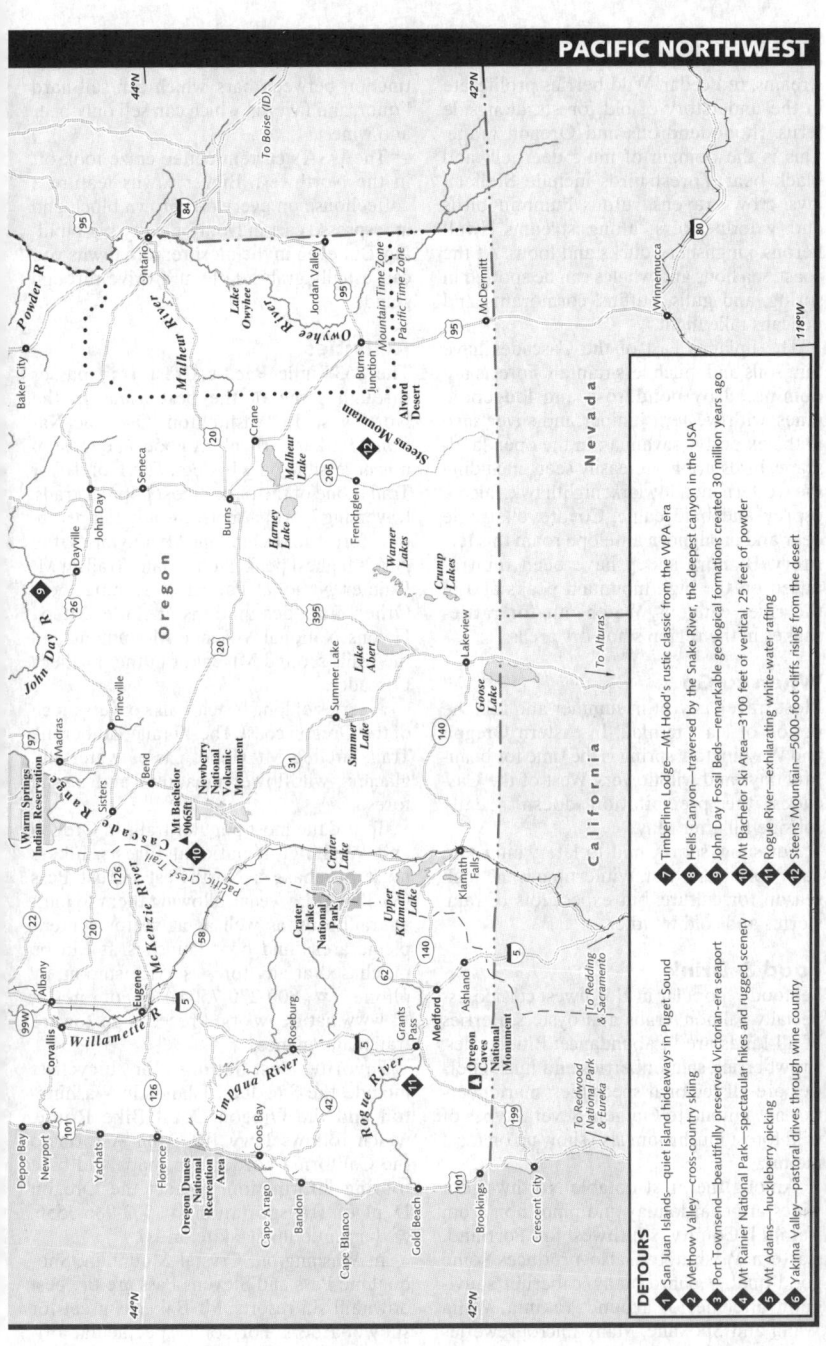

PACIFIC NORTHWEST

DETOURS

1. San Juan Islands—quiet island hideaways in Puget Sound
2. Methow Valley—cross-country skiing
3. Port Townsend—beautifully preserved Victorian-era seaport
4. Mt Rainier National Park—spectacular hikes and rugged scenery
5. Mt Adams—huckleberry picking
6. Yakima Valley—pastoral drives through wine country
7. Timberline Lodge—Mt Hood's rustic classic from the WPA era
8. Hells Canyon—traversed by the Snake River, the deepest canyon in the USA
9. John Day Fossil Beds—remarkable geological formations created 30 million years ago
10. Mt Bachelor Ski Area—3100 feet of vertical, 25 feet of powder
11. Rogue River—exhilarating white-water rafting
12. Steens Mountain—5000-foot cliffs rising from the desert

with Douglas fir, Sitka spruce, western hemlock, maples, oaks and, especially along streams, red cedar. Wild berries proliferate in the understory of old forests, alongside ferns, rhododendrons and Oregon grape. This is the domain of mule deer, elk and black bear. Forest birds include Steller's jays, crows, ravens, rufous hummingbirds and woodpeckers; along streams dwell herons, kingfishers, ducks and loons. At the coast, sea lions and whales can be spotted in spring, and gulls, puffins, cormorants and pelicans take flight.

The uplands east of the Cascades have thin soils and much less rainfall. Forests are dominated by ponderosa and lodgepole pines, with western juniper and silver sage in the extensive savannas. In the open landscape, birds are more easily seen, including the western meadowlark, nighthawk, falcon, osprey and bald eagle. Coyote, elk, mule deer and pronghorn antelope roam this territory. Bighorn sheep have been reintroduced on the high mountain peaks and in the river canyons. Watch out for rattlesnakes in the region's hot, dry areas.

When to Go

Most travelers visit in summer and fall, the period of least rainfall. In eastern Oregon and Washington, spring is the time for beautiful days and wildflowers. West of the Cascades, the precipitation doesn't really subside till after May.

For snow sports, mid to late winter and early spring are best. Wintertime is the high season for culture, but expect lots of rain, storms and cold weather.

Food & Drink

Seafood is popular in Northwest cuisine, especially salmon, crabs and oysters. Berries of all kinds are in abundance: Blueberries, strawberries, salmonberries and huckleberries are all regional specialties; marionberries are unique to Oregon. Several types of wild forest mushroom also show up on local menus.

Among the most notable Northwestern wines are chardonnay and pinot noir from Yamhill County, southwest of Portland. Eastern Washington also produces some good-quality chardonnay, cabernet sauvignon and merlot around Yakima, Walla Walla and Spokane. Many microbreweries in the region provide a broad choice of beers and ales. Note that there is a legal distinction between bars, which can sell hard liquor, and taverns, which can sell only beer and wine.

The USA's current coffee craze took off in the Northwest. Bigger towns feature a coffeehouse on every downtown block and an espresso cart in front of every big building. But even in the most remote towns you can usually grab a latte at a drive-through stand.

Activities

The 2638-mile Pacific Crest Trail passes through some of the best areas in the Northwest. In Washington, Olympic National Park is particularly good, and most of it is accessible only by foot. The Hoh River Trail is one of the park's most popular trails, traversing North America's only temperate rain forest and climbing Mt Olympus, the park's highest peak. Wonderland Trail, in Mt Rainier National Park, is a 93-mile loop. Other fine destinations include Mt St Helens National Volcanic Monument and the trails around Mt Baker in the northern Cascades.

A series of long beach walks covers much of the Oregon coast. The 40-mile Timberline Trail, circling Mt Hood, passes waterfalls, glaciers, wildflower meadows and alpine forests.

To use the most popular trails in Oregon and Washington national forests, hikers must purchase a Northwest Forest Pass ($5/30 per day/year), allowing them to park at trailheads, as well as at visitor centers, picnic areas and boat launches. It can be purchased at any forest service station, by phone (☎ 800-270-7504) or online at Ⓦ www.naturenw.org. Proceeds go toward trail maintenance.

Favorite destinations for bicyclists include the San Juan Islands in Washington and the Oregon Coast Bike Route, which follows Hwy 101 from Astoria to the California border. For maps and bike touring information, contact the Oregon Dept of Transportation (☎ 503-986-3556, ⓔ daryl.m.bonitz@state.or.us).

In Washington, Crystal Mountain, Snoqualmie Pass and Stevens Pass are the best downhill ski resorts; Mt Baker is great for snowboarders. For some spectacular off-the-beaten-path cross-country skiing, try Mt St Helens, Mt Rainier, the Methow area and Olympic National Park.

In Oregon, the Timberline resort at Mt Hood offers downhill skiing nearly year-round, and Mt Bachelor is famous for powder snow. The Rim Drive around Crater Lake is popular with cross-country skiers.

The Skagit, Yakima and Wenatchee Rivers in Washington all offer good white-water rafting. Sea kayaking is excellent in Puget Sound, especially if combined with whale-watching. In Oregon, the Deschutes and the Rogue Rivers both offer good paddling.

Getting There & Around

Air Sea-Tac (Seattle-Tacoma) is the main airport in the Northwest, with daily service to Europe, Asia and points throughout the USA and Canada.

Bus Greyhound provides service along the I-5 corridor and the main east-west routes, with links to some other communities. Local public transit systems in both Oregon and Washington link urban hubs with outlying districts, but they usually are oriented toward commuters, so weekend service is minimal.

Train Amtrak trains to, from and around the Northwest include the following:

Coast Starlight – daily along the US West Coast between Seattle and Los Angeles via Portland and Klamath Falls, Oregon, and Olympia and Tacoma, Washington.

Empire Builder – daily between Chicago and Seattle or Portland, with stops in Wisconsin, Minnesota, North Dakota, Montana and Idaho. This service offers two routes west of Spokane – either to Portland along the Columbia River Gorge, or to Seattle across the Cascade Range.

Cascades – European-style Talgo trains run between Seattle and Portland four times daily. Amtrak's Thruway bus service extends this line north to Vancouver, British Columbia (BC), and south to Eugene, Oregon. One train a day operates between Seattle and Vancouver.

Car & Motorcycle The entire Pacific Coast is a scenic route if it's not shrouded in mist, and the Cascade Range has innumerable lovely drives. Roads skirt both sides of the dramatic Columbia River Gorge, with remnants of the old Columbia River Hwy

retaining some early-20th-century design features. Driving your own vehicle is the most convenient way to tour the Pacific Northwest; major rental agencies can be found throughout the region.

Boat Both passenger-only and car ferries operate around Puget Sound and across to Vancouver Island in British Columbia. Washington State Ferries (☎ 206-464-6400) link Seattle with Bremerton, Bainbridge and Vashon Islands. Other WSF routes cross from Whidbey Island to Port Townsend on the Olympic Peninsula, and from Anacortes, Washington, through the San Juan Islands to Sidney, BC.

Washington

Washington has a postindustrial, trendsetting status in everything from wilderness values to high-tech innovation. Culturally, it runs the gamut from indigenous art to grunge rock. Glaciated peaks overlook dynamic cities and misty harbors. To the east, the arid uplands get 300 days of sunshine a year and offer all-season recreation.

History

The first US settlement in Washington was at Tumwater, on the southern edge of Puget Sound, in 1845. Both Seattle and Port Townsend were established in 1851 and quickly became logging centers. Lumber was shipped at great profit to San Francisco, the boomtown of the California Gold Rush.

In 1853, Washington separated from the Oregon territory. With the massacre at the Whitman mission still fresh in the memories of some settlers, Congress ratified treaties that reduced the land shares open to native hunting and fishing and opened up the eastern part of the state to settlement. The arrival of rail links in the last decades of the century created a readily accessible market for the products of the Pacific Northwest and brought in floods of settlers.

Washington was admitted to the union in 1889, and Seattle began to flourish in 1897, when it became the principal port en route to the Alaska and Yukon goldfields. The construction of the Bonneville Dam (1937) and Grand Coulee Dam (1947) accelerated the region's industrial and agricultural

Washington

Nicknames: Evergreen State, Chinook State

Population: 5,894,100 (15th)

Area: 71,302 sq miles (18th)

Admitted to Union: November 11, 1889 (42nd)

Capital city: Olympia (population 42,500)

Other cities: Seattle (563,400; metro area 3.55 million), Spokane (195,600), Tacoma (193,600), Vancouver (143,600), Bellevue (109,600)

Birthplace of: novelist and social critic Mary McCarthy (1912–89), Jimi Hendrix (1942–70), *Far Side* cartoonist Gary Larson (b 1950)

Famous for: Jumbo jets, apples, Microsoft, Pearl Jam, caffeine culture

development by providing cheap hydro-electric power and irrigation.

The rapid postwar urbanization of the Puget Sound region has created an enormous metropolitan area linked by jammed-up freeways that mar the waterfront vistas. This era has seen Seattle in particular become larger, more affluent and widely recognized as one of the nation's most attractive cities. Most recently, software giant Microsoft, Seattle's music scene and even the Starbucks coffee chain have contributed to Washington's status as a cutting-edge destination.

Government & Politics

Washington has progressive, somewhat maverick politics. With a relatively high proportion of swing voters, the state can support Democrats or Republicans, and votes for third parties will sometimes determine the outcome.

Economy

The traditional engines of the regional economy have been logging and fishing. Boeing, the world's largest aircraft manufacturer, remains the chief economic force of western Washington despite its decision in 2001 to relocate its corporate headquar-

ters to Chicago. The presence of Microsoft has spawned the growth of other large high-tech firms.

Washington is the nation's fifth-largest exporting state, and one in four jobs depends on international trade. Seattle and Tacoma are among the largest ports on the West Coast; Tacoma is the financial center of the Northwest.

Information

The Washington State Tourism Office (☎ 360-725-5052, 🅆 www.tourism.wa.gov) sends out information. Washington State Parks (☎ 360-902-8500, 800-233-0321, 🅆 www.parks.wa.gov) is a useful source for camping and outdoor activities. For winter highway conditions, call ☎ 206-368-4499 in Seattle or ☎ 800-695-7623 elsewhere in Washington. State sales tax is 6.5%, but county and city taxes can bring that up to 8% or more.

Western Washington has switched to a 10-digit dialing system for local calls. To make a local call within the 206, 253, 425, 360 and 564 area codes, you must dial the area code first (without dialing 1 first, as for long-distance calls).

SEATTLE

Washington's largest city (population 563,374) sits on a slim isthmus between two bodies of water, Puget Sound to the west and Lake Washington to the east. This once conservative and tranquil town now boasts solid success as a trade, manufacturing and high-tech center (computer giant Microsoft dominates life in the sprawling suburb of Redmond). One of the fastest-growing metropolitan areas in the USA, the 'Emerald City' has become an exporter of trends. Seattle has made coffee a national obsession; its homegrown grunge rock swept the nation in the 1990s; and TV series and movies base themselves in Seattle in order to partake of the city's hip but quirky cultural and social life. The coastal mountains and the many islands and fingers of land and water that make up the complex geography of Puget Sound give Seattle one of the most beautiful settings of any US city.

History

The Lake Washington area was originally home to the Duwamish, a Salish tribe. The seaport potential of the sound attracted a group of settlers led by David Denny in 1851. They first settled on Alki Point, in present-day West Seattle. The colony was named Seattle for the Duwamish chief Sealth.

In 1893 Seattle was linked to the rest of the country by rail. During this decade the city became the provisioning point for prospectors headed to the Yukon gold territory, and the banking center for the fortunes made there. The boom continued through WWI, when Northwest lumber was in great demand and the Puget Sound area prospered as a shipbuilding center. In 1916 William Boeing founded the aircraft manufacturing business that would become one of the largest employers in Seattle, attracting tens of thousands of newcomers to the region during WWII.

In more recent years, the growth of Microsoft and other software developers has made it increasingly difficult to find someone who isn't a contractor, caterer or car dealer for the Microsoft crowd.

A series of calamitous events around the turn of the millennium seemed calculated to deflate the confidence of even the most upbeat Seattleites. In November 1999, the city drew attention as protesters and police clashed violently outside a World Trade Organization summit. In June 2000 a federal judge ruled that Microsoft should be split up as a result of its monopolistic business practices (the decision was later overturned). Then, on February 28, 2001, a 6.8-magnitude earthquake near the state capital caused billions of dollars' worth of damages (though, miraculously, little loss of life). Just a few weeks later came the ultimate kick in the teeth: Boeing announced its intention to relocate its headquarters to Chicago.

Orientation

The historic downtown area, Pioneer Square, includes the area between Cherry and S King Sts, along 1st to 3rd Ave. The main shopping area is along 4th and 5th Aves from Olive Way down to University St. Just north of downtown is Seattle Center, with many of the city's cultural and sporting facilities, as well as the Space Needle. Alaskan Way is the Waterfront's main drag; the Waterfront Streetcar runs the length of it.

Information

The visitor center (☎ 206-461-5840) is at the Washington State Convention & Trade Center at 7th Ave and Pike St. A good

---

Bill Gates: Richest Guy on Earth

William Gates III, born October 28, 1955, grew up in Seattle's upper-class Laurelhurst neighborhood and began developing software at the age of 13. In college at Harvard, Gates hung out in the computer lab and whipped up programming language for the world's first microcomputer.

Eventually Gates dropped out of Harvard and hooked up with his buddy Paul Allen; the two went on to develop DOS, then the Windows operating systems. At the age of 37, Gates became the second-richest man in the USA and, soon after, the richest man not only in the country but in the world, with a fortune estimated at $48 billion.

Few Bill Gates stories generate more tongue wagging than that of the Gates mansion in Medina, on Lake Washington. Built to represent the ultimate in high-tech living, this 48,000-sq-foot structure boasts such features as walls made of video monitors and music sensors that are electronically programmed to play selected tunes as one wanders from room to room. The price tag? An estimated $40 million. From Luther Burbank Park on the northeast corner of Mercer Island, you can see the mansion across the lake if you know where to look.

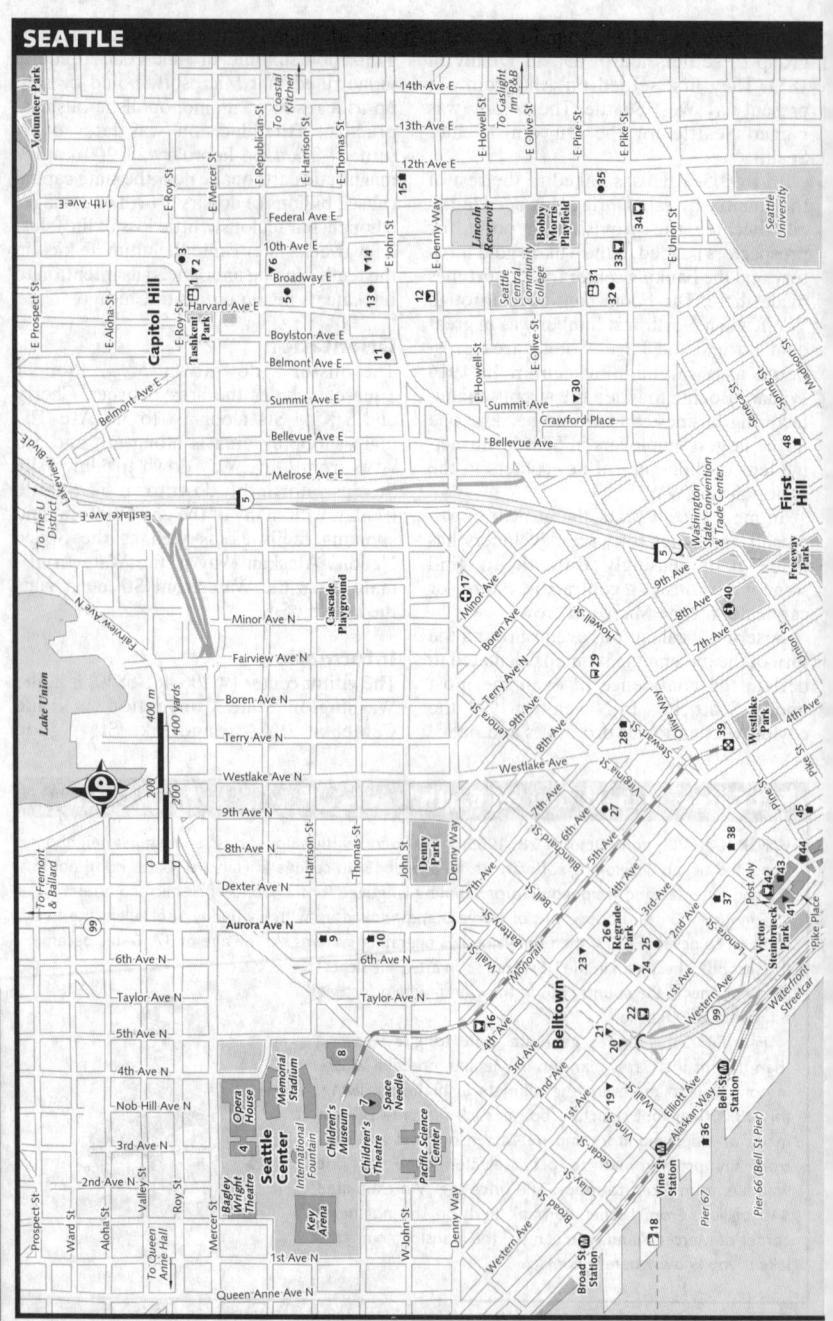

SEATTLE

SEATTLE

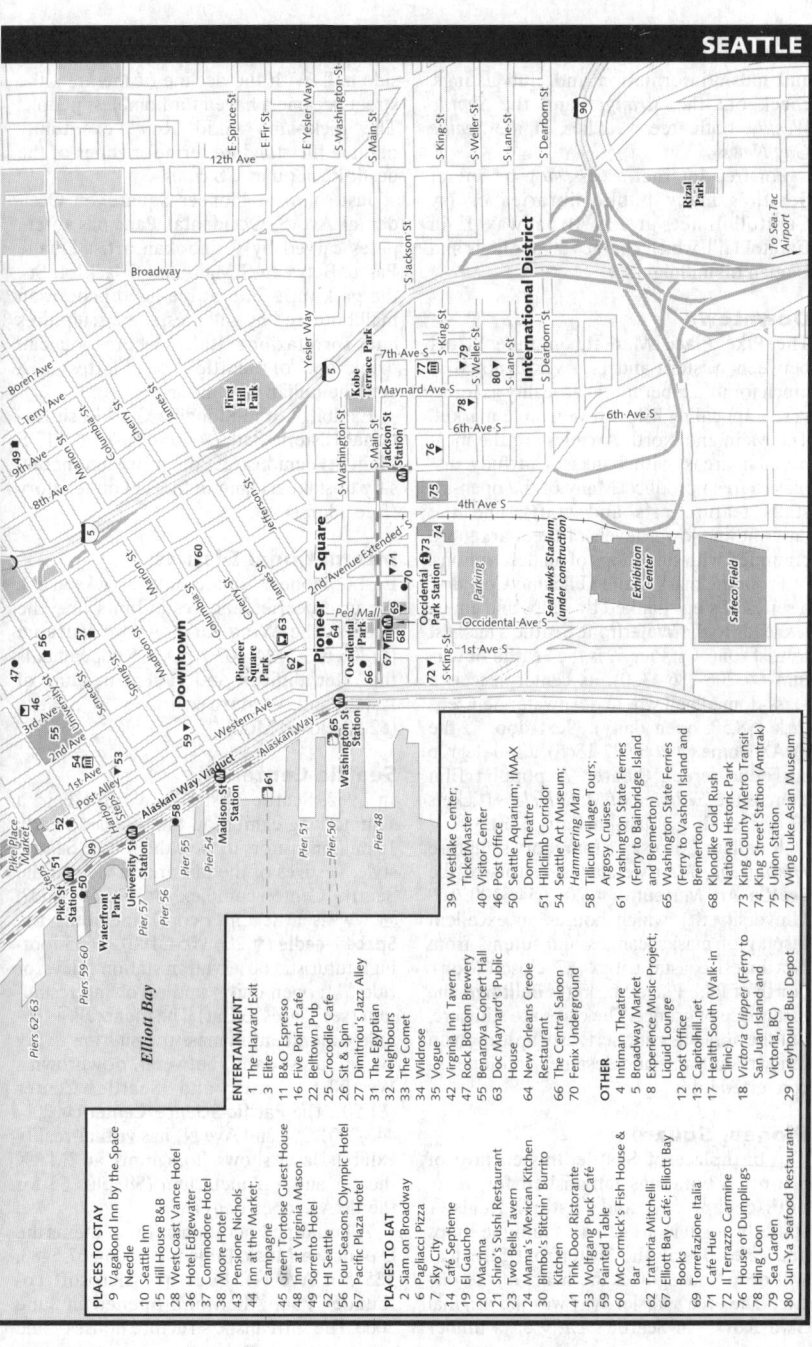

PACIFIC NORTHWEST

PLACES TO STAY
9 Vagabond Inn by the Space Needle
10 Seattle Inn
15 Hill House B&B
28 WestCoast Vance Hotel
36 Hotel Edgewater
37 Commodore Hotel
38 Moore Hotel
43 Pensione Nichols
44 Inn at the Market; Campagne
45 Green Tortoise Guest House
48 Inn at Virginia Mason
49 Sorrento Hotel
52 HI Seattle
56 Four Seasons Olympic Hotel
57 Pacific Plaza Hotel

PLACES TO EAT
2 Siam on Broadway
6 Pagliacci Pizza
7 Sky City
14 Café Septieme
19 El Gaucho
20 Macrina
23 Shiro's Sushi Restaurant
24 Two Bells Tavern
30 Mama's Mexican Kitchen
34 Bimbo's Bitchin' Burrito Kitchen
41 Pink Door Ristorante
53 Wolfgang Puck Café
59 Painted Table
60 McCormick's Fish House & Bar
62 Trattoria Mitchelli
67 Elliott Bay Café; Elliott Bay Books
69 Torrefazione Italia
71 Cafe Hue
72 Il Terrazzo Carmine
76 House of Dumplings
78 Hing Loon
79 Sea Garden
80 Sun-Ya Seafood Restaurant

ENTERTAINMENT
1 The Harvard Exit
3 Elite
11 B&O Espresso
16 Five Point Cafe
22 Belltown Pub
26 Crocodile Cafe
27 Sit & Spin
27 Dimitriou's Jazz Alley
31 The Egyptian
32 Neighbours
33 The Comet
35 Vogue
42 Virginia Inn Tavern
47 Rock Bottom Brewery
55 Benaroya Concert Hall
63 Doc Maynard's Public House
64 New Orleans Creole Restaurant
66 The Central Saloon
70 Fenix Underground

OTHER
4 Intiman Theatre
5 Broadway Market
8 Experience Music Project; Liquid Lounge
12 Post Office
13 Capitolhill.net
17 Health South (Walk-in Clinic)
18 Victoria Clipper (Ferry to San Juan Island and Victoria, BC)
29 Greyhound Bus Depot
39 Westlake Center; TicketMaster
40 Visitor Center
46 Post Office
50 Seattle Aquarium; IMAX Dome Theatre
51 Hillclimb Corridor
54 Seattle Art Museum; Hammering Man
58 Tillicum Village Tours; Argosy Cruises
61 Washington State Ferries (Ferry to Bainbridge Island and Bremerton)
65 Washington State Ferries (Ferry to Vashon Island and Bremerton)
68 Klondike Gold Rush National Historic Park
73 King County Metro Transit
74 King Street Station (Amtrak)
75 Union Station
77 Wing Luke Asian Museum

source for entertainment listings is 'The Ticket,' in Thursday's *Seattle Times*. For film and music information and club listings, check out the *Stranger* and the *Seattle Weekly*, both free weeklies, or the *Seattle Gay News*.

For free Internet access, stop by any of Seattle's many public libraries or try Capitolhill.net, at 219 Broadway E in Capitol Hill, which charges $6 per hour and is open till midnight.

Downtown

The **Pike Place Market**, on Pike Street between Western and 1st Aves, is noted as much for its exuberant theatricality as for its vastly appealing fish and vegetable market. The Main and North Arcades are the most popular areas, with banks of artfully displayed fresh produce. Many of the open-air stalls feature arts and crafts, and the labyrinthine lower levels of the market are crammed with tiny shops of all descriptions.

From the market, the Hillclimb Corridor, a series of steps flanked by shops and eateries, leads to the **Waterfront**, Seattle's tackiest tourist zone. On Pier 59 is the **Seattle Aquarium** (☎ 206-386-4320); its centerpiece is a glass-domed hall where deepwater denizens lurk ($8.50; open daily). Next door is the **IMAX Dome** (☎ 206-622-1868), a 180-degree surround-screen theater. A popular film there is the *Eruption of Mt St Helens* (tickets $7 or, including aquarium entry, $13).

Jonathan Borofsky's four-story sculpture *Hammering Man* welcomes visitors to the **Seattle Art Museum** (☎ 206-654-3100, 100 University St), which houses an excellent display of masks, canoes and totems from Northwest coastal tribes ($7; closed Mon). North of Pike Place Market is **Belltown**, the birthplace of grunge. The clubs are still here, but the area has gone seriously upscale, with fancy restaurants and designer boutiques in converted lofts.

Pioneer Square

The birthplace of Seattle, this enclave of red-brick buildings languished for years until cheap rents and Historic Register status brought in art galleries, antique shops and cafes. Today the Waterfront Streetcar will drop you right in the heart of the district. The area's Yesler Way was the original Skid Row – in Seattle's early days timber would 'skid' down the road from a logging camp above town to Henry Yesler's pier-side mill. With the decline of the area, the street became a haven for homeless people. The nickname 'Skid Row' eventually became the standard term for zones of the destitute in other US cities.

Just south of Pioneer Square, on Occidental Ave S, **Occidental Park** has totem poles carved by Chinookan artist Duane Pasco. Between S Main and S Jackson Sts, the park turns into a tree-lined pedestrian mall bordered by galleries, some sculptures and Torrefazione Italia, where you can drink one of Seattle's best lattes in a genuine Italian ceramic *tazza*.

Exhibits at the **Klondike Gold Rush National Historic Park** (☎ 206-553-7220, 117 S Main St) demonstrate the provisions necessary to stake a claim in the Yukon territory (free admission).

International District

East of Pioneer Square (take S Jackson St), Asian groceries and restaurants line the streets. The **Wing Luke Asian Museum** (☎ 206-623-5124, 407 7th Ave S) documents the often difficult and violent meeting of Asian and Western cultures in Seattle ($2.50; closed Mon).

Seattle Center

In 1962, Seattle hosted a World's Fair, a summerlong exhibition that enticed nearly 10 million visitors to view the future, Seattle style. Vestiges of the fair are on view at the Seattle Center complex (☎ 206-684-8582, Ⓦ www.seattlecenter.com), including the **Space Needle** (☎ 206-905-2100), a 605-foot-high futuristic observation station (elevator ride $11; open daily) and revolving restaurant (see Places to Eat). The **monorail**, a 1½-mile experiment in mass transit, runs every 10 minutes daily between downtown's Westlake Center and Seattle Center ($1.50). The **Pacific Science Center** (☎ 206-443-2001, 200 2nd Ave N) has virtual-reality exhibits, laser shows, holograms, an IMAX theater and a planetarium ($8, plus $3 for the IMAX; open daily).

A brand-new addition to the center is the **Experience Music Project** (☎ 206-367-5483, 325 5th Ave N), built by Microsoft co-founder Paul Allen and opened in June 2000. The surrealistic structure houses some

80,000 artifacts of music memorabilia, including handwritten lyrics by Nirvana's Kurt Cobain and a Fender Stratocaster demolished by Jimi Hendrix ($20).

Capitol Hill
This area has long been a countercultural oasis, and as the principal gay and lesbian neighborhood, it has an unmatched vitality. Capitol Hill is about 1.5 miles northeast of downtown. Take bus No 7 or 10 and get off at **Broadway**. The junction of Broadway and E John St (the continuation of Olive Way) is the core of activity. Continue north to stately **Volunteer Park**, on E Prospect St, originally Seattle's cemetery. The **Seattle Asian Art Museum** (☎ 206-654-3100), within the park, houses an extensive collection of paintings, sculptures, ceramics and textiles of Japan, China and Korea ($3, ticket also valid at the Seattle Art Museum downtown; closed Mon). Also in Volunteer Park is the glass-sided Victorian **conservatory**, filled with palms, cacti and tropical plants (free admission).

If you're driving, your best bet is to park in the pay lot on Harvard Ave E, behind the Broadway Market.

Fremont
Fun-loving Fremont, about 2 miles north of the Seattle Center, is known for its unorthodox public sculpture, junk stores, summer outdoor film festival and general high spirits. **Fremont Ave N** is the main strip. Probably the most discussed piece of public art in the city, *Waiting for the Interurban* is a cast aluminum statue of ordinary people awaiting a train that never comes; the Interurban linking Seattle and Everett stopped running in the 1930s (in 2001 Sound Transit trains resumed the long dormant run). The *Fremont Troll,* a mammoth cement figure consuming an entire VW bug carcass, lives under the Aurora Bridge.

The U District
The University of Washington campus sits at the edge of this busy commercial area about 3 miles northeast of downtown. The main streets are University Way, also known as **'the Ave,'** and NE 45th St, both with inexpensive restaurants, bars, cinemas and bookstores. The center of the campus is

Central Plaza, known as Red Square because of its base of red brick. Get information and a campus map at the visitor center (☎ 206-543-9198, 4014 University Way). Near the junction of 16th Ave NE and NE 45th St is the **Burke Museum**, with an excellent collection of Northwest Coast Indian artifacts ($5.50; open daily). At the corner of 15th Ave NE and NE 41st St is the **Henry Art Gallery** (☎ 206-543-2280), with some of the most intelligent exhibits in Seattle ($5; closed Mon).

More than 5500 plant species grow in the wild and lovely **Washington Park Arboretum** (☎ 206-543-8800), just south of the campus. Get trail guides at the visitor center, 2300 Arboretum Dr E (free tours Sun at 1pm). At the northern edge of the arboretum is a wonderful **wetlands trail** around Foster Island in Lake Washington's Union Bay.

Ballard & the Canal
Northwest of Seattle, the waters of Lake Washington and Lake Union flow through the 8-mile-long Lake Washington Ship Canal and into Puget Sound. Construction of the canal began in 1911; today 100,000 boats a year pass through the **Hiram M Chittenden Locks**. Viewing the vessels as they traverse the two locks is a popular pastime. On the southern side of the locks is a **fish ladder** that enables salmon to make their way to spawning grounds in the Cascade headwaters of the Sammamish River, which feeds Lake Washington. Visitors can watch the fish from underwater glass-sided tanks. The locks are at 3015 NW 54th St, about a half mile west of Ballard off NW Market St.

The community of Ballard is often referred to as the Viking North because of its early-20th-century settlement by Scandinavians, who established Seattle's fishing fleet.

Today's fishing fleet resides at **Fishermen's Terminal**, on the south end of the Ballard Bridge at 19th Ave and W Nickerson St. Within the terminal buildings are several restaurants that offer the freshest seafood in Seattle.

Activities
You can go **hiking** through old-growth forest at Seward Park, dominating the Bailey Peninsula that juts into Lake Washington, or

on longer trails in 534-acre Discovery Park, northwest of Seattle at the mouth of Chittenden Locks. Hikers and bikers use the Burke-Gilman Trail, which extends for 16½ miles from Gas Works Park on the northern shores of Lake Washington north to Kenmore. Rent a **bicycle** at Al Young Bike and Ski (☎ 206-524-2642, 3615 NE 45th St), or at Gregg's Greenlake Cycle (☎ 206-523-1822, 7007 Woodlawn Ave NE).

The Sierra Club (☎ 206-523-2019) leads day-hiking and car-camping trips on weekends; most day trips are free. The outdoor-gear outfitter REI organizes year-round recreational activities; call REI Adventure Travel (☎ 206-223-1944, 800-622-2236).

Northwest Outdoor Center Inc (☎ 206-281-9694, 2100 Westlake Ave N), on Lake Union, rents kayaks and offers tours and instruction in sea and white-water **kayaking**. The UW Waterfront Activities Center (☎ 206-543-9433), at the southeast corner of the Husky Stadium parking lot, off Montake Blvd NE, rents canoes and rowboats. Bring along an ID or passport.

Green Lake and Lake Washington are popular for **windsurfing**. Green Lake Boat Rentals (☎ 206-527-0171, 7351 E Green Lake Dr) provides lessons and rentals.

Organized Tours
Gray Line of Seattle (☎ 206-626-5208, W www.graylineofseattle.com) and Show Me Seattle (☎ 206-633-2489, W www.showmeseattle.com) both run city tours. Argosy Cruises (☎ 206-623-1445), at Pier 56, has cruises from $15.

Seattle's Underground Tour explores a network of subterranean chambers that predate the Great Fire and subsequent rebuilding of the district above the tide flats. Tours leave daily from Doc Maynard's Public House (☎ 206-682-4646, 610 1st Ave), in Pioneer Square ($8; reservations are advised).

Special Events
Chinese New Year (☎ 206-382-1197) is celebrated with parades, fireworks and food in the International District (Jan or late Feb). The Northwest Folklife Festival (☎ 206-684-7300) includes international music, dance, crafts, food and family activities at the Seattle Center (Memorial Day weekend in May).

Seafair (☎ 206-728-0123, W www.seafair.com) has hydroplane races, a torchlight parade, an air show, music and a carnival (late July and Aug). Bumbershoot (☎ 206-281-8111, W www.bumbershoot.com) is a major arts and cultural event at Seattle Center (Labor Day weekend, in Sept).

Places to Stay
The Seattle Hotel Hotline (☎ 206-461-5882) has a free reservation service. For a list of bed and breakfast inns, try the Seattle B&B Association (☎ 206-547-1020), PO Box 31772, Seattle, WA 98103-1772.

Downtown For hostelers, *HI Seattle* (☎ 206-622-5443, e reserve@hiseattle.org, 84 Union St) is central to the Waterfront and Pike Place Market ($17 members; $20 non-members). *Green Tortoise Guest House* (☎ 206-340-1222, 1525 2nd Ave) has dorm beds for $17 and private rooms for $40.

Near Pike Place Market, the charming *Pensione Nichols* (☎ 206-441-7125, 1923 1st Ave) has B&B-style lodging from $75/95 singles/doubles.

Pricier but well located is *Pacific Plaza Hotel* (☎ 206-623-3900, 400 Spring St), from $110. Rooms at the *WestCoast Vance Hotel* (☎ 206-441-4200, 620 Stewart St) start at $120 (less in winter). The *Inn at Virginia Mason* (☎ 206-583-6453, 1006 Spring St), on First Hill just above downtown, has a nice rooftop garden and quiet rooms from $125.

Right in the thick of Pike Place, the *Inn at the Market* (☎ 206-443-3600, 86 Pine St) offers rooms from $190, most with views over Puget Sound. Several historic hotels provide atmospheric lodging in the center of town: *Sorrento Hotel* (☎ 206-622-6400, W www.hotelsorrento.com, 900 Madison St), with rooms from $215, and the *Four Seasons Olympic Hotel* (☎ 206-621-1700, 411 University St), from $195.

Belltown Some of the best deals in the city are found in Belltown. Rooms at the once grand *Moore Hotel* (☎ 206-448-4851, 1926 2nd Ave) start at $39/49 singles/doubles. The newly renovated *Commodore Hotel* (☎ 206-448-8868, 2013 2nd Ave) has rooms from $59, including breakfast.

On Aurora Ave N are the *Seattle Inn* (☎ 206-728-7666), with rooms from $79, and the *Vagabond Inn by the Space Needle*

(☎ 206-441-0400, 800-522-1555), with singles/doubles from $94/105. *Hotel Edgewater* (☎ 206-728-7000, 2411 Alaskan Way) faces onto Elliott Bay. A waterfront suite can set you back as much as $425 in peak season; rooms off the water are about $100 less.

Capitol Hill & The U District On Capitol Hill, *Gaslight Inn B&B* (☎ 206-325-3654, 1727 15th Ave E), with a pool and hot tub, has rooms from $78. *Hill House B&B* (☎ 206-720-7161, 1113 E John St), in a restored 1903 home, charges $80/95 and up for rooms with shared/private bath.

Off I-5 exit 169 are a number of moderately priced motels near the University of Washington. For rooms between $70 and $105, try *University Plaza Hotel* (☎ 206-634-0100, 400 NE 45th St), or *University Inn* (☎ 206-632-5055, 4140 Roosevelt Way NE).

Places to Eat
Downtown For cheap eats, go to the food court at Westlake Center, 4th Ave and Pine St. *McCormick's Fish House & Bar* (722 4th Ave) has daily inexpensive fresh fish specials. The *Painted Table* (92 Madison St) is an unpretentious restaurant in the Alexis Hotel featuring Pacific Rim cuisine.

Head to Pike Place Market for a wide selection of fresh produce, bakery products, deli items and take-out ethnic foods. *Copacabana Cafe*, in the Triangle Building, has inexpensive Andean dishes. The mid-priced *Place Pigalle* (81 Pike St) offers great views over the bay and inventive Latin- and Asian-influenced dishes. *Pink Door Ristorante* (1919 Post Alley) has pasta lunch dishes for $8. On the street just below the market is the popular *Typhoon!* (1400 Western Ave), featuring Thai food artistry. Also outside the market and recommended is *Wolfgang Puck Café* (1225 1st Ave), with pizza, salads and pasta. *Campagne* (86 Pine St), inside the Inn at the Market, is Seattle's best traditional French restaurant (entrées $25-35). *Chez Shea* (94 Pike St) is a treasure with great views over the sound and four courses for $40.

Belltown & Seattle Center Belltown is the uncontested center of fine dining in Seattle. Fortunately, there's still an abundance of delis and inexpensive taverns in the area. *Mama's Mexican Kitchen* (2234 2nd Ave) has $6 burritos. The venerable *Two Bells Tavern* (2313 4th Ave) serves some of Seattle's best burgers. For excellent, well-priced sushi, head to *Shiro's Sushi Restaurant* (2401 2nd Ave). On 1st Ave at Battery St there's *Macrina*, an artsy bakery that also serves light lunches. *El Gaucho* (2505 1st Ave) is a modern, hip re-creation of a 1950s supper club, with massive steaks and a stylish clientele. A contender for Seattle's best formal Italian restaurant, *Lampreia* (☎ 206-443-3301, 2400 1st Ave) specializes in grilled meat and poultry.

Head to Seattle Center for dinner in the Space Needle tower at *Sky City* (☎ 206-443-2111). The restaurant is expensive, but the elevator is free, and the views are priceless.

Pioneer Square Stop by *Cafe Hue* (312 2nd Ave S), an inexpensive Vietnamese restaurant with colonial French influences. *Elliott Bay Café* (☎ 206-682-6664, 101 S Main St), downstairs from Elliott Bay Books, is a cozy place for soup, salad and sandwiches. *Trattoria Mitchelli* (84 Yesler Way) serves good pasta till 4am (entrées from $10; Tue-Sat). *Il Terrazzo Carmine* (☎ 206-467-7797, 411 1st Ave S) is a showcase of European luxury, serving excellent many-coursed Italian meals.

International District This neighborhood's best deals are found at the many Vietnamese, Thai and Chinese restaurants that line S Jackson St between 6th and 12th Aves. *Hing Loon* (628 S Weller St) specializes in seafood dishes; garlic prawns cost $9.25. A bit pricier but of higher quality is *Sea Garden* (509 7th Ave S). For the best dim sum, try *Sun-Ya Seafood Restaurant* (605 7th Ave). For a cheap snack or meal, there's *House of Dumplings* (510 S King St).

Capitol Hill & the U District Broadway has no end of good, inexpensive places to eat. *Siam on Broadway* (616 E Broadway) is a Thai food favorite; *Pagliacci Pizza* (426 E Broadway) is a by-the-slice place; and *Café Septieme* (214 E Broadway) is a trendy space with unfussy homemade grub. *Bimbo's Bitchin' Burrito Kitchen* (506 E Pine St) serves huge $5 burritos till 2am. East of Broadway, *Coastal Kitchen* (429 15th Ave E) offers an eclectic mix of Cajun, Mayan and Mexican inspirations.

PACIFIC NORTHWEST

Adjacent to the University of Washington is University Way, with loads of cheap restaurants and cafes. Recommended are *Schultzy's Sausages (4142 University Way)*; *Araya's Place (4732 University Way)* for vegetarian Thai fare; and *Tandoor (5024 University Way)*.

Entertainment

Consult the *Seattle Weekly,* the *Stranger* or the arts sections of the daily papers for entertainment listings. Tickets for most events are available at TicketMaster (☎ 206-628-0888), which operates a discount ticket booth at Westlake Center (☎ 206-233-1111). Day-of-performance tickets are extra cheap.

Coffeehouses Seattle's java fanaticism has revitalized the coffeehouse as a social space that offers poetry readings, drama and acoustic music. In Belltown, *Sit & Spin (2219 4th Ave)* is a combination coffeehouse, bar, live music venue and Laundromat. *Uptown Espresso Bar (525 Queen Anne Ave N),* between Mercer and Republican Sts, is an after-show place.

On Capitol Hill are *B&O Espresso (204 Belmont Ave E),* a pleasant spot for some postcard scribbling, and the *Globe Cafe (1531 14th Ave),* south of Pine St, with music and readings. Near the university are *Café Allegro (4214 University Way NE)* and *Grand Illusion (1405 NE 50th Ave).*

Bars & Brew Pubs If you're looking for late-night action, make for Capitol Hill's **Pike-Pine Corridor**, extending from Broadway to about 12th Ave, home to a plethora of arty live-music clubs and taverns. *The Comet (☎ 206-323-9853, 922 E Pike St)* is a no-frills institution with cheap beer and loyal locals.

The Corridor is also the main gay nightlife district, with a number of gay-oriented dance clubs and coffeehouses. *Wildrose (☎ 206-324-9210, 1021 E Pike St)* is a comfortable lesbian bar.

For a good overview of the club scene in Pioneer Square, spring for the $5 joint cover ($10 Fri and Sat) that lets you in to about 10 clubs, many with live jazz and blues. Pay the cover and pick up a list of participating clubs at the Central or New Orleans Creole Restaurant (see Live Music, below). Most of the participating clubs are on 1st Ave S.

The *Rock Bottom Brewery (☎ 206-623-3070, 1333 5th Ave),* in Rainier Square, is downtown's only brew pub. In Belltown, the *Virginia Inn Tavern (☎ 206-728-1937, 1937 1st Ave)* and the *Belltown Pub (☎ 206-728-4311, 2322 1st Ave)* are both friendly bars with tons of atmosphere.

Near Seattle Center is *Five Point Cafe (☎ 206-448-9993, 415 Cedar St),* in Tillicum Square, a popular hangout for old-timers as well as bikers and young hipsters. The *Liquid Lounge (☎ 206-770-2777, 325 5th Ave N),* upstairs at the Experience Music Project, is a cool spot with live acts Tue to Sat nights and no cover.

In the U District is the rowdy *Big Time Microbrew & Music (4133 University Way NE). Blue Moon Tavern (712 NE 45th St)* is a dive made famous by the people who hung out there, like Jack Kerouac and Allen Ginsberg.

Live Music & Dance Clubs The cult of grunge rock is generally considered passé now, but it did force Seattle's club scene into existence. The city's live-music venues host a spectrum of sounds, from world music to folk to jazz to rock & roll. Don't miss *Crocodile Cafe (☎ 206-441-5611, 2200 2nd Ave)* in Belltown, a genuine institution and springboard for local bands. The center for clubbing in Pioneer Square is the *Fenix Underground (☎ 206-467-1111, 315 2nd Ave S).* In Ballard, try *Tractor Tavern (☎ 206-789-3599, 5213 Ballard Ave NW).* For jazz, head to *Dimitriou's Jazz Alley (☎ 206-441-9729, 2033 6th Ave),* at Lenora St, or *New Orleans Creole Restaurant (☎ 206-622-2563, 114 1st Ave S),* near Pioneer Square. Just down the street is the city's best blues club, the *Central Saloon (☎ 206-622-0209, 207 1st Ave S).*

Vogue (☎ 206-324-5778, 1516 11th Ave N) has varied DJ-driven music. For a mostly gay male disco scene, head to *Neighbours (☎ 206-324-5358, 1509 Broadway Ave E)* – enter in the alley – or *Elite (☎ 206-324-4470, 622 Broadway Ave E).*

Theater Seattle boasts one of the most vibrant theater scenes on the West Coast. *A Contemporary Theatre (☎ 206-292-7676, 700 Union St)*, at Kreielsheimer Place, produces excellent performances year round. Seattle Repertory Theatre performs at the *Bagley Wright Theatre (☎ 206-443-2222)*, and Intiman Theatre Company, Seattle's oldest, takes the stage at the *Intiman Playhouse (☎ 206-269-1900)*. Both theaters front on Mercer St, the north side of Seattle Center.

Classical Music & Dance The *Seattle Symphony (☎ 206-215-4747)* has risen to prominence as a major regional ensemble; it plays at the Benaroya Concert Hall, downtown at 2nd Ave and University St. The *Seattle Opera (☎ 206-389-7676)* isn't afraid to tackle weighty or nontraditional works. Performances are at the Opera House in Seattle Center, also home to the *Pacific Northwest Ballet (☎ 206-441-9411)*.

Cinemas At opposite ends of Capitol Hill are two of the city's best art cinemas, the *Egyptian (☎ 206-323-4978, 805 E Pine St)* and the *Harvard Exit (☎ 206-323-8986, 807 E Roy St)*. Both are key venues during the three-week Seattle International Film Festival *(☎ 206-464-5830)*, in late May/early June.

Spectator Sports

Seattle has a full complement of professional teams; for tickets, try TicketMaster (☎ 206-628-0888). The Seattle Mariners baseball team (☎ 206-628-3555) plays in the new Safeco Field just south of downtown. The Seattle Seahawks (☎ 206-827-9777) pro football club temporarily uses UW's Husky Stadium, pending construction of their new stadium. The Supersonics, Seattle's National Basketball Association franchise (☎ 206-283-3865), draws huge crowds at Seattle Center's Key Arena. The Huskies are the enormously popular University of Washington football team; for information and tickets, call ☎ 206-543-2200.

Getting There & Away

Air Seattle's airport, known as Sea-Tac, is 13 miles south of Seattle on I-5. Sea-Tac has daily service to Europe, Asia and points throughout the USA and Canada, with fre-

quent flights to/from Portland and Vancouver, British Columbia. Small commuter airlines link Seattle to the San Juan Islands, Bellingham, Wenatchee, Yakima and Spokane.

Bus The Greyhound station (☎ 206-628-5561), at 8th Ave and Stewart St, has connections to Portland, Oregon, and other cities on the I-5 corridor, as well as east to Spokane and on to Chicago. Regular service includes the following destinations:

Portland – $22; 4 hours; 10 daily
San Francisco – $59; from 19 hours; 5 daily
Spokane – $28; from 5½ hours; 4 daily
Vancouver, BC – $20.50; 4 hours; 9 daily
Yakima – $23; 3½ hours; 3 daily

The Quick Shuttle (☎ 800-665-2122) has daily express runs between Seattle and Vancouver, British Columbia. Pickup is either at the airport ($39 to Vancouver) or the City Center Travelodge, at 2213 8th Ave ($31).

Train Amtrak (☎ 800-872-7245, 303 S Jackson St) serves the following destinations. Fares vary widely, depending on advance purchase, season and availability; average fares are given here:

Chicago – via Spokane, WA; $276; 2 days; 1 daily
Portland – $26; from 3½ hours; 4 daily
San Francisco – $133; 23 hours; 1 daily
Vancouver, BC – via Bellingham, WA; $34; 4 hours; 1 daily

Car & Motorcycle Taxes make renting a car in Seattle expensive. That said, most national car rental agencies have booths at the airport and downtown. The following agencies are downtown: Avis (☎ 206-448-1700), Budget (☎ 206-448-1940), Dollar (☎ 206-682-1316), Hertz (☎ 206-903-6260), National (☎ 206-448-7368), Rent A Wreck (☎ 800-876-4670) and Thrifty (☎ 206-625-1133).

Boat Washington State Ferries (☎ 206-464-6400, in Washington only ☎ 800-843-3779) operates routes to many Washington destinations, including Bremerton and Bainbridge Island, and to Sidney, BC. Clipper Navigation (☎ 206-448-5000) runs the passenger-only *Victoria Clipper*, which departs Pier 69 for Victoria four times daily in summer ($66/109 one way/roundtrip; 3 hours), with the first departure making a stop at San Juan Island.

Getting Around

Gray Line runs an Airport Express (☎ 206-626-6088) between Sea-Tac and major downtown hotels every 15 minutes from 5am to 11pm ($8.50/14 one-way/roundtrip). Or, catch Metro Transit bus No 174 or 194 ($1.75) outside the baggage claim area.

Metro Transit (☎ 206-553-3000, 800-542-7876) serves the greater Seattle metropolitan area. All bus rides are free 6am-7pm in the area between 6th Ave and the Waterfront, and between Pioneer Square and Battery St in Belltown (note that Seattle Center is not within the ride-free zone). Fares are $1.50/1.25 during peak (6-9am and 3-6pm)/off-peak hours. Buy tickets in advance and get a system map at the King County Metro Transit office (201 S Jackson St), or at the Westlake Center bus tunnel station. Route information is also available on Metro Transit's Web site: ⓦ transit.metrokc.gov.

Vintage Australian streetcars run along the waterfront from Broad Street (a 10-minute walk from Seattle Center) to South Main and branch east to the International District. Fares are the same as for Metro buses.

Seattle traffic is among the worst in the country. Add to that the steep one-way streets and expensive parking and you might consider using public transit within the city. If you do drive, take a friend. Some Seattle freeways have High-Occupancy Vehicle (HOV) lanes for vehicles carrying two or more people.

For a cab, call Farwest Taxi (☎ 206-622-1717), or try Yellow Cabs (☎ 206-622-6500).

Rent bikes at Al Young Bike & Ski (☎ 206-524-2642, 3615 NE 45th St). Near Green Lake, you can rent bicycles and in-line skates at Gregg's Greenlake Cycle (☎ 206-523-1822, 7007 Woodlawn Ave NE).

AROUND SEATTLE

The Washington State Ferry to Winslow, the primary town of **Bainbridge Island**, is popular for the great views of Seattle it offers as it crosses Elliott Bay. At Winslow is the Bainbridge Island Winery (☎ 206-842-9463). Ferries leave at least once an hour from Pier 52 for the 35-minute trip ($4.50 per passenger, $10 per car and driver).

In **Blake Island State Park** is Tillicum Village (☎ 206-443-1244), with its Northwest Coast Indian Cultural Center & Restaurant. Boats depart from Piers 55 and 56 in Seattle for a four-hour tour of the waterfront and Blake Island ($65). The package includes a traditional Indian salmon bake, dancing and a film about Northwest Native Americans. There's time for a short hike after the meal.

Near the city of Everett is the **Boeing Factory** (☎ 206-544-1264), where the 747, 767 and 777 jets are assembled in one of the world's most capacious buildings. Tours are popular and can be booked up. Call ☎ 800-464-1476 to reserve a space ($5; open 8am-4pm Mon-Fri). To reach the Boeing factory, follow I-5 north of Seattle to exit 189, turn west and drive 3 miles on Hwy 526.

TACOMA

For years, Tacoma (population 193,556) was known as a beleaguered mill town with little to recommend it. However, an influx of artists and the renovation of notable downtown buildings are heralding Tacoma's renaissance. The city's setting – backed up against the foothills of Mt Rainier and facing onto the fjords of Puget Sound and the jagged peaks of the Olympic Mountains – is another reason to visit. The visitor center (☎ 253-305-1000, 800-272-2662, ⓦ www.traveltacoma.com) is at 1001 Pacific Ave, suite 400. For an Internet connection, visit the Tacoma Public Library (1102 Tacoma Ave S); an access card costs $2 for each day of Internet use.

The enormous copper-domed neo-baroque **Union Station** (1911), designed by the architects who built New York's Grand Central Station, was renovated in the early 1990s. It now houses the federal courts. Next door is the **Washington State History Museum** (☎ 888-238-4373, 1911 Pacific Ave), with good exhibits on the tribes of the Northwest Coast ($7; open 10am-5pm Mon-Sat, 11am-5pm Sun). The **Tacoma Art Museum** (☎ 253-272-4258, 1123 Pacific Ave) features Tacoma artist Dale Chihuly's glasswork ($5; closed Mon). The ornate **Pantages Theater** (☎ 253-591-5894, 901 Broadway), once an elaborate vaudeville hall, is now Tacoma's premier performance stage. Directly north of 9th St on Broadway is **Antique Row**, a maze of collectibles shops.

In Tacoma's Stadium District, at the corner of N 1st St and Broadway, is the turreted, ivy-wrapped **Stadium High School**, which initially was conceived as a monumental luxury hotel.

Five miles northeast of downtown Tacoma (off Hwy 509) is *Dash Point State Park* (☎ 253-593-2206), a beachfront recreation area with tent/RV sites for $13/19. For bed and breakfast inns, call the Greater Tacoma B&B Reservation Service (☎ 253-759-4088). About the least expensive lodging near the center is *Travel Inn Motel* (☎ 253-383-8853, 2512 Pacific Ave) with singles/doubles for $39/50. Other moderately priced options are scattered along Pacific Highway in Fife, a western suburb, and south of the center between I-5 exits 128 and 129.

The *Freighthouse Square Market*, a converted railroad warehouse at S 25th and East D St alongside the Tacoma Dome (the world's largest wooden domed structure), has a range of inexpensive ethnic eateries. *Harmon Pub & Brewery* (1938 Pacific Ave S), opposite the history museum, draws its own homemade ales, some of which go into hearty entrées ($9-14). *Harbor Lights* (☎ 253-752-8600, 2761 Ruston Way) has excellent seafood.

Greyhound (☎ 253-383-4621, 510 Puyallup Ave), behind the Tacoma Dome, links Tacoma to Seattle ($5) and other cities along the I-5 corridor. Sound Transit bus routes 590 and 594, which also use the Tacoma Dome station, provide a cheaper way to reach Seattle ($2.50). The free Downtown Connector service makes a loop between the station and Seattle city center every 15 minutes.

Amtrak links Tacoma to Seattle and Portland from the station at 1001 Puyallup Ave (☎ 253-627-8141). Ferry rides to Vashon Island are $2.90 per passenger, $13 per vehicle and driver. For a taxi, call Yellow Cab (☎ 253-472-3303).

OLYMPIA

The state capital (population 42,514) has a strong alternative feel, partly attributable to Evergreen State College, an innovative public university noted for its interdisciplinary academic programs and student-centered approach. Situated at the southern end of Puget Sound, Olympia and the neighboring towns of Lacey and Tumwater constitute an urban entity known as the South Sound.

The State Capitol Visitors Center (☎ 360-586-3460), at 14th Ave and Capitol Way, provides information on both the capitol campus and the Olympia area.

At the **Washington State Capitol** campus is the vast, domed 1927 Legislative Building. Due to the 6.8 earthquake of March 2001, which damaged some of the columns underlying the dome, the building will be closed for renovation from 2002 till as late as 2006. Visitors can still tour the campus (free admission) and visit the Temple of Justice and Capitol Conservatory, housing a large collection of tropical plants. Guided tours of the grounds are offered (1:30pm daily June-Aug).

The **State Capital Museum** (☎ 360-753-2580, 211 W 21st Ave) has exhibits on the Nisqually Indians ($2; closed Mon). The **Olympia Farmers Market** (☎ 360-352-9096), at the north end of Capitol Way, has fresh local produce, crafts and food booths (open 10am-3pm Thur-Sun Apr-Oct, Sat-Sun Nov-Dec).

The **Tumwater Brewery** (☎ 360-754-5217), east of I-5 exit 103 in Tumwater, has produced beer since 1896. The facility once made Olympia Beer; in 1999 it was acquired by Miller Brewing to produce its popular Lite beer, among other brands. A 45-minute tour leads visitors past the fermentation tanks to the tasting room (free admission; closed Sun). Nearby is **Tumwater Historical Park**, the site of Olympia's original pioneer settlement, with a nature trail and several museums. The 1905 Henderson House Museum contains artifacts and displays of pioneer life and early industry (1-4pm Thurs, Fri, Sun). Adjacent 1858 Crosby House was the home of one of Olympia's first families (1pm-3pm Thurs and Sun, mid-Mar to mid-Oct).

Olympia Campground (☎ 360-352-2551, 1441 83rd Ave SW), off I-5 exit 101, has tent sites/hookups for $17/23. Six miles farther south, *Millersylvania State Park* (☎ 360-753-1519) charges $11/15. Downtown, *Golden Gavel Motel* (☎ 360-352-8533, 909 Capitol Way S) offers carefully maintained singles/doubles for $50/57. The similarly priced *Carriage Inn Motel* (☎ 360-943-4710,

*1211 Quince St SE), off I-5 exit 105, has an outdoor pool. In a quiet neighborhood east of the center, **Swantown Inn** (☎ 360-753-9123, 1431 11th Ave SE) offers B&B-style accommodations from $80.

Urban Onion (116 Legion Way E) has lunchtime salad and quiche for $7. **Otto's** (114 4th Ave E) offers fresh bagels and espresso drinks. Try the inexpensive Indian lunch buffet at **Santosh** (116 4th Ave). For home-brewed English-style ales and fine pub fare, stop in to the **Fishbowl Brewpub** (515 Jefferson St SE). **Gardner's** (☎ 360-786-8466, 111 W Thurston Ave) serves the city's best seafood, pasta and steaks.

Greyhound (☎ 360-357-5541, 107 7th Ave E) links Olympia to Seattle ($8; 1¾ hours; 6 daily) and other I-5-corridor cities. Intercity Transit's (IT; ☎ 360-786-1881) Olympia Express travels to/from Tacoma ($1.50; 1 hour), with connections to Seattle by Sound Transit. IT buses arrive at and depart from the downtown transit center at State Ave and Washington Street. Grays Harbor Transportation Authority (☎ 360-532-2770) offers bus service to Aberdeen.

Amtrak (☎ 360-923-4602) operates daily links to Seattle ($13) and Portland ($16). Bus No 64 shuttles between the station and downtown Olympia. For a cab, call Capital City Taxi (☎ 360-357-4949).

OLYMPIC PENINSULA

The Olympic Peninsula is a rugged, remote area characterized by wild coastlines, deep old-growth forests and craggy mountains. Seafaring Native Americans have lived here for thousands of years. Only one road, US 101, rings the Olympic Peninsula. Although the highway is in excellent condition, distances are great, and visitors often find it takes a lot longer than expected to get where they're going. From Seattle, the fastest access to the peninsula is by ferry to Bainbridge Island or via Edmonds to Kingston, continuing by car or bus over the Hood Canal bridge. See the Port Townsend section for details of the ferry-bus connection. See the Port Angeles and Port Townsend sections for more information on these routes.

Olympic National Park

One of the most popular US national parks, Olympic is noted for its wilderness hiking, dramatic scenery and widely varying ecosystems. The heavily glaciated Olympic Mountains rise to nearly 8000 feet. Few roads penetrate more than a few miles into the park proper, but visitors willing to hike a few miles will encounter magnificent waterfalls, wide-open alpine meadows, moss-bearded forests and remote lakes. Most lower valley trails are passable year-round, but expect rain, or at least clouds, at any time.

The park headquarters is in Port Angeles. The entry fee is $5/10 per person/vehicle, valid for one week; campsite fees are $8-12. Many park visitor centers double as USFS ranger stations, where you can pick up permits for wilderness camping ($5 per group, valid up to 14 days, plus $2 per person per night).

Northern Entrances The most popular access to the park is from the north. From Port Angeles, an 18-mile road leads to extensive wildflower meadows and expansive vistas at **Hurricane Ridge**. The Olympic National Park Visitor Center (☎ 360-565-3130, 3002 Mt Angeles Rd) is open daily. The closest campground is **Heart O' the Hills**, 5 miles south of Port Angeles on Hurricane Ridge Rd.

Popular for boating and fishing is **Lake Crescent**. From Storm King Information Station (☎ 360-928-3380) on the lake's south shore, a 1-mile hike climbs through old-growth forest to Marymere Falls. **Fairholm Campground**, at the lake's west end, has tent and RV sites for $10. Adjacent to the ranger station, the upscale **Lake Crescent Lodge** (☎ 360-928-3211, ⓦ www.olypen.com/lakecrescentlodge) has a restaurant and bar and rooms from $69 (closed Nov-Apr). On the north shore is **Log Cabin Resort** (☎ 360-928-3325, ⓦ www.logcabinresort.net, 3183 E Beach Rd), with a restaurant and cabins from $58 for two (closed Nov-Mar).

Along the Sol Duc River, the **Sol Duc Hot Springs Resort** (☎ 360-327-3583, ⓦ www.northolympic.com/solduc) has studio cabins from $105 and RV sites for $16 (closed Oct to mid-May). Apart from the hot springs ($10), this area has some of the best day hiking in the Olympics. There's camping upstream from the resort for $12.

Eastern Entrances The graveled Dosewallips River Rd follows the river from US 101 for 15 miles to **Dosewallips Ranger Station**, where the trails begin. There aren't many short loop trails here, but hiking portions of the two long-distance paths – with increasingly impressive views of heavily glaciated **Mt Anderson** – is reason enough to visit the valley. Another eastern entry for hikers is the **Staircase Ranger Station** (☎ 360-877-5569), just inside the national park boundary, 15 miles from Hoodsport on US 101. Two state parks along the eastern edge of the national park are popular with campers: **Dosewallips State Park** (☎ 360-796-4415) and **Lake Cushman State Park** (☎ 360-877-5491). Both have running water, flush toilets and some RV hookups.

Western Entrances Isolated by distance and inclement weather, the Pacific side of the Olympics remains its wildest; only US 101 offers access to its noted temperate rain forests. Leading out from the **Hoh River Rain Forest** visitor center and campground (☎ 360-374-6925), at the end of Hoh River Rd, are several excellent day hikes into virgin rain forest.

The **Queets River Valley** is the most remote, and hence the most pristine, part of the park. Queets River Rd ends at primitive *Queets Campground* and Ranger Station. **Sam's River Loop Trail**, a gentle, 3-mile day hike, starts here.

Lake Quinault is a beautiful glacial lake surrounded by forested peaks; it's popular for fishing, boating and swimming. A number of short trails begin just below *Lake Quinault Lodge* (☎ 360-288-2900, 🖩 www.visitlakequinault.com), on South Shore Rd, an antique hideaway with heated pool, lake-view dining and rooms from $110. *Rain Forest Resort Village* (☎ 360-288-2535, 🖩 www.rfrv.com, 516 South Shore Rd) has motel rooms/cabins from $90/130, and RV hookups.

The **Enchanted Valley Trail** climbs up to a large meadow (a former glacial lakebed) that's resplendent with wildflowers and copses of alder trees. The 13-mile hike to the aptly named valley begins from the Graves Creek Ranger Station at the end of the South Shore Rd, 19 miles from US 101.

Port Townsend

One of the best-preserved Victorian-era seaports in the USA, Port Townsend (population 8334) experienced a building boom in 1890 followed by an immediate bust, leaving its architectural splendor largely intact.

The visitor center (☎ 360-385-2722) is at 2437 E Sims Way. Internet access is available at Port Townsend Library, uptown at 1220 Lawrence St.

Historic **Fort Worden** (☎ 360-344-4400), 2 miles north of the ferry landing, has been refurbished; it was featured in the film *An Officer and a Gentleman*. Within the complex are the Commanding Officer's Quarters, a restored Victorian-era home ($1; open daily June-Aug, Sat-Sun only Mar-May and Sept-Oct), and the Coast Artillery Museum ($2; open Tue-Sun June-Aug, Sat-Sun only Apr-May). Sections of the fort serve as venues for summer arts festivals; call ☎ 360-385-3102 for details.

At *Fort Worden State Park* (☎ 360-344-4431), tent and RV sites are $20, and the *HI Olympic Hostel* (☎ 360-385-0655, 🖩 olyhost@olympus.net) charges from $12. *Point Hudson Resort & Marina* (☎ 360-385-2828, 🖩 pthudson@olypen.com, 103 Hudson St), at the east end of Water Street, has simple quarters from $49/59 with shared/private bath, as well as RV sites ($22 with hookup). The *Waterstreet Hotel* (☎ 360-385-5467, 635 Water St), in the center of town, offers old-world charm at reasonable rates: from $55 with shared bath.

The turreted *Manresa Castle* (☎ 360-385-5750), at 7th and Sheridan Sts, has rooms from $85 and the town's most romantic restaurant. The center of Port Townsend is packed with trendy cafes and restaurants. Join the local marina folk for breakfast at *Landfall Restaurant (412 Water St). Silverwater Café* (☎ 360-385-6448, 237 Taylor St) provides a romantic setting for creative Northwest dishes.

To reach Port Townsend, take the ferry from downtown Seattle to Bainbridge Island. At the ferry dock catch the No 90 Kitsap Transit bus (☎ 360-373-2877) to Poulsbo ($1; 20 minutes), then pick up a Jefferson Transit No 7 bus (☎ 360-385-4777) to Port Townsend ($1; 1 hour). Call for schedules, as service is infrequent. Washington State Ferries (☎ 206-464-6400) has trips to

Keystone, on Whidbey Island ($2 per passenger, $8.75 per car and driver).

For car rentals, Budget (☎ 360-385-7766) is at 518 Logan St. For a cab, call Peninsula Taxi (☎ 360-385-1872).

Port Angeles

This town (population 18,397) is a good base for exploring the Olympic Peninsula. Port Angeles Visitors Center (☎ 360-452-2363) is adjacent to the ferry terminal; the visitor center for Olympic National Park (☎ 360-565-3130) is a mile south of town, off Race St. Rent outdoor gear at Olympic Mountaineering (☎ 360-452-0240, 140 W Front St).

Pitch a tent for $10 at *Lincoln Park* (☎ 360-417-4550), off Lauridsen Blvd by the county fairgrounds (open June-Sept), or at *Salt Creek County Park* (☎ 360-928-3441), 16 miles west on Hwy 112, with stunning views of the Strait of Juan de Fuca. The amiably managed *Thor Town International Hostel* (☎ 360-452-0931, W www.thortown.com, 316 N Race St) has dorm-style accommodations and a few private rooms for $14 per person. *Tudor Inn B&B* (☎ 360-452-3138, 1108 S Oak St) starts at $85.

First Street Haven (107 E 1st St) is the place for hearty country breakfasts. *Thai Peppers* (222 N Lincoln St) offers an array of vegetarian dishes.

Two ferries run from Port Angeles to Victoria, BC: the Coho Vehicle Ferry (☎ 360-457-4491) costs $7.50 each way per passenger, $29.50 per car and driver (1½ hours); the passenger-only Victoria Express (☎ 360-452-8088) operates from May to September ($12.50; 1 hour).

Olympic Bus Lines (☎ 360-417-0700) runs twice daily to Seattle from the public transit center at the corner of Oak and Front Sts ($29/49 one-way/roundtrip). Clallam Transit buses (☎ 360-452-4511) go to Forks, Neah Bay and Sequim. Budget Rent-a-Car (☎ 360-452-4774) is across from the ferry terminal and at Fairchild International Airport (☎ 360-457-4246). For a taxi, call Blue Top (☎ 360-452-2223).

Northwest Peninsula

Several Indian reservations cling to this corner of the continent, and they welcome respectful visitors. On Hwy 112, 75 miles west of Port Angeles, is **Neah Bay**, the center of the Makah Indian Reservation. The **Makah Cultural & Research Center** (☎ 360-645-2711) is the sole repository of artifacts from nearby Ozette, which document the day-to-day life of the ancient Makah ($4; open daily June to mid-Sept, Wed-Sun rest of year). Seven miles beyond, a short boardwalk trail leads to Cape Flattery, a 300-foot promontory that marks the most northwesterly point in the lower 48 states.

The Makah run the year-round *Best Bay* lodging (☎ 360-645-2201), about 2 miles west of Neah Bay on Hwy 112, with dormitory-style units from $42. *Silver Salmon Resort* (☎ 360-645-2388), on Hwy 112, has rooms from $52. On the waterfront is the *Makah Maiden Restaurant*.

Convenient to the Hoh Rain Forest and the Olympic coastline is **Forks**, 57 miles from Neah Bay. *Bogachiel State Park* (☎ 360-374-6356), 6 miles south of Forks on US 101, has campsites, running water and toilets. A bed at the *Rain Forest Hostel* (☎ 360-374-2270), on US 101 8 miles south of the turnoff for the Hoh Rain Forest, is $12.

A tiny fishing village at the mouth of the Quillayute River, **La Push** is the principal settlement in the Quileute Indian Reservation (☎ 360-374-6163). *La Push Ocean Park Resort* (☎ 360-374-5267, W www.lapushwa .com) is tribally owned and operated, with cabins from $63 and motel units from $69. There's also tent and RV camping. La Push has no restaurant, but there's a small market, and fresh seafood is available near the harbor.

Pacific Coast

The extensive sandy beaches here are the closest ones to Puget Sound population centers and consequently can be very busy. **Ocean Shores** is what's left of a huge development gone bust. The coastline gets more rugged and picturesque as you go farther north on Hwy 109 toward Moclips, with a number of desultory beach towns and beach access points along the way. *Pacific Beach State Park* (☎ 360-276-4297), 2 miles south of Moclips, has tent and RV sites for $14/20. Farther north at Sunset Beach is the pleasant *Ocean Crest Resort* (☎ 360-276-4465); rooms cost from $65, and there's a restaurant.

From the marina at Ocean Shores, a passenger ferry crosses to Westport between

May and September ($8 roundtrip). Call ☎ 360-268-0047 for schedules.

NORTHWEST WASHINGTON

Offshore islands are the primary attraction in this marine-oriented corner of the state. The San Juans, reached only by ferry and air, pepper the northern Puget Sound. More accessible, Whidbey Island features beautiful Deception Pass State Park and the quaint, oyster-rich village of Coupeville. Back on the mainland is the lively university town of Bellingham.

Whidbey Island

Green, low-lying and much visited Whidbey Island snakes 41 miles along the Washington mainland from the northern suburbs of Seattle to Deception Pass. On discovering the treacherous chasm that separates Whidbey from Fidalgo Island to the north, Captain George Vancouver realized he had been 'deceived' by the misconception that Whidbey was attached to the mainland. **Deception Pass State Park**, with forest trails, lakes and more than 17 miles of saltwater shoreline, encompasses the narrow channel traversed by a dramatic bridge that links the two islands. Standard/primitive campsites are $14/6 (running water, flush toilets).

Whidbey's largest town is charmless Oak Harbor. More worthy of a visit is historic **Coupeville**, 10 miles south, with its attractive seafront, antique stores and old inns. The Visitor Information Center (☎ 360-678-5434, 120 S Main St) is open 10am-5pm daily. The Victorian-era **Inn at Penn Cove** (☎ 360-678-8000, 702 N Main St) has B&B-style rooms from $60. Charming **Captain Whidbey Inn** (☎ 360-678-4097, 2072 W Captain Whidbey Inn Rd), 3 miles west of Coupeville on Madrona Way, has singles/doubles from $75/85 and a romantic dining room. Sample local oysters and mussels at the **Captain's Galley** (10 Front St). Ten miles south of Coupeville on Hwy 525 is **Whidbey's Greenbank Berry Farm** (☎ 360-678-7700), noted for its loganberry liqueur.

The most popular getaway on Whidbey Island is **Langley**, an attractive artists' colony that is nevertheless overrun with cutesy commercialism. The Visitor Information Center (☎ 360-221-6765) is at 208 Anthes Ave. One of many B&Bs is **Eagles Nest** (☎ 360-221-5331, 4680 E Saratoga Rd), with views of Saratoga Passage and Mt Baker and rooms from $95. **Cafe Langley** (113 1st St) has Mediterranean cuisine, often pepped up with fresh Northwest seafood.

Harbor Airlines (☎ 800-359-3220, Ⓦ www.harborair.com) has daily links from Oak Harbor Airport to Sea-Tac Airport and the San Juan Islands. Bellair Airporter Shuttle (☎ 800-235-5247, Ⓦ www.airporter.com) has buses from Sea-Tac and Bellingham to Oak Harbor. Washington State Ferries link Clinton to Mukilteo every 30 minutes ($2.70/6.25 passenger/car and driver; 20 minutes) and Keystone to Port Townsend every 45 minutes ($2/9.75; 30 minutes). Island Transit buses (☎ 360-678-7771, 800-240-8747) run the length of Whidbey every hour daily except Sun, from the Clinton ferry dock (free).

Anacortes

Pleasant Anacortes (population 14,557), on Fidalgo Island, is noted principally as the departure point for the San Juan Island ferries. The chamber of commerce (☎ 360-293-3832) is at 819 Commercial Ave.

All sorts of lodgings line Hwy 20 along its southern approach. Cheapest is **Gateway Motel** (☎ 360-293-2655, 2019 Commercial Ave) with singles/doubles for $44/49. **Anacortes Inn** (☎ 360-293-3153, 3006 Commercial Ave), with standard motel amenities, is $55/60. Downtown is **Cap Sante Inn** (☎ 360-293-0602, 906 9th St), charging $72/81. **Rockfish Grill/Anacortes Brewery** (320 Commercial Ave) has good wood-fired pizzas ($7-10).

The Bellair Airporter Shuttle (☎ 800-423-4219, Ⓦ www.airporter.com) links Anacortes to the I-5 corridor at Mount Vernon ($6.50; 18 miles; 8 departures daily) and to connections for Bellingham and Sea-Tac Airport. Skagit Transit bus No 410 (☎ 360-757-4433) travels hourly between Anacortes (10th St and Commercial Ave) and the San Juan ferry terminal (50¢).

Bellingham

The handsome, old port city of Bellingham (population 67,171), 18 miles south of the US-Canadian border, is home to Western Washington University, a busy nightlife scene and plenty of good restaurants. The visitor center (☎ 360-671-3990, 800-487-2032, Ⓦ www.bellingham.org) is at 904 Potter St.

PACIFIC NORTHWEST

Victoria/San Juan Cruises (☎ 360-738-8099) has whale-watching trips to Victoria, BC, via the San Juan Islands. Boats leave from the Bellingham Cruise Terminal in the hip, historic district of Fairhaven, 3 miles from downtown.

Just south of the US-Canadian border, *HI Birch Bay Hostel* (☎ 360-371-2180, ℮ bbhostel@az.com, 7467 Gemini St) offers both dorms and private rooms for up to four people (check in 5-10pm; open May-Sept). Rates are $14/17 for members/nonmembers. For B&Bs, contact the B&B Guild of Whatcom County (☎ 360-676-4560). Most of the inexpensive motels are on Samish Way, off I-5 exit 252. Downtown are the remodeled *Shangri-La Downtown Motel* (☎ 360-733-7050, 611 E Holly St), and *Bellingham Inn* (☎ 360-734-1900, 202 E Holly St), both offering rooms in the low $40s. *Fairhaven Village Inn* (☎ 360-733-1311, ⓦ www.nwcountryinns.com/fairhaven, 1200 10th St) is a new boutique hotel in Fairhaven. Bay-view rooms start at $149.

For organic produce and health foods, go to the *Community Food Co-op* (1220 N Forest St). Get fresh bagels and lattes at *The Bagelry* (1319 Railroad Ave). For good Tex-Mex, try *Pepper Sisters* (1055 N State St), with nightly specials from $7. *Boundary Bay Brewery* (1107 Railroad Ave) is an excellent microbrewery and restaurant that serves moderately priced Northwest-influenced fare. In Fairhaven is the trendy *Colophon Cafe* (1208 11th St), at Village Books, with scrumptious pastries and big sandwiches ($6-8).

Greyhound (☎ 360-733-5252) travels daily to Vancouver, British Columbia ($12.50; 2 hours), and Seattle ($16.50; 2 hours). The bus depot/Amtrak station is located at the end of Harris Ave near the ferry terminal.

Alaska Marine Highway Ferries (☎ 360-676-0212, 800-642-0066, ⓦ www.ak.gov/ferry) go to Skagway (from $277) and other southeast Alaskan ports. San Juan Islands Shuttle Express (☎ 360-671-1137, 888-373-8522) offers daily summer service to Orcas and the San Juan Islands.

The Bellair Airporter Shuttle (☎ 800-423-4219, ⓦ www.airporter.com) runs to Sea-Tac airport with connections en route to Anacortes and Whidbey Island.

SAN JUAN ISLANDS

The San Juan archipelago sprawls across 750 sq miles of Pacific waters where Puget Sound and the Straits of Juan de Fuca and Georgia meet. Long considered an inaccessible backwater of farmers and fishers, the islands are today economically dependent on tourism; even so, they retain their bucolic charm. During July and August, accommodations reservations are essential; try All Island Reservations (☎ 360-378-6977). For information on the islands, contact the San Juan Islands Visitor Information Center (☎ 360-468-3663, ⓦ www.guidetosanjuans.com).

An increasingly popular means of exploring the shores of the San Juans is by sea kayak. Kayaks are available for rent on Lopez, Orcas and San Juan Islands. Expect a guided half-day trip to cost around $30-45. Note that most beach access is barred by private property, except at state or county parks.

Airlines serving the San Juan Islands include Harbor Air Lines (☎ 800-359-3220, ⓦ www.harborair.com), Kenmore Air (☎ 800-543-9595) and West Isle Air (☎ 800-874-4434). Flights from Seattle to the San Juans start at $75 one way. Public transport is nonexistent, but most motels will pick up guests at the ferry landing with advance notice, and bike rentals are available.

Washington State Ferries (☎ 206-464-6400, in Washington only ☎ 800-843-3779, ⓦ www.wsdot.wa.gov/ferries) leave Anacortes for the San Juans; some continue to Sidney, BC, near Victoria. To Lopez Island it's 45 minutes ($6.80/21.25 per passenger/car and driver); to Friday Harbor on San Juan Island it's 1¼ hours ($6.80/28.25). Fares are roundtrip and collected on westbound journeys only (except those returning from Sidney, BC). To visit all the islands, it's cheapest to go to Friday Harbor first and work your way back through the other islands; interisland ferries are free. Keep in mind, however, that *not all ferries stop at all the islands*.

Private ferries (summer only) include San Juan Shuttle Express (☎ 888-373-8522), with service from Bellingham to Orcas and Friday Harbor; the *Victoria Clipper* (☎ 206-448-5000), from Seattle to Friday Harbor and Orcas; and Puget Sound Express (☎ 360-385-5288), from Port Townsend to the San Juans.

Lopez Island

The most agricultural of the San Juan Islands, Lopez is also the closest to the mainland. For pastoral charm, it's a hard place to beat. South of the ferry landing (1.3 miles) is *Odlin County Park* (☎ 360-468-2496), with standard campsites from $15. The 1920s *MacKaye Harbor Inn* (☎ 360-468-2253, 949 MacKaye Harbor Rd) has B&B-style lodging from $99.

Orcas Island

Ruggedly beautiful Orcas Island is the largest of the San Juans. The ferry terminal is at Orcas Landing, 13½ miles south of the main population center, Eastsound. On the island's eastern lobe is **Moran State Park** (☎ 360-376-2326), dominated by Mt Constitution (2409 feet). Cascade and Mountain Lakes offer campgrounds, trout fishing and swimming beaches. The park has 40 miles of trails; get a map from the park headquarters.

For assistance with accommodations, call the Orcas Chamber of Commerce (☎ 360-376-8888). At the ferry landing, the historic *Orcas Hotel* (☎ 360-376-4300) has refurbished rooms from $79. The lovely *Turtle-*

back Farm Inn (☎ 360-376-4914, 1981 Crow Valley Road) charges $80-235. The least expensive option in Eastsound is the *Outlook Inn* (☎ 360-376-2200), on Main Street, with doubles from $84. The countercultural *Doe Bay Village Resort & Retreat* (☎ 360-376-2291, Ⓦ www.doebay.com), on the island's easternmost shore, has hostel beds for $16.

For bike rentals, head to Wildlife Cycles (☎ 360-376-4708, 350 North Beach Rd) in Eastsound. Orcas Island Taxi (☎ 360-376-8294) can transport visitors (and their bikes) to/from the ferry.

San Juan Island

San Juan offers the most hospitable blend of sophisticated amenities and rural landscapes. The main settlement is **Friday Harbor**, where the visitor center (☎ 360-378-5240) is at Front and Spring Sts. **San Juan Island National Historical Park** (☎ 360-378-2240), commemorating a mid-19th century British-US territorial conflict that started over a pig, consists of two former military camps on opposite ends of the island. Both of these day-use sites contain remnants of the old officers' quarters; the American

---

Mystery of the Orcas

Every summer a community of orcas migrates down from Vancouver Island to feed on the millions of salmon that make their way into Puget Sound. The orcas, also called killer whales (they're actually very large carnivorous dolphins) are a seasonal draw for tourists and cruise operators on the sound. But it appears this whale community is dwindling, and no one knows why.

Researchers keeping a close watch on the 'southern residents' orca community (another group resides in the waters around the northern half of Vancouver Island) have noted a steady population decline since 1992. As of 2001 there were 78 whales in the community, 21% fewer than six years earlier. The worrisome reduction could be due to the concurrent drop in salmon stocks, or it could be the result of the high level of toxic PCBs in the waters of the sound, which have been detected in the bloodstreams of the whales. Another possibility is that the numerous whale watch tours operating around the San Juan Islands are somehow disturbing the orcas' ability to communicate with one another, a requirement for team foraging. Though evidence to support any of these theories remains sparse, it's safe to say that if the orca population continues its recent waning trend, there won't be any left to watch by next century.

Camp, on the island's southeast end, features a splendid hike up Mt Finlayson, from which three mountain ranges can be glimpsed on a clear day. On the western shore, **Lime Kiln Point State Park** is devoted to whale watching.

Camp from April to September at *Lakedale Resort* (☎ 360-378-2350, 4313 Roche Harbor Rd), from $8. *Wayfarer's Rest* (☎ 360-378-6428, 35 Malcolm St) in Friday Harbor is a backpackers' hostel with dormitory beds for $20. *Roche Harbor Resort* (☎ 360-378-2155), a splendid seaside village on the island's northwest corner, has rooms from $79. Friday Harbor's great places to eat include *Blue Dolphin Café*, *Front St Ale House & San Juan Brewing Company*, both near the ferry landing, *Thai Kitchen* (42 1st St) and *Springtree Café* (310 Spring St).

CASCADE RANGE

Mighty peaks, spectacular hikes and rugged scenery make the mountains of the Cascade Range an outdoor enthusiast's heaven. Summer days can turn blustery in an instant, so pack a warm sweater and rain gear.

North Cascades

As with the Olympic Mountains, the most dramatic points in the rocky, glaciated North Cascades are reached by foot, by hiking the numerous trails or climbing to the crests of mountain ridges. Only one road, Hwy 20, cuts through the 781-sq-mile North Cascades National Park, and the route is usually closed from late November to April. Pick up backcountry permits at park headquarters (☎ 360-856-5700) in Sedro Woolley, well to the west of the mountains, at 2105 Hwy 20.

Upper Skagit River Valley From the town of Sedro Woolley, Hwy 20 makes its subtle ascent east along this pretty Cascade river valley toward North Cascades National Park. **Concrete**, 23 miles east of Sedro Woolley, has motels and is a base for Baker Lake and for climbs around 10,781-foot Mt Baker.

Rockport, at the junction of Hwys 20 and 530, is a prime bald eagle viewing site. Stop for gas and snacks at Marblemount, where the Wilderness Information Center (☎ 360-873-4500 ext 39) issues backcountry permits.

Eight *campgrounds* (☎ 877-444-6777) flank Baker Lake. *Rockport State Park* (☎ 360-853-8461), a lush old-growth forest, has several hiking trails and tent/RV sites for $14/20. *A Cab in the Woods* (☎ 360-873-4106), on Hwy 20 about 3 miles west of Marblemount, rents log cabins for $85/515 per night/week.

North Cascades NP Hundreds of great backcountry hikes crisscross this park. Campgrounds abound, with 19 facilities accessible from Hwy 20, but bring food and supplies. **Newhalem**, a dam-workers' town, is the jumping-off point for recreation; the visitor center (☎ 206-386-4495) has information on trails and camping as well as tours of the Diablo and Ross Dams and rafting on the Skagit River, both popular pursuits. A National Park Service campground is nearby. The park's Web site, Ⓦ www.nps.gov/noca, is another good resource. Tours of Diablo and Ross Dams and rafting on the Skagit River are popular pursuits.

Methow Valley The Methow (**met**-how) River valley has plenty of hiking, mountain biking, rafting and fishing, but is best known for cross-country skiing. Snows block Hwy 20 between Marblemount and Mazama (east of the park) from mid-November to mid-April (call ☎ 888-766-4636 for a road report), so Methow-bound skiers approach from western Washington by taking US 2 to Wenatchee, then heading north to Twisp. Three USFS campgrounds are just off Hwy 20 on Early Winters Creek. Inquire at the USFS visitor center (☎ 509-996-4000), west of Winthrop, about conditions. For other lodgings, call Methow Valley Central Reservations (☎ 509-996-2148), or check the Web site: Ⓦ www.methow.com/lodging.

The steep-walled Methow Valley opens up as it hits the Old West–themed town of Winthrop. Just to the east of town are the charming *Farmhouse Inn* (☎ 509-996-2191, Ⓦ www.farmhouse-inn.com, 709 Hwy 20) with rooms from $45, and a rambling, riverside *KOA* (☎ 509-996-2258), with secluded tent sites at $20. To the north, *Pearrygin Lake State Park* (☎ 509-996-2370), on Pearrygin Lake Rd 5 miles northeast of town (follow the signs from Hwy 20) has campsites for $14. Twisp, 8 miles south of Winthrop, is a more genuine version of the West than its false-fronted neighbor. There are several campgrounds in the surrounding area.

Lake Chelan The third-deepest lake in the USA, long, slender Lake Chelan is central Washington's playground. *Lake Chelan State Park* (☎ 509-687-3710), on South Shore Rd, has 144 campsites; a number of lakeshore campgrounds are accessible only by boat. The **town of Chelan**, at the lake's southeastern tip, is the primary base for accommodations and services. There's a USFS ranger station (☎ 509-682-2549) at 428 Woodin Ave. Reasonable lodgings include the *Parkway Motel* (☎ 509-682-2822, 402 Manson Hwy), from $40/68 single/double, and laid-back *Mom's Montlake Motel* (☎ 509-682-5715, 823 Wapato Ave), from $49/60. Link Transit buses (☎ 509-662-1155, W www.linktransit.com) connect Chelan with Wenatchee and Leavenworth ($1).

Beautiful **Stehekin**, on the northern tip of Lake Chelan, is accessible only by boat (☎ 509-682-4584, W www.ladyofthelake.com; $16/25 one way/round trip), seaplane (☎ 509-682-5555; $120 round trip from Chelan) or a long hike, most often across Cascade Pass, 28 miles from the lake. Most facilities are open mid-June to mid-September only. The National Park Service maintains a dozen primitive campsites along the Stehekin Valley Rd and runs a shuttle van up and down this road three times daily in summer ($12). *North Cascades Stehekin Lodge* (☎ 509-682-4494) offers lakefront rooms from $90.

Mt Rainier National Park

At 14,410 feet, Mt Rainier, 95 miles southeast of Seattle, is the highest peak in the Cascades. The park has four entrances: Nisqually, on Hwy 706 via Ashford, near the park's southwest corner; Ohanapecosh, via Hwy 123; White River, off Hwy 410; and Carbon River, the most remote entryway, at the northwest corner. Only the Nisqually entrance is open in winter, when it's used by cross-country skiers.

For information, contact the superintendent's office (☎ 360-569-2211 ext 3314) or consult the Web site at www.nps.gov/mora. Park entry is $10/5 per car/pedestrian. For overnight trips, get a wilderness camping permit (free) from ranger stations or visitor centers. Reservations are strongly advised

during summer months and can be made up to two months in advance by phone or fax (☎ 360-569-4453, fax 360-569-3131); get a reservation form via the Internet at W www .nps.gov/mora/recreation/rsvpform.htm.

The six campgrounds in the park have running water and toilets, but no RV hookups. The Rainer Shuttle (☎ 360-569-2331) runs between Sea-Tac Airport and Paradise three times daily ($46). Gray Line (☎ 206-624-5077, W www.graylineseattle.com) runs tours from Seattle ($54; 10 hours).

Nisqually Entrance The park's main entrance gives access to lovely countryside, from lush old-growth forests near **Longmire** to alpine meadows at **Paradise**, which has the most popular route up to the summit of Mt Rainier. Rainier Mountaineering (☎ 253-627-6242, summer only ☎ 360-569-2227, W www.rmiguides.com) has guided summit climbs ($551 for a two-day climb). Get trail information and backcountry permits at the Longmire Hiker Information Center (☎ 360-569-2211 ext 3317) and the Jackson Visitor Center (☎ 360-569-2211 ext 2328) at Paradise. There are several campgrounds. *Longmire National Park Inn* (open year round) and *Paradise Inn* (open late May to early Oct) have rooms from $75; for reservations, call ☎ 360-569-2275 or go to W www.guestservices.com/rainier. In Ashford, bunk beds are available for $25 at *Whittaker's Bunkhouse* (☎ 360-569-2439, 30205 Rte 706 East).

Other Entrances Packwood (on US 12) is the closest town to the **White River** and **Ohanapecosh** entrances, both of which have campsites. The Packwood Ranger Station (☎ 360-494-0600) is near the east end of town. *Hotel Packwood* (☎ 360-494-5431, 104 Main St) has clean, charming rooms from $20 and a mountain-view veranda. The Ohanapecosh Visitor Center (☎ 360-569-2211 ext 6046), on Hwy 123 at the park's southeastern corner, is open daily in summer (camping $15). The White River entrance affords some of the best views of Mt Rainier; the ranger station here (☎ 360-663-2273) issues backcountry permits.

The remote **Carbon River** entrance gives access to the park's inland rain forest. The ranger station (☎ 360-829-9639), just inside the entrance, is open daily in summer. There's camping at the end of Carbon River Rd ($6), but no drinkable water. The closest motel is the ***Mountain View Inn*** (☎ 360-829-1100), at the junction of Hwys 165 and 410 in the town of Buckley.

Mt St Helens National Volcanic Monument

On May 18, 1980, Mt St Helens erupted with the force of a 24-megaton blast, leveling hundreds of square miles of forest and blowing 1300 feet off its peak. Slowly recovering from the devastation, the 171 sq miles of volcano-wracked wilderness can now be visited as a day trip from either Portland or Seattle.

The **Mt St Helens Visitor Center** (☎ 360-274-2100), just off I-5 exit 49 near Castle Rock, presents an overview of the site's history and geology. Forty-three miles east of Castle Rock on Hwy 504, the **Coldwater Ridge Visitors Center** (☎ 360-274-2131) provides views directly into the mouth of Mt St Helens' north-facing crater, as well as interpretive talks and hikes year-round. A more remote vista point, with good views of the lava dome inside the crater, is on the northeastern side of the mountain along **Windy Ridge**, the terminus of USFS Rd 99.

Admission is $3/6 for a single/multiple-site pass. Some viewpoints and trails on the volcano's east side require a Northwest Forest Pass (see Activities at the beginning

When Mt St Helens Erupted

In March 1980, the Mt St Helens eruption was heralded by small steam clouds building above the mountain and earthquakes that rocked the area. Initially, geologists thought that the pyrotechnics were simply the result of groundwater reaching the molten core of the mountain and didn't realize until quite late that a major eruption was imminent.

Molten rock was rising toward the surface, heavily infused with water pressurized at temperatures of more than 750°F. As the piston of lava and its explosive charge of superheated steam pushed closer and closer to the surface, a bulge formed on the north side of the peak, growing larger and more unstable every day.

On May 18, the mountain gave way and a

mass of rock, ash, steam and gas blasted 15 miles into the air. The entire north face of Mt St Helens disintegrated and collapsed in what geologists believe was the largest landslide in recorded history. A 200mph rush of mud, snow, ice and rock consumed Spirit Lake and engulfed 17 miles of the North Fork Toutle River valley. Poisonous gases exploded north of the crater, leveling 150 sq miles of forest in an instant.

Huge deposits of mud and ash closed shipping channels on the Columbia River for weeks, and several inches of ash settled between Yakima and Spokane. Many years later, drifts of ash left by the region's snowplows were still visible along the roadsides. You can see 100-foot banks of dredged white ash, now covered with gorse, along the Toutle River near I-5 exit 52.

Nearby residents were given ample warning – perhaps too much, as quite a few returned to their homes when the volcano did not erupt on cue. Some 59 people were killed when it finally blew. The most famous casualty was Harry Truman – not the US president but the proprietor of a resort on Spirit Lake – who had lived in the area for many years and simply refused to leave. His lodge and all of Spirit Lake were buried beneath 200 feet of mud, ash and debris. Mt St Helens has remained calm since 1980, but geologists concur that another explosion is only a matter of time.

of this chapter) for entry, obtainable at the USFS ranger station in Randle, on Hwy 12 north of the park.

A couple of diners and motels are in Castle Rock, but most people camp or visit on a day trip. Campsites are most abundant on the south side of Mt St Helens, including Cougar, Beaver Bay and Swift. To the north (on USFS Rd 25 near the junction with USFS Rd 26) is *Iron Creek Campground* (☎ *360-569-0519*), charging from $12.50 for tent sites. To the east, opposite the Mt St Helens Visitor Center, is *Seaquest State Park* (☎ *206-274-8633*), open year round.

Mt Adams

Mt Adams (12,276 feet) is one of the most beautiful of the Cascade peaks, with some enchanting hikes and an easy summit ascent. A unique activity in the area is huckleberry picking (permits required). For information on hiking or climbing, inquire at the ranger station in Trout Lake (☎ 509-395-3400, 2455 Hwy 141) or in Randle (☎ 509-497-1100), on Hwy 12. There are numerous campgrounds around Mt Adams, and B&Bs in Trout Lake.

Be aware that the eastern slope is part of the Yakama Indian Reservation and mostly closed to nontribal members. A notable exception is the 3-mile **Bird Creek Meadow Trail**, one of the best-loved hikes in the Northwest. The 3-mile loop trail gently climbs to an alpine meadow showered by waterfalls and ablaze with wildflowers; looming above are the glaciers of Mt Adams' summit. It begins in a small, western portion of the reservation that is open to non-Yakamas ($10 vehicle fee). Near Bird Creek Meadows are three lakeside campgrounds (☎ 509-865-5121 ext 657).

The easiest access to Mt Adams is from the Columbia River Gorge, from either I-84 or Hwy 14. From Hood River, take Hwy 141 to Trout Lake, the head of recreation in the area.

CENTRAL & EASTERN WASHINGTON

The rugged, dramatic landscape of the Columbia Basin, scoured by ice-age floods, characterizes the central and eastern regions of the state. The setting affords a dramatic backdrop for the massive Grand Coulee Dam hydroelectric project. Spokane, just inside the border with Idaho, is a surprisingly appealing metropolitan center and a good place to start exploring the area. Farther south, near the border with Oregon, is Walla Walla, site of the 1847 Whitman Mission massacre and today the lively domain of Whitman College. In central Washington, the Yakima Valley Hwy (old US 12) parallels the freeway east of Yakima city, providing a pastoral alternative to I-82 and giving access to the region's wineries.

Spokane

The largest city between Seattle and Minneapolis, Spokane (population 195,629) feels closer in spirit to the latter than the former. As the prosperous trade center of the Inland Northwest, it's the only place hereabouts where you have a chance of seeing the opera or eating a decent Thai meal. The visitor center (☎ 509-747-3230, W www.visitspokane.com) is at 201 W Main St. Internet access is free at the Spokane Public Library, downtown at the corner of Lincoln and Main Sts.

Developed just for the 1974 World's Fair and Exposition, **Riverfront Park** features gardens, playgrounds and a fun vintage carousel. A gondola at the park's west end glides over the multitiered **Spokane Falls** ($4.75; operates Apr-Sept). Local wineries produce good merlots, which you can taste at Arbor Crest Wine Cellars (☎ 509-927-9894, 4705 N Fruithill Rd).

The pleasant *Riverside State Park* (☎ *509-456-3964*), 6 miles northwest off Hwy 291, has campsites for $14. Plenty of mid-priced chain motels lie along Division St near the malls and along Sunset Blvd on the way out to the airport. Downtown are *Trade Winds Motel* (☎ *509-838-8504, 509-838-2091*), with terraced singles/doubles from $43/48, and *Budget Inn* (☎ *509-838-6101, 110 E 4th Ave*), off I-90 exit 281, from $40 a double.

Frank's Diner (1516 W 2nd Ave), inside a vintage railway car, is a must for breakfast. Open till midnight, *Europa Pizzaria & Bakery* (125 South Wall St) serves pizza and pasta ($10-15) in a cozy salon. *Milford's* (☎ *509-326-7251, 719 N Monroe St*) is Spokane's best seafood restaurant (entrées $19-25).

Buses and trains depart from the Spokane Intermodal Transportation Station,

221 W 1st Ave. Greyhound and Northwestern Trailways (☎ 509-624-5252) run to Seattle ($28) and other destinations. Amtrak (☎ 509-624-5144) has daily service westbound to Seattle and Portland ($38 each) and eastbound to Chicago.

Spokane Transit trolley-buses pick up from the west side of the Plaza transit center on Wall St at W Sprague Ave and loop clockwise around Riverfront Park (25¢). For a taxi, call Spokane Cab (☎ 509-568-8000).

Grand Coulee Dam
Construction of the Grand Coulee Dam, 225 miles from Seattle, commenced in 1933 as a massive Works Progress Administration (WPA) project. The dam disrupted the Columbia River's ecology and displaced the Colville Confederated Tribes from their riverfront land; it now provides irrigation to 781 sq miles of farmland and is the world's third-largest hydropower producer. Three small, rather drab towns cluster around the dam: Grand Coulee and Electric City are just above it; directly below is Coulee Dam, the best bet for a motel room. The Colville Indian Reservation has its southern boundary in Coulee Dam.

The Grand Coulee Visitor Arrival Center (☎ 509-633-9265), open daily, has historical exhibits and films on the dam's construction and geology of the region. Tours of the generator and power plants are given hourly and take 35 minutes (free admission; open 10am-4pm daily).

Yakima & Around
Yakima (population 71,845) is the trading center of an immense agricultural area. A single block makes up Yakima's much touted historic district. The visitor center (☎ 509-575-1300) is at 10 N 8th St.

The excellent **Yakima Valley Museum** (☎ 509-248-0747, 2105 Tieton Dr) has exhibits on native Yakama culture. There are *campsites* ($11) at Sportsman State Park (☎ 509-575-2774, 904 Keyes Rd). Inexpensive motels (from $30) and fast-food outlets abound on N 1st St.

Numerous wineries lie between Yakima and Benton City, and the valley is home to the Yakama Indian Reservation, the state's largest. At Toppenish, the **Yakama Indian Nation Cultural Center** (☎ 509-865-2800) has displays on tribal life ($4; open 8am-5pm daily). Toppenish is also known for its murals depicting events from Yakama and Northwest history.

Walla Walla
This town (population 29,686) has one of the most significant enclaves of historic architecture in eastern Washington. The chamber of commerce (☎ 509-525-0850) is located at 29 E Sumach St. More than 30 wineries grace the Walla Walla valley; sample their chardonnays at several tasting rooms on Main St.

The museum at the 1856 **Fort Walla Walla** (☎ 509-525-7703) includes an old blacksmith shop, a schoolhouse and arguably the biggest model of a mule team on earth ($5; open Tue-Sun, Apr-Oct). The remains of the 1836 **Whitman Mission** are 7 miles west of Walla Walla off US 12. A monument commemorates Marcus Whitman and the 14 missionaries who died at the hands of Cayuse Indians in 1847. The visitor center (☎ 509-529-2761) has exhibits on the events that led up to the massacre ($2).

The *Capri Motel* (☎ *509-525-1130, 2003 Melrose St)*, at the east end of town, has spacious singles/doubles for $36/50. Opposite Whitman College, *Travelodge* (☎ *509-529-4940, 421 E Main St)* charges $50/60.

Oregon

With its rugged Pacific coastline, glaciated volcanic peaks, high-desert plains cut by deep river canyons, and dramatic mountain ranges, Oregon's landscape is epic in its variety and drama.

Just as varied are the Oregonians themselves, who run the gamut from pro-logging, anti-gay conservatives to tree-hugging, dope-growing, ex-hippie liberals – all fiercely proud of their state and ready to defend it against all comers.

History
An ad hoc collection of New England missionaries and French and British trappers, Oregon officially became a US territory in 1848, achieving statehood in 1859. Settlers had populated most of the coastal and central region by the 1860s, many having made the arduous six-month journey across the continent on the Oregon Trail. The new Oregonians proceeded to appro-

Oregon

Nickname: Beaver State

Population: 3,421,400 (28th)

Area: 98,386 sq miles (9th)

Admitted to Union: February 14, 1859 (33rd)

Capital city: Salem (population 131,400)

Other cities: Portland (529,100), Eugene (137,900), Gresham (90,200), Beaverton (76,100)

Birthplace of: scientist, antinuclear activist and double Noble laureate Linus Pauling (1901–94); *The Simpsons* creator, Matt Groening (b 1954); mountaineering and adventure novelist Jon Krakauer (b 1954)

Famous for: forests, the Oregon Trail, recycling (the 'Bottle Bill'), Nike

priate the homelands of the various Native American groups, and after a series of battles in the 1850s most of the Native Americans were confined to a few reservations. Gold discoveries in 1852 and 1861 accelerated settlement and sealed the Indians' fate.

Portland flourished as the trade conduit for agricultural products of the fertile inland valleys. The railroad reached Portland in 1883, and grain poured in from the Columbia Basin and as far away as Montana. By 1890 it was one of the world's largest wheat-shipment points.

The world wars brought further economic expansion to Oregon, much of it related to resource exploitation, especially logging. Post-WWII Oregon grew with a new kind of immigrant, as idealistic baby boomers flooded in from California and the eastern states, seeking alternative lifestyles, natural surroundings and other new opportunities. These arrivals brought the state pace-setting policies on many environmental and social issues. Oregon continues to lure immigrants and is one of the fastest-growing states in the country.

Government & Politics

Since the 1960s, Portland and western Oregon have been particularly influenced by the new, politically progressive settlers, while small towns and rural areas have remained conservative. Social and economic changes in the 1990s saw a right-wing resurgence, with the state divided on issues ranging from gay rights to forest conservation. Largely because of its ballot-initiative system, which gives Oregonians the opportunity to advance citizen-proposed laws to the ballot box, Oregon has become a stage for political dramas on divisive issues in which the whole country has an interest. The legalization of physician-assisted suicide and marijuana for medicinal purposes are some of the more recent laws advanced by Oregon's citizens.

Arts

Summer brings a host of music festivals, outdoor theater productions and art shows to the state. Progressive arts funding has endowed Portland with a bounty of public art and a well-regarded symphony and opera. Ashland, in southern Oregon, hosts the renowned Oregon Shakespeare Festival.

Information

The helpful Oregon Tourism Commission (☎ 503-986-0000, 800-547-7842, W www.traveloregon.com; 775 Summer St NE, Salem, OR 97310), has publications on accommodations, camping, state parks and outfitters for outdoor activities. Get information about Oregon's state parks at ☎ 800-551-6949, W www.prd.state.or.us. For highway information, call ☎ 800-977-6368. Oregon has no state sales tax, but most towns have a local 'lodging tax' on accommodations.

Oregon has a 10-digit dialing system for local calls. To make a local call, you must dial the area code first (without preceding it by 1).

PORTLAND

Oregon's largest city (population 529,121) lies at the confluence of two great rivers, the Columbia and the Willamette. Portland's friendly sophistication and beautiful setting amid forests and ancient volcanoes ensure that it remains near the top of the list of the USA's 'most livable cities.' The city is known nationally for its progressive politics, its easygoing pace and its love of the outdoors. A vibrant downtown, fine architecture and an extensive park system make it a great place to spend a few days.

PACIFIC NORTHWEST

PORTLAND

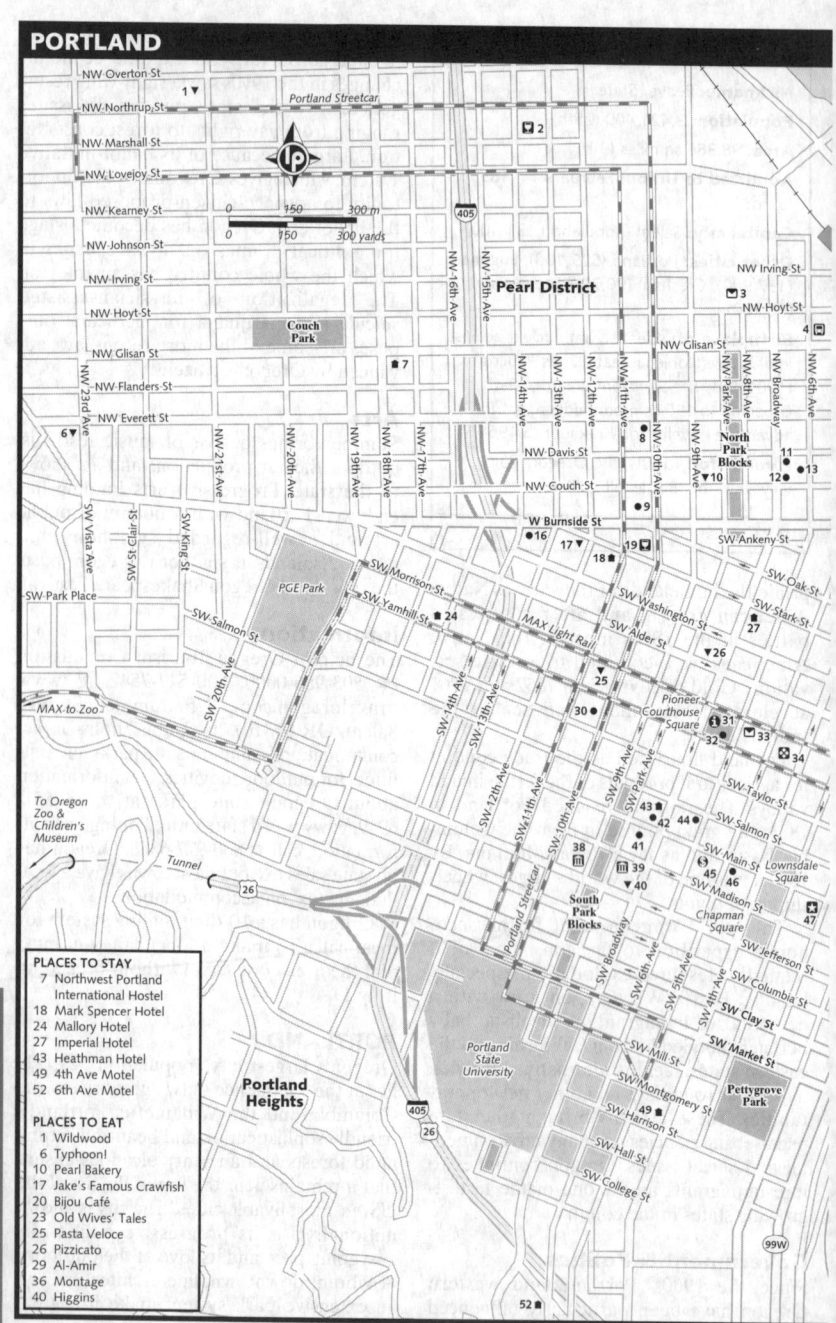

PLACES TO STAY
7 Northwest Portland
  International Hostel
18 Mark Spencer Hotel
24 Mallory Hotel
27 Imperial Hotel
43 Heathman Hotel
49 4th Ave Motel
52 6th Ave Motel

PLACES TO EAT
1 Wildwood
6 Typhoon!
10 Pearl Bakery
17 Jake's Famous Crawfish
20 Bijou Café
23 Old Wives' Tales
25 Pasta Veloce
26 Pizzicato
29 Al-Amir
36 Montage
40 Higgins

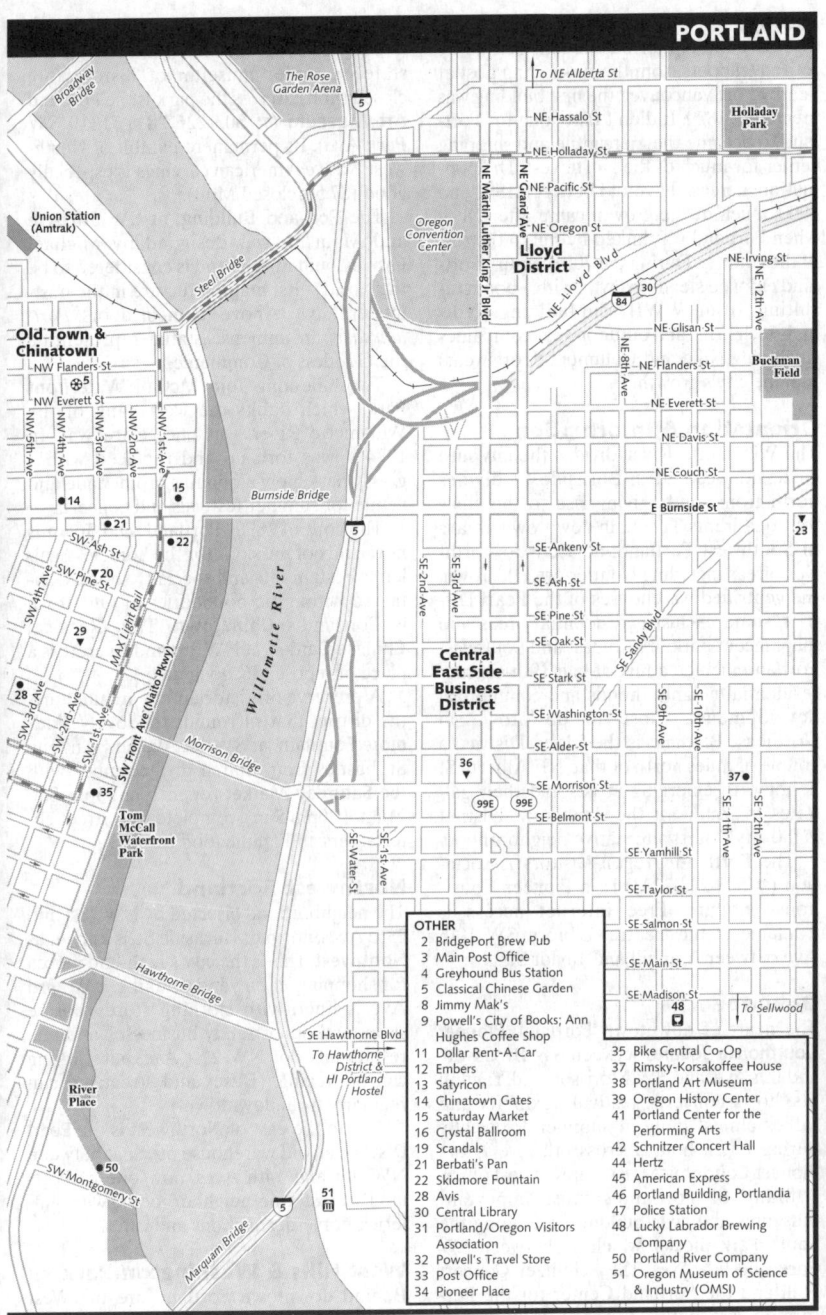

PORTLAND

OTHER
2   BridgePort Brew Pub
3   Main Post Office
4   Greyhound Bus Station
5   Classical Chinese Garden
8   Jimmy Mak's
9   Powell's City of Books; Ann
    Hughes Coffee Shop
11 Dollar Rent-A-Car
12 Embers
13 Satyricon
14 Chinatown Gates
15 Saturday Market
16 Crystal Ballroom
19 Scandals
21 Berbati's Pan
22 Skidmore Fountain
28 Avis
30 Central Library
31 Portland/Oregon Visitors
    Association
32 Powell's Travel Store
33 Post Office
34 Pioneer Place
35 Bike Central Co-Op
37 Rimsky-Korsakoffee House
38 Portland Art Museum
39 Oregon History Center
41 Portland Center for the
    Performing Arts
42 Schnitzer Concert Hall
44 Hertz
45 American Express
46 Portland Building, Portlandia
47 Police Station
48 Lucky Labrador Brewing
    Company
50 Portland River Company
51 Oregon Museum of Science
    & Industry (OMSI)

History

The Portland region was initially settled by retired trappers from the fur-trading post at nearby Fort Vancouver; the first building was erected in 1829. It didn't take long for Portland to became the mercantile and shipping center for much of the Northwest. The population increased fivefold between 1880 and 1900; much of the growth came after 1883, when Portland was linked by rail to the rest of the country. During the 20th century Portland enjoyed steady growth, with a boom resulting from WWII shipbuilding. Now high-tech firms and outdoor-gear companies (including Nike and Columbia Sportswear) fuel the city's growth.

Orientation & Information

The Willamette River divides the city into east and west sides; Burnside St divides north from south, giving rise to the city's four quadrants. The main downtown area is in Southwest Portland, adjacent to northwest areas including frontier-era Old Town, the gentrified warehouses of the Pearl District, some exclusive residential areas and magnificent parks. Northeast and Southeast Portland include a mix of late-19th-century residential neighborhoods and commercial developments. Close to downtown in Northeast Portland is the Lloyd District; a couple of miles north of that, NE Alberta St is home to emerging artists and their galleries. In Southeast, the Hawthorne District is the city's most alternative neighborhood.

The Portland/Oregon Visitors Association (☎ 503-222-2223) is in Pioneer Courthouse Square. Free internet access is available at the Central Library, SW 10th Ave between Yamhill and Taylor Sts.

Downtown

The heart of downtown Portland, **Pioneer Courthouse Square**, between SW Broadway and 6th Ave, and SW Morrison and Yamhill Sts, hosts concerts, festivals, exhibits and rallies almost daily in summer, especially during lunch hour. Across 6th Ave is the **Pioneer Courthouse** (1875), now a post office.

Many of Portland's most important museums and civic buildings are along the **South Park Blocks**, which lie between SW Park and 9th Aves. The Schnitzer Concert Hall and the Portland Center for the Performing Arts both face onto SW Main St at

Broadway. The **Oregon History Center** (☎ 503-222-1741, 1200 SW Park Ave) is the state's premier museum of history ($6; closed Mon). Across the park is the **Portland Art Museum** (☎ 503-226-2811, 1219 SW Park Ave). Its permanent exhibit of Northwest Native American carvings is especially good ($7.50; closed Mon).

The **Portland Building**, at SW 5th Ave and Main St, was designed by Michael Graves, built in 1980 and is considered to be the world's first major structure in the postmodern style. Above its main doors, *Portlandia* is an immense statue representing the Goddess of Commerce.

Two-mile-long **Tom McCall Waterfront Park**, which flanks the west bank of the Willamette River, was once a freeway. In 1974 it was torn up and replaced with a grassy park, now a popular promenade and venue for summer festivals and concerts.

The core of 1890s Portland, **Old Town** is now a mix of missions for the homeless, galleries, restaurants and specialty shops. Contained within the boundaries of Old Town is Portland's **Chinatown**. The **Classical Chinese Garden**, at NW 3rd and Everett, is a place of repose ($6; open daily).

A preserve of Victorian-era architecture, the district that surrounds the lovely **Skidmore Fountain**, at SW 1st Ave and Ankeny St, bustles from March to December with the **Saturday Market** (open 10am-5pm Sat, 11am-4:30pm Sun), complete with street entertainers and ethnic food carts.

Northwest Portland

The neighborhood bisected by NW 21st and 23rd Aves, north of Burnside St, is known as **Northwest**. This is the city's high-end mecca for shopping, eating and drinking. NW 23rd Ave is lined with clothing stores, coffee shops and other trendy businesses, and fine restaurants dot NW 21st Ave, but parking can be vexing. (Buses and streetcars run regularly from downtown.)

Just to the east of Northwest is the **Pearl District**, an old warehouse precinct between NW 9th and 14th Aves, now one of Portland's most chic neighborhoods, with galleries, home-decor shops and cafes.

West Hills & Washington Park

Behind downtown Portland are the West Hills, a ridge of ancient volcanic peaks that divide Portland from its westerly suburbs. The huge Washington Park complex contains the **International Rose Test Gardens**, with 400 types of rose, including many rare varieties (free admission; open daily). Farther uphill is the tranquil **Japanese Garden** ($6). In summer, the Zoo Train connects the Rose Gardens with the **Oregon Zoo** (☎ 503-226-1561, 4001 SW Canyon Rd), which has one of the world's most successful elephant breeding programs ($5.50; open daily); inquire about summer concerts on the zoo's lawns. Near the zoo is the **Children's Museum** (☎ 503-223-6500, 4015 SW Canyon Rd; $5; open daily).

East Side

Across the Willamette in Northeast Portland, the **Lloyd District** is the neighborhood surrounding the nation's first full-blown shopping mall, the Lloyd Center. Gentrification of surrounding streets, especially NE Broadway between 12th and 21st Aves, has brought an influx of good restaurants and specialty shops. Along NE Alberta St between 14th and 33rd Aves you'll find galleries, vegan restaurants, performance spaces and a food co-op.

The **Oregon Museum of Science & Industry** (OMSI; ☎ 503-797-4000, 1945 SE Water Ave), which has an Omnimax theater, is on the river ($9.50; closed Mon).

The lively **Hawthorne District** is full of bookstores, brew pubs and restaurants, especially along SE Hawthorne Blvd between 30th and 45th Aves. Southeast of downtown is **Sellwood**, an antique-store ghetto, especially along SE 13th Ave between Tacoma and Bybee Sts.

Activities

Hikers will find more than 50 miles of **hiking** trails in Forest Park. Pick up a map of the park at the Hoyt Arboretum Visitor Center (4000 Fairview Blvd). The Wildwood Trail starts in the zoo/Children's Museum complex at the arboretum and winds through 30 miles of forest. The many spur trails allow for loop hikes. For good **mountain biking**, head uphill to the western end of NW Thurman St and continue past the gate onto Leif Erikson Drive, an old dirt logging road leading 11 miles into Forest Park. (Don't bike on the hiking trails!)

Organized Tours

Ecotours of Oregon (☎ 503-245-1428) specializes in naturalist tours in northwest Oregon. Evergreen Trailways Gray Line (☎ 503-285-9845) has city bus tours in summer. Paddle the Willamette River in kayaks with Portland River Company (☎ 503-229-0551, 0315 SW Montgomery St) year round ($35).

Special Events

Parades, a riverfront carnival, ships full of sailors, a Rose Queen and lots of blooming roses make the Portland Rose Festival (☎ 503-227-2681, 𝕎 www.rosefestival.org) the city's biggest celebration (early June). March through downtown with dykes on bikes, the chief of police and 10,000 others during the Gay Pride Parade and celebration (☎ 503-295-9788) in late June.

Chamber Music Northwest (☎ 503-223-3202, 𝕎 www.cmnw.org) is an exceptionally good summer series of chamber music concerts held at the Reed College campus and Catlin Gabel School (late June-July). The Waterfront Blues Festival (☎ 503-282-0555) brings music and partying to Waterfront Park, with proceeds going to the Oregon Food Bank (July 4th weekend). Quaff microbrews from near and far during the Waterfront Park Oregon Brewers Festival (☎ 503-241-7179) in late July.

Places to Stay

The majority of central Portland's hotels are downtown or in Northeast, near the Lloyd District and convention center. On NE Airport Way, at I-205 exit 24, are several chain motels, and freeway exits around the outskirts of town are good places to find budget motels. Make summer reservations well in advance. An 11% bed tax is added to the room rate.

The best place to camp near Portland is **Oxbow Park** (☎ *503-663-4708, 3010 SE Oxbow Parkway*), in Gresham, just east of town. Tent/RV sites are $13. Pets are not allowed. The popular **HI Portland Hostel** (☎ *503-236-3380, 3031 SE Hawthorne Blvd*) is in a fun area and has good facilities and decent dorm beds for $15. Take bus No 14 from downtown. **HI Portland, Northwest** (☎ *503-241-2783, 1818 NW Glisan*) is another good base; it's between the Pearl District and NW Portland. Beds are $16.

The **4th Ave Motel** (☎ 503-226-7646, 1889 SW 4th Ave) is just to the south of the city center. Singles/doubles are $45/55. Also convenient, **6th Ave Motel** (☎ 503-226-2979, 2221 SW 6th Ave) has rooms for $55/65. **Edgefield** (☎ 503-669-8610, 2126 SW Halsey St), a handsome brick building east of Portland in Troutdale, was once the county poor farm and is now a B&B (from $50).

In NE Portland, the **Hojo Inn** (☎ 503-288-6891, 3939 NE Hancock St) is in a pleasant neighborhood a short ride on the MAX light-rail train to downtown ($55/65). The **Lion & the Rose** (☎ 503-287-9245, 1810 NE 15th Ave) is a turreted Queen Anne–style mansion B&B with rooms from $85. The less prissy **Kennedy School** (☎ 503-249-3983, 5736 NE 33rd Ave) was once a grade school; now it's a B&B with a bar in the former principal's office (rooms are $99-109).

The **Mark Spencer Hotel** (☎ 503-224-3293, 409 SW 11th Ave) is a good deal downtown, where rooms with full kitchens are $89. **Mallory Hotel** (☎ 503-223-6311, 729 SW 15th Ave) is handy to the city center and has free parking ($90/95). The face-lifted **Imperial Hotel** (☎ 503-228-7221, 400 SW Broadway) has rooms for $100/110. The fine **Heathman Hotel** (☎ 503-241-4100, 1001 SW Broadway) has rooms from $145.

Places to Eat

Downtown, the **food carts** at SW 6th Ave and Washington St offer cheap lunches. Downstairs at **Pioneer Place Mall**, at SW 6th Ave and Taylor St, is a food court. **Bijou Café** (132 SW 3rd Ave) is a favorite downtown breakfast place. **Pizzicato** (705 SW Alder St) has good pizza; the pasta is cheap and tasty at **Pasta Veloce** (1022 SW Morrison St).

Al-Amir (223 SW Stark St) serves delicious Lebanese food at moderate prices in a delightful old building. Fresh seafood, steak and a vibrant bar scene make **Jake's Famous Crawfish** (☎ 503-226-1419, 401 SW 12th Ave) perennially popular. **Higgins** (☎ 503-222-9070, 1239 SW Broadway) is a bit more high end, offering fresh, often organically grown ingredients and innovative preparations, including many vegetarian options.

In the Northwest, you can lunch for under $5 at the **Pearl Bakery** (102 NW 9th Ave), near Powell's Books. It also has delicious pastries and sandwiches. **Typhoon!** (2310 NW Everett St) has excellent Thai cuisine at prices just higher than average ($8-15 for dinner). Eat in the dining room (spendy) or at the bar (less so) at **Wildwood** (☎ 503-248-9663, 1221 NW 21st Ave), one of the proving grounds for trendy Northwest cuisine.

In the Northeast, the **Grand Central Bakery** (1444 NE Weidler St) has great breads and pastries. Soup, pizza and light entrées are also good and reasonably priced. For a full breakfast, **Cadillac Café** (914 NE Broadway) is excellent. **Vita Cafe** (3024 NE Alberta St) is a vegan joint that also serves burgers!

In the Southeast, home to many good inexpensive restaurants, try **Montage** (301 SE Morrison St), a Creole nightspot with delicious, inexpensive dishes. The Tex-Mex food at **Esparza's** (2715 SE Ankeny St) has people lined up out the door. **Old Wives' Tales** (1300 E Burnside St) has good international comfort food and is especially kid friendly. **Hoda's** (3401 SE Belmont St) serves cheap Middle-Eastern food (no credit cards). **Bread & Ink Café** (3610 SE Hawthorne Blvd) is the quintessential Portland cafe; blintzes are a standby, and the salmon sandwich is also good. At **Assaggio** (7742 SE 13th Ave), in Sellwood, pasta dishes are the stronghold, but they're not the kind of pasta dinners you're likely to cook up at home. Many are vegetarian.

Entertainment

The best guide to local entertainment is *Willamette Week*, out on Wednesday.

Coffeehouses In Powell's Books, **Ann Hughes Coffee Shop** (1005 W Burnside St) serves caffeine to book lovers. In Southeast Portland, **Café Lena** (2239 SE Hawthorne Blvd) hosts acoustic-guitar performances and open-mic poetry. The eccentric **Rimsky-Korsakoffee House** (707 SE 12th Ave), which has no sign, often has live classical musicians. **Tao of Tea** (3430 SE Belmont St) is an Asian countryside tea hut dropped down in Southeast Portland. It's a great escape on a rainy afternoon.

Bars & Brew Pubs All of these places have snacks, light meals or even full lunch and dinner service. ***BridgePort Brew Pub*** (☎ *503-241-7179, 1313 NW Marshall St*) is in an old red-brick warehouse. The same brewery's ***Hawthorne Street Ale House*** (☎ *503-233-6540, 3632 SE Hawthorne Blvd*) has outstanding food. ***Lucky Labrador Brewing Company*** (☎ *503-236-3555, 915 SE Hawthorne Ave*) is very friendly, with seating for humans and dogs out back.

Live Music & Dance Clubs Nightspots include ***Satyricon*** (☎ *503-243-2380, 125 NW 6th Ave*), for punk and alternative rock; ***Berbati's Pan*** (☎ *503-248-4579, 10 SW 3rd Ave*), which is eclectically hip; and ***Jimmy Mak's*** (☎ *503-295-6542, 300 NW 10th Ave*), for jazz.

The historic ***Crystal Ballroom*** (☎ *503-778-5625, 1332 W Burnside St*) has a 'floating' dance floor; it's underlaid with rockers (like a rocking chair) that are outfitted with ball bearings, so the floor appears to float on the bearings. It's a great place to see touring bands.

Gay & Lesbian Venues The hub of Portland's gay nightlife is found in the neighborhood flanking Stark St and SW 11th Ave; try ***Scandals*** (*1038 SW Stark St*), a friendly laidback place, and ***Embers*** (*110 NW Broadway*) for dancing. Women should check out the ***Egyptian Room*** (*3701 SE Division St*). Hawthorne Blvd is pretty much regarded as Lesbian Central.

Performing Arts The showcase theater is ***Portland Center for the Performing Arts*** (☎ *503-796-9293, 1111 SW Broadway*). The century-old Oregon Symphony performs in the beautiful, if not acoustically brilliant, ***Schnitzer Concert Hall*** (☎ *503-228-1353*), on the corner of Broadway and SW Main St. The Portland Opera (☎ *503-241-1802*) stages five performances a year at the ***Keller Auditorium*** (*222 SW Clay St*). Oregon Ballet Theatre (☎ *503-222-5538*) is Portland's resident dance troupe, with classical and contemporary dance programs performed on stages around town.

Spectator Sports
The Portland Trail Blazers play basketball at the Rose Garden Arena, on N Williams Ave at Hassalo St; call ☎ 503-231-8000 for tickets, which usually sell out to local obsessives.

It's a little easier to see the Portland Winter Hawks (☎ 503-238-6366) play pro hockey, or the Portland Fire women's basketballers (☎ 503-233-9622), also in the Rose Garden Arena.

Getting There & Around
Air Horizon Air flies several times a day between Portland International Airport (PDX) and Seattle, and there are frequent flights to/from San Francisco and Seattle on United and Alaska Airlines. Tri-Met's MAX light-rail train runs between PDX and downtown ($1.55); in the reverse direction, catch it outbound along Yamhill St. A taxi costs up to $25.

Bus Greyhound (☎ 503-243-2357, 550 NW 6th Ave) connects Portland with cities along I-5 and I-84. Regular service includes the following destinations: San Francisco ($55; 18½ hours); Seattle ($22; 4 hours); Vancouver, British Columbia ($42; 10 hours); Boise, Idaho ($40; 10 hours).

Local buses are run by Tri-Met (☎ 503-238-7433), which has an information bureau (☎ 503-231-3198) at Pioneer Courthouse Square. Tri-Met also operates a light-rail system called Metropolitan Area Express (MAX). A streetcar runs from Portland State University, south of downtown, through the Pearl District to NW 23. Within the downtown core, public transportation is free; outside downtown, fares run about $1.25.

Train Amtrak (☎ 503-241-4290) serves Union Station, NW 6th Ave at Hoyt St. Trains run regularly to and from the following destinations: Seattle ($26; 4 hours; four trains a day), Los Angeles ($135; 26 hours; one train a day) and Chicago ($234; 2 days; one train a day).

Car & Motorcycle Major car-rental agencies have outlets at PDX airport. Downtown there's Avis (☎ 503-227-0220), at SW 4th Ave and Washington St; Budget (☎ 503-249-6500); Dollar (☎ 503-228-3540), at NW Broadway and Davis St; and Hertz (☎ 503-249-5727), at SW 6th Ave and Salmon St.

Bicycle Rent a bike from Bike Central Co-Op (☎ 503-227-4439, 732 SW 1st Ave), downtown, or Fat Tire Farm (☎ 503-222-3276, 2714

PACIFIC NORTHWEST

NW Thurman St). A map of metro-area bike routes is available from bike shops or from Powell's Travel Store (☎ 503-226-4849, 701 SW 6th Ave).

COLUMBIA RIVER GORGE

The enormous canyon of the Columbia River, which divides Washington and Oregon, is one of the Pacific Northwest's most dramatic and scenic destinations. Immediately south of the gorge rises Mt Hood, Oregon's highest peak, a magnet for hikers, skiers and climbers. Two highways pass through the gorge: river-level I-84 (Oregon side) is the quickest route, providing access to the most popular sites and activities. Washington's Hwy 14, although much slower, offers spectacular vistas. Remains of the historic Columbia River Hwy (US 30) exist between Troutdale and Warrendale, and between Mosier and the Dalles. Hood River and the Dalles are the major commercial centers; of the two, Hood River is the livelier base. Campers will find state parks on both sides of the river; on summer weekends, campsites are scarce and traffic noise can be bothersome.

Historic Columbia River Hwy

The remarkable highway between Troutdale, just east of Portland, and Hood River opened in 1915. To reach it, take exit 17 or 35 off I-84. Famous as the western entry to the gorge, the **Crown Point** viewpoint and interpretive center sit atop a craggy cliff of basalt.

Bike, walk or jog along two stretches of the old highway that have been renovated for nonautomotive use. The western section of the trail runs between Tanner Creek (at the Bonneville Dam exit from I-84) and Eagle Creek; another, longer stretch runs 4½ miles from Hood River to Mosier.

Waterfalls and hiking trails line the Oregon side of the gorge. Stop at **Multnomah Falls** to ogle the 642-foot, two-tiered falls and hike to the top. The Forest Service visitor center next door to the gift shop is a good place to get information on other gorge hikes.

Ainsworth State Park (☎ 503-731-3411), 3 miles east of Multnomah Falls, has campsites ($18 for full hookups or tent sites). The best place to stay or eat in the western Columbia River Gorge is *Edgefield* (☎ 503-669-8610, 2126 SW Halsey), in Troutdale, with hostel beds for $20, rooms from $50 and your choice of inexpensive ex-hippie pub food or fancier fare.

Hood River & Around

Hood River (population 5831), 63 miles east of Portland on I-84, is the center for recreation in the gorge. The Columbia River here is a windsurfing hot spot. There's great mountain biking south of town off Hwy 35 and Forest Rd 44. A section of the historic highway heading east from Hood River has been refurbished as a bike path.

The chamber of commerce (☎ 541-386-2000) is by the Expo Center. Discover Bicycles (☎ 541-386-4820, 1020 Wasco Ave) rents mountain bikes.

Viento State Park (☎ 541-374-8811), 8 miles west of Hood River, is popular with windsurfers and has campsites for $16.

Gorge View B&B (☎ 541-386-5770, 1009 Columbia St) has a dorm-style room ($35). The *Vagabond Lodge* (☎ 541-386-2992), on Westcliffe Drive next to the huge, swanky Columbia Gorge Hotel, has river-view motel rooms from $45.

Cross the Columbia to Bingen, Washington, where the *Bingen School Inn* (☎ 509-493-3363), at the corner of Cedar and Franklin Sts, has dorm beds/doubles for $14/35. Just upriver, in Lyle, Washington, the renovated *Lyle Hotel* (☎ 509-365-5953, 100 7th St) has rooms for $50.

Big City Chicks (1303 13th St) is good for chicken, and *North Oak Brasserie* (113 3rd St) is recommended for its salads and Italian food.

Greyhound (☎ 541-386-1212, 1205 B St) runs daily buses to Portland ($11) and points east.

MT HOOD

The state's highest peak, 11,240-foot Mt Hood is visible on a sunny day from much of northern Oregon. It is accessible year round via US 26 from Portland, and from Hood River via Hwy 35. Together with the Columbia River Hwy, these routes constitute the **Mt Hood Loop**, one of the finest scenic-road excursions in the USA.

The settlement of **Government Camp**, 56 miles from Portland and 44 miles from Hood River, is at the pass over Mt Hood. Most facilities for travelers are on the western side of the mountain. The Mt Hood Information Center (☎ 503-622-4822, 68260 E Welches Rd) is in Welches.

A masterpiece of the WPA era, the 1930s **Timberline Lodge** (☎ 503-272-3311) was built and decorated in grand rustic style as a hotel, ski resort and restaurant. It's 5 miles north of US 26 from Government Camp. The horror movie *The Shining* was filmed here.

Mt Hood Meadows (☎ 503-337-2222), 76 miles from Portland, is the largest ski area on Mt Hood and often has the best conditions. **Mt Hood SkiBowl** (☎ 503-272-3206), off US 26 just west of Government Camp, is the USA's largest night-ski area, and the closest one to Portland. **Timberline** (☎ 503-622-0717) has skiing almost year round.

Hikers should get the free USFS pamphlet *Day Hikes Around Mt Hood.* After Japan's Mt Fuji, Mt Hood is the world's most-climbed peak over 10,000 feet, with a typical route from Timberline Lodge taking about 10 to 12 hours roundtrip (for experienced climbers). Timberline Mountain Guides (☎ 541-312-9242) is a well-established guide service and climbing school. Climbing is best from May to mid-July.

Reservations for some campgrounds can be made by calling ☎ 877-444-6777. Site fees are $12, reservation fees another $8.65. *Mt Hood RV Village* (☎ 503-622-4011, 65000 E US 26), near Brightwood, is a huge resort complex where hookups cost $32.

At Government Camp, *Cascade Ski Club Lodge* (☎ 503-272-9204) has beds for $22. *Mazama Lodge* (☎ 503-272-9214), the Government Camp base for the Mazamas mountaineering club, sometimes has bunks available for nonmembers, at $17. *Huckleberry Inn* (☎ 503-272-3325, 88611 E Government Camp Loop) is conveniently located and far from fancy, with rooms from $60. The tidy *Shamrock Motel* (☎ 503-622-4911, 59550 E US 26), down the mountain a ways, has basic rooms from $39.

For real ambience, go for the *Timberline Lodge* (☎ 503-272-3311), where basic rooms start at $75 and a large room with a fireplace is $170.

WILLAMETTE VALLEY

The incredibly fertile Willamette Valley, between Portland and Eugene, was the destination of the Oregon Trail pioneers. Historic sites in the northern valley and the Yamhill County vineyards are within easy reach of Portland for day trips. In the mid-valley is Salem, the state capital. The small college cities of Corvallis and Eugene, in the southern valley, are both dynamic and engaging, with good inexpensive food and lodging.

Yamhill County Wine Country

For information about the 30-plus wineries in Yamhill County, contact the Yamhill County Wineries Association (☎ 503-646-2985, PO Box 871, McMinnville, OR 97218). The **Oregon Wine Tasting Room** (☎ 503-843-3787) is 9 miles southwest of McMinnville on Hwy 18 at Bellevue. Grape Escape (☎ 503-282-4262) specializes in wine-country tours departing from Portland. The **Spruce Goose**, the world's largest wood-framed airplane, is housed in a museum near McMinnville (open daily).

Salem

Oregon's state capital, Salem (population 136,924), is a sprawling and somewhat soulless city of gray buildings and bureaucrats. Get details from the visitors association (☎ 503-581-4325, 1313 Mill St SE).

The 1935 **Oregon State Capitol** (☎ 503-986-1388), at Court and Capitol Sts, has Bauhaus and art deco influences. Rambling 19th-century Bush House is an Italianate mansion now preserved as a museum (closed Monday) within **Bush Pasture Park** (☎ 503-363-4714, 600 Mission St SE), a lovely public garden. Twenty-six miles east of Salem on Hwy 214 is **Silver Falls State Park** (☎ 503-873-8681), with waterfalls you can hike behind.

The closest camping is at *Salem Campground & RV* (☎ 503-581-6736, 3700 Hagers Grove Rd SE), with tent/RV sites from $15/21. To stay close to the capitol, try *Travelodge* (☎ 503-581-2466, 1555 State St), with singles/doubles for $60/65 and an outdoor pool, or *Cottonwood Cottage* (☎ 503-362-3979, 960 E St NE), which has two B&B rooms from $65. *Motel 6* (☎ 503-371-8024, 1401 Hawthorne Ave NE), at I-5 exit 256, has rooms for $42/49.

The *Arbor Café (380 High St NE)* is Salem's best lunch spot. Casual *DaVinci's (180 High St SE)* is popular for Italian.

Greyhound goes to Portland ($8), Bend and Eugene from the station at 450 Church

St NE (☎ 503-362-2407). Amtrak has daily trains north and south from the station at 13th and Oak Sts (☎ 503-588-1551).

Corvallis

Home to Oregon State University, Corvallis (population 49,322) is a pleasant town at the base of the Coast Range, 43 miles from Eugene. The old tree-lined downtown is filled with bakeries, bookstores and cafes. The visitor center (☎ 541-757-1544) is at 420 NW 2nd St.

Founded in 1852 and just west of downtown is the green and leafy OSU campus. Visit the student union for its bookstore and flag-draped vestibule.

Camping feels transient in the grassy field at **Willamette Park** (☎ 541-757-6918), south of town (sites $7). **Corvallis/Albany KOA** (☎ 541-967-8521, 33775 Oakville Rd), just a few miles east, offers full services for RVs. **Towne House Motor Inn** (☎ 541-753-4496, 350 SW 4th St), between the university and downtown, charges $41/48 for singles/doubles.

Mexican food is tasty at whimsical **Bombs Away Café** (2527 NW Monroe Way). Casual **Big River Restaurant** (☎ 541-757-0694, 101 NW Jackson) is more upscale. Local bands and rock bands play at the collegiate **Peacock Tavern** (☎ 541-754-8522, 125 SW 2nd St).

The town's bus station (☎ 541-757-1797, 153 NW 4th St), has Greyhound connections to Portland ($13) and Eugene ($7); Amtrak Thruway buses go to Newport ($12). Call Action Taxi (☎ 541-754-1111) for a cab.

Eugene

Life in Eugene (population 137,893) seems to be a denial that the 1960s have passed. Many of the city's successful businesses are owned by former 'radicals,' and activism is still de rigueur here. The city receives much of its character from the University of Oregon, the state's largest. Eugene is also famous for track and field champions and is the birthplace of Nike.

The visitor center (☎ 541-484-5307) is at 115 W 8th Ave, suite 190.

At E 5th Ave between Pearl and High Sts, **Fifth St Public Market** is the heart of a small but lively shopping and cafe district. The famous waffle iron used to make the first Nike soles is displayed at the Nike

Eugene Store. Housed in a replica of a Native American longhouse, the University of Oregon's **Museum of Natural History** (☎ 541-346-3024, 1680 E 15th Ave), has the state's best display of Native American artifacts ($2 donation; closed Mon).

The Oregon Country Fair (☎ 541-343-4298), in July, is a riotous three-day celebration of Eugene's folksy, hippie past and present. It's held on a farm 13 miles west of Eugene on Hwy 126, near Veneta.

Eugene Kamping World (☎ 541-343-4832), 6 miles north of town at I-5 exit 199, costs $15/17.50 for tents/RVs. **Eugene International Hostel** (☎ 541-349-0589, 2352 Willamette St) is a real flophouse (dorms $13). **Courtesy Inn** (☎ 541-345-3391, 345 W 6th Ave), with singles/doubles at $44/61, and **Timbers Motel** (☎ 541-345-3345, 1015 Pearl St), with rooms for $38/40, are both decent motels convenient to downtown.

Fifth Street Market has a great bakery and a number of small ethnic restaurants. Try **Ring of Fire** (1099 Chambers St) for Thai food; **Cafe Navarro** (454 Willamette St) for eclectic Caribbean, Latin and African; and **West Brother's Bar-B-Que** (844 Olive St) for barbecue and Cajun (all moderately priced with some budget-priced items).

The Eugene Opera, Symphony and Ballet perform at the **Hult Center for the Performing Arts**, at 6th Ave and Willamette St. You can reach the concert line at ☎ 541-682-5746. Find acoustic music at the **WOW Hall** (☎ 541-687-2746, 8th Ave) or **Sam Bond's Garage** (☎ 541-343-2635, 407 Blair Blvd).

The bus station (☎ 541-344-6265, 987 Pearl St) has connections to Portland ($13), San Francisco ($48) and Bend ($22). The Amtrak station (☎ 541-687-1383) at E 4th Ave and Willamette St has trains north to Vancouver, British Columbia ($45; 12 hours) and south to San Francisco ($90; 16 hours).

McKenzie River Valley

The single term *McKenzie* identifies a river, a 5325-foot mountain pass, the historic and spectacular **Old McKenzie Hwy** (Hwy 242), and one of Oregon's most wonderful natural areas. There's great fishing, easy hikes and fun rafting trips. Contact the McKenzie River Chamber of Commerce (☎ 541-896-3330) on Hwy 126 in Leaburg.

McKenzie Bridge, 50 miles east of Eugene on Hwy 126, offers campgrounds and cabins at the gateway to lava-laden McKenzie Pass. Up on the pass, the Dee Wright Observatory offers good views of volcanoes in the adjoining **Three Sisters Wilderness**. The scenic **McKenzie National Recreation Trail** follows the river north from McKenzie Bridge to Fish Lake. From Eugene, take bus No 91 ($1) to reach the trailhead across from the McKenzie River Ranger Station (☎ 541-822-3381, 57600 Hwy 126). *Paradise Campground* has perfect campsites ($10) near the Hwy 242 junction.

CENTRAL & EASTERN OREGON

It's impossible to ignore the geography of central and eastern Oregon. Volcanic power and persistent erosion have decorated the landscape with spectacular formations.

Hells Canyon

The Snake River has been flowing through Hells Canyon for nearly 13 million years, cutting an 8000-foot-deep trench – the deepest canyon in North America. The Wallowa Mountains Visitor Center (☎ 541-426-5546, 88401 Hwy 82), in Enterprise, is a good source of information about Hells Canyon. Another information center is at the Hells Canyon Dam (☎ 541-785-3395).

The little campground community of **Copperfield** is a crossroads of activity for recreation on the Snake. The *Copperfield Campground* (☎ 541-785-3323), on Hwy 26 at the Oregon/Idaho border, has riverside tent and RV sites. The real action is below Hells Canyon Dam, 28 miles north (downriver) from Copperfield. **Hells Canyon Adventures** (☎ 541-785-3352, 800-422-3568, 4200 Hells Canyon Dam Rd), in Oxbow, runs daylong raft trips ($150) as well as less expensive but noisy jet-boat tours.

It's 23 miles from Imnaha along USFS Rd 4240 to the spectacular lookout at **Hat Point**, where there are a few primitive campsites. Allow at least two hours for the drive out. The road is generally open from late May till snowfall; phone ☎ 541-426-5546 for details.

Wallowa Mountains

Tritely called 'Oregon's Alps,' these stunningly beautiful glacier-hewn peaks have spectacular but remote backcountry hikes in the Eagle Cap Wilderness. Just north of the mountains, in the Wallowa Valley, two small towns off Hwy 82, Enterprise and Joseph, have lodging and food. Joseph is known for its bronze galleries and western art and is quite crowded in the summer.

Camp at the busy *Wallowa Lake State Park* (☎ 541-432-4185), off Hwy 82, with sites from $18, or stay in Joseph at the equally popular *Indian Lodge Motel* (☎ 541-432-2651, 201 S Main) for $50.

Warm Springs Indian Reservation

Home to three groups, the Wasco, the Tenino and the Northern Paiute (the Confederated Tribes), Warm Springs Reservation stretches east and west from the banks of the Deschutes River to the peaks of the Cascades. Contact the Confederated Tribes of the Warm Springs Reservation (☎ 541-553-1161, W www.warmsprings.com) to learn more about the reservation's residents and events.

The **Warm Springs Museum** (☎ 541-553-3331), on Hwy 26 just west of Warm Springs, evokes traditional Native American life and culture with artifacts, audio-visuals and re-created villages ($6; open daily). The Kah-Nee-Ta Resort (☎ 541-553-1112), 11 miles north of Warm Springs on Simnasho Rd, has a giant hot-springs-fed **swimming pool** (day passes $7, parking $4) among other amenities, and is a great stopover for travelers.

John Day Fossil Beds National Monument

This monument encompasses 22 sq miles at three sites. Only Sheep Rock, 10 miles northwest of Dayville (take Hwy 19 north from US 26), has a staffed visitor center (☎ 541-987-2333), with exhibits explaining the complex geology. Be sure to take the short hike up the Blue Basin trail for stunning scenery and fossil exhibits.

The Painted Hills Unit, near the town of Mitchell, consists of low-slung, colorfully banded hills formed about 30 million years ago.

The Clarno Unit is the oldest and most remote of the fossil beds, exposing mud flows that washed over an Eocene-era forest. The Clarno Formation eroded into distinctive, sheer-white cliffs topped with spires and turrets of stone.

PACIFIC NORTHWEST

Several campgrounds provide relatively easy access to the fossil beds. Two nice ones, *Lone Pine* and *Big Bend*, are on the North Fork John Day River near the Sheep Rock Unit. In Dayville, the *Fish House Inn* (☎ 541-987-2124, 110 E Franklin St) has B&B rooms from $45.

Service Creek B&B (☎ 541-468-3331), 20 miles southeast of the charming town of Fossil on the John Day River, has rooms from $60, a cafe and raft rentals in case you want to float the generally placid John Day.

Bend & Mt Bachelor Area

Bend is a swaggering little city (population 52,029) with tons of superb recreation right out its back door. The Central Oregon Welcome Center (☎ 541-389-8799) is at 63085 N US 97.

Lava Lands Visitor Center (☎ 541-593-2421), on US 97 about 11 miles south of Bend, has exhibits revealing the geology, wildlife and archeology of the **Newberry National Volcanic Monument**. Nearby is the Lava Butte, rising 500 feet above the surrounding lava flows. Bring a flashlight to explore Lava River Cave, about a mile south of the visitor center.

Twenty-two miles southwest of Bend, 9065-foot **Mt Bachelor** has Oregon's best skiing, with 3100 feet of vertical and nearly 300 inches of snow per year; it's known for fine dry powder. The season begins in November and can last until June. Day tickets cost $43. Call the resort (☎ 541-382-2442, 800-829-2442) for more information.

Drive the Cascade Lakes Hwy (Hwy 46) past Mt Bachelor to mountain lakes, campgrounds and hiking trails into the **Three Sisters Wilderness**.

Central Oregon Recreation Association (☎ 541-382-8334) can help with accommodations, and the Bend Ranger Station (☎ 541-388-5664, 1230 NE 3rd St) can advise about camping. *Bend Cascade Hostel* (☎ 541-389-3813, 19 SW Century Dr), a mile west of downtown, is well kept ($15). *Mill Inn B&B* (☎ 541-389-9198, 642 NW Colorado Ave) is an easy walk from downtown and has comfortable, unfussy rooms from $59. There's a motel strip along US 97 (here called 3rd St), where *Sonoma Lodge* (☎ 541-382-4891, 450 SE 3rd St) is clean and friendly, with in-room microwaves and refrigerators.

It's easy to find a good meal in downtown Bend, which is much nicer than the Hwy 97 strip through town would lead you to believe. Try Wall or Bond Sts, home to inexpensive eateries like *Baja Norte (801 Bond St)*, *Deschutes Brewery* and *Public House (1044 NW Bond St)*. The local Greyhound station (☎ 541-382-2151, 63076 N Hwy 97) has buses to Portland via Madras and Redmond.

SOUTHERN OREGON

Some of Oregon's most magical sites, including Crater Lake National Park, are in the valleys of the Rogue and Umpqua Rivers and the Klamath Basin. The city of Ashland hosts a renowned Shakespeare festival.

Siskiyou Pass, on I-5 between Oregon and California, is known for treacherous winter driving. Call ☎ 800-977-6368 for a road report.

Ashland

The cultural center of southern Oregon, Ashland (population 19,522) is famous for its Oregon Shakespeare Festival (OSF), held from February to October. Contact the chamber of commerce (☎ 541-482-3486, 110 E Main St) for information. Call the Southern Oregon Reservation Center (☎ 541-488-1011) for room reservations, Shakespeare tickets and ski and recreation packages.

Though the core of the **Oregon Shakespeare Festival** repertoire is Shakespearean and Elizabethan drama, it also features contemporary theater from around the world. There are three festival theaters: the outdoor Elizabethan Theatre, the Angus Bowmer Theatre and the intimate New Theatre. The only way to get last-minute tickets is to wait at the box office (☎ 541-482-4331, 15 S Pioneer St) for unclaimed tickets ($28 to $47), released at 9:30am and 6pm daily.

Swans glide across the pond at beautiful **Lithia Park**, which serves as a venue for summer concerts and events.

Glenyan Campground (☎ 541-488-1785, 5310 Hwy 66) is a shady RV campground with some tent sites ($17.50), 4 miles out of Ashland near Emigrant Lake.

Rooms are booked solid throughout the summer. The *Ashland Hostel* (☎ 541-482-9217, 150 N Main St) is only blocks from downtown (dorms $20). The quaint *Manor Motel* (☎ *541-482-2246, 476 N Main St)*, the modern *Timbers Motel* (☎ *541-482-4242, 1450 Ashland St)* and the European-style *Columbia Hotel* (☎ *541-482-3726, 262½ E Main St)* all start at around $65 and are within half a mile of the theaters. If you get stuck for accommodations, try Medford, only 10 miles away. The Ashland B&B Clearinghouse (☎ 541-488-0338) can help locate a B&B.

Eat cheap downtown at *Ashland Bakery & Café (38 E Main St)* or at *Pilaf's (10 Guanajuato Way)*, on Ashland Creek. Ashland is the only place in Oregon with a restaurant tax (5%).

Amtrak Thruway buses stop right downtown. Greyhound stops at the I-5 freeway exit, a few miles north of town.

Grants Pass

This town (population 23,000) is a portal to adventures, especially rafting, on the Rogue and Illinois Rivers, and in the Kalmiopsis Wilderness. The chamber of commerce (☎ 541-476-7717, 1995 NW Vine St) is near I-5 exit 58. The Siskiyou National Forest supervisor's office (☎ 541-471-6500) is at 200 Greenfield Rd. The *Riverpark RV Resort* (☎ *541-479-0046, 2956 Rogue River Hwy)*, on Hwy 99, has hookups right on the river ($22.50). Budget motels along 6th and 7th Sts have rooms from $35 to $50. *Motel 6* (☎ *541-474-1331, 1800 NE 7th)* is one of the nicest.

There are daily Greyhound and Amtrak Thruway buses from the station (☎ 541-476-4513, 460 NE Agness Ave).

Wild Rogue Wilderness Area

The Wild Rogue Wilderness is famous for challenging white-water rafting and a 40-mile long-distance trail through a roadless canyon dotted with rustic lodges. Galice, west of Grants Pass on Merlin-Galice Rd, accesses the eastern edge of the canyon. For raft permits and backpacking advice, contact the BLM's Rand Visitor Center (☎ 541-479-3735, 14335 Galice Rd, Merlin, OR 97532). A three-day organized raft trip costs upward of $500. Lodging averages $75 per person; try *Black Bar Lodge* (☎ *541-479-6507)* or *Marial Lodge* (☎ *541-474-4923 ext 7718)*.

Rogue River War

The Rogue River Indians, who called themselves the Takelma, received their popular name from French beaver trappers early in the 19th century, who termed them *coquins,* or 'rogues,' because of their open hostility toward whites. This fierce tribe earned its nickname in 1846, when a group of adventurous pioneers led by Jesse and Lindsay Applegate seeking an all-land route to the Willamette Valley opened up southern Oregon to the settlers. The Takelma attacked immigrant parties traveling the new South Road and refused to negotiate with the army to allow passage through their land.

The discovery of gold near Jacksonville in 1852 exacerbated tensions, and as disenchanted gold panners from California streamed into the region a series of conflicts developed among the Takelma, the army and settlers, with plenty of tit-for-tat butchery. The Table Rock Treaty, signed in 1853, kept the peace until 1855. War broke out after miners attacked and killed a large number of Takelma women and children. The Takelma raided the mining camp in retaliation, killing 16 people.

The Takelma eluded the army by retreating into the remote canyons of the western Rogue Valley in late fall 1855, but gave themselves up after several winter months of skirmishing with little food or shelter. They were sent north to the Grand Ronde Reservation on the Yamhill River.

Oregon Caves
National Monument

In the Illinois River valley, the 'Oregon Caves' (there's actually only one) feature 3 miles of chambers with a fast-moving stream, the River Styx, running the length of the cave. Guided tours ($7.50) leave daily; dress warmly and be prepared to get a little wet. True spelunkers may want to consider 'off-trail' caving. From Grants Pass, take US 199 south to tiny Cave Junction and travel 20 miles east on Hwy 46. The Illinois Valley Visitor Information Center (☎ 541-592-2631) is in Cave Junction.

Rooms at the *Oregon Caves Chateau* (☎ *541-592-3400)*, at the entrance to the monument, start at $75. There are USFS campgrounds just outside the cave; closest is *Cave Creek Campground* ($8). Off the beaten path in nearby Takilma is *Out 'n' About Treesort (☎ 541-592-2208),* with lodging in rustic treehouses ($85).

Crater Lake National Park

Perfectly symmetrical and uncannily blue, Crater Lake National Park offers hiking and cross-country skiing trails, a boat ride to a rugged island and scenic drives around the lip of the crater. The park can be reached from Medford (72 miles) or from Klamath Falls (73 miles) on Hwy 62. The popular south entrance is open year round. Most facilities are closed from October to June, but people still come for cross-country skiing. A $10 vehicle fee is charged in summer. For information, contact the park headquarters (☎ 541-594-2211, PO Box 7, Crater Lake, OR 97604).

Facilities are limited. Many travelers day trip from Medford, Roseburg, or Klamath Falls. If park lodging is booked up, try lodges and USFS campgrounds around Union Creek and Prospect, west on Hwy 62. *Mazama Campground,* near the park's south entrance, costs $13. In the park, choose between *Mazama Village Motor Inn* ($104) and the grand old *Crater Lake Lodge* (from $124). Call ☎ 541-830-8700 for reservations at either.

Steens Mountain

The highest peak in southeastern Oregon (9773 feet), Steens Mountain is part of a massive, 30-mile fault-block range. On the west slope of the range, Ice Age glaciers bulldozed massive U-shaped valleys into the flanks of the mountain. To the east, 'the Steens' maintain delicate alpine meadows and lakes and drop off dizzyingly to the Alvord Desert, 5000 feet below. Beginning in Frenchglen, the gravel Steens Mountain Loop Rd offers access to Steens Mountain Recreation Area but is open only from late June to November, depending on the weather.

Four miles from Frenchglen along the Loop Rd is *Page Springs Campground,* on the Blitzen River. Next door, the *Steens Mountain Resort (☎ 541-493-2415)* has RV and tent sites and a few cabins ($50). Farther up the mountain are two more iso-

lated campsites: *Fish Lake* and *Jackman Park. Frenchglen Hotel (☎ 541-493-2825)* is old-fashioned and austere, but friendly, and is popular with bird-watchers. Rooms with shared bath are $60.

OREGON COAST

Oregon's most famous beach resorts are on the north coast, between the Columbia River and Newport. Much of the southern coast, from Florence to the California border, approaches pristine wilderness. Oregon's beaches are open to the public, even in developed areas, and the coastline is dotted with state parks.

US 101 stretches the length of the coast for a classic scenic drive or bike ride, generally from north to south with the prevailing winds. The segments from Yachats to Florence and from Port Orford to Brookings are the most spectacular.

Bus transport along the coast is disjointed, with few real bus depots and little information. Greyhound's coast route travels from Portland to San Francisco via Lincoln City, but there are also other routes on other carriers, including Amtrak. Call local bus stations (staffed by Greyhound) to find out exactly who goes where. Available connections include Portland to Astoria or Lincoln City; Corvallis (Albany) to Newport; Eugene to Florence; and Kelso, Washington, to Astoria. Travel between the coast towns is relatively easy on community buses.

Astoria

Astoria (population 9813) sits at the mouth of the Columbia River, where the 4.1-mile Astoria Bridge crosses over to Washington. The city has a great deal of history and scruffy charm. John Jacob Astor and his Pacific Fur Trading Company established a small fort here in the spring of 1811, making this the first US settlement in the West. The helpful visitor center (☎ 503-325-6311) is at 111 W Marine Dr.

Astoria has some of the most lovingly restored and precipitously poised Victorian homes outside of San Francisco. Tour the ornate Flavel House (☎ 503-325-2203, 441 8th St) to get a feel for these magnificent residences, dating back to the 1880s ($5; open daily). At the Columbia River Maritime Museum (☎ 503-325-2323, 1792

Marine Dr), Astoria's 150-year-old seafaring heritage is well exhibited ($5; open daily). Head out to the South Jetty in Fort Stevens State Park to watch the Columbia River pour into the ocean.

Reconstructed **Fort Clatsop** (☎ 503-861-2471), 8 miles south of Astoria off US 101, is well worth a stop ($2; open daily). The Lewis and Clark party spent a miserable winter here in 1805–6. Come spring, they returned up the Columbia, Snake and Clearwater Rivers, eventually arriving in St Louis, where their stories of the Northwest became legend. The small fort was named after a local Native American community who befriended them.

On Clatsop Spit and close to the beaches is *Fort Stevens State Park* (☎ 503-861-1671, reservations ☎ 800-452-5687), in Hammond, Oregon's largest state park campground (sites $17, yurts $35). Across the street is *Astoria-Seaside KOA* (☎ 503-861-2606, 1100 NW Ridge Rd), with campsites ($22) and cabins ($37).

Most motels are along US 30 and can be noisy. In the $60 range are the older-style *Lamplighter* (☎ 503-325-4051, 131 W Marine Dr) and the *Rivershore Motel* (☎ 503-325-2921, 59 W Marine Dr). *Rosebriar Hotel* (☎ 503-325-7427, 636 14th St) offers European-style lodging in 11 rooms (from $75). *Clementine's B&B* (☎ 503-325-2005, 847 Exchange St) occupies an 1888 Italianate mansion (from $70).

Big ships float by the *Cannery Cafe*, which overlooks the river from the end of 6th St. The *Columbian Cafe* (1114 Marine Dr) offers a daily fresh fish selection and other entrées for $17-21.

The Amtrak Thruway bus from Portland ($16) stops at the Mini Mart (☎ 503-325-4162), at 95 W Marine Dr, as does the Pacific Trails bus to Kelso, Washington. Pick up local connections to Seaside or Long Beach, Washington, on Duane St downtown.

Seaside

At its best, Seaside (population 5900), 76 miles to the northwest of Portland, seems pleasantly old-fashioned, but it gets crowded and is very commercial. The visitor center (☎ 503-738-6391) is at 7 North Roosevelt Dr.

Circle Creek Campground (☎ 503-738-6070), a mile south of town, has riverside tent/RV sites for $17/22. *HI Seaside Hostel*

(☎ 503-738-7911, 930 N Holladay Dr) offers dorm beds from $15. *Night Cap Inn* (☎ 503-738-7473, 24 Ave U), a few blocks from the beach, has clean rooms from $55.

Pacific Bento (111 Broadway) prepares smoothies and pastries. At *Dooger's* (505 Broadway), there's a good selection of fresh fish in the $8-14 range.

Amtrak Thruway buses from Portland ($16) stop at Tony's True Value Hardware (☎ 503-738-5966, 34 N Holladay Dr).

Cannon Beach

Miles of sandy beaches, broken by immense basalt promontories and rocky tide pools, stretch north and south of Cannon Beach (population 1588), 9 miles south of Seaside. Some of the coast's premier hotels are here, as well as interesting shops and galleries. Watch glassblowers at work at IceFire Glassworks, 116 E Gower. The visitor center (☎ 503-436-2623) is on 2nd St. On the community's renowned Sandcastle Day, on a Saturday in June, teams compete for originality and execution in sand sculpture.

Sea Ranch RV Park (☎ 503-436-2815), near the entrance to Ecola State Park, has tent/RV sites for $19/21. Wheelbarrows are provided for hauling gear to walk-in tent sites ($14) at *Oswald West State Park* (☎ 503-368-5154), 10 miles south of town. Both parks are popular for trails and surf beaches.

The cheapest rooms start at $70. *McBee Motel* (☎ 503-436-2569, 888 S Hemlock St) and older *Blue Gull Inn Motel* (☎ 503-436-2714, 487 S Hemlock St) are both pleasant. Famous *Pizza A Fetta* (231 N Hemlock) serves by the slice.

Amtrak Thruway buses (☎ 503-436-0515) travel daily to Portland ($15). Local buses to Seaside and Astoria leave with more frequency from the visitor center.

Depoe Bay

Pounding waves battered a narrow channel through basalt cliffs to create Depoe Bay, 10 miles north of Newport. The tiny fishing village here (population 1174) is busily occupied with whale-watching trips ($20) and charter fishing.

Charming *Whale Inn* (☎ 541-765-2789, 416 US 101 N) has rooms from $62. Clifftop *Tidal Raves* (☎ 541-765-2995, 279 US 101) has affordable seafood. Greyhound and

PACIFIC NORTHWEST

local Lincoln County Transit (☎ 541-265-4900) buses travel to Depoe Bay from Newport.

Newport

Marine-based nature tourism dominates Newport (population 9532), but the old downtown still features lively seafood markets. The visitor center (☎ 541-265-8801) is at 555 SW Coast Hwy. The **Oregon Coast Aquarium** (☎ 541-867-3474, 2820 SE Ferry Slip Rd) is famous for arresting marine exhibits such as an enormous, plexiglass tunnel through a shark tank ($9.25; open daily).

There's access to **Nye Beach** along Coast St. *South Beach State Park* (☎ 541-867-4715, 800-452-5687 for reservations), 2 miles south of Newport on US 101, also has good beach access, and campsites ($19). *Sylvia Beach Hotel* (☎ 541-265-5428, 267 NW Cliff St) offers dorm beds and guest rooms ($27/75, breakfast included) in an old hotel for bibliophiles; rooms are decorated after famous authors. Next door, *Nye Beach Hotel* (☎ 541-265-3334) is a restored 1910s inn with rooms from $75 and a good cafe. There are plenty of older, well-kept motels along US 101 north of Newport, most around $50; try *Penny Saver Motel* (☎ 541-265-6631, 710 N Coast Hwy). *The Coffeehouse* (156 SW Bay Blvd) is excellent for breakfast and lunch. Newport's most convivial seafood restaurant is the *Whale's Tale* (452 SW Bay Blvd).

Yachats

Volcanic intrusions south of Yachats (population 617) form some of Oregon's most dramatic and beautiful shoreline. Surf explodes against the shore at **Cape Perpetua**, which offers enjoyable prowling among intertidal rocks and sandy inlets and a fantastic viewpoint. Ten miles south of Yachats, the 1894 Heceta Head Lighthouse towers precipitously above the churning ocean; a trail there leads from enchanting Devil's Elbow State Park. Enormous **Sea Lion Caves** (☎ 541-547-3111), filled with smelly, shrieking sea lions, is a highlight of the central Oregon coast ($6.50; open daily).

Sites at *Cape Perpetua Campground* are $11. Seven miles south of Yachats is *Sea Perch Campground* (☎ 541-547-3505), with ocean-view sites for $28. *Dublin House* (☎ 541-547-3200), at the northern end of Yachats, has an indoor pool and rooms from $70. Six miles south is the *See Vue Motel* (☎ 541-547-3227), an old charmer with ocean-view rooms from $57. Food is good in Yachats at the *Drift Inn*, a friendly cafe and watering hole.

Oregon Dunes

Fifty miles of shifting sand between Florence and Coos Bay form the largest expanse of coastal dunes in the USA. Hiking trails, bridle paths, and boating and swimming areas have been established, and the entire region has abundant wildlife, especially birds. Unfortunately, dune buggies and dirt bikes scream up and down the dunes, especially the stretch south of Reedsport (see 'Dune Buggy Danger'). The northern stretch has the most hiking trails. Oregon Dunes National Recreation Area headquarters (☎ 541-271-3611) is at 855 Highway Ave in logged-out Reedsport. This town hosts chainsaw carving championships in June.

Popular *Jessie M Honeyman State Park* (☎ 541-997-3641, 800-452-5687 for reservations), 3 miles south of Florence on US 101, is handy for recreation in the dunes (campsites cost $16-20). *Umpqua Lighthouse State Park* (☎ 503-271-4118, 800-452-5687 for reservations) has campsites ($13) and deluxe yurts (from $35) with TVs, VCR, and refrigerators a mile south of Winchester Bay. USFS campgrounds like *Eel Creek*, 10 miles south of Reedsport, offer the best dune access (sites cost $13).

Dune Buggy Danger

Designated off-road vehicle (ORV) and non-ORV areas are set up to restrict ORVs, not hikers, who have full freedom to explore any public areas of the dunes. However, hikers venturing into ORV territory need to remain keen to the direction of ORV traffic. Climbing toward the crest of a high dune is an especially bad place to be when a dune buggy comes flying over the top. Red (sometimes orange) flags waving above the dunes indicate oncoming ORVs.

Cape Arago

The dramatic **Conde McCullough Bridge** soars over the harbor at Coos Bay, the coast's largest city (population 15,374). Five miles west is **Cape Arago**, with beaches, trails, a botanical garden and great wildlife viewing contained in a trio of state parks. Coos Bay's visitor center (☎ 541-269-0215, 50 E Central Ave) has information. Campsites and cabins at *Bastendorff Beach County Park (☎ 541-888-5353)*, close to Charleston, run $10-25.

Bandon

Little Bandon (population 2833) is considered a real jewel (though a lackluster one), with an Old Town full of cafes, gift shops and taverns and a reputation for being a center of alternative spirituality. Ask about medical marijuana at the visitor center (☎ 541-347-9616), 2nd St and Chicago Ave – locals do.

Beach Loop Drive leads south of town to Bandon's best beaches, with towering seastacks and monoliths that host large numbers of seabirds. Bluffs like **Coquille Point**, at the end of 11th St, are a popular place to spot migrating whales in winter and spring.

Two miles north of Bandon off US 101, *Bullards Beach State Park (☎ 541-347-2209)* has ocean-access sites from $13. The *HI Sea Star Hostel (☎ 541-347-9632, 375 2nd St)*, in Old Town, has dorms/rooms from $13/28. Motels here are nothing fancy. Those along Beach Loop Rd have beach access and ocean views. Charming *Table Rock Motel (☎ 541-347-2700, 840 Beach Loop Rd)*, on a shrubby bluff, has rooms from $48. Modern *Driftwood Motel (☎ 541-347-9022, 460 US 101)* is downtown with singles/doubles for $64/74.

In Old Town, *Harp's (130 Chicago Ave)* is recommended for bay-view dining. Greyhound stops at the Sea Star Hostel.

Gold Beach

Jet boats from Gold Beach (population 1897) zip up the Rogue River to the Wild Rogue Wilderness Area, though fishing is the main attraction of this largely utilitarian town. The visitor center (☎ 541-247-7526) is at the Gold Beach Ranger Station (29279 S Ellensburg Ave).

On the Rogue River's south bank, *Indian Creek Recreation Park (☎ 541-247-7704, 94680 Jerry's Flat Rd)* has tent/RV sites for $15/22. There are more campgrounds upriver. Unappealing *City Center Motel (☎ 541-247-6675, 94200 Harlow St)* offers the only cheap rooms ($40). The Greyhound station (☎ 541-247-7710) is on Colvin St, across from the restaurant *Grant's (29790 Ellensburg Ave)*.

Brookings

Just 6 miles north of the California-Oregon border on US 101 is the balmy harbor town of Brookings (population 5447). The chamber of commerce (☎ 541-469-3181) is at 16330 Lower Harbor Rd. Greyhound (☎ 541-469-3326) stops at the Fiji Island Tan building (601 Railroad St).

Roads lead inland from Brookings along the Chetco River to the western edge of remote **Kalmiopsis Wilderness Area**, the state's largest. Oregon's only redwood forests are found up the Chetco River; some groves are preserved in **Alfred A Loeb State Park** (☎ 541-469-2021, ☎ 800-452-5687 reservations), also known for its myrtle trees (campsites cost $16).

North of town is **Samuel H Boardman State Park**, with 11 miles of Oregon's most beautiful coastline, its sheer cliffs, nice beaches and tiny island chains home to shorebirds and sea lions. *Harris Beach State Park (☎ 541-469-2021, ☎ 800-452-5687 reservations)*, 2 miles north of Brookings on US 101, has sites from $16. *Pacific Sunset Inn (☎ 541-469-2141, 1144 Chetco Ave)*, on US 101, has rooms for $45.

Alaska

Alaska

Alaska is a major side trip for most visitors to the USA, but it's worth it. The state offers such unique experiences as a cruise through the fjords of the Inside Passage, walks through unspoiled wilderness and close encounters with wildlife.

Southeast Alaska is the state's most accessible region, and it's also one of the most interesting. A two- to three-week side trip from Seattle will be a highlight of any visit to the USA, and can be done for as little as $1500 with camping and hostel accommodations, an Alaska Marine Hwy ferry ticket to Haines, and a flight back to Seattle.

If you want to see more of the state, take a flight to the Southcentral region, where you can enjoy Prince William Sound and the Kenai Peninsula. Then you can head north to Denali National Park. Allow an extra week for each place, and accept the risk that you'll blow all your time and money in Alaska.

History

The indigenous Alaskans – the Athabascans, Aleuts, Inuit, and coastal tribes of Tlingits and Haidas – are descended from people who migrated over the 900-mile Bering Strait land bridge during the last Ice Age.

Spanish, British and French explorers touched on Alaska's coasts, but Russia became the dominant power. Russian fur merchants overran the Aleutian Islands and Kodiak Island in the 18th century, competing murderously with each other and almost annihilating the peaceful Aleuts. When the fur colonies were depleted, the Russians moved to the Southeast, ruthlessly subduing the Tlingits and using immense fur profits to make Sitka 'an American Paris in Alaska.'

By the 1860s the Russians were badly overextended due to the Napoleonic Wars in Europe and the declining fur industry. In 1867 Russia signed a treaty with US Secretary of State William H Seward for the USA to purchase the territory for $7.2 million, less than 2¢ an acre. There was a public uproar over 'Seward's Ice Box' (also known as 'Seward's Folly'), but Congress eventually approved the deal. The riches of the remote,

Highlights

- The Inside Passage – a spectacular sea trip past islands, fjords, glaciers and isolated towns

- Alaskan wildlife – opportunities for bear watching, whale cruises, salmon fishing

- Mt McKinley – the tallest peak in North America

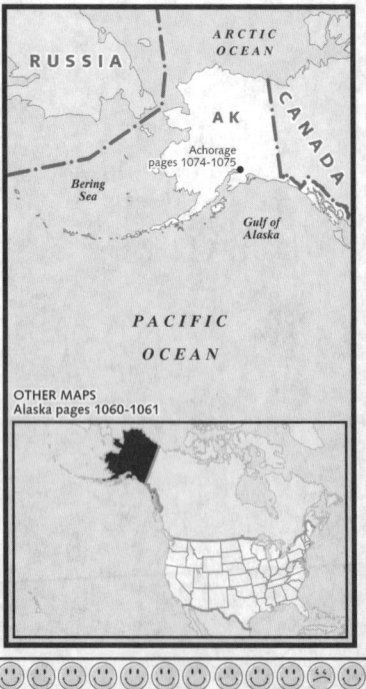

lawless territory were gradually uncovered – first whales, then the phenomenal salmon runs, then gold.

Gold-rush towns like Juneau and Douglas sprang up in the 1880s, Circle City in 1893, followed by the Klondike gold rush, 'the last grand adventure.' From the boomtown of Skagway, almost 30,000 prospectors tackled the steep Chilkoot Trail, then rafted down to the gold fields. In the 1900s, miners shifted to Nome and then to Fairbanks.

When the Japanese attacked some Alaskan islands in WWII, large military bases were built and thousands of personnel came to run them. Fearing future naval and air attacks, the military built the famous Alcan (Alaska-Canada) Hwy. The road finally linked the remote territory with the rest of the USA and contributed greatly to the postwar development of Alaska, which became a state in 1959.

On Good Friday in 1964, a powerful earthquake (9.2 on the Richter scale) hit Southcentral Alaska, leaving the new state in shambles. Recovery was boosted in 1968 when massive oil deposits were discovered under Prudhoe Bay in the Arctic Ocean. The 1971 Alaska Native Claims Settlement Act opened the way for construction of a 789-mile pipeline to the ice-free port of Valdez, and the boom years of pipeline construction saw Anchorage become a full-fledged modern city.

For a time Alaska had the highest per-capita income in the country, but the party ended in 1986, when oil prices dropped. The hangover came in 1989 when the *Exxon Valdez* fuel tanker hit a reef and spilled 11 million gallons of crude into Prince William Sound, eventually contaminating 1560 miles of shoreline.

As Prudhoe Bay oil production began to decline, big oil and pipeline companies laid off workers, while US military cutbacks and the closure of several lumber mills spelled more bad news for the economy. To help offset the decrease in oil royalties, the state is now considering a sales or income tax (there currently is neither in Alaska), while user fees at parks, campgrounds and trails have risen sharply in recent years. The best hope for economic revival is the construction of a natural-gas line from the Arctic Slope to the 'Lower 48' states via Canada, and the opening of the Arctic National Wildlife Refuge (ANWR) to oil production. Environmentalists have been fighting hard to protect the 1.5-million-acre refuge from oil rigs and were successful when President Clinton was in office. But with the arrival of President George W Bush, a former Texas oil man, there seems little hope this wilderness will remain pristine.

Geography

At latitudes spanning the Arctic Circle, the main body of Alaska is about 800 miles square, with the long arc of the Aleutian Island chain stretching some 1600 miles south and west, and a 'panhandle' strip running 600 miles southeast down the North American coast. The panhandle and Southcentral coasts are heavily indented by glaciation, with fjords, channels and coastal islands. The Brooks Range crosses the north of the state, and its North Slope goes to the Arctic Ocean. The central Plateau area drains to the west via the Yukon River from several mountain ranges extending east from northern Canada.

Environment

Due to Alaska's huge tracts of remaining wilderness, its environmental concerns are not just regional conflicts but usually national debates. Opening the coastal plain of ANWR to oil drilling is just one of the prominent issues. Others include the state's decision to embark on a program of wolf management (killing wolves to ensure there are enough moose and caribou for hunters), clear-cutting of the Tongass National Forest and overfishing by fleets of factory ships. Perhaps the environmental issue that affects tourists most is Alaska's desire to build roads, including a proposed road to connect Juneau with Skagway.

Alaska

Nickname: The Last Frontier

Population: 626,900 (48th)

Area: 591,004 sq miles (1st)

Admitted to Union: January 3, 1959 (49th)

Capital city: Juneau (population 31,000)

Other cities: Anchorage (260,000), Fairbanks (82,000), Ketchikan (14,000), Kodiak (14,000)

State flower: forget-me-not

State motto: North to the Future

State sport: mushing

Birthplace of: Olympic gold medallist (skiing) Tommy Moe

Famous for: its size (if split in half, Alaska would still be the largest two states in the USA), Eskimos (Inuit)

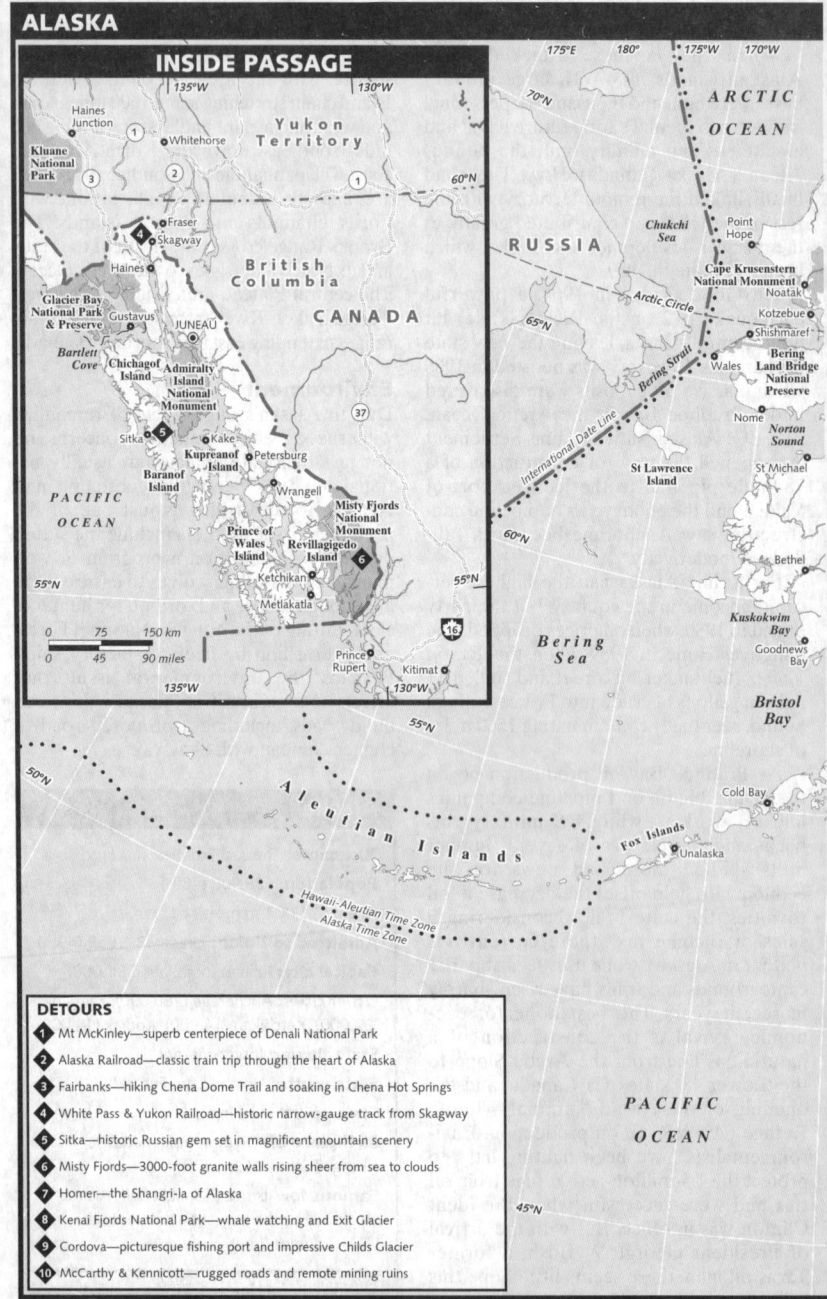

ALASKA

ALASKA

INSIDE PASSAGE

- Haines Junction
- Whitehorse
- Yukon Territory
- Kluane National Park
- Fraser
- Skagway
- British Columbia
- Haines
- Glacier Bay National Park & Preserve
- Gustavus
- JUNEAU
- Bartlett Cove
- Chichagof Island
- Admiralty Island National Monument
- CANADA
- Sitka
- Kake
- Kupreanof Island
- Petersburg
- Baranof Island
- Wrangell
- Misty Fjords National Monument
- Prince of Wales Island
- Revillagigedo Island
- Ketchikan
- Metlakatla
- PACIFIC OCEAN
- Prince Rupert
- Kitimat

0   75   150 km
0   45   90 miles

ARCTIC OCEAN

RUSSIA

Chukchi Sea

Point Hope

Cape Krusenstern National Monument

Noatak

Arctic Circle

Kotzebue

Shishmaref

Bering Strait

Wales

Bering Land Bridge National Preserve

International Date Line

Nome

Norton Sound

St Lawrence Island

St Michael

Bering Sea

Bethel

Kuskokwim Bay

Goodnews Bay

Bristol Bay

Aleutian Islands

Cold Bay

Fox Islands

Unalaska

Hawaii-Aleutian Time Zone
Alaska Time Zone

PACIFIC OCEAN

DETOURS

1 Mt McKinley—superb centerpiece of Denali National Park

2 Alaska Railroad—classic train trip through the heart of Alaska

3 Fairbanks—hiking Chena Dome Trail and soaking in Chena Hot Springs

4 White Pass & Yukon Railroad—historic narrow-gauge track from Skagway

5 Sitka—historic Russian gem set in magnificent mountain scenery

6 Misty Fjords—3000-foot granite walls rising sheer from sea to clouds

7 Homer—the Shangri-la of Alaska

8 Kenai Fjords National Park—whale watching and Exit Glacier

9 Cordova—picturesque fishing port and impressive Childs Glacier

10 McCarthy & Kennicott—rugged roads and remote mining ruins

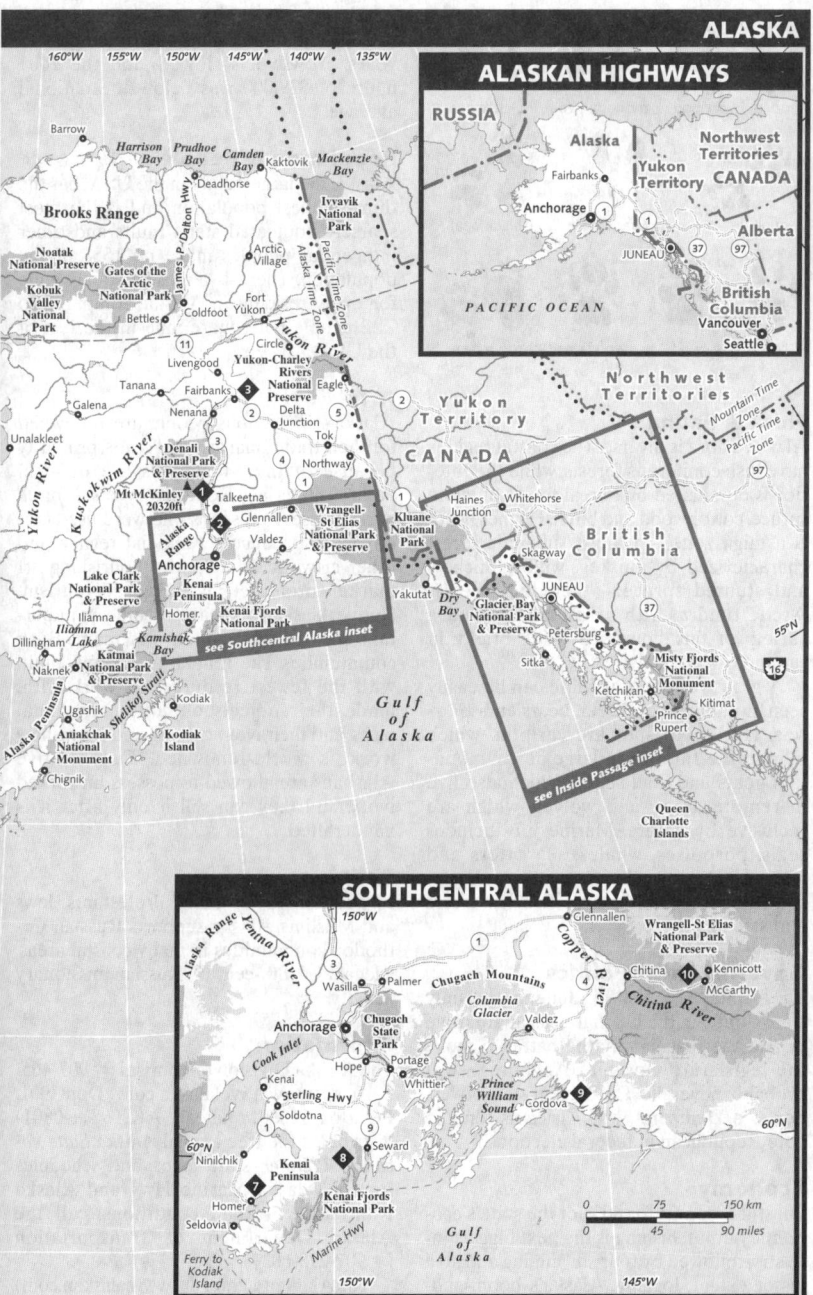

ALASKA

moose   caribou   mountain goat   Dall sheep

mink   snowshoe hare   black bear

lynx   wolf   wolverine   brown bear

Flora & Fauna
Alaska's flora is diverse. The coastal regions have lush coniferous forests, while the Interior is dominated by boreal forest of white spruce, cottonwood and birch. Farther north is a taiga zone – a moist subarctic forest characterized by muskeg, willow thickets and stunted spruce – then the treeless Arctic tundra, with grass, mosses and a variety of tiny flowers thriving briefly in summer.

A great variety of wildlife can be easily seen, notably moose, deer, bears and squirrels. Harder to spot are caribou, which inhabit the Interior in large herds; mountain goats and Dall sheep, which also live in remote areas; and wolves, which are reclusive by nature. Marine life includes seals, porpoises, whales, sea otters and walrus. During the summer salmon-spawning run, millions of fish fill rivers and streams.

Government & Politics
The capital of Alaska is Juneau, the only state capital in the US that you cannot drive to and the reason why the battle to move the legislature closer to Anchorage will probably never die. The current state governor is a Democrat, but Alaskans tend to vote Republican in federal elections.

Economy
Oil still accounts for 80% of the state's economic output. Fishing is the next biggest industry, followed by tourism, mining and, to a lesser extent, logging. Alaska's boom-and-bust economy peaked in 1986, when

Alaskans' per-capita income was over $20,000, the nation's highest. In the past 15 years, growth has slowed, and the 2001 figure of $29,000 was below the national average.

Population & People
Alaska, the largest state in the USA, has the third-smallest population and is the most sparsely populated state. Inuits and other indigenous peoples make up 15% of the population. There is almost a square mile for every resident in Alaska, compared to 71.2 people per square mile in the rest of the USA.

Arts
Alaska's indigenous people are renowned for their traditional arts and crafts, primarily because of their ingenious use of local natural materials. Roots, ivory tusks, birch bark, grasses and soapstone were used creatively to produce ceremonial regalia and other artwork. Thanks to a flourishing art market, prompted by increased tourism, Native Alaskan arts have become an important slice of the economy in many Bush communities. The Inupiat and Yupik Inuit, with the fewest resources to work with, made their objects out of sea-mammal parts, and their ivory carving and scrimshaw work is world-renowned. Only Native Alaskans are allowed to possess unworked ivory, and they can sell it only after it is handcrafted.

Religion
In addition to Catholics, Protestants, Jews and Muslims, Alaska supports Russian Orthodox communities in many coastal areas, a legacy of 18th-century Russian missionary activity.

Information
The Alaska Division of Tourism (☎ 907-465-2010, Ⓦ www.travelalaska.com, Dept 901, PO Box 110801, Juneau, AK 99811-0801) distributes the free annual *Alaska State Vacation Planner*, state maps, and schedules for the Alaska Marine Hwy and Alaska Railroad. For road conditions, call the Alaska Department of Transportation (☎ 907-273-6037).

The Alaskan Center (Ⓦ www.alaskan.com) has background information as well as bus, ferry, air and train schedules. There are several Alaskan Internet travel sites, including Alaska One (W www.AlaskaOne.com) and Alaska Guidebook (W www.AlaskaGuidebook.com). All 13 national parks in Alaska have pages on the Web and can be reached through W www.nps.gov (for Denali National Park, it's W www.nps.gov/dena).

There is no state sales tax, but most cities will have a local sales tax and often a bed tax that supports their visitor bureau. The combination of these often increases the cost of a bed in a hotel, motel or B&B by 4% to 12%.

When to Go
The peak tourist season is early July to mid-August, when the best-known parks are very crowded and it's essential to make reservations for ferries, transport and accommodations. May and September still have mild weather, everything is less crowded, and prices are lower. Late April is slushy and muddy in the Interior but OK in the Southcentral areas, and you get big off-season discounts. In winter expect long nights, minus-50°F temperatures and the fantastic northern lights.

Accommodations
Most mid-range hotels cost $80 and up for a double room, with B&Bs charging around $70. There are several HI-AYH hostels and a growing number of independent hostels, but anyone on a tight budget should bring a tent and make use of the many campgrounds. USFS cabins (see 'Alaska's Forest Service Cabins') in remote areas cost around $35 and sleep at least four people. They provide a great experience, but you often need a reservation, as well as a charter flight to reach them.

In Southeast Alaska, reservations are a good idea in summer. Each town has a different set of taxes, which will add about 10% to 12% to accommodation costs. The region is well supplied with hostels and campgrounds.

Activities
Hiking opportunities are boundless and a sure way to get away from summer crowds. For more information, see Lonely Planet's *Hiking in Alaska*. Mountain bikes are great in many areas and can be carried on ferries.

Alaska's Forest Service Cabins

The USFS cabin program offers more than shelter in the mountains or a cheap lodging option in this land of high prices. When you rent a USFS cabin ($35-50 a night), you're renting your own slice of wilderness.

Although some cabins can be reached on foot or by boat, the vast majority require a flight on a floatplane, ensuring that your party will be the only people in the area until the next group is flown in. The fishing can be outstanding, the chances of seeing wildlife are excellent and your wilderness solitude is guaranteed.

This is Alaskan wilderness at its easiest and cheapest; but remember that a USFS cabin is not a suite at the Hilton, or even a room at Motel 6. The cabin provides security from the weather, a wood-burning stove, an outhouse, and often a small rowboat, but you need to pack sleeping bags, food, a water filter and a cooking stove.

Of the 190 USFS cabins, 150 are in Tongass National Forest, which covers most of Southeast Alaska, and there are another 40 in Chugach National Forest, in the Prince William Sound area. For a list, call the Alaska Public Lands Information Center (☎ 907-271-2737). Cabins can be reserved 179 days in advance through the National Forest Reservation Center (☎ 877-444-6777, W www.reserveusa.com).

In addition to the nightly fee, you need to budget the cost of the floatplane, paying a bush pilot for both a drop-off and a pickup. For cabins within 15 to 20 minutes from major towns like Juneau or Ketchikan, budget $300-400 for a party of two or three.

Paddlers have a choice of coastal kayaking amid otters and icebergs, or running river rapids. Rental equipment is widely available (from $35 per day).

Getting There & Around
Air Anchorage is the major regional air hub, with direct flights from Seattle ($300 roundtrip), Chicago ($750 roundtrip) and several other cities. Try Alaska Airlines (☎ 800-426-0333, W www.alaskaair.com), Delta, Northwest, American Airlines, or

United. Many small regional airlines serve small towns, and 'bush planes' can be chartered to the most remote areas.

Bus Reliable bus services link all the main towns in Alaska, with connections to the Lower 48. Busing it is not cheaper than flying, but you do get to experience the Alaska Hwy. From Seattle, Washington (via Vancouver), and Prince George, Dawson and Whitehorse in Canada, it takes four days by bus to reach Anchorage ($550 one way).

Train The Alaska Railroad (☎ 907-265-2494, 800-544-0552, W www.akrr.com) has one main route, from Seward on the Gulf of Alaska to Anchorage ($55 one way), and north from there via Denali ($125) to Fairbanks ($175). Book early on this popular train.

The narrow-gauge 1890s White Pass & Yukon Railroad (☎ 800-343-7373, W www .whitepassrailroad.com) links Skagway to Fraser, British Columbia, with connections to Whitehorse on the Alcan Hwy (Hwy 2), but for most travelers the train is a day trip from Skagway.

Car & Motorcycle Allow at least a week to drive from the northern US through Canada to Fairbanks on the mostly paved Alcan Hwy. It's not worth it unless you can make some stops on the way and spend a few weeks in Alaska. Local car rentals are handy to get around the countryside, starting at $50 a day with 100 miles free.

Southeast Alaska

The Southeast is the part of Alaska closest to the continental USA, linked to Bellingham, in northwest Washington, by the ferries of the Alaska Marine 'Highway.' It's possible to fly into Southeast Alaskan towns, but the best option is a cruise through the Inside Passage.

Getting There & Around
Alaska Airlines has daily north- and southbound flights year round, with stops at all main towns. Roundtrip advance-purchase fares include Seattle-Juneau ($300), Juneau-Anchorage ($225) and Ketchikan-Juneau

($175). Smaller airlines serving the region include LAB (☎ 907-766-2222, 800-426-0543), Taquan Air (☎ 907-225-9668, 800-770-8800) and Wings of Alaska (☎ 907-789-0790).

The scenic White Pass & Yukon Railroad (☎ 800-343-7373) runs between Skagway and Fraser, with connections to Whitehorse on the Alcan Hwy ($95).

It's possible to take a car on the Alaska Marine Hwy ferries, but it costs a lot and space must be reserved months ahead. In several towns you can rent cars to visit surrounding attractions. See individual town sections for details.

Alaska Marine Hwy (☎ 907-645-3941, 800-642-0066) runs ferries north and south along the Inside Passage, calling at the main towns almost daily in summer. Smaller boats make less frequent calls to minor settlements. The complete trip, from Bellingham, Washington, to Juneau costs $249 per person; this permits stops at ports on the way if you arrange it in advance. Fares for trips within the Inside Passage include Prince Rupert–Haines ($134), Ketchikan-Petersburg ($42), Petersburg-Sitka ($290), Sitka-Juneau ($290) and Juneau-Haines ($26).

It is now possible to take a state-run ferry across the Gulf of Alaska from Juneau in the Southeast to Seward on the Kenai Peninsula. The service began in 1998 on the ferry *Kennicott*. The one-way fare from Juneau to Seward is $148 for the five-day trip. Ferries can be heavily booked in summer. If you can't get on a ferry in Bellingham, take alternative transport to Prince Rupert, British Columbia, which has more departures.

INSIDE PASSAGE
The Inside Passage is a waterway made up of thousands of islands, fjords and mountainous coastlines. You can take a cruise, stopping at some of the 14 ports along the way for sightseeing, side trips, hiking, kayaking, whale-watching and so on.

Ketchikan
The Alaska Marine Hwy ferry's first Alaskan stop is Ketchikan, a fishing and timber town with frontier character. The visitor bureau (☎ 907-225-6166, 800-770-3300, W www.visit-ketchikan.com), on the City Dock, arranges tours, gives out a

walking-tour map and has city bus information. For details on trails, cabins and outdoor activities, pay a visit to the Southeast Alaska Discover Center (☎ 907-228-6220, 50 Main St), with an impressive theater and exhibit hall ($3).

The former red-light district of Creek St features Dolly's House, the parlor of Ketchikan's most famous madam ($4). The Totem Heritage Center (☎ 907-225-5900), on Deermont St, restores Tlingit totem poles ($3). At nearby Deer Mountain Tribal Hatchery and Eagle Center (☎ 907-225-5158), also on Deermont St, biologists annually raise 300,000 salmon for release ($6).

The 3.1-mile **Deer Mountain Trail** begins near the city center, providing access to a USFS cabin ($35 per night). More trails are in the Ward Lake Recreation Area (see below). Southeast Exposure (☎ 907-225-8829, 515 Water St) rents kayaks and runs tours (from $50).

The closest camping is available at the three USFS campgrounds, 10 miles north of Ketchikan, in the Ward Lake Recreation Area on Ward Lake Rd. The rustic campgrounds are *Signal Creek*, *Last Chance* and *Three C* ($10). Bustling but basic *HI-AYH Ketchikan Hostel* (☎ 907-225-3319, 400 Main St), in the United Methodist Church, charges $10/13 members/nonmembers (open Memorial Day to Labor Day).

Renovated *Gilmore Hotel* (☎ 907-225-9423, 326 Front St) has some historic flavor (from $75/85 singles/doubles). *New York Hotel* (☎ 907-225-0246, 207 Stedman St) has waterfront views ($79/89). Ketchikan Reservation Service (☎ 907-247-5337, 800-987-5337) books B&B rooms (from $65). There are 30 USFS cabins (☎ 877-444-6777, Ⓦ www.reserveusa.com) in the area, most involving air charter.

In the Gilmore Mall, 1920s-style *Annabelle's* (326 Front St) has chowders and pancakes from $5. Local seafood and waterfront dining is enjoyed at *Streamers on the Dock* (76 Front St), and affordable Mexican at *Chico's* (435 Dock St). Internet access and lattes are at *Cyber By The Sea* (5 Salmon Landing), while next door to the Plaza Mall is *Carr's* (2417 Tongass Ave), a 24-hour supermarket.

Sprawling *First City Saloon* (803 Water St) features giant-screen TVs, pool tables and live music. The fishing crowd frequents *Potlatch Bar* (126 Thomas St), but *Eagles Club*, on Creek St, serves cheaper beer.

The MV *Aurora* (☎ 907-225-6181) sails to Metlakatla ($15 one way) and Hollis on Prince of Wales Island ($22). Alaska Car Rental (☎ 907-225-5123, 800-662-0007) has compacts for $47 a day (unlimited mileage).

Around Ketchikan

Some 2 miles south of Ketchikan, **Saxman Totem Park** has the world's largest standing collection of totem poles, as well as a cultural center (☎ 907-225-5163). Ten miles north of Ketchikan, **Totem Bight State Historical Park** contains 14 restored totem poles and a colorful community house (free admission).

Misty Fjords National Monument begins 22 miles east of Ketchikan, offering wildlife and spectacular views. Kayaking is popular. Alaska Cruises (☎ 907-225-6044) runs an 11-hour trip for $145; alternatively, try a two-hour sightseeing flight with Island Wings (☎ 907-225-2444, 888-854-2444), for $179.

Prince of Wales Island

The third-largest island in the USA, Prince of Wales Island features Native American villages, logging camps, 900 miles of coast and the Southeast's most extensive road network (mostly unpaved). The island's chamber of commerce (☎ 907-826-3870) is in Craig. The USFS has offices in Craig (☎ 907-826-3271) and Thorne Bay (☎ 907-828-3304). Two USFS cabins are accessible from the road.

Ferries arrive at Hollis, and the fishing and timber community of Craig is 31 miles southwest. Camp in the city park or try *Ruthann's Hotel* (☎ 907-826-3378), on Main St, from $90, or *TLC Laundry & Rooms* (☎ 907-826-2966, 333 Cold Storage Rd), with bunks for $40 and Internet access. There are several restaurants and bars.

The ferry *Aurora* (☎ 907-225-6181) visits Hollis most days ($22 from Ketchikan). Sea Otter Taxi (☎ 907-755-2362) of Klawock will meet the ferry in Hollis ($25). Rental cars are available in Craig and Klawock or can be brought from Ketchikan on the ferry ($28).

Wrangell

Founded by Russians in 1834, leased to the British in 1840 and then taken over by Americans with the purchase of Alaska, the Russian town of Redoubt St Dionysius was renamed Fort Wrangell in 1868. It thrived as first a fur-trading and then a gold-mining supply center. The visitor center (☎ 907-874-3901, 800-367-9745, ⓦ www.wrangell.com) is in front of the city hall. There's a local USFS office (☎ 907-874-2323, 525 Bennett St). Practical Rent-A-Car (☎ 907-874-3975) is at the airport.

Displays of indigenous artifacts, petroglyphs and a collection of Alaskan art are at the **Wrangell Museum** (☎ 907-874-3770, 318 Church St), which also provides tour details for the **Shakes Community House**, an upper-caste tribal house ($3 each site). There are about 20 petroglyphs around Wrangell, as well as several hiking trails.

The *City Park Campground*, 1¾ miles south of the ferry terminal on Zimovia Hwy, is for tents only, with a one-night limit (free). Three miles farther south, the *Shoemaker Bay Recreation Area* has a 10-day limit (tents free, RVs from $10). *Wrangell Hostel (☎ 907-874-3534, 220 Church St)* charges $15. Local B&Bs include *Rooney's Roost (☎ 907-874-2026, 206 McKinnon St)*, at $60/65 singles/doubles, and *The Anchor (☎ 907-874-2078, 325 Church)*, at $70/80.

Stikine Inn (☎ 907-874-3388, 107 Stikine Ave) charges $85/90. A mile south of town, *Hardings Old Sourdough Lodge (☎ 907-874-3613, 800-874-3613, 1104 Peninsula St)* offers sauna, meals and free ferry/airport transport and charges $85/95.

There are 20 USFS cabins (☎ 877-444-6777, ⓦ www.reserveusa.com) around Wrangell. The six on the Stikine River flats, 12 to 15 miles from Wrangell, are accessible by canoe or bush plane.

The cheapest spot to eat is *Diamond C Café (223 Front St)*. At the City Dock, *J&W's (120 Front St)* stays open later. Wrangell's best is Stikine Inn's *Waterfront Grill*, featuring local seafood. A full dinner is close to $20.

Mingle with locals at *Totem Bar (116 Front St)* or dance with them at *Stikine Inn Lounge (107 Stikine Ave)*, featuring Wrangell's only dance floor.

Petersburg

At the north end of spectacular Wrangell Narrows lies the picturesque community of Petersburg, a town known for Norwegian heritage. Petersburg is also known as being the home of Alaska's largest halibut fleet.

The visitor center (☎ 907-772-4636, ⓦ www.petersburg.org) is at Fram and 1st Sts. The center also has USFS information; you can also visit the USFS office (☎ 907-772-3871), in the Federal Building on Nordic Dr.

The center of old Petersburg was **Sing Lee Alley**, which winds past weathered homes and boathouses perched on pilings above the water. The **Clausen Memorial Museum** (☎ 907-772-3598, 203 Fram St) features local artifacts and relics ($3).

There are **kayaking** opportunities for day paddles and weeklong blue-water adventures. Tongass Kayak Adventures (☎ 907-772-4600, ⓦ www.alaska.net/~tonkayak, 106 N Nordic Dr) offers rentals and drop-off transportation. Its four-day guided paddle to LeConte Glacier is $708 per person.

On Haugen Dr half a mile northwest of the airport, *Tent City* is crowded in summer ($5). Central *LeConte RV Park (☎ 907-772-4680)*, at 4th St and Haugen Dr, has $7 tent sites. *Petersburg Bunk & Breakfast Hostel (☎ 907-772-3632, ⓦ www.rentahostel.net)* is 1½ miles from the ferry terminal and has nine beds ($25 per person). Call in advance for directions. Petersburg also has several B&Bs at around $75/85 singles/doubles; ask at the visitor center. *Tides Inn (☎ 907-772-4288, 800-665-8433, 307 1st St)* has rooms for $70/85.

Near the ferry terminal, good Chinese dishes and fish dinners are enjoyed at *Joan Mei (1130 Nordic Dr)* for $10-14. *Helse Health Foods & Deli (17 Sing Lee Alley)* is cheap and wholesome. The best seafood is at *Coastal Cold Storage (306 Nordic Dr)*.

Locals drink at *Harbor Bar (310 Nordic Dr)*. *Kito's Kave (11 Sing Lee Alley)* has live music and dancing, and it can get wild at times.

Le Conte ferry (☎ 907-465-3941) leaves for Juneau on Tuesday ($48 one way), stopping at Kake, Sitka, Angoon, Tenakee and Hoonah. Tides Inn (see above) rents midsize cars ($66 a day).

Sitka

Russians established Southeast Alaska's first nonindigenous settlement here in 1799, and the town flourished on fur. After the US purchase of Alaska, the town was given its present name, Sitka, and was the territorial capital until 1900. A gem in a beautiful setting, Sitka sees itself as the cultural center of the Southeast.

The visitor bureau (☎ 907-747-5940, W www.sitka.org, 330 Harbor Dr) is in the Centennial Building. USFS (☎ 907-747-6671, 204 Siginaka Way) provides hiking and kayaking information.

On Lincoln St, **St Michael's Cathedral** is a replica of the original 1840s Russian Orthodox cathedral destroyed by fire in 1966; priceless treasures were salvaged by residents ($2). **Castle Hill** is the site of Baranof's Castle, where Alaska was officially transferred from Russia to the USA. Built in 1842, the **Russian Bishop's House**, on Lincoln St, is Sitka's oldest intact Russian building and now a museum managed by the National Park Service ($3). **Sheldon Jackson Museum** (☎ 907-747-8981, 104 College Dr), on the college campus, houses an excellent indigenous-culture collection ($3). The colorful **Katlian St fishing quarter**, at the west end of town, is a photographer's delight.

The top attraction is **Sitka National Historical Park** (☎ 907-747-6281), at the east end of Lincoln St. A trail winds past 15 totem poles, while the visitor center shows Russian and indigenous artifacts and presents traditional carving demonstrations (free admission).

Sitka has superb **hiking**, and the Gaven Hill Trail into the mountains is accessible from the downtown area. There are also many **kayaking** trips around Baranof and Chichagof Islands. Baidarka Boats (☎ 907-747-8996, W www.kayaksite.com, 320 Seward St) rent kayaks and run guided trips. Singles/doubles are $50/55 per day. Sitka Tours (☎ 907-747-8443) runs short tours for ferry passengers waiting in Sitka for tide changes ($8).

There are two campgrounds in the Sitka area, but neither is close to town. *Starrigavan Campground*, three-quarters of a mile north of the ferry terminal on Halibut Point Rd, was renovated in 2001 ($8). *Sawmill Creek Campground*, on Blue Lake Rd, is 6 miles east of Sitka and offers free tent sites.

The basic *HI-AYH Sitka Youth Hostel* (☎ 907-747-8661, 303 Kimsham St) charges $11/14 for members/nonmembers. Numerous B&Bs offer singles/doubles for around $55/60; call the visitor bureau. About the most affordable hotel is *Sitka Hotel* (☎ 907-747-3288, 118 Lincoln St), at $70/75.

Several *USFS cabins* (☎ 877-444-6777, W www.reserveusa.com) are accessible by air in 30 minutes or less.

Good coffee, espresso drinks for under $4, fresh bagels and Internet access are available at *Highliner Coffee* (215 Kimsham Rd). *Victoria's* (118 Lincoln St) serves breakfast ($6-10) all day. Large portions and great hamburgers are at *Rookies Sports Grill* (1617 Sawmill Creek Rd), which also boasts Sitka's only dance floor. *Channel Club* (2906 Halibut Point Rd) has local seafood and Sitka's best steaks (from $12). Hang out with the loggers and fishermen at *Pioneer Bar* (212 Katlian St).

Allstar Rental (☎ 907-966-2552), at Sitka Airport, has subcompact vehicles for $45 per day (unlimited mileage). During the summer, Alaska Marine Hwy ferries (☎ 907-747-8737) stop almost daily at the terminal, 7 miles north of town.

Secondary Ports

Between Sitka and Juneau, the ferry *Le Conte* (☎ 907-465-3941) services small ports, offering a chance to experience untouristed Alaska. Wings of Alaska (☎ 907-785-6466), LAB (☎ 907-785-6435) and Bellair (☎ 907-785-6411) fly to these places.

On Kupreanof Island, the Indian beachfront community of **Kake** boasts Alaska's tallest totem pole and serves as the departure point for Tebenkof Bay kayaking trips. Rustic **Tenakee Springs** (population 150) is known for its relaxed pace, alternative lifestyle and 108°F hot springs. Twice monthly, *Le Conte* travels to the lively fishing town of **Pelican**, on Chichagof Island, a unique day trip from Juneau ($70). Built on pilings over tidelands, Pelican's main street is a mile-long wooden boardwalk.

Juneau

Alaska's scenic capital has narrow streets, a bustling waterfront and a snowcapped-mountain backdrop. It's also the gateway to Glacier Bay National Park and Admiralty Island National Monument (see those sections later).

Site of Alaska's first major gold strike, the town was named 'Juneau' in 1881 and became the territory capital in 1906. Downtown Juneau clings to a mountainside; the rest of the city is spread north into the Mendenhall Valley.

The main visitor center is Davis Log Cabin (☎ 907-586-2201, W www.traveljuneau .com, 134 3rd St). The USFS information center (☎ 907-586-8751, 101 Egan Dr) is in Centennial Hall and has details on cabins, hiking, Glacier Bay, Admiralty Island and Tongass National Forest. The Juneau Public Library (☎ 907-586-5249, 292 Marine Way) provides Internet access. The information kiosk in Marine Park, at the southern end of Egan Dr, has walking-tour maps.

Things to See & Do Historic **South Franklin St** is lined with shops, bars and restaurants and bustles with tourists. On 5th St, **St Nicholas Russian Orthodox Church** is the Southeast's oldest church (dating from 1894).

The **Juneau-Douglas City Museum** (☎ 907-586-3572), at 4th and Main Sts, highlights the area's gold-mining history ($3); pick up the *Perseverance Trail* booklet and 'Treadwell Mine Historic Trail' brochure for self-guided walks. The **Last Chance Mining Museum** (☎ 907-586-5338, 1001 Basin Rd) is an impressive complex of railroad lines, ore cars and repair sheds ($3). The **Treadwell Mine ruins** near Douglas are also interesting.

The **Alaska State Museum** (☎ 907-465-2901, 393 Whittier St) has historical displays and indigenous artifacts, plus a full-size eagle's nest atop a two-story tree ($5).

Three miles north of downtown, the **Macauley Salmon Hatchery Visitor Center** (☎ 907-463-4810, 2697 Channel Dr) has underwater-viewing windows that allow you to see fish spawning and climbing ladders. Displays explain the salmon life cycle and hatchery operations ($3).

The area's numerous glaciers include **Mendenhall**, the 'drive-in' glacier; the informative visitor center (☎ 907-789-0097) is 13 miles from the city at the end of Glacier Spur Rd. Capital Transit buses from the city center cost $1.25. Mendenhall Glacier Transport (☎ 907-789-5460) city tours include the glacier ($17.50).

The top attraction is **hiking**, and some trails access USFS cabins. The most stunning scenery is along the West Glacier Trail, which sidles by the Mendenhall Glacier.

The Mt Roberts Trail is the most popular hike to the Alpine country above Juneau. Or you can skip the hike and just jump on the **Mt Roberts Tram** (☎ 800-461-8726, 490 S Franklin St), which takes passengers from the dock to the tree line ($20). Juneau Parks & Recreation (☎ 907-586-5226, 155 S Seward St) offers organized hikes. Buy topographic maps at the Foggy Mountain Shop (☎ 907-586-6780, 134 N Franklin St).

For **kayaking**, the area is good for day trips and longer paddles. Juneau Outdoor Center (☎ 907-586-8220, 101 Dock St), in Douglas, rents boats, and Alaska Discovery (☎ 800-586-1911, 5310 Glacier Hwy) runs guided three-day paddles in Berners Bay ($495).

The steep-sided fjord of Tracy Arm, 50 miles southeast of Juneau, makes an excellent day trip. Auk Nu Tours (☎ 907-789-5701, 888-305-2515, 79 Egan Dr) charges $110, and Adventure Bound Alaska (☎ 907-463-2509, 800-228-3875, 215 Ferry Way) charges $99.

Places to Stay Downtown accommodations are heavily booked during summer. The USFS runs beautiful *Mendenhall Lake Campground*, 13 miles from downtown on Montana Creek Rd, and *Auke Village*, 2 miles from the ferry terminal on Glacier Hwy (both $8). *Juneau International Hostel* (☎ 907-586-9559, 614 Harris St) is one of Alaska's best ($10). Juneau has more than 50 B&Bs (from $65); stop at the visitor center to find one, or call the Alaska B&B Association (☎ 907-586-2959).

Alaskan Hotel (☎ 907-586-1000, 800-327-9347, 167 S Franklin St) dates from 1913 ($60/80 for shared/private bath). Rooms with kitchen and private bath are available at *Cashen Quarters* (☎ 907-586-9863, 315 Gold St) for $95. *Driftwood Lodge* (☎ 907-586-2280, 800-544-2239, 435 Willoughby Ave), near the Alaska State Museum, has an airport/ferry courtesy van and charges $85/104. *Inn at the Waterfront* (☎ 907-586-2050, 455 S Franklin St) once appeared in Charles Kuralt's *On the Road* show (rooms begin at $55). There are also motels near the airport.

Places to Eat Juneau has an excellent range of restaurants. The best salmon bake is at *Thane Ore House* (☎ 907-586-3442,

4400 Thane Rd), 4 miles south of town ($19). The cheapest for breakfast or lunch is the *Cafeteria,* on the 2nd floor of the Federal Building (open 7am-3:30pm). Cheap pizza downtown is at *Bullwinkle's Pizza Parlor (318 Willoughby Ave),* across from the state office building (from $12).

Popular *Fiddlehead Restaurant (429 W Willoughby Ave)* serves seafood and Juneau's best vegetarian cuisine (from $11). Of the handful of Mexican restaurants downtown, *Armadillo Tex-Mex Café (431 S Franklin St)* is the best. Fresh-baked bagels and deli sandwiches are at *Silverbow Inn Bakery (120 2nd St),* and for good espresso there's *Heritage Coffee Company (625 W 7th St).* The *Carr's* supermarket, at Egan Hwy and Vintage Blvd, offers some prepared foods (open 24 hours), while *The Cookhouse (200 Admiral Way)* boasts Alaska's largest hamburgers.

Entertainment South Franklin St is Juneau's drinking sector. The (in)famous *Red Dog Saloon (278 S Franklin St)* has a sawdust floor and relic-covered walls. Hidden in *Alaskan Hotel* (see Places to Stay) is a unique bar with historic ambience and folk or jazz music. Southeast Alaska's largest selection of microbrew beers and waterfront views are at *Hangar on the Wharf (2 Marine Way).*

Getting There & Around The main airlines serving Juneau are Alaska (☎ 907-789-0600) and Air North (☎ 907-789-2007). Smaller companies like Wings of Alaska (☎ 907-789-0790, 8421 Livingston Way) provide service to isolated communities.

The ferry terminal is 14 miles from downtown; *Le Conte* (☎ 907-465-3941) runs to Hoonah, Angoon and Tenakee Springs. There are no state ferries to Gustavus (and neighboring Glacier Bay), but Auk Nu Tours (☎ 907-789-5701, 888-305-2515, 79 Egan Dr) runs a catamaran daily ($85 roundtrip, kayaks $40). Mendenhall Glacier Transport buses (☎ 907-789-5460) meet the ferries ($6).

Capital Transit (☎ 907-789-6901) runs Juneau's public buses ($1.25). Numerous car rental places offer pickup/drop-off and unlimited mileage. Rent-A-Wreck (☎ 907-789-4111, 9099 Glacier Hwy) has a $40 special, while Evergreen Ford (☎ 907-789-9386, 888-267-9300, 8895 Mallard St) rents $45 compacts.

Admiralty Island National Monument

Fifteen miles southeast of Juneau, this island has 1406 sq miles of designated wilderness with bears, eagles, humpback whales, harbor seals, porpoises and sea lions. Obtain supplies in Juneau and information from the USFS office (☎ 907-586-8751, 101 Egan Dr) or the Admiralty Island National Monument office (☎ 907-586-8790, 8461 Old Dairy Rd) in Mendenhall Valley.

The single settlement on Admiralty Island, **Angoon**, is the starting point for paddling trips, including the 32-mile Cross Admiralty Canoe Route to Mole Harbor. *Favorite Bay Inn* (☎ 907-788-3123) is 2 miles from the ferry terminal ($89/129 singles/doubles). *Kootznahoo Lodge* (☎ 907-788-3501), on Kootznahoo Rd, is a half-mile from the ferry terminal ($85 singles or doubles). Angoon is a dry community with only one cafe.

The best bear-viewing area in Southeast Alaska is at **Pack Creek**, on the eastern side of Admiralty Island. The bears are most abundant July to August, when the salmon are running, and visitors watch them feed from a sand spit or an observation tower along the creek reached by a mile-long trail. Most people reach Pack Creek via guiding companies. Alaska Discovery (☎ 800-586-1911) offers a one-day tour from Juneau ($475 per person) and a three-day trip ($900).

Glacier Bay National Park

Sixteen tidewater glaciers spill from the mountains and fill the sea with icebergs around the famous wilderness of **Glacier Bay National Park & Preserve**. To see the glaciers most visitors join a cruise on the *Spirit of Adventure* (☎ 800-451-5952) for a nine-hour trip up the West Arm of Glacier Bay ($157).

The only developed trails are in Bartlett Cove, but there is excellent kayaking; rent equipment from Glacier Bay Sea Kayaks (☎ 907-697-2257). Alaska Discovery (☎ 800-586-1911 in Juneau) runs guided day trips from Bartlett Cove ($125). Spirit Walker Expeditions (☎ 907-697-2266, 800-529-2937) offers a day paddle to Pleasant Island ($115).

The park is served by the settlement of **Gustavus**. Near the Salmon River Bridge, *Salmon River Cabins* (☎ 907-697-2245), charges $70 for two. Also renting cabins are

Puffin B&B (☎ *907-697-2260)*, from $90, and *Tri B&B* (☎ *907-697-2425)*, from $75.

Gustavus Inn (☎ *907-697-2254, 800-649-5220)* charges $140 per person, including gourmet meals. A quarter-mile south of the Salmon River Bridge is *Strawberry Point Café*. Next door *Beartrack Mercantile* sells groceries at outrageous prices. It's best to bring your food from Juneau.

Site of the park headquarters (☎ 907-697-2230), **Bartlett Cove** has a restaurant and a free campground. The visitor center, at the dock, provides backcountry permits, maps and information. *Glacier Bay Lodge* (☎ *800-451-5952)* has $165 doubles and $28 dorm bunks.

Air Excursions (☎ 907-697-2375) has daily flights between Gustavus and Juneau ($100 roundtrip). The Glacier Bay Lodge bus meets flights ($10). Auk Nu Tours (☎ 907-789-5701, 888-305-2515) runs boats from Juneau ($85 roundtrip). Glacier Bay Tours & Cruises (☎ 800-451-5952, Ⓦ www .glacierbaytours.com) offers two-day, one-night package tours from Juneau with accommodations at Glacier Bay Lodge. With a dorm bunk it's $426 per person, with a room $481.

Haines

Providing access to Canada's Yukon Territory and Interior Alaska, Haines is surrounded by mountains. The Northwest Trading Company arrived in 1878, followed by missionaries and gold prospectors. WWII saw construction of the Haines Hwy, linking the city to the Alcan Hwy.

Haines has a visitor bureau (☎ 907-766-2234, 800-458-3579, Ⓦ www.haines.ak.us) at 2nd Ave and Willard St, and a State Parks office (☎ 907-766-2292) on Main St.

The **Sheldon Museum** (☎ 907-766-2366, 11 Main St) features indigenous artifacts and gold-rush-era relics ($3). The **American Bald Eagle Foundation** (☎ 907-766-3094, 113 Haines Hwy) displays over 100 species in natural habitat.

Fort Seward, a national historical site, is undergoing renovation; get walking-tour maps from Hotel Halsingland. Within the fort is the **Alaska Indian Arts Tribal House** (☎ 907-766-2160), which stages nightly dance and productions ($10) and has carving and weaving demonstrations.

Haines offers two major **hiking** trail systems (the visitor bureau has the details)

and numerous **rafting** trips. Chilkat Guides (☎ 907-766-2491) runs a four-hour Chilkat River float ($82), while Chilkat Guides and Alaska Discovery (☎ 907-586-1911) offer an exciting 10-day Tatshenshinin/Alsek River raft trip for around $2100.

The closest state campground is *Portage Cove*, half a mile southeast of Fort Seward ($6). Seven miles southeast of town, *Chilkat State Park*, on Mud Bay Rd, has glacier views ($6). *Salmon Run Campground* (☎ *907-766-4229, Mile 7 Lutak Rd)* is 1¾ miles from the ferry terminal and has tent sites ($13) and cabins ($45).

Bear Creek Camp & International Hostel (☎ *907-766-2259)*, on Small Tract Rd, is 2½ miles south of town and has bunks ($15), tent sites ($12 for two) and two-person cabins ($38).

There are several B&Bs in the fort. *Officers' Inn* (☎ *907-766-2000, 800-542-6363, 13 Fort Seward Dr)* has economy singles/doubles for $50/55, and *Fort Seward Lodge* (☎ *907-766-2009, 800-478-7772, 1 Fort Seward Dr)* is cheap at $50/60. *Chilkat Eagle B&B* (☎ *907-766-2763, 67 Tower Rd)* charges $70/80 and has Internet access.

Near the fort entrance, *Mountain View Motel* (☎ *907-766-2900, 800-478-2902, 57 Mud Bay Rd)* has rooms with kitchenettes ($70/75). In town, *Thunderbird Motel* (☎ *907-766-2131, 216 Dalton St)* charges $70/80.

Standard breakfasts are available at *Bamboo Room (11 2nd Ave)* for $6-8, and the best pizza in town is at *Grizzly Greg's Pizzeria (223 Main St)*. Nearby *Bear-Rittos (8 Main St)* serves local seafood with a Mexican twist. There's a nightly salmon bake at *Port Chilkoot Potlatch*, in Fort Seward ($22).

Haines is a hard-drinking town: *Fogcutter Bar (122 Main St)* and *Pioneer Bar (13 2nd Ave)* get lively at night, while Fort Seward has *Hotel Halsingland Pub*.

Several air charter companies service Haines; the cheapest is Wings of Alaska (☎ 907-766-2030). Also check with Haines Airways (☎ 907-766-2646) and LAB Flying Service (☎ 907-766-2222). A Juneau-Haines ticket is around $75. All also offer Glacier Bay National Park sightseeing flights (about $200 for two).

Alaskon Express discontinued its bus service to Haines in 2000. Ask at the visitor center if somebody has picked up the Haines-Fairbanks route. Haines-Skagway Water Taxi (☎ 907-766-3395, 800-766-3395) runs day trips to Skagway ($35 roundtrip).

Eagle Nest Car Rentals (☎ 907-766-2891, 800-354-6009, 1183 Haines Hwy), in the Eagle Nest Motel, has cars for as low as $45. There's also Affordable Car Rental (☎ 907-766-3111, 108 2nd Ave), at $69 per day.

Around Haines

The 75-sq-mile **Alaska Chilkat Bald Eagle Preserve**, along the Chilkat River, protects the world's largest known gathering of bald eagles. The most birds are seen December and January, but you can see eagles here anytime during the summer. Lookouts on the Haines Hwy, particularly between Miles 18 and 22, allow motorists to view the birds. Alaska Nature Tours (☎ 907-766-2876) offers a three-hour tour of the preserve ($50).

Skagway

The northern terminus of the Alaska Marine Hwy, Skagway was a gold-rush town infamous for its lawlessness. In 1887 the population was two; by 1897 Skagway was Alaska's largest city, with 20,000 residents. Construction of a railroad over the White Pass Trail began in 1898, and the narrow-gauge track reached Whitehorse two years later. Today Skagway survives almost entirely on tourism and gets crowded when the cruise ships pull in.

The National Park Service visitor center (☎ 907-983-2921, 154 Broadway St) provides information on the Chilkoot Trail, local trails and camping. The Skagway Visitor Center (☎ 907-983-2854, W www.skagway.org, 245 Broadway St) is in the driftwood-covered Arctic Brotherhood Hall.

A seven-block corridor along Broadway St, part of the historical district, features the restored buildings, false fronts and wooden sidewalks of Skagway's golden era. At the visitor center for the **Klondike Gold Rush National Historic Park** (154 Broadway St), watch the excellent 30-minute movie on the gold-rush days.

The **Trail of '98 Museum** (700 Spring St), jammed with gold-rush relics ($3), is in the Skagway City Hall. On 5th Ave is **Moore's Cabin**, Skagway's oldest building (1887),

while **Mascot Saloon** (290 Broadway St) is now a museum devoted to Skagway's heyday as the 'roughest place in the world.' The best tour is a three-hour Summit Excursion on the **White Pass & Yukon Railroad** (☎ 907-983-2217), which climbs the high White Pass in the historic narrow-gauge train ($82).

Near the ferry terminal, *Pullen Creek Park Campground* (☎ 907-983-2768) caters to RVs ($24) but has tent sites ($10). *Skagway Mountain View RV Park* (☎ 907-983-3333, 1450 Broadway St) charges $14-23 for RVs and $13 for tents. Nine miles north of Skagway, *Dyea Camping Area* is free, but there's no water.

Skagway Home Hostel (☎ 907-983-2131, 480 3rd Ave) has bunks ($15) and a couples' room ($40). Singles/doubles at the Victorian *Skagway Inn B&B* (☎ 907-983-2289, 655 Broadway St) cost $85/115. Stop at the visitor center for other B&Bs.

Alaska's oldest hotel, *Golden North Hotel* (☎ 907-983-2451, 888-222-1898, 299 Broadway St) has economy rooms for $65/75. *Sgt Preston's Lodge* (☎ 907-983-2521, 370 6th Ave) has rooms for $70/75.

For breakfast, try *Sweet Tooth Café (315 Broadway St)*, which opens at 6am. *Corner Café (421 State St)* offers seafood dinners (around $15). *Northern Lights Pizzeria (435 Broadway St)* serves huge portions of pasta, Greek or Mexican food (from $9). *Ristorante Portobello (111 Broadway St)* has the best pasta in town and an Internet cafe. *Stowaway Café (☎ 907-983-3463, 205 Congress Way)*, near the Harbor Master's office, is Skagway's best (from $16).

Red Onion Saloon (205 Broadway St) is a former brothel and now Skagway's liveliest bar. Handcrafted beer is at *Skagway Brewing Company*, in the Golden North Hotel.

LAB Flying Service (☎ 907-983-2471), Wings of Alaska (☎ 907-983-2442) and Skagway Air (☎ 907-983-2218) have regular flights between Skagway and Juneau ($80 one way), Haines ($40) and Glacier Bay; Skagway Air is generally cheapest.

Northbound, Alaskon Express buses (☎ 907-983-2241) depart at 8:45am daily for Whitehorse ($46), with connections to Fairbanks ($216) or Anchorage ($219).

Historic White Pass & Yukon Railroad (☎ 800-343-7373, W www.whitepassrailroad.com) goes to Fraser, British Columbia

($67), where there's a bus connection to Whitehorse ($95 for the whole trip).

Alaska Marine Hwy ferries (☎ 907-983-2841) depart every day in summer. Haines-Skagway Water Taxis run twice daily to Haines (at 10:45am and 5pm); buy tickets on the boat ($35 roundtrip).

Sourdough Car Rentals (☎ 907-983-2523) charges $45-55 a day (100 free miles).

Southcentral Alaska

This area is similar to Southeast Alaska, with its spectacular scenery. One feature that sets it apart is a road system linking many of the towns, making Southcentral Alaska one of the cheapest, most accessible and most popular areas in the state to visit.

ANCHORAGE

Anchorage offers the comforts and problems of a large US city within 30 minutes' drive of the Alaskan wilderness. Founded in 1914 as a work camp for the Alaska Railroad, the city was devastated by the 1964 Good Friday Earthquake. The oil boom made it an industry headquarters, and oil money has paid for the most modern amenities.

Information

The Alaska Convention and Visitors Bureau maintains the Log Cabin Visitors Center (☎ 907-274-3531, Ⓦ www.anchorage.net, 524 W 4th Ave), which distributes a visitor guide and walking-tour map and lists events (☎ 907-276-3200 for event information). Nearby, the Alaska Public Lands Information Center (☎ 907-271-2737, 605 W 4th Ave) has park, trail and cabin information as well as excellent displays.

Shop for outdoor equipment on Northern Lights Blvd between Minnesota Dr and New Seward Hwy. Access the Internet at ZJ Loussac Public Library (☎ 907-261-2845, 3600 Denali St).

Things to See & Do

The Cadastral Survey Monument, at E St and 2nd Ave, traces Anchorage's development as a city. On K St is *The Last Blue Whale*, an eye-catching statue. Captain Cook Monument, in nearby Resolution Park, marks the 200th anniversary of Cook's visit to Cook Inlet and offers great views of the inlet. The wood-frame Oscar Anderson House (☎ 907-274-2336), at Elderberry Park on M St, is Anchorage's only home museum ($3).

The impressive Anchorage Historical & Fine Arts Museum (☎ 907-343-4326, 121 W 7th St) features Alaskan history and indigenous culture ($5). The Heritage Library Museum (☎ 907-265-2834, 301 W Northern Lights Blvd) displays Native Alaskan costumes, weapons and artwork (free admission).

Beautiful city parks include Earthquake Park, Russian Jack Springs Park (the Municipal Greenhouse) and the 4000-acre Far North Bi-Centennial Park, where the Hilltop Ski Area becomes a mountain biker's oasis in the summer (bike rentals available).

Activities include cycling on 122 miles of paved paths; the Knowles Coastal Trail is the most scenic. It begins at the west end of 2nd Ave. Bikes are available for $29 a day at Downtown Bicycle Rental (☎ 907-279-5293), at W 4th Ave and C St. Alaska's most climbed peak is Flattop Mountain, a three-to four-hour hike from a trailhead on the outskirts of Anchorage. Maps are available at the Alaska Public Lands Information Center (see Information).

Organized Tours

Anchorage Historical Properties takes visitors on hourlong downtown walking tours ($5) at 1pm beginning from the Old City Hall on 4th Ave. For half-day city tours ($30), try Gray Line (☎ 907-277-5581, 745 W 4th Ave). Gray Line's 10-hour tour includes the city and a trip out to Portage Glacier ($89).

'Flightseeing' – touring in a small plane – is popular in Anchorage. Tours are short and expensive, but aerial views offer a sense of Alaska's grandeur. Rust's Flying Service (☎ 907-243-1595, 800-544-2299) offers half-hour tours ($69) and a three-hour flight to view Mt McKinley ($249).

Alaska Railroad (☎ 907-265-2494) has interesting Denali National Park packages ($269). Gray Line will take you for two days, one night, to Nome and Kotzebue ($520).

Native Culture in Anchorage

The first phase of the $15-million Alaska Native Heritage Center (☎ 800-315-6608, 8800 Heritage Center Dr) opened in 1999 in Anchorage, off Muldoon Rd, north of Glenn Hwy. The Welcome House has a theater and exhibition space devoted to the history, lifestyle and arts of Native Alaskans, as well as open studios where artists carve baleen or sew skin boats. A half-mile trail leads past a smokehouse, covered carving shed and other traditional village structures.

Around the lake, in five replicate village settings – Athabascan, Yupik, Inupiat, Aleut and Tlingit/Haida – people will be involved in such traditional activities as splitting and drying salmon, tanning hides or building kayaks ($20; open 9am-6pm daily).

Another excellent Native culture experience is at the Alaska Native Medical Center (ANMC; ☎ 907-563-2662, 4315 Diplomace Dr), near Tudor Rd and Boniface Pkwy, where the hospital's art collection displays 4-foot-high grass baskets, baleen carvings, raincoats of seal intestine, spirit masks and soapstone carvings. The fascinating ANMC gift shop (☎ 907-729-1122) sells fine pieces on consignment, and most of the money goes back to the person who carved the ivory earrings, wove the baleen basket or sewed the sealskin slippers (free admission; open 10am-2pm Mon-Fri).

Places to Stay

The city maintains two campgrounds (☎ 907-343-4474). The **Centennial Park Campground** is 4½ miles from downtown on Glenn Hwy ($15; seven-day limit), and **Lion's Camper Park** is in Russian Jack Springs Park ($15).

HI-AYH Anchorage International Hostel (☎ 907-276-3635, 700 H St) is large but reservations are recommended in summer ($16/19 members/nonmembers). Friendly **Spenard Hostel** (☎ 907-248-5036, 2845 W 42nd Place) charges $15. Delightful **Anchorage Guest House** (☎ 907-274-0408, 200 Hillcrest Dr) has bunks ($22) and rooms ($40).

B&Bs (from $75) have blossomed; inquire at the visitor center or B&B Hotline (☎ 907-272-5909).

Many of the town's 50 hotels/motels offer free airport/station pickup. **Puffin Inn** (☎ 907-243-4044, 800-478-3346, 4400 Spenard Rd), handy to the airport, charges $99/119 for singles/doubles. Downtown, **Caribou Inn** (☎ 907-272-0444, 800-272-5878, 501 L St) starts at $75. Amid 5th Ave's cluster of motels is **Econo Lodge** (☎ 907-274-1515, 642 5th Ave), at $114/124. **Midtown Lodge** (☎ 907-258-7778, 604 W 26th Ave) has shared-bath rooms from $60/70.

Places on the city outskirts are generally cheaper. **Brown Bear Motel** (☎ 907-653-7000, Mile 103 Seward Hwy) is 20 minutes south of Anchorage and charges $40.

Places to Eat

The downtown has wonderful eateries, including **Blondie's Café** (333 W 4th Ave), open 24 hours. **Downtown Deli** (425 W 4th Ave) is Anchorage's best-known spot. **Sack's Café** (☎ 907-276-3546, 328 W G St) is recommended for shellfish. **Humpy's** (610 W 6th Ave) has more than 40 beers on tap and great halibut tacos ($7). Near Anchorage International Hostel, **Wings & Things** (529 I St) has spicy chicken wings and cheap subs.

Glacier Brew House (737 W 5th Ave) has handcrafted beers, seafood pastas ($16-18) and wood-grilled chops and ribs ($18-22). In midtown, **Moose's Tooth Pub** (3300 Old Seward Hwy) is another brew pub, with the best pizza in Anchorage.

The bizarre, pig-obsessed **Hogg Brothers Café** (1049 W Northern Lights Blvd) serves all-day breakfasts. **Twin Dragon** (612 E 15th Ave) has the best Mongolian barbecue in town ($12).

Entertainment

Check the *Anchorage Press* for entertainment listings. Colorful **Chilkoot Charlie's** (2435 Spenard Rd) features bands and dancing. Nearby **Mr Whitekeys Fly by Nite Club** (☎ 907-279-7726, 3300 Spenard Rd) plays jazz, blues and rock but is best known for the 'Whale-Fat Follies' musical act (from $12). **Humpy's** has live music nightly, and **Hot Rods** (4848 Old Seward Hwy) is a 1950s-style nightclub and billiards hall.

ALASKA

ANCHORAGE

PLACES TO STAY
2 Centennial Park Campground
3 Lion's Camper Park
4 Anchorage Guest House
10 Midtown Lodge
17 Spenard Hostel
18 Puffin Inn
37 Caribou Inn
45 Econo Lodge
46 Anchorage International Hostel

PLACES TO EAT
6 Twin Dragon
9 Hogg Brothers Café
14 Moose's Tooth Pub
27 Sack's Café
30 Downtown Deli
33 Blondie's Cafe
36 Glacier Brew House
38 Wings & Things
41 Humpy's

OTHER
1 Alaska Native Heritage Center
5 Denali Car Rental
7 Alaska Regional Hospital
8 Chilkoot Charlie's
11 Heritage Library Museum
12 Medical Park Family Clinic
13 Mr Whitekeys Fly by Night Club
15 University of Alaska
16 ZJ Loussac Public Library
19 Affordable Car Rental

20 Hot Rods
21 Alaska Native Medical Center
22 Alaska Railroad Train Station
23 Captain Cook Monument
24 Cadastral Survey Monument
25 Oscar Anderson House
26 The Last Blue Whale
28 Alaska Public Lands
    Information Center
29 Gray Line

31 Log Cabin Visitors Center
32 Old City Hall
34 Post Office
35 Downtown Bicycle Rental
39 Transit Center
40 City Hall
42 Police Station
43 Fire Station
44 Anchorage Historical & Fine
    Arts Museum

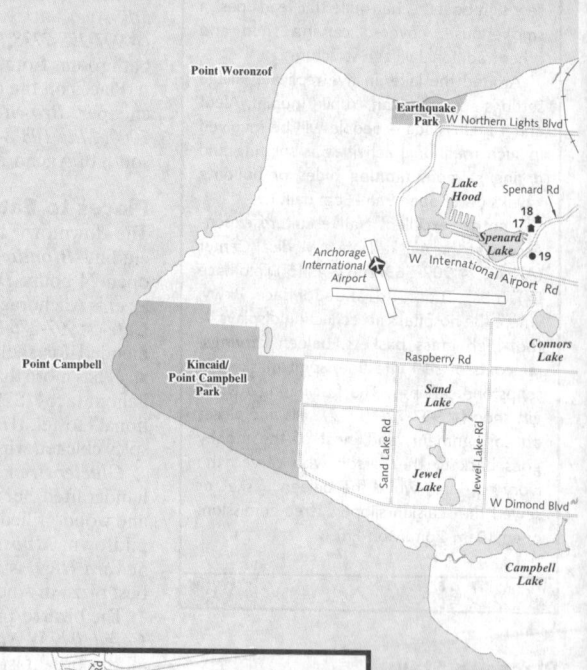

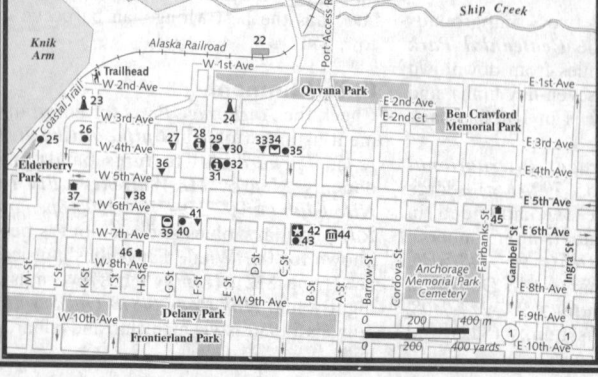

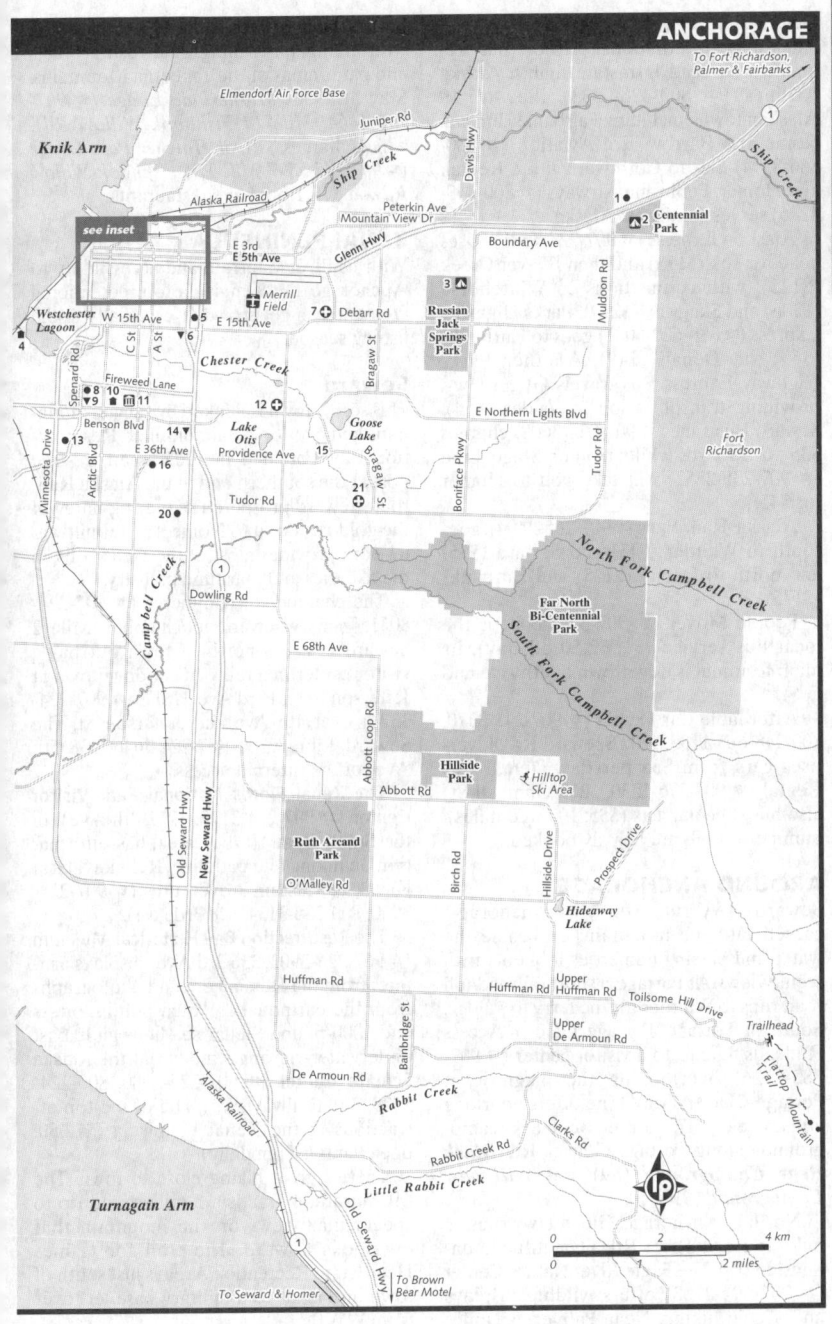

ALASKA

Getting There & Around

Anchorage International Airport has frequent inter- and intrastate flights. Alaska Airlines (☎ 800-426-0333) flies to 19 Alaskan towns, including Fairbanks, Juneau, Nome and Barrow. Era Aviation (☎ 800-866-8394) flies to Cordova, Valdez, Kodiak and Homer. Peninsula Airways (☎ 800-448-4226) serves southwest Alaska.

Alaskon Express (☎ 907-227-5581) buses head for Tok ($113) and then Beaver Creek ($122), with connections to Whitehorse ($206) and Skagway ($219). Parks Highway Express (☎ 888-600-6001) goes to Fairbanks ($69) via Denali ($49). Another Parks Highway Express Bus travels Glenn Hwy, providing transportation to Valdez ($54). Seward Bus Line (☎ 907-224-3608) charges $35 to Seward, while Homer Stage Line (☎ 907-235-2252) will take you to Homer for $45.

Alaska Railroad (☎ 907-265-2494) goes south to Whittier ($45) and Seward ($55) and north to Denali ($125) and Fairbanks ($175).

People Mover (☎ 907-343-6543) is the local bus service ($1; $2.50 all day); its main terminal is downtown at 6th Ave and G St.

Affordable Car Rental (☎ 907-243-3370, 800-248-685-1155, 4707 Spenard Rd) advertises cars from $35 per day. Denali Car Rental (☎ 907-276-1230, 1209 Gambell St) also has subcompacts ($35; 100 free miles). Summer rentals are heavily booked.

AROUND ANCHORAGE

Seward Hwy runs south of Anchorage, carved into the mountainside beside the water and passing numerous lookouts with scenic views. At Portage, a short railroad/toll road runs to Whittier for the ferry to Valdez. South of Portage, Portage Glacier Access Rd leads 5 miles to a visitor center (☎ 907-783-2326) overlooking the magnificent **Portage Glacier**. Gray Line offers hourlong cruises ($25). There are two USFS campgrounds along Portage Glacier Rd: *Black Bear Campground* ($9) and *Williwaw Campground* ($10-15).

North of Anchorage, Glenn Hwy runs 13 miles to Eagle River Rd, a beautiful mountainside trip. The **Eagle River Nature Center** (☎ 907-694-2108) offers wildlife displays and scenic hiking. Near Palmer, 35 miles north, **Hatcher Pass** is an Alpine paradise, with hiking, parasailing, gold-rush artifacts and panoramas of the Takeetna Mountains. Stay at 1930s *Motherlode Lodge* (☎ 907-746-1464, Mile 14 Fishhook-Willow Rd), which charges $70, or *Hatcher Pass Lodge* (☎ 907-745-5897, Mile 17.5 Fishhook-Willow Rd), at $75. Both have restaurants.

KENAI PENINSULA

With its diverse terrain and accessibility to Anchorage, the Kenai is a top recreational area and can get crowded, especially in the fishing season.

Seward

This scenic town is flanked by rugged mountains and overlooks salmon-filled Resurrection Bay. Founded in 1903 as an ice-free port at the southern end of the Alaska Railroad, Seward prospered as the beginning of the gold-rush trail to Nome. The rebuilt waterfront provides most of the area's jobs, in the fisheries and maritime industry.

The chamber of commerce (☎ 907-224-8051, W www.seward.net/chamber, Mile 2 Seward Hwy) is north of town but has a visitor center in a railroad car downtown at Jefferson St and 3rd Ave. USFS (☎ 907-224-3374) is at 4th Ave and Jefferson St. The Seward Library (☎ 907-224-3646, 238 5th Ave) offers Internet access.

The **Kenai Fjords National Park Visitor Center** (☎ 907-224-3175, 1212 4th Ave), in the Small Boat Harbor area, has information on hiking and paddling. Rent kayaks at Kayak & Custom Adventures (☎ 907-224-3960, 800-288-3134, 328 3rd Ave).

The **Resurrection Bay Historical Museum** (☎ 907-224-3902, 336 3rd Ave) displays artifacts from the Russian era and photographs from the earthquake. Watch puffins, otters and 1000-pound Stellar sea lions glide past underwater-viewing windows at the **Alaska SeaLife Center** (☎ 907-224-3080, 800-224-2525, 301 Railway Ave), one of the top attractions in the Kenai Peninsula ($12.50; open 9am-9:30pm daily).

There's great **hiking** close to town. The Mt Marathon Trail is a 3-mile roundtrip to spectacular views on the mountain that overlooks Seward. The trail for Caines Head State Recreation Area is just south of town and leads to a military base left over from WWII.

The *Waterfront Campground* (☎ *907-224-3331*), on Ballaine Blvd, overlooks the bay, with grassy tent/RV sites ($6/10).

Moby Dick Hostel (☎ *907-224-7072, 432 3rd Ave*) has $15 bunks. North of town, *Kate's Roadhouse* (☎ *907-224-5888, Mile 5.5 Seward Hwy*) has beds for $17.

Downtown *Seward Waterfront Lodging* (☎ *907-224-5563, 550 Railway Ave*) offers $97 doubles, while nearby *Falcon's Way B&B* (☎ *907-224-5757, 611 4th Ave*) charges $55/70 for singles/doubles.

Motels in the Small Boat Harbor area include *Murphy's Motel* (☎ *907-224-8090, 911 4th Ave*), charging $80/90, and nicer *Breeze Inn* (☎ *907-224-5237, 1306 Seward Hwy*), for $110/120. Downtown there's historical 1916 *Van Guilder Hotel* (☎ *907-224-3525, 800-204-6835, 307 Adam St*), with some 'pension' rooms ($75), and *Taroka Inn* (☎ *907-224-8975, 235 3rd Ave*), with rooms starting at $85.

For the cheapest fare, *Don's Kitchen* (*405 Washington St*) is open 24 hours. Nearby *Apollo* (*229 4th Ave*) serves pizza, Greek dishes and pasta, with dinners beginning around $8. The best seafood in town is at *Ray's Waterfront* (*1316 4th Ave*), with waterfront dinning in the Small Boat Harbor.

Yukon Bar, 4th Ave at Washington St, and *Tony's Bar* (*135 4th Ave*) both have live music and can get loud at night. Head to *Resurrect Art Galley and Coffee House* (*320 3rd Ave*) for a latte and a quieter atmosphere.

Seward Bus Lines (☎ 907-224-3608) run daily to Anchorage ($35). In summer, daily Alaska Railroad trains take a spectacular route to Anchorage ($55). From the ferry terminal (☎ 907-224-5485), semiweekly ferries go to Kodiak ($59), Valdez ($64) and Homer ($106).

Kenai Fjords National Park

Seward is the gateway to Kenai Fjords National Park and shelters the visitor center (see Seward earlier). The park's main features are the 917-sq-mile Harding Icefield and the tidewater glaciers calving into the sea. **Exit Glacier**, at the end of Exit Glacier Rd, is the most popular attraction. There's a visitor center and a paved quarter-mile trail to a glacier overlook.

Glacier Quest Eco-Tours (☎ 907-224-5770, 877-444-5770) offers daily tours ($20).

Hikers can climb a difficult 5 miles to the edge of the ice field – worth it for spectacular views. The best marine-wildlife cruises in the state are the tour boats that run into Kenai Fjords past calving glaciers. Kenai Fjords Tours (☎ 907-224-8068, 800-478-3346) offers a six-hour cruise into the park for $99.

Sterling Highway

This paved route (Hwy 1) makes an arc around the peninsula, and a side road heads north to the quaint old mining town of **Hope**. The main road goes east, past the Kenai National Wildlife Refuge, with wildlife and a plague of anglers. Soldotna is strictly a service town. Turn north to **Kenai**, with good views and some Russian history, and continue to Captain Cook Strait Recreation Area, which is off the fishing circuit. South of Soldotna, the scenic highway hugs the coastline, passing through small villages with campgrounds and great clamming beaches. Scenic **Ninilchik** has a Russian accent, and *HI Eagle Watch Hostel* (☎ *907-567-3905, Mile 3 Oil Well Rd*) is 3 miles east in a gorgeous rural setting.

Homer

Charming, colorful Homer, at the end of Sterling Hwy, sits on beautiful Kachemak Bay amid incredible mountains. Coal was the first industry, followed by fishing. The town attracted alternative types starting in the 1960s and is now home to artists and aging hippies. The visitor center (☎ 907-235-7740, W www.homeralaska.org, 135 Sterling Hwy) has courtesy phones to book rooms or tours. Homer Public Library (☎ 907-235-3180, 141 W Pioneer Ave) has Internet access.

The **Pratt Museum** (☎ 907-235-8635, 3779 Bartlett St) features native Alaskan artifacts, marine-life exhibits and the best display anywhere on the Exxon oil spill ($5). **Homer Spit** is a 5-mile sandbar with clamming, beach camping and a small-boat harbor.

The best **hiking** is across the Kachemak Bay at Kachemak Bay State Park. St Augustine's Kayak & Tours (☎ 907-235-6126) transports backpackers for $45 roundtrip. From the drop-off spot it's an easy 3½-mile hike to Grewingk Glacier, where you can camp on a beach lined with icebergs.

There's beach camping at *Homer Spit Campground*, at the end of the Spit (tents $3). *Karen Hornaday Memorial Campground* (☎ 907-235-8206), on Bartlett St, is on a wooded hill overlooking town and bay ($3). *Seaside Farms* (☎ 907-235-7850, 40904 Seaside Farms Rd) is 5 miles east off E End Rd and has backpacker bunks ($15) and cabins ($55), but you can do better staying in town. *Sunspin Guest House* (☎ 907-235-6677, 358 E Lee St) has bunk beds ($28) and five rooms (from $70).

The visitor center lists over 40 B&Bs ($60-120); alternatively, call the Homer B&B Association (☎ 907-235-6677). A dozen hotels/motels cost $70-100; book in summer. Delightful *Driftwood Inn* (☎ 907-235-8019, 800-478-8019, 435 W Bunnell Ave) is the most affordable (from $54/64 singles/doubles).

Assorted cafes and bakeries serve sandwiches and cappuccinos. Among the coffeehouses is *Two Sisters Bakery (106 W Bunnell Ave)*, with tables on a porch overlooking the bay. Places on Pioneer Ave include affordable *Neon Coyote (435 E Pioneer Ave)*; *Café Cups (162 W Pioneer Ave)*, which doubles as an art gallery; and vegetarian *Smoky Bay Natural Foods (248 W Pioneer Ave)*. Cheap eats at the end of the Spit include *Glacier Drive-In*, while nearby is the *Salty Dawg Saloon*, Homer's best-known watering hole. Other venues offer live music and dancing.

ERA Aviation (☎ 907-235-7565, 800-866-8394) flies frequently from Anchorage ($75). Kachemak Bay Transit (☎ 907-235-3795, 877-235-9101) and Homer Stage Lines (☎ 907-235-2252) provide bus service to Anchorage ($45). The ferry *Tustumena* (☎ 907-235-8449) goes twice weekly to Seldovia ($20) and Kodiak ($57). Polar Car Rental (☎ 907-235-0734) rents subcompacts ($60; 100 free miles).

PRINCE WILLIAM SOUND

Prince William Sound is the northern extent of the Gulf of Alaska, flanked by mountains and featuring abundant wildlife, including whales, sea lions, harbor seals, otters, eagles and bears. Annual rainfall averages over 100 inches. Alaska Marine Hwy ferries link Cordova, Valdez, Whittier and Seward.

Whittier

At the western end of Prince William Sound, Whittier was built by the military as a WWII warm-water port. Rail tunnels were drilled west through solid rock to connect with the main line of the Alaska Railroad. In 2000 the tunnel was converted to handle vehicles also, and many see Whittier booming in the future with visitors and tour groups. The Whittier Visitor Center (☎ 907-472-2379) is in a railroad car near the Small Boat Harbor and has information about hiking and kayaking.

Camp at *Whittier Public Campground*, behind the Begich Towers ($5). *Anchor Inn* (☎ 907-472-2354, 100 Whittier St) and *Sportsman Inn* (☎ 907-472-2352, 888 Frontier St) offer doubles ($75), food and drink. Local eateries do burgers, pizza and beer.

A train leaves Whittier daily for Anchorage ($45). The MV *Bartlett* ferry goes east to Valdez and Cordova six times weekly.

Valdez

Just 25 miles east of the Columbia Glacier, the ice-free port of Valdez is the southern terminus of the Trans-Alaska Pipeline. Bustling Small Boat Harbor has a pleasant boardwalk and scenic mountain backdrop – excellent at night.

Valdez first boomed in 1897 and '98, when 4000 gold seekers passed through for the Klondike. The treacherous Valdez Trail cost hundreds of lives, until army captain William Abercrombie brought some order. After the 1964 earthquake the city was rebuilt 4 miles farther east. The visitor center (☎ 907-835-4636, 800-770-5954, W www.valdezalaska.org, 200 Fairbanks Dr) has area information and courtesy phones to book accommodations. The Valdez Public Library (☎ 907-835-4632, 212 Fairbanks St) has Internet access.

Though the *Exxon Valdez* oil spill was an environmental disaster, the cleanup created a cash bonanza, especially for opportunists who became known as the 'spillionaires.' The Valdez Museum (☎ 907-835-2764, 217 Egan Dr) is packed with displays, including oil-spill exhibits and a model of the pipeline.

The magnificent Columbia Glacier is retreating, but its 3-mile-wide face can be seen from Alaska Marine Hwy ferries going to or from Whittier. For a longer and much closer look at it, contact Prince William Sound Tours Charters (☎ 907-835-4731, 800-992-1297, W www.princewilliamsound.com, 101 N Harbor Dr), the largest tour operator; six-hour boat tours cost $74.

Eight miles from town via Richardson Hwy, Dayville Rd and scenic Solomon Gulch is the remarkable **oil pipeline terminal**. The visitor center explains the project, and Valdez Tours (☎ 907-835-2686, 212 Tatitlek Ave) offers a two-hour trip ($15); it's oil-company PR, but interesting.

There are few developed trails in the area and no USFS office. **Paddling**, however, has more potential. Keystone Adventures (☎ 907-835-2606, 800-328-8460, W www.alaskawhitewater.com) runs 1½-hour Lowe River raft trips ($35). Shoup Bay offers a popular overnight kayak trip amid icebergs, seals and other sea life; Anadyr Adventures (☎ 907-835-2814, 800-865-2925, W www.anadyradventures.com, 225 Harbor Dr) rents kayaks (singles $45 per day) and offers guided day trips to Shoup Bay.

The *Bear Paw RV Campground* (☎ 907-835-2530, 101 N Harbor Dr), near the Small Boat Harbor, has wooded tent sites ($17). *Valdez Hostel* (☎ 907-835-2155, 139 Alatna St) offers bunks ($22).

More than 30 B&Bs around town charge about $60/75 for singles/doubles; the visitor center has listings and a speed-dial phone. *Downtown Inn* (☎ 800-835-2791, 113 Galina Dr) has shared-bath rooms from $85.

Try *Oscars* (143 N Harbor Dr) for breakfast ($6-8), burgers and chowder ($7). *Alaskan Halibut House* (208 Meals Ave) has halibut, chips and salad ($7). *Mike's Palace* (201 N Harbor Dr) specializes in pasta and seafood ($11-16), while *Kung Fu* (207 Kobuk St) has killer Chinese for lunch ($8) and dinner (from $11).

ERA Aviation (☎ 907-835-2636) flies daily to Anchorage ($75-85). Alaskon Express (☎ 907-835-4445) and Parks Highway Express (☎ 888-600-6001) have buses to Anchorage. Parks Highway Express is cheaper ($59 one way). Alaska Marine Hwy ferries (☎ 907-835-4436) sail regularly to Whittier ($64), Seward ($64), Homer ($152) and Cordova ($33).

Cordova

At the eastern end of the sound, this beautiful little town's population of 2600 doubles in summer as fishing and cannery workers arrive.

First settled by the nomadic Eyak, who lived on the enormous salmon runs, Cordova became a fish-packing center in 1889. In 1906 a dramatic railroad connected the town to the Kennicott copper mine. When the mine closed, Cordova again turned to fishing. The chamber of commerce office (☎ 907-424-7260, W www.cordovachamber.com), on 1st St, has information on the area.

The interesting **Cordova Museum** (☎ 907-424-6666, 622 1st Ave), in the Centennial Building, offers cassettes for self-guided town tours and will also store packs during the day. It has displays on history, marine life and mining.

Activity centers on the Small Boat Harbor during summer. **Mt Eyak Ski Area** (☎ 907-424-7766), east of town, has a vintage chairlift to a wonderful panorama ($7). The most stunning scenery, which includes **Childs Glacier** calving into the Copper River, is along the 50-mile Copper River Hwy. Rent a car at Reluctant Fishermen Hotel (☎ 907-424-3272, 800-770-3272), for $75 per day, or book a tour through Cooper River/Northwest Tours (☎ 907-424-5356), at $35 per person. The USFS (☎ 907-424-7661, 612 2nd St) has free maps to trails accessible from the road.

The *Odiak Camper Park* (☎ 907-424-6200), on Whitshed Rd half a mile east of town, has tent sites ($3) but can be dismal. The visitor center at Cordova Museum lists a dozen B&Bs ($60-70). *Alaskan Hotel & Bar* (☎ 907-424-3288, 600 1st St) charges $40/60 for doubles with shared/private bath. *Cannery Bunkhouse* (☎ 907-424-5920, 1 Cannery Row) has singles/doubles ($50/55) when the fish processing plant next door doesn't take it over for the summer. *Prince William Sound Motel* (☎ 907-424-3201, 888-796-6835, 502 2nd St) costs $80/90.

Don't pass up funky *Baja Taco Wagon*, on Nicholoff Way, a converted school bus across from the harbor where you can enjoy a plate of tacos ($8) outdoors. *Killer Whale Café* (507 1st St) serves sandwiches ($7-8) and has a view. Formerly a cannery canteen, *Cookhouse Café* (1 Cannery Row) serves pancakes, pastries and $13 seafood dinners. *Powder House Bar (Mile 1.5 Copper River Hwy)* features food and folk and country music.

Alaska Airlines (☎ 907-424-7151) flies daily from Anchorage ($90 one way). In summer, the MV *Bartlett* ferry arrives every couple of days from Valdez ($33) or Whittier ($64).

Wrangell–St Elias National Park

Part of a 31,250-sq-mile wilderness area, this park is a crossroads of mountain ranges: the Wrangell, Chugachs and St Elias. Extensive ice fields and 100 major glaciers spill from the peaks.

From Valdez, the **Richardson Highway** is an incredibly scenic route to Glennallen, with canyons, mountain passes and glaciers. The main headquarters for Wrangell–St Elias National Park (☎ 907-822-5234, Ⓦ www.nps.gov/wrst, Mile 105 Old Richardson Hwy) is in Copper Center.

A side road at Tonsina goes east to Chitina, where a log-cabin visitor center (☎ 907-823-2205, Mile 33 Edgerton Hwy) is open in summer. Nearby are a gas station, grocery store, two restaurants and some campgrounds. From there, the rugged Mt McCarthy Rd follows former railroad tracks 60 miles east through the stunning Chugach Mountains and across the mighty Copper River to historic McCarthy. You can park a mile before McCarthy and cross the Kennicott River footbridge to the abandoned copper-mining town of Kennicott, in the national park.

McCarthy & Kennicott

Attractively decrepit little McCarthy was the Wild West counterpart to the Kennicott company town.

In 1900 Sourdough miners discovered the incredibly rich Kennicott copper deposit, and a syndicate built 196 miles of railroad through the wilderness to bring the ore to Cordova. From 1911 to 1938 the company town of Kennicott worked 24 hours a day. In November 1938, faced with falling copper prices and a possible labor strike, management closed the mine, giving workers two hours to catch the last train out. Despite some pilferage, Kennicott remains a remarkably preserved piece of US mining history.

There's some good **hiking** around the glaciers, peaks and mines, as well as **rafting** on the Kennicott River. Local Chris Richards (☎ 907-544-4444, 800-644-4537) provides colorful two-hour guided walks around the mines ($25). St Elias Alpine Guides (☎ 907-544-4445) offers day trips from McCarthy, and the McCarthy Museum has a $1 walking-tour map. McCarthy Air (☎ 907-544-4440) and Wrangell Mountain Air (☎ 907-544-4400) offer scenic flights (from $50). A one-hour flight around Mt Blackburn and Mt Wrangell costs $100; it's worth every penny if the weather is clear.

You can camp along the west side of the river ($5), though it can get crowded and dusty. Also on the river's west side is *Kennicott River Lodge and Hostel (☎ 907-544-4441)*, with bunks for $25. In McCarthy, *McCarthy Lodge (☎ 907-554-4402)* offers meals ($17-22), showers ($5) and cold beer ($4). It also runs the renovated 1916 *Ma Johnson's Hotel*, with singles/doubles for $95/110. *Kennicott Glacier Lodge (☎ 800-478-2350 within Alaska, ☎ 800-582-5128 outside the state)* costs $149/169; the $12 breakfast is a good value.

Backcountry Connections (☎ 907-822-5292) buses leave Glennallen most days for McCarthy via Chitina ($55). In McCarthy there's a five-hour layover to visit Kennicott; this long day trip costs $99. St Elias Alpine Guides (see above) rents mountain bikes ($35).

KODIAK ISLAND

Southwest of the Kenai Peninsula, Kodiak Island is most famous for Kodiak brown bears, which grow huge gorging on salmon. Accommodations and transport are expensive, but camping gear and a mountain bike could make Kodiak affordable.

The visitor center (☎ 907-486-4782, 800-789-4782, Ⓦ www.kodiak.org, 100 Marine Way) has lists of accommodations (including 20 B&Bs). The Homes Johnson Library (☎ 907-486-8686, 319 Lower Mill Rd) has Internet access.

Bear watching is best July to September but usually involves a charter flight to a remote salmon stream ($300-500 per person). Mythos Expeditions (☎ 907-486-5536) rents kayaks and offers superb guided day trips (from $50).

Alaska Airlines (☎ 907-487-4363) and ERA (☎ 907-487-2663) both have six flights daily from Anchorage, and the ferry MV *Tustumena* (☎ 907-486-3800) connects Kodiak three times weekly with Homer ($53) and Seward ($59). Rent a car to explore rough roads into the wilderness.

The Interior

The 'great big broad land' of Alaska's Interior is a central plateau drained by great rivers and bordered by the rugged Alaska Range to the south and the Brooks Range to the north. Alaska's major highways (rarely more than two-lane roads) crisscross the region.

The main route is George Parks Hwy (Hwy 3), which winds 358 miles from Anchorage to Fairbanks, passing Denali National Park. The Alaska Hwy (Hwy 2) extends southeast from Fairbanks via Delta Junction and Tok to become the Alcan Hwy, connecting to Haines Junction and Whitehorse. All the Interior roads are lined with turnoffs, campgrounds, hiking trails and wildlife-spotting possibilities. Towns are small service centers with gas stations, motels and cafes, and a few retain rustic gold-rush frontier flavor.

GEORGE PARKS HIGHWAY

North of Anchorage, George Parks Hwy passes through the dormitory suburb of Wasilla, just past the Glenn Hwy (Hwy 1) turnoff. A dramatic detour, the Fishook-Willow Rd between Palmer and Willow, goes through **Hatcher Pass**, an alpine paradise with foot trails, gold-mining artifacts and panoramas of the Talkeetna Mountains.

Talkeetna

At Mile 98.7, a side road heads north to this interesting and colorful town. It was a miners' supply center in 1901 and later a riverboat station and railroad-construction headquarters. Since the 1950s, Mt McKinley mountaineers have made Talkeetna their staging post. The Talkeetna Denali Visitor Center (☎ 800-660-2688), on George Parks Hwy, has information about the area.

The new **Mountaineering Ranger Station** (☎ 907-733-2231), on B St, handles expeditions going to Mt McKinley and has

videos and displays for nonclimbers. The four restored buildings of the **Talkeetna Historical Society Museum** (☎ 907-733-2487) are a block south of Main St and house exhibits on bush pilots and McKinley climbs.

For scenic flights to view Mt McKinley ($80-150), check Doug Geeting Aviation (☎ 907-733-2366, 800-770-2366), Hudson Air Service (☎ 907-733-2333) or K2 Aviation (☎ 907-733-2291, 800-764-2291). If the day is clear, be prepared for a long wait and an unforgettable flight.

The *River Park Campground*, at the end of Main St, has sites near the river ($8). *Talkeetna Hostel International* (☎ 907-733-4678, I St) has bunks for $22. *Fairview Inn* (☎ 907-733-2423, 101 Main St) offers noisy singles/doubles with shared bath ($53/63). More upscale and quieter is *Latitude 62 Lodge* (☎ 907-733-2262, Mile 13.5 Talkeetna Spur Rd), at $65/75.

Talkeetna Roadhouse, on Main St, does hearty breakfasts ($9) and dinners ($10-15). Across the street, the *McKinley Deli & Espresso Bar* serves sandwiches ($7) and pizzas ($13) until 11pm.

The Alaska Railroad stops daily in summer from Anchorage ($75) and heads north to Denali National Park ($70) and Fairbanks ($100). Parks Highway Express (☎ 800-600-6001) picks up at the Talkeetna Spur Hwy junction on George Parks Hwy on its way to Denali and Fairbanks ($54).

Denali National Park

This breathtakingly brilliant wilderness area, which includes North America's highest mountain, attracts a million visitors a year. A single road curves 91 miles through the heart of the park, with campsites, trailheads, wildlife and stunning panoramas. This road can be used only by official shuttle buses, which have limited seating. Numbers in the campsites and wilderness zones are also strictly limited. This means Disneyland-like crowds at the entrance but relative solitude once you're inside.

Wildlife, including mammals from marmots to moose, is easy to spot. Caribou, wolves and brown bears are crowd favorites. The main attraction is still magnificent Mt McKinley, a 3-mile-high pyramid of rock, snow and glaciers rising from the valley floor. Clouds will obscure McKinley more often than not, so be prepared to wait for the big view.

Information The park entrance is at Mile 237.3 George Parks Hwy. Entry costs $5/10 per person/family per week. The highway north and south of the park entrance is a touristy strip of private campgrounds, lodges, restaurants and facilities. The Visitor Access Center (VAC; ☎ 907-683-1266, 683-2294, ⓦ www.nps.gov/dena) is the place to organize your trip into the park, pick up permits and purchase maps (open 7am-8pm daily in summer). If possible, plan the exact days you will be in the park, and reserve bus seats and campsites ahead through the Denali National Park Reservation Service (☎ 907-272-7275, 800-622-7275).

Shuttle buses provide access for day hiking and sightseeing, and can be reserved by phone beginning in late February for that summer. In the backcountry you can get on or off buses, at any point along their routes. Buses leave the VAC regularly 6:30am-2pm for Eielson Visitor Center ($23; 4 hours) and Wonder Lake ($30; 5½ hours). Special campers' shuttle buses, with space for backpacks and mountain bikes, charge $19 to any point on the road.

Activities For **day hiking**, get off the shuttle bus at any valley, riverbed or ridge that takes your fancy (no permit needed). For a guided walk, book at the VAC one or two days ahead.

For **backcountry camping** inside the park, you must get a backcountry permit from the VAC one day in advance. The park is divided into 43 zones, each with a regulated number of visitors. Some are more popular than others. Watch the Backcountry Simulator Program video at the VAC, covering bears, rivers and backcountry safety, and check the quota board for an area you can access. You then go to the counter to book a camper shuttle bus and buy your maps.

Most bikers book campsites at the VAC and then carry their bikes on the camper shuttle. **Bicycling** is permitted only on roads. Rent bikes for $37 per day for two days or longer from Denali Outdoor Center (☎ 907-638-1925, ⓦ www.denalioutdoor center .com, Mile 238.5 Parks Hwy).

Several **rafting** companies offer daily floats on the Nenana River; Denali Raft Adventures (☎ 907-683-2234, 800-683-2234, Mile 238 Parks Hwy) offers a canyon run through the gorge, as well as a milder Mt McKinley run ($50).

Places to Stay Campsites inside the park cost $6 or $12, and most can be reserved for a $4 fee. It can be difficult to get a place in the campground of your choice, so take anything available and change campgrounds later. At the park entrance, **Riley Creek Campground** is open year round and overrun by RVs ($12). **Morino Campground** is a walk-in backpackers' campground near the train station ($6). Other campgrounds are spaced along the park road; the nicest is **Wonder Lake**, with 26 tent sites ($12) overlooking Mt McKinley.

The private campgrounds and accommodations north and south of the park entrance usually provide transport to the park. Six miles south of the entrance, **Denali Grizzly Bear Campground** (☎ 907-683-2696, Mile 231 Parks Hwy) has tent sites for $17 and platform tents for $23. Near Healy, 11 miles north, **McKinley KOA** (☎ 907-683-2379, Mile 248.4 Parks Hwy) charges $17/23 for tents/RVs.

There are two hostels in the area. In Healy, **Denali Hostel** (☎ 907-683-1295), on Otter Lake Rd, has bunks for $24. To the south of the park, **Denali Mountain Hostel** (☎ 907-683-7503, Mile 224 Parks Hwy) has bunks ($22), Internet access and gear storage.

Rent a cabin near the entrance at **Sourdough Cabins** (☎ 907-683-2773, 800-354-6020, ⓦ www.denalisourdoughcabins.com, Mile 238.8 Parks Hwy) for $165/$175 per triple/quad. South of the entrance, **Denali River Cabins** (☎ 907-683-2500, 800-230-7275, Mile 231 Parks Hwy) cost $100/156 for doubles/quads. Farther south, **Carlo Creek Lodge** (☎ 907-683-2576, Mile 224 Parks Hwy) has creekside cabins (from $90) and tent sites ($15).

Places to Eat The only food inside the park entrance area is **McKinley Mercantile**, which sells fresh, dried and canned food. It's better to stock up on supplies in Fairbanks or Anchorage.

Outside the park, **Lynx Creek Pizza** (Mile 238.6 Parks Hwy) has excellent offerings, including beer on tap and large pizzas

($17). **Denali Salmon Bake** *(Mile 238.5 Parks Hwy)* offers Alaskan salmon dinners ($20). There are espresso drinks and Internet access at **Black Bear Coffee House** *(Mile 238.5 Parks Hwy)*.

Getting There & Around From the VAC, Parks Highway Express (☎ 888-600-6001) makes the run back to Anchorage ($49) and Fairbanks ($34).

The Alaska Railroad departs from a depot near Riley Creek campground and is expensive but very scenic. The one-way trip to Fairbanks is $50, to Anchorage $125.

FAIRBANKS
A spread-out low-rise city, Fairbanks features log cabins, sled dogs and extremes of climate. Summer days average 70°F and can reach 90°F. 'Downtown' is roughly centered on Golden Heart Park, and Cushman St is more or less the main street. Downtown motels, B&Bs and restaurants are 15 minutes' walk from the train station. Buses will drop you off downtown.

Fairbanks was founded in 1901, when a trader could get his riverboat no farther up the Chena River. A gold strike 12 miles north made Fairbanks a boomtown, with 18,000 people by 1908, but by 1920 it had slumped to 1000. When the Alaska Railroad reached Fairbanks in 1923, major mining companies introduced mechanized dredges to extract ore from the frozen ground. WWII, the Alcan Hwy and military bases produced minor booms, but the town took off as a construction base for the Trans-Alaska oil pipeline and still serves as a gateway to the North Slope.

Information
The Visitors Bureau Log Cabin (☎ 907-456-5774, Ⓦ www.explorefairbanks.com, 550 1st Ave) overlooks the Chena River and has courtesy phones to motels and B&Bs. A recording (☎ 907-456-4636) lists the daily events/attractions. The Alaska Public Lands Information Center (☎ 907-456-0531, 250 Cushman St) has maps, information and displays on parks, wildlife refuges and recreation areas. There's Internet access at Café Latte (☎ 907-455-4898, 519 6th Ave).

Things to See & Do
The Golden Heart Plaza is a pleasant riverside park. The biggest attraction is **Alaskaland** (☎ 907-459-1087), on Airport Way, a 44-acre pioneer theme park with historical

LIBRARY OF CONGRESS

Sled dogs howl at a cloudy moon (1920).

displays, an old stern-wheeler and a railroad car. At the University of Alaska – Fairbanks (UAF), the excellent **University Museum** (☎ 907-474-7211) has sections on geology and history, including a 36,000-year-old bison found preserved in the permafrost ($5). Eight miles north of the city along Steese Hwy is the **Alyeska Pipeline Visitor Center**, where you can view the Trans-Alaska Pipeline and read outdoor displays on it.

For **hiking**, head out to Chena River State Recreational Area, with short walks or the 29-mile Chena Dome Trail. Chena Hot Springs Resorts (☎ 907-369-4111) offers a one-day tour that includes transport and soaking in hot springs ($33). **Canoeing** options range from afternoon paddles to overnight trips; ask at 7 Bridges Boats & Bikes (☎ 907-479-0751, 4321 Birch Lane), at 7 Gables Inn. Alternatively, cruise the Chena River ($40) on board the historic stern wheeler *Riverboat Discovery,* (☎ 907-479-6673, 1975 Discovery Dr).

Places to Stay

The public **Chena River State Campground**, on University Ave, is just north of Airport Way ($15). There are also many private campgrounds in the city; **River's Edge Resort** (☎ 907-474-0286, 4140 Boat St) has tent sites ($16).

Fairbanks has more hostels than any other city in Alaska. The best in the area is **Billie's Backpackers** (☎ 907-479-2034, 2895 Mack Rd), with $20 bunks and $7 breakfasts. Some others are **Fairbanks Shelter & Shower** (☎ 907-479-5016, 248 Madcap Lane), with bunks ($15) and tent sites ($10), and **Fairbanks Hostel** (☎ 907-479-5016, 248 Madcap Lane), next to the university, with bunks for $18. See the visitor-bureau brochure for Fairbanks' 100-plus B&Bs, mostly from $65/75 for singles/doubles. Downtown hotels include **Fairbanks Hotel** (☎ 907-456-6411, 888-329-4685, 517 3rd Ave), with rooms from $60 and bike rentals. Nearby is **Northern Lights Hotel** (☎ 907-452-4456, 427 1st Ave), where rooms are $85-95. **Golden North Hotel** (☎ 907-479-6201, 4888 Airport Way) has small rooms (from $69) and free van service. **Super 8 Motel** (☎ 907-451-8888, 1909 Airport Way) has big, clean rooms from $99/$110.

Places to Eat & Drink

The inexpensive **Co-op Diner** (535 2nd Ave), in the Co-op Plaza, offers hamburgers, sandwiches and Thai specials ($8). **Soapy Smith's** (543 2nd Ave) has good burgers ($7), sandwiches and chowder in a saloon atmosphere. Go to **Gambardella's Pasta Bella** (706 2nd Ave) for homemade pizzas ($13-17) in a delightful outdoor setting. Walk south on Cushman St to find more restaurants, including **Thai House** (526 5th Ave). Fast-food franchises proliferate on Airport Way and in the university area.

The **Palace Saloon** at Alaskaland has honky-tonk piano and cancan dancers in its Golden Heart Revue. Several saloons offer live music and bar games.

Getting There & Around

Alaska Airlines (☎ 907-474-0481) has eight daily flights to Anchorage ($100-150), with occasional bargains. For travel into Arctic Alaska, there's Frontier Flying Service (☎ 907-474-0014, 800-478-6779).

Departing from Fairbanks, Alaskon Express (☎ 907-456-6835) buses stop at Tok ($73) and Beaver Creek ($94), with connections to Whitehorse ($173). Parks Highway Express (☎ 888-600-6001) offers daily connections to Denali National Park ($34) and Anchorage ($69). It also departs Fairbanks for Valdez ($79) and Dawson City ($125).

Alaska Railroad (☎ 907-456-4155) trains depart at 8:30am daily for Denali National Park ($50) and Anchorage ($175).

The Metropolitan Area Commuter Service (MACS; ☎ 907-459-1011) provides local bus service in Fairbanks on weekdays (day passes $3).

Affordable Car Rental (☎ 907-452-4279, 800-471-3101) offers cheap rentals ($40). There's also Rent-A-Wreck (☎ 907-452-1606, 800-478-1606).

The Bush

The Bush is the vast area of Alaska that is not readily accessible by road or ferry. It includes Arctic Alaska, the Brooks Range, the Alaska Peninsula–Aleutian Islands chain and the Bering Sea coast. Traveling to the Bush usually involves small, expensive chartered aircraft ('bush planes'). Facilities for travelers are also pricey and very limited. If you're planning to visit small, isolated communities, it's best to be accompanied by a local contact or tour guide.

To visit **Arctic Alaska**, take the Dalton Hwy, a rough gravel road that goes some 490 miles north from Fairbanks to Deadhorse, near Prudhoe Bay. You can tour the oil complex at Prudhoe, but you can't stay on the shores of the Arctic Ocean. It's not really worth going north of **Atigun Pass**, 300 miles from Fairbanks, where there's a good view over the plains of the North Slope. Dalton Highway Express (☎ 907-452-2031) makes the run twice a week to Prudhoe Bay. It's $100 roundtrip to go to the Arctic Circle, where you can camp at a *BLM campground*, and $250 to Prudhoe Bay.

The Dalton Hwy passes the remote **Gates of the Arctic National Park**, with great hiking and paddling, but the park is best accessed from the town of Bettles, which can be reached only by air. For information, contact the national park ranger station (☎ 907-692-5494) or call Sourdough Outfitters (☎ 907-692-5252).

Isolated settlements on the **Aleutian Islands** can be reached by the ferry MV *Tustumena*, which makes six trips along the archipelago every summer. It's a superbly scenic trip when the weather is clear, and the ferry stops at five ports beyond Kodiak, for just long enough to look around. It costs over $550 from Seward to Dutch Harbor and back. If you want to stay longer on the islands, you'll probably have to fly.

On the Bering Sea coast, the storied old gold-rush town of **Nome** is friendly and interesting. The visitor center (☎ 907-443-5535, Ⓦ www.nomealaska.org) has information about accommodations and trips in the surrounding area. You can camp at no cost on the Golden Sands Beach, where in 1899 gold was discovered and is still being panned. An advance-purchase Air Alaska ticket costs $350-400 from Anchorage.

Hawaii

Hawaii

With its year-round balmy weather, Hawaii is one of the top vacation destinations for US citizens. Volcanic in origin, the Hawaiian Islands are high and rugged, lushly green and cut by spectacular gorges and valleys. From coastal deserts to Alpine mountaintops, barren lava flows to tropical rainforests, bleached white beaches to jet-black sands, the Hawaiian terrain startles and amazes. Some 2500 miles from the nearest landmass, the islands are so isolated that of the thousands of species of flora and fauna that have evolved here, more than 90% exist nowhere else on earth.

Despite the heavy tourism in some areas, you can find scores of quiet spots and secluded beaches. The world's top surfing and windsurfing, as well as excellent conditions for snorkeling, swimming, diving, bodysurfing and most other water sports, lure enthusiasts from around the world. For those who prefer their feet on the ground, there's fantastic hiking to cascading waterfalls, remote rainforest valleys and quiet backcountry camping spots.

Oahu is the most crowded and developed of the islands; the high-rise beach resort of Waikiki contains almost half the tourist accommodations in Hawaii. Oahu also boasts the only royal palace in the USA and Hawaii's most awesome surf.

Maui is the second largest and second most developed of the islands, but it has plenty of unspoiled places well off the beaten path. Maui is also the best island for watching humpback whales.

The Big Island of Hawaii has two things the others don't: snow and erupting volcanoes, the latter the centerpiece of the astonishing Hawaii Volcanoes National Park.

Kauai has Hawaii's greenest scenery, a deeply cut canyon resembling a mini–Grand Canyon and the famous razorback cliffs of the Na Pali Coast. The least developed of the four largest islands, it's a mecca for hikers and other outdoor enthusiasts.

Molokai, the most Hawaiian of the islands, is rural, slow-paced and only lightly visited by tourists. Lanai, the smallest main island, has moved from growing pineapples to becoming a luxury resort destination.

Most visitors to Hawaii have a favorite island. However, the more you explore, the harder it may become to favor just one.

History

Hawaii's first inhabitants were Polynesians who arrived from the Marquesas Islands between AD 500 and 700. Tahitians conquered the islands in about 1000, introducing human sacrifice and *kapu*, a practice of taboos that strictly regulated all social inter-

Highlights

- Killer surf – winter waves up to 35 feet high on Oahu's North Shore
- Fiery lava – Hawaii Volcanoes National Park, where the Big Island gets bigger
- Sea-cliff hiking – Kauai's spectacular Na Pali Coast

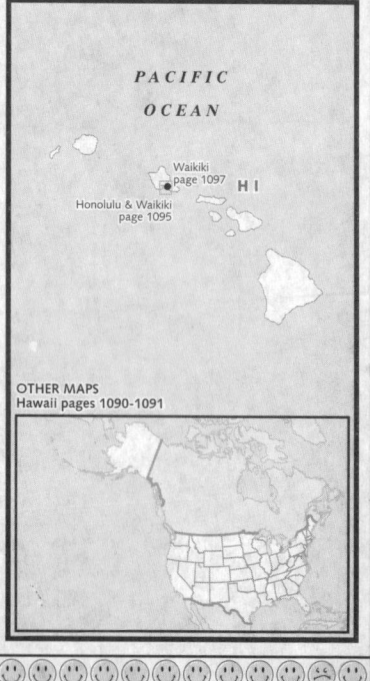

PACIFIC

OCEAN

Waikiki
page 1097

H I

Honolulu & Waikiki
page 1095

OTHER MAPS
Hawaii pages 1090-1091

action. The Tahitians also built the rock temples called *heiau,* some of which can still be seen (including Keaiwa Heiau on Oahu and Mookini Heiau on the Big Island).

British explorer Captain James Cook spotted the Hawaiian archipelago on January 18, 1778. He was met favorably by the islanders, but was killed in a melee on a later visit. The islands' separate warring chiefdoms were united in 1810 by King Kamehameha the Great, chief of the Big Island. Following his death in 1819, his wife, Queen Kaahumanu, felt so stymied by the kapus that she purposely began to undermine that system, extinguishing Hawaii's old religion.

Cook's crew introduced the first of many foreign diseases that decimated the native Hawaiians. During the 1820s the first Christian missionaries arrived and quickly became a powerful influence on Hawaiian society. Foreigners gained control of vast tracts of land and established a sugar industry.

In 1852 American plantation owners began recruiting laborers from overseas, bringing in some 350,000 Japanese, Chinese, Filipinos and Europeans. Immigrants soon came to outnumber native Hawaiians, but together they created modern Hawaii's multiethnic culture. Within a few decades, westerners owned 80% of Hawaii's privately held lands, while the Hawaiians drifted into ghettos in the larger towns. By the end of the 19th century the native population had been reduced from an estimated 300,000 to less than 50,000.

As the sugar barons became more powerful, they advocated the annexation of Hawaii to the USA. When Queen Liliuokalani (1891–93) tried to strengthen the monarchy, they overthrew her. In January 1893 they announced a provisional government led by Sanford Dole, son of a pioneer missionary. Hawaii was annexed on July 7, 1898. Soon afterward, the US Navy set up a huge Pacific headquarters at Pearl Harbor and built Schofield Barracks, the largest US Army base anywhere.

Hawaii was relatively untouched by WWI, but the surprise Japanese attack on Pearl Harbor on December 7, 1941, jolted the USA into WWII. In 1959 Hawaiians voted, by a 93% majority, to become a US state.

In 1993 President Clinton formally apologized to native Hawaiians 'for the overthrow of the Kingdom of Hawaii' and expressed a commitment to 'provide a proper foundation for reconciliation.' A Hawaiian sovereignty movement, favoring some form of a nation-within-a-nation model, is being debated, but native Hawaiians are widely divided on the specifics.

In 2000 the US Supreme Court struck down a Hawaii law that had allowed only native Hawaiians to select trustees for the Office of Hawaiian Affairs, the leading organization that provides social and economic benefits to people of Hawaiian ancestry. The conservative court ruled that native Hawaiians are a racial group, not a tribe that has a political relationship with the USA. The consequences could be far-reaching, from impacting sovereignty issues to jeopardizing an array of government-funded programs aimed at bettering the lot of native Hawaiians.

Geography

Hawaii is the world's most isolated archipelago, 2500 miles from the nearest landmass, North America. Volcanic in origin, the six main islands all have splendid scenery. Their leeward (southwestern) coasts are sunny, dry and desertlike, with white sands and turquoise waters. The mountainous windward (northeastern) sides have tropical jungles, cascading waterfalls and pounding surf. The uplands are cool and green, with rolling pastures, small farms and ranches.

Hawaii

Nickname: Aloha State

Population: 1,211,500 (42nd)

Area: 10,930 sq miles (43rd)

Admitted to Union: August 21, 1959 (50th)

Capital city: Honolulu (population 400,000)

Other cities: Pearl City (45,000), Kailua (39,000)

State fish: *humuhumunukunukuapuaa* (rectangular triggerfish)

Birthplace of: surfing, Olympic gold medallist and 'father of modern surfing' Duke Kahanamoku (1890–1968), the ukulele ('flea' in Hawaiian)

HAWAII

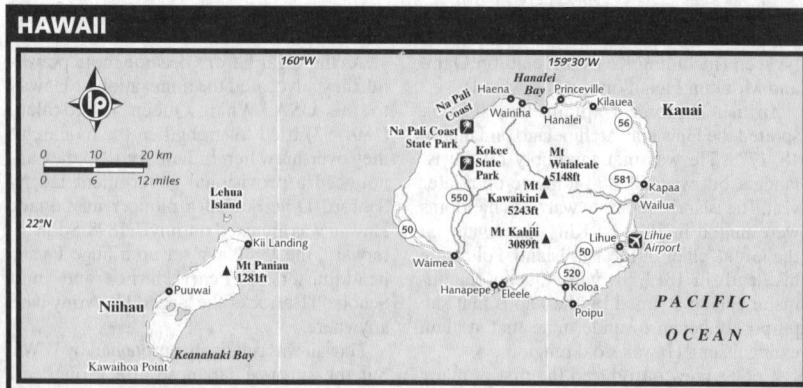

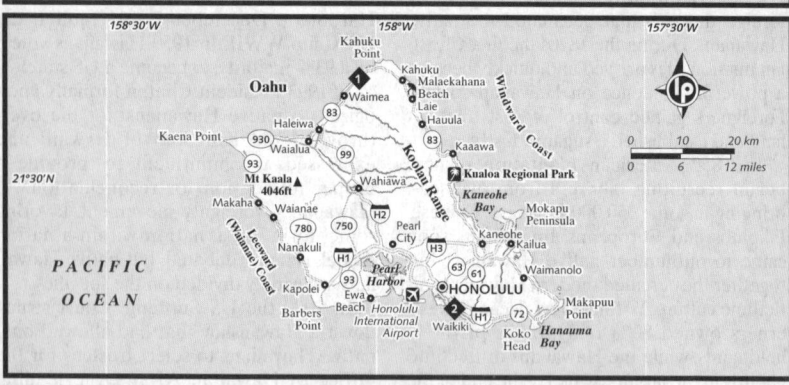

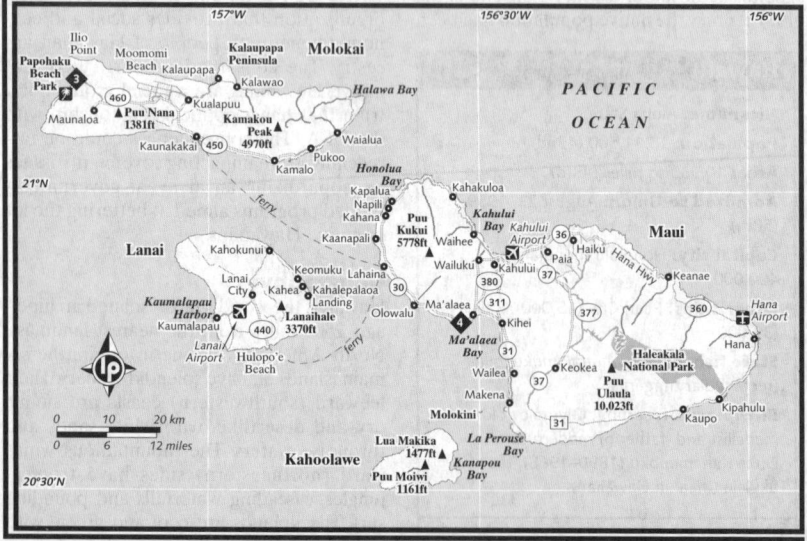

HAWAII

DETOURS

1. Sunset at Sunset Beach—coral clouds and a hard-core surf scene

2. Honolulu's Chinatown—herbalists and temples, cheap restaurants and noodle factories

3. Papohaku Beach—2½ magnificent miles of golden sand and crashing surf

4. Papawai Point—a prime spot for whale-watching

5. Kealakekua Bay—the best snorkeling on the Big Island

6. Chain of Craters Road—an awesome drive passing volcanic craters and ending at an active lava flow

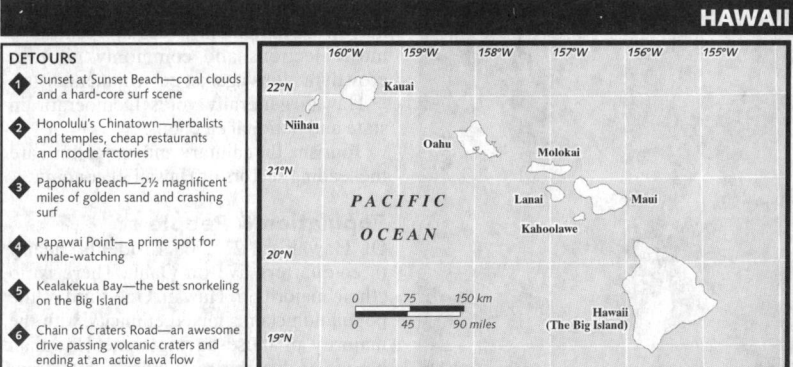

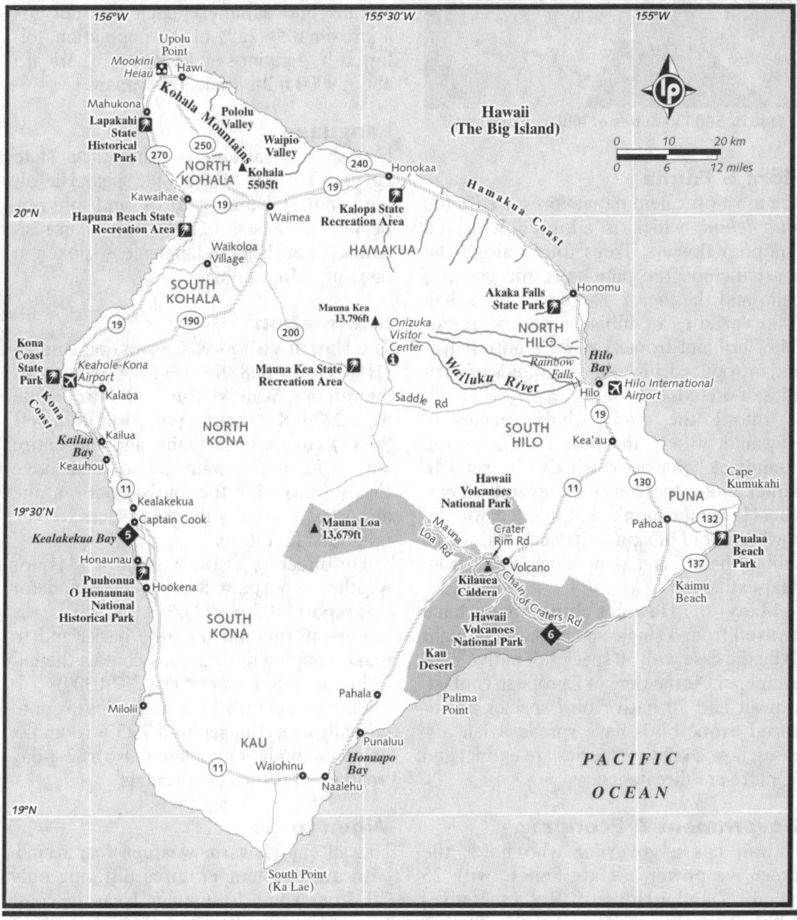

One of 5000 varieties of hibiscus in Hawaii

Flora & Fauna

The most prevalent native forest tree is the *ohia lehua,* which is adorned with red pompom flowers. Trees found along the coast include the pandanus, the coconut palm and the *kiawe.* There are more than 5000 varieties of hibiscus and scores of other brilliant tropical flowers, both native and introduced, including hundreds of varieties of orchids.

Among the many whale species in Hawaiian waters, the best known are the humpback whales, which can be seen in winter along the coasts of several islands. The Hawaiian monk seal, named for the cowl-like fold of skin at its neck and for its solitary habits, is making a comeback from near-extinction.

Many of Hawaii's birds may have evolved from a single species, as is thought to be the case with 30 species of native honeycreeper. At the time of European contact, Hawaii had 70 native bird species. Introduced exotic birds have spread avian diseases; now 24 native species are extinct and 36 more are threatened.

Government & Economy

Hawaii has a governor who holds the executive power, a state Senate with 25 members, and a House of Representatives with 51 members. The state is further divided into four counties, each led by a mayor. Development issues are central to most elections and commonly pit pro-growth factions against environmentalists.

Hawaii generally votes Democratic in state and national elections.

Tourism, the military and agriculture are the leading sectors of Hawaii's economy.

Population & People

Of Hawaii's 1,211,500 residents, nearly three-quarters live on Oahu. There is no ethnic majority in Hawaii. One-third of the population claims mixed ethnicity, with the majority of those having some Hawaiian blood. As for the remainder, white Caucasians and Japanese each account for approximately 22% of the population, followed by Filipinos and Chinese. There are about 9000 full-blooded Hawaiians.

Language

English and Hawaiian are the official state languages. About 9000 people speak Hawaiian, and Hawaiian words and phrases pepper the speech of most Hawaiian residents. A non-English language is spoken in one out of four homes.

Information

The Hawaii Visitors & Convention Bureau (HVCB; ☎ 808-923-1811, Ⓦ www.visit .hawaii.org, Waikiki Business Plaza, suite 801, 2270 Kalakaua Ave, Honolulu, HI 96815) covers both Oahu and the entire state. The other main islands also have tourist offices, but the tourist booths at the airports are usually the best places to pick up tourist literature.

For directory assistance, dial ☎ 1441; for weather reports, ☎ 808-973-4381; and for surf reports, ☎ 808-973-4383.

For information on state parks and to make camping reservations, contact the Division of State Parks (☎ 808-587-0300).

Hawaii tacks a 4.17% state sales tax onto virtually everything, plus a 7.25% room tax on accommodations. There's also a $2-a-day 'road use' tax on all car rentals.

When to Go

Hawaii enjoys warm weather year round, with average temperatures differing only 7°F from winter to summer. Near the coast the daily temperatures average a high of

83°F and a low of 68°F. Summer and fall are the driest seasons, winter the wettest. December to March is also the busiest tourist season, so that's when you can expect the most competition for affordable rooms. Fall and spring are slow seasons and offer better discounts.

Accommodations

If you want to stay in an expensive resort hotel, consider booking a holiday package. For B&Bs, try All-Islands Bed & Breakfast (☎ 808-263-2342) or Bed & Breakfast Hawaii (☎ 808-822-7771).

For budget travelers there are hostels and campgrounds. Permits, required for camping in all county and state parks, cost $5 for state parks and range from free to $3 for county parks; they can be picked up at state and county park offices. Campers should never leave possessions unattended in any park, and occasionally campers have been harassed at campgrounds – so inquire about safety when you get your permit. As a general rule, state and national parks are generally safer.

Activities

All of the state's beaches are publicly owned, so even beaches adjacent to exclusive properties have public access.

Hawaii is a great place to surf, windsurf, dive or snorkel. Equipment rental and lessons for beginners are available on the main islands. There are also fine opportunities for kayaking, fishing, hiking, mountain biking and jogging.

Getting There & Around

Honolulu is a major Pacific hub and an intermediate stop on many flights between the US mainland and Asia, Australia, New Zealand and the South Pacific. Passengers on any of these routes can often make a free stopover. From Europe, ask about an add-on fare from the US West Coast or perhaps a round-the-world ticket. From the US mainland, the cheapest fares generally start at $600-900 (depending on the season) from the East Coast, $300-500 from California.

Most flights arrive in Honolulu; travelers to other islands must then make the short hop to their final destination. Interisland travel is inexpensive; fares between the main islands are $55-95. Ask about discount coupons and air passes. The largest airlines, Hawaiian (☎ 808-838-1555) and Aloha (☎ 808-484-1111), have frequent flights. Island Air (☎ 808-484-2222) services the smaller airports.

The only ferry services in the state are between Maui and Lanai and between Maui and Molokai. See those sections, later, for details.

An excellent bus service goes around Oahu, and the Big Island and Kauai have limited public buses. Some scenic mountain routes can be narrow and winding, but main roads are generally good. Rental cars are available on all the main islands and cost $30-50 a day, $150-200 a week. It's wise to book a car before you arrive. Phone a few companies to find the best price. You might find some companies have a minimum-age requirement of 25.

Each island offers half- and full-day sightseeing bus tours that are advertised in the free tourist booklets. Specialized tours include whale-watching cruises, bicycle tours, snorkel trips, overnight tours and helicopter tours. All can be booked after arrival in Hawaii.

Oahu

Oahu is the most developed of the Hawaiian Islands. Around Honolulu it's an urban scene, with highways, high-rises and crowds, but these quickly give way to pineapple fields and mountains. Oahu also has excellent beaches and offers a full range of activities, from water sports to hiking and horseback riding.

Getting Around

Oahu's extensive public bus system, TheBus (☎ 808-848-5555), has some 80 routes that collectively cover most of Oahu. The one-way fare for all rides is $1.50, with free transfers to connecting routes (ask when you board). Four-day ($10) and monthly ($27) passes are available at any of the ubiquitous ABC shops. The *Honolulu & Oahu by TheBus* map ($5) shows bus routes and major attractions with bus stops and numbers. TheBus also distributes a simple, free schematic route map. Bus Nos 52 and 55 can be combined for a cheap circle-island tour ($1.50; 4 hours).

HAWAII

The State Department of Transportation's *Bike Oahu* map can be found at the HVCB in Waikiki and at bike shops. The Hawaii Bicycling League (☎ 808-735-5756) holds a variety of free bike rides (open to the public) around Oahu nearly every weekend. Most public buses have bike racks.

Conventional all-day circle-island tours are offered by Roberts Hawaii (☎ 808-539-9400) for $42.

HONOLULU & WAIKIKI

Honolulu (Sheltered Harbor) is a modern city blending eastern and western influences and featuring fine city beaches and parks. Waikiki, Honolulu's famous beachside suburb, is crowded with package tourists, mostly from Japan and the US mainland. It's an enclave of restaurants, bars, clubs, upscale stores, kitschy shops, hotels and condos.

Information

You can pick up tourist brochures from the HVCB visitor office (☎ 808-924-0266), on the 4th floor of the Royal Hawaiian Shopping Center in Waikiki.

There are branch post offices in Waikiki and downtown Honolulu, but to pick up general-delivery mail you must go to the main post office (3600 Aolele St), opposite the airport's interisland terminal.

Fishbowl Internet Cafe (☎ 808-922-7562, 2463 Kuhio St), in Waikiki, has Internet service for $6 an hour; most hostels also have Internet access.

Good bookshops include Waldenbooks at the Waikiki Shopping Plaza (2270 Kalakaua Ave, Waikiki) and Borders Books & Music (Ward Center, 1200 Ala Moana Blvd, Honolulu).

Downtown

Downtown Honolulu is a hodgepodge of past and present. Built for King Kalakaua in 1882, **Iolani Palace** (☎ 808-522-0832), at S King and Richards Sts, is the only royal palace in the USA; tours ($15) are given 9am-2:15pm Tuesday to Saturday. At the adjacent **State Capitol**, visitors can wander through the rotunda without charge.

Built of coral slabs, **Kawaiahao Church**, Oahu's oldest church (1838), is at the corner of Punchbowl and S King Sts. Nearby is the

Mission Houses Museum (553 S King St), which comprises three original buildings and many artifacts of the Sandwich Islands Mission headquarters ($8; open Tue-Sat). The **Honolulu Academy of Arts** (900 S Beretania St) has exceptional art collections, including a small but choice Hawaiian section ($7; closed Mon).

Down by the harbor at Pier 9, the observation deck of the landmark **Aloha Tower** has sweeping, although not particularly scenic, views of the commercial harbor and downtown. The **Hawaii Maritime Center**, at Pier 7, has a museum ($7.50) with a good whaling-era section and the berth for the double-hulled canoe *Hokulea,* which has made several voyages retracing the routes of early Polynesian seafarers.

Between downtown and Waikiki, **Ala Moana Beach Park** is frequented by city residents for laid-back picnicking and swimming – minus the tourists.

Chinatown

This busy and colorful district, immediately north of downtown Honolulu, was settled around 1860 by Chinese immigrants who had worked off their sugarcane plantation contracts. Its bustling heart is the 1904 Oahu Market, at Kekaulike and N King Sts. You can get tattooed, consult with an herbalist, explore the temples and antique shops or eat at inexpensive restaurants. While Chinatown is a fun place to explore during the day, walking around at night is not recommended due to drug and gang activity.

Waikiki

Bustling 2-mile **Waikiki Beach** is good for swimming, boogie boarding, surfing, sailing and other beach activities. (Some stretches of Waikiki Beach are also known by other names, such as Kahanamoku Beach, Fort DeRussy Beach and Gray's Beach.) The 200-acre Kapiolani Park contains the informative **Waikiki Aquarium** ($7) and **Honolulu Zoo** ($6). The park is also the venue for many community events, including the famous, if touristy, **Kodak Hula Show** (free admission).

Other Attractions

The **Bishop Museum** (1525 Bernice St) is possibly the world's best Polynesian anthropological museum ($15). It covers the cultural

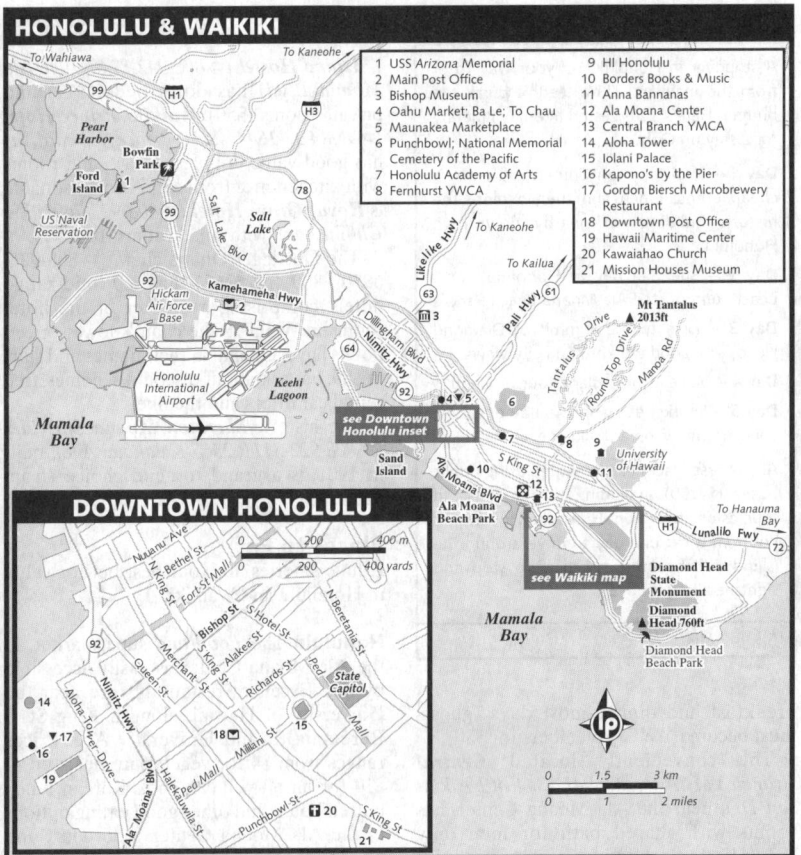

HONOLULU & WAIKIKI

1 USS *Arizona* Memorial
2 Main Post Office
3 Bishop Museum
4 Oahu Market; Ba Le; To Chau
5 Maunakea Marketplace
6 Punchbowl; National Memorial Cemetery of the Pacific
7 Honolulu Academy of Arts
8 Fernhurst YWCA
9 HI Honolulu
10 Borders Books & Music
11 Anna Bannanas
12 Ala Moana Center
13 Central Branch YMCA
14 Aloha Tower
15 Iolani Palace
16 Kapono's by the Pier
17 Gordon Biersch Microbrewery Restaurant
18 Downtown Post Office
19 Hawaii Maritime Center
20 Kawaiahao Church
21 Mission Houses Museum

HAWAII

DOWNTOWN HONOLULU

history of Hawaii and also has a planetarium, daily hula shows and special exhibits for children.

Perched above downtown Honolulu is **Punchbowl**, the bowl-shaped remains of a long-extinct volcanic crater, with a panoramic view of the city. This is the site of the National Memorial Cemetery of the Pacific, where over 25,000 US servicepeople are buried.

Activities

Surfboards, windsurfing equipment and snorkel gear can be rented right on the beach in Waikiki. There are several **hiking** trails and lookouts with sweeping views in the lush Upper Manoa, Tantalus and Makiki Valleys, and in the hills above the University

of Hawaii. Some trailheads are accessible by bus. Guided hikes ($3) are offered on weekends by the Sierra Club (☎ 808-538-6616).

Places to Stay

Although Oahu isn't known for its low prices, it's usually not too difficult to find a good-value place to stay in the Honolulu area.

Honolulu Friendly *HI Honolulu* (☎ 808-946-0591, 2323 Seaview Ave), near the University of Hawaii and several bus routes, can accommodate 42 travelers in bunk beds ($14/17 members/nonmembers) and two private rooms ($10 extra). *Fernhurst YWCA* (☎ 808-941-2231, 1566 Wilder Ave), near Punahou, has twin rooms for women only at $25 per person or $30 for singles, including

HAWAII

Honolulu Stopover

A stopover in Honolulu on your way to or from the mainland USA needn't break the budget. Here's a suggested five-day itinerary for a stay on Oahu:

Day 1 – Stroll through Chinatown, enjoy a cheap ethnic lunch and then explore the historic buildings of nearby downtown Honolulu.

Day 2 – Spend a day at Honolulu's best beach, untouristed Ala Moana Beach Park.

Day 3 – Hike to the summit of Diamond Head for a good workout and city views.

Day 4 – Make a circle-island tour of Oahu.

Day 5 – Snorkel at Hanauma Bay or take a windsurfing lesson at Kailua Beach Park.

All of these places can be visited using public buses ($1.50), including the circle-island tour, as day trips from Honolulu. However, if you rent a car one day to drive around the island, it'll be more practical to stop and sightseeing along the way.

breakfast and dinner most days (guests must become YWCA members for $30).

The conveniently located **Central Branch YMCA** (☎ 808-941-3344, 401 Atkinson Dr), near the Ala Moana Center, has rooms with shared bath for men only ($30/41 singles/doubles); doubles with private bath for men or women cost $53.

Waikiki Kalakaua Ave, the main beach-front strip, is lined largely with high-rise hotels and $150-plus rooms. Better values are found at the smaller hostelries on the back streets, in the Kuhio Ave area, and up near the Ala Wai Canal, all a short walk from the beach.

Central **HI Waikiki** (☎ 808-926-8313, 2417 Prince Edward St) can accommodate 60 travelers in dorm beds ($17/20 members/nonmembers) and private rooms ($40/46).

The largest of the many private hostels is multistoried **Banana Bungalow Waikiki Beach** (☎ 808-924-5074, 2463 Kuhio Ave), with dorm beds ($18) and private rooms (from $54). Nearby **InterClub Hostel Waikiki** (☎ 808-924-2636, 2413 Kuhio Ave)

has dorm beds ($18) and private rooms ($65).

Island Hostel (☎ 808-942-8748, 1946 Ala Moana Blvd) has dorm beds ($17) and private rooms ($50). **Waikiki Prince Hotel** (☎ 808-922-1544, 2431 Prince Edward St) has good-value doubles for $45 and rooms with kitchenettes from $55. Also reasonable is **Royal Grove Hotel** (☎ 808-923-7691, 151 Uluniu Ave), with small rooms from $43.

The Outrigger/Ohana chain (☎ 808-921-6870, 800-462-6262) has 20 mid-range hotels, comprising a quarter of the hotel rooms in Waikiki. The chain's lower-priced hotels have 'Ohana' in their names and start at $89, but ask about discount schemes, free rental car offers and the like.

The historic **Sheraton Moana Surfrider** (☎ 808-922-3111, 2365 Kalakaua Ave), built in 1901, is a grand top-end choice (from $265).

Places to Eat

Ethnic eateries are your best bet for value in Honolulu and Waikiki.

Honolulu The **Foodland** supermarket, in the Ala Moana Center, is easily accessible by bus. Excellent restaurants are near the University of Hawaii, along S King St, S Beretania St and University Ave. Prices ranges from $4 for vegetarian meals up to $10 for an all-you-can-cook Korean lunch buffet. You'll find other good eating options in the Ala Moana Center food court and nearby Ward Center and Ward Warehouse shopping complexes on Ala Moana Blvd.

In Chinatown a fun local dining option is the food court in **Maunakea Marketplace**, on N Hotel St. Nearby **Ba Le** (150 N King St) has good snacks for breakfast and lunch, while Vietnamese **To Chau** (1007 River St) is highly recommended for its *pho* ($4), a rich noodle soup.

The waterfront **Gordon Biersch Microbrewery Restaurant**, beside the Aloha Tower on Ala Moana Blvd, specializes in bistro fare and fresh brew.

Waikiki The best place to get groceries is **Food Pantry** (2370 Kuhio Ave), open 24 hours. **Patisserie**, offering pastries and coffee, has two locations, one at 2330 Kuhio Ave and one on Beach Walk in the Ohana Edgewater hotel.

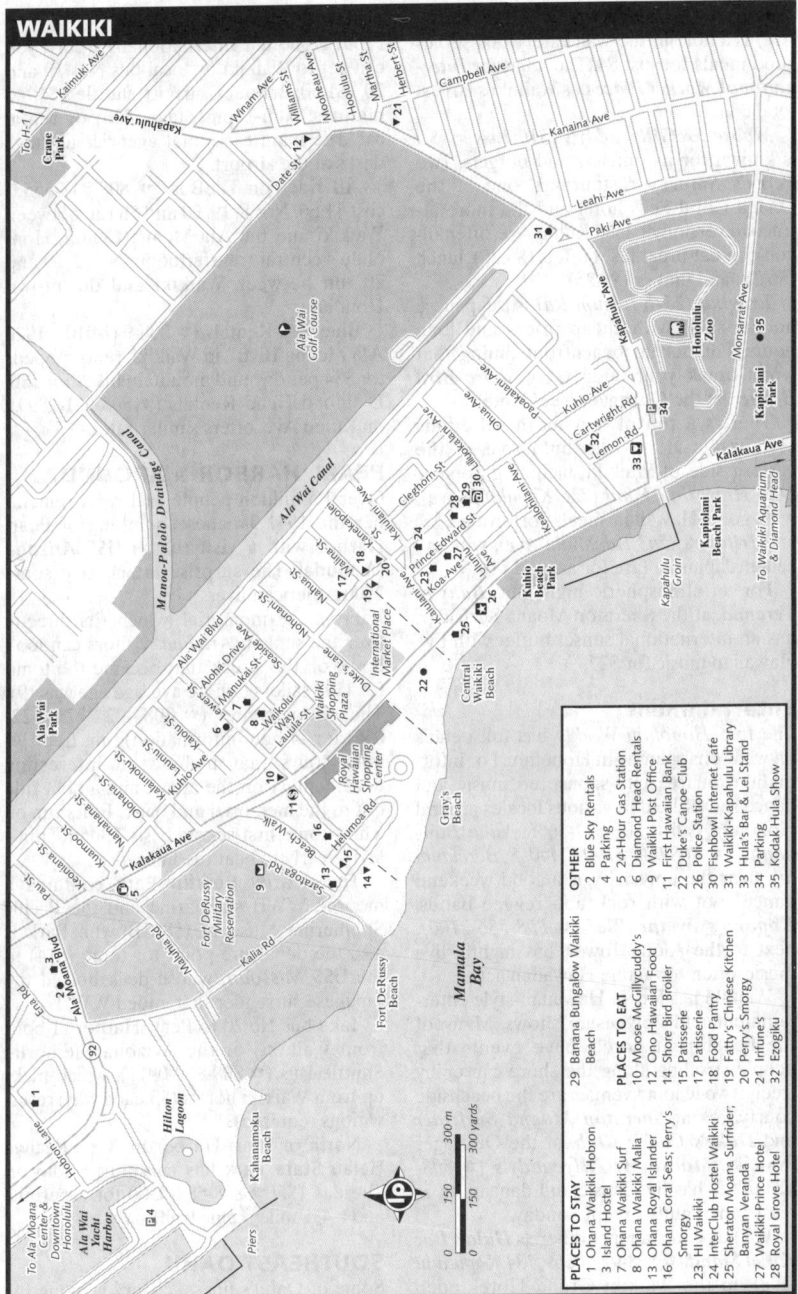

WAIKIKI

HAWAII

PLACES TO STAY
1 Ohana Waikiki Hobron
3 Island Hostel
7 Ohana Waikiki Surf
8 Ohana Waikiki Malia
13 Ohana Royal Islander
16 Ohana Coral Seas; Perry's Smorgy
23 HI Waikiki
24 InterClub Hostel Waikiki
25 Sheraton Moana Surfrider; Banyan Veranda
27 Waikiki Prince Hotel
28 Royal Grove Hotel

29 Banana Bungalow Waikiki Beach

PLACES TO EAT
10 Moose McGillycuddy's
12 Ono Hawaiian Food
14 Shore Bird Broiler
15 Patisserie
17 Patisserie
18 Food Pantry
19 Fatty's Chinese Kitchen
20 Perry's Smorgy
21 Irifune's
32 Ezogiku

OTHER
2 Blue Sky Rentals
4 Parking
5 24-Hour Gas Station
6 Diamond Head Rentals
9 Waikiki Post Office
11 First Hawaiian Bank
22 Duke's Canoe Club
26 Police Station
30 Fishbowl Internet Cafe
31 Waikiki-Kapahulu Library
33 Hula's Bar & Lei Stand
34 Parking
35 Kodak Hula Show

Fatty's Chinese Kitchen (2345 Kuhio Ave) is a hole-in-the-wall eatery that serves good meals for just $4. The adjacent *International Market Place* has Waikiki's largest food court.

Moose McGillycuddy's (310 Lewers St) is known for its omelets and burgers. Two *Perry's Smorgy* restaurants, one at the Ohana Coral Seas hotel and the more attractive version at 2380 Kuhio Ave, offer all-you-can-eat breakfast buffets ($5.25), lunch ($6.25)and dinner ($9.25).

Ezogiku (2546 Lemon Rd) is a Japanese noodle shop with cheap prices and long hours. For decent beachfront dining that won't break your budget, try *Shore Bird Broiler*, at the Outrigger Reef Hotel.

There's a run of neighborhood ethnic restaurants along Kapahulu Ave, at the eastern side of Waikiki, including popular *Ono Hawaiian Food (726 Kapahulu Ave)*, with good Hawaiian meals for around $8, and *Irifune's (563 Kapahulu Ave)*, with excellent Japanese fare for around $10.

For an atmospheric night out, *Banyan Veranda*, at the Sheraton Moana Surfrider, has an international sunset buffet with live Hawaiian music for $27.

Entertainment

The free *Honolulu Weekly* has full details on what's happening in Honolulu. For information on free city-sponsored music and dance shows, held in various locales around Honolulu, call ☎ 808-527-5666. *Anna Bannanas (☎ 808-946-5190, 2440 S Beretania St)*, near the university, is a good weekend dance spot with rock and reggae bands. *Kapono's by the Pier (☎ 808-536-2100)*, next to the Aloha Tower, has nightly live music, often top-name Hawaiian acts.

Waikiki has lots of Hawaiian-style entertainment and Polynesian shows. Many of the beachfront hotels have events that people strolling along the shore can enjoy freely; two leading venues are the beachside courtyards at *Sheraton Moana Surfrider* and *Duke's Canoe Club*, at the Outrigger Waikiki. *Moose McGillycuddy's (☎ 808-923-0751)* has live music and dancing to at least 1am nightly except Sunday.

For gay entertainment there's *Hula's Bar & Lei Stand (☎ 808-923-0669, 134 Kapahulu Ave)*, in the Waikiki Grand Hotel, open 10am-2am.

Getting Around

From Honolulu International Airport, you can get to Waikiki by local bus Nos 19 and 20 ($1.50; 1 hour), airport shuttle ($6; 45 minutes; 6am-10pm), taxi ($20) or rental car. The main car rental agencies all have desks at the airport.

All rides on TheBus (☎ 808-848-5555) cost $1.50. Nos 8, 19, 20 and 58 run between Waikiki and the Ala Moana Center, Honolulu's central transfer point. Nos 2, 19 and 20 run between Waikiki and downtown Honolulu.

Blue Sky Rentals (☎ 808-947-0101, 1920 Ala Moana Blvd), in Waikiki, rents mopeds for $34 per day and mountain bikes for $20. Diamond Head Rentals (☎ 808-921-2899), on Kuhio Ave, offers similar rates.

PEARL HARBOR & AROUND

Over 1.5 million people each year remember the 1941 Japanese bombing of Pearl Harbor with a visit to the **USS Arizona Memorial**. The surprise attack cost some 2500 American lives.

From the memorial, which sits directly over the sunken *Arizona,* visitors can look down on the wreck that became the tomb for 1177 sailors (whose average age was 19). The visitor center (☎ 808-422-2771, 422-0561 for 24-hour information) runs free 1¼-hour tours that include an interesting documentary on the attack and a boat ride out to the memorial and back. Tours run on a first-come, first-served basis 7:30am-5pm – arrive early to beat the lines.

The nearby **Bowfin Park** contains a moored WWII submarine and the Pacific Submarine Museum ($8). Bowfin Park is also the departure point for tours ($14) to the **USS *Missouri***, whose deck hosted the Japanese surrender that ended WWII.

Take bus No 20 to Pearl Harbor (1 hour from Waikiki) or the Arizona Memorial Shuttle Bus (☎ 808-839-0911), which picks up from Waikiki hotels ($3 each way; reservations required).

North of Pearl Harbor in Aiea, **Keaiwa Heiau State Park** has camping Friday to Tuesday ($5; ☎ 808-587-0300 for a permit) and a 4½-mile scenic trail.

SOUTHEAST OAHU

Some of Oahu's finest scenery is along the southeast coast, which curves around the tip of the Koolau Range. To make the loop around southeast Oahu from Waikiki, take bus No 58 to Sea Life Park and then No 57 up to Kailua and back into Honolulu.

Diamond Head State Monument

Visitors can climb this extinct volcano (760 feet) along a fairly steep **hiking** trail to the crater rim ($1 entry fee). The trail (1½ miles roundtrip) goes through some of the tunnels built by the US Army early in the 20th century. At the top are sweeping views of Waikiki. Take bus No 22 or 58 from Waikiki.

Koko Head Regional Park

The entire Koko Head area is a county regional park, featuring volcanic tuff cones and other curious rock formations, Sandy Beach (a top spot for experienced bodysurfers) and a blowhole that gushes during incoming tides. A splendid upmarket area restaurant is *Roy's* (☎ 808-396-7697), in the Hawaii Kai Corporate Plaza on Hwy 72, with Pacific Rim cuisine.

Hanauma Bay Beach Park

This very popular park encircles a wide, sheltered bay of sapphire and turquoise waters set in a rugged volcanic ring. There's excellent snorkeling and diving year round, though heavy use of the bay has damaged the coral on the shallow reef ($3; closed Tue). A concession stand rents snorkel gear. Take bus No 22 from Waikiki.

Makapuu Point

North of Sandy Beach, 647-foot Makapuu Point and its lighthouse mark the easternmost point of Oahu. **Makapuu Beach** is one of the island's top winter spots for experienced bodysurfers. Opposite the beach is **Sea Life Park** (☎ 808-259-7933), Hawaii's only marine park ($25/12.50 adults/kids), with aquariums and dolphin shows; there's no charge for the adjacent Whaling Museum. Take bus Nos 22 or 57 'Kailua/Sea Life Park.'

WINDWARD COAST

Scenic Pali Hwy (Hwy 61) runs between Honolulu and Kailua, cutting through the spectacular Koolau Range. **Nuuanu Pali Lookout** (1200 feet) is where Kamehameha the Great's invading troops, in 1795, forced hundreds of Oahu warriors over the cliff (some hundred years later, more than 500 skulls were discovered at the base of the cliffs).

Windward Oahu, the island's eastern side, follows the Koolau Range along its entire length, from Kahuku Point in the north to Makapuu Point in the south. The coast is exposed to the northeast trade winds, creating ideal conditions for windsurfing.

Kailua

This ordinary middle-class community shelters lovely **Kailua Beach**, the island's top **windsurfing** spot (gear rental and lessons available weekdays on the beach). Popoia Island, an offshore bird sanctuary, is a popular destination for kayakers.

Kailua has no hotels, but there are many furnished beachfront cottages, studios and B&B-style rooms in private homes. For reservations, contact Affordable Paradise Bed & Breakfast (☎ 808-261-1693). In addition, Naish Hawaii (☎ 808-262-6068) books windsurfing vacations in Kailua.

Kaneohe

Kaneohe Bay is the state's largest bay and reef-sheltered lagoon. The near-constant trade winds are ideal for sailing. Free weekend camping (some of the island's safest) is allowed in **Hoomaluhia Park** (permit required; ☎ 808-233-7323), in the uplands of Kaneohe. This 400-acre park contains a lush botanical garden.

Off the Kahekili Hwy, 1½ miles north of Haiku Rd, is the Valley of the Temples, an interdenominational cemetery. The main attraction here is the Japanese Buddhist **Byodo-In**, the 'Temple of Equality,' which sits against the scenic Koolau Range ($2).

Kualoa Regional Park

This is a nice beach park in a scenic setting just south of Kaaawa. Apua Pond, a brackish salt marsh on the point, is a nesting area for the endangered aeo (Hawaiian stilt). Camping is free Friday to Tuesday (permit required; ☎ 808-523-4525).

Laie

Laie is the site of a stately 1919 **Mormon Temple**, the first built outside the mainland USA (the temple interior is off-limits to tourists). The Mormon-run **Polynesian**

HAWAII

Cultural Center (☎ 808-293-3333), Oahu's second-most-visited attraction, re-creates seven theme villages representing Samoa, New Zealand, Fiji, Tahiti, Tonga, the Marquesas and Hawaii ($27; closed Sun). *Best Inn Hukilau Resort (☎ 808-293-9282),* outside the Polynesian Cultural Center, offers rooms for $84, including continental breakfast.

Malaekahana Beach
Attractive Malaekahana Beach, between Laie and Kahuku, is good for swimming, bodysurfing, board surfing and windsurfing. Mokuauia, a state bird sanctuary just offshore, has a nice sandy cove with good snorkeling.

Malaekahana State Recreation Area, at the beach, has the best campgrounds on this end of the windward coast. You can camp in the park's main Kalanai Point section ($5) with a permit (☎ 808-587-0300), or rent a rustic cabin ($70) in the Makahoa Point section (☎ 808-293-1736), which is privately operated.

NORTH SHORE
Oahu's North Shore is synonymous with surfing and prime winter waves. Sunset Beach, the Banzai Pipeline and Waimea Bay are among the world's top surf spots and attract some of the best international surfers.

Waikiki surfers started taking on North Shore breakers in the late 1950s, and big-time surf competitions followed a few years later. Each December the North Shore hosts three major surf competitions, collectively known as the Triple Crown, with prize purses reaching six figures.

Haleiwa
This is the gateway to the North Shore, with a picturesque boat harbor bounded by beach parks. It's also the main setting for the TV show *Baywatch Hawaii.* **Haleiwa Alii Beach Park** is the site of several surfing tournaments in the winter, when northern swells can bring waves as high as 20 feet. The county (☎ 808-637-5051) gives free **surfing lessons** here on weekend mornings in winter. Surf-N-Sea (☎ 808-637-9887) rents boards and equipment for other water sports and also offers lessons.

Camping with a permit (☎ 808-523-4525) is allowed in *Kaiaka Beach Park,* about a

mile west of town, and *Mokuleia Beach Park,* farther west. In town, the casual *Surfhouse Hawaii (☎ 808-637-7146)* has a cabin with dorm beds ($15), tent spaces on the lawn ($9) and a private room ($45). Other people occasionally rent out rooms in their homes; check the bulletin boards at Coffee Gallery, Celestial Natural Foods and Haleiwa Super Market.

Most Haleiwa restaurants, including the famous surfer haunt *Cafe Haleiwa,* are lined up along Kamehameha Ave, the main drag.

Waimea
The **Waimea Bay Beach Park** is the North Shore's most popular beach. Winter belongs to surfers. Summer is usually the only time the water is calm enough for swimming and snorkeling. Across the highway, **Waimea Valley Adventure Park** (☎ 808-638-8511) is a botanical garden, cultural preserve and tourist park all in one. Admission is steep ($24), but if you come after 4pm the rate drops to $10.

Along the highway, **Pupukea Beach Park** is a long beach that includes the Three Tables area (so named for stone ledges) on the left and Shark's Cove on the right. Both have good snorkeling and diving in summer only, and Shark's Cove has Oahu's most popular cavern dive. In the middle is Old Quarry, where a wonderful array of jagged rock formations and tidal pools are exposed at low tide.

Killer Waves

Hawaii lies smack in the path of all the major swells that run unimpeded across the Pacific, and they hit hardest in winter, breaking along the north shore. Waimea Bay holds the record for the highest waves ever ridden in international competition. When the surf's up, crowds of spectators throng to watch Waimea surfers perform their near-suicidal feats on winter waves reaching up to 35 feet.

'The Quiksilver in Memory of Eddi Aikau' contest, which attracts the world's top surfers, is named for a local surfing legend who died in a rescue attempt in 1978. The current record holder is Noah Johnson, who rode a 25-foot wave to victory in 1999.

The main reason people come to Ekuhai Beach Park is to watch the pros surf the world-famous **Banzai Pipeline**, a few hundred feet to the left of the park. Just south of mile marker 9, **Sunset Beach Park** is Oahu's classic winter surf spot, with incredible waves and challenging breaks. Backyards, the surf break off Sunset Point at the northern end of the beach, draws a lot of top windsurfers.

Opposite Three Tables, *Backpackers* (☎ 808-638-7838) is pretty much a surfers' hangout, with bunks ($20) and doubles ($60). You can get fast food and plate lunches at *Sunset Diner*, opposite Sunset Beach Park. *Starbucks*, at the Foodland supermarket opposite Pupukea Beach, has good coffee and pastries.

LEEWARD (WAIANAE) COAST

The road doesn't connect around the far western tip of the island (Kaena Point). It's a big detour to the leeward (west) coast, which has few attractions other than watching surfers or hitting the waves yourself at **Makaha Beach Park**. The Waianae Coast remains the island's least-touristed side, and the area has a history of resisting development and a reputation for being unreceptive to outsiders.

Some of the long stretches of white-sand beaches are quite attractive, others a bit trashed. Although the towns themselves are ordinary, the cliffs and valleys cutting into the Waianae Range form a lovely backdrop. At road's end, there's a mile-long undeveloped beach and a coastal hike to **Kaena Point**, which has been designated a natural area reserve because of its unique ecosystem. The extensive, dry and windswept coastal dunes that rise above the point are the habitat of many rare native plants. Don't leave anything valuable in your car.

Hawaii (The Big Island)

The island of Hawaii is suitably dubbed the 'Big Island,' as it's larger than all the other Hawaiian islands combined. It encompasses an amazingly varied geography that includes active volcanoes, coastal deserts, lush rainforests and snowy mountaintops. Some

of the most impressive scenery is at Hawaii Volcanoes National Park, where you can drive or cycle around the rim of Kilauea's huge caldera and walk across still-steaming crater floors. There are plenty of beaches, some with white coral sand and others with black lava sand, and the island has numerous historic sites to explore.

Getting There & Around

The airports in Kailua and Hilo both have car rental booths and taxi stands. Most flights into these airports are from other islands, but United Airlines offers a few nonstop flights to Kailua from California.

Hele-On (☎ 808-961-8744), the county public bus system, connects Hilo and Kailua ($5.25), Kailua and Waimea ($3), and Waimea and Hilo ($4.50). There are four other routes: Pahoa to Hilo, Honokaa to Hilo, Waiohinu to Hilo via Volcano, and Hilo to the Waikoloa hotels in the South Kohala district. Service is infrequent, so call ahead for schedules.

KAILUA

The Kona Coast is the dry, sunny west coast of the Big Island, but the name 'Kona' is also used to refer to this coast's largest town, Kailua, which is also called 'Kailua-Kona.'

The largest vacation destination on the Big Island, Kailua has year-round good weather and outdoor activities ranging from world-class deep-sea fishing to snorkeling cruises. Every October 1500 athletes from 50 countries descend on the city to compete in the Ironman Triathlon.

The grounds of King Kamehameha's Kona Beach Hotel at **Kamakahonu** beach were once the site of Kamehameha the Great's royal residence. They include the **Ahuena Heiau**, a temple once used for human sacrifice.

A few minutes away on Alii Dr is the lava-rock **Mokuaikaua Church** (1836). **Hulihee Palace** (1838), opposite, is a museum with good Hawaiian artifacts ($5). **Kahaluu Beach**, on Alii Dr in Keauhou at the south side of Kailua, has the island's best easy-access snorkeling; gear rental ($6) is available from an on-site vendor.

Hostel-like *Patey's Place* (☎ 808-326-7018, 75-195 Ala-Ona Ona) has dorm beds ($20) and singles/doubles ($32/42); airport transfers ($5) are available. Budget hotels include popular **Kona Tiki Hotel** (☎ *808-329-1425, 75-5968 Alii Dr*), from $59, and **Kona Bay Hotel** (☎ *808-329-1393, 75-5739 Alii Dr*), from $79.

Unassuming **Ocean View Inn**, in the town center, has good, inexpensive Chinese, American and Hawaiian food. **Quinn's**, a bar opposite King Kamehameha's Kona Beach Hotel, serves Kona's best fresh fish. **Island Java Java**, at Alii Sunset Plaza, is a great little coffee and sandwich shop and often has music in the evenings.

Happy-hour specials abound in the open-air restaurants along Alii Dr. There's dancing nightly at **Huggo's** (☎ *808-329-1493*), next to the Royal Kona Resort.

The Alii Shuttle (☎ 808-775-7121) runs between Kailua and Keauhou ($2 each way, $5 for a day pass). Bike rentals are available from Dave's Triathlon Shop (☎ 808-329-4522) and Hawaiian Pedals (☎ 808-329-2294).

SOUTH KONA COAST
Aquatic explorations and Hawaiian history are the highlights of this area.

A side road off Hwy 11 leads to the mile-wide Kealakekua Bay. **Kealakekua Bay State Historical Park** is at the bay's south end, and an obelisk at its north end marks the spot where Captain Cook was killed. The bay's north end has some of the best **snorkeling** on the Big Island but can be reached only by sea or by hiking along a dirt trail (1½ hours). Fairwind (☎ 808-322-2788) offers 3½-hour snorkeling cruises from Keauhou ($50).

Manago Hotel (☎ *808-323-2642*), on Hwy 11 in the town of Captain Cook, offers simple singles/doubles with shared bath ($25/28) and the town's favorite restaurant (closed Mon).

Four miles south of Kealakekua Bay, **Puuhonua O Honaunau National Historical Park** (☎ 808-328-2288), also called the Place of Refuge, includes ancient temples, royal grounds and a *puu-honua* – 'sanc-tuary' ($2/4 per person/family). A self-guided walk is de-tailed in the park brochure.

There's terrific snorkeling and diving near the small boat ramp immediately north of the park.

There's no food service in the park, but nearby on Hwy 160 is pleasant **Wakefield Botanical Gardens**, with a simple lunch menu.

NORTH KONA COAST
Beautiful secluded beaches, most accessible only by foot, lie on the north Kona Coast (which incorporates the districts of North Kona and South Kohala), but there's vehicle access to undeveloped **Kona Coast State Park** (closed Wed). Most of the Big Island's fanciest resorts are farther north, in the Waikoloa area of the South Kohala district. South Kohala was an important area in Hawaiian history, and it shelters *heiau* (ancient stone temples), fishponds, petro-glyphs and ancient **trails** that can be fun to explore. The popular **Hapuna Beach State Recreation Area** has a snack bar and A-frame cabins ($20 for up to four); make reservations at any state park office (☎ 808-974-6200 on the Big Island).

NORTH KOHALA
The northwest tip of the Big Island is domi-nated by a central ridge, the Kohala Moun-tains. Off Hwy 270, just south of mile marker 14, are the remains of a 600-year-old de-serted fishing village, now **Lapakahi State Historical Park** (closed holidays). **Mookini Heiau**, on the desolate northern tip of the Big Island, is one of the oldest and most histori-cally significant temples in Hawaii. A stone enclosure nearby marks the birth site of Kamehameha the Great. Hwy 270 ends at a viewpoint that overlooks secluded **Pololu Valley** and the trailhead for a 20-minute walk down to the valley.

Camping is allowed at **Keokea Beach Park** (☎ *808-961-8311*) with a permit ($5). In downtown Hawi, **Kohala Village Inn** (☎ *808-889-0419*) has doubles from $50. Hawi's best food is at **Bamboo**, on Hwy 270, open for lunch and dinner.

WAIMEA & SADDLE ROAD
Waimea (also known as 'Kamuela') has a pretty setting in the foothills of the Kohala Mountains. It has a couple of good dining spots and some local museums worth a short visit. The 50-mile Saddle Rd (Hwy 200),

Hawaii's most remote, cuts across the 'saddle' between the two highest points on the island, Mauna Kea and Mauna Loa. Although the road is paved, most car rental contracts prohibit travel on it, and there are no gas stations or other facilities along the way.

Hawaii's highest mountain, **Mauna Kea** (13,796 feet) is topped with a cluster of world-class astronomical observatories on its summit. The Onizuka Visitor Center (☎ 808-961-2180) offers displays, free astronomy presentations, stargazing and summit tours. A rugged 6-mile hiking trail from the visitor center to the summit begins at 9300 feet and takes four to five hours; start early in the day, bring warm clothing and be prepared for severe weather conditions. Mauna Kea Summit Tours (☎ 888-322-2366) conducts sunset and stargazing tours ($144); Arnott's Lodge (☎ 808-969-7097) in Hilo offers its hostel guests a day outing on Mauna Kea ($48). *Mauna Kea State Park (☎ 808-974-6200)* has cabins with heat at $55 for up to four people.

HAMAKUA COAST

The Hamakua Coast offers some of the Big Island's most gorgeous scenery.

At the end of Hwy 240, the large, lush, spectacular amphitheater of **Waipio Valley** is a mix of tangled jungle, flowering plants, taro patches and waterfalls, fronted by a black-sand beach. The 45-minute hike down from the lookout to the valley floor is steep, so expect a good workout. A couple of tour companies go into the valley by 4WD (☎ 808-775-7121; $42) or mule-drawn wagon (☎ 808-775-9518; $40) daily except Sunday.

Backcountry camping is allowed by permit in Waimanu Valley (☎ 808-974-4221), a seven-hour hike northwest from Waipio Valley. In Honokaa, 8 miles east of Waipio, is *Hotel Honokaa Club (☎ 808-775-0678)*, on Mamane St, with dorm beds from $15 and private rooms from $25.

Akaka Falls State Park has the Big Island's most impressive easy-to-view waterfall, with a couple of stunning lookouts along a short rainforest loop trail. *Akiko's Buddhist Bed & Breakfast (☎ 808-963-6422)*, a mile north of Honomu and 15 miles north of Hilo, has simple singles/doubles from $40/55.

Between Honomu and Hilo is the delightful 4-mile **Pepeekeo Scenic Dr** off Hwy 19 through lush tropical jungle. Along the way is the Hawaii Tropical Botanical Garden ($15).

HILO

In terms of lush natural beauty, Hilo, the county capital, beats Kailua any day – the only catch is finding a dry one. The city's reputation for wet weather (it's the rainiest city in the USA) has put a damper on tourism, helping to protect this unspoiled corner of Hawaii from invasive development. Despite the scenic setting, nature hasn't always been kind to Hilo: Two devastating tsunamis have hit the capital in the last 50 years, and in 1984 a lava flow from Mauna Loa stopped just 8 miles above town. The city is ethnically diverse and features a thriving alternative community of back-to-the-earth folks attracted by Hilo's affordable land prices.

The tourist office (☎ 808-961-5797), on the corner of Haili and Keawe Sts, has a free, informative walking-tour brochure.

Downtown Hilo is an intriguing mishmash of classic old buildings and aging wooden storefronts. The excellent **Lyman House Memorial Museum** (276 Haili St) offers insight into Hawaii's history ($7; closed Sun). Morning is the best time to see rainbows at **Rainbow Falls**, off Waianuenue Ave. Another 1½ miles up the avenue, **Peepee Falls** drop from a sheer rock face into bubbling pools known as the Boiling Pots.

A great place to meet other travelers is *Arnott's Lodge (☎ 808-969-7097, 98 Apapane Rd)*, with tent sites ($9), dorm beds ($17) and private rooms ($47). In downtown Hilo, convenient *Wild Ginger Inn (☎ 808-935-5556, 100 Puueo St)* charges $45 including breakfast, while the popular *Dolphin Bay Hotel (☎ 808-935-1466, 333 Iliahi St)* has singles/doubles for $66/69.

Soup or Roll (77 Kilauea Ave), in the Kaikoo Mall, is a family-run place with good Vietnamese food for around $5. For a thoroughly local experience, head to inexpensive *Cafe 100 (969 Kilauea Ave)*. *Bears' Coffee (106 Keawe St)* is popular for a light lunch or breakfast.

PUNA

The district of Puna, the diamond-shaped easternmost point of the Big Island, sees little tourism. At its heart is **Pahoa**, a funky little town with cowboy architecture. If you'd like to stay in town, inquire at Pahoa Natural Foods about apartments they rent. *Luquin's*, on Main St, serves authentic Mexican fare ($6).

The usual route beyond Pahoa is a triangle that goes down Hwy 132 past **Lava Tree State Park** to Kapoho, then continues on Hwy 137, which ends abruptly at Kaimu Beach on the eastern edge of Kalapana (a village entirely buried by lava in 1990). The route then comes back to Pahoa via Hwy 130. One of Puna's few protected swimming spots is **Ahalanui Beach Park**, on Hwy 137, with a lovely thermal spring-fed pool set in lava rock; don't leave anything valuable in your car, as the place has a history of rip-offs.

HAWAII VOLCANOES NATIONAL PARK

This huge park contains two active volcanoes and terrain ranging from tropical beaches to the subarctic summit of Mauna Loa (13,679 feet). The centerpiece is Kilauea Caldera, the still-steaming sunken center of Kilauea Volcano.

The park's 24-hour hotline (☎ 808-985-6000) has information on current volcanic activity and directions to the best viewing sites ($10 per car, $5 per person/bicycle). Rangers at the Kilauea Visitor Center, near the park entrance, can provide the lowdown on guided walks, trail conditions and the like.

The park experiences a wide range of climatic conditions, and it's a good idea to wear clothing in layers. Stay on marked trails and take all warning signs seriously.

Crater Rim Road

This amazing 11-mile loop road skirts the rim of Kilauea Caldera with marked stops at steam vents and crater lookouts. Short trails and trailheads provide starting points for longer hikes into and around the caldera. **Jaggar Museum** is worth a visit for its displays and fine view of Halemaumau Crater.

The Halemaumau Overlook, perched on the crater rim, is at the start of the **Halemaumau Trail**, which runs 3 miles across Kilauea Caldera. Crater Rim Rd continues across the barren Kau Desert and then through the fallout area of the 1959 eruption of Kilauea Iki Crater. **Devastation Trail** is a fascinating half-mile walk across a former rainforest devastated by cinder and

pumice from that eruption. The tunnel-like **Thurston Lava Tube** is almost big enough to run a train through.

Chain of Craters Road

Once a through route to Puna, this road, which winds 20 miles down the slopes of Kilauea Volcano, now ends abruptly near the coast, where recent eruptions have buried it in lava. At the road's end you can see steam plumes shooting up as the molten lava flows into the sea, and if you wait till dark the hillside glows a fiery red. It's a good, paved two-lane road, but there are no services, so bring water and check the gas tank before striking out.

Mauna Loa Road

About 1½ miles up this road you'll find the **Kipuka Puaulu Loop Trail**, which runs through a curious sanctuary of native Hawaiian forest. The rugged 18-mile **Mauna Loa Trail**, which ascends 6600 feet up the slopes of Mauna Loa, begins at the end of the road.

Places to Stay & Eat

Hiking shelters and simple cabins are available at no charge along some of the park's longer backcountry trails. There are two primitive camping areas, at *Apua Point* and the *Napau Crater*. Overnight hikers must register no more than one day ahead and obtain a free permit at the visitor center before heading out. Camping is also free at two roadside campgrounds: *Namakani Paio*, just off Hwy 11, and *Kulanaokuaiki*, about 5 miles down Hilina Pali Rd, off Chain of Craters Rd; there's no registration or reservation system.

Volcano House (☎ 808-967-7321), opposite the visitor center, has rooms from $85 and also manages the 10 dreary *Namakani Paio Cabins* in the park ($40 for up to four people). It also maintains a pricey restaurant with ordinary fare and a small snack bar.

Another option is to stay in the nondescript village of Volcano, just east of the park. *HI Holo Holo In* (☎ 808-967-7950, 19-4036 Kalani Honua Rd) is a friendly little hostel with dorms/private rooms for $17/40. Also in Volcano are *My Island B&B* (☎ 808-967-7216), offering singles/doubles from $45/60, and *Kilauea Lodge*

(☎ 808-967-7366,) with upmarket rooms and cabins for $125.

Volcano village has some decent eating options – *Lava Rock Cafe*, with good breakfasts and lunches ($6), and *Surt's*, with interesting Asian fare at higher prices.

Getting There & Away
The public bus (☎ 808-961-8744) between Hilo and Waiohinu stops at the visitor center (and at Volcano village) once in each direction weekdays ($2.25; 1 hour).

KAU
The Kau district stretches from South Kona along the southern flanks of Mauna Loa, taking in the entire southern tip of the island. It is sparsely populated, and much of it is dry and desertlike. Camping ($5) is allowed with a permit (☎ 808-961-8311) at **Whittington Beach Park** on Honuapo Bay and at **Punaluu Beach Park**, just north of Naalehu along Hwy 11.

Maui

Maui has much to lure visitors, including superb scenery, diverse landscapes, world-class windsurfing and excellent conditions for most other water sports. The island's warm coastal waters are the main wintering grounds for North Pacific humpback whales, making for wonderful whale-watching. Not surprisingly, Maui has become the most visited and developed of the Neighbor Islands (that is, the main Hawaiian islands other than Oahu). But it's quite easy to escape the West Maui scene, where most tourism is centered, by heading to the quieter east coast or upcountry to the slopes of Haleakala Volcano.

Getting There & Around
The main airport is in Kahului, with two smaller ones at Kapalua and Hana. All the major car rental companies have booths at Kahului's airport. Maui has no public bus service, but TransHawaiian (☎ 808-877-0380) operates a shuttle service ($13) from the airport to Lahaina and Kaanapali every 30 minutes 9am-4pm.

The ferry *Molokai Princess* (☎ 808-667-6165) runs between Lahaina, on Maui's west coast, and Kaunakakai every day but Sunday ($40 one way). The Expeditions ferry (☎ 808-661-3756) plies the waters between Lahaina and Lanai five times each day ($25).

LAHAINA & KAANAPALI
The former whaling port of Lahaina is abuzz with commercial activity, but it has plenty of historic buildings that can be fun to poke around. The main drag and tourist strip is Front St, with its bustling harbor backed by the whaling-era **Pioneer Inn** and a park boasting the largest **banyan tree** in the USA. The replica square-rigger ship *Carthaginian,* in the harbor, can be visited for $3. In winter, Papawai Point, a roadside area between Lahaina and Maalaea, is a prime **whale-watching** spot.

To the north, Kaanapali is a high-rise resort community with 3 miles of sandy beach open to the public. Kaanapali's main attractions are the snorkeling at Black Rock and the **Whaling Museum** (free admission) in the Whalers Village mall. The West Maui Shopping Express runs shuttles between Lahaina and Kaanapali ($1).

The *Camp Pecusa (☎ 808-661-4303)* in Olowalu, 6 miles south of Lahaina, has a 'tentground' available on a first-come, first-served basis ($5; arrive before 5pm). In Lahaina, you couldn't be more in the middle of the action than at the harborside *Best Western Pioneer Inn (☎ 808-661-3636),* with rooms for $130.

Lahaina has lots of restaurants and fast-food outlets in its malls. *Westside Natural Foods & Deli (193 Lahainaluna Rd)* sells vegetarian dishes by weight. Reasonably priced are oceanfront *Aloha Cantina (839 Front St)* for Mexican fare and *Cheeseburger in Paradise (811 Front St),* with creative burgers and live music. *Maui Brews (900*

HAWAII

Maui's Home

According to legend, the Polynesian demigod Maui was wandering the Pacific on a fishing expedition when his fishhook snagged the sea floor. He tugged with such force that the islands of Hawaii were yanked to the surface. He then claimed the island of Maui and made it his home.

Front St), a lively sports bar, has happy-hour specials and numerous beers on tap.

KIHEI, WAILEA & MAKENA

Maui's fastest-growing community, Kihei is fringed with sandy beaches and has long attracted sunbathers, boogie boarders and windsurfers. *Dolphin House Bed and Breakfast* (☎ 808-874-0126, 69 Kalola Place, Kihei), not far from the beach, has good-value singles/doubles ($55/65). Nearby *Wailana Kai* (☎ 808-877-5796, 34 Wailana Place) has 10 pleasant condo units for $70. *Panda Express*, in the Azeka Place shopping center, has good multi-item meals ($5). Nearby *Hapa's Brew Haus* (☎ 808-879-9001) is the place for nightly music and dancing.

The manicured lava-rock coastline around upmarket Wailea is broken by attractive gold-sand beaches, with good swimming and snorkeling, and superb shoreline whale-watching in winter. Accommodations in the area aren't cheap: Destination Resorts (☎ 808-879-1595) books condo units from a hefty $150, and Wailea hotels start at double that! A free shuttle bus runs every 30 minutes around the Wailea resort.

Makena has two knockout undeveloped beaches – **Big Beach** and the secluded **Little Beach**. After Big Beach, Makena Rd goes through the **Ahihi-Kinau Natural Area Reserve**, with its lava tide pools, before ending just short of La Perouse Bay.

KAHULUI-WAILUKU & AROUND

Kahului and Wailuku, Maui's two largest communities, flow together in one urban sprawl. Except for mall shopping, there's not much to do in Kahului. The more historic Wailuku makes for a good stroll, especially along Market St. The Maui Visitors Bureau (☎ 808-244-3530) is at 1727 Wili Pa Loop. Three miles out of Wailuku, **Iao Valley State Park** is nestled in the mountains and centers on the stunning Iao Needle rock pinnacle, which rises 1200 feet from the valley floor.

In Wailuku, *Northshore Inn* (☎ 808-242-8999, 2080 Vineyard St) is popular with European travelers (bunk beds $16, singles/doubles $29/38). Nearby *Banana Bungalow* (☎ 808-244-5090, 310 Lower Market St) has dorm beds for $16 and rooms for $29/40; it runs a free shuttle to the beach.

In Kahului, there are fast-food eateries at the **Kaahumanu Center** food court and **Maui Marketplace**. Wailuku has a range of reasonably priced ethnic restaurants near the intersection of Vineyard and Market Sts.

PAIA

This old sugar town has a more international flavor than any other small town in Hawaii. In the 1980s, windsurfers began discovering nearby **Hookipa Beach**, and Paia was dubbed the 'Windsurfing Capital of the World.' *Mana Foods*, a top-notch health-food store on Baldwin Ave, has a bulletin board with rental ads. *Picnics* and *Peach's & Crumble Cafe & Bakery* both prepare box lunches ($8) for the road to Hana. *Wunderbar* has good fish meals and doubles as Paia's main watering hole.

HANA HIGHWAY

The Hana Hwy (Hwy 360) ranks as *the* most spectacular coastal drive in Hawaii. It's a cliff-hugger, winding its way deep into lush valleys and back out above a rugged coastline. In **Keanae**, *YMCA Camp* (☎ 808-242-9007) offers hostel-style beds in guest cabins for only $15, but advance reservations are required; you can also set up your tent here. **Waianapanapa State Park**, just north of Hana, shelters two impressive lava-tube caves with clear mineral waters. Tent camping is allowed with a permit (☎ 808-984-8109).

HANA & AROUND

Hana's isolation has protected it from development. Surfers head to Waikoloa Beach, while nude sunbathers favor gorgeous Kaihalulu (Red Sand) Beach, reached by trail from the end of Uakea Rd. There's free tent camping (no permit necessary) at *Oheo Gulch*, 10 miles south of Hana. *Joe's Place* (☎ 808-248-7033), on Uakea Rd, has rooms from $45, while *Aloha Cottages* (☎ 808-248-8420), on Keawa Place, has studios from $65. *Tutu's*, a grill at Hana Beach Park, has the best food values in Hana.

The road south from Hana is also incredibly beautiful. Oheo Stream dramatically cuts its way through **Oheo Gulch** to a lovely series of wide pools and waterfalls, each tumbling into the one below. At the end of the road is Kipahulu, burial site of aviator Charles Lindbergh.

UPCOUNTRY

Upcountry, the highland area of East Maui on the western slopes of Haleakala, is un-crowded and dotted with small towns. In the center of **Makawao** is a cluster of restaurants; check the bulletin board at the health-food store for room rentals. On the mountainside above Kula (just off Hwy 37) are the delightful cloud forests of the **Polipoli** state recreation area, with trails and remote *camping (☎ 808-984-8109)*.

HALEAKALA NATIONAL PARK

Haleakala Crater resembles the surface of the moon, with a seemingly lifeless floor dotted with high, majestic cinder cones. Haleakala (House of the Sun) is the world's largest dormant volcano: Its crater is so big that the island of Manhattan could fit inside. The park centers on the crater, offering impressive views from its rim and several hikes across the crater floor. For the best crater views, arrive for sunrise – the sunlight illuminating the crater floor is awesome.

Check on weather conditions and sunrise times (☎ 808-871-5054) before heading up to the park ($10 per car, $5 per person). Park headquarters (☎ 808-572-4400) provides permits for camping in the crater and can give you details on free guided hikes and nature talks. The park never closes, but the visitor center is open only from sunrise to 3pm.

Free tent camping is allowed at *Hosmer Grove*, near the main entrance (three-night maximum), but permits (first-come, first-served, from the park headquarters) are required for the two *backcountry campgrounds* inside Haleakala Crater. The park also has primitive cabins, but demand for these is so high they hold a monthly lottery (write to Cabin Lottery Request, Haleakala National Park, Box 369, Makawao, HI 96768).

Kauai

Kauai, the least developed of Hawaii's four major islands, offers stunning natural beauty. Its central volcanic peak, Mt Waialeale, is the rainiest place on earth and feeds scores of scenic waterfalls and a unique rainforest. On the northwest coast of Kauai are the spectacular Na Pali cliffs, Hawaii's foremost hiking destination.

Getting There & Around

Kauai's main airport is in Lihue. All the major car rental companies maintain booths there, and taxis line up outside the arrival area. Kauai has rather a limited public bus service (☎ 808-241-6410), which does not serve the airport ($1 all routes; daily except Sun).

LIHUE

Lihue is the island's capital. Seek information at the tourist office (☎ 808-245-3971, 4334 Rice St). The **Kauai Museum** (4428 Rice St) traces Kauai's history ($5; closed Sun).

There are accommodations at *Motel Lani (☎ 808-245-2965, 4240 Rice St)* from $35, *Tip Top Motel (☎ 808-245-2333, 3173 Akahi St)* at $45 and *Garden Island Inn (☎ 808-245-7227, 3445 Wilcox Rd)* from $75 – the latter only a few minutes from the beach.

Hamura Saimin (2956 Kress St) is a local favorite with noodle soup from $3.50, and *The Fish Express*, on Hwy 50 near the hospital, has unbeatable fresh fish dishes ($7).

EAST SIDE

The 3-mile stretch of Kuhio Hwy (Hwy 56) from Wailua to Kapaa, with Waipouli in between, is a run of shopping centers, restaurants, hotels and condos. Popular activities include the riverboat tour up the Wailua River to Fern Grotto. Smith's Motor Boat Service (☎ 808-821-6892) and Waialeale Boat Tours (☎ 808-822-4908) both charge $15 for a 1½-hour tour.

Kauai International Hostel (☎ 808-823-6142, 4532 Lehua St, Kapaa) offers bunk beds ($20) and airport pickup. Nearby *Kapaa BeachHouse (☎ 808-822-3424, 1552 Kuhio Hwy, Kapaa)*, a casual hostel-style guesthouse, also has $20 bunks. For fancier digs there's *Hotel Coral Reef (☎ 808-822-4481, 1516 Kuhio Hwy, Kapaa)*, with $65 rooms, simple breakfast included.

Wailua has several places to eat in *Coconut Marketplace*. *Bubba's*, near the hostel in Kapaa, has burgers for under $5; alternatively, try Kapaa's *Pono Market*, which has good takeout sushi at bargain prices.

NA PALI COAST & NORTH SHORE

Kauai's lush and mountainous North Shore features incredible scenery and good water-sports options. At Kilauea Point are a picturesque lighthouse and a thriving seabird sanctuary.

Hanalei, on a magnificent bay, has sports shops renting out kayaks for paddling up the Hanalei River. Camping is allowed at *Hanalei Beach Park* (☎ *808-241-6660*) with a permit ($3). *Historic B&B* (☎ *808-826-4622*) is pleasant (from $75). For snacks, try *Hanalei Gourmet*, in the Hanalei Center.

At the end of the road is lovely **Kee Beach**, with some excellent snorkeling possibilities. Camping ($3) is allowed with a permit at nearby *Haena Beach Park* (☎ *808-241-6660*), which is close to the Kalalau trailhead.

The awesome 11-mile **Kalalau Trail** runs along the high Na Pali cliffs and winds up and down a series of lush valleys. The scenery is breathtaking, with sheer green cliffs dropping into brilliant turquoise waters. You need a permit (☎ 808-274-3444) for hiking beyond the first valley (Hanakapiai) and for camping ($10), which is allowed in three valleys. This is a rugged backcountry adventure, so you'll need good hiking boots and backpacking gear – give yourself three or four days to do it without rushing.

SOUTH SHORE
Kauai's main beach-resort area is **Poipu**. It's typically sunny, good for swimming and snorkeling year round and for surfing in summer. *Koloa Landing Cottages* (☎ *808-742-1470, 2704B Hoonani Rd*) has studios from $60. In nearby Koloa, *Kahili Mountain Park* (☎ *808-742-9921*) offers cabins from $45 (reservations recommended). *Taqueria Nortenos*, in the Poipu Plaza, has simple Mexican fare for under $5.

WEST SIDE
The top destinations here are adjacent **Waimea Canyon**, with its 2785-foot-deep river-cut gorge, and **Kokee State Park**. Both feature spectacular views and a vast network of hiking trails. Waimea Canyon Dr (Hwy 550) starts in Waimea and boasts plenty of scenic lookouts along the way to the park. At Kokee, pick up information on trail conditions at the Kokee Museum (☎ 808-335-9975).

There's camping ($5) with a permit at Kokee State Park (☎ 808-274-3444). *Kokee Lodge* (☎ *808-335-6061*) rents older one-room cabins ($35) and cedar cabins with two bedrooms ($45); it serves food till 3:30pm.

Molokai

As you come from the airport you'll see a casually written sign that says it all: 'Slow Down – This is Molokai.' If you're itching to get off the trodden tourist track, Molokai's a good choice.

In population and atmosphere, Molokai is the most Hawaiian of any island (except Niihau, which isn't open to visitors). It's sparsely populated, has only a few small resorts, and offers quiet hikes and deserted beaches. Molokai's impenetrable North Shore, from Kalaupapa to Halawa, features the world's highest sea cliffs (3300 feet).

Getting There & Around
In the center of the island, Molokai Airport (also called Hoolehua Airport) has limited car rentals, so book early.

The ferry *Molokai Princess* (☎ 808-667-6165) runs between Kaunakakai and Lahaina, Maui ($40; Mon-Sat).

Molokai has no public bus service. Kukui Tours & Limousines (☎ 808-552-2282) offer taxi services and airport transfers ($10 per person to Kaunakakai or the West End) if you book ahead.

KAUNAKAKAI
Molokai's biggest town hasn't changed its face at all for tourism. Most of its businesses are along broad Ala Malama St. The Molokai Visitors Association (☎ 808-553-3876) is on Kamoi St in the town center behind the post office. Camping is allowed with a $3 permit at nearby *One Alii Beach Park* (☎ *808-553-3204*). Waterfront *Hotel Molokai* (☎ *808-553-5347*) has rooms from $75. The inexpensive restaurant in the back of *Kanemitsu Bakery* offers good breakfasts and lunches.

EAST MOLOKAI
The 28-mile south-coast drive from Kaunakakai to Halawa Valley takes about 1½ hours one way and rewards you with a delightful glimpse of rural Hawaii. The only place to eat en route is *Neighborhood Store 'N' Counter* in Pukoo, which makes an

unbeatable $4 chicken teriyaki sandwich. The last part of the road is very narrow, with lots of hairpin bends and coastal views, winding up to a great panorama of **Halawa Valley**. The road then runs down to a popular surfing spot, **Halawa Beach Park**.

CENTRAL MOLOKAI

Central Molokai takes in the Hoolehua Plains, which stretch from windswept Moomomi Beach in the west to the former plantation town of Kualapuu. The central part of the island includes **Kamakou Preserve**, with rainforests and the island's highest point, Kamakou Peak (4970 feet).

Palaau State Park (☎ 808-567-6891) features camping with a permit ($5), but it can be damp and there's no drinking water. In Kualapuu, *Kamuela's Cookhouse* serves reasonably priced meals (closed Sun).

Set at the base of majestic and formidable cliffs, the **Kalaupapa Peninsula** has been a leprosy settlement for more than a century. Today fewer than 100 patients live here. To minimize the impact on residents, the park requires all visitors to join a guided tour. Access is via a steep trail by mule ($135) with Molokai Mule Ride (☎ 800-567-7550) or on foot; if you hike you'll need to join up with Damien Tours (☎ 808-567-6171) once you reach the peninsula (tours $30).

The Kalaupapa Overlook, in Palaau State Park, affords a breathtaking view of the peninsula. A marked trail from the overlook leads to a phallic rock, which plays a role in local legend.

WEST MOLOKAI

Maunaloa Hwy (Hwy 460) heads west from Kaunakakai through high grassy rangeland to the small town of Maunaloa, with its well-known Big Wind Kite Factory. A side road leads down to the low-key Kaluakoi Resort and magnificent **Papohaku Beach**, with 2½ miles of golden sand and crashing surf – a choice site for camping (☎ 808-553-3204 for a $3 permit).

Other Islands

LANAI

A former pineapple plantation, Lanai is now pushing for the luxury-resort market and can be quite expensive. It shelters some obscure archaeological sites and petroglyphs, as well as Hawaii's last native dryland forest, the Kanepuu Preserve. Many of the sights are a good distance from **Lanai City**, the island's only town, along rutted dirt roads that require a 4WD vehicle.

A good, inexpensive way to experience a slice of Lanai is to take the Expeditions ferry (☎ 808-661-3756; $25 one way) from Lahaina (Maui) in the morning, spend the day snorkeling at Hulopoe Bay, with Lanai's finest beach, and take a return ferry in the afternoon.

KAHOOLAWE

This uninhabited island, 7 miles off the southwest coast of Maui, was used exclusively by the US military as a bombing target from WWII until 1990, and continues to be off-limits.

NIIHAU

The smallest of the inhabited Hawaiian Islands and a native Hawaiian preserve, Niihau (population 230) has long been closed to outsiders, earning it the nickname 'The Forbidden Island.' No other place in Hawaii has more successfully turned its back on change: There are no paved roads, no airport, no islandwide electricity and no telephones. Niihau Helicopters (☎ 808-335-3500), in Kauai, offers helicopter tours ($250), which you should arrange well in advance.

NORTHWESTERN HAWAIIAN ISLANDS

These 10 island clusters, also known as the Leeward Islands, stretch from Kauai nearly 1300 miles across the Pacific in an almost

Selfless Mission

The trip to the Kalaupapa peninsula is a pilgrimage of sorts for admirers of Father Damien (Joseph de Veuster), the Belgian priest who devoted much of his life to helping people with leprosy. He nursed the sick, buried the dead and built 300 homes and a church, before dying in 1889 of the disease himself.

straight northwesterly line. Volcanic in origin, the islands are slowly slipping back into the sea as a result of a sagging of the ocean floor and the ongoing forces of erosion.

One group of them, the **Midway Islands**, can be visited on guided package tours (from $1700; 5 days) from Kauai. Midway Dive-N-Snorkel (☎ 888-329-9559), in Lihue, offers dive tours to Midway. For ecology tours, contact Oceanic Society Expeditions (☎ 415-441-1106), in San Francisco.

Glossary

4WD – four-wheel-drive vehicle
24/7 – 24 hours a day, seven days a week

AAA – the American Automobile Association, also called 'Triple A' or the 'Auto Club' (see AAA Membership in the Getting Around chapter); a federal organization with affiliates in every state
adobe – a traditional Spanish-Mexican building material of sun-baked bricks made with mud and straw; a structure built with this type of brick
Acela – high-speed train operating in the Northeast
aka – also known as
alien – official term for a non-US citizen, visiting or resident in the USA (as in 'resident alien,' 'illegal alien,' etc)
Amtrak – national government-supported passenger railroad company
Angeleno/Angelena – a resident of Los Angeles
antebellum – of the period before the Civil War; pre-1861
antojito – (Spanish) an appetizer, snack or light meal
Arts and Crafts – an architecture and design movement that gained popularity in the USA just after the start of the 20th century; the style emphasizes simple craftsmanship and functional design, and emerged as a reaction to the perceived shoddiness of machine-made goods; also called (American) craftsman
ATM – automated teller machine; also called Tyme machines, Cashpoints, etc; most of them are connected to at least one of the Star, Cirrus, Plus, Interlink or Maestro networks
ATF – Bureau of Alcohol, Tobacco & Firearms; powerful federal law enforcement agency, concerned mainly with taxing drinkers and smokers
ATV – all-terrain vehicle, used for off-road transportation and recreation, often resulting in environmental destruction

back east – to Californians, the East is 'back east,' even if they've never been there
backpacker – one who hikes or camps out overnight; less commonly, a young, low-budget traveler

BLM – Bureau of Land Management, an agency of the federal Department of the Interior that controls large areas of public land
blue book – a guide that lists the average prices of used cars by year, make and model; available in most libraries
bluegrass – a form of Appalachian folk music that evolved in the bluegrass country of Kentucky and Tennessee
bodega – especially in New York City, a small local store selling liquor, food and other basics
boomtown – a town that has experienced rapid economic and population growth; many areas experienced such a boom during a gold rush, then 'busted' when the gold ran out, becoming 'ghost towns'
booster – a person who promotes the interests and growth of his/her town or city, usually with a view to advancing personal business interests at the same time
burro – a small donkey used as a pack animal
Bush – the greater part of Alaska, inaccessible by road or sea; to get there, charter a 'bush plane'; the US president

Cajun – corruption of 'Acadia,' the area of eastern Canada from which French speakers were exiled in the 18th century; people and culture descended from the Arcadians who came to Louisiana
camper – pickup truck with a detachable roof or shell fitted out for camping
carded – if you have to show your ID to get into a bar, you've been carded
carpetbaggers – exploitative Northerners who migrated to the South following the Civil War
CCC – Civilian Conservation Corps, a Depression-era federal program established in 1933 to employ unskilled young men, mainly on projects aimed at the conservation of US wildlands
CDW – collision/damage waiver; optional insurance against damaging a rental car
cell – cellular phone (mobile phone)
chamber of commerce – association of local businesses that often provides a tourist information service; many chambers of

commerce are closed on weekends and do not have information about cheap establishments that are not chamber members

Chicano/Chicana – a Mexican American man/woman

CNN – Cable News Network, a cable TV station based in Atlanta, Georgia, providing continuous bulletins of US and international news

coach fare – economical fare on an airplane or train

coed – coeducational, open to both males and females; often used in noneducational contexts (eg, hostel dorms)

conestoga – big covered wagon drawn by horses or oxen, the vehicle of westward migration; also called a 'prairie schooner'

Confederacy – the 11 Southern states that seceded from the USA in 1860–61

contiguous states – all states except Alaska and Hawaii; also called the Lower 48

cot – camp-bed (babies sleep in cribs)

country & western – an amalgamation of rock and folk music of the southern and western USA; line dancing and the two-step are dances associated with this music

coyote – a small wild dog, native to the central and western North American lowlands; also, a person who assists illegal immigrants to cross the Mexican border into the USA

cracker – in the South, a derogatory term for a poor white person

CVB – convention and visitors bureau, run by many cities to promote tourism and assist visitors

Dixie – the South; the states south of the Mason-Dixon Line

DEA – Drug Enforcement Agency, the federal body responsible for enforcing US drug laws

Deep South – in this book, the states of Louisiana, Mississippi and Alabama

DMV – Department of Motor Vehicles, the state agency that administers the registration of vehicles and the licensing of drivers

docent – a guide or attendant at a museum

dog, to ride the – to travel by Greyhound bus

downtown – the center of a city, central business district; in the direction of downtown (eg, a downtown bus)

DUI – driving under the influence of alcohol and/or drugs; sometimes called a DWI (driving while intoxicated)

East – generally, the states east of the Mississippi River

efficiency – a small furnished apartment with a kitchen, often for short-term rental

Emancipation – in 1863, Abraham Lincoln's Emancipation Proclamation was a largely political move that nominally freed all slaves in the Confederate-controlled states; slavery was completely abolished in the USA when the 13th Amendment to the US Constitution was enacted in 1865

entrée – the main course of a meal

express bus/train – bus or train that stops only at selected stations, and not at 'local' stations

express stop/station – stop/station served by express buses/trains as well as local ones

flag stop – a place where the bus only stops if you flag it down

foldaway – portable folding bed, available at most lodgings to accommodate an extra person in a room, for an extra charge

forty-niners – immigrants to California during the 1849 gold rush; also, San Francisco's pro-football team (49ers)

gallery – in the USA, a commercial establishment where artwork is sold; institutions that exhibit an art collection are usually called museums

gated community – walled residential area accessible only through security gates; usually these are recent, upmarket real-estate developments

general delivery – poste restante

GOP – Grand Old Party, nickname of the Republican party

graduate study – advanced-degree study, after completing a bachelor's degree

green card – technically, a Registration Receipt Card, issued to holders of immigrant visas; it's actually pink, and it allows the holder to live and work legally in the USA

HI-AYH – Hostelling International-American Youth Hostels, a term given to hostels affiliated with Hostelling International, a member group of IYHF (International Youth Hostel Federation)

Hispanic – of Latin American descent or culture (often used interchangeably with Latino)

hookup – a facility at an RV camping site for connecting (hooking up) a vehicle to electricity, water, sewer or even cable TV

IMAX – giant-screen movies filmed using a technique that permits a great level of detail; viewed in specialized theaters with high-fidelity sound systems

Interstate – an Interstate Highway, part of the national, federally funded highway system

INS – Immigration & Naturalization Service, the federal body, reporting to the Department of Justice, that's responsible for immigration and naturalization of aliens

IRS – Internal Revenue Service, a branch of the US Treasury Department responsible for administering and enforcing internal revenue laws (ie, the tax collectors)

Jim Crow laws – in the post-Civil War South, laws intended to limit the civil or voting rights of blacks; Jim Crow is an old pejorative term for a black person

Joshua tree – a tall, treelike type of yucca plant, common to the arid Southwest

kiva – round underground chamber built by Southwestern Native American cultures for ceremonial and everyday purposes

KOA – Kampgrounds of America, a private chain of campgrounds throughout the USA, with extensive amenities and moderate- to high-priced sites for RVs and tents

Labor Day – public holiday on the first Monday in September; end of the summer holiday season

Latino/Latina – a man/woman of Latin American descent; Hispanic

LDS – from the Church of Jesus Christ of Latter-Day Saints, the formal name of the Mormon church

live oak – hardwood, evergreen oak native to the South; dead live oaks make excellent boat-building timber

local – a train or bus that stops at every station or bus stop, compared to an express, which stops only at designated 'express' stations or stops

Lower 48 – the 48 contiguous states of continental USA; all states except Alaska and Hawaii

Mason-Dixon Line – border between Pennsylvania and Maryland delineated by Royal Surveyors Charles Mason and Jeremiah Dixon between 1763 and 1767; later regarded as the boundary between free and slave states in the period before the Civil War

Memorial Day – public holiday commemorating soldiers who died in battle; the last Monday in May; start of the summer holiday season

MLS – Major League Soccer, the professional soccer league

moonshine – illegal liquor, usually corn whiskey, associated with backwoods stills in the Appalachian Mountains

morteros – hollows in rocks used by Native Americans for grinding seeds; also called mortar holes

NAACP – National Association for the Advancement of Colored People

National Guard – each state's federally supported military reserves, used most often in civil emergencies; the National Guard can be called into action either by the state's governor or by congress for federal service

National Recreation Area – term used to describe National Park Service areas of scenic or ecological importance that have been modified by human activity, such as by major dam projects

National Register of Historic Places – listing of historic sites designated by the National Park Service, based on evidence supporting a structure's significance in the development of a community; being listed on the register restricts property owners from making major structural changes to buildings but also provides tax incentives for their preservation

NBA – National Basketball Association, the professional men's basketball league

NCAA – National Collegiate Athletic Association, the body that regulates the huge business of intercollegiate sports

New Deal – domestic program introduced by President Franklin D Roosevelt (1933–8) to counteract the effects of the Depression; the many and varied policies included bank regulation, grants to states and extensive new public works

NFL – National Football League, the professional football league – that's American football, of course!

NHL – National Hockey League, the professional ice hockey league, which comprises 16 US and eight Canadian teams

NHS – National Historic Site

NM – National Monument

NOW – National Organization for Women, strong proponent of women's issues, using education, politics and legal action to improve the political and economic status of American women

NPR – National Public Radio, a noncommercial, listener-supported broadcast organization that produces and distributes news, public affairs and cultural programming via a network of loosely affiliated radio stations throughout the USA

NPS – National Park Service, a division of the Department of the Interior that administers US national parks and monuments

NRA – National Recreation Area; also National Rifle Association, an influential lobby opposed to gun-control legislation

NWR – National Wildlife Refuge

OHV or **ORV** – off-highway vehicle or off-road vehicle

outfitter – business providing supplies, equipment, transport, guides, etc, for fishing, canoeing, rafting and hiking trips

out west – the opposite of 'back east'; anywhere west of the speaker or the Mississippi River

panhandle – a narrow piece of land projecting from the main body of a state (eg, the Florida, Texas and Idaho panhandles); also, to beg from passersby

parking lot/garage – paved area/building for parking cars (the word 'carpark' is not used)

PBS – Public Broadcasting System, a noncommercial TV network known for nature shows, British imports and Pavarotti; the TV equivalent of NPR

PC – politically correct; personal computer

petroglyph – a work of rock art in which the design is pecked, chipped or abraded into the surface of the rock

PGA – Professional Golfers' Association

pickup – small truck

pictograph – work of rock art in which the design is painted on a rock surface with one or more colors

po'boy – a fat sandwich on a bread roll

pound symbol – in the USA, # is known as the pound symbol (or pound key on a telephone), not £

powwow – gathering of Native American people

Presidents' Day – public holiday commemorating Washington and Lincoln; third Monday in February

pueblo – Native American village of the Southwest, with adjoining dwellings of adobe or stone

ranchero – a Mexican rancher; a Mexican American musical style blending German and Spanish influences

rancho – a small ranch (Mexican Spanish)

raw bar – a restaurant counter that serves raw shellfish

Reconstruction – period after the Civil War, when secessionist states were placed under federal control before they were readmitted to the Union

redneck – derogatory term for a working-class right-winger, characterized by jingoism and intolerance for liberal views

RV – recreational vehicle, also known as a motor home

scalawags – Southern whites with Northern sympathies who profited under Reconstruction after the Civil War

schlep – carry awkwardly or with difficulty (Yiddish)

schlock – cheap, trashy products (another great Yiddish word)

shotgun shack – a small timber house with three or four adjoining rooms arranged so you could fire a shotgun straight through the doors from front to back; once-common dwellings for poor whites and blacks in the South

sierra – (Spanish) mountain range

SoCal – Southern California

soul food – food (such as chitterlings, ham hocks and collard greens) traditionally eaten by Southern black Americans

SSN – Social Security number, a nine-digit ID code required for employment and receiving Social Security benefits

stick, stick shift – manually operated gearshift; car with manual transmission ('Can you drive a stick?')

strip mall – a collection of businesses and stores arranged around a parking lot, in an often-tacky, neon-lit row, square or 'strip'

SUV – sports utility vehicle, a large but comfortable vehicle, ostensibly for work and off-road use; SUVs are exempt from the usual fuel-economy requirements, and are the nation's leading gas-guzzlers

trailer – transportable dwelling, often sited permanently in a 'trailer park' and providing low-cost housing

TTY, TDD – telecommunications devices for the deaf

two-by-four – standard-size timber, 2 inches thick and 4 inches wide; the basic component of timber-frame buildings since the 1840s

Union, the – the United States; in the Civil War, the Union means 'the North,' the Northern states at war with the Confederate states of the South

USAF – United States Air Force

USFS – United States Forest Service, a division of the Department of Agriculture that implements policies on federal forest lands on the principles of 'multiple use,' including timber cutting, wildlife management, camping and recreation

USGS – United States Geological Survey, an agency of the Department of the Interior responsible for, among other things, detailed topographic maps of the entire country (USGS maps are particularly popular with hikers and backpackers)

USMC – United States Marine Corps, a branch of the armed forces that enforces US policy abroad; though reporting to the Department of the Navy, the Marines have their own ships, artillery and aircraft, and are usually the first US forces dispatched to any foreign trouble spot

USN – United States Navy

wash – a watercourse in the desert, usually dry but subject to flash flooding

well drinks – drinks containing hard liquor, straight or mixed; these drinks use less expensive liquor than 'top-shelf' drinks

WNBA – Women's National Basketball Association

WPA – Works Progress (later, Works Projects) Administration, a Depression-era program established under the Roosevelt administration in 1935 as part of the New Deal to increase employment by funding public works projects, including road and building construction, beautification of public structures (especially post offices) and the publication of a well-respected series of state and regional guidebooks

zip code – a five- or nine-digit postal code introduced under the Zone Improvement Program to expedite the sorting and delivery of US mail

Thanks

Many thanks to the travelers who used the last edition and wrote to us with helpful hints, useful advice and anecdotes. Your names follow:

Hilary Abel, Andrew Adams, Tina Adcock, Armin Ahrleg, Lysa Allman-Baldwin, Raymond Alvarez, Claire Anderson, Warren Anderson, Emanuela Appetiti, Sonia Archer, Christina Arnold, P Ashcroft, John Atchison, Jessie Attri, Saeed Azam, Neil Bage, Magdalena Balcerek, Cliff Barnes, Jenny Barnfield, Julie Bauer, Ralph Bauer, Mehdi Bazargan, Cesar Becerra, Alison Beck, Tony Beck, Jen Bervin, Paul Blakeman, Christian Bosselmann, Robin Brass, Kevin Broughton, Jessica Brown, Brad Burkman, Mark Burnell, Mark Burton, Marianne Busch, Craig Butz, Natasha Calvey, John Cassella, Nicole Castelijn, Emma Chippendale, James Clark, Jim Clark, Bethany Collings, Mary Condon, David Cope, Frances Copping, Simon Cox, Jerry and Tanya Coyd, Rob Curry, Rod Daldry, A Dean, Andrew Dennis RN, Lisa Doan, Fiona Dogrrill, Alan Dorin, James Downey, Christine Dowzer, Charlie Doyle, Jean-Marc Dumont, Paul and Alex Dunlea, Brett A Dunn, Clay Durham, Andrew Dykstra, Jennifer Edwards, Christina Eliason, Yesim Evrensel, Jim Feist, Annette Ferguson, Nicole and Pete Finlayson, Pernille and Kennet Foh, William Folk, Tracey Ford, Andrew Forin, Chris Forster-Brown, Barbara Friedrich, Don Gates, Susan Gauthier, Tom Genway, Teneal Gerry, Mark Girshovich, Val and Bill Goodman, James Gordon, Peter Gradwell, Bernie Grayson, Aisling Greene, Rebecca Griffin, Mr and Mrs Charles L Groff, Todd and Wendy Gunter, Sarah Havenell, Mike Heinz, Bernd Heisele, Renate Heygster, Roger B Hicks, Rachel and Richard Higgins, Oliver Hofmann, Helen Ibbott, Dafydd James, Rainald Jirsch, Cherie Johnson, Felicity Johnson, Peter Johnson, Anna Jordan, Karles Karwin, Alaska Keirsey, Andrew Kelham, Chad Kelly, Ellen Keohane, Matt Kerr, Karen Kester, Eva Knoche, Ulker Kocak, Lisa Krohne, Maija Kurkela, Tim Lamacraft, Jochen Lambers, Stephen Lambert, David Lay, Dominik Lehmann, Lasse Leick, Kath Leishman, John Leopold, Josh Levin, Tim Lewis, Dave Linton, Gail Lloyd, RC Loesch, Jeroen Looijen, Ross Maloney, Edward Marriott, Clive and Jean Marshall, Tim Marshall, Clara Mazzi, Patti McCullough, David McIntosh, Alex Mears, Pierre Meunier, Christoph Meyer, Skye Migan, Marlene Miller, Melina Mingari, Stephanie Minns, Tommy Miron, Martin Moll, Catherine Mollan, Matthew J Moore, Deb Moore-Marchant, Anita Morav, Angela Morgan, Fiona Morris, Ross Mote, John Paul Mowberry, Susan Murphy, Roberta Murray, Katherine Ogburn, James Oliver, Edward O'Loughlin, Dr William Olver, Pete W Onni, Nick Pace, Jake Page, Kate Palmer, Ornella Panzera, Edward H Parish, James Parry, Andrew Pearson, Dennis Phelan, Bob Phyllis, David Pinder, Lisa Polec, Angela and John Pos, Marcelo Horacio Pozzo, Lee Preece, Jenny Raven, John Rees, Sofia Rehn, Mary Richards, Judy Roberts, Andrica Rogge, Lucie Russell, Danny Ryan, Bill Sanders, Carol and Rick Sarchet, Sylvia Sepura, Gloria Ser, Mick and Liz Sharry, Peter and Florence Shaw, Christy Shuler, Paolo Simeone, Chris Simon, Neil Simpson, John Sinclair, Valerie Slade, James Slezak, Dawn Smith, Vivianne Smith, Jennie So, Andy Sparrow, Mark Spinelli, Lloyd Spivak, Hans de Roo Sr, Dave Stanton, Rob Stevens, Kim Stuart, Esther Studer, David Thomson, Bjorn Thorngren, Igor Tikhonov, Sarah Tilley, Loredana Tsamaidis, Twyla Urasaki, Jerry Van Belle, Willy Visser, Peter Vogl, Line von Gersdorff, Naomi Wall, Neil Ware, Aimee Wassong, Philip Weate, Julie Webb, Christine Weber, Jeff Weir, David Wignall, Tanya Withers, Renee Wolfson, Norman C Wood, Jeff Woods, Shaun Wylie, Joy Young

LONELY PLANET

You already know that Lonely Planet produces more than this one guidebook, but you might not be aware of the other products we have on this region. Here is a selection of titles that you may want to check out as well:

San Francisco city map
ISBN 1 86450 014 X
US$5.95 • UK£3.99

Los Angeles city map
ISBN 1 86450 258 4
US$5.99 • UK£3.99

Chicago city map
ISBN 1 86450 006 9
US$5.95 • UK£3.99

New York City
ISBN 1 86450 180 4
US$16.99 • UK£10.99

New Orleans
ISBN 0 86442 782 4
US$15.95 • UK£9.99

Las Vegas
ISBN 1 86450 086 7
US$15.95 • UK£9.99

Available wherever books are sold.

LONELY PLANET

Guides by Region

Lonely Planet is known worldwide for publishing practical, reliable and no-nonsense travel information in our guides and on our Web site. The Lonely Planet list covers just about every accessible part of the world. Currently there are 16 series: Travel guides, Shoestring guides, Condensed guides, Phrasebooks, Read This First, Healthy Travel, Walking guides, Cycling guides, Watching Wildlife guides, Pisces Diving & Snorkeling guides, City Maps, Road Atlases, Out to Eat, World Food, Journeys travel literature and Pictorials.

AFRICA Africa on a shoestring • Botswana • Cairo • Cairo City Map • Cape Town • Cape Town City Map • East Africa • Egypt • Egyptian Arabic phrasebook • Ethiopia, Eritrea & Djibouti • Ethiopian Amharic phrasebook • The Gambia & Senegal • Healthy Travel Africa • Kenya • Malawi • Morocco • Moroccan Arabic phrasebook • Mozambique • Namibia • Read This First: Africa • South Africa, Lesotho & Swaziland • Southern Africa • Southern Africa Road Atlas • Swahili phrasebook • Tanzania, Zanzibar & Pemba • Trekking in East Africa • Tunisia • Watching Wildlife East Africa • Watching Wildlife Southern Africa • West Africa • World Food Morocco • Zambia • Zimbabwe, Botswana & Namibia
Travel Literature: Mali Blues: Traveling to an African Beat • The Rainbird: A Central African Journey • Songs to an African Sunset: A Zimbabwean Story

AUSTRALIA & THE PACIFIC Aboriginal Australia & the Torres Strait Islands • Auckland • Australia • Australian phrasebook • Australia Road Atlas • Cycling Australia • Cycling New Zealand • Fiji • Fijian phrasebook • Healthy Travel Australia, NZ and the Pacific • Islands of Australia's Great Barrier Reef • Melbourne • Melbourne City Map • Micronesia • New Caledonia • New South Wales • New Zealand • Northern Territory • Outback Australia • Out to Eat – Melbourne • Out to Eat – Sydney • Papua New Guinea • Pidgin phrasebook • Queensland • Rarotonga & the Cook Islands • Samoa • Solomon Islands • South Australia • South Pacific • South Pacific phrasebook • Sydney • Sydney City Map • Sydney Condensed • Tahiti & French Polynesia • Tasmania • Tonga • Tramping in New Zealand • Vanuatu • Victoria • Walking in Australia • Watching Wildlife Australia • Western Australia
Travel Literature: Islands in the Clouds: Travel in the Highlands of New Guinea • Kiwi Tracks: A New Zealand Journey • Sean & David's Long Drive

CENTRAL AMERICA & THE CARIBBEAN Bahamas, Turks & Caicos • Baja California • Belize, Guatemala & Yucatán • Bermuda • Central America on a shoestring • Costa Rica • Costa Rica Spanish phrasebook • Cuba • Cycling Cuba • Dominican Republic & Haiti • Eastern Caribbean • Guatemala • Havana • Healthy Travel Central & South America • Jamaica • Mexico • Mexico City • Panama • Puerto Rico • Read This First: Central & South America • Virgin Islands • World Food Caribbean • World Food Mexico • Yucatán
Travel Literature: Green Dreams: Travels in Central America

EUROPE Amsterdam • Amsterdam City Map • Amsterdam Condensed • Andalucía • Athens • Austria • Baltic States phrasebook • Barcelona • Barcelona City Map • Belgium & Luxembourg • Berlin • Berlin City Map • Britain • British phrasebook • Brussels, Bruges & Antwerp • Brussels City Map • Budapest • Budapest City Map • Canary Islands • Catalunya & the Costa Brava • Central Europe • Central Europe phrasebook • Copenhagen • Corfu & the Ionians • Corsica • Crete • Crete Condensed • Croatia • Cycling Britain • Cycling France • Cyprus • Czech & Slovak Republics • Czech phrasebook • Denmark • Dublin • Dublin City Map • Dublin Condensed • Eastern Europe • Eastern Europe phrasebook • Edinburgh • Edinburgh City Map • England • Estonia, Latvia & Lithuania • Europe on a shoestring • Europe phrasebook • Finland • Florence • Florence City Map • France • Frankfurt City Map • Frankfurt Condensed • French phrasebook • Georgia, Armenia & Azerbaijan • Germany • German phrasebook • Greece • Greek Islands • Greek phrasebook • Hungary • Iceland, Greenland & the Faroe Islands • Ireland • Italian phrasebook • Italy • Kraków • Lisbon • The Loire • London • London City Map • London Condensed • Madrid • Madrid City Map • Malta • Mediterranean Europe • Milan, Turin & Genoa • Moscow • Munich • Netherlands • Normandy • Norway • Out to Eat – London • Out to Eat – Paris • Paris • Paris City Map • Paris Condensed • Poland • Polish phrasebook • Portugal • Portuguese phrasebook • Prague • Prague City Map • Provence & the Côte d'Azur • Read This First: Europe • Rhodes & the Dodecanese • Romania & Moldova • Rome • Rome City Map • Rome Condensed • Russia, Ukraine & Belarus • Russian phrasebook • Scandinavian & Baltic Europe • Scandinavian phrasebook • Scotland • Sicily • Slovenia • South-West France • Spain • Spanish phrasebook • Stockholm • St Petersburg • St Petersburg City Map • Sweden • Switzerland • Tuscany • Ukrainian phrasebook • Venice • Vienna • Wales • Walking in Britain • Walking in France • Walking in Ireland • Walking in Italy • Walking in Scotland • Walking in Spain • Walking in Switzerland • Western Europe • World Food France • World Food Greece • World Food Ireland • World Food Italy • World Food Spain **Travel Literature:** After Yugoslavia • Love and War in the Apennines • The Olive Grove: Travels in Greece • On the Shores of the Mediterranean • Round Ireland in Low Gear • A Small Place in Italy

LONELY PLANET

Mail Order

Lonely Planet products are distributed worldwide. They are also available by mail order from Lonely Planet, so if you have difficulty finding a title please write to us. North and South American residents should write to 150 Linden St, Oakland, CA 94607, USA; European and African residents should write to 10a Spring Place, London NW5 3BH, UK; and residents of other countries to Locked Bag 1, Footscray, Victoria 3011, Australia.

INDIAN SUBCONTINENT & THE INDIAN OCEAN Bangladesh • Bengali phrasebook • Bhutan • Delhi • Goa • Healthy Travel Asia & India • Hindi & Urdu phrasebook • India • India & Bangladesh City Map • Indian Himalaya • Karakoram Highway • Kathmandu City Map • Kerala • Madagascar • Maldives • Mauritius, Réunion & Seychelles • Mumbai (Bombay) • Nepal • Nepali phrasebook • North India • Pakistan • Rajasthan • Read This First: Asia & India • South India • Sri Lanka • Sri Lanka phrasebook • Tibet • Tibetan phrasebook • Trekking in the Indian Himalaya • Trekking in the Karakoram & Hindukush • Trekking in the Nepal Himalaya • World Food India **Travel Literature:** The Age of Kali: Indian Travels and Encounters • Hello Goodnight: A Life of Goa • In Rajasthan • Maverick in Madagascar • A Season in Heaven: True Tales from the Road to Kathmandu • Shopping for Buddhas • A Short Walk in the Hindu Kush • Slowly Down the Ganges

MIDDLE EAST & CENTRAL ASIA Bahrain, Kuwait & Qatar • Central Asia • Central Asia phrasebook • Dubai • Farsi (Persian) phrasebook • Hebrew phrasebook • Iran • Israel & the Palestinian Territories • Istanbul • Istanbul City Map • Istanbul to Cairo • Istanbul to Kathmandu • Jerusalem • Jerusalem City Map • Jordan • Lebanon • Middle East • Oman & the United Arab Emirates • Syria • Turkey • Turkish phrasebook • World Food Turkey • Yemen **Travel Literature:** Black on Black: Iran Revisited • Breaking Ranks: Turbulent Travels in the Promised Land • The Gates of Damascus • Kingdom of the Film Stars: Journey into Jordan

NORTH AMERICA Alaska • Boston • Boston City Map • Boston Condensed • British Columbia • California & Nevada • California Condensed • Canada • Chicago • Chicago City Map • Chicago Condensed • Florida • Georgia & the Carolinas • Great Lakes • Hawaii • Hiking in Alaska • Hiking in the USA • Honolulu & Oahu City Map • Las Vegas • Los Angeles • Los Angeles City Map • Louisiana & the Deep South • Miami • Miami City Map • Montréal • New England • New Orleans • New Orleans City Map • New York City • New York City Map • New York City Condensed • New York, New Jersey & Pennsylvania • Oahu • Out to Eat – San Francisco • Pacific Northwest • Rocky Mountains • San Diego & Tijuana • San Francisco • San Francisco City Map • Seattle • Seattle City Map • Southwest • Texas • Toronto • USA • USA phrasebook • Vancouver • Vancouver City Map • Virginia & the Capital Region • Washington, DC • Washington, DC City Map • World Food New Orleans **Travel Literature:** Caught Inside: A Surfer's Year on the California Coast • Drive Thru America

NORTH-EAST ASIA Beijing • Beijing City Map • Cantonese phrasebook • China • Hiking in Japan • Hong Kong & Macau • Hong Kong City Map • Hong Kong Condensed • Japan • Japanese phrasebook • Korea • Korean phrasebook • Kyoto • Mandarin phrasebook • Mongolia • Mongolian phrasebook • Seoul • Shanghai • South-West China • Taiwan • Tokyo • World Food Hong Kong • World Food Japan **Travel Literature:** In Xanadu: A Quest • Lost Japan

SOUTH AMERICA Argentina, Uruguay & Paraguay • Bolivia • Brazil • Brazilian phrasebook • Buenos Aires • Buenos Aires City Map • Chile & Easter Island • Colombia • Ecuador & the Galápagos Islands • Healthy Travel Central & South America • Latin American Spanish phrasebook • Peru • Quechua phrasebook • Read This First: Central & South America • Rio de Janeiro • Rio de Janeiro City Map • Santiago de Chile • South America on a shoestring • Trekking in the Patagonian Andes • Venezuela **Travel Literature:** Full Circle: A South American Journey

SOUTH-EAST ASIA Bali & Lombok • Bangkok • Bangkok City Map • Burmese phrasebook • Cambodia • Cycling Vietnam, Laos & Cambodia • East Timor phrasebook • Hanoi • Healthy Travel Asia & India • Hill Tribes phrasebook • Ho Chi Minh City (Saigon) • Indonesia • Indonesian phrasebook • Indonesia's Eastern Islands • Java • Lao phrasebook • Laos • Malay phrasebook • Malaysia, Singapore & Brunei • Myanmar (Burma) • Philippines • Pilipino (Tagalog) phrasebook • Read This First: Asia & India • Singapore • Singapore City Map • South-East Asia on a shoestring • South-East Asia phrasebook • Thailand • Thailand's Islands & Beaches • Thailand, Vietnam, Laos & Cambodia Road Atlas • Thai phrasebook • Vietnam • Vietnamese phrasebook • World Food Indonesia • World Food Thailand • World Food Vietnam

ALSO AVAILABLE: Antarctica • The Arctic • The Blue Man: Tales of Travel, Love and Coffee • Brief Encounters: Stories of Love, Sex & Travel • Buddhist Stupas in Asia: The Shape of Perfection • Chasing Rickshaws • The Last Grain Race • Lonely Planet...On the Edge: Adventurous Escapades from Around the World • Lonely Planet Unpacked • Lonely Planet Unpacked Again • Not the Only Planet: Science Fiction Travel Stories • Ports of Call: A Journey by Sea • Sacred India • Travel Photography: A Guide to Taking Better Pictures • Travel with Children • Tuvalu: Portrait of an Island Nation

Notes

Index

Abbreviations

AK	– Alaska	KY	– Kentucky	NY	– New York		
AL	– Alabama	LA	– Louisiana	OH	– Ohio		
AR	– Arkansas	MA	– Massachusetts	OK	– Oklahoma		
AZ	– Arizona	MD	– Maryland	OR	– Oregon		
CA	– California	ME	– Maine	PA	– Pennsylvania		
CO	– Colorado	MI	– Michigan	RI	– Rhode Island		
CT	– Connecticut	MN	– Minnesota	SC	– South Carolina		
DC	– District of Columbia	MO	– Missouri	SD	– South Dakota		
DE	– Delaware	MS	– Mississippi	TN	– Tennessee		
FL	– Florida	MT	– Montana	TX	– Texas		
GA	– Georgia	NC	– North Carolina	UT	– Utah		
HI	– Hawaii	ND	– North Dakota	VA	– Virginia		
IA	– Iowa	NE	– Nebraska	VT	– Vermont		
ID	– Idaho	NH	– New Hampshire	WA	– Washington		
IL	– Illinois	NJ	– New Jersey	WI	– Wisconsin		
IN	– Indiana	NM	– New Mexico	WV	– West Virginia		
KS	– Kansas	NV	– Nevada	WY	– Wyoming		

Text

A

AAA. *See* American Automobile Association
Abbeville (LA) 570
Abilene (KS) 735
Abingdon (VA) 373–4
Abiquiu (NM) 857–8
Absaroka Beartooth Wilderness (MT) 815–6
Acadia National Park (ME) 327
Acadians 568–9
accommodations 119–23. *See also individual locations*
B&Bs 121
camping 119–20
costs 87–8
hostels 83, 120–1
motels & hotels 121–3
resorts & lodges 123
university 121
YMCAs & YWCAs 121
Acoma Pueblo (NM) 844
activities 94, 112–8. *See also individual activities*

Bold indicates maps.

Acute Mountain Sickness (AMS) 102
The Adirondacks (NY) 42, 222–3
Admiralty Island National Monument (AK) 1069
Adventure Island (FL) 645
African Americans. *See also* slavery
books 95
dialects 72
history 36, 40, 95, 196, 268, 360, 399, 492–3, 520, 522, 537–8, 730, 735, 742
music 59, 346, 552
population 54
religion 72
Agate Fossil Beds National Monument (NE) 747
agriculture 46–7
AIDS 41, 81–2, 102–3, 128, 970
air pollution 47
air travel
airlines 133, 143
airports 97, 133, 160–1
domestic 143–6
glossary 136

international 133–41, 144
routes **145**
Akron (OH) 432
Alabama 536–42, **490**
The Alamo (TX) 680, 681
Alamogordo (NM) 853
Alamosa (CO) 795
Alaska 1058–85, **1060–1**
Alaska Chilkat Bald Eagle Preserve (AK) 1071
Albany (NY) 220–1
The Albermarle (NC) 502–3
Albuquerque (NM) 838–42, **839, 843**
Alcatraz (CA) 978
alcoholic drinks 109, 127, 598
Alcott, Louisa May 265, 277
Aleutian Islands (AK) 1085
Aleuts 1058, 1073
Alexandria (VA) 354
Allegheny National Forest (PA) 255–6
Allen, Woody 184, 233
Alpine (TX) 700
Alturas (CA) 1000
Amador City (CA) 997
Amagansett (NY) 217
Amana Colonies (IA) 739

Bold indicates maps.

Haleiwa (HI) 1100
Half Dome (CA) 1003, 1004
Half Moon Bay (CA) 987
Hamakua Coast (HI) 1103
Hamilton (MT) 818
Hampton (VA) 366
Hampton Beach (NH) 311
Hampton Roads (VA) 366–7
The Hamptons (NY) 216–7
Hana (HI) 1106
Hanalei (HI) 1108
Hanauma Bay Beach Park (HI) 1099
handicrafts 132, 391
hang gliding 494, 504
Hanksville (UT) 900
Hannibal (MO) 714–5
Hanover (NH) 318–9
Harbor Springs (MI) 452
Hardin (MT) 816
Harlem. See New York City (NY)
Harmony (CA) 964
Harpers Ferry (WV) 392–3
Harriman State Park (NY) 218
Harrisburg (PA) 248
Harrodsburg (KY) 603
Hartford (CT) 296–7
Harvard University (MA) 269
Havasupai 873–4
Hawaii (island) 1088, 1101–5, **1091**
Hawaii (state) 1088–110, **1090–1**
Hawaii Volcanoes National Park (HI) 1104–5
Hays (KS) 735
Healdsburg (CA) 991
health 99–103
  bites & stings 103
  diseases 102–3
  environmental hazards 101–2
  food & drink 100
  insurance 83, 100
  travel-related problems 100–1
Hearst Castle (CA) 964
Heber City (UT) 892
Helen (GA) 527–8
Helena (AR) 578
Helena (MT) 816–7

Hells Canyon (ID, OR) 827, 1049
Hemingway, Ernest 56, 452
Henry Ford Museum (MI) 448
The Hermitage (TN) 588
Hershey (PA) 248
Hibbing (MN) 484
Hidatsa 757, 759, 761
High Uintas Wilderness Area (UT) 894
highways 157. See also Pacific Coast Hwy (Hwy 1)
hiking & backpacking 113–4
  Alaska 1063, 1065, 1067, 1068, 1070, 1076, 1077, 1080, 1082, 1084
  California 923–4, 969, 1001–2, 1004, 1006
  Capital Region 336, 347, 373, 393
  Florida 611, 623, 645
  Great Lakes 403, 451
  Great Plains 706, 716, 752, 753, 756, 760
  guides 94
  Hawaii 1093, 1095, 1099, 1102, 1104, 1108
  Mid-Atlantic States 165, 168, 223
  New England 262, 294, 305, 308, 315, 316, 324, 329
  Pacific Northwest 1014, 1021–2, 1029, 1034–5, 1037, 1043, 1047, 1048–9
  Rocky Mountains 769, 779–80, 781–2, 784, 790, 791, 792, 793, 794, 797, 809, 811, 817, 818–9, 820, 824, 826
  safety 112–3
  The South 494, 502, 527
  Southwest 836, 840–1, 846, 851, 858, 861, 871, 872, 873, 880, 891, 899, 901, 903–4
  Texas 663, 696, 699
Hill City (SD) 755
Hill Country (TX) 677–9
Hilo (HI) 1103
Hilton Head Island (SC) 515

Hinton (WV) 395
hip-hop 60–1
Hirshhorn Museum (DC) 343
Historic Columbia River Highway (OR) 1046
history 21–41. See also Civil War; Revolutionary War; *individual locations*
  books 94–5
  chronology of 22–3
  indigenous peoples 21, 24, **25**
  European exploration & settlement 24, 26–8, **27**
  French & Indian War 28–9, 165
  colonial discontent 29
  Revolutionary War 29–30
  ratification of US Constitution 30
  territorial expansion 30–2, **31**
  War of 1812 30, 32, 337, 384
  Mexican War 32, 659, 919
  Civil War 32–4
  from Civil War to WWI 34–7
  WWI 37
  Roaring '20s 37
  Great Depression 37–8
  New Deal 38
  WWII 38, 1098
  Cold War 39–40
  Korean War 39
  civil-rights movement & social justice 40–1
  Vietnam War 39
  Persian Gulf War 39
hitchhiking 160
HIV 81–2, 102–3
Hoboken (NJ) 230–1
hockey 131
Hocking County (OH) 435
Hodgenville (KY) 598
Hohokam 21, 830, 860
Holbrook (AZ) 876
Holiday, Billie 59, 60, 616
holidays 110–1
Holly, Buddy 60, 695
Holly Springs (MS) 545
Hollywood (CA) 931–3, 937, 939, **932**
homeless people 108–9
Homer (AK) 1077–8

Bold indicates maps.

Bold indicates maps.

Bold indicates maps.

Bold indicates maps.

Boxed Text

MAP LEGEND

ROUTES

City   Regional

............................Freeway
............................Toll Freeway
............................Primary Road
............................Secondary Road
............................Tertiary Road
............................Dirt Road

............................Pedestrian Mall
............................Steps
............................Tunnel
............................Trail
............................Walking Tour
............................Path

TRANSPORTATION

............................Train
............................Metro

............................Bus Route
............................Ferry

BOUNDARIES

............................International
............................State
............................Fortified Wall

............................County
............................Disputed

ROUTE SHIELDS

USA
80 ... Interstate Freeway
101 ... US Highway
95 ... State Highway

G4 ... County Road
1 ... California State Highway
95 ... Nevada State Highway

CANADA
1 ... Trans-Canada Highway
17 ... Canadian Highway
99 ... Provincial Highway

MEXICO
MEX 1 ... Mexican Highway
MEX 1D ... Mexican Toll Highway

HYDROGRAPHY

............................River; Creek
............................Canal
............................Reef
............................Water
............................Spring; Rapids
............................Waterfalls
............................Dry Lake
............................Salt Flat

AREAS

............................Beach
............................Building
............................Campus
............................Cemetery
............................Forest
............................Garden; Zoo
............................Golf Course
............................Park
............................Plaza
............................Reservation
............................Sports Field
............................Swamp; Mangrove

POPULATION SYMBOLS

⊕ NATIONAL CAPITAL ... National Capital
◉ STATE CAPITAL ... State Capital

● Large City ... Large City
● Medium City ... Medium City

● Small City ... Small City
● Town; Village ... Town; Village

MAP SYMBOLS

■ .... Place to Stay
▼ .... Place to Eat
● .... Point of Interest

............Airfield
............Airport
............Archeological Site; Ruin
............Bank
............Baseball Stadium
............Battlefield
............Beach
............Border Crossing
............Buddhist Temple
............Bus Terminal
............Cable Car; Chairlift
............Campground
............Castle
............Cathedral; Church
............Cave
............Church; Cathedral

............Cinema
............Dive Site
............Embassy; Consulate
............Ferry Terminal
............Footbridge
............Fountain
............Gas Station
............Hindu Temple
............Hospital
............Information
............Internet Café
............Lighthouse
............Lookout
............Mine
............Mission
............Monument

............Mountain
............Museum
............Observatory
............Park
............Parking Area
............Pass
............Picnic Area
............Police Station
............Pool
............Post Office
............Pub; Bar
............Pueblo
............RV Park
............Shipwreck
............Shopping Mall
............Skiing - Cross Country

............Skiing - Downhill
............Stately Home
............Surfing
............Synagogue
............Taoist Temple
............Taxi
............Telephone
............Theater
............Toilet - Public
............Tomb
............Trailhead
............Tram Stop
............Transportation
............Volcano
............Windsurfing
............Winery

Note: Not all symbols displayed above appear in this book.

LONELY PLANET OFFICES

Australia
Locked Bag 1, Footscray, Victoria 3011
☎ 03 8379 8000 fax 03 8379 8111
email talk2us@lonelyplanet.com.au

USA
150 Linden Street, Oakland, California 94607
☎ 510 893 8555, TOLL FREE 800 275 8555
fax 510 893 8572
email info@lonelyplanet.com

UK
10a Spring Place, London NW5 3BH
☎ 020 7428 4800 fax 020 7428 4828
email go@lonelyplanet.co.uk

France
1 rue du Dahomey, 75011 Paris
☎ 01 55 25 33 00 fax 01 55 25 33 01
email bip@lonelyplanet.fr
www.lonelyplanet.fr

World Wide Web: www.lonelyplanet.com *or* AOL keyword: lp
Lonely Planet Images: lpi@lonelyplanet.com.au